masculin	**m**	masculine
mathématique	**Math**	mathematics
médecine	**Med, Méd**	medicine
météorologie	**Met, Mét**	meteorology
métallurgie	**Metal, Métal**	metallurgy
masculin et féminin	**mf**	masculine and feminine
militaire	**Mil**	military
mines	**Min**	mining
minéralogie	**Miner, Minér**	mineralogy
masculin pluriel	**mpl**	masculine plural
musique	**Mus**	music
mythologie	**Myth**	mythology
nom	**n**	noun
nord de l'Angleterre	**N Angl**	North of England
nautique	**Naut**	nautical, naval
négatif	**neg, nég**	negative
nord de l'Angleterre	**N Engl**	North of England
nom féminin	**nf**	feminine noun
nom masculin	**nm**	masculine noun
nom masculin et féminin	**nmf, nm,f**	masculine and feminine noun
physique nucléaire	**Nucl Phys**	nuclear physics
numéral	**num**	numerical
objet	**obj**	object
opposé	**opp**	opposite
optique	**Opt**	optics
ornithologie	**Orn**	ornithology
	o.s.	oneself
parlement	**Parl**	parliament
passif	**pass**	passive
péjoratif	**pej, péj**	pejorative
personnel	**pers**	personal
pharmacie	**Pharm**	pharmacy
philatélie	**Philat**	philately
philosophie	**Philos**	philosophy
photographie	**Phot**	photography
	phr vb elem	phrasal verb element
physique	**Phys**	physics
physiologie	**Physiol**	physiology
pluriel	**pl**	plural
politique	**Pol**	politics
possessif	**poss**	possessive
préfixe	**pref, préf**	prefix
préposition	**prep, prép**	preposition
prétérit	**pret, prét**	preterite
pronom	**pron**	pronoun
proverbe	**Prov**	proverb
participe présent	**prp**	present participle
psychiatrie, psychologie	**Psych**	psychology, psychiatry
participe passé	**ptp**	past participle
quelque chose	**qch**	
quelqu'un	**qn**	
marque déposée	**®**	registered trademark
radio	**Rad**	radio
chemin de fer	**Rail**	rail(ways)
relatif	**rel**	relative
religion	**Rel**	religion
	sb	somebody, someone
sciences	**Sci**	science
école	**Scol**	school
écossais, Écosse	**Scot**	Scottish, Scotland
sculpture	**Sculp**	sculpture
séparable	**sep**	separable
singulier	**sg**	singular
ski	**Ski**	skiing
argot	**sl**	slang
sociologie	**Soc, Sociol**	sociology, social work
Bourse	**St Ex**	Stock Exchange
	sth	something
subjonctif	**subj**	subjunctive
suffixe	**suf**	suffix
superlatif	**superl**	superlative
chirurgie	**Surg**	surgery
arpentage	**Surv**	surveying
terme de spécialiste	**T**	specialist's term
technique	**Tech**	technical
télécommunication	**Telec, Téléc**	telecommunications
industrie textile	**Tex**	textiles
théâtre	**Theat, Théât**	theatre
télévision	**TV**	television
typographie	**Typ**	typography
non comptable	**U**	uncountable
université	**Univ**	university
américain, États-Unis	**US**	American, United States
voir	**V**	see
verbe	**vb**	verb
médecine vétérinaire	**Vet, Vét**	veterinary medicine
verbe intransitif	**vi**	intransitive verb
verbe pronominal	**vpr**	pronominal verb
verbe transitif	**vt**	transitive verb
verbe transitif et intransitif	**vti**	transitive and intransitive verb
verbe transitif indirect	**vt indir**	
zoologie	**Zool**	zoology
voir page xviii	* ‡ ❖	see page xviii
voir page xviii	† ††	see page xviii

DICTIONNAIRE FRANÇAIS~ANGLAIS ANGLAIS~FRANÇAIS
FRENCH~ENGLISH ENGLISH~FRENCH DICTIONARY

ROBERT · COLLINS
DICTIONNAIRE
FRANÇAIS - ANGLAIS
ANGLAIS - FRANÇAIS

Avec la collaboration
du comité du Robert
sous la présidence de Paul Robert

Société du Nouveau Littré
Paris

COLLINS · ROBERT FRENCH ~ ENGLISH ENGLISH ~ FRENCH DICTIONARY

by

Beryl T. Atkins

Alain Duval Rosemary C. Milne

and

Pierre-Henri Cousin

Hélène M. A. Lewis Lorna A. Sinclair

Renée O. Birks Marie-Noëlle Lamy

Collins

London & Glasgow

Cleveland & Toronto

First published 1978

Collins Publishers
P.O. Box, Glasgow, G4 0NB, Great Britain
2080 West 117th Street, Cleveland, Ohio 44111, U.S.A.
100 Lesmill Road, Don Mills, Ontario M3B 2T5, Canada

ISBN 0 00 433478 7
with thumb index ISBN 0 00 433479 5

S.N.L. Dictionnaire Le Robert
107, av. Parmentier, 75011 PARIS

ISBN 2-85036-008-2

Computer typeset by G. A. Pindar & Son Ltd, Scarborough, England
Manufactured in the United States of America by Rand McNally & Company

TABLE DES MATIÈRES

CONTENTS

PRÉFACE

VOICI une œuvre faite en commun dans les deux vieux pays pour aider à la communication entre les anglophones et les francophones de l'ancien et du nouveau monde.

L'amour passionné que j'ai toujours porté au français n'a point nui à celui que j'éprouve pour l'anglais. Alors que je travaillais à mon *Dictionnaire alphabétique et analogique de la langue française*, je rêvais de faire, ou de contribuer à faire, le même effort pour la langue anglaise. Par mes ancêtres acadiens, je suis moi-même l'enfant de deux continents. Le génie des deux langues et celui des deux nations qui les ont répandues dans l'univers, sont pour moi cordialement liés; je veux dire liés par le cœur autant que par l'esprit. Or ce dictionnaire se veut moyen de transmission autant pour le cœur que pour l'esprit. Nous avons souhaité qu'il se distinguât des autres par la facilité qu'il donnerait aux usagers de transposer, en les maintenant vivants, les sentiments et de traduire, derrière les pensées, les arrière-pensées, les intentions, et même les passions.

Il fallait pour cela réunir une équipe de spécialistes — de Britanniques connaissant le français, de Français connaissant l'anglais — astreints à n'écrire, dans ce dictionnaire, que dans leur langue maternelle. Ceci afin qu'ils aient à leur disposition, dans la langue qui n'est pas la leur, le mot juste: celui qu'un Britannique emploie naturellement dans sa propre langue, un Français dans la sienne; non seulement le mot, mais l'expression juste, afin même qu'ils puissent, dans la langue étrangère, pousser le cri du cœur, de leur cœur.

Pour ce faire, j'ai été heureux d'abord de mettre à la disposition de l'admirable équipe de francophones et d'anglophones réunie par Collins dès 1962, le *Grand Robert*, le *Petit Robert* et le *Micro Robert*. Puis, quand le projet d'une collaboration plus directe prit corps, avec mon ami Jan Collins, je songeai à réunir une équipe capable, à Paris, de faire une lecture critique du manuscrit. En 1972, je m'assurai pour cela de la collaboration d'une Française, Marie-Christine de Montoussé, et d'un Français, Robert Mengin, que plus d'un quart de siècle d'expérience désignait pour cela. Ils avaient vécu en Grande-Bretagne, aux États-Unis et au Canada avant, pendant et après la guerre. En même temps, ils étaient parisiens, et traducteurs en français des genres les plus divers, les plus vivants: romans d'auteurs contemporains, anglais et américains; dialogues de théâtre et de cinéma. Je leur confiai la tâche principale du comité qui a fonctionné depuis 1973.

Voici cette tâche terminée. Cependant, il faudra la poursuivre, dans les années qui viennent. Car nos deux langues vivent, et il faut vivre avec elles.

PAUL ROBERT

Comité du Robert
Martine Bercot, Gilberte Gagnon, Maryline Hira
Lucette Jourdan, Denis Keen, Jean Mambrino
Jacques Mengin, Robert Mengin, Marie Christine de Montoussé
Alain Rey, Josette Rey-Debove
Colette Thompson, Elaine Williamson

PREFACE

THIS book is the second in a major series of bilingual dictionaries. Like its predecessor, COLLINS SPANISH DICTIONARY, which was received with acclaim when it appeared in 1971, it embodies a fresh approach to bilingual lexicography, with its emphasis on the current, living language of everyday communication.

A team of British and French lexicographers has planned, worked, and polished over a period of 15 years to fashion this Dictionary into as perfect a tool as possible to promote accurate and easy communication between the speakers of two great world languages. We have tried to define and meet the needs of a wide range of users, from those with an academic or professional commitment—teachers at all levels, translators, students of French or English, as the case may be—through business people whose affairs demand an ability to conduct discussion or correspondence in both languages, to the large numbers of people of each nationality who are interested in the language, literature and culture of the other and know that only the best possible dictionary is a good enough tool.

In realizing this aim we in Collins count ourselves singularly fortunate to have secured the wholehearted collaboration of Paul Robert and la Société du Nouveau Littré, whose magistral *Dictionnaire alphabétique et analogique de la langue française* first appeared in 1953. The publication of *Le Grand Robert*, *Le Petit Robert* and *Le Micro Robert* made an immediate and outstanding contribution to French lexicography, and Collins are happy to have as a source for this bilingual dictionary the Robert range with its leading reputation. The resulting COLLINS-ROBERT FRENCH DICTIONARY, a true co-publication, brings a new dimension in authenticity and reliability to bilingual lexicography.

This collaboration, the availability to our lexicographers of the archives of the Dictionnaire le Robert and the skills of its lexicographers, added to our rigorous policy that every French word in the Dictionary was created and vetted by *French* lexicographers and every English word by *English* lexicographers, with constant and full discussion between them, means that French-speaking and English-speaking users can approach this Dictionary with equal confidence. It is truly an international Dictionary.

We offer this new Dictionary in the confident hope that this basic strength, and the many other features described in the pages that follow, will establish it in the appreciation of all who use it.

I must, in conclusion, express my keen appreciation of the work of the many compilers and collaborators whose skill and insight have helped to make the Dictionary the book it is, and in particular, of course, the General Editors, who have lived with and laboured on the text of the Dictionary for so many years.

JAN COLLINS

Compiling Staff
John Scullard, Edwin Carpenter, Margaret Curtin
Kenneth Gibson, Gerry Kilroy, Michael Janes
Anthony Linforth, Trevor Peach, Elise Thomson

Collins Staff
William T. McLeod, Richard Thomas
Barbara Christie, Carol Purdon

INTRODUCTION

LE DICTIONNAIRE ROBERT–COLLINS est avant tout un outil qui cherche à répondre à un besoin pratique: permettre la communication entre le français et l'anglais de façon simple, rapide et sûre. Ses caractéristiques principales, notamment l'étendue et la nature du vocabulaire traité et l'agencement des indications servant à guider le lecteur, découlent directement de cette conception fonctionnelle d'un dictionnaire bilingue.

Étendue et nature du vocabulaire

L'accent est mis résolument sur la langue contemporaine. Le corpus très étendu (plus de 100.000 mots et composés, plus de 100.000 exemples et expressions idiomatiques) s'attache à présenter au lecteur une image fidèle de la langue telle qu'elle est pratiquée quotidiennement, lue dans les journaux et les revues, parlée en société, entendue dans la rue.

Pour éviter un ouvrage trop long et peu maniable, il a fallu opérer un certain choix. Les mots trop rares, les sens trop spécialisés ont donc été écartés au profit d'emplois nouveaux et de nombreux néologismes absents des dictionnaires bilingues et parfois monolingues existants, mais qui sont indispensables si l'on veut rendre compte de la pratique courante de la langue actuelle.

Une place non négligeable a été également réservée à la langue littéraire, au vocabulaire scientifique et aux domaines marquants de notre époque, tels que la sociologie, l'électronique, l'éducation, les voyages et la politique.

Une autre préoccupation fondamentale a été de faire un dictionnaire qui s'adresse aussi bien au lecteur de langue française qu'à celui de langue anglaise. Suivant une politique rigoureuse, chaque mot français a été écrit et vérifié par des rédacteurs de langue française et chaque mot anglais par des rédacteurs de langue anglaise, travaillant en étroite collaboration pour s'assurer de la justesse de leurs traductions. Les utilisateurs de l'une ou l'autre langue peuvent donc se servir de ce dictionnaire avec une confiance égale: les auteurs ont veillé à ce que chacune des deux parties soit également valable dans le sens thème et dans le sens version, ce qui est d'une importance capitale.

La langue décrite ne se limite pas au français de France, à l'anglais de Grande-Bretagne: les emplois courants de l'anglais d'Amérique, ainsi que les termes les plus répandus du français du Canada sont également traités.

Indications servant à guider le lecteur

Un dictionnaire, si riche soit-il, perd une grande partie de sa valeur lorsque l'utilisateur ne peut pas trouver rapidement et sans incertitude ce qu'il cherche. Sachant combien il est facile, surtout pour un dictionnaire bilingue, de tomber dans cette ornière, les auteurs du présent ouvrage ont soigneusement étudié cet aspect fondamental, et consacré une part importante de la place précieuse dont ils disposaient à l'établissement d'un système très complet d'indications qui guident le lecteur.

Tout article complexe est clairement divisé en catégories sémantiques introduites par une indication qui en fait ressortir le sens général. De plus, les variations de sens à l'intérieur de ces catégories sont soigneusement mises en évidence à l'aide de renseignements supplémentaires précisant chaque nuance. L'utilisation cohérente de ce système d'indications, sous forme de synonymes, de définitions partielles ou de compléments à valeur typique, est l'une des caractéristiques essentielles de ce dictionnaire. Les auteurs espèrent combler ainsi une lacune majeure de beaucoup d'ouvrages de ce type.

Les complexités et les subtilités de registre tendent à celui qui étudie une langue étrangère des pièges sournois. Les expressions qu'il utilise peuvent se trouver tout à fait déplacées — et parfois de façon grotesque — dans la situation du moment. Il est difficile d'acquérir une maîtrise parfaite des niveaux de langue à partir d'une page de dictionnaire, mais les auteurs ont tenté de créer un code très précis qui renseigne le lecteur, et indique pour chaque mot et expression, tant dans la langue de départ que dans la langue d'arrivée, les restrictions stylistiques qui s'imposent.

Les mots et expressions dont le niveau de style n'est pas précisé seront considérés comme neutres et pourront s'utiliser normalement dans les situations courantes. Chaque fois qu'il n'en est pas ainsi, une précision est apportée sur la nature de la restriction: par exemple langue soutenue ou littéraire, emploi américain, argot militaire, connotation humoristique ou péjorative.

Les auteurs se sont en particulier attachés à élaborer un système aussi efficace que possible qui indique les différents degrés dans la familiarité, depuis les expressions légèrement familières jusqu'à celles qui sont ressenties comme très vulgaires. Un, deux ou trois astérisques avertissent le lecteur étranger. De même une croix ou une double croix indique que le mot est vieilli ou archaïque.

Ce système d'indications offre à l'utilisateur une amélioration importante par rapport aux dictionnaires bilingues existants.

Un autre écueil des ouvrages traditionnels est constitué par le manque de renseignements d'ordre grammatical, ce qui ne permet généralement pas au lecteur étranger d'insérer correctement la traduction dans une structure plus complexe. Les auteurs ont donc tenu ici à indiquer soigneusement les exigences syntaxiques des deux langues en apportant toujours les précisions nécessaires (telles que la notation des constructions verbales ou des prépositions liées aux noms ou aux adjectifs). De nombreux exemples viennent en outre enrichir le contenu des articles, et montrent que le mot n'a pas d'existence en dehors de la phrase, et que les traductions ne sont pas fixes, mais peuvent changer suivant le contexte. Mettre le mot en situation permet de plus d'introduire les expressions idiomatiques nécessaires pour s'exprimer dans une langue authentique et éviter les erreurs d'usage.

Les pages qui suivent décrivent avec plus de détails les caractéristiques principales du dictionnaire.

INTRODUCTION

THE COLLINS–ROBERT FRENCH DICTIONARY is first and foremost a practical tool designed for a specific function: to facilitate easy, rapid, and reliable communication between French and English. Its major characteristics spring directly from this concept of the function of a bilingual dictionary. In particular, this has shaped two fundamental aspects: the scope and nature of the language treated; and the arrangement of the information presented and helps provided.

The scope and nature of the language treated

The emphasis is firmly placed on contemporary language. The range is wide: over 100,000 headwords and compounds, over 100,000 phrases and idioms have been selected and arranged to present the user with the authentic language he will meet daily in newspapers, journals, books, in society and in the street.

The desire to avoid an unduly lengthy and unwieldy volume has involved a certain choice. Hence uncommon words, specialized terms and meanings have been omitted in favour of numerous recent coinages and new meanings, not found in existing bilingual dictionaries and even absent from some monolingual volumes, but essential if the Dictionary is truly to reflect current, living language as it is spoken and written today.

Space has been found, too, for a considerable representation of the vocabulary of literature and science, and especially of those areas which have contributed notably to the modern consciousness — sociology, electronics, education, travel, politics, and so on.

One of our primary concerns has been to make the Dictionary equally valid for French-speaking and English-speaking users. Our rigorous policy that every French word in the Dictionary has been created and vetted by *French* lexicographers and every English word by *English* lexicographers, with constant discussion between them, means that French-speaking and English-speaking users can approach this Dictionary with equal confidence. In addition, we have taken care that each side of the Dictionary is equally helpful for translation from and into the foreign language, a point of fundamental concern to all users.

The spread of language treated is not confined to British English or metropolitan French: American English and Canadian French are given due attention.

Arrangement and helps

However well-chosen the content of a dictionary may be, much of its value is instantly lost if the user cannot easily and quickly find his way to the meaning that meets his needs. Conscious of how easy it is for a dictionary, especially a bilingual dictionary, to fall short of the ideal in this respect, the editors and compilers of the present work have devoted much time and thought — and not a little of their precious space — to devising and implementing a comprehensive system of indicating material.

Not only are all entries of any complexity clearly divided into separate areas of meaning, but the sense of each area is signposted by 'indicators' which immediately highlight the group of meanings in that category. In addition, variations of meaning within each category are precisely pinpointed by further indicating material attached to each sense. The *systematic* and consistent use throughout the Dictionary of indicating material, which may take the form of field labels, synonyms, typical subjects or objects of verbs, and so on, is a feature of the Dictionary to which we attach the greatest importance, as it completely supplies a want that has for long disfigured bilingual dictionaries.

One of the most insidious linguistic traps that besets the student of any foreign language is to use words or expressions inappropriate — occasionally grotesquely so — to the context of the moment. The complexities and subtleties of register, especially of social overtones, are hardly to be acquired from the printed page, but we have created for this Dictionary a range of 'style labels' that accurately characterize the stylistic restrictions that should be placed on any word or expression in the text — both in source language and in target language.

Words and expressions that are unmarked for style or register in source or target language are to be taken as standard language appropriate to any normal context or situation. Wherever this is not the case the nature of the restriction is indicated: formal, literary, US, military slang, humorous, pejorative, and so on.

In particular we gave much thought to how best to indicate the degrees of colloquialism ranging from expressions that are slightly informal through slang to those that are widely regarded as taboo. The foreign user of each language is warned by a label of one, two, or three asterisks of the degrees of care he must exercise in the use of expressions so marked. Similarly, a dagger and double dagger indicate words that are old-fashioned and obsolete.

We believe that in this system of marking language we offer the user a significant improvement on existing bilingual dictionaries.

Another feature of this Dictionary is the wealth of phrases provided within many entries. These examples greatly expand the validity of the information provided by showing how translation and sometimes structure change in different contexts and by giving examples of the idioms and set expressions relating to the headword.

The pages that follow describe these and other features of the Dictionary in greater detail.

apparat [apaʀa] *nm* **(a)** (*pompe*) pomp. **d'~** *dîner, habit, discours* ceremonial; *V* **grand. (b)** (*Littérat*) **~ critique** critical apparatus.

appareil [apaʀɛj] **1** *nm* **(a)** (*machine, instrument*) (*gén*) piece of apparatus, device; (*électrique, ménager*) appliance; (*Rad, TV: poste*) set; (*Phot*) camera; (*téléphone*) (tele)phone. **qui est à l'~?** who's speaking?; **Paul à l'~** Paul speaking.

(b) (*Aviat*) (aero)plane, aircraft.

(c) (*Méd*) (*dentier*) brace; (*pour fracture*) splint.

division claire en catégories sémantiques

(d) (*Anat*) apparatus, system. **~ digestif/urogénital** digestive/urogenital system *ou* apparatus; **~ phonateur** vocal apparatus *ou* organs (*pl*).

clear division into semantic categories

(e) (*structure administrative*) machinery. **l'~ policier** the police machinery; **l'~ du parti** the party apparatus *ou* machinery; **l'~ des lois** the machinery of the law.

(f) (*littér*) (*dehors fastueux*) air of pomp; (*cérémonie fastueuse*) ceremony. **l'~ magnifique de la royauté** the trappings *ou* splendour of royalty; *V* **simple.**

(g) (*Archit: agencement des pierres*) bond.

composés

2: appareil critique critical apparatus; **appareil de levage** lifting appliance; **appareil orthopédique** orthopaedic appliance; **appareil-photo** *nm, pl* **appareils-photos, appareil photographique** camera; **appareil à sous** (*distributeur*) slot machine; (*jeu*) fruit machine, one-armed bandit.

compound words

appareillage [apaʀɛjaʒ] *nm* **(a)** (*Naut*) (*départ*) casting off, getting under way; (*manœuvres*) preparations for casting off *ou* getting under way. **(b)** (*équipement*) equipment.

champ sémantique

appareiller [apaʀeje] (1) **1** *vi* (*Naut*) to cast off, get under way. **2** *vt* **(a)** (*Naut*) *navire* to rig, fit out. **(b)** (*Archit: tailler*) *pierre* to draft. **(c)** (*coupler*) to pair; (*assortir*) to match up; (*accoupler*) to mate (*avec* with).

field labels

apparemment [apaʀamɑ̃] *adv* apparently.

apparence [apaʀɑ̃s] *nf* **(a)** (*aspect*) *[maison, personne]* appearance, aspect. **ce bâtiment a (une) belle ~** it's a fine-looking building; **il a une ~ négligée** he is shabby-looking, he has a slovenly look about him.

(b) (*fig: extérieur*) appearance. **sous cette ~ souriante** under that smiling exterior; **sous l'~ de la générosité** under this (outward) show *ou* apparent display of generosity; **ce n'est qu'une (fausse) ~** it's a mere façade; **il ne faut pas prendre les ~s pour la réalité** one mustn't mistake appearance(s) for reality; **se fier aux/sauver les ~s** to trust/keep up appearances.

nombreux exemples

(c) (*semblant, vestige*) semblance. **il n'a plus une ~ de respect pour** he no longer has a semblance of respect for.

extensive illustrative phrases

(d) (*Philos*) appearance.

(e) (*loc*) **malgré l'~** *ou* **les ~s** in spite of appearances; **contre toute ~** against all expectations; **selon toute ~** in all probability; **en ~** apparently, seemingly, on the face of it; **des propos en ~ si contradictoires/si anodins** words apparently so contradictory/harmless; **ce n'est qu'en ~ qu'il est heureux** it's only on the surface *ou* outwardly that he's happy.

apparent, e [apaʀɑ̃, ɑ̃t] *adj* **(a)** (*visible*) *appréhension, gêne* obvious, noticeable; *ruse* obvious. **de façon ~e** visibly, conspicuously; **sans raison/cause ~e** without apparent *ou* obvious reason/cause; **plafond avec poutres ~es** ceiling with visible beams *ou* beams showing; **coutures ~es** topstitched seams.

(b) (*superficiel*) *solidité, causes, contradictions* apparent (*épith*).

apparentement [apaʀɑ̃tmɑ̃] *nm* (*Pol*) grouping of electoral lists (*in proportional representation system*).

verbes pronominaux

apparenter (s') [apaʀɑ̃te] (1) *vpr*: **s'~ à** (*Pol*) to ally o.s. with (*in elections*); (*par mariage*) to marry into; (*ressembler à*) to be similar to, have certain similarities to.

pronominal verbs

appariement [apaʀimɑ̃] *nm* (*V* **apparier**) matching; pairing; mating.

renvoi au tableau de conjugaisons

apparier [apaʀje] (7) *vt* (*littér*) (*assortir*) to match; (*coupler*) to pair; (*accoupler*) to mate.

all French verbs referred to verb tables

appariteur [apaʀitœʀ] *nm* (*Univ*) attendant (*in French Universities*). (*hum*) **~ musclé** strong-arm porter *ou* attendant (*hired at times of student unrest*).

apparition [apaʀisjɔ̃] *nf* **(a)** (*manifestation*) *[étoile, symptôme, signe]* appearance; *[personne]* appearance, arrival; *[boutons, fièvre]* outbreak. **faire son ~** *[personne]* to make one's appearance, turn up, appear; *[symptômes]* to appear; **il n'a fait qu'une ~** he only put in a brief appearance.

(b) (*vision*) apparition; (*fantôme*) apparition, spectre. **avoir des ~s** to see *ou* have visions.

anglais de Grande-Bretagne et des U.S.A.

apparoir [apaʀwaʀ] *vb impers* (*frm, hum*) **il appert (de ces résultats) que** it appears *ou* is evident (from these results) that.

British and American English

français du Canada

appartement [apaʀtəmɑ̃] *nm* **(a)** flat (*Brit*), apartment (*US*); *[hôtel]* suite; *V* **chien, plante. (b)** (*Can*) room.

French Canadian usage

indications syntaxiques

appartenance [apaʀtənɑ̃s] *nf* **(a)** *[race, famille]* belonging (*à* to), membership (*à* of); *[parti]* adherence (*à* to), membership (*à* of). (*Math*) **~ à un ensemble** membership of a set. **(b)** (*Jur*) **~s** appurtenances.

grammatical constructions

glose, lorsqu'il n'est pas possible de traduire — *explanation when no equivalent*

bob[1] [bɒb] **1** *vi* **(a)** se balancer, monter et descendre, s'agiter, sautiller; (*in the air*) pendiller. **to ~ (up and down) in** *or* **on the water** danser sur l'eau; **to ~ for apples** *essayer d'attraper avec les dents des pommes flottant sur l'eau.*
(b) (*curtsy*) faire une (petite) révérence.
2 *n* (*curtsy*) (petite) révérence *f*; (*nod*) (bref) salut *m* de tête; (*jerky movement*) petite secousse, petit coup.

verbes à particule — *phrasal verbs*

bob down *vi* **(a)** (*duck*) baisser la tête; (*straight*) se baisser subitement.
(b) (*: be quiet*) la fermer*.
bob up *vi* remonter brusquement. (*fig*) **he bobbed up again in London** il s'est repointé* à Londres.

chiffres distinguant les homographes — *superior numbers mark homographs*

bob[2]* [bɒb] *n, pl inv* (*Brit*) shilling *m.*

division claire en catégories sémantiques — *clear division into grammatical categories*

bob[3] [bɒb] **1** *n* (*curl*) boucle *f*, mèche courte; (*haircut*) coiffure courte; (*straight*) coiffure à la Jeanne d'Arc; (*horse's tail*) queue écourtée; (*weight*) *[pendulum]* poids *m*; *[plumbline]* plomb *m*; *[ribbons]* nœud *m*; (*float*) bouchon *m*; (*bait*) paquet *m* de vers.
2 *vt hair* couper court; *horse's tail* écourter.
3 *vi* (*Fishing*) pêcher à la ligne flottante.
4 *cpd*: (*US*) **bobcat** lynx *m*; **bobtail** (*tail*) queue écourtée (*V* **rag**[1]); (*horse/dog*) cheval/chien écourté; **bobtailed** à (la) queue écourtée.
bob[4] [bɒb] *n* (*sleigh: also* **~sled, ~sleigh**) bobsleigh *m*; (*runner*) patin *m.*
bobbin ['bɒbɪn] *n [thread, wire]* bobine *f*; *[sewing machine]* bobine *f*; *[lace]* fuseau *m.* **~ lace** dentelle *f* aux fuseaux.

noms propres — *proper names*

Bobby ['bɒbɪ] *n* (*dim of* **Robert**) Bobby *m.*
bobby* ['bɒbɪ] *n* flic* *m.*

anglais des U.S.A. — *American English*

bobby pin ['bɒbɪpɪn] *n* (*esp US*) pince *f* à cheveux, barrette *f.*
bobbysocks* ['bɒbɪsɒks] *n* (*US*) socquettes *fpl* (*portées par les filles*).
bock [bɒk] *n* **(a)** (*U*) bière allemande. **(b)** (*glass of beer*) bock *m.*

astérisques marquant un emploi familier — *asterisks mark informal usage*

bod* [bɒd] *n* (*Brit*) type* *m*; *V* **odd.**
bode [bəʊd] **1** *vi*: **to ~ well** être de bon augure (*for* pour); **it ~s ill (for)** cela est de mauvais augure (pour), cela ne présage rien de bon (pour). **2** *vt* présager, annoncer, augurer.
bodice ['bɒdɪs] *n* **(a)** *[dress]* corsage *m*; *[peasant's dress]* corselet *m.* **(b)** (*vest*) cache-corset *m.*

renvois — *cross references*

-bodied ['bɒdɪd] *adj ending in cpds* *V* **able, full** *etc.*
bodiless ['bɒdɪlɪs] *adj* (*lit*) sans corps; (*insubstantial*) incorporel.

transcription phonétique selon la notation de l'API — *phonetics in IPA*

bodily ['bɒdɪlɪ] **1** *adv* **(a)** (*in the flesh*) physiquement, corporellement. **they were carried ~ to the door** ils ont été portés à bras-le-corps jusqu'à la porte.
(b) (*in person*) en personne. **he appeared ~** il apparut en personne.
(c) (*all together*) tout entier, en masse.
2 *adj* (*physical*) physique, corporel, matériel; *pain* physique. **~ illness** troubles *mpl* physiques; **~ needs** *or* **wants** besoins matériels; **~ harm** blessure *f.*

croix marquant un emploi vieilli — *daggers mark older usage*

bodkin ['bɒdkɪn] *n* (*for threading tape*) passe-lacet *m*; (*for leather*) poinçon *m*; (*††: hairpin*) épingle *f* à cheveux.
body ['bɒdɪ] **1** *n* **(a)** *[man, animal]* corps *m.* **just enough to keep ~ and soul together** juste assez pour subsister; **to belong to sb ~ and soul** appartenir à qn corps et âme; *V* **sound**[2].
(b) (*corpse*) corps *m*, cadavre *m.*

indications guidant l'usager — *detailed indicating words pinpoint meaning*

(c) (*main part of structure*) *[dress]* corsage *m*, corps *m* (de robe); *[car]* carrosserie *f*; *[plane]* fuselage *m*; *[ship]* coque *f*; *[church]* nef *f*; *[speech, document]* fond *m*, corps. (*Brit Parl*) **in the ~ of the House** au centre de la Chambre.

indication du genre — *French genders marked*

(d) (*group, mass*) masse *f*, ensemble *m*, corps *m.* **~ of troops** corps de troupes; **the main ~ of the army** le gros de l'armée; **the great ~ of readers** la masse des lecteurs; **a large ~ of people** une masse de gens, une foule nombreuse; **in a ~** en masse; **taken in a ~** pris ensemble, dans leur ensemble; **the ~ politic** le corps politique; **legislative ~** corps législatif; **a large ~ of water** une grande masse d'eau; **a strong ~ of evidence** une forte accumulation de preuves.
(e) (*) (*man*) bonhomme* *m*; (*woman*) bonne femme*. **an inquisitive old ~** une vieille fouine; **a pleasant little ~** une gentille petite dame.
(f) (*Chem etc: piece of matter*) corps *m.* **heavenly ~** corps céleste; *V* **foreign.**

emploi 'non comptable' — *uncountable uses marked*

(g) (*U*) *[wine, paper]* corps *m.* **this wine has not enough ~** ce vin n'a pas assez de corps; **to give one's hair ~** donner du volume à ses cheveux.

composés — *compound words*

2 *cpd*: **bodybuilder** (*Aut*) carrossier *m*; (*food*) aliment *m* énergétique; (*apparatus*) extenseur *m*; **body-building** culturisme *m*; **body-building exercises** exercices *mpl* de culturisme *or* de musculation; **bodyguard** garde *m* du corps; **body repairs** travaux *mpl* de carrosserie; **body (repair) shop** atelier *m* de carrosserie; (*Hist*) **body snatcher** déterreur *m* de cadavres; (*Space*) **body-waste disposal** évacuation *f* des matières organiques; (*Aut*) **bodywork** carrosserie *f.*

Comment utiliser le dictionnaire

1.1 Ordre des mots Le principe général est l'ordre alphabétique. Les variantes orthographiques qui ne se suivent pas immédiatement dans l'ordre alphabétique figurent à leur place dans la nomenclature avec un renvoi à la forme qui est traitée.

khalife ... *nm* = **calife.**
callipers ... *npl* = **calipers.**

1.2 Les variantes orthographiques américaines sont traitées de la même manière.

honor ... *n* (*US*) = **honour.**

1.3 Les noms propres figurent à leur place dans l'ordre alphabétique général.

1.4 Les termes français que l'anglais a adoptés tels quels, sans changement de sens (ex.: savoir-faire), ne figurent pas en principe à la nomenclature anglaise. Ils sont traités lorsqu'il s'est produit un glissement sémantique (ex.: table d'hôte).

1.5 Les homographes sont suivis d'un chiffre qui permet de les distinguer, ex.: **raie**[1], **raie**[2]; **blow**[1], **blow**[2].

2.1 Les composés Pour les besoins de ce dictionnaire, le terme 'composé' regroupe non seulement les mots formés de termes reliés par un trait d'union (ex.: camion-citerne, arrière-pensée, body-building), mais également les expressions anglaises formées à l'aide de noms adjectivés (ex.: boat train, freedom fighter) ou d'autres collocations similaires figées par la langue (ex.: grand ensemble, modèle déposé, air traffic control, ear nose and throat specialist). Ils sont rassemblés et traités dans une catégorie à part suivant un ordre strictement alphabétique.

2.2 Les composés français formés de termes soudés sont considérés comme mots à part entière et traités selon l'ordre alphabétique général (ex.: portemanteau, portefeuille). Les composés anglais formés de termes soudés figurent dans la catégorie des composés et ne font pas l'objet d'articles séparés (ex.: bodyguard); toutefois les vocables formés avec un suffixe (ex.: childhood, friendship) sont traités dans la nomenclature à leur place alphabétique normale.

2.3 Les composés français formés à l'aide de préfixes d'origine verbale sont en général regroupés sous le verbe

lave- ... *préf V* **laver.**

et à l'article laver

laver ... **3: lave-glace**

2.4 Dans la nomenclature anglaise, la catégorie

Using the Dictionary

1.1 Word Order Alphabetical order is followed throughout. If two variant spellings are not alphabetically adjacent each is treated as a separate headword and there is a cross-reference to the form treated in depth.

1.2 American variations in spelling are treated in the same fashion.

1.3 Proper names will be found in their alphabetical place in the word list.

1.4 French words which have been adopted in English (eg savoir-faire) are not normally included in the English word list if their meaning and usage is the same in both languages. Where these differ however (eg table d'hôte) the word is treated in full.

1.5 Superior numbers are used to separate words of like spelling, eg **raie**[1], **raie**[2]; **blow**[1], **blow**[2].

2.1 Compounds and set phrases For the purposes of this dictionary the term 'compound' is taken to cover not only solid and hyphenated compounds (eg camion-citerne, arrière-pensée, body-building), but also attributive uses of English nouns (eg boat train, freedom fighter), and other collocations which function in a similar way (eg grand ensemble, modèle déposé, air traffic control, ear nose and throat specialist). All of the above are normally treated in the compound section of the entry in alphabetical order.

2.2 Solid compounds in French (eg portefeuille, portemanteau) are treated as headwords. Solid compounds in English (eg bodyguard) are normally treated in the compound section. However English words of the pattern *full word* + *suffix* (eg childhood, friendship) are not considered to be compounds: these are treated as headwords.

2.3 French compounds of the pattern *verb root* + *noun* generally occur under the verb

lave- ... *préf V* **laver.**

and in the entry for laver

laver ... **3: lave-glace**

2.4 In English parts of speech are indicated for

grammaticale des composés est donnée lorsqu'elle n'est pas évidente ou que la forme composée appartient à plusieurs catégories grammaticales.

compounds in cases where the user might otherwise be confused.

daredevil (*n*) casse-cou *m inv* ...; (*adj*) *behaviour* de casse-cou; *adventure* fou (*f* folle) ...

Pour le français, la catégorie grammaticale et s'il y a lieu le genre des composés avec trait d'union sont donnés; ils sont aussi indiqués lorsqu'il y a risque d'erreur ou lorsque le terme traité appartient à plusieurs catégories grammaticales.

In French the part of speech, and if appropriate the gender, is given for all hyphenated compounds. It will also be given of course when the compound has several grammatical categories or if there is any risk of confusion.

2.5 Lorsque, pour des raisons pratiques, un composé anglais a été traité comme mot à part entière et doit être cherché à sa place dans la liste alphabétique générale, un renvoi prévient le lecteur.

2.5 When for practical reasons an English compound is treated as a headword in its alphabetical place, a cross-reference always makes this plain.

house ... **2** *cpd* ... **housewife** *V* **housewife**;

2.6 Les composés sont placés sous le premier élément, 'grand ensemble' sous grand, 'pont d'envol' sous pont, 'freedom fighter' sous freedom, 'general post office' sous general. Lorsque pour des raisons pratiques ce principe n'a pas été appliqué, un renvoi prévient le lecteur.

2.6 Compounds are placed under the first element, 'grand ensemble' under grand, 'pont d'envol' under pont, 'freedom fighter' under freedom, 'general post office' under general. Where for practical reasons an exception has been made to this rule a cross-reference alerts the user.

2.7 Les formules figées et les expressions idiomatiques figurent sous le premier terme qui reste inchangé, quelles que soient les modifications que l'on apporte à l'expression en question.

'Monter sur ses grands chevaux' et 'monter un bateau à quelqu'un' sont traités sous **monter**. 'Savoir quelque chose sur le bout du doigt' est placé sous **bout** parce que l'on peut dire également 'connaître quelque chose sur le bout du doigt'.
Lorsque ce principe a été abandonné, un renvoi prévient l'utilisateur.

2.7 Set phrases and idiomatic expressions are also placed under the first element or the first word in the phrase which remains constant despite minor variations in the phrase itself.

'To break somebody's heart' and 'to break a record' are both included under **break**. 'To lend somebody a hand' is however under **hand** because it is equally possible to say 'to give somebody a hand'.
Where this 'first element' principle has been abandoned a cross-reference alerts the user.

2.8 Un certain nombre de verbes français et anglais servent à former un très grand nombre de locutions verbales.

2.8 Certain very common French and English verbs form the basis of a very large number of phrases.

faire honneur à, faire du ski, faire la tête, etc.
to make sense of something, to make an appointment, to make a mistake, etc.

En pareil cas l'expression figurera sous le second élément: 'faire la tête' sous **tête**, 'to make sense of something' sous **sense**.
La liste qui suit indique les verbes que nous avons considérés comme 'vides' à cet égard:
en français: avoir, être, faire, donner, mettre, passer, porter, prendre, remettre, reprendre, tenir, tirer.
en anglais: be, become, come, do, get, give, go, have, lay, make, put, set, take.

We have considered such verbs to have a diminished meaning and in such cases the set phrases will be found under the second element, eg 'faire la tête' under **tête**, 'to make sense of something' under **sense**.
The following is a list of the verbs which we consider to have such a diminished meaning content:
French—avoir, être, faire, donner, mettre, passer, porter, prendre, remettre, reprendre, tenir, tirer.
English—be, become, come, do, get, give, go, have, lay, make, put, set, take.

3.1 Répétition du mot dans l'article Par souci d'économie de place, le mot est remplacé par le signe ~ lorsqu'il est répété dans le corps de l'article sans subir de modification orthographique.

3.1 Repetition of the headword within the entry To save space, where the headword occurs in its full form within the entry it is replaced by ~.

age ... **she stayed for ~s**
carry ... **to ~ the can** ... *but* **he carried his audience with him**

3.2 Les verbes conjugués français sont repris en toutes lettres (ex.: porter ... il porte ... ils porteront), ainsi que les composés dans les deux langues et que les verbes anglais à particule.

3.2 Inflected forms of French verbs are shown in full (eg porter ... il porte ... ils porteront), as are compounds in both languages and phrasal verbs in English.

4.1 Pluriel Les formes plurielles qui présentent des difficultés sont données dans la langue de départ.

4.1 Plurals Irregular plural forms of English words are given in the English-French side, those of French words and compounds in the French-English side.

4.2 En français, les pluriels autres que ceux qui se forment par le simple ajout du *-s* sont indiqués ex. cheval, -aux; celui des composés avec trait d'union est toujours donné.

4.2 In French, all plurals which do not consist of *headword* + *s* are shown, eg cheval, -aux. The plural form of hyphenated compounds is always given.

4.3 En anglais, les pluriels formés régulièrement ne sont pas donnés.
4.3.1 La plupart des noms prennent *-s* au pluriel: *bed-s, site-s.*
4.3.2 Les noms se terminant par *-s, -x, -z, -sh* et *-ch* [tʃ] prennent *-es* au pluriel: *boss-es, box-es, dish-es, patch-es.*
4.3.3 Les noms se terminant par *-y* non précédé d'une voyelle changent au pluriel le *-y* en *-ies*: *lady-ladies, berry-berries* (mais *tray-s, key-s*).

4.3 In English a knowledge of the basic rules is assumed.
4.3.1 Most English nouns take *-s* in the plural: *bed-s, site-s.*
4.3.2 Nouns that end in *-s, -x, -z, -sh* and some in *-ch* [tʃ] take *-es* in the plural: *boss-es, box-es, dish-es, patch-es.*
4.3.3 Nouns that end in *-y* not preceded by a vowel change the *-y* to *-ies* in the plural: *lady-ladies, berry-berries* (but *tray-s, key-s*).

4.4 Quand le pluriel d'un mot est très différent du singulier, il figure à sa place dans la nomenclature générale avec un renvoi; il est répété sous le singulier.

4.4 Plural forms of the headword which differ substantially from the singular form are listed in their alphabetical place in the word list with a cross-reference, and repeated under the singular form.

yeux ... *nmpl de* **œil.**
œil, *pl* **yeux** ... *nm*
children ... *npl of* **child.**
child, *pl* **children** ... *n*

4.5 Dans la partie anglais-français, seul le pluriel invariable des mots français est indiqué.

4.5 French invariable plurals are marked on the English-French side for ease of reference.

5.1 Genre Les formes féminines des mots français qui ne suivent pas directement le masculin dans l'ordre alphabétique sont données à leur place normale dans la nomenclature, avec un renvoi au masculin; elles sont répétées sous celui-ci.

5.1 Genders Feminine forms in French which are separated alphabetically from the masculine form in the word list are shown as separate headwords with a cross-reference to the masculine form.

belle ... *V* **beau.**

5.2 Un mot féminin exigeant une traduction différente du masculin fait l'objet soit d'un article séparé

5.2 A feminine headword requiring a different translation from its masculine form is given either a separate entry

chien ... *nm* ... dog.
chienne ... *nf* bitch.
coiffeur ... *nm [dames]* hairdresser; *[hommes]* hairdresser, barber.
coiffeuse ... *nf* (*personne*) hairdresser; (*meuble*) ...

soit d'une catégorie bien individualisée dans le cas d'articles complexes.

or a separate category in the case of complex entries.

cadet, -ette … **1** *adj* … **2** *nm* … **3 cadette** *nf*

5.3 Dans la partie anglais-français, le féminin des adjectifs français se construisant régulièrement n'est pas indiqué. Sont considérées comme régulières les formes suivantes:

5.3 In the English-French side of the dictionary the feminine forms of French adjectives are given only where these are not regular. The following are considered regular adjective inflections:

-, e; -ef, -ève; -eil, -eille; -er, -ère; -et, -ette; -eur, -euse; -eux, -euse; -ien, -ienne; -ier, -ière; -if, -ive; -il, -ille; -on, -onne; -ot, -otte.

Par contre quand un nom anglais peut recevoir une traduction au masculin ou au féminin, selon le sexe, la forme du féminin est toujours mentionnée.

When the translation of an English noun could be either masculine or feminine, according to sex, the feminine form of the French noun translation is always given.

singer … *n* chanteur *m*, -euse *f*.

5.4 Dans la partie anglais-français, le genre d'un nom français n'est pas spécifié quand l'adjectif ou l'article qui accompagne celui-ci le rend évident.

5.4 In the English-French side of the dictionary the gender of a French noun is not specified where this is made clear by an accompanying adjective or definite or indefinite article.

airline ligne aérienne

empty threats menaces vaines

6.1 Les indications guidant le lecteur sont imprimées en italiques et prennent les formes suivantes.

6.1 General indicating material in the dictionary is printed in italics and takes the following forms.

6.2 Entre parenthèses ( )

6.2 In parentheses ( )

6.2.1 Les synonymes et définitions partielles.

6.2.1 Synonyms and partial definitions.

décent, e … *adj* (*bienséant*) decent, proper; (*discret, digne*) proper; (*acceptable*) reasonable, decent.

dyke … *n* (*channel*) fosse *m*; (*wall, barrier*) digue *f*; (*causeway*) levée *f*, chaussée *f*; …

6.2.2 Les autres précisions et explications susceptibles de guider l'usager.

6.2.2 Other information and hints which guide the user.

décaper … *vt* (*gén*) to clean, cleanse; (*à l'abrasif*) to scour; … (*à la brosse*) to scrub; …

employment … *n* … (*a job*) emploi *m*, travail *m*; (*modest*) place *f*; (*important*) situation *f*.

6.2.3 Les indications d'ordre grammatical permettant au lecteur étranger d'utiliser le mot correctement. Elles sont données après la traduction.

6.2.3 Syntactical information to allow the non-native speaker to use the word correctly. This is given after the translation.

différer … *vi* … to differ, be different (*de* from, *en, par* in).

dissimuler … *vt* … to conceal, hide (*à qn* from sb).

order … *vt* … ordonner (*sb to do* à qn de faire).

6.3 Entre crochets [ ]

6.3 In square brackets [ ]

6.3.1 Dans un article traitant un verbe, les noms sujets éclairant le sens.

6.3.1 Within verb entries, typical noun subjects of the headword.

décroître … *vi [nombre, population]* to decrease, diminish, decline; … *[eaux, crue]* to subside, go down; *[popularité]* to decline, drop; …

fade … *vi [flower]* se faner, se flétrir; *[light]* baisser, diminuer, s'affaiblir; *[colour]* passer, perdre son éclat; *[material]* passer, se décolorer; …

6.3.2 Dans un article traitant un nom, les noms compléments.

6.3.2 Within noun entries, typical noun complements of the headword.

défiguration ... *nf [vérité]* distortion; *[texte, tableau]* mutilation; *[visage]* disfigurement.

branch ... *n* ... *[tree]* branche *f*; ... *[mountain chain]* ramification *f*; ... *[subject, science etc]* branche.

[vérité] doit se lire 'de la vérité'.

In such instances *[tree]* should be read as 'of tree'.

6.4 Sans parenthèses

6.4 Unbracketed indicating material

6.4.1 Les compléments d'objet des verbes transitifs.

6.4.1 Typical objects of transitive verbs.

défaire ... *vt* ... *couture, tricot* to undo, unpick; *écheveau* to undo, unravel; *corde, nœud, ruban* to undo, untie; *valise, bagages* to unpack.

impair ... *vt abilities, faculties* détériorer, diminuer; *negotiations, relations* porter atteinte à; *health* abîmer, détériorer; *sight, hearing* affaiblir, abîmer; ...

6.4.2 Les noms que peut qualifier l'adjectif.

6.4.2 Typical noun complements of adjectives.

élancé, e ... *adj clocher, colonne, taille* slender.

distinct ... *adj landmark, voice, memory* distinct, clair, net; *promise, offer* précis, formel; *preference, likeness* marqué, net; ...

6.4.3 Les verbes ou adjectifs modifiés par l'adverbe.

6.4.3 Typical verb or adjective complements of adverbs.

bien ... *adv* ... (*de façon satisfaisante*) *jouer, dormir, travailler* well; *conseiller, choisir* well, wisely; *fonctionner* properly, well.

briskly ... *adv move* vivement; *walk* d'un bon pas; *speak* brusquement; *act* sans tarder.

6.5 Le symbole *U* signifie 'non comptable'. Il est utilisé pour indiquer qu'un nom ne s'emploie pas normalement au pluriel et ne se construit pas, en règle générale, avec l'article indéfini ou un numéral. Ce symbole a pour but d'avertir le lecteur étranger dans les cas où celui-ci risquerait d'employer le mot de manière incorrecte; mais notre propos n'est nullement de donner une liste exhaustive de ces mots en anglais. Ce symbole est parfois utilisé comme indication dans la langue de départ, lorsque c'est le seul moyen de distinguer emplois 'non comptables' et 'comptables'.

6.5 The symbol *U* stands for 'uncountable' and serves to mark nouns which are not normally used in the plural or with the indefinite article or with numerals. The symbol occurs only as a warning device in cases where a non-native speaker might otherwise use the word wrongly. There has been no attempt to give an exhaustive account of 'uncountability' in English. The symbol has also been used as an indicator to distinguish meanings in the source language.

astuce ... *nf* **(a)** (*U*) shrewdness, astuteness. **(b)** (*moyen, truc*) (clever) way, trick.

clignement ... *nm* ... blinking (*U*).

bracken ... *n* (*U*) fougère *f*.

implement ... *n* ... **~s** (*U*) équipement *m* (*U*), matériel *m*.

6.6 Le symbole *T* signifie 'terme de spécialiste'.

6.6 The symbol *T* stands for 'technical term'.

tympan ... *nm* eardrum, tympanum (*T*).

Cela veut dire que le mot anglais d'usage courant est 'eardrum' et que 'tympanum' ne se rencontre que dans le vocabulaire des spécialistes.

This indicates that the common English word is 'eardrum' and that 'tympanum' is restricted to the vocabulary of specialists.

6.7 ≃ introduit une équivalence culturelle,

6.7 ≃ is used when the source language head-

lorsque ce que représente le terme de la langue de départ n'existe pas ou n'a pas d'équivalent exact dans la langue d'arrivée, et n'est donc pas à proprement parler traduisible.

word or phrase has no equivalent in the target language and is therefore untranslatable. In such cases the nearest cultural equivalent is given.

borne ... *nf* ... (*kilométrique*) kilometre-marker, ≃ **milestone.**

the Health Service ≃ la Sécurité sociale.

Une glose explicative accompagne généralement l'équivalent culturel choisi; elle peut être donnée seule lorsqu'il n'existe pas d'équivalent culturel assez proche dans la langue d'arrivée.

Sometimes it is accompanied by an explanatory gloss (in italics). Such a gloss may be given alone in cases where there is no cultural equivalent in the target language.

image d'Épinal (*lit*) *popular 18th or 19th century print depicting traditional scenes of French life.*

Yorkshire pudding *pâte à crêpe cuite qui accompagne un rôti de bœuf.*

6.8 On a eu recours aux petites majuscules pour indiquer, dans certaines expressions anglaises, l'accent d'insistance qui rend, ou requiert, une nuance particulière du français.

6.8 Small capitals are used to indicate the spoken stress in certain English expressions.

mais enfin! je viens de te le dire! but I've just TOLD you!

I know HER but I've never seen HIM je la connais, elle, mais lui je ne l'ai jamais vu.

7.1 Les champs sémantiques sont mentionnés dans les cas suivants:

7.1 Field labels occur in such cases as the following:

7.1.1 Pour indiquer les différents sens d'un terme et introduire les traductions appropriées.

7.1.1 To differentiate various meanings of the headword.

cuirasse ... *nf* (*Hist*) [*chevalier*] cuirass, breastplate; (*Naut*) armour (-plate *ou* -plating); (*Zool*) cuirass.

eagle ... *n* (*Orn*) aigle *mf* (*gen m*); (*Rel: lectern*) aigle *m*; (*Her, Hist, Mil*) aigle *f*; (*Golf*) eagle *m*.

7.1.2 Quand le terme de la langue de départ n'est pas ambigu, mais que la traduction peut l'être.

7.1.2 When the meaning in the departure language is clear but may be ambiguous in the target language.

comprimé ... *nm* (*Pharm*) tablet.

parabola ... *n* parabole *f* (*Math*).

7.2 La liste des champs sémantiques apparaissant sous forme abrégée figure à la page xxviii.

7.2 A full list of the abbreviated field labels is given on page xxviii.

8.1 Niveaux de langue Les mots et expressions qui ne sont pas stylistiquement neutres ont été indiqués suivant deux registres.

(i) de la langue soutenue à la langue familière
(ii) style littéraire, langue vieillie ou archaïque

Ces indications sont données aussi bien dans la langue de départ que dans la langue d'arrivée, et constituent avant tout un avertissement au lecteur utilisant la langue étrangère.

8.1 Style labels All words and phrases which are not standard language have been labelled according to two separate registers.

(i) formal and informal usage
(ii) old-fashioned and literary usage

This labelling is given for both source and target languages and serves primarily to provide a warning to the non-native speaker.

8.2 Langue soutenue et langue familière

8.2 Formal and informal usage

8.2.1 *frm* indique le style administratif, les formules officielles, la langue soignée.

8.2.1 ***frm*** **denotes formal language such as that used on official forms, in pronouncements and other formal communications.**

agréer ... (*frm*) **1** *vt* (*accepter*) *excuses* to accept.

(*frm*) **heretofore** jusque-là, jusqu'ici, ci-devant.

8.2.2 * marque la majeure partie des expressions familières et les incorrections de langage employées dans la langue de tous les jours. Ce signe conseille au lecteur d'être prudent.

8.2.2 * indicates that the expression, while not forming part of standard language, is used by all educated speakers in a relaxed situation but would not be used in a formal essay or letter, or on an occasion when the speaker wishes to impress.

charabia* ... *nm* gibberish, gobbledygook*.
c'est du gâteau* it's a piece of cake* (*Brit*), it's a walkover*.
to make a bolt for it* filer* *or* se sauver à toutes jambes.
he's pretty hot* at football il est très calé en foot*.

8.2.3 ‡ marque les expressions très familières qui sont à employer avec la plus grande prudence par le lecteur étranger, qui devra posséder une grande maîtrise de la langue et savoir dans quel contexte elles peuvent être utilisées.

8.2.3 ‡ indicates that the expression is used by some but not all educated speakers in a very relaxed situation. Such words should be handled with extreme care by the non-native speaker unless he is very fluent in the language and is very sure of his company.

se faire pigeonner‡ to be done‡, be taken for a ride‡, be had‡.
bigwig‡ grosse légume‡, huile‡ *f*.

8.2.4 ☠ marque le petit nombre d'expressions courantes que le lecteur étranger doit pouvoir reconnaître, mais dont l'emploi est ressenti comme fortement indécent ou injurieux.

8.2.4 ☠ means 'Danger!' Such words are either 'swear words' or highly indecent or offensive expressions which should be avoided by the non-native speaker.

baiser ... *vt* ... **(b)**(☠) to screw☠.
you bloody fool!☠ espèce de con!☠

8.3 Style littéraire et langue vieillie ou archaïque

8.3 Old-fashioned and literary usage

8.3.1 † marque les termes ou expressions démodés, qui ont quitté l'usage courant mais que l'étranger peut encore rencontrer au cours de ses lectures.

8.3.1 † denotes old-fashioned terms which are no longer in wide current use but which the foreign user will certainly find in reading.

indéfrisable† ... *nf* perm.
beau† ... *n* (*dandy*) élégant *m*, dandy *m*.

8.3.2 †† marque les termes ou expressions archaïques, que le lecteur ne rencontrera en principe que dans les œuvres classiques.

8.3.2 †† denotes obsolete words which the user will normally find only in classical literature.

gageure ... *nf* ... **(b)** (††: *pari*) wager.
burthen†† ... = **burden.**

On évitera de confondre ces signes avec l'indication *Hist*, qui ne marque pas le niveau de langue du mot lui-même (*signifiant*) mais souligne que l'objet désigné (*signifié*) ne se rencontre que dans un contexte historiquement daté.

The use of † and †† should not be confused with the label *Hist. Hist* does not apply to the expression itself (*signifiant*) but denotes the historical context of the object so named (*signifié*).

ordalie ... *nf* (*Hist*) ordeal.

8.3.3 *littér, liter* marquent les expressions de style poétique ou littéraire.

8.3.3 *liter, littér* denote an expression which belongs to literary or poetic language.

ostentatoire ... *adj* (*littér*) ostentatious.
beseech ... *vt* (*liter*) **(a)** (*ask for*) ... **(b)** (*entreat*) ...

Le lecteur veillera à ne pas confondre ces indications avec (*lit*) d'une part (sens propre, emploi littéral) et *Littérat*, *Literat* de l'autre (domaine de la littérature).

The user should not confuse the style labels *liter, littér* with the field labels *Literat, Littérat* which indicate that the expression belongs to the field of literature. Similarly the user should note that the abbreviation *lit* indicates the literal, as opposed to the figurative, meaning of a word.

8.4 Les indications *arg* (argot) et *sl* (slang) désignent les termes appartenant au vocabulaire de groupes restreints (tels que les écoliers, les militaires) et l'indication du champ sémantique approprié leur est adjoint dans la langue de départ.

8.4 For the purpose of this dictionary the indicators *sl* (slang) and *arg* (argot) mark specific areas of vocabulary restricted to clearly defined groups of speakers (eg schoolchildren, soldiers, etc) and for this reason a field label is added to the label *sl* or *arg* marking the departure language expression.

(*arg Drogue*) **se camer** to get high (*arg*)
(*Mil sl*) **glasshouse** trou *m* (*sl*)

8.5 Les indications de niveau de langue peuvent soit s'attacher à un terme ou à une expression isolés, soit marquer une catégorie entière ou même un article complet.

8.5 The labels and symbols above are used to mark either an individual word or phrase, or a whole category, or even a complete entry.

9.1 Ponctuation Une virgule sépare les traductions qui sont considérées comme étant pratiquement équivalentes, alors qu'un point-virgule indique un changement notable de sens.

9.1. Punctuation In a list of equivalents in the target language a comma is used to separate translations which have very similar senses, whereas a semi-colon indicates a distinct shift in meaning.

gamin, e ... *adj* (*espiègle*) mischievous, playful; (*puéril*) childish.
bill[1] ... *n* (*account*) note *f*, facture *f*; (*esp Brit*) *[restaurant]* addition *f*; *[hotel]* note.

9.2 Dans la traduction d'expressions, les variantes correspondant à l'expression entière sont séparées par une virgule; celles qui ne correspondent qu'à une partie de l'expression à traduire peuvent suivre ou précéder un tronc commun, et sont alors séparées par *ou* ou par *or*.

9.2 In the translation of phrases a comma separates two possible translations of the whole phrase, an alternative translation of only part of the phrase being preceded by the word *or* or *ou*.

se tenir à distance to keep one's distance, stand aloof
il n'a pas dit un mot he hasn't said *ou* spoken *ou* uttered a (single) word
from an early age dès l'enfance, de bonne heure
in his early youth dans sa première *or* prime jeunesse

9.3 Le trait oblique / permet de regrouper des expressions de sens différent ayant un élément en commun, lorsque cette structure est reflétée dans la langue d'arrivée.

9.3 An oblique / indicates alternatives in the departure language which are reflected exactly in the target language.

to run in/out/past entrer/sortir/passer en courant

9.4 Les parenthèses figurant à l'intérieur des expressions ou de leur traduction indiquent que les mots qu'elles contiennent sont facultatifs.

9.4 Parentheses within illustrative phrases or their translations indicate that the material so contained is optional.

dans les limites de mes moyens within (the limits of) my means
at an early hour (of the morning) à une heure matinale

Ces parenthèses peuvent figurer en corrélation.

Such parentheses may be given for phrases in both source and target language.

faire ses achats (de Noël) to do one's (Christmas) shopping

10.1 Les renvois sont utilisés dans les cas suivants:

10.1.1 Pour éviter d'avoir à répéter un ensemble

10.1 Cross-references are used in the following instances:

10.1.1 To avoid repeating indicating material

d'indications, lorsqu'un mot a été traité en profondeur et que ses dérivés ont des divisions de sens correspondantes. Ceci se produit notamment pour les adverbes dérivés d'adjectifs et les nominalisations (voir aussi 11.3).

where one word has been treated in depth and derivatives of that word have corresponding semantic divisions, eg adverbs which are cross-referred to adjectives, nouns which are cross-referred to verbs (see also para 11.3).

diffuser ... *vt lumière, chaleur* to diffuse; *bruit, idée* to spread (abroad), circulate, diffuse; *livres* to distribute; *émission* to broadcast.

diffusion ... *nf* (*V* **diffuser**) diffusion; spreading; circulation; distribution; broadcast.

10.1.2 Pour renvoyer le lecteur à l'article dans lequel est traitée une certaine expression, où figure un certain composé.

10.1.2 To refer the user to the headword under which a certain compound or idiom has been treated (see para 2 above).

10.1.3 Pour attirer l'attention de l'usager sur certains mots-clés qui ont été traités en profondeur: pour les numéraux, six, sixième et soixante; pour les jours de la semaine, samedi; pour les mois de l'année, septembre. Dans la nomenclature anglaise, ce seront les mots six, sixth, sixty, Saturday, September.

10.1.3 To draw the user's attention to the full treatment of such words as numerals, days of the week, and months of the year under certain key words. The key words which have been treated in depth are: French - six, sixième, soixante, samedi, septembre. English - six, sixth, sixty, Saturday, September.

Friday ... *for other phrases V* **Saturday**.
vendredi ... *pour autres loc V* **samedi**.

11.1 Verbes Les tables de conjugaison des verbes français et anglais sont données en annexe, aux pages 758 et 773. Dans la nomenclature française, chaque verbe est suivi d'un numéro entre parenthèses qui renvoie le lecteur à ces tables. Les formes passées des verbes forts anglais sont données après le verbe dans le corps de l'article.

11.1 Verbs Tables of French and English verbs are included in the supplements on pages 758 and 773. At each verb headword in the French-English side of the dictionary, a number in parentheses refers the user to these verb tables. Parts of English strong verbs are given at the main verb entry.

11.2 Dans la partie français-anglais, les emplois véritablement pronominaux des verbes sont traités dans une catégorie à part.

11.2 In the French-English part of the dictionary verbs which are true pronominals are treated in a separate grammatical category.

baisser ... **3 se baisser** *vpr* (*pour ramasser qch*) to bend down, stoop; (*pour éviter qch*) to duck.

Les emplois pronominaux à valeur réciproque, réfléchie ou passive, ne figurent que lorsque la traduction l'exige. En pareil cas, ils peuvent être simplement donnés dans la catégorie appropriée du verbe transitif, à titre d'exemple.

Pronominal uses which indicate a reciprocal, reflexive or passive sense are shown only if the translation requires it. In such cases they may be given within the transitive category of the verb as an illustrative phrase.

grandir ... *vt* ... (*faire paraître grand*) ... **ces chaussures te grandissent** those shoes make you (look) taller; **il se grandit en se mettant sur la pointe des pieds** he made himself taller by standing on tiptoe.

11.3 Les nominalisations des verbes français (mots en *-age, -ation, -ement* etc) reçoivent souvent des traductions qui ne sont données qu'à titre indicatif; ces traductions doivent être utilisées avec prudence, l'usager étant supposé savoir que dans de nombreux cas une construction verbale est plus courante en anglais.

11.3 French nouns formed from the *verb root* + *-ation* or *-age* or *-ement* etc are sometimes given only token translations. These translations must be treated with care by the user, who is assumed to know that in many cases a verbal construction is more common in English.

11.4 Si la traduction d'un participe passé ne peut se déduire directement à partir du verbe, ou si le participe a pris une valeur adjective, il est traité comme mot à part entière et figure à sa place alphabétique dans la nomenclature.

11.4 If the translation of a past participle cannot be reached directly from the verb entry or if the past participle has adjectival value then the past participle is treated as a headword.

étendu, e ... (*ptp de* **étendre**) **1** *adj* **(a)** (*vaste*) ... **(b)** (*allongé*) ...

broken ... **1** *ptp of* **break. 2** *adj* **(a)** (*lit*) cassé, brisé; ... **(b)** (*uneven*) ...; **(c)** (*interrupted*) ...; **(d)** (*spoilt, ruined*) ...

11.5 Les verbes anglais à particule sont divisés en trois catégories: l'une pour les verbes intransitifs, les deux autres pour les verbes à fonction transitive.

11.5 Phrasal verbs in English have been treated in three grammatical categories: one intransitive and two transitive.

11.5.1 Verbes à fonction intransitive: *vi*

11.5.1 Intransitive: *vi*

boil over *vi* **(a)** *[water]* déborder; *[milk]* se sauver, déborder. **the kettle boiled over** (l'eau dans) la bouilloire a débordé. **(b)** (*: *with rage*) bouillir (*with* de).

11.5.2 Verbes à fonction transitive: *vt sep*

11.5.2 Transitive: *vt sep*

block up *vt sep gangway* encombrer; *pipe* bloquer, obstruer; *window, entrance* murer, condamner; *hole* boucher, bloquer.

vt sep (= séparable) indique que le complément d'objet s'il s'agit d'un nom peut s'insérer entre le verbe et sa particule, ceci étant la place obligatoire d'un pronom objet: 'the rubbish *blocked* the pipe *up*', 'the rubbish *blocked up* the pipe', 'the rubbish *blocked* it *up*', mais jamais 'the rubbish *blocked up* it'.

vt sep (= separable) shows that the object of the verb, if a noun, may be inserted between the two parts of the phrasal verb: 'the rubbish *blocked* the pipe *up*', 'the rubbish *blocked up* the pipe'. On the other hand if the object is a pronoun it must be placed between the two parts of the phrasal verb: 'the rubbish *blocked* it *up*', never 'the rubbish blocked up it'.

11.5.3 Verbes à fonction transitive: *vt fus*

11.5.3 Transitive: *vt fus*

break into *vt fus* **(a)** (*enter illegally*) *house* entrer par effraction dans ... **(b)** (*use part of*) *savings* entamer ... **(c)** (*begin suddenly*) commencer à, se mettre à ...

vt fus (= fusionné) indique que le complément d'objet, qu'il soit nom ou pronom, suit obligatoirement la particule: 'he *broke into* the safe easily', 'he *broke into* it easily', mais jamais 'he *broke* it *into* easily'. Quelques *vt fus* sont composés de trois éléments: 'to *come up with* a good idea' etc.

vt fus (= fused) shows that the object of the verb, whether noun or pronoun, must follow the second element of the phrasal verb: 'he *broke into* the safe easily', 'he *broke into* it easily', never 'he broke it into easily'. Some *vt fus* phrasal verbs have three elements: 'to *come up with* a good idea' etc.

11.5.4 Lorsqu'un verbe à particule s'utilise exactement comme le verbe simple, dans un sens donné, il figure normalement dans la catégorie appropriée du verbe simple.

11.5.4 Where the phrasal verb form in all its usages is identical in meaning to one category of the main verb it is normally included in the main verb.

bandage ... **2** *vt* (*also* ~ **up**) *broken limb* bander; *wound* mettre un pansement sur; *person* mettre un pansement *or* un bandage à.

11.5.5 Lorsque le verbe présente un certain nombre de formes à particule du type *verbe + adverbe de direction*, celles-ci ne sont pas traitées dans un article indépendant mais figurent en général sous la catégorie *vt* ou *vi* du verbe simple.

11.5.5 When the phrasal verb consists simply of *verb + adverb of direction* it will normally be treated under the main headword in the *vi* or *vt* category.

dash ... *vi* **(a)** (*rush*) se précipiter, filer*. **to ~ away/back/up** *etc* s'en aller/revenir/monter *etc* à toute allure *or* en coup de vent ...

Comme il est possible de former de nombreux verbes de cette façon, ces formes composées ne sont pas toutes données.

This layout must be taken to mean that other directional phrasal verbs may be formed in similar fashion, eg 'to dash across', 'to dash round', 'to dash through' etc.

PRONUNCIATION OF FRENCH

1.1 Transcription The symbols used to record the pronunciation of French are those of the International Phonetic Association. The variety of French transcribed is that shown in *Le Robert*, i.e. standard Parisian speech. Within this variety of French, variant pronunciations are to be observed. In particular, there is a marked tendency among speakers today to make no appreciable distinction between: [a] and [ɑ], *patte* [pat] and *pâte* [pɑt] both tending towards the pronunciation [pat]; [ɛ̃] and [œ̃], *brin* [bʀɛ̃] and *brun* [bʀœ̃] both tending towards the pronunciation [bʀɛ̃]. The distinction between these sounds is maintained in the transcription.

1.2 Headwords Each headword is transcribed with its pronunciation between square brackets. In the case of words having a variant pronunciation (e.g. *tandis* [tɑ̃di], [tɑ̃dis]), the one pronunciation given is that regarded by the editorial team as preferable, often on grounds of frequency.

1.3 Morphological variations of headwords are shown phonetically where necessary, without repetition of the root (e.g. *journal*, pl *-aux* [ʒuʀnal, o]).

1.4 Compound words derived from headwords and shown within an entry are given without phonetic transcription (e.g. *passer* [pɑse], but *passe-lacet, passe-montagne*). The pronunciation of compounds is usually predictable, being that of the citation form of each element, associated with the final syllable stress characteristic of the language (see following paragraph).

1.5 Syllable stress In normal, unemphatic speech, the final syllable of a word, or the final syllable of a sense group, carries a moderate degree of stress. The syllable stressed is given extra prominence by greater length and intensity. The exception to this rule is a final syllable containing a mute *e*, which is never stressed. In view of this simple rule, it has not been considered necessary to indicate the position of a stressed syllable of a word by a stress mark in the phonetic transcription.

1.6 Vowel length As vowel length is not a discriminating factor in French, the length mark (ː) has not been used in transcription.

1.7 Closing of [ɛ] Under the influence of stressed [y], [i], or [e] vowels, an [ɛ] in an open syllable tends towards a closer [e] sound, even in careful speech. In such cases, the change has been indicated: *aimant* [ɛmɑ̃], but *aimer* [eme]; *bête* [bɛt], but *bêtise* [betiz].

1.8 Opening of [e] As the result of the dropping of an [ə] within a word, an [e] may occur in a closed syllable. If so, it tends towards [ɛ], as the transcription shows (e.g. *événement* [evɛnmɑ̃]; *élevage* [ɛlvaʒ]).

1.9 Mute e [ə] Within isolated words, a mute *e* [ə] preceded by a single pronounced consonant is regularly dropped (e.g. *follement* [fɔlmɑ̃]; *samedi* [samdi]). In connected speech, the possible retention or omission of mute *e* is shown by (ə): e.g. *table* [tabl(ə)]; *fenêtre* [f(ə)nɛtʀ(ə)].

1.10 Aspirate h Initial *h* in the spelling of a French word does not imply strong expulsion of breath, except in the case of certain interjections. Initial *h* is called 'aspirate' when it is incompatible with liaison (*des haricots* [de'aʀiko]) or elision (*le haricot* [lə'aʀiko]). Aspirate *h* is shown in transcriptions by an apostrophe placed just before the word (e.g. *hibou* ['ibu]).

1.11 Consonants and assimilation Within a word and in normal speech, a voiceless consonant may be voiced when followed by a voiced consonant (e.g. example [ɛgzɑ̃pl(ə)]), and a voiced consonant may be devoiced when followed by a voiceless consonant (e.g. *absolument* [apsɔlymɑ̃]). When this phenomenon is regular in a word, it is shown in transcription (e.g. *abside* [apsid]). In speech, its frequency varies from speaker to speaker. Thus, while the citation form of *tasse* is [tɑs], the group *une tasse de thé* may be heard pronounced [yntɑsdəte] or [yntɑzdəte].

1.12 Sentence stress Unlike the stress pattern of English associated with meaning, sentence stress in French is associated with rhythm. The stress falls on the final syllable of the sense groups of which the sentence is formed (see 1.5). In the following example: *quand il m'a vu, il a traversé la rue en courant pour me dire un mot*, composed of three sense groups, the syllables *vu*, *-rant* and *mot* carry the stress, being slightly lengthened.

1.13 French intonation is less mobile than English, and is closely associated with sentence stress. It occurs normally on the final syllable of sense groups. Thus, in the sentence given above (1.12), the syllables *vu* and *-rant* are spoken with a slight rise (indicating continuity), while the syllable *mot* is accompanied by a fall in the voice (indicating finality). In the case of a question, the final syllable will normally also be spoken with rising voice.

Phonetic Transcription of French

Phonetic alphabet used

Vowels

[i]	**il, vie, lyre**
[e]	**blé, jouer**
[ɛ]	**lait, jouet, merci**
[a]	**plat, patte**
[ɑ]	**bas, pâte**
[ɔ]	**mort, donner**
[o]	**mot, dôme, eau, gauche**
[u]	**genou, roue**
[y]	**rue, vêtu**
[ø]	**peu, deux**
[œ]	**peur, meuble**
[ə]	**le, premier**
[ɛ̃]	**matin, plein**
[ɑ̃]	**sans, vent**
[ɔ̃]	**bon, ombre**
[œ̃]	**lundi, brun**

Semi-consonants

[j]	**yeux, paille, pied**
[w]	**oui, nouer**
[ɥ]	**huile, lui**

Consonants

[p]	**père, soupe**
[t]	**terre, vite**
[k]	**cou, qui, sac, képi**
[b]	**bon, robe**
[d]	**dans, aide**
[g]	**gare, bague**
[f]	**feu, neuf, photo**
[s]	**sale, celui, ça, dessous, tasse, nation**
[ʃ]	**chat, tache**
[v]	**vous, rêve**
[z]	**zéro, maison, rose**
[ʒ]	**je, gilet, geôle**
[l]	**lent, sol**
[ʀ]	**rue, venir**
[m]	**main, femme**
[n]	**nous, tonne, animal**
[ɲ]	**agneau, vigne**
[h]	**hop! (exclamative)**
[']	**haricot (no liaison)**
[ŋ]	**words borrowed from English: camping**
[x]	**words borrowed from Spanish or Arabic: jota**

PRONONCIATION DE L'ANGLAIS

1.1 La notation adoptée est celle de l'Association Phonétique Internationale. L'ouvrage de base qui nous a servi constamment d'outil de référence est l'*English Pronouncing Dictionary* de Daniel Jones, qui, mis à jour par le Professeur A. C. Gimson, continue de faire autorité en France et partout ailleurs où l'on apprend l'anglais britannique.

1.2 La transcription correspond à la *Received Pronunciation (R.P.)*, variété de l'anglais britannique la plus généralement étudiée dans le monde d'aujourd'hui. Elle correspond également, à quelques exceptions près, à celle de la 14e édition de l'*English Pronouncing Dictionary (EPD)* (Dent, 1977). Ce système de transcription présente, par rapport à celui de l'édition précédente, l'avantage d'utiliser des signes qui indiquent clairement la distinction à la fois quantitative et qualitative qui existe entre les voyelles tendues et relâchées (par exemple: 13e édition: [iː], [i]; [əː], [ə]; 14e édition: [iː], [ɪ]; [ɜː], [ə].

1.3 Pour des raisons d'économie de place, une seule prononciation est donnée pour chaque mot, à l'exclusion des variantes éventuelles et connues. La prononciation ainsi transcrite est celle la plus fréquemment entendue selon l'*EPD*, ou, dans le cas de néologismes et de mots nouveaux, selon les membres de l'équipe Collins-Le Robert.

1.4 Il a été jugé inutile de compliquer la tâche de l'utilisateur en indiquant au moyen de symboles appropriés la prononciation de mots sortant du cadre du vocabulaire britannique. Ainsi, *aluminium*, *aluminum* sont transcrits: [ˌæljʊˈmɪnɪəm], [əˈluːmɪnəm], bien que la seconde forme, exclusivement américaine, ne s'entende normalement qu'avec un accent américain. Il s'agit, dans de tels cas, d'une approximation qui ne met pas en cause la compréhension du mot employé.

1.5 Les formes réduites Certains mots monosyllabiques, en nombre limité, ayant une fonction plus structurale que lexicale, sont sujets, surtout à l'intérieur d'un énoncé, à une réduction vocalique plus ou moins importante. Le mot *and*, isolé, se prononce [ænd]; mais, dans la chaîne parlée, il se prononcera, à moins d'être accentué, [ənd, ən, n] selon le débit du locuteur et selon le contexte. Les mots qui sont le plus souvent touchés par cette réduction vocalique sont les suivants: a, an, and, as, at, but, for, from, of, some, than, that, the, them, to, us, am, is, are, was, were, must, will, would, shall, should, have, has, had, do, does, can, could.

1.6 L'accent tonique Tout mot anglais, isolé, de deux syllabes ou plus, porte un accent tonique. Cet accent est noté au moyen du signe (ˈ) placé devant la syllabe intéressée; par exemple: *composer* [kəmˈpəʊzəʳ]. Le Français doit veiller à bien placer l'accent tonique sous peine de poser de sérieux problèmes de compréhension à ses interlocuteurs. Le tableau suivant indique un certain nombre de suffixes qui permettent de prévoir la place de l'accent tonique sur de nombreux mots. Ce tableau est donné à titre indicatif et ne cherche pas à être exhaustif.

Tableau des suffixes déterminant la position de l'accent tonique

Suffixe	*Exemple*	*Exceptions*	*Remarques*
1. Accent sur syllabe finale			
-ee	refuˈgee	ˈcoffee, ˈtoffee, comˈmittee, ˈpedigree	
-eer	engiˈneer		
-ese	Japanese		
-esque	pictuˈresque		
-ette	quarˈtette	ˈetiquette, ˈomelette	
-ate	creˈate		*Verbes de 2 syllabes*
-fy	deˈfy		*Verbes de 2 syllabes*
-ise, ize	adˈvise		*Verbes de 2 syllabes*

Suffixe	*Exemple*	*Exceptions*	*Remarques*
2. Accent sur pénultième			
-ial	comˈmercial		
-ian	Iˈtalian		
-ic, -ics	ecoˈnomics	ˈArabic, aˈrithmetic, (ˈCatholic) ˈheretic, ˈlunatic, ˈpolitics	*Les suffixes* -ical, -ically *ne modifient pas la place de l'accent tonique, et n'admettent pas d'exceptions. Par exemple:* poˈlitical, poˈlitically, arithˈmetical.
-ion	inforˈmation	ˈdandelion, (ˈtelevision)	
-ish	diˈminish	imˈpoverish	*Verbes en* -ish
-itis	appendiˈcitis		
-osis	diagˈnosis	(metaˈmorphosis)	
3. Accent sur antépénultième			
-ety	soˈciety		
-ity	sinˈcerity		
-itive	comˈpetitive		
-itude	ˈattitude		
-grapher	phoˈtographer		
-graphy	phoˈtography		
-logy	biˈology		
-ate	apˈpreciate		
-fy	ˈpacify		*Pour les verbes de 2 syllabes, voir plus haut*
-ise, ize	ˈadvertise	characterize, ˈregularize, (ˈliberalize, ˈnationalize)	*Pour les verbes de 2 syllabes, voir plus haut*

N.B. ***Les mots placés entre parenthèses ont aussi une accentuation conforme au modèle.***

1.7 L'accent secondaire Dans un mot, toute syllabe accentuée en plus de celle qui porte l'accent tonique porte un accent secondaire, c'est-à-dire un accent ayant moins d'intensité que l'accent tonique. L'accent secondaire est noté au moyen du signe (ˌ) devant la syllabe intéressée: Par exemple: *composition* [ˌkɒmpəˈzɪʃən] (accent secondaire sur [ˌkɒm]; accent tonique sur [ˈzɪʃ]).

1.8 Les composés La prononciation des mots ou groupes de mots rassemblés dans la catégorie *cpd* d'un article n'est pas indiquée, car elle correspond à celle du mot-souche suivie de celle du mot ou des mots formant le reste du composé mais avec une restriction importante: pour des raisons pratiques, on considérera que la grande majorité des composés à deux éléments ne sont accentués que sur le premier élément, cette accentuation s'accompagnant d'une chute de la voix. Exemple: ˈfoodstuffs, ˈfood prices.

1.9 L'accent de phrase À la différence du français dont l'accent de phrase (syllabe allongée) tombe normalement sur la dernière syllabe des groupes de souffle, l'anglais met en relief la syllabe accentuée de chaque mot apportant un nouvel élément d'information. Dans la pratique cela veut dire que les mots lexicaux reçoivent un accent de phrase, tandis que les mots grammaticaux n'en reçoivent pas (voir 1.5). Il est logique, dans un tel système, que même les mots lexicaux ne soient pas accentués s'ils n'apportent pas de nouveaux éléments d'information; c'est le cas, notamment, de mots ou de concepts répétés dans une même séquence; ils sont accentués une première fois, mais ils perdent leur accent par la suite. De même, lorsqu'une idée est répétée dans une même séquence, les mots qui l'expriment ne sont plus mis en relief lors de sa réapparition. Par contre, les éléments contrastifs de la phrase anglaise sont toujours fortement accentués.
Exemple: ***John's recently bought himself a car, and Peter's got a new one too.***
Accents sur: ***John, recently, bought, car, Peter, too.***
Accents contrastifs sur: ***John*** (facultatif) et ***Peter***.
Absence d'accent sur: ***'s got a new one,*** qui n'apporte aucun nouvel élément d'information et pourrait être supprimé: (***and Peter, too.***)

1.10 L'intonation en anglais, beaucoup plus qu'en français, révèle le sentiment du locuteur vis-à-vis des propos qu'il tient. Dans les deux langues, l'intonation est liée à l'accent de phrase. L'intonation française, tout comme l'accent de phrase, se manifeste sur la dernière syllabe des groupes de souffle: légère montée de la voix à l'intérieur de la phrase, avec une chute ou une montée sur la syllabe finale, selon qu'il s'agit d'une déclarative ou d'une interrogative. En anglais, l'intonation est liée au sens, et se manifeste sur toutes les syllabes accentuées de la phrase (voir 1.9). La phrase anglaise type présente une intonation commençant relativement haut, et descendant vers le grave progressivement sur les syllabes accentuées. Sur la dernière syllabe accentuée de la phrase, la voix marque soit une chute, soit une montée, plus importante qu'en français, selon le type de phrase: une chute, s'il s'agit d'une indication de finalité (déclaratives, impératives, etc.); une montée s'il s'agit d'une invitation au dialogue (interrogatives, requêtes polies, etc.). Plus le discours est animé et plus l'écart entre l'aigu et le grave se creuse. Des mots ayant un sens affectif intense tendent à faire monter la voix beaucoup plus haut que n'exigent les habitudes du discours français.

Transcription phonétique de l'anglais

Alphabet phonétique et valeur des signes

Voyelles et diphtongues

[iː]	bead, see
[ɑː]	bard, calm
[ɔː]	born, cork
[uː]	boon, fool
[ɜː]	burn, fern, work
[ɪ]	sit, pity
[e]	set, less
[æ]	sat, apple
[ʌ]	fun, come
[ɒ]	fond, wash
[ʊ]	full, soot
[ə]	composer, above
[eɪ]	bay, fate
[aɪ]	buy, lie
[ɔɪ]	boy, voice
[əʊ]	no, ago
[aʊ]	now, plough
[ɪə]	tier, beer
[ɛə]	tare, fair
[ʊə]	tour

Consonnes

[p]	pat, pope
[b]	bat, baby
[t]	tab, strut
[d]	dab, mended
[k]	cot, kiss, chord
[g]	got, agog
[f]	fine, raffle
[v]	vine, river
[s]	pots, sit, rice
[z]	pods, buzz
[θ]	thin, maths
[ð]	this, other
[ʃ]	ship, sugar
[ʒ]	measure
[tʃ]	chance
[dʒ]	just, edge
[l]	little, place
[r]	ran, stirring
[m]	ram, mummy
[n]	ran, nut
[ŋ]	rang, bank
[h]	hat, reheat
[j]	yet, million
[w]	wet, bewail
[x]	loch

Divers

Un caractère en italique représente un son qui peut ne pas être prononcé.

[ʳ]	représente un [r] entendu s'il forme une liaison avec la voyelle du mot suivant
[ˈ]	accent tonique
[ˌ]	accent secondaire

Remerciements

Les auteurs tiennent à exprimer leurs remerciements à tous ceux qui ont apporté leur collaboration tout au long de la rédaction de cet ouvrage, et en particulier à Tom McArthur, dont les travaux sur les verbes anglais à particule ont été d'une aide précieuse; à Richard Wakely, qui a bien voulu les faire bénéficier de son concours pour le traitement des auxiliaires de mode anglais; à Colin Smith, qui leur a montré la voie; à Duncan McMillan pour ses conseils et sa collaboration à un stade avancé de la rédaction; à Guy Rondeau pour son contours lors de la compilation des emplois du français du Canada; enfin à tous ceux dont l'aide a concouru au parachèvement du texte.

Il faut aussi signaler et remercier les nombreux auxiliaires de rédaction, les correcteurs et les dactylographes qui ont permis de transformer en ouvrage imprimé un manuscrit volumineux — tout particulièrement Michèle Rodger, qui a dactylographié la majeure partie du dictionnaire.

Les auteurs tiennent enfin à exprimer leur gratitude à Geneviève McMillan pour sa longue et précieuse collaboration.

Les auteurs

Acknowledgements

The Editors are indebted to the following:

Tom McArthur for his original approach to English phrasal verbs; Richard Wakely for help with modal verbs in English; Colin Smith, Editor of Collins Spanish Dictionary, for his inspiring example; Duncan McMillan for advice and help in the later stages of the book; Guy Rondeau for help with French Canadian usage; the many other individuals and organizations who helped on specific translation points.

Our thanks go also to the numerous copy editors and proofreaders who assisted in the conversion of our handwritten manuscript to the printed page, and especially to Michèle Rodger who typed most of the dictionary.

Finally we would like to express our gratitude to Geneviève McMillan for all that she contributed to this dictionary over a period of many years.

The Editors

Les Marques Déposées

Les termes qui constituent à notre connaissance une marque déposée ont été désignés comme tels. La présence ou l'absence de cette désignation ne peut toutefois être considérée comme ayant valeur juridique.

Note on Trademarks

Entered words which we have reason to believe constitute trademarks have been designated as such. However, neither the presence nor the absence of such designation should be regarded as affecting the legal status of any trademark.

Abréviations grammaticales et niveaux de langue

La plupart des abréviations figurent de manière identique dans les deux parties du dictionnaire car elles peuvent s'appliquer aux deux langues. Lorsque pour des raisons d'orthographe ou d'usage, il n'a pas été possible de trouver une forme commune aux deux langues pour une indication grammaticale, un champ sémantique, etc, deux formes différentes ont été utilisées, l'une correspondant aux habitudes du français dans la partie français-anglais, l'autre correspondant aux habitudes de l'anglais dans la partie anglais-français.

Abbreviations, Field labels and Style labels

Most abbreviations used in the text are applicable to both languages and appear in both parts of the dictionary. When for reasons of spelling or usage it has not been possible to provide one abbreviation suitable for both languages two different forms have been used, a French one in the French-English side, an English abbreviation in the English-French side.

Abréviations grammaticales et niveaux de langue

Abbreviations, field labels and style labels

abréviation	abbr, abrév	abbreviated, abbreviation
adjectif	adj	adjective
administration	Admin	administration
adverbe	adv	adverb
agriculture	Agr	agriculture
anatomie	Anat	anatomy
antiquité	Antiq	ancient history
approximativement	approx	approximately
archéologie	Archeol, Archéol	archaeology
architecture	Archit	architecture
argot	arg	slang
article	art	article
astrologie	Astrol	astrology
astronomie	Astron	astronomy
attribut	attrib	predicative
automobile	Aut	automobiles
auxiliaire	aux	auxiliary
aviation	Aviat	aviation
biologie	Bio	biology
botanique	Bot	botany
britannique, Grande-Bretagne	Brit	British, Great Britain
canadien, Canada	Can	Canadian, Canada
chimie	Chem, Chim	chemistry
cinéma	Cine, Ciné	cinema
commerce	Comm	commerce
comparatif	comp	comparative
conditionnel	cond	conditional
conjonction	conj	conjunction
construction	Constr	building trade
mots composés	cpd	compound, in compounds
cuisine	Culin	cookery
défini	def, déf	definite
démonstratif	dem, dém	demonstrative
dialectal, régional	dial	dialect
diminutif	dim	diminutive
direct	dir	direct
écologie	Ecol	ecology
économique	Econ, Écon	economics
écossais, Écosse	Écos	Scottish, Scotland
par exemple	eg	for example
électricité, électronique	Elec, Élec	electricity, electronics
épithète	épith	before noun
surtout	esp	especially
et cetera	etc	etcetera
euphémisme	euph	euphemism
par exemple	ex	for example
exclamation	excl	exclamation
féminin	f	feminine
figuré	fig	figuratively
finance	Fin	finance
féminin pluriel	fpl	feminine plural
formel, langue soignée	frm	formal language
football	Ftbl	football
fusionné	fus	fused
futur	fut	future
en général, généralement	gen, gén	in general, generally
géographie	Geog, Géog	geography
géologie	Geol, Géol	geology
géométrie	Geom, Géom	geometry
grammaire	Gram	grammar
gymnastique	Gym	gymnastics
héraldique	Her, Hér	heraldry
histoire	Hist	history
humoristique	hum	humorous
impératif	imper, impér	imperative
impersonnel	impers	impersonal
industrie	Ind	industry
indéfini	indef, indéf	indefinite
indicatif	indic	indicative
indirect	indir	indirect
infinitif	infin	infinitive
inséparable	insep	inseparable
interrogatif	interrog	interrogative
invariable	inv	invariable
irlandais, Irlande	Ir	Irish, Ireland
ironique	iro	ironic
irrégulier	irrég	irregular
droit, juridique	Jur	law, legal
linguistique	Ling	linguistics
littéral, au sens propre	lit	literally
littéraire	liter	literary
littérature	Literat	literature
littéraire	littér	literary
littérature	Littérat	literature
locutions	loc	locution

masculin	**m**	masculine
mathématique	**Math**	mathematics
médecine	**Med, Méd**	medicine
météorologie	**Met, Mét**	meteorology
métallurgie	**Metal, Métal**	metallurgy
masculin et féminin	**mf**	masculine and feminine
militaire	**Mil**	military
mines	**Min**	mining
minéralogie	**Miner, Minér**	mineralogy
masculin pluriel	**mpl**	masculine plural
musique	**Mus**	music
mythologie	**Myth**	mythology
nom	**n**	noun
nord de l'Angleterre	**N Angl**	North of England
nautique	**Naut**	nautical, naval
négatif	**neg, nég**	negative
nord de l'Angleterre	**N Engl**	North of England
nom féminin	**nf**	feminine noun
nom masculin	**nm**	masculine noun
nom masculin et féminin	**nmf, nm,f**	masculine and feminine noun
physique nucléaire	**Nucl Phys**	nuclear physics
numéral	**num**	numerical
objet	**obj**	object
opposé	**opp**	opposite
optique	**Opt**	optics
ornithologie	**Orn**	ornithology
	o.s.	oneself
parlement	**Parl**	parliament
passif	**pass**	passive
péjoratif	**pej, péj**	pejorative
personnel	**pers**	personal
pharmacie	**Pharm**	pharmacy
philatélie	**Philat**	philately
philosophie	**Philos**	philosophy
photographie	**Phot**	photography
	phr vb elem	phrasal verb element
physique	**Phys**	physics
physiologie	**Physiol**	physiology
pluriel	**pl**	plural
politique	**Pol**	politics
possessif	**poss**	possessive
préfixe	**pref, préf**	prefix
préposition	**prep, prép**	preposition
prétérit	**pret, prét**	preterite
pronom	**pron**	pronoun
proverbe	**Prov**	proverb
participe présent	**prp**	present participle
psychiatrie, psychologie	**Psych**	psychology, psychiatry
participe passé	**ptp**	past participle
quelque chose	**qch**	
quelqu'un	**qn**	
marque déposée	®	registered trademark
radio	**Rad**	radio
chemin de fer	**Rail**	rail(ways)
relatif	**rel**	relative
religion	**Rel**	religion
	sb	somebody, someone
sciences	**Sci**	science
école	**Scol**	school
écossais, Écosse	**Scot**	Scottish, Scotland
sculpture	**Sculp**	sculpture
séparable	**sep**	separable
singulier	**sg**	singular
ski	**Ski**	skiing
argot	**sl**	slang
sociologie	**Soc, Sociol**	sociology, social work
Bourse	**St Ex**	Stock Exchange
	sth	something
subjonctif	**subj**	subjunctive
suffixe	**suf**	suffix
superlatif	superl	superlative
chirurgie	**Surg**	surgery
arpentage	**Surv**	surveying
terme de spécialiste	**T**	specialist's term
technique	**Tech**	technical
télécommunication	**Telec, Téléc**	telecommunications
industrie textile	**Tex**	textiles
théâtre	**Theat, Théât**	theatre
télévision	**TV**	television
typographie	**Typ**	typography
non comptable	**U**	uncountable
université	**Univ**	university
américain, États-Unis	**US**	American, United States
voir	**V**	see
verbe	**vb**	verb
médecine vétérinaire	**Vet, Vét**	veterinary medicine
verbe intransitif	**vi**	intransitive verb
verbe pronominal	**vpr**	pronominal verb
verbe transitif	**vt**	transitive verb
verbe transitif et intransitif	**vti**	transitive and intransitive verb
verbe transitif indirect	**vt indir**	
zoologie	**Zool**	zoology
voir page xviii	* ‡ **	see page xviii
voir page xviii	† ††	see page xviii

DICTIONNAIRE FRANÇAIS-ANGLAIS
FRENCH-ENGLISH DICTIONARY

A

A, a [ɑ] *nm* (*lettre*) A, a. **de A (jusqu')à Z** from A to Z; **prouver qch par a plus b** to prove sth conclusively.

à [a] *prép* (*contraction avec le, les*: **au, aux**) **(a)** (*copule introduisant compléments après vb, loc verbale, adj, n*) **obéir/pardonner ~ qn** to obey/forgive sb; **rêver ~ qch** to dream of *ou* about sth; **se mettre ~ faire** to begin to do, set about *ou* start doing; **se décider ~ faire** to make up one's mind to do, decide (up)on doing; **s'habituer ~ faire** to get *ou* become *ou* grow used to doing; **prendre plaisir ~ faire** to take pleasure in doing, derive pleasure from doing; **c'est facile/difficile ~ faire** it's easy/difficult to do; **il est lent ~ s'habiller** he takes a long time dressing, he's slow at dressing (himself); **son aptitude ~ faire/au travail** his aptitude for doing/for work; **son empressement ~ aider** his eagerness *ou* willingness to help; **depuis son accession au trône/admission au club** since his accession to the throne/admission to the club; **je consens ~ ce que vous partiez** I consent *ou* agree to your leaving *ou* to your departure; *V vb, n, adj appropriés.*

(b) (*déplacement, direction*) (*vers*) to; (*dans*) into. **aller** *ou* **se rendre ~ Paris/ ~ Bornéo/au Canada/aux Açores** to go to Paris/Borneo/Canada/the Azores; **le train de Paris ~ Reims** the train from Paris to Rheims; **aller ~ l'école/~ l'église/au marché/au théâtre** to go to school/church/(the) market/the theatre; **aller ~ la chasse/pêche** to go hunting/fishing; **aller** *ou* **partir ~ la recherche de qch** to go looking *ou* go and look for sth; **raconte ton voyage ~ Londres** tell us about your trip to London; **entrez donc au salon** (do) come into the lounge; **mets-toi ~ l'ombre** get into *ou* in the shade; **au lit/travail les enfants!** time for bed/work children!, off to bed/work children!

(c) (*position, localisation*) at; (*à l'intérieur de*) in; (*à la surface de*) on. **habiter ~ Carpentras/~ Paris/au Canada/aux Açores** to live at *ou* in Carpentras/in Paris/in Canada/in the Azores; **elle habite au 4e (étage)** she lives on the 4th floor; **être ~ l'école/~ la maison/au bureau/au théâtre** to be at school/home/the office/the theatre; **travailler ~ l'étranger/~ domicile** to work abroad/at home; **il faisait très chaud ~ l'église/au théâtre** it was very hot in church/the theatre; **Paris est ~ 400 km de Londres** Paris is 400 km from London; **il est seul au monde** he is (all) alone in the world; **c'est ~ 3 km/5 minutes (d'ici)** it's 3 km/5 minutes away (from here); **2e rue ~ droite/gauche** 2nd street on the right/left; **elle était assise ~ la fenêtre** she was sitting at *ou* by the window; **le magasin au coin de la rue** the shop *ou* store (*US*) on *ou* at the corner, the corner shop (*Brit*); **debout le dos au feu** standing with one's back to the fire; **j'ai froid aux jambes/aux mains** my legs/hands are cold, I've got cold legs/hands; **prendre qn au cou/~ la gorge** to take sb by the neck/throat; **il a été blessé ~ l'épaule/au genou** he was injured in the shoulder/knee; **il entra le sourire aux lèvres** he came in with a smile on his face; **il a de l'eau (jusqu')aux genoux** the water comes up to his knees, he's knee-deep in water; **regardez ~ la page 4** look at *ou* up page 4; **~ la télévision/radio** on television/the radio; *V* **à-côté, bord, bout** *etc.*

(d) (*temps*) (*moment précis*) at; (*jour, date*) on; (*époque*) at, during; (*jusqu'à*) to, till, until. **~ quelle heure vient-il?— ~ 6 heures** what time is he coming? — at 6 *ou* (at) 6 o'clock; **je n'étais pas là ~ leur arrivée** I wasn't there when they arrived; **ils partirent au matin/le 3 au soir** they left in the morning/on the evening of the 3rd; **au printemps** in spring; **~ l'automne** in autumn; **la poésie au 19e siècle** poetry in the 19th century, 19th-century poetry; **aux grandes vacances/~ l'époque des fêtes il y a du monde** in the summer holidays/during the festive season it's very crowded; **je vous verrai aux vacances/~ Noël/au retour** I'll see you in the holidays/at Christmas/when we come back; **~ demain/l'an prochain/dans un mois/samedi** see you tomorrow/next year/in a month's time/on Saturday; **le docteur reçoit de 2 ~ 4** the doctor has his surgery (*Brit*) *ou* sees patients from 2 to *ou* till 4; **remettre ~ huitaine** to postpone *ou* defer for a week *ou* until the next *ou* following week.

(e) (*condition, situation*) in, on, at. **être/rester au chaud/au froid/au vent/~ l'humidité** to be/stay in the warm/cold/wind/damp; **être ~ genoux/quatre pattes** to be on one's knees/on all fours; **il est ~ ménager/plaindre** he is to be handled carefully/pitied; **ils en sont ~ leurs derniers sous** they're down to their last few pence (*Brit*) *ou* pennies (*US*); **elle n'est pas femme ~ faire cela** she is not the sort (of woman) to do that; **ce n'est pas le genre de docteur ~ oublier** he's not the sort of doctor to forget *ou* who would forget; **être/rester ~ travailler** to be/stay working *ou* at one's work; **il est toujours (là) ~ se plaindre** he's forever complaining; **il a été le premier ~ le dire, mais ils sont plusieurs ~ le penser** he was the first to say so, but there are quite a few who think like him *ou* the same; **ils sont 2 ~ l'avoir fait** there were 2 of them that did it; *V* **à-coup, bout, cran** *etc.*

(f) (*rapport, évaluation, distribution etc*) by, per; (*approximation*) to. **faire du 50 ~ l'heure** to do 50 km an *ou* per hour; **consommer 9 litres aux 100 km** to use 9 litres to the *ou* per 100 km, do 100 km to 9 litres; **être payé ~ la semaine/l'heure** to be paid by the week/the hour; **vendre au détail/poids/mètre/kilo** to sell retail/by weight/by the metre/by the kilo; **il leur faut 4 ~ 5 heures/kilos/mètres** they need 4 to 5 hours/kilos/metres; **entrer un ~ un/deux ~ deux** to come in one by one/two by two, come in one/two at a time; **~ chaque coup** every *ou* each time; **~ chaque pas** at each *ou* every step; **~ chaque page** on each *ou* every page; *V* **bout, heure** *etc.*

(g) (*appartenance*) to, of. **être** *ou* **appartenir ~ qn/qch** to belong to sb/sth; **ce livre est ~ Pierre** this book belongs to Peter *ou* is Peter's; **le sac est ~ moi/~ elle** the bag is mine/hers; **c'est une amie ~ lui/eux** she is a friend of his/theirs; **ils n'ont pas de maison ~ eux** they haven't a house of their own; **le couteau ~ Jean*** John's knife; **c'est ~ lui de protester** (*sa responsabilité*) it's up to him *ou* it's his job to protest; (*son tour*) it's his turn to protest; **l'ananas a un goût bien ~ lui** pineapple has a flavour all (of) its own *ou* a distinctive flavour; **ce n'est pas ~ moi de le dire** it's not for me to say, it's not up to me to say; **c'est très gentil** *ou* **aimable ~ vous** that's very kind of you.

(h) (*avec vt à double complément*) (*attribution etc*) to (*souvent omis*); (*provenance*) from, out of; (*comparaison, préférence*) to. **donner/prêter/enseigner qch ~ qn** to give/lend/teach sb sth, give/lend/teach sth to sb; **prendre de l'eau au puits/~ la rivière/au seau** to take water from the well/from the river/out of *ou* from the bucket; **il préfère le vin ~ la bière** he prefers wine to beer; *V* **aider, conseiller**[1], **emprunter, offrir** *etc.*

(i) (*moyen*) on, by, with. **faire qch ~ la machine/~ la main** to do sth by machine/hand; **la cuisinière marche au gaz/au charbon/~ l'électricité** the cooker runs on *ou* uses gas/coal/electricity; **aller ~ bicyclette/~ pied/~ cheval** to cycle/walk/ride, go by bicycle/on foot/on horseback; **examiner qch au microscope/~ la loupe/~ l'œil nu** to examine sth under *ou* with a microscope/with a magnifying glass/with the naked eye; **il nous a joué l'air au piano/violon** he played us the tune on the piano/violin.

(j) (*manière: souvent traduit par adv*) at, in. **il est parti ~ toute allure/au galop** he rushed/galloped off, he left at full tilt*/at a gallop; **vivre ~ l'américaine** to live like an American *ou* in the American style; **une histoire ~ la (manière de) Tolstoï** a story in the style of Tolstoy *ou* à la Tolstoy; **elle fait la cuisine ~ l'huile/au beurre** she cooks with oil/butter; (*Culin*) **canard aux petits pois/aux pruneaux** duck with peas/prunes; **il l'a fait ~ sa manière** he did it in his own way; **il l'a fait ~ lui tout seul** he did it (all) on his own *ou* (all) by himself *ou* single-handed; **ils couchent ~ 3 dans la même chambre** they sleep 3 to a room; **ils ont fait le travail ~ 3/~ eux tous** they did the work between the 3 of them/between them (all).

(k) (*caractérisation: avec n*) with (*souvent omis*). **pompe ~ eau/essence** water/petrol (*Brit*) *ou* gasoline (*US*) pump; **bête ~ plumes/~ fourrure** feathered/furry creature; **enfant aux yeux bleus/aux cheveux longs** blue-eyed/long-haired child, child with blue eyes/long hair; **robe ~ manches** dress with sleeves; **robe ~ manches courtes** short-sleeved dress; **canne ~ bout ferré** metal-tipped stick, stick with a metal tip; **bons ~ 10 ans** 10-year bonds; **la dame au chapeau vert** the lady in *ou* with the green hat.

(l) (*destination*) (*avec n*) for (*souvent omis*); (*avec vb*) to; (*dédicace*) to. **tasse ~ thé** teacup; **pot ~ lait** milk jug; **j'ai une maison ~ vendre/louer** I have a house to sell *ou* for sale/to let *ou* for letting; **donner une robe ~ nettoyer** to take a dress to be cleaned, take a dress in for cleaning; **il a un bouton ~ recoudre** he's got a button to sew on *ou* that needs sewing on; **je n'ai rien ~ lire/faire** I have nothing to read/do; **avez-vous ~ manger/boire?** have you anything to eat/drink?; **je peux vous donner ~ déjeuner/dîner** I can give you (some) lunch/dinner.

(m) (+ *infin: au point de: conséquence, intensité*) **s'ennuyer ~ mourir** to be bored to death *ou* tears; **il est laid ~ faire peur** he is as ugly as sin; **ce bruit est ~ vous rendre fou** this noise is enough to drive you mad; **c'est ~ se demander s'il est complètement idiot** it makes you wonder if he isn't an utter idiot.

(n) (+ *infin: valeur de gérondif: cause, hypothèse etc*) **~ le voir si maigre, j'ai eu pitié** (on) seeing him *ou* when I saw him so thin I took pity on him; **vous le buterez ~ le punir ainsi** you'll antagonize him if you punish him like that; **je me fatigue ~**

répéter I'm wearing myself out repeating; **il nous fait peur ~ conduire si vite** he frightens us (by) driving *ou* when he drives so fast; **~ bien considérer la chose, ~ bien réfléchir** if you think about it; **s'ennuyer ~ ne rien faire** to get bored doing nothing; *V* **force.**

(o) (*conséquence, résultat*) to; (*cause*) at; (*d'après*) according to, from. **~ sa consternation** to his dismay; **~ leur grande surprise** much to their surprise, to their great surprise; **~ la demande de certains** at the request of certain people; **~ sa pâleur, on devinait son trouble** one could see *ou* tell by his paleness that he was distressed; **~ la nouvelle, il y eut des protestations** the news was greeted with protests; **~ ce qu'il prétend** according to what he says; **~ ce que j'ai compris** from what I understood; **c'est aux résultats qu'on le jugera** he will be judged on his results, it'll be on his results that he's judged.

(p) (*loc*) **~ ta *ou* votre santé!, ~ la tienne! *ou* la vôtre!** cheers!, your (good) health!; **aux absents!** to absent friends!; **~ la porte!** (get) out!; **~ la poubelle!** (it's) rubbish!, (let's) throw it out!; **au voleur!** stop thief!; **au feu!** fire!; *V* **abordage, boire, souhait.**

(q) (*Prov*) **~ bon chat bon rat** tit for tat (*Prov*); **~ bon entendeur, salut** a word to the wise is enough; **~ chacun sa chacune*** every Jack has his Jill; **~ chacun selon son mérite** to each according to his merits; **~ chacun son métier** every man to his own trade; **~ chaque jour suffit sa peine** sufficient unto the day is the evil thereof (*Prov*); **~ cœur vaillant rien d'impossible** nothing is impossible to a willing heart (*Prov*); **aux grands maux les grands remèdes** desperate ills demand desperate measures; **~ l'impossible nul n'est tenu** no one is bound to do the impossible; **~ père avare, enfant prodigue** a miser will father a spendthrift son; **~ quelque chose malheur est bon** every cloud has a silver lining (*Prov*); **au royaume des aveugles les borgnes sont rois** in the kingdom of the blind the one-eyed man is king (*Prov*); **~ la Sainte Luce, les jours croissent du saut d'une puce** Lucy light, the shortest day and the longest night (*Prov*); **~ tout seigneur tout honneur** honour to whom honour is due.

abaissant, e [abɛsɑ̃, ɑ̃t] *adj* degrading.

abaisse [abɛs] *nf* rolled-out pastry.

abaisse-langue [abɛslɑ̃g] *nm inv* spatula (*Brit*), tongue depressor.

abaissement [abɛsmɑ̃] *nm* **(a)** (*action d'abaisser*) pulling down; pushing down; lowering; bringing down; reduction (*de* in); carrying; dropping; humiliation; debasing; humbling.

(b) (*fait de s'abaisser*) *[température, valeur, taux]* fall, drop (*de* in); *[terrain]* downward slope. **l'~ de la moralité** the moral decline *ou* degeneration, the decline in morals.

(c) (*conduite obséquieuse*) subservience, self-abasement; (*conduite choquante*) degradation.

abaisser [abese] (1) **1** *vt* **(a)** *levier* (*tirer*) to pull down; (*pousser*) to push down; *store* to lower, pull down. (*littér*) **~ les yeux sur qn** to deign to look upon sb; **cette vitre s'abaisse-t-elle?** does this window lower? *ou* go down?

(b) *température, valeur, taux* to lower, reduce, bring down; *niveau, mur* to lower.

(c) (*Math*) *chiffre* to bring down, carry; *perpendiculaire* to drop.

(d) (*rabaisser*) *[personne]* to humiliate; *[vice]* to debase; (*Rel*) to humble. **~ la puissance des nobles** to bring down the nobles, reduce the power of the nobles.

(e) (*Culin*) *pâte* to roll out.

2 s'abaisser *vpr* **(a)** (*diminuer*) *[température, valeur, taux]* to fall, drop, go down; *[terrain]* to slope down; (*Théât*) *[rideau]* to fall (*sur* on).

(b) (*s'humilier*) to humble o.s. **s'~ à** to stoop *ou* descend to.

abaisseur [abɛsœʀ] *adj m, nm*: **(muscle) ~** depressor.

abandon [abɑ̃dɔ̃] *nm* **(a)** (*délaissement*) *[personne, lieu]* desertion, abandonment. **~ de poste** desertion of one's post.

(b) *[idée, responsabilité, privilège, fonction]* giving up; *[droit]* relinquishment, renunciation; *[course]* withdrawal, retiral (*de* from). **faire ~ de ses biens à qn** to make over one's property to sb; **faire ~ de ses droits sur** to relinquish *ou* renounce one's right(s) to; (*fig*) **~ de soi-même** self-abnegation.

(c) (*manque de soin*) neglected state, neglect. **l'(état d')~ où se trouvait la ferme** the neglected state (that) the farm was in; **jardin à l'~** neglected garden, garden run wild *ou* in a state of neglect; **laisser qch à l'~** to neglect sth.

(d) (*confiance*) lack of constraint. **parler avec ~** to talk freely *ou* without constraint; **dans ses moments d'~** in his moments of abandon *ou* his more expansive moments.

(e) (*nonchalance*) *[style]* easy flow. **étendu sur le sofa avec ~** stretched out luxuriously on the sofa; **l'~ de son attitude/ses manières** his relaxed *ou* easy-going attitude/manners.

abandonné, e [abɑ̃dɔne] (*ptp de* **abandonner**) *adj* **(a)** *attitude, position* relaxed; (*avec volupté*) abandoned. **(b)** *route, usine, jardin* disused.

abandonner [abɑ̃dɔne] (1) **1** *vt* **(a)** (*délaisser*) *lieu* to desert, abandon; *personne* (*gén*) to leave, abandon; (*intentionnellement*) to desert, abandon, forsake (*littér*); *technique, appareil* to abandon, give up. **vieille maison abandonnée** deserted old house; **son courage l'abandonna** his courage failed *ou* deserted *ou* forsook (*littér*) him; **ses forces l'abandonnèrent** his strength failed *ou* deserted him; **l'ennemi a abandonné ses positions** the enemy abandoned their positions; (*Mil*) **~ son poste** to desert one's post; **~ le terrain** (*lit, Mil*) to take flight; (*fig*) to give up.

(b) (*se retirer de*) *fonction* to give up, relinquish; *études, recherches* to give up, abandon; *droit, privilèges* to give up, relinquish, renounce; *course* to give up, withdraw *ou* retire from; *projet, hypothèse, espoir* to give up, abandon. **~ le pouvoir** to retire from *ou* give up *ou* leave office; (*lit, fig*) **~ la lutte *ou* la partie** to give up the fight *ou* struggle; **j'abandonne!** I give up!

(c) (*donner ou laisser*) **~ à** (*gén*) to give *ou* leave to; **~ ses biens à une bonne œuvre** to leave *ou* donate *ou* give one's wealth to a good cause; **elle lui abandonna sa main** she let him take her hand; **~ à qn le soin de faire qch** to leave it up to sb to do sth; **~ qn à son sort** to leave *ou* abandon (*littér*) sb to his fate; **~ au pillage/à la destruction/à la mort** to leave to be pillaged/to be destroyed/to die; **~ son corps au bien-être** to give o.s. up *ou* abandon o.s. to a sense of well-being.

2 s'abandonner *vpr* **(a)** (*se relâcher, se confier*) to let o.s. go. **il s'abandonna, me confia ses problèmes** he let himself go *ou* opened up and told me his problems; **elle s'abandonna dans mes bras** she sank into my arms.

(b) (*se laisser aller*) **s'~ à** *désespoir, passion, joie* to abandon o.s. to, give way to, give o.s. up to; *paresse* to give way to; *débauche* to give o.s. up to; **s'~ à la rêverie/au bien-être** to indulge in *ou* give o.s. up to daydreaming/a sense of well-being; **il s'abandonna au sommeil** he let sleep overcome him, he let himself sink into sleep.

(c) (*s'en remettre à*) **s'~ à** to commit o.s. to, put o.s. in the hands of.

(d) (†: *se donner sexuellement*) to give o.s. (*à* to).

abaque [abak] *nm* abacus.

abasourdir [abazuʀdiʀ] (2) *vt* **(a)** (*étonner*) to stun, dumbfound. **être abasourdi** to be stunned *ou* dumbfounded *ou* staggered*. **(b)** (*étourdir*) *[bruit]* to stun, daze.

abasourdissement [abazuʀdismɑ̃] *nm* bewilderment, stupefaction.

abat- [aba] *préf V* **abattre.**

abâtardir [abɑtaʀdiʀ] (2) **1** *vt race, vertu* to cause to degenerate; *qualité* to debase. **2 s'abâtardir** *vpr [race, vertu]* to degenerate; *[qualité]* to become debased.

abâtardissement [abɑtaʀdismɑ̃] *nm* (*V* **abâtardir**) degeneration; debasement.

abats [aba] *nmpl [volaille]* giblets; *[bœuf, porc]* offal.

abattage [abataʒ] *nm* **(a)** *[animal]* slaughter, slaughtering; *[arbre]* felling, cutting (down); (*Min*) extracting. **(b)** (*) **avoir de l'~** (*entrain*) to be dynamic, have plenty of go*; (*force*) **il a de l'~** he's a strapping fellow.

abattant [abatɑ̃] *nm* flap, leaf (*of table, desk*).

abattement [abatmɑ̃] *nm* **(a)** (*dépression*) dejection, despondency. **être dans un extrême ~** to be in very low spirits. **(b)** (*fatigue*) exhaustion; (*faiblesse*) enfeeblement. **(c)** (*Fin*) (*rabais*) reduction; (*fiscal*) (tax) allowance.

abattis [abati] **1** *nmpl [volaille]* giblets; (*: *bras et jambes*) limbs; *V* **numéroter. 2** *nm* (*Can: terrain déboisé*) brushwood. **faire un ~** to untimber land.

abattoir [abatwaʀ] *nm* slaughterhouse, abattoir. (*fig*) **envoyer des hommes à l'~*** to send men to be slaughtered *ou* massacred.

abattre [abatʀ(ə)] (41) **1** *vt* **(a)** (*faire tomber*) *maison, mur* to pull *ou* knock down; *arbre* to cut down, fell; *adversaire* to fell, floor, knock down; *roche, minerai* to break away, hew; *quilles* to knock down; *avion* to bring *ou* shoot down. **le vent a abattu la cheminée** the wind blew the chimney down; **la pluie abat la poussière** the rain settles the dust; **il abattit son bâton sur ma tête** he brought his stick down on my head.

(b) (*tuer*) *personne, oiseau* to shoot down; *fauve* to shoot, kill; *animal domestique* to destroy, put down; *animal de boucherie* to slaughter.

(c) (*fig: ébranler*) *[fièvre, maladie]* to weaken, drain (of energy); *[mauvaise nouvelle, échec]* to demoralize, shatter*; *[efforts]* to tire out, wear out. **la maladie l'a abattu** (the) illness left him prostrate, (the) illness drained him of energy; **être abattu par la fatigue/la chaleur** to be overcome by tiredness/the heat; **se laisser ~ par des échecs** to be demoralized by failures, let failures get one down; **ne te laisse pas ~** keep your spirits up, don't let things get you down.

(d) (*fig: affaiblir*) *courage* to weaken; *forces* to drain, sap; *fierté* to humble.

(e) *carte* to lay down. **~ son jeu *ou* ses cartes** (*lit*) to lay *ou* put one's cards on the table, lay down one's hand; (*fig*) to show one's hand *ou* cards, lay *ou* put one's cards on the table.

(f) ~ du travail to get through a lot of work.

2 s'abattre *vpr* **(a)** (*tomber*) *[personne]* to fall (down), collapse; *[cheminée]* to fall *ou* crash down. **le mât s'abattit** the mast came *ou* went crashing down.

(b) s'~ sur *[pluie]* to beat down on(to); *[ennemi]* to swoop down on, fall on; *[oiseau de proie]* to swoop down on; *[moineaux]* to sweep down on(to); (*fig*) *[coups, injures]* to rain on.

3: abat-jour *nm inv [lampe]* lampshade; (*Archit*) splay; **abat-son** *nm inv* louver *ou* luffer-boarding (*to deflect sound downwards*); **abat-vent** *nm inv [cheminée]* chimney cowl; *[fenêtre, ouverture]* louver boarding; (*Agr*) wind screen.

abattu, e [abaty] (*ptp de* **abattre**) *adj* (*fatigué*) worn out, exhausted; (*faible*) *malade* very weak, feeble, prostrate; (*déprimé*) downcast, demoralized, despondent; *V* **bride.**

abbatial, e, *mpl* **-aux** [abasjal, o] **1** *adj* abbey (*épith*). **2 abbatiale** *nf* abbey-church.

abbaye [abei] *nf* abbey.

abbé [abe] *nm [abbaye]* abbot; (*prêtre*) priest. **~ mitré** mitred abbot; *V* **monsieur.**

abbesse [abɛs] *nf* abbess.

abc [abese] *nm* (*livre*) ABC *ou* alphabet book; (*rudiments*) ABC, fundamentals (*pl*), rudiments (*pl*). **c'est l'~ du métier** it's the most elementary *ou* the first requirement of the job.

abcès [apsɛ] *nm* (*Méd*) abscess; *[gencive]* gumboil, abscess. (*fig*) **il faut vider l'~!** we must root out the evil!

abdication [abdikɑsjɔ̃] *nf* (*lit, fig*) abdication. (*fig*) **l'~ des**

parents devant leurs enfants parents' abdication of authority over their children.

abdiquer [abdike] (1) **1** *vi [roi]* to abdicate. **la justice abdique devant le terrorisme** justice gives way in the face of *ou* before terrorism; **dans ces conditions j'abdique*** in that case I give up.
2 *vt*: ~ **la couronne** to abdicate the throne; ~ **ses croyances/son autorité** to give up *ou* renounce one's beliefs/one's authority.

abdomen [abdɔmɛn] *nm* abdomen.

abdominal, e, *mpl* **-aux** [abdɔminal, o] **1** *adj* abdominal. **2** *nmpl*: ~**aux** stomach *ou* abdominal muscles; (*Sport*) **faire des ~aux** to do exercises for the *ou* exercise one's stomach muscles.

abécédaire [abesedɛʀ] *nm* alphabet primer.

abeille [abɛj] *nf* bee. ~ **maçonne** mason bee; *V* **nid, reine.**

aber [abɛʀ] *nm* aber (*deep estuary*).

aberrant, e [abɛʀɑ̃, ɑ̃t] *adj* **(a)** (*insensé*) *conduite* aberrant; *histoire* absurd, nonsensical. **il est ~ qu'il parte** it is absolutely absurd *ou* it is sheer nonsense that he should go. **(b)** (*Bio*) aberrant, abnormal, deviant; (*Ling*) irregular.

aberration [abɛʀɑsjɔ̃] *nf* (*gén*) (mental) aberration; (*Astron, Phys*) aberration. **dans un moment** *ou* **instant d'~** in a moment of aberration; **par quelle ~ a-t-il accepté?** whatever possessed him to accept?

abêtir *vt*, **s'abêtir** *vpr* [abetiʀ] (2) to turn into a moron *ou* half-wit.

abêtissant, e [abetisɑ̃, ɑ̃t] *adj travail* which makes one dull *ou* half-witted.

abêtissement [abetismɑ̃] *nm* (*état*) stupidity, mindlessness. (*action*) **l'~ des masses par la télévision** the stupefying effect of television on the masses.

abhorrer [abɔʀe] (1) *vt* (*littér*) to abhor, loathe.

abîme [abim] *nm* **(a)** abyss, gulf, chasm. (*fig*) **l'~ qui nous sépare** the gulf *ou* chasm between us.
(b) (*loc*) **au bord de l'~** *pays, banquier* on the brink *ou* verge of ruin; *personne* on the brink *ou* verge of despair; **être au fond de l'~** *[personne]* to be in the depths of despair *ou* at one's lowest ebb; *[pays]* to have reached rock-bottom; (*littér*) **les ~s de l'enfer/de la nuit/du temps** the depths of hell/night/time; **être plongé dans un ~ de perplexité** to be utterly *ou* deeply perplexed; **c'est un ~ de bêtise** he's abysmally *ou* incredibly stupid.

abîmer [abime] (1) **1** *vt* **(a)** (*ébrécher*) to damage, spoil; (*rayer, tacher*) to spoil. **la pluie a complètement abîmé mon chapeau** the rain has ruined my hat.
(b) (‡: *frapper*) ~ **qn** to beat sb up; ~ **le portrait à qn** to smash* *ou* bash* sb's face in.
2 s'abîmer *vpr* **(a)** *[objet]* to get spoilt *ou* damaged; *[fruits]* to go bad, spoil. **s'~ les yeux** to ruin *ou* strain one's eyes, spoil one's eyesight.
(b) (*littér*) *[navire]* to sink, founder. *[personne]* **s'~ dans la réflexion** to be deep *ou* sunk *ou* plunged in thought; **s'~ dans la douleur** to lose o.s. in grief.

abject, e [abʒɛkt] *adj* despicable, contemptible, abject. **être ~ envers qn** to treat sb in a despicable manner, behave despicably towards sb.

abjection [abʒɛksjɔ̃] *nf* abjection, abjectness.

abjuration [abʒyʀɑsjɔ̃] *nf* abjuration, renunciation, recantation (*de* of). **faire ~ de** to abjure.

abjurer [abʒyʀe] (1) *vt* to abjure, renounce, recant.

ablatif [ablatif] *nm* ablative. ~ **absolu** ablative absolute.

ablation [ablɑsjɔ̃] *nf* (*Méd*) removal, ablation (*T*); (*Géol*) ablation.

ablette [ablɛt] *nf* bleak.

ablutions [ablysjɔ̃] *nfpl* (*gén*) ablutions. **faire ses ~** to perform one's ablutions.

abnégation [abnegɑsjɔ̃] *nf* (self-)abnegation, self-denial, self-sacrifice. **avec ~** selflessly.

aboiement [abwamɑ̃] *nm* **(a)** *[chien]* bark. ~**s** barking (*U*). **(b)** (*péj*) (*cri*) cry. (*critiques, exhortations*) ~**s** rantings, snarlings.

abois [abwa] *nmpl* baying. **aux ~** (*Chasse*) at bay; (*fig*) at bay, with one's back to the wall, in a desperate plight.

abolir [abɔliʀ] (2) *vt coutume, loi* to abolish, do away with.

abolition [abɔlisjɔ̃] *nf* abolition.

abolitionnisme [abɔlisjɔnism(ə)] *nm* abolitionism.

abolitionniste [abɔlisjɔnist(ə)] *adj, nmf* abolitionist.

abominable [abɔminabl(ə)] *adj* abominable, horrible; (*sens affaibli*) awful, frightful, terrible. **l'~ homme des neiges** the abominable snowman.

abominablement [abɔminabləmɑ̃] *adv s'habiller* abominably. ~ **cher** frightfully *ou* terribly expensive; ~ **laid** frightfully *ou* horribly ugly.

abomination [abɔminɑsjɔ̃] *nf* **(a)** (*horreur, crime*) abomination. **(b)** (*loc*) **avoir qn/qch en ~** to loathe *ou* abominate (*rare*) sb/sth; **c'est une ~!** it's abominable!; **l'~ de la désolation** the abomination of desolation; **dire des ~s** to say abominable *ou* outrageous things.

abominer [abɔmine] (1) *vt* (*littér: exécrer*) to loathe, abominate (*rare*).

abondamment [abɔ̃damɑ̃] *adv* abundantly, plentifully; *écrire* prolifically; *manger, boire* copiously. **prouver ~ qch** to provide ample proof *ou* evidence of sth.

abondance [abɔ̃dɑ̃s] *nf* **(a)** (*profusion*) abundance. **des fruits en ~** plenty of *ou* an abundance of fruit, fruit in abundance *ou* in plenty; **larmes qui coulent en ~** tears falling in profusion *ou* profusely; **il y a (une) ~ de** there are plenty of, there is an abundance of; **année d'~** year of plenty; (*Prov*) **~ de biens ne nuit pas** an abundance of goods does no harm; *V* **corne.**
(b) (*richesses*) wealth, prosperity, affluence. **vivre dans l'~** to live in affluence; **~ d'idées** wealth of ideas.
(c) parler d'~ (*improviser*) to improvise, extemporize; (*parler beaucoup*) to speak at length.

abondant, e [abɔ̃dɑ̃, ɑ̃t] *adj récolte* good; *réserves* plentiful; *végétation* lush, luxuriant; *chevelure* thick, abundant (*frm*); *larmes* profuse, copious; *repas* copious, hearty (*épith*); *style* rich. **il me fit d'~es recommandations** he gave me copious advice, he lavished advice on me; **illustré d'~es photographies** illustrated with numerous photographs, richly *ou* lavishly illustrated with photographs; **la récolte est ~e cette année** there is a rich *ou* good *ou* fine harvest this year; **les pêches sont ~es sur le marché** peaches are in plentiful *ou* good *ou* generous supply; **il lui faut une nourriture ~e** he must have plenty to eat *ou* plenty of food.

abonder [abɔ̃de] (1) *vi* **(a)** to abound, be plentiful. **les légumes abondent cette année** there are plenty of vegetables this year, vegetables are plentiful *ou* in good supply this year.
(b) ~ en to be full of, abound in; **les forêts/rivières abondent en gibier/poissons** the forests/rivers are full of *ou* teeming with game/fish; **son œuvre abonde en images** his work is rich in *ou* is full of images.
(c) il abonda dans notre sens he was in complete *ou* thorough *ou* full agreement with us.

abonné, e [abɔne] (*ptp de* **abonner**) **1** *adj*: **être ~ à un journal** to subscribe to a paper; **être ~ au téléphone** to be on the phone (*Brit*), have a phone; **être ~ au gaz** to have gas, be a gas consumer; (*fig*) **il y est ~!*** he's making (quite) a habit of it!
2 *nm,f* (*Presse, Téléc*) subscriber; (*Élec, Gaz*) consumer; (*Rail, Sport, Théât*) season-ticket holder.

abonnement [abɔnmɑ̃] *nm* (*Presse*) subscription; (*Téléc*) rental; (*Rail, Sport, Théât*) season ticket. **prendre un ~ à un journal** to subscribe to *ou* take out a subscription to a paper.

abonner [abɔne] (1) **1** *vt*: ~ **qn (à qch)** (*Presse*) to take out a subscription (to sth) for sb; (*Sport, Théât*) to buy sb a season ticket (for sth).
2 s'abonner *vpr* (*Presse*) to subscribe, take out a subscription (*à* to); (*Sport, Théât*) to buy a season ticket (*à* for).

abord [abɔʀ] *nm* **(a)** (*environs*) ~**s** (*gén*) surroundings; *[ville, village]* outskirts, surroundings; **aux ~s de** in the area around *ou* surrounding; **dans ce quartier et aux ~s** in this area and round about.
(b) (*manière d'accueillir*) manner. **être d'un ~** *ou* **avoir l'~ rude/rébarbatif** to have a rough/an off-putting (*surtout Brit*) manner; **être d'un ~ facile/difficile** to be approachable/unapproachable.
(c) (*accès*) access, approach. **lieu d'un ~ difficile** place with difficult means of access, place that is difficult to get to; **lecture d'un ~ difficile** reading matter which is difficult to get into *ou* difficult to get to grips with.
(d) (*loc*) **d'~**: (*en premier lieu*) **allons d'~ chez le boucher** let's go to the butcher's first; (*au commencement*) **il fut (tout) d'~ poli, puis il devint grossier** he was polite at first *ou* initially, and then became rude; (*introduisant une restriction*) **d'~, il n'a même pas 18 ans** for a start *ou* in the first place, he's not even 18; **dès l'~** from the outset, from the very beginning; **au premier ~** at first sight, initially; *V* **prime, tout.**

abordable [abɔʀdabl(ə)] *adj prix* reasonable; *marchandise* reasonable, reasonably priced; *personne* approachable; *lieu* accessible.

abordage [abɔʀdaʒ] *nm* **(a)** (*assaut*) attacking. **à l'~!** up lads and at 'em!, away boarders! **(b)** (*accident*) collision; *V* **sabre.**

aborder [abɔʀde] (1) **1** *vt* **(a)** (*arriver à*) *rivage* to reach; *contrée* to arrive in *ou* at, reach; *tournant, montée* to reach. **les coureurs abordent la ligne droite** the runners are entering the home straight; (*fig*) ~ **la vieillesse avec inquiétude** to approach old age with misgivings.
(b) (*approcher*) *personne* to approach, go *ou* come up to, accost. **il m'a abordé avec un sourire** he came up to me *ou* approached me with a smile.
(c) (*entreprendre*) *sujet* to start on, take up, tackle; *problème* to tackle. **il n'a abordé le roman que vers la quarantaine** he didn't take up writing *ou* move on to writing novels until he was nearly forty; **c'est le genre de question qu'il ne faut jamais ~ avec lui** that's the sort of question you should never get on to *ou* touch on with him.
(d) (*Naut*) (*attaquer*) to board; (*heurter*) to collide with.
2 *vi* (*Naut*) to land, touch *ou* reach land. ~ **dans** *ou* **sur une île** to land on an island.

aborigène [abɔʀiʒɛn] (*indigène*) **1** *adj* aboriginal, indigenous. **2** *nmf* aborigine, native. **les ~s d'Australie** the Australian aborigines, the Aborigines.

abortif, -ive [abɔʀtif, iv] (*Méd*) **1** *adj* abortive. **2** *nm* abortifacient (*T*).

abouchement [abuʃmɑ̃] *nm* (*Tech*) joining up end to end; (*Anat*) anastomosis.

aboucher [abuʃe] (1) **1** *vt* (*Tech*) to join up (end to end). (*fig*) ~ **qn avec** to put sb in contact *ou* in touch with. **2 s'aboucher** *vpr*: **s'~ avec qn** to get in touch with sb, make contact with sb.

abouler‡ [abule] (1) **1** *vt* (*donner*) to hand over. **aboule!** hand over!*, give it here!*, let's have it!* **2 s'abouler** *vpr* (*venir*) to come. **aboule-toi!** come (over) here!

aboulie [abuli] *nf* ab(o)ulia.

aboulique [abulik] **1** *adj* ab(o)ulic (*T*). **2** *nmf* (*Méd*) person suffering from ab(o)ulia. (*fig*) **son mari est un ~** her husband is utterly apathetic *ou* (totally) lacking in will power.

about [abu] *nm* (*Tech*) butt.

aboutement [abutmɑ̃] *nm* (*action*) joining (end to end); (*état*) join.

abouter [abute] (1) *vt* to join (up) (end to end).

aboutir [abutiʀ] (2) *vi* **(a)** (*réussir*) *[démarche]* to succeed, come off*; *[personne]* to succeed. **ses efforts/tentatives n'ont**

pas abouti his efforts/attempts have had no effect *ou* have failed *ou* didn't come off*; **faire ~ des négociations/un projet** to bring negotiations/a project to a successful conclusion.

(b) (*arriver à, déboucher sur*) ~ **à** *ou* **dans** to end (up) in *ou* at; **la route aboutit à un cul-de-sac** the road ends in a cul-de-sac; **une telle philosophie aboutit au désespoir** such a philosophy results in *ou* leads to despair; ~ **en prison** to end up in prison; **les négociations n'ont abouti à rien** the negotiations have come to nothing, nothing has come of the negotiations; **en additionnant le tout, j'aboutis à 12 F** adding it all up I get 12 francs *ou* I get it to come to 12 francs; **il n'aboutira jamais à rien dans la vie** he'll never get anywhere in life.

(c) (*Méd*) *[abcès]* to come to a head.

aboutissants [abutisɑ̃] *nmpl V* **tenant.**

aboutissement [abutismɑ̃] *nm* (*résultat*) *[efforts, opération]* outcome, result; (*succès*) *[plan]* success.

aboyer [abwaje] (8) *vi* to bark; (*péj: crier*) to shout, yell. ~ **après** *ou* **contre qn** to bark *ou* yell at sb; *V* **chien.**

aboyeur† [abwajœʀ] *nm* (*Théât*) barker.

abracadabra [abʀakadabʀa] *nm* abracadabra.

abracadabrant, e [abʀakadabʀɑ̃, ɑ̃t] *adj* incredible, fantastic, preposterous.

abrasif, -ive [abʀazif, iv] *adj, nm* abrasive.

abrasion [abʀazjɔ̃] *nf* (*gén, Géog*) abrasion.

abrégé [abʀeʒe] *nm [livre, discours]* summary, synopsis; *[texte]* summary, précis. **faire un ~ de** to summarize, précis; **en ~** (*en miniature*) in miniature; (*en bref*) in brief, in a nutshell; **répéter qch en ~** to repeat sth in a few words; **mot/phrase en ~** word/sentence in a shortened *ou* an abbreviated form; **voilà, en ~, de quoi il s'agissait** briefly *ou* to cut a long story short, this is what it was all about.

abrégement [abʀɛʒmɑ̃] *nm [durée]* cutting short, shortening; *[texte]* abridgement.

abréger [abʀeʒe] (3 *et* 6) *vt vie* to shorten; *souffrances* to cut short; *durée, visite* to cut short, shorten; *texte* to shorten, abridge; *mot* to abbreviate, shorten. **pour ~ les longues soirées d'hiver** to while away the long winter evenings, to make the long winter evenings pass more quickly; **abrège!*** come *ou* get to the point!

abreuver [abʀœve] (1) **1** *vt* **(a)** *animal* to water.

(b) (*fig*) ~ **qn de** to overwhelm *ou* shower sb with; ~ **qn d'injures** to heap *ou* shower insults on sb; **le public est abreuvé de films d'horreur** (*inondé*) the public is swamped with horror films; (*saturé*) the public has had its fill of *ou* has had enough of horror films.

(c) (*imbiber*) (*gén*) to soak, drench (*de* with); (*Tech*) to prime. **terre abreuvée d'eau** sodden *ou* waterlogged ground.

2 s'abreuver *vpr [animal]* to drink; (*) *[personne]* to quench one's thirst, wet one's whistle*.

abreuvoir [abʀœvwaʀ] *nm* (*mare*) watering place; (*récipient*) drinking trough.

abréviation [abʀevjasjɔ̃] *nf* abbreviation.

abri [abʀi] *nm* **(a)** (*refuge, cabane*) shelter. ~ **à vélos** bicycle shed; (*Mil*) ~ **souterrain/antiatomique** air-raid/fallout shelter; (*hum*) **tous aux ~s!** take cover!, run for cover!; **construire un ~ pour sa voiture** to build a carport.

(b) (*fig: protection*) refuge (*contre* from), protection (*contre* against).

(c) (*loc*) **à l'~: être/mettre à l'~** (*des intempéries*) to be/put under cover; (*du vol, de la curiosité*) to be/put in a safe place; **se mettre à l'~** to shelter, take cover; **être à l'~ de** (*protégé de*) *pluie, vent, soleil* to be sheltered from; *danger, soupçons* to be safe *ou* shielded from; *regards* to be safe *ou* hidden from; (*protégé par*) *mur, feuillage* to be sheltered *ou* protected *ou* shielded by; **je ne suis pas à l'~ d'une erreur** I'm not above making a mistake; **elle est à l'~ du besoin** she is free from financial worries; **se mettre à l'~ de** *pluie, vent, soleil* to take shelter from; *regards* to hide from, take cover from; *soupçons* to safeguard o.s. against; **se mettre à l'~ du mur/du feuillage** to take cover *ou* shelter behind the wall/under the trees; **pour se mettre à l'~ d'une mauvaise surprise** to safeguard o.s. against an unpleasant surprise; **mettre qch à l'~ de** *intempéries* to shelter sth from; *regards* to hide *ou* shield sth from; **mettre qch à l'~ d'un mur** to put sth in the shelter of a wall.

abricot [abʀiko] **1** *nm* (*Bot*) apricot; *V* **pêche**[1]. **2** *adj inv* apricot (-coloured).

abricoté, e [abʀikɔte] *adj gâteau* apricot (*épith*); *V* **pêche**[1].

abricotier [abʀikɔtje] *nm* apricot tree.

abriter [abʀite] (1) **1** *vt* (*de la pluie, du vent*) to shelter (*de* from); (*du soleil*) to shade (*de* from); (*de radiations*) to screen (*de* from). **le bâtiment peut ~ 20 personnes** the building can accommodate 20 people; **abritant ses yeux de sa main** shading his eyes with his hand; **le côté abrité** (*de la pluie*) the sheltered side; (*du soleil*) the shady side; **maison abritée** house in a sheltered spot, sheltered house.

2 s'abriter *vpr* to (take) shelter (*de* from), take cover. (*fig*) **s'~ derrière la tradition** to shield o.s. *ou* hide behind tradition, use tradition as a shield; (*fig*) **s'~ derrière son chef/le règlement** to take cover behind one's boss/the rules.

abrogation [abʀɔgasjɔ̃] *nf* repeal, abrogation.

abrogeable [abʀɔʒabl(ə)] *adj* repealable.

abroger [abʀɔʒe] (3) *vt* to repeal, abrogate.

abrupt, e [abʀypt, pt(ə)] **1** *adj pente* abrupt, steep; *falaise* sheer; *personne* abrupt; *manières* abrupt, brusque. **2** *nm* steep slope.

abruptement [abʀyptəmɑ̃] *adv descendre* steeply, abruptly; *annoncer* abruptly.

abruti, e [abʀyti] (*ptp de* **abrutir**) **1** *adj* **(a)** (*hébété*) stunned, dazed (*de* with). ~ **par l'alcool** besotted *ou* stupefied with drink.

(b) (*: *bête*) idiotic*, moronic‡. **2** *nm,f* (‡) idiot*, moron‡.

abrutir [abʀytiʀ] (2) *vt* **(a)** (*fatiguer*) to exhaust. **la chaleur m'abrutit** the heat makes me feel quite stupid; ~ **qn de travail** to work sb silly *ou* stupid; **ces discussions m'ont abruti** these discussions have left me quite dazed; **s'~ à travailler** to work o.s. silly; **leur professeur les abrutit de travail** their teacher drives them stupid with work; **tu vas t'~ à force de lire** you'll overtax *ou* exhaust yourself reading so much.

(b) (*abêtir*) ~ **qn** to deaden sb's mind; **l'alcool l'avait abruti** he was stupefied *ou* besotted with drink; **s'~ à regarder la télévision** to become quite moronic *ou* mindless through watching (too much) television.

abrutissant, e [abʀytisɑ̃, ɑ̃t] *adj bruit* stunning, thought-destroying; *travail* mind-destroying. **ce bruit est ~** this noise drives you silly *ou* stupid *ou* wears you down.

abrutissement [abʀytismɑ̃] *nm* (*fatigue extrême*) (mental) exhaustion; (*abêtissement*) mindless *ou* moronic state. **l'~ des masses par la télévision** the stupefying effect of television on the masses.

abscisse [apsis] *nf* abscissa.

abscons, e [apskɔ̃, ɔ̃s] *adj* abstruse, recondite.

absence [apsɑ̃s] *nf* **(a)** (*gén, Jur*) *[personne]* absence. **son ~ à la réunion** his absence *ou* non-attendance at the meeting; (*Admin, Scol*) **3 ~s successives** 3 absences in succession; **cet élève/employé accumule les ~s** this pupil/employee is persistently absent.

(b) (*manque*) absence, lack (*de* of). **~ de goût/de réflexion/d'affection** lack of taste/thought/affection; **l'~ de rideaux** the absence of curtains; **il constata l'~ de sa valise** he noticed that his case was missing *ou* wasn't there *ou* had gone.

(c) (*défaillance*) ~ **(de mémoire)** mental blank; **il a des ~s** at times his mind goes blank *ou* is elsewhere.

(d) en l'~ de in the absence of; **en l'~ de sa mère, c'est Anne qui fait la cuisine** in her mother's absence *ou* while her mother's away, Anne is *ou* it's Anne who is doing the cooking; **en l'~ de preuves** in the absence of proof.

absent, e [apsɑ̃, ɑ̃t] **1** *adj* **(a)** *personne* (*gén*) away (*de* from); (*pour maladie*) absent (*de* from), off*. **être ~ de son travail** to be absent from work, be off work*; **il est ~ de Paris/de son bureau en ce moment** he's out of *ou* away from Paris/his office at the moment; **conférence internationale dont la France était ~e** international conference from which France was absent.

(b) *sentiment* lacking; *objet* missing. **discours d'où toute émotion était ~e** speech in which there was no trace of emotion; **il constata que sa valise était ~e** he noticed that his case was missing *ou* had gone.

(c) (*distrait*) *air* vacant.

(d) (*Jur*) missing.

2 *nm,f* (*Scol Admin*) absentee; (*littér: mort, en voyage*) absent one (*littér*); (*disparu*) missing person. **le ministre/le champion a été le grand ~ de la réunion** the minister/the champion was the most notable absentee at the meeting; (*Prov*) **les ~s ont toujours tort** the absent are always in the wrong.

absentéisme [apsɑ̃teism(ə)] *nm* (*Agr, Écon, Ind*) absenteeism.

absentéiste [apsɑ̃teist(ə)] *nmf* (*Agr*) absentee. (*gén*) **c'est un ~, il est du genre ~** he is always *ou* regularly absent *ou* off*; **propriétaire ~** absentee landlord.

absenter (s') [apsɑ̃te] (1) *vpr* (*gén*) to go out, leave; (*Mil*) to go absent. **s'~ de** *pièce* to go out of, leave; *ville* to leave; **s'~ quelques instants** to go out for a few moments; **je m'étais absenté de Paris** I was away from *ou* out of Paris; **elle s'absente souvent de son travail** she is frequently off work* *ou* away from work; **élève qui s'absente trop souvent** pupil who is too often absent *ou* away (from school) *ou* off school.

abside [apsid] *nf* apse.

absidial, e, *mpl* **-iaux** [apsidjal, jo] *adj* apsidal.

absidiole [apsidjɔl] *nf* apsidiole.

absinthe [apsɛ̃t] *nf* (*liqueur*) absinth(e); (*Bot*) wormwood, absinth(e).

absolu, e [apsɔly] **1** *adj* **(a)** (*total*) absolute. **en cas d'~e nécessité** if absolutely essential; **être dans l'impossibilité ~e de faire qch** to find it absolutely impossible to do sth; **c'est une règle ~e** it's an absolutely unbreakable rule, it's a hard-and-fast rule; **j'ai la preuve ~e de sa trahison** I have absolute *ou* positive proof of his betrayal; *V* **alcool.**

(b) (*entier*) *ton* peremptory; *jugement, caractère* rigid, uncompromising.

(c) (*opposé à* **relatif**) *valeur, température* absolute. **considérer qch de manière ~e** to consider sth absolutely *ou* in absolute terms.

(d) (*Hist, Pol*) *majorité, roi, pouvoir* absolute.

(e) (*Ling*) *construction* absolute. **verbe employé de manière ~e** verb used absolutely *ou* in the absolute; **génitif/ablatif ~** genitive/ablative absolute; *V* **superlatif.**

2 *nm*: **l'~** the absolute; **juger dans l'~** to judge out of context *ou* in the absolute.

absolument [apsɔlymɑ̃] *adv* **(a)** (*entièrement*) absolutely. **avoir ~ tort** to be quite *ou* absolutely *ou* entirely wrong; **s'opposer ~ à qch** to be entirely *ou* absolutely opposed to sth, be completely *ou* dead* against sth; **il a tort! — ~!** he's wrong! — absolutely!; **vous êtes sûr? — ~!** are you sure? — positive! *ou* absolutely!; **~ pas!** certainly not!; **~ rien!** absolutely nothing!, nothing whatever.

(b) (*à tout prix*) absolutely, positively. **vous devez ~** you absolutely *ou* positively *ou* simply must; **il veut ~ revenir** he (absolutely) insists upon returning.

(c) (*Ling*) absolutely.

absolution [apsɔlysjɔ̃] *nf* **(a)** (*Rel*) absolution (*de* from). **donner l'~ à qn** to give sb absolution. **(b)** (*Jur*) dismissal (*of case, when defendant is considered to have no case to answer*).

absolutisme [apsɔlytism(ə)] *nm* absolutism.

absolutiste [apsɔlytist(ə)] **1** *adj* absolutistic. **2** *nmf* absolutist.
absorbable [apsɔʀbabl(ə)] *adj* absorbable.
absorbant, e [apsɔʀbɑ̃, ɑ̃t] **1** *adj matière* absorbent; *tâche* absorbing, engrossing; (*Bot, Zool*) *fonction, racines* absorptive. **2** *nm* absorbent.
absorbé, e [apsɔʀbe] (*ptp de* **absorber**) *adj*: **avoir un air ~** to look engrossed *ou* absorbed (in one's thoughts *etc*).
absorber [apsɔʀbe] (1) **1** *vt* **(a)** (*avaler*) *médicament, aliment* to take; (*fig*) *parti, groupe* to absorb; (*Écon*) *firme* to take over, absorb.
(b) (*résorber*) (*gén*) to absorb; *liquide* to absorb, soak up; *tache* to remove, lift; (*Fin*) *dette* to absorb; *bruit* to deaden, absorb. **le noir absorbe la lumière** black absorbs light; **cet achat a absorbé presque toutes mes économies** I used up *ou* spent nearly all my savings on that purchase.
(c) (*accaparer*) *attention, temps* to occupy, take up. **mon travail m'absorbe beaucoup, je suis très absorbé par mon travail** my work takes up *ou* claims a lot of my time; **absorbé par son travail il ne m'entendit pas** he was engrossed in *ou* absorbed in his work and he didn't hear me; **cette pensée absorbait mon esprit, j'avais l'esprit absorbé par cette pensée** my mind was completely taken up with this thought.
2 s'absorber *vpr* (*se plonger*) **s'~/être absorbé dans une lecture** to become/be absorbed *ou* engrossed in reading; **s'~/être absorbé dans une profonde méditation** to become lost in/be plunged deep in thought.
absorption [apsɔʀpsjɔ̃] *nf* **(a)** (*V* **absorber**) taking; absorption; takeover; removal. **(b)** (*méditation*) absorption.
absoudre [apsudʀ(ə)] (51) *vt* (*Rel*) to absolve (*de* from); (*littér*) to absolve (*de* from), pardon (*de* for); (*Jur*) to dismiss.
absoute [apsut] *nf [office des morts]* absolution; *[jeudi saint]* general absolution.
abstenir (s') [apstəniʀ] (22) *vpr* **(a) s'~ de qch** to refrain *ou* abstain from sth; **s'~ de faire** to refrain from doing; **s'~ de vin, s'~ de boire du vin** to abstain from wine, refrain from drinking wine; **s'~ de tout commentaire, s'~ de faire des commentaires** to refrain from (making) any comment, refrain from commenting; **dans ces conditions je préfère m'~** in that case I'd rather not; *V* **doute.**
(b) (*Pol*) to abstain (*de voter* from voting).
abstention [apstɑ̃sjɔ̃] *nf* abstention; (*non-intervention*) non-participation.
abstentionnisme [apstɑ̃sjɔnism(ə)] *nm* abstentionism.
abstentionniste [apstɑ̃sjɔnist(ə)] *adj, nmf* abstentionist.
abstinence [apstinɑ̃s] *nf* abstinence. **faire ~** to abstain (*from meat on Fridays*).
abstinent, e [apstinɑ̃, ɑ̃t] *adj* abstinent.
abstraction [apstʀaksjɔ̃] *nf* (*fait d'abstraire*) abstraction; (*idée abstraite*) abstraction, abstract idea. **faire ~ de** to set *ou* leave aside, disregard; **en faisant ~** *ou* **~ faite des difficultés** setting aside *ou* leaving aside *ou* disregarding the difficulties.
abstraire [apstʀɛʀ] (50) **1** *vt* (*isoler*) to abstract (*de* from), isolate (*de* from); (*conceptualiser*) to abstract. **2 s'abstraire** *vpr* to cut o.s. off (*de* from).
abstrait, e [apstʀɛ, ɛt] **1** *adj* abstract. **2** *nm* **(a)** (*artiste*) abstract painter. (*genre*) **l'~** abstract art. **(b)** (*Philos*) **l'~** the abstract; **dans l'~** in the abstract.
abstraitement [apstʀɛtmɑ̃] *adv* abstractly, in the abstract.
abstrus, e [apstʀy, yz] *adj* abstruse, recondite.
absurde [apsyʀd(ə)] **1** *adj* (*Philos*) absurd; (*illogique*) absurd, preposterous; (*ridicule*) absurd, ridiculous, ludicrous. **ne sois pas ~!** don't talk such nonsense!, don't be ridiculous! *ou* absurd!
2 *nm* (*Littérat, Philos*) **l'~** the absurd; *V* **prouver.**
absurdement [apsyʀdəmɑ̃] *adv* (*V* **absurde**) absurdly; preposterously; ridiculously; ludicrously.
absurdité [apsyʀdite] *nf* **(a)** (*V* **absurde**) absurdity; preposterousness; ridiculousness; ludicrousness.
(b) (*parole, acte*) absurdity. **il vient de dire une ~** he has just said something (quite) absurd *ou* ridiculous; **dire des ~s** to talk nonsense.
abus [aby] **1** *nm* **(a)** (*excès*) *[médicaments, alcool]* abuse; *[force, autorité]* abuse, misuse. **faire ~ de** *sa force, son pouvoir* to abuse; **faire ~ de cigarettes** to smoke excessively; **l'~ (qu'il fait) d'aspirine** (his) excessive use *ou* (his) overuse of aspirin; **~ de boisson** excessive drinking, drinking to excess; **nous avons fait des** *ou* **quelques ~ hier soir** we overdid it *ou* things *ou* we overindulged last night; **il y a de l'~!*** that's going a bit too far!*, that's a bit steep!* (*Brit*).
(b) (*injustice*) abuse, social injustice.
2: abus d'autorité abuse *ou* misuse of authority; **abus de confiance** abuse of confidence, breach of trust; (*escroquerie*) confidence trick; **abus de pouvoir** abuse *ou* misuse of power.
abuser [abyze] (1) **1 abuser de** *vt indir* **(a)** (*exploiter*) *situation, crédulité* to exploit, take advantage of; *autorité, puissance* to abuse, misuse; *hospitalité, amabilité, confiance* to abuse; *ami, victime* to take advantage of. **~ de sa force** to misuse one's strength; **je ne veux pas ~ de votre temps** I don't want to encroach on *ou* take up *ou* waste your time; **je ne voudrais pas ~ (de votre gentillesse)** I don't want to impose (upon your kindness); (*euph*) **~ d'une femme** to take advantage of a woman (*euph*); **alors là, tu abuses!** now you're going too far! *ou* overstepping the mark!; **je suis compréhensif, mais il ne faudrait pas ~** I'm an understanding sort of person but don't try taking advantage *ou* don't push me too far; **elle abuse de la situation** she's trying it on a bit*.
(b) (*user avec excès*) *médicaments, citations* to overuse. **~ de l'alcool** to drink too much *ou* excessively, drink to excess; **~ de ses forces** to overexert o.s., overtax one's strength, overdo it*; **il ne faut pas ~ des bonnes choses** one mustn't overindulge in good things, enough is as good as a feast (*Prov*); **il use et (il) abuse de métaphores** he's too fond *ou* overfond of metaphors.
2 *vt [escroc]* to deceive; *[ressemblance]* to mislead. **se laisser ~ par de belles paroles** to be taken in *ou* misled by fine *ou* fair words.
3 s'abuser *vpr* (*frm*) (*se tromper*) to be mistaken, make a mistake; (*se faire des illusions*) to delude o.s. **si je ne m'abuse** if I'm not mistaken.
abusif, -ive [abyzif, iv] *adj pratique* improper; *mère, père* over-possessive; *prix* exorbitant, excessive; *punition* excessive. **usage ~ de son autorité** improper use *ou* misuse of one's authority; **usage ~ d'un mot** misuse *ou* improper use *ou* wrong use of a word; **c'est peut-être ~ de dire cela** it's perhaps putting it a bit strongly to say that.
abusivement [abyzivmɑ̃] *adv* (*Ling: improprement*) wrongly, improperly; (*excessivement*) excessively, to excess. **il s'est servi ~ de lui** he took unfair advantage of him.
abyssal, e, *mpl* **-aux** [abisal, o] *adj* abyssal.
abysse [abis] *nm* (*Géog*) abyssal zone.
abyssin, e [abisɛ̃, in] = **abyssinien.**
Abyssinie [abisini] *nf* Abyssinia.
abyssinien, -ienne [abisinjɛ̃, jɛn] **1** *adj* Abyssinian. **2** *nm,f*: **A~(ne)** Abyssinian.
acabit [akabi] *nm* (*péj*) **être du même ~** to be cast in the same mould; **ils sont tous du même ~** they're all tarred with the same brush; **fréquenter des gens de cet ~** to mix with people of that type *ou* like that.
acacia [akasja] *nm* (*gén: faux acacia, robinier*) locust tree, false acacia; (*Bot: mimosacée*) acacia.
académicien, -ienne [akademisjɛ̃, jɛn] *nm,f* (*gén*) academician; *[Académie française] member of the French Academy,* Academician; (*Antiq*) academic.
académie [akademi] *nf* **(a)** (*société savante*) learned society; (*Antiq*) academy. **l'A~ royale de** the Royal Academy of; **l'A~ des Sciences** the Academy of Science; **l'A~ (française)** the (French) Academy.
(b) (*école*) academy. **~ de dessin/danse** art/dancing school, academy of art/dancing.
(c) (*Univ*) ≈ regional (education) authority.
(d) (*Art: nu*) nude; (*: *anatomie*) anatomy (*hum*).
académique [akademik] *adj* (*péj, Art, littér*) academic; *[Académie française]* of the French Academy; (*Univ*) ≈ of the regional (education) authority, regional authority (*épith*). (*Belgique, Can, Suisse*) **année ~** academic year; *V* **inspection, palme.**
académisme [akademism(ə)] *nm* (*péj*) academicism.
Acadie [akadi] *nf* (*Hist*) Acadia. (*Géog*) **l'~** the Maritime Provinces.
acadien, -ienne [akadjɛ̃, jɛn] **1** *adj* Acadian. **2** *nm* (*Ling*) Acadian. **3** *nm,f*: **A~(ne)** Acadian.
acajou [akaʒu] **1** *nm* (*à bois rouge*) mahogany; (*anacardier*) cashew. **2** *adj inv* mahogany (*épith*).
acanthe [akɑ̃t] *nf* (*Bot*) acanthus. (*Archit*) **(feuille d')~** acanthus.
acariâtre [akaʀjɑtʀ(ə)] *adj caractère* sour, cantankerous; *femme* shrewish. **d'humeur ~** sour-tempered.
accablant, e [akɑblɑ̃, ɑ̃t] *adj chaleur* exhausting, oppressive; *témoignage* overwhelming, damning; *responsabilité* overwhelming; *douleur* excruciating; *travail* exhausting.
accablement [akɑbləmɑ̃] *nm* (*abattement*) despondency, depression; (*oppression*) exhaustion. **être dans l'~ du désespoir** to be in the depths of despair; **être dans l'~ de la douleur** to be prostrate with grief.
accabler [akɑble] (1) *vt* **(a)** *[chaleur, fatigue]* to overwhelm, overcome; (*littér*) *[fardeau]* to weigh down. **accablé de chagrin** prostrate *ou* overwhelmed with grief; **les troupes, accablées sous le nombre** the troops, overwhelmed *ou* overpowered by numbers.
(b) *[témoignage]* to condemn, damn. **sa déposition m'accable** his evidence is overwhelmingly against me.
(c) (*faire subir*) **~ qn d'injures** to heap *ou* shower abuse on sb; **~ qn de reproches/critiques** to heap reproaches/criticism on sb; **il m'accabla de son mépris** he poured contempt upon me; **~ qn d'impôts** to overburden sb with taxes; **~ qn de travail** to overburden sb with work, pile work on sb; **~ qn de questions** to overwhelm *ou* shower sb with questions; (*iro*) **il nous accablait de conseils** he overwhelmed us with advice.
accalmie [akalmi] *nf* (*gén*) lull; *[vent, tempête]* lull (*de* in); *[fièvre]* respite (*dans* in), remission (*dans* of); (*Comm*) *[affaires, transactions]* slack period; *[combat]* lull, break; *[crise politique ou morale]* period of calm, lull, calm spell (*de* in). **profiter d'une ~ pour sortir** to take advantage of a calm spell *ou* of a lull (in the wind) to go out; **nous n'avons pas eu un seul moment d'~ pendant la journée** we didn't have a single quiet moment during the whole day, there was no lull (in the activity) throughout the entire day.
accaparant, e [akapaʀɑ̃, ɑ̃t] *adj métier, enfant* that claims *ou* takes up a great deal of one's time and energy.
accaparement [akapaʀmɑ̃] *nm* (*V* **accaparer**) *[pouvoir, production]* monopolizing; *[médecin etc]* involvement (*par* in).
accaparer [akapaʀe] (1) *vt* **(a)** (*monopoliser*) *production, pouvoir, conversation, hôte* to monopolize. **les enfants l'ont tout de suite accaparée** the children claimed all her attention straight away; **ces élèves brillants qui accaparent les prix** those bright pupils who carry off *ou* grab* all the prizes.
(b) (*absorber*) *[soucis, travail]* to take up the time and energy of. **accaparé par sa profession/les soucis** completely taken up by *ou* wrapped up in his job/worries; **les enfants l'accaparent** the children take up all her time (and energy).

accapareur, -euse [akapaʀœʀ, øz] **1** *adj* monopolistic, grabbing* (*épith*). **2** *nm,f* (*péj*) monopolizer, grabber*.
accéder [aksede] (6) **accéder à** *vt indir* **(a)** (*atteindre*) *lieu, sommet* to reach, get to; *honneur, indépendance* to attain; *grade* to rise to; *responsabilité* to accede to. ~ **directement à** to have direct access to; **on accède au château par le jardin** you (can) get to the castle through the garden, (the) access to the castle is through the garden; ~ **au trône** to accede to the throne.
(b) (*frm: exaucer*) *requête, prière* to grant, accede to (*frm*); *vœux* to meet, comply with.
accélérateur, -trice [akseleʀatœʀ, tʀis] **1** *adj* accelerating. **2** *nm* (*Aut, Phot, Phys*) accelerator.
accélération [akseleʀɑsjɔ̃] *nf* (*Aut, Tech*) acceleration; *[travail]* speeding up; *[pouls]* quickening.
accéléré [akseleʀe] *nm* (*Ciné*) speeded-up motion. **film en** ~ speeded-up film.
accélérer [akseleʀe] (6) **1** *vt rythme* to speed up, accelerate; *travail* to speed up; *vitesse* to increase. ~ **le pas** to quicken *ou* speed up one's pace; (*fig*) ~ **le mouvement** to get things moving, hurry *ou* speed things up; **son pouls s'accéléra** his pulse quickened.
2 *vi* (*Aut, fig*) to accelerate, speed up. **accélère!*** hurry up!, get a move on!*
accent [aksɑ̃] **1** *nm* **(a)** (*prononciation*) accent. **avoir l'~ paysan/du Midi** to have a country/southern (French) accent; **parler sans** ~ to speak without an accent.
(b) (*Orthographe*) accent. **e** ~ **grave/aigu** e grave/acute; ~ **circonflexe** circumflex (accent).
(c) (*Phonétique*) accent, stress; (*fig*) stress. **mettre l'~ sur** (*lit*) to stress, put the stress *ou* accent on; (*fig*) to stress, emphasize; **l'~ est mis sur la production** (the) emphasis *ou* accent is (placed *ou* put) on production.
(d) (*inflexion*) tone (of voice). ~ **suppliant/plaintif** beseeching/plaintive tone; ~ **de sincérité/de détresse** note of sincerity/of distress; **récit qui a l'~ de la sincérité** story which has a ring of sincerity; **avec des ~s de rage (dans la voix)** in accents of rage; **les ~s de cette musique** the strains of this music; **les ~s de l'espoir/de l'amour** the accents of hope/love; **les ~s déchirants de ce poète** the heartrending accents of this poet.
2: **accent de hauteur** pitch; **accent d'intensité** tonic *ou* main stress; **accent de mot** word stress; **accent nasillard** nasal twang; **accent de phrase** sentence stress; **accent tonique** = **accent d'intensité**; **accent traînant** drawl.
accentuable [aksɑ̃tɥabl(ə)] *adj lettre* that can take an accent; *syllabe* that can be stressed *ou* accented.
accentuation [aksɑ̃tɥɑsjɔ̃] *nf* (*V* **accentuer**) accentuation; stressing, emphasizing; intensification; marked increase. (*Phonétique*) **les règles de l'~** the rules of stress.
accentué, e [aksɑ̃tɥe] (*ptp de* **accentuer**) *adj* (*marqué*) marked, pronounced; (*croissant*) increased.
accentuel, -elle [aksɑ̃tɥɛl] *adj* (*Ling*) stressed, accented. **système ~ d'une langue** stress *ou* accentual system of a language.
accentuer [aksɑ̃tɥe] (1) **1** *vt* **(a)** *lettre* to accent; *syllabe* to stress, accent. **syllabe (non) accentuée** (un)stressed *ou* (un)accented syllable.
(b) (*souligner*) *silhouette, contraste* to emphasize, accentuate; *goût* to bring out; (*augmenter*) *effort, poussée* to increase, intensify.
2 s'accentuer *vpr [tendance, hausse]* to become more marked *ou* pronounced, increase; *[contraste, traits]* to become more marked *ou* pronounced. **l'inflation s'accentue** inflation is becoming more pronounced *ou* acute; **le froid s'accentue** it's becoming noticeably colder.
acceptable [aksɛptabl(ə)] *adj* **(a)** (*passable*) *résultats, travail* satisfactory, fair. **ce café/vin est** ~ this coffee/wine is reasonable *ou* quite decent* *ou* quite acceptable. **(b)** (*recevable*) *condition* acceptable.
acceptation [aksɛptɑsjɔ̃] *nf* (*gén*) acceptance.
accepter [aksɛpte] (1) *vt* **(a)** (*gén, Comm*) to accept; *proposition, condition* to agree to, accept; *pari* to take on, accept. **elle accepte tout de sa fille** she puts up with *ou* takes anything from her daughter; (*littér, hum*) **j'en accepte l'augure** I'd like to believe it; ~ **le combat** *ou* **le défi** to take up *ou* accept the challenge; **il n'accepte pas que la vie soit une routine** he won't accept that life should be a routine.
(b) (*être d'accord*) to agree (*de faire* to do). **je n'accepterai pas que tu partes** I shall not agree to your leaving, I won't let you leave.
acception [aksɛpsjɔ̃] *nf* (*Ling*) meaning, sense, acceptation. **dans toute l'~ du mot** *ou* **terme** in every sense *ou* in the full meaning of the word, using the word in its fullest sense; **sans** ~ **de** without distinction of.
accès [aksɛ] *nm* **(a)** (*possibilité d'approche*) access (*U*). **une grande porte interdisait l'~ du jardin** a big gate barred entry *ou* prevented access to the garden; ~ **interdit à toute personne étrangère aux travaux** no entry *ou* no admittance to unauthorized persons; **d'~ facile** *lieu, port* (easily) accessible; *personne* approachable; *traité, manuel* easily understood; *style* accessible; **d'~ difficile** hard to get to, difficult of access; unapproachable; not easily understood.
(b) (*voie*) **tous les ~ de la ville sont bloqués** all approaches to *ou* means of access to the town are blocked; **les ~ de l'immeuble étaient gardés** the entrances to the building were guarded; '~ **aux quais**' 'to the trains'.
(c) (*loc*) **avoir ~ à qch** to have access to sth; **avoir ~ auprès de qn** to be able *ou* in a position to approach sb, have access to sb; **donner ~ à** *lieu* to give access to, (*en montant*) to lead up to; *carrière* to open the door *ou* way to.
(d) (*crise*) *[colère, folie]* fit; *[fièvre]* attack, bout; *[enthousiasme]* burst. ~ **de toux** fit *ou* bout of coughing; **être pris d'un ~ de mélancolie/de tristesse** to be overcome by melancholy/sadness.
accessibilité [aksesibilite] *nf* accessibility (*à* to).
accessible [aksesibl(ə)] *adj lieu* accessible (*à* to), get-at-able*; *personne* approachable; *but* attainable. **parc ~ au public** gardens open to the public; **elle n'est ~ qu'à ses amies** only her friends are able *ou* allowed to see her; **ces études sont ~s à tous** (*gén*) this course is open to everyone; (*financièrement*) this course is within everyone's pocket; (*intellectuellement*) this course is within the reach of everyone; **être ~ à la pitié** to be capable of pity.
accession [aksɛsjɔ̃] *nf* **(a)** ~ **à** *pouvoir, fonction* accession to; *indépendance* attainment of; *rang* rise to; **mouvement d'~ à la propriété** trend towards home ownership.
(b) (*littér: accord*) ~ **à** *requête, désir* granting of, compliance with.
accessit [aksesit] *nm* (*Scol*) ≈ certificate of merit.
accessoire [akseswaʀ] **1** *adj idée* of secondary importance; *clause* secondary; *frais* additional, incidental. **l'un des avantages ~s de ce projet** one of the added *ou* incidental advantages of this plan; **c'est d'un intérêt tout ~** this is only of minor *ou* incidental interest.
2 *nm* **(a)** (*Théât*) prop; (*Aut, Habillement*) accessory. **~s de toilette** toilet requisites; *V* **magasin**.
(b) (*Philos*) **l'~** the unessential, unessentials.
accessoirement [akseswaʀmɑ̃] *adv* (*secondairement*) secondarily, incidentally; (*si besoin est*) if need be, if necessary.
accessoiriste [akseswaʀist(ə)] **1** *nm* property man *ou* master. **2** *nf* property girl *ou* mistress.
accident [aksidɑ̃] **1** *nm* **(a)** (*entraînant des blessures*) (*gén*) accident; (*Aut, Rail*) accident, crash; (*Aviat*) crash. (*Admin*) **il n'y a pas eu d'~ de personnes** there were no casualties, no one was injured; **il y a eu plusieurs ~s mortels sur la route** there have been several road deaths *ou* several fatalities on the roads.
(b) (*mésaventure*) **les ~s de sa carrière** the setbacks in his career; **les ~s de la vie** life's ups and downs, life's trials; **les ~s qui ont entravé la réalisation du projet** the setbacks *ou* hitches which held up the realization of the plan; **cette mauvaise note n'est qu'un ~** this bad mark is only an isolated one; **il a déchiré son manteau, c'est un petit ~** he's torn his coat but it's not very serious; **c'est un simple ~, il ne l'a pas fait exprès** it was just an accident, he didn't do it on purpose; **elle a eu un petit ~ de santé** she's had a little trouble with her health.
(c) (*Méd*) illness, trouble. ~ **secondaire** minor complication.
(d) (*Philos*) accident.
(e) (*littér*) (*hasard*) (pure) accident; (*fait mineur*) minor event. **par ~** by chance, by accident; **si par ~ tu ...** if by chance you ..., if you happen to ... .
(f) (*Mus*) accidental.
2: **accident d'avion** air *ou* plane crash; **accident de la circulation** road accident; **accident de montagne** mountaineering *ou* climbing accident; **accident de parcours** chance mishap; **accident de la route** = **accident de la circulation**; **accident de terrain** accident (*T*), undulation; **les accidents de terrain** the unevenness of the ground; **accident du travail** industrial injury, accident at work; **accident de voiture** car accident *ou* crash.
accidenté, e [aksidɑ̃te] (*ptp de* **accidenter**) **1** *adj* **(a)** *région* undulating, hilly; *terrain* uneven, bumpy; *vie, carrière* chequered, eventful. **(b)** *véhicule* damaged. **2** *nm,f* casualty, injured person.
accidentel, -elle [aksidɑ̃tɛl] *adj* (*fortuit*) *événement* accidental, fortuitous; (*par accident*) *mort* accidental.
accidentellement [aksidɑ̃tɛlmɑ̃] *adv* **(a)** (*par hasard*) accidentally, by accident *ou* chance. **il était là ~** he just happened to be there. **(b)** *mourir* in an accident.
accidenter [aksidɑ̃te] (1) *vt personne* to injure, hurt; *véhicule* to damage.
acclamation [aklamɑsjɔ̃] *nf*: **~s** cheers, cheering; **élire qn par ~** to elect sb by acclamation.
acclamer [aklame] (1) *vt* to cheer, acclaim. **on l'acclama roi** they acclaimed him king.
acclimatable [aklimatabl(ə)] *adj* acclimatizable, acclimatable (*US*).
acclimatation [aklimatɑsjɔ̃] *nf* acclimatization, acclimation (*US*); *V* **jardin**.
acclimatement [aklimatmɑ̃] *nm* acclimatization, acclimation (*US*).
acclimater [aklimate] (1) **1** *vt* (*Bot, Zool*) to acclimatize, acclimate (*US*); (*fig*) *idée, usage* to introduce.
2 s'acclimater *vpr [personne, animal, plante]* to become acclimatized, adapt (o.s. *ou* itself) (*à* to); (*fig*) *[usage, idée]* to become established *ou* accepted.
accointances [akwɛ̃tɑ̃s] *nfpl* contacts, links. **avoir des ~** to have contacts (*avec* with, *dans* in, among).
accolade [akɔlad] *nf* **(a)** (*embrassade*) embrace (*on formal occasion*); (*Hist: coup d'épée*) accolade. **donner/recevoir l'~** to embrace/be embraced.
(b) (*Typ*) brace. **mots (mis) en ~** words bracketed together.
(c) (*Archit, Mus*) accolade.
accoler [akɔle] (1) *vt* (*gén*) to place side by side; (*Typ*) to bracket together. ~ **une chose à une autre** to place a thing beside *ou* next to another; **il avait accolé à son nom celui de sa mère** he had joined *ou* added his mother's maiden name to his surname.
accommodant, e [akɔmɔdɑ̃, ɑ̃t] *adj* accommodating.
accommodation [akɔmɔdɑsjɔ̃] *nf* (*Opt*) accommodation; (*adaptation*) adaptation.

accommodement [akɔmɔdmɑ̃] *nm* (*littér: arrangement*) compromise, accommodation (*littér*). **trouver des ~s** (*hum*) **avec le ciel/avec sa conscience** to come to an arrangement with the powers on high (*hum*)/with one's conscience.

accommoder [akɔmɔde] (1) **1** *vt* **(a)** (*Culin*) *plat* to prepare (*à* in, with). **savoir ~ les restes** to be good at making the most of *ou* using up the left-overs.

(b) (*concilier*) **~ le travail avec le plaisir** to combine business with pleasure; **~ ses principes aux circonstances** to adapt *ou* alter one's principles to suit the circumstances.

(c) (††) (*arranger*) *affaire* to arrange; *querelle* to put right; (*réconcilier*) *ennemis* to reconcile, bring together; (*malmener*) to give harsh treatment to. (*installer confortablement*) **~ qn** to make sb comfortable.

2 *vi* (*Opt*) to focus (*sur* on).

3 s'accommoder *vpr* **(a)** (†: *s'adapter à*) **s'~ à** *[personne]* to adapt (o.s.) to; *[chose]* to adapt to.

(b) (*supporter*) **s'~ de** to put up with; **il lui a bien fallu s'en ~** he just had to put up with it *ou* accept it, he just had to make the best of a bad job; **je m'accommode de peu** I'm content *ou* I can make do with little; **elle s'accommode de tout** she can make do with anything.

(c) (††: *s'arranger avec*) **s'~ avec qn** to come to an agreement *ou* arrangement with sb (*sur* about).

accompagnateur, -trice [akɔ̃paɲatœʀ, tʀis] *nm,f* (*Mus*) accompanist; (*guide*) guide; (*Scol*) accompanying adult; *[voyage organisé]* courier.

accompagnement [akɔ̃paɲmɑ̃] *nm* **(a)** (*Mus*) accompaniment. **sans ~** unaccompanied.

(b) (*Culin*) accompanying vegetables, trimmings*.

(c) (*escorte*) escort; (*fig*) accompaniment; (*conséquence*) result, consequence; *V* **tir**.

accompagner [akɔ̃paɲe] (1) *vt* **(a)** (*escorter*) to accompany, go with, come with. **~ un enfant à l'école** to take a child to school; **~ qn chez lui/à la gare** to go home/to the station with sb, see sb home/to the station; **il s'était fait ~ de sa mère** he had got his mother to go with him *ou* to accompany him; **être accompagné de** *ou* **par qn** to be with sb, be accompanied by sb; **est-ce que vous êtes accompagné?** is there anybody with you?; **tous nos vœux vous accompagnent** all our good wishes go with you; **~ qn de ses huées** to accompany sb with cat calls.

(b) (*assortir*) to accompany, go (together) with. **il accompagna ce mot d'une mimique expressive** he gestured expressively as he said the word; **une lettre accompagnait les fleurs** a letter came with the flowers; **crise de nerfs accompagnée de sanglots** hysteria accompanied by sobbing; **l'agitation qui accompagna son arrivée** the stir *ou* fuss that accompanied his arrival; **la guerre s'accompagne toujours de privations** war is always accompanied by *ou* always brings hardship.

(c) (*Mus*) to accompany (*à* on). **il s'accompagna (lui-même) à la guitare** he accompanied himself on the guitar.

(d) (*Culin*) **du chou accompagnait le rôti** cabbage was served with the roast; **le poisson s'accompagne d'un vin blanc sec** fish is served with a dry white wine; **le beaujolais est ce qui accompagne le mieux cette viande** a Beaujolais goes best with this meat, Beaujolais is the best wine to serve with this meat.

accompli, e [akɔ̃pli] (*ptp de* **accomplir**) *adj* **(a)** (*parfait, expérimenté*) accomplished. **(b)** (*révolu*) **avoir 60 ans ~s** to be over *ou* turned 60; *V* **fait**.

accomplir [akɔ̃pliʀ] (2) *vt* **(a)** (*réaliser*) *devoir, promesse* to fulfil, carry out; *mauvaise action* to commit; *tâche, mission* to perform, carry out, accomplish; *exploit* to perform, achieve. **~ des merveilles** to work wonders, perform miracles; **il a enfin pu ~ ce qu'il avait décidé de faire** at last he managed to achieve *ou* accomplish what he had decided to do; **la volonté de Dieu s'est accomplie** God's will was done.

(b) *apprentissage, service militaire* (*faire*) to do; (*terminer*) to complete, finish.

accomplissement [akɔ̃plismɑ̃] *nm* (*V* **accomplir**) fulfilment; accomplishment; committing; completion.

accord [akɔʀ] *nm* **(a)** (*entente*) agreement; (*concorde*) harmony. **l'~ fut général sur ce point** there was general agreement on this point; **le bon ~ régna pendant 10 ans** harmony prevailed for 10 years; *V* **commun**.

(b) (*traité*) agreement. **passer un ~ avec qn** to make an agreement with sb; **~ à l'amiable** mutual agreement; **~-cadre** outline agreement; **~ de principe** agreement in principle.

(c) (*permission*) consent, agreement.

(d) (*harmonie*) *[couleurs]* harmony. **en ~ avec le paysage** in harmony *ou* in keeping with the landscape.

(e) (*Gram*) *[adjectif, participe]* agreement. **~ en genre/nombre** agreement in gender/number.

(f) (*Mus*) (*notes*) chord; (*réglage*) tuning. **~ parfait** triad; **~ de tierce** third; **~ de quarte** fourth.

(g) (*loc*) **d'~: être d'~** to agree; **se mettre** *ou* **tomber d'~ avec qn** to agree *ou* come to an agreement with sb; **être d'~ pour faire** to agree *ou* be in agreement to do; **essayer de mettre 2 personnes d'~** to try to make 2 people come to *ou* reach an agreement *ou* agree with each other, try to make 2 people see eye to eye; **je les ai mis d'~ en leur donnant tort à tous les deux** I ended their disagreement by pointing out that they were both wrong; **c'est d'~** (we're) agreed, all right; **c'est d'~ pour demain** it's agreed for tomorrow, O.K. for tomorrow*; **d'~!** O.K.!*, (all) right!, right ho!* (*surtout Brit*); **alors là, (je ne suis) pas d'~!*** I don't agree on that point! *ou* about that!, I don't go along with you on this!; *V* **commun**.

accordable [akɔʀdabl(ə)] *adj* (*Mus*) tunable; *faveur* which can be granted.

accordage [akɔʀdaʒ] *nm*, **accordement** [akɔʀdmɑ̃] *nm* tuning.

accordéon [akɔʀdeɔ̃] *nm* accordion. **en ~*** *voiture* crumpled up; *pantalon, chaussette* wrinkled (up).

accordéoniste [akɔʀdeɔnist(ə)] *nmf* accordionist.

accorder [akɔʀde] (1) **1** *vt* **(a)** (*donner*) *faveur, permission, demande* to grant; *allocation, pension* to give, award (*à* to). **on lui a accordé un congé exceptionnel** he's been given *ou* granted special leave; **il ne s'accorde jamais de répit** he never gives himself a rest, he never lets up*; **elle accorde à ses enfants tout ce qu'ils demandent** she lets her children have *ou* she gives her children anything they ask for; *V* **main**.

(b) (*admettre*) **~ à qn que** to admit (to sb) that; **vous m'accorderez que j'avais raison** you'll admit *ou* concede I was right; **je vous l'accorde, j'avais tort** I admit *ou* accept *ou* concede that I was wrong, I was wrong I'll grant you that.

(c) (*attribuer*) **~ de l'importance à qch** to attach importance to sth; **~ de la valeur à qch** to attach value to sth, value sth.

(d) (*Mus*) *instrument* to tune. (*fig*) **ils ont accordé leurs violons** they came to *ou* reached an agreement.

(e) (*Gram*) **(faire) ~ un verbe/un adjectif** to make a verb/an adjective agree (*avec* with).

(f) (*mettre en harmonie*) *personnes* to bring together. **~ ses actions avec ses opinions** to match one's actions to one's opinions, act in accordance with one's opinions; **~ la couleur du tapis avec celle des rideaux** to match the colour of the carpet with (that of) the curtains, make the carpet match the curtains in colour.

2 s'accorder *vpr* **(a)** (*être d'accord*) to agree, be agreed; (*se mettre d'accord*) to agree. **ils s'accordent pour dire que le film est mauvais** they agree that it's a poor film; **ils se sont accordés pour le faire élire** they agreed to get him elected.

(b) (*s'entendre*) *[personnes]* to get on together. **(bien/mal) s'~ avec qn** to get on (well/badly) with sb.

(c) (*être en harmonie*) *[couleurs]* to match, go together; *[opinions]* to agree; *[sentiments, caractères]* to be in harmony. **s'~ avec** *[opinion]* to agree with; *[sentiments]* to be in harmony *ou* in keeping with; *[couleur]* to match, go with; **il faut que nos actions s'accordent avec nos opinions** one's actions must be in keeping with one's opinions, one must act in accordance with one's opinions.

(d) (*Ling*) to agree (*avec* with).

accordeur [akɔʀdœʀ] *nm* (*Mus*) tuner.

accordoir [akɔʀdwaʀ] *nm* tuning hammer *ou* wrench.

accorte [akɔʀt(ə)] *adj f* (*hum*) winsome, comely.

accostable [akɔstabl(ə)] *adj*: **le rivage n'est pas ~** you can't get near the shore.

accostage [akɔstaʒ] *nm* (*Naut*) coming alongside; *[personne]* accosting.

accoster [akɔste] (1) *vt* **(a)** (*gén, péj*) *personne* to accost. **(b)** (*Naut*) *quai, navire* to come *ou* draw alongside; (*emploi absolu*) to berth.

accotement [akɔtmɑ̃] *nm* (*Aut*) shoulder, verge; (*Rail*) shoulder. **~ non stabilisé** soft verge (*Brit*) *ou* shoulder (*US*); **~ stabilisé** hard shoulder.

accoter [akɔte] (1) **1** *vt tête, échelle* to lean, rest (*contre* against, *sur* on). **2 s'accoter** *vpr*: **s'~ à** *ou* **contre** to lean against.

accotoir [akɔtwaʀ] *nm [bras]* armrest; *[tête]* headrest.

accouchée [akuʃe] *nf* (new) mother.

accouchement [akuʃmɑ̃] *nm* (child)birth, delivery; (*travail*) labour, confinement. **~ dirigé** induced delivery; **~ à terme** delivery at full term, full-term delivery; **~ avant terme** early delivery, delivery before full term; **~ naturel** natural childbirth; **~ prématuré** premature birth; **~ sans douleur** painless childbirth; **pendant l'~** during the delivery.

accoucher [akuʃe] (1) **1** *vt*: **~ qn** to deliver sb's baby, deliver sb.

2 *vi* **(a)** (*être en travail*) to be in labour; (*donner naissance*) to have a baby, give birth. **où avez-vous accouché?** where did you have your baby?; **elle accouchera en octobre** her baby is due in October; **~ avant terme** to have one's baby prematurely *ou* early *ou* before it is due; **~ d'un garçon** to give birth to a boy, have a (baby) boy.

(b) (*fig hum*) **~ de** *roman* to bring forth (*hum*), produce (*with difficulty*); **accouche!:** spit it out!:, out with it!*

accoucheur, -euse [akuʃœʀ, øz] **1** *nm,f*: **(médecin) ~** obstetrician. **2 accoucheuse** *nf* (*sage-femme*) midwife.

accouder (s') [akude] (1) *vpr* to lean (on one's elbows). **s'~ sur** *ou* **à** to lean (one's elbows) on, rest one's elbows on; **accoudé à la fenêtre** leaning (on one's elbows) at the window.

accoudoir [akudwaʀ] *nm* armrest.

accouplement [akupləmɑ̃] *nm* (*V* **accoupler**) yoking; coupling (up); hitching (up); joining (up); connecting (up); bringing together; mating; coupling.

accoupler [akuple] (1) **1** *vt* **(a)** (*ensemble*) *animaux de trait* to yoke; *roues* to couple (up); *wagons* to couple (up), hitch (up); *générateurs* to connect (up); *tuyaux* to join (up), connect (up); *moteurs* to couple, connect (up); (*fig*) *mots, images* to bring together, link. **ils sont bizarrement accouplés*** they make a strange couple, they're an odd match.

(b) **~ une remorque/un cheval à** to hitch a trailer/horse (up) to; **~ un moteur/un tuyau à** to connect an engine/a pipe to.

(c) (*faire copuler*) to mate (*à, avec, et* with).

2 s'accoupler *vpr [animaux]* to mate, couple; (*hum péj*) *[humains]* to mate.

accourir [akuʀiʀ] (11) *vi* (*lit*) to rush up, run up (*à, vers* to); (*fig*) to hurry, hasten, rush (*à, vers* to). **à mon appel il accourut immédiatement** (*du salon*) at my call he ran up *ou* rushed up immediately; (*de province*) when I called on him he rushed *ou* hastened to see me immediately; **ils sont accourus (pour) le féliciter** they rushed up *ou* hurried to congratulate him.

accoutrement [akutʀəmɑ̃] *nm* (*péj*) getup*, rig-out* (*Brit*).

accoutrer [akutʀe] (1) (*péj*) **1** *vt* (*habiller*) to get up*, rig out* (*de* in).

2 s'accoutrer *vpr* to get o.s. up*, rig o.s. out* (*de* in). **il était bizarrement accoutré** he was strangely rigged out* *ou* got up*, he was wearing the oddest rig-out* (*Brit*).

accoutumance [akutymɑ̃s] *nf* (*habitude*) habituation (*à* to); (*besoin*) addiction (*à* to).

accoutumé, e [akutyme] (*ptp de* **accoutumer**) *adj* usual. **comme à l'~e** as usual.

accoutumer [akutyme] (1) **1** *vt*: **~ qn à qch/à faire qch** to accustom sb *ou* get sb used to sth/to doing sth; **on l'a accoutumé à** *ou* **il a été accoutumé à se lever tôt** he has been used *ou* accustomed to getting up early.

2 s'accoutumer *vpr*: **s'~ à qch/à faire qch** to get used *ou* accustomed to sth/to doing sth; **il s'est lentement accoutumé** he gradually got used *ou* accustomed to it.

accréditer [akʀedite] (1) **1** *vt rumeur* to substantiate, give substance to; *personne* to accredit (*auprès de* to). **2 s'accréditer** *vpr [rumeur]* to gain ground.

accroc [akʀo] *nm* **(a)** (*déchirure*) tear. **faire un ~ à** to make a tear in, tear. **(b)** (*fig*) *[réputation]* blot (*à* on); *[règle]* breach, infringement (*à* of). **faire un ~ à** *règle* to twist, bend*; *réputation* to blot. **(c)** (*anicroche*) hitch, snag. **sans ~s** without a hitch, smoothly.

accrochage [akʀɔʃaʒ] *nm* **(a)** (*Aut: collision*) collision, bump*; (*Mil: combat*) encounter, engagement; (*Boxe*) clinch; (*fig: dispute*) clash, brush.

(b) (*action*) *[tableau]* hanging; *[wagons]* coupling, hitching (up) (*à* to).

accroche-cœur, *pl* **accroche-cœurs** [akʀɔʃkœʀ] *nm* kiss curl.

accrocher [akʀɔʃe] (1) **1** *vt* **(a)** (*suspendre*) *chapeau, tableau* to hang (up) (*à* on); (*attacher*) *wagons* to couple, hitch together. **~ un wagon/une remorque à** to hitch *ou* couple a carriage/a trailer (up) to; **~ un ver à l'hameçon** to put a worm on the hook; *V* **cœur.**

(b) (*accidentellement*) *jupe, collant* to catch (*à* on); *aile de voiture* to catch (*à* on), bump (*à* against); *voiture* to bump into; *piéton* to hit; *pile de livres, meuble* to catch (on). **rester accroché aux barbelés** to be caught on (the) barbed wire.

(c) (*attirer*) **~ le regard** to catch the eye; **vitrine qui accroche les clients** window which attracts customers; **film qui accroche le public** picture that draws (in) *ou* pulls in the public.

(d) (*: *saisir*) *occasion* to get; *personne* to get hold of; *mots, fragments de conversation* to catch.

(e) (*Mil*) to engage; (*Boxe*) to clinch.

2 *vi* **(a)** *[fermeture éclair]* to stick, jam; (*fig*) *[pourparlers]* to come up against a hitch *ou* snag. (*fig*) **cette traduction accroche par endroits** this translation is a bit rough in places, there are one or two places where this translation does not run smoothly; **cette planche accroche quand on l'essuie** this board catches on the cloth when you wipe it.

(b) (*plaire*) *disque, slogan* to catch on. **ça accroche entre eux** they hit it off together*.

3 s'accrocher *vpr* **(a)** (*se cramponner*) to hang on. **s'~ à** (*lit*) *branche* to cling to, hang on to; (*fig*) *espoir, personne* to cling to; **accroche-toi bien!** hold on tight!; (*littér*) **les vignes s'accrochent au flanc du coteau** the vineyards cling to the hillside.

(b) (*: *être tenace*) *[malade]* to cling on, hang on; *[étudiant]* to stick at it, stick in*; *[importun]* to cling.

(c) (*entrer en collision*) *[voitures]* to bump (each other), touch *ou* clip each other, have a bump; (*Boxe*) to go *ou* get into a clinch; (*Mil*) to engage; (*fig: se disputer*) to have a clash *ou* a brush (*avec* with). **ils s'accrochent tout le temps** they are always at loggerheads *ou* always quarrelling.

(d) (‡: *en faire son deuil*) **se l'~: tu peux te l'~** you can say goodbye to it, you've got a hope* (*iro*).

accrocheur, -euse [akʀɔʃœʀ, øz] *adj* **(a)** *joueur, concurrent* tenacious; *vendeur, représentant* persistent. **c'est un ~** he's a sticker* *ou* fighter.

(b) *affiche, titre,* eye-catching; *méthode* calculated to appeal; *slogan* catchy; *prix* very attractive; *film* which (really) pulls the crowds *ou* pulls them in*.

accroire [akʀwaʀ] *vt* (*frm, hum*) **faire** *ou* **laisser ~ à qn qch/que** to delude sb into believing sth/that; **et tu veux me faire ~ que ...** and you want me to believe that ...; **il veut nous en faire ~** he's trying to deceive us *ou* take us in; **il ne s'en est pas laissé ~** he didn't let himself be taken in *ou* be led up the garden path*.

accroissement [akʀwasmɑ̃] *nm* (*gén*) increase (*de* in); *[nombre, production]* growth (*de* in), increase (*de* in).

accroître [akʀwatʀ(ə)] (55) **1** *vt* (*gén*) to increase; *somme, plaisir, confusion* to increase, add to; *réputation* to enhance; *gloire* to increase, heighten.

2 s'accroître *vpr* to increase, grow. **sa part s'accrut de celle de son frère** his share was increased by the addition of (what had been) his brother's.

accroupi, e [akʀupi] (*ptp de* **s'accroupir**) *adj* squatting *ou* crouching (down).

accroupir (s') [akʀupiʀ] (2) *vpr* to squat *ou* crouch (down).

accroupissement [akʀupismɑ̃] *nm* squatting, crouching.

accu* [aky] *nm* (*abrév de* **accumulateur**) (*Aut etc*) battery. (*fig*) **recharger ses ~s** to recharge one's batteries.

accueil [akœj] *nm* (*gén: réception*) welcome, reception; *[sinistrés, idée]* reception. **rien n'a été prévu pour l'~ des touristes** no plans have *ou* no provision has been made for accommodating the tourists *ou* putting up the tourists; **quel ~ a-t-on fait à ses idées?** what sort of reception did his ideas get?, how were his ideas received?; **faire bon ~ à** *idée, proposition* to welcome; **faire bon ~ à qn** to welcome sb, make sb (feel) welcome; **faire mauvais ~ à** *idée, suggestion* to receive badly; **faire mauvais ~ à qn** to make sb feel unwelcome, give sb a bad reception; **d'~** *centre, organisation* reception (*épith*); *paroles, cérémonie* welcoming, of welcome; *V* **terre.**

accueillant, e [akœjɑ̃, ɑ̃t] *adj maison, personne* welcoming, friendly.

accueillir [akœjiʀ] (12) *vt* **(a)** (*aller chercher*) to meet, collect; (*recevoir*) to welcome, greet; (*donner l'hospitalité à*) to welcome, take in; (*pouvoir héberger*) to accommodate. **j'ai été l'~ à la gare** I went to meet *ou* collect him at the station; **il m'a bien accueilli** he made me (most) welcome, he gave me a good reception; **il m'a mal accueilli** he gave me a bad reception *ou* a poor welcome; **pendant la guerre il m'a accueilli sous son toit/ dans sa famille** during the war he welcomed me into his house/his family; **cet hôtel peut ~ 80 touristes** this hotel can accommodate 80 tourists; **ils se sont fait ~ par des coups de feu/des huées, des coups de feu/des huées les ont accueillis** they were greeted with shots/jeers *ou* cat calls.

(b) *idée, demande, nouvelle* to receive. **il accueillit ma suggestion avec un sourire** he greeted *ou* received my suggestion with a smile; **cette décision a été très mal accueillie (par l'opinion)** this decision was badly received (by the public), this decision met with a very bad reception (from the public).

acculer [akyle] (1) *vt*: **~ qn à** *mur* to drive sb back against; (*fig*) *ruine, désespoir* to drive sb to the brink of; (*fig*) *choix, aveu* to force sb into; **acculé à la mer** driven back to the edge of the sea; **~ qn contre** to drive sb back to *ou* against; **~ qn dans** *impasse, pièce* to corner sb in; (*lit, fig*) **nous sommes acculés — nous devons céder** we're cornered, we must give in.

accumulateur [akymylatœʀ] *nm* accumulator, (storage) battery.

accumulation [akymylɑsjɔ̃] *nf* **(a)** (*action, processus: V* **accumuler**) accumulation; amassing; building up; piling up; stockpiling; accruing; (*tas*) heap, accumulation.

(b) (*Élec*) storage. **à ~ (nocturne)** (night-)storage (*épith*).

accumuler [akymyle] (1) **1** *vt documents, richesses, preuves, erreurs* to accumulate, amass; *marchandises* to accumulate, build up (a stock of), stockpile. (*Fin*) **les intérêts accumulés pendant un an** the interest accrued over a year.

2 s'accumuler *vpr* to accumulate, pile up; (*Fin*) to accrue.

accusateur, -trice [akyzatœʀ, tʀis] **1** *adj doigt, regard* accusing; *documents, preuves* accusatory, incriminating. **2** *nm,f* accuser. (*Hist*) **~ public** public prosecutor (*during the French Revolution*).

accusatif [akyzatif] *nm* (*Ling*) accusative (case).

accusation [akyzɑsjɔ̃] *nf* (*gén*) accusation; (*Jur*) charge, indictment. (*le procureur etc*) **l'~** the prosecution; **porter** *ou* **lancer une ~ contre** to bring an accusation against; **mettre en ~** to indict; **mise en ~** indictment; **une terrible ~ contre notre société** a terrible indictment of our society; (*Jur*) **abandonner l'~** to drop the charge; *V* **acte, chambre.**

accusatoire [akyzatwaʀ] *adj* (*Jur*) accusatory.

accusé, e [akyze] (*ptp de* **accuser**) **1** *adj* (*marqué*) marked, pronounced. **2** *nm,f* accused; *[procès]* defendant. **~ levez-vous!** ≃ the defendant will rise; *V* **banc. 3**: **accusé de réception** acknowledgement of receipt.

accuser [akyze] (1) **1** *vt* **(a)** *personne* (*gén*) to accuse (*de* of). (*Jur*) **~ de** to accuse of, charge with, indict for; **~ qn d'ingratitude** to tax sb with *ou* accuse sb of ingratitude; **~ qn d'avoir volé de l'argent** to accuse sb of stealing *ou* having stolen money; **tout l'accuse** everything points to his guilt *ou* his being guilty.

(b) (*rendre responsable*) *pratique, malchance, personne* to blame (*de* for). **accusant son mari de ne pas s'être réveillé à temps** blaming her husband for not waking up in time; **accusant le médecin d'incompétence pour avoir causé la mort de l'enfant** blaming the doctor's incompetence for having caused the child's death, blaming the child's death on the doctor's incompetence.

(c) (*souligner*) *effet, contraste* to emphasize, accentuate, bring out. **robe qui accuse la sveltesse du corps** dress which accentuates *ou* emphasizes the slimness of the body.

(d) (*montrer*) to show. **la balance accusait 80 kg** the scales read 80 kg; **~ la quarantaine** to show (all of) one's forty years; (*lit, fig*) **~ le coup** to stagger under the blow, show that the blow has struck home; **elle accuse la fatigue de ces derniers mois** she's showing the strain of these last few months; **~ réception** to acknowledge receipt (*de* of).

2 s'accuser *vpr* **(a) s'~ de qch/d'avoir fait** (*se déclarer coupable*) to admit to sth/to having done; (*se rendre responsable de*) to blame o.s. for sth/for having done; (*Rel*) **mon père, je m'accuse (d'avoir péché)** Father, I have sinned; **en protestant, il s'accuse** by objecting, he is pointing to *ou* admitting his guilt.

(b) (*s'accentuer*) *[tendance]* to become more marked *ou* pronounced.

acerbe [asɛʀb(ə)] *adj* caustic, acid. **d'une manière ~** caustically, acidly.

acéré, e [aseʀe] *adj griffe, pointe* sharp; *lame* sharp, keen; *raillerie, réplique* scathing, biting, cutting. (*fig*) **critique à la plume ~e** critic with a scathing pen.

acétate [asetat] *nm* acetate.

acétique [asetik] *adj* acetic.

acétone [asetɔn] *nf* acetone.

acétylène [asetilɛn] *nm* acetylene; *V* **lampe.**

achalandé, e [aʃalɑ̃de] *adj*: **bien ~** (*bien fourni*) well-stocked; (†: *très fréquenté*) well-patronized.

acharné, e [aʃaʀne] (*ptp de* **s'acharner**) *adj combat, concurrence, adversaire* fierce, bitter; *travail, efforts* relentless, unremitting, strenuous; *poursuivant, poursuite* relentless;

joueur, travailleur relentless, determined. ~ **à faire** set *ou* bent *ou* intent on doing, determined to do; ~ **contre** set against; ~ **à sa destruction** set *ou* bent on destroying him, set *ou* bent on his destruction.

acharnement [aʃaʀnəmɑ̃] *nm [combattant, résistant]* fierceness, fury; *[poursuivant]* relentlessness; *[travailleur]* determination, unremitting effort. **son ~ au travail** the determination with which he tackles his work; **avec ~** *poursuivre* relentlessly; *travailler* relentlessly, furiously; *combattre* bitterly, fiercely; *résister* fiercely; **se battant avec ~** fighting tooth and nail.

acharner (s') [aʃaʀne] (1) *vpr*: **s'~ sur** *victime, proie* to go at fiercely and unrelentingly; **s'~ contre qn** *[malchance]* to dog sb; *[adversaire]* to set o.s. against sb, have got one's knife into sb; **elle s'acharne après cet enfant** she's always hounding this child *ou* chasing this child (up); **il s'acharne à prouver que c'est vrai** he is trying desperately to prove that it is true; **il s'acharne à son tableau** he is working furiously away at *ou* on his painting; **je m'acharne à le leur faire comprendre** I'm desperately trying to explain it to them; **il s'acharne inutilement, il n'y arrivera jamais** he's wasting his efforts, he'll never make it.

achat [aʃa] *nm* **(a)** (*action*) purchase, purchasing, buying; (*chose achetée*) purchase. **faire l'~ de qch** to purchase *ou* buy sth; **faire un ~** to make a purchase; **il est allé faire quelques ~s** he has gone out to buy a few things *ou* to do some shopping; **faire des ~s** to shop, go shopping; **faire ses ~s (de Noël)** to do one's (Christmas) shopping; **c'est cher à l'~ mais c'est de bonne qualité** it's expensive to buy but it's good quality; **il a fait un ~ judicieux** he made a wise buy *ou* purchase.

(b) (*Bourse, Comm*) buying. **la livre vaut 8 F à l'~** the buying rate for sterling is 8 francs.

acheminement [aʃminmɑ̃] *nm* (*V* **acheminer**) forwarding, dispatch; conveying, transporting; routing; sending. **l'~ du courrier est rendu difficile par les récentes chutes de neige** the distribution *ou* transport of mail has been made difficult by the recent snowfalls.

acheminer [aʃmine] (1) **1** *vt courrier, colis* to forward, dispatch (*vers* to); *troupes* to convey, transport (*vers* to). **~ des trains sur** *ou* **vers** to route trains to; **~ un train supplémentaire sur Dijon** to put on *ou* send an extra train for Dijon; (*fig*) **~ le pays vers la ruine** to set the country on the road to ruin.

2 s'acheminer *vpr*: **s'~ vers** *endroit* to make one's way towards, head for; *conclusion, solution* to move towards; *destruction, ruine* to head for.

acheter [aʃte] (5) *vt* **(a)** to buy, purchase. **~ qch à qn** (*à un vendeur*) to buy *ou* purchase sth from sb; (*pour un ami*) to buy sth for sb, buy sb sth; **je lui ai acheté une robe pour son anniversaire** I bought her a dress for her birthday; **~ qch d'occasion** to buy sth secondhand; **(s')~ une conduite** to turn over a new leaf, mend one's ways; *V* **comptant, crédit, détail** *etc.*

(b) (*péj*) *vote, appui* to buy; *électeur, juge* to bribe, buy. **se laisser ~** to let o.s. be bribed *ou* bought.

acheteur, -euse [aʃtœʀ, øz] *nm,f* buyer, purchaser; (*Jur*) vendee; (*Comm: professionnel*) buyer. **il est ~** he's prepared to buy it; **il n'a pas encore trouvé d'~ pour sa voiture** he hasn't yet found anyone to buy his car, he hasn't yet found a buyer for his car; **article qui ne trouve pas d'~** item which does not sell; **la foule des ~s** the crowd of shoppers.

achevé, e [aʃve] (*ptp de* **achever**) *adj canaille* downright, out-and-out, thorough; *artiste* accomplished; *art, grâce* perfect. **d'un ridicule ~** perfectly ridiculous; **tableau d'un mauvais goût ~** picture in thorough(ly) bad taste.

achèvement [aʃɛvmɑ̃] *nm [travaux]* completion; (*littér: perfection*) culmination; *V* **voie.**

achever [aʃve] (5) **1** *vt* **(a)** (*terminer*) *discours, repas* to finish, end; *livre* to finish, reach the end of; (*parachever*) *tâche, tableau* to complete, finish. **~ ses jours à la campagne** to end one's days in the country; (*littér*) **le soleil achève sa course** the sun completes its course; **~ (de parler)** to finish (speaking); **il partit sans ~ (sa phrase)** he left in mid sentence *ou* without finishing his sentence; **~ de se raser/de se préparer** to finish shaving/getting ready; **le pays achevait de se reconstruire** the country was just finishing its *ou* coming to the end of its rebuilding.

(b) (*porter à son comble*) **~ de: cette remarque acheva de l'exaspérer** this remark really brought his irritation to a head, this last remark really did make him cross; **cette révélation acheva de nous plonger dans la confusion** this revelation was all we needed to complete our confusion.

(c) (*tuer*) *blessé* to finish off; *cheval* to destroy; (*fatiguer, décourager*) to finish (off). **cette mauvaise nouvelle acheva son père malade** this bad news finished (off) his sick father; **cette longue promenade m'a achevé!** that long walk was the end of me! *ou* finished me!

2 s'achever *vpr* (*se terminer*) to end (*par, sur* with); (*littér*) *[jour, vie]* to come to an end, draw to a close. (*TV*) **ainsi s'achèvent nos émissions de la journée** that brings to an end our programmes for the day.

achigan [aʃigɑ̃] *nm* (*Can*) (black) bass. **~ à grande bouche** large-mouth bass; **~ à petite bouche** small-mouth bass; **~ de roche** rock bass.

Achille [aʃil] *nm* Achilles.

achoppement [aʃɔpmɑ̃] *nm V* **pierre.**

achopper [aʃɔpe] (1) *vi*: **~ sur** *difficulté* to stumble over; (*littér*) *pierre* to stumble against *ou* over.

achromatique [akʀɔmatik] *adj* achromatic.

acide [asid] **1** *adj* (*lit, fig*) acid, sharp, tart; (*Chim*) acid. **2** *nm* acid. **~ aminé** amino-acid.

acidificateur [asidifikatœʀ] *nm* acidifying agent, acidifier.

acidification [asidifikasjɔ̃] *nf* acidification.

acidifier *vt*, **s'acidifier** *vpr* [asidifje] (7) to acidify.

acidité [asidite] *nf* (*lit, fig*) acidity, sharpness, tartness; (*Chim*) acidity.

acidulé, e [asidyle] *adj goût* slightly acid; *V* **bonbon.**

acier [asje] *nm* steel. **~ inoxydable/trempé** stainless/tempered steel; **~ rapide** high-speed steel; **d'~** *poutre, colonne* steel (*épith*), of steel; (*fig*) *regard* steely; (*fig*) **muscles d'~** muscles of steel; *V* **gris.**

aciérie [asjeʀi] *nf* steelworks.

acmé [akme] *nf* (*littér: apogée*) acme, summit; (*Méd*) crisis.

acné [akne] *nf* acne. **~ juvénile** teenage acne.

acolyte [akɔlit] *nm* (*péj: associé*) confederate, associate; (*Rel*) acolyte, server.

acompte [akɔ̃t] *nm* (*arrhes*) deposit; (*sur somme due*) down payment; (*versement régulier*) instalment; (*sur salaire*) advance. (*sur somme due*) **un ~ de 10 F** 10 francs on account, a down payment of 10 francs; (*sur somme due*) **recevoir un ~** to receive something on account, receive a down payment; (*fig*) **ce week-end à la mer, c'était un petit ~ sur nos vacances** this weekend at the seaside was like snatching a bit of our holidays in advance.

acoquiner (s') [akɔkine] (1) *vpr* (*péj*) to get together, team up (*avec* with).

Açores [asɔʀ] *nfpl*: **les ~** the Azores.

à-côté, *pl* à-côtés [akote] *nm [problème]* side issue; *[situation]* side aspect; (*gain, dépense secondaire*) extra. **avec ce boulot, il se fait des petits ~s*** with this job, he makes something *ou* a bit on the side*.

à-coup, *pl* à-coups [aku] *nm [moteur]* hiccough; *[machine]* jolt, jerk; *[économie, organisation]* jolt. **travailler par ~s** to work by *ou* in fits and starts; **avancer par ~s** to move forward in *ou* by fits and starts, jerk *ou* jolt forward *ou* along; **sans ~s** smoothly; **le moteur eut quelques ~s** the engine gave a few (hic)coughs *ou* hiccoughed a bit.

acoustique [akustik] **1** *adj* acoustic; *V* **cornet. 2** *nf* (*science*) acoustics (*sg*); (*sonorité*) acoustics (*pl*). **il y a une mauvaise ~** the acoustics are bad.

acquéreur [akeʀœʀ] *nm* buyer, purchaser. **j'ai trouvé/ je n'ai pas trouvé ~ pour mon appartement** I have/I haven't found a purchaser *ou* buyer for my flat, I've found someone/I haven't found anyone to buy my flat; **cet objet n'a pas encore trouvé ~** this object has not yet found a purchaser *ou* buyer; **se porter ~ (de qch)** to announce one's intention of buying *ou* purchasing (sth); **se rendre ~ de qch** to purchase *ou* buy sth.

acquérir [akeʀiʀ] (21) *vt* **(a)** *propriété, meuble* to acquire, purchase, buy. **~ qch par succession** to come into sth, inherit sth; *V* **bien.**

(b) (*obtenir*) *faveur, célébrité* to win, gain; *habileté, autorité, habitude* to acquire; *importance, valeur, expérience* to acquire, gain. **~ la certitude de** to become certain of; **c'est une chose qui s'acquiert facilement** it's something that's easy to pick up; **~ la preuve de** to gain *ou* obtain (the) proof of; **les certitudes que nous avions acquises** the facts we had clearly established.

(c) (*valoir, procurer*) to win, gain. **ceci lui acquit une excellente réputation** this won *ou* gained him an excellent reputation; **il s'est acquis l'estime/l'appui de ses chefs** he won *ou* gained his superiors' esteem/support.

acquêt [akɛ] *nm* acquest; *V* **communauté.**

acquiescement [akjɛsmɑ̃] *nm* **(a)** (*approbation*) approval, agreement. **il leva la main en signe d'~** he raised his hand in a sign of approval *ou* agreement.

(b) (*consentement*) acquiescence, assent. **donner son ~ à qch** to give one's assent to sth.

acquiescer [akjese] (3) *vi* **(a)** (*approuver*) to approve, agree. **il acquiesça d'un signe de tête** he nodded his approval *ou* agreement. **(b)** (*consentir*) to acquiesce, assent. **~ à une demande** to acquiesce to *ou* in a request, assent to a request.

acquis, e [aki, iz] (*ptp de* **acquérir**) **1** *adj* **(a)** *fortune, qualité, droit* acquired. (*Bio*) **caractères ~** acquired characteristics; *V* **vitesse.**

(b) *fait* established, accepted. **tenir qch pour ~** (*comme allant de soi*) to take sth for granted; (*comme décidé*) to take sth as settled *ou* agreed; **il est maintenant ~ que** it has now been established that, it is now accepted that.

(c) être ~ à qn: ce droit nous est ~ we have now established this right as ours; **ses faveurs nous sont ~es** we can count on *ou* be sure of his favour; **être ~ à un projet/qn** to be completely behind a plan/sb.

2 *nm* (*savoir*) experience. **avoir de l'~** to have experience; **grâce à l'~ qu'il a obtenu en travaillant chez un patron** thanks to the experience he got *ou* the knowledge he acquired working for an employer; **la connaissance qu'il a de l'anglais représente pour lui un ~ précieux** his knowledge of English is a valuable asset (to him).

acquisition [akizisjɔ̃] *nf* (*action, processus*) acquisition, acquiring; (*objet*) acquisition; (*par achat*) purchase. **faire l'~ de qch** to acquire sth; (*par achat*) to purchase sth.

acquit [aki] *nm* **(a)** (*Comm: décharge*) receipt. **'pour ~'** 'received'. **(b) par ~ de conscience** to set one's mind at rest, to be quite sure. **(c) ~-à-caution** bond note.

acquittement [akitmɑ̃] *nm* (*V* **acquitter**) acquittal; payment; discharge; settlement; fulfilment. (*Jur*) **verdict d'~** verdict of not guilty.

acquitter [akite] (1) **1** *vt* **(a)** *accusé* to acquit.

(b) *droit, impôt* to pay; *dette* to pay (off), settle, discharge; *facture* (*gén*) to pay, settle; (*Comm*) to receipt.

(c) (*rendre quitte*) **~ qn de** *dette, obligation* to release sb from.

2 s'acquitter *vpr*: **s'~ de** *dette* to pay (off), discharge, settle; *dette morale, devoir* to discharge; *promesse* to fulfil, carry out;

obligation to fulfil, discharge; *fonction, tâche* to fulfil, carry out, perform; **comment m'~ (envers vous)?** how can I ever repay you? (*de* for).

acre [akʀ(ə)] 1 *nf* (*Hist*) ≃ acre. 2 *nm* (*Can*) acre (*4.046,86m²*).

âcre [ɑkʀ(ə)] *adj odeur, saveur* acrid, pungent; (*fig littér*) acrid.

âcreté [ɑkʀəte] *nf [odeur, saveur]* acridness, acridity, pungency; (*fig littér*) acridness, acridity.

acrimonie [akʀimɔni] *nf* acrimony, acrimoniousness.

acrimonieux, -euse [akʀimɔnjø, øz] *adj* acrimonious.

acrobate [akʀɔbat] *nmf* (*lit, fig*) acrobat.

acrobatie [akʀɔbasi] *nf* (*tour*) acrobatic feat; (*art, fig*) acrobatics (*sg*). ~ **aérienne** aerobatics; (*lit, fig*) **faire des ~s** to perform acrobatics; (*fig*) **mon emploi du temps tient de l'~*** I have to tie myself in knots* to cope with my timetable.

acrobatique [akʀɔbatik] *adj* (*lit, fig*) acrobatic.

Acropole [akʀɔpɔl] *nf*: **l'~** the Acropolis.

acrostiche [akʀɔstiʃ] *nm* acrostic.

acte [akt(ə)] 1 *nm* **(a)** (*action*) action, act. ~ **instinctif/réflexe** instinctive/reflex action; **moins de paroles — des ~s** (let's have) less talk and more action, we want more action and less talk; **plusieurs ~s de terrorisme ont été commis** several acts of terrorism have been committed; ~ **de bravoure/de lâcheté/de cruauté** act of bravery/cowardice/cruelty, brave/cowardly/cruel act *ou* action *ou* deed; **ce crime est un ~ de folie/l'~ d'un fou** this crime is an act of madness/the act *ou* deed of a madman; **après avoir menacé en paroles il passa aux ~s** having proffered verbal threats he proceeded to carry them out; (*Philos*) **en ~** in actuality.

(b) (*Jur*) *[notaire]* deed; *[état civil]* certificate.

(c) (*Théât, fig*) act. **comédie/pièce en un ~** one-act comedy/play; **le dernier ~ du conflit se joua en Orient** the final act of the struggle was played out in the East.

(d) *[congrès etc]* **~s** proceedings.

(e) (*loc*) **demander ~ que/de qch** to ask for formal acknowledgement that/of sth; **donner ~ que/de qch** to acknowledge formally that/sth; **faire ~ de citoyen/d'honnête homme** to act *ou* behave as a citizen/an honest man; **faire ~ d'autorité/d'énergie** to make a show of authority/energy; **faire ~ de candidature** to apply, submit an application; **faire ~ de présence** to put in a token appearance, put in an appearance; **il a au moins fait ~ de bonne volonté** he has at least shown goodwill *ou* willingness; **prendre ~ que** to record formally that; **nous prenons ~ de votre promesse/proposition** we have noted *ou* taken note of your promise/proposal.

2: **acte d'accusation** bill of indictment; **acte d'amnistie** amnesty (*act*); **les Actes des Apôtres** the Acts of the Apostles; **acte d'association** partnership agreement *ou* deed, articles of partnership; **acte authentique** = **acte notarié**; **acte de banditisme** criminal act; **acte de baptême** baptismal certificate; **acte de charité** act of charity; **acte de commerce** commercial act *ou* deed; **acte de contrition** act of contrition; **acte de décès** death certificate; **acte d'espérance** act of hope; **acte de l'état civil** *birth, marriage or death certificate*; **acte de foi** act of faith; **acte gratuit** acte gratuit, gratuitous act; **acte de guerre** act of war; **acte de mariage** marriage certificate; **acte médical** (medical) consultation, medical treatment (*U*); **acte de naissance** birth certificate; **acte notarié** notarial deed, deed executed by notary; **acte sous seing privé** private agreement (*document, not legally certified*); **acte de succession** attestation of inheritance; **acte de vente** bill of sale.

acteur [aktœʀ] *nm* (*Théât, fig*) actor; *V* **actrice**.

actif, -ive [aktif, iv] 1 *adj personne, participation* active; *poison, médicament* active, potent; (*Phys*) *substance* activated, active; (*Ling*) active. **prendre une part ~ive à qch** to take an active part in sth; *V* **armée²**, **charbon** *etc.*

2 *nm* **(a)** (*Ling*) active (voice).

(b) (*Fin*) assets; *[succession]* credits. **porter une somme à l'~** to put a sum on the assets side; (*fig*) **sa gentillesse est à mettre à son ~** his kindness is a point in his favour, on the credit *ou* positive *ou* plus* side there is his kindness (to consider); (*fig*) **il a plusieurs crimes à son ~** he has several crimes to his name; **il a plusieurs records à son ~** he has several records to his credit *ou* name.

3 **active** *nf* (*Mil*) **l'~** the regular army.

action [aksjɔ̃] 1 *nf* **(a)** (*acte*) action, act. **faire une bonne ~** to do a good deed; ~ **audacieuse** act *ou* deed of daring, bold deed *ou* action; **vous avez commis là une mauvaise ~** you've done something (very) wrong, you've behaved badly.

(b) (*activité*) action. **être en ~** to be at work; **passer à l'~** to take action; **le moment est venu de passer à l'~** the time has come for action; (*Mil*) **passer à l'~, engager l'~** to go into battle *ou* action; **entrer en ~** *[troupes, canon]* to go into action; **mettre un plan en ~** to put a plan into action; **le dispositif de sécurité se mit en ~** the security measures were put into operation; *V* **champ, feu¹, homme**.

(c) (*effet*) *[éléments naturels, loi, machine]* action; *[médicament]* action, effect. **ce médicament est sans ~** this medicine is ineffective *ou* has no effect; **sous l'~ du gel** under the action of frost, through the agency of frost; **machine à double ~** double-acting machine *ou* engine.

(d) (*initiative*) action. **c'est grâce à l'~ d'amis que nous avons réussi** it is thanks to the action of *ou* it is through *ou* by the agency of friends that we have succeeded; **engager une ~ commune** to take concerted action; **recourir à l'~ directe** to resort to *ou* have recourse to direct action.

(e) *[pièce, film]* (*mouvement, péripéties*) action; (*intrigue*) plot. **l'~ se passe en Grèce** the action takes place in Greece; **film d'~** action film; **roman d'~** action-packed novel.

(f) (*Jur*) action (at law), lawsuit. ~ **juridique/civile** legal/civil action; *V* **intenter**.

(g) (*Fin*) share. **~s** shares, stocks; ~ **ordinaire** ordinary share; **~s nominatives/au porteur** registered/bearer shares; **société par ~s** (joint) stock company; ~ **de chasse** hunting rights (*pl*); (*fig*) **ses ~s sont en hausse/baisse** things are looking up/are not looking so good for him.

2: (*Jur*) **action en diffamation** libel action; **action d'éclat** dazzling *ou* brilliant feat *ou* deed; **action de grâce(s)** thanksgiving; **action revendicative** *[ouvriers]* industrial action (*U*); *[ménagères, étudiants]* protest (*U*).

actionnaire [aksjɔnɛʀ] *nmf* shareholder.

actionnariat [aksjɔnaʀja] *nm* shareholding.

actionnement [aksjɔnmɑ̃] *nm [mécanisme]* activating, activation.

actionner [aksjɔne] (1) *vt* **(a)** *dispositif, mécanisme* to activate; *moteur, machine* to drive, work. **moteur actionné par la vapeur** steam-powered *ou* -driven engine; ~ **la sonnette** to ring the bell.

(b) (*Jur*) to sue, bring an action against. ~ **qn en dommages et intérêts** to sue sb for damages.

activation [aktivɑsjɔ̃] *nf* (*Chim, Phys*) activation; (*Bio*) initiation of development.

activement [aktivmɑ̃] *adv* actively. **participer ~ à qch** to take an active part *ou* be actively involved in sth.

activer [aktive] (1) 1 *vt* **(a)** (*accélérer*) *processus, travaux* to speed up; (*aviver*) *feu* to stoke, pep up*.

(b) (*Chim*) to activate.

2 *vi* (*: *se dépêcher*) to get a move on*, get moving*.

3 **s'activer** *vpr* (*s'affairer*) to bustle about. **s'~ à faire** to be busy doing; **active-toi!*** get a move on!*

activisme [aktivism(ə)] *nm* activism.

activiste [aktivist(ə)] *adj, nmf* activist.

activité [aktivite] *nf* (*gén*) activity. **les rues sont pleines d'~** the streets are bustling with activity *ou* are very busy; **l'~ de la rue** the bustle of the street; **le passage de l'~ à la retraite** passing from active life into retirement; (*Mil*) transfer from the active to the retired list; **être en ~** *[usine]* to function, be in operation; *[volcan]* to be active; *[fonctionnaire]* to be in active life; **être en pleine ~** *[usine, bureau]* to be operating at full strength, be in full operation; *[club]* to be running full-time; *[personne]* to be fully active; (*hum*) to be hard at it*.

actrice [aktʀis] *nf* (*Théât, fig*) actress.

actuaire [aktɥɛʀ] *nmf* actuary.

actualisation [aktɥalizɑsjɔ̃] *nf* (*V* **actualiser**) actualization; updating.

actualiser [aktɥalize] (1) *vt* (*Ling, Philos*) to actualize; (*mettre à jour*) to update.

actualité [aktɥalite] *nf* **(a)** *[livre, sujet]* topicality. **livre d'~** topical book.

(b) (*événements*) **l'~** current events; **l'~ sportive** the sports scene; (*rubrique*) sporting *ou* sports news.

(c) (*Ciné, Presse*) **les ~s** the news; **les ~s télévisées** (the) television news.

(d) (*Philos*) actuality.

actuariel, -elle [aktɥaʀjɛl] *adj* actuarial.

actuel, -elle [aktɥɛl] *adj* **(a)** (*présent*) present, current. **à l'heure ~le** at the present time; **à l'époque ~le** nowadays, in this day and age; **le monde ~** the world today.

(b) (*d'actualité*) *livre, problème* topical.

(c) (*Philos, Rel*) actual.

actuellement [aktɥɛlmɑ̃] *adv* at the moment, at present.

acuité [akɥite] *nf [son]* shrillness; *[douleur]* acuteness, intensity; *[sens]* sharpness, acuteness; *[crise politique]* acuteness.

acuponcteur, acupuncteur [akypɔ̃ktœʀ] *nm* acupuncturist.

acuponcture, acupuncture [akypɔ̃ktyʀ] *nf* acupuncture.

adage [adaʒ] *nm* adage.

Adam [adɑ̃] *nm* Adam; *V* **pomme**.

adamantin, e [adamɑ̃tɛ̃, in] *adj* (*littér*) adamantine.

adaptable [adaptabl(ə)] *adj* adaptable.

adaptateur, -trice [adaptatœʀ, tʀis] 1 *nm,f* (*Ciné, Théât*) adapter. 2 *nm* (*Tech*) adapter.

adaptation [adaptɑsjɔ̃] *nf* (*gén, Ciné, Théât*) adaptation. **faire un effort d'~** to try to adapt.

adapter [adapte] (1) 1 *vt* **(a)** (*appliquer*) ~ **une prise/un mécanisme à** to fit a plug/a mechanism to; **ces mesures sont-elles bien adaptées à la situation?** are these measures really suited to the situation?; ~ **la musique aux paroles** to fit the music to the words.

(b) (*modifier*) *conduite, méthode, organisation* to adapt (*à* to); *roman, pièce* to adapt (*pour* for).

2 **s'adapter** *vpr* **(a)** (*s'habituer*) to adapt (o.s.) (*à* to).

(b) (*s'appliquer*) *[objet, prise]* **s'~ à** to fit.

addenda [adɛ̃da] *nm inv* addenda.

additif, -ive [aditif, iv] 1 *adj* (*Math*) additive. 2 *nm* (*note, clause*) additional clause, rider; (*substance*) additive.

addition [adisjɔ̃] *nf* (*gén*) addition; (*problème*) addition, sum; (*facture*) bill, check (*US*). **par ~ de** by adding, by the addition of.

additionnel, -elle [adisjɔnɛl] *adj* additional; *V* **centime**.

additionner [adisjɔne] (1) 1 *vt* (*lit, fig*) to add up. **~ qch à** to add sth to; **~ le vin de sucre** to add sugar to the wine, mix sugar with the wine; (*sur étiquette*) **additionné d'alcool** with alcohol added.

2 **s'additionner** *vpr* to add up.

adducteur [adyktœʀ] *adj m, nm*: **(canal) ~** feeder (canal); **(muscle) ~** adductor *ou* adducent muscle.

adduction [adyksjɔ̃] *nf* (*Anat*) adduction. (*Tech*) **~ d'eau** water conveyance; **travaux d'~ d'eau** laying on water.

adepte [adɛpt(ə)] *nmf* follower. **faire des ~s** to win over *ou* gain followers.

adéquat, e [adekwa, at] *adj* appropriate, suitable, fitting. **utiliser le vocabulaire ~** to use the appropriate vocabulary; **ces installations ne sont pas ~es** these facilities are not suitable.

adéquation [adekwɑsjɔ̃] *nf* appropriateness.

adhérence [adeʀɑ̃s] *nf* (*gén*) adhesion (*à* to); *[pneus, semelles]* grip (*à* on), adhesion (*à* to). *[voiture]* **~ (à la route)** roadholding.

adhérent, e [adeʀɑ̃, ɑ̃t] **1** *adj*: **~ à** which sticks *ou* adheres to. **2** *nm,f* member, adherent.

adhérer [adeʀe] (6) **adhérer à** *vt indir* **(a)** (*coller*) to stick to, adhere to. **~ à la route** *[pneu]* to grip the road; *[voiture]* to hold *ou* grip the road; **ça adhère bien** it sticks *ou* adheres well; it grips the road well.

(b) (*se rallier à*) *point de vue* to support, adhere to (*frm*); *idéal* to adhere to.

(c) (*devenir membre de*) to join; (*être membre de*) to be a member of, belong to.

adhésif, -ive [adezif, iv] **1** *adj* adhesive, sticky. **2** *nm* adhesive.

adhésion [adezjɔ̃] *nf* **(a)** (*accord*) support (*à* for), adhesion (*frm*) (*à* to).

(b) (*inscription*) joining; (*fait d'être membre*) membership (*à* of). **son ~ au club** his joining the club; **bulletin/campagne d'~** membership form/drive; **il y a 3 nouvelles ~s cette semaine** 3 new members joined this week, there have been 3 new memberships this week.

ad hoc [adɔk] *adj inv* ad hoc.

adieu, *pl* **~x** [adjø] **1** *nm* **(a)** (*salut*) farewell, goodbye. (*lit, fig*) **dire ~ à** to say goodbye *ou* farewell to; **baiser d'~** farewell kiss.

(b) (*séparation*) **~x** farewells; **faire ses ~x (à qn)** to say one's farewells (to sb).

2 *excl* (*au revoir*) goodbye, cheerio* (*Brit*), farewell (*frm*, ††), adieu (*frm*); (*dial: bonjour*) hullo, hi*. (*fig*) **~ la tranquillité/les vacances** goodbye to (our) peace and quiet/our holidays.

à-Dieu-va(t) [adjøva(t)] *excl* it's all in God's hands!

adipeux, -euse [adipø, øz] *adj* (*Anat*) adipose; *visage* bloated, fleshy.

adiposité [adipozite] *nf* adiposity.

adjacent, e [adʒasɑ̃, ɑ̃t] *adj* adjacent, adjoining. **~ à** adjacent to, adjoining; *V* **angle.**

adjectif, -ive [adʒɛktif, iv] **1** *adj* adjectival, adjective (*épith*). **2** *nm* adjective. **~ substantivé/qualificatif** nominalized/qualifying adjective.

adjectival, e, *mpl* **-aux** [adʒɛktival, o] *adj* adjectival.

adjectivé, e [adʒɛktive] *adj* used as an adjective.

adjectivement [adʒɛktivmɑ̃] *adv* adjectivally, as an adjective.

adjoindre [adʒwɛ̃dʀ(ə)] (49) *vt* **(a)** (*associer*) **~ un collaborateur à qn** to appoint sb as an assistant to sb; **~ qn à un comité** to appoint sb to a committee; **s'~ un collaborateur** to take on *ou* appoint an assistant.

(b) (*ajouter*) **~ une pièce/un dispositif à qch** to attach *ou* affix a part/device to sth; **~ un chapitre à un ouvrage** to add a chapter to a book; (*à la fin*) to append a chapter to a book.

adjoint, e [adʒwɛ̃, wɛ̃t] (*ptp de* **adjoindre**) **1** *adj*: **commissaire** *etc* **~** assistant commissioner *etc*; *V* **professeur. 2** *nm,f* assistant. **~ au maire** deputy mayor. **3** *nm* (*Ling*) adjunct.

adjonction [adʒɔ̃ksjɔ̃] *nf* **(a)** (*action*) *[collaborateur]* addition; *[article, chapitre]* addition, (*à la fin*) appending (*à* to); *[dispositif]* attaching, affixing (*à* to). **l'~ de 2 secrétaires à l'équipe** the addition of 2 secretaries to the team, the appointment of 2 extra *ou* additional secretaries to the team.

(b) (*chose ajoutée*) addition.

adjudant [adʒydɑ̃] *nm* warrant officer. **~ chef** (*Armée*) ≃ warrant officer (*Brit*), (chief) warrant officer (*US*); (*Armée de l'air*) ≃ flight sergeant (*Brit*), warrant officer (*US*).

adjudicataire [adʒydikatɛʀ] *nmf* (*aux enchères*) purchaser; (*soumissionnaire*) successful tenderer. **qui est l'~ du contrat?** who won *ou* secured the contract?, who is the successful tenderer?

adjudicateur, -trice [adʒydikatœʀ, tʀis] *nm,f [enchères] official offering goods at auction*; *[contrat]* awarder.

adjudication [adʒydikɑsjɔ̃] *nf* **(a)** (*vente aux enchères*) sale by auction; (*marché administratif*) invitation to tender, putting up for tender. **par (voie d')~** by auction; by tender; **mettre en vente par ~** to put up for sale by auction; **offrir par ~** to put up for tender.

(b) (*attribution*) *[contrat]* awarding (*à* to); *[meuble, tableau]* auctioning (*à* to).

adjuger [adʒyʒe] (3) **1** *vt* **(a)** (*aux enchères*) to knock down, auction (*à* to). **une fois, deux fois, trois fois, adjugé, (vendu)!** going, going, gone!; **ceci fut adjugé pour 30 F** this went for *ou* was sold for 30 francs.

(b) (*attribuer*) *contrat, avantage, récompense* to award; (*: *donner*) *place, objet* to give.

2 s'adjuger *vpr* (*obtenir*) *contrat, récompense* to win; (*s'approprier*) to take for o.s. **il s'est adjugé la meilleure place** he has taken the best seat for himself, he has grabbed* *ou* nabbed* the best seat.

adjuration [adʒyʀɑsjɔ̃] *nf* entreaty, plea, adjuration (*frm*).

adjurer [adʒyʀe] (1) *vt*: **~ qn de faire** to implore *ou* beg *ou* adjure (*frm*) sb to do.

adjuvant [adʒyvɑ̃] *nm* (*médicament*) adjuvant; (*additif*) additive; (*stimulant*) stimulant.

ad lib(itum) [adlib(itɔm)] *adv* ad lib.

admettre [admɛtʀ(ə)] (56) *vt* **(a)** (*laisser entrer*) *visiteur, démarcheur* to admit, let in. **la salle ne pouvait ~ que 50 personnes** the room could only accommodate *ou* seat *ou* admit 50 people; **les chiens ne sont pas admis dans le magasin** dogs are not allowed in the shop; (*sur écriteau*) no dogs (allowed); **il fut admis dans une grande pièce** he was ushered *ou* shown *ou* admitted into a large room; (*Tech*) **l'air/le liquide est admis dans le cylindre** the air/the liquid is allowed to pass into the cylinder.

(b) (*recevoir*) *hôte* to receive; *nouveau membre* to admit. **~ qn à sa table** to receive sb at one's table; **il a été admis chez le ministre** he was received by the minister, he was admitted to see the minister; **se faire ~ dans un club** to gain admittance to *ou* be admitted to a club.

(c) (*Scol, Univ*) (*à un examen*) to pass; (*dans une classe*) to admit, accept. **ils ont admis 30 candidats** they passed 30 of the candidates; **il a été admis au concours** he passed *ou* got through the exam; **il a été admis dans un bon rang au concours** he came out well in *ou* got a good place in the exam; **il a/il n'a pas été admis en classe supérieure** he will move up into *ou* he will be admitted to/he didn't get into *ou* won't be admitted to the next class; **lire la liste des admis au concours** to read the list of successful candidates in *ou* of those who passed the (competitive) exam.

(d) (*convenir de*) *défaite, erreur* to admit, acknowledge. **il n'admet jamais ses torts** he'll never accept *ou* admit he's in the wrong.

(e) (*accepter*) *excuses, raisons* to accept; (*Jur*) *pourvoi* to accept. **je suis prêt à ~ que vous aviez raison** I'm ready to accept *ou* admit *ou* concede *ou* acknowledge that you were right; **il est admis que, c'est chose admise que** it's an accepted fact that, it's generally admitted that.

(f) (*supposer*) to suppose, assume. **en admettant que** supposing *ou* assuming that.

(g) (*tolérer*) *ton, attitude, indiscipline* to allow, accept. **je n'admets pas qu'il se conduise ainsi** I won't allow *ou* permit him to behave like that, I won't stand for *ou* accept such behaviour (from him); (*Admin*) **~ qn à siéger** to admit sb (*as a new member*); (*Admin*) **admis à faire valoir ses droits à la retraite** entitled to retire.

(h) (*laisser place à*) to admit of. **ton qui n'admet pas de réplique** a tone which brooks no reply; **règle qui n'admet aucune exception** rule which allows of *ou* admits of no exception; **règle qui admet plusieurs exceptions** rule which allows for several exceptions.

administrateur, -trice [administʀatœʀ, tʀis] *nm,f* (*gén*) administrator; *[banque, entreprise]* director; *[fondation]* trustee. (*Jur*) **~/~trice d'un bien** administrator/administratrix of an estate.

administratif, -ive [administʀatif, iv] *adj* administrative.

administration [administʀɑsjɔ̃] *nf* **(a)** (*gérance*: *V* **administrer**) management; running; administration; government. **je laisse l'~ de mes affaires à mon notaire** I leave my lawyer to deal with my affairs, I leave my affairs in the hands of my lawyer, I leave the handling of my affairs to my lawyer; **~ légale** guardianship (*parental*); *V* **conseil.**

(b) *[médicament, sacrement]* administering, administration.

(c) (*service public*) branch (of the public services). **l'A~** ≃ the Civil Service; **l'~ locale** local government; **être** *ou* **travailler dans l'~** to work in the government services; **l'~ des Douanes** ≃ the Customs and Excise; **l'~ des Eaux et forêts** ≃ the Forestry Commission; **l'~ des Impôts** the tax department, ≃ the Inland Revenue (*Brit*), the Internal Revenue (*US*).

administrativement [administʀativmɑ̃] *adv* administratively. **interné ~** officially committed (to mental hospital).

administré, e [administʀe] *nm,f* ≃ citizen.

administrer [administʀe] (1) *vt* **(a)** (*gérer*) *affaires, entreprise* to manage, run; *fondation* to administer; *pays* to run, govern; *commune* to run.

(b) (*dispenser*) *justice, remède, sacrement* to administer; *coup, gifle* to deal, administer; (*Jur*) *preuve* to produce.

admirable [admiʀabl(ə)] *adj* admirable, wonderful. **être ~ de courage** to show admirable *ou* wonderful courage; **portrait ~ de vérité** portrait showing a wonderful likeness.

admirablement [admiʀabləmɑ̃] *adv* admirably, wonderfully.

admirateur, -trice [admiʀatœʀ, tʀis] *nm,f* admirer.

admiratif, -ive [admiʀatif, iv] *adj* admiring.

admiration [admiʀɑsjɔ̃] *nf* admiration. **faire l'~ de qn, remplir qn d'~** to fill sb with admiration; **tomber/être en ~ devant qch/qn** to be filled with/lost in admiration for sth/sb.

admirativement [admiʀativmɑ̃] *adv* admiringly.

admirer [admiʀe] (1) *vt* to admire; (*iro*) to admire, marvel at.

admissibilité [admisibilite] *nf [postulant]* eligibility (*à* for); (*Scol, Univ*) *eligibility to sit the oral part of an exam.*

admissible [admisibl(ə)] **1** *adj* **(a)** (*tolérable*) *conduite, procédé* admissible, acceptable; *excuse* acceptable. **ce comportement n'est pas ~** this behaviour is quite inadmissible *ou* unacceptable. **(b)** *postulant* eligible (*à* for); (*Scol, Univ*) *having passed the written part of an exam.* **2** *nmf* eligible candidate.

admission [admisjɔ̃] *nf* **(a)** (*dans un lieu, club*) admission, admittance, entry (*à* to). (*Univ*) **~ à un concours** gaining a place in an exam, passing an exam; (*Scol, Univ*) **~ à une école** (gaining) acceptance *ou* entrance to a school; **son ~ (au club) a été obtenue non sans mal** he had some difficulty in gaining admission *ou* entry (to the club); **faire une demande d'~ à un club** to apply to join *ou* make application to join a club, apply for membership of a club; (*Douane*) **~ temporaire d'un véhicule** temporary importation of a vehicle; (*Univ*) **le nombre des ~s au concours a augmenté** the number of successful candidates in this exam has gone up.

(b) (*Tech: introduction*) intake; (*Aut*) induction; *V* **soupape.**

admonestation [admɔnɛstɑsjɔ̃] *nf* (*littér*) admonition, admonishment.

admonester [admɔnɛste] (1) *vt* (*gén, Jur*) to admonish.

admonition [admɔnisjɔ̃] *nf* (*littér, Jur*) admonition, admonishment.

adolescence [adɔlesɑ̃s] *nf* adolescence. **ses années d'~** his adolescent *ou* teenage years.

adolescent, e [adɔlesɑ̃, ɑ̃t] **1** *adj (littér)* adolescent *(épith)*. **2** *nm,f* adolescent, teenager; *(Méd, Psych)* adolescent.

Adonis [adɔnis] *nm (Myth, fig)* Adonis.

adonner (s') [adɔne] (1) *vpr*: **s'~ à** *art, études* to devote o.s. to; *sport, hobby* to devote o.s. to, go in for; *boisson, vice* to give o.s. over to, take to; **adonné au jeu** addicted to gambling.

adopter [adɔpte] (1) *vt* **(a)** *enfant* to adopt; *(fig: accueillir)* to adopt. **(b)** *attitude, religion, nom, mesure* to adopt; *cause* to take up, adopt. **(c)** *loi* to pass; *motion* to pass, adopt.

adoptif, -ive [adɔptif, iv] *adj enfant, patrie* adopted; *parent* adoptive.

adoption [adɔpsjɔ̃] *nf (V* **adopter***)* adoption; passing. **pays d'~** country of adoption; **un Londonien d'~** a Londoner by adoption.

adorable [adɔʀabl(ə)] *adj personne* adorable, delightful; *robe, village* lovely, delightful.

adorablement [adɔʀabləmɑ̃] *adv* delightfully, adorably.

adorateur, -trice [adɔʀatœʀ, tʀis] *nm,f (Rel, fig)* worshipper.

adoration [adɔʀɑsjɔ̃] *nf* adoration; *(Rel)* worship, adoration. **être en ~ devant** to dote (up)on, worship, idolize.

adorer [adɔʀe] (1) *vt personne, chose* to adore, love, be crazy* about *ou* mad* about; *(Rel)* to worship, adore; *V* **brûler.**

adosser [adose] (1) **1** *vt*: **~ à** *ou* **contre qch** *meuble* to stand against sth; *échelle* to stand *ou* lean against sth; *bâtiment* to build against *ou* onto sth; **il était adossé au pilier** he was leaning with his back against the pillar, he was standing with his back against the pillar.

2 s'adosser *vpr*: **s'~ à** *ou* **contre qch** *[personne]* to lean with one's back against sth; *[bâtiment]* to be built (hard) against sth, back onto sth.

adoubement [adubmɑ̃] *nm (Hist)* dubbing.

adouber [adube] (1) *vt (Hist)* to dub; *(Dames, Échecs)* to adjust.

adoucir [adusiʀ] (2) **1** *vt* **(a)** *saveur, acidité* to make milder *ou* smoother; *(avec sucre)* to sweeten; *rudesse, voix, peau* to soften; *couleur, contraste* to soften, tone down; *aspérités, surface* to smooth out; *caractère, personne* to mellow; *chagrin* to soothe, allay, ease; *conditions pénibles, épreuve* to ease, alleviate; *dureté, remarque* to mitigate, soften. **pour ~ ses vieux jours** to comfort (him in) his old age; **pour ~ sa solitude** to ease his loneliness; **cette averse a adouci la température** this shower has brought the temperature down; **~ la condamnation de qn** to reduce sb's sentence; *V* **musique.**

(b) *(Tech) eau* to soften.

2 s'adoucir *vpr [saveur, acidité]* to become milder *ou* smoother; *(avec sucre)* to become sweeter; *[voix, couleur, peau]* to soften; *[caractère, personne]* to mellow. **la température s'est adoucie** the weather has got milder; **vers le haut la pente s'adoucit** towards the top the slope became gentler *ou* less steep.

adoucissement [adusismɑ̃] *nm (V* **adoucir***)* sweetening; softening; toning-down; smoothing-out; mellowing; soothing; allaying; alleviation. **on espère un ~ de la température** we are hoping for milder weather *ou* a slight rise in the temperature; **apporter des ~s aux conditions de vie des prisonniers** to make the living conditions of the prisoners less harsh, alleviate the living conditions of the prisoners.

adoucisseur [adusisœʀ] *nm*: **~ (d'eau)** water softener.

ad patres [adpatʀes] *adv (hum)* **expédier** *ou* **envoyer qn ~** to bump sb off*.

adrénaline [adʀenalin] *nf* adrenalin.

adressage [adʀɛsaʒ] *nm* mailing.

adresse[1] [adʀɛs] *nf* **(a)** *(domicile)* address. **partir sans laisser d'~** to leave without giving a forwarding address; **à Paris je connais quelques bonnes ~s de restaurants** in Paris I know (the names *ou* addresses of) some good restaurants; *V* **carnet.**

(b) *(frm: message)* address. **à l'~ de** for the benefit of.

(c) *(Lexicographie)* headword; *(Ordinateur)* address.

adresse[2] [adʀɛs] *nf (habileté)* deftness, dexterity, skill; *(subtilité, finesse)* shrewdness, skill, cleverness; *(tact)* adroitness. **jeu/exercice d'~** game/exercise of skill; **il eut l'~ de ne rien révéler** he was adroit enough *ou* shrewd enough not to say anything; *V* **tour.**

adresser [adʀese] (1) **1** *vt* **(a) ~ une lettre/un colis à** *(envoyer)* to send a letter/parcel to; *(écrire l'adresse)* to address a letter/parcel to; **la lettre m'était personnellement adressée** the letter was addressed to me personally; **mon médecin m'a adressé à un spécialiste** my doctor sent *ou* referred me to a specialist; **machine à ~ (le courrier)** Addressograph ®.

(b) ~ une remarque/une requête à to address a remark/a request to; **~ une accusation/un reproche à** to level an accusation/a reproach at *ou* against, aim an accusation/a reproach at; **~ une allusion/un coup à** to aim a remark/a blow at; **~ un compliment/ses respects à** to pay a compliment/one's respects to; **~ une prière à** to address a prayer to; *(à Dieu)* to offer (up) a prayer to; **~ un regard furieux à qn** to direct an angry look at sb; **il m'adressa un signe de tête/un geste de la main** he nodded/waved at me; **~ un sourire à qn** to give sb a smile, smile at sb; **~ la parole à qn** to speak to *ou* address sb; **il m'adressa une critique acerbe** he criticized me harshly.

2 s'adresser *vpr* **(a)** *(adresser la parole à)* **s'~ à qn** to speak to sb, address sb; *(fig)* **il s'adresse à un public féminin** *[discours, magazine]* it is intended for *ou* aimed at a female audience; *[auteur]* he writes for *ou* is addressing a female audience; *(fig)* **ce livre s'adresse à notre générosité** this book is directed at *ou* appeals to our generosity.

(b) *(aller trouver)* **s'~ à** *personne* to go and see; *(Admin) personne, bureau* to apply to; **adressez-vous au concierge** go and see (*ou* ask, tell *etc*) the concierge; **adressez-vous au secrétariat** enquire at the office, go and ask at the office.

adret [adʀɛ] *nm (Géog)* south-facing slope, adret *(T)*.

adroit, e [adʀwa, wat] *adj (habile)* skilful, dext(e)rous, deft; *(subtil)* shrewd, skilled, clever; *(plein de tact)* adroit. **~ de ses mains** clever with one's hands, dext(e)rous.

adroitement [adʀwatmɑ̃] *adv (V* **adroit***)* skilfully; deftly; dext(e)rously; shrewdly; cleverly; adroitly.

adulateur, -trice [adylatœʀ, tʀis] *nm,f (littér) (admirateur)* adulator; *(flatteur)* sycophant.

adulation [adylɑsjɔ̃] *nf (littér) (admiration)* adulation; *(flatterie)* sycophancy.

aduler [adyle] (1) *vt (littér) (admirer)* to adulate; *(flatter)* to flatter.

adulte [adylt(ə)] **1** *adj personne* adult *(épith)*; *animal, plante* fully-grown, mature; *V* **âge. 2** *nmf* adult, grown-up.

adultère [adyltɛʀ] **1** *adj relations, désir* adulterous. **femme ~** adulteress; **homme ~** adulterer. **2** *nm (acte)* adultery; *V* **constat.**

adultérin, e [adylteʀɛ̃, in] *adj (Jur) enfant* born of adultery, adulterine.

advenir [advəniʀ] (22) **1** *vb impers* **(a)** *(survenir)* **~ que** to happen that, come to pass that *(littér)*; **~ à** to happen to, befall *(littér)*; **qu'est-il advenu au prisonnier?** what has happened to the prisoner?; **il m'advient de faire** I sometimes happen to do; **advienne que pourra** come what may; **quoi qu'il advienne** whatever happens *ou* may happen.

(b) *(devenir, résulter de)* **~ de** to become of; **qu'est-il advenu du prisonnier/du projet?** what has become of the prisoner/the project? **on ne sait pas ce qu'il en adviendra** nobody knows what will come of it *ou* how it will turn out.

2 *vi (arriver)* to happen.

adventice [advɑ̃tis] *adj (Bot)* self-propagating; *(Philos, littér: accessoire)* adventitious.

adventiste [advɑ̃tist(ə)] *nmf (Rel)* Adventist.

adverbe [advɛʀb(ə)] *nm* adverb.

adverbial, e, *mpl* **-aux** [advɛʀbjal, o] *adj* adverbial.

adverbialement [advɛʀbjalmɑ̃] *adv* adverbially.

adversaire [advɛʀsɛʀ] *nmf (gén)* opponent, adversary; *(Mil)* adversary, enemy; *[théorie]* opponent.

adversatif, -ive [advɛʀsatif, iv] *adj* adversative.

adverse [advɛʀs(ə)] *adj partie, forces, bloc* opposing. *(littér)* **la fortune ~** adverse fortune.

adversité [advɛʀsite] *nf* adversity.

ad vitam æternam* [advitametɛʀnam] *loc adv* till kingdom come.

aède [aɛd] *nm* (Greek) bard.

aérage [aeʀaʒ] *nm* ventilation.

aérateur [aeʀatœʀ] *nm* ventilator.

aération [aeʀɑsjɔ̃] *nf [pièce, literie]* airing; *[terre, racine]* aeration; *(circulation d'air)* ventilation; *V* **conduit.**

aéré, e [aeʀe] *(ptp de* **aérer***) adj pièce* airy, well-ventilated; *page* well spaced out; *V* **centre.**

aérer [aeʀe] (6) **1** *vt pièce, literie* to air; *terre, racine* to aerate; *(fig: alléger) exposé, présentation* to lighten. **2 s'aérer** *vpr [personne]* to get some fresh air. **s'~ les idées** to clear one's mind.

aérien, -ienne [aeʀjɛ̃, jɛn] **1** *adj* **(a)** *(Aviat) espace, droit* air *(épith)*; *navigation, photographie* aerial *(épith)*; *attaque* aerial *(épith)*, air *(épith)*. **base ~ne** air base; *V* **compagnie, ligne, métro.**

(b) *(léger) silhouette* sylphlike; *démarche* light, floating; *musique, poésie* ethereal.

(c) *(Bot) racine* aerial; *(Téléc) circuit, câble* overhead *(épith)*; *(Géog) courant, mouvement* air *(épith)*.

2 *nm (Rad: antenne)* aerial.

aérium [aeʀjɔm] *nm* sanatorium, sanitarium *(US)*.

aérobie [aeʀɔbi] *adj* aerobic.

aéro-club [aeʀoklœb] *nm* flying club.

aérodrome [aeʀɔdʀom] *nm* aerodrome *(Brit)*, airfield.

aérodynamique [aeʀɔdinamik] **1** *adj soufflerie, expérience* aerodynamics *(épith)*; *ligne, véhicule* streamlined, aerodynamic. **2** *nf* aerodynamics *(sg)*.

aérofrein [aeʀofʀɛ̃] *nm* air brake.

aérogare [aeʀɔgaʀ] *nf [aéroport]* airport (buildings); *(en ville)* air terminal.

aéroglisseur [aeʀɔglisœʀ] *nm* hovercraft.

aérogramme [aeʀɔgʀam] *nm* airmail letter.

aérolit(h)e [aeʀɔlit] *nm* aerolite, aerolith.

aéromodélisme [aeʀɔmɔdelism(ə)] *nm* model aircraft making.

aéronaute [aeʀɔnot] *nmf* aeronaut.

aéronautique [aeʀɔnotik] **1** *adj* aeronautical. **2** *nf* aeronautics *(sg)*.

aéronaval, e, *pl* **~s** [aeʀɔnaval] *adj forces* air and sea *(épith)*. **l'A~e** ≃ the Fleet Air Arm.

aéronef† [aeʀɔnɛf] *nm* aircraft.

aérophagie [aeʀɔfaʒi] *nf* aerophagy *(T)*. **il a** *ou* **fait de l'~** he suffers from air in the stomach *ou* wind.

aéroplane† [aeʀɔplan] *nm* aeroplane *(Brit)*, airplane *(US)*.

aéroport [aeʀɔpɔʀ] *nm* airport.

aéroporté, e [aeʀɔpɔʀte] *adj troupes* airborne; *matériel* airlifted, brought *ou* ferried by air *(attrib)*.

aéropostal, e, *mpl* **-aux** [aeʀɔpɔstal, o] *adj* airmail *(épith)*. *(Hist)* **l'A~e** the (French) airmail service.

aérosol [aeʀɔsɔl] *nm* aerosol. **déodorant en ~** deodorant spray, spray-on *ou* aerosol deodorant.

aérospatial, e, *mpl* **-aux** [aeʀɔspasjal, o] **1** *adj* aerospace *(épith)*. **2 aérospatiale** *nf* aerospace science.

aérostat [aeʀɔsta] *nm* aerostat.

aérostatique [aeʀɔstatik] **1** *adj* aerostatic. **2** *nf* aerostatics *(sg)*.

aérotrain [aeʀɔtʀɛ̃] *nm* ® hovertrain.
affabilité [afabilite] *nf* affability.
affable [afabl(ə)] *adj* affable.
affablement [afabləmɑ̃] *adv* affably.
affabulateur, -trice [afabylatœʀ, tʀis] *nm,f* inveterate liar, storyteller.
affabulation [afabylɑsjɔ̃] *nf* **(a)** (*mensonges*) **c'est de l'~, ce sont des ~s** it's all made up, it's pure fabrication. **(b)** *[roman]* (construction of the) plot.
affabuler [afabyle] (1) *vi* to invent *ou* make up stories.
affadir [afadiʀ] (2) **1** *vt aliment, mets* to make tasteless *ou* insipid; *couleur, conversation, style* to make dull *ou* uninteresting *ou* colourless.
2 s'affadir *vpr [conversation, couleur, style]* to become dull, pall; *[aliment, saveur]* to lose (its) flavour, become tasteless *ou* insipid.
affadissant, e [afadisɑ̃, ɑ̃t] *adj influence* dulling.
affadissement [afadismɑ̃] *nm [aliment]* loss of flavour (*de* in, from); *[saveur, style]* loss of strength (*de* in), weakening (*de* of); *[couleurs, sensations]* dulling (*de* of).
affaiblir [afebliʀ] (2) **1** *vt* (*gén*) to weaken.
2 s'affaiblir *vpr [personne, autorité, résolution, facultés]* to weaken, grow *ou* become weaker; *[vue]* to grow *ou* get dim *ou* weaker; *[son]* to fade (away), grow fainter; *[intérêt]* to wane; *[vent, tempête]* to abate, die down. **le sens de ce mot s'est affaibli** the meaning of this word has got weaker.
affaiblissement [afeblismɑ̃] *nm* (*gén*) weakening; *[bruit]* fading (away).
affaire [afɛʀ] **1** *nf* **(a)** (*problème*) matter, business. **j'ai à régler deux ou trois ~s urgentes** I've got two or three urgent matters to settle; **ce n'est pas une petite** *ou* **une mince ~** it's no small matter; **il faut tirer cette ~ au clair** we must get to the bottom of this business, we must sort out this business; **il m'a tiré d'~** he helped me out, he got me out of a spot*; **il est assez grand pour se tirer d'~ tout seul** he's big enough to manage on his own *ou* to sort it out by himself; **c'est une ~ d'hommes** it's a man's business; **c'est mon ~, non la tienne** it's my business *ou* affair, not yours; **ce n'est pas ton ~** it's none of your business; **j'en fais mon ~** I'll deal with that; **c'était une ~ bâclée en cinq minutes** it was a botched and hurried job.
(b) (*ce qui convient*) **j'ai là votre ~** I've got (just) what you want; **cet employé fera/ne fait pas l'~** this employee will do nicely/won't do (for the job); **ça fait mon ~** that's (just) what I want *ou* need; **cela fera bien l'~ de quelqu'un** that will (certainly) come in handy for somebody, that'll do nicely for somebody.
(c) (*scandale*) business, affair, matter. **on a voulu étouffer l'~** they wanted to hush the business *ou* matter up; **il a essayé d'arranger l'~** he tried to straighten out *ou* settle the matter; **c'est une sale ~** it's a nasty business; **l'~ Dreyfus** the Dreyfus affair; **l'~ de Suez** the Suez crisis; **une grave ~ de corruption/d'espionnage** a serious affair of corruption/espionage, a serious corruption/spy case; **c'est une ~ de gros sous** there's big money involved; **c'est une ~ à suivre** it's something *ou* a matter worth watching *ou* keeping an eye on.
(d) (*Jur, Police*) case. **l'~ X** the X case; **être sur une ~** to be on a case; **une ~ de vol** a case of theft; **son ~ est claire** it's an open and shut case.
(e) (*transaction*) deal, bargain, transaction. **une (bonne) ~** a good deal, a (good) bargain; **une mauvaise ~** a bad deal *ou* bargain; **faire ~ avec qn** to settle a bargain with sb, conclude *ou* clinch a deal with sb; **ils font des ~s (d'or)** they're pulling in the money, they're raking it in*; **ils font beaucoup d'~s** they do a lot of business; **l'~ est faite!** *ou* **conclue!** that's the deal settled!; **l'~ est dans le sac*** it's in the bag*.
(f) (*firme*) business, concern. **c'est une ~ qui marche/en or** it's a going concern/a gold mine; **il a repris l'~ de son père** he has taken on *ou* over his father's business.
(g) (*intérêts publics et privés*) **~s** affairs; **les ~s culturelles/de la municipalité/étrangères/publiques** cultural/municipal/foreign/public affairs; (*Can*) **A~s extérieures** External Affairs (*Can*); (*Québec*) **A~s intergouvernementales** Intergovernmental Affairs (*Can*), Foreign Affairs; **mettre de l'ordre dans ses ~s** to put one's affairs in order; **occupe-toi de tes ~s** mind your own business; **se mêler des ~s des autres** to interfere in other people's business *ou* affairs; **il raconte ses ~s à tout le monde** he tells everyone about his affairs.
(h) (*activités commerciales*) **les ~s** business; **être dans les ~s** to be in business; **parler (d')~s** to talk *ou* discuss business; **il est venu pour ~s** he came on business; **il est dur en ~s** he's a tough businessman; **les ~s sont les ~s** business is business; **d'~s** *déjeuner, rendez-vous etc* business (*épith*); *V* **cabinet, carré, chiffre.**
(i) **~s** (*habits*) clothes, things; (*objets, effets personnels*) things, belongings; **range tes ~s!** put away *ou* tidy up your things!
(j) (*loc*) **avoir ~ à** *cas, problème* to be faced with, have to deal with; *personne* (*s'occuper de*) to be dealing with; (*être servi ou examiné par*) to be dealt with by; (*ton menaçant*) **tu auras ~ à moi/lui** you'll be hearing from me/him; **nous avons ~ à un dangereux criminel** we are dealing here with a dangerous criminal; **être à son ~** to be in one's element; **il n'est pas à son ~** he doesn't feel at ease, he is self-conscious; **faire son ~ à qn*** to do sb in*; **cela ne fait rien à l'~** that's got nothing to do with it; **en voilà une ~!** what a (complicated) business!; **ce n'est pas une ~!** it's nothing to get worked up about!; **c'est toute une ~ (que d'aller à Glasgow)** it's quite a business (getting to Glasgow); **il en a fait toute une ~** he blew it up out of all proportion, he made a dreadful fuss about it, he made a great song and dance about it; **se faire une ~ de qch** to make a fuss about sth; **c'est une tout autre ~** that's quite another matter *ou* quite another kettle of fish; **toutes ~s cessantes** forthwith; **c'est (une) ~ de goût/de mode** it's a matter of taste/fashion; **c'est l'~ de quelques minutes/quelques clous** it's a matter of a few minutes/a few nails; *V* **beau, connaître.**
2: **affaire de cœur** love affair; (*Pol*) **affaire d'État** affair of state; **il en a fait une affaire d'état*** he made a song and dance about it *ou* a great issue of it; **affaire d'honneur** affair of honour; **affaire de mœurs** (*gén*) sex scandal; (*Jur*) sex case.
affairé, e [afeʀe] (*ptp de* **s'affairer**) *adj* busy.
affairement [afɛʀmɑ̃] *nm* bustling activity.
affairer (s') [afeʀe] (1) *vpr* to busy o.s., bustle about. **s'~ auprès** *ou* **autour de qn** to fuss around sb; **s'~ à faire** to busy o.s. doing, bustle about doing.
affairisme [afeʀism(ə)] *nm* (political) racketeering.
affairiste [afeʀist(ə)] *nm* racketeer. **sous ce régime il n'y a pas de place pour l'~** there is no place under this government for political racketeering *ou* for those who want to use politics to line their purse.
affaissement [afɛsmɑ̃] *nm* (*V* **affaisser**) subsidence; sagging; sinking. **~ de terrain** subsidence (*U*).
affaisser [afese] (1) **1 s'affaisser** *vpr* **(a)** (*fléchir*) *[route, sol]* to subside, sink; *[corps, poutre]* to sag; *[plancher]* to cave in, give way; (*fig*) *[forces, volonté]* to sink. **le sol était affaissé par endroits** the ground had subsided *ou* sunk in places.
(b) (*s'écrouler*) *[personne]* to collapse. **il s'était affaissé sur le sol** he had collapsed *ou* crumpled in a heap on the ground; **il était affaissé dans un fauteuil/sur le sol** he was slumped in an armchair/on the ground.
2 *vt route, sol* to cause to subside.
affaler (s') [afale] (1) *vpr* (*tomber*) to collapse, fall; (*se laisser tomber*) to collapse, flop, slump. **affalé dans un fauteuil** slumped in an armchair; (*Naut*) **s'~ le long d'un cordage** to slide down a rope.
affamé, e [afame] (*ptp de* **affamer**) *adj* starving, famished, ravenous. (*fig*) **~ de gloire** hungry *ou* greedy for fame; *V* **ventre.**
affamer [afame] (1) *vt personne, ville* to starve.
affameur, -euse [afamœʀ, øz] *nm,f* (*péj*) tight-fisted employer (*who pays starvation wages*).
affectation [afɛktɑsjɔ̃] *nf* **(a)** *[immeuble, somme]* allocation, allotment, assignment (*à* to, for). **l'~ du signe + à un nombre** the addition of the plus sign to a number, the modification of a number by the plus sign.
(b) (*nomination*) (*à un poste*) appointment; (*à une région, un pays*) posting. **rejoindre son ~** to take up one's appointment; to take up one's posting.
(c) (*manque de naturel*) affectation, affectedness. **avec ~** affectedly, with affectation *ou* affectedness.
(d) (*simulation*) affectation, show. **avec une ~ de** with an affectation *ou* show of.
affecté, e [afɛkte] (*ptp de* **affecter**) *adj* (*feint*) affected, feigned, assumed; (*maniéré*) affected.
affecter [afɛkte] (1) *vt* **(a)** (*feindre*) to affect, feign. **~ de faire qch** to pretend to do sth; **~ le bonheur/un grand chagrin** to affect *ou* feign happiness/great sorrow, put on a show of happiness/great sorrow; (*littér*) **~ un langage poétique** to affect *ou* favour a poetic style of language; **il affecta de ne pas s'y intéresser** he affected *ou* pretended not to be interested in it; **~ une forme** to take on *ou* assume a shape.
(b) (*destiner*) to allocate, allot, assign (*à* to, for). **~ des crédits à la recherche** to earmark funds for research, allocate *ou* allot *ou* assign funds to *ou* for research.
(c) (*nommer*) (*à une fonction, un bureau*) to appoint; (*à une région, un pays*) to post (*à* to).
(d) (*émouvoir*) to affect, move, touch; (*concerner*) to affect. **il a été très affecté par leur mort** he was deeply affected *ou* moved by their deaths.
(e) (*Math*) to modify. **nombre affecté du coefficient 2/du signe +** number modified by *ou* bearing the coefficient 2/a plus sign.
affectif, -ive [afɛktif, iv] *adj* (*gén*) *vie* emotional; *terme, nuance* affective, emotional; (*Psych*) affective.
affection [afɛksjɔ̃] *nf* **(a)** (*tendresse*) affection. **avoir de l'~ pour** to feel affection for, be fond of; **prendre en ~** to become fond of *ou* attached to. **(b)** (*Méd*) ailment, affection. **(c)** (*Psych*) affection.
affectionné, e [afɛksjɔne] (*ptp de* **affectionner**) *adj* (*frm*) **votre fils ~/fille ~e** your loving *ou* beloved son/daughter; **votre ~** yours affectionately.
affectionner [afɛksjɔne] (1) *vt chose* to have a liking for, be fond of; *personne* to have affection *ou* an attachment for.
affectivité [afɛktivite] *nf* affectivity.
affectueusement [afɛktɥøzmɑ̃] *adv* affectionately, fondly.
affectueux, -euse [afɛktɥø, øz] *adj personne* affectionate; *pensée, regard* affectionate, fond.
afférent, e [afeʀɑ̃, ɑ̃t] *adj* **(a)** (*Admin*) **~ à** *fonction* pertaining to, relating to; **questions ~es** related questions; (*Jur*) **part ~e à** portion accruing to. **(b)** (*Méd*) afferent.
affermage [afɛʀmaʒ] *nm* (*V* **affermer**) leasing; renting.
affermer [afɛʀme] (1) *vt [propriétaire]* to lease, let out on lease; *[fermier]* to rent, take on lease.
affermir [afɛʀmiʀ] (2) *vt pouvoir, position* to consolidate, strengthen; *muscles, chairs* to tone up; *prise, charge, coiffure* to make firm *ou* firmer; *arrimage* to tighten, make firm *ou* firmer. **~ sa voix** to steady one's voice; **cela l'affermit dans sa résolution** that strengthened him in his resolution; **après cet événement son autorité s'est affermie** his authority was strengthened after that event.

affermissement [afɛʀmismɑ̃] *nm* strengthening.
affété, e [afete] *adj* (*littér*) precious, affected, mannered.
afféterie [afetʀi] *nf* (*littér*) preciosity, affectation (*U*).
affichage [afiʃaʒ] *nm* (*V* **afficher**) putting *ou* posting *ou* sticking up; billing. **l'~** billsticking, billposting; **~ interdit** (stick *ou* post) no bills; **interdit à l'~** *magazine* not for public display; *V* **panneau, tableau.**
affiche [afiʃ] *nf* **(a)** (*officielle*) public notice; (*Admin, Théât*) bill; (*publicité, Art*) poster; (*électorale etc*) poster. **la vente a été annoncée par voie d'~** the sale was advertised by public notice, posters have gone up *ou* have been put up advertising the sale; **~ de théâtre** (play)bill; **par voie d'~** by (means of) public notices.
(b) (*Théât*) **mettre à l'~** to bill; **quitter l'~** to come off, close; **tenir longtemps l'~** to have a long run; **la pièce a tenu l'~ pendant 6 mois** the play ran for 6 months *ou* had a 6-month run; *V* **tête.**
afficher [afiʃe] (1) **1** *vt* **(a)** *affiche, résultat* to put *ou* post *ou* stick up; (*Théât*) to bill. **défense d'~** (stick *ou* post) no bills.
(b) (*péj*) *émotion, mépris* to exhibit, display; *qualité, vice* to flaunt, parade, display. **~ sa maîtresse** to parade one's mistress.
2 s'afficher *vpr [personne]* to flaunt o.s. **s'~ avec sa maîtresse** to parade o.s. *ou* show o.s. off with one's mistress; **l'hypocrisie qui s'affiche sur tous les visages** the hypocrisy which is plain to see *ou* flaunted *ou* displayed on everybody's face.
affichette [afiʃɛt] *nf* (*V* **affiche**) small public notice; small bill; small poster.
afficheur [afiʃœʀ] *nm* billsticker, billposter.
affichiste [afiʃist(ə)] *nmf* poster designer *ou* artist.
affidé, e [afide] *nm,f* (*péj*) confederate, accomplice, henchman.
affilage [afilaʒ] *nm* (*V* **affiler**) sharpening; whetting; honing.
affilé, e[1] [afile] (*ptp de* **affiler**) *adj outil, couteau* sharp; *intelligence* keen; *V* **langue.**
affilée[2] [afile] *nf*: **d'~** at a stretch, running. **8 heures d'~** 8 hours at a stretch *ou* on end *ou* solid *ou* running; **boire plusieurs verres d'~** to drink several glasses at a stretch *ou* one after the other.
affiler [afile] (1) *vt couteau, outil* to sharpen, whet; *rasoir* to sharpen, hone.
affiliation [afiljɑsjɔ̃] *nf* affiliation.
affilié, e [afilje] (*ptp de* **affilier**) *nm,f* affiliated member.
affilier [afilje] (7) **1** *vt* to affiliate (*à* to). **2 s'affilier** *vpr* to become affiliated, affiliate o.s. (*ou* itself) (*à* to).
affiloir [afilwaʀ] *nm* (*outil*) sharpener; (*pierre*) whetstone; *[boucher, couteau à découper]* steel.
affinage [afinaʒ] *nm [métal]* refining; *[verre]* fining; *[fromage]* maturing.
affinement [afinmɑ̃] *nm [goût, manières, style]* refinement.
affiner [afine] (1) *vt* **(a)** *métal* to refine; *verre* to fine; *fromage* to complete the maturing (process) of. **(b)** *esprit, mœurs* to refine; *style* to polish, refine; *sens* to make keener, sharpen. **son goût s'est affiné** his taste has become more refined.
affineur, -euse [afinœʀ, øz] *nm,f [métal]* refiner; *[verre]* finer; *[fromage] person in charge of the last stages of the maturing process.*
affinité [afinite] *nf* (*gén*) affinity.
affirmatif, -ive [afiʀmatif, iv] **1** *adj réponse, proposition* affirmative; *personne, ton* assertive, affirmative. **il a été ~ à ce sujet** he was quite positive on that score *ou* about that; *V* **signe.**
2 affirmative *nf* affirmative. **répondre par l'~ive** to answer yes *ou* in the affirmative; **dans l'~ive** in the event of the answer being yes *ou* of an affirmative reply (*frm*); **nous espérons que vous viendrez: dans l'~ive, faites-le-nous savoir** we hope you'll come and if you do *ou* can please let us know.
affirmation [afiʀmɑsjɔ̃] *nf* **(a)** (*allégation*) assertion. **(b)** (*Gram*) assertion. **(c)** (*manifestation*) *[talent, autorité]* assertion, affirmation.
affirmativement [afiʀmativmɑ̃] *adv* in the affirmative, affirmatively.
affirmer [afiʀme] (1) *vt* **(a)** (*soutenir*) to maintain, assert. **tu affirmes toujours tout sans savoir** you always assert everything *ou* you are always positive about everything without really knowing; **il affirme l'avoir vu s'enfuir** he maintains *ou* asserts that *ou* claims that he saw him run off; **il affirme que c'est de votre faute** he contends *ou* maintains *ou* asserts that it is your fault; **pouvez-vous l'~?** can you swear to it?, can you be positive about it?; **on ne peut rien ~ encore** we can't say anything positive *ou* for sure yet, we can't affirm anything yet; **~ qch sur l'honneur** to maintain *ou* affirm sth on one's word of honour; **~ sur l'honneur que** to give one's word of honour that, maintain *ou* affirm on one's word of honour that.
(b) (*manifester*) *originalité, autorité, position* to assert. **talent/personnalité qui s'affirme** talent/personality which is asserting itself; **il s'affirme comme l'un de nos meilleurs romanciers** he is asserting himself *ou* establishing himself as one of our best novelists.
(c) (*frm: proclamer*) to affirm, assert. **le président a affirmé sa volonté de régler cette affaire** the president affirmed *ou* asserted his wish to settle this matter.
affixe [afiks(ə)] *nm* affix.
affleurement [aflœʀmɑ̃] *nm* (*Géol*) outcrop; (*fig*) emergence; (*Tech*) flushing.
affleurer [aflœʀe] (1) **1** *vi [rocs, récifs]* to show on the surface; *[filon, couche]* to show on *ou* through the surface, outcrop (*T*); (*fig*) *[sentiment, sensualité]* to show through the surface, come *ou* rise to the surface. **quelques récifs affleuraient (à la surface de l'eau)** a few reefs showed on the surface (of the water).
2 *vt* (*Tech*) to make flush, flush.
afflictif, -ive [afliktif, iv] *adj* (*Jur*) corporal.
affliction [afliksjɔ̃] *nf* (*littér*) affliction. **être dans l'~** to be in (a state of) affliction.
affligé, e [afliʒe] (*ptp de* **affliger**) *adj*: **être ~ de** *maladie* to be afflicted with; (*fig*) **il était ~ d'une femme acariâtre** he was afflicted *ou* cursed with a cantankerous wife; (*littér*) **les ~s** the afflicted.
affligeant, e [afliʒɑ̃, ɑ̃t] *adj* distressing; (*iro*) pathetic (*iro*).
affliger [afliʒe] (3) *vt* (*attrister*) to distress, grieve, afflict; (*littér: accabler*) to smite (*littér*) (*de* with). **s'~ de qch** to be grieved *ou* distressed about sth; (*hum*) **la nature l'avait affligé d'un nez crochu** nature had afflicted *ou* cursed him with a hooked nose.
affluence [aflyɑ̃s] *nf [gens]* crowds (*pl*), throng (*littér*); *V* **heure.**
affluent [aflyɑ̃] *nm* tributary, affluent (*T*).
affluer [aflye] (1) *vi [fluide, sang]* to rush, flow (*à, vers* to); *[foule]* to flock. **les dons affluaient de partout** the donations were flooding in *ou* rolling in from all parts; **les télégrammes affluaient sur sa table** telegrams were pouring onto his table; **l'argent afflue dans les caisses de la banque** money is flowing *ou* flooding into the coffers of the bank.
afflux [afly] *nm [fluide]* rush, flow, afflux (*T*); *[argent, foule]* influx, flood; (*Elec*) flow.
affolant, e [afɔlɑ̃, ɑ̃t] *adj* (*effrayant*) frightening; (*littér: troublant*) *situation, nouvelle* distressing, disturbing. **c'est ~!*** it's alarming!*; **à une vitesse ~e** at an alarming speed.
affolé, e [afɔle] (*ptp de* **affoler**) *adj* **(a)** (*effrayé*) panic- *ou* terror-stricken; (*littér: troublé*) driven wild *ou* crazy. **je suis ~ de voir ça*** I'm appalled *ou* horrified at that; **air ~** look of panic, panic-stricken look.
(b) *boussole* wildly fluctuating.
affolement [afɔlmɑ̃] *nm* **(a)** (*effroi*) panic; (*littér: trouble*) (wild) turmoil. **pas d'~!*** no panic!, don't panic! **(b)** *[boussole]* wild fluctuations.
affoler [afɔle] (1) **1** *vt* (*effrayer*) to throw into a panic, terrify; (*littér: troubler*) to drive wild, throw into a turmoil.
2 s'affoler *vpr* to lose one's head. **ne nous affolons pas*** don't let's panic *ou* get in a panic*, let's keep our heads.
affouillement [afujmɑ̃] *nm* undermining (*by water*).
affouiller [afuje] (1) *vt* to undermine (*T*).
affranchi, e [afʀɑ̃ʃi] (*ptp de* **affranchir**) *nm,f* (*esclave*) emancipated *ou* freed slave; (*libertin*) emancipated man (*ou* woman).
affranchir [afʀɑ̃ʃiʀ] (2) *vt* **(a)** (*avec des timbres*) to put a stamp *ou* stamps on, stamp; (*à la machine*) to frank. **lettre affranchie/non affranchie** stamped/unstamped letter; franked/unfranked letter; **j'ai reçu une lettre insuffisamment affranchie** I received a letter with insufficient postage on it.
(b) *esclave* to enfranchise, emancipate, (set) free; *peuple, pays* to free; (*fig*) *esprit, personne* to free, emancipate. (*fig*) **~ qn de** *contrainte* to free sb from, set sb free from; **s'~ d'une domination étrangère/des convenances** to free o.s. from foreign domination/from convention.
(c) (*arg Crime: mettre au courant*) **~ qn** to give sb the low-down:, put sb in the picture*.
(d) (*Cartes*) to clear.
affranchissement [afʀɑ̃ʃismɑ̃] *nm* **(a)** (*U: V* **affranchir**) stamping; franking; emancipation; enfranchisement; freeing. **(b)** (*Poste: prix payé*) postage.
affres [afʀ(ə)] *nfpl* (*littér*) **les ~ de** the pangs *ou* the torments of; **être dans les ~ de la mort** to be in the throes of death.
affrètement [afʀɛtmɑ̃] *nm* (*V* **affréter**) chartering; hiring.
affréter [afʀete] (6) *vt* (*Aviat, Naut*) to charter; (*Aut*) to hire, charter.
affréteur [afʀetœʀ] *nm* (*Aviat, Naut*) charterer; (*Aut*) hirer.
affreusement [afʀøzmɑ̃] *adv souffrir, blesser* horribly. **~ laid** hideously ugly; **pâlir ~** to turn ghastly pale; **ce plat est ~ mauvais** this dish is really horrible *ou* horrid; **on est ~ mal assis/en retard*** we're dreadfully (*surtout Brit*) *ou* awfully (*surtout Brit*) badly seated/late.
affreux, -euse [afʀø, øz] **1** *adj* (*très laid*) hideous, horrible, horrid, ghastly; (*effroyable, abominable*) dreadful, awful, horrible. **quel temps ~!** what ghastly (*surtout Brit*) *ou* dreadful *ou* horrible weather!; **j'ai un mal de tête ~** I've got a splitting *ou* a dreadful *ou* an awful *ou* a horrible headache.
2 *nm* (*arg Mil*) (white) mercenary (*gen serving in Africa*).
affriander [afʀijɑ̃de] (1) *vt* (*littér*) to attract, allure, entice.
affriolant, e [afʀijɔlɑ̃, ɑ̃t] *adj perspective, programme* enticing, appealing, tempting, exciting; *femme* enticing, inviting; *habit féminin* titillating, alluring.
affrioler [afʀijɔle] (1) *vt* to tempt, excite, arouse.
affriqué, e [afʀike] **1** *adj* affricative. **2 affriquée** *nf* affricate.
affront [afʀɔ̃] *nm* (*frm: insulte*) affront. **faire (un) ~ à** to affront, offer an affront to.
affrontement [afʀɔ̃tmɑ̃] *nm* (*Mil, Pol*) confrontation.
affronter [afʀɔ̃te] (1) **1** *vt adversaire, danger* to confront, face, meet. **~ la mort** to face *ou* brave death; **~ le mauvais temps** to brave the bad weather.
2 s'affronter *vpr [adversaires]* to confront each other, be in confrontation. **ces deux théories s'affrontent** these two theories are in confrontation.
affublement [afybləmɑ̃] *nm* (*péj*) attire, apparel†, rig-out* (*Brit*).
affubler [afyble] (1) *vt*: **~ qn de** *vêtement* to rig* *ou* deck sb out in; **~ qn d'un sobriquet** to attach a nickname to sb; **il s'affubla d'un vieux manteau** he rigged* himself out *ou* got* himself up in an old coat; **affublé d'un vieux chapeau** wearing an old hat.

affût [afy] *nm* **(a)** ~ **(de canon)** (gun) carriage. **(b)** (*Chasse*) hide. **chasser à l'~** to lie in wait for game, hunt game from a hide; **être à l'~** to be (lying) in wait; **se mettre à l'~** to be in wait, hide out; (*fig*) **être à l'~ de qch** to be on the look-out for sth.
affûtage [afytaʒ] *nm* sharpening, grinding.
affûter [afyte] (1) *vt* to sharpen, grind.
affûteur [afytœʀ] *nm* grinder, sharpener.
affûteuse [afytøz] *nf* grinder.
affûtiaux [afytjo] *nmpl* (††, *hum*) garments, raiment†† (*U*).
afghan, e [afgɑ̃, an] **1** *adj* Afghan. **2** *nm,f*: **A~(e)** Afghan.
Afghanistan [afganistɑ̃] *nm* Afghanistan.
afin [afɛ̃] *prép*: **~ de** to, in order to, so as to; **~ que** + *subj* so that, in order that.
a fortiori [afɔʀsjɔʀi] *loc adv* a fortiori, all the more.
africain, e [afʀikɛ̃, ɛn] **1** *adj* African. **2** *nm,f*: **A~(e)** African.
africanisation [afʀikanizɑsjɔ̃] *nf* Africanization.
africaniste [afʀikanist(ə)] *nmf* Africanist.
afrikaans [afʀikɑ̃] *nm, adj inv* Afrikaans.
afrikander [afʀikɑ̃dɛʀ] *nm* Afrikaner.
Afrique [afʀik] *nf* Africa. **l'~ australe/du Nord/du Sud** southern/North/South Africa.
afro-asiatique [afʀɔazjatik] **1** *adj* Afro-Asian. **2** *nmf*: **A~** Afro-Asian.
agaçant, e [agasɑ̃, ɑ̃t] *adj* irritating, aggravating*, annoying.
agacement [agasmɑ̃] *nm* irritation, annoyance.
agacer [agase] (3) *vt* **(a)** **~ qn** (*énerver*) to get on sb's nerves, irritate *ou* aggravate* sb; (*taquiner*) to pester *ou* tease sb; **~ les dents de qn** to set sb's teeth on edge; **~ les nerfs de qn** to get on sb's nerves; **ça m'agace!** it's getting on my nerves!; **agacé par le bruit** irritated *ou* annoyed by the noise; **agacé de l'entendre** irritated at hearing him.
(b) (*littér: aguicher*) to excite, lead on.
agaceries [agasʀi] *nfpl* coquetries, provocative gestures.
agapes [agap] *nfpl* (*hum*) banquet, feast.
agate [agat] *nf* agate.
agave [agav] *nm* agave.
âge [ɑʒ] **1** *nm* **(a)** (*gén*) age. **quel ~ avez-vous?** how old are you?, what age are you?; **à l'~ de 8 ans** at the age of 8; **j'ai votre ~** I'm your age, I'm the same age as you; **ils sont du même ~** they're the same age; (*hum*) **il est d'un ~ canonique** he's a venerable age (*hum*); **elle est d'un ~ avancé** she is getting on in age *ou* years, she is quite elderly; **d'~ moyen** middle-aged; **il ne paraît pas son ~** he doesn't look his age; **elle porte bien son ~** she looks well for her age, she carries her years well; **il fait plus vieux que son ~** he looks older than he is *ou* than his years; **sans ~, qui n'a pas d'~** ageless; **il a vieilli avant l'~** he has got *ou* is old before his time; **il a pris de l'~** he has got older, he has aged; **amusez-vous, c'est de votre ~** enjoy yourself — you should (do) at your age; **j'ai passé l'~ de le faire** I've passed the age for doing it, I'm too old to do it; **avec l'~ il se calmera** as he grows *ou* gets older he'll settle down; **des gens de tout ~** people of all ages; **être en ~ de se marier** to be of marriageable age, be old enough to get married; **être en ~ de combattre** to be old enough to fight; *V* **bas, moyen** *etc*.
(b) (*ère*) age. **l'~ de (la) pierre/du bronze/du fer** the Stone/Bronze/Iron Age.
2: **l'âge adulte** (*gén*) adulthood; (*homme*) manhood; (*femme*) womanhood; **l'âge critique** the change of life; **l'âge d'homme** manhood; **l'âge ingrat** the awkward *ou* difficult age; **l'âge légal** the legal age; **avoir l'âge légal** to be of age; **il n'a pas encore l'âge légal** he's under age; **l'âge mûr** maturity, middle age; **l'âge d'or** the golden age; **l'âge de la pierre polie** the neolithic age; **l'âge de la pierre taillée** the palaeolithic age; **l'âge de raison** the age of reason; **l'âge de la retraite** retiring age; **l'âge tendre** the tender years *ou* age; **l'âge viril** = **l'âge d'homme**.
âgé, e [ɑʒe] *adj*: **être ~** to be old, be elderly (*euph*); **être ~ de 9 ans** to be 9 (years old), be 9 years of age; **enfant ~ de 4 ans** 4-year-old child; **dame ~e** elderly lady; **les personnes ~es** the elderly, old people.
agence [aʒɑ̃s] *nf* (*succursale*) branch (office); (*bureaux*) offices (*pl*); (*organisme*) agency, bureau, office. **~ immobilière** estate agent's (office); **~ matrimoniale** marriage bureau; **~ de placement** employment agency *ou* bureau; **~ de presse** news *ou* press agency; **~ de publicité** advertising *ou* publicity agency; **~ de renseignements** information bureau *ou* office; **~ de voyages** travel agency.
agencé, e [aʒɑ̃se] (*ptp de* **agencer**) *adj*: **local bien/mal ~** (*conçu*) well-/badly-laid-out *ou* -arranged premises; (*meublé*) well-/badly-equipped premises; **phrase bien ~e** well-put-together *ou* well-constructed sentence; **éléments bien ~s** well-organized elements.
agencement [aʒɑ̃smɑ̃] *nm* [*éléments*] organization, ordering; [*phrase, roman*] construction, organization; [*local*] (*disposition*) arrangement, lay-out; (*équipement*) equipment. **muni d'~s modernes** provided with modern fittings, fitted with modern equipment.
agencer [aʒɑ̃se] (3) *vt éléments* to put together, organize, order; *couleurs* to harmonize; *phrase, roman* to put together, construct; *local* to lay out, arrange.
agenda [aʒɛ̃da] *nm* diary.
agenouillement [aʒnujmɑ̃] *nm* (*littér*) kneeling.
agenouiller (s') [aʒnuje] (1) *vpr* to kneel (down). **être agenouillé** to be kneeling; (*fig*) **s'~ devant l'autorité** to bow before authority.
agenouilloir [aʒnujwaʀ] *nm* (*escabeau*) hassock, kneeling stool; (*planche*) kneeling plank.
agent [aʒɑ̃] **1** *nm* **(a)** **~ (de police)** policeman, (police) constable; **~ de la circulation** ≈ policeman on traffic duty; **pardon monsieur l'~** excuse me, officer *ou* constable.
(b) (*Chim, Gram, Sci*) agent; *V* **complément**.
(c) (*Comm, Pol: représentant*) agent; (*Admin*) officer, official. **les ~s du lycée/de l'hôpital** the ancillary staff of the school/hospital; **arrêter un ~ ennemi** to arrest an enemy agent; **~ consulaire/de publicité** *etc* consular/publicity *ou* advertising *etc* agent.
2: **agent d'assurances** insurance broker; **agent de change** stockbroker; **agent commercial** (sales) representative; **agent comptable** accountant; **agent double** double agent; **agent électoral** campaign organizer *ou* aide; **agent de la force publique** member of the police force; **agent du gouvernement** government official; **agent immobilier** estate agent (*Brit*), real estate agent (*US*); (*Mil*) **agent de liaison** liaison officer; **agent de maîtrise** supervisor; **agent maritime** shipping agent; **agent provocateur** agent provocateur; **agent de renseignements** intelligence officer; **agent secret** secret agent; **agent technique** chief technician; (*Mil*) **agent de transmission** despatch rider, messenger; **agent voyer** ≈ borough surveyor.
agglomérat [aglɔmeʀa] *nm* (*Géol: volcanique*) agglomerate.
agglomération [aglɔmeʀɑsjɔ̃] *nf* **(a)** (*Admin*) (*ville*) town; (*Aut*) built-up area. **l'~ parisienne** Paris and its suburbs, the urban area of Paris. **(b)** [*nations, idées*] conglomeration; [*matériaux*] conglomeration, agglomeration.
aggloméré [aglɔmeʀe] *nm* (*charbon*) briquette; (*bois*) chipboard; (*pierre*) conglomerate.
agglomérer [aglɔmeʀe] (6) **1** *vt* (*amonceler*) to pile up. (*Tech*) *charbon* to briquette; *bois, pierre* to compress.
2 s'agglomérer *vpr* (*Tech*) to agglomerate; (*s'amonceler*) to pile up; (*se rassembler*) to conglomerate, gather. (*Admin*) **population agglomérée** dense population.
agglutinant, e [aglytinɑ̃, ɑ̃t] **1** *adj substance* agglutinating, agglutinative; (*Bio*) *sérum* which causes agglutination; (*Ling*) agglutinative. **2** *nm* agglutinant.
agglutination [aglytinɑsjɔ̃] *nf* (*Bio, Ling*) agglutination.
agglutiner [aglytine] (1) *vt* to stick together; (*Bio*) to agglutinate. (*fig*) **les passants s'agglutinent devant la vitrine** the passers-by congregate in front of the window.
agglutinine [aglytinin] *nf* agglutinin.
agglutinogène [aglytinɔʒɛn] *nm* agglutinogen.
aggravante [agʀavɑ̃t] *adj f V* **circonstance**.
aggravation [agʀavɑsjɔ̃] *nf* [*mal, situation*] worsening, aggravation; [*impôt, chômage*] increase.
aggraver [agʀave] (1) **1** *vt* (*faire empirer*) to make worse, worsen, aggravate; (*renforcer*) to increase. **2 s'aggraver** *vpr* (*empirer*) to get worse; (*se renforcer*) to increase.
agile [aʒil] *adj* (*physiquement, mentalement*) agile, nimble. **être ~ de ses mains** to be nimble with one's hands; **d'un geste ~** with an agile *ou* a nimble *ou* quick gesture; **~ comme un singe** as nimble as a goat.
agilement [aʒilmɑ̃] *adv* nimbly, agilely.
agilité [aʒilite] *nf* agility, nimbleness.
agio [aʒjo] *nm* Exchange premium, *premium on money in exchange*.
agiotage [aʒjɔtaʒ] *nm* (*Hist*) speculation on exchange business.
agioteur [aʒjɔtœʀ] *nm* (*Hist*) speculator on exchange business.
agir [aʒiʀ] (2) **1** *vi* **(a)** (*gén*) to act; (*se comporter*) to behave, act. **il faut ~ tout de suite** we must act *ou* do something at once, we must take action at once; **il a agi de son plein gré/en toute liberté** he acted quite willingly/freely; **il agit comme un enfant** he acts *ou* behaves like a child; **il a bien/mal agi envers sa mère** he behaved well/badly towards his mother; **il a sagement agi** he did the right thing, he acted wisely; **le syndicat a décidé d'~** the union has decided to take action *ou* to act; **~ en ami** to behave *ou* act like a friend; **~ au nom de** to act on behalf of; *V* **façon, manière**.
(b) (*exercer une influence*) **~ sur qch** to act on sth; **~ sur qn** to bring pressure to bear on sb; (*Bourse*) **~ sur le marché** to influence the market; **~ auprès de qn** to use one's influence with sb.
(c) faire ~: **faire ~ la loi** to put *ou* set the law in motion; **il a fait ~ son syndicat/ses amis** he got his union/friends to act *ou* take action; **je ne sais pas ce qui le fait ~ ainsi** I don't know what prompts him to *ou* makes him act like that.
(d) (*opérer*) [*médicament*] to act, work; [*influence*] to have an effect (*sur* on). **le remède agit lentement** the remedy is slow to take effect, the remedy acts *ou* works slowly; **laisser ~ la nature** to let nature take its course; **la lumière agit sur les plantes** light acts on *ou* has an effect on plants.
2 s'agir *vb impers* **(a)** (*il est question de*) **il s'agit de** it is a matter *ou* question of; **dans ce film il s'agit de 3 bandits** this film is about 3 gangsters; **décide-toi, il s'agit de ton avenir** make up your mind, it's your future that's at stake; **les livres/personnes** *etc* **dont il s'agit** the books/people *etc* in question; **quand il s'agit de manger, il est toujours là** when it's a matter of eating, he's always there; **quand il s'agit de travailler, il n'est jamais là** when there's any work to be done, he's never there *ou* around; **on a trouvé des colonnes: il s'agirait/il s'agit d'un temple grec** some columns have been found: it would appear to be/it is a Greek temple; **de quoi s'agit-il?** what is it?, what's it (all) about?, what's the matter?; **voilà ce dont il s'agit** that's what it's (all) about; **il ne s'agit pas d'argent** it's not a question *ou* matter of money; **il ne s'agit pas de ça!** that's not it! *ou* the point!; (*iro*) **il s'agit bien de ça!** that's hardly the problem!
(b) (*il est nécessaire de faire*) **il s'agit de faire: il s'agit de faire vite** we must act quickly, the thing (to do) is to act quickly; **il s'agit pour lui de réussir** what he has to do is succeed; **maintenant, il ne s'agit pas de plaisanter** this is no time for joking; **avec ça, il ne s'agit pas de plaisanter** that's no joking matter; **maintenant il s'agit de garder notre avance** now it's a matter *ou* question of maintaining our lead, now what we have to do *ou*

must do is maintain our lead; **il s'agit de s'entendre: tu viens ou tu ne viens pas?** let's get one thing clear *ou* straight — are you coming or aren't you?; **il s'agit de savoir ce qu'il va faire** the question is — what is he going to do, what we have to establish is what he's going to do.

(c) (†*loc*) **s'agissant de qn/qch** as regards sb/sth; **s'agissant de sommes aussi importantes, il faut être prudent** when such large amounts are involved, one must be careful.

agissant, e [aʒisɑ̃, ɑ̃t] *adj* (*actif*) active; (*efficace*) efficacious, effective. **minorité ~e** active *ou* influential minority.

agissements [aʒismɑ̃] *nmpl* (*péj*) schemes, intrigues. **surveiller les ~ de qn** to keep an eye on what sb is up to*.

agitateur, -trice [aʒitatœʀ, tʀis] **1** *nm,f* (*Pol*) agitator. **2** *nm* (*Chim*) stirring rod.

agitation [aʒitɑsjɔ̃] *nf* **(a)** *[mer]* roughness, choppiness; *[air]* turbulence; *[personne]* (*ayant la bougeotte*) restlessness, fidgetiness; (*affairé*) bustle; (*troublé*) agitation, nervousness; *[lieu, rue etc]* bustle, stir.

(b) (*Pol*) unrest, agitation.

agité, e [aʒite] (*ptp de* **agiter**) *adj* **(a)** *personne* (*ayant la bougeotte*) restless, fidgety; (*affairé*) bustling (*épith*); (*troublé*) agitated, troubled, perturbed. (*Psych*) **les ~s** manic persons.

(b) *mer* rough, choppy; *vie* hectic; *époque* troubled. **avoir le sommeil ~** to toss about in one's sleep, have broken sleep; **une nuit ~e** a restless night; **être ~ par la fièvre** to be restless with fever.

agiter [aʒite] (1) **1** *vt* **(a)** (*secouer*) *bras, mouchoir* to wave; *ailes* to flap, flutter; *queue* to wag; *bouteille, liquide* to shake; (*fig*) *menace* to brandish. **~ avant l'emploi** shake (well) before use *ou* using; **~ l'air de ses bras** to fan the air with one's arms; **le vent agite doucement les branches** the wind stirs *ou* sways the branches (gently); **le vent agite violemment les branches** the wind shakes the branches; **les feuilles, agitées par le vent** the leaves, quivering *ou* stirring in the wind; **bateau agité par les vagues** boat tossed *ou* rocked by the waves.

(b) (*inquiéter*) to trouble, perturb, agitate.

(c) (*débattre*) *question, problème* to discuss, debate, air.

2 s'agiter *vpr [employé, serveur]* to bustle about; *[malade]* to move about *ou* toss restlessly; *[enfant, élève]* to fidget; *[foule, mer]* to stir. **s'~ dans son sommeil** to toss and turn in one's sleep; **les pensées qui s'agitent dans ma tête** the thoughts that are stirring *ou* dancing about in my head; **le peuple s'agite** the masses are stirring *ou* getting restless; **s'~ sur sa chaise** to wriggle about on one's chair.

agneau, *pl* **~x** [aɲo] *nm* lamb; (*fourrure*) lambskin. (*fig*) **son mari est un véritable ~** her husband is as meek as a lamb; (*iro*) **mes ~x** my dears (*iro*); (*Rel*) **~ pascal** paschal lamb; (*Rel*) **l'~ sans tache** the lamb without stain; *V* **doux, innocent.**

agnelage [aɲlaʒ] *nm* (*mise bas*) lambing; (*époque*) lambing season.

agneler [aɲle] (5) *vt* to lamb.

agnelet [aɲlɛ] *nm* small lamb, lambkin†.

agneline [aɲlin] *nf* lamb's wool.

agnelle [aɲɛl] *nf* (she) lamb.

Agnès [aɲɛs] *nf* Agnes.

agnosticisme [agnɔstisism(ə)] *nm* agnosticism.

agnostique [agnɔstik] *adj, nmf* agnostic.

agonie [agɔni] *nf* (*Méd*) mortal agony. **entrer en ~** to begin to suffer the agony *ou* pangs of death, begin one's mortal agony (*frm*); **être à l'~** to be at death's door *ou* at the point of death; **longue ~** slow death; **son ~ fut longue** he died a slow death, he suffered the long agony of death (*frm*); (*fig*) **l'~ d'un régime** the death throes of a régime.

agonir [agɔniʀ] (2) *vt* to revile. **~ qn d'injures** to hurl insults *ou* abuse at sb, heap insults *ou* abuse on sb.

agonisant, e [agɔnizɑ̃, ɑ̃t] *adj* (*littér, fig*) dying. **la prière des ~s** prayers for the dying, last rites (*pl*).

agoniser [agɔnize] (1) *vi* (*littér, fig*) to be dying. **un blessé agonisait dans un fossé** a wounded man lay dying in a ditch.

agoraphobie [agɔʀafɔbi] *nf* agoraphobia.

agrafage [agʀafaʒ] *nm [vêtement]* hooking (up), fastening (up); *[papiers]* stapling; (*Méd*) putting in of clips.

agrafe [agʀaf] *nf [vêtement]* hook, fastener; *[papiers]* staple; (*Méd*) clip.

agrafer [agʀafe] (1) *vt vêtement* to hook (up), fasten (up); *papiers* to staple; (*: *arrêter*) to nab*, grab*.

agrafeuse [agʀaføz] *nf* stapler.

agraire [agʀɛʀ] *adj politique, lois* agrarian; *mesure, surface* land (*épith*); *V* **réforme.**

agrammatical, e, *mpl* **-aux** [agʀamatikal, o] *adj* ungrammatical.

agrandir [agʀɑ̃diʀ] (2) **1** *vt* **(a)** (*rendre plus grand*) *passage* to widen; *usine, domaine* to enlarge, extend; *écart* to increase; *photographie, dessin, trou* to enlarge, blow up*; (*à la loupe*) to magnify. **ce miroir agrandit la pièce** this mirror makes the room look bigger *ou* larger; **(faire) ~ sa maison** to extend one's house.

(b) (*développer*) to extend, expand. **pour ~ le cercle de ses activités** to widen *ou* extend *ou* expand the scope of one's activities.

(c) (*ennoblir*) *âme* to uplift, elevate, ennoble.

2 s'agrandir *vpr [ville, famille]* to grow, expand; *[écart]* to widen, grow, get bigger; *[passage]* to get wider; *[trou]* to get larger. **il nous a fallu nous ~** we had to expand, we had to find a bigger place; **ses yeux s'agrandirent sous le coup de la surprise** his eyes widened *ou* grew wide with surprise.

agrandissement [agʀɑ̃dismɑ̃] *nm [local]* extension; *[puissance, ville]* expansion; (*Phot*) (*action*) enlargement; (*photo*) enlargement, blow-up*.

agrandisseur [agʀɑ̃disœʀ] *nm* enlarger.

agraphie [agʀafi] *nf* agraphia.

agrarien, -ienne [agʀaʀjɛ̃, jɛn] *adj, nm* (*Hist, Pol*) agrarian.

agréable [agʀeabl(ə)] *adj* pleasant, agreeable. **~ à voir** nice to see; **~ à l'œil** pleasing to the eye; **~ à vivre** *personne* easy *ou* pleasant to live with; *lieu* pleasant to live in; **il est toujours ~ de** it is always pleasant *ou* nice *ou* agreeable to; **ce que j'ai à dire n'est pas ~** what I have to say isn't (very) pleasant; **si ça peut lui être ~** if he finds that agreeable, if that is agreeable to him; **il me serait ~ de** it would be a pleasure for me to, I should be pleased to; **être ~ de sa personne**† to be pleasant-looking *ou* personable†; **l'~ de la chose** the pleasant *ou* nice thing about it; *V* **joindre.**

agréablement [agʀeabləmɑ̃] *adv* pleasantly, agreeably. **nous avons ~ passé la soirée** we spent a pleasant *ou* an agreeable *ou* a nice evening, we spent the evening pleasantly *ou* agreeably; **~ surpris** pleasantly surprised.

agréé [agʀee] *nm* attorney, solicitor (*appearing for parties before a 'tribunal de commerce'*).

agréer [agʀee] (1) (*frm*) **1** *vt* (*accepter*) *demande, excuses* to accept. **veuillez ~, Monsieur (*ou* Madame), l'expression de mes sentiments distingués** yours faithfully; **veuillez ~ mes meilleures *ou* sincères salutations** yours sincerely; **fournisseur agréé** registered dealer.

2 agréer à *vt indir personne* to please, suit. **si cela vous agrée** if it suits *ou* pleases you, if you are agreeable.

agrèg [agʀɛg] *nf* (*arg Univ*) *abrév de* **agrégation.**

agrégat [agʀega] *nm* (*Constr, Écon, Géol*) aggregate; (*péj*) *[idées]* medley.

agrégatif, -ive [agʀegatif, iv] *nm,f candidate for the agrégation.*

agrégation [agʀegɑsjɔ̃] *nf* **(a)** (*Univ*) agrégation, *highest competitive examination for teachers in France.* **(b)** *[particules]* aggregation.

agrégé, e [agʀeʒe] (*ptp de* **agréger**) *nm,f* agrégé, *successful candidate in the agrégation*; *V* **professeur.**

agréger [agʀeʒe] (3 *et* 6) *vt particules* to aggregate. (*fig*) **~ qn à un groupe** to incorporate sb into a group; **s'~ à un groupe** to incorporate o.s. into a group.

agrément [agʀemɑ̃] *nm* **(a)** (*littér: charme*) *[personne]* charm; *[visage]* attractiveness, charm; *[conversation]* charm, pleasantness, agreeableness; *[lieu, climat]* pleasantness, agreeableness, amenity (*littér*). **sa compagnie est pleine d'~** his company is very enjoyable *ou* pleasant *ou* agreeable; **ville/maison sans ~** unattractive town/house, town/house with no agreeable *ou* attractive features; **les ~s de la vie** the pleasures of life, the pleasant things in life; **faire un voyage d'~** to go on *ou* make a pleasure trip; **voyages d'~** travelling for pleasure; *V* **art, jardin.**

(b) (*frm: consentement*) consent, approval; (*Jur*) assent.

(c) (*Mus*) ornament.

agrémenter [agʀemɑ̃te] (1) *vt*: **~ qch de** (*décorer*) to embellish *ou* adorn sth with; (*varier, relever*) to accompany sth with; **agrémenté de broderies** trimmed *ou* embellished *ou* adorned with embroidery; **conférence agrémentée de projections** lecture supplemented with *ou* accompanied by slides; **il agrémentait son récit d'anecdotes** he peppered *ou* accompanied *ou* enlivened his story with anecdotes; (*iro*) **dispute agrémentée de coups** argument complete with blows (*iro*).

agrès [agʀɛ] *nmpl* (*Aviat, Naut*) tackle; (*Sport*) (gymnastics) apparatus. **exercices aux ~** exercises on the apparatus, apparatus work.

agresser [agʀese] (1) *vt* to attack.

agresseur [agʀɛsœʀ] *nm* attacker, assailant, aggressor. **(pays) ~** aggressor.

agressif, -ive [agʀɛsif, iv] *adj* (*gén*) aggressive.

agression [agʀɛsjɔ̃] *nf* (*contre une personne*) attack; (*contre un pays*) aggression; (*Psych*) aggression. **~ nocturne** attack *ou* assault at night; **les agressions de la vie moderne** the brutal stresses *ou* strains of modern living *ou* life.

agressivement [agʀɛsivmɑ̃] *adv* aggressively.

agressivité [agʀɛsivite] *nf* aggressiveness.

agreste [agʀɛst(ə)] *adj* (*littér*) rustic.

agricole [agʀikɔl] *adj ressources, enseignement* agricultural; *ouvrier, produits, travaux* farm (*épith*), agricultural; *population, peuple* farming (*épith*), agricultural; *V* **comice, exploitation.**

agriculteur [agʀikyltœʀ] *nm* farmer.

agriculture [agʀikyltyʀ] *nf* agriculture, farming.

agripper [agʀipe] (1) **1** *vt* (*se retenir à*) to grab *ou* clutch hold of; (*arracher*) to snatch, grab. **2 s'agripper** *vpr*: **s'~ à qch** to cling on to sth, clutch *ou* grip sth; **ne t'agrippe pas à moi** don't cling on to *ou* hang on to me.

agronome [agʀɔnɔm] *nm* agronomist. **ingénieur ~** agricultural engineer.

agronomie [agʀɔnɔmi] *nf* agronomy, agronomics (*sg*).

agronomique [agʀɔnɔmik] *adj* agronomic(al).

agrumes [agʀym] *nmpl* citrus fruits.

aguerrir [ageʀiʀ] (2) *vt* to harden. **~ qn contre** to harden sb to *ou* against, inure sb to; **des troupes aguerries** (*au combat*) seasoned troops; (*à l'effort*) trained troops; **s'~** to become hardened; **s'~ contre** to become hardened to *ou* against, inure o.s. to.

aguets [agɛ] *nmpl*: **aux ~** on the look-out, on the watch.

aguichant, e [agiʃɑ̃, ɑ̃t] *adj* enticing, tantalizing.

aguicher [agiʃe] (1) *vt* to entice, lead on, tantalize.

aguicheur, -euse [agiʃœʀ, øz] **1** *adj* enticing, tantalizing. **2** *nm* (*rare: enjôleur*) seducer. **3 aguicheuse** *nf* (*allumeuse*) teaser, vamp.

ah [ɑ] **1** *excl* **(a)** (*réponse, réaction exclamative*) ah!, oh!, ooh! (*question*) **~?, ~ bon?, ~ oui?** really?, is that so?; (*résignation*)

~ **bon** oh *ou* ah well; (*insistance*) ~ **oui** oh yes, yes indeed; (*insistance*) ~ **non** oh no, certainly *ou* definitely not.
(b) (*intensif*) ~ **j'allais oublier** oh! *ou* ah! I nearly forgot; ~, ~! **je t'y prends** aha! *ou* oho! I've caught you at it; ~, **qu'il est lent!** oh how slow he is!
2 *nm*: **pousser un ~ de soulagement** to sigh with relief, give a sigh of relief; **des ~s d'allégresse** oohs and ahs of joy.

ahan†† [aɑ̃] *nm* V **grand.**

ahaner [aane] (1) *vi* (††, *littér*) to labour, make great efforts. **ahanant sous le fardeau** labouring under (the weight of) the burden.

ahuri, e [ayʀi] (*ptp de* **ahurir**) **1** *adj* (*stupéfait*) stunned, flabbergasted; (*hébété, stupide*) stupefied, vacant. **avoir l'air ~** to have a stupefied look. **2** *nm,f* (*péj*) blockhead*, nitwit*.

ahurir [ayʀiʀ] (2) *vt* to dumbfound, astound, stun.

ahurissant, e [ayʀisɑ̃, ɑ̃t] *adj* stupefying, astounding; (*sens affaibli*) staggering.

ahurissement [ayʀismɑ̃] *nm* stupefaction.

aï [ai] *nm* (*Zool*) ai.

aiche [ɛʃ] *nf* = **èche.**

aide [ɛd] **1** *nf* **(a)** (*assistance*) help, assistance. **apporter son ~ à qn** to bring help *ou* assistance to sb; **son ~ nous a été précieuse** he was a great help *ou* of great help *ou* assistance to us, his help was invaluable to us; **appeler/crier à l'~** to call/shout for help; **appeler qn à son ~** to call for help from sb, call to sb for help; **venir/aller à l'~ de qn** to come/go to sb's aid *ou* assistance, come/go to help sb; **venir en ~ à qn** to help sb, come to sb's assistance *ou* aid; **à l'~!** help!; **sans l'~ de personne** without (any) help *ou* assistance, (completely) unassisted *ou* unaided, single-handed.
(b) (*secours financier*) aid.
(c) **à l'~ de** with the help *ou* aid of.
(d) (*Équitation*) ~s aids.
2 *nm,f* assistant. **~-chimiste/-chirurgien** assistant chemist/surgeon.
3: **aide de camp** *nm* aide-de-camp; **aide-comptable** *nm, pl* **aides-comptables** accountant's assistant; **aide de cuisine** *nm* kitchen hand; **aide-électricien** *nm, pl* **aides-électriciens** electrician's mate (*surtout Brit*) *ou* helper (*US*); **aide familiale** mother's help, home help; **aide-jardinier** *nm, pl* **aides-jardiniers** gardener's help *ou* mate (*surtout Brit*), under-gardener; **aide de laboratoire** *nmf* laboratory assistant; **aide-maçon** *nm, pl* **aides-maçons** builder's mate (*surtout Brit*) *ou* labourer; **aide maternelle** = **aide familiale**; **aide médicale (gratuite)** (free) medical aid; (*Ciné*) **aide-opérateur** *nm, pl* **aides-opérateurs** assistant cameraman; **aide sociale** ≃ social security, welfare; **aide soignante** auxiliary nurse.

aide-mémoire [ɛdmemwaʀ] *nm inv* crib (*Scol*), memorandum.

aider [ede] (1) **1** *vt* to help. ~ **qn (à faire qch)** to help sb (to do sth); ~ **qn à monter/à descendre/à traverser** to help sb up/down/across *ou* over; **il l'a aidé à sortir de la voiture** he helped him out of the car; ~ **qn de ses conseils** to help *ou* assist sb with one's advice; ~ **qn financièrement** to help sb (out) *ou* assist sb financially, give sb financial help *ou* aid; **il m'aide beaucoup** he helps me a lot, he's a great help to me; **je me suis fait ~ par** *ou* **de mon frère** I got my brother to help *ou* assist me *ou* to give me a hand*; **elle ne se déplace qu'aidée de sa canne** she can only get about with the help *ou* aid of her walking stick.
2 *vi* to help. **elle est venue pour ~** she came to help (out) *ou* to give *ou* lend a hand; ~ **à la cuisine** to help (out) in *ou* give a hand in the kitchen; **le débat aiderait à la compréhension du problème** discussion would help (towards) *ou* contribute towards an understanding of the problem, discussion would help (one) to understand the problem; **ça aide à passer le temps** it helps to pass (the) time; **l'alcool aidant, il se mit à parler** helped on by the alcohol *ou* with the help of alcohol, he began to speak; *V* **dieu.**
3 s'aider *vpr* **(a)** **s'~ de** to use, make use of. **atteindre le placard en s'aidant d'un escabeau** to reach the cupboard by using a stool *ou* with the aid of a stool; **en s'aidant de ses bras** using his arms to help him.
(b) (*loc*) **entre voisins il faut s'~** we neighbours should help each other (out); (*Prov*) **aide-toi, le Ciel t'aidera** God helps those who help themselves (*Prov*).

aïe [aj] *excl* (*douleur*) ouch!, ow! ~ ~ ~!, **ça se présente mal** dear oh dear, things don't look too good!

aïeul [ajœl] *nm* (*littér*) grandfather. **les ~s** the grandparents.

aïeule [ajœl] *nf* (*littér*) grandmother.

aïeux [ajø] *nmpl* (*littér*) forefathers, forbears, ancestors. **mes ~!*** my godfathers!* (†, *hum*), by jingo!*

aigle [ɛgl(ə)] **1** *nm* (*Zool, lutrin*) eagle; ~ **royal** golden eagle; (*fig*) **regard d'~** eagle look; **ce n'est pas un ~*** he's no genius. **2** *nf* (*Mil, Zool*) eagle.

aiglefin [ɛgləfɛ̃] *nm* haddock.

aiglon, -onne [ɛglɔ̃, ɔn] *nm,f* eaglet. (*Hist*) **l'A~** Napoleon II.

aigre [ɛgʀ(ə)] **1** *adj* **(a)** *fruit* sour, sharp; *vin* vinegary, sour, acid; *goût, odeur, lait* sour.
(b) *son* shrill, piercing, sharp; *voix* sharp, cutting (*épith*).
(c) *froid, vent* bitter, keen, cutting (*épith*).
(d) *propos, critique* cutting (*épith*), harsh, acrid; *V* **tourner.**
2: **aigre-doux, aigre-douce,** *mpl* **aigres-doux** *adj sauce* sweet and sour; *fruit* bitter-sweet; (*fig*) *propos* bitter-sweet.

aigrefin [ɛgʀəfɛ̃] *nm* swindler, crook.

aigrelet, -ette [ɛgʀəlɛ, ɛt] *adj petit-lait, pomme* sourish; *vin* vinegarish; *voix, son* shrillish.

aigrement [ɛgʀəmɑ̃] *adv répondre, dire* sourly.

aigrette [ɛgʀɛt] *nf* **(a)** *[oiseau]* egret, aigrette; *[chapeau]* aigrette. **(b)** (*Orn*) egret; (*Bot*) aigrette, pappus; (*Phys*) brush discharge.

aigreur [ɛgʀœʀ] *nf* **(a)** (*acidité*) *[petit-lait]* sourness; *[vin]* sourness, acidity; *[pomme]* sourness, sharpness. **(b)** ~**s**: **avoir des ~s d'estomac** to have heartburn. **(c)** (*acrimonie*) sharpness, harshness.

aigri, e [egʀi] (*ptp de* **aigrir**) *adj* embittered, bitter.

aigrir [egʀiʀ] (2) **1** *vt personne* to embitter; *caractère* to sour. **2 s'aigrir** *vpr [aliment]* to turn sour; *[caractère]* to sour. **il s'est aigri** he has become embittered.

aigu, -uë [egy] **1** *adj* **(a)** *son, voix* high-pitched, shrill; *note* high-pitched, high. **(b)** *crise, phase* acute; *douleur* acute, sharp; *intelligence* keen, acute, sharp. **(c)** (*pointu*) sharp, pointed; *V* **accent, angle. 2** *nm* (*Mus*) **les ~s** the high notes; **passer du grave à l'~** to go from low to high pitch.

aigue-marine, *pl* **aigues-marines** [ɛgmaʀin] *nf* aquamarine.

aiguière [ɛgjɛʀ] *nf* ewer.

aiguillage [egɥijaʒ] *nm* (*Rail*) (*action*) shunting (*Brit*), switching (*US*); (*instrument*) points (*pl*) (*Brit*), switch (*US*). **le déraillement est dû à une erreur d'~** the derailment was due to faulty shunting (*Brit*) *ou* switching (*US*); (*fig*) **il y a eu un mauvais ~** *ou* **une erreur d'~** we took a wrong course; *V* **cabine.**

aiguille [egɥij] **1** *nf* **(a)** (*Bot, Couture, Méd*) needle. ~ **à coudre/à tricoter/à repriser** sewing/knitting/darning needle; **travail à l'~** needlework; *V* **chercher, fil, tirer.**
(b) *[compteur, boussole, gramophone]* needle; *[horloge]* hand; *[balance]* pointer, needle; *[cadran solaire]* pointer, index; *[clocher]* spire; (*Rail*) point (*Brit*), switch (*US*); (*Géog*) (*pointe*) needle; (*cime*) peak. **en forme d'aiguille** needle-shaped; **la petite/grande ~** the hour/minute hand, the little/big hand.
2: **aiguille de glace** icicle; **aiguille de pin** pine needle.

aiguillée [egɥije] *nf* length of thread (*for use with needle at any one time*).

aiguiller [egɥije] (1) *vt* **(a)** (*orienter*) to direct. ~ **un enfant vers le technique** to direct *ou* orientate *ou* steer a child towards technical studies; (*Scol*) **on l'a mal aiguillé** he was orientated *ou* steered in the wrong direction, he was misdirected; ~ **la conversation sur un autre sujet** to direct *ou* steer *ou* shunt* the conversation onto another subject; ~ **la police sur une mauvaise piste** to direct *ou* put the police onto the wrong track.
(b) (*Rail*) shunt (*Brit*), switch (*US*).

aiguillette [egɥijɛt] *nf [pourpoint]* aglet; (*Culin, Mil*) aiguillette.

aiguilleur [egɥijœʀ] *nm* (*Rail*) pointsman (*Brit*), switchman.

aiguillon [egɥijɔ̃] *nm [insecte]* sting; *[bouvier]* goad; (*Bot*) thorn; (*fig*) spur, stimulus.

aiguillonner [egɥijɔne] (1) *vt bœuf* to goad; (*fig*) to spur *ou* goad on.

aiguisage [egizaʒ] *nm* sharpening; grinding.

aiguiser [egize] (1) *vt* **(a)** *couteau, outil* to sharpen, grind; *rasoir* to sharpen. **(b)** (*fig*) *appétit* to whet, stimulate; *sens* to excite, stimulate; *esprit* to sharpen; *style* to polish.

aiguiseur [egizœʀ] *nm* (*ouvrier*) sharpener, grinder.

aiguisoir [egizwaʀ] *nm* sharpener, sharpening tool.

ail, *pl* **~s, aulx** [aj, o] *nm* garlic; *V* **gousse, saucisson, tête.**

aile [ɛl] *nf* **(a)** (*gén*) wing; *[moulin]* sail; *[hélice, ventilateur]* blade, vane; *[nez, papilionacées]* ala, wing. ~ **marchante** (*Mil*) wheeling flank; (*fig*) *[groupe]* active element.
(b) (*loc*) **l'oiseau disparut d'un coup d'~** the bird disappeared with a flap of its wings; **d'un coup d'~ nous avons gagné Orly** we reached Orly in the twinkling of an eye *ou* in a trice; **avoir des ~s** to have wings, fly (*fig*); **l'espoir lui donnait des ~s** hope lent *ou* gave him wings (*littér*); **prendre sous son ~ (protectrice)** to take under one's wing; **sous l'~ maternelle** under one's mother's *ou* the maternal wing; *V* **peur, plomb, tire-d'aile(s)** *etc.*

ailé, e [ele] *adj* (*fig littér*) winged.

aileron [ɛlʀɔ̃] *nm* (*Zool*) *[requin, raie]* fin; *[oiseau]* pinion; (*Aviat*) aileron; (*Aut: de stabilisation*) aerofoil; (*Archit*) console.

ailette [ɛlɛt] *nf [missile, radiateur]* fin; *[turbine, ventilateur]* blade.

ailier [elje] *nm* winger.

aillade [ajad] *nf* garlic dressing *ou* sauce.

ailler [aje] (1) *vt* to flavour with garlic.

ailleurs [ajœʀ] *adv* **(a)** somewhere else, elsewhere. **nulle part ~** nowhere else; **partout ~** everywhere else; **il est ~, il a l'esprit ~** his thoughts are *ou* his mind is elsewhere, he's miles away (*fig*); **ils viennent d'~** they come from somewhere else; **j'ai gagné là ce que j'ai perdu (par) ~** I gained on this what I lost elsewhere; **nous sommes passés (par) ~** we went another way; **je l'ai su par ~** I heard of it from another source.
(b) **par ~** (*autrement*) otherwise, in other respects; (*en outre*) moreover, furthermore; **d'~** besides, moreover; **d'~ il faut avouer que ...** anyway *ou* besides *ou* moreover we have to confess that ...; **ce vin, d'~ très bon, n'est ...** this wine, which I may add is very good *ou* which is very good by the way, is not ...; **lui non plus d'~** neither does (*ou* is, has *etc*) he, for that matter.

ailloli [ajɔli] *nm* garlic mayonnaise.

aimable [ɛmabl(ə)] *adj* **(a)** (*gentil*) *parole* kind, nice; *personne* kind, nice, amiable (*frm*). **c'est un homme ~** he's a (very) nice man; **tu es bien ~ de m'avoir attendu** it was very nice *ou* kind of you to wait for me; **c'est très ~ à vous** it's most kind of you; (*frm*) **soyez assez ~ pour** be so kind *ou* good as to (*frm*); ~ **comme une porte de prison** like a bear with a sore head.
(b) (†: *agréable*) *endroit, moment* pleasant.
(c) (††: *digne d'amour*) lovable, amiable††.

aimablement [ɛmabləmɑ̃] *adv agir* kindly, nicely; *répondre, recevoir* amiably, nicely; *refuser* politely. **il m'a offert ~ à boire** he kindly offered me a drink.

aimant[1] [ɛmɑ̃] *nm* magnet. ~ **(naturel)** magnetite (*U*).

aimant[2]**, e** [ɛmɑ̃, ɑ̃t] *adj* loving, affectionate.
aimantation [ɛmɑ̃tɑsjɔ̃] *nf* magnetization.
aimanté, e [ɛmɑ̃te] (*ptp de* **aimanter**) *adj aiguille, champs* magnetic.
aimanter [ɛmɑ̃te] (1) *vt* to magnetize.
aimer [eme] (1) **1** *vt* **(a)** (*d'amour*) to love, be in love with; (*d'amitié, attachement, goût*) to like, be fond of. **~ beaucoup** *personne* to like very much *ou* a lot, be very fond of; *animaux, choses* to like very much *ou* a lot, be very keen on *ou* fond of, love; **~ bien** to like, be fond of; **il l'aime d'amour** he loves her; **il l'aime à la folie** he adores her, he's crazy about her*; **j'aime une bonne tasse de café après déjeuner** I like *ou* enjoy *ou* love a good cup of coffee after lunch; **les hortensias aiment l'ombre** hydrangeas like shade; **tous ces trucs-là, tu aimes, toi?*** do you go in for all that kind of stuff?*; **je n'aime pas beaucoup cet acteur** I don't care for *ou* I don't like that actor very much, I'm not very keen on that actor, I don't go much for that actor*; **elle n'aime pas le tennis** she doesn't like tennis *ou* care for tennis, she's not keen on tennis; **les enfants aiment qu'on s'occupe d'eux** children like *ou* love attention; **elle n'aime pas qu'il sorte le soir** she doesn't like him going out *ou* him to go out at night; **~ faire,** (*littér*) **~ à faire** to like doing *ou* to do; (*frm, hum*) **j'aime à penser** *ou* **à croire que ...** I like to think that ...; *V* **qui.**

(b) (*avec assez, autant, mieux*) **~ autant: j'aime autant vous dire que je n'irai pas!** I may as well tell you that I won't go!; **il aime** *ou* **aimerait autant ne pas sortir aujourd'hui** he'd just as soon not go out today, he'd be just as happy not going out today; **j'aimerais autant que ce soit elle qui m'écrive** I'd rather it was she who wrote to me; **j'aime autant qu'elle ne soit pas venue** I'm just as happy *ou* it's (probably) just as well she didn't come; **j'aime autant ça!*** (*menace*) that sounds more like it!*; (*soulagement*) what a relief!; **~ mieux: on lui apporte des fleurs, elle aimerait mieux des livres** they bring her flowers and she would rather *ou* sooner have *ou* she would prefer books; **il aurait mieux aimé se reposer que d'aller au cinéma** he would rather have rested than *ou* he would have preferred to rest than go to the cinema; **~ assez: elle aime assez** *ou* **bien bavarder avec les commerçants** she quite *ou* rather likes chatting with the tradesmen.

(c) (*au conditionnel = vouloir*) **aimeriez-vous une tasse de thé?** would you like a cup of tea?, would you care for a cup of tea?; **elle aimerait bien aller se promener** she would like to go for a walk; **j'aimerais vraiment venir** I'd really like to come, I'd love to come; **je n'aimerais pas être dehors par ce temps** I wouldn't want *ou* like to be out in this (sort of) weather; **j'aimerais assez/je n'aimerais pas ce genre de manteau** I would rather like/wouldn't like a coat like that.

2 s'aimer *vpr* **(a) ils s'aiment** they are in love, they love each other; **aimez-vous les uns les autres** love one another; **ces deux collègues ne s'aiment guère** there's no love lost between those two colleagues; **se faire ~ de quelqu'un de riche** *etc* to get somebody rich *etc* to fall in love with one; **essayer de se faire ~ de qn** to try to win the love *ou* affection of sb; **je ne m'aime pas avec ce chapeau** I don't like myself in that hat.

(b) (*faire l'amour*) to make love.
aine [ɛn] *nf* groin (*Anat*).
aîné, e [ene] **1** *adj* (*plus âgé*) elder, older; (*le plus âgé*) eldest, oldest.

2 *nm* **(a)** *[famille]* **l'~** the oldest child *ou* one; **l'~ des garçons** the eldest boy *ou* son; **mon (frère) ~** my elder *ou* older brother; **l'~ des mes frères** my eldest *ou* oldest brother; **le père était fier de son ~** the father was proud of his eldest boy.

(b) (*relation d'âges*) **il est mon ~** he's older than me; **il est mon ~ de 2 ans** he's 2 years older than me, he's 2 years my senior; (*littér*) **respectez vos ~s** respect your elders.

3 aînée *nf* **(a) l'~e** the eldest child *ou* one; **l'~e des filles** the eldest girl *ou* daughter; **ma sœur ~e, mon ~e** my elder *ou* older sister.

(b) elle est mon ~e she's older than me; **elle est mon ~e de 2 ans** she's 2 years older than me, she's 2 years my senior.
aînesse [ɛnɛs] *nf V* **droit.**
ainsi [ɛ̃si] *adv* **(a)** (*de cette façon*) in this way *ou* manner. **je préfère agir ~** I prefer to act in this way *ou* manner *ou* to act thus; **il faut procéder ~** you have to proceed as follows *ou* thus *ou* in this manner; **c'est ~ que ça s'est passé** that's the way *ou* how it happened; **est-ce ~ que tu me traites?** is this the way *ou* is this how you treat me?, is this the manner in which you treat me?; **pourquoi me traites-tu ~?** why do you treat me thus?†, why do you treat me like this? *ou* in this way?; **~ finit son grand amour** thus ended his great love; **il n'en est pas ~ pour tout le monde** it's not so *ou* the case for everyone; **s'il en est ~** *ou* **puisque c'est ~, je m'en vais** if *ou* since this is the way things are *ou* how things are, I am leaving, if *ou* since this is the case, I am leaving; **s'il en était ~** if this were the case; **il en sera ~ et pas autrement** this is how *ou* the way it *ou* things will be and no other way.

(b) (*littér: en conséquence*) thus; (*donc*) so. **ils ont perdu le procès, ~ ils sont ruinés** they lost the case and so they are ruined; **~ tu vas partir!** so, you're going to leave!

(c) (*littér: de même*) so, in the same way. **comme le berger mène ses moutons, ~ le pasteur guide ses ouailles** just as the shepherd leads his sheep, so *ou* in the same way does the minister guide his flock (*littér*).

(d) ~ que (just) as; (*littér*) **~ qu'il vous plaira** (just) as it pleases you; **~ que nous avons dit hier** just as we said yesterday; **la jalousie, ~ qu'un poison subtil, s'insinuait en lui** jealousy, (just) like a subtle poison, was slowly worming its way into him; **sa beauté ~ que sa candeur me frappèrent** I was struck by her beauty as well as her innocence.

(e) (*loc*) **pour ~ dire** so to speak, as it were; **ils sont pour ~ dire ruinés** they are ruined, so to speak *ou* as it were, you might say they are ruined; **~ soit-il** (*gén*) so be it; (*Rel*) amen; **et ~ de suite** and so on (and so forth); **~ va le monde** that's the way of the world.
air[1] [ɛʀ] **1** *nm* **(a)** (*gaz*) air; (*brise*) air, (light) breeze; (*courant d'air*) draught. **l'~ de la campagne/de la mer** the country/sea air; **l'~ de la ville ne lui convient pas** town air *ou* the air of the town doesn't suit him; **une pièce sans ~** a stuffy room; **on manque d'~ ici** there's no air (in) here, it's stuffy (in) here; **donnez-nous un peu d'~** give us some (fresh) air; **sortir à l'~ libre** to come out into the open air; **jouer à l'~** to play in the open air *ou* outdoors; **mettre la literie à l'~** to put the bedclothes (out) to air *ou* out for an airing, air the bedclothes; **sortir prendre l'~** to go out for some *ou* a breath of (fresh) air; (*Naut*) **il y a des ~s** there is a wind (up); **il y a un peu d'~ aujourd'hui** there's a light *ou* slight breeze today; **on sent de l'~ qui vient de la porte** you can feel a draught (*Brit*) *ou* draft (*US*) from the door; *V* **bol, chambre, courant** *etc.*

(b) (*espace*) air. **s'élever dans l'~** *ou* **dans les ~s** to rise (up) into the skies *ou* the air; **regarder en l'~** to look into the air; **avoir le nez en l'~** to gaze vacantly into the air *ou* about one; **jeter qch en l'~** to throw sth (up) into the air; **transports par ~** air transport, transport by air; **l'avion a pris l'~** the plane has taken off; **de l'~** *hôtesse, ministère* air (*épith*); *V* **armée, école, mal.**

(c) (*fig: atmosphère, ambiance*) atmosphere. **dans l'~: ces idées étaient dans l'~ à cette époque** those ideas were in the air at that time; **il y a de la bagarre dans l'~** there's a quarrel in the wind *ou* brewing; **il y a de l'orage dans l'~** there's a storm brewing; **la grippe est dans l'~** there's flu about; **il est allé prendre l'~ du bureau** he has gone to see how things look *ou* what things look like at the office; **tout le monde se dispute, l'~ de la maison est irrespirable** everyone's quarrelling and the atmosphere in the house is unbearable; **il a besoin de l'~ de la ville** he needs the atmosphere of the town.

(d) (*loc*) **en l'~** *paroles, promesses* idle, empty; *agir* rashly; **ce ne sont encore que des projets en l'~** these plans are still very much in the air; **en l'~** (*en désordre*) upside down, in a mess; **flanquer*** *ou* **ficher*** *ou* **foutre‡ tout en l'~** (*jeter*) to chuck* *ou* sling* it all away *ou* out; (*abandonner*) to chuck it all up‡ *ou* in‡; **ce contretemps a fichu en l'~ mes vacances*** this hitch has (completely) messed up my holidays*; **en courant, il a flanqué le vase en l'~*** as he was running he knocked over the vase; **vivre** *ou* **se nourrir de l'air du temps** to live on air *ou* on nothing at all; *V* **parler.**

2: air comprimé compressed air; **air conditionné** air conditioning; **air liquide** liquid air; (*Mil*) **air-sol** *adj inv* air-to-ground.
air[2] [ɛʀ] *nm* **(a)** (*apparence, manière*) air. **d'un ~ décidé** in a resolute manner; **sous son ~ calme c'est un homme énergique** beneath his calm appearance he is a forceful man; **un garçon à l'~ éveillé** a lively-looking boy; **ils ont un ~ de famille** there's a family likeness between them; **ça lui donne l'~ d'un clochard** it makes him look like a tramp; *V* **faux, grand.**

(b) (*expression*) look, air. **d'un ~ perplexe** with a look *ou* an air of perplexity, with a perplexed air *ou* look; **je lui trouve un drôle d'~ ce matin** I think he looks funny *ou* very odd this morning; **prendre un ~ éploré** to put on *ou* adopt a tearful expression; **elle a pris son petit ~ futé pour me dire** she told me in her sly little manner, she put on that rather sly look she has *ou* of hers to tell me; **prendre un ~ entendu** to adopt a knowing air.

(c) (*loc*) **avoir l'~: elle a l'~ d'une enfant** she looks like a child; **ça m'a l'~ d'un mensonge** it looks to me *ou* sounds to me like a lie; **ça m'a l'~ d'être assez facile** it strikes me as being fairly easy, it looks fairly easy to me; **elle a l'~ intelligente** she looks *ou* seems intelligent, she has an intelligent look; **il a eu l'~ de ne pas comprendre** he looked as if *ou* as though he didn't understand, he didn't seem to understand; (*faire semblant*) he pretended not to understand, he behaved as if he didn't understand; **elle n'avait pas l'~ de vouloir travailler** she didn't look as if *ou* as though she wanted to work; **il est très ambitieux sans en avoir l'~** he might not look it but he's very ambitious, he's very ambitious although he might not *ou* doesn't really look it; **ça (m')a tout l'~ d'être une fausse alerte** it looks (to me) as if it's a false alarm; **il a l'~ de vouloir neiger** it looks like snow; **de quoi j'ai l'~ maintenant!*, j'ai l'~ fin maintenant!*** I really look like (a bit of) a fool *ou* like a fine one *ou* like a right one now*; **il n'a l'~ de rien, mais il sait ce qu'il fait** you wouldn't think it to look at him but he knows what he's doing; **cette plante n'a l'~ de rien, pourtant elle donne de très jolies fleurs** this plant doesn't look much but it has very pretty flowers; **sans avoir l'~ de rien, filons discrètement** let's just behave naturally and slip away unnoticed.
air[3] [ɛʀ] *nm [opéra]* aria; (*mélodie*) tune, air. **l'~ d'une chanson** the tune of a song; **~ d'opéra** operatic aria; **~ de danse** dance tune; (*lit, fig*) **~ connu** familiar tune; **chanter des slogans sur l'~ des lampions** to chant slogans.
airain [ɛʀɛ̃] *nm* (*littér*) bronze.
aire [ɛʀ] *nf* (*zone*) area, zone; (*Math*) area; *[aigle]* eyrie. **~ d'atterrissage** landing strip; (*pour hélicoptère*) landing patch; (*Agr*) **~ de battage** threshing floor; (*Géol*) **~s continentales** continental shields; **~ d'embarquement** boarding area; (*Bio*) **~ embryonnaire** germinal area; **~ de lancement** launching site; **~ de stationnement** parking area; (*Naut*) **~ de vent** rhumb; **suivant l'~ de vent** following the rhumb-line route, taking a rhumb-line course.
airelle [ɛʀɛl] *nf* (*myrtille*) bilberry, whortleberry. **~ (rouge)** (type of) cranberry.
ais†† [ɛ] *nm* (*planche*) plank, board.

aisance [ɛzɑ̃s] *nf* **(a)** (*facilité*) ease. **s'exprimer avec une rare** *ou* **parfaite** ~ to have great facility *ou* ease of expression, express o.s. with great ease *ou* facility; **il patinait avec une rare** *ou* **parfaite** ~ he skated along with the greatest of ease *ou* with great ease; **il y a beaucoup d'~ dans son style** he has an easy *ou* a flowing style *ou* a very fluent style.
(b) (*richesse*) affluence. **vivre dans l'~** to be comfortably off *ou* well-off, live comfortably *ou* in easy circumstances.
(c) (*Couture*) **redonner de l'~ sous les bras** to give more freedom of movement *ou* more fullness under the arms; *V* **pli.**
(d) *V* **fosse, lieu.**

aise [ɛz] **1** *nf* **(a)** (*littér*) joy, pleasure, satisfaction. **j'ai tant d'~ à vous voir** I'm overjoyed to see you, it gives me such joy *ou* pleasure *ou* satisfaction to see you; **sourire d'~** to smile with pleasure; **tous ces compliments la comblaient d'~** all these compliments made her overjoyed *ou* filled her with great joy *ou* satisfaction.
(b) (*loc*) **être à l'~, être à son ~** (*dans une situation*) to be *ou* feel at ease; (*dans un vêtement, fauteuil*) to feel *ou* be comfortable; (*être riche*) to be comfortably off *ou* comfortable; **être mal à l'~, être mal à son ~** (*dans une situation*) to be *ou* feel ill at ease; (*dans un vêtement, fauteuil*) to feel *ou* be uncomfortable; **mettez-vous à l'~** *ou* **à votre ~** make yourself comfortable, make yourself at home; **leur hôtesse les mit tout de suite à l'~** their hostess immediately put them at (their) ease *ou* made them feel immediately at home; **en prendre à son ~ avec qch** to make free with sth, do exactly as one likes with sth; **vous en prenez à votre ~!** taking things nice and easy!; **tu en parles à ton ~!** it's easy (enough) *ou* it's all right for you to talk!; **à votre ~!** please yourself!, just as you like!; **on tient à 4 à l'~ dans cette voiture** this car holds 4 (quite) comfortably, 4 can get in this car (quite) comfortably.
(c) **~s: aimer ses ~s** to like *ou* be fond of (one's) creature comforts *ou* one's comforts; (*iro*) **tu prends tes ~s!** you're making yourself comfortable all right! (*iro*).
2 *adj* (*littér*) **être bien ~ d'avoir fini son travail** to be delighted *ou* most pleased to have finished one's work.

aisé, e [eze] *adj* **(a)** (*facile*) easy. **(b)** (*dégagé*) *démarche* easy, graceful; *style* flowing, fluent. **(c)** (*riche*) well-to-do, comfortably off (*attrib*), well-off.

aisément [ezemɑ̃] *adv* (*sans peine*) easily; (*sans réserves*) readily; (*dans la richesse*) comfortably.

aisselle [ɛsɛl] *nf* (*Anat*) armpit; (*Bot*) axil.

ajonc [aʒɔ̃] *nm* gorse (*U*), furze (*U*).

ajour [aʒuʀ] *nm* (*gén pl*) *[broderie, sculpture]* openwork (*U*).

ajouré, e [aʒuʀe] (*ptp de* **ajourer**) *adj mouchoir* openwork (*épith*), hemstitched; *bijou, sculpture* which has an openwork design.

ajourer [aʒuʀe] (1) *vt sculpture* to ornament with openwork; *mouchoir* to hemstitch.

ajournement [aʒuʀnəmɑ̃] *nm* (*V* **ajourner**) adjournment; deferment; postponement; referring; summons.

ajourner [aʒuʀne] (1) **1** *vt réunion, assemblée* to adjourn, *élection, décision* to defer, postpone, adjourn; *date* to postpone, put off, delay; *candidat* to refer; *conscrit* to defer; (*Jur: convoquer*) to summon. **réunion ajournée d'une semaine/au lundi suivant** meeting adjourned *ou* delayed for a week/until the following Monday.
2 s'ajourner *vpr* (*Pol*) to adjourn.

ajout [aʒu] *nm [texte]* addition.

ajouter [aʒute] (1) **1** *vt* **(a)** to add. **ajoute un peu de sel** put in *ou* add a bit more salt; **je dois ~ que** I should add that; **sans ~ un mot** without (saying *ou* adding) another word; **ajoutez à cela qu'il pleuvait** on top of that *ou* in addition to that *ou* what's more, it was raining; **ajoutez à cela sa maladresse naturelle** add to that his natural clumsiness.
(b) **~ foi aux dires de qn** to lend *ou* give credence to sb's statements, believe sb's statements.
2 ajouter à *vt indir* (*littér*) to add to, increase; **ton arrivée ajoute à mon bonheur** your arrival adds to *ou* increases my happiness.
3 s'ajouter *vpr*: **s'~ à** to add to; **ces malheurs venant s'~ à leur pauvreté** these misfortunes adding further to their poverty; **ceci, venant s'~ à ses difficultés** this coming on top of *ou* to add further to his difficulties; **à ces dépenses viennent s'~ les impôts** on top of *ou* in addition to these expenses there are taxes.

ajustage [aʒystaʒ] *nm* (*Tech*) fitting.

ajustement [aʒystəmɑ̃] *nm [statistique, prix]* adjustment; (*Tech*) fit.

ajuster [aʒyste] (1) **1** *vt* **(a)** (*régler*) *ceinture, salaires* to adjust; *vêtement* to alter; *pièce réglable* to adjust, regulate. **robe ajustée** close-fitting dress; **il leur est difficile d'~ leurs vues** it is difficult for them to make their views agree *ou* to reconcile their views.
(b) (*adapter*) **~ qch à** to fit sth to; **~ un tuyau au robinet** to fit a hose onto the tap (*Brit*) *ou* faucet (*US*); **~ son style à un sujet** to fit *ou* adapt one's style to a subject.
(c) *tir* to aim. **~ son coup** to aim one's shot; **~ qn** to aim at sb.
(d) (†) *coiffure* to tidy, arrange; *tenue* to arrange.
2 s'ajuster *vpr* **(a)** (*Tech*) (*s'emboîter*) to fit (together); (*s'adapter*) to be adjustable. **s'~ à** to fit.
(b) (†: *se rajuster*) to arrange *ou* tidy one's dress†.

ajusteur [aʒystœʀ] *nm* metal worker.

alacrité [alakʀite] *nf* (*littér*) alacrity.

Aladin [aladɛ̃] *nm* Aladdin.

alaise [alɛz] *nf* undersheet, drawsheet.

alambic [alɑ̃bik] *nm* still (*Chim*).

alambiqué, e [alɑ̃bike] *adj* (*péj*) *style, discours* convoluted (*péj*), involved; *personne, esprit* over-subtle (*péj*).

alangui, e [alɑ̃gi] (*ptp de* **alanguir**) *adj attitude, geste* languid; *rythme, style* languid, lifeless.

alanguir [alɑ̃giʀ] (2) **1** *vt* **(a)** *[fièvre]* to make feeble *ou* languid, enfeeble; *[chaleur]* to make listless *ou* languid; *[plaisirs, vie paresseuse]* to make indolent *ou* languid. **être tout alangui par la chaleur** to feel listless *ou* languid with the heat.
(b) *récit* to make nerveless *ou* lifeless.
2 s'alanguir *vpr* to grow languid *ou* weak, languish.

alanguissement [alɑ̃gismɑ̃] *nm* languidness, languor.

alarmant, e [alaʀmɑ̃, ɑ̃t] *adj* alarming.

alarme [alaʀm(ə)] *nf* **(a)** (*signal de danger*) alarm, alert. **donner** *ou* **sonner l'~** to give *ou* sound *ou* raise the alarm, give the alert; *V* **signal, sirène, sonnette.**
(b) (*inquiétude*) alarm. **jeter l'~** to cause (great) alarm; **à la première ~** at the first sign of danger.

alarmer [alaʀme] (1) **1** *vt* to alarm. **2 s'alarmer** *vpr* to become alarmed (*de, pour* about, at). **il n'a aucune raison de s'~** he has *ou* there is no cause for alarm.

alarmiste [alaʀmist(ə)] *adj, nmf* alarmist.

albanais, e [albanɛ, ɛz] **1** *adj* Albanian. **2** *nm* (*Ling*) Albanian. **3** *nm,f*: **A~(e)** Albanian.

Albanie [albani] *nf* Albania.

albâtre [albɑtʀ(ə)] *nm* alabaster.

albatros [albatʀos] *nm* albatross.

albertain, e [albɛʀtɛ̃, ɛn] **1** *adj* Albertan. **2** *nm,f*: **A~(e)** Albertan.

albigeois, e [albiʒwa, waz] **1** *adj* **(a)** (*Géog*) of *ou* from Albi. **(b)** (*Hist*) Albigensian. **2** *nm,f*: **A~(e)** inhabitant *ou* native of Albi. **3** *nmpl* (*Hist*) **les ~** the Albigenses, the Albigensians; *V* **croisade.**

albinisme [albinism(ə)] *nm* albinism.

albinos [albinos] *nmf, adj inv* albino.

Albion [albjɔ̃] *nf*: **(la perfide) ~** (perfidious) Albion.

album [albɔm] *nm* album. **~ de timbres** stamp album; **~ à colorier** colouring *ou* painting book.

albumen [albymɛn] *nm* albumen.

albumine [albymin] *nf* albumin.

albumineux, -euse [albyminø, øz] *adj* albuminous.

albuminoïde [albyminɔid] *adj, nm* albuminoid.

albuminurie [albyminyʀi] *nf* albuminuria.

albuminurique [albyminyʀik] *adj* albuminuric.

alcade [alkad] *nm* alcalde.

alcaïque [alkaik] *adj* Alcaic. **vers ~s** Alcaics.

alcali [alkali] *nm* alkali. **~ volatil** ammonia.

alcalin, e [alkalɛ̃, in] *adj* alkaline.

alcalinité [alkalinite] *nf* alkalinity.

alcaloïde [alkalɔid] *nm* alkaloid.

alchimie [alʃimi] *nf* alchemy.

alchimique [alʃimik] *adj* alchemic(al).

alchimiste [alʃimist(ə)] *nm* alchemist.

alcool [alkɔl] *nm* **(a)** (*Chim*) alcohol. **~ absolu** pure alcohol; **~ à brûler** methylated spirits; **~ camphré** camphorated alcohol; **~ à 90°** surgical spirit; **lampe à ~** spirit lamp.
(b) (*boisson*) alcohol (*U*). **boire de l'~** (*gén*) to drink alcohol; (*eau de vie*) to drink spirits; **il ne prend jamais d'~** he never drinks *ou* he never touches alcohol; **le cognac est un ~** cognac is a brandy *ou* spirit; **vous prendrez bien un petit ~** you won't say no to a little brandy *ou* liqueur; **~ de prune/poire** plum/pear brandy; **~ de menthe** medicinal mint spirit.

alcoolémie [alkɔlemi] *nf*: **taux d'~** alcohol level (in the blood).

alcoolique [alkɔlik] *adj, nmf* alcoholic.

alcoolisation [alkɔlizɑsjɔ̃] *nf* alcoholization.

alcooliser [alkɔlize] (1) **1** *vt* to alcoholize. **boissons alcoolisées** alcoholic drinks. **2 s'alcooliser** *vpr* to become an alcoholic; (*hum: s'enivrer*) to get drunk.

alcoolisme [alkɔlism(ə)] *nm* alcoholism.

alcoo(l)test [alkɔ(l)tɛst] *nm* (*objet*) Breathalyser; (*épreuve*) breath test. **faire subir l'~ à qn** to breathalyse sb, give sb a breath test.

alcoomètre [alkɔmɛtʀ(ə)] *nm* alcoholometer.

alcôve [alkov] *nf* alcove, recess (*in a bedroom*). (*fig*) **d'~** bedroom (*épith*), intimate; *V* **secret.**

alcyon [alsjɔ̃] *nm* (*Myth*) Halcyon.

aléa [alea] *nm* hazard. **en comptant avec tous les ~s** taking all the risks *ou* the unknown factors into account; **les ~s de l'examen** the hazards of the exam; **après bien des ~s** after many ups and downs *ou* many hazards.

aléatoire [aleatwaʀ] *adj gains, succès* uncertain; *marché* chancy, risky, uncertain; *V* **contrat.**

alémanique [alemanik] *adj, nm* (*Ling*) Alemannic; *V* **suisse.**

alêne [alɛn] *nf* awl.

alentour [alɑ̃tuʀ] *adv* around, round about. **tout ~** *ou* **à l'entour††** all around; **~ de qch** (a)round sth; **les villages d'~** the villages around *ou* round about, the neighbouring *ou* surrounding villages.

alentours [alɑ̃tuʀ] *nmpl* **(a)** (*environs*) *[ville]* surroundings, neighbourhood. **les ~ sont très pittoresques** the surroundings *ou* environs are very picturesque; **dans les ~** in the vicinity *ou* neighbourhood; **aux ~ de Dijon** in the vicinity *ou* neighbourhood of Dijon; (*fig*) **étudier les ~ d'un problème** to study the side issues of a problem; **il gagne aux ~ de 1.000 F** he earns (something) in the region *ou* neighbourhood of 1,000 francs, he earns round about 1,000 francs; **aux ~ de 8 heures** round about 8 (o'clock), some time around 8 (o'clock).
(b) (*Art*) *[tapisserie]* border.

alerte [alɛʀt(ə)] **1** *adj personne, geste* agile, nimble; *esprit* alert, agile, nimble; *vieillard* spry, agile; *style* brisk, lively.
2 *nf* **(a)** (*signal de danger, durée du danger*) alert, alarm. **donner l'~** to give the alert *ou* alarm; **donner l'~ à qn** to alert

sb; ~ **aérienne** air raid warning; **systèmes d'**~ alarm systems; **les nuits d'**~ nights on alert *ou* with an alert; *V* **état, faux.**

(b) (*fig*) (*avertissement*) warning sign; (*inquiétude*) alarm. **à la première** ~ at the first warning sign; **l'**~ **a été chaude** *ou* **vive** there was intense *ou* considerable alarm.

3 *excl*: ~! watch out!

alertement [alɛʀt(ə)mɑ̃] *adv* (*V* **alerte**) agilely; nimbly; alertly; spryly; briskly.

alerter [alɛʀte] (1) *vt* (*donner l'alarme*) to alert; (*informer*) to inform, notify; (*prévenir*) to warn. **les pouvoirs publics ont été alertés** the authorities have been informed *ou* notified, it has been brought to the attention of the authorities.

alésage [alezaʒ] *nm* (*action*) reaming; (*diamètre*) bore.

alèse [alɛz] *nf* = **alaise.**

aléser [aleze] (6) *vt* to ream.

alevin [alvɛ̃] *nm* alevin, young fish (*bred artificially*).

alevinage [alvinaʒ] *nm* (*action*) stocking with alevins *ou* young fish; (*pisciculture*) pisciculture, fish farming.

aleviner [alvine] (1) **1** *vt* (*empoissonner*) to stock with alevins *ou* young fish. **2** *vi* (*pondre*) to spawn.

Alexandre [alɛksɑ̃dʀ(ə)] *nm* Alexander.

alexandrin, e [alɛksɑ̃dʀɛ̃, in] **1** *adj art, poésie,* (*Hist*) Alexandrian; *prosodie* alexandrine. **2** *nm* alexandrine.

alezan, e [alzɑ̃, an] *adj, nm,f* chestnut (*horse*). ~ **clair** sorrel.

alfa [alfa] *nm* (*herbe*) Esparto (grass); (*papier*) Esparto paper.

Alfred [alfʀɛd] *nm* Alfred.

algarade [algaʀad] *nf* (*gronderie*) angry outburst, rating; (*dispute*) row; (*Hist: attaque*) incursion. **avoir une** ~ **avec qn** to row *ou* have a row with sb.

algèbre [alʒɛbʀ(ə)] *nf* (*Math*) algebra. **par l'**~ algebraically; **c'est de l'**~* it's (all) Greek to me*.

algébrique [alʒebʀik] *adj* algebraic.

algébriquement [alʒebʀikmɑ̃] *adv* algebraically.

algébriste [alʒebʀist(ə)] *nmf* algebraist.

Alger [alʒe] *n* Algiers.

Algérie [alʒeʀi] *nf* Algeria.

algérien, -ienne [alʒeʀjɛ̃, jɛn] **1** *adj* Algerian. **2** *nm,f*: **A**~**(ne)** Algerian.

algérois, e [alʒeʀwa, waz] **1** *adj* of *ou* from Algiers. **2** *nm,f*: **A**~**(e)** inhabitant *ou* native of Algiers. **3** *nm* (*région*) **l'A**~ the Algiers region.

algorithme [algɔʀitm(ə)] *nm* algorithm.

algorithmique [algɔʀitmik] *adj* algorithmic.

alguazil [algwazil] *nm* (*Hist*) alguazil; (*hum péj*) cop*.

algue [alg(ə)] *nf* (*gén*) seaweed (*U*); (*Bot*) alga. ~**s** (*gén*) seaweed; (*Bot*) algae.

alias [aljɑs] *adv* alias.

alibi [alibi] *nm* alibi.

Alice [alis] *nf* Alice.

aliénabilité [aljenabilite] *nf* alienability.

aliénable [aljenabl(ə)] *adj* alienable.

aliénataire [aljenatɛʀ] *nm* alienee.

aliénateur, -trice [aljenatœʀ, tʀis] *nm,f* (*Jur*) alienator.

aliénation [aljenɑsjɔ̃] *nf* (*gén*) alienation. (*Méd*) ~ **(mentale)** (mental) derangement, alienation (*T*).

aliéné, e [aljene] (*ptp de* **aliéner**) *nm,f* insane person, lunatic (*péj*); *V* **asile.**

aliéner [aljene] (6) *vt* **(a)** (*Jur: céder*) to alienate; *droits, liberté* to give up. ~ **sa liberté entre les mains de qn** to give (up) one's freedom into the hands of sb; **un traité qui aliène leur liberté** a treaty which alienates their freedom.

(b) (*rendre hostile*) *partisans, opinion publique* to alienate (*à qn* from sb). **cette mesure (lui) a aliéné les esprits** this measure alienated people (from him); **s'**~ **ses partisans/l'opinion publique** to alienate one's supporters/public opinion; **s'**~ **un ami** to alienate *ou* estrange a friend; **s'**~ **l'affection de qn** to alienate sb's affections, estrange sb.

(c) (*Philos, Sociol*) ~ **qn** to alienate sb.

aliéniste [aljenist(ə)] *nmf* specialist in mental illness, alienist††.

alignement [aliɲmɑ̃] *nm* **(a)** (*action*) aligning, lining up, bringing into alignment; (*rangée*) alignment, line. **les** ~**s de Carnac** the Carnac menhirs *ou* alignments (*T*).

(b) (*Mil*) **être à l'**~ to be in line; **se mettre à l'**~ to fall into line, line up; **sortir de l'**~ to step out of line (*lit*); **à droite/gauche,** ~! right/left, dress!

(c) *[rue]* building line; (*Pol*) alignment; (*Fin*) alignment. ~ **monétaire** monetary alignment *ou* adjustment; **maison frappée d'**~ house hit by the road widening scheme; *V* **non.**

aligner [aliɲe] (1) **1** *vt* **(a)** *objets* to align, line up, bring into alignment (*sur* with); (*fig*) *chiffres* to string together, string up a line of; (*fig*) *arguments* to reel off; (*Mil*) to form into lines, draw up in lines. **il alignait des cubes/allumettes sur la table** he was lining up *ou* making lines of building blocks/matches on the table; **des peupliers étaient alignés le long de la route** poplars stood in a straight line along the roadside; (*payer*) **pour acheter cette voiture, il va falloir les** ~**:** you'll have to lay out* *ou* cough up: a lot to buy this car.

(b) *rue* to modify the (statutory) building line of; (*Fin, Pol*) to bring into alignment (*sur* with). (*fig*) ~ **sa conduite sur** to bring one's behaviour into line with, modify one's behaviour to conform with.

2 s'aligner *vpr [soldats]* to fall into line, line up. (*Pol*) **s'**~ **sur** *politique* to conform to the line of; *pays, parti* to align o.s. with; **tu peux toujours t'aligner!:** just try and match *ou* beat that!*

aliment [alimɑ̃] *nm* **(a)** (*nourriture*) food. **c'est un** ~ **riche** it's a rich food; **un** ~ **pauvre** a food with low nutritional value; **bien mâcher les** ~**s** to chew one's food well; **le pain est un** ~ bread is (a) food *ou* a type of food; **le pain et le lait sont des** ~**s** bread and milk are (kinds of) food *ou* foods; **comment conserver vos** ~**s** how to keep (your) food *ou* foodstuffs fresh; ~ **complet/liquide** whole/liquid food; (*fig*) **fournir un** ~ **à la curiosité de qn** to feed sb's curiosity, give sb's curiosity something to work on; **ça a fourni un** ~ **à la conversation** it gave us something to talk about.

(b) (*Jur*) ~**s** maintenance.

alimentaire [alimɑ̃tɛʀ] *adj* **(a)** *besoins* food (*épith*). **produits** *ou* **denrées** ~**s** foodstuffs; *V* **bol, pâte, pension.**

(b) (*péj*) *besogne, littérature* done to earn a living *ou* some cash. **c'est de la littérature** ~ this sort of book is written as a potboiler *ou* as a money-spinner *ou* is written to earn a living.

alimentation [alimɑ̃tɑsjɔ̃] *nf* **(a)** (*action*) *[personne, chaudière]* feeding; *[moteur, circuit]* supplying, feeding. **l'**~ **en eau du moteur/des grandes villes** supplying water to *ou* the supply of water to the engine/large towns; *V* **tuyau.**

(b) (*régime*) diet. ~ **de base** staple diet; **il lui faut une** ~ **lactée** he must have milky food(s) *ou* a milk diet.

(c) (*Comm*) food trade; (*enseigne*) *[magasin]* grocery (store), groceries; *[rayon]* groceries.

alimenter [alimɑ̃te] (1) *vt personne, animal, chaudière* to feed; *conversation* to sustain, keep going, nourish; *curiosité* to feed, sustain; *moteur, circuit* to supply, feed. **le réservoir alimente le moteur en essence** the tank supplies the engine with petrol (*Brit*) *ou* gasoline (*US*) *ou* feeds *ou* supplies petrol *etc* to the engine; ~ **une ville en gaz/électricité** to supply a town with gas/electricity; **le malade recommence à s'**~ the patient is starting to eat again *ou* to take food again.

alinéa [alinea] *nm* (*passage*) paragraph; (*ligne*) indented line (*at the beginning of a paragraph*). **nouvel** ~ new line.

alitement [alitmɑ̃] *nm* confinement to (one's) bed.

aliter [alite] (1) **1** *vt* to confine to (one's) bed. **rester alité** to remain confined to (one's) bed, remain bedridden; **infirme alité** bedridden invalid. **2 s'aliter** *vpr* to take to one's bed.

alizé [alize] *adj m, nm*: **(vent)** ~ trade wind.

Allah [ala] *nm* Allah.

allaitement [alɛtmɑ̃] *nm* **(a)** (*action: V* **allaiter**) feeding; suckling; nursing. ~ **maternel** breast-feeding; ~ **mixte** mixed feeding; ~ **au biberon** bottle-feeding. **(b)** (*période*) breast-feeding.

allaiter [alete] (1) *vt [femme]* to (breast-)feed, give the breast to, suckle†, nurse; *[animal]* to suckle. ~ **au biberon** to bottle-feed; **elle allaite encore** she's still (breast-)feeding (the baby).

allant, e [alɑ̃, ɑ̃t] **1** *adj* (*littér: alerte*) sprightly, active. **musique** ~**e** lively music. **2** *nm* (*dynamisme*) drive, energy. **avoir de l'**~ to have plenty of drive *ou* energy; **avec** ~ energetically.

alléchant, e [aleʃɑ̃, ɑ̃t] *adj* (*V* **allécher**) mouth-watering; enticing; tempting; alluring.

allécher [aleʃe] (6) *vt [odeur]* to make one's mouth water, tempt; (*fig*) *[proposition]* to entice, tempt, lure. **alléché par l'odeur** one's mouth watering at the smell, tempted by the smell.

allée [ale] *nf* **(a)** *[forêt]* lane, path; *[ville]* avenue; *[jardin]* path; *[parc]* path, walk, (*plus large*) avenue; (*menant à une maison*) drive, driveway; *[cinéma, autobus]* aisle. ~ **cavalière** bridle path.

(b) ~**s et venues** comings and goings; **que signifient ces** ~**s et venues dans le couloir?** what is the meaning of these comings and goings in the corridor?; **ceci l'oblige à de constantes** ~**s et venues (entre Paris et la province)** this forces him to go constantly back and forth *ou* backwards and forwards *ou* he is forced to be constantly coming and going (between Paris and the provinces); **j'ai perdu mon temps en** ~**s et venues pour avoir ce renseignement** I've wasted my time going back and forth *ou* to-ing and fro-ing to get this information; **le malade l'obligeait à de constantes** ~**s et venues** the patient kept her constantly on the run *ou* running about (for him).

allégation [alegɑsjɔ̃] *nf* allegation.

allégeance [aleʒɑ̃s] *nf* allegiance.

allégement [alɛʒmɑ̃] *nm* (*V* **alléger**) lightening; alleviation; reduction; mitigation; trimming. ~ **fiscal** reducing the tax burden.

alléger [aleʒe] (6 *et* 3) *vt poids* to lighten; *bagages, véhicule* to make lighter; *douleur* to alleviate, relieve, soothe; *impôts, responsabilités* to reduce, lighten; *châtiment* to mitigate. ~ **les programmes scolaires** to lighten *ou* trim the school syllabus.

allégorie [alegɔʀi] *nf* allegory.

allégorique [alegɔʀik] *adj* allegorical.

allégoriquement [alegɔʀikmɑ̃] *adv* allegorically.

allègre [alɛgʀ(ə)] *adj personne, humeur* gay, cheerful, light-hearted; *démarche* lively, jaunty; *musique* lively, merry. **il descendait la rue d'un pas** ~ he was walking gaily *ou* cheerfully *ou* briskly down the street.

allégrement, allègrement [alɛgʀəmɑ̃] *adv* (*V* **allègre**) gaily, cheerfully; light-heartedly; jauntily; merrily; (**hum*) blithely, cheerfully.

allégresse [alegʀɛs] *nf* elation, exhilaration. **ce fut l'**~ **générale** there was general rejoicing.

alléguer [alege] (6) *vt* **(a)** *fait* to put forward (as proof *ou* as an excuse *ou* as a pretext); *excuse, prétexte, raison, preuve* to put forward. **il allégua comme prétexte que ...** he put forward as a pretext that ...; **ils refusèrent de m'écouter, alléguant (comme raison) que ...** they refused to listen to me, arguing that ... *ou* proffering the argument that ... *ou* alleging that ... .

(b) (*littér: citer*) to cite, quote.

alléluia [aleluja] *nm, excl* (*Rel*) alleluia, hallelujah.

Allemagne [almaɲ] *nf* Germany. **l'**~ **fédérale** *ou* **de l'Ouest** the Federal German Republic; ~ **de l'Ouest/de l'Est** West/East Germany.

allemand, e [almɑ̃, ɑ̃d] **1** *adj* German. **2** *nm* (*Ling*) German; *V* **bas, haut. 3** *nm,f*: **A**~**(e)** German. **4 allemande** *nf* (*Danse, Mus*) allemande.

aller [ale] (9) 1 *vi* **(a)** (*se déplacer*) to go. ~ **à grands pas** to stride along; ~ **deux par deux** to go *ou* walk in twos *ou* pairs; **il va sans but par les rues** he wanders (aimlessly) through the streets; **il allait trop vite quand il a eu son accident (d'auto)** he was driving *ou* going too fast when he had his (car) accident; **en ville, on va plus vite à pied qu'en voiture** in town it is quicker to walk than to go by car, in town it is quicker to get around on foot than in a car; ~ **et venir** to come and go.

(b) (*se rendre à*) ~ **à/vers** to go to/towards *ou* in the direction of; ~ **loin** to go a long way, go far (afield); ~ **à Paris/en Allemagne/à la campagne/chez le boucher** to go to Paris/to Germany/to the country/to the butcher's; **penses-tu y** ~**?** do you think you'll be going (there)?; ~ **au lit/à l'église/à l'école** to go to bed/to church/to school; ~ **à la chasse/à la pêche** to go hunting/fishing; ~ **aux champignons** to go mushroom-picking, go collecting mushrooms; ~ **à Paris en voiture/à** *ou* **en bicyclette/en avion** to drive/cycle/fly to Paris; **vas-tu à pied?** will you walk? *ou* go on foot?; ~ **sur Paris** to go in the direction of Paris, go towards Paris; ~ **aux renseignements/aux nouvelles** to go and inquire/and find out the news; (*fig*) **j'irai jusqu'au ministre** I'll take it to the minister; **il ira loin** he'll go far; **il est allé trop loin** he went too far; **on va à la catastrophe** we're heading for disaster; **il est allé jusqu'à dire** he went as *ou* so far as to say; ~ **sur ses 30 ans** to be getting *ou* going on for 30, be nearly 30; **où allons-nous?** what are things coming to?; **on ne va pas loin avec 100 F** you won't get far on 100 francs; **ce travail lui déplaît mais il ira jusqu'au bout** he doesn't like this job but he'll see it through.

(c) (*mener, s'étendre*) to go (*à* to). **cette route doit** ~ **quelque part** this road must go somewhere; **son champ va jusqu'à la forêt** his field goes *ou* stretches as far as *ou* to the forest; **l'affaire pourrait** ~ **loin** this matter could turn out to be very serious.

(d) (*état de santé*) **comment allez-vous?** how are you?; **(comment) ça va?*** *ou* **comment va la santé?*** — **ça va*** how's things?* *ou* how are you keeping?* — fine *ou* not so bad*; **ça va mieux maintenant** I'm feeling better now; **comment va ton frère?** — **il va bien/mal** how's your brother? — he's well *ou* fine*/he isn't well *ou* he's unwell *ou* he's ill; **ça va?*** — **faudra bien que ça aille*** you all right?* — I'll have to be*.

(e) (*situation*) **(comment) ça va?*** — **ça va*** how's life?* *ou* how are you getting on?* — fine* *ou* not so bad*; **ça va, la réparation?*** — **faudra bien que ça aille*** is the repair all right? — it'll have to be*; **comment vont les affaires?** — **elles vont bien/mal** how's business? — (it's) fine/not too good; **ça va mal en Asie/à la maison** things aren't going too well *ou* things aren't looking so good in Asia/at home; **ça va mieux pour lui maintenant** things are looking better for him now, things are looking more hopeful for him now; **ça ne va pas mieux! il refuse d'obéir** whatever next! he's refusing to obey; **ça va mal** ~ **si tu continues** if you carry on, there's going to be trouble; **est-ce que ta pendule va bien?** *ou* **juste?** is your clock right?; **ça ne va pas sans difficulté** it's no easy job, there are problems; *V* **chemin, cœur, main.**

(f) (*convenir*) ~ **à qn** *[forme, mesure]* to fit sb; *[style, genre]* to suit sb; ~ **(bien) avec** to go (well) with; ~ **bien ensemble** to go well together; **ce tableau va bien/mal sur ce mur** this picture goes well/doesn't go well on this wall; **la clef ne va pas dans la serrure** the key won't go in *ou* doesn't fit the lock; **cette robe lui va bien** (*couleur, style*) this dress suits her; (*pour la taille*) this dress fits her; **vos projets me vont parfaitement** your plans suit me fine; **rendez-vous demain 4 heures?** — **ça me va*** see you tomorrow at 4? — (it) suits me* *ou* it's all right by me; **ce climat ne leur va pas** this climate doesn't suit them *ou* agree with them; **les ciseaux ne vont pas pour couper du carton** scissors won't do *ou* are no good for cutting cardboard; **votre plan ne va pas** your plan won't do *ou* work; **ça lui va mal** *ou* (*hum*) **bien de critiquer les autres*** he's got a nerve* criticizing other people, he's a fine one* to criticize other people.

(g) (*Méd*) ~ **(à la selle** *ou* **aux cabinets)** to have a bowel movement; **le malade est-il allé à la selle?** have the patient's bowels moved?; **cela fait** ~***** it keeps the bowels open, it clears you out* (*hum*).

(h) (*avec participe présent: pour exprimer la progression*) ~ **en empirant** to get worse and worse; **le bruit va croissant** the noise is getting louder and louder.

(i) (*excl*) (*stimulation*) **allons!, allez!** go on!, come on!; (*incrédulité*) **allons donc!** really?, come on now!, come off it!*; (*agacement*) **allons bon! qu'est-ce qui t'est encore arrivé?** NOW what's happened!; (*impatience*) **allons, cesse de m'ennuyer!** will you just stop bothering me!; (*encouragement*) **allons, allons, il ne faut pas pleurer** come on now *ou* come, come, you mustn't cry; **ça va, ça va!*** all right, that's enough!, O.K., O.K.*, don't go on!*; **allez, au revoir!** cheerio then! (*surtout Brit*), 'bye then!, ta ta then* (*surtout Brit*); ~ **de soi** to be self-evident, be obvious; **cela va de soi** it's obvious, it stands to reason, it goes without saying; **cela va sans dire** it goes without saying; **il va sans dire qu'il accepta** needless to say *ou* it goes without saying, he accepted; **va pour une nouvelle voiture!*** all right we'll HAVE a new car!; **va donc, eh imbécile!‡** get lost, you twit‡; **allez, allez, circulez** come on now, move along.

(j) (*avec en*) **il en va de: il en va de même pour tous les autres** the same applies to all the others; **il en va de cette affaire comme de la précédente** the same goes for this matter as for the previous one.

(k) (*avec y*) **on y va?*** shall we go?, are we off then?*; **allons-y!** let's go!; **allez-y, c'est votre tour** go on *ou* on you go, it's your turn; **allez-y, vous ne risquez rien** go ahead *ou* go on *ou* on you go, you've nothing to lose; **comme vous y allez!** you're going a bit far!*; **tu y vas mal!*** *ou* **un peu fort!*** you're going a bit far*; **vas-y doucement*** *ou* **mollo‡** gently does it, go gently; (*impers*) **y** ~ **de: il y va de votre vie/de votre santé** your life/your health is at stake *ou* depends on it; **il y est allé de sa petite chanson*** he gave us his little song; **elle y va toujours de son porte-monnaie** she's always the one who forks out‡; **il y est allé de sa petite larme*** he had a little weep.

2 *vb aux* (+ *infin*) **(a)** (*futur immédiat*) to be going to. **tu vas être en retard** you are going to be late, you'll be late; **il va descendre dans une minute** he'll be (coming) down in a minute; **ils allaient commencer** they were going to start, they were on the point of starting, they were about to start; **ça va prendre un quart d'heure** that'll take *ou* it's going to take a quarter of an hour.

(b) (*lit*) ~ **faire qch** to go and do sth; **il est allé me chercher mes lunettes** he went *ou* has gone to fetch my glasses; ~ **voir qn à l'hôpital** to go and visit sb in hospital; **je suis allé en courant chercher le docteur** I ran to fetch the doctor; ~ **faire le** *ou* **son marché** to go to the market.

(c) (*intensif*) ~ **se faire du souci inutilement** to go and worry for no reason at all; **allez donc voir si c'est vrai!** (well) you can believe it if you like!, you'll never know if it's true!; **n'allez pas vous imaginer que** don't you go imagining that; **pourvu qu'il n'aille pas penser que** as long as he doesn't go and think that.

3 s'en aller *vpr* **(a)** (*partir*) to go (away); (*déménager*) to move, leave. **s'en** ~ **subrepticement** to steal *ou* sneak away; **elle s'en va en vacances demain** she goes *ou* is going away on holiday tomorrow; **ils s'en vont à Paris** they are going *ou* off to Paris; **il s'en est allé furieux, il s'est en allé furieux*** he went away *ou* off in a huff, he left in a huff; **bon, je m'en vais** right, I'm off *ou* I'll be going; **ils s'en vont du quartier** they are leaving the district, they are moving (away from the district).

(b) (*mourir*) to die. **il s'en va** he's sinking *ou* going; **il s'en est allé paisiblement** he passed away peacefully.

(c) (*prendre sa retraite*) to retire. **il s'en va cette année** he's retiring *ou* leaving this year.

(d) (*disparaître*) *[tache]* to come off; *[temps, années]* to pass, go by. **ça s'en ira au lavage** it'll wash off, it'll come off in the wash; **tous nos projets s'en vont en fumée** all our plans are going up in smoke; **tout son argent s'en va en disques** all his money goes on records.

(e) (*loc*) **je m'en vais leur montrer de quoi je suis capable** I'll show them what I'm made of!; **va-t'en voir si c'est vrai!*** (well) you can believe it if you like!, you'll never know if it's true!

4 *nm* (*trajet*) outward journey; (*billet*) single (*Brit*) *ou* one-way (*US*) (ticket). **l'**~ **s'est bien passé** the (outward) journey went off well; **j'irai vous voir à l'**~ I'll come and see you on the way there; **je ne fais que l'**~**-retour** I'm just going there and back; **3** ~**s (simples) pour Tours** 3 singles (*Brit*) *ou* one-way tickets (*US*) to Tours; **prendre un** ~**-retour** to buy a return (*Brit*) *ou* round-trip (*US*) (ticket).

allergie [alɛʀʒi] *nf* allergy.

allergique [alɛʀʒik] *adj* (*lit, fig*) allergic (*à* to).

alliacé, e [aljase] *adj* alliaceous.

alliage [aljaʒ] *nm* alloy. (*fig péj*) **un** ~ **disparate de doctrines** a hotchpotch of doctrines.

alliance [aljɑ̃s] **1** *nf* **(a)** (*pacte*) (*Pol*) alliance; (*entente*) union; (*Bible*) covenant. **faire** *ou* **conclure une** ~ **avec un pays** to enter into an alliance with a country; **il a fait** ~ **avec nos ennemis** he has allied himself with our enemies; **une étroite** ~ **s'était établie entre le vieillard et les enfants** a close bond had established itself between the old man and the children; **l'**~ **de la musique et de la poésie dans cet opéra** the union of music and poetry in this opera; *V* **saint, triple.**

(b) (*frm: mariage*) union, marriage. **neveu/oncle par** ~ nephew/uncle by marriage; **entrer par** ~ **dans une famille, faire** ~ **avec une famille** to marry into a family, become united by marriage with a family.

(c) (*bague*) (wedding) ring.

(d) (*fig: mélange*) combination.

2: **l'alliance française** the Alliance Française, ≈ the British Council; (*Littérat*) **alliance de mots** bold juxtaposition (of words), oxymoron.

allié, e [alje] (*ptp de* **allier**) **1** *adj pays* allied. **famille** ~**e** family *ou* relations by marriage. **2** *nm,f* (*pays*) ally; (*fig: ami, soutien*) ally; (*parent*) relative by marriage. (*Pol*) **les A**~**s** the Allies.

allier [alje] (7) **1** *vt efforts* to combine, unite; *couleurs* to match; *familles* to ally, unite by marriage; (*Pol*) to ally; (*Tech*) to alloy. **elle allie l'élégance à la simplicité** she combines elegance with simplicity; **ils sont alliés à une puissante famille** they are allied to *ou* related by marriage to a powerful family.

2 s'allier *vpr [efforts]* to combine, unite; *[couleurs]* to match; (*frm*) *[familles]* to become united by marriage, become allied; (*Pol*) to become allies *ou* allied; (*Tech*) to alloy. **s'**~ **à une famille riche** to become allied to *ou* with a wealthy family, marry into a wealthy family; **la France s'allia à l'Angleterre** France became allied to *ou* with England *ou* allied itself to *ou* with England.

alligator [aligatɔʀ] *nm* alligator.

allitération [aliteʀasjɔ̃] *nf* alliteration.

allô [alo] *excl* (*Téléc*) hullo! *ou* hallo!

allocataire [alɔkatɛʀ] *nmf* beneficiary.

allocation [alɔkasjɔ̃] **1** *nf* **(a)** (*V* **allouer**) allocation; granting; allotment. **(b)** (*somme*) allowance. **toucher les allocations*** to draw *ou* get family allowance(s). **2: allocation de chômage** unemployment benefit (*U*), dole (money)* (*U*); **allocations familiales** family allowance(s), child benefits; **allocation de logement** rent allowance *ou* subsidy; **allocation de maternité** maternity allowance *ou* benefit.

allocution [alɔkysjɔ̃] *nf* short speech. ~ **télévisée** short televised speech.

allogène [alɔʒɛn] *adj population* non-native; *(fig) éléments* foreign. **ces gens forment un groupe ~ en Grande-Bretagne** these people form a non-native racial group in Britain.
allonge [alɔ̃ʒ] *nf* (*Tech*) extension; *[table]* leaf; *[boucherie]* hook; (*Boxe*) reach. **avoir une bonne ~** to have a long reach.
allongé, e [alɔ̃ʒe] (*ptp de* **allonger**) *adj* **(a)** (*étendu*) **être ~** to be stretched out, be lying; **rester ~** *[blessé, malade]* to stay lying down, be lying down *ou* flat; (*se reposer*) to be lying down, have one's feet up, be resting; **~ sur son lit** lying on one's bed; **~ sur le dos** stretched out on *ou* lying on one's back, supine (*littér*); **les (malades) ~s** the recumbent patients; (*Art*) **une figure ~e** a recumbent figure.
(b) (*long*) long; (*étiré*) elongated; (*oblong*) oblong. **faire une mine ~e** to pull *ou* make a long face.
allongement [alɔ̃ʒmɑ̃] *nm* **(a)** (*Anat, Métal*) elongation; (*Ling*) lengthening; (*Aviat*) aspect ratio.
(b) (*V* **allonger**) *[distance, vêtement]* lengthening; *[route, voie ferrée, congés, vie]* lengthening, extension. **l'~ des jours** the lengthening of the days, the longer days.
allonger [alɔ̃ʒe] (3) **1** *vt* **(a)** (*rendre plus long*) *vêtement, trajet* to lengthen, make longer; *route, congés, vie* to lengthen, extend; *visite, discours* to lengthen, prolong. **~ le pas** to hasten one's step(s); (*fig*) **cette coiffure lui allonge le visage** this hair style makes her face look longer *ou* long.
(b) (*étendre*) *bras, jambe* to stretch (out); *malade* to lay *ou* stretch out. **~ le cou (pour apercevoir qch)** to crane *ou* stretch one's neck (to see sth); **la jambe allongée sur une chaise** with one leg up on *ou* stretched out on a chair.
(c) (*: donner*) *somme* to dish out*, hand out; *coup, gifle* to deal, land*. **~ qn** to knock sb flat; **il va falloir les ~** we'll (*ou* you'll *etc*) have to lay out a lot* *ou* cough up*.
(d) (*Culin*) *sauce* to thin (down). (*fig*) **~ la sauce*** to spin it out.
2 *vi*: **les jours allongent** the days are growing longer *ou* drawing out.
3 s'allonger *vpr* **(a)** (*devenir ou paraître plus long*) *[ombres, jours]* to get longer, lengthen; *[enfant]* to grow taller; *[discours, visite]* to drag on. (*fig*) **son visage s'allongea à ces mots** at these words he pulled *ou* made a long face *ou* his face fell; **la route s'allongeait devant eux** the road stretched away before them.
(b) (*s'étendre*) to lie down (*full length*), stretch o.s. out. **s'~ dans l'herbe** to lie down on the grass, stretch o.s. out on the grass; (*pour dormir*) **je vais m'~ quelques minutes** I'm going to lie down for a few minutes.
allopathe [alɔpat] **1** *adj* allopathic. **2** *nmf* allopath, allopathist.
allopathie [alɔpati] *nf* allopathy.
allotropie [alɔtʀɔpi] *nf* allotropy.
allotropique [alɔtʀɔpik] *adj* allotropic.
allouer [alwe] (1) *vt argent* to allocate; *indemnité* to grant; (*Fin*) *actions* to allot; *temps* to allot, allow, allocate. **pendant le temps alloué** during the allotted *ou* allowed time, during the time allowed *ou* allocated.
allumage [alymaʒ] *nm* **(a)** (*action*) *[feu]* lighting, kindling; *[poêle]* lighting; *[électricité]* putting *ou* switching *ou* turning on; *[gaz]* lighting, putting *ou* turning on.
(b) (*Aut*) ignition. **avance/retard à l'~** ignition advance/retard; *V* **auto-allumage.**
allume-cigare [alymsigaʀ] *nm inv* cigar lighter.
allume-gaz [alymgɑz] *nm inv* gas lighter (*for cooker*).
allumer [alyme] (1) **1** *vt* **(a)** *feu* to light, kindle; *bougie, poêle* to light; *cigare, pipe* to light (up); *incendie* to start, light. **il alluma sa cigarette à celle de son voisin** he lit (up) his cigarette from his neighbour's, he got a light from his neighbour's cigarette; **le feu était allumé** the fire was lit *ou* alight, the fire was going*; **laisse le poêle allumé** leave the stove on *ou* lit *ou* alight.
(b) *électricité, lampe, radio* to put *ou* switch *ou* turn on; *gaz* to light, put *ou* turn on. **laisse la lumière allumée** leave the light on; **allume dans la cuisine** put *ou* switch *ou* turn the kitchen light(s) on, put *ou* switch *ou* turn the lights on in the kitchen; **le bouton n'allume pas, ça n'allume pas** the light doesn't come on *ou* work.
(c) ~ une pièce to put *ou* switch *ou* turn the light(s) on in a room; **sa fenêtre était allumée** there was a light (on) at his window, his window was lit (up); **laisse le salon allumé** leave the light(s) on in the sitting-room, leave the sitting room light(s) on.
(d) *colère, envie, haine* to arouse, stir up, kindle; *guerre* to stir up; *amour* to kindle. **elle sait ~ les hommes** she knows how to excite men *ou* to turn men on*.
2 s'allumer *vpr [incendie]* to blaze, flare up; *[lumière]* to come *ou* go on; *[radiateur]* to switch (itself) on; *[sentiment]* to be aroused; *[guerre]* to break out. **le désir s'alluma dans ses yeux** his eyes lit up with desire, the light of desire shone in his eyes; **ses yeux s'allumèrent/son regard s'alluma** his eyes/face lit up; **ce bois s'allume bien** this wood catches fire *ou* burns easily; **la pièce s'alluma** the light(s) came *ou* went on in the room, the room lit up; **sa fenêtre s'alluma** a light came *ou* went on at his window, his window lit up.
allumette [alymɛt] *nf* **(a)** match; (*morceau de bois*) match-(stick). **~ de sûreté** *ou* **suédoise** safety match; **~ tison** fuse. **(b)** (*Culin*) flaky pastry finger. **~ au fromage** cheese straw.
allumeur [alymœʀ] *nm* (*Aut*) distributor; (*Tech*) igniter. (*Hist*) **~ de réverbères** lamplighter.
allumeuse [alymøz] *nf* (*péj*) teaser, vamp.
allure [alyʀ] *nf* **(a)** (*vitesse*) *[véhicule]* speed; *[piéton]* pace. **rouler** *ou* **aller à grande/faible ~** to drive *ou* go at (a) great/slow speed; **à toute ~** at top *ou* full speed, at full tilt.
(b) (*démarche*) walk, gait (*littér*); (*prestance*) bearing; (*attitude*) air, look; (*: aspect*) *[objet, individu]* look, appearance. **avoir de l'~** to have style, have a certain elegance; **avoir fière** *ou* **grande/piètre ~** to cut a fine/shabby figure; **avoir une drôle d'~/bonne ~** to look odd *ou* funny/fine; **d'~ louche/bizarre** fishy-/odd-looking; **les choses prennent une drôle d'~** things are taking a funny *ou* an odd turn.
(c) (*comportement*) **~s** ways; **choquer par sa liberté d'~s** to shock people with *ou* by the freedom of one's ways; **il a des ~s de voyou** he behaves *ou* carries on* like a hooligan.
(d) (*Équitation*) gait; (*Naut*) trim.
allusif, -ive [alyzif, iv] *adj* allusive.
allusion [alyzjɔ̃] *nf* (*référence*) allusion (*à* to); (*avec sous-entendu*) hint (*à* at). **~ malveillante** innuendo; **faire ~ à** to allude *ou* refer to, hint at, make allusions to; **par ~** allusively.
alluvial, e, *mpl* **-aux** [alyvjal, o] *adj* alluvial.
alluvionnement [alyvjɔnmɑ̃] *nm* alluviation.
alluvions [alyvjɔ̃] *nfpl* alluvial deposits, alluvium (*sg*).
almanach [almana] *nm* almanac.
almée [alme] *nf* almah.
aloès [alɔɛs] *nm* aloe.
aloi [alwa] *nm*: **de bon ~** *plaisanterie, gaieté* honest, respectable; *individu* worthy, of sterling *ou* genuine worth; *produit* sound, worthy, of sterling *ou* genuine quality *ou* worth; **de mauvais ~** *plaisanterie, gaieté* unsavoury, unwholesome; *individu* of little worth, of doubtful reputation; *produit* of doubtful quality.
alors [alɔʀ] *adv* **(a)** (*à cette époque*) then, in those days, at that time. **il était ~ étudiant** he was a student then *ou* at that time *ou* in those days; **les femmes d'~ portaient la crinoline** the women in *ou* of those days *ou* at *ou* of that time wore crinolines; **le ministre d'~ M Dupont** the then minister Mr Dupont, the minister at that time, Mr Dupont; *V* **jusque.**
(b) (*en conséquence*) then, in that case, so. **vous ne voulez pas de mon aide? ~ je vous laisse** you don't want my help? then *ou* in that case *ou* so I'll leave you *ou* I'll leave you then; **il ne connaissait pas l'affaire, ~ on l'a mis au courant** he wasn't familiar with the matter so they put him in the picture; **~ qu'est-ce qu'on va faire?** what are we going to do then?, so what are we going to do?
(c) ~ que (*simultanéité*) while, when; (*opposition*) whereas; **~ même que** (*même si*) even if, even though; (*au moment où*) while, just when; **on a sonné ~ que j'étais dans mon bain** the bell rang while *ou* when I was in my bath; **elle est sortie ~ que le docteur le lui avait interdit** she went out although *ou* even though the doctor had told her not to; **il est parti travailler à Paris ~ que son frère est resté au village** he went to work in Paris whereas *ou* while his brother stayed behind in the village; **~ même qu'il me supplierait** even if he begged me, even if *ou* though he were to beg me.
(d) (*) **~ tu viens (oui ou non)?** well (then), are you coming (or not)?, are you coming then (or not)?; **~ là je ne peux pas vous répondre** well then, I can really give you no answer; **et (puis) ~?** and then what (happened)?; **il pleut — et ~?** it's raining — so (what)?; *V* **non.**
alose [aloz] *nf* shad.
alouette [alwɛt] *nf* lark, skylark, meadowlark (*Can*). **attendre que les ~s vous tombent toutes rôties dans la bouche** to wait for things to fall into one's lap; *V* **miroir.**
alourdir [aluʀdiʀ] (2) **1** *vt objet, véhicule* to weigh *ou* load down, make heavy; *style, phrase* to make heavy *ou* cumbersome; *démarche, traits* to make heavy; *impôts* to increase; *esprit* to dull. **avoir la tête alourdie par le sommeil** to be heavy with sleep *ou* heavy-eyed; **vêtements alourdis par la pluie** clothes heavy with rain; **les odeurs d'essence alourdissaient l'air** petrol fumes hung heavy on the air, the air was heavy with petrol fumes.
2 s'alourdir *vpr* to become *ou* grow heavy. **sa taille/elle s'est alourdie** her waist/she has thickened out; **ses paupières s'alourdissaient** his eyes were growing *ou* becoming heavy.
alourdissement [aluʀdismɑ̃] *nm [véhicule, objet]* increased weight, heaviness; *[phrase, style, pas]* heaviness; *[impôts]* increase (*de* in); *[esprit]* dullness, dulling; *[taille]* thickening.
aloyau [alwajo] *nm* sirloin.
alpaga [alpaga] *nm* (*Tex, Zool*) alpaca.
alpage [alpaʒ] *nm* (*pré*) high mountain pasture; (*époque*) *season spent by sheep etc in mountain pasture.*
alpe [alp(ə)] *nf* **(a) les A~s** the Alps. **(b)** (*pré*) alpine pasture.
alpestre [alpɛstʀ(ə)] *adj* alpine.
alpha [alfa] *nm* alpha. (*Rel, fig*) **l'~ et l'oméga** the alpha and omega.
alphabet [alfabɛ] *nm* (*système*) alphabet; (*livre*) alphabet *ou* ABC book. **~ morse** Morse code.
alphabétique [alfabetik] *adj* alphabetic(al). **par ordre ~** in alphabetical order, alphabetically.
alphabétiquement [alfabetikmɑ̃] *adv* alphabetically.
alphabétisation [alfabetizɑsjɔ̃] *nf* elimination of illiteracy (*de* in). **l'~ d'une population** teaching a population to read and write; **campagne d'~** literacy campaign.
alphabétiser [alfabetize] (1) *vt pays* to eliminate illiteracy in. **~ une population/des adultes** to teach a population/adults to read and write.
Alphonse [alfɔ̃s] *nm* Alphonse, Alphonso.
alpin, e [alpɛ̃, in] *adj* alpine.
alpinisme [alpinism(ə)] *nm* mountaineering, climbing.
alpiniste [alpinist(ə)] *nmf* mountaineer, climber.
Alsace [alzas] *nf* Alsace.
alsacien, -ienne [alzasjɛ̃, jɛn] **1** *adj* Alsatian. **2** *nm* (*Ling*) Alsatian. **3** *nm,f*: **A~(ne)** Alsatian.
altérabilité [alteʀabilite] *nf* alterability.
altérable [alteʀabl(ə)] *adj* alterable. **~ à l'air** liable to oxidization.
altérant, e [alteʀɑ̃, ɑ̃t] *adj* thirst-making.

altération [alteʀasjɔ̃] *nf* **(a)** (*action: V* **altérer**) distortion, falsification; alteration; adulteration; debasement; change; modification.

(b) (*V* **s'altérer**) debasement; alteration; distortion; impairment. **l'~ de sa santé** the change for the worse in *ou* the deterioration of *ou* in his health. **l'~ de son visage/de sa voix** his distorted features/broken voice.

(c) (*Mus*) accidental; (*Géol*) weathering.

altercation [altɛʀkɑsjɔ̃] *nf* altercation, dispute.

altérer [alteʀe] (6) **1** *vt* **(a)** (*assoiffer*) to make thirsty. (*littér*) **altéré d'honneurs** thirsty for *ou* thirsting after (*littér*) honours; **fauve altéré de sang** wild animal thirsting for blood; **il était altéré** his thirst was great, his throat was parched.

(b) (*fausser*) *texte, faits, vérité* to distort, falsify, alter, tamper with; *monnaie* to falsify; (*Comm*) *vin, aliments, qualité* to adulterate.

(c) (*abîmer*) *vin, aliments, qualité* to spoil, debase; *matière* to alter, debase; *sentiments* to alter, spoil; *couleur* to alter; *visage, voix* to distort; *santé, relations* to impair, affect. **la chaleur altère la viande** heat makes meat go off *ou* spoils the meat; **ceci n'a pas altéré mon amour pour elle** this has not spoilt *ou* altered my love for her.

(d) (*modifier*) to alter, change, modify.

2 s'altérer *vpr [vin]* to become spoiled; *[viande]* to go off; *[matière]* to become altered *ou* debased; *[couleur]* to become altered; *[visage]* to change, become distorted; *[sentiments]* to alter, be spoilt; *[santé, relations]* to deteriorate. **sa santé s'altère de plus en plus** his health is deteriorating further *ou* is getting progressively worse; **sa voix s'altéra sous le coup de la douleur** grief made his voice break, grief distorted his voice.

altérité [alteʀite] *nf* otherness, alterity.

alternance [altɛʀnɑ̃s] *nf* (*gén, Bio, Ling*) alternation; (*Agr*) alternation, rotation. **en ~: cette émission reprendra en ~ avec d'autres programmes** this broadcast will alternate with other programmes; **ils présentèrent le spectacle en ~** they took turns to present the show, they presented the show alternately.

alternant, e [altɛʀnɑ̃, ɑ̃t] *adj* alternating; (*Agr*) alternating, rotating. **pouls ~** pulsus alternans.

alternateur [altɛʀnatœʀ] *nm* alternator.

alternatif, -ive[1] [altɛʀnatif, iv] *adj* (*périodique*) alternate; (*Philos*) alternative; (*Élec*) alternating.

alternative[2] [altɛʀnativ] *nf* (*dilemme*) alternative; (*: *possibilité*) alternative, option; (*Philos*) alternative. **être dans une ~** to be faced with only one alternative; **passer par des ~s de douleur et de joie** to alternate between pleasure and pain.

alternativement [altɛʀnativmɑ̃] *adv* alternately, in turn.

alterne [altɛʀn(ə)] *adj* (*Bot, Math*) alternate.

alterné, e [altɛʀne] (*ptp de* **alterner**) *adj rimes* alternate.

alterner [altɛʀne] (1) **1** *vt choses* to alternate; *cultures* to rotate, alternate. **2** *vi* to alternate (*avec* with). **ils alternèrent à la présidence** they took (it in) turns in the chair.

altesse [altɛs] *nf* (*titre*) highness. **Son A~ Sérénissime** (*prince*) His Serene Highness; (*princesse*) Her Serene Highness; **j'en ai vu entrer des ~s!** I saw lots of princes and princesses go in.

altier, -ière [altje, jɛʀ] *adj caractère* haughty. (*littér*) **cimes ~ières** lofty peaks (*littér*).

altimètre [altimɛtʀ(ə)] *nm* altimeter.

altimétrie [altimetʀi] *nf* altimetry.

altiste [altist(ə)] *nmf* viola player, violist.

altitude [altityd] *nf* **(a)** (*par rapport à la mer*) altitude, height above sea level; (*par rapport au sol*) height. (*fig*) **~s** heights; **être à 500 mètres d'~** to be at a height *ou* altitude of 500 metres, be 500 metres above sea level; **en ~** at high altitude, high up; **l'air des ~s** the mountain air.

(b) (*Aviat*) **perdre de l'~** to lose altitude *ou* height; **prendre de l'~** to gain altitude; **il volait à basse/haute ~** he was flying at low/high altitude.

alto [alto] **1** *nm* (*instrument*) viola. **2** *nf* = **contralto.**

altruisme [altʀɥism(ə)] *nm* altruism.

altruiste [altʀɥist(ə)] **1** *adj* altruistic. **2** *nmf* altruist.

alu [aly] *nm abrév de* **aluminium.**

aluminate [alyminat] *nm* aluminate.

alumine [alymin] *nf* alumina.

aluminium [alyminjɔm] *nm* aluminium (*Brit*), aluminum (*US*).

alun [alœ̃] *nm* alum.

alunir [alyniʀ] (2) *vi* to land on the moon.

alunissage [alynisaʒ] *nm* (moon) landing.

alvéolaire [alveolɛʀ] *adj* alveolar.

alvéole [alveɔl] *nf ou* (*rare*) *nm [ruche]* alveolus, cell (*of a honeycomb*); (*Géol*) cavity. (*Méd*) **~ dentaire** tooth socket, alveolus (*T*); **~s dentaires** alveolar ridge, teeth ridge, alveoli (*T*); **~ pulmonaire** air cell, alveolus (*T*).

alvéolé, e [alveɔle] *adj* honeycombed, alveolate (*T*).

amabilité [amabilite] *nf* kindness. **ayez l'~ de** be so kind *ou* good as to; **plein d'~ envers moi** extremely kind *ou* polite to me; **faire des ~s à qn** to show politeness *ou* courtesy to sb.

amadou [amadu] *nm* touchwood, amadou.

amadouer [amadwe] (1) *vt* (*enjôler*) to coax, cajole; (*adoucir*) to mollify, soothe. **~ qn pour qu'il fasse qch** to coax *ou* wheedle *ou* cajole sb into doing sth.

amaigrir [amegʀiʀ] (2) **1** *vt* **(a)** to make thin *ou* thinner. **joues amaigries par l'âge** cheeks wasted with age; **je l'ai trouvé très amaigri** I found him much thinner, I thought he looked much thinner; **10 années de prison l'ont beaucoup amaigri** 10 years in prison have left him very much thinner.

(b) (*Tech*) to thin down, reduce.

2 s'amaigrir *vpr* to get *ou* become thin *ou* thinner.

amaigrissant, e [amegʀisɑ̃, ɑ̃t] *adj régime* slimming.

amaigrissement [amegʀismɑ̃] *nm* **(a)** (*pathologique*) *[corps]* loss of weight, thinness; *[visage, membres]* thinness. **(b)** (*volontaire*) slimming. **un ~ de 3 kg** a loss (in weight) of 3 kg.

amalgamation [amalgamɑsjɔ̃] *nf* (*Métal*) amalgamation.

amalgame [amalgam] *nm* (*péj: mélange*) (strange) mixture *ou* blend; (*Métal*) amalgam. **un ~ d'idées** a hotchpotch *ou* (strange) mixture of ideas.

amalgamer [amalgame] (1) **1** *vt* (*fig: mélanger*) to combine; (*Métal*) to amalgamate. **2 s'amalgamer** *vpr* (*fig: s'unir*) to combine; (*Métal*) to be amalgamated.

amande [amɑ̃d] *nf* **(a)** (*fruit*) almond. **en ~** almond-shaped, almond (*épith*); *V* **pâte. (b)** *[noyau]* kernel.

amandier [amɑ̃dje] *nm* almond (tree).

amanite [amanit] *nf any mushroom of the genus Amanita.* **~ phalloïde** death cap; **~ tue-mouches** fly agaric.

amant [amɑ̃] *nm* lover. **~ de passage** casual lover; **les deux ~s** the two lovers.

amante†† [amɑ̃t] *nf* (*fiancée*) betrothed†.

amarante [amaʀɑ̃t] **1** *nf* amaranth. **2** *adj inv* amaranthine.

amariner [amaʀine] (1) *vt* **(a)** *navire ennemi* to take over and man. **(b)** *matelot* to season (*gén ptp*), accustom to life at sea. **elle n'est pas *ou* ne s'est pas encore amarinée** she has not got used to the sea *ou* not found her sea legs yet.

amarrage [amaʀaʒ] *nm* (*Naut*) mooring. **être à l'~** to be moored.

amarre [amaʀ] *nf* (*Naut: cordage*) rope *ou* line *ou* cable (for mooring). **les ~s** moorings; *V* **larguer, rompre.**

amarrer [amaʀe] (1) *vt navire* to moor, make fast; *cordage* to make fast, belay; (*fig*) *paquet, valise* to tie down, make fast.

amas [amɑ] *nm* **(a)** (*lit: tas*) heap, pile, mass; (*fig*) *[souvenirs, idées]* mass. **tout un ~ de** a whole heap *ou* pile *ou* mass of. **(b)** (*Astron*) star cluster. **(c)** (*Min*) mass.

amasser [amɑse] (1) **1** *vt* **(a)** (*amonceler*) *choses* to pile *ou* store up, amass, accumulate; *fortune* to amass, accumulate. **il ne pense qu'à ~ (de l'argent)** all he thinks of is amassing *ou* accumulating wealth.

(b) (*rassembler*) *preuves, données* to amass, gather (together); *V* **pierre.**

2 s'amasser *vpr [choses, preuves]* to pile up, accumulate; *[foule]* to gather, mass, muster. **les preuves s'amassent contre lui** the evidence is building up *ou* piling up against him.

amateur [amatœʀ] *nm* **(a)** (*non-professionnel*) amateur. **équipe ~** amateur team; **talent d'~** amateur talent; **c'est un peintre/musicien ~** he's an amateur painter/musician.

(b) (*connaisseur*) **~ de** lover of; **~ d'art/de musique** art/music lover; **être ~ de films/de concerts** to be a keen film-/concert-goer, be keen on films/concerts; **elle est très ~ de framboises** she is very fond of *ou* she loves raspberries.

(c) (*: *disposé à acheter etc*) taker; (*disposé à faire*) volunteer; *V* **trouver.**

(d) (*péj*) dilettante, mere amateur. **travail/talent d'~** amateurish work/talent; **faire qch en ~** to do sth amateurishly *ou* as a mere amateur.

amateurisme [amatœʀism(ə)] *nm* (*Sport*) amateurism; (*péj*) amateurishness. **c'est de l'~!** it's amateurish!

Amazone [amazon] **1** *nm* (*Géog*) Amazon. **2** *nf* (*Myth*) Amazon; (*fig*) amazon.

amazone [amazon] *nf* **(a)** (*écuyère*) horsewoman. **tenue d'~** woman's riding habit; **monter en ~** to ride sidesaddle. **(b)** (*jupe*) long riding skirt.

ambages [ɑ̃baʒ] *nfpl*: **sans ~** without beating about the bush, in plain language.

ambassade [ɑ̃basad] *nf* **(a)** (*institution, bâtiment*) embassy; (*charge*) ambassadorship, embassy; (*personnel*) embassy staff *ou* officials (*pl*), embassy. **(b)** (*fig: mission*) mission. **être envoyé en ~ auprès de qn** to be sent on a mission to sb.

ambassadeur [ɑ̃basadœʀ] *nm* (*Pol, fig*) ambassador. **~ extraordinaire** ambassador extraordinary (*auprès de* to); **l'~ de la pensée française** the representative *ou* ambassador of French thought.

ambassadrice [ɑ̃basadʀis] *nf* (*diplomate*) ambassador (*auprès de* to); (*femme de diplomate*) ambassador's wife, ambassadress; (*fig*) ambassador, ambassadress.

ambiance [ɑ̃bjɑ̃s] *nf* (*climat, atmosphère*) atmosphere; (*environnement*) surroundings (*pl*); *[famille, équipe]* atmosphere. **l'~ de la salle** the atmosphere in the house, the mood of the audience; **il vit dans une ~ calme** he lives in calm *ou* peaceful surroundings; **il y a de l'~!*** there's a great atmosphere here!*

ambiant, e [ɑ̃bjɑ̃, ɑ̃t] *adj air* surrounding, ambient; *température* ambient. (*fig*) **déprimé par l'atmosphère ~e** depressed by the atmosphere around him.

ambidextre [ɑ̃bidɛkstʀ(ə)] *adj* ambidextrous.

ambigu, -uë [ɑ̃bigy] *adj* ambiguous.

ambiguïté [ɑ̃bigɥite] *nf* **(a)** (*U*) ambiguousness, ambiguity. **une réponse sans ~** an unequivocal *ou* unambiguous reply; **parler/répondre sans ~** to speak/reply unambiguously *ou* without ambiguity. **(b)** (*terme*) ambiguity.

ambitieusement [ɑ̃bisjøzmɑ̃] *adv* ambitiously.

ambitieux, -euse [ɑ̃bisjø, øz] *adj* ambitious. **c'est un ~** he's an ambitious man; (*littér*) **~ de plaire** desirous of pleasing (*littér*).

ambition [ɑ̃bisjɔ̃] *nf* ambition. **il met toute son ~ à faire** he makes it his sole aim to do.

ambitionner [ɑ̃bisjɔne] (1) *vt* to seek *ou* strive after. **il ambitionne d'escalader l'Everest** it's his ambition to *ou* his ambition is to climb Everest.

ambivalence [ɑ̃bivalɑ̃s] *nf* ambivalence.

ambivalent, e [ɑ̃bivalɑ̃, ɑ̃t] *adj* ambivalent.

amble [ɑ̃bl(ə)] *nm [cheval]* amble. **aller l'~** to amble.

ambler [ɑ̃ble] (1) *vi [cheval]* to amble.

ambre [ɑ̃bʀ(ə)] *nm*: **~ (jaune)** amber; **~ gris** ambergris; **couleur d'~** amber(-coloured).

ambré, e [ɑ̃bʀe] *adj couleur* amber; *parfum* perfumed with ambergris.
Ambroise [ɑ̃bʀwaz] *nm* Ambrose.
ambroisie [ɑ̃bʀwazi] *nf* (*Bot, Myth*) ambrosia. (*fig*) **c'est de l'~!** this is food fit for the gods!
ambrosiaque [ɑ̃bʀozjak] *adj* ambrosial.
ambulance [ɑ̃bylɑ̃s] *nf* ambulance.
ambulancier [ɑ̃bylɑ̃sje] *nm* (*conducteur*) ambulance driver; (*infirmier*) ambulance man.
ambulancière [ɑ̃bylɑ̃sjɛʀ] *nf* ambulance driver; (*infirmière*) ambulance woman.
ambulant, e [ɑ̃bylɑ̃, ɑ̃t] *adj comédien, musicien* itinerant, strolling, travelling. (*fig*) **c'est un squelette/dictionnaire ~*** he's a walking skeleton/dictionary; *V* **marchand.**
ambulatoire [ɑ̃bylatwaʀ] *adj* (*Méd*) ambulatory.
âme [ɑm] *nf* **(a)** (*gén, Philos, Rel*) soul. **(que) Dieu ait son ~** (may) God rest his soul; (*fig*) **avoir l'~ chevillée au corps** to hang on to life, have nine lives (*fig*); **sur mon ~††** upon my word†; *V* **recommander, rendre.**
(b) (*centre de qualités intellectuelles et morales*) heart, soul, mind. **avoir** *ou* **être une ~ généreuse** to have great generosity of spirit; **avoir** *ou* **être une ~ basse** *ou* **vile** to have an evil heart *ou* mind, be evil-hearted *ou* evil-minded; **grandeur** *ou* (*frm*) **noblesse d'~** high- *ou* noble-mindedness; **en mon ~ et conscience** in all conscience *ou* honesty; (*littér*) **de toute mon ~** with all my soul; **il y a mis toute son ~** he put his heart and soul into it.
(c) (*centre psychique et émotif*) soul. **faire qch avec ~** to do sth with feeling; **ému jusqu'au fond de l'~** profoundly moved; **c'est un corps sans ~** he has no soul; **il est musicien dans l'~** he's a musician to the core; **il a la technique mais son jeu est sans ~** he has the technique but he plays without feeling *ou* his playing is soulless.
(d) (*personne*) soul. (*frm*) **un village de 600 ~s** a village of 600 souls; **on ne voyait ~ qui vive** you couldn't see a (living *ou* mortal) soul, there wasn't a (living *ou* mortal) soul to be seen; **bonne ~*** kind soul; **est-ce qu'il n'y aura pas une bonne ~ pour m'aider?** won't some kind soul give me a hand?; (*iro*) **il y a toujours de bonnes ~s pour critiquer** there's always some kind soul ready to criticize (*iro*); (*gén péj*) **~ charitable** kind(ly) *ou* well-meaning soul (*iro*); **il est là/il erre comme une ~ en peine** he looks like/he is wandering about like a lost soul; **être l'~ damnée de qn** to be sb's henchman *ou* tool; **il a trouvé l'~ sœur** he has found a soul mate.
(e) (*principe qui anime*) soul, spirit. **l'~ d'un peuple** the soul *ou* spirit of a nation; **l'~ d'un complot** the moving spirit in a plot; **être l'~ d'un parti** to be the soul *ou* leading light of a party; **elle a une ~ de sœur de charité** she is the very soul *ou* spirit of charity; **elle a une ~ de chef** she has the soul of a leader.
(f) (*Tech*) *[canon]* bore; *[aimant]* core; *[violon]* soundpost; *V* **charge, état, fendre** *etc.*
Amélie [ameli] *nf* Amelia.
améliorable [ameljɔʀabl(ə)] *adj* improvable.
améliorant, e [ameljɔʀɑ̃, ɑ̃t] *adj* (*Agr*) soil-improving.
amélioration [ameljɔʀɑsjɔ̃] *nf* **(a)** (*U: V* **améliorer**) improvement; betterment; amelioration. **l'~ de son état de santé** the improvement of *ou* in *ou* the change for the better in his health.
(b) improvement. **faire des ~s dans, apporter des ~s à** to make *ou* carry out improvements to.
améliorer [ameljɔʀe] (1) **1** *vt* (*gén*) to improve; *situation, sort, statut* to improve, better, ameliorate (*frm*); *domaine, immeuble* to improve. **~ sa situation** to better *ou* improve o.s. *ou* one's situation. **2 s'améliorer** *vpr* to improve.
amen [amɛn] *adv* (*Rel*) amen. **dire ~ à qch/à tout** to say amen to sth/everything, agree religiously to sth/everything.
aménagement [amenaʒmɑ̃] *nm* (*V* **aménager**) fitting-out; laying-out; converting, conversion; fitting-up; putting-in; fixing-up; developing; planning; adjusting. **l'~ du territoire** national and regional development, ≈ town and country planning (*Brit*); **les nouveaux ~s d'un quartier/d'un centre hospitalier** the new developments in *ou* improvements to *ou* in a neighbourhood/hospital; **demander des ~s financiers/d'horaire** to request certain financial adjustments/adjustments to one's timetable.
aménager [amenaʒe] (3) *vt local, bateau* to fit out; *parc, plan d'eau* to lay out; *mansarde, vieille ferme* to convert; *gradins, coin-cuisine, placards* to fit up, put in; *territoire* to develop; *horaire* (*gén*) to plan, work out; (*modifier*) to adjust; *forêt* to manage. **~ un bureau dans une chambre** to fit *ou* fix up a study in a bedroom; **~ une chambre en bureau** to convert a bedroom into a study, fit out a bedroom as a study.
amendable [amɑ̃dabl(ə)] *adj* (*Pol*) amendable; (*Agr*) which can be enriched.
amende [amɑ̃d] *nf* fine. **mettre à l'~** to penalize; **il a eu 5 F d'~** he got a 5-franc fine, he was fined 5 francs; **défense d'entrer sous peine d'~** trespassers will be prosecuted *ou* fined; **faire ~ honorable** to make amends.
amendement [amɑ̃dmɑ̃] *nm* (*Pol*) amendment; (*Agr*) (*opération*) enrichment; (*substance*) enriching agent.
amender [amɑ̃de] (1) **1** *vt* (*Pol*) to amend; (*Agr*) to enrich; *conduite* to improve, amend. **2 s'amender** *vpr* to mend one's ways, amend.
amène [amɛn] *adj* (*littér: aimable*) *propos, visage* affable; *personne, caractère* amiable, affable. **des propos peu ~s** unkind words.
amener [amne] (5) **1** *vt* **(a)** (*faire venir*) *personne, objet* to bring (along); (*acheminer*) *cargaison* to bring, convey. **on nous amène les enfants tous les matins** they bring the children (along) to us every morning, the children are brought (along) to us every morning; **amène-la à la maison** bring her round *ou* along (to the house), bring her home; **le sable est amené à Paris par péniche** sand is brought *ou* conveyed to Paris by barges; **qu'est-ce qui vous amène ici?** what brings you here?; **amène-le une fois au cinéma** do bring him with you to the cinema (*Brit*) *ou* movies (*US*) some time; *V* **bon[1], mandat.**
(b) (*provoquer*) to bring about, cause. **~ la disette** to bring about *ou* cause a shortage; **~ le typhus** to cause typhus.
(c) (*inciter*) **~ qn à faire qch** *[circonstances]* to induce *ou* lead *ou* bring sb to do sth; *[personne]* to bring sb round to doing sth, get sb to do sth; (*par un discours persuasif*) to talk sb into doing sth; **la crise pourrait ~ le gouvernement à agir** the crisis might induce *ou* lead *ou* bring the government to take action; **elle a été finalement amenée à renoncer à son voyage** she was finally induced *ou* driven to give up her trip; **je suis amené à croire que** I am led to believe *ou* think that; **c'est ce qui m'a amené à cette conclusion** that is what led *ou* brought me to that conclusion.
(d) (*diriger*) to bring. **~ qn à ses propres idées/à une autre opinion** to bring sb round to one's own ideas/another way of thinking; **~ la conversation sur un sujet** to bring the conversation round to a subject, lead the conversation on to a subject; **système amené à un haut degré de complexité** system brought to a high degree of complexity.
(e) *transition, conclusion, dénouement* to present, introduce. **exemple bien amené** well-introduced example.
(f) (*Pêche*) *poisson* to draw in; (*Naut*) *voile, pavillon* to strike. (*Mil*) **~ les couleurs** to strike colours.
(g) (*Dés*) *paire, brelan* to throw.
2 s'amener* *vpr* (*venir*) to come along. **allez-vous ~?** are you going to get a move on?*, come along!; **il s'est amené avec toute sa bande** he came along *ou* turned up *ou* showed up* with the whole gang.
aménité [amenite] *nf* (*amabilité*) *[propos]* affability; *[personne, caractère]* amiability, affability. **sans ~** unkindly; (*iro*) **se dire des ~s** to exchange uncomplimentary remarks.
amenuisement [amənɥizmɑ̃] *nm [valeur, avance, espoir]* dwindling; *[chances]* lessening; *[ressources]* diminishing, dwindling.
amenuiser [amənɥize] (1) **1 s'amenuiser** *vpr [valeur, avance, espoir]* to dwindle; *[chances]* to grow slimmer, lessen; *[provisions, ressources]* to run low, diminish, dwindle; *[temps]* to run out; *[planche]* to get thinner.
2 *vt objet* to thin down; (*fig*) to reduce.
amer[1] [amɛʀ] *nm* (*Naut*) seamark.
amer[2], -ère [amɛʀ] *adj* (*lit, fig*) bitter. **~ comme chicotin*** as bitter as wormwood; **avoir la bouche ~ère** to have a bitter taste in one's mouth.
amèrement [amɛʀmɑ̃] *adv* bitterly.
américain, e [ameʀikɛ̃, ɛn] **1** *adj* American. **à l'~e** (*gén*) in the American style; (*Culin*) à l'Américaine; *V* **œil. 2** *nm* (*Ling*) American (English). **3** *nm,f*: **A~(e)** American. **4 américaine** *nf* (*automobile*) American car.
américanisation [ameʀikanizɑsjɔ̃] *nf* americanization.
américaniser [ameʀikanize] (1) **1** *vt* to americanize. **2 s'américaniser** *vpr* to become americanized.
américanisme [ameʀikanism(ə)] *nm* americanism.
américaniste [ameʀikanist(ə)] *nmf* Americanist, American specialist.
amérindien, -ienne [ameʀɛ̃djɛ̃, jɛn] *adj* Amerindian, American Indian.
Amérique [ameʀik] *nf* America. **~ centrale/latine/du Nord/du Sud** Central/Latin/North/South America.
Amerloque: [amɛʀlɔk] *nmf*, **Amerlo(t):** [amɛʀlo] *nm* Yankee*, Yank*.
amerrir [ameʀiʀ] (2) *vi* (*Aviat*) to land (on the sea); (*Espace*) to splash down.
amerrissage [ameʀisaʒ] *nm* (*Aviat*) (sea) landing; (*Espace*) splashdown.
amertume [amɛʀtym] *nf* (*lit, fig*) bitterness. **plein d'~** full of bitterness, very bitter.
améthyste [ametist(ə)] *nf, adj inv* amethyst.
ameublement [amœbləmɑ̃] *nm* (*meubles*) furniture; (*action*) furnishing. **articles d'~** furnishings; **commerce d'~** furniture trade.
ameublir [amœbliʀ] (2) *vt* (*Agr*) to loosen, break down.
ameuter [amøte] (1) **1** *vt* **(a)** (*attrouper*) *curieux, passants* to bring *ou* draw a crowd of; *voisins* to bring out; (*soulever*) *foule* to rouse, stir up, incite (*contre* against). **ses cris ameutèrent les passants** his shouts brought *ou* drew a crowd of passers-by; **tais-toi, tu vas ~ toute la rue!*** be quiet, you'll have the whole street out!
(b) *chiens* to form into a pack.
2 s'ameuter *vpr* (*s'attrouper*) *[passants]* to gather, mass; *[voisins]* to come out; (*se soulever*) to band together (with riotous intent), gather into a mob. **des passants s'ameutèrent** a crowd of passers-by gathered (angrily).
ami, e [ami] **1** *nm,f* **(a)** friend. **c'est un vieil ~ de la famille** *ou* **de la maison** he's an old friend of the family; **c'est un/mon ~ d'enfance** he's a/my childhood friend; **~ intime** (very) close *ou* intimate friend, bosom friend; **il m'a présenté son ~e** he introduced his girlfriend to me; **elle est sortie avec ses ~es** she's out with her (girl)friends; **se faire un ~ de qn** to make *ou* become friends with sb, become a friend of sb; **faire ~ avec qn*** to make friends with sb; **nous sommes entre ~s** (*2 personnes*) we're friends; (*plus de 2*) we're all friends; **je vous dis ça en ~** I'm telling you this as a friend; **~s des bêtes/de la nature** animal/nature lovers; **société** *ou* **club des ~s de Balzac** Balzac club *ou* society; **un célibataire/professeur de mes ~s** a bachelor/teacher friend of mine; **être sans ~s** to be friendless, have no

friends; **parents et ~s** friends and relations *ou* relatives; **~ des arts** patron of the arts; **l'~ de l'homme** man's best friend.
(b) (*euph*) (*amant*) boyfriend (*euph*); (*maîtresse*) girlfriend (*euph*). **l'~e de l'assassin** the murderer's lady-friend (*euph*); *V* **bon**[1], **petit.**
(c) (*interpellation*) **mes chers ~s** gentlemen; (*auditoire mixte*) ladies and gentlemen; **mon cher ~** my dear fellow *ou* chap (*Brit*); **ça, mon (petit) ~** now look here; **ben mon ~!* si j'avais su** blimey!* (*Brit*) *ou* crikey!* (*Brit*) if I had known that; (*entre époux*) **oui mon ~!** yes my dear.
2 *adj visage, pays* friendly; *regard* kindly, friendly. **tendre à qn une main ~e** to lend *ou* give sb a friendly *ou* helping hand; **être très ~ avec qn** to be very friendly *ou* (very) great *ou* good friends with sb; **nous sommes très ~s** we're very close *ou* good friends, we're very friendly; **être ~ de l'ordre** to be a lover of order.

amiable [amjabl(ə)] *adj* (*Jur*) amicable. **à l'~: vente à l'~** private sale, sale by private agreement; **partage à l'~** private *ou* amicable partition; **accord** *ou* **règlement à l'~** friendly *ou* amicable agreement *ou* arrangement; **régler** *ou* **liquider une affaire à l'~** to settle a difference out of court.

amiante [amjɑ̃t] *nm* asbestos. **plaque/fils d'~** asbestos sheet *ou* plate/thread.

amibe [amib] *nf* amoeba.

amibiase [amibjaz] *nf* amoebiasis.

amibien, -ienne [amibjɛ̃, jɛn] **1** *adj maladie* amoebic. **2** *nmpl*: **~s** Amoebae.

amical, e, *mpl* **-aux** [amikal, o] **1** *adj* friendly. **peu ~** unfriendly. **2 amicale** *nf* association (*of people having the same interest*). **~e des anciens élèves** old boys' association.

amicalement [amikalmɑ̃] *adv* in a friendly way. **il m'a salué ~** he gave me a friendly wave; (*formule épistolaire*) **(bien) ~** kind regards, best wishes, yours (ever).

amidon [amidɔ̃] *nm* starch.

amidonnage [amidɔnaʒ] *nm* starching.

amidonner [amidɔne] (1) *vt* to starch.

amincir [amɛ̃siʀ] (2) **1** *vt* (*en rabotant, par laminage, usure etc*) to thin (down). **cette robe l'amincit/amincit ta taille** this dress makes her/your waist look slim(mer) *ou* thin(ner); **visage aminci par la tension** face drawn with tension *ou* hollow with anxiety.
2 s'amincir *vpr [couche de glace, épaisseur de tissu]* to get thinner.

amincissement [amɛ̃sismɑ̃] *nm* thinning (down). **j'ai remarqué l'~ de sa taille** I noticed her slim(mer) waist, I noticed her waist had got thinner; **l'~ de la couche de glace a causé l'accident** the thinning of the layer of ice was the cause of the accident; **cure d'~** slimming treatment (*U*).

aminé, e [amine] *adj V* **acide.**

amiral, e, *mpl* **-aux** [amiʀal, o] **1** *adj*: **vaisseau** *ou* **bateau ~** flagship. **2** *nm* (*hum*) admiral; *V* **contre, vice-. 3 amirale** *nf* admiral's wife.

amirauté [amiʀote] *nf* admiralty.

amitié [amitje] *nf* **(a)** (*sentiment*) friendship. **prendre qn en ~, se prendre d'~ pour qn** to take a liking to sb, befriend sb; **se lier d'~ avec qn,** (*littér*) **nouer une ~ avec qn** to strike up a friendship with sb; **avoir de l'~ pour qn** to be fond of sb, have a liking for sb; **faites-moi l'~ de venir** do me the kindness *ou* favour of coming; **l'~ franco-britannique** Anglo-French *ou* Franco-British friendship; **~ particulière** (*entre hommes*) homosexual relationship; (*entre femmes*) lesbian relationship.
(b) (*formule épistolaire*) **~s** all the very best, very best wishes *ou* regards; **(affectueuses) ~s, Paul** love (from) Paul; **~s, Paul** kind regards, Paul, yours, Paul; **elle vous fait** *ou* **transmet toutes ses ~s** she sends her best wishes *ou* regards.
(c) (†: *civilités*) **faire mille ~s à qn** to give sb a warm and friendly welcome.

ammoniac, -aque [amɔnjak] **1** *adj* ammoniac. **sel ~** sal ammoniac; **gomme ammoniaque** gum ammoniac. **2** *nm* (*gaz*) ammonia. **3 ammoniaque** *nf* ammonia (water).

ammoniacal, e, *mpl* **-aux** [amɔnjakal, o] *adj* ammoniacal.

ammonite [amɔnit] *nf* (*Zool*) ammonite.

ammonium [amɔnjɔm] *nm* ammonium.

amnésie [amnezi] *nf* amnesia.

amnésique [amnezik] **1** *adj* amnesic. **2** *nmf* amnesiac.

amnistie [amnisti] *nf* amnesty. **loi d'~** law of amnesty.

amnistier [amnistje] (7) *vt* to amnesty, grant an amnesty to. **les amnistiés** the amnestied prisoners.

amocher‡ [amɔʃe] (1) *vt objet, personne* to mess up*, make a mess of*; *véhicule* to bash up*. **tu l'as drôlement amoché** you've made a terrible mess of him*, you've messed him up something terrible*; **se faire ~ dans un accident/une bagarre** to get messed up* in an accident/a fight; **il/la voiture était drôlement amoché(e)** he/the car was a terrible mess*; **il s'est drôlement amoché en tombant** he gave himself a terrible bash* *ou* made a real mess of himself* when he fell.

amoindrir [amwɛ̃dʀiʀ] (2) **1** *vt autorité* to lessen, weaken; *forces* to weaken; *fortune, quantité* to diminish, reduce; *personne* (*physiquement*) to make weaker, weaken; (*moralement, mentalement*) to diminish. **~ qn (aux yeux des autres)** to belittle sb (in the eyes of others).
2 s'amoindrir *vpr [autorité, facultés]* to grow weaker, weaken, diminish; *[forces]* to weaken, grow weaker; *[quantité, fortune]* to diminish, grow less.

amoindrissement [amwɛ̃dʀismɑ̃] *nm* (*V* **amoindrir**) lessening; weakening; diminishing; reduction.

amollir [amɔliʀ] (2) **1** *vt chose* to soften, make soft; *personne* (*moralement*) to soften; (*physiquement*) to weaken, make weak; *volonté, forces, résolution* to weaken. **cette chaleur vous amollit** this heat makes one feel (quite) limp *ou* weak.
2 s'amollir *vpr [chose]* to go soft; (*s'affaiblir*) *[courage, énergie]* to weaken; *[jambes]* to go weak; *[personne] (perdre courage, énergie)* to grow soft, weaken; (*s'attendrir*) to soften, relent.

amollissant, e [amɔlisɑ̃, ɑ̃t] *adj climat, plaisirs* enervating.

amollissement [amɔlismɑ̃] *nm* (*V* **amollir**) softening; weakening. **l'~ général est dû à ...** the general weakening of purpose *ou* loss of stamina is due to ... .

amonceler [amɔ̃sle] (4) **1** *vt choses* to pile *ou* heap up; *richesses* to amass, accumulate; *difficultés* to accumulate; *documents, preuves* to pile up, accumulate, amass.
2 s'amonceler *vpr [choses]* to pile *ou* heap up; *[courrier, demandes]* to pile up, accumulate; *[nuages]* to bank up; *[neige]* to drift into banks, bank up. **les preuves s'amoncellent contre lui** the evidence is building up *ou* piling up against him.

amoncellement [amɔ̃sɛlmɑ̃] *nm* **(a)** (*V* **amonceler**) piling up; heaping up; banking up; amassing; accumulating. **(b)** *[choses]* pile, heap, mass; *[idées]* accumulation.

amont [amɔ̃] *nm [cours d'eau]* upstream water; *[pente]* uphill slope. **en ~** upstream, upriver; uphill; **en ~ de** upstream *ou* upriver from; uphill from, above; **les rapides/l'écluse d'~** the upstream rapids/lock; **l'~ était coupé de rapides** the river upstream was a succession of rapids; **le skieur/le ski ~** the uphill skier/ski.

amoral, e, *mpl* **-aux** [amɔʀal, o] *adj* amoral.

amoralisme [amɔʀalism(ə)] *nm* amorality.

amorçage [amɔʀsaʒ] *nm* **(a)** (*action: V* **amorcer**) baiting; ground baiting; priming; energizing. **(b)** (*dispositif*) priming cap, primer.

amorce [amɔʀs(ə)] *nf* **(a)** (*Pêche*) *[hameçon]* bait; *[emplacement]* ground bait.
(b) (*explosif*) *[cartouche]* cap, primer, priming; *[obus]* percussion cap; *[mine]* priming; *[pistolet d'enfant]* cap.
(c) (*début*) *[route]* initial section; *[trou]* start; (*Ciné*) leader; *[conversations, négociations]* beginning; *[idée, projet]* beginning, germ. **l'~ d'une réforme/d'un changement** the beginnings (*pl*) of a reform/change.

amorcer [amɔʀse] (3) *vt* **(a)** *hameçon, ligne* to bait. **il amorce au ver de vase** (*ligne*) he baits his line with worms; (*emplacement*) he uses worms as ground bait.
(b) *pompe* to prime; *dynamo* to energize; *syphon, obus* to prime.
(c) *route, tunnel, travaux* to start *ou* begin (building); *trou* to begin *ou* start to bore. **la construction est amorcée depuis 2 mois** work has been in progress *ou* been under way for 2 months.
(d) (*commencer*) *réformes, évolution* to initiate, begin; *virage* to begin. **il amorça un geste pour prendre la tasse** he made as if to take the cup; **~ la rentrée dans l'atmosphère** to initiate re-entry into the earth's atmosphere; **une descente s'amorce après le virage** after the bend the road starts to go down.
(e) (*Pol: entamer*) *conversations* to start (up); *négociations* to start, begin. **une détente est amorcée** *ou* **s'amorce** there are signs of (the beginnings of) a détente.
(f) (†: *attirer*) *client* to allure, entice.

amorphe [amɔʀf(ə)] *adj* **(a)** (*apathique*) *personne* passive, lifeless, spiritless; *esprit, caractère, attitude* passive. **(b)** (*Minér*) amorphous.

amorti, e [amɔʀti] (*ptp de* **amortir**) *nm,f* **(a)** (*Ftbl*) **faire un ~** to trap the ball; (*Tennis*) **un(e) ~(e)** a drop shot. **(b)** (‡: *personne âgée*) old fogey*.

amortir [amɔʀtiʀ] (2) *vt* **(a)** (*diminuer*) *choc* to absorb, cushion; *coup, chute* to cushion, soften; *bruit* to deaden, muffle; *passions, douleur* to deaden, dull.
(b) (*Fin*) *dette* to pay off, amortize (*T*); *action* to redeem; *matériel* to write off, depreciate (*T*). (*gén*) **il utilise sa voiture le plus souvent possible pour l'~** he uses his car as often as possible to make it pay *ou* to recoup the cost to himself; **maintenant, notre équipement est amorti** now we have written off the (capital) cost of the equipment.
(c) (*Archit*) to put an amortizement on.

amortissable [amɔʀtisabl(ə)] *adj* (*Fin*) redeemable.

amortissement [amɔʀtismɑ̃] *nm* **(a)** (*Fin*) *[dette] (remboursement)* paying off; (*jeu d'écritures*) writing off; *[action]* redemption; *[matériel] (jeu d'écritures)* depreciation; (*montant*) reserve *ou* provision for depreciation. (*gén*) **l'~ de ce matériel se fait en 3 ans** this equipment takes 3 years to pay for itself, it takes 3 years for the cost of this equipment to write itself off.
(b) (*rare: diminution*) (*V* **amortir**) absorption; cushioning; softening; deadening; muffling; dulling; (*Phys*) damping.
(c) (*Archit*) amortizement.

amortisseur [amɔʀtisœʀ] *nm* shock absorber.

amour [amuʀ] **1** *nm* **(a)** (*sentiment*) love. **parler d'~** to speak of love; **se nourrir** *ou* **vivre d'~ et d'eau fraîche*** to live on love alone; **~ platonique** platonic love; **lettre/mariage/roman d'~** love letter/match/story; **fou d'~** madly *ou* wildly in love; **~ fou** wild love *ou* passion, mad love; **ce n'est plus de l'~, c'est de la rage*** it's not love, it's raving madness!*; *V* **filer, saison.**
(b) (*acte*) love-making (*U*). **pendant l'~, elle murmurait des mots tendres** while they were making love *ou* during their love-making, she murmured tender words; **l'~ libre** free love; **l'~ physique** physical love; **faire l'~** to make love (*avec* to, with).
(c) (*personne*) love; (*aventure*) love affair. **premier ~** (*personne*) first love; (*aventure*) first love (affair); **ses ~s de jeunesse** (*aventures*) the love affairs *ou* loves of his youth; (*personnes*) the loves *ou* lovers of his youth; **c'est un ~ de jeunesse** she's one of his old loves *ou* flames*†; **des ~s de rencontre** casual love affairs; (*hum*) **à tes ~s!*** (*quand on*

trinque) here's to you!; (*quand on éternue*) bless you!; (*hum*) **comment vont tes ~s?*** how's your love life?* (*hum*).

(d) (*terme d'affection*) **mon ~** my love, my sweet; **cet enfant est un ~** that child's a real darling; **passe-moi l'eau, tu seras un ~** be a darling *ou* dear and pass me the water, pass me the water, there's a darling *ou* a dear; **un ~ de bébé/de petite robe** a lovely *ou* sweet little baby/dress.

(e) (*Art*) cupid. (*Myth*) **(le dieu) A~** Eros, Cupid.

(f) (*loc*) **pour l'~ de Dieu** for God's sake, for the love of God; **pour l'~ de votre mère** for your mother's sake; **faire qch pour l'~ de l'art*** to do sth for the love of it *ou* for love*; **avoir l'~ du travail bien fait** to have a great love for work well done, love to see work well done; **faire qch avec ~** to do sth with loving care.

2 *nfpl* (*littér*) **~s** (*personnes*) loves; (*aventures*) love affairs; (*hum*) **~s ancillaires** amorous adventures with the servants.

3: amour-propre *nm* self-esteem, pride. **blessure d'amour-propre** wound to one's self-esteem *ou* pride.

amouracher (s') [amuʀaʃe] (1) *vpr* (*péj*) **s'~ de** to become infatuated with (*péj*).

amourette [amuʀɛt] *nf* passing fancy, passing love affair.

amoureusement [amuʀøzmɑ̃] *adv* lovingly, amorously.

amoureux, -euse [amuʀø, øz] **1** *adj* **(a)** (*épris*) *personne* in love (*de* with). **être ~ de la musique/la nature** to be passionately fond of *ou* a lover of music/nature; (*fig hum*) **il est ~ de sa voiture** he's in love with his car (*hum*); *V* **tomber**.

(b) (*d'amour*) *aventures* amorous, love (*épith*). **déboires ~** disappointments in love; **vie ~euse** love life.

(c) (*ardent*) *tempérament, personne* amorous; *regard* (*tendre*) loving; (*voluptueux*) amorous.

2 *nm,f* (†: *soupirant*) lover, love†, sweetheart†. (*fig*) **~ de** lover of; **un ~ de la nature** a nature lover, a lover of nature; **~ transi** bashful lover.

amovibilité [amɔvibilite] *nf* (*Jur*) removability.

amovible [amɔvibl(ə)] *adj doublure, housse, panneau* removable, detachable; (*Jur*) removable.

ampère [ɑ̃pɛʀ] *nm* ampere, amp.

ampèremètre [ɑ̃pɛʀmɛtʀ(ə)] *nm* ammeter.

amphétamine [ɑ̃fetamin] *nf* amphetamine.

amphi [ɑ̃fi] *nm* (*arg Univ*) *abrév de* **amphithéâtre.**

amphibie [ɑ̃fibi] **1** *adj* amphibious. **2** *nm* amphibian.

amphibiens [ɑ̃fibjɛ̃] *nmpl* amphibia, amphibians.

amphigouri [ɑ̃figuʀi] *nm* amphigory.

amphithéâtre [ɑ̃fiteɑtʀ(ə)] *nm* (*Archit*) amphitheatre; (*Univ*) lecture hall *ou* theatre; (*Théât*) (upper) gallery. (*Géol*) **~ morainique** morainic cirque *ou* amphitheatre.

amphitryon [ɑ̃fitʀijɔ̃] *nm* (*hum, littér: hôte*) host.

amphore [ɑ̃fɔʀ] *nf* amphora.

ample [ɑ̃pl(ə)] *adj manteau* roomy, ample; *jupe* full, ample; *manche* broad, ample; *geste* bountiful, liberal; *voix* full; *style* spacious; *projet* vast; *vues, sujet* wide-ranging, extensive. **faire ~(s) provision(s) de** to gather a bountiful supply *ou* a liberal stock of; **donner ~ matériel à discussion** to give ample material for discussion; (*frm*) **jusqu'à plus ~ informé** until fuller *ou* further information is available; **pour plus ~ informé je tenais à vous dire ...** for your further information I should tell you ... .

amplement [ɑ̃pləmɑ̃] *adv expliquer, mériter* fully, amply. **il a fait ~ ce qu'on lui demandait** he has more than done what was asked of him; **gagner ~ sa vie** to earn a very good *ou* ample living; **ça suffit ~, c'est ~ suffisant** that's more than enough, that's ample.

ampleur [ɑ̃plœʀ] *nf* **(a)** *[vêtement, voix]* fullness; *[geste]* liberalness; *[style, récit]* opulence; *[vues, sujet, problème]* extent, scope, range; *[projet]* vastness, scope. **donner de l'~ à une robe** to give fullness to a dress.

(b) (*importance*) *[crise]* scale, extent; *[dégâts]* extent. **devant l'~ de la catastrophe** in the face of the sheer scale *ou* extent of the catastrophe; **vu l'~ des dégâts ...** in view of the widespread damage *ou* the extent of the damage ...; **l'~ des moyens mis en œuvre** the sheer size *ou* the massive scale of the measures implemented; **sans grande ~** of limited scope, small-scale (*épith*); **ces manifestations prennent de l'~** these demonstrations are growing *ou* increasing in scale *ou* extent *ou* are becoming more extensive.

ampli [ɑ̃pli] *nm abrév de* **amplificateur.**

amplificateur [ɑ̃plifikatœʀ] *nm* (*Phys, Rad*) amplifier; (*Phot*) enlarger (*permitting only fixed enlarging*).

amplification [ɑ̃plifikɑsjɔ̃] *nf* (*V* **amplifier**) development; expansion; increase; amplification; magnification; (*Phot*) enlarging; (*Opt*) magnifying.

amplifier [ɑ̃plifje] (7) **1** *vt* **(a)** (*accentuer, développer*) *tendance* to develop, accentuate; *mouvement, échanges, coopération* to expand, increase, develop; *pensée* to expand, develop, amplify; (*péj*) *incident* to magnify, exaggerate.

(b) (*Tech*) *son, courant* to amplify; *image* to magnify.

2 s'amplifier *vpr [mouvement, tendance, échange]* to grow, increase; *[pensée]* to expand, develop.

amplitude [ɑ̃plityd] *nf* **(a)** (*Astron, Phys*) amplitude. (*Géom*) **l'~ d'un arc** the length of the chord subtending an arc. **(b)** *[températures]* range. **(c)** (*fig: importance*) **l'~ de la catastrophe** the magnitude of the catastrophe.

ampoule [ɑ̃pul] *nf* (*Élec*) bulb; (*Pharm*) phial; (*Méd*) *[main, pied]* blister.

ampoulé, e [ɑ̃pule] *adj style* turgid, pompous, bombastic.

amputation [ɑ̃pytɑsjɔ̃] *nf* (*Anat*) amputation; (*fig*) *[texte, roman, fortune]* drastic cut *ou* reduction (*de* in); *[budget]* drastic cutback *ou* reduction (*de* in).

amputer [ɑ̃pyte] (1) *vt* **(a)** (*Anat*) to amputate. **il est amputé d'une jambe** he has had a leg amputated; **c'est un amputé** he has lost an arm (*ou* a leg), he has had an arm (*ou* a leg) off*.

(b) (*fig*) *texte, roman, fortune* to cut *ou* reduce drastically; *budget* to cut back *ou* reduce drastically (*de* by). **~ un pays d'une partie de son territoire** to sever a country of a part of its territory.

amuïr (s') [amɥiʀ] (2) *vpr* (*Phonétique*) to become mute, drop (*in pronunciation*).

amuïssement [amɥismɑ̃] *nm* (*Phonétique*) *dropping of a phoneme in pronunciation.*

amulette [amylɛt] *nf* amulet.

amure [amyʀ] *nf* (*Naut*) tack. **aller bâbord/tribord ~s** to go on the port/starboard tack.

amurer [amyʀe] (1) *vt voile* to haul aboard the tack of, tack.

amusant, e [amyzɑ̃, ɑ̃t] *adj* (*distrayant*) *jeu* amusing, entertaining; (*drôle*) *film, remarque, convive* amusing, funny. **c'est (très) ~** (*distrayant*) it's (great) fun *ou* (very) entertaining; (*surprenant*) it's (very) amusing *ou* funny; **l'~ de l'histoire c'est que** the funny part of the story is that, the amusing part about it all is that.

amuse-gueule, *pl* **amuse-gueules** [amyzgœl] *nm* appetizer, snack.

amusement [amyzmɑ̃] *nm* **(a)** (*divertissement*) amusement (*U*). **pour l'~ des enfants** for the children's amusement *ou* entertainment, to amuse *ou* entertain the children; **prendre de l'~ à faire qch** to get enjoyment out of doing sth.

(b) (*jeu*) toy; (*activité*) diversion, pastime.

(c) (*hilarité*) amusement (*U*).

amuser [amyze] (1) **1** *vt* **(a)** (*divertir*) to amuse, entertain; (*non intentionnellement*) to amuse.

(b) (*faire rire*) *histoire drôle* to amuse. **ces remarques ne m'amusent pas du tout** I don't find these remarks in the least bit funny *ou* amusing, I'm not in the least amused by such remarks; **toi tu m'amuses avec tes grandes théories** you make me laugh *ou* you amuse me with your great theories; **faire le pitre pour ~ la galerie** *ou* **le tapis** to clown about and play to the crowd, clown about to amuse the crowd.

(c) (*plaire*) **ça ne m'amuse pas de devoir aller leur rehdre visite** I don't enjoy having to go and visit them; **si tu crois que ces réunions m'amusent** if you think I enjoy these meetings.

(d) (*détourner l'attention de*) *ennemi, caissier* to distract (the attention of), divert the attention of. **pendant que tu l'amuses, je prends l'argent** while you keep him busy *ou* distract his attention, I'll take the money.

(e) (*tromper: par promesses etc*) to delude, beguile.

2 s'amuser *vpr* **(a)** (*jouer*) *[enfants]* to play. **s'~ avec** *jouet, personne, chien* to play with; *stylo, ficelle* to play *ou* fiddle *ou* toy with; **s'~ à un jeu** to play a game; **s'~ à faire** to amuse o.s. doing, play at doing; **pour s'~ ils allumèrent un grand feu de joie** they lit a big bonfire for a lark; (*fig*) **ne t'amuse pas à recommencer, sinon!** don't you do *ou* start that again, or else!

(b) (*se divertir*) to have fun *ou* a good time, enjoy o.s.; (*rire*) to have a good laugh. **s' ~ à faire** to play about *ou* have fun doing; **nous nous sommes amusés comme des fous à écouter ses histoires** we laughed ourselves silly listening to his jokes; **nous nous sommes bien amusés** we had great fun *ou* a great time*; **qu'est-ce qu'on s'amuse!** this is great fun!; **j'aime autant te dire qu'on ne s'est pas amusés** it wasn't much fun, I can tell you; **on ne va pas s'~ à cette réunion** we're not going to have much fun *ou* enjoy it much at this meeting; **on ne faisait rien de mal, c'était juste pour s'~** we weren't doing any harm, it was just for fun *ou* for a laugh.

(c) (*batifoler*) to mess about. **il ne faut pas qu'on s'amuse** (*il faut se dépêcher*) we mustn't dawdle; (*il faut travailler dur*) we mustn't idle.

(d) (*littér: se jouer de*) **s'~ de qn** to make a fool of sb.

amusette [amyzɛt] *nf* diversion. **elle n'a été pour lui qu'une ~** she was mere sport to him, she was just a passing fancy for him; **au lieu de perdre ton temps à des ~s tu ferais mieux de travailler** instead of frittering your time away on idle pleasures you'd do better to work.

amuseur, -euse [amyzœʀ, øz] *nm,f* entertainer. (*péj*) **ce n'est qu'un ~** he's just a clown.

amygdale [amidal] *nf* tonsil.

amygdalite [amidalit] *nf* tonsillitis.

amylacé, e [amilase] *adj* starchy, amylaceous (*T*).

amylase [amilɑz] *nf* amylase.

an [ɑ̃] *nm* **(a)** (*durée*) year. **après 5 ~s de prison** after 5 years in prison; **dans 3 ~s** in 3 years, in 3 years' time; **une amitié de 20 ~s** a friendship of 20 years' standing.

(b) (*âge*) year. **un enfant de six ~s** a six-year-old child, a six-year-old; **il a 22 ~s** he is 22 (years old); **il n'a pas encore 10 ~s** he's not yet 10.

(c) (*point dans le temps*) year. **4 fois par ~** 4 times a year; **il reçoit tant par ~** he gets so much a year *ou* annually *ou* per annum; **le jour** *ou* **le premier de l'~, le nouvel ~** New Year's Day; **en l'~ 300 de Rome** in the Roman year 300; **en l'~ 300 de notre ère/avant Jésus-Christ** in (the year) 300 A.D./B.C.; (*frm, hum*) **en l'~ de grâce ...** in the year of grace ...; **je m'en moque** *ou* **je m'en soucie comme de l'~ quarante** I couldn't care, less (about it); *V* **bon**[1].

(d) (*littér*) **~s: les ~s l'ont courbé** he has become bowed *ou* hunched with age; **l'outrage des ~s** the ravages of time; **courbé sous le poids des ~s** bent under the weight of years *ou* age.

ana [ana] *nm* ana.

anabaptisme [anabatism(ə)] *nm* anabaptism.

anabaptiste [anabatist(ə)] *adj, nmf* anabaptist.

anabolisme [anabɔlism(ə)] *nm* anabolism.

anacarde [anakaʀd(ə)] *nm* cashew (nut).

anacardier [anakaʀdje] *nm* cashew (tree).

anachorète [anakɔʀɛt] *nm* anchorite.

anachronique [anakʀɔnik] *adj* anachronistic, anachronous.
anachronisme [anakʀɔnism(ə)] *nm* anachronism.
anacoluthe [anakɔlyt] *nf* anacoluthon.
anaconda [anakɔ̃da] *nm* anaconda.
anacréontique [anakʀeɔ̃tik] *adj* anacreontic.
anaérobie [anaeʀɔbi] **1** *adj* anaerobic. **2** *nm* anaerobe.
anagrammatique [anagʀamatik] *adj* anagrammatical.
anagramme [anagʀam] *nf* anagram.
anal, e, *mpl* **-aux** [anal, o] *adj* anal.
analgésie [analʒezi] *nf* analgesia.
analgésique [analʒezik] *adj, nm* analgesic.
analogie [analɔʒi] *nf* analogy. **par ~ avec** by analogy with.
analogique [analɔʒik] *adj* analogical.
analogiquement [analɔʒikmɑ̃] *adv* analogically.
analogue [analɔg] **1** *adj* analogous, similar (*à* to). **2** *nm* analogue.
analphabète [analfabɛt] **1** *adj* illiterate, analphabetic. **2** *nmf* illiterate.
analphabétisme [analfabetism(ə)] *nm* illiteracy.
analysable [analizabl(ə)] *adj* analysable (*Brit*), analyzable (*US*).
analyse [analiz] **1** *nf* **(a)** (*Chim, Gram, Logique: examen*) analysis. **faire l'~ de** *pensées, désirs, craintes* to analyse; *ouvrage scientifique* to make an analysis of, analyse (*Brit*), analyze (*US*); *phrase* to analyse; (*analyse traditionnelle ou scolaire*) to parse; **ce qu'il soutient ne résiste pas à l'~** what he maintains doesn't stand up to analysis; **avoir l'esprit d'~** to have an analytic(al) mind.
(b) (*Méd*) test. **~ de sang/d'urine** blood/urine test; **se faire faire des ~s** to have some tests (done); *V* **laboratoire.**
(c) (*Psych*) psychoanalysis, analysis. **il poursuit une ~** he's undergoing *ou* having psychoanalysis *ou* analysis.
(d) (*Math*) (*discipline*) calculus; (*exercice*) analysis.
2: analyse combinatoire combinatorial analysis; **analyse grammaticale** parsing; **analyse logique** sentence analysis; **analyse de marché** market analysis; **analyse spectrale** spectrum analysis; **analyse du travail** job analysis.
analyser [analize] (1) *vt* (*gén*) to analyse; (*Méd*) *sang, urine* to test; (*analyse grammaticale, traditionnelle ou scolaire*) to parse.
analyste [analist(ə)] *nmf* (*gén, Math*) analyst; (*psychanalyste*) psychoanalyst, analyst. **~-programmeur** systems analyst.
analytique [analitik] **1** *adj* analytic(al). **2** *nf* analytics (*sg*).
analytiquement [analitikmɑ̃] *adv* analytically.
ananas [anana(s)] *nm* (*fruit, plante*) pineapple.
anapeste [anapɛst(ə)] *nm* anapaest.
anaphore [anafɔʀ] *nf* anaphora.
anaphorique [anafɔʀik] *adj* anaphoric.
anar* [anaʀ] *nmf abrév de* **anarchiste.**
anarchie [anaʀʃi] *nf* (*Pol, fig*) anarchy.
anarchique [anaʀʃik] *adj* anarchic(al).
anarchiquement [anaʀʃikmɑ̃] *adv* anarchically.
anarchisant, e [anaʀʃizɑ̃, ɑ̃t] *adj personne, groupe* with anarchic leanings (*attrib*); *théories, tendances* anarchistic.
anarchisme [anaʀʃism(ə)] *nm* anarchism.
anarchiste [anaʀʃist(ə)] **1** *adj* anarchistic. **2** *nmf* anarchist.
anarcho-syndicalisme [anaʀʃɔsɛ̃dikalism(ə)] *nm* anarcho-syndicalism.
anarcho-syndicaliste, *pl* **anarcho-syndicalistes** [anaʀʃɔsɛ̃dikalist(ə)] *nmf* anarcho-syndicalist.
anastigmat [anastigma] *adj m, nm:* **(objectif) ~** anastigmat, anastigmatic lens.
anastigmatique [anastigmatik] *adj* anastigmatic.
anastrophe [anastʀɔf] *nf* anastrophe.
anathématiser [anatematize] (1) *vt* (*lit, fig*) to anathematize.
anathème [anatɛm] *nm* (*excommunication, excommunié*) anathema. (*fig*) **jeter l'~ sur** to anathematize, curse; (*Rel*) **prononcer un ~ contre qn, frapper qn d'un ~** to excommunicate sb, anathematize sb.
anatomie [anatɔmi] *nf* **(a)** (*science*) anatomy.
(b) (*corps*) anatomy. **elle a une belle ~*** she has a smashing figure*.
(c) (††: *dissection*) (*Méd*) anatomy; (*fig*) analysis. **faire l'~ de** to dissect (*fig*), analyse; **pièce d'~** anatomical subject.
anatomique [anatɔmik] *adj* anatomical, anatomic.
anatomiquement [anatɔmikmɑ̃] *adv* anatomically.
anatomiste [anatɔmist(ə)] *nmf* anatomist.
ancestral, e, *mpl* **-aux** [ɑ̃sɛstʀal, o] *adj* ancestral.
ancêtre [ɑ̃sɛtʀ(ə)] *nmf* **(a)** (*aïeul*) ancestor; (*: *vieillard*) old man (*ou* woman). **nos ~s du Moyen Âge** our ancestors *ou* forefathers *ou* forbears of the Middle Ages.
(b) (*fig: précurseur*) *[personne, objet]* ancestor, forerunner, precursor. **c'est l'~ de la littérature moderne** he's the father of modern literature.
anche [ɑ̃ʃ] *nf* (*Mus*) reed.
anchois [ɑ̃ʃwa] *nm* anchovy.
ancien, -ienne [ɑ̃sjɛ̃, jɛn] **1** *adj* **(a)** (*vieux*) *coutume, château, loi* ancient; *livre, mobilier, objet d'art* antique. **les plus ~nes familles de la région** the oldest families in the region; **il est plus ~ que moi dans la maison** he has been with *ou* in the firm longer than me; **une ~ne amitié** an old friendship, a friendship of long standing; *V* **testament.**
(b) (*avant n: précédent*) former, old. **son ~ne femme** his ex-wife, his former *ou* previous wife; **c'est mon ~ quartier/~ne école** it's my old neighbourhood/school, that's where I used to live/go to school.
(c) (*passé, de l'antiquité*) *langue, civilisation* ancient. **les peuples ~s** the ancients; **dans l'~ temps** in the olden *ou* old days; **dans les temps ~s** in ancient times; **la Grèce/l'Égypte ~ne** ancient Greece/Egypt; **l'A~ Régime** the Ancien Régime.
2 *nm* (*mobilier ancien*) **l'~** antiques (*pl*).
3 *nm,f* (*personne*) **(a)** (*, †: *par l'âge*) elder, old man (*ou* woman). (*hum*) **et le respect pour les ~s?** and where's your respect for your elders?; **les ~s du village** the village elders.
(b) (*par l'expérience*) senior person, experienced person; (*Mil*) old soldier. **c'est un ~ dans la maison/dans le gouvernement** he has been with *ou* in the firm/in the government a long time.
(c) (*Hist*) **les A~s** the Ancients; (*Littérat*) **les A~s et les Modernes** the Ancients and the Moderns.
4: ancien combattant war veteran, ex-serviceman; **ancien (élève)** old boy (*surtout Brit*), alumnus (*US*), former pupil; **ancienne (élève)** old girl (*surtout Brit*), alumna (*US*), former pupil.
anciennement [ɑ̃sjɛnmɑ̃] *adv* (*autrefois*) formerly.
ancienneté [ɑ̃sjɛnte] *nf* **(a)** (*durée de service*) (length of) service; (*privilèges obtenus*) seniority. **à l'~** by seniority; **il a 10 ans d'~ dans la maison** he has been with *ou* in the firm (for) 10 years.
(b) *[maison]* oldness, (great) age, ancientness; *[statue, famille, objet d'art]* age, antiquity; *[loi, tradition]* ancientness. **de toute ~** since time immemorial.
ancillaire [ɑ̃silɛʀ] *adj V* **amour.**
ancrage [ɑ̃kʀaʒ] *nm* **(a)** (*Naut*) *[grand bateau]* anchorage; *[petit bateau]* moorage, moorings (*pl*). **(b)** (*attache*) *[poteau, câble]* anchoring; *[mur]* cramping.
ancre [ɑ̃kʀ(ə)] *nf* **(a)** (*Naut*) anchor. **être à l'~** to be *ou* lie *ou* ride at anchor; **jeter/lever l'~** to cast *ou* drop/weigh anchor.
(b) (*Constr*) cramp(-iron), anchor; (*Horlogerie*) anchor escapement, recoil escapement.
ancrer [ɑ̃kʀe] (1) **1** *vt* **(a)** (*Naut*) to anchor.
(b) (*Tech*) *poteau, câble* to anchor; *mur* to cramp.
(c) (*fig*) to root. **~ qch dans la tête de qn** to fix sth firmly in sb's mind, get sth (to sink) into sb's head; **il a cette idée ancrée dans la tête** he's got this idea firmly fixed *ou* rooted in his head.
2 s'ancrer *vpr* **(a)** (*Naut*) to anchor, cast *ou* drop anchor.
(b) (*fig: s'incruster*) **il a l'habitude de s'~ chez les gens** when he visits people he usually stays for ages *ou* settles in for a good long while; **quand une idée s'ancre dans l'esprit des gens** when an idea takes root *ou* becomes fixed in people's minds; **il s'est ancré dans la tête que ...** he got it into *ou* fixed in his head that ...
andain [ɑ̃dɛ̃] *nm* swath.
andalou, -ouse [ɑ̃dalu, uz] **1** *adj* Andalusian. **2** *nm,f*: **A~(se)** Andalusian.
Andalousie [ɑ̃daluzi] *nf* Andalusia.
Andes [ɑ̃d] *nfpl*: **les ~** the Andes.
andin, e [ɑ̃dɛ̃, in] *adj* Andean.
andouille [ɑ̃duj] *nf* **(a)** (*Culin*) andouille (*sausage made of chitterlings*). **(b)** (*: *imbécile*) clot*, nit*: (*Brit*), fool. **faire l'~** to act the fool; **espèce d'~!, triple ~!** you (stupid) clot!* *ou* nit!*:
andouiller [ɑ̃duje] *nm* tine, (branch of) antler.
andouillette [ɑ̃dujɛt] *nf* andouillette (*small sausage made of chitterlings*).
André [ɑ̃dʀe] *nm* Andrew.
androgyne [ɑ̃dʀɔʒin] **1** *adj* androgynous. **2** *nm* hermaphrodite, androgyne.
Andromaque [ɑ̃dʀɔmak] *nf* Andromache.
âne [ɑn] *nm* **(a)** (*Zool*) donkey, ass. **être comme l'~ de Buridan** to be unable to decide between two alternatives; (*hum*) **il y a plus d'un ~ qui s'appelle Martin** we (*ou* they) are all of a kind; *V* **dos.**
(b) (*fig*) ass, fool. **faire l'~ pour avoir du son** to act *ou* play dumb to find out what one wants to know; **~ bâté†** stupid ass; *V* **bonnet, pont.**
anéantir [aneɑ̃tiʀ] (2) **1** *vt* **(a)** (*détruire*) *ville, armée* to annihilate, wipe out; *efforts* to wreck, ruin, destroy; *espoirs* to dash, ruin, destroy; *sentiment* to obliterate, destroy.
(b) (*déprimer, gén pass*) *[chaleur]* to overwhelm, overcome; *[fatigue]* to exhaust, wear out; *[chagrin]* to crush, prostrate; *[mauvaise nouvelle]* to overwhelm, crush.
2 s'anéantir *vpr* to vanish utterly; *[espoir]* to be dashed.
anéantissement [aneɑ̃tismɑ̃] *nm* **(a)** (*destruction: V* **anéantir**) annihilation, wiping out; wrecking; ruin; destruction; dashing, obliteration. **c'est l'~ de tous mes espoirs** that's the end of *ou* that has wrecked all my hopes; **ce régime vise à l'~ de l'individu** this régime aims at the complete suppression *ou* annihilation of the individual('s rights).
(b) (*fatigue*) state of exhaustion, exhaustion; (*abattement*) state of dejection, dejection.
anecdote [anɛkdɔt] *nf* (*gén, littér*) anecdote. **l'~** trivial detail *ou* details; (*péj*) **cet historien ne s'élève pas au-dessus de l'~** this historian doesn't rise above mere detail.
anecdotique [anɛkdɔtik] *adj histoire, description* anecdotal; *peinture* exclusively concerned with detail (*attrib*).
anémie [anemi] *nf* (*Méd*) anaemia; (*fig*) deficiency. **~ pernicieuse** pernicious anaemia.
anémié, e [anemje] (*ptp de* **anémier**) *adj* (*Méd*) anaemic; (*fig*) weakened, enfeebled.
anémier [anemje] (7) **1** *vt* (*Méd*) to make anaemic; (*fig*) to weaken. **2 s'anémier** *vpr* (*Méd*) to become anaemic.
anémique [anemik] *adj* (*Méd, fig*) anaemic.
anémomètre [anemɔmɛtʀ(ə)] *nm* *[fluide]* anemometer; *[vent]* anemometer, wind gauge.
anémone [anemɔn] *nf* anemone. **~ de mer** sea anemone.
ânerie [ɑnʀi] *nf* **(a)** (*U*) stupidity. **il est d'une ~!** he's a real ass!*
(b) (*parole*) stupid *ou* idiotic remark; (*action*) stupid mistake, blunder. **arrête de dire des ~s!** stop talking rubbish!; **faire une ~** to make a blunder, do something silly.
anéroïde [aneʀɔid] *adj V* **baromètre.**

ânesse [ɑnɛs] *nf* she-ass.

anesthésie [anɛstezi] *nf* (*état d'insensibilité, technique*) anaesthesia; (*opération*) anaesthetic. **sous ~** under the anaesthetic, under anaesthesia; **je vais vous faire une ~** I'm going to give you an anaesthetic.

anesthésier [anɛstezje] (7) *vt* (*Méd*) *organe* to anaesthetize; *personne* to give an anaesthetic to, anaesthetize; (*fig*) to deaden, benumb, anaesthetize.

anesthésique [anɛstezik] *adj, nm* anaesthetic.

anesthésiste [anɛstezist(ə)] *nmf* anaesthetist.

anévrisme [anevʀism(ə)] *nm* aneurism.

anfractuosité [ɑ̃fʀaktɥozite] *nf [falaise, mur, sol]* crevice.

ange [ɑ̃ʒ] **1** *nm* **(a)** (*Rel*) angel. **bon/mauvais ~** good/bad angel; (*fig*) **être le bon ~ de qn** to be sb's good *ou* guardian angel; (*fig*) **être le mauvais ~ de qn** to be an evil influence over *ou* on sb.
(b) (*personne*) angel. **oui mon ~** yes, darling; **va me chercher mes lunettes tu seras un ~** be an angel *ou* a darling and fetch me my glasses, go and look for my glasses, there's an angel *ou* a dear; **il est sage comme un ~** he's an absolute angel, he's as good as gold; **il est beau comme un ~** he's as pretty as a picture *ou* an angel, he looks quite angelic; **avoir une patience d'~** to have the patience of a saint; **c'est un ~ de douceur/de bonté** he's the soul of meekness/goodness.
(c) (*Zool*) angel fish.
(d) (*loc*) **un ~ passa** there was an awkward pause *ou* silence (in the conversation); **être aux ~s** to be in (the) seventh heaven.
2: (*Rel*) **ange déchu** fallen angel; (*Rel*) **l'ange exterminateur** the exterminating angel; **ange gardien** (*Rel, fig*) guardian angel; (*fig: garde du corps*) bodyguard; *V* **cheveux, faiseur, rire.**

angélique[1] [ɑ̃ʒelik] *adj* (*Rel, fig*) angelic(al).

angélique[2] [ɑ̃ʒelik] *nf* (*Bot, Culin*) angelica.

angéliquement [ɑ̃ʒelikmɑ̃] *adv* angelically, like an angel.

angélisme [ɑ̃ʒelism(ə)] *nm* (*Rel*) angelism; (*fig péj*) otherworldliness.

angelot [ɑ̃ʒlo] *nm* (*Art*) cherub.

angélus [ɑ̃ʒelys] *nm* angelus.

angevin, e [ɑ̃ʒvɛ̃, in] **1** *adj* Angevin (*épith*), of *ou* from Anjou. **2** *nm,f*: **A~(e)** *[province]* inhabitant *ou* native of Anjou; *[ville]* inhabitant *ou* native of Angers.

angine [ɑ̃ʒin] *nf* (*amygdalite*) tonsillitis; (*pharyngite*) pharyngitis. **avoir une ~** to have a sore throat; **~ de poitrine** angina (pectoris); **~ couenneuse, ~ diphtérique** diphtheria.

angineux, -euse [ɑ̃ʒinø, øz] *adj* anginal.

anglais, e [ɑ̃glɛ, ɛz] **1** *adj* English; *V* **assiette, broderie, crème.**
2 *nm* **(a) A~** Englishman; **les A~** (*en général*) English people, the English; (*hommes*) Englishmen.
(b) (*Ling*) English. **~ canadien** Canadian English.
3 anglaise *nf* **(a) A~e** Englishwoman.
(b) (*Coiffure*) **~es** ringlets.
(c) (*Écriture*) ≃ modern English handwriting.
(d) à l'~e *légumes* boiled; *V* **filer, jardin.**
4 *adv*: **parler ~** to speak English.

angle [ɑ̃gl(ə)] **1** *nm* **(a)** (*encoignure*) *[meuble, rue]* corner. **à l'~ de ces deux rues** at *ou* on the corner of these two streets; **le magasin qui fait l'~** the shop on the corner; **la maison est en ~** the house forms the corner *ou* stands directly on the corner; **rues qui se coupent à ~ droit** streets which cross *ou* intersect at right angles.
(b) (*Math*) angle. **~ saillant/rentrant** salient/re-entrant angle; **~ aigu/obtus** acute/obtuse angle; **~s alternes externes/internes** exterior/interior alternate angles.
(c) (*aspect*) angle, point of view. **vu sous cet ~** seen from *ou* looked at from that angle *ou* point of view.
(d) (*fig*) *[caractère, personne]* rough edge; *V* **arrondir.**
2: **angles adjacents** adjacent angles; **angle de braquage** lock; **angle dièdre** dihedral angle; **angle droit** right angle; **angle facial** facial angle; **angle d'incidence** angle of incidence; **angle d'inclinaison** angle of inclination; **angle inscrit (à un cercle)** inscribed angle (of a circle); **angle de marche** = **angle de route**; **angle mort** dead angle; **angle optique** optic angle; **angle de réfraction** angle of refraction; (*Mil*) **angle de route** bearing, direction of march; **angle de tir** firing angle; **angle visuel** visual angle; *V* **grand.**

Angleterre [ɑ̃glətɛʀ] *nf* England.

anglican, e [ɑ̃glikɑ̃, an] *adj, nm,f* Anglican.

anglicanisme [ɑ̃glikanism(ə)] *nm* Anglicanism.

anglicisant, e [ɑ̃glisizɑ̃, ɑ̃t] *nm,f* (*étudiant*) student of English (*language and civilization*); (*spécialiste*) anglicist, English specialist.

angliciser [ɑ̃glisize] (1) **1** *vt* to anglicize. **2 s'angliciser** *vpr* to become anglicized.

anglicisme [ɑ̃glisism(ə)] *nm* anglicism.

angliciste [ɑ̃glisist(ə)] *nmf* (*étudiant*) student of English (*language and civilization*); (*spécialiste*) anglicist, English specialist.

anglo- [ɑ̃glɔ] *préf* anglo-.

anglo-américain [ɑ̃glɔameʀikɛ̃] *nm* (*Ling*) American English.

anglo-arabe [ɑ̃glɔaʀab] *adj, nmf* (*cheval*) Anglo-Arab.

anglo-canadien, -ienne [ɑ̃glɔkanadjɛ̃, jɛn] **1** *adj* Anglo-Canadian. **2** *nm* (*Ling*) Canadian English. **3** *nm,f*: **A~(ne)** English Canadian.

anglomane [ɑ̃glɔman] *nmf* anglomaniac.

anglomanie [ɑ̃glɔmani] *nf* anglomania.

anglo-normand, e [ɑ̃glɔnɔʀmɑ̃, ɑ̃d] **1** *adj* Anglo-Norman; *V* **île. 2** *nm* (*Ling*) Anglo-Norman. **3** *nm,f* (*cheval*) Anglo-Norman (horse).

anglophile [ɑ̃glɔfil] **1** *adj* anglophilic. **2** *nmf* anglophile.

anglophilie [ɑ̃glɔfili] *nf* anglophilia.

anglophobe [ɑ̃glɔfɔb] **1** *adj* anglophobic. **2** *nmf* anglophobe.

anglophobie [ɑ̃glɔfɔbi] *nf* anglophobia.

anglophone [ɑ̃glɔfɔn] **1** *adj* English-speaking. **2** *nmf* English-speaker, Anglophone (*Can*).

anglo-saxon, -onne [ɑ̃glɔsaksɔ̃, ɔn] **1** *adj* Anglo-Saxon. **2** (*Ling*) Anglo-Saxon. **3** *nm,f*: **A~(ne)** Anglo-Saxon.

angoissant, e [ɑ̃gwasɑ̃, ɑ̃t] *adj situation, silence* harrowing, agonizing. **nous avons vécu des jours ~s** we went through *ou* suffered days of anguish *ou* agony.

angoisse [ɑ̃gwas] *nf* **(a)** (*U*) (*gén, Psych*) anguish, distress. (*Philos*) **l'~ métaphysique** metaphysical anguish, Angst; **une étrange ~ le saisit** a strange feeling of anguish gripped him; **l'~ de la mort** the anguish of death; **il vivait dans l'~/dans l'~ d'un accident** he lived in anguish/in fear and dread of an accident; **ils ont vécu des jours d'~** they went through *ou* suffered days of anguish *ou* agony.
(b) (*peur*) dread (*U*), fear. (*rare: sensation d'étouffement*) **avoir des ~s** to choke with anguish.

angoissé, e [ɑ̃gwase] (*ptp de* **angoisser**) *adj geste, visage, voix* anguished; *question, silence* agonized. **regard/cri ~** look/cry of anguish; **être ~** (*inquiet*) to be distressed *ou* in anguish; (*oppressé*) to feel choked.

angoisser [ɑ̃gwase] (1) *vt* (*inquiéter*) to harrow, cause anguish *ou* distress to; (*oppresser*) to choke.

angora [ɑ̃gɔʀa] *adj, nm* angora.

angstrœm [aŋstʀœm] *nm* angstrom (unit).

anguille [ɑ̃gij] *nf* (*Culin, Zool*) eel. **~ de mer** conger eel, conger; **il m'a filé entre les doigts comme une ~** he slipped right through my fingers, he wriggled out of my clutches; **il y a ~ sous roche** there's something in the wind.

angulaire [ɑ̃gylɛʀ] *adj* angular; *V* **pierre.**

anguleux, -euse [ɑ̃gylø, øz] *adj menton, visage* angular, bony; *coude* bony.

anharmonique [anaʀmɔnik] *adj* anharmonic.

anhydre [anidʀ(ə)] *adj* anhydrous.

anhydride [anidʀid] *nm* anhydride.

anicroche* [anikʀɔʃ] *nf* hitch, snag. **sans ~s** smoothly, without a hitch.

ânier, -ière [ɑnje, jɛʀ] *nm,f* donkey-driver.

aniline [anilin] *nf* aniline.

animal, e, *mpl* **-aux** [animal, o] **1** *adj* (*Bio, fig*) animal (*épith*). (*péj: bestial*) **ses instincts ~aux** his animal instincts; **sa confiance était aveugle, ~e** his confidence was blind, instinctive; *V* **esprit.**
2 *nm* (*Bio, fig*) animal. **quel ~!*** what a lout!

animalcule [animalkyl] *nm* animalcule.

animalier [animalje] **1** *adj m peintre, sculpteur* animal (*épith*). **2** *nm* (*peintre*) painter of animals, animal painter; (*sculpteur*) sculptor of animals, animal sculptor.

animalité [animalite] *nf* animality.

animateur, -trice [animatœʀ, tʀis] *nm,f* **(a)** (*personne dynamique*) **l'~ de cette entreprise** the driving force behind *ou* the prime mover in this undertaking; **l'~ de ces congrès scientifiques** the driving *ou* dynamic force behind these scientific congresses.
(b) (*professionnel*) (*Music Hall, TV*) compère; *[centres culturels]* leader, organizer. **~ de jeunes/groupes** youth/group leader.
(c) (*Ciné: technicien*) animator.

animation [animɑsjɔ̃] *nf* **(a)** (*vie*) *[quartier, regard, personne]* life, liveliness; *[discussion]* animation, liveliness; (*affairement*) *[rue, quartier, bureau]* (hustle and) bustle. **son arrivée provoqua une grande ~** his arrival caused a great deal of excitement; **parler avec ~** to speak with great animation; **mettre de l'~ dans** *ou* **donner de l'~ à une réunion** to put some life into a meeting, liven a meeting up.
(b) (*Ciné*) animation; *V* **cinéma.**

animé, e [anime] (*ptp de* **animer**) *adj* **(a)** *rue, quartier* (*affairé*) busy; (*plein de vie*) lively; *regard, visage* lively; *discussion* animated, lively, spirited; (*Comm*) *enchères, marché* brisk.
(b) (*Ling, Philos*) animate.
(c) *V* **dessin.**

animer [anime] (1) **1** *vt* **(a)** (*être l'élément dynamique de, mener*) *débat, discussion, groupe* to lead; *réunion* to conduct; *entreprise* to lead, be prime mover in, mastermind; (*Rad, TV*) *spectacle* to compère. **~ une course** to set the pace in a race.
(b) (*pousser*) *[haine]* to drive, impel; *[foi]* to impel; *[espoir]* to nourish, sustain. **animé seulement par le** *ou* **du désir de vous être utile** prompted only by the desire to be of service to you.
(c) (*stimuler*) *soldat* to rouse; *coureur* to urge *ou* cheer *ou* egg* on; *courage* to arouse. **la foi qui animait son regard** the faith which shone in his eyes.
(d) (*mouvoir*) to drive. **la fusée animée d'un mouvement ascendant** the rocket propelled *ou* driven by an upward thrust; **le balancier était animée d'un mouvement régulier** the pendulum was moving in a steady rhythm.
(e) (*donner de la vie à*) *ville, soirée, conversation* to liven up; *yeux* to put a sparkle into; *regard, visage* to put life into, light up; (*Art*) *peinture, statue* to bring to life; (*Philos*) *nature, matière* to animate.
2 s'animer *vpr [personne, rue]* to come to life, liven up; *[conversation]* to become animated, liven up; *[foule, objet inanimé]* to come to life; *[yeux, traits]* to light up.

animisme [animism(ə)] *nm* animism.

animiste [animist(ə)] **1** *adj théorie* animist(ic); *philosophe* animist. **2** *nmf* animist.

animosité [animozite] *nf* (*hostilité*) animosity (*contre* towards, against).

anion [anjɔ̃] *nm* anion.

anis [ani(s)] *nm* (*plante*) anise; (*Culin*) aniseed; (*bonbon*) aniseed ball. **à l'~** aniseed (*épith*).
aniser [anize] (1) *vt* to flavour with aniseed. **goût anisé** taste of aniseed.
anisette [anizɛt] *nf* anisette.
ankylose [ɑ̃kiloz] *nf* ankylosis.
ankyloser [ɑ̃kiloze] (1) **1** *vt* to stiffen, ankylose (*T*); (*fig*) to benumb. **être tout ankylosé** to be stiff all over; **mon bras ankylosé** my stiff arm. **2 s'ankyloser** *vpr* to get stiff, ankylose (*T*); (*fig*) to become numb.
annales [anal] *nfpl* annals. **ça restera dans les ~*** that'll go down in history (*hum*).
annamite† [anamit] **1** *adj* Annamese, Annamite. **2** *nmf*: **A~** Annamese, Annamite.
Anne [an] *nf* Ann, Anne.
anneau, *pl* **~x** [ano] **1** *nm* **(a)** (*gén: cercle*) ring; (*bague*) ring; *[chaîne]* link. **~ de rideau/de porte-clefs** curtain/key ring.
(b) (*Algèbre*) ring; (*Géom*) ring, annulus; *[colonne]* annulet; *[champignon]* annulus; *[ver]* segment, metamere.
(c) (*Sport*) **~x** rings; **exercices aux ~x** ring exercises.
2: (*Opt*) **anneaux colorés** Newton's rings; **anneau épiscopal** bishop's ring; **anneau nuptial** wedding ring; (*Opt*) **anneau oculaire** eye ring; **anneau de Saturne** Saturn's ring; (*Géom*) **anneau sphérique** (spherical) annulus *ou* ring.
année [ane] **1** *nf* **(a)** (*durée*) year. **il y a bien des ~s qu'il est parti** he has been gone for many years, it's many years since he has been gone; **la récolte d'une ~** a *ou* one year's harvest; **tout au long de l'~** the whole year (round); **payé à l'~** paid annually; **l'~ universitaire/scolaire** the academic/school year; **~ sabbatique** sabbatical year.
(b) (*âge, grade*) year. **il est dans sa vingtième ~** he is in his twentieth year; (*Scol*) **de première/deuxième ~** first-/second-year (*épith*).
(c) (*point dans le temps*) year. **les ~s de guerre** the war years; **~ de naissance** year of birth; **les ~s 20/30** the 20s/30s; **d'une ~ à l'autre** from one year to the next; **d'~ en ~** from year to year; (*littér*) **en l'~ 700 de notre ère/avant Jésus-Christ** in (the year) 700 A.D./B.C.; *V* **bon**[1], **souhaiter.**
2: **année bissextile** leap year; **année civile** calendar year; **année-lumière** *nf, pl* **années-lumières** light year.
annelé, e [anle] *adj* ringed; (*Bot, Zool*) annulate; (*Archit*) annulated.
annexe [anɛks(ə)] **1** *adj document* annexed, appended. **les bâtiments ~s** the annexes. **2** *nf* (*Constr*) annex(e); *[document]* annex (*de* to).
annexer [anɛkse] (1) **1** *vt territoire* to annex; *document* to append, annex (*à* to). **2 s'annexer*** *vpr personne, privilège* to hog*, monopolize.
annexion [anɛksjɔ̃] *nf* (*Pol*) annexation.
annexionnisme [anɛksjɔnism(ə)] *nm* annexationism.
annexionniste [anɛksjɔnist(ə)] *adj, nmf* annexationist.
Annibal [anibal] *nm* Hannibal.
annihilation [aniilɑsjɔ̃] *nf* **(a)** (*V* **annihiler**) annihilation; wrecking; ruin; destruction; dashing; crushing. **(b)** (*Phys*) annihilation.
annihiler [aniile] (1) *vt efforts* to wreck, ruin, destroy; *espoirs* to dash, ruin, destroy; *résistance* to wipe out, destroy, annihilate; *personne, esprit* to crush. **le chef, par sa forte personnalité, annihile complètement ses collaborateurs** because of his strong personality, the boss completely overwhelms *ou* overshadows his colleagues.
anniversaire [anivɛʀsɛʀ] **1** *adj* anniversary (*épith*). **le jour ~ de leur mariage** on the anniversary of their marriage. **2** *nm [naissance]* birthday; *[événement, mariage, mort]* anniversary. **cadeau/carte d'~** birthday present/card.
annonce [anɔ̃s] *nf* **(a)** announcement; (*publicité*) advertisement (*in newspaper*); (*Bridge*) declaration. **petites ~s** classified advertisements *ou* ads*, small ads*; **~ personnelle** personal message; **~ judiciaire** *ou* **légale** legal notice.
(b) (*fig: indice*) sign, indication. **ce chômage grandissant est l'~ d'une crise économique** this growing unemployment heralds *ou* foreshadows an economic crisis.
annoncer [anɔ̃se] (3) **1** *vt* **(a)** (*informer de*) *fait, décision, nouvelle* to announce (*à* to). **~ à qn que** to announce to sb that, tell sb that; **on m'a annoncé par lettre que** I was informed *ou* advised by letter that; **je lui ai annoncé la nouvelle** (*gén*) I announced the news to her, I told her the news; (*mauvaise nouvelle*) I broke the news to her; **on annonce l'ouverture d'un nouveau magasin** they're advertising the opening of a new shop; **on annonce la sortie prochaine de ce film** the forthcoming release of this film has been announced; **les journaux ont annoncé leur mariage** their marriage has been announced in the papers; **on annonce un important arrivage de poisson** a large catch (of fish) is reported to have been landed.
(b) (*prédire*) *pluie, chômage* to forecast. **on annonce un ralentissement économique dans les mois à venir** a slowing-down in the economy is forecast *ou* predicted for the coming months.
(c) (*signaler*) *[présage]* to foreshadow, foretell; *[signe avant-coureur]* to herald; *[sonnerie, pas]* to announce, herald. **les nuages qui annoncent une tempête** the clouds that herald a storm; **ça n'annonce rien de bon** it bodes no good; **ce radoucissement annonce la pluie/le printemps** this warmer weather means that *ou* is a sign that rain/spring is on the way; **la cloche qui annonce la fin des cours** the bell announcing *ou* signalling the end of classes; **il s'annonçait toujours en frappant 3 fois** he always announced himself by knocking 3 times.
(d) (*dénoter*) to bespeak (of), indicate, point to.
(e) (*introduire*) *personne* to announce. **il entra sans se faire ~** he went in without having himself announced *ou* without announcing himself; **annoncez-vous au concierge en arrivant** announce *ou* say who you are to the concierge when you arrive; **vous auriez pu vous ~!** you might have said you were there! *ou* made your presence known!; **qui dois-je ~?** what name shall I say?, whom shall I announce?
(f) (*Cartes*) to declare, (*fig*) **~ la couleur** to lay one's cards on the table, say where one stands.
2 s'annoncer *vpr* **(a)** (*se présenter*) *[situation]* to shape up. **comment est-ce que ça s'annonce?** how is it shaping up? *ou* looking?; **le temps s'annonce orageux** the weather looks like being stormy; **ça s'annonce bien** that looks promising, that looks like a promising *ou* good start.
(b) (*arriver*) to approach. **la révolution qui s'annonçait** the signs of the coming revolution; **l'hiver s'annonçait** winter was on its way.
annonceur [anɔ̃sœʀ] *nm* (*publicité*) advertiser; (*Rad, TV: speaker*) announcer.
annonciateur, -trice [anɔ̃sjatœʀ, tʀis] **1** *adj*: **~ de** *événement favorable* heralding; *événement défavorable* foreboding; **signe ~ de** portent of. **2** *nm,f* herald, harbinger (*littér*).
Annonciation [anɔ̃sjɑsjɔ̃] *nf*: **l'~** (*événement*) the Annunciation; (*jour*) Annunciation Day, Lady Day.
annotateur, -trice [anɔtatœʀ, tʀis] *nm,f* annotator.
annotation [anɔtɑsjɔ̃] *nf* annotation.
annoter [anɔte] (1) *vt* to annotate.
annuaire [anɥɛʀ] *nm* yearbook, annual; *[téléphone]* (telephone) directory, phone book*.
annualité [anɥalite] *nf* (*gén*) yearly recurrence. **l'~ du budget/de l'impôt** yearly budgeting/taxation.
annuel, -elle [anɥɛl] *adj* annual, yearly; *V* **plante**[1].
annuellement [anɥɛlmɑ̃] *adv* annually, once a year, yearly.
annuité [anɥite] *nf* (*gén*) annual instalment (*Brit*) *ou* installment (*US*), annual payment; *[dette]* annual repayment. *[pension]* **avoir toutes ses ~s** to have (made) all one's years' contributions.
annulable [anylabl(ə)] *adj* annullable, liable to annulment (*attrib*).
annulaire [anylɛʀ] **1** *adj* annular, ring-shaped. **2** *nm* ring finger, third finger.
annulation [anylɑsjɔ̃] *nf* (*V* **annuler**) invalidation; nullification; quashing; cancellation; annulment.
annuler [anyle] (1) **1** *vt contrat* to invalidate, void, nullify; *jugement, décision* to quash; *engagement* to cancel, call off; *élection, acte, examen* to nullify, declare void; *mariage* to annul; *commande* to cancel, withdraw.
2 s'annuler *vpr [poussées, efforts]* to cancel each other out, nullify each other.
anoblir [anɔbliʀ] (2) *vt* to ennoble, confer a title of nobility on.
anoblissement [anɔblismɑ̃] *nm* ennoblement.
anode [anɔd] *nf* anode.
anodin, e [anɔdɛ̃, in] *adj personne* insignificant; *détail* trivial, trifling, insignificant; *critique* unimportant; *blessure* harmless; *propos* harmless, innocuous; (†† *Méd*) anodyne; *remède* ineffectual.
anodique [anɔdik] *adj* anodic.
anomal, e, *mpl* **-aux** [anɔmal, o] *adj* (*Gram*) anomalous.
anomalie [anɔmali] *nf* (*gén, Astron, Gram*) anomaly; (*Bio*) abnormality; (*Tech*) (technical) fault.
ânon [ɑnɔ̃] *nm* (*petit de l'âne*) ass's foal; (*petit âne*) little ass *ou* donkey.
anone [anɔn] *nf* annona.
ânonnement [ɑnɔnmɑ̃] *nm* (*V* **ânonner**) drone; faltering *ou* mumbling (speech).
ânonner [ɑnɔne] (1) *vti* (*de manière inexpressive*) to read *ou* recite in a drone; (*en hésitant*) to read *ou* recite in a fumbling manner. **~ sa leçon** (*sans expression*) to drone out one's lesson; (*en hésitant*) to stumble *ou* fumble (one's way) through one's lesson.
anonymat [anɔnima] *nm* anonymity. **sous le couvert de l'~** anonymously; **garder l'~** to remain anonymous, preserve one's anonymity.
anonyme [anɔnim] *adj* (*sans nom*) anonymous; (*impersonnel*) *décor, meubles* impersonal.
anonymement [anɔnimmɑ̃] *adv* anonymously.
anophèle [anɔfɛl] *nm* anopheles.
anorak [anɔʀak] *nm* anorak.
anorexie [anɔʀɛksi] *nf* anorexia.
anormal, e, *mpl* **-aux** [anɔʀmal, o] **1** *adj* (*Bio, Méd, Sci*) abnormal; (*insolite*) unusual, abnormal; (*injuste*) abnormal. **il est ~ qu'il n'ait pas les mêmes droits** it isn't normal *ou* it's abnormal for him not to have the same rights.
2 *nm,f* (*Méd*) abnormal person.
anormalement [anɔʀmalmɑ̃] *adv se développer* abnormally; *se conduire, agir* unusually, abnormally. **~ chaud/grand** unusually *ou* abnormally hot/tall.
anse [ɑ̃s] *nf [panier, tasse]* handle; (*Géog*) cove; (*Anat*) loop, flexura (*T*). (*Archit*) **~ (de panier)** basket-handle arch; (*hum*) **faire danser** *ou* **valser l'~ du panier** to make a bit out of the shopping money*.
antagonique [ɑ̃tagɔnik] *adj* antagonistic.
antagonisme [ɑ̃tagɔnism(ə)] *nm* antagonism.
antagoniste [ɑ̃tagɔnist(ə)] **1** *adj forces, propositions* antagonistic; (*Anat*) *muscles* antagonist. **2** *nmf* antagonist.
antan [ɑ̃tɑ̃] *nm* (*littér*) **d'~** of yesteryear, of long ago; **ma jeunesse d'~** my long-lost youth, my youth of long ago; **ma force d'~** my strength of former days *ou* of days gone by *ou* of yesteryear; **mes plaisirs d'~** my erstwhile pleasures.
antarctique [ɑ̃taʀktik] **1** *adj* antarctic. **2** *nm*: **l'A~** the Antarctic, Antarctica.
antécédence [ɑ̃tesedɑ̃s] *nf* antecedence.

antécédent, e [ɑ̃tesedɑ̃, ɑ̃t] **1** *adj* antecedent.
2 *nm* **(a)** (*Gram, Math, Philos*) antecedent; (*Méd*) past *ou* previous history.
(b) ~s *[personne]* past *ou* previous history, antecedents; *[affaire]* past *ou* previous history; **avoir de bons/mauvais** ~s to have a good/bad previous history.
antéchrist [ɑ̃tekʀist] *nm* Antichrist.
antédiluvien, -ienne [ɑ̃tedilyvjɛ̃, jɛn] *adj* (*lit, fig*) antediluvian.
antenne [ɑ̃tɛn] *nf* **(a)** (*Zool*) antenna, feeler. (*fig*) **avoir des** ~s to have a sixth sense; (*fig*) **avoir des** ~**s dans un ministère** to have contacts in a ministry.
(b) (*pour capter*) (*Rad*) aerial, antenna; (*TV*) aerial; *[radar]* antenna.
(c) (*Rad, TV: écoute*) **être sur l'**~ to be on the air; **passer à l'**~ to go on the air; **gardez l'**~ stay tuned in; **je donne l'**~ **à Paris** we'll go over to Paris now; **je rends l'**~ **au studio** I'll return you to the studio; **vous avez droit à 2 heures d'**~ you are entitled to 2 hours' broadcasting time *ou* to 2 hours on the air; **hors** ~, **le ministre a déclaré que** off the air, the minister declared that; **sur les** ~**s de notre station** on our station.
(d) (*Naut: vergue*) lateen yard.
(e) (*petite succursale*) sub-branch, agency; (*Mil: poste avancé*) outpost. ~ **chirurgicale** (*Mil*) advanced surgical unit; (*Aut*) emergency unit.
antépénultième [ɑ̃tepenyltjɛm] **1** *adj* antepenultimate. **2** *nf* antepenultimate syllable, antepenult.
antéposé, e [ɑ̃tepoze] *adj* (*Gram*) placed *ou* put in front of the word (*attrib*).
antérieur, e [ɑ̃teʀjœʀ] *adj* **(a)** (*dans le temps*) *époque, situation* previous, earlier. **c'est** ~ **à la guerre** it was prior to the war; **cette décision était** ~**e à son départ** that decision was prior *ou* previous to his departure, that decision preceded his departure; **nous ne voulons pas revenir à la situation** ~**e** we don't want to return to the former *ou* previous situation; **dans une vie** ~**e** in a former life.
(b) (*dans l'espace*) *partie* front (*épith*). **membre** ~ forelimb; **patte** ~**e** forefoot.
(c) (*Ling*) *voyelle* front (*épith*); *V* **futur, passé.**
antérieurement [ɑ̃teʀjœʀmɑ̃] *adv* earlier. ~ **à** prior *ou* previous to.
antériorité [ɑ̃teʀjɔʀite] *nf [événement, phénomène]* precedence; (*Gram*) anteriority.
anthologie [ɑ̃tɔlɔʒi] *nf* anthology.
anthozoaires [ɑ̃tɔzɔɛʀ] *nmpl*: **les** ~ the Anthozoa.
anthracite [ɑ̃tʀasit] **1** *nm* anthracite. **2** *adj inv* dark grey (*Brit*) *ou* gray (*US*), charcoal grey.
anthrax [ɑ̃tʀaks] *nm inv* (*tumeur*) carbuncle.
anthropocentrique [ɑ̃tʀɔpɔsɑ̃tʀik] *adj* anthropocentric.
anthropocentrisme [ɑ̃tʀɔpɔsɑ̃tʀism(ə)] *nm* anthropocentrism.
anthropoïde [ɑ̃tʀɔpɔid] **1** *adj* anthropoid. **2** *nm* anthropoid (ape).
anthropologie [ɑ̃tʀɔpɔlɔʒi] *nf* anthropology.
anthropologique [ɑ̃tʀɔpɔlɔʒik] *adj* anthropological.
anthropologiste [ɑ̃tʀɔpɔlɔʒist(ə)] *nmf*, **anthropologue** [ɑ̃tʀɔpɔlɔg] *nmf* anthropologist.
anthropométrie [ɑ̃tʀɔpɔmetʀi] *nf* anthropometry.
anthropométrique [ɑ̃tʀɔpɔmetʀik] *adj* anthropometric(al).
anthropomorphisme [ɑ̃tʀɔpɔmɔʀfism(ə)] *nm* anthropomorphism.
anthropomorphiste [ɑ̃tʀɔpɔmɔʀfist(ə)] **1** *adj* anthropomorphist, anthropomorphic. **2** *nmf* anthropomorphist.
anthroponymie [ɑ̃tʀɔpɔnimi] *nf* (*Ling*) anthroponomy.
anthropophage [ɑ̃tʀɔpɔfaʒ] **1** *adj* cannibalistic, cannibal (*épith*), anthropophagous (*T*). **2** *nm* cannibal, anthropophagite (*T*).
anthropophagie [ɑ̃tʀɔpɔfaʒi] *nf* cannibalism, anthropophagy (*T*).
anthropopithèque [ɑ̃tʀɔpɔpitɛk] *nm* anthropopithecus.
anti [ɑ̃ti] **1** *préf* **anti(-)** **(a)** (*rapport d'hostilité, d'opposition*) anti-; (*contraire à l'esprit de*) un-. **partis/vues** ~**démocratiques** anti-democratic parties/views; **ambiance/mesure** ~**démocratique** undemocratic atmosphere/measure; **campagne** ~**voitures/pollution** anti-car/-pollution campaign; **campagne** ~**bruit** noise abatement campaign; **propagande** ~**tabac** anti-smoking propaganda.
(b) (*négation, contraire, inversion*) **style** ~**scientifique/poétique/érotique** unscientific/unpoetic/unerotic style; **démarche** ~**rationnelle** counter-rational approach; **l'**~**-art/-théâtre** anti-art/-theatre; **une** ~**-école** an alternative school.
(c) (*protection*) anti-. **mesures** ~**inflationnistes** anti- *ou* counter-inflationary measures; **mesures** ~**natalistes** birth-rate control measures; **dispositif** ~**friction/halo** anti-friction/-halo device; **dispositif** ~**radiations** radiation protection device; **crème** ~**solaire/(-)moustiques** sun/anti-mosquito cream; **(médicament)** ~**dépresseur** anti-depressant (drug); ~**éblouissant/transpirant** anti-dazzle/-perspirant; **produits/traitement** ~**cellulite** fat-reducing products/treatment.
2 *nm* (*hum*) **le parti des** ~**s** those who are anti *ou* against, the anti crowd*.
antiaérien, -ienne [ɑ̃tiaeʀjɛ̃, jɛn] *adj batterie, canon* anti-aircraft; *abri* air-raid (*épith*).
antialcoolique [ɑ̃tialkɔlik] *adj*: **campagne** ~ campaign against alcohol; **ligue** ~ temperance league.
antiatomique [ɑ̃tiatɔmik] *adj* anti-radiation. **abri** ~ fallout shelter.
anti-aveuglant, e [ɑ̃tiavœglɑ̃, ɑ̃t] *adj* (*Aut*) anti-dazzle.
antibiotique [ɑ̃tibjɔtik] *adj, nm* antibiotic.
antibois [ɑ̃tibwa] *nm* chair-rail.
antibrouillard [ɑ̃tibʀujaʀ] *adj, nm* (*Aut*) **(phare)** ~ fog lamp (*Brit*), fog light (*US*).
antibuée [ɑ̃tibɥe] *adj inv*: **dispositif** ~ demister; **bombe/liquide** ~ anti-mist spray/liquid.
anticancéreux, -euse [ɑ̃tikɑ̃seʀø, øz] *adj* cancer (*épith*). **centre** ~ (*laboratoire*) cancer research centre; (*hôpital*) cancer hospital.
anticasseur [ɑ̃tikasœʀ] *adj*: **loi** ~**(s), mesures** ~**(s)** *law, measures designed to prevent damage to property by demonstrators.*
antichambre [ɑ̃tiʃɑ̃bʀ(ə)] *nf* antechamber, anteroom. **faire** ~† to wait humbly *ou* patiently (for an audience with sb).
antichar [ɑ̃tiʃaʀ] *adj* anti-tank.
antichoc [ɑ̃tiʃɔk] *adj montre etc* shockproof.
anticipation [ɑ̃tisipasjɔ̃] *nf* **(a)** (*Fin*) ~ **de paiement, paiement par** ~ payment in advance *ou* anticipation, advance payment. **(b)** (*Littérat*) **littérature d'**~ science fiction; **roman d'**~ science fiction novel.
anticipé, e [ɑ̃tisipe] (*ptp de* **anticiper**) *adj retour* early (*épith*). **remboursement** ~ repayment before due date; **recevez mes remerciements** ~**s** thanking you in advance *ou* anticipation.
anticiper [ɑ̃tisipe] (1) **1** *vi* **(a)** (*prévoir, calculer*) to anticipate; (*en imaginant*) to look *ou* think ahead, anticipate what will happen; (*en racontant*) to jump ahead. **n'anticipons pas!** don't let's look *ou* think too far ahead, don't let's anticipate.
(b) ~ **sur** *récit, rapport* to anticipate; ~ **sur l'avenir** to anticipate the *ou* look into the future; **sans vouloir** ~ **sur ce que je dirai tout à l'heure** without wishing to go into *ou* launch into what I shall say later.
2 *vt* (*Comm*) *paiement* to anticipate, pay before due; (*littér*) *avenir, événement* to anticipate, foresee.
anticlérical, e, *mpl* -aux [ɑ̃tikleʀikal, o] **1** *adj* anticlerical. **2** *nm,f* anticleric(al).
anticléricalisme [ɑ̃tikleʀikalism(ə)] *nm* anticlericalism.
anticlinal, e, *mpl* -aux [ɑ̃tiklinal, o] *adj, nm* anticlinal.
anticoagulant, e [ɑ̃tikɔagylɑ̃, ɑ̃t] *adj, nm* anticoagulant.
anticolonialisme [ɑ̃tikɔlɔnjalism(ə)] *nm* anticolonialism.
anticolonialiste [ɑ̃tikɔlɔnjalist(ə)] *adj, nmf* anticolonialist.
anticommunisme [ɑ̃tikɔmynism(ə)] *nm* anticommunism.
anticommuniste [ɑ̃tikɔmynist(ə)] *adj, nmf* anticommunist.
anticonceptionnel, -elle [ɑ̃tikɔ̃sɛpsjɔnɛl] *adj* contraceptive. **propagande** ~**le** birth-control propaganda; **moyens** ~**s** contraceptive methods, methods of birth control.
anticonformisme [ɑ̃tikɔ̃fɔʀmism(ə)] *nm* nonconformism.
anticonformiste [ɑ̃tikɔ̃fɔʀmist(ə)] *adj, nmf* nonconformist.
anticonstitutionnel, -elle [ɑ̃tikɔ̃stitysjɔnɛl] *adj* unconstitutional.
anticonstitutionnellement [ɑ̃ntikɔ̃stitysjɔnɛlmɑ̃] *adv* unconstitutionally.
anticorps [ɑ̃tikɔʀ] *nm* antibody.
anticyclone [ɑ̃tisiklon] *nm* anticyclone.
antidater [ɑ̃tidate] (1) *vt* to backdate, predate, antedate.
antidémocratique [ɑ̃tidemɔkʀatik] *adj* (*opposé à la démocratie*) antidemocratic; (*peu démocratique*) undemocratic.
antidérapant, e [ɑ̃tideʀapɑ̃, ɑ̃t] *adj* non-skid.
antidétonant, e [ɑ̃tidetɔnɑ̃, ɑ̃t] *adj, nm* anti-knock.
antidiphtérique [ɑ̃tidifteʀik] *adj sérum* diphtheria (*épith*).
antidoping [ɑ̃tidɔpiŋ] *adj*, **antidopage** [ɑ̃tidɔpaʒ] *adj loi* anti-doping (*épith*); *contrôle* dope (*épith*).
antidote [ɑ̃tidɔt] *nm* (*lit, fig*) antidote (*contre, de* for, against).
antiéconomique [ɑ̃tiekɔnɔmik] *adj* uneconomical.
antiengin [ɑ̃tiɑ̃ʒɛ̃] *adj* antimissile.
antienne [ɑ̃tjɛn] *nf* (*Rel*) antiphon; (*fig littér*) chant, refrain.
antiesclavagisme [ɑ̃tiɛsklavaʒism(ə)] *nm* abolition (of slavery); (*US Hist*) abolitionism.
antiesclavagiste [ɑ̃tiɛsklavaʒist(ə)] **1** *adj* antislavery, opposed to slavery (*attrib*); (*US Hist*) abolitionist. **2** *nmf* opponent of slavery; abolitionist.
antifasciste [ɑ̃tifaʃist(ə)] *adj, nmf* antifascist.
anti-g [ɑ̃tiʒe] *adj inv*: **combinaison** ~ G-suit.
antigang [ɑ̃tigɑ̃] *adj inv*: **brigade** ~ (police) commando squad.
antigel [ɑ̃tiʒɛl] *nm* antifreeze.
antigène [ɑ̃tiʒɛn] *nm* antigen.
Antigone [ɑ̃tigɔn] *nf* Antigone.
antigouvernemental, e, *mpl* -aux [ɑ̃tiguvɛʀnəmɑ̃tal, o] *adj* antigovernment(al).
antihéros [ɑ̃tieʀo] *nm* anti-hero.
antihistaminique [ɑ̃tiistaminik] *adj, nm* antihistamine.
antihygiénique [ɑ̃tiiʒjenik] *adj* unhygienic.
antillais, e [ɑ̃tijɛ, ɛz] **1** *adj* West Indian. **2** *nm,f*: **A**~**(e)** West Indian.
Antilles [ɑ̃tij] *nfpl*: **les** ~ the West Indies.
antilope [ɑ̃tilɔp] *nf* antelope.
antimatière [ɑ̃timatjɛʀ] *nf* antimatter.
antimilitarisme [ɑ̃timilitaʀism(ə)] *nm* antimilitarism.
antimilitariste [ɑ̃timilitaʀist(ə)] *adj, nmf* antimilitarist.
antimissile [ɑ̃timisil] *adj* antimissile.
antimite [ɑ̃timit] **1** *adj* (anti-)moth (*épith*). **2** *nm* mothproofing agent, moth repellent; (*boules de naphtaline*) mothballs.
antimoine [ɑ̃timwan] *nm* antimony.
antimonarchique [ɑ̃timɔnaʀʃik] *adj* antimonarchist, antimonarchic(al).
antimonarchiste [ɑ̃timɔnaʀʃist(ə)] *nmf* antimonarchist.
antinational, e, *mpl* -aux [ɑ̃tinasjɔnal, o] *adj* antinational.
antinomie [ɑ̃tinɔmi] *nf* antinomy.
antinomique [ɑ̃tinɔmik] *adj* antinomic(al).
antipape [ɑ̃tipap] *nm* antipope.
antiparasitage [ɑ̃tipaʀazitaʒ] *nm* fitting of a suppressor to.

antiparasite [ɑ̃tiparazit] *adj* anti-interference. **dispositif ~** suppressor.

antiparasiter [ɑ̃tiparazite] (1) *vt* to fit a suppressor to.

antiparlementaire [ɑ̃tiparləmɑ̃tɛr] *adj* antiparliamentary.

antiparlementarisme [ɑ̃tiparləmɑ̃tarism(ə)] *nm* antiparliamentarianism.

antipathie [ɑ̃tipati] *nf* antipathy. **l'~ entre ces deux communautés** the hostility *ou* antipathy between these two communities.

antipathique [ɑ̃tipatik] *adj personne* disagreeable, unpleasant; *endroit* unpleasant. **il m'est ~** I don't like him, I find him disagreeable.

antipatriotique [ɑ̃tipatrijɔtik] *adj* antipatriotic; (*peu patriote*) unpatriotic.

antipatriotisme [ɑ̃tipatrijɔtism(ə)] *nm* antipatriotism.

antipersonnel [ɑ̃tipɛrsɔnɛl] *adj inv* antipersonnel.

antiphrase [ɑ̃tifrɑz] *nf* antiphrasis. **par ~** ironically.

antipode [ɑ̃tipɔd] *nm* (*Géog*) **les ~s** the antipodes; (*Géog*) **être à l'~** *ou* **aux ~s** to be on the other side of the world (*de* from, to); (*fig*) **votre théorie est aux ~s de la mienne** our theories are poles apart, your theory is the opposite extreme of mine.

antipoétique [ɑ̃tipɔetik] *adj* unpoetic.

antipoliomyélitique [ɑ̃tipɔljɔmjelitik] *adj* polio (*épith*).

antiprotectionniste [ɑ̃tiprɔtɛksjɔnist(ə)] **1** *adj* free-trade (*épith*). **2** *nmf* free trader.

antipsychiatrie [ɑ̃tipsikjatri] *nf* anti-psychiatry.

antipyrétique [ɑ̃tipiretik] *adj* antipyretic.

antipyrine [ɑ̃tipirin] *nf* antipyrine.

antiquaille [ɑ̃tikɑj] *nf* (*péj*) piece of old junk.

antiquaire [ɑ̃tikɛr] *nmf* antique dealer.

antique [ɑ̃tik] *adj* (*de l'antiquité*) *vase, objet* antique, ancient; *style* ancient; (*littér: très ancien*) *coutume, objet* ancient; (*péj*) *véhicule, chapeau* antiquated. **style imitant l'~** mock-antique style; **il aime l'~** he is a lover of the art and style of antiquity.

antiquité [ɑ̃tikite] *nf* **(a)** (*période*) **l'~** antiquity.

(b) (*ancienneté*) antiquity, (great) age. **de toute ~** from the beginning of time, from time immemorial.

(c) ~s (*œuvres de l'antiquité*) antiquities; (*meubles anciens etc*) antiques; **marchand d'~s** antique dealer.

antirachitique [ɑ̃tiraʃitik] *adj* antirachitic.

antiraciste [ɑ̃tirasist(ə)] *adj* antiracist, antiracialist.

antireflet [ɑ̃tir(ə)flɛ] *adj inv* non-reflecting.

antireligieux, -euse [ɑ̃tirliʒjø, øz] *adj* antireligious.

antirépublicain, e [ɑ̃tirepyblikɛ̃, ɛn] *adj* antirepublican.

antirévolutionnaire [ɑ̃tirevɔlysjɔnɛr] *adj* antirevolutionary.

antirides [ɑ̃tirid] *adj inv* anti-wrinkle.

antirouille [ɑ̃tiruj] *adj inv* anti-rust.

anti-roulis [ɑ̃tiruli] *adj inv* anti-roll (*épith*).

antiscorbutique [ɑ̃tiskɔrbytik] *adj* antiscorbutic.

antiségrégationniste [ɑ̃tisegregasjɔnist(ə)] *adj* antisegregationist.

antisémite [ɑ̃tisemit] **1** *adj* anti-semitic. **2** *nmf* anti-semite.

antisémitisme [ɑ̃tisemitism(ə)] *nm* anti-semitism.

antisepsie [ɑ̃tisɛpsi] *nf* antisepsis.

antiseptique [ɑ̃tisɛptik] *adj, nm* antiseptic.

antisocial, e, *mpl* **-aux** [ɑ̃tisɔsjal, o] *adj* (*Pol*) antisocial.

anti-sous-marin, e [ɑ̃tisumarɛ̃, in] *adj* anti-submarine.

antispasmodique [ɑ̃tispasmɔdik] *adj, nm* antispasmodic.

antisportif, -ive [ɑ̃tispɔrtif, iv] *adj* (*opposé au sport*) antisport; (*peu élégant*) unsporting, unsportsmanlike.

antistrophe [ɑ̃tistrɔf] *nf* antistrophe.

anti-subversif, -ive [ɑ̃tisybvɛrsif, iv] *adj* counter-subversive.

antitétanique [ɑ̃titetanik] *adj sérum etc* tetanus (*épith*).

antithèse [ɑ̃titɛz] *nf* (*lit, fig*) antithesis.

antithétique [ɑ̃titetik] *adj* antithetic(al).

antitoxine [ɑ̃titɔksin] *nf* antitoxin.

antitoxique [ɑ̃titɔksik] *adj* antitoxic.

antitrust [ɑ̃titrœst] *adj inv loi, mesures* anti-monopoly (*Brit*), anti-trust (*US*).

antituberculeux, -euse [ɑ̃titybɛrkylø, øz] *adj sérum* tuberculosis (*épith*).

antivénéneux, -euse [ɑ̃tivenenø, øz] *adj* alexipharmic, antidotal.

antivenimeux, -euse [ɑ̃tivənimø, øz] *adj*: **sérum ~, substance ~euse** antivenom, antivenin.

antivol [ɑ̃tivɔl] *nm, adj inv*: **(dispositif) ~** anti-theft device.

Antoine [ɑ̃twan] *nm* Ant(h)ony.

antonomase [ɑ̃tɔnɔmɑz] *nf* antonomasia.

antonyme [ɑ̃tɔnim] *nm* antonym.

antonymie [ɑ̃tɔnimi] *nf* antonymy.

antre [ɑ̃tr(ə)] *nm* (*littér: caverne*) cave; *[animal]* den, lair; (*fig*) den; (*Anat*) antrum.

anus [anys] *nm* anus.

Anvers [ɑ̃vɛr] *n* Antwerp.

anxiété [ɑ̃ksjete] *nf* (*inquiétude, Méd*) anxiety. **avec ~** with anxiety *ou* great concern; **être dans l'~** to be very anxious *ou* worried.

anxieusement [ɑ̃ksjøzmɑ̃] *adv* anxiously.

anxieux, -euse [ɑ̃ksjø, øz] **1** *adj personne, regard* anxious, worried; *attente* anxious. (*Méd*) **crises ~euses** crises of anxiety; **~ de** anxious to. **2** *nm,f* worrier.

aoriste [aɔrist(ə)] *nm* aorist.

aorte [aɔrt(ə)] *nf* aorta.

aortique [aɔrtik] *adj* aortic.

août [u] *nm* August; *pour loc V* **septembre** *et* **quinze.**

aoûtat [auta] *nm* harvest tick *ou* mite.

aoûtien, -ienne* [ausjɛ̃, jɛn] *nm,f* August holiday-maker.

apache [apaʃ] *nm* **(a)** (*indien*) **A~** Apache. **(b)** (†: *voyou*) ruffian, tough. **il a une allure ~** he has a tough *ou* vicious look about him.

apaisant, e [apɛzɑ̃, ɑ̃t] *adj* (*chassant la tristesse, les soucis*) soothing; (*calmant les esprits*) mollifying, pacifying.

apaisement [apɛzmɑ̃] *nm* (*V* **s'apaiser**) calming *ou* quietening down; cooling *ou* calming down; subsiding; abating; going *ou* dying down; appeasement; allaying. **donner des ~s à qn** to give assurances to sb, reassure sb; **cela lui procura un certain ~** this brought him some relief.

apaiser [apeze] (1) **1** *vt* **(a)** *personne, foule* to calm (down), pacify, placate.

(b) *désir, faim* to appease, assuage; *soif* to slake; *passion, excitation* to calm, quell, soothe; *conscience* to salve; *scrupules* to allay; *douleur* to soothe.

2 s'apaiser *vpr* **(a)** *[personne, malade]* to calm *ou* quieten down; *[coléreux]* to cool *ou* calm down.

(b) *[vacarme, excitation, tempête]* to die down, subside; *[vagues, douleur]* to go *ou* die down; *[passion, désir, soif, faim]* to be satisfied *ou* appeased; *[scrupules]* to be allayed.

apalachien, -ienne [apalaʃjɛ̃, jɛn] *adj* Appalachian.

apanage [apanaʒ] *nm* (*privilège*) **être l'~ de qn/qch** to be the privilege *ou* prerogative of sb/sth; **le pessimisme est le triste ~ des savants** it's the scholar's sorry privilege to be pessimistic; **avoir l'~ de qch** to have the sole *ou* exclusive right to sth, possess sth exclusively; **il croit avoir l'~ du bon sens** he thinks he's the only one with any common sense.

aparté [aparte] *nm* (*entretien*) private conversation (*in a group*); (*Théât, gén: remarque*) aside. **en ~** in an aside, in a stage whisper; (*Théât*) in an aside.

apathie [apati] *nf* apathy.

apathique [apatik] *adj* apathetic.

apathiquement [apatikmɑ̃] *adv* apathetically.

apatride [apatrid] *nmf* stateless person.

aperception [apɛrsɛpsjɔ̃] *nf* apperception.

apercevoir [apɛrsəvwar] (28) **1** *vt* **(a)** (*voir*) to see; (*brièvement*) to catch a glimpse of; (*remarquer*) to notice, see. **on apercevait au loin un clocher** a church tower could be seen in the distance; **ça s'aperçoit à peine, c'est très bien réparé** it's hardly noticeable *ou* you can hardly see it, it's very well repaired.

(b) (*se rendre compte de*) *danger, contradictions* to see, perceive; *difficultés* to see, foresee. **si on fait cela, j'aperçois des problèmes** if we do that, I (can) see problems ahead *ou* I (can) foresee problems.

2 s'apercevoir *vpr*: **s'~ de** *erreur, omission* to notice; *présence, méfiance* to notice, become aware of; *dessein, manège* to notice, see through, become aware of; **s'~ que** to notice *ou* realize that; **sans s'en ~** without realizing, inadvertently.

aperçu [apɛrsy] *nm* **(a)** (*idée générale*) general survey. **~ sommaire** brief survey; **cela vous donnera un bon ~ de ce que vous allez visiter** that will give you a good idea *ou* a general idea *ou* picture of what you are about to visit.

(b) (*point de vue personnel*) insight (*sur* into).

apéritif, -ive [aperitif, iv] **1** *adj* (*littér*) *boisson* that stimulates the appetite. **ils firent une promenade ~ive** they took a walk to get up an appetite. **2** *nm* aperitif, aperitive. **prendre l'~** to have an aperitif *ou* aperitive.

apéro* [apero] *nm* (*abrév de apéritif*) aperitif, aperitive.

aperture [apɛrtyr] *nf* (*Ling*) aperture.

apesanteur [apəzɑ̃tœr] *nf* weightlessness.

à-peu-près [apøprɛ] *nm inv* vague approximation; *V* **près.**

apeuré, e [apœre] *adj* frightened, scared.

apex [apɛks] *nm* (*Astron, Bot, Sci*) apex; (*Ling*) *[langue]* apex, tip; (*accent latin*) macron.

aphasie [afazi] *nf* aphasia.

aphasique [afazik] *adj, nmf* aphasic.

aphérèse [aferɛz] *nf* aphaeresis.

aphone [afɔn] *adj* voiceless, aphonic (*T*). **je suis presque ~ d'avoir trop crié** I've nearly lost my voice *ou* I'm hoarse from so much shouting.

aphonie [afɔni] *nf* aphonia.

aphorisme [afɔrism(ə)] *nm* aphorism.

aphrodisiaque [afrɔdizjak] *adj, nm* aphrodisiac.

Aphrodite [afrɔdit] *nf* Aphrodite.

aphte [aft(ə)] *nm* mouth ulcer, aphtha (*T*).

aphteux, -euse [aftø, øz] *adj* aphthous; *V* **fièvre.**

api [api] *V* **pomme.**

apical, e, *mpl* **-aux** [apikal, o] *adj* apical.

apico-alvéolaire [apikoalveɔlɛr] *adj, nf* apico-alveolar.

apico-dental, e, *mpl* **-aux** [apikodɑ̃tal, o] **1** *adj* apico-dental. **2 apico-dentale** *nf* apico-dental.

apicole [apikɔl] *adj* beekeeping (*épith*), apiarian (*T*).

apiculteur, -trice [apikyltœr, tris] *nm,f* beekeeper, apiarist (*T*).

apiculture [apikyltyr] *nf* beekeeping, apiculture (*T*).

apitoiement [apitwamɑ̃] *nm* (*pitié*) pity, compassion.

apitoyer [apitwaje] (8) **1** *vt* to move to pity. **~ qn sur le sort de qn** to move sb to pity for *ou* make sb feel sorry for sb's lot; **n'essaie pas de m'~** don't try and make me feel sorry for you, don't try to get round me.

2 s'apitoyer *vpr*: **s'~ sur (qn/le sort de qn)** to feel pity *ou* compassion for (sb/sb's lot); **s'~ sur son propre sort** to feel sorry for o.s.

aplanir [aplanir] (2) **1** *vt terrain* to level; *difficultés* to smooth away *ou* out, iron out; *obstacles* to smooth away. **~ le chemin devant qn** to smooth sb's path *ou* way.

2 s'aplanir *vpr [terrain]* to become level. **les difficultés se sont aplanies** the difficulties smoothed themselves out *ou* were ironed out.

aplanissement [aplanismɑ̃] *nm* (*V* **aplanir**) levelling; smoothing away; ironing out.

aplati, e [aplati] (*ptp de* **aplatir**) *adj forme, objet, nez* flat. **c'est ~ sur le dessus/à son extrémité** it's flat on top/at one end.

aplatir [aplatiʀ] (2) **1** *vt objet* to flatten; *couture* to press flat; *cheveux* to smooth down, flatten; *pli* to smooth (out); *surface* to flatten (out). **~ qch à coups de marteau** to hammer sth flat; **~ qn*** to flatten sb*.

2 s'aplatir *vpr* **(a)** *[personne]* **s'~ contre un mur** to flatten o.s. against a wall; **s'~ par terre** (*s'étendre*) to lie flat on the ground; (*: *tomber*) to fall flat on one's face; (*fig: s'humilier*) **s'~ devant qn** to crawl to sb, grovel before sb.

(b) *[choses]* (*devenir plus plat*) to become flatter; (*être écrasé*), to be flattened *ou* squashed. (*s'écraser*) **s'~ contre*** to smash against.

aplatissement [aplatismɑ̃] *nm* (*gén*) flattening; (*fig: humiliation*) grovelling. **l'~ de la terre aux pôles** the flattening-out *ou* -off of the earth at the poles.

aplomb [aplɔ̃] *nm* **(a)** (*assurance*) self-assurance; (*péj: insolence*) nerve, audacity, cheek*.

(b) (*équilibre*) balance, equilibrium; (*verticalité*) perpendicular, plumb. *[personne]* **perdre l'~ *ou* son ~** to lose one's balance; **à l'~ du mur** at the base of the wall.

(c) (*Équitation*) **~s** stand.

(d) d'~ *corps* steady, balanced; *bâtiment, mur* plumb; **se tenir d'~ (sur ses jambes)** to be steady on one's feet; **être (posé) d'~** to be balanced *ou* level; **tu n'as pas l'air d'~*** you look off-colour* (*Brit*) *ou* out of sorts; **se remettre d'~ après une maladie*** to pick up *ou* get back on one's feet again after an illness; **ça va te remettre d'~*** that'll put you right *ou* on your feet again; **le soleil tombait d'~** the sun was beating straight down.

apocalypse [apɔkalips(ə)] *nf* (*Rel*) apocalypse. **l'A~** Revelation, the Apocalypse; **atmosphère d'~** doom-laden *ou* end-of-the-world atmosphere; **paysage/vision d'~** landscape/vision of doom.

apocalyptique [apɔkaliptik] *adj* (*Rel*) apocalyptic; (*fig*) *paysage* of doom; *vision* apocalyptic, of doom.

apocope [apɔkɔp] *nf* apocope.

apocryphe [apɔkʀif] **1** *adj* apocryphal, of doubtful authenticity; (*Rel*) Apocryphal. **2** *nm* apocryphal book. **les ~s** the Apocrypha.

apodictique [apɔdiktik] *adj* apodictic.

apogée [apɔʒe] *nm* (*Astron*) apogee; (*fig*) peak, apogee.

apolitique [apɔlitik] *adj* (*indifférent*) apolitical, unpolitical; (*indépendant*) non-political.

apolitisme [apɔlitism(ə)] *nm* (*V* **apolitique**) *[personne]* apolitical *ou* unpolitical attitude; non-political stand; *[organisme]* non-political character.

Apollon [apɔlɔ̃] *nm* (*Myth*) Apollo; (*fig*) Apollo, Greek god.

apologétique [apɔlɔʒetik] **1** *adj* (*Philos, Rel*) apologetic. **2** *nf* apologetics (*sg*).

apologie [apɔlɔʒi] *nf* apology, apologia. **faire l'~ de** (*gén*) to praise; (*Jur*) to vindicate.

apologiste [apɔlɔʒist(ə)] *nmf* apologist.

apologue [apɔlɔg] *nm* apologue.

apophyse [apɔfiz] *nf* apophysis.

apoplectique [apɔplɛktik] *adj* apoplectic.

apoplexie [apɔplɛksi] *nf* apoplexy.

apostasie [apɔstazi] *nf* apostasy.

apostasier [apɔstazje] (7) *vi* to apostatize, renounce the faith.

apostat, e [apɔsta, at] *adj, nm,f* apostate, renegade.

a posteriori [apɔsteʀjɔʀi] *loc adv, adj* (*Philos*) a posteriori; (*gén*) after the event. **il est facile, ~, de dire que ...** it is easy enough, after the event *ou* with hindsight, to say that ... .

apostille [apɔstij] *nf* apostil.

apostiller [apɔstije] (1) *vt* to add an apostil to.

apostolat [apɔstɔla] *nm* (*Bible*) apostolate, discipleship; (*prosélytisme*) proselytism, preaching, evangelism. (*fig*) **ce métier est un ~** this job requires total devotion *ou* has to be a vocation.

apostolique [apɔstɔlik] *adj* apostolic; *V* **nonce.**

apostoliquement [apɔstɔlikmɑ̃] *adv* apostolically.

apostrophe [apɔstʀɔf] *nf* (*Gram, Rhétorique*) apostrophe; (*interpellation*) rude remark (*shouted at sb*). **mot mis en ~** word used in apostrophe; **lancer des ~s à qn** to shout rude remarks at sb.

apostropher [apɔstʀɔfe] (1) *vt* (*interpeller*) to shout at, address sharply.

apothème [apɔtɛm] *nm* apothem.

apothéose [apɔteoz] *nf* **(a)** (*consécration*) pinnacle (of achievement). **cette nomination est pour lui une ~** this appointment is a supreme honour for him; **les tragédies de Racine sont l'~ de l'art classique** Racine's tragedies are the apotheosis *ou* pinnacle of classical art.

(b) (*Théât, gén: bouquet*) grand finale. **finir dans une ~** to end in a blaze of glory.

(c) (*Antiq: déification*) apotheosis.

apothicaire†† [apɔtikɛʀ] *nm* apothecary††.

apôtre [apotʀ(ə)] *nm* (*Hist, Rel, fig*) apostle, disciple. **faire le bon ~** to play the saint.

Appalaches [apalaʃ] *npl*: **les ~** the Appalachian Mountains.

appalachien, -ienne [apalaʃjɛ̃, jɛn] *adj* Appalachian.

apparaître [apaʀɛtʀ(ə)] (57) *vi* **(a)** (*se montrer*) *[jour, personne, fantôme]* to appear (*à* to); *[difficulté, vérité]* to appear, come to light; *[signes, obstacles]* to appear; *[fièvre, boutons]* to break out. **la vérité lui apparut soudain** the truth suddenly dawned on him; **la silhouette qui apparaît/les problèmes qui apparaissent à l'horizon** the figure/the problems looming up on the horizon.

(b) (*sembler*) to seem, appear (*à* to). **ces remarques m'apparaissent fort judicieuses** these seem *ou* sound very judicious remarks to me; **je dois t'~ comme un monstre** I must seem like *ou* appear a monster to you; **ça m'apparaît comme suspect** it seems slightly suspicious *ou* odd to me; **il apparaît que** it appears *ou* turns out that.

apparat [apaʀa] *nm* **(a)** (*pompe*) pomp. **d'~** *dîner, habit, discours* ceremonial; *V* **grand. (b)** (*Littérat*) **~ critique** critical apparatus.

appareil [apaʀɛj] **1** *nm* **(a)** (*machine, instrument*) (*gén*) piece of apparatus, device; (*électrique, ménager*) appliance; (*Rad, TV: poste*) set; (*Phot*) camera; (*téléphone*) (tele)phone. **qui est à l'~?** who's speaking?; **Paul à l'~** Paul speaking.

(b) (*Aviat*) (aero)plane, aircraft.

(c) (*Méd*) (*dentier*) brace; (*pour fracture*) splint.

(d) (*Anat*) apparatus, system. **~ digestif/urogénital** digestive/urogenital system *ou* apparatus; **~ phonateur** vocal apparatus *ou* organs (*pl*).

(e) (*structure administrative*) machinery. **l'~ policier** the police machinery; **l'~ du parti** the party apparatus *ou* machinery; **l'~ des lois** the machinery of the law.

(f) (*littér*) (*dehors fastueux*) air of pomp; (*cérémonie fastueuse*) ceremony. **l'~ magnifique de la royauté** the trappings *ou* splendour of royalty; *V* **simple.**

(g) (*Archit: agencement des pierres*) bond.

2: appareil critique critical apparatus; **appareil de levage** lifting appliance; **appareil orthopédique** orthopaedic appliance; **appareil-photo** *nm, pl* **appareils-photos, appareil photographique** camera; **appareil à sous** (*distributeur*) slot machine; (*jeu*) fruit machine, one-armed bandit.

appareillage [apaʀɛjaʒ] *nm* **(a)** (*Naut*) (*départ*) casting off, getting under way; (*manœuvres*) preparations for casting off *ou* getting under way. **(b)** (*équipement*) equipment.

appareiller [apaʀeje] (1) **1** *vi* (*Naut*) to cast off, get under way. **2** *vt* **(a)** (*Naut*) *navire* to rig, fit out. **(b)** (*Archit: tailler*) *pierre* to draft. **(c)** (*coupler*) to pair; (*assortir*) to match up; (*accoupler*) to mate (*avec* with).

apparemment [apaʀamɑ̃] *adv* apparently.

apparence [apaʀɑ̃s] *nf* **(a)** (*aspect*) *[maison, personne]* appearance, aspect. **ce bâtiment a (une) belle ~** it's a fine-looking building; **il a une ~ négligée** he is shabby-looking, he has a slovenly look about him.

(b) (*fig: extérieur*) appearance. **sous cette ~ souriante** under that smiling exterior; **sous l'~ de la générosité** under this (outward) show *ou* apparent display of generosity; **ce n'est qu'une (fausse) ~** it's a mere façade; **il ne faut pas prendre les ~s pour la réalité** one mustn't mistake appearance(s) for reality; **se fier aux/sauver les ~s** to trust/keep up appearances.

(c) (*semblant, vestige*) semblance. **il n'a plus une ~ de respect pour** he no longer has a semblance of respect for.

(d) (*Philos*) appearance.

(e) (*loc*) **malgré l'~ *ou* les ~s** in spite of appearances; **contre toute ~** against all expectations; **selon toute ~** in all probability; **en ~** apparently, seemingly, on the face of it; **des propos en ~ si contradictoires/si anodins** words apparently so contradictory/harmless; **ce n'est qu'en ~ qu'il est heureux** it's only on the surface *ou* outwardly that he's happy.

apparent, e [apaʀɑ̃, ɑ̃t] *adj* **(a)** (*visible*) *appréhension, gêne* obvious, noticeable; *ruse* obvious. **de façon ~e** visibly, conspicuously; **sans raison/cause ~e** without apparent *ou* obvious reason/cause; **plafond avec poutres ~es** ceiling with visible beams *ou* beams showing; **coutures ~es** topstitched seams.

(b) (*superficiel*) *solidité, causes, contradictions* apparent (*épith*).

apparentement [apaʀɑ̃tmɑ̃] *nm* (*Pol*) grouping of electoral lists (*in proportional representation system*).

apparenter (s') [apaʀɑ̃te] (1) *vpr*: **s'~ à** (*Pol*) to ally o.s. with (*in elections*); (*par mariage*) to marry into; (*ressembler à*) to be similar to, have certain similarities to.

appariement [apaʀimɑ̃] *nm* (*V* **apparier**) matching; pairing; mating.

apparier [apaʀje] (7) *vt* (*littér*) (*assortir*) to match; (*coupler*) to pair; (*accoupler*) to mate.

appariteur [apaʀitœʀ] *nm* (*Univ*) attendant (*in French Universities*). (*hum*) **~ musclé** strong-arm porter *ou* attendant (*hired at times of student unrest*).

apparition [apaʀisjɔ̃] *nf* **(a)** (*manifestation*) *[étoile, symptôme, signe]* appearance; *[personne]* appearance, arrival; *[boutons, fièvre]* outbreak. **faire son ~** *[personne]* to make one's appearance, turn up, appear; *[symptômes]* to appear; **il n'a fait qu'une ~** he only put in a brief appearance.

(b) (*vision*) apparition; (*fantôme*) apparition, spectre. **avoir des ~s** to see *ou* have visions.

apparoir [apaʀwaʀ] *vb impers* (*frm, hum*) **il appert (de ces résultats) que** it appears *ou* is evident (from these results) that.

appartement [apaʀtəmɑ̃] *nm* **(a)** flat (*Brit*), apartment (*US*); *[hôtel]* suite; *V* **chien, plante. (b)** (*Can*) room.

appartenance [apaʀtənɑ̃s] *nf* **(a)** *[race, famille]* belonging (*à* to), membership (*à* of); *[parti]* adherence (*à* to), membership (*à* of). (*Math*) **~ à un ensemble** membership of a set. **(b)** (*Jur*) **~s** appurtenances.

appartenir [apaʀtəniʀ] (22) **1 appartenir à** *vt indir* **(a)** (*être la possession de*) to belong to; **ceci m'appartient** this is mine, this belongs to me; (*fig*) **pour des raisons qui m'appartiennent** for reasons of my own *ou* which concern me (alone); **un médicin ne s'appartient pas** a doctor's time *ou* life is not his own.

(b) (*faire partie de*) *famille, race, parti* to belong to, be a member of.

2 *vb impers*: **il appartient/n'appartient pas au comité de décider si ...** it is for *ou* up to/not for *ou* up to the committee to decide if ..., it is/is not the committee's business to decide if ... .

appas [apɑ] *nmpl* (*littér*) charms.

appât [apɑ] *nm* (*Pêche*) bait; (*fig*) lure, bait. **mettre un ~ à l'hameçon** to bait one's hook; **mordre à l'~** (*fig*) to rise to the bait, bite; (*Pêche*) to bite; **l'~ du gain/d'une récompense** the lure of gain/a reward.

appâter [apɑte] (1) *vt* **(a)** (*pour attraper*) *poissons, gibier* to lure, entice; *piège, hameçon* to bait; (*fig*) *personne* to lure, entice. **(b)** (*engraisser*) *petits oiseaux* to feed (up); *volailles* to fatten (up).

appauvrir [apovʀiʀ] (2) **1** *vt personne, sol, langue* to impoverish; *sang* to make thin **2 s'appauvrir** *vpr [personne, sol, langue]* to grow poorer, become (more) impoverished; *[sang]* to become thin; *[race]* to degenerate.

appauvrissement [apovʀismɑ̃] *nm* (*V* **appauvrir, s'appauvrir**) impoverishment; thinning; degeneration.

appeau, *pl* **~x** [apo] *nm* (*instrument*) bird call; (*oiseau, fig*) decoy. **servir d'~ à qn** to act as a decoy *ou* a stool pigeon for sb.

appel [apɛl] **1** *nm* **(a)** (*cri*) call; (*demande pressante*) appeal. **accourir à l'~ de qn** to run in answer to sb's call; **~ à l'aide** *ou* **au secours** call for help; **elle a entendu des ~s** *ou* **des cris d'~** she heard someone calling out, she heard cries; **à son ~, elle se retourna** she turned round when he called; **~ à l'insurrection/aux armes/aux urnes** call to insurrection/to arms/to vote; **~ au calme** appeal *ou* call for calm; **il me fit un ~ du regard** he gave me a meaningful glance; **il a fait un ~ du pied au chef de l'autre parti** he made covert advances to the leader of the other party; **faire l'~ nominal des candidats** to call out the candidates' names; **faire un ~ de phares** to flash one's headlights.

(b) faire ~ à (*invoquer*) to appeal to; (*avoir recours à*) to call on, resort to; (*fig: nécessiter*) to require; **faire ~ au bon sens/à la générosité de qn** to appeal to sb's common sense/generosity; **faire ~ à ses souvenirs** to call up one's memories; **il a dû faire ~ à tout son courage** he had to summon up *ou* muster all his courage; **on a dû faire ~ aux pompiers** they had to call on (the help of) the firemen; **ils ont fait ~ au président pour que ...** they appealed to *ou* called on the president to ...; **ce problème fait ~ à des connaissances qu'il n'a pas** this problem calls for *ou* requires knowledge he hasn't got.

(c) (*fig: voix*) call. **l'~ du devoir/de la religion** the call of duty/of religion; **l'~ de la raison/de sa conscience** the voice of reason/of one's conscience.

(d) (*vérification de présence*) roll call, register (*Scol*). **faire l'~** (*Scol*) to call the register; (*Mil*) to call the roll; **absent/présent à l'~** (*Scol*) absent/present (for the register); (*Mil*) absent/present at roll call; (*Jur*) **l'~ des causes** reading of the roll of cases (*to be heard*); *V* **manquer, numéro.**

(e) (*Jur: recours*) appeal (*contre* against, from). **faire ~ d'un jugement** to appeal against a judgment; **faire ~** to appeal, lodge an appeal; **juger en ~/sans ~** to judge on appeal/without appeal; (*fig*) **sans ~** (*adj*) final; (*adv*) irrevocably; *V* **cour.**

(f) (*Mil: mobilisation*) **~ de la classe 1967** 1967 call-up, call-up of the class of 1967; *V* **devancer.**

(g) (*Cartes*) signal (*à* for). **faire un ~ à pique** to signal for a spade.

(h) (*Athlétisme: élan*) take-off. **pied d'~** take-off foot.

2: appel d'air in-draught (*Brit*), in-draft (*US*), intake of air; **appel de fonds** call for capital; **faire un appel de fonds** to call up capital; **appel à maxima** *appeal by prosecution against the harshness of a sentence*; **appel à minima** *appeal by prosecution against the leniency of a sentence*; (*Comm*) **appel d'offres** invitation to tender; **appel au peuple** appeal *ou* call to the people; **appel téléphonique** (tele)phone call.

appelé [aple] *nm* (*Mil*) conscript, draftee (*US*). (*Rel, fig*) **il y a beaucoup d'~s et peu d'élus** many are called but few are chosen.

appeler [aple] (4) **1** *vt* **(a)** (*interpeller*) *personne, chien* to call; (*téléphoner à*) *personne* to ring (up), phone (up), call (up); *numéro* to dial, call, phone. **~ le nom de qn** to call out sb's name; (*Jur*) **~ une cause** to call (out) a case; **en attendant que notre cause soit appelée** waiting for our case to come up *ou* be called; **~ qn à l'aide** *ou* **au secours** to call to sb for help; **~ qn (d'un geste) de la main** to beckon (to) sb; **je vais ~ vos noms** I'm going to call (out) your names.

(b) (*faire venir*) *médecin, taxi, police* to call, send for, summon; *ascenseur* to call, summon. **~ les fidèles à la prière** to summon the faithful to prayer; **~ le peuple aux armes** to call the people to arms; (*Jur*) **~ qn en justice** to summon sb before the court; (*Jur*) **~ qn à comparaître comme témoin** to summon sb as a witness; (*Mil*) **~ une classe (sous les drapeaux)** to call up a class (of recruits); (*frm, hum*) **Dieu/la République vous appelle** God/the Republic is calling you; **les pompiers ont été appelés plusieurs fois dans la nuit** the firemen were called out several times during the night; **il a été appelé auprès de sa mère malade** he was called *ou* summoned to his sick mother's side; **~ la colère du ciel sur qn** to call down the wrath of heaven upon sb; **~ la bénédiction de Dieu sur qn** to confer God's blessing upon sb.

(c) (*nommer*) to call. **~ qn un imbécile** to call sb an imbecile; **j'appelle ceci une table/du bon travail** I call this a table/good work; **~ qn par son prénom** to call *ou* address sb by his first name; **nous nous appelons par nos prénoms** we are on first-name terms, we call each other by our first names; **~ qn Monsieur/Madame** to call sb Sir/Madam; **~ les choses par leur nom** to call things by their rightful name; **~ un chat un chat** to call a spade a spade; **voilà ce que j'appelle écrire!** that's what I call writing!

(d) (*désigner*) **~ qn à** *poste* to appoint *ou* assign sb to; **être appelé à de hautes/nouvelles fonctions** to be assigned important/new duties; **sa nouvelle fonction l'appelle à jouer un rôle important** his new function will require him to play an important part; **être appelé à un brillant avenir** to be destined for a brilliant future; **la méthode est appelée à se généraliser** the method is bound to become general.

(e) (*réclamer*) *[situation, conduite]* to call for, demand. **j'appelle votre attention sur ce problème** I call your attention to this problem; **les affaires l'appellent à Lyon** business calls him to Lyons.

(f) (*entraîner*) **une lâcheté en appelle une autre** one act of cowardice leads to *ou* begets another.

2 *vi* **(a)** (*crier*) **~ à l'aide** *ou* **au secours** to call for help; **elle appelait, personne ne venait** she called (out) but nobody came.

(b) en ~ à to appeal to; **en ~ de** to appeal against; **j'en appelle à votre bon sens** I appeal to your common sense.

3 s'appeler *vpr* (*être nommé*) to be called. **il s'appelle Paul** his name is Paul, he's called Paul; **comment s'appelle cet oiseau?** what's the name of this bird?, what's this bird called?; **comment cela s'appelle-t-il en français?** what's that (called) in French?; **voilà ce qui s'appelle une gaffe/être à l'heure!** that's what's called a blunder/being on time!

appellatif [apelatif] *adj m, nm* (*Ling*) **(nom) ~** appellative.

appellation [apelɑsjɔ̃] *nf* designation, appellation; (*littér: mot*) term, name. **~ d'origine** mark of the country of manufacture *ou* origin; **~ (d'origine) contrôlée** appellation contrôlée (*mark guaranteeing the quality of wine*).

appendice [apɛ̃dis] *nm [livre]* appendix; (*Anat*) (*gén*) appendage, appendix. *[intestin]* **l'~** the appendix; (*hum: nez*) **~ nasal** proboscis (*hum*).

appendicite [apɛ̃disit] *nf* appendicitis.

appentis [apɑ̃ti] *nm* (*petit bâtiment*) lean-to; (*toit en auvent*) penthouse (roof), sloping roof.

appert [apɛʀ] *V* **apparoir.**

appesantir [apəzɑ̃tiʀ] (2) **1** *vt tête, paupières* to weigh down; *objet* to make heavier; *gestes, pas* to slow (down); *esprit* to dull. (*fig*) **~ son bras** *ou* **autorité sur** to strengthen one's authority over.

2 s'appesantir *vpr [tête]* to grow heavier; *[gestes, pas]* to become slower; *[esprit]* to grow duller; *[autorité]* to grow stronger. **s'~ sur un sujet/des détails** to dwell at length on a subject/on details; **leur autorité s'est appesantie sur le peuple opprimé** their control over the oppressed nation has been strengthened.

appesantissement [apəzɑ̃tismɑ̃] *nm [démarche]* heaviness; *[esprit]* dullness.

appétence [apetɑ̃s] *nf* appetence (*de* for).

appétissant, e [apetisɑ̃, ɑ̃t] *adj nourriture* appetizing, mouth-watering; *femme* delectable.

appétit [apeti] *nm* **(a)** (*pour la nourriture*) appetite. **avoir de l'~, avoir bon ~** to have a good *ou* hearty appetite; **perdre l'~** to lose one's appetite, go off one's food* (*Brit*); **il n'a pas d'~** he's got no appetite; **donner de l'~ à qn** to give sb an appetite; (*lit*) **mettre qn en ~** to give sb an appetite; (*fig*) **ce premier essai m'a mis en ~** this first attempt gave me an appetite *ou* a taste for it; **avoir un ~ d'oiseau** to eat like a bird; **manger avec ~** to eat heartily; **avoir un ~ de loup** *ou* **d'ogre** to eat like a horse; **l'~ vient en mangeant** (*lit*) eating whets the appetite; (*fig*) the more you have the more you want; *V* **bon**[1], **rester.**

(b) (*désir naturel*) appetite; *[bonheur, connaissances]* appetite, thirst (*de* for).

applaudimètre [aplodimɛtʀ(ə)] *nm* clapometer (*Brit*), applause meter.

applaudir [aplodiʀ] (2) **1** *vt* to applaud, clap. (*fig littér: approuver*) to applaud, commend. **applaudissons notre sympathique gagnant** let's give the winner a big hand.

2 *vi* to applaud, clap. **~ à tout rompre** to bring the house down.

3 applaudir à *vt indir* (*littér: approuver*) *initiative* to applaud, commend. **~ des deux mains à qch** to approve heartily of sth, commend sth warmly.

4 s'applaudir *vpr* (*se réjouir de*) **je m'applaudis de n'y être pas allé!** I'm congratulating myself *ou* patting myself on the back for not having gone!

applaudissement [aplodismɑ̃] *nm* **(a)** (*acclamations*) **~s** applause (*U*), clapping (*U*); **des ~s nourris éclatèrent** loud applause *ou* clapping broke out; **un tonnerre d'~s** thunderous applause.

(b) (*littér: approbation*) approbation, commendation.

applicabilité [aplikabilite] *nf* applicability.

applicable [aplikabl(ə)] *adj* applicable. *[loi etc]* **être ~ à** to apply to, be applicable to.

applicateur [aplikatœʀ] **1** *adj m* applicator (*épith*). **2** *nm* (*dispositif*) applicator.

application [aplikɑsjɔ̃] *nf* **(a)** (*V* **appliquer**) application; use; enforcement; implementation; administration. **mettre en ~** *décision, loi* to put into practice, implement, apply; **mise en ~** *[décision, loi]* implementation, application; **mesures prises en ~ de la loi** measures taken to implement the law.

(b) ~s *[théorie, méthode]* applications; **les ~s de cette théorie sont très nombreuses** the (possible) applications of this theory are numerous.

(c) (*attention*) application, industry. **~ à qch** application to sth; **travailler avec ~** to work industriously.

(d) (*Couture*) appliqué (work). **~ de dentelles** appliqué lace; **~ de velours** velvet appliqué.

(e) (*Math*) mapping.

applique [aplik] *nf* (*lampe*) wall lamp; (*Couture*) appliqué.

appliqué, e [aplike] (*ptp de* **appliquer**) *adj personne* industrious, assiduous; *écriture* careful. **bien ~** *baiser* firm; *coup* well-aimed; **linguistique** *etc* **~e** applied linguistics *etc.*

appliquer [aplike] (1) **1** *vt* **(a)** (*poser*) *peinture, revêtement, cataplasme* to apply. (*Géom*) **~ une figure sur une autre** to apply one figure on another; **~ une échelle sur** *ou* **contre un**

mur to put *ou* lean a ladder against a wall; ~ **son oreille sur** *ou* **à une porte** to put one's ear to a door.

(b) (*mettre en pratique*) *théorème* to apply; *peine* to enforce; *loi, règlement, décision* to implement, apply, put into practice; *remède* to administer; *recette* to use. ~ **un traitement à une maladie** to apply a treatment to an illness.

(c) (*consacrer*) ~ **son esprit à l'étude** to apply one's mind to study; ~ **toutes ses forces à faire qch** to put all one's strength into doing sth.

(d) (*donner*) *gifle, châtiment* to give; *épithète, qualificatif* to apply. ~ **un baiser/sobriquet à qn** to give sb a kiss/nickname; **je lui ai appliqué ma main sur la figure** I struck *ou* slapped him across the face, I struck *ou* slapped his face; **il s'est toujours appliqué cette maxime** he has always applied this maxim to himself.

2 s'appliquer *vpr* **(a)** (*coïncider avec*) s'~ **sur** to fit over; **le calque s'applique exactement sur son modèle** the tracing fits exactly on top of *ou* over its model.

(b) (*correspondre à*) s'~ **à** to apply to; **cette remarque ne s'applique pas à vous** this remark doesn't apply to you.

(c) (*se consacrer à*) s'~ **à** to apply o.s. to; **s'~ à cultiver son esprit** to apply o.s. to cultivating one's mind; **s'~ à l'étude de** to apply o.s. to the study of; **s'~ à paraître à la mode** to take pains to appear fashionable; **élève qui s'applique** pupil who applies himself.

appoggiature [apɔʒjatyʀ] *nf* appoggiatura.

appoint [apwɛ̃] *nm* **(a)** (*monnaie*) **l'~** the right money *ou* change; **faire l'~** to give the right money *ou* change.

(b) (*ressource, aide complémentaire*) (extra) contribution, (extra) help. **salaire d'~** secondary *ou* extra income; **radiateur d'~** back-up *ou* extra heater.

appointements [apwɛ̃tmɑ̃] *nmpl* salary.

appointer [apwɛ̃te] (1) *vt* to pay a salary to. **être appointé à l'année/au mois** to be paid yearly/monthly.

appontage [apɔ̃taʒ] *nm* landing (*on an aircraft carrier*).

appontement [apɔ̃tmɑ̃] *nm* landing stage, wharf.

apponter [apɔ̃te] (1) *vi* to land (*on an aircraft carrier*).

apport [apɔʀ] *nm* **(a)** (*approvisionnement*) *[capitaux]* contribution, supply; (*Tech*) *[chaleur, air frais, eau potable]* supply. **le tourisme grâce à son ~ de devises** tourism, thanks to the currency it brings in; **leur ~ financier/intellectuel** their financial/intellectual contribution; **terrain rendu plus fertile par l'~ d'alluvions d'une rivière** land made more fertile by the alluvia brought *ou* carried down by a river; **l'~ de** *ou* **en vitamines d'un aliment** the vitamins provided by a food.

(b) (*contribution*) contribution. **l'~ de notre civilisation à l'humanité** our civilization's contribution to humanity.

(c) (*Jur*) ~**s** property; ~**s en communauté** *goods contributed by man and wife to the joint estate*; (*Fin*) ~**s en société** capital invested.

apporter [apɔʀte] (1) *vt* **(a)** *objet* to bring. **apporte-le-moi** bring it to me, bring me it; **apporte-le-lui** take it to him; **apporte-le en montant** bring it up with you, bring it up when you come; **apporte-le en venant** bring it with you (when you come), bring it along; **qui a apporté toute cette boue?** who brought in all this mud?; **le vent d'ouest nous apporte toutes les fumées d'usine** the west wind blows *ou* sends *ou* carries all the factory fumes our way; **vent qui apporte la pluie** wind that brings rain.

(b) *satisfaction, repos, soulagement* to bring, give; *ennuis, nouvelles* to bring; *modification* to bring about; *preuve, solution* to supply, provide, give; *argent, dot* to bring. ~ **sa contribution à qch** to make one's contribution to sth; ~ **du soin à qch/à faire qch** to exercise care in sth/in doing sth; ~ **de l'attention à qch/à faire qch** to bring one's attention to bear on sth/on doing sth; **elle y a apporté toute son énergie** she put all her energy into it; **son livre n'apporte rien de nouveau** his book contributes *ou* says nothing new, his book has nothing new to contribute *ou* say.

apposer [apoze] (1) *vt* (*frm*) *sceau, timbre, plaque* to affix; *signature* to append (*frm*); (*Jur*) *clause* to insert. (*Jur*) ~ **les scellés** to affix the seals (*to prevent unlawful entry*).

apposition [apozisjɔ̃] *nf* **(a)** (*Gram*) apposition. **en ~** in apposition. **(b)** (*V* **apposer**) affixing; appending; insertion.

appréciable [apʀesjabl(ə)] *adj* (*évaluable*) appreciable, noticeable; (*assez important*) appreciable. **un nombre ~ de** a good many *ou* few, an appreciable number of.

appréciateur, -trice [apʀesjatœʀ, tʀis] *nm,f* judge, appreciator.

appréciatif, -ive [apʀesjatif, iv] *adj* (*estimatif*) appraising, evaluative; (*admiratif*) appreciative; *V* **état**.

appréciation [apʀesjɑsjɔ̃] *nf* (*V* **apprécier**) valuation; assessment; appraisal; estimation. **je le laisse à votre ~** I leave you to judge for yourself, I leave it to your judgment *ou* assessment; **les ~s du professeur sur un élève** a teacher's assessment *ou* appraisal of a pupil.

apprécier [apʀesje] (7) *vt* **(a)** (*évaluer*) *distance, importance* to estimate, assess, appraise; (*expertiser*) *objet* to value, assess the value of.

(b) (*discerner*) *nuance* to perceive, appreciate.

(c) (*goûter*) *qualité, repas* to appreciate. ~ **qn** (*le trouver sympathique*) to have a liking for sb; (*reconnaître ses qualités*) to appreciate sb; **un mets très apprécié** a much appreciated dish, a highly-rated dish; **son discours n'a pas été apprécié par la droite** his speech was not appreciated by the right wing; **il n'a pas apprécié!*** he didn't appreciate that!, he didn't much care for that!

appréhender [apʀeɑ̃de] (1) *vt* **(a)** (*arrêter*) to apprehend. **(b)** (*redouter*) to dread. ~ **(de faire) qch** to dread (doing) sth; ~ **que** to fear that. **(c)** (*Philos*) to apprehend.

appréhensif, -ive [apʀeɑ̃sif, iv] *adj* apprehensive, fearful (*de* of).

appréhension [apʀeɑ̃sjɔ̃] *nf* **(a)** (*crainte*) apprehension. **envisager qch avec ~** to be apprehensive about sth, dread sth; **avoir de l'~/un peu d'~** to be apprehensive/ a little apprehensive; **son ~ de l'examen/d'un malheur** his apprehension about the exam/of a disaster.

(b) (*littér, Philos*) apprehension.

apprendre [apʀɑ̃dʀ(ə)] (58) *vt* **(a)** *sujet, leçon, métier* to learn. ~ **que/à lire/à nager** to learn that/to read/to swim *ou* how to swim; ~ **à se servir de** to learn (how) to use; ~ **à connaître** to get to know; **l'espagnol s'apprend facilement** Spanish is easy to learn; **ce jeu s'apprend vite** this game is quickly learnt; *V* **cœur**.

(b) *nouvelle* to hear, learn; *événement, fait* to hear of, learn of; *secret* to learn (of) (*de qn* from sb). **j'ai appris hier que ...** I heard *ou* learnt *ou* it came to my knowledge (*frm*) yesterday that ...; **j'ai appris son arrivée par des amis/par la radio** I heard of *ou* learnt of his arrival through friends/on the radio; **apprenez que je ne me laisserai pas faire!** be warned that *ou* let me make it quite clear that I won't be trifled with!

(c) (*annoncer*) ~ **qch à qn** to tell sb (of) sth; **il m'a appris la nouvelle** he told me the news; **il m'apprend à l'instant son départ/qu'il va partir** he has just told me of his departure/that he's going to leave; **vous ne m'apprenez rien!** you're not telling me anything new! *ou* anything I don't know already!, that's no news to me!

(d) (*enseigner*) ~ **qch à qn** to teach sb sth, teach sth to sb; ~ **à qn à faire** to teach sb (how) to do; **il a appris à son chien à obéir/qu'il doit obéir** he taught his dog to obey/that he must obey; (*iro*) **je vais lui ~ à répondre de cette façon** I'll teach him to answer back like that; (*iro*) **je vais lui ~ à vivre** I'll teach him a thing or two, I'll sort (*Brit*) *ou* straighten him out; (*iro*) **ça lui apprendra (à vivre)!** that'll teach him (a lesson)!; **on n'apprend pas à un vieux singe à faire des grimaces** you can't teach an old dog new tricks.

apprenti, e [apʀɑ̃ti] *nm,f [métier]* apprentice; (*débutant*) novice, beginner. ~ **mécanicien** apprentice mechanic, mechanic's apprentice; (*péj*) ~ **philosophe** novice philosopher; ~ **sorcier** sorcerer's apprentice.

apprentissage [apʀɑ̃tisaʒ] *nm* apprenticeship; (*fig*) initiation, learning. **mettre qn en ~** to apprentice sb (*chez* to); **être en ~** to be apprenticed *ou* an apprentice (*chez* to); **faire son ~** to serve one's apprenticeship (*chez* with); **école** *ou* **centre d'~** training school; **faire l'~ de** (*lit*) *métier* to serve one's apprenticeship to; (*fig*) *douleur etc* to have one's first experience of, be initiated into; *V* **contrat**.

apprêt [apʀɛ] *nm* **(a)** (*Tech: opération*) *[cuir, tissu]* dressing; *[papier]* finishing; (*Peinture*) sizing. (*fig*) **sans ~** unaffectedly.

(b) (*Tech: substance*) *[cuir, tissu]* dressing; (*Peinture*) size.

(c) (*préparatifs*) ~**s** *[voyage etc]* preparations (*de* for).

apprêtage [apʀɛtaʒ] *nm* (*V* **apprêt**) dressing; finishing; sizing.

apprêté, e [apʀete] (*ptp de* **apprêter**) *adj* (*affecté*) *manière, style* affected.

apprêter [apʀete] (1) **1** *vt* **(a)** *nourriture* to prepare, get ready. (*habiller*) ~ **un enfant/une mariée** to get a child/bride ready, dress a child/bride.

(b) (*Tech*) *peau, papier, tissu* to dress, finish; (*Peinture*) to size.

2 s'apprêter *vpr* **(a)** s'~ **à qch/à faire qch** to get ready for sth/to do sth, prepare (o.s.) for sth/to do sth; **nous nous apprêtions à partir** we were getting ready *ou* preparing to leave.

(b) (*faire sa toilette*) to dress o.s., prepare o.s.

apprivoisable [apʀivwazabl(ə)] *adj* tameable.

apprivoisé, e [apʀivwaze] (*ptp de* **apprivoiser**) *adj* tame, tamed.

apprivoisement [apʀivwazmɑ̃] *nm* (*action*) taming; (*état*) tameness.

apprivoiser [apʀivwaze] (1) *vt* to tame. **le renard finit par s'~** the fox was finally tamed *ou* finally became tame.

approbateur, -trice [apʀɔbatœʀ, tʀis] **1** *adj* approving. **signe de tête ~** nod of approval, approving nod. **2** *nm,f* (*littér*) approver.

approbatif, -ive [apʀɔbatif, iv] *adj* = **approbateur**.

approbation [apʀɔbɑsjɔ̃] *nf* (*jugement favorable*) approval, approbation (*frm*); (*acceptation*) approval. **donner son ~ à un projet** to give one's approval to a project; **ce livre a rencontré l'~ du grand public** this book has been well received by the public; **conduite/travail digne d'~** commendable behaviour/work.

approbativement [apʀɔbativmɑ̃] *adv* approvingly.

approchable [apʀɔʃabl(ə)] *adj* *chose* accessible; *personne* approachable. **il n'est pas ~ aujourd'hui, il est de mauvaise humeur** don't go near him today, he's in a bad mood; **le ministre est difficilement ~** the minister is rather inaccessible *ou* is not very accessible.

approchant, e [apʀɔʃɑ̃, ɑ̃t] *adj* *style, genre* similar (*de* to); *résultat* close (*de* to). **quelque chose d'~** something like that, something similar; **rien d'~** nothing like that.

approche [apʀɔʃ] *nf* **(a)** (*arrivée*) *[personne, véhicule, événement]* approach. **à mon ~ il sourit** he smiled as I drew nearer *ou* approached; **à l'~ de l'hiver/de la date prévue** at the approach of winter/the arranged date, as winter/the arranged date drew near *ou* approached; **pour empêcher l'~ de l'ennemi** to prevent the enemy's approaching *ou* the enemy from approaching; **s'enfuir à l'~ du danger** to flee at the approach of danger; **à l'~** *ou* **aux ~s de la cinquantaine** as he neared *ou* approached fifty, as fifty drew nearer.

(b) (*abord*) **être d'~ difficile/aisée** *[personne]* to be unapproachable/approachable, be difficult/easy of approach; *[lieu]* to be inaccessible/(easily) accessible, be difficult/easy of approach; *[musique, auteur]* to be difficult/easy to understand; **manœuvres** *ou* **travaux d'~** (*Mil*) approaches, saps; (*fig*) manoeuvres, manoeuvrings.

(c) (*parages*) **les ~s de** *ville, côte, région* the surrounding area of, the area (immediately) surrounding; **aux ~s de la ville il y avait ...** as we (*ou* he *etc*) neared *ou* approached the town there was ... .

(d) (*façon d'aborder*) approach. **l'~de ce problème** the approach to this problem; **ce n'est qu'une ~ sommaire de la question** this is only an outline approach to the question.

(e) (*Typ*) (*espace*) spacing; (*faute*) spacing error; (*signe*) close-up mark; *V* **lunette.**

approché, e [apʀɔʃe] (*ptp de* **approcher**) *adj résultat, idée* approximate.

approcher [apʀɔʃe] (1) **1** *vt* **(a)** *objet* to put near, move near, draw up. **~ un fauteuil/une table de la fenêtre** to move an armchair/a table near to the window; **approche ta chaise** draw *ou* bring up your chair; **il approcha les 2 chaises l'une de l'autre** he moved the 2 chairs close together; **il approcha le verre de ses lèvres** he lifted *ou* raised the glass to his lips; **elle approcha son visage du sien** she moved her face near to his; **ce mouvement l'approcha d'elle** this movement drew *ou* brought him near *ou* close to her.

(b) *personne* (*lit*) to go near, come near, approach; (*fig*) to approach. (*lit*) **ne l'approchez pas!** don't go near him!, keep away from him!; (*fig*) **il approche tous les jours les plus hautes personnalités** he is in contact every day with the top people; (*fig*) **essaie de l'~ ce soir pour lui parler de notre plan** try to approach him tonight about our plan.

2 *vi* **(a)** *[date, saison]* to approach, draw near, draw on; *[personne, orage]* to approach, come nearer; *[nuit, jour]* to approach, draw on. **le jour approche où** the day is near when; **approche que je t'examine** come here and let me look at you.

(b) ~ de qch: ~ d'un lieu to near a place, get *ou* draw near to a place; **~ du but/du résultat** to draw near to *ou* to near the goal/result; **~ de la perfection** to come close to perfection, approach perfection; **il approche de la cinquantaine** he's getting on for *ou* approaching fifty; **devoir qui approche de la moyenne** exercise that is just below a pass mark; **l'aiguille du compteur approchait du 80** the needle on the speedometer was approaching *ou* nearing 80.

3 s'approcher *vpr* (*venir*) to come near, approach; (*aller*) to go near, approach. **un homme s'est approché pour me parler** a man came up to speak to me; **l'enfant s'approcha de moi** the child came up to me *ou* came close to *ou* near me; **ne t'approche pas de moi** don't come near me; **dis-lui de s'~ du micro** (*venir*) tell him to go up to the mike; (*se rapprocher*) tell him to get close to *ou* near (to) the mike; **approche-toi!** come here!; **approchez-vous du feu** come near (to) the fire; **à aucun moment ce roman ne s'approche de la réalité** at no time does this novel come anywhere near to *ou* approach reality; **il s'approcha du lit à pas de loup** he crept up to the bed.

approfondi, e [apʀɔfɔ̃di] (*ptp de* **approfondir**) *adj connaissances, étude* thorough, detailed.

approfondir [apʀɔfɔ̃diʀ] (2) *vt canal, puits* to deepen, make deeper; (*fig*) *question, étude* to go (deeper) into; *connaissances* to deepen, increase. **la rivière s'est approfondie** the river has become deeper *ou* has deepened; **il vaut mieux ne pas ~ le sujet** it's better not to go into the matter too closely; **sans ~** superficially.

approfondissement [apʀɔfɔ̃dismɑ̃] *nm [canal, puits]* deepening (*U*); *[connaissances]* deepening (*U*), increasing (*U*). **l'~ de la question/de cette étude serait souhaitable** it would be a good idea to go deeper into the question/this study.

appropriation [apʀɔpʀijɑsjɔ̃] *nf* **(a)** (*Jur*) appropriation. **l'~ des terres par les conquérants** the appropriation of territory by the conquerors. **(b)** (*adaptation*) suitability, appropriateness.

approprié, e [apʀɔpʀije] (*ptp de* **approprier**) *adj réponse, méthode, remède* appropriate, suitable; *place* proper, right, appropriate. **il faut des remèdes ~s au mal** we need remedies that are suited *ou* appropriate to the evil; **fournir une réponse ~e à la question** to provide an apt *ou* a suitable *ou* an appropriate reply to the question.

approprier [apʀɔpʀije] (7) **1** *vt* (*adapter*) to suit, fit, adapt (*à* to). **~ son style à l'auditoire** to suit one's style to the audience, adapt one's style to (suit) the audience.

2 s'approprier *vpr* **(a)** (*s'adjuger*) *bien* to appropriate; *pouvoir, droit, propriété* to take over, appropriate. **s'~ l'idée/la découverte de quelqu'un d'autre** to appropriate somebody else's idea/discovery.

(b) (*s'adapter à*) **s'~ à** to be appropriate to, fit, suit; **cette musique s'approprie à ma mélancolie** this music is in keeping with *ou* suits *ou* fits my melancholy mood.

approuver [apʀuve] (1) *vt* **(a)** *personne* to agree with. **il a démissionné et je l'approuve** he resigned, and I agree with him *ou* approve (of his doing so); **je l'approuve d'avoir démissionné** I approve of his resigning *ou* his having resigned; **on a besoin de se sentir approuvé** one needs to feel the approval of others.

(b) (*trouver louable*) *politique, prudence, décision, plan* to approve of. **nous n'approuvons pas ce genre d'attitude** we do not approve of that kind of behaviour; **je n'approuve pas qu'il parte maintenant** I don't approve of his leaving now.

(c) (*formellement*) (*en votant*) *projet de loi* to approve, pass; (*par décret*) *méthode, médicament* to approve; (*en signant*) *contrat* to ratify; *procès-verbal* to approve; *V* **lire**[1].

approvisionnement [apʀɔvizjɔnmɑ̃] *nm* (*action*) supplying (*en, de* of). (*réserves*) **~s** supplies, provisions, stock; **l'~ en légumes de la ville** supplying the town with vegetables, (the) supplying (of) vegetables to the town; **il avait tout un ~ d'alcool** he was well stocked with spirits, he had a large stock of spirits.

approvisionner [apʀɔvizjɔne] (1) **1** *vt magasin, commerçant* to supply (*en, de* with); (*Fin*) *compte* to pay funds into; *fusil* to load. **commerçant bien approvisionné en fruits** tradesman well supplied *ou* stocked with fruit.

2 s'approvisionner *vpr* to stock up (*en* with), lay in supplies (*en* of). **s'~ en bois chez le grossiste** to stock up with wood *ou* get supplies of wood at the wholesaler's; **s'~ au supermarché le plus proche** to shop at the nearest supermarket.

approvisionneur, -euse [apʀɔvizjɔnœʀ, øz] *nm,f* supplier.

approximatif, -ive [apʀɔksimatif, iv] *adj calcul, évaluation* rough; *nombre* approximate; *termes* vague.

approximation [apʀɔksimɑsjɔ̃] *nf* (*gén*) approximation, (rough) estimate; (*Math*) approximation.

approximativement [apʀɔksimativmɑ̃] *adv* (*V* **approximatif**) roughly; approximately; vaguely.

appui [apɥi] **1** *nm* **(a)** (*lit, fig*) support. **prendre ~ sur** *[personne]* to lean on; *[objet]* to rest on; **son pied trouva un ~** he found a foothold; **avoir besoin d'~** to need (some) support; **trouver un ~** to find (some) support; **avoir l'~ de qn** to have sb's support; **il a des ~s au ministère** he has connections in the ministry; *V* **barre, point**[1].

(b) (*Mus*) *[voix]* placing. (*Poésie*) **consonne d'~** supporting consonant; **voyelle d'~** support vowel.

(c) à l'~ in support of this, to back this up; **il me dit comment tapisser une pièce avec démonstration à l'~** he told me how to wallpaper a room and backed this up with a demonstration; **à l'~ de son témoignage il présenta cet écrit** in support of his testimony he presented this document.

2: (*Mil*) **appui aérien** air support; **appui-bras** *nm, pl* **appuis-bras, appuie-bras** *nm inv* armrest; **appui de la fenêtre** window-sill, window ledge; **appui-main** *nm, pl* **appuis-main, appuie-main** *nm inv* maulstick; (*Mil*) **appui tactique** tactical support; **appui-tête** *nm, pl* **appuis-tête, appuie-tête** *nm inv [voiture, fauteuil de dentiste]* headrest; *[fauteuil]* antimacassar.

appuie- [apɥi] *préf V* **appui.**

appuyé, e [apɥije] (*ptp de* **appuyer**) *adj* (*insistant*) *regard* fixed, intent; *geste* emphatic; (*excessif*) *politesse* overdone; *compliment* laboured, overdone.

appuyer [apɥije] (8) **1** *vt* **(a)** (*poser*) **~ qch contre qch** to lean *ou* rest sth against sth; **~ une échelle contre un mur** to lean *ou* rest *ou* stand a ladder against a wall, prop a ladder up against a wall; **~ les coudes sur la table/son front contre la vitre** to rest *ou* lean one's elbows on the table/one's forehead against the window; **~ sa main sur l'épaule/la tête de qn** to rest one's hand on sb's shoulder/head.

(b) (*presser*) to press. **~ le pied sur l'accélérateur** to press *ou* put one's foot down on the accelerator; **il dut ~ son genou sur la valise pour la fermer** he had to press *ou* push the case down with his knee to close it; **appuie ton doigt sur le pansement** put *ou* press your finger on the dressing; (*fig*) **~ son regard sur qn** to stare intently at sb.

(c) (*étayer*) **~ un mur par qch** to support *ou* prop up a wall with sth.

(d) (*fig: soutenir*) *personne, candidature, politique* to support, back (up). **il a appuyé sa thèse de documents convaincants** he backed up *ou* supported his thesis with convincing documents; **~ la demande de qn** to support sb's request.

(e) (*Mil*) *attaque* to back up. **l'offensive sera appuyée par l'aviation** the offensive will be backed up from the air *ou* given air support.

2 *vi* **(a)** (*presser sur*) **~ sur** *sonnette, bouton* to press, push; *frein* to press on, press down; *levier* to press (down *etc*); (*Aut*) **~ sur le champignon*** to step on it*, put one's foot down.

(b) (*reposer sur*) **~ sur** to rest on; **la voûte appuie sur des colonnes** the vault rests on columns *ou* is supported by columns.

(c) ~ sur (*insister sur*) *mot, argument* to stress, emphasize; (*accentuer*) *syllabe* to stress, emphasize, accentuate; (*Mus*) *note* to accentuate, accent; **n'appuyez pas trop** don't press the point; **~ sur la chanterelle** to harp on.

(d) (*se diriger*) **~ sur la droite** *ou* **à droite** to bear to the right.

3 s'appuyer *vpr* **(a)** (*s'accoter sur*) **s'~ sur/contre** to lean on/against; **appuie-toi sur mon épaule/à mon bras** lean on my shoulder/arm.

(b) (*fig: compter sur*) **s'~ sur qn/l'amitié de qn** to lean on sb/on sb's friendship; (*Pol*) **il s'appuie sur les groupements de gauche** he relies on the support of the groups of the left; **s'~ sur l'autorité de qn** to lean on sb's authority; **s'~ sur des découvertes récentes pour démontrer ...** to use recent discoveries to demonstrate ..., rely on recent discoveries in order to demonstrate ... .

(c) (*: *faire, subir*) *importun, discours ennuyeux* to put up with*; *corvée* to take on. **qui va s'~ la vaisselle?** who'll take on the washing-up?; **chaque fois c'est nous qui nous appuyons toutes les corvées** it's always us who get stuck* *ou* landed* with all the chores; **il s'est appuyé le voyage de nuit** he had to put up with travelling at night, he jolly well (*Brit*) had to travel by night*.

âpre [ɑpʀ(ə)] *adj* **(a)** *goût, vin* pungent, acrid; *hiver, vent* bitter; *temps* raw; *son, voix, ton* harsh.

(b) (*dur*) *vie* harsh; *combat, discussion* bitter, grim; *caractère* acrid; *détermination, résolution* grim; *concurrence, critique* fierce.

(c) ~ au gain grasping, greedy.

âprement [ɑpʀəmɑ̃] *adv lutter* bitterly, grimly; *critiquer* fiercely.

après [apʀɛ] **1** *prép* **(a)** (*temps*) after. **il est entré ~ le début/~ elle** he came in after it started *ou* after the start/after her; **ne venez pas ~ 8 heures** don't come after 8; **cela s'est passé bien/peu ~ la guerre** this took place long *ou* a good while/shortly *ou* soon *ou* a short time after the war; ~ **beaucoup d'hésitations il a accepté** after much hesitation he accepted; **on l'a servie ~ moi** she was served after me; ~ **cela il ne peut plus refuser** after that he can no longer refuse; (*hum*) ~ **nous le déluge!** *ou* **la fin du monde!** after us the heavens can fall!; ~ **coup** after the event, afterwards; **il n'a compris qu'~ coup** he did not understand until after the event *ou* afterwards; **elle l'a grondé, ~ quoi il a été sage** she gave him a scolding after which *ou* and afterwards he behaved himself; **nuit ~ nuit les bombes tombaient** bombs fell night after night; **page ~ page** page after page, page upon page; ~ **tout** after all; ~ **tout, il peut bien attendre** after all he can wait; ~ **tout, ce n'est qu'un enfant** after all *ou* when all is said and done he is only a child; *V* **Jésus.**

(b) (*espace*) (*plus loin que*) after, past; (*derrière*) behind, after. **j'étais ~ elle dans la queue** I was behind *ou* after her in the queue; **sa maison est (juste) ~ la mairie** his house is (just) past *ou* beyond the town hall; **elle traîne toujours ~ elle 2 petits chiens** she always trails 2 little dogs along behind her.

(c) (*espace: sur*) on. **c'est resté collé ~ le mur** it has stayed stuck on the wall; **grimper ~ un arbre** to climb (up) a tree; **sa jupe s'accrochait ~ les ronces** her skirt kept catching on *ou* in the brambles; **son chapeau est ~ le porte-manteau** his hat is on the peg.

(d) (*ordre d'importance*) after. **sa famille passe ~ ses malades** he puts his family after his patients; ~ **le capitaine vient le lieutenant** after captain comes lieutenant; ~ **vous, je vous prie** after you.

(e) (*poursuite*) after; (*aggressivité*) at. **courir ~ un ballon** to run after a ball; **aboyer/crier ~ qn** to bark/shout at sb; **il est furieux ~ ses enfants** he is furious with *ou* at* his children; ~ **qui en a-t-il?** who is he after?, who has he got it in for?*; **elle est toujours ~ lui** she's always (going) on at* *ou* nagging (at) him, she keeps on at him all the time*; *V* **courir, demander.**

(f) ~ + *infin* after; ~ **que** + *indic* after; ~ **manger** after meals *ou* food; ~ **s'être reposé il reprit la route** after resting *ou* after he had rested *ou* (after) having rested he went on his way; **une heure ~ que je l'eus quittée elle me téléphona** an hour after I had left her she phoned me; **venez me voir ~ que vous lui aurez parlé** come and see me after *ou* when you have spoken to him.

(g) d'~ lui/elle according to him/her, in his/her opinion; **d'~ moi** in my opinion; **(à en juger) d'~ son regard/ce qu'il a dit** (to judge) from the look he gave/what he said; **ne jugez pas d'~ les apparences/ce qu'il dit** don't go by *ou* on appearances/what he says, don't judge by appearances/what he says; **d'~ le baromètre/les journaux** according to the barometer/the papers; **d'~ ma montre** by my watch, according to my watch; **portrait peint d'~ nature** portrait painted from life; **dessin d'~ Ingres** drawing after Ingres, drawing in the style *ou* manner of Ingres; **d'~ Balzac** adapted from Balzac.

2 *adv* **(a)** (*temps*) (*ensuite*) afterwards, after, next; (*plus tard*) later. **venez me voir ~** come and see me afterwards; **aussitôt/longtemps ~** immediately *ou* straight/long *ou* a long time after(wards); **2 heures/jours/semaines ~** 2 hours/days/weeks later.

(b) (*ordre d'importance, poursuite, espace*) **il pense surtout à ses malades, sa famille passe ~** he thinks of his patients first, his family comes second *ou* afterwards; ~ **nous avons des articles moins chers** otherwise we have cheaper things; **l'autobus démarra et il courut ~** as the bus started he ran after it; **va chercher le cintre, ton manteau est ~** fetch the coat hanger, your coat is on it; **laisse ta sœur tranquille, tu cries tout le temps ~** leave your sister alone, you're always (going) on at her*; **qu'est-ce qui vient ~?** what comes next?, what's to follow?; **et (puis) ~?** (*lit*) and then what?; (*fig*) so what?*, what of it?; ~ **tu iras dire que ...** next you'll be saying that ...; **la semaine/le mois d'~** the following *ou* next week/month, the week/month after; **qu'allons-nous faire ~?** what are we going to do next? *ou* afterwards?; **la page d'~** the next *ou* following page; **le train d'~ est plus rapide** the next train is faster.

3: **après-demain** *adv* the day after tomorrow; **après-gaullisme** *nm* post-Gaullism; **après-guerre** *nm, pl* **après-guerres** post-war years; **d'après-guerre** *adj* post-war; **après-midi** *nm ou nf inv* afternoon; **après-rasage** *nm inv* after-shave; **lotion d'après-rasage** after-shave lotion; **après-ski** *nm inv* (*soulier*) snow boot; (*loisirs*) **l'après-ski** the après-ski; **après-vente** *adj V* **service.**

âpreté [ɑpʀəte] *nf* (*V* **âpre**) pungency; acridity; bitterness; rawness; harshness, grimness; fierceness.

a priori [apʀijɔʀi] 1 *loc adv, adj* a priori. 2 *nm* apriorism.

apriorisme [apʀiɔʀism(ə)] *nm* apriority.

aprioriste [apʀijɔʀist(ə)] 1 *adj* aprioristic, apriorist (*épith*). 2 *nmf* a priori reasoner, apriorist.

à-propos [apʀɔpo] *nm [remarque, acte]* aptness. **avec beaucoup d'~ le gouvernement a annoncé ...** the government has very aptly announced that ...; **répondre avec ~** to make an apt *ou* a suitable reply; **avoir beaucoup d'~** (*dans ses réponses*) to have the knack of saying the right thing *ou* of making an apt reply; (*dans ses actes*) to have the knack of doing the right thing; **en cette circonstance imprévue, il a fait preuve d'~** in this unforeseen situation he showed great presence of mind; **il a manqué d'~** *ou* **il n'a pas su répondre avec ~ devant cette question brusque** he was unable to make an apt *ou* a suitable reply to this sudden question; **son manque d'~ lui nuit** his inability to say *ou* do the right thing is doing him harm; *V* **esprit.**

apte [apt(ə)] *adj* **(a)** ~ **à qch** capable of sth; ~ **à faire** capable of doing, able to do; ~ **à exercer une profession** (suitably) qualified for a job; **je ne suis pas ~ à juger** I'm not able to judge *ou* capable of judging, I'm no fit judge; (*Mil*) ~ **(au service)** fit for service.

(b) (*Jur*) ~ à fit to *ou* for.

aptéryx [apteʀiks] *nm* apterix.

aptitude [aptityd] *nf* **(a)** (*disposition, faculté*) aptitude, ability. **son ~ à étudier** *ou* **à** *ou* **pour l'étude** his aptitude for study *ou* studying, his ability to study; **avoir des ~s variées** to have varied gifts *ou* talents; **avoir de grandes ~s** to be very gifted *ou* talented. **(b)** (*Jur*) fitness.

apurement [apyʀmɑ̃] *nm* auditing, audit.

apurer [apyʀe] (1) *vt* to audit.

aquaplanage [akwaplanaʒ] *nm* aquaplaning.

aquaplane [akwaplan] *nm* aquaplane.

aquaplaning [akwaplaniŋ] *nm* = **aquaplanage.**

aquarelle [akwaʀɛl] *nf* watercolours (*pl*), aquarelle.

aquarelliste [akwaʀelist(ə)] *nmf* painter in watercolours, aquarellist.

aquarium [akwaʀjɔm] *nm* aquarium, fish tank.

aquatique [akwatik] *adj plante, animal* aquatic. **oiseau ~** water bird, aquatic bird; **paysage ~** (*sous l'eau*) underwater landscape; (*marécageux*) watery landscape.

aqueduc [akdyk] *nm* aqueduct; (*Anat*) duct.

aqueux, -euse [akø, øz] *adj* aqueous; *V* **humeur.**

à quia [akɥija] *loc adv* (*littér*) **mettre qn ~** to nonplus sb; **être ~** to be at a loss for a reply.

aquifère [akɥifɛʀ] *adj* aquiferous.

aquilin, e [akilɛ̃, in] *adj* aquiline.

aquilon [akilɔ̃] *nm* (*Poésie*) north wind.

ara [aʀa] *nm* macaw.

arabe [aʀab] 1 *adj désert, cheval* Arabian; *nation, peuple* Arab; *art, langue, littérature* Arabic, Arab; *V* **république.** 2 *nm* (*Ling*) Arabic. **l'~ littéral** written Arabic. 3 *nmf*: **A~** Arab.

arabesque [aʀabɛsk(ə)] *nf* arabesque. ~ **de style** stylistic ornament, ornament of style.

Arabie [aʀabi] *nf* Arabia. ~ **Saoudite, ~ Séoudite** Saudi Arabia.

arabique [aʀabik] *adj V* **gomme.**

arabisant, e [aʀabizɑ̃, ɑ̃t] *nm,f* Arabist, Arabic scholar.

arabisation [aʀabizɑsjɔ̃] *nf* arabization.

arabiser [aʀabize] (1) *vt* to arabize.

arable [aʀabl(ə)] *adj* arable.

arac [aʀak] *nm* = **arack.**

arachide [aʀaʃid] *nf* (*plante*) groundnut (plant); (*graine*) peanut, monkey nut (*Brit*), groundnut. **huile d'~** groundnut *ou* peanut oil; (*Can*) **beurre d'~** peanut butter.

arachnéen, -enne [aʀakneɛ̃, ɛn] *adj* (*littér: léger*) gossamer (*épith*), of gossamer, gossamery; (*Zool*) arachnidan.

arachnoïde [aʀaknɔid] *nf* arachnoid (membrane).

arachnoïdien, -ienne [aʀaknɔidjɛ̃, jɛn] *adj* arachnoid.

arack [aʀak] *nm* a(r)rack.

araignée [aʀeɲe] *nf* **(a)** (*animal*) spider. ~ **de mer** spider crab; **il a une ~ dans le plafond*** *ou* **au plafond*** he's got a screw loose*; *V* **toile. (b)** (*crochet*) grapnel.

araire [aʀɛʀ] *nm* swing plough.

araméen, -enne [aʀameɛ̃, ɛn] 1 *adj* Aram(a)ean, Aramaic. 2 *nm* (*Ling*) Aramaic, Aram(a)ean. 3 *nm,f*: **A~(ne)** Aram(a)ean.

arasement [aʀɑzmɑ̃] *nm* (*V* **araser**) levelling; planing(-down); erosion.

araser [aʀɑze] (1) *vt mur* to level; (*Menuiserie*) to plane (down) (*the piece which is to fit into another*); (*Géol*) *relief* to erode away.

aratoire [aʀatwaʀ] *adj* ploughing (*épith*). **travaux ~s** ploughing; **instrument ~** ploughing implement.

arbalète [aʀbalɛt] *nf* crossbow.

arbalétrier [aʀbaletʀije] *nm* crossbowman.

arbitrage [aʀbitʀaʒ] *nm* **(a)** (*Comm, Pol: action*) arbitration; (*Bourse*) arbitrage; (*sentence*) arbitrament. ~ **obligatoire** compulsory arbitration.

(b) (*Sport: V* **arbitre**) refereeing; umpiring. **erreur d'~** refereeing *ou* referee's error; umpiring *ou* umpire's error.

arbitraire [aʀbitʀɛʀ] 1 *adj* (*despotique, contingent*) arbitrary.

2 *nm*: **l'~: le règne de l'~** the reign of the arbitrary; **l'~ du signe linguistique/d'une décision** the arbitrary nature *ou* the arbitrariness of the linguistic sign/of a decision.

arbitrairement [aʀbitʀɛʀmɑ̃] *adv* arbitrarily.

arbitral, e, *mpl* **-aux** [aʀbitʀal, o] *adj* **(a)** (*Jur*) arbitral. **(b)** (*Sport: V* **arbitre**) referee's (*épith*); umpire's (*épith*). **décision ~e** referee's decision *ou* ruling.

arbitralement [aʀbitʀalmɑ̃] *adv* (*Jur*) by arbitrators; (*Sport: V* **arbitre**) by the referee; by the umpire.

arbitre [aʀbitʀ(ə)] *nm* **(a)** (*Jur*) arbitrator; (*gén*) arbiter, judge. **(b)** (*Sport*) (*Boxe, Ftbl, Rugby*) referee, ref*; (*Cricket, Hockey, Tennis*) umpire; *V* **libre.**

arbitrer [aʀbitʀe] (1) *vt* **(a)** *conflit, litige* to arbitrate; *personnes* to arbitrate between. **(b)** (*Boxe, Ftbl, Rugby*) to referee, ref*; (*Cricket, Hockey, Tennis*) to umpire.

arborer [aʀbɔʀe] (1) *vt vêtement* to sport; *sourire* to wear; *air* to display; *décoration, médaille* to sport, display; *drapeau* to bear, display; *bannière* to bear. **le journal arbore un gros titre** the paper is carrying a big headline; (*fig*) ~ **l'étendard de la révolte** to bear the standard of revolt.

arborescence [aʀbɔʀesɑ̃s] *nf* arborescence.

arborescent, e [aʀbɔʀesɑ̃, ɑ̃t] *adj* arborescent, treelike. **fougère ~e** tree fern.

arboricole [aʀbɔʀikɔl] *adj technique etc* arboricultural; *animal* arboreal.

arboriculteur, -trice [aʀbɔʀikyltœʀ, tʀis] *nm,f* arboriculturist.

arboriculture [aʀbɔʀikyltyʀ] *nf* arboriculture.

arborisation [aʀbɔʀizɑsjɔ̃] *nf* arborization.

arborisé, e [aʀbɔʀize] *adj* arborized.

arbouse [aʀbuz] *nf* arbutus berry.

arbousier [aʀbuzje] *nm* arbutus, strawberry tree.

arbre [aʀbʀ(ə)] **1** *nm* **(a)** (*Bot*) tree. ~ **fruitier/d'agrément** fruit/ornamental tree; (*fig*) **les ~s vous cachent la forêt** you can't see the wood for the trees; (*Prov*) **entre l'~ et l'écorce il ne faut pas mettre le doigt** do not meddle in other people's family affairs.
(b) (*Tech*) shaft.
2: **arbre à cames** camshaft; **avec arbre à cames en tête** with overhead camshaft; **arbre de couche** driving shaft; **arbre d'entraînement** drive shaft; **arbre généalogique** family tree; **arbre d'hélice** propeller shaft; **arbre de mai** may tree; **arbre-manivelle** *nm, pl* **arbres-manivelles** crankshaft; **arbre moteur** driving shaft; **arbre de Noël** (*décoration, aussi Tech*) Christmas tree; **arbre à pain** breadfruit tree; **arbre de transmission** propeller shaft; **arbre de vie** (*Anat*) arbor vitae, tree of life; (*Bible*) tree of life.
arbrisseau, *pl* ~**x** [aʀbʀiso] *nm* shrub.
arbuste [aʀbyst(ə)] *nm* small shrub, bush.
arc [aʀk] **1** *nm* (*arme*) bow; (*Géom*) arc; (*Anat, Archit*) arch. **l'~ de ses sourcils** the arch of her eyebrows; **la côte formait un ~** the coastline formed an arc; *V* **corde, lampe, soudure, tir.**
2: **arc brisé** gothic arch; (*Géom*) **arc de cercle** arc of a circle; (*gén*) **ça forme un arc de cercle** it forms a curve *ou* an arc; **en arc de cercle** in a circular arc; **arc-en-ciel** *nm, pl* **arcs-en-ciel** rainbow; **arc électrique** electric arc; **arc outrepassé** Moorish arch; **arc en plein cintre** Roman arch; **arc-rampant** *nm, pl* **arcs-rampants** rampant arch; **arc de triomphe** triumphal arch; **arc voltaïque** = **arc électrique.**
arcade [aʀkad] *nf* (*Archit*) arch, archway. ~**s** arcade, arches; **les ~s d'un cloître/d'un pont** the arches *ou* arcade of a cloister/of a bridge; **se promener sous les ~s** to walk through the arcade *ou* underneath the arches; ~ **dentaire** dental arch; ~ **sourcilière** arch of the eyebrows.
arcane [aʀkan] *nm* **(a)** (*fig gén pl: mystère*) mystery. **(b)** (*Alchimie*) arcanum.
arcature [aʀkatyʀ] *nf* arcature.
arc-boutant, *pl* **arcs-boutants** [aʀkbutɑ̃] *nm* (*Archit*) flying buttress.
arc-bouter [aʀkbute] (1) **1** *vt* (*Archit*) to buttress. **2 s'arc-bouter** *vpr* to lean, press (*à, contre* (up) against, *sur* on). **arc-bouté contre le mur, il essayait de pousser la table** pressed *ou* braced up against the wall, he tried to push the table.
arceau, *pl* ~**x** [aʀso] *nm* (*Archit*) arch; (*Croquet*) hoop; (*Méd*) cradle.
archaïque [aʀkaik] *adj* archaic.
archaïsant, e [aʀkaizɑ̃, ɑ̃t] **1** *adj* archaistic. **2** *nm,f* archaist.
archaïsme [aʀkaism(ə)] *nm* archaism.
archange [aʀkɑ̃ʒ] *nm* archangel.
arche [aʀʃ(ə)] *nf* **(a)** (*Archit*) arch. **(b)** (*Rel*) ark. **l'~ de Noé** Noah's Ark; **l'~ d'alliance** the Ark of the Covenant.
archéologie [aʀkeɔlɔʒi] *nf* archaeology.
archéologique [aʀkeɔlɔʒik] *adj* archaeological.
archéologue [aʀkeɔlɔg] *nmf* archaeologist.
archer [aʀʃe] *nm* archer, bowman.
archet [aʀʃɛ] *nm* (*Mus, gén*) bow.
archétype [aʀketip] **1** *nm* (*gén*) archetype; (*Bio*) prototype. **2** *adj* (*gén*) archetypal; (*Bio*) prototypal, prototypic.
archevêché [aʀʃəveʃe] *nm* (*territoire*) archdiocese, archbishopric; (*charge*) archbishopric; (*palais*) archbishop's palace.
archevêque [aʀʃəvɛk] *nm* archbishop.
archi... [aʀʃi] **1** *préf* **(a)** (*: *extrêmement*) tremendously, enormously. ~**bondé,** ~**comble,** ~**plein** chock-a-block*; ~**connu** tremendously *ou* enormously well-known; ~**difficile** tremendously *ou* enormously difficult; ~**millionnaire** millionaire several times over.
(b) (*dans un titre*) arch ... . ~**diacre** archdeacon; ~**duc** archduke.
2: (*Ling*) **archiphonème** archiphoneme.
archidiaconat [aʀʃidjakɔna] *nm* archdeaconry.
archidiaconé [aʀʃidjakɔne] *nm* archdeaconry.
archidiacre [aʀʃidjakʀ(ə)] *nm* archdeacon.
archidiocèse [aʀʃidjɔsɛz] *nm* archdiocese.
archiduc [aʀʃidyk] *nm* archduke.
archiduchesse [aʀʃidyʃɛs] *nf* archduchess.
archiépiscopal, e, *mpl* **-aux** [aʀʃiepiskɔpal, o] *adj* archiepiscopal.
archiépiscopat [aʀʃiepiskɔpa] *nm* archbishopric (*office*), archiepiscopate.
archimandrite [aʀʃimɑ̃dʀit] *nm* archimandrite.
Archimède [aʀʃimɛd] *nm* Archimedes; *V* **principe, vis**[1].
archipel [aʀʃipɛl] *nm* archipelago.
archiprêtre [aʀʃipʀɛtʀ(ə)] *nm* archpriest.
architecte [aʀʃitɛkt(ə)] *nm* (*lit, fig*) architect.
architectonique [aʀʃitɛktɔnik] **1** *adj* architectonic. **2** *nf* architectonics (*sg*).
architectural, e, *mpl* **-aux** [aʀʃitɛktyʀal, o] *adj* architectural.
architecture [aʀʃitɛktyʀ] *nf* (*lit, fig*) architecture.
architrave [aʀʃitʀav] *nf* architrave.
archives [aʀʃiv] *nfpl* archives. **les A~ Nationales** the National Archives, ≈ the Public Record Office (*Brit*); **ça restera dans les ~!*** that will go down in history!
archiviste [aʀʃivist(ə)] *nmf* archivist.
archivolte [aʀʃivɔlt(ə)] *nf* archivolt.
arçon [aʀsɔ̃] *nm* (*d'avant*) pommel, horn; (*d'arrière*) cantle; *V* **cheval, pistolet, vider.**
arctique [aʀktik] **1** *adj* (*Géog*) arctic. **2** *nm*: **l'~** the Arctic.
ardemment [aʀdamɑ̃] *adv* ardently, fervently.
ardent, e [aʀdɑ̃, ɑ̃t] *adj* **(a)** (*brûlant*) *tison* burning, glowing; *flambeau* burning; *feu* blazing; *yeux* burning, fiery (*de* with); *couleur* flaming, fiery; *chaleur, soleil* burning, blazing, scorching; *fièvre* burning, raging; *soif* raging; *V* **buisson, chapelle, charbon.**
(b) (*vif*) *conviction, foi* fervent, passionate; *colère* burning, raging; *passion, désir* burning, ardent; *piété, haine* fervent, ardent; *lutte* ardent, passionate; *discours* impassioned, inflamed; *prière, espoir* fervent.
(c) (*bouillant*) *amant* ardent, hot-blooded; *jeunesse, caractère* fiery, passionate; *joueur* keen; *partisan* ardent, keen; *cheval* mettlesome, fiery. **être ~ au travail/au combat** to be a zealous worker/an ardent fighter.
ardeur [aʀdœʀ] *nf* (*V* **ardent**) fervour; passion; raging, ardour; hot-bloodedness; fieriness; keenness. (*littér*) **les ~s de l'amour/de la haine** the ardour of love/hatred; (*littér, hum*) **modérez vos ~s!** control yourself!; **défendre une cause avec ~** to defend a cause ardently *ou* fervently; **son ~ au travail** *ou* **à travailler** his enthusiasm for work; **l'~ du soleil** the heat of the sun; (*littér*) **les ~s de l'été** the heat of summer.
ardillon [aʀdijɔ̃] *nm* [*boucle*] tongue.
ardoise [aʀdwaz] **1** *nf* (*roche, plaque, tablette*) slate; (†: *dette*) unpaid bill. **toit d'~s** slate roof; **couvrir un toit d'~(s)** to slate a roof; (*fig*) **avoir une ~ chez l'épicier** to have credit at the grocer's. **2** *adj inv* (*couleur*) slate-grey.
ardoisé, e [aʀdwaze] *adj* slate-grey.
ardoisier, -ière[1] [aʀdwazje, jɛʀ] **1** *adj gisement* slaty; *industrie* slate (*épith*). **2** *nm* (*ouvrier*) slate-quarry worker; (*propriétaire*) slate-quarry owner.
ardoisière[2] [aʀdwazjɛʀ] *nf* slate quarry.
ardu, e [aʀdy] *adj travail* arduous, laborious; *problème* difficult; *pente* steep.
are [aʀ] *nm* are, one hundred square metres.
areligieux, -euse [aʀəliʒjø, øz] *adj* areligious.
aréna [aʀena] *nf* (*Can Sport*) arena, (skating) rink.
arène [aʀɛn] *nf* (*piste*) arena; (*Géol*) sand, arenite. (*Archit*) ~**s** amphitheatre; (*fig*) **l'~ politique** the political arena; (*Géol*) ~ **granitique** granitic sand; *V* **descendre.**
aréomètre [aʀeɔmɛtʀ(ə)] *nm* hydrometer.
aréométrie [aʀeɔmetʀi] *nf* hydrometry.
aréopage [aʀeɔpaʒ] *nm* (*fig*) learned assembly. (*Hist*) **l'A~** the Areopagus.
arête [aʀɛt] *nf* **(a)** (*Zool*) (fish)bone. ~ **centrale** backbone; **c'est plein d'~s** it's full of bones, it's very bony; **enlever les ~s d'un poisson** to bone a fish.
(b) (*bord*) (*gén*) [*cube, pierre*] edge (*where two faces meet*); [*toit*] arris; [*voûte*] groin; [*montagne*] ridge; [*nez*] bridge.
(c) (*Bot*) [*seigle, orge*] beard. ~**s** beard.
argent [aʀʒɑ̃] *nm* **(a)** (*métal*) silver. **en ~, d' ~** silver; *V* **noce, parole, vif**[1].
(b) (*couleur*) silver. **cheveux/reflets (d')~** silvery hair/glints; **des souliers ~** silver *ou* silvery shoes.
(c) (*Fin*) money (*U*). **il a de l'~** he's got money, he's well off; ~ **liquide** ready money, (ready) cash; ~ **de poche** pocket money; **il l'a fait pour de l'~** he did it for money; **il se fait un ~ fou*** he makes lots *ou* loads* of money; **les puissances d'~** the power of money; **payer ~ comptant** to pay cash; *V* **couleur, manger.**
(d) (*loc*) **l'~ leur fond dans les mains** they spend money like water; **j'en ai/j'en veux pour mon ~** I've got/I want (to get) my money's worth; **on en a pour son ~** we get good value (for money), it's worth every penny; **faire ~ de tout** to turn everything into cash, make money out of anything; **jeter** *ou* **flanquer* l'~ par la fenêtre** to throw *ou* chuck* money away, throw money down the drain; **prendre qch/les paroles de qn pour ~ comptant** to take sth/what sb says at (its) face value; (*Prov*) **l'~ n'a pas d'odeur** money has no smell; (*Prov*) **l'~ ne fait pas le bonheur** money can't buy happiness; (*Prov*) **point d'~, point de Suisse** nothing for nothing.
(e) (*Hér*) argent.
argenté, e [aʀʒɑ̃te] (*ptp de* **argenter**) *adj couleur, reflets, cheveux* silver, silvery; *couverts, objet* silver-plated, silvered. **je ne suis pas très ~ en ce moment*** I'm (rather) broke at the moment*, I'm not too well-off just now; **ils ne sont pas très ~s*** they're not very well-off; *V* **renard.**
argenter [aʀʒɑ̃te] (1) *vt miroir* to silver; *couverts* to silver (-plate); (*fig littér*) to give a silvery sheen to, silver (*littér*).
argenterie [aʀʒɑ̃tʀi] *nf* silverware; (*de métal argenté*) silver plate.
argenteur [aʀʒɑ̃tœʀ] *nm* silverer.
argentier [aʀʒɑ̃tje] *nm* (*hum: ministre*) Minister of Finance; (*Hist*) Superintendent of Finance; (*meuble*) silver cabinet.
argentifère [aʀʒɑ̃tifɛʀ] *adj* silver-bearing, argentiferous (*T*).
argentin, e[1] [aʀʒɑ̃tɛ̃, in] *adj* silvery.
argentin, e[2] [aʀʒɑ̃tɛ̃, in] **1** *adj* Argentinian, Argentine (*épith*). **2** *nm,f*: **A~(e)** Argentinian, Argentine.
Argentine [aʀʒɑ̃tin] *nf*: l' ~ Argentina, the Argentine.
argenture [aʀʒɑ̃tyʀ] *nf* [*miroir*] silvering; [*couverts*] silver-plating, silvering.
argien, -ienne [aʀʒjɛ̃, jɛn] **1** *adj* Argos (*épith*), of Argos. **2** *nm, f*: **A~(ne)** inhabitant *ou* native of Argos.
argile [aʀʒil] *nf* clay; *V* **colosse.**
argileux, -euse [aʀʒilø, øz] *adj* clayey.
argon [aʀgɔ̃] *nm* argon.
argonaute [aʀgɔnot] *nm* (*Myth*) Argonaut; (*Zool*) argonaut, paper nautilus.
argot [aʀgo] *nm* slang. ~ **de métier** trade slang.
argotique [aʀgɔtik] *adj* (*de l'argot*) slang; (*très familier*) slangy.
argotisme [aʀgɔtism(ə)] *nm* slang term.
argousin†† [aʀguzɛ̃] *nm* (*péj hum: agent de police*) rozzer† (*péj*), bluebottle† (*péj*).
arguer [aʀgɥe] (1) (*littér*) **1** *vt* **(a)** (*déduire*) to deduce. **il ne**

peut rien ~ de ces faits he can draw no conclusion from these facts.

(b) (*prétexter*) **~ que** to put forward the reason that; **il argua qu'il n'avait rien entendu** he protested that he had heard nothing.

2 arguer de *vt indir*: **il refusa, arguant de leur manque de ressources** he refused, putting forward their lack of resources as an excuse *ou* as a reason.

argument [aʀgymɑ̃] *nm* (*raison, preuve, Littérat, Math*) argument. **tirer ~ de** to use as an argument *ou* excuse; **~ frappant** convincing argument; (*hum: coup*) blow; **~ massue** sledgehammer argument.

argumentateur, -trice [aʀgymɑ̃tatœʀ, tʀis] *adj* argumentative.

argumentation [aʀgymɑ̃tɑsjɔ̃] *nf* argumentation.

argumenter [aʀgymɑ̃te] (1) *vi* to argue. **discours bien argumenté** well-argued speech.

argus [aʀgys] *nm*: **l'~** ≈ Glass's directory (*Brit*) (*guide to secondhand car prices*).

argutie [aʀgysi] *nf* (*littér: gén péj*) quibble. **~s** pettifoggery, quibbles, quibbling.

aria[1] [aʀja] *nm* (†, *dial*) bother (*U*), nuisance (*U*).

aria[2] [aʀja] *nf* (*Mus*) aria.

Ariane [aʀjan] *nf* Ariadne; *V* **fil.**

aride [aʀid] *adj* **(a)** (*stérile*) *terre, climat* arid; *esprit* sterile, infertile; *sujet* dry, arid, barren; *travail* thankless (*épith*). **cœur ~** heart of stone. **(b)** (*sec*) *terre* arid, parched; *climat* arid, dry; *vent* dry.

aridité [aʀidite] *nf* (*V* **aride**) aridity; sterility; infertility; dryness; barrenness; thanklessness; parchedness. **~ du cœur** stony-heartedness.

ariette [aʀjɛt] *nf* arietta, ariette.

Arioste [aʀjɔst] *nm*: **l'~** Ariosto.

aristo: [aʀisto] *nmf* (*abrév péj de* **aristocrate**) toff*† (*Brit*).

aristocrate [aʀistɔkʀat] *nmf* aristocrat.

aristocratie [aʀistɔkʀasi] *nf* aristocracy.

aristocratique [aʀistɔkʀatik] *adj* aristocratic.

aristocratiquement [aʀistɔkʀatikmɑ̃] *adv* aristocratically.

Aristophane [aʀistɔfan] *nm* Aristophanes.

Aristote [aʀistɔt] *nm* Aristotle.

aristotélicien, -ienne [aʀistɔtelisjɛ̃, jɛn] *adj, nm,f* Aristotelian.

arithméticien, -ienne [aʀitmetisjɛ̃, jɛn] *nm,f* arithmetician.

arithmétique [aʀitmetik] **1** *nf* (*science*) arithmetic; (*livre*) arithmetic book. **2** *adj* arithmetic(al).

arithmétiquement [aʀitmetikmɑ̃] *adv* arithmetically.

arlequin [aʀləkɛ̃] *nm* (*Théât*) Harlequin. **bas (d')~** harlequin stockings; *V* **habit.**

arlequinade [aʀləkinad] *nf* (*fig*) buffoonery; (*Théât*) harlequinade.

armagnac [aʀmaɲak] *nm* armagnac.

armateur [aʀmatœʀ] *nm* (*propriétaire*) shipowner; (*exploitant*) ship's manager.

armature [aʀmatyʀ] *nf* **(a)** (*gén: carcasse*) *[tente, montage, parapluie]* frame; (*Constr*) framework, armature (*T*); (*fig: infrastructure*) framework. **~ de corset** corset bones *ou* stays; **soutien-gorge à ~** underwired bra.

(b) (*Mus*) key signature.

(c) (*Phys*) *[condensateur]* electrode; *[aimant]* armature.

arme [aʀm(ə)] *nf* **(a)** (*instrument*) (*gén*) weapon, arm; (*fusil, revolver*) gun. **fabrique d'~s** arms factory; **on a retrouvé l'~ du crime** the weapon used in the crime has been found; **il braqua** *ou* **dirigea son ~ vers** *ou* **contre moi** he aimed *ou* pointed his gun at me; **des policiers sans ~(s)** unarmed police; **se battre à l'~ blanche** to fight with blades; **~ atomique/biologique** atomic/biological weapon; **~ à feu** firearm; **~s de jet** projectiles; **l'~ absolue** the ultimate weapon; *V* **bretelle, maniement, port**[2].

(b) (*élément d'une armée*) arm. **l'~ de l'infanterie** the infantry arm; **dans quelle ~ sert-il?** which section is he in?; **les 3 ~s** the 3 services.

(c) (*Mil*) **la carrière** *ou* **le métier des ~s** soldiering; (*littér*) **le succès de nos ~s** the success of our armies; **être sous les ~s** to be a soldier; **appeler un régiment sous les ~s** to call up a regiment; **soldats en ~s** soldiers at arms; **un peuple en ~s** a people up in arms; **aux ~s!** to arms!; **compagnon** *ou* **frère d'~s** comrade-in-arms; *V* **homme, place, prise.**

(d) (*fig: moyen d'action*) weapon. **donner** *ou* **fournir des ~s à qn** to give sb weapons (*contre* against); **le silence peut être une ~ puissante** silence can be a powerful weapon; **une ~ à double tranchant** a double-edged blade *ou* weapon; **il est sans ~ contre ce genre d'accusation** he's defenceless (*Brit*) *ou* defenseless (*US*) against that sort of accusation.

(e) (*Escrime*) **les ~s** fencing; **faire des ~s** to fence, do fencing; *V* **maître, passe**[1]**, salle.**

(f) (*Hér*) **~s** arms, coat of arms; **aux ~s de** bearing the arms of; *V* **héraut.**

(g) (*loc*) **à ~s égales** on equal terms; **déposer** *ou* **mettre bas les ~s** to lay down (one's) arms; **rendre les ~s** to lay down one's arms, surrender; **faire ses premières ~s** to make one's début (*dans* in); **passer qn par les ~s** to shoot sb (*firing squad*); **partir avec ~s et bagages** to pack up and go; **passer l'~ à gauche**: to kick the bucket:; **prendre le pouvoir/régler un différend par les ~s** to take power/settle a dispute by force; **porter les ~s** to be a soldier; **prendre les ~s** (*se soulever*) to rise up in arms; (*pour défendre son pays etc*) to take up arms; **avoir l'~ au bras** to be in arms; **~ à la bretelle!** ≈ slope arms!; **~ sur l'épaule!** shoulder arms!; **~ au pied!** attention! (*with rifle on ground*); **portez ~!** shoulder arms!; **présentez ~!** present arms!; **reposez ~!** order arms!; *V* **appel, fait**[1]**, gens**[1]**, pris, suspension.**

armé, e[1] [aʀme] (*ptp de* **armer**) **1** *adj personne, forces, conflit* armed. **~ jusqu'aux dents** armed to the teeth; **bien ~ contre le froid** well-armed *ou* -equipped against the cold; **attention, il est ~!** careful, he's armed!; **~ d'un bâton/d'un dictionnaire** armed with a stick/a dictionary; **être bien ~ pour passer un examen** to be well-equipped to take an examination; (*fig*) **il est bien ~ pour se défendre** he is well-equipped for life; **il est bien ~ contre leurs arguments** he's well-armed against their arguments; **cactus ~ de piquants** cactus armed with spikes; **canne ~e d'un bout ferré** stick fitted with an iron tip, stick tipped with iron; *V* **béton, ciment, force, main.**

2 *nm* (*position*) cock.

armée[2] [aʀme] **1** *nf* army. **~ de mercenaires/d'occupation/régulière** mercenary/occupying/regular army; **être dans l'~** to be in the army; **les ~s alliées** the allied armies; (*fig*) **une ~ de domestiques/rats** an army of servants/rats; (*péj*) **regardez-moi cette armée (d'incapables)** just look at this hopeless bunch* *ou* crew*; *V* **corps, grand, zone.**

2: armée active regular army; **l'armée de l'air** the Air Force; **l'armée de mer** the Navy; **armée de réserve** reserve; **l'Armée Rouge** the Red Army; **l'Armée du Salut** the Salvation Army; **l'armée de terre** the Army.

armement [aʀməmɑ̃] *nm* **(a)** (*action*) *[pays, armée]* armament; *[personne]* arming; *[fusil]* cocking; *[appareil-photo]* winding-on; *[navire]* fitting-out, equipping.

(b) (*armes*) *[soldat]* arms, weapons; *[pays, troupe, avion, navire]* arms, armament(s). **usine d'~** arms factory; **la réduction des ~s** the reduction of arms; **dépenses d'~s de la France** France's expenditure on arms; **vendre des ~s aux rebelles** to sell weapons *ou* arms to the rebels; *V* **course.**

Arménie [aʀmeni] *nf* Armenia; *V* **papier.**

arménien, -ienne [aʀmenjɛ̃, jɛn] **1** *adj* Armenian. **2** *nm* (*Ling*) Armenian. **3** *nm,f*: **A~(ne)** Armenian.

armer [aʀme] (1) **1** *vt* **(a)** *pays, forteresse, personne* to arm (*de* with). **~ des rebelles contre un gouvernement** to arm rebels against a government; (*fig*) **~ le gouvernement de pouvoirs exceptionnels** to arm *ou* equip the government with exceptional powers; (*fig*) **~ qn contre les difficultés de la vie** to arm sb against life's difficulties, arm *ou* equip sb to deal with the difficulties of life.

(b) (*Hist*) **~ qn chevalier** to dub sb knight.

(c) (*Naut*) *navire* to fit out, equip.

(d) *fusil* to cock; *appareil-photo* to wind on.

(e) (*renforcer*) *béton, poutre* to reinforce (*de* with). **~ qch de** to fit sth with; **~ un bâton d'une pointe d'acier** to fit a stick with a steel tip, fit a steel tip on(to) a stick.

2 s'armer *vpr* (*s'équiper*) to arm o.s. (*de* with, *contre* against). **s'~ d'un fusil/d'un dictionnaire** to arm o.s. with a gun/a dictionary; (*fig*) **s'~ de courage/de patience** to arm o.s. with courage/patience.

armistice [aʀmistis] *nm* armistice.

armoire [aʀmwaʀ] *nf* (*gén*) (tall) cupboard; (*penderie*) wardrobe. **~ à pharmacie** medicine chest *ou* cabinet; **~ frigorifique** cold room *ou* store; **~ à linge** linen cupboard (*Brit*) *ou* closet (*US*); **~ normande** large wardrobe; **~ à glace** (*lit*) wardrobe with a mirror; (**fig: costaud*) hulking great brute*.

armoiries [aʀmwaʀi] *nfpl* coat of arms, armorial bearings.

armorial, e, *mpl* **-aux** [aʀmɔʀjal, o] *adj, nm* armorial.

armoricain, e [aʀmɔʀikɛ̃, ɛn] **1** *adj* Armorican. **2** *nm,f* (*Hist*) **A~(e)** Armorican.

armorier [aʀmɔʀje] (7) *vt* to emblazon.

armure [aʀmyʀ] *nf* (*Mil, Zool*) armour; (*fig*) defence; (*Phys*) armature; (*Tex*) weave.

armurerie [aʀmyʀʀi] *nf* (*V* **armurier**) (*fabrique*) arms factory; (*magasin*) gunsmith's; armourer's; (*profession*) arms trade.

armurier [aʀmyʀje] *nm* (*fabricant, marchand*) *[armes à feu]* gunsmith; *[armes blanches]* armourer; (*Mil*) armourer.

arnaquer: [aʀnake] (1) *vt* (*escroquer*) to do:, diddle*, swindle*; (*arrêter*) to nab*. **on s'est fait ~ dans ce restaurant** we were fleeced* *ou* diddled* in that restaurant.

arnaqueur, -euse [aʀnakœʀ, øz] *nm,f* swindler, cheat.

arnica [aʀnika] *nf* arnica.

aromate [aʀɔmat] *nm* seasoning (*U*). **ajoutez quelques ~s** add (some) seasoning *ou* a few herbs (*ou* spices).

aromatique [aʀɔmatik] *adj* (*gén, Chim*) aromatic.

aromatiser [aʀɔmatize] (1) *vt* to flavour.

arôme, arome [aʀom] *nm [plat]* aroma; *[café, vin]* aroma, fragrance; *[fleur]* fragrance.

aronde†† [aʀɔ̃d] *nf* swallow; *V* **queue.**

arpège [aʀpɛʒ] *nm* arpeggio.

arpéger [aʀpeʒe] (6 *et* 3) *vt passage* to play in arpeggios; *accord* to play as an arpeggio, spread.

arpent [aʀpɑ̃] *nm* (*Hist*) arpent (*about an acre*). (*fig*) **il a quelques ~s de terre en province** he's got a few acres in the country.

arpentage [aʀpɑ̃taʒ] *nm* (*technique*) (land) surveying; (*mesure*) measuring, surveying.

arpenter [aʀpɑ̃te] (1) *vt* to pace (up and down); (*Tech*) *terrain* to measure, survey.

arpenteur [aʀpɑ̃tœʀ] *nm* (land) surveyor; *V* **chaîne.**

arpète* [aʀpɛt] *nmf* apprentice.

arpion: [aʀpjɔ̃] *nm* hoof:.

arqué, e [aʀke] (*ptp de* **arquer**) *adj forme, objet* curved, arched; *sourcils* arched, curved; *jambes* bow (*épith*), bandy. **avoir le dos ~** to be humpbacked *ou* hunchbacked; **le dos ~ sous l'effort** his back arched under the strain; **il a les jambes ~es** he's bandy(-legged) *ou* bow-legged; **nez ~** hooknose, hooked nose.

arquebuse [aʀkəbyz] *nf* (h)arquebus.

arquebusier [aʀkəbyzje] *nm* (*soldat*) (h)arquebusier.

arquer [aʀke] (1) **1** *vt objet, tige* to curve; *dos* to arch. **2** *vi [objet]* to bend, curve; *[poutre]* to sag. **il ne peut plus ~‡** he can't walk any more. **3 s'arquer** *vpr* to curve.

arrachage [aʀaʃaʒ] *nm* (*V* **arracher**) lifting; pulling up; uprooting; extraction; pulling; pulling out. **~ des mauvaises herbes** weeding.

arrache- [aʀaʃ] *préf V* **arracher.**

arraché [aʀaʃe] *nm* (*Sport*) snatch. (*fig*) **obtenir la victoire à l'~** to snatch victory; **ils ont eu le contrat à l'~** they just managed to snatch the contract.

arrachement [aʀaʃmɑ̃] *nm* **(a)** (*chagrin*) wrench. **quel ~ de le voir partir!** it was a terrible wrench to see him leave! **(b)** (*V* **arracher**) pulling out; tearing off.

arracher [aʀaʃe] (1) **1** *vt* **(a)** (*extraire*) *légume* to lift; *souche, plante* to pull up, uproot; *mauvaises herbes* to pull up; *dent* to take out, extract, pull (*US*); *poil, clou* to pull out. **il est parti ~ les mauvaises herbes** he's out weeding; **je vais me faire ~ une dent** I'm going to have a tooth out *ou* extracted.

(b) (*déchirer*) *chemise, affiche, membre* to tear off; *cheveux* to tear *ou* pull out; *feuille, page* to tear *ou* pull out (*de* of). (*fig*) **je vais lui ~ les yeux** I'll scratch *ou* claw his eyes out; (*fig*) **j'ai arraché son voile** *ou* **masque** I have torn down his mask, I've unmasked him; (*fig*) **ce spectacle lui arracha le cœur** the sight of it broke his heart, it was a heartrending sight for him.

(c) (*enlever*) **~ à qn** *portefeuille, arme* to snatch *ou* grab from sb; (*fig*) *argent* to extract from sb, get out of sb; *applaudissements, larmes* to wring from sb; *victoire* to wrest from sb; **il lui arracha son sac à main** he snatched *ou* grabbed her handbag from her; **je lui ai arraché cette promesse/ces aveux/la vérité** I dragged this promise/confession/the truth out of him, I wrung *ou* wrested this promise/this confession/the truth out of *ou* from him.

(d) (*soustraire*) **~ qn à** *famille, pays* to tear *ou* drag sb away from; *passion, vice, soucis* to rescue sb from; *sommeil, rêve* to drag *ou* snatch sb out of; *ou* from; *sort, mort* to snatch sb from; *habitudes, méditation* to force sb out of; **~ qn des mains d'un ennemi** to snatch sb from (out of) the hands of an enemy; **la mort nous l'a arraché** death has snatched *ou* torn him from us; **il m'a arraché du lit à 6 heures** he got *ou* dragged me out of bed at 6 o'clock.

2 s'arracher *vpr* **(a)** (*se déchirer*) **tu t'es encore arraché (les vêtements) après le grillage** you've torn your clothes on the fence again; **s'~ les cheveux** (*lit*) to tear *ou* pull out one's hair; (*fig*) to tear one's hair; (*fig*) **s'~ les yeux** to scratch each other's eyes out.

(b) s'~ qn/qch to fight over sb/sth; (*hum*) **on se m'arrache‡** they're all fighting over me* (*hum*).

(c) s'~ de *ou* **à** *pays, famille* to tear o.s. away from; *habitude, méditation, passion* to force o.s. out of; *lit* to drag o.s. from, force o.s. out of.

3: arrache-clou *nm, pl* **arrache-clous** nail wrench; **arrache-pied: d'arrache-pied** *adv* relentlessly.

arracheur [aʀaʃœʀ] *nm V* **mentir.**

arracheuse [aʀaʃøz] *nf* (*Agr*) lifter, grubber.

arraisonnement [aʀɛzɔnmɑ̃] *nm* (*Naut*) inspection.

arraisonner [aʀɛzɔne] (1) *vt* (*Naut*) to inspect.

arrangeant, e [aʀɑ̃ʒɑ̃, ɑ̃t] *adj* accommodating, obliging.

arrangement [aʀɑ̃ʒmɑ̃] *nm* **(a)** (*action*) *[fleurs, coiffure, voyage]* arrangement.

(b) (*agencement*) *[mobilier, maison]* layout, arrangement; *[fiches]* order, arrangement; *[mots]* order. **l'~ de sa coiffure** the way her hair is done *ou* arranged; **l'~ de sa toilette** the way she is dressed.

(c) (*accord*) agreement, settlement, arrangement. **arriver** *ou* **parvenir à un ~** to reach an agreement *ou* a settlement, come to an arrangement; (*Jur*) **~ de famille** family settlement (*in financial matters*).

(d) (*Mus*) arrangement. **~ pour guitare** arrangement for guitar.

(e) (*Math*) arrangement.

(f) (*préparatifs*) **~s** arrangements.

arranger [aʀɑ̃ʒe] (3) **1** *vt* **(a)** (*disposer*) *fleurs, coiffure, chambre* to arrange. **~ sa cravate/sa jupe** to straighten (up) one's tie/skirt, set one's tie/skirt straight.

(b) (*organiser*) *voyage, réunion* to arrange, organize; *rencontre, entrevue* to arrange, fix (up). **~ sa vie/ses affaires** to organize one's life/one's affairs; **il a tout arrangé pour ce soir** he has seen to *ou* he has arranged everything for tonight; **ce combat de catch était arrangé à l'avance** this wrestling match was fixed (in advance) *ou* was a put-up job*.

(c) (*régler*) *différend* to settle. **je vais essayer d'~ les choses** I'll try to sort things out; **tout est arrangé, le malentendu est dissipé** everything is settled *ou* sorted out, the disagreement is over; **et ce qui n'arrange rien, il est en retard!** and he's late, which doesn't help matters!; **ce contretemps n'arrange pas nos affaires** this setback doesn't help our affairs.

(d) (*contenter*) to suit, be convenient for. **ça ne m'arrange pas tellement** that doesn't really suit me; **cela m'arrange bien** that suits me nicely *ou* fine; **à 6 heures si ça vous arrange** at 6 o'clock if that suits you *ou* if that's convenient (for you); **tu le crois parce que ça t'arrange** you believe him because it suits you (to do so).

(e) (*réparer*) *voiture, montre* to fix, put right; *robe* (*recoudre*) to fix, mend; (*modifier*) to alter. **il faudrait ~ votre devoir, il est confus** you'll have to sort out your exercise as it's rather muddled.

(f) (**: malmener*) to sort out‡ (*Brit*). **il s'est drôlement fait ~** he got a real working over*, they really sorted him out‡ (*Brit*); **te voilà bien arrangé!** what a state *ou* mess you've got yourself in!*

(g) (*Littérat, Mus*) to arrange.

2 s'arranger *vpr* **(a)** (*se mettre d'accord*) to come to an agreement *ou* arrangement. **arrangez-vous avec le patron** you'll have to come to an agreement *ou* arrangement with the boss *ou* sort it out with the boss; **s'~ à l'amiable** to come to a friendly *ou* an amicable agreement.

(b) (*s'améliorer*) *[querelle]* to be settled; *[situation]* to work out, sort itself out (*Brit*); *[santé]* to get better. **le temps n'a pas l'air de s'~** it doesn't look as though the weather is getting any better; **tout va s'~** everything will work out (all right) *ou* sort itself out, it'll all work out (all right) *ou* sort itself out; **les choses s'arrangèrent d'elles-mêmes** things sorted (*Brit*) *ou* worked themselves out unaided; **ça ne s'arrange pas*, il est plus brouillon que jamais** things are no better, he's more muddled than ever; **alors, ça s'arrange entre eux?** are things getting (any) better between them?

(c) (*se débrouiller*) **arrangez-vous comme vous voudrez mais je les veux demain** I don't mind how you do it but I want them for tomorrow; (*iro*) **tu t'arranges toujours pour avoir des taches!** you always manage to get grubby! (*iro*); **je ne sais pas comment tu t'arranges, mais tu as toujours des taches** I don't know how you manage (it), but you're always grubby; **il va s'~ pour finir le travail avant demain** he'll see to it that *ou* he'll make sure (that) he finishes the job before tomorrow; **il s'est arrangé pour avoir des places gratuites** he has seen to it that he has got *ou* he has managed to get some free seats; **arrangez-vous pour venir me chercher à la gare** arrange it so that you can *ou* see to it that you can come and meet me at the station.

(d) s'~ de to make do with; **il s'est arrangé du fauteuil pour dormir** he made do with the armchair to sleep in.

(e) (*se classer*) to be arranged. **ses arguments s'arrangent logiquement** his arguments are logically arranged.

(f) (*se rajuster*) to tidy o.s. up. **elle s'arrange les cheveux** she's tidying her hair.

(g) (**: se faire mal*) **tu t'es bien arrangé!** you've got yourself in a fine state!, you DO look a mess!*

arrangeur [aʀɑ̃ʒœʀ] *nm* (*Mus*) arranger.

arrérages [aʀeʀaʒ] *nmpl* arrears.

arrestation [aʀɛstɑsjɔ̃] **1** *nf* arrest. **procéder à l'~ de qn** to arrest sb, take sb into custody; **être en état d'~** to be under arrest; **mettre en état d'~** to place *ou* put under arrest, take into custody; **mise en ~** arrest; **ils ont procédé à une douzaine d'~s** they made a dozen arrests.

2: arrestation préventive ≈ arrest; **arrestation provisoire** taking into preventive custody.

arrêt [aʀɛ] **1** *nm* **(a)** *[machine, véhicule]* stopping; *[développement, croissance]* stopping, checking, arrest; *[hémorragie]* stopping, arrest. **attendez l'~ complet (du train/de l'avion)** wait until the train stops/until the aircraft has come to a standstill; **5 minutes d'~** 5 minutes' stop, a 5-minute stop; **véhicule à l'~** stationary vehicle; **faire un ~** *[train]* to stop, make a stop; *[gardien de but]* to make a save; **le train fit un ~ brusque** the train suddenly stopped *ou* came to a sudden stop *ou* standstill; **nous avons fait plusieurs ~s** we made several stops *ou* halts; *V* **chien.**

(b) (*lieu*) stop. **~ d'autobus** bus stop; **~ fixe/facultatif** compulsory/request stop; **ne descendez pas, ce n'est pas l'~** don't get out, this isn't the stop.

(c) (*Mil*) **~s** arrest; **~s simples/de rigueur** open/close arrest; **~s de forteresse** confinement (*in military prison*); **mettre qn aux ~s** to put sb under arrest; *V* **maison, mandat.**

(d) (*Jur: décision, jugement*) judgment, decision. (†, *littér*) **les ~s du destin** the decrees of destiny (*littér*).

(e) (*Couture*) **faire un ~** to fasten off the thread; *V* **point**[2].

(f) (*Tech*) *[machine]* stop mechanism; *[serrure]* ward; *[fusil]* safety catch. **appuyez sur l'~** press the stop button.

(g) (*loc*) (*Jur*) **faire ~ sur les appointements** to issue a writ of attachment (on debtor's salary); **rester** *ou* **tomber en ~** (*Chasse*) to point; (*fig*) to stop short; **marquer un ~ avant de continuer à parler** to pause *ou* make a pause before going on; **sans ~** (*sans interruption*) *travailler, pleuvoir* without stopping, non-stop; (*très fréquemment*) *se produire, se détraquer* continually, constantly; (*Rail*) **'sans ~ jusqu'à Perpignan'** 'non-stop to Perpignan', 'through train to Perpignan'; **ce train est sans ~ jusqu'à Lyon** this train is non-stop to Lyons, this is the through train to Lyons.

2: arrêt du cœur cardiac arrest; **l'arrêt des hostilités** the cessation of hostilities; (*Sport*) **arrêt du jeu** stoppage; **arrêt de mort** sentence of death, death sentence *ou* penalty; **arrêt de travail** stoppage (of work).

arrêté, e [aʀete] (*ptp de* **arrêter**) **1** *adj décision, volonté* firm, immutable; *idée, opinion* fixed, firm. **c'est une chose ~e** the matter *ou* it is settled.

2 *nm* (*décision administrative*) order, decree (*frm*). **~ ministériel** departmental *ou* ministerial order; **~ municipal** ≈ by(e)-law; **~ préfectoral** order of the prefect; **~ de compte** (*fermeture*) settlement of account; (*relevé*) statement of account (*to date*).

arrêter [aʀete] (1) **1** *vt* **(a)** (*immobiliser*) *personne, machine, montre* to stop; *cheval* to stop, pull up; *moteur* to switch off, stop. **arrêtez-moi près de la poste** drop me by the post office; **il m'a arrêté dans le couloir pour me parler** he stopped me in the corridor to speak to me; (*dans la conversation*) **ici, je vous arrête!** I must stop *ou* interrupt you there!; **arrête ton char‡** (*parler*) shut up!*, belt up!‡; (*se vanter*) stop swanking!*

(b) (*entraver*) *développement, croissance* to stop, check, arrest; *foule, ennemi* to stop, halt; *hémorragie* to stop, arrest. **le trafic ferroviaire est arrêté à cause de la grève** rail traffic is at a standstill *ou* all the trains have been cancelled *ou* halted because of the strike; **rien n'arrête la marche de l'histoire**

nothing can stop ou check ou halt the march of history; (hum) on n'arrête pas le progrès there's no stopping progress; nous avons été arrêtés par un embouteillage we were held up ou stopped by a traffic jam; seul le prix l'arrête it's only the price that stops him; rien ne l'arrête there's nothing to stop him.

(c) (abandonner) étude to give up; (Sport) compétition to give up; (Théât) représentations to cancel. ~ ses études/le tennis to give up one's studies/tennis, stop studying/playing tennis; ~ la fabrication d'un produit to discontinue (the manufacture of) a product; on a dû ~ les travaux à cause de la neige we had to stop work ou call a halt to the work because of the snow.

(d) (faire prisonnier) to arrest. il s'est fait ~ hier he got himself arrested yesterday.

(e) (Fin) compte (fermer) to settle; (relever) to make up. les comptes sont arrêtés chaque fin de mois statements (of account) are made up at the end of every month.

(f) (Couture) point to fasten off.

(g) (fixer) jour, lieu to appoint, decide on; plan to decide on. ~ son attention/ses regards sur to fix one's attention/gaze on; ~ un marché to settle a deal; il a arrêté son choix he has made his choice; ma décision est arrêtée my mind is made up; (Admin) ~ que to rule that.

2 vi to stop. il n'arrête pas he's never still, he's always on the go; il n'arrête pas de critiquer tout le monde he never stops criticizing everyone; arrête de parler! stop talking!; il a arrêté de fumer après sa maladie he gave up ou stopped smoking after his illness.

3 s'arrêter vpr (a) (s'immobiliser) [personne, machine, montre] to stop; [train, voiture] to stop, come to a stop ou a halt ou a standstill. nous nous arrêtâmes sur le bas-côté/dans un village we pulled up ou stopped by the roadside/at a village; le train s'arrêta brusquement the train came to a sudden stop ou halt, the train stopped suddenly; s'~ court ou net [personne] to stop dead ou short; [bruit] to stop suddenly; nous nous sommes arrêtés 10 jours à Lyon we stayed ou stopped* 10 days in Lyons.

(b) (s'interrompre) to stop, break off. s'~ de travailler/de parler to stop working/speaking; s'~ pour se reposer/pour manger to break off ou stop for a rest/to eat; arrête-toi un peu, tu vas t'épuiser stop for a while ou take a break ou you'll wear yourself out; les ouvriers se sont arrêtés à 17 heures (grève) the workmen downed tools (surtout Brit) ou stopped work at 5 o'clock; (heure de fermeture) the workmen finished (work) ou stopped work at 5 o'clock; sans s'~ without stopping, without a break.

(c) (cesser) [développement, croissance] to stop, come to a halt, come to a standstill; [hémorragie] to stop. le travail s'est arrêté dans l'usine en grève work has stopped in the striking factory, the striking factory is at a standstill; s'~ de manger/marcher to stop eating/walking; s'~ de fumer/boire to give up ou stop smoking/drinking.

(d) s'~ sur [choix, regard] to fall on; il ne faut pas s'~ aux apparences one must always look beneath appearances; s'~ à des détails to pay too much attention to details; s'~ à un projet to settle ou fix on a plan.

arrhes [aʀ] nfpl deposit.

arrière [aʀjɛʀ] 1 nm (a) [voiture] back; [bateau] stern; [train] rear. (Naut) à l'~ aft, at the stern; à l'~ de at the stern of, abaft; se balancer d'avant en ~ to rock backwards and forwards; avec le moteur à l'~ with the engine at the back; (en temps de guerre) l'~ (du pays) the civilian zone (behind the line of fighting); l'~ tient bon morale behind the lines is high.

(b) (Sport: joueur) fullback.

(c) (Mil) les ~s the rear; attaquer les ~s de l'ennemi to attack the enemy in the rear; assurer ou protéger ses ~s (lit) to protect the rear; (fig) to keep one's options open.

(d) en ~ (derrière) behind; (vers l'arrière) backwards; être/rester en ~ to be/lag ou drop behind; regarder en ~ to look back ou behind; faire un pas en ~ to step back(wards), take a step back; aller/marcher en ~ to go/walk backwards; se pencher en ~ to lean back(wards); (Naut) en ~ toute! full astern!; 100 ans en ~ 100 years ago ou back; il faut remonter loin en ~ pour trouver une telle sécheresse we have to go a long way back (in time) to find a similar drought; revenir en ~ [marcheur] to go back, retrace one's steps; [orateur] to go back over what has been said; [civilisation] to regress; (avec magnétophone) to rewind; (avec ses souvenirs) to go back in time (fig), look back; renverser la tête en ~ to tilt one's head back(wards); le chapeau en ~ his hat tilted back(wards); être peigné ou avoir les cheveux en ~ to have ou wear one's hair brushed ou combed back(wards).

(e) (lit, fig) en ~ de behind; rester ou se tenir en ~ de qch to stay behind sth; il est très en ~ des autres élèves he's a long way behind the other pupils.

2 adj inv: roue/feu ~ rear wheel/light; siège ~ back seat; [moto] pillion; V machine[3], marche[1], vent.

3 excl: en ~! vous gênez stand ou get back! you're in the way; ~, misérable!† behind me, wretch†!

4: arrière-ban nm, pl arrière-bans V ban; arrière-bouche nf, pl arrière-bouches back of the mouth; arrière-boutique nf, pl arrière-boutiques back shop; arrière-cour nf, pl arrière-cours backyard; arrière-cuisine nf, pl arrière-cuisines scullery; arrière-garde nf, pl arrière-gardes rearguard; arrière-gorge nf, pl arrière-gorges back of the throat; (lit, fig) arrière-goût nm, pl arrière-goûts aftertaste; arrière-grand-mère nf, pl arrière-grand-mères great-grandmother; arrière-grand-oncle nm, pl arrière-grands-oncles great-great-uncle; arrière-grands-parents nmpl great-grandparents; arrière-grand-père nm, pl arrière-grands-pères great-grandfather; arrière-grand-tante nf, pl arrière-grand-tantes great-great-aunt; arrière-pays nm inv hinterland; arrière-pensée nf, pl arrière-pensées (raison intéressée) ulterior motive; (réserves, doute) mental reservation; arrière-petits-enfants nmpl great-grandchildren; arrière-petite-fille nf, pl arrière-petites-filles great-granddaughter; arrière-petit-fils nm, pl arrière-petits-fils great-grandson; arrière-plan nm, pl arrière-plans background; (lit, fig) à l'arrière-plan in the background; arrière-saison nf, pl arrière-saisons end of autumn, late autumn; arrière-salle nf, pl arrière-salles back room, inner room (esp of restaurant); arrière-train nm, pl arrière-trains [animal], (hum) [personne] hindquarters.

arriéré, e [aʀjeʀe] 1 adj (a) (Comm) paiement overdue, in arrears (attrib); dette outstanding.

(b) (Psych) enfant, personne backward, retarded; région, pays backward, behind the times (attrib); croyances, méthodes, personne out-of-date, behind the times (attrib).

2 nm (choses à faire, travail) backlog; (paiement) arrears (pl). il voulait régler l'~ de sa dette he wanted to settle the arrears on his debt.

arriérer [aʀjeʀe] (6) (Fin) 1 vt paiement to defer. 2 s'arriérer vpr to fall into arrears, fall behind with payments.

arrimage [aʀimaʒ] nm (Naut) stowage, stowing.

arrimer [aʀime] (1) vt (Naut) cargaison to stow; (gén) colis to lash down, secure.

arrimeur [aʀimœʀ] nm stevedore.

arrivage [aʀivaʒ] nm [marchandises] arrival; (fig hum) [touristes] fresh load (hum) ou influx.

arrivant, e [aʀivɑ̃, ɑ̃t] nm,f newcomer. nouvel ~ newcomer, new arrival; combien d'~s y avait-il hier? how many new arrivals were there yesterday?, how many newcomers ou people arrived yesterday?; les premiers ~s de la saison the first arrivals of the season.

arrivée [aʀive] nf (a) [personne, train, courrier] arrival; [printemps, neige, hirondelles] arrival, coming; [course, skieur] finish. à mon ~, je ... when I arrived ou upon my arrival, I ...; à son ~ chez lui on (his) arrival ou arriving home, when he arrived home; attendant l'~ du courrier waiting for the post to come ou arrive, waiting for the arrival of the post; c'est l'~ des abricots sur le marché apricots are beginning to arrive in ou are coming into the shops; V gare[1], juge, ligne[1].

(b) (Tech) ~ d'air/d'eau/de gaz (robinet) air/water/gas inlet; (processus) inflow of air/water/gas.

arriver [aʀive] (1) 1 vi (a) (au terme d'un voyage) [train, personne] to arrive. ~ à ville to arrive at, get to, reach; ~ de ville, pays to arrive from; ~ en France to reach France; ~ chez des amis to arrive at friends'; ~ chez soi to arrive ou get ou reach home; ~ à destination to arrive at one's ou its destination; ~ à bon port to arrive safe and sound; nous sommes arrivés we've arrived; le train doit ~ à 6 heures the train is due (to arrive) ou scheduled to arrive ou is due in at 6 o'clock; il est arrivé par le train/en voiture he arrived by train/by car ou in a car; nous sommes presque arrivés, nous arrivons we're almost there, we've almost arrived; cette lettre m'est arrivée hier this letter reached me yesterday; ~ le premier (course) to come in first; (soirée, réception) to be the first to arrive, arrive first; les premiers arrivés the first to arrive, the first arrivals; (fig) ~ comme mars en carême to come as sure as night follows day.

(b) (approcher) [saison, nuit, personne, véhicule] to come; ~ à grands pas/en courant to stride up/run up; j'arrive! (I'm) coming!, just coming!; le train arrive en gare the train is pulling ou coming into the station; la voici qui arrive here she comes (now); allez, arrive, je suis pressé! hurry up ou come on, I'm in a hurry!; ton tour arrivera bientôt it'll soon be your turn, your turn won't be long (in) coming; on va commencer à manger, ça va peut-être faire ~ ton père we'll start eating, perhaps that will make your father come; pour faire ~ l'eau jusqu'à la maison ... to lay the water on for ou to bring the water (up) to the house ...; l'air/l'eau arrive par ce trou the air/water comes in through this hole; pour qu'arrive plus vite le moment où il la reverrait to hasten ou to bring nearer the moment when ou to bring the moment closer when he would see her again; V chien.

(c) (atteindre) ~ à niveau, lieu to reach, get to, arrive at; personne, âge to reach, get to; poste, rang to attain, reach; résultat, but, conclusion to reach, arrive at; la nouvelle est arrivée jusqu'à nous the news has reached us ou got to us; le bruit arrivait jusqu'à nous the noise reached us; je n'ai pas pu ~ jusqu'au chef I wasn't able to get right to the boss; comment arrive-t-on chez eux? how do you get to their house?; le lierre arrive jusqu'au 1er étage the ivy goes up to ou goes up as far as the 1st floor; l'eau lui arrivait (jusqu')aux genoux the water came up to his knees; et le problème des salaires? — j'y arrive and what about the wages problem? — I'm just coming to that; (fig) il ne t'arrive pas à la cheville he's not a patch on you (Brit), he can't hold a candle to you; ~ au pouvoir to come to power.

(d) (réussir à) ~ à faire qch to succeed in doing sth, manage to do sth; pour ~ à lui faire comprendre qu'il a tort to get him to ou to succeed in making him understand he's wrong; il n'arrive pas à le comprendre he just doesn't understand it; je n'arrive pas à comprendre son attitude I just don't ou can't understand ou I fail to understand his attitude; je n'arrive pas à faire ce devoir I (just) can't manage (to do) this exercise; tu y arrives? — je n'y arrive pas can you do it? ou can you manage (to do) it? — I can't (manage it); ~ à ses fins to achieve one's ends; il n'arrivera jamais à rien he'll never get anywhere, he'll never achieve anything; on n'arrivera jamais à rien avec lui it's impossible to get anywhere with him.

(e) (réussir socialement) to succeed (in life), get on (in life). il veut ~ he wants to get on ou succeed (in life); il se croit arrivé he thinks he has made it* ou he has arrived.

(f) (*se produire*) to happen. **c'est arrivé hier** it took place *ou* happened *ou* occurred yesterday; **ce genre d'accident n'arrive qu'à lui!** that sort of accident only (ever) happens to him!; **ce sont des choses qui arrivent** these things (will) happen; **cela peut ~ à n'importe qui** it could *ou* can happen to anyone; **cela ne m'arrivera plus!** it won't happen again!; **il croit que c'est arrivé*** he thinks he has made it*; **cela devait lui ~** he had it coming to him*; **faire ~ un accident** to bring about an accident; **tu vas nous faire ~ des ennuis** you'll get us into trouble *ou* bring trouble upon our heads.

(g) (*finir par*) **en ~ à** to come to; **on n'en est pas encore arrivé là!** we've not come to that (stage) yet!; **on en arrive à se demander si ...** we're beginning to wonder whether ...; **il faudra bien en ~ là!** it'll have to come to that (eventually); **c'est triste d'en ~ là** it's sad to be reduced to that.

2 *vb impers* **(a) il est arrivé un accident** there has been an accident; **il (lui) est arrivé un malheur** something dreadful has happened (to him); **il lui est arrivé un accident/un malheur** he has had an accident/a misfortune, he has met with an accident/a misfortune; **il est arrivé un télégramme** a telegram has come *ou* arrived; **il lui arrivera des ennuis** he'll get (himself) into trouble; **il m'arrive toujours des aventures incroyables** incredible things are always happening to me, I'm always getting involved in incredible adventures; **quoiqu'il arrive** whatever happens; **elle est parfois arrogante comme il arrive souvent aux timides** she is sometimes arrogant as is often the case with shy people.

(b) il arrive que + *subj*, **il arrive de: il m'arrive d'oublier, il arrive que j'oublie** I sometimes forget; **il peut ~ qu'elle se trompe, il peut lui ~ de se tromper** she does occasionally make a mistake, it occasionally happens that she makes a mistake; **il peut ~ qu'elle se trompe mais ce n'est pas une raison pour la critiquer** she may (indeed) make mistakes but that's not a reason for criticizing her; **il pourrait ~ qu'ils soient sortis** they might *ou* could just have gone out; **s'il lui arrive** *ou* **arrivait de faire une erreur, prévenez-moi** if she should happen *ou* if she happens to make a mistake, let me know; **il m'est arrivé plusieurs fois de le voir/faire** I have seen him/done it several times; **il ne lui arrive pas souvent de mentir** it is not often that he lies, he does not often lie.

arrivisme [aʀivism(ə)] *nm* ambitiousness, pushfulness.

arriviste [aʀivist(ə)] *nmf* go-getter*.

arrogamment [aʀɔgamɑ̃] *adv* arrogantly.

arrogance [aʀɔgɑ̃s] *nf* arrogance.

arrogant, e [aʀɔgɑ̃, ɑ̃t] *adj* arrogant.

arroger (s') [aʀɔʒe] (3) *vpr pouvoirs, privilèges* to assume (without right); *titre* to claim (falsely), claim (without right), assume. **s'~ le droit de ...** to assume the right to ..., take it upon o.s. to ... .

arroi [aʀwa] *nm* (*littér*) array. (*fig*) **être en mauvais ~** to be in a sorry state.

arrondi, e [aʀɔ̃di] (*ptp de* **arrondir**) **1** *adj objet, forme, relief* round, rounded; *visage* round; *voyelle* rounded. **2** *nm* (*gén: contour*) roundness; (*Aviat*) flare-out, flared landing; (*Couture*) hemline (*of skirt*).

arrondir [aʀɔ̃diʀ] (2) **1** *vt* **(a)** *objet, contour* to round, make round; *rebord, angle* to round off; *phrases* to polish, round out; *gestes* to make smoother; *caractère* to make more agreeable, smooth the rough edges off; *voyelle* to round, make rounded; *jupe* to level; *visage, taille, ventre* to fill out, round out. (*fig*) **essayer d'~ les angles** to try to smooth things over.

(b) (*accroître*) *fortune* to swell; *domaine* to increase, enlarge. **~ ses fins de mois** to supplement one's income.

(c) (*simplifier*) *somme, nombre* to round off. **~ au franc supérieur** to round up to the nearest franc; **~ au franc inférieur** to round off to the nearest franc down.

2 s'arrondir *vpr* [*relief*] to become round(ed); [*taille, joues, ventre*] to fill out, round out; [*fortune*] to swell.

arrondissement [aʀɔ̃dismɑ̃] *nm* **(a)** (*Admin*) ≈ district. **(b)** [*voyelle*] rounding; [*fortune*] swelling; [*taille, ventre*] rounding, filling out.

arrosage [aʀozaʒ] *nm* [*pelouse*] watering; [*voie publique*] spraying; *V* **lance, tuyau.**

arroser [aʀoze] (1) *vt* **(a)** [*personne*] *plante, terre* (*gén*) to water; (*avec un tuyau*) to hose, water, spray; (*légèrement*) to sprinkle; *rôti* to baste. **~ qch d'essence** to pour petrol over sth.

(b) [*pluie*] *terre* to water; *personne* (*légèrement*) to make wet; (*fortement*) to drench, soak. **Rouen est la ville la plus arrosée de France** Rouen is the wettest city in France; **se faire ~** to get drenched *ou* soaked.

(c) (*Géog*) [*fleuve*] to water.

(d) (*Mil*) (*avec fusil, balles*) to spray (*de* with); (*avec canon*) to bombard (*de* with). **leurs mitrailleuses/projectiles arrosèrent notre patrouille** they sprayed *ou* peppered our patrol with machine-gun fire/bullets.

(e) (*) *événement, succès* to drink to; *repas* to wash down (with wine)*; *café* to lace (with a spirit). **après un repas bien arrosé** after a meal washed down with plenty of wine; **tu as gagné, ça s'arrose!** you've won – that deserves a drink! *ou* we must drink to that!

(f) (*: *soudoyer*) to grease *ou* oil the palm of.

(g) (*littér*) [*sang*] to soak. **visage arrosé de larmes** face bathed in *ou* awash with (*littér*) tears; **~ de ses larmes une photographie** to bathe a photograph in tears, let one's tears fall upon a photograph; **terre arrosée de sang** blood-soaked earth.

arroseur [aʀozœʀ] *nm* **(a)** [*jardin*] waterer; [*rue*] water cartman. **(b)** (*tourniquet*) sprinkler.

arroseuse [aʀozøz] *nf* [*rue*] water cart.

arrosoir [aʀozwaʀ] *nm* watering can.

arsenal, *pl* -aux [aʀsənal, o] *nm* (*stock, manufacture d'armes*) arsenal; (*: *attirail*) gear* (*U*), paraphernalia (*U*). **l'~ du pêcheur/du photographe** the gear *ou* paraphernalia of the fisherman/photographer; **tout un ~ de vieux outils** a huge collection *ou* assortment of old tools; (*Naut*) **~ (de la marine** *ou* **maritime)** naval dockyard.

arsenic [aʀsənik] *nm* arsenic. **empoisonnement à l'~** arsenic poisoning.

arsenical, e, *mpl* -aux [aʀsənikal, o] *adj substance* arsenical.

arsénieux [aʀsenjø] *adj m* arsenic (*épith*). **oxyde** *ou* **anhydride ~** arsenic trioxide, arsenic.

arsouille† [aʀsuj] *nm ou nf* (*voyou*) ruffian. **il a un air ~** he looks like a ruffian.

art [aʀ] **1** *nm* **(a)** (*esthétique*) art. **l'~ espagnol/populaire** Spanish/popular art; **les ~s plastiques** the visual arts, the fine arts; **l'~ pour l'~** art for art's sake; **livre/critique d'~** art book/critic; **aimer/protéger les ~s** to love/protect the arts; (*hum*) **c'est du grand ~!** and they call that (great) art! (*hum*); *V* **amateur, beau, huitième** *etc.*

(b) (*technique*) art. **~ culinaire/militaire/oratoire** the art of cooking/of warfare/of public speaking; **il est passé maître dans l'~ de faire rire** he's a past master in the art of making people laugh; **un homme/les gens de l'~** a man/the people in the profession; **demandons à un homme de l'~!** let's ask a professional!; *V* **règle.**

(c) (*adresse*) [*artisan*] skill, artistry; [*poète*] skill, art, artistry. **faire qch avec un ~ consommé** to do sth with consummate skill; **il faut tout un ~ pour faire cela** doing that is quite an art, there's quite an art (involved) in doing that; **il a l'~ et la manière** he's got the know-how and he does it in style, he has both (great) skill and (great) style in what he does.

(d) l'~ de faire qch the art of doing sth, a talent *ou* flair for doing sth, the knack of doing sth*; **il a l'~ de me mettre en colère** he has a flair *ou* a talent for *ou* a knack of making me angry; **ce style a l'~ de me plaire** this style appeals to me; (*iro*) **ça a l'~ de m'endormir** it has the knack of sending me to sleep; **il y a un ~ de faire ceci** there's quite an art to doing this; **réapprendre l'~ de marcher** to re-learn the art of walking.

2: arts d'agrément accomplishments; **arts décoratifs** decorative arts; **l'art dramatique** dramatic art; **les arts du feu** ceramics; **les arts libéraux** the (seven) liberal arts; **arts mécaniques** mechanical arts; **arts ménagers** (*technique*) homecraft (*U*), domestic science; **les Arts Ménagers** (*salon*) ≈ the Ideal Home Exhibition; **arts et métiers** applied *ou* industrial arts and crafts; **art nouveau** art nouveau; **art poétique** (*technique*) poetic art; (*doctrine*) ars poetica, poetics (*sg*); **art de vivre** art of living.

artère [aʀtɛʀ] *nf* (*Anat*) artery. (*Aut*) **(grande) ~** main road.

artériel, -ielle [aʀteʀjɛl] *adj* (*Anat*) arterial; *V* **tension.**

artériosclérose [aʀteʀjɔskleʀoz] *nf* arteriosclerosis.

artérite [aʀteʀit] *nf* arteritis.

artésien, -ienne [aʀtezjɛ̃, jɛn] *adj* Artois (*épith*), of *ou* from Artois; *V* **puits.**

arthrite [aʀtʀit] *nf* arthritis.

arthritique [aʀtʀitik] *adj, nmf* arthritic.

arthritisme [aʀtʀitism(ə)] *nm* arthritism.

arthrose [aʀtʀoz] *nf* (degenerative) osteoarthritis.

Arthur [aʀtyʀ] *nm* Arthur.

artichaut [aʀtiʃo] *nm* artichoke; *V* **cœur.**

article [aʀtikl(ə)] **1** *nm* **(a)** (*Comm*) item, article. **baisse sur tous nos ~s** all (our) stock reduced, reduction on all items; **~ d'importation** imported product; **nous ne faisons plus cet ~** we don't stock that item *ou* product any more; **faire l'~** (*lit*) to sing the praises of a product, give the sales patter; (*fig*) to praise sb *ou* sth up, beat the drum.

(b) (*Presse*) [*revue, journal*] article; [*dictionnaire*] entry.

(c) (*chapitre*) point; [*loi, traité*] article. **les 2 derniers ~s de cette lettre** the last 2 points in this letter; **pour** *ou* **sur cet ~** on this point; **sur l'~ de** in the matter of, in matters of.

(d) (*Gram*) article. **~ contracté/défini/élidé/indéfini/partitif** contracted/definite/elided/indefinite/partitive article.

(e) à l'~ de la mort at the point of death.

2: articles de bureau office accessories; **article de foi** article of faith; **il prend ces recommandations pour articles de foi** for him these recommendations are articles of faith; **article de fond** feature article; **articles de luxe** luxury goods; **articles de mode** fashion accessories; **articles de Paris** fancy goods; **article réclame** special offer; **articles de toilette** toiletries, toilet requisites *ou* articles; **articles de voyage** travel goods *ou* requisites.

articulaire [aʀtikylɛʀ] *adj* articular; *V* **rhumatisme.**

articulation [aʀtikylɑsjɔ̃] *nf* **(a)** (*Anat*) joint; (*Tech*) articulation. **~s des doigts** knuckles, joints of the fingers.

(b) (*fig*) [*discours, raisonnement*] linking sentence. **la bonne ~ des parties de son discours** the cohesiveness *ou* cohesion of his speech.

(c) (*Ling*) articulation. **point d'~** point of articulation.

(d) (*Jur*) enumeration, setting forth.

articulatoire [aʀtikylatwaʀ] *adj* articulatory.

articulé, e [aʀtikyle] (*ptp de* **articuler**) **1** *adj langage* articulate(d); *membre* jointed, articulated; *objet* jointed; *poupée* with movable joints (*épith*). **2** *nmpl* (*Zool*) **les ~s** the Arthropoda.

articuler [aʀtikyle] (1) *vt* **(a)** *mot* (*prononcer clairement*) to articulate, pronounce clearly; (*dire*) to pronounce, utter. **il articule bien/mal ses phrases** he articulates *ou* speaks/doesn't articulate *ou* speak clearly; **il articule mal** he doesn't articulate (his words) *ou* speak clearly; **articule!** speak clearly!

(b) (*joindre*) *mécanismes, os* to articulate, joint; *idées* to link (up *ou* together). **élément/os qui s'articule sur un autre** element/bone that articulates *ou* is articulated with *ou* is jointed to another; **les parties de son discours s'articulent bien**

the different sections of his speech are well linked *ou* hang together well.

(c) (*Jur*) *faits, griefs* to enumerate, set out.

artifice [aʀtifis] *nm* (artful *ou* clever *ou* ingenious) device, trick; (*péj*) trick, artifice. ~ **de calcul** (clever) trick of arithmetic; ~ **de style** stylistic device *ou* trick; **les femmes usent d'~s pour paraître belles** women use artful *ou* ingenious devices *ou* tricks to make themselves look beautiful; **l'~ est une nécessité de l'art** art cannot exist without (some) artifice; *V* **feu**[1].

artificiel, -ielle [aʀtifisjɛl] *adj* (*gén*) artificial; *fibre* man-made; *soie* artificial; *colorant* artificial, synthetic; *dent* false; *bijou, fleur* artificial, imitation; *raisonnement, style* artificial, contrived; *vie, besoins* artificial; *gaieté* forced, unnatural.

artificiellement [aʀtifisjɛlmɑ̃] *adv* artificially. **fabriqué** ~ man-made, synthetically made.

artificier [aʀtifisje] *nm* pyrotechnist.

artificieusement [aʀtifisjøzmɑ̃] *adv* (*littér*) guilefully, deceitfully.

artificieux, -ieuse [aʀtifisjø, jøz] *adj* (*littér*) guileful, deceitful.

artillerie [aʀtijʀi] *nf* artillery, ordnance. ~ **de campagne** field artillery; ~ **de marine** naval guns; **pièce d'~** piece of artillery, ordnance (*U*); **tir d'~** artillery fire.

artilleur [aʀtijœʀ] *nm* artilleryman, gunner.

artimon [aʀtimɔ̃] *nm* (*voile*) mizzen; (*mât*) mizzen(mast); *V* **mât**.

artisan [aʀtizɑ̃] *nm* (self-employed) craftsman, artisan. **être l'~ de la victoire** to be the architect of victory; **il est l'~ de sa propre ruine** he has brought about *ou* he is the author of his own ruin.

artisanal, e, *mpl* **-aux** [aʀtizanal, o] *adj*: **profession** ~**e** craft, craft industry; **retraite** ~**e** pension for self-employed craftsmen; **la fabrication se fait encore de manière très** ~**e** production is still carried on in a very unsophisticated way *ou* very much in the style of a cottage industry.

artisanalement [aʀtizanalmɑ̃] *adv* by craftsmen.

artisanat [aʀtizana] *nm* (*métier*) cottage industry, arts and crafts; (*classe sociale*) artisans, artisan class.

artiste [aʀtist(ə)] **1** *nmf* **(a)** (*gén: musicien, cantatrice, sculpteur etc*) artist. ~ **peintre** artist, painter; (*hum*) ~ **capillaire** hair artiste; **les** ~**s quittèrent la salle de concert** the performers *ou* artists left the concert hall.

(b) (*Ciné, Théât*) (*acteur*) actor (*ou* actress); (*chanteur*) singer; (*fantaisiste*) entertainer; *[music-hall, cirque]* artiste, entertainer. ~ **dramatique/de cinéma** stage/film actor; **les** ~**s saluèrent** the performers took a bow; *V* **entrée**.

(c) (*péj: bohème*) bohemian.

2 *adj personne, style* artistic. (*péj*) **il est du genre** ~ he's the artistic type.

artistement [aʀtistəmɑ̃] *adv* artistically.

artistique [aʀtistik] *adj* artistic.

artistiquement [aʀtistikmɑ̃] *adv* artistically.

arum [aʀɔm] *nm* arum (lily).

aryen, -yenne [aʀjɛ̃, jɛn] **1** *adj* Aryan. **2** *nm,f*: **A~(ne)** Aryan.

arythmie [aʀitmi] *nf* arrhythmia.

as [ɑs] *nm* **(a)** (*carte, dé*) ace.

(b) (*fig: champion*) ace*. **un** ~ **de la route/du ciel** a crack driver/pilot; **l'~ de l'école** the school's star pupil.

(c) (*loc*) **être ficelé** *ou* **fagoté comme l'~ de pique*** to be dressed (all) anyhow*; **être (plein) aux ~‡** to be loaded*, be rolling in it*; **passer à l'~‡: avec toutes les dépenses qu'on a faites, les vacances sont passées à l'~** with all the expense we'd had the holidays had to go by the board *ou* the holidays were completely written off*; **cet appareil ne marche pas, voilà 200 F passés à l'~** this camera doesn't work so that's 200 francs written off* *ou* 200 francs down the drain*.

asbeste [asbɛst(ə)] *nm* asbestos.

ascendance [asɑ̃dɑ̃s] *nf* **(a)** (*généalogique*) ancestry. **son** ~ **paternelle** his paternal ancestry; **être d'~ bourgeoise** to be of middle-class descent. **(b)** (*Astron*) rising, ascent. (*Phys*) ~ **thermique** thermal.

ascendant, e [asɑ̃dɑ̃, ɑ̃t] **1** *adj astre* rising, ascending; *mouvement, direction* upward; *progression* ascending; *trait* rising, mounting; (*Généalogie*) *ligne* ancestral. **mouvement** ~ **du piston** upstroke of the piston.

2 *nm* **(a)** (*influence*) (powerful) influence, ascendancy (*sur* over). **subir l'~ de qn** to be under sb's influence.

(b) (*Admin*) ~**s** ascendants.

(c) (*Astron*) rising star; (*Astrol*) ascendant.

ascenseur [asɑ̃sœʀ] *nm* lift (*Brit*), elevator (*US*).

ascension [asɑ̃sjɔ̃] *nf* **(a)** *[ballon]* ascent, rising; *[fusée]* ascent; (*fig: sociale*) rise. (*Rel*) **l'A~** the Ascension; (*jour férié*) Ascension (Day); (*Astron*) ~ **droite** right ascension.

(b) *[montagne]* ascent. **faire l'~ d'une montagne** to climb a mountain, make the ascent of a mountain; **la première** ~ **de l'Everest** the first ascent of Everest; **c'est une** ~ **difficile** it's a difficult climb; **faire des** ~**s** to go (mountain) climbing.

ascensionnel, -elle [asɑ̃sjɔnɛl] *adj mouvement* upward; *force* upward, elevatory. **vitesse** ~**le** climbing speed.

ascèse [asɛz] *nf* asceticism.

ascète [asɛt] *nmf* ascetic.

ascétisme [asetism(ə)] *nm* asceticism.

ascorbique [askɔʀbik] *adj acide* ascorbic.

asepsie [asɛpsi] *nf* asepsis.

aseptique [asɛptik] *adj* aseptic.

aseptisation [asɛptizɑsjɔ̃] *nf* (*V* **aseptiser**) fumigation; sterilization; disinfection.

aseptiser [asɛptize] (1) *vt pièce* to fumigate; *pansement, ustensile* to sterilize; *plaie* to disinfect.

asexué, e [asɛksɥe] *adj* (*Bio*) asexual; *personne* sexless, asexual.

Asiate [azjat] *nmf* Asian, Asiatic.

asiatique [azjatik] **1** *adj* Asian, Asiatic. **2** *nmf*: **A~** Asian, Asiatic.

Asie [azi] *nf* Asia. ~ **Mineure** Asia Minor.

asile [azil] *nm* **(a)** (*institution*) ~ **(de vieillards)** (old people's) home; ~ **(d'aliénés)** (lunatic) asylum; ~ **de nuit** night shelter, hostel, doss house* (*Brit*).

(b) (*lit, fig: refuge*) refuge, sanctuary; (*Pol*) asylum. **sans** ~ homeless; **droit d'~** (*Hist*) right of sanctuary; (*Pol*) right of asylum; ~ **de paix** haven of peace, peaceful retreat; **demander/donner** ~ to seek/provide sanctuary (*Hist*) *ou* asylum (*Pol*) *ou* refuge (*gén*).

asocial, e, *mpl* **-aux** [asɔsjal, o] *adj comportement, personne* antisocial.

asparagus [aspaʀagys] *nm* asparagus fern.

aspect [aspɛ] *nm* **(a)** (*allure*) *[personne]* look, appearance; *[objet, paysage]* appearance, look. **homme d'~ sinistre** sinister-looking man, man of sinister appearance *ou* aspect; **l'intérieur de cette grotte a l'~ d'une église** the inside of this cave resembles *ou* looks like a church; **les nuages prenaient l'~ de montagnes** the clouds took on the appearance of mountains; **ce château a un** ~ **mystérieux** this castle has a look *ou* an air of mystery (about it).

(b) (*angle*) *[question]* aspect, side. **vu sous cet** ~ seen from that angle *ou* side, seen in that light; **sous tous ses** ~**s** in all its aspects, from all its sides.

(c) (*Astrol, Ling*) aspect.

(d) (*littér: vue*) sight. **à l'~ de** at the sight of.

asperge [aspɛʀʒ(ə)] *nf* **(a)** asparagus; *V* **pointe**. **(b)** (*: *personne*) **(grande)** ~ beanpole*.

asperger [aspɛʀʒe] (3) *vt surface* to spray, (*légèrement*) to sprinkle; *personne* to splash (*de* with). **s'~ le visage** to splash one's face with water; **le bus nous a aspergés au passage*** the bus splashed us *ou* sprayed water over us as it went past; **se faire** ~* (*par une voiture*) to get splashed.

aspérité [aspeʀite] *nf* **(a)** (*partie saillante*) bump. **les** ~**s de la table** the bumps on the table, the rough patches on the surface of the table. **(b)** (*littér*) *[caractère, remarques, voix]* harshness.

aspersion [aspɛʀsjɔ̃] *nf* spraying, sprinkling; (*Rel*) sprinkling of holy water, aspersion.

asphaltage [asfaltaʒ] *nm* asphalting.

asphalte [asfalt(ə)] *nm* asphalt.

asphalter [asfalte] (1) *vt* to asphalt.

asphodèle [asfɔdɛl] *nm* asphodel.

asphyxiant, e [asfiksjɑ̃, ɑ̃t] *adj* suffocating, asphyxiating; (*fig*) stifling, suffocating; *V* **gaz**.

asphyxie [asfiksi] *nf* (*gén*) suffocation, asphyxiation; (*Méd*) asphyxia; *[plante]* asphyxiation; (*fig*) *[personne]* suffocation; *[industrie]* strangulation, stifling.

asphyxier [asfiksje] (7) **1** *vt* (*lit*) to suffocate, asphyxiate; (*fig*) *industrie, esprit* to stifle. **mourir asphyxié** to die of suffocation *ou* asphyxiation.

2 s'asphyxier *vpr* (*accident*) to suffocate, asphyxiate, be asphyxiated; (*suicide*) to suffocate o.s.; (*fig*) to suffocate. **il s'est asphyxié au gaz** he gassed himself.

aspic [aspik] *nm* (*Zool*) asp; (*Bot*) aspic; (*Culin*) meat (*ou* fish *etc*) in aspic. ~ **de volaille** chicken in aspic.

aspirant, e [aspiʀɑ̃, ɑ̃t] **1** *adj* suction (*épith*), vacuum (*épith*); *V* **pompe**[1]. **2** *nm,f* (*candidat*) candidate (*à* for). **3** *nm* (*Mil*) officer cadet; (*Naut*) midshipman.

aspirateur, -trice [aspiʀatœʀ, tʀis] **1** *adj* aspiratory.

2 *nm* (*domestique*) vacuum cleaner, hoover ® (*Brit*); (*Constr, Méd etc*) aspirator. **passer les tapis à l'~** to vacuum *ou* hoover the carpets, run the vacuum cleaner *ou* hoover over the carpets.

aspiration [aspiʀɑsjɔ̃] *nf* **(a)** (*en inspirant*) inhaling (*U*), inhalation, breathing in (*U*); (*Ling*) aspiration. **de longues** ~**s** long deep breaths.

(b) *[liquide]* (*avec une paille*) sucking (up); (*gén, Tech: avec une pompe etc*) sucking up, drawing up, suction.

(c) (*ambition*) aspiration (*vers, à* for, after); (*souhait*) desire, longing (*vers, à* for).

aspiré, e [aspiʀe] (*ptp de* **aspirer**) **1** *adj* (*Ling*) aspirated. **h** ~ aspirate h. **2 aspirée** *nf* aspirate.

aspirer [aspiʀe] (1) **1** *vt* **(a)** *air, odeur* to inhale, breathe in; *liquide* (*avec une paille*) to suck (up); (*Tech: avec une pompe etc*) to suck *ou* draw up. ~ **et refouler** to pump in and out.

(b) (*Ling*) to aspirate.

2 aspirer à *vt indir honneur, titre* to aspire to; *genre de vie, tranquillité* to desire, long for. **aspirant à quitter cette vie surexcitée** longing to leave this hectic life; ~ **à la main de qn**† to be sb's suitor†, aspire to sb's hand†.

aspirine [aspiʀin] *nf* aspirin; *V* **blanc**.

assagir [asaʒiʀ] (2) **1** *vt* **(a)** (*calmer*) *personne* to quieten down, sober down; *enfant* to quieten down; *passion* to assuage, temper, quieten. **n'arrivant pas à** ~ **ses cheveux rebelles** not managing to tame her rebellious hair.

(b) (*littér: rendre plus sage*) to make wiser.

2 s'assagir *vpr [personne]* to quieten down, sober down; *[style, passions]* to become subdued.

assagissement [asaʒismɑ̃] *nm [personne]* quietening down, sobering down; *[passions]* abatement.

assaillant, e [asajɑ̃, ɑ̃t] *nm,f* assailant, attacker.

assaillir [asajiʀ] (13) *vt* (*lit*) to assail, attack; (*fig*) to assail (*de* with). **il fut assailli de questions** he was assailed *ou* bombarded with questions.

assainir [aseniʀ] (2) *vt quartier, logement* to clean up, improve the living conditions in; *marécage* to drain; *air, eau* to purify, decontaminate; (*lit, fig*) *atmosphère* to clear; *finances, marché* to stabilize; *monnaie* to rehabilitate, re-establish. **la situation s'est assainie** the situation has become healthier.

assainissement [asenismɑ̃] *nm* (*V* **assainir**) cleaning up; purification; decontamination; stabilization. ~ **monétaire** rehabilitation *ou* re-establishment of the currency.

assaisonnement [asɛzɔnmɑ̃] *nm* (*méthode*) *[salade]* dressing, seasoning; *[plat]* seasoning; (*ingrédient*) seasoning.

assaisonner [asɛzɔne] (1) *vt* (*Culin*) to season, add seasoning to; *salade* to dress, season; (*fig*) *conversation etc* to spice, give zest to. **le citron assaisonne bien la salade** lemon is a good dressing for *ou* on a salad; ~ **qn:** (*physiquement*) to knock sb about*, give sb a thumping‡; (*verbalement*) to give sb a telling off*, tell sb off*, bawl sb out*; (*financièrement*) to clobber sb‡, sting sb‡.

assassin, e [asasɛ̃, in] **1** *adj œillade, mouche*. fatal, provocative. **2** *nm* (*gén*) murderer; (*Pol*) assassin; (*Presse etc*) killer*, murderer. **l'~ court toujours** the killer* *ou* murderer is still at large; **à l'~!** murder!

assassinat [asasina] *nm* murder; (*Pol*) assassination.

assassiner [asasine] (1) *vt* to murder; (*Pol*) to assassinate. **mes créanciers m'assassinent!*** my creditors are bleeding me white!*

assaut [aso] *nm* (*Mil*) assault (*de* on), attack (*de* on); (*Boxe, Escrime*) bout. **donner l'~ à** to storm, attack; **ils donnent l'~** they're attacking; **résister aux ~s de l'ennemi** to resist the enemy's attacks *ou* onslaughts; **partir à l'~ de** (*lit*) to attack, charge; (*fig*) **de petites firmes qui sont parties à l'~ d'un marché international** small firms who have set out to take the international market by storm *ou* to capture the international market; **prendre d'~** to take by storm, assault; (*fig*) **prendre une place d'~** to grab a seat; **les librairies étaient prises d'~** the bookshops were stormed by the public; **ils faisaient ~ de politesse** they were vying with each other *ou* rivalling each other in politeness; *V* **char.**

assèchement [asɛʃmɑ̃] *nm* (*V* **assécher**) draining; drainage, emptying; drying (out); drying (up).

assécher [aseʃe] (6) *vt terrain* to drain; *réservoir* to drain, empty; *[vent, évaporation] terrain* to dry (out); *réservoir* to dry (up).

assemblage [asɑ̃blaʒ] *nm* **(a)** (*action*) *[éléments, parties]* assembling, putting together; (*Menuiserie*) assembling, jointing; *[meuble, maquette, machine]* assembling, assembly; (*Typ*) *[feuilles]* gathering; (*Couture*) *[pièces]* sewing together; *[robe, pull-over]* sewing together *ou* up, making up. ~ **de pièces par soudure/collage** soldering/glueing together of parts.

(b) (*Menuiserie: jointure*) joint. ~ **à vis/par rivets/à onglet** screwed/rivet(ed)/mitre joint.

(c) (*structure*) **une charpente est un ~ de poutres** the framework of a roof is an assembly of beams; **toit fait d'~s métalliques** roof made of metal structures.

(d) (*réunion*) *[couleurs, choses, personnes]* collection.

(e) (*Art: tableau etc*) assemblage.

assemblé [asɑ̃ble] *nm* (*Danse*) assemblé.

assemblée [asɑ̃ble] *nf* (*gén: réunion, foule*) gathering; (*réunion convoquée*) meeting; (*Pol*) assembly. (*Rel*) **l'~ des fidèles** the congregation; ~ **mensuelle/extraordinaire** monthly/extraordinary meeting; **réunis en ~** gathered *ou* assembled for a meeting; **à la grande joie de l'~** to the great joy of the assembled company *ou* of those present; **l'A~ nationale** the French National Assembly; (*Pol*) ~ **délibérante** deliberating assembly.

assembler [asɑ̃ble] (1) **1** *vt* **(a)** (*réunir*) *données, matériaux* to gather (together), collect (together); (*Pol*) *comité* to convene, assemble; (†) *personnes* to assemble, gather (together); (*Typ*) *feuilles* to gather. (*Pol*) **les chambres assemblées ont voté la loi** the assembled chambers passed the law; (*Danse*) ~ **les pieds** to take up third position; **l'amour les assemble**† love unites them (together) *ou* binds them together.

(b) (*joindre*) *idées, meuble, machine, puzzle* to assemble, put together; *pull, robe* to sew together *ou* up, make up; (*Menuiserie*) to assemble, to joint; *couleurs, sons* to put together. ~ **par soudure/collage** to solder/glue together.

2 s'assembler *vpr [foule]* to gather, collect; *[participants, conseil, groupe]* to assemble, gather; (*fig*) *[nuages]* to gather; *V* **qui.**

assembleur, -euse [asɑ̃blœʀ, øz] **1** *nm,f* (*ouvrier*) (*gén*) assembler, fitter; (*Typ*) gatherer. **2 assembleuse** *nf* (*Typ: machine*) gathering machine.

assener, asséner [asene] (5) *vt coup* to strike, deal; (*fig*) *argument* to thrust forward; *propagande* to deal out; *réplique* to thrust *ou* fling back.

assentiment [asɑ̃timɑ̃] *nm* (*consentement*) assent, consent; (*approbation*) approval. **donner son ~ à** to give one's assent *ou* consent *ou* approval to.

asseoir [aswaʀ] (26) **1** *vt* **(a)** ~ **qn** (*personne debout*) to sit sb down; (*personne couchée*) to sit sb up; ~ **qn sur une chaise/dans un fauteuil** to sit *ou* put sb on a chair/in an armchair, seat sb on a chair/in an armchair; ~ **un enfant sur ses genoux** to sit *ou* take a child on one's knee; (*fig*) ~ **un prince sur le trône** to put *ou* set a prince on the throne.

(b) faire ~ qn to ask sb to sit down; **faire ~ ses invités** to ask one's guests to sit down *ou* to take a seat; **je leur ai parlé après les avoir fait ~** I talked to them after asking them to sit down; **fais-la ~, elle est fatiguée** get her to sit down, she is tired.

(c) être assis to be sitting *ou* seated; **reste assis!** (*ne bouge pas*) sit still!; (*ne te lève pas*) don't get up!; **nous sommes restés assis pendant des heures** we sat *ou* remained seated for hours; **ils restèrent assis quand on a joué l'hymne national** they remained seated when the national anthem was played; **nous étions très bien/mal assis** (*sur des chaises*) we had very comfortable/uncomfortable seats; (*par terre*) we were very comfortably/uncomfortably seated, we were sitting very comfortably/uncomfortably; **assis en tailleur** sitting cross-legged; **assis à califourchon sur** sitting astride, straddling; (*fig*) **être assis entre deux chaises** to be in an awkward position, be in a predicament.

(d) (*frm*) (*affermir*) *réputation* to establish, assure; *autorité, théorie* to establish. ~ **une maison sur du granit** to build a house on granite; ~ **les fondations sur** to lay *ou* build the foundations on; ~ **sa réputation sur qch** to build one's reputation on sth; **pour ~ son autorité/sa réputation** to establish his authority/reputation; ~ **une théorie sur des faits** to base a theory on facts; ~ **son jugement sur des témoignages dignes de foi** to base one's judgment on reliable evidence.

(e) (*: *stupéfier*) to stagger, stun. **son inconscience m'assoit** his foolishness staggers me, I'm stunned by his foolishness; **j'en suis** *ou* **reste assis de voir que** I'm staggered *ou* stunned *ou* flabbergasted* to see that.

(f) (*Fin*) ~ **un impôt** to base a tax, fix a tax.

2 s'asseoir *vpr* to sit (o.s.) down; *[personne couchée]* to sit up. **asseyez-vous donc** do sit down, do have *ou* take a seat; **asseyez-vous par terre** sit (down) on the floor; **il n'y a rien pour s'~** there is nothing to sit on; **le règlement, je m'assieds dessus!‡** you know what you can do with the rule!‡; **s'~ à califourchon (sur qch)** to sit (down) astride (sth); **s'~ en tailleur** to sit (down) cross-legged.

assermenté, e [asɛʀmɑ̃te] *adj témoin, policier* sworn, on oath (*attrib*); *médecin, expert* officially designated.

assertion [asɛʀsjɔ̃] *nf* assertion.

asservi, e [asɛʀvi] (*ptp de* **asservir**) *adj peuple* enslaved; *presse* subservient. **moteur ~** servomotor.

asservir [asɛʀviʀ] (2) *vt* (*assujettir*) *personne* to enslave; *pays* to reduce to slavery, subjugate; (*littér: maîtriser*) *passions, nature* to overcome, master. **être asservi à** to be a slave to.

asservissement [asɛʀvismɑ̃] *nm* (*action*) enslavement; (*lit, fig: état*) slavery, subservience (*à* to); (*Élec*) servo-control (*U*) (*à* by).

assesseur [asesœʀ] *nm* assessor.

assez [ase] *adv* **(a)** (*suffisamment, avec vb*) enough; (*devant adj, adv*) enough, sufficiently. **bien ~** quite enough, plenty; **tu as (bien) ~ mangé** you've had *ou* eaten (quite) enough, you've had (quite) enough *ou* plenty to eat; **c'est bien ~ grand** it's quite big enough; **plus qu'~** more than enough; **je n'ai pas ~ travaillé** I haven't worked (hard) enough, I haven't worked sufficiently (hard); **la maison est grande mais elle ne l'est pas ~ pour nous** the house is big but it is not big enough for us; **il ne vérifie pas ~ souvent** he does not check often enough; **tu travailles depuis ~ longtemps** you've been working (for) long enough; **ça a ~ duré!** it has gone on long enough!; **combien voulez-vous? est-ce que 5 F c'est ~? — c'est bien ~** how much do you want? is 5 francs enough? *ou* will 5 francs do? — that will be plenty *ou* ample *ou* that will be quite *ou* easily enough; **il a juste ~ pour s'acheter ce livre** he has just enough to buy himself that book; *V* **peu.**

(b) ~ de (*quantité, nombre*) enough; **avez-vous acheté ~ de pain/d'oranges?** have you bought enough *ou* sufficient bread/enough oranges?; **il n'y a pas ~ de viande pour tout le monde** there is not enough meat to go round *ou* for everyone; **c'est ~ de lui à me critiquer sans que tu t'en mêles** it's quite enough his criticizing me without your joining in (too); **ils sont ~ de deux pour ce travail** the two of them are enough *ou* will do* for this job; **j'en ai ~ de 3** 3 will be enough for me *ou* will do (for) me*; **n'apportez pas de pain/verres, il y en a ~** don't bring any bread/glasses, there is/are enough *ou* we have enough.

(c) (*en corrélation avec pour*) enough. **as-tu trouvé une boîte ~ grande pour tout mettre?** have you found a big enough box *ou* a box big enough to put it all in?; **le village est ~ près pour qu'elle puisse y aller à pied** the village is near enough for her to walk there; **je n'ai pas ~ d'argent pour m'offrir cette voiture** I can't afford (to buy myself) this car, I haven't enough money to buy myself this car; **il est ~ idiot pour refuser!** he's stupid enough to refuse!; **il n'est pas ~ sot pour le croire** he is not so stupid as to believe him.

(d) (*intensif*) rather, quite, fairly, pretty*. **la situation est ~ inquiétante** the situation is rather *ou* somewhat *ou* pretty* disturbing; **ce serait ~ agréable d'avoir un jour de congé** it would be rather *ou* quite nice to have a day off; **il était ~ tard quand ils sont partis** it was quite *ou* fairly *ou* pretty* late when they left; **j'ai oublié son adresse, est-ce ~ bête!** how stupid (of me), I've forgotten his address!; **je l'ai ~ vu!** I have seen (more than) enough of him!; **elle était déjà ~ malade il y a 2 ans** she was already quite ill 2 years ago.

(e) (*loc*) **en voilà ~!, c'est ~!, c'en est ~!** I've had enough!, enough is enough!; **~!** that will do!, that's (quite) enough!; ~ **parlé** *ou* **de discours, des actes!** enough talk *ou* enough said, let's have some action!; **(en) avoir ~ de qch/qn** to have (had) enough *ou* be sick* of sth/sb, be fed up with sth/sb*; **j'en ai ~ de toi et de tes jérémiades*** I've had enough of *ou* I'm sick (and tired) of* *ou* I'm fed up with* you and your moaning.

assidu, e [asidy] *adj* **(a)** (*ponctuel*) *présence* regular. **c'est un élève ~** he's a regular (and attentive) pupil; **ouvrier ~** workman who is regular in his work.

(b) (*appliqué*) *soin, effort* assiduous, unremitting; *travail* assiduous, constant; painstaking; *personne* assiduous, painstaking.

(c) (*empressé*) *personne* assiduous *ou* unremitting in one's attention (*auprès de* to). **faire une cour ~e à qn** to be assiduous in one's attentions to sb, woo sb assiduously.

assiduité [asidɥite] *nf* (*ponctualité*) regularity; (*empressement*) attentiveness, assiduity (*à* to). **son ~ aux cours** his regular attendance at classes; **fréquenter le bistrot avec ~** to be a regular at the pub (*Brit*) *ou* bar (*US*); (*frm, hum*) **poursuivre**

une femme de ses ~s to pester a woman with one's assiduous attentions (*hum*).
assidûment [asidymɑ̃] *adv fréquenter* faithfully, assiduously; *travailler* assiduously.
assiégeant, e [asjeʒɑ̃, ɑ̃t] *nm,f* besieger. **les troupes ~es** the besieging troops.
assiéger [asjeʒe] (3 *et* 6) *vt* (*Mil*) *ville* to besiege, lay siege to; *armée* to besiege; (*fig*) (*entourer*) *guichet, porte, personne* to mob, besiege; (*harceler*) to beset. **la garnison assiégée** the beleaguered *ou* besieged garrison; **assiégé par l'eau/les flammes** hemmed in by water/flames; **à Noël les magasins étaient assiégés** the shops (*Brit*) *ou* stores (*US*) were mobbed at Christmas; **ces pensées/tentations qui m'assiègent** these thoughts/temptations that beset me.
assiette [asjɛt] **1** *nf* **(a)** (*vaisselle, quantité*) plate. **le nez dans son ~** with his head bowed over his plate.
(b) (*équilibre*) (*Équitation*) *[cavalier]* seat; (*Naut*) *[navire]* trim; (*Archit*) *[colonne]* seating. (*Équitation*) **perdre son ~** to lose one's seat, be unseated; (*Équitation*) **avoir une bonne ~** to have a good seat, sit one's horse well; (*fig*) **il n'est pas dans son ~ aujourd'hui** he's not feeling (quite) himself today, he's (feeling) a bit off-colour (*Brit*) today.
(c) (*Jur*) *[impôt]* (basis of) assessment, subject matter of assessment; *[hypothèque]* property *ou* estate on which a mortgage is secured.
2: assiette anglaise assorted cold roast meats; (*fig*) **c'est l'assiette au beurre** it's a plum job; **assiette de charcuterie** assorted cold meats; **assiette creuse** (soup) dish, soup plate; **assiette à dessert** dessert plate, side plate; **assiette plate** (dinner) plate; **assiette à soupe** = **assiette creuse**.
assiettée [asjete] *nf* (*gén*) plate(ful); *[soupe]* plate(ful), dish.
assignable [asiɲabl(ə)] *adj* (*attribuable*) *cause, origine* ascribable, attributable (*à* to).
assignat [asiɲa] *nm bank note used during the French Revolution.*
assignation [asiɲɑsjɔ̃] *nf* (*Jur*) *[parts]* assignation, allocation. **~ (à comparaître)** *[prévenu]* summons; *[témoin]* subpoena; **~ en justice** ≃ subpoena, writ of summons; **~ à résidence** assignation to a forced residence.
assigner [asiɲe] (1) *vt* **(a)** (*attribuer*) *part, place, rôle* to assign, allocate, allot; *valeur, importance* to attach, ascribe, allot; *cause, origine* to ascribe, attribute (*à* to).
(b) (*affecter*) *somme, crédit* to allot, allocate (*à* to), earmark (*à* for).
(c) (*fixer*) *limite, terme* to set, fix (*à* to). **~ un objectif à qn** to set sb a goal.
(d) (*Jur*) **~ (à comparaître)** *prévenu* to summons; *témoin* to subpoena, cite, summon; **~ qn en justice** to issue a writ against sb, serve a writ on sb; **~ qn à résidence** to assign a forced residence to sb.
assimilable [asimilabl(ə)] *adj* **(a)** *immigrant* easily assimilated; *connaissances* easily assimilated *ou* absorbed; *nourriture* assimilable, easily assimilated. **ces connaissances ne sont pas ~s par un enfant** this knowledge could not be assimilated by a child, a child could not assimilate *ou* absorb *ou* take in this knowledge.
(b) (*comparable à*) **~ à** comparable to; **ce poste est ~ à celui de contremaître** this job is comparable to *ou* may be considered like that of a foreman.
assimilateur, -trice [asimilatœʀ, tʀis] *adj* assimilative, assimilating. **c'est un admirable ~** he has fine powers of assimilation.
assimilation [asimilɑsjɔ̃] *nf* **(a)** (*absorption*) *[immigrants, connaissances]* assimilation, absorption; (*Bio, Ling*) assimilation. **~ chlorophyllienne** photosynthesis.
(b) (*comparaison*) **l'~ de ce bandit à un héros/à Napoléon est un scandale** it's a scandal making this criminal out to be a hero/to liken *ou* compare this criminal to Napoleon; **l'~ des techniciens supérieurs aux ingénieurs** the classification of top-ranking technicians as engineers, the inclusion of top-ranking technicians in the same category as engineers.
assimilé, e [asimile] (*ptp de* **assimiler**) **1** *adj* (*similaire*) **ce procédé et les autres méthodes ~es** this process and the other comparable methods.
2 *nm* (*Mil*) *non-combatant ranking with the combatants.* **les fonctionnaires et ~s** civil servants and comparable categories.
assimiler [asimile] (1) **1** *vt* **(a)** *aliments* to assimilate, absorb; *connaissances* to assimilate, take in, absorb. **un élève qui assimile bien** a pupil who assimilates *ou* takes things in easily; **ses idées sont du Nietzsche mal assimilé** his ideas are just a few ill-digested notions (taken) from Nietzsche.
(b) *immigrants,* (*Bio*) *substance* to assimilate, absorb; (*fig*) *style, idée* to assimilate.
(c) ~ qn/qch à (*comparer à*) to liken *ou* compare sb/sth to; (*classer comme*) to class sb/sth as, put sb/sth into the category of; (*faire ressembler à*) to make sb/sth similar to; **il s'assimila, dans son discours, aux plus grands savants** in his speech, he likened himself to *ou* classed himself alongside the greatest scientists; **les jardinières d'enfants demandent à être assimilées à des institutrices** kindergarten teachers are asking to be classed as *ou* given the same status as primary school teachers.
2 s'assimiler *vpr* **(a)** (*être absorbé*) *[aliments]* to assimilate, be assimilated.
(b) (*s'intégrer*) *[immigrants]* to be assimilated (*à* into, by), be absorbed (*à* into).
assis, e[1] [asi, iz] (*ptp de* **asseoir**) *adj* **(a)** *personne* sitting (down), seated. **position ~e** sitting position; **demeurer** *ou* **rester ~** to remain seated; **restez ~** (please) don't get up; **être ~** *V* asseoir; *V* **magistrature, place**.
(b) (*fig*) *situation* stable, firm; *personne* stable; *autorité* (well-)established.
assise[2] [asiz] *nf* (*Constr*) course; (*Bio, Géol*) stratum; (*fig*) basis, foundation.
Assise [asiz] *n* Assisi.
assises [asiz] *nfpl* (*Jur*) assizes; (*fig*) meeting; *[parti politique]* conference. **tenir ses ~** to hold one's meeting; **ce parti tient ses ~ à Nancy** this party holds its annual meeting *ou* conference at Nancy; *V* **cour**.
assistanat [asistana] *nm* assistantship.
assistance [asistɑ̃s] **1** *nf* **(a)** (*assemblée*) *[conférence]* audience; *[débat]* audience, house; *[meeting]* house; *[cérémonie]* gathering, audience.
(b) (*aide*) assistance. **donner/prêter ~ à qn** to give/lend sb assistance.
(c) (*présence*) attendance.
2: assistance judiciaire legal aid; **assistance médicale (gratuite)** (free) medical care; **l'Assistance publique** ≃ National Assistance†; **être à l'Assistance publique** to be in care (*in State institution*); **enfant de l'Assistance (publique)** child in care; **assistance sociale** social aid; **assistance technique** technical aid.
assistant, e [asistɑ̃, ɑ̃t] **1** *nm,f* (*gén, Scol*) assistant; (*Univ*) ≃ assistant lecturer. **~e sociale** social worker; *V* **maître**. **2** *nmpl*: **les ~s** those present.
assisté, e [asiste] (*ptp de* **assister**) *adj* (*Jur, Méd, Sociol*) receiving (State) aid. **enfant ~** child in care.
assister [asiste] (1) **1 assister à** *vt indir* (*être présent à*) *cérémonie, conférence, messe* to be (present) at, attend; *match, spectacle* to be at; *événement* to be present at, witness.
2 *vt* (*aider*) to assist. (*frm*) **~ qn dans ses derniers moments** to succour (*frm*) *ou* comfort sb in his last hour; **~ les pauvres**† to minister to† *ou* assist the poor.
associatif, -ive [asɔsjatif, iv] *adj* associative. (*Math*) **opération ~ive** associative operation.
association [asɔsjɑsjɔ̃] *nf* **(a)** (*gén: société*) association, society; (*Comm, Écon*) partnership. (*Jur*) **~ de malfaiteurs** conspiracy, combination (*US*); **~ sportive** sports association; **~ syndicale** property owners' syndicate.
(b) *[idées, images]* association; *[couleurs, intérêts]* combination.
(c) (*participation*) association, partnership. **l'~ de ces deux écrivains a été fructueuse** these two writers have had a very fruitful partnership; **son ~ à nos travaux dépendra de ...** his joining us in our undertaking will depend on ... .
associationnisme [asɔsjɑsjɔnism(ə)] *nm* (*Philos*) associationism.
associationniste [asɔsjɑsjɔnist(ə)] *adj, nmf* associationist.
associé, e [asɔsje] (*ptp de* **associer**) *nm,f* (*gén*) associate; (*Comm, Fin*) partner, associate. **~ principal** senior partner; *V* **membre**.
associer [asɔsje] (7) **1** *vt* **(a)** (*faire participer à*) **~ qn à** *profits* to give sb a share of; *affaire* to make sb a partner in; **~ qn à son triomphe** to include sb else in one's triumph.
(b) ~ qch à (*rendre solidaire de*) to associate *ou* link sth with; (*allier à*) to combine sth with; **il associe la paresse à la malhonnêteté** he combines laziness with dishonesty.
(c) (*grouper*) *idées, images, mots* to associate; *couleurs, intérêts* to combine (*à* with).
2 s'associer *vpr* **(a)** (*s'unir*) *[firmes]* to join together, form an association; *[personnes]* (*gén*) to join forces, join together; (*Comm*) to form a partnership; *[pays]* to form an alliance. **s'~ à** *ou* **avec** *firme* to join with, form an association with; *personne* (*gén*) to join (forces) with; (*Comm*) to go into partnership with; *pays* to form an alliance with; *bandits* to fall in with.
(b) (*participer à*) **il s'est associé à nos projets** he joined us in our projects; **il finit par s'~ à notre point de vue** he finally came round to our point of view; **s'~ à la douleur/aux difficultés de qn** to share in sb's grief/difficulties, feel for sb in his grief/difficulties; **je m'associe aux compliments que l'on vous fait** I should like to join with those who have complimented you.
(c) (*s'allier*) *[couleurs, qualités]* to be combined (*à* with). **ces 2 couleurs s'associent à merveille** these 2 colours go together beautifully.
(d) (*s'adjoindre*) **s'~ qn** to take sb on as a partner.
assoiffant, e [aswafɑ̃, ɑ̃t] *adj chaleur, travail* thirsty (*épith*), thirst-giving.
assoiffé, e [aswafe] *adj* (*fig*) **~ de** thirsting for *ou* after (*littér*); (*littér, hum*) **monstre ~ de sang** bloodthirsty monster.
assoiffer [aswafe] (1) *vt [temps, course]* to make thirsty.
assolement [asɔlmɑ̃] *nm* (systematic) rotation (of crops).
assoler [asɔle] (1) *vt champ* to rotate crops on.
assombri, e [asɔ̃bʀi] (*ptp de* **assombrir**) *adj ciel* darkened, sombre; *visage, regard* gloomy, sombre. **les couleurs ~es du crépuscule** the sombre shades of dusk.
assombrir [asɔ̃bʀiʀ] (2) **1** *vt* **(a)** *ciel* to darken; *pièce* (*obscurcir*) to darken, make dark *ou* dull; (*rendre triste*) to make gloomy *ou* sombre; *couleur* to make sombre, darken.
(b) (*attrister*) *personne* to fill with gloom; *assistance* to cast a gloom over; *visage, vie, voyage* to cast a shadow over. **les malheurs ont assombri son caractère** misfortune has given him a gloomy *ou* sombre outlook on life *ou* has made him a gloomier person.
2 s'assombrir *vpr* **(a)** *[ciel, pièce]* to darken, grow dark; *[couleur]* to grow sombre, darken.
(b) *[personne, caractère]* to become gloomy *ou* morose; *[visage, regard]* to cloud over. **la situation politique s'est assombrie** the political situation has become gloomier.
assombrissement [asɔ̃bʀismɑ̃] *nm [ciel, pièce]* darkening. **ses amis s'inquiètent de l'~ progressif de son caractère** his friends

are worried at the increasing gloominess of his attitude to life.
assommant, e* [asɔmɑ̃, ɑ̃t] *adj* (*ennuyeux*) deadly (boring)*, deadly (dull)*. **il est ~** he's a deadly* *ou* an excruciating bore, he's deadly (dull *ou* boring)*.
assommer [asɔme] (1) *vt* (*lit*) (*tuer*) to batter to death; (*étourdir*) *animal* to knock out, stun; *personne* to knock out, knock senseless, stun; (**fig: ennuyer*) to bore stiff* *ou* to death*. **être assommé par le bruit/la chaleur** to be overwhelmed by the noise/overcome by the heat; **si je lui mets la main dessus je l'assomme*** if I can lay my hands on him I'll beat his brains out.
assommoir†† [asɔmwaʀ] *nm* (*massue*) club; (*café*) grogshop†.
Assomption [asɔ̃psjɔ̃] *nf* Assumption.
assonance [asɔnɑ̃s] *nf* assonance.
assonant, e [asɔnɑ̃, ɑ̃t] *adj* assonant, assonantal.
assorti, e [asɔʀti] (*ptp de* **assortir**) *adj* **(a)** (*en harmonie*) **des époux bien/mal ~s** a well/badly-matched *ou* suited couple, a good/bad match; **nos amis sont mal ~s** our friends are a mixed bunch; **être ~ à** *couleur* to match.
(b) *bonbons* assorted. **'hors-d'œuvre/fromages ~s'** 'assortment of hors d'œuvres/cheeses'; **magasin bien/mal ~** well/poorly-stocked shop.
(c) être ~ de *conditions, conseils* to be accompanied with.
assortiment [asɔʀtimɑ̃] *nm* **(a)** (*gamme, série*) *[bonbons, hors-d'œuvre]* assortment; *[livres]* collection; *[vaisselle]* set. **je vous fais un ~?** shall I give you an assortment?; **il y avait tout un ~ d'outils** there was a whole set *ou* collection of tools.
(b) (*association, harmonie*) *[couleurs, formes]* arrangement, ensemble.
(c) (*Comm: lot, stock*) stock, selection.
assortir [asɔʀtiʀ] (2) **1** *vt* **(a)** (*accorder*) *couleurs, motifs* to match (*à, avec* to, with). **elle assortit la couleur de son écharpe à celle de ses yeux** she chose the colour of her scarf to match her eyes, she matched the colour of her scarf to her eyes; **elle avait su ~ ses invités** she had mixed *ou* matched her guests cleverly.
(b) (*accompagner de*) **~ qch de** *conseils, commentaires* to accompany sth with; **ce livre s'assortit de notes** this book has accompanying notes *ou* has notes with it.
(c) (*Comm: approvisionner*) *commerçant* to supply; *magasin* to stock (*de* with).
2 s'assortir *vpr [couleurs, motifs]* to match, go (well) together; *[caractères]* to go together, harmonize (with each other). **le papier s'assortit aux rideaux** the wallpaper matches *ou* goes (well) with the curtains.
assoupi, e [asupi] (*ptp de* **assoupir**) *adj personne* dozing, sleeping; *sens* (be)numbed; *intérêt, douleur* dulled; *haine* stilled, quietened, lulled.
assoupir [asupiʀ] (2) **1** *vt* (*endormir*) to make drowsy; (*fig*) *sens* to numb, dull; *facultés, intérêt, sentiment* to dull; *douleur* to deaden; *passion* to lull, quieten, still.
2 s'assoupir *vpr* (*s'endormir*) to doze off; *[sens]* to grow numb, be numbed; *[facultés, intérêt, douleur]* to be dulled; *[passions]* to die down, be stilled *ou* lulled.
assoupissement [asupismɑ̃] *nm* **(a)** (*sommeil*) doze; (*fig: somnolence*) drowsiness. **être au bord de l'~** to be about to doze off. **(b)** (*action*) *[sens]* numbing; *[facultés, intérêt]* dulling; *[douleur]* deadening; *[chagrin]* lulling.
assouplir [asupliʀ] (2) **1** *vt cuir* to soften, make supple, make pliable; *membres, corps* to make supple; *règlements, mesures* to relax; *principes* to make more flexible, relax. **~ le caractère de qn** to make sb more manageable.
2 s'assouplir *vpr* to soften; to become supple; to become pliable; to relax; to become more flexible. **son caractère s'est assoupli** he has become more manageable.
assouplissement [asuplismɑ̃] *nm* (*V* **assouplir**) softening; suppling up; relaxing. **faire des exercices d'~** to limber up, do (some) limbering up exercises.
assourdir [asuʀdiʀ] (2) **1** *vt* **(a)** (*rendre sourd*) *personne* to deafen. **(b)** (*amortir*) *bruit* to deaden, muffle. **2 s'assourdir** *vpr* (*Ling*) to become voiceless, become unvoiced.
assourdissant, e [asuʀdisɑ̃, ɑ̃t] *adj* deafening.
assourdissement [asuʀdismɑ̃] *nm* **(a)** *[personne]* (*état*) (temporary) deafness; (*action*) deafening. **(b)** *[bruit]* deadening, muffling. **(c)** (*Ling*) devoicing.
assouvir [asuviʀ] (2) *vt faim, passion* to satisfy, appease.
assouvissement [asuvismɑ̃] *nm* satisfaction, satisfying, appeasement.
assujetti, e [asyʒeti] (*ptp de* **assujettir**) *adj peuple* subject, subjugated. **~ à** *règle* subject to; *taxe* liable *ou* subject to; (*Admin*) **les personnes ~es à l'impôt** persons liable to tax *ou* affected by tax.
assujettir [asyʒetiʀ] (2) **1** *vt* (*contraindre*) *peuple* to subjugate, bring into subjection; (*fixer*) *planches, tableau* to secure, make fast. **~ qn à une règle** to subject sb to a rule. **2 s'assujettir** *vpr* (*à une règle*) to submit (*à* to).
assujettissant, e [asyʒetisɑ̃, ɑ̃t] *adj travail, emploi* demanding, exacting.
assujettissement [asyʒetismɑ̃] *nm* (*contrainte*) constraint; (*dépendance*) subjection. **~ à l'impôt** tax liability.
assumer [asyme] (1) **1** *vt* **(a)** (*prendre*) *responsabilité, tâche* to assume, take on, shoulder; *commandement* to assume, take over; *rôle, fonction* to take on, assume; *poste* to take up. **j'assume la responsabilité de faire ...** I'll take it upon myself to do ... .
(b) (*remplir*) *poste* to hold; *rôle* to fulfil; (*supporter*) *responsabilités* to shoulder. **après avoir assumé ce poste pendant 2 ans** having held this post for 2 years.
(c) (*accepter*) *conséquence, situation, (Philos) condition* to accept; *douleur* to accept, shoulder.
2 s'assumer *vpr* to come to terms with o.s.
assurable [asyʀabl(ə)] *adj* insurable.
assurage [asyʀaʒ] *nm* (*Alpinisme*) belaying.
assurance [asyʀɑ̃s] **1** *nf* **(a)** (*confiance en soi*) self-confidence, (self-)assurance. **avoir de l'~** to be self-confident *ou* (self-)assured; **prendre de l'~** to gain (self-)confidence *ou* (self-)assurance; **parler avec ~** to speak with assurance *ou* confidence.
(b) (*garantie*) assurance, undertaking. **donner à qn l'~ formelle que** to give sb a formal assurance *ou* undertaking that; (*formule épistolaire*) **veuillez agréer l'~ de ma considération distinguée** *ou* **de mes sentiments dévoués** ≈ yours faithfully *ou* truly.
(c) (*contrat*) insurance (policy); (*firme*) insurance company. **contracter** *ou* **prendre une ~ contre** to take out insurance *ou* an insurance policy against; **il est dans les ~s** he's in insurance, he's in the insurance business; *V* **police**[2], **prime**[1].
(d) (*Alpinisme*) = **assurage.**
2: assurance-automobile *nf, pl* **assurances-automobile** car insurance; (*Can*) **assurance-chômage** *nf, pl* **assurances-chômage** unemployment insurance; **assurance-incendie** *nf, pl* **assurances-incendie** fire insurance; **assurance invalidité-vieillesse** disablement insurance; **assurance maladie** health insurance; **assurance maritime** marine insurance; **assurance responsabilité-civile = assurance au tiers; assurances sociales** ≈ National Insurance; **il est (inscrit) aux assurances sociales** he's on the health service; **assurance au tiers** third-party insurance; (*Aut*) **assurance tous risques** comprehensive insurance; **assurance-vie** *nf, pl* **assurances-vie, assurance sur la vie** life assurance *ou* insurance; **assurance-vieillesse** *nf, pl* **assurances-vieillesse** state pension scheme; **assurance contre le vol** insurance against theft.
assuré, e [asyʀe] (*ptp de* **assurer**) **1** *adj* **(a)** *réussite, échec* certain, sure; *situation, fortune* assured. **son avenir est ~ maintenant** his future is certain *ou* assured now; **entreprise ~e du succès** undertaking (which is) heading for certain success *ou* which is sure of success.
(b) *air, voix, démarche* assured, (self-)confident; *main, pas* steady. **mal ~** *voix, pas* uncertain, unsteady; **il est mal ~ sur ses jambes** he's unsteady on his legs.
(c) (*loc*) **tenir pour ~ que** to be confident that, take it as certain that; **il se dit ~ de** he says he is confident of; **tenez pour ~ que** rest assured that.
2 *nm,f* (*Assurance*) *[assurance-vie]* assured person; *[autres assurances]* insured person, policyholder. **l'~** the assured, the policyholder; **~ social** ≈ member of the National Insurance scheme (*Brit*) *ou* Social Security (*US*).
assurément [asyʀemɑ̃] *adv* (*frm*) assuredly, most certainly. **~, ceci présente des difficultés** this does indeed present difficulties; **(oui) ~** yes indeed, (yes) most certainly; **~ il viendra** assuredly he'll come, he will most certainly come.
assurer [asyʀe] (1) **1** *vt* **(a)** (*certifier*) **~ à qn que** to assure sb that; **~ que** to affirm *ou* contend *ou* assert that; **cela vaut la peine, je vous assure** it's worth it, I assure you.
(b) (*confirmer*) **~ qn de** *amitié, bonne foi* to assure sb of; **sa participation nous est assurée** we have been assured of his participation, we're guaranteed that he'll take part.
(c) (*Fin: par contrat*) *maison, bijoux* to insure (*contre* against); *personne* to assure. **~ qn sur la vie** to give sb (a) life assurance *ou* insurance, assure sb's life; **faire ~ qch** to insure sth, have *ou* get sth insured; **être assuré** to be insured.
(d) (*fournir*) *fonctionnement* to maintain; *surveillance* to provide, maintain; *service* to operate, provide. **pendant la grève, les mineurs n'assureront que les travaux d'entretien** during the strike the miners will carry out *ou* undertake maintenance work only; **on utilise des appareils électroniques pour ~ la surveillance des locaux** electronic apparatus is used to guard *ou* for guarding the premises; **l'avion qui assure la liaison entre Genève et Aberdeen** the plane that links Geneva and Aberdeen; **l'armée a dû ~ le ravitaillement des sinistrés** the army has had (to be moved in) to provide supplies for the victims.
(e) (*procurer, garantir*) **~ une situation à son fils** to secure a position for one's son; **cela devrait leur ~ une vie aisée** that should ensure that they lead a comfortable life *ou* ensure a comfortable life for them; **ça lui a assuré la victoire** that ensured his victory *ou* made his victory certain.
(f) (*rendre sûr*) *bonheur, succès, paix* to ensure; *fortune* to secure; *avenir* to make certain. (*Mil*) **~ les frontières contre** to make the frontiers secure from; (*fig*) **~ ses arrières** to keep one's options open, ensure one has something to fall back on.
(g) (*affermir*) *pas, prise, échelle* to steady; (*fixer*) *échelle, volet* to secure; (*Alpinisme*) to belay. **il assura ses lunettes sur son nez** he fixed his glasses firmly on his nose.
2 s'assurer *vpr* **(a)** (*vérifier*) **s'~ que/de qch** to make sure that/of sth, check that/sth, ascertain that/sth; **assure-toi qu'on n'a rien volé** make sure *ou* check *ou* ascertain that nothing has been stolen; **assure-toi si le robinet est fermé** check if *ou* make sure the tap (*Brit*) *ou* faucet (*US*) is off; **je vais m'en ~** I'll make sure *ou* check.
(b) (*contracter une assurance*) to insure o.s. (*contre* against). (*se prémunir*) **s'~ contre** *attaque, éventualité* to insure (o.s.) against; **s'~ sur la vie** to insure one's life, take out (a) life assurance *ou* insurance.
(c) (*se procurer*) **~ l'aide de qn/la victoire** to secure *ou* ensure sb's help/victory; **il s'est ainsi assuré un revenu** he thus ensured *ou* secured himself an income; **cela m'assure un toit pour les vacances** that assures me of *ou* that ensures me a roof over my head for the holidays; **s'~ l'accès de** to secure access to.
(d) (*s'affermir*) to steady o.s. (*sur* on); (*Alpinisme*) to belay

o.s. **s'~ sur sa selle/ses jambes** to steady o.s. in one's saddle/on one's legs.

(e) (*littér: arrêter*) **s'~ d'un voleur** to apprehend a thief.

assureur [asyʀœʀ] *nm* (*agent*) insurance agent; (*société*) insurance company; (*Jur: partie*) insurers (*pl*); *[entreprise]* underwriters.

Assyrie [asiʀi] *nf* Assyria.

assyrien, -ienne [asiʀjɛ̃, jɛn] **1** *adj* Assyrian. **2** *nm,f*: **A~(ne)** Assyrian.

aster [astɛʀ] *nm* aster.

astérisque [asteʀisk(ə)] *nm* asterisk.

astéroïde [asteʀɔid] *nm* asteroid.

asthénie [asteni] *nf* asthenia.

asthénique [astenik] *adj, nmf* asthenic.

asthmatique [asmatik] *adj, nmf* asthmatic.

asthme [asm(ə)] *nm* asthma.

asticot [astiko] *nm* (*gén*) maggot; (*: *type*) bloke* (*Brit*), guy (*US*).

asticoter* [astikɔte] (1) *vt* to needle, get at*. **cesse donc d'~ ta sœur!** stop getting at* *ou* plaguing *ou* needling your sister!

astigmate [astigmat] **1** *adj* astigmatic. **2** *nmf* astigmat(ic).

astigmatisme [astigmatism(ə)] *nm* astigmatism.

astiquage [astikaʒ] *nm* polishing.

astiquer [astike] (1) *vt arme, meuble, parquet* to polish; *bottes, métal* to polish, shine, rub up.

astragale [astʀagal] *nm* (*Anat, Bot*) astragalus; (*Archit*) astragal.

astrakan [astʀakɑ̃] *nm* astrakhan.

astral, e, *mpl* **-aux** [astʀal, o] *adj* astral.

astre [astʀ(ə)] *nm* star. (*littér*) **l'~ du jour/de la nuit** the day-/night star (*littér*).

astreignant, e [astʀɛɲɑ̃, ɑ̃t] *adj travail* exacting, demanding.

astreindre [astʀɛ̃dʀ(ə)] (49) **1** *vt*: **~ qn à faire** to compel *ou* oblige *ou* force sb to do; **~ qn à un travail pénible/une discipline sévère** to force a trying task/a strict code of discipline upon sb.

2 s'astreindre *vpr*: **s'~ à faire** to force *ou* compel o.s. to do; **elle s'astreignait à un régime sévère** she forced herself to keep to a strict diet; **astreignez-vous à une vérification rigoureuse** apply yourself to a thorough check (*frm*), make yourself carry out a thorough check.

astreinte [astʀɛ̃t] *nf* (*littér: obligation*) constraint, obligation; (*Jur*) penalty, damages (*pl*) (*imposed on daily basis for non-completion of contract*).

astringence [astʀɛ̃ʒɑ̃s] *nf* astringency.

astringent, e [astʀɛ̃ʒɑ̃, ɑ̃t] *adj, nm* astringent.

astrolabe [astʀɔlab] *nm* astrolabe.

astrologie [astʀɔlɔʒi] *nf* astrology.

astrologique [astʀɔlɔʒik] *adj* astrologic(al).

astrologue [astʀɔlɔg] *nm* astrologer.

astronaute [astʀɔnot] *nmf* astronaut.

astronautique [astʀɔnotik] *nf* astronautics (*sg*).

astronef† [astʀɔnɛf] *nm* spaceship, spacecraft.

astronome [astʀɔnɔm] *nm* astronomer.

astronomie [astʀɔnɔmi] *nf* astronomy.

astronomique [astʀɔnɔmik] *adj* (*lit, fig*) astronomical, astronomic.

astronomiquement [astʀɔnɔmikmɑ̃] *adv* astronomically.

astrophysicien, -ienne [astʀɔfizisjɛ̃, jɛn] *nm,f* astrophysicist.

astrophysique [astʀɔfizik] **1** *adj* astrophysical. **2** *nf* astrophysics (*sg*).

astuce [astys] *nf* **(a)** (*U*) shrewdness, astuteness. **il a beaucoup d'~** he is very shrewd *ou* astute.

(b) (*moyen, truc*) (clever) way, trick. **là, l'~ c'est d'utiliser de l'eau au lieu de pétrole** now the trick *ou* the clever bit here is to use water instead of oil; **les ~s du métier** the tricks of the trade; **c'est ça l'~!** that's the trick! *ou* the clever bit!

(c) (*) (*jeu de mot*) pun; (*plaisanterie*) wisecrack*. **faire des ~s** to make wisecracks*; **~ vaseuse** lousy* pun.

astucieusement [astysjøzmɑ̃] *adv* cleverly, astutely.

astucieux, -ieuse [astysjø, jøz] *adj personne, réponse, raisonnement* shrewd, astute; *visage* shrewd, astute-looking; *moyen, solution* shrewd, clever.

asymétrie [asimetʀi] *nf* asymmetry.

asymétrique [asimetʀik] *adj* asymmetric(al).

asymptote [asɛ̃ptɔt] **1** *adj* asymptotic. **2** *nf* asymptote.

asymptotique [asɛ̃ptɔtik] *adj* asymptotic.

asynchrone [asɛ̃kʀɔn] *adj* asynchronous.

asyndète [asɛ̃dɛt] *nf* asyndeton.

atavique [atavik] *adj* atavistic.

atavisme [atavism(ə)] *nm* atavism. **c'est de l'~!** it's heredity coming out!, it's an atavistic trait!

atèle [atɛl] *nm* spider monkey.

atelier [atəlje] *nm* **(a)** (*local*) *[artisan]* workshop; *[artiste]* studio; *[couturières]* workroom; *[haute couture]* atelier. **~ de fabrication** workshop.

(b) (*groupe*) (*Art*) studio; (*Scol*) work-group.

(c) (*Ind*) *[usine]* shop, workshop; *V* **chef**[1].

atemporel, -elle [atɑ̃pɔʀɛl] *adj vérité* timeless.

atermoiement [atɛʀmwamɑ̃] *nm* prevarication, procrastination (*U*).

atermoyer [atɛʀmwaje] (8) *vi* (*tergiverser*) to procrastinate, temporize.

athée [ate] **1** *adj* atheistic. **2** *nmf* atheist.

athéisme [ateism(ə)] *nm* atheism.

Athéna [atena] *nf* Athena, (Pallas) Athene.

Athènes [atɛn] *n* Athens.

athénien, -ienne [atenjɛ̃, jɛn] **1** *adj* Athenian. **2** *nm,f*: **A~(ne)** Athenian.

athlète [atlɛt] *nmf* athlete. **corps d'~** athletic body; (*hum*) **regarde l'~!, quel ~!** just look at muscleman! (*hum*).

athlétique [atletik] *adj* athletic.

athlétisme [atletism(ə)] *nm* athletics (*sg*).

Atlantide [atlɑ̃tid] *nf* Atlantis.

atlantique [atlɑ̃tik] **1** *adj* Atlantic. (*Can*) **les Provinces ~** the Atlantic Provinces; *V* **heure**. **2** *nm*: **l'A~** the Atlantic (Ocean).

atlantisme [atlɑ̃tism(ə)] *nm* support for the Atlantic Alliance.

atlantiste [atlɑ̃tist(ə)] **1** *adj, politique etc* which promotes the Atlantic Alliance. **2** *nmf* supporter of the Atlantic Alliance.

atlas [atlɑs] *nm* (*livre, Anat*) atlas. (*Myth*) **A~** Atlas; (*Géog*) **l'A~** the Atlas Mountains.

atmosphère [atmɔsfɛʀ] *nf* (*lit, fig*) atmosphere.

atmosphérique [atmɔsfeʀik] *adj* atmospheric; *V* **courant, perturbation**.

atoca* [atɔka] *nm* (*Can: canneberge*) cranberry, atoca† (*Can*).

atoll [atɔl] *nm* atoll.

atome [atom] *nm* atom. **il n'a pas un ~ de bon sens** he hasn't an iota *ou* atom of sense; (*fig*) **avoir des ~s crochus avec qn** to have things in common with sb, hit it off with sb*.

atomique [atɔmik] *adj* (*Chim, Phys*) atomic; (*Mil, Pol*) atomic, nuclear; *V* **bombe**.

atomiser [atɔmize] (1) *vt* (*gén*) to atomize; (*Mil*) to destroy by atomic *ou* nuclear weapons. **les atomisés d'Hiroshima** the victims of the Hiroshima atom bomb.

atomiseur [atɔmizœʀ] *nm* (*gén*) spray; *[parfum]* atomizer.

atomiste [atɔmist(ə)] *nmf* (*aussi* **savant, ingénieur** *etc* **~**) atomic scientist.

atomistique [atɔmistik] **1** *adj*: **théorie ~** atomic theory. **2** *nf* atomic theory; (*Sci*) atomology.

atonal, e, *mpl* **~s** [atɔnal] *adj* atonal.

atonalité [atɔnalite] *nf* atonality.

atone [atɔn] *adj* **(a)** (*sans vitalité*) *être* lifeless; (*sans expression*) *regard* expressionless; (*Méd*) atonic. **(b)** (*Ling*) unstressed, unaccented, atonic.

atonie [atɔni] *nf* (*Ling, Méd*) atony; (*manque de vitalité*) lifelessness.

atours [atuʀ] *nmpl* (†, *hum*) attire, finery. **dans ses plus beaux ~** in her loveliest attire (†, *hum*), in all her finery (†, *hum*).

atout [atu] *nm* **(a)** (*Cartes*) trump. **jouer ~** to play a trump; (*en commençant*) to lead trumps; **~ cœur** hearts are trumps; **~ maître** master trump.

(b) (*fig*) (*avantage*) asset; (*carte maîtresse*) trump card. **l'avoir dans l'équipe est un ~** it's a great advantage having him in the team, he is an asset to our team; **avoir tous les ~s (dans son jeu)** to hold all the trumps *ou* winning cards.

atoxique [atɔksik] *adj* non-poisonous.

atrabilaire [atʀabilɛʀ] *adj* (††, *hum*) bilious, atrabilious.

âtre [ɑtʀ(ə)] *nm* (*littér*) hearth.

atroce [atʀɔs] *adj* **(a)** *crime* atrocious, heinous, foul; *douleur* excruciating; *spectacle* atrocious, ghastly, horrifying; *mort, sort, vengeance* dreadful, terrible.

(b) (*sens affaibli*) *goût, odeur, temps* ghastly, atrocious, foul; *livre, acteur* atrocious, dreadful; *laideur, bêtise* dreadful.

atrocement [atʀɔsmɑ̃] *adv* **(a)** *souffrir* atrociously, horribly; *défigurer* horribly. **il s'est vengé ~** he wreaked a terrible *ou* dreadful revenge; **elle avait ~ peur** she was terror-stricken.

(b) (*sens affaibli*) *laid* atrociously, dreadfully; *bête* dreadfully; *mauvais, ennuyeux* excruciatingly, dreadfully. **loucher ~** to have a dreadful squint.

atrocité [atʀɔsite] *nf* **(a)** (*qualité*) *[crime, action]* atrocity, atrociousness; *[spectacle]* ghastliness.

(b) (*acte*) atrocity, outrage. **dire des ~s sur qn** to say wicked things about sb; **cette nouvelle tour est une ~** this new tower is an atrocity *ou* an eyesore.

atrophie [atʀɔfi] *nf* (*Méd*) atrophy; (*fig*) degeneration, atrophy.

atrophier [atʀɔfje] (7) **1** *vt* (*Méd*) to atrophy; (*fig*) to atrophy, cause the degeneration of. **2 s'atrophier** *vpr [membres, muscle]* to waste away, atrophy (*T*); (*fig*) to atrophy, degenerate.

attabler (s') [atable] (1) *vpr* (*pour manger*) to sit down at (the) table. **s'~ autour d'une bonne bouteille (avec des amis)** to sit (down) at the table *ou* settle down round (*Brit*) *ou* around (*US*) the table for a drink (with friends); **il retourna s'~ à la terrasse du café** he went back to sit at a table outside the café; **il traversa la salle et vint s'~ avec eux** he crossed the room and came to sit at their table; **les clients attablés** the seated customers.

attachant, e [ataʃɑ̃, ɑ̃t] *adj livre* captivating, engaging; *caractère, personne* likeable, engaging; *enfant* engaging, lovable.

attache [ataʃ] *nf* **(a)** (*en ficelle*) (piece of) string; (*en métal*) clip, fastener; (*courroie*) strap.

(b) (*Anat*) **~s** (*épaules*) shoulders; (*aines*) groins; (*poignets et chevilles*) wrists and ankles.

(c) (*fig*) (*lien*) tie. (*connaissances*) **~s** ties, connections; **avoir des ~s dans une région** to have family ties *ou* connections in a region.

(d) (*Bot*) tendril.

(e) (*loc*) **à l'~** *animal* tied up; (*fig*) *personne* tied; *bateau* moored; *V* **point**[1], **port**[1].

attaché, e [ataʃe] (*ptp de* **attacher**) **1** *adj* **(a)** (*tenir à*) **être ~ à** *personne, région, tableau* to be attached to; *habitude* to be tied *ou* attached to; **~ à la vie** attached to life.

(b) (*frm: être affecté à*) **être ~ au service de qn** to be in sb's personal service; **les avantages ~s à ce poste** the benefits connected with *ou* attached to this position; **son nom restera ~ à cette découverte** his name will always be linked with this discovery.

2 *nm* attaché. **~ d'ambassade/de presse/militaire** embassy/press/military attaché; **~ d'administration** administrative assistant.

3: attaché-case [kɛz] *nm inv* attaché case.

attachement [ataʃmɑ̃] *nm* **(a)** (*à une personne*) affection (*à* for), attachment (*à* to); (*à un lieu, à une doctrine, à la vie*) attachment (*à* to). **(b)** (*Constr*) daily statement (*of work done and expenses incurred*).

attacher [ataʃe] (1) **1** *vt* **(a)** *animal, plante* to tie up; (*avec une chaîne*) to chain up; *volets* to fasten, secure. ~ **une étiquette à un arbre/à une valise** to tie a label to a tree/on(to) a case; **attachez donc votre chien** please tie up your dog *ou* get your dog tied up; **il attacha sa victime sur une chaise** he tied his victim to a chair; **il a attaché son nom à cette découverte** he has linked *ou* put his name to this discovery; **s'~ à une corde** to tie o.s. with a rope; **s'~ à son siège** to fasten o.s. to one's seat.

(b) *paquet, colis* to tie up; *prisonnier* to tie up, bind; *plusieurs choses ensemble* to tie together, bind together. ~ **les mains d'un prisonnier** to tie a prisoner's hands together, bind a prisoner's hands (together); **la ficelle qui attachait le paquet** the string that was round the parcel; **est-ce bien attaché?** is it well *ou* securely tied (up)?; **il ne les attache pas avec des saucisses*** he's a bit tight-fisted.

(c) *ceinture* to do up, fasten; *robe* (*à boutons*) to do up, button up, fasten; (*à fermeture éclair*) to do up, zip up; *lacets* to do up, tie up; *fermeture, bouton* to do up. **attache tes chaussures** do up *ou* tie up your shoes; (*Aviat*) **veuillez ~ vos ceintures** (please) fasten your seatbelts.

(d) *papiers* (*épingler*) to pin together, attach; (*agrafer*) to staple together, attach. ~ **à** to pin to; to staple onto; ~ **une notice au mur avec du scotch** to stick a notice up on the wall with sellotape (*Brit*) *ou* Scotch tape, sellotape (*Brit*) *ou* Scotch-tape a notice to the wall.

(e) (*fig: lier à*) **des souvenirs l'attachent à ce village** (*qu'il a quitté*) he still feels attached to the village because of his memories; (*qu'il habite*) his memories keep him here in this village; **il a su s'~ ses étudiants** he has won the loyalty of his students; **plus rien ne l'attachait à la vie** nothing held her to life any more.

(f) (*attribuer*) ~ **de l'importance à qch** to attach importance to sth; ~ **de la valeur** *ou* **du prix à qch** to attach great value to sth, set great store by sth; ~ **un certain sens à** to attach *ou* attribute a certain meaning to.

(g) (*frm: adjoindre*) ~ **des gardes à qn** to give sb a personal guard; ~ **qn à son service** to engage sb, take sb into one's service.

(h) (*fixer*) ~ **son regard** *ou* **ses yeux sur** to fix one's eyes upon.

2 *vi* (*Culin*) to stick. **les pommes de terre ont attaché** the potatoes have stuck; **une poêle qui n'attache pas** a non-stick frying pan.

3 s'attacher *vpr* **(a)** (*gén*) to do up, fasten (up) (*avec, par* with); *[robe]* (*à boutons*) to button up, do up; (*à fermeture éclair*) to zip up, do up; *[fermeture, bouton]* to do up. **ça s'attache derrière** it does up (at) the back, it fastens (up) at the back.

(b) (*se prendre d'affection pour*) **s'~ à** to become attached to; **cet enfant s'attache vite** this child soon becomes attached to people.

(c) (*accompagner*) **s'~ aux pas de qn** to follow sb closely, dog sb's footsteps; **les souvenirs qui s'attachent à cette maison** the memories attached to *ou* associated with that house.

attaquable [atakabl(ə)] *adj* (*Mil*) open to attack; *testament* contestable.

attaquant, e [atakɑ̃, ɑ̃t] *nm,f* (*Mil, Sport*) attacker; (*Ftbl*) striker, forward. **l'avantage est à l'~** the advantage is on the attacking side.

attaque [atak] **1** *nf* **(a)** (*Mil, Police, Sport, fig*) attack. **aller à l'~** to go into the attack; **passer à l'~** to move into the attack; ~ **d'artillerie** *etc* artillery *etc* attack.

(b) (*Méd*) (*gén*) attack; *[épilepsie]* fit, attack (*de* of). **avoir une ~** (*cardiaque*) to have a heart attack, have a stroke; (*apoplexie*) to have a seizure.

(c) (*Mus*) striking up.

(d) (**loc*) **d'~** on form, in top form; **il est particulièrement d'~ ce soir** he is in particularly fine form tonight; **il n'est pas d'~ ce matin** he's a bit off form this morning; **se sentir** *ou* **être assez d'~ pour faire** to feel up to doing.

2: attaque aérienne air raid, air attack; **attaque d'apoplexie** apoplectic attack *ou* seizure; **attaque cardiaque** heart attack; **attaque à main armée** armed attack; **attaque de nerfs** fit of hysterics.

attaquer [atake] (1) **1** *vt* **(a)** (*assaillir*) *pays* to attack, make *ou* launch an attack upon; *passant, jeune fille* to attack, assault, set upon; (*fig*) *abus, réputation, personne* to attack. **l'armée prussienne/l'équipe adverse attaqua** the Prussian army/the opposing team attacked *ou* went into the attack; ~ **de front/par derrière** to attack from the front/from behind *ou* from the rear; ~ **(qn) par surprise** to make a surprise attack ((up)on sb).

(b) (*endommager*) *[rouille, acide]* to attack; (*Méd*) *[infection]* to affect, attack. **l'humidité a attaqué les peintures** damp has attacked *ou* damaged the paintings; **la pollution attaque notre environnement** pollution is having a damaging effect on *ou* is damaging our environment; **l'acide attaque le fer** acid attacks *ou* eats into iron.

(c) (*aborder*) *difficulté, obstacle* to tackle, attack; *chapitre* to tackle; *discours* to launch upon; *travail* to set about, buckle down to, get down to; (*Mus*) *morceau* to strike up, launch into; *note* to attack. **il attaqua les hors-d'œuvre*** he tucked into* *ou* got going on* the hors d'œuvres.

(d) (*Jur*) ~ **qn en justice** to bring an action against sb; ~ **un testament** to contest a will.

2 s'attaquer *vpr*: **s'~ à** *personne, abus, mal* to attack; *problème* to tackle, attack; **s'~ à plus fort que soi** to take on more than one's match.

attardé, e [ataRde] *adj* **(a)** (*Psych*) *enfant* backward. **(b)** (*en retard*) *promeneur* late, belated (*littér*). **(c)** (*démodé*) *personne, goût* old-fashioned, behind the times (*attrib*).

attarder [ataRde] (1) **1** *vt* to make late.

2 s'attarder *vpr* **(a)** (*se mettre en retard*) to linger (behind). **s'~ chez des amis** to stay on at friends'; **s'~ à boire** to linger over drinks *ou* a drink; **il s'est attardé au bureau pour finir un rapport** he has stayed on at the office to finish a report; **s'~ au café** to linger at the café; **s'~ pour cueillir des fleurs** to stay behind to pick flowers; **elle s'est attardée en route** she dawdled *ou* lingered *ou* tarried (*littér*) on the way; **s'~ derrière les autres** to lag behind the others; **ne nous attardons pas ici** let's not linger *ou* hang about* here.

(b) (*fig*) **s'~ sur une description** to linger over a description; **s'~ à des détails** to linger over *ou* dwell (up)on details.

atteindre [atɛ̃dR(ə)] (49) **1** *vt* **(a)** (*parvenir à*) *lieu, limite* to reach; *objet haut placé* to reach, get at; *objectif* to reach, arrive at, attain. **il ne m'atteint pas l'épaule** he doesn't come up to *ou* reach my shoulder; **la Seine a atteint la cote d'alerte** the Seine has risen to *ou* reached danger level; **cette tour atteint 30 mètres** this tower is 30 metres high; **les peupliers peuvent ~ une très grande hauteur** poplars can grow to *ou* reach a very great height; **il a atteint son but** he has reached his goal, he has achieved his aim *ou* end; *V* **bave**.

(b) (*contacter*) *personne* to get in touch with, contact, reach.

(c) (*toucher*) *[pierre, balle, tireur]* to hit (*à* in); *[événement, maladie, reproches]* to affect. **il a eu l'œil atteint par un éclat d'obus** he was hit in the eye by a bit of shrapnel; **la maladie a atteint ses facultés mentales** the illness has affected *ou* impaired his mental faculties; **les reproches ne l'atteignent pas** reproaches don't affect him, he is unaffected by reproaches; **le malheur qui vient de l'~** the misfortune which has just struck him; **il a été atteint dans son amour-propre/ses sentiments** his pride has/his feelings have been hurt *ou* wounded.

2 atteindre à *vt indir* (*littér: parvenir à*) *but* to reach, achieve. ~ **à la perfection** to attain (to) *ou* achieve perfection.

atteint, e[1] [atɛ̃, ɛ̃t] *adj* **(a)** (*malade*) **être ~ de** to be suffering from; **le poumon** *etc* **est gravement/légèrement ~** the lung *etc* is badly/slightly affected; **il est gravement/légèrement ~** he is seriously/only slightly ill, he is a serious/mild case; **les malades les plus ~s** the worst cases, the worst affected.

(b) (**: fou*) touched*, cracked*.

atteinte[2] [atɛ̃t] *nf* **(a)** (*préjudice*) attack (*à* on). (*Jur*) ~ **à l'ordre public** breach of the peace; **porter ~ à** to strike a blow at, undermine.

(b) (*Méd: crise*) attack (*de* of). **les premières ~s du mal** the first effects of the illness; *V* **hors**.

attelage [atlaʒ] *nm* **(a)** (*V* **atteler**) harnessing; hitching up; yoking; coupling.

(b) (*harnachement, chaînes*) *[chevaux]* harness; *[bœuf]* yoke; *[remorque]* coupling, attachment; (*Rail*) coupling.

(c) (*équipage*) *[chevaux]* team; *[bœufs]* team, *[deux bœufs]* yoke.

atteler [atle] (4) **1** *vt* *cheval* to harness, hitch up; *bœuf* to yoke, hitch up; *charrette, remorque* to hitch up; (*Rail*) *wagon* to couple on; *wagons* to couple. **le cocher était en train d'~** the coachman was in the process of getting the horses harnessed *ou* of harnessing up; (*fig*) ~ **qn à un travail** to put sb on a job.

2 s'atteler *vpr*: **s'~ à** *travail, tâche* to get *ou* buckle down to; *problème* to get down to; **il est attelé à ce travail depuis ce matin** he has been working away at this job since this morning.

attelle [atɛl] *nf [cheval]* hame; (*Méd*) splint.

attenant, e [atnɑ̃, ɑ̃t] *adj* (*contigu*) adjoining. **jardin ~ à la maison** garden adjoining the house.

attendre [atɑ̃dR(ə)] (41) **1** *vt* **(a)** *[personne] personne, événement* to wait for, await (*littér*). **maintenant, nous attendons qu'il vienne/de savoir** we are now waiting for him to come/to find out; **attendez qu'il vienne/de savoir pour partir** wait until he comes/you know before you leave, wait for him to come/wait and find out before you leave; ~ **la fin du film** to wait until the film is over *ou* until the end of the film; **(aller/venir) ~ un train/qn au train** to meet a train/sb off the train; **j'attends le** *ou* **mon train** I'm waiting for the *ou* my train; ~ **le moment favorable** to wait for the right moment; ~ **les vacances avec impatience** to look forward eagerly to the holidays, long for the holidays; **nous n'attendons plus que lui pour commencer** we're only waiting for him to start, there's only him to come and then we can start; **il faut ~ un autre jour/moment pour lui parler** we'll have to wait till another day/time to speak to him; **je n'attends qu'une chose, c'est qu'elle s'en aille** I (just) can't wait for her to go; **il n'attendait que ça!** that's just what he was waiting for!; **qu'attendez-vous pour réclamer?** what are you waiting for? why don't you (go ahead and) complain?

(b) *[voiture]* to be waiting for; *[maison]* to be ready for; *[mauvaise surprise]* to be in store for, await, wait for; *[gloire]* to be in store for, await. **il ne sait pas encore le sort qui l'attend!** he doesn't know yet what's in store for him! *ou* awaiting him!, he does not yet know what fate awaits him!; **une brillante carrière l'attend** he has a brilliant career in store (for him) *ou* ahead of him; **le dîner vous attend** dinner's ready (when you are).

(c) (*sans objet*) *[personne, chose]* to wait; *[chose]* (*se conserver*) to keep. **attendez un instant** wait a moment, hang on a minute*; **j'ai attendu 2 heures** I waited (for) 2 hours; **attendez voir*** let me *ou* let's see *ou* think*; **attendez un peu** let's see, wait a second; (*menace*) just (you) wait!; (*iro*) **tu peux toujours ~!** you've got a hope!, you'll be lucky!; **ce travail attendra/peut ~** this work will wait/can wait; **ces fruits ne peuvent pas ~ (à demain)** this fruit won't keep (until tomorrow).

(d) faire ~ qn to keep sb waiting; **se faire ~** to keep people waiting, be a long time coming; **le conférencier se fait ~** the speaker is late *ou* is a long time coming; **il aime se faire ~** he likes to keep you *ou* people waiting; **excusez-moi de m'être fait ~** sorry to have kept you (waiting); **la paix se fait ~** peace is a long time coming; **la riposte ne se fit pas ~** the retort was not long in coming *ou* was quick to follow.

(e) (*escompter, prévoir*) *personne, chose* to expect. **~ qch de qn/qch** to expect sth from sb/sth; **il n'attendait pas un tel accueil** he wasn't expecting such a welcome; **elle est arrivée alors qu'on ne l'attendait plus** she came when she was no longer expected *ou* when they had given her up; **on attendait beaucoup de ces pourparlers** they had great hopes *ou* they expected great things* of these negotiations; **j'attendais mieux de cet élève** I expected better of this child, I expected this child to do better.

(f) (*loc*) **~ de pied ferme** to wait resolutely; **~ son tour** to wait one's turn; **~ un enfant** to be expecting a baby, be expecting*; **il attend son heure!** he's biding his time; **il m'attendait au tournant*** he waited for the chance to trip me up; **attendez-moi sous l'orme!**† you can wait for me till the cows come home!; **en attendant** (*pendant ce temps*) meanwhile, in the meantime; (*en dépit de cela*) all the same, be that as it may; **en attendant, j'ai le temps de finir le ménage** meanwhile *ou* in the meantime I've time to finish the housework; **en attendant, il est (quand même) très courageux** all the same *ou* be that as it may, he's (nonetheless) very brave; **il a pris froid en attendant** he caught cold while (he was) waiting; **en attendant l'heure de partir, il jouait aux cartes** he used to play cards (while he waited) until it was time to go; **on ne peut rien faire en attendant de recevoir sa lettre** we can't do anything until we get his letter; **en attendant qu'il vienne, je vais vite faire une course** while I'm waiting for him to come I'm going to nip down* (*Brit*) *ou* pop down* to the shop.

2 attendre après* *vt indir chose* to be in a hurry for, be anxious for; *personne* to be waiting for, hang about waiting for*. **ne vous pressez pas de me rendre cet argent, je n'attends pas après** there's no rush to pay me the money, I'm in no hurry for it; **je n'attends pas après lui/son aide!** I can get along without him/his help!

3 s'attendre *vpr* (*escompter, prévoir*) **s'~ à qch** to expect sth (*de* from); **il ne s'attendait pas à gagner** he wasn't expecting to win; **est-ce que tu t'attends vraiment à ce qu'il écrive?** do you really expect him to write?; **on ne s'attendait pas à cela de lui** we didn't expect that of him.

attendri, e [atɑ̃dʀi] (*ptp de* **attendrir**) *adj air, regard* melting (*épith*), tender.

attendrir [atɑ̃dʀiʀ] (2) **1** *vt viande* to tenderize; (*fig*) *personne* to move (to pity); *cœur* to soften, melt. **il se laissa ~ par ses prières** he let her pleadings make him relent *ou* yield.

2 s'attendrir *vpr* to be moved *ou* touched (*sur* by); to sigh, get emotional (*sur* over). **s'~ sur (le sort de) qn** to feel (sorry *ou* pity *ou* sympathy) for sb; **s'~ sur soi-même** to feel sorry for o.s.

attendrissant, e [atɑ̃dʀisɑ̃, ɑ̃t] *adj* moving, touching.

attendrissement [atɑ̃dʀismɑ̃] *nm* (*tendre*) emotion, tender feelings; (*apitoyé*) pity. **ce fut l'~ général** everybody got emotional; **pas d'~!** no soft-heartedness!, no displays of emotion!

attendrisseur [atɑ̃dʀisœʀ] *nm* (*Boucherie*) tenderizer. **viande passée à l'~** tenderized meat.

attendu, e [atɑ̃dy] (*ptp de* **attendre**) **1** *adj personne, événement, jour* long-awaited; (*prévu*) expected.

2 *prép* (*étant donné*) given, considering. **~ que** seeing that, since, given *ou* considering that; (*Jur*) whereas.

3 *nm* (*Jur*) **~s d'un jugement** reasons adduced for a judgment.

attentat [atɑ̃ta] *nm* (*gén: contre une personne*) murder attempt; (*Pol*) assassination attempt; (*contre un bâtiment*) attack (*contre* on). **~ à la bombe** bomb attack; **un ~ a été perpétré contre M Dupont** an attempt has been made on the life of M Dupont; **~ aux droits/à la liberté** violation of rights/of liberty; **~ contre la sûreté de l'État** conspiracy against the security of the State; (*Jur*) **~ aux mœurs** offence against public morals; (*Jur*) **~ à la pudeur** indecent exposure.

attentatoire [atɑ̃tatwaʀ] *adj* prejudicial (*à* to), detrimental (*à* to).

attente [atɑ̃t] *nf* **(a)** wait, waiting (*U*) **cette ~ fut très pénible** it was a trying wait; **l'~ est ce qu'il y a de plus pénible** it's the waiting which is hardest to bear; **l'~ des résultats devenait insupportable** waiting for the results was becoming unbearable; **l'~ se prolongeait** the wait was growing longer and longer; **vivre dans l'~ d'une nouvelle** to spend one's time waiting for (a piece of) news; **dans l'~ de vos nouvelles** looking forward to hearing *ou* hoping to hear from you; *V* **salle**.

(b) (*espoir*) expectation. **répondre à l'~ de qn** to come up to sb's expectations; **contre toute ~** contrary to (all) expectation(s).

attenter [atɑ̃te] (1) *vi* **(a) ~ à la vie de qn** to make an attempt on sb's life; **~ à ses jours** to attempt suicide, make an attempt on one's life; **~ à la sûreté de l'État** to conspire against the security of the State. **(b)** (*fig: violer*) **~ à** *liberté, droits* to violate.

attentif, -ive [atɑ̃tif, iv] *adj* **(a)** (*vigilant*) *personne, air* attentive. **regarder qn d'un œil ~** to look at sb attentively; **écouter d'une oreille ~ive** to listen attentively; **être ~ à tout ce qui se passe** to pay attention to all that goes on, heed all that goes on; **sois donc ~** pay attention!

(b) (*scrupuleux*) *examen* careful, close, searching; *travail* careful; *soin* scrupulous. **~ à son travail** careful *ou* painstaking in one's work; **~ à ses devoirs** heedful *ou* mindful of one's duties; **~ à ne blesser personne** careful *ou* cautious not to hurt anyone.

(c) (*prévenant*) *soins* thoughtful; *prévenance* watchful. **~ à plaire** anxious to please; **~ à ce que tout se passe bien** keeping a close watch to see that all goes (off) well.

attention [atɑ̃sjɔ̃] *nf* **(a)** (*concentration*) attention; (*soin*) care. **avec ~** *écouter* carefully, attentively; *examiner* carefully, closely; **attirer/détourner l'~ de qn** to attract/divert *ou* distract sb's attention; **ce cas/projet mérite toute notre ~** this case/project deserves our undivided attention; **'à l'~ de M Dupont'** 'for the attention of M Dupont'; **je demande toute votre ~** can I have your full attention?; *V* **signaler**.

(b) faire *ou* **prêter ~ à** to pay attention *ou* heed to; **as-tu fait ~ à ce qu'il a dit?** did you pay attention to *ou* attend *ou* listen carefully to what he said?; **il n'a même pas fait ~ à moi/à ce changement** he didn't (even) take any notice of me/the change; **tu vas faire ~ quand il entrera et tu verras** look carefully *ou* have a good look when he comes in and you'll see what I mean; **ne faites pas ~ à lui** pay no attention to him, take no notice of him, never mind him.

(c) faire ~ (*prendre garde*) to be careful, take care; **(fais) ~ à ta ligne** watch *ou* mind your waistline; **fais ~ à ne pas trop manger** mind *ou* be careful you don't eat too much; **fais ~ (à ce) que la porte soit fermée** be *ou* make sure *ou* mind the door's shut.

(d) (*loc*) **~! tu vas tomber** watch! *ou* mind (out)! *ou* careful!, you're going to fall! *ou* you'll fall!; **~ chien méchant** beware of the dog; **~ travaux** caution, work in progress; **~ à la marche** mind the step; **~! je n'ai pas dit cela** careful! *ou* watch it!*, I didn't say that; **~ à la peinture** (caution) wet paint.

(e) (*prévenance*) attention, thoughtfulness (*U*). **être plein d'~s pour qn** to be very thoughtful *ou* attentive towards sb; **ses ~s me touchaient** I was touched by his attentions *ou* thoughtfulness; **quelle charmante ~!** how very thoughtful!, what a lovely thought!

attentionné, e [atɑ̃sjɔne] *adj* (*prévenant*) thoughtful, considerate (*pour, auprès de* towards).

attentisme [atɑ̃tism(ə)] *nm* wait-and-see policy, waiting-game.

attentiste [atɑ̃tist(ə)] **1** *nmf* partisan of a wait-and-see policy. **2** *adj politique* wait-and-see (*épith*).

attentivement [atɑ̃tivmɑ̃] *adv lire, écouter* attentively, carefully; *examiner* carefully, closely.

atténuantes [atenɥɑ̃t] *adj fpl V* **circonstance**.

atténuation [atenɥɑsjɔ̃] *nf* **(a)** (*V* **atténuer**) alleviation, easing; mollifying; appeasement, toning down; palliation (*frm*); lightening; watering down; subduing; dimming; softening; toning down; (*Jur*) *[peine]* mitigation.

(b) (*V* **s'atténuer**) dying down; easing; subsiding, abatement; softening.

atténuer [atenɥe] (1) **1** *vt* **(a)** *douleur* to alleviate, ease; *rancœur* to mollify, appease; *propos, reproches* to tone down; *faute* to palliate (*frm*), mitigate; *responsabilité* to lighten; *punition* to lighten, mitigate; *faits* to water down.

(b) *lumière* to subdue, dim; *couleur, son* to soften, tone down.

2 s'atténuer *vpr* **(a)** *[douleur]* to ease, die down; *[sensation]* to die down; *[violence, crise]* to subside, abate.

(b) *[bruit]* to die down; *[couleur]* to soften. **leurs cris s'atténuèrent** their cries grew quieter *ou* died down.

atterrer [ateʀe] (1) *vt* to dismay, appal (*Brit*), appall (*US*), shatter. **il était atterré par cette nouvelle** he was aghast *ou* shattered at this piece of news; **sa bêtise m'atterre** his stupidity appals me, I am appalled by his stupidity; **on devinait à son air atterré que ...** we could tell by his look of utter dismay that ... .

atterrir [ateʀiʀ] (2) *vi* (*Aviat*) to land, touch down. **~ sur le ventre** *[personne]* to land (up) flat on one's face; *[avion]* to make a belly landing, bellyland; (*fig*) **~ en prison/dans un village perdu*** to land up* in prison/in a village in the middle of nowhere.

atterrissage [ateʀisaʒ] *nm* (*Aviat*) landing. **au moment de l'~** at the moment of landing, at touchdown; **~ en catastrophe/sur le ventre/sans visibilité** crash/belly/blind landing; **~ forcé** emergency *ou* forced landing; *V* **piste, terrain, train**.

attestation [atɛstɑsjɔ̃] *nf* **(a)** *[fait]* attestation. **(b)** (*document*) certificate. **~ médicale** doctor's certificate.

attester [atɛste] (1) *vt* **(a)** (*certifier*) *fait* to testify to, vouch for. **~ que** to testify that, vouch for the fact that, attest that; *[témoin]* to attest that; **~ (de) l'innocence de qn** to testify to *ou* vouch for sb's innocence; **ce fait est attesté par tous les témoins** this fact is borne out *ou* is attested by all the witnesses.

(b) (*démontrer*) *[preuve, chose]* to attest, testify to. **cette attitude atteste son intelligence** *ou* **atteste qu'il est intelligent** his intelligence is attested to by this attitude, this attitude attests to *ou* testifies to his intelligence.

(c) (*littér: prendre à témoin*) **j'atteste les dieux que ...** I call the gods to witness that ... .

attiédir [atjediʀ] (2) **1** *vt* (*littér*) *eau* to make lukewarm; *climat* to make more temperate, temper; *désir, ardeur* to temper, cool.

2 s'attiédir *vpr [eau]* to become lukewarm; *[climat]* to become more temperate; (*littér*) *[désir, ardeur]* to cool down, wane. **l'eau s'est attiédie** (*plus chaude*) the water has got warmer *ou* has warmed up; (*moins chaude*) the water has got cooler *ou* has cooled down.

attiédissement [atjedismɑ̃] *nm [climat]* tempering; (*littér*) *[désir]* cooling, waning.

attifer* [atife] (1) **1** *vt* (*habiller*) *femme* to get up*, doll up*; *homme* to get up* (*de* in). **regardez comme elle est attifée!** look at her getup!*

2 s'attifer *vpr [femme]* to get *ou* doll o.s. up*; *[homme]* to get o.s. up* (*de* in).

attiger: [atiʒe] (3) *vi* to go a bit far*, overstep the mark.

Attila [atila] *nm* Attila.

attique[1] [atik] *adj* (*Antiq*) Attic. **finesse/sel ~** Attic wit/salt.

attique[2] [atik] *nm* (*Constr*) attic (storey).

attirail* [atiʀaj] *nm* gear*, paraphernalia.

attirance [atiʀɑ̃s] *nf* attraction (*pour, envers* for). **éprouver de l'~ pour qch/qn** to be *ou* feel drawn towards sth/sb, be attracted to sth/sb; **l'~ du vide** the lure *ou* tug of the abyss.

attirant, e [atiʀɑ̃, ɑ̃t] *adj* attractive, appealing. **une femme très ~e** an alluring *ou* a very attractive woman.

attirer [atiʀe] (1) *vt* **(a)** (*gén, Phys*) to attract; (*en appâtant*) to lure, entice. **il m'attrapa et m'attira dans un coin** he caught hold of me and drew me into a corner; **~ qn dans un piège/par des promesses** to lure *ou* entice sb into a trap/with promises; **spectacle fait pour ~ la foule** show guaranteed to bring in *ou* draw *ou* attract the crowds; **être attiré par une doctrine/qn** to be attracted *ou* drawn to a doctrine/sb; **~ l'attention de qn sur qch** to draw sb's attention to sth; **il essaya d'~ son attention** he tried to attract *ou* catch his attention; **robe qui attire les regards** eye-catching dress; **elle/son charme attire les hommes** she/her charm appeals to *ou* attracts men.

(b) (*causer*) **~ des ennuis à qn** to cause *ou* bring sb difficulties; **cela va lui ~ des ennuis** that's going to cause *ou* give him problems; **cela a attiré sur lui toute la colère de la ville** this brought the anger of the entire town down on him; **ses discours lui ont attiré des sympathies** his speeches won *ou* gained *ou* earned him sympathy; **s'~ des critiques/la colère de qn** to incur criticism/sb's anger, bring criticism on/sb's anger down on o.s.; **s'~ des ennemis** to make enemies for o.s.; **tu vas t'attirer des ennuis** you're going to cause trouble for yourself *ou* bring trouble upon yourself; **je me suis attiré sa gratitude** I won *ou* earned his gratitude.

attiser [atize] (1) *vt feu* to poke (up), stir up; *désir, querelle* to stir up, fan the flame of. **pour ~ la flamme** to make the fire burn up.

attitré, e [atitʀe] *adj* (*habituel*) *marchand* regular, usual; (*agréé*) *marchand* accredited, appointed, registered; *journaliste* accredited. **fournisseur ~ d'un chef d'état** purveyors by appointment to a head of state.

attitude [atityd] *nf* (*maintien*) bearing; (*comportement*) attitude; (*point de vue*) standpoint; (*affectation*) attitude, façade. **prendre des ~s gracieuses** to adopt graceful poses; **avoir une ~ décidée** to have an air of firmness; **prendre une ~ ferme** to adopt a firm standpoint *ou* attitude; **le socialisme chez lui ce n'est qu'une ~** his socialism is only a façade.

attouchement [atuʃmɑ̃] *nm* touch, touching (*U*); (*Méd*) palpation. **se livrer à des ~s sur qn** (*gén*) to fondle *ou* stroke sb; (*Jur*) to interfere with sb.

attractif, -ive [atʀaktif, iv] *adj* (*Phys*) *phénomène* attractive.

attraction [atʀaksjɔ̃] *nf* **(a)** (*gén: attirance, Ling, Phys*) attraction.

(b) (*centre d'intérêt*) attraction; (*partie d'un spectacle*) attraction; (*numéro d'un artiste*) number. **il est l'~ numéro un au programme** he is the star attraction on the programme; (*boîte de nuit*) **quand passent les ~s?** when is the cabaret on?; (*cirque etc*) **ils ont renouvelé leurs ~s** they have changed their programme (of attractions *ou* entertainments); *V* **parc.**

attrait [atʀɛ] *nm* **(a)** (*séduction*) *[femme, paysage, doctrine]* appeal, attraction; *[danger, aventure]* appeal; *[honneurs, plaisirs]* attraction, allurement. **ses romans ont pour moi beaucoup d'~** I find his novels very appealing *ou* attractive, his novels appeal to me very much; **éprouver un ~ *ou* de l'~ pour qch** to be attracted to sth, find sth attractive *ou* appealing.

(b) (*charmes*) **~s** attractions.

attrapade* [atʀapad] *nf* row*, telling off*.

attrape [atʀap] *nf* (*farce*) trick; *V* **farce**[1].

attrape- [atʀap] *préf V* **attraper.**

attraper [atʀape] (1) **1** *vt* **(a)** *ballon* to catch; (**fig*) *train* to catch, get; *contravention, gifle* to get; *journal, crayon* to pick up.

(b) *personne, voleur* to catch. **si je t'attrape!** if I catch you!; **~ qn à faire qch** to catch sb doing sth; **que je t'y attrape!*** don't let me catch you doing that!, if I catch you doing that!

(c) *maladie* to catch, get. **tu vas ~ froid *ou* du mal** you'll catch cold; **j'ai attrapé un rhume/son rhume** I've caught a cold/a cold from him *ou* his cold; **j'ai attrapé mal à la gorge** I've got a sore throat; **tu vas ~ la mort** you'll catch your death (of cold); **la grippe s'attrape facilement** flu is very catching.

(d) (*intercepter*) *mots* to pick up.

(e) (*acquérir*) *style, accent* to pick up.

(f) (*gronder*) to tell off*. **se faire ~ (par qn)** to be told off (by sb)*, get a telling off (from sb)*; **mes parents vont m'~** I'll get it: from my parents, my parents will give me a telling off*; **ils se sont attrapés pendant une heure** they went at each other for a whole hour*

(g) (*tromper*) to take in. **se laisser ~** to be had* *ou* taken in; **tu as été bien attrapé** (*trompé*) you were had all right*; (*surpris*) you were caught out there all right!

2: attrape-mouche *nm, pl* **attrape-mouche (s)** (*Bot*) fly trap; (*Orn*) flycatcher; (*piège*) flypaper; **attrape-nigaud*** *nm, pl* **attrape-nigaud(s)** con*.

attrayant, e [atʀɛjɑ̃, ɑ̃t] *adj* (*agréable, beau*) attractive; (*séduisant*) *idée* appealing, attractive. **c'est une lecture ~e** it makes *ou* it's pleasant reading; **peu ~** *travail* unappealing; *paysage* unattractive; *proposition* unattractive, unappealing.

attribuable [atʀibɥabl(ə)] *adj* attributable (*à* to).

attribuer [atʀibɥe] (1) *vt* **(a)** (*allouer*) *prix* to award; *avantages, privilèges* to grant, accord; *place, rôle* to allocate, assign; *biens, part* to allocate (*à* to). **s'~ le meilleur rôle/la meilleure part** to give o.s. the best role/the biggest share, claim the best role/the biggest share for o.s.

(b) (*imputer*) *faute* to attribute, impute; *pensée, intention* to attribute, ascribe (*à* to). **à quoi attribuez-vous cet échec/accident?** what do you put this failure/accident down to?, what do you attribute *ou* ascribe this failure/accident to?

(c) (*accorder*) *invention, mérite* to attribute (*à* to). **on lui attribue l'invention de l'imprimerie** the invention of printing has been attributed to him, he has been credited with the invention of printing; **la critique n'attribue que peu d'intérêt à son livre** the critics find little of interest in his book *ou* consider his book of little interest; **~ de l'importance à qch** to attach importance to sth; **s'~ tout le mérite** to claim all the merit for o.s.

attribut [atʀiby] *nm* (*caractéristique, symbole*) attribute; (*Gram*) complement. **nom/adjectif ~** noun/adjectival complement.

attribution [atʀibysjɔ̃] *nf* **(a)** *[prix]* awarding; *[place, rôle, part]* allocation; *[œuvre, invention]* attribution. **(b)** (*prérogatives, pouvoirs*) **~s** attributions.

attristant, e [atʀistɑ̃, ɑ̃t] *adj nouvelle, spectacle* saddening.

attrister [atʀiste] (1) **1** *vt* to sadden. **cette nouvelle nous a profondément attristés** we were greatly saddened by *ou* grieved at this news.

2 s'attrister *vpr* to be saddened (*de* by), become sad (*de qch* at sth, *de voir que* at seeing that).

attroupement [atʀupmɑ̃] *nm [foule]* gathering; (*groupe*) crowd, mob (*péj*).

attrouper (s') [atʀupe] (1) *vpr* to gather (together), flock together, form a crowd.

au [o] *V* **à.**

aubade [obad] *nf* dawn serenade. **donner une ~ à qn** to serenade sb at dawn.

aubaine [obɛn] *nf* godsend; (*financière*) windfall. **profiter de l'~** to make the most of one's good fortune *ou* of the opportunity.

aube[1] [ob] *nf* **(a)** dawn, daybreak, first light. **à l'~** at dawn *ou* daybreak *ou* first light; **avant l'~** before dawn *ou* daybreak. **(b)** (*fig*) dawn, beginning. **à l'~ de** at the dawn of.

aube[2] [ob] *nf* (*Rel*) alb.

aube[3] [ob] *nf* (*Tech*) *[bateau]* paddle, blade; *[moulin]* vane; *[ventilateur]* blade, vane. **roue à ~s** paddle wheel.

aubépine [obepin] *nf* hawthorn. **fleurs d'~** may (blossom), hawthorn blossom.

auberge [obɛʀʒ(ə)] *nf* inn. **il prend la maison pour une ~!*, il se croit à l'~!*** he uses this place as a hotel!; **~ de (la) jeunesse** youth hostel; *V* **sortir.**

aubergine [obɛʀʒin] **1** *nf* **(a)** (*légume*) aubergine, eggplant. **(b)** (*: *contractuelle*) traffic warden (*Brit*). **2** *adj inv* aubergine (-coloured).

aubergiste [obɛʀʒist(ə)] *nmf [hôtel]* hotel-keeper; *[auberge]* innkeeper, landlord. *[auberge de jeunesse]* **père ~, mère ~** (youth-hostel) warden.

aubier [obje] *nm* sapwood, alburnum.

auburn [obœʀn] *adj inv* auburn.

aucun, e [okœ̃, yn] **1** *adj* **(a)** (*nég*) no, not any. **~ commerçant ne le connaît** no tradesman (*Brit*) knows him; **il n'a ~e preuve** he has no proof, he hasn't any proof; **sans faire ~ bruit** without making a noise *ou* any noise; **sans ~ doute** without (any) doubt, undoubtedly; **en ~e façon** in no way; **ils ne prennent ~ soin de leurs vêtements** they don't take care of their clothes (at all); **ils n'ont eu ~ mal à trouver le chemin** they had no trouble finding the way, they found the way without any trouble.

(b) (*positif*) any. **il lit plus qu'~ autre enfant** he reads more than any other child; **croyez-vous qu'~ auditeur aurait osé le contredire?** do you think that any listener would have dared to contradict him?

2 *pron* **(a)** (*nég*) **il n'aime ~ de ces films** he doesn't like any of these films; **~ de ses enfants ne lui ressemble** none of his children are like him; **je ne pense pas qu'~ d'entre nous puisse y aller** I don't think any of us can go; **combien de réponses avez-vous eues? — ~e** how many answers did you get? — not one *ou* none.

(b) (*positif*) any, any one. **il aime ses chiens plus qu'~ de ses enfants** he is fonder of his dogs than of any (one) of his children; **pensez-vous qu'~ ait compris?** do you think anyone *ou* anybody understood?

(c) (*littér*) **d'~s** some; **d'~s aiment raconter que ...** there are some who like to say that ... .

aucunement [okynmɑ̃] *adv* in no way, not in the least, not in the slightest. **il n'est ~ à blâmer** he's not in the slightest *ou* least to blame, he's in no way *ou* not in any way to blame; **accepterez-vous? — ~** are you going to accept? — indeed no *ou* (most) certainly not.

audace [odas] *nf* **(a)** (*U*) (*témérité*) daring, boldness, audacity; (*Art: originalité*) daring; (*effronterie*) audacity, effrontery. **avoir l'~ de** to have the audacity to, dare to.

(b) (*geste osé*) daring gesture; (*innovation*) daring idea *ou* touch. **elle lui en voulait de ses ~s** she held his boldness *ou* his bold behaviour against him; **une ~ de génie** a daring touch of genius; **~s de style** daring innovations of style; **les ~s de la mode** the daring inventions *ou* creations of high fashion.

audacieusement [odasjøzmɑ̃] *adv* (*V* **audacieux**) daringly; boldly; audaciously.

audacieux, -ieuse [odasjø, jøz] *adj soldat, action* daring, bold; *artiste, projet* daring; *geste* audacious, bold; *V* **fortune.**

au-deçà, au-dedans, au-dehors *V* **deçà, dedans, dehors.**

au-delà [odla] **1** *loc adv V* **delà. 2** *nm*: **l'~** the beyond.

au-dessous, au-dessus *V* **dessous, dessus.**

au-devant [od(ə)vɑ̃] **1** *loc prép*: **~ de** ahead of; **aller ~ de qn** to go and meet sb; **aller ~ des désirs de qn** to anticipate sb's wishes. **2** *loc adv* ahead.

audibilité [odibilite] *nf* audibility.

audible [odibl(ə)] *adj* audible.

audience [odjɑ̃s] *nf* **(a)** (*frm: entretien*) interview, audience. **donner ~ à qn** to give audience to sb.

(b) (*Jur: séance*) hearing.

(c) (*attention*) (interested) attention. **ce projet eut beaucoup d'~** this project aroused much interest; **cet écrivain a trouvé ~ auprès des étudiants** this author has had a favourable reception from students.
(d) (*spectateurs, auditeurs*) audience.

audiomètre [odjɔmɛtʀ(ə)] *nm* audiometer.

audio-visuel, -elle [odjɔvizɥɛl] **1** *adj* audio-visual. **2** *nm* (*équipement*) audio-visual aids; (*méthodes*) audio-visual techniques *ou* methods.

auditeur, -trice [oditœʀ, tʀis] *nm,f* (*gén, Rad*) listener; (*Ling*) hearer. **le conférencier avait charmé ses ~s** the lecturer had captivated his audience; (*Univ*) **~ libre** unregistered student (*who is allowed to attend lectures*); (*Admin*) **~ à la Cour des comptes** junior official (*at the Cour des Comptes*).

auditif, -ive [oditif, iv] *adj* auditory. **appareil ~ de correction** hearing aid; **c'est un ~** he remembers things when he hears them.

audition [odisjɔ̃] *nf* **(a)** (*Mus, Théât*) (*essai*) audition; (*récital*) recital; (*concert d'élèves*) concert (*de* by).
(b) (*Jur*) **procéder à l'~ d'un témoin** to examine the witness.
(c) (*écoute*) *[musique, disque]* hearing. **salle conçue pour l'~ de la musique** room designed for listening to music; **avec l'orage l'~ est très mauvaise** with the storm the sound is very bad.
(d) (*ouïe*) hearing.

auditionner [odisjɔne] (1) **1** *vt* to audition, give an audition to. **2** *vi* to be auditioned, audition.

auditoire [oditwaʀ] *nm* audience.

auditorium [oditɔʀjɔm] *nm* (*Rad*) public studio.

auge [oʒ] *nf* (*Agr, Constr*) trough. (*Géog*) **vallée en ~** U-shaped valley, trough; (*hum*) **passe ton ~!*** give us your plate!*

augmentatif, -ive [ɔgmɑ̃tatif, iv] *adj* (*Gram*) augmentative.

augmentation [ɔgmɑ̃tɑsjɔ̃] *nf* (*accroissement*) (*gén*) increase; *[prix, population, production]* increase, rise (*de* in). **~ de salaire/prix** pay/price rise, salary/price increase, increase in salary/price; (*Fin*) **~ de capital** increase in capital; **l'~ des salaires par la direction** the management's raising of salaries; **l'~ des prix par les commerçants** the raising *ou* putting up of prices by shopkeepers (*Brit*) *ou* storekeepers (*US*).

augmenter [ɔgmɑ̃te] (1) **1** *vt* **(a)** *salaire, prix, impôts* to increase, raise, put up; *nombre* to increase, raise, augment; *production, quantité, dose* to increase, step up, raise; *durée* to increase; *difficulté, inquiétude* to add to, increase; *intérêt* to heighten. **~ les prix de 10%** to increase *ou* raise *ou* put up prices by 10%; **il augmente ses revenus en faisant des heures supplémentaires** he augments *ou* supplements his income by working overtime; **sa collection s'est augmentée d'un nouveau tableau** he has extended *ou* enlarged his collection with a new painting, he has added a new painting to his collection; (*Tricot*) **~ (de 5 mailles)** to increase (5 stitches); **ceci ne fit qu'augmenter sa colère** this only added to his anger; *V* **édition.**
(b) ~ qn (de 50 F) to increase sb's salary (by 50 francs), give sb a (50-franc) rise; **il n'a pas été augmenté depuis 2 ans** he has not had *ou* has not been given a rise *ou* a salary increase for 2 years.
2 *vi* (*grandir*) *[salaire, prix, impôts]* to increase, rise, go up; *[loyer, marchandises]* to go up; *[poids, quantité]* to increase; *[population, production]* to grow, increase, rise; *[douleur]* to grow *ou* get worse, increase; *[difficulté, inquiétude]* to grow, increase. **~ de poids/volume** to increase in weight/volume; *V* **vie.**

augure [ɔgyʀ] *nm* **(a)** (*devin*) (*Hist*) augur; (*fig hum*) soothsayer, oracle. **consulter les ~s** to consult the oracle.
(b) (*présage*) omen; (*Hist*) augury. **être de bon ~** to be of good omen, augur well; **être de mauvais ~** to be ominous *ou* of ill omen, augur ill; **cela me paraît de bon/mauvais ~** that's a good/bad sign, that augurs well/badly; *V* **accepter, oiseau.**

augurer [ɔgyʀe] (1) *vt*: **que faut-il ~ de son silence?** what must we gather *ou* understand from his silence?; **je n'augure rien de bon de cela** I don't foresee *ou* see any good coming from *ou* out of it; **cela augure bien/mal de la suite** that augurs well/ill (for what is to follow).

Auguste [ɔgyst(ə)] *nm* Augustus. (*Antiq*) **le siècle d'~** the Augustan age.

auguste [ɔgyst(ə)] **1** *adj personnage, assemblée* august; *geste* noble, majestic. **2** *nm*: **A~** ≃ Coco the clown.

augustin, e [ɔgystɛ̃, in] *nm,f* (*Rel*) Augustinian.

augustinien, -ienne [ɔgystinjɛ̃, jɛn] *adj* Augustinian.

aujourd'hui [oʒuʀdɥi] *adv* **(a)** (*ce jour-ci*) today. **~ en huit** a week today, today week (*Brit*); **il y a ~ 10 jours que** it's 10 days ago today that; **c'est tout pour ~** that's all *ou* that's it *ou* that's the lot* (*Brit*) for today; **à dater** *ou* **à partir d'~** (as) from today, from today onwards; **~ après-midi** this afternoon; **je le ferai dès ~** I'll do it this very day; *V* **jour.**
(b) (*de nos jours*) today, nowadays, these days. **ça ne date pas d'~** *[objet]* it's not exactly new; *[situation, attitude]* it's nothing new; **les jeunes d'~** young people nowadays, (the) young people of today.

aulne [on] *nm* alder.

aulx [o] *nmpl V* **ail.**

aumône [ɔmon] *nf* (*don*) charity (*U*), alms; (*action de donner*) almsgiving. **vivre d'~(s)** to live on charity; **demander l'~** (*lit*) to ask *ou* beg for charity *ou* alms; (*fig*) to beg (for money *etc*); **faire l'~** to give alms (*à* to); **cinquante francs! c'est une ~** fifty francs, that's a beggarly sum (from him)!; (*fig*) **faire** *ou* **accorder l'~ d'un sourire à qn** to favour sb with a smile, spare sb a smile.

aumônerie [ɔmonʀi] *nf* chaplaincy.

aumônier [ɔmonje] *nm* chaplain.

aumônière [ɔmonjɛʀ] *nf* (*Hist, Rel*) purse.

aune[1] [on] *nm* = **aulne.**

aune[2] [on] *nf* ≃ ell. (*fig*) **il fit un nez long d'une ~, son visage s'allongea d'une ~** he pulled a long face *ou* a face as long as a fiddle (*Brit*).

auparavant [opaʀavɑ̃] *adv* (*d'abord*) before(hand), first. (*avant*) **2 mois ~** 2 months before(hand) *ou* previously.

auprès [opʀɛ] **1** *prép*: **~ de (a)** (*près de, à côté de*) next to, close to, by; (*au chevet de, aux côtés de*) with. **rester ~ d'un malade** to stay with an invalid; **s'asseoir ~ de la fenêtre/de qn** to sit down by *ou* close to the window/by *ou* next to *ou* close to sb.
(b) (*comparé à*) compared with, in comparison with, next to. **notre revenu est élevé ~ du leur** our income is high compared with *ou* in comparison with *ou* next to theirs.
(c) (*s'adressant à*) with, to. **faire une demande ~ des autorités** to apply to the authorities, lodge a request with the authorities; **faire une démarche ~ du ministre** to approach the minister, apply to the minister; **déposer une plainte ~ des tribunaux** to instigate legal proceedings; **avoir accès ~ de qn** to have access to sb; **ambassadeur ~ du Vatican** ambassador to the Vatican.
(d) (*dans l'opinion de*) in the view of, in the opinion of. **il passe pour un incompétent ~ de ses collègues** he is incompetent in the view *ou* opinion of his colleagues; **jouir ~ de qn de beaucoup d'influence** to have *ou* carry much weight with sb.
2 *adv* (*littér*) nearby.

auquel [okɛl] *V* **lequel.**

aura [ɔʀa] *nf* aura.

auréole [ɔʀeɔl] *nf* **(a)** (*Art, Astron*) halo, aureole. (*fig*) **entouré de l'~ du succès** surrounded by a glow of success; (*fig*) **paré de l'~ du martyre** wearing a martyr's crown *ou* the crown of martyrdom; **parer qn d'une ~** to glorify sb.
(b) (*tache*) ring.

auréoler [ɔʀeɔle] (1) **1** *vt* (*gén ptp*) (*glorifier*) to glorify; (*Art*) to encircle with a halo. **tête auréolée de cheveux blancs** head with a halo of white hair; **être auréolé de gloire** to be wreathed in *ou* crowned with glory; **être auréolé de prestige** to have an aura of prestige.
2 s'auréoler *vpr*: **s'~ de** to take on an aura of.

auréomycine [ɔʀeɔmisin] *nf* aureomycin (*Brit*), Aureomycin ® (*US*).

auriculaire [ɔʀikylɛʀ] **1** *nm* little finger. **2** *adj* auricular; *V* **témoin.**

aurifère [ɔʀifɛʀ] *adj* gold-bearing.

aurification [ɔʀifikɑsjɔ̃] *nf [dent]* filling with gold.

aurifier [ɔʀifje] (7) *vt dent* to fill with gold.

Aurigny [ɔʀiɲi] *nf* Alderney.

aurochs [ɔʀɔk(s)] *nm* aurochs.

aurore [ɔʀɔʀ] *nf* **(a)** dawn, daybreak, first light. **à l'~** at dawn *ou* first light *ou* daybreak; **avant l'~** before dawn *ou* daybreak; **~ australe** aurora australis; **~ boréale** northern lights, aurora borealis; **~ polaire** polar lights.
(b) (*fig*) dawn, beginning. **à l'~ de** at the dawn of.

auscultation [ɔskyltɑsjɔ̃] *nf* auscultation.

ausculter [ɔskylte] (1) *vt* to auscultate.

auspices [ɔspis] *nmpl* **(a)** (*Antiq*) auspices. **(b) sous de bons/mauvais ~s** under favourable/unfavourable auspices; **sous les ~s de qn** under the patronage *ou* auspices of sb.

aussi [osi] **1** *adv* **(a)** (*également*) too, also. **je suis fatigué et lui/eux ~** I'm tired and so is he/are they, I'm tired and he is/they are too; **il travaille bien et moi ~** he works well and so do I; **il parle ~ l'anglais** he also speaks ENGLISH, he speaks ENGLISH as well, he speaks ENGLISH too; **lui ~ parle l'anglais** HE speaks English too *ou* as well, he too speaks English; **il parle l'italien et ~ l'anglais** he speaks Italian and English too *ou* as well, he speaks Italian and also English; **il a la grippe — lui ~?** he's got flu — him too?* *ou* him as well?, he has flu — he too? (*frm*); **c'est ~ mon avis** I think so too *ou* as well, that's my view too *ou* as well; **faites bon voyage — vous ~** have a good journey — you too *ou* (the) same to you; **il ne suffit pas d'être doué, il faut ~ travailler** it's not enough to be talented, you also have to work; **toi ~, tu as peur?** so you too are afraid?, so you are afraid too? *ou* as well?
(b) (*comparaison*) **~ grand** *etc* **que** as tall *etc* as; **il est ~ bête que méchant** *ou* **qu'il est méchant** he's as stupid as he is ill-natured; **viens ~ souvent que tu voudras** come as often as you like; **s'il pleut ~ peu que l'an dernier** if it rains as little as last year; **il devint ~ riche qu'il l'avait rêvé** he became as rich as he had dreamt he would; **la piqûre m'a fait ~ mal que la blessure** the injection hurt me as much as the injury (did); **~ vite que possible** as quickly as possible; **d'~ loin qu'il nous vit il cria** far away though he was he shouted as soon as he saw us.
(c) (*si, tellement*) so. **je ne te savais pas ~ bête** I didn't think you were so *ou* that* stupid; **comment peut-on laisser passer une ~ bonne occasion?** how can one let slip such a good opportunity? *ou* so good an opportunity?; **je ne savais pas que cela se faisait ~ facilement (que ça)** I didn't know that could be done as easily (as that) *ou* so easily *ou* that easily*; **~ léger qu'il fût** light though he was; **~ idiot que ça puisse paraître** silly though *ou* as it may seem.
(d) (*tout autant*) **~ bien** just as well, just as easily; **tu peux ~ bien dire non** you can just as easily *ou* well say no; (*littér*) **puisqu'~ bien tout est fini** since, moreover, everything is finished; **mon tableau peut ~ bien représenter une montagne qu'un animal** my picture could just as well *ou* easily represent a mountain as an animal; **~ sec*** on the spot*, quick as a flash.
2 *conj* (*en conséquence*) therefore, consequently; (*d'ailleurs*) well, moreover. **je suis faible, ~ ai-je besoin d'aide** I'm weak, therefore *ou* consequently I need help; **tu n'as pas compris, ~ c'est ta faute: tu n'écoutais pas** you haven't understood, well, it's your own fault — you weren't listening.

aussitôt [osito] **1** *adv* straight away, immediately. ~ **arrivé/descendu il s'attabla** as soon as he arrived/came down he sat down at table; ~ **le train arrêté, elle descendit** as soon as *ou* immediately (*surtout Brit*) the train stopped she got out; ~ **dit,** ~ **fait** no sooner said than done; ~ **après son retour** straight *ou* directly *ou* immediately after his return; **il est parti** ~ **après** he left straight *ou* directly *ou* immediately after; ~ **que** as soon as; ~ **que je le vis** as soon as *ou* the moment I saw him.

2 *prép*: ~ **mon arrivée, je lui ai téléphoné** immediately (up)on my arrival I phoned him, immediately (*surtout Brit*) I arrived I phoned him.

austère [ɔstɛʀ] *adj personne, vie, style, monument* austere; *livre, lecture* dry. **coupe** ~ **d'un manteau** severe cut of a coat.

austèrement [ɔstɛʀmɑ̃] *adv* austerely.

austérité [ɔsteʀite] *nf* (*V* **austère**) austerity; dryness. (*Rel*) ~**s** austerities.

austral, e, *mpl* ~**s** [ɔstʀal] *adj* southern, austral (*T*). **pôle** ~ south pole; *V* **aurore.**

Australie [ɔstʀali] *nf* Australia.

australien, -ienne [ɔstʀaljɛ̃, jɛn] **1** *adj* Australian. **2** *nm,f*: **A~(ne)** Australian.

australopithèque [ɔstʀalɔpitɛk] *nm* Australopithecus.

autant [otɑ̃] *adv* **(a)** ~ **de** (*quantité*) as much (*que* as); (*nombre*) as many (*que* as); **il y a** ~ **de place ici (que là-bas)** there's (just) as much room here (as over there); **il n'y a pas** ~ **de neige que l'année dernière** there isn't as much *ou* there's not so much snow as last year; **nous employons** ~ **d'hommes qu'eux** we employ as many men as they do *ou* as them; **nous sommes** ~ **qu'eux** we are as many as they are *ou* as them, there are as many of us as of them; **il nous prêtera** ~ **de livres qu'il pourra** he'll lend us as many books as he can; **ils ont** ~ **de mérite/de talents l'un que l'autre** they have equal merit/talents; **elle mange deux fois** ~ **que lui** she eats twice as much as him *ou* as he does; **tous ces enfants sont** ~ **de petits menteurs** all these children are so many little liars; **tous** ~ **que vous êtes** the whole lot of you.

(b) (*intensité*) as much (*que* as). **il travaille toujours** ~ he works as hard as ever, he's still working as hard; **pourquoi travaille-t-il** ~**?** why does he work so much? *ou* so hard?; **rien ne lui plaît** ~ **que de regarder les autres travailler** there is nothing he likes so much as *ou* likes better than watching others work; **intelligent, il l'est** ~ **que vous** he's as clever as you are; **il peut crier** ~ **qu'il veut** he can scream as much as he likes; **cet avertissement vaut pour vous** ~ **que pour lui** this warning applies to you as much as to him; **courageux** ~ **que compétent** courageous as well as competent, as courageous as he is competent; ~ **prévenir la police** it would be as well to tell the police; *V* **aimer.**

(c) (*tant*) (*quantité*) so much, such; (*nombre*) so many, such a lot of. **elle ne pensait pas qu'il aurait** ~ **de succès/qu'il mangerait** ~ she never thought that he would have so much *ou* such success/that he would eat so much *ou* such a lot; **vous invitez toujours** ~ **de gens?** do you always invite so many people? *ou* such a lot of people?; **j'ai rarement vu** ~ **de monde** I've seldom seen such a crowd *ou* so many people.

(d) (*avec en: la même chose*) the same. **je ne peux pas en dire** ~ I can't say the same (for myself); **je ne peux pas en faire** ~ I can't do as much *ou* the same.

(e) (*avec de: exprimant une proportion*) **d'~: ce sera augmenté d'~** it will be increased accordingly *ou* in proportion; **d'~ que, d'~ plus que** all the more so since *ou* because; **c'est d'~ plus dangereux qu'il n'y a pas de parapet** it's all the more dangerous since *ou* because there is no parapet; **écrivez-lui, d'~ que** *ou* **d'~ plus que je ne suis pas sûr qu'il vienne demain** you'd better write to him especially since I'm not sure if he's coming tomorrow; **cela se gardera d'~ mieux (que ...)** it will keep even better *ou* all the better (since ...); **nous le voyons d'~ moins qu'il habite très loin maintenant** we see him even less *ou* all the less now that he lives a long way away.

(f) (*loc*) ~ **il est généreux,** ~ **elle est avare** he is as generous as she is miserly; ~ **il aime les chiens,** ~ **il déteste les chats** he likes dogs as much as he hates cats; ~ **que possible** as much *ou* as far as possible; **il voudrait,** ~ **que possible, éviter les grandes routes** he would like to avoid the major roads as much *ou* as far as possible; (*Prov*) ~ **d'hommes,** ~ **d'avis** every man to his own opinion; **(pour)** ~ **que je** (*ou* **qu'il** *etc*) **sache** as far as I know (*ou* he *etc* knows), to the best of my (*ou* his *etc*) knowledge; **c'est** ~ **de gagné** *ou* **de pris** at least that's something; **c'est** ~ **de fait** that's that done at least; ~ **dire qu'il ne sait rien/qu'il est fou** you *ou* one might as well say that he doesn't know anything/that he's mad; **pour** ~ for all that; **vous l'avez aidé mais il ne vous remerciera pas pour** ~ you helped him but for all that you won't get any thanks from him; **il ne le fera qu'~ qu'il saura que vous êtes d'accord** he'll only do it in so far (*Brit*) as he knows you agree.

autarcie [otaʀsi] *nf* autarky.

autarcique [otaʀsik] *adj* autarkical.

autel [ɔtɛl] *nm* **(a)** (*Rel*) altar. **le trône et l'~** the Church and the Crown; (*fig*) **conduire** *ou* **mener sa fille à l'~** to give one's daughter away (in marriage). **(b)** (*fig littér*) altar. **dresser un** ~ *ou* **des** ~**s à qn** to worship sb, put sb on a pedestal; **sacrifier qch sur l'~ de** to sacrifice sth on the altar of.

auteur [otœʀ] *nm* **(a)** *[invention, plan, crime]* author; *[texte, roman]* author, writer; *[opéra, concerto]* composer; *[procédé]* originator, author. **il/elle en est l'~** (*invention*) he/she invented it; (*texte*) he/she wrote it, he's/she's the author (of it); **l'~ de cette plaisanterie** the author of this prank, the person who played this prank; **l'~ de l'accident s'est enfui** the person who caused the accident ran off; **l'~ de ce tableau** the painter of this picture, the artist who painted this picture; **qui est l'~ de cette affiche?** who designed this poster?; (*musée*) '~ **inconnu**' 'anonymous', 'artist unknown'; **il fut l'~ de sa propre ruine** he was the author of his own ruin; **Prévert est l'~ des paroles, Kosma de la musique** Prévert wrote the words *ou* lyrics and Kosma composed the music; (†, *hum*) **l'~ de mes jours** my noble progenitor (†, *hum*); (*Mus*) ~**-compositeur** composer-songwriter; *V* **droit³.**

(b) (*écrivain*) author. (*femme*) **c'est un** ~ **connu** she is a well-known author *ou* authoress; *V* **femme.**

authenticité [ɔtɑ̃tisite] *nf* (*V* **authentique**) authenticity; genuineness.

authentifier [ɔtɑ̃tifje] (7) *vt* to authenticate.

authentique [ɔtɑ̃tik] *adj œuvre d'art, récit* authentic, genuine; *signature, document* authentic; *sentiment* genuine; *V* **acte.**

authentiquement [ɔtɑ̃tikmɑ̃] *adv* genuinely, authentically; *rapporter* faithfully.

autisme [ɔtism(ə)] *nm* autism.

autistique [ɔtistik] *adj* autistic.

auto [ɔto] **1** *nf* (*voiture*) car, automobile (*US*). ~**s tamponneuses** dodgems, bumper cars; *V* **salon, train.**

2 *adj inv*: **assurance** ~ car *ou* motor (*Brit*) *ou* automobile (*US*) insurance; **frais** ~ running costs (*of a car*).

auto ... [ɔto] *préf* **(a)** (*fait sur soi*) self-. ~**(-) censure/mutilation** self-censorship/-mutilation; ~**discipline** self-discipline; **s'~gérer/financer** to be self-managing *ou* -running/self-financing; **organisme** ~**géré** self-managed *ou* -run body; **tendances** ~**destructrices** self-destructive tendencies.

(b) (*qui se fait tout seul*) self-. ~**(-)contrôle** automatic control; ~**(-)régulation** self-regulating system; ~**(-)nettoyant/adhésif** self-cleaning/adhesive.

(c) (*se rapportant à l'automobile*) **train** ~**-couchettes** car sleeper train; ~**(-)radio** car radio.

auto-allumage [ɔtoalymaʒ] *nm* preignition.

autoberge [ɔtobɛʀʒ(ə)] *nm* embankment expressway.

autobiographie [ɔtobjɔgʀafi] *nf* autobiography.

autobiographique [ɔtobjɔgʀafik] *adj* autobiographic(al).

autobus [ɔtobys] *nm* bus. (*Hist*) ~ **à impériale** open-topped bus.

autocar [ɔtokaʀ] *nm* coach (*Brit*), bus (*US*); (†) country bus.

autochenille [ɔtoʃnij] *nf* half-track.

autochtone [ɔtɔktɔn] **1** *adj* native, autochthonous (*T*); (*Géol*) autochthonous. **2** *nmf* native, autochton (*T*).

autoclave [ɔtoklav] *adj, nm* (*Méd, Tech*) (**appareil** *m* *ou* **marmite** *f*) ~ autoclave.

autocollant, e [ɔtokolɑ̃, ɑ̃t] **1** *adj étiquette* self-adhesive, self-sticking; *papier* self-adhesive; *enveloppe* self-seal, self-adhesive. **2** *nm* sticker.

autocrate [ɔtokʀat] *nm* autocrat.

autocratie [ɔtokʀasi] *nf* autocracy.

autocratique [ɔtokʀatik] *adj* autocratic.

autocratiquement [ɔtokʀatikmɑ̃] *adv* autocratically.

autocritique [ɔtokʀitik] *nf* self-criticism. **faire son** ~ to criticize oneself.

autocuiseur [ɔtokɥizœʀ] *nm* pressure cooker.

autodafé [ɔtodafe] *nm* auto-da-fé.

autodéfense [ɔtodefɑ̃s] *nf* self-defence. **groupe d'~** vigilance committee.

autodestruction [ɔtodɛstʀyksjɔ̃] *nf* self-destruction.

autodétermination [ɔtodetɛʀminɑsjɔ̃] *nf* self-determination.

autodidacte [ɔtodidakt(ə)] *adj* self-taught. **c'est un** ~ he is self-taught, he is a self-taught man.

autodrome [ɔtodʀom] *nm* motor-racing track.

auto-école [ɔtoekɔl] *nf* driving school. **moniteur d'~** driving instructor.

auto-érotique [ɔtoeʀɔtik] *adj* auto-erotic.

auto-érotisme [ɔtoeʀɔtism(ə)] *nm* auto-eroticism, auto-erotism.

autofécondation [ɔtofekɔ̃dɑsjɔ̃] *nf* (*Bio*) self-fertilization.

autofinancement [ɔtofinɑ̃smɑ̃] *nm* self-financing.

autogène [ɔtoʒɛn] *adj V* **soudure.**

autogestion [ɔtoʒɛstjɔ̃] *nf* self-management.

autogire [ɔtoʒiʀ] *nm* autogiro, autogyro.

autographe [ɔtogʀaf] *adj, nm* autograph.

autoguidage [ɔtogidaʒ] *nm* self-steering.

autoguidé, e [ɔtogide] *adj* self-guided.

auto-induction [ɔtoɛ̃dyksjɔ̃] *nf* (*Phys*) self-induction.

auto-intoxication [ɔtoɛ̃tɔksikɑsjɔ̃] *nf* auto-intoxication.

automate [ɔtomat] *nm* (*lit, fig*) automaton. **marcher comme un** ~ to walk like a robot.

automation [ɔtomɑsjɔ̃] *nf* automation.

automatique [ɔtomatik] **1** *adj* automatic. **2** *nm* (*Téléc*) ≃ subscriber trunk dialling (*Brit*), STD (*Brit*), direct dialing (*US*); (*revolver*) automatic (*pistol etc*); *V* **distributeur.**

automatiquement [ɔtomatikmɑ̃] *adv* automatically.

automatisation [ɔtomatizɑsjɔ̃] *nf* automation.

automatiser [ɔtomatize] (1) *vt* to automate.

automatisme [ɔtomatism(ə)] *nm* automatism; *[machine]* automatic functioning, automatism.

automédon [ɔtomedɔ̃] *nm* (†, *hum*) coachman.

automitrailleuse [ɔtomitʀɑjøz] *nf* armoured car.

automnal, e, *mpl* **-aux** [ɔto(m)nal, o] *adj* autumnal.

automne [ɔtɔn] *nm* autumn, fall (*US*). (*fig*) **c'est l'~ de ses jours** he's in the autumn of his life.

automobile [ɔtomɔbil] **1** *adj véhicule* self-propelled, motor (*épith*); *course, sport* motor (*épith*); *assurance, industrie* motor, car, automobile (*US*); *V* **canot.**

2 *nf* (*voiture*) motor car (*Brit*), automobile (*US*). (*industrie*) **l'~** the car *ou* motor industry, the automobile industry (*US*); (*Sport, conduite*) **l'~** motoring; **termes d'~** motoring terms; **être passionné d'~** to be a car fanatic; **aimer les courses d'~s** to like motor racing.

automobiliste [ɔtɔmɔbilist(ə)] *nmf* motorist.

automoteur, -trice [ɔtɔmɔtœʀ, tʀis] **1** *adj* self-propelled, motorized, motor (*épith*). **2 automotrice** *nf* electric railcar.

autoneige [ɔtonɛʒ] *nf* (*Can*) snowmobile (*US, Can*), snowcat.

autonome [ɔtɔnɔm] *adj* **(a)** *port* independent, autonomous; *territoire* autonomous, self-governed. **(b)** *personne* self-sufficient; (*Philos*) *volonté* autonomous; *V* **scaphandre.**

autonomie [ɔtɔnɔmi] *nf* (*Admin, Fin, Philos, Pol*) autonomy; (*Aut, Aviat*) range. **certains Corses/Bretons veulent l'~** some Corsicans/Bretons want home rule *ou* autonomy *ou* self-government.

autonomiste [ɔtɔnɔmist(ə)] *nmf* (*Pol*) autonomist.

autopont [ɔtɔpɔ̃] *nm* flyover (*Brit*), overpass (*US*).

autoportrait [ɔtɔpɔʀtʀɛ] *nm* self-portrait.

autopropulsé, e [ɔtɔpʀɔpylse] *adj* self-propelled.

autopropulsion [ɔtɔpʀɔpylsjɔ̃] *nf* self-propulsion.

autopsie [ɔtɔpsi] *nf* autopsy, post-mortem (examination); (*fig*) dissection.

autopsier [ɔtɔpsje] (7) *vt* to carry out an autopsy *ou* a post-mortem (examination) on.

autopunition [ɔtɔpynisjɔ̃] *nf* self-punishment.

autorail [ɔtɔʀɑj] *nm* railcar.

autorisation [ɔtɔʀizɑsjɔ̃] *nf* (*permission*) permission, authorization (*frm*) (*de qch* for sth, *de faire* to do); (*permis*) permit. **nous avions l'~ du professeur** we had the teacher's permission; **avoir l'~ de faire qch** to have permission *ou* be allowed to do sth; (*Admin*) to be authorized to do sth; **le projet doit recevoir l'~ du comité** the project must be passed by the committee.

autorisé, e [ɔtɔʀize] (*ptp de* **autoriser**) *adj agent, version* authorized; *opinion* authoritative. **dans les milieux ~s** in official circles; **nous apprenons de source ~e que ...** we have learnt from official sources that ... .

autoriser [ɔtɔʀize] (1) **1** *vt* **(a) ~ qn à faire** (*donner la permission de*) to give *ou* grant sb permission to do, authorize sb to do; (*habiliter à*) *[personne, décret]* to give sb authority to do, authorize sb to do; **il nous a autorisés à sortir** he has given *ou* granted us permission to go out, we have his permission to go out; **sa faute ne t'autorise pas à le condamner** his mistake does not entitle you *ou* give you the right to pass judgment on him; **tout nous autorise à croire que ...** everything leads us to believe that ...; **se croire autorisé à dire que ...** to feel one is entitled *ou* think one has the right to say that ... .

(b) (*permettre*) *[personne] manifestation, sortie* to authorize, give permission for; *projet* to pass, authorize.

(c) (*rendre possible*) *[chose]* to admit of, allow (of), sanction. **l'imprécision de cette loi autorise les abus** the imprecisions in this law admit of *ou* allow of *ou* appear to sanction abuses; **expression autorisée par l'usage** expression sanctioned *ou* made acceptable by use.

(d) (*littér: justifier*) to justify.

2 s'autoriser *vpr*: **s'~ de qch pour faire** (*idée de prétexte*) to use sth as an excuse to do; (*invoquer*) **je m'autorise de notre amitié pour** in view of our friendship I permit myself to.

autoritaire [ɔtɔʀitɛʀ] *adj, nmf* authoritarian.

autoritairement [ɔtɔʀitɛʀmɑ̃] *adv* in an authoritarian way.

autoritarisme [ɔtɔʀitaʀism(ə)] *nm* authoritarianism.

autorité [ɔtɔʀite] *nf* **(a)** (*pouvoir*) authority (*sur* over). **l'~ que lui confère son expérience/âge** the authority conferred upon him by experience/age; **avoir de l'~ sur qn** to have authority over sb; **être sous l'~ de qn** to be under sb's authority; **avoir ~ pour faire** to have authority to do; **ton/air d'~** authoritative tone/air, tone/air of authority.

(b) (*expert, ouvrage*) authority. **c'est l'une des grandes ~s en la matière** it *ou* he is one of the great authorities on the subject.

(c) (*Admin*) **l'~** those in authority, the powers that be (*gén iro*); **les ~s** the authorities; **l'~ militaire/législative** *etc* the military/legislative *etc* authorities; **les ~s civiles et religieuses/locales** the civil and religious/local authorities; **agent** *ou* **représentant de l'~** representative of authority; **adressez-vous à l'~** *ou* **aux ~s compétente(s)** apply to the proper authorities.

(d) (*Jur*) **l'~ de la loi** the authority *ou* power of the law; **l'~ de la chose jugée** res judicata; **être déchu de son ~ paternelle** to be divested of one's paternal authority; **fermé/vendu par ~ de justice** closed/sold by order of the court.

(e) (*loc*) **d'~** (*de façon impérative*) on one's own authority; (*sans réflexion*) out of hand, straight off, unhesitatingly; **de sa propre ~** on one's own authority; **faire ~** *[livre, expert]* to be accepted as an authority, be authoritative.

autoroute [ɔtɔʀut] *nf* motorway (*Brit*), expressway (*US*), highway (*US*). **~ de dégagement** *toll-free stretch of motorway leading out of a big city*; **~ de liaison** *toll motorway* (*Brit*) *ou turnpike* (*US*) *linking the main cities.*

autoroutier, -ière [ɔtɔʀutje, jɛʀ] *adj* motorway (*Brit*) (*épith*), expressway (*US*) (*épith*).

autosatisfaction [ɔtɔsatisfaksjɔ̃] *nf* self-satisfaction.

auto-stop [ɔtɔstɔp] *nm* hitch-hiking, hitching*. **l'~ est dangereux** hitch-hiking *ou* hitching* is dangerous; **pour rentrer, il a fait de l'~** (*long voyage*) he hitched* *ou* hitch-hiked home; (*courte distance*) he thumbed *ou* hitched* a lift home; **il a fait le tour du monde en ~** he hitch-hiked round the world, he hitched* his way round the world; **j'ai pris quelqu'un en ~** I picked up *ou* gave a lift to a hitch-hiker *ou* hitcher*; **il nous a pris en ~** he picked us up, he gave us a lift.

auto-stoppeur, -euse [ɔtɔstɔpœʀ, øz] *nm,f* hitch-hiker, hitcher*. **prendre un ~** to pick up a hitch-hiker *ou* hitcher*.

autostrade† [ɔtɔstʀad] *nf* motorway (*Brit*), expressway (*US*), highway (*US*).

autosuggestion [ɔtɔsygʒɛstjɔ̃] *nf* autosuggestion.

autour¹ [otuʀ] **1** *adv* around. **tout ~** all around; **une maison avec un jardin ~** a house surrounded by a garden, a house with a garden around *ou* round (*Brit*) it.

2 *prép*: **~ de** *lieu* around, round (*Brit*); *temps, somme* about, around, round about; **regarder ~ de soi** to look around *ou* about one; *V* **tourner.**

autour² [otuʀ] *nm* (*Orn*) goshawk.

autovaccin [ɔtɔvaksɛ̃] *nm* auto(genous) vaccine.

autre [otʀ(ə)] **1** *adj indéf* **(a)** (*différent*) other, different. **ils ont un (tout) ~ mode de vie/point de vue** they have a (completely) different way of life/point of view; **c'est une ~ question/un ~ problème** that's another *ou* a different question/problem; **c'est (tout) ~ chose** that's a different *ou* another matter (altogether); **parlons d'~ chose** let's talk about something else *ou* different; **revenez une ~ fois/un ~ jour** come back some other *ou* another time/another *ou* some other day; **je fais cela d'une ~ façon** I do it a different way *ou* another way *ou* differently; **il n'y a pas d'~ moyen d'entrer que de forcer la porte** there's no other way *ou* there isn't any other way of getting in but to force open the door; **vous ne le reconnaîtrez pas, il est (devenu) tout ~** you won't know him, he's completely different *ou* he is a changed man; **après ce bain je me sens un ~ homme** after that swim, I feel a new man; (*Prov*) **~s temps ~s mœurs** customs change with the times, autres temps autres mœurs; *V* **part.**

(b) (*supplémentaire*) other. **elle a 2 ~s enfants** she has 2 other *ou* 2 more children; **donnez-moi un ~ kilo/une ~ tasse de thé** give me another kilo/cup of tea; **il y a beaucoup d'~s solutions** there are many other *ou* many more solutions; **c'est un ~ Versailles** it's another Versailles; **c'est un ~ moi-même** he's my alter ego; **des couteaux, des verres et ~s objets indispensables** knives, glasses and other necessary articles *ou* necessary items.

(c) (*de deux: marque une opposition*) other. **il habite de l'~ côté de la rue/dans l'~ sens** he lives on the other *ou* opposite side of the street/in the other *ou* opposite direction; **mets l'~ manteau** put on the other coat; **mets ton ~ manteau** put on your other coat.

(d) (*loc*) **l'~ jour** the other day; **nous/vous ~s*: faut pas nous raconter des histoires, à nous ~s!*** there's no point telling fibs to US!; **nous ~s*, on est prudents** WE are *ou* WE'RE cautious; **taisez-vous, vous ~s*** be quiet, you lot* (*Brit*) *ou* you people; **et vous ~s qu'en pensez-vous?** what do you people *ou* you lot* (*Brit*) think?; **nous ~ Français, nous aimons la bonne cuisine** we Frenchmen like good cooking; **j'aimerais bien entendre un ~ son de cloche** I'd like to have a second opinion; **c'est un ~ son de cloche** that's quite another story; **j'ai d'~s chats à fouetter** I've other fish to fry; **vous êtes de l'~ côté de la barrière** you see it from the other side; **c'est cela et pas ~ chose** it's that or nothing; **~ chose, Madame?** anything *ou* something else, madam?; **ce n'est pas ~ chose que de la jalousie** that's just jealousy, that's nothing but jealousy; **une chose est de rédiger un rapport, ~ chose est d'écrire un livre** it's one thing to draw up a report, but quite another thing *ou* but another thing altogether to write a book; **~ part** somewhere else; **d'~ part** on the other hand; (*de plus*) moreover; **c'est une ~ paire de manches*** that's another kettle of fish, that's another story; (*Rel*) **l'~ monde** the next world.

2 *pron indéf* **(a)** (*qui est différent*) another (one). **d'~s** others; **aucun ~, nul ~, personne d'~** no one else, nobody else; **prendre qn pour un ~/une chose pour une ~** to take sb for sb else/sth for sth else; **envoyez-moi bien ce livre je n'en veux pas d'~** make sure you send me this book, I don't want any other (one) *ou* I want no other; **à d'~s!*** (go and) tell that to the marines!*, (that's) a likely story!; **il n'en fait jamais d'~s!** that's just typical of him!, that's just what he always does!; **un ~ que moi/lui aurait refusé** anyone else (but me/him) would have refused; **il en a vu d'~s!** he's seen worse!; **les deux ~s** the other two, the two others; **vous en êtes un ~!*†** you're a fool!; **X, Y, Z, et ~s** X, Y, Z and others *ou* etc; **d'~s diraient que ...** others would say that ...; *V* **entre, rien.**

(b) (*qui vient en plus*) **deux enfants, c'est assez, je n'en veux pas d'~/d'~s** two children are enough, I don't want another (one)/(any) more; **donnez m'en un ~** give me another (one) *ou* one more; **qui/quoi d'~?** who/what else?; **rien/personne d'~** nothing/nobody else.

(c) (*marque une opposition*) **l'~** the other (one); **les ~s** (*choses*) the others, the other ones; (*personnes*) the others; **les ~s ne veulent pas venir** the others don't want to come; **penser du mal des ~s** to think ill of others *ou* of other people; **avec toi, c'est toujours les ~s qui ont tort** with you, it's always the others who are *ou* the other person who is in the wrong; **d'une minute/semaine à l'~** (*sous peu*) any minute/week (now); (*à tout moment*) from one minute/week to the next; *V* **côté, ni.**

3 *nm* (*Philos*) **l'~** the other.

autrefois [otʀəfwa] *adv* in the past, in bygone days (*littér*). **d'~** of the past, of old, past; **~ ils s'éclairaient à la bougie** in the past *ou* in bygone days they used candles for lighting; **~ je préférais le vin** (in the past) I used to prefer wine.

autrement [otʀəmɑ̃] *adv* **(a)** (*d'une manière différente*) differently. **il faut s'y prendre (tout) ~** we'll have to go about it in (quite) another way *ou* (quite) differently; **avec ce climat il ne peut en être ~** with this climate it can't be any other way *ou* how else could it be!; **cela ne peut s'être passé ~** it can't have happened any other way; **agir ~ que d'habitude** *ou* **qu'on ne fait d'habitude** to act differently from usual; **comment aller à Londres ~ que par le train?** how can we get to London other than by train?; **~ appelé** otherwise known as.

(b) faire ~: il n'y a pas moyen de faire ~, on ne peut pas faire ~ it's impossible to do otherwise *ou* to do anything else; **il n'a pas pu faire ~ que de me voir** he couldn't help seeing me *ou* help but see me; **quand il voit une pâtisserie il ne peut pas faire ~ que d'y entrer** whenever he sees a cake-shop he can't help going in *ou* he just HAS to go in; **elle a fait ~ que je lui avais dit** she did something different from what I told her.

(c) (*sinon*) otherwise; (*idée de menace*) otherwise, or else. **travaille bien, ~ tu auras de mes nouvelles!** work hard, otherwise *ou* or else you'll be hearing a few things from me!

(d) (*: *à part cela*) otherwise, apart from that. **la viande était bonne, ~ le repas était quelconque** the meat was good but apart from that *ou* but otherwise the meal was pretty nondescript.

(e) (*: *comparatif*) far (more). **il est ~ intelligent** he is far more intelligent, he is more intelligent by far; **c'est ~ meilleur** it's far better, it's better by far (*que* than).

(f) (*: *pas spécialement*) **pas ~** not particularly *ou* especially; **cela ne m'a pas ~ surpris** that didn't particularly surprise me.

(g) **~ dit** (*en d'autres mots*) in other words; (*c'est-à-dire*) that is.

Autriche [otʀiʃ] *nf* Austria.

autrichien, -ienne [otʀiʃjɛ̃, jɛn] **1** *adj* Austrian. **2** *nm,f*: **A~(ne)** Austrian.

autruche [otʀyʃ] *nf* ostrich. (*fig*) **faire l'~** to bury one's head in the sand; *V* **estomac, politique.**

autrui [otʀɥi] *pron* (*littér*) others. **respecter le bien d'~** to respect the property of others *ou* other people's property.

auvent [ovɑ̃] *nm [maison]* canopy; *[tente]* awning, canopy.

auvergnat, e [ɔvɛʀɲa, at] **1** *adj* of *ou* from Auvergne. **2** *nm* (*Ling*) Auvergne dialect. **3** *nm,f*: **A~(e)** inhabitant *ou* native of Auvergne.

aux [o] *V* **à.**

auxiliaire [ɔksiljɛʀ] **1** *adj* (*Ling, Mil, gén*) auxiliary (*épith*); *cause, raison* secondary, subsidiary; (*Scol*) assistant (*épith*). **bureau ~** sub-office.

2 *nmf* (*assistant*) assistant, helper. (*Jur*) **~ de la justice** representative of the law; **~ médical** medical auxiliary.

3 *nm* (*Gram, Mil*) auxiliary.

auxiliairement [ɔksiljɛʀmɑ̃] *adv* (*Ling*) as an auxiliary; (*fig: secondairement*) secondarily, less importantly.

avachi, e [avaʃi] (*ptp de* **avachir**) *adj* **(a)** *cuir, feutre* limp; *chaussure, vêtement* out of shape. **un pantalon ~** baggy trousers.

(b) *personne* (*par la chaleur*) limp; (*moralement*) flabby, sloppy. **~ sur son pupitre** slumped on his desk.

avachir [avaʃiʀ] (2) **1** *vt* **(a)** *cuir, feutre* to make limp; *chaussure, vêtement* to make shapeless, put out of shape.

(b) (*état*) *personne* (*physiquement*) to make limp; (*moralement*) to make flabby *ou* sloppy.

2 s'avachir *vpr* **(a)** *[cuir]* to become limp; *[vêtement]* to go out of shape, become shapeless.

(b) *[personne]* (*physiquement*) to become limp; (*moralement*) to become flabby *ou* sloppy.

avachissement [avaʃismɑ̃] *nm* **(a)** *[vêtement, cuir]* loss of shape. *[personne]* **leur ~ faisait peine à voir** it was a shame to see them becoming so sloppy *ou* to see them letting themselves go like this.

(b) *[personne]* (*physiquement*) limpness; (*moralement*) sloppiness, flabbiness.

aval[1] [aval] *nm [cours d'eau]* downstream water; *[pente]* downhill slope. **en ~** below, downstream, down-river; downhill; **en ~ de** below, downstream *ou* down-river from; downhill from; **les rapides/l'écluse d'~** the downstream rapids/lock; **l'~ était coupé de rapides** the river downstream was a succession of rapids; **le skieur/ski ~** the downhill skier/ski.

aval[2], *pl* **~s** [aval] *nm* (*fig: soutien*) backing, support; (*Comm, Jur*) guarantee. **donner son ~ à qn** to give sb one's support, back sb.

avalanche [avalɑ̃ʃ] *nf* (*Géog*) avalanche; *[coups]* shower; *[compliments]* flood, torrent; *[réclamations, prospectus]* avalanche; *V* **couloir.**

avalancheux, -euse [avalɑ̃ʃø, øz] *adj zone, pente* avalanche-prone.

avaler [avale] (1) *vt* **(a)** *nourriture* to swallow (down); *repas* to swallow; *boisson* to swallow (down), drink (down); (*fig*) *roman* to devour. *[fumeur]* **~ la fumée** to inhale (the smoke); **~ qch d'un trait** *ou* **d'un seul coup** to swallow sth in one gulp, down sth in one*; **~ son café à petites gorgées** to sip one's coffee; **~ sa salive** to gulp, swallow hard; **il a avalé de travers** it went down the wrong way; **il n'a rien avalé depuis 2 jours*** he hasn't eaten a thing *ou* had a thing to eat for 2 days.

(b) *mensonge, histoire* to swallow; *affront* to swallow, take; *mauvaise nouvelle* to accept. **on lui ferait ~ n'importe quoi** he would swallow anything; **~ la pilule** to take it lying down; **~ des couleuvres** (*affront*) to swallow an affront; (*mensonge*) to swallow a lie, be taken in; **j'ai cru qu'il allait m'~ tout cru** I thought he was going to eat me alive; **c'est un ambitieux qui veut tout ~** he's an ambitious man who thinks he can take on anything; **~ ses mots** to mumble; (*Sport*) **~ l'obstacle** to make short work of the obstacle, take the obstacle in one's stride.

(c) (*loc fig*) **tu as avalé ta langue?** have you lost your tongue?; **on dirait qu'il a avalé son parapluie** he's so (stiff and) starchy.

avaleur, -euse [avalœʀ, øz] *nm,f*: **~ de sabres** sword swallower.

avaliser [avalize] (1) *vt plan, entreprise* to back, support; (*Comm, Jur*) to endorse, guarantee.

avance [avɑ̃s] *nf* **(a)** (*marche, progression*) advance. **accélérer/ralentir son ~** to speed up/slow down one's advance.

(b) (*sur un concurrent etc*) lead. **avoir/prendre de l'~ sur qn** to have/take the lead over sb; **10 minutes/km d'~** a 10-minute/km lead; **l'~ des Russes dans le domaine scientifique** the Russians' lead in the world of science; **perdre son ~** to lose one's *ou* the lead; **cet élève est tombé malade et a perdu son avance** this pupil fell ill and lost the lead he had (on the rest of the class).

(c) (*sur un horaire*) **avoir/prendre de l'~** to be/get ahead of schedule; **avoir beaucoup d'~/une ~ de 2 ans** to be well/2 years ahead of schedule; **avoir/prendre de l'~ dans son travail** to be/get ahead in *ou* with one's work; **le train a 10 minutes d'~** the train is 10 minutes early; **le train a pris de l'~/10 minutes d'~** the train has got ahead/has got 10 minutes ahead of schedule; **le train a perdu son ~** the train has lost the time it had gained; (*Aut, Tech*) **~ à l'allumage** ignition advance; **ma montre a 10 minutes d'~** my watch is 10 minutes fast; **ma montre prend de l'~** my watch is gaining *ou* gains; **ma montre prend beaucoup d'~** my watch gains a lot.

(d) (*Comm, Fin: acompte*) advance. **~ de fonds** advance; **faire une ~ de 100 F à qn** to advance sb 100 francs, make sb an advance of 100 francs; **donner à qn une ~ sur son salaire** to give sb an advance on his salary.

(e) (*ouvertures*) **~s** overtures, (*galantes*) advances; **faire des ~s à qn** to make overtures *ou* advances to sb.

(f) **en ~** (*sur l'heure fixée*) early; (*sur l'horaire etc*) ahead of schedule; **être en ~ sur qn** to be ahead of sb; **être en ~ d'une heure** (*sur l'heure fixée*) to be an hour early; (*sur l'horaire*) to be an hour ahead of schedule; **dépêche-toi, tu n'es pas en ~!** hurry up, you've not got much time! *ou* you're running out of time!; **les crocus sont en ~ cette année** the crocuses are early this year; **leur fils est très en ~ dans ses études/sur les autres enfants** their son is well ahead in his studies/of the other children; **il est en ~ pour son âge** he is advanced for his age, he is ahead of his age-group; **leur pays est en ~ dans le domaine scientifique** their country leads *ou* is ahead in the field of science; **ses idées étaient/il était très en ~ sur son temps** *ou* **son époque** his ideas were/he was well ahead of *ou* in advance of his time.

(g) (*loc*) **à l'~** in advance, beforehand; **réserver une place un mois à l'~** to book a seat one month ahead *ou* in advance; **prévenir qn 2 heures à l'~** to give sb 2 hours' notice, notify *ou* warn sb 2 hours beforehand *ou* in advance; **je vous remercie à l'~** *ou* **d'~** thanking you in advance *ou* in anticipation; **merci d'~** thanks (in advance); **d'~** in advance; **d'~ je peux vous dire que ...** I can tell you in advance *ou* right now that ...; **d'~ il pouvait deviner** already *ou* even then he could guess; **il faut payer d'~** one must pay in advance; **ça a été arrangé d'~** it was prearranged, it was arranged beforehand *ou* in advance; **par ~** in advance; **je peux vous dire par ~ ce qui va arriver** I can tell you in advance *ou* even now what will happen.

avancé, e[1] [avɑ̃se] (*ptp de* **avancer**) *adj* **(a)** *élève, civilisation, technique* advanced. **la saison/journée était ~e** it was late in the season/day; **la nuit était ~e** it was well into the night; **il est très ~ dans son travail** he is well on with his work; **à une heure ~e de la nuit** well on into the night; **son roman est déjà assez ~** he's already quite a long way on *ou* quite far ahead with his novel; **cet enfant n'est vraiment pas ~ pour son âge** this child is rather backward *ou* is not at all advanced for his age; **être d'un âge ~** to be advanced in years *ou* well on in years; **dans un état ~ de ...** in an advanced state of ...; **après toutes ses démarches, il n'en est pas plus ~** after all the steps he has taken, he's no further on than he was; (*iro*) **nous voilà bien ~s!*** a long way that's got us! (*iro*), a (fat) lot of good that's done us!* (*iro*); *V* **heure.**

(b) (*d'avant-garde*) *opinion, idée* progressive, advanced.

(c) (*qui se gâte*) *fruit, fromage* overripe. **ce poisson est ~** this fish is going off (*surtout Brit*).

(d) (*Mil*) *poste* advanced.

avancée[2] [avɑ̃se] *nf* overhang.

avancement [avɑ̃smɑ̃] *nm* **(a)** (*promotion*) promotion. **avoir** *ou* **prendre de l'~** to be promoted, get promotion.

(b) (*progrès*) *[travaux]* progress; *[sciences, techniques]* advancement.

(c) (*mouvement*) forward movement.

(d) (*Jur*) **~ d'hoirie** advancement.

avancer [avɑ̃se] (3) **1** *vt* **(a)** (*porter en avant*) *objet* to move *ou* bring forward; *tête* to move forward; *main* to hold out, put out (*vers* to); *pion* to move forward. **~ le cou** to crane one's neck; **~ un siège à qn** to draw up *ou* bring forward a seat for sb; **le blessé avança les lèvres pour boire** the injured man put his lips forward to drink; (†, *hum*) **la voiture de Madame est avancée** Madam's carriage awaits (†, *hum*); **~ (les aiguilles d')une pendule** to put (the hands of) a clock forward *ou* on (*surtout Brit*).

(b) (*fig*) *opinion, hypothèse* to put forward, advance. **ce qu'il avance paraît vraisemblable** what he is putting forward *ou* suggesting seems quite plausible.

(c) *date, départ* to bring forward. **il a dû ~ son retour** he had to bring forward the date of his return.

(d) (*faire progresser*) *travail* to speed up. **est-ce que cela vous avancera si je vous aide?** will it speed things up (for you) *ou* will you get on more quickly if I lend you a hand?; **ça n'avance pas nos affaires** that doesn't improve matters for us; **cela t'avancera à quoi** *ou* **cela ne t'avancera à rien de crier*** shouting won't get you anywhere, you won't get anywhere by shouting.

(e) *somme d'argent, fonds* to advance; (*: *prêter*) to lend.

2 *vi* **(a)** (*progresser*) to advance, move forward; *[bateau]* to make headway. **l'armée avance sur Paris** the army is advancing on Paris; **il avança d'un pas** he took *ou* moved a step forward; **il avança d'un mètre** he moved three feet forward, he came three feet nearer; **mais avance donc!** move on *ou* forward *ou* up, will you!; **le paysan essayait de faire ~ son âne** the peasant tried to get his donkey to move (on) *ou* to make his donkey move (on).

(b) (*fig*) to make progress. **la nuit avance** night is wearing on;

faire ~ *travail* to speed up; *élève* to bring on, help to make progress; *science* to further; **~ vite/lentement dans son travail** to make good/slow progress in one's work; **~ péniblement dans son travail** to plod on slowly with *ou* make halting progress in one's work; **~ en âge** to be getting on (in years); **~ en grade** to be promoted, get promotion; **son livre n'avance guère** he's not making much headway *ou* progress with his book; **tout cela n'avance à rien** that doesn't get us any further *ou* anywhere; **je travaille mais il me semble que je n'avance pas** I'm working but I don't seem to be getting anywhere.

(c) *[montre, horloge]* to gain. **~ de 10 minutes par jour** to gain 10 minutes a day; **ma montre avance** *ou* **j'avance (de 10 minutes)** my watch is *ou* I'm (10 minutes) fast.

(d) *[cap, promontoire]* to project, jut out (*dans* into); *[lèvre, menton]* to protrude. **un balcon qui avance (de 3 mètres) sur la rue** a balcony that juts out *ou* projects (3 metres) over the street.

3 s'avancer *vpr* **(a)** (*aller en avant*) to move forward; (*progresser*) to advance. **il s'avança vers nous** he came towards us; **la procession s'avançait lentement** the procession advanced slowly *ou* moved slowly forward.

(b) (*fig: s'engager*) to commit o.s. **il n'aime pas beaucoup s'~** he does not like to commit himself *ou* stick his neck out*; **je ne peux pas m'~ sans connaître la question** I don't know enough about it to venture *ou* hazard an opinion, I can't commit myself without knowing more about it.

avanie [avani] *nf*: **subir une ~** to be snubbed; **faire** *ou* **infliger des ~s à qn** to snub sb; **les ~s qu'il avait subies** the snubs he had received.

avant [avɑ̃] **1** *prép* **(a)** (*temps, lieu*) before; (*avec limite de temps*) by, before. **il est parti ~ la pluie/la fin** he left before the rain started/the end; **il est parti ~ nous** he left before us; **cela s'est passé bien/peu ~ son mariage** this took place long *ou* a good while/shortly *ou* a short time before he was *ou* got married *ou* before his marriage; **ne venez pas ~ 10 heures** don't come until *ou* before 10; **il n'arrivera pas ~ une demi-heure** he won't be here for another half hour (yet) *ou* for half an hour (yet); **~ cela il était très gai** before that *ou* (up) until then he had been very cheerful; **j'étais ~ lui dans la queue mais on l'a servi ~ moi** I was in front of him *ou* before him in the queue (*Brit*) *ou* line (*US*) but he was served before me *ou* before I was; **il me le faut ~ demain/minuit** I must have it by *ou* before tomorrow/midnight; **il me le faut ~ une semaine/un mois** I must have it within a week/a month; **~ peu** shortly; **sa maison est (juste) ~ la mairie** his house is (just) before *ou* this side of the town hall; **X, ce féministe (bien) ~ la lettre** X, a feminist (long) before the term existed *ou* had been coined; *V* **Jésus.**

(b) (*priorité*) before, in front of, above. **~ tout** above all, first and foremost; **le travail passe ~ tout** work comes before everything; **~ tout, il faut éviter la guerre** above all (things) war must be avoided; **il faut ~ tout vérifier l'état du toit** first and foremost *ou* above all else we must see what state the roof is in; **en classe, elle est ~ sa sœur** at school she is ahead of her sister; **il met sa santé ~ sa carrière** he puts his health before *ou* above his career, he values his health above his career; **le capitaine est ~ le lieutenant** captain comes before lieutenant.

(c) ~ de + *infin* before; **~ que** + *subj* before; **à prendre ~ (de) manger** to be taken before food *ou* meals; **dînez donc ~ de partir** do have a meal before you go; **consultez-moi ~ de prendre une décision** consult me before making your decision *ou* before you decide; **je veux lire sa lettre ~ qu'elle (ne) l'envoie** I want to read her letter before she sends it (off); **n'envoyez pas cette lettre ~ que je (ne) l'aie lue** don't send this letter before *ou* until I have read it; **la poste est juste ~ d'arriver à la gare** the post office is just before you come to the station.

2 *adv* **(a)** (*temps*) before, beforehand. **le voyage sera long, mangez ~** it's going to be a long journey so have something to eat beforehand *ou* before you go; **quelques semaines/mois ~** a few *ou* some weeks/months before (hand) *ou* previously *ou* earlier; **peu de temps/longtemps ~** shortly/well *ou* long before(hand); **la semaine/le mois d'~** the week/month before, the previous week/month; **fort ~ dans la nuit** far *ou* well into the night; **les gens d'~ étaient plus aimables** the previous people were nicer, the people who were there before were nicer; **réfléchis ~, tu parleras après** think before you speak, think first then (you can) speak; **le train d'~ était plein** the earlier *ou* previous train was full; **~ je préférais le bateau au train** (before) I used to prefer the boat to the train; **venez me parler ~** come and talk to me beforehand.

(b) (*lieu: fig*) before; (*avec mouvement*) forward, ahead. **tu vois la gare? il habite juste ~** (you) see the station? he lives just this side (of it) *ou* before it; **n'avancez pas trop** *ou* **plus ~, c'est dangereux** don't go any further (forward), it's dangerous; **il s'était engagé trop ~ dans le bois** he had gone too far *ou* too deep into the wood; (*fig*) **il s'est engagé trop ~** he has got* *ou* become too involved, he has committed himself too deeply; **n'hésitez pas à aller plus ~** don't hesitate to go further *ou* on; **ils sont assez ~ dans leurs recherches** they are well into *ou* well advanced in *ou* far ahead in their research.

(c) en ~ (*mouvement*) forward; (*temps, position*) in front, ahead (*de* of); **en ~, marche!** forward march!; (*Naut*) **en ~ toute!** full steam ahead!; **la voiture fit un bond en ~** the car lurched forward; **être en ~** (*d'un groupe de personnes*) to be (out) in front; **marcher en ~ de la procession** to walk in front of the procession; **les enfants sont partis en ~** the children have gone on ahead *ou* in front; **partez en ~, on vous rejoindra** you go on (ahead *ou* in front), we'll catch you up; (*fig*) **regarder en ~** to look ahead; (*fig*) **mettre qch en ~** to put sth forward, advance sth; (*fig*) **mettre qn en ~** (*pour se couvrir*) to use sb as a front; (*pour aider qn*) to push sb forward *ou* to the front; (*fig*) **il aime se mettre en ~** he likes to push himself forward, he likes to be in the forefront.

3 *nm* **(a)** *[voiture, train]* front; *[navire]* bow(s), stem. **voyager à l'~ du train** to travel in the front of the train; **dans cette voiture on est mieux à l'~** it's more comfortable in the front of this car; (*fig*) **aller de l'~** to forge ahead.

(b) (*Sport: joueur*) forward. **la ligne des ~s** the forward line.

(c) (*Mil*) front.

4 *adj inv roue* front; *marche* forward. **traction ~** front-wheel drive; **la partie ~** the front part.

5: avant-bras *nm inv* forearm; **avant-centre** *nm, pl* **avant-centres** centre-forward; **avant-coureur** *adj inv* precursory, premonitory; **signe avant-coureur** forerunner, harbinger (*littér*); **avant-dernier** (*f* **-ière**), *mpl* **avant-derniers** *nm(f), adj* next to last, last but one, (*sg seulement*) penultimate; **avant-garde** *nf, pl* **avant-gardes** (*Mil*) vanguard; (*Art, Pol*) avant-garde; **art/poésie/idées d'avant-garde** avant-garde art/poetry/ideas; **avant-goût** *nm* foretaste; **avant-guerre** *nm* pre-war years; **d'avant-guerre** *adj* pre-war; **avant-hier** *adv* the day before yesterday; (*Belgique, Can*) **avant-midi*** *nm ou nf inv* morning; **avant-port** *nm, pl* **avant-ports** outer harbour; **avant-poste** *nm, pl* **avant-postes** outpost; **avant-première** *nf, pl* **avant-premières** preview; **avant-projet** *nm, pl* **avant-projets** pilot study; **avant-propos** *nm inv* foreword; (*Théât*) **avant-scène** *nf, pl* **avant-scènes** (*scène*) apron, proscenium; (*loge*) box (*at the front of the house*); **avant-train** *nm, pl* **avant-trains** *[animal]* foreparts, forequarters; *[véhicule]* front axle assembly *ou* unit; **avant-veille** *nf*: **l'avant-veille** two days before *ou* previously; **c'était l'avant-veille de Noël** it was the day before Christmas Eve *ou* two days before Christmas.

avantage [avɑ̃taʒ] *nm* **(a)** (*intérêt*) advantage. **cette solution a l'~ de ne léser personne** this solution has the advantage of not hurting anyone; **il a ~ à y aller** it will be to his advantage to go, it will be worth his while to go; **j'ai ~ à acheter en gros** it's worth my while to *ou* it's worth it for me to buy in bulk; **tirer ~ de la situation** to take advantage of the situation, turn the situation to one's advantage; **tu aurais ~ à te tenir tranquille*** you'd be *ou* do better to keep quiet*, you'd do well to keep quiet.

(b) (*supériorité*) advantage. **avoir un ~ sur qn** to have an advantage over sb; **j'ai sur vous l'~ de l'expérience** I have the advantage of experience over you; **ils ont l'~ du nombre sur leurs adversaires** they have the advantage of numbers over their enemies.

(c) (*Fin: gain*) benefit. **~s en nature** benefits in kind; **gros ~s matériels d'un métier** overall material benefits of a job; **~ pécuniaire** financial benefit; **~s sociaux** fringe benefits.

(d) (*Mil, Sport, fig*) advantage; (*Tennis*) vantage (*Brit*), advantage. **avoir l'~** to have the advantage, have the upper hand, be one up*; (*Tennis*) **~ service/dehors** vantage in/out (*Brit*), advantage in/out; **~ détruit** deuce (*again*).

(e) (*frm: plaisir*) **j'ai (l'honneur et) l'~ de vous présenter M X** I have the (honour and) privilege of introducing Mr X to you (*frm*); **que me vaut l'~ de votre visite?** to what do I owe the pleasure *ou* honour of your visit? (*frm*).

(f) (*loc*) **être à son ~** (*sur une photo*) to look one's best; (*dans une conversation*) to be at one's best; **elle est à son ~ avec cette coiffure** she looks her best with that hair style, that hair style flatters her; **il s'est montré à son ~** he was seen in a favourable light *ou* to advantage; **c'est (tout) à ton ~** it's (entirely) to your advantage; **changer à son ~** to change for the better.

avantager [avɑ̃taʒe] (3) *vt* **(a)** (*donner un avantage à*) to favour, give an advantage to. **elle a été avantagée par la nature** she was favoured by nature; **il a été avantagé par rapport à ses frères** he has been given an advantage over his brothers.

(b) (*mettre en valeur*) to flatter. **ce chapeau l'avantage** that hat flatters her, she looks good in that hat.

avantageusement [avɑ̃taʒøzmɑ̃] *adv vendre* at a good price; *décrire* favourably, flatteringly. **la situation se présente ~** the situation looks favourable; **une robe qui découvrait ~ ses épaules magnifiques** a dress which showed off her lovely shoulders to great advantage.

avantageux, -euse [avɑ̃taʒø, øz] *adj* **(a)** (*profitable*) *affaire* worthwhile, profitable; *prix* attractive. **ce serait plus ~ de faire comme cela** it would be more profitable *ou* worthwhile to do it this way; **c'est une occasion ~euse** it's an attractive *ou* a good bargain. **(b)** (*présomptueux*) *air, personne* conceited. **(c)** (*qui flatte*) *portrait, chapeau* flattering.

avare [avaʀ] **1** *adj* **(a)** *personne* miserly, avaricious, tight-fisted*. **il est ~ de paroles** he's sparing of words; **il est ~ de compliments** he's sparing with his compliments *ou* sparing of compliments; *V* **à.**

(b) (*littér: peu abondant*) *terre* meagre. **une lumière ~ pénétrait dans la pièce** a dim *ou* weak light filtered into the room.

2 *nmf* miser.

avarice [avaʀis] *nf* miserliness, avarice.

avaricieux, -ieuse [avaʀisjø, jøz] (*littér*) **1** *adj miserly, niggardly, stingy.* **2** *nm* miser, niggard, skinflint.

avarie [avaʀi] *nf [navire, véhicule]* damage (*U*); (*Tech*) *[cargaison, changement]* damage (*U*) (in transit), average (*T*).

avarié, e [avaʀje] (*ptp de* **avarier**) *adj aliment* rotting; *navire* damaged. **une cargaison de viande ~e** a cargo of rotting meat; **cette viande est ~e** this meat has gone off (*Brit*) *ou* gone bad.

avarier [avaʀje] (7) **1** *vt* to spoil, damage. **2 s'avarier** *vpr [fruits, viande]* to go bad, rot.

avatar [avataʀ] *nm* (*Rel*) avatar; (*fig*) metamorphosis. (*péripéties*) **~s*** misadventures.

Avé [ave] *nm inv* (*prière: aussi* **~ Maria**) Hail Mary, Ave Maria.

avec [avɛk] **1** *prép* **(a)** (*accompagnement, accord*) with. **elle est sortie ~ les enfants** she is out *ou* has gone out with the children; **son mariage** ~ **X a duré 8 ans** her marriage to X lasted (for) 8 years; **ils ont les syndicats** ~ **eux** they've got the unions on their side *ou* behind them.

(b) (*comportement: envers*) to, towards, with. **comment se comportent-ils** ~ **vous?** how do they behave towards *ou* with you?; **il est très doux** ~ **les animaux** he is very gentle with animals; **il a été très gentil** ~ **nous** he was very kind to us.

(c) (*moyen, manière*) with; (*ingrédient*) with, from, out of. **vous prenez votre thé** ~ **du lait ou du citron?** do you have *ou* take your tea with milk or (with) lemon?, do you have *ou* take milk or lemon in your tea?; **boire** ~ **une paille** to drink with a straw; **une maison** ~ **jardin** a house with a garden; **faire qch** ~ **(grande) facilité** to do sth with (great) ease *ou* (very) easily; **parler** ~ **colère/bonté/lenteur** to speak angrily *ou* with anger/kindly/slowly; **chambre** ~ **salle de bain** room with a bathroom *ou* its own bathroom; **couteau** ~ **(un) manche en bois** knife with a wooden handle, wooden-handled knife; **gâteau fait** ~ **du beurre** cake made with butter; **ragoût fait** ~ **des restes** stew made out of *ou* from (the) left-overs; **c'est fait (entièrement)** ~ **du plomb** it's made (entirely) of lead.

(d) (*cause, simultanéité, contraste etc*) with. **on oublie tout** ~ **le temps** one forgets everything in time *ou* in the course of time *ou* with the passing of time; ~ **les élections, on ne parle plus que politique** with the elections (on) no one talks anything but politics; ~ **l'inflation et le prix de l'essence, les voitures se vendent mal** what with inflation and the price of petrol, cars aren't selling very well; **il est difficile de marcher** ~ **ce vent** it is difficult to walk in *ou* with this wind; ~ **un peu de travail, il aurait gagné le prix** with a little work *ou* if (only) he had done a little work he would have won the prize; ~ **toute ma bonne volonté, je ne suis pas parvenu à l'aider** with the best will in the world *ou* for all my goodwill I did not manage to help him; **se lever** ~ **le jour** to get up *ou* rise with the sun *ou* dawn, get up at daybreak; **ils sont partis** ~ **la pluie** they left in the rain.

(e) (*opposition*) with. **rivaliser/combattre** ~ **qn** to vie/fight with sb; **elle s'est fâchée** ~ **tous leurs amis** she has fallen out with all their friends.

(f) **d'**~: **séparer/distinguer qch d'**~ **qch d'autre** to separate/distinguish sth from sth else; **divorcer d'**~ **qn** to divorce sb; **se séparer d'**~ **qn** to leave sb, part from sb (*littér*); **elle s'est séparée d'**~ **X** she has separated from X.

(g) ~ **cela***: (*dans un magasin*) **et** ~ **ça, madame?** anything else?; **il conduit mal et** ~ **ça il conduit trop vite** he drives badly and what's more *ou* on top of that he drives too fast; ~ **cela que tu ne le savais pas!** what do you mean you didn't know!, as if you didn't know!; (*iro*) **et** ~ **ça qu'il est complaisant!** and it's not as if he were helpful (either *ou* at that)!, and he's not exactly *ou* even helpful either! *ou* at that!; ~ **tout ça j'ai oublié le pain** in the midst of all this I forgot about the bread.

2 *adv* (*) **tiens mes gants, je ne peux pas conduire** ~ hold my gloves, I can't drive with them on; **rends-moi mon stylo, tu allais partir** ~**!** give me back my pen, you were going to walk off with it!

aven [avɛn] *nm* swallow hole (*Brit*), sinkhole, pothole.

avenant, e [avnɑ̃, ɑ̃t] **1** *adj personne* pleasant, welcoming; *manières* pleasant, pleasing; *maison* of pleasing appearance.

2 *nm* **(a)** **à l'**~ in keeping (*de* with); **la maison était luxueuse, et le mobilier était à l'**~ the house was luxurious, and the furniture was in keeping (with it).

(b) (*Jur*) *[police d'assurance]* endorsement. **faire un** ~ **à** to endorse, make out an endorsement for.

avènement [avɛnmɑ̃] *nm [roi]* accession, succession (*à* to); *[régime, politique, idée]* advent; *[Messie]* Advent, Coming.

avenir[1] [avniʀ] *nm* **(a)** (*futur*) future; (*postérité*) future generations. **avoir des projets d'**~ to have plans for the future, have future plans; **dans un proche** ~ in the near future.

(b) (*bien-être*) future (well-being). **assurer l'**~ **de ses enfants** to take care of *ou* ensure one's children's future.

(c) (*carrière*) future, prospects. **il a de l'**~**, c'est un homme d'**~ he's a man with a future *ou* with good prospects, he's an up-and-coming man; **métier d'**~ job with a future *ou* with prospects; **il n'y a aucun** ~ **dans ce métier** there's no future in this job, this is a dead-end job; **projet sans** ~ project without prospects of success *ou* without a future.

(d) (*dorénavant*) **à l'**~ from now on, in future.

avenir[2] [avniʀ] *nm* (*Jur*) writ of summons (*from one counsel to another*).

Avent [avɑ̃] *nm*: **l'**~ Advent.

aventure [avɑ̃tyʀ] *nf* **(a)** (*péripétie, incident*) adventure; (*entreprise*) venture; (*liaison amoureuse*) affair. **fâcheuse** ~ unfortunate experience; **une** ~ **effrayante** a terrifying experience; **film/roman d'**~**s** adventure film/story; **une** ~ **sentimentale** a love affair; **avoir une** ~ **(galante) avec qn** to have an affair with sb.

(b) **l'**~ adventure; **esprit d'**~ spirit of adventure; *V* **dire, diseuse.**

(c) (*loc*) **marcher à l'**~ to walk aimlessly; (*littér*) **si, par** ~ *ou* **d'**~ if by any chance; **quand, par** ~ *ou* **d'**~ when by chance.

aventuré, e [avɑ̃tyʀe] (*ptp de* **aventurer**) *adj entreprise* risky, chancy; *hypothèse* risky, venturesome.

aventurer [avɑ̃tyʀe] (1) **1** *vt somme, réputation, vie* to risk, put at stake, chance; *remarque, opinion* to venture.

2 s'aventurer *vpr* to venture (*dans* into, *sur* onto). **s'**~ **à faire qch** to venture to do sth, risk doing sth; (*fig*) **s'**~ **en terrain** *ou* **sur un chemin glissant** to tread on dangerous ground, skate on thin ice.

aventureusement [avɑ̃tyʀøzmɑ̃] *adv* adventurously, riskily.

aventureux, -euse [avɑ̃tyʀø, øz] *adj personne, esprit* adventurous, enterprising, venturesome; *imagination* bold; *projet, entreprise* risky, rash, chancy; *vie* adventurous.

aventurier [avɑ̃tyʀje] *nm* adventurer.

aventurière [avɑ̃tyʀjɛʀ] *nf* (*péj*) adventuress (*péj*).

aventurisme [avɑ̃tyʀism(ə)] *nm* (*Pol*) adventurism.

aventuriste [avɑ̃tyʀist(ə)] *adj* (*Pol*) adventurist.

avenu, e[1] [avny] *adj V* **nul.**

avenue[2] [avny] *nf [ville]* (*boulevard*) avenue; *[parc]* (*allée*) drive, avenue. (*littér*) **les** ~**s du pouvoir** the avenues of *ou* to power.

avéré, e [aveʀe] (*ptp de* **s'avérer**) *adj fait* known, recognized. **il est** ~ **que** it is a known *ou* recognized fact that.

avérer (s') [aveʀe] (6) *vpr*: **il s'avère que** it turns out that; **ce remède s'avéra inefficace** this remedy proved (to be) *ou* turned out to be ineffective; **il s'est avéré un employé consciencieux** he proved (to be) *ou* turned out to be *ou* showed himself to be a conscientious employee.

avers [avɛʀ] *nm* obverse (*of coin, medal*).

averse [avɛʀs(ə)] *nf* (*pluie*) shower (of rain); (*fig*) *[insultes, pierres]* shower. **forte** ~ heavy shower, downpour; ~ **orageuse** thundery shower; **être pris par** *ou* **recevoir une** ~ to be caught in a shower.

aversion [avɛʀsjɔ̃] *nf* aversion (*pour* to), loathing (*pour* for). **avoir en** ~, **avoir de l'**~ **pour** to have an aversion to, have a loathing *ou* a strong dislike for, loathe; **prendre en** ~ to take a (violent) dislike to.

averti, e [avɛʀti] (*ptp de* **avertir**) *adj public* informed, mature; *connaisseur, expert* well-informed. **c'est un film réservé à des spectateurs** ~**s** it's a film suitable for a mature *ou* informed audience; ~ **de** *problèmes etc* aware of; **être très** ~ **des travaux cinématographiques contemporains** to be very well up on *ou* well informed about the contemporary film scene; *V* **homme.**

avertir [avɛʀtiʀ] (2) *vt* (*mettre en garde*) to warn (*de qch* of sth); (*renseigner*) to inform (*de qch* of sth). **avertissez-le de ne pas recommencer** warn him not to do it again; **tenez-vous pour averti** be warned, don't say you haven't been warned; **avertissez-moi dès que possible** let me know as soon as possible.

avertissement [avɛʀtismɑ̃] *nm* (*avis*) warning; (*présage*) warning, warning sign; (*réprimande*) (*Sport*) warning, caution; (*Scol*) admonition. (*préface*) ~ **(au lecteur)** foreword; (*Jur*) ~ **sans frais** notice of assessment.

avertisseur, -euse [avɛʀtisœʀ, øz] **1** *adj* warning. **2** *nm* (*Aut*) horn, hooter. ~ **(d'incendie)** (fire) alarm.

aveu, *pl* ~**x** [avø] *nm* **(a)** *[crime, amour]* confession, avowal (*littér*); *[fait]* acknowledgement, admission; *[faiblesse]* admission, confession. **faire l'**~ **d'un crime** to confess to a crime; **faire des** ~**x complets** to make a full confession; **passer aux** ~**x** to make a confession.

(b) (*frm: selon*) **de l'**~ **de qn** according to sb; **de l'**~ **même du témoin** on the witness's own testimony.

(c) (*frm*) **sans** ~ *homme, politicien* disreputable.

(d) (*littér: assentiment*) consent. **sans l'**~ **de qn** without sb's authorization *ou* consent.

aveuglant, e [avœglɑ̃, ɑ̃t] *adj lumière* blinding, dazzling; *vérité* blinding, overwhelming.

aveugle [avœgl(ə)] **1** *adj personne* blind, sightless (*épith*); (*fig*) *passion, dévouement, obéissance* blind; *fenêtre* blind. **devenir** ~ to go blind; ~ **d'un œil** blind in one eye; **il est** ~ **de naissance** he was born blind, he has been blind from birth; **son amour le rend** ~ love is blinding him, he is blinded by love; **avoir une confiance** ~ **en qn** to trust sb blindly *ou* implicitly; **une confiance** ~ **dans la parole de qn** an implicit trust *ou* faith in sb's word; **être** ~ **aux défauts de qn** to be blind to sb's faults; **l'**~ **instrument du destin** the blind *ou* unwitting instrument of fate.

2 *nmf* blind man (*ou* woman). **les** ~**s** the blind; **faire qch en** ~ to do sth blindly; *V* **à.**

aveuglement [avœgləmɑ̃] *nm* (*littér: égarement*) blindness.

aveuglément [avœglemɑ̃] *adv* (*fidèlement*) blindly; (*inconsidérément*) blindly, blindfold.

aveugler [avœgle] (1) **1** *vt* **(a)** (*lit, fig*) (*rendre aveugle*) to blind; (*éblouir*) to dazzle, blind. **(b)** *fenêtre* to block *ou* brick up; *voie d'eau* to stop up. **2 s'aveugler** *vpr*: **s'**~ **sur qn** to be blind to *ou* shut one's eyes to sb's defects.

aveuglette [avœglɛt] *nf*: **avancer à l'**~ to grope (one's way) along, feel one's way along; **descendre à l'**~ to grope one's way down; **prendre des décisions à l'**~ to take decisions in the dark *ou* blindly.

aveulir [avøliʀ] (2) **1** *vt* to enfeeble, enervate. **2 s'aveulir** *vpr* to lose one's will (power), degenerate.

aveulissement [avølismɑ̃] *nm* enfeeblement, enervation; loss of will (power).

aviateur [avjatœʀ] *nm* airman, aviator, pilot.

aviation [avjɑsjɔ̃] **1** *nf* (*Mil*) (*corps d'armée*) air force; (*avions*) aircraft, air force. **l'**~ (*sport, métier de pilote*) flying; (*secteur commercial*) aviation; (*moyen de tranport*) air travel; **coupe/meeting d'**~ flying cup/meeting; **usine d'**~ aircraft factory; **services/base d'**~ air services/base; *V* **champ, ligne**[1]**, terrain.**

2: **aviation de chasse** fighter force; **aviation navale** fleet air arm (*Brit*), naval air force (*US*).

aviatrice [avjatʀis] *nf* woman pilot, aviator.

avicole [avikɔl] *adj* (*V* **aviculture**) *élevage* bird (*épith*); poultry (*épith*); *établissement* bird-breeding; poultry farming *ou* breeding; *ferme* poultry.

aviculteur, -trice [avikyltœʀ, tʀis] *nm,f* (*V* **aviculture**) poultry farmer *ou* breeder; aviculturist (*T*), bird breeder, bird fancier.

aviculture [avikyltyʀ] *nf* (*volailles*) poultry farming *ou* breeding; (*oiseaux*) aviculture (*T*), bird breeding, bird fancying.

avide [avid] *adj* (*par intensité*) eager; (*par cupidité*) greedy, grasping (*épith*); *lecteur* avid, eager. ~ **de** *plaisir, sensation* eager *ou* avid for; *argent, nourriture* greedy for; *pouvoir, honneurs* greedy *ou* avid for; ~ **de faire qch** eager to do sth; ~ **de sang** *ou* **de carnage** bloodthirsty (*épith*), thirsting for blood (*attrib*).

avidement [avidmɑ̃] *adv* (*V* **avide**) eagerly; greedily; avidly.

avidité [avidite] *nf* (*V* **avide**) eagerness; greed; greediness; avidity (*de* for).

avilir [aviliʀ] (2) **1** *vt personne* to degrade, debase, demean; *monnaie* to debase; *marchandise* to depreciate. **2 s'avilir** *vpr* [*personne*] to degrade o.s., debase o.s., demean o.s.; [*monnaie, marchandise*] to depreciate.

avilissant, e [avilisɑ̃, ɑ̃t] *adj spectacle* degrading, shameful, shaming (*épith*); *conduite, situation, travail* degrading, demeaning.

avilissement [avilismɑ̃] *nm* (*V* **avilir**) degradation; debasement; depreciation.

aviné, e [avine] *adj* (*littér*) *personne* inebriated, intoxicated; *voix* drunken. **il a l'haleine** ~**e** his breath smells of alcohol.

avion [avjɔ̃] **1** *nm* (*appareil*) aeroplane (*Brit*), plane, airplane (*US*), aircraft (*pl inv*). (*sport*) **l'**~ flying; **défense/batterie contre** ~**s** anti-aircraft defence/battery; **il est allé à Paris en** ~ he went to Paris by air *ou* by plane, he flew to Paris; **par** ~ by air(mail).

2: avion de bombardement bomber; **avion-cargo** *nm, pl* **avions-cargos** (air) freighter, cargo aircraft; **avion de chasse** interceptor, fighter; **avion-cible** *nm, pl* **avions-cibles** target aircraft; **avion-citerne** *nm, pl* **avions-citernes** air tanker; **avion commercial** commercial aircraft; **avion-fusée** *nm, pl* **avions-fusées** rocket-propelled plane; **avion de ligne** airliner; **avion postal** mail plane; **avion à réaction** jet (plane); **avion de reconnaissance** reconnaissance aircraft; **avion-suicide** *nm, pl* **avions-suicide** suicide plane; **avion-taxi** *nm, pl* **avions-taxis** taxiplane (*US*); **avion de transport** transport aircraft.

aviron [aviʀɔ̃] *nm* **(a)** (*rame*) oar; (*sport*) rowing. **faire de l'**~ to row. **(b)** (*Can*) paddle.

avironner [aviʀɔne] (1) *vt* (*Can*) to paddle.

avis [avi] **1** *nm* **(a)** (*opinion*) opinion. **donner son** ~ to give one's opinion *ou* views (*sur* on, about); **les** ~ **sont partagés** opinion is divided; **être du même** ~ **que qn, être de l'**~ **de qn** to be of the same opinion *ou* of the same mind as sb, share the view of sb; **je ne suis pas de votre** ~ I'm not of your opinion *ou* view; **à mon** ~ **c'est ...** in my opinion *ou* to my mind it is ...; **si tu veux mon** ~**, il est ...** if you ask me *ou* if you want my opinion he is ...; (*iro*) **à mon humble** ~ in my humble opinion; **de l'**~ **de tous, il ne sera pas élu** the general opinion is that he won't be elected; *V* **changer, deux.**

(b) (*conseil*) advice (*U*). **un** ~ **amical** a friendly piece of advice, a piece of friendly advice, some friendly advice; **suivre l'**~ *ou* **les** ~ **de qn** to take *ou* follow sb's advice; **sur l'**~ **de qn** on sb's advice; **suivant l'**~ **donné** following the advice given.

(c) (*notification*) notice; (*Fin*) advice. **lettre d'**~ letter of advice; ~ **de crédit/de débit** credit/debit advice; **sans** ~ **préalable** without prior notice; **jusqu'à nouvel** ~ until further notice; **sauf** ~ **contraire** unless otherwise informed, unless one hears to the contrary; (*sur étiquette, dans préface etc*) unless otherwise indicated; **donner** ~ **de/que**† to give notice of/that.

(d) (*Admin: consultation officielle*) opinion. **les membres ont émis un** ~ the members put forward an opinion; **on a pris l'**~ **du conseil** they took the opinion of the council.

(e) (*loc*) **être d'**~ **que/de: il était d'**~ **de partir** *ou* **qu'on parte immédiatement** he thought we should leave immediately, he was of the opinion that we should leave at once, he was for leaving at once*; **je suis d'**~ **qu'il vaut mieux attendre** I think *ou* I am of the opinion that it is better to wait; (†, *hum*) **m'est** ~ **que** methinks (†, *hum*).

2: avis de décès announcement of death, death notice*; **avis au lecteur** foreword; **avis de mobilisation** mobilization notice; **avis au public** public notice; (*en-tête*) notice to the public.

avisé, e [avize] (*ptp de* **aviser**) *adj* sensible, wise. **bien** ~ well-advised; **mal** ~ rash, ill-advised.

aviser [avize] (1) **1** *vt* **(a)** (*frm, littér: avertir*) to advise, inform (*de* of), notify (*de* of, about). **il ne m'en a pas avisé** he didn't notify me of *ou* about it.

(b) (*littér: apercevoir*) to catch sight of, notice.

2 *vi*: **cela fait, nous aviserons** once that's done, we'll see where we are *ou* where we stand *ou* we'll take stock; **sur place, nous aviserons** once (we're) there, we'll try and sort (*Brit*) *ou* work something out *ou* we'll assess the situation; **il va falloir** ~ well, we'll have to think about it *ou* give it some thought; ~ **à qch** to see to sth; **nous aviserons au nécessaire** we shall see to the necessary *ou* do what is necessary.

3 s'aviser *vpr* **(a)** (*remarquer*) **s'**~ **de qch** to become suddenly aware of sth, realize sth suddenly; **il s'avisa que ...** he suddenly realized that ... .

(b) (*s'aventurer à*) **s'**~ **de faire qch** to dare to do sth, take it into one's head to do sth; **et ne t'avise pas d'aller lui dire** and don't you dare go and tell him, and don't you take it into your head to go and tell him.

avitaminose [avitaminoz] *nf* vitamin deficiency, avitaminosis (*T*).

aviver [avive] (1) **1** *vt* **(a)** *douleur physique, appétit* to sharpen; *regrets, chagrin* to deepen; *intérêt, désir* to kindle, arouse; *colère* to stir up; *souvenirs* to stir up, revive; *querelle* to stir up, add fuel to; *passion* to arouse, excite, stir up; *regard* to brighten; *couleur* to revive, brighten (up); *feu* to revive, stir up. **l'air frais leur avait avivé le teint** the fresh air had given them some colour *ou* put colour into their cheeks.

(b) (*Méd*) *plaie* to open up; (*Tech*) *bronze* to burnish; *poutre* to square off.

2 s'aviver *vpr* (*V* **aviver**) to sharpen; to deepen; to be kindled; to be aroused; to be stirred up; to be excited; to brighten; to revive, be revived; to brighten up.

avocaillon [avɔkajɔ̃] *nm* (*péj*) pettifogging lawyer, small-town lawyer.

avocasserie [avɔkasʀi] *nf* (*péj*) pettifoggery, chicanery.

avocassier, -ière [avɔkasje, jɛʀ] *adj* (*péj*) pettifogging, chicaning.

avocat[1]**, e** [avɔka, at] **1** *nm,f* **(a)** (*Jur: personne inscrite au barreau*) barrister, advocate (*Écos*), attorney(-at-law) (*US*). **consulter son** ~ to consult one's lawyer; **l'accusé et son** ~ the accused and his counsel.

(b) (*fig: défenseur*) advocate, champion. **se faire l'**~ **d'une cause** to advocate *ou* champion *ou* plead a cause; **fais-toi mon** ~ **auprès de lui** plead with him on my behalf.

2: avocat d'affaires business lawyer; **avocat-conseil** *nm, pl* **avocats-conseils** ≃ consulting barrister, ≃ counsel-in-chambers; **l'avocat de la défense** the counsel for the defence *ou* defendant, the defending counsel; (*Rel, fig*) **l'avocat du diable** the devil's advocate; **avocat général** assistant public prosecutor, assistant procurator fiscal (*Écos*); **l'avocat de la partie civile** the counsel for the plaintiff; **avocat plaidant** court lawyer; **avocat sans cause** briefless barrister (*Brit*) *ou* attorney (*US*).

avocat[2] [avɔka] *nm* avocado (pear).

avocatier [avɔkatje] *nm* avocado (tree), avocado pear tree.

avoine [avwan] *nf* oats; *V* **farine, flocon, fou.**

avoir [avwaʀ] (34) **1** *vt* **(a)** (*posséder, disposer de*) *maison, patron, frère* to have. **il n'a pas d'argent** he has no money, he hasn't got any money; **on ne peut pas tout** ~ you can't have everything; **avez-vous du feu?** have you got a light?; **j'ai (tout) le temps de le faire** I have *ou* have got (plenty of) time to do it; ~ **qn pour ami** to have sb as a friend; **pour tout mobilier ils ont deux chaises et une table** the only furniture they have is two chairs and a table.

(b) (*obtenir, attraper*) *renseignement, prix, train* to get. **j'ai eu un coup de téléphone de Richard** I had *ou* got a phone call from Richard; **il a eu sa licence en 1939** he graduated in 1939, he got his degree in 1939; **nous avons très bien la BBC** we (can) get the BBC very clearly; **pouvez-vous nous** ~ **ce livre?** can you get this book for us?, can you get us this book?; **elle a eu 3 pommes pour un franc** she got 3 apples for one franc; **j'avais Jean au téléphone quand on nous a coupés** I was on the phone to John when we were cut off; **essayez de m'**~ **Paris (au téléphone)** could you put me through to Paris *ou* get me Paris; **je n'arrive pas à** ~ **Paris** I can't get through to Paris.

(c) (*souffrir de*) *rhume, maladie* to have. ~ **de la fièvre** to have *ou* run a high temperature; **il a la rougeole** he's got measles; **il a eu la rougeole à 10 ans** he had *ou* got measles at the age of 10.

(d) (*porter*) *vêtements* to have on, wear. **la femme qui a le chapeau bleu et une canne** the woman with the blue hat and a stick.

(e) *caractéristiques physiques ou morales* to have. **il a les yeux bleus** he has *ou* has got blue eyes; **il a du courage/de l'ambition/du toupet** he has (got) courage/ambition/cheek, he is courageous/ambitious/cheeky; **son regard a quelque chose de méchant, il a quelque chose de méchant dans le regard** he's got a nasty look in his eye; ~ **la tête qui tourne** to feel giddy; **j'ai le cœur qui bat** my heart is thumping; **regardez, il a les mains qui tremblent** look, his hands are shaking.

(f) *âge* to be. **quel âge avez-vous?** how old are you?; **il a dix ans** he is ten (years old); **ils ont le même âge** they are the same age.

(g) *formes, dimensions, couleur* to be. ~ **3 mètres de haut/4 mètres de long** to be 3 metres high/4 metres long; **cette armoire a une jolie ligne** this cupboard is a nice shape; **qu'est-ce qu'elle a comme tour de taille?** what's her waist measurement?, what waist is she?; **la maison a 5 étages** the house has 5 floors; **la voiture qui a cette couleur** the car which is that colour.

(h) (*éprouver*) *joie, chagrin* to feel; *intérêt* to show. ~ **faim/froid/honte** to be *ou* feel hungry/cold/ashamed; ~ **le sentiment/l'impression que** to have the feeling/the impression that; **qu'est-ce qu'il a?** what's the matter with him?, what's wrong with him?; **il a sûrement quelque chose** there's certainly something the matter with him, there's certainly something wrong with him; **il a qu'il est furieux** he's furious, that's what's wrong *ou* the matter with him; **qu'est-ce qu'il a à pleurer?** what's he crying for?; *V* **besoin, envie, mal** *etc.*

(i) *idées, raisons* to have; *opinion* to hold, have. **cela n'a aucun intérêt pour eux** it is of no interest to them; **la danse n'a aucun charme pour moi** dancing doesn't appeal to me at all; *V* **raison, tort.**

(j) *geste* to make; *rire* to give; *cri* to utter. **elle eut un sourire malin** she gave a knowing smile, she smiled knowingly; **il eut une grimace de douleur** he winced; **ils ont eu des remarques malheureuses** they made *ou* passed some unfortunate remarks; *V* **mot.**

(k) (*recevoir*) *visites, amis* to have. **il aime** ~ **des amis** he likes to have friends round, he likes to entertain friends; ~ **des amis à dîner** to have friends to dinner.

(l) *obligation, activité, conversation* to have. **ils ont des soirées 2 ou 3 fois par semaine** they have parties 2 or 3 times a week; **je n'ai rien ce soir** I've nothing on this evening, I'm not doing anything this evening; (*Scol*) **j'ai le français à 10 heures** I've got French at 10.

(m) (*: *vaincre*) **on les aura!** we'll have *ou* get them!*; **ils ont fini par** ~ **le coupable** they got the culprit in the end; **je t'aurai!** I'll get you!*; **dans la fusillade, ils ont eu le chef de la bande** in the shoot-out they got the gang leader*.

(n) (*: *duper*) *personne* to take in, take for a ride‡, con‡. **je les ai eus** I took them in, I took them for a ride‡, I conned them‡; **ils m'ont eu** I've been had*; **se faire ~** to be had*, be taken in, be taken for a ride‡.

(o) (*loc*) **en ~ à*** *ou* **après*** *ou* **contre qn*** to have a down on sb; **après qui en as-tu?*** who have you got a grudge against?; **en ~ pour son argent** to have *ou* get one's money's worth; **j'en ai pour 100 F** it will cost me *ou* set me back* 100 francs; **il en a pour 2 heures** it will take him 2 hours; **il en a pour 2 secondes** it won't take him 2 seconds; **tu en as pour combien de temps?** how long are you going to be?, how long will it take you?; **en ~ assez*** *ou* **par-dessus la tête*** *ou* **plein le dos*** to be fed up*, be cheesed off* *ou* browned off* (*de qch* with sth); **on en a encore pour 20 km de cette mauvaise route** there's another 20 km of this awful road; **quand il se met à pleuvoir, on en a pour 3 jours** once it starts raining, it sets in for 3 days; *V* **estime, horreur.**

2 *vb aux* **(a)** (*avec ptp*) **j'étais pressé, j'ai couru** I was in a hurry so I ran; **j'ai déjà couru 10 km** I've already run 10 km; **quand il eut** *ou* **a eu parlé** when he had spoken; **il n'est pas bien, il a dû trop manger** he is not well, he must have eaten too much; **nous aurons terminé demain** we shall have finished tomorrow; **si je l'avais vu** if I had seen him; **il a été tué hier** he was killed yesterday; **il a été renvoyé deux fois** he has been dismissed twice; **il aura été retardé par la pluie** he must *ou* will have been held up by the rain; *V* **vouloir.**

(b) (+ *infin: devoir*) **~ qch à faire** to have sth to do; **j'ai des lettres à écrire** I've (got) some letters to write; **j'ai à travailler** I have to work, I must work; **il n'a pas à se plaindre** he can't complain; **vous aurez à parler** you will have to speak; **vous n'avez pas à vous en soucier** you mustn't *ou* needn't worry about it; *V* **maille, rien, voir.**

(c) **n'~ qu'à: tu n'as qu'à me téléphoner demain** just give me a ring tomorrow, why don't you ring me up tomorrow?; **tu n'as qu'à appuyer sur le bouton, et ça se met en marche** (you) just press the knob, and it starts up; **il n'a qu'un mot à dire pour nous sauver** he need only say the word, and we're saved; **c'est simple, vous n'avez qu'à lui écrire** it's simple, just write to him *ou* you need only write to him *ou* you've only (got) to write to him; **tu n'avais qu'à ne pas y aller** you shouldn't have gone (in the first place); **tu n'as qu'à faire attention/te débrouiller** you'll just have to take care/sort (*Brit*) *ou* work it out for yourself; **s'il n'est pas content, il n'a qu'à partir** if he doesn't like it, he can just go.

(d) **ils ont eu leurs carreaux cassés par la grêle** they had their windows broken by the hail; **vous aurez votre robe nettoyée gratuitement** your dress will be cleaned free of charge.

3 *vb impers* **(a)** **il y a** (*avec sg*) there is; (*avec pl*) there are; **il y a eu 3 blessés** 3 people were injured, there were 3 injured; **il n'y avait que moi** I was the only one; **il y avait une fois ...** once upon a time, there was ...; **il y en a pour dire** *ou* **qui disent** there are some *ou* those who say, some say; **il y a enfant et enfant** there are children and children!; **il y en a, je vous jure*** some people, honestly!*, really, some people!*; **il n'y a pas de quoi** don't mention it; **qu'y a-t-il?, qu'est-ce qu'il y a?** what is it?, what's the matter?, what's up?*; **il y a que nous sommes mécontents*** we're annoyed, that's what*; **il n'y a que lui pour faire cela!** only he would do that!, trust him to do that!, it takes him to do that!; **il n'y a pas que nous à le dire** we're not the only ones who say *ou* to say that; **il n'y a pas à dire*, il est très intelligent** there's no denying he's very intelligent; **il doit/peut y ~ une raison** there must/may be a reason; **il n'y a qu'à les laisser partir** just let them go; **il n'y a qu'à protester** we shall just have to protest, why don't we protest; **quand il n'y en a plus, il y en a encore!** there's plenty more where that came from!*; **il n'y a pas que toi** you're not the only one!; **il n'y en a que pour mon petit frère, à la maison** my little brother gets all the attention at home.

(b) (*pour exprimer le temps écoulé*) **il y a 10 ans que je le connais** I have known him (for) 10 years; **il y aura 10 ans demain que je ne l'ai vu** it will be 10 years tomorrow since I last saw him; **il y avait longtemps qu'elle désirait ce livre** she had wanted this book for a long time; **il y a 10 ans, nous étions à Paris** 10 years ago we were in Paris; **il y a 10 jours que nous sommes rentrés** we got back 10 days ago, we have been back 10 days.

(c) (*pour exprimer la distance*) **il y a 10 km d'ici à Paris** it is 10 km from here to Paris; **combien y a-t-il d'ici à Paris?** how far is it from here to Paris?

4 *nm* **(a)** (*bien*) assets, resources. **son ~ était bien peu de chose** what he had wasn't much.

(b) (*Comm*) (*actif*) credit (side); (*billet de crédit*) credit note. (*Fin*) **~ fiscal** tax credit; *V* **doit.**

(c) ~s holdings, assets; **~s à l'étranger** foreign assets *ou* holdings.

avoisinant, e [avwazinɑ̃, ɑ̃t] *adj région, pays* neighbouring; *rue, ferme* nearby, neighbouring. **dans les rues ~es** in the nearby streets, in the streets close by *ou* nearby.

avoisiner [avwazine] (1) *vt lieu* to be near *ou* close to, border on; (*fig*) to border *ou* verge on *ou* upon.

avortement [avɔʀtəmɑ̃] *nm* (*Méd*) abortion. (*fig*) **~ de** failure of.

avorter [avɔʀte] (1) *vi* **(a)** (*Méd*) to have an abortion, abort. **faire ~ qn** *[personne]* to give sb an abortion, abort sb; *[remède etc]* to make sb abort; **se faire ~** to have an abortion.

(b) (*fig*) to fail, come to nothing. **faire ~ un projet** to frustrate *ou* wreck a plan; **projet avorté** abortive plan.

avorteur, -euse [avɔʀtœʀ, øz] *nm,f* abortionist.

avorton [avɔʀtɔ̃] *nm* (*péj: personne*) little runt (*péj*); (*arbre, plante*) puny *ou* stunted specimen; (*animal*) puny specimen.

avouable [avwabl(ə)] *adj* blameless, worthy (*épith*), respectable. **il a utilisé des procédés peu ~s** he used pretty disreputable methods *ou* methods which don't bear mentioning.

avoué, e [avwe] (*ptp de* **avouer**) **1** *adj ennemi, revenu, but* avowed. **2** *nm* ≈ solicitor, attorney-at-law (*US*).

avouer [avwe] (1) **1** *vt amour* to confess, avow (*littér*); *crime* to confess (to), own up to, avow (*littér*); *fait* to acknowledge, admit; *faiblesse, vice* to admit to, confess to. **~ avoir menti** to admit *ou* confess that one has lied, admit *ou* own up to lying; **~ que** to admit *ou* confess that; **elle est douée, je l'avoue** she is gifted, I must admit; *V* **faute.**

2 *vi* **(a)** (*se confesser*) *[coupable]* to confess, own up.

(b) (*admettre*) to admit, confess. **tu avoueras, c'est un peu fort!** you must admit *ou* confess, it is a bit much!

3 **s'avouer** *vpr*: **s'~ coupable** to admit *ou* confess one's guilt; **s'~ vaincu** to admit *ou* acknowledge defeat; **s'~ déçu** to admit to being disappointed, confess o.s. disappointed.

avril [avʀil] *nm* April. (*Prov*) **en ~ ne te découvre pas d'un fil** ≈ never cast a clout till May is out (*Prov*); *pour autres loc V* **septembre** *et* **poisson, premier.**

avunculaire [avɔ̃kylɛʀ] *adj* avuncular.

axe [aks(ə)] *nm* **(a)** (*Tech*) axle; (*Anat, Astron, Bot, Math*) axis.

(b) (*route*) trunk road (*Brit*). **les grands ~s (routiers)** the major trunk roads (*Brit*), the main roads; **l'~ Paris-Marseille** the main Paris-Marseilles road, the main road between Paris and Marseilles.

(c) (*fig*) *[débat, théorie, politique]* main line.

(d) (*Hist*) **l'A~** the Axis.

(e) (*dans le prolongement*) **dans l'~: cette rue est dans l'~ du boulevard** this street is on the same line as the boulevard; **mets-toi bien dans l'~ (de la cible)** line up on the target, get directly in line with the target.

axer [akse] (1) *vt*: **~ qch sur/autour de** to centre sth on/round.

axial, e, *mpl* **-iaux** [aksjal, jo] *adj* axial. **éclairage ~** central overhead lighting.

axiomatique [aksjɔmatik] **1** *adj* axiomatic. **2** *nf* axiomatics (*sg*).

axiome [aksjom] *nm* axiom.

axis [aksis] *nm* axis (vertebra).

ayant cause, *pl* **ayants cause** [ɛjɑ̃koz] *nm* (*Jur*) assignee, assign.

ayant droit, *pl* **ayants droit** [ɛjɑ̃dʀwa] *nm* **(a)** (*Jur*) = **ayant cause. (b)** *[prestation, pension]* eligible party. **~ à** party entitled to *ou* eligible for.

azalée [azale] *nf* azalea.

azimut [azimyt] *nm* azimuth. **chercher qn dans tous les ~s*** to look all over the place for sb*.

azimutal, e, *mpl* **-aux** [azimytal, o] *adj* azimuthal.

azote [azɔt] *nf* nitrogen.

azoté, e [azɔte] *adj* nitrogenous; *V* **engrais.**

aztèque [aztɛk] **1** *adj* Aztec. **2** *nmf*: **A~** Aztec.

azur [azyʀ] *nm* (*littér*) (*couleur*) azure, sky blue; (*ciel*) skies, sky; *V* **côte.**

azuré, e [azyʀe] (*ptp de* **azurer**) *adj* azure.

azurer [azyʀe] (1) *vt linge* to blue; (*littér*) to azure, tinge with blue.

azyme [azim] *adj* unleavened; *V* **pain.**

B

B, b [be] *nm* (*lettre*) B, b.
baba[1] [baba] *nm* (*Culin*) baba. ~ **au rhum** rum baba.
baba[2] [baba] **1** *nm*: **il l'a eu dans le ~‡** that loused things up for him all right‡. **2** *adj inv* (*) **en être** *ou* **en rester** ~ to be flabbergasted* *ou* dumbfounded; **j'en suis resté** ~ you could have knocked me down with a feather*.
B.A.-BA [beaba] *nm sg* A.B.C.-stage.
Babel [babɛl] *n V* **tour**[1].
Babette [babɛt] *nf* Betty, Bess.
babeurre [babœʀ] *nm* buttermilk.
babil [babi(l)] *nm* (*littér*) (*V* **babillard**) babble; prattle; twitter; chatter.
babillage [babijaʒ] *nm* (*V* **babillard**) babble, babbling; prattling; twitter(ing); chatter(ing).
babillard, e [babijaʀ, aʀd(ə)] **1** *adj* (*littér*) *personne* prattling, chattering; *bébé* babbling; *oiseau* twittering; *ruisseau* babbling, chattering. **2** *nm,f* chatterbox. **3 babillarde*** *nf* (*lettre*) letter, note.
babiller [babije] (1) *vi* (*V* **babillard**) to prattle; to chatter; to babble; to twitter.
babines [babin] *nfpl* (*Zool*) (pendulous) lips; *[chien]* chops; (*: *lèvres*) lips, chops‡.
babiole [babjɔl] *nf* (*bibelot*) trinket, knick-knack; (*fig: vétille*) trifle, triviality. (*cadeau sans importance*) **offrir une** ~ to give a small token *ou* a little something.
bâbord [babɔʀ] *nm* (*Naut*) port (side). **par** *ou* **à** ~ on the port side, to port.
babouche [babuʃ] *nf* babouche, Turkish *ou* oriental slipper.
babouin [babwɛ̃] *nm* baboon.
Babylone [babilɔn] *n* Babylon.
babylonien, -ienne [babilɔnjɛ, jɛn] **1** *adj* Babylonian. **2** *nm,f*: **B~(ne)** inhabitant *ou* native of Babylon.
bac[1]* [bak] *nm* (*Scol*) *abrév de* **baccalauréat.**
bac[2] [bak] *nm* **(a)** (*bateau*) ferry, ferryboat. ~ **à voitures** carferry.
(b) (*récipient*) tub; (*abreuvoir*) trough; (*Ind*) tank, vat; (*Peinture, Phot*) tray; *[évier]* sink. **évier avec deux ~s** double sink unit; ~ **à glace** ice-tray; ~ **à laver** washtub, (deep) sink; ~ **à légumes** vegetable compartment *ou* tray.
baccalauréat [bakalɔʀea] *nm Secondary School examination giving university entrance qualification* ≃ G.C.E. A-levels (*Brit*). (*Jur*) ~ **en droit** ≃ degree of Bachelor of Laws.
baccara [bakaʀa] *nm* baccara(t).
baccarat [bakaʀa] *nm*: **(cristal de)** ~ Baccarat crystal.
bacchanale [bakanal] *nf* **(a)** (*danse*) bacchanalian *ou* drunken dance; (†: *orgie*) orgy, drunken revel. **(b)** (*Antiq*) **~s** Bacchanalia.
bacchante [bakɑ̃t] *nf* **(a)** (*Antiq*) bacchante. **(b) ~s*** moustache, whiskers (*hum*).
bacchus [bakys] *nm* Bacchus.
bâchage [bɑʃaʒ] *nm* covering, sheeting over.
bâche [bɑʃ] *nf* canvas cover *ou* sheet. ~ **goudronnée** tarpaulin.
bachelier, -ière [baʃəlje, jɛʀ] *nm,f person who has passed the baccalauréat.* (*Jur*) ~ **en droit** ≃ Bachelor of Laws.
bâcher [bɑʃe] (1) *vt* to cover (with a canvas sheet *ou* a tarpaulin), put a canvas sheet *ou* a tarpaulin over. **camion bâché** covered lorry.
bachique [baʃik] *adj* (*Antiq, fig*) Bacchic. **chanson** ~ drinking song.
bachot[1]* [baʃo] *nm* (*Scol*) = **baccalauréat**; *V* **boîte.**
bachot[2] [baʃo] *nm* (small) boat, skiff.
bachotage [baʃɔtaʒ] *nm* (*Scol*) cramming. **faire du** ~ to cram (for an exam).
bachoter [baʃɔte] (1) *vi* (*Scol*) to cram (for an exam).
bacillaire [basilɛʀ] *adj maladie* bacillary; *malade* tubercular. **les ~s** tubercular cases *ou* patients.
bacille [basil] *nm* (*gén*) germ, bacillus (*T*).
bacillose [basiloz] *nf* (*gén*) bacillus infection; (*tuberculose*) tuberculosis.
bâclage [bɑklaʒ] *nm* botching, scamping.
bâcler [bɑkle] (1) *vt travail, devoir* to botch (up), scamp; *ouvrage* to throw together; *cérémonie* to skip through, hurry over. ~ **sa toilette** to have a quick wash, give o.s. a lick and a promise; **c'est du travail bâclé** it's slapdash work.
bactéricide [bakteʀisid] *adj* bactericidal.
bactérie [bakteʀi] *nf* bacterium.
bactérien, -ienne [bakteʀjɛ̃, jɛn] *adj* bacterial.
bactériologie [bakteʀjɔlɔʒi] *nf* bacteriology.
bactériologique [bakteʀjɔlɔʒik] *adj* bacteriological.
bactériologiste [bakteʀjɔlɔʒist(ə)] *nmf* bacteriologist.
bactériophage [bakteʀjɔfaʒ] *nm* bacteriophage.
badaud, e [bado, od] **1** *adj*: **les Parisiens sont très ~s** Parisians love to stop and stare *ou* are full of idle curiosity. **2** *nm,f* (*qui regarde*) curious *ou* gaping (*péj*) *ou* gawking (*péj*) onlooker; (*qui se promène*) stroller.
badauder [badode] (1) *vi* (*V* **badaud**) to stroll (*dans* about); to gawk (*devant* at).
badauderie [badodʀi] *nf* (idle) curiosity.
baderne [badɛʀn(ə)] *nf* (*péj*) **(vieille)** ~ old fogey*.
badigeon [badiʒɔ̃] *nm* (*V* **badigeonner**) distemper; whitewash; colourwash (*Brit*). **donner un coup de** ~ to give a coat of distemper *ou* whitewash.
badigeonnage [badiʒɔnaʒ] *nm* (*V* **badigeonner**) distempering; whitewashing; colourwashing; painting.
badigeonner [badiʒɔne] (1) *vt* **(a)** *mur intérieur* to distemper; *mur extérieur* to whitewash (*Brit*); (*en couleur*) to colourwash (*Brit*), give a colourwash (*Brit*) to; (*barbouiller*) *visage, surface* to smear, daub, cover (*de* with).
(b) (*Méd*) *plaie* to paint (*à, avec* with). **se ~ la gorge** to paint one's throat (*à* with).
(c) (*Culin*) to brush (*de* with).
badigeonneur [badiʒɔnœʀ] *nm* (*péj*) dauber (*péj*); (*Tech*) painter.
badin[1], **e**[1]† [badɛ̃, in] *adj* (*gai*) light-hearted, jocular; (*taquin*) playful. **sur un** *ou* **d'un ton** ~ light-heartedly, jocularly; playfully.
badin[2] [badɛ̃] *nm* (*Aviat*) airspeed indicator.
badinage [badinaʒ] *nm* (*propos légers*) banter (*U*), jesting talk (*U*). **sur un ton de** ~ in a jesting *ou* bantering *ou* light-hearted tone.
badine[2] [badin] *nf* switch.
badiner [badine] (1) *vi* **(a)** (†: *plaisanter*) to exchange banter, jest†. **pour** ~ for a jest†, in jest.
(b) c'est quelqu'un qui ne badine pas he's not a man to be trifled with; **il ne badine pas sur la discipline** he's a stickler for discipline, he has strict ideas about discipline; **il ne faut pas ~ avec ce genre de maladie** this sort of illness is not to be treated lightly, an illness of this sort should be taken seriously; **et je ne badine pas!** I'm in no mood for joking!, I'm not joking!
badinerie† [badinʀi] *nf* jest†.
baffe* [baf] *nf* slap, clout*. **tu veux une ~?** do you want your face slapped? *ou* want a clip on the ear?*
bafouer [bafwe] (1) *vt* to hold up to ridicule.
bafouillage [bafujaʒ] *nm* (*bredouillage*) spluttering, stammering; (*propos stupides*) gibberish (*U*), babble (*U*).
bafouille* [bafuj] *nf* (*lettre*) letter, note.
bafouiller [bafuje] (1) **1** *vi [personne]* (*bredouiller*) to splutter, stammer; (*tenir des propos stupides*) to talk gibberish, babble; *[moteur]* to splutter, misfire.
2 *vt* to splutter (out), stammer (out). **qu'est-ce qu'il bafouille?** what's he babbling *ou* jabbering on about?*
bafouilleur, -euse [bafujœʀ, øz] *nm,f* splutterer, stammerer.
bâfrer‡ [bɑfʀe] (1) **1** *vi* to guzzle*, gobble, wolf*. **2** *vt* to guzzle (down)*, gobble (down), bolt (down), wolf (down)*.
bâfreur, -euse‡ [bɑfʀœʀ, øz] *nm,f* greedy guts*, guzzler*.
bagage [bagaʒ] *nm* **(a)** (*gén pl: valises*) luggage (*U*), baggage (*U*). **faire/défaire ses ~s** to pack/unpack (one's luggage), do one's packing/unpacking; **envoyer qch en ~s accompagnés** to send sth as registered luggage; **~s à main** hand luggage.
(b) (*valise*) bag, piece of luggage; (*Mil*) kit. **il avait pour tout ~ une serviette** his only luggage was a briefcase.
(c) (*fig*) (*connaissances*) stock of knowledge; (*diplômes*) qualifications. **son ~ intellectuel/littéraire** his stock *ou* store of general/literary knowledge.
bagagiste [bagaʒist(ə)] *nm* porter, luggage *ou* baggage handler.
bagarre [bagaʀ] *nf* **(a)** (*U*) fighting. **il veut** *ou* **cherche la** ~ he wants *ou* is looking for a fight; **il aime la** ~ he loves fighting *ou* a fight.
(b) (*rixe*) fight, scuffle, brawl; (*fig: entre deux orateurs*) set-to, clash, barney*; (*Sport*) fight, battle (*fig*). ~ **générale** free-for-all; **violentes ~s** rioting.
bagarrer* [bagaʀe] (1) **1** *vi* (*se disputer*) to argue, wrangle; (*lutter*) to fight. **2 se bagarrer** *vpr* (*se battre*) to fight, scuffle, scrap*; (*se disputer*) to have a set-to *ou* a barney*. **ça s'est bagarré (dur) dans les rues** there was (heavy *ou* violent) rioting in the streets.
bagarreur, -euse* [bagaʀœʀ, øz] **1** *adj caractère* aggressive, fighting (*épith*). **il est** ~ he loves a fight. **2** *nm,f* (*pour arriver dans la vie*) fighter; (*Sport*) battler.
bagatelle [bagatɛl] *nf* **(a)** (*chose de peu de prix*) small thing, trinket; (†: *bibelot*) knick-knack, trinket.
(b) (*petite somme*) small *ou* paltry sum, trifle. **je l'ai eu pour une** ~ I got it for next to nothing; (*iro*) **un accident qui m'a coûté la ~ de 3.000 F** an accident which cost me the paltry sum of 3,000 francs *ou* a mere 3,000 francs (*iro*).
(c) (*fig: vétille*) trifle. **s'amuser à** *ou* **perdre son temps à des ~s** to fritter away one's time.
(d) († *ou hum: amour*) philandering. **être porté sur la** ~ *[homme]* to be a bit of a philanderer *ou* womanizer; *[femme]* to be a bit of a lass.
(e) (††) **~s!** fiddlesticks!†
bagnard [baɲaʀ] *nm* convict.
bagne [baɲ] *nm* (*Hist*) (*prison*) penal colony; (*peine*) penal servitude, hard labour. **être condamné au** ~ to be sentenced to

hard labour; (*fig*) **quel ~!*, c'est un vrai ~!*** it's a hard grind!, it's sheer slavery!

bagnole* [baɲɔl] *nf* motorcar, buggy‡. **vieille ~** old banger* (*Brit*), jalopy*.

bagou(t)* [bagu] *nm* volubility, glibness (*péj*). **avoir du ~** to have the gift of the gab, have a glib tongue (*péj*).

baguage [bagaʒ] *nm [oiseau, arbre]* ringing.

bague [bag] *nf (bijou)* ring; *[cigare]* band; *[oiseau]* ring; (*Tech*) collar. **elle lui a mis la ~ au doigt*** she has hooked him*; **~ de serrage** jubilee clip.

baguenaude* [bagnod] *nf*: **être en ~** to be gallivanting about.

baguenauder (se)* [bagnode] (1) *vpr (faire un tour)* to go for a stroll, go for a jaunt; (*traîner*) to mooch about* (*Brit*), trail around.

baguer [bage] (1) *vt* **(a)** *oiseau, arbre* to ring; (*Tech*) to collar. **elle avait les mains baguées** she had rings on her fingers; **cigare bagué** cigar with a band round it. **(b)** (*Couture*) to baste, tack.

baguette [bagɛt] **1** *nf* **(a)** (*bâton*) switch, stick. (*pour manger*) **~s** chopsticks; **~ de chef d'orchestre** (conductor's) baton; **sous la ~ de X** conducted by X, with X conducting; (*fig*) **mener** *ou* **faire marcher qn à la ~** to rule sb with an iron hand, keep a strong hand on sb.

(b) (*pain*) loaf *ou* stick of French bread.

(c) (*Constr*) bead(ing), strip of wood; (*Élec: cache-fils*) wood casing *ou* strip.

(d) (*Habillement*) clock.

2: baguette de coudrier hazel stick *ou* switch, divining rod; **baguette de fée** magic wand; **baguette de fusil** ramrod; **baguette magique** = **baguette de fée**; **baguette de sourcier** divining rod; **baguette de tambour** drumstick; **cheveux en baguettes de tambour** dead straight hair.

bah [ba] *excl* (*indifférence*) pooh!; (*doute*) well ...!, really!

Bahamas [baamas] *nfpl*: **les (îles) ~** the Bahamas.

bahut [bay] *nm* **(a)** (*coffre*) chest; (*buffet*) sideboard. **(b)** (*arg Scol*) school.

bai, e[1] [bɛ] *adj cheval* bay.

baie[2] [bɛ] *nf* **(a)** (*Géog*) bay. **(b)** (*Archit*) opening. (*fenêtre*) **~ (vitrée)** picture window.

baie[3] [bɛ] *nf* (*Bot*) berry.

baignade [bɛɲad] *nf* (*action*) bathing; (*bain*) bathe; swim; (*lieu*) bathing place. **~ interdite** no bathing; **c'est l'heure de la ~** it's time for a bathe *ou* a swim.

baigner [beɲe] (1) **1** *vt* **(a)** *bébé, chien* to bath; *pieds, visage, yeux* to bathe. **des larmes baignaient ses joues** his face was bathed in tears.

(b) baigné de bathed in; (*trempé de*) soaked with; **visage baigné de larmes/sueur** face bathed in tears/sweat; **chemise baignée de sang/sueur** shirt soaked with blood/sweat, blood-/sweat-soaked shirt; **forêt baignée de lumière** forest bathed in *ou* flooded with light.

(c) *[mer, rivière]* to wash, bathe; *[lumière]* to bathe, flood.

2 *vi* **(a)** (*tremper dans l'eau*) *[linge]* to soak, lie soaking (*dans* in); (*tremper dans l'alcool*) *[fruits]* to steep, soak (*dans* in). **la viande baignait dans la graisse** the meat was swimming in fat *ou* lay in a pool of fat; **la victime baignant dans son sang** the victim lying in a pool of blood; (*fig*) **la ville baigne dans la brume** the town is shrouded *ou* wrapped in mist; (*fig*) **tout baigne dans l'huile*** everything's hunky-dory*, everything's looking great*.

(b) (*fig: être plongé dans*) **il baigne dans la joie** his joy knows no bounds, he is bursting with joy; **~ dans le mystère** *[affaire]* to be shrouded *ou* wrapped *ou* steeped in mystery; *[personnes]* to be completely mystified *ou* baffled.

3 se baigner *vpr* (*dans la mer, une rivière*) to go bathing *ou* swimming, have a bathe *ou* a swim; (*dans une piscine*) to go swimming, have a swim; (*dans une baignoire*) to have a bath.

baigneur, -euse [bɛɲœʀ, øz] **1** *nm,f* bather, swimmer. **2** *nm* (*jouet*) dolly, baby doll.

baignoire [bɛɲwaʀ] *nf* **(a)** bath(tub). **~ sabot** = hip-bath. **(b)** (*Théât*) ground floor box, baignoire. **(c)** *[sous-marin]* conning tower.

bail [baj], *pl* **baux** [bo] **1** *nm* **(a)** (*Jur*) lease. **prendre à ~** to lease, take out a lease on; **donner à ~** to lease (out); **faire/passer un ~** to draw up/enter into a lease.

(b) (*fig*) **ça fait un ~!*** it's ages* (*que* since).

2: bail commercial commercial lease; **bail à ferme** farming lease; **bail à loyer** (house-)letting lease.

baille [baj] *nf* (*Naut*) (wooden) bucket. **à la ~!*** into the drink (with him)!*

bâillement [bajmɑ̃] *nm* **(a)** *[personne]* yawn. **(b)** *[col]* gaping *ou* loose fit.

bailler [baje] (1) *vt* (†† *ou hum*) to give (*fig*). **vous me la baillez belle!** *ou* **bonne!** that's a tall tale!

bâiller [baje] (1) *vi* **(a)** *[personne]* to yawn. **~ d'ennui** to yawn with *ou* from boredom; **~ à s'en décrocher la mâchoire** to yawn one's head off.

(b) (*être trop large*) *[col, décolleté]* to hang *ou* sit loose, gape; *[soulier]* to gape.

(c) (*être entr'ouvert*) *[couture, boutonnage]* to gape; *[porte]* to be ajar *ou* half-open; *[soulier]* to gape, be split open.

bailleur, bailleresse [bajœʀ, bajʀɛs] *nm,f* lessor. **~ de fonds** backer, sponsor.

bailli [baji] *nm* bailiff.

bailliage [bajaʒ] *nm* bailiwick.

bâillon [bajɔ̃] *nm* (*lit, fig*) gag. **mettre un ~ à qn** to gag sb.

bâillonnement [bajɔnmɑ̃] *nm* (*V* **bâillonner**) gagging; stifling.

bâillonner [bajɔne] (1) *vt personne* to gag; (*fig*) *presse, opposition, opinion* to gag, stifle.

bain [bɛ̃] **1** *nm* **(a)** (*dans une baignoire*) bath; (*dans une piscine*) swim; (*dans la mer*) bathe. **~ de boue/sang** mud/blood bath; (*fig*) **ce séjour à la campagne fut pour elle un ~ de fraîcheur** that stay in the country put new life into her *ou* revitalized her; **prendre un ~** (*dans une baignoire*) to have a bath; (*dans la mer, une rivière*) to have a swim *ou* bathe; (*dans une piscine*) to have a swim.

(b) (*liquide*) bath(water); (*Chim, Phot*) bath. **fais chauffer mon ~** heat my bath *ou* bathwater; **fais couler mon ~** run my bath (for me); (*Phot*) **~ de fixateur/de révélateur** fixing/developing bath.

(c) (*récipient*) (*baignoire*) bath(tub); *[teinturier]* vat.

(d) (*piscine*) **petit/grand ~** shallow/deep end; (*lieu*) **~s** baths; **~s publics/romains** public/Roman baths.

(e) (**loc*) **mettre qn dans le ~** (*informer*) to put sb in the picture; (*compromettre*) to incriminate sb, implicate sb; **en avouant, il nous a tous mis dans le ~** by owning up, he has involved us all (in it); **nous sommes tous dans le même ~** we're all in the same boat, we're in this together; **tu seras vite dans le ~** you'll soon pick it up *ou* get the hang of it* *ou* find your feet (*Brit*).

2: bains douches municipaux public baths (with showers); **bain de foule** walkabout; **prendre un bain de foule** to mingle with the crowd, go on a walkabout; **j'ai pris un bain de jouvence** it was a rejuvenating experience, it made me feel years younger; **bain-marie** *nm, pl* **bains-marie** (hot water in) double boiler, bain-marie; **faire chauffer au bain-marie** *sauce* to heat in a bain-marie *ou* a double boiler; *boîte de conserve* to immerse in boiling water; **bains de mer** sea bathing; **bain de mousse** bubble *ou* foam bath; **bain de pieds** (*récipient*) foot-bath; (*baignade*) paddle; **bain de siège** sitzbath; **prendre un bain de siège** to have a sitzbath, have a hip-bath; (*hum*) to sit at the edge of the water; **prendre un bain de soleil** to sunbathe; **les bains de soleil lui sont déconseillés** he has been advised against sunbathing; **bain turc** Turkish bath; **bain de vapeur** steam bath.

baïonnette [bajɔnɛt] *nf* (*Élec, Mil*) bayonet. **charge à la ~** bayonet charge; **charger ~ au canon** to charge with fixed bayonets.

baisemain [bɛzmɛ̃] *nm*: **il lui fit le ~** he kissed her hand; **le ~ ne se pratique plus** it is no longer the custom to kiss a woman's hand.

baisement [bɛzmɑ̃] *nm* (*Rel*) kissing.

baiser [beze] **1** *nm* kiss. **gros ~** smacking kiss*, smacker*; **~ rapide** quick kiss, peck; (*fin de lettre*) **bons ~s** love (and kisses); **~ de paix** kiss of peace.

2 (1) *vt* **(a)** (*frm*) *main, visage* to kiss.

(b) (∵) to screw∵, lay∵, fuck∵.

(c) (‡: *avoir, l'emporter sur*) to outdo, have‡. **il a été baisé, il s'est fait ~** he was really had‡.

3 *vi* (∵) to screw∵, fuck∵. **elle baise bien** she's a good fuck∵.

baisse [bɛs] *nf [température, prix, provisions]* fall, drop; *[baromètre]* fall; (*Bourse*) fall; *[pression, régime d'un moteur]* drop; *[niveau]* fall, drop, lowering; *[eaux]* drop, fall; *[popularité]* decline, drop, lessening (*de* in). **être en ~** to be falling; to be dropping; to be sinking; to be declining *ou* lessening; (*Comm*) **cette semaine ~ sur le beurre** this week butter down in price *ou* reduced.

baisser [bese] (1) **1** *vt* **(a)** *objet* to lower; *store* to lower, pull down; *vitre* to lower, let down; (*à l'aide d'une manivelle*) to wind down; *col* to turn down; (*Théât*) *rideau* to lower, ring down. **baisse la branche pour que je puisse l'attraper** pull the branch down so (that) I can reach it; **~ pavillon** (*Naut*) to lower *ou* strike the flag; (*fig*) to show the white flag, give in.

(b) *main, bras* to lower. **~ la tête** to lower *ou* bend one's head; (*de chagrin, honte*) to hang *ou* bow one's head (*de* in); (*) *[plantes]* to wilt, droop; **~ les yeux** to look down, lower one's eyes; **elle entra, les yeux baissés** she came in with downcast eyes; **faire ~ les yeux à qn** to outstare sb, stare sb out of countenance; **~ le nez*** (*de honte*) to hang one's head; **~ le nez dans son livre*** to bury one's nose in one's book; **~ le nez dans son assiette*** to bend over one's plate; (*fig*) **~ les bras** to give up, throw in the sponge*.

(c) *chauffage, lampe, radio* to turn down, turn low; *voix, ton* to lower. (*Aut*) **~ ses phares** to dip one's headlights; **~ le ton** (*lit*) to modify one's tone; (*fig*) to climb down; **baisse un peu le ton!*** pipe down!*

(d) *prix* to lower, bring down, reduce.

(e) *mur* to lower.

2 *vi* **(a)** *[température]* to fall, drop, go down; *[baromètre]* to fall; *[pression]* to drop, fall; *[marée]* to go out, ebb; *[eaux]* to subside, go down, sink; *[réserves, provisions]* to run *ou* get low; *[prix]* to come down, go down, drop, fall; (*Bourse*) to fall, drop; *[popularité]* to decline, lessen, drop; *[soleil]* to go down, sink. **il a baissé dans mon estime** he has sunk *ou* gone down *ou* dropped in my estimation.

(b) *[vue, mémoire, forces, santé]* to fail, dwindle; *[talent]* to decline, drop, fall off. **le jour baisse** the light is failing *ou* dwindling, it is getting dark; **il a beaucoup baissé ces derniers temps** (*physiquement*) he has got a lot weaker recently; (*mentalement*) his mind has got a lot weaker recently.

3 se baisser *vpr* (*pour ramasser qch*) to bend down, stoop; (*pour éviter qch*) to duck. **il n'y a qu'à se ~ pour les ramasser*** there are loads* of them, they are lying thick on the ground.

4 *nm* (*Théât*) final curtain. **avant le/au ~ du rideau** before/when the curtain falls, before/at the final curtain.

baissier [besje] *nm* (*Bourse*) bear.

bajoues [baʒu] *nfpl* (*Zool*) chaps, chops; (*fig: joues*) heavy *ou* flabby (*péj*) cheeks.

Bakélite [bakelit] *nf* ® Bakelite ®.

bal, *pl* **~s** [bal] **1** *nm* (*réunion*) dance; (*habillé*) ball; (*lieu*) dance hall. **aller au ~** to go dancing; **~ champêtre** open-air dance; ~ **costumé/masqué** fancy dress/masked ball; ~ **populaire** dance, hop*. **2: bal musette** popular dance (*to the accordion*); **bal travesti** costume ball.

balade* [balad] *nf* (*à pied*) walk, stroll; (*en auto*) drive, run. **être en** ~ to be out for a walk (*ou* a drive); **faire une** ~, **aller en** ~ to go for a walk (*ou* a drive).

balader* [balade] (1) **1** *vt* **(a)** (*traîner*) *chose* to trail round, carry about; *personne* to trail round.

(b) (*promener*) *personne, animal* to take for a walk.

2 se balader *vpr* (*à pied*) to go for a walk *ou* a stroll *ou* a saunter; (*en auto*) to go for a drive; (*traîner*) to traipse round. **aller se** ~ **en Afrique** to go touring *ou* gallivanting round Africa; **la lettre s'est baladée de bureau en bureau** the letter has been pushed round from one office to another.

baladeur, -euse [baladœʀ, øz] **1** *adj* wandering, roving. **avoir la main** ~**euse** *ou* **les mains** ~**euses** to have wandering *ou* roving hands. **2 baladeuse** *nf* (*lampe*) inspection lamp.

baladin† [baladɛ̃] *nm* wandering entertainer *ou* actor.

balafre [balafʀ(ə)] *nf* (*blessure*) gash; (*intentionnelle*) slash; (*cicatrice*) scar.

balafrer [balafʀe] (1) *vt* (*V* **balafre**) to gash; to slash; to scar. **il s'est balafré** he gashed his face.

balai [balɛ] **1** *nm* (*gén*) broom, brush; *[bruyère, genêt]* besom, broom; (*Élec*) brush; (*Aut*) *[essuie-glace]* blade. **passer le** ~ to sweep the floor, give the floor a sweep; **donner un coup de** ~ (*lit*) to give the floor a (quick) sweep; (*fig*) to make a clean sweep.

2: balai-brosse *nm, pl* **balai-brosses** (long-handled) scrubbing brush; **balai de crin** horsehair brush; **balai éponge** squeezy mop; **balai mécanique** carpet sweeper.

balaise‡ [balɛz] *adj* = **balèze‡**.

balance [balɑ̃s] **1** *nf* **(a)** (*instrument*) pair of scales; (*à bascule*) weighing machine; (*pour salle de bains*) (bathroom) scales (*pl*); (*pour cuisine*) (kitchen) scales (*pl*); (*Chim, Phys*) balance.

(b) (*loc*) **(main)tenir la** ~ **égale entre 2 rivaux** to hold the scales even between 2 rivals; **être en** ~ *[proposition]* to hang in the balance; *[candidat]* to be under consideration; **être en** ~ **entre 2 idées** to be wavering between 2 ideas; **mettre dans la** *ou* **en** ~ **le pour et le contre** to weigh up the pros and cons; **il a mis** *ou* **jeté toute son autorité dans la** ~ he used his authority to tip the scales; **si on met dans la** ~ **son ancienneté** if you take his seniority into account, if you include his seniority in his favour.

(c) (*Comm, Écon, Élec, Pol*) balance. ~ **de l'actif et du passif** balance of assets and liabilities.

(d) (*Astron*) **la B**~ Libra, the Balance. **être de la B**~ to be Libra *ou* a Libran.

(e) (*Pêche*) drop-net.

2: balance automatique shop scales (*pl*); **balance à bascule** (*à marchandises*) weighbridge; (*à personnes*) weighing machine; **balance du commerce** *ou* **commerciale** balance of trade; **balance des comptes** balance of payments; **balance des forces** balance of power; **balance de ménage** kitchen scales (*pl*); **balance des paiements** = **balance des comptes**; **balance des pouvoirs** balance of power; **balance de précision** precision balance; **balance de Roberval** (Roberval's) balance; **balance romaine** steelyard.

balancé, e [balɑ̃se] (*ptp de* **balancer**) *adj*: **phrase bien/harmonieusement** ~**e** well-turned/nicely balanced phrase; *[personne]* **être bien** ~* to be well-built; **elle est bien** ~**e*** she's got a smashing figure*, she's got what it takes*.

balancelle [balɑ̃sɛl] *nf* (*dans un jardin*) couch hammock.

balancement [balɑ̃smɑ̃] *nm* **(a)** (*mouvement*) *[corps]* sway; *[bras]* swing(ing); *[bateau]* motion; *[hanches, branches]* swaying. **(b)** (*Littérat, Mus*) balance.

balancer [balɑ̃se] (3) **1** *vt* **(a)** *chose, bras, jambe* to swing; *bateau, bébé* to rock; (*sur une balançoire*) to swing, push, give a push to. **veux-tu que je te balance?** do you want me to push you? *ou* give you a push?; **le vent balance les branches** the wind rocks the branches *ou* sets the branches swaying.

(b) (‡: *lancer*) to fling, chuck*. **balance-moi mon crayon** fling *ou* chuck* me over my pencil; ~ **qch à la tête de qn** to fling *ou* chuck* sth at sb's head; (*fig*) **qu'est-ce qu'il leur a balancé!** he didn't half give them a telling-off!*, he didn't half bawl them out!‡

(c) (‡: *se débarrasser de*) *vieux meubles* to chuck out* *ou* away*. ~ **qn** to give sb the push‡ *ou* the boot‡, chuck sb out*; **balance-ça à la poubelle** chuck it in the dustbin*; **il s'est fait** ~ **du lycée** he got kicked out* *ou* chucked out* of school; **j'ai envie de tout** ~ (*métier, travail*) I feel like chucking it all up‡; (*vieux objets*) I feel like chucking the whole lot out* *ou* away*.

(d) (*équilibrer*) *compte, phrases, paquets* to balance. ~ **le pour et le contre**† to weigh (up) the pros and cons; **tout bien balancé** everything considered.

2 *vi* **(a)** (†: *hésiter*) to waver, hesitate, dither. (*hum*) **entre les deux mon cœur balance** I can't bring myself to choose (between them).

(b) (*osciller*) *[objet]* to swing.

3 se balancer *vpr* **(a)** (*osciller*) *[bras, jambes]* to swing; *[bateau]* to rock; *[branches]* to sway; *[personne]* (*sur une balançoire*) to swing, have a swing; (*sur une bascule*) to seesaw, play on a seesaw. **se** ~ **sur ses jambes** *ou* **sur un pied** to sway about, sway from side to side; **ne te balance pas sur ta chaise!** don't tip back on your chair!; (*Naut*) **se** ~ **sur ses ancres** to ride at anchor.

(b) (*: *se ficher de*) **se** ~ **de** not to give a darn about*; **je m'en balance** I couldn't give a darn* (about it), I couldn't care less (about it).

balancier [balɑ̃sje] *nm* *[pendule]* pendulum; *[montre]* balance wheel; *[équilibriste]* (balancing) pole.

balançoire [balɑ̃swaʀ] *nf* (*suspendue*) swing; (*sur pivot*) seesaw. **faire de la** ~ to have (a go on) a swing *ou* a seesaw.

balayage [balɛjaʒ] *nm* sweeping; (*Élec, Rad*) scanning.

balayer [baleje] (8) *vt* **(a)** (*ramasser*) *poussière, feuilles mortes* to sweep up, brush up.

(b) (*nettoyer*) *pièce* to sweep (out); *trottoir* to sweep. (*fig*) **le vent balaie la plaine** the wind sweeps across the plain.

(c) (*chasser*) *feuilles* to sweep away; *soucis, obstacles* to sweep away, get rid of; *personnel* to sack*, fire*. **l'armée balayant tout sur son passage** the army sweeping aside all that lies (*ou* lay) in its path; **le gouvernement a été balayé par ce nouveau scandale** the government was swept out of office by this new scandal.

(d) (*Tech*) *[phares]* to sweep (across); *[vague]* to sweep over; (*Élec, Rad*) *[radar]* to scan; *[tir]* to sweep (across).

balayette [balɛjɛt] *nf* small (hand)brush.

balayeur, -euse [balɛjœʀ, øz] **1** *nm,f* roadsweeper. **2 balayeuse** *nf* roadsweeping machine, roadsweeper.

balayures [balejyʀ] *nfpl* sweepings.

balbutiement [balbysimɑ̃] *nm* (*paroles confuses*) stammering, mumbling; *[bébé]* babbling. **les premiers** ~**s de l'enfant** the child's first faltering attempts at speech; (*fig: débuts*) ~**s** beginnings; **cette science en est à ses premiers** ~**s** this science is still in its infancy.

balbutier [balbysje] (7) **1** *vi* (*bredouiller*) to stammer, mumble. **2** *vt* to stammer (out), falter out, mumble.

balcon [balkɔ̃] *nm* (*Constr*) balcony. (*Théât*) **(premier)** ~ dress circle; **deuxième** ~ upper circle; **loge/fauteuil de** ~ box/seat in the dress circle.

baldaquin [baldakɛ̃] *nm* (*dais*) baldaquin, canopy; *[lit]* tester, canopy.

Bâle [bɑl] *n* Basle.

Baléares [baleaʀ] *nfpl*: **les** ~ the Balearic Islands, the Baleares.

baleine [balɛn] *nf* **(a)** whale. **(b)** (*fanon*) (piece of) whalebone, baleen; (*pour renforcer*) stiffener. ~ **de corset** (corset-)stay; ~ **de parapluie** umbrella rib.

baleiné, e [balene] *adj col* stiffened; *gaine, soutien-gorge* boned.

baleineau, *pl* ~**x** [balɛno] *nm* whale calf.

baleinier, -ière [balenje, jɛʀ] **1** *adj* whaling. **2** *nm* (*pêcheur, bateau*) whaler. **3 baleinière** *nf* whaler *ou* whaling boat.

balèze‡ [balɛz] *adj* (*musclé*) brawny, hefty*; (*doué*) terrific*, great* (*en* at).

balisage [balizaʒ] *nm* (*V* **balise**) **(a)** (*action*) beaconing; marking-out. **(b)** (*signaux*) beacons, buoys; runway lights; (road)signs; markers.

balise [baliz] *nf* (*Naut*) beacon, (marker) buoy; (*Aviat*) beacon, runway light; (*Aut*) (road)sign; *[piste de ski]* marker.

baliser [balize] (1) *vt* (*V* **balise**) to mark out with beacons *ou* buoys *ou* lights; to signpost, put signs (up) on; to mark out.

baliseur [balizœʀ] *nm* (*personne*) ≃ (Trinity House) buoy-keeper; (*bateau*) ≃ Trinity House boat.

balistique [balistik] **1** *adj* ballistic. **2** *nf* ballistics (*sg*).

baliverne [balivɛʀn] *nf*: ~**s** twaddle, nonsense; **dire des** ~**s** to talk nonsense *ou* twaddle; **s'amuser à des** ~**s** to fool around; ~**s!**† nonsense!, balderdash!†, fiddlesticks!†

balkanique [balkanik] *adj* Balkan.

Balkans [balkɑ̃] *nmpl*: **les** ~ the Balkans.

ballade [balad] *nf* (*poème court, Mus*) ballade; (*poème long*) ballad.

ballant, e [balɑ̃, ɑ̃t] **1** *adj*: **les bras** ~**s** with arms dangling, with swinging arms; **les jambes** ~**es** with dangling legs; **ne reste pas là, les bras** ~**s*** don't stand there looking helpless *ou* with your arms dangling at your sides.

2 *nm* (*mou*) *[câble]* slack, play; *[chargement]* sway, roll. **avoir du** ~ *[câble]* to be slack; *[chargement]* to be slack *ou* loose; **donner du** ~ **(à un filin)** to give some slack *ou* play (to a rope).

ballast [balast] *nm* (*Rail*) ballast; (*Naut*) ballast tank.

balle[1] [bal] *nf* **(a)** (*projectile*) bullet. ~ **dum-dum/explosive/traçante** dum-dum/explosive/tracer bullet; ~ **perdue** stray bullet; **percé** *ou* **criblé de** ~**s** *chose* full of *ou* riddled with bullet holes; *personne* riddled with bullet holes *ou* bullets; **prendre une** ~ **dans la peau*** to get shot *ou* plugged‡; **finir avec douze** ~**s dans la peau*** to end up in front of a firing squad; (*fig*) **saisir la** ~ **au bond** to jump at the opportunity.

(b) (*Sport*) ball. ~ **de golf/de ping-pong** golf/table tennis ball; **jouer à la** ~ to play (with a) ball; **à toi la** ~**!** catch!

(c) (*Sport*) shot, ball. **c'est une** ~ **bien placée** *ou* **une belle** ~ that's a well placed *ou* good shot; **faire des** *ou* **quelques** ~**s** to have a knock-up; (*Tennis*) ~ **de jeu/match/set** game/match/set point.

(d) ~**s*** francs.

balle[2] [bal] *nf* (*Agr, Bot*) husk, chaff.

balle[3] [bal] *nf* *[coton, laine]* bale.

balle[4]* [bal] *nf* chubby face. **il a une bonne** ~ he has a jolly face.

baller [bale] (1) *vi* *[bras, jambes]* to dangle, hang loosely; *[tête]* to hang; *[chargement]* to be slack *ou* loose.

ballerine [balʀin] *nf* (*danseuse*) ballerina, ballet dancer; (*soulier*) ballet shoe, ballerina.

ballet [balɛ] *nm* (*danse, spectacle*) ballet; (*musique*) ballet music. (*compagnie*) **les B**~**s russes** the Russian Ballet.

ballon [balɔ̃] **1** *nm* **(a)** (*Sport*) ball. ~ **de football** football; ~ **de rugby** rugby ball; (*fig*) **le** ~ **rond** soccer; **le** ~ **ovale** rugger.

(b) ~ **(en baudruche)** (child's toy) balloon.

(c) (*Aviat*) balloon. **monter en** ~ to go up in a balloon; **voyager en** ~ to travel by balloon.

(d) (*Géog*) round-topped mountain, balloon.

(e) (*verre*) wineglass, brandy glass; (*contenu*) glass (of wine).

(f) **avoir le** ~**‡** to be expecting*, be in the family way*.

2: **ballon de barrage** barrage balloon; **ballon captif** captive balloon; **ballon dirigeable** airship; **ballon d'eau chaude** hot-water tank; **ballon d'essai** (*Mét*) pilot balloon; (*fig*) test of public opinion, feeler; **ballon d'oxygène** oxygen bottle; **ballon-sonde** *nm, pl* **ballons-sondes** sounding balloon.
ballonnement [balɔnmɑ̃] *nm* feeling of distension, flatulence; (*Vét*) bloat.
ballonner [balɔne] (1) *vt ventre* to distend; *personne* to blow out; (*Vét*) *animal* to cause bloat in. **j'ai le ventre ballonné, je me sens ballonné, je suis ballonné** I feel bloated, my stomach feels distended.
ballonnet [balɔnɛ] *nm* (*gén, Aviat, Mét*) (small) balloon.
ballot [balo] *nm* **(a)** (*paquet*) bundle, package. **(b)** (*: *nigaud*) nitwit*, silly ass*. **tu es/c'est ~ de l'avoir oublié** you're/it's a bit daft to have forgotten it*.
ballottage [balɔtaʒ] *nm* (*Pol*) **il y a ~** there will have to be a second ballot, people will have to vote again; **M Dupont est en ~** M Dupont has to stand again at the second ballot.
ballottement [balɔtmɑ̃] *nm* (*V* **ballotter**) banging about; rolling; lolling; bouncing; tossing, bobbing; shaking.
ballotter [balɔte] (1) **1** *vi [objet]* to roll around, bang about; *[tête, membres]* to loll; *[poitrine]* to bounce; *[bateau]* to toss, bob about.
2 *vt* (*gén pass*) *personne* to shake about, jolt; *bateau* to toss (about). **on est ballotté dans ce train** you get shaken about *ou* thrown about in this train; (*fig*) **être ballotté entre 2 sentiments contraires** to be tossed between 2 conflicting feelings; **cet enfant a été ballotté entre plusieurs écoles** this child has been shifted around *ou* shunted around* from school to school.
ballottine [balɔtin] *nf* (*Culin*) ≃ meat loaf (*made with poultry*).
balluchon [balyʃɔ̃] *nm* (†) bundle (*of clothes*); (*) belongings. **faire son ~*** to pack up one's traps.
balnéaire [balneɛʀ] *adj* bathing; *V* **station.**
balourd, e [baluʀ, uʀd(ə)] **1** *nm,f* (*: *lourdaud*) dolt, fathead*, clumsy oaf*. **qu'il est ~!** what a dolt he is! **2** *nm* (*Tech*) unbalance.
balourdise [baluʀdiz] *nf* **(a)** (*maladresse manuelle*) clumsiness; (*manque de finesse*) fatheadedness*, doltishness. **(b)** (*gaffe*) blunder, boob*.
balsa [balza] *nm* balsa (wood).
balsamier [balzamje] *nm* balsam tree.
balsamine [balzamin] *nf* balsam.
balsamique [balzamik] *adj* balsamic.
balte [balt] *adj pays, peuple* Baltic.
balthazar [baltazaʀ] *nm* **(a)** (*Antiq, Rel*) **B~** Belshazzar. **(b)** (†: *banquet*) feast, banquet. **(c)** (*bouteille*) balthazar.
baltique [baltik] **1** *adj mer, région* Baltic. **2** *nf*: **la (mer) B~** the Baltic (Sea).
baluchon [balyʃɔ̃] *nm* = **balluchon.**
balustrade [balystʀad] *nf* (*Archit*) balustrade; (*garde-fou*) railing, handrail.
balustre [balystʀ(ə)] *nm* (*Archit*) baluster; *[siège]* spoke.
balzacien, -ienne [balzasjɛ̃, jɛn] *adj* Balzacian.
balzan, e [balzɑ̃, an] **1** *adj cheval* with white stockings. **2 balzane** *nf* white stocking.
bambin [bɑ̃bɛ̃] *nm* small child, little lad*.
bambochard, e [bɑ̃bɔʃaʀ, aʀd(ə)] = **bambocheur.**
bambocher* [bɑ̃bɔʃe] (1) *vi* (*faire la noce*) to live it up*, have a wild time.
bambocheur, -euse [bɑ̃bɔʃœʀ, øz] **1** *adj tempérament* revelling. **2** *nm,f* (*: *noceur*) reveller, fast liver.
bambou [bɑ̃bu] *nm* bamboo; (*canne*) bamboo (walking) stick.
bamboula* [bɑ̃bula] *nf*: **faire la ~** to live it up*, have a wild time.
ban [bɑ̃] *nm* **(a)** *[mariage]* **~s** banns.
(b) *[applaudissements]* round of applause, cheer; *[tambour]* drum roll; *[clairon]* bugle call, fanfare. **faire un ~ à qn** to applaud *ou* cheer sb; **un ~ pour X!, ouvrez le ~!** (let's have) a hand for* *ou* a round of applause for X!, ≃ three cheers for X!
(c) (*Hist*) proclamation.
(d) (*loc*) (*Hist*) **être/mettre au ~ de l'Empire** to be banished/banish from the Empire; (*fig*) **être/mettre au ~ de la société** to be outlawed/outlaw from society; (*Hist*) **le ~ et l'arrière ~** the barons and vassals; **le ~ et l'arrière ~ de sa famille/de ses amis** every last one of *ou* the entire collection of his relatives/his friends.
banal, e[1], *mpl* **~s** [banal] *adj* (*ordinaire*) *roman, conversation* banal, trite; *idée* banal, trite, well-worn; *vie* humdrum, banal; *personne* run-of-the-mill, ordinary; *nouvelle, incident* (*courant*) commonplace, everyday (*épith*); (*insignifiant*) trivial. **il n'y a rien là que de très ~** there is nothing at all unusual *ou* out of the ordinary about that; **une grippe ~e** a common or garden case of flu; **un personnage peu ~** an unusual character; **haïr le ~** to hate what is banal *ou* what is trite.
banal, e[2], *mpl* **-aux** [banal, o] *adj* (*Hist*) **four/moulin ~** communal *ou* village oven/mill.
banalement [banalmɑ̃] *adv* (*V* **banal**[1]) tritely; in a humdrum way. **tout ~** quite simply; **c'est arrivé très ~** it happened in the most ordinary way.
banalisation [banalizɑsjɔ̃] *nf* (*Univ*) opening to the police.
banaliser [banalize] (1) *vt* **(a)** *expression* to make commonplace *ou* trite; *vie* to rob of its originality. **ce qui banalise la vie quotidienne** what makes life humdrum *ou* robs life of its excitement.
(b) *voiture de police* to disguise; *campus* to open to the police. (*Police*) **voiture banalisée** unmarked police vehicle.
banalité [banalite] *nf* (*V* **banal**[1]) **(a)** (*caractère*) banality; triteness; ordinariness; triviality. **(b)** (*propos*) truism, platitude, trite remark.
banane [banan] *nf* **(a)** (*fruit*) banana. **(b)** (*Aut*) overrider. **(c)** (*Coiffure*) French plait. **(d)** (*arg Mil*) medal, decoration, gong*. **(e)** (*arg Aviat*) twin-rotor helicopter, chopper*. **(f)** *[skieur]* waist-bag.
bananeraie [bananʀɛ] *nf* banana plantation.
bananier [bananje] *nm* (*arbre*) banana tree; (*bateau*) banana boat.
banc [bɑ̃] **1** *nm* **(a)** (*siège*) seat, bench. **~ (d'école)** (desk) seat; **nous nous sommes connus sur les ~s de l'école** we've known each other since we were at school together.
(b) (*Géol*) (*couche*) layer, bed; *[coraux]* reef. **~ de sable/vase** sand/mudbank; (*Can*) **~ de neige** snowdrift, snowbank.
(c) *[poissons]* shoal.
(d) (*Tech*) (work)bench.
(e) (*Mét*) bank, patch.
2: (*Jur*) **banc des accusés** dock, bar; (*Jur*) **banc des avocats** bar; **banc d'église** pew; **banc d'essai** (*Tech*) test bed; (*fig*) testing ground; **émission qui sert de banc d'essai pour jeunes chanteurs** programme that gives young singers a chance to show their talents; (*Parl*) **banc des ministres** government front bench; (*Rel*) **banc d'œuvre** ≃ churchwardens' pew; (*Can*) **Cour du Banc de la Reine** Queen's Bench; (*Jur*) **banc des témoins** witness box (*Brit*), witness stand (*US*).
bancable [bɑ̃kabl(ə)] *adj* bankable.
bancaire [bɑ̃kɛʀ] *adj* banking. **chèque ~** (bank) cheque.
bancal, e, *mpl* **~s** [bɑ̃kal] *adj* **(a)** *personne* (*boiteux*) limping, wobbly*; (*aux jambes arquées*) bandy-legged. **(b)** *table, chaise* wobbly, rickety. **(c)** *idée, raisonnement* shaky, unsound.
banco [bɑ̃ko] *nm* banco. **faire ~** to go banco.
bandage [bɑ̃daʒ] *nm* **(a)** (*objet*) *[blessé]* bandage; *[roue]* (*en métal*) band, hoop; (*en caoutchouc*) tyre. **~ herniaire** truss. **(b)** (*action*) *[blessé]* bandaging; *[ressort]* stretching; *[arc]* bending.
bandagiste [bɑ̃daʒist(ə)] *nmf* truss maker *ou* manufacturer.
bande[1] [bɑ̃d] **1** *nf* **(a)** (*ruban*) (*en tissu, métal*) band, strip; (*en papier*) strip; (*de sable*) strip, tongue; (*Ciné*) film; *[magnétophone]* tape; (*Presse*) wrapper; (*Méd*) bandage. (*Mil*) **~ (de mitrailleuse)** (ammunition) belt; **journal sous ~** mailed newspaper.
(b) (*dessin, motif*) stripe; *[chaussée]* line; *[assiette]* band; (*Hér*) bend.
(c) (*Billard*) cushion. **jouer la ~** to play (the ball) off the cushion; (*fig*) **faire/obtenir qch par la ~** to do/get sth by devious means *ou* in a roundabout way; **apprendre qch par la ~** to hear of sth indirectly *ou* through the grapevine*.
(d) (*Naut*) list. **donner de la ~** to list.
2: (*Phys*) **bande d'absorption** absorption band; **bande dessinée** comic strip, strip cartoon; (*Rad*) **bande de fréquence** waveband; **bande illustrée** = **bande dessinée**; **bande magnétique** magnetic tape; **bande molletière** puttee; **bande perforée** punched *ou* perforated tape; **bande de roulement** *[pneu]* tread; (*Ciné*) **bande sonore** sound track; **bande de terre** strip *ou* tongue of land; (*Méd*) **bande Velpeau** crêpe bandage.
bande[2] [bɑ̃d] *nf* **(a)** (*groupe*) *[gens]* band, group, gang*; *[oiseaux]* flock. **~ de loups/chiens** pack of wolves/dogs; **~ de lions** troop *ou* pride (*littér*) of lions; **~ de singes** troop of monkeys; **ils sont partis en ~** they set off in a group, they all went off together.
(b) (*groupe constitué*) set, gang; *[pirates]* band; *[voleurs]* gang, band. **~ armée** armed band *ou* gang; **il ne fait pas partie de leur ~** he's not in their crowd *ou* set *ou* gang; **ils sont toute une ~ d'amis** they make up a whole crowd *ou* group of friends; **faire ~ à part** (*lit*) to keep aloof *ou* apart, make a separate group; (*fig*) *[une personne]* to be a lone wolf; *[une ou plusieurs personnes]* to keep to o.s.
(c) (*: *groupe de*) **~ de** bunch of*, pack of*; **~ d'imbéciles!** pack of idiots!*, bunch of fools!*; **c'est une ~ de paresseux** they're a lazy lot *ou* bunch* *ou* crowd*.
bandeau, *pl* **~x** [bɑ̃do] *nm* **(a)** (*ruban*) headband, bandeau; (*pansement*) head bandage; (*pour les yeux*) blindfold. **mettre un ~ à qn** to blindfold sb; **avoir un ~ sur l'œil** to wear an eye patch; (*fig*) **avoir un ~ sur les yeux** to be blind.
(b) (*Coiffure*) **porter les cheveux en ~** to wear one's hair coiled round one's head.
bandelette [bɑ̃dlɛt] *nf* strip of cloth, (narrow) bandage; *[momie]* wrapping, bandage.
bander [bɑ̃de] (1) **1** *vt* **(a)** (*entourer*) *genou, plaie* to bandage. **~ les yeux à qn** to blindfold sb; **les yeux bandés** blindfold(ed).
(b) (*tendre*) *corde* to strain, tauten; *arc* to bend; *ressort* to stretch, tauten; *muscles* to tense.
2 *vi* (**) to have an erection, have a hard-on**.
banderille [bɑ̃dʀij] *nf* banderilla.
banderole [bɑ̃dʀɔl] *nf* (*drapeau*) banderole. **~ publicitaire** streamer.
bandit [bɑ̃di] *nm* (*voleur*) gangster, thief; (*assassin*) gangster; (*brigand*) bandit; (*fig: escroc*) crook, shark*; (*: *enfant*) rascal. **~ armé** gunman; **~ de grand chemin** highwayman.
banditisme [bɑ̃ditism(ə)] *nm* (*actions criminelles*) crime. (*fig*) **300 F pour cette réparation, c'est du ~!** 300 francs for this repair job – it's daylight robbery!
bandoulière [bɑ̃duljɛʀ] *nf* (*gén*) shoulder strap; (*Mil*) bandoleer, bandolier. **en ~** slung across the shoulder.
bang [bɑ̃g] **1** *nm inv*: **~ (supersonique)** supersonic bang, sonic boom. **2** *excl* bang!, crash!
banjo [bɑ̃ʒo] *nm* banjo.
banlieue [bɑ̃ljø] *nf* suburbs, outskirts. **proche/moyenne/grande ~** inner *ou* immediate/inner *ou* near/outer suburbs; **Paris et sa (grande) ~** greater Paris; **la grande ~ de Paris** the outer suburbs of Paris, the commuter belt of Paris; **la ~ rouge** the Communist-controlled suburbs of Paris; **habiter en ~** to live in

the suburbs; **de** ~ *maison, ligne de chemin de fer* suburban (*épith*); *train* commuter (*épith*).
banlieusard, e [bɑ̃ljøzaʀ, aʀd(ə)] *nm,f* suburbanite, (suburban) commuter.
banni, e [bani] (*ptp de* **bannir**) *nm,f* exile.
bannière [banjɛʀ] *nf* **(a)** banner. (*fig*) **se battre** *ou* **se ranger sous la** ~ **de qn** to fight on sb's side *ou* under sb's banner. **(b)** (*: *pan de chemise*) shirttail. **il se promène toujours en** ~ he's always walking round with his shirttail hanging out.
bannir [baniʀ] (2) *vt citoyen* to banish; *pensée* to banish, dismiss; *mot, sujet, aliment* to banish, exclude (*de* from); *usage* to prohibit, put a ban on. (*frm*) **je l'ai banni de ma maison** I forbade him to darken my door (*frm*), I told him never to set foot in my house again.
bannissement [banismɑ̃] *nm* banishment.
banque [bɑ̃k] **1** *nf* **(a)** (*établissement*) bank; (*ensemble*) banks. **il a 3 millions en** *ou* **à la** ~ he's got 3 million in the bank; **mettre** *ou* **porter des chèques à la** ~ to bank cheques; **la grande** ~ **appuie sa candidature** the big banks are backing his candidature.
(b) (*activité, métier*) banking.
(c) (*Jeux*) bank. **tenir la** ~ to be (the) banker.
2: banque d'affaires commercial *ou* mercantile bank; **banque de dépôt** deposit bank; **banque de données** data bank; **banque d'émission** bank of issue; **banque d'escompte** discount bank; **banque d'information(s), banque de l'informatique** = **banque de données**; (*Méd*) **banque du sang/des yeux** blood/eye bank.
banqueroute [bɑ̃kʀut] *nf* (*Fin*) (fraudulent) bankruptcy; (*Pol*) bankruptcy; (*fig littér*) failure. **faire** ~ to go bankrupt.
banqueroutier, -ière [bɑ̃kʀutje, jɛʀ] *nm,f* (fraudulent) bankrupt.
banquet [bɑ̃kɛ] *nm* dinner; (*d'apparat*) banquet.
banqueter [bɑ̃kte] (4) *vi* (*lit*) to banquet; (*festoyer*) to feast.
banquette [bɑ̃kɛt] *nf* **(a)** *[train]* seat; *[auto]* (bench) seat; *[restaurant]* (wall) seat; *[piano]* (duet) stool. **(b)** (*Archit*) window seat. **(c)** (*Mil*) ~ **de tir** banquette, fire-step.
banquier [bɑ̃kje] *nm* (*Fin, Jeux*) banker.
banquise [bɑ̃kiz] *nf* ice field; (*flottante*) ice floe.
baobab [baɔbab] *nm* baobab.
baptême [batɛm] **1** *nm* **(a)** (*sacrement*) baptism; (*cérémonie*) christening, baptism. **donner le** ~ **à** to baptize, christen; **recevoir le** ~ to be baptized *ou* christened.
(b) *[cloche]* blessing, dedication; *[navire]* naming, christening.
2: baptême de l'air first flight; **baptême du feu** baptism of fire; (*Naut*) **baptême de la ligne** (first) crossing of the line.
baptiser [batize] (1) *vt* **(a)** (*Rel*) to baptize, christen.
(b) *cloche* to bless, dedicate; *navire* to name, christen.
(c) (*appeler*) to call, christen, name. **on le baptisa Paul** he was christened Paul; **on baptisa la rue du nom du maire** the street was named *ou* called after the mayor.
(d) (*: *surnommer*) to christen, dub. (*hum*) **la pièce qu'il baptisait pompeusement salon** the room which he pompously dubbed the drawing room, the room to which he gave the pompous title of drawing room.
(e) (**fig*) *vin, lait* to water down.
baptismal, e, *mpl* **-aux** [batismal, o] *adj* baptismal.
baptisme [batism(ə)] *nm* baptism.
baptiste [batist(ə)] *nmf* Baptist.
baptistère [batistɛʀ] *nm* baptistry.
baquet [bakɛ] *nm* tub; *V* **siège**[1].
bar[1] [baʀ] *nm* (*établissement, comptoir*) bar.
bar[2] [baʀ] *nm* (*poisson*) bass, sea perch.
bar[3] [baʀ] *nm* (*Phys*) bar.
barachois [baʀaʃwa] *nm* (*Can*) lagoon.
baragouin* [baʀagwɛ̃] *nm* gibberish, double Dutch.
baragouinage* [baʀagwinaʒ] *nm* (*façon de parler*) gibbering; (*propos*) gibberish, double Dutch.
baragouiner* [baʀagwine] (1) **1** *vi* to gibber, talk gibberish *ou* double Dutch.
2 *vt langue* to speak badly; *discours, paroles* to jabber out, gabble. **il baragouine un peu l'espagnol** he can speak a bit of Spanish; (*péj*) **qu'est-ce qu'il baragouine?** what's he jabbering on about?*
baragouineur, -euse* [baʀagwinœʀ, øz] *nm,f* jabberer.
barakaꜝ [baʀaka] *nf* luck. **avoir la** ~ to be lucky.
baraque [baʀak] *nf* **(a)** (*abri en planches*) shed, hut; (*servant de boutique*) stand, stall. ~ **foraine** fairground stall.
(b) (*: *maison*) place*, shack*; (*appartement*) padꜝ, place*; (*péj: maison, entreprise etc*) dump*, holeꜝ. **une belle** ~ a smart place*; **quand je suis rentré à la** ~ when I got back to my place* *ou* shackꜝ *ou* padꜝ; **quelle (sale)** ~! what a lousy dump!ꜝ, what a hole!ꜝ
baraqué, e* [baʀake] *adj*: **bien** ~ *homme* hefty, well-built; *femme* well-built.
baraquement [baʀakmɑ̃] *nm*: ~**(s)** group of huts; (*Mil*) camp.
baratin* [baʀatɛ̃] *nm* (*boniment*) sweet talk*, smooth talk*; (*verbiage*) chatter, hot airꜝ; (*Comm*) patter*, sales talk. **assez de** ~! cut the chat!* *ou* the cackle!*; (*gén*) **faire son** *ou* **du** ~ **à qn** to sweet-talk sbꜝ, chat sb up* (*Brit*); (*Comm*) **faire son** *ou* **le** ~ **à un client** to give a customer the sales talk *ou* patter*; **avoir du** ~ to have all the patter*, be a smooth talker.
baratiner* [baʀatine] (1) **1** *vt* (*amadouer par un boniment*) to chat up* (*Brit*), sweet-talk*; (*draguer*) to chat up* (*Brit*). (*Comm*) ~ **(le client)** to give a customer the sales talk *ou* patter*. **2** *vi* (*bavarder*) to natter*.
baratineur, -euse* [baʀatinœʀ, øz] **1** *nm,f* (*beau parleur, menteur*) smooth talker; (*bavard*) gasbagꜝ, windbagꜝ. **2** *nm* (*dragueur*) smooth talker.
baratte [baʀat] *nf [beurre]* churn.
baratter [baʀate] (1) *vt* to churn.
Barbade [baʀbad] *nf*: **la** ~ Barbados.
barbant, e* [baʀbɑ̃, ɑ̃t] *adj* (*ennuyeux*) boring, deadly dull. **qu'il est/que c'est** ~! what a bore he/it is!, he's/it's dead boring!*
barbaqueꜝ [baʀbak] *nf* (*péj*) meat.
barbare [baʀbaʀ] **1** *adj invasion, peuple* barbarian, barbaric; *mœurs, musique, crime* barbarous, barbaric. **2** *nm* (*Hist, fig*) barbarian.
barbarement [baʀbaʀmɑ̃] *adv* barbarously, barbarically.
barbaresque [baʀbaʀɛsk(ə)] *adj* (*Hist: d'Afrique du Nord*) *régions, peuples, pirate* Barbary Coast (*épith*).
barbarie [baʀbaʀi] *nf* (*manque de civilisation*) barbarism; (*cruauté*) barbarity, barbarousness.
Barbarie [baʀbaʀi] *nf*: **la** ~ the Barbary Coast.
barbarisme [baʀbaʀism(ə)] *nm* (*Gram*) barbarism.
barbe[1] [baʀb(ə)] **1** *nf* **(a)** (*Anat*) beard. **une** ~ **de 3 mois** 3 months' (growth of) beard; **il a une** ~ **de 3 jours** he has got 3 days' stubble on his chin; **sans** ~ *adulte* clean-shaven, beardless; *adolescent* (*imberbe*) beardless; **il a de la** ~ **(au menton)** *[adulte]* he needs a shave; *[adolescent]* he has already a few hairs on his chin; **avoir une** ~, **porter la** *ou* **une** ~ to have a beard, be bearded; **faire la** ~ **à qn** to trim sb's beard; (*fig hum*) **il n'a pas encore de** ~ **au menton et il croit tout savoir** he's still in short pants and he thinks he knows it all.
(b) *[chèvre, singe, oiseau]* beard.
(c) *[plume]* barb; *[poisson]* barbel, wattle; *[orge]* beard (*U*). ~**s** whiskers.
(d) (*aspérités*) ~**s** *[papier]* ragged edge; *[métal]* jagged edge.
(e) (*loc*) **à la** ~ **de qn** under sb's nose; **dérober qch à la** ~ **de qn** to pinch* sth from under sb's nose; **vieille** ~* old stick-in-the-mud*, old fogey*; **marmonner dans sa** ~ to mumble *ou* mutter into one's beard; **rire dans sa** ~ to laugh up one's sleeve; **la** ~!* damn (it)!ꜝ, blast!*; **il faut que j'y retourne, quelle** ~!* I've got to go back – what a drag!*; **oh toi, la** ~!* oh shut up, you!*, shut your mouth, you!ꜝ
2: Barbe bleue *nm* Bluebeard; **barbe de capucin** wild chicory; **barbe à papa** candy-floss (*Brit*), cotton candy (*US*).
barbe[2] [baʀb(ə)] *nm* (*Zool*) **(cheval)** ~ barb.
barbeau, *pl* ~**x** [baʀbo] *nm* (*Zool*) barbel; (*Bot*) cornflower; (ꜝ: *souteneur*) pimp, ponce.
barbecue [baʀbəkju] *nm* barbecue.
barbelé, e [baʀbəle] *adj, nm*: **(fil de fer)** ~ barbed wire (*U*); **les** ~**s** the barbed wire fence *ou* fencing; **s'égratigner après les** ~**s** to get scratched on the barbed wire; **derrière les** ~**s** in a P.O.W. camp.
barber* [baʀbe] (1) **1** *vt* to bore stiff*, bore to tears*. **2 se barber** *vpr* to be bored stiff*, be bored to tears* (*à faire qch* doing sth).
Barberousse [baʀbəʀus] *nm* Barbarossa.
barbet [baʀbɛ] *nm*: **(chien)** ~ water spaniel.
barbiche [baʀbiʃ] *nf* goatee (beard).
barbichette* [baʀbiʃɛt] *nf* (small) goatee (beard).
barbier [baʀbje] *nm* (††) barber; (*Can*) (men's) hairdresser.
barbillon [baʀbijɔ̃] *nm* **(a)** *[plume, hameçon]* barb; *[poisson]* barbel. *[bœuf, cheval]* ~**s** barbs. **(b)** (*Zool: petit barbeau*) (small) barbel.
barbiturique [baʀbityʀik] **1** *adj* barbituric. **2** *nm* barbiturate.
barbon [baʀbɔ̃] *nm* (†† *ou péj*) **(vieux)** ~ greybeard, old fogey*.
barbotage [baʀbɔtaʒ] *nm* (*V* **barboter**) pinching*; filching*; paddling, splashing about, squelching around; bubbling.
barboter [baʀbɔte] (1) **1** *vt* (*: *voler*) to pinch*, filch (*à* from, off*). **elle lui a barboté son briquet** she has pinched* his lighter.
2 *vi* **(a)** (*patauger*) *[canard]* to dabble; *[enfant]* to paddle; (*en éclaboussant*) to splash about. ~ **dans la boue** to squelch around in *ou* paddle through the mud.
(b) *[gaz]* to bubble.
barboteur, -euse[1] [baʀbɔtœʀ, øz] **1** *adj* (*) **il est (du genre)** ~, **c'est un** ~ he's a bit light-fingered. **2** *nm* (*Chim*) bubble chamber.
barboteuse[2] [baʀbɔtøz] *nf* (*vêtement*) rompers.
barbouillage [baʀbujaʒ] *nm* **(a)** (*peinture*) daub; (*écriture*) scribble, scrawl. **(b)** (*action*) daubing; scribbling, scrawling.
barbouiller [baʀbuje] (1) *vt* **(a)** (*couvrir, salir*) to smear, daub (*de* with), cover (*de* with, in). **il a le visage tout barbouillé de chocolat** he's got chocolate (smeared) all over his face, he's got his face covered in chocolate.
(b) (*péj: peindre*) *mur* to daub *ou* slap paint on. **il barbouille (des toiles) de temps en temps** he does an odd bit of painting from time to time; **il barbouille des toiles en amateur** he messes about with paints and canvas, he does a bit of painting on the side.
(c) (*péj: écrire, dessiner*) to scribble (*sur* on). ~ **une feuille de dessins** to scribble *ou* scrawl drawings on a piece of paper; ~ **du papier** to cover a piece of paper with scrawls, scrawl all over a piece of paper; ~ **un slogan sur un mur** to daub a slogan on a wall.
(d) (*) ~ **l'estomac** to upset the stomach; **être barbouillé, avoir l'estomac** *ou* **le cœur barbouillé** to feel queasy *ou* sick.
barbouilleur, -euse [baʀbujœʀ, øz] *nm,f* **(a)** (*péj: artiste*) dauber; (*péj: peintre en bâtiment*) bad *ou* slapdash painter. **(b)** ~ **de papier** hack (writer).
barbouillis [baʀbuji] *nm* (*écriture*) scribble, scrawl; (*peinture*) daub.
barbouze* [baʀbuz] *nf* **(a)** beard. **(b)** (*policier*) secret (government) police agent; (*garde du corps*) bodyguard.
barbu, e [baʀby] **1** *adj* bearded. **un** ~ a bearded man, a man with a beard. **2 barbue** *nf* (*Zool*) brill.
barcarolle [baʀkaʀɔl] *nf* barcarolle.
barcasse [baʀkas] *nf* lighter, tender.
Barcelone [baʀsəlɔn] *n* Barcelona.

barda* [baʀda] *nm* gear*; (*Mil*) kit. **il a tout un ~ dans la voiture** he's got a whole load of stuff* in the car.

barde¹ [baʀd(ə)] *nm* (*poète*) bard.

barde² [baʀd(ə)] *nf* (*Culin, Mil*) bard.

bardeau¹, *pl* **~x** [baʀdo] *nm* shingle.

bardeau², *pl* **~x** [baʀdo] *nm* = **bardot.**

barder [baʀde] (1) **1** *vt* **(a)** (*Culin*) to bard.

(b) (*Mil*) *cheval* to bard. **bardé de fer** *cheval* barded; *soldat* armour-clad; *porte* with iron bars; **discours bardé de citations** speech packed *ou* larded with quotations; **poitrine bardée de décorations** chest covered with medals.

(c) (*fig*) **être bardé (contre)** to be immune (to).

2 *vb impers* (*) **ça va ~** things are going to get hot; **ça a bardé!** (*dans une réunion*) the sparks really flew!; (*dans les rues*) things got hot!

bardot [baʀdo] *nm* hinny.

barème [baʀɛm] *nm* (*table de référence*) table, list; (*tarif*) (*Comm*) scale of charges, price list; (*Rail*) fare schedule. **~ des salaires** salary scale; **~ des impôts** tax scale.

barge [baʀʒ(ə)] *nf* (*Naut*) barge.

barguigner [baʀgiɲe] (1) *vi* (*littér, hum*) **sans ~** without humming and hawing, without shilly-shallying.

baril [baʀi(l)] *nm* *[pétrole]* barrel; *[vin]* barrel, cask; *[poudre]* keg, cask; *[harengs]* barrel. **~ de lessive** drum of detergent.

barillet [baʀijɛ] *nm* **(a)** (*petit baril*) small barrel *ou* cask. **(b)** (*Tech*) *[serrure, revolver]* cylinder; *[pendule]* barrel.

bariolage [baʀjɔlaʒ] *nm* (*résultat*) riot *ou* medley of colours; (*action*) daubing.

bariolé, e [baʀjɔle] (*ptp de* **barioler**) *adj* *vêtement* many-coloured, rainbow-coloured, gaudy (*péj*); *groupe* colourfully dressed, gaily-coloured.

barioler [baʀjɔle] (1) *vt* to splash *ou* daub bright colours on, streak with bright colours.

bariolure [baʀjɔlyʀ] *nf* gay *ou* gaudy (*péj*) colours.

baromètre [baʀɔmɛtʀ(ə)] *nm* (*lit, fig*) barometer; (*lit*) glass. **le ~ baisse** the glass *ou* barometer is falling; **le ~ est au beau fixe/à la pluie** the barometer is set at fair/is pointing to rain; (*fig*) **le ~ est au beau (fixe)*** things are looking good*; **~ enregistreur/anéroïde** recording/aneroid barometer.

barométrique [baʀɔmetʀik] *adj* barometric(al).

baron [baʀɔ̃] *nm* **(a)** (*titre*) baron; *V* **monsieur. (b)** (*fig: magnat*) baron, lord. **les ~s de la presse** the press lords *ou* barons.

baronnage [baʀɔnaʒ] *nm* (*titre*) barony; (*corps des barons*) baronage.

baronne [baʀɔn] *nf* baroness; *V* **madame.**

baronnet [baʀɔnɛ] *nm* baronet.

baronnie [baʀɔni] *nf* barony.

baroque [baʀɔk] **1** *adj* *idée* weird, strange, wild; (*Archit, Art*) baroque. **2** *nm* baroque.

baroud [baʀud] *nm* (*arg Mil*) fighting. **~ d'honneur** last-ditch struggle, gallant last stand.

baroudeur [baʀudœʀ] *nm* (*arg Mil*) firebrand, scrapper*.

barouf(le)‡ [baʀuf(lə)] *nm* (*vacarme*) row*, din*, racket*. **faire du ~** to kick up a din*, make a row*; (*protester*) to kick up a fuss* *ou* stink‡.

barque [baʀk(ə)] *nf* small boat, small craft. **~ à moteur** (small) motorboat; **~ de pêche** small fishing boat.

barquette [baʀkɛt] *nf* (*Culin*) pastry boat, small tart.

barrage [baʀaʒ] *nm* **(a)** *[rivière, lac]* dam, barrage, (*petit*) weir.

(b) (*barrière*) barrier; (*Mil†*) barrage. **~ de police** (*gén*) (police) roadblock; (*cordon d'agents*) police cordon; (*chevaux de frise*) (police) barricade; **faire ~ à** to hinder, stand in the way of.

(c) (*action de barrer*) *[vallée]* damming; *[port]* blockading; blocking; *[rue]* barricading, closure, blocking.

(d) (*Cartes*) pre-emptive bid, pre-empt.

barre [baʀ] **1** *nf* **(a)** (*gén, Hér: tige, morceau*) bar; (*de fer*) rod, bar; (*de bois*) piece, rod; (*Ftbl, Rugby*) crossbar. **~ de chocolat** bar of chocolate; **~ de savon** cake *ou* bar of soap.

(b) (*Danse*) barre. **exercices à la ~** exercises at the barre, barre exercises.

(c) (*Naut*) helm; *[petit bateau]* tiller. (*lit, fig*) **être à la** *ou* **tenir la ~** to be at the helm; (*lit, fig*) **prendre la ~** to take the helm.

(d) (*Jur*) **~ du tribunal** bar; **~ (des témoins)** witness box (*Brit*), witness stand (*US*); **être appelé à la ~** to be called as a witness; **comparaître à la ~** to appear as a witness.

(e) (*Géog: houle*) (*gén*) race; (*à l'estuaire*) bore; (*banc de sable*) (sand) bar; (*crête de montagne*) ridge.

(f) (*trait*) line, dash, stroke; (*du t, f*) stroke. **faire** *ou* **tirer des ~s** to draw lines (on a page); **mets une ~ à ton t** cross your t; (*Math*) **~ de fraction/d'addition** *etc* fraction/addition *etc* line.

(g) (†: *jeu*) **~s** ≈ prisoners' base; (*frm*) **avoir ~(s) sur qn** (*avantage*) to have an advantage over sb; (*pouvoir*) to have power *ou* a hold over sb.

(h) (*Zool*) *[cheval]* bar.

2: (*Aut*) **barre d'accouplement** tie-rod; **barre d'appui** (window) rail; (*Sport*) **barre fixe** horizontal bar; (*Mus*) **barre de mesure** bar line; (*Tech*) **barre à mine** crowbar; (*Sport*) **barres parallèles** parallel bars.

barreau, *pl* **~x** [baʀo] *nm* **(a)** *[échelle]* rung; *[cage, fenêtre]* bar. **être derrière les ~x** *[prisonnier]* to be behind bars; **~ de chaise** (*lit*) (chair) rung *ou* crossbar; (*: *cigare*) fat cigar. **(b)** (*Jur*) bar. **entrer** *ou* **être admis** *ou* **reçu au ~** to be called to the bar.

barrement [baʀmɑ̃] *nm* *[chèque]* crossing.

barrer [baʀe] (1) **1** *vt* **(a)** (*obstruer*) *porte* to bar; *fenêtre* to bar up; *chemin, route* (*par accident*) to block; (*pour travaux, par la police*) to close (off), shut off. **~ le passage** *ou* **la route à qn** (*lit*) to stand in sb's way, block sb's way, stop sb getting past; (*fig*) to stand in sb's way; **des rochers nous barraient la route** rocks blocked *ou* barred our way.

(b) (*rayer*) *mot, phrase* to cross out, score out; *surface, feuille* to cross. **~ un chèque** to cross (*Brit*) a cheque; **chèque barré/non barré** crossed (*Brit*)/open *ou* uncrossed (*Brit*) cheque; **les rides qui barraient son front** the wrinkles which lined his forehead.

(c) (*Naut*) to steer. (*Sport*) **quatre barré** coxed four.

2 *vi* (*Naut*) to steer, take the helm.

3 se barrer‡ *vpr* (*s'enfuir*) to clear off*, clear out*. **barre-toi!** clear off!*, beat it!*, scram!‡, hop it!*

barrette [baʀɛt] *nf* **(a)** (*pour cheveux*) (hair) slide; (*bijou*) brooch; *[médaille]* bar. **(b)** (*Rel*) biretta. **recevoir la ~** to receive the red hat, become a cardinal.

barreur, -euse [baʀœʀ, øz] *nm,f* (*gén*) helmsman, coxswain; (*Aviron*) cox(swain). **quatre avec/sans ~** coxed/coxless four.

barricade [baʀikad] *nf* barricade; *V* **côté.**

barricader [baʀikade] (1) **1** *vt* *porte, fenêtre, rue* to barricade.

2 se barricader *vpr*: **se ~ dans/derrière** to barricade o.s. in/behind; (*fig*) **se ~ chez soi** to lock *ou* shut o.s. in.

barrière [baʀjɛʀ] **1** *nf* (*clôture*) fence; (*porte*) gate; (*lit, fig: obstacle*) barrier; (*Hist: octroi*) tollgate.

2: **barrière de dégel** *restrictions on heavy vehicles during a thaw*; **barrière douanière** trade *ou* tariff barrier; **barrière naturelle** natural barrier; **barrière (de passage à niveau)** level (*Brit*) *ou* grade (*US*) crossing gate.

barrique [baʀik] *nf* barrel, cask; *V* **plein.**

barrir [baʀiʀ] (2) *vi* to trumpet.

barrissement [baʀismɑ̃] *nm* trumpeting.

bartavelle [baʀtavɛl] *nf* rock partridge.

Barthélemy [baʀtelemi] *nm* Bartholomew.

baryton [baʀitɔ̃] *adj, nm* baritone.

baryum [baʀjɔm] *nm* barium.

bas¹, basse [bɑ, bɑs] **1** *adj* **(a)** *siège, colline, voix,* (*Mus*) *note* low; *maison* low-roofed; *terrain* low(-lying). **le soleil est ~ sur l'horizon** the sun is low on the horizon; **pièce basse de plafond** room with a low ceiling; **le feu est ~** the fire is low; **les basses branches** *ou* **les branches basses d'un arbre** the lower *ou* bottom branches of a tree; **les branches de cet arbre sont basses** the branches of this tree hang low; **~ sur pattes** short-legged, stumpy-legged; **il parle sur un ton trop ~** he speaks too softly; *V* **main, messe, oreille** *etc.*

(b) *prix, baromètre, altitude, chiffre* low; (*Élec*) *fréquence* low. **je l'ai eu à ~ prix** I got it cheap *ou* for a small sum.

(c) *marée, fleuve* low. **c'est la basse mer, c'est (la) marée basse** the tide is low *ou* out, it's low tide; **à marée basse** at low tide *ou* water; **pendant les basses eaux** when the waters are low, when the water level is low.

(d) (*humble*) *condition, naissance* low, lowly; (*subalterne*) menial; (*mesquin*) *jalousie, vengeance* base, petty; (*abject*) *action* base, mean, low. **basses besognes** menial tasks, dirty work.

(e) (*Hist, Ling*) **le B~ Empire** the late Empire; **le ~ latin** low Latin; **le ~ allemand** Low German, plattdeutsch (*T*).

(f) (*Géog*) **la Basse Seine** the Lower Seine; **le B~ Languedoc** Lower Languedoc; **les B~ Bretons** the inhabitants of Lower Britanny; (*Hist Can*) **le B~ Canada** Lower Canada.

(g) (*loc*) **être au plus ~** *[personne]* to be very low, be at a very low ebb; *[prix]* to have reached rock bottom, be at their lowest; **au ~ mot** at the very least, at the lowest estimate; **en ce ~ monde** here below; **de ~ étage** (*humble*) lowborn; (*médiocre*) poor, second-rate; **un enfant en ~ âge** a young *ou* small child.

2 *adv* **(a)** **très/trop** *etc* **~** very/too *etc* low; **mettez vos livres plus ~** put your books lower down; **comme l'auteur le dit plus ~** as the author says further on *ou* says below; **voir plus ~** see below.

(b) *parler, dire* softly, in a low voice. **mettez la radio/le chauffage plus ~** turn the radio/heating down *ou* low; **parler tout ~** to speak in a whisper *ou* in a very low voice.

(c) (*fig*) **mettre** *ou* **traiter qn plus ~ que terre** to treat sb like dirt; **son moral est (tombé) très ~** his morale is very low *ou* is at a low ebb, he's in very low spirits; **le malade est bien ~** the patient is very weak *ou* low; **les prix n'ont jamais été** *ou* **ne sont jamais tombés aussi ~** prices have reached a new low *ou* an all-time low.

(d) (*loc*) (*Vét*) **mettre ~** to give birth, drop; **mettre ~ les armes** (*Mil*) to lay down one's arms; (*fig*) to throw in the sponge; **mettre ~ qch†** to lay sth down; **~ les mains*** *ou* **les pattes!‡** hands off!*, (keep your) paws off!‡; (*à un chien*) **~ les pattes!** down!; **à ~ le fascisme!** down with fascism!; *V* **chapeau, jeter.**

3 *nm* **(a)** *[page, escalier, colline]* foot, bottom; *[visage]* lower part; *[mur]* foot; *[pantalon]* bottom; *[jupe]* hem, bottom. **dans le ~** at the bottom; **au ~ de la page** at the foot *ou* bottom of the page; **l'étagère/le tiroir du ~** the bottom shelf/drawer; **les appartements du ~** the downstairs flats, the flats downstairs *ou* down below; **au ~ de l'échelle sociale** at the bottom of the social ladder; **compter/lire de ~ en haut** to count/read starting at the bottom *ou* from the bottom up.

(b) **en ~**: **il habite en ~** he lives downstairs *ou* down below; **marcher la tête en ~** to walk on one's hands; **le bruit vient d'en ~** the noise is coming from downstairs *ou* from down below; **les voleurs sont passés par en ~** the thieves got in downstairs; **en ~ de la côte** at the bottom *ou* foot of the hill; *V* **haut.**

4 basse *nf* (*Mus*) (*chanteur*) bass; (*voix*) bass (voice); (*instrument*) (double) bass. **basse continue** (basso) continuo.

5: (*Typ*) **bas de casse** *nm* lower case; (*Rel*) **le bas clergé** the lower clergy; **bas-côté** *nm, pl* **bas-côtés** *[route]* verge; *[église]* (side) aisle; (*Can*) penthouse, lean-to extension; **basse-cour** *nf, pl* **basses-cours** (*lieu*) farmyard; (*volaille*) poultry (*U*); (*Naut*) **bas-fond** *nm, pl* **bas-fonds** shallow, shoal; **les bas-fonds de la**

société the lowest depths *ou* the dregs of society; **les bas-fonds de la ville** the seediest *ou* slummiest parts of the town; **basse-fosse** *nf, pl* **basses-fosses** *V* **cul**; (*Boucherie*) **les bas morceaux** the cheap cuts; **le bas peuple** the lower classes; **les bas quartiers de la ville** the seedy *ou* poor parts of the town; **bas-relief** *nm, pl* **bas-reliefs** bas relief, low relief; (*Tourisme*) **basse saison** low season, off season; (*Mus*) **basse-taille** *nf, pl* **basses-tailles** bass baritone; **bas-ventre** *nm, pl* **bas-ventres** stomach, guts.

bas² [bɑ] *nm* stocking. ~ **fins** sheer stockings; ~ **de nylon** nylon stockings, nylons; ~ **sans couture** seamless stockings; ~ **de laine** (*lit*) woollen stockings; (*fig*) savings, nest egg (*fig*); (*péj*) ~**-bleu** bluestocking.

basal, e, *mpl* **-aux** [bɑzal, o] *adj* basal.

basalte [bazalt(ə)] *nm* basalt.

basaltique [bazaltik] *adj* basalt(ic).

basané, e [bazane] *adj teint, visage [vacancier]* (sun)tanned, sunburnt; *[marin]* tanned, weather-beaten; *[indigène]* swarthy.

basculant, e [baskylɑ̃, ɑ̃t] *adj V* **benne.**

bascule [baskyl] *nf* **(a)** (*balance*) *[marchandises]* weighing machine. *[personne]* ~ **(automatique)** scales (*pl*); *V* **pont.**

(b) (*balançoire*) **(jeu de)** ~ seesaw; **cheval/fauteuil à** ~ rocking horse/chair; **faire tomber qn/qch par un mouvement de** ~ to topple sb/sth over; **pratiquer une politique de** ~ to have a policy of maintaining the balance of power.

(c) (*mécanisme*) bascule.

basculer [baskyle] (1) **1** *vi [personne]* to fall over, overbalance; *[objet]* to fall *ou* tip over; *[benne, planche, wagon]* to tip up; *[tas]* to topple (over). **il bascula dans le vide** he toppled over the edge; (*fig, Pol*) ~ **dans l'opposition** to swing *ou* go over to the opposition.

2 *vt* (*plus gén* **faire** ~) *benne* to tip up; *contenu* to tip out; *personne* to knock off balance, topple over.

basculeur [baskylœʀ] *nm* **(a)** (*Élec*) rocker switch. **(b)** (*benne*) tipper.

base [bɑz] **1** *nf* **(a)** *[bâtiment, colonne, triangle]* base; *[montagne]* base, foot; (*Anat, Chim, Math*) base.

(b) (*Mil etc: lieu*) base. ~ **navale/aérienne** naval/air base; **rentrer à sa** *ou* **la** ~ to return to base.

(c) (*Pol*) **la** ~ the rank and file, the grass roots.

(d) (*principe fondamental*) basis. ~**s** basis, foundations; ~**s d'un traité/accord** basis of a treaty/an agreement; **raisonnement fondé sur des** ~**s solides** argument based on solid facts; **il a des** ~**s solides en anglais** he has a good grounding in English *ou* a sound basic knowledge of English; **saper/renverser les** ~**s de...** to undermine/destroy the foundations of...; **établir** *ou* **jeter** *ou* **poser les** ~**s de...** to lay the foundations of... .

(e) (*loc*) **à** ~ **de**: **un produit à** ~ **de soude** a soda-based product; **être à la** ~ **de** to be at the root of; **sur la** ~ **de ces renseignements** on the basis of this information; **de** ~ basic, fundamental; **ouvrage/règles de** ~ basic work/rules; **le français de** ~ basic French.

2: (*fig*) **base de départ** starting point (*fig*); **base de lancement** launching site; **base de maquillage** make-up base; **base d'opération** base of operations, operations base; **base de ravitaillement** supply base.

base-ball [bɛzbol] *nm* baseball.

baser [bɑze] (1) *vt opinion, théorie* to base (*sur* on). (*Mil*) **être basé à/dans/sur** to be based at/in/on; **sur quoi vous basez-vous pour le dire?** (*preuves*) what basis *ou* grounds have you for saying that?; (*données*) what are you basing your argument on?, what is the basis of your argument?

basilic [bazilik] *nm* (*Bot*) basil; (*Zool*) basilisk.

basilique [bazilik] *nf* basilica.

basique [bɑzik] *adj* (*Chim*) basic.

basket* [baskɛt] *nm* basketball. ~**s** basketball boots, sneakers*.

basket-ball [baskɛtbol] *nm* basketball.

basketteur, -euse [baskɛtœʀ, øz] *nm,f* basketball player.

basquais, e [baskɛ, ɛz] **1** *adj* (*Culin*) **poulet/sauce** ~**e basquaise** chicken/sauce. **2** *nf*: **B**~**e** Basque (woman).

basque¹ [bask(ə)] **1** *adj* Basque. **2** *nm* (*Ling*) Basque. **3** *nmf*: **B**~ Basque.

basque² [bask(ə)] *nf [habit]* skirt(s); *[robe]* basque; *V* **pendu.**

basse [bɑs] *V* **bas¹.**

bassement [bɑsmɑ̃] *adv* basely, meanly, despicably.

bassesse [bɑsɛs] *nf* **(a)** (*U*) (*servilité*) servility; (*mesquinerie*) meanness, baseness, lowness; (*vulgarité*) vulgarity, vileness.

(b) (*acte servile*) servile act; (*acte mesquin*) low *ou* mean *ou* base act. **faire des** ~**s à qn pour obtenir** to kowtow to sb *ou* grovel in order to get; **faire des** ~**s à un ennemi** to play underhand tricks on an enemy.

basset [bɑsɛ] *nm* (*Zool*) basset (hound).

bassin [basɛ̃] *nm* **(a)** (*pièce d'eau*) ornamental lake, pond; *[piscine]* pool; *[fontaine]* basin. **(b)** (*cuvette*) bowl; (*Méd*) bedpan. **(c)** (*Géog*) basin. ~ **houiller/minier** coal/mineral field *ou* basin. **(d)** (*Anat*) pelvis. **(e)** (*Naut*) dock. ~ **de radoub** dry dock.

bassine [basin] *nf* **(a)** (*cuvette*) bowl, basin. ~ **à confiture** preserving pan. **(b)** (*contenu*) bowl(ful).

bassiner [basine] (1) *vt* **(a)** *plaie* to bathe; (*Agr*) to sprinkle *ou* spray (water on). **(b)** *lit* to warm (with a warming pan). **(c)** (*: *ennuyer*) to bore. **elle nous bassine** she's a pain in the neck*.

bassinoire [basinwaʀ] *nf* (*Hist*) warming pan; (*) bore, pain in the neck*.

bassiste [bɑsist(ə)] *nmf* (double) bass player.

basson [bɑsɔ̃] *nm* (*instrument*) bassoon; (*musicien*) bassoonist.

bassoniste [basɔnist(ə)] *nmf* bassoonist.

baste†† [bast] *excl* (*indifférence*) never mind!, who cares?; (*dédain*) pooh!

bastide [bastid] *nf* **(a)** (country) house (*in Provence*). **(b)** (*Hist*) walled town (*in S.W. France*).

bastille [bastij] *nf* fortress, castle. (*Hist*) **la B**~ the Bastille.

bastingage [bastɛ̃gaʒ] *nm* (*Naut*) (ship's) rail; (*Hist*) bulwark.

bastion [bastjɔ̃] *nm* bastion; (*fig*) bastion, stronghold.

bastonnade†† [bastɔnad] *nf* drubbing, beating.

bastringue* [bastʀɛ̃g] *nm* **(a)** (*objets*) junk*, clobber‡. **(b)** (*bruit*) racket*, din*. **(c)** (*bal*) (local) dance hall; (*orchestre*) band.

bât [bɑ] *nm* packsaddle. (*fig*) **c'est là où le** ~ **le blesse** that's where the shoe pinches.

bataclan* [bataklɑ̃] *nm* junk*, clobber‡. **...et tout le** ~ ...and everything else, ...and whatnot*, ...and what have you*.

bataille [bataj] **1** *nf* **(a)** (*Mil*) battle; (*rixe*) fight; (*fig*) fight, struggle; (*controverse*) fight, dispute. ~ **de rue** street fighting (*U*); **la vie est une dure** ~ life is a hard fight *ou* struggle.

(b) (*Cartes*) beggar-my-neighbour.

(c) (*loc*) **en** ~ (*Mil, Naut*) in battle order *ou* formation; **il a les cheveux en** ~ his hair's all dishevelled *ou* tousled; **le chapeau en** ~ with his hat on askew *ou* on the skew-whiff*.

2: **bataille aérienne** air battle; **bataille de boules de neige** snowball fight; **bataille électorale** election contest *ou* fight; **bataille navale** naval battle; **bataille rangée** pitched battle.

batailler [bataje] (1) *vi* (*fig: lutter*) to fight, battle.

batailleur, -euse [batajœʀ, øz] *adj* pugnacious, aggressive. **il est** ~ he loves a fight.

bataillon [batajɔ̃] *nm* (*Mil*) battalion; (*fig*) crowd, herd.

bâtard, e [bɑtaʀ, aʀd(ə)] **1** *adj enfant* illegitimate, bastard† (*épith*); (*fig*) *œuvre, solution* hybrid (*épith*). **chien** ~ mongrel. **2** *nm,f* (*personne*) illegitimate child, bastard† (*péj*); (*chien*) mongrel. **3** *nm* (*Boulangerie*) ≈ Vienna roll. **4 bâtarde** *nf* (*Typ*: *aussi* **écriture** ~**e**) slanting round-hand.

bâtardise [bɑtaʀdiz] *nf* bastardy†, illegitimacy.

batavia [batavja] *nf* Webb lettuce.

bateau, *pl* ~**x** [bato] **1** *nm* **(a)** (*gén*) boat; (*grand*) ship. ~ **à moteur/à rames/à voiles** motor/rowing/sailing boat; **prendre le** ~ (*embarquer*) to embark, take the boat (*à* at); (*voyager*) to go by boat, sail; **aller en** ~ to go by boat, sail; **faire du** ~ (*à voiles*) to go sailing; (*à rames etc*) to go boating.

(b) *[trottoir]* driveway entrance (*depression in kerb*).

2 *adj inv* (‡: *banal*) hackneyed. **c'est (un sujet** *ou* **thème)** ~ it's the same old theme* *ou* the favourite topic (that crops up every time).

3: **bateau amiral** flagship; **bateau-citerne** *nm, pl* **bateaux-citernes** tanker (*Naut*); **bateau de commerce** merchant ship *ou* vessel; **bateau-école** *nm, pl* **bateaux-écoles** training ship; **bateau-feu** *nm, pl* **bateaux-feux** lightship; **bateau de guerre** warship, battleship; **bateau-lavoir** *nm, pl* **bateaux-lavoirs** wash-shed (on river); (*péj*) **capitaine** *ou* **amiral de bateau-lavoir** freshwater sailor; **bateau-mouche** *nm, pl* **bateaux-mouches** pleasure steamer, river boat (*on the Seine*); **bateau de pêche** fishing boat; **bateau-phare** *nm, pl* **bateaux-phares** lightship; **bateau-pilote** *nm, pl* **bateaux-pilotes** pilot boat; **bateau de plaisance** pleasure boat; **bateau-pompe** *nm, pl* **bateaux-pompes** fireboat; **bateau de sauvetage** lifeboat; **bateau à vapeur** steamer, steamship.

bateleur, -euse [batlœʀ, øz] *nm,f* (†) tumbler; (*péj*) buffoon.

batelier [batəlje] *nm* boatman, waterman; *[bac]* ferryman.

batelière [batəljɛʀ] *nf* boatwoman; *[bac]* ferrywoman.

batellerie [batɛlʀi] *nf* **(a)** (*transport*) inland water transport *ou* navigation, canal transport. **(b)** (*bateaux*) river and canal craft.

bâter [bɑte] (1) *vt* to put a packsaddle on.

bat-flanc [baflɑ̃] *nm inv* boards (*pl*) (*in army huts etc, for sleeping on*).

bathymètre [batimɛtʀ(ə)] *nm* bathometer, bathymeter.

bathymétrie [batimetʀi] *nf* bathometry, bathymetry.

bathymétrique [batimetʀik] *adj* bathymetric.

bathyscaphe [batiskaf] *nm* bathyscaphe.

bathysphère [batisfɛʀ] *nf* bathysphere.

bâti, e [bɑti] (*ptp de* **bâtir**) **1** *adj* **(a) être bien/mal** ~ *personne* to be well-built/of clumsy build; *dissertation* to be well/badly constructed.

(b) terrain ~**/non** ~ developed/undeveloped site.

2 *nm* **(a)** (*Couture*) tacking (*U*). **point de** ~ tacking stitch.

(b) (*Constr*) *[porte]* frame; *[machine]* stand, support, frame.

batifolage [batifɔlaʒ] *nm* (*V* **batifoler**) frolicking about; larking about; dallying; flirting.

batifoler [batifɔle] (1) *vi* (†, *hum*) **(a)** (*folâtrer*) to lark *ou* frolic about; (*péj: perdre son temps*) to dally, lark about. **(b)** (*flirter*) to dally, flirt (*avec* with).

bâtiment [bɑtimɑ̃] *nm* **(a)** (*édifice*) building. **(b)** (*industrie*) **le** ~ the building industry *ou* trade; **être dans le** ~ to be in the building trade, be a builder. **(c)** (*Naut*) ship, vessel.

bâtir [bɑtiʀ] (2) *vt* **(a)** (*Constr*) to build. **(se) faire** ~ **une maison** to have a house built; **se** ~ **une maison** to build o.s. a house; **la maison s'est bâtie en 3 jours** the house was built *ou* put up in 3 days; ~ **sur le roc/sable** to build on rock/sand; **terrain/pierre à** ~ building land/stone.

(b) (*fig*) *hypothèse* to build (up); *phrase* to construct, build; *fortune* to amass, build up; *réputation* to build (up), make (*sur* on); *plan* to draw up.

(c) (*Couture*) to tack, baste. **fil/coton à** ~ tacking thread/cotton.

bâtisse [bɑtis] *nf* **(a)** (*maison*) building; (*péj*) great pile *ou* edifice. **(b)** (*Tech*) masonry.

bâtisseur, -euse [bɑtisœʀ, øz] *nm,f* builder.

batiste [batist(ə)] *nf* batiste, cambric, lawn.

bâton [bɑtɔ̃] **1** *nm* **(a)** (*canne*) stick, staff (*littér*); (*Rel: insigne*) staff; (*trique*) club, cudgel; (*à deux mains*) staff.

(b) (*morceau*) *[craie etc]* stick. **~ de rouge (à lèvres)** lipstick.
(c) (*trait*) vertical line *ou* stroke. (*Scol*) **faire des ~s** to draw vertical lines (*when learning to write*).
(d) (*loc*) **il m'a mis des ~s dans les roues** he put a spoke in my wheel, he put a spanner in the works (for me); **parler à ~s rompus** to talk on about this and that; (*fig hum*) **il est mon ~ de vieillesse** he is the prop *ou* staff of my old age (*hum*).
2: **bâton de berger** shepherd's crook; **bâton blanc**† (*d'agent de police*) policeman's baton; **bâton de chaise** chair rung; **bâton de chef d'orchestre** conductor's baton; (*lit*) **bâton de maréchal** marshal's baton; (*fig*) **ce poste, c'est son bâton de maréchal** that's as high as he'll go in that job; (*Rel*) **bâton de pèlerin** pilgrim's staff; (*fig*) **prendre son bâton de pèlerin** to set out on a peace mission; **bâton de ski** ski stick.

bâtonner†† [bɑtɔne] (1) *vt* to hit *ou* beat with a stick.

bâtonnet [bɑtɔnɛ] *nm* short stick *ou* rod; (*Opt*) rod.

bâtonnier [bɑtɔnje] *nm* ≈ president of the Bar.

batracien [batʀasjɛ̃] *nm* batrachian.

battage [bataʒ] *nm* **(a)** *[tapis, or]* beating; *[céréales]* threshing.
(b) (*: *publicité*) publicity campaign. **faire du ~ autour de qch** to plug sth*, push sth*, sell sth hard*; **faire du ~ autour de qn** to give sb a plug*, sell sb hard*.

battant, e [batɑ̃, ɑ̃t] **1** *adj V* **battre, pluie, tambour.**
2 *nm* **(a)** *[cloche]* clapper, tongue. **~ (de porte)** left-hand *ou* right-hand flap *ou* door (*of a double door*); **~ (de fenêtre)** (left-hand *ou* right-hand) window; *[volet]* shutter, flap; **porte à double ~** double door; **ouvrir une porte à deux ~s** to open both sides *ou* doors (*of a double door*).
(b) (*personne*) fighter (*fig*).

batte [bat] *nf* **(a)** (*outil*) (*à beurre*) dasher; *[blanchisseuse]* washboard; (*Sport*) bat; (*sabre de bois*) wooden sword. **(b)** (*battage*) beating.

battement [batmɑ̃] *nm* **(a)** (*claquement*) *[porte, volet]* banging (*U*); *[marteau]* banging (*U*), thud; *[pluie]* beating (*U*), (pitter-) patter (*U*); *[tambour]* beating (*U*), rattle (*U*); *[voile, toile]* flapping (*U*).
(b) (*mouvement*) *[ailes]* flapping (*U*), flutter (*U*), beating (*U*); *[cils]* fluttering (*U*); *[rames]* plash (*U*), splash (*U*). **~ de paupières** blinking of eyelids (*U*); **~s de jambes** leg movement; **accueillir qn avec des ~s de mains** to greet sb with clapping *ou* applause.
(c) (*Méd*) *[cœur]* beat, beating (*U*); *[pouls]* beat, throbbing (*U*), beating (*U*); (*irrégulier*) fluttering (*U*); *[tempes]* throbbing (*U*). **avoir des ~s de cœur** to get *ou* have palpitations; **cela m'a donné des ~s de cœur** it set my heart beating, it gave me palpitations, it set me all of a flutter*.
(d) (*intervalle*) interval. **2 minutes de ~** (*pause*) a 2-minute break; (*attente*) 2 minutes' wait; (*temps libre*) 2 minutes to spare; **j'ai une heure de ~ de 10 à 11** I'm free for an hour *ou* I've got an hour to spare between 10 and 11.
(e) (*Rad*) beat.

batterie [batʀi] *nf* **(a)** (*Mil*) battery. **mettre des canons en ~** to unlimber guns; **~ de canons** battery of artillery; **~ antichars/de D.C.A** anti-tank/anti-aircraft battery; **~ côtière** coastal battery; (*fig*) **changer/dresser ses ~s** to change/lay *ou* make one's plans; (*fig*) **démasquer** *ou* **dévoiler ses ~s** to unmask one's guns.
(b) (*Mus: percussion*) percussion (instruments); (*Jazz*) drum kit. **X à la ~ X** on drums *ou* percussion.
(c) (*Aut, Élec*) battery.
(d) (*groupe*) *[tests, chaudières]* battery. **~ de projecteurs** bank of spotlights.
(e) ~ de cuisine (*Culin*) pots and pans, kitchen utensils; (*: *décorations*) gongs*, ironmongery*; **toute la ~ de cuisine*** everything but the kitchen sink, the whole caboodle*.

batteur [batœʀ] *nm* **(a)** (*Culin*) whisk, beater. **(b)** (*Mus*) drummer, percussionist. **(c)** (*métier*) (*Agr*) thresher; (*Métal*) beater; (*Sport*) batsman; (*Baseball*) striker.

batteuse [batøz] *nf* **(a)** (*Agr*) threshing machine; *V* **moissonneuse. (b)** (*Métal*) beater.

battoir [batwaʀ] *nm* **(a)** *[laveuse]* beetle, battledore; (*à tapis*) (carpet) beater. **(b)** (*grandes mains*) **~s*** (great) mitts‡ *ou* paws‡.

battre [batʀ(ə)] (41) **1** *vt* **(a)** *personne* to beat, strike, hit. **elle ne bat jamais ses enfants** she never hits *ou* smacks her children; **~ qn comme plâtre*** to beat the living daylights out of sb*, thrash *ou* beat sb soundly; **~ qn à mort** to batter *ou* beat sb to death; **regard de chien battu** cowering look.
(b) (*vaincre*) *adversaire, équipe* to beat, defeat; *record* to beat. **se faire ~** to be beaten *ou* defeated; **il ne se tient pas pour battu** he doesn't consider himself beaten *ou* defeated; (*Sport*) **~ qn (par) 6 à 3** to beat sb 6–3; **~ qn à plate(s) couture(s)** to beat sb hollow.
(c) (*frapper*) *tapis, linge, fer, or* to beat; *blé* to thresh. (*Prov*) **~ le fer pendant qu'il est chaud** to strike while the iron is hot (*Prov*); **il battit l'air/l'eau des bras** his arms thrashed the air/water; **~ le fer à froid** to cold hammer iron; **son manteau lui bat les talons** his coat is flapping round his ankles; **~ le briquet**† to strike a light.
(d) (*agiter*) *beurre* to churn; *blanc d'œuf* to beat (up), whip, whisk; *crème* to whip; *cartes* to shuffle. **œufs battus en neige** stiff egg whites, stiffly-beaten egg whites.
(e) (*parcourir*) *région* to scour, comb. **~ le pays** to scour the countryside; (*Chasse*) **~ les buissons/les taillis** to beat the bushes/undergrowth (for game); **hors des chemins battus** off the beaten track; (*fig*) **~ la campagne** to wander in one's mind; **~ le pavé** to wander aimlessly about *ou* around.
(f) (*heurter*) *[pluie]* to beat *ou* lash against; *[mer]* to beat *ou* dash against; (*Mil*) *positions, ennemis* to batter. **littoral battu par les tempêtes** storm-lashed coast.
(g) (*Mus*) **~ la mesure** to beat time; (*Mil*) **~ le tambour** (*lit*) to beat the drum; (*fig*) to shout from the housetops; **~ le rappel** to call to arms; (*fig*) **~ le rappel de ses souvenirs** to summon up one's old memories; **~ le rappel de ses amis** to rally one's friends; (*Mil*) **~ la retraite** to sound the retreat.
(h) (*loc*) **~ la breloque**† *[appareil]* to be on the blink*, be erratic; *[cœur]* to be giving out; **son cœur battait la chamade** his heart was pounding *ou* beating wildly; **~ en brèche une théorie** to demolish a theory; **~ froid à qn** to cold-shoulder sb, give sb the cold shoulder; **~ son plein** *[saison touristique]* to be at its height; *[fête]* to be going full swing; **~ la semelle** to stamp one's feet (to keep warm); (*Naut*) **~ pavillon britannique** to fly the British flag, sail under the British flag; (*Fin*) **~ monnaie** to strike *ou* mint coins; (*Rel*) **~ sa coulpe** to beat one's breast (*fig*).
2 *vi* **(a)** *[cœur, pouls]* to beat; *[montre, métronome]* to tick; *[pluie]* to beat, lash (*contre* against); *[porte, volets]* to bang, rattle; *[voile, drapeau]* to flap; *[tambour]* to beat. (*fig hum*) **son cœur bat pour lui** he is her heart-throb; **son cœur battait d'émotion** his heart was beating wildly *ou* pounding *ou* thudding with emotion; **le cœur battant** with beating heart.
(b) ~ en retraite to beat a retreat, fall back.
3 battre de *vt indir:* **~ des mains** to clap one's hands; (*fig*) to dance for joy, exult; **~ du tambour** to beat the drum; **l'oiseau bat des ailes** the bird is beating *ou* flapping its wings; (*fig*) **~ de l'aile** to be in a bad *ou* in a dicky (*Brit*) *ou* shaky state*.
4 se battre *vpr* **(a)** (*dans une guerre, un combat*) to fight (*avec* with, *contre* against); (*se disputer*) to fall out; (*fig*) to fight, battle, struggle (*contre* against). **se ~ comme des chiffonniers** to fight like cat and dog; **se ~ au couteau/à la baïonnette** to fight with knives/bayonets; **nos troupes se sont bien battues** our troops fought well *ou* put up a good fight; **se ~ en duel** to fight a duel; (*fig*) **se ~ contre les préjugés** to battle *ou* fight *ou* struggle against prejudice; **se ~ contre des moulins à vent** to tilt at windmills; **il faut se ~ pour arriver à obtenir quelque chose** you have to fight to get what you want; **voilà une heure qu'il se bat avec ce problème** he's been struggling *ou* battling with that problem for an hour now.
(b) se ~ la poitrine to beat one's breast; (*fig*) **se ~ les flancs** to flog a dead horse.
(c) je m'en bats l'œil‡ I don't care a fig* *ou* a damn‡.

battu, e[1] [baty] (*ptp de* **battre**) *adj V* **jeté, œil, pas**[1]**, terre, battre.**

battue[2] [baty] *nf* (*Chasse*) battue, beat.

batture [batyʀ] *nf* (*Can*) sand bar, strand.

bau, *pl* **~x** [bo] *nm* (*Naut*) beam.

baudelairien, -ienne [bodlɛʀjɛ̃, jɛn] *adj* Baudelairean.

baudet [bodɛ] *nm* **(a)** (*Zool*) donkey, ass. **(b)** (*Menuiserie*) trestle, sawhorse.

baudrier [bodʀije] *nm [épée]* baldric; *[drapeau]* shoulder-belt.

baudruche [bodʀyʃ] *nf* (*personne*) windbag*; (*théorie*) empty theory, humbug*.

bauge [boʒ] *nf [sanglier, porc]* wallow.

baume [bom] *nm* (*lit*) balm, balsam; (*fig*) balm. **ça lui a mis du ~ dans le cœur** it heartened him.

Baumé [bome] *nm V* **degré.**

baux [bo] *nmpl de* **bail, bau.**

bauxite [boksit] *nf* bauxite.

bavard, e [bavaʀ, aʀd(ə)] **1** *adj personne* talkative, garrulous; *discours, récit* long-winded, wordy. **2** *nm,f* chatterbox*, talkative person, prattler; (*péj*) gossip, blabbermouth*.

bavardage [bavaʀdaʒ] *nm* **(a)** (*action*) chattering; (*péj*) gossiping. **(b)** (*propos*) (idle) chatter (*U*) *ou* prattle (*U*); (*papotages*) gossip (*U*), tittle-tattle* (*U*); (*indiscrétion*) gossip (*U*), blabbering* (*U*).

bavarder [bavaʀde] (1) *vi* to chat, chatter, prattle; (*papoter*) to gossip, tittle-tattle*; (*divulguer un secret*) to blab*, give the game away, talk.

bavarois, e [bavaʀwa, waz] **1** *adj* Bavarian. **2** *nm,f*: **B~(e)** Bavarian. **3 bavaroise** *nf* (*Culin*) ≈ mousse.

bavasser* [bavase] (1) *vi* (*bavarder*) to natter* (*surtout Brit*), gas‡.

bave [bav] *nf [personne]* dribble; *[animal]* slaver, slobber; *[chien enragé]* foam, froth; *[escargot]* slime; *[crapaud]* spittle; (*fig*) venom, malicious words. **la ~ du crapaud n'atteint pas la blanche colombe!** your spiteful words can't touch me!

baver [bave] (1) **1** *vi* **(a)** *[personne]* to dribble, (*beaucoup*) to slobber, drool; *[animal]* to slaver, slobber; *[chien enragé]* to foam *ou* froth at the mouth; *[stylo]* to leak; *[pinceau]* to drip; *[liquide]* to run.
(b) (*loc*) **en ~ d'admiration*** to gasp in admiration; **en ~‡** to have a rough *ou* hard time of it*; **il m'en a fait ~‡** he really made me sweat*.
(c) (*littér*) **~ sur la réputation de qn** to besmear *ou* besmirch sb's reputation.
2 *vt:* **il en a bavé des ronds de chapeau‡** his eyes nearly popped out of his head*.

bavette [bavɛt] *nf* **(a)** *[tablier, enfant]* bib. **(b)** (*Culin*) undercut; *V* **tailler.**

baveux, -euse [bavø, øz] **1** *adj bouche* dribbling, slobbery; *enfant* dribbling. **omelette ~euse** runny omelette; (*Typ*) **lettre ~euse** blurred *ou* smeared letter. **2** *nm* (‡) (news)paper, rag*.

Bavière [bavjɛʀ] *nf* Bavaria.

bavoir [bavwaʀ] *nm* bib.

bavure [bavyʀ] *nf* (*tache*) smudge, smear; (*Tech*) burr; (*fig*) hitch, flaw; (*Admin euph*) unfortunate mistake (*euph*). (*fig*) **sans ~** (*adj*) flawless, faultless; (*adv*) flawlessly, faultlessly.

bayadère [bajadɛʀ] **1** *nf* bayadère. **2** *adj tissu* colourfully striped.

bayer [baje] (1) *vi:* **~ aux corneilles** to stand gaping, stand and gawp.

bazar [bazaʀ] *nm* **(a)** (*magasin*) general store; (*oriental*) bazaar.
(b) (*: *effets personnels*) junk* (*U*), gear: (*U*), things*.
(c) (*: *désordre*) clutter, jumble, shambles (*U*). **quel ~!** what a shambles!*; **et tout le ~** and whatnot*, and what have you*, the whole caboodle*.

bazarder* [bazaʀde] (1) *vt* (*jeter*) to get rid of, chuck out*, ditch*; (*vendre*) to flog:, get rid of, sell off.

bazooka [bazuka] *nm* bazooka.

bê [bɛ] *excl* baa!

béant, e [beɑ̃, ɑ̃t] *adj blessure* gaping, open; *bouche* gaping, wide open; *yeux* wide open; *gouffre* gaping, yawning; *personne* wide-eyed, open-mouthed (*de* with, in), gaping (*de* in).

béarnais, e [bearnɛ, ɛz] 1 *adj personne* from the Béarn. (*Culin*) **(sauce** *f*) **~e** Béarnaise sauce. 2 *nm,f*: **B~(e)** inhabitant *ou* native of the Béarn.

béat, e [bea, at] *adj* (*hum*) *personne* blissfully happy; (*content de soi*) smug, self-satisfied, complacent; *sourire, air* (*niaisement heureux*) beatific, blissful. **optimisme ~** smug optimism; **admiration ~e** blind *ou* dumb admiration; **être ~ d'admiration** to be struck dumb with admiration; **regarder qn d'un air ~** to look at sb in open-eyed wonder *ou* with dumb admiration.

béatement [beatmɑ̃] *adv* (*V* **béat**) smugly; complacently; beatifically, blissfully.

béatification [beatifikɑsjɔ̃] *nf* beatification.

béatifier [beatifje] (7) *vt* to beatify.

béatitude [beatityd] *nf* (*Rel*) beatitude; (*bonheur*) bliss.

beau [bo], **bel** *devant n commençant par voyelle ou h muet*, **belle** [bɛl] *f, mpl* **beaux** [bo] 1 *adj* **(a)** (*qui plaît au regard, à l'oreille*) *objet, paysage* beautiful, lovely; *femme* beautiful, fine-looking, lovely; *homme* handsome, good-looking. **les belles dames et les beaux messieurs** the smart ladies and gentlemen; **les beaux quartiers** the smart *ou* posh* districts; **il est ~ comme le jour** *ou* **comme un dieu** he's like a Greek god; **mettre ses beaux habits** to put on one's best clothes; **il est ~ garçon** he's good-looking, he's a good-looking lad*; **il est ~ gosse*** he's a good looker*.
(b) (*qui plaît à l'esprit, digne d'admiration*) *discours, match* fine; *poème, roman* fine, beautiful. **il a un ~ talent** he has a fine gift, he's very talented *ou* gifted; **une belle mort** a fine death; **une belle âme** a fine *ou* noble nature; **un ~ geste** a noble act; **toutes ces belles paroles/tous ces beaux discours n'ont convaincu personne** all these fine(-sounding) words/all these grand speeches failed to convince anybody.
(c) (*agréable*) *temps* fine, beautiful; *voyage* lovely. **aux beaux jours** in (the) summertime; **par une belle soirée d'été** on a beautiful *ou* fine summer's evening; **il fait (très) ~ (temps)** the weather's very good, it's beautiful weather, it's very fine; **la mer était belle** the sea was calm; **c'est le bel âge** those are the best years of life; **c'est la belle vie!** this is the (good) life!; (*Hist*) **la Belle Époque** the Belle Époque, the Edwardian era.
(d) (*: *intensif*) *revenu, profit* handsome, tidy*; *résultat, occasion* excellent, fine. **il a une belle situation** he has an excellent position; **cela fait une belle somme!** that's a tidy* sum of money!; **il en reste un ~ morceau** there's still a good bit (of it) left; **95 ans, c'est un bel âge** it's a good age, 95; **un ~ jour** (*passé*) one (fine) day; (*futur*) one of these (fine) days, one (fine) day; **il est arrivé un ~ matin/jour** he came one morning/day.
(e) (*iro: déplaisant*) **il a attrapé une belle bronchite** he's got a nasty attack of bronchitis; **une belle gifle** a good slap; **une belle brûlure/peur** a nasty burn/fright; **ton frère est un ~ menteur** your brother is a terrible *ou* the most awful liar; **un ~ désordre** *ou* **gâchis** a fine mess; **un ~ vacarme** a terrible din; **la belle affaire!** big deal!*, so what?*; **en faire de belles** to get up to mischief; **embarquez tout ce ~ monde!** cart this fine crew* *ou* bunch* away!; (*iro*) **en apprendre/dire de belles sur qn*** to hear/say some nice things about sb (*iro*); **être dans un ~ pétrin** *ou* **dans de beaux draps** to be in a fine old mess*.
(f) (*loc*) **ce n'est pas ~ de mentir** it isn't nice to tell lies; **ça me fait une belle jambe!*** a fat lot of good it does me!*; (*iro*) **c'est du ~ travail!** well done! (*iro*); **de plus belle** all the more, more than ever, even more; **crier de plus belle** to shout louder than ever *ou* all the louder *ou* even louder; **recommencer de plus belle** to start off *ou* up again, start up even worse than before *ou* ever; **dormir** *ou* **coucher à la belle étoile** to sleep out in the open; **il y a belle lurette de cela** that was ages ago *ou* donkey's years* ago; **il y a belle lurette que** it is ages *ou* donkey's years* since; **il l'a eu(e) belle de s'échapper** they really made it child's play for him to escape; **faire qch pour les beaux yeux de qn** to do sth just for sb *ou* just to please sb; **tout ~, tout ~!**† steady on!, easy does it!; **le plus ~ de l'histoire, c'est que...** the best bit of it *ou* part about it is that ...; **c'est trop ~ pour être vrai** it's too good to be true; **ce serait trop ~!** that would be too much to hope for!; **avoir ~ jeu de** to have every opportunity to; **avoir le ~ rôle** to show o.s. in a good light, come off best (in a situation); **se faire ~** to get spruced *ou* dressed up; **se faire belle** to get dressed up; **se mettre ~** to get dressed up; (*littér*) **porter ~** to look dapper; **avoir ~**: **on a ~ faire/dire ils n'apprennent rien** whatever you do/say they won't learn anything, try as you may they won't learn anything; **on a ~ protester, personne n'écoute** however much you protest no one listens; **on a ~ dire, il n'est pas bête** say what you like, he is not stupid; **il eut ~ essayer** however much *ou* whatever he tried, try as he might; **il ferait ~ voir qu'il mente!** he'd better not be lying!; **bel et bien** well and truly; **ils sont bel et bien entrés par la fenêtre** they really did get in through the window, they got in through the window all right *ou* no doubt about it *ou* no doubt about that; **il s'est bel et bien trompé** he got it well and truly wrong; *V* **bailler, échapper.**
2 *nm* **(a) le ~** the beautiful; **le culte du ~** the cult of beauty; **elle n'aime que le ~** she only likes what is beautiful; **elle n'achète que le ~** she only buys the best quality.
(b) (*loc*) **faire le ~** *[chien]* to sit up and beg; (*péj*) *[personne]* to curry favour (*devant* with); **être au ~** *[temps]* to be fine, be set fair; *[baromètre]* to be set fair; **c'est du ~!** (*reproche*) that was a fine thing to do! (*iro*); (*consternation*) this is a fine business! (*iro*) *ou* a fine mess! (*iro*).
3 **belle** *nf* **(a)** beauty, belle; (*compagne*) lady friend. **ma belle!*** my girl!; **la Belle au bois dormant** Sleeping Beauty.
(b) (*Jeux, Sport*) decider, deciding match.
4: **les beaux-arts** *nmpl* (*Art*) the fine arts; (*école*) the Art School; **bel esprit** wit; **faire le bel esprit** to show off one's wit; **belle-famille** *nf, pl* **belles-familles** *[homme]* wife's family, in-laws*; *[femme]* husband's family, in-laws*; **belle-fille** *nf, pl* **belles-filles** (*bru*) daughter-in-law; (*remariage*) stepdaughter; **beau-fils** *nm, pl* **beaux-fils** (*gendre*) son-in-law; (*remariage*) stepson; **beau-frère** *nm, pl* **beaux-frères** brother-in-law; **belle-de-jour** *nf, pl* **belles-de-jour** (*Bot*) convolvulus, morning glory; (*: *prostituée*) prostitute; **belles-lettres** *nfpl* great literature; **belle-maman*** *nf, pl* **belles-mamans** mother-in-law, mum-in-law*; **belle-mère** *nf, pl* **belles-mères** mother-in-law; (*nouvelle épouse du père*) stepmother; **le beau monde** high society; **fréquenter du beau monde** to move in high society; **belle-de-nuit** *nf, pl* **belles-de-nuit** (*Bot*) marvel of Peru; (*: *prostituée*) prostitute; **beau-papa*** *nm, pl* **beaux-papas** father-in-law, dad-in-law*; **beaux-parents** *nmpl* *[homme]* wife's family, in-laws*; *[femme]* husband's family, in-laws*; **beau parleur** glib talker; **beau-père** *nm, pl* **beaux-pères** father-in-law; (*nouveau mari de la mère*) stepfather; **le beau sexe** the fair sex; **belle-sœur** *nf, pl* **belles-sœurs** sister-in-law; (*hum*) **beau ténébreux** dashing young man with a sombre air.

beauceron, -onne [bosʀɔ̃, ɔn] 1 *adj* of *ou* from the Beauce. 2 *nm,f*: **B~(ne)** inhabitant *ou* native of the Beauce.

beaucoup [boku] *adv* **(a)** a lot, (very) much, a great deal. **il mange ~** he eats a lot; **elle lit ~** she reads a great deal *ou* a lot; **elle ne lit pas ~** she doesn't read much *ou* a great deal *ou* a lot; **la pièce ne m'a pas ~ plu** I didn't like the play very much, I didn't greatly like the play; **il s'intéresse ~ à la peinture** he is very *ou* greatly interested in painting, he takes a lot *ou* a great deal of interest in painting; **il y a ~ à faire/voir** there's a lot to do/see; **il a ~ voyagé/lu** he has travelled/read a lot *ou* extensively *ou* a great deal.
(b) ~ de (*quantité*) a great deal of, a lot of, much; (*nombre*) many, a lot of, a good many; **~ de monde** a lot of people, a great *ou* good many people; **avec ~ de soin/plaisir** with great care/pleasure; **il ne reste pas ~ de pain** there isn't a lot of *ou* isn't (very) much bread left; **j'ai ~ (de choses) à faire** I have a lot (of things) to do; **pour ce qui est de l'argent/du lait, il en reste ~/il n'en reste pas ~** as for money/milk, there is a lot left/there isn't a lot *ou* much left; **vous attendiez des touristes, y en a-t-il eu ~? — oui (il y en a eu) ~** you were expecting tourists and were there many *ou* a lot (of them)? — yes there were (a good many *ou* a lot of them); **j'en connais ~ qui pensent que** I know a great many (people) *ou* a lot of people who think that; **il a ~ d'influence** he has a great deal *ou* a lot of influence, he is very influential; **il a eu ~ de chance** he's been very lucky.
(c) (*employé seul: personnes*) many. **ils sont ~ à croire que ..., ~ croient que ...** many *ou* a lot of people think that...; **~ d'entre eux sont partis** a lot *ou* many of them have left.
(d) (*modifiant adv trop, plus, moins, mieux et adj*) much, far, a good deal; (*nombre*) a lot. **~ plus rapide** much *ou* a good deal *ou* a lot quicker; **elle travaille ~ trop** she works far too much; **elle travaille ~ trop lentement** she works much *ou* far too slowly; **se sentir ~ mieux** to feel much *ou* miles* better; **~ plus d'eau** much *ou* a lot *ou* far more water; **~ moins de gens** many *ou* a lot *ou* far fewer people; **il est susceptible, il l'est même ~** he's touchy, in fact very much so.
(e) de ~ by far, by a long way, by a long chalk* (*Brit*); **elle est de ~ la meilleure élève** she is by far *ou* is far and away the best pupil, she's the best pupil by far *ou* by a long chalk* (*Brit*); **il l'a battu de ~** he beat him by miles* *ou* by a long way; **il est de ~ ton aîné** he is very much *ou* is a great deal older than you; **il est de ~ supérieur** he is greatly *ou* far superior; **il préférerait de ~ s'en aller** he'd much *ou* far rather go; **il s'en faut de ~ qu'il soit au niveau** he is far from being up to standard.
(f) (*loc*) **c'est déjà ~ de l'avoir fait** *ou* **qu'il l'ait fait** it was quite something for him to do it at all; **à ~ près** far from it; **c'est ~ dire** that's an exaggeration *ou* an overstatement, that's putting it a bit strong*; **être pour ~ dans une décision/une nomination** to be largely responsible for a decision/an appointment, have a big hand in making a decision/an appointment; **il y est pour ~** he's largely responsible for it, he's had a lot to do with it, he had a big hand in it.

beaupré [bopʀe] *nm* bowsprit.

beauté [bote] *nf* **(a)** (*gén*) beauty; *[femme]* beauty, loveliness; *[homme]* handsomeness. **de toute ~** very beautiful, magnificent; **se (re)faire une ~** to powder one's nose, do one's face*; **finir** *ou* **terminer qch en ~** to complete sth brilliantly, finish sth with a flourish; **finir en ~** to end with a flourish, finish brilliantly; **la ~ du diable** youthful beauty *ou* bloom.
(b) (*belle femme*) beauty.
(c) ~s beauties; **les ~s de Rome** the beauties *ou* sights of Rome.

bébé [bebe] *nm* (*enfant, animal*) baby; (*poupée*) dolly. **faire le ~** to behave *ou* act like a baby; **c'est un vrai ~** he's a real baby; **il est resté très ~** he has stayed very babyish; **~ éléphant/girafe** baby elephant/giraffe; **~-éprouvette** test-tube baby.

bébête* [bebɛt] *adj* silly.

bec [bɛk] 1 *nm* **(a)** (*Orn*) beak, bill. **oiseau qui se fait le ~**

(contre) bird that sharpens its beak (on); **(nez en)** ~ **d'aigle** hook nose.
(b) (*pointe*) *[plume]* nib; *[carafe, casserole]* lip; *[théière]* spout; *[flûte, trompette]* mouthpiece; (*Géog*) bill, headland.
(c) (*: *bouche*) mouth. **ouvre ton** ~ open your mouth!, mouth open!*; **ferme ton** ~! shut your trap!‡, just shut up!*; **il n'a pas ouvert le** ~ he never opened his mouth, he didn't say a word; **la pipe au** ~ with his pipe stuck* in his mouth; **clore** *ou* **clouer le** ~ **à qn** to reduce sb to silence, shut sb up*; *V* **prise.**
(d) (*loc*) **tomber sur un** ~ **(de gaz)*** to be stymied*, come unstuck*; **être** *ou* **rester le** ~ **dans l'eau*** to be left high and dry.
2: **bec Auer** Welsbach burner; **bec Bunsen** Bunsen burner; **bec-de-cane** *nm, pl* **becs-de-cane** (*poignée*) doorhandle; (*serrure*) catch; **bec de cygne** type of tap; **bec fin*** gourmet; **bec à gaz** gas burner *ou* jet; **bec de gaz** lamppost, gaslamp; (*Méd*) **bec-de-lièvre** *nm, pl* **becs-de-lièvre** harelip; **bec verseur** pourer, pouring lip.

bécane* [bekan] *nf* bike*.

bécarre [bekaʀ] *nm* (*Mus*) natural. **sol** ~ G natural.

bécasse [bekas] *nf* (*Zool*) woodcock; (*: *sotte*) (silly) goose*.

bécasseau, *pl* ~**x** [bekaso] *nm* sandpiper; (*petit de la bécasse*) young woodcock.

bécassine [bekasin] *nf* snipe.

bêchage [bɛʃaʒ] *nm* digging, turning over.

béchamel [beʃamɛl] *nf*: **(sauce)** ~ béchamel (sauce), white sauce.

bêche [bɛʃ] *nf* spade.

bêcher [beʃe] (1) *vt* (*Agr*) to dig, turn over; (‡*fig*) to pick to pieces.

bêcheur, -euse‡ [bɛʃœʀ, øz] **1** *adj* stuck-up*, toffee-nosed*. **2** *nm,f* stuck-up person*, toffee-nosed person*.

bécot* [beko] *nm* kiss, peck. **gros** ~ smacker*.

bécoter* [bekɔte] (1) **1** *vt* to kiss. **2 se bécoter*** *vpr* to smooch.

becquée [beke] *nf* beakful. **donner la** ~ **à** to feed.

becqueter [bɛkte] (4) *vt* (*Orn*) to peck (at); (‡) to eat. **qu'y a-t-il à** ~ **ce soir?** what's for grub tonight?‡, what's tonight's nosh?‡ *ou* grub?‡

bedaine* [bədɛn] *nf* paunch, corporation, potbelly‡.

bedeau, *pl* ~**x** [bədo] *nm* (*Rel*) beadle, verger.

bedon* [bədɔ̃] *nm* corporation, potbelly‡, paunch.

bedonnant, e* [bədɔnɑ̃, ɑ̃t] *adj* potbellied‡, paunchy, portly.

bedonner* [bədɔne] (1) *vi* to get a paunch *ou* corporation, get potbellied‡.

bédouin, e [bedwɛ̃, in] **1** *adj* Bedouin. **2** *nm,f*: **B**~**(e)** Bedouin.

bée [be] *adj*: **être** *ou* **rester bouche** ~ to stand open-mouthed *ou* gaping; **elle est bouche** ~ **devant lui** she is lost in wonder *ou* left gaping in wonder at him.

béer [bee] (1) *vi* **(a)** to be (wide) open. **(b)** ~ **d'admiration/d'étonnement** to gape in admiration/amazement, stand gaping in admiration/amazement.

beethovénien, -ienne [betɔvenjɛ̃, jɛn] *adj* Beethovenian.

beffroi [befʀwa] *nm* belfry.

bégaiement, bégayement [begɛmɑ̃] *nm* (*lit*) stammering, stuttering. (*fig: débuts*) ~**s** faltering *ou* hesitant beginnings.

bégayer [begeje] (8) **1** *vi* to stammer, stutter, have a stammer. **2** *vt* to stammer (out), falter (out).

bégonia [begɔnja] *nm* begonia.

bègue [bɛg] *nmf* stammerer, stutterer. **être** ~ to stammer, have a stammer.

bégueule [begœl] **1** *nf* prude. **2** *adj* prudish.

bégueulerie [begœlʀi] *nf* prudishness, prudery.

béguin [begɛ̃] *nm* **(a)** (‡: *toquade*) **avoir le** ~ **pour qn** to have a crush on sb*, be sweet on sb*; **elle a eu le** ~ **pour cette petite ferme** she took a great fancy to that little farmhouse. **(b)** (*bonnet*) bonnet.

béguinage [beginaʒ] *nm* (*Rel*) Beguine convent.

béguine [begin] *nf* (*Rel*) Beguine.

behaviorisme [biavjɔʀism(ə)] *nm* behaviourism.

beige [bɛʒ] *adj, nm* beige.

beigne[1]‡ [bɛɲ] *nf* slap, clout*. **donner une** ~ **à qn** to clout sb *, give sb a clout*.

beigne[2] [bɛɲ] *nm* (*Can*) doughnut.

beignet [bɛɲɛ] *nm* *[fruits, légumes]* fritter; (*pâte frite*) doughnut.

bel [bɛl] *adj V* **beau.**

bêlement [bɛlmɑ̃] *nm* (*Zool, fig*) bleat(ing).

bêler [bele] (1) *vi* (*Zool, fig*) to bleat.

belette [bəlɛt] *nf* weasel.

belge [bɛlʒ(ə)] **1** *adj* Belgian. **2** *nmf*: **B**~ Belgian.

Belgique [bɛlʒik] *nf* Belgium.

bélier [belje] *nm* (*Zool*) ram; (*Tech*) ram, pile driver; (*Mil*) (battering) ram. ~ **hydraulique** hydraulic ram; (*Astron*) **le B**~ Aries, the Ram; **être (du) B**~ to be Aries *ou* an Arian.

bélître†† [belitʀ(ə)] *nm* rascal, knave†.

belladone [beladɔn] *nf* (*Bot*) belladonna, deadly nightshade; (*Méd*) belladonna.

bellâtre [bɛlɑtʀ(ə)] *nm* buck, swell*.

belle [bɛl] *V* **beau.**

bellement [bɛlmɑ̃] *adv* (*bel et bien*) well and truly; (†: *avec art*) nicely, gently.

bellicisme [belisism(ə)] *nm* bellicosity, warmongering.

belliciste [belisist(ə)] **1** *adj* warmongering, bellicose. **2** *nmf* warmonger.

belligérance [beliʒeʀɑ̃s] *nf* belligerence, belligerency.

belligérant, e [beliʒeʀɑ̃, ɑ̃t] *adj, nm,f* belligerent.

belliqueux, -euse [belikø, øz] *adj* *humeur, personne* quarrelsome, aggressive; *politique, peuple* warlike, bellicose, aggressive.

bellot, -otte*† [bɛlo, ɔt] *adj* *enfant* bonny.

belon [bəlɔ̃] *nm ou nf* Belon oyster.

belote [bəlɔt] *nf* belote.

belvédère [bɛlvedɛʀ] *nm* belvedere.

bémol [bemɔl] *nm* (*Mus*) flat. **en si** ~ in B flat.

bénédicité [benedisite] *nm* grace. **dire le** ~ to say grace.

bénédictin, e [benediktɛ̃, in] **1** *adj* Benedictine. **2** *nm,f* Benedictine; *V* **travail[1]**. **3** *nf*: **Bénédictine** (*liqueur*) Benedictine.

bénédiction [benediksjɔ̃] *nf* **(a)** (*Rel: consécration*) benediction, blessing; *[église]* consecration; *[drapeau, bateau]* blessing. **recevoir la** ~ to be given a blessing; **donner la** ~ **à** to bless; ~ **nuptiale** marriage blessing; **la** ~ **nuptiale leur sera donnée ...** the marriage ceremony will take place ... .
(b) (*assentiment, faveur*) blessing. **donner sa** ~ **à** to give one's blessing to.
(c) (*: *aubaine*) blessing, godsend. **c'est une** ~ **(du ciel)!** it's a blessing! *ou* a godsend!

bénef‡ [benɛf] *nm* (*abrév de* **bénéfice**) profit.

bénéfice [benefis] **1** *nm* **(a)** (*Comm*) profit. **vendre à** ~ to sell at a profit; **réaliser de gros** ~**s** to make a big profit *ou* big profits; **faire du** ~ to make a profit.
(b) (*avantage*) advantage, benefit. (*Jur*) **il a obtenu un divorce à son** ~ he obtained a divorce in his favour; **il perd tout le** ~ **de sa bonne conduite** he loses all the benefits he has gained from his good behaviour; **concert donné au** ~ **des aveugles** concert given to raise funds for *ou* in aid of the blind; **conclure une affaire à son** ~ to complete a deal to one's advantage; **il a tiré un** ~ **certain de ses efforts** his efforts certainly paid off; **quel** ~ **as-tu à le nier?** what's the point of (your) denying it?, what good is there in (your) denying it?; **laissons-lui le** ~ **du doute** let us give him the benefit of the doubt; (*Jur*) **au** ~ **de l'âge** by prerogative of age.
(c) (*Rel*) benefice, living.
2: (*Jur*) **bénéfice des circonstances atténuantes** benefit of mitigating circumstances; (*Jur*) **sous bénéfice d'inventaire** without liability to debts beyond assets descended.

bénéficiaire [benefisjɛʀ] **1** *adj* *opération* profit-making, profitable; *V* **marge. 2** *nmf* (*gén*) beneficiary; *[testament]* beneficiary; *[chèque]* payee. **être le** ~ **d'une nouvelle mesure** to benefit by a new measure.

bénéficier [benefisje] (7) **bénéficier de** *vt indir* (*jouir de*) to have, enjoy; (*obtenir*) to get, have; (*tirer profit de*) to benefit by *ou* from, gain by. ~ **de certains avantages** to have *ou* enjoy certain advantages; ~ **d'une remise** to get a reduction *ou* discount; ~ **d'un préjugé favorable** to be favourably considered; ~ **d'une mesure/d'une situation** to benefit by *ou* gain by a measure/situation; (*Jur*) ~ **d'un non-lieu** to be (unconditionally) discharged; (*Jur*) ~ **de circonstances atténuantes** to be granted mitigating circumstances; **faire** ~ **qn de certains avantages** to enable sb to enjoy certain advantages; **faire** ~ **qn d'une remise** to give *ou* allow sb a discount.

bénéfique [benefik] *adj* beneficial.

Bénélux [benelyks] *nm*: **le** ~ the Benelux countries.

benêt [bənɛ] **1** *nm* simpleton, silly. **grand** ~ great silly*, stupid lump‡; **faire le** ~ to act stupid *ou* daft‡. **2** *adj m* simple, simple(-minded), silly.

bénévole [benevɔl] *adj* *aide, travail, personne* voluntary, unpaid.

bénévolement [benevɔlmɑ̃] *adv* *travailler* voluntarily, for nothing.

Bengale [bɛ̃gal] *nm* Bengal; *V* **feu[1]**.

bengali [bɛ̃gali] **1** *adj* Bengali, Bengalese. **2** *nm* (*Ling*) Bengali; (*oiseau*) waxbill. **3** *nmf*: **B**~ Bengali, Bengalese.

bénigne [beniɲ] *adj f V* **bénin.**

bénignement [beniɲmɑ̃] *adv* (*littér*) benignly, in a kindly way.

bénignité [beniɲite] *nf* *[maladie]* mildness; (*littér*) *[personne]* benignity, kindness.

bénin, -igne [benɛ̃, iɲ] *adj* **(a)** *accident* slight, minor; *punition* mild; *maladie, remède* mild, harmless; *tumeur* benign. **(b)** (*littér*) *humeur, critique* benign, kindly.

béni-oui-oui* [beniwiwi] *nmf inv* (*péj*) yes man* (*péj*).

bénir [beniʀ] (2) *vt* **(a)** (*Rel*) *fidèle, objet* to bless; *mariage* to bless, solemnize; *V* **dieu.**
(b) (*remercier*) to be eternally grateful to, thank God for. **il bénissait l'arrivée providentielle de ses amis** he thanked God for *ou* was eternally grateful for the providential arrival of his friends; **soyez béni!** bless you!; (*iro*) **ah, toi, je te bénis!** oh curse you! *ou* damn you!‡; ~ **le ciel de qch** to thank God for sth; **béni soit le jour où ...** thank God for the day (when) ...; **je bénis cette coïncidence** (I) thank God for this coincidence.

bénit, e [beni, it] *adj* *pain, cierge* consecrated; *eau* holy.

bénitier [benitje] *nm* (*Rel*) stoup, font; *V* **diable, grenouille.**

benjamin [bɛ̃ʒamɛ̃] *nm* youngest son, youngest child.

benjamine [bɛ̃ʒamin] *nf* youngest daughter, youngest child.

benjoin [bɛ̃ʒwɛ̃] *nm* benzoin.

benne [bɛn] *nf* **(a)** (*Min*) skip, truck, tub. **(b)** *[camion]* (*basculante*) tipper (lorry), dump truck; (*amovible*) skip; *[grue]* scoop, bucket; *[téléphérique]* (cable-)car.

Benoist, Benoît [bənwa] *nm* Benedict.

benoît, e [bənwa, wat] *adj* (*littér*) bland, ingratiating.

benoîtement [bənwatmɑ̃] *adv* (*littér*) blandly, ingratiatingly.

benzène [bɛ̃zɛn] *nm* benzene.

benzine [bɛ̃zin] *nf* benzine.

benzol [bɛ̃zɔl] *nm* benzol.

béotien, -ienne* [beɔsjɛ̃, jɛn] **1** *adj* Boeotian. **2** *nm* **(a)** philistine. **(b)** (*Ling*) Boeotian. **3** *nm,f*: **B**~**(ne)** Boeotian.

béquille [bekij] *nf* **(a)** *[infirme]* crutch. **marcher avec des** ~**s** to walk *ou* be on crutches. **(b)** *[motocyclette, mitrailleuse]* stand; (*Aviat*) tail skid; (*Naut*) shore, prop. **mettre une** ~ **sous qch** to prop *ou* shore sth up. **(c)** *[serrure]* handle.

béquiller [bekije] (1) **1** *vt* (*Naut*) to shore up. **2** *vi* (*) to walk with *ou* on crutches.

ber [bɛʀ] *nm* (*Can: berceau*) cradle.

berbère [bɛʀbɛʀ] **1** *adj* Berber. **2** *nmf*: **B~** Berber.

bercail [bɛʀkaj] *nm* (*Rel, fig*) fold. **rentrer au ~*** to return to the fold.

berçante [bɛʀsɑ̃t] *nf* (*Can*: aussi* **chaise ~**) rocking chair.

berceau, *pl* **~x** [bɛʀso] *nm* **(a)** (*lit*) cradle, crib; (*lieu d'origine*) birthplace. **dès le ~** from birth, from the cradle; **il les prend au ~!*** he snatches them straight from the cradle!, he's a baby *ou* cradle snatcher! **(b)** (*Archit*) barrel vault; (*charmille*) bower, arbour; (*Naut*) cradle.

bercelonnette [bɛʀsəlɔnɛt] *nf* rocking cradle, cradle on rockers.

bercement [bɛʀsəmɑ̃] *nm* rocking (movement).

bercer [bɛʀse] (3) **1** *vt* **(a)** *bébé* to rock; (*dans ses bras*) to rock, cradle; *navire* to rock. **il a été bercé au son du canon** he was reared with the sound of battle in his ears.

(b) (*apaiser*) *douleur* to lull, soothe.

(c) (*tromper*) **~ de** to delude with.

2 se bercer *vpr*: **se ~ de** to delude o.s. with; **se ~ d'illusions** to harbour illusions, delude o.s.

berceur, -euse [bɛʀsœʀ, øz] **1** *adj rythme* lulling, soothing. **2 berceuse** *nf* **(a)** (*chanson*) lullaby, cradlesong; (*Mus*) berceuse. **(b)** (*fauteuil*) rocking chair.

béret [beʀɛ] *nm* beret.

bergamasque [bɛʀgamask(ə)] *nf* bergamask.

bergamote [bɛʀgamɔt] *nf* bergamot orange.

bergamotier [bɛʀgamɔtje] *nm* bergamot.

berge [bɛʀʒ(ə)] *nf* [*rivière*] bank. (‡: *année*) **il a 50 ~s** he's 50 (years old).

berger [bɛʀʒe] *nm* (*lit, Rel*) shepherd. **(chien de) ~** sheepdog; **~ allemand** alsatian; *V* **étoile.**

bergère [bɛʀʒɛʀ] *nf* **(a)** (*personne*) shepherdess. **(b)** (*fauteuil*) wing chair, easy chair.

bergerie [bɛʀʒəʀi] *nf* **(a)** sheepfold, sheep pen; *V* **loup. (b)** (*Littérat*) **~s** pastorals.

bergeronnette [bɛʀʒəʀɔnɛt] *nf* wagtail.

béribéri [beʀibeʀi] *nm* beriberi.

berlander* [bɛʀlɑ̃de] (1) *vi* (*Can*) to prevaricate, equivocate.

Berlin [bɛʀlɛ̃] *n* Berlin. **~-Est/-Ouest** East/West Berlin.

berline [bɛʀlin] *nf* **(a)** (*Aut*) saloon (car) (*Brit*), sedan (*US*); (††: *à chevaux*) berlin. **(b)** (*Min*) truck.

berlingot [bɛʀlɛ̃go] *nm* **(a)** (*bonbon*) boiled sweet, humbug. **(b)** (*emballage*) (pyramid-shaped) carton.

berlinois, e [bɛʀlinwa, waz] **1** *adj* of *ou* from Berlin. **2** *nm,f*: **B~(e)** Berliner.

berlot [bɛʀlo] *nm* (*Can*) sleigh.

berlue [bɛʀly] *nf*: **avoir la ~** to be seeing things.

berme [bɛʀm(ə)] *nf* [*canal*] path; [*fossé*] verge.

bermuda(s) [bɛʀmyda] *nm* bermuda shorts, bermudas.

Bermudes [bɛʀmyd] *nfpl* Bermuda.

bernardin, e [bɛʀnaʀdɛ̃, in] *nm,f* Bernardine, Cistercian.

bernard-l'(h)ermite [bɛʀnaʀlɛʀmit] *nm inv* hermit crab.

berne [bɛʀn(ə)] *nf*: **en ~** ≃ at half-mast; **mettre en ~** ≃ to half-mast.

Berne [bɛʀn(ə)] *n* Berne.

berner [bɛʀne] (1) *vt* (*littér: tromper*) to fool, hoax; (*Hist*) *personne* to toss in a blanket.

bernique[1] [bɛʀnik] *nf* limpet.

bernique[2]* [bɛʀnik] *excl* (*rien à faire*) nothing doing!*, not a chance! *ou* hope!

bernois, e [bɛʀnwa, waz] **1** *adj* Bernese. **2** *nm,f*: **B~(e)** Bernese.

berrichon, -onne [bɛʀiʃɔ̃, ɔn] **1** *adj* of *ou* from the Berry. **2** *nm,f*: **B~(ne)** inhabitant *ou* native of the Berry.

Berthe [bɛʀt(ə)] *nf* Bertha.

Bertrand [bɛʀtʀɑ̃] *nm* Bertrand, Bertram.

béryl [beʀil] *nm* beryl.

besace [bəzas] *nf* scrip, beggar's bag *ou* pouch.

bésef‡ [bezɛf] *adv*: **il n'y en a pas ~** (*quantité*) there's not much (of it) *ou* a lot (of it); (*nombre*) there aren't many (of them) *ou* a lot (of them).

besicles [bezikl(ə)] *nfpl* (*Hist*) spectacles; (*hum*) glasses, specs*.

bésigue [bezig] *nm* bezique.

besogne [bəzɔɲ] *nf* (*travail*) work (*U*), job. **se mettre à la ~** to set to work; **c'est de la belle ~** (*lit*) it's nice work; (*iro*) it's a nice mess; **une sale ~** a nasty job.

besogner [b(ə)zɔɲe] (1) *vi* to toil (away), drudge.

besogneux, -euse [b(ə)zɔɲø, øz] *adj* (*miséreux, mal payé*) needy, poor; (*travailleur*) industrious, hard-working.

besoin [bəzwɛ̃] *nm* **(a)** (*exigence*) need (*de* for). **subvenir** *ou* **pourvoir aux ~s de qn** to provide for sb's needs; **il a de grands/petits ~s** his needs are great/small; **éprouver le ~ de faire qch** to feel the need to do sth; **mentir est devenu un ~ chez lui** lying has become compulsive *ou* a need with him.

(b) (*pauvreté*) **le ~** need, want; **être dans le ~** to be in need *ou* want; **cela les met à l'abri du ~** that will keep the wolf from their door; **une famille dans le ~** a needy family; **pour ceux qui sont dans le ~** for the needy, for those in straitened circumstances.

(c) (*euph*) **~s naturels** nature's needs; **faire ses ~s** [*personne*] to relieve o.s., spend a penny* (*Brit*), go to the john* (*US*); [*animal domestique*] to do its business; **satisfaire un ~ pressant** to relieve o.s.

(d) (*avec avoir*) **avoir ~ de qch** to need sth, be in need of sth, want sth; **avoir ~ de faire qch** to need to do sth; **il n'a pas ~ de venir** he doesn't need *ou* have to come, there's no need for him to come; **il a ~ que vous l'aidiez** he needs your help *ou* you to help him; **pas ~ de dire qu'il ne m'a pas cru** it goes without saying *ou* needless to say he didn't believe me; **je n'ai pas ~ de vous rappeler que ...** there's no need (for me) to remind you that ...; **ce tapis a ~ d'être nettoyé** this carpet needs *ou* wants cleaning; **vous pouvez jouer mais il n'y a pas ~ de faire autant de bruit** you can play but you don't have *ou* need to be so noisy; **il a grand ~ d'aide** he needs help badly, he's badly in need of help; (*iro*) **il avait bien ~ de ça!** that's just what he needed! (*iro*); **est-ce que tu avais ~ d'y aller?*** why on earth did you go?, did you really have to go?, what did you want to go for anyway!*

(e) (*avec être: littér*) **si ~ est, s'il en est ~** if need(s) be, if necessary; **il n'est pas ~ de mentionner que ...** there is no need to mention that ... .

(f) (*loc*) **au ~** if necessary, if need(s) be; **si le ~ s'en fait sentir** if the need arises, if it's felt to be necessary; **en cas de ~** if the need arises, in case of necessity; **pour les ~s de la cause** for the purpose in hand.

bestiaire [bɛstjɛʀ] *nm* **(a)** (*livre*) bestiary. **(b)** (*gladiateur*) gladiator.

bestial, e, *mpl* **-aux** [bɛstjal, o] *adj* bestial, brutish.

bestialement [bɛstjalmɑ̃] *adv* bestially, brutishly.

bestialité [bɛstjalite] *nf* (*sauvagerie*) bestiality, brutishness; (*perversion*) bestiality.

bestiaux [bɛstjo] *nmpl* (*gén*) livestock; (*bovins*) cattle.

bestiole [bɛstjɔl] *nf* (tiny) creature.

bêta[1], **-asse*** [bɛta, ɑs] **1** *adj* silly, stupid. **2** *nm,f* goose*, silly billy*. **gros ~!** great silly!*, silly goose!*

bêta[2] [bɛta] *nm* (*Ling, Phys*) beta.

bétail [betaj] *nm* (*gén*) livestock; (*bovins, fig*) cattle. **gros ~** cattle; **le ~ humain qu'on entasse dans les camps** the people who are crammed like cattle into the camps.

bétaillère [betajɛʀ] *nf* cattle truck.

bête [bɛt] **1** *nf* **(a)** (*animal*) animal; (*insecte*) insect, bug*, creature. **~ (sauvage)** (wild) beast; **nos amies les ~s** our friends the animals, our four-legged friends; **aller soigner les ~s** to go and see to the animals; **gladiateur livré aux ~s** gladiator flung to the beasts; **pauvre petite ~** poor little thing* *ou* creature; **ce chien est une belle ~** this dog is a fine animal *ou* beast; **tu as une petite ~ sur ta manche** there's an insect *ou* a crawly thing* on your sleeve; **ces sales ~s ont mangé mes salades** those wretched creatures have been eating my lettuces.

(b) (*personne*) (*bestial*) beast; (†: *stupide*) fool. **c'est une méchante ~** he is a wicked creature; **quelle sale ~!** (*enfant*) what a wretched pest!; (*adulte*) what a horrible creature!, what a beast!; (*hum*) **c'est une brave** *ou* **une bonne ~!** he is a good-natured sort *ou* soul; (*terme d'affection*) **grande** *ou* **grosse ~!*** you big silly!*; **faire la ~** to act stupid *ou* daft*, play the fool.

2 *adj* **(a)** (*stupide*) *personne, idée, sourire* stupid, silly, foolish, idiotic. **ce qu'il peut être ~!** what a fool he is!; **il est plus ~ que méchant** he may be stupid but he's not malicious, he's stupid rather than really nasty; **il est loin d'être ~** he's far from stupid *ou* from being a fool, he's quite the reverse of stupid; **être ~ comme ses pieds‡** to be too stupid for words, be an absolute fool *ou* ass; **lui, pas si ~, est parti à temps** knowing better *ou* being no fool, he left in time; **ce film est ~ à pleurer** this film is too stupid for words; **c'est ~, on n'a pas ce qu'il faut pour faire des crêpes** it's a shame *ou* it's stupid we haven't got what we need for making pancakes; **que je suis ~!** how silly *ou* stupid of me!, what a fool I am!; **ce n'est pas ~** that's not a bad idea.

(b) (*: *très simple*) **c'est tout ~** it's quite *ou* dead* simple; **~ comme chou** simplicity itself, as easy as pie* *ou* as winking*.

3: bête à bon dieu ladybird; **bête à cornes** horned animal; (*hum*) snail; (*iro*) **bête curieuse** queer *ou* strange animal; **regarder qn comme une bête curieuse** to stand and stare at sb; **bête fauve** big cat, wild beast; **bête féroce** wild animal; **bête noire: c'est ma bête noire** [*chose*] that's my pet hate *ou* bête noire; [*personne*] I just can't stand him; **bête de race** pedigree animal; **bête sauvage** = **bête féroce**; **bête de somme** beast of burden; **bête de trait** draught animal.

bétel [betɛl] *nm* betel.

bêtement [bɛtmɑ̃] *adv* stupidly, foolishly, idiotically. **tout ~** quite simply.

Bethléem [bɛtleɛm] *n* Bethlehem.

Bethsabée [bɛtsabe] *nf* Bathsheba.

bêtifiant, e [betifjɑ̃, ɑ̃t] *adj livre, film* idiotic.

bêtifier [betifje] (7) *vi* to prattle stupidly, talk twaddle.

bêtise [betiz] *nf* **(a)** (*U: stupidité*) stupidity, foolishness, folly. **être d'une ~ crasse** to be incredibly stupid; **j'ai eu la ~ d'accepter** I was foolish enough to accept; **c'était de la ~ d'accepter** it was folly to accept.

(b) (*action stupide*) silly *ou* stupid thing; (*erreur*) blunder; (*frasque*) stupid prank. **ne dis pas de ~s** don't talk nonsense *ou* rubbish; **ne faites pas de ~s, les enfants** don't do anything silly children, don't get into *ou* up to mischief children; **faire une ~** (*action stupide, frasque*) to do something stupid; (*erreur*) to make a blunder, boob*.

(c) (*bagatelle*) trifle, triviality. **dépenser son argent en ~s** to spend *ou* squander one's money on rubbish.

(d) ~ de Cambrai ≃ mint humbug.

(e) (*Can*) **~s*** insults, rude remarks.

béton [betɔ̃] *nm* concrete. **~ armé** reinforced concrete; (*Ftbl*) **faire** *ou* **jouer le ~** to play defensively.

bétonnage [betɔnaʒ] *nm* (*V* **bétonner**) concreting; defensive play.

bétonner [betɔne] (1) **1** *vt* (*Constr*) to concrete. **2** *vi* (*Ftbl*) to play defensively.

bétonnière [betɔnjɛʀ] *nf* cement mixer.

bette [bɛt] *nf* beet.

betterave [bɛtʀav] *nf*: ~ **fourragère** mangel-wurzel, beet; ~ **(rouge)** beetroot (*Brit*), beet (*US*); ~ **sucrière** sugar beet.
betteravier, -ière [bɛtʀavje, jɛʀ] 1 *adj* beetroot (*épith*), of beetroots (*Brit*) *ou* beets (*US*). 2 *nm* beet grower.
beuglant* [bøglɑ̃] *nm* honky-tonk*.
beuglante: [bøglɑ̃t] *nf* (*cri*) yell, holler*; (*chanson*) song. **pousser une** ~ to yell, give a yell *ou* holler*.
beuglement [bøgləmɑ̃] *nm* (*V* **beugler**) lowing (*U*), mooing (*U*); bellowing (*U*); bawling (*U*), hollering* (*U*); blaring (*U*). **pousser des** ~**s** to bawl, bellow.
beugler [bøgle] (1) 1 *vi* **(a)** *[vache]* to low, moo; *[taureau]* to bellow. **(b)** (*) *[personne]* to bawl, bellow, holler*; *[radio]* to blare. **faire** ~ **sa télé** to have one's TV on (at) full blast*. 2 *vt* (*péj*) *chanson* to bellow out, belt out*.
beurre [bœʀ] 1 *nm* **(a)** (*laitier*) butter. ~ **salé/demi-sel** salted/slightly salted butter; **au** ~ *plat* (cooked) in butter; *pâtisserie* made with butter; **faire la cuisine au** ~ to cook with butter; *V* **inventer, motte, œil** *etc.*
(b) (*Culin*) paste. ~ **d'anchois/d'écrevisses** anchovy/shrimp paste; (*substance végétale*) ~ **de cacao/de cacahuètes** cocoa/peanut butter.
(c) (*:loc*) **entrer comme dans du** ~ to go *ou* get in with the greatest (of) ease; **le couteau entre dans cette viande comme dans du** ~ this meat is like butter to cut; **ce rôti, c'est du** ~! this is a very tender joint; **ça va mettre du** ~ **dans les épinards** that will add a little to the kitty; **faire son** ~ to make a packet* *ou* one's pile*, feather one's nest; *V* **compter.**
2: **beurre-frais** *adj inv* (*couleur*) buttercup yellow; (*Culin*) **beurre noir** brown (butter) sauce; **beurre persillé** *ou* **d'escargots** garlic and parsley butter; **beurre roux** roux.
beurré, e [bœʀe] (*ptp de* **beurrer**) 1 *adj* (*: ivre*) canned:, plastered:. 2 *nm* butter-pear, beurré. 3 **beurrée** *nf* (*Can*†) slice of bread and butter.
beurrer [bœʀe] (1) 1 *vt* **(a)** to butter. **tartine beurrée** slice of bread and butter. **(b)** (*Can*) to smear. 2 **se beurrer:** *vpr* to get canned: *ou* plastered:.
beurrier, -ière [bœʀje, jɛʀ] 1 *adj industrie, production* butter (*épith*). **région** ~**ière** butter-producing region. 2 *nm* butter dish.
beuverie [bœvʀi] *nf* drinking bout *ou* session, binge*.
bévue [bevy] *nf* blunder.
bey [bɛ] *nm* bey.
bézef: [bezɛf] *adv* = **bésef:**.
bi... [bi] *préf* bi... .
biacide [biasid] *adj, nm* diacid.
biais [bjɛ] *nm* **(a)** (*détour, artifice*) device, expedient, dodge*. **chercher un** ~ **pour obtenir qch** to find some means of getting sth *ou* expedient for getting sth; **il a trouvé le** *ou* **un** ~ **(pour se faire exempter)** he found a dodge (to get himself exempted); **par quel** ~ **vais-je m'en tirer?** what means can I use to get out of it?, how on earth* am I going to get out of it?; **par le** ~ **de** by means of, using the expedient of.
(b) (*aspect*) angle, way. **c'est par ce** ~ **qu'il faut aborder le problème** the problem should be approached from this angle *ou* in this way.
(c) (*Tex*) (*sens*) bias; (*bande*) piece of cloth cut on the bias *ou* the cross. **coupé** *ou* **taillé dans le** ~ cut on the bias *ou* the cross.
(d) (*ligne oblique*) slant.
(e) (*loc*) **en** ~, **de** ~ slantwise, at an angle; **une allée traverse le jardin en** ~ a path cuts diagonally across the garden; **regarder qn de** ~ to give sb a sidelong glance; **prendre une question de** ~ to tackle a question indirectly *ou* in a roundabout way.
biaiser [bjeze] (1) *vi* **(a)** (*louvoyer*) to sidestep the issue, prevaricate. **(b)** (*obliquer*) to change direction.
bibelot [biblo] *nm* (*objet sans valeur*) trinket, knick-knack; (*de valeur*) bibelot, curio.
biberon [bibʀɔ̃] *nm* feeding bottle, baby's bottle. **élevé au** ~ bottle-fed; **l'heure du** ~ (baby's) feeding time; **élever** *ou* **nourrir au** ~ to bottle-feed.
biberonner: [bibʀɔne] (1) *vi* to tipple*, booze:.
bibi[1]* [bibi] *nm* woman's hat.
bibi[2]: [bibi] *pron* me, yours truly (*hum*).
bibine [bibin] *nf* (weak) beer, dishwater (*hum*). **une infâme** ~ a loathsome brew.
bible [bibl(ə)] *nf* (*livre, fig*) bible. **la B**~ the Bible.
bibliobus [biblijɔbys] *nm* mobile library.
bibliographe [biblijɔgʀaf] *nmf* bibliographer.
bibliographie [biblijɔgʀafi] *nf* bibliography.
bibliographique [biblijɔgʀafik] *adj* bibliographic(al).
bibliomane [biblijɔman] *nmf* booklover.
bibliomanie [biblijɔmani] *nf* bibliomania.
bibliophile [biblijɔfil] *nmf* bibliophile, booklover.
bibliophilie [biblijɔfili] *nf* bibliophilism, love of books.
bibliothécaire [biblijɔtekɛʀ] *nmf* librarian.
bibliothèque [biblijɔtɛk] *nf* (*édifice, pièce*) library; (*meuble*) bookcase; (*collection*) library, collection (of books). ~ **de gare** station bookstall (*Brit*) *ou* newsstand (*US*); ~ **de prêt** lending library.
biblique [biblik] *adj* biblical.
bicaméral, e, *mpl* **-aux** [bikameʀal, o] *adj* bicameral, two-chamber (*épith*).
bicaméralisme [bikameʀalism(ə)] *nm*, **bicamérisme** [bikameʀism(ə)] *nm* bicameral *ou* two-chamber system.
bicarbonate [bikaʀbɔnat] *nm* bicarbonate. ~ **de soude** bicarbonate of soda, sodium bicarbonate, baking soda.
bicarré, e [bikaʀe] *adj* (*Math*) biquadratic.
bicéphale [bisefal] *adj* two-headed, bicephalous (*T*).
biceps [bisɛps] *nm* biceps. **avoir des** *ou* **du** ~* to have a strong *ou* good pair of arms.
biche [biʃ] *nf* hind, doe. **un regard** *ou* **des yeux de** ~ **aux abois** frightened doe-like eyes; (*fig*) **ma** ~ darling, pet.
bicher* [biʃe] (1) *vi* **(a)** *[personnes]* to be pleased with o.s. **(b)** **ça biche?** how's things?*, things O.K. with you?*
bichlorure [biklɔʀyʀ] *nm* bichloride.
bichon, -onne [biʃɔ̃, ɔn] *nm,f* (*chien*) toy dog. **mon** ~* pet, love.
bichonnage [biʃɔnaʒ] *nm* titivation.
bichonner [biʃɔne] (1) *vt* **(a)** (*pomponner*) to dress up, doll up*. (*péj*) **elle est en train de se** ~ **dans sa chambre** she's sprucing herself up *ou* she's titivating (herself) *ou* getting dolled up* in her room. **(b)** (*prendre soin de*) ~ **qn** to wait on sb hand and foot, cosset sb.
bichromate [bikʀɔmat] *nm* bichromate.
bicolore [bikɔlɔʀ] *adj* bicolour(ed), two-colour(ed), two-tone; (*Cartes*) two-suited.
biconcave [bikɔ̃kav] *adj* biconcave.
biconvexe [bikɔ̃vɛks] *adj* biconvex.
bicoque [bikɔk] *nf* (*péj*) shack*, dump*; (*: *maison*) shack*, place*.
bicorne [bikɔʀn(ə)] 1 *nm* cocked hat. 2 *adj* two-horned.
bicot [biko] *nm* (*péj*) wog (*péj*), North African Arab.
bicycle [bisikl(ə)] *nm* (*Can*) bicycle.
bicyclette [bisiklɛt] *nf* **(a)** bicycle, bike*. **aller à la ville à** *ou* **en** ~ to go to town by bicycle, cycle to town; **faire de la** ~ to go cycling, cycle; **sais-tu faire de la** ~? can you cycle?, can you ride a bike?*; ~ **à moteur** motorized pedal cycle, moped (*Brit*).
(b) (*Sport*) cycling.
bidasse* [bidas] *nm* (*conscrit*) soldier, swaddy (*arg Mil*).
bide [bid] *nm* **(a)** (*: ventre*) belly:. **(b)** (*arg Théât*) **être** *ou* **faire un** ~ to be a flop *ou* a washout.
bidet [bidɛ] *nm* **(a)** bidet. **(b)** (*cheval*) (old) nag.
bidoche: [bidɔʃ] *nf* meat.
bidon [bidɔ̃] 1 *nm* **(a)** (*gén*) can, tin; (*à huile*) can; (*à peinture*) tin; *[campeur, soldat]* water bottle, flask. ~ **à lait** milk-churn.
(b) (*: ventre*) belly:.
(c) (*: bluff*) **c'est du** ~ that's a load of codswallop: (*Brit*) *ou* rubbish; **ce n'est pas du** ~ I'm (*ou* he's *etc*) not kidding!:, that's the God's honest truth*.
2 *adj inv* (*: simulé*) *attentat, attaque* mock. **une société** ~ a ghost company.
bidonnant, e: [bidɔnɑ̃, ɑ̃t] *adj* hilarious. **c'était** ~ it was a hell: of a laugh, it had us (*ou* them *etc*) doubled up.
bidonner (se): [bidɔne] (1) *vpr* to split one's sides laughing*, be doubled up with laughter.
bidonville [bidɔ̃vil] *nm* shanty town.
bidous [bidu] *nmpl* (*Can*) money.
bidule* [bidyl] *nm* (*machin*) thingummy* (*Brit*), thingumabob*, contraption, (*petit*) gadget.
bief [bjɛf] *nm* **(a)** *[canal]* reach. **(b)** *[moulin]* ~ **d'amont** mill race; ~ **d'aval** tail race *ou* water.
bielle [bjɛl] *nf* connecting rod; (*Aut*) connecting rod, con rod*.
bien [bjɛ̃] 1 *adv* **(a)** (*de façon satisfaisante*) *jouer, dormir, travailler* well; *conseiller, choisir* well, wisely; *fonctionner* properly, well. **aller** *ou* **se porter** ~, **être** ~ **portant** to be well, be in good health; **il a** ~ **réussi** he's done well (for himself); **cette porte ferme** ~ this door shuts properly *ou* well; **la télé* ne marche pas** ~ the telly* isn't working properly *ou* right; **il s'habille** ~ he dresses well *ou* smartly; **il parle** ~ **l'anglais** he speaks good English, he speaks English well; **elle est** ~ **coiffée aujourd'hui** her hair looks nice *ou* is nicely done today; **nous sommes** ~ **nourris à l'hôtel** we get good food *ou* we are well fed at the hotel; **il a** ~ **pris ce que je lui ai dit** he took what I had to say in good part *ou* quite well; **il s'y est** ~ **pris (pour le faire)** he went about it the right way; **si je me rappelle** ~ if I remember right *ou* correctly; **ils vivent très** ~ **avec son salaire** they live very comfortably *ou* get along very well on his salary; **on vit** ~ **dans ce pays** life is pleasant in these parts.
(b) (*selon les convenances, la morale, la raison*) *se conduire, agir* well, decently. **il pensait** ~ **faire** he thought he was doing the right thing; **vous avez** ~ **fait** you did the right thing, you did right; **se tenir** ~ **à table** to behave properly *ou* well at table; **il faut te tenir particulièrement** ~ **aujourd'hui** you must behave especially well *ou* be especially good today, you must be on your best behaviour today; **pour** ~ **faire, il faudrait ...** (in order) to do it *ou* to do things properly one should ...; **faire** ~ **les choses** to do things properly *ou* in style; **vous faites** ~ **de me le dire!** you've done well to tell me!, it's a good thing you've told me!; **vous feriez** ~ **de partir tôt** you'd do well *ou* you'd be well advised to leave early.
(c) (*sans difficulté*) *supporter* well; *se rappeler* well, clearly. **on comprend** ~**/très** ~ **pourquoi** one can quite/very easily understand *ou* see why; **il peut très** ~ **le faire** he can quite easily do it.
(d) (*exprimant le degré*) (*très*) very, really, awfully*; (*beaucoup*) very much, thoroughly; (*trop*) rather, jolly* (*Brit*), pretty*. ~ **mieux** much better; ~ **souvent** quite often; **nous sommes** ~ **contents de vous voir** we're very glad *ou* awfully* pleased to see you; ~ **plus heureux/cher** far *ou* much happier/more expensive; **c'est un** ~ **beau pays** it's a really *ou* truly beautiful country; **nous avons** ~ **ri** we had a good laugh; **les enfants se sont** ~ **amusés** the children thoroughly enjoyed themselves *ou* had great fun; **vos œufs sont** ~ **frais?** are your eggs really *ou* quite fresh?; **question** ~ **délicate** highly sensitive question; ~ **trop bête** far too stupid; **tout cela est** ~ **joli mais** that's all very well but; **elle est** ~ **jeune (pour se marier)** she is very *ou* rather young (to be getting married); **nous avons** ~ **travaillé aujourd'hui** we've done some good work today; **c'est** ~ **moderne pour mes goûts** it's rather too modern for my taste; **il me paraît** ~ **sûr de lui** he seems to me to be rather *ou* jolly* (*Brit*) *ou* pretty* sure of himself.

(e) (*effectivement*) indeed, definitely; (*interrog: réellement*) really. **nous savons ~ où il se cache** we know perfectly well *ou* quite well where he's hiding; **j'avais ~ dit que je ne viendrais pas** I DID say *ou* I certainly did say that I wouldn't come; **je trouve ~ que c'est un peu cher mais tant pis** I DO think it's rather dear *ou* I agree it's rather dear but too bad; **je sais ~ mais ...** I know (full well) but ..., I agree but ...; **c'est ~ une erreur** it's definitely *ou* certainly a mistake; **c'est ~ à ton frère que je pensais** it was indeed your brother I was thinking of; **ce n'est pas lui mais ~ son frère qui est docteur** it's not he but his brother who is a doctor, it's his brother not he who is a doctor; **dis-lui ~ que** be sure to *ou* and tell him that, make sure you tell him that; **je vous avais ~ averti** I gave you due *ou* ample warning; **est-ce ~ mon manteau?** is it really my coat?; **était-ce ~ une erreur?** was it really *ou* in fact a mistake?

(f) (*exclamatif: vraiment, justement*) **il s'agit ~ de cela!** as if that's the point!; **voilà ~ les femmes!** how like women!, that's just like women!, that's women all over!; **c'est ~ ma veine!*** (it's) just my luck!; **c'était ~ la peine!** after all that trouble!, it wasn't worth the trouble!; **c'est ~ cela, on t'invite et tu te décommandes!** that's right *ou* that's just like it! – you're invited and you call off!

(g) (*intensif*) **ferme ~ la porte** shut the door properly, make sure you shut the door; **tourne ~ ton volant à droite** turn your wheel hard to the right; **écoute-moi ~** listen to me carefully; **regardez ~ ce qu'il va faire** watch what he does carefully; **mets-toi ~ en face** stand right *ou* straight opposite; **percer un trou ~ au milieu** to knock a hole right *ou* bang* in the centre; **tiens-toi ~ droit** stand quite straight; **ça m'est ~ égal** it's all one *ou* the same to me; **il est mort et ~ mort** he is dead and buried *ou* gone; **c'est ~ compris?** is that clearly *ou* quite understood?; **c'est ~ promis?** is that a firm promise?; **il arrivera ~ à se débrouiller** he'll manage to cope all right; **ça finira ~ par s'arranger** it's bound to work out all right in the end; **j'espère ~!** I should hope so (too)!; **on verra ~** we'll see, time will tell; **où peut-il ~ être?** where on earth* can he be?, where CAN he be?; **il se pourrait ~ qu'il pleuve** it could well rain.

(h) (*malgré tout*) **il fallait ~ que ça se fasse** it had to be done; **il fallait ~ que ça arrive** it was bound to happen; **j'étais ~ obligé d'accepter** I was more or less *ou* pretty well* obliged *ou* bound to accept; **il faut ~ le supporter** one just has to put up with it; **il pourrait ~ venir nous voir de temps en temps!** he could at least come and see us now and then!

(i) (*volontiers*) **je mangerais ~ un morceau** I wouldn't mind something to eat; **il partirait ~ en vacances mais il a trop de travail** he would gladly go *ou* he'd be only too glad to go on holiday but he has too much work to do; **j'irais ~ mais ...** I'd willingly *ou* happily *ou* gladly go but ...; **je voudrais ~ t'y voir!** I wouldn't half† like to see you do it!; **je verrais très ~ un vase sur la cheminée** I think a vase on the mantelpiece might look very nice.

(j) (*au moins*) at least. **il y a ~ 3 jours que je ne l'ai vu** I haven't seen him for at least 3 days; **cela vaut ~ ce prix là** it's well worth the price *ou* that much, it's worth at least that price.

(k) **~ des ...** a good many ..., many a ...; **~ du, ~ de la** a great deal of; **je connais ~ des gens qui auraient protesté** I know a good many *ou* quite a few who would have protested; **ils ont eu ~ de la chance** they were really very lucky; **elle a eu ~ du mal ou de la peine à élever ses enfants** she had a good *ou* great deal of difficulty in bringing up her children; **ça fait ~ du monde** that makes an awful lot of people.

(l) **~ que** although, though; **~ que je ne puisse pas venir** although *ou* though I can't come.

(m) (*loc*) **ah ~ (ça) alors!** (*surprise*) well, well!, just fancy!; (*indignation*) well really!; **ah ~ oui** well of course; **~ entendu, ~ sûr, ~ évidemment** of course; (*dans une lettre*) **~ à vous** yours; **ni ~ ni mal** so-so*; **~ lui en a pris** it was just as well he did it; (*iro*) a lot of good it has done him; **c'est ~ fait (pour lui)** it serves him right.

2 *adj inv* **(a)** (*satisfaisant*) *personne* good; *film, tableau, livre* good, fine. **elle est très ~ comme secrétaire** she's a very good *ou* competent secretary; **donnez-lui quelque chose de ~** give him something really good; **ce serait ~ s'il venait** it would be good if he were to come; (*approbation*) **~!** good!, fine!; (*exaspération*) **~! ~!, c'est ~!** all right!, all right!, O.K.!, O.K.!*

(b) (*en bonne forme*) well, in good form *ou* health *ou* shape. **il n'était pas très ~ ce matin** he was out of sorts *ou* off colour* (*Brit*) *ou* he wasn't in very good form this morning.

(c) (*beau*) *personne* good-looking, nice-looking; *chose* nice. **elle était très ~ quand elle était jeune** she was very attractive *ou* good-looking when she was young; **il est ~ de sa personne** he's a good-looking man *ou* a fine figure of a man; **ils ont une maison tout ce qu'il y a de ~*** they've got a smashing* *ou* really lovely *ou* nice house; **ce bouquet fait ~ sur la cheminée** the flowers look nice on the mantelpiece.

(d) (*à l'aise*) **il est ~ partout** he is *ou* feels at home anywhere; **on est ~ à l'ombre** it's pleasant *ou* nice in the shade; **on est ~ ici** it's nice here, we like it here; **je suis ~ dans ce fauteuil** I'm very comfortable in this chair; **elle se trouve ~ dans son nouveau poste** she's very happy in her new job; **laisse-le, il est ~ où il est!** leave him alone — he's quite all right where he is *ou* he's fine where he is; (*iro*) **vous voilà ~!** now you've done it!, you're in a fine mess now!

(e) (*moralement, socialement acceptable*) nice **c'est pas ~ de dire ça** it's not nice to say that; **ce n'est pas ~ de faire ça** it's not nice to do that, it's wrong to do that; **c'est ~ ce qu'il a fait là** it was very good *ou* decent *ou* nice of him to do that; **c'est ~ à vous de les aider** it's good *ou* nice of you to help them; **c'est un type ~*** he's a decent *ou* nice fellow; **trouves-tu ~ qu'il ait fait cela?** do you think it was very nice of him to do that?; **c'est une femme ~** she's a very nice woman; **des gens ~** very nice *ou* decent people.

(f) (*en bons termes*) **être ~ avec qn** to be on good terms *ou* get on well with sb; **ils sont ~ ensemble** they're on the best of terms; **se mettre ~ avec qn** to get on the good *ou* right side of sb, get into sb's good books*.

3 *nm* **(a)** (*ce qui est avantageux, agréable*) good. **le ~ public** the public good; **pour le ~ de l'humanité** for the good of humanity; **c'est pour ton ~!** it's for your own good!; **pour son (plus grand) ~** for his (greater) benefit; **finalement cet échec temporaire a été un ~** in the end this setback was a good thing; **je trouve qu'il a changé en ~** I find he has changed for the better *ou* he has improved; **faire du ~ à qch/qn** to do sth/sb good; **ses paroles m'ont fait du ~** his words did me good, I took comfort from his words; **dire du ~ de** to speak well of; **parler en ~ de qn** to speak favourably *ou* well of sb; **vouloir du ~ à qn** to wish sb well; (*iro*) **un ami qui vous veut du ~** a well-wisher; **on a dit le plus grand ~ de ce livre/de cet acteur** this book/this actor has been highly praised, people spoke very highly *ou* favourably of this book/this actor; **on dit beaucoup de ~ de ce restaurant** this restaurant has got a very good name, people speak very highly of this restaurant; **grand ~ vous fasse!** much good may it do you!, you're welcome to it!; (*littér*) **être du dernier ~ avec qn** to be on the closest terms possible *ou* on intimate terms with sb.

(b) (*ce qui a une valeur morale*) **savoir discerner le ~ du mal** to be able to tell good from evil *ou* right from wrong; **faire le ~** to do good; **rendre le ~ pour le mal** to return good for evil.

(c) (*gén: possession*) possession, property (*U*); (*argent*) fortune; (*terres*) estate. **~s** goods, possessions, property; **cette bibliothèque est son ~ le plus cher** this bookcase is his most treasured possession; **la tranquillité est le seul ~ qu'il désire** peace of mind is all he asks for; **il considère tout comme son ~** he regards everything as being his property *ou* his own; **il est très attaché aux ~s de ce monde** he lays great store by worldly goods *ou* possessions; (*Prov*) **~ mal acquis ne profite jamais** ill gotten ill spent, ill-gotten goods *ou* gains seldom prosper; **il a dépensé tout son ~** he has gone through all his fortune; **avoir du ~ (au soleil)** to have property; **laisser tous ses ~s à ...** to leave all one's (worldly) goods *ou* possessions to ... .

4: bien-aimé(e) *adj, nm(f), pl* **bien-aimé(e)s** beloved; **biens de consommation** consumer goods; **bien-être** *nm* (*physique*) well-being; (*matériel*) comfort, material well-being; **bien de famille** family estate; **biens fonciers** = **biens immeubles**; **bien-fondé** *nm [opinion, assertion]* validity; (*Jur*) *[plainte]* cogency; **biens immeubles, biens immobiliers** real estate *ou* property, landed property; **biens meubles, biens mobiliers** personal property *ou* estate, movables; **bien pensant** *adj* (*Rel*) God-fearing; (*Pol, gén*) right-thinking; (*péj*) **les bien-pensants** right-thinking people; **biens privés** private property; **biens publics** public property.

bienfaisance [bjɛ̃fəzɑ̃s] *nf* charity. **association** *ou* **œuvre de ~** charitable organization; **l'argent sera donné à des œuvres de ~** the money will be given to charity.

bienfaisant, e [bjɛ̃fəzɑ̃, ɑ̃t] *adj* **(a)** *climat, cure, influence* salutary, beneficial; *pluie* refreshing, beneficial. **(b)** *personne* beneficent, kind, kindly.

bienfait [bjɛ̃fɛ] *nm* kindness. **c'est un ~ du ciel!** it's a godsend! *ou* a blessing!; **les ~s de la science** the benefits of science; **les ~s d'un traitement** the beneficial action *ou* effects of a treatment; **il commence à ressentir les ~s de son séjour à la campagne** he is beginning to feel the beneficial effects *ou* the benefit of his stay in the country *ou* the good his stay in the country has done him.

bienfaiteur [bjɛ̃fɛtœʀ] *nm* benefactor.

bienfaitrice [bjɛ̃fɛtʀis] *nf* benefactress.

bienheureux, -euse [bjɛ̃nœʀø, øz] *adj* **(a)** (*Rel*) blessed, blest. **les ~** the blessed, the blest. **(b)** happy.

biennal, e, *mpl* **-aux** [bjenal, o] **1** *adj* biennial. **2 biennale** *nf* biennial event.

bienpensant, e [bjɛ̃pɑ̃sɑ̃, ɑ̃t] adj *V* **bien.**

bienséance [bjɛ̃seɑ̃s] *nf* propriety, decorum. **les ~s** the proprieties, the rules of etiquette.

bienséant, e [bjɛ̃seɑ̃, ɑ̃t] *adj action, conduite* proper, seemly, becoming. **il n'est pas ~ de bâiller** it is unbecoming *ou* unseemly to yawn, it isn't the done thing to yawn.

bientôt [bjɛ̃to] *adv* soon. **à ~!** see you soon!, 'bye for now!*; **c'est ~ dit** it's easier said than done, it's easy to say; **on est ~ arrivé** we'll soon be there, we'll be there shortly; **on ne pourra ~ plus circuler dans Paris** before long it will be impossible to drive in Paris; **c'est pour ~?** is it due soon?, any chance of its being ready soon?; (*naissance*) is the baby expected *ou* due soon?; **il est ~ minuit** it's nearly midnight; **il aura ~ 30 ans** he'll soon be 30, it will soon be his 30th birthday; **il eut ~ fait de finir son travail**† he finished his work in no time, he lost no time in finishing his work.

bienveillance [bjɛ̃vɛjɑ̃s] *nf* benevolence, kindness (*envers* to). **par ~** out of kindness; **examiner un cas avec ~** to give favourable consideration to a case; (*Admin*) **je sollicite de votre haute ~ ...** I beg (leave) to request ... .

bienveillant, e [bjɛ̃vɛjɑ̃, ɑ̃t] *adj* benevolent, kindly.

bienvenu, e [bjɛ̃vny] **1** *adj*: **remarque ~e** apposite *ou* well-chosen remark.

2 *nm,f*: **vous êtes le ~, soyez le ~** you are very welcome, pleased to see you*; **une tasse de café serait la ~e** a cup of coffee would be (most) welcome.

3 bienvenue *nf* welcome. **souhaiter la ~e à qn** to welcome sb; **~e à vous!** welcome (to you)!, you are most welcome!; **allocution de ~e** welcoming speech; (*Can*) **~e!** welcome!

bière[1] [bjɛʀ] *nf* beer. **garçon, 2 ~s!** waiter, 2 beers!; **~ blonde**

lager; ~ **brune** brown ale, stout; ~ **(à la) pression** draught beer.

bière² [bjɛʀ] *nf* coffin. **mettre qn en** ~ to put *ou* place sb in his coffin; **la mise en** ~ **a eu lieu ce matin** the body was placed in the coffin this morning.

biffage [bifaʒ] *nm* crossing out.

biffer [bife] (1) *vt* to cross out, strike out. ~ **à l'encre/au crayon** to ink/pencil out.

biffure [bifyʀ] *nf* crossing out.

bifocal, e, *mpl* **-aux** [bifɔkal, o] *adj* bifocal. **lunettes** ~**es** bifocals.

bifteck [biftɛk] *nm* (piece of) steak. ~ **de cheval** horsemeat steak.

bifurcation [bifyʀkɑsjɔ̃] *nf [route]* fork, branching off, junction; (*Rail*) fork, branching off; *[artère, tige]* branching; (*fig*) change, branching off.

bifurquer [bifyʀke] (1) *vi* **(a)** *[route, voie ferrée]* to fork, branch off. **(b)** *[véhicule]* to turn off (*vers, sur* for); (*fig*) *[personne]* to branch off (*vers* into). ~ **sur la droite** to bear right.

bigame [bigam] **1** *adj* bigamous. **2** *nmf* bigamist.

bigamie [bigami] *nf* bigamy.

bigarré, e [bigaʀe] (*ptp de* **bigarrer**) *adj* **(a)** (*bariolé*) *vêtement* many-coloured, rainbow-coloured; *groupe* colourfully dressed, gaily coloured. **(b)** (*fig*) *foule* motley (*épith*); *société, peuple* heterogeneous, mixed.

bigarreau, *pl* ~**x** [bigaʀo] *nm* bigarreau, bigaroon (cherry).

bigarrer [bigaʀe] (1) *vt* to mottle, variegate.

bigarrure [bigaʀyʀ] *nf* coloured pattern. **la** ~ *ou* **les** ~**s d'un tissu** the medley of colours in a piece of cloth, the gaily-coloured pattern of a piece of cloth.

bigle† [bigl(ə)] *adj* (*hum*) squint(-eyed), cross-eyed.

bigler‡ [bigle] (1) **1** *vt femme* to eye up*; *objet* to take a squint at*. **2** *vi* (*loucher*) to squint, have a squint. **arrête de** ~ **sur** *ou* **dans mon jeu** stop squinting at my cards*, take your beady eyes off my cards*.

bigleux, -euse* [biglø, øz] *adj* (*myope*) short-sighted. **quel** ~ **tu fais!** you need glasses!

bigophone* [bigɔfɔn] *nm* phone*, blower‡. **passer un coup de** ~ **à qn** to get sb on the blower‡, give sb a ring.

bigorneau, *pl* ~**x** [bigɔʀno] *nm* winkle.

bigorner‡ [bigɔʀne] (1) **1** *vt voiture* to smash up. **2 se bigorner** *vpr* (*se battre*) to come to blows, scrap* (*avec* with); (*se disputer*) to have a brush *ou* an argument *ou* a barney‡ (*avec* with).

bigot, e [bigo, ɔt] **1** *adj* over-pious, bigoted, holier-than-thou. **2** *nm,f* (religious) bigot.

bigoterie [bigɔtʀi] *nf* (*péj*) (religious) bigotry, pietism.

bigoudi [bigudi] *nm* (hair-)curler *ou* roller. **une femme en** ~**s** a woman (with her hair) in curlers *ou* rollers.

bigre [bigʀ(ə)] *excl* (*hum*) gosh!*, holy smoke!*

bigrement [bigʀəmɑ̃] *adv chaud, bon* dashed*, jolly*; *changer* a heck of a lot*. **on a** ~ **bien mangé** we had a jolly good meal*.

bihebdomadaire [biɛbdɔmadɛʀ] *adj* twice-weekly.

bijou, *pl* ~**x** [biʒu] *nm* jewel; (*chef d'œuvre*) gem. **un** ~ **de précision** a marvel of precision; (*terme d'affection*) **mon** ~ my love, pet; **les** ~**x d'une femme** a woman's jewels *ou* jewellery.

bijouterie [biʒutʀi] *nf* (*boutique*) jeweller's (shop); (*commerce*) jewellery business *ou* trade; (*art*) jewellery-making; (*bijoux*) jewellery.

bijoutier, -ière [biʒutje, jɛʀ] *nm,f* jeweller.

bikini [bikini] *nm* bikini.

bilabial, e, *mpl* **-aux** [bilabjal, o] (*Ling*) **1** *adj* bilabial. **2 bilabiale** *nf* bilabial.

bilame [bilam] *nf* (*Phys*) bimetallic strip.

bilan [bilɑ̃] *nm* **(a)** (*évaluation*) appraisal, assessment; (*résultats*) results; (*conséquences*) consequences. **le** ~ **d'une catastrophe** the final toll of a disaster; **faire le** ~ **d'une situation** to take stock of *ou* assess a situation; **'camion fou sur l'autoroute,** ~**: 3 morts'** 'runaway lorry on motorway: 3 dead'; (*Méd*) ~ **de santé** checkup; **se faire faire un** ~ **de santé** to go for *ou* have a checkup.

(b) (*Fin*) balance sheet, statement of accounts. **dresser** *ou* **établir son** ~ to draw up the balance sheet; ~ **de liquidation** statement of affairs (*in a bankruptcy petition*).

bilatéral, e, *mpl* **-aux** [bilateʀal, o] *adj* bilateral. **stationnement** ~ parking on both sides (of the road).

bilboquet [bilbɔkɛ] *nm* cup-and-ball game.

bile [bil] *nf* (*Anat, fig: amertume*) bile. (*fig*) **se faire de la** ~ **(pour)** to get worried (about), worry o.s. sick (about)*.

biler (se)* [bile] (1) *vpr* (*gén nég*) to worry o.s. sick* (*pour* about). **ne vous bilez pas!** don't get all worked up!* *ou* het up!*, don't get yourself all worried!

bileux, -euse* [bilø, øz] *adj* easily upset *ou* worried. **il n'est pas** ~**!, ce n'est pas un** ~**!** he's not one to worry *ou* to let things bother him, he doesn't let things bother him; **quel** ~ **tu fais!** what a fretter* *ou* worrier you are!

biliaire [biljɛʀ] *adj* biliary; *V* **calcul, vésicule.**

bilieux, -ieuse [biljø, jøz] *adj teint* bilious, yellowish; *personne, tempérament* irritable, testy, irascible.

bilingue [bilɛ̃g] *adj* bilingual.

bilinguisme [bilɛ̃gɥism(ə)] *nm* bilingualism.

billard [bijaʀ] *nm* **(a)** (*jeu*) billiards (*sg*); (*table*) billiard table; (*salle*) billiard room. **boule de** ~ billiard ball; **faire un** ~ to play a game of billiards; ~ **japonais** pinball, pin table.

(b) (**loc*) **passer sur le** ~ to be operated on, have an operation; **c'est du** ~ it's dead easy*, it's a piece of cake* (*Brit*) *ou* a cinch*; **cette route est un vrai** ~ this road is like a billiard table.

bille [bij] *nf* **(a)** (*boule*) *[enfant]* marble; *[billard]* (billiard) ball. **jouer aux** ~**s** to play marbles, have a game of marbles.

(b) ~ **de bois** billet, block of wood.

(c) (*: *visage*) mug‡, face. **il a fait une drôle de** ~**!** you should have seen his face!; ~ **de clown** funny face; **il a une bonne** ~ he's got a jolly face.

billet [bijɛ] **1** *nm* **(a)** ticket. ~ **de quai/train/loterie** platform/train/lottery ticket; ~ **circulaire/collectif** round-trip/group ticket; **est-ce que tu as ton** ~ **de retour?** have you got your return (*Brit*) *ou* round trip (*US*) ticket?; **prendre un** ~ **aller/aller-retour** to take a single (*Brit*) *ou* one-way (*US*)/return (*Brit*) *ou* round-trip (*US*) ticket.

(b) (*Banque, Fin*) note, bill (*US*); (*: *1.000 anciens francs ou 10 nouveaux francs*) ≃ quid*. ~ **de 10 francs** 10-franc note; *V* **faux²**.

(c) (*littér ou* †: *lettre*) note, short letter.

(d) (*loc*) **je te fiche** *ou* **flanque mon** ~ **qu'il ne viendra pas!‡** I bet you my bottom dollar* *ou* a pound to a penny* (*Brit*) *ou* a dollar to a doughnut* (*US*) he won't come.

2: billet de banque banknote; **billet de commerce** promissory note; **billet doux** billet doux, love letter; **billet de faveur** complimentary ticket; (*Mil*) **billet de logement** billet; **billet à ordre** promissory note, bill of exchange; **billet de parterre*†: prendre** *ou* **ramasser un billet de parterre** to come a cropper*, fall flat on one's face; **billet au porteur** bearer order; **billet de retard** *note from public transport authorities attesting late running of train etc.*

billevesées [bijvəze] *nfpl* (*littér: sornettes*) nonsense (*U*).

billion [biljɔ̃] *nm* (*million de millions*) billion (*Brit*), trillion (*US*); (†: *milliard*) milliard (*Brit*), billion (*US*).

billot [bijo] *nm [boucher, bourreau, cordonnier]* block; (*Can*) log (of wood). (*fig*) **j'en mettrais ma tête sur le** ~ I'd stake my life on it.

bilobé, e [bilɔbe] *adj* bilobed.

bimbeloterie [bɛ̃blɔtʀi] *nf* (*objets*) knick-knacks, fancy goods (*Brit*); (*commerce*) fancy goods business (*Brit*).

bimbelotier, -ière [bɛ̃blɔtje, jɛʀ] *nm,f* (*fabricant*) fancy goods manufacturer (*Brit*); (*marchand*) fancy goods dealer (*Brit*).

bimensuel, -elle [bimɑ̃sɥɛl] *adj* fortnightly (*surtout Brit*), bimonthly.

bimensuellement [bimɑ̃sɥɛlmɑ̃] *adv* fortnightly (*surtout Brit*), twice a month.

bimétallique [bimetalik] *adj* bimetallic.

bimétallisme [bimetalism(ə)] *nm* bimetallism.

bimoteur [bimɔtœʀ] **1** *adj* twin-engined. **2** *nm* twin-engined plane.

binage [binaʒ] *nm* hoeing, harrowing.

binaire [binɛʀ] *adj* binary.

biner [bine] (1) *vt* to hoe, harrow.

binette [binɛt] *nf* **(a)** (*Agr*) hoe. **(b)** (*: *visage*) face, dial‡.

bing [biŋ] *excl* smack!, thwack!

biniou [binju] *nm* (*Mus*) (Breton) bagpipes; (*: *téléphone*) phone, blower‡.

binocle [binɔkl(ə)] *nm* pince-nez.

binoculaire [binɔkylɛʀ] *adj* binocular.

binôme [binom] *nm* binomial.

biochimie [bjɔʃimi] *nf* biochemistry.

biochimique [bjɔʃimik] *adj* biochemical.

biographe [bjɔgʀaf] *nmf* biographer.

biographie [bjɔgʀafi] *nf* biography. ~ **romancée** biographical novel.

biographique [bjɔgʀafik] *adj* biographical.

biologie [bjɔlɔʒi] *nf* biology.

biologique [bjɔlɔʒik] *adj* biological; *produits, aliments* natural, organic.

biologiste [bjɔlɔʒist(ə)] *nmf* biologist.

biophysique [bjɔfizik] *nf* biophysics (*sg*).

biopsie [bjɔpsi] *nf* biopsy.

biosphère [bjɔsfɛʀ] *nf* biosphere.

bioxyde [biɔksid] *nm* dioxide.

bipale [bipal] *adj* twin-bladed.

biparti, e, bipartite [bipaʀti] *adj*, **bipartite** [bipaʀtit] *adj* (*Bot*) bipartite; (*Pol*) two-party, bipartite.

bipède [bipɛd] *adj, nm* biped.

biphasé, e [bifaze] *adj* diphase, two-phase.

biplace [biplas] *adj, nm* two-seater.

biplan [biplɑ̃] **1** *adj*: **avion** ~ biplane. **2** *nm* biplane.

bipolaire [bipɔlɛʀ] *adj* bipolar.

bipolarité [bipɔlaʀite] *nf* bipolarity.

bique [bik] *nf* nanny-goat. (*péj*) **vieille** ~ old hag, old trout* (*Brit*), old witch*.

biquet, -ette [bikɛ, ɛt] *nm,f* (*Zool*) kid. (*terme d'affection*) **mon** ~ love, ducky* (*Brit*).

biquotidien, -ienne [bikɔtidjɛ̃, jɛn] *adj* twice-daily.

birbe [biʀb(ə)] *nm* (*péj*) **vieux** ~ old fuddy-duddy‡, old fogey*.

biréacteur [biʀeaktœʀ] *nm* twin-engined jet.

biréfringence [biʀefʀɛ̃ʒɑ̃s] *nf* birefringence.

biréfringent, e [biʀefʀɛ̃ʒɑ̃, ɑ̃t] *adj* birefringent.

birème [biʀɛm] *nf* (*Antiq*) bireme.

birman, e [biʀmɑ̃, an] **1** *adj* Burmese. **2** *nm* (*Ling*) Burmese. **3** *nm,f*: **B**~**(e)** Burmese.

Birmanie [biʀmani] *nf* Burma.

bis¹ [bis] **1** *adv*: ~**!** (*Théât*) encore!; (*Mus: sur partition*) repeat, twice; (*numéro*) 12 ~ 12a. **2** *nm* (*Théât*) encore.

bis², e [bi, biz] *adj* greyish-brown, brownish-grey; *V* **pain.**

bisaïeul [bizajœl] *nm* great-grandfather.

bisaïeule [bizajœl] *nf* great-grandmother.

bisannuel, -elle [bizanɥɛl] *adj* biennial.

bisbille* [bisbij] *nf* squabble, tiff. **être en** ~ **avec qn** to be at loggerheads *ou* at odds *ou* at variance with sb.

Biscaye [biskɛ] *n*: **le golfe de** ~ the Bay of Biscay.

biscornu, e [biskɔʀny] *adj forme* irregular, crooked; *idée,*

esprit cranky, peculiar; *raisonnement* tortuous, cranky. **un chapeau ~** a shapeless hat.
biscoteaux* [biskɔto] *nmpl* biceps. **avoir des ~** to have a good pair of biceps.
biscotte [biskɔt] *nf* rusk.
biscuit [biskɥi] **1** *nm* **(a)** (*Culin*) sponge cake. **~ (sec)** biscuit (*Brit*), cracker (*US*). **(b)** (*céramique*) biscuit, bisque. **2: biscuit de chien** dog biscuit; **biscuit à la cuiller** sponge finger; **biscuit de Savoie** sponge cake.
biscuiterie [biskɥitʀi] *nf* (*usine*) biscuit factory; (*commerce*) biscuit trade.
bise[1] [biz] *nf* North wind.
bise[2] [biz] *nf* kiss. **faire une ~ à qn** to kiss sb, give sb a kiss; **il lui a fait une petite ~ rapide** he gave her a quick peck* *ou* kiss.
biseau, *pl* **~x** [bizo] *nm* (*bord*) *[glace, vitre]* bevel, bevelled edge; (*Menuiserie*) chamfer, chamfered edge; (*outil*) bevel. **en ~** bevelled, with a bevelled edge; chamfered, with a chamfered edge.
biseautage [bizotaʒ] *nm* (*V* **biseau**) bevelling; chamfering.
biseauter [bizote] (1) *vt glace, vitre* to bevel; (*Menuiserie*) to chamfer; *cartes* to mark.
bisexué, e [bisɛksɥe] *adj* bisexual.
bismuth [bismyt] *nm* bismuth.
bison [bizɔ̃] *nm* bison, American buffalo.
bisque [bisk(ə)] *nf* (*Culin*) bisk, bisque. **~ de homard** lobster soup, bisque of lobster.
bisquer* [biske] (1) *vi* to be riled* *ou* nettled. **faire ~ qn** to rile* *ou* nettle sb.
bissac†† [bisak] *nm* shoulder bag.
bissecteur, -trice [bisɛktœʀ, tʀis] **1** *adj* bisecting. **2 bissectrice** *nf* bisector, bisecting line.
bisser [bise] (1) *vt* (*faire rejouer*) *acteur, chanson* to encore; (*rejouer*) *morceau* to play again, sing again.
bissextile [bisɛkstil] *adj f V* **année.**
bissexué, e [bisɛksɥe] *adj* = **bisexué.**
bistouri [bistuʀi] *nm* lancet, (surgeon's) knife, bistoury (*T*).
bistre [bistʀ(ə)] **1** *adj couleur* blackish-brown, bistre; *objet* bistre-coloured, blackish-brown; *peau, teint* swarthy. **2** *nm* bistre.
bistré, e [bistʀe] (*ptp de* **bistrer**) *adj teint* tanned, swarthy.
bistrer [bistʀe] (1) *vt objet* to colour with bistre; *peau* to tan.
bistro(t) [bistʀo] *nm* **(a)** (*: *café*) = pub (*Brit*), bar (*US*), café. **(b)** (†: *cafetier*) = publican (*Brit*), bartender (*US*), café owner.
bitte [bit] *nf* **(a)** *[navire]* bitt. **~ (d'amarrage)** *[quai]* mooring post, bollard. **(b)** (**) prick**, cock**, tool**.
bitterois, e [bitɛʀwa, wɑz] **1** *adj* of *ou* from Béziers. **2** *nm,f*: **B~(e)** inhabitant *ou* native of Béziers.
bitture: [bityʀ] *nf* = **biture:.**
bitumage [bitymaʒ] *nm* asphalting.
bitume [bitym] *nm* (*Chim, Min*) bitumen; (*revêtement*) asphalt, Tarmac ®.
bitumé, e [bityme] (*ptp de* **bitumer**) *adj route* asphalted, asphalt, tarmac (*épith*); *carton* bitumized.
bitum(in)er [bitym(in)e] (1) *vt* to asphalt, tarmac.
bitum(in)eux, -euse [bitym(in)ø, øz] *adj* bituminous.
biture: [bityʀ] *nf*: **prendre une ~** to get drunk *ou* canned: *ou* plastered:; **il tient une de ces ~s** he's plastered:, he's blind drunk*.
biturer (se): [bityʀe] (1) *vpr* to get drunk *ou* canned: *ou* plastered:.
biunivoque [biynivɔk] *adj* (*fig*) one-to-one; (*Math*) *V* **correspondance.**
bivalent, e [bivalɑ̃, ɑ̃t] *adj* bivalent.
bivalve [bivalv(ə)] *adj, nm* bivalve.
bivouac [bivwak] *nm* bivouac.
bivouaquer [bivwake] (1) *vi* to bivouac.
bizarre [bizaʀ] **1** *adj personne, conduite* strange, odd, peculiar; *idée, raisonnement, temps* odd, queer, strange, funny*; *vêtement* strange *ou* funny(-looking). **tiens, c'est ~** that's odd *ou* queer *ou* funny*.
2 *nm*: **le ~** the bizarre; **le ~ dans tout cela ...** what is strange *ou* odd *ou* queer *ou* peculiar about all that ..., the strange *ou* odd part about it all ... .
bizarrement [bizaʀmɑ̃] *adv* strangely, oddly, peculiarly, queerly.
bizarrerie [bizaʀʀi] *nf [personne]* odd *ou* strange *ou* peculiar ways; *[idée]* strangeness, oddness, queerness; *[situation, humeur]* queer *ou* strange *ou* odd nature. **~s** *[langue, règlement]* peculiarities, oddities, vagaries.
bizut(h) [bizy] *nm* (*arg Scol*) fresher (*arg*), first-year student *ou* scholar.
bizutage [bizytaʒ] *nm* (*arg Scol*) ragging (*of new student etc*).
bizuter [bizyte] (1) *vt* (*arg Scol*) to rag (*new student etc*).
blablabla* [blablabla] *nm* blah*, claptrap*, waffle*.
blackboulage [blakbulaʒ] *nm* blackballing.
blackbouler [blakbule] (1) *vt* (*à une élection*) to blackball; (*: *à un examen*) to fail, plough*.
black-out [blakawt] *nm* (*Élec, Mil*) blackout.
blafard, e [blafaʀ, aʀd(ə)] *adj teint* pale, pallid, wan; *couleur, lumière, soleil* wan, pale. **l'aube ~e** the pale light of dawn.
blague [blag] *nf* **(a)** (*) (*histoire, plaisanterie*) joke; (*farce*) practical joke, trick. **faire une ~ à qn** to play a trick *ou* a joke on sb; **sans ~?** really?, you're kidding!:, you don't say!*; **sans ~, ~ à part** seriously, joking apart; **il prend tout à la ~** he can never take anything seriously; **ne me raconte pas de ~s!** stop having me on!* *ou* kidding me!:, pull the other one!:
(b) (*: erreur) silly thing, blunder, stupid mistake. **faire une ~** to make a blunder *ou* a stupid mistake; **faire des ~s** to do silly *ou* stupid things.
(c) ~ (à tabac) (tobacco) pouch.
blaguer* [blage] (1) **1** *vi* to be joking *ou* kidding:. **j'ai dit cela pour ~** I said it for a lark*. **2** *vt* to tease, make fun of, kid:, take the mickey out of: (*Brit*).
blagueur, -euse [blagœʀ, øz] **1** *adj sourire, air* ironical, teasing. **2** *nm,f* joker, comedian.
blair: [blɛʀ] *nm* nose, hooter: (*Brit*), beak:.
blaireau, *pl* **~x** [blɛʀo] *nm* **(a)** (*Zool*) badger. **(b)** (*pour barbe*) shaving brush.
blairer: [blɛʀe] (1) *vt*: **je ne peux pas le ~** he gives me the creeps:, I can't stand *ou* bear him.
blâmable [blɑmabl(ə)] *adj* blameful.
blâme [blɑm] *nm* **(a)** (*désapprobation*) blame; (*réprimande*) reprimand, rebuke. **(b)** (*punition: Admin, Sport*) reprimand. **donner un ~** to reprimand, administer a reprimand; **recevoir un ~** to be reprimanded, incur a reprimand.
blâmer [blɑme] (1) *vt* (*désavouer*) to blame; (*réprimander*) to reprimand, rebuke. **je ne te blâme pas de** *ou* **pour l'avoir fait** I don't blame you for having done it.
blanc, blanche [blɑ̃, blɑ̃ʃ] **1** *adj* **(a)** (*de couleur blanche*) white. **il était ~ à 30 ans** he had white hair at 30; **ils sont rentrés de vacances ~s comme ils sont partis** they came back from holiday as pale as when they left; **elle avait honte de ses jambes blanches** she was ashamed of her lily-white (*hum*) *ou* pale legs; **~ de colère/de peur** white with anger/fear; **~ comme neige** (as) white as snow, snow-white; **~ comme un cachet d'aspirine** white as a sheet; **il devint ~ comme un linge** he went *ou* turned as white as a sheet; *V* **arme, bois, bonnet** *etc.*
(b) (*non imprimé*) *page, bulletin de vote* blank; *papier* unlined, plain, blank. (*Scol*) **il a rendu copie blanche** *ou* **sa feuille blanche** he handed in a blank paper; *V* **carte, examen** *etc.*
(c) (*innocent*) pure, innocent. **~ comme neige** *ou* **comme la blanche hermine** as pure as the driven snow.
(d) (*de la race blanche*) *domination, justice* white. **l'Afrique blanche** white Africa.
2 *nm* **(a)** (*couleur*) white. **peindre qch en ~** to paint sth white; **le ~ de sa robe tranchait sur sa peau brune** her white dress *ou* the white of her dress contrasted sharply with her dark skin; *V* **but.**
(b) (*linge*) **laver séparément le ~ et la couleur** to wash whites and coloureds separately; **vente de ~** white sale, sale of household linen; **magasin de ~** linen shop; **la quinzaine du ~** (annual) sale of household linen, (annual) white sale.
(c) (*cosmétique*) **elle se met du ~** she wears white powder.
(d) (*espace non écrit*) blank, space; *[bande magnétique]* blank; *[domino]* blank. **laisser un ~** to leave a blank *ou* space; **il faut laisser le nom en ~** the name must be left blank *ou* must not be filled in; *V* **chèque, signer.**
(e) (*vin*) white wine.
(f) (*Culin*) **~ (d'œuf)** (egg) white; **~ (de poulet)** white (meat), breast of chicken; **elle n'aime pas le ~** she doesn't like the white (meat) *ou* the breast.
(g) le ~ (de l'œil) the white (of the eye); *V* **regarder, rougir.**
(h) (*homme blanc*) **un B~** a White, a white man; **les B~s** the Whites, white men.
(i) (*loc*) **à ~** *charger* with blanks; **tirer à ~** to fire blanks; **cartouche à ~** blank (cartridge); *V* **chauffer, saigner.**
3 blanche *nf* **(a)** (*femme*) **une B~e** a white woman.
(b) (*Mus*) minim.
(c) (*Billard*) white (ball).
4: blanc de baleine spermaceti; **blanc bec*** greenhorn*, tenderfoot*; **blanc de blanc(s)** blanc de blanc(s); **blanc cassé** off-white; **blanc-cassis** *nm, pl* **blancs-cassis** (apéritif of) white wine and blackcurrant liqueur; **blanc de céruse** white lead; **blanc de chaux** whitewash; **blanc d'Espagne** whiting, whitening; (*Culin*) **blanc-manger** *nm, pl* **blancs-mangers** blancmange; **Blanche-Neige** Snow White; (*lit*) **blanc seing** signature to a blank document; (*fig*) **donner un blanc seing à qn** to give sb a free rein *ou* free hand; **blanc de zinc** zinc oxide.
blanchâtre [blɑ̃ʃɑtʀ(ə)] *adj* whitish, off-white.
blanche [blɑ̃ʃ] *V* **blanc.**
blancheur [blɑ̃ʃœʀ] *nf* whiteness.
blanchiment [blɑ̃ʃimɑ̃] *nm* (*décoloration*) bleaching; (*badigeonnage*) whitewashing.
blanchir [blɑ̃ʃiʀ] (2) **1** *vt* **(a)** (*gén*) to whiten, lighten; *mur* to whitewash; *cheveux* to turn grey *ou* white; *toile* to bleach. **le soleil blanchit l'horizon** the sun is lighting up the horizon; **la neige blanchit les collines** the snow is turning the hills white; **~ à la chaux** to whitewash.
(b) (*nettoyer*) *linge* to launder. **il est logé, nourri et blanchi** he gets bed and board and his washing *ou* his laundry is done for him.
(c) (*disculper*) *personne* to exonerate, absolve, clear; *réputation* to clear. **il en est sorti blanchi** he cleared his name.
(d) (faire) ~ (*Culin*) *légume* to blanch; (*Agr*) to blanch.
2 *vi [personne, cheveux]* to turn *ou* go grey *ou* white; *[couleur, horizon]* to become lighter. **son teint a blanchi** he's looking *ou* got paler, he has lost colour; **~ de peur** to blanch *ou* go white with fear.
3 se blanchir *vpr* to exonerate o.s. (*de* from), clear one's name.
blanchissage [blɑ̃ʃisaʒ] *nm [linge]* laundering; *[sucre]* refining. **donner du linge au ~** to send linen to the laundry; **note de ~** laundry bill.
blanchissement [blɑ̃ʃismɑ̃] *nm* whitening. **ce shampooing retarde le ~ des cheveux** this shampoo stops your hair going grey *ou* white.
blanchisserie [blɑ̃ʃisʀi] *nf* laundry.
blanchisseur [blɑ̃ʃisœʀ] *nm* launderer.
blanchisseuse [blɑ̃ʃisøz] *nf* laundress.

blanquette [blɑ̃kɛt] *nf* **(a)** (*Culin*) ~ **de veau/d'agneau** blanquette of veal/of lamb, veal/lamb in white sauce. **(b)** (*vin*) sparkling white wine.
blasé, e [blaze] (*ptp de* **blaser**) **1** *adj* blasé. **2** *nm,f* blasé person. **faire le** ~ to affect a blasé indifference to everything.
blaser [blaze] (1) **1** *vt* to make blasé *ou* indifferent. **être blasé de** to be bored with *ou* tired of. **2 se blaser** *vpr* to become bored (*de* with), become tired (*de* of), become blasé (*de* about).
blason [blazɔ̃] *nm* **(a)** (*armoiries*) coat of arms, blazon. **(b)** (*science*) heraldry. **(c)** (*Littérat: poème*) blazon.
blasphémateur, -trice [blasfematœʀ, tʀis] **1** *adj personne* blaspheming, blasphemous. **2** *nm,f* blasphemer.
blasphématoire [blasfematwaʀ] *adj parole* blasphemous.
blasphème [blasfɛm] *nm* blasphemy.
blasphémer [blasfeme] (6) *vti* to blaspheme.
blatte [blat] *nf* cockroach.
blé [ble] *nm* wheat, corn (*Brit*). **le** ~ **en herbe** (*Agr*) corn on the blade; (*fig*) young shoots, young bloods; ~ **dur** hard wheat, durum wheat; ~ **noir** buckwheat; (*Can*) ~ **d'Inde*** maize, (Indian) corn (*US, Can*).
bled [blɛd] *nm* **(a)** (*) village; (*péj*) hole*, godforsaken place*, dump‡. **c'est un** ~ **perdu** *ou* **paumé** it's a godforsaken place* *ou* hole* (in the middle of nowhere).
(b) (*Afrique du Nord*) **le** ~ the interior (of North Africa). (*fig*) **habiter dans le** ~* to live in the middle of nowhere *ou* at the back of beyond.
blême [blɛm] *adj teint* pallid, deathly pale, wan; *lumière* pale, wan. ~ **de rage/de colère** livid *ou* white with rage/anger.
blêmir [blemiʀ] (2) *vi [personne]* to turn *ou* go pale, pale; *[lumière]* to grow pale. ~ **de colère** to go livid *ou* white with anger.
blêmissement [blemismɑ̃] *nm [teint, lumière]* paling.
blende [blɛ̃d] *nf* blende.
blennorragie [blenɔʀaʒi] *nf* blennorrhoea, gonorrhoea.
blèsement [blɛzmɑ̃] *nm* lisping.
bléser [bleze] (6) *vi* to lisp.
blessant, e [blɛsɑ̃, ɑ̃t] *adj* (*offensant*) cutting, biting, hurtful.
blessé, e [blese] (*ptp de* **blesser**) **1** *adj* injured, wounded; *soldat* wounded; (*offensé*) hurt, upset. **être** ~ **à la tête/au bras** to have a head/an arm injury *ou* wound.
2 *nm* wounded *ou* injured man, casualty; (*Mil*) wounded soldier, casualty. **les** ~**s** (*gén*) the injured; (*Mil*) the wounded; **l'accident a fait 10** ~**s** 10 people were injured *ou* hurt in the accident.
3 blessée *nf* wounded *ou* injured woman, casualty.
4: **grand blessé, blessé grave** seriously *ou* severely injured *ou* wounded person; **blessé de guerre** person who was wounded in the war; **les blessés de guerre** the war wounded; **blessé léger** slightly injured person; **blessés de la route** road casualties, people *ou* persons injured in road accidents.
blesser [blese] (1) *vt* **(a)** (*gén*) to hurt, injure; (*Mil*) to wound. **il a été blessé d'un coup de couteau** he received a knife wound, he was stabbed (with a knife); **être blessé dans un accident de voiture** to be injured in a car accident; **il s'est blessé en tombant** he fell and injured himself; **il s'est blessé (à) la jambe** he has injured *ou* hurt his leg.
(b) (*faire mal*) (*lit*) to hurt, make sore; (*fig*) to offend. **ses souliers lui blessent le talon** his shoes hurt his heel *ou* make his heel sore; **sons qui blessent l'oreille** sounds which offend the ear *ou* grate on the ear; **couleurs qui blessent la vue** colours which offend *ou* shock the eye.
(c) (*offenser*) to hurt (the feelings of), upset, wound. ~ **qn au vif** to cut sb to the quick; **il s'est senti blessé dans son orgueil** his pride was hurt, he felt wounded in his pride; **des paroles qui blessent** cutting words, wounding *ou* cutting remarks; **il se blesse pour un rien** he's easily hurt *ou* offended, he's quick to take offence.
(d) (*littér: porter préjudice à*) *règles, convenances* to offend against; *intérêts* to go against, harm. **cela blesse son sens de la justice** that offends his sense of justice.
blessure [blesyʀ] *nf* (*V* **blesser**) injury; wound; (*fig*) wound. **cela a été pour lui une** ~ **d'amour-propre** his pride was hurt *ou* wounded.
blet, blette[1] [blɛ, blɛt] *adj fruit* overripe, soft.
blette[2] [blɛt] *nf* = **bette.**
blettir [bletiʀ] (2) *vi* to become overripe *ou* soft.
blettissement [bletismɑ̃] *nm* overripeness.
bleu, e [blø] **1** *adj couleur* blue; *steak* very rare, underdone. ~ **de froid** blue with cold; **être** ~ **de colère** to be livid *ou* purple with rage; *V* **enfant, fleur, peur** *etc.*
2 *nm* **(a)** (*couleur*) blue. (*fig*) **il n'y a vu que du** ~ he didn't twig* (*Brit*), he didn't smell a rat*; **regarde le** ~ **de ce ciel** look at the blueness of that sky, look how blue the sky is.
(b) ~ **(de lessive)** (dolly) blue; **passer le linge au** ~ to blue the laundry.
(c) (*marque sur la peau*) bruise. **être couvert de** ~**s** to be covered in bruises, be black and blue*.
(d) (*vêtement*) ~**(s) (de travail)** dungarees, overalls; ~ **(de chauffe** *ou* **de mécanicien)** boiler suit (*Brit*), overalls; ~ **de chauffe** (*Mode*) dungarees.
(e) (*arg Mil: recrue*) rookie (*arg*), new *ou* raw recruit; (*gén: débutant*) beginner, greenhorn*. **tu me prends pour un** ~? do you think I was born yesterday?*
(f) (*fromage*) blue(-veined) cheese.
(g) (*Culin*) **truite au** ~ trout au bleu.
(h) (*Can*) **les B**~**s** the Conservatives.
3: **bleu ardoise** slaty *ou* slate-blue; **bleu canard** peacock blue; **bleu ciel** sky blue; **bleu de cobalt** cobalt blue; **bleu horizon** sky blue; **bleu lavande** lavender blue; **bleu marine** navy blue; (*Méd*) **bleu de méthylène** methylene blue; **bleu noir** blue-black; **bleu nuit** midnight blue; **bleu outremer** ultramarine; **bleu pétrole** airforce blue; **bleu de Prusse** Prussian blue; **bleu roi** royal blue; **bleu vert** blue-green.
bleuâtre [bløɑtʀ(ə)] *adj* bluish.
bleuet [bløɛ] *nm* cornflower; (*Can*) blueberry.
bleuir [bløiʀ] (2) *vti* to turn blue.
bleuissement [bløismɑ̃] *nm* turning blue.
bleuté, e [bløte] *adj reflet* bluish; *verre* blue-tinted.
bleuetière [bløɛtjɛʀ] *nf* (*Can*) blueberry grove.
blindage [blɛ̃daʒ] *nm* (*V* **blinder**) armour plating; screening; timbering, shoring up.
blindé, e [blɛ̃de] (*ptp de* **blinder**) **1** *adj* **(a)** (*Mil*) *division* armoured; *engin, train* armoured, armour-plated; *abri* bombproof; *porte* reinforced.
(b) (*: *endurci*) immune, hardened (*contre* to). **il a essayé de me faire peur mais je suis** ~ he tried to frighten me but I'm too thickskinned*.
(c) (‡: *ivre*) stewed‡, canned‡, plastered‡.
2 *nm* (*Mil*) armoured car, tank. **les** ~**s** the armour.
blinder [blɛ̃de] (1) *vt* **(a)** (*Mil*) to armour, put armour plating on; (*Élec*) to screen; (*Constr*) to shore up, timber. **(b)** (*: *endurcir*) to harden, make immune (*contre* to). **(c)** (‡: *soûler*) to make *ou* get drunk *ou* plastered‡ *ou* canned‡.
blizzard [blizaʀ] *nm* blizzard.
bloc [blɔk] **1** *nm* **(a)** *[pierre, marbre, bois]* block. **table faite d'un seul** ~ table made in one piece.
(b) (*papeterie*) pad. ~ **de bureau** office notepad, desk pad; ~ **de papier à lettres** writing pad.
(c) (*système d'éléments*) unit. **ces éléments forment (un)** ~ these elements make up a unit.
(d) (*groupe, union*) group; (*Pol*) bloc. **ces entreprises forment un** ~ these companies make up a group; (*Pol*) **le** ~ **communiste/des pays capitalistes** the communist/capitalist bloc; (*Pol*) **pays divisé en deux** ~**s adverses** country split into two opposing blocks *ou* factions; (*Fin*) ~ **monétaire** monetary bloc.
(e) (‡: *prison*) **mettre qn au** ~ to clap sb in clink‡ *ou* jug‡; **j'ai eu 10 jours de** ~ I got 10 days in clink‡ *ou* jug‡.
(f) (*loc*) **faire** ~ **avec qn** to join sides *ou* unite with sb; **faire** ~ **contre qn** to unite against sb; **à** ~: **serrer** *ou* **visser qch à** ~ to screw sth up as tight as possible *ou* as far as it will go; **fermer un robinet à** ~ to turn a tap right *ou* hard off; **en** ~: **acheter/vendre qch en** ~ to buy/sell sth as a whole; **il refuse en** ~ **tous mes arguments** he rejects all my arguments out of hand *ou* outright; **les pays du Marché commun ont condamné en** ~ **l'attitude des USA** the Common Market countries were united *ou* unanimous in their condemnation of the US attitude; **se retourner tout d'un** ~ to swivel round; *V* **freiner, gonflé.**
2: **bloc-calendrier** *nm, pl* **blocs-calendriers** tear-off calendar; **bloc-cuisine** *nm, pl* **blocs-cuisines** kitchen unit; **bloc de culasse** breech-block; (*Aut*) **bloc-cylindres** *nm, pl* **blocs-cylindres** cylinder block; (*Géog*) **bloc-diagramme** *nm, pl* **blocs-diagrammes** block diagram; **bloc-évier** *nm, pl* **blocs-éviers** sink unit; (*Aut*) **bloc-moteur** *nm, pl* **blocs-moteurs** engine block; **bloc-notes** *nm, pl* **blocs-notes** desk pad; (*Méd*) **bloc opératoire** operating theatre suite; (*Ciné*) **bloc sonore** sound unit; (*Rail*) **bloc-système** *nm,pl* **blocs-systèmes** block system.
blocage [blɔkaʒ] *nm* **(a)** *[prix, salaires]* freeze, freezing; *[compte bancaire]* freezing. **(b)** (*Constr*) rubble. **(c)** (*Psych*) block. **(d)** *[frein, roues]* locking; *[écrou]* overtightening.
blocaille [blɔkaj] *nf* (*Constr*) rubble.
blockhaus [blɔkos] *nm* (*Mil*) blockhouse, pillbox.
blocus [blɔkys] *nm* blockade. (*Hist*) **le** ~ **continental** the Continental System; **lever/forcer le** ~ to raise/run the blockade; **faire le** ~ **de** to blockade.
blond, e [blɔ̃, ɔ̃d] **1** *adj cheveux* fair, blond; *personne* fair, fair-haired, blond; *blé, sable* golden. ~ **cendré** ash-blond; ~ **roux** sandy, light auburn; **tabac** ~ mild *ou* Virginia tobacco; **bière** ~**e** lager.
2 *nm* (*couleur*) blond, light gold; (*homme*) fair-haired man.
3 blonde *nf* (*bière*) lager; (*cigarette*) Virginia cigarette; (*femme*) blonde; (*Can**) girl friend, sweetheart; ~**e incendiaire** blond bombshell (*hum*); ~**e oxygénée** peroxide blonde.
blondasse [blɔ̃das] *adj* (*péj*) tow-coloured.
blondeur [blɔ̃dœʀ] *nf* (*littér*) *[cheveux]* fairness; *[blés]* gold.
blondin [blɔ̃dɛ̃] *nm* fair-haired child *ou* young man; (††: *élégant*) dandy.
blondine [blɔ̃din] *nf* fair-haired child *ou* young girl.
blondinet [blɔ̃dinɛ] *nm* light-haired boy.
blondinette [blɔ̃dinɛt] *nf* light-haired girl.
blondir [blɔ̃diʀ] (2) *vi [cheveux]* to go fairer; (*littér*) *[blés]* to turn golden.
bloquer [blɔke] (1) **1** *vt* **(a)** (*grouper*) to lump together, put *ou* group together, combine. ~ **ses jours de congé** to lump one's days off together; ~ **les notes en fin de volume** to put *ou* group all the notes together at the end of the book.
(b) (*immobiliser*) *machine* to jam; *écrou* to overtighten; *roue* (*accidentellement*) to lock; (*exprès*) to put a block under, chock; *porte* to jam, wedge. ~ **les freins** to jam on the brakes; ~ **qn contre un mur** to pin sb against a wall; **être bloqué par les glaces** to be stuck in the ice, be icebound; **être bloqué par un accident/la foule** to be held up by an accident/the crowd.
(c) (*obstruer*) to block (up); (*Mil*) to blockade. **port bloqué/route bloquée par la glace** icebound port/road, port/road blocked by ice; **un camion bloque la route** a truck is blocking the road, the road is blocked by a truck; **des travaux bloquent la route** there are road works in *ou* blocking the way; **les enfants bloquent le passage** the children are standing in *ou* blocking the way, the children are stopping me (*ou us etc*) getting past.
(d) (*Sport*) *ballon* to block; (*Billard*) *bille* to jam, wedge.

(e) *marchandises* to stop, hold up; *crédit, salaires* to freeze; *compte en banque* to stop, freeze.
2 se bloquer *vpr [porte]* to jam, get stuck, stick; *[machine]* to jam; *[roue]* to lock; *[frein]* to jam, lock on.
bloqueur [blɔkœʀ] *nm* (*Can Ftbl*) lineman.
blottir (se) [blɔtiʀ] (2) *vpr* to curl up, snuggle up, huddle up. **se ~ contre qn** to snuggle up to sb; **se ~ dans les bras de qn** to snuggle up in sb's arms; **blottis les uns contre les autres** curled up *ou* huddled up (close) against one another; **blotti parmi les arbres** nestling *ou* huddling among the trees.
blousant, e [bluzɑ̃, ɑ̃t] *adj robe* loose-fitting.
blouse [bluz] *nf* (*tablier*) overall; (*chemisier*) blouse, smock; *[médecin]* (white) coat; *[paysan]* smock.
blouser[1] [bluze] (1) *vi [robe]* to be loose-fitting.
blouser[2]‡ [bluze] (1) **1** *vt* to con‡, trick, pull a fast one on‡. **se faire ~** to be had* *ou* conned‡. **2 se blouser** *vpr* to make a mistake *ou* a blunder.
blouson [bluzɔ̃] *nm* lumber jacket, windjammer. **les ~s dorés** rich delinquents; **~ noir** ≃ teddy-boy.
blue-jean, *pl* **blue-jeans** [bludʒin] *nm* (pair of) jeans.
blues [bluz] *nm inv* (*Mus*) blues.
bluet [blyɛ] *nm* (*Can*) blueberry.
bluff* [blœf] *nm* bluff. **c'est du ~!** he's just bluffing!, he's just trying it on!‡ (*surtout Brit*).
bluffer* [blœfe] (1) **1** *vi* to bluff, try it on‡ (*surtout Brit*); (*Cartes*) to bluff. **2** *vt* to fool, have (*Brit*) *ou* put on‡; (*Cartes*) to bluff.
bluffeur, -euse [blœfœʀ, øz] *nm,f* bluffer.
blutage [blytaʒ] *nm* bolting (*of flour*).
boa [bɔa] *nm* (*Habillement, Zool*) boa. **~ constricteur** boa constrictor.
bobard* [bɔbaʀ] *nm* (*mensonge*) lie, fib*; (*histoire*) tall story, yarn.
bobèche [bɔbɛʃ] *nf* **(a)** candle-ring. **(b)** (*) *[personne]* head, nut*.
bobinage [bɔbinaʒ] *nm* (*gén: action*) winding; (*Élec: ensemble*) coil(s).
bobine [bɔbin] *nf* **(a)** *[fil]* reel, bobbin; *[métier à tisser]* bobbin, spool; *[machine à écrire]* spool; (*Phot*) spool; (*Ciné*) reel; (*Élec*) coil. (*Aut*) **~ (d'allumage)** coil; (*Phot*) **~ de pellicule** roll of film. **(b)** (*: *visage*) dial‡. **il a fait une drôle de ~!** what a face he pulled!; **tu en fais une drôle de ~!** you look a bit put out!*
bobiner [bɔbine] (1) *vt* to wind.
bobinette†† [bɔbinɛt] *nf* (wooden) latch.
bobineuse [bɔbinøz] *nf* winding machine.
bobinoir [bɔbinwaʀ] *nm* winding machine.
bobo [bobo] *nm* (*langage enfantin*) (*plaie*) sore; (*coupure*) cut. **avoir ~** to be hurt, have a pain; **avoir ~ à la gorge** to have a sore throat; **ça (te) fait ~?** does it hurt?, is it sore?
bobonne*† [bɔbɔn] *nf*: **il est sorti avec (sa) ~** he's gone out with his old woman‡ *ou* his missus*; (*hum*) **oui ~** yes love* *ou* dearie*.
bocage [bɔkaʒ] *nm* **(a)** (*Géog*) bocage, *farmland criss-crossed by hedges and trees.* **(b)** (*littér: bois*) grove, copse.
bocager, -ère [bɔkaʒe, ɛʀ] *adj* (*littér: boisé*) wooded. (*Géog*) **paysage ~** bocage landscape.
bocal, *pl* **-aux** [bɔkal, o] *nm* jar. **~ à poissons rouges** goldfish bowl; **mettre en ~aux** *fruits* to preserve, bottle.
Boccace [bɔkas] *nm* Boccaccio.
boche [bɔʃ] (*péj*) **1** *adj* Boche. **2** *nm*: **B~** Jerry, Boche, Hun.
bock [bɔk] *nm* (*verre*) beer glass; (*bière*) glass of beer, ≃ half (a pint)*.
Boers [buʀ] *nmpl*: **les ~** the Boers.
bœuf [bœf], *pl* **~s** [bø] **1** *nm* **(a)** (*bête*) ox; (*de boucherie*) bullock, steer; (*viande*) beef. **~s de boucherie** beef cattle; **~-mode** stewed beef with carrots; *V* **charrue, fort, qui** *etc.* **(b)** (*arg Mus*) jam session. **2** *adj inv*: **effet/succès~*** tremendous* *ou* fantastic* effect/success.
bog(g)ie [bɔʒi] *nm* (*Rail*) bogie.
Bohême, Bohème [bɔɛm] *nf* Bohemia.
bohème [bɔɛm] **1** *adj* bohemian, happy-go-lucky, unconventional. **2** *nmf* bohemian, happy-go-lucky person. **mener une vie de ~** to lead a bohemian life. **3** *nf* (*milieu*) **la B~** Bohemia.
bohémien, -ienne [bɔemjɛ̃, jɛn] **1** *adj* Bohemian. **2** *nm,f* (*gitan*) gipsy. (*de Bohême*) **B~(ne)** Bohemian.
boire [bwaʀ] (53) **1** *vt* **(a)** to drink. **~ un verre, ~ un coup*** to have a drink; **aller ~ un coup*** to go for a drink; **~ qch à longs traits** to take great gulps of sth, gulp sth down; **offrir/donner à ~ à qn** to get sb/give sb sth to drink *ou* a drink; **~ à la santé/au succès de qn** to drink sb's health/to sb's success; **~ en Suisse** to drink on one's own; **on a bu une bouteille à nous deux** we drank a (whole) bottle between the two of us; **ce vin se boit bien** this wine goes down nicely*, this wine is very drinkable.
(b) faire ~ un enfant to give a child something to drink; **faire ~ un cheval** to water a horse.
(c) (*gén emploi absolu: boire trop*) to drink. **~ comme un trou*** to drink like a fish; **~ sans soif** to drink heavily; **c'est un homme qui boit (sec)** he's a (heavy) drinker; **il s'est mis à ~** he has taken to drink, he has started drinking; **il a bu, c'est évident** he has obviously been drinking.
(d) (*absorber*) to soak up, absorb. **ce papier boit l'encre** the ink soaks into this paper; **ce buvard boit bien l'encre** this blotter soaks up the ink well; **la plante a déjà tout bu** the plant has already soaked up all the water.
(e) (*loc*) **~ les paroles de qn** to drink in sb's words, lap up what sb says*; **~ le calice jusqu'à la lie** to drain one's cup to the (last) dregs *ou* last drop; **~ un bouillon*** (*revers de fortune*) to make a big loss, be ruined; (*en se baignant*) to swallow *ou* get a mouthful; **~ la tasse*** to swallow *ou* get a mouthful; **~ du (petit) lait** to lap it up*; **il y a à ~ et à manger là-dedans** (*dans une boisson*) there are bits floating about in it; (*fig*) (*qualités et défauts*) it's got its good points and its bad; (*vérités et mensonges*) you have to pick and choose what to believe.
2 *nm*: **le boire et le manger** food and drink.
bois [bwa] **1** *nm* **(a)** (*forêt, matériau*) wood. **c'est en ~** it's made of wood; **chaise de** *ou* **en ~** wooden chair; **ramasser du petit ~** to collect sticks *ou* kindling; (*fig*) **son visage était de ~** his face was impassive, he was poker-faced; (*fig*) **je ne suis pas de ~** I'm only human.
(b) (*objet en bois*) (*gravure*) woodcut; (*manche*) shaft, handle; (*Golf*) wood.
(c) (*Zool*) antler.
(d) (*Mus*) **les ~** the woodwind (instruments *ou* section *etc*).
(e) (*loc*) (*Tennis*) **faire un ~** to hit the ball off the wood; **je ne suis pas du ~ dont on fait les flûtes** I'm not going to let myself be pushed around, I'm not just anyone's fool; **il va voir de quel ~ je me chauffe!** I'll show him (what I'm made of)!, just let me get my hands on him!; **il fait feu** *ou* **flèche de tout ~** all's grist that comes to his mill, he'll use any means available to him.
2: bois blanc whitewood, deal; (*Can* †) **bois-brûlé, e** *nm,f, mpl* **bois-brûlés** half-breed Indian, bois-brûlé (*Can*); **bois à brûler** firewood; **bois de charpente** timber; **bois de chauffage** firewood; (*Can*) **bois debout** standing timber; **bois d'ébène** (*Hist péj: esclaves*) black gold; **bois exotique, bois des îles** exotic wood; **bois de lit** bedstead; **bois de menuiserie** timber; **bois mort** deadwood; (*Can*) **bois rond** unhewn timber; **bois de rose** rosewood; **bois vert** green wood; (*Menuiserie*) unseasoned *ou* green timber.
boisage [bwazaʒ] *nm* (*action*) timbering; (*matière*) timber work.
boisé, e [bwaze] (*ptp de* **boiser**) *adj* wooded, woody. **pays ~** woodland(s), wooded *ou* woody countryside.
boisement [bwazmɑ̃] *nm* afforestation.
boiser [bwaze] (1) *vt région* to afforest, plant with trees; *galerie* to timber.
boiserie [bwazʀi] *nf*: **~(s)** panelling, wainscot(t)ing.
boisseau, *pl* **~x** [bwaso] *nm* (††) ≃ bushel; (*Can*) bushel (*36,36 litres*). **il est embêtant comme un ~ de puces!*** he's a menace!* *ou* a pest!*; **garder** *ou* **laisser** *ou* **mettre qch sous le ~** to keep sth dark *ou* in the dark.
boisson [bwasɔ̃] *nf* drink; (*Can**) hard liquor, spirits. **ils apportent la ~** they are bringing the drinks; **usé par la ~** worn out with drinking; (*littér*) **être pris de ~** to be drunk, be under the influence; **~ alcoolisée** alcoholic beverage (*frm*) *ou* drink; **~ non alcoolisée** soft drink.
boîte [bwat] **1** *nf* **(a)** (*récipient*) (*en carton, bois*) box; (*en métal*) box, tin; *[conserves]* tin (*Brit*), can (*US*). **mettre des haricots en ~** to can beans; **des tomates en ~** tinned (*Brit*) *ou* canned (*US*) tomatoes; (*fig*) **mettre qn en ~*** to pull sb's leg*, take the mickey out of sb‡ (*Brit*); **il a mangé toute la ~ de caramels** he ate the whole box of toffees.
(b) (*: *cabaret*) night club; (*: *lieu de travail*) (*firme*) firm, company; (*bureau*) office; (*école*) school. **quelle (sale)~!** what a joint!‡ *ou* dump!‡, what a crummy hole!‡; **je veux changer de ~** (*usine*) I want to change my job; (*lycée*) I want to change schools; **il s'est fait renvoyer de la ~** he got chucked out‡.
2: boîte d'allumettes box of matches; (*péj*) **boîte à bachot** cramming school; **boîte à bijoux** jewel box; **boîte de conserve** tin (*Brit*) *ou* can (*US*) of food; **boîte de couleurs** box of paints, paintbox; (*Anat*) **boîte crânienne** cranium, brainpan; (*Aut*) **boîte à gants** glove locker (*Brit*) *ou* compartment; **boîte à** *ou* **aux lettres** (*publique*) pillar box (*Brit*), mailbox (*US*), letterbox; (*privée*) letterbox; (*fig: personne*) go-between; **boîte à musique** musical box; (*Aviat*) **boîte noire** flight recorder, black box; **boîte de nuit** night club; **boîte à ordures** dustbin (*Brit*), garbage *ou* trash can (*US*); **boîte à outils** toolbox; **boîte à ouvrage** *ou* **à couture** sewing box, workbox; **boîte postale 150** P.O. Box 150 (*Brit*); (*Aut*) **boîte de vitesses** gearbox.
boitement [bwatmɑ̃] *nm* limping.
boiter [bwate] (1) *vi [personne]* to limp, walk with a limp; *[meuble]* to wobble; *[raisonnement]* to be unsound *ou* shaky. **~ bas** to limp badly; **~ de la jambe gauche** to limp with one's left leg.
boiteux, -euse [bwatø, øz] *adj personne* lame, who limps; *meuble* wobbly, rickety; *paix, projet* shaky; *union* ill-assorted; *raisonnement* unsound, shaky; *explication* lame, clumsy, weak; *vers* faulty; *phrase* (*incorrecte*) grammatically wrong, (*mal équilibrée*) unbalanced, clumsy.
boîtier [bwatje] *nm* case. **~ électrique** electric torch (*Brit*), flashlight (*US*); **~ de montre** watchcase.
boitillement [bwatijmɑ̃] *nm* slight limp, hobble.
boitiller [bwatije] (1) *vi* to limp slightly, have a slight limp, hobble.
bol [bɔl] *nm* **(a)** bowl. (*fig*) **prendre un (bon) ~ d'air** to get a good breath of fresh air. **(b)** (*Pharm*) bolus. (*Méd*) **~ alimentaire** bolus. **(c)** (‡*loc*) **avoir du ~** to be lucky; **pas de ~!** no luck! **(d)** (*Can**) = **bolle***.
bolchevique [bɔlʃəvik] *adj, nmf* Bolshevik, Bolshevist.
bolchevisme [bɔlʃəvism(ə)] *nm* Bolchevism.
bolcheviste [bɔlʃəvist(ə)] = **bolchevique.**
bolée [bɔle] *nf* bowl(ful).
boléro [bɔleʀo] *nm* (*Habillement, Mus*) bolero.
bolet [bɔlɛ] *nm* mushroom, boletus (*T*).
bolide [bɔlid] *nm* (*Astron*) meteor, bolide (*T*); (*voiture*) (high-powered) racing car. **comme un ~** *arriver, passer* at top speed; *s'éloigner* like a rocket.
Bolivie [bɔlivi] *nf* Bolivia.
bolivien, -ienne [bɔlivjɛ̃, jɛn] **1** *adj* Bolivian. **2** *nm,f*: **B~(ne)** Bolivian.
bollard [bɔlaʀ] *nm* (*Naut*) bollard.

bolle* [bɔl] *nf (Can)* head. **j'ai mal à la ~** I have a headache.
Bologne [bɔlɔɲ] *n* Bologna.
bolognais, e [bɔlɔɲɛ, ɛz] **1** *adj* Bolognese; *(Culin)* bolognese. **2** *nm,f*: **B~(e)** Bolognese.
bombance*† [bɔ̃bɑ̃s] *nf* feast, revel, beanfeast* *(Brit)*. **faire ~** to revel, have a beanfeast* *(Brit)*.
bombarde [bɔ̃baʀd(ə)] *nf (Mil)* bombard.
bombardement [bɔ̃baʀdəmɑ̃] *nm* (*V* **bombarder**) *(Mil)* bombardment; bombing; shelling; *(fig)* pelting; showering; bombarding; *(Phys)* bombardment. **~ aérien** air raid, aerial bombing *(U)*; **~ atomique** *(Mil)* atom-bomb attack; *(Phys)* atomic bombardment.
bombarder [bɔ̃baʀde] (1) *vt (Mil)* to bombard; *(avec bombes)* to bomb; *(par obus)* to shell; *(Phys)* to bombard. *(fig)* **~ de** *cailloux, tomates* to pelt with; *questions* to bombard with; *lettres* to shower with, inundate with; **on l'a bombardé directeur*** he was suddenly thrust into *ou* pitchforked into the position of director.
bombardier [bɔ̃baʀdje] *nm (avion)* bomber; *(aviateur)* bomb-aimer, bombardier *(US)*.
bombe [bɔ̃b] **1** *nf* **(a)** *(Mil)* bomb. **attentat à la ~** bomb *ou* bombing attack; *(fig)* **comme une ~** unexpectedly, (like a bolt) out of the blue; **la nouvelle a éclaté comme une ~** the news came as a bombshell *ou* was like a bolt out of the blue.
(b) *(atomiseur)* spray.
(c) *(Équitation)* riding cap *ou* hat.
(d) *(loc)* **faire la ~*** to go on a spree *ou* a binge*.
2: bombe atomique atom(ic) bomb; *(Méd)* **bombe au cobalt** cobalt therapy unit, telecobalt machine; **bombe déodorante** spray deodorant; *(Culin)* **bombe glacée** bombe glacée, ice pudding; **bombe H** H-bomb; **bombe à hydrogène** hydrogen bomb; **bombe incendiaire** incendiary bomb; **bombe insecticide** fly spray; **bombe lacrymogène** teargas grenade; **bombe de laque** hair spray; **bombe au plastic** plastic bomb; **bombe à retardement** time bomb; *(Géol)* **bombe volcanique** volcanic bomb.
bombé, e [bɔ̃be] *(ptp de* **bomber**) *adj forme* rounded, convex; *cuiller* heaped, rounded; *poitrine* thrown out; *front* domed; *mur* bulging; *dos* humped, hunched; *route* steeply cambered. **verre ~** balloon-shaped glass.
bombement [bɔ̃bmɑ̃] *nm [forme]* convexity; *[route]* camber; *[front]* bulge.
bomber [bɔ̃be] (1) **1** *vt*: **~ le torse** *ou* **la poitrine** (*lit*) to stick out *ou* throw out one's chest; *(fig)* to puff out one's chest, swagger about. **2** *vi [route]* to camber; *[mur]* to bulge; *(Menuiserie)* to warp.
bombonne [bɔ̃bɔn] *nf* = **bonbonne.**
bombyx [bɔ̃biks] *nm* bombyx.
bon[1], **bonne**[1] [bɔ̃, bɔn] **1** *adj* **(a)** *(de qualité)* *(gén)* good; *fauteuil, lit* good, comfortable. **il a une bonne vue** *ou* **de ~s yeux** he has good eyesight, his eyesight is good; **il a de bonnes jambes** he has a good *ou* strong pair of legs; **il a fait du ~ travail** he has done a good job of work; **marchandises/outils de bonne qualité** good quality goods/tools; **si j'ai bonne mémoire, si ma mémoire est bonne** if my memory is correct *ou* serves me well.
(b) *(compétent) docteur, élève, employé* good; *(efficace) instrument, système, remède* good, reliable; *(sage) conseil* good, sound; *(valable) excuse, raison* good, valid, sound; *(sain, sûr) placement, monnaie, entreprise* sound. **être ~ en anglais** to be good at English; **une personne de ~ conseil** a man of sound judgment; **pour le ~ fonctionnement du moteur** for the efficient working of the motor, for the motor to work efficiently *ou* properly; **quand on veut réussir tous les moyens sont ~s** anything goes when one wants to succeed; **tout lui est ~ pour me discréditer** he'll stop at nothing to discredit me.
(c) *(agréable) odeur, vacances, surprise, repas* good, pleasant, nice. **un ~ petit vin** a nice (little) wine; **elle aime les bonnes choses** she likes the good things in life; **nous avons passé une bonne soirée** we had a pleasant *ou* nice evening; **c'était vraiment ~** *(à manger, à boire)* it was *ou* tasted really good *ou* nice; **l'eau est bonne** the water is warm *ou* fine *ou* nice; **il a la bonne vie** he's got it easy*, life's a bed of roses for him; **être en bonne compagnie** to be in good company *ou* with pleasant companions; *(littér)* **être de bonne compagnie** to be pleasant *ou* good company.
(d) *(moralement ou socialement irréprochable) lectures, fréquentations, pensées, famille* good. **il est ~ père et ~ fils** he's a good father and a good son; **libéré pour bonne conduite** released for good conduct; **de bonne renommée** of good repute; **d'un ~ milieu social** from a good social background; **dans la bonne société** in polite society.
(e) *(charitable) personne* good, kind(-hearted), kindly; *action* good, kind, kindly; *parole* kind, comforting, kindly. **la bonne action** *ou* **la b.a. quotidienne de l'éclaireur** the scout's good deed for the day; **il a eu un ~ mouvement** he made a nice gesture; **être ~ pour les animaux** to be kind to animals; **avoir ~ cœur** to have a good *ou* kind heart, be kind- *ou* good-hearted; **vous êtes bien** *ou* **trop ~** you are really too kind, it's really too kind *ou* good of you; **il est ~ comme du ~ pain** he has a heart of gold; **elle est bonne fille** she's a nice *ou* good-hearted girl, she's a good sort*; **une bonne âme** a good soul; *(iro)* **vous êtes ~, vous, avec vos idées impossibles!*** you're a great help with your wild ideas!; *(péj)* **c'est un ~ pigeon** *ou* **une bonne poire** he is a bit of a sucker: ou mug: *(Brit)* *ou* dope*.
(f) *(valable, utilisable) billet, passeport, timbre* valid. **médicament/yaourt ~ jusqu'au 5 mai** medicine/yoghurt to be used before 5th May; **est-ce que la soupe va être encore bonne avec cette chaleur?** will the soup have kept *ou* will the soup still be all right in this heat?; **ce joint de caoutchouc n'est plus ~** this rubber washer is perished; **est-ce que ce pneu/ce vernis est encore ~?** is this tyre/varnish still fit to be used? *ou* still usable?
(g) *(favorable) opinion, rapport* good, favourable; *(Scol) bulletin, note* good. **dans le ~ sens du terme** in the favourable sense of the word.
(h) *(recommandé) alimentation* good. **~ pour la santé/pour le mal de tête** good for one's health/for headaches; **ces champignons ne sont pas ~s (à manger)** these mushrooms aren't safe (to eat); **est-ce que cette eau est bonne?** is this water fit *ou* all right to drink?, is this water drinkable?; **est-ce bien ~ de fumer tant?** is it very wise to smoke so much?; **ce serait une bonne chose s'il restait là-bas** it would be a good thing if he stayed there; **il serait ~ que vous les préveniez** you would do well *ou* it would be a good idea to let them know; **il est ~ de louer de bonne heure** it's as well *ou* it's advisable to book early; **croire** *ou* **juger** *ou* **trouver ~ de faire** to think *ou* see fit to do; **il semblerait ~ de** it would seem sensible *ou* a good idea to; **trouvez-vous ~ qu'il y aille?** do you think it's a good thing for him to go?; **quand/comme vous le jugerez ~** when/as you see fit; **quand/comme ~ vous semble** when/as you think best; **allez-y si ~ vous semble** go ahead if you think it best.
(i) ~ pour: *(Mil)* **~ pour le service** fit for service; **il est ~ pour la casse*** *[objet détérioré]* it's only fit for the dustbin *ou* the scrap heap; *[personne]* he's on his last legs*, he's ready for the scrap heap; **le voilà ~ pour une contravention*** he's let himself in for a fine; **le voilà ~ pour recommencer** now he'll have to start all over again; **la télévision, c'est ~ pour ceux qui n'ont rien à faire** television is all right *ou* fine for people who have nothing to do; **cette solution, c'est ~ pour toi, mais pas pour moi** that may be a solution for you but it won't do for me.
(j) ~ à: cet enfant n'est ~ à rien this child is no good *ou* use at anything; **cet appareil n'est ~ à rien/n'est pas ~ à grand-chose** this instrument is useless/isn't much good *ou* use for anything; **c'est ~ à jeter** it's fit for the dustbin, it might as well be thrown out; **c'est (tout juste) ~ à nous créer des ennuis** it will only create problems for us, all it will do is (to) create problems for us; **ce drap est (tout juste) ~ à faire des torchons** this sheet is (just) about good enough for *ou* is only fit for dusters; **c'est ~ à savoir** it's useful *ou* just as well to know that, that's worth knowing; **c'est toujours ~ à prendre** there's no reason to turn it down, it's better than nothing; **tout n'est pas ~ à dire** some things are better left unsaid; **puis-je vous être ~ à quelque chose?** can I be of any use *ou* help to you?, can I do anything for you?
(k) *(correct) solution, méthode, réponse, calcul* right, correct. **au ~ moment** at the right *ou* proper time; **le ~ numéro/cheval** the right number/horse; **sur le ~ côté de la route** on the right *ou* proper side of the road; **le ~ côté du couteau** the cutting *ou* sharp edge of the knife; **le ~ usage** correct usage (of language); *(fig)* **ils sont sur la bonne route** they're on the right track; *(Prov)* **les ~s comptes font les ~s amis** bad debts make bad friends.
(l) *(intensif de quantité)* good. **un ~ kilomètre** a good kilometre; **une bonne livre/semaine/heure** a good pound/week/hour; **une bonne raclée*** a thorough *ou* sound hiding; **un ~ savon*** a thorough *ou* sound telling-off*; **il a reçu une bonne paire de claques** he got a smart clip on the ear*; **la voiture en a pris un ~ coup*** the car has got *ou* had a real bash*; **ça fait un ~ bout de chemin!** that's quite a good way! *ou* a step!, that's quite some way!; **il est tombé une bonne averse/couche de neige** there has been a heavy shower/fall of snow; **après un ~ moment** after quite some time *ou* a good while; **laissez une bonne marge** leave a good *ou* wide margin; **il faudrait une bonne gelée pour tuer la vermine** what is needed is a hard frost to kill off the vermin; **ça aurait besoin d'une bonne couche de peinture/d'un ~ coup de balai** it needs *ou* would need a good coat of paint/a good sweep-out; **ça fait un ~ poids à traîner!** that's quite a *ou* some load to drag round!; **d'un ~ pas** at a good pace *ou* speed; **faire ~ poids/bonne mesure** to give good weight/measure; **il faudrait qu'il pleuve une bonne fois** what's needed is a good downpour; **je te le dis une bonne fois (pour toutes)** I'm telling you once and for all, I'll tell you one last time; **(un) ~ nombre de** a good many; **arriver ~ premier** to come in an easy first, come in well ahead of everyone else; **arriver ~ dernier** to finish last by a long way, come in a long way *ou* well behind the others.
(m) *(intensif de qualité)* **une bonne paire de souliers** a good (strong) pair of shoes; **une bonne robe de laine** a nice warm woollen dress; **une bonne tasse de thé** a nice (hot) cup of tea; **un ~ bain chaud** a nice hot bath; **le ~ vieux temps** the good old days; **c'était le ~ temps!** those were the days!
(n) mon ~ monsieur my good man; **ma bonne dame** my good woman; **les bonnes gens** good *ou* honest people; **mon ~ ami** my dear *ou* good friend; **une bonne dame m'a fait entrer** some good woman let me in.
(o) *(souhaits)* **bonne (et heureuse) année!** happy New Year!; **~ anniversaire!** happy birthday!; **~ appétit!** have a nice meal!, enjoy your meal!; **bonne chance!** good luck!, all the best!; **~ courage!** good luck!; **~ dimanche!** have a good time on Sunday!, have a nice Sunday!; **bonne fin de semaine!** enjoy the rest of the week!, have a good weekend!; **bonne nuit!** good night!; **bonne rentrée!** I hope you get back all right! *ou* safely!, safe return!; *(Scol)* I hope the new term starts well!; **~ retour!** safe journey back!, safe return!; **bonne route!** safe journey!; **bonne santé!** (I) hope you keep well!; **bonnes vacances!** have a good holiday!; **~ voyage!** safe journey!, have a good journey!; **au revoir et bonne continuation** goodbye and I hope all goes well (for you) *ou* and all the best!
(p) *(amical) ambiance* good, pleasant, nice; *regard, sourire* warm, pleasant. **relations de ~ voisinage** good neighbourly relations; **un ~ (gros) rire** a hearty *ou* cheery laugh; **c'est un ~ camarade** he's a good friend.

(q) (*loc*) ~! right!, O.K.!*; ~! ~! all right! all right!; **c'est ~! je le ferai moi-même** (all) right then I'll do it myself; **~ Dieu!***, **~ sang (de bonsoir)!** damn (it) and blast it!ː; **à ~ droit** with good reason, legitimately; **~s baisers** much love, love and kisses; **~ débarras!** good riddance!; **~ vent!** good riddance!, go to blazes!*; **~ an mal an** taking one year with another, on average; **~ gré mal gré** whether you (*ou* they *etc*) like it or not, willy-nilly; **à bonne fin** to a successful conclusion; **être en bonnes mains** to be in good hands; **(à) ~ marché** *acheter* cheap; **de ~ cœur** *manger, rire* heartily; *faire, accepter* willingly, readily; **être de bonne composition** to be biddable, be easy to deal with; **à ~ compte** *obtenir* (on the) cheap, for very little, for a song; **s'en tirer à ~ compte** to get off lightly; **à la bonne franquette*** informally; **de bonne heure** early; **à la bonne heure!** that's fine!; (*iro*) that's a fine idea! (*iro*); **manger de ~ appétit** to eat heartily; **de ~ matin** early; **une bonne pâte** an easy-going fellow, a good sort; **avoir ~ pied ~ œil** to be as fit as a fiddle, be hale and hearty; **cette fois-ci, on est ~!*** this time we've had it!*; **c'est de bonne guerre** that's fair enough; (*iro*) **elle est bien bonne celle-là** that's a good one!; (*littér*) **faire bonne chère** to eat well, have a good meal; (*littér*) **faire ~ visage à qn** to put on a pleasant face for sb; **faire le ~ apôtre** to have a holier-than-thou attitude; **tenir le ~ bout*** to be getting near the end of one's work, be past the worst; **garder qch pour la bonne bouche** to save sth till the end *ou* till last; (*hum*) **pour la bonne cause**† with honourable motives *ou* intentions; **voilà une bonne chose de faite** that's one good job got out of the way *ou* done; (*Prov*) **~ chien chasse de race** like father like son (*Prov*); (*Prov*) **bonne renommée vaut mieux que ceinture dorée** a good name is better than riches; (*Prov*) **~ sang ne saurait mentir** what's bred in the bone will (come) out in the flesh (*Prov*); **prendre du ~ temps** to enjoy o.s., have a good time; *V* **allure, vent.**

2 *adv*: **il fait ~ ici** it's nice *ou* pleasant here; **il fait ~ au soleil** it's nice and warm in the sun; **il fait ~ vivre à la campagne** it's a nice life in the country; **il fait ~ vivre** it's good to be alive; **il ne ferait pas ~ le contredire** we (*ou* you *etc*) would be ill-advised to contradict him.

3 *nm* **(a)** (*personne*) good *ou* upright person, welldoer. **les ~s et les méchants** good people and wicked people, welldoers and evildoers; (*westerns*) the goodies and the baddies (*Brit*), the good guys and the bad guys (*US*).

(b) (*morceau, partie*) **mange le ~ et laisse le mauvais** eat what's good *ou* the good part and leave what's bad *ou* the bad part.

(c) (*loc*) **avoir du ~: cette solution a du ~** this solution has its advantages *ou* its (good) points; **il y a du ~: il y a du ~ dans ce qu'il dit** there are some good points in what he says; **il y a du ~ et du mauvais** it has its good and its bad points; **il y a du ~ et du moins ~** parts of it are good and parts of it are not so good, some bits are better than others.

4 bonne *nf*: **en voilà une bonne!** that's a good one!; (*iro*) **tu en as de bonnes, toi!*** you're kidding!ː, you must be joking!*; **avoir qn à la bonne*** to like sb; **il m'a à la bonne*** I'm in his good books*.

5: (*hum*) **bonne amie**† girlfriend, sweetheart; **le Bon Dieu** God, the good *ou* dear Lord; **bon enfant** *adj inv* good-natured; **bonne étoile** lucky star; (*péj: femme*) **bonne femme** woman; (*péj: épouse*) **sa bonne femme** his old womanː, his missus*; **bonne maman*** granny*, grandma; **bon marché** *adj inv* cheap, inexpensive; **bon mot** witty remark, witticism; **bonnes œuvres** charity; **bon papa*** grandpa, grandad*; (*Rel*) **la bonne parole** (*lit*) the word of God; (*fig*) the gospel (*fig*); (*Scol*) **bon point** star; (*fig*) **un bon point pour vous!** that's a point in your favour!; **bon public: être bon public** to be appreciative, be an appreciative audience; **bon à rien, bonne à rien** *nm,f* good-for-nothing, ne'er-do-well; (*Bible, fig*) **bon Samaritain** good Samaritan; **bon sens** common sense; **bonne sœur*** nun; **bon teint** *couleur* fast; (*fig*) staunch, dyed-in-the-wool* (*fig*); **le bon ton** good form, good manners; **il est de bon ton de** it is good form *ou* good manners to; **bon vivant** (*adj*) jovial; (*nm*) jovial fellow.

bon[2] [bɔ̃] **1** *nm* (*formulaire*) slip, form; (*coupon d'échange*) coupon, voucher; (*Fin: titre*) bond.

2: **bon de caisse** cash voucher; **bon de commande** order form; **bon d'épargne** savings certificate; **bon d'essence** petrol coupon; **bon de garantie** guarantee (slip); **bon de livraison** delivery slip; **bon de réduction** reduction coupon *ou* voucher; (*Typ*) **bon à tirer** (*adj*) passed for press; (*nm*) final corrected proof; **donner le bon à tirer** to pass for press; **bon du Trésor** (Government) Treasury bill.

bonapartisme [bɔnapaʀtism(ə)] *nm* Bonapartism.

bonapartiste [bɔnapaʀtist(ə)] *adj, nmf* Bonapartist.

bonasse [bɔnas] *adj* meek (and mild), soft*, easy-going.

bonbon [bɔ̃bɔ̃] **1** *nm* sweet (*Brit*), sweetie* (*Brit*), candy (*US*).

2: **bonbon acidulé** acid drop; **bonbon anglais** fruit drop (*Brit*); **un bonbon au chocolat** a chocolate; **bonbon fourré** sweet (*Brit*) with soft centre; **bonbon à la menthe** mint, humbug; **bonbon au miel** honey drop.

bonbonne [bɔ̃bɔn] *nf* (*recouverte d'osier*) demijohn; (*à usage industriel*) carboy.

bonbonnière [bɔ̃bɔnjɛʀ] *nf* (*boîte*) sweet box, bonbonnière; (*fig: appartement*) bijou flat (*Brit*) *ou* apartment (*US*), bijou residence (*hum*).

bond [bɔ̃] *nm [personne, animal]* leap, bound, jump, spring; *[balle]* bounce. **faire des ~s** (*sauter*) to leap *ou* spring up *ou* into the air; (*gambader*) to leap *ou* jump about; **faire un ~ d'indignation** to leap *ou* jump up in indignation *ou* indignantly; **faire un ~ de surprise** to start with surprise; **franchir qch d'un ~** to clear sth at one jump *ou* bound; **se lever d'un ~** to leap *ou* jump *ou* spring up; **il ne fit qu'un ~ jusqu'à l'hôpital** he rushed *ou* dashed off to the hospital, he was at the hospital in a trice; **progresser par ~s** to progress by leaps and bounds; (*Mil*) to advance by successive dashes; **l'économie nationale a fait un ~ (en avant)** the country's economy has leapt forward, there has been a boom in the country's economy; **les prix ont fait un ~** prices have shot up *ou* soared; *V* **balle[1], faux[2].**

bonde [bɔ̃d] *nf* **(a)** (*bouchon*) *[tonneau]* bung, stopper; *[évier, baignoire]* plug; *[étang]* sluice gate. **(b)** (*trou*) *[tonneau]* bung-hole; *[évier, baignoire]* plughole.

bondé, e [bɔ̃de] *adj* packed(-full), cram-full, jam-packed*.

bondieuserie [bɔ̃djøzʀi] *nf* (*péj*) (*piété*) religiosity, devoutness; (*bibelot*) religious trinket *ou* bric-à-brac (*U*).

bondir [bɔ̃diʀ] (2) *vi* **(a)** (*sauter*) *[homme, animal]* to jump *ou* leap *ou* spring up; *[balle]* to bounce (up). **~ de joie** to jump *ou* leap for joy; **~ de colère** to fume with anger; (*fig*) **cela me fait ~*** it makes me hopping mad*, it makes my blood boil*; **il bondit d'indignation** he leapt up indignantly.

(b) (*gambader*) to jump *ou* leap about.

(c) (*sursauter*) to start. **~ de surprise/de frayeur** to start with surprise/fright.

(d) (*se précipiter*) **~ vers** *ou* **jusqu'à** to dash *ou* rush to; **~ sur sa proie** to pounce on one's prey.

bondissement [bɔ̃dismɑ̃] *nm* bound, leap. **regarder les ~s d'une chèvre** to watch a goat bounding *ou* leaping *ou* skipping about.

bonheur [bɔnœʀ] **1** *nm* **(a)** (*U: félicité*) happiness, bliss.

(b) (*joie*) joy (*U*), source of happiness *ou* joy. **le ~ de vivre/d'aimer** the joy of living/of loving; **avoir le ~ de voir son fils réussir** to have the joy of seeing one's son succeed; **faire le ~ de qn** to make sb happy, bring happiness to sb; **si ce ruban peut faire ton ~, prends-le*** if this ribbon is what you're looking for *ou* can be any use to you take it; **des vacances! quel ~!** holidays! what bliss! *ou* what a delight!; **quel ~ de vous revoir!** what a pleasure it is to see you again!

(c) (*chance*) (good) luck, good fortune. **avoir le ~ de faire** to be lucky enough *ou* have the good fortune to do; **il ne connaît pas son ~!** he doesn't know *ou* realize (just) how lucky he is!, he doesn't know *ou* realize his luck!*; **il eut le rare ~ de gagner 3 fois** he had the unusual good fortune *ou* luck of winning *ou* to win 3 times; **porter ~ à qn** to bring sb luck; **par ~** fortunately, luckily; **par un ~ inespéré** by an unhoped-for stroke of luck *ou* good fortune.

(d) (*loc*) (*littér*) **avec ~** felicitously; **mêler avec ~ le tragique et le comique** to make a happy *ou* skilful blend of the tragic and the comic; **au petit ~ (la chance)** haphazardly, any old how*.

2: **bonheur-du-jour** *nm, pl* **bonheurs-du-jour** escritoire, writing desk.

bonhomie [bɔnɔmi] *nf* good-naturedness, good-heartedness, bonhomie.

bonhomme [bɔnɔm], *pl* **bonshommes** [bɔ̃zɔm] **1** *nm* (*) (*homme*) chap*, fellow*, bloke* (*Brit*), guy*; (*mari*) old manː; (ː*Can: père*) old manː, father. **dessiner des bonshommes** to draw little men; **un petit ~ de 4 ans** a little chap* *ou* lad* *ou* fellow* of 4; **dis-moi, mon ~** tell me, sonny* *ou* little fellow*; (*fig*) **aller** *ou* **suivre son petit ~ de chemin** to carry on *ou* go on in one's own sweet way.

2 *adj inv*: **air/regard ~** good-natured expression/look.

3: **bonhomme de neige** snowman; **bonhomme de pain d'épice** gingerbread man.

boni† [bɔni] *nm* (*bénéfice*) profit. **100 F de ~** a 100-franc profit.

boniche [bɔniʃ] *nf* (*péj*) servant (maid).

bonification [bɔnifikɑsjɔ̃] *nf* **(a)** (*amélioration*) *[terre, vins]* improvement. **(b)** (*en compétition*) bonus (points); (*avantage*) advantage, start.

bonifier *vt*, **se bonifier** *vpr* [bɔnifje] (7) to improve.

boniment [bɔnimɑ̃] *nm* (*baratin*) sales talk, patter* (*U*); (*mensonge*) tall story, humbug (*U*).

bonjour [bɔ̃ʒuʀ] *nm* (*gén*) hello, how d'you do?; (*matin*) (good) morning; (*après-midi*) (good) afternoon; (*au revoir*) good day (*frm*), good morning, good afternoon. **donnez-lui le ~ de ma part** give him my regards, remember me to him; **j'ai un ~ à vous donner de M X** Mr X asked me to give *ou* sends his regards.

bonne[2] [bɔn] *nf* maid, domestic. **~ d'enfants** nanny (*Brit*), child's nurse (*US*); **~ à tout faire** general help; (*hum*) maid of all work; *V aussi* **bon[1]**.

bonnement [bɔnmɑ̃] *adv*: **tout ~** just, (quite) simply; **dire tout ~ que** to say (quite) frankly *ou* openly *ou* plainly that.

bonnet [bɔnɛ] **1** *nm* **(a)** (*coiffure*) bonnet, hat; *[bébé]* bonnet.

(b) *[soutien-gorge]* cup.

(c) (*Zool*) reticulum.

(d) (*loc*) **prendre qch sous son ~** to make sth one's concern *ou* responsibility, take it upon o.s. to do sth; **c'est ~ blanc et blanc ~** it's six of one and half a dozen of the other; *V* **jeter.**

2: **bonnet d'âne** dunce's cap; **bonnet de bain** bathing cap; **bonnet de nuit** (*Habillement*) nightcap; (**fig*) wet blanket*, killjoy, spoilsport; **bonnet phrygien** Phrygian cap; **bonnet à poils** bearskin; **bonnet de police** forage cap, garrison *ou* overseas cap (*US*).

bonneterie [bɔnɛtʀi] *nf* (*objets*) hosiery; (*magasin*) hosier's shop, hosiery; (*commerce*) hosiery trade.

bonnetier, -ière [bɔntje, jɛʀ] *nm,f* hosier.

bonnette [bɔnɛt] *nf* (*Phot*) supplementary lens; (*Naut*) studding sail, stuns'l; (*Mil*) *[fortification]* bonnet.

bonniche [bɔniʃ] *nf* = **boniche.**

bonsoir [bɔ̃swaʀ] *nm* (*en arrivant*) hello, good evening; (*en partant*) good evening, good night; (*en se couchant*) good night. **souhaiter le ~** to say good night; **~!*** (that's just) too bad!*; (*rien à faire*) nothing doing!*, not a chance!*, not on your life!*

bonté [bɔ̃te] *nf* **(a)** (*U*) kindness, goodness. **ayez la ~ de faire**

would you be so kind *ou* good as to do?; **faire qch par pure ~ d'âme** to do sth out of the goodness of one's heart; **~ divine!** good heavens!*
(b) (act of) kindness. **merci de toutes vos ~s** thank you for all your kindnesses to me *ou* for all the kindness you've shown me.
bonze [bɔ̃z] *nm* (*Rel*) bonze; (*: *personnage important*) bigwig*. **vieux ~:** old fossil:.
bonzerie [bɔ̃zʀi] *nf* Buddhist monastery.
bonzesse [bɔ̃zɛs] *nf* bonze.
boom [bum] *nm* (*expansion*) boom.
boomerang [bumʀɑ̃g] *nm* (*lit, fig*) boomerang.
boqueteau, *pl* **~x** [bɔkto] *nm* copse.
borborygme [bɔʀbɔʀigm(ə)] *nm* rumble, rumbling noise (in one's stomach).
bord [bɔʀ] *nm* **(a)** *[route]* side, edge; *[rivière]* side, bank; *[lac]* edge, side, shore; *[cratère]* edge, rim, lip; *[forêt, table, assiette]* edge; *[précipice]* edge, brink; *[verre, tasse]* brim, rim; *[plaie]* edge. **le ~ de la mer** the seashore; **~ du trottoir** edge of the pavement, kerb (*Brit*), curb (*US*); **une maison au ~ du lac** a house by the lake *ou* at the lakeside, a lakeside house; **se promener au ~ de la rivière** to go for a walk along the riverside *ou* the river bank *ou* by the river; **passer ses vacances au ~ de la mer** to spend one's holidays at the seaside *ou* by the sea, go to the seaside for one's holidays; **pique-niquer au ~ *ou* sur le ~ de la route** to (have a) picnic at *ou* by the roadside; **au ~ de l'eau** at the water's edge; **se promener au ~ de l'eau** to go for a walk by the lake *ou* river *ou* sea; **en été les ~s du lac sont envahis de touristes** in summer the shores of the lake are overrun by tourists; **il a regagné le ~ à la nage** (*dans la mer*) he swam ashore *ou* to the shore; (*dans une piscine*) he swam to the side; **verre rempli jusqu'au ~ *ou* à ras ~** glass full *ou* filled to the brim.
(b) *[vêtement, mouchoir]* edge, border; *[chapeau]* brim. **chapeau à large(s) ~(s)** wide *ou* broad-brimmed hat; **le ~ ourlé *ou* roulotté d'un mouchoir** the rolled hem of a handkerchief; **veste ~ à ~** single-breasted jacket; **coller du papier ~ à ~** to hang wallpaper edge to edge.
(c) (*Naut*) side. **les hommes du ~** the crew; (*Aviat, Naut*) **à ~** on board, aboard; **monter à ~** to go on board *ou* aboard; **prendre qn à son ~** to take sb aboard *ou* on board; **monter à ~ d'un navire** to board a ship, go on board *ou* aboard ship; (*Naut*) **passer/jeter par-dessus ~** to hand/throw overboard; (*Aut*) **M X, à ~ d'une voiture bleue** Mr X, driving *ou* in a blue car; (*Naut*) **journal *ou* livre de ~** log(book), ship's log.
(d) (*Naut: bordée*) tack. **tirer des ~s** to tack, make tacks; **tirer un ~** to tack, make a tack.
(e) (*Can**) side. **de mon ~** on my side; **prendre le ~** to make off.
(f) (*loc*) **être au ~ de la ruine/du désespoir** to be on the verge *ou* brink of ruin/despair; **au ~ de la tombe** on the brink of death, at death's door; **au ~ des larmes, elle sortit** she went out, on the verge of tears *ou* almost in tears; **nous sommes du même ~** we are on the same side, we are of the same opinion; (*socialement*) we are all of a kind; **à pleins ~s** abundantly, freely; **sur les ~s*: il est un peu fantaisiste sur les ~s*** he's a shade eccentric *ou* a bit of an eccentric.
bordage [bɔʀdaʒ] *nm* **(a)** (*Couture*), edging, bordering. **(b)** (*Naut*) **~s** (*en bois*) planks, planking; (*en fer*) plates, plating. **(c)** (*Can*) **~s** inshore ice.
bordé [bɔʀde] *nm* **(a)** (*Couture*) braid, trimming. **(b)** (*Naut*) (*en bois*) planking; (*en fer*) plating.
bordeaux [bɔʀdo] **1** *nm* Bordeaux (wine). **~ rouge** claret. **2** *adj inv* maroon, burgundy.
bordée [bɔʀde] *nf* **1 (a)** (*salve*) broadside. (*fig*) **~ d'injures** torrent *ou* volley of abuse.
(b) (*Naut: quart*) watch.
(c) (*parcours*) tack. **tirer des ~s** to tack, make tacks; (*fig*) **tirer une ~** to go on a spree* *ou* binge*.
2 (*Can**) **une bordée de neige** a heavy snowfall.
bordel: [bɔʀdɛl] *nm* brothel, whorehouse*†. (*fig*) **quel ~!** what a bloody (*Brit*) shambles!:; **ce ~ de ...** this bloody ...:; **~!** bloody hell!: (*Brit*), hell!:
bordelais, e [bɔʀdəlɛ, ɛz] **1** *adj* of *ou* from Bordeaux, Bordeaux (*épith*). **2** *nm,f*: **B~(e)** inhabitant *ou* native of Bordeaux. **3** *nm* (*région*) **le B~** the Bordeaux region.
border [bɔʀde] (1) *vt* **(a)** (*Couture*) (*entourer*) to edge, trim (*de* with); (*ourler*) to hem, put a hem on.
(b) *rue, rivière [arbres, immeubles, maisons]* to line; *[sentier]* to run alongside. **allée bordée de fleurs** path edged *ou* bordered with flowers; **rue bordée de maisons** road lined with houses; **rue bordée d'arbres** tree-lined road.
(c) *personne* to tuck in *ou* up; *couverture* to tuck in. **~ un lit** to tuck the blankets in.
(d) (*Naut*) (*en bois*) to plank; (*en fer*) to plate.
(e) (*Naut*) *voile* to haul on, pull on; *avirons* to ship.
bordereau, *pl* **~x** [bɔʀdəʀo] **1** *nm* (*formulaire*) note, slip; (*relevé*) statement, summary; (*facture*) invoice.
2: bordereau d'achat purchase note; **bordereau d'envoi** dispatch note; **bordereau de livraison** delivery slip *ou* note; **bordereau de salaire** salary advice; **bordereau de versement** pay(ing)-in slip.
bordure [bɔʀdyʀ] *nf* (*bord*) edge; (*cadre*) surround, frame; (*de gazon, fleurs*) border; (*d'arbres*) line; (*Couture*) border, edging, edge. **~ de pavés** kerb (*Brit*), curb (*US*), kerbstones; **en ~ de** (*le long de*) running along, alongside, along the edge of; (*à côté de*) next to, by; (*près de*) near (to); **papier à ~ noire** black-edged paper, paper with a black edge.
bore [bɔʀ] *nm* boron.
boréal, e, *mpl* **-aux** [bɔʀeal, o] *adj* boreal.
borgne [bɔʀɲ(ə)] *adj* **(a)** *personne* one-eyed, blind in one eye. *fenêtre* **~** obstructed window. **(b)** (*fig: louche*) *hôtel, rue* shady.
borique [bɔʀik] *adj* boric.
bornage [bɔʀnaʒ] *nm [champ]* boundary marking, demarcation.
borne [bɔʀn(ə)] **1** *nf* **(a)** (*kilométrique*) kilometre-marker, ≃ milestone; *[terrain]* boundary stone *ou* marker; (*autour d'un monument etc*) block of stone. **ne reste pas là planté comme une ~!*** don't just stand there like a statue!
(b) (*fig*) **~s** limit(s), bounds; **il n'y a pas de ~s à la bêtise humaine** human folly knows no bounds; **franchir *ou* dépasser les ~s** to go too far, overdo it; **sans ~s** limitless, unlimited, boundless; **mettre des ~s à** to limit.
(c) (*) kilometre.
(d) (*Elec*) terminal.
2: (*Can*) **borne-fontaine** *nf, pl* **borne-fontaines** fire hydrant.
borné, e [bɔʀne] (*ptp de* **borner**) *adj personne* narrow-minded, short-sighted; *esprit, vie* narrow; *intelligence* limited.
Bornéo [bɔʀneo] *n* Borneo.
borner [bɔʀne] (1) **1** *vt* **(a)** *ambitions, besoins, enquête* to limit, restrict (*à faire* to doing, *à qch* to sth).
(b) *terrain* to mark out *ou* off, mark the boundary of. **arbres qui bornent un champ** trees which border a field; **immeubles qui bornent la vue** buildings which limit *ou* restrict one's view.
2 se borner *vpr* (*se contenter de*) **se ~ à faire** to content o.s. with doing, be content to do; **se ~ à qch** to content o.s. with sth; (*se limiter à*) **se ~ à faire/à qch** *[personne]* to restrict *ou* confine *ou* limit o.s. to doing/to sth; *[visite, exposé]* to be limited *ou* restricted *ou* confined to doing/to sth; **je me borne à vous faire remarquer que ...** I would just *ou* merely like to point out to you that ...; **il s'est borné à resserrer les vis** he merely tightened up the screws, he contented himself with tightening up the screws.
bosniaque [bɔznjak] **1** *adj* Bosnian. **2** *nmf*: **B~** Bosnian.
bosnien, -ienne [bɔznjɛ̃, jɛn] **1** *adj* Bosnian. **2** *nm,f*: **B~(ne)** Bosnian.
Bosphore [bɔsfɔʀ] *nm*: **le ~** the Bosphorus.
bosquet [bɔskɛ] *nm* copse, grove.
bossage [bɔsaʒ] *nm* (*Archit*) boss. **~s** bosses, bossage.
bosse [bɔs] *nf* **(a)** *[chameau, bossu]* hump; (*en se cognant*) bump, lump; (*éminence*) bump. **se faire une ~ au front** to get a bump on one's forehead; **route pleine de ~s** (very) bumpy road.
(b) (**loc*) **avoir la ~ des maths** to have a good head for maths, be good at maths; **avoir la ~ du théâtre** to have a flair for acting, be a born actor; **avoir la ~ du commerce** to be a born businessman (*ou* businesswoman).
bosselage [bɔslaʒ] *nm* embossment.
bosseler [bɔsle] (4) *vt* (*déformer*) to dent, bash about; (*marteler*) to emboss. **tout bosselé** *théière* battered, badly dented, all bashed* about *ou* in (*attrib*); *front* covered in bumps; *sol* bumpy.
bossellement [bɔsɛlmɑ̃] *nm* embossing.
bosselure [bɔslyʀ] *nf* (*défaut*) dent; (*relief*) embossment.
bosser* [bɔse] (1) **1** *vi* (*travailler*) to work; (*travailler dur*) (*intellectuellement*) to swot, work hard, slog away*; (*physiquement*) to slave away, work one's guts out:.
2 *vt examen* to swot for. **~ son anglais** to swot up *ou* slog away at* one's English.
bosseur, -euse [bɔsœʀ, øz] *nm,f* slogger*, hard worker.
bossoir [bɔswaʀ] *nm [bateau]* davit; *[ancre]* cathead.
bossu, e [bɔsy] **1** *adj personne* hunchbacked. **dos ~** hunch(ed) back; **redresse-toi, tu es tout ~** sit up, you're getting round-shouldered. **2** *nm,f* hunchback; *V* **rire.**
boston [bɔstɔ̃] *nm* (*danse, jeu*) boston.
bostonnais, e [bɔstɔnɛ, ɛz] *nm,f* (*Can Hist*) Bostonian, American.
bot, e [bo, ɔt] *adj*: **main ~e** club-hand; **pied ~** club-foot.
botanique [bɔtanik] **1** *adj* botanical. **2** *nf* botany.
botaniste [bɔtanist(ə)] *nmf* botanist.
botte¹ [bɔt] *nf* (high) boot. **~ de caoutchouc** wellington (boot), gumboot, welly:; **~ de cheval, ~ de cavalier** riding boot; **~ d'égoutier** wader; **être à la ~ de qn** to be sb's puppet; **être sous la ~ de l'ennemi** to be under the enemy's heel; *V* **lécher.**
botte² [bɔt] *nf [fleurs, légumes]* bunch; *[foin]* (*en gerbe*) bundle, sheaf; (*au carré*) bale.
botte³ [bɔt] *nf* (*Escrime*) thrust. **porter une ~ à** (*lit*) to make a thrust at; (*fig*) to hit out at; (*fig*) **~ secrète** artful thrust.
botte⁴ [bɔt] *nf* (*arg Scol: École Polytechnique*) **sortir dans la ~** to be among the top students in one's year.
botter [bɔte] (1) **1** *vt* **(a)** (*mettre des bottes à*) to put boots on; (*vendre des bottes à*) to sell boots to. **se ~** to put one's boots on; **il se botte chez X** he buys his boots at X's; **botté de cuir** with leather boots on, wearing leather boots.
(b) ~ les fesses *ou* le derrière de qn: to kick *ou* boot: sb in the behind*, give sb a kick up the backside: *ou* in the pants:.
(c) ça me botte* I fancy* (*surtout Brit*) *ou* like *ou* dig: that; **ce film m'a botté*** I really liked *ou* went for* that film.
(d) (*Ftbl*) to kick.
2 *vi* (*Ftbl*) to kick the ball.
bottier [bɔtje] *nm [bottes]* bootmaker; *[chaussures]* shoemaker.
bottillon [bɔtijɔ̃] *nm* ankle boot, bootee; *[bébé]* bootee.
Bottin [bɔtɛ̃] *nm* ® directory, phonebook.
bottine [bɔtin] *nf* (ankle) boot, bootee. **~ à boutons** button-boot.
bouc [buk] *nm* (*Zool*) (billy) goat; (*barbe*) goatee (beard). **sentir *ou* puer le ~:** to stink*, pong:; (*fig*) **~ émissaire** scapegoat, fall guy (*surtout US*).
boucan* [bukɑ̃] *nm* din*, racket*. **faire du ~** (*bruit*) to kick up* a din* *ou* a racket*; (*protestation*) to kick up* a fuss *ou* a shindy*.

boucane‡ [bukan] *nf* (*Can*) smoke.
boucaner [bukane] (1) *vt viande* to smoke, cure; *peau* to tan.
boucanier [bukanje] *nm* (*pirate*) buccaneer.
bouchage [buʃaʒ] *nm* (*V* **boucher**) corking; filling up *ou* in; plugging; stopping; blocking (up); choking up.
bouche [buʃ] **1** *nf* **(a)** (*Anat*) mouth; *[volcan, fleuve, four]* mouth. **embrasser à pleine ~** to kiss full on the lips; **parler la ~ pleine** to talk with one's mouth full; **avoir la ~ amère** to have a bitter taste in one's mouth; **j'ai la ~ sèche** my mouth feels *ou* is dry; **j'ai la ~ pâteuse** my tongue feels thick *ou* coated; (*fig*) **il a 5 ~s à nourrir** he has 5 mouths to feed; **il faut se débarrasser des ~s inutiles** we must get rid of all the non-active *ou* unproductive population.
(b) (*organe de la communication*) mouth. **fermer la ~ à qn** to shut sb up; **garder la ~ close** to keep one's mouth shut; **dans sa ~, ce mot choque** coming from him *ou* when he says *ou* uses it, that word sounds offensive; **il a toujours l'injure à la ~** he's always ready with an insult; **il n'a que ce mot-là à la ~** that word is never off his lips; **de ~ à oreille** by word of mouth, confidentially; **ta ~ (bébé)!‡** shut your mouth!‡ *ou* trap!‡; **~ cousue!*** don't breathe a word!, mum's the word!*; **l'histoire est dans toutes les ~s** the story is on everyone's lips, everyone's talking about it; **son nom est dans toutes les ~s** his name is a household word *ou* is on everyone's lips; **aller *ou* passer de ~ en ~** to be rumoured about; **il a la ~ pleine de cet acteur** he can talk of nothing but this actor; **il en a plein la ~** he really lays off‡ about it, he can talk of nothing else; **nos sentiments s'expriment par sa ~** our feelings are expressed by him *ou* by what he says.
(c) (*loc*) **s'embrasser à ~ que veux-tu** to kiss eagerly; **faire la fine *ou* petite ~** to turn one's nose up (*fig*); **avoir la ~ en cœur** to simper; **avoir la ~ en cul-de-poule** to purse one's lips; **être *ou* rester ~ bée** to be flabbergasted.
2: **bouche d'aération** air vent *ou* inlet; **bouche à bouche** *nm inv* kiss of life; **bouche de chaleur** hot-air vent *ou* inlet; **bouche d'égout** manhole; (*Hist*) **bouche à feu** piece (of ordnance), gun; **bouche d'incendie** fire hydrant; **bouche de métro** metro *ou* tube (*Brit*) entrance.
bouché, e[1] [buʃe] (*ptp de* **boucher**) *adj temps* cloudy, overcast; (‡*fig*) *personne* stupid, thick‡. **~ à l'émeri** *flacon* with a ground glass stopper; (*) *personne* thick as a brick‡ (*surtout Brit*); **les mathématiques sont ~es** there is no future in maths.
bouchée[2] [buʃe] *nf* **(a)** mouthful. (*fig*) **pour une ~ de pain** for a song, for next to nothing; (*fig*) **mettre les ~s doubles** to get stuck in*, put on a spurt; **ne faire qu'une ~ d'un plat** to gobble up *ou* polish off a dish in next to no time; (*fig*) **ne faire qu'une ~ d'un adversaire** to make short work of an opponent.
(b) (*Culin*) **une ~ (au chocolat)** a chocolate; **~ à la reine** chicken vol-au-vent.
boucher[1] [buʃe] (1) **1** *vt* **(a)** *bouteille* to cork, put the *ou* a cork in; *trou, fente* to fill up *ou* in; *fuite* to plug, stop; *fenêtre* to block (up); *lavabo* to block (up), choke (up). **sécrétions qui bouchent les pores** secretions which block up *ou* clog up the pores; **j'ai les oreilles bouchées** my ears are blocked (up); **j'ai le nez bouché** my nose is blocked (up) *ou* stuffed up; **~ le passage** to be *ou* stand in the way; **~ le passage à qn** to be *ou* stand in sb's way, block sb's way; **~ la vue** to block the view; **tu me bouches le jour** you're in my *ou* the light.
(b) **ça/elle lui en a bouché un coin‡** it/she has left him floored*, that/she took the wind out of his sails.
2 se boucher *vpr [évier]* to get blocked *ou* choked *ou* clogged up; *[temps]* to get cloudy, become overcast. **se ~ le nez** to hold one's nose; **se ~ les oreilles** to put one's fingers in one's ears; **se ~ les yeux** to put one's hands over one's eyes, hide one's eyes.
boucher[2] [buʃe] *nm* (*lit, fig*) butcher.
bouchère [buʃɛʀ] *nf* (woman) butcher; (*épouse*) butcher's wife.
boucherie [buʃʀi] *nf* (*magasin*) butcher's (shop); (*métier*) butchery (trade); (*fig*) slaughter. **~ chevaline** horse(meat) butcher's.
bouche-trou, *pl* **bouche-trous** [buʃtʀu] *nm* (*personne*) fill-in, stopgap, stand-in; (*chose*) stopgap.
bouchon [buʃɔ̃] *nm* **(a)** (*en liège*) cork; (*en verre*) stopper; (*en plastique*) stopper, top; (*en chiffon, papier*) plug, bung; *[bidon, réservoir]* cap; *[tube]* top; *[évier]* plug. **vin qui sent le ~** corked wine.
(b) (*Pêche*) float.
(c) **~ (de paille)** wisp.
(d) (*Aut*) holdup, traffic jam.
bouchonnage [buʃɔnaʒ] *nm [cheval]* rubbing-down, wisping-down.
bouchonner [buʃɔne] (1) *vt cheval* to rub down, wisp down; (**fig*) to cosset.
bouchot [buʃo] *nm* mussel bed.
bouclage [buklaʒ] *nm* (*: *mise sous clefs*) locking up *ou* away, imprisonment; (*encerclement*) surrounding, sealing off.
boucle [bukl(ə)] *nf [ceinture, soulier]* buckle; *[cheveux]* curl, lock; *[ruban, voie ferrée, rivière]* loop; (*Sport*) lap; (*Aviat*) loop; (*Ordinateurs*) loop. **fais une ~ à ton j** put a loop on your j; **fais une ~ à ton lacet** tie your shoelace in a bow; **~ d'oreille** earring.
bouclé, e [bukle] (*ptp de* **boucler**) *adj cheveux, fourrure* curly. **il avait la tête ~e** his hair was curly *ou* all curls.
boucler [bukle] (1) **1** *vt* **(a)** (*fermer*) *ceinture* to buckle, fasten (up); (*) *porte* to shut, close. **~ sa valise** (*lit*) to fasten one's suitcase; (*fig*) to pack one's bags; **tu vas la ~!‡** will you belt up!‡, will you shut your trap!‡
(b) (*fig: terminer*) *affaire* to finish off, get through with, settle; *circuit* to complete, go round; *budget* to balance. (*Aviat*) **~ la boucle** to loop the loop; (*fig*) **on est revenu par l'Espagne pour ~ la boucle** we came back through Spain to make (it) a round trip; (*fig*) **nous revoilà dans ce village, on a bouclé la boucle** we're back in the village, so we've come full circle; **dans le cycle de production la boucle est bouclée** the cycle of production is now completed.
(c) (*: *enfermer*) to shut up *ou* away, lock up, put inside*. **ils ont bouclé le coupable** they've locked up the criminal *ou* put the criminal under lock and key; **être bouclé chez soi** to be cooped up *ou* stuck* at home.
(d) (*Mil, Police: encercler*) to surround, seal off. **la police a bouclé le quartier** the police surrounded the area *ou* sealed off the area.
2 *vi* to curl, be curly.
bouclette [buklɛt] *nf* small curl.
bouclier [buklije] *nm* (*Mil, fig*) shield. **faire un ~ de son corps à qn** to shield sb with one's body; (*Espace*) **~ thermique** heat shield.
Bouddha [buda] *nm* Buddha. (*statuette*) **b~** Buddha.
bouddhique [budik] *adj* Buddhistic.
bouddhisme [budism(ə)] *nm* Buddhism.
bouddhiste [budist(ə)] *adj, nmf* Buddhist.
bouder [bude] (1) **1** *vi* to sulk, have a sulk *ou* the sulks*. **2** *vt personne* to refuse to talk to *ou* have anything to do with; *chose* to refuse to have anything to do with, keep away from. **ils se boudent** they're not on speaking terms.
bouderie [budʀi] *nf* (*état*) sulkiness (*U*); (*action*) sulk.
boudeur, -euse [budœʀ, øz] *adj* sulky, sullen.
boudin [budɛ̃] *nm* **(a)** (*Culin*) **~ (noir)** ≃ black pudding (*Brit*); **~ blanc** ≃ white pudding (*Brit*). **(b)** (*bourrelet*) roll; (*doigt*) podgy *ou* fat finger.
boudiné, e [budine] (*ptp de* **boudiner**) *adj* **(a)** *doigt* podgy. **(b)** (*serré*) **~ dans** squeezed into, bursting out of; **~ dans un corset** strapped into *ou* bulging out of a tight-fitting corset.
boudiner [budine] (1) **1** *vt* (*Tex*) to rove; *fil* to coil. **sa robe la boudine** her dress makes her look all bulges. **2 se boudiner** *vpr*: **se ~ dans ses vêtements** to squeeze o.s. into one's clothes, wear too tight-fitting clothes.
boudoir [budwaʀ] *nm* (*salon*) boudoir; (*biscuit*) sponge (*Brit*) *ou* lady (*US*) finger.
boue [bu] *nf* (*gén*) mud; *[mer, canal]* sludge, silt; (*dépôt*) sediment. (*Méd*) **~s activées** activated sludge; (*fig*) **traîner qn dans la ~** to drag sb in the mud; (*fig*) **couvrir qn de ~** to throw mud at sb.
bouée [bwe] *nf* buoy; *[baigneur]* rubber ring. **~ de sauvetage** (*lit*) lifebuoy; (*fig*) lifeline; **~ sonore** radio buoy.
boueux, -euse [bwø, øz] **1** *adj* muddy; (*Typ*) blurred, smudged. **2** *nm* dustman (*Brit*), refuse collector (*Brit Admin*), garbage collector (*US*).
bouffant, e [bufɑ̃, ɑ̃t] *adj manche* puffed-out, full; *cheveux* bouffant. **pantalon ~** baggy breeches.
bouffarde* [bufaʀd(ə)] *nf* pipe.
bouffe[1] [buf] *adj V* **opéra**.
bouffe[2]**‡** [buf] *nf* grub‡. **il ne pense qu'à la ~** he only thinks of his stomach *ou* of his grub‡ *ou* nosh‡.
bouffée [bufe] *nf [parfum]* whiff; *[pipe, cigarette]* puff, drag*; *[colère]* outburst; *[orgueil]* fit. **~ d'air *ou* de vent** puff *ou* breath *ou* gust of wind; (*lit, fig*) **une ~ d'air pur** a breath of fresh air; **~ de chaleur** (*Méd*) hot flush; (*gén*) gust *ou* blast of hot air; **par ~s** in gusts.
bouffer[1] [bufe] (1) *vi [jupe, manche]* to puff *ou* fill out; *[cheveux]* to be bouffant.
bouffer[2]***** [bufe] (1) *vt* **(a)** to eat, gobble up*. **cette voiture bouffe de l'essence** this car drinks petrol; **se ~ le nez** to have a go at one another*, scratch each other's eyes out*; **~ du curé** to be violently anti-church *ou* anticlerical. **(b)** (*emploi absolu*) to eat, nosh‡. **on bouffe mal ici** the grub‡ here isn't up to much; **on a bien bouffé ici** the grub was great here‡.
bouffetance‡ [buftɑ̃s] *nf* = **bouffe**[2].
bouffi, e [bufi] (*ptp de* **bouffir**) *adj visage* puffed up, bloated; *yeux* swollen, puffy; (*fig*) swollen, puffed up (*de* with).
bouffir [bufiʀ] (2) **1** *vt* to puff up. **2** *vi* to become bloated, puff up.
bouffissure [bufisyʀ] *nf* puffiness (*U*), bloatedness (*U*); puffy swelling.
bouffon, -onne [bufɔ̃, ɔn] **1** *adj* farcical, comical. **2** *nm* (*pitre*) buffoon, clown; (*Hist*) jester.
bouffonnerie [bufɔnʀi] *nf* **(a)** (*U*) *[personne]* clowning, sense of the burlesque; *[action]* drollery. **(b)** **~s** (*comportement*) antics, foolery, buffoonery; (*paroles*) jesting; **faire des ~s** to clown about, play the fool.
bougainvillée [bugɛ̃vile] *nf*, **bougainvillier** [bugɛ̃vilje] *nm* bougainvillea.
bouge [buʒ] *nm* (*taudis*) hovel, dump*; (*bar louche*) low dive*.
bougeoir [buʒwaʀ] *nm* (*bas*) candle-holder; (*haut*) candlestick.
bougeotte* [buʒɔt] *nf* fidgets*. **avoir la ~** (*voyager*) to be always on the move; (*remuer*) to fidget (about), have the fidgets*, have ants in one's pants‡.
bouger [buʒe] (3) **1** *vi* **(a)** (*remuer*) to move, stir; *[peuple, grévistes]* to stir. **ne bouge pas** keep still, don't move *ou* budge; **il n'a pas bougé (de chez lui)** he stayed in *ou* at home, he didn't stir out.
(b) (*loc*) **ne pas ~** to stay the same, not to alter; **ce tissu ne bouge pas** (*gén*) this cloth wears *ou* will wear well; (*dimension*) this cloth is shrink-resistant; (*couleur*) this cloth will not fade; **ses idées n'ont pas bougé** his ideas haven't altered, he hasn't changed his ideas; **les prix n'ont pas bougé** prices have stayed put* *ou* the same.
2 *vt* (*) *objet* to move, shift*. **il n'a pas bougé le petit doigt** he didn't lift a finger (to help).
3 se bouger‡ *vpr* to move. **bouge-toi de là!** shift over!‡, shift out of the way!‡; **il faut se ~ pour obtenir satisfaction** you have to put yourself out to get satisfaction.
bougie [buʒi] *nf* **(a)** (*chandelle*) candle; (*Aut*) spark(ing) plug,

plug*. **ampoule de 40 ~s** 40-watt bulb. **(b)** (*: *visage*) dial*. **faire une drôle de ~** to pull a (wry) face.

bougna(t)* [buɲ a] *nm* (*charbonnier*) coalman; (*marchand de charbon*) coal merchant (*who also runs a small café*).

bougon, -onne [bugɔ̃, ɔn] **1** *adj* grumpy, grouchy*. **2** *nm,f* grumbler, grouch*.

bougonnement [bugɔnmɑ̃] *nm* grumbling, grouching.

bougonner [bugɔne] (1) *vi* to grouch (away) (to o.s.), grumble.

bougran [bugʀɑ̃] *nm* buckram.

bougre* [bugʀ(ə)] *nm* **(a)** (*type*) chap*, fellow*, blighter* (*Brit*); (*enfant*) (little) rascal. **bon ~** good sort* *ou* chap*; **pauvre ~** poor devil* *ou* blighter*; **ce ~ d'homme** that confounded man; **~ d'idiot!** *ou* **d'animal!** stupid *ou* confounded idiot!*, silly blighter!* (*Brit*).
(b) *excl* good Lord!*, strewth!*

bougrement* [bugʀəmɑ̃] *adv* (*hum*) damn*, damned*.

bougresse: [bugʀɛs] *nf* woman; (*péj*) hussy, bitch:.

boui-boui, *pl* **bouis-bouis** [bwibwi] *nm* (*café*) small (dingy) café *ou* restaurant.

bouif*† [bwif] *nm* cobbler.

bouillabaisse [bujabɛs] *nf* bouillabaisse, fish soup.

bouillant, e [bujɑ̃, ɑ̃t] *adj* (*brûlant*) *boisson* boiling (hot), scalding; (*qui bout*) *eau, huile* boiling; (*fig*) *tempérament* fiery; *personne* fiery-natured, hotheaded. **~ de colère** seething *ou* boiling with anger.

bouille* [buj] *nf* (*visage*) face, mug: (*péj*). **avoir une bonne ~** to have a cheerful friendly face.

bouilleur [bujœʀ] *nm* (*distillateur*) distiller. **~ de cru** home distiller.

bouillie [buji] *nf* [*bébé*] baby's cereal; [*vieillard*] gruel, porridge. **mettre en ~** to pulp, mash *ou* reduce to a pulp; (*fig*) **c'est de la ~ pour les chats** it's a (proper) dog's dinner*; **réduit en ~** (*lit*) *légumes* cooked to a pulp *ou* mush; (*fig*) *adversaire* crushed to a pulp.

bouillir [bujiʀ] (15) **1** *vi* **(a)** (*lit*) to boil, be boiling. **commencer à ~** to reach boiling point, be nearly boiling; **l'eau bout** the water is boiling; **l'eau ne bout plus** the water has gone *ou* is off the boil; **faire ~ de l'eau** to boil water, bring water to the boil; **faire ~ du linge/des poireaux** to boil clothes/leeks; **faire ~ un biberon** to sterilize a (baby's) bottle by boiling; **~ à gros bouillons** to boil fast; (*fig*) **avoir de quoi faire ~ la marmite** to have enough to keep the pot boiling.
(b) (*fig*) to boil. **à voir ça, je bous!** seeing that makes my blood boil!, I boil at seeing that!; **faire ~ qn** to make sb's blood boil, make sb mad*; **~ d'impatience** to seethe with impatience; **~ de rage/de haine** to seethe *ou* boil with anger/hatred.
2 *vt eau, linge* to boil.

bouilloire [bujwaʀ] *nf* kettle.

bouillon [bujɔ̃] **1** *nm* **(a)** (*soupe*) broth, stock. **~ de légumes/poulet** vegetable/chicken stock; **prendre** *ou* **boire un ~*** (*en nageant*) to swallow *ou* get a mouthful; (*Fin*) to make a big loss, be ruined.
(b) (*bouillonnement*) bubble (in boiling liquid). **au premier ~** as soon as it boils; **couler à gros ~s** to gush out, come gushing out.
(c) (*arg Presse*) **~s** unsold copies, returns.
(d) (*Couture*) puff.
2: bouillon cube stock cube; (*Bio*) **bouillon de culture** (culture) medium; **bouillon gras** meat stock; **bouillon de légumes** vegetable stock; **bouillon d'onze heures** poisoned drink, lethal potion.

bouillonnant, e [bujɔnɑ̃, ɑ̃t] *adj* (*V* **bouillonner**) bubbling; seething; foaming, frothing.

bouillonnement [bujɔnmɑ̃] *nm* (*V* **bouillonner**) bubbling; seething; foaming, frothing.

bouillonner [bujɔne] (1) *vi* [*liquide chaud*] to bubble, seethe; [*torrent*] to foam, froth; [*idées*] to bubble up; [*esprit*] to seethe. (*fig*) **~ de colère** to seethe *ou* boil with anger; **il bouillonne d'idées** his mind is teeming with ideas.

bouillotte [bujɔt] *nf* hot-water bottle.

boulange* [bulɑ̃ʒ] *nf* bakery trade. **être dans la ~** to be a baker (by trade).

boulanger [bulɑ̃ʒe] *nm* baker.

boulangère [bulɑ̃ʒɛʀ] *nf* (woman) baker; (*épouse*) baker's wife.

boulangerie [bulɑ̃ʒʀi] *nf* (*magasin*) baker's (shop), bakery; (*commerce*) bakery trade. **~ pâtisserie** baker's and confectioner's (shop).

boule[1] [bul] *nf* **1** **(a)** (*Billard, Croquet*) ball; (*Boules*) bowl. **jouer aux ~s** to play bowls; (*Casino*) **jouer à la ~** to play (at) boule; **roulé en ~** *animal* curled up in a ball; *paquet* rolled up in a ball.
(b) (*loc*) (*fig*) **avoir une ~ dans la gorge** to have a lump in one's throat; **perdre la ~*** to go bonkers: (*Brit*) *ou* nuts*, go off one's rocker:; **être en ~*** to be in a temper *ou* paddy*; **se mettre en ~*** to fly off the handle*; **cela me met en ~*** that makes me mad* *ou* gets my goat: *ou* gets me:.
2: boule de billard billiard ball; **boule de cristal** crystal ball; **boule de gomme** (*Pharm*) throat pastille; (*bonbon*) fruit pastille *ou* gum; **boule de neige** snowball; **boule-de-neige** *nf, pl* **boules-de-neige** (*fleur*) guelder-rose; (*arbre*) snowball tree; (*fig*) **faire boule de neige** to snowball; ® **boule Quiès** earplug.

boule[2] [bul] *nm* (*Menuiserie*) boule, buhl. **commode ~** boule *ou* buhl chest of drawers.

bouleau, *pl* **~x** [bulo] *nm* (silver) birch.

bouledogue [buldɔg] *nm* bulldog.

bouler [bule] (1) *vi* to roll along. **envoyer ~ qn*** to send sb packing*, send sb away with a flea in his ear*.

boulet [bulɛ] *nm* **(a)** [*forçat*] ball and chain. **~ (de canon)** cannonball; (*fig*) **traîner un ~** to have a millstone round one's neck; **c'est un (véritable) ~ pour ses parents** he is a millstone round his parents' neck; **arriver comme un ~ de canon** to come bursting in *ou* crashing in; **tirer à ~s rouges sur qn** to lay into sb tooth and nail.
(b) [*charbon*] (coal) nut.
(c) (*Vét*) fetlock.

boulette [bulɛt] *nf* **(a)** [*papier*] pellet; (*Culin*) meat croquette, meatball; (*empoisonnée*) poison ball. **(b)** (**fig*) blunder, bloomer*. **faire une ~** to make a blunder *ou* bloomer*, drop a brick* *ou* clanger* (*Brit*).

boulevard [bulvaʀ] *nm* boulevard. **les ~s extérieurs** the outer boulevards of Paris; **les grands ~s** the grand boulevards; **pièce** *ou* **comédie de ~** light comedy; *V* **théâtre**.

bouleversant, e [bulvɛʀsɑ̃, ɑ̃t] *adj spectacle, récit* deeply moving; *nouvelle* shattering, overwhelming.

bouleversement [bulvɛʀsəmɑ̃] *nm* [*habitudes, vie politique etc*] upheaval, disruption. **le ~ de son visage** the utter distress on his face, his distraught face.

bouleverser [bulvɛʀse] (1) *vt* **(a)** (*déranger*) to turn upside down.
(b) (*modifier*) to disrupt, change completely *ou* drastically.
(c) (*émouvoir*) to distress deeply; (*causer un choc*) to overwhelm, bowl over, shatter. **bouleversé par l'angoisse/la peur** distraught with anxiety/fear; **la nouvelle les a bouleversés** they were shattered *ou* deeply distressed by the news.

boulier [bulje] *nm* (*calcul*) abacus; (*Billard*) scoring board.

boulimie [bulimi] *nf* bulimia (*T*). **il fait de la ~*** he is a compulsive eater.

boulimique [bulimik] **1** *adj* bulimic (*T*). **2** *nmf* bulimiac (*T*), compulsive eater.

boulingrin [bulɛ̃gʀɛ̃] *nm* lawn.

bouliste [bulist(ə)] *nmf* bowls player.

boulle [bul] *nm* = **boule[2]**.

boulodrome [bulɔdʀom] *nm* bowling pitch.

boulon [bulɔ̃] *nm* bolt; (*avec son écrou*) nut and bolt.

boulonnage [bulɔnaʒ] *nm* (*V* **boulonner**) bolting (on); bolting (down).

boulonner [bulɔne] (1) **1** *vt* (*serrer à force*) to bolt (down); (*assembler*) to bolt (on). **2** *vi* (*) to work. **~ (dur)** to slog* *ou* slave* away.

boulot[1], -otte [bulo, ɔt] *adj* plump, tubby*.

boulot[2]* [bulo] *nm* (*travail*) work (*U*); (*dur labeur*) grind* (*U*); (*emploi*) job, work (*U*); (*lieu de travail*) work (*U*), place of work. **elle a 4 enfants à élever, quel ~!** she has 4 children to bring up, what a job!; **il a trouvé du ~** *ou* **un ~** he's found work *ou* a job; **allons, au ~!** let's get cracking!*

boulotter* [bulɔte] (1) **1** *vi* to eat, nosh:. **on a bien boulotté** we had a good meal *ou* nosh:. **2** *vt* to eat.

boum [bum] *excl* [*chute*] bang!, wallop!; [*explosion*] bang. **~ par terre!** whoops a daisy!; **on entendit un grand ~** there was an enormous bang *ou* thump; (*loc*) **être en plein ~:** to be in full swing, be going full blast*; **il fait un ~ terrible dans son travail** he's going great guns in his job*.

boumer: [bume] (1) *vi*: **ça boume** everything's going fine *ou* swell* (*US*); **ça boume?** how's things?* *ou* tricks?*

bouquet[1] [bukɛ] *nm* **(a)** (*Bot*) **~ (de fleurs)** bunch (of flowers); (*soigneusement composé*) (*grand*) bouquet, (*petit*) posy; **~ d'arbres** clump of trees; **faire un ~** to make up a bouquet; **le ~ de mariée** the bride's bouquet; **~ de persil/thym** bunch of parsley/thyme; (*Culin*) **~ garni** bouquet garni, bunch of mixed herbs; (*Can:*) **~s** (garden *ou* cut) flowers; (house) plants.
(b) [*feu d'artifice*] finishing *ou* crowning piece (*in a firework display*). (*fig*) **c'est le ~!*** that takes the cake!* *ou* the biscuit!* (*Brit*), that's the last straw!
(c) [*vin*] bouquet. **vin qui a du ~** wine which has a good bouquet *ou* nose.

bouquet[2] [bukɛ] *nm* (*Zool: crevette*) prawn.

bouquetière [buktjɛʀ] *nf* flower seller, flower girl.

bouquetin [buktɛ̃] *nm* ibex.

bouquin* [bukɛ̃] *nm* book.

bouquiner* [bukine] (1) *vti* to read. **il passe son temps à ~** he always has his nose in a book.

bouquiniste [bukinist(ə)] *nmf* secondhand bookseller (*esp along the Seine in Paris*).

bourbe [buʀb(ə)] *nf* mire, mud.

bourbeux, -euse [buʀbø, øz] *adj* miry, muddy.

bourbier [buʀbje] *nm* (quag)mire; (*fig*) mess; (*entreprise*) unsavoury *ou* nasty business, quagmire.

bourde* [buʀd(ə)] *nf* (*gaffe*) blunder, bloomer*, boob*; (*faute*) slip, mistake, bloomer*; howler* (*surtout Scol*). **faire une ~** (*gaffe*) to boob*, blunder, drop a clanger* (*Brit*); (*faute*) to make a (silly) mistake.

bourdon[1] [buʀdɔ̃] *nm* **(a)** (*Zool*) bumblebee, humble-bee. **avoir le ~*** to have the blues*; *V* **faux[2]**. **(b)** (*Mus*) (*cloche*) great bell; [*cornemuse*] bourdon, drone; [*orgue*] bourdon; *V* **faux[2]**.

bourdon[2] [buʀdɔ̃] *nm* (*Typ*) omission, out.

bourdon[3] [buʀdɔ̃] *nm* pilgrim's staff.

bourdonnement [buʀdɔnmɑ̃] *nm* [*insecte*] humming (*U*), buzzing (*U*), drone (*U*); [*voix*] buzz (*U*), hum (*U*); [*moteur*] hum (*U*), humming (*U*), drone (*U*); [*avion*] drone (*U*). **avoir un ~ dans les oreilles** *ou* **des ~s d'oreilles** to have a singing *ou* buzzing noise in one's ears.

bourdonner [buʀdɔne] (1) *vi* (*V* **bourdonnement**) to hum; to buzz; to drone; to sing.

bourg [buʀ] *nm* market town, (*petit*) village. **au ~, dans le ~** in town, in the village.

bourgade [buʀgad] *nf* (large) village, (small) town.

bourgeois, e [buʀʒwa, waz] **1** *adj* **(a)** middle-class; *appartement* comfortable, snug. **quartier ~** middle-class *ou* residential district.

(b) (*gén péj: conventionnel*) *culture, préjugé* bourgeois, middle-class; *valeurs, goûts* bourgeois, middle-class, conventional; *respectabilité* bourgeois, middle-class, smug. **avoir l'esprit (petit) ~** to have a conventional *ou* narrow outlook; **mener une petite vie ~e** to live a humdrum existence; *V* **petit.**

2 *nm,f* **(a)** bourgeois, middle-class person. **grand ~** upper middle-class person; (*péj*) **les ~** the wealthy (classes); **sortir en ~*†** to go out in mufti*† *ou* in civvies*; *V* **épater.**

(b) (*Hist*) (*citoyen*) burgess; (*riche roturier*) bourgeois.

3 *nm* (*Can*) head of household, master.

4 bourgeoise* *nf* (*hum: épouse*) **la** *ou* **ma ~e** the wife*, the missus*.

bourgeoisement [buʀʒwazmɑ̃] *adv penser, réagir* conventionally; *vivre* comfortably.

bourgeoisie [buʀʒwazi] *nf* **(a)** middle class(es), bourgeoisie. **petite/moyenne/haute ~** lower middle/middle/upper middle class. **(b)** (*Hist: citoyenneté*) bourgeoisie, burgesses.

bourgeon [buʀʒɔ̃] *nm* (*Bot*) bud; († *fig*) spot, pimple.

bourgeonnement [buʀʒɔnmɑ̃] *nm* (*Bot*) budding; (*Méd*) granulation.

bourgeonner [buʀʒɔne] (1) *vi* (*Bot*) to (come into) bud; (*Méd*) *[plaie]* to granulate. (*fig*) **son visage bourgeonne** he's getting spots *ou* pimples on his face.

bourgmestre [buʀgmɛstʀ(ə)] *nm* burgomaster.

bourgogne [buʀgɔɲ] **1** *nm* (*vin*) burgundy. **2** *nf* (*région*) **la B~** Burgundy.

bourguignon, -onne [buʀgiɲɔ̃, ɔn] **1** *adj* Burgundian. (*Culin*) **bœuf ~** bœuf bourguignon. **2** *nm,f*: **B~(ne)** Burgundian.

bourlinguer [buʀlɛ̃ge] (1) *vi* **(a)** (*naviguer*) to sail; (*: *voyager*) to get around a lot*, knock about a lot*. **(b)** (*Naut*) to labour.

bourrache [buʀaʃ] *nf* borage.

bourrade [buʀad] *nf* (*du poing*) thump; (*du coude*) dig, poke, prod.

bourrage [buʀaʒ] *nm [coussin]* stuffing; *[poêle, pipe]* filling; *[fusil]* wadding. **~ de crâne*** brainwashing; (*récits exagérés*) eyewash*; (*Scol*) cramming.

bourrasque [buʀask(ə)] *nf* gust of wind, squall. **~ de neige** flurry of snow; **le vent souffle en ~** the wind is blowing in gusts.

bourrasser* [buʀase] (1) *vt* (*Can*) to browbeat, bully.

bourratif, -ive [buʀatif, iv] *adj* filling, stodgy.

bourre[1] [buʀ] *nf [coussin]* stuffing; (*en poils*) hair; (*en laine, coton*) wadding, flock; *[bourgeon]* down; *[fusil]* wad. **à la ~:** late.

bourre[2]**:** [buʀ] *nm* (*policier*) cop*. **les ~s** the fuzz:, the cops*.

bourré, e[1] [buʀe] (*ptp de* **bourrer**) *adj* **(a)** (*plein à craquer*) *salle, sac, compartiment* packed, crammed (*de* with). **portefeuille ~ de billets** wallet cram-full of *ou* stuffed with notes; **devoir ~ de fautes** exercise packed *ou* crammed with mistakes.

(b) (:: *ivre*) tight*, canned:, plastered:.

bourreau, *pl* **~x** [buʀo] **1** *nm* **(a)** (*tortionnaire*) torturer.

(b) (*Hist*) *[guillotine]* executioner, headsman; *[pendaison]* executioner, hangman.

2: bourreau des cœurs ladykiller; **bourreau d'enfants** child-beater; **bourreau de travail** glutton for work*, eager beaver*.

bourrée[2] [buʀe] *nf* (*Mus*) bourrée.

bourreler [buʀle] (4) *vt*: **bourrelé de remords** racked by remorse.

bourrelet [buʀlɛ] *nm* **(a)** *[porte, fenêtre]* draught excluder (*Brit*), weather strip (*US*). **(b) ~ (de chair)** fold *ou* roll of flesh; **~ de graisse** roll of fat, spare tyre*.

bourrelier [buʀəlje] *nm* saddler.

bourrellerie [buʀɛlʀi] *nf* saddlery.

bourrer [buʀe] (1) *vt* **(a)** (*remplir*) *coussin* to stuff; *pipe, poêle* to fill; *valise* to stuff *ou* cram full; (*Mil, Min*) to ram home. **~ une dissertation de citations** to cram an essay with quotations; **~ un sac de papiers** to stuff *ou* cram papers into a bag.

(b) ~ qn de nourriture to stuff sb with food; **ne te bourre pas de frites** don't stuff* yourself *ou* fill yourself up* with chips; **les frites, ça bourre!** chips are very filling!

(c) (*loc*) **~ le crâne à qn*** (*endoctriner*) to stuff* sb's head full of ideas, brainwash sb; (*en faire accroire*) to feed sb a lot of eyewash*; (*Scol*) to cram sb; **~ qn de coups** to pummel sb, beat sb up, hammer blows on sb; **se faire ~ la gueule♥** to get one's head bashed in:; **se ~ la gueule♥** (*se battre*) to bash one another up:; (*se soûler*) to get sloshed: *ou* pissed♥ (*surtout Brit*) *ou* plastered:; *V* **mou**[2].

bourriche [buʀiʃ] *nf [huîtres]* hamper, basket; (*Pêche*) keep-net.

bourrichon* [buʀiʃɔ̃] *nm*: **se monter le ~** to get a notion in one's head; **monter le ~ à qn** to put ideas into sb's head, stir sb up (*contre* against).

bourricot [buʀiko] *nm* (small) donkey.

bourrin* [buʀɛ̃] *nm* horse, nag*.

bourrique [buʀik] *nf* **(a)** (*Zool*) (*âne*) donkey, ass; (*ânesse*) she-ass. **(b)** (**fig*) (*imbécile*) ass, blockhead*; (*têtu*) pigheaded* person. **faire tourner qn en ~** to drive sb to distraction *ou* up the wall*; *V* **têtu.**

bourriquot [buʀiko] *nm* = **bourricot.**

bourru, e [buʀy] *adj personne, air* surly; *voix* gruff.

bourrure [buʀyʀ] *nf* (*Can*) stuffing (*in saddle etc*).

bourse [buʀs(ə)] **1** *nf* **(a)** (*porte-monnaie*) purse. **la ~ ou la vie!** your money or your life!, stand and deliver!; **sans ~ délier** without spending a penny; **avoir la ~ dégarnie/bien garnie** to have an empty/a well-lined purse; **ils font ~ commune** they share expenses, they pool their resources; **ils font ~ à part** they keep separate accounts, they keep their finances separate; **il nous a ouvert sa ~** he lent us some money, he helped us out with a loan; **devoir faire appel à la ~ de qn** to have to ask sb for a loan; *V* **cordon.**

(b) (*Bourse*) **la B~** the Stock Exchange *ou* Market (*US*); *[Paris]* the Bourse; *[Londres]* the (London) Stock Exchange; *[New York]* Wall Street; **la B~ monte/descend** share (*Brit*) *ou* stock (*US*) prices are going up/down, the market is going up/down; **valoir tant en B~** to be worth so much on the Stock Exchange *ou* Market; **jouer à la B~** to speculate *ou* gamble on the Stock Exchange.

(c) (*Univ*) **~ (d'études)** (student's) grant; **~ d'état/d'entretien** state/maintenance grant.

(d) (*Anat*) **~s** scrotum.

2: bourse du commerce *ou* **des marchandises** produce exchange, commodity market; (*Ind*) **Bourse du travail** (*lieu de réunion des syndicats*) ≃ trades union centre; **bourse des valeurs** Stock Market, Stock *ou* Securities Exchange.

boursicotage [buʀsikɔtaʒ] *nm* (*Bourse*) speculation (on a small scale), dabbling on the Stock Exchange.

boursicoter [buʀsikɔte] (1) *vi* (*Bourse*) to speculate in a small way, dabble on the Stock Exchange.

boursicotier, -ière [buʀsikɔtje, jɛʀ] *nm,f*, **boursicoteur, -euse** [buʀsikɔtœʀ, øz] *nm,f* (*Bourse*) small-time speculator.

boursier, -ière [buʀsje, jɛʀ] **1** *adj* **(a)** (*Univ*) **étudiant ~** student receiving a grant, grant-holder. **(b)** (*Bourse*) Stock Market (*épith*). **2** *nm,f* (*Univ*) grant-holder.

boursouflage [buʀsuflaʒ] *nm [visage]* swelling, puffing-up; *[style]* turgidity.

boursouflé, e [buʀsufle] (*ptp de* **boursoufler**) *adj visage* puffy, swollen, bloated; *surface peinte* blistered; (*fig*) *style, discours* bombastic, turgid.

boursouflement [buʀsufləmɑ̃] *nm* = **boursouflage.**

boursoufler [buʀsufle] (1) **1** *vt* to puff up, bloat. **2 se boursoufler** *vpr [peinture]* to blister.

boursouflure [buʀsuflyʀ] *nf [visage]* puffiness; *[style]* turgidity, pomposity; (*cloque*) blister.

bouscaud, e [busko, od] *adj* (*Can*) thickset.

bouscueil [buskœj] *nm* (*Can*) break-up of ice (in rivers and lakes).

bousculade [buskylad] *nf* (*remous*) hustle, jostle, crush; (*hâte*) rush, scramble.

bousculer [buskyle] (1) **1** *vt* **(a)** *personne* (*pousser*) to jostle, shove; (*heurter*) to bump into *ou* against, knock into *ou* against; (*presser*) to rush, hurry (up); (*Mil*) to drive from the field. (*fig*) **être (très) bousculé** to be rushed off one's feet.

(b) *objet* (*heurter*) to knock *ou* bump into; (*faire tomber*) to knock over; (*déranger*) to knock about.

2 se bousculer *vpr* (*se heurter*) to jostle each other; (*: *se dépêcher*) to get a move on*. **ça se bouscule au portillon*** he can't get his words out fast enough.

bouse [buz] *nf* (cow *ou* cattle) dung (*U*), cow pat.

bouseux: [buzø] *nm* (*péj*) bumpkin, yokel.

bousier [buzje] *nm* dung-beetle.

bousillage [buzijaʒ] *nm* **(a)** (*: *V* **bousiller**) botching; bungling; wrecking; busting-up:; smashing-up*; pranging* (*Brit*). **(b)** (*Constr*) cob.

bousiller* [buzije] (1) *vt travail* to botch, bungle, louse up:; *appareil* to wreck, bust up: *ou* in:; *moteur* to bust up:, wreck; *voiture* to smash up*, prang* (*Brit*); *avion* to prang*; *personne* to bump off:, do in:. **se faire ~** to get done in: *ou* bumped off:.

bousilleur, -euse* [buzijœʀ, øz] *nm,f* bungler, botcher.

boussole [busɔl] *nf* compass. (*fig*) **perdre la ~*** to lose one's head.

boustifaille: [bustifaj] *nf* grub:, nosh:, chow:.

bout [bu] **1** *nm* **(a)** (*extrémité*) *[ficelle, planche, perche]* end; *[nez, doigt, langue, oreille]* tip; *[table]* end; *[canne]* end, tip. **~ du sein** nipple; **à ~ rond/carré** round-/square-ended; **à ~ ferré** *canne* with a steel *ou* metal tip; *souliers* with a steel toecap; **cigarette à ~ de liège** cork-tipped cigarette; **il écarta les feuilles mortes du ~ du pied** he pushed aside the dead leaves with his toe; **à ~ de bras** at arm's length; (*fig*) **du ~ des lèvres** reluctantly, half-heartedly; (*fig*) **avoir qch sur le ~ de la langue** to have sth on the tip of one's tongue; **il est artiste jusqu'au ~ des ongles** he is an artist to his fingertips; **savoir** *ou* **connaître qch sur le ~ du doigt** to have sth at one's fingertips; **regarder** *ou* **voir les choses par le petit ~ de la lorgnette** to take a narrow view of things; **il a mis le ~ du nez à** *ou* **passé le ~ du nez par la porte et il a disparu** he popped his head round the door *ou* he just showed his face then disappeared; *V* **manger, montrer, savoir.**

(b) *[espace, durée]* end. **au ~ de la rue** at the end of the street; **à l'autre ~ de la pièce** at the far *ou* other end of the room; **au ~ du jardin** at the bottom *ou* end of the garden; **au ~ d'un mois** at the end of a month, after a month, a month later; **au ~ d'un moment** after a while; **à l'autre ~ de** at the other *ou* far end of; **on n'en voit pas le ~** there doesn't seem to be any end to it; **d'un ~ à l'autre de la ville** from one end of the town to the other; **d'un ~ à l'autre de ses œuvres** throughout *ou* all through his works; **d'un ~ de l'année à l'autre** all the year round, from one year's end to the next; **d'un ~ à l'autre du voyage** from the beginning of the journey to the end, throughout *ou* right through the journey; (*fig*) **ce n'est pas le ~ du monde!** it's not the end of the world!; **si tu as 5 F à payer c'est (tout) le ~ du monde*** 5 francs is the very most it might cost you, at the (very) worst it might cost you 5 francs; **commençons par un ~ et nous verrons** let's get started *ou* make a start and then we'll see.

(c) (*morceau*) *[ficelle]* piece, bit; *[pain, papier]* piece, bit, scrap; (*Naut*) (length of) rope. **on a fait un ~ de chemin ensemble** we walked part of the way *ou* some of the way *ou* a bit of the way together; **il m'a fait un ~ de conduite** he went part of the way with me; **jusqu'à Paris, cela fait un ~*** it's some distance *ou* quite a long way to Paris; **il est resté un (bon) ~ de temps** he stayed a while *ou* quite some time; **écrivez-moi un ~ de lettre** drop me a line *ou* a note; **avoir un ~ de rôle dans une pièce** to have a small *ou* bit part in a play; **un ~ de terrain** a patch *ou* plot of land; **un ~ de pelouse** a patch of lawn; **un ~ de ciel bleu** a patch of blue sky; **un petit ~ d'homme*** a (mere) scrap of a man; **un petit ~ de femme** a slip of a woman; **un petit ~ de chou*** a little kid* *ou* nipper*; *V* **connaître.**

(d) à ~: **être à ~** (*fatigué*) to be all in*, be at the end of one's tether; (*en colère*) to have had enough, be at the end of one's patience; **ma patience est à ~** my patience is exhausted; **être à ~ de souffle** to be out of breath; **être à ~ de force(s)/ressources** to have no strength/money left; **être à ~ d'arguments** to have run out of arguments; **être à ~ de nerfs** to be at the end of one's tether, be just about at breaking *ou* screaming* point; **mettre** *ou* **pousser qn à ~** to push sb to the limit (of his patience).

(e) (*loc*) **au ~ du compte** in the last analysis, all things considered; **être au ~ de son rouleau*** (*n'avoir plus rien à dire*) to have run out of ideas; (*être sans ressources*) to be running short (of money); (*être épuisé*) to be at the end of one's tether; (*être près de la mort*) to have come to the end of the road; **il n'est pas au ~ de ses peines** he's not out of the wood (*Brit*) *ou* woods (*US*) yet, his troubles still aren't over; **je suis** *ou* **j'arrive au ~ de mes peines** I am out of the wood (*Brit*) *ou* woods (*US*), the worst of my troubles are over; **jusqu'au ~:** **nous sommes restés jusqu'au ~** we stayed right to the end; **ils ont combattu jusqu'au ~** they fought to the bitter end; **rebelle jusqu'au ~** rebel to the end *ou* the last; **il faut aller jusqu'au ~ de ce qu'on entreprend** if you take something on you must see it through (to the end); **aller jusqu'au ~ de ses idées** to follow one's ideas through to their logical conclusion; **~ à ~** end to end; **mettre des planches/cordes ~ à ~** to put planks/ropes end to end; **de ~ en ~:** **lire un livre de ~ en ~** to read a book from cover to cover *ou* right through *ou* from start to finish; **parcourir une rue de ~ en ~** to go from one end of a street to the other; **à ~ portant** point-blank, at point-blank range; **mettre les ~s:** to hop it: (*Brit*), skedaddle*, scarper:; *V* **bon¹, brûler, joindre** *etc.*

2: (*Rel*) **bout de l'an** memorial service (*held on the first anniversary of a person's death*); (*Naut*) **bout-dehors** *nm, pl* **bouts-dehors** boom; (*Ciné*) **bout d'essai** screen test; **bout filtre** *nm* filter tip; **cigarettes (à) bout filtre** filter tip cigarettes, tipped cigarettes; (*Littérat*) **bout-rimé** *nm, pl* **bouts-rimés** bouts rimés, poem in set rhymes.

boutade [butad] *nf* **(a)** (*plaisanterie*) jest, sally. **(b)** (*caprice*) whim. **par ~** as the whim takes him (*ou* her *etc*), by fits and starts.

boute-en-train [butɑ̃tʀɛ̃] *nm inv* live wire*. **c'était le ~ de la soirée** he was the life and soul of the party.

bouteille [butɛj] *nf* **(a)** (*récipient*) bottle; (*contenu*) bottle(ful). **~ d'air comprimé/de butane** cylinder of compressed air/of butane gas; ® **~ Thermos** Thermos ® (flask); **~ d'un litre/de 2 litres** litre/2-litre bottle; **~ de vin** (*récipient*) wine bottle; (*contenu*) bottle of wine; **bière en ~** bottled beer; **mettre du vin en ~s** to bottle wine; **vin qui a 10 ans de ~** wine that has been in (the) bottle for 10 years.

(b) (*loc*) **prendre de la ~*** to be getting on in years, be getting long in the tooth* (*hum*); **boire une (bonne) ~** to drink *ou* have a bottle of (good) wine; (*gén hum*) **aimer la ~** to be fond of drink *ou* the bottle, like one's tipple*; **c'est la ~ à l'encre** the whole business is about as clear as mud, you can't make head nor tail of it.

bouter†† [bute] (1) *vt* to drive, push (*hors de* out of).

boutique [butik] *nf* shop, store (*surtout US*); [*grand couturier*] boutique; (*:fig*) dump:. **~ en plein vent** open-air stall; **quelle sale ~!** what a crummy: place! *ou* dump!:; *V* **fermer.**

boutiquier, -ière [butikje, jɛʀ] *nm,f* shopkeeper.

boutoir [butwaʀ] *nm* [*sanglier*] snout; *V* **coup.**

bouton [butɔ̃] **1** *nm* **(a)** (*Couture*) button.

(b) (*mécanisme*) (*Élec*) switch; [*porte, radio*] knob; [*sonnette*] (push-)button.

(c) (*Bot*) bud. **en ~** in bud; **~ de rose** rosebud.

(d) (*Méd*) spot, pimple. **avoir des ~s** to have spots *ou* pimples, have a pimply face.

2: **bouton de col** collar stud; **bouton de manchette** cufflink; **bouton-d'or** *nm, pl* **boutons-d'or** buttercup; **bouton-pression** *nm, pl* **boutons-pression** press stud, snap fastener.

boutonnage [butɔnaʒ] *nm* buttoning(-up).

boutonner [butɔne] (1) **1** *vt* **(a)** *vêtement* to button *ou* fasten (up). **(b)** (*Escrime*) to button. **2 se boutonner** *vpr* [*vêtement*] to button (up); [*personne*] to button (up) one's coat *ou* trousers *etc.*

boutonneux, -euse [butɔnø, øz] *adj* pimply, spotty.

boutonnière [butɔnjɛʀ] *nf* buttonhole. **avoir une fleur à la ~** to wear a flower in one's buttonhole, wear a buttonhole (*Brit*) *ou* boutonniere (*US*); **porter une décoration à la ~** to wear a decoration on one's lapel.

bouturage [butyʀaʒ] *nm* taking (of) cuttings, propagation (by cuttings).

bouture [butyʀ] *nf* cutting. **faire des ~s** to take cuttings.

bouturer [butyʀe] (1) **1** *vt* to take a cutting from, propagate (by cuttings). **2** *vi* to put out suckers.

bouvet [buvɛ] *nm* (*Menuiserie*) rabbet plane.

bouvier [buvje] *nm* [*troupeau*] herdsman, cattleman; [*charrue*] ploughman.

bouvreuil [buvʀœj] *nm* bullfinch.

bovidés [bɔvide] *nmpl* bovines, bovidae (*T*).

bovin, e [bɔvɛ̃, in] **1** *adj* (*lit, fig*) bovine. **2** *nmpl*: **~s** cattle.

bowling [bɔliŋ] *nm* (*jeu*) (tenpin) bowling; (*salle*) bowling alley.

box, *pl* **boxes** [bɔks] *nm* [*hôpital, dortoir*] cubicle; [*écurie*] loose-box; [*porcherie*] stall, pen; (*garage*) lock-up (garage). (*Jur*) **~ des accusés** dock.

box-calf [bɔkskalf] *nm* box calf.

boxe [bɔks(ə)] *nf* boxing. **match de ~** boxing match.

boxer¹ [bɔkse] (1) **1** *vi* to box, be a boxer. **~ contre** to box against, fight. **2** *vt* (*Sport*) to box against, fight; (*: frapper*) to thump*, punch.

boxer² [bɔksɛʀ] *nm* boxer (dog).

boxeur [bɔksœʀ] *nm* boxer.

boxon: [bɔksɔ̃] *nm* brothel, whorehouse*†. **c'est le ~!** it's a shambolic mess!:

boy [bɔj] *nm* (native) servant boy, boy.

boyard [bɔjaʀ] *nm* (*Hist*) boyar(d).

boyau, *pl* **~x** [bwajo] *nm* **(a)** (*intestins*) **~x** [*animal*] guts, entrails; (*) [*homme*] insides*, guts*; *V* **tripe.**

(b) (*corde*) **~ (de chat)** (cat)gut.

(c) (*passage*) (narrow) passageway; (*tuyau*) narrow pipe; (*Mil*) communication trench, sap; (*Min*) (narrow) gallery.

(d) [*bicyclette*] (racing) tyre, tubeless tyre .

boycottage [bɔjkɔtaʒ] *nm* boycotting (*U*), boycott.

boycotter [bɔjkɔte] (1) *vt* to boycott.

boy-scout, *pl* **boy(s)-scouts** [bɔjskut] *nm* (boy) scout. **avoir une mentalité de ~*** to have a (rather) naïve *ou* ingenuous outlook.

brabançon, -onne [bʀabɑ̃sɔ̃, ɔn] **1** *adj* of *ou* from Brabant. **2** *nm,f*: **B~(ne)** inhabitant *ou* native of Brabant. **3** *nf*: **la Brabançonne** the Belgian national anthem.

brabant [bʀabɑ̃] *nm* **(a)** (*Agr: aussi* **double ~**) swivel plough, turnwrest plow (*US*). **(b)** (*Géog*) **le B~** the Brabant.

bracelet [bʀaslɛ] **1** *nm* [*poignet*] bracelet; [*bras, cheville*] bangle; [*montre*] strap, bracelet. **2: bracelet de force** (leather) wristband; **bracelet-montre** *nm, pl* **bracelets-montres** wrist (let) watch.

brachial, e, *mpl* **-iaux** [bʀakjal, jo] *adj* brachial.

brachiopode [bʀakjɔpɔd] *nm* brachiopod.

brachycéphale [bʀakisefal] **1** *adj* brachycephalic. **2** *nmf* brachycephalic person.

brachycéphalie [bʀakisefali] *nf* brachycephaly.

braconnage [bʀakɔnaʒ] *nm* poaching.

braconner [bʀakɔne] (1) *vi* to poach.

braconnier [bʀakɔnje] *nm* poacher.

brader [bʀade] (1) **1** *vt* to sell cheaply *ou* for a song*; (*Comm, fig*) to sell off. **2** *vi* (*Comm*) to have a clearance sale.

braderie [bʀadʀi] *nf* (open-air *ou* market) clearance sale.

braguette [bʀagɛt] *nf* fly, flies (*of trousers*); (*Hist*) codpiece.

brahmane [bʀɑman] *nm* Brahmin, Brahman.

brahmanique [bʀɑmanik] *adj* Brahminical.

brahmanisme [bʀɑmanism(ə)] *nm* Brahminism, Brahmanism.

brahmine [bʀɑmin] *nf* Brahmani, Brahmanee.

brai [bʀɛ] *nm* pitch, tar.

braies [bʀɛ] *nfpl* (*Hist*) breeches (*worn by Gauls*).

braillard, e [bʀɑjaʀ, aʀd(ə)] (*V* **brailler**) **1** *adj* bawling (*épith*); yelling (*épith*); howling (*épith*); squalling (*épith*). **2** *nm,f* bawler.

braille [bʀɑj] *nm* Braille.

braillement [bʀɑjmɑ̃] *nm* (*V* **brailler**) bawl(ing); yelling; howl(ing); squall(ing).

brailler [bʀɑje] (1) **1** *vi* (*crier*) to bawl, yell; (*pleurer*) to bawl, howl, squall. **2** *vt chanson, slogan* to bawl out.

brailleur, -euse [bʀɑjœʀ, øz] = **braillard.**

braiment [bʀɛmɑ̃] *nm* bray(ing).

braire [bʀɛʀ] (50) *vi* (*lit, fig*) to bray. **faire ~ qn:** to get on sb's wick:.

braise [bʀɛz] *nf* **(a)** [*feu*] **la ~, les ~s** the (glowing) embers; (*charbon de bois*) live charcoal; (*fig*) **être sur la ~** to be on tenterhooks; **yeux de ~** fiery eyes, eyes like coals. **(b)** (*: argent*) cash*, dough:.

braiser [bʀeze] (1) *vt* to braise.

bramement [bʀɑmmɑ̃] *nm* (*V* **bramer**) bell, troat; wailing.

bramer [bʀɑme] (1) *vi* [*cerf*] to bell, troat; (**fig*) to wail.

bran [bʀɑ̃] *nm* bran. **~ de scie** sawdust.

brancard [bʀɑ̃kaʀ] *nm* **(a)** (*bras*) [*charrette*] shaft; [*civière*] shaft, pole; *V* **ruer.** **(b)** (*civière*) stretcher.

brancardier, -ière [bʀɑ̃kaʀdje, jɛʀ] *nm,f* stretcher-bearer.

branchage [bʀɑ̃ʃaʒ] *nm* branches, boughs. **~s** fallen *ou* lopped-off branches, lops.

branche [bʀɑ̃ʃ] *nf* **(a)** (*Bot*) branch, bough. **~ mère** main branch; **sauter de ~ en ~** to leap from branch to branch; **asperges en ~s** whole asparagus, asparagus spears; **céleri en ~s** (sticks of) celery; *V* **vieux.**

(b) (*ramification*) [*nerfs, veines*] branch, ramification; [*rivière, canalisation, bois de cerf*] branch; [*lunettes*] sidepiece; [*compas*] leg; [*ciseaux*] blade; [*fer à cheval*] half; [*famille*] branch. **la ~ aînée** the older *ou* eldest branch of the family; **la ~ maternelle** the maternal branch of the family, the mother's side of the family; *V* **chandelier.**

(c) (*secteur*) branch. **les ~s de la science moderne** the different branches of modern science; **notre fils s'orientera vers une ~ technique** our son will go in for the technical side.

branchement [bʀɑ̃ʃmɑ̃] *nm* (*action: V* **brancher**) plugging-in; connecting-up; linking-up; (*objet*) connection, installation; (*Rail*) branch line.

brancher [bʀɑ̃ʃe] (1) *vt* **(a)** *appareil électrique* to plug in; (*installer*) to connect up; *appareil à gaz, tuyau* to connect up; *téléphone* to connect (up); *réseau* to link up (*sur* with). **~ qch sur qch** to plug sth into sth; to connect sth up with sth; **où est-ce que ça se branche?** where does that plug in?; **où est-ce que je peux me ~?** where can I plug (it) in?

(b) (*fig*) **~ qn sur un sujet** to start sb off on a subject; **être**

branché* to be in the know; **quand on l'a branché** *ou* **quand il est branché là-dessus il est intarissable** when he's launched on that *ou* when somebody gets him started on that he can go on forever; **le journal est branché en direct sur ce qui se passe** the paper is in close touch with current events.
branchette [brɑ̃ʃɛt] *nf* small branch, twig.
branchial, e, *mpl* **-aux** [brɑ̃ʃjal, o] *adj* branchial.
branchies [brɑ̃ʃi] *nfpl (Zool)* branchiae (*T*), gills.
branchiopode [brɑ̃ʃjɔpɔd] *nm* branchiopod.
branchu, e [brɑ̃ʃy] *adj* branchy.
brandade [brɑ̃dad] *nf*: **~ (de morue)** brandade (*dish made with cod*).
brande [brɑ̃d] *nf* (*lande*) heath(land); (*plantes*) heath, heather, brush.
brandebourg [brɑ̃dbur] *nm* (*Habillement*) frog. **à ~(s)** frogged.
brandebourgeois, e [brɑ̃dburʒwa, waz] **1** *adj* Brandenburg (*épith*). **2** *nm,f*: **B~(e)** inhabitant *ou* native of Brandenburg.
brandir [brɑ̃dir] (2) *vt arme, document* to brandish, flourish.
brandon [brɑ̃dɔ̃] *nm* firebrand.
branlant, e [brɑ̃lɑ̃, ɑ̃t] *adj dent* loose; *mur* shaky; *escalier, meuble* rickety, shaky; *pas* unsteady, tottering, shaky; (*fig*) *régime* tottering, shaky; *raison* shaky.
branle [brɑ̃l] *nm [cloche]* swing. **mettre en ~** *cloche* to swing, set swinging; (*fig*) *forces* to set in motion, set off, get moving; **donner le ~ à** to set in motion, set rolling; **se mettre en ~** to get going *ou* moving.
branle-bas [brɑ̃lbɑ] *nm inv* bustle, commotion, pandemonium. **dans le ~ du départ** in the confusion *ou* bustle of (the) departure; **être en ~** to be in a state of commotion; **mettre qch en ~** to turn sth upside down, cause commotion in sth; (*Naut*) **~ de combat** (*manœuvre*) preparations for action; (*ordre*) 'action stations!'; **sonner le ~ de combat** to sound action stations; **mettre en ~ de combat** to clear the decks (for action).
branlement [brɑ̃lmɑ̃] *nm [tête]* wagging, shaking.
branler [brɑ̃le] (1) **1** *vt* (a): **~ la tête** *ou* (*hum*) **du chef** to shake *ou* wag one's head.
(b) (**) **qu'est ce qu'ils branlent?** what the hell are they up to?‡
2 *vi [échafaudage]* to be shaky *ou* unsteady; *[meuble]* to be shaky *ou* rickety; *[dent]* to be loose. (*fig*) **~ dans le manche** to be shaky *ou* precarious, be in a shaky position.
3 se branler** *vpr* to wank** (*Brit*), jerk off** (*US*). (*fig*) **je m'en branle** I don't give a fuck**.
branleux, -euse‡ [brɑ̃lø, øz] *adj* (*Can*) equivocating, slow, shilly-shallying*.
braquage [brakaʒ] *nm* (*Aut*) (steering) lock; (*arg Crime*) stickup (*arg*); *V* **angle, rayon.**
braque [brak] **1** *adj* (*) barmy* (*Brit*), crackers*. **2** *nm* (*Zool*) pointer.
braquer [brake] (1) **1** *vt* (a) **~ une arme** *etc* **sur** to point *ou* aim *ou* level a weapon *etc* at; **~ un télescope** *etc* **sur** to train a telescope *etc* on; **~ son regard/attention** *etc* **sur** to turn one's gaze/attention *etc* towards, fix one's gaze/attention *etc* on; **~ les yeux sur qch** to fix one's eyes on sth, stare hard at sth.
(b) (*Aut*) *roue* to turn.
(c) (*fig: buter*) **~ qn** to put sb's back up*, make sb dig in his heels; **~ qn contre qch** to turn sb against sth; **il est braqué** he's not to be budged.
2 *vi* (*Aut*) to turn the (steering) wheel. *[voiture]* **~ bien/mal** to have a good/bad lock; **braquez vers la gauche/la droite!** left hand/right hand down!
3 se braquer *vpr* to dig one's heels in. **se ~ contre** to set one's face against.
braquet [brakɛ] *nm [bicyclette]* gear ratio.
bras [bra] **1** *nm* (a) arm. **une serviette sous le ~** with a briefcase under one's arm; **un panier au ~** with a basket on one's arm; **donner le ~ à qn** to give sb one's arm; **prendre le ~ de qn** to take sb's arm; **être au ~ de qn** to be on sb's arm; **se donner le ~** to link arms; **~ dessus, ~ dessous** arm in arm; (*lit*) **les ~ croisés** with one's arms folded; (*fig*) **rester les ~ croisés** to sit idly by; **tendre** *ou* **allonger le ~ vers qch** to reach out for sth, stretch out one's hand *ou* arm for sth; *V* **arme, force, plein** *etc*.
(b) (*travailleur*) hand, worker. **manquer de ~** to be short-handed, be short of manpower *ou* labour; **c'est lui la tête, moi je suis le ~** he does the thinking and I do the (actual) work, he supplies the brain and I supply the brawn.
(c) (*pouvoir*) **le ~ de la justice** the arm of the law; (*Rel*) **le ~ séculier** the secular arm.
(d) *[manivelle, outil, pompe]* handle; *[fauteuil]* arm(rest); *[grue]* jib; *[sémaphore, ancre, électrophone]* arm; *[moulin]* sail, arm; *[croix]* limb; *[aviron, brancard]* shaft; (*Naut*) *[vergue]* brace.
(e) *[fleuve]* branch.
(f) *[cheval]* shoulder; *[mollusque]* tentacle.
(g) (*loc*) **en ~ de chemise** in (one's) shirt sleeves; **saisir qn à ~ le corps** to seize sb round the waist, seize sb bodily; (*fig*) **avoir le ~ long** to have a long arm; (*lit, fig*) **à ~ ouverts, les ~ ouverts** with open arms (*lit, fig*); **à ~ tendus** with outstretched arms; **tomber sur qn à ~ raccourcis*** to set (up)on sb, pitch into sb*; **lever les ~ au ciel** to throw up one's arms; **les ~ m'en tombent** I'm flabbergasted* *ou* stunned; **avoir qch/qn sur les ~*** to have sth/sb on one's hands, be stuck* *ou* landed* with sth/sb; **il a une nombreuse famille sur les ~*** he's got a large family to look after; **avoir une sale histoire sur les ~*** to have a nasty business on one's hands; (*hum*) **(être) dans les ~ de Morphée** (to be) in the arms of Morpheus; *V* **bout, couper, gros** *etc*.
2: (*fig*) **bras droit** right-hand man; (*Sport*) **bras de fer** Indian wrestling (*U*); **bras de levier** lever arm; **bras de mer** arm of the sea, sound; **bras mort** oxbow lake, cutoff.
brasage [brazaʒ] *nm* brazing.
braser [braze] (1) *vt* to braze.
brasero [brazero] *nm* brazier.
brasier [brazje] *nm* (*incendie*) (blazing) inferno, furnace; (*fig: foyer de guerre*) inferno. **son cœur/esprit était un ~** his heart/mind was on fire *ou* ablaze.
brassage [brasaʒ] *nm* (a) *[bière]* brewing. (b) (*mélange*) mixing. **~ de races** intermixing of races; (*Aut*) **~ des gaz** mixing. (c) (*Naut*) bracing.
brassard [brasar] *nm* armband. **~ de deuil** black armband.
brasse [bras] *nf* (a) (*Sport*) breast-stroke. **~ coulée** breast-stroke; **~ papillon** butterfly(-stroke); **nager la ~** to swim breast-stroke. (b) (††: *mesure*) ≈ 5 feet; (*Naut*) fathom.
brassée [brase] *nf* armful. **par ~s** in armfuls; (*Can‡*) *[machine à laver etc]* load.
brasser [brase] (1) *vt* (a) (*remuer*) to stir (up); (*mélanger*) to mix; *pâte* to knead; *salade* to toss; *cartes* to shuffle; *argent* to handle a lot of. **~ des affaires** to be in big business. (b) *bière* to brew. (c) (*Naut*) to brace.
brasserie [brasri] *nf* (a) (*café*) ≈ pub (*Brit*), bar (*US*), brasserie. (b) (*fabrique de bière*) brewery; (*industrie*) brewing industry.
brasseur, -euse [brasœr, øz] *nm,f* (a) *[bière]* brewer. (b) (*Comm*) **~ d'affaires** big businessman.
brassière [brasjɛr] *nf* (a) *[bébé]* (baby's) vest (*Brit*) *ou* undershirt (*US*). **~ (de sauvetage)** life jacket. (b) (*Can: soutien-gorge*) bra, brassière.
brasure [brazyr] *nf* (*procédé*) brazing; (*résultat*) brazed joint, braze; (*métal*) brazing metal.
bravache [bravaʃ] **1** *nm* braggart, blusterer. **faire le ~** to swagger about. **2** *adj* swaggering, blustering.
bravade [bravad] *nf* act of bravado. **par ~** out of bravado.
brave [brav] *adj* (a) (*courageux*) *personne, action* brave, courageous, gallant (*littér*). **faire le ~** to act brave, put on a bold front.
(b) (*avant n: bon*) good, nice, fine; (*honnête*) decent, honest. **c'est une ~ fille** she's a nice girl; **c'est un ~ garçon** he's a good *ou* nice lad; **ce sont de ~s gens** they're good *ou* decent people *ou* souls; **il est bien ~** he's not a bad chap* (*surtout Brit*) *ou* guy* (*US*), he's a nice enough fellow; **mon ~ (homme)** my good man *ou* fellow; **ma ~ dame** my good woman.
bravement [bravmɑ̃] *adv* (*courageusement*) bravely, courageously, gallantly (*littér*); (*résolument*) boldly, unhesitatingly.
braver [brave] (1) *vt* (*défier*) *autorité, parents* to stand up to, hold out against, defy; *règle* to defy, disobey; *danger, mort* to brave. **~ l'opinion** to fly in the face of (public) opinion.
bravo [bravo] **1** *excl* (*félicitation*) well done!, bravo!; (*approbation*) hear! hear! **2** *nm* cheer.
bravoure [bravur] *nf* bravery, braveness, gallantry; *V* **morceau.**
break [brɛk] *nm* (*Aut*) estate (car) (*Brit*), shooting brake† (*Brit*), station wagon (*US*).
brebis [brəbi] *nf* (*Zool*) ewe; (*Rel: pl*) flock. **~ égarée** stray *ou* lost sheep; **~ galeuse** black sheep; **à ~ tondue Dieu mesure le vent** the Lord tempers the wind to the shorn lamb.
brèche [brɛʃ] *nf [mur]* breach, opening, gap; (*Mil*) breach; *[lame]* notch, nick. (*Mil*) **faire** *ou* **ouvrir une ~ dans le front ennemi** to make a breach in *ou* breach the enemy line; (*fig*) **faire une ~ à sa fortune** to make a hole in one's fortune; (*fig*) **être toujours sur la ~** to be always hard at it*; *V* **battre.**
brechtien, -ienne [brɛʃtjɛ̃, jɛn] *adj* Brechtian.
bredouillage [brədujaʒ] *nm* spluttering, mumbling.
bredouille [brəduj] *adj* (*gén*) empty-handed. (*Chasse, Pêche*) **rentrer ~** to go *ou* come home empty-handed *ou* with an empty bag.
bredouillement [brədujmɑ̃] *nm* = **bredouillage.**
bredouiller [brəduje] (1) **1** *vi* to stammer, mumble. **2** *vt* to mumble, stammer (out), falter out. **~ une excuse** to splutter out *ou* falter out *ou* stammer an excuse.
bredouilleur, -euse [brədujœr, øz] **1** *adj* mumbling, stammering. **2** *nm,f* mumbler, stammerer.
bref, brève [brɛf, ɛv] **1** *adj rencontre, discours, lettre* brief, short; *voyelle, syllabe* short. **d'un ton ~** sharply, curtly; **soyez ~ et précis** be brief and to the point; **à ~ délai** shortly.
2 *adv*: **(enfin)** **~** (*pour résumer*) to cut a long story short, in short, in brief; (*passons*) let's not waste any more time; (*donc*) anyway; **en ~** in short, in brief.
3 *nm* (*Rel*) (papal) brief.
4 brève *nf* (*syllabe*) short syllable; (*voyelle*) short vowel.
bréhaigne [breɛɲ] *adj* (*Zool*†) barren, sterile.
brelan [brəlɑ̃] *nm* (*Cartes*) three of a kind. **~ d'as** three aces.
breloque [brəlɔk] *nf* (bracelet) charm; *V* **battre.**
brème [brɛm] *nf* (a) (*Zool*) bream. (b) (*arg Cartes*) card.
Brésil [brezil] *nm* Brazil.
brésil [brezil] *nm* brazil (wood).
brésilien, -ienne [breziljɛ̃, jɛn] **1** *adj* Brazilian. **2** *nm,f*: **B~(ne)** Brazilian.
bressan, e [brɛsɑ̃, an] **1** *adj* of *ou* from Bresse. **2** *nm,f*: **B~(e)** inhabitant *ou* native of Bresse.
Bretagne [brətaɲ] *nf* Brittany; *V* **grand.**
bretèche [brətɛʃ] *nf* gatehouse, bartizan.
bretelle [brətɛl] *nf* (a) *[sac]* (shoulder) strap; *[lingerie]* strap; *[fusil]* sling. *[pantalon]* **~s** braces (*Brit*), suspenders (*US*); **porter l'arme** *ou* **le fusil à la ~** to carry one's weapon slung over one's shoulder. (b) (*Rail*) crossover; (*Aut*) link road (*Brit*); *[autoroute]* motorway link (road) (*Brit*). **~ de raccordement** access road (*Brit*); **~ de contournement** motorway (*Brit*) bypass.
breton, -onne [brətɔ̃, ɔn] **1** *adj* Breton. **2** *nm* (*Ling*) Breton. **3** *nm,f*: **B~(ne)** Breton.

bretonnant, e [bʀətɔnɑ̃, ɑ̃t] *adj* Breton-speaking. **la Bretagne ~e** Breton-speaking Brittany.
bretteur [bʀetœʀ] *nm* (††) swashbuckler; (*duelliste*) duellist.
bretteux, -euse: [bʀɛtø, øz] *adj* (*Can*) idling, dawdling. **un ~** an idler, a slowcoach (*Brit*), a slowpoke (*US*).
bretzel [bʀɛdzɛl] *nm* pretzel.
breuvage [bʀœvaʒ] *nm* drink, beverage; (*magique*) potion.
brève [bʀɛv] *V* **bref.**
brevet [bʀəvɛ] **1** *nm* **(a)** (*diplôme*) diploma, certificate; (*Hist: note royale*) royal warrant; (*Scol*) *exam taken at end of 4th form* ≃ (G.C.E.) 'O' level (*Brit*). (*Scol*) **avoir son ~** ≃ to have (passed) one's 'O' levels (*Brit*).
(b) (*Naut*) certificate, ticket. **~ de capitaine** master's certificate *ou* ticket; (*Mil*) **~ de commandant** major's brevet.
(c) (*Jur*) **~ (d'invention)** letters patent, patent.
(d) (*fig: garantie*) guarantee. **donner à qn un ~ d'honnêteté** to testify to *ou* guarantee sb's honesty; **on peut lui décerner un ~ de persévérance** you could give him a medal for perseverance.
2: **brevet d'apprentissage** ≃ certificate of apprenticeship; (*Scol*) **brevet d'études du premier cycle** *exam taken at end of 4th form* ≃ (G.C.E.) 'O' level; **brevet de pilote** pilot's licence.
brevetable [bʀəvtabl(ə)] *adj* patentable.
breveté, e [bʀəvte] (*ptp de* **breveter**) *adj* **(a)** *invention* patented. **(b)** (*diplômé*) *technicien* qualified, certificated; (*Mil*) *officier* commissioned.
breveter [bʀəvte] (4) *vt invention* to patent. **faire ~ qch** to take out a patent for sth.
bréviaire [bʀevjɛʀ] *nm* (*Rel*) breviary; (*fig*) bible.
briard, e [bʀijaʀ, aʀd(ə)] **1** *adj* of *ou* from Brie. **2** *nm,f*: **B~(e)** inhabitant *ou* native of Brie.
bribe [bʀib] *nf* (*fragment*) bit, scrap. **~s de conversation** snatches of conversation; **~s de nourriture** scraps of food; **les ~s de sa fortune** the remnants of his fortune; **par ~s** in snatches, piecemeal.
bric-à-brac [bʀikabʀak] *nm inv* **(a)** (*objets*) bric-a-brac, odds and ends; (*fig*) bric-a-brac, trimmings. **(b)** (*magasin*) junk shop.
bric et de broc [bʀikedbʀɔk] *loc adv*: **de ~** (*de manière disparate*) in any old way*, any old how*; **meublé de ~** furnished with bits and pieces *ou* with odds and ends.
brick [bʀik] *nm* (*Naut*) brig.
bricolage [bʀikɔlaʒ] *nm* **(a)** (*passe-temps*) tinkering about, do-it-yourself, D.I.Y.* (*Brit*); (*travaux*) odd jobs. **j'ai du ~ à faire** I've got a few (odd) jobs to do; **rayon ~** do-it-yourself department.
(b) (*réparation*) makeshift repair *ou* job.
bricole [bʀikɔl] *nf* **(a)** (*) (*babiole*) trifle; (*cadeau*) something small, token; (*menu travail*) easy job, small matter. **il ne reste que des ~s** there are only a few bits and pieces *ou* a few odds and ends left; **ça coûte 10 F et des ~s** it costs 10 francs odd*.
(b) *[cheval]* breast harness.
(c) (*Can*) **~s*** braces (*Brit*), suspenders (*US*).
bricoler [bʀikɔle] (1) **1** *vi* (*menus travaux*) to do odd jobs, potter about; (*réparations*) to do odd repairs, do odd jobs; (*passe-temps*) to tinker about *ou* around.
2 *vt* (*réparer*) to fix (up), mend; (*mal réparer*) to tinker *ou* mess (about) with; (*fabriquer*) to knock up*.
bricoleur [bʀikɔlœʀ] *nm* handyman, D.I.Y. man* (*Brit*), do-it-yourselfer*. **il est ~** he is good with his hands, he's very handy*; **je ne suis pas très ~** I'm not much of a handyman.
bricoleuse [bʀikɔløz] *nf* handywoman, D.I.Y. woman* (*Brit*), do-it-yourselfer*.
bride [bʀid] *nf* **(a)** (*Équitation*) bridle. **tenir un cheval en ~** to curb a horse; (*fig*) **tenir ses passions/une personne en ~** to keep one's passions/a person in check, keep a tight hand *ou* rein on one's passions/a person; **jeter** *ou* **laisser** *ou* **mettre la ~ sur le cou** *ou* **col à un cheval** to give a horse the reins, give a horse his head; (*fig*) **laisser la ~ sur le cou à qn** to give *ou* leave sb a free hand; **les jeunes ont maintenant la ~ sur le cou** young people have free rein to do as they like nowadays; **tenir la ~ haute à un cheval** to rein in a horse; (*fig*) **tenir la ~ haute à qn** to keep a tight rein on sb; **aller à ~ abattue** *ou* **à toute ~** to ride flat out*, ride hell for leather*; *V* **lâcher, tourner.**
(b) *[bonnet]* string; (*en cuir*) strap.
(c) (*Couture*) *[boutonnière]* bar; *[bouton]* loop; *[dentelle]* bride.
(d) (*Tech*) *[bielle]* strap; *[tuyau]* flange.
bridé, e [bʀide] (*ptp de* **brider**) *adj*: **avoir les yeux ~s** to have slanting *ou* slit eyes.
brider [bʀide] (1) *vt* **(a)** *cheval* to bridle; (*fig*) *impulsion, colère* to bridle, restrain, keep in check, quell; *personne* to keep in check, hold back. (*fig*) **il est bridé dans son costume, son costume le bride** his suit is too tight for him. **(b)** (*Culin*) to truss. **(c)** *boutonnière* to bind; *tuyau* to clamp, flange; (*Naut*) to lash together.
bridge [bʀidʒ(ə)] *nm* (*Cartes*) bridge; (*prothèse dentaire*) bridge. **~ contrat** contract bridge; **~ aux enchères** auction bridge; **faire un ~** to play *ou* have a game of bridge.
bridger [bʀidʒe] (3) *vi* to play bridge.
bridgeur, -euse [bʀidʒœʀ, øz] *nm,f* bridge player.
bridon [bʀidɔ̃] *nm* snaffle.
brie [bʀi] *nm* Brie (cheese).
brièvement [bʀijɛvmɑ̃] *adv* briefly, concisely.
brièveté [bʀijɛvte] *nf* brevity, briefness.
brigade [bʀigad] *nf* (*Mil*) brigade; (*Police*) squad; (*gén: équipe*) gang, team. **~ des mœurs** vice squad; **~ des stupéfiants** drug squad; **~ volante** flying squad,;u4 **~ anti-gang** (police) commando squad, anti-terrorist squad.
brigadier [bʀigadje] *nm* (*Police*) sergeant; (*Mil*) *[artillerie]* bombardier; *[blindés, cavalerie, train]* corporal. **~-chef** ≃ lance sergeant (*Brit*).
brigand [bʀigɑ̃] *nm* (†: *bandit*) brigand, bandit; (*péj: filou*) twister (*Brit*), sharpie* (*US*), crook; (*hum: enfant*) rascal, imp.
brigandage [bʀigɑ̃daʒ] *nm* (armed) robbery, banditry; (†) brigandage. **commettre des actes de ~** to engage in robbery with violence; (*fig*) **c'est du ~!** it's daylight robbery!
brigantine [bʀigɑ̃tin] *nf* (*Naut*) spanker.
brigue [bʀig] *nf* (*littér*) intrigue. **obtenir qch par ~** to get sth by intrigue.
briguer [bʀige] (1) *vt emploi* to covet, aspire to, bid for; *honneur, faveur* to aspire after, crave; *amitié* to court, solicit; *suffrages* to solicit, canvass (for).
brillamment [bʀijamɑ̃] *adv* brilliantly. **réussir ~ un examen** to pass an exam with flying colours.
brillance [bʀijɑ̃s] *nf* (*Astron*) brilliance.
brillant, e [bʀijɑ̃, ɑ̃t] **1** *adj* **(a)** (*luisant*) shiny, glossy; (*étincelant*) sparkling, bright; *chaussures* well-polished, shiny; *couleur* bright, brilliant. **elle avait les yeux ~s de fièvre/d'impatience** her eyes were bright with fever/impatience; **il avait les yeux ~s de convoitise/colère** his eyes glittered with envy/anger; *V* **peinture, sou.**
(b) (*remarquable*) brilliant, outstanding; *situation* excellent, brilliant; *succès* brilliant, dazzling, outstanding; *avenir* brilliant, bright; *conversation* brilliant, sparkling. **avoir une intelligence ~e** to be outstandingly intelligent, be brilliant; **sa santé n'est pas ~e** his health isn't too good; **ce n'est pas ~** it's not up to much, it's not too good, it's not fantastic*.
2 *nm* **(a)** (*U: éclat*) (*étincelant*) sparkle, brightness; (*luisant*) shine, glossiness; *[couleur]* brightness, brilliance; *[étoffe]* sheen; (*par usure*) shine. (*fig*) **le ~ de son esprit/style** the brilliance of his mind/style; **il a du ~ mais peu de connaissances réelles** he has a certain brilliance but not much serious knowledge; **donner du ~ à un cuir** to polish up a piece of leather.
(b) (*diamant*) brilliant. **taillé/monté en ~** cut/mounted as a brilliant.
brillantine [bʀijɑ̃tin] *nf* brilliantine.
briller [bʀije] (1) *vi* **(a)** (*gén*) *[lumière, soleil]* to shine; *[diamant, eau]* to sparkle, glitter; *[étoile]* to twinkle, shine (brightly); *[métal]* to glint, shine; *[feu, braises]* to glow (brightly); *[flammes]* to blaze; *[éclair]* to flash; *[chaussures]* to shine; *[surface polie, humide]* to shine, glisten. **faire ~ les meubles/l'argenterie** to polish the furniture/the silver; **faire ~ ses chaussures** to shine *ou* polish one's shoes; *V* **tout.**
(b) *[yeux]* to shine, sparkle; *[nez]* to be shiny; *[larmes]* to glisten. **ses yeux brillaient de joie** his eyes sparkled with joy; **ses yeux brillaient de convoitise** his eyes glinted greedily.
(c) *[personne]* to shine, stand out. **~ en société** to be a success in society; **~ à un examen** to come out (on) top in *ou* do brilliantly in an exam; **~ par son talent/éloquence** to be outstandingly talented/eloquent; **il ne brille pas par le courage/la modestie** courage/modesty is not his strong point; **~ par son absence** to be conspicuous by one's absence; **le désir de ~** the longing to stand out (from the crowd), the desire to be the centre of attention; **faire ~ les avantages de qch à qn** to paint a glowing picture of sth to sb.
brimade [bʀimad] *nf* (*vexation*) vexation; (*Mil, Scol: d'initiation*) ragging (*U*) (*Brit*). **faire subir des ~s à qn** to harry sb, harass sb; (*Mil, Scol*) to rag sb (*Brit*).
brimbalement* [bʀɛ̃balmɑ̃] *nm* shaking (about); (*bruit*) rattle.
brimbaler* [bʀɛ̃bale] (1) = **bringuebaler*.**
brimborion [bʀɛ̃bɔʀjɔ̃] *nm* (*colifichet*) bauble, trinket.
brimer [bʀime] (1) *vt* (*soumettre à des vexations*) to aggravate, bully; (*Mil, Scol*) *nouveaux* to rag (*Brit*). **se sentir brimé** to feel one's being got at* *ou* being done down* (*Brit*); **je suis brimé*** I'm being got at* *ou* done down* (*Brit*).
brin [bʀɛ̃] *nm* **(a)** *[blé, herbe]* blade; *[bruyère, mimosa, muguet]* sprig; *[osier]* twig; *[paille]* wisp. (*fig*) **un beau ~ de fille** a fine-looking girl.
(b) *[chanvre, lin]* yarn, fibre; *[corde, fil, laine]* strand.
(c) (*un peu*) **un ~ de** a touch *ou* grain *ou* bit of; **il n'a pas un ~ de bon sens** he hasn't got an ounce *ou* a grain of common sense; **avec un ~ de nostalgie** with a touch *ou* hint of nostalgia; **il y a en lui un ~ de folie/méchanceté** there's a touch of madness/malice in him; **faire un ~ de causette** to have a bit of a chat*; **faire un ~ de toilette** to have a lick and a promise, have a quick wash; **il n'y a pas un ~ de vent** there isn't a breath of wind; **un ~ +** *adj* a shade *ou* bit *ou* little + *adj*; **un ~ plus grand/haut** a bit *ou* a little *ou* a fraction *ou* a shade bigger/higher; **je suis un ~ embêté*** I'm a trifle *ou* a shade worried.
(d) (*Rad*) *[antenne]* wire.
brindille [bʀɛ̃dij] *nf* twig.
bringue[1]* [bʀɛ̃g] *nf*: **grande ~** beanpole*.
bringue[2]* [bʀɛ̃g] *nf* (*beuverie*) binge*; (*débauche*) spree. **faire la ~** to go on a binge* *ou* a spree.
bringuebaler* [bʀɛ̃gbale] (1), **brinquebaler*** [bʀɛ̃kbale] (1) **1** *vi* *[tête]* to shake about, joggle; *[voiture]* to shake *ou* rock about, joggle; (*avec bruit*) to rattle. **une vieille auto toute bringuebalante** a ramshackle *ou* broken-down old car; **il y a quelque chose qui bringuebale dans ce paquet** something is rattling in this packet.
2 *vt* to cart (about).
brio [bʀijo] *nm* (*virtuosité*) brilliance; (*Mus*) brio. **faire qch avec ~** to do sth brilliantly, carry sth off with great panache.
brioche [bʀijɔʃ] *nf* brioche (*sort of bun*). (*fig*) **prendre de la ~*** to develop a paunch *ou* a corporation, get a bit of a tummy*.
brioché, e [bʀijɔʃe] *adj* (baked) like a brioche; *V* **pain.**
brique [bʀik] **1** *nf* **(a)** (*Constr*) brick; *[savon]* bar, cake; *[tourbe]*

slab. **mur de** *ou* **en ~(s)** brick wall; **~ pleine/creuse** solid/hollow brick; (*fig*) **bouffer des ~s**‡ to have nothing to eat.
(b) (*) a million (old) francs.
(c) (*Naut*) **~ à pont** holystone.
2 *adj inv* brick red.
briquer [bʀike] (1) *vt* (*) to polish up; (*Naut*) to holystone, scrub down.
briquet[1] [bʀikɛ] *nm* (cigarette) lighter. **~-tempête** windproof lighter; *V* **battre.**
briquet[2] [bʀikɛ] *nm* (*Zool*) beagle.
briquetage [bʀiktaʒ] *nm* (*mur*) brickwork; (*enduit*) imitation brickwork.
briqueter [bʀikte] (4) *vt* **(a)** (*bâtir*) to brick, build with bricks. **(b)** (*peindre*) to face with imitation brickwork.
briqueterie [bʀikt(ə)ʀi] *nf* brickyard, brickfield.
briqueteur [bʀiktœʀ] *nm* bricklayer.
briquetier [bʀiktje] *nm* (*ouvrier*) brickyard worker, brickmaker; (*entrepreneur*) brickseller.
briquette [bʀikɛt] *nf* briquette.
bris [bʀi] *nm* breaking. (*Jur*) **~ de clôture** trespass, breaking-in; (*Aut*) **~ de glaces** broken windows; (*Jur*) **~ de scellés** breaking of seals; (*Jur*) **~ de prison** prison breaking.
brisant, e [bʀizɑ̃,ɑ̃t] **1** *adj* high-explosive (*épith*). **obus ~** high-explosive shell. **2** *nm* **(a)** (*vague*) breaker. **(b)** (*écueil*) shoal, reef. **(c)** (*brise-lames*) groyne, breakwater.
briscard [bʀiskaʀ] *nm* (*Hist Mil*) veteran, old soldier.
brise [bʀiz] *nf* breeze.
brise- [bʀiz] *préf V* **briser.**
brisé, e [bʀize] (*ptp de* **briser**) *adj*: **~ (de fatigue)** worn out, exhausted; **~ (de chagrin)** overcome by sorrow; *V* **arc, ligne[1], pâte.**
brisées [bʀize] *nfpl*: **marcher sur les ~ de qn** to poach on sb's preserves (*fig*).
briser [bʀize] (1) **1** *vt* **(a)** (*casser*) *objet* to break, smash; *mottes de terre* to break up; *chaîne, fers* to break. **~ qch en mille morceaux** to smash sth to smithereens, break sth into little pieces *ou* bits, shatter sth (into little pieces); (*lit, fig*) **~ la glace** to break the ice.
(b) (*saper, détruire*) *carrière, vie* to ruin, wreck; *personne* (*épuiser*) to tire out, exhaust; (*abattre la volonté de*) to break, crush; *espérance* to smash, shatter, crush; *cœur, courage* to break; *traité, accord* to break; *amitié* to break up, bring to an end. **d'une voix brisée par l'émotion** in a voice choked with emotion; **ces épreuves l'ont brisé** these trials and tribulations have left him a broken man; **il en a eu le cœur brisé** it broke his heart, he was heartbroken about it.
(c) (*avoir raison de*) *volonté* to break, crush; *rebelle* to crush, subdue; *opposition, résistance* to crush, break down; *grève* to break (up); *révolte* to crush, quell. **il était décidé à ~ les menées de ces conspirateurs** he was determined to put paid to *ou* put a stop to the schemings of these conspirators.
(d) (†: *mettre fin à*) *entretien* to break off.
2 *vi* (*littér*) **(a)** (*rompre*) **~ avec qn** to break with sb; **brisons là!**† enough said!
(b) (*déferler*) *[vagues]* to break.
3 se briser *vpr* **(a)** *[vitre, verre]* to break, shatter, smash; *[bâton, canne]* to break, snap.
(b) *[vagues]* to break (*contre* against).
(c) *[résistance]* to break down, snap; *[assaut]* to break up (*sur* on, *contre* against); *[espoir]* to be dashed. **nos efforts se sont brisés sur cette difficulté** our efforts were frustrated *ou* thwarted by this difficulty.
(d) *[cœur]* to break, be broken; *[voix]* to falter, break.
4: brise-bise *nm inv* half-curtain (*on window*); **brise-fer** *nm inv* (*enfant*) wrecker; **brise-glace** *nm inv* (*navire*) icebreaker; *[pont]* icebreaker, ice apron; **brise-jet** *nm inv* tap swirl; **brise-lames** *nm inv* breakwater, mole; **brise-mottes** *nm inv* harrow; **brise-tout** *nm inv* = **brise-fer**; **brise-vent** *nm inv* windbreak.
briseur, -euse [bʀizœʀ, øz] *nm,f* breaker, wrecker. **~ de grève** strikebreaker.
brisquard [bʀiskaʀ] *nm* = **briscard.**
bristol [bʀistɔl] *nm* (*papier*) Bristol board; (*carte de visite*) visiting card.
brisure [bʀizyʀ] *nf* (*cassure*) break, crack; *[charnière]* joint, break; (*Hér*) mark of cadency, brisure.
britannique [bʀitanik] **1** *adj* British. **2** *nmf*: **B~** Briton, British person, Britisher (*US*); **c'est un B~** he's British *ou* a Britisher (*US*); **les B~s** the British (people).
broc [bʀo] *nm* pitcher, ewer.
brocante [bʀɔkɑ̃t] *nf* (*commerce*) secondhand (furniture) trade, secondhand market; (*objets*) secondhand goods (*esp furniture*). **il est dans la ~** he deals in secondhand goods; **acheter qch à la ~** to buy sth on the flea market.
brocanter [bʀɔkɑ̃te] (1) *vi* to deal in secondhand goods (*esp furniture*).
brocanteur, -euse [bʀɔkɑ̃tœʀ, øz] *nm,f* secondhand (furniture) dealer.
brocard[1] [bʀɔkaʀ] *nm* (*Zool*) brocket.
brocard[2] [bʀɔkaʀ] *nm* (*littér*, †) gibe, taunt.
brocarder [bʀɔkaʀde] (1) *vt* (*littér*, †) to gibe at, taunt.
brocart [bʀɔkaʀ] *nm* brocade.
brochage [bʀɔʃaʒ] *nm* (*V* **brocher**) binding (*with paper*); brocading.
broche [bʀɔʃ] *nf* **(a)** (*bijou*) brooch. **(b)** (*Culin*) spit; (*Tex*) spindle; (*Tech*) drift, pin; (*Élec*) pin; (*Méd*) pin. (*Culin*) **faire cuire à la ~** to spit-roast.
broché [bʀɔʃe] **1** *nm* (*Tex*) (*procédé*) brocading; (*tissu*) brocade. **2** *adj m*: **livre ~** book with paper binding, paperback (book).
brocher [bʀɔʃe] (1) *vt* **(a)** *livre* to bind (*with paper*), put a paper binding on. **(b)** (*Tex*) to brocade. **tissu broché d'or** gold brocade.
brochet [bʀɔʃɛ] *nm* (*Zool*) pike.
brochette [bʀɔʃɛt] *nf* (*Culin: ustensile*) skewer; (*plat*) kebab, brochette. (*fig*) **~ de décorations** row of medals; (*fig*) **~ de personnalités** bevy *ou* band of VIPs.
brocheur, -euse [bʀɔʃœʀ, øz] **1** *nm,f* (*V* **brocher**) book binder; brocade weaver. **2** *nm* brocade loom. **3 brocheuse** *nf* binder, binding machine.
brochure [bʀɔʃyʀ] *nf* **(a)** (*magazine*) brochure, booklet, pamphlet. **(b)** *[livre]* (paper) binding. **(c)** (*Tex*) brocaded pattern *ou* figures.
brocoli [bʀɔkɔli] *nm* broccoli.
brodequin [bʀɔdkɛ̃] *nm* (laced) boot; (*Hist Théât*) buskin, sock. (*Hist: supplice*) **les ~s** the boot.
broder [bʀɔde] (1) **1** *vt tissu* to embroider (*de* with); (*fig*) *récit* to embroider. **2** *vi* (*exagérer*) to embroider, embellish; (*trop développer*) to elaborate. **~ sur un sujet** to elaborate on a subject.
broderie [bʀɔdʀi] *nf* (*art*) embroidery; (*objet*) piece of embroidery, embroidery (*U*); (*industrie*) embroidery trade. **faire de la ~** to embroider, do embroidery; **~ anglaise** broderie anglaise.
brodeur [bʀɔdœʀ] *nm* embroiderer.
brodeuse [bʀɔdøz] *nf* (*ouvrière*) embroideress; (*machine*) embroidery machine.
broiement [bʀwamɑ̃] *nm* = **broyage.**
bromate [bʀɔmat] *nm* bromate.
brome [bʀom] *nm* (*Chim*) bromine.
bromique [bʀɔmik] *adj* bromic.
bromure [bʀɔmyʀ] *nm* bromide. **~ d'argent/de potassium** silver/potassium bromide.
bronche [bʀɔ̃ʃ] *nf* bronchus (*T*). **les ~s** the bronchial tubes; **il est faible des ~s** he has a weak chest.
broncher [bʀɔ̃ʃe] (1) *vi [cheval]* to stumble. **personne n'osait ~*** no one dared move a muscle *ou* say a word; **le premier qui bronche ...!*** the first person to budge ...!* *ou* make a move ...!; **sans ~** (*sans peur*) without turning a hair, without flinching; (*: *sans protester*) uncomplainingly, meekly; (*sans se tromper*) faultlessly, without faltering.
bronchique [bʀɔ̃ʃik] *adj* bronchial.
bronchite [bʀɔ̃ʃit] *nf* bronchitis (*U*). **avoir une bonne ~** to have (got) a bad bout *ou* attack of bronchitis.
bronchitique [bʀɔ̃ʃitik] *adj* bronchitic (*T*). **il est ~** he suffers from bronchitis.
broncho-pneumonie, *pl* **broncho-pneumonies** [bʀɔ̃kɔpnømɔni] *nf* broncho-pneumonia (*U*).
brontosaure [bʀɔ̃tozɔʀ] *nm* brontosaurus.
bronzage [bʀɔ̃zaʒ] *nm* (*V* **bronzer**) (sun)tan; bronzing.
bronze [bʀɔ̃z] *nm* (*métal, objet*) bronze.
bronzé, e [bʀɔ̃ze] (*ptp de* **bronzer**) *adj* (sun)tanned, sunburnt.
bronzer [bʀɔ̃ze] (1) **1** *vt peau* to tan; *métal* to bronze. **2** *vi [peau, personne]* to get a tan. **les gens qui (se) bronzent sur la plage** people who sunbathe on the beach.
bronzeur [bʀɔ̃zœʀ] *nm* (*fondeur*) bronze-smelter; (*fabricant*) bronze-smith.
broquette [bʀɔkɛt] *nf* (tin)tack.
brossage [bʀɔsaʒ] *nm* brushing.
brosse [bʀɔs] **1** *nf* **(a)** brush; *[peintre]* (paint)brush. (*fig hum*) **l'art de manier la ~ à reluire** the art of sucking up to people* *ou* buttering people up; **donne un coup de ~ à ta veste** give your jacket a brush; **passer le tapis à la ~** to give the carpet a brush; **passer le carrelage à la ~** to give the (stone) floor a scrub.
(b) (*Coiffure*) crew-cut. **avoir les cheveux en ~** to have a crew-cut.
(c) (*Can*) **prendre une ~**‡ to get drunk *ou* smashed‡.
2: brosse à chaussures shoebrush; **brosse à cheveux** hairbrush; **brosse en chiendent** scrubbing brush; **brosse à dents** toothbrush; **brosse à habits** clothesbrush; **brosse à ongles** nailbrush; **brosse métallique** wire brush.
brosser [bʀɔse] (1) **1** *vt* **(a)** (*nettoyer*) to brush; *cheval* to brush down; *plancher, carrelage* to scrub. **~ qn** to brush sb's clothes.
(b) (*Art, fig*) to paint.
(c) (*Sport*) to put spin on.
2 se brosser *vpr* **(a)** to brush one's clothes, give one's clothes a brush. **se ~ les dents** to brush *ou* clean one's teeth; **se ~ les cheveux** to brush one's hair.
(b) (‡) **se ~ le ventre** to go without food; **tu peux (toujours) te ~!** you'll have to do without!, nothing doing!‡, you can whistle for it!‡
brosserie [bʀɔsʀi] *nf* (*usine*) brush factory; (*commerce*) brush trade.
brossier [bʀɔsje] *nm* (*ouvrier*) brush maker; (*commerçant*) brush dealer.
brou [bʀu] *nm* (*écorce*) husk, shuck (*US*). **~ de noix** (*Menuiserie*) walnut stain; (*liqueur*) walnut liqueur.
brouet‡ [bʀu] *nf* (*Can*) *[bière]* froth; *[mer]* foam.
brouet [bʀuɛ] *nm* (††: *potage*) gruel; (*péj, hum*) brew.
brouette [bʀuɛt] *nf* wheelbarrow.
brouettée [bʀuete] *nf* (wheel)barrowful.
brouetter [bʀuete] (1) *vt* to (carry in a) wheelbarrow.
brouhaha [bʀuaa] *nm* (*tintamarre*) hubbub.
brouillage [bʀujaʒ] *nm* (*Rad*) (*intentionnel*) jamming; (*accidentel*) interference.
brouillard [bʀujaʀ] *nm* **(a)** (*dense*) fog; (*léger*) mist; (*mêlé de fumée*) smog. **~ de chaleur** heat haze; **~ à couper au couteau** thick *ou* dense fog, peasouper*; **il fait** *ou* **il y a du ~** it's foggy; (*fig*) **être dans le ~** to be lost, be all at sea.
(b) (*Comm*) daybook.
brouillasser [bʀujase] (1) *vi* to drizzle.

brouille [bʀuj] *nf* disagreement, breach, quarrel. ~ **légère** tiff; **être en** ~ **avec qn** to have fallen out with sb, be on bad terms with sb.

brouillé, e [bʀuje] (*ptp de* **brouiller**) *adj* **(a)** (*fâché*) **être** ~ **avec qn** to have fallen out with sb, be on bad terms with sb; **être** ~ **avec les dates/l'orthographe/les maths*** to be hopeless *ou* useless* at dates/spelling/maths.
(b) avoir le teint ~ to have a muddy complexion; *V* **œuf.**

brouiller [bʀuje] (1) **1** *vt* **(a)** (*troubler*) *contour, vue, yeux* to blur; *papiers, idées* to mix *ou* muddle up; *message, combinaison de coffre* to scramble. **la buée brouille les verres de mes lunettes** my glasses are misting up; **la pluie a brouillé l'adresse** the rain has smudged *ou* blurred the address; **son accident lui a brouillé la cervelle*** since he had that accident his mind has been a bit muddled *ou* confused; (*fig*) ~ **les pistes** *ou* **cartes** to cloud the issue, draw a red herring across the trail.
(b) (*fâcher*) to set at odds, put on bad terms. **cet incident l'a brouillé avec sa famille** this incident set him at odds with *ou* put him on bad terms with his family.
(c) (*Rad*) *émission* (*avec intention*) to jam; (*par accident*) to cause interference to.
2 se brouiller *vpr* **(a)** (*se troubler*) *[vue]* to become blurred; *[souvenirs, idées]* to get mixed *ou* muddled up, become confused. **tout se brouilla dans sa tête** everything became confused *ou* muddled in his mind.
(b) (*se fâcher*) **se** ~ **avec qn** to fall out *ou* quarrel with sb; **depuis qu'ils se sont brouillés** since they fell out (with each other).
(c) (*Mét*) *[ciel]* to cloud over. **le temps se brouille** it's going *ou* turning cloudy, the weather is breaking.

brouillerie [bʀujʀi] *nf* = **brouille.**

brouillon, -onne [bʀujɔ̃, ɔn] **1** *adj* (*qui manque de soin*) untidy; (*qui manque d'organisation*) unmethodical, unsystematic, muddle-headed. **élève** ~ careless pupil; **avoir l'esprit** ~ to be muddle-headed.
2 *nm,f* muddler, muddlehead.
3 *nm [lettre, devoir]* rough copy; (*ébauche*) (rough) draft; (*calculs, notes etc*) rough work. **(papier)** ~ rough paper; **prendre qch au** ~ to make a rough copy of sth; *V* **cahier.**

broussaille [bʀusaj] *nf*: ~**s** undergrowth, brushwood, scrub; **avoir les cheveux en** ~ to have unkempt *ou* untidy *ou* tousled hair.

broussailleux, -euse [bʀusajø, øz] *adj terrain, sous-bois* bushy, scrubby; *ronces* brambly; *jardin* overgrown; *sourcils, barbe* bushy; *cheveux* bushy, tousled.

brousse [bʀus] *nf*: **la** ~ the bush; (*fig*) **c'est en pleine** ~***** it's at the back of beyond* (*Brit*), it's in the middle of nowhere.

broutement [bʀutmɑ̃] *nm*, **broutage** [bʀutaʒ] *nm* (*V* **brouter**) grazing; nibbling; browsing; chattering; grabbing; juddering.

brouter [bʀute] (1) **1** *vt herbe* to graze (on); *[lapin]* to nibble. (*fig*) **il nous les broute!**‡ he's a pain in the neck!‡, he's a bloody nuisance‡.
2 *vi* **(a)** *[mouton]* to graze; *[vache, cerf]* to browse; *[lapin]* to nibble.
(b) (*Tech*) *[rabot]* to chatter; (*Aut*) *[freins]* to grab; *[embrayage]* to judder.

broutille [bʀutij] *nf* (*bagatelle*) trifle. **c'est de la** ~***** (*de mauvaise qualité*) it's cheap rubbish; (*sans importance*) it's not worth mentioning, it's nothing of any consequence.

broyage [bʀwajaʒ] *nm* (*V* **broyer**) grinding; crushing; braking.

broyer [bʀwaje] (8) *vt pierre, sucre, os* to grind (to powder), crush; *chanvre, lin* to brake; *poivre, blé* to grind; *aliments* to grind, break up; *couleurs* to grind; *doigt, main* to crush. (*fig*) ~ **du noir** to be in the doldrums *ou* down in the dumps*.

broyeur, -euse [bʀwajœʀ, øz] **1** *adj* crushing, grinding. **2** *nm* (*ouvrier*) grinder, crusher; (*machine*) grinder, crusher; *[chanvre, lin]* brake. ~ **(de cailloux)** pebble grinder.

brrr [bʀʀ] *excl* brr!

bru [bʀy] *nf* daughter-in-law.

brucelles [bʀysɛl] *nfpl* tweezers.

brugnon [bʀyɲɔ̃] *nm* nectarine.

brugnonier [bʀyɲɔnje] *nm* nectarine tree.

bruine [bʀɥin] *nf* (fine) drizzle, Scotch mist.

bruiner [bʀɥine] (1) *vi* to drizzle.

bruire [bʀɥiʀ] (2) *vi [feuilles, tissu, vent]* to rustle; *[ruisseau]* to murmur; *[insects]* to buzz, hum.

bruissement [bʀɥismɑ̃] *nm* (*V* **bruire**) rustle, rustling; murmur; buzz(ing), humming.

bruit [bʀɥi] *nm* **(a)** (*gén*) sound, noise; (*avec idée d'intensité désagréable*) noise. **j'entendis un** ~ I heard a noise; **un** ~ **de vaisselle** the clatter of dishes; **un** ~ **de moteur/voix** the sound of an engine/voices; **un** ~ **de verre brisé** the tinkle *ou* sound of broken glass; **un** ~ **de pas** (the sound of) footsteps; **le** ~ **d'un plongeon** (the sound of) a splash; **le** ~ **de la pluie contre les vitres** the sound *ou* patter of the rain against the windows; **le** ~ **des radios** the noise *ou* blare of radios; **les** ~**s de la rue** street noises; **un** ~ *ou* **des** ~**s de marteau** (the sound of) hammering; ~ **de fond** background noise; **le** ~ **familier des camions** the familiar rumble of the lorries; ~ **sourd** thud; ~ **strident** screech, shriek; **on n'entend aucun** ~ **d'ici** you can't hear a sound from here.
(b) (*opposé à silence*) **le** ~ noise; **on ne peut pas travailler dans le** ~ one cannot work against noise; **le** ~ **est insupportable ici** the noise is unbearable here; **cette machine fait un** ~ **infernal** this machine makes a dreadful noise *ou* racket*; **sans** ~ noiselessly, without a sound, silently.
(c) il y a trop de ~ there's too much noise, it's too noisy; **s'il y a du** ~ **je ne peux pas travailler** if there's (a) noise I can't work; **les enfants font du** ~**, c'est normal** it's natural that children are noisy; **arrêtez de faire du** ~ stop making a noise *ou* being (so) noisy; **faites du** ~ **pour chasser les pigeons** make a *ou* some noise to scare the pigeons away; **j'entendis du** ~ I heard a noise.
(d) (*fig*) **beaucoup de** ~ **pour rien** much ado about nothing, a lot of fuss about nothing; **faire grand** ~ *ou* **beaucoup de** ~ **autour de qch** to make a great fuss *ou* to-do about sth; **il fait plus de** ~ **que de mal** his bark is worse than his bite.
(e) (*nouvelle*) rumour. **le** ~ **de son départ ...** the rumour of his leaving ...; **le** ~ **court qu'il doit partir** there is a rumour going about *ou* rumour has it that he is to go; **c'est un** ~ **qui court** it's a rumour that's going round; **répandre de faux** ~**s (sur)** to spread false rumours *ou* tales (about); **les** ~**s de couloir à l'Assemblée nationale** parliamentary rumours; (††) **il n'est** ~ **dans la ville que de son arrivée** his arrival is the talk of the town, his arrival has set the town agog.
(f) (*Téléc*) noise. (*Méd*) ~ **de souffle** murmur.

bruitage [bʀɥitaʒ] *nm* sound effects.

bruiteur [bʀɥitœʀ] *nm* sound-effects engineer.

brûlage [bʀylaʒ] *nm [cheveux]* singeing; *[café]* roasting; *[herbes]* burning. **faire un** ~ **à qn** to singe sb's hair.

brûlant, e [bʀylɑ̃, ɑ̃t] *adj* **(a)** (*chaud*) *objet* burning (hot), red-hot; *plat* piping hot; *liquide* boiling (hot), scalding; *soleil* scorching, blazing; *air* burning. **il a le front** ~ **(de fièvre)** his forehead is burning (with fever).
(b) (*passionné*) *regard, pages* fiery, impassioned.
(c) (*controversé*) *sujet* ticklish. **être sur un terrain** ~ to touch on a hotly debated issue; **c'est d'une actualité** ~**e** it's the burning question of the hour.

brûle- [bʀyl] *préf V* **brûler.**

brûlé, e [bʀyle] (*ptp de* **brûler**) **1** *adj* (*) *espion, agent* blown (*attrib*). **il est** ~ his cover is blown*. *V* **crème, terre, tête. 2** *nm* **(a) ça sent le** ~ (*lit*) there's a smell of burning; (*fig*) trouble's brewing; **cela a un goût de** ~ it tastes burnt *ou* has a burnt taste.
(b) (*personne*) **grand** ~ victim of third-degree burns, badly burnt person.

brûler [bʀyle] (1) **1** *vt* **(a)** (*détruire*) *objet, ordures, corps* to burn; *maison* to burn down. **être brûlé vif** (*accident*) to be burnt alive *ou* burnt to death; (*supplice*) to be burnt at the stake; (*fig*) **il a brûlé ses dernières cartouches** he has shot his bolt; (*fig*) ~ **ses vaisseaux** to burn one's boats (*Brit*); ~ **le pavé**† to ride *ou* run *etc* hell for leather*; (*Théât*) ~ **les planches** to give a spirited performance; ~ **ce qu'on a adoré** to burn one's old idols.
(b) (*endommager*) [*flamme*] (*gén*) to burn; *cheveux* to singe; [eau bouillante] to scald; *[fer à repasser]* to singe, scorch; *[soleil] herbe* to scorch; *peau* to burn; *[gel] bourgeon* to nip, damage; *[acide] peau* to burn, sear; *métal* to burn, attack, corrode. **il a la peau brûlée par le soleil** (*bronzage*) his skin is sunburnt *ou* tanned; (*lésion*) his skin *ou* he has been burnt by the sun; **le soleil nous brûle** the sun is scorching *ou* burning.
(c) (*traiter*) *café* to roast; (*Méd*) to cauterize.
(d) (*consommer*) *électricité, charbon* to burn, use; *cierge, chandelle* to burn. **ils ont brûlé tout leur bois** they've burnt up *ou* used up all their wood; ~ **la chandelle par les deux bouts** to burn the candle at both ends; ~ **de l'encens** to burn incense.
(e) (*dépasser*) (*Aut*) ~ **un stop** to ignore a stop sign; ~ **un feu rouge** to go through a red light (without stopping); (*Rail*) ~ **un signal/une station** to go through *ou* past a signal/a station (without stopping); ~ **une étape** to cut out a stop; (*fig*) ~ **les étapes** (*réussir rapidement*) to shoot ahead; (*trop se précipiter*) to cut corners, take short cuts; ~ **la politesse à qn** to leave sb abruptly (without saying goodbye).
(f) (*donner une sensation de brûlure*) to burn. **le radiateur me brûlait le dos** the radiator was burning my back; **j'ai les yeux qui me brûlent, les yeux me brûlent** my eyes are smarting *ou* stinging; **j'ai la figure qui (me) brûle** my face is burning; **la gorge lui brûle** he's got a burning sensation in his throat; (*fig*) **l'argent lui brûle les doigts** money burns a hole in his pocket.
(g) (*fig: consumer*) **le désir de l'aventure le brûlait, il était brûlé du désir de l'aventure** he was burning *ou* longing for adventure.
2 *vi* **(a)** *[charbon, feu]* to burn; *[maison, forêt]* to be on fire; (*Culin*) to burn. **on a laissé** ~ **l'électricité** *ou* **l'électricité a brûlé toute la journée** the lights have been left on *ou* have been burning away all day; **ce bois brûle très vite** this wood burns (up) very quickly; *V* **torchon.**
(b) (*être brûlant*) to be burning (hot) *ou* scalding. **son front brûle de fièvre** his forehead is burning; **ne touche pas, ça brûle** don't touch that, you'll burn yourself *ou* you'll get burnt; (*jeu, devinette*) **tu brûles!** you're getting hot!
(c) (*fig*) ~ **de faire qch** to be burning *ou* be dying to do sth; ~ **d'impatience** to seethe with impatience; († *ou hum*) ~ **(d'amour) pour qn** to be infatuated *ou* madly in love with sb; ~ **d'envie** *ou* **du désir de faire qch** to be dying *ou* longing to do sth.
3 se brûler *vpr* **(a)** to burn o.s.; (*se tuer*) to set o.s. on fire; (*s'ébouillanter*) to scald o.s. **se** ~ **les doigts** (*lit*) to burn one's fingers; (*fig*) to get one's fingers burnt (*fig*); **le papillon s'est brûlé les ailes à la flamme** the butterfly burnt its wings in the flame; (*se compromettre*) **se** ~ **les ailes**† to burn one's fingers; **se** ~ **la cervelle** to blow one's brains out.
(b) (**Can*) to exhaust o.s., wear o.s. out.
4: brûle-gueule *nm inv* short (clay) pipe; **brûle-parfum** *nm inv* perfume burner; **brûle-pourpoint** *adv*: **à brûle-pourpoint** point-blank; (†: *à bout portant*) at point-blank range.

brûlerie [bʀylʀi] *nf [café]* coffee-roasting plant *ou* shop; *[alcool]* (brandy) distillery.

brûleur [bʀylœʀ] *nm* (*dispositif*) burner.

brûloir [bʀylwaʀ] *nm* coffee roaster (*machine*).

brûlot [bʀylo] *nm* **(a)** (*Hist Naut*) fire ship; (*personne*) fire-brand. **(b)** (*Can*) midge, gnat.

brûlure [bRylyR] *nf* (*lésion*) burn; (*sensation*) burning sensation. ~ **(d'eau bouillante)** scald; ~ **de cigarette** cigarette burn; ~ **du premier degré** first-degree burn; ~**s d'estomac** heartburn.

brumaire [bRymɛR] *nm* Brumaire (*second month of French Republican calendar*).

brumasser [bRymase] (1) *vb impers*: **il brumasse** it's a bit misty, there's a slight mist.

brume [bRym] *nf* (*gén*) mist; (*dense*) fog; (*Mét*) mist; (*Naut*) fog. ~ **légère** haze; ~ **de chaleur** *ou* **de beau temps** heat haze; *V* **corne.**

brumeux, -euse [bRymø, øz] *adj* misty, foggy; (*fig*) obscure, hazy.

brun, e [bRœ̃, yn] **1** *adj yeux, couleur* brown; *cheveux* brown, dark; *peau* dusky, swarthy; (*bronzé*) tanned, brown; *tabac* dark; *bière* brown. **il est** ~ (*cheveux*) he's dark-haired; (*bronzé*) he's tanned; **il est** ~ **(de peau)** he's dark-skinned; ~ **roux** (dark) auburn.
 2 *nm* (*couleur*) brown; (*homme*) dark-haired man.
 3 brune *nf* **(a)** (*bière*) brown ale, stout.
 (b) (*femme*) brunette.
 (c) (*littér*) **à la** ~ at twilight, at dusk.

brunante [bRynɑ̃t] *nf* (*Can*) **à la** ~ at dusk, at nightfall.

brunâtre [bRynɑtR(ə)] *adj* brownish.

brunette [bRynɛt] *nf* brunette.

brunir [bRyniR] (2) **1** *vi [personne, peau]* to get sunburnt, get a tan; *[cheveux]* to go darker; *[caramel]* to brown. **2** *vt* **(a)** *peau* to tan; *cheveux* to darken. **(b)** *métal* to burnish, polish.

brunissage [bRynisaʒ] *nm* burnishing.

brunissement [bRynismɑ̃] *nm [peau]* tanning.

brunissure [bRynisyR] *nf [métal]* burnish; (*Agr*) potato rot; *[vigne]* brown rust.

brushing [bRœʃiŋ] *nm* blow-dry.

brusque [bRysk(ə)] *adj* **(a)** (*rude, sec*) *personne, manières* brusque, abrupt, blunt; *geste* brusque, abrupt, rough; *ton* curt, abrupt, blunt. **être** ~ **avec qn** to be curt *ou* abrupt with sb.
 (b) (*soudain*) *départ, changement* abrupt, sudden; *virage* sharp; *envie* sudden.

brusquement [bRyskəmɑ̃] *adj* (*V* **brusque**) brusquely; abruptly; bluntly; roughly; curtly; suddenly; sharply.

brusquer [bRyske] (1) *vt* **(a)** (*précipiter*) to rush, hasten. **attaque brusquée** surprise attack; **il ne faut rien** ~ we musn't rush things. **(b)** *personne* to rush, chivvy*.

brusquerie [bRyskəRi] *nf* brusqueness, abruptness.

brut, e[1] [bRyt] **1** *adj* **(a)** *diamant* uncut, rough; *pétrole* crude; *minerai* crude, raw; *sucre* unrefined; *soie, métal* raw; *toile* unbleached; *laine* untreated; *champagne* brut, extra dry; (*fig*) *fait* crude; *idée* crude, raw. **à l'état** ~ (*lit*) *matière* untreated, in the rough; (*fig*) *idées* in the rough.
 (b) (*Comm*) *bénéfice, poids, traitement* gross. **produire** ~ **un million** to gross a million; **ça fait 100 F/100 kg** ~, **ça fait** ~ **100 F/100 kg** that makes 100 francs/100 kg gross; *V* **produit.**
 2 *nm* crude (oil).

brutal, e, *mpl* **-aux** [bRytal, o] *adj* **(a)** (*violent*) *personne, caractère* rough, brutal, violent; *instinct* savage; *jeu* rough. **être** ~ **avec qn** to be rough with sb; **force** ~**e** brute force.
 (b) (*choquant*) *langage, franchise* blunt; *vérité* plain, unvarnished; *réalité* stark. **il a été très** ~ **dans sa réponse** he was very outspoken in his answer, he gave a very blunt answer.
 (c) (*soudain*) *mort* sudden; *choc, coup* brutal.

brutalement [bRytalmɑ̃] *adv* (*V* **brutal**) roughly; brutally; violently; bluntly; plainly; suddenly.

brutaliser [bRytalize] (1) *vt personne* to bully, knock about, handle roughly, manhandle; *machine* to ill-treat.

brutalité [bRytalite] *nf* (*U: violence*) brutality, violence, roughness; (*acte brutal*) brutality; (*Sport*) rough play (*U*); (*U: soudaineté*) suddenness. ~**s policières** police brutality.

brute[2] [bRyt] *nf* (*homme brutal*) brute, animal; (*homme grossier*) boor, lout; (*littér: animal*) brute, beast. **taper sur qch comme une** ~* to bash* away at sth (savagely); **frapper qn comme une** ~ to hit out at sb brutishly; ~ **épaisse*** brutish lout; **tu es une grosse** ~**!*** you're a big bully!

Bruxelles [bRysɛl] *n* Brussels; *V* **chou**[1].

bruyamment [bRɥijamɑ̃] *adv rire, parler* noisily, loudly; *protester* loudly.

bruyant, e [bRɥijɑ̃, ɑ̃t] *adj personne, réunion* noisy, boisterous; *rue* noisy; *rire* loud; *succès* resounding (*épith*). **ils ont accueilli la nouvelle avec une joie** ~**e** they greeted the news with whoops* *ou* with loud cries of joy.

bruyère [bRyjɛR] *nf* (*plante*) heather; (*terrain*) heath(land). **pipe en (racine de)** ~ briar pipe; *V* **coq**[1].

bu, e [by] *ptp de* **boire.**

buanderie [bɥɑ̃dRi] *nf* wash house, laundry; (*Can: blanchisserie*) laundry.

bubon [bybɔ̃] *nm* bubo.

bubonique [bybɔnik] *adj* bubonic.

buccal, e, *mpl* **-aux** [bykal, o] *adj* buccal; *V* **voie.**

bûche [byʃ] *nf* **(a)** *[bois]* log. (*Culin*) ~ **de Noël** Yule log. **(b)** (*: *lourdaud*) blockhead‡, clot‡, lump*. **(c)** (*: *chute*) fall, spill. **ramasser une** ~ to come a cropper*.

bûcher[1] [byʃe] *nm* **(a)** (*remise*) woodshed. **(b)** (*funéraire*) (funeral) pyre; (*supplice*) stake. **être condamné au** ~ to be condemned to (be burnt at) the stake.

bûcher[2]* [byʃe] (1) **1** *vt* to swot up*, slog away at*, bone up on*. **2** *vi* to swot*, slog away*.

bûcher[3] [byʃe] (1) (*Can*) **1** *vt arbres* to fell, cut down, chop down. **2** *vi* to fell trees.

bûcheron [byʃRɔ̃] *nm* woodcutter, lumberjack, lumberman (*US*).

bûchette [byʃɛt] *nf* (dry) twig, stick (of wood); (*pour compter*) rod, stick.

bûcheur, -euse* [byʃœR, øz] **1** *adj* hard-working. **2** *nm,f* slogger*.

bucolique [bykɔlik] **1** *adj* bucolic, pastoral. **2** *nf* bucolic, pastoral (poem).

budget [bydʒɛ] *nm* budget; *V* **boucler.**

budgétaire [bydʒetɛR] *adj dépenses, crise* budgetary. **prévisions** ~**s** budget forecasts; **année** ~ financial year.

budgétisation [bydʒetizasjɔ̃] *nf* inclusion in the budget.

budgétiser [bydʒetize] (1) *vt* (*Fin*) to include in the budget, budget for.

buée [bɥe] *nf [haleine]* condensation, steam; *[eau chaude]* steam; (*sur vitre*) mist, steam, condensation; (*sur miroir*) mist, blur. **couvert de** ~ misted up, steamed up; **faire de la** ~ to make steam.

buffet [byfɛ] *nm* **(a)** (*meuble*) *[salle à manger]* sideboard. ~ **de cuisine** kitchen dresser *ou* cabinet; *V* **danser.**
 (b) *[réception]* (*table*) buffet; (*repas*) buffet (meal). ~ **(de gare)** station buffet, refreshment room.
 (c) (‡*fig: ventre*) stomach, belly‡. **il n'a rien dans le** ~ he hasn't had anything to eat; (*manque de courage*) he has no guts*.
 (d) ~ **(d'orgue)** (organ) case.

buffle [byfl(ə)] *nm* buffalo.

bugle[1] [bygl(ə)] *nm* (*Mus*) bugle.

bugle[2] [bygl(ə)] *nf* (*Bot*) bugle.

buire [bɥiR] *nf* ewer.

buis [bɥi] *nm* (*arbre*) box(wood) (*U*), box tree; (*bois*) box(wood).

buisson [bɥisɔ̃] *nm* (*Bot*) bush. (*Culin*) ~ **de langoustines** scampi en buisson *ou* in a bush; (*Bible*) ~ **ardent** burning bush.

buissonneux, -euse [bɥisɔnø, øz] *adj terrain* bushy, full of bushes; *végétation* scrubby.

buissonnière [bɥisɔnjɛR] *adj f V* **école.**

bulbe [bylb(ə)] *nm* (*Bot*) bulb, corm; (*Anat*) bulb; (*Archit*) onion-shaped dome.

bulbeux, -euse [bylbø, øz] *adj* (*Bot*) bulbous; *forme* bulbous, onion-shaped.

bulgare [bylgaR] **1** *adj* Bulgarian. **2** *nm* (*Ling*) Bulgarian. **3** *nmf*: **B**~ Bulgarian, Bulgar.

Bulgarie [bylgaRi] *nf* Bulgaria.

bulldozer [buldozœR] *nm* bulldozer.

bulle [byl] *nf* **(a)** *[air, savon, verre]* bubble; (*Méd*) blister; *[bande dessinée]* balloon. **faire des** ~**s** to blow bubbles. **(b)** (*Rel*) bull.

bulletin [byltɛ̃] **1** *nm* (*reportage, communiqué*) bulletin, report; (*magazine*) bulletin; (*formulaire*) form; (*certificat*) certificate; (*billet*) ticket; (*Scol*) report; (*Pol*) ballot paper.
 2: bulletin de bagage luggage ticket; (*Pol*) **bulletin blanc** blank vote; **bulletin de consigne** left-luggage ticket; **bulletin d'état civil** identity document (*issued by local authorities*); **bulletin d'information** news bulletin; **bulletin météorologique** weather forecast *ou* report; **bulletin de naissance** birth certificate; (*Pol*) **bulletin nul** spoilt ballot paper; **bulletin-réponse** *nm, pl* **bulletins-réponses** reply-paid coupon; **bulletin de salaire** salary advice, pay-slip; **bulletin de santé** medical bulletin; (*Scol*) **bulletin trimestriel** end-of-term report; (*Pol*) **bulletin de vote** ballot paper.

bungalow [bœ̃galo] *nm* (*petit pavillon*) bungalow; *[motel]* chalet.

buraliste [byRalist(ə)] *nmf [bureau de tabac]* tobacconist; *[poste]* clerk.

bure [byR] *nf* (*étoffe*) frieze, homespun; (*vêtement*) *[moine]* frock, cowl. **porter la** ~ to be a monk.

bureau, *pl* ~**x** [byRo] **1** *nm* **(a)** (*meuble*) desk.
 (b) (*cabinet de travail*) study.
 (c) (*lieu de travail: pièce, édifice*) office. **le** ~ **du directeur** the manager's office; **pendant les heures de** ~ during office hours; **nos** ~**x seront fermés** our premises *ou* the office will be closed; *V* **chef**[1]**, deuxième, employé.**
 (d) (*section*) department; (*Mil*) branch, department.
 (e) (*comité*) committee; (*exécutif*) board. **aller à une réunion du** ~ to go to a committee meeting.
 2: bureau de bienfaisance welfare office; **bureau de change** (foreign) exchange office, bureau de change; **bureau des contributions** tax office; **bureau à cylindre** roll-top desk; **bureau de douane** customs house; **bureau d'études** research department *ou* unit; (*entreprise indépendante*) research consultancy, research organization; **bureau de location** booking *ou* box office; **bureau ministre** pedestal desk; **bureau des objets trouvés** lost property office; **bureau-paysage** landscaped office; **bureau de placement** employment agency; **bureau postal d'origine** dispatching (post) office; **bureau de poste** post office; **bureau de tabac** tobacconist's (shop); **bureau de tri** sorting office; **bureau de vote** polling station.

bureaucrate [byRokRat] *nmf* bureaucrat.

bureaucratie [byRokRasi] *nf* (*péj*) (*système*) bureaucracy, red tape*; (*employés*) officials, officialdom.

bureaucratique [byRokRatik] *adj* bureaucratic.

bureaucratisation [byRokRatizasjɔ̃] *nf* bureaucratization.

bureaucratiser [byRokRatize] (1) *vt* to bureaucratize.

burette [byRɛt] *nf* (*Chim*) burette; (*Culin, Rel*) cruet; *[mécanicien]* oilcan.

burgrave [byRgRav] *nm* burgrave.

burin [byRɛ̃] *nm* (*Art*) (*outil*) burin, graver; (*gravure*) engraving, print; (*Tech*) (cold) chisel.

buriné, e [byRine] (*ptp de* **buriner**) *adj* (*fig*) *visage* seamed, craggy.

buriner [byRine] (1) *vt* (*Art*) to engrave; (*Tech*) to chisel, chip.

burlesque [byRlɛsk(ə)] *adj* (*Théât*) burlesque; (*comique*) comical, funny; (*ridicule*) ludicrous, ridiculous, absurd. **le ~** the burlesque.

burnous [byʀnu(s)] *nm [Arabe]* burnous(e); *[bébé]* baby's cape; *V* **suer.**

bus* [bys] *nm* bus.

busard [byzaʀ] *nm* (*Orn*) harrier.

buse¹ [byz] *nf* (*Orn*) buzzard; (*: *imbécile*) dolt*.

buse² [byz] *nf* tube, duct; *[tuyau]* nozzle; (*Aut*) choke tube. **~ d'aération** ventilation duct; **~ de haut fourneau** blast nozzle; **~ d'injection** injector (nozzle).

business: [biznɛs] *nm* (*truc, machin*) thingummy* (*Brit*), thingumajig, whatnot*; (*affaire louche*) piece of funny business*. **qu'est-ce que c'est que ce ~?** what's all this business about?

busqué, e [byske] *adj*: **avoir le nez ~** to have a hooked *ou* a hook nose.

buste [byst(ə)] *nm* (*torse*) chest; (*seins*) bust; (*sculpture*) bust.

bustier [bystje] *nm* long-line (strapless) bra.

but [by] *nm* **(a)** (*destination*) goal. **prenons comme ~ (de promenade) le château** let's go (for a walk) as far as the castle, let's aim to walk as far as the castle; **leur ~ de promenade favori** their favourite walk; **aller *ou* errer sans ~** to wander aimlessly about.

(b) (*objectif*) aim, goal, objective. **il n'a aucun ~ dans la vie** he has no aim in life; **il a pour ~ *ou* il s'est donné pour ~ de faire** his aim is to do, he is aiming to do; **aller droit au ~** to come *ou* go straight to the point; **nous touchons au ~** the end *ou* our goal is in sight; **être encore loin du ~** to have a long way to go.

(c) (*intention*) aim, purpose, object; (*raison*) reason. **dans le ~ de faire** with the intention of doing, in order to do; **je lui écris dans le ~ de ...** my aim in writing to him is to ...; **je fais ceci dans le seul ~ de ...** my sole aim in doing this is to ...; **c'est dans ce ~ que nous partons** it's with this aim in view that we're leaving; **faire qch dans un ~ déterminé** to do sth for a definite reason *ou* aim, do sth with one object in view; **c'était le ~ de l'opération** that was the object *ou* point of the operation.

(d) (*Sport*) (*Ftbl etc*) goal; (*Tir*) target, mark; (*Pétanque: cochonnet*) jack. **gagner/perdre (par) 3 ~s à 2** to win/lose by 3 goals to 2.

(e) de ~ en blanc suddenly, point-blank, just like that*; **comment puis-je te répondre de ~ en blanc?** how can I possibly give you an answer on the spur of the moment? *ou* just like that?*; **il me demanda de ~ en blanc si ...** he asked me point-blank if ... .

butane [bytan] *nm* (*Camping, Ind*) butane; (*usage domestique*) calor gas.

buté, e¹ [byte] (*ptp de* **buter**) *adj personne, air* stubborn, obstinate, mulish.

butée² [byte] *nf* **(a)** (*Archit*) abutment. **(b)** (*Tech*) stop; *[piscine]* end wall.

buter [byte] (1) **1** *vi* **(a)** to stumble, trip. **~ contre qch** (*trébucher*) to stumble over sth, catch one's foot on sth; (*cogner*) to bump *ou* bang into *ou* against sth; (*s'appuyer*) to be supported by sth, rest against sth; (*fig*) **~ contre une difficulté** to come up against a difficulty, hit a snag*; **nous butons sur ce problème depuis le début** it's a problem which has balked *ou* stymied* us from the start.

(b) (*Ftbl*) to score a goal.

2 *vt* **(a)** *personne* to antagonize. **cela l'a buté** it made him dig his heels in.

(b) (*renforcer*) *mur, colonne* to prop up.

(c) (*: *tuer*) to bump off:, do in:.

3 se buter *vpr* **(a)** (*s'entêter*) to dig one's heels in, get obstinate *ou* mulish.

(b) (*se heurter*) **se ~ à une personne** to bump into a person; **se ~ à une difficulté** to come up against a difficulty, hit a snag*.

buteur [bytœʀ] *nm* **(a)** (*Ftbl*) striker. **(b)** (*: *tueur*) killer.

butin [bytɛ̃] *nm* **(a)** *[armée]* spoils, booty, plunder; *[voleur]* loot; (*fig*) booty. **~ de guerre** spoils of war. **(b)** (**Can*) linen, calico; (*tissu*) material; (*vêtements*) clothes.

butiner [bytine] (1) **1** *vi [abeilles]* to gather nectar. **2** *vt [abeilles] nectar* to gather; (*fig*) to gather, glean, pick up.

butoir [bytwaʀ] *nm* (*Rail*) buffer; (*Tech*) stop. **~ de porte** doorstop, door stopper.

butor [bytɔʀ] *nm* (*péj: malotru*) boor, lout, yob:; (*Orn*) bittern.

buttage [bytaʒ] *nm* earthing-up.

butte [byt] *nf* (*tertre*) mound, hillock. **~ de tir** butts; **~-témoin** outlier; (*fig*) **être en ~ à** to be exposed to.

butter [byte] (1) *vt* **(a)** (*Agr*) *plante* to earth up; *terre* to ridge. **(b)** (*: *tuer*) to bump off:, do in:.

buvable [byvabl(ə)] *adj* drinkable, fit to drink. (*fig*) **c'est ~!*** it's not too bad!; (*Méd*) **ampoule ~** phial to be taken orally.

buvard [byvaʀ] *nm* (*papier*) blotting paper; (*sous-main*) blotter.

buvette [byvɛt] *nf* **(a)** (*café*) refreshment room; (*en plein air*) refreshment stall. **(b)** *[ville d'eau]* pump room.

buveur, -euse [byvœʀ, øz] *nm,f* **(a)** (*ivrogne*) drinker. **(b)** (*consommateur*) drinker; *[café]* customer. **~ de bière** beer drinker.

byronien, -ienne [biʀɔnjɛ̃, jɛn] *adj* Byronic.

Byzance [bizɑ̃s] *n* Byzantium.

byzantin, e [bizɑ̃tɛ̃, in] *adj* (*Hist*) Byzantine; (*fig*) protracted and trivial, wrangling.

byzantinisme [bizɑ̃tinism(ə)] *nm* argumentativeness, logic-chopping, (love of) hair-splitting.

byzantiniste [bizɑ̃tinist(ə)] *nmf* Byzantinist, specialist in Byzantine art.

C

C, c [se] *nm* (*lettre*) C, c.

c' [s] *abrév de* **ce.**

ça¹ [sa] *nm* (*Psych: inconscient*) id.

ça² [sa] *pron dém* (= **cela** *mais plus courant et plus familier*) **(a)** (*gén*) that, it; (*: *pour désigner*) (*près*) this; (*plus loin*) that. **je veux ~, non pas ~, ~ là dans le coin** I want that, no, not this, that over there in the corner; **qu'est-ce que ~ veut dire?** what does that *ou* it *ou* this mean?; **on ne s'attendait pas à ~** that was (quite) unexpected, we weren't expecting that; **~ n'est pas très facile** that's not very easy; **~ m'agace de l'entendre se plaindre** it gets on my nerves hearing him complain; **~ vaut la peine qu'il essaie** it's worth his having a go; **~ donne bien du souci, les enfants** children are a lot of worry; **faire des études, ~ ne le tentait guère** studying didn't really appeal to him.

(b) (*péj: désignant qn*) he, she, they. **et ~ va à l'église!** and (then) he (*ou* she *etc*) goes to church!

(c) (*renforçant qui, pourquoi, comment etc*) **il ne veut pas venir — pourquoi ~?** he won't come — why not? *ou* why's that? *ou* why won't he?; **j'ai vu X — qui ~?/quand ~?/où ~?** I've seen X — who (do you mean)? *ou* who's that?/when was that?/where was that?

(d) ~ fait 10 jours/longtemps qu'il est parti it's 10 days/a long time since he left, he has been gone 10 days/a long time; **voilà, Madame, ~ (vous) fait 10 F** here you are, Madam, that will be 10 francs.

(e) (*loc*) **tu crois ~! *ou* cela!, on croit ~! *ou* cela!** that's what YOU think!; **~ ne fait rien** it doesn't matter; **on dit ~! *ou* cela!** that's what they (*ou* you *etc*) SAY!; **voyez-vous ~!** how do you like that!, did you ever hear of such a thing!; **~ va? *ou* marche?** *etc* how are things?*, how goes it?*; **oui ~ va, continuez comme ~** yes that's fine *ou* O.K.*, carry on like that; **(ah) ~ non!** most certainly not!; **(ah) ~ oui!** absolutely!, (yes) definitely!; (*iro*) **c'est ~, continue!** that's right, just you carry on!* (*iro*); **~ par exemple!** (*indignation*) well!, well really!; (*surprise*) well I never!; **~ alors!** you don't say!; **me faire ~ à moi!** fancy doing that to me (of all people)!

çà [sa] *adv* **(a) ~ et là** here and there. **(b)** (††: *ici*) hither (†† *ou hum*).

cabale [kabal] *nf* **(a)** (*complot, comploteurs*) cabal. **(b)** (*Hist*) cab(b)ala.

cabalistique [kabalistik] *adj* (*mystérieux*) *signe* cabalistic, arcane; (*Hist*) cabalistic.

caban [kabɑ̃] *nm* (*veste longue*) car coat, three-quarter (length) coat; *[marin]* reefer (jacket).

cabane [kaban] **1** *nf* **(a)** (*en bois*) hut, cabin; (*en terre*) hut; (*pour rangements, animaux*) shed.

(b) (*péj: bicoque*) shack.

(c) (*: *prison*) **en ~** in (the) clink:, in the nick: (*Brit*), in jug:; **3 ans de ~** 3 years in (the) clink: *ou* in the nick: (*Brit*) *ou* in jug:.

2: cabane à lapins (*lit*) rabbit hutch; (*fig*) box; **cabane à outils** toolshed; **cabane de rondins** log cabin; (*Can*) **cabane à sucre*** sap house (*Can*).

cabanon [kabanɔ̃] *nm* **(a)** (*en Provence: maisonnette*) *[campagne]* (country) cottage; *[littoral]* cabin, chalet. **(b)** (*remise*) shed, hut. **(c)** (*cellule*) *[aliénés]* padded cell. **il est bon pour le ~*** he should be locked up, he's practically certifiable*.

cabaret [kabaʀɛ] *nm* (*boîte de nuit*) night club, cabaret; (†: *café*) tavern, inn; *V* **danseuse.**

cabaretier, -ière† [kabaʀtje, jɛʀ] *nm,f* innkeeper.

cabas [kabɑ] *nm* (*sac*) shopping bag.

cabestan [kabɛstɑ̃] *nm* capstan; *V* **virer.**

cabillaud [kabijo] *nm* (fresh) cod.

cabine [kabin] **1** *nf [navire, véhicule spatial]* cabin; *[avion]* cockpit; *[train, grue]* cab; *[piscine]* cubicle; *[laboratoire de langues]* booth; (*Can*) motel room, cabin (*US, Can*).
2: **cabine d'aiguillage** signal box; **cabine (d'ascenseur)** lift (cage); **cabine de bain** (bathing *ou* beach) hut; **cabine d'essayage** fitting room; **cabine de pilotage** cockpit; **cabine de projection** projection room; **cabine téléphonique** call *ou* (tele)-phone box, telephone booth *ou* kiosk.
cabinet [kabinɛ] **1** *nm* **(a)** (*réduit*) closet†.
(b) (*toilettes*) ~s toilet, loo* (*Brit*), lav* (*Brit*).
(c) (*local professionnel*) *[dentiste]* surgery (*Brit*), office (*US*); *[médecin]* surgery (*Brit*), office (*US*), consulting-room; *[notaire]* office; *[avocat]* chambers (*pl*); *[agent immobilier]* agency.
(d) (*clientèle*) *[avocat, médecin]* practice.
(e) (*Pol*) (*gouvernement*) cabinet; *[ministre]* advisers (*pl*); *V* **chef**[1].
(f) *[exposition]* exhibition room.
(g) (*meuble*) cabinet.
(h) (†: *bureau*) study.
2: **cabinet d'affaires** business consultancy; **cabinet d'aisances**† water closet† (*Brit*), lavatory; **cabinet de consultation** surgery (*Brit*), consulting-room; **cabinet de débarras** box room (*Brit*), storage room (*US*), lumber room, glory hole* (*Brit*); **cabinet d'étude**† study; **cabinet de lecture**† reading room; **cabinet particulier** private dining room; **cabinet de toilette** toilet; **cabinet de travail** study.
câblage [kɑblaʒ] *nm* **(a)** (*V* **câbler**) cabling; twisting together. **(b)** (*Élec: ensemble de fils*) wiring.
câble [kɑbl(ə)] **1** *nm* (*gén*) cable. ~ **métallique** wire cable. **2**: **câble d'amarrage** mooring line; **câble électrique** (electric) cable; **câble de frein** brake cable; **câble de halage** towrope; (*Élec*) **câble hertzien** radio link (*by hertzian waves*).
câbler [kɑble] (1) *vt* **(a)** *dépêche, message* to cable. **(b)** (*Tech*) *torons* to twist together (into a cable).
câblerie [kɑbləʀi] *nf* cable-manufacturing plant.
câblier [kɑblije] *nm* (*navire*) cable ship.
câblodistribution [kɑblɔdistʀibysjɔ̃] *nf* (*Québec*) cable television *ou* vision, community antenna television (*US*).
cabochard, e* [kabɔʃaʀ, aʀd(ə)] *adj* (*têtu*) pigheaded*, mulish. **c'est un** ~ he's pigheaded*.
caboche [kabɔʃ] *nf* **(a)** (*: *tête*) noddle*, nut*, head. **mets-toi ça dans la** ~ get that into your head *ou* noddle* *ou* thick skull*; **quand il a quelque chose dans la** ~ when he has something in his head; **il a la** ~ **solide** he must have a thick skull; **quelle** ~ **il a!** he's so pigheaded!*
(b) (*clou*) hobnail.
cabochon [kabɔʃɔ̃] *nm* **(a)** (*bouchon*) *[carafe]* stopper; (*brillant*) cabochon. **(b)** (*clou*) stud.
cabosser [kabɔse] (1) *vt* (*bosseler*) to dent. **une casserole toute cabossée** a battered *ou* badly dented saucepan.
cabot [kabo] **1** *nm* **(a)** (*péj: chien*) dog, tyke (*péj*), cur (*péj*). **(b)** (*arg Mil: caporal*) ≃ corp (*arg Mil Brit*). **2** *adj, nm* = **cabotin**.
cabotage [kabɔtaʒ] *nm* (*Naut*) coastal navigation. **petit/grand** ~ inshore/seagoing navigation.
caboter [kabɔte] (1) *vi* (*Naut*) to coast, ply (along the coast). ~ **le long des côtes d'Afrique** to ply along the African coast.
caboteur [kabɔtœʀ] *nm* (*bateau*) tramp, coaster.
cabotin, e [kabɔtɛ̃, in] **1** *adj* (*péj*) theatrical. **il est très** ~ he likes to show off *ou* hold the centre of the stage. **2** *nm,f* (*péj*) (*personne maniérée*) show-off, poseur; (*acteur*) ham (actor).
cabotinage [kabɔtinaʒ] *nm [personne, enfant]* showing off, playacting; *[acteur]* ham *ou* third-rate acting.
cabotiner [kabɔtine] (1) *vi [élève, m'as-tu-vu]* to playact.
caboulot [kabulo] *nm* (*péj: bistro*) sleazy* *ou* seedy* dive* (*péj*) *ou* pub.
cabré, e [kɑbʀe] (*ptp de* **cabrer**) *adj attitude* unbending, obstinate.
cabrer [kɑbʀe] (1) **1** *vt cheval* to rear up; *avion* to nose up. **faire** ~ **son cheval** to make one's horse rear up; (*fig*) ~ **qn** to put sb's back up; (*fig*) ~ **qn contre qn** to turn *ou* set sb against sb.
2 se cabrer *vpr [cheval]* to rear up; *[avion]* to nose up; (*fig*) *[personne, orgueil]* to revolt, rebel. **se** ~ **contre qn** to turn *ou* rebel against sb; se ~ **à** *ou* **devant** to jib at.
cabri [kabʀi] *nm* (*Zool*) kid.
cabriole [kabʀijɔl] *nf* (*bond*) *[enfant, chevreau]* caper; (*culbute*) *[clown, gymnaste]* somersault; (*Danse*) cabriole; (*Équitation*) capriole, spring; (*fig*) *[politicien]* skilful manoeuvre, clever caper. **faire des** ~**s** *[chevreau, enfant]* to caper *ou* cavort (about); *[cheval]* to cavort.
cabrioler [kabʀijɔle] (1) *vi* (*gambader*) to caper *ou* cavort about.
cabriolet [kabʀijɔlɛ] *nm* (*Hist*) cabriolet; (*voiture décapotable*) convertible.
cabus [kaby] *nm V* **chou**[1].
caca* [kaka] *nm* (*langage enfantin*) **faire** ~ to do a pooh* (*langage enfantin Brit*) *ou* job (*langage enfantin*); **il a marché dans du** ~/**dans le** ~ **du chien** he stepped on some dirt/on the dog's dirt; (*couleur*) ~ **d'oie** greenish-yellow.
cacah(o)uète, cacahouette [kakawɛt] *nf* peanut, monkey nut (*Brit*); *V* **beurre**.
cacao [kakao] *nm* (*Culin*) (*poudre*) cocoa (powder); (*boisson*) cocoa, (drinking) chocolate; (*Bot*) cocoa bean.
cacaoté, e [kakaɔte] *adj farine* cocoa- *ou* chocolate-flavoured.
cacaotier [kakaɔtje] *nm*, **cacaoyer** [kakaɔje] *nm* cacao (tree).
cacaoui [kakawi] *nm* (*Can*) old squaw (duck), cockawee (*Can rare*).
cacatoès [kakatɔɛs] *nm* (*oiseau*) cockatoo.
cacatois [kakatwa] *nm* (*Naut*) (*voile*) royal; (*aussi* **mât de** ~) royal mast. **grand/petit** ~ main/fore royal.
cachalot [kaʃalo] *nm* sperm whale.
cache[1] [kaʃ] *nm* (*Ciné, Phot*) mask; (*gén*) card (*for covering one eye, masking out a section of text*).
cache[2] [kaʃ] *nf* (†: *cachette*) hiding place; (*pour butin*) cache.
cache- [kaʃ] *préf V* **cacher**.
caché, e [kaʃe] (*ptp de* **cacher**) *adj trésor* hidden; *asile* secluded, hidden; *sentiments* inner(most), secret; *sens* hidden, secret; *charmes, vertus* hidden. **je n'ai rien de** ~ **pour eux** I have no secrets from them; **mener une vie** ~**e** (*secrète*) to have a secret *ou* hidden life; (*retirée*) to lead a secluded life.
cachemire [kaʃmiʀ] *nm* (*laine*) cashmere. **motif** *ou* **impression** *ou* **dessin** ~ paisley pattern; **écharpe en** ~ cashmere scarf; **écharpe** ~ paisley(-pattern) stole.
cacher [kaʃe] (1) **1** *vt* **(a)** (*dissimuler volontairement*) *objet* to hide, conceal; *malfaiteur* to hide. **le chien est allé** ~ **son os** the dog has gone (away) to bury its bone; ~ **ses cartes** *ou* **son jeu** (*lit*) to keep one's cards up, play a close game; (*fig*) to keep one's cards close to one's chest, hide one's game.
(b) (*masquer*) *accident de terrain, trait de caractère* to hide, conceal. **les arbres nous cachent le fleuve** the trees hide *ou* conceal the river from our view *ou* from us; **tu me caches la lumière** you're in my light; **son silence cache quelque chose** he's hiding something by his silence; **les mauvaises herbes cachent les fleurs** you can't see the flowers for the weeds; **ces terrains cachent des trésors minéraux** mineral treasures lie hidden in this ground; *V* **arbre**.
(c) (*garder secret*) *fait, sentiment* to hide, conceal (*à qn* from sb). ~ **son âge** to keep one's age a secret; **on ne peut plus lui** ~ **la nouvelle** you can't keep *ou* hide *ou* conceal the news from her any longer; **il ne m'a pas caché qu'il désire partir** he hasn't hidden *ou* concealed it from me that he wants to leave, he hasn't kept it (a secret) from me that he wants to leave; **il n'a pas caché que** he made no secret (of the fact) that.
2 se cacher *vpr* **(a)** (*volontairement*) *[personne, soleil]* to hide. **va te** ~**!** get out of my sight!, be gone!*; **se** ~ **de qn** to hide from sb; **il se cache pour fumer** he goes and hides to have a smoke; **il se cache d'elle pour boire** he drinks behind her back; (*littér*) **se** ~ **de ses sentiments** to hide *ou* conceal one's feelings; **je ne m'en cache pas** I am quite open about it, I make no secret of it, I do not hide *ou* conceal it.
(b) (*être caché*) *[personne]* to be hiding; *[malfaiteur, évadé]* to be in hiding; *[chose]* to be hiding *ou* hidden. **il se cache de peur d'être puni** he is keeping out of sight *ou* he's hiding for fear of being punished.
(c) (*être masqué*) *[accident de terrain, trait de caractère]* to be concealed. **la maison se cache derrière le rideau d'arbres** the house is concealed *ou* hidden behind the line of trees.
(d) sans se ~**: faire qch sans se** ~ *ou* **s'en** ~ to do sth openly, do sth without hiding *ou* concealing the fact, do sth and make no secret of it; **il l'a fait sans se** ~ **de nous** he did it without hiding *ou* concealing it from us.
3: **cache-cache** *nm inv* (*lit, fig*) hide-and-seek; **cache-col** *nm inv*, **cache-nez** *nm inv* scarf, muffler; **cache-pot** *nm inv* flowerpot holder; **cache-radiateur** *nm inv* radiator cover; **cache-sexe** *nm inv* G-string; **cache-tampon** *nm inv* hunt-the-thimble, hide-the thimble.
cachet [kaʃɛ] *nm* **(a)** (*Pharm*) (*gén: comprimé*) tablet; (††: *enveloppe*) cachet. **un** ~ **d'aspirine** an aspirin (tablet).
(b) (*timbre*) stamp; (*sceau*) seal. ~ **(de la poste)** postmark; **sa lettre porte le** ~ **de Paris** his letter is postmarked from Paris *ou* has a Paris postmark; *V* **lettre**.
(c) (*fig: style, caractère*) style, character. **cette petite église avait du** ~ there was something very characterful about that little church, that little church had (great) character *ou* style; **une robe qui a du** ~ a stylish *ou* chic dress, a dress with some style about it; **ça porte le** ~ **de l'originalité/du génie** it bears the stamp of originality/genius, it has the mark of originality/genius on it.
(d) (*rétribution*) fee; *V* **courir**.
cachetage [kaʃtaʒ] *nm* sealing.
cacheter [kaʃte] (4) *vt* to seal; *V* **cire**.
cachette [kaʃɛt] *nf [objet]* hiding-place; *[personne]* hideout, hiding-place. **en** ~ *agir, fumer* on the sly *ou* quiet; *rire* to oneself, up one's sleeve; *économiser* secretly; **en** ~ **de qn** (*action répréhensible*) behind sb's back; (*action non répréhensible*) unknown to sb.
cachot [kaʃo] *nm* (*cellule*) dungeon; (*punition*) solitary confinement.
cachotterie [kaʃɔtʀi] *nf* (*secret*) mystery. **c'est une nouvelle** ~ **de sa part** it's another of his (little) mysteries; **faire des** ~**s** to be secretive, act secretively, make mysteries about things; **faire des** ~**s à qn** to make a mystery of sth to sb, be secretive about sth to sb.
cachottier, -ière [kaʃɔtje, jɛʀ] *adj* secretive. **cet enfant est (un)** ~ he's a secretive child.
cachou [kaʃu] *nm* (*bonbon*) cachou.
cacique [kasik] *nm* (*Ethnologie*) cacique. (*arg Scol*) **c'était le** ~ he came first, he got first place.
cacochyme [kakɔʃim] *adj* († *ou hum*) **un vieillard** ~ a doddery old man.
cacophonie [kakɔfɔni] *nf* cacophony.
cacophonique [kakɔfɔnik] *adj* cacophonous.
cactée [kakte] *nf*, **cactacée** [kaktase] *nf* cactacea.
cactus [kaktys] *nm inv* cactus.
cadastral, e, *mpl* **-aux** [kadastʀal, o] *adj* cadastral.
cadastre [kadastʀ(ə)] *nm* (*registre*) cadastre; (*service*) cadastral survey.
cadastrer [kadastʀe] (1) *vt* to survey and register (*in the cadastre*).
cadavéreux, -euse [kadɑveʀø, øz] *adj teint* deathly (pale),

deadly pale; *pâleur* deathly. **les blessés au teint ~** the deathly-looking *ou* deathly pale injured.

cadavérique [kadaveʀik] *adj teint* deathly (pale), deadly pale; *pâleur* deathly; *V* **rigidité.**

cadavre [kadavʀ(ə)] *nm* **(a)** (*humain*) corpse, (dead) body; (*animal*) carcass, body. (*fig*) **c'est un ~ ambulant** he's a living corpse.

(b) (*: *bouteille vide, de vin etc*) empty (bottle), dead man* *ou* soldier*. **on avait rangé les ~s dans un coin** we had lined up the empties in a corner.

cadeau, *pl* **~x** [kado] *nm* **(a)** present, gift (*de qn* from sb). **faire un ~ à qn** to give sb a present *ou* gift; **~ de mariage/de Noël** wedding/Christmas present.

(b) (*loc*) **faire ~ de qch à qn** (*offrir*) to make sb a present of sth, give sb sth as a present; (*laisser*) to let sb keep sth, give sb sth; **il a décidé d'en faire ~ (à qn)** he decided to give it away (to sb); **ils ne font pas de ~x** *[examinateurs etc]* they don't let you off lightly; **en ~** as a present; **garde la monnaie, je t'en fais ~** keep the change, I'm giving it to you; (*hum, iro*) **les petits ~x entretiennent l'amitié** there's nothing like a little present between friends (*iro*).

cadenas [kadna] *nm* padlock. **fermer au ~** to padlock.

cadenasser [kadnase] (1) *vt* to padlock.

cadence [kadɑ̃s] *nf* **(a)** (*rythme*) *[vers, chant, danse]* rhythm. **marquer la ~** to accentuate the rhythm.

(b) (*vitesse, taux*) rate, pace. **~ de tir/de production** rate of fire/of production; **à la ~ de 10 par jour** at the rate of 10 a day; **à une bonne ~** at a good pace *ou* rate; (*fig*) **forcer la ~** to force the pace.

(c) (*Mus*) *[succession d'accords]* cadence; *[concerto]* cadenza.

(d) (*loc*) **en ~** (*régulièrement*) rhythmically; (*ensemble, en mesure*) in time.

cadencé, e [kadɑ̃se] (*ptp de* **cadencer**) *adj* (*rythmé*) rhythmic(al); *V* **pas**[1].

cadencer [kadɑ̃se] (3) *vt débit, phrases, allure, marche* to put rhythm into, give rhythm to.

cadet, -ette [kadɛ, ɛt] **1** *adj* (*plus jeune*) younger; (*le plus jeune*) youngest.

2 *nm* **(a)** *[famille]* **le ~** the youngest child *ou* one; **le ~ des garçons** the youngest boy *ou* son; **mon (frère) ~** my younger brother; **le ~ de mes frères** my youngest brother; **le père avait un faible pour son ~** the father had a soft spot for his youngest boy.

(b) (*relation d'âges*) **il est mon ~** he's younger than me; **il est mon ~ de 2 ans** he's 2 years younger than me, he's 2 years my junior, he's my junior by 2 years; **c'est le ~ de mes soucis** it's the least of my worries.

(c) (*Sport*) minor (*15-17 years*); (*Hist*) cadet (*gentleman who entered the army to acquire military skill and eventually a commission*).

3 cadette *nf* **(a) la ~te** the youngest child *ou* one; **la ~te des filles** the youngest girl *ou* daughter; **ma (sœur) ~te** my younger sister.

(b) elle est ma ~te she's younger than me.

(c) (*Sport*) minor (*15-17 years*).

cadogan [kadɔgɑ̃] *nm* = **catogan.**

cadrage [kadʀaʒ] *nm* (*Phot*) centring (of image).

cadran [kadʀɑ̃] **1** *nm [téléphone, boussole, compteur]* dial; *[montre, horloge]* dial, face; *[baromètre]* face; *V* **tour**[2]. **2: cadran solaire** sundial.

cadre [kadʀ(ə)] *nm* **(a)** *[tableau, porte, bicyclette]* frame. **mettre un ~ à un tableau** to put a picture in a frame, frame a picture; **il roulait à bicyclette avec son copain sur le ~** he was riding along with his pal on the crossbar.

(b) (*caisse*) **~ (d'emballage** *ou* **de déménagement)** crate, packing case; **~-conteneur** *ou* **-container** container.

(c) (*sur formulaire*) space, box. **ne rien écrire dans ce ~** do not write in this space, leave this space blank.

(d) (*décor*) setting; (*entourage*) surroundings. **vivre dans un ~ luxueux** to live in luxurious surroundings; **son enfance s'écoula dans un ~ austère** he spent his childhood in austere surroundings; **une maison située dans un ~ de verdure** a house surrounded by greenery; **sortir du ~ étroit de la vie quotidienne** to get out of the strait jacket *ou* the narrow confines of everyday life; **quel ~ magnifique!** what a magnificent setting!

(e) (*limites*) scope. **rester/être dans le ~ de** to remain/be *ou* fall within the scope of; **cette décision sort du ~ de notre accord** this decision is outside *ou* beyond the scope of our agreement; **il est sorti du ~ de ses fonctions** he went beyond the scope of *ou* overstepped the limits of his responsibilities; **respecter le ~ de la légalité** to remain within (the bounds of) the law; *V* **loi.**

(f) (*contexte*) **dans le ~ des réformes/des recherches** within the context of *ou* the framework of the reforms/research; **une manifestation qui aura lieu dans le ~ du festival** an event which will take place within the context *ou* framework of the festival *ou* as part of the festival.

(g) (*structure*) scope. **le ~** *ou* **les ~s de la mémoire/de l'inconscient** the framework of memory/the unconscious.

(h) (*chef, responsable*) executive, manager; (*Mil*) officer. **les ~s** the managerial staff; **elle est passée ~** she has been upgraded to a managerial position *ou* to the rank of manager, she's been made an executive; **jeune ~** junior executive; **~ supérieur** executive, senior manager; **~ moyen** middle executive.

(i) (*Admin: liste du personnel*) **entrer dans/figurer sur les ~s (d'une compagnie)** to be (placed) on/be on the books (of a company); **être rayé des ~s** (*licencié*) to be dismissed; (*libéré*) to be discharged; *V* **hors.**

(j) *[radio]* frame antenna.

cadrer [kadʀe] (1) **1** *vi* (*coïncider*) to tally (*avec* with), conform (*avec* to, with). **2** *vt* (*Ciné, Phot*) to centre.

cadreur [kadʀœʀ] *nm* (*Ciné*) cameraman.

caduc, caduque [kadyk] *adj* **(a)** (*Bot*) deciduous. **(b)** (*Jur*) null and void. **devenir ~** to lapse; **rendre ~** to render null and void, invalidate. **(c)** (*périmé*) *théorie* outmoded, obsolete. **(d)** (*Ling*) **e ~** mute e. **(e) âge ~** declining years.

caducée [kadyse] *nm* caduceus.

cæcum [sekɔm] *nm* caecum.

cafard[1] [kafaʀ] *nm* **(a)** (*insecte*) cockroach. **(b)** (*: *mélancolie*) **un accès de ~** a fit of depression *ou* of the blues*; **avoir le ~** to be down in the dumps*, be feeling gloomy *ou* blue* *ou* low*; **ça lui donne le ~** that depresses him, that gets him down*.

cafard[2], **e** [kafaʀ, aʀd(ə)] *nm,f* (*péj*) (*rapporteur*) sneak, telltale, tattletale (*US*); (*rare: tartufe*) hypocrite.

cafardage* [kafaʀdaʒ] *nm* (*rapportage*) sneaking, taletelling.

cafarder* [kafaʀde] (1) **1** *vt* (*rapporter*) to tell tales on, sneak on. **2** *vi* to tell tales, sneak.

cafardeur, -euse[1] [kafaʀdœʀ, øz] *nm,f* (*péj*) sneak, telltale, tattletale (*US*).

cafardeux, -euse[2] [kafaʀdø, øz] *adj* (*déprimé*) *personne* down in the dumps* (*attrib*), gloomy, feeling blue* (*attrib*); *tempérament* gloomy, melancholy.

café [kafe] **1** *nm* **(a)** (*plante, boisson, produit*) coffee.

(b) (*moment du repas*) coffee. **au ~, on parlait politique** we talked politics over coffee; **il est arrivé au ~** he came in when we were having coffee.

(c) (*lieu*) café, ≃ pub.

2: café bar café (*serving spirits, coffee, snacks*); **café complet** ≃ continental breakfast; (*Hist*) **café-concert** *nm, pl* **cafés-concerts, caf'conc'** *café where singers etc entertain customers*; **café crème** white coffee; **café express** espresso coffee; **café filtre** filter(ed) coffee; **café en grains** coffee beans; **café au lait** (*nm*) white coffee (*Brit*), coffee with milk; (*adj inv*) coffee-coloured; **café liégeois** coffee ice cream (*with crème Chantilly*); **café noir** *ou* **nature** black coffee; **café en poudre** instant coffee; **café-restaurant** *nm, pl* **cafés-restaurants** restaurant, *café serving meals*; **café soluble** = **café en poudre**; **café tabac** *tobacconist's also serving coffee and spirits*; **café théâtre** theatre workshop; **café turc** Turkish coffee; **café vert** unroasted coffee.

caféier [kafeje] *nm* coffee tree.

caféière [kafejɛʀ] *nf* coffee plantation.

caféine [kafein] *nf* caffeine.

cafetan [kaftɑ̃] *nm* caftan.

cafétéria [kafeteʀja] *nf* cafeteria.

cafetier, -ière [kaftje, jɛʀ] **1** *nm,f* café-owner. **2 cafetière** *nf* **(a)** (*pot*) coffeepot; (*percolateur*) coffee-maker. **(b)** (*: *tête*) nut*, noddle* (*surtout Brit*), noodle* (*US*).

cafouillage* [kafujaʒ] *nm* muddle, shambles (*sg*).

cafouiller* [kafuje] (1) *vi [organisation, administration, gouvernement]* to be in *ou* get into a (state of) shambles *ou* a mess; *[discussion]* to turn into a shambles, fall apart; *[équipe]* to get into a shambles, go to pieces; *[candidat]* to flounder; *[moteur, appareil]* to work in fits and starts. **dans cette affaire le gouvernement cafouille** the government's in a real shambles over this business; (*Sport*) **~ (avec) le ballon** to fumble the ball.

cafouilleur, -euse* [kafujœʀ, øz], **cafouilleux, -euse*** [kafujø, øz] **1** *adj organisation, discussion* shambolic*, chaotic. **il est ~** he always gets (things) into a muddle, he's a bungler *ou* muddler.

2 *nm,f* muddler, bungler.

cafre [kafʀ(ə)] **1** *adj* kaf(f)ir. **2** *nmf*: **C~** Kaf(f)ir.

cage [kaʒ] **1** *nf* **(a)** *[animaux]* cage. **mettre en ~** (*lit*) to put in a cage; (*fig*) *voleur* to lock up; **dans ce bureau, je me sens comme un animal en ~** in this office I feel caged up *ou* in.

(b) (*Tech*) *[roulement à billes, pendule]* casing; *[maison]* shell; (*Sport*: buts*) goal.

2: cage d'ascenseur lift shaft; **cage d'escalier** (stair)well; (*Min*) **cage d'extraction** cage; (*Élec*) **cage de Faraday** Faraday cage; **cage à lapins** (*lit*) (rabbit) hutch; (*fig péj: maison*) poky little hole*, box; **cage à poules** (*lit*) hen-coop; (*fig péj: maison*) shack, poky little hole*, box; **cage thoracique** rib cage.

cageot [kaʒo] *nm [légumes, fruits]* crate.

cagibi* [kaʒibi] *nm* (*débarras*) box room (*Brit*), storage room (*US*), glory hole* (*Brit*); (*remise*) shed.

cagne [kaɲ] *nf* (*arg Scol*) *Arts class preparing entrance exam for the École normale supérieure.*

cagneux, -euse[1] [kaɲø, øz] *adj cheval, personne* knock-kneed; *jambes* crooked. **genoux ~** knock knees.

cagneux, -euse[2] [kaɲø, øz] *nm,f* (*arg Scol*) *pupil in the 'cagne'*; *V* **cagne.**

cagnotte [kaɲɔt] *nf* (*caisse commune*) kitty; (*: *économies*) nest egg.

cagot, e [kago, ɔt] (†† *ou péj*) **1** *adj allure, air* sanctimonious. **2** *nm,f* sanctimonious *ou* canting hypocrite.

cagoule [kagul] *nf [moine]* cowl; *[pénitent]* hood; *[bandit]* hood, mask; *[alpiniste]* cagoule.

cahier [kaje] **1** *nm* (*Scol*) notebook, exercise book; (*Typ*) gathering; (*revue littéraire*) journal.

2: cahier de brouillon roughbook (*Brit*); (*Jur*) **cahier des charges** schedule (of conditions); **cahier de cours** notebook, exercise book; **cahier de devoirs** (home) exercise book, homework book; (*Hist*) **cahier de doléances** register of grievances; **cahier d'exercices** exercise book; **cahier de textes** homework notebook.

cahin-caha* [kaɛ̃kaa] *adv*: **aller ~** *[troupe, marcheur]* to jog along; *[vie, affaires]* to jog *ou* struggle along; *[santé]* to be so-so, have its ups and downs; **alors ça va?** — ~ how are you? — (I'm) so-so *ou* middling*.

cahot [kao] *nm* (*secousse*) jolt, bump. (*fig*) ~s ups and downs.

cahotant, e [kaɔtɑ̃, ɑ̃t] *adj route* bumpy, rough; *véhicule* bumpy, jolting.

cahotement [kaɔtmɑ̃] *nm* bumping, jolting.

cahoter [kaɔte] (1) **1** *vt voyageurs* to jolt, bump about; *véhicule* to jolt; (*fig*) *[vicissitudes]* to buffet about. **une famille cahotée par la guerre** a family buffeted *ou* tossed about by the war.

2 *vi [véhicule]* to jog *ou* trundle along. **le petit train cahotait le long du canal** the little train jogged *ou* trundled along by the canal.

cahoteux, -euse [kaɔtø, øz] *adj route* bumpy, rough.

cahute [kayt] *nf* (*cabane*) shack, hut; (*péj*) shack.

caïd [kaid] *nm* **(a)** (*meneur*) *[pègre]* boss, big chief*, top man; (*) *[classe, bureau]* big shot*. (*as, crack*) **le ~ de l'équipe*** the star of the team, the team's top man; **en maths/en mécanique, c'est un ~*** he's an ace* at maths/at mechanics.

(b) (*en Afrique du Nord: fonctionnaire*) kaid.

caillasse [kajas] *nf* (*pierraille*) loose stones. **pente couverte de ~** scree-covered slope, slope covered with loose stones; (*péj*) **ce n'est pas du sable ni de la terre, ce n'est que de la ~** it's neither sand nor soil, it's just like gravel *ou* it's just loose stones.

caille [kɑj] *nf* (*oiseau*) quail. **chaud comme une ~** snug as a bug in a rug; **rond comme une ~** plump as a partridge.

caillé [kɑje] *nm* curds.

caillebotis [kɑjbɔti] *nm* (*treillis*) grating; (*plancher*) duckboard.

caillement [kɑjmɑ̃] *nm* (*V* **cailler**) curdling; coagulating, clotting.

cailler [kɑje] (1) **1** *vt* (*plus courant* **faire** *ou* **laisser ~**) *lait* to curdle.

2 *vi,* **se cailler** *vpr* **(a)** *[lait]* to curdle; *[sang]* to coagulate, clot; *V* **lait**.

(b) (*:) (*avoir froid*) to be cold. (*faire froid*) **ça caille** it's freezing; **qu'est-ce qu'on (se) caille*** it's freezing cold *ou* perishing* (cold).

caillette [kajɛt] *nf* (*Zool*) rennet stomach, abomasum (*T*).

caillot [kajo] *nm* (blood) clot.

caillou, *pl* **~x** [kaju] *nm* (*gén*) stone; (*petit galet*) pebble; (*grosse pierre*) boulder; (*: *tête, crâne*) head, nut*; (*: *diamant etc*) stone. **des tas de ~x d'empierrement** heaps of road metal, heaps of chips for the road; **on ne peut rien faire pousser ici, c'est du ~** you can't get anything to grow here, it's nothing but stones; (*fig*) **il a un ~ à la place du cœur** he has a heart of stone; **il n'a pas un poil** *ou* **cheveu sur le ~*** he's as bald as a coot *ou* an egg.

cailloutage [kajutaʒ] *nm* (*action*) metalling; (*cailloux*) (road) metal.

caillouter [kajute] (1) *vt* (*empierrer*) to metal.

caillouteux, -euse [kajutø, øz] *adj route, terrain* stony; *plage* pebbly, shingly.

cailloutis [kajuti] *nm* (*gén*) gravel; *[route]* (road) metal.

caïman [kaimɑ̃] *nm* cayman, caiman.

Caire [kɛʀ] *n*: **le ~** Cairo.

cairn [kɛʀn] *nm* cairn.

caisse [kɛs] **1** *nf* **(a)** (*container*) box; *[fruits, légumes]* crate; *[plantes]* box. **mettre des arbres en ~** to plant trees in boxes *ou* tubs.

(b) (*Tech: boîte, carcasse*) *[horloge]* casing; *[orgue]* case; *[véhicule]* bodywork; *[tambour]* cylinder.

(c) (*contenant de l'argent*) cashbox; (*tiroir*) till; (*machine*) cash register, till. **avoir de l'argent en ~** to have ready cash; **ils n'ont plus un sou en ~** they haven't a penny left in the bank; **faire la ~** to count up the money in the till, do the till; **être à la ~** (*temporairement*) to be at *ou* on the cashdesk; (*être caissier*) to be the cashier; **tenir la ~** to be the cashier; (*fig hum*) to hold the purse strings; **les ~s (de l'état) sont vides** the coffers (of the state) are empty; **voler la ~, partir avec la ~** to steal *ou* make off with the contents of the till *ou* the takings; *V* **bon**[2], **livre**[1].

(d) (*guichet*) *[boutique]* cashdesk; *[banque]* teller's desk; *[supermarché]* check-out. **passer à la ~** (*lit*) to go to the cashdesk *ou* cashier; (*être payé*) to collect one's money; (*être licencié*) to get paid off, get one's books (*Brit*) *ou* cards* (*Brit*); **on l'a prié de passer à la ~** he was asked to take his cards (*Brit*) and go.

(e) (*établissement, bureau*) office; (*organisme*) fund. **~ de retraite/d'entraide** pension/mutual aid fund; **il travaille à la ~ de la Sécurité sociale** he works at the Social Security office.

(f) (*Mus: tambour*) drum; *V* **gros**.

(g) (*: *poitrine*) chest. **il s'en va** *ou* **part de la ~** his lungs are giving out.

2: (*Mus*) **caisse claire** side *ou* snare drum; **caisse comptable = caisse enregistreuse**; (*Naut, Rail*) **caisse à eau** water tank; **caisse d'emballage** packing case; **caisse enregistreuse** cash register; **caisse d'épargne** savings bank; **caisse noire** secret funds; **caisse à outils** toolbox; **caisse de résonance** resonance chamber; **caisse à savon** (*lit*) soapbox; (*péj: meuble*) old box; **caisse du tympan** middle ear, tympanic cavity (*T*).

caissette [kɛsɛt] *nf* (small) box.

caissier, -ière [kesje, jɛʀ] *nm,f [banque]* cashier, teller, bank clerk; *[magasin]* cashier; *[supermarché]* check-out assistant; *[cinéma]* cashier, box-office assistant.

caisson [kɛsɔ̃] *nm* **(a)** (*caisse*) box, case; *[bouteilles]* crate; (*coffrage*) casing; (*Mil: chariot*) caisson.

(b) (*Tech: immergé*) caisson. **le mal** *ou* **la maladie des ~s** caisson disease, the bends*.

(c) *[plafond]* caisson, coffer; *V* **plafond, sauter**.

cajoler [kaʒɔle] (1) *vt* (*câliner*) to pet, make a lot of, make a fuss of; (†: *amadouer*) to wheedle, coax, cajole. **~ qn pour qu'il donne qch** to try to wheedle sb into giving sth; **~ qn pour obtenir qch** to try to wheedle sth out of sb, cajole sb to try and get sth from him.

cajolerie [kaʒɔlʀi] *nf* (*flatterie*) wheedling (*U*), coaxing (*U*), cajoling (*U*). **faire des ~s à qn** to pet sb, make a lot *ou* a fuss of sb; **arracher une promesse à qn à force de ~s** to coax *ou* wheedle a promise out of sb.

cajoleur, -euse [kaʒɔlœʀ, øz] **1** *adj* (*câlin*) *mère* affectionate; (*flatteur*) *voix, personne* wheedling, coaxing. **2** *nm,f* (*flatteur*) wheedler, coaxer.

cajou [kaʒu] *nm* cashew nut.

cake [kɛk] *nm* fruit cake.

cal [kal] *nm* (*Bot, Méd*) callus.

calage [kalaʒ] *nm* (*V* **caler**) wedging; chocking; keying; locking.

calamar [kalamaʀ] *nm* = **calmar**.

calamine [kalamin] *nf* **(a)** (*Minér*) calamine. **(b)** (*Aut: résidu*) carbon deposits.

calaminer (se) [kalamine] (1) *vpr cylindre etc* to coke up (*Brit*), get coked up (*Brit*).

calamistré, e [kalamistʀe] *adj cheveux* waved and brillian-tined.

calamité [kalamite] *nf* (*malheur*) calamity. (*hum*) **ce type est une ~*** this bloke* (*Brit*) *ou* guy* is a (walking) disaster; **quelle ~!*** what a disaster!

calamiteux, -euse [kalamitø, øz] *adj* calamitous.

calandre [kalɑ̃dʀ(ə)] *nf [automobile]* radiator grill; (*machine*) calender.

calanque [kalɑ̃k] *nf* (*crique: en Méditerranée*) rocky inlet.

calcaire [kalkɛʀ] **1** *adj* **(a)** (*qui contient de la chaux*) *sol, terrain* chalky, calcareous (*T*); *eau* hard.

(b) (*Géol*) *roche, plateau, relief* limestone (*épith*).

(c) (*Méd*) *dégénérescence* calcareous; (*Chim*) *sels* calcium (*épith*).

2 *nm* (*Géol*) limestone; *[bouilloire]* fur.

calcanéum [kalkaneɔm] *nm* calcaneum.

calcification [kalsifikasjɔ̃] *nf* (*Méd*) calcification.

calcination [kalsinasjɔ̃] *nf* calcination.

calciné, e [kalsine] (*ptp de* **calciner**) *adj débris, os* burned to ashes (*attrib*); *rôti* burned to a cinder (*attrib*). (*littér*) **la plaine ~e par le soleil** the plain scorched by the sun, the sun-scorched *ou* sun-baked plain.

calciner [kalsine] (1) **1** *vt* (*Tech: brûler*) *pierre, bois, métal* to calcine; *rôti* to burn to a cinder. **2 se calciner** *vpr [rôti]* to burn to a cinder; *[débris]* to burn to ashes.

calcium [kalsjɔm] *nm* calcium.

calcul [kalkyl] **1** *nm* **(a)** (*opération*) calculation; (*exercice scolaire*) sum. **se tromper dans ses ~s, faire une erreur de ~** to miscalculate, make a miscalculation, make a mistake in one's calculations; *V* **règle**.

(b) (*discipline*) **le ~** arithmetic; **fort en ~** good at arithmetic *ou* sums; **le ~ différentiel/intégral** differential/integral calculus.

(c) (*estimation*) reckoning(s), calculations, computations. **tous ~s faits** with all factors reckoned up, having done all the reckonings *ou* calculations; **d'après mes ~s** by my reckoning, according to my calculations *ou* computations.

(d) (*plan*) calculation (*U*). **par ~** with an ulterior motive, out of (calculated) self-interest; **sans (aucun) ~** without any ulterior motive *ou* (any) self-interest; **faire un bon ~** to calculate correctly *ou* right; **faire un mauvais ~** to miscalculate, make a miscalculation; **c'est le ~ d'un arriviste** it's the calculation of an arriviste; **~s intéressés** self-interested motives.

(e) (*Méd*) stone, calculus (*T*).

2: **calcul algébrique** calculus; (*Méd*) **calcul biliaire** gallstone; **calcul mental** (*discipline*) mental arithmetic; (*opération*) mental calculation; **calcul des probabilités** probability theory; (*Méd*) **calcul rénal** stone in the kidney, renal calculus (*T*).

calculable [kalkylabl(ə)] *adj* calculable, which can be calculated *ou* worked out.

calculateur, -trice [kalkylatœʀ, tʀis] **1** *adj* (*intéressé*) calculating.

2 *nm* (*machine*) **~ électromagnétique** electromechanical computer; **~ électronique** electronic computer; **~ de poche** pocket calculator.

3 calculatrice *nf* (*machine*) adding machine.

4 *nm,f* (*personne*) calculator. **c'est un bon ~** he's good at counting *ou* at figures *ou* at calculations.

calculer [kalkyle] (1) **1** *vt* **(a)** *prix, quantité* to work out, calculate, reckon; *surface* to work out, calculate. **apprendre à ~** to learn to calculate; **il calcule vite** he calculates quickly, he's quick at figures *ou* at calculating; **~ (un prix) de tête** *ou* **mentalement** to work out *ou* reckon *ou* calculate (a price) in one's head; *V* **machine**[3], **règle**.

(b) (*évaluer, estimer*) *chances, conséquences* to calculate, work out, weigh up. (*Sport*) **~ son élan** to judge one's run-up; **~ que** to work out *ou* calculate that; **tout bien calculé** when you work it all out *ou* weigh everything up; *V* **risque**.

(c) (*combiner*) *geste, attitude, effets* to plan, calculate; *plan, action* to plan. **elle calcule continuellement** she's always calculating; **~ son coup** to plan one's move (carefully); **avec une gentillesse calculée** with calculated kindness.

2 *vi* (*économiser, compter*) to budget carefully, count the pennies. (*péj*) **ces gens qui calculent** those (people) who are always counting their pennies *ou* who work out every penny (*péj*).

cale[1] [kal] *nf* **(a)** (*Naut: soute*) hold; *V* **fond**. **(b)** (*chantier, plan incliné*): **cale de chargement** slipway; **cale de construction**

slipway; **cale de halage** slipway; **cale de radoub** graving dock; **cale sèche** dry dock.

cale[2] [kal] *nf* (*coin*) *[meuble, caisse, tonneau]* wedge; *[roue]* chock, wedge. **mettre une voiture sur ~s** to put a car on blocks.

calé, e* [kale] (*ptp de* **caler**) *adj* **(a)** (*savant*) *personne* bright. **être ~ en maths** to be a wizard* at maths. **(b)** (*ardu*) *problème* tough. **c'est drôlement ~ ce qu'il a fait** what he did was terribly clever.

calebasse [kalbɑs] *nf* (*récipient*) calabash, gourde.

calèche [kalɛʃ] *nf* barouche.

caleçon [kalsɔ̃] *nm* pair of underpants. **3 ~s** 3 pairs of underpants; **où sont tes ~s?** where are your underpants?; **~(s) de bain** bathing trunks; **~(s) long(s)** long johns*.

calédonien, -ienne [kaledɔnjɛ̃, jɛn] *adj* Caledonian.

calembour [kalɑ̃buʀ] *nm* pun, play on words (*U*).

calembredaine [kalɑ̃bʀədɛn] *nf* (*plaisanterie*) silly joke. (*balivernes*) **~s** balderdash (*U*), nonsense.

calendes [kalɑ̃d] *nfpl* (*Antiq*) calends; *V* **renvoyer.**

calendrier [kalɑ̃dʀije] *nm* (*jours et mois*) calendar; (*programme*) timetable. **~ à effeuiller/perpétuel** tear-off/everlasting calendar; **~ des examens** exam timetable; **~ de travail** work schedule *ou* programme; *V* **bloc.**

cale-pied [kalpje] *nm inv [vélo]* toe clip.

calepin [kalpɛ̃] *nm* notebook.

caler [kale] (1) **1** *vt* **(a)** (*avec une cale, un coin*) *meuble* to put a wedge under, wedge; *fenêtre, porte* to wedge; *roue* to chock, wedge.

(b) (*avec une vis, une goupille*) *poulie* to key; *cheville, objet pivotant* to wedge, lock.

(c) (*avec des coussins etc*) *malade* to prop up. **~ sa tête sur l'oreiller** to prop *ou* rest one's head on the pillow; **des coussins lui calaient la tête, il avait la tête (bien) calée par des coussins** his head was (well) propped up on *ou* supported by cushions.

(d) (*appuyer*) *pile de livres, de linge* to prop up. **~ dans un coin/contre** to prop up in a corner/against.

(e) *moteur, véhicule* to stall.

(f) (*Naut: baisser*) *mât* to house.

(g) (*: *bourrer*) **ça vous cale l'estomac** it fills you up; **je suis calé pour un bon moment** that's me full up for a while*.

2 *vi* **(a)** *[véhicule, moteur, conducteur]* to stall.

(b) (*) (*céder*) to give in; (*abandonner*) to give up. **il a calé avant le dessert** he gave up before the dessert; **il a calé sur le dessert** he couldn't finish his dessert.

(c) (*Naut*) **~ trop** to have too great a draught; **~ 8 mètres** to draw 8 metres of water.

3 se caler *vpr*: **se ~ dans un fauteuil** to plant o.s. firmly *ou* settle o.s. comfortably in an armchair; **se ~ les joues*** to have a good tuck-in* (*Brit*).

caleter‡ *vi*, **se caleter**‡ *vpr* [kalte] (1) = **calter**‡.

calfatage [kalfataʒ] *nm* ca(u)lking.

calfater [kalfate] (1) *vt* (*Naut*) to ca(u)lk.

calfeutrage [kalføtʀaʒ] *nm* (*V* **calfeutrer**) draughtproofing; filling, stopping-up.

calfeutrer [kalføtʀe] (1) **1** *vt pièce, porte* to (make) draughtproof; *fissure* to fill, stop up. **2 se calfeutrer** *vpr* (*s'enfermer*) to shut o.s. up *ou* away; (*pour être au chaud*) to hole (o.s.) up, make o.s. snug.

calibrage [kalibʀaʒ] *nm* (*V* **calibrer**) grading; gauging; measuring.

calibre [kalibʀ(ə)] *nm* **(a)** (*diamètre*) *[fusil, canon]* calibre, bore; *[conduite, tuyau]* bore, diameter; *[obus, balle]* calibre; *[cylindre]* bore; *[câble]* diameter; *[œufs, fruits]* grade; *[boule]* size. **de gros ~** *pistolet* large-bore (*épith*); *obus* large-calibre (*épith*); **pistolet de ~ 7,35** 7.35 mm pistol.

(b) (*arg Crime: pistolet*) rod (*arg*), gat (*arg*).

(c) (*instrument*) (*gradué et ajustable*) gauge; (*réplique*) template.

(d) (*fig: envergure*) calibre. **son frère est d'un autre ~** his brother is of another calibre altogether; **c'est rare un égoïsme de ce ~** you don't often see selfishness on such a scale.

calibrer [kalibʀe] (1) *vt* **(a)** (*mesurer*) *œufs, fruits, charbon* to grade; *conduit, cylindre, fusil* to gauge, measure. **(b)** (*finir*) *pièce travaillée* to gauge.

calice [kalis] *nm* (*Rel*) chalice; (*Bot, Physiol*) calyx; *V* **boire.**

calicot [kaliko] *nm* **(a)** (*tissu*) calico; (*banderole*) banner. **(b)** (†: *vendeur*) draper's assistant (*Brit*).

califat [kalifa] *nm* caliphate.

calife [kalif] *nm* caliph.

Californie [kalifɔʀni] *nf* California.

californien, -ienne [kalifɔʀnjɛ̃, jɛn] **1** *adj* Californian. **2** *nm,f*: **C~(ne)** Californian.

califourchon [kalifuʀʃɔ̃] *nm*: **à ~** astride; **s'asseoir à ~ sur qch** to straddle sth, sit astride sth; **être à ~ sur qch** to bestride sth, be astride sth; (*Equitation*) **monter à ~** to ride astride.

câlin, e [kɑlɛ̃, in] **1** *adj* (*qui aime les caresses*) *enfant, chat* cuddly, cuddlesome; (*qui câline*) *mère, ton, regard* tender, loving. **2** *nm* cuddle. **faire un (petit) ~ à qn** to give sb a cuddle.

câliner [kɑline] (1) *vt* (*cajoler*) to fondle, cuddle.

câlinerie [kɑlinʀi] *nf* (*tendresse*) tenderness. (*caresses, cajoleries*) **~s** caresses; **faire des ~s à qn** to fondle *ou* cuddle sb.

calisson [kalisɔ̃] *nm* calisson (*lozenge-shaped sweet made of ground almonds*).

calleux, -euse [kalø, øz] *adj peau* horny, callous.

calligraphe [kaligʀaf] *nmf* calligrapher, calligraphist.

calligraphie [kaligʀafi] *nf* (*technique*) calligraphy, art of handwriting. **c'est de la ~** it's lovely handwriting, the (hand)-writing is beautiful.

calligraphier [kaligʀafje] (7) *vt titre, phrase* to write artistically, calligraph (*T*).

calligraphique [kaligʀafik] *adj* calligraphic.

callosité [kalozite] *nf* callosity.

calmant, e [kalmɑ̃, ɑ̃t] **1** *adj* **(a)** (*Pharm*) (*tranquillisant*) tranquillizing (*épith*); (*contre la douleur*) painkilling (*épith*). **(b)** (*apaisant*) *paroles* soothing. **2** *nm* (*Pharm*) tranquillizer, sedative; painkiller.

calmar [kalmaʀ] *nm* squid.

calme [kalm(ə)] **1** *adj vie, journée, endroit, atmosphère* quiet, peaceful; *nuit, air, ciel* still; *personne* (*temporairement*) quiet, calm; (*par nature*) calm, peaceful; *mer* calm, quiet; (*Fin*) *bourse, marché, affaires* quiet. **malgré leurs provocations il restait très ~** he remained quite calm *ou* cool *ou* unruffled in spite of their taunts; **le malade a eu une nuit ~** the invalid has had a quiet *ou* peaceful night.

2 *nm* **(a)** quietness, peacefulness; stillness, still (*littér*); calm, calmness. **garder son ~** to keep cool *ou* calm, keep one's cool* *ou* head; **perdre son ~** to lose one's composure; **avec un ~ incroyable** with incredible sangfroid *ou* coolness; **recouvrant son ~** recovering his equanimity.

(b) (*tranquillité*) **le ~** quietness, peace (and quiet); **chercher le ~** to look for (some) peace and quiet; **le ~ de la campagne** the peace (and quiet) of the countryside; **il me faut du ~ pour travailler** I need quietness *ou* peace to work; **du ~!** (*restez tranquille*) let's have some quiet!, quieten down! (*Brit*), quiet down! (*US*); (*pas de panique*) keep cool! *ou* calm!; *[malade]* **rester au ~** to avoid excitement, take things quietly; (*Pol*) **ramener le ~** to restore order; **le ~ avant la tempête** the lull before the storm.

(c) (*Naut*) **calme plat** dead calm; (*fig*) **en août c'est le ~ plat dans les affaires** in August business is dead quiet *ou* at a stand-still; (*fig*) **depuis que je lui ai envoyé cette lettre c'est le calme plat** since I sent him that letter I haven't heard a thing *ou* a squeak; **calmes équatoriaux** doldrums (*lit*).

calmement [kalməmɑ̃] *adv agir* calmly. **la journée s'est passée ~** the day passed quietly.

calmer [kalme] (1) **1** *vt* **(a)** (*apaiser*) *personne* to calm (down), pacify; *querelle, discussion* to quieten down (*Brit*), quiet down (*US*); *sédition, révolte* to calm; (*littér*) *tempête, flots* to calm. **~ les esprits** to calm people down, pacify people; **attends un peu, je vais te ~!*** just you wait, I'll (soon) quieten (*Brit*) *ou* quiet (*US*) you down!

(b) (*réduire*) *douleur, inquiétude* to soothe, ease; *nerfs, agitation, crainte, colère* to calm, soothe; *fièvre* to bring down, reduce, soothe; *impatience* to curb; *faim* to appease; *soif* to quench; *désir, ardeur* to cool, subdue.

2 se calmer *vpr* **(a)** *[personne]* (*s'apaiser*) to calm down, cool down; (*faire moins de bruit*) to quieten down (*Brit*), quiet down (*US*); (*se tranquilliser*) to calm down; *[discussion, querelle]* to quieten down (*Brit*), quiet down (*US*); *[tempête]* to calm down, die down; *[mer]* to calm down.

(b) (*diminuer*) *[douleur]* to ease, subside; *[faim, soif, inquiétude]* to ease; *[crainte, impatience, fièvre]* to subside; *[colère, désir, ardeur]* to cool, subside.

calomel [kalɔmɛl] *nm* calomel.

calomniateur, -trice [kalɔmnjatœʀ, tʀis] (*V* **calomnier**) **1** *adj* slanderous; libellous. **2** *nm,f* slanderer; libeller.

calomnie [kalɔmni] *nf* slander, calumny; (*écrite*) libel; (*sens affaibli*) maligning (*U*). **cette ~ l'avait profondément blessé** he'd been deeply hurt by this slander *ou* calumny; **écrire une ~/des ~s** to write something libellous/libellous things; **dire une ~/des ~s** to say something slanderous/slanderous things.

calomnier [kalɔmnje] (7) *vt* (*diffamer*) to slander; (*par écrit*) to libel; (*sens affaibli: vilipender*) to malign.

calomnieux, -euse [kalɔmnjø, øz] *adj* (*V* **calomnier**) slanderous; libellous.

calorie [kalɔʀi] *nf* calorie. **aliment riche/pauvre en ~s** food with a high/low calorie content, high-/low-calorie food; **ça donne des ~s*** it warms you up; **tu aurais besoin de ~s!*** you need building up!

calorifère [kalɔʀifɛʀ] **1** *adj* heat-giving. **2** *nm* (†) stove.

calorifique [kalɔʀifik] *adj* calorific.

calorifuge [kalɔʀifyʒ] *adj* (heat-)insulating, heat-retaining.

calorifugeage [kalɔʀifyʒaʒ] *nm* lagging, insulation, insulating.

calorifuger [kalɔʀifyʒe] (3) *vt* to lag, insulate (against loss of heat).

calorimètre [kalɔʀimɛtʀ(ə)] *nm* calorimeter.

calorimétrie [kalɔʀimetʀi] *nf* calorimetry.

calorimétrique [kalɔʀimetʀik] *adj* calorimetric(al).

calot [kalo] *nm* **(a)** (*coiffure*) forage cap. **(b)** (*bille*) (large) marble.

calotin, e [kalɔtɛ̃, in] (*péj*) **1** *adj* sanctimonious, churchy. **2** *nm, f* (*bigot*) bigot, sanctimonious churchgoer.

calotte [kalɔt] **1** *nf* **(a)** (*bonnet*) skullcap.

(b) (*péj*) **la ~** (*le clergé*) the priests, the cloth; (*le parti dévot*) the church party.

(c) (*partie supérieure*) *[chapeau]* crown; (*Archit*) *[voûte]* calotte.

(d) (*: *gifle*) slap. **il m'a donné une ~** he gave me a slap *ou* a box on the ears*.

2: la calotte des cieux the dome *ou* vault of heaven; (*Anat*) **calotte crânienne** top of the skull; (*Géog*) **calotte glaciaire** icecap; **calotte sphérique** segment of a sphere.

calotter* [kalɔte] (1) *vt* (*gifler*) to cuff, box the ears of, clout*.

calquage [kalkaʒ] *nm* tracing.

calque [kalk(ə)] *nm* **(a)** (*dessin*) tracing. **prendre un ~ d'un plan** to trace a plan.

(b) (**papier-)~** tracing paper.

(c) (*fig: reproduction*) *[œuvre d'art]* exact copy; *[incident, événement]* carbon copy; *[personne]* spitting image.

(d) (*Ling*) calque.

calquer [kalke] (1) *vt* (*copier*) *plan, dessin* to trace; (*fig*) to copy exactly; (*Ling*) to translate literally *ou* by calque, use a calque to translate. ~ **son comportement sur celui de son voisin** to model one's behaviour on that of one's neighbour, copy one's neighbour's behaviour exactly.

calter‡ *vi*, **se calter‡** *vpr* [kalte] (1) (*décamper*) to scarper‡ (*Brit*), make o.s. scarce‡, buzz off‡ (*Brit*).

calumet [kalymɛ] *nm* calumet. **fumer le ~ de la paix** (*lit*) to smoke the pipe of peace; (*fig*) to bury the hatchet.

calva* [kalva] *nm abrév de* **calvados.**

calvados [kalvados] *nm* (*eau-de-vie*) calvados.

calvaire [kalvɛʀ] *nm* **(a)** (*croix*) (*au bord de la route*) wayside cross *ou* crucifix, calvary; (*peinture*) Calvary, road *ou* way to the Cross.

(b) (*épreuve*) suffering, martyrdom. **le ~ du Christ** Christ's martyrdom *ou* suffering (on the cross); **sa vie fut un long ~** his life was one long martyrdom *ou* agony *ou* tale of suffering; **un enfant comme ça, c'est un ~ pour la mère** a child like that must be a sore *ou* bitter trial *ou* sore burden to his mother.

(c) (*Rel*) **Le C~** Calvary.

calvinisme [kalvinism(ə)] *nm* Calvinism.

calviniste [kalvinist(ə)] **1** *adj* Calvinist, Calvinistic. **2** *nmf* Calvinist.

calvitie [kalvisi] *nf* baldness (*U*). **~ précoce** premature baldness (*U*).

camaïeu [kamajø] *nm* (*peinture*) monochrome. **en ~** *paysage, motif* monochrome (*épith*), en camaïeu; **en ~ bleu** in blue monochrome; **peint en ~** painted in monochrome *ou* en camaïeu.

camail [kamaj] *nm* (*Rel*) cappa magna.

camarade [kamaʀad] **1** *nmf* companion, friend, mate*, pal*. (*Pol*) **le ~ X** comrade X; **elle voyait en lui un bon ~** she saw him as a good companion.

2: camarade d'atelier workmate; **camarade d'école** schoolmate, school friend; **camarade d'étude** fellow student; **camarade de jeu** playmate; **camarade de régiment** mate from one's army days, army mate.

camaraderie [kamaʀadʀi] *nf* good-companionship, good-fellowship, camaraderie. **la ~ mène à l'amitié** good-companionship *ou* a sense of companionship leads to friendship.

camard, e [kamaʀ, aʀd(ə)] *adj nez* pug (*épith*); *personne* pug-nosed.

camarguais, e [kamaʀgɛ, ɛz] **1** *adj* of *ou* from the Camargue. **2** *nm,f*: **C~(e)** inhabitant *ou* native of the Camargue.

cambiste [kɑ̃bist(ə)] *nm* foreign exchange broker *ou* dealer; *[devises des touristes]* moneychanger.

Cambodge [kɑ̃bɔdʒ] *nm* Cambodia.

cambodgien, -ienne [kɑ̃bɔdʒjɛ̃, jɛn] **1** *adj* Cambodian. **2** *nm,f*: **C~(ne)** Cambodian.

cambouis [kɑ̃bwi] *nm* dirty oil *ou* grease.

cambrage [kɑ̃bʀaʒ] *nm* (*Tech*: *V* **cambrer**) bending; curving; arching.

cambré, e [kɑ̃bʀe] (*ptp de* **cambrer**) *adj*: **avoir les reins ~s** to have an arched back; **avoir le pied très ~** to have very high insteps *ou* arches; **chaussures ~es** shoes with a high instep.

cambrement [kɑ̃bʀəmɑ̃] *nm* = **cambrage.**

cambrer [kɑ̃bʀe] (1) **1** *vt* **(a)** *pied* to arch. **~ la taille** *ou* **le corps** *ou* **les reins** to throw back one's shoulders, arch one's back.

(b) (*Tech*) *pièce de bois* to bend; *métal* to curve; *tige, semelle* to arch.

2 se cambrer *vpr* (*se redresser*) to throw back one's shoulders, arch one's back.

cambrien, -ienne [kɑ̃bʀijɛ̃, ijɛn] *adj, nm* Cambrian.

cambriolage [kɑ̃bʀijɔlaʒ] *nm* (*activité, méthode*) burglary, housebreaking, breaking and entering (*Jur*); (*coup*) break-in, burglary.

cambrioler [kɑ̃bʀijɔle] (1) *vt* to break into, burgle, burglarize (*US*).

cambrioleur [kɑ̃bʀijɔlœʀ] *nm* burglar, housebreaker.

cambrouse‡ [kɑ̃bʀuz] *nf*, **cambrousse‡** [kɑ̃bʀus] *nf* (*campagne*) country. **en pleine ~** in the middle of nowhere, at the back of beyond; (*péj*) **frais arrivé de sa ~** fresh from the backwoods.

cambrure [kɑ̃bʀyʀ] *nf* **(a)** (*courbe, forme*) *[poutre, taille, reins]* curve; *[semelle, pied]* arch; *[route]* camber. **sa ~ de militaire** his military bearing.

(b) (*partie*) **~ du pied** instep; **~ des reins** small *ou* hollow of the back; **pieds qui ont une forte ~** feet with a high instep; **reins qui ont une forte ~** back which is very hollow *ou* arched.

cambuse [kɑ̃byz] *nf* **(a)** (‡) (*chambre*) dump‡, hole‡; (*péj*: *maison*) hovel. **(b)** (*Naut*) storeroom.

came[1] [kam] *nf* (*Tech*) cam; *V* **arbre.**

came[2] [kam] *nf* (*arg Drogue*) snow (*arg*), junk (*arg*), stuff (*arg*); (‡: *marchandise*) stuff*; (*péj*: *pacotille*) junk*, trash*.

camé, e[1] [kame] *nm,f* (*arg Drogue*) junkie (*arg*).

camée[2] [kame] *nm* cameo.

caméléon [kameleɔ̃] *nm* (*Zool*) chameleon; (*fig*) chameleon, turncoat.

camélia [kamelja] *nm* camellia.

camelot [kamlo] *nm* street pedlar *ou* vendor. (*Hist*) **les C~s du roi** *militant royalist group in 1930s.*

camelote [kamlɔt] *nf* (*pacotille*) junk*, trash*, rubbish; (*: *marchandise*) stuff*.

camembert [kamɑ̃bɛʀ] *nm* Camembert (cheese).

caméra [kameʀa] *nf* (*Ciné, TV*) camera; *[amateur]* cine-camera, movie camera (*US*).

cameriste [kameʀist(ə)] *nf* (*femme de chambre*) chambermaid; (*Hist*) lady-in-waiting.

Cameroun [kamʀun] *nm* Cameroon; (*Hist*) Cameroons.

camerounais, e [kamʀunɛ, ɛz] **1** *adj* Cameroonian. **2** *nm,f*: **C~(e)** Cameroonian.

camion [kamjɔ̃] **1** *nm* **(a)** (*véhicule*) (*ouvert*) lorry (*Brit*), truck (*US*); (*fermé*) van, truck (*US*).

(b) (*chariot*) wag(g)on, dray.

(c) *[peintre]* (*seau*) (paint-)pail.

2: camion-citerne *nm, pl* **camions-citernes** tanker (lorry) (*Brit*), tank truck (*US*); **camion de déménagement** removal van, pantechnicon (*Brit*); **camion (à) remorque** lorry (*Brit*) *ou* truck (*US*) with a trailer; **camion (à) semi-remorque** articulated lorry (*Brit*), trailer truck (*US*).

camionnage [kamjɔnaʒ] *nm* haulage, transport.

camionnette [kamjɔnɛt] *nf* (small) van.

camionneur [kamjɔnœʀ] *nm* (*chauffeur*) lorry (*Brit*) *ou* truck (*US*) driver; van driver; (*entrepreneur*) haulage contractor (*Brit*), road haulier (*Brit*).

camisole [kamizɔl] **1** *nf* (††) (*blouse*) camisole†; (*chemise de nuit*) nightshirt. **2: camisole de force** strait jacket.

camomille [kamɔmij] *nf* (*Bot*) camomile; (*tisane*) camomile tea.

camouflage [kamuflaʒ] *nm* **(a)** (*Mil*) (*action*) camouflaging; (*résultat*) camouflage. **(b)** (*gén*) *[argent]* concealing, hiding; *[erreur]* camouflaging, covering-up. **le ~ d'un crime en accident** disguising a crime as an accident.

camoufler [kamufle] (1) *vt* (*Mil*) to camouflage; (*fig*) (*cacher*) *argent* to conceal, hide; *erreur, embarras* to conceal, cover up; (*déguiser*) *défaite, intentions* to disguise. **~ un crime en accident** to disguise a crime as an accident *ou* to look like an accident.

camouflet [kamuflɛ] *nm* (*littér*) snub. **donner un ~ à qn** to snub sb.

camp [kɑ̃] **1** *nm* **(a)** (*Mil, Sport, emplacement*) camp. **~ de prisonniers/de réfugiés/de vacances** prison/refugee/holiday (*Brit*) camp; **rentrer au ~** to come *ou* go back to camp; *V* **aide, feu[1]** *etc.*

(b) (*séjour*) **faire un ~ d'une semaine dans les Pyrénées** to go camping for a week *ou* go for a week's camping holiday (*Brit*) *ou* vacation (*US*) in the Pyrenees; **le ~ vous fait découvrir beaucoup de choses** camping lets you discover lots of things.

(c) (*parti, faction*) (*Jeu, Sport*) side; (*Pol*) camp. **changer de ~** *[joueur]* to change sides; *[soldat]* to go over to the other side; (*fig*) **à cette nouvelle la consternation/l'espoir changea de ~** on hearing this, it was the other side which began to feel dismay/hopeful; **dans le ~ opposé/victorieux** in the opposite/winning camp; **passer au ~ adverse** to go over to the opposite camp.

2: camp de base base camp; **camp de concentration** concentration camp; **camp d'extermination** death camp; (*Mil*) **camp retranché** fortified camp; **camp de toile** campsite, camping site; **camp volant** camping tour *ou* trip; (*Mil*) temporary camp; (*fig*) **vivre** *ou* **être en camp volant** to live out of a suitcase.

campagnard, e [kɑ̃paɲaʀ, aʀd(ə)] **1** *adj vie, allure, manières* country (*épith*); (*péj*) rustic (*péj*); *V* **gentilhomme. 2** *nm* countryman, country fellow; (*péj*) rustic (*péj*). **~s** countryfolk; (*péj*) rustics (*péj*). **3 campagnarde** *nf* countrywoman, country lass.

campagne [kɑ̃paɲ] *nf* **(a)** (*gén*: *habitat*) country; (*paysage*) countryside; (*Agr*: *champs ouverts*) open country. **la ville et la ~** town and country; **la ~ anglaise** the English countryside; **dans la ~ environnante** in the surrounding countryside; **nous sommes tombés en panne en pleine ~** we broke down right in the middle of the country(-side) *ou* away out in the country; **à la ~** in the country; **auberge/chemin de ~** country inn/lane; **les travaux de la ~** farm *ou* agricultural work; *V* **battre, maison** *etc.*

(b) (*Mil*) campaign. **faire ~** to fight (a campaign); **les troupes en ~** the troops on campaign *ou* in the field; **entrer en ~** to embark on a campaign; **la ~ d'Italie/de Russie** the Italian/Russian campaign; **artillerie/canon de ~** field artillery/gun; *V* **tenue.**

(c) (*Pol, Presse etc*) campaign (*pour* for, *contre* against). **~ électorale** election campaign; **~ commerciale** marketing *ou* sales campaign, sales drive; (*Pol*) **faire ~ pour un candidat** to campaign *ou* canvass for *ou* on behalf of a candidate; **partir en ~** to launch a campaign (*contre* against); **mener une ~ pour/contre** to campaign for/against, lead a campaign for/against; **tout le monde se mit en ~ pour lui trouver une maison** everybody set to work *ou* got busy to find him a house.

campagnol [kɑ̃paɲɔl] *nm* vole.

campanile [kɑ̃panil] *nm* *[église]* campanile; (*clocheton*) bell-tower.

campanule [kɑ̃panyl] *nf* bellflower, campanula.

campement [kɑ̃pmɑ̃] *nm* (*camp*) camp, encampment. **matériel de ~** camping equipment; **chercher un ~ pour la nuit** to look for somewhere to set up camp *ou* for a camping place for the night; **établir son ~ sur les bords d'un fleuve** to set up one's camp on the bank of a river; **~ de nomades/d'Indiens** camp *ou* encampment of nomads/of Indians; (*Mil*) **revenir à son ~** to return to camp; (*hum*) **on était en ~ dans le salon** we were camping out in the lounge.

camper [kɑ̃pe] (1) **1** *vi* (*lit*) to camp. (*fig hum*) **on campait à l'hôtel/dans le salon** we were camping out at *ou* in a hotel/in the lounge.

2 *vt* **(a)** *troupes* to camp out. **campés pour 2 semaines près du village** camped (out) for 2 weeks by the village.

(b) (*fig*: *esquisser*) *caractère, personnage* to portray; *récit* to construct; *portrait* to fashion, shape. **personnage bien campé** vividly sketched *ou* portrayed character.

(c) (*fig*: *poser*) **~ sa casquette sur l'oreille** to pull *ou* clap one's cap on firmly over one ear; **se ~ des lunettes sur le nez** to plant* a pair of glasses on one's nose.

3 se camper *vpr*: **se ~ devant** to plant o.s. in front of; **se ~ sur ses jambes** to plant o.s. *ou* stand firmly on one's feet.

campeur, -euse [kɑ̃pœʀ, øz] *nm,f* camper.

camphre [kɑ̃fʀ(ə)] *nm* camphor.

camphré, e [kɑ̃fʀe] *adj* camphorated; *V* **alcool.**

camphrier [kɑ̃fʀije] *nm* camphor tree.

camping [kɑ̃piŋ] *nm* **(a)** (*activité*) **le ~** camping; **faire du ~** to go camping. **(b)** (*lieu*) campsite, camping site.

campos† [kɑ̃po] *nm*: **demain on a ~** tomorrow is a day off, we've got tomorrow off *ou* free; **on a eu** *ou* **on nous a donné ~ à 4 heures** we were free *ou* told to go at 4 o'clock, we were free from 4 o'clock.

campus [kɑ̃pys] *nm* campus.

camus, e [kamy, yz] *adj nez* pug (*épith*); *personne* pug-nosed.

Canada [kanada] *nm* Canada.

canadianisme [kanadjanism(ə)] *nm* Canadianism.

canadien, -ienne [kanadjɛ̃, jɛn] **1** *adj* Canadian. **2** *nm,f*: **C~(ne)** Canadian; **C~(ne) français(e)** French Canadian. **3 canadienne** *nf* (*veste*) fur-lined jacket; (*canoë*) (Canadian) canoe; (*tente*) (ridge) tent.

canaille [kanɑj] **1** *adj inv air, manières* low, cheap, coarse. **sous ses airs ~s, il est sérieux** despite his spiv-like (*Brit*) *ou* flashy appearance he is reliable.

2 *nf* (*péj*) (*salaud*) bastard**:** (*péj*); (*escroc*) scoundrel, crook (*péj*); (*hum: enfant*) rascal, rogue, (little) devil. (*la populace*) **la ~†** the rabble (*péj*), the riffraff (*péj*).

canaillerie [kanɑjʀi] *nf* **(a)** *[allure, ton, manières]* lowness, cheapness, coarseness. **(b)** (*malhonnêteté*) *[procédés, personne]* crookedness. **(c)** (*action malhonnête*) dirty *ou* low trick.

canal, *pl* **-aux** [kanal, o] **1** *nm* **(a)** (*artificiel*) canal; (*détroit*) channel; (*tuyau, fossé*) conduit, duct; (*Anat*) canal, duct; (*TV*) channel.

(b) (*intermédiaire*) **par le ~ d'un collègue** through *ou* via a colleague; **par le ~ de la presse** through the medium of the press; (*littér*) **par un ~ amical** through a friendly channel.

2: **canal d'amenée** feeder canal; (*Anat*) **canal biliaire** biliary canal, bile duct; **canal déférent** vas deferens; **canal de dérivation** diversion canal; **canal de fuite** tail-race; **canal d'irrigation** irrigation canal; **canal maritime** ship canal; (*Anat, Bot*) **canal médullaire** medullary cavity *ou* canal; **canal de navigation** ship canal; **le Canal de Suez** the Suez Canal.

canalisation [kanalizɑsjɔ̃] *nf* **(a)** (*tuyau*) (main) pipe. **~s** (*réseau*) pipes, piping; (*Élec*) cables. **(b)** (*aménagement*) *[cours d'eau]* canalization.

canaliser [kanalize] (1) *vt* **(a)** *foule, demandes, pensées* to channel. **(b)** *fleuve* to canalize; *région, plaine* to provide with a network of canals.

cananéen, -éenne [kananeɛ̃, eɛn] **1** *adj* Canaanite. **2** *nm* (*Ling*) Canaanite. **3** *nm,f*: **C~(ne)** Canaanite.

canapé [kanape] *nm* **(a)** (*meuble*) sofa, settee, couch. **~ transformable** *ou* **convertible, ~-lit** bed settee, day bed.

(b) (*Culin*) open sandwich, canapé. **crevettes sur ~** shrimp canapé, canapé of shrimps.

canard [kanaʀ] **1** *nm* **(a)** (*oiseau, Culin*) duck; (*mâle*) drake; *V* **froid, mare.**

(b) (*) (*journal*) rag*; (*fausse nouvelle*) false report, rumour, canard.

(c) (*Mus: couac*) false note. **faire un ~** to hit a false note.

(d) (*terme d'affection*) **mon (petit) ~** pet, poppet* (*Brit*).

(e) (*: *sucre arrosé*) *sugar lump dipped in brandy or coffee.* **tu veux (prendre) un ~?** would you like to dip a sugar lump (in the brandy *etc*)?

2: **canard de Barbarie** Muscovy *ou* musk duck; (*Culin*) **canard à l'orange** duck in orange sauce.

canardeau, *pl* **~x** [kanaʀdo] *nm* duckling.

canarder* [kanaʀde] (1) *vt* (*au fusil*) to snipe at, take potshots at; (*avec des pierres etc*) to pelt (*avec* with). **~ qn avec des boules de neige** to pelt sb with snowballs; **ça canardait de tous les côtés** there was firing *ou* firing was going on on all sides.

canardière [kanaʀdjɛʀ] *nf* (*mare*) duck-pond; (*fusil*) punt gun.

canari [kanaʀi] *nm* canary. **(jaune) ~** canary (yellow).

Canaries [kanaʀi] *nfpl*: **les (îles) ~** the Canary Islands.

canasson [kanasɔ̃] *nm* (*péj: cheval*) nag (*péj*).

canasta [kanasta] *nf* canasta.

cancan [kɑ̃kɑ̃] *nm* **(a)** (*racontar*) piece of gossip. **~s** gossip; **dire des ~s (sur qn)** to spread gossip *ou* stories (about sb), tittle-tattle (about sb). **(b)** (*danse*) cancan.

cancaner [kɑ̃kane] (1) *vi* **(a)** (*bavarder*) to gossip; (*médire*) to spread scandal *ou* gossip, tittle-tattle. **(b)** *[canard]* to quack.

cancanier, -ière [kɑ̃kanje, jɛʀ] **1** *adj* gossipy, scandal-mongering (*épith*), tittle-tattling (*épith*). **2** *nm,f* gossip, scandalmonger, tittle-tattle.

cancer [kɑ̃sɛʀ] *nm* **(a)** (*Méd, fig*) cancer. **avoir un ~ du sein/du poumon** to have breast/lung cancer; **~ du sang** leukaemia. **(b)** (*Astron*) **le C~** Cancer, the Crab; **être (du) C~** to be Cancer *ou* a Cancerian.

cancéreux, -euse [kɑ̃seʀø, øz] **1** *adj tumeur* cancerous; *personne* with cancer. **2** *nm,f* person with cancer; (*à l'hôpital*) cancer patient.

cancérigène [kɑ̃seʀiʒɛn] *adj*, **cancérogène** [kɑ̃seʀɔʒɛn] *adj* carcinogenic, cancer-producing.

cancérologie [kɑ̃seʀɔlɔʒi] *nf* cancerology.

cancérologue [kɑ̃seʀɔlɔg] *nmf* cancerologist.

cancre [kɑ̃kʀ(ə)] *nm* (*péj: élève*) dunce.

cancrelat [kɑ̃kʀəla] *nm* cockroach.

candélabre [kɑ̃delabʀ(ə)] *nm* (*chandelier*) candelabra, candelabrum.

candeur [kɑ̃dœʀ] *nf* ingenuousness, guilelessness, naïvety.

candi [kɑ̃di] *adj m V* **sucre.**

candidat, e [kɑ̃dida, at] *nm,f [examen, élection]* candidate (*à* at); *[poste]* applicant, candidate (*à* for). **être ~ à la députation** ≈ to stand for Parliament (*Brit*), ≈ run for congress (*US*); **être ~ à un poste** to be an applicant *ou* a candidate for a job, have applied for a job; **se porter ~ à un poste** to apply for a job, put o.s. forward for a job.

candidature [kɑ̃didatyʀ] *nf* (*Pol*) candidature, candidacy (*US*); *[poste]* application (*à* for). **poser sa ~ à** *poste* to apply for, submit one's application for; *élection* to stand (*Brit*) *ou* put o.s. forward as a candidate in.

candide [kɑ̃did] *adj* ingenuous, guileless, naïve.

candidement [kɑ̃didmɑ̃] *adv* ingenuously, guilelessly, naïvely.

candir [kɑ̃diʀ] (2) *vi*: **faire ~** to candy.

cane [kan] *nf* (female) duck.

caner: [kane] (1) *vi* (*mourir*) to kick the bucket**:**, snuff it**:**; (*flancher*) to chicken out**:**, funk it**:** (*devant* in the face of).

caneton [kantɔ̃] *nm* duckling.

canette¹ [kanɛt] *nf* duckling.

canette² [kanɛt] *nf [machine à coudre]* spool; (*bouteille*) bottle (of beer).

canevas [kanva] *nm* **(a)** *[livre, discours]* framework, basic structure. **(b)** (*Couture*) (*toile*) canvas; (*ouvrage*) tapestry (work). **(c)** (*Cartographie*) network.

caniche [kaniʃ] *nm* poodle. **~ nain** toy poodle.

caniculaire [kanikylɛʀ] *adj chaleur, jour* scorching. **une journée ~** a scorcher*, a scorching (hot) day.

canicule [kanikyl] *nf* (*forte chaleur*) scorching heat. **une ~ qui dure depuis 3 jours** a heatwave which has been going on for 3 days; (*spécialement juillet-août*) **la ~** the midsummer heat, the dog days; **cette ~ précoce** this early (summer) heatwave; **aujourd'hui c'est la ~** today is *ou* it's a scorcher.

canif [kanif] *nm* penknife, pocket knife.

canin, e [kanɛ̃, in] **1** *adj espèce* canine; *exposition* dog (*épith*). **2 canine** *nf* (*dent*) canine (tooth), eye tooth.

caniveau, *pl* **~x** [kanivo] *nm* gutter (*in roadway etc*).

cannage [kanaʒ] *nm* (*partie cannée*) canework; (*opération*) caning.

canne [kan] **1** *nf* (*bâton*) (walking) stick, cane; *[souffleur de verre]* rod; *V* **sucre. 2**: **canne-épée** *nf, pl* **cannes-épées** sword-stick; **canne à pêche** fishing rod; **canne à sucre** sugar cane.

canné, e [kane] (*ptp de* **canner**) *adj siège* cane (*épith*).

cannelé, e [kanle] (*ptp de* **canneler**) *adj colonne* fluted.

canneler [kanle] (4) *vt* to flute.

cannelier [kanəlje] *nm* cinnamon tree.

cannelle [kanɛl] *nf* (*Culin*) cinnamon; (*robinet*) tap, spigot.

cannelure [kanlyʀ] *nf [meuble, colonne]* flute; *[plante]* striation. **~s** *[colonne]* fluting; *[neige]* corrugation; (*Géol*) **~s glaciaires** striae, striations.

canner [kane] (1) *vt chaise* to cane.

cannette [kanɛt] *nf* = **canette².**

canneur, -euse [kanœʀ, øz] *nm,f* cane worker, caner.

cannibale [kanibal] **1** *adj tribu, animal* cannibal (*épith*). **2** *nmf* cannibal, man-eater.

cannibalisme [kanibalism(ə)] *nm* cannibalism.

canoë [kanɔe] *nm* canoe. **faire du ~** to go canoeing, canoe.

canoéiste [kanɔeist(ə)] *nmf* canoeist.

canon¹ [kanɔ̃] **1** *nm* **(a)** (*arme*) gun; (*Hist*) cannon. **~ de 75/125** 75/125-mm gun; *V* **chair, coup.**

(b) (*tube*) *[fusil, revolver]* barrel. **à deux ~s** double-barrelled; *V* **baïonnette.**

(c) (*Tech*) *[clef, seringue]* barrel; *[arrosoir]* spout.

(d) (*Vét*) *[bœuf, cheval]* cannonbone.

(e) (*Hist Habillement*) canion.

(f) (*: *verre*) glass (of wine).

2: (*Mil*) **canon anti-aérien** anti-aircraft *ou* A.A. gun; (*Mil*) **canon anti-char** anti-tank gun; **canon anti-grêle** anti-hail gun; (*Phys*) **canon à électrons** electron gun; **canon lisse** smooth bore; **canon de marine** naval gun; **canon rayé** rifled barrel.

canon² [kanɔ̃] *nm* **(a)** (*norme, modèle*) model, perfect example. (*normes, code*) **~s** canons. **(b)** (*Rel*) (*loi*) canon; *[messe, Nouveau Testament]* canon; *V* **droit³.**

canon³ [kanɔ̃] *nm* (*Mus*) **~ à 2 voix** canon for 2 voices; **chanter en ~** to sing in a round *ou* in canon.

cañon [kaɲɔ̃] *nm* canyon, cañon.

canonique [kanɔnik] *adj* canonical; *V* **âge.**

canonisation [kanɔnizɑsjɔ̃] *nf* canonization.

canoniser [kanɔnize] (1) *vt* to canonize.

canonnade [kanɔnad] *nf* cannonade. **le bruit d'une ~** the noise of a cannonade *ou* of (heavy) gunfire.

canonner [kanɔne] (1) *vt* to bombard, shell.

canonnier [kanɔnje] *nm* gunner.

canonnière [kanɔnjɛʀ] *nf* gunboat.

canot [kano] *nm* (*barque*) (small *ou* open) boat, ding(h)y; (*Can*) Canadian canoe. **~ automobile** motorboat; **~ de pêche** (open) fishing boat; **~ pneumatique** rubber *ou* inflatable ding(h)y; **~ de sauvetage** lifeboat.

canotage [kanɔtaʒ] *nm* boating, rowing; (*Can*) canoeing. **faire du ~** to go boating *ou* rowing; (*Can*) to go canoeing.

canoter [kanɔte] (1) *vi* to go boating *ou* rowing *ou* (*Can*) canoeing.

canoteur [kanɔtœʀ] *nm* rower.

canotier [kanɔtje] *nm* (*chapeau*) boater.

cantaloup [kɑ̃talu] *nm* cantaloup, muskmelon.

cantate [kɑ̃tat] *nf* cantata.

cantatrice [kɑ̃tatʀis] *nf [opéra]* (opera) singer, prima donna; *[chants classiques]* (professional) singer.

cantilène [kɑ̃tilɛn] *nf* song, cantilena.

cantine [kɑ̃tin] *nf* **(a)** (*réfectoire*) *[usine]* canteen; *[école]* (*lieu*)

dining hall; (*service*) school meals *ou* dinners. **manger à la ~** to eat in the canteen; to have school meals. **(b)** (*malle*) tin trunk.
cantinière [kɑ̃tinjɛʀ] *nf* (*Hist Mil*) canteen woman.
cantique [kɑ̃tik] *nm* (*chant*) hymn; *[Bible]* canticle. **le ~ des ~s** the Song of Songs, the Song of Solomon.
canton [kɑ̃tɔ̃] *nm* **(a)** (*Pol*) (*en France*) canton, ≃ district; (*en Suisse*) canton. **(b)** (*section*) *[voie ferrée, route]* section. **(c)** (†: *région*) district; (*Can*) township.
cantonade [kɑ̃tɔnad] *nf*: **à la ~** (*à personne en particulier*) to everyone in general; (*sur les toits, à tout venant*) **crier à la ~ que** to tell the whole world that, shout from the housetops *ou* rooftops that; (*Théât*) **parler à la ~** to speak off.
cantonais, e [kɑ̃tɔnɛ, ɛz] **1** *adj* Cantonese. **2** *nm* (*Ling*) Cantonese. **3** *nm,f*: **C~(e)** Cantonese.
cantonal, e, *mpl* **-aux** [kɑ̃tɔnal, o] *adj* (*en France*) cantonal, ≃ district (*épith*); (*en Suisse*) cantonal. **sur le plan ~** at (the) local level; at the level of the cantons.
cantonnement [kɑ̃tɔnmɑ̃] *nm* (*V* **cantonner**) (*Mil*) (*action*) stationing; billeting, quartering; (*lieu*) quarters (*pl*), billet; camp. **établir un ~ en pleine nature** to set up (a) camp in the wilds.
cantonner [kɑ̃tɔne] (1) **1** *vt* (*Mil*) to station; (*chez l'habitant etc*) to quarter, billet (*chez, dans* on). (*fig*) **~ qn dans un travail** to confine sb to a job. **2** *vi* (*Mil*) *[troupe]* to be quartered *ou* billetted; be stationed (*à, dans* at). **3 se cantonner** *vpr*: **se ~ dans** (*s'isoler dans, se limiter à*) to confine o.s. to.
cantonnier [kɑ̃tɔnje] *nm* (*ouvrier*) roadmender, roadman.
cantonnière [kɑ̃tɔnjɛʀ] *nf* (*tenture*) pelmet.
canular [kanylaʀ] *nm* (*farce, mystification*) hoax. **monter un ~** to think up *ou* plan a hoax; **faire un ~ à qn** to hoax sb, play a hoax on sb.
canule [kanyl] *nf* cannula.
canuler‡ [kanyle] (1) *vt* (*ennuyer*) to bore; (*agacer*) to pester. **qu'est-ce qu'il est canulant avec ses histoires** what a pain (in the neck) he is‡ *ou* he really gets you down with his stories.
canut, -use [kany, yz] *nm,f* (*† rare*) silk worker (*at Lyons*).
caoutchouc [kautʃu] *nm* **(a)** (*matière*) rubber. **en ~** rubber (*épith*); ® **~ mousse** foam *ou* sponge rubber; **une balle en ~ mousse** a rubber *ou* sponge ball; *V* **botte**[1].
(b) (*élastique*) rubber *ou* elastic band.
(c) (†) (*imperméable*) waterproof. (*chaussures*) **~s** overshoes, galoshes.
caoutchouter [kautʃute] (1) *vt* to rubberize, coat with rubber.
caoutchouteux, -euse [kautʃutø, øz] *adj* rubbery.
cap [kap] **1** *nm* **(a)** (*Géog*) cape; (*promontoire*) point, headland. **le ~ Horn** Cape Horn; **le ~ de Bonne Espérance** the Cape of Good Hope; (*Naut*) **passer** *ou* **doubler un ~** to round a cape; *[malade etc]* **il a passé le ~** he's over the hump *ou* the worst; **il a passé le ~ de l'examen** he has got over the hurdle of the exam; **dépasser** *ou* **franchir le ~ des 40 ans** to turn 40; **dépasser** *ou* **franchir le ~ des 50 millions** to pass the 50-million mark.
(b) (*direction*) (*lit, fig*) **changer de ~** to change course; (*Naut*) **mettre le ~ au vent** to head into the wind; **mettre le ~ au large** to stand out to sea; (*Aut, Naut*) **mettre le ~ sur** to head for, steer for; *V* **pied.**
2: cap-hornier *nm, pl* **cap-horniers** Cape Horner.
capable [kapabl(ə)] *adj* **(a)** (*compétent*) able, capable.
(b) (*apte à*) **~ de faire** capable of doing; **te sens-tu ~ de tout manger?** do you feel you can eat it all?, do you feel up to eating it all?; **tu n'en es pas ~** you're not up to it, you're not capable of it; **viens te battre si tu en es ~** come and fight if you've got it in you *ou* if you dare; **cette conférence est ~ d'intéresser beaucoup de gens** this lecture is liable to interest *ou* likely to interest a lot of people.
(c) (*qui peut faire preuve de*) **~ de** *dévouement, courage, éclat, incartade* capable of; **il est ~ du pire comme du meilleur** he's capable of (doing) the worst as well as the best; **il est ~ de tout** he'll stop at nothing, he's capable of anything.
(d) (*) **il est ~ de l'avoir perdu/de réussir** he's quite likely to have lost it/to succeed; **il est bien ~ d'en réchapper** he may well get over it.
(e) (*Jur*) competent.
capacité [kapasite] **1** *nf* **(a)** (*contenance, potentiel*) capacity; (*Élec*) *[accumulateur]* capacitance, capacity.
(b) (*aptitude*) ability. **d'une très grande ~** of very great ability; **~s intellectuelles** intellectual abilities *ou* capacities; **en-dehors de mes ~s** beyond my capabilities *ou* capacities; **sa ~ d'analyse/d'analyser les faits** his capacity for analysis/analysing facts.
(c) (*Jur*) capacity. **avoir ~ pour** to be (legally) entitled to.
2: (*Jur*) **capacité civile** civil capacity; **capacité en droit** *basic legal qualification*; **capacité électrostatique** capacitance; **capacité légale** legal capacity; (*Méd*) **capacité thoracique** vital capacity.
caparaçon [kapaʀasɔ̃] *nm* (*Hist*) caparison.
caparaçonner [kapaʀasɔne] (1) *vt* (*Hist*) *cheval* to caparison. (*fig hum*) **caparaçonné de cuir** all clad in leather.
cape [kap] *nf* (*Habillement*) (*courte*) cape; (*longue*) cloak. **roman/film de ~ et d'épée** swashbuckling novel/film; *V* **rire.**
capeline [kaplin] *nf* wide-brimmed hat.
capésien, -ienne [kapesjɛ̃, jɛn] *nm,f* student preparing the C.A.P.E.S.; holder of the C.A.P.E.S, ≃ qualified graduate teacher.
capétien, -ienne [kapesjɛ̃, jɛn] *adj, nm,f* Capetian.
capharnaüm* [kafaʀnaɔm] *nm* (*bric-à-brac, désordre*) shambles* (*U*), pigsty. **quel ~ dans le grenier** what a pigsty the attic is, what a shambles in the attic.
capillaire [kapilɛʀ] **1** *adj* (*Anat, Bot, Phys*) capillary; *soins, lotion* hair (*épith*); *V* **artiste, vaisseau. 2** *nm* (*Anat*) capillary; (*Bot: fougère*) maidenhair fern.
capillarité [kapilaʀite] *nf* capillarity.
capilliculteur [kapilikyltœʀ] *nm* specialist in hair care.
capilotade [kapilɔtad] *nf*: **en ~** *gâteau* in crumbs; *fruits, visage* in a pulp; *objet cassable* in smithereens; **mettre en ~** (*écraser*) *gâteau* to squash to bits; *fruits* to squash to a pulp; *adversaire* to beat to a pulp; (*casser*) to smash to smithereens; **il avait les reins/les jambes en ~** his back was/his legs were aching like hell‡ *ou* giving him hell‡.
capitaine [kapitɛn] **1** *nm* (*Mil*) (*armée de terre*) captain; (*armée de l'air*) flight lieutenant; (*Naut*) *[grand bateau]* captain, master; *[bateau de pêche etc]* captain, skipper; (*Sport*) captain, skipper*; (*littér: chef militaire*) (military) leader; *V* **instructeur, mon.**
2: capitaine de corvette lieutenant commander; **capitaine de frégate** commander; **capitaine de gendarmerie** ≃ police inspector; **capitaine d'industrie** captain of industry; **capitaine au long cours** master mariner; **capitaine de la marine marchande** captain in the merchant navy; **capitaine des pompiers** fire chief, firemaster (*Brit*); **capitaine de port** harbour master; **capitaine de vaisseau** captain.
capital, e, *mpl* **-aux** [kapital, o] **1** *adj* **(a)** (*fondamental*) *œuvre* major (*épith*), main (*épith*); *point, erreur, question* major (*épith*), chief (*épith*), fundamental; *rôle* cardinal, major (*épith*), fundamental; *importance* cardinal, capital. **d'une importance ~e** of cardinal *ou* capital importance; **lettre ~e** *V* 3; *V* **péché, sept.**
(b) (*principal*) major, main. **c'est l'œuvre ~e de X** it is X's major work; **son erreur ~e est d'avoir ...** his major *ou* chief mistake was to have ... .
(c) (*essentiel*) **il est ~ d'y aller** *ou* **que nous y allions** it is of paramount importance *ou* it is absolutely essential that we go there.
(d) (*Jur*) capital; *V* **peine.**
2 *nm* **(a)** (*Fin: avoirs*) capital. **50 millions de francs de ~** a 50-million-franc capital, a capital of 50 million francs; **au ~ de** with a capital of; *V* **augmentation.**
(b) (*placements*) **~aux** money, capital; **investir des ~aux dans une affaire** to invest money *ou* capital in a business; **la circulation/fuite des ~aux** the circulation/flight of money *ou* capital.
(c) (*possédants*) **le ~** capital; **le ~ et le travail** capital and labour; *V* **grand.**
(d) (*fig: fonds, richesse*) stock, fund. **le ~ de connaissances acquis à l'école** the stock *ou* fund of knowledge acquired at school; **la connaissance d'une langue constitue un ~ appréciable** knowing a language is a significant *ou* major asset; **le ~ artistique du pays** the artistic wealth *ou* resources of the country; **accroître son ~-santé** to build up one's reserves of health.
3 capitale *nf* **(a)** (*Typ*) **(lettre) ~e** capital (letter); **en grandes/petites ~es** in large/small capitals; **en ~es d'imprimerie** in block letters *ou* block capitals.
(b) (*métropole*) capital (city). **Paris est la ~e de la France** Paris is the capital (city) of France; **le dimanche, les Parisiens quittent la ~e** on Sundays Parisians leave the capital; **grande/petite ~e régionale** large/small regional capital; (*fig*) **la ~e du vin/de la soie** the capital of winegrowing/of the silk industry.
4: capital circulant working capital, circulating capital; **capital constant** constant capital; **capital d'exploitation** working capital; **capital fixe** fixed (capital) assets; **capitaux flottants** *ou* **fébriles** hot money; **capital social** authorized capital; **capital variable** variable capital.
capitalisable [kapitalizabl(ə)] *adj* capitalizable.
capitalisation [kapitalizɑsjɔ̃] *nf* capitalization.
capitaliser [kapitalize] (1) **1** *vt* **(a)** (*amasser*) *somme* to amass; (*fig*) *expériences, connaissances* to build up, accumulate. **l'intérêt capitalisé pendant un an** interest accrued *ou* accumulated in a year. **(b)** (*Fin: ajouter au capital*) *intérêts* to capitalize. **(c)** (*calculer le capital de*) *rente* to capitalize. **2** *vi* to save, put money by.
capitalisme [kapitalism(ə)] *nm* capitalism.
capitaliste [kapitalist(ə)] *adj, nmf* capitalist.
capitation [kapitɑsjɔ̃] *nf* (*Hist*) poll tax, capitation.
capiteux, -euse [kapitø, øz] *adj vin, parfum* heady; *femme, beauté* intoxicating, alluring.
capiton [kapitɔ̃] *nm* (*bourre*) padding.
capitonnage [kapitɔnaʒ] *nm* padding.
capitonner [kapitɔne] (1) *vt siège, porte* to pad (*de* with). (*fig*) **capitonné de** lined with; **nid capitonné de plumes** feather-lined nest.
capitulaire [kapitylɛʀ] *adj* (*Rel*) capitular. **salle ~** chapter house.
capitulard, e [kapitylaʀ, aʀd(ə)] (*péj*) **1** *adj* (*Mil*) partisan of surrender; (*fig*) defeatist. **2** *nm,f* (*Mil*) advocate of surrender; (*fig*) defeatist.
capitulation [kapitylɑsjɔ̃] *nf* (*Mil*) (*reddition*) capitulation, surrender; (*traité*) capitulation (treaty); (*fig: défaite, abandon*) capitulation, surrender. **~ sans conditions** unconditional surrender.
capituler [kapityle] (1) *vi* (*Mil: se rendre*) to capitulate, surrender; (*fig: céder*) to surrender, give in, capitulate.
capon, -onne†† [kapɔ̃, ɔn] **1** *adj* cowardly. **2** *nm,f* coward.
caporal, *pl* **-aux** [kapɔʀal, o] *nm* **(a)** (*Mil*) corporal. **~ d'ordinaire** *ou* **de cuisine** mess corporal; **~-chef** corporal. **(b)** (*tabac*) caporal.
caporalisme [kapɔʀalism(ə)] *nm* *[personne, régime]* authoritarianism; (petty) officiousness.
capot [kapo] **1** *nm* **(a)** *[véhicule, moteur]* bonnet (*Brit*), hood (*US*). **(b)** (*Naut*) (*bâche de protection*) cover; (*trou d'homme*)

companion hatch. 2 *adj inv* (*Cartes*) **être** ~ to have lost all the tricks; **il nous a mis** ~ he took all the tricks.
capotage [kapɔtaʒ] *nm [avion, véhicule]* overturning.
capote [kapɔt] *nf* **(a)** *[voiture]* hood (*Brit*), top (*US*). **(b)** (*gén Mil: manteau*) greatcoat. **(c)** (‡) ~ **(anglaise)** French letter‡ (*Brit*), rubber‡, safe‡ (*US*). **(d)** (†: *chapeau*) bonnet.
capoter [kapɔte] (1) **1** *vi [avion, véhicule]* to overturn. **2** *vt* (*Aut*) (*garnir d'une capote*) to fit with a hood, put a hood on; (*abaisser la capote*) to put the hood (up) over.
câpre [kɑpʀ(ə)] *nf* (*Culin*) caper.
caprice [kapʀis] *nm* **(a)** (*lubie*) whim, caprice, capriciousness (*U*); (*toquade amoureuse*) (passing) fancy. **agir par** ~ to act out of caprice *ou* capriciousness; **ne lui cède pas, c'est seulement un** ~ don't give in to him it's only a whim; **faire un** ~ to throw a tantrum; **cet enfant fait des** ~**s** this child is being awkward *ou* capricious; **cet arbre est un vrai** ~ **de la nature** this tree is a real freak of nature; **une récolte exceptionnelle due à quelque** ~ **de la nature** an exceptional crop due to some quirk *ou* trick of nature.
(b) (*variations*) ~**s** (*littér*) *[nuages, vent]* caprices, fickle play; *[chemin]* wanderings, windings; **les** ~**s de la mode** the vagaries *ou* whims of fashion; **les** ~**s du sort** *ou* **du hasard** the quirks of fate.
capricieusement [kapʀisjøzmɑ̃] *adv* capriciously, whimsically.
capricieux, -ieuse [kapʀisjø, jøz] *adj* (*fantasque*) *personne, humeur, destinée* capricious; *personne, esprit* whimsical; (*péj*) *personne, voiture, appareil* temperamental; (*littér*) *brise* capricious; *chemin* winding. **cet enfant est (un)** ~ this child is awkward *ou* capricious, this child throws tantrums.
capricorne [kapʀikɔʀn(ə)] *nm* **(a)** (*Astron*) **le C**~ Capricorn, the Goat; **être (du) C**~ to be (a) Capricorn; *V* **tropique**. **(b)** (*Zool*) capricorn beetle.
câprier [kɑpʀije] *nm* caper (bush *ou* shrub).
caprin, e [kapʀɛ̃, in] *adj* (*Zool*) *espèce* goat (*épith*), caprine (*T*); *allure* goat-like.
capsulage [kapsylaʒ] *nm* capsuling.
capsule [kapsyl] *nf* **(a)** (*Anat, Bot, Pharm*) capsule. ~ **spatiale** space capsule. **(b)** *[bouteille]* capsule, cap. **(c)** *[arme à feu]* (percussion) cap, primer; *[pistolet d'enfant]* cap; *V* **pistolet**.
capsuler [kapsyle] (1) *vt* to put a capsule *ou* cap on.
captage [kaptaʒ] *nm [cours d'eau]* harnessing; *[message, émission]* picking up.
capteur, -trice [kaptatœʀ, tʀis] *nm,f* (*Jur*) ~ **de testament** *ou* **de succession** legacy hunter.
captation [kaptɑsjɔ̃] *nf* (*Jur*) improper sollicitation of a legacy.
capter [kapte] (1) *vt* **(a)** *suffrages, attention* to win, capture; *confiance, faveur, bienveillance* to win, gain. **(b)** (*Téléc*) *message, émission* to pick up. **(c)** *source, cours d'eau* to harness. **(d)** (*Élec*) *courant* to tap.
captieusement [kapsjøzmɑ̃] *adv* (*littér*) speciously.
captieux, -euse [kapsjø, øz] *adj* specious.
captif, -ive [kaptif, iv] **1** *adj soldat, personne* captive; (*Géol*) *nappe d'eau* confined; *V* **ballon**. **2** *nm,f* (*lit, fig*) captive, prisoner.
captivant, e [kaptivɑ̃, ɑ̃t] *adj film, lecture* gripping, enthralling, captivating; *personne* fascinating, captivating.
captiver [kaptive] (1) *vt personne* to fascinate, enthrall, captivate; *attention, esprit* to captivate.
captivité [kaptivite] *nf* captivity.
capture [kaptyʀ] *nf* **(a)** (*action: V* **capturer**) capture; catching. **(b)** (*animal*) catch; (*personne*) capture.
capturer [kaptyʀe] (1) *vt malfaiteur, animal* to catch, capture; *navire* to capture.
capuche [kapyʃ] *nf* hood.
capuchon [kapyʃɔ̃] *nm* **(a)** (*Couture*) hood; (*Rel*) cowl; (*pèlerine*) hooded raincoat. **(b)** *[stylo]* top, cap. **(c)** *[cheminée]* cowl.
capucin [kapysɛ̃] *nm* (*Rel*) Capuchin; (*Zool: singe*) capuchin; *V* **barbe**[1].
capucine [kapysin] *nf* (*Bot*) nasturtium; (*Rel*) Capuchin nun.
caque [kak] *nf* herring barrel. (*Prov*) **la** ~ **sent toujours le hareng** what's bred in the bone will (come) out in the flesh (*Prov*).
caquelon [kaklɔ̃] *nm* earthenware fondue-dish.
caquet [kakɛ] *nm* (*) *[personne]* blether*, gossip, prattle; *[poule]* cackle, cackling. **rabattre** *ou* **rabaisser le** ~ **de** *ou* **à qn*** to bring *ou* pull sb down a peg or two.
caquetage [kaktaʒ] *nm* (*V* **caqueter**) cackle, cackling, blether*.
caqueter [kakte] (4) *vi [personne]* to gossip, cackle, blether*; *[poule]* to cackle.
car[1] [kaʀ] *nm* coach (*Brit*), bus (*US*). ~ **de police** police van; ~ **de (radio-)reportage** outside-broadcasting van.
car[2] [kaʀ] *conj* because, for.
carabin [kaʀabɛ̃] *nm* (*arg Méd*) medical student, medic*.
carabine [kaʀabin] *nf* carbine, rifle. ~ **à air comprimé** air rifle *ou* gun.
carabiné, e* [kaʀabine] *adj fièvre, vent, orage* raging, violent; *cocktail, facture, punition* stiff. **amende** ~**e** heavy *ou* stiff fine; **rhume** ~ stinking‡ *ou* shocking* cold; **mal de tête** ~ splitting *ou* blinding headache; **mal de dents** ~ raging *ou* screaming* (*Brit*) toothache.
carabinier [kaʀabinje] *nm* (*en Espagne*) carabinero, customs officer; (*en Italie*) carabinieri, police officer; (*Hist Mil*) carabineer.
carabosse [kaʀabɔs] *nf V* **fée**.
caraco† [kaʀako] *nm* (woman's) loose blouse.
caracoler [kaʀakɔle] (1) *vi [cheval]* to caracole, prance; *[cavalier]* to caracole; (*fig: gambader*) to gambol *ou* caper about.

caractère [kaʀaktɛʀ] *nm* **(a)** (*tempérament*) character, nature. **être d'un** *ou* **avoir un** ~ **ouvert/fermé** to have an outgoing/withdrawn nature; **être d'un** *ou* **avoir un** ~ **froid/passionné** to be a cold(-natured)/passionate(-natured) person; **avoir bon/mauvais** ~ to be good-/ill-natured, be good-/bad-tempered; **il est très jeune de** ~ *[adolescent]* he's very immature; *[adulte]* he has a very youthful outlook; **son** ~ **a changé** his character has changed; **les chats ont un** ~ **sournois** cats have a sly nature; **il a** *ou* **c'est un heureux** ~ he has a happy nature; **ce n'est pas dans son** ~ **de faire, il n'a pas un** ~ **à faire** it is not in his nature to do, it is not like him to do; **le** ~ **méditerranéen/latin** the Mediterranean/Latin character; **il a un sale** ~* he is a difficult *ou* pig-headed customer; **il a un** ~ **de cochon*** he is an awkward *ou* a cussed* so-and-so*; **il a un** ~ **en or** he's very good-natured, he has a delightful nature.
(b) (*nature, aspect*) nature. **sa présence confère à la réception un** ~ **officiel** his being here gives an official character *ou* flavour to the reception; **la crise n'a aucun** ~ **de gravité** the crisis shows no sign *ou* evidence of seriousness; **le** ~ **difficile de cette mission est évident** the difficult nature of this mission is quite clear; **le récit a le** ~ **d'un plaidoyer** the story is (in the nature of) a passionate plea.
(c) (*fermeté*) character. **il a du** ~ he has *ou* he's got* character; **il n'a pas de** ~ he has no character *ou* spirit *ou* backbone; **un style sans** ~ a characterless style.
(d) (*cachet, individualité*) character. **la maison/cette vieille rue a du** ~ the house/this old street has (got) character.
(e) (*littér: personne*) character. **ces** ~**s ne sont pas faciles à vivre** these characters are not easy to live with; *V* **comique**.
(f) (*gén pl: caractéristique*) characteristic, feature; *[personne]* trait. ~**s nationaux/d'une race** national/racial characteristics *ou* features *ou* traits; ~ **héréditaire/acquis** hereditary/acquired characteristic *ou* feature.
(g) (*Écriture, Typ*) character. ~ **gras/maigre** heavy-/light-faced letter; (*Typ*) ~**s gras** bold type (*U*); **écrire en gros/petits** ~**s** to write in large/small characters; **écrivez en** ~**s d'imprimerie** write in block capitals; **les** ~**s de ce livre sont agréables à l'œil** the print of this book is easy on the eye.
caractériel, -elle [kaʀaktɛʀjɛl] *adj traits* character (*épith*), of character. **troubles** ~**s** emotional disturbance; **un (enfant)** ~ an emotionally disturbed child, a problem child.
caractérisation [kaʀakteʀizɑsjɔ̃] *nf* characterization.
caractérisé, e [kaʀakteʀize] (*ptp de* **caractériser**) *adj erreur* downright. **une rubéole** ~**e** a clear *ou* straightforward case of German measles; **c'est de l'insubordination** ~**e** it's sheer *ou* downright insubordination.
caractériser [kaʀakteʀize] (1) *vt* (*être typique de*) to characterize, be characteristic of; (*décrire*) to characterize. **avec le toupet qui le caractérise** with his characteristic cheek; **ça se caractérise par** it is characterized *ou* distinguished by; **l'art de** ~ **un paysage** the knack of picking out the main features of a landscape; **ce qui caractérise ce paysage** the main *ou* characteristic features of this landscape.
caractéristique [kaʀakteʀistik] **1** *adj* characteristic (*de* of). **2** *nf* characteristic, (typical) feature.
caractérologie [kaʀaktɛʀɔlɔʒi] *nf* characterology.
carafe [kaʀaf] *nf* decanter; *[eau, vin ordinaire]* carafe; *V* **rester**.
carafon [kaʀafɔ̃] *nm* (*V* **carafe**) small decanter; small carafe.
caraïbe [kaʀaib] *adj* Caribbean. **les C**~**s** the Caribbean.
carambolage [kaʀɑ̃bɔlaʒ] *nm [autos]* multiple crash, pileup; (*Billard*) cannon.
caramboler [kaʀɑ̃bɔle] (1) **1** *vt* to collide with, go *ou* cannon into. **5 voitures se sont carambolées** there was a pileup of 5 cars, 5 cars ran into each other *ou* collided. **2** *vi* (*Billard*) to cannon, get *ou* make a cannon.
caramel [kaʀamɛl] *nm* (*sucre fondu*) caramel; (*bonbon*) (*mou*) caramel, fudge; (*dur*) toffee.
caramélisation [kaʀamelizɑsjɔ̃] *nf* caramelization.
caraméliser [kaʀamelize] (1) **1** *vt sucre* to caramelize; *moule, pâtisserie* to coat with caramel; *boisson, aliment* to flavour with caramel. **2** *vi*, **se caraméliser** *vpr [sucre]* to caramelize.
carapace [kaʀapas] *nf [crabe, tortue]* shell, carapace. **sommet recouvert d'une** ~ **de glace** summit encased in a sheath of ice; **il est difficile de pénétrer sa** ~ **d'égoïsme** it's difficult to penetrate the armour of his egoism *ou* his thickskinned self-centredness.
carapater (se)* [kaʀapate] (1) *vpr* to skedaddle*, hop it*, take to one's heels, run off.
carat [kaʀa] *nm* carat. **or à 18** ~**s** 18-carat gold.
caravane [kaʀavan] *nf* (*convoi*) caravan; (*véhicule*) caravan, trailer (*US*). **une** ~ **de voitures** a procession *ou* stream of cars; **une** ~ **de touristes** a stream of tourists; *V* **chien**.
caravanier, -ière [kaʀavanje, jɛʀ] **1** *adj itinéraire, chemin* caravan (*épith*). **tourisme** ~ caravanning. **2** *nm* **(a)** (*conducteur de caravane*) caravaneer. **(b)** (*vacancier*) caravanner.
caravaning [kaʀavaniŋ] *nm* (*mode de déplacement*) caravanning; (*emplacement*) caravan site.
caravansérail [kaʀavɑ̃seʀaj] *nm* (*lit, fig*) caravanserai.
caravelle [kaʀavɛl] *nf* (*Hist Naut*) caravel. (*Aviat*) ® **C**~ Caravelle.
carbochimie [kaʀbɔʃimi] *nf* organic chemistry.
carbonate [kaʀbɔnat] *nm* carbonate. ~ **de soude** sodium carbonate, washing soda.
carbone [kaʀbɔn] *nm* carbon; *V* **papier**.
carbonifère [kaʀbɔnifɛʀ] **1** *adj* (*Minér*) carboniferous; (*Géol*) Carboniferous. **2** *nm* Carboniferous.
carbonique [kaʀbɔnik] *adj* carbonic; *V* **gaz, neige** *etc.*
carbonisation [kaʀbɔnizɑsjɔ̃] *nf* carbonization.

carbonisé, e [karbɔnize] (*ptp de* **carboniser**) *adj arbre, restes* charred. **il est mort** ~ he was burned to death.
carboniser [karbɔnize] (1) *vt bois, substance* to carbonize; *forêt, maison* to burn to the ground, reduce to ashes; *rôti* to burn to a cinder.
carbon(n)ade [karbɔnad] *nf* (*méthode*) grilling (of meat) on charcoal; (*mets*) meat (*U*) grilled on charcoal.
carburant [karbyrɑ̃] **1** *adj m*: **mélange** ~ mixture (of petrol and air) (*in internal combustion engine*). **2** *nm* fuel.
carburateur [karbyratœr] *nm* carburettor.
carburation [karbyrasjɔ̃] *nf [essence]* carburation; *[fer]* carburization.
carbure [karbyr] *nm* carbide; *V* **lampe.**
carburé, e [karbyre] (*ptp de* **carburer**) *adj air, mélange* carburetted; *métal* carburized.
carburer [karbyre] (1) **1** *vi* **(a)** *[moteur]* **ça carbure bien/mal** it's well/badly tuned.
(b) (:) **alors, ça carbure?** well, are things going O.K.?; **il carbure au rouge** red wine is his tipple; **ça carbure sec ici!** they're really knocking it back in here!
2 *vt air* to carburet; *métal* to carburize.
carcajou [karkaʒu] *nm* wolverine, carcajou.
carcan [karkɑ̃] *nm* (*Hist*) iron collar; (*fig: contrainte*) yoke, shackles. **ce col est un vrai** ~ this collar is like a vice.
carcasse [karkas] *nf* **(a)** *[animal]*, (*) *[personne]* carcass. **je vais réchauffer ma** ~ **au soleil*** I'm going to toast myself in the sun*. **(b)** (*armature*) *[abat-jour]* frame; *[bateau, immeuble]* skeleton.
carcéral, e, *mpl* **-aux** [karseral, o] *adj* prison (*épith*).
cardage [kardaʒ] *nm* carding.
cardan [kardɑ̃] *nm* universal joint; *V* **joint.**
carder [karde] (1) *vt* to card.
cardeur, -euse [kardœr, øz] **1** *nm,f* carder. **2 cardeuse** *nf* (*machine*) carding machine.
cardiaque [kardjak] **1** *adj* (*Anat*) cardiac. **malade** ~ heart case *ou* patient; **être** ~ to suffer from *ou* have a heart condition; *V* **crise. 2** *nmf* heart case *ou* patient.
cardinal, e, *mpl* **-aux** [kardinal, o] **1** *adj nombre* cardinal; (*littér: capital*) cardinal; *V* **point**[1].
2 *nm* **(a)** (*Rel*) cardinal. ~**-évêque** cardinal bishop; ~**-prêtre** cardinal priest.
(b) (*nombre*) cardinal number.
(c) (*Orn*) cardinal (bird).
cardinalat [kardinala] *nm* cardinalship.
cardinalice [kardinalis] *adj* of a cardinal. **conférer à qn la dignité** ~ to make sb a cardinal, raise sb to the purple; *V* **pourpre.**
cardiogramme [kardjɔgram] *nm* cardiogram.
cardiographe [kardjɔgraf] *nm* cardiograph.
cardiographie [kardjɔgrafi] *nf* cardiography.
cardiologie [kardjɔlɔʒi] *nf* cardiology.
cardiologue [kardjɔlɔg] *nmf* cardiologist, heart specialist.
cardio-vasculaire [kardjɔvaskylɛr] *adj* cardiovascular.
cardite [kardit] *nf* (*Méd*) carditis.
cardon [kardɔ̃] *nm* (*Culin*) cardoon.
carême [karɛm] **1** *nm* (*jeûne*) fast. (*Rel: période*) **le C**~ Lent; **sermon de** ~ Lenten sermon; **faire** ~ to observe *ou* keep Lent, be fasting; **rompre le** ~ to break the Lent(en) fast *ou* the fast of Lent; (*fig*) **le** ~ **qu'il s'est imposé** the fast he has undertaken.
2: carême-prenant†† Shrovetide.
carénage [karenaʒ] *nm* **(a)** (*Naut*) (*action*) careening; (*lieu*) careenage. **(b)** *[véhicule]* streamlining.
carence [karɑ̃s] *nf* **(a)** (*Méd: manque*) deficiency. **maladie de** *ou* **par** ~ deficiency disease; ~ **vitaminique** *ou* **en vitamines** vitamin deficiency; (*fig*) **une grave** ~ **en personnel qualifié** a grave deficiency *ou* shortage of qualified staff.
(b) (*U: incompétence*) *[gouvernement]* shortcomings (*pl*), incompetence; *[parents]* inadequacy.
(c) (*Jur*) insolvency.
carène [karɛn] *nf* **(a)** (*Naut*) (lower part of the) hull. **mettre en** ~ to careen. **(b)** (*Bot*) carina, keel.
caréner [karene] (6) *vt* **(a)** (*Naut*) to careen. **(b)** (*Tech*) *véhicule* to streamline.
caressant, e [karesɑ̃, ɑ̃t] *adj enfant, animal* affectionate; *regard, voix* caressing, tender; *brise* caressing.
caresse [karɛs] *nf* **(a)** caress; (*à un animal*) stroke. **faire des** ~**s à** *personne* to caress, fondle; *animal* to stroke, fondle; (*littér*) **la** ~ **de la brise/des vagues** the caress of the breeze/of the waves.
(b) (††: *flatterie*) cajolery (*U*), flattery (*U*). **endormir la méfiance de qn par des** ~**s** to use cajolery to allay *ou* quieten sb's suspicions.
caresser [karese] (1) *vt* **(a)** *personne* to caress, fondle, stroke; *animal* to stroke, fondle; *objet* to stroke. **il lui caressait les jambes/les seins** he was stroking *ou* caressing her legs/ fondling her breasts; **il caressait les touches du piano** he stroked *ou* caressed the keys of the piano; ~ **qn du regard** to give sb a fond *ou* caressing look, look lovingly *ou* fondly at sb; (*hum*) **je vais lui** ~ **les côtes*** I'm going to give him a drubbing.
(b) *projet, espoir* to entertain, toy with. ~ **le projet de faire qch** to toy with the idea of doing sth.
(c) (††: *flatter*) to flatter, cajole, fawn on.
cargaison [kargɛzɔ̃] *nf* **(a)** (*Aviat, Naut*) cargo, freight. **une** ~ **de bananes** a cargo of bananas. **(b)** (*) load, stock. **des** ~**s de touristes** busloads *ou* shiploads *etc* of tourists.
cargo [kargo] *nm* cargo boat, freighter. ~ **mixte** cargo and passenger vessel.
cargue [karg(ə)] *nf* (*Naut*) brail.
carguer [karge] (1) *vt voiles* to brail, furl.
cari [kari] *nm* = **curry.**
cariatide [karjatid] *nf* caryatid.
caribou [karibu] *nm* caribou.
caricatural, e, *mpl* **-aux** [karikatyral, o] (*ridicule*) *aspect, traits* ridiculous, grotesque; (*exagéré*) *description, interprétation* caricatured.
caricature [karikatyr] *nf* **(a)** (*dessin, description*) caricature; (*dessin à intention politique*) cartoon. **faire la** ~ **de** to make a caricature of, caricature; **ce n'est qu'une** ~ **de procès** it's a mere mockery of a trial; **ce n'est qu'une** ~ **de la vérité** it's a caricature *ou* gross distortion of the truth.
(b) (*: *personne laide*) fright*.
caricaturer [karikatyre] (1) *vt* to caricature.
caricaturiste [karikatyrist(ə)] *nmf* caricaturist; (*à intention politique*) (satirical) cartoonist.
carie [kari] *nf* **(a)** (*Méd*) *[dents, os]* caries (*U*). **la** ~ **dentaire** tooth decay, (dental) caries; **j'ai une** ~ I've got a bad tooth *ou* a hole in my tooth. **(b)** (*Bot*) *[arbre]* blight; *[blé]* smut, bunt.
carier [karje] (7) **1** *vt* to decay, cause to decay. **dent cariée** bad *ou* decayed tooth. **2 se carier** *vpr* to decay.
carillon [karijɔ̃] *nm* **(a)** *[église]* (*cloches*) (peal *ou* set of) bells; (*air*) chimes. **on entendait le** ~ **de St Pierre/des** ~**s joyeux** we could hear the chimes of St Pierre/hear joyful chimes. **(b)** *[horloge]* (*système de sonnerie*) chime; (*air*) chimes. **une horloge à** ~, **un** ~ a chiming clock. **(c)** *[vestibule, entrée]* (door) chime.
carillonner [karijɔne] (1) **1** *vi* **(a)** *[cloches]* to ring, chime.
(b) (*à la porte*) to ring very loudly. **ça ne sert à rien de** ~, **il n'y a personne** it's no use jangling *ou* ringing the doorbell like that — there's no one in.
2 *vt fête* to announce with a peal of bells; *heure* to chime, ring; (*fig*) *nouvelle* to broadcast.
carillonneur [karijɔnœr] *nm* bell ringer.
carlin [karlɛ̃] *nm* pug(dog).
carlingue [karlɛ̃g] *nf* (*Aviat*) cabin; (*Naut*) keelson.
carliste [karlist(ə)] *adj, nmf* Carlist.
carmagnole [karmaɲɔl] *nf* (*chanson, danse*) carmagnole; (*Hist: veste*) short jacket (*worn during the French revolution*).
carme [karm(ə)] *nm* Carmelite, White Friar.
carmel [karmɛl] *nm* (*ordre*) **le C**~ the Carmelite order; (*monastère*) *[carmes]* Carmelite monastery; *[carmélites]* Carmelite convent.
carmélite [karmelit] *nf* Carmelite nun.
carmin [karmɛ̃] **1** *nm* (*colorant*) cochineal; (*couleur*) carmine, crimson. **2** *adj inv* carmine, crimson.
carminé, e [karmine] *adj* carmine, crimson.
carnage [karnaʒ] *nm* (*lit, fig*) carnage, slaughter.
carnassier, -ière [karnasje, jɛr] **1** *adj animal* carnivorous, flesh-eating; *dent* carnassial. **2** *nm* carnivore. ~**s** carnivores, carnivora (*T*). **3 carnassière** *nf* (*dent*) carnassial; (*gibecière*) gamebag.
carnation [karnasjɔ̃] *nf* (*teint*) complexion; (*Peinture: gén pl*) flesh tints.
carnaval, *pl* ~**s** [karnaval] *nm* (*fête*) carnival; (*période*) carnival (time). (*mannequin*) **(Sa Majesté) C**~ King Carnival; (*fig: excentrique*) **une espèce de** ~ a sort of gaudily-dressed person *ou* clown; **de** ~ *tenue, ambiance* carnival (*épith*).
carnavalesque [karnavalɛsk(ə)] *adj* (*grotesque*) carnivalesque; (*relatif au carnaval*) of the carnival.
carne [karn(ə)] *nf* (*péj*) (*: *viande*) tough *ou* leathery meat; (†: *cheval*) nag, hack. (*fig*) **quelle** ~**!:** (*homme*) what a swine!: *ou* bastard!:; (*femme*) what a bitch!:
carné, e [karne] *adj* **(a)** *alimentation* meat (*épith*). **(b)** *fleur* flesh-coloured.
carnet [karnɛ] **1** *nm* (*calepin*) notebook; (*liasse*) book.
2: carnet d'adresses address book; **carnet de bal** dance card; **carnet de billets** book of tickets; **carnet de chèques** cheque book; **carnet de commandes** order book; (*Scol*) **carnet de notes** school report; **avoir un bon carnet (de notes)** to have a good report; **carnet à souches** counterfoil book; **carnet de timbres** book of stamps.
carnier [karnje] *nm* gamebag.
carnivore [karnivɔr] **1** *adj animal* carnivorous, flesh-eating; *insecte, plante* carnivorous. **2** *nm* carnivore. ~**s** carnivores, carnivora (*T*).
carolingien, -ienne [karɔlɛ̃ʒjɛ̃, jɛn] **1** *adj* Carolingian. **2** *nm,f*: **C**~**(ne)** Carolingian.
carotide [karɔtid] *adj, nf* carotid.
carottage: [karɔtaʒ] *nm* (*vol*) swiping:, nicking: (*Brit*), pinching*.
carotte [karɔt] **1** *nf* **(a)** (*Bot, Culin*) carrot. (*fig*) **les** ~**s sont cuites!*** they've (*ou* we've *etc*) had it!*, it's all up with them (*ou* us *etc*):; *V* **poil.**
(b) (*: *promesse*) carrot.
(c) (*Tech*) core.
(d) *[tabac]* plug; (*enseigne*) tobacconist's sign.
2 *adj inv cheveux* red, carroty* (*péj*); *couleur* carroty. **objet (couleur)** ~ carrot-coloured object; **rouge** ~ carrot red.
carotter: [karɔte] (1) **1** *vt* (*voler*) *objet* to swipe:, nick: (*Brit*), pinch*; *client* to do*. ~ **qch à qn** to nick: sth from sb; **il m'a carotté (de) 5 F, je me suis fait** ~ **(de) 5 F** he did* *ou* diddled* me out of 5 francs.
2 *vi*: ~ **sur: elle carotte sur l'argent des commissions** she fiddles the shopping money.
carotteur, -euse: [karɔtœr, øz] *nm,f* pincher*, diddler*.
caroube [karub] *nf* carob (*fruit*).
caroubier [karubje] *nm* carob (tree).
Carpathes [karpat] *nfpl*: **les** ~ the Carpathians.
carpe[1] [karp(ə)] *nf* (*Zool*) carp; *V* **saut.**
carpe[2] [karp(ə)] *nm* (*Anat*) carpus.
carpeau, *pl* ~**x** [karpo] *nm* young carp.
carpette [karpɛt] *nf* (*tapis*) rug; (*péj: personne servile*) fawning *ou* servile person, doormat (*fig*). **s'aplatir comme une**

~ **devant qn** to fawn on sb.
carpien, -ienne [kaʀpjɛ̃, jɛn] *adj* carpal.
carquois [kaʀkwa] *nm* quiver.
carrare [kaʀaʀ] *nm* (*marbre*) Carrara (marble).
carre [kaʀ] *nf [ski]* edge. (*Ski*) **faire mordre les** ~**s** to dig in the edges of one's skis.
carré, e [kaʀe] (*ptp de* **carrer**) **1** *adj* **(a)** *table, jardin, menton* square; *V* **partie**[2].
(b) (*Math*) square. **mètre/kilomètre** ~ square metre/kilometre; **il n'y avait pas un centimètre** ~ **de place** there wasn't a square inch of room, there wasn't room *ou* there was no room to swing a cat (*Brit*); *V* **racine.**
(c) (*fig: franc*) *personne* forthright, straightforward; *réponse* straight, straightforward. **être** ~ **en affaires** to be aboveboard *ou* forthright in one's (business) dealings.
2 *nm* **(a)** (*gén*) square. **découper qch en petits** ~**s** to cut sth up into little squares; **un** ~ **de soie** a silk square; **un** ~ **de terre** a patch *ou* plot (of land); **un** ~ **de choux/de salades** a cabbage/lettuce patch.
(b) (*Mil: disposition*) square; *V* **former.**
(c) (*Naut: mess, salon*) wardroom. **le** ~ **des officiers** the (officers') wardroom.
(d) (*Math*) square. **le** ~ **de 4** 4 squared, the square of 4; **3 au carré** 3 squared; **élever** *ou* **mettre** *ou* **porter un nombre au** ~ to square a number.
(e) (*Cartes*) **un** ~ **d'as** four aces.
(f) (*Culin*) ~ **de l'Est** *type of cheese*; (*Boucherie*) ~ **d'agneau** loin of lamb.
3 carrée *nf* (‡: *chambre*) pad‡; (*Hist Mus*) breve.
carreau, *pl* ~**x** [kaʀo] *nm* **(a)** (*par terre*) (floor) tile; (*au mur*) (wall) tile.
(b) (*carrelage, sol*) (tiled) floor.
(c) (*vitre*) (window) pane. **remplacer un** ~ to replace a pane; **regarder au** ~ to look out of the window; **des vandales ont cassé les** ~**x** vandals have smashed the windows; (*: *lunettes*) **enlève tes** ~**x** take off your specs* (*Brit*).
(d) (*sur un tissu*) check; (*sur du papier*) square. **à** ~**x** check (*épith*), checked; **veste à grands/petits** ~**x** jacket with a large/small check; (*Scol*) **laisser 3** ~**x de marge** leave 3 squares' margin, leave a margin of 3 squares; (*Tech*) **mettre un plan au** ~ to square a plan.
(e) (*Cartes*) diamond.
(f) *[mine]* bank. **le** ~ **des Halles** the floor of les Halles.
(g) (*Hist: flèche*) bolt.
(h) (**loc*) **laisser qn sur le** ~ (*bagarre*) to lay sb out cold*; **rester sur le** ~ (*bagarre*) to be laid out cold*; (*examen*) **le candidat est resté sur le** ~ the candidate didn't make the grade; **se tenir à** ~ to lie low, keep one's nose clean‡.
carrefour [kaʀfuʀ] *nm* **(a)** *[routes, rues]* crossroads. (*fig*) **la Belgique,** ~ **de l'Europe** Belgium, the crossroads of Europe; (*fig*) **Marseille,** ~ **de la drogue** Marseilles, the crossroads of the drug traffic; (*fig*) **discipline au** ~ **de plusieurs sciences** subject at the junction *ou* meeting point of many different sciences; (*fig*) **cette manifestation est un** ~ **d'idées** this event is a forum for ideas.
(b) (*situation de choix multiple*) crossroads. **se trouver à un** ~ **(de sa vie/carrière)** to be at a crossroads (in one's life/career).
(c) (*rencontre, forum*) forum, symposium.
carrelage [kaʀlaʒ] *nm* (*action*) tiling; (*carreaux*) tiles, tiling. **poser un** ~ to lay a tiled floor.
carreler [kaʀle] (4) *vt mur, sol* to tile; *papier* to square.
carrelet [kaʀlɛ] *nm* **(a)** (*poisson*) plaice. **(b)** (*filet*) *square fishing net.* **(c)** (*Tech*) *[bourrelier]* half-moon needle; *[dessinateur]* square ruler.
carreleur [kaʀlœʀ] *nm* tiler.
carrément [kaʀemɑ̃] *adv* **(a)** (*franchement*) bluntly, straight out. **je lui ai dit** ~ **ce que je pensais** I told him bluntly *ou* straight out what I thought.
(b) (*sans hésiter*) straight. **il a** ~ **écrit au directeur** he wrote straight to the headmaster; **vas-y** ~ go right ahead; **j'ai pris** ~ **à travers champs** I resolutely struck across fields.
(c) (*intensif*) **il est** ~ **timbré*** he's definitely cracked*; **cela nous fait gagner** ~ **10 km/2 heures** it saves us 10 whole km *ou* the whole of 10 km/a whole 2 hours *ou* 2 full hours *ou* the whole of 2 hours.
(d) (*rare: d'aplomb*) squarely, firmly.
carrer [kaʀe] (1) **1** *vt* (*Math, Tech*) to square. **2 se carrer** *vpr* to settle (o.s.) comfortably *ou* firmly, ensconce o.s. (*dans* in).
carrier [kaʀje] *nm* (*ouvrier*) quarryman, quarrier; (*propriétaire*) quarry owner. **maître** ~ quarry master.
carrière[1] [kaʀjɛʀ] *nf [sable]* (sand)pit; *[roches etc]* quarry.
carrière[2] [kaʀjɛʀ] *nf* **(a)** (*profession*) career. **en début/fin de** ~ at the beginning/end of one's career; **les** ~**s du droit** the legal careers; (*Pol*) **la** ~ the diplomatic service; **embrasser la** ~ **des armes**† to embark on the career of arms†; **faire** ~ **dans l'enseignement** to make one's career in teaching; **il est entré dans l'industrie et y a fait (rapidement)** ~ he went into industry and (quickly) made a career for himself (in it); *V* **militaire.**
(b) (*littér: cours*) **le jour achève sa** ~ the day is drawing to a close *ou* has run its course; **donner (libre)** ~ **à** to give free rein to, give scope for.
carriériste [kaʀjeʀist(ə)] *nmf* (*péj*) careerist.
carriole [kaʀjɔl] *nf* **(a)** (*péj*) (ramshackle) cart. **(b)** (*Can*) sleigh, ca(r)riole (*US, Can*), carryall (*US, Can*).
carrossable [kaʀɔsabl(ə)] *adj route etc* suitable for (motor) vehicles.
carrosse [kaʀɔs] *nm* coach (*horse-drawn*). ~ **d'apparat** state coach; *V* **rouler.**
carrosser [kaʀɔse] (1) *vt* (*Aut*) (*mettre une carrosserie à*) to fit a body to; (*dessiner la carrosserie de*) to design a body for *ou* the body of. **voiture bien carrossée** car with a well-designed body; **elle est bien carrossée‡** she's got curves in all the right places.
carrosserie [kaʀɔsʀi] *nf* (*Aut*) (*coque*) body, coachwork; (*métier*) coachbuilding (*Brit*). **atelier de** ~ coachbuilder's workshop (*Brit*).
carrossier [kaʀɔsje] *nm* (*constructeur*) coachbuilder (*Brit*); (*dessinateur*) car designer. **ma voiture est chez le** ~ my car is at the coachbuilder's.
carrousel [kaʀusɛl] *nm* (*Équitation*) carrousel; (*fig: tourbillon*) merry-go-round. **un** ~ **d'avions dans le ciel** planes weaving patterns in the sky.
carrure [kaʀyʀ] *nf* **(a)** (*largeur d'épaules*) *[personne]* build; *[vêtement]* breadth across the shoulders. **manteau un peu trop étroit de** ~ coat a little tight across the shoulders; **une** ~ **d'athlète** an athlete's build; **homme de belle/forte** ~ well-built/burly man.
(b) (*forme carrée, massive*) *[mâchoire, bâtiment]* squareness.
(c) (*fig: envergure*) calibre, stature.
carry [kaʀi] *nm* = **curry.**
cartable [kaʀtabl(ə)] *nm [écolier]* (*à poignée*) (school)bag; (*à bretelles*) satchel.
carte [kaʀt(ə)] **1** *nf* **(a)** (*Jeux*) ~ **(à jouer)** (playing) card; **battre** *ou* **brasser** *ou* **mêler les** ~**s** to shuffle the cards; **donner les** ~**s** to deal (the cards); **faire** *ou* **tirer les** ~**s à qn** to read sb's cards; ~ **maîtresse** (*lit*) master (card); (*fig*) trump card; ~ **forcée** (*lit*) forced card; (*fig*) **c'est la** ~ **forcée!** we've no choice!, it's Hobson's choice!; (*lit, fig*) ~**s sur table** cards on the table; *V* **brouiller, château** *etc.*
(b) (*Géog*) map; (*Astron, Mét, Naut*) chart. ~ **du relief/géologique** relief/geological map; ~ **routière** roadmap; ~ **du ciel** sky chart; ~ **de la lune** chart *ou* map of the moon.
(c) (*au restaurant*) menu. **manger à la** ~ to eat à la carte; **repas à la** ~ à la carte meal; **une très bonne/très petite** ~ a very good/very small menu *ou* choice of dishes; (*fig*) **programme à la** ~ free-choice curriculum, curriculum allowing pupils a choice of subjects.
(d) ~ **(postale)** (post)card.
(e) ~ **(de visite)** (visiting) card, (calling) card (*US*).
(f) (*loc*) **en** ~: **fille** *ou* **femme en** ~ registered prostitute.
2: carte d'alimentation = **carte de rationnement; carte blanche: avoir carte blanche** to have carte blanche *ou* a free hand; **donner carte blanche à qn** to give sb carte blanche *ou* a free hand; **carte de chemin de fer** railway (*Brit*) *ou* train (*US*) season ticket; **carte de correspondance** (plain) postcard; **carte de crédit** credit card; **carte d'électeur** elector's card; **carte d'état-major** Ordnance Survey map (*Brit*); **carte d'étudiant** student card; **carte de famille nombreuse** *card issued to members of large families, allowing reduced fares etc;* **carte grise** ≈ (car) registration book (*Brit*), logbook; **carte d'identité** identity card; **carte d'invitation** invitation card; **carte de lecteur** library *ou* reader's (*Brit*) ticket; **carte-lettre** *nf, pl* **cartes-lettres** letter-card; **carte mécanographique** = **carte perforée; carte de Noël** Christmas card; **carte orange** monthly *ou* yearly season ticket (*for all types of transport*); **carte perforée** punch card; **carte de rationnement** ration card; **carte syndicale** union card; **carte vermeille** ≈ O.A.P. *ou* senior citizen's rail pass; (*Aut*) **carte verte** green card (*Brit*); **carte des vins** wine list; **carte de vœux** New Year(s) card.
cartel [kaʀtɛl] *nm* **(a)** (*Pol*) cartel, coalition; (*Écon*) cartel, combine. **(b)** (*pendule*) wall clock. **(c)** (*Hist: défi*) cartel.
cartellisation [kaʀtelizɑsjɔ̃] *nf* (*Écon*) formation of combines.
carter [kaʀtɛʀ] *nm [bicyclette]* chain guard; (*Aut*) *[huile]* sump; *[boîte de vitesses]* (gearbox) casing; *[différentiel]* cage; *[moteur]* crankcase.
cartésianisme [kaʀtezjanism(ə)] *nm* Cartesianism.
cartésien, -ienne [kaʀtezjɛ̃, jɛn] *adj, nm,f* Cartesian.
Carthage [kaʀtɑʒ] *n* Carthage.
carthaginois, e [kaʀtaʒinwa, waz] **1** *adj* Carthaginian. **2** *nm,f*: **C**~**(e)** Carthaginian.
cartilage [kaʀtilaʒ] *nm* (*Anat*) cartilage; *[viande]* gristle.
cartilagineux, -euse [kaʀtilaʒinø, øz] *adj* (*Anat*) cartilaginous; *viande* gristly.
cartographe [kaʀtɔgʀaf] *nmf* cartographer.
cartographie [kaʀtɔgʀafi] *nf* cartography, map-making.
cartographique [kaʀtɔgʀafik] *adj* cartographic(al).
cartomancie [kaʀtɔmɑ̃si] *nf* fortunetelling (*with cards*), cartomancy.
cartomancien, -ienne [kaʀtɔmɑ̃sjɛ̃, jɛn] *nm,f* fortuneteller (*who uses cards*).
carton [kaʀtɔ̃] **1** *nm* **(a)** (*matière*) cardboard. **écrit/collé sur un** ~ written/pasted on (a piece of) cardboard; **masque de** *ou* **en** ~ cardboard mask.
(b) (*boîte*) (cardboard) box, carton (*US*); (*cartable*) (school)bag, satchel. (*fig*) **c'est quelque part dans mes** ~**s** it's somewhere in my files; *V* **taper.**
(c) (*cible*) target. **faire un** ~ (*à la fête*) to have a go at the rifle range; (*: *sur l'ennemi*) to take a potshot* (*sur* at); **faire un bon** ~ to make a good score, do a good shoot (*Brit*).
(d) (*Peinture*) sketch; (*Géog*) inset map; *[tapisserie, mosaïque]* cartoon.
2: carton à chapeau hatbox; **carton à chaussures** shoebox; **carton à dessin** portfolio; **carton pâte** pasteboard; **de carton pâte** *décor,* (*fig*) *personnages* cardboard (*épith*).
cartonnage [kaʀtɔnaʒ] *nm* **(a)** (*industrie*) cardboard industry. **(b)** (*emballage*) cardboard (packing). **(c)** (*Reliure*) (*action*)

boarding. (*couverture*) ~ **pleine toile** cloth binding; ~ **souple** limp cover.

cartonner [kaʀtɔne] (1) *vt* to bind in boards. **livre cartonné** hardback (book).

cartonnerie [kaʀtɔnʀi] *nf* (*industrie*) cardboard industry; (*usine*) cardboard factory.

cartonnier [kaʀtɔnje] *nm* **(a)** (*artiste*) tapestry *ou* mosaic designer. **(b)** (*meuble*) filing cabinet.

cartouche[1] [kaʀtuʃ] *nf [fusil, stylo, magnétophone]* cartridge; *[cigarettes]* carton.

cartouche[2] [kaʀtuʃ] *nm* (*Archéol, Archit*) cartouche.

cartoucherie [kaʀtuʃʀi] *nf* (*fabrique*) cartridge factory; (*dépôt*) cartridge depot.

cartouchière [kaʀtuʃjɛʀ] *nf* (*ceinture*) cartridge belt; (*sac*) cartridge pouch.

caryatide [kaʀjatid] *nf* = **cariatide.**

cas [kɑ] **1** *nm* **(a)** (*situation*) case, situation; (*événement*) occurrence. ~ **tragique/spécial** tragic/special case; **un** ~ **imprévu** an unforeseen case *ou* situation; ~ **urgent** urgent case, emergency; **comme c'est son** ~ as is the case with him; **il neige à Nice, et c'est un** ~ **très rare** it's snowing in Nice and it's a very rare occurrence; **exposez-lui votre** ~ state your case, explain your position; (*à un médecin*) describe your symptoms; **il s'est mis dans un mauvais** ~ he's got himself into a tricky situation *ou* position; **dans le premier** ~ in the first case *ou* instance.

(b) (*Jur*) case. ~ **d'homicide/de divorce** murder/divorce case; **l'adultère est un** ~ **de divorce** adultery is grounds for divorce; **soumettre un** ~ **au juge** to submit a case to the judge; (*hum*) **c'est un** ~ **pendable** he deserves to be shot (*hum*).

(c) (*Méd, Sociol*) case. **il y a plusieurs** ~ **de variole dans le pays** there are several cases of smallpox in the country; (*fig*) **c'est vraiment un** ~**!** he's (*ou* she's) a real case!*

(d) (*Ling*) case.

(e) (*loc*) **faire (grand)** ~ **de/peu de** ~ **de** to attach great/little importance to, set great/little store by; **il ne fait jamais aucun** ~ **de nos observations** he never pays any attention to *ou* takes any notice of our comments; **c'est bien le** ~ **de le dire** you've said it; **c'est le** ~ **ou jamais de réclamer** if ever there was a case for complaint this is it; **au** ~ *ou* **dans le** ~ **où il pleuvrait, en** ~ **qu'il pleuve**† in case it rains, in case it should rain; **je prends un parapluie au** ~ **où*** *ou* **en** ~* I am taking an umbrella (just) in case; **dans ce** ~**-là** *ou* **en ce** ~ **téléphonez-nous** in that case give us a ring; **le** ~ **échéant** if the case arises; **en** ~ **de** in case of, in the event of; **en** ~ **de réclamation/d'absence** in case of *ou* in the event of complaint/absence; **en** ~ **de besoin nous pouvons vous loger** if need be we can put you up; **en** ~ **d'urgence** in an emergency, in emergencies; **en aucun** ~ **vous ne devez vous arrêter** on no account *ou* under no circumstances are you to stop; **en tout** ~, **en** *ou* **dans tous les** ~ in any case, at any rate; **mettre qn dans le** ~ **d'avoir à faire** to put sb in the situation *ou* position of having to do; **il accepte ou il refuse selon les** ~ he accepts or refuses as the case may be.

2: cas de conscience matter *ou* case of conscience; **il a un cas de conscience** he's in a moral dilemma; **cas d'égalité des triangles** congruence of triangles; **cas d'espèce** individual case; **cas de force majeure** case of absolute necessity; **cas de légitime défense** case of legitimate self-defense; **cas limite** borderline case.

casanier, -ière [kazanje, jɛʀ] **1** *adj personne, habitudes, vie* stay-at-home (*épith*). **2** *nm,f* stay-at-home, homebody (*US*).

casaque [kazak] *nf [jockey]* blouse; (†) *[femme]* overblouse; (*Hist*) *[mousquetaire]* tabard; *V* **tourner.**

casbah [kazba] *nf* kasbah.

cascade [kaskad] *nf* waterfall, cascade; (*fig*) *[mots, événements, chiffres]* stream, torrent, spate; *[rires]* peal. (*fig*) **des démissions en** ~ a chain *ou* spate of resignations; *V* **montage.**

cascader [kaskade] (1) *vi* (*littér*) to cascade.

cascadeur [kaskadœʀ] *nm [film]* stuntman; *[cirque]* acrobat.

cascadeuse [kaskadøz] *nf [film]* stuntgirl; *[cirque]* acrobat.

case [kɑz] *nf* **(a)** (*sur papier*) square, space; *[échiquier]* square.

(b) *[pupitre]* compartment, shelf; *[courrier]* pigeonhole; *[boîte, tiroir]* compartment. ~ **postale** post-office box; **il a une** ~ **vide*, il lui manque une** ~* he has a screw loose*.

(c) (*hutte*) hut, cabin.

caséeux, -euse [kazeø, øz] *adj* caseous.

caséine [kazein] *nf* casein.

casemate [kazmat] *nf* blockhouse.

caser* [kaze] (1) **1** *vt* **(a)** (*placer*) *objets* to put; (*loger*) *amis* to put up. **il a casé les chaussures dans une poche** he tucked *ou* stuffed the shoes into a pocket.

(b) (*marier*) *fille* to find a husband for; (*pourvoir d'une situation*) to find a job for. **il a casé son fils dans une grosse maison d'édition** he got his son a job *ou* got his son set up in a big publishing house; **ses enfants sont casés maintenant** (*emploi*) his children have got jobs now *ou* are fixed up now; (*mariage*) his children are (married and) off his hands now.

2 se caser *vpr* (*se marier*) to settle down; (*trouver un emploi*) to find a (steady) job; (*se loger*) to find a place (to live).

caserne [kazɛʀn(ə)] *nf* (*Mil, fig*) barracks. ~ **de pompiers** fire station; **la** ~ **est à 5 minutes de la gare** the barracks is *ou* are 5 minutes from the station; **ce H.L.M. est une vraie** ~ this council block (*Brit*) looks like a barracks.

casernement [kazɛʀnəmɑ̃] *nm* (*Mil*) (*action*) quartering in barracks; (*bâtiments*) barrack buildings.

caserner [kazɛʀne] (1) *vt* (*Mil*) to barrack, quarter in barracks.

casernier [kazɛʀnje] *nm* barrack quartermaster.

cash* [kaʃ] *adv* (*comptant*) **payer** ~ to pay cash down; **il m'a donné 40.000 F** ~ he gave me 40,000 francs cash down *ou* on the nail* (*Brit*) *ou* on the barrel* (*US*).

cash-flow [kaʃflo] *nm* cash flow.

casier [kɑzje] **1** *nm* **(a)** (*compartiment*) compartment; (*tiroir*) drawer, (*fermant à clef*) locker; *[courrier]* pigeonhole.

(b) (*meuble*) set of compartments *ou* pigeonholes; (*à tiroirs*) filing cabinet.

(c) (*Pêche*) (lobster *etc*) pot. **poser des** ~**s** to put out lobster pots.

2: casier à bouteilles bottle rack; **casier à homards** lobster pot; **casier judiciaire** police record; **avoir un casier judiciaire vierge** to have no *ou* a clean (police) record; **casier à musique** music cabinet.

casino [kazino] *nm* casino.

casoar [kazɔaʀ] *nm* (*Orn*) cassowary; (*plumet*) plume.

casque [kask(ə)] **1** *nm* **(a)** (*qui protège*) *[soldat, alpiniste, ouvrier]* helmet; *[motocycliste etc]* crash helmet.

(b) (*pour sécher les cheveux*) (hair-)drier.

(c) *[radiotélégraphiste]* ~ **(à écouteurs)** headphones, headset (*US*).

(d) (*Zool*) casque.

(e) (*Bot*) helmet, galea.

2: les Casques bleus the U.N. peace-keeping force *ou* troops; **casque colonial** sun *ou* tropical helmet, topee; **casque à pointe** spiked helmet.

casqué, e [kaske] **1** *ptp de* **casquer*.** **2** *adj motocycliste, soldat* wearing a helmet, helmeted. ~ **de cuir** wearing a leather helmet.

casquer* [kaske] (1) *vi* (*payer*) to cough up*, fork out*.

casquette [kaskɛt] *nf* cap. ~ **d'officier** officer's (peaked) cap.

cassable [kɑsabl(ə)] *adj* breakable.

cassage [kɑsaʒ] *nm* breaking. ~ **de gueule**‡ punch-up‡.

cassandre [kasɑ̃dʀ(ə)] **1** *nf* (*Myth*) **C**~ Cassandra. **2** *nmf* (*fig*) prophet of doom.

cassant, e [kɑsɑ̃, ɑ̃t] *adj* **(a)** *glace, substance* brittle; *métal* short; *bois* easily broken *ou* snapped. **(b)** (*fig*) *ton* curt, abrupt, brusque; *attitude, manières* brusque, abrupt. **(c) ce n'est pas** ~* it's not exactly tiring work.

cassate [kasat] *nf* cassata.

cassation [kɑsɑsjɔ̃] *nf* **(a)** (*Jur*) cassation; *V* **cour, pourvoir.** **(b)** (*Mil*) reduction to the ranks.

casse [kɑs] **1** *nf* **(a)** (*action*) breaking, breakage; (*objets cassés*) damage, breakages. **la** ~ **d'une assiette est sans importance** breaking a plate doesn't matter; **il y a eu beaucoup de** ~ **pendant le déménagement** there were a lot of things broken *ou* a lot of breakages during the move; **payer la** ~ to pay for the damage *ou* breakages; **il va y avoir de la** ~* there's going to be (some) rough stuff*; **pas de** ~**!** (*lit*) don't break anything!; (**fig*) no rough stuff!*

(b) (*récupération*) **mettre à la** ~ to scrap; **vendre à la** ~ to sell for scrap; **bon pour la** ~ fit for scrap, ready for the scrap heap; **envoyer une voiture à la** ~ to send a car to the breakers.

(c) (*Typ*) **lettres du haut de/du bas de** ~ upper-case/lower-case letters.

(d) (*Bot*) cassia.

2 *nm* (*arg Crime: cambriolage*) break-in.

casse- [kɑs] *préf V* **casser.**

cassé, e [kɑse] (*ptp de* **casser**) *adj voix* broken, cracked; *vieillard* bent; *V* **blanc, col.**

cassement [kɑsmɑ̃] *nm* **(a)** ~ **de tête** headache (*fig*), worry. **(b)** = **casse 2.**

casser [kɑse] (1) **1** *vt* **(a)** (*briser*) *objet* to break; *volonté, moral* to break; *noix* to crack; *latte, branche* to snap, break; (*) *appareil* to bust*. ~ **une dent/un bras à qn** to break sb's tooth/arm; ~ **qch en deux/en morceaux** to break sth in two/into pieces; ~ **un morceau de chocolat** to break off *ou* snap off a piece of chocolate; ~ **un carreau** (*volontairement*) to smash a pane; (*accidentellement*) to break a pane; **il s'est mis à tout** ~ **autour de lui** he started smashing *ou* breaking everything about him; **cette bonne casse tout** *ou* **beaucoup** this maid is always breaking things; **cette maladie lui a cassé la voix** this illness has ruined his voice.

(b) (*dégrader*) *personne* (*Mil*) to reduce to the ranks, break; (*Admin*) to demote.

(c) (*Admin, Jur: annuler*) *jugement* to quash; *mariage* to annul; *arrêt* to nullify, annul. **faire** ~ **un jugement pour vice de forme** to have a sentence quashed on a technicality.

(d) (*Comm*) ~ **les prix** to slash prices.

(e) (‡: *tuer*) ~ **du Viet/du Boche** to go Viet-/Jerry-smashing.

(f) (*loc*) (*Aviat*) ~ **du bois** to smash up one's plane; ~ **la croûte*** *ou* **la graine*** to have a bite *ou* something to eat; ~ **la figure*** *ou* **la gueule**‡ **à qn** to smash sb's face in‡; ~ **le morceau**‡ (*avouer*) to spill the beans, come clean; (*trahir*) to blow the gaff* (*Brit*); ~ **les pieds à qn*** (*fatiguer*) to wear sb out, bore sb stiff; (*irriter*) to get on sb's nerves; **il nous les casse!**‡ he's a pain (in the neck)!‡; ~ **sa pipe*** to kick the bucket‡; **ça/il ne casse rien, ça/il ne casse pas trois pattes à un canard** it's/he's nothing special, it's/he's nothing to shout about; ~ **du sucre sur le dos de qn** to talk about sb behind his back; **il nous casse la tête** *ou* **les oreilles*** **avec sa trompette** he deafens us with his trumpet; **il nous casse la tête avec ses histoires*** he bores us stiff with his stories; ~ **les vitres*** to kick up* *ou* create a stir; **à tout** ~* (*extraordinaire*) *film, repas* stupendous, fantastic; (*tout au plus*) **tu en auras pour 100 F à tout** ~ that'll cost you at the outside *ou* at the most 100 francs; *V* **omelette.**

2 *vi* (*se briser*) *[objet]* to break; *[baguette, plaque]* to break, snap. **la corde a cassé** the rope has broken *ou* snapped; **ça casse facilement** it breaks easily; **ça casse comme du verre** it breaks like glass; **le pantalon doit** ~ **sur la chaussure** the trouser (leg) should rest on the instep.

3 se casser *vpr* **(a)** (*se briser*) *[objet]* to break. **la tasse s'est cassée en tombant** the cup fell and broke; **l'anse s'est cassée** the handle came off *ou* broke (off); **se ~ net** to break clean off *ou* through.

(b) *[personne]* **se ~ la jambe/une jambe/une dent** to break one's leg/a leg/a tooth; (*fig*) **se ~ le cou** *ou* **la figure*** *ou* **la gueule‡** (*tomber*) to come a cropper; (*d'une certaine hauteur*) to crash down; (*faire faillite*) to come a cropper; (*se tuer*) to smash o.s. up*; **se ~ la figure contre** to crash into; (*fig*) **se ~ le nez** (*trouver porte close*) to find no one in; (*échouer*) to come a cropper; (*fig*) **il ne s'est pas cassé la tête*** *ou* **la nénette‡** he didn't overtax himself *ou* overdo it; (*fig*) **cela fait 2 jours que je me casse la tête sur ce problème** I've been racking my brains for 2 days over this problem.

(c) (*: *se fatiguer*) **il ne s'est rien cassé** *ou* **il ne s'est pas cassé pour écrire cet article** he didn't strain himself writing this article.

4: casse-cou* *nmf inv* (*sportif etc*) daredevil, reckless person; (*en affaires*) reckless person; **il/elle est casse-cou** he/she is reckless *ou* a daredevil; **crier casse-cou à qn** to warn sb; **casse-croûte** *nm inv* snack, lunch (*US*); (*Can*) snack bar; **prendre/emporter un petit casse-croûte** to have/take along a bite to eat *ou* a snack; **casse-gueule‡** (*adj inv*) *sentier* dangerous, treacherous; *opération, entreprise* dicey* (*surtout Brit*), dangerous; (*nm inv*) (*opération, entreprise*) dicey* (*surtout Brit*) business; (*endroit*) dangerous *ou* nasty spot; **aller au casse-gueule***† to go to war (to be killed); **casse-noisettes** *nm inv*, **casse-noix** *nm inv* nutcrackers (*Brit*), nutcracker (*US*); **as-tu un casse-noisettes?** have you got a pair of nutcrackers? (*Brit*) *ou* a nutcracker? (*US*); **le casse-noisettes est sur la table** the nutcrackers (*Brit*) are *ou* the nutcracker (*US*) is on the table; **casse-pieds*** *nmf inv* (*importun*) nuisance, pain in the neck‡; (*ennuyeux*) bore; **ce qu'elle est casse-pieds*!** (*importune*) she's a pain in the neck!‡; (*ennuyeuse*) what a bore she is!; **casse-pipes*** *nm inv*: **aller au casse-pipes** to go to the front (to be killed); **casse-tête** *nm inv* (*problème difficile*) headache (*fig*); (*jeu*) puzzle, brain teaser; (*Hist: massue*) club.

casserole [kasʀɔl] *nf* **(a)** (*Culin*) (*ustensile*) saucepan; (*contenu*) saucepan(ful). **du veau à la** *ou* **en ~** braised veal.

(b) (*péj*) **c'est une vraie ~** *[piano]* it's a tinny piano; *[voiture]* it's a tinny car.

(c) (*arg Ciné*) projector.

(d) (‡*loc*) **passer à la ~** *fille* to screw**, do‡, lay**; *prisonnier* (*tuer*) to bump off‡; **elle est passée à la ~** she got screwed** *ou* done‡ *ou* laid**.

cassette [kasɛt] *nf* **(a)** (*coffret*) casket; (*trésor*) *[roi]* privy purse. (*hum*) **il a pris l'argent sur sa ~ personnelle** he took the money *ou* paid out of his own pocket. **(b)** *[magnétophone]* cassette; *V* **magnétophone.**

casseur [kɑsœʀ] *nm* (*: *bravache*) tough *ou* big guy*; (*Aut: ferrailleur*) scrap merchant (*surtout Brit*) *ou* dealer; (*Pol: manifestant*) demonstrator who damages property; (‡: *cambrioleur*) burglar. **jouer les ~s*** to come the rough stuff*; **~ de pierres** stone breaker; **~ de vitres** troublemaker.

cassis [kasis] *nm* **(a)** (*fruit*) blackcurrant; (*arbuste*) blackcurrant (bush); (*liqueur*) blackcurrant liqueur; *V* **blanc. (b)** (‡: *tête*) nut*, block*. **(c)** *[route]* bump, ridge.

cassonade [kasɔnad] *nf* brown sugar.

cassoulet [kasulɛ] *nm* cassoulet (*casserole dish of S.W. France*).

cassure [kɑsyʀ] *nf* **(a)** (*lit, fig*) break; *[col]* fold. **à la ~ du pantalon** where the trousers rest on the shoe. **(b)** (*Géol*) (*gén*) break; (*fissure*) crack; (*faille*) fault.

castagnettes [kastaɲɛt] *nfpl* castanets. **avoir les dents/les genoux qui jouent des ~*** to feel one's teeth rattling/knees knocking.

caste [kast(ə)] *nf* (*lit, péj*) caste; *V* **esprit.**

castel [kastɛl] *nm* mansion, small castle.

castillan, e [kastijɑ̃, an] **1** *adj* Castilian. **2** *nm* (*Ling*) Castilian. **3** *nm,f*: **C~(e)** Castilian.

Castille [kastij] *nf* Castile.

castor [kastɔʀ] *nm* (*Zool, fourrure*) beaver.

castrat [kastʀa] *nm* (*chanteur*) castrato.

castration [kastʀɑsjɔ̃] *nf* (*V* **castrer**) castration; spaying; gelding; doctoring.

castrer [kastʀe] (1) *vt* (*gén*) *homme, animal mâle* to castrate; *animal femelle* to castrate, spay; *cheval* to geld; *chat, chien* to doctor.

castriste [kastʀist(ə)] **1** *adj* Castro (*épith*). **2** *nmf* supporter *ou* follower of Castro.

casuel, -elle [kɑzɥɛl] **1** *adj* **(a)** (*Ling*) **désinences ~les** case endings. **(b)** (*littér*) fortuitous. **2** *nm* (†) (*gain variable*) commission money; *[curé]* casual offerings (*pl*).

casuiste [kɑzɥist(ə)] *nm* (*Rel, péj*) casuist.

casuistique [kɑzɥistik] *nf* (*Rel, péj*) casuistry.

catabolisme [katabɔlism(ə)] *nm* catabolism.

catachrèse [katakʀɛz] *nf* catachresis.

cataclysme [kataklism(ə)] *nm* cataclysm.

cataclysmique [kataklismik] *adj* cataclysmic, cataclysmal.

catacombes [katakɔ̃b(ə)] *nfpl* catacombs.

catadioptre [katadjɔptʀ(ə)] *nm* reflector (*Aut*).

catafalque [katafalk(ə)] *nm* catafalque.

catalan, e [katalɑ̃, an] **1** *adj* Catalan, Catalonian. **2** *nm* (*Ling*) Catalan. **3** *nm,f*: **C~(e)** Catalan.

catalepsie [katalɛpsi] *nf* catalepsy. **tomber en ~** to have a cataleptic fit.

cataleptique [katalɛptik] *adj, nmf* cataleptic.

Catalogne [katalɔɲ] *nf* Catalonia.

catalogne [katalɔɲ] *nf* (*Can Artisanat*) *piece of cloth woven into drapes, covers and rugs.*

catalogue [katalɔg] *nm* catalogue. **prix de ~** list price; **faire le ~ de** to catalogue, list.

cataloguer [katalɔge] (1) *vt articles, objets* to catalogue, list; *bibliothèque, musée* to catalogue; (*) *personne* to label, put a label on.

catalyse [kataliz] *nf* catalysis.

catalyser [katalize] (1) *vt* (*Chim, fig*) to catalyse.

catalyseur [katalizœʀ] *nm* (*Chim, fig*) catalyst.

catalytique [katalitik] *adj* catalytic.

catamaran [katamaʀɑ̃] *nm* (*voilier*) catamaran; *[hydravion]* floats.

cataphote [katafɔt] *nm* ® = **catadioptre.**

cataplasme [kataplasm(ə)] *nm* (*Méd*) poultice. **~ sinapisé** mustard poultice *ou* plaster; (*fig*) **cet entremets est un véritable ~ sur l'estomac** the dessert lies like a lead weight *ou* lies heavily on the stomach.

catapultage [katapyltaʒ] *nm* (*lit, fig*) catapulting; (*Aviat*) catapult launch.

catapulte [katapylt(ə)] *nf* (*Aviat, Hist*) catapult.

catapulter [katapylte] (1) *vt* (*lit, fig*) to catapult.

cataracte [kataʀakt(ə)] *nf* **(a)** (*chute d'eau*) cataract. (*fig*) **des ~s de pluie** torrents of rain. **(b)** (*Méd: U*) cataract. **il a été opéré de la ~** he's had a cataract operation, he's been operated on for (a) cataract.

catarrhal, e, *mpl* **-aux** [kataʀal, o] *adj* catarrhal.

catarrhe [kataʀ] *nm* catarrh.

catarrheux, -euse [kataʀø, øz] *adj voix* catarrhal, thick. **vieillard ~** wheezing old man.

catastrophe [katastʀɔf] *nf* disaster, catastrophe. **~! le prof est arrivé!*** panic stations! the teacher's here!; **en ~: atterrir en ~** to make a forced *ou* an emergency landing; **ils sont partis en ~** they left in a terrible *ou* mad rush.

catastrophé, e* [katastʀɔfe] *adj personne, air* stunned. **être ~** to be shattered *ou* stunned.

catastropher* [katastʀɔfe] (1) *vt* to shatter, stun.

catastrophique [katastʀɔfik] *adj* disastrous, catastrophic.

catch [katʃ] *nm* (all-in) wrestling. **il fait du ~** he's an all-in wrestler, he's a wrestler.

catcheur, -euse [katʃœʀ, øz] *nm,f* (all-in) wrestler.

catéchèse [kateʃɛz] *nf* catechetics (*pl*), catechesis.

catéchisation [kateʃizɑsjɔ̃] *nf* catechization.

catéchiser [kateʃize] (1) *vt* (*Rel*) to catechize; (*endoctriner*) to indoctrinate, catechize; (*sermonner*) to lecture.

catéchisme [kateʃism(ə)] *nm* (*enseignement, livre, fig*) catechism. **aller au ~** to go to catechism (class), ≃ go to Sunday school.

catéchiste [kateʃist(ə)] *nmf* catechist; *V* **dame.**

catéchumène [katekymɛn] *nmf* (*Rel*) catechumen; (*fig*) novice.

catégorie [kategɔʀi] *nf* (*gén, Philos*) category; (*Boxe, Hôtellerie*) class; (*Admin*) *[personnel]* grade. (*Boucherie*) **morceaux de première/deuxième ~** prime/second cuts; **ranger par ~** to categorize; **il est de la ~ de ceux qui ...** he comes in *ou* he belongs to the category of those who ... .

catégoriel, -elle [kategɔʀjɛl] *adj* **(a)** (*Pol, Syndicats*) **revendications ~les** differential claims. **(b)** (*Gram*) **indice ~** category index.

catégorique [kategɔʀik] *adj* **(a)** (*net*) *ton, personne* categorical, dogmatic; *démenti, refus* flat (*épith*), categorical. **(b)** (*Philos*) categorical.

catégoriquement [kategɔʀikmɑ̃] *adv* (*V* **catégorique**) categorically; dogmatically; flatly.

catégorisation [kategɔʀizɑsjɔ̃] *nf* (*gén*) categorization; (*Admin*) grading.

catégoriser [kategɔʀize] (1) *vt* to categorize. **le risque de ~ à outrance** the risk of over-categorizing.

caténaire [katenɛʀ] *adj, nf* (*Rail*) catenary.

catgut [katgyt] *nm* (*Méd*) catgut.

catharsis [kataʀsis] *nf* (*Littérat, Psych*) catharsis.

cathédrale [katedʀal] *nf* cathedral; *V* **verre.**

Catherine [katʀin] *nf* Catherine, Katherine.

catherinette [katʀinɛt] *nf unmarried girl of 25 and over.*

cathéter [kateteʀ] *nm* catheter.

cathode [katɔd] *nf* cathode.

cathodique [katɔdik] *adj* (*Phys*) cathodic; *V* **rayon.**

catholicisme [katɔlisism(ə)] *nm* (Roman) Catholicism.

catholicité [katɔlisite] *nf* **(a)** (*fidèles*) **la ~** the (Roman) Catholic Church. **(b)** (*orthodoxie*) catholicity.

catholique [katɔlik] **1** *adj* **(a)** (*Rel*) *foi, dogme* (Roman) Catholic. **(b)** (*) **pas (très) ~** fishy*, shady, a bit doubtful. **2** *nmf* (Roman) Catholic.

catimini [katimini] *adv*: **en ~** on the sly *ou* q.t.; **sortir en ~** to steal *ou* sneak out; **il me l'a dit en ~** he whispered it in my ear.

catin† [katɛ̃] *nf* (*prostituée*) trollop†.

cation [katjɔ̃] *nm* cation.

catogan [katɔgɑ̃] *nm bow tying hair on the neck.*

Caucase [kokaz] *nm*: **le ~** the Caucasus.

caucasien, -ienne [kokazjɛ̃, jɛn] **1** *adj* Caucasian. **2** *nm,f*: **C~(ne)** Caucasian.

cauchemar [koʃmaʀ] *nm* nightmare. (*fig*) **l'analyse grammaticale était son ~** parsing was a nightmare to him; **vision de ~** nightmarish sight.

cauchemardesque [koʃmaʀdɛsk(ə)] *adj impression, expérience* nightmarish.

cauchemardeux, -euse [koʃmaʀdø, øz] *adj* **(a)** = **cauchemardesque. (b) sommeil ~** sleep full of nightmares.

caudal, e, *mpl* **-aux** [kodal, o] *adj* caudal.

causal, e [kozal] *adj* causal.

causalité [kozalite] *nf* causality.

causant, e [kozɑ̃, ɑ̃t] *adj* talkative, chatty. **il n'est pas très ~** he doesn't say very much, he's not very forthcoming *ou* talkative.

causatif, -ive [kozatif, iv] *adj* (*Gram*) *conjonction* causal; *construction, verbe* causative.

cause [koz] *nf* **(a)** (*motif, raison*) cause. **quelle est la ~ de l'accident?** what caused the accident?, what was the cause of the accident?; **on ne connaît pas la ~ de son absence** the reason for *ou* the cause of his absence is not known; **être (la) ~ de qch** to be the cause of sth; **la chaleur en est la ~** it is caused by the heat; **les ~s qui l'ont poussé à agir** the reasons that caused him to act; être ~ que†: **cet accident est ~ que nous sommes en retard** this accident is the cause of our being late; **elle est ~ que nous sommes en retard** she is responsible for our being late; *V* **relation.**

(b) (*Jur*) lawsuit, case; (*à plaider*) brief. **~ civile** civil action; **~ criminelle** criminal proceedings; **la ~ est entendue** (*lit*) the sides have been heard; (*fig*) there's no doubt in our minds; **~ célèbre** cause célèbre, famous trial *ou* case; **plaider sa ~** to plead one's case; **un avocat sans ~(s)** a briefless barrister; *V* **connaissance.**

(c) (*ensemble d'intérêts*) cause. **une juste ~** a just cause; **une ~ perdue** a lost cause; **faire ~ commune avec qn** to make common cause with sb, side *ou* take sides with sb.

(d) (*Philos*) cause. **~ première/seconde/finale** primary/secondary/final cause.

(e) (*loc*) **à ~ de** (*en raison de*) because of, owing to; (*par égard pour*) because of, for the sake of; **à ~ de cet incident technique** owing to *ou* because of this technical failure; **c'est à ~ de lui que nous nous sommes perdus** it's because of him we got lost, he is responsible for our getting lost; **à ~ de son âge** on account of *ou* because of his age; **il est venu à ~ de vous** he came for your sake *ou* because of you; (*iro*) **ce n'est pas à ~ de lui que j'y suis arrivé!** it's no thanks to him I managed to do it!; **être en ~** *[personne]* to be involved *ou* concerned; *[intérêts etc]* to be at stake, be involved; **son honnêteté n'est pas en ~** there is no question about his honesty, his honesty is not in question; **mettre en ~** *projet, nécessité* to call into question; *personne* to implicate; **remettre en ~** *principe, tradition* to question, challenge; **sa démission remet tout en ~** his resignation re-opens the whole question, we're back to square one* (*Brit*) *ou* where we started from because of his resignation; **mettre qn hors de ~** to clear *ou* exonerate sb; **c'est hors de ~** it is out of the question; **pour ~ de** on account of; **fermé pour ~ d'inventaire/de maladie** closed for stocktaking/on account of illness; **et pour ~!** and for (a very) good reason!; **non sans ~!** not without (good) reason!; **ils le regrettent — non sans ~!** they are sorry — as well they might be! *ou* not without reason!

causer[1] [koze] (1) *vt* (*provoquer*) to cause; (*entraîner*) to bring about. **~ des ennuis à qn** to get sb into trouble, bring trouble to sb; **~ de la peine à qn** to hurt sb; **~ du plaisir à qn** to give pleasure to sb.

causer[2] [koze] (1) *vti* **(a)** (*s'entretenir*) to chat, talk; (*: *discourir*) to speak, talk. **~ de qch** to talk about sth; (*propos futiles*) to chat about sth; **~ politique/travail** to talk politics/shop; **elles causaient chiffons** they were chatting *ou* discussing clothes; **~ à qn*** to talk *ou* speak to sb; (*iro*) **cause toujours, tu m'intéresses!** keep going *ou* talking, I couldn't care less.

(b) (*jaser*) to talk, gossip (*sur qn* about sb).

(c) (*: *avouer*) to talk. **pour le faire ~** to loosen his tongue, to make him talk.

causerie [kozʀi] *nf* (*conférence*) talk; (*conversation*) chat.

causette [kozɛt] *nf*: **faire la ~, faire un brin de ~** to have a chat* *ou* natter* (*avec* with).

causeur, -euse [kozœʀ, øz] **1** *adj* (*rare*) talkative, chatty. **2** *nm,f* talker, conversationalist. **3 causeuse** *nf* (*siège*) causeuse, love seat.

causse [kos] *nm* causse, *limestone plateau* (*in south-central France*).

causticité [kostisite] *nf* (*lit, fig*) causticity.

caustique [kostik] *adj, nmf* (*Sci, fig*) caustic.

caustiquement [kostikmɑ̃] *adv* caustically.

cautèle [kotɛl] *nf* (*littér*) cunning, guile.

cauteleusement [kotløzmɑ̃] *adv* in a wily way.

cauteleux, -euse [kotlø, øz] *adj* wily.

cautère [kɔtɛʀ] *nm* cautery. **c'est un ~ sur une jambe de bois** it's as much use as a poultice on a wooden leg.

cautérisation [kɔteʀizɑsjɔ̃] *nf* cauterization.

cautériser [kɔteʀize] (1) *vt* to cauterize.

caution [kosjɔ̃] *nf* **(a)** (*somme d'argent*) (*Fin*) guarantee, security; (*Jur*) bail (bond). **verser une ~ (de 1.000 F)** to put *ou* lay down a security *ou* a guarantee (of 1,000 francs); **mettre qn en liberté sous ~** to release *ou* free sb on bail; **libéré sous ~** freed *ou* released *ou* out on bail; **payer la ~ de qn** to stand (*Brit*) *ou* go (*US*) bail for sb, bail sb out.

(b) (*fig: garantie morale*) guarantee. **sa parole est ma ~** his word is my guarantee.

(c) (*appui*) backing, support. **avoir la ~ d'un parti/de son chef** to have the backing *ou* support of a party/one's boss.

(d) (*personne, garant*) **se porter ~ pour qn** to stand security (*Brit*) *ou* surety for sb; *V* **sujet.**

cautionnement [kosjɔnmɑ̃] *nm* (*somme*) guaranty, guarantee, security; (*contrat*) surety bond.

cautionner [kosjɔne] (1) *vt* **(a)** (*répondre de*) (*moralement*) to answer for, guarantee; (*financièrement*) to guarantee, stand surety *ou* guarantor for. **(b)** *politique, gouvernement* to support, give one's support *ou* backing to.

cavaillon [kavajɔ̃] *nm* cavaillon melon.

cavalcade [kavalkad] *nf* **(a)** (*course tumultueuse*) stampede; (*: *troupe désordonnée*) stampede, stream. **(b)** *[cavaliers]* cavalcade. **(c)** (*défilé, procession*) cavalcade, procession.

cavalcader [kavalkade] (1) *vi* (*gambader, courir*) to stream, swarm, stampede; (†: *chevaucher*) to cavalcade, ride in a cavalcade.

cavale [kaval] *nf* **(a)** (*littér*) mare. **(b)** (*arg Prison: évasion*) **être en ~** to be on the run.

cavaler‡ [kavale] (1) **1** *vi* (*courir*) to run. **il fallait le voir ~!** you should have seen him run!; **j'ai dû ~ dans tout Londres pour le trouver** I had to rush all round London to find it.

2 *vt* (*ennuyer*) to bore, annoy. **il commence à nous ~** we're beginning to get cheesed off* (*Brit*) *ou* browned off* (*Brit*) *ou* teed off* (*US*) with him, he's beginning to get on our wick‡ (*Brit*).

3 se cavaler *vpr* (*se sauver*) to clear off‡, get the hell out of it‡. **les animaux se sont cavalés** the animals have done a bunk* (*Brit*); **il s'est cavalé à la maison** he belted* to the house.

cavalerie [kavalʀi] *nf* (*Mil*) cavalry; *[cirque]* stable (of circus horses). (*Mil*) **~ légère** light cavalry *ou* horse; (*: *articles massifs*) **c'est de la grosse ~** it's the heavy stuff.

cavaleur‡ [kavalœʀ] *nm* wolf, womanizer. **il est ~** he's always after the women, he chases anything in skirts.

cavaleuse‡ [kavaløz] *nf* hot piece‡. **elle est ~** she's always after the men, she chases anything in trousers *ou* in pants*.

cavalier, -ière [kavalje, jɛʀ] **1** *adj* **(a)** (*impertinent*) cavalier, offhand. **je trouve que c'est un peu ~ de sa part (de faire cela)** I think he's being a bit offhand (doing that).

(b) allée/piste ~ière riding path/track.

2 *nm,f* **(a)** (*Équitation*) rider. (*fig*) **faire ~ seul** to go it alone, be a loner*.

(b) (*partenaire: au bal etc*) partner.

3 *nm* **(a)** (*Mil*) trooper, cavalryman. **une troupe de 20 ~s** a troop of 20 horses.

(b) (*accompagnateur*) escort; (*Can**) boyfriend, beau (*US*). **être le ~ d'une dame** to escort a lady.

(c) (*Échecs*) knight.

(d) (*clou*) staple; *[balance]* rider; *[dossier]* tab.

(e) (*Hist Brit*) cavalier.

(f) (††: *gentilhomme*) gentleman.

cavalièrement [kavaljɛʀmɑ̃] *adv* in cavalier fashion, offhandedly.

cavatine [kavatin] *nf* (*Mus*) cavatina.

cave[1] [kav] *nf* **(a)** (*pièce*) cellar, vault; (*cabaret*) cellar nightclub. **(b)** (*Vin*) cellar. **avoir une bonne ~** to have *ou* keep a fine cellar. **(c)** (*coffret à liqueurs*) liqueur cabinet. **(d)** (*Can*) *[maison]* basement.

cave[2] [kav] *adj* (*creux*) *yeux, joues* hollow, sunken; *V* **veine.**

cave[3]**‡** [kav] *nm* **(a)** *someone who does not belong to the underworld.*

(b) (*imbécile*) sucker‡. **il est ~** he's a sucker‡.

caveau, *pl* **~x** [kavo] *nm* (*sépulture*) vault, tomb; (*cabaret*) nightclub; (*cave*) (small) cellar. **~ de famille** family vault.

caverne [kavɛʀn(ə)] *nf* **(a)** (*grotte*) cave, cavern; *V* **homme. (b)** (*Anat*) cavity.

caverneux, -euse [kavɛʀnø, øz] *adj* **(a)** *voix* cavernous. **(b)** (*Anat, Méd*) *respiration* cavernous; *poumon* with cavitations, with a cavernous lesion; *V* **corps. (c)** (*littér*) *montagne, tronc* cavernous.

cavernicole [kavɛʀnikɔl] *adj* cavernicolous.

caviar [kavjaʀ] *nm* **(a)** (*Culin*) caviar. **~ rouge** salmon roe. **(b)** (*Presse*) **passer au ~** to blue-pencil, censor.

caviarder [kavjaʀde] (1) *vt* (*Presse*) to censor, blue-pencil.

caviste [kavist(ə)] *nm* cellarman.

cavité [kavite] *nf* cavity. **~ articulaire** socket (*of bone*).

Cayenne [kajɛn] *n* Cayenne; *V* **poivre.**

ce [sə], **cet** [sɛt] *devant voyelle ou h muet au masculin,* **cette** [sɛt] *f,* **ces** [se] *pl* **1** *adj dém* **(a)** (*proximité*) this; (*pl*) these; (*non-proximité*) that; (*pl*) those. **ce chapeau(-ci)/(-là)** this/that hat; **si seulement ce mal de tête s'en allait** if only this headache would go away; **un de ces films sans queue ni tête** one of those films without beginning or end; **ah ces promenades dans la campagne anglaise!** (*en se promenant*) ah these walks in the English countryside!; (*évocation*) ah those walks in the English countryside!; **je ne peux pas voir cet homme** I can't stand (the sight of) that man; **cet imbécile d'enfant a perdu ses lunettes** this *ou* that stupid child has lost his glasses; **et ce rhume/cette jambe, comment ça va?*** and how's the cold/leg (doing)?*

(b) (*loc de temps*) **venez ce soir/cet après-midi** come tonight *ou* this evening/this afternoon; **cette nuit** (*qui vient*) tonight; (*passée*) last night; **ce mois(-ci)** this month; **ce mois-là** that month; **il faudra mieux travailler ce trimestre(-ci)** you'll have to work harder this term; **il a fait très beau ces jours(-ci)** the weather's been very fine lately *ou* these last few days; **en ces temps troublés** (*de nos jours*) in these troubled days; (*dans le passé*) in those troubled days; **j'irai la voir un de ces jours** I'll call on her one of these days.

(c) (*intensif*) **comment peut-il raconter ces mensonges!** how can he tell such lies!; **aurait-il vraiment ce courage?** would he really have that sort of *ou* that much courage?; **cette idée!** what an idea!; **ce toupet!*** what (a) cheek!*, such cheek!*; **cette générosité me semble suspecte** such *ou* this generosity looks suspicious to me; **elle a de ces initiatives!** she gets hold of *ou* has some *ou* these wild ideas!; *V* **un.**

(d) (*frm*) **si ces dames veulent bien me suivre** if the ladies will be so kind as to follow me; **ces messieurs sont en réunion** the gentlemen are in a meeting.

(e) (*avec qui, que*) **cette amie chez qui elle habite est docteur** the friend she's living with is a doctor; **elle n'est pas de ces femmes qui se plaignent toujours** she's not one of those *ou* these women who are always complaining; **c'est un de ces livres que l'on lit en vacances** it's one of those books *ou* the sort of book you read on holiday; **il a cette manie qu'ont les jeunes**

de ... he has this *ou* that habit common to young people of ... *ou* that young people have of ... .

2 *pron dém* (a) c'est, ce sont: qui est-ce? *ou* c'est?* — c'est un médecin/l'instituteur (*en désignant*) who's he? *ou* who's that? — he is a doctor/the schoolteacher; (*au téléphone, à la porte*) who is it? — it's a doctor/the schoolteacher; c'est la camionnette du boucher it's *ou* that's the butcher's van; ce sont des hôtesses de l'air/de bons souvenirs they are air hostesses/happy memories; c'est la plus intelligente de la classe she is the most intelligent in the class; c'est une voiture rapide it's a fast car; c'était le bon temps! those were the days!; je vais acheter des pêches, ce n'est pas cher en ce moment I am going to buy some peaches — they're quite cheap just now; qui est-ce *ou* c'est* qui a crié? — c'est lui who shouted? — HE did *ou* it was him; à qui est ce livre? — c'est à elle/à ma sœur whose book is this? — it's hers/my sister's; c'est impossible à faire it's impossible to do; c'est impossible de le faire* it's impossible to do it.

(b) (*tournure emphatique*) c'est le vent qui a emporté la toiture it was the wind that blew the roof off; c'est eux* *ou* ce sont eux *ou* c'étaient eux qui mentaient they are the ones who *ou* it's they who were lying; c'est vous qui devez décider, c'est à vous de décider it's up to you to decide, it's you who must decide; c'est toi qui le dis! that's what YOU say!; c'est avec plaisir que nous acceptons we accept with pleasure; c'est une bonne voiture que vous avez là that's a good car you've got there; un hôtel pas cher, c'est difficile à trouver a cheap hotel isn't easy to find; c'est à se demander s'il n'est pas fou you really wonder *ou* it makes you wonder if he isn't mad.

(c) ce qui, ce que what; (*reprenant une proposition*) which; ce qui est important c'est ... what really matters is ...; elle fait ce qu'on lui dit she does what she is told *ou* as she is told; il ne sait pas ce que sont devenus ses amis he doesn't know what has become of his friends; il ne comprenait pas ce à quoi on faisait allusion/ce dont on l'accusait he didn't understand what they were hinting at/what he was being accused of; nous n'avons pas de jardin, ce qui est dommage we haven't got a garden, which is a pity; il faut être diplômé, ce qu'il n'est pas you have to have qualifications, which he hasn't; il a été reçu à son examen, ce à quoi il s'attendait fort peu he passed his exam, which he wasn't expecting (to do); voilà tout ce que je sais that's all I know.

(d) à ce que, de ce que: on ne s'attendait pas à ce qu'il parle they were not expecting him *ou* he was not expected to speak; il se plaint de ce qu'on ne l'ait pas prévenu he is complaining that no one warned him.

(e) (*: *intensif*) ce que *ou* qu'est-ce que ce film est lent! how slow this film is!, what a slow film this is!; ce qu'on peut s'amuser! what fun (we are having)!; ce qu'il parle bien! what a good speaker he is!, how well he speaks!; ce que c'est que le destin! that's fate for you!; voilà ce que c'est que de conduire trop vite that's what comes of driving too fast.

(f) (*explication*) c'est que: quand il/s'il écrit, c'est qu'il a besoin d'argent when he/if he writes, it means *ou* it'll mean (that) *ou* it's *ou* it'll be because he needs money; c'est qu'elle n'entend rien, la pauvre! but the poor woman can't hear a thing!, but she can't hear, poor woman!; ce n'est pas qu'elle soit bête, mais elle ne travaille pas it's not that she's stupid, but she just doesn't work.

(g) (*loc*) c'est (vous) dire s'il a eu peur that shows you how frightened he was; c'est tout dire that (just) shows; à ce qu'on dit/que j'ai appris from what they say/what I've heard; qu'est-ce à dire?† what does that mean?; ce faisant in so doing, in the process; ce disant so saying, saying this; pour ce faire to this end, with this end in view; (*frm*) et ce: il a refusé, et ce, après toutes nos prières he refused, (and this) after all our entreaties.

céans†† [seɑ̃] *adv* here, in this house; *V* maître.

ceci [səsi] *pron dém* this. ce cas a ~ de surprenant que ... this case is surprising in that ..., there is one surprising thing about this case which is that ...; à ~ près que except that, with the *ou* this exception that; ~ compense cela one thing makes up for another.

cécité [sesite] *nf* blindness. ~ verbale word blindness; frappé de ~ à l'âge de 5 ans struck blind *ou* stricken with blindness at the age of 5.

cédant, e [sedɑ̃, ɑ̃t] (*Jur*) 1 *adj* assigning. 2 *nm,f* assignor.

céder [sede] (6) 1 *vt* (a) (*donner*) *part, place, tour* to give up. ~ qch à qn to let sb have sth, give sth up to sb; je m'en vais, je vous cède ma place *ou* je cède la place I'm going so you can have my place *ou* I'll let you have my place; (*Rad*) et maintenant je cède l'antenne à notre correspondant à Paris now over to our Paris correspondent; (*Jur*) ~ ses biens to make over *ou* transfer one's property.

(b) (*vendre*) *commerce* to sell, dispose of. ~ qch à qn to let sb have sth, sell sth to sb; le fermier m'a cédé un litre de lait the farmer let me have a litre of milk; ~ à bail to lease; il a bien voulu ~ un bout de terrain he agreed to part with a plot of ground.

(c) (*loc*) ~ le pas à qn/qch to give precedence to sb/sth; ~ la place (à qn) to let sb take one's place; (*lit*) ~ du terrain (à l'ennemi) to yield ground (to the enemy), fall back (before the enemy); (*fig*) ils finiront par ~ du terrain in the end they'll make concessions; (*fig*) l'épidémie cède du terrain devant les efforts des docteurs the epidemic is receding before the doctors' efforts; le ~ à qn en qch: son courage ne le cède en rien à son intelligence he's as brave as he is intelligent; il ne le cède à personne en égoïsme as far as selfishness is concerned he's second to none.

2 *vi* (a) (*capituler*) to give in. ~ par faiblesse/lassitude to give in out of weakness/tiredness; aucun ne veut ~ no one wants to give in *ou* give way.

(b) ~ à (*succomber à*) to give way to, yield to; (*consentir*) to give in to; ~ à la force/tentation to give way *ou* yield to force/temptation; ~ à qn (*à ses raisons, ses avances*) to give in *ou* yield to sb; ~ aux caprices/prières de qn to give in to sb's whims/entreaties; il cède facilement à la colère he gives way easily to anger.

(c) (*se rompre*) [*digue, chaise, branche*] to give way; (*fléchir, tomber*) [*fièvre, colère*] to subside. la glace a cédé sous le poids the ice gave (way) under the weight.

cédille [sedij] *nf* cedilla.

cédrat [sedʀa] *nm* (*fruit*) citron; (*arbre*) citron (tree).

cèdre [sɛdʀ(ə)] *nm* (*arbre*) cedar (tree); (*Can: thuya*) cedar, arbor vitae; (*bois*) cedar (wood).

cédrière [sedʀjɛʀ(ə)] *nf* (*Can*) cedar grove.

cédulaire [sedylɛʀ] *adj* (*Jur*) impôts ~s scheduled taxes.

cédule [sedyl] *nf* (*Impôts*) schedule.

cégétiste [seʒetist(ə)] 1 *adj* C.G.T. (*épith*). 2 *nmf* member of the C.G.T.

ceindre [sɛ̃dʀ(ə)] (52) *vt* (*littér*) (a) (*entourer*) ~ sa tête d'un bandeau to put a band round one's head; la tête ceinte d'un diadème wearing a diadem; ~ une ville de murailles to encircle a town with walls; (*Bible*) se ~ les reins to gird one's loins.

(b) (*mettre*) *armure, insigne d'autorité* to don, put on. ~ son épée to buckle *ou* gird on one's sword; (*lit, fig*) ~ l'écharpe municipale ≃ to put on *ou* don the mayoral chain; (*lit, fig*) ~ la couronne to assume the crown.

ceint, e [sɛ̃, ɛ̃t] *ptp de* ceindre.

ceinture [sɛ̃tyʀ] 1 *nf* (a) [*manteau, pantalon*] belt; [*pyjamas, robe de chambre*] cord; (*écharpe*) sash; (*gaine, corset*) girdle. se mettre *ou* se serrer la ~* to tighten *ou* pull in one's belt (*fig*).

(b) (*Couture: taille*) [*pantalon, jupe*] waistband.

(c) (*Anat*) waist. nu jusqu'à la ~ stripped to the waist; l'eau lui arrivait (jusqu')à la ~ the water came up to his waist, he was waist-deep in *ou* up to his waist in water.

(d) (*Sport*) (*prise*) waistlock. (*Judo*) ~ noire black belt; (*Boxe, fig*) coup au-dessous de la ~ blow below the belt.

(e) [*fortifications, murailles*] ring; [*arbres, montagnes*] belt.

(f) (*métro, bus*) circle line. petite/grande ~ inner/outer circle.

2: ceinture de chasteté chastity belt; ceinture de flanelle flannel binder; (*Can*) ceinture fléchée arrow sash; ceinture de grossesse maternity girdle *ou* support; ceinture herniaire truss; ceinture médicale = ceinture orthopédique; ceinture de natation swimming ring; ceinture orthopédique surgical corset; (*Anat*) ceinture pelvienne pelvic girdle; ceinture de sauvetage lifebelt; (*Anat*) ceinture scapulaire pectoral girdle; ceinture de sécurité seat *ou* safety belt; ceinture verte green belt.

ceinturer [sɛ̃tyʀe] (1) *vt personne* (*gén*) to grasp *ou* seize round the waist; (*Sport*) to tackle (round the waist); *ville* to surround, encircle.

ceinturon [sɛ̃tyʀɔ̃] *nm* [*uniforme*] belt.

cela [s(ə)la] *pron dém* (a) (*gén, en opposition à ceci*) that; (*en sujet apparent*) it. qu'est-ce que ~ veut dire? what does that *ou* this mean?; on ne s'attendait pas à ~ that was (quite) unexpected, we weren't expecting that; ~ n'est pas très facile that's not very easy; ~ m'agace de l'entendre se plaindre it annoys me to hear him complain; ~ vaut la peine qu'il essaie it's worth his trying; ~ me donne du souci it *ou* that gives me a lot of worry; faire des études, ~ ne le tentait guère studying did not really appeal to him.

(b) (*renforce comment, où, pourquoi etc*) il ne veut pas venir — pourquoi ~? he won't come — why not? *ou* why won't he?; j'ai vu X — qui ~?/quand ~?/où ~? I've seen X — who (do you mean)? *ou* who is that?/when was that?/where was that?

(c) ~ fait 10 jours/longtemps qu'il est parti it is 10 days/a long time since he left, he has been gone 10 days/a long time.

(d) (*loc*) voyez-vous ~! did you ever hear of such a thing!; ~ ne fait rien it *ou* that does not matter; et en dehors de *ou* à part ~? apart from that?; à ~ près que except that, with the exception that; avec eux, il y a ~ de bien qu'ils ... there's one thing to their credit and that's that they ..., I'll say this *ou* that for them, they ... .

céladon [seladɔ̃] *nm, adj inv*: (vert) ~ celadon.

célébrant [selebʀɑ̃] (*Rel*) 1 *adj m* officiating. 2 *nm* celebrant.

célébration [selebʀɑsjɔ̃] *nf* celebration.

célèbre [selɛbʀ(ə)] *adj* famous, celebrated (*par* for). cet escroc, tristement ~ par ses vols this crook, notorious for his robberies; se rendre ~ par to achieve celebrity for *ou* on account of.

célébrer [selebʀe] (6) *vt* (a) *anniversaire, fête* to celebrate; *cérémonie* to hold; *mariage* to celebrate, solemnize. ~ la messe to celebrate mass; ~ les Jeux olympiques to hold the Olympic Games.

(b) (*glorifier*) to celebrate, extol. ~ les louanges de qn to sing sb's praises.

célébrité [selebʀite] *nf* (*renommée*) fame, celebrity; (*personne*) celebrity. parvenir à la ~ to rise to fame.

celer [s(ə)le] (5) *vt* († *ou littér*) to conceal (*à qn* from sb).

céleri [sɛlʀi] *nm*: ~ en branche(s) celery; ~(-rave) celeriac; ~ rémoulade celeriac in remoulade (dressing); *V* pied.

célérité [seleʀite] *nf* promptness, speed, swiftness. avec ~ promptly, swiftly.

célesta [selɛsta] *nm* celeste, celesta.

céleste [selɛst(ə)] *adj* (a) (*du ciel, divin*) celestial, heavenly. colère/puissance ~ celestial anger/power, anger/power of heaven; le C~ Empire the Celestial Empire. (b) (*fig: merveilleux*) heavenly.

célibat [seliba] *nm* [*homme*] bachelorhood, celibacy; [*femme*] spinsterhood; (*par abstinence*) (period of) celibacy; [*prêtre*] celibacy. **vivre dans le ~** (*gén*) to live a single life, be unmarried; *[prêtre]* to be celibate.

célibataire [selibatɛʀ] **1** *adj* single, unmarried; (*Admin*) single. **mère ~** unmarried mother.

2 *nm* (*homme*) bachelor; (*Admin*) single man. **la vie de ~** (the) single life, the bachelor's life.

3 *nf* (*femme jeune*) single girl, unmarried woman; (*moins jeune*) spinster; (*Admin*) single woman. **la vie de ~** (the) single life.

celle [sɛl] *pron dém V* **celui.**

cellier [selje] *nm* storeroom (*for wine and food*).

cellophane [selɔfan] *nf* ® cellophane ®.

cellulaire [selylɛʀ] *adj* **(a)** (*Bio*) cellular. **(b) régime ~** confinement; **voiture** *ou* **fourgon ~** prison van.

cellule [selyl] *nf* (*Bio, Bot, Jur, Mil, Phot, Pol*) cell; *[avion]* airframe; *[électrophone]* cartridge. (*Mil*) **6 jours de ~** 6 days in the cells, 6 days' cells.

cellulite [selylit] *nf* cellulitis.

celluloïd [selylɔid] *nm* celluloid.

cellulose [selyloz] *nf* cellulose.

cellulosique [selylozik] *adj* cellulose (*épith*).

celte [sɛlt(ə)] **1** *adj* Celtic. **2** *nmf*: **C~** Celt.

celtique [sɛltik] *adj, nm* Celtic.

celui [səlɥi], **celle** [sɛl], *mpl* **ceux** [sø], *fpl* **celles** [sɛl] *pron dém* **(a)** (*fonction démonstrative*) **celui-ci, celle-ci** this one; **ceux-ci, celles-ci** these (ones); **celui-là, celle-là** that one; **ceux-là, celles-là** those (ones); **j'hésite entre les deux chaises, celle-ci est plus élégante, mais on est mieux sur celle-là** I hesitate between the two chairs — this one's more elegant, but that one's more comfortable; **une autre citation, plus littéraire celle-là** another quotation, this time a more literary one *ou* this next one is more literary.

(b) (*référence à un antécédent*) **j'ai rendu visite à mon frère et à mon oncle: celui-ci était malade et celui-là très déprimé** I visited my brother and my uncle — the latter was ill and the former very depressed; **elle écrivit à son frère: celui-ci ne répondit pas** she wrote to her brother, who did not answer *ou* but he did not answer; **ceux-là, ils auront de mes nouvelles** that lot* *ou* as for them, I'll give them a piece of my mind; **il a vraiment de la chance, celui-là!** that chap* (*Brit*) *ou* guy* certainly has a lot of luck!; **elle est forte** *ou* **bien bonne, celle-là!** that's a bit much! *ou* steep!* *ou* stiff!*

(c) (+ *de*) **celui de: je n'aime pas cette pièce, celle de X est meilleure** I don't like this play, X's is better; **c'est celui des 3 frères que je connais le mieux** of the 3 brothers he's the one I know (the) best, he's the one I know (the) best of the 3 brothers; **il n'a qu'un désir, celui de devenir ministre** he only wants one thing — (that's) to become a minister; **s'il cherche un appartement, celui d'en-dessous est libre** if he's looking for a flat, the one below is free; **ce livre est pour celui/pour ceux d'entre vous que la peinture intéresse** this book is for whichever one of you who is/is for those among you *ou* any of you who are interested in painting.

(d) celui qui/que/dont: ses romans sont ceux qui se vendent le mieux his novels are the ones *ou* those that sell best; **c'est celle que l'on accuse** she is the one who is being accused; **donnez-lui le ballon jaune, c'est celui qu'il préfère** give him the yellow ball — it's *ou* that's the one he likes best; **celui dont je t'ai parlé** the one I told you about.

(e) (*: *avec adj, participe*) **cette marque est celle recommandée par X** this brand is the one recommended by X, this is the brand recommended by X; **celui proche de la fontaine** the one near the fountain; **tous ceux ayant le même âge** all those of the same age.

cément [semɑ̃] *nm* (*Métal*) cement; *[dents]* cementum, cement.

cénacle [senakl(ə)] *nm* (*réunion, cercle*) (literary) coterie *ou* set; (*Rel*) cenacle.

cendre [sɑ̃dʀ(ə)] *nf* (*gén: substance*) ash, ashes. *[charbon]* **~**, **~s** ash, ashes, cinders; *[mort]* **~s** ashes; **~ de bois** wood ash; **des ~s** *ou* **de la ~ (de cigarette)** (cigarette) ash; **réduire en ~s** to reduce to ashes; **couleur de ~** ashen, ash-coloured; **le jour des C~s, les C~s** Ash Wednesday; **cuire qch sous la ~** to cook sth in (the) embers; (*Géol*) **~s volcaniques** volcanic ash; *V* **couver, renaître.**

cendré, e [sɑ̃dʀe] **1** *adj* ashen; *V* **blond. 2 cendrée** *nf* (*piste*) cinder track. (*Chasse, Pêche*) **de la ~e** dust shot.

cendreux, -euse [sɑ̃dʀø, øz] *adj terrain, substance* ashy; *couleur* ash (*épith*), ashy; *teint* ashen.

cendrier [sɑ̃dʀije] *nm [fumeur]* ashtray; *[poêle]* ash pan. *[locomotive]* **~ de foyer** ash box.

cendrillon [sɑ̃dʀijɔ̃] *nf* (†: *humble servante*) Cinderella. **C~** Cinderella.

cène [sɛn] *nf* (Holy) Communion, Lord's Supper, Lord's Table. (*Peinture, Rel*) **la C~** the Last Supper.

cénesthésie [senɛstezi] *nf* coen(a)esthesia.

cénesthésique [senɛstezik] *adj* cenesthesic, cenesthetic.

cénobite [senɔbit] *nm* coenobite.

cénotaphe [senɔtaf] *nm* cenotaph.

cens [sɑ̃s] *nm* (*Hist*) (*quotité imposable*) taxable quota *ou* rating (*as an electoral qualification*); (*redevance féodale*) rent (*paid by tenant of a piece of land to feudal superior*); (*recensement*) census. **~ électoral** (electoral) property qualification.

censé, e [sɑ̃se] *adj*: **être ~ faire qch** to be supposed to do sth; **je suis ~ travailler** I'm supposed to be *ou* I should be working; **nul n'est ~ ignorer la loi** ignorance of the law is no excuse.

censément [sɑ̃semɑ̃] *adv* (*en principe*) supposedly; (*pratiquement*) virtually; (*pour ainsi dire*) to all intents and purposes.

censeur [sɑ̃sœʀ] *nm* **(a)** (*Ciné, Presse*) censor. **(b)** (*fig: critique*) critic. **(c)** (*Scol*) ≈ deputy *ou* assistant head. **(d)** (*Hist*) censor.

censitaire [sɑ̃sitɛʀ] **1** *adj*: **suffrage** *ou* **système ~** suffrage based on property qualification. **2** *nm*: **(électeur) ~** eligible voter (*through payment of the 'cens'*).

censurable† [sɑ̃syʀabl(ə)] *adj* censurable.

censure [sɑ̃syʀ] *nf* **(a)** (*Ciné, Presse*) (*examen*) censorship; (*censeurs*) (board of) censors; (*Psych*) censor. **(b)** (†: *critique*) censure (*U*); (*Jur, Pol: réprimande*) censure. **les ~s de l'Église** the censure of the Church; *V* **motion.**

censurer [sɑ̃syʀe] (1) *vt* **(a)** (*Ciné, Presse*) *spectacle, journal* to censor. **(b)** (*critiquer: Jur, Pol, Rel*) to censure.

cent[1] [sɑ̃] **1** *adj* **(a)** (*cardinal: gén*) a hundred; (*100 exactement*) one hundred, a hundred. (*multiplié par un nombre*) **quatre ~s** four hundred; **quatre ~ un/treize** four hundred and one/thirteen; **~/deux ~s chaises** a hundred/two hundred chairs.

(b) (*ordinal: inv*) **page ~** page one hundred *ou* a hundred; **numéro/page quatre ~** number/page four hundred; **en l'an treize ~** in the year thirteen hundred.

(c) (*beaucoup de*) **il a eu ~ occasions de le faire** he has had hundreds of opportunities to do it; **je te l'ai dit ~ fois** I've told you a hundred times, if I've told you once I've told you a hundred times; **il a ~ fois raison** he's absolutely right; **~ fois mieux/pire** a hundred times better/worse; **je préférerais ~ fois faire votre travail** I'd far rather do your job, I'd rather do your job any day*; *V* **mot.**

(d) (*loc*) **il est aux ~ coups** he is frantic, he doesn't know which way to turn; **faire les ~ pas** to pace up and down; (*Sport*) **(course des) quatre ~s mètres haies** the 400 metres hurdles; **tu ne vas pas attendre ~ sept ans*** you can't wait for ever; (*Hist*) **les C~ jours** the Hundred Days; **je vous le donne en ~** I'll give you a hundred guesses, you'll never guess; **s'ennuyer** *ou* **s'emmerder‡ à ~ sous l'heure*** to be bored to tears*, be screaming with boredom; *V* **quatre.**

2 *nm* **(a)** (*nombre*) a hundred. **il habite au (numéro) ~ de la rue des Plantes, il habite ~ rue des Plantes** he lives at (number) 100 rue des Plantes; **il y a ~ contre un à parier que ...** it's a hundred to one that ...; *V* **gagner.**

(b) pour ~ per cent; **argent placé à 5 pour ~** money invested at 5 per cent; (*fig*) **être ~ pour ~ français, être français (à) ~ pour ~** to be a hundred per cent French *ou* French through and through; **je suis ~ pour ~ sûr** I'm a hundred per cent certain.

(c) (*Comm: centaine*) **un ~** a *ou* one hundred; **un ~ de billes/d'œufs** a *ou* one hundred marbles/eggs; **c'est 12 F le ~** they're 12 francs a hundred; *pour autres loc V* **six.**

cent[2] [sɛnt], (*Can*) [sɛn] *nm* (*US, Can: monnaie*) cent. (*Can*†) **quinze-~** cheap store, dime store (*US, Can*), five-and-ten (*US, Can*).

centaine [sɑ̃tɛn] *nf* **(a)** (*environ cent*) **une ~ de** about a hundred, a hundred or so; **la ~ de spectateurs qui ...** the hundred or so spectators who ...; **plusieurs ~s (de)** several hundred; **des ~s de personnes** hundreds of people; **ils vinrent par ~s** they came in (their) hundreds.

(b) (*cent unités*) hundred. **10 F la ~** 10 francs a hundred; **atteindre la ~** (*âge*) to live to be a hundred; (*collection etc*) to reach the (one) hundred mark; **il les vend à la ~** he sells them by the hundred; (*Math*) **la colonne des ~s** the hundreds column; *pour autres loc V* **soixantaine.**

centaure [sɑ̃tɔʀ] *nm* centaur.

centenaire [sɑ̃tnɛʀ] **1** *adj* hundred-year-old (*épith*). **cet arbre est ~** this tree is a hundred years old, this is a hundred-year-old tree. **2** *nmf* (*personne*) centenarian. **3** *nm* (*anniversaire*) centenary.

centenier [sɑ̃tənje] *nm* (*Hist*) centurion.

centésimal, e, *mpl* **-aux** [sɑ̃tezimal, o] *adj* centesimal.

centiare [sɑ̃tjaʀ] *nm* centiare.

centième [sɑ̃tjɛm] **1** *adj, nmf* hundredth; *pour loc V* **sixième. 2** *nf* (*Théât*) hundredth performance.

centigrade [sɑ̃tigʀad] *adj* centigrade.

centigramme [sɑ̃tigʀam] *nm* centigramme.

centilitre [sɑ̃tilitʀ(ə)] *nm* centilitre.

centime [sɑ̃tim] *nm* centime. (*fig*) **je n'ai pas un ~** I haven't got a penny *ou* a cent (*US*); **~ additionnel** ≈ local rates.

centimètre [sɑ̃timɛtʀ(ə)] *nm* (*mesure*) centimetre; (*ruban*) tape measure, measuring tape.

centrage [sɑ̃tʀaʒ] *nm* (*action de centrer*) centring; (*Math: détermination du centre*) centring.

central, e, *mpl* **-aux** [sɑ̃tʀal, o] **1** *adj* **(a)** (*du centre*) *quartier* central; *partie, point* centre (*épith*), central. **mon appartement occupe une position très ~e** my flat is very central; **Amérique/Asie ~e** Central America/Asia; *V* **chauffage.**

(b) (*le plus important*) *problème, idée* central; *bureau* head (*épith*), main (*épith*), central (*épith*).

(c) (*Jur*) *pouvoir, administration* central.

2 *nm* (*Téléc*) **~ (téléphonique)** (telephone) exchange, central (*US*†).

3 centrale *nf* **(a) ~e (électrique)** power station.

(b) ~e syndicale *ou* **ouvrière** *group of affiliated trade unions.*

(c) (*prison*) (central) prison.

(d) C~e = École c~e des arts et manufactures.

centralisateur, -trice [sɑ̃tʀalizatœʀ, tʀis] *adj* centralizing (*épith*).

centralisation [sɑ̃tʀalizɑsjɔ̃] *nf* centralization.

centraliser [sɑ̃tʀalize] (1) *vt* to centralize.

centre [sɑ̃tʀ(ə)] **1** *nm* **(a)** (*gén, Géom*) centre; (*fig*) *[problème]* centre, heart. **le C~ (de la France)** central France, the central region *ou* area of France; **il habite en plein ~ (de la ville)** he lives right in the centre (of town); **~-ville** town centre, city centre; **il se croit le ~ du monde** he thinks the universe revolves around him; **au ~ du débat** at the centre of the debate; **mot ~** key word.

(b) (*lieu d'activités*) centre; (*bureau*) office, centre; (*bâti-

ment, services) centre. **les grands ~s urbains/industriels/universitaires** the great urban/industrial/academic centres.

(c) (*Pol*) centre. **~ gauche/droit** centre left/right; **député du ~** deputy of the centre.

(d) (*Ftbl*) (†: *joueur*) centre (half *ou* forward)†; (*passe*) centre; *V* **avant.**

2: **centre aéré** day holiday centre; **centre d'attraction** centre of attraction; **centre commercial** shopping centre; (*Phys*) **centre de gravité** centre of gravity; **centre hospitalier** hospital complex; **centre d'influence** centre of influence; **centre d'intérêt** centre of interest; **centre médical** medical centre; (*Physiol, fig*) **centres nerveux** nerve centres; (*Poste*) **centre de tri** sorting office; **centres vitaux** (*Physiol*) vital organs, vitals; (*fig*) *[entreprise]* vital organs (*fig*).

centrer [sɑ̃tʀe] (1) *vt* (*Sport, Tech*) to centre. (*fig*) **~ une pièce/une discussion sur** to focus a play/a discussion (up)on.

centrifugation [sɑ̃tʀifygɑsjɔ̃] *nf* centrifugation.

centrifuge [sɑ̃tʀifyʒ] *adj* centrifugal.

centrifuger [sɑ̃tʀifyʒe] (3) *vt* to centrifuge.

centrifugeur [sɑ̃tʀifyʒœʀ] *nm*, **centrifugeuse** [sɑ̃tʀifyʒøz] *nf* centrifuge.

centripète [sɑ̃tʀipɛt] *adj* centripetal.

centrisme [sɑ̃tʀism(ə)] *nm* (*Pol*) centrism, centrist policies.

centriste [sɑ̃tʀist(ə)] *adj, nmf* centrist.

centuple [sɑ̃typl(ə)] **1** *adj* a hundred times as large (*de* as). **mille est un nombre ~ de dix** a thousand is a hundred times ten.

2 *nm*: **le ~ de 10** a hundred times 10; **au ~** a hundredfold; **on lui a donné le ~ de ce qu'il mérite** he was given a hundred times more than he deserves.

centupler [sɑ̃typle] (1) *vti* to increase a hundred times *ou* a hundredfold. **~ un nombre** to multiply a number by a hundred.

centurie [sɑ̃tyʀi] *nf* (*Hist Mil*) century.

centurion [sɑ̃tyʀjɔ̃] *nm* centurion.

cep [sɛp] *nm* **(a) ~ (de vigne)** (vine) stock. **(b)** *[charrue]* stock.

cépage [sepaʒ] *nm* (type of) vine.

cèpe [sɛp] *nm* (*Culin*) cepe; (*Bot*) (edible) boletus.

cependant [s(ə)pɑ̃dɑ̃] *conj* **(a)** (*pourtant*) nevertheless, however. **ce travail est dangereux, nous allons ~ essayer de le faire** this job is dangerous — however *ou* nevertheless we shall try *ou* we shall nevertheless try *ou* we shall try nevertheless to do it; **c'est incroyable et ~ c'est vrai** it's incredible, yet *ou* but nevertheless it is true *ou* but it's true nevertheless.

(b) (*littér*) (*pendant ce temps*) meanwhile, in the meantime. (*tandis que*) **~ que** while.

céphalique [sefalik] *adj* cephalic.

céphalopode [sefalɔpɔd] *nm* cephalopod. **~s** cephalopods, Cephalopoda (*T*).

céphalo-rachidien, -ienne [sefalɔʀaʃidjɛ̃, jɛn] *adj* cephalorachidian (*T*), cerebrospinal.

céramique [seʀamik] **1** *adj* ceramic. **2** *nf* (*matière*) ceramic; (*objet*) ceramic (*ornament etc*). (*art*) **la ~** ceramics, pottery; **vase en ~** ceramic *ou* pottery vase; **la ~ dentaire** dental ceramics.

céramiste [seʀamist(ə)] *nmf* ceramist.

cerbère [sɛʀbɛʀ] *nm* (*fig péj*) fierce watchdog (*person*). (*Myth*) **C~** Cerberus.

cerceau, *pl* **~x** [sɛʀso] *nm [enfant, tonneau, crinoline]* hoop; *[capote, tonnelle]* half-hoop. **jouer au ~** to bowl a hoop, play with a hoop.

cerclage [sɛʀklaʒ] *nm* hooping.

cercle [sɛʀkl(ə)] **1** *nm* **(a)** (*forme, figure*) circle, ring; (*Géog, Géom*) circle. **l'avion décrivait des ~s** the plane was circling (overhead); **itinéraire décrivant un ~** circular itinerary; **entourer d'un ~ le chiffre correct** to circle *ou* ring *ou* put a circle *ou* ring round the correct number; **faire ~ (autour de qn/qch)** to gather round (sb/sth) in a circle *ou* ring, make a circle *ou* ring (round sb/sth); **~s imprimés sur la table par les (fonds de) verres** rings left on the table by the glasses; **un ~ de badauds/de chaises** a circle *ou* ring of onlookers/chairs; *V* **arc, quadrature.**

(b) (*fig: étendue*) scope, circle, range. **le ~ des connaissances humaines** the scope *ou* range of human knowledge; **étendre le ~ de ses relations/de ses amis** to widen the circle of one's acquaintances/one's circle of friends.

(c) (*groupe*) circle. **le ~ de famille** the family circle; **un ~ d'amis** a circle of friends.

(d) (*cerceau*) hoop, band. **~ de tonneau** barrel hoop *ou* band; **~ de roue** tyre (*made of metal*).

(e) (*club*) society, club. **~ littéraire** literary circle *ou* society; **~ d'études philologiques** philological society *ou* circle; **aller/dîner au ~** to go to dine at the club.

(f) (*instrument*) protractor.

2: **cercle horaire** horary circle; **cercle polaire** polar circle; **cercle polaire arctique** Arctic Circle; **cercle polaire austral** Antarctic Circle; (*fig*) **cercle vicieux** vicious circle.

cercler [sɛʀkle] (1) *vt* (*gén*) to ring; *tonneau* to hoop; *roue* to tyre (*de* with). **lunettes cerclées d'écaille** horn-rimmed spectacles.

cercueil [sɛʀkœj] *nm* coffin, casket (*US*).

céréale [seʀeal] *nf* cereal (*Bot*).

céréalier, -ière [seʀealje, jɛʀ] **1** *adj* cereal (*épith*). **2** *nm* (*producteur*) cereal grower. **(navire) ~** grain carrier *ou* ship.

cérébelleux, -euse [seʀebelø, øz] *adj* cerebellar.

cérébral, e, *mpl* **-aux** [seʀebʀal, o] *adj* (*Méd*) cerebral; (*intellectuel*) *travail* mental. **c'est un ~** he's a cerebral type.

cérébro-spinal, e, *mpl* **-aux** [seʀebʀospinal, o] *adj* cerebrospinal.

cérémonial, *pl* **~s** [seʀemɔnjal] *nm* ceremonial.

cérémonie [seʀemɔni] *nf* ceremony. **sans ~** *manger* informally; *proposer* without ceremony, unceremoniously; *réception* informal; **avec ~** ceremoniously; **faire des ~s** to stand on ceremony, make a to-do* *ou* fuss*; **tenue** *ou* **habit de ~** formal dress (*U*), ceremonial dress (*U*); (*Mil*) **tenue de ~** dress uniform; *V* **maître.**

cérémonieusement [seʀemɔnjøzmɑ̃] *adv* ceremoniously, formally.

cérémonieux, -euse [seʀemɔnjø, øz] *adj ton, accueil, personne* ceremonious, formal. **il est très ~** he's very formal *ou* ceremonious in his manner.

cerf [sɛʀ] *nm* stag, hart (*littér*).

cerfeuil [sɛʀfœj] *nm* chervil.

cerf-volant, *pl* **cerfs-volants** [sɛʀvɔlɑ̃] *nm* **(a)** (*jouet*) kite. **jouer au ~** to fly a kite. **(b)** (*Zool*) stag beetle.

cerisaie [s(ə)ʀizɛ] *nf* cherry orchard.

cerise [s(ə)ʀiz] **1** *nf* cherry. **2** *adj inv* cherry(-red), cerise; *V* **rouge.**

cerisier [s(ə)ʀizje] *nm* (*arbre*) cherry (tree); (*bois*) cherry (wood).

cérium [seʀjɔm] *nm* cerium.

cerne [sɛʀn(ə)] *nm [yeux, lune]* ring; (*tache*) ring, mark. **les ~s de** *ou* **sous ses yeux** the (dark) rings *ou* shadows under his eyes.

cerné, e [sɛʀne] *adj*: **avoir les yeux ~s** to have (dark) shadows *ou* rings under one's eyes; **ses yeux ~s trahissaient sa fatigue** the dark shadows *ou* rings under his eyes revealed his tiredness.

cerneau, *pl* **~x** [sɛʀno] *nm* unripe walnut; (*Culin*) half shelled walnut.

cerner [sɛʀne] (1) *vt* **(a)** (*entourer*) to encircle, surround; (*Peinture*) *visage, silhouette* to outline (*de* with, in). **ils étaient cernés de toute(s) part(s)** they were surrounded on all sides, they were completely surrounded *ou* encircled.

(b) *problème* to delimit, define.

(c) *noix* to shell (*while unripe*); *arbre* to ring.

certain, e [sɛʀtɛ̃, ɛn] **1** *adj* **(a)** (*après n: incontestable*) *fait, succès, événement* certain; *indice* sure; *preuve* positive, sure; *cause* undoubted, sure. **c'est la raison ~e de son départ** it's undoubtedly the reason for his going; **ils vont à une mort ~e** they're heading for certain death; **il a fait des progrès ~s** he has made definite *ou* undoubted progress; **la victoire est ~e** victory is assured *ou* certain; **c'est une chose ~e** it's absolutely certain; **c'est ~** there's no doubt about it *ou* that, that's quite certain, that's for sure*; **il est maintenant ~ qu'elle ne reviendra plus** it's now (quite) certain that she won't come back, she's sure *ou* certain not to come back now; **il est aujourd'hui ~ que la terre tourne autour du soleil** there is nowadays no doubt that *ou* today it is a known fact that the earth revolves around the sun; **je le tiens pour ~!** I'm certain *ou* sure of it!; **il est ~ que ce film ne convient guère à des enfants** this film is undoubtedly not suitable *ou* is certainly unsuitable for children.

(b) (*convaincu, sûr*) *personne* sure, certain (*de qch* of sth, *de faire* of doing); convinced (*de qch* of sth, *que* that). **es-tu ~ de rentrer ce soir?** are you sure *ou* certain you'll be back this evening? *ou* of being back this evening?; **il est ~ de leur honnêteté** he's certain *ou* convinced *ou* sure of their honesty; **on n'est jamais ~ du lendemain** you can never be sure *ou* tell what tomorrow will bring; **elle est ~e qu'ils viendront** she's sure *ou* certain *ou* convinced (that) they'll come; *V* **sûr.**

(c) (*Comm: déterminé*) *date, prix* definite.

2 *adj indéf* (*avant n*) **(a)** (*plus ou moins défini*) **un ~** a certain, some; **elle a un ~ charme** she's got a certain charm; **dans une ~e mesure** to some extent; **il y a un ~ village où** there is a certain *ou* some village where; **dans un ~ sens, je le comprends** in a way *ou* in a certain sense *ou* in some senses I can see his point; **jusqu'à un ~ point** up to a (certain) point; **il a manifesté un ~ intérêt** he showed a certain (amount of) *ou* some interest; **un ~ nombre d'éléments font penser que ...** a (certain) number of things lead one to think that ... .

(b) (*parfois péj: personne*) **un ~** a (certain), one; **un ~ M X vous a demandé** a *ou* one Mr X asked for you; **il y a un ~ Robert dans la classe** there is a certain Robert in the class; **un ~ ministre disait même que** a certain minister even said that.

(c) (*intensif*) some. **il a un ~ âge** he is getting on; **une personne d'un ~ âge** an oldish person; **c'est à une ~e distance d'ici** it's quite a *ou* some distance from here; **cela demande une ~e patience** it takes a fair amount of patience; **ça demande un ~ toupet!*** it takes some cheek!*; **au bout d'un ~ temps** after a while *ou* some time.

(d) (*pl: quelques*) **~s** some, certain; **dans ~s cas** in some *ou* certain cases; **~es personnes ne l'aiment pas** some people don't like him; **~es fois, à ~s moments** at (certain) times; **sans ~es notions de base** without some *ou* certain (of the) basic notions.

3 *pron indéf pl*: **~s** (*personnes*) some (people); (*choses*) some; **dans ~s de ces cas** in certain *ou* some of these cases; **parmi ses récits ~s sont amusants** some of his stories are amusing; **pour ~s** for some (people); **~s disent que** some say that; **~s d'entre vous** some of you; **il y en a ~s qui** there are some (people) *ou* there are those who.

certainement [sɛʀtɛnmɑ̃] *adv* (*très probablement*) most probably, most likely, surely; (*sans conteste*) certainly; (*bien sûr*) certainly, of course. **il va ~ venir ce soir** he'll certainly *ou* most probably *ou* most likely come tonight; **il est ~ le plus intelligent** he's certainly *ou* without doubt the most intelligent; **il y a ~ un moyen de s'en tirer** there must certainly *ou* surely be some way out; **puis-je emprunter votre stylo? — ~** can I borrow your pen? — certainly *ou* of course.

certes [sɛʀt(ə)] *adv* **(a)** (*de concession*) (*sans doute*) certainly, admittedly; (*bien sûr*) of course. **il est ~ le plus fort, mais ...** he is admittedly *ou* certainly the strongest, but ...; **~ je n'irai pas**

jusqu'à le renvoyer mais ... of course I shan't *ou* I certainly shan't go as far as dismissing him but ... .

(b) (*d'affirmation*) indeed, most certainly. **l'avez-vous apprécié? — ~** did you like it? — I did indeed *ou* I most certainly did.

certificat [sɛʀtifika] **1** *nm* (*attestation*) certificate, attestation; (*diplôme*) certificate, diploma; (*recommandation*) *[domestique]* testimonial; (*fig*) guarantee.

2: certificat d'aptitude pédagogique teaching diploma; **certificat d'aptitude professionnelle** *diploma obtained after vocational training*; **certificat de bonne vie et mœurs** character reference, certificate of good conduct; **certificat d'études primaires** primary leaving certificate; (*Univ*†) **certificat de licence** ≃ *part of first degree;* **certificat médical** medical *ou* doctor's certificate; **certificat de navigabilité** (*Naut*) certificate of seaworthiness; (*Aviat*) certificate of airworthiness; (*Comm*) **certificat d'origine** certificate of origin; (*Admin*) **certificat de résidence** certificate of residence *ou* domicile; **certificat de scolarité** attestation of attendance at school *ou* university; **certificat de travail** attestation of employment.

certification [sɛʀtifikɑsjɔ̃] *nf* (*Jur: assurance*) attestation, witnessing. **~ de signature** attestation of signature.

certifié, e [sɛʀtifje] (*ptp de* **certifier**) *nm,f* secondary school *ou* high-school (*US*) teacher (*holder of C.A.P.E.S. or C.A.P.E.T.*).

certifier [sɛʀtifje] (7) *vt* **(a)** (*assurer*) **~ qch à qn** to assure sb of sth, guarantee sb sth *ou* sth to sb; **je te certifie qu'ils vont avoir affaire à moi!** I can assure you *ou* I'm telling you* they'll have ME to reckon with!

(b) (*Jur: authentifier*) *document* to certify, guarantee; *signature* to attest, witness; *caution* to counter-secure. **copie certifiée conforme à l'original** certified copy of the original.

certitude [sɛʀtityd] *nf* certainty, certitude (*rare*). **c'est une ~/une ~ absolue** it's certain *ou* a certainty/absolutely certain *ou* an absolute certainty; **avoir la ~ de qch/de faire** to be certain *ou* (quite) sure *ou* confident of sth/of doing; **j'ai la ~ d'être le plus fort** I am certain *ou* (quite) sure of being *ou* that I am the stronger, I am convinced that I am the stronger.

cérumen [seʀymɛn] *nm* (ear)wax, cerumen (*T*).

céruse [seʀyz] *nf* ceruse.

cerveau, *pl* **~x** [sɛʀvo] **1** *nm* **(a)** (*Anat*) brain; (*fig: intelligence*) brain(s), mind; (*fig: centre de direction*) brain(s). **avoir un ~ étroit/puissant** to have limited mental powers/a powerful mind; **ce bureau est le ~ de l'entreprise** this department is the brain(s) of the company; **avoir le ~ dérangé** *ou* (*hum*) **fêlé** to be deranged *ou* (a bit) touched* *ou* cracked*; *V* **rhume, transport.**

(b) (*fig: personne*) brain, mind. **c'est un (grand) ~** he has a great brain *ou* mind, he is a mastermind; **c'était le ~ de l'affaire** he masterminded the job, he was the brain(s) *ou* mastermind behind the job; **c'est le ~ de la bande** he's the brain(s) *ou* the mastermind of the gang; **la fuite** *ou* **l'exode des ~x** the brain-drain.

2: cerveau antérieur forebrain; **cerveau électronique** electronic brain; **cerveau moyen** midbrain; **cerveau postérieur** hindbrain.

cervelas [sɛʀvəla] *nm* saveloy.

cervelet [sɛʀvəlɛ] *nm* cerebellum.

cervelle [sɛʀvɛl] *nf* (*Anat*) brain; (*Culin*) brains. (*Culin*) **~ d'agneau** lamb's brains; **se brûler** *ou* **se faire sauter la ~** to blow one's brains out; **quand il a quelque chose dans la ~** when he gets something into his head; **avoir une ~ d'oiseau** to be feather-brained; **toutes ces ~s folles** (all) these scatterbrains; *V* **creuser, trotter.**

cervical, e, *mpl* **-aux** [sɛʀvikal, o] *adj* cervical.

cervidé [sɛʀvide] *nm*: **~s** cervidae (*T*); **le daim est un ~** the deer is a member of *ou* is one of the cervidae family *ou* species.

cervier [sɛʀvje] *adj m V* **loup.**

cervoise [sɛʀvwaz] *nf* barley beer.

ces [se] *pron dém V* **ce.**

César [sezaʀ] *nm* Caesar.

césarien, -ienne [sezaʀjɛ̃, jɛn] **1** *adj* (*Hist*) Caesarean. **2 césarienne** *nf* (*Méd*) Caesarean (section). **elle a eu** *ou* **on lui a fait une ~ne** she had a Caesarean.

cessant, e [sɛsɑ̃, ɑ̃t] *adj V* **affaire.**

cessation [sɛsɑsjɔ̃] *nf* (*frm*) *[activité, pourparlers]* cessation; *[hostilités]* cessation, suspension; *[paiements]* suspension. (*Ind*) **~ de travail** stoppage (*of work*).

cesse [sɛs] *nf* **(a) sans ~** (*tout le temps*) continually, constantly, incessantly; (*sans interruption*) continuously, without ceasing, incessantly; **elle est sans ~ après lui** she's continually *ou* constantly nagging (at) him, she keeps *ou* is forever nagging (at) him; **la pluie tombe sans ~ depuis hier** it has been raining continuously *ou* non-stop since yesterday.

(b) il n'a de ~ que ... he will not rest until ...; **il n'a eu de ~ qu'elle ne lui cède** he gave her no peace *ou* rest until she gave in to him.

cesser [sese] (1) **1** *vt* **(a)** *bavardage, bruit, activité* to stop, cease (*frm ou* †); *relations* to (bring to an) end, break off. **nous avons cessé la fabrication de cet article** we have stopped making this item, this line has been discontinued; (*Admin*) **~ ses fonctions** to relinquish *ou* give up (one's) office; (*Fin*) **~ ses paiements** to stop *ou* discontinue payment; (*Mil*) **~ le combat** to stop (the) fighting; **~ le travail** to stop work *ou* working.

(b) faire ~ *bruit* to put a stop to, stop; *scandale* to put an end *ou* a stop to; (*Jur*) **pour faire ~ les poursuites** in order to have the action *ou* proceedings dropped.

(c) ~ de faire qch to stop doing sth, cease doing sth; **il a cessé de fumer** he's given up *ou* stopped smoking; **il a cessé de venir il y a un an** he ceased *ou* gave up *ou* left off* coming a year ago; **il n'a pas cessé de pleuvoir de toute la journée** it hasn't stopped raining all day; **la compagnie a cessé d'exister en 1943** the company ceased to exist in 1943; **quand cesseras-tu** *ou* **tu vas bientôt ~ de faire le clown?** when are you going to give up *ou* leave off* *ou* stop acting the fool?; **son effet n'a pas cessé de se faire sentir** its effect is still making itself felt.

(d) (*frm: répétition fastidieuse*) **ne ~ de: il ne cesse de m'importuner** he's continually *ou* incessantly worrying me; **il ne cesse de dire que ...** he is constantly *ou* continually saying that ..., he keeps repeating (endlessly) that ... .

2 *vi [bavardage, bruit, activités, combat]* to stop, cease; *[relations, fonctions]* to come to an end; *[douleur]* to stop; *[fièvre]* to pass, die down. **le vent a cessé** the wind has stopped (blowing); **tout travail a cessé** all work has stopped *ou* come to a halt *ou* a standstill.

cessez-le-feu [seselfø] *nm inv* ceasefire.

cessible [sesibl(ə)] *adj* (*Jur*) transferable, assignable.

cession [sɛsjɔ̃] *nf [bail, biens, droit]* transfer. **faire ~ de** to transfer, assign.

cessionnaire [sɛsjɔnɛʀ] *nm* (*Jur*) *[bien, droit]* transferee, assignee.

c'est-à-dire [setadiʀ] *conj* **(a)** (*à savoir*) that is (to say), i.e. **un lexicographe, ~ quelqu'un qui fait un dictionnaire** a lexicographer, that is (to say), someone who compiles a dictionary.

(b) ~ que (*en conséquence*): **l'usine a fermé, ~ que son frère est maintenant en chômage** the factory has shut down which means that his brother is unemployed now; (*manière d'excuse*) **viendras-tu dimanche? — ~ que j'ai arrangé un pique-nique avec mes amis** will you come on Sunday? — well actually *ou* well the thing is *ou* I'm afraid I've arranged a picnic with my friends; (*rectification*) **je suis fatigué — ~ que tu as trop bu hier** I'm tired — you mean *ou* what you mean is you had too much to drink yesterday.

césure [sezyʀ] *nf* caesura.

cet [sɛt] *adj dém V* **ce.**

cétacé [setase] *nm* cetacean.

ceux [sø] *pron dém V* **celui.**

cévenol, e [sevnɔl] **1** *adj* of *ou* from the Cévennes (region). **2** *nm,f*: **C~(e)** inhabitant *ou* native of the Cévennes (region).

Ceylan [selɑ̃] *nm* Ceylon.

chacal, *pl* **~s** [ʃakal] *nm* jackal.

chaconne [ʃakɔn] *nf* chaconne.

chacun, e [ʃakœ̃, yn] *pron indéf* **(a)** (*d'un ensemble bien défini*) each (one). **~ de** each (one) *ou* every one of; **~ d'entre eux** each (one) of them, every one of them; **~ des deux** each *ou* both of them, each of the two; **ils me donnèrent ~ 10 F/leur chapeau** they each (of them) gave me 10 francs/their hat, each (one) of them gave me 10 francs/their hat; **il leur donna (à) ~ 10 F** *ou* **10 F (à) ~** he gave them 10 francs each, he gave them each 10 francs, he gave each (one) of them 10 francs; **il remit les livres ~ à sa** *ou* **leur place** he put back each of the books in its (own) place; **nous sommes entrés ~ à notre tour** we each went in in turn *ou* went in each in turn.

(b) (*d'un ensemble indéfini: tout le monde*) everyone, everybody. **comme ~ le sait** as everyone *ou* everybody *ou* each person knows; **~ son tour!** everyone in turn!, each in turn!; **~ son goût** *ou* **ses goûts** every man to his (own) taste; **~ pour soi (et Dieu pour tous!)** every man for himself (and God for us all!); *V* **à, tout.**

chafouin, e [ʃafwɛ̃, in] *adj visage* sly(-looking), foxy(-looking). **à la mine ~e** sly- *ou* foxy-looking, with a sly expression.

chagrin[1]**, e** [ʃagʀɛ̃, in] **1** *adj* (*littér*) (*triste*) *air, humeur, personne* despondent, woeful, dejected; (*bougon*) *personne* ill-humoured, morose. **les esprits ~s disent que ...** disgruntled people say that ... .

2 *nm* **(a)** (*affliction*) grief, sorrow. **un ~ d'enfant** a child's disappointment *ou* distress *ou* sorrow; (*à un enfant*) **alors, on a un gros ~!** well, we do look sorry for ourselves! *ou* unhappy! *ou* woeful!; **avoir un ~ d'amour** to have an unhappy love affair, be disappointed in love; **plonger qn dans un profond ~** to plunge sb deep in grief; **faire du ~ à qn** to grieve *ou* distress sb, cause sb grief *ou* distress *ou* sorrow; **avoir du ~** to be grieved *ou* distressed; *V* **noyer**[2]**.**

(b) (††: *mélancolie*) ill-humour.

chagrin[2] [ʃagʀɛ̃] *nm* (*cuir*) shagreen; *V* **peau.**

chagrinant, e [ʃagʀinɑ̃, ɑ̃t] *adj* distressing, grievous.

chagriner [ʃagʀine] (1) *vt* (*désoler*) to grieve, distress, upset; (*tracasser*) to worry, bother.

chah [ʃa] *nm* = **shah.**

chahut* [ʃay] *nm* (*tapage*) uproar, rumpus*, hullabaloo*; (*Scol*) uproar. **faire du ~** to kick up* *ou* make *ou* create a rumpus* *ou* a hullabaloo*; (*Scol*) to make *ou* create an uproar.

chahuter [ʃayte] (1) **1** *vi* (*Scol: faire du bruit*) to make *ou* create an uproar; (*faire les fous*) to kick up* *ou* create a rumpus*, make a commotion.

2 *vt* **(a)** *professeur* to rag, bait; (†) *fille*, to tease. **un professeur chahuté** a teacher who is baited *ou* ragged (by his pupils).

(b) (*: *cahoter*) *objet* to knock about.

chahuteur, -euse [ʃaytœʀ, øz] **1** *adj* rowdy, unruly. **2** *nm,f* rowdy, ragger.

chai [ʃɛ] *nm* wine and spirit store(house).

chaîne [ʃɛn] **1** *nf* **(a)** (*de métal, ornementale*) chain. **~ de bicyclette/de montre** bicycle/watch chain; **attacher un chien à une ~** to chain up a dog, put a dog on a chain; (*Aut*) **~s** (snow) chains.

(b) (*fig: esclavage*) **~s** chains, bonds, fetters, shackles; **les travailleurs ont brisé leurs ~s** the workers have cast off their chains *ou* bonds *ou* shackles.

(c) (*suite, succession*) (*gén, Anat, Chim, Méd*) chain; (*Géog*) *[montagnes]* chain, range. **la ~ des Alpes** the alpine range; (*fig*) **faire la ~** to form a (human) chain; *V* **réaction.**

(d) (*Ind*) **~ (de fabrication)** production line; **produire qch à la**

~ to mass-produce sth, make sth on an assembly line *ou* a production line; (*fig*) **il produit des romans à la ~** he churns out* one novel after another; *V* **travail**[1].

(e) (*TV: longueur d'onde*) channel. **première/deuxième ~** first/second channel.

(f) (*Rad: appareil*) system. **~ hi-fi/stéréophonique** hi-fi/stereophonic system.

(g) (*Comm*) *[journaux]* string; *[magasins]* chain, string.

(h) (*Tex*) warp.

2: (*Écologie*) **chaîne alimentaire** food chain; (*Tech*) **chaîne d'arpenteur** (surveyor's) chain, chain measure; (*Ind*) **chaîne de fabrication** production line; (*Ind*) **chaîne de montage** assembly line; (*Ling*) **chaîne parlée** spoken sequence; **chaîne de sûreté** (*gén*) safety chain; *[porte]* door *ou* safety chain.

chaînette [ʃɛnɛt] *nf* (small) chain. (*Math*) **courbe** *ou* **arc en ~** catenary curve; *V* **point**[2].

chaînon [ʃɛnɔ̃] *nm* (*lit, fig*) *[chaîne]* link; *[filet]* loop; (*Géog*) secondary range (of mountains).

chair [ʃɛʀ] *nf* **(a)** *[homme, animal, fruit]* flesh. **les ~s, la ~ vive** the flesh; **en ~ et en os** in the flesh, as large as life (*hum*); **être ni ~ ni poisson** (*indécis*) to have an indecisive character; (*de caractère flou*) to be neither one thing nor the other; **collant (couleur) ~** flesh-coloured tights; **l'ogre aime la ~ fraîche** the ogre likes a diet of warm young flesh; (*hum*) **il aime la ~ fraîche** (*des jeunes femmes*) he likes firm young flesh *ou* bodies; **avoir/donner la ~ de poule** (*froid*) to have/give goosepimples *ou* gooseflesh; *[chose effrayante]* **ça vous donne** *ou* **on en a la ~ de poule** it makes your flesh creep, it gives you gooseflesh; (*fig*) **~ à canon** cannon fodder; (*Culin*) **~ (à saucisse)** sausage meat; (*fig*) **je vais en faire de la ~ à pâté** *ou* **le transformer en ~ à pâté** I'm going to make mincemeat of him; **bien en ~** well-padded (*hum*), plump.

(b) (*littér, Rel: opposé à l'esprit*) flesh. **souffrir dans/mortifier sa ~** to suffer in/mortify the flesh; **fils/parents selon la ~** natural son/parents; **sa propre ~, la ~ de sa ~** his own flesh and blood; **la ~ est faible** the flesh is weak.

(c) (*Peinture*) **~s** flesh tones *ou* tints.

chaire [ʃɛʀ] *nf* **(a)** (*estrade*) *[prédicateur]* pulpit; *[professeur]* rostrum. **monter en ~** to go up into the pulpit. **(b)** (*Univ: poste*) chair. **créer une ~ de français** to create a chair of French. **(c) la ~ pontificale** the papal throne.

chaise [ʃɛz] **1** *nf* chair. **faire la ~** (*pour porter un blessé*) to link arms to make a seat *ou* chair.

2: **chaise de bébé** highchair; **chaise de cuisine** kitchen chair; **chaise électrique** electric chair; **chaise de jardin** garden chair; **chaise longue** (*siège pliant*) deckchair; (*canapé*) chaise longue; **faire de la chaise longue** to lie back *ou* relax in a deck-chair; (*se reposer*) to put one's feet up; **chaise percée** commode; **chaise (à porteurs)** sedan(-chair); **chaise de poste** poste chaise; **chaise roulante** wheelchair, bathchair†.

chaisière [ʃɛzjɛʀ] *nf* (female) chair attendant.

chaland[1] [ʃalɑ̃] *nm* (*Naut*) barge.

chaland[2], **e**† [ʃalɑ̃, ɑ̃d] *nm,f* (*client*) customer.

Chaldée [kalde] *nf* Chaldea.

chaldéen, -enne [kaldeɛ̃, ɛn] **1** *adj* Chaldean, Chaldee. **2** *nm* (*Ling*) Chaldean. **3** *nm,f*: **C~(ne)** Chaldean, Chaldee.

châle [ʃɑl] *nm* shawl.

chalet [ʃalɛ] *nm* chalet; (*Can*) summer cottage. **~ de nécessité**†† public convenience.

chaleur [ʃalœʀ] *nf* **(a)** (*gén, Phys*) heat; (*modérée, agréable*) warmth. **il fait une ~ accablante** the heat is oppressive, it is oppressively hot; **il faisait une ~ lourde** the air was sultry, it was very close; **les grandes ~s (de l'été)** the hot (summer) days *ou* weather; (*sur étiquette*) **'craint la ~'** 'keep *ou* to be kept in a cool place'; **~ massique** *ou* **spécifique/latente** specific/latent heat.

(b) (*fig*) *[discussion, passion]* heat; *[accueil, voix, couleur]* warmth; *[convictions]* fervour. **prêcher avec ~** to preach with fire *ou* fervour; **défendre une cause/un ami avec ~** to defend a cause/a friend hotly *ou* heatedly *ou* fervently.

(c) (*Zool: excitation sexuelle*) **la période des ~s** the heat; **en ~** on *ou* in heat.

(d) (†: *malaise*) flush. **éprouver des ~s** to have hot flushes; *V* **bouffée.**

chaleureusement [ʃalœʀøzmɑ̃] *adv* warmly.

chaleureux, -euse [ʃalœʀø, øz] *adj accueil, applaudissements, remerciements* warm; *félicitations* hearty, warm. **il parla de lui en termes ~** he spoke of him most warmly.

châlit [ʃɑli] *nm* bedstead.

challenge [ʃalɑ̃ʒ] *nm* (*épreuve*) contest, tournament (*in which a trophy is at stake*); (*trophée*) trophy.

challengeur [ʃalɑ̃ʒœʀ], **challenger** [ʃalɑ̃ʒɛʀ] *nm* challenger.

chaloir [ʃalwaʀ] *vi V* **chaut.**

chaloupe [ʃalup] *nf* launch; (*Can**) rowing boat (*Brit*), rowboat (*US, Can*). **~ de sauvetage** lifeboat.

chaloupé, e [ʃalupe] *adj danse* swaying. **démarche ~e** rolling gait.

chalumeau, *pl* **~x** [ʃalymo] *nm* **(a)** (*Tech*) blowlamp (*Brit*), blowtorch (*US*). **~ oxyacétylénique** oxyacetylene torch; **ils ont découpé le coffre-fort au ~** they used a blowlamp to cut through the safe.

(b) (*Mus*) pipe.

(c) (†: *paille*) (drinking) straw.

(d) (*Can*) spout (fixed at the sugar maple-tree) for collecting maple sap.

chalut [ʃaly] *nm* trawl (net). **pêcher au ~** to trawl.

chalutage [ʃalytaʒ] *nm* trawling.

chalutier [ʃalytje] *nm* (*bateau*) trawler; (*pêcheur*) trawlerman.

chamade [ʃamad] *nf V* **battre.**

chamaille [ʃamɑj] *nf* squabble, (petty) quarrel.

chamailler (se)* [ʃamɑje] (1) *vpr* to squabble, bicker.

chamaillerie* [ʃamɑjʀi] *nf* (*gén pl*) squabble, (petty) quarrel. **~s** squabbling (*U*), bickering (*U*).

chamailleur, -euse [ʃamɑjœʀ, øz] *adj* quarrelsome. **c'est un ~** he's a quarrelsome one, he's a squabbler.

chamarré, e [ʃamaʀe] (*ptp de* **chamarrer**) *adj étoffe, rideaux* richly coloured *ou* brocaded. **~ d'or/de pourpre** bedecked *ou* bedizened (*littér*) with gold/purple; **des généraux ~s de décorations** generals laden *ou* aglitter with medals.

chamarrer [ʃamaʀe] (1) *vt* (*littér: orner*) to bedeck, adorn, bedizen (*littér*).

chamarrure [ʃamaʀyʀ] *nf* (*gén pl*) *[étoffe]* rich *ou* flashy (*péj*) pattern; *[habit, uniforme]* rich trimming.

chambard* [ʃɑ̃baʀ] *nm* (*vacarme*) racket*, row*, rumpus*; (*protestation*) rumpus*, row*, shindy*; (*bagarre*) scuffle, brawl; (*désordre*) shambles* (*sg*), mess; (*bouleversement*) upheaval. **faire du ~** (*protester*) to kick up a rumpus* *ou* a row* *ou* a shindy*; **ça va faire du ~!** there'll be a row* *ou* a rumpus* over that!

chambardement* [ʃɑ̃baʀdəmɑ̃] *nm* (*bouleversement*) upheaval; (*nettoyage*) clear-out.

chambarder* [ʃɑ̃baʀde] (1) *vt* (*bouleverser*) *objets* to turn upside down; *projets, habitudes* to turn upside down, upset; (*se débarrasser de*) to chuck out‡, throw out, get rid of. **il a tout chambardé** (*bouleversé*) he turned everything upside down; (*liquidé*) he chucked‡ *ou* threw the whole lot out, he got rid of the whole lot.

chambellan [ʃɑ̃belɑ̃] *nm* chamberlain.

chamboulement* [ʃɑ̃bulmɑ̃] *nm* (*désordre*) chaos, confusion; (*bouleversement*) upheaval.

chambouler* [ʃɑ̃bule] (1) *vt* (*bouleverser*) *objets* to turn upside down (*fig*); *projets* to mess up*, make a mess of*, cause chaos in. **cela a chamboulé nos projets** that caused chaos in *ou* messed up* our plans *ou* threw our plans right out*; **il a tout chamboulé dans la maison** he has turned the (whole) house upside down; **pour bien faire, il faudrait tout ~** to do things properly we should have to turn the whole thing *ou* everything upside down.

chambranle [ʃɑ̃bʀɑ̃l] *nm* *[porte]* (door) frame, casing; *[fenêtre]* (window) frame, casing; *[cheminée]* mantelpiece. **il s'appuya au ~** he leant against the doorpost.

chambre [ʃɑ̃bʀ(ə)] **1** *nf* **(a)** (*pour dormir*) bedroom; (††: *pièce*) chamber††, room. **~ à un lit/à deux lits** single-/twin-bedded room; **va dans ta ~!** go to your (bed)room!; **faire ~ à part** to sleep apart *ou* in separate rooms; *V* **femme, robe.**

(b) (*Pol*) House, Chamber. **à la C~** in the House; **système à deux ~s** two-house *ou* -chamber system; **C~ Haute/Basse** Upper/Lower House *ou* Chamber.

(c) (*Jur: section judiciaire*) division; (*Admin: assemblée, groupement*) chamber. **première/deuxième ~** upper/lower chamber.

(d) (*Tech*) *[fusil, mine, canon]* chamber.

(e) (*loc*) **en ~: travailler en ~** to work at home; **couturière en ~** dressmaker working at home; (*iro*) **stratège/alpiniste en ~** armchair strategist/mountaineer; *V* **musique, orchestre.**

2: (*Jur*) **chambre d'accusation** court of criminal appeal; (*Aut*) **chambre à air** (inner) tube; **sans chambre à air** tubeless; **chambre d'amis** spare *ou* guest room; **chambre de bonne** maid's room; (*Naut*) **chambre des cartes** chart-house; **chambre à cartouches** (cartridge) chamber; (*Aut*) **chambre de combustion** combustion chamber; (*Comm*) **Chambre de commerce** Chamber of Commerce; (*Brit Pol*) **la Chambre des Communes** the House of Commons; (*Comm*) **chambre de compensation** clearing house; (*Jur*) **chambre correctionnelle** ≃ police *ou* magistrates' court; **chambre à coucher** (*pièce*) bedroom; (*mobilier*) bedroom suite; (*Jur*) **chambre criminelle** court of criminal appeal (*in the Cour de Cassation*); (*Pol*) **la Chambre des députés** the Chamber of Deputies; **chambre d'enfant** child's (bed)room, nursery; **chambre d'explosion** = **chambre de combustion; chambre forte** strongroom; **chambre froide** *ou* **frigorifique** cold room; **mettre qch en chambre froide** *ou* **frigorifique** to put sth into cold storage *ou* in the cold room; **chambre à gaz** gas chamber; (*Brit Pol*) **la Chambre des Lords** the House of Lords; (*Naut*) **chambre des machines** engine-room; **chambre des métiers** guild chamber; **chambre meublée** furnished room, bed-sitter; (*Phot*) **chambre noire** dark room; (*Anat*) **les chambres de l'œil** the aqueous chambers of the eye; (*Jur*) **chambre des requêtes** (preliminary) civil appeal court; **chambre syndicale** employers' federation.

chambrée [ʃɑ̃bʀe] *nf* (*pièce, occupants*) room; *[soldats]* barrack-room.

chambrer [ʃɑ̃bʀe] (1) *vt vin* to bring to room temperature, chambré; *personne* (*prendre à l'écart*) to corner, collar*; (*tenir enfermé*) to keep in, confine, keep cloistered. **les organisateurs ont chambré l'invité d'honneur** the organisers kept the V.I.P. guest out of circulation *ou* to themselves.

chambrette [ʃɑ̃bʀɛt] *nf* small bedroom.

chambrière [ʃɑ̃bʀijɛʀ] *nf* (*béquille de charrette*) cart-prop; (†: *servante*) chambermaid.

chameau, *pl* **~x** [ʃamo] *nm* **(a)** (*Zool*) camel; *V* **poil. (b)** (**péj*) beast*. **elle devient ~ avec l'âge** the older she gets the more beastly she becomes.

chamelier [ʃaməlje] *nm* camel driver, cameleer.

chamelle [ʃamɛl] *nf* **(a)** (*Zool*) she-camel. **(b) = chameau b.**

chamois [ʃamwa] **1** *nm* chamois; *V* **peau. 2** *adj inv* fawn, buff(-coloured).

champ [ʃɑ̃] **1** *nm* **(a)** (*Agr*) field. **~ de blé** cornfield, field of corn; **~ d'avoine/de trèfle** field of oats/clover; **travailler aux ~s** to work in the fields; **on s'est retrouvé en plein(s) ~(s)** we found ourselves in the middle of *ou* surrounded by fields.

(b) (*campagne*) **~s** country(side); **la vie aux ~s** life in the country, country life; **fleurs des ~s** wild flowers, flowers of the countryside; *V* **clef, travers**[2].

(c) (*fig: domaine*) field, area. **il a dû élargir le ~ de ses recherches** he had to widen *ou* extend the field *ou* area of his research *ou* his investigations.

(d) (*Élec, Ling, Phys*) field.

(e) (*Ciné, Phot*) **dans le ~** in (the) shot *ou* the picture; **être dans le ~** to be in shot; **sortir du ~** to go out of shot; **pas assez de ~** not enough depth of focus; *V* **profondeur.**

(f) (*Hér*) *[écu, médaille]* field.

(g) (*loc*) **avoir du ~** to have elbowroom *ou* room to move; **laisser du ~ à qn** to leave sb room to manoeuvre; **laisser le ~ libre** to leave the field open *ou* clear; **vous avez le ~ libre** I'll (*ou* we'll *etc*) leave you to it, it's all clear for you; **laisser le ~ libre à qn** to leave sb a clear field; **prendre du ~** (*lit*) to step back, draw back; (*fig*) to draw back; (*Mil*) **sonner aux ~s!** to sound the general salute; *V* **sur**[1], **tout.**

2: **champ d'action** sphere of activity; (*Aviat*) **champ d'aviation** airfield; (*Mil, fig*) **champ de bataille** battlefield; **champ clos** combat area; (*fig*) **en champ clos** behind closed doors; **champ de courses** racecourse; **champ de foire** fairground; (*Mil*) **champ d'honneur** field of honour; **mourir** *ou* **tomber au champ d'honneur** to be killed in action; (*Phys*) **champ magnétique** magnetic field; (*Mil*) **champ de manœuvre** parade ground; **champ de Mars** ≃ military esplanade; **champ de mines** minefield; **champ de neige** snowfield; (*Méd*) **champ opératoire** operative field; (*Phys*) **champ optique** optical field; (*Agr*) **champ ouvert** open field; (*Ling*) **champ sémantique** semantic field; **champ de tir** (*terrain*) rifle *ou* shooting range, practice ground; (*zone*) field of fire; **champ visuel** *ou* **de vision** field of vision *ou* view, visual field.

champagne [ʃɑ̃paɲ] **1** *nm* champagne. **2** *nf*: **la C~** Champagne, the Champagne region; *V* **fine**[2].

champagnisation [ʃɑ̃paɲizɑsjɔ̃] *nf [vin]* champagnization.

champagniser [ʃɑ̃paɲize] (1) *vt vin* to champagnize.

champenois, e [ʃɑ̃pənwa, waz] **1** *adj* of *ou* from Champagne. (*Vin*) **méthode ~e** champagne method; **vin (mousseux) méthode ~e** champagne-type *ou* sparkling wine. **2** *nm,f*: **C~(e)** inhabitant *ou* native of Champagne.

champêtre [ʃɑ̃pɛtʀ(ə)] *adj* (*rural*) (*gén*) rural; *vie* country (*épith*), rural; *odeur* country (*épith*); *bal, fête* village (*épith*); *V* **garde**[2].

champignon [ʃɑ̃piɲɔ̃] *nm* **(a)** (*gén*) mushroom; (*terme générique*) fungus; (*vénéneux*) toadstool, poisonous mushroom *ou* fungus; (*Méd*) fungus. **~ comestible** (edible) mushroom, edible fungus; **certains ~s sont comestibles** some fungi are edible; **~ de Paris** *ou* **de couche** cultivated mushroom; *V* **ville.**

(b) (*aussi* **~ atomique**) mushroom (cloud).

(c) ((*Aut**) accelerator; *V* **appuyer.**

champignonnière [ʃɑ̃piɲɔnjɛʀ] *nf* mushroom bed.

champion, -onne [ʃɑ̃pjɔ̃, ɔn] **1** *adj* (*) A1, first-rate. **c'est ~!** that's great! *ou* first-rate! *ou* top-class! (*Brit*).

2 *nm,f* (*Sport, défenseur*) champion. **~ du monde de boxe** world boxing champion; **se faire le ~ d'une cause** to champion a cause; (*hum*) **c'est le ~ de la gaffe** there's no one to beat him for tactlessness.

championnat [ʃɑ̃pjɔna] *nm* championship. **~ du monde/d'Europe** world/European championship.

chançard, e* [ʃɑ̃saʀ, aʀd(ə)] **1** *adj* lucky. **2** *nm,f* lucky devil*, lucky dog*.

chance [ʃɑ̃s] *nf* **(a)** (*bonne fortune*) (good) luck. **tu as de la ~ d'y aller** you're lucky *ou* fortunate to be going; **il a la ~ d'y aller** he's lucky *ou* fortunate enough to be going, he has the good luck *ou* good fortune to be going; **avec un peu de ~** with a bit of luck; **quelle ~!** what a bit *ou* stroke of (good) luck!, how lucky!; **c'est une ~ que ...** it's lucky *ou* fortunate that ..., it's a bit of *ou* a stroke of luck that ...; **la ~ a voulu qu'il y eût un médecin sur place** by a stroke of luck *ou* luckily there was a doctor on the spot; **par ~** luckily, fortunately; **pas de ~!** hard *ou* bad *ou* tough* luck!, hard lines!*; (*iro*) **c'est bien ma ~** (that's) just my luck!; *V* **coup, porter.**

(b) (*hasard, fortune*) luck, chance. **courir** *ou* **tenter sa ~** to try one's luck; **la ~ a tourné** his (*ou* her *etc*) luck has changed; **la ~ lui sourit** luck favours him, (good) fortune smiles on him; **mettre la ~** *ou* **toutes les ~s de son côté** to take no chances; **sa mauvaise ~ le poursuit** he is dogged by ill-luck, bad luck dogs his footsteps (*littér*); *V* **bon**[1].

(c) (*possibilité de succès*) chance. **donner sa ~** *ou* **ses ~s à qn** to give sb his chance; **quelles sont ses ~s (de réussir** *ou* **de succès)?** what are his chances *ou* what chance has he got (of succeeding *ou* of success)?; **il a ses** *ou* **des ~s (de gagner)** he's got *ou* stands a *ou* some chance (of winning); **il n'a aucune ~** he hasn't got *ou* doesn't stand a (dog's) chance; **il y a une ~ sur cent (pour) que ...** there's one chance in a hundred *ou* a one-in-a-hundred chance that ...; **il y a peu de ~s (pour) qu'il la voie** there's little chance (that) he'll see her, there's little chance of his seeing her, the chances of his seeing her are slim; **il y a toutes les ~s que ...** there's every chance that ..., the chances are that ...; **ils ont des ~s égales** they have equal chances *ou* an equal chance; **elle a une ~ sur deux de s'en sortir** she's got a fifty-fifty chance of pulling through.

chancelant, e [ʃɑ̃slɑ̃, ɑ̃t] *adj démarche, pas* unsteady, faltering, tottering; *meuble, objet* wobbly, unsteady; *mémoire, santé* uncertain, shaky; *conviction, courage, résolution* wavering, faltering, shaky; *autorité* tottering, wavering, shaky. **dynasties ~es** tottering dynasties.

chanceler [ʃɑ̃sle] (4) *vi [personne]* to totter; (*d'émotion*) to reel; *[objet]* to wobble, totter; *[autorité]* to totter, falter; *[conviction, résolution, courage]* to waver, falter. **il s'avança en chancelant** he tottered forward; **une société qui chancelle sur ses bases** a society which is tottering upon its foundations; **il chancela dans sa résolution** he wavered in his resolve.

chancelier [ʃɑ̃səlje] *nm [Allemagne, Autriche]* chancellor; *[ambassade]* secretary; (*Hist*) chancellor. **le C~ de l'Échiquier** the Chancellor of the Exchequer.

chancelière [ʃɑ̃səljɛʀ] *nf* foot-muff (*Brit*).

chancellerie [ʃɑ̃sɛlʀi] *nf [ambassade, consulat]* chancellery, chancery; (*Hist*) chancellery.

chanceux, -euse [ʃɑ̃sø, øz] *adj* lucky, fortunate; (††: *hasardeux*) hazardous.

chancre [ʃɑ̃kʀ(ə)] *nm* (*Bot, Méd, fig: abcès*) canker. **~ syphilitique** chancre; **~ mou** chancroid, soft chancre; **manger** *ou* **bouffer comme un ~**‡ to pig oneself‡ (*Brit*), stuff oneself like a pig*.

chandail [ʃɑ̃daj] *nm* (thick) jumper (*Brit*), (thick) sweater.

chandelier [ʃɑ̃dəlje] *nm* (*à une branche*) candlestick; (*à plusieurs branches*) candelabra.

Chandeleur [ʃɑ̃dlœʀ] *nf*: **la ~** Candlemas.

chandelle [ʃɑ̃dɛl] *nf* **(a)** (*bougie*) (tallow) candle. **dîner aux ~s** dinner by candlelight.

(b) (*fig*) (*Aviat*) chandelle; (*Rugby*) up-and-under; (*Tennis*) lob; (*Gym*) shoulder stand; (‡: *au nez*) trickle of snot*. (*fusée d'artifice*) **~ romaine** roman candle.

(c) (*loc*) (*hum*) **tenir la ~** to play gooseberry (*Brit*); (*Aviat*) **monter en ~** to climb vertically; *V* **économie, jeu.**

chanfrein [ʃɑ̃fʀɛ̃] *nm* **(a)** (*Tech*) chamfer, bevelled edge. **(b)** *[cheval]* nose.

change [ʃɑ̃ʒ] *nm* **(a)** (*Fin*) *[devises]* exchange. (*Banque*) **faire le ~** to exchange money; **opération de ~** (foreign) exchange transaction; *V* **agent, bureau** *etc.*

(b) (*Fin: taux d'échange*) exchange rate. **le ~ est avantageux** the exchange rate is favourable; **la cote des ~s** the (list of) exchange rates.

(c) (*loc*) **gagner/perdre au ~** to gain/lose on the exchange *ou* deal; **donner le ~** to allay suspicion, put people off the scent; **donner le ~ à qn** to throw sb off the scent, put sb off the track.

changeable [ʃɑ̃ʒabl(ə)] *adj* (*transformable*) changeable, alterable.

changeant, e [ʃɑ̃ʒɑ̃, ɑ̃t] *adj personne, fortune, humeur* changeable, fickle, changing (*épith*); *couleur, paysage* changing (*épith*); *temps* changeable, unsettled. **son humeur est ~e** he's a man of many moods *ou* of uneven temper.

changement [ʃɑ̃ʒmɑ̃] *nm* **(a)** (*remplacement*) changing. **le ~ de la roue nous a coûté 100 F** the wheel change cost us 100 francs; **le ~ de la roue nous a pris une heure** changing the wheel *ou* the wheel change took us an hour, it took us an hour to change the wheel.

(b) (*fait de se transformer*) change (*de* in, of). **le ~ soudain de la température/de la direction du vent** the sudden change in *ou* of temperature/(the) direction of the wind.

(c) (*transformation*) change, alteration. **il n'aime pas le(s) ~(s)** he doesn't like change(s); **elle a trouvé de grands ~s dans le village** she found great changes in the village, she found the village greatly changed *ou* altered; **la situation reste sans ~** there has been no change in the situation, the situation remains unchanged *ou* unaltered; **~ en bien** *ou* **en mieux** change for the better.

(d) (*V* **changer 2**) **~ de** change of; **~ d'adresse/d'air/de ministère** change of address/air/government; **~ de programme** (*projet*) change of plan *ou* in the plan(s); (*spectacle etc*) change of programme *ou* in the programme; **~ de direction** (*sens*) change of course *ou* direction; (*dirigeants*) change of management; (*sur un écriteau*) under new management; **il y a eu un ~ de propriétaire** it has changed hands, it has come under new ownership; (*Mus*) **~ de ton** change of key; **~ de décor** (*paysage*) change of scenery; (*Théât*) scene-change; (*Théât*) **~ à vue** transformation (scene).

(e) (*Admin: mutation*) transfer. **demander son ~** to apply for a transfer.

(f) (*Aut*) **~ de vitesse** (*dispositif*) gears, gear lever, gear change; (*action*) change of gears, gear changing (*U*), gear change; *[bicyclette]* gear(s).

(g) (*Rail*) change. **il y a 2 ~s pour aller de X à Y** you have to change twice *ou* make 2 changes to get from X to Y.

changer [ʃɑ̃ʒe] (3) **1** *vt* **(a)** (*modifier*) *projets, personne* to change, alter. **on ne le changera pas** nothing will change him, nothing will make him change; **ce chapeau la change** this hat makes her look different; **cela change tout!** that makes all the difference!, that changes everything!; **~ qch à: une promenade lui changera les idées** a walk will take his mind off things; **il n'a pas changé une virgule au rapport** he hasn't changed *ou* altered a comma in the report; **il ne veut rien ~ à ses habitudes** he doesn't want to change *ou* alter his habits in any way; **cela ne change rien à l'affaire** it doesn't make the slightest difference, it doesn't alter things a bit; **cela ne change rien au fait que** it doesn't change *ou* alter the fact that.

(b) (*remplacer, échanger*) to change; (*Théât*) *décor* to change, shift; (*Fin*) *argent, billet* to change. **~ 100 F contre des livres** to change 100 francs into pounds, exchange 100 francs for pounds; **~ les draps/une ampoule** to change the sheets/a bulb; **il a changé sa voiture pour** *ou* **contre une nouvelle** he changed his car for a new one; **ce manteau était trop petit, j'ai dû le ~** that coat was too small — I had to change *ou* exchange it; **j'ai changé ma place contre la sienne** I changed *ou* swapped* places with him, I exchanged my place for his; **il a changé sa montre contre celle de son ami** he exchanged his watch for his friend's, he swapped* watches with his friend.

(c) (*déplacer*) **~ qn de poste** to move sb to a different job; **~ qn/qch de place** to move sb/sth to a different place, shift sb/sth;

ils ont changé tous les meubles de place they've changed *ou* moved all the furniture round, they've shifted all the furniture (about); (*fig*) ~ **son fusil d'épaule** to change *ou* alter one's stand.

(d) (*transformer*) ~ **qch/qn en** to change *ou* turn sth/sb into; **la citrouille fut changée en carrosse** the pumpkin was changed *ou* turned into a carriage.

(e) ~ **un enfant/malade** to change a child/patient; ~ **ses couches à un enfant** to change a child's nappies (*Brit*) *ou* diapers (*US*).

(f) (*procurer un changement à*) **cela nous a changés agréablement de ne plus entendre de bruit** it was a pleasant *ou* nice change for us not to hear any noise; **ils vont en Italie, cela les changera de leur pays pluvieux** they are going to Italy — it will be *ou* make a change for them from their rainy country.

2 changer de *vt indir* **(a)** (*remplacer*) to change; (*modifier*) to change, alter. ~ **d'adresse/de nom/de voiture** to change one's address/name/car; ~ **de domicile** *ou* **d'appartement** to move (house); ~ **de peau** (*lit*) to shed one's skin; (*fig*) to become a different person; ~ **de vêtements** *ou* **de toilette** to change (one's clothes); **elle a changé de coiffure** she has changed *ou* altered her hair style; ~ **d'avis** *ou* **d'idée/de ton** to change one's mind/tune; **elle a changé de couleur quand elle m'a vu** she changed colour when she saw me; **la rivière a changé de cours** the river has altered *ou* shifted its course; **elle a changé de visage** her face has changed *ou* altered; (*d'émotion*) her expression changed *ou* altered; **change de disque!‡** put another record on!‡, don't keep (harping) on *ou* don't go on about it!*

(b) (*passer dans une autre situation*) to change. ~ **de train/compartiment/pays** to change trains/compartments/countries; ~ **de camp** *[victoire, soldat]* to change camps *ou* sides; (*Aut*) ~ **de vitesse** to change gear; **changeons de crémerie‡** *ou* **d'auberge‡** let's take our custom elsewhere; ~ **de position** to alter *ou* shift *ou* change one's position; ~ **de côté** (*gén*) to go over *ou* across to the other side, change sides; (*dans la rue*) to cross over (to the other side); ~ **de propriétaire** *ou* **de mains** to change hands; **changeons de sujet** let's change the subject; **il a changé de route pour m'éviter** he went a different way *ou* changed his route to avoid me; (*Naut*) ~ **de cap** to change *ou* alter course.

(c) (*échanger*) to exchange, change, swap* (*avec qn* with sb). ~ **de place avec qn** to change *ou* exchange *ou* swap* places with sb; **j'aime bien ton sac, tu changes avec moi?*** I like your bag — will you swap* (with me)? *ou* will you exchange *ou* do a swap* (with me)?

3 *vi* **(a)** (*se transformer*) to change, alter. ~ **en bien** *ou* **en mieux/en mal** *ou* **en pire** to change for the better/the worse; **il n'a pas du tout changé** he hasn't changed *ou* altered at all *ou* a bit; **les temps ont bien changé!** *ou* **sont bien changés!** (how) times have changed!; **le vent a changé** the wind has changed (direction) *ou* has veered round.

(b) (*Aviat, Rail etc*) to change. **j'ai dû** ~ **à Rome** I had to change at Rome.

(c) (*lit, iro*) **pour** ~! (just) for a change!, by way of a change!; **et pour (pas)** ~ **c'est nous qui faisons le travail*** and as per usual* *ou* and just by way of a change (*iro*) we'll be doing the work.

(d) (*procurer un changement*) **ça change des films à l'eau de rose** it makes a change from these sugary *ou* sentimental films.

4 se changer *vpr* **(a)** (*mettre d'autres vêtements*) to change (one's clothes). **va te** ~ **avant de sortir** go and change (your clothes) before you go out.

(b) se ~ **en** to change *ou* turn into.

changeur [ʃɑ̃ʒœʀ] *nm* **(a)** (*personne*) moneychanger. **(b)** (*machine*) ~ **(de disques)** record changer; ~ **de monnaie** change machine.

chanoine [ʃanwan] *nm* (*Rel*) canon (*person*); *V* **gras.**

chanoinesse [ʃanwanɛs] *nf* (*Rel*) canoness.

chanson [ʃɑ̃sɔ̃] **1** *nf* song. ~ **d'amour/à boire/de marche/populaire** love/drinking/marching/popular song; ~ **enfantine/d'étudiant** children's/student song; (*fig*) **c'est toujours la même** ~ it's always the same old story; ~**s que tout cela!††**, fiddle-de-dee!††, poppycock!††; **ça, c'est une autre** ~ that's quite a different matter *ou* quite another story; *V* **connaître.**

2: chanson folklorique folksong; (*Littérat*) **chanson de geste** chanson de geste; **chanson de marin** (sea) shanty; **chanson de Noël** (Christmas) carol; **la Chanson de Roland** the Chanson de Roland, the Song of Roland; (*Littérat*) **chanson de toile** chanson de toile.

chansonnette [ʃɑ̃sɔnɛt] *nf* ditty, light-hearted song.

chansonnier [ʃɑ̃sɔnje] *nm* (*artiste*) chansonnier, cabaret singer (*specializing in political satire*); (*livre*) song-book.

chant[1] [ʃɑ̃] *nm* **(a)** (*sons*) *[personne]* singing; *[oiseau]* singing, warbling; (*mélodie habituelle*) song; *[insecte]* chirp(ing); *[coq]* crow(ing); *[mer, vent, instrument]* song. **entendre des** ~**s mélodieux** to hear melodious singing; **au** ~ **du coq** at cockcrow; (*fig*) **le** ~ **du cygne d'un artiste** *etc* an artist's *etc* swan song.

(b) (*chanson*) song. ~ **patriotique/populaire** patriotic/popular song; ~ **de Noël** (Christmas) carol; ~ **religieux** *ou* **sacré** *ou* **d'Eglise** hymn; ~ **de guerre** battle song.

(c) (*action de chanter, art*) singing. **nous allons continuer par le** ~ **d'un cantique** we shall continue by singing a hymn; **cours/professeur de** ~ singing lessons/teacher; **apprendre le** ~ to learn singing; **j'aime le** ~ **choral** I like choral *ou* choir singing; ~ **grégorien** Gregorian chant; ~ **à une/à plusieurs voix** song for one voice/several voices.

(d) (*mélodie*) melody.

(e) (*Poésie*) (*genre*) ode; (*division*) canto. ~ **funèbre** funeral song *ou* lament; ~ **nuptial** nuptial song *ou* poem; **épopée en douze** ~**s** epic in twelve cantos; (*fig*) **le** ~ **désespéré de ce poète** the despairing song of this poet.

chant[2] [ʃɑ̃] *nm* edge. **de** *ou* **sur** ~ on edge, edgewise.

chantable [ʃɑ̃tabl(ə)] *adj* (*souvent nég*) singable. **je doute que cet air soit** ~ I doubt if this tune can be sung.

chantage [ʃɑ̃taʒ] *nm* blackmail. **se livrer à un** *ou* **exercer un** ~ **sur qn** to blackmail sb; **faire du** ~ to use *ou* apply blackmail; **on lui a extorqué des millions à coup de** ~ they blackmailed him into parting with millions; **il (nous) a fait le** ~ **au suicide** he threatened suicide to blackmail us, he blackmailed us with the threat of *ou* by threatening suicide.

chantant, e [ʃɑ̃tɑ̃, ɑ̃t] *adj* **(a)** (*mélodieux*) *accent, voix* singsong, lilting. **(b)** (*qui se chante aisément*) *air, musique* tuneful, catchy*.

chanter [ʃɑ̃te] (1) **1** *vt* **(a)** (*chanson, opéra* to sing; (*Rel*) *messe, vêpres* to sing. **l'oiseau chante ses trilles** the bird sings *ou* warbles *ou* chirrups its song; **chante-nous quelque chose!** sing us a song!

(b) (*célébrer*) to sing of, sing. ~ **les exploits de qn** to sing (of) sb's exploits; ~ **l'amour** to sing of love; (*fig*) ~ **les louanges de qn** to sing sb's praises; *V* **victoire.**

(c) (*: *raconter*) **qu'est-ce qu'il nous chante là?** what's this he's telling us?, what's he on about now?*; ~ **qch sur tous les tons** to harp on about sth, go on about sth*.

2 *vi* **(a)** *[personne]* to sing; (**fig: de douleur*) to yell (out), sing out*; *[oiseau]* to sing, warble; *[coq]* to crow; *[poule]* to cackle; *[ruisseau]* to babble; *[bouilloire]* to sing; *[eau qui bout]* to hiss. ~ **juste/faux** to sing in tune/out of tune *ou* flat; ~ **pour endormir un enfant** to sing a child to sleep; **chantez donc plus fort!** sing up!; **c'est comme si on chantait*** it's like talking to a deaf man, it's a waste of breath; **il chante en parlant** he's got a lilting *ou* singsong voice *ou* accent, he speaks with a lilt.

(b) (*par chantage*) **faire** ~ **qn** to blackmail sb.

(c) (*: *plaire*) **vas-y si le programme te chante** (you) go if the programme appeals to you *ou* if you fancy the programme; **cela ne me chante guère de sortir ce soir** I don't really feel like *ou* fancy going out *ou* I am not very keen on going out tonight; **il vient quand** *ou* **si** *ou* **comme ça lui chante** he comes when *ou* if *ou* as the fancy takes him.

chanterelle [ʃɑ̃tʀɛl] *nf* **(a)** (*Bot*) chanterelle. **(b)** (*Mus*) E-string; *V* **appuyer. (c)** (*oiseau*) decoy (bird).

chanteur, -euse [ʃɑ̃tœʀ, øz] *nm,f* singer. ~ **de charme** crooner; ~ **de(s) rues** street singer; (*devant théâtres, cinémas*) busker; *V* **maître, oiseau.**

chantier [ʃɑ̃tje] **1** *nm* **(a)** (*Constr*) building site; (*Ponts et Chaussées*) roadworks (*pl*); (*Can**†: *exploitation forestière*) logging *ou* lumbering industry (*US, Can*); (*Can*; **Hist: habitation de bûcherons*) lumber camp (*US, Can*), shanty (*Can*). **le matin il est au** ~ he's on the (building *etc*) site in the mornings; **devant nous il y avait un** ~ there were roadworks in front of us; (*écriteau*) '~ **interdit au public**' 'no entry *ou* admittance (to the public)'; (*écriteau*) **'fin de** ~' 'road clear'.

(b) (*entrepôt*) depot, yard.

(c) (**fig: désordre*) shambles*. **quel** ~ **dans ta chambre!** what a shambles* *ou* mess in your room!

(d) (*loc*) **en** ~, **sur le** ~: **il a 2 livres en** ~ *ou* **sur le** ~ he has 2 books in hand, he's working on 2 books; **mettre un ouvrage en** ~ *ou* **sur le** ~ to put a piece of work in hand; **dans l'appartement, nous sommes en** ~ **depuis 2 mois** we've had work *ou* alterations going on in the flat for 2 months now.

2: chantier de démolition demolition site; **chantier d'exploitation forestière** tree-felling *ou* lumber site; (*Min*) **chantier d'exploitation** opencast working; **chantier naval** shipyard, shipbuilding yard.

chantonnement [ʃɑ̃tɔnmɑ̃] *nm* (soft) singing, humming, crooning.

chantonner [ʃɑ̃tɔne] (1) **1** *vi [personne]* to sing to oneself, hum, croon; *[eau qui bout]* to sing. ~ **pour endormir un bébé** to croon *ou* sing a baby to sleep. **2** *vt* to sing, hum. ~ **une mélodie** to sing *ou* hum a tune (to oneself); ~ **une berceuse à** *ou* **pour un bébé** to croon *ou* sing a lullaby to a baby.

chantoung [ʃɑ̃tuŋ] *nm* Shantung (silk).

chantourner [ʃɑ̃tuʀne] (1) *vt* to jig-saw; *V* **scie.**

chantre [ʃɑ̃tʀ(ə)] *nm* (*Rel*) cantor; (*fig littér*) (*poète*) bard, minstrel; (*laudateur*) exalter, eulogist. (*littér*) **les** ~**s des bois** the songsters; *V* **grand.**

chanvre [ʃɑ̃vʀ(ə)] *nm* (*Bot, Tex*) hemp. **de** ~ hemp (*épith*), hempen (*épith*); ~ **du Bengale** jute; ~ **indien** Indian hemp; ~ **de Manille** Manila hemp, abaca; *V* **cravate.**

chanvrier, -ière [ʃɑ̃vʀije, ijɛʀ] **1** *adj* hemp (*épith*). **2** *nm,f* (*cultivateur*) hemp-grower; (*ouvrier*) hemp dresser.

chaos [kao] *nm* (*lit, fig*) chaos. **dans le** ~ in (a state of) chaos.

chaotique [kaɔtik] *adj* chaotic.

chapardage* [ʃapaʀdaʒ] *nm* petty theft, pilfering (*U*).

chaparder* [ʃapaʀde] (1) *vti* to pinch, pilfer (*à* from).

chapardeur, -euse* [ʃapaʀdœʀ, øz] **1** *adj* light-fingered. **2** *nm,f* pilferer, petty thief.

chape [ʃap] *nf* **(a)** (*Rel*) cope. **(b)** (*Tech*) *[pneu]* tread; *[bielle]* strap; *[poulie]* shell; *[voûte]* coating.

chapeau, *pl* ~**x** [ʃapo] *nm* **1 (a)** (*coiffure*) hat. **saluer qn** ~ **bas** to doff one's hat to sb; **tirer son** ~ **à qn*** to take off one's hat to sb; **il a réussi? eh bien** ~ **!*** he managed it? hats off to him!; ~, **mon vieux!*** well done *ou* jolly good, old man!* (*Brit*).

(b) (*Tech*) *[palier]* cap. (*Aut*) ~ **de roue** hub cap; **démarrer sur les** ~**x de roues*** *[véhicule, personne]* to shoot off at top speed, take off like a shot; *[affaire, soirée]* to get off to a good start; **prendre un virage sur les** ~**x de roues** to screech round a corner.

(c) (*Presse*) *[article]* introductory paragraph.

(d) (*Bot*) *[champignon]* cap; (*Culin*) *[vol-au-vent]* lid, top.

2: (*Mus*) **chapeau chinois** crescent, jingling Johnny; **chapeau cloche** cloche (hat); **chapeau de gendarme** (*en papier*) (folded) paper hat; **chapeau haut-de-forme** top hat, topper*; **chapeau melon** bowler (hat); **chapeau mou** trilby, fedora (*US*); **chapeau de paille** straw hat; **chapeau de plage** *ou* **de soleil** sun hat; **chapeau tyrolien** Tyrolean hat.
chapeauté, e [ʃapote] **1** *ptp de* **chapeauter**. **2** *adj* with a hat on, wearing a hat.
chapeauter [ʃapote] (1) *vt* (*Admin etc*) to head, oversee.
chapelain [ʃaplɛ̃] *nm* chaplain.
chapelet [ʃaplɛ] *nm* **(a)** (*objet*) rosary, beads; (*prières*) rosary. **réciter** *ou* **dire son ~** to say the rosary, tell *ou* say one's beads†; **le ~ a lieu à 5 heures** the rosary is at 5 o'clock; (*fig*) **dévider** *ou* **défiler son ~*** to recite one's grievances.
(b) (*fig: succession, chaîne*) **~ d'oignons/d'injures/d'îles** string of onions/of insults/of islands; **~ de bombes** stick of bombs.
chapelier, -ière [ʃapəlje, jɛʀ] **1** *adj* hat (*épith*). **2** *nm,f* hatter.
chapelle [ʃapɛl] *nf* **(a)** (*Rel*) (*lieu*) chapel; (*Mus: chœur*) chapel. **~ absidiale/latérale** absidial/side chapel; **~ de la Sainte Vierge** Lady Chapel; **~ ardente** chapel of rest; *V* **maître**. **(b)** (*coterie*) coterie, clique.
chapellerie [ʃapɛlʀi] *nf* (*magasin*) hat shop, hatter('s); (*commerce*) hat trade, hat industry.
chapelure [ʃaplyʀ] *nf* (*Culin*) (dried) bread-crumbs.
chaperon [ʃapʀɔ̃] *nm* **(a)** (*personne*) chaperon. **(b)** (*Constr*) *[mur]* coping. **(c)** (†: *capuchon*) hood. **le petit ~ rouge** Little Red Riding Hood.
chaperonner [ʃapʀɔne] (1) *vt* **(a)** *personne* to chaperon. **(b)** (*Constr*) *mur* to cope.
chapiteau, *pl* **~x** [ʃapito] *nm* **(a)** *[colonne]* capital. **(b)** *[cirque]* big top, marquee. **sous le ~** under the big top. **(c)** *[alambic]* head.
chapitre [ʃapitʀ(ə)] *nm* **(a)** *[livre, traité]* chapter; *[budget, statuts]* section, item. (*fig*) **c'était un nouveau ~ de sa vie qui commençait** a new chapter of *ou* in his life was beginning.
(b) (*fig: sujet, rubrique*) subject, matter. **il est imbattable sur ce ~** he's unbeatable on that subject *ou* score; **il est très strict sur le ~ de la discipline** he's very strict in the matter of discipline *ou* about discipline; **au ~ des faits divers** under the heading of news in brief; **on pourrait dire sur ce ~ que ...** one might say on that score *ou* subject that ... .
(c) (*Rel: assemblée*) chapter; *V* **salle, voix.**
chapitrer [ʃapitʀe] (1) *vt* **(a)** (*réprimander*) to admonish, reprimand; (*sermonner*) to lecture. **(b)** *texte* to divide into chapters; *budget* to divide into headings, itemize.
chapon [ʃapɔ̃] *nm* capon.
chapska [ʃapska] *nm* schapska.
chaptalisation [ʃaptalizɑsjɔ̃] *nf [vin]* chaptalization.
chaptaliser [ʃaptalize] (1) *vt vin* to chaptalize.
chaque [ʃak] *adj* **(a)** (*d'un ensemble bien défini*) every, each. **~ élève (de la classe)** every *ou* each pupil (in the class); **ils coûtent 10 F ~*** they're 10 francs each *ou* apiece.
(b) (*d'un ensemble indéfini*) every. **~ homme naît libre** every man is born free; **il m'interrompt à ~ instant** he interrupts me every other second, he keeps interrupting me; **~ 10 minutes, il éternuait*** he sneezed every 10 minutes; **~ chose à sa place** everything in its place; *V* **à**.
char [ʃaʀ] **1** *nm* **(a)** (*Mil*) tank. **régiment de ~s** tank regiment.
(b) *[carnaval]* (carnival) float. **le défilé des ~s fleuris** the procession of flower-decked floats.
(c) (†: *charrette*) waggon, cart. **les ~s de foin rentraient** the hay waggons *ou* carts were returning.
(d) (*Can*†) car, automobile (*US*).
(e) (*Antiq*) chariot. (*littér*) **le ~ de l'Aurore** the chariot of the dawn (*littér*); (*fig*) **le ~ de l'État** the ship of state; *V* **arrêter.**
2: (*Mil*) **char d'assaut** tank; **char à banc** charabanc, char-à-banc; **char à bœufs** oxcart; (*Mil*) **char de combat** = **char d'assaut**; **char funèbre** hearse.
charabia* [ʃaʀabja] *nm* gibberish, gobbledygook*.
charade [ʃaʀad] *nf* (*parlée*) riddle, word puzzle; (*mimée*) charade.
charançon [ʃaʀɑ̃sɔ̃] *nm* weevil.
charançonné, e [ʃaʀɑ̃sɔne] *adj* weevilly, weevilled.
charbon [ʃaʀbɔ̃] **1** *nm* **(a)** (*combustible*) coal (*U*). **faire cuire qch sur des ~s** to cook sth over a coal fire; **recevoir un ~ dans l'œil** to get a speck of soot *ou* a bit of grit in one's eye; (*fig*) **être sur des ~s ardents** to be like a cat on hot bricks.
(b) (*maladie*) *[blé]* smut, black rust; *[bête, homme]* anthrax.
(c) (*Peinture*) (*instrument*) piece of charcoal; (*dessin*) charcoal drawing.
(d) (*Pharm*) charcoal. **pastilles au ~** charcoal tablets.
(e) (*Élec*) *[arc électrique]* carbon.
2: **charbon actif** *ou* **activé** active *ou* activated carbon; **charbon animal** animal black; **charbon de bois** charcoal; **charbon de terre**†† coal.
charbonnage [ʃaʀbɔnaʒ] *nm* (*gén pl: houillère*) colliery, coalmine. **les C~s (de France)** the (French) Coal Board.
charbonner [ʃaʀbɔne] (1) **1** *vt* (*noircir*) *inscription* to scrawl in charcoal. **~ un mur de dessins** to scrawl (charcoal) drawings on a wall; **avoir les yeux charbonnés** to have eyes heavily rimmed with black; **se ~ le visage** to blacken *ou* black one's face.
2 *vi [lampe, poêle, rôti]* to char, go black; (*Naut*) to take on coal.
charbonneux, -euse [ʃaʀbɔnø, øz] *adj* **(a)** *apparence, texture* coal-like; (*littér: noirci, souillé*) sooty. **(b)** (*Méd*) **tumeur ~euse** anthracoid *ou* anthrasic tumour; **mouche ~euse** anthrax-carrying fly.
charbonnier, -ière [ʃaʀbɔnje, jɛʀ] **1** *adj* coal (*épith*). **navire ~** collier, coaler; *V* **mésange**. **2** *nm* (*personne*) coalman; (††: *fabriquant de charbon de bois*) charcoal burner. (*Prov*) **~ est maître dans sa maison** *ou* **chez soi** a man is master in his own home; *V* **foi**.
charcuter* [ʃaʀkyte] (1) *vt personne* to hack about*, butcher*. (*hum*) **se ~** to dig holes in o.s.
charcuterie [ʃaʀkytʀi] *nf* (*magasin*) pork butcher's shop and delicatessen; (*produits*) cooked pork meats; (*commerce*) pork meat trade; delicatessen trade.
charcutier, -ière [ʃaʀkytje, jɛʀ] *nm,f* pork butcher; (*traiteur*) delicatessen dealer; (**fig: chirurgien*) butcher* (*fig*).
chardon [ʃaʀdɔ̃] *nm* (*Bot*) thistle. *[grille, mur]* **~s** spikes.
chardonneret [ʃaʀdɔnʀɛ] *nm* goldfinch.
charentais, e [ʃaʀɑ̃tɛ, ɛz] **1** *adj* of *ou* from Charente. **2** *nm,f*: **C~(e)** inhabitant *ou* native of Charente.
charge [ʃaʀʒ(ə)] **1** *nf* **(a)** (*lit, fig: fardeau*) burden; *[véhicule]* load; *[navire]* freight, cargo; (*Archit: poussée*) load. **fléchir** *ou* **plier sous la ~** to bend under the load *ou* burden; (*fig*) **l'éducation des enfants est une lourde ~ pour eux** educating the children is a heavy burden for them; (*fig*) **leur mère infirme est une ~ pour eux** their invalid mother is a burden to *ou* upon them.
(b) (*rôle, fonction*) responsibility; (*Admin*) office; (*Jur*) practice. **les hautes ~s qu'il occupe** the high office that he holds; **les devoirs de la ~** the duties of (the) office; **on lui a confié la ~ de (faire) l'enquête** he was given the responsibility of (carrying out) the inquiry; *V* **femme**.
(c) (*obligations financières*) **~s** *[commerçant]* expenses, costs, outgoings; *[locataire]* maintenance *ou* service charges (and tenant's rates); **il a de grosses ~s familiales** his family expenses *ou* outgoings are high; **dans ce commerce, nous avons de lourdes ~s** we have heavy expenses *ou* costs *ou* our overheads are high in this trade; **les ~s de l'État** government expenditure; *V* **cahier**.
(d) (*Jur*) charge. **les ~s qui pèsent contre lui** the charges against him; *V* **témoin**.
(e) (*Mil: attaque*) charge; *V* **pas¹, revenir, sonner.**
(f) (*Tech*) *[fusil]* (*action*) loading, charging; (*explosifs*) charge; (*Élec*) (*action*) charging; (*quantité*) charge. (*Élec*) **conducteur en ~** live conductor; (*Élec*) **mettre une batterie en ~** to charge a battery, put a battery on charge; **la batterie est en ~** the battery is being charged *ou* is on charge.
(g) (*caricature, satire*) caricature; *V* **portrait**.
(h) (*Naut: chargement*) loading.
(i) (*loc*) **être à la ~ de qn** *[frais, réparations]* to be chargeable to sb, be payable by sb; *[personne, enfant]* to be dependent upon sb, be a charge on sb, be supported by sb; **les frais sont à la ~ de l'entreprise** the costs will be borne by the firm, the firm will pay the expenses; **il a sa mère à (sa) ~** he has a dependent mother, he has his mother to support; **enfants à ~** dependent children; **les enfants confiés à sa ~** the children in his care; (*littér*) **être à ~ à qn** to be a burden to *ou* upon sb; **avoir la ~ de qn** to be responsible for sb, have charge of sb; **à ~ pour lui de payer** on condition that he meets the costs; **il a la ~ de faire, il a pour ~ de faire** the onus is upon him to do, he is responsible for doing; **j'accepte ton aide, à ~ de revanche** I accept your help on condition *ou* provided that you'll let me do the same for you one day *ou* for you in return; **prendre en ~** (*recueillir*) *[personne]* to take charge of; *[Assistance publique]* to take into care; (*payer*) *frais, remboursement* to take care of; (*transporter*) *[bus, taxi]* to take on; **prise en ~** *[taxi etc]* minimum (standard) charge; *[Sécurité sociale]* acceptance (of financial liability); **avoir ~ d'âmes** *[prêtre]* to be responsible for people's spiritual welfare, have the care of souls; *[père, conducteur]* to be responsible for (the) welfare of children, passengers *etc*, have lives in one's care; *V* **pris**.
2: (*Mil*) **charge creuse** hollow-charge; **charge d'explosifs** explosive charge; **charges de famille** dependents; **charges fiscales** taxation burden; **charges locatives** maintenance *ou* service charges (and tenant's rates); **charge maximale** maximum load; (*Admin*) **charge publique** public office; **charges sociales** social security contributions; **charge utile** live load; **charge à vide** weight (when) empty, empty weight.
chargé, e [ʃaʀʒe] (*ptp de* **charger**) **1** *adj* **(a)** (*lit*) *personne, véhicule* loaded, laden (*de* with). **être ~ comme un mulet*** *ou* **une bourrique*** to be loaded *ou* laden (down) like a mule.
(b) (*responsable de*) **~ de** *travail, enfants* in charge of.
(c) (*fig: rempli de*) **~ de: un homme ~ d'honneurs** a man laden with honours; (*littér*) **~ d'ans** *ou* **d'années** weighed down by (the) years (*littér*), ancient in years (*littér*); **passage/mot ~ de sens** passage/word full of *ou* pregnant with meaning; **un regard ~ de menaces** a look full of threats; **nuage ~ de neige** snow-laden cloud, cloud laden *ou* heavy with snow; **air ~ de parfums** air heavy with fragrance (*littér*), air heavy with sweet smells.
(d) (*occupé*) *emploi du temps, journée* full, heavy. **notre programme est très ~ en ce moment** we have a very busy schedule *ou* a very full programme *ou* we are very busy at the moment.
(e) (*fig: lourd*) *conscience* troubled; *ciel* overcast, heavy; *style* overelaborate, intricate. **hérédité ~e** tainted heredity; **j'ai la conscience ~e de my conscience** is burdened *ou* troubled with; **c'est un homme qui a un passé ~** he is a man with a past.
(f) (*Méd*) *estomac* overloaded. **avoir la langue ~e** to have a coated *ou* furred tongue.
(g) (*Tech*) *arme, appareil* loaded.
2: **chargé d'affaires** *nm* chargé d'affaires; **chargé de cours** *adj, nm* ≃ (part-time) lecturer; **chargé de famille** *adj* with family commitments *ou* responsibilities; **chargé de mission** *nm* (official) representative.
chargement [ʃaʀʒəmɑ̃] *nm* **(a)** (*action*) loading. **le ~ d'un**

camion the loading(-up) of a lorry; **le ~ des bagages** the loading of the luggage.

(b) (*gén: marchandises*) load; *[navire]* freight, cargo. **le ~ a basculé** the load toppled over.

(c) (*Comm*) (*remise*) registering; (*paquet*) registered parcel.

(d) *[arme, caméra]* loading; *[chaudière]* stoking.

charger [ʃaʀʒe] (3) **1** *vt* **(a)** (*lit, fig*) *animal, personne, véhicule* to load; *table, rayonnage* to load. **~ qn de paquets** to load sb up *ou* weigh sb down with parcels; **je vais ~ la voiture** I'll go and load the car (up); **on a trop chargé cette voiture** this car has been overloaded; **table chargée de mets appétissants** table laden with mouth-watering dishes; **~ le peuple d'impôts** to burden the people with *ou* weigh the people down with taxes; **~ sa mémoire (de faits)/un texte de citations** to overload one's memory (with facts)/a text with quotations; **un plat qui charge l'estomac** a dish that lies heavy on *ou* overloads the stomach; **ne lui chargez pas l'estomac** don't overload his stomach.

(b) (*placer, prendre*) *objet* to load. **~ les bagages dans le coffre** to load the luggage into the boot; **il a chargé le sac/le cageot sur son épaule** he loaded the sack/the crate onto his shoulder, he heaved the sack over/the crate onto his shoulder; *[taxi]* **~ un client** to pick up a passenger *ou* a fare.

(c) *fusil, caméra* to load; (*Élec*) *batterie* to charge; *chaudière* to stoke, fire; (*Couture*) *bobine, canette* to load *ou* fill with thread.

(d) (*donner une responsabilité*) **~ qn de qch** to put sb in charge of sth; **~ qn de faire** to give sb the responsibility *ou* job of doing, ask sb to do; **il m'a chargé d'un petit travail** he gave me a little job to do; **on l'a chargé d'une mission importante** he was assigned an important mission; **on l'a chargé de la surveillance des enfants** *ou* **de surveiller les enfants** he was put in charge of the children, he was given the job of looking after the children; **il m'a chargé de mettre une lettre à la poste** he asked me to post a letter; **on m'a chargé d'appliquer le règlement** I've been instructed to apply the rule; **il m'a chargé de m'occuper de la correspondance** he gave me the responsibility *ou* job of seeing to the correspondence; **il m'a chargé de ses amitiés pour vous** *ou* **de vous transmettre ses amitiés** he sends you his regards, he asked me to give you his regards *ou* to convey his regards.

(e) (*accuser*) *personne* to bring all possible evidence against. (*littér*) **~ qn de** *crime* to charge sb with.

(f) (*Mil: attaquer*) *ennemi* to charge (at). **chargez!** charge!; **il a chargé dans le tas*** he charged into them*.

(g) (*caricaturer*) *portrait* to make a caricature of; *description* to overdo, exaggerate; (*Théât*) *rôle* to overact, ham (up)*. **il a tendance à ~** he has a tendency to overdo it *ou* to exaggerate.

2 se charger *vpr*: **se ~ de** *tâche* to see to, take care *ou* charge of; *enfant, prisonnier, élève,* (*iro*) *ennemi* to see to, attend to, take care of; **se ~ de faire** to undertake to do, take it upon o.s. to do; **il s'est chargé des enfants** he is seeing to *ou* taking care *ou* charge of the children; **d'accord je m'en charge** O.K., I'll see to it *ou* I'll take care of that; **je me charge de m'occuper de lui** leave it to me to look after him, I'll undertake to look after him; **je me charge de le faire venir** I'll make sure he comes, I'll make it my business to see that he comes.

chargeur [ʃaʀʒœʀ] *nm* **(a)** (*personne*) (*gén, Mil*) loader; (*Naut: négociant*) shipper. **(b)** (*dispositif*) *[arme à feu]* clip; (*Phot*) cartridge. **il vida son ~ sur les gendarmes** he emptied his magazine at the police; (*Élec*) **~ de batterie** (battery) charger.

chariot [ʃaʀjo] *nm* (*charrette*) waggon (*Brit*), wagon, (*plus petit*) truck, cart; (*table, panier à roulettes*) trolley (*Brit*), cart (*US*); (*appareil de manutention*) truck, float (*Brit*); (*Tech*) *[machine à écrire, machine-outil]* carriage; *[hôpital]* trolley. *[gare, aéroport]* **~ (à bagages)** (luggage) trolley; (*Ciné*) **~ (de caméra)** dolly; **~ élévateur (à fourche)** fork-lift truck; (*Astron*) **le petit/grand C~** the Little/Great Bear.

charitable [ʃaʀitabl(ə)] *adj* (*qui fait preuve de charité*) charitable (*envers* towards); (*gentil*) kind (*envers* to, towards). (*iro*) **... et c'est un conseil ~** ... that's just a friendly *ou* kindly bit of advice (*iro*); *V* **âme**.

charitablement [ʃaʀitabləmɑ̃] *adv* (*V* **charitable**) charitably; kindly. (*iro*) **je vous avertis ~ que la prochaine fois ...** let me give you a friendly *ou* kindly warning that the next time ... .

charité [ʃaʀite] *nf* **(a)** (*gén: bonté, amour*) charity; (*gentillesse*) kindness; (*Rel*) charity, love. **il a eu la ~ de faire** he was kind enough to do; **faites-moi la ~ de, ayez la ~ de** have the kindness to, be so kind as to, be kind enough to; **ce serait une ~ à lui faire que de** it would be doing him a kindness *ou* a good turn to; *V* **dame, sœur.**

(b) (*aumône*) charity. **demander la ~** (*lit*) to ask *ou* beg for charity; (*fig*) to come begging; **faire la ~** to give to charity, do charitable works; **faire la ~ à** *mendiant, déshérités* to give (something) to; **je ne veux pas qu'on me fasse la ~** I don't want charity; **la ~, ma bonne dame!** have you got a penny, kind lady?; **vivre de la ~ publique** to live on (public) charity; **vivre des ~s de ses voisins** to live on the charity of one's neighbours; (*Prov*) **~ bien ordonnée commence par soi-même** charity begins at home (*Prov*); **fête de ~** fête in aid of charity; **vente de ~** sale of work (in aid of charity).

charivari [ʃaʀivaʀi] *nm* hullabaloo.

charlatan [ʃaʀlatɑ̃] *nm* (*péj*) (*médecin*) quack, charlatan; (*pharmacien, vendeur*) mountebank; (*politicien*) charlatan, trickster; *V* **remède.**

charlatanerie [ʃaʀlatanʀi] *nf* = **charlatanisme.**

charlatanesque [ʃaʀlatanɛsk(ə)] *adj* (*de guérisseur*) *remède, méthodes* quack (*épith*); (*de démagogue, d'escroc*) *méthodes* phoney, bogus.

charlatanisme [ʃaʀlatanism(ə)] *nm* *[guérisseur]* quackery, charlatanism; *[politicien etc]* charlatanism, trickery.

Charles [ʃaʀl] *nm* Charles. **~ le Téméraire** Charles the Bold; **~-Quint** Charles the Fifth (of Spain).

charleston [ʃaʀlɛstɔn] *nm* (*danse*) charleston.

Charlot [ʃaʀlo] *nm* (*Ciné*) Charlie Chaplin.

charlotte [ʃaʀlɔt] *nf* (*Culin*) charlotte; (*coiffure*) mobcap.

charmant, e [ʃaʀmɑ̃, ɑ̃t] *adj* **(a)** (*aimable*) *hôte, jeune fille, employé* charming; *enfant* sweet, delightful; *sourire, manières* charming, engaging. **il s'est montré ~ et nous a aidé du mieux qu'il a pu** he was quite charming and helped us as much as he could; **c'est un collaborateur ~** he is a charming *ou* delightful man to work with; *V* **prince.**

(b) (*très agréable*) *séjour, soirée* delightful, lovely. (*iro*) **eh bien c'est ~** charming! (*iro*); (*iro*) **~e soirée delightful time!** (*iro*).

(c) (*ravissant*) *robe, village, jeune fille, film, sourire* lovely, charming.

charme[1] [ʃaʀm(ə)] *nm* (*Bot*) hornbeam.

charme[2] [ʃaʀm(ə)] *nm* **(a)** (*attrait*) *[personne, musique, paysage]* charm. **le ~ de la nouveauté** the attraction(s) of novelty; **elle a beaucoup de ~** she has great charm; **ça lui donne un certain ~** that gives him a certain charm *ou* appeal; **cette vieille maison a son ~** this old house has its charm; **c'est ce qui en fait (tout) le ~** that's where its attraction lies, that's what is so delightful about it; **ça ne manque pas de ~** it's not without (a certain) charm; **ça a peut-être du ~ pour vous, mais** it may appeal to you but; (*hum, iro*) **je suis assez peu sensible aux ~s d'une promenade sous la pluie** a walk in the rain holds few attractions for me.

(b) (*hum: attraits d'une femme*) **~s** charms (*hum*); *V* **commerce.**

(c) (*envoûtement*) spell. **subir le ~ de qn** to be under sb's spell, be captivated by sb; **exercer un ~ sur qn** to have sb under one's spell; **il est tombé sous son ~** he has fallen beneath her spell; **être sous le ~ de** to be held spellbound by, be under the spell of; **tenir qn sous le ~ (de)** to captivate sb (with), hold sb spellbound (with); **le ~ est rompu** the spell is broken; *V* **chanteur.**

(d) (*loc*) **faire du ~** to turn on the charm; **faire du ~ à qn** to make eyes at sb; **aller** *ou* **se porter comme un ~** to be *ou* feel as fit as a fiddle.

charmé, e [ʃaʀme] (*ptp de* **charmer**) *adj*: **être ~ de faire** to be delighted to do.

charmer [ʃaʀme] (1) *vt* *public* to charm, enchant; *serpents* to charm; (†, *littér*) *peine, douleur* to charm away. **elle a des manières qui charment** she has charming *ou* delightful ways; **spectacle qui charme l'oreille et le regard** performance that charms *ou* enchants both the ear and the eye.

charmeur, -euse [ʃaʀmœʀ, øz] **1** *adj sourire, manières* winning, engaging. **2** *nm,f* (*séducteur*) charmer. **~ de serpent** snake charmer.

charmille [ʃaʀmij] *nf* arbour; (*allée d'arbres*) tree-covered walk.

charnel, -elle [ʃaʀnɛl] *adj* (*frm*) *passions, instincts* carnal; *désirs* carnal, fleshly. **l'acte ~, l'union ~le** the carnal act (*frm*); **un être ~** an earthly creature, a creature of blood *ou* flesh; **liens ~s** blood ties.

charnellement [ʃaʀnɛlmɑ̃] *adv* (*frm, littér*) **convoiter** *ou* **désirer qn ~** to desire sb sexually; **connaître ~** to have carnal knowledge of; **pécher ~** to commit the sin of the flesh.

charnier [ʃaʀnje] *nm* *[victimes]* mass grave; (††: *ossuaire*) charnel-house.

charnière [ʃaʀnjɛʀ] *nf* **(a)** *[porte, fenêtre, coquille]* hinge; *[timbre de collection]* (stamp) hinge; *V* **nom.**

(b) (*fig*) turning point; (*Mil*) pivot. **la ~ de notre équipe** the pivot of our team; **à la ~ de deux époques** at the turning point between two eras; **une discipline-~** an interlinking field of study; **un roman-~** a novel marking a turning point *ou* a transition; **une époque-~** a transition period.

charnu, e [ʃaʀny] *adj lèvres* fleshy, thick; *fruit, bras* plump, fleshy. **les parties ~es du corps** the fleshy parts of the body; (*hum*) **sur la partie ~e de son individu** on that fleshy part of his person (*hum*).

charognard [ʃaʀɔɲaʀ] *nm* (*lit*) vulture, carrion crow; (*fig*) vulture.

charogne [ʃaʀɔɲ] *nf* (*cadavre*) carrion, decaying carcass; (**:** *salaud*) (*femme*) bitch**:**; (*homme*) bastard**:**, sod**:** (*Brit*).

charolais, e [ʃaʀɔlɛ, ɛz] **1** *adj* of *ou* from the Charolais. **2** *nm*: **le C~** the Charolais. **3** *nm,f* (*bétail*) Charolais.

charpente [ʃaʀpɑ̃t] *nf* **(a)** *[maison, bâtiment]* frame(work), skeleton; *V* **bois.**

(b) (*fig: structure*) *[feuille]* skeleton; *[roman, pièce de théâtre]* structure, framework. **le squelette est la ~ du corps** the skeleton is the framework of the body.

(c) (*carrure*) build, frame. **quelle solide ~!** what a solid build (he is)!, what a strong frame he has!; **~ fragile/forte/épaisse** fragile/strong/stocky build.

charpenté, e [ʃaʀpɑ̃te] *adj*: **bien/solidement/puissament ~** *personne* well/solidly/powerfully built; *texte* well/solidly/powerfully constructed.

charpentier [ʃaʀpɑ̃tje] *nm* (*Constr*) carpenter; (*Naut*) shipwright.

charpie [ʃaʀpi] *nf* **(a)** (††: *pansement*) shredded linen (*used to dress wounds*).

(b) (*loc*) **cette viande est trop cuite, c'est de la ~** this meat has been cooked to shreds; **ces vêtements sont tombés en ~** these clothes are (all) in shreds *ou* ribbons, these clothes are falling to bits; **mettre** *ou* **réduire en ~** *papier, vêtements* (*déchirer*) to tear to shreds; *viande* (*hacher menu*) to mince; **je vais le mettre en ~!** I'll tear him to shreds!, mincemeat of him!; **il s'est fait mettre en ~ par le train** he was mashed up* *ou* hacked to pieces by the train.

charretée [ʃaʀte] *nf* (*lit*) cartload (*de* of). (**fig: grande quantité de*) **une ~ de, des ~s de** loads* *ou* stacks* of.

charretier, -ière [ʃaʀtje, jɛʀ] **1** *adj chemin* cart (*épith*). **porte ~ière** carriage gate. **2** *nm* carter. (*péj*) **de ~** *langage, manières* coarse; *V* **jurer.**

charrette [ʃaʀɛt] *nf* cart. **~ à bras** handcart, barrow. **~ des condamnés** tumbrel.

charriage [ʃaʀjaʒ] *nm* **(a)** (*transport*) carriage, cartage. **(b)** (*Géol: déplacement*) overthrusting; *V* **nappe.**

charrier [ʃaʀje] (7) **1** *vt* **(a)** (*transporter*) *[personne]* (*avec brouette etc*) to cart (along), trundle along, wheel (along); (*sur le dos*) to hump (*Brit*) *ou* lug along, heave (along), cart (along); *[camion etc]* to carry, cart. **on a passé des heures à ~ du charbon** we spent hours heaving *ou* carting coal.

(b) (*entraîner*) *[fleuve]* to carry (along), wash along, sweep (along); *[coulée, avalanche]* to carry (along), sweep (along). (*littér*) **le ciel** *ou* **le vent charriait de lourds nuages** the sky *ou* the wind carried past *ou* along heavy clouds.

(c) (‡: *se moquer de*) **~ qn** to take sb for a ride‡, kid sb on‡ (*Brit*), have sb on‡ (*Brit*), put sb on‡ (*US*); **se faire ~ par ses amis** to be kidded on‡ (*Brit*) *ou* had on‡ (*Brit*) *ou* put on‡ (*US*) by one's friends.

2 *vi* (‡) (*abuser*) to go too far, overstep the mark; (*plaisanter*) to be kidding‡, be joking*. **vraiment il charrie** he's really going too far, he's really overstepping the mark; **tu charries, elle n'est pas si vieille!** you must be kidding‡ *ou* you must be joking – she's not that old!, pull the other one* (*Brit*) – she's not that old!; **faudrait pas ~** hold on a minute!, what do you think I am?*

charrieur, -euse‡ [ʃaʀjœʀ, øz] *nm,f*: **c'est un ~** (*il abuse*) he's always going too far *ou* overstepping the mark; (*il plaisante*) he's always having (*Brit*) *ou* kidding (*Brit*) *ou* putting (*US*) people on‡; **il est un peu ~** he's a bit of a joker*.

charroi†† [ʃaʀwa] *nm* (*transport*) cartage.

charron [ʃaʀɔ̃] *nm* cartwright, wheelwright.

charroyer [ʃaʀwaje] (8) *vt* (*littér*) (*transporter par charrette*) to cart; (*transporter laborieusement*) to cart (along), heave (along).

charrue [ʃaʀy] *nf* plough (*Brit*), plow (*US*). (*fig*) **mettre la ~ devant** *ou* **avant les bœufs** to put the cart before the horse.

charte [ʃaʀt(ə)] *nf* (*Hist, Pol: convention*) charter; (*Hist: titre, contrat*) title, deed. (*Hist*) **accorder une ~ à** to grant a charter to, charter; (*Pol*) **la C~ des Nations Unies** the Charter of the United Nations.

charter [tʃaʀtœʀ, ʃaʀtɛʀ] **1** *nm* (*vol*) charter flight; (*avion*) chartered plane. **2** *adj inv vol, billet, prix* charter (*épith*). **avion ~** chartered plane.

chartisme [ʃaʀtism(ə)] *nm* (*Pol Brit*) Chartism.

chartiste [ʃaʀtist(ə)] **1** *adj, nmf* (*Hist*) Chartist. **2** *nmf* (*élève*) student of the École des Chartes (*in Paris*).

chartreuse [ʃaʀtʀøz] *nf* (*liqueur*) chartreuse; (*couvent*) Charterhouse, Carthusian monastery; (*religieuse*) Carthusian nun.

chartreux [ʃaʀtʀø] *nm* (*religieux*) Carthusian monk.

Charybde [kaʀibd] *n V* **tomber.**

chas [ʃa] *nm* eye (*of needle*).

chasse¹ [ʃas] **1** *nf* **(a)** (*gén*) hunting; (*au fusil*) shooting, hunting. **aller à la ~** to go hunting; **aller à la ~ aux papillons** to go butterfly-hunting; **air/habits de ~** hunting tune/clothes; **~ au faisan** pheasant shooting; **~ au lapin** rabbit shooting, rabbiting; **~ au renard/au chamois/au gros gibier** fox/chamois/big game hunting; *V* **chien, cor¹, fusil** *etc.*

(b) (*période*) hunting season, shooting season. **la ~ est ouverte/fermée** it is the open/close season.

(c) (*gibier tué*) **manger/partager la ~** to eat/share the game; **faire (une) bonne ~** to get a good bag; **~ gardée** (*lit*) private hunting (ground), private shooting; (*fig*) private ground; **c'est ~ gardée!** no poaching on *ou* keep off our (*ou* their *etc*) preserve!, out of bounds!

(d) (*terrain, domaine*) hunting ground. **louer une ~** to rent land to shoot *ou* hunt on; **une ~ giboyeuse** well-stocked hunting ground; *V* **action.**

(e) (*chasseurs*) **la ~** the hunt.

(f) (*Aviat*) **la ~** the fighters (*pl*); *V* **avion, pilote.**

(g) (*poursuite*) chase. **une ~ effrénée dans les rues de la ville** a frantic chase through the streets of the town.

(h) (*loc*) **faire la ~ aux souris/aux moustiques** to hunt down *ou* chase mice/mosquitoes; **faire la ~ aux abus/erreurs** to hunt down *ou* track down abuses/errors; **faire la ~ aux appartements/occasions** to be *ou* go flat-/bargain-hunting; **faire la ~ au mari** to be hunting for a husband, be on the hunt for a husband*; **prendre en ~, donner la ~ à** *fuyard, voiture* to give chase to, chase after; *avion, navire, ennemi* to give chase to; (*Aviat, Mil, Naut*) **donner la ~** to give chase; **se mettre en ~ pour trouver qch** to go hunting for sth.

2: chasse à l'affût hunting (from a hide); **chasse au chevreuil** deer hunting, deer-stalking; **chasse à courre** hunting; **chasse au furet** ferreting; **chasse au fusil** shooting; **chasse à l'homme** manhunt; (*Pol*) **chasse aux sorcières** witch hunt; **chasse sous-marine** harpooning, harpoon fishing.

chasse² [ʃas] *nf*: **~ (d'eau** *ou* **des cabinets)** (toilet) flush; **actionner** *ou* **tirer la ~** to pull the chain (*Brit*), flush the toilet *ou* lavatory (*surtout Brit*).

châsse [ʃɑs] *nf* (*reliquaire*) reliquary, shrine.

chasse- [ʃas] *préf V* **chasser.**

chassé [ʃase] **1** *nm* (*danse*) chassé.

2: chassé-croisé *nm, pl* **chassés-croisés** (*Danse*) chassé-croisé, set to partners; (*fig*) **avec tous ces chassés-croisés nous ne nous sommes pas vus depuis 6 mois** amid *ou* with all these to-ings and fro-ings we haven't seen each other for 6 months; (*fig*) **par suite d'un chassé-croisé nous nous sommes manqués** we missed each other because of a mix-up *ou* confusion about where to meet.

chasselas [ʃasla] *nm* chasselas grape.

chassepot [ʃaspo] *nm* (*Hist*) chassepot (rifle).

chasser [ʃase] (1) **1** *vt* **(a)** (*gén*) to hunt; (*au fusil*) to shoot, hunt. **~ à l'affût/au filet** to hunt from a hide/with a net; **~ le faisan/le renard** to go pheasant-shooting/foxhunting; **~ le lapin au furet** to go ferreting; **il chasse le lion en Afrique** he is shooting lions *ou* lion-shooting in Africa; (*fig*) **il est ministre, comme son père et son grand-père: il chasse de race** he's a minister like his father and grandfather before him — it runs in the family *ou* he carries on the family tradition; *V* **bon¹.**

(b) (*faire partir*) *importun, animal, ennemi* to drive away, drive out, chase out, chase away; (*congédier*) *ouvrier, domestique* to send packing, turn out; (*expulser*) *fils indigne, manifestant* to send packing, turn out; *immigrant* to drive out, expel; (*fig: faire fuir*) *touristes, clients* to drive away, chase away. **chassant de la main les insectes** brushing away (the) insects with his hand; **il a chassé les gamins du jardin** he chased *ou* drove the lads out of the garden; **mon père m'a chassé de la maison** my father has turned me out of the house *ou* has sent me packing; **le brouillard nous a chassés de la plage** we were driven away from *ou* off the beach by the fog; **ces touristes, ils vont finir par nous ~ de chez nous** these tourists will end up driving us away from *ou* out of *ou* hounding us from our own homes; **il a été chassé de son pays par le nazisme** he was forced by Nazism to flee his country, Nazism drove him from his country; (*Prov*) **chassez le naturel, il revient au galop** what's bred in the bone comes out in the flesh; *V* **faim.**

(c) (*dissiper*) *odeur* to dispel, drive away; *idée* to dismiss, chase away; *souci, doute* to dispel, drive away, chase away. **essayant de ~ ces images obsédantes** trying to chase away *ou* dismiss these haunting images; **il faut ~ cette idée de ta tête** you must get that idea out of your head *ou* dismiss that idea from your mind; **le vent a chassé le brouillard** the wind dispelled *ou* blew away the fog.

(d) (*pousser*) *troupeau, nuages, pluie* to drive; (*Tech*) *clou* to drive in.

(e) (*éjecter*) *douille, eau d'un tuyau* to drive out; *V* **clou.**

2 *vi* **(a)** (*aller à la chasse*) (*gén*) to go hunting; (*au fusil*) to go shooting.

(b) (*déraper*) *[véhicule, roues]* to skid; *[ancre]* to drag. (*Naut*) **~ sur ses ancres** to drag its anchors.

3: chasse-clou *nm, pl* **chasse-clous** nail punch; **chasse-mouches** *nm inv* flyswatter, fly whisk; **chasse-neige** *nm inv* (*instrument, Ski*) snowplough; **descendre en chasse-neige** (*Ski*) to snowplough; **chasse-pierres** *nm inv* cowcatcher.

chasseresse [ʃasʀɛs] *nf* (*littér*) huntress; *V* **Diane.**

chasseur [ʃasœʀ] **1** *nm* **(a)** (*gén*) hunter; (*à courre*) hunter, huntsman. **c'est un très bon ~** (*gibier à poil*) he's a very good hunter; (*gibier à plume*) he's an excellent shot; **c'est un grand ~ de perdrix** he's a great one for partridge-shooting; **c'est un grand ~ de renards** he's a great one for foxhunting, he's a great foxhunter.

(b) (*Mil*) (*soldat*) chasseur. (*régiment*) **le 3e ~** the 3rd (regiment of) chasseurs.

(c) (*Mil*) (*avion*) fighter; (*bateau*) (submarine) chaser.

(d) (*garçon d'hôtel*) page (boy), messenger (boy), bellboy (*US*).

2: (*Mil*) **chasseur alpin** mountain infantryman; (*troupe*) **les chasseurs alpins** the mountain infantry, the alpine chasseurs; (*Aviat, Mil*) **chasseur-bombardier** *nm, pl* **chasseurs-bombardiers** fighter-bomber; (*Hist Mil*) **chasseur à cheval** cavalryman; (*troupe*) **les chasseurs à cheval** the cavalry; **chasseur d'images/de son** roving photographic/recording enthusiast; (*Hist Mil*) **chasseur à pied** infantryman; (*troupe*) **les chasseurs à pied** the infantry; (*Aviat*) **chasseur à réaction** jet fighter; **chasseur de têtes** headhunter.

chasseuse [ʃasøz] *nf* (*rare*) huntswoman, hunter, huntress (*littér*).

chassie [ʃasi] *nf [yeux]* sticky matter (*in eye*).

chassieux, -euse [ʃasjø, øz] *adj yeux* sticky, gummy; *personne, animal* gummy- *ou* sticky-eyed.

châssis [ʃɑsi] *nm* **(a)** *[véhicule]* chassis, subframe; *[machine]* sub- *ou* under-frame.

(b) (*encadrement*) *[fenêtre]* frame; *[toile, tableau]* stretcher; (*Typ*) chase; (*Phot*) (printing) frame. **~ mobile/dormant** opening/fixed frame.

(c) (‡) (*corps féminin*) body, figure; (*jolie fille*) nice piece‡. **elle a un beau ~!** what a smashing figure she's got!*

(d) (*Agr*) cold frame.

chaste [ʃast(ə)] *adj personne, pensées, amour, baiser* chaste; *yeux, oreilles* innocent. **de ~s jeunes filles** chaste *ou* innocent young girls.

chastement [ʃastəmɑ̃] *adv* chastely, innocently.

chasteté [ʃastəte] *nf* chastity; *V* **ceinture.**

chasuble [ʃazybl(ə)] *nf* chasuble; *V* **robe.**

chat [ʃa] **1** *nm* **(a)** (*animal*) (*gén*) cat; (*mâle*) tomcat. **~ persan/siamois** Persian/Siamese cat; **petit ~** kitten; (*terme d'affection*) **mon petit ~** (*à un enfant*) pet*, poppet*; (*à une femme*) sweetie*, lovie*.

(b) (*jeu*) tig (*Brit*), tag. **jouer à ~** to play tig (*Brit*) *ou* tag, have a game of tig (*Brit*) *ou* tag; **(c'est toi le) ~!** you're it! *ou* he!

(c) (*loc*) **il n'y avait pas un ~ dehors** there wasn't a soul outside; **avoir un ~ dans la gorge** to have a frog in one's throat; (*Prov*) **~ échaudé craint l'eau froide** once bitten, twice shy (*Prov*); *V* **appeler, chien, fouetter** *etc.*

2: le Chat Botté Puss in Boots; **chat de gouttière** ordinary cat, alley cat (*péj*); (*Zool*) **chat-huant** *nm, pl* **chats-huants** screech owl, barn owl; (*Hist Naut*) **chat à neuf queues** cat-o'-nine-tails; (*jeu*) **chat perché** 'off-ground' tag *ou* tig; **chat sauvage** wildcat; **chat-tigre** *nm, pl* **chats-tigres** tiger cat.

châtaigne [ʃɑtɛɲ] *nf* **(a)** (*fruit*) chestnut. ~ **d'eau** water chestnut. **(b)** (*: *coup de poing*) clout*, biff*. **flanquer une** ~ **à qn** to clout* *ou* biff* sb, give sb a clout* *ou* biff*.

châtaigneraie [ʃɑtɛɲʀɛ] *nf* chestnut grove.

châtaignier [ʃɑteɲe] *nm* (*arbre*) chestnut (tree); (*bois*) chestnut.

châtain [ʃɑtɛ̃] **1** *nm* chestnut brown. **2** *adj inv* *cheveux* chestnut (brown); *personne* brown-haired. **elle est** ~ **clair/roux** she has light brown hair/auburn hair.

château, *pl* ~**x** [ʃɑto] **1** *nm* (*forteresse*) castle; (*résidence royale*) palace, castle; (*manoir, gentilhommière*) mansion, stately home; (*en France*) château. **les** ~**x de la Loire** the Loire châteaux; (*vignobles*) **les** ~**x du Bordelais** the châteaux of the Bordeaux region; (*fig*) **bâtir** *ou* **faire des** ~**x en Espagne** to build castles in the air *ou* in Spain; *V* **vie.**

2: (*Naut*) **château d'arrière** aftercastle; (*Naut*) **château d'avant** forecastle, fo'c'sle; (*Cartes, fig*) **château de cartes** house of cards; **château d'eau** water tower; **château fort** stronghold, fortified castle; **Château-la-Pompe**† *nm inv* Adam's ale†; (*Naut*) **château de poupe** = **château d'arrière**; (*Naut*) **château de proue** = **château d'avant.**

chateaubriand, châteaubriant [ʃɑtobʀijɑ̃] *nm* (*Culin*) chateaubriand, chateaubriant.

châtelain [ʃɑtlɛ̃] *nm* **(a)** (*Hist: seigneur*) (feudal) lord. **le** ~ the lord of the manor.

(b) (*propriétaire d'un manoir*) (*d'ancienne date*) squire; (*nouveau riche*) owner of a manor. **le** ~ **vint nous ouvrir** the owner of the manor *ou* the squire came to the door.

châtelaine [ʃɑtlɛn] *nf* **(a)** (*propriétaire d'un manoir*) owner of a manor. **la** ~ **vint nous recevoir** the lady of the manor came to greet us.

(b) (*épouse du châtelain*) lady (of the manor), chatelaine.

(c) (*ceinture*) chatelaine, châtelaine.

châtié, e [ʃɑtje] (*ptp de* **châtier**) *adj style* polished, refined; *langage* refined.

châtier [ʃɑtje] (7) *vt* **(a)** (*littér: punir*) *coupable* to chastise (*littér*), castigate (*littér*), punish; *faute* to punish; (*Rel*) *corps* to chasten, mortify. ~ **l'insolence de qn** to chastise *ou* punish sb for his insolence; *V* **qui.**

(b) (*soigner, corriger*) *style* to polish, refine, perfect; *langage* to refine.

chatière [ʃatjɛʀ] *nf* (*porte*) cat-flap; (*trou d'aération*) (air-) vent, ventilation hole; (*piège*) cat-trap.

châtiment [ʃɑtimɑ̃] *nm* (*littér*) chastisement (*littér*), castigation (*littér*), punishment. ~ **corporel** corporal punishment; **subir un** ~ to receive *ou* undergo punishment.

chatoiement [ʃatwamɑ̃] *nm* (*V* **chatoyant**) glistening; shimmer(ing); sparkle.

chaton[1] [ʃatɔ̃] *nm* **(a)** (*Zool*) kitten. **(b)** (*Bot*) catkin. ~**s de saule** pussy willows; (*fig*) ~**s de poussière** balls of fluff.

chaton[2] [ʃatɔ̃] *nm* (*monture*) bezel, setting; (*pierre*) stone.

chatouille* [ʃatuj] *nf* tickle. **faire des** ~**s à qn** to tickle sb; **craindre les** ~**s** *ou* **la** ~ to be ticklish.

chatouillement [ʃatujmɑ̃] *nm* (*gén*) tickling; (*dans le nez, la gorge*) tickle. **des** ~**s la faisaient se trémousser** a tickling sensation made her fidget.

chatouiller [ʃatuje] (1) *vt* **(a)** (*lit*) to tickle. **arrête, ça chatouille!** don't, that tickles! *ou* you're tickling! **(b)** (*fig*) *amour-propre, curiosité* to tickle, titillate; *palais, odorat* to titillate. **(c)** († *hum*) ~ **les côtes à qn** to tan sb's hide.

chatouilleux, -euse [ʃatujø, øz] *adj* **(a)** (*lit*) ticklish.

(b) (*fig: susceptible*) *personne, caractère* touchy, (over)-sensitive. **individu à l'amour-propre** ~ person who easily takes offence *ou* whose pride is sensitive; **être** ~ **sur l'honneur/l'étiquette** to be touchy *ou* sensitive on points of honour/etiquette.

chatouillis [ʃatuji] *nm* (*sensation*) light tickling, gentle tickling. **faire des** ~**s à qn** to tickle sb lightly *ou* gently.

chatoyant, e [ʃatwajɑ̃, ɑ̃t] *adj* *vitraux* glistening; *reflet, étoffe* shimmering; *bijoux, plumage* glistening, shimmering; *couleurs, style* sparkling. **l'éclat** ~ **des pierreries** the glistening *ou* shimmering of the gems.

chatoyer [ʃatwaje] (8) *vi* (*V* **chatoyant**) to glisten; to shimmer; to sparkle.

châtré‡ [ʃɑtʀe] *nm* (*homme à voix aigüe*) squeaker; (*pleutre*) weakling, woman (*fig péj*). **voix de** ~ squeaky little voice.

châtrer [ʃɑtʀe] (1) *vt* *taureau, cheval* to castrate, geld; *chat* to neuter, castrate; *homme* to castrate, emasculate; (*fig littér*) *texte* to mutilate, bowdlerize.

chatte [ʃat] *nf* (she-)cat. **elle est très** ~ she's very kittenish; (*terme d'affection*) **ma (petite)** ~ (my) pet*, sweetie(-pie)*.

chatterie [ʃatʀi] *nf* **(a)** (*caresses*) ~**s** playful attentions *ou* caresses; (*minauderies*) kittenish ways; **faire des** ~**s à qn** to pet sb. **(b)** (*friandise*) titbit, dainty morsel. **aimer les** ~**s** to love a little delicacy *ou* a dainty morsel.

chatterton [ʃatɛʀtɔn] *nm* (*Élec*) (adhesive) insulating tape.

chaud, e [ʃo, od] **1** *adj* **(a)** warm; (*très chaud*) hot. **les climats** ~**s** warm climates; (*très chaud*) hot climates; **l'eau du lac n'est pas assez** ~**e pour se baigner** the water in the lake is not warm enough for bathing; **bois ton thé pendant qu'il est** ~ drink your tea while it's hot; **tous les plats étaient servis très** ~**s** all the dishes were served up piping hot; **cela sort tout** ~ **du four** it's (piping) hot from the oven; (*fig*) **il a des nouvelles toutes** ~**es** he's got some news hot from the press (*fig*) *ou* some hot news; *V* **battre, main** *etc.*

(b) (*qui tient chaud*) *couverture, vêtement* warm, cosy.

(c) (*vif, passionné*) *félicitations* warm, hearty; (*littér*) *amitié* warm; *partisan* keen, ardent; *admirateur* warm, ardent; *discussion* heated. **la bataille a été** ~**e** it was a fierce battle, the battle was fast and furious; **être** ~ **(pour faire/pour qch)*** to be keen (on doing/on sth); **il n'est pas très** ~ **pour conduire de nuit*** he is not very *ou* too keen on driving at night.

(d) (*dangereux*) **l'alerte a été** ~**e** it was a near *ou* close thing; **les points** ~**s du globe** the world's hot spots; **les journaux prévoient un été '**~**'** newspapers forecast a long hot summer (of violence).

(e) *voix, couleur* warm.

(f) (*: *sensuel*) *personne, tempérament* hot.

2 *nm* **(a)** (*chaleur*) **le** ~ (the) heat, the warmth; **elle souffre autant du** ~ **que du froid** she suffers as much from the heat as from the cold; **restez donc au** ~ stay in the warmth, stay where it's warm; **garder qch au** ~ to keep sth warm *ou* hot; **garder un enfant enrhumé au** ~ to keep a child with a cold (indoors) in the warmth; **être bien au** ~ to be nice and warm.

(b) **à** ~ *opération* emergency; (*Tech*) *travailler* under heat; **il a été opéré à** ~ he had an emergency operation; *V* **souder.**

3 *adv*: *avoir* ~ to be warm, feel warm; (*très chaud*) to be hot, feel hot; **avez-vous assez** ~**?** are you warm enough?; **on a trop** ~ **ici** it's too hot *ou* too warm in here; (*fig*) **ma voiture a dérapé, j'ai eu** ~**!*** my car skidded, I got a real fright *ou* it gave me a nasty fright; **il fait** ~ it is hot *ou* warm; (*iro*) **il fera** ~ **le jour où il voudra bien travailler*** that will be the day when he decides to work (*iro*); **ça ne me fait ni** ~ **ni froid** I couldn't care less either way; **manger** ~ to have a hot meal, eat something hot; **boire** ~ to have *ou* take hot drinks; **il a fallu tellement attendre qu'on n'a pas pu manger** ~ we had to wait so long the food was no longer hot; **servir** ~ serve hot; **tenir** ~ **à qn** to keep sb warm; *V* **ni, souffler.**

4 chaude *nf* (†: *flambée*) blaze.

5: (*Méd*) **chaud et froid** chill; (*Culin*) **chaud-froid** *nm, pl* **chauds-froids** chaudfroid; **chaud lapin‡** randy (*surtout Brit*) *ou* horny devil‡; **chaude-pisse‡** *nf inv* clap‡.

chaudement [ʃodmɑ̃] *adv* (*contre le froid*) *s'habiller* warmly; (*chaleureusement*) *féliciter, recommander* warmly, heartily; (*avec passion, acharnement*) heatedly, hotly. ~ **disputé** hotly disputed; (*hum*) **comment ça va? —** ~**!** how are you? — (I'm) hot! (*hum*).

chaudière [ʃodjɛʀ] *nf* [*locomotive, chauffage central*] boiler.

chaudron [ʃodʀɔ̃] *nm* cauldron.

chaudronnerie [ʃodʀɔnʀi] *nf* **(a)** (*métier*) boilermaking, boilerwork; (*industrie*) boilermaking industry.

(b) (*boutique*) coppersmith's workshop; (*usine*) boilerworks.

(c) (*produits*) **grosse** ~ industrial boilers; **petite** ~ pots and pans, hollowware (*Brit*).

chaudronnier [ʃodʀɔnje] *nm* (*artisan*) coppersmith; (*ouvrier*) boilermaker.

chauffage [ʃofaʒ] *nm* (*action*) heating; (*appareils*) heating (system). **il y a le** ~**?** is there any heating?, is it heated?; **avoir un bon** ~ to have a good heating system; ~ **au charbon/au gaz/à l'électricité** solid fuel/gas/electric heating; ~ **central** central heating; ~ **par le sol** under-floor heating; ~ **urbain** urban *ou* district heating system; *V* **bois.**

chauffant, e [ʃofɑ̃, ɑ̃t] *adj* *surface, élément* heating (*épith*); *V* **couverture, plaque.**

chauffard [ʃofaʀ] *nm* (*péj*) reckless driver. **(espèce de)** ~**!** roadhog!; **c'est un vrai** ~ he's a real menace *ou* maniac on the roads; **il a été renversé/tué par un** ~ he was run over/killed by a reckless driver; **on n'a pas retrouvé le** ~ **responsable de l'accident** the driver responsible for the accident has not yet been found; **il pourrait s'agir d'un** ~ the police are looking for a hit-and-run driver.

chauffe [ʃof] *nf* (*lieu*) fire-chamber; (*processus*) stoking. **surface de** ~ heating-surface, fire surface; (*Naut*) **chambre de** ~ stokehold; *V* **bleu.**

chauffe- [ʃof] *préf* *V* **chauffer.**

chauffer [ʃofe] (1) **1** *vt* **(a)** (*plus gén* **faire** ~**, mettre à** ~) *soupe* to warm up, heat up; *assiette* to warm, heat; *eau du bain* to heat (up); *eau du thé* to boil, heat up. ~ **qch au four** to heat sth up in the oven, put sth in the oven to heat up; (*hum*) **faites** ~ **la colle!** bring out the glue! (*when sb has broken sth*).

(b) *appartement* to heat. **chez eux, ils chauffent au charbon** their house is heated by coal, in their house they use coal for heating; **le mazout chauffe bien** oil gives (out) a good heat; **on va** ~ **un peu la pièce** we'll heat (up) the room a bit.

(c) [*soleil*] to warm, make warm; [*soleil brûlant*] to heat, make hot.

(d) (*Tech*) *métal, verre, liquide* to heat; *chaudière, locomotive* to stoke (up), fire. (*lit, fig*) ~ **qch à blanc** to make sth white-hot; (*fig*) ~ **qn à blanc** to fire sb into action.

(e) (*: *préparer*) *candidat* to cram; *commando* to train up.

(f) (†*: *voler*) to pinch*, whip*, swipe*.

2 *vi* **(a)** (*être sur le feu*) [*aliment, eau du bain*] to be heating up, be warming up; [*assiette*] to be heating (up), be warming (up); [*eau du thé*] to be heating up. **mets l'eau/les assiettes à** ~ put the water on/the plates in to heat up.

(b) (*devenir chaud*) [*moteur, télévision*] to warm up; [*four*] to heat up; [*chaudière, locomotive*] to get up steam.

(c) (*devenir trop chaud*) [*freins, appareil, moteur*] to overheat.

(d) (**loc*) **ça chauffe dans le coin!** things are getting heated over there!, sparks are about to fly over there!; **ça va** ~**!** sparks will fly!; (*Sport*) **le but/l'essai chauffe** there must be a goal/try now!, they're on the brink of a goal/try; (*cache-tampon*) **tu chauffes!** you're getting warm(er)!

3 se chauffer *vpr* **(a)** (*près du feu*) to warm o.s.; (*: *en faisant des exercices*) to warm o.s. up. **se** ~ **au soleil** to warm o.s. in the sun.

(b) se ~ au bois/charbon to burn wood/coal, use wood/coal for heating; **se ~ à l'électricité** to have electric heating, use electricity for heating; *V* **bois.**

4: chauffe-assiettes *nm inv* plate-warmer; **chauffe-bain** *nm, pl* **chauffe-bains** water-heater; **chauffe-biberon** *nm inv* bottle-warmer; **chauffe-eau** *nm inv* water-heater; (*à élément chauffant*) immersion heater, immerser; **chauffe-pieds** *nm inv* foot-warmer; **chauffe-plats** *nm inv* dish-warmer, chafing dish.

chaufferette [ʃofʀɛt] *nf* (*chauffe-pieds*) foot-warmer.

chaufferie [ʃofʀi] *nf [usine]* boiler room; *[navire]* stokehold.

chauffeur [ʃofœʀ] **1** *nm* **(a)** (*conducteur*) (*gén*) driver; (*privé*) chauffeur. **~ d'autobus** bus driver; **voiture avec/sans ~** chauffeur-driven/self-drive car.

(b) *[chaudière]* fireman, stoker.

2: chauffeur de camion lorry (*Brit*) *ou* truck (*US*) driver; (*hum*) **chauffeur du dimanche** Sunday driver, weekend motorist; **chauffeur de maître** chauffeur; **chauffeur de taxi** taxi driver, cab driver.

chauffeuse [ʃoføz] *nf* low armless chair, unit chair.

chaulage [ʃolaʒ] *nm* (*V* **chauler**) liming; whitewashing.

chauler [ʃole] (1) *vt sol, arbre, raisins* to lime; *mur* to whitewash.

chaume [ʃom] *nm* **(a)** (*reste des tiges*) stubble. (*littér: champs*) **les ~s** the stubble fields. **(b)** (*couverture de toit*) thatch. **couvrir de ~** to thatch; *V* **toit. (c)** (*rare: tige*) *[graminée, céréale]* culm.

chaumer [ʃome] (1) **1** *vt* to clear stubble from. **2** *vi* to clear the stubble.

chaumière [ʃomjɛʀ] *nf* (*littér, hum: maison*) (little) cottage; (*maison à toit de chaume*) thatched cottage. **on en parlera encore longtemps dans les ~s** it will be talked of in the countryside *ou* in the villages for a long time to come; **un feuilleton qui fait pleurer dans les ~s** a serial which will bring tears to the eyes of all simple folk.

chaumine [ʃomin] *nf* (*littér ou* †) little cottage (*often thatched*), cot (*Poésie*).

chaussant, e [ʃosɑ̃, ɑ̃t] *adj* (*confortable*) well-fitting, snug-fitting. **ces souliers sont très ~s** these shoes are a very good fit *ou* fit very well.

chausse [ʃos] *nf V* **chausses.**

chausse- [ʃos] *préf V* **chausser.**

chaussée [ʃose] *nf* **(a)** (*route, rue*) road, roadway. **s'élancer sur la ~** to rush out into the road *ou* onto the roadway; **traverser la ~** to cross the road; **ne reste pas sur la ~** don't stay in *ou* on the road *ou* on the roadway; **l'entretien de la ~** the maintenance of the roadway, road maintenance; **~ pavée** cobbled street; (*route*) cobbled *ou* flagged road; **~ bombée** cambered road; '**~ glissante**' 'slippery road'; '**~ déformée**' 'uneven road surface'; *V* **pont.**

(b) (*chemin surélevé*) causeway; (*digue*) embankment. **la ~ des Géants** the Giants' Causeway.

chausser [ʃose] (1) **1** *vt* **(a)** (*mettre des chaussures à*) *enfant* to put shoes on. **chausse les enfants pour sortir** put the children's shoes on (for them) and we'll go out; **se ~** to put one's shoes on; **se faire ~ par** to have one's shoes put on by; **~ qn de bottes** to put boots on sb; **chaussé de bottes/sandales** with boots/sandals on; *V* **cordonnier.**

(b) (*mettre*) *souliers, lunettes* to put on. **~ du 40** to take size 40 in shoes, take a (size) 40 shoe; **~ des bottes à un client** to put boots on a customer; (*Équitation*) **~ les étriers** to put one's feet into the stirrups.

(c) (*fournir en chaussures*) **ce marchand nous chausse depuis 10 ans** this shoemaker has been supplying us with shoes for 10 years; **se (faire) ~ chez ...** to buy *ou* get one's shoes at ...; **se (faire) ~ sur mesure** to have one's shoes made to measure.

(d) *[chaussure]* to fit. **ces chaussures chaussent large** these shoes come in a wide fitting (*Brit*) *ou* size (*US*), these are wide-fitting shoes; **ces chaussures vous chaussent bien** those shoes fit you well *ou* are a good fit; **ces souliers chaussent bien (le pied)** these are well-fitting shoes.

(e) (*Agr*) *arbre* to earth up.

(f) (*Aut*) *voiture* to fit tyres on. **voiture bien chaussée** car with good tyres.

2: chausse-pied *nm, pl* **chausse-pieds** shoehorn; (*lit, fig*) **chausse-trappe** *nf, pl* **chausse-trappes** trap; **tomber dans/éviter une chausse-trappe** to fall into/avoid a trap.

chausses [ʃos] *nfpl* (*Hist Habillement*) chausses; *V* **haut.**

chaussette [ʃosɛt] *nf* sock. **j'étais en ~s** I was in my socks; **~s à clous**‡ *[agent de police]* (policeman's) hobnailed boots; **~s russes** foot-bindings.

chausseur [ʃosœʀ] *nm* (*fabricant*) shoemaker; (*fournisseur*) footwear specialist, shoemaker. **mon ~ m'a déconseillé cette marque** my shoemaker has advised me against that make.

chausson [ʃosɔ̃] *nm* **(a)** (*pantoufle*) slipper; *[bébé]* bootee; *[danseur]* ballet shoe *ou* pump; *V* **point**². **(b)** (*Culin*) turnover.

chaussure [ʃosyʀ] **1** *nf* **(a)** (*soulier*) shoe. **la ~ est une partie importante de l'habillement** footwear is *ou* shoes are an important part of one's dress; **rayon (des) ~s** shoe *ou* footwear department.

(b) (*industrie*) shoe industry; (*commerce*) shoe trade (*surtout Brit*) *ou* business.

2: chaussures basses flat shoes; **chaussures cloutées** *ou* **à clous** hobnailed boots; **chaussures montantes** ankle boots; **chaussures de ski** ski boots.

chaut [ʃo] *vi* (†† *ou hum*) **peu me ~** it matters little to me, it is of no import (†† *ou hum*) *ou* matter† to me.

chauve [ʃov] **1** *adj personne* bald(-headed); *crâne* bald; (*fig littér*) *colline, sommet* bare. **~ comme un œuf*** *ou* **une bille*** *ou* **mon genou*** as bald as a coot. **2:** (*Zool*) **chauve-souris** *nf, pl* **chauves-souris** bat.

chauvin, e [ʃovɛ̃, in] **1** *adj* chauvinistic.

2 *nm,f* chauvinist.

chauvinisme [ʃovinism(ə)] *nm* chauvinism.

chauviniste [ʃovinist(ə)] **1** *adj* chauvinistic.

2 *nmf* chauvinist.

chaux [ʃo] *nf* lime. **~ vive/éteinte** quick/slaked lime; **blanchi** *ou* **passé à la ~** whitewashed.

chavirer [ʃaviʀe] (1) **1** *vi* **(a)** *[bateau]* to capsize, keel over, overturn; (*fig*) *[gouvernement]* to founder, crumble, sink. **faire ~ un bateau** to keel a boat over, capsize *ou* overturn a boat.

(b) *[pile d'objets]* to keel over, overturn; *[charrette]* to overturn, tip over; (*fig*) *[yeux]* to roll; *[paysage, chambre]* to reel, spin; *[esprit]* to reel; *[cœur]* to turn over (*fig*).

2 *vt* **(a)** (*renverser*) *bateau [vagues]* to capsize, overturn; (*Tech: en cale sèche*) to keel over; *meubles* to overturn.

(b) (*bouleverser*) *personne* to bowl over. **j'en suis toute chavirée*** I'm completely shattered by it, it has left me all of a flutter*; **musique qui chavire l'âme** music that tugs at the heartstrings.

chéchia [ʃeʃja] *nf* tarboosh, fez.

check-up [(t)ʃɛkœp] *nm inv* check-up.

chef¹ [ʃɛf] **1** *nm* **(a)** (*patron, dirigeant*) head, boss*, top man*; *[tribu]* chief(tain), headman. **il a l'estime de ses ~s** he is highly thought of by his superiors *ou* bosses*.

(b) *[expédition, révolte, syndicat]* leader. (*: *as*) **tu es un ~** you're the greatest*, you're the tops*; **avoir une âme** *ou* **un tempérament de ~** to be a born leader.

(c) (*Mil: au sergent*) **oui, ~!** yes, Sarge!

(d) (*Culin*) **~ (de cuisine** *ou* **cuisinier)** chef; **spécialité du ~** chef's speciality; **pâté du ~** chef's special pâté.

(e) en ~: commandant en ~ commander-in-chief; **général en ~** general-in-chief; **ingénieur/rédacteur en ~** chief engineer/editor; **le général commandait en ~ les troupes alliées** the general was the commander-in-chief of the allied troops.

2 *adj inv*: **gardien/médecin ~** chief warden/consultant.

3: chef d'atelier (shop) foreman; **chef de bande** gang leader; **chef de bataillon** major; **chef de bureau** head clerk; (*Admin*) **chef de cabinet** principal private secretary; **chef de chantier** (works (*Brit*) *ou* factory) foreman; (*Mus*) **chef des chœurs** choirmaster; **chef de clinique** senior hospital lecturer; **chef comptable** chief accountant; **chef de dépôt** shed *ou* yard master; (*Art, Littérat*) **chef d'école** leader of a school; **chef d'entreprise** company manager *ou* head; **chef d'équipe** foreman; (*Sport*) captain; **chef d'escadron** major; **chef d'État** head of state; **le chef de l'État** the Chief of State; (*Mil*) **chef d'état-major** chief of staff; **chef de famille** head of the family; (*Admin*) householder; **chef de file** leader; (*Pol*) party leader; (*Naut*) leading ship; (*Rail*) **chef de gare** station master; (*Jur*) **chef des jurés** foreman of the jury; (*Admin, Géog*) **chef-lieu** *nm, pl* **chef-lieux** ≃ county town; **chef mécanicien** chief mechanic; (*Rail*) head driver (*Brit*), chief engineer (*US*); **chef de musique** bandmaster; **chef de nage** stroke (oar); **chef-d'œuvre** *nm, pl* **chefs-d'œuvre** masterpiece, chef d'œuvre; (*Mus*) **chef d'orchestre** conductor; **chef de patrouille** patrol leader; (*Mil*) **chef de pièce** captain of a gun; (*Comm*) **chef de rayon** department(al) supervisor, departmental manager; (*Admin*) **chef de service** section *ou* departmental head; (*Rail*) **chef de train** guard (*Brit*), conductor (*US*).

chef² [ʃɛf] *nm* **(a)** (†† *ou hum: tête*) head. (*Jur*) **~ d'accusation** charge, count (of indictment).

(b) (*loc*) (*Jur*) **du ~ de sa femme** in one's wife's right; (*frm*) **de son propre ~** on his own initiative, on his own authority; (*littér*) **au premier ~** greatly, exceedingly; (*littér*) **de ce ~** accordingly, hence.

cheftaine [ʃɛftɛn] *nf [louveteaux]* cubmistress (*Brit*), den mother (*US*); *[jeunes éclaireuses]* Brown Owl (*Brit*), den mother (*US*); *[éclaireuses]* (guide) captain.

cheik [ʃɛk] *nm* sheik.

chelem [ʃlɛm] *nm* (*Cartes*) slam. **petit/grand ~** small/grand slam.

chemin [ʃ(ə)mɛ̃] **1** *nm* **(a)** (*gén*) path; *[campagne]* lane, path; (*à peine tracé*) track; *V* **croisée**², **voleur** *etc.*

(b) (*parcours, trajet, direction*) way (*de, pour* to). **demander/trouver le** *ou* **son ~** to ask/find the *ou* one's way; **montrer le ~ à qn** to show sb the way; **il y a bien une heure de ~** it's a good hour's walk; **quel ~ a-t-elle pris?** which way did she go?; **de bon matin, ils prirent le ~ de X** they set out *ou* off for X early in the morning; **le ~ le plus court entre deux points** the shortest distance between two points; **ils ont fait tout le ~ à pied/en bicyclette** they walked/cycled all the way *ou* the whole way; **on a fait du ~ depuis une heure** we've come quite a (good) way in an hour; **se mettre en ~** to set out *ou* off; **poursuivre son ~** to carry on *ou* keep on one's way; (*littér*) **passez votre ~** go your way (*littér*), be on your way; **~ faisant, en ~** on the way; **pour venir, nous avons pris le ~ des écoliers** we came the long way round; (*fig*) **aller son ~** to go one's own sweet way; *V* **rebrousser.**

(c) (*fig*) path, way, road. **le ~ de l'honneur/de la gloire** the path *ou* way of honour/to glory; **le ~ de la ruine** the road to ruin; *V* **droit**².

(d) (*loc*) **il a encore du ~ à faire** he's still got a long way to go, he's not there yet; (*iro*) there's still room for improvement; **faire son ~ dans la vie** to make one's way in life; **se mettre dans** *ou* **sur le ~ de qn** to stand *ou* get in sb's way, stand in sb's path; **il a fait du ~!** (*arriviste, jeune cadre*) he has come up in the world; (*savant, chercheur*) he has come a long way; **cette idée a fait du ~** this idea has gained ground; (*concession*) **faire la moitié du ~** to go half-way (to meet sb); **montrer le ~** to lead the way; **cela n'en prend pas le ~** it doesn't look likely; **il ne doit pas s'arrêter en si beau ~** he mustn't stop (now) when he's doing so well *ou* after such a good start; **il n'y arrivera pas par ce ~** he won't achieve anything this way, he won't get far if he goes about it this way; **être sur le bon ~** to be on the right track *ou* lines; **être toujours sur les ~s** to be always on the road, be always gadding about; **trouver des difficultés sur son ~** to meet difficulties on one's path; **est-ce qu'il va réussir? — il n'en prend pas le ~** will he succeed? — he's not going the right way about it.

2: chemin creux sunken lane; (*Rel*) **le chemin de (la) croix** the Way of the Cross; (*Rail*) **chemin de fer** railway (*Brit*), railroad (*US*); (*moyen de transport*) rail; (*Admin*) Railways (*Brit*), Railroad (*US*); **par chemin de fer** by rail; **chemin de halage** towpath; (*Archit*) **chemin de ronde** covered way; **chemin de table** table runner; **chemin de terre** dirt track; **chemin de traverse** path across *ou* through the fields; **chemin vicinal** country road *ou* lane, minor road.

chemineau, *pl* **~x** [ʃ(ə)mino] *nm* (*littér ou* ††: *vagabond*) vagabond, tramp.

cheminée [ʃ(ə)mine] **1** *nf* **(a)** (*extérieure*) *[maison, usine]* chimney (stack); *[paquebot, locomotive]* funnel, smokestack.

(b) (*intérieure*) fireplace; (*foyer*) fireplace, hearth; (*encadrement*) mantelpiece, chimney piece. **un feu pétillait dans la ~** a fire was crackling in the hearth *ou* fireplace *ou* grate; *V* **feu**[1].

(c) (*Alpinisme*) chimney; *[lampe]* chimney.

2: cheminée d'aération ventilation shaft; **cheminée prussienne** (closed) stove; **cheminée d'usine** factory chimney.

cheminement [ʃ(ə)minmɑ̃] *nm* (*progression*) *[caravane, marcheurs]* progress, advance; (*Mil*) *[troupes]* advance (under cover); *[sentier, itinéraire, eau]* course, way; (*fig*) *[idées, pensée]* development, progression.

cheminer [ʃ(ə)mine] (1) *vi* (*littér*) **(a)** (*marcher, Mil: avancer à couvert*) to walk (along). **~ péniblement** to trudge (wearily) along; **après avoir longtemps cheminé** having plodded along for ages; **nous cheminions vers la ville** we wended (*littér*) *ou* made our way towards the town.

(b) (*progresser*) *[sentier]* to make its way (*dans* along); *[eau]* to make its way, follow its course (*dans* along); *[idées]* to follow their course. **sa pensée cheminait de façon tortueuse** his thoughts followed a tortuous course; **les eaux de la Durance cheminent pendant des kilomètres entre des falaises** the waters of the Durance flow for miles between cliffs *ou* make their way between cliffs for miles (and miles).

cheminot [ʃ(ə)mino] *nm* railwayman (*Brit*), railroad man (*US*).

chemisage [ʃ(ə)mizaʒ] *nm* (*intérieur*) lining; (*extérieur*) jacketing.

chemise [ʃ(ə)miz] **1** *nf* **(a)** (*Habillement*) *[homme]* shirt; (††) *[femme]* chemise††, shift†; *[bébé]* vest. **~ de soirée/de sport** dress/sports shirt; **être en manches** *ou* **bras de ~** to be in one's shirt sleeves; **col/manchette de ~** shirt collar/cuff; **s'en moquer** *ou* **s'en soucier comme de sa première ~** not to care twopence (*Brit*) *ou* a fig.

(b) *[dossier]* folder; (*Tech*) (*revêtement intérieur*) lining; (*revêtement extérieur*) jacket. (*Aut*) **~ de cylindre** cylinder liner.

2: chemise (américaine) (woman's) vest (*Brit*) *ou* undershirt (*US*); (*Hist*) **chemises brunes** Brownshirts; **chemise d'homme** man's shirt; **chemise de maçonnerie** facing; (*Hist*) **chemises noires** Blackshirts; **chemise de nuit** *[femme]* nightdress, nightgown, nightie*; *[homme]* nightshirt; (*Hist*) **chemises rouges** Redshirts.

chemiser [ʃ(ə)mize] (1) *vt intérieur* to line; *extérieur* to jacket.

chemiserie [ʃ(ə)mizʀi] *nf* (*magasin*) (gentlemen's) outfitters' (*Brit*), man's shop; (*rayon*) shirt department; (*commerce*) shirt(-making) trade (*surtout Brit*) *ou* business.

chemisette [ʃ(ə)mizɛt] *nf* *[homme]* short-sleeved shirt; *[femme]* short-sleeved blouse.

chemisier [ʃ(ə)mizje] *nm* **(a)** (*marchand*) (gentlemen's) shirtmaker; (*fabricant*) shirtmaker.

(b) (*vêtement*) blouse; *V* **robe.**

chênaie [ʃɛnɛ] *nf* oak grove.

chenal, *pl* **-aux** [ʃənal, o] **1** *nm* (*canal*) channel, fairway; (*rigole*) channel; *[moulin]* millrace; *[forge, usine]* flume. **2:** (*Ind*) **chenal de coulée** gate, runner; (*Géol*) **chenal proglaciaire** glaciated valley.

chenapan [ʃ(ə)napɑ̃] *nm* (*hum: garnement*) scallywag (*hum*), rascal (*hum*); (*péj: vaurien*) scoundrel, rogue.

chêne [ʃɛn] **1** *nm* (*arbre*) oak (tree); (*bois*) oak. **2: chêne-liège** *nm, pl* **chênes-lièges** cork-oak; **chêne vert** holm oak, ilex.

chéneau, *pl* **~x** [ʃeno] *nm* *[toit]* gutter.

chenet [ʃ(ə)nɛ] *nm* fire-dog, andiron.

chènevis [ʃɛnvi] *nm* hempseed.

chenil [ʃ(ə)ni(l)] *nm* kennels.

chenille [ʃ(ə)nij] **1** *nf* **(a)** (*Aut, Zool*) caterpillar. **véhicule à ~s** tracked vehicle. **(b)** (*Tex*) chenille. **2: chenille du mûrier** silkworm; **chenille processionnaire** processionary caterpillar.

chenillé, e [ʃ(ə)nije] *adj véhicule* with caterpillar tracks, tracked.

chenillette [ʃ(ə)nijɛt] *nf* (*véhicule*) tracker vehicle.

chenu, e [ʃəny] *adj* (*littér*) *vieillard, tête* hoary; *arbre* leafless with age.

cheptel [ʃɛptɛl] **1** *nm* (*bétail*) livestock; (*Jur*) livestock (*leased*). **~ ovin/porcin d'une région** sheep/pig *ou* swine population of an area; *V* **bail. 2:** (*Jur*) **cheptel mort** farm implements; (*Jur*) **cheptel vif** livestock.

chèque [ʃɛk] **1** *nm* **(a)** (*Banque*) cheque (*Brit*), check (*US*). **faire/toucher un ~** to write/cash a cheque; **~ de 100 F** cheque for 100 francs.

(b) (*bon*) voucher. **~-repas** luncheon voucher (*Brit*); **~-cadeau** gift token; **~-essence** petrol (*Brit*) *ou* gasoline (*US*) coupon *ou* voucher.

2: chèque bancaire cheque; **chèque barré** crossed cheque (*Brit*); (*lit, fig*) **chèque en blanc** blank cheque; **chèque certifié** certified cheque; **chèque à ordre** cheque to order, order cheque; **chèque au porteur** cheque to bearer; **chèque postal** ≃ (Post Office) Girocheque; **chèque sans provision** bad *ou* dud* cheque; **chèque de voyage** traveller's cheque.

chéquier [ʃekje] *nm* cheque book.

cher, chère[1] [ʃɛʀ] **1** *adj* **(a)** (*gén après n: aimé*) *personne, souvenir, vœu* dear (*à* to). **ceux qui nous sont ~s** our nearest and dearest, our dear ones; **des souvenirs ~s** fond memories; **des souvenirs ~s à mon cœur** memories dear to my heart; **les êtres ~s** the loved ones; **c'est mon vœu le plus ~** it's my fondest *ou* dearest wish; **mon désir le plus ~** *ou* **mon plus ~ désir est de** my greatest *ou* most cherished desire is to; **l'honneur est le bien le plus ~** honour is one's most precious possession, one's honour is to be treasured above all else.

(b) (*avant n*) dear. **(mes) ~s auditeurs** dear listeners; (*Rel*) **mes bien ~s frères** my dear(est) brethren; **Monsieur et ~ collègue** dear colleague; **ce ~ (vieux) Louis!*** dear old Louis!*; (*hum*) **le ~ homme n'y entendait pas malice** the dear man didn't mean any harm by it; **retrouver ses ~s parents/chères pantoufles** to find one's beloved parents/slippers again; **retrouver ses chères habitudes** to slip back into one's dear old habits.

(c) (*coûteux: après n*) *marchandise* expensive, dear, costly; *boutique, commerçant* expensive, dear. **un petit restaurant pas ~** an inexpensive *ou* reasonably priced little restaurant; **la vie est chère à Paris** the cost of living is high in Paris, Paris is an expensive place to live; **c'est moins ~ qu'en face** it's cheaper than *ou* less expensive than in the shop opposite; **cet épicier est trop ~** this grocer is too expensive *ou* too dear *ou* charges too much; *V* **vie.**

2 *nm,f* (*frm, hum*) **mon ~, ma chère** my dear; **oui, très ~** yes, dearest.

3 *adv valoir, coûter, payer* a lot (of money), a great deal (of money). **article qui vaut** *ou* **coûte ~** expensive item, item that costs a lot *ou* a great deal; **as-tu payé ~ ton costume?** did you pay much *ou* a lot for your suit?, was your suit (very) expensive? *ou* (very) dear?; **il se fait payer ~, il prend ~** he charges high rates, his rates are high, he's expensive; **il vend ~** his prices are high, he charges high prices; **ça s'est vendu ~** it went for *ou* fetched a high price *ou* a lot (of money); **je ne l'ai pas acheté ~, je l'ai eu pour pas ~*** I bought it very cheaply *ou* bought it cheap*, I didn't pay much for it; (*fig*) **garnement qui ne vaut pas ~** ne'er-do-well, good-for-nothing; (*fig*) **tu ne vaux pas plus ~ que lui** you're no better than him, you're just as bad as he is; (*fig*) **son imprudence lui a coûté ~** his rashness cost him dear; (*fig*) **il a payé ~ son imprudence** he paid dearly for his rashness.

chercher [ʃɛʀʃe] (1) **1** *vt* **(a)** (*essayer de trouver*) *personne, chose égarée, emploi* to look for, search for, try to find, hunt for; *solution, moyen* to look for, seek, try to find; *ombre, lumière, tranquillité* to seek; *citation, heure de train* to look up; *nom, mot* to try to find, try to think of; *raison, excuse* to cast about for, try to find, look for. **~ qn du regard** *ou* **des yeux** to look (around) for sb; **~ qch à tâtons** to grope *ou* fumble for sth; **attends, je cherche** wait a minute, I'm trying to think; **il n'a pas bien cherché** he didn't look *ou* search very hard; **~ partout qch/qn** to search *ou* hunt everywhere for sth/sb; **~ sa voie** to look for *ou* seek a path in life; **~ ses mots** to search for words; (*à un chien*) **cherche! cherche!** find it, boy!

(b) (*viser à*) *gloire, succès* to seek (after); (*rechercher*) *alliance, faveur* to seek. **il ne cherche que son intérêt** he is concerned only with his own interest.

(c) (*provoquer*) *danger, mort* to court. **~ la difficulté** to look for difficulties; **~ la bagarre** to be looking *ou* spoiling for a fight; **tu l'auras cherché!** you've been asking for it!; **si on me cherche, on me trouve*** if anyone asks for it, they'll get it*; **~ le contact avec l'ennemi** to try to engage the enemy in combat.

(d) (*prendre, acheter*) **aller ~ qch/qn** to go for sth/sb, go and fetch *ou* get sth/sb; **il est venu ~ Paul** he called *ou* came for Paul, he came to fetch *ou* to get Paul; **il est allé me ~ de la monnaie** he has gone to get some change for me; **va me ~ mon sac** go and fetch *ou* get me my bag; **qu'est-ce que tu vas ~? je n'ai rien dit!** whatever do you mean? *ou* whatever are you trying to read into it? I didn't say a thing!; **où est-ce qu'il va ~ toutes ces idées idiotes!** where does he get all those stupid ideas from!; **monter/descendre ~ qch** to go up/down for sth *ou* to get sth; **il est allé/venu le ~ à la gare** he went/came to meet *ou* collect him at the station; **aller ~ les enfants à l'école** to go to fetch *ou* get *ou* collect the children from school; **envoyer (qn) ~ le médecin** to send (sb) for the doctor; (*fig*) **ça va ~ dans les 300 F/dans les 5 ans de prison*** it'll add up to *ou* come to something like 300 francs/a 5-year jail sentence.

(e) ~ à faire to try to do, attempt to do; **~ à comprendre** to try to understand; **faut pas ~ à comprendre*** don't (even) try and understand, don't seek to understand; **~ à faire plaisir à qn** to try *ou* endeavour to please sb; **~ à obtenir qch** to try to obtain sth; **~ à savoir qch** to try *ou* attempt to find out sth.

(f) (*loc*) **~ des crosses à qn*** to try and pick a fight with sb; **~ fortune** to seek one's fortune; **~ des histoires à qn** to try to make trouble for sb; **~ midi à quatorze heures** to complicate the issue, look for complications; **~ noise à qn** to seek a quarrel with sb; **~ la petite bête** to split hairs; **~ une aiguille dans une botte** *ou* **meule de foin** to look for a needle in a haystack; **~ des poux dans la tête de qn** to try and make trouble for sb; **~ querelle à qn** to seek a quarrel with sb; **~ son salut dans la fuite** to seek *ou* take refuge in flight; **cherchez la femme!** cherchez la femme!

2 se chercher *vpr* (*chercher sa voie*) to search for an identity.

chercheur, -euse [ʃɛʀʃœʀ, øz] **1** *adj esprit* inquiring; *V* **tête**.

2 *nm* (*Tech*) *[télescope]* finder; *[détecteur à galène]* cat's whisker. **~ de fuites** gas-leak detector.

3 *nm,f* (*personne qui étudie, cherche*) researcher; (*Univ: chargé de recherches*) researcher, research worker. (*personne qui cherche qch*) **~ de** seeker of; **~ d'aventure(s)** adventure seeker, seeker after adventure; **~ d'or** gold digger; **~ de trésors** treasure hunter.

chère[2] [ʃɛʀ] *nf* (†† *ou hum*) food, fare. **faire bonne ~** to eat well.

chèrement [ʃɛʀmɑ̃] *adv* **(a)** (*avec affection*) *aimer* dearly, fondly. **conserver ~ des lettres** to keep letters lovingly, treasure letters; **conserver ~ le souvenir de qn/qch** to treasure *ou* cherish the memory of sb/sth.

(b) (*non sans pertes, difficultés*) **~ acquis** *ou* **payé** *avantage, victoire, succès* dearly bought *ou* won; **vendre** *ou* **faire payer ~ sa vie** to sell one's life dearly.

(c) (†: *au prix fort*) *vendre* at a high price, dearly†.

chéri, e [ʃeʀi] (*ptp de* **chérir**) **1** *adj* (*bien-aimé*) beloved, darling, dear(est). **quand il a revu son fils ~** when he saw his beloved son again; **dis-moi, maman ~e** tell me, mother dear *ou* mother darling; (*sur tombe*) **à notre père ~** to our beloved father.

2 *nm,f* **(a)** (*terme d'affection*) darling. **mon (grand) ~** (my) darling, my (little) darling; (*hum*) **bonjour mes ~s** hullo (my) darlings (*hum*).

(b) (*péj: chouchou*) **c'est le ~ à sa maman** he's mummy's little darling *ou* mummy's blue-eyed boy, his mother dotes on him; **c'est le ~ de ses parents** his parents dote on him, he's the apple of his parents' eye.

chérir [ʃeʀiʀ] (2) *vt* (*littér*) *personne* to cherish, love dearly; *liberté, idée* to cherish, hold dear; *souvenir* to cherish, treasure.

chérot* [ʃeʀo] *adj m* (*coûteux*) pricey* (*Brit*).

cherry [ʃeʀi] *nm*, **cherry brandy** [ʃeʀibʀɑ̃di] *nm* cherry brandy.

cherté [ʃɛʀte] *nf [article]* high price, dearness; *[époque, région]* high prices (*de* in). **la ~ de la vie** the high cost of living, the cost of things*.

chérubin [ʃeʀybɛ̃] *nm* (*lit, fig*) cherub. **~s** cherubs; (*Rel*) cherubim.

chétif, -ive [ʃetif, iv] *adj* **(a)** (*malingre*) *enfant* puny, sickly; *adulte* puny; *arbuste, plante* puny, stunted. **enfant/végétaux à l'aspect ~** puny-looking child/plants.

(b) (*minable*) *récolte* meagre, poor; *existence* meagre, mean; *repas* skimpy, scanty; *raisonnement* paltry, feeble.

chétivement [ʃetivmɑ̃] *adv pousser* punily.

chevaine [ʃ(ə)vɛn] *nm* = **chevesne**.

cheval, -aux [ʃ(ə)val, o] **1** *nm* **(a)** (*animal*) horse. **carosse à deux/à six ~aux** coach and pair/and six; (*péj*) **c'est un grand ~, cette fille** she's built like a cart-horse (*Brit péj*), she's a great horse of a girl (*péj*); **au travail, c'est un vrai ~** he works like a cart-horse (*Brit*), he works like a Trojan; (*fig*) **ce n'est pas le mauvais ~** he's not a bad sort *ou* soul.

(b) (*Aut*) horsepower (*U*). **elle fait combien de ~aux?** what horsepower is it?; **c'est une 6 ~aux** it's a 6 horsepower car.

(c) (*loc*) **à ~** on horseback; **se tenir bien à ~** to have a good seat, sit well on horseback; **être à ~ sur une chaise** to be (sitting) astride a chair, be straddling a chair; **village à ~ sur deux départements** village straddling two departments; **à ~ sur deux mois** overlapping two (different) months, running from one month into the next; **être (très) à ~ sur le règlement/les principes** to be a (real) stickler for the rules/for principles; **de ~*** *remède* drastic; *fièvre* raging.

2: cheval d'arçons (vaulting) horse; **cheval d'attelage** plough horse; **cheval à bascule** rocking horse; (*Mil*) **cheval de bataille** battle horse, charger; (*fig*) **il a ressorti son cheval de bataille** he's back on his hobby-horse *ou* his favourite theme again; **cheval de bois** wooden horse; **monter** *ou* **aller sur les chevaux de bois** to go on the roundabout (*Brit*) *ou* merry-go-round; († *ou hum*) **déjeuner** *ou* **dîner** *ou* **manger avec les chevaux de bois** to miss a meal, go dinnerless; **cheval de chasse** hunter; **cheval de cirque** circus horse; **cheval de course** racehorse; **cheval de fiacre** carriage horse; **cheval fiscal** horsepower (*for tax purposes*); **chevaux de frise** chevaux-de-frise; **cheval de labour** cart-horse, plough horse; **cheval de manège** school horse; **cheval marin** *ou* **de mer** sea horse; **cheval de poste** *ou* **de relais** post horse; **cheval de renfort** remount; **(vieux) cheval de retour** old lag* (*surtout Brit*); **cheval de selle** saddle horse; **cheval de trait** draught horse; (*lit, fig*) **cheval de Troie** Trojan horse; **cheval vapeur** horsepower.

chevalement [ʃ(ə)valmɑ̃] *nm [mur]* shoring; *[galerie]* (pit)head frame.

chevaler [ʃ(ə)vale] (1) *vt mur* to shore up.

chevaleresque [ʃ(ə)valʀɛsk(ə)] *adj caractère, conduite* chivalrous, gentlemanly. **règles ~s** rules of chivalry; **l'honneur ~** the honour of a knight, knightly honour; *V* **littérature**.

chevalerie [ʃ(ə)valʀi] *nf* (*Hist: institution*) chivalry; (*dignité, chevaliers*) knighthood; *V* **roman**[1].

chevalet [ʃ(ə)valɛ] *nm [peintre]* easel; (*Menuiserie*) trestle, sawhorse; *[violon etc]* bridge; (*Hist: torture*) rack.

chevalier [ʃ(ə)valje] **1** *nm* **(a)** (*Hist*) knight. **faire qn ~** to knight sb, dub sb knight; **'je te fais ~'** 'I dub you knight'.

(b) (*oiseau*) sandpiper.

2: chevalier errant knight-errant; **chevalier d'industrie** crook, swindler; **chevalier de la Légion d'honneur** chevalier of the Legion of Honour; **chevalier servant** (attentive) escort; **chevalier de la Table ronde** Knight of the Round Table; **le chevalier de la Triste Figure** the Knight of the Sorrowful Countenance.

chevalière [ʃ(ə)valjɛʀ] *nf* signet ring.

chevalin, e [ʃ(ə)valɛ̃, in] *adj race* of horses, equine; *visage, œil* horsy; *V* **boucherie**.

chevauchant, e [ʃ(ə)voʃɑ̃, ɑ̃t] *adj pans, tuiles, dents* overlapping.

chevauchée [ʃ(ə)voʃe] *nf* (*course*) ride; (*cavaliers, cavalcade*) cavalcade.

chevauchement [ʃ(ə)voʃmɑ̃] *nm* (*gén*) overlapping; (*Géol*) thrust fault.

chevaucher [ʃ(ə)voʃe] (1) **1** *vt* **(a)** (*être à cheval sur*) *cheval, âne* to be astride; *chaise* to sit astride, straddle, bestride. (*fig*) **de grosses lunettes lui chevauchaient le nez** a large pair of glasses sat on his nose; (*fig*) **le pont chevauche l'abîme** the bridge spans the abyss.

(b) (*recouvrir partiellement*) *ardoise, pan* to overlap, lap over.

2 se chevaucher *vpr* (*se recouvrir partiellement*) *[dents, tuiles, lettres]* to overlap (each other); (*Géol*) *[couches]* to overthrust, override.

3 *vi* **(a)** († *ou littér: aller à cheval*) to ride (on horseback).

(b) = **se chevaucher**.

chevau-léger, *pl* **chevau-légers** [ʃ(ə)voleʒe] *nm* (*Hist*) (*soldat*) member of the Household Cavalry. (*troupe*) **~s** Household Cavalry.

chevelu, e [ʃəvly] *adj personne* (*gén*) with a good crop of *ou* long mane of hair, long-haired; (*péj*) hairy (*péj*), long-haired (*péj*); *tête* hairy; (*fig*) *épi* tufted; *racine* bearded; *V* **cuir**.

chevelure [ʃəvlyʀ] *nf* **(a)** (*cheveux*) hair (*U*). **une ~ malade/terne** unhealthy/dull hair; **elle avait une ~ abondante/une flamboyante ~ rousse** she had thick hair *ou* a thick head of hair/a shock of flaming red hair; **sa ~ était magnifique** her hair was magnificent. **(b)** *[comète]* tail.

chevesne [ʃ(ə)vɛn] *nm* dace.

chevet [ʃ(ə)vɛ] *nm* **(a)** *[lit]* bed(head). **au ~ de qn** at sb's bedside; *V* **lampe, livre**[1], **table**. **(b)** (*Archit*) *[église]* chevet.

cheveu, *pl* **~x** [ʃ(ə)vø] **1** *nm* **(a)** (*gén pl*) hair. (*chevelure*) **~x** hair (*U*); (*collectif*) **il a le ~ rare** he is balding, his hair is going thin; **une femme aux ~x blonds/frisés** a fair-haired/curly-haired woman, a woman with fair/curly hair; **avoir les ~x en désordre** *ou* **en bataille** *ou* **hirsutes** to have untidy *ou* tousled hair, be dishevelled; **(les) ~x au vent** hair hanging loose; **elle s'est trouvé 2 ~x blancs** she has found 2 white hairs; **épingle/brosse/filet à ~x** hairpin/brush/net; **en ~x†** hatless†, bareheaded; **il n'a pas un ~ sur la tête*** *ou* **le caillou*** he hasn't a (single) hair on his head; *V* **coupe**[2].

(b) (*loc*) **tenir à un ~: leur survie n'a tenu qu'à un ~** their survival hung by a thread, they survived but it was a very close thing; **son accord n'a tenu qu'à un ~** it was touch and go whether he would agree; **il s'en faut d'un ~ qu'il ne change d'avis** it's touch and go whether he'll change his mind; **il s'en est fallu d'un ~ qu'ils ne se tuent** they escaped death by the skin of their teeth *ou* by a hair's breadth, they were within an ace of being killed; **si vous osez toucher à un ~ de cet enfant** if you dare touch a hair of this child's head; **avoir un ~* (sur la langue)** to have a lisp; **se faire des ~x* (blancs)** to worry o.s. grey *ou* stiff*; **comme un ~ sur la soupe*** *arriver* at the most awkward moment, just at the right time (*iro*); **ça arrive** *ou* **ça vient comme un ~ sur la soupe, ce que tu dis** that remark is completely irrelevant *ou* quite out of place; **tiré par les ~x** *histoire* far-fetched; **il y a un ~*** there's a hitch* *ou* snag*; **il va y trouver un ~*** he's not going to like it one bit; **se prendre aux ~x** to come to blows; *V* **arracher, couper** *etc*.

2: cheveux d'ange (*vermicelle*) fine vermicelli; (*décoration*) silver floss (*for Christmas tree*).

cheville [ʃ(ə)vij] *nf* **(a)** (*Anat*) ankle. **l'eau lui venait** *ou* **arrivait à la ~** *ou* **aux ~s** he was ankle-deep in water, the water came up to his ankles; (*fig*) **aucun ne lui arrive à la ~** he is head and shoulders above the others, there's no one to touch him.

(b) (*fiche*) (*pour joindre*) dowel, peg, pin; (*pour y enfoncer un clou*) plug; (*Mus*) *[instrument à cordes]* peg; (*Boucherie: crochet*) hook. **~ ouvrière** (*Aut*) kingpin; (*fig*) kingpin, mainspring.

(c) (*Littérat*) *[poème]* cheville; (*péj: remplissage*) padding (*U*).

(d) (*loc*) **être en ~ avec qn** to be in league with sb.

cheviller [ʃ(ə)vije] (1) *vt* (*Menuiserie*) to peg; *V* **âme**.

chèvre [ʃɛvʀ(ə)] **1** *nf* **(a)** (*Zool*) (*gén*) goat; (*femelle*) she-goat, nanny-goat. (*fig*) **rendre** *ou* **faire devenir qn ~*** to drive sb up the wall*; *V* **fromage** *etc*.

(b) (*Tech*) (*treuil*) hoist, gin; (*chevalet*) sawhorse, trestle.

2 *nm* (*fromage*) goat cheese, goat's-milk cheese.

chevreau, *pl* **~x** [ʃəvʀo] *nm* (*animal, peau*) kid. **bondir comme un ~** to frisk like a lamb.

chèvrefeuille [ʃɛvʀəfœj] *nm* honeysuckle.

chevrette [ʃəvʀɛt] *nf* **(a)** (*jeune chèvre*) kid, young she-goat. **(b)** (*chevreuil femelle*) roe, doe; (*fourrure*) goatskin. **(c)** (*trépied*) (metal) tripod.

chevreuil [ʃəvʀœj] *nm* (*Zool*) roe deer; (*mâle*) roebuck; (*Can**: *cerf de Virginie*) deer; (*Culin*) venison.

chevrier [ʃəvʀije] *nm* (*berger*) goatherd; (*haricot*) (type of) kidney bean.

chevrière [ʃəvʀijɛʀ] *nf* (*rare*) goat-girl.

chevron [ʃəvʀɔ̃] *nm* (*poutre*) rafter; (*galon*) stripe, chevron; (*motif*) chevron, V(-shape). **~s** herringbone (pattern), chevron pattern; **à ~s** (*petits*) herringbone; (*grands*) chevron-patterned; *V* **engrenage**.

chevronné, e [ʃəvʀɔne] *adj alpiniste* practised, seasoned, experienced; *soldat* seasoned, veteran; *conducteur* experienced, practised. **un parlementaire ~** a parliamentary veteran, an old parliamentary hand.

chevrotant, e [ʃəvʀɔtɑ̃, ɑ̃t] *adj voix* quavering, shaking; *vieillard* with a quavering voice.

chevrotement [ʃəvʀɔtmɑ̃] *nm [voix]* quavering, shaking; *[vieillard]* quavering (voice).

chevroter [ʃəvʀɔte] (1) *vi [personne]* to quaver; *[voix]* to quaver, shake.

chevrotine [ʃəvʀɔtin] *nf* buckshot (*U*).

chewing-gum, *pl* **chewing-gums** [ʃwiŋgɔm] *nm* chewing gum (*U*).

chez [ʃe] *prép* **(a)** (*à la maison*) **~ soi** at home; **être/rester ~ soi** to be/stay at home, be/stay in; **est-ce qu'elle sera ~ elle aujourd'hui?** will she be at home *ou* in today?; **nous rentrons ~ nous** we are going home; **j'ai des nouvelles de ~ moi** I have news from home; **faites comme ~ vous** make yourself at home; **on n'est plus ~ soi avec tous ces étrangers!** it doesn't feel like home any more with all these foreigners about!; **je l'ai accompagné ~ lui** I saw *ou* walked him home; **nous l'avons trouvée ~ elle** we found her at home; **avoir un ~ soi** to have a home to call one's own.

(b) ~ qn (*maison*) at sb's house *ou* place; (*appartement*) at sb's place *ou* flat (*Brit*); (*famille*) in sb's family *ou* home; (*sur une adresse*) c/o sb; **~ moi nous sommes 6** there are 6 of us in my *ou* our family; **près de/devant/de ~ qn** near/in front of/from sb's place *ou* house; **de/près de ~ nous** from/near (our) home *ou* our place *ou* our house; **~ Robert/le voisin** at Robert's (house)/the neighbour's (house); **~ moi/son frère, c'est tout petit** my/his brother's place *ou* flat (*Brit*) is tiny; **je vais ~ lui/Robert** I'm going to his place/to Robert's (place); **il séjourne ~ moi** he is staying at my place *ou* with me; **la personne ~ qui je suis allé** the person to whose house I went; **passons par ~ eux/mon frère** let's drop in on them/my brother, let's drop by their place/my brother's place; (*enseigne de café*) **~ Rosalie** Rosalie's, chez Rosalie; **~ nous** (*pays*) in our country, at home, back home*; **c'est une paysanne/coutume (bien) de ~ nous** she/it is one of our typical local country girls/customs; **~ eux/vous, il n'y a pas de parlement** in their/your country there's no parliament; **il a été élevé ~ les Jésuites** he was brought up in a Jesuit school *ou* by the Jesuits.

(c) ~ l'épicier/le coiffeur/le docteur at the grocer's/the hairdresser's/the doctor's; **je vais ~ le boucher** I'm going to the butcher's; **il va ~ le dentiste/le docteur** he's going to the dentist('s)/the doctor('s).

(d) (*avec peuple, groupe humain ou animal*) among. **~ les Français/les Sioux/les Romains** among the French/the Sioux/the Romans; **~ l'ennemi, les pertes ont été élevées** the enemy's losses were heavy; **~ les fourmis/le singe** among (the) ants/(the) monkeys; **on trouve cet instinct ~ les animaux** you find this instinct in animals; **~ les politiciens** among politicians.

(e) (*avec personne, œuvre*) **~ Balzac/Picasso on trouve de tout** in Balzac/Picasso you find a bit of everything; **c'est rare ~ un enfant de cet âge** it's rare in a child of that age; **~ lui, c'est une manie/une habitude** it's a mania/a habit with *ou* for him; **~ lui c'est le foie qui ne va pas** it's his liver that gives him trouble.

chiadé, e [ʃjade] (*ptp de* **chiader**) *adj* (*arg Scol*) (*difficile*) *problème* tough*, stiff*; (*approfondi*) *exposé, leçon* brainy*, powerful*; (*perfectionné*) *appareil* clever, nifty*.

chiader [ʃjade] (1) **1** *vt* (*arg Scol*) *leçon* to swot up* (*Brit Scol*); *examen* to swot for* (*Brit*), cram for*; *exposé* to work on. **2** *vi* (*travailler*) to swot* (*Brit*), slog away*.

chialer‡ [ʃjale] (1) *vi* (*pleurer*) to blubber*.

chialeur, -euse‡ [ʃjalœʀ, øz] *nm,f* crybaby*, blubberer*.

chiant, e∵ [ʃjɑ̃, ɑ̃t] *adj* (*ennuyeux*) *personne, problème, difficulté* bloody (*Brit*) *ou* damn annoying‡. **ce roman est ~** this novel's a bloody (*Brit*) *ou* damn pain‡; **c'est ~, je vais être en retard** it's a bloody (*Brit*) *ou* damn nuisance‡ *ou* it's bloody (*Brit*) *ou* damn annoying *ou* sickening‡, I'm going to be late.

chiasme [kjasm(ə)] *nm* (*Littérat*) chiasmus; (*Anat*) chiasm.

chiasse [ʃjas] **1** *nf* (∵) **(a)** (*colique*) runs*, trots*, skitters‡; (*fig: peur*) willies*, funk‡. **avoir/attraper la ~** (*lit*) to have/get the runs* *ou* the trots*; (*fig*) to have/get the willies*, be/get shit-scared∵, be/get in a funk‡; **ça lui donne la ~** (*lit*) it gives him the runs*; (*fig*) it gets him shit-scared∵.

(b) (*poisse*) **c'est la ~, quelle ~** what a bloody (*Brit*) *ou* damn pain‡, what a bloody (*Brit*) *ou* damn drag‡.

2: chiasse(s) de mouche(s) fly speck(s).

chic [ʃik] **1** *nm* **(a)** (*élégance*) *[toilette, chapeau]* stylishness; *[personne]* style. **avoir du ~** *[toilette, chapeau]* to have style, be stylish; *[personne]* to have (great) style; **être habillé avec ~** to be stylishly dressed.

(b) (*loc*) **avoir le ~ pour faire qch** to have the knack of doing sth; **de ~** *peindre, dessiner* without a model, from memory; **traduire/écrire qch de ~** to translate/write sth off the cuff.

2 *adj inv* **(a)** (*élégant*) *chapeau, toilette, personne* stylish, smart.

(b) (*de la bonne société*) *dîner* smart, posh*. **2 messieurs ~** 2 well-to-do *ou* smart(-looking) gentlemen; **les gens ~ vont à l'opéra le vendredi** the smart set go to the opera on Fridays; **elle travaille chez des gens ~** she's working for some posh* *ou* well-to-do people.

(c) (*: *gentil, généreux*) decent*, nice. **c'est une ~ fille** she's a decent sort* *ou* a nice girl; **c'est un ~ type** he's a decent sort* *ou* a nice bloke* (*Brit*) *ou* a nice guy*; **elle a été très ~ avec moi** she's been very nice *ou* decent to me; **c'est très ~ de sa part** that's very decent *ou* nice of him.

3 *excl*: **~ (alors), on va au cinéma** terrific!* *ou* great!* we're going to the cinema.

chicane [ʃikan] *nf* **(a)** (*zigzag*) *[barrage routier]* ins and outs, twists and turns; *[circuit automobile]* chicane; *[gymkhana]* in and out, zigzag. **des camions stationnés en ~ gênaient la circulation** lorries parked at intervals on both sides of the street held up the traffic.

(b) († *Jur*) (*objection*) quibble; (*querelle*) squabble, petty quarrel. **aimer la ~** (*disputes*) to enjoy picking quarrels with people, enjoy bickering; (*procès*) to enjoy pettifogging *ou* bickering over points of procedure; **faire des ~s à qn** to pick petty quarrels with sb; **gens de ~** pettifoggers.

chicaner [ʃikane] (1) **1** *vt* **(a)** († *ou littér*) (*mesurer*) **~ qch à qn** to quibble *ou* haggle with sb over sth; (*contester*) **nul ne lui chicane son courage** no one disputes *ou* denies his courage *ou* calls his courage into question.

(b) († *ou littér: chercher querelle à*) **~ qn (sur *ou* au sujet de qch)** to quibble *ou* squabble with sb (over sth); **ils se chicanent continuellement** they wrangle (*littér*) constantly (with each other), they are constantly bickering.

2 *vi* **(a)** (*ergoter sur*) **~ sur** to quibble about, haggle over.

(b) († *Jur*) to chicane†, pettifog†.

chicanerie [ʃikanʀi] *nf* (†) (*disputes*) wrangling (*littér*), petty quarrelling (*U*); (*tendance à ergoter*) (constant) quibbling. **toutes ces ~s** all this quibbling *ou* haggling.

chicaneur, -euse [ʃikanœʀ, øz] (*ergoteur*) **1** *adj* argumentative, pettifogging. **2** *nm,f* quibbler.

chicanier, -ière [ʃikanje, jɛʀ] **1** *adj* quibbling. **2** *nm,f* quibbler.

chiche¹ [ʃiʃ] *adj V* **pois.**

chiche² [ʃiʃ] *adj* **(a)** (*mesquin*) *personne* niggardly, mean; *rétribution* niggardly, paltry, mean; *repas* scanty, meagre. **comme cadeau, c'est un peu ~** it's a rather mean *ou* paltry gift; **être ~ de paroles/compliments** to be sparing with one's words/compliments.

(b) (*: *capable de*) **être ~ de faire qch** to be able to do sth *ou* capable of doing sth; **tu n'es pas ~ (de le faire)** you couldn't (do that); **~ que je le fais!** I bet you I do it!*, (I) bet you I will!*; **~?** — **~!** am I on?* *ou* are you game?* — you're on!*

chichement [ʃiʃmɑ̃] *adv récompenser, nourrir* meanly, meagrely; *vivre, se nourrir* (*pauvrement*) poorly; (*mesquinement*) meanly.

chichi* [ʃiʃi] *nm*: **~(s)** (*embarras*) fuss (*U*), carry-on* (*U*); (*manières*) fuss (*U*); **faire des ~s *ou* du ~** (*embarras*) to fuss, make a fuss; (*manières*) to make a fuss; **ce sont des gens à ~(s)** they're the sort of people who make a fuss; **on vous invite sans ~(s)** we're inviting you informally.

chichiteux, -euse* [ʃiʃitø, øz] *adj* (*péj*) (*faiseur d'embarras*) troublesome; (*maniéré*) affected, fussy.

chicorée [ʃikɔʀe] *nf* (*salade*) endive; (*à café*) chicory. **~ frisée** curly endive (lettuce).

chicot [ʃiko] *nm* (*dent*) stump; (*rare: souche*) (tree) stump. **elle souriait, découvrant des ~s jaunis par le tabac** she smiled, revealing the stumps of her nicotine-stained teeth.

chicotin [ʃikɔtɛ̃] *nm V* **amer².**

chié, e¹‡ [ʃje] *adj* (*réussi, calé*) bloody good‡. (*iro*) **c'est ~ comme bled!** it's a bloody dump!∵; **il est ~ ce problème** it's a hell of a problem‡.

chiée²∵ [ʃje] *nf*: **une ~ de, des ~s de** a hell of a lot of‡.

chien [ʃjɛ̃] **1** *nm* **(a)** (*animal*) dog. **petit ~** (*jeune*) pup, puppy; (*de petite taille*) small dog; **'(attention) ~ méchant'** 'beware of the dog'; **ne fais pas le ~ fou** calm down a bit.

(b) *[fusil]* hammer.

(c) (††: *injure*) **~!** (you) cur!††.

(d) (*loc*) **coiffée à la ~** wearing a fringe; **en ~ de fusil** curled up; **quel ~ de temps!** *ou* **temps de ~!** what filthy *ou* foul weather!; **vie de ~** dog's life; **ce métier de ~** this rotten job; **comme un ~** *mourir, traiter* like a dog; **elle a du ~*** she has a certain something*, she's very attractive; **entre ~ et loup** in the twilight *ou* dusk; **c'est pas fait pour les ~s!*** it's there to be used; **être *ou* vivre *ou* s'entendre comme ~ et chat** to fight like cat and dog, always be at one another's throats; **arriver comme un ~ dans un jeu de quilles** to turn up when least needed *ou* wanted; **recevoir qn comme un ~ dans un jeu de quilles** to give sb a cold reception; (*Prov*) **un ~ regarde bien un évêque** a cat may look at a king (*Prov*); (*Prov*) **les ~s aboient, la caravane passe** let the world say what it will.

2 *adj inv* **(a)** (*avare*) mean, stingy*.

(b) (*méchant*) rotten. **elle n'a pas été ~ avec toi** she was quite decent to you.

3: chien d'appartement house dog; **chien d'arrêt** pointer; **chien assis** (*Constr*) dormer window; **chien d'aveugle** guide dog, blind dog; **chien de berger** sheepdog; **chien de chasse** retriever, gun-dog; **chien couchant** setter; **faire le chien couchant** to toady; **chien courant** hound; **chien de garde** guard dog; **chien-loup** *nm, pl* **chiens-loups** wolfhound; **chien de manchon** lapdog; **chien de mer** dogfish; **chien polaire = chien de traîneau**; **chien policier** police dog; **chien de race** pedigree dog; **chien de salon = chien de manchon**; **chien savant** (*lit*) performing dog; (*fig*) know-all; **chien de traîneau** husky.

chien-chien [ʃjɛ̃ʃjɛ̃] *nm* (*langage enfantin*) doggy (*langage enfantin*). **oh le beau ~** nice doggy!, good doggy!

chiendent [ʃjɛ̃dɑ̃] *nm* **(a)** (*Bot*) couch grass, quitch (grass); *V* **brosse. (b)** (†*: *l'ennui*) **le ~** the trouble *ou* rub (†, *hum*).

chienlit [ʃjɑ̃li] *nf* **(a)** (*pagaille*) havoc. **(b)** (†: *mascarade*) fancy-dress parade.

chienne [ʃjɛn] *nf* bitch. (††: *injure*) **~!** (you) trollop!††; **quelle ~ de vie!** what a dog's life!

chier∵ [ʃje] (7) *vi* **(a)** to shit∵, crap∵. **~ un coup** to have a crap∵ *ou* shit∵.

(b) (*loc*) **faire ~ qn** *[personne]* (*ennuyer*) to give sb a pain in the arse∵ (*Brit*) *ou* ass∵ (*US*), bore the pants off sb‡; (*tracasser, harceler*) to get up sb's nose‡ (*Brit*), bug sb‡; **ça me fait ~** it's a *ou* it gives me a pain in the arse✡; **envoyer ~ qn** to tell sb to piss off✡ (*Brit*) *ou* bugger off✡ (*Brit*) *ou* fuck off✡; **se faire ~: je me suis fait ~ pendant 3 heures à réparer la voiture** I sweated my guts out‡ for 3 hours repairing the car; **qu'est-ce qu'on se fait ~ à ses conférences** what a bloody bore‡ his lectures are, his lectures bore the pants off you‡; **ça va ~** there'll be one hell of a (bloody) row!‡; **y a pas à ~, c'est lui le meilleur** say what you bloody *ou* damn well like✡, he's the best!

chiffe [ʃif] *nf* **(a)** (*personne sans volonté*) spineless individual, wet*, drip*. **être une ~ (molle)** to be spineless *ou* wet*; **je suis comme une ~ (molle)** (*fatigué*) I feel like a wet rag; *V* **mou**[1]. **(b)** (*rare: chiffon*) rag.

chiffon [ʃifɔ̃] **1** *nm* **(a)** (*tissu usagé*) (piece of) rag. **jeter de vieux ~s** to throw out old rags; (*fig*) **ce devoir est un vrai ~** this exercise is extremely messy *ou* a dreadful mess; **mettre ses vêtements en ~** to throw down one's clothes in a crumpled heap; **parler ~s*** to talk (about) clothes*.

(b) (*Papeterie*) **le ~** rag; **fait avec du ~** made from rags (*linen, cotton etc*); *V* **papier**.

2: chiffon à chaussures shoe cloth *ou* duster *ou* rag; **chiffon à meubles = chiffon à poussière; chiffon de papier: écrire qch sur un chiffon de papier** to write sth (down) on a (crumpled) scrap of paper; **ce traité n'est qu'un chiffon de papier** this treaty isn't worth the paper it's written on *ou* is no more than a useless scrap of paper; **chiffon à poussière** duster.

chiffonné, e [ʃifɔne] (*ptp de* **chiffonner**) *adj* **(a)** (*fatigué*) *visage* worn-looking.

(b) un petit minois/nez ~ an irregular but not unattractive little face/nose.

chiffonner [ʃifɔne] (1) *vt* **(a)** (*lit*) *papier* to crumple; *habits* to crease, rumple, crumple; *étoffe* to crease, crumple. **ce tissu se chiffonne facilement** this material creases *ou* crumples easily *ou* is easily creased.

(b) (*: *contrarier*) **ça me chiffonne** it bothers *ou* worries me; **qu'est-ce qui te chiffonne?** what's the matter (with you)?, what's bothering *ou* worrying you?

chiffonnier [ʃifɔnje] *nm* **(a)** (*personne*) ragman, rag-and-bone man (*Brit*). **se battre/se disputer comme des ~s** to fight/quarrel like fishwives. **(b)** (*meuble*) chiffonier.

chiffrable [ʃifʀabl(ə)] *adj*: **ce n'est pas ~** one can't put a figure to it; **c'est ~ à des millions** it runs into seven figures.

chiffrage [ʃifʀaʒ] *nm* (*V* **chiffrer**) (en)coding, ciphering; assessing; numbering; marking; figuring.

chiffre [ʃifʀ(ə)] *nm* **(a)** (*caractère*) figure, numeral, digit (*Math*). **~ arabe/romain** Arab/Roman numeral; **nombre** *ou* **numéro de 7 ~s** 7-figure *ou* 7-digit number; **écrire un nombre en ~s** to write out a number in figures; **science des ~s** science of numbers; **employé qui aligne des ~s toute la journée** clerk who spends all day adding long columns of figures; **il aime les ~s** he likes working with figures.

(b) (*montant*) [*dépenses*] total, sum. **en ~s ronds** in round figures; **ça atteint des ~s astronomiques** it reaches an astronomical figure *ou* sum; **le ~ des naissances** the total *ou* number of births *ou* the birth total; **le ~ des chômeurs** the unemployment figures *ou* total, the total *ou* figure of those unemployed.

(c) (*Comm*) **~ (d'affaires)** turnover; **il fait un ~ (d'affaires) de 3 millions** he has a turnover of 3 million francs; **~ net/brut** net/gross figure *ou* sum; *V* **impôt**.

(d) (*code*) [*message*] code, cipher; [*coffre-fort*] combination. **écrire une lettre en ~s** to write a letter in code *ou* cipher; **on a trouvé leur ~** their code has been broken; **le (service du) ~** the cipher office.

(e) (*initiales*) (set of) initials, monogram. **mouchoir brodé à son ~** handkerchief embroidered with one's initials *ou* monogram.

(f) (*Mus: indice*) figure.

chiffrement [ʃifʀəmɑ̃] *nm* [*texte*] (en)coding, ciphering.

chiffrer [ʃifʀe] (1) **1** *vt* **(a)** (*coder*) *message* to (en)code, cipher; (*Informatique*) *données, télégramme* to encode; *V* **message**.

(b) (*évaluer*) *dépenses* to put a figure to, assess (the amount of).

(c) (*numéroter*) *pages* to number.

(d) (*marquer*) *effets personnels, linge* to mark (with one's initials).

(e) (*Mus*) *accord* to figure. **basse chiffrée** figured bass.

2 *vi*, **se chiffrer** *vpr*: **(se) ~** à to add up to, amount to, come to; **ça (se) chiffre à combien?** what *ou* how much does that add up to? *ou* amount to? *ou* come to?; **ça (se) chiffre par millions** that adds up to *ou* amounts to *ou* comes to millions; **ça finit par ~*** it adds up to *ou* amounts to *ou* comes to quite a lot in the end.

chiffreur [ʃifʀœʀ] *nm* coder.

chignole [ʃiɲɔl] *nf* (*outil*) (*à main*) (hand) drill; (*électrique*) (electric) drill; (*: *voiture*) jalopy* (*hum*).

chignon [ʃiɲɔ̃] *nm* bun, chignon. **cheveux tordus en ~** hair twisted into a bun *ou* chignon; *V* **crêper**.

Chili [ʃili] *nm* Chile.

chilien, -ienne [ʃiljɛ̃, jɛn] **1** *adj* Chilean. **2** *nm,f*: **C~(ne)** Chilean.

chimère [ʃimɛʀ] *nf* **(a)** (*utopie*) (wild) dream, chimera; (*illusion, rêve*) pipe dream, (idle) fancy. **le bonheur est une ~** happiness is a figment of the imagination *ou* is just a (wild) dream *ou* is a chimera; **c'est une ~ que de croire ...** it is fanciful *ou* unrealistic to believe ...; **ce projet de voyage est une ~ de plus** these travel plans are just another pipe dream *ou* (idle) fancy; **se repaître de ~s** to live on dreams *ou* in a fool's paradise; **se forger des ~s** to fabricate wild *ou* impossible dreams; **tes grands projets, ~s (que tout cela)!** your grand plans are nothing but pipe dreams *ou* (idle) fancies; **un monde peuplé de vagues ~s** a world filled with vague imaginings.

(b) (*Myth*) chim(a)era, Chim(a)era.

chimérique [ʃimeʀik] *adj* **(a)** (*utopique*) *esprit, projet, idée* fanciful; *rêve* wild (*épith*), idle (*épith*). **c'est un esprit ~** he's very fanciful, he's a great dreamer. **(b)** (*imaginaire*) *personnage* imaginary, chimerical.

chimie [ʃimi] *nf* chemistry. **~ organique/minérale** organic/inorganic chemistry; **cours/expérience de ~** chemistry class/experiment.

chimiothérapie [ʃimjɔteʀapi] *nf* chemotherapy.

chimique [ʃimik] *adj* chemical; *V* **produit**.

chimiquement [ʃimikmɑ̃] *adv* chemically.

chimiste [ʃimist(ə)] *nmf* chemist (*scientist*); *V* **ingénieur**.

chimpanzé [ʃɛ̃pɑ̃ze] *nm* chimpanzee, chimp*.

chinchilla [ʃɛ̃ʃila] *nm* (*Zool, fourrure*) chinchilla.

Chine [ʃin] *nf* China. **~ populaire/nationaliste** red *ou* communist/nationalist China; *V* **crêpe**[2], **encre** *etc*.

chine [ʃin] *nm* **(a)** (*papier*) Chinese *ou* rice paper. **(b)** (*vase*) china vase; (*U: porcelaine*) china.

chiner [ʃine] (1) *vt* **(a)** (*Tex*) *étoffe* to dye the warp of. **manteau/tissu chiné** chiné coat/fabric.

(b) (*: *taquiner*) to kid (*Brit*) *ou* have (*Brit*) on*, rag*. **tu ne vois pas qu'il te chine** don't you see he's kidding you on (*Brit*) *ou* ragging* you *ou* having you on* (*Brit*); **je n'aime pas qu'on me chine** I don't like being ragged*.

Chinetoque [ʃintɔk] *nmf* (*péj: Chinois*) Chink* (*péj*).

chinois, e [ʃinwa, waz] **1** *adj* **(a)** (*de Chine*) Chinese; *V* **ombre**[1].

(b) (*péj: pointilleux*) *personne* pernickety (*péj*), fussy (*péj*); *règlement* hair-splitting (*péj*).

2 *nm* **(a)** (*Ling*) Chinese. (*péj*) **c'est du ~*** it's double Dutch* (*Brit*), it's all Greek to me*.

(b) C~ Chinese, Chinese man, Chinaman (*hum*); **les C~** the Chinese.

(c) (**péj: maniaque*) hair-splitter (*péj*).

3 *nf*: **Chinoise** Chinese, Chinese woman.

chinoiserie [ʃinwazʀi] *nf* **(a)** (*subtilité excessive*) hair-splitting (*U*).

(b) (*complications*) **~s** unnecessary complications *ou* fuss. **les ~s de l'administration** red tape; **tout ça, ce sont des ~s** that is all nothing but unnecessary complications.

(c) (*Art*) (*décoration*) chinoiserie; (*objet*) Chinese ornament, Chinese curio.

chintz [ʃints] *nm* (*Tex*) chintz.

chiot [ʃjo] *nm* pup(py).

chiotte [ʃjɔt] *nf* **(a)** (*W.-C.*) **~s**✡ bog‡ (*Brit*), john‡ (*US*); *V* **corvée**. **(b)** (‡: *voiture*) jalopy* (*hum*).

chiourme [ʃjuʀm(ə)] *nf V* **garder**.

chiper* [ʃipe] (1) *vt* (*voler*) *portefeuille, idée* to pinch*, filch*; *rhume* to catch.

chipeur, -euse* [ʃipœʀ, øz] *adj gamin* thieving.

chipie [ʃipi] *nf* vixen (*péj*).

chipolata [ʃipɔlata] *nf* chipolata.

chipotage* [ʃipɔtaʒ] *nm* (*marchandage*) haggling; (*ergotage*) quibbling; (*pour manger*) picking *ou* nibbling (at one's food).

chipoter* [ʃipɔte] (1) *vi* (*manger*) to nibble at *ou* pick at one's food; (*ergoter*) to quibble (*sur* over); (*marchander*) to haggle (*sur* over). **~ sur sa nourriture** to nibble *ou* pick at one's food.

chipoteur, -euse* [ʃipɔtœʀ, øz] **1** *adj* (*marchandeur*) haggling; (*ergoteur*) quibbling. **2** *nm,f* (*marchandeur*) haggler; (*ergoteur*) quibbler. (*en mangeant*) **quel ~!, il est vraiment ~** how he picks *ou* nibbles at his food!

chips [ʃip(s)] *nmpl* (*Culin*) crisps; *V* **pomme**.

chique [ʃik] *nf* (*tabac*) quid, chew; (*: *enflure*) (facial) swelling, lump (on the cheek); *V* **couper**.

chiqué* [ʃike] *nm* **(a)** (*bluff*) pretence (*U*), bluffing (*U*). **il a fait ça au ~** he bluffed it out; **il prétend que cela le laisse froid mais c'est du ~** he pretends it leaves him cold but it's all put on* *ou* a great pretence.

(b) (*factice*) sham (*U*). **ces combats de catch c'est du ~** these wrestling matches are all sham *ou* all put on* *ou* are faked; **combat sans ~** fight that's for real*; **~!, remboursez!** what a sham!, give us our money back!

(c) (*manières*) putting on airs (*U*), airs and graces (*pl*). **faire du ~** to put on airs (and graces).

chiquement* [ʃikmɑ̃] *adv s'habiller* smartly, stylishly; *traiter, accueillir* kindly, decently.

chiquenaude [ʃiknod] *nf* (*pichenette*) flick, flip. **il l'écarta d'une ~** he flicked *ou* flipped it off; (*fig*) **une ~ suffirait à renverser le gouvernement** the government could be overturned by a flick *ou* snap of the fingers.

chiquer [ʃike] (1) **1** *vt tabac* to chew; *V* **tabac**. **2** *vi* to chew tobacco.

chiqueur, -euse [ʃikœʀ, øz] *nm,f* tobacco-chewer.

chiromancie [kiʀɔmɑ̃si] *nf* palmistry, chiromancy (*T*).

chiromancien, -ienne [kiʀɔmɑ̃sjɛ̃, jɛn] *nm,f* palmist, chiromancer (*T*).

chiropracteur [kiʀɔpʀaktœʀ] *nm* chiropractor.

chiropractie [kiʀɔpʀakti] *nf*, **chiropraxie** [kiʀɔpʀaksi] *nf* chiropractic.

chirurgical, e, *mpl* **-aux** [ʃiʀyʀʒikal, o] *adj* surgical.

chirurgie [ʃiʀyʀʒi] *nf* surgery (*science*). **~ esthétique/dentaire** plastic/dental surgery.

chirurgien [ʃiʀyʀʒjɛ̃] *nm* surgeon. **~-dentiste** dental surgeon; (*Mil*) **~-major** army surgeon.

chiure [ʃjyʀ] *nf*: **~(s) de mouche(s)** fly speck(s).

chleuh [ʃlø] (*péj*) **1** *adj* Boche. **2** *nm*: **C~** Boche, Jerry†.

chlorate [klɔʀat] *nm* chlorate.

chlore [klɔʀ] *nm* chlorine.

chloré, e [klɔʀe] (*ptp de* **chlorer**) *adj* chlorinated.

chlorer [klɔʀe] (1) *vt* to chlorinate.

chlorhydrique [klɔʀidʀik] *adj* hydrochloric.
chlorique [klɔʀik] *adj* chloric.
chloroforme [klɔʀɔfɔʀm(ə)] *nm* chloroform.
chloroformer [klɔʀɔfɔʀme] (1) *vt* to chloroform.
chlorophylle [klɔʀɔfil] *nf* chlorophyll.
chlorophyllien, -ienne [klɔʀɔfiljɛ̃, jɛn] *adj* chlorophyllous.
chlorure [klɔʀyʀ] *nm* chloride. ~ **de sodium** sodium chloride; ~ **de chaux** chloride of lime.
chlorurer [klɔʀyʀe] (1) *vt* = **chlorer.**
choc [ʃɔk] **1** *nm* **(a)** (*heurt*) *[objets]* impact, shock; *[vagues]* crash, shock. **le ~ de billes d'acier qui se heurtent** the impact of steel balls as they collide; **cela se brise au moindre ~** it breaks at the slightest bump *ou* knock; **'résiste au(x) ~(s)'** 'shock-resistant'; **la résistance au ~ d'un matériau** a material's resistance to shock; **la carosserie se déforma sous le ~** the coachwork twisted with *ou* under the impact; **la corde se rompit sous le ~** the sudden wrench made the rope snap *ou* snapped the rope.
(b) (*collision*) *[véhicules]* crash, smash; *[personnes]* blow, bump. **le ~ entre les véhicules fut très violent** the vehicles crashed together with a tremendous impact; **encore un ~ meurtrier sur la RN7** another fatal crash *ou* smash on the RN7; **il tituba sous le ~** the blow *ou* bump put *ou* sent him off balance.
(c) (*bruit d'impact*) (*violent*) crash, smash; (*sourd*) thud, thump; (*métallique*) clang, clash; (*cristallin*) clink, chink; *[gouttes, grêlons]* (*sur du verre*) rapping (*U*); (*sur de la tôle*) drumming (*U*). **le ~ sourd des obus** the thud of shellfire; **j'entendais au loin le ~ des pesants marteaux d'acier** in the distance I could hear the clang *ou* clash of the heavy steel hammers.
(d) (*affrontement*) *[troupes, émeutiers]* clash; (*fig*) *[intérêts, passions]* clash, collision. **il y a eu un ~ sanglant entre la police et les émeutiers** there has been a violent clash between police and rioters; **la petite armée ne put résister au ~** the little army could not stand up to the onslaught.
(e) (*émotion brutale*) shock. **il ne s'est pas remis du ~** he hasn't got over the shock *ou* recovered from the shock; **ça m'a fait un drôle de ~ de le voir dans cet état** it gave me a nasty shock *ou* quite a turn* to see him in that state; *V* **état.**
(f) de ~ *troupe, unité* shock; *traitement, thérapeutique, tactique* shock; *enseignement* avant-garde, futuristic; *évêque, patron* high-powered, supercharged*.
2 *adj inv* (*à sensation*) **argument/discours/formule(-)~** shock argument/speech/formula; **film/photo(-)~** shock film/photo; **mesures(-)~** shock measures; **'prix(-)~'** 'amazing *ou* drastic reductions'; **'notre prix-~: 99 F'** 'OUR price *ou* our special price: 99 francs'.
3: choc électrique electric shock; **choc nerveux** (nervous) shock; **choc opératoire** post-operative shock; **choc en retour** (*Élec*) return shock; (*fig*) backlash.
chocolat [ʃɔkɔla] **1** *nm* **(a)** (*substance*) chocolate; (*bonbon*) chocolate, choc* (*Brit*); (*boisson*) (drinking) chocolate. **'un ~ s'il vous plaît'** 'a cup of chocolate please'; **mousse/crème au ~** chocolate mousse/cream; **~ au lait/aux noisettes** milk/hazelnut chocolate; *V* **barre, plaque** *etc.*
(b) (*couleur*) chocolate (brown), dark brown.
(c) être ~*† to be thwarted *ou* foiled.
2 *adj inv* chocolate(-coloured).
3: chocolat blanc white chocolate; **chocolat chaud** hot chocolate; **chocolat à croquer** plain (eating) chocolate; **chocolat à cuire** cooking chocolate; **chocolat fondant** fondant chocolate; **chocolat liégeois** chocolate ice cream (*with crème Chantilly*); **chocolat de ménage = chocolat à cuire; chocolat en poudre** drinking chocolate.
chocolaté, e [ʃɔkɔlate] *adj* (*additionné de chocolat*) chocolate-flavoured, chocolate (*épith*); (*au goût de chocolat*) chocolate-flavoured, chocolat(e)y*.
chocolaterie [ʃɔkɔlatʀi] *nf* (*fabrique*) chocolate factory; (*magasin*) (quality) chocolate shop.
chocolatier, -ière [ʃɔkɔlatje, jɛʀ] **1** *adj*: **l'industrie ~ière** the chocolate industry. **2** *nm,f* (*fabricant*) chocolate maker; (*commerçant*) chocolate seller.
chocottes‡ [ʃɔkɔt] *nfpl* gnashers*. (*avoir peur*) **avoir les ~** to have the jitters* *ou* heebie-jeebies*.
chœur [kœʀ] *nm* **(a)** (*chanteurs*) (*gén, Rel*) choir; *[opéra, oratorio etc]* chorus.
(b) (*Théât: récitants*) chorus.
(c) (*fig*) (*concert*) **un ~ de récriminations** a chorus of recriminations; (*groupe*) **le ~ des mécontents** the band of malcontents.
(d) (*Archit*) choir, chancel; *V* **enfant.**
(e) (*Mus: composition*) chorus; (*hymne*) chorale; (*Théât: texte*) chorus. **~ à 4 parties** (*opéra*) 4-part chorus; (*Rel*) 4-part chorale.
(f) (*loc*) **en ~** (*Mus*) in chorus; (*fig: ensemble*) *chanter* in chorus; *répondre, crier* in chorus *ou* unison; (*fig hum*) **on s'ennuyait en ~** we were all getting bored (together); **tous en ~!** all together now!
choir [ʃwaʀ] *vi* (*littér ou † ou hum*) to fall. **faire ~** to cause to fall; **laisser ~ un objet** to drop an object; (*fig*) **laisser ~ ses amis** to let one's friends down; **se laisser ~ dans un fauteuil** to sink into an armchair.
choisi, e [ʃwazi] (*ptp de* **choisir**) *adj* **(a)** (*sélectionné*) *morceaux, passages* selected. **(b)** (*raffiné*) *langage, termes* carefully chosen; *clientèle, société* select.
choisir [ʃwaziʀ] (2) *vt* **(a)** (*gén*) to choose. **nous avons choisi ces articles pour nos clients** we have selected these items for our customers; **des 2 solutions, j'ai choisi la première** I chose *ou* picked the first *ou* I plumped (*Brit*) for the first of the 2 solutions; **il faut savoir ~ ses amis** you must know how to pick *ou* choose your friends; **dans les soldes, il faut savoir ~** in the sales, you've got to know what to choose *ou* you've got to know how to be selective; **se ~ un mari** to choose a husband; **on l'a choisi parmi des douzaines de candidats** he was picked (out) *ou* selected *ou* chosen from among dozens of applicants.
(b) ~ de faire qch to choose to do sth; **à toi de ~ si et quand tu veux partir** it's up to you to choose if and when you want to leave.
choix [ʃwa] *nm* **(a)** (*sélection faite ou à faire*) choice. **il a fait un bon/mauvais ~** he has made a good/bad choice, he has chosen well/badly; **un aménagement de son ~** alterations of one's (own) choosing; **ce ~ de poèmes plaira aux plus exigeants** this selection of poems will appeal to the most demanding reader; **le ~ d'un cadeau est souvent difficile** choosing a gift *ou* the choice of a gift is often difficult; *V* **embarras.**
(b) (*variété*) choice, selection, variety. **ce magasin offre un grand ~** this shop has a wide *ou* large selection (of goods); **il y a du ~** there is a choice; **il y a tout le ~ qu'on veut** there is plenty of choice, there are plenty to choose from; **il n'y a pas beaucoup de ~** there isn't a great deal of *ou* much choice, there isn't a great selection (to choose from).
(c) (*échantillonnage de*) **~ de** selection of; **il avait apporté un ~ de livres** he had brought a selection *ou* collection of books.
(d) (*qualité*) **de ~** choice, selected; **morceau de ~** (*viande*) prime cut; **de premier ~** *fruits* class *ou* grade one; *viande* top grade; **de ~ courant** standard quality; **de second ~** *fruits, viande* class *ou* grade two; **articles de second ~** seconds.
(e) (*loc*) **au ~: vous pouvez prendre, au ~, fruits ou fromages** you may have fruit or cheese, as you wish *ou* prefer, you have a choice between *ou* of fruit or cheese; **'dessert au ~'** 'choice of desserts'; **avancement au ~** promotion on merit *ou* by selection; **au ~ du client** as the customer chooses, according to (the customer's) preference; **faire son ~** to take *ou* make one's choice, take one's pick*; **mon ~ est fait** my choice is made; **avoir le ~** to have a *ou* the choice; **je n'avais pas le ~** I had no option *ou* choice; (*frm*) **faire ~ de qch** to select sth; **laisser le ~ à qn (de faire)** to leave sb (free) to choose (to do); **donner le ~ à qn (de faire)** to give sb the choice (of doing); **arrêter *ou* fixer *ou* porter son ~ sur qch** to fix one's choice (up)on sth, settle on sth; **il lit sans (faire de) ~** he's an indiscriminate reader, he reads indiscriminately.
choléra [kɔleʀa] *nm* cholera.
cholérique [kɔleʀik] **1** *adj* choleraic. **2** *nmf* cholera patient *ou* case.
cholestérol [kɔlɛsteʀɔl] *nm* cholesterol.
chômage [ʃomaʒ] **1** *nm [travailleurs]* unemployment; (*rare*) *[usine, industrie]* inactivity. **~ saisonnier/chronique** seasonal/chronic unemployment; **de ~** *allocation, indemnité* unemployment (*épith*); **(être) en *ou* au ~** (to be) unemployed *ou* out of work; **être/s'inscrire au ~** to be/sign on the dole* (*Brit*), receive/apply for unemployment benefit; **mettre qn au *ou* en ~** to make sb redundant (*Brit*), put sb out of work *ou* a job, pay sb off*; **beaucoup ont été mis en ~** many have been made redundant (*Brit*) *ou* have been put out of work *ou* a job, there have been many redundancies (*Brit*).
2: chômage partiel short-time working; **mettre qn en *ou* au chômage partiel** to put sb on short-time (working); **chômage structurel** structural unemployment; **chômage technique** layoffs (*pl*); **mettre en chômage technique** to lay off employees; **le nombre de travailleurs en chômage technique** the number of workers laid off.
chômé, e [ʃome] (*ptp de* **chômer**) *adj*: **jour ~, fête ~e** public holiday.
chômer [ʃome] (1) **1** *vi* **(a)** (*fig: être inactif*) *[capital, équipements]* to be unemployed, be idle, lie idle; *[esprit, imagination]* to be idle, be inactive. **son imagination ne chômait pas** his imagination was not idle *ou* inactive; **ses mains ne chômaient pas** his hands were not idle *ou* inactive; **j'aime autant te dire qu'on n'a pas chômé** I don't need to tell you that we didn't just sit around idly *ou* we weren't idle.
(b) (*être sans travail*) *[travailleur]* to be unemployed, be out of work *ou* a job; *[usine, installation]* to be *ou* stand idle, be at a standstill; *[industrie]* to be at a standstill.
(c) (*††: être en congé*) to have a holiday, be on holiday.
2 *vt* (*††*) *jour férié* to keep.
chômeur, -euse [ʃomœʀ, øz] *nm,f* (*gén*) unemployed person *ou* worker; (*mis au chômage*) redundant worker (*Brit*). **les ~s** the unemployed; **le nombre des ~s** the number of unemployed, the number of people out of work; **un million de/3.000 ~s** a million/3,000 unemployed *ou* out of work; **un ~ n'a pas droit à ces prestations** an unemployed person is not entitled to these benefits.
chope [ʃɔp] *nf* (*récipient*) tankard, (beer)mug; (*contenu*) pint.
choper‡ [ʃɔpe] (1) *vt* **(a)** (*voler*) to pinch*, nick* (*Brit*). **(b)** (*attraper*) *rhume* to catch; *voleur* to nab*. **se faire ~ (par la police/par le vendeur)** to get nabbed* (by the police/shopkeeper).
chopine [ʃɔpin] *nf* (*: *bouteille*) bottle (of wine); (*††: mesure*) half-litre, pint; (*Can:* ½ *pinte, 0,568 l*) pint. **on a été boire une ~*** we went for *ou* we had a drink (of wine).
choquant, e [ʃɔkɑ̃, ɑ̃t] *adj* (*qui heurte le goût*) shocking, appalling; (*qui heurte le sens de la justice*) outrageous, scandalous; (*qui heurte la pudeur*) shocking. **le spectacle ~ de ces blessés** the harrowing *ou* horrifying sight of those injured people; **c'est un film ~, même pour les adultes** it's a film that shocks even adults.
choquer [ʃɔke] (1) **1** *vt* **(a)** (*scandaliser*) to shock, (*plus fort*) appal; (*heurter, blesser*) to offend, shock. **ça m'a choqué de le voir dans cet état** I was shocked *ou* appalled to see him in that state; **de tels films me choquent** I find such films shocking, I am

shocked by films like that; **ce roman risque de ~** this novel may well be offensive *ou* shocking (to some people), people may find this novel offensive *ou* shocking; **j'ai été vraiment choqué par son indifférence** I was really shocked *ou* appalled by his indifference; **ne vous choquez pas de ma question** don't be shocked at *ou* by my question; **il a été très choqué de ne pas être invité** he was most offended *ou* very put out at not being invited *ou* not to be invited; **ce film/cette scène m'a beaucoup choqué** I was deeply shocked by that film/scene.

(b) (*aller à l'encontre de*) *délicatesse, pudeur, goût* to offend against; *bon sens, raison* to offend against, go against; *vue* to offend; *oreilles [son, musique]* to jar on, offend; *[propos]* to shock, offend. **cette question a choqué sa susceptibilité** that question made him take umbrage.

(c) (*commotionner*) *[chute]* to shake (up); *[accident]* to shake (up), shock; *[deuil, maladie]* to shake. **il sortit du véhicule, durement choqué** he climbed out of the vehicle badly shaken *ou* shocked; **la mort de sa mère l'a beaucoup choqué** the death of his mother has shaken him badly, he has been badly shaken by his mother's death.

(d) (*taper, heurter*) (*gén*) to knock (against); *verres* to clink. **choquant leurs verres, ils trinquèrent** clinking glasses they drank a toast; **il entendait les ancres se ~ dans le petit port** he could hear the anchors clanking against each other in the little harbour; **choquant son verre contre le** *ou* **au mien** clinking his glass against mine.

2 se choquer *vpr* (*s'offusquer*) to be shocked. **il se choque facilement** he's easily shocked.

choral, e, *mpl* **~s** [kɔʀal] **1** *adj* choral. **2** *nm* choral(e). **3 chorale** *nf* choral society, choir.

chorégraphe [kɔʀegʀaf] *nmf* choreographer.

chorégraphie [kɔʀegʀafi] *nf* choreography.

chorégraphique [kɔʀegʀafik] *adj* choreographic.

choreute [kɔʀøt] *nm* chorist.

choriste [kɔʀist(ə)] *nmf [chœur]* choir member, chorister; *[opéra, théâtre antique]* member of the chorus. **les ~s** the choir; the chorus.

chorus [kɔʀys] *nm*: **faire ~** to chorus *ou* voice one's agreement *ou* approval; **faire ~ avec qn** to voice one's agreement with sb; **ils ont fait ~ avec lui pour condamner ces mesures** they joined with him in voicing their condemnation of the measures.

chose [ʃoz] **1** *nf* **(a)** thing. **on m'a raconté une ~ extraordinaire** I was told an extraordinary thing; **j'ai pensé (à) une ~** I thought of one thing; **il a un tas de ~s à faire à Paris** he has a lot of things *ou* lots to do in Paris; **il n'y a pas une seule ~ de vraie là-dedans** there isn't a (single) word of truth in it; **critiquer est une ~, faire le travail en est une autre** criticizing is one thing, doing the work is another (matter); **ce n'est pas ~ facile** *ou* **aisée de ...** it's not an easy thing *ou* easy to ...; **~ étrange** *ou* **curieuse, il a accepté** strangely *ou* curiously enough, he accepted, the strange *ou* curious thing is (that) he accepted; **c'est une ~ admise que ...** it's an accepted fact that ... .

(b) (*événements, activités etc*) **les ~s** things; **les ~s se sont passées ainsi** it (all) happened like this; **les ~s vont mal** things are going badly; **dans l'état actuel des ~s, au point où en sont les ~s** as things *ou* matters stand at present, the way things stand at present; **ce sont des ~s qui arrivent** it's one of those things, these things (just) happen; **regarder les ~s en face** to face up to things; **prendre les ~s à cœur/comme elles sont** to take things to heart/as they come; **mettons les ~s au point** let's get things clear *ou* straight; **en mettant les ~s au mieux/au pire** at best/worst; **parler/discuter de ~(s) et d'autre(s)** to talk about/discuss this and that *ou* one thing and another; *V* **force, leçon, ordre**[1].

(c) (*ce dont il s'agit*) **la ~: la ~ est d'importance** it's no trivial matter, it's a matter of some importance; **la ~ dont j'ai peur, c'est que** what *ou* the thing I'm afraid of is that; **il va vous expliquer la ~** he'll tell you all about it *ou* what it's all about; **la ~ en question, la ~ dont je parle** the matter in hand, the case in point, what we are discussing; **il a très bien pris la ~** he took it all very well; **c'est la ~ à ne pas faire** that's the one thing *ou* the very thing not to do.

(d) (*réalités matérielles*) **les ~s** things; **les bonnes/belles ~s** good/beautiful things; **les ~s de ce monde** the things of this world; **chez eux, quand ils reçoivent, ils font bien les ~s** when they have guests they really go to town* *ou* do things in style; *V* **demi**[1].

(e) (*parole*) thing. **j'ai plusieurs ~s à vous dire** I've got several things to tell you; **vous lui direz bien des ~s de ma part** give him my regards.

(f) (*objet*) thing. *[personne]* **être la ~ de qn** to be sb's creature.

(g) (*Jur*) **la ~ jugée** the res judicata, the final decision; (*Pol*) **la ~ publique** the state *ou* nation; († *ou hum*) **la ~ imprimée** the printed word.

(h) (*loc*) **c'est (tout) autre ~** that's another *ou* a different matter (altogether); **c'est ~ faite** it's done; **c'est bien peu de ~** it's nothing really; **(très) peu de ~** nothing much, very little; **avant toute ~** above all (else); **de deux ~s l'une** it's got to be one thing or the other; (*Prov*) **~ promise, ~ due** promises are made to be kept; *V* **porté**.

2 *nm* (*) **(a)** (*truc, machin*) thing, contraption, thingumajig*. **qu'est-ce que c'est que ce ~?** what's this thing here?, what's this thingumajig?*

(b) (*personne*) what's-his-name*, thingumajig*. **j'ai vu le petit ~** I saw young what's-his-name* *ou* what do you call him; **Monsieur C~** Mr what's-his-name* *ou* thingumajig*; **eh! C~** hey, you.

3 *adj inv*: **être/se sentir tout ~** (*bizarre*) to be/feel not quite oneself, feel a bit peculiar; (*malade*) to be/feel out of sorts *ou* under the weather; **ça l'a rendu tout ~ d'apprendre cette nouvelle** hearing that piece of news made him go all funny.

chosifier [ʃozifje] (7) *vt* to thingify.

chosisme [ʃozism(ə)] *nm* thingism.

chou[1], *pl* **~x** [ʃu] **1** *nm* **(a)** (*Bot*) cabbage.

(b) (*ruban*) rosette.

(c) (*Culin*) puff; *V* **pâte**.

(d) (**loc*) **être dans les ~x** *[projet]* to be up the spout* (*Brit*), be a write-off; (*Sport*) to be last in the field, be right out of the running; *[candidat]* to have had it; **faire ~ blanc** to draw a blank; **ils vont faire leurs ~x gras de ces vieux vêtements** they'll be only too glad to make use of these old clothes.

2: chou de Bruxelles Brussels sprout; **chou cabus** white cabbage; (*Culin*) **chou à la crème** cream puff; **chou-fleur** *nm, pl* **choux-fleurs** cauliflower; **chou frisé** kale; **chou-navet** *nm, pl* **choux-navets** swede; **chou-palmiste** *nm, pl* **choux-palmistes** cabbage tree; **chou-rave** *nm, pl* **choux-raves** kohlrabi; **chou rouge** red cabbage.

chou[2], **-te***, *mpl* **~x** [ʃu, ʃut, ʃu] **1** *nm,f* (*amour, trésor*) darling. **c'est un ~** he's a darling *ou* a dear; **oui ma ~te** yes darling *ou* honey (*US*).

2 *adj inv* (*ravissant*) delightful, cute* (*surtout US*). **ce que c'est ~, cet appartement** what a delightful *ou* lovely little flat, what an absolute darling of a flat; **ce qu'elle est ~ dans ce manteau** doesn't she look just (too) delightful *ou* adorable in this coat?

choucas [ʃuka] *nm* jackdaw.

chouchou, -te* [ʃuʃu, ut] *nm,f* pet, darling, blue-eyed boy (*ou* girl). **le ~ du prof** the teacher's pet.

chouchouter* [ʃuʃute] (1) *vt* to pamper, coddle, pet.

choucroute [ʃukʀut] *nf* sauerkraut. **~ garnie** *sauerkraut with meat*.

chouette[1]* [ʃwɛt] *adj* **(a)** (*beau*) *objet, personne* smashing*, great*, cute* (*surtout US*). **(b)** (*gentil*) nice; (*sympathique*) smashing* (*Brit*), great*. **sois ~, prête-moi 100 F** be a dear *ou* sport* and lend me 100 francs. **(c)** (*tant mieux*) **~ (alors)!** smashing!* (*Brit*), great!*

chouette[2] [ʃwɛt] *nf* (*Zool*) owl. (*fig péj*) **quelle vieille ~!** what an old harpy!

chow-chow, *pl* **chows-chows** [ʃuʃu] *nm* chow (*dog*).

choyer [ʃwaje] (8) *vt* (*frm: dorloter*) to cherish; (*avec excès*) to pamper; (*fig*) *idée* to cherish.

chrême [kʀɛm] *nm* chrism, holy oil.

chrétien, -ienne [kʀetjɛ̃, jɛn] **1** *adj* Christian. **2** *nm,f*: **C~(ne)** Christian.

chrétiennement [kʀetjɛnmɑ̃] *adv agir* in a Christian way. **mourir ~** to die as a Christian, die like a good Christian.

chrétienté [kʀetjɛ̃te] *nf* Christendom.

christ [kʀist] *nm* **(a) le C~** Christ. **(b)** (*Art*) Christ (*on the cross*). **un grand ~ en** *ou* **de bois** a large wooden figure of Christ on the cross; **peindre un ~** to paint a figure of Christ.

christiania [kʀistjanja] *nm* (parallel) christie.

christianisation [kʀistjanizasjɔ̃] *nf* conversion to Christianity.

christianiser [kʀistjanize] (1) *vt* to convert to Christianity.

christianisme [kʀistjanism(ə)] *nm* Christianity.

Christophe [kʀistɔf] *nm* Christopher.

chromage [kʀomaʒ] *nm* chromium-plating.

chromate [kʀɔmat] *nm* chromate.

chromatique [kʀɔmatik] *adj* (*Mus, Peinture*) chromatic; (*Bio*) chromosomal.

chromatisme [kʀɔmatism(ə)] *nm* (*Mus*) chromaticism; (*Peinture: aberration chromatique*) chromatum, chromatic aberration; (*coloration*) colourings.

chrome [kʀom] *nm* (*Chim*) chromium. (*Peinture*) **jaune/vert de ~** chrome yellow/green; (*Aut*) **faire les ~s*** to polish the chrome.

chromer [kʀome] (1) *vt* to chromium-plate. **métal chromé** chromium-plated metal.

chromo [kʀɔmo] *nm* chromo.

chromosome [kʀɔmozom] *nm* chromosome.

chromosomique [kʀɔmozomik] *adj* chromosomal.

chronicité [kʀɔnisite] *nf* chronicity.

chronique [kʀɔnik] **1** *adj* chronic. **2** *nf* (*Littérat*) chronicle; (*Presse*) column, page. **~ financière** financial column *ou* page; **~ locale** local news and gossip; *V* **défrayer**.

chroniquement [kʀɔnikmɑ̃] *adv* chronically.

chroniqueur [kʀɔnikœʀ] *nm* (*Littérat*) chronicler; (*Presse, gén*) columnist. **~ parlementaire/sportif** parliamentary/sports editor; **~ dramatique** drama critic.

chrono* [kʀɔno] *nm* (*abrév de* **chronomètre**) stopwatch. (*Aut*) **faire du 80 (km/h) ~** *ou* **au ~** to be timed *ou* clocked at 80; (*temps chronométré*) **faire un bon ~** to do a good time.

chronologie [kʀɔnɔlɔʒi] *nf* chronology.

chronologique [kʀɔnɔlɔʒik] *adj* chronological.

chronologiquement [kʀɔnɔlɔʒikmɑ̃] *adv* chronologically.

chronométrage [kʀɔnɔmetʀaʒ] *nm* (*Sport*) timing.

chronomètre [kʀɔnɔmɛtʀ(ə)] *nm* (*montre de précision*) chronometer; (*Sport*) stopwatch. **~ de marine** marine *ou* box chronometer.

chronométrer [kʀɔnɔmetʀe] (6) *vt* to time.

chronométreur [kʀɔnɔmetʀœʀ] *nm* timekeeper.

chronométrique [kʀɔnɔmetʀik] *adj* chronometric.

chrysalide [kʀizalid] *nf* chrysalis. (*fig*) **sortir de sa ~** to blossom out, come out of one's shell.

chrysanthème [kʀizɑ̃tɛm] *nm* chrysanthemum.

chrysolithe [kʀizɔlit] *nf* chrysolite, olivine.

chu [ʃy] *ptp de* **choir**.

chuchotement [ʃyʃɔtmɑ̃] *nm* (*V* **chuchoter**) whisper, whispering (*U*); murmur.

chuchoter [ʃyʃɔte] (1) *vti [personne, vent, feuilles]* to whisper; *[ruisseau]* to murmur. ~ **qch à l'oreille de qn** to whisper *ou* murmur sth in sb's ear.
chuchoteur, -euse [ʃyʃɔtœʀ, øz] **1** *adj* whispering. **2** *nm,f* whisperer.
chuintant, e [ʃɥɛ̃tɑ̃, ɑ̃t] *adj, nf (Ling)* **(consonne)** ~e palato-alveolar fricative, hushing sound.
chuintement [ʃɥɛ̃tmɑ̃] *nm (Ling)* pronunciation of *s* sound as *sh*; *(bruit)* soft *ou* gentle hiss.
chuinter [ʃɥɛ̃te] (1) *vi* **(a)** *(Ling)* to pronounce *s* as *sh.* **(b)** *[chouette]* to hoot, screech. **(c)** *(siffler)* to hiss softly *ou* gently.
chut [ʃyt] *excl* sh!
chute [ʃyt] *nf* **(a)** *[pierre etc]* fall; *(Théât) [rideau]* fall. **faire une** ~ *[personne]* to (have a) fall; *[chose]* to fall; **faire une** ~ **de 3 mètres** to fall 3 metres; **faire une** ~ **de cheval/de vélo** to fall off *ou* tumble off *ou* come off a horse/bicycle; **loi de la** ~ **des corps** law of gravity; ~ **libre** free fall; **économie en** ~ **libre** plummeting economy; **attention,** ~ **de pierres** danger, falling rocks; *V* **point**[1].
(b) *[cheveux]* loss; *[feuilles]* fall(ing). **lotion contre la** ~ **des cheveux** lotion which prevents hair loss *ou* prevents hair from falling out.
(c) *(fig: ruine) [empire]* fall, collapse; *[commerce]* collapse; *[roi, ministère]* (down)fall; *[femme séduite]* downfall; *(Mil) [ville]* fall; *(Fin) [monnaie, cours]* fall, drop *(de* in); *(Théât) [pièce, auteur]* failure. *(Rel)* **la** ~ the Fall; **il a entraîné le régime dans sa** ~ he dragged the régime down with him (in his fall); **plus dure sera la** ~ the harder the fall.
(d) *(Géog)* fall. ~ **d'eau** waterfall; **les** ~**s du Niagara/Zambèze** the Niagara/Victoria Falls; *(Élec)* **barrage de basse/moyenne/haute** ~ weir with a low/medium/high head; **de fortes** ~**s de pluie/neige** heavy falls of rain/snow, heavy rainfalls/snowfalls.
(e) *(baisse) [température, pression]* drop, fall *(de* in).
(f) *(déchet) [papier, tissu]* clipping, scrap; *[bois]* off-cut.
(g) *[toit]* pitch, slope; *[vers]* cadence. **la** ~ **des reins** the small of the back; ~ **du jour** nightfall.
(h) *(Cartes)* **faire 3 (plis) de** ~ to be 3 (tricks) down.
chuter [ʃyte] (1) *vi* **(a)** (*) *(tomber)* to fall; *(fig: échouer)* to come a cropper*. *(lit, fig)* **faire** ~ **qn** to bring sb down. **(b)** *(Théât)* to flop. **(c)** *(Cartes)* ~ **de deux (levées)** to go down two.
Chypre [ʃipʀ(ə)] *n* Cyprus.
chypriote [ʃipʀiɔt] = **cypriote.**
ci [si] **1** *adv* **(a)** *(dans l'espace)* **celui-**~, **celle-**~ this one; **ceux-**~ these (ones); **ce livre-**~ this book; **cette table-**~ this table; **cet enfant-**~ this child; **ces livres-/tables-**~ these books/tables.
(b) *(dans le temps)* **à cette heure-**~ *(à une heure déterminée)* at this time; *(à une heure indue)* at this hour of the day, at this time of night; *(à l'heure actuelle)* by now, at this moment; **ces jours-**~ *(avenir)* one of these days, in the next few days; *(passé)* these past few days, in the last few days; *(présent)* these days; **ce dimanche-**~**/cet après-midi-**~ **je ne suis pas libre** I'm not free this Sunday/this afternoon; **non, je pars cette nuit-**~ no, it's tonight I'm leaving.
(c) de ~ **de là** here and there; *V* **comme, par-ci par-là.**
2: ci-après below; **ci-contre** opposite; **ci-dessous** below; **ci-dessus** above; **ci-devant** *(adv)* formerly; *(nmf) (Hist)* ci-devant *(aristocrat who lost his title in the French Revolution)*; **ci-gît** here lies; **ci-inclus une enveloppe** envelope enclosed; **l'enveloppe ci-incluse** the enclosed envelope; **ci-joint: vous trouverez ci-joint les papiers que vous avez demandés** you will find enclosed the papers which you asked for; **les papiers ci-joints** the enclosed papers.
cibiche* [sibiʃ] *nf (cigarette)* fag* *(Brit)*, cig*.
cible [sibl(ə)] *nf (lit)* target. *(lit, fig)* **être la** ~ **de, servir de** ~ **à** to be a target for, be the target of; *(lit, fig)* **prendre pour** ~ to take as one's target.
ciboire [sibwaʀ] *nm (Rel)* ciborium *(vessel)*.
ciboule [sibul] *nf (Bot)* (larger) chive; *(Culin)* chives.
ciboulette [sibulɛt] *nf (Bot)* (smaller) chive; *(Culin)* chives.
ciboulot‡ [sibulo] *nm (tête, cerveau)* head, nut*. **il s'est mis dans le** ~ **de ...** he got it into his head *ou* nut* to ... .
cicatrice [sikatʀis] *nf (lit, fig)* scar.
cicatriciel, -ielle [sikatʀisjɛl] *adj* cicatricial; *V* **tissu**[1].
cicatrisant, e [sikatʀizɑ̃, ɑ̃t] **1** *adj* healing. **2** *nm* healing substance.
cicatrisation [sikatʀizɑsjɔ̃] *nf [égratignure]* healing; *[plaie profonde]* closing up, healing.
cicatriser [sikatʀize] (1) **1** *vt (lit, fig)* to heal (over). **sa jambe est cicatrisée** his leg has healed. **2 se cicatriser** *vpr* to heal (up), form a scar.
Cicéron [siseʀɔ̃] *nm* Cicero.
cicérone [siseʀɔn] *nm (hum)* guide, cicerone. **faire le** ~ to act as a guide *ou* cicerone.
cicéronien, -ienne [siseʀɔnjɛ̃, jɛn] *adj éloquence, discours* Ciceronian.
cidre [sidʀ(ə)] *nm* cider. ~ **bouché** *fine bottled cider.*
cidrerie [sidʀəʀi] *nf (industrie)* cider-making; *(usine)* cider factory.
ciel [sjɛl] **1** *nm* **(a)** *(espace: pl littér* **cieux)** sky, heavens *(littér)*. **il resta là, les bras tendus/les yeux tournés vers le** ~ he remained there, (with) his arms stretched out/gazing towards the sky *ou* heavenwards *(littér)*; **haut dans le** ~ *ou (littér)* **dans les cieux** high (up) in the sky, high in the heavens; **suspendu entre** ~ **et terre** *personne, objet* suspended in mid-air; *village* suspended between sky and earth; **sous un** ~ **plus clément, sous des cieux plus cléments** *(littér: climat)* beneath more clement skies *ou* a more clement sky; *(fig hum: endroit moins dangereux)* in *ou* into healthier climes; **sous d'autres cieux** *(littér)* beneath other skies; *(hum)* in other climes; **sous le** ~ **de Paris/de Provence** beneath the Parisian/Provençal sky; *(fig)* **sous le** ~ beneath the heavens *(littér)*, on earth; *V* **septième.**
(b) *(paysage, Peinture: pl* **ciels)** sky. **les** ~**s de Grèce** the skies of Greece; **les** ~**s de Turner** Turner's skies.
(c) *(séjour de puissances surnaturelles: pl* **cieux)** heaven. **il est au** ~ he is in heaven; **le royaume des cieux** the kingdom of heaven; **notre Père qui es aux cieux** our Father which art in heaven.
(d) *(divinité, providence)* heaven. **le** ~ **a écouté leurs prières** heaven heard their prayers; ~**!, juste** ~**!** good heavens!; **le** ~ **m'est témoin que ...** heaven knows that ...; **le** ~ **soit loué!** thank heavens!; **c'est le** ~ **qui vous envoie!** you're heaven-sent!
(e) à ~ **ouvert** *égout* open; *piscine* open-air; *mine* opencast.
2: ciel de carrière quarry ceiling; **ciel de lit** canopy, tester.
cierge [sjɛʀʒ(ə)] *nm (Rel)* candle; *(Bot)* cereus; *V* **brûler.**
cieux [sjø] *nmpl de* **ciel.**
cigale [sigal] *nf* cicada.
cigare [sigaʀ] *nm (lit)* cigar; (**fig: tête)* head, nut*.
cigarette [sigaʀɛt] *nf* cigarette. ~ **(à) bout filtre** filter tip, filter-tip(ped) cigarette; **la** ~ **du condamné** the condemned man's last smoke *ou* cigarette.
cigarillo [sigaʀijo] *nm* cigarillo.
cigogne [sigɔɲ] *nf (Orn)* stork; *(Tech)* crank brace.
ciguë [sigy] *nf (Bot, poison)* hemlock.
cil [sil] *nm (Anat)* eyelash. *(Bio)* ~**s vibratiles** cilia.
cilice [silis] *nm* hair shirt.
cillement [sijmɑ̃] *nm* blinking.
ciller [sije] (1) *vi:* ~ **(des yeux)** to blink (one's eyes); *(fig)* **personne n'ose** ~ **devant lui** nobody dares move a muscle in his presence.
cimaise [simɛz] *nf (Peinture)* picture rail, picture moulding; *(Archit)* cyma; *V* **honneur.**
cime [sim] *nf [montagne]* summit; *(pic)* peak; *[arbre]* top; *(fig) [gloire]* peak, height.
ciment [simɑ̃] *nm* cement. ~ **armé** reinforced concrete.
cimenter [simɑ̃te] (1) *vt* **(a)** *(Constr) sol* to cement, cover with concrete; *bassin* to cement, line with cement; *piton, anneau, pierres* to cement.
(b) *(fig) amitié, accord, paix* to cement. **l'amour qui cimente leur union** the love which binds them together.
cimenterie [simɑ̃tʀi] *nf* cement works.
cimeterre [simtɛʀ] *nm* scimitar.
cimetière [simtjɛʀ] *nm [ville]* cemetery; *[église]* graveyard, churchyard. ~ **de voitures** scrapyard.
ciné [sine] **1** *nm* (*: *abrév de* **cinéma)** flicks*, pictures, movies *(US)*.
2: ciné-club *nm, pl* **ciné-clubs** film society *ou* club; *(Québec)* **ciné-parc** *nm, pl* **ciné-parcs** drive-in (cinema); **ciné-roman** *nm, pl* **ciné-romans** film story.
cinéaste [sineast(ə)] *nmf* film-maker.
cinéma [sinema] **1** *nm* **(a)** *(procédé, art, industrie)* cinema; *(salle)* cinema, picture house, movie theater *(US)*. **roman adapté pour le** ~ novel adapted for the cinema *ou* the screen; **faire du** ~ to be a film actor *(ou* actress); **de** ~ *technicien, producteur, studio, plateau* film *(épith)*; *projecteur, écran* cinema *(épith)*; **acteur/vedette de** ~ film *ou* movie *(US)* actor/star; **être dans le** ~ to be in the film business *ou* in films; **aller au** ~ to go to the cinema *ou* pictures *ou* movies *(US)*.
(b) (**fig: frime)* **c'est du** ~ it's all put on*, it's all an act; **arrête ton** ~ cut out the acting*; **faire tout un** ~ to put on a great act*.
(c) (*: *embarras, complication)* fuss. **c'est toujours le même** ~ it's always the same old to-do *ou* business; **tu ne vas pas nous faire ton** ~**!** you're not going to make a fuss *ou* a great scene *ou* a song and dance* about it!
2: le cinéma d'animation the cartoon film; **cinéma d'art et d'essai** avant-garde *ou* experimental films *ou* cinema; *(salle)* arts cinema; **cinéma muet** silent films; **cinéma parlant** talking films, talkies*; **cinéma permanent** continuous performance; **cinéma-vérité** *nm* cinéma-vérité, ciné vérité.
cinémascope [sinemaskɔp] *nm* ® Cinemascope ®.
cinémathèque [sinematɛk] *nf* film archives *ou* library; *(salle)* film theatre.
cinématique [sinematik] *nf* kinematics *(sg)*.
cinématographe [sinematɔgʀaf] *nm* cinematograph.
cinématographie [sinematɔgʀafi] *nf* film-making, cinematography.
cinématographier [sinematɔgʀafje] (7) *vt* to film.
cinématographique [sinematɔgʀafik] *adj* film *(épith)*, cinema *(épith)*.
cinéphile [sinefil] *nmf* film *ou* cinema enthusiast, cineaste.
cinéraire [sineʀɛʀ] **1** *adj vase* cinerary. **2** *nf (Bot)* cineraria.
cinétique [sinetik] **1** *adj* kinetic. **2** *nf* kinetics *(sg)*.
cing(h)alais, e [sɛ̃galɛ, ɛz] **1** *adj* Sin(g)halese. **2** *nm (Ling)* Sin(g)halese. **3** *nm,f:* **C**~**(e)** Sin(g)halese.
cinglant, e [sɛ̃glɑ̃, ɑ̃t] *adj vent* biting, bitter; *pluie* lashing, driving; *propos, ironie* biting, scathing, cutting.
cinglé, e* [sɛ̃gle] *(ptp de* **cingler)** *adj* nutty*, screwy*, cracked*. **c'est un** ~ he's a crackpot* *ou* a nut*.
cingler [sɛ̃gle] (1) **1** *vt [personne] corps, cheval* to lash; *[vent, pluie, branche] visage, jambe* to sting, whip (against); *[pluie] vitre* to lash (against); *(fig)* to lash, sting. **il cingla l'air de son fouet** he lashed the air with his whip.
2 *vi (Naut)* ~ **vers** to make for.
cinoque‡ [sinɔk] *adj* = **sinoque‡.**
cinq [sɛ̃k] *adj, nm* five. **dire les** ~ **lettres** to use bad language; *(euph)* **je lui ai dit les** ~ **lettres** I told him where to go *(euph)*; **en** ~ **sec*** in a flash, in two ticks* *(Brit)*, before you could say Jack Robinson*; *pour autres loc V* **six.**

cinq-dix-quinze†: [sɛ̃diskɛ̃z] *nm (Can)* cheap store, dime store (*US, Can*), five-and-ten (*US, Can*).
cinquantaine [sɛ̃kɑ̃tɛn] *nf (âge, nombre)* about fifty; *pour loc V* **soixantaine.**
cinquante [sɛ̃kɑ̃t] *adj inv, nm inv* fifty; *pour loc V* **six.**
cinquantenaire [sɛ̃kɑ̃tnɛʀ] **1** *adj arbre etc* fifty-year-old (*épith*), fifty years old. **il est ~** it *ou* he is fifty years old. **2** *nm* (*anniversaire*) fiftieth anniversary, golden jubilee.
cinquantième [sɛ̃kɑ̃tjɛm] *adj, nmf* fiftieth; *pour loc V* **sixième.**
cinquantièmement [sɛ̃kɑ̃tjɛmmɑ̃] *adv* in the fiftieth place.
cinquième [sɛ̃kjɛm] **1** *adj, nmf* fifth. **être la ~ roue du carrosse*** to be just there for decoration, be of no real use; **~ colonne** fifth column; *pour autres loc V* **sixième. 2** *nf* (*Scol*) second form *ou* year.
cinquièmement [sɛ̃kjɛmmɑ̃] *adv* in the fifth place.
cintrage [sɛ̃tʀaʒ] *nm [tôle, bois]* bending.
cintre [sɛ̃tʀ(ə)] *nm* **(a)** (*Archit*) arch; *V* **voûte. (b)** (*portemanteau*) coat hanger. **(c)** (*Théât*) **les ~s** the flies.
cintré, e [sɛ̃tʀe] (*ptp de* **cintrer**) *adj porte, fenêtre* arched; *galerie* vaulted, arched; *veste* waisted; (*‡fig: fou*) nuts*, crackers*. **chemise ~e** close- *ou* slim-fitting shirt.
cintrer [sɛ̃tʀe] (1) *vt* (*Archit*) *porte* to arch, make into an arch; *galerie* to vault, give a vaulted *ou* arched roof to; (*Tech*) to bend, curve; (*Habillement*) to take in at the waist.
cirage [siʀaʒ] *nm* **(a)** (*produit*) (shoe) polish.
(b) (*action*) *[souliers]* polishing; *[parquets]* polishing, waxing.
(c) (*fig*) **être dans le ~*** (*malaise*) to be dazed *ou* in a stupor; (*ne rien comprendre*) to be in a fog* *ou* all at sea*; (*arg Aviat*) to be flying blind. **quand il est sorti du ~** when he got on his feet again; *V* **noir.**
circoncire [siʀkɔ̃siʀ] (37) *vt* to circumcize.
circoncision [siʀkɔ̃sizjɔ̃] *nf* circumcision.
circonférence [siʀkɔ̃feʀɑ̃s] *nf* circumference.
circonflexe [siʀkɔ̃flɛks(ə)] *adj*: **accent ~** circumflex.
circonlocution [siʀkɔ̃lɔkysjɔ̃] *nf* circumlocution. **employer des ~s pour annoncer qch** to announce sth in a roundabout way.
circonscription [siʀkɔ̃skʀipsjɔ̃] *nf (Admin, Mil)* district, area. **~ (électorale)** *[député]* constituency; *[conseiller municipal]* district, ward.
circonscrire [siʀkɔ̃skʀiʀ] (39) *vt feu, épidémie* to contain, confine; *territoire* to mark out; *sujet* to define, delimit. (*Math*) **~ un cercle/carré à** to draw a circle/square round; **le débat s'est circonscrit à** *ou* **autour de cette seule question** the debate limited *ou* restricted itself to *ou* was centred round that one question; **les recherches sont circonscrites au village** the search is being limited *ou* confined to the village.
circonspect, e [siʀkɔ̃spɛ(kt), ɛkt(ə)] *adj personne* circumspect, cautious, wary; *silence, remarque* prudent, cautious.
circonspection [siʀkɔ̃spɛksjɔ̃] *nf* caution, wariness, circumspection.
circonstance [siʀkɔ̃stɑ̃s] *nf* **(a)** (*occasion*) occasion. **en la ~** in this case, on this occasion, given the present circumstances; **en pareille ~** in such a case, in such circumstances; **il a profité de la ~ pour me rencontrer** he took advantage of the occasion to meet me; *V* **concours.**
(b) (*situation*) **~s** circumstances; (*Écon*) **~s économiques** economic circumstances; **être à la hauteur des ~s** to be equal to the occasion; **du fait** *ou* **en raison des ~s, étant donné les ~s** in view of *ou* given the circumstances; **dans ces ~s** under *ou* in these circumstances; **dans les ~s présentes** *ou* **actuelles** in the present circumstances; **il a honteusement profité des ~s** he took shameful advantage of the situation.
(c) *[crime, accident]* circumstance. (*Jur*) **~s atténuantes** mitigating *ou* extenuating circumstances; **~ aggravante** aggravation; **il y a une ~ troublante** there's one disturbing circumstance *ou* point; **dans des ~s encore mal définies** in circumstances which are still unclear.
(d) de ~ *parole, mine, conseil* appropriate, apt, fitting; *œuvre, poésie* occasional (*épith*); *habit* appropriate, suitable.
circonstancié, e [siʀkɔ̃stɑ̃sje] *adj rapport* detailed.
circonstanciel, -ielle [siʀkɔ̃stɑ̃sjɛl] *adj* adverbial. **complément ~ de lieu/temps** adverbial phrase of place/time.
circonvenir [siʀkɔ̃vniʀ] (22) *vt (frm) personne* to circumvent (*frm*), get round.
circonvoisin, e [siʀkɔ̃vwazɛ̃, in] *adj* (*littér*) surrounding, neighbouring.
circonvolution [siʀkɔ̃vɔlysjɔ̃] *nf (Anat)* convolution; *[rivière, itinéraire]* twist, convolution (*frm*). **décrire des ~s** *[rivière]* to meander, twist and turn; *[route]* to twist and turn; **~ cérébrale** cerebral convolution.
circuit [siʀkɥi] **1** *nm* **(a)** (*itinéraire touristique*) tour, (round) trip. **~ d'autocar** coach (*Brit*) tour *ou* trip, bus trip; **on a fait un grand ~ à travers la Bourgogne** we did a grand tour of *ou* a great trip round Burgundy; **il y a un très joli ~ (à faire) à travers bois** there's a very nice trip *ou* run (one can go) through the woods; **faire le ~ des volcans d'Auvergne** to tour round *ou* go on a tour of the volcanoes in Auvergne.
(b) (*parcours compliqué*) roundabout *ou* circuitous route. **il faut emprunter un ~ assez compliqué pour y arriver** you have to take a rather circuitous *ou* roundabout route *ou* you have to go a rather complicated way to get there; **l'autre grille du parc était fermée et j'ai dû refaire tout le ~ en sens inverse** the other park gate was shut and I had to go right back round the way I'd come *ou* make the whole journey back the way I'd come.
(c) (*Sport*) circuit.
(d) (*Elec*) circuit. **couper/rétablir le ~** to break/restore the circuit; **mettre qch en ~** to connect sth up.
(e) (*Écon*) circulation.
(f) (*enceinte*) *[ville]* circumference.
(g) (**loc*) **être dans le ~** to be around; **est-ce qu'il est toujours dans le ~?** is he still around?, is he still on the go?*; **mettre qch dans le ~** to put sth into circulation, feed sth into the system.
2: (*Comm*) **circuit de distribution** distribution network *ou* channels; **circuit électrique** (*Élec*) electric(al) circuit; *[train miniature]* (electric) track; **circuit fermé** (*Élec, fig*) closed circuit; **vivre en circuit fermé** to live in a closed world; **ces publications circulent en circuit fermé** this literature has a limited *ou* restricted circulation; **circuit imprimé** printed circuit; **circuit intégré** integrated circuit.
circulaire [siʀkylɛʀ] *adj, nf (gén)* circular; *V* **billet.**
circulairement [siʀkylɛʀmɑ̃] *adv* in a circle.
circulation [siʀkylɑsjɔ̃] *nf [air, sang, argent]* circulation; *[marchandises]* movement; *[nouvelle]* spread; *[trains]* running; (*Aut*) traffic. **la ~ (du sang)** the circulation; **la libre ~ des travailleurs** the free movement of labour; (*Aut*) **pour rendre la ~ plus fluide** to improve traffic flow; **mettre en ~** *argent* to put into circulation; *livre, journal, produit* to bring *ou* put out, put on the market; *voiture* to put on the market, bring *ou* put out; *fausse nouvelle* to circulate, spread (about); **mise en ~** *[argent]* circulation; *[livre, produit, voiture]* marketing; *[fausse nouvelle]* spreading, circulation; **~ aérienne** air traffic; (*Fin*) **~ monétaire** money *ou* currency circulation; (*Aut*) **~ interdite** no vehicular traffic; *V* **accident, agent.**
circulatoire [siʀkylatwaʀ] *adj* circulation (*épith*), circulatory. **avoir des troubles ~s** to have trouble with one's circulation, have circulatory trouble.
circuler [siʀkyle] (1) *vi* **(a)** *[sang, air, marchandises, argent]* to circulate; *[rumeur]* to circulate, go round *ou* about. **il circule bien des bruits à son propos** there's a lot of gossip going round about him, there's a lot being said about him; **faire ~** *air, sang* to circulate; *marchandises* to put into circulation; *argent* to circulate; **faire ~ des bruits au sujet de** to put rumours about concerning, spread rumours concerning.
(b) *[voiture]* to go, move; *[train]* to go, run; *[passant]* to walk; *[foule]* to move (along); *[plat, bonbons, lettre]* to be passed *ou* handed round. **circulez!** move along!; **faire ~** *voitures, piétons* to move on; *plat, bonbons, document, pétition* to hand *ou* pass round.
circumnavigation [siʀkɔmnavigɑsjɔ̃] *nf* circumnavigation.
circumpolaire [siʀkɔmpɔlɛʀ] *adj* circumpolar.
cire [siʀ] *nf (gén)* wax; (*pour meubles, parquets*) polish; (*Méd*) *[oreille]* (ear)wax. **~ d'abeille** beeswax; **~ à cacheter** sealing wax.
ciré [siʀe] *nm* (*Habillement*) oilskin.
cirer [siʀe] (1) *vt* to polish; *V* **toile.**
cireur, -euse [siʀœʀ, øz] **1** *nm,f* (*personne*) *[souliers]* bootblack; *[planchers]* (floor-)polisher. **2 cireuse** *nf* (*appareil*) floor polisher.
cireux, -euse [siʀø, øz] *adj matière* waxy; *teint* waxen.
ciron [siʀɔ̃] *nm* (*littér, Zool*) mite.
cirque [siʀk(ə)] *nm* **(a)** (*spectacle*) circus.
(b) (*Antiq: arène*) amphitheatre; *V* **jeu.**
(c) (*Géog*) cirque.
(d) (*‡: complication, embarras*) **quel ~ il a fait quand il a appris la nouvelle** what a scene *ou* to-do he made when he heard the news; **quel ~ pour garer sa voiture ici!** what a carry-on* (*Brit*) *ou* performance* to get the car parked here!
(e) (*: *désordre*) chaos. **c'est un vrai ~ ici aujourd'hui** it's absolute chaos here today, this place is like a bear garden today.
cirrhose [siʀoz] *nf* cirrhosis. **~ du foie** cirrhosis of the liver (*T*).
cirro-cumulus [siʀɔkymylys] *nm* cirrocumulus.
cirro-stratus [siʀɔstʀatys] *nm* cirrostratus.
cirrus [siʀys] *nm* cirrus.
cisaille *nf*, **cisailles** *nfpl* [sizɑj] *[métal]* shears; *[fil métallique]* wire cutters; *[jardinier]* (gardening) shears.
cisaillement [sizɑjmɑ̃] *nm* (*V* **cisailler**) cutting; clipping, pruning; shearing off.
cisailler [sizɑje] (1) *vt* **(a)** (*couper*) *métal* to cut; *arbuste* to clip, prune.
(b) (*user*) *rivet* to shear off.
(c) (*: *tailler maladroitement*) *tissu, planche, cheveux* to hack.
(d) (*: *empêcher la promotion*) *personne* to cripple the career of; *carrière* to cripple.
cisalpin, e [sizalpɛ̃, in] *adj* cisalpine.
ciseau, *pl* **~x** [sizo] *nm* **(a) (paire *f* de) ~x** (*gén*) *[tissu, papier]* (pair of) scissors; *[métal, laine]* shears; *[fil métallique]* wire cutters; **~x de brodeuse** embroidery scissors; **~x de couturière** dressmaking shears *ou* scissors; **~x à ongles** nail scissors. **(b)** (*Sculp, Tech*) chisel. **~ à froid** cold chisel. **(c)** (*Sport: prise*) scissors (hold *ou* grip); *V* **sauter.**
ciselage [sizlaʒ] *nm* chiselling.
ciseler [sizle] (5) *vt* (*lit*) *pierre* to chisel, carve; *métal* to chase, chisel; (*fig*) *style* to polish. (*fig*) **les traits finement ciselés de son visage** his finely chiselled features.
ciseleur [sizlœʀ] *nm* (*V* **ciselure**) carver; engraver.
ciselure [sizlyʀ] *nf* **(a)** *[bois, marbre]* carving, chiselling; *[orfèvrerie]* engraving, chasing. **(b)** (*dessin*) *[bois]* carving; *[orfèvrerie]* engraved *ou* chased pattern *ou* design, engraving.
cistercien, -ienne [sistɛʀsjɛ̃, jɛn] *adj, nm* Cistercian.
citadelle [sitadɛl] *nf* (*lit, fig*) citadel.
citadin, e [sitadɛ̃, in] **1** *adj* (*gén*) town (*épith*), urban; *[grande ville]* city (*épith*), urban. **2** *nm,f* city dweller.
citation [sitɑsjɔ̃] *nf [auteur]* quotation; (*Jur*) summons. (*Jur*) **~ à comparaître** (*à accusé*) summons to appear; (*à témoin*) subpoena; (*Mil*) **~ à l'ordre du jour** *ou* **de l'armée** mention in dispatches.

cité [site] **1** *nf* (*littér*) (*Antiq, grande ville*) city; (*petite ville*) town; *V* **droit**[3].

2: cité-dortoir *nf, pl* **cités-dortoirs** dormitory town; **cité-jardin** *nf, pl* **cités-jardins** garden city; **cité ouvrière** ≈ (workers') housing estate (*Brit*) *ou* development (*US*); **cité universitaire** (student) halls of residence.

citer [site] (1) *vt* **(a)** (*rapporter*) *texte, exemples, faits* to quote, cite. ~ **(du) Shakespeare** to quote from Shakespeare; **il n'a pas pu ~ 3 pièces de Sartre** he couldn't name *ou* quote 3 plays by Sartre.

(b) ~ **(en exemple)** *personne* to hold up as an example; **il a été cité (en exemple) pour son courage** he has been held up as an example for his courage; (*Mil*) ~ **un soldat (à l'ordre du jour** *ou* **de l'armée)** to mention a soldier in dispatches.

(c) (*Jur*) to summon. ~ **(à comparaître)** *accusé* to summon to appear; *témoin* to subpoena.

citerne [sitɛʀn(ə)] *nf* tank; (*à eau*) water tank; *V* **camion.**

cithare [sitaʀ] *nf* zither; (*Antiq*) cithara.

citoyen, -enne [sitwajɛ̃, ɛn] **1** *nm,f* citizen. ~ **d'honneur d'une ville** freeman of a city *ou* town. **2** *nm* (*: *type*) bloke* (*Brit*), guy*. **drôle de ~** queer customer *ou* fellow.

citoyenneté [sitwajɛnte] *nf* citizenship.

citrique [sitʀik] *adj* citric.

citron [sitʀɔ̃] **1** *nm* (*fruit*) lemon; (*: *tête*) nut*. **un** *ou* **du ~ pressé** a (fresh) lemon juice; *V* **thé. 2** *adj inv* lemon (-coloured).

citronnade [sitʀɔnad] *nf* lemon squash, still lemonade (*Brit*).

citronné, e [sitʀɔne] *adj goût, odeur* lemony; *gâteau* lemon (-flavoured); *liquide* with lemon juice added, lemon-flavoured; *eau de toilette* lemon-scented.

citronnelle [sitʀɔnɛl] *nf* (*Bot, huile*) citronella; (*liqueur*) lemon liqueur.

citronnier [sitʀɔnje] *nm* lemon tree.

citrouille [sitʀuj] *nf* pumpkin; (*: *hum: tête*) nut*.

cive [siv] *nf* (*Bot*) chive; (*Culin*) chives.

civet [sivɛ] *nm* stew. **un lièvre en ~, un ~ de lièvre** ≈ jugged hare.

civette[1] [sivɛt] *nf* (*Zool*) civet (cat); (*parfum*) civet.

civette[2] [sivɛt] *nf* (*Bot*) chive; (*Culin*) chives.

civière [sivjɛʀ] *nf* stretcher.

civil, e [sivil] **1** *adj* **(a)** (*entre citoyens, Jur*), *guerre, mariage* civil; *V* **code, partie**[2] *etc.*

(b) (*non militaire*) civilian.

(c) (*littér: poli*) civil, courteous.

2 *nm* **(a)** (*non militaire*) civilian. **se mettre en ~** *[soldat]* to dress in civilian clothes, wear civvies*; *[policier]* to dress in plain clothes; **policier en ~** plain-clothes policeman, policeman in plain clothes; **soldat en ~** soldier in civvies* *ou* in civilian clothes; **dans le ~** in civilian life, in civvy street*.

(b) (*Jur*) **poursuivre qn au ~** to take civil action against sb, sue sb in the civil courts.

civilement [sivilmɑ̃] *adv* **(a)** (*Jur*) **poursuivre qn ~** to take civil action against sb, sue sb in the (civil) courts; **être ~ responsable** to be legally responsible; **se marier ~** to have a civil wedding, ≈ get married in a registry office (*Brit*). **(b)** (*littér*) civilly.

civilisable [sivilizabl(ə)] *adj* civilizable.

civilisateur, -trice [sivilizatœʀ, tʀis] **1** *adj* civilizing. **2** *nm,f* civilizer.

civilisation [sivilizɑsjɔ̃] *nf* civilization.

civiliser [sivilize] (1) **1** *vt peuple,* (*) *personne* to civilize. **2 se civiliser** *vpr [peuple]* to become civilized; (*) *[personne]* to become more civilized.

civilité [sivilite] *nf* (*politesse*) civility. (*frm: compliments*) ~**s** civilities; **faire** *ou* **présenter ses ~s à** to pay one's compliments to.

civique [sivik] *adj* civic. **avoir le sens ~** to have a sense of civic responsibility; *V* **instruction.**

civisme [sivism(ə)] *nm* public-spiritedness. **cours de ~** civics (*sg*).

clabaudage [klabodaʒ] *nm* gossip; *[chien]* yapping.

clabauder [klabode] (1) *vi* (*médire*) to gossip; *[chien]* to yap. ~ **contre qn** to make denigrating remarks about sb.

clabauderie [klabodʀi] *nf* = **clabaudage.**

clabaudeur, -euse [klabodœʀ, øz] **1** *adj* (*médisant*) gossiping; (*aboyant*) yapping. **2** *nm,f* (*cancanier*) gossip.

clac [klak] *excl [porte]* slam!; *[élastique, stylo etc]* snap!; *[fouet]* crack!; *V* **clic.**

clafoutis [klafuti] *nm* clafoutis (*fruit, esp cherries, cooked in batter*).

claie [klɛ] *nf [fruit, fromage]* grid; (*crible*) riddle; (*clôture*) hurdle.

clair, e[1] [klɛʀ] **1** *adj* **(a)** (*lumineux*) *pièce* bright, light; *ciel* clear; *couleur, flamme* bright. **par temps ~** on a clear day, in clear weather.

(b) (*pâle*) *teint, couleur* light; *tissu, robe* light-coloured. **bleu/vert ~** light blue/green.

(c) (*lit, fig: limpide*) *eau, son, conscience* clear. **d'une voix ~e** in a clear voice; **des vitres propres et ~es** clean and sparkling *ou* clean bright windows.

(d) (*peu consistant*) *sauce, soupe* thin; *cheveux* thin, sparse; *tissu usé* thin; *tissu peu serré* light, thin; *blés* sparse.

(e) (*sans ambiguïté*) *exposé, pensée, position, attitude* clear. **voilà qui est ~!** well, that's clear anyway!; **cette affaire n'est pas ~e** there's something slightly suspicious *ou* not quite clear about this affair; **avoir un esprit ~** to be a clear thinker.

(f) (*évident*) clear, obvious, plain. **le plus ~ de l'histoire** the most obvious thing in the story; **il est ~ qu'il se trompe** it is clear *ou* obvious *ou* plain that he's mistaken; **son affaire est ~e, il est coupable** it's quite clear *ou* obvious that he's guilty; **c'est ~ comme le jour** *ou* **comme de l'eau de roche** it's as clear as daylight, it's crystal-clear; **il passe le plus ~ de son temps à rêver** he spends most of his time daydreaming; **il dépense le plus ~ de son argent en cigarettes** he spends the better part of his money on cigarettes.

2 *adv parler, voir* clearly. **il fait ~** it is daylight; **il ne fait guère ~ dans cette pièce** it's not very light in this room; **il fait aussi ~** *ou* **on voit aussi ~ qu'en plein jour** it's as bright as daylight.

3 *nm* **(a)** (*loc*) **tirer qch au ~** to clear sth up, clarify sth; **en ~** (*c'est-à-dire*) to put it plainly; (*non codé*) in clear; *V* **sabre.**

(b) (*partie usée d'une chaussette etc*) ~**s** worn parts, thin patches.

(c) (*Art*) ~**s** light (*U*), light areas; **les ~s et les ombres** the light and shade.

4: clair de lune moonlight; **au clair de lune** in the moonlight; **promenade au clair de lune** moonlight saunter, stroll in the moonlight; **clair-obscur** *nm, pl* **clairs-obscurs** (*Art*) chiaroscuro; (*gén*) twilight; **claire-voie** *nf, pl* **claires-voies** (*clôture*) openwork fence; *[église]* clerestory; **à claire-voie** openwork (*épith*).

claire[2] [klɛʀ] *nf* (*parc*) oyster bed. **(huître de) ~** fattened oyster; *V* **fine**[2].

clairement [klɛʀmɑ̃] *adv* clearly.

clairet, -ette [klɛʀɛ, ɛt] **1** *adj soupe* thin; *voix* high-pitched. **(vin) ~** light red wine. **2 clairette** *nf* light sparkling wine.

clairière [klɛʀjɛʀ] *nf* clearing, glade.

clairon [klɛʀɔ̃] *nm* (*instrument*) bugle; (*joueur*) bugler; *[orgue]* clarion (stop).

claironnant, e [klɛʀɔnɑ̃, ɑ̃t] *adj voix* strident, resonant, like a foghorn.

claironner [klɛʀɔne] (1) **1** *vt succès, nouvelle* to trumpet, shout from the rooftops. **2** *vi* (*parler fort*) to speak at the top of one's voice.

clairsemé, e [klɛʀsəme] *adj arbres, maisons, applaudissements, auditoire* scattered; *cheveux* thin, sparse; *blés, gazon* sparse; *population* sparse, scattered.

clairvoyance [klɛʀvwajɑ̃s] *nf* (*discernement*) *[personne]* clear-sightedness, perceptiveness; *[esprit]* perceptiveness.

clairvoyant, e [klɛʀvwajɑ̃, ɑ̃t] *adj* **(a)** (*perspicace*) *personne* clear-sighted, perceptive; *œil, esprit* perceptive. **(b)** (*doué de vision*) **les aveugles et les ~s** the blind and the sighted.

clam [klam] *nm* (*Zool*) clam.

clamecer: [klamse] (3) *vi* (*mourir*) to kick the bucket:, snuff it: (*Brit*).

clamer [klame] (1) *vt* to shout out, proclaim. ~ **son innocence/son indignation** to proclaim one's innocence/one's indignation.

clameur [klamœʀ] *nf* clamour. **les ~s de la foule** the clamour of the crowd; (*fig*) **les ~s des mécontents** the protests of the discontented.

clamser: [klamse] (1) *vi* = **clamecer**:.

clan [klɑ̃] *nm* (*lit, fig*) clan.

clandestin, e [klɑ̃dɛstɛ̃, in] *adj réunion* secret, clandestine; *revue, mouvement* underground (*épith*); *commerce* clandestine, illicit. **(passager) ~** stowaway.

clandestinement [klɑ̃dɛstinmɑ̃] *adv* (*V* **clandestin**) secretly; clandestinely; illicitly.

clandestinité [klɑ̃dɛstinite] *nf* **(a)** *[activité etc]* secret nature. **dans la ~** (*en secret*) *travailler, imprimer* in secret, clandestinely; (*en se cachant*) *vivre* underground; **entrer dans la ~** to go underground; **le journal interdit a continué de paraître dans la ~** the banned newspaper went on being published underground *ou* clandestinely.

(b) (*Hist: la Résistance*) **la ~** the Resistance.

clapet [klapɛ] *nm* **(a)** (*Tech*) valve; (*Élec*) rectifier. (*Aut*) ~ **d'admission/d'échappement** induction/exhaust valve. **(b)** (*: *bouche*) **ferme ton ~** hold your peace *ou* tongue*; **quel ~!** what a chatterbox! *ou* gasbag!*

clapier [klapje] *nm* **(a)** (*cabane à lapins*) hutch; (*péj: logement surpeuplé*) dump:, hole*. **(b)** (*éboulis*) scree.

clapotement [klapɔtmɑ̃] *nm* lap(ping) (*U*).

clapoter [klapɔte] (1) *vi [eau]* to lap.

clapotis [klapɔti] *nm* lap(ping) (*U*).

clappement [klapmɑ̃] *nm* click(ing) (*U*).

clapper [klape] (1) *vi*: ~ **de la langue** to click one's tongue.

claquage [klakaʒ] *nm* (*action*) pulling *ou* straining (of a muscle); (*blessure*) pulled *ou* strained muscle. **se faire un ~** to pull *ou* strain a muscle.

claquant, e* [klakɑ̃, ɑ̃t] *adj* (*fatigant*) killing*, exhausting.

claque[1] [klak] *nf* **(a)** (*gifle*) slap. **donner** *ou* **flanquer* une ~ à qn** to slap sb, give sb a slap *ou* clout*; *V* **tête. (b)** (*loc*) **il en a sa ~*** (*excédé*) he's fed up to the back teeth* (*Brit*) *ou* to the teeth* (*US*); (*épuisé*) he's dead beat* *ou* all in*. **(c)** (*Théât*) claque.

claque[2] [klak] *adj, nm*: **(chapeau) ~** opera hat.

claqué, e* [klake] (*ptp de* **claquer**) *adj* (*fatigué*) all in*, dead beat*.

claquement [klakmɑ̃] *nm* (*bruit répété*) *[porte]* banging (*U*), slamming (*U*); *[fouet]* cracking (*U*); *[langue]* clicking (*U*); *[doigts]* snap(ping) (*U*); *[talons]* click(ing) (*U*); *[drapeau]* flapping (*U*); (*bruit isolé*) *[porte]* bang, slam; *[fouet]* crack; *[langue]* click. **la corde cassa avec un ~ sec** the rope broke with a sharp snap; **le ~ de deux morceaux de bois frappés l'un contre l'autre** the sound of two pieces of wood being rapped *ou* banged against one another.

claquemurer [klakmyʀe] (1) **1** *vt* to coop up. **il reste claquemuré dans son bureau toute la journée** he stays shut up *ou* shut away in his office all day. **2 se claquemurer** *vpr* to shut o.s. away *ou* up.

claquer [klake] (1) **1** *vi* **(a)** *[porte, volet]* to bang; *[drapeau]* to flap; *[fouet]* to crack; *[coup de feu]* to ring out. **faire ~ une porte**

to bang *ou* slam a door; **faire ~ son fouet** to crack one's whip.

(b) ~ des doigts to snap one's fingers; **~ des *ou* dans ses mains** to clap (one's hands); (*Mil*) **~ des talons** to click one's heels; (*fig*) **~ du bec**ː to be famished; **il claquait des dents** his teeth were chattering; **faire ~ ses doigts** to snap one's fingers; **faire ~ sa langue** to click one's tongue.

(c) (ː: *mourir*)) to snuff itː (*Brit*), kick the bucketː; (*: *tomber hors d'usage*) *[télévision, moteur, lampe électrique]* to conk outː, go phut* (*Brit*), pack in*; *[ficelle, élastique]* to snap. **~ dans les mains de qn** *[malade]* to die on sb; *[élastique]* to snap in sb's hands; *[appareil]* to bust* *ou* go phut* (*Brit*) in sb's hands; *[entreprise, affaire]* to go bust in sb's hands *ou* on sb*; **il a claqué d'une crise cardiaque** a heart attack finished him off.

2 *vt* **(a)** (*gifler*) *enfant* to slap.

(b) (*refermer avec bruit*) *livre* to snap shut. **~ la porte** (*lit*) to slam the door; (*fig*) to leave *ou* walk out in a huff; **il m'a claqué la porte au nez** (*lit*) he slammed the door in my face; (*fig*) he refused to listen to me.

(c) (*: *fatiguer*) *[travail]* to exhaust, tire out. **le voyage m'a claqué** I felt whacked* (*Brit*) *ou* dead tired after the journey; **~ son cheval** to wear out *ou* exhaust one's horse; **ne travaille pas tant, tu vas te ~** don't work so hard or you'll knock *ou* wear yourself out *ou* kill yourself.

(d) (*: *casser*) to bust*. (*Sport*) **se ~ un muscle** to pull *ou* strain a muscle.

(e) (ː: *dépenser*) *argent* to blow*, blue*.

claquette [klakɛt] *nf* **(a)** (*danse*) **~s** tap-dancing; *V* **danseur.** **(b)** (*claquoir*) clapper; (*Ciné*) clapperboard.

claquoir [klakwaʀ] *nm* clapper.

clarification [klaʀifikɑsjɔ̃] *nf* (*lit, fig*) clarification.

clarifier *vt*, **se clarifier** *vpr* [klaʀifje] (7) (*lit, fig*) to clarify. **la situation se clarifie** the situation is clarifying itself *ou* is becoming clear(er).

clarine [klaʀin] *nf* cowbell.

clarinette [klaʀinɛt] *nf* clarinet.

clarinettiste [klaʀinetist(ə)] *nmf* clarinettist.

clarté [klaʀte] *nf* **(a)** (*gén: lumière*) light; *[lampe, crépuscule, astre]* light. **~ douce/vive/faible** soft/bright/weak light; **~ de la lune** light of the moon, moonlight; **à la ~ de la lampe** in the lamplight, in *ou* by the light of the lamp.

(b) (*transparence, luminosité*) *[flamme, pièce, jour, ciel]* brightness; *[eau, son, verre]* clearness; *[teint]* (*pureté*) clearness; (*pâleur*) lightness.

(c) (*fig: netteté*) *[explication, pensée, attitude, conférencier]* clarity. **~ d'esprit** clear thinking.

(d) (*fig: précisions*) **~s: avoir des ~s sur une question** to have some (further *ou* bright) ideas on a subject; **cela projette quelques ~s sur la question** this throws some light on the subject.

classe [klɑs] *nf* **(a)** (*catégorie sociale*) class. (*Démographie*) **~s creuses** *age groups depleted by war deaths or low natality;* **les ~s moyennes** the middle classes; **les basses/hautes ~s (sociales)** the lower/upper (social) classes; **la ~ laborieuse *ou* ouvrière** the working class; **selon sa ~ sociale** according to one's social status *ou* social class; **(société) sans ~** classless (society).

(b) (*gén, Sci: espèce*) class; (*Admin: rang*) grade. **cela s'adresse à toutes les ~s d'utilisateurs** it is aimed at every category of user; (*fig*) **il est vraiment à mettre dans une ~ à part** he's really in a class of his own *ou* a class apart; (*Admin*) **cadre de première/deuxième ~** first/second grade manager; (*Comm*) **hôtel de première ~** first class hotel; (*Gram*) **~ grammaticale *ou* de mots** grammatical category, part of speech; **~ d'âge** age group.

(c) (*Aviat, Rail*) class. **compartiment/billet de 1ère/2e ~** 1st/2nd class compartment/ticket; **voyager en 1ère ~** to travel 1st class; (*Aviat*) **~ touriste** economy class.

(d) (*gén, Sport: valeur*) class. **liqueur/artiste de (grande) ~** liqueur/artist of great distinction; **de ~ internationale** of international status, in the international class; **elle a de la ~** she's got class; **ils ne sont pas de la même ~, ils n'ont pas la même ~** they're not in the same class.

(e) (*Scol: ensemble d'élèves*) form (*Brit*), class; (*division administrative*) form; (*année d'études secondaires*) year. **les grandes ~s, les ~s supérieures** the senior school, the upper forms (*Brit*) *ou* classes (*US*); **les petites ~s** the junior school, the lower forms (*Brit*) *ou* classes (*US*); **il est en ~ de 6e** he is in the 1st year; **toutes les ~s de 1ère** all the 6th forms (*Brit*), all the 6th year; **monter de ~** to go up a class; **il est (le) premier/(le) dernier de la ~** he is top/bottom of the form (*Brit*) *ou* class; **~ enfantine** play-school; *V* **redoubler.**

(f) (*Scol*) (*cours, leçon*) class. (*l'école*) **la ~** school; **la ~ d'histoire/de français** the history/French class; **aller en ~** to go to school; **pendant/après la ~ *ou* les heures de ~** during/after school *ou* school hours; **à l'école primaire la ~ se termine *ou* les élèves sortent de ~ à 16 heures** school finishes *ou* classes finish at 4 o'clock in primary school; **il est en ~** (*en cours*) *[professeur]* he is in class, he is teaching; *[élève]* he is in class *ou* at lessons; (*à l'école*) *[élève]* he is at school; **faire la ~: c'est M X qui leur fait la ~** Mr X is their (primary school) teacher, Mr X takes them at (primary) school.

(g) (*Scol: salle*) classroom. **il est turbulent en ~** he's disruptive in class *ou* in the classroom; **les élèves viennent d'entrer en ~** the pupils have just gone into class.

(h) (*Mil*) (*rang*) **militaire *ou* soldat de 1ère ~** (*armée de terre*) ≃ private (*Brit*), private first class (*US*); (*armée de l'air*) ≃ leading aircraftman (*Brit*), airman first class (*US*); **militaire *ou* soldat de 2e ~** (*terre*) private (soldier); (*air*) aircraftman (*Brit*), airman basic (*US*); (*contingent*) **la ~ de 1972** the 1972 class; **ils sont de la même ~** they were called up at the same time; **faire ses ~s** to do one's recruit training.

classé, e [klɑse] *adj bâtiment, monument etc* listed, with a preservation order on it; *vins* classified. **joueur ~** ≃ (*Tennis*) officially graded player; (*Bridge*) graded *ou* master player.

classement [klɑsmɑ̃] *nm* **(a)** (*rangement*) *[papiers]* filing; *[livres]* classification; *[fruits]* grading. **faire un ~ par ordre de taille** to grade by size; **faire un ~ par sujet** to classify by subject matter; **j'ai fait du ~ toute la journée** I've spent all day filing *ou* classifying; **~ alphabétique** alphabetical classification.

(b) (*classification*) *[fonctionnaire, élève]* grading; *[joueur]* grading, ranking; *[hôtel]* grading, classification. **on devrait supprimer le ~ des élèves** they ought to stop grading pupils.

(c) (*rang*) *[élève]* place (in class), position in class; *[coureur]* placing. **aitir un bon ~** to be well placed; **le ~ des coureurs à l'arrivée** the placing of the runners at the finishing line.

(d) (*liste*) *[élèves]* class list (in order of merit); *[coureurs]* finishing list. **je vais vous lire le ~** I'm going to read you your (final) placings (in class); (*Cyclisme*) **premier au ~ général/au ~ de l'étape** first overall/for the stage; (*Sport*) **~ général** overall placing(s).

(e) (*clôture*) *[affaire]* closing.

classer [klɑse] (1) **1** *vt* **(a)** (*ranger*) *papiers* to file; *livres* to classify; *documents* to file, classify. **~ des livres par sujet** to classify books by *ou* according to subject (matter).

(b) (*Sci: classifier*) *animaux, plantes* to classify.

(c) (*hiérarchiser*) *employé, fruits* to grade; *élève, joueur, copie* to grade; *hôtel* to grade, classify. **~ des copies de composition (par ordre de mérite)** to arrange *ou* grade exam papers in order of merit; **X, que l'on classe parmi les meilleurs violonistes** X, who ranks among the top violin players.

(d) (*clore*) *affaire, dossier* to close. **c'est une affaire classée maintenant** that matter is closed now.

(e) (*péj: cataloguer*) *personne* to size up*, categorize.

2 se classer *vpr*: **se ~ premier/parmi les premiers** to be *ou* come first/among the first; (*Courses*) **le favori s'est classé 3e** the favourite finished *ou* came 3rd; **ce livre se classe au nombre des grands chefs-d'œuvre littéraires** this book ranks among the great works of literature.

classeur [klɑsœʀ] *nm* (*meuble*) filing cabinet; (*dossier*) (loose-leaf) file.

classicisme [klasisism(ə)] *nm* (*Art*) classicism; (*gén: conformisme*) conventionality.

classificateur, -trice [klasifikatœʀ, tʀis] **1** *adj procédé, méthode* classifying; (*fig: méthodique*) *esprit* methodical, orderly. **obsession ~trice** mania for categorizing *ou* classifying things. **2** *nm,f* classifier.

classification [klasifikɑsjɔ̃] *nf* classification.

classifier [klasifje] (7) *vt* to classify.

classique [klasik] **1** *adj* **(a)** (*Art*) *auteur, genre, musique* classical; (*Ling*) *langue* classical. **il préfère le ~** he prefers classical music (*ou* literature, painting *etc*).

(b) (*sobre*) *coupe, vêtement, ameublement, décoration* classic, classical. **j'aime mieux le ~ que tous ces meubles modernes** I prefer a classic *ou* classical style of furniture to any of these modern styles.

(c) (*habituel*) *argument, réponse, méthode* standard, classic; *conséquence* usual; *symptôme* usual, classic. **c'est ~!** it's the usual *ou* classic situation!; **c'est le coup ~!*** it's the usual thing; **c'est la question/la plaisanterie ~ dans ces cas-là** it's the classic question/joke on those occasions; **son mari buvait, alors elle l'a quitté, c'est ~** her husband drank, so she left him — it's the usual *ou* classic situation; **le cambriolage s'est déroulé suivant le plan ~** the burglary followed the standard *ou* recognized pattern.

(d) (*banal*) *situation, maladie* classic, standard. **grâce à une opération maintenant ~, on peut guérir cette infirmité** thanks to an operation which is now quite usual *ou* standard, this disability can be cured.

(e) (*Scol: littéraire*) **faire des études ~s** to do classical studies, study classics; **il est en section ~** he's in the classics stream; *V* **lettre.**

2 *nm* **(a)** (*auteur*) (*Antiq*) classical author; (*classicisme français*) classic, classicist. (*grand écrivain*) **(auteur) ~** classic (author); **bien qu'il soit encore vivant, cet écrivain est déjà un ~** although he's still alive, this author is already a classic.

(b) (*ouvrage*) classic. **un ~ du cinéma** a classic of the cinema; **c'est un ~ du genre** it's a classic of its kind; (*hum*) **je connais mes ~s!*** I know my classics!

classiquement [klasikmɑ̃] *adv* classically.

claudication [klodikɑsjɔ̃] *nf* (*littér*) limp.

claudiquer [klodike] (1) *vi* (*littér*) to limp.

clause [kloz] *nf* (*Gram, Jur*) clause. **~ pénale** penalty clause; **~ de style** standard *ou* set clause.

claustral, e, *mpl* **-aux** [klostʀal, o] *adj* monastic.

claustration [klostʀɑsjɔ̃] *nf* confinement.

claustrer [klostʀe] (1) **1** *vt* (*enfermer*) to confine. **2 se claustrer** *vpr* to shut o.s. up *ou* away. (*fig*) **se ~ dans** to wrap *ou* enclose o.s. in.

claustrophobie [klostʀɔfɔbi] *nf* claustrophobia.

clausule [klozyl] *nf* clausula.

clavecin [klavsɛ̃] *nm* harpsichord.

claveciniste [klavsinist(ə)] *nmf* harpsichordist.

clavette [klavɛt] *nf* (*Tech*) *[boulon etc]* key, cotter pin.

clavicorde [klavikɔʀd(ə)] *nm* clavichord.

clavicule [klavikyl] *nf* collarbone, clavicle (*T*).

clavier [klavje] *nm* (*lit*) keyboard; (*fig: registre*) range. **à un/deux ~(s)** *orgue, clavecin* single-/double-manual (*épith*).

clayette [klɛjɛt] *nf* (*gén*) wicker *ou* wire tray *ou* rack; (*cageot à fruits*) tray.

clayon [klɛjɔ̃] *nm [fromage]* wicker tray; *[pâtisserie]* pastry-cook's wire tray.

clé [kle] = **clef.**

clébard* [klebaʀ] *nm,* **clebs*** [klɛps] *nm* (*péj: chien*) dog, hound (*hum*).

clef [kle] **1** *nf* **(a)** *[serrure, pendule, boîte de conserve]* key; *[poêle]* damper; (*fig*) *[mystère, réussite, code]* key (*de* to); (*position stratégique*) key. **la ~ de la porte d'entrée** the door key; **la ~ est sur la porte** the key is in the door; **Avignon, ~ de la Provence** Avignon, the key to Provence; *V* **fermer, tour²**.

(b) (*Tech*) spanner. **un jeu de ~s** a set of spanners.

(c) (*Mus*) *[guitare, violon]* peg; *[clarinette]* key; *[gamme]* clef; *[accordeur]* key. **~ de fa/de sol/d'ut** bass *ou* F/treble *ou* G/alto *ou* C clef; **trois dièses à la ~** 3 sharps; **avec une altération à la ~** with a change in the key signature.

(d) (*loc*) **personnage à ~s** real-life character disguised under a fictitious name; **roman** *ou* **livre à ~s** roman à clef, *novel in which actual persons appear as fictitious characters*; (*Comm*) **acheter un appartement ~s en main** to buy a flat ready for immediate occupation *ou* with immediate entry; **prix ~s en main** *[voiture]* price on the road; *[appartement]* price with immediate entry *ou* possession; (*fig*) **à la ~*: il y a une récompense à la ~** there's a reward at the end of it all *ou* at the end of the day; **je vais les mettre en retenue, avec un devoir à la ~** I'll keep them behind, and give them an exercise into the bargain; **mettre sous ~** (*à l'abri, en prison*) to put under lock and key; (*fig*) **mettre la ~ sous la porte** *ou* **le paillasson** to do a bunk* (*Brit*), clear out; **prendre la ~ des champs** *[criminel]* to take to the country, clear out; (*gén*) to run away *ou* off; **donner la ~ des champs à qn/un animal** to let sb/an animal go, give sb/an animal his/its freedom.

2 *adj inv* key (*épith*). **position-/industrie-~** key position/industry; *V* **mot.**

3: clef anglaise (monkey) wrench; (*Aut*) **clef de contact** ignition key; **clef forée** pipe key; **clef à molette** adjustable wrench *ou* spanner; **clef à pipe** box spanner (*Brit*), box wrench (*US*); **clef plate** spanner (*Brit*), wrench (*US*); (*Archit, fig*) **clef de voûte** keystone.

clématite [klematit] *nf* clematis.

clémence [klemɑ̃s] *nf* (*douceur*) *[temps]* mildness, clemency (*frm*); (*indulgence*) *[juge etc]* clemency, leniency.

clément, e [klemɑ̃, ɑ̃t] *adj* (*doux*) *temps* mild, clement (*frm*); (*indulgent*) *juge etc* lenient. (*hum, littér*) **sous un ciel plus ~** in milder climes; **se montrer ~** to show clemency.

clémentine [klemɑ̃tin] *nf* clementine.

clenche [klɑ̃ʃ] *nf* latch.

Cléopâtre [kleɔpatʀ] *nf* Cleopatra.

cleptomane [klɛptɔman] *nmf* = **kleptomane.**

cleptomanie [klɛptɔmani] *nf* = **kleptomanie.**

clerc [klɛʀ] *nm* **(a)** *[notaire etc]* clerk; *V* **pas¹**.

(b) (*Rel*) cleric.

(c) (†: *lettré*) (learned) scholar. **être (grand) ~ en la matière** to be an expert on the subject; **on n'a pas besoin d'être grand ~ pour deviner ce qui s'est passé!** you don't need to be a genius to guess what happened!

clergé [klɛʀʒe] *nm* clergy.

clérical, e, *mpl* **-aux** [kleʀikal, o] **1** *adj* (*Rel*) clerical. **2** *nm,f* clerical, supporter of the clergy.

cléricalisme [kleʀikalism(ə)] *nm* clericalism.

clic [klik] *nm* click. **le ~-clac des sabots de cheval** the clip(pety)-clop of the horses' hooves; **le ~-clac de talons sur le parquet** the tap *ou* the clickety-clack of heels on the wooden floor.

cliché [kliʃe] *nm* (*lieu commun*) cliché; (*Phot*) negative; (*Typ*) plate.

client, e [klijɑ̃, ɑ̃t] *nm,f* **(a)** *[magasin, restaurant]* customer; *[coiffeur]* client, customer; *[avocat]* client; *[hôtel]* guest, patron; *[médecin]* patient; *[taxi]* fare. **être ~ d'un magasin** to patronize a shop, be a regular customer at a shop; **le boucher me sert bien parce que je suis (une) ~e** the butcher gives me good service as I'm a regular customer (of his) *ou* as I'm one of his regulars; (*Écon*) **la France est un gros ~ de l'Allemagne** France is a large trading customer of Germany.

(b) (**péj: individu*) bloke* (*Brit*), guy*. **c'est un drôle de ~** he's an odd customer *ou* bloke*; **pour le titre de champion du monde, X est un ~ sérieux** X is a hot contender for *ou* X is making a strong bid for the title of world champion.

(c) (*Antiq: protégé*) client.

clientèle [klijɑ̃tɛl] *nf* **(a)** (*ensemble des clients*) *[restaurant, hôtel, coiffeur]* clientèle; *[magasin]* customers, clientèle; *[avocat, médecin]* practice; *[taxi]* fares. **le boucher a une nombreuse ~** the butcher has a large clientèle *ou* has many customers; (*Pol, fig*) **le candidat a conservé sa ~ électorale au 2e tour** the candidate held on to his voters at the second round; **la ~ d'un parti politique** the supporters of a political party.

(b) (*fait d'être client*) custom. **accorder sa ~ à qn** to give sb one's custom, patronize sb; **retirer sa ~ à qn** to withdraw one's custom from sb.

(c) (*Antiq: protégés*) clients.

clignement [kliɲmɑ̃] *nm* blinking (*U*). **cela l'obligeait à des ~s d'yeux continuels** it made him blink continually; **un ~ d'œil** a wink.

cligner [kliɲe] (1) *vt, vt indir:* **~ les** *ou* **des yeux** (*clignoter*) to blink; (*fermer à moitié*) to screw up one's eyes; **~ de l'œil** to wink (*en direction de* at).

clignotant, e [kliɲɔtɑ̃, ɑ̃t] **1** *adj lumière* (*vacillant*) flickering; (*intermittent, pour signal*) flashing, winking. **il entra, les yeux ~s** he came in blinking (his eyes). **2** *nm* (*Aut*) indicator, trafficator; (*Écon fig: indice de danger*) warning light (*fig*). (*Aut*) **mettre son ~ pour tourner** to indicate that one is about to turn.

clignotement [kliɲɔtmɑ̃] *nm* (*V* **clignoter**) blinking; twinkling; flickering; flashing, winking. **les ~s de la lampe** the flickering of the lamplight.

clignoter [kliɲɔte] (1) *vi [yeux]* to blink; *[étoile]* to twinkle; *[lumière]* (*vaciller*) to flicker; (*vu de loin*) to twinkle; (*de manière intermittente, pour signal*) to flash, wink. **~ des yeux** to blink.

climat [klima] *nm* (*lit, fig*) climate; (*littér: contrée*) clime (*littér*).

climatique [klimatik] *adj* climatic; *V* **station.**

climatisation [klimatizɑsjɔ̃] *nf* air conditioning.

climatiser [klimatize] (1) *vt pièce, atmosphère* to air-condition; (*Tech*) *appareil* to adapt for use in severe conditions.

climatiseur [klimatizœʀ] *nm* air conditioner.

climatologie [klimatɔlɔʒi] *nf* climatology.

climatologique [klimatɔlɔʒik] *adj* climatological.

clin [klɛ̃] *nm:* **~ d'œil** wink; **des ~s d'œil** *ou* **d'yeux** winks; **faire un ~ d'œil** to wink (*à* at); **en un ~ d'œil** in a flash, in the twinkling of an eye.

clinfoc [klɛ̃fɔk] *nm* flying jib.

clinicien [klinisjɛ̃] *nm* clinician.

clinique [klinik] **1** *adj* clinical. **2** *nf* **(a)** (*établissement*) nursing home, private hospital, private clinic; (*section d'hôpital*) clinic. **~ d'accouchement** maternity home; *V* **chef¹**. **(b)** (*enseignement*) clinic.

clinquant, e [klɛ̃kɑ̃, ɑ̃t] **1** *adj bijoux, décor, langage* flashy. **2** *nm* (*lamelles brillantes*) tinsel; (*faux bijoux*) imitation *ou* tawdry jewellery; (*fig*) *[opéra, style]* flashiness.

clip [klip] *nm* brooch.

clique [klik] *nf* **(a)** (*péj: bande*) clique, set. **(b)** (*Mil: orchestre*) band (of bugles and drums). **(c) prendre ses ~s et ses claques (et s'en aller)** to pack up (and go), pack one's bags (and leave).

cliquet [klikɛ] *nm* pawl.

cliqueter [klikte] (4) *vi [monnaie]* to jingle, clink, chink; *[dés]* to rattle; *[vaisselle]* to clatter; *[verres]* to clink, chink; *[chaînes]* to clank; *[ferraille]* to jangle; *[mécanisme]* to go clickety-clack; *[armes]* to clash; (*Aut*) *[moteur]* to pink, knock. **j'entends quelque chose qui cliquette** I (can) hear something clinking.

cliquetis [klikti] *nm [clefs]* jingle (*U*), clink (*U*); jingling (*U*), clinking (*U*); *[vaisselle]* clatter (*U*); *[verres]* clink (*U*), clinking (*U*); *[chaînes]* clank (*U*), clanking (*U*); *[ferraille]* jangle (*U*), jangling (*U*); *[mécanisme]* clickety-clack (*U*); *[armes]* clash (*U*); (*Aut*) *[moteur]* pinking *ou* knocking sound, pinking (*U*); *[machine à écrire]* rattle (*U*), clicking (*U*). **on entendait un ~** *ou* **des ~ de vaisselle** we could hear the clatter of dishes; **des ~ se firent entendre** clinking noises could be heard; **un ~ de mots** a jingle of words.

clisse [klis] *nf* **(a)** *[fromage]* wicker tray. **(b)** *[bouteille]* wicker covering.

clisser [klise] (1) *vt bouteille* to cover with wicker(work).

clitoridien, -ienne [klitɔʀidjɛ̃, jɛn] *adj* clitoral.

clitoris [klitɔʀis] *nm* clitoris.

clivage [klivaʒ] *nm* (*Géol: fissure*) cleavage; (*Minér*) (*action*) cleaving; (*résultat*) cleavage; (*fig*) *[groupes]* cleavage, split, division; *[idées]* distinction, split (*de* in).

cliver *vt,* **se cliver** *vpr* [klive] (1) (*Minér*) to cleave.

cloaque [klɔak] *nm* (*fig: égout*) cesspool, cesspit; (*Zool*) cloaca.

clochard, e* [klɔʃaʀ, aʀd(ə)] *nm,f* down-and-out, tramp.

cloche [klɔʃ] **1** *nf* **(a)** *[église etc]* bell. **en forme de ~** bell-shaped; **courbe en ~** bell-shaped curve; *V* **son²**.

(b) (*couvercle*) *[plat]* dishcover, lid; *[plantes, légumes]* cloche.

(c) (*) (*imbécile*) clot* (*Brit*), lout; (*clochard*) tramp, down-and-out. **la ~** (*les clochards*) (the) down-and-outs; (*l'existence de clochard*) a tramp's life.

(d) (*Chim*) bell jar.

(e) (*chapeau*) cloche (hat).

2 *adj* **(a)** (*évasé*) *jupe* bell-shaped. **chapeau ~** cloche hat.

(b) (*: *idiot*) idiotic, silly. **qu'il est ~ ce type!** what a (silly) clot* (*Brit*) *ou* lout he is!

3: cloche à fromage cheese-cover; **cloche à plongeur** diving bell.

cloche-pied [klɔʃpje] *adv:* **à ~** hopping; **il partit (en sautant) à ~** he hopped away *ou* off.

clocher¹ [klɔʃe] *nm* **(a)** (*Archit*) (*en pointe*) steeple; (*quadrangulaire*) church tower. **(b)** (*fig: paroisse*) **revoir son ~** to see one's native heath again; **de ~** *mentalité* parochial, small-town (*épith*); *rivalités* local, parochial; *V* **esprit.**

clocher² [klɔʃe] (1) *vi* **(a)** (*: *être défectueux*) *[raisonnement]* to be cockeyed*. **qu'est-ce qui cloche donc?** what's up (with you)?*; **pourvu que rien ne cloche** provided nothing goes wrong *ou* there are no hitches; **il y a quelque chose qui cloche (dans ce qu'il dit)** there's something which doesn't quite fit *ou* something not quite right in what he says; **il y a quelque chose qui cloche dans le moteur** there's something not quite right *ou* there's something up* with the engine.

(b) (*rare: boiter*) to limp.

clocheton [klɔʃtɔ̃] *nm* (*Archit*) pinnacle.

clochette [klɔʃɛt] *nf* (small) bell; (*Bot*) (*partie de fleur*) bell; (*fleur*) bellflower.

cloison [klwazɔ̃] *nf* **(a)** (*Constr*) partition (wall).

(b) (*Anat, Bot*) septum, partition.

(c) (*Naut*) bulkhead. **~ étanche** (*lit*) watertight compartment; (*fig*) impenetrable barrier.

(d) (*fig*) barrier. **les ~s entre les différentes classes sociales** the barriers between the different social classes.

cloisonnage [klwazɔnaʒ] *nm* partitioning.

cloisonné, e [klwazɔne] (*ptp de* **cloisonner**) *adj:* **être ~** *[sciences, services administratifs]* to be (highly) compartmentalized, be cut off from one another; **se sentir ~** to feel shut *ou* cut off; **nous vivons dans un monde ~** we live in a compartmentalized world.

cloisonnement [klwazɔnmɑ̃] *nm* (*V* **cloisonner**: *action, résultat*) dividing up; partitioning (off); compartmentalization.

cloisonner [klwazɔne] (1) *vt maison* to divide up, partition; *tiroir* to divide up; (*fig: compartimenter*) *activités, secteurs* to compartmentalize.

cloître [klwatʀ(ə)] *nm* cloister.

cloîtrer [klwatʀe] (1) **1** *vt* (*enfermer*) to shut away (*dans* in); (*Rel*) to cloister. **~ une jeune fille** (*lit*) to put a girl in a convent; (*fig*) to keep a girl shut away (from the rest of society); **couvent/religieux cloîtré** enclosed order/monk.

2 se cloîtrer *vpr* (*s'enfermer*) to shut o.s. up *ou* away, cloister o.s. (*dans* in); (*Rel*) to enter a convent *ou* monastery. **il est resté cloîtré dans sa chambre pendant 2 jours** he stayed shut up *ou* away in his room for 2 days; **ils vivent cloîtrés chez eux sans jamais voir personne** they cut themselves off from the world *ou* they live cloistered lives and never see anyone.

clope* [klɔp] *nm* fag* (*Brit*), cig*.

clopin-clopant [klɔpɛ̃klɔpɑ̃] *adv* **(a)** (*en boitillant*) **marcher ~** to hobble along; **il vint vers nous ~** he hobbled towards us; **sortir/entrer ~** to hobble out/in.

(b) (*fig*) **les affaires allaient ~** business was struggling along *ou* was just ticking over; **comment ça va? — ~** how are things? — so-so.

clopiner [klɔpine] (1) *vi* (*boitiller*) to hobble *ou* limp along. **~ vers** to hobble *ou* limp to(wards).

cloporte [klɔpɔʀt(ə)] *nm* (*Zool*) woodlouse; (*fig péj*) creep*.

cloque [klɔk] *nf* [*peau, peinture*] blister; (*Bot*) peach leaf curl *ou* blister.

cloqué, e [klɔke] (*ptp de* **cloquer**) **1** *adj*: **étoffe ~e** seersucker (*U*). **2** *nm* (*Tex*) seersucker.

cloquer [klɔke] (1) **1** *vi* [*peau, peinture*] to blister. **2** *vt étoffe* to crinkle.

clore [klɔʀ] (45) *vt* **(a)** (*clôturer*) *liste, débat* to close; *livre, discours* to end, conclude; (*Fin*) *compte* to close. **la séance est close** the meeting is closed *ou* finished; **l'incident est clos** the matter is closed; **le débat s'est clos sur cette remarque** the discussion ended *ou* closed with that remark.

(b) (*être la fin de*) *spectacle, discours* to end, conclude; *livre* to end. **une description clôt le chapitre** the chapter closes *ou* ends *ou* concludes with a description.

(c) († *ou littér: conclure*) *accord, marché* to conclude.

(d) (*littér: entourer*) *terrain, ville* to enclose (*de* with).

(e) (*littér: fermer*) *porte, volets* to close, shut; *lettre* to seal; *chemin, passage* to close off, seal off. (*fig*) **~ le bec*** *ou* **la bouche à qn** to shut sb up*, make sb be quiet.

clos, e [klo, oz] (*ptp de* **clore**) **1** *adj système, ensemble* closed; *espace* enclosed. **les yeux ~** *ou* **les paupières ~es, il ...** with his eyes closed *ou* shut, he ...; *V* **huis, maison** *etc.*

2 *nm* (*pré*) (enclosed) field; (*vignoble*) vineyard. **un ~ de pommiers** an apple orchard.

Clotilde [klɔtild(ə)] *nf* Clotilda.

clôture [klotyʀ] *nf* **(a)** (*enceinte*) (*en planches*) fence, paling; (*en fil de fer*) (wire) fence; (*haies, arbustes etc*) hedge; (*en ciment*) wall. **mur/grille de ~** outer *ou* surrounding wall/railing; *V* **bris.**

(b) (*fermeture*) [*débat, liste, compte*] closing, closure; [*bureaux, magasins*] closing. (*Ciné, Théât*) **~ annuelle** annual closure; **il faut y aller avant la ~** (*du festival*) we must go before it ends *ou* is over; (*d'une pièce*) we must go before it closes *ou* ends; (*du magasin*) we must go before it closes *ou* shuts; **séance/date** *etc* **de ~** closing session/date *etc.*

(c) [*monastère*] enclosure.

clôturer [klotyʀe] (1) *vt* **(a)** *jardin, champ* to enclose, close off.

(b) *débats, liste, compte* to close; *inscriptions* to close (the list of).

clou [klu] **1** *nm* **(a)** (*gén*) nail; (*décoratif*) stud. **fixe-le avec un ~** nail it up (*ou* down *ou* on); **pendre son chapeau à un ~** to hang one's hat on a nail.

(b) [*chaussée*] stud. **traverser dans les ~s, prendre les ~s (pour traverser)** to cross at the pedestrian *ou* zebra crossing.

(c) (*Méd*)) boil.

(d) (*attraction principale*) [*spectacle*] star attraction *ou* turn. **le ~ de la soirée** the highlight *ou* the star turn of the evening.

(e) (*: *mont-de-piété*) pawnshop. **mettre sa montre au ~** to pawn one's watch, put one's watch in hock*.

(f) (*: *vieil instrument*) ancient machine *ou* implement *etc.* **(vieux) ~** (*voiture*) old banger‡ (*Brit*) *ou* crock* (*Brit*) *ou* jalopy*; (*vélo*) old boneshaker* (*Brit*).

(g) (*arg Mil: prison*) clink (*arg*), cooler (*arg*). **mettre qn au ~** to put sb in (the) clink *ou* in the cooler.

(h) (*loc*) **des ~s!‡** no go!*, nothing doing!*, not on your nelly!‡ (*Brit*); (*Prov*) **un ~ chasse l'autre** one man goes and another steps in *ou* another takes his place.

2: **clou à crochet** hook; (*Culin*) **clou de girofle** clove; **clou à souliers** tack; **clou de tapissier** (upholstery) tack; **clou sans tête** brad; **clou en U** staple.

clouage [kluaʒ] *nm* [*planches*] nailing down; [*tapis*] tacking *ou* nailing down; [*tapisserie*] nailing up.

clouer [klue] (1) *vt* **(a)** *planches, couvercle, caisse* to nail down; *tapis* to tack *ou* nail down; *tapisserie* to nail up. **il l'a cloué au sol d'un coup d'épée** he pinned him to the ground with a thrust of his sword.

(b) (*fig: immobiliser*) *ennemi, armée* to pin down. [*étonnement, peur*] **~ qn sur place** to nail *ou* root *ou* glue sb to the spot; [*maladie*] **~ qn au lit** to keep sb stuck in bed* *ou* confined to bed; (*Échecs*) **~ une pièce** to pin a piece; **être** *ou* **rester cloué de stupeur** to be glued *ou* rooted to the spot with amazement; **~ le bec à qn*** to shut sb up*.

clouté, e [klute] *adj ceinture, porte etc* studded; *souliers* hobnailed; *V* **passage.**

clouterie [klutʀi] *nf* nail factory.

clovisse [klɔvis] *nf* clam.

clown [klun] *nm* clown. **faire le ~** to clown (about), play the fool; **c'est un vrai ~** he's a real comic.

clownerie [klunʀi] *nf* clowning (*U*), silly trick. **faire des ~s** to clown (about), play the fool; **arrête tes ~s** stop your (silly) antics.

clownesque [klunɛsk(ə)] *adj comportement* clownish; *situation* farcical.

club [klœb] *nm* (*société, aussi Golf: crosse*) club; *V* **fauteuil.**

cluse [klyz] *nf* (*Géog*) transverse valley (in the Jura), cluse (*T*).

clystère†† [klistɛʀ] *nm* clyster††.

coaccusé, e [kɔakyze] *nm,f* codefendant.

coacquéreur [kɔakeʀœʀ] *nm* joint purchaser.

coadjuteur [kɔadʒytœʀ] *nm* coadjutor.

coadjutrice [kɔadʒytʀis] *nf* coadjutress.

coadministrateur [kɔadministʀatœʀ] *nm* (*Comm*) co-director; (*Jur*) co-trustee.

coagulable [kɔagylabl(ə)] *adj* which can coagulate.

coagulant, e [kɔagylɑ̃, ɑ̃t] **1** *adj* coagulative. **2** *nm* coagulant.

coagulateur, -trice [kɔagylatœʀ, tʀis] *adj* coagulative.

coagulation [kɔagylɑsjɔ̃] *nf* coagulation.

coaguler *vti*, **se coaguler** *vpr* [kɔagyle] (1) to coagulate; [*sang*] to coagulate (*T*), clot, congeal; [*lait*] to curdle.

coalisé, e [kɔalize] (*ptp de* **coaliser**) *adj* (*allié*) *pays* allied; (*conjoint*) *efforts, sentiments* united. **les ~s** the members of the coalition.

coaliser [kɔalize] (1) **1** *vt* to unite (in a coalition).

2 se coaliser *vpr* (*se liguer*) (*gén*) to unite; [*pays*] to form a coalition, unite (in a coalition). **deux des commerçants se sont coalisés contre un troisième** two of the shopkeepers joined forces *ou* united against a third; (*fig*) **tout se coalise contre moi!** everything seems to be stacked against me!, everything is conspiring against me!

coalition [kɔalisjɔ̃] *nf* coalition. (*Pol*) **ministère de ~** coalition government.

coassement [kɔasmɑ̃] *nm* croaking (*U*).

coasser [kɔase] (1) *vi* to croak.

coassocié, e [kɔasɔsje] *nm,f* copartner.

coassurance [kɔasyʀɑ̃s] *nf* mutual assurance.

coauteur [kootœʀ] *nm* **(a)** (*Littérat*) (*homme*) co-author, joint author; (*femme*) co-authoress, joint authoress. **(b)** (*Jur*) accomplice.

cobalt [kɔbalt] *nm* cobalt.

cobaye [kɔbaj] *nm* (*lit, fig*) guinea-pig. **servir de ~ à** to act as *ou* be used as a guinea-pig for.

cobelligérant, e [kɔbeliʒeʀɑ̃, ɑ̃t] *adj* cobelligerent. **les ~s** the cobelligerent nations *ou* states *etc.*

cobra [kɔbʀa] *nm* cobra.

coca [kɔka] **1** *nm* **(a)** (*: *abrév de* **Coca-Cola** ®) Coke ®. **(b)** (*aussi nf*) (*Bot: arbrisseau*) coca. **2** *nf* (*substance*) coca extract.

cocagne [kɔkaɲ] *nf V* **mât, pays**[1].

cocaïne [kɔkain] *nf* cocaine.

cocaïnomane [kɔkainɔman] *nmf* cocaine addict.

cocarde [kɔkaʀd(ə)] *nf* (*en tissu*) rosette; (*Hist: sur la coiffure*) cockade; [*avion*] roundel. (*sur voiture officielle etc*) **~ (tricolore)** ≃ official sticker; (*fig*) **changer de ~** to change sides.

cocardier, -ière [kɔkaʀdje, jɛʀ] **1** *adj* jingoist(ic), chauvinistic. **2** *nm,f* jingo(ist), chauvinist.

cocasse [kɔkas] *adj* comical, funny.

cocasserie [kɔkasʀi] *nf* comicalness, funniness; (*histoire*) comical *ou* funny story. **c'était d'une ~!** it was so funny! *ou* comical!

coccinelle [kɔksinɛl] *nf* ladybird.

coccyx [kɔksis] *nm* coccyx.

coche [kɔʃ] *nm* (*diligence*) (stage)coach. (*Hist*) **~ d'eau** horse-drawn barge; *V* **manquer, mouche.**

cochenille [kɔʃnij] *nf* cochineal.

cocher[1] [kɔʃe] (1) *vt* (*au crayon*) to tick (off); (*d'une entaille*) to notch.

cocher[2] [kɔʃe] *nm* coachman, coach driver; [*fiacre*] cabman, cabby*.

cochère [kɔʃɛʀ] *adj f V* **porte.**

Cochinchine [kɔʃɛ̃ʃin] *nf* Cochin-China.

cochon[1] [kɔʃɔ̃] *nm* **(a)** (*animal*) pig; (*: *viande*) pork (*U*). **~ d'Inde** guinea-pig; **~ de lait** (*gén*) piglet; (*Culin*) sucking-pig; *V* **manger.**

(b) (*loc*) (*hum*) **(et) ~ qui s'en dédit*** let's shake (hands) on it, cross my heart (and hope to die)*; **un ~ n'y retrouverait pas ses petits** it's like a pigsty in there, it's a real mess in there; **tout homme a dans son cœur un ~ qui sommeille** there's a bit of the animal in every man; *V* **confiture, copain** *etc.*

cochon[2], **-onne** [kɔʃɔ̃, ɔn] **1** *adj* **(a)** (‡: *obscène*) *chanson, histoire* dirty, blue, smutty; *personne* dirty-minded.

(b) **c'est pas ~!‡** (*c'est bon*) it's not at all bad; (*il n'y en a pas beaucoup*) there's precious little there.

2 *nm,f* (‡*péj: personne*) **c'est un ~!** (*sale, vicieux*) he's a dirty pig‡ *ou* beast‡; (*salaud*) he's a bastard‡ *ou* swine‡; **tu es une vraie petite ~ne, va te laver!** you're a dirty little pig‡, go and get washed!; **ce ~ de voisin/de commerçant** that swine‡ of a neighbour/shopkeeper; **quel ~ de temps!** *ou* **temps de ~!** what lousy *ou* filthy weather!*; (*: *terme amical*) **eh bien, mon ~, tu l'as échappé belle!** you had a narrow escape, you old devil!*

cochonnaille* [kɔʃɔnaj] *nf* (*charcuterie*) pork. **assiette de ~** selection of cold pork *ou* ham *etc.*

cochonner* [kɔʃɔne] (1) *vt* (*mal faire*) *travail etc* to botch (up), bungle; (*salir*) *vêtements etc* to mess up*, make filthy.

cochonnerie* [kɔʃɔnʀi] *nf* (*nourriture*) disgusting *ou* foul food, pigswill* (*U*); (*marchandise*) rubbish (*U*), trash (*U*); (*plaisanterie*) smutty *ou* dirty joke; (*tour*) dirty *ou* low trick; (*saleté*) filth (*U*), filthiness (*U*). **faire une ~ à qn** to play a dirty trick on sb; **ne fais pas de ~s dans la cuisine, elle est toute propre** don't make a mess in the kitchen, it's clean.

cochonnet [kɔʃɔnɛ] *nm* (*Zool*) piglet; (*Boules*) jack.

cocktail [kɔktɛl] *nm* (*réunion*) cocktail party; (*boisson*) cocktail; (*fig*) mixture, potpourri.

coco[1] [koko] *nm* **(a)** (*langage enfantin: œuf*) eggie (*langage enfantin*).
(b) (*terme d'affection*) pet, darling, poppet*. **oui, mon ~** yes, darling.
(c) (*‡péj: type*) bloke* (*Brit*), guy*. **un drôle de ~** an odd bloke* (*Brit*) *ou* guy*.
(d) (*péj: communiste*) commie*.
(e) (*‡: estomac*) **n'avoir rien dans le ~** to have an empty belly‡.
(f) (*poudre de réglisse*) liquorice powder; (*boisson*) liquorice water.
(g) (†: *noix*) coconut. **beurre/lait de ~** coconut butter/milk; *V* **noix.**

coco[2] [koko] *nf* (*arg Drogue: cocaïne*) snow (*arg*), coke (*arg*).

cocon [kɔkɔ̃] *nm* cocoon; (*fig*) shell.

cocorico [kɔkɔʀiko] *nm, excl* cock-a-doodle-do.

cocoter‡ [kɔkɔte] (4) *vi* (*sentir mauvais*) to pong‡ (*Brit*), stink.

cocotier [kɔkɔtje] *nm* coconut palm *ou* tree.

cocotte [kɔkɔt] **1** *nf* **(a)** (*langage enfantin: poule*) hen, cluck-cluck (*langage enfantin*).
(b) (**péj: femme*) tart*.
(c) (*à un cheval*) **allez ~!, hue ~!** gee up!
(d) (*terme d'affection*) **ma ~*** pet, sweetie*.
(e) (*marmite*) casserole. **faire un poulet à la ~** to casserole a chicken; **poulet/veau (à la) ~** casserole of chicken/veal.
2: cocotte minute ® pressure cooker; **cocotte en papier** paper shape.

cocu, e‡ [kɔky] **1** *adj* cuckold†. **elle l'a fait ~** she was unfaithful to him, she cuckolded him†. **2** *nm,f* cuckold†; *V* **veine.**

cocuage‡ [kɔkyaʒ] *nm* cuckoldry.

cocufier‡ [kɔkyfje] (7) *vt* to cuckold†, be unfaithful to.

coda [kɔda] *nf* (*Mus*) coda.

codage [kɔdaʒ] *nm* coding, encoding.

code [kɔd] *nm* **(a)** (*Jur*) code. **~ civil** civil code, ≃ common law; **~ pénal** penal code; **~ maritime/de commerce** maritime/commercial law; (*Aut*) **C~ de la route** highway code; (*Aut*) **il a eu le ~, mais pas la conduite** he passed on the highway code but not on the driving.
(b) (*fig: règles*) code. **~ de la politesse/de l'honneur** code of politeness/honour.
(c) *[message]* (*gén, Sci*) code. **~ (secret)** (secret) code; **écrire qch en ~** to write sth in code; **mettre qch en ~** to code *ou* encode sth, put sth in code.
(d) (*Aut*) **(phares)** ~ dipped (head)lights (*Brit*), low beams (*US*); **mettre ses ~s, se mettre en ~** to dip one's (head)lights (*Brit*), put on the low beams (*US*); **rouler en ~** to drive on dipped (head)lights (*Brit*) *ou* low beams (*US*).

codébiteur, -trice [kodebitœʀ, tʀis] *nm,f* joint debtor.

codemandeur, -eresse [kodmɑ̃dœʀ, dʀɛs] *nm,f* joint plaintiff.

coder [kɔde] (1) *vt* to code.

codétenteur, -trice [kodetɑ̃tœʀ, tʀis] *nm,f* (*Jur*) joint holder; (*Sport*) *[record, titre]* joint holder.

codétenu, e [kodɛtny] *nm,f* prisoner, inmate. **avec ses ~s** with his fellow prisoners *ou* inmates.

codex [kɔdɛks] *nm*: **C~** pharmacopoeia (*officially approved*).

codicillaire [kɔdisilɛʀ] *adj* (*Jur*) codicillary.

codicille [kɔdisil] *nm* (*Jur*) codicil.

codificateur, -trice [kɔdifikatœʀ, tʀis] **1** *adj tendance, esprit* codifying. **2** *nm,f* codifier.

codification [kɔdifikasjɔ̃] *nf* codification.

codifier [kɔdifje] (7) *vt* (*Jur, systématiser*) to codify.

codirecteur, -trice [kodiʀɛktœʀ, tʀis] *nm,f* co-director, joint manager (*ou* manageress).

coefficient [kɔefisjɑ̃] *nm* (*Scol*) *[note] relative importance given to a particular mark when calculating an average.* (*Math, Phys*) coefficient. **~ d'erreur** margin of error; **~ de sécurité** safety margin; **~ d'élasticité** modulus of elasticity; **~ de dilatation** coefficient of expansion.

cœnesthésie [senɛstezi] *nf* = **cénesthésie.**

coéquipier, -ière [koekipje, jɛʀ] *nm,f* team mate.

coercitif, -ive [kɔɛʀsitif, iv] *adj* coercive.

coercition [kɔɛʀsisjɔ̃] *nf* coercion.

cœur [kœʀ] *nm* **(a)** (*Anat*) heart. (*lit, hum*) **c'est une chance que j'ai le ~ solide** it's a good thing I haven't got a weak heart; **il faut avoir le ~ bien accroché pour risquer ainsi sa vie** you need guts* *ou* a strong stomach to risk your life like that; **serrer *ou* presser qn contre *ou* sur son ~** to hold *ou* clasp *ou* press sb to one's heart *ou* breast; **opération à ~ ouvert** open-heart operation; **on l'a opéré à ~ ouvert** he had an open-heart operation; **maladie de ~** heart complaint *ou* trouble; **avoir le ~ malade** to have a weak heart *ou* a heart condition; *V* **battement, greffe**[1].
(b) (*fig: estomac*) **avoir mal au ~** to feel sick; **cela me soulève le ~** it nauseates me, it makes me (feel) sick; **ça vous fait mal au ~ de penser que** it is sickening to think that; **une odeur/un spectacle qui soulève le ~** a nauseating *ou* sickening smell/sight; *V* **haut.**
(c) (*siège des sentiments, de l'amour*) heart. (*forme d'adresse*) **mon ~**† dear heart†; (*à un enfant*) sweetheart; **avoir un *ou* le ~ sensible** to be sensitive *ou* tender-hearted; **un dur au ~ tendre** someone whose bark is worse than his bite; **elle lui a donné son ~** she has lost her heart to him *ou* given him her heart; **mon ~ se serre/se brise *ou* se fend à cette pensée** my heart sinks/breaks at the thought; **chagrin qui brise le ~** heartbreaking grief *ou* sorrow; **un spectacle à vous fendre le ~** a heartrending *ou* heartbreaking sight; **avoir le ~ gros *ou* serré** to have a heavy heart; **il avait la rage au ~** he was inwardly seething with anger; **cela m'a réchauffé le ~ de les voir** it did my heart good *ou* it was heartwarming to see them; **ce geste lui est allé (droit) au ~** he was (deeply) moved *ou* touched by this gesture, this gesture went straight to his heart; *V* **affaire, courrier** *etc.*
(d) (*bonté, générosité*) **avoir bon ~** to be kind-hearted; **avoir le ~ sur la main** to be open-handed; **manquer de ~** to be unfeeling *ou* heartless; **il a du ~** he is a good-hearted man, his heart is in the right place; **c'est un (homme) sans ~, il n'a pas de ~** he is a heartless man; **il a *ou* c'est un ~ de pierre/d'or** he has a heart of stone/gold; **un homme/une femme de ~** a noble-hearted man/woman.
(e) (*humeur*) **avoir le ~ gai *ou* joyeux/léger/triste** to feel happy/light-hearted/sad *ou* sad at heart; **je n'ai pas le ~ à rire/à sortir** I do not feel like laughing/going out, I am not in the mood for laughing/going out; **il n'a plus le ~ à rien** his heart isn't in anything any more; **si le ~ vous en dit** if you feel like it, if you are in the mood.
(f) (*âme, pensées intimes*) **c'est un ~ pur *ou* candide** he is a candid soul; **la noirceur de son ~** his blackness of heart; **la noblesse de son ~** his noble-heartedness; **connaître le fond du ~ de qn** to know sb's innermost feelings; **des paroles venues (du fond) du ~** words (coming) from the heart, heartfelt words; **dévoiler son ~ à qn** to open one's heart to sb; **elle a vidé son ~** she poured out her heart; **au fond de son ~** in his heart of hearts; **il m'a parlé à ~ ouvert** he had a heart-to-heart talk with me; *V* **cri.**
(g) (*courage, ardeur*) heart, courage. **le ~ lui manqua (pour faire)** his heart *ou* courage failed him (when it came to doing); **mettre tout son ~ dans qch *ou* à faire qch** to put all one's heart into sth *ou* into doing sth; **comment peut-on avoir le ~ de refuser?** how can one have *ou* find the heart to refuse?; **donner du ~ au ventre à qn*** to buck sb up*; **avoir du ~ au ventre*** to have guts*; **avoir du ~ à l'ouvrage** to put one's heart into one's work; **il travaille mais le ~ n'y est pas** he does the work but his heart isn't in it; **cela m'a redonné du ~** that gave me new heart.
(h) (*partie centrale*) *[chou]* heart; *[arbre, bois]* heart, core; *[fruit, pile atomique]* core; *[problème, ville]* heart. **au ~ de** *région, ville, forêt* in the heart of; **aller au ~ du sujet** to get to the heart of the matter; **au ~ de l'été** in the height of summer; **au ~ de l'hiver** in the depth *ou* heart of winter; **fromage fait à ~** fully ripe cheese; **~ de palmier** heart of palm; (*lit*) **~ d'artichaut** artichoke heart; (*fig*) **il a un ~ d'artichaut** he falls in love with every girl he meets.
(i) (*objet*) heart. **en (forme de) ~** heart-shaped; **volets percés de ~s** shutters with heart-shaped holes; *V* **bouche.**
(j) (*Cartes*) heart. **valet/as de ~** knave/ace of hearts; **avez-vous du ~?** have you any hearts?; *V* **atout, joli.**
(k) (*loc*) **par ~** *réciter, apprendre* by heart; **je la connais par ~** I know her inside out, I know her like the back of my hand; **dîner/déjeuner par ~**† to have to do without dinner/lunch; **sur le ~: ce qu'il m'a dit, je l'ai sur le ~ *ou* ça m'est resté sur le ~** what he told me still rankles with me, I still feel sore about what he told me; **je vais lui dire ce que j'ai sur le ~** I'm going to tell him what's on my mind; **à ~ joie** to one's heart's content; **de tout mon ~** with all my heart; **je vous souhaite de tout mon ~ de réussir** I wish you success with all my heart *ou* from the bottom of my heart; **être de tout ~ avec qn dans la joie/une épreuve** to share (in) sb's happiness/sorrow; **je suis de tout ~ avec vous** I DO sympathize with you; **ne pas porter qn dans son ~** to have no great liking for sb; **je veux en avoir le ~ net** I want to be clear in my own mind (about it); **avoir à ~ de faire** to make a point of doing; **prendre les choses à ~** to take things to heart; **prendre à ~ de faire** to set one's heart on doing; **ce voyage me tient à ~** I have set my heart on this journey; **ce sujet me tient à ~** this subject is close to my heart; **trouver un ami selon son ~** to find a friend after one's own heart.

coexistence [kɔɛgzistɑ̃s] *nf* coexistence. **~ pacifique** peaceful coexistence.

coexister [kɔɛgziste] (1) *vi* to coexist.

coffrage [kɔfʀaʒ] *nm* (*pour protéger, cacher*) boxing (*U*); *[galerie, tranchée]* (*dispositif, action*) coffering (*U*); *[béton]* (*dispositif*) form, formwork (*U*), shuttering; (*action*) framing.

coffre [kɔfʀ(ə)] **1** *nm* **(a)** (*meuble*) chest. **~ à linge/à outils** linen/tool chest.
(b) (*Aut*) boot (*Brit*), trunk (*US*). **~ avant/arrière** front/rear boot.
(c) (*coffrage*) (*gén*) case; *[piano]* case; *[radio etc]* cabinet.
(d) (*Hist, fig: cassette*) coffer. **les ~s de l'État** the coffers of the state; **~(-fort)** safe.
(e) (*: *poitrine*) **le ~** the chest; **il a du ~** he's got a lot of puff* (*Brit*) *ou* blow*.
2: coffre-fort *nm, pl* **coffres-forts** safe; **coffre à jouets** toybox; **coffre de voyage**† trunk.

coffrer [kɔfʀe] (1) *vt* **(a)** (*: *emprisonner*) to throw *ou* put inside*. **(b)** (*Tech*) *béton* to place a frame *ou* form for; *tranchée, galerie* to coffer.

coffret [kɔfʀɛ] *nm* casket. **~ à bijoux** jewel box, jewellery case.

cogérant [kɔʒeʀɑ̃] *nm* joint manager.

cogérante [kɔʒeʀɑ̃t] *nf* joint manageress.

cogestion [kɔʒɛstjɔ̃] *nf* co-management.

cogitation [kɔʒitɑsjɔ̃] *nf* (*hum*) cogitation.

cogiter [kɔʒite] (1) *vi* (*hum: réfléchir*) to cogitate. **qu'est-ce qu'il cogite?** what's he thinking up?

cognac [kɔɲak] *nm* cognac, (French) brandy.
cognassier [kɔɲasje] *nm* quince (tree).
cogne‡ [kɔɲ] *nm* (*policier*) cop*. **les ~s** the cops*, the fuzz‡.
cognée [kɔɲe] *nf* felling axe; *V* **jeter.**
cognement [kɔɲmɑ̃] *nm* (*V* **cogner**) banging; knocking; rapping; (*Aut*) knocking.
cogner [kɔɲe] (1) **1** *vt* **(a)** (*heurter*) to knock. **fais attention à ne pas ~ les verres** mind you don't knock the glasses against anything; **quelqu'un m'a cogné en passant** somebody knocked (into) me as he went by.
(b) (‡: *battre*) to beat up. **ils se sont cognés** they had a punch-up* (*surtout Brit*) *ou* fist fight.
2 *vi* **(a)** *[personne] (taper)* **~ sur** *clou, piquet* to hammer; *mur* to bang *ou* knock on; (*fort*) to hammer *ou* rap on; **~ du poing sur la table** to bang *ou* thump one's fist on the table; **~ à la porte/au plafond** to knock at the door/on the ceiling; (*fort*) to bang *ou* rap at the door/on the ceiling.
(b) *[volet, battant]* to bang (*contre* against). *[objet lancé, caillou]* **~ contre** to hit, strike; **un caillou est venu ~ contre le pare-brise** a stone hit the windscreen; **il y a un volet qui cogne (contre le mur)** there's a shutter banging (against the wall); (*Aut*) **le moteur cogne** the engine's knocking.
(c) (*) *[boxeur, bagarreur]* to hit out; (*fig*) *[soleil]* to beat down. **ça va ~ à la manif*** there's going to be some rough stuff at the demo*; **ce boxeur-là, il cogne dur** that boxer's a hard hitter, that boxer hits hard.
3 se cogner *vpr*: **se ~ contre un mur** to bang o.s. on *ou* against a wall; **se ~ la tête/le genou contre un poteau** to bang one's head/knee on *ou* against a post; (*fig*) **c'est à se ~ la tête contre les murs** it's enough to drive you up the wall.
cogneur* [kɔɲœʀ] *nm* (*bagarreur, boxeur*) bruiser*.
cognitif, -ive [kɔgnitif, iv] *adj* cognitive.
cognition [kɔgnisjɔ̃] *nf* cognition.
cohabitation [kɔabitɑsjɔ̃] *nf* living together, living under the same roof. **le caractère de son mari rendait la ~ impossible** her husband's character made living together *ou* living under the same roof impossible.
cohabiter [kɔabite] (1) *vi* to live together, live under the same roof. **la crise du logement les oblige à ~ avec leurs grands-parents** the shortage of accommodation forces them to live with their grandparents.
cohérence [kɔeʀɑ̃s] *nf* (*V* **cohérent**) coherence; consistency. **la ~ de l'équipe laisse à désirer** the team is not as well-knit as one would like.
cohérent, e [kɔeʀɑ̃, ɑ̃t] *adj ensemble, arguments* coherent, consistent; *conduite, roman* consistent; *équipe* well-knit.
cohéritier [kɔeʀitje] *nm* joint heir, coheir.
cohéritière [kɔeʀitjɛʀ] *nf* joint heiress, coheiress.
cohésif, -ive [kɔezif, iv] *adj* cohesive.
cohésion [kɔezjɔ̃] *nf* cohesion.
cohorte [kɔɔʀt(ə)] *nf* (*groupe*) troop; (*Hist Mil*) cohort.
cohue [kɔy] *nf* (*foule*) crowd; (*bousculade*) crush.
coi, coite [kwa, kwat] *adj*: **se tenir ~, rester ~** to remain silent; **en rester ~** to be rendered speechless.
coiffe [kwaf] *nf* **(a)** *[costume régional, religieuse]* headdress.
(b) *[chapeau]* lining; (*Tech*) *[fusée]* cap; (*Anat*) *[nouveau-né]* caul.
coiffé, e [kwafe] (*ptp de* **coiffer**) *adj* **(a)** (*peigné*) **est-ce que tu es ~?** have you done your hair?; **il est toujours mal/bien ~** his hair always looks untidy/nice; **être ~ en brosse** to have a crew-cut; **être coiffé en chien fou** to have dishevelled hair; **il était ~ en arrière** he had his hair brushed *ou* combed back; *V* **né.**
(b) (*couvert*) **(il était) ~ d'un béret** (he was) wearing a beret; **le clown entra ~ d'une casserole** the clown came in with a saucepan on his head.
(c) (*entiché*) **être ~ de** to be infatuated with.
coiffer [kwafe] (1) **1** *vt* **(a)** (*arranger les cheveux de*) **~ qn** to do sb's hair; **X coiffe bien** X is a good hairdresser; **(aller) se faire ~** to (go and) have one's hair done.
(b) (*couvrir la tête de*) **~ (la tête d')un bébé d'un bonnet** to put a bonnet on a baby's head; **sa mère la coiffe de chapeaux ridicules** her mother makes her wear ridiculous hats; **ce chapeau la coiffe bien** that hat suits her; **le béret qui la coiffait** the beret she had on *ou* was wearing; **elle allait bientôt ~ Sainte Catherine** she would soon be 25 and still unmarried.
(c) (*fournir en chapeaux*) **c'est Mme X qui la coiffe** Mme X makes her hats, her hats come from Mme X.
(d) (*mettre*) *chapeau* to put on.
(e) (*surmonter*) **de lourds nuages coiffaient le sommet** heavy clouds covered the summit, the summit was topped with heavy clouds; **pic coiffé de neige** snow-capped peak.
(f) (*être à la tête de*) *organismes, services* to have overall responsibility for.
(g) (*: *dépasser*) **se faire ~** to be overtaken; **~ qn à l'arrivée** to pip sb at the post*.
2 se coiffer *vpr* **(a)** (*arranger ses cheveux*) to do one's hair.
(b) (*mettre comme coiffure*) **se ~ d'une casquette** to put on a cap; **d'habitude, elle se coiffe d'un chapeau de paille** she usually wears a straw hat.
(c) (*se fournir en chapeaux*) **se ~ chez X** to buy one's hats from X.
(d) (*péj: s'enticher de*) **se ~ de qn** to become infatuated with sb.
coiffeur [kwafœʀ] *nm [dames]* hairdresser; *[hommes]* hairdresser, barber.
coiffeuse [kwaføz] *nf* (*personne*) hairdresser; (*meuble*) dressing table.
coiffure [kwafyʀ] *nf* (*façon d'être peigné*) hair style, hairdo*; (*chapeau*) hat, headgear* (*U*). (*métier*) **la ~** hairdressing; *V* **salon.**
coin [kwɛ̃] *nm* **(a)** (*angle*) *[objet, chambre]* corner. **armoire/place de ~** corner cupboard/seat; (*Scol*) **va au ~!** go and stand in the corner!; (*Rail*) **~(-)fenêtre/(-)couloir** seat by the window/by the door.
(b) *[rue]* corner. **au ~ (de la rue)** at *ou* on the corner (of the street); **la blanchisserie fait le ~** the laundry is right on the corner; **le magasin du ~** the corner shop; **le boucher du ~** the butcher('s) at *ou* round the corner; **à tous les ~s de rue** on every street corner.
(c) *[yeux, bouche]* corner. **sourire en ~** half smile; **regard en ~** side glance; **regarder/surveiller qn du ~ de l'œil** to look at/watch sb out of the corner of one's eye.
(d) (*espace restreint*) *[plage, village, maison]* corner. (*dans un journal, magasin*) **le ~ du bricoleur** the handyman's corner; **un ~ de terre/ciel bleu** a patch of land/blue sky; **dans un ~ de sa mémoire** in a corner of her memory; **dans quel ~ l'as-tu mis?** where on earth did you put it?; **je l'ai mis dans un ~, je ne sais plus où** I put it somewhere but I can't remember where; **j'ai cherché dans tous les ~s (et recoins)** I looked in every nook and cranny; **~-bureau/-cuisine/-repas** work/kitchen/dining area; *V* **petit.**
(e) (*lieu de résidence*) area. **dans quel ~ habitez-vous?** whereabouts do you live?; **vous êtes du ~?** do you live locally? *ou* round here? *ou* in the area?; **l'épicier du ~** the local grocer; **un ~ perdu** *ou* **paumé*** a place miles from anywhere; **il y a beaucoup de pêche dans ce ~-là** there's a lot of fishing in that area; **on a trouvé un petit ~ pas cher/tranquille pour les vacances** we found somewhere nice and cheap/nice and quiet for the holidays, we found a nice inexpensive/quiet little spot for the holidays.
(f) (*objet triangulaire*) *[reliure, cartable, sous-main]* corner (piece); (*pour coincer, écarter*) wedge; (*pour graver*) die; (*poinçon*) hallmark. (*Typ*) **~ (de serrage)** quoin; (*fig*) **frappé** *ou* **marqué au ~ du bon sens** bearing the stamp of common sense.
(g) (*loc*) **je n'aimerais pas le rencontrer au ~ d'un bois** I wouldn't like to meet him on a dark night; **au ~ du feu** by the fireside, in the chimney-corner; **causerie/rêverie au ~ du feu** fireside chat/reverie.
coinçage [kwɛ̃saʒ] *nm* wedging.
coincement [kwɛ̃smɑ̃] *nm* jamming.
coincer [kwɛ̃se] (3) **1** *vt* **(a)** (*bloquer*) (*intentionnellement*) to wedge; (*accidentellement*) *tiroir, fermeture éclair* to jam. **le tiroir est coincé** the drawer is stuck *ou* jammed; **(le corps de) l'enfant était coincé sous le camion** the child('s body) was pinned under the lorry; **il se trouva coincé contre un mur par la foule** he was pinned against a wall by the crowd; **il m'a coincé entre deux portes pour me dire ...** he cornered me to tell me ...; **nous étions coincés dans le couloir/dans l'ascenseur** we were stuck *ou* jammed in the corridor/in the lift; **ils ont coincé l'armoire en voulant la faire passer par la porte** they got the wardrobe jammed *ou* stuck trying to get it through the door.
(b) (**fig: attraper*) *voleur* to pinch*, nab*; *faussaire, fraudeur* to catch up with. **je me suis fait ~** *ou* **ils m'ont coincé sur cette question** they got me on *ou* caught me out on that question, I was caught out on that question; **coincé entre son désir et la peur** caught between his desire and fear; **nous sommes coincés, nous ne pouvons rien faire** we are stuck *ou* cornered *ou* in a corner and we can't do anything.
2 se coincer *vpr* to jam, stick, get jammed *ou* stuck.
coïncidence [kɔɛ̃sidɑ̃s] *nf* (*gén, Géom*) coincidence.
coïncident, e [kɔɛ̃sidɑ̃, ɑ̃t] *adj surfaces, faits* coincident.
coïncider [kɔɛ̃side] (1) *vi [surfaces, témoignages, dates]* to coincide (*avec* with). **faire ~ l'extrémité de deux conduits** to make the ends of two pipes meet exactly; **nous sommes arrivés à faire ~ nos dates de vacances** we've managed to get the dates of our holidays to coincide.
coin-coin [kwɛ̃kwɛ̃] *nm inv [canard]* quack. **~!** quack! quack!
coïnculpé, e [kɔɛ̃kylpe] *nm,f* co-defendant.
coing [kwɛ̃] *nm* quince (*fruit*).
coït [kɔit] *nm* coitus, coition. **~ interrompu** coitus interruptus.
coite [kwat] *adj f V* **coi.**
coke [kɔk] *nm* coke.
cokéfaction [kɔkefaksjɔ̃] *nf* coking.
cokéfier [kɔkefje] (7) *vt* to coke.
cokerie [kɔkʀi] *nf* cokeworks, coking works.
col [kɔl] **1** *nm* **(a)** *[chemise, manteau]* collar. **ça bâille du ~** it gapes at the neck; **pull à ~ roulé/rond** polo-/round-neck jumper; *V* **faux**².
(b) (*Géog*) pass.
(c) (*partie étroite*) *[carafe, vase]* neck. **~ du fémur/de la vessie** neck of the thighbone/of the bladder; **elle s'est cassé le col du fémur** she has broken her hip, she fractured the neck of her thighbone; **~ de l'utérus** neck of the womb, cervix.
(d) († *ou littér: encolure, cou*) neck. **un homme au ~ de taureau** a man with a neck like a bull, a bull-necked man.
2: col blanc (*personne*) white-collar worker; **col bleu** (*ouvrier*) blue-collar worker; (*marin*) bluejacket; **col cassé** wing collar; **col-de-cygne** *nm, pl* **cols-de-cygne** *[plomberie]* swan neck; *[mobilier]* swan('s) neck; **col dur** stiff collar; **col Mao** Mao collar; **col marin** sailor's collar; **col mou** soft collar; **col officier** mandarin collar; **col roulé** polo-neck.
cola [kɔla] *nm* cola, kola.
colchique [kɔlʃik] *nm* autumn crocus, meadow saffron, colchicum (*T*).
colégataire [kɔlegatɛʀ] *nmf* joint legatee.
coléoptère [kɔleɔptɛʀ] *nm* coleopteron (*T*), coleopterous insect (*T*), beetle. **~s** coleoptera (*T*).

colère [kɔlɛʀ] **1** *nf* **(a)** (*irritation*) anger. **la ~ est mauvaise conseillère** anger is a bad counsellor; **être en ~** to be angry; **se mettre en ~** to get angry; **mettre qn en ~** to make sb angry; **passer sa ~ sur qn** to work off one's anger on sb; **en ~ contre moi-même** angry with myself, mad at myself*; **dit-il avec ~** he said angrily.
(b) (*accès d'irritation*) (fit of) rage. **il fait des ~s terribles** he has terrible fits of anger *ou* rage; **il est entré dans une ~ noire** he flew into a white rage; **faire** *ou* **piquer une ~** to throw a tantrum.
(c) (*littér*) wrath. **la ~ divine** divine wrath; **la ~ des flots/du vent** *etc* the rage *ou* wrath of the sea/of the wind *etc.*
2 *adj inv* (†) (*coléreux*) irascible; (*en colère*) irate.
coléreux, -euse [kɔleʀø, øz] *adj*, **colérique** [kɔleʀik] *adj caractère* quick-tempered, irascible; *enfant* quick-tempered, easily angered; *vieillard* quick-tempered, peppery, irascible.
colibacille [kɔlibasil] *nm* colon bacillus.
colibacillose [kɔlibasiloz] *nf* colibacillosis.
colibri [kɔlibʀi] *nm* hummingbird.
colifichet [kɔlifiʃɛ] *nm* (*bijou fantaisie*) trinket, bauble; (*babiole*) knick-knack.
colimaçon [kɔlimasɔ̃] *nm* (†) snail. (*fig*) **escalier en ~** spiral staircase.
colin [kɔlɛ̃] *nm* hake.
colineau, *pl* **~x** [kɔlino] *nm* = **colinot.**
colin-maillard [kɔlɛ̃majaʀ] *nm* blind man's buff.
colinot [kɔlino] *nm* codling.
colique [kɔlik] *nf* **(a)** (*diarrhée*) diarrhoea. **avoir la ~** (*lit*) to have diarrhoea; (*fig: peur*) to be scared stiff; (*fig*) **il me donne la ~**‡ he bores me out of my mind*.
(b) (*douleur intestinale, gén pl*) stomach pain, colic pain, colic (*U*). **être pris de violentes ~s** to have violent stomach pains; **~s hépatiques/néphrétiques** biliary/renal colic; **quelle ~!**‡ (*personne*) what a pain in the neck!‡; (*chose*) what a drag!‡
colis [kɔli] *nm* parcel. **envoyer/recevoir un ~ postal** to send/receive a parcel through the post (*Brit*) *ou* mail; **par ~ postal** by parcel post (*Brit*).
Colisée [kɔlize] *nm*: **le ~** the Coliseum.
colistier [kɔlistje] *nm* (*Pol*) fellow candidate.
colite [kɔlit] *nf* colitis.
collaborateur, -trice [kɔlabɔʀatœʀ, tʀis] *nm,f* [*personne*] colleague; [*journal, revue*] contributor; [*livre, publication*] collaborator; (*Pol*) [*ennemi*] collaborateur, collaborationist.
collaboration [kɔlabɔʀɑsjɔ̃] *nf* (*Pol, à un travail, un livre*) collaboration (*à* on); (*à un journal*) contribution (*à* to). **s'assurer la ~ de qn** to enlist the services of sb; **en ~ avec** in collaboration with.
collaborer [kɔlabɔʀe] (1) *vi* **(a)** **~ avec qn** to collaborate *ou* work with sb; **~ à** *travail, livre* to collaborate on; *journal* to contribute to. **(b)** (*Pol*) to collaborate.
collage [kɔlaʒ] *nm* **(a)** (*action*) [*objets, éléments*] sticking, gluing; pasting; [*étiquettes etc*] sticking. **~ de papiers peints** paperhanging; **~ d'affiches** billposting. **(b)** (*Art*) collage. **(c)** (*apprêt*) [*vin*] fining; [*papier*] sizing. **(d)** (*péj: concubinage*) affair. **c'est un ~** they're having an affair.
collant, e [kɔlɑ̃, ɑ̃t] **1** *adj* (*ajusté*) *vêtement* skintight, tight-fitting, clinging; (*poisseux*) sticky. (*importun*) **être ~*** to cling, stick like a leech; *V* **papier.**
2 *nm* (*maillot*) [*femme*] body stocking; [*danseur, acrobate*] leotard; (*bas*) tights.
3 collante *nf* (*arg Scol: convocation*) exam notification.
collatéral, e, *mpl* **-aux** [kɔlateʀal, o] *adj parent, artère* collateral. (**nef**) **~e** (side) aisle; **les ~aux** (*parents*) collaterals; (*Archit*) (side) aisles.
collation [kɔlɑsjɔ̃] *nf* **(a)** (*repas*) light meal, light refreshment, collation†; (*goûter*) snack. **(b)** (*V* **collationner**) collation; checking. **(c)** (*frm*) [*titre, grade*] conferment.
collationnement [kɔlɑsjɔnmɑ̃] *nm* (*V* **collationner**) collation; checking.
collationner [kɔlɑsjɔne] (1) *vt* (*comparer*) *manuscrits etc* to collate (*avec* with); (*vérifier*) *liste* to check; (*Typ*) to collate.
colle [kɔl] *nf* **(a)** (*gén*) glue; [*papiers peints*] wallpaper paste; (*apprêt*) size. **~ (blanche** *ou* **d'écolier** *ou* **de pâte)** paste; **~ (forte)** (strong) glue, adhesive; **~ (gomme)** gum; **~ à bois** wood glue; **~ de bureau** glue; **~ de poisson** fish glue; (*fig*) **ce riz, c'est de la vraie ~ (de pâte)** this rice is like paste *ou* is a gluey *ou* sticky mass; *V* **chauffer, pot.**
(b) (*: *question*) poser*, teaser. **poser une ~ à qn** to set sb a poser*; **là, vous me posez une ~** you've stumped me there*.
(c) (*arg Scol*) (*examen blanc*) mock oral exam; (*retenue*) detention. **mettre une ~ à qn** to give sb detention; **j'ai eu 3 heures de ~** I was kept in for 3 hours.
(d) (‡) **vivre** *ou* **être à la ~** to live together, shack up together‡.
collecte [kɔlɛkt(ə)] *nf* (*quête*) collection; (*Rel: prière*) collect.
collecter [kɔlɛkte] (1) *vt* to collect.
collecteur, -trice [kɔlɛktœʀ, tʀis] **1** *nm,f* (*personne*) collector. **~ d'impôts** tax collector; **~ de fonds** fund-raiser. **2** *nm* (*Aut*) manifold; (*Élec*) commutator. (*Rad*) **~ d'ondes** aerial; (**égout**) **~, (grand) ~** main sewer.
collectif, -ive [kɔlɛktif, iv] **1** *adj travail, responsabilité, punition* collective; *billet, réservation* group (*épith*); *hystérie, licenciements* mass (*épith*); *installations* public; (*Ling*) *terme, sens* collective. **faire une démarche ~ive auprès de qn** to approach sb collectively *ou* as a group; *V* **convention, ferme².**
2 *nm* (*immeuble*) (large) block (of flats) (*Brit*), apartment building (*US*); (*Gram: mot*) collective noun. (*Fin*) **~ budgétaire** ≃ Finance Bill.
collection [kɔlɛksjɔ̃] *nf* **(a)** [*timbres, papillons etc*] collection; (*Comm*) [*échantillons*] line; (*hum: groupe*) collection. **faire (la) ~ de** to collect; *V* **pièce.**
(b) (*Mode*) collection.
(c) (*Presse: série*) series, collection. **notre ~ 'jeunes auteurs'** our 'young authors' series *ou* collection; **il a toute la ~ des œuvres de X** he's got the complete collection *ou* set of X's works.
collectionner [kɔlɛksjɔne] (1) *vt* (*gén, hum*) to collect.
collectionneur, -euse [kɔlɛksjɔnœʀ, øz] *nm,f* collector.
collectivement [kɔlɛktivmɑ̃] *adv* (*gén*) collectively; *démissionner, protester* in a body, collectively.
collectivisation [kɔlɛktivizɑsjɔ̃] *nf* collectivization.
collectiviser [kɔlɛktivize] (1) *vt* to collectivize.
collectivisme [kɔlɛktivism(ə)] *nm* collectivism.
collectiviste [kɔlɛktivist(ə)] *adj, nmf* collectivist.
collectivité [kɔlɛktivite] *nf* **(a)** (*groupement*) group. (*le public, l'ensemble des citoyens*) **la ~** the community; **la ~ nationale** the Nation (as a community); (*Admin*) **les ~s locales** ≃ the local communities; **~s professionnelles** professional bodies *ou* organizations; **la ~ des habitants/des citoyens** the inhabitants/the citizens as a whole *ou* a body.
(b) (*vie en communauté*) **la ~** communal life *ou* living; **vivre en ~** to lead a communal life.
(c) (*possession commune*) collective ownership.
collège [kɔlɛʒ] *nm* **(a)** (*Scol*) (*école secondaire*) secondary school, high school (*US*); (†: *école privée*) private school. **~ d'enseignement secondaire/technique** secondary modern/technical school; (*Can*) **C~ d'enseignement général et professionnel** general and vocational college (*Can*).
(b) (*Pol, Rel: assemblée*) college. **~ électoral** body of electors, electorate, ≃ electoral college (*US*); *V* **sacré.**
collégial, e, *mpl* **-iaux** [kɔleʒjal, jo] *adj* (*Rel*) collegiate; (*Pol*) collegial, collegiate. (**église**) **~e** collegiate church.
collégialité [kɔleʒjalite] *nf* (*Pol*) collegial administration; (*Rel*) collegiality.
collégien [kɔleʒjɛ̃] *nm* schoolboy. (*fig: novice*) **c'est un ~** he's an innocent.
collégienne [kɔleʒjɛn] *nf* schoolgirl.
collègue [kɔlɛg] *nmf* colleague; *V* **Monsieur.**
coller [kɔle] (1) **1** *vt* **(a)** (*lit*) *étiquette, timbre* to stick (*sur* on); *affiche* to stick up (*à, sur* on); *enveloppe* to stick down; *papier peint* to hang. **colle-la** (*étiquette*) stick it on; (*affiche*) stick it up; (*enveloppe*) stick it down; **~ 2 morceaux (ensemble)** to stick *ou* glue *ou* paste 2 pieces together; **~ qch à** *ou* **sur qch** to stick sth on(to) sth; **les cheveux collés de sang** his hair stuck together *ou* matted with blood; **les yeux encore collés de sommeil** his eyes still half-shut with sleep.
(b) (*appliquer*) **~ son oreille à la porte/son nez contre la vitre** to press one's ear to *ou* against the door/one's nose against the window; **il colla l'armoire contre le mur** he stood the wardrobe right against the wall; **il se colla contre le mur pour les laisser passer** he pressed himself against the wall to let them pass; (*Mil*) **ils l'ont collé au mur** they stuck him up against the wall.
(c) (*: *mettre*) to stick*, shove*. **colle tes valises dans un coin** stick* *ou* plonk* *ou* shove* *ou* dump* your bags in a corner; **il en colle des pages** he writes reams; **dans ses devoirs il colle n'importe quoi** he puts *ou* sticks* *ou* shoves* any old thing (down) in his homework; **ils se collent devant la télé dès qu'ils rentrent** they're glued to the telly* as soon as they come in, they plonk themselves* in front of the telly* as soon as they come in; **ils l'ont collé ministre** they've gone and made him a minister*; *V* **poing.**
(d) (*: *donner*) **on m'a collé une fausse pièce** I've been palmed off with a dud coin; **il m'a collé une contravention/une punition/une gifle** he gave me a fine/a punishment/a clout; **on lui a collé 3 ans de prison** they've stuck him in prison for 3 years*, they've given him 3 years; **on lui a collé la responsabilité/la belle-mère** he's got (himself) stuck* *ou* landed* *ou* lumbered‡ with the responsibility/his mother-in-law.
(e) (*arg Scol*) (*consigner*) to put in detention, keep in; (*recaler, ajourner*) to fail, plough*. **se faire ~** (*en retenue*) to be put in detention, be given a detention; (*à l'examen*) to be failed, be ploughed*.
(f) (*: *embarrasser par une question*) to catch out.
(g) (*: *suivre*) *personne* to cling to. **la voiture qui nous suit nous colle de trop près** the car behind is sticking too close *ou* is sitting right on our tail*; **il m'a collé (après) toute la journée** he clung to me all day.
(h) (*apprêter*) *vin* to fine; *papier* to size.
2 *vi* **(a)** (*être poisseux*) to be sticky; (*adhérer*) to stick (*à* to).
(b) (*fig*) to cling to. **pour ne pas être distancé, le cycliste collait au peloton de tête** so as not to be outdistanced, the cyclist clung *ou* stuck close to the leaders; **robe qui colle au corps** tight-fitting *ou* clinging dress; **ils nous collent au derrière*** they're right on our tail*; **voiture qui colle à la route** car that grips the road; **un rôle qui lui colle à la peau** a part tailor-made for him, a part which fits him like a glove; **~ au sujet** to stick to the subject; **ce roman colle à la réalité** this novel sticks *ou* is faithful to reality; **mot qui colle à une idée** word which fits an idea closely.
(c) (*: *bien marcher*) **ça colle?** O.K.?*; **ça ne colle pas entre eux/nous** they/we aren't hitting it off* *ou* getting on together; **il y a quelque chose qui ne colle pas** there's something wrong *ou* amiss *ou* not right here; **ça ne colle pas, je ne suis pas libre** that's no good *ou* that won't do, I am not free; **son histoire ne colle pas** his story doesn't hold together.
3 se coller *vpr* **(a)** (‡: *subir*) *tâche, personne* to be *ou* get stuck with*, be *ou* get landed with*, be *ou* get lumbered with‡. **il va falloir se ~ la belle-mère pendant 3 jours!** we'll have to put up with the mother-in-law for 3 days!

(b) (‡: *se mettre à*) **se ~ à (faire) qch** to get stuck into (doing) sth*, get down to (doing) sth, set about (doing) sth; (*jeux d'enfants*) **c'est à toi de t'y ~** it's your turn to be it.

(c) (*s'accrocher à*) **se ~ à qn** *[danseur]* to press o.s. against sb, cling to sb; *[importun]* to stick to sb like glue *ou* like a leech; **elle dansait collée à lui** she was dancing tightly pressed against him *ou* clinging tight to him; **ces deux-là sont toujours collés ensemble‡** those two *ou* that pair always go around together *ou* are never apart.

(d) (‡: *se mettre en concubinage*) **se ~ ensemble** to live together, shack up together‡; **ils sont collés ensemble depuis 2 mois** they've been living together *ou* shacking up‡ together *ou* shacked up‡ together for 2 months.

collerette [kɔlʀɛt] *nf* (*col*) collaret; (*Hist: fraise*) ruff; (*Bot*) *[champignon]* ring, annulus; (*Tech*) *[tuyau]* flange.

collet [kɔlɛ] *nm* (*piège*) snare, noose; (*petite cape*) short cape; (*Méd*) *[dent]* neck; (*Boucherie*) neck; (*Tech*) collar, flange; (*Bot*) neck. **prendre** *ou* **saisir qn au ~** to seize sb by the collar, grab sb by the throat; (*fig*) **mettre la main au ~ de qn** to get hold of sb, collar sb; **elle est très ~ monté** she's very strait-laced.

colleter [kɔlte] (4) **1** *vt adversaire* to seize by the collar, grab by the throat. **il s'est fait ~ (par la police) en sortant du bar*** he was collared (by the police) as he came out of the bar.

2 se colleter* *vpr* (*se battre*) to have a tussle, tussle. (*lit, fig*) **se ~ avec** to wrestle *ou* grapple *ou* tussle with.

colleur, -euse [kɔlœʀ, øz] **1** *nm,f* **(a) ~ d'affiches** billsticker, billposter; **~ de papiers peints** wallpaperer. **(b)** (*arg Scol*) *mock oral examiner.* **2 colleuse** *nf* (*Ciné*) splicer.

collier [kɔlje] *nm* **(a)** *[femme]* necklace; *[chevalier, maire]* chain; *[chien, cheval, chat]* (*courroie, pelage*) collar. **~ de fleurs** garland, chain of flowers; **~ de misère** yoke of misery; **reprendre le ~*** to get back into harness; *V* **coup, franc**[1].

(b) (*barbe*) **~ (de barbe)** *narrow beard along the line of the jaw.*

(c) (*Tech*) **~ de serrage** clamp collar.

collimateur [kɔlimatœʀ] *nm* (*lunette*) collimator. (*fig*) **avoir qn/qch dans son ~** to have sb/sth in one's sights.

colline [kɔlin] *nf* hill.

collision [kɔlizjɔ̃] *nf* *[véhicules, bateaux]* collision; (*fig*) *[intérêts, manifestants]* clash. **entrer en ~** to collide, clash (*avec* with).

collocation [kɔlɔkɑsjɔ̃] *nf* (*Jur*) *classification of creditors in order of priority*; (*Ling*) collocation.

collodion [kɔlɔdjɔ̃] *nm* collodion.

colloïdal, e, *mpl* **-aux** [kɔlɔidal, o] *adj* (*Chim*) colloidal.

colloïde [kɔlɔid] *nm* (*Chim*) colloid.

colloque [kɔlɔk] *nm* colloquium, symposium; (*hum*) confab*.

collusion [kɔlyzjɔ̃] *nf* (*complicité*) collusion.

collutoire [kɔlytwaʀ] *nm* (*Méd*) oral medication (*U*); (*en bombe*) throat spray.

collyre [kɔliʀ] *nm* eye lotion, collyrium (*T*).

colmatage [kɔlmataʒ] *nm* (*V* **colmater**) sealing(-off); plugging; filling-in; closing; warping.

colmater [kɔlmate] (1) *vt* **(a)** *fuite* to seal (off), plug; *fissure, trou* to fill in, plug. (*fig, Mil*) **~ une brèche** to seal *ou* close a gap; **la fissure s'est colmatée toute seule** the crack has filled itself in *ou* sealed itself. **(b)** (*Agr*) *terrain* to warp.

colocataire [kɔlɔkatɛʀ] *nmf* *[locataire]* fellow tenant, cotenant; *[logement]* tenant, co-tenant, joint tenant.

Cologne [kɔlɔɲ] *n* Cologne; *V* **eau.**

Colomb [kɔlɔ̃] *nm* Columbus.

colombage [kɔlɔ̃baʒ] *nm* half-timbering. **maison à ~** half-timbered house.

colombe [kɔlɔ̃b] *nf* (*Orn, fig, Pol*) dove.

Colombie [kɔlɔ̃bi] *nf* Colombia.

colombien, -ienne [kɔlɔ̃bjɛ̃, jɛn] **1** *adj* Colombian. **2** *nm,f*: **C~(ne)** Colombian.

colombier [kɔlɔ̃bje] *nm* dovecote.

colombin‡ [kɔlɔ̃bɛ̃] *nm* (*étron*) turd**.

colombophile [kɔlɔ̃bɔfil] **1** *adj* pigeon-fancying, pigeon-fanciers'. **2** *nmf* pigeon-fancier.

colombophilie [kɔlɔ̃bɔfili] *nf* pigeon-fancying.

colon [kɔlɔ̃] *nm* **(a)** (*pionnier*) settler, colonist. **(b)** (*enfant*) *[colonie]* child, boarder; *[pénitencier]* child, inmate. **(c)** (*arg Mil*) colonel. **eh bien, mon ~!*** heck!*, blimey!* (*Brit*).

côlon [kolɔ̃] *nm* (*Anat*) colon.

colonel [kɔlɔnɛl] *nm* colonel; (*armée de l'air*) group captain.

colonelle [kɔlɔnɛl] *nf* (*V* **colonel**) colonel's wife; group captain's wife.

colonial, e, *mpl* **-aux** [kɔlɔnjal, o] **1** *adj* colonial; *V* **casque. 2** *nm* (*soldat*) soldier of the colonial troops; (*habitant*) colonial. **3** *nf*: **la coloniale** the (French) Colonial Army.

colonialisme [kɔlɔnjalism(ə)] *nm* colonialism.

colonialiste [kɔlɔnjalist(ə)] *adj, nmf* colonialist.

colonie [kɔlɔni] *nf* (*gén*) colony. **~ de vacances** holiday camp (*Brit*), vacation camp (*US*) (*for children*); **~ pénitentiaire**† penal settlement *ou* colony††.

colonisateur, -trice [kɔlɔnizatœʀ, tʀis] **1** *adj* colonizing (*épith*). **2** *nm,f* colonizer.

colonisation [kɔlɔnizɑsjɔ̃] *nf* colonization, settlement.

coloniser [kɔlɔnize] (1) *vt* to colonize, settle. **les colonisés** the colonized peoples.

colonnade [kɔlɔnad] *nf* colonnade.

colonne [kɔlɔn] **1** *nf* (*gén*) column; (*Archit*) column, pillar. **en ~ par deux** in double file; **mettez-vous en ~ par huit** get into eights; *V* **cinquième.**

2: colonne barométrique barometric column; **colonne blindée** armoured column; **les Colonnes d'Hercule** the Pillars of Hercules; **colonne montante** rising main; **colonne Morris** (pillar-shaped) billboard; **colonne de secours** rescue party; **colonne vertébrale** spine, spinal *ou* vertebral column (*T*).

colonnette [kɔlɔnɛt] *nf* small column.

colophane [kɔlɔfan] *nf* rosin, colophony.

coloquinte [kɔlɔkɛ̃t] *nf* (*Bot*) colocynth (*T*), bitter apple; (type of) gourd; (‡†: *tête*) nut*, bonce‡.

colorant, e [kɔlɔʀɑ̃, ɑ̃t] *adj, nm* colouring; *V* **shampooing.**

coloration [kɔlɔʀɑsjɔ̃] *nf* **(a)** (*V* **colorer**) colouring; dyeing; staining. **(b)** (*couleur, nuance*) colouring, colour, shade; *[peau]* colouring; (*fig*) *[voix, ton]* coloration.

coloré, e [kɔlɔʀe] (*ptp de* **colorer**) *adj teint* florid, ruddy; *objet* coloured; *foule* colourful; *style, description, récit* vivid, colourful.

colorer [kɔlɔʀe] (1) **1** *vt* **(a)** (*teindre*) *substance* to colour; *tissu* to dye; *bois* to stain. **~ qch en bleu** to colour (*ou* dye *ou* stain) sth blue; (*littér*) **le soleil colore les cimes neigeuses** the sun tinges the snowy peaks with colour.

(b) (*littér: enjoliver*) *récit, sentiments* to colour (*de* with).

2 se colorer *vpr* **(a)** (*prendre de la couleur*) *[tomate etc]* to turn red. **le ciel se colore de rose** the sky takes on a rosy tinge *ou* colour; **son teint se colora** her face became flushed, her colour rose.

(b) (*être empreint de*) **se ~ de** to be coloured *ou* tinged with.

coloriage [kɔlɔʀjaʒ] *nm* (*action*) colouring (*U*); (*dessin*) coloured drawing.

colorier [kɔlɔʀje] (7) *vt carte, dessin* to colour (in). **images à ~** pictures to colour (in); *V* **album.**

coloris [kɔlɔʀi] *nm* (*gén*) colour, shade; *[visage, peau]* colouring. (*Comm*) **carte de ~** shade card.

coloriste [kɔlɔʀist(ə)] **1** *nmf* (*peintre*) colourist; (*enlumineur*) colourer. **2** *nf* (*coiffeuse*) hairdresser (specializing in tinting and rinsing).

colossal, e, *mpl* **-aux** [kɔlɔsal, o] *adj* colossal, huge.

colossalement [kɔlɔsalmɑ̃] *adv* colossally, hugely.

colosse [kɔlɔs] *nm* (*personne*) giant (*fig*); (*institution, état*) colossus, giant. **le ~ de Rhodes** the Colossus of Rhodes; **~ aux pieds d'argile** idol with feet of clay.

colportage [kɔlpɔʀtaʒ] *nm* *[marchandises, ragots]* hawking, peddling; *V* **littérature.**

colporter [kɔlpɔʀte] (1) *vt marchandises, ragots* to hawk, peddle.

colporteur, -euse [kɔlpɔʀtœʀ, øz] *nm,f* (*vendeur*) hawker, pedlar. **~ de fausses nouvelles** newsmonger; **~ de rumeurs** *ou* **ragots*** gossipmonger.

colt [kɔlt] *nm* (*revolver*) gun, Colt.

coltiner [kɔltine] (1) **1** *vt fardeau, colis* to carry, hump* (*Brit*) *ou* lug* around.

2 se coltiner* *vpr colis* to hump* (*Brit*) *ou* lug* around, carry; (‡) *travail, personne* to be *ou* get stuck* *ou* landed* with. **il va falloir se ~ ta sœur pendant toutes les vacances‡** we'll have to put up with your sister for the whole of the holidays*.

columbarium [kɔlɔ̃baʀjɔm] *nm* (*cimetière*) columbarium.

colza [kɔlza] *nm* rape(seed), colza.

coma [kɔma] *nm* (*Méd*) coma. **être/entrer dans le ~** to be in/go into a coma.

comateux, -euse [kɔmatø, øz] *adj* comatose. **état ~** state of coma; **un ~** a patient in a coma.

combat [kɔ̃ba] **1** *nm* **(a)** (*bataille*) fight, fighting (*U*). **~s aériens** air-battles; **~s d'arrière-garde** rearguard fighting; **aller au ~** to go into battle, enter the fray (*littér*); **les ~s continuent** the fighting goes on; *V* **branle-bas, char, hors.**

(b) (*genre de bataille*) **~ défensif/offensif** defensive/offensive action; **~ aérien** aerial combat (*U*), dogfight; **~ naval** naval action; (*lit, fig*) **~ d'arrière-garde/de retardement** rearguard/delaying action.

(c) (*fig: lutte*) fight (*contre* against, *pour* for). **des ~s continuels entre parents et enfants** endless fighting between parents and children; **engager le ~ contre la vie chère** to take up the fight against the high cost of living; **la vie est un ~ de tous les jours** life is a daily struggle.

(d) (*Sport*) match, fight. **~ de boxe/de catch** boxing/wrestling match; **il y a 3 ~s au programme de ce soir** there are 3 fights *ou* matches in this evening's programme.

(e) (*littér: concours*) **ce fut entre eux un ~ de générosité/d'esprit** they vied with each other in generosity/wit.

2: combat de coqs cockfight, cockfighting (*U*); **combat de gladiateurs** gladiatorial combat *ou* contest; **combat rapproché** close combat; **combat de rues** street fighting (*U*); **combat singulier** single combat.

combatif, -ive [kɔ̃batif, iv] *adj troupes, soldat* ready to fight; *personne* of a fighting spirit; *esprit, humeur* fighting (*épith*). **les troupes fraîches sont plus ~ives** fresh troops show greater readiness to fight; **c'est un ~** he's a battler *ou* fighter.

combativité [kɔ̃bativite] *nf* *[troupe]* readiness to fight; *[personne]* fighting spirit.

combattant, e [kɔ̃batɑ̃, ɑ̃t] **1** *adj troupe* fighting (*épith*), combatant (*épith*). **2** *nm,f* *[guerre]* combatant; *[bagarre]* brawler; *V* **ancien.**

combattre [kɔ̃batʀ(ə)] (41) **1** *vt incendie, adversaire* to fight; *théorie, politique, inflation, vice* to combat, fight (against); *maladie [malade]* to fight against; *[médecin]* to fight, combat. **2** *vi* to fight (*contre* against, *pour* for).

combe [kɔ̃b] *nf* (*Géog*) coomb, comb(e).

combien [kɔ̃bjɛ̃] **1** *adv* **(a) ~ de** (*quantité*) how much; (*nombre*) how many; **~ de lait/de bouteilles as-tu acheté/achetées?** how much milk/many bottles have you bought?; **~ en a-t-il (en moins)?** (*quantité*) how much (less) is there (of it)?; (*nombre*) how many (fewer) are there (of them)?; **~ de temps?** how long?; **tu en as pour ~ de temps?** how long will you be?; **depuis ~ de temps travaillez-vous ici?** how long have you been working here?; ~ **de fois?** (*nombre*) how many times?; (*fréquence*) how often?

(b) ~ **(d'entre eux)** how many (of them); ~ **n'ouvrent jamais un livre!** how many (people) never open a book!; ~ **sont-ils?** how many (of them) are there?, how many are they?

(c) (*frm: à quel point, comme*) **si tu savais** ~/~**peu**/~ **plus je travaille maintenant!** if you (only) knew how much/how little/how much more I work now!; **tu vois** ~ **il est paresseux/inefficace** you can see how lazy/inefficient he is; **c'est étonnant de voir** ~ **il a changé** it is surprising to see how changed he is *ou* how (much) he has changed; ~ **précieux m'est ce souvenir** how dear to me this memory is; ~ **vous avez raison!** how right you are!; († *ou hum*) **il est bête, ô** ~! he is stupid, (oh) so stupid!; ~ **d'ennui je vous cause** what a lot of trouble I'm causing you.

(d) (*tellement*) ~ **peu de gens** how few people; ~ **moins de gens/d'argent** how many fewer people/much less money; ~ **plus de gens/d'argent** how many more people/much more money; **c'est plus long à faire mais** ~ **meilleur!** it takes (a lot) longer to do but how much better it is!

(e) (*quelle somme, distance etc*) ~ **est-ce?**, ~ **ça coûte?**, **ça fait** ~**?*** how much is it?; ~ **pèses-tu?** *ou* **fais-tu?** how heavy are you?, how much do you weigh?; ~ **pèse ce colis?** how much does this parcel weigh?, how heavy is this parcel?; ~ **mesure-t-il?** *[personne]* how tall is he?; *[colis]* how big is it?; ~ **cela mesure-t-il?** (*gén*) how big is it?; (*longueur*) how long is it?, what length is it?; **vous le voulez en** ~ **de large?** what width do you want (it)?, how wide do you want it?; **ça va augmenter de** ~? how much more will it go up? *ou* be?; **ça va faire une différence de** ~? what will the difference be?; ~ **y a-t-il d'ici à la ville?** how far is it from here to the town?; ~ **cela mesure-t-il en hauteur/largeur?, ça a** *ou* **fait** ~ **de hauteur/largeur?*** how high/wide is it?, what height/width is it?; (*Sport*) **il a fait** ~ **aux essais?** what was his time at the trial run?

2 *nm* (*) (*rang*) **le** ~ **êtes-vous?** where did you come?*, where were you placed?; (*date*) **le** ~ **sommes-nous?** what's the date?, what date is it?; (*fréquence*) **il y en a tous les** ~? how often do they come? *ou* run?

combientième* [kɔ̃bjɛ̃tjɛm] **1** *adj*: **Lincoln était le** ~ **président des USA?** what number president of the USA was Lincoln?*; **c'est le** ~ **accident qu'il a eu en 2 ans?** that's how many accidents he's had in 2 years?; **c'est la** ~ **fois que ça arrive!** how many times has that happened now!

2 *nmf* **(a)** (*rang*) **il est le** ~? where was he placed?; **ce coureur est arrivé le** ~? where did this runner come?

(b) (*énumération*) **encore un attentat, c'est le** ~ **depuis le début du mois?** another attack, how many does that make *ou* is that since the beginning of the month?; **donne-moi le troisième — le** ~? give me the third one — which one did you say?

(c) (*date*) **on est le** ~ **aujourd'hui?** what's the date today?, what date is it today?

combinaison [kɔ̃binɛzɔ̃] *nf* **(a)** (*action*) combining; (*Math*) *[éléments, sons, chiffres]* combination. (*Pol*) ~ **(ministérielle)** government (ministers); (*Chim*) ~ **(chimique)** (*entre plusieurs corps*) combination; (*corps composé*) compound.

(b) *[coffre-fort]* combination.

(c) (*vêtement*) *[femme]* slip; *[aviateur]* flying suit; *[mécanicien]* boiler suit (*Brit*), (one-piece) overalls (*US*).

(d) (*astuce*) device; (*manigance*) scheme. **des** ~**s louches** shady schemes *ou* scheming.

combinard, e [kɔ̃binaʀ, aʀd(ə)] *adj, nm,f* (*péj*) **il est** ~, **c'est un** ~ (*astuces, trucs*) he knows all the tricks; (*manigances*) he's a schemer, he's on to all the fiddles*.

combinat [kɔ̃bina] *nm* (industrial) complex.

combinatoire [kɔ̃binatwaʀ] *adj* (*Ling*) combinative; (*Math*) combinatorial, combinatory.

combine [kɔ̃bin] *nf* (*astuce, truc*) trick; (*péj: manigance*) scheme. **la** ~ scheming; **il est dans la** ~ he knows (all) about it, he's in on it*.

combiné [kɔ̃bine] *nm* (*Chim*) compound; *[téléphone]* receiver. (*vêtement*) ~ **(gaine-soutien-gorge)** corselette; (*Rad*) ~ **(radio-tourne-disque)** radiogram; (*Tech*) ~ **(batteur-mixeur)** mixer and liquidizer, blender; (*Ski*) ~ **alpin/nordique** alpine/nordic combination; **il est 3e au** ~ he's 3rd overall.

combiner [kɔ̃bine] (1) **1** *vt* **(a)** (*grouper*) *éléments, sons, chiffres* to combine. **opération combinée** joint *ou* combined operation; **l'oxygène combiné à l'hydrogène** oxygen combined with hydrogen; **l'oxygène et l'hydrogène combinés** oxygen and hydrogen combined; **l'inquiétude et la fatigue combinées** a combination of anxiety and tiredness.

(b) (*méditer, élaborer*) *affaire, mauvais coup, plan* to devise, work out, think up; *horaire, emploi du temps* to devise, plan. **bien combiné** well devised.

2 se combiner *vpr [éléments]* to combine (*avec* with).

comble [kɔ̃bl(ə)] **1** *adj salle, autobus* packed (full), jam-packed*; *V* **mesure, salle.**

2 *nm* **(a)** (*degré extrême*) height. **c'est le** ~ **du ridicule!** that's the height of absurdity!; **être au** ~ **de la joie** to be overjoyed; **elle était au** ~ **du désespoir** she was in the depths of despair; *[joie, colère etc]* **être à son** ~ to be at its peak *ou* height; **ceci mit le** ~ **à sa fureur/son désespoir** this brought his anger/his despair to its climax *ou* a peak; **cela mit le** ~ **à sa joie** that crowned his joy; **pour** ~ **de malheur il ...** to cap *ou* crown it all he ... .

(b) (*loc*) **c'est le** ~!, **c'est un** ~! that's the last straw!, that beats all!*, that takes the cake!* *ou* biscuit!* (*Brit*); **le** ~, **c'est qu'il est parti sans payer** what beats all* was that he left without paying; **et pour** ~, **il est parti sans payer** and to cap *ou* crown it all, he left without paying.

(c) (*charpente*) roof trussing (*T*), roof timbers. ~ **mansardé** mansard roof; **les** ~**s** the attic, the loft; **loger (dans une chambre) sous les** ~**s** to live in a garret *ou* an attic; *V* **fond.**

comblement [kɔ̃bləmɑ̃] *nm [cavité]* filling(-in).

combler [kɔ̃ble] (1) *vt* **(a)** (*boucher*) *trou, fente, creux* to fill in. (*fig*) **ça comblera un trou dans nos finances** that'll fill a gap in our finances.

(b) (*résorber*) *déficit* to make good, make up; *lacune, vide* to fill. ~ **son retard** to make up lost time.

(c) (*satisfaire*) *désir, espoir* to fulfil; *besoin* to fulfil, fill; *personne* to gratify. **parents comblés par la naissance d'un fils** parents overjoyed at the birth of a son; **c'est une femme comblée** she has all that she could wish for.

(d) (*couvrir qn de*) ~ **qn de** *cadeaux, honneurs* to shower sb with; **il mourut comblé d'honneurs** he died laden with honours; **vous me comblez d'aise** *ou* **de joie** you fill me with joy; **vraiment, vous nous comblez!** really you're too good to us!

combustibilité [kɔ̃bystibilite] *nf* combustibility.

combustible [kɔ̃bystibl(ə)] **1** *adj* combustible. **2** *nm* fuel. **les** ~**s** fuels, kinds of fuel.

combustion [kɔ̃bystjɔ̃] *nf* combustion. **poêle à** ~ **lente** slow-burning stove.

comédie [kɔmedi] **1** *nf* **(a)** (*Théât*) comedy. ~ **de mœurs/d'intrigue** comedy of manners/of intrigue; ~ **de caractères/de situation** character/situation comedy; **de** ~ *personnage, situation* (*Théât*) comedy (*épith*); (*fig*) comic.

(b) (*fig: simulation*) playacting. **c'est de la** ~ it's all an act, it's all sham; **jouer la** ~ to put on an act.

(c) (*) palaver, fuss. **c'est toujours la même** ~ it's always the same palaver; **allons, pas de** ~ come on, no nonsense *ou* fuss; **faire la** ~ to make a fuss *ou* a scene.

2: (*Théât*) **la Comédie-Française** the Comédie-Française; **la comédie humaine** the comédie humaine; **comédie musicale** musical.

comédien, -ienne [kɔmedjɛ̃, jɛn] **1** *nm,f* **(a)** (*fig: hypocrite*) sham. **être** ~ to be a sham. **(b)** (*fig: pitre*) show-off. **2** *nm* (*acteur*) actor; (*acteur comique*) comedy actor, comedian. **3 comédienne** *nf* (*actrice*) actress; (*actrice comique*) comedy actress, comedienne.

comestible [kɔmɛstibl(ə)] **1** *adj* edible. **2** *nmpl*: ~**s** (fine) foods, delicatessen; **magasin de** ~**s** ≃ delicatessen (shop).

comète [kɔmɛt] *nf* (*Astron*) comet; *V* **plan**[1].

cométique [kɔmetik] *nm* (*Can*) Eskimo sledge, komatik (*US, Can*).

comice [kɔmis] *nm*: ~**(s) agricole(s)**† agricultural show *ou* meeting.

comique [kɔmik] **1** *adj* (*Théât*) *acteur, film, genre* comic; (*fig*) *incident, personnage* comical; *V* **opéra.**

2 *nm* **(a)** (*U*) *[situation, habillement]* comic aspect *ou* character. **c'est d'un** ~ **irrésistible** it's hilariously *ou* irresistibly funny; **le** ~ **de la chose, c'est que ...** the funny *ou* amusing thing about it is that ... .

(b) (*Littérat*) **le** ~ comedy; ~ **de caractère/de situation** character/situation comedy; ~ **troupier** coarse comedy; **avoir le sens du** ~ to have a sense of the comic.

(c) (*artiste, amuseur*) comic, comedian; (*dramaturge*) comedy writer.

comiquement [kɔmikmɑ̃] *adv* comically.

comité [kɔmite] **1** *nm* (*groupement, ligue*) committee; (*permanent, élu*) board, committee. ~ **consultatif/exécutif/restreint/secret** advisory/executive/select/closed committee; **se grouper en** ~ **pour faire** to form a committee to do; (*fig*) **se réunir en petit** ~ to meet in a select group, have a small get-together*.

2: **comité directeur** management committee; **comité d'entreprise** work's council; **comité des fêtes** gala *ou* festival committee; **comité de gestion** board of management; **comité de lecture** reading panel *ou* committee.

commandant [kɔmɑ̃dɑ̃] **1** *nm* **(a)** (*armée de terre*) major; (*armée de l'air*) squadron leader (*Brit*); (*gén: dans toute fonction de commandement*) commander, commandant.

(b) (*Aviat, Naut*) captain.

2: (*Aviat*) **commandant de bord** captain; **commandant en chef** commander-in-chief; **commandant en second** second in command.

commandante [kɔmɑ̃dɑ̃t] *nf* (*V* **commandant**) major's wife; squadron leader's wife; commander's wife; captain's wife.

commande [kɔmɑ̃d] *nf* **(a)** (*Comm*) order. **passer une** ~ to put in an order (*de* for); **on vous livrera vos** ~**s jeudi** your order will be delivered to you on Thursday; **payable à la** ~ cash with order; **cet article est en** ~ the article is on order; **fait sur** ~ made to order; **carnet/bulletin de** ~**s** order book/form.

(b) (*Aviat, Tech: gén pl*) (*action*) control, controlling; (*dispositif*) controls. **les organes** *ou* **leviers de** ~, **les** ~**s** the controls; ~ **à distance** remote control; **moteur à** ~ **électrique** electrically ignited engine; **câble de** ~ control cable; **véhicule à double** ~ dual control vehicle, vehicle with dual controls; **se mettre aux** ~**s, prendre les** ~**s** (*lit*) to take control, take (over) the controls; (*fig*) to take control; (*lit, fig*) **passer les** ~**s à qn** to hand over control to sb, hand over the controls to sb; **être aux** ~**s, tenir les** ~**s** (*lit*) to be in control, be at the controls; (*fig*) to be in control; *V* **levier, tableau.**

(c) (*loc*) **de** ~ *sourire* forced, affected; *zèle* affected; **agir sur** ~ to act on orders; **je ne peux pas jouer ce rôle/m'amuser sur** ~ I can't act the role/enjoy myself to order; **ouvrage écrit/composé sur** ~ commissioned work/composition.

commandement [kɔmɑ̃dmɑ̃] *nm* **(a)** (*direction*) *[armée, navire]* command. **avoir/prendre le** ~ **de** to be in *ou* have/take command of; **sur un ton de** ~ in a commanding tone; **avoir l'habitude du** ~ to be used to being in command; *V* **poste**[2].

(b) (*état-major*) command. **le ~ a décidé que ...** it has been decided at higher command that ...; *V* **haut.**
(c) (*Rel*) commandment.
(d) (*ordre*) command. (*Mil*) **à mon ~, marche!** on my command, march!; **avoir ~ de faire qch**† to have orders to do sth.
(e) (*Jur*) *[huissier]* summons.

commander [kɔmɑ̃de] (1) **1** *vt* **(a)** (*ordonner*) *obéissance, attaque* to order, command. **~ à qn de faire** to order *ou* command sb to do; **il me commanda le silence** he ordered *ou* commanded me to keep quiet; **l'amitié ne se commande pas** you can't make friends to order; **je ne peux pas le sentir, ça ne se commande pas** I can't stand him — you can't help these things; **le devoir commande** duty calls.
(b) (*imposer*) **~ le respect/l'admiration** to command *ou* compel respect/admiration.
(c) (*requérir*) *[événements, circonstances]* to demand. **la prudence commande que ...** prudence demands that ... .
(d) (*Comm*) *marchandise, repas* to order; (*Art*) *tableau, œuvre* to commission. (*au café*) **avez-vous déjà commandé?** has your order been taken?, have you ordered?; (*hum*) **nous avons commandé le soleil** we've ordered the sun to shine (*hum*).
(e) (*diriger*) *armée, navire, expédition, attaque* to command; (*emploi absolu*) to be in command, be in charge. (*Mil*) **~ le feu** to give the order to shoot *ou* to (open) fire; **c'est lui qui commande ici** he's in charge here; **je n'aime pas qu'on me commande** I don't like to be ordered about *ou* to be given orders; **à la maison, c'est elle qui commande** she's the boss at home, she is the one who gives the orders at home.
(f) (*contrôler*) to control. **ce bouton commande la sirène** this switch controls the siren; **forteresse qui commande l'entrée du détroit** fortress which commands the entrance to the straits.
2 commander à *vt indir passions, instincts* to have command *ou* control over. **il ne commande plus à sa jambe gauche** he no longer has any control over his left leg; **~ à sa colère** to have command *ou* control over one's anger; **il ne sait pas se ~** he cannot control himself.
3 se commander *vpr* (*communiquer*) *[pièces, chambres]* to lead into one another.

commandeur [kɔmɑ̃dœʀ] *nm* commander (*of an Order*).

commanditaire [kɔmɑ̃ditɛʀ] *nm* (*Comm*) limited *ou* sleeping (*Brit*) *ou* silent (*US*) partner.

commandite [kɔmɑ̃dit] *nf* (*Comm*) (*fonds*) share (*of limited partner*). **(société en) ~** limited partnership.

commanditer [kɔmɑ̃dite] (1) *vt* (*Comm: financer*) to finance.

commando [kɔmɑ̃do] *nm* commando (group). **les membres du ~** the commando members, the commandos.

comme [kɔm] **1** *conj* **(a)** (*temps*) as. **elle entra (juste) ~ le rideau se levait** she came in (just) as the curtain was rising.
(b) (*cause*) as, since, seeing that. **~ il pleut, je prends la voiture** I'll take the car seeing that it's raining *ou* as *ou* since it's raining; **~ il est lâche, il n'a pas osé parler** being a coward *ou* coward that he is *ou* as he is a coward, he did not dare speak out.
(c) (*comparaison*) as, like (*devant n et pron*); (*avec idée de manière*) as, the way*. **elle a soigné son chien ~ elle aurait soigné un enfant** she nursed her dog as she would have done a child; **il pense ~ nous** he thinks as we do *ou* like us; **c'est un homme ~ lui qu'il nous faut** we need a man like him *ou* such as him; **ce pantalon est pratique pour le travail ~ pour les loisirs** these trousers are practical for work as well as leisure; **il s'ennuie en ville ~ à la campagne** he gets bored both in town and in the country, he gets bored in town as he does in the country; (*Rel*) **sur la terre ~ au ciel** on earth as it is in heaven; **il écrit ~ il parle** he writes as *ou* the way he speaks; **il voudrait une moto ~ son frère*** *ou* **celle de son frère/la mienne** he would like a motorbike like his brother's/mine; **il voudrait une moto, ~ son frère** he would like a motorbike (just) like his brother; **le héros du film n'agit pas ~ dans la pièce** the hero in the film does not act as he does *ou* the way he does in the play; **si, ~ nous pensons, il a oublié** if, as we think (he did), he forgot; **faites ~ vous voulez** do as you like; **choisissez ~ pour vous** choose as you would for yourself, choose as if it were for yourself; **dur ~ du fer** (as) hard as iron.
(d) (*en tant que*) as. **nous l'avons eu ~ président** we had him as (our) president; **~ étudiant, il est assez médiocre** as a student, he is rather poor.
(e) (*tel que*) like, such as. **les fleurs ~ la rose et l'œillet sont fragiles** flowers such as *ou* like roses and carnations *ou* such flowers as roses and carnations are fragile; **bête ~ il est ...** stupid as he is ...; **elle n'a jamais vu de maison ~ la nôtre** she's never seen a house like ours *ou* such as ours.
(f) (*devant adj, ptp*) as though, as if. **il était ~ fasciné par ces oiseaux** it was as though *ou* as if he were fascinated by these birds, he was as though *ou* as if fascinated by these birds; **il était ~ fou** he was like a madman; **il était ~ perdu dans cette foule** it was as though *ou* as if he were lost in this crowd; **~ se parlant à lui-même** as if *ou* as though talking to himself; **il y eut ~ une hésitation/lueur** there was a sort *ou* kind of hesitation/light.
(g) ~ si as if, as though; **~ pour faire** as if to do; **~ quoi** (*disant que*) to the effect that; (*d'où il s'ensuit que*) which goes to show that, which shows that; **il se conduit ~ si de rien n'était** he behaves as if *ou* as though nothing had happened; **~ si nous ne savions pas!** as if we didn't know!; **ce n'est pas ~ si on ne l'avait pas prévenu!** it's not as if *ou* as though he hadn't been warned!; **il fit un geste ~ pour la frapper** he made (a gesture) as if to strike her; **il écrit une lettre ~ quoi il retire sa candidature** he is writing a letter to the effect that he is withdrawing his candidature; **~ quoi il ne fallait pas l'écouter** which shows *ou* goes to show that you shouldn't have listened to him.
(h) ~ cela, ~ ça like that; **~ ci ~ ça** so-so, (fair to) middling; **vous aimeriez une robe ~ ça?** would you like a dress like that?, would you like that sort of dress?; **alors, ~ ça, vous nous quittez?** so you're leaving us just like that?; **je l'ai enfermé, ~ ça il ne peut pas nous suivre** I locked him in, so he can't follow us, I locked him in — like that *ou* that way he can't follow us; **il a pêché un saumon ~ ça!** he caught a salmon that *ou* this size! *ou* a salmon like that! *ou* this!; **comment l'as-tu trouvé? — ~ ça *ou* ~ ci ~ ça** how did you find him? — so-so *ou* (fair to) middling; **c'est ~ ça, un point c'est tout** that's the way it is, and that's all there is to it; **il m'a dit ~ ça qu'il n'était pas d'accord*** he told me just like that that he didn't agree; (*admiratif*) **~ ça!*** fantastic!*, terrific!*
(i) (*loc*) **~ il vous plaira** as you wish; **~ de juste** naturally, needless to say; (*iro*) **~ par hasard, il était absent** he just HAPPENED to be away (*iro*); (*Prov*) **~ on fait son lit, on se couche** you (*ou* he *etc*) have (*ou* has *etc*) made your (*ou* his *etc*) bed, now you (*ou* he *etc*) must lie on it; **~ il faut** properly; **mange/tiens-toi ~ il faut** eat/sit up properly; († *ou hum*) **une personne très ~ il faut** a decent well-bred person; **elle est mignonne ~ tout** she's as sweet as can be; **c'est facile ~ tout** it's as easy as can be *ou* as easy as winking; **c'était amusant ~ tout** it was terribly funny *ou* as funny as can be; **il est menteur ~ tout** he's a terrible *ou* dreadful liar; **~ dit l'autre*** as they say; **~ qui dirait*** as you might say; *V* **tout.**
2 *adv* how. **~ ces enfants sont bruyants!** how noisy these children are!, these children are so noisy!; **~ il fait beau!** what a lovely day!, what lovely weather!; **tu sais ~ elle est** you know how she is *ou* what she is like; **écoute ~ elle chante bien** listen (to) how beautifully she sings; **~ vous y allez, vous!*** (now) hold on a minute!*, don't get carried away!; *V* **voir.**

commémoratif, -ive [kɔmemɔʀatif, iv] *adj cérémonie, plaque* commemorative (*épith*), memorial (*épith*); *service* memorial (*épith*). **monument ~** memorial.

commémoration [kɔmemɔʀɑsjɔ̃] *nf* commemoration. **en ~ de** in commemoration of.

commémorer [kɔmemɔʀe] (1) *vt* to commemorate.

commençant, e [kɔmɑ̃sɑ̃, ɑ̃t] **1** *adj* beginning (*épith*). **2** *nm,f* (*débutant*) beginner.

commencement [kɔmɑ̃smɑ̃] *nm* **(a)** (*début*) beginning, commencement (*frm*); (*départ*) start. **il y a eu un ~ d'incendie** there has been the beginning(s) of a fire; **un bon/mauvais ~** a good/bad start *ou* beginning; (*Jur*) **~ d'exécution** *initial steps in the commission of a crime*; (*Jur*) **~ de preuve** prima facie evidence; **au/dès le ~** in/from the beginning, at/from the outset *ou* start; **du ~ à la fin** from beginning to end, from start to finish; **c'est le ~ de la fin** it's the beginning of the end; **il y a un ~ à tout** you've (always) got to start somewhere, there's always a beginning.
(b) ~s *[science, métier]* (*premiers temps*) beginnings; (*rudiments*) basic knowledge. **les ~s ont été durs** the beginning was hard.

commencer [kɔmɑ̃se] (3) **1** *vt* **(a)** (*entreprendre*) *travail, opération, repas* to begin, start, commence (*frm*). **ils ont commencé les travaux de l'autoroute** they've started *ou* begun work on the motorway; **j'ai commencé un nouveau chapitre** I have started *ou* begun on a new chapter; **quelle façon de ~ l'année!** what a way to begin *ou* start the (new) year!; **commençons par le commencement** let's begin at the beginning.
(b) (*Scol*) **~ un élève (en maths)** to start a pupil (off) (in maths), ground a pupil (in maths); **il a été très bien/mal commencé (en maths)** he was given a good/bad start (in maths), he got a good/bad grounding (in maths).
(c) *[chose]* to begin. **mot/phrase qui commence un chapitre** word/sentence which begins a chapter, opening word/sentence of a chapter; **une heure de prières commence la journée** the day begins with an hour of prayers.
2 *vi* **(a)** (*débuter*) to begin, start, commence (*frm*). **le concert va ~** the concert is about to begin *ou* start *ou* commence (*frm*); (*lit, iro*) **ça commence bien!** that's a good start!, we're off to a good start!; **pour ~** (*lit*) to begin *ou* start with; (*fig*) to begin *ou* start with, for a start; **elle commence demain chez X** she starts *ou* commences (*frm*) (work) tomorrow at X's.
(b) ~ à (*ou* **de**) **faire** to begin *ou* start to do, begin *ou* start doing; **il commençait à neiger** it was beginning *ou* starting to snow, snow was setting in; **il commençait à s'inquiéter/à s'impatienter** he was getting nervous/impatient; **je commence à en avoir assez*** I've had just about enough (of it); **ça commence à bien faire*** it's getting a bit much*.
(c) ~ par qch to start *ou* begin with sth; **~ par faire qch** to start *ou* begin by doing sth; **par quoi voulez-vous ~?** what would you like to begin *ou* start with?; **commence par faire tes devoirs, on verra après** do your homework for a start, and then we'll see.

commensal, e, *mpl* **-aux** [kɔmɑ̃sal, o] *nm,f* (*littér: personne*) companion at table, table companion; (*Zool*) commensal.

commensalisme [kɔmɑ̃salism(ə)] *nm* (*Zool*) commensalism.

commensurable [kɔmɑ̃syʀabl(ə)] *adj* commensurable.

comment [kɔmɑ̃] **1** *adv* **(a)** (*de quelle façon*) how; (*rare: pourquoi*) how is that?, how come?. **~ a-t-il fait?** how did he do it?, how did he manage that?; **je ne sais pas ~ il a fait cela** I don't know how he did it; **~ a-t-il osé!** how did he dare!; **~ s'appelle-t-il?** what's his name?; **~ appelles-tu cela?** what do you call that?; **~ allez-vous?** *ou* **vas-tu?** how are you?; **~ est-il, ce type?*** what sort of fellow* is he?, what's that fellow* like?; **~ va-t-il?** how is he?; **~ faire?** how shall we do it? *ou* go about it?; **~ se fait-il que ...?** how is it that ...?, how come that ...?*; **~ se peut-il que ...?** how can it be that ...?
(b) (*excl*) **~?** (I beg your) pardon?, sorry?, what?*; **~ cela?** what do you mean?; **~, il est mort?** what! is he dead?; **vous avez assez mangé? — et ~!** have you had enough to eat? — we (most)

certainly have! *ou* I should say so! *ou* and how!*; **avez-vous bien travaillé? — et ~!** did you work well? — I should say so! *ou* not half!* *ou* and how!*; **~ donc!** by all means!, of course!

2 *nm*: le ~ the how; **les ~(s)** the hows; *V* **pourquoi.**

commentaire [kɔmɑ̃tɛʀ] *nm* **(a)** (*remarque*) comment (*sur* on). **quel a été son ~** *ou* **quels ont été ses ~s sur ce qui s'est passé?** what was his comment *ou* what were his comments on what happened?; **~s de presse** press comments; **je vous dispense de vos ~s** I can do without your comments *ou* remarks, I don't want (to hear) any comments *ou* remarks from you; **tu feras comme je te l'ordonne, et pas de ~s!** you will do as I say and that's final! *ou* and that's all there is to it!; **son attitude/une telle action se passe de ~s** *ou* **est sans ~** his attitude/such an action speaks for itself; **vous avez entendu ce qu'il a dit! — sans ~!** did you hear him! — enough said! *ou* no comment!

(b) (*péj*) ~s comments; **sa conduite donne lieu à bien des ~s!** his behaviour gives rise to a lot of comment!; **ils vont faire des ~s sur ce qui se passe chez nous** they'll have a lot to say *ou* a lot of comments to make about what's going on at home.

(c) (*exposé*) commentary (*de* on). (*Littérat: mémoires*) **les 'C~s' de César** Caesar's 'Commentaries'; **un bref ~ de la séance** a brief commentary *ou* some brief comments on the meeting.

(d) (*Littérat: explication*) commentary. **faire le ~ d'un texte** to do *ou* give a commentary on *ou* comment (on) a text; **édition avec ~(s)** annotated edition.

commentateur, -trice [kɔmɑ̃tatœʀ, tʀis] *nm,f* (*glossateur, journaliste*) commentator, correspondent; (*Rad, TV*) *[politique, économie etc]* correspondent; *[football]* commentator.

commenter [kɔmɑ̃te] (1) *vt poème* to comment (on), do *ou* give a commentary on; *conduite* to make comments on, comment upon; *événement, actualité* to comment on *ou* upon. **le match sera commenté par X** the commentary on the match will be given by X, the match will be covered by X.

commérage [kɔmeʀaʒ] *nm* piece of gossip. **~s** gossip, gossiping.

commerçant, e [kɔmɛʀsɑ̃, ɑ̃t] **1** *adj* **(a)** *nation* trading (*épith*), commercial; *ville* commercial; *rue, quartier* shopping (*épith*). **rue très ~e** busy shopping street, street with many shops.

(b) (*habile*) *personne, procédé* commercially shrewd. **il est très ~** he's got good business sense.

2 *nm* shopkeeper, tradesman (*surtout Brit*). **~ en détail** shopkeeper, retail merchant; **~ en gros** wholesale dealer; **les ~s du quartier** (the) local tradesmen (*surtout Brit*) *ou* shopkeepers.

3 commerçante *nf* shopkeeper.

commerce [kɔmɛʀs(ə)] *nm* **(a)** (*activités commerciales*) **le ~** trade, commerce; (*affaires*) **le ~** business, trade; **le ~ n'y est pas encore très développé** commerce *ou* trade isn't very highly developed there yet; **depuis quelques mois le ~ ne marche pas très bien** business *ou* trade has been bad for a few months; **opération/maison/traité de ~** commercial operation/firm/treaty; **~ en** *ou* **de gros/demi-gros/détail** wholesale/retail-wholesale/retail trade; **~ intérieur/extérieur** domestic *ou* home/foreign trade *ou* commerce; **faire du ~ (avec)** to trade (with); **être dans le ~** to be in trade; **faire ~ de**† to trade in; (*fig péj*) **faire ~ de ses charmes/son nom** to trade on one's charms/name; *V* **effet.**

(b) (*circuit commercial*) **dans le ~** *objet* in the shops; **vendu hors-~** not sold in shops (*Brit*) *ou* stores (*US*), sold directly to the public.

(c) (*commerçants*) **le ~** tradespeople (*Brit*), traders, shopkeepers; **le petit ~** small shopowners *ou* traders; **le monde du ~** the trading world, trading *ou* commercial circles.

(d) (*boutique*) business. **tenir** *ou* **avoir un ~ d'épicerie** to have a grocery business; **un gros/petit ~** a big/small business.

(e) († *ou littér*) (*fréquentation*) (social) intercourse; (*compagnie*) company; (*rapport*) dealings. **être d'un ~ agréable** to be pleasant company; **avoir ~ avec qn** to have dealings with sb.

commercer [kɔmɛʀse] (3) *vi* to trade (*avec* with).

commercial, e, *mpl* **-iaux** [kɔmɛʀsjal, jo] **1** *adj* (*gén*) commercial; *activité, société, port* commercial, trading (*épith*). (*péj*) **avoir un sourire ~** to have the polite professional smile of the shopkeeper; (*Aut*) **une 2 CV ~e** a 2 CV van.

2 commerciale *nf* (*véhicule*) (light) van.

commercialement [kɔmɛʀsjalmɑ̃] *adv* commercially.

commercialisation [kɔmɛʀsjalizasjɔ̃] *nf [produit]* marketing.

commercialiser [kɔmɛʀsjalize] (1) *vt brevet, produit, idée* to market.

commère [kɔmɛʀ] *nf* (*péj: bavarde*) gossip.

commérer† [kɔmeʀe] (6) *vi* to gossip.

commettre [kɔmɛtʀ(ə)] (56) **1** *vt* **(a)** (*perpétrer*) *crime, faute, injustice* to commit; *erreur* to make. (*hum*) **il a commis 2 ou 3 romans** he's perpetrated 2 or 3 novels (*hum*).

(b) (*littér: confier*) **~ qch à qn** to commit sth to sb, entrust sth to sb.

(c) (*frm: nommer*) **~ qn à une charge** to appoint *ou* nominate sb to an office; (*Jur*) **~ un arbitre** to nominate *ou* appoint an arbitrator; **avocat commis d'office** barrister (*Brit*) *ou* counselor (*US*) appointed by the court.

(d) (†: *compromettre*) *réputation* to endanger, compromise.

2 se commettre *vpr* (*péj, frm*) to endanger one's reputation, lower o.s. **se ~ avec des gens peu recommandables** to associate with rather undesirable people.

comminatoire [kɔminatwaʀ] *adj ton, lettre* threatening; (*Jur*) *appointing a penalty for non-compliance.*

commis [kɔmi] *nm* (*gén: vendeur*) (shop *ou* store (*US*)) assistant. **~ de bureau** office clerk; **~ aux écritures** book-keeper; **~-greffier** assistant to the clerk of the court; **~ de magasin** shop assistant (*Brit*), store assistant (*US*); (*Naut*) **~ aux vivres** ship's steward; **~ voyageur** commercial traveller; *V* **grand.**

commisération [kɔmizeʀasjɔ̃] *nf* commiseration.

commissaire [kɔmisɛʀ] **1** *nm* **(a) ~ (de police)** (police) superintendent; **~ principal** chief superintendent; **~ divisionnaire** ≃ Chief Constable (*Brit*), Commissioner (*US*).

(b) (*surveillant*) *[rencontre sportive, fête]* steward.

(c) (*envoyé*) representative; *V* **haut.**

(d) *[commission]* commission member, commissioner.

2: commissaire de l'Air chief administrator (*in Air Force*); (*Naut*) **commissaire du bord** purser; (*Fin*) **commissaire aux comptes** auditor; **commissaire du gouvernement** government commissioner; (*Can*) **commissaire aux langues officielles** Commissioner of Official Languages (*Can*); **commissaire de la Marine** chief administrator (*in Navy*); **commissaire-priseur** *nm, pl* **commissaires-priseurs** auctioneer.

commissariat [kɔmisaʀja] *nm* **(a)** (*poste*) **~ (de police)** police station.

(b) (*Admin: fonction*) commissionership. **~ du bord** pursership; **~ aux comptes** auditorship.

(c) (*corps*) **~ maritime** ≃ Admiralty Board; **~ de l'air** ≃ Air Force Board; *V* **haut.**

commission [kɔmisjɔ̃] **1** *nf* **(a)** (*bureau nommé*) commission; (*comité restreint*) committee. (*Pol*) **la ~ du budget** the Budget committee; **les membres sont en ~** the members are in committee; **travail en ~** work in committee; (*Pol*) **renvoi d'un texte en ~** committal *ou* commitment of a bill.

(b) (*message*) message. **est-ce qu'on vous a fait la ~?** did you get *ou* were you given the message?

(c) (*course*) errand. **faire des ~s (pour)** to run errands (for); **on l'a chargé d'une ~** he was sent on an errand; (*fig: langage enfantin*) **la petite/grosse ~** number 1/2 (*langage enfantin*).

(d) (*emplettes*) **~s** shopping; **faire les/des ~s** to do the/some shopping; **partir en ~s** to go shopping; **l'argent des ~s** the shopping money.

(e) (*pourcentage*) commission. **toucher 10% de ~** to get 10% commission (*sur* on); **travailler à la ~** to work on commission.

(f) (*Comm, Jur: mandat*) commission. **avoir la ~ de faire** to be empowered *ou* commissioned to do.

2: commission d'arbitrage arbitration committee; **commission d'armistice** armistice council; **commission d'enquête** committee *ou* board *ou* commission of inquiry; **commission d'examen** board of examiners; **commission militaire** army exemption tribunal; **commission paritaire** joint commission (with equal representation of the sides); **commission parlementaire** parliamentary commission, parliamentary committee; **commission permanente** permanent commission, standing committee; (*Jur*) **commission rogatoire** letters rogatory.

commissionnaire [kɔmisjɔnɛʀ] *nm* **(a)** (*livreur*) delivery boy, (*adulte*) delivery man; (*messager*) messenger boy, (*adulte*) messenger; (*chasseur*) page (boy) (*in hotel*), (*adulte*) commissionaire.

(b) (*intermédiaire*) agent, broker. **~ en douane** customs agent *ou* broker; **~ de transport** forwarding agent; **~ de roulage** carrier, haulage contractor (*Brit*), haulier (*Brit*).

commissionner [kɔmisjɔne] (1) *vt* (*Comm, Jur: mandater*) to commission.

commissure [kɔmisyʀ] *nf [bouche]* corner; (*Anat, Bot*) commissure.

commode [kɔmɔd] **1** *adj* **(a)** (*pratique*) *appartement, meuble* convenient; *outil* handy (*pour* for, *pour faire* for doing); *itinéraire* handy, convenient.

(b) (*facile*) easy. **ce n'est pas ~** it's not easy (*à faire* to do); **ce serait trop ~!** that would be too easy!

(c) *morale* easy-going; (†) *caractère* easy-going. **~ à vivre** easy to get on with; **il n'est pas ~** he's an awkward customer.

2 *nf* (*meuble*) chest of drawers.

commodément [kɔmɔdemɑ̃] *adv* (*confortablement*) comfortably.

commodité [kɔmɔdite] *nf* **(a)** (*agrément, confort*) convenience. **pour plus de ~** for greater convenience; **les ~s de la vie moderne** the conveniences *ou* comforts of modern life. **(b)** (††: *toilettes*) **~s** toilets.

commotion [kɔmosjɔ̃] *nf* (*secousse*) shock. (*Méd*) **~ cérébrale** concussion; (*fig*) **les grandes ~s sociales** the great social upheavals.

commotionner [kɔmosjɔne] (1) *vt [secousse, nouvelle]* **~ qn** to give sb a shock, shake sb; **être fortement commotionné par qch** to be badly *ou* severely shocked *ou* shaken by sth.

commuable [kɔmɥabl(ə)] *adj peine* commutable.

commuer [kɔmɥe] (1) *vt peine* to commute (*en* to).

commun, e[1] [kɔmœ̃, yn] **1** *adj* **(a)** (*collectif, de tous*) common; (*fait ensemble*) *effort, réunion* joint (*épith*). **pour le bien ~** for the common good; **dans l'intérêt ~** in the common interest; **ils ont une langue ~e qui est l'anglais** they have English as a common language; **d'un ~ accord** of a common accord, of one accord.

(b) (*partagé*) *élément* common; *pièce, cuisine* communal, shared; (*Math*) *dénominateur, facteur, angle* common (*à* to). **ces deux maisons ont un jardin ~** these two houses have a shared garden; *[chose]* **être ~ à** to be shared by; **le jardin est ~ aux deux maisons** the garden is common to *ou* shared by the two houses; **tout est ~ entre eux** they share everything; **un ami ~** a mutual friend; **la vie ~e** *[couple]* conjugal life, life together; *[communauté]* communal life.

(c) (*comparable*) *goût, intérêt, caractère* common (*épith*). **ils n'ont rien de ~** they have nothing in common; **ce métal n'a rien de ~ avec l'argent** this metal has nothing in common with *ou* is nothing like silver; **il n'y a pas de ~e mesure entre eux** there's no possible comparison between them; *V* **nom.**

(d) en ~ in common; **faire la cuisine/les achats en ~** to share (in) the cooking/the shopping; **vivre en ~** to live communally; **faire une démarche en ~** to take joint steps; **mettre ses ressources en ~** to share *ou* pool one's resources; **tout mettre en ~** to share everything; **ces plantes ont en ~ de pousser sur les hauteurs** these plants have in common the fact that they grow at high altitudes.
(e) (*habituel, ordinaire*) *accident, erreur* common; *opinion* commonly held, widespread; *métal* common. **peu ~** out of the ordinary, uncommon; **il est d'une force peu ~e pour son âge** he is unusually *ou* uncommonly strong for his age; **il est ~ de voir des daims traverser la route** it is quite common *ou* quite a common thing to see deer crossing the road.
(f) (*péj: vulgaire*) *manière, voix, personne* common.
2 *nm* **(a) le ~ des mortels** the common run of people; **cet hôtel n'est pas pour le ~ des mortels** this hotel is not for ordinary mortals like myself (*ou* ourselves) *ou* is not for the common run of people; († *péj*) **le ~, les gens du ~** the common people *ou* herd; **hors du ~** out of the ordinary.
(b) (*bâtiments*) **les ~s** the outbuildings, the outhouses.
3 commune *nf V* **commune**².
communal, e, *mpl* **-aux** [kɔmynal, o] *adj dépenses* council (*épith*); *fête, aménagements [ville]* local (*épith*); *[campagne]* village (*épith*). **l'école ~e, la ~e** the local (primary) school.
communard, e [kɔmynaʀ, aʀd(ə)] **1** *adj* (*Hist*) of the Commune. **2** *nm,f* (*Hist*) communard; (*péj: communiste*) red (*péj*), commie* (*péj*).
communautaire [kɔmynotɛʀ] *adj* community (*épith*); (*Pol*) *droit, politique* Community (*épith*).
communauté [kɔmynote] *nf* **(a)** (*identité*) *[idées, sentiments]* identity; *[intérêts, langue, culture]* community.
(b) (*Pol, Rel etc: groupe*) community. **servir la ~** to serve the community; **~ urbaine** urban community; **vivre en ~** to live communally; **mettre qch en ~** to pool sth.
(c) (*Jur: entre époux*) **biens qui appartiennent à la ~** joint estate (*of husband and wife*); **mariés sous le régime de la ~ (des biens)** married with a communal estate settlement; **~ légale** communal estate; **~ réduite aux acquêts** communal estate comprising only property acquired after marriage.
(d) (*Pol*) **la C~ Économique Européenne (C.E.E.)** the European Economic Community (E.E.C.).
commune² [kɔmyn] *nf* **(a)** (*Admin*) commune; (*rurale*) ≃ rural district; (*plus petite*) ≃ parish; (*urbaine*) ≃ district borough. **les travaux sont à la charge de la ~** the district *ou* borough council is responsible for the cost of the work. **(b)** (*groupe*) commune. **(c)** (*Hist*) **la C~** the Commune. **(d)** (*Brit Pol*) **la Chambre des C~s, les C~s** the (House of) Commons.
communément [kɔmynemɑ̃] *adv* commonly.
communiant, e [kɔmynjɑ̃, ɑ̃t] *nm,f* (*Rel*) communicant. **(premier) ~** child making his first communion.
communicable [kɔmynikabl(ə)] *adj expérience, sentiment* which can be communicated; (*Jur*) *droit* transferable; *dossier* which may be made available. **ces renseignements ne sont pas ~s par téléphone** this information cannot be given over the telephone.
communicant, e [kɔmynikɑ̃, ɑ̃t] *adj pièces, salles* communicating (*épith*); *V* **vase**¹.
communicateur, -trice [kɔmynikatœʀ, tʀis] *adj* (*Tech*) *fil, pièce* connecting (*épith*).
communicatif, -ive [kɔmynikatif, iv] *adj rire, ennui* infectious; *personne* communicative.
communication [kɔmynikɑsjɔ̃] *nf* **(a)** (*gén, Philos: relation*) communication. **la ~ est très difficile avec lui, il est si timide** communication (with him) is very difficult because he's so shy; **être en ~ avec** *ami, société savante* to be in communication *ou* contact with; *esprit* to communicate *ou* be in communication with; **mettre qn en ~ avec qn** to put sb in touch *ou* contact with sb; **théorie des ~s** communications theory.
(b) (*fait de transmettre*) *[fait, nouvelle]* communication; *[dossier]* transmission. **avoir ~ d'un fait** to be informed of a fact; **demander ~ d'un dossier/d'un livre** to ask for a file/a book; **donner ~ d'une pièce (à qn)** to communicate a document (to sb).
(c) (*message*) message, communication; (*Univ: exposé*) paper. **faire une ~** to read *ou* give a paper.
(d) ~ (téléphonique) (telephone) call, (phone) call. **mettre qn en ~ (avec)** to put sb through (to), connect sb (with); **~ interurbaine** trunk call; **~ à longue distance** long-distance call; **~ en PCV** reverse charge call (*Brit*), collect call (*US*); **~ avec préavis** personal call; **vous avez la ~** you are through; **je n'ai pas pu avoir la ~** I couldn't get through.
(e) (*moyen de liaison*) communication. **porte de ~** communicating door; **les (voies de) ~s ont été coupées par les chutes de neige** communications *ou* the lines of communication were cut off by the snow(fall); **moyens de ~** means of communication.
communier [kɔmynje] (7) *vi* (*Rel*) to receive communion. **~ sous les deux espèces** to receive communion under both kinds; (*fig*) **~ dans** *sentiment* to be united in; (*fig*) **~ avec** *sentiment* to share.
communion [kɔmynjɔ̃] *nf* (*Rel, fig*) communion. **faire sa (première) ~** to make one's first communion; **faire sa ~ solennelle** to make one's solemn communion; **pour la (première) ~ de ma fille, il pleuvait** it rained on the day of my daughter's first communion; (*fig*) **être en ~ avec** *personne* to be in communion with; *sentiments* to be in sympathy with; **être en ~ d'idées avec qn** to be in sympathy with sb's ideas; **être en ~ d'esprit avec qn** to be of the same intellectual outlook as sb; **nous sommes en ~ d'esprit** we are of the same (intellectual) outlook, we are kindred spirits; **la ~ des saints** the communion of the saints.
communiqué [kɔmynike] *nm* communiqué. **~ de presse** press release.
communiquer [kɔmynike] (1) **1** *vt* **(a)** *nouvelle, renseignement, demande* to pass on, communicate, convey (*à* to); *dossier, document* (*donner*) to give (*à* to); (*envoyer*) to send, transmit (*à* to). **~ un fait à qn** to inform sb of a fact; **le livre est déjà communiqué** the book is already out; **se ~ des renseignements** to pass on information to one another.
(b) *enthousiasme, peur* to communicate, pass on (*à* to); (*Méd*) *maladie* to pass on, give (*à qn* to sb).
(c) *[chose] mouvement* to communicate, transmit, impart (*à* to); *[soleil] lumière, chaleur* to transmit (*à* to).
2 *vi* **(a)** (*correspondre*) to communicate (*avec* with). **les sourds-muets communiquent par signes** deaf-mutes communicate by signs; **~ avec qn par lettre/téléphone** to communicate with sb by letter/phone.
(b) *[pièces, salles]* to communicate (*avec* with). **des pièces qui communiquent** communicating rooms, rooms which communicate with one another; **couloir qui fait ~ les chambres** corridor that links *ou* connects the rooms.
3 se communiquer *vpr* **(a)** (*se propager*) **se ~ à** *[feu, maladie]* to spread to.
(b) (*se livrer*) **personne réservée qui se communique peu** reserved and rather uncommunicative person.
communisant, e [kɔmynizɑ̃, ɑ̃t] **1** *adj* communistic. **2** *nm,f* communist sympathizer, fellow traveller (*fig*).
communisme [kɔmynism(ə)] *nm* communism.
communiste [kɔmynist(ə)] *adj, nmf* communist.
commutable [kɔmytabl(ə)] *adj* = **commuable.**
commutateur [kɔmytatœʀ] *nm* (*Élec*) (changeover) switch, commutator; (*Téléc*) commutation switch; (*bouton*) (light) switch.
commutatif, -ive [kɔmytatif, iv] *adj* (*Jur, Ling, Math*) commutative.
commutation [kɔmytɑsjɔ̃] *nf* (*Jur, Math*) commutation; (*Ling*) substitution, commutation.
commutativité [kɔmytativite] *nf [élément]* commutative property, commutability; *[addition]* commutative nature.
commuter [kɔmyte] (1) *vt* (*Math*) *éléments* to commute; (*Ling*) *termes* to substitute, commute.
Comores [kɔmɔʀ] *nfpl*: **les (îles) ~** the Comoro Islands.
compacité [kɔ̃pasite] *nf* (*V* **compact**) density; compactness.
compact, e [kɔ̃pakt, akt(ə)] *adj* (*dense*) *foule, substance* dense; *quartier* closely *ou* densely built-up; (*de faible encombrement*) *véhicule, appareil* compact. (*Pol*) **une majorité ~e** a solid majority.
compagne [kɔ̃paɲ] *nf* (*camarade, littér: épouse*) companion; (*maîtresse*) (lady)friend; *[animal]* mate. **~ de classe** classmate; **~ de jeu** playmate.
compagnie [kɔ̃paɲi] **1** *nf* **(a)** (*présence, société*) company. **il n'a pour toute ~ que sa vieille maman** he has only his old mother for company; **ce n'est pas une ~ pour lui** he *ou* she is not fit company *ou* is no company for him; **en ~ de** *personne* in the company of; *chose* alongside, along with; **il n'est heureux qu'en ~ de ses livres** he's only happy when (he's) surrounded by his books; **en bonne/mauvaise/joyeuse ~** in good/bad/cheerful company; **tenir ~ à qn** to keep sb company; **être d'une ~ agréable** to be pleasant company; (*frm*) **être de bonne/mauvaise ~** to be well-/ill-bred; **nous voyageâmes de ~** we travelled together *ou* in company; **ça va de ~ avec** it goes hand in hand with; *V* **fausser.**
(b) (*réunion*) gathering, company (*U*). **bonsoir la ~!** goodnight all!
(c) (*Comm*) company; (*groupe de savants, écrivains*) body. **~ d'assurances/théâtrale/aérienne** insurance/theatrical/airline company; **la banque X et ~** the X and company bank, the bank of X and company; **tout ça, c'est voleurs et ~** they're all the same thieving lot* *ou* crowd* *ou* bunch‡; **la ~, l'illustre ~** the French Academy.
(d) (*Mil*) company.
2: (*Mil*) **compagnie de discipline** punishment company (*made up of convicted soldiers*); (*Hist*) **la Compagnie des Indes** the East India Company; (*Rel*) **la Compagnie de Jésus** the Society of Jesus; (*Chasse*) **compagnie de perdreaux** covey of partridges; (*Police*) **compagnies républicaines de sécurité** *state security police force in France.*
compagnon [kɔ̃paɲɔ̃] **1** *nm* **(a)** (*camarade, littér: époux*) companion; (*écuyer*) companion. **~ d'études/de travail** fellow student/worker; **~ d'exil/de misère/d'infortune** companion in exile/in suffering/in misfortune.
(b) (*ouvrier*) craftsman, journeyman.
(c) (*franc-maçon*) companion.
2: compagnon d'armes companion- *ou* comrade-in-arms; **compagnon de bord** shipmate; **compagnon de jeu** playmate; **compagnon de route** fellow traveller (*lit*); **compagnon de table** companion at table, table companion; **compagnon de voyage** travelling companion, fellow traveller (*lit*); (*Hist*) **compagnon du voyage** *ou* **du Tour de France** journeyman (*touring France after his apprenticeship*).
compagnonnage [kɔ̃paɲɔnaʒ] *nm* (*Hist: association d'ouvriers*) ≃ (trade) guild.
comparable [kɔ̃paʀabl(ə)] *adj grandeur, élément* comparable (*à* to, *avec* with). **ce n'est pas ~** there's (just) no comparison, you can't compare them.
comparaison [kɔ̃paʀɛzɔ̃] *nf* **(a)** (*gén*) comparison (*à* to, *avec* with). **mettre qch en ~ avec** to compare sth with; **vous n'avez qu'à faire la ~** you only need to compare them; **il n'y a pas de ~ (possible) (entre)** there is no (possible) comparison (between); **ça ne soutient pas la ~** that doesn't bear *ou* stand comparison.

(b) (*Gram*) comparison. **adjectif/adverbe de ~** comparative adjective/adverb.

(c) (*Littérat*) simile, comparison.

(d) (*loc*) **en ~ (de)** in comparison (with); **par ~** by comparison (*avec, à* with); **il est sans ~ le meilleur** he is far and away the best; **c'est sans ~ avec** it cannot be compared with; (*Prov*) **~ n'est pas raison** comparisons are odious.

comparaître [kɔ̃paʀɛtʀ(ə)] (57) *vi* (*Jur*) to appear. (*fig littér*) **il fait ~ dans ses nouvelles toutes sortes de personnages** he brings all sorts of characters into his short stories; *V* **citation, citer.**

comparatif, -ive [kɔ̃paʀatif, iv] *adj, nm* comparative. (*Gram*) **au ~** in the comparative; **~ d'infériorité/de supériorité** comparative of lesser/greater degree.

comparatiste [kɔ̃paʀatist(ə)] *nmf* (*Ling*) specialist in comparative linguistics; (*Littérat*) specialist in comparative literature.

comparativement [kɔ̃paʀativmɑ̃] *adv* comparatively, by comparison. **~ à** by comparison with, compared to *ou* with.

comparé, e [kɔ̃paʀe] (*ptp de* **comparer**) *adj étude, littérature* comparative.

comparer [kɔ̃paʀe] (1) *vt* **(a)** (*confronter*) to compare (*à, avec* with). **~ deux choses (entre elles)** to compare two things; **vous n'avez qu'à ~** you've only to compare.

(b) (*identifier*) to compare, liken (*à* to). **Molière peut se ~ *ou* être comparé à Shakespeare** Molière can be compared *ou* likened to Shakespeare; **c'est un bon écrivain mais il ne peut quand même pas se ~ à X** he's a good writer but he still can't compare with X; **ça ne se compare pas** there's no comparison, they can't be compared.

comparse [kɔ̃paʀs(ə)] *nmf* (*Théât*) supernumerary, walk-on; (*péj*) associate, stooge*. **rôle de ~** (*Théât*) walk-on part; (*péj, fig*) minor part; **nous n'avons là que les ~s, il nous faut le vrai chef** we've only the small fry here, we want the real leader.

compartiment [kɔ̃paʀtimɑ̃] *nm* (*casier, Rail*) compartment; *[damier]* square; *[parterre]* bed.

compartimentage [kɔ̃paʀtimɑ̃taʒ] *nm [armoire]* partitioning, compartmentation; *[administration, problème]* compartmentalization.

compartimenter [kɔ̃paʀtimɑ̃te] (1) *vt armoire* to partition, divide into compartments, put compartments in; *problème, administration* to compartmentalize.

comparution [kɔ̃paʀysjɔ̃] *nf* (*Jur*) appearance; *V* **non.**

compas [kɔ̃pa] **1** *nm* (*Géom*) (pair of) compasses; (*Naut*) compass. (*fig*) **avoir le ~ dans l'œil** to have an accurate eye; *V* **naviguer. 2: compas d'épaisseur** spring-adjusting callipers; **compas à pointes sèches** dividers; **compas quart de cercle** wing compass.

compassé, e [kɔ̃pɑse] (*ptp de* **compasser**) *adj* (*guindé*) formal, stuffy*, starchy.

compasser [kɔ̃pɑse] (1) *vt* (*littér*) *attitude, démarche* to control rigidly, make (seem) stiff and unnatural.

compassion [kɔ̃pɑsjɔ̃] *nf* compassion. **avec ~** compassionately.

compatibilité [kɔ̃patibilite] *nf* compatibility.

compatible [kɔ̃patibl(ə)] *adj* compatible.

compatir [kɔ̃patiʀ] (2) *vi* to sympathize. **~ à la douleur de qn** to sympathize *ou* share *ou* commiserate with sb in his grief.

compatissant, e [kɔ̃patisɑ̃, ɑ̃t] *adj* compassionate, sympathetic.

compatriote [kɔ̃patʀijɔt] **1** *nm* compatriot, fellow countryman. **2** *nf* compatriot, fellow countrywoman.

compensateur, -trice [kɔ̃pɑ̃satœʀ, tʀis] **1** *adj indemnité, élément, mouvement* compensatory, compensating (*épith*). **2** *nm*: **(pendule) ~** compensation pendulum.

compensation [kɔ̃pɑ̃sɑsjɔ̃] *nf* **(a)** (*dédommagement*) compensation. **donner qch en ~ d'autre chose** to give sth in compensation for something else, make up for something with sth else; **en ~ (des dégâts), à titre de ~ (pour les dégâts)** in compensation *ou* by way of compensation (for the damage); **c'est une piètre ~ de le savoir** it's not much (of a) compensation to know that; **il y en a peu mais en ~ c'est bon** there's not much of it but what there is is good *ou* but on the other hand *ou* but to make up for that it's good.

(b) (*équilibre*) balance; (*neutralisation*) balancing; (*Phys*) *[forces]* compensation; (*Méd*) *[maladie, infirmité]* compensation; (*Naut*) *[compas]* correction; (*Psych*) compensation; (*Fin*) *[dette]* set-off. **il y a ~ entre gains et pertes** gains and losses cancel each other out; (*Math*) **loi de ~** law of large numbers; (*Jur*) **~ des dépens** division *ou* sharing of the costs; *V* **chambre.**

compensatoire [kɔ̃pɑ̃satwaʀ] *adj* compensatory, compensating.

compensé, e [kɔ̃pɑ̃se] (*ptp de* **compenser**) *adj semelles* platform (*épith*); *gouvernail* balanced; *horloge* compensated. **chaussures à semelles ~es** platform shoes, shoes with platform soles.

compenser [kɔ̃pɑ̃se] (1) *vt* to make good, compensate for, offset; *perte, dégâts* to compensate for, make up for; (*Méd*) *infirmité* to compensate (for); (*Naut*) *compas* to correct; (*Fin*) *dette* to set off. **~ une peine par une joie** to make up for a painful experience with a happy one; **ses qualités et ses défauts se compensent** his qualities compensate for *ou* make up for his faults; **pour ~** to compensate, to make up for it, as a compensation; (*Jur*) **~ les dépens** to divide *ou* share the costs, tax each party for its own costs; (*Phys*) **forces qui se compensent** compensating forces; *V* **ceci.**

compère [kɔ̃pɛʀ] *nm* **(a)** (*gén: complice*) accomplice; (*aux enchères*) puffer. **(b)**(†) (*ami*) crony*, comrade; (*personne, type*) fellow.

compère-loriot, *pl* **compères-loriots** [kɔ̃pɛʀlɔʀjo] *nm* (*Méd: orgelet*) sty(e); (*Orn*) golden oriole.

compétence [kɔ̃petɑ̃s] *nf* **(a)** (*expérience, habileté*) competence. **~s** abilities; **avoir de la ~** to be competent; **manquer de ~** to lack competence; **faire qch avec ~** to do sth competently; **faire appel à la ~ *ou* aux ~s d'un spécialiste** to call (up)on the skills *ou* the skilled advice of a specialist; **savoir utiliser les ~s** to know how to put people's skills *ou* abilities to the best use.

(b) (*rayon d'activité*) (*Jur*) competence. (*Jur*) **c'est de la ~ de ce tribunal** it's within the competence of this court; **ce n'est pas de ma ~, cela n'entre pas dans mes ~s** that's not (in) my sphere *ou* domain, that falls outside the scope of my activities.

compétent, e [kɔ̃petɑ̃, ɑ̃t] *adj* (*capable, qualifié*) competent, capable; (*Jur*) competent. **~ en** competent in; **~ en la matière** competent in the subject; **adressez-vous à l'autorité ~e** apply to the authority concerned.

compétiteur, -trice [kɔ̃petitœʀ, tʀis] *nm,f* competitor.

compétitif, -ive [kɔ̃petitif, iv] *adj* competitive.

compétition [kɔ̃petisjɔ̃] *nf* **(a)** (*Sport: activité*) **la ~** competitive sport; **faire de la ~** to go in for competitive sport; **la ~ automobile** motor racing; **abandonner la ~** *[coureur]* to retire from *ou* give up competitive running; **sport de ~** competitive sport.

(b) (*Sport: épreuve*) event. **~ sportive** sporting event; **une ~ automobile** a motor racing event.

(c) (*gén, Sport: rivalité, concurrence*) competition (*U*); (*Comm, Pol*) rivalry, competition. **entrer en ~ avec** to compete with; **être en ~** to be competing, be in competition (*avec* with).

compétitivité [kɔ̃petitivite] *nf* competitiveness.

compilateur, -trice [kɔ̃pilatœʀ, tʀis] **1** *nm,f* (*souvent péj*) compiler. **2** *nm* (*Ordinateurs*) compiler.

compilation [kɔ̃pilɑsjɔ̃] *nf* (*action*) compiling, compilation; (*souvent péj: ouvrage*) compilation.

compiler [kɔ̃pile] (1) *vt* to compile.

complainte [kɔ̃plɛ̃t] *nf* (*Littérat, Mus*) lament.

complaire [kɔ̃plɛʀ] (54) **1 complaire à** *vt indir* to (try to) please. **2 se complaire** *vpr*: **se ~ dans qch/à faire qch** to take pleasure in sth/in doing sth, delight *ou* revel in sth/in doing sth.

complaisamment [kɔ̃plɛzamɑ̃] *adv* (*V* **complaisant**) obligingly, kindly; accommodatingly; smugly, complacently.

complaisance [kɔ̃plɛzɑ̃s] *nf* **(a)** (*obligeance*) kindness, complaisance (*envers* to, towards); (*esprit accommodant*) accommodating attitude. (*frm*) **il a eu la ~ de m'accompagner** he was kind *ou* good enough to *ou* he was so kind as to accompany me; **par ~** out of kindness *ou* complaisance.

(b) (*indulgence coupable*) indulgence, leniency; (*connivence malhonnête*) connivance; (*servilité*) servility, subservience. **la ~ de ce mari trompé** the complacency of this deceived husband; **avoir des ~s pour qn** to treat sb indulgently; **sourire de ~** polite smile; **certificat *ou* attestation de ~** false certificate of ill health (*produced to oblige a patient*); (*Comm*) **billet de ~** accommodation bill.

(c) (*fatuité*) self-satisfaction, complacency. **il parlait avec ~ de ses succès** he spoke smugly about his successes.

complaisant, e [kɔ̃plɛzɑ̃, ɑ̃t] *adj* **(a)** (*obligeant*) kind, obliging, complaisant; (*arrangeant*) accommodating.

(b) (*trop indulgent*) indulgent, lenient; (*trop arrangeant*) over-obliging; (*servile*) servile, subservient. **c'est un mari ~** he turns a blind eye to his wife's goings-on; **prêter une oreille ~e à qn/qch** to listen to sb/sth readily, lend a willing ear to sb/sth.

(c) (*fat*) self-satisfied, smug, complacent.

complément [kɔ̃plemɑ̃] *nm* **(a)** (*gén, Bio, Math*) complement; (*reste*) rest, remainder. **~ d'information** supplementary *ou* further *ou* additional information (*U*).

(b) (*Gram*) (*gén*) complement; (*complément d'objet*) object. **~ circonstanciel de lieu/de temps** *etc* adverbial phrase of place/time *etc*; **~ (d'objet) direct/indirect** direct/indirect object; **~ d'agent** agent; **~ de nom** possessive phrase.

complémentaire [kɔ̃plemɑ̃tɛʀ] *adj* (*gén, Math*) complementary; (*additionnel*) supplementary. **pour tout renseignement ~** for any supplementary *ou* further *ou* additional information (*U*); *V* **cours.**

complémentarité [kɔ̃plemɑ̃taʀite] *nf* complementarity, complementary nature.

complet, -ète [kɔ̃plɛ, ɛt] **1** *adj* **(a)** (*exhaustif, entier*) (*gén*) complete, full; *rapport, analyse* comprehensive, full. **procéder à un examen ~ de qch** to make a full *ou* thorough examination of sth; **il reste encore 3 tours/jours ~s** there are still 3 complete *ou* full laps/days to go; **il a fait des études ~ètes de pharmacien** he has done a complete *ou* full course in pharmacy; **pour vous donner une idée ~ète de la situation** to give you a complete *ou* full idea of the situation; **les œuvres ~ètes de Voltaire** the complete works of Voltaire; **le dossier est-il ~?** is the file complete?; **il en possède une collection très ~ète** he has a very full collection (of it *ou* them); **la lecture ~ète de ce livre prend 2 heures** it takes 2 hours to read this book right through *ou* from cover to cover; *V* **aliment, pension.**

(b) (*total*) *échec, obscurité* complete, total, utter; *découragement* complete, total. **dans la misère la plus ~ète** in the most abject poverty.

(c) (*consommé, achevé: après n*) *homme, acteur* complete. **c'est un athlète ~** he's an all-round athlete, he's the complete athlete.

(d) (*plein*) *autobus, train* full, full up (*attrib*). (*écriteau*) '~' *[hôtel]* 'no vacancies'; *[parking]* 'full (up)'; *[cinéma]* 'full house'; *[match]* 'ground full'; **le théâtre affiche ~ tous les soirs** the theatre has a full house every evening.

(e) (*) **eh bien! c'est ~!** well, that's the end! *ou* the limit!, that's all we needed!

2 *nm* **(a) au (grand) ~: maintenant que nous sommes au ~** now that we are all here; **la famille au grand ~ s'était rassemblée** the whole *ou* entire family had got together.

(b) (*costume*) suit. **~-veston** suit.

complètement [kɔ̃plɛtmɑ̃] *adv* **(a)** (*en entier*) *démonter, nettoyer, repeindre* completely; *lire un article etc* right through; *lire un livre* from cover to cover; *citer* in full. **~ nu** completely *ou* stark naked; **~ trempé/terminé** completely soaked/finished; **écouter ~ un disque** to listen to a record right through, listen to the whole of a record (*Brit*).

(b) (*absolument*) **~ fou** completely mad, absolutely crazy; **~ faux** completely *ou* absolutely *ou* utterly false; **~ découragé** completely *ou* totally discouraged.

(c) (*à fond*) *étudier qch, faire une enquête* fully, thoroughly.

compléter [kɔ̃plete] (6) **1** *vt* **(a)** (*terminer, porter au total voulu*) *somme, effectifs* to make up; *mobilier, collection, dossier* to complete. **pour ~ votre travail/l'ensemble ...** to complete your work/the whole ...; **elle compléta ses études en suivant un cours de dactylographie** she completed *ou* rounded off *ou* finished off her studies by taking a course in typing; **un délicieux café compléta le repas** a delightful cup of coffee rounded off the meal; (*fig*) **sa dernière gaffe complète le tableau: il est vraiment incorrigible** his latest blunder crowns it – he never learns; (*fig*) **et pour ~ le tableau, il arriva en retard!** and to crown it all *ou* as a finishing touch he arrived late!

(b) (*augmenter, agrémenter*) *études, formation* to complement, supplement; *connaissances, documentation, collection* to supplement, add to; *mobilier, garde-robe* to add to. **sa collection se complète lentement** his collection is slowly building up.

2 se compléter *vpr* [*caractères, partenaires, fonctions*] to complement one another.

complétif, -ive [kɔ̃pletif, iv] **1** *adj* substantival. **2 complétive** *nf*: **(proposition) ~ive** noun *ou* substantival clause; **relative ~ive** relative clause.

complexe [kɔ̃plɛks(ə)] **1** *adj* (*gén: compliqué*) complex, complicated; (*Ling, Math*) *nombre, quantité, phrase* complex. **sujet ~** compound subject.

2 *nm* **(a)** (*Psych*) complex. **~ d'Œdipe/d'infériorité/de supériorité** Oedipus/inferiority/superiority complex; **être bourré de ~s*** to have loads of hang-ups*, be full of complexes.

(b) (*Econ*) *industriel, universitaire etc* complex.

(c) (*Chim, Math*) complex.

complexer [kɔ̃plɛkse] (1) *vt*: **ça le complexe terriblement** it gives him a terrible complex; **être très complexé** to have awful complexes, be very hung-up* *ou* mixed up*.

complexion†† [kɔ̃plɛksjɔ̃] *nf* (*constitution*) constitution; (*teint*) complexion; (*humeur*) disposition, temperament.

complexité [kɔ̃plɛksite] *nf* complexity, intricacy; [*calcul*] complexity.

complication [kɔ̃plikɑsjɔ̃] *nf* (*complexité*) complexity, intricacy; (*ennui*) complication. (*Méd*) **~s** complications; **faire des ~s** to make life difficult *ou* complicated.

complice [kɔ̃plis] **1** *adj* **(a) être ~ de qch** to be (a) party to sth.

(b) *regard* knowing (*épith*); *attitude* conniving. (*littér*) **la nuit ~ protégeait leur fuite** the friendly night conspired to shelter their flight (*littér*).

2 *nmf* **(a)** (*criminel*) accomplice. **être (le) ~ de qn** to be sb's accomplice, be in collusion with sb.

(b) (*adultère*) (*Jur*) co-respondent; (*amant*) lover; (*maîtresse*) mistress.

complicité [kɔ̃plisite] *nf* (*Jur, fig*) complicity. **agir en ~ avec** to act in complicity *ou* collusion with.

complies [kɔ̃pli] *nfpl* compline.

compliment [kɔ̃plimɑ̃] *nm* **(a)** (*félicitations*) **~s** congratulations; **recevoir les ~s de qn** to receive sb's congratulations, be congratulated by sb; **faire des ~s à qn (pour)** to compliment *ou* congratulate sb (on); (*lit, iro*) **je vous fais mes ~s!** congratulations!, let me congratulate you!

(b) (*louange*) compliment. **elle rougit sous le ~** she blushed at the compliment; **faire des ~s à qn sur sa bonne mine, faire ~ à qn de sa bonne mine** to compliment sb on his healthy appearance; **il lui fait sans cesse des ~s** he's always paying her compliments.

(c) (*formule de politesse*) **~s** compliments; **faites-lui mes ~s** give him my compliments *ou* regards; **avec les ~s de la direction** with the compliments of the management.

(d) (*petit discours*) congratulatory speech.

complimenter [kɔ̃plimɑ̃te] (1) *vt* to congratulate, compliment (*pour, sur, de* on).

complimenteur, -euse [kɔ̃plimɑ̃tœʀ, øz] **1** *adj* obsequious. **2** *nm,f* complimenter; (*péj*) flatterer.

compliqué, e [kɔ̃plike] (*ptp de* **compliquer**) *adj mécanisme* complicated, intricate; *affaire, explication, phrase* complicated, involved; *histoire, esprit* tortuous; *personne* complicated; (*Méd*) *fracture* compound (*épith*). **ne sois pas si ~!** don't be so complicated!; **puisque tu refuses, ce n'est pas ~, moi je pars** since you refuse, there's no problem *ou* that makes it easy *ou* that simplifies the problem — I'm leaving.

compliquer [kɔ̃plike] (1) **1** *vt* to complicate. **il nous complique l'existence** he DOES make life difficult *ou* complicated for us; **se ~ l'existence** to make life difficult *ou* complicated for o.s.

2 se compliquer *vpr* to become *ou* get complicated. **ça se complique** things are getting more and more complicated; **la maladie se complique** complications have set in.

complot [kɔ̃plo] *nm* (*conspiration*) plot. **mettre qn dans le ~*** to let sb in on the plot*.

comploter [kɔ̃plɔte] (1) *vti* to plot (*de faire* to do, *contre* against). **qu'est-ce que vous complotez?*** what are you hatching?

comploteur [kɔ̃plɔtœʀ] *nm* plotter.

componction [kɔ̃pɔ̃ksjɔ̃] *nf* (*péj*) (affected) gravity; (*Rel*) contrition. **avec ~** solemnly, with a great show of dignity.

comportement [kɔ̃pɔʀtəmɑ̃] *nm* (*gén*) behaviour (*envers, avec* towards). **le bon ~ de ces pneus sur chaussée verglacée** the excellent performance *ou* behaviour of these tyres on icy roads.

comporter [kɔ̃pɔʀte] (1) **1** *vt* **(a)** (*consister en*) to be composed of, be made up of, consist of, comprise. **ce roman comporte 2 parties** this novel is made up of *ou* is composed of *ou* comprises 2 parts; **la maison comporte 5 pièces et une cuisine** the house comprises 5 rooms and a kitchen.

(b) (*être muni de*) to have, include. **son livre comporte une préface** his book has *ou* includes a preface; **cette machine ne comporte aucun dispositif de sécurité** this machine has no safety mechanism, there is no safety mechanism included in this machine; **cette règle comporte des exceptions** this rule has certain exceptions.

(c) (*impliquer*) *risques etc* to entail, involve. **je dois accepter cette solution, avec tout ce que cela comporte (de désavantages/d'imprévu)** I must accept this solution with all (the disadvantages/unexpected consequences) that it entails *ou* involves.

2 se comporter *vpr* **(a)** (*se conduire*) to behave. **se ~ en** *ou* **comme un enfant gâté** to behave like a spoilt child; **il s'est comporté d'une façon odieuse (avec sa mère)** he behaved in a horrible way (towards his mother).

(b) (*réagir*) [*personne*] to behave; [*machine, voiture*] to perform. **comment s'est-il comporté après l'accident?** how did he behave after the accident?; **notre équipe s'est très bien comportée hier** our team played very well yesterday, our team put up a good performance yesterday; **comment le matériel s'est-il comporté en altitude?** how did the equipment stand up to the high altitude?; **ces pneus se comportent très bien sur chaussée glissante** these tyres behave *ou* perform very well on slippery roads.

composant, e [kɔ̃pozɑ̃, ɑ̃t] **1** *adj, nm* component, constituent. **2 composante** *nf* (*Phys, gén*) component.

composé, e [kɔ̃poze] (*ptp de* **composer**) **1** *adj* **(a)** (*Chim, Gram, Math, Mus*) compound (*épith*); (*Bot*) *fleur* composite (*épith*); *feuille* compound (*épith*); *V* **passé**.

(b) (*guindé, affecté*) *maintien, attitude* studied.

2 *nm* (*Chim, Gram*) compound. (*fig*) **c'est un ~ étrange de douceur et de violence** he's a strange combination *ou* mixture of gentleness and violence.

3 *nf* (*Bot*) **composées** compositae (*T*), composites.

composer [kɔ̃poze] (1) **1** *vt* **(a)** (*confectionner*) *plat, médicament* to make (up); *équipe de football etc* to select; *assemblée, équipe scientifique* to form, set up. **l'étalagiste compose une belle vitrine** the window dresser is arranging *ou* laying out *ou* setting up a fine display.

(b) (*élaborer*) *poème, lettre, roman* to write, compose; *symphonie* to compose; *tableau* to paint; *numéro de téléphone* to dial; *projet, programme* to work out, draw up; *couleurs, éléments d'un tableau* to arrange harmoniously; *bouquet* to arrange, make up.

(c) (*constituer*) *ensemble, produit, groupe* to make up; *assemblée* to form, make up. **pièces qui composent une machine** parts which (go to) make up a machine; **ces objets composent un ensemble harmonieux** these objects form *ou* make a harmonious group.

(d) (*Typ*) to set.

(e) (*frm: étudier artificiellement*) **~ son visage** to assume an affected expression; **~ ses gestes** to use affected gestures; **attitudes/allures composées** studied behaviour/manners; **il s'était composé un personnage de dandy** he had established his image as that of a dandy; **se ~ un visage de circonstance** to assume a suitable expression.

2 *vi* **(a)** (*Scol*) **~ en anglais** to sit (*surtout Brit*) *ou* take an English test; **les élèves sont en train de ~** the pupils are (in the middle of) doing a test *ou* an exam.

(b) (*traiter*) to compromise. **~ avec** *adversaire etc* to come to terms with, compromise with.

3 se composer *vpr* (*consister en*) **se ~ de** *ou* **être composé de** to be composed of, be made up of, consist of, comprise; **la vitrine se compose** *ou* **est composée de robes** the window display is made up of *ou* composed of dresses.

composite [kɔ̃pozit] **1** *adj* **(a)** (*hétérogène*) *éléments, mobilier* heterogeneous; *foule* motley (*épith*). **(b)** (*Archit*) composite. **2** *nm* (*Archit*) composite order.

compositeur, -trice [kɔ̃pozitœʀ, tʀis] *nm,f* (*Mus*) composer; (*Typ*) compositor, typesetter.

composition [kɔ̃pozisjɔ̃] *nf* **(a)** (*confection*) [*plat, médicament*] making(-up); [*assemblée*] formation, setting-up; [*équipe sportive*] selection; [*équipe de chercheurs etc*] setting-up.

(b) (*élaboration*) [*roman, lettre, poème*] writing, composition; [*symphonie*] composition; [*tableau*] painting. **une œuvre de ma ~** a work of my own composition, one of my own compositions.

(c) (*œuvre*) (*musicale, picturale*) composition; (*architecturale*) structure.

(d) (*structure*) [*plan, ensemble*] structure. **quelle est la ~ du passage?** what is the structure of the passage?; **la répartition des masses dans le tableau forme une ~ harmonieuse** the distribution of the masses in the picture forms *ou* makes a harmonious composition.

(e) (*constituants*) [*mélange, équipe*] composition. **quelle est la ~ du gâteau?** what is the cake made of?, what ingredients go into the cake?

(f) (*Scol: examen*) **~ trimestrielle** end-of-term test, term exam; ~ **de français** (*en classe*) French test *ou* exam; (*à l'examen*) French paper; (*rédaction*) ~ **française** French essay *ou* composition.

(g) (*Typ*) typesetting, composition.

(h) (*loc*) **venir à** ~ to come to terms; **amener qn à** ~ to get sb to come to terms; *V* **bon**[1].

compost [kɔ̃pɔst] *nm* compost.

compostage [kɔ̃pɔstaʒ] *nm* (*V* **composter**) (date) stamping; punching.

composter [kɔ̃pɔste] (1) *vt* (*dater*) to (date) stamp; (*poinçonner*) to punch.

composteur [kɔ̃pɔstœʀ] *nm* (*timbre dateur*) date stamp; (*poinçon*) punch; (*Typ*) composing stick.

compote [kɔ̃pɔt] *nf* (*Culin*) stewed fruit, compote. ~ **de pommes/de poires** stewed apples/pears, compote of apples/pears; (*fig*) **j'ai les jambes en** ~* (*de fatigue*) my legs are aching (all over); (*par l'émotion, la maladie*) my legs are like jelly *ou* cotton wool; **il a le visage en** ~* his face is black and blue *ou* is a mass of bruises.

compotier [kɔ̃pɔtje] *nm* fruit dish *ou* bowl.

compréhensibilité [kɔ̃pʀeɑ̃sibilite] *nf [texte]* comprehensibility.

compréhensible [kɔ̃pʀeɑ̃sibl(ə)] *adj* (*clair*) comprehensible, easily understood; (*concevable*) understandable.

compréhensif, -ive [kɔ̃pʀeɑ̃sif, iv] *adj* (*tolérant*) understanding; (*Logique*) comprehensive.

compréhension [kɔ̃pʀeɑ̃sjɔ̃] *nf* (*indulgence*) understanding; (*fait ou faculté de comprendre*) understanding, comprehension; (*clarté*) understanding, intelligibility; (*Logique*) comprehension. **la** ~ **d'un terme** the area covered by a term, the comprehension of a term.

comprendre [kɔ̃pʀɑ̃dʀ(ə)] (58) *vt* **(a)** (*être composé de*) to be composed of, be made up of, consist of, comprise; (*être muni de, inclure*) to include. **ce manuel comprend 3 parties** this textbook is composed of *ou* is made up of *ou* comprises 3 parts; **cet appareil comprend en outre un flash** this camera also has *ou* comes with* a flash, (also) included with this camera is a flash; **le loyer ne comprend pas le chauffage** the rent doesn't include *ou* cover (the) heating, the rent is not inclusive of heating; **je n'ai pas compris là-dedans les frais de déménagement** I haven't included the removal expenses in that.

(b) *problème, langue* to understand; *plaisanterie* to understand, get*; *personne* (*ce qu'elle dit ou écrit*) to understand. **je ne le comprends pas/je ne comprends pas ce qu'il dit, il parle trop vite** I can't understand him/I can't make out what he says, he speaks too quickly; **vous m'avez mal compris** you've misunderstood me; **il ne comprend pas l'allemand** he doesn't understand German; ~ **la vie/les choses** to understand life/things; **il ne comprend pas la plaisanterie** he can't take a joke; **il ne comprend rien à rien** he hasn't a clue about anything, he doesn't understand a thing (about anything); **c'est à n'y rien** ~ it (just) baffles me, it's (just) beyond me, I (just) can't understand it; **se faire** ~ to make o.s. understood; **j'espère que je me suis bien fait** ~ *ou* **que c'est compris** I hope I've made myself quite clear; **il comprend vite** he's quick, he catches on quickly*; **tu comprends, ce que je veux c'est ...** you see, what I want is ...; **il a bien su me faire** ~ **que je le gênais** he made it quite clear *ou* plain to me that I was annoying him; **dois-je** ~ **que ...?** am I to take it *ou* understand that ...?

(c) (*être compréhensif envers*) *personne* to understand. **j'espère qu'il comprendra** I hope he'll understand; ~ **les jeunes/les enfants** to understand young people/children; **je le comprends, il en avait assez** I (can) understand him *ou* I know (just) how he feels — he'd had enough.

(d) (*concevoir*) *attitude, point de vue* to understand. **il ne veut pas** ~ **mon point de vue** he refuses to *ou* he won't understand *ou* see my point of view; **je comprends mal son attitude** I find it hard to understand his attitude; **c'est comme ça que je comprends les vacances** that's what I understand by *ou* think of as holidays; **c'est comme ça que je comprends le rôle de Hamlet** that's how I see *ou* understand the role of Hamlet; **ça se comprend, il voulait partir** it's quite understandable *ou* it's perfectly natural, he wanted to go; **nous comprenons vos difficultés mais nous ne pouvons rien faire** we understand *ou* appreciate your difficulties but there's nothing we can do.

(e) (*se rendre compte de, saisir*) to realize, understand (*pourquoi* why, *comment* how). **il n'a pas encore compris la gravité de son acte** he hasn't yet realized *ou* understood *ou* grasped the seriousness of his action; **il m'a fait** ~ **que je devais faire attention** he made me realize that I should be careful; **il a enfin compris qu'elle ne voulait pas revenir** he realized *ou* understood at last that she didn't want to come back.

comprenette* [kɔ̃pʀənɛt] *nf*: **il est dur** *ou* **lent à la** ~, **il a la** ~ **difficile** *ou* **dure** he's slow on the uptake*, he's slow to catch on*.

compresse [kɔ̃pʀɛs] *nf* compress.

compresseur [kɔ̃pʀesœʀ] *nm* compressor; *V* **rouleau**.

compressibilité [kɔ̃pʀesibilite] *nf* (*Phys*) compressibility. (*Fin*) **la** ~ **des dépenses** the extent to which expenses can be reduced *ou* cut.

compressible [kɔ̃pʀesibl(ə)] *adj* (*Phys*) compressible; *dépenses* reducible. (*Fin*) **ces dépenses ne sont pas** ~**s à l'infini** these costs cannot be reduced *ou* cut down indefinitely.

compressif, -ive [kɔ̃pʀesif, iv] *adj* (*Méd*) compressive; (†*fig*) repressive.

compression [kɔ̃pʀesjɔ̃] *nf* **(a)** (*action de comprimer*) *[gaz, substance]* compression; *[dépenses, personnel]* reduction, cutback, cutting-down (*de* in). **procéder à des** ~**s de crédits** to set up credit restrictions *ou* a credit squeeze; **des** ~**s budgétaires** cutbacks in spending, budget restrictions; **des mesures de** ~ **sont nécessaires** restrictions *ou* cutbacks are needed.

(b) (*Aut, Phys: pression*) compression. **pompe de** ~ compression pump; **meurtri par** ~ bruised by crushing.

comprimé [kɔ̃pʀime] *nm* (*Pharm*) tablet.

comprimer [kɔ̃pʀime] (1) *vt* **(a)** (*presser*) *air, gaz* to compress; *artère* to compress; *substance à emballer etc* to press *ou* pack tightly together *ou* into blocks *etc*. **sa ceinture lui comprimait l'estomac** his belt was pressing *ou* digging into his stomach; **nous étions tous comprimés dans l'ascenseur** we were all jammed together* *ou* packed tightly together in the lift; *V* **air**[1].

(b) (*réduire*) *dépenses, personnel* to cut down *ou* back, reduce.

(c) (*contenir*) *larmes* to hold back; *colère, sentiments* to hold back, repress, restrain.

compris, e [kɔ̃pʀi, iz] (*ptp de* **comprendre**) *adj* **(a)** (*inclus*) **10 F emballage** ~ 10 francs inclusive of *ou* including packaging, 10 francs packaging included; **10 F emballage non** ~ 10 francs exclusive of *ou* excluding *ou* not including packaging; (*sur menu etc*) **service** ~ service included; **service non** ~ service not included, service extra; **tout** ~ all inclusive, everything included; **c'est 10 F tout** ~ it's 10 francs all inclusive *ou* all in*; **il va vendre ses terres, la ferme** ~**e/non** ~**e** he's selling his land including/excluding the farm.

(b) y ~: **100 F y** ~ **l'électricité** *ou* **l'électricité y** ~**e 100 francs** including electricity *ou* electricity included.

(c) (*situé*) **être** ~ **entre** to be contained between *ou* by, be bounded by; **la zone** ~**e entre les falaises et la mer** the area (lying) between the cliffs and the sea, the area contained *ou* bounded by the cliffs and the sea; **il possède la portion de terrain** ~**e entre ces deux rues** he owns the piece of ground between these two streets *ou* contained *ou* bounded by these two streets; **lisez tous les chapitres qui sont** ~ **entre les pages 12 et 145** read all the chapters (which are) contained *ou* included in pages 12 to 145.

(d) (*d'accord*) **(c'est)** ~! (it's) agreed!; **alors c'est** ~, **on se voit demain** so it's agreed then, we'll see each other tomorrow; **tu vas aller te coucher tout de suite,** ~! you're going to go to bed immediately, understand? *ou* is that understood?

compromettant, e [kɔ̃pʀɔmetɑ̃, ɑ̃t] *adj* compromising. **signer cette pétition, ce n'est pas très** ~ you won't commit yourself to very much by signing this petition, there's no great commitment involved in signing this petition; (*péj*) **un homme** ~ an undesirable associate.

compromettre [kɔ̃pʀɔmɛtʀ(ə)] (56) **1** *vt personne, réputation* to compromise; *avenir, chances, santé* to compromise, jeopardize. **2 se compromettre** *vpr* (*s'avancer*) to commit o.s.; (*se discréditer*) to compromise o.s.

compromis, e [kɔ̃pʀɔmi, iz] (*ptp de* **compromettre**) **1** *adj*: **être** ~ *[personne, réputation]* to be compromised; *[avenir, projet, chances]* to be jeopardized *ou* in jeopardy. **2** *nm* compromise. **solution de** ~ compromise solution.

compromission [kɔ̃pʀɔmisjɔ̃] *nf* compromise, (shady) deal. **c'est là une** ~ **avec votre conscience** now you're compromising with your conscience.

comptabilisation [kɔ̃tabilizɑsjɔ̃] *nf* (*Fin*) posting.

comptabiliser [kɔ̃tabilize] (1) *vt* (*Fin*) to post.

comptabilité [kɔ̃tabilite] *nf* (*science*) accountancy, accounting; (*d'une petite entreprise*) book-keeping; (*comptes*) accounts, books; (*bureau, service*) accounts office *ou* department; (*profession*) accountancy. **il s'occupe de la** ~ **de notre entreprise** he does the accounting *ou* keeps the books for our firm; ~ **publique** public finance; ~ **à partie simple/double** single/double entry book-keeping; ~ **industrielle** industrial book-keeping; *V* **chef**[1].

comptable [kɔ̃tabl(ə)] **1** *adj* **(a)** (*Fin*) accounts (*épith*); *V* **machine**[3]. **(b)** (*responsable*) accountable (*de* for). **2** *nmf* accountant. (*Can*) ~ **agréé** *ou* **du Trésor** chartered accountant; *V* **chef**[1], **expert**.

comptage [kɔ̃taʒ] *nm* counting.

comptant [kɔ̃tɑ̃] **1** *adv payer* cash, in cash; *acheter, vendre* for cash. **verser 10 F** ~ to pay 10 francs down, put down 10 francs. **2** *nm* (*argent*) cash. **au** ~ *payer* cash; *acheter, vendre* for cash; **achat/vente au** ~ cash purchase/sale; *V* **argent**.

compte [kɔ̃t] **1** *nm* **(a)** (*calcul*) count. **faire le** ~ **des prisonniers** to count (up) the prisoners, make a count of the prisoners; **l'as-tu inclus dans le** ~? have you counted *ou* included him?, did you include him in the count?; **faire le** ~ **des dépenses/de sa fortune** to calculate *ou* work out the expenditure/one's wealth.

(b) (*nombre exact*) (right) number. **le** ~ **y est** (*paiement*) that's the right amount; (*inventaire*) that's the right number, they're all there; **ça ne fait pas le** ~ (*paiement*) that's not the right amount; (*inventaire*) there's (still) something missing, they're not all there; **avez-vous le bon** *ou* **votre** ~ **de chaises?** have you got the right number of chairs? *ou* the number of chairs you want?; **cela fait un** ~ **rond** it makes a round number *ou* figure; **je n'arrive jamais au même** ~ I never get the same figure *ou* number *ou* total twice; **nous sommes loin du** ~ we are a long way short of the target.

(c) (*comptabilité*) account. **faire ses** ~**s** to do one's accounts *ou* books; **tenir les** ~**s du ménage** to keep the household accounts; **tenir les** ~**s d'une firme** to keep the books *ou* accounts of a firm; **publier à** ~ **d'auteur** to publish at the author's expense; (*hum*) ~**s d'apothicaire** careful accounting; **approuver/liquider un** ~ to approve/clear *ou* settle an account; **passer en** ~ to place *ou* pass to account; *V* **laissé-pour-compte, ligne**[1] *etc*.

(d) (*Banque*) ~ **(en banque** *ou* **bancaire)** (bank) account; **avoir de l'argent en** ~ to have money in an account; ~ **courant/de dépôt** current/deposit account; **porter une somme au** ~ **débiteur/créditeur de qn** to debit/credit a sum to sb's account; **à ~** on account; **être en ~ avec qn** to have an *ou* be in account with sb.

(e) (*dû*) **donner** *ou* **régler son ~ à un employé** (*lit*) to settle up with an employee; (*fig: renvoyer*) to give an employee his cards* (*Brit*) *ou* books* (*Brit*) *ou* pink slip* (*US*); (*fig*) **il avait son ~*** (*fatigué*) he'd had as much as he could take; (*mort*) he'd had it*, he was done for; (*soûl*) he'd had more than he could hold; (*fig*) **son ~ est bon** he's had it*, he's for it*; *V* **régler.**

(f) (*Comm: facture, addition*) (*gén*) account, invoice, bill; *[hôtel, restaurant]* bill (*Brit*), check (*US*).

(g) (*explications, justifications*) **~s** explanation; **devoir/rendre des ~s à qn** to owe/give sb an explanation; **demander** *ou* **réclamer des ~s à qn** to ask sb for an explanation; **il me doit des ~s à propos de cette perte** he owes me an explanation for this loss, he will have to account to me for this loss; *V* **rendre.**

(h) (*avantage, bien*) **cela fait mon ~** that suits me; **il y a trouvé son ~** he's got something out of it, he did well out of it; **chacun y trouve son ~** it has got *ou* there is something in it for everybody.

(i) (*loc*) (*Boxe*) **envoyer qn/aller au tapis** *ou* **à terre pour le ~** to floor sb/go down for the count; **tenir ~ de qch** to take sth into account; **il n'a pas tenu ~ de nos avertissements** he didn't take any notice of our warnings, he disregarded *ou* ignored our warnings; **~ tenu de** considering, in view of; **tenir ~ à qn de son dévouement** to take sb's devotion into account; **on lui a tenu ~ de son passé honorable** they took his honourable past into account *ou* consideration; **en prendre pour son ~*** to take a hiding; **prendre qch à son ~** (*payer*) to pay for sth; (*en assumer la responsabilité*) to take responsibility for sth; **je reprends cette maxime à mon ~** I adopt this maxim as my own; **il a repris la boutique à son ~** he's taken over the shop on his own account *ou* in his own name; **être/s'établir** *ou* **s'installer à son ~** to be/set up in business for o.s., have/set up one's own business; **à ce ~-là** (*dans ce cas*) in this case; (*à ce train-là*) at this rate; **tout ~ fait** all things considered, when all is said and done; **mettre qch sur le ~ de** to put sth down to, attribute *ou* ascribe sth to; **dire/apprendre qch sur le ~ de qn** to say/learn sth about sb; **pour le ~ de** (*au nom de*) on behalf of; **pour mon ~ (personnel)** (*en ce qui me concerne*) personally; (*pour mon propre usage*) for my own use.

2: (*Fin*) **compte chèque postal** = Giro account (*Brit*); (*Fin*) **compte numéroté** *ou* **à numéro** numbered account; (*Fin*) **compte des profits et pertes** profit and loss account; (*Espace, fig*) **compte à rebours** countdown; **compte rendu** (*rapport*) (*gén*) account, report; *[livre, film]* review; **faire le compte rendu d'un match/d'une réunion** to give an account *ou* a report of a match/meeting, give a run-down of a match/meeting.

compte- [kɔ̃t] *préf V* **compter.**

compter [kɔ̃te] (1) **1** *vt* **(a)** (*calculer*) *choses, personnes, argent, jours* to count. **combien en avez-vous compté?** how many did you count?, how many did you make it?; **40 cm? j'avais compté 30** 40 cm? I made it 30; **il a 50 ans bien comptés** he's a good 50 (years old); **on peut ~ (sur les doigts de la main) les auditeurs qui comprennent vraiment** you can count (on the fingers of one hand) the members of the audience who understand; **on ne compte plus ses gaffes, ses gaffes ne se comptent plus** we've lost (all) count of *ou* we can't keep count of his blunders.

(b) (*escompter, prévoir*) to allow, reckon. **combien as-tu compté qu'il nous fallait de chaises?** how many chairs did you reckon we'd need?; **j'ai compté qu'il nous en fallait 10** I reckoned we'd need 10; **combien de temps/d'argent comptez-vous pour finir les travaux?** how much time/money do you reckon it'll take to finish the work?, how much time/money are you allowing to finish the work?; **il faut (bien) ~ 10 jours/10 F** you must allow (a good) 10 days/10 francs, you must reckon on it taking (a good) 10 days/10 francs; **j'ai compté 90 cm pour le frigo, j'espère que ça suffira** I've allowed 90 cm for the fridge, I hope that'll do.

(c) (*tenir compte de*) to take into account; (*inclure*) to include. **on te comptera ta bonne volonté** your goodwill *ou* helpfulness will be taken into account; **cela fait 1 mètre en comptant l'ourlet** that makes 1 metre counting *ou* including *ou* if you include the hem; **t'es-tu compté?** did you count *ou* include yourself?; **ne me comptez pas** don't include me; **nous étions 10, sans ~ l'instituteur** we were 10, not counting the teacher; **ils nous apportèrent leurs connaissances, sans ~ leur bonne volonté** they gave us their knowledge, not to mention *ou* to say nothing of their goodwill *ou* helpfulness; **sans ~ que** (*et de plus* ...) not to mention that; (*d'autant plus que*) **il aurait dû venir, sans ~ qu'il n'avait rien à faire** he ought to have come especially since he had nothing to do.

(d) (*facturer*) to charge for. **~ qch à qn** to charge sb for sth; **ils n'ont pas compté le café** they didn't charge for the coffee; **combien vous ont-ils compté le café?** how much did they charge you for the coffee?; **ils nous l'ont compté trop cher/10 F/au prix de gros** they charged us too much/10 francs/the wholesale price for it.

(e) (*avoir*) to have. **la ville compte quelques très beaux monuments** the town has some very beautiful monuments; **il compte 2 ans de règne/de service** he has been reigning/in the firm for 2 years; **il ne compte pas d'ennemis** he has no enemies; **cette famille compte trois musiciens parmi ses membres** this family has *ou* boasts three musicians among its members.

(f) (*classer, ranger*) to consider. **on compte ce livre parmi les meilleurs de l'année** this book is considered (to be) *ou* ranks among the best of the year; **il le compte au nombre de ses amis** he considers him one of his friends, he numbers him among his friends.

(g) (*verser*) to pay. **le caissier va vous ~ 600 F** the cashier will pay you 600 francs; **vous lui compterez 100 F pour les heures supplémentaires** you will pay him 100 francs' overtime.

(h) (*donner avec parcimonie*) **il compte chaque sou qu'il nous donne** he counts every penny he gives us; **les permissions leur sont comptées** their leave is rationed; **il ne compte pas sa peine** he spares no trouble; **ses jours sont comptés** his days are numbered.

(i) (*avoir l'intention de*) to intend, plan, mean (*faire* to do); (*s'attendre à*) to reckon, expect. **ils comptent partir demain** they plan *ou* mean to go tomorrow, they reckon on going tomorrow; **je compte recevoir la convocation demain** I'm expecting to receive the summons tomorrow; **~ que: je ne compte pas qu'il vienne aujourd'hui** I am not expecting him to come today.

2 *vi* **(a)** (*calculer*) to count. **il sait ~ (jusqu'à 10)** he can count (up to 10); **tu as mal compté** you counted wrong, you miscounted; **à ~ de** (starting *ou* as) from.

(b) (*être économe*) to economize. **avec la montée des prix, il faut ~ sans cesse** with the rise in prices you have to watch every penny (you spend); **dépenser sans ~** (*être dépensier*) to spend extravagantly; (*donner généreusement*) to give without counting the cost; **il s'est dépensé sans ~ pour cette cause** he spared no effort in furthering that cause, he gave himself wholeheartedly to that cause.

(c) (*avoir de l'importance*) to count, matter. **c'est le résultat/le geste qui compte** it's the result/the gesture that counts *ou* matters; **35 ans de mariage, ça compte!** 35 years of marriage, that's quite something!; **c'est un succès qui compte** it's an important success; **ce qui compte c'est de savoir dès maintenant** the main thing is to find out right away.

(d) (*tenir compte de*) **~ avec qch** to reckon with sth, take account of sth, allow for sth; **il faut ~ avec l'opinion** you've got to reckon with *ou* take account of public opinion; **il faut ~ avec le temps incertain** you have to allow for changeable weather; **un nouveau parti avec lequel il faut ~** a new party to be reckoned with; **on avait compté sans la grève** we hadn't reckoned on there being a strike, we hadn't allowed for the strike.

(e) (*figurer*) **~ parmi** to be *ou* rank among; **~ au nombre de** to be one of; **~ pour: il compte pour 2** he's worth 2 men; **cela compte pour beaucoup/ne compte pour rien dans sa réussite/dans sa décision** that has a lot/has nothing to do with his success/his decision; **cela compte pour (du) beurre*** that counts for nothing, that doesn't count.

(f) (*valoir*) to count. **pour la retraite, les années de guerre comptent double** for the purposes of retirement, war service counts double; **après 60 ans les années comptent double** after 60 every year counts double.

(g) (*se fier à*) **~ sur** to count on, rely on; **~ sur la discrétion/la bonne volonté de qn** to count on *ou* rely on sb's discretion/goodwill; **nous comptons sur vous (pour) demain** we're expecting you (to come) tomorrow, we're relying on your coming tomorrow; **j'y compte bien!** I should hope so!, so I should hope!; **n'y comptez pas trop, ne comptez pas trop là-dessus** don't bank on it, don't count too much on it; **je compte sur vous** I'm counting *ou* relying on you; **vous pouvez ~ là-dessus** you can depend upon it; **ne comptez pas sur moi** (you can) count me out; **compte (là-)dessus et bois de l'eau‡** you've got a hope!, you'll be lucky!, you've got a fat chance!*

3: (*Tech*) **compte-fils** *nm inv* linen tester; **compte-gouttes** *nm inv* (*pipette*) dropper; **au compte-gouttes** (*fig: avec parcimonie*) sparingly; **ils les distribuent au compte-gouttes** they dole them out sparingly; **compte-tours** *nm inv* (*Aut*) rev *ou* revolution counter, tachometer; (*Tech*) rev *ou* revolution counter.

compteur [kɔ̃tœʀ] *nm* meter. **~ d'eau/d'électricité/à gaz** water/electricity/gas meter; **~ Geiger** Geiger counter; **~ (kilométrique)** milometer, odometer; **~ (de vitesse)** speedometer.

comptine [kɔ̃tin] *nf* (*gén: chanson*) nursery rhyme; (*pour compter*) counting rhyme *ou* song.

comptoir [kɔ̃twaʀ] *nm* **(a)** *[magasin]* counter; *[bar]* bar. **(b)** (*colonial*) trading post. **(c)** (*Comm: cartel*) syndicate (*for marketing*). **(d)** (*Fin: agence*) branch.

compulser [kɔ̃pylse] (1) *vt* to consult, examine.

comte [kɔ̃t] *nm* count; (*Brit*) earl.

comté [kɔ̃te] *nm* **(a)** (*Hist*) earldom; (*Admin Brit, Can*) county. **(b)** (*fromage*) comté (*kind of gruyère cheese*).

comtesse [kɔ̃tɛs] *nf* countess.

comtois, e [kɔ̃twa, waz] **1** *adj* of *ou* from Franche-Comté. **2** *nm,f*: **C~(e)** inhabitant *ou* native of Franche-Comté.

con, conne [kɔ̃, kɔn] **1** *adj* (*f aussi inv*) (‡: *stupide*) bloody stupid‡ (*Brit*). **qu'il est ~!** what a damned *ou* bloody (*Brit*) fool‡ (he is)!; **il est ~ comme la lune** *ou* **comme un balai** he's a bloody fool‡ *ou* idiot‡.

2 *nm,f* (‡: *crétin*) damn fool‡, bloody (*Brit*) idiot‡. **quel ~ ce mec** what a damn fool‡ *ou* bloody idiot‡ this guy* is; **bande de ~s** load of cretins‡ *ou* bloody idiots‡; **faire le ~** to ass about‡; **dispositif/gouvernement à la ~** lousy‡ *ou* crummy‡ device/government.

3 *nm* (*‡: vagin*) cunt*‡.

conard‡ [kɔnaʀ] *nm* = **connard‡.**

conasse‡ [kɔnas] *nf* = **connasse‡.**

concassage [kɔ̃kɑsaʒ] *nm* (*V* **concasser**) crushing; grinding.

concasser [kɔ̃kɑse] (1) *vt pierre, sucre, céréales* to crush; *poivre* to grind.

concasseur [kɔ̃kɑsœʀ] **1** *adj m* crushing. **2** *nm* crusher.

concaténation [kɔ̃katenɑsjɔ̃] *nf* concatenation.

concave [kɔ̃kav] *adj* concave.

concavité [kɔ̃kavite] *nf* (*Opt*) concavity; (*gén: cavité*) hollow,

cavity. **les ~s d'un rocher** the hollows *ou* cavities in a rock.
concéder [kɔ̃sede] (6) *vt privilège, droit, exploitation* to grant; *point* to concede; (*Sport*) *but, corner* to concede, give away. **je vous concède que** I'll grant you that.
concentration [kɔ̃sɑ̃tʀɑsjɔ̃] *nf* **(a)** (*gén, Chim*) *[rayons, troupes, acide]* concentration. **les grandes ~s urbaines des Midlands** the great conurbations of the Midlands; *V* **camp**.
(b) (*Écon*) **la ~ des entreprises** merging of businesses; **~ horizontale/verticale** horizontal/vertical integration.
(c) ~ (d'esprit) concentration.
concentrationnaire [kɔ̃sɑ̃tʀɑsjɔnɛʀ] *adj* of *ou* in concentration camps, concentration camp (*épith*).
concentré, e [kɔ̃sɑ̃tʀe] (*ptp de* **concentrer**) **1** *adj* **(a)** *acide* concentrated; *lait* condensed.
(b) *candidat, athlète* in a state of concentration, concentrating hard (*attrib*).
2 *nm* (*chimique*) concentrated solution; (*bouillon*) concentrate, extract. **~ de tomates** tomato purée.
concentrer [kɔ̃sɑ̃tʀe] (1) **1** *vt* (*gén*) to concentrate. **~ son attention sur** to concentrate *ou* focus one's attention on.
2 se concentrer *vpr [foule, troupes]* to concentrate. **le candidat se concentra avant de répondre** the candidate gathered his thoughts *ou* thought hard before replying; **je me concentre!** I'm concentrating!; **se ~ sur un problème** to concentrate on a problem; **les regards se concentrèrent sur moi** everybody's gaze was fixed *ou* focused on me, all eyes turned on me.
concentrique [kɔ̃sɑ̃tʀik] *adj cercle* concentric.
concentriquement [kɔ̃sɑ̃tʀikmɑ̃] *adv* concentrically.
concept [kɔ̃sɛpt] *nm* concept.
conception [kɔ̃sɛpsjɔ̃] *nf* **(a)** (*Bio*) conception; *V* **immaculé**.
(b) (*action*) *[idée]* conception, conceiving. **la ~ d'un tel plan est géniale** it is a brilliantly conceived plan; **la ~ de cette idée m'est venue hier** this idea came to me yesterday; **voilà quelle est ma ~ de la chose** this is how I see it; **machine d'une ~ révolutionnaire** machine conceived on revolutionary lines, machine of revolutionary design.
(c) (*idée*) notion, idea; (*réalisation*) creation.
conceptualisation [kɔ̃sɛptɥalizɑsjɔ̃] *nf* conceptualization.
conceptualiser [kɔ̃sɛptɥalize] (1) *vt* to conceptualize.
conceptuel, -elle [kɔ̃sɛptɥɛl] *adj* conceptual.
concernant [kɔ̃sɛʀnɑ̃] *prép* **(a)** (*se rapportant à*) concerning, relating to, regarding. **des mesures ~ ce problème seront bientôt prises** steps will soon be taken concerning *ou* relating to *ou* regarding this problem.
(b) (*en ce qui concerne*) with regard to, as regards. **~ ce problème, des mesures seront bientôt prises** with regard to this problem *ou* as regards this problem *ou* as far as this problem is concerned, steps will soon be taken to resolve it.
concerner [kɔ̃sɛʀne] (1) *vt* to concern. **cela ne vous concerne pas** it's no concern of yours, it doesn't concern you; **en ce qui concerne cette question** with regard to this question, as regards this question, as far as this question is concerned; **en ce qui me concerne** as far as I'm concerned; (*Admin*) **pour affaire vous concernant** to discuss a matter which concerns you *ou* a matter concerning you.
concert [kɔ̃sɛʀ] *nm* **(a)** (*Mus*) concert. **~ spirituel** concert of sacred music; (*fig*) **~ de louanges/de lamentations/d'invectives** chorus of praise/lamentation(s)/invective; **l'embouteillage se prolongeant, on entendit un ~ d'avertisseurs** as the traffic jam got worse a chorus of horns started up; *V* **café, salle**.
(b) (*littér*) (*harmonie*) chorus; (*accord*) entente, accord. **un ~ de voix** a chorus of voices; **le ~ des grandes puissances** the entente *ou* accord between the great powers.
(c) de ~ (*ensemble*) *partir* together; *rire* in unison; *agir* together, in unison; (*d'un commun accord*) *décider* unanimously; *agir* in concert; **ils ont agi de ~ pour éviter ...** they took concerted action to avoid ...; **de ~ avec** (*en accord avec*) in cooperation *ou* conjunction with; (*ensemble*) together with.
concertant, e [kɔ̃sɛʀtɑ̃, ɑ̃t] *adj V* **symphonie**.
concertation [kɔ̃sɛʀtɑsjɔ̃] *nf* (*échange de vues, dialogue*) dialogue; (*rencontre*) meeting. (*principe*) **la ~** dialogue; **suggérer une ~ des pays industriels** to suggest setting up *ou* creating a dialogue between industrial nations; **sans ~ préalable** without preliminary consultation(s).
concerté, e [kɔ̃sɛʀte] (*ptp de* **concerter**) *adj* concerted.
concerter [kɔ̃sɛʀte] (1) **1** *vt* (*organiser*) *plan, entreprise, projet* to devise. **2 se concerter** *vpr* (*délibérer*) to consult (each other), take counsel together.
concertina [kɔ̃sɛʀtina] *nm* concertina.
concertino [kɔ̃sɛʀtino] *nm* concertino.
concertiste [kɔ̃sɛʀtist(ə)] *nmf* concert artiste *ou* performer.
concerto [kɔ̃sɛʀto] *nm* concerto. **~ pour piano (et orchestre)** piano concerto, concerto for piano and orchestra.
concessif, -ive [kɔ̃sesif, iv] (*Gram*) **1** *adj* concessive. **2 concessive** *nf* concessive clause.
concession [kɔ̃sesjɔ̃] *nf* **(a)** (*faveur*) concession (*à* to). **faire des ~s** to make concessions. **(b)** (*cession*) *[terrain, exploitation]* concession. **faire la ~ d'un terrain** to grant a piece of land. **(c)** (*exploitation, terrain, territoire*) concession; *[cimetière]* plot. **~ minière** mining concession; **~ à perpétuité** plot held in perpetuity.
concessionnaire [kɔ̃sesjɔnɛʀ] **1** *adj*: **la société ~** the concessionary company. **2** *nmf* (*marchand agréé*) agent, dealer, franchise holder; (*bénéficiaire d'une concession*) concessionaire, concessionary.
concevable [kɔ̃svabl(ə)] *adj* (*compréhensible*) conceivable. **il est très ~ que** it's quite conceivable that.
concevoir [kɔ̃s(ə)vwaʀ] (28) **1** *vt* **(a)** (*penser*) to imagine; *fait, concept, idée* to conceive of. **je n'arrive pas à ~ que c'est fini** I can't conceive *ou* believe that it's finished.
(b) (*élaborer, étudier*) *solution, projet, moyen* to conceive, devise, think up. **leur maison est bien/mal conçue** their house is well/badly designed *ou* planned.
(c) (*envisager*) *question* to see, view. **voilà comment je conçois la chose** that's how I see it *ou* view it *ou* look at it; **ils concevaient la question différemment** they viewed the question differently; **ce qui se conçoit bien s'énonce clairement** what is clearly understood can be clearly expressed.
(d) (*comprendre*) to understand. **je conçois sa déception** *ou* **qu'il soit déçu** I can understand his disappointment *ou* his being disappointed; **cela se conçoit facilement** it's quite understandable, it's easy to understand; **il ne conçoit pas qu'on puisse souffrir de la faim** he cannot imagine *ou* conceive that people can suffer from starvation; **on concevrait mal qu'il puisse refuser** they would find it difficult to understand his refusal.
(e) (*rédiger*) *lettre, réponse* to set out, express. **ainsi conçu, conçu en ces termes** expressed *ou* couched in these terms.
(f) (*littér: éprouver*) **je conçois des doutes quant à son intégrité** I have *ou* feel some doubts as to his integrity; **il en conçut une terrible jalousie** he conceived a terrible feeling of jealousy (*littér*); **il conçut de l'amitié pour moi** he took a liking to me.
(g) (*engendrer*) to conceive.
2 *vi* (*engendrer*) to conceive.
concierge [kɔ̃sjɛʀʒ(ə)] *nmf* caretaker (*Brit*), janitor (*US*); (*en France*) concierge. (*fig*) **c'est un(e) vrai(e) ~** he (*ou* she) is a real gossip.
conciergerie [kɔ̃sjɛʀʒəʀi] *nf [lycée, château]* caretaker's *ou* janitor's lodge; (*Can*) apartment house. (*Hist*) **la C~** the Conciergerie.
concile [kɔ̃sil] *nm* (*Rel*) council, synod. **~ œcuménique** ecumenical council.
conciliable [kɔ̃siljabl(ə)] *adj* (*compatible*) reconcilable.
conciliabule [kɔ̃siljabyl] *nm* **(a)** (*entretien*) confabulation (*littér*), confab*. (*iro*) **tenir de grands ~s** to have great confabs*. **(b)** (†: *réunion*) secret meeting.
conciliaire [kɔ̃siljɛʀ] *adj* conciliar. **les pères ~s** the fathers of the council.
conciliant, e [kɔ̃siljɑ̃, ɑ̃t] *adj* conciliatory, conciliating.
conciliateur, -trice [kɔ̃siljatœʀ, tʀis] **1** *adj* conciliatory, conciliating. **2** *nm,f* (*médiateur*) conciliator.
conciliation [kɔ̃siljɑsjɔ̃] *nf* conciliation. **esprit de ~** spirit of conciliation; **comité de ~** arbitration committee; **la ~ d'intérêts opposés** the reconciliation *ou* reconciling of conflicting interests; *V* **procédure**.
conciliatoire [kɔ̃siljatwaʀ] *adj* (*Jur*) conciliatory.
concilier [kɔ̃silje] (7) **1** *vt* **(a)** (*rendre compatible*) *exigences, opinions, sentiments* to reconcile (*avec* with).
(b) (*ménager, attirer*) to win, gain. **sa bonté lui a concilié les électeurs** his kindness won *ou* gained him the support of the voters *ou* won over the voters.
(c) (*littér, Jur: réconcilier*) *ennemis* to reconcile, conciliate.
2 se concilier *vpr* (*se ménager, s'attirer*) to win, gain. **se ~ les bonnes grâces de qn** to win *ou* gain sb's favour.
concis, e [kɔ̃si, iz] *adj* concise. **en termes ~** concisely.
concision [kɔ̃sizjɔ̃] *nf* concision, conciseness, succinctness.
concitoyen, -yenne [kɔ̃sitwajɛ̃, jɛn] *nm,f* fellow citizen.
conclave [kɔ̃klav] *nm* conclave (*for the election of the pope*).
concluant, e [kɔ̃klyɑ̃, ɑ̃t] *adj* conclusive.
conclure [kɔ̃klyʀ] (35) **1** *vt* **(a)** (*signer*) *affaire, accord* to conclude. **~ un marché** to conclude *ou* clinch a deal; **marché conclu!** it's a deal!
(b) (*terminer*) *débat, discours, texte* to conclude, end. **et pour ~** and to conclude; **on vous demande de ~** will you please bring your discussion *etc* to a close, will you please wind up your discussion *etc*; **il conclut par ces mots/en disant ...** he concluded with these words/by saying ... .
(c) (*déduire*) to conclude (*qch de qch* sth from sth).
2 *vi* **(a) ~ de: j'en conclus que** I therefore concluded that.
(b) ~ à: ils ont conclu à son innocence/au suicide they concluded that he was innocent/that it was suicide, they pronounced him to be innocent/that it was suicide; **les juges ont conclu à l'acquittement** the judges decided on an acquittal.
(c) (*Jur*) **~ contre qn** *[témoignage]* to convict sb.
conclusion [kɔ̃klyzjɔ̃] *nf* (*gén*) conclusion; *[discours]* close. **~s** (*Jur*) *[demandeur]* pleadings, submissions; *[avocat]* summing-up; *[jury]* findings, conclusions; **en ~** in conclusion; **~*, on s'était trompé** in a word, we had made a mistake.
concocter* [kɔ̃kɔkte] (1) *vt* (*élaborer*) *breuvage, mélange* to concoct; *discours, loi* to elaborate, devise.
concombre [kɔ̃kɔ̃bʀ(ə)] *nm* cucumber.
concomitamment [kɔ̃kɔmitamɑ̃] *adv* concomitantly.
concomitance [kɔ̃kɔmitɑ̃s] *nf* concomitance.
concomitant, e [kɔ̃kɔmitɑ̃, ɑ̃t] *adj* concomitant.
concordance [kɔ̃kɔʀdɑ̃s] *nf* **(a)** (*gén*) agreement. **la ~ de 2 témoignages** the agreement of 2 testimonies, the fact that 2 testimonies tally *ou* agree; **la ~ de 2 résultats/situations** the similarity of *ou* between 2 results/situations; **mettre ses actes en ~ avec ses principes** to act in accordance with one's principles.
(b) (*index*) *[Bible etc]* concordance; (*Géol*) conformability. (*Gram*) **~ des temps** sequence of tenses; (*Phys*) **~ de phases** synchronization of phases.
concordant, e [kɔ̃kɔʀdɑ̃, ɑ̃t] *adj faits* (*coïncidents*) in agreement (*attrib*); (*analogues*) (virtually) the same (*attrib*); (*Géol*) conformable. **2 témoignages ~s** 2 testimonies which agree *ou* which are in agreement *ou* which tally.
concordat [kɔ̃kɔʀda] *nm* (*Rel*) concordat; (*Comm*) composition.
concorde [kɔ̃kɔʀd(ə)] *nf* (*littér: harmonie*) concord.
concorder [kɔ̃kɔʀde] (1) *vi [faits, dates, témoignages]* to agree,

tally; *[idées]* to coincide, match; *[caractères]* to match. **faire ~ des chiffres** to make figures agree *ou* tally; **ses actes concordent-ils avec ses idées?** is his behaviour in accordance with his ideas?

concourant, e [kɔ̃kuʀɑ̃, ɑ̃t] *adj* (*convergent*) *droites* convergent; *efforts* concerted (*épith*), united, cooperative.

concourir [kɔ̃kuʀiʀ] (11) *vi* **(a)** *[concurrent]* to compete (*pour* for). **(b)** (*Math: converger*) to converge (*vers* towards, on). **(c)** (*coopérer pour*) **~ à qch/à faire qch** to work towards sth/ towards doing sth.

concours [kɔ̃kuʀ] *nm* **(a)** (*gén: jeu, compétition*) competition; (*Scol: examen*) competitive examination. **~ hippique/agricole** horse/agricultural show; (*Admin*) **promotion par (voie de) ~** promotion by (competitive) examination; **~ de beauté** beauty contest; (*Scol*) **~ d'entrée (à)** (competitive) entrance examination (for); (*Scol*) **~ général** *competitive examination with prizes, open to secondary school children*; *V* **hors.**
(b) (*participation*) aid, help. **prêter son ~ à qch** to lend one's support to sth; **avec le ~ de** with the aid *ou* help *ou* assistance of; **il a fallu le ~ des pompiers** the firemen's help was needed.
(c) (*rencontre*) **~ de circonstances** combination of circumstances; **un grand ~ de peuple**† a large concourse† *ou* throng of people.

concret, -ète [kɔ̃kʀɛ, ɛt] *adj* (*tous sens: réel*) concrete. **esprit ~** down-to-earth mind; **le ~ et l'abstrait** the concrete and the abstract; **ce que je veux, c'est du ~** I want something concrete; **il en a tiré des avantages ~s** he got *ou* it gave him certain real *ou* positive advantages; *V* **musique.**

concrètement [kɔ̃kʀɛtmɑ̃] *adv* in concrete terms. **je me représente très ~ la situation** I can visualize the situation very clearly; **~, à quoi ça va servir?** what practical use will it have?, in concrete terms, what use will it be?

concrétion [kɔ̃kʀesjɔ̃] *nf* (*Géol, Méd*) concretion.

concrétiser [kɔ̃kʀetize] (1) **1** *vt* to put in concrete form. **2 se concrétiser** *vpr [espoir, projet, rêve]* to materialize. **ses promesses/menaces ne se sont pas concrétisées** his promises/ threats didn't come to anything *ou* didn't materialize; **le projet commence à se ~** the project is beginning to take shape.

concubin, e [kɔ̃kybɛ̃, in] *nm,f* (*Jur*) cohabitant; (*maîtresse*) concubine.

concubinage [kɔ̃kybinaʒ] *nm* cohabitation; concubinage. **ils vivent en ~** they're living together *ou* as husband and wife; (*Jur*) **~ notoire** common law marriage.

concupiscence [kɔ̃kypisɑ̃s] *nf* (*littér*) concupiscence.

concupiscent, e [kɔ̃kypisɑ̃, ɑ̃t] *adj* (*littér*) concupiscent.

concurremment [kɔ̃kyʀamɑ̃] *adv* **(a)** (*conjointement*) jointly. **il agit ~ avec le président** he acts jointly with *ou* in conjunction with the president. **(b)** (*en même temps*) concurrently.

concurrence [kɔ̃kyʀɑ̃s] *nf* (*gén, Comm*) competition. **un prix défiant toute ~** an absolutely unbeatable price, a rock-bottom price; **~ déloyale** unfair trading *ou* competition; **faire ~ à qn, être en ~ avec qn** to be in competition with sb, compete with sb; **jusqu'à ~ de ...** up to ..., to a limit of ... .

concurrencer [kɔ̃kyʀɑ̃se] (3) *vt* to compete with. **il nous concurrence dangereusement** he is a serious threat *ou* challenge to us; **leurs produits risquent de ~ les nôtres** their products could well pose a serious threat *ou* challenge to ours *ou* could well seriously challenge ours.

concurrent, e [kɔ̃kyʀɑ̃, ɑ̃t] **1** *adj* (†: *concourant*) *forces, actions* concurrent, cooperative. **2** *nm,f* (*Comm, Sport*) competitor; (*Scol*) *[concours]* candidate.

concurrentiel, -elle [kɔ̃kyʀɑ̃sjɛl] *adj* (*Écon*) competitive.

concussion [kɔ̃kysjɔ̃] *nf* misappropriation of public funds.

condamnable [kɔ̃dɑnabl(ə)] *adj action, opinion* reprehensible, blameworthy. **il n'est pas ~ d'avoir pensé à ses intérêts** he cannot be blamed for having thought of his own interests.

condamnation [kɔ̃dɑnɑsjɔ̃] *nf* **(a)** (*Jur*) *[coupable]* (*action*) sentencing (*à* to, *pour* for); (*peine*) sentence. **il a 3 ~s à son actif** he (already) has 3 convictions; **~ à mort** death sentence, sentence of death; **~ à une amende** imposition of a fine; **~ à 5 ans de prison** 5-year (prison) sentence; **~ (aux travaux forcés) à perpétuité** life sentence (of hard labour); **~ aux dépens** order to pay the costs; **~ par défaut/par contumace** decree by default/in one's absence; **~ pour meurtre** sentence for murder.
(b) (*interdiction, punition*) *[livre, délit]* condemnation, condemning.
(c) (*blâme*) *[conduite, idée]* condemnation.
(d) (*faillite*) *[espoir, théorie, projet]* end. **c'est la ~ du petit commerce** it means the end of *ou* it spells the end for the small trader.

condamné, e [kɔ̃dɑne] (*ptp de* **condamner**) *nm,f* sentenced person, convict; (*à mort*) condemned person. **un ~ à mort s'est échappé** a man under sentence of death *ou* a condemned man has escaped; *V* **cigarette.**

condamner [kɔ̃dɑne] (1) *vt* **(a)** (*Jur*) *coupable* to sentence (*à* to, *pour* for). **~ à mort** to sentence to death; **~ qn à une amende** to fine sb; **~ qn à 5 ans de prison** to sentence sb to 5 years' imprisonment, pass a 5-year (prison) sentence on sb; **~ aux dépens** to be ordered to pay costs; **~ qn par défaut/par contumace** to sentence sb by default/in his absence *ou* in absentia; **~ pour meurtre** to sentence for murder; **X, plusieurs fois condamné pour vol ...** X, several times convicted of theft ... .
(b) (*interdire, punir*) *délit, livre* to condemn. **la loi condamne l'usage de stupéfiants** the law condemns the use of drugs; **ces délits sont sévèrement condamnés** these offences carry heavy sentences *ou* penalties.
(c) (*blâmer*) *action, idées,* (*Ling*) *impropriété* to condemn. **il ne faut pas le ~ d'avoir fait cela** you mustn't condemn *ou* blame him for doing that; (*Ling*) **expression condamnée par les grammairiens** expression condemned by grammarians.
(d) (*accuser*) to condemn. **sa rougeur le condamne** his blushes condemn him.
(e) (*Méd*) *malade* to give up (hope for); (*fig*) *théorie, projet, espoir* to put an end to. **il était condamné depuis longtemps** there had been no hope for him *ou* he had been doomed for a long time.
(f) (*obliger, vouer*) **~ à: ~ qn au silence/à l'attente** to condemn sb to silence/to waiting; **je suis condamné *ou* ça me condamne à me lever tôt** I'm condemned to get up early; **c'est condamné à sombrer dans l'oubli** it's doomed to sink into oblivion.
(g) *porte, fenêtre* (*gén*) to fill in, block up; (*avec briques*) to brick up; (*avec planches etc*) to board up; *pièce* to lock up. (*fig*) **~ sa porte à qn** to bar one's door to sb.

condensable [kɔ̃dɑ̃sabl(ə)] *adj* condensable.

condensateur [kɔ̃dɑ̃satœʀ] *nm* (*Élec*) capacitor, condenser; (*Opt*) condenser.

condensation [kɔ̃dɑ̃sɑsjɔ̃] *nf* condensation.

condensé [kɔ̃dɑ̃se] *nm* (*Presse*) digest.

condenser [kɔ̃dɑ̃se] (1) **1** *vt gaz, vapeur* to condense; *exposé, pensée* to condense, compress; *V* **lait. 2 se condenser** *vpr [vapeur]* to condense.

condenseur [kɔ̃dɑ̃sœʀ] *nm* (*Opt, Phys*) condenser.

condescendance [kɔ̃desɑ̃dɑ̃s] *nf* condescension.

condescendant, e [kɔ̃desɑ̃dɑ̃, ɑ̃t] *adj* condescending.

condescendre [kɔ̃desɑ̃dʀ(ə)] (41) *vi*: **~ à** to condescend to; **~ à faire** to condescend *ou* deign to do.

condiment [kɔ̃dimɑ̃] *nm* condiment (*including pickles, spices, and any other seasoning*).

condisciple [kɔ̃disipl(ə)] *nm* (*Scol*) schoolfellow, schoolmate; (*Univ*) fellow student.

condition [kɔ̃disjɔ̃] *nf* **(a)** (*circonstances*) **~s** conditions; **~s atmosphériques/sociologiques** atmospheric/sociological conditions; **~s de travail/vie** working/living conditions; **dans ces ~s, je refuse** under these conditions, I refuse; **dans les ~s actuelles** in *ou* under (the) present conditions.
(b) (*stipulation*) *[traité]* condition; (*exigence*) *[acceptation]* condition, requirement. **~ préalable** prerequisite; **la ~ nécessaire et suffisante pour que ...** the necessary and sufficient condition for ...; **l'endurance est une ~ essentielle** endurance is an essential requirement; **~s d'un traité** conditions of a treaty; **l'honnêteté est la ~ du succès** honesty is the (prime) requirement for *ou* condition of success; **dicter/poser ses ~s** to state/lay down one's conditions; **il ne remplit pas les ~s requises (pour le poste)** he doesn't fulfil the requirements (for the job); **~s d'admission (dans une société)** terms *ou* conditions of admission *ou* entry (to a society); **sans ~(s)** (*adj*) unconditional; (*adv*) unconditionally.
(c) (*Comm*) term. **~s de vente/d'achat** terms of sale/of purchase; **~s de paiement** terms (of payment); **obtenir des ~s intéressantes** to get favourable terms; **faire ses ~s** to make *ou* name one's (own) terms; **acheter/envoyer à *ou* sous ~** to buy/send on approval *ou* on appro*.
(d) (*état*) **en bonne ~** *aliments, envoi* in good condition; **en bonne *ou* grande ~ (physique)** in condition, fit; **en mauvaise ~ (physique)** out of condition, unfit; **mettre en ~** (*physique*) to get into condition, make *ou* get fit; (*mentale*) to get into condition *ou* form; (*psychologique*) to condition; **la mise en ~ des téléspectateurs** the conditioning of television viewers; **se mettre en ~** to get fit, get into condition *ou* form.
(e) (*rang social*) station, condition. **vivre selon sa ~** to live according to one's station; **un étudiant de ~ modeste** a student from a modest home *ou* background; **ce n'est pas pour un homme de sa ~** it doesn't befit a man of his station; **personne de ~**†† person of quality.
(f) (*situation*) conditions. **améliorer la ~ des ouvriers** to improve the conditions of the workers; **la ~ de prêtre** (the) priesthood.
(g) (*loc*) **entrer en/être de *ou* en ~ chez qn**†† to enter sb's service/be in service with sb; **à une ~** on one condition; **je viendrai, à ~ d'être prévenu à temps** I'll come provided (that) *ou* providing (that) I'm told in time; **tu peux rester, à ~ d'être sage *ou* à ~ que tu sois sage** you can stay provided (that) *ou* providing (that) *ou* on condition that you're good; **sous ~** conditionally.

conditionnel, -elle [kɔ̃disjɔnɛl] *adj, nm* (*tous sens*) conditional.

conditionnellement [kɔ̃disjɔnɛlmɑ̃] *adv* conditionally.

conditionnement [kɔdisjɔnmɑ̃] *nm* (*emballage*) packaging; *[air, personne, textile]* conditioning.

conditionner [kɔ̃disjɔne] (1) *vt* (*emballer*) to package, prepack; (*influencer*) to condition; *textiles, blé* to condition. **ceci conditionne notre départ** our departure will be dependent on *ou* conditioned by this; *V* **air**[1], **réflexe.**

condoléances [kɔ̃dɔleɑ̃s] *nfpl* condolences. **offrir *ou* faire ses ~ à qn** to offer sb one's sympathy *ou* condolences; **toutes mes ~** (please accept) all my condolences *ou* my deepest sympathy; **une lettre de ~** a letter of condolence.

condominium [kɔ̃dɔminjɔm] *nm* condominium.

condor [kɔ̃dɔʀ] *nm* condor.

conductance [kɔ̃dyktɑ̃s] *nf* conductance.

conducteur, -trice [kɔ̃dyktœʀ, tʀis] **1** *adj* (*Élec*) conductive, conducting; *V* **fil. 2** *nm,f* (*Aut, Rail*) driver; *[machine]* operator. **~ de bestiaux** herdsman, drover; **~ d'hommes** leader; **~ de travaux** clerk of works. **3** *nm* (*Élec*) conductor.

conductibilité [kɔ̃dyktibilite] *nf* conductivity.

conductible [kɔ̃dyktibl(ə)] *adj* conductive.

conduction [kɔ̃dyksjɔ̃] (*Méd, Phys*) conduction.

conduire [kɔ̃dɥiʀ] (38) **1** *vt* **(a)** (*emmener*) **~ qn quelque part** to take sb somewhere; (*en voiture*) to take *ou* drive sb somewhere;

~ **un enfant à l'école/chez le docteur** to take a child to school/to the doctor; ~ **la voiture au garage** to take the car to the garage; ~ **les bêtes aux champs** to take *ou* drive the animals to the fields; ~ **qn à la gare** (*en voiture*) to take *ou* drive sb to the station; (*à pied*) to walk *ou* see sb to the station; **il me conduisit à ma chambre** he showed me *ou* took me to my room.

(b) (*guider*) to lead. **il conduisit les hommes à l'assaut** he led the men into the attack; **le guide nous conduisait** the guide was leading us; **il nous a conduits à travers Paris** he guided us through Paris.

(c) (*piloter*) *véhicule* to drive; *embarcation* to steer; *avion* to pilot; *cheval [cavalier]* to ride; *[cocher]* to drive. ~ **un cheval par la bride** to lead a horse by the bridle.

(d) (*Aut: emploi absolu*) to drive. **il conduit bien/mal** he is a good/bad driver, he drives well/badly; *V* **permis.**

(e) (*mener*) ~ **qn quelque part** *[véhicule]* to take sb somewhere; *[route, traces]* to lead *ou* take sb somewhere; *[études, événement]* to lead sb somewhere; **la sociologie ne conduit à rien** sociology doesn't lead to anything *ou* leads nowhere; **où cela va-t-il nous** ~? where will all this lead us?; **cela nous conduit à penser que** that leads us to think that; **cet escalier conduit à la cave** this staircase leads (down) to the cellar; **où ce chemin conduit-il?** where does this road lead? *ou* go?; **ses dérèglements l'ont conduit en prison** his profligacy landed him in prison.

(f) (*diriger*) *affaires* to run, manage; *travaux* to supervise; *pays* to run, lead; *négociations, enquête* to lead, conduct; *orchestre [chef d'orchestre]* to conduct; *[premier violon]* to lead. **les fouilles sont conduites par X** the excavation is being led *ou* directed by X.

(g) (*transmettre*) *chaleur, électricité* to conduct; (*transporter*) to carry. **un aqueduc conduit l'eau à la ville** an aqueduct carries water to the town.

2 se conduire *vpr* to behave. **il sait se** ~ **(en société)** he knows how to behave (in polite company); **ce ne sont pas des façons de se** ~ that's no way to behave; **conduisez-vous comme il faut!** behave properly!; **il s'est mal conduit** he behaved badly.

conduit [kɔ̃dɥi] **1** *nm* **(a)** (*Tech*) conduit, pipe. ~ **de fumée** flue; ~ **d'air** *ou* **de ventilation** ventilation shaft; ~ **d'alimentation** supply pipe; ~ **d'aération** air duct.

(b) (*Anat*) duct, canal.

2: **conduit auditif** auditory canal; **conduit lacrymal** lachrymal (*T*) *ou* tear duct; **conduit urinaire** ureter, urinary canal.

conduite [kɔ̃dɥit] **1** *nf* **(a)** (*pilotage*) *[véhicule]* driving; *[embarcation]* steering; *[avion]* piloting. **la** ~ **d'un gros camion demande de l'habileté** driving a big truck takes a lot of skill; **en Angleterre la** ~ **est à gauche** in England, you drive on the left; **voiture avec** ~ **à gauche/à droite** left-hand-drive/right-hand-drive car; **faire un brin de** ~ **à qn*** to go *ou* walk part of the way with sb, walk along with sb for a bit.

(b) (*direction*) *[affaires]* running, management; *[travaux]* supervision; *[pays]* running, leading; *[négociations, enquête]* leading, conducting; (*Littérat*) *[intrigue]* conducting. **sous la** ~ **de** *homme politique, capitaine, guide* under the leadership of; *instituteur* under the supervision of; *chef d'orchestre* under the baton *ou* leadership of.

(c) (*comportement*) behaviour; (*Scol*) conduct. **avoir une** ~ **bizarre** to behave strangely; **quelle** ~ **adopter?** what course of action shall we take?; (*Scol*) **zéro de** ~ no marks *ou* nought for conduct; (*Scol*) **tu as combien en** *ou* **pour la** ~? what did you get for conduct?; (*Prison*) **relâché pour bonne** ~ released for good conduct; *V* **acheter, écart, ligne**[1].

(d) (*tuyau*) pipe. ~ **d'eau/de gaz** water/gas main.

2: (*Psych*) **conduite d'échec** defeatist behaviour; (*Hydro-Électricité*) **conduite forcée** pressure pipeline; (*Aut*) **conduite intérieure** saloon (car) (*Brit*), sedan (*US*); **conduite montante** rising main; **conduite de refus** consumer resistance.

cône [kon] *nm* (*Anat, Bot, Math, Tech*) cone; *[volcan]* cone. **en forme de** ~ cone-shaped; ~ **de déjection** alluvial cone; ~ **d'ombre/de lumière** cone of shadow/light.

confection [kɔ̃fɛksjɔ̃] *nf* **(a)** (*exécution*) *[appareil, vêtement]* making; *[repas]* making, preparation, preparing.

(b) (*Habillement*) **la** ~ the clothing industry, the rag trade*; **être dans la** ~ to be in the ready-made clothes business; **vêtement de** ~ ready-made garment; **il achète tout en** ~ he buys everything off-the-peg (*surtout Brit*) *ou* ready-to-wear; *V* **magasin.**

confectionner [kɔ̃fɛksjɔne] (1) *vt mets* to prepare, make; *appareil, vêtement* to make.

confédéral, e, *mpl* **-aux** [kɔ̃fedeʀal, o] *adj* confederal.

confédération [kɔ̃fedeʀasjɔ̃] *nf* confederation, confederacy.

confédéré, e [kɔ̃fedeʀe] (*ptp de* **confédérer**) **1** *adj nations* confederate. **2** *nmpl* (*US Hist*) **les C~s** the Confederates.

confédérer [kɔ̃fedeʀe] (6) *vt* to confederate.

conférence [kɔ̃feʀɑ̃s] *nf* **(a)** (*exposé*) lecture; *V* **salle, maître.**

(b) (*réunion*) conference, meeting. **être en** ~ to be in conference *ou* in a *ou* at a meeting; ~ **au sommet** summit (conference); ~ **de presse** press conference.

conférencier, -ière [kɔ̃feʀɑ̃sje, jɛʀ] *nm,f* speaker, lecturer.

conférer [kɔ̃feʀe] (6) **1** *vt* **(a)** (*décerner*) *dignité* to confer (*à* on); *baptême, ordres sacrés* to give. (*frm: donner*) ~ **un certain sens/aspect à qch** to endow sth with a certain meaning/look, give sth a certain meaning/look; **ce titre lui confère un grand prestige** that title confers great prestige on him.

(b) (*collationner*) to collate, compare.

2 *vi* (*s'entretenir*) to confer (*sur* on, about).

confesse [kɔ̃fɛs] *nf*: **être/aller à** ~ to be at/go to confession.

confesser [kɔ̃fese] (1) **1** *vt* **(a)** (*avouer, Rel*) *péchés, erreur* to confess. ~ **que** to confess that; ~ **sa foi** to confess one's faith.

(b) ~ **qn** (*Rel*) to hear sb's confession, confess sb; (*: *faire parler*) to draw the truth out of sb, make sb talk; **l'abbé X confesse de 4 à 6** Father X hears confessions from 4 to 6.

2 se confesser *vpr* (*Rel*) to go to confession. **se** ~ **à** *prêtre* to confess to, make confession to; *ami* to confess to; **se** ~ **de** *péchés, (littér) méfait* to confess.

confesseur [kɔ̃fesœʀ] *nm* confessor.

confession [kɔ̃fɛsjɔ̃] *nf* (*aveu*) confession; (*acte du prêtre*) hearing of confession; (*religion*) denomination; *V* **donner.**

confessionnal, *pl* **-aux** [kɔ̃fɛsjɔnal, o] *nm* confessional.

confessionnel, -elle [kɔ̃fɛsjɔnɛl] *adj* denominational. **querelle** ~**le** interdenominational dispute.

confetti [kɔ̃feti] *nm* confetti (*U*).

confiance [kɔ̃fjɑ̃s] *nf* (*en l'honnêteté de qn*) confidence, trust; (*en la valeur de qn, le succès de qch, la solidité d'un appareil*) confidence, faith (*en* in). **avoir** ~ **en** *ou* **dans, faire** ~ **à** to have confidence *ou* faith in, trust; (*Pol*) **voter la** ~ **(au gouvernement)** to pass a vote of confidence (in the government); **il faut avoir** ~ one must have confidence; **je n'ai pas** ~ **dans leur matériel** I've no faith *ou* confidence in their equipment; **il a toute ma** ~ he has my complete trust *ou* confidence; **mettre qn en** ~ to win sb's trust; **placer** *ou* **mettre sa** ~ **dans** to place one's confidence in; **avec** ~ *se confier* trustingly; *espérer* confidently; **en (toute)** ~, **de** ~ *acheter* with confidence; **de** ~ *homme, maison* trustworthy, reliable; **un poste de** ~ a position of trust; ~ **en soi** self-confidence; *V* **abus, question.**

confiant, e [kɔ̃fjɑ̃, ɑ̃t] *adj* **(a)** (*assuré, plein d'espoir*) confident; (*en soi-même*) (self-)confident, (self-)assured. **(b)** (*sans défiance*) *caractère, regard* confiding.

confidence [kɔ̃fidɑ̃s] *nf* (*secret*) confidence, little (personal) secret. **faire une** ~ **à qn** to confide sth to sb, trust sb with a secret; **faire des** ~**s à qn** to share a secret with sb, confide in sb; **en** ~ in confidence; **mettre qn dans la** ~ to let sb into the secret; ~**s sur l'oreiller** intimate confidences, pillow talk.

confident [kɔ̃fidɑ̃] *nm* confidant.

confidente [kɔ̃fidɑ̃t] *nf* confidante.

confidentiel, -ielle [kɔ̃fidɑ̃sjɛl] *adj* confidential; (*sur une enveloppe*) private (and confidential).

confidentiellement [kɔ̃fidɑ̃sjɛlmɑ̃] *adv* confidentially.

confier [kɔ̃fje] (7) **1** *vt* **(a)** (*dire en secret*) to confide (*à* to). **il me confie ses projets** he confides his projects to me, he tells me about his projects; **il me confie tous ses secrets** he shares all his secrets with me; **dans ce livre il confie ses joies et ses peines** in this book he tells of *ou* reveals his sorrows and his joys.

(b) (*laisser aux soins de qn*) to confide, entrust (*à* to). ~ **qn/qch aux soins/à la garde de qn** to confide *ou* entrust sb/sth to sb's care/safe keeping; **je vous confie le soin de le faire** I entrust you with the task of doing it.

2 se confier *vpr* **(a)** (*dire un secret*) **se** ~ **à qn** to confide in sb; **ils se confièrent l'un à l'autre leur chagrin** they confided their grief to each other; (*littér*) **qu'il est doux de se** ~! how nice it is to confide in somebody!

(b) (*se fier à*) **se** ~ **à** *ou* **en qn** to place o.s. in sb's hands.

configuration [kɔ̃figyʀasjɔ̃] *nf* (general) shape, configuration (*T*). **la** ~ **des lieux** the layout of the premises; **suivant la** ~ **du terrain** following the lie of the land.

confiné, e [kɔ̃fine] (*ptp de* **confiner**) *adj* **(a)** (*enfermé*) **vivre** ~ **chez soi** to live shut away in one's own home. **(b)** (*renfermé*) *atmosphère* enclosed; *air* stale.

confinement [kɔ̃finmɑ̃] *nm* (*V* **confiner**) confining.

confiner [kɔ̃fine] (1) **1** *vt* (*enfermer*) ~ **qn à** *ou* **dans** to confine sb to *ou* in.

2 confiner à *vt indir* (*toucher à*) (*lit*) to border on, adjoin; (*fig*) to border *ou* verge on.

3 se confiner *vpr* to confine o.s. (*à* to). **se** ~ **chez soi** to confine o.s. to the house, shut o.s. up at home.

confins [kɔ̃fɛ̃] *nmpl* borders. **aux** ~ **de la Bretagne et de la Normandie/du rêve et de la réalité** on the borders of Brittany and Normandy/dream and reality; **aux** ~ **de la Bretagne/la science** at the outermost *ou* furthermost bounds of Brittany/science.

confire [kɔ̃fiʀ] (37) *vt* (*au sucre*) to preserve; (*au vinaigre*) to pickle; *V* **confit.**

confirmand, e [kɔ̃fiʀmɑ̃, ɑ̃d] *nm,f* confirmand (*T*), confirmation candidate.

confirmation [kɔ̃fiʀmasjɔ̃] *nf* (*gén, Rel*) confirmation. **en** ~ **de** confirming, in confirmation of; **apporter** ~ **de** to confirm, provide confirmation of; **c'est la** ~ **de** it confirms, it provides *ou* is confirmation of; **j'en attends** ~ I'm waiting for confirmation of it.

confirmer [kɔ̃fiʀme] (1) *vt* (*gén, Rel*) to confirm. **il m'a confirmé que** he confirmed to me that; **cela l'a confirmé dans ses idées** it confirmed *ou* strengthened him in his ideas; **la nouvelle se confirme** there is some confirmation of the news; *V* **exception.**

confiscable [kɔ̃fiskabl(ə)] *adj* confiscable.

confiscation [kɔ̃fiskasjɔ̃] *nf* confiscation.

confiserie [kɔ̃fizʀi] *nf* (*magasin*) confectioner's (shop), sweetshop (*Brit*), candy store (*US*); (*métier*) confectionery; (*bonbons*) confectionery (*U*), sweets (*Brit*), candy (*U*) (*US*). **manger une** ~**/des** ~**s** to eat a sweet/sweets (*Brit*) *ou* candy (*US*).

confiseur, -euse [kɔ̃fizœʀ, øz] *nm,f* confectioner.

confisquer [kɔ̃fiske] (1) *vt* (*gén, Jur*) to confiscate.

confit, e [kɔ̃fi, it] (*ptp de* **confire**) **1** *adj fruit* crystallized, candied; *cornichon etc* pickled. (*fig*) ~ **de** *ou* **en dévotion** steeped in piety. **2** *nm*: ~ **d'oie/de canard** conserve of goose/duck.

confiture [kɔ̃fityʀ] *nf* jam. ~ **de prunes/d'abricots** plum/apricot jam; ~ **d'oranges** (orange) marmalade; ~ **de citrons** lemon marmalade; **veux-tu de la** ~? *ou* **des** ~**s?** do you want (some) jam?; (*fig*) **donner de la** ~ **aux cochons** to throw pearls before swine.

confiturerie [kɔ̃fityʀʀi] *nf* jam factory.

conflagration [kɔ̃flagʀɑsjɔ̃] *nf* (*frm: conflit*) cataclysm.

conflit [kɔ̃fli] *nm* (*gén, Mil*) conflict, clash; (*Psych*) conflict; (*Jur*) conflict. **pour éviter le ~** to avoid (a) conflict *ou* a clash; **entrer en ~ avec qn** to come into conflict with sb, clash with sb; **être en ~ avec qn** to be in conflict with sb, clash with sb; **~ d'intérêts** conflict *ou* clash of interests; **~ armé** armed conflict.

confluence [kɔ̃flyɑ̃s] *nf* (*action*) *[cours d'eau]* confluence, flowing together; (*fig*) mingling, merging.

confluent [kɔ̃flyɑ̃] *nm* (*endroit*) confluence.

confluer [kɔ̃flye] (1) *vi [cours d'eau]* to join, flow together; (*littér*) *[foule, troupes]* to converge (*vers* on). **~ avec** to flow into, join.

confondre [kɔ̃fɔ̃dʀ(ə)] (41) **1** *vt* **(a)** (*mêler*) *choses, dates* to mix up, confuse. **on confond toujours ces deux frères** people always mix up *ou* confuse these two brothers *ou* get these two brothers mixed up *ou* muddled up; **les deux sœurs se ressemblent au point qu'on les confond** the two sisters are so alike that you take *ou* mistake one for the other; **il confond toujours le Chili et** *ou* **avec le Mexique** he keeps mixing up *ou* confusing Chile and *ou* with Mexico; **~ qch/qn avec qch/qn d'autre** to mistake sth/sb for sth/sb else; **elle a confondu sa valise avec la mienne** she mistook my case for hers; **je croyais que c'était son frère, j'ai dû ~** I thought it was his brother but I must have made a mistake *ou* I must have been mistaken; **mes réserves ne sont pas de la lâcheté, il ne faudrait pas ~** my reservations aren't cowardice, let there be no mistake about that *ou* you shouldn't confuse the two.

(b) (*déconcerter*) to astound. **il me confondit par l'étendue de ses connaissances** he astounded me with the extent of his knowledge; **son insolence a de quoi vous ~** his insolence is astounding *ou* is enough to leave you speechless; **je suis confondu devant** *ou* **de tant d'amabilité** I'm overcome by such kindness; **être confondu de reconnaissance** to be overcome with gratitude.

(c) (*réduire au silence*) *détracteur, ennemi, menteur* to confound.

(d) (*réunir, fusionner*) to join, meet. **deux rivières qui confondent leurs eaux** two rivers which flow together *ou* join.

2 se confondre *vpr* **(a)** (*ne faire plus qu'un*) to merge; (*se rejoindre*) to meet. **les silhouettes se confondaient dans la brume** the silhouettes merged (together) in the mist; **les couleurs se confondent de loin** the colours merge in the distance; **tout se confondait dans sa mémoire** everything became confused in his memory; **les deux événements se confondirent (en un seul) dans sa mémoire** the two events merged into one in his memory, the two events became confused (as one) in his memory; **nos intérêts se confondent** our interests are one and the same; **les deux fleuves se confondent à cet endroit** the two rivers flow together *ou* join here.

(b) se ~ en excuses to apologize profusely; **se ~ en remerciements** to offer profuse thanks, be effusive in one's thanks; **il se confondit en remerciements** he thanked me (*ou* them *etc*) profusely *ou* effusively.

conformation [kɔ̃fɔʀmɑsjɔ̃] *nf* conformation; *V* **vice**.

conforme [kɔ̃fɔʀm(ə)] *adj* **(a)** (*semblable*) true (*à* to). **~ à l'original/au modèle** true to the original/pattern; **c'est ~ à l'échantillon** it matches the sample; **c'est peu ~ à ce que j'ai dit** it bears little resemblance to what I said; **cette copie est bien ~, n'est-ce pas?** it's a true *ou* good replica, isn't it?; *V* **copie**.

(b) (*fidèle*) in accordance (*à* with). **l'exécution des travaux est ~ au plan prévu** the work is being carried out in accordance with the agreed plan; **~ à la loi** in accordance *ou* conformity with the law; **~ à la règle/à la norme** in accordance with the rule/norm.

(c) (*en harmonie avec*) **~ à** in keeping with, consonant with. **un niveau de vie ~ à nos moyens** a standard of living in keeping *ou* consonant with our means; **il a des vues ~s aux miennes** his views are in keeping with mine, we have similar views.

conformé, e [kɔ̃fɔʀme] (*ptp de* **conformer**) *adj corps, enfant* **bien/mal ~** well/ill-formed; **bizarrement ~** strangely shaped *ou* formed.

conformément [kɔ̃fɔʀmemɑ̃] *adv* **~ à (a)** (*en respectant*) in conformity with, in accordance with. **~ à la loi, j'ai décidé que** in accordance *ou* conformity with the law, I have decided that; **les travaux se sont déroulés ~ au plan prévu** the work was carried out in accordance with *ou* according to the proposed plan; **ce travail a été exécuté ~ au modèle/à l'original** this piece of work was done to conform to the pattern/original *ou* to match the pattern/original exactly.

(b) (*suivant*) in accordance with. **~ à ce que j'avais promis/prédit** in accordance with what I had promised/predicted.

conformer [kɔ̃fɔʀme] (1) **1** *vt* (*calquer*) **~ qch à** to model sth on. **~ sa conduite à celle d'une autre personne** to model one's (own) conduct on somebody else's; **~ sa conduite à ses principes** to match one's conduct to one's principles.

2 se conformer *vpr*: **se ~ à** to conform to.

conformisme [kɔ̃fɔʀmism(ə)] *nm* (*gén, Rel*) conformity.

conformiste [kɔ̃fɔʀmist(ə)] *adj, nmf* (*gén, Rel*) conformist.

conformité [kɔ̃fɔʀmite] *nf* **(a)** (*identité*) similarity, correspondence (*à* to). **la ~ de deux choses** the similarity of *ou* between two things, the close correspondence of *ou* between two things; **en ~ avec le modèle** in accordance with the pattern.

(b) (*fidélité*) faithfulness (*à* to). **~ à la règle/aux ordres reçus** compliance with the rules/orders received; **en ~ avec le plan prévu/avec les ordres reçus** in accordance *ou* conformity with the proposed plan/orders received.

(c) (*harmonie*) conformity, agreement (*avec* with). **la ~ de nos vues sur la question, notre ~ de vues sur la question** the agreement of our views on the question; **sa conduite est en ~ avec ses idées** his conduct is in keeping *ou* in conformity *ou* in agreement with his ideas.

confort [kɔ̃fɔʀ] *nm* comfort. **appartement tout ~** *ou* **avec (tout) le ~ moderne** flat with all mod cons (*surtout Brit*); **y a-t-il (tout) le ~?** does it have all mod cons? (*surtout Brit*); **il aime le** *ou* **son ~** he likes his creature comforts *ou* his comfort; **dès que ça dérange son ~ personnel il refuse de nous aider** as soon as it puts him out he refuses to help us.

confortable [kɔ̃fɔʀtabl(ə)] *adj* **(a)** (*douillet*) *appartement, vêtement, vie* comfortable, comfy*. **fauteuil peu ~** rather uncomfortable armchair.

(b) (*opulent*) *fortune, retraite* comfortable; *métier, situation* comfortable, cushy*.

(c) (*important*) comfortable (*épith*). **prendre une avance ~ sur ses rivaux** to get a comfortable lead over one's rivals.

confortablement [kɔ̃fɔʀtabləmɑ̃] *adv* comfortably. **vivre ~** (*dans le confort*) to live in comfort; (*dans la richesse*) to live very comfortably, lead a comfortable existence.

conforter [kɔ̃fɔʀte] (1) *vt* to reinforce, confirm.

confraternel, -elle [kɔ̃fʀatɛʀnɛl] *adj* brotherly, fraternal.

confraternité [kɔ̃fʀatɛʀnite] *nf* brotherliness.

confrère [kɔ̃fʀɛʀ] *nm [profession]* colleague, confrère (*frm*); *[association]* fellow member, confrère (*frm*); (*journal*) (fellow) newspaper. **mon cher ~** dear colleague.

confrérie [kɔ̃fʀeʀi] *nf* brotherhood.

confrontation [kɔ̃fʀɔ̃tɑsjɔ̃] *nf [opinions, personnes]* confrontation; *[textes]* comparison, collation.

confronter [kɔ̃fʀɔ̃te] (1) *vt* (*opposer*) *opinions, personnes* to confront; (*comparer*) *textes* to compare, collate.

confucianisme [kɔ̃fysjanism(ə)] *nm* Confucianism.

confus, e [kɔ̃fy, yz] *adj* **(a)** (*peu clair*) *bruit, texte, souvenir* confused; *esprit, personne* confused, muddled; *mélange, amas d'objets* confused. **cette affaire est très ~e** this business is very confused *ou* muddled.

(b) (*honteux*) *personne* ashamed, embarrassed. **il était ~ d'avoir fait cela** he was embarrassed at having done that; **vous avez fait des folies, nous sommes ~!** you've been far too kind, we're quite overwhelmed! *ou* you make us feel quite ashamed!; **je suis tout ~ de mon erreur** I'm quite ashamed of my mistake, I don't know what to say about my mistake.

confusément [kɔ̃fyzemɑ̃] *adv distinguer* vaguely; *comprendre, ressentir* vaguely, in a confused way; *parler* unintelligibly, confusedly.

confusion [kɔ̃fyzjɔ̃] *nf* **(a)** (*honte*) embarrassment; (*trouble, embarras*) confusion. **à ma grande ~** to my great embarrassment; to my great confusion.

(b) (*erreur*) *[noms, personnes, dates]* confusion (*de* in). **vous avez fait une ~** you've made a mistake, you've got things confused.

(c) (*désordre*) *[esprits, idées]* confusion; *[assemblée, pièce, papiers]* confusion, disorder (*de* in). **c'était dans une telle ~** it was in such confusion *ou* disorder; **mettre** *ou* **jeter la ~ dans les esprits/l'assemblée** to throw people/the audience into confusion.

(d) (*Jur*) **~ des dettes** confusion; **~ de part** *ou* **de paternité** doubt over paternity; **~ des peines** concurrency of sentences; **~ des pouvoirs** *non-separation of legislature, executive and judiciary*.

confusionnisme [kɔ̃fyzjɔnism(ə)] *nm* (*Psych*) *confused thinking of a child*; (*Pol*) *policy of spreading confusion in people's minds*.

congé [kɔ̃ʒe] **1** *nm* **(a)** (*vacances*) holiday (*surtout Brit*), vacation (*US*); (*Mil: permission*) leave. **3 jours de ~ pour** *ou* **à Noël** 3 days' holiday (*Brit*) *ou* vacation (*US*) *ou* 3 days off at Christmas; **en ~** *écolier, employé* on holiday (*Brit*) *ou* vacation (*US*); *soldat* on leave; **avoir ~: quel jour avez-vous ~?** which day do you have off? *ou* are you off?; **quand avez-vous ~ en été?** when are you off *ou* when do you get a holiday (*Brit*) *ou* vacation (*US*) in the summer?; **avoir ~ le mercredi** to have Wednesdays off, be off on Wednesdays *ou* on a Wednesday; **il me reste 3 jours de ~ à prendre** I've got 3 days (holiday) still to come.

(b) (*arrêt momentané de travail*) time off (*U*), leave (*U*). **prendre/donner du ~** to take/give time off *ou* some leave; **prendre un ~ d'une semaine** to take a week off *ou* a week's leave; **~ sans traitement** *ou* **solde** unpaid leave, time off without pay; **demander à être mis en ~ sans traitement** *ou* **solde pendant un an** to ask for a year's unpaid leave, ask for a year off without pay.

(c) (*avis de départ*) notice; (*renvoi*) notice (to quit *ou* leave). **donner son ~** *[employé]* to hand in *ou* give in one's notice (*à* to); *[locataire]* to give notice (*à* to); **donner (son) ~ à un locataire/employé** to give a lodger/an employee (his) notice; **il faut donner ~ 8 jours à l'avance** one must give a week's notice; **il a demandé son ~** he's asked to leave.

(d) (*adieu*) **prendre ~ (de qn)** to take one's leave (of sb); **donner ~ à qn à la fin d'un entretien** to dismiss (*frm*) sb at the end of a conversation.

(e) (*Admin: autorisation*) clearance certificate; *[transports d'alcool]* release (*of wine etc from bond*). (*Naut*) **~ (de navigation)** clearance.

2: congé annuel annual holiday (*Brit*) *ou* vacation (*US*) *ou* leave; **congé de maladie** sick leave; **congé de maternité** maternity leave; **les congés payés** (*vacances*) (annual) paid holidays (*Brit*) *ou* vacation (*US*) *ou* leave; (*péj: vacanciers*) the rank and file (holiday-makers (*Brit*) *ou* vacationers (*US*)); **congés scolaires** school holidays (*Brit*) *ou* vacation (*US*).

congédiable [kɔ̃ʒedjabl(ə)] *adj* (*Mil*) due for discharge; (*gén*) able to be dismissed. **le personnel non titulaire est ~ à tout moment** non-tenured staff can be dismissed at any time.

congédier [kɔ̃ʒedje] (7) *vt* to dismiss.
congelable [kɔ̃ʒlabl(ə)] *adj* which can be easily frozen.
congélateur [kɔ̃ʒelatœʀ] *nm* (*meuble*) deep-freeze; (*compartiment*) freezer compartment.
congélation [kɔ̃ʒelɑsjɔ̃] *nf [eau, aliments]* freezing; *[huile]* congealing; *V* **point**[1].
congeler [kɔ̃ʒle] (5) **1** *vt eau, huile* to freeze; *aliments* to (deep-)freeze. **les produits congelés** (deep-)frozen foods, deep-freeze foods. **2 se congeler** *vpr* to freeze.
congénère [kɔ̃ʒenɛʀ] **1** *adj* congeneric. **2** *nmf* (*semblable*) fellow, fellow creature. **toi et tes ~s** you and your like.
congénital, e, *mpl* **-aux** [kɔ̃ʒenital, o] *adj* congenital.
congère [kɔ̃ʒɛʀ] *nf* snowdrift.
congestif, -ive [kɔ̃ʒɛstif, iv] *adj* congestive.
congestion [kɔ̃ʒɛstjɔ̃] *nf* congestion. **~ (cérébrale)** stroke; **~ (pulmonaire)** congestion of the lungs.
congestionner [kɔ̃ʒɛstjɔne] (1) *vt rue* to congest; *personne, visage* to flush, make flushed. **être congestionné** *[personne, visage]* to be flushed; *[rue]* to be congested.
conglomérat [kɔ̃glɔmeʀa] *nm* (*lit*) conglomerate; (*fig*) conglomeration.
conglomération [kɔ̃glɔmeʀɑsjɔ̃] *nf* conglomeration.
conglomérer [kɔ̃glɔmeʀe] (6) *vt* to conglomerate.
Congo [kɔ̃go] *nm*: **le ~** (*pays, fleuve*) the Congo.
congolais, e [kɔ̃gɔlɛ, ɛz] **1** *adj* Congolese. **2** *nm,f*: **C~(e)** Congolese.
congratulations [kɔ̃gʀatylɑsjɔ̃] *nfpl* († *ou hum*) congratulations.
congratuler [kɔ̃gʀatyle] (1) († *ou hum*) *vt* to congratulate.
congre [kɔ̃gʀ(ə)] *nm* conger (eel).
congrégation [kɔ̃gʀegɑsjɔ̃] *nf* (*Rel*) congregation; (*fig*) assembly.
congrès [kɔ̃gʀɛ] *nm* congress. (*US Pol*) **le C~** Congress; **membre du C~** congressman, member of Congress.
congressiste [kɔ̃gʀesist(ə)] *nmf* participant at a congress.
congru, e [kɔ̃gʀy] *adj* **(a)** *V* **portion. (b) = congruent.**
congruence [kɔ̃gʀyɑ̃s] *nf* (*Math*) congruence.
congruent, e [kɔ̃gʀyɑ̃, ɑ̃t] *adj* (*Math*) congruent.
conifère [kɔnifɛʀ] *nm* conifer.
conique [kɔnik] **1** *adj* conical. **de forme ~** cone-shaped, coniform. **2** *nf* conic (section).
conjectural, e, *mpl* **-aux** [kɔ̃ʒɛktyʀal, o] *adj* conjectural.
conjecturalement [kɔ̃ʒɛktyʀalmɑ̃] *adv* conjecturally.
conjecture [kɔ̃ʒɛktyʀ] *nf* conjecture. **se perdre en ~s quant à qch** to lose o.s. in conjectures about sth; **nous en sommes réduits aux ~s** we can only conjecture *ou* guess (about this).
conjecturer [kɔ̃ʒɛktyʀe] (1) *vt* to conjecture. **on ne peut rien ~ sur cette situation** one can't conjecture anything about that situation.
conjoint, e [kɔ̃ʒwɛ̃, wɛ̃t] **1** *adj démarche, action,* (*Fin*) *débiteurs, legs* joint (*épith*); *problèmes* linked, related.
2 *nm,f* (*Admin: époux*) spouse. **lui et sa ~e** he and his spouse; **le maire a félicité les ~s** the mayor congratulated the couple; **les (deux) ~s** the husband and wife; **les futurs ~s** the bride and groom to be.
conjointement [kɔ̃ʒwɛ̃tmɑ̃] *adv* jointly. **~ avec** together with; **la notice explicative vous sera expédiée ~ (avec l'appareil)** the explanatory notice will be enclosed (with the machine).
conjonctif, -ive [kɔ̃ʒɔ̃ktif, iv] **1** *adj* (*Gram*) conjunctive; (*Anat*) connective. **2 conjonctive** *nf* (*Anat*) conjunctiva.
conjonction [kɔ̃ʒɔ̃ksjɔ̃] *nf* **(a)** (*Astron, Gram*) conjunction. (*Ling*) **~ de coordination/de subordination** coordinating/subordinating conjunction. **(b)** (*frm: union*) union, conjunction.
conjonctivite [kɔ̃ʒɔ̃ktivit] *nf* conjunctivitis.
conjoncture [kɔ̃ʒɔ̃ktyʀ] *nf* (*circonstances*) circumstances. **dans la ~ (économique) actuelle** in the present (economic) circumstances; **crise de ~** economic crisis (due to a number of factors); **étude de ~** study of the overall economic climate *ou* of the present state of the economy.
conjoncturel, -elle [kɔ̃ʒɔ̃ktyʀɛl] *adj*: **crises/fluctuations ~les** economic crises/fluctuations arising out of certain economic conditions.
conjugable [kɔ̃ʒygabl(ə)] *adj* which can be conjugated.
conjugaison [kɔ̃ʒygɛzɔ̃] *nf* (*Bio, Gram*) conjugation; (*frm: union*) union, uniting. **grâce à la ~ de nos efforts** by our joint efforts.
conjugal, e, *mpl* **-aux** [kɔ̃ʒygal, o] *adj amour, union* conjugal. **vie ~e** married *ou* conjugal life; *V* **domicile, foyer.**
conjugalement [kɔ̃ʒygalmɑ̃] *adv*: **vivre ~** to live (together) as a (lawfully) married couple.
conjugué, e [kɔ̃ʒyge] (*ptp de* **conjuguer**) **1** *adj* (*Bot, Math*) conjugate; *efforts, actions* joint, combined. **2** *nfpl* (*Bot*) **conjuguées** conjugatae.
conjuguer [kɔ̃ʒyge] (1) **1** *vt* (*Gram*) to conjugate; (*combiner*) to combine. **ce verbe se conjugue avec avoir** this verb is conjugated with avoir. **2 se conjuguer** *vpr [efforts]* to combine.
conjuration [kɔ̃ʒyʀɑsjɔ̃] *nf* (*complot*) conspiracy; (*rite*) conjuration. **c'est une véritable ~!*** it's a conspiracy!, it's all a big plot!
conjuré, e [kɔ̃ʒyʀe] (*ptp de* **conjurer**) *nm,f* conspirator.
conjurer [kɔ̃ʒyʀe] (1) **1** *vt* **(a)** (*éviter*) *danger, échec* to avert.
(b) (*littér: exorciser*) *démons, diable* to ward off, cast out. **essayer de ~ le sort** to try to ward off *ou* evade ill fortune.
(c) (*prier, implorer*) **~ qn de faire qch** to beseech *ou* entreat *ou* beg sb to do sth; **je vous en conjure** I beseech *ou* entreat *ou* beg you.
(d) (††: *conspirer*) *mort, perte de qn* to plot. **~ contre qn** to plot *ou* conspire against sb.
2 se conjurer *vpr* (*s'unir*) *[circonstances]* to conspire; *[conspirateurs]* to plot, conspire (*contre* against). (*frm, hum*) **vous vous êtes tous conjurés contre moi!** you're all conspiring against me!, you're all in league against me!
connaissable [kɔnɛsabl(ə)] *adj* knowable. **le ~** the knowable.
connaissance [kɔnɛsɑ̃s] *nf* **(a)** (*savoir*) **la ~ de qch** (the) knowledge of sth; **la ~** knowledge; **la ~ intuitive/expérimentale** intuitive/experimental knowledge; **sa ~ de l'anglais** his knowledge of English, his acquaintance with English; **il a une bonne ~ des affaires** he has a good *ou* sound knowledge of business matters; **une profonde ~ du cœur humain** a deep understanding of the human heart; **la ~ de soi** self-knowledge.
(b) (*choses connues, science*) **~s** knowledge; **faire étalage de ses ~s** to display one's knowledge *ou* learning; **approfondir/enrichir ses ~s** to deepen *ou* broaden/enhance one's knowledge; **avoir *ou* posséder des ~s de** to be acquainted with, have some knowledge of; **c'est un garçon qui a des ~s** he's a knowledgeable fellow; **il a de vagues ~s de physique** he has a vague knowledge of *ou* a nodding acquaintance with physics.
(c) (*personne*) acquaintance. **c'est une vieille/simple ~** he is an old/a mere acquaintance; **faire de nouvelles ~s** to make new acquaintances, meet new people; **il a de nombreuses ~s** he has many acquaintances, he knows a great number of people.
(d) (*conscience, lucidité*) consciousness. **avoir toute sa ~** to be fully conscious; **être sans ~** to be unconscious; **perdre ~** to lose consciousness; **reprendre ~** to regain consciousness, come round*.
(e) (*loc*) **à ma/sa/leur ~** to (the best of) my/his/their knowledge, as far as I know/he knows/they know; **pas à ma ~** not to my knowledge, not as far as I know; **venir à la ~ de qn** to come to sb's knowledge; **donner ~ de qch à qn** to inform *ou* notify sb of sth; **porter qch à la ~ de qn** to notify sb of sth, bring sth to sb's attention; **avoir ~ d'un fait** to be aware of a fact; **en ~ de cause** with full knowledge of the facts; **nous sommes parmi gens de ~** we are among familiar faces; **un visage de ~** a familiar face; **en pays de ~** (*gens qu'on connaît*) among familiar faces; (*branche, sujet qu'on connaît*) on familiar ground *ou* territory; **il avait amené quelqu'un de sa ~** he had brought along an acquaintance of his *ou* someone he knew; **faire ~ avec qn, faire la ~ de qn** (*rencontrer*) to meet sb, make sb's acquaintance; (*apprendre à connaître*) to get to know sb; **prendre ~ de qch** to read *ou* peruse sth; **nous avons fait ~ à Paris** we met in Paris; **je leur ai fait faire ~** I introduced them (to each other).
connaissement [kɔnɛsmɑ̃] *nm* (*Comm*) bill of lading.
connaisseur, -euse [kɔnɛsœʀ, øz] **1** *adj coup d'œil, air* expert. **2** *nm,f* connoisseur. **être ~ en vins** to be a connoisseur of wines; **il juge en ~** his opinion is that of a connoisseur.
connaître [kɔnɛtʀ(ə)] (57) **1** *vt* **(a)** *date, nom, adresse* to know; *fait* to know, be acquainted with; *personne* (*gén*) to know, be acquainted with; (*rencontrer*) to meet; (††: *sens biblique*) to know. **connaît-il la nouvelle?** has he heard *ou* does he know the news?; **connais-tu un bon restaurant près d'ici?** do you know of a good restaurant near here?; **~ qn de vue/nom/réputation** to know sb by sight/by name/by repute; **chercher à ~ qn** to try to get to know sb; **apprendre à ~ qn** to get to know sb; **il l'a connu à l'université** he met *ou* knew him at university; **je l'ai connu enfant *ou* tout petit** I knew him when he was a child; (*je le vois encore*) I have known him since he was a child; **vous connaissez la dernière (nouvelle)?** have you heard the latest (news)?; (*hum*) **si tu te conduis comme ça je ne te connais plus!** if you behave like that (I'll pretend) I'm not with you; **je ne lui connaissais pas ce chapeau/ces talents** I didn't know he had that hat/these talents; **je ne lui connais pas de défauts/d'ennemis** I'm not aware of his having any faults/enemies; **je ne le connais ni d'Ève ni d'Adam** I don't know him from Adam.
(b) *langue, science* to know; *méthode, auteur, texte* to know, be acquainted with. **~ les oiseaux/les plantes** to know about birds/plants; **tu connais la mécanique/la musique?** do you know anything *ou* much about engineering/music?; **~ un texte** to know a text, be familiar with a text; **il connaît son affaire** he knows what he's talking about. **il connaît son métier** he (really) knows his job; **il en connaît un bout* *ou* un rayon*** he knows a thing or two about it*; **un poète qui connaît la vie/l'amour** a poet who knows what life/love is *ou* knows (about) life/love; **elle attendit longtemps de ~ l'amour** she waited a long time to discover what love is; **il ne connaît pas grand-chose à cette machine** he doesn't know (very) much about this machine; **elle n'y connaît rien** she doesn't know anything *ou* a thing about it, she hasn't a clue about it*; **je ne connais pas bien les coutumes du pays** I'm not really familiar with *ou* I'm not (very) well acquainted with the customs of the country, I'm not very well up on the customs of the country*; (*fig*) **je connais la chanson *ou* la musique*** I've heard it all before; **il ne connaît pas sa force** he doesn't know *ou* realize his own strength; **il ne connaît que son devoir** duty first is his motto.
(c) (*éprouver*) *[personne] faim, privations* to know, experience; *[pays, institution] crise* to experience. **il ne connaît pas la pitié** he knows no pity; **ils ont connu des temps meilleurs** they have known *ou* seen better days; **nous connaissons de tristes heures** we are going through sad times; **le pays connaît une crise économique grave** the country is going through *ou* experiencing a serious economic crisis.
(d) (*avoir*) *succès* to enjoy, have; *sort* to experience. **sa patience ne connaît pas de bornes** his patience knows no bounds.
(e) faire ~ *idée, sentiment* to make known; **faire ~ qn** *[pièce, livre]* to make sb's name *ou* make sb known; *[personne]* to make sb known, make a name for sb; **faire ~ qn à qn** to introduce sb to sb; **il m'a fait ~ les joies de la pêche** he introduced me to *ou* initiated me in(to) the joys of fishing; **se faire ~** (*par le succès*) to make a name for o.s., make one's name; (*aller voir qn*) to introduce o.s., make o.s. known.

(f) (*Jur*) ~ **de** to take *ou* have cognizance of.
(g) (*loc*) **il la connaît dans les coins*** he knows it backwards* *ou* inside out*; **ça le/me connaît!*** he knows/I know all about it!; **je ne connais que lui/que ça!** do I know him/it!*, don't I know him/it!*; **une bonne tasse de café après le repas, je ne connais que ça** there's nothing like a good cup of coffee after a meal; **je ne le connais ni d'Ève ni d'Adam** I don't know him from Adam.
2 se connaître *vpr* **(a) se ~ (soi-même)** to know o.s.; **connais-toi toi-même** know thyself; (*fig*) **il ne se connaît plus** he's beside himself (*with joy or rage etc*).
(b) (*se rencontrer*) to meet. **ils se sont connus en Grèce** they met *ou* became acquainted in Greece.
(c) s'y ~ *ou* **se ~**† **à** *ou* **en qch** to know (a lot) about sth, be well up on* *ou* well versed in sth; **il s'y connaît en voitures** he knows (all) about cars, he's an expert on cars.
connard‡ [kɔnaʀ] *nm* (silly) bugger‡, damn fool‡.
connarde‡ [kɔnaʀd(ə)] *nf*, **connasse‡** [kɔnas] *nf* (silly) bitch‡ *ou* cow‡.
conne [kɔn] *V* **con.**
connecter [kɔnɛkte] (1) *vt* to connect.
connerie‡ [kɔnʀi] *nf* **(a)** (*U*) bloody (*Brit*) *ou* damned stupidity‡.
(b) (*remarque, acte*) bloody (*Brit*) *ou* damned stupid thing to say *ou* do‡; (*livre, film*) bullshit‡ (*U*), bloody (*Brit*) *ou* damned rubbish‡ (*U*). **arrête de dire des ~s** stop talking (such) bullshit‡ *ou* such bloody (*Brit*) *ou* damned rubbish‡; **il a encore fait une ~** he's gone and done another damned stupid thing‡.
connétable [kɔnetabl(ə)] *nm* (*Hist*) constable.
connexe [kɔnɛks(ə)] *adj* (closely) related.
connexion [kɔnɛksjɔ̃] *nf* (*gén*) link, connection; (*Élec*) connection.
connivence [kɔnivɑ̃s] *nf* connivance. **être/agir de ~ avec qn** to be/act in connivance with sb; **un sourire de ~** a smile of complicity.
connotation [kɔnɔtɑsjɔ̃] *nf* connotation.
connoter [kɔnɔte] (1) *vt* to connote, imply; (*Ling*) to connote.
connu, e [kɔny] (*ptp de* **connaître**) *adj* (*non ignoré*) *terre, animal* known; (*répandu, courant*) *idée, méthode* widely-known, well-known; (*fameux*) *auteur, livre* well-known. **(bien) ~** well-known; **très ~** very well-known, famous; **ces faits sont mal ~s** these facts are not well-known *ou* widely-known; **il est ~ comme le loup blanc** everybody knows him; *V* **ni.**
conque [kɔ̃k] *nf* (*coquille*) conch; (*Anat*) concha. (*littér*) **la main en ~** cupping his hand round *ou* to his ear.
conquérant, e [kɔ̃keʀɑ̃, ɑ̃t] **1** *adj pays, peuple* conquering; *ardeur* masterful; *air, regard* swaggering. **2** *nm,f* conqueror.
conquérir [kɔ̃keʀiʀ] (21) *vt pays, place forte, montagne* to conquer; (*littér*) *femme, cœur* to conquer (*littér*), win; (*littér*) *estime, respect* to win, gain; (*littér*) *supérieur, personnage influent* to win over. **conquis à une doctrine** won over to a doctrine; **il a conquis ses galons sur le champ de bataille** he won his stripes on the battlefield; *V* **pays**[1].
conquête [kɔ̃kɛt] *nf* conquest. **faire la ~ de** *pays, montagne* to conquer; *femme* to conquer (*littér*), win; *supérieur, personnage influent* to win over; (*hum*) **faire des ~s** to make a few conquests (*hum*).
conquis, e [kɔ̃ki, iz] *ptp de* **conquérir.**
conquistador [kɔ̃kistadɔʀ] *nm* conquistador.
consacré, e [kɔ̃sakʀe] (*ptp de* **consacrer**) *adj* **(a)** (*béni*) *hostie, église* consecrated; *lieu* consecrated, hallowed.
(b) (*habituel, accepté*) *expression* accepted; *coutume* established, accepted; *itinéraire, visite* traditional; *écrivain* established, recognized.
(c) (*destiné à*) **~ à** given over to; **talents ~s à faire le bien** talents given over to *ou* dedicated to doing good.
consacrer [kɔ̃sakʀe] (1) *vt* **(a) ~ à** (*destiner, dédier à*) to devote to, dedicate to, consecrate to; (*affecter à, utiliser pour*) to devote to, give (over) to; **~ sa vie à Dieu** to devote *ou* dedicate *ou* consecrate one's life to God; **il consacre toutes ses forces/tout son temps à son travail** he devotes all his energies/time to his work, he gives all his energies/time (over) to his work; **pouvez-vous me ~ un instant?** can you give *ou* spare me a moment?; **se ~ à une profession/à Dieu** to dedicate *ou* devote o.s. to a profession/God, give o.s. to a profession/God.
(b) (*Rel*) *reliques, lieu* to consecrate, hallow (*littér*); *église, évêque, hostie* to consecrate. **temple consacré à Apollon** temple consecrated *ou* dedicated to Apollo; (*littér*) **leur mort a consacré cette terre** their death has made this ground hallowed.
(c) (*entériner*) *coutume, droit* to establish; *abus* to sanction. **expression consacrée par l'usage** expression sanctioned by use *ou* which has become accepted through use; **consacré par le temps** time-honoured (*épith*); **la fuite de l'ennemi consacre notre victoire** the enemy's flight makes our victory complete.
consanguin, e [kɔ̃sɑ̃gɛ̃, in] **1** *adj*: **frère ~** half-brother (*on the father's side*); **mariage ~** marriage between blood relations; **les mariages ~s sont à déconseiller** marriages between blood relations should be discouraged, inbreeding (*T*) should be discouraged.
2 *nmpl*: **les ~s** blood relations.
consanguinité [kɔ̃sɑ̃gɥinite] *nf* (*du même père, d'ancêtre commun*) consanguinity; (*Bio: union consanguine*) inbreeding.
consciemment [kɔ̃sjamɑ̃] *adv* consciously, knowingly.
conscience [kɔ̃sjɑ̃s] *nf* **(a)** (*faculté psychologique*) **la ~ de qch** the awareness *ou* consciousness of sth; (*Philos, Psych*) **la ~** consciousness; **~ de soi** self-awareness; **~ collective/de classe** collective/class consciousness; **~ linguistique** linguistic awareness; **avoir ~ que** to be aware *ou* conscious that; **avoir ~ de sa faiblesse/de l'importance de qch** to be aware *ou* conscious of one's own weakness/of the importance of sth; **prendre ~ de qch** to become aware of sth, realize sth, awake to sth; **il prit soudain ~ d'avoir dit ce qu'il ne fallait pas** he was suddenly aware that *ou* he suddenly realized that he had said something he shouldn't have; *V* **pris.**
(b) (*état de veille, faculté de sensation*) consciousness. **perdre/reprendre ~** to lose/regain consciousness.
(c) (*faculté morale*) conscience. **avoir la ~ tranquille/chargée** to have a clear/guilty conscience; **il n'a pas la ~ tranquille** he has a guilty *ou* an uneasy conscience, his conscience is troubling him; **avoir qch sur la ~** to have sth on one's conscience; **avoir bonne/mauvaise ~** to have a good *ou* clear/bad *ou* guilty conscience; **agir selon sa ~** to act according to one's conscience *ou* as one's conscience dictates; **sans ~** without conscience; **en (toute) ~** in all conscience *ou* honesty; **étouffer les ~s** to stifle consciences *ou* people's conscience; (*fig*) **il a sorti tout ce qu'il avait sur la ~** he came out with all he had on his conscience; (*fig*) **son déjeuner lui est resté sur la ~*** his lunch is lying heavy on his stomach; *V* **acquit, objecteur.**
(d) ~ (professionnelle) conscientiousness; **faire un travail avec beaucoup de ~** to do a piece of work conscientiously.
consciencieusement [kɔ̃sjɑ̃sjøzmɑ̃] *adv* conscientiously.
consciencieux, -ieuse [kɔ̃sjɑ̃sjø, jøz] *adj* conscientious.
conscient, e [kɔ̃sjɑ̃, ɑ̃t] *adj* (*non évanoui*) conscious; (*lucide*) *personne* lucid; *mouvement, décision* conscious. **~ de** conscious *ou* aware of.
conscription [kɔ̃skʀipsjɔ̃] *nf* conscription, draft (*US*).
conscrit [kɔ̃skʀi] *nm* conscript, draftee (*US*). **se faire avoir comme un ~*** to be taken in like a newborn babe *ou* like a real sucker*.
consécration [kɔ̃sekʀɑsjɔ̃] *nf [lieu, église]* consecration; *[coutume, droit]* establishment; *[abus]* sanctioning. **la ~ d'un temple à un culte** the consecration *ou* dedication of a temple to a religion; **la ~ du temps** time's sanction; **la ~ d'une œuvre par le succès** the consecration of a work by its success *ou* by the success it has; (*Rel*) **la ~** the consecration.
consécutif, -ive [kɔ̃sekytif, iv] *adj* consecutive. **pendant trois jours ~s** for three days running, for three consecutive days; **~ à** following upon; *V* **proposition.**
consécutivement [kɔ̃sekytivmɑ̃] *adv* consecutively. **elle eut ~ deux accidents** she had two consecutive accidents, she had two accidents one after the other; **~ à** following upon.
conseil [kɔ̃sɛj] **1** *nm* **(a)** (*recommandation*) piece of advice, advice (*U*); (*simple suggestion*) hint. **donner un ~/des ~s à qn** to give sb (a piece of) advice/sb advice; **écouter/suivre le ~ de qn** to listen to/follow sb's advice; **demander ~ à qn** to ask *ou* seek sb's advice, ask sb for advice; **prendre ~ de qn** to take advice from sb; **je lui ai donné le ~ d'attendre** I advised him to wait; **un petit ~** a word *ou* a few words *ou* a bit of advice, a hint *ou* tip; **ne pars pas, c'est un ~ d'ami** don't go — that's (just) a friendly piece of advice *ou* hint; **écoutez mon ~** take my advice, listen to my advice; **un bon ~** a sound piece of advice; **ne suivez pas les ~s de la colère** don't let yourself be guided by the promptings *ou* dictates of anger; **les ~s que nous donne l'expérience** everything that experience teaches us; (*littér*) **un homme de bon ~** a good counsellor, a man of sound advice; (*Admin, Comm*) **~s à ...** advice to ...; **~s à la ménagère/au débutant** hints *ou* tips for the housewife/the beginner; *V* **nuit.**
(b) (*en apposition: personne*) **ingénieur-~** consulting engineer; **avocat-/esthéticienne-~** legal/beauty consultant.
(c) (*groupe, assemblée*) *[entreprise]* board; *[organisme politique ou professionnel]* council, committee; (*séance, délibération*) meeting. **tenir ~** (*se réunir*) to hold a meeting; (*délibérer*) to deliberate.
2: conseil d'administration *[société anonyme etc]* board of directors; *[hôpital, école]* board of governors; (*Scol*) **conseil de classe** staff meeting (*to discuss the progress of individual members of a class*); (*Scol, Univ*) **conseil de discipline** disciplinary committee; (*Jur*) **Conseil d'État** Council of State; (*Rel*) **conseil de fabrique** fabric committee; (*Jur*) **conseil de famille** board of guardians; (*Admin*) **conseil général** regional council; (*Mil*) **conseil de guerre** court-martial; **passer en conseil de guerre** to be court-martialled; **faire passer qn en conseil de guerre** to court-martial sb; (*Pol*) **le Conseil des ministres** (*en Grande-Bretagne*) the Cabinet; (*en France*) the (French) Cabinet, the council of ministers; (*Admin*) **conseil municipal** town council; (*Jur*) **conseil des prud'hommes** industrial arbitration court, ≃ industrial tribunal (*with wide administrative and advisory powers*); (*Mil*) **conseil de révision** recruiting board, draft board (*US*); **Conseil de Sécurité** Security Council.
conseiller[1] [kɔ̃seje] (1) *vt* **(a)** (*recommander*) *prudence, méthode, bonne adresse* to recommend (*à qn* to sb). **il m'a conseillé ce docteur** he advised me to go to this doctor, he recommended this doctor to me; **~ à qn de faire qch** to advise sb to do sth; **je vous conseille vivement de ...** I strongly advise you to ...; **la peur/prudence lui conseilla de ...** fear/prudence prompted him to ...; **il est conseillé de s'inscrire à l'avance** it is advisable to enrol in advance; **il est conseillé aux parents de ...** parents are advised to ... .
(b) (*guider*) to advise, give advice to, counsel. **~ un étudiant dans ses lectures** to advise *ou* counsel a student in his reading; **il a été bien/mal conseillé** he has been given good/bad advice, he has been well/badly advised.
conseiller[2]**, -ère** [kɔ̃seje, kɔ̃sɛjɛʀ] **1** *nm,f* **(a)** (*expert*) adviser; (*guide, personne d'expérience*) counsellor, adviser. **~ juridique/technique** legal/technical adviser; (*fig*) **que ta conscience soit ta ~ère** may your conscience be your guide; *V* **colère.**
(b) (*Admin, Pol: fonctionnaire*) council member, councillor.
2: conseiller d'État senior member of the Council of State; **conseiller matrimonial** marriage guidance counsellor; **conseiller municipal** town councillor.

conseilleur, -euse [kɔ̃sɛjœʀ, øz] *nm,f* (*péj*) dispenser of advice. (*Prov*) **les ~s ne sont pas les payeurs** givers of advice don't pay the price.
consensus [kɔ̃sɛ̃sys] *nm* consensus (of opinion).
consentant, e [kɔ̃sɑ̃tɑ̃, ɑ̃t] *adj amoureuse* willing; (*frm*) *personnes, parties* in agreement, agreeable; (*Jur*) *parties, partenaire* consenting. **le mariage ne peut avoir lieu que si les parents sont ~s** the marriage can only take place with the parents' consent *ou* if the parents consent to it.
consentement [kɔ̃sɑ̃tmɑ̃] *nm* consent. **son ~ à leur mariage était nécessaire** his consent to their marriage was needed; **donner son ~ à qch** to consent to sth, give one's consent to sth; (*littér*) **le ~ universel** universal *ou* common assent.
consentir [kɔ̃sɑ̃tiʀ] (16) **1** *vi* (*accepter*) to agree, consent (*à* to). **~ à faire qch** to agree to do(ing) sth; **~ (à ce) que qn fasse qch** to consent *ou* agree to sb's doing sth; **espérons qu'il va (y) ~** let's hope he'll agree *ou* consent to it; *V* **qui.**
2 *vt* (*accorder*) *permission, délai, prêt* to grant (*à* to).
conséquemment [kɔ̃sekamɑ̃] *adv* (*littér: par suite*) consequently; († *ou littér: avec cohérence, logique*) consequentially. **~ à** as a result of, following on.
conséquence [kɔ̃sekɑ̃s] *nf* **(a)** (*effet, résultat*) result, outcome (*U*), consequence. **cela pourrait avoir** *ou* **entraîner des ~s graves pour ...** this could have serious consequences for *ou* repercussions on ...; **cela a eu pour ~ de l'obliger à réfléchir** the result *ou* consequence of this was that he was forced to think; **accepter/subir les ~s de ses actions** to accept/suffer the consequences of one's actions; **incident gros** *ou* **lourd de ~s** incident fraught with consequences; **avoir d'heureuses ~s** to have a happy outcome *ou* happy results.
(b) (*Philos: suite logique*) consequence; *V* **proposition, voie.**
(c) (*conclusion, déduction*) inference, conclusion (*de* to be drawn from). **tirer les ~s** to draw conclusions *ou* inferences (*de* from).
(d) (*loc*) **de ~** *affaire, personne* of (some) consequence *ou* importance; **en ~** (*par suite*) consequently; (*comme il convient*) accordingly; **en ~ de** (*par suite de*) in consequence of, as a result of; (*selon*) according to; **sans ~** (*sans suite fâcheuse*) without repercussions; (*sans importance*) of no consequence *ou* importance; **cela ne tire pas à ~** it's of no consequence, that's unlikely to have any repercussions.
conséquent, e [kɔ̃sekɑ̃, ɑ̃t] **1** *adj* **(a)** (*logique*) logical, rational; (*doué d'esprit de suite*) consistent. (*littér*) **~ à** consistent with, in keeping *ou* conformity with; **~ avec soi-même** consistent (with o.s.); **~ dans ses actions** consistent in one's actions.
(b) (*: *important*) sizeable.
(c) (*Géol*) *rivière, percée* consequent.
(d) (*Mus*) **(partie) ~e** consequent, answer.
(e) par ~ consequently, therefore.
2 *nm* (*Ling, Logique, Math*) consequent; (*Mus*) consequent, answer.
conservateur, -trice [kɔ̃sɛʀvatœʀ, tʀis] **1** *adj* (*gén*) conservative; (*Brit Pol*) Conservative, Tory*. (*Can*) **le parti ~** the Progressive-Conservative Party (*Can*).
2 *nm,f* **(a)** (*gardien*) *[musée]* curator; *[bibliothèque]* librarian. **~ des Eaux et forêts** ≃ forestry commissioner; **~ des hypothèques** ≃ land registrar.
(b) (*Pol*) conservative; (*Brit Pol*) Conservative, Tory*; (*Can*) Conservative (*Can*).
conservation [kɔ̃sɛʀvasjɔ̃] *nf* **(a)** (*action*) *[aliments]* preserving; *[monuments]* preserving, preservation; *[archives]* keeping; *[accent, souplesse]* retention, retaining, keeping; *[habitudes]* keeping up; *V* **instinct.**
(b) (*état*) *[aliments, monuments]* preservation. **en bon état de ~** *fruits* well-preserved; *monument* well-preserved, in a good state of preservation.
(c) (*Admin: charge*) **~ des Eaux et forêts** ≃ Forestry Commission; **~ des hypothèques** ≃ Land Registry.
conservatisme [kɔ̃sɛʀvatism(ə)] *nm* conservatism.
conservatoire [kɔ̃sɛʀvatwaʀ] **1** *adj* (*Jur*) protective; *V* **saisie.**
2 *nm* school, academy (*of music, drama etc*). **le C~ (de musique et de déclamation)** the (Paris) Conservatoire; **le C~ des arts et métiers** the Conservatoire *ou* Conservatory of Arts and Crafts.
conserve [kɔ̃sɛʀv(ə)] **1** *nf*: **les ~s** tinned (*Brit*) *ou* canned food(s); **~s de viande/poisson** tinned (*Brit*) *ou* canned meat/fish; **l'industrie de la ~** the canning industry; **lait/poulet de ~** canned *ou* tinned (*Brit*) milk/chicken; **en ~** canned, tinned (*Brit*); **mettre en ~** to can; **se nourrir de ~s** to live out of tins (*Brit*) *ou* cans; *V* **boîte.**
2 *adv* (*ensemble*) **de ~** *naviguer* in convoy; *agir* in concert.
conservé, e [kɔ̃sɛʀve] (*ptp de* **conserver**) *adj*: **bien ~** *personne* well-preserved.
conserver [kɔ̃sɛʀve] (1) **1** *vt* **(a)** (*garder dans un endroit*) *objets, papiers* to keep. '**~ à l'abri de la lumière**' 'keep *ou* store away from light'.
(b) (*ne pas perdre*) (*gén*) to retain, keep; *usage, habitude* to keep up; *espoir* to retain; *qualité, droits* to conserve, retain; *son calme, ses amis, ses cheveux* to keep. **ça conserve tout son sens** it retains its full meaning; **~ la vie** to conserve life; **il a conservé toute sa tête** (*calme*) he kept his head *ou* cool*; (*lucidité*) he still has his wits about him; (*Naut*) **~ l'allure** to maintain speed; (*Mil*) **~ sa position** to hold one's position.
(c) (*maintenir en bon état*) *aliments, santé, monument* to preserve. **la vie au grand air, ça conserve!*** (the) open-air life keeps you young; **bien conservé pour son âge** well-preserved for one's age.
(d) (*Culin*) to preserve. **~ (dans du vinaigre)** to pickle; **~ en bocal** to bottle.
2 se conserver *vpr [aliments]* to keep.
conserverie [kɔ̃sɛʀvəʀi] *nf* (*usine*) canning factory; (*industrie*) canning industry.
considérable [kɔ̃sideʀabl(ə)] *adj somme, foule, retard, travail* considerable; *rôle, succès, changement* considerable, significant; *dégâts, surface* considerable, extensive; († *ou littér*) *personnage, situation* eminent, important. **saisi d'une émotion ~** considerably *ou* deeply moved.
considérablement [kɔ̃sideʀabləmɑ̃] *adv* (*V* **considérable**) considerably; significantly; extensively. **ceci nous a ~ retardés** this delayed us considerably; **ceci a ~ modifié la situation** this modified the situation to a considerable *ou* significant extent, this modified the situation considerably *ou* significantly.
considérant [kɔ̃sideʀɑ̃] *nm* (*Jur*) *[loi, jugement]* preamble.
considération [kɔ̃sideʀasjɔ̃] *nf* **(a)** (*examen*) *[problème etc]* consideration. **ceci mérite ~** this is worth considering *ou* consideration *ou* looking into; **prendre qch en ~** to take sth into consideration *ou* account.
(b) (*motif, aspect*) consideration, factor. **n'entrons pas dans ces ~s** don't let's go into these considerations; **c'est une ~ dont je n'imagine pas qu'il faille se préoccuper** it's a question *ou* factor I don't think we need bother ourselves with.
(c) (*remarques, observations*) **~s** reflections; **il se lança dans des ~s interminables sur l'infériorité des femmes** he launched into lengthy reflections on the inferiority of women.
(d) (*respect*) esteem, respect. **jouir de la ~ de tous** to enjoy everyone's esteem *ou* respect; (*formule épistolaire*) '**veuillez agréer l'assurance de ma ~ distinguée**' 'yours faithfully *ou* truly'.
(e) (*loc*) **en ~ de** (*en raison de*) because of, given; (*par rapport à*) considering; **sans ~ de** *dangers, conséquences, prix* heedless *ou* regardless of; **sans ~ de personne** without taking personalities into account *ou* consideration; **par ~ pour** out of respect *ou* regard for.
considérer [kɔ̃sideʀe] (6) *vt* **(a)** (*envisager*) *problème etc* to consider. **il faut ~ (les) avantages et (les) inconvénients** one must consider *ou* take into account the advantages and disadvantages; **~ le pour et le contre** to consider the pros and cons; **considère bien ceci** think about this carefully, consider this well; **il ne considère que son intérêt** he only thinks about *ou* considers his own interests; **tout bien considéré** all things considered, taking everything into consideration *ou* account; **c'est à ~** (*pour en tenir compte*) this has to be considered *ou* borne in mind *ou* taken into account; (*à étudier*) this must be gone into *ou* examined.
(b) (*assimiler à*) **~ comme** to look upon as, regard as, consider (to be); **je le considère comme mon fils** I look upon him as *ou* regard him as my son, I consider him (to be) my son; **il se considère comme un personnage important** he sees himself as an important person, he considers himself (to be) an important person.
(c) (*juger*) to consider, deem (*frm*). **je le considère intelligent** I consider him intelligent, I deem him to be intelligent (*frm*); **je considère qu'il a raison** I consider that he is right; **c'est très mal considéré (d'agir ainsi)** it's very bad form (to act like that); **considérant que** considering that.
(d) (*frm: regarder*) to consider, study.
(e) (*respecter: gén ptp*) to respect, have a high regard for. **il est hautement considéré** *ou* **on le considère hautement** he is highly regarded *ou* respected, he is held in high regard *ou* high esteem; **le besoin d'être considéré** the need to have people's respect *ou* esteem.
consignataire [kɔ̃siɲatɛʀ] *nm* (*Comm*) *[biens, marchandises]* consignee; *[navire]* consignee, forwarding agent; (*Jur*) *[somme]* depositary.
consignation [kɔ̃siɲasjɔ̃] *nf* (*Jur: dépôt d'argent*) deposit; (*Comm: dépôt de marchandise*) consignment. **la ~ d'un emballage** charging a deposit on a container.
consigne [kɔ̃siɲ] *nf* **(a)** (*instructions*) orders. **donner/recevoir/observer la ~** to give/get *ou* be given/obey orders; **c'est la ~** those are the orders.
(b) (*punition*) (*Mil*) confinement to barracks; (*Scol* †) detention.
(c) (*pour les bagages*) left-luggage (office) (*Brit*), checkroom (*US*). **~ automatique** left-luggage lockers.
(d) (*Comm: somme remboursable*) deposit. **il y a 30 centimes de ~ sur la bouteille** there's a 30-centime deposit *ou* a deposit of 30 centimes on the bottle.
consigné, e [kɔ̃siɲe] (*ptp de* **consigner**) *adj* (*Comm*) *bouteille, emballage* returnable. **non ~** non-returnable.
consigner [kɔ̃siɲe] (1) *vt* **(a)** (*mettre par écrit*) *fait, pensée, incident* to record.
(b) (*interdire de sortir à*) *troupe, soldat* to confine to barracks; *élève* to give detention to, keep in (after school); (*interdire l'accès de*) *salle, établissement* to bar entrance to. **consigné à la caserne** confined to barracks; **établissement consigné aux militaires** establishment out of bounds to troops.
(c) (*mettre en dépôt*) *somme, marchandise* to deposit; *navire* to consign; *bagages* to deposit *ou* put in the left-luggage (office) (*Brit*) *ou* checkroom (*US*).
(d) (*facturer provisoirement*) *emballage, bouteille* to put a deposit on. **je vous le consigne** I'm giving it to you on a deposit.
consistance [kɔ̃sistɑ̃s] *nf [sauce, neige, terre]* consistency; (*fig*) *[caractère]* solidity. **~ sirupeuse/élastique** syrupy/elastic consistency; **manquer de ~** to lack consistency; **prendre ~** *[liquide]* to thicken; **sans ~** *caractère* spineless, lacking in solidity (*attrib*); *nouvelle, rumeur* ill-founded, groundless; *substance* lacking in consistency (*attrib*); **cette rumeur prend de la ~** this rumour is gaining ground.
consistant, e [kɔ̃sistɑ̃, ɑ̃t] *adj repas* solid (*épith*), substantial;

nourriture solid (*épith*); *mélange, peinture, sirop* thick; (*fig*) *rumeur* well-founded; (*fig*) *argument* solid, sound.
consister [kɔ̃siste] (1) *vi* **(a)** (*se composer de*) ~ **en** to consist of, be made up of; **le village consiste en 30 maisons et une église** the village consists of *ou* is made up of 30 houses and a church; **en quoi consiste votre travail?** what does your work consist of?
(b) (*résider dans*) ~ **dans** to consist in; **le salut consistait dans l'arrivée immédiate de renforts** their salvation consisted *ou* lay in the immediate arrival of reinforcements; ~ **à faire** to consist in doing.
consistoire [kɔ̃sistwaʀ] *nm* consistory.
consœur [kɔ̃sœʀ] *nf* (*hum*) (lady) colleague.
consolable [kɔ̃sɔlabl(ə)] *adj* consolable.
consolant, e [kɔ̃sɔlɑ̃, ɑ̃t] *adj* consoling, comforting.
consolateur, -trice [kɔ̃sɔlatœʀ, tʀis] **1** *adj* consolatory. **2** *nm,f* (*littér*) comforter.
consolation [kɔ̃sɔlɑsjɔ̃] *nf* (*action*) consoling, consolation; (*réconfort*) consolation (*U*), comfort (*U*), solace (*U: littér*). **nous prodiguant ses** ~**s** offering us comfort; **paroles de** ~ words of consolation *ou* comfort; **elle est sa** ~ she is his consolation *ou* comfort *ou* solace (*littér*); **enfin, il n'y a pas de dégâts, c'est une** ~ anyway, (at least) there's no damage, that's one consolation *ou* comfort; *V* **prix.**
console [kɔ̃sɔl] *nf* **(a)** (*table*) console (table); (*Archit*) console. **(b)** (*Mus*) *[harpe]* neck; *[orgue]* console; (*Ordinateurs, Tech: d'enregistrement*) console.
consoler [kɔ̃sɔle] (1) **1** *vt personne* to console, solace (*littér*); *chagrin* to soothe. **ça me consolera de mes pertes** that will console me for my losses; **je ne peux pas le** ~ **de sa peine** I cannot console *ou* comfort him in his grief; **si ça peut te** ~ ... if it is of any consolation *ou* comfort to you ...; **le temps console** time heals.
2 se consoler *vpr* to console o.s., find consolation. **se** ~ **d'une perte/de son échec** to be consoled for *ou* to get over a loss/one's failure; (*hum*) **il s'est vite consolé avec une autre*** he soon consoled himself with another woman, he soon found comfort *ou* consolation with another woman; **il ne s'en consolera jamais** he'll never be consoled, he'll never get over it.
consolidation [kɔ̃sɔlidɑsjɔ̃] *nf* (*V* **consolider, se consolider**) (*gén*) strengthening; reinforcement; consolidation; knitting; (*Fin*) funding.
consolidé, e [kɔ̃sɔlide] (*ptp de* **consolider**) (*Fin*) **1** *adj* funded. **2** *nmpl* consols.
consolider [kɔ̃sɔlide] (1) **1** *vt* **(a)** *maison, table* to strengthen, reinforce; (*Méd*) *fracture* to knit.
(b) *accord, amitié, parti, fortune* to consolidate; (*Écon*) *monnaie* to strengthen.
(c) (*Fin*) *rente, emprunt* to guarantee. **rentes consolidées** funded income.
2 se consolider *vpr [régime, parti]* to strengthen *ou* consolidate its position; *[fracture]* to knit. **la position de la gauche/droite s'est encore consolidée** the position of the left/right has been further consolidated *ou* strengthened; **le régime ne s'est pas consolidé** the regime has not strengthened *ou* consolidated its position.
consommable [kɔ̃sɔmabl(ə)] *adj solide* edible; *liquide* drinkable. **cette viande n'est** ~ **que bouillie** this meat can only be eaten boiled.
consommateur, -trice [kɔ̃sɔmatœʀ, tʀis] *nm,f* (*acheteur*) consumer; (*client d'un café*) customer.
consommation [kɔ̃sɔmɑsjɔ̃] *nf* **(a)** *[nourriture, gaz, matière première]* consumption; (*Aut*) *[essence, huile]* consumption. **il fait une grande** ~ **de papier** he goes through* *ou* uses (up) a lot of paper; (*Aut*) ~ **aux 100 km** (fuel) consumption per 100 km, ≃ miles per gallon.
(b) (*Écon*) **la** ~ consumption. **de** ~ *biens, société* consumer (*épith*).
(c) (*dans un café*) drink. **le garçon prend les** ~**s** the waiter takes the orders.
(d) (*frm*) *[mariage]* consummation; *[crime]* perpetration (*frm*), committing. **jusqu'à la** ~ **des siècles** until the end of the age(s).
consommé, e [kɔ̃sɔme] (*ptp de* **consommer**) **1** *adj habileté* consummate (*épith*); *écrivain etc* accomplished. **tableau qui témoigne d'un art** ~ picture revealing consummate artistry.
2 *nm* consommé. ~ **de poulet** chicken consommé, consommé of chicken.
consommer [kɔ̃sɔme] (1) *vt* **(a)** *nourriture* to eat, consume (*frm*); *boissons* to drink, consume (*frm*). **on consomme beaucoup de fruits chez nous** we eat a lot of fruit in our family; **la France est le pays où l'on consomme** *ou* **où il se consomme le plus de vin** France is the country with the greatest wine consumption *ou* where the most wine is consumed *ou* drunk; **il est interdit de** ~ **à la terrasse** drinks are not allowed *ou* drinking is not allowed *ou* drinks may not be consumed outside.
(b) *combustible, carburant, matière première* to use, consume; (*quantité spécifiée*) to use (up), go through*, consume. **cette machine consomme beaucoup d'eau** this machine uses (up) *ou* goes through* a lot of water; **gâteau qui consomme beaucoup de farine** a cake which uses *ou* takes *ou* needs a lot of flour; (*Aut*) **combien consommez-vous aux 100 km?** how much (petrol) do you use per 100 km?, what's your petrol consumption?, ≃ how many miles per gallon do you get?; (*Aut*) **elle consomme beaucoup d'essence/d'huile** it's heavy on petrol/oil, it uses a lot of petrol/oil.
(c) (*frm: accomplir*) *acte sexuel* to consummate (*frm*); *crime* to perpetrate (*frm*), commit. **le mariage n'a pas été consommé** the marriage has not been consummated; **cela a consommé sa ruine** this finally confirmed his downfall.
consomption [kɔ̃sɔ̃psjɔ̃] *nf* († *ou littér: dépérissement*) wasting; (†: *tuberculose*) consumption†.
consonance [kɔ̃sɔnɑ̃s] *nf* consonance (*U*). **nom aux** ~**s étrangères/douces** foreign-/sweet-sounding name.
consonant, e [kɔ̃sɔnɑ̃, ɑ̃t] *adj* consonant.
consonantique [kɔ̃sɔnɑ̃tik] *adj* consonantal, consonant (*épith*).
consonantisme [kɔ̃sɔnɑ̃tism(ə)] *nm* consonant system.
consonne [kɔ̃sɔn] *nf* consonant.
consort [kɔ̃sɔʀ] **1** *adj V* **prince. 2** *nmpl* (*péj*) **X et** ~**s** (*acolytes*) X and company (*péj*), X and his bunch* (*péj*); (*pareils*) X and his like (*péj*).
consortium [kɔ̃sɔʀsjɔm] *nm* consortium.
conspirateur, -trice [kɔ̃spiʀatœʀ, tʀis] **1** *adj* conspiratorial. **2** *nm,f* conspirer, conspirator, plotter.
conspiration [kɔ̃spiʀɑsjɔ̃] *nf* conspiracy.
conspirer [kɔ̃spiʀe] (1) **1** *vi* (*comploter*) to conspire, plot (*contre* against).
2 conspirer à *vt indir* (*concourir à*) ~ **à faire** to conspire to do; **tout semblait** ~ **à notre succès** everything seemed to be conspiring to bring about our success.
3 *vt* (†) *mort, ruine de qn* to conspire († *ou littér*), plot.
conspuer [kɔ̃spɥe] (1) *vt* to boo, shout down.
constamment [kɔ̃stamɑ̃] *adv* (*sans trêve*) constantly, continuously; (*très souvent*) constantly, continually.
constance [kɔ̃stɑ̃s] *nf* **(a)** (*permanence*) consistency, constancy.
(b) (*littér: persévérance, fidélité*) constancy, steadfastness. **travailler avec** ~ to work steadfastly; (*iro*) **vous avez de la constance!** you don't give up easily (I'll say that for you)!
(c) (†: *courage*) fortitude, steadfastness.
constant, e [kɔ̃stɑ̃, ɑ̃t] **1** *adj* **(a)** (*invariable*) constant; (*continu*) constant, continuous; (*très fréquent*) constant, continual.
(b) (*littér: persévérant*) *effort* steadfast; *travail* constant. **être** ~ **dans ses efforts** to be steadfast *ou* constant in one's efforts.
2 constante *nf* (*Math*) constant.
Constantin [kɔ̃stɑ̃tɛ̃] *nm* Constantine.
Constantinople [kɔ̃stɑ̃tinɔpl(ə)] *n* Constantinople.
constat [kɔ̃sta] *nm*: ~ **(d'huissier)** certified report (*by bailiff*); ~ **(d'accident)** (accident) report; ~ **d'adultère** recording of adultery; (*fig*) ~ **d'échec/d'impuissance** acknowledgement of failure/impotence.
constatation [kɔ̃statɑsjɔ̃] *nf* **(a)** (*U: V* **constater**) noting; noticing; seeing; taking note; recording; certifying. **(b)** (*gén*) observation. ~**s** *[enquête]* findings; (*Police*) **procéder aux** ~**s d'usage** to make a *ou* one's routine report.
constater [kɔ̃state] (1) *vt* **(a)** (*remarquer*) *fait* to note, notice; *erreur* to see, notice; *dégâts* to note, take note of. **il constata la disparition de son carnet** he noticed *ou* saw that his notebook had disappeared; **je ne critique pas: je ne fais que** ~ I'm not criticizing, I'm merely stating a fact *ou* I'm merely making a statement (of fact) *ou* an observation; **je constate que vous n'êtes pas pressé de tenir vos promesses** I see *ou* notice *ou* note that you aren't in a hurry to keep your promises; **vous pouvez** ~ **pour vous-même les erreurs** you can see the mistakes for yourself.
(b) (*frm: consigner*) *effraction, état de fait, authenticité* to record; *décès* to certify. **le médecin a constaté le décès** the doctor certified that death had taken place *ou* occurred.
constellation [kɔ̃stelɑsjɔ̃] *nf* (*Astron*) constellation. (*fig littér*) ~ **de** *lumières, poètes* constellation *ou* galaxy of.
constellé, e [kɔ̃stele] (*ptp de* **consteller**) *adj*: ~ **(d'étoiles)** star-studded, star-spangled; ~ **de** *astres, joyaux, lumières* spangled *ou* studded with; *taches* spotted *ou* dotted with.
consteller [kɔ̃stele] (1) *vt*: **des lumières constellaient le ciel** the sky was spangled *ou* studded with lights; **des taches constellaient le tapis** the carpet was spotted *ou* dotted with marks.
consternant, e [kɔ̃stɛʀnɑ̃, ɑ̃t] *adj* dismaying, disquieting.
consternation [kɔ̃stɛʀnɑsjɔ̃] *nf* consternation, dismay.
consterner [kɔ̃stɛʀne] (1) *vt* to dismay, fill with consternation *ou* dismay. **air consterné** air of consternation *ou* dismay.
constipation [kɔ̃stipɑsjɔ̃] *nf* constipation.
constipé, e [kɔ̃stipe] (*ptp de* **constiper**) *adj* (*Méd*) constipated. (*péj: contraint, embarrassé*) **avoir l'air** *ou* **être** ~ to look stiff *ou* ill-at-ease, be stiff.
constiper [kɔ̃stipe] (1) *vt* to constipate.
constituant, e [kɔ̃stitɥɑ̃, ɑ̃t] **1** *adj* **(a)** *élément* constituent.
(b) (*Pol*) **assemblée** ~**e** constituent assembly; (*Hist*) **l'assemblée** ~**e, la C**~**e** the Constituent Assembly; (*Hist*) **les** ~**s** the members of the Constituent Assembly.
2 constituante *nf* (*Québec*) *[université]* branch.
constitué, e [kɔ̃stitɥe] (*ptp de* **constituer**) *adj* **(a)** (*Méd*) **bien/mal** ~ of sound/unsound constitution. **(b)** (*Pol*) *V* **corps.**
constituer [kɔ̃stitɥe] (1) **1** *vt* **(a)** (*fonder*) *comité, ministère, gouvernement, société anonyme* to set up, form; *bibliothèque* to build up; *collection* to build up, put together; *dossier* to make up, put together.
(b) (*composer*) to make up, constitute, compose. **les pièces qui constituent cette collection** the pieces that (go to) make up *ou* that constitute this collection; **sa collection est surtout constituée de porcelaines** his collection is made up *ou* is composed *ou* consists mainly of pieces of porcelain.
(c) (*être, représenter*) to constitute. **ceci constitue un délit/ne constitue pas un motif** that constitutes an offence/does not constitute a motive; **ce billet de 10 F constitue toute ma fortune** this 10-franc note constitutes *ou* represents my entire fortune; **ils constituent un groupe homogène** they make up *ou* form a well-knit group.
(d) (*Jur: établir*) *rente, pension, dot* to settle (*à* on); *avocat* to retain. ~ **qn son héritier** to appoint sb one's heir; ~ **qn à la**

garde des enfants to appoint sb *ou* take sb on to look after one's children.

2 se constituer *vpr* **(a)** **se ~ prisonnier** to give o.s. up; **se ~ témoin** to come forward as a witness; **se ~ partie civile** *to associate in an action with the public prosecutor.*

(b) (*Comm*) **se ~ en société** to form o.s. into a company.

constitutif, -ive [kɔ̃stitytif, iv] *adj* constituent, component.

constitution [kɔ̃stitysjɔ̃] *nf* **(a)** (*U: V* **constituer**) setting-up, formation, forming; building-up; putting together; making-up; settlement, settling; retaining. (*Jur*) **~ de partie civile** *association with the public prosecutor.*

(b) (*éléments, composition*) *[substance]* composition, make-up; *[ensemble, organisation]* make-up, composition; *[équipe, comité]* composition.

(c) (*Méd: conformation, santé*) constitution. **il a une robuste ~** he has a sturdy constitution.

(d) (*Pol: charte*) constitution.

constitutionnaliser [kɔ̃stitysjɔnalize] (1) *vt* to constitutionalize.

constitutionnalité [kɔ̃stitysjɔnalite] *nf* constitutionality.

constitutionnel, -elle [kɔ̃stitysjɔnɛl] *adj* constitutional; *V* **droit³**.

constitutionnellement [kɔ̃stitysjɔnɛlmɑ̃] *adv* constitutionally.

constricteur [kɔ̃stʀiktœʀ] *adj m, nm* (*Anat*) **(muscle) ~** constrictor (muscle); *V* **boa.**

constriction [kɔ̃stʀiksjɔ̃] *nf* constriction.

constrictor [kɔ̃stʀiktɔʀ] *adj, nm:* **(boa) ~** (boa) constrictor.

constructeur, -trice [kɔ̃stʀyktœʀ, tʀis] **1** *adj* (*Zool*) home-making (*épith*); (*fig*) *imagination* constructive.

2 *nm* (*fabricant*) maker; (*bâtisseur*) builder, constructor. **~ d'automobiles** car manufacturer; **~ de navires** shipbuilder.

constructif, -ive [kɔ̃stʀyktif, iv] *adj* constructive.

construction [kɔ̃stʀyksjɔ̃] *nf* **(a)** (*action: V* **construire**) building; construction. **la ~ de l'immeuble/du navire a pris 2 ans** building the flats/ship *ou* the construction of the flats/ship took 2 years, it took 2 years to build the flats/ship; **c'est de la ~ robuste** it is solidly built, it is of solid construction; **les ~s navales/aéronautiques européennes sont menacées** European shipbuilding *ou* the European shipbuilding industry/the European aircraft industry is threatened; **cela va bien dans la ~** things are going well in the building trade (*Brit*) *ou* construction business; **matériaux de ~** building materials; **de ~ française/anglaise** *bateau, voiture* French/British built; **en ~** under construction, in the course of construction; *V* **jeu.**

(b) (*structure*) *[roman, thèse]* construction; *[phrase]* structure. **c'est une simple ~ de l'esprit** it's (a) pure hypothesis.

(c) (*édifice, bâtiment*) building, construction.

(d) (*Ling: expression, tournure*) construction, structure.

(e) (*Géom: figure*) figure, construction.

construire [kɔ̃stʀɥiʀ] (38) *vt machine, bâtiment, route, navire, chemin de fer* to build, construct; *figure géométrique* to construct; *théorie, phrase, intrigue* to construct, put together, build up. **on a *ou* ça s'est beaucoup construit ici depuis la guerre** there's been a lot of building here since the war; (*Ling*) **ça se construit avec le subjonctif** it takes the subjunctive, it takes a subjunctive construction.

consubstantialité [kɔ̃sypstɑ̃sjalite] *nf* consubstantiality.

consubstantiation [kɔ̃sypstɑ̃sjɑsjɔ̃] *nf* consubstantiation.

consubstantiel, -elle [kɔ̃sypstɑ̃sjɛl] *adj* consubstantial (*à, avec* with).

consul [kɔ̃syl] *nm* consul. **~ général** consul general; **~ de France** French Consul.

consulaire [kɔ̃sylɛʀ] *adj* consular.

consulat [kɔ̃syla] *nm* **(a)** (*bureaux*) consulate; (*charge*) consulate, consulship. **(b)** (*Hist française*) **le C~** the Consulate.

consultable [kɔ̃syltabl(ə)] *adj* (*disponible*) *ouvrage, livre* available for consultation, which may be consulted. (*utilisable*) **cette carte est trop grande pour être aisément ~** this map is too big to be used easily.

consultant, e [kɔ̃syltɑ̃, ɑ̃t] *adj avocat* consultant (*épith*). **(médecin) ~** consulting physician.

consultatif, -ive [kɔ̃syltatif, iv] *adj* consultative, advisory. **à titre ~** in an advisory capacity.

consultation [kɔ̃syltɑsjɔ̃] *nf* **(a)** (*action*) consulting, consultation. **pour faciliter la ~ du dictionnaire/de l'horaire** to make the dictionary/timetable easier *ou* easy to consult; **après ~ de son agenda** (after) having consulted his diary; **ouvrage de référence d'une ~ difficile** reference work that is difficult to consult.

(b) (*séance: chez le médecin, un expert*) consultation. (*Méd*) **aller à la ~** to go to the surgery (*Brit*) *ou* doctor's office (*US*); **donner une ~/des ~s gratuites** to give a consultation/free consultations; (*Méd*) **les heures de ~** surgery (*Brit*) *ou* consulting hours; (*Méd*) **il y avait du monde à la ~** there were a lot of people at the surgery (*Brit*) *ou* doctor's office (*US*).

(c) (*échange de vues*) consultation. **être en ~ avec des spécialistes** to be in consultation with specialists.

(d) (*frm: avis donné*) professional advice (*U*).

consulter [kɔ̃sylte] (1) **1** *vt médecin* to consult; *expert, avocat, parent* to consult, seek advice from; *dictionnaire, livre, horaire* to consult, refer to; *boussole, baromètre* to consult. **ne ~ que sa raison/son intérêt** to be guided only by one's reason/self-interest, look only to one's reason/self-interest.

2 *vi [médecin] (recevoir)* to hold surgery (*Brit*); (*conférer*) to hold a consultation.

3 se consulter *vpr* (*s'entretenir*) to confer, consult each other. **ils se consultèrent du regard** they looked questioningly at each other.

consumer [kɔ̃syme] (1) **1** *vt* **(a)** (*brûler*) to consume, burn. **l'incendie a tout consumé** the fire consumed everything; **des débris à demi consumés** charred debris; **une bûche se consumait dans l'âtre** a log was burning in the hearth; **le bois s'est consumé entièrement** the wood was completely destroyed (by fire).

(b) (*fig: dévorer*) *[fièvre, mal]* to consume, devour. **consumé par l'ambition** consumed with *ou* devoured by ambition.

(c) (*littér: dépenser*) *forces* to expend; *fortune* to squander. **il consume sa vie en plaisirs frivoles** he fritters away his life in idle pleasures.

2 se consumer *vpr* (*littér: dépérir*) to waste away. (*se ronger de*) **se ~ de chagrin/de désespoir** to be consumed with sorrow/despair; **il se consume à petit feu** he is slowly wasting away.

contact [kɔ̃takt] *nm* **(a)** (*toucher*) touch, contact. **le ~ de 2 surfaces** contact between *ou* of 2 surfaces; **un ~ très doux** a very gentle touch; (*Méd*) **ça s'attrape par le ~** it's contagious, it can be caught by contact; **le ~ de la soie est doux** silk is soft to the touch; **au point de ~ des deux lignes** at the point of contact *ou* the meeting point of the two lines; *V* **verre.**

(b) (*Aut, Élec*) contact. (*Aut*) **mettre/couper le ~** to switch on/off the ignition; **~ électrique** electrical contact; **appuyer sur le ~** to press the contact button *ou* lever; *V* **clef.**

(c) (*rapport d'affaires etc*) contact. **il a beaucoup de ~s (avec l'étranger)** he has got a lot of contacts *ou* connections (abroad); **dès le premier ~, ils ...** from their first meeting, they ...; **en ~ étroit avec** in close touch *ou* contact with; (*Mil*) **établir/rompre le ~ (avec)** to make/break off contact (with).

(d) (*loc*) **prendre ~, entrer en** (*Aviat, Mil, Rad*) to make contact (*avec* with); (*rapport d'affaires*) to get in touch *ou* contact (*avec* with); **rester/être en ~** (*Aviat, Mil, Rad*) to remain in/be in contact (*avec* with); (*rapport d'affaires*) to remain in/be in touch (*avec* with), remain in/be in contact (*avec* with); **se mettre en ~ avec la tour de contrôle/qn** to make contact with *ou* to contact the control tower/sb; **entrer/être en ~** *[objets]* to come into/be in contact; *[fils électriques]* to make/be making contact; **mettre en ~** *objets* to bring into contact; *relations d'affaires* to put in touch; (*Aviat, Rad*) to put in contact; **prise de ~** (*première entrevue*) first meeting; (*Mil*) first contact; **au ~ de: au ~ de sa main** at the touch of his hand; **au ~ de ces jeunes gens il a acquis de l'assurance** through his contact *ou* association with these young people he has gained self-assurance; **métal qui s'oxyde au ~ de l'air/de l'eau** metal that oxydises in contact with air/water.

contacter [kɔ̃takte] (1) *vt* to contact, get in touch with.

contagieux, -euse [kɔ̃taʒjø, øz] *adj maladie* (*gén*) infectious, catching (*attrib*); (*par le contact*) contagious; *personne* infectious; contagious; (*fig*) *enthousiasme, peur, rire* infectious, contagious, catching (*attrib*). **l'isolement des ~** the isolation of contagious patients *ou* cases *ou* of patients with contagious diseases.

contagion [kɔ̃taʒjɔ̃] *nf* (*Méd*) contagion, contagiousness; (*fig*) infectiousness, contagion. **être exposé à la ~** to be in danger of becoming infected; **les ravages de la ~ parmi les vieillards** the ravages of the disease among the old.

contagionner [kɔ̃taʒjɔne] (1) *vt* to infect.

container [kɔ̃tɛnɛʀ] *nm* (freight) container.

contamination [kɔ̃taminɑsjɔ̃] *nf* contamination.

contaminer [kɔ̃tamine] (1) *vt* to contaminate.

conte [kɔ̃t] *nm* (*récit*) tale, story; († *ou littér: histoire mensongère*) (tall) story. (*lit, fig*) **~ de fée** fairy tale *ou* story.

contemplateur, -trice [kɔ̃tɑ̃platœʀ, tʀis] *nm,f* contemplator.

contemplatif, -ive [kɔ̃tɑ̃platif, iv] *adj air, esprit* contemplative, meditative; (*Rel*) *ordre* contemplative. (*Rel*) **un ~** a contemplative.

contemplation [kɔ̃tɑ̃plɑsjɔ̃] *nf* (*action*) contemplation. **la ~** (*Philos*) contemplation, meditation; (*Rel*) contemplation.

contempler [kɔ̃tɑ̃ple] (1) *vt* to contemplate, gaze at, gaze upon (*littér*).

contemporain, e [kɔ̃tɑ̃pɔʀɛ̃, ɛn] *adj* **(a)** (*de la même époque*) *personne* contemporary; *événement* contemporaneous, contemporary (*de* with). **ses ~s** his contemporaries. **(b)** (*actuel*) contemporary, present-day (*épith*).

contemporanéité [kɔ̃tɑ̃pɔʀaneite] *nf* contemporaneousness.

contempteur, -trice [kɔ̃tɑ̃ptœʀ, tʀis] *nm,f* (*littér*) denigrator, contemnor (*littér*).

contenance [kɔ̃tnɑ̃s] *nf* **(a)** (*capacité*) *[bouteille, réservoir]* capacity; *[navire]* (carrying) capacity. **avoir une ~ de 45 litres** to have a capacity of 45 litres, take *ou* hold 45 litres.

(b) (*attitude*) bearing, attitude. **~ humble/fière** humble/proud bearing; **~ gênée** embarrassed attitude; **il fumait pour se donner une ~** he was smoking to give an impression of composure *ou* to disguise his lack of composure; **faire bonne ~ (devant)** to put on a bold front (in the face of); **perdre ~** to lose one's composure.

contenant [kɔ̃tnɑ̃] *nm:* **le ~ (et le contenu)** the container (and the contents).

contenir [kɔ̃tniʀ] (22) **1** *vt* **(a)** (*avoir une capacité de*) *[récipient]* to hold, take; *[cinéma, avion, autocar]* to seat, hold.

(b) (*renfermer*) *[récipient, livre, minerai]* to contain. **ce minerai contient beaucoup de fer** this ore contains a lot of iron *ou* has a lot of iron in it; **discours contenant de grandes vérités** speech containing *ou* embodying great truths.

(c) (*maîtriser*) *surprise* to contain; *colère* to contain, suppress; *sanglots, larmes* to contain, hold back; *foule* to contain, restrain, hold in check. (*Mil*) **~ l'ennemi** to contain the enemy, hold the enemy in check.

2 se contenir *vpr* to contain o.s., control one's emotions.

content, e [kɔ̃tɑ̃, ɑ̃t] **1** *adj* **(a)** (*heureux, ravi*) pleased, glad, happy. **l'air ~** with a pleased expression; **je serais ~ que vous veniez** I'd be pleased *ou* glad *ou* happy if you came; **je suis ~ d'apprendre cela** I'm pleased *ou* glad about this news, I'm pleased *ou* glad *ou* happy to hear this news; **il était très ~ de ce changement** he was very pleased *ou* glad about *ou* at the change; **je suis très ~ ici** I'm very happy *ou* contented here.

(b) (*satisfait de*) **~ de** *élève, voiture, situation* pleased *ou* happy with; **être ~ de peu** to be content with little, be easily satisfied; **être ~ de soi** to be pleased with o.s.

(c) non ~ d'être/d'avoir fait ... not content with being/with having done ... .

2 *nm*: **avoir (tout) son ~ de qch** to have had one's fill of sth.

contentement [kɔ̃tɑ̃tmɑ̃] *nm* (*action de contenter*) satisfaction, satisfying; (*état*) contentment, satisfaction. **éprouver un profond ~ à la vue de ...** to feel great contentment *ou* deep satisfaction at the sight of ...; **~ d'esprit** spiritual contentment; **~ de soi** self-satisfaction; (*Prov*) **~ passe richesse** happiness is worth more than riches.

contenter [kɔ̃tɑ̃te] (1) **1** *vt personne, besoin, envie, curiosité* to satisfy. **facile à ~** easy to please, easily pleased *ou* satisfied; **cette explication l'a contenté** he was satisfied *ou* happy with this explanation, this explanation satisfied him; **il est difficile de ~ tout le monde** it's difficult to please *ou* satisfy everyone.

2 se contenter *vpr*: **se ~ de qch/de faire qch** to content o.s. with sth/with doing sth; **il a dû se ~ d'un repas par jour/de manger les restes** he had to content himself *ou* make do* with one meal a day/with eating the left-overs; **il se contenta d'un sourire/de sourire** he contented himself with a smile/with smiling, he merely gave a smile/smiled.

contentieux, -euse [kɔ̃tɑ̃sjø, øz] **1** *adj* (*Jur*) contentious. **2** *nm* (*litiges*) (*Comm*) litigation; (*Pol*) disputes; (*service*) legal department. **~ administratif/commercial** administrative/commercial actions *ou* litigation.

contenu, e [kɔ̃tny] (*ptp de* **contenir**) **1** *adj colère, sentiments* restrained, suppressed.

2 *nm [récipient, dossier]* contents; *[loi, texte]* content. **la table des matières indique le ~ du livre** the table shows the contents of the book; **le ~ subversif de ce livre** the subversive content of this book.

conter [kɔ̃te] (1) *vt* **(a)** (*littér*) *histoire* to recount, relate. (*hum*) **contez-nous vos malheurs** well let's hear your problems, tell us all about it.

(b) (*loc*) **que me contez-vous là?** what are you trying to tell me?, what yarn are you trying to spin me?*; **il lui en a conté de belles!** he really spun him some yarns!* *ou* told him some incredible stories!; **elle ne s'en laisse pas ~** she's not easily taken in, she doesn't let herself be taken in (easily); **il ne faut pas lui en ~** it's no use trying it on with him*, don't bother trying those stories on him; († *ou hum*) **~ fleurette à qn** to murmur sweet nothings to sb († *ou hum*).

contestable [kɔ̃tɛstabl(ə)] *adj théorie, idée* questionable, disputable; *raisonnement* questionable, doubtful.

contestataire [kɔ̃tɛstatɛʀ] **1** *adj journal, étudiants, tendances* anti-establishment. **2** *nmf*: **c'est un ~** he's anti-establishment; **les ~s ont été expulsés** the protesters were expelled.

contestation [kɔ̃tɛstasjɔ̃] *nf* **(a)** (*U: V* **contester**) contesting; questioning; disputing. **(b)** (*discussion*) dispute. **sans ~ possible** beyond dispute; **élever une ~** to raise an objection (*sur* to); **il y a matière à ~** there are grounds for contention *ou* dispute. **(c)** (*gén Pol: opposition*) **la ~** anti-establishment activity; **faire de la ~** to (actively) oppose the establishment, protest (against the establishment).

conteste [kɔ̃tɛst(ə)] *nf*: **sans ~** unquestionably, indisputably.

contester [kɔ̃tɛste] (1) **1** *vt* (*Jur*) *succession, droit, compétence* to contest; *fait, raisonnement, vérité* to question, dispute, contest. **je ne conteste pas que vous ayez raison** I don't dispute that you're right; **je ne lui conteste pas ce droit** I don't question *ou* dispute *ou* contest his right; **ce roman/cet écrivain est très contesté** this novel/writer is very controversial.

2 *vi* to take issue (*sur* over); (*Pol etc*) to protest. **il ne conteste jamais** he never takes issue over anything; **il conteste toujours sur des points de détail** he's always taking issue over points of detail; **maintenant les jeunes ne pensent qu'à ~** young people nowadays think only about protesting.

conteur, -euse [kɔ̃tœʀ, øz] *nm,f* (*écrivain*) storywriter; (*narrateur*) storyteller.

contexte [kɔ̃tɛkst(ə)] *nm* context.

contexture [kɔ̃tɛkstyʀ] *nf [tissu, organisme]* texture; *[roman, œuvre]* structure.

contigu, -uë [kɔ̃tigy] *adj choses* adjoining, adjacent, contiguous (*frm*); (*fig*) *domaines, sujets* (closely) related. **être ~ à qch** to be adjacent *ou* next *ou* contiguous (*frm*) to sth.

contiguïté [kɔ̃tigɥite] *nf [choses]* proximity, contiguity (*frm*); (*fig*) *[sujets]* relatedness. **la ~ de nos jardins est très commode** it's very handy that our gardens are next to each other *ou* adjacent *ou* adjoining; **la ~ de ces deux sujets** the fact that these two subjects are (closely) related, the relatedness of these two subjects.

continence [kɔ̃tinɑ̃s] *nf* continence, continency.

continent[1], e [kɔ̃tinɑ̃, ɑ̃t] *adj* continent.

continent[2] [kɔ̃tinɑ̃] *nm* (*gén, Géog*) continent; (*par rapport à une île*) mainland.

continental, e, *mpl* **-aux** [kɔ̃tinɑ̃tal, o] *adj* continental.

contingence [kɔ̃tɛ̃ʒɑ̃s] *nf* **(a)** (*Philos*) contingency.

(b) les ~s contingencies; **les ~s de tous les jours** (little) everyday occurrences *ou* contingencies; **les ~s de la vie** the (little) chance happenings of life; **tenir compte des ~s** to take account of all contingencies *ou* eventualities.

contingent, e [kɔ̃tɛ̃ʒɑ̃, ɑ̃t] **1** *adj* contingent. **2** *nm* **(a)** (*Mil: groupe*) contingent. (*en France*) **le ~** *the conscripts called up for national service*, the draft (*US*). **(b)** (*Comm: quota*) quota. **(c)** (*part, contribution*) share.

contingentement [kɔ̃tɛ̃ʒɑ̃tmɑ̃] *nm*: **le ~ des exportations/importations** the fixing *ou* establishing of export/import quotas, the placing of quotas on exports/imports.

contingenter [kɔ̃tɛ̃ʒɑ̃te] (1) *vt* (*Comm*) *importations, exportations* to place *ou* fix a quota on; *produits, matière première* to distribute by a system of quotas.

continu, e [kɔ̃tiny] **1** *adj mouvement, série, bruit* continuous; (*Math*) continuous; *ligne, silence* unbroken, continuous; *effort* continuous, unremitting; *souffrance* endless; *V* **jet[1], journée**. **2** *nm* (*Math, Philos, Phys*) continuum; (*Élec*) direct current.

continuateur, -trice [kɔ̃tinɥatœʀ, tʀis] *nm,f [œuvre littéraire]* continuator; *[innovateur, précurseur]* successor. **les ~s de cette réforme** those who carried on (*ou* carry on *etc*) the reform.

continuation [kɔ̃tinɥasjɔ̃] *nf* continuation. **nous comptons sur la ~ de cette entente** we count on our continuing agreement; *V* **bon[1]**.

continuel, -elle [kɔ̃tinɥɛl] *adj* (*continu*) continuous; (*qui se répète*) continual, constant.

continuellement [kɔ̃tinɥɛlmɑ̃] *adv* (*V* **continuel**) continuously; continually, constantly.

continuer [kɔ̃tinɥe] (1) **1** *vt* **(a)** (*poursuivre*) *démarches, politique* to continue (with), carry on with; *tradition* to continue, carry on; *travaux, études* to continue (with), carry on with, go on with. **~ son chemin** to continue on *ou* along one's way, go on; **~ l'œuvre de son maître** to carry on *ou* continue the work of one's master; **Pompidou continua de Gaulle** Pompidou carried on *ou* continued where de Gaulle left off.

(b) (*prolonger*) *droite, route* to continue.

2 *vi* **(a)** *[bruit, spectacle, guerre]* to continue, go on. **la route (se) continue jusqu'à la gare** the road goes (on) *ou* continues as far as the station.

(b) *[voyageur]* to go on, continue on one's way.

(c) ~ de *ou* **à marcher/manger** *etc* to go on *ou* keep on *ou* continue walking/eating *etc*, continue to walk/eat *etc*, walk/eat *etc* on; **continue le travail!** go on *ou* keep on *ou* continue working!; **'mais' continua-t-il** 'but' he went on *ou* continued; **dis-le, continue!** go on, say it!; **s'il continue, je vais ...** if he goes on *ou* keeps on *ou* continues, I'm going to ... .

continuité [kɔ̃tinɥite] *nf [politique, tradition]* continuation; *[action]* continuity. **assurer la ~ d'une politique** to ensure continuity in applying a policy, ensure the continuation of a policy; *V* **solution**.

continûment [kɔ̃tinymɑ̃] *adv* continuously.

continuum [kɔ̃tinɥɔm] *nm* continuum. **le ~ espace-temps** the four-dimensional *ou* space-time continuum.

contondant, e [kɔ̃tɔ̃dɑ̃, ɑ̃t] *adj instrument* blunt. **arme ~e** blunt instrument.

contorsion [kɔ̃tɔʀsjɔ̃] *nf* contortion.

contorsionner (se) [kɔ̃tɔʀsjɔne] (1) *vpr* (*lit*) *[acrobate]* to contort o.s.; (*fig, péj*) to contort o.s. **il se contorsionnait pour essayer de se défaire de ses liens** he was writhing about *ou* contorting himself in an attempt to free himself from his bonds.

contorsionniste [kɔ̃tɔʀsjɔnist(ə)] *nmf* contortionist.

contour [kɔ̃tuʀ] *nm* **(a)** *[objet]* outline; *[montagne, visage, corps]* outline, line, contour. **(b)** *[route, rivière]* **~s** windings.

contourné, e [kɔ̃tuʀne] (*ptp de* **contourner**) *adj* (*péj*) *raisonnement, style* tortuous; (*péj*) *colonne, pied de table* (over)elaborate; *jambes, pieds* twisted, crooked.

contourner [kɔ̃tuʀne] (1) *vt* **(a)** *ville* to skirt round, bypass; *montagne* to skirt round, walk (*ou* drive *etc*) round; *mur, véhicule* to walk (*ou* drive *etc*) round; (*fig*) *règle, difficulté* to circumvent, bypass.

(b) (*façonner*) *arabesques* to trace (out); *vase* to fashion.

(c) (*déformer*) to twist, contort.

contraceptif, -ive [kɔ̃tʀasɛptif, iv] *adj, nm* contraceptive.

contraception [kɔ̃tʀasɛpsjɔ̃] *nf* contraception.

contractant, e [kɔ̃tʀaktɑ̃, ɑ̃t] **1** *adj* (*Jur*) contracting. **2** *nm,f* contracting party.

contracté, e [kɔ̃tʀakte] (*ptp de* **contracter**) *adj* **(a)** (*Ling*) contracted. **(b)** *personne* tense, tensed up.

contracter[1] [kɔ̃tʀakte] (1) **1** *vt* **(a)** (*raidir*) *muscle* to tense, contract; *traits, visage* to tense; (*fig*) *personne* to make tense. **la peur lui contracta la gorge** fear gripped his throat; **l'émotion lui contracta la gorge** his throat tightened with emotion; **les traits contractés par la souffrance** his features drawn with suffering; **un sourire forcé contracta son visage** his face stiffened into a forced smile.

(b) (*Phys: réduire*) **~ un corps/fluide** to make a body/fluid contract.

2 se contracter *vpr [muscle]* to tense (up), contract; *[gorge]* to tighten; *[traits, visage]* to tense (up); *[cœur]* to contract; (*fig*) *[personne]* to become tense, get tensed up; (*Phys*) *[corps]* to contract; (*Ling*) *[mot, syllabe]* to be (able to be) contracted.

contracter[2] [kɔ̃tʀakte] (1) *vt* **(a)** *dette, obligation* to contract, incur; *alliance* to contract, enter into. **~ une assurance** to take out an insurance (policy); (*Admin*) **~ mariage avec** to contract (a) marriage with. **(b)** *maladie* to contract; *manie, habitude* to acquire, contract.

contractile [kɔ̃tʀaktil] *adj* contractile.

contractilité [kɔ̃tʀaktilite] *nf* contractility.

contraction [kɔ̃tʀaksjɔ̃] *nf* **(a)** (*U: action*) *[corps, liquide]* contraction; *[muscle]* tensing, contraction. **(b)** (*U: état*) *[muscles, traits, visage]* tenseness. **(c)** (*spasme*) contraction.

contractuel, -elle [kɔ̃tʀaktɥɛl] **1** *adj* contractual. **2** *nm,f [parking]* ≃ traffic warden (*Brit*). **(agent) ~** contract (public) employee.

contracture [kɔ̃tʀaktyʀ] *nf* (*Archit*) contracture; (*Physiol*) spasm, (prolonged) contraction.

contradicteur [kɔ̃tʀadiktœʀ] *nm* contradictor.

contradiction [kɔ̃tʀadiksjɔ̃] *nf* **(a)** (*U: contestation*) **la ~** argument, debate; **porter la ~ dans un débat** to introduce counter-arguments in a debate, add a dissenting voice to a debate; **je ne supporte pas la ~** I can't bear to be contradicted; *V* **esprit.**

(b) (*discordance*) contradiction, inconsistency. **texte plein de ~s** text full of contradictions *ou* inconsistencies; **le monde est plein de ~s** the world is full of contradictions; **~ dans les termes** contradiction in terms; **il y a ~ entre ...** there is a contradiction between ...; **être en ~ avec soi-même** to contradict o.s.; **il est en ~ avec ce qu'il a dit précédemment** he's contradicting what he said before.

(c) (*Jur*) *fact of hearing all parties to a case.*

contradictoire [kɔ̃tʀadiktwaʀ] *adj idées, théories, récits* contradictory, conflicting. **débat ~** debate; **réunion politique ~** political meeting with an open debate; **~ à** in contradiction to, in conflict with; (*Jur*) **arrêt/jugement ~** order/judgment given after due hearing of the parties.

contradictoirement [kɔ̃tʀadiktwaʀmɑ̃] *adv* (*Jur*) after due hearing of the parties.

contraignant, e [kɔ̃tʀɛɲɑ̃, ɑ̃t] *adj horaire* restricting, constraining; *obligation, occupation* restricting.

contraindre [kɔ̃tʀɛ̃dʀ(ə)] (52) *vt*: **~ qn à faire qch** to force *ou* compel sb to do sth; **contraint à démissionner** forced *ou* compelled *ou* constrained to resign; **il/cela m'a contraint au silence/au repos** he/this forced *ou* compelled me to be silent/to rest; **se ~ avec peine** to restrain o.s. with difficulty; **se ~ à être aimable** to force o.s. to be polite, make o.s. be polite; (*Jur*) **~ par voie de justice** to constrain by law (*to pay debt*).

contraint, e[1] [kɔ̃tʀɛ̃, ɛ̃t] (*ptp de* **contraindre**) *adj* **(a)** (*gêné*) constrained, forced. **d'un air ~** with an air of constraint, constrainedly. **(b) ~ et forcé** under constraint *ou* duress.

contrainte[2] [kɔ̃tʀɛ̃t] *nf* **(a)** (*violence*) constraint. (*littér*) **vivre dans la ~** to live in bondage; **par ~** *ou* **sous la ~** under constraint *ou* duress; **empêcher qn d'agir par la ~** to prevent sb from acting by force, forcibly prevent sb from acting.

(b) (*gêne*) constraint, restraint. **sans ~** unrestrainedly, unconstrainedly.

(c) (*Jur*) **~ par corps** civil imprisonment.

contraire [kɔ̃tʀɛʀ] **1** *adj* **(a)** (*opposé, inverse*) *sens, effet, avis* opposite; (*Naut*) *vent* contrary, adverse; (*contradictoire*) *opinions* conflicting, opposite; *propositions, intérêts* conflicting; *mouvements, forces* opposite; *V* **avis.**

(b) (*nuisible*) *vent, forces, action* contrary; *destin* adverse. **l'alcool m'est ~** alcohol doesn't agree with me; **le sort lui fut ~** fate was against him *ou* opposed him; **~ à la santé** bad for the health, injurious *ou* prejudicial to the health (*frm*).

2 *nm* **(a)** *[mot, concept]* opposite. **c'est le ~ de son frère** he's the opposite *ou* the antithesis of his brother; **et pourtant c'est tout le ~** and yet it's just the reverse *ou* opposite; **il fait toujours le ~ de ce qu'on lui dit** he always does the opposite *ou* contrary of what he's told; **je ne vous dis pas le ~** I'm not saying anything to the contrary, I'm not disputing *ou* denying it.

(b) au ~, bien au ~, tout au ~ on the contrary; **au ~ des autres** unlike the others, as opposed to the others.

contrairement [kɔ̃tʀɛʀmɑ̃] *adv*: **~ à** contrary to; (*dans une comparaison*) **~ aux autres ...** unlike the others ... .

contralto [kɔ̃tʀalto] *nm* contralto.

contrariant, e [kɔ̃tʀaʀjɑ̃, ɑ̃t] *adj personne* perverse, contrary; *incident* tiresome, annoying, irksome.

contrarier [kɔ̃tʀaʀje] (7) *vt* **(a)** (*irriter*) to annoy; (*ennuyer*) to bother. **il cherche à vous ~** he's trying to annoy you.

(b) (*gêner*) *projets* to frustrate, thwart; *amour* to thwart. (*Naut*) **~ la marche d'un bateau** to impede a ship's progress; (*Mil*) **~ les mouvements de l'ennemi** to impede the enemy's movements.

(c) (*contraster*) to juxtapose *ou* alternate (for contrast).

contrariété [kɔ̃tʀaʀjete] *nf* (*irritation*) annoyance, vexation. **éprouver une ~** to feel annoyed *ou* vexed; **un geste de ~** a gesture of annoyance; **toutes ces ~s l'ont rendu furieux** all these annoyances *ou* vexations made him furious.

contrastant, e [kɔ̃tʀastɑ̃, ɑ̃t] *adj couleurs, figures, effets* contrasting (*épith*).

contraste [kɔ̃tʀast(ə)] *nm* (*gén, TV*) contrast. **par ~** by contrast; **faire ~ avec** to contrast with; **en ~ avec** in contrast to; **mettre en ~** to contrast.

contrasté, e [kɔ̃tʀaste] (*ptp de* **contraster**) *adj couleurs* contrasted, contrasting; *composition, photo, style* with some contrast. **une photographie trop/pas assez ~e** a photograph with too much/not enough contrast.

contraster [kɔ̃tʀaste] (1) **1** *vt éléments, caractères* to contrast; *photographie* to give contrast to, put contrast into. **ce peintre contraste à peine son sujet** this painter hardly brings out his subject (at all) *ou* hardly makes his subject stand out.

2 *vi* to contrast (*avec* with).

contrat [kɔ̃tʀa] *nm* (*convention, document*) contract, agreement; (*fig: accord, pacte*) agreement. **~ d'apprentissage** apprenticeship contract; **~ de mariage** marriage contract; **~ de travail** work contract; **~ collectif** collective agreement; **~ administratif** public service contract; **~ d'assurance** contract of insurance; (*Hist, Pol*) **~ social** social contract; **réaliser** *ou* **remplir son ~** (*Bridge*) to make one's contract; (*fig: Pol etc*) to fulfil one's pledges; (*Jur*) **~ aléatoire** aleatory contract; *V* **bridge.**

contravention [kɔ̃tʀavɑ̃sjɔ̃] *nf* **(a)** (*Aut*) (*pour infraction au code*) fine; (*pour stationnement interdit*) (*amende*) (parking) fine; (*procès-verbal*) parking ticket. **dresser ~ (à qn)** (*stationnement interdit*) to write out *ou* issue a parking ticket (for sb); (*autres infractions*) to book sb*, take down sb's particulars; **donner** *ou* **flanquer* une ~ à qn** to book sb* for parking, give sb a parking ticket; to book sb.

(b) (*Jur: infraction*) **~ à** contravention *ou* infraction of; **être en (état de) ~** to be contravening the law; **être en ~ à** to be in contravention of.

contre [kɔ̃tʀ(ə)] **1** *prép* **(a)** (*contact, juxtaposition*) against. **se mettre ~ le mur** to (go and) stand against the wall; **s'appuyer ~ un arbre** to lean against a tree; **la face ~ terre** face downwards; **appuyez-vous ~** lean *ou* press against *ou* on it; **serrer qn ~ sa poitrine** *ou* **son cœur** to hug sb (to one), hug *ou* clasp sb to one's breast *ou* bosom (*littér*); **pousse la table ~ la fenêtre** push the table (up) against the window; **son garage est juste ~ notre maison** his garage is built onto our house; **elle se blottit ~ sa mère** she nestled *ou* cuddled up to her mother; **elle s'assit (tout) ~ lui** she sat down (right) next to *ou* beside him; **il s'est cogné la tête ~ le mur** he banged his head against *ou* on the wall; **joue ~ joue** cheek to cheek; **les voitures étaient pare-chocs ~ pare-chocs** the cars were bumper to bumper; *V* **ci.**

(b) (*opposition, hostilité*) against. **se battre/voter ~ qn** to fight/vote against sb; (*Sport*) **Poitiers ~ Lyon** Poitiers versus Lyons; **être furieux/en colère ~ qn** to be furious/angry with sb; **jeter une pierre ~ la fenêtre** to throw a stone at the window; **agir ~ l'avis/les ordres de qn** to act contrary to *ou* counter to *ou* against sb's advice/orders; **aller/nager ~ le courant** to go/swim against the current; **acte ~ nature** unnatural act, act contrary to *ou* against nature; **je n'ai rien ~ (cela)** *ou* (*frm*) **là ~** I have nothing against it; **il a les ouvriers ~ lui** he's got the workers against him; **je suis (tout à fait) ~!** I'm (completely) against it!; *V* **envers**[1], **gré, vent.**

(c) (*défense, protection*) **s'abriter ~ le vent/la pluie** to shelter from the wind/rain; **des comprimés ~ la grippe** flu tablets, tablets for flu; **sirop ~ la toux** cough mixture *ou* syrup; **s'assurer ~ les accidents/l'incendie** to insure (o.s.) against *ou* for accidents/fire.

(d) (*échange*) (in exchange) for. **échanger** *ou* **troquer qch ~** to exchange *ou* swap* sth for; **donner qch ~** to give sth (in exchange) for; **il a cédé ~ la promesse/l'assurance que ...** he agreed in return for the promise/assurance that ...; **envoi ~ remboursement** cash on delivery, C.O.D.

(e) (*proportion, rapport*) **il y a un étudiant qui s'intéresse ~ neuf qui bâillent!** for every one interested student there are nine who are bored; **9 voix ~ 4** 9 votes to 4; **à 100 ~ 1** at 100 to 1.

(f) (*loc: contrairement à*) **~ toute attente** *ou* **toute prévision** contrary to (all) expectations *ou* to expectation; **~ toute apparence** despite (all) appearances to the contrary; **par ~** on the other hand.

2 *nm* **(a)** *V* **pour.**

(b) (*fig: riposte*) counter, retort; (*Billard*) rebound; (*Cartes*) double. **l'art du ~** the art of repartee.

3: contre-accusation *nf, pl* **contre-accusations** countercharge; **contre-alizé** *nm, pl* **contre-alizés** anti-trade (wind); **contre-allée** *nf, pl* **contre-allées** (*en ville*) service road; (*dans un parc*) side path (*running parallel to the main drive*); **contre-amiral** *nm, pl* **contre-amiraux** rear admiral; **contre-analyse** *nf, pl* **contre-analyses** second analysis, counteranalysis; **contre-attaque** *nf, pl* **contre-attaques** counter-attack; **contre-attaquer** *vi* to counter-attack; **contre-autopsie** *nf, pl* **contre-autopsies** control autopsy, second autopsy; **contre-avion(s)** *adj V* **défense**[1]; **contre-boutant** *nm, pl* **contre-boutants** (*en bois*) shore; (*en pierre*) buttress; **contre-braquage** *nm, pl* **contre-braquages** steering into the skid (*U*); **grâce à ce contre-braquage instantané** thanks to his having immediately steered into the skid; **contre-braquer** *vi* to steer into the skid; **contre-butement** *nm* = **contre-boutant**; **contre-chant** *nm* counterpoint; **contre-courant** *nm, pl* **contre-courants** *[cours d'eau]* counter-current; **à contre-courant** (*lit*) upstream, against the current; (*fig*) against the current *ou* tide; **contre-écrou** *nm, pl* **contre-écrous** lock nut; **contre-éléctromotrice** *adj f V* **force**; **contre-enquête** *nf, pl* **contre-enquêtes** counter-inquiry; **contre-épreuve** *nf, pl* **contre-épreuves** (*Typ*) counter-proof; (*vérification*) countercheck; **contre-espionnage** *nm* counter-espionage; **contre-essai** *nm, pl* **contre-essais** second test, repetition test; **contre-expertise** *nf, pl* **contre-expertises** second (expert) assessment; **contre-fer** *nm, pl* **contre-fers** iron cap; **contre-feu** *nm, pl* **contre-feux** (*plaque*) fire-back; (*feu*) backfire; **contre-fil** *nm* (*Menuiserie*) **à contre-fil** against the grain; **contre-filet** *nm* sirloin; **contre-fugue** *nf* counter-fugue; **contre-gouvernement** *nm, pl* **contre-gouvernements** (*administration*) shadow government (*surtout Brit*); (*cabinet*) shadow Cabinet (*surtout Brit*); **contre-haut: en contre-haut** *adj, adv* (up) above; **en contre-haut de** *prép* above; **contre-indication** *nf, pl* **contre-indications** (*Méd, Pharm*) contraindication; **contre-indiqué, e** *adj* (*Méd*) contraindicated; (*déconseillé*) unadvisable, ill-advised; **contre-indiquer** *vt* to contraindicate; **contre-interrogatoire** *nm, pl* **contre-interrogatoires** cross-examination; **faire subir un contre-interrogatoire à qn** to cross-examine sb; **contre-jour** *nm, pl* **contre-jours** (*éclairage*) backlighting (*U*), contre-jour (*U*); (*photographie*) backlit *ou* contre-jour shot; **à contre-jour** *se profiler, se détacher* against the sunlight; *photographier* into the light; *travailler, lire* with one's back to the light; **contre-manifestant, e** *nm,f, mpl* **contre-manifestants** counter demonstrator; **contre-manifestation** *nf, pl* **contre-manifestations** counter demonstration; **contre-manifester** *vi* to hold a counter demonstration; **contre-mesure** *nf, pl* **contre-mesures** (*action*) counter-measure; (*Mus*) **à contre-mesure** against the beat, offbeat; **contre la montre** *adj* against the clock; **épreuve contre la montre** time-trial; **contre-offensive** *nf, pl* **contre-offensives** counter-offensive; **contre-pas** *nm* half pace; **contre-pente** *nf,* *pl* **contre-pentes** opposite slope; **contre-performance** *nf, pl* **contre-performances** (*Sport*) below-average *ou* substandard performance; **contre-pied** *nm [opinion, attitude]* (exact) opposite; **prendre le contre-pied de** *opinion* to take the opposing *ou* opposite view of; *action* to take the opposite course to; **il a pris le contre-pied de ce qu'on lui demandait** he did the exact opposite of what he was asked; (*Sport*) **à contre-pied** on the wrong foot; **prendre qn à contre-pied** (*lit*) to wrong foot sb; (*fig*) to catch sb on the wrong foot; **contre-plaqué** *nm* plywood; **contre-plongée** *nf, pl* **contre-plongées** low-angle shot; **filmer en contre-plongée** to film from below; **contre-poil: à contre-poil** *adv* (*lit, fig*) the wrong way; **contre-porte** *nf, pl* **contre-portes** inner door; **contre-projet** *nm, pl* **contre-projets** counterplan; **contre-propagande** *nf* counter-propaganda; **contre-proposition** *nf, pl* **contre-propositions** counterproposal, counterproposition; **contre-rail** *nm, pl* **contre-rails** checkrail (*Brit*), guard-rail; **contre-réforme** *nf* Counter-Reformation; **contre-révolution** *nf, pl* **contre-révolutions** counter-revolution; **contre-révolutionnaire** *adj, nmf, pl* **contre-révolutionnaires** counter-revolutionary; **contre-terrorisme** *nm* counter-terrorism; **contre-terroriste** *adj, nmf, pl* **contre-terroristes** counter-terrorist; **contre-torpilleur** *nm, pl* **contre-torpilleurs** destroyer; **contre-ut** *nm* top *ou* high C; **contre-valeur** *nf* exchange value; **contre-vérité** *nf, pl* **contre-vérités** untruth, falsehood; **contre-visite** *nf, pl* **contre-visites** second (medical) opinion; **à contre-voie** *adv* (*en sens inverse*) on the wrong track; (*du mauvais côté*) on the wrong side (of the train).

contrebalancer [kɔ̃tʀəbalɑ̃se] (3) **1** *vt [poids]* to counterbalance; (*fig: égaler, compenser*) to offset. **2 se contrebalancer*** *vpr*: **se ~ de** not to give a darn* about; **je m'en contrebalance** I don't give a darn* (about it), I couldn't care a hoot* (about it).

contrebande [kɔ̃tʀəbɑ̃d] *nf* (*activité*) contraband, smuggling; (*marchandises*) contraband, smuggled goods. **faire de la ~** to do some smuggling; **faire la ~ du tabac** to smuggle tobacco; **produits de ~** contraband, smuggled goods.

contrebandier, -ière [kɔ̃tʀəbɑ̃dje, jɛʀ] *nm,f* smuggler. **navire ~** smugglers' ship.

contrebas [kɔ̃tʀəbɑ] *nm*: **en ~** (down) below; **en ~ de** below.

contrebasse [kɔ̃tʀəbɑs] *nf* (*instrument*) (double) bass; (*musicien*) (double) bass player.

contrebassiste [kɔ̃tʀəbɑsist(ə)] *nmf* (double) bass player.

contrebasson [kɔ̃tʀəbɑsɔ̃] *nm* contrabassoon, double bassoon.

contrecarrer [kɔ̃tʀəkaʀe] (1) *vt projets*, (†) *personne* to thwart.

contrechamp [kɔ̃tʀəʃɑ̃] *nm* (*Ciné*) reverse shot.

contrechâssis [kɔ̃tʀəʃɑsi] *nm* double (window) frame.

contreclef [kɔ̃tʀəkle] *nf* voussoir adjoining the keystones.

contrecœur[1] [kɔ̃tʀəkœʀ] *adv*: **à ~** (be)grudgingly, reluctantly.

contrecœur[2] [kɔ̃tʀəkœʀ] *nm* **(a)** (*fond de cheminée*) fire-back. **(b)** (*Rail*) guard-rail, checkrail (*Brit*).

contrecoup [kɔ̃tʀəku] *nm* (*répercussions*) repercussions, indirect consequence. **le ~ d'un accident** the repercussions of an accident; **la révolution a eu des ~s en Asie** the revolution has had (its) repercussions in Asia; **par ~** as an indirect consequence.

contredanse [kɔ̃tʀədɑ̃s] *nf* **(a)** (*) (*gén*) fine; (*pour stationnement interdit*) (parking) ticket. **(b)** (††: *danse, air*) quadrille.

contredire [kɔ̃tʀədiʀ] (37) *vt [personne]* to contradict; *[faits]* to be at variance with, refute.

contredit [kɔ̃tʀədi] *nm*: **sans ~** unquestionably, without question.

contrée [kɔ̃tʀe] *nf* (*littér*) (*pays*) land; (*région*) region.

contrefaçon [kɔ̃tʀəfasɔ̃] *nf* **(a)** (*U: V* **contrefaire**) counterfeiting; forgery, forging.

(b) (*faux*) (*édition etc*) unauthorized *ou* pirated edition; (*produit*) imitation; (*billets, signature*) forgery, counterfeit. (*Comm*) **méfiez-vous des ~s** beware of imitations.

contrefacteur [kɔ̃tʀəfaktœʀ] *nm* (*Jur*) forger, counterfeiter.

contrefaire [kɔ̃tʀəfɛʀ] (60) *vt* **(a)** (*littér: imiter*) to imitate; (*ridiculiser*) to mimic, imitate.

(b) (*déguiser*) *voix* to disguise.

(c) (*falsifier*) *argent, signature* to counterfeit, forge; *produits, édition* to counterfeit.

(d) (†: *feindre*) to feign († *ou littér*), counterfeit.

(e) (†: *rendre difforme*) to deform.

contrefait, e [kɔ̃tʀəfɛ, ɛt] (*ptp de* **contrefaire**) *adj* (*difforme*) misshapen, deformed.

contreficher (se)* [kɔ̃tʀəfiʃe] (1) *vpr*: **se ~ de** not to give a darn* about; **je m'en contrefiche** I couldn't care a hoot* (about it), I don't give a darn* (about it).

contrefort [kɔ̃tʀəfɔʀ] *nm* **(a)** (*Archit*) *[voûte, terrasse]* buttress. **(b)** *[soulier]* stiffener. **(c)** (*Géog*) *[arête]* spur. *[chaîne]* **~s** foothills.

contrefoutre (se): [kɔ̃tʀəfutʀ(ə)] *vpr*: **je m'en/tu t'en contrefous** I/you don't give a damn: (about it).

contremaître [kɔ̃tʀəmɛtʀ(ə)] *nm* foreman.

contremaîtresse [kɔ̃tʀəmɛtʀɛs] *nf* forewoman.

contremarche [kɔ̃tʀəmaʀʃ(ə)] *nf* **(a)** (*Mil*) countermarch. **(b)** *[marche d'escalier]* riser.

contremarque [kɔ̃tʀəmaʀk(ə)] *nf* **(a)** (*Comm: marque*) countermark. **(b)** (*Ciné, Théât: ticket*) passout ticket.

contrepartie [kɔ̃tʀəpaʀti] *nf* **(a)** (*compensation: lit, fig*) compensation. **en ~** (*en échange, en retour*) in return; (*en revanche*) in compensation, to make up for it.

(b) (*littér: contre-pied*) opposing view.

(c) (*Comm*) (*registre*) duplicate register; (*écritures*) counterpart entries.

contrepet [kɔ̃tʀəpɛ] *nm*, **contrepèterie** [kɔ̃tʀəpetʀi] *nf* spoonerism.

contrepoids [kɔ̃tʀəpwa] *nm* (*lit*) counterweight, counterbalance; *[acrobate]* balancing-pole. **faire ~** to act as a counterbalance; **porter un panier à chaque main pour faire ~** to carry a basket in each hand to balance oneself; (*fig*) **servir de ~ à, apporter un ~ à** to counterbalance.

contrepoint [kɔ̃tʀəpwɛ̃] *nm* counterpoint.

contrepoison [kɔ̃tʀəpwazɔ̃] *nm* antidote, counterpoison.

contrer [kɔ̃tʀe] (1) **1** *vt* **(a)** *personne, menées* to counter. **(b)** (*Cartes*) to double. **2** *vi* (*Cartes*) to double.

contrescarpe [kɔ̃tʀɛskaʀp(ə)] *nf* (*Mil*) counterscarp.

contreseing [kɔ̃tʀəsɛ̃] *nm* (*Jur*) countersignature.

contresens [kɔ̃tʀəsɑ̃s] *nm* (*erreur*) misinterpretation; (*de traduction*) mistranslation; (*absurdité*) nonsense (*U*), piece of nonsense. **à ~** (*Aut*) the wrong way; (*Couture*) against the grain; **à ~ de** against; **il a pris mes paroles à ~, il a pris le ~ de mes paroles** he misinterpreted what I said; **le traducteur a fait un ~** the translator has been guilty of a mistranslation.

contresigner [kɔ̃tʀəsiɲe] (1) *vt* to countersign.

contretemps [kɔ̃tʀətɑ̃] *nm* **(a)** (*complication, retard*) hitch, contretemps. **(b)** (*Mus*) off-beat rhythm. **(c) à ~** (*Mus*) off the beat; (*fig*) at an inopportune moment.

contrevenant, e [kɔ̃tʀəvnɑ̃, ɑ̃t] (*Jur*) **1** *adj* offending. **2** *nm,f* offender.

contrevenir [kɔ̃tʀəvniʀ] (22) **contrevenir à** *vt indir* (*Jur, littér*) *loi, règlement* to contravene.

contrevent [kɔ̃tʀəvɑ̃] *nm* **(a)** (*volet*) shutter. **(b)** *[charpente]* brace, strut.

contribuable [kɔ̃tʀibɥabl(ə)] *nmf* taxpayer.

contribuer [kɔ̃tʀibɥe] (1) **contribuer à** *vt indir résultat, effet* to contribute to(wards); *effort, dépense* to contribute towards. **de nombreux facteurs ont contribué au déclin de .../à réduire le ...** numerous factors contributed to(wards) the decline in .../ to(wards) the reduction in the ... *ou* to reducing the ...

contributif, -ive [kɔ̃tʀibytif, iv] *adj* (*Jur*) *part* contributory.

contribution [kɔ̃tʀibysjɔ̃] *nf* **(a)** (*participation*) contribution. **mettre qn à ~** to call upon sb's services, make use of sb; **mettre qch à ~** to make use of sth; **apporter sa ~ à qch** to make one's contribution to sth.

(b) (*impôts*) **~s** (*à la commune*) rates; (*à l'état*) taxes; **~s directes/indirectes** direct/indirect taxation.

(c) (*administration*) **~s** tax office, ≃ Inland Revenue (*Brit*), ≃ Internal Revenue (*US*); **travailler aux ~s** to work for *ou* in the Inland Revenue (*Brit*) *ou* Internal Revenue (*US*), work in the tax office.

contrister [kɔ̃tʀiste] (1) *vt* (*littér*) to grieve, sadden.

contrit, e [kɔ̃tʀi, it] *adj* contrite.

contrition [kɔ̃tʀisjɔ̃] *nf* contrition; *V* **acte**.

contrôlable [kɔ̃tʀolabl(ə)] *adj opération* that can be checked; *affirmation* that can be checked *ou* verified, verifiable; *sentiment* that can be controlled, controllable. **un billet ~ à l'arrivée** a ticket that is inspected *ou* checked on arrival.

contrôle [kɔ̃tʀol] *nm* **(a)** (*vérification: V* **contrôler**) checking (*U*), check; inspecting (*U*), inspection; controlling (*U*), control; verifying (*U*), verification. (*Police*) **~ d'identité** identity check; (*Méd*) **visite de ~** (routine) checkup, medical*; (*Comm*) **~s de qualité** quality checks *ou* controls.

(b) (*surveillance: V* **contrôler**) controlling; supervising, supervision; monitoring. **exercer un ~ sévère sur les agissements de qn** to maintain strict control over sb's actions; (*Fin*) **~ des changes** exchange control; (*Fin*) **~ économique** *ou* **des prix** price control; (*organisme*) ≃ Prices Board; (*Sociol*) **~ des naissances** birth control.

(c) (*maîtrise*) control. **~ de soi-même** self-control; **garder le ~ de sa voiture** to remain in control of one's vehicle.

(d) (*bureau*) (*gén*) office; (*Théât*) (advance) booking office (*surtout Brit*), reservation office (*US*).

(e) (*Mil: registres*) **~s** rolls, lists; **rayé des ~s de l'armée** removed from the army lists.

(f) (*poinçon*) hallmark.

contrôler [kɔ̃tʀole] (1) **1** *vt* **(a)** (*vérifier*) *billets, passeports* to inspect, check; *comptes* to check, inspect, control; *texte, traduction* to check (*sur* against); *régularité de qch* to check; *qualité de qch* to control, check; *affirmations* to check, verify.

(b) (*surveiller*) *opérations, agissements, gestion* to control, supervise; *subordonnés, employés* to supervise; *prix, loyers* to monitor, control.

(c) (*maîtriser*) *colère, réactions, nerfs* to control; (*Mil*) *zone, pays* to be in control of; (*Écon*) *secteur, firme* to control; (*Sport*) *ballon, skis, jeu* to control.

(d) (*Orfèvrerie*) to hallmark.

2 se contrôler *vpr* to control o.s. **il ne se contrôlait plus** he was no longer in control of himself, he could control himself no longer.

contrôleur [kɔ̃tʀolœʀ] *nm* **(a)** *[autobus]* (bus) conductor; (*Rail*) (*dans le train*) (ticket) inspector; (*sur le quai*) ticket collector. **~ de la navigation aérienne** air traffic controller.

(b) (*Fin*) *[comptabilité]* auditor; *[contributions]* inspector.

(c) (*Tech*) regulator. **~ de ronde** time-clock, tell-tale.

contrordre [kɔ̃tʀɔʀdʀ(ə)] *nm* counter-order, countermand. **ordres et ~s** orders and counter-orders; **il y a ~** there has been a change of orders; **sauf ~** unless orders to the contrary are given, unless otherwise directed.

controuvé, e [kɔ̃tʀuve] *adj* (*littér*) *fait, nouvelle* fabricated; *histoire, anecdote* fabricated, concocted.

controversable [kɔ̃tʀɔvɛʀsabl(ə)] *adj* debatable.

controverse [kɔ̃tʀɔvɛʀs(ə)] *nf* controversy. **prêter à ~** to be debatable.

controversé, e [kɔ̃tʀɔvɛʀse] *adj théorie, question* much debated.

contumace [kɔ̃tymas] **1** *adj* (*rare*) in default, defaulting. **2** *nf* (*Jur*) **par ~** in his (*ou* her *etc*) absence.

contusion [kɔ̃tyzjɔ̃] *nf* bruise, contusion (*T*).

contusionner [kɔ̃tyzjɔne] (1) *vt* to bruise, contuse (*T*).

conurbation [konyʀbɑsjɔ̃] *nf* conurbation.

convaincant, e [kɔ̃vɛ̃kɑ̃, ɑ̃t] *adj* convincing.

convaincre [kɔ̃vɛ̃kʀ(ə)] (42) *vt* **(a)** *sceptique* to convince (*de qch* of sth); *hésitant* to persuade (*de faire qch* to do sth). **je ne suis pas convaincu par son explication** I'm not convinced by his explanation; **je ne demande qu'à me laisser convaincre** I'm open to persuasion *ou* conviction; **il m'a finalement convaincu de renoncer à cette idée** he finally persuaded me to give up that idea, he finally talked me into giving up that idea, he finally convinced me (that) I should give up that idea; **se laisser ~** to let o.s. be persuaded, let o.s. be talked into it.
(b) (*déclarer coupable*) **~ qn de meurtre/trahison** to prove sb guilty of *ou* convict sb of murder/treason.

convaincu, e [kɔ̃vɛ̃ky] (*ptp de* **convaincre**) *adj* convinced. **d'un ton ~** in a tone of conviction, with conviction.

convalescence [kɔ̃valesɑ̃s] *nf* convalescence. **être en ~** to be convalescing; **entrer en ~** to start one's convalescence; **période de ~** (period of) convalescence; **maison de ~** convalescent home.

convalescent, e [kɔ̃valesɑ̃, ɑ̃t] *adj, nm,f* convalescent.

convection [kɔ̃vɛksjɔ̃] *nf* convection.

convenable [kɔ̃vnabl(ə)] *adj* **(a)** (*approprié*) *parti* fitting, suitable; *moment, endroit* fitting, suitable, appropriate.
(b) (*décent*) *manières* acceptable, correct, proper; *vêtements* decent, respectable; *invité, jeune homme* acceptable. **peu ~** *manières* improper, unseemly; *vêtements* improper; **ne montre pas du doigt, ce n'est pas ~** don't point — it's not polite, it's bad manners to point.
(c) (*acceptable*) *devoir* adequate, passable; *salaire, logement* decent, acceptable, adequate. **salaire à peine ~** scarcely acceptable *ou* adequate salary.

convenablement [kɔ̃vnabləmɑ̃] *adv placé, choisi* suitably, appropriately; *s'habiller, s'exprimer* correctly, properly, acceptably, decently; *payé, logé* adequately, decently. **tout ce que je vous demande c'est de travailler ~** all I'm asking of you is to work adequately *ou* in an acceptable fashion.

convenance [kɔ̃vnɑ̃s] *nf* **(a)** (*ce qui convient*) (*frm*) **consulter les ~s de qn** to consult sb's preferences; **trouver qch à sa ~** to find sth to one's liking, find sth suitable; **choisissez un jour à votre ~** choose a day to suit your convenience; **pour des raisons de ~(s) personnelle(s)** for personal reasons; *V* **mariage.**
(b) (*normes sociales*) **les ~s** propriety, the proprieties; **contraire aux ~s** contrary to the proprieties.
(c) (*littér*) (*harmonie*) *[goûts, caractères]* affinity; (†: *caractère adéquat*) *[terme, équipement]* appropriateness, suitability.

convenir [kɔ̃vniʀ] (22) **1 convenir à** *vt indir* (*être approprié à*) to suit, be suitable for; (*être utile à*) to suit, be convenient for; (*être agréable à*) to be agreeable to, suit. **ce chapeau ne convient pas à la circonstance** this hat is not suitable for the occasion *ou* does not suit the occasion; **le climat ne lui convient pas** the climate does not suit him *ou* does not agree with him; **oui, cette chambre me convient très bien** yes, this room suits me very well; **cette chambre convient à des adolescents** this room is suitable for teenagers; **j'irai si cela me convient** I'll go if it is convenient (for me); (*ton péremptoire*) I'll go if it suits me; **si l'heure/la date (vous) convient** if the time/date is convenient (for you) *ou* is agreeable to you *ou* suits you; **c'est tout à fait ce qui me convient** this is exactly what I need *ou* want.
2 convenir de *vt indir* **(a)** (*avouer, reconnaître*) to admit (to), acknowledge. **il convint d'avoir été un peu brusque** he admitted (to) having been *ou* owned to having been a little abrupt, he acknowledged (that) he'd been a bit abrupt.
(b) (*s'accorder sur*) to agree upon. **~ d'une date/d'un lieu** to agree upon a date/place; **une date a été convenue** a date has been agreed upon; **comme convenu** as agreed.
3 *vt*: **~ que** (*avouer, reconnaître*) to admit that, acknowledge the fact that; (*s'accorder sur*) to agree that; **il est convenu que nous nous réunissons demain** it is agreed that we (shall) meet tomorrow.
4 *vb impers*: **il convient de faire** (*il vaut mieux*) it's advisable to do; (*il est bienséant de*) it would be proper to do; **il convient d'être prudent** caution is advised, it is advisable to be prudent; **il convient qu'elle remercie ses hôtes de leur hospitalité** it is proper *ou* right for her to thank her host and hostess for their hospitality; (*frm*) **il convient de faire remarquer** we should point out.

convention [kɔ̃vɑ̃sjɔ̃] *nf* **(a)** (*pacte*) (*gén*) agreement, covenant (*frm, Admin*); (*Pol*) convention. (*Ind*) **~ collective** collective agreement; **cela n'entre pas dans nos ~s** that doesn't enter into our agreement.
(b) (*accord tacite*) (*gén*) understanding; (*Art, Littérat*) convention. **les ~s (sociales)** convention, social conventions; (*Littérat, Théât*) **décor/personnage/langage de ~** conventional set/character/language; **mots/amabilité de ~** conventional words/kindness.
(c) (*assemblée*) (*US Pol*) Convention. (*Hist française*) **la C~** the Convention.

conventionné, e [kɔ̃vɑ̃sjɔne] *adj établissement, médecin* ≃ National Health (*épith*).

conventionnel, -elle [kɔ̃vɑ̃sjɔnɛl] **1** *adj* (*gén*) conventional; (*Jur*) *acte, clause* contractual. **2** *nm* (*Hist française*) **les ~s** the members of the Convention.

conventionnellement [kɔ̃vɑ̃sjɔnɛlmɑ̃] *adv* conventionally.

conventionnement [kɔ̃vɑ̃sjɔnmɑ̃] *nm* ≃ National Health contract.

conventuel, -elle [kɔ̃vɑ̃tɥɛl] *adj vie, règle [moines]* monastic; *[nonnes]* convent (*épith*), conventual; *bâtiment* monastery (*épith*); convent (*épith*); *simplicité, sérénité* monastic; convent-like.

convenu, e [kɔ̃vny] (*ptp de* **convenir**) *adj* **(a)** (*décidé*) *heure, prix, mot* agreed. **(b)** (*littér péj: conventionnel*) conventional.

convergence [kɔ̃vɛʀʒɑ̃s] *nf* convergence.

convergent, e [kɔ̃vɛʀʒɑ̃, ɑ̃t] *adj* convergent.

converger [kɔ̃vɛʀʒe] (3) *vi [lignes, rayons, routes]* to converge. *[regards]* **~ sur** to focus on; **nos pensées convergent vers la même solution** our thoughts are leading towards *ou* converging on the same solution.

convers, e [kɔ̃vɛʀ, ɛʀs(ə)] *adj* (*Rel*) lay (*épith*).

conversation [kɔ̃vɛʀsɑsjɔ̃] *nf* **(a)** (*entretien*) (*gén*) conversation, chat*; (*politique, diplomatique*) talk. **la ~** conversation; **lors d'une ~ téléphonique** during a telephone conversation *ou* a chat* on the telephone; **les ~s téléphoniques sont surveillées** telephone conversations are tapped; **en (grande) ~ avec** (deep) in conversation with; **faire la ~ à** to make conversation with; *V* **frais**[2].
(b) (*art de parler*) **il a une ~ brillante** he is a brilliant conversationalist; **il n'a pas de ~** he's got no conversation; **avoir de la ~** to be a good conversationalist.
(c) (*langage familier*) **dans la ~ courante** in informal *ou* conversational talk *ou* speech; **employer le style de la ~** to use a conversational style.

converser [kɔ̃vɛʀse] (1) *vi* to converse (*avec* with).

conversion [kɔ̃vɛʀsjɔ̃] *nf* **(a)** (*V* **convertir**) conversion (*à* to, *en* into); winning over (*à* to); (*V* **se convertir**) conversion (*à* to). **faire une ~ de fractions en ...** to convert fractions into ... . **(b)** (*demi-tour*) (*Mil*) wheel; (*Ski*) kick turn.

converti, e [kɔ̃vɛʀti] (*ptp de* **convertir**) **1** *adj* converted. **2** *nm,f* convert; *V* **prêcher.**

convertibilité [kɔ̃vɛʀtibilite] *nf* (*Fin*) convertibility.

convertible [kɔ̃vɛʀtibl(ə)] **1** *adj* convertible (*en* into). **2** *nm* (*avion*) convertiplane; (*canapé*) bed-settee.

convertir [kɔ̃vɛʀtiʀ] (2) **1** *vt* **(a)** (*rallier*) (*à une religion*) to convert (*à* to); (*à une théorie*) to win over, convert (*à* to). **(b)** (*transformer*) **~ en** (*gén, Fin, Math*) to convert into. **2 se convertir** *vpr* (*Rel; à une théorie etc*) to be converted (*à* to).

convertissage [kɔ̃vɛʀtisaʒ] *nm* (*Métal*) conversion.

convertissement [kɔ̃vɛʀtismɑ̃] *nm* (*Fin*) conversion.

convertisseur [kɔ̃vɛʀtisœʀ] *nm* (*Élec, Métal*) converter. **~ Bessemer** Bessemer converter; (*Élec*) **~ d'images** image converter.

convexe [kɔ̃vɛks(ə)] *adj* convex.

convexion [kɔ̃vɛksjɔ̃] *nf* = **convection.**

convexité [kɔ̃vɛksite] *nf* convexity.

conviction [kɔ̃viksjɔ̃] *nf* **(a)** (*certitude*) conviction, (firm) belief. **j'en ai la ~** I'm convinced of it; **parler avec ~** to speak with conviction.
(b) (*sérieux, enthousiasme*) conviction. **faire qch avec/sans ~** to do sth with/without conviction; **manquer de ~** to lack conviction.
(c) (*opinions*) **~s** beliefs, convictions.
(d) *V* **pièce.**

convier [kɔ̃vje] (7) *vt* (*frm*) **~ à** *soirée etc* to invite to; **~ qn à faire qch** to urge sb to do sth; **la chaleur conviait à la baignade** the hot weather was an invitation to swim.

convive [kɔ̃viv] *nmf* guest (*at a meal*).

convocation [kɔ̃vɔkɑsjɔ̃] *nf* **(a)** (*U: V* **convoquer**) convening, convoking; inviting; summoning. **la ~ des membres doit se faire longtemps à l'avance** members must be invited a long time in advance; **cette ~ chez le directeur l'intriguait** this summons to appear before the director intrigued him; **la ~ des membres/candidats doit se faire par écrit** members/candidates must be given written notification to attend.
(b) (*lettre, carte*) (letter of) notification to appear *ou* attend; (*Jur*) summons.

convoi [kɔ̃vwa] *nm* **(a)** (*cortège funèbre*) funeral procession. **(b)** (*train*) train. **~ de marchandises** goods train. **(c)** (*suite de véhicules, navires, prisonniers*) convoy.

convoiement [kɔ̃vwamɑ̃] *nm* (*V* **convoyer**) escorting; convoying.

convoiter [kɔ̃vwate] (1) *vt héritage, objet, femme* to covet, lust after; *poste* to covet.

convoitise [kɔ̃vwatiz] *nf* (*U: désir*) (*gén*) covetousness; (*pour une femme*) lust, desire. **la ~ des richesses** the lust for wealth; **la ~ de la chair** the lusts of the flesh; **l'objet de sa ~** the object of his desire; **regarder avec ~** *objet* to cast covetous looks on; *femme* to cast lustful looks on; **un regard brillant de ~** a covetous look; **l'objet des ~s de tous** the object of everyone's desire.

convoler [kɔ̃vɔle] (1) *vi* († *ou hum*) **~ (en justes noces)** to be wed († *ou hum*).

convoquer [kɔ̃vɔke] (1) *vt assemblée* to convene, convoke; *membre de club etc* to invite (*à* to); *candidat* to ask to attend; *témoin, prévenu, subordonné* to summon. **il va falloir ~ les membres** we're going to have to call a meeting of the members *ou* call the members together; **as-tu été convoqué pour l'assemblée annuelle?** have you been invited to (attend) the AGM? (*Brit*); **j'ai été convoqué à 10 heures (pour mon oral)** I've been asked to attend at 10 o'clock (for my oral); **le chef m'a convoqué** I was summoned by *ou* called before the boss; **le chef m'a convoqué dans son bureau** the boss called *ou* summoned me to his office; **le juge m'a convoqué** I was summoned to appear before the judge, I was called before the judge.

convoyage [kɔ̃vwajaʒ] *nm* = **convoiement.**

convoyer [kɔ̃vwaje] (8) *vt* (*gén*) to escort; (*Mil, Naut*) to escort, convoy.

convoyeur [kɔ̃vwajœʀ] *nm* (*navire*) convoy, escort ship; (*per-*

sonne) escort; (*Tech*) conveyor. ~ **de fonds** security guard (*transferring banknotes etc*).
convulser [kɔ̃vylse] (1) *vt visage* to convulse, distort; *corps* to convulse. **la douleur lui convulsa le visage** his face was distorted *ou* convulsed by *ou* with pain; **son visage se convulsait** his face was distorted.
convulsif, -ive [kɔ̃vylsif, iv] *adj* convulsive.
convulsion [kɔ̃vylsjɔ̃] *nf* (*gén, Méd, fig*) convulsion.
convulsionnaire [kɔ̃vylsjɔnɛʀ] *nmf* convulsionary.
convulsionner [kɔ̃vylsjɔne] (1) *vt* to convulse. **visage convulsionné** distorted *ou* convulsed face.
convulsivement [kɔ̃vylsivmɑ̃] *adv* convulsively.
coobligé, e [kɔɔbliʒe] *nm,f* (*Jur*) joint obligor.
coolie [kuli] *nm* coolie.
coopé [kɔpe] *nf* (*abrév de* **coopérative**) co-op.
coopérant [kɔɔpeʀɑ̃] *nm* ≈ *person serving on VSO* (*Brit*) *ou in the Peace Corps* (*US*).
coopérateur, -trice [kɔɔpeʀatœʀ, tʀis] **1** *adj* cooperative. **2** *nm,f* **(a)** (*associé*) collaborator, cooperator. **(b)** (*membre d'une coopérative*) member of a cooperative, cooperator.
coopératif, -ive [kɔɔpeʀatif, iv] *adj* cooperative.
coopération [kɔɔpeʀɑsjɔ̃] *nf* **(a)** (*gén: collaboration*) cooperation. **apporter sa ~ à une entreprise** to cooperate *ou* collaborate in an undertaking.
(b) (*Pol*) ≈ Voluntary Service Overseas (*Brit*) *ou* Peace Corps (*US*) (*usually as form of military service*). **il a été envoyé en Afrique comme professeur au titre de la ~** ≈ he was sent to Africa as a VSO teacher.
coopératisme [kɔɔpeʀatism(ə)] *nm* (*Écon*) cooperation.
coopérative [kɔɔpeʀativ] *nf* (*organisme*) cooperative; (*magasin*) co-op.
coopérer [kɔɔpeʀe] (6) **1** *vi* to cooperate. **2 coopérer à** *vt indir* to cooperate in.
cooptation [kɔɔptɑsjɔ̃] *nf* coopting, cooptation.
coopter [kɔɔpte] (1) *vt* to coopt.
coordinateur, -trice [kɔɔʀdinatœʀ, tʀis] = **coordonnateur.**
coordination [kɔɔʀdinɑsjɔ̃] *nf* coordination; *V* **conjonction.**
coordonnateur, -trice [kɔɔʀdɔnatœʀ, tʀis] **1** *adj* coordinating. **2** *nm,f* coordinator.
coordonné, e [kɔɔʀdɔne] (*ptp de* **coordonner**) **1** *adj* coordinated. (*Ling*) **(proposition) ~e** coordinate clause.
2 *nmpl* (*Habillement*) **~s** coordinates.
3 coordonnées *nfpl* (*Math*) coordinates. (*fig*) **donnez-moi vos ~es*** tell me how and where I can get in touch with you, give me some details of when you'll be where*.
coordonner [kɔɔʀdɔne] (1) *vt* to coordinate.
copain *ou* **copin** (*rare*), **copine** [kɔpɛ̃, in] *nm,f* pal*, friend, mate* (*surtout Brit*), buddy* (*US*). **de bons ~s** good friends, great pals*; **il est très ~ avec le patron** he's (very) pally‡ (*Brit*) with the boss, he's really in with the boss*; **avec eux, c'est** *ou* **on est ~ ~*** we're dead pally‡ (*Brit*) *ou* dead chummy* *ou* great buddies* with them; **ils sont ~s comme cochons*** they are bosom buddies*.
coparticipant, e [kɔpaʀtisipɑ̃, ɑ̃t] (*Jur*) **1** *adj* in copartnership *ou* joint account. **2** *nm,f* copartner.
coparticipation [kɔpaʀtisipɑsjɔ̃] *nf* (*Jur*) copartnership. **~ aux bénéfices** profit-sharing.
copeau, *pl* **~x** [kɔpo] *nm* [*bois*] shaving; [*métal*] turning. **brûler des ~x** to burn wood shavings.
Copenhague [kɔpənag] *n* Copenhagen.
copiage [kɔpjaʒ] *nm* (*gén*) copying; (*Scol*) copying, cribbing (*arg Scol*).
copie [kɔpi] *nf* **(a)** (*U: V* **copier**) copying; reproduction; making of a replica; transcription. **la ~ au net de cette traduction m'a pris du temps** it took me a lot of time to do the fair copy of this translation.
(b) (*reproduction, exemplaire*) [*diplôme, film etc*] copy; [*tableau*] copy, reproduction; [*sculpture*] copy, reproduction, replica. (*Admin*) **~ certifiée conforme** certified copy; (*Admin*) **pour ~ conforme** certified accurate; **je veux la ~ au net de vos traductions demain** I want the fair copy of your translations tomorrow; **prendre ~ de** to make a copy of; **œuvre qui n'est que la pâle ~ d'une autre** work which is only a pale imitation of another; **c'est la ~ de sa mère** she's the replica *ou* (spitting) image of her mother.
(c) (*Scol*) (*feuille de papier*) sheet (of paper), paper; (*devoir*) exercise; (*composition, examen*) paper, script.
(d) (*Typ*) copy.
(e) (*Presse*) copy, material; *V* **pisseur.**
copier [kɔpje] (7) **1** *vt* **(a)** (*recopier*) *écrit, texte,* (*Jur*) *acte* to copy, make a copy of; *tableau, sculpture* to copy, reproduce; *musique* to copy. **~ qch au propre** *ou* **au net** to make a fair copy of sth, copy sth out neatly; **~ une leçon 3 fois** to copy out a lesson 3 times.
(b) (*Scol: tricher*) to copy, crib (*arg Scol*). **~ (sur) le voisin** to copy *ou* crib from one's neighbour.
(c) (*imiter*) *style, démarche, auteur* to copy.
(d) vous me la copierez* well, we won't forget that in a hurry!*, well, that's one to remember!
2 *vi* (*Scol*) to copy, crib (*arg Scol*) (*sur* from).
copieur, -euse [kɔpjœʀ, øz] *nm,f* (*Scol*) copier, cribber (*arg Scol*).
copieusement [kɔpjøzmɑ̃] *adv manger, boire* copiously, heartily. **un repas ~ arrosé** a meal generously washed down with wine; **on s'est fait ~ arroser/engueuler*** we got thoroughly *ou* well and truly soaked/told off*; **~ illustré/annoté** copiously illustrated/annotated.
copieux, -euse [kɔpjø, øz] *adj repas* copious, hearty; *portion* generous; *notes, exemples* copious.
copilote [kɔpilɔt] *nmf* co-pilot; (*Aut*) navigator.
copinage* [kɔpinaʒ] *nm* = **copinerie*.**
copine [kɔpin] *nf V* **copain.**
copiner* [kɔpine] (1) *vi* to be pally‡ (*Brit*) *ou* great buddies* (*avec* with).
copinerie* [kɔpinʀi] *nf* (*péj*) pallyness‡ (*Brit*), matiness*.
copiste [kɔpist(ə)] *nmf* (*Hist, Littérat*) copyist, transcriber.
coposséder [kɔpɔsede] (6) *vt* to own jointly, be co-owner *ou* joint owner of.
copossession [kɔpɔsɛsjɔ̃] *nf* co-ownership, joint ownership.
copra(h) [kɔpʀa] *nm* copra.
coprin [kɔpʀɛ̃] *nm* ink cap, coprinus (*T*).
coproduction [kɔpʀɔdyksjɔ̃] *nf* (*Ciné, TV*) coproduction, joint production. **une ~ franco-italienne** a joint French-Italian production.
copropriétaire [kɔpʀɔpʀijetɛʀ] *nmf* co-owner, joint owner.
copropriété [kɔpʀɔpʀijete] *nf* co-ownership, joint ownership. **immeuble en ~** block of flats in co-ownership.
copte [kɔpt(ə)] **1** *adj* Coptic. **2** *nm* (*Ling*) Coptic. **3** *nmf*: **C~** Copt.
copulatif, -ive [kɔpylatif, iv] *adj* (*Ling*) copulative.
copulation [kɔpylɑsjɔ̃] *nf* copulation.
copule [kɔpyl] *nf* (*Ling*) copulative verb, copula.
copuler [kɔpyle] (1) *vi* to copulate.
copyright [kɔpiʀajt] *nm* copyright.
coq[1] [kɔk] **1** *nm* [*basse-cour*] cock, rooster. (*oiseau mâle*) **~ faisan/de perdrix** cock pheasant/partridge; **jeune ~** cockerel; (*Boxe*) **~, poids ~** bantam-weight; **être comme un ~ en pâte** to be *ou* live in clover; (*fig*) **jambes** *ou* **mollets de ~** wiry legs; *V* **chant**[1], **rouge.**
2: coq-à-l'âne *nm inv* abrupt change of subject; **sauter du coq-à-l'âne** to jump from one subject to another; **coq de bruyère** capercaillie, woodgrouse; **coq de clocher** weather cock; **coq de combat** fighting cock; **le coq gaulois** the French cockerel (*emblem of the Frenchman's fighting spirit*); **coq nain** bantam cock; **coq de roche** cock of the rock; (*fig*) **coq du village** cock of the walk; (*Culin*) **coq au vin** coq au vin.
coq[2] [kɔk] *nm* (*Naut*) (ship's) cook.
coquart‡ [kɔkaʀ] *nm* shiner‡.
coque [kɔk] *nf* **(a)** [*bateau*] hull; [*avion*] fuselage; [*auto*] shell, body. **(b)** [*noix, amande*], (†) [*œuf*] shell. (*Culin*) **à la ~** boiled. **(c)** (*mollusque*) cockle.
coquelet [kɔklɛ] *nm* (*Culin*) cockerel.
coquelicot [kɔkliko] *nm* poppy; *V* **rouge.**
coqueluche [kɔklyʃ] *nf* (*Méd*) whooping cough. (*fig*) **être la ~ de** to be the idol *ou* darling of.
coquemar [kɔkmaʀ] *nm* cauldron, big kettle.
coquerico [kɔkʀiko] = **cocorico.**
coquerie [kɔkʀi] *nf* (*Naut*) (*à bord*) (ship's) galley, caboose (*Brit*); (*à terre*) cookhouse.
coquet, -ette [kɔkɛ, ɛt] *adj* **(a)** (*flirteur*) flirtatious. **c'est une ~te** she's a coquette *ou* a flirt, she's very coquettish *ou* flirtatious.
(b) (*bien habillé*) appearance-conscious, clothes-conscious, interested in one's appearance (*attrib*). **homme trop ~** man who takes too much interest in *ou* who is too particular about his appearance *ou* who is too clothes-conscious.
(c) *ville* pretty, charming; *logement* smart, charming, stylish.
(d) (*: *intensif*) *somme d'argent, revenu* tidy* (*épith*).
coquetier [kɔktje] *nm* (*godet*) egg cup; (††: *marchand*) poultry seller. **gagner le ~*†** to hit the jackpot*.
coquettement [kɔkɛtmɑ̃] *adv sourire, regarder* coquettishly; *s'habiller* smartly, stylishly; *meubler* prettily, stylishly.
coquetterie [kɔkɛtʀi] *nf* **(a)** (*goût d'une mise soignée*) [*personne*] interest in one's appearance, consciousness of one's appearance; [*toilette, coiffure*] smartness, stylishness.
(b) (*galanterie*) coquetry, flirtatiousness (*U*). (*littér: amour propre*) **il mettait sa ~ à marcher sans canne/parler sans notes** he prided himself on *ou* made a point of walking without a stick/talking without notes.
(c) avoir une ~ dans l'œil* to have a cast (in one's eye).
coquillage [kɔkijaʒ] *nm* (*mollusque*) shellfish (*U*); (*coquille*) shell.
coquille [kɔkij] **1** *nf* **(a)** [*mollusque, œuf, noix*] shell. (*fig*) **rentrer dans/sortir de sa ~** to go *ou* withdraw into/come out of one's shell.
(b) (*récipient*) (shell-shaped) dish, scallop. (*Culin: mets*) **~ de poisson/crabe** scallop of fish/crab, fish/crab served in scallop shells.
(c) (*décorative*) scallop; [*épée*] coquille, shell.
(d) (*Typ*) misprint.
(e) (*Sport: protectrice*) box; (*Méd: plâtre*) spinal bed.
2: coquille de beurre shell of butter; (*Naut*) **coquille de noix*** cockleshell; **coquille Saint-Jacques** (*animal*) scallop; (*carapace*) scallop shell.
coquillettes [kɔkijɛt] *nfpl* pasta shells.
coquillier, ière [kɔkije, jɛʀ] **1** *adj* conchiferous (*T*). **2** *nm* (†) shell collection.
coquin, e [kɔkɛ̃, in] **1** *adj* **(a)** (*malicieux*) *enfant* mischievous, rascally; *air* mischievous, roguish. **~ de sort!*** the devil!*, the deuce!*†
(b) (*polisson*) *histoire, regard* naughty, suggestive.
2 *nm,f* (*enfant*) rascal, mischief.
3 *nm* (††: *gredin*) rascal, rogue, rascally fellow†.
4 coquine†† *nf* (*débauchée*) loose woman, strumpet††.
coquinerie [kɔkinʀi] *nf* **(a)** (*U: caractère*) [*enfant*] mischievousness, roguishness. **(b)** (*action*) [*enfant*] mischievous trick; [*personne peu honnête*] low-down *ou* rascally trick.
cor[1] [kɔʀ] *nm* (*Mus*) horn. **~ anglais** cor anglais; **~ de chasse**

hunting horn; ~ **d'harmonie** French horn; ~ **à piston** valve horn; ~ **de basset** bass clarinet; (*fig*) **réclamer** *ou* **demander qch/qn à** ~ **et à cri** to clamour for sth/sb.
cor² [kɔʀ] *nm* (*Méd*) ~ **(au pied)** corn.
cor³ [kɔʀ] *nm [cerf]* tine. **un (cerf) 10** ~**s** a 10-point stag, a 10-pointer.
corail, *pl* **-aux** [kɔʀaj, o] *nm* coral. (*littér*) **de** ~**, couleur** ~ coral (pink).
corallien, -ienne [kɔʀaljɛ̃, jɛn] *adj* coralline (*littér*), coral (*épith*).
coran [kɔʀɑ̃] *nm* Koran; (*fig rare: livre de chevet*) bedside reading (*U*).
coranique [kɔʀanik] *adj* Koranic.
corbeau, *pl* ~**x** [kɔʀbo] *nm* **(a)** (*oiseau*) (*gén*) crow. **(grand)** ~ raven; ~ **freux** rook; ~ **corneille** crow. **(b)** († *péj: prêtre*) black-coat († *péj*), priest. **(c)** (*Archit*) corbel.
corbeille [kɔʀbɛj] **1** *nf* **(a)** (*panier*) basket.
(b) (*Théât*) (dress) circle.
(c) (*Archit*) *[chapiteau]* bell, basket.
(d) (*Bourse*) stockbrokers' central enclosure (*in Paris Stock Exchange*).
2: (*Bot*)**corbeille d'argent** sweet alyssum; (*fig*) **corbeille de mariage** wedding presents; (*Bot*) **corbeille d'or** golden alyssum; **corbeille à ouvrage** workbasket; **corbeille à pain** breadbasket; **corbeille à papiers** wastepaper basket *ou* bin.
corbillard [kɔʀbijaʀ] *nm* hearse.
cordage [kɔʀdaʒ] *nm* **(a)** (*corde, lien*) rope. ~**s** (*gén*) ropes, rigging; (*Naut: de voilure*) rigging. **(b)** (*U*) *[raquette de tennis]* stringing.
corde [kɔʀd(ə)] **1** *nf* **(a)** (*gén: câble, cordage*) rope. (*fig*) **la** ~† hanging, the gallows, the hangman's rope; (*fig*) **mériter la** ~† to deserve to be hanged; **attacher qn avec une** ~ *ou* **de la** ~ to tie up sb with a (piece of) rope; **attacher** *ou* **lier qn à un arbre avec une** ~ to rope sb to a tree, tie sb to a tree with a (piece of) rope; **en** ~**, de** ~ *semelle* rope (*épith*); *tapis* whipcord (*épith*); **grimper** *ou* **monter à la** ~ to climb a rope, pull o.s. up a rope; *V* **danseur, sauter.**
(b) (*Mus*) string. **les instruments à** ~**s** the stringed instruments; **les** ~**s** the strings; **orchestre/quatuor à** ~**s** string orchestra/quartet.
(c) (*Sport*) *[raquette, arc]* string. ~**s** (*Boxe*) ropes; (*Courses*) rails; (*Boxe*) **être envoyé dans les** ~**s** to be thrown against the ropes.
(d) (*trame d'un tissu*) thread; *V* **user.**
(e) (*Math*) chord.
(f) (†: *mesure*) cord.
(g) (*loc*) **avoir/se mettre la** ~ **au cou** to have/put one's head in the noose; (*lit, fig*) **être** *ou* **marcher** *ou* **danser sur la** ~ **raide** to walk a tightrope; **politique de la** ~ **raide** brinkmanship; (*fig*) **parler de (la)** ~ **dans la maison du pendu** to bring up a sore point, make a tactless remark; **avoir plus d'une** ~ *ou* **plusieurs** ~**s à son arc** to have more than one string to one's bow; **c'est dans ses** ~**s** it's right up his street, it's in his line; **ce n'est pas dans mes** ~**s** it's not my line (of country); (*Courses*) **tenir la** ~ to be on the inside (lane); (*Aut*) **prendre un virage à la** ~ to hug the bend; **tirer sur la** ~ to push one's luck a bit*, go too far; **toucher** *ou* **faire vibrer la** ~ **sensible** to touch the right chord; **il pleut** *ou* **il tombe des** ~**s*** it's bucketing (down)* (*Brit*) *ou* raining cats and dogs*; *V* **sac¹.**
2: **corde cervicale** cervical nerve; **corde dorsale** spinal cord; **corde à linge** clothes line, washing line; (*Sport*) **corde lisse** (climbing) rope; (*Sport*) **corde à nœuds** knotted climbing rope; **corde raide** tightrope; **corde à sauter** skipping rope; **corde du tympan** chorda tympani; **cordes vocales** vocal cords.
cordeau, *pl* ~**x** [kɔʀdo] *nm* **(a)** (*corde*) string, line. ~ **de jardinier** gardener's line; (*fig*) **fait** *ou* **tiré au** ~ as straight as a die. **(b)** (*mèche*) fuse. ~ **Bickford** Bickford fuse, safety fuse; ~ **détonant** detonator fuse. **(c)** (*Pêche*) paternoster.
cordée [kɔʀde] *nf* **(a)** *[alpinistes]* rope, roped party; *V* **premier. (b)** *[bois]* cord. **(c)** (*Pêche*) hook length.
cordelette [kɔʀdəlɛt] *nf* cord.
Cordelier [kɔʀdəlje] *nm* (*religieux*) Cordelier.
cordelière [kɔʀdəljɛʀ] *nf* **(a)** (*corde*) cord. **(b)** (*Archit*) cable moulding. **(c)** (*religieuse*) **C**~ Franciscan nun.
corder [kɔʀde] (1) *vt* **(a)** (*Tech*) *chanvre, tabac* to twist. **(b)** (*rare: lier*) *malle* to tie up (with rope), rope up. **(c)** (*mesurer*) *bois* to cord. **(d)** *raquette* to string.
corderie [kɔʀd(ə)ʀi] *nf* (*industrie*) ropemaking industry; (*atelier*) rope factory.
cordial, e, *mpl* **-iaux** [kɔʀdjal, jo] **1** *adj accueil* hearty, warm, cordial; *sentiment, personne* warm; *manières* cordial; *antipathie, haine* cordial, hearty; *V* **entente. 2** *nm* heart tonic, stimulant.
cordialement [kɔʀdjalmɑ̃] *adv* (*V* **cordial**) heartily; warmly; cordially. **haïr qn** ~ to detest sb cordially *ou* heartily; (*en fin de lettre*) ~ **(vôtre)** ever yours.
cordialité [kɔʀdjalite] *nf* (*V* **cordial**) heartiness; warmth; cordiality.
cordier [kɔʀdje] *nm* **(a)** (*fabricant*) ropemaker. **(b)** (*Mus*) tailpiece.
cordillère [kɔʀdijɛʀ] *nf* mountain range, cordillera. **la** ~ **des Andes** the Andes cordillera.
cordon [kɔʀdɔ̃] **1** *nm* **(a)** *[sonnette, rideau]* cord; *[tablier]* tie; *[sac, bourse]* string; *[souliers]* lace. ~ **de sonnette** bell-pull; (*fig*) **tenir les** ~**s de la bourse** to hold the purse strings; **tenir les** ~**s du poêle** to be a pallbearer.
(b) *[soldats]* cordon.
(c) (*Archit*) string-course, cordon.
(d) (*décoration*) sash. ~ **du Saint-Esprit** the ribbon of the order of the Holy Ghost; ~ **de la Légion d'honneur** sash *ou* cordon of the Légion d'Honneur.
2: **cordon Bickford** Bickford fuse, safety fuse; **cordon-bleu** *nm, pl* **cordons-bleus** (*Culin**) cordon-bleu cook; (*décoration*) cordon bleu; **cordon littoral** offshore bar; **cordon médullaire** spinal cord; **cordon ombilical** umbilical cord; (*Méd, Pol*) **cordon sanitaire** quarantine line, cordon sanitaire.
cordonner [kɔʀdɔne] (1) *vt soie, cheveux* to twist.
cordonnerie [kɔʀdɔnʀi] *nf* (*boutique*) shoe-repairer's (shop), shoemender's (shop), cobbler's (shop); (*métier*) shoe-repairing, shoemending, cobbling.
cordonnet [kɔʀdɔnɛ] *nm* (*petit cordon*) braid, cord.
cordonnier, -ière [kɔʀdɔnje, jɛʀ] *nm,f* (*réparateur*) shoe-repairer, shoemender, cobbler; (†: *fabricant*) shoemaker. (*Prov*) **les** ~**s sont toujours les plus mal chaussés** shoemaker's children are the worst shod.
cordouan, e [kɔʀduɑ̃, an] *adj* Cordovan.
Cordoue [kɔʀdu] *n* Cordoba.
Corée [kɔʀe] *nf* Korea. **C**~ **du Sud/du Nord** South/North Korea.
coréen, -enne [kɔʀeɛ̃, ɛn] **1** *adj* Korean. **2** *nm* (*Ling*) Korean. **3** *nm,f:* **C**~**(ne)** Korean.
coreligionnaire [kɔʀəliʒjɔnɛʀ] *nmf [Arabe, Juif etc]* fellow Arab *ou* Jew *etc*, co-religionist.
Corfou [kɔʀfu] *n* Corfu.
coriace [kɔʀjas] *adj* (*lit, fig*) tough. **il est** ~ **en affaires** he's a hard-headed *ou* tough businessman.
coriandre [kɔʀjɑ̃dʀ(ə)] *nf* coriander.
coricide [kɔʀisid] *nm* (*Pharm*) corn remover.
corindon [kɔʀɛ̃dɔ̃] *nm* corundum.
Corinthe [kɔʀɛ̃t] *n* Corinth; *V* **raisin.**
corinthien, -ienne [kɔʀɛ̃tjɛ̃, jɛn] *adj* Corinthian.
Coriolan [kɔʀiɔlɑ̃] *nm* Coriolanus.
cormier [kɔʀmje] *nm* (*arbre*) service tree; (*bois*) service wood.
cormoran [kɔʀmɔʀɑ̃] *nm* cormorant.
cornac [kɔʀnak] *nm [éléphant]* mahout, elephant driver.
cornage [kɔʀnaʒ] *nm* (*Méd, Vét*) *[cheval, âne]* roaring (*U*), wheezing (*U*); *[malade]* wheeze, wheezing (*U*).
cornard‡ [kɔʀnaʀ] *nm* cuckold†.
corne [kɔʀn(ə)] **1** *nf* **(a)** *[animal, escargot]* horn; *[cerf]* antler. **à** ~**s** horned; **donner un coup de** ~ **à qn** to butt sb; **blesser qn d'un coup de** ~ to gore sb; (*fig*) **avoir** *ou* **porter des** ~**s*** to be (a) cuckold†; (*fig*) **faire les** ~**s à qn** to make a face at sb, make a jeering gesture at sb; *V* **bête, taureau.**
(b) (*U: substance*) horn.
(c) (*instrument*) horn; (*Chasse*) hunting horn; (*Aut*†: *avertisseur*) hooter†, horn.
(d) (*coin*) *[page]* dog-ear. **faire une** ~ **à la page d'un cahier** to turn down the corner of the page in a book.
(e) (**U: peau dure*) (patch of) hard skin.
2: **corne d'abondance** horn of plenty, cornucopia; **corne de brume** foghorn; **corne à chaussures** shoehorn.
cornée [kɔʀne] *nf* cornea.
cornéen, -enne [kɔʀneɛ̃, ɛn] *adj* corneal; *V* **lentille.**
corneille [kɔʀnɛj] *nf* crow; *V* **bayer.**
cornélien, -ienne [kɔʀneljɛ̃, jɛn] *adj* (*Littérat*) Cornelian; (*fig*) *where love and duty conflict.*
cornemuse [kɔʀnəmyz] *nf* bagpipes. **joueur de** ~ bagpiper.
corner¹ [kɔʀne] (1) **1** *vt* **(a)** *livre, carte* to make *ou* get dog-eared; *page* to turn down the corner of.
(b) (*rare: claironner*) *nouvelle* to blare out. **arrête de nous** ~ **(cette nouvelle) aux oreilles*** stop deafening* us (with your news).
2 *vi [chasseur]* to sound *ou* wind (*Brit*) a horn; *[automobiliste]* to hoot (*Brit*) *ou* sound one's horn; *[sirène]* to sound. **les oreilles me cornent** my ears are ringing.
corner² [kɔʀnɛʀ] *nm* (*Ftbl*) corner (kick).
cornet [kɔʀnɛ] **1** *nm* **(a)** (*récipient*) ~ **(de papier)** paper cone; ~ **de dragées/de frites** cornet *ou* paper cone of sweets/chips, ≃ bag of sweets/chips; ~ **de crème glacée** ice-cream cone *ou* cornet; **mettre sa main en** ~ to cup one's hand to one's ear.
(b) (*Mus*) *[orgue]* cornet stop.
2: **cornet acoustique** ear trumpet; **cornet à dés** dice cup; (*Anat*) **cornets du nez** turbinate bones; (*Mus*) **cornet (à pistons)** cornet.
cornette [kɔʀnɛt] *nf [religieuse]* cornet; (*Naut: pavillon*) burgee.
cornettiste [kɔʀnetist(ə)] *nmf* cornet player.
corniaud [kɔʀnjo] *nm* (*chien*) mongrel; (‡: *imbécile*) nitwit*, nincompoop*, twit* (*Brit*).
corniche¹ [kɔʀniʃ] *nf* **(a)** (*Archit*) cornice. **(b) (route en)** ~ coast road, cliff road. **(c)** (*neigeuse*) cornice.
corniche² [kɔʀniʃ] *nf* (*arg Scol*) *class preparing for the school of Saint-Cyr.*
cornichon [kɔʀniʃɔ̃] *nm* (*concombre*) gherkin; (*: *personne*) nitwit*, greenhorn, nincompoop*; (*arg Scol*) *pupil in the class preparing for Saint-Cyr.*
cornière [kɔʀnjɛʀ] *nf* (*pièce métallique*) corner iron; (*d'écoulement*) valley.
cornique [kɔʀnik] **1** *adj* (*rare*) Cornish. **2** *nm* (*Ling*) Cornish.
corniste [kɔʀnist(ə)] *nmf* horn player.
Cornouailles [kɔʀnwaj] *nf* Cornwall.
cornu, e [kɔʀny] **1** *adj animal, démon* horned. **2 cornue** *nf* (*récipient*) retort; (*Tech: four*) retort.
corollaire [kɔʀɔlɛʀ] *nm* (*Logique, Math*) corollary; (*gén: conséquence*) consequence, corollary. **et ceci a pour** ~ ... and this has as a consequence ..., and the corollary of this is ... .
corolle [kɔʀɔl] *nf* corolla.
coron [kɔʀɔ̃] *nm* (*maison*) mining cottage; (*quartier*) mining village.
coronaire [kɔʀɔnɛʀ] *adj* (*Anat*) coronary.

corporatif, -ive [kɔʀpɔʀatif, iv] *adj mouvement, système* corporative; *esprit* corporate.
corporation [kɔʀpɔʀɑsjɔ̃] *nf [notaires, médecins]* corporate body; (*Hist*) guild.
corporatisme [kɔʀpɔʀatism(ə)] *nm* corporatism.
corporel, -elle [kɔʀpɔʀɛl] *adj châtiment* corporal; *besoin* bodily. (*Jur*) **bien ~** corporeal property.
corps [kɔʀ] **1** *nm* **(a)** (*Anat*) body; (*cadavre*) corpse, (dead) body. **frissonner** *ou* **trembler de tout son ~** to tremble all over; **jusqu'au milieu du ~** up to the waist; **n'avoir rien dans le ~** to have an empty stomach; (*fig*) **c'est un drôle de ~!*†** he's a strange character *ou* bod* (*Brit*); *V* **contrainte²**, **diable** *etc.*
(b) (*Chim, Phys: objet, substance*) body. **~ simples/composés** simple/compound bodies; *V* **chute.**
(c) (*partie essentielle*) body; *[bâtiment, lettre, article, ouvrage]* (main) body; *[meuble]* main part, body; *[pompe]* barrel; (*Typ*) body.
(d) *[vêtement]* body, bodice; *[armure]* cors(e)let.
(e) (*consistance*) *[étoffe, papier, vin]* body. **ce vin a du ~** this wine is full-bodied *ou* has (got) body.
(f) (*groupe de personnes*) body, corps; (*Mil*) corps. **~ de sapeurs-pompiers** fire brigade; *V* **esprit.**
(g) (*recueil de textes*) corpus, body. **~ de doctrines** body of doctrines.
(h) (*loc*) **se donner ~ et âme à qch** to give o.s. heart and soul to sth; **perdu ~ et biens** lost with all hands; **s'élancer** *ou* **se jeter à ~ perdu dans une entreprise** to throw o.s. headlong into an undertaking; **donner ~ à qch** to give substance to sth; **faire ~** *[idées]* to form one body (*avec* with); *[choses concrètes]* to be joined (*avec* to); **prendre ~** to take shape; **s'ils veulent faire cela, il faudra qu'ils me passent sur le ~** if they want to do that, they'll have to do it over my dead body; **pour avoir ce qu'il veut, il vous passerait sur le ~** he'd trample you underfoot to get his own way; **faire qch à son ~ défendant** to do sth against one's will *ou* unwillingly; **mais qu'est-ce qu'il a dans le ~?** what HAS got into him?; **j'aimerais bien savoir ce qu'il a dans le ~** I'd like to know what makes him tick.
2: corps d'armée army corps; **corps de ballet** corps de ballet; **corps de bâtiment** main body (of a building); **corps caverneux** erectile tissue (of the penis); **corps céleste** celestial *ou* heavenly body; **corps constitués** constituent bodies; **corps à corps** (*adv*) hand-to-hand; (*nm*) clinch; (*Jur*) **corps du délit** corpus delicti; **corps diplomatique** diplomatic corps; **corps électoral** electorate; **le corps enseignant** the teaching profession; (*Méd*) **corps étranger** foreign body; **corps expéditionnaire** task force; **corps franc** irregular force; (*Mil*) **corps de garde** (*local*) guardroom; (*rare: troupe*) guard; (*péj*) **plaisanteries de corps de garde** guardroom jokes; **corps gras** glyceride; (*Physiol*) **corps jaune** yellow body, corpus luteum (*T*); **corps législatif** legislative body; **corps de logis** main building, central building; **le corps médical** the medical profession; **corps de métier** trade association, guild; **corps mort** moorings; (*Phys*) **corps noir** black body; **corps politique** body politic; **corps de troupe** unit (of troops).
corpulence [kɔʀpylɑ̃s] *nf* stoutness, corpulence. **(être) de forte/moyenne ~** (to be) of stout/medium build; **avoir de la ~** to be stout *ou* corpulent.
corpulent, e [kɔʀpylɑ̃, ɑ̃t] *adj* stout, corpulent.
corpus [kɔʀpys] *nm* (*Jur: recueil, Ling*) corpus.
corpusculaire [kɔʀpyskylɛʀ] *adj* (*Anat, Phys*) corpuscular.
corpuscule [kɔʀpyskyl] *nm* (*Anat, Phys*) corpuscle.
correct, e [kɔʀɛkt, ɛkt(ə)] *adj* **(a)** (*exact*) *plan, copie* accurate; *phrase* correct, right; *emploi, fonctionnement* proper, correct. (*en réponse*) **~!** correct!, right! **(b)** (*convenable*) *tenue* proper, correct; *conduite, personne* correct. **il est ~ en affaires** he's very correct in business matters. **(c)** (**: acceptable*) adequate.
correctement [kɔʀɛktəmɑ̃] *adv* (*V* **correct**) accurately; correctly; properly; adequately.
correcteur, -trice [kɔʀɛktœʀ, tʀis] **1** *adj dispositif* corrective; *V* **verre. 2** *nm,f [examen]* examiner, marker; (*Typ*) proofreader. **3** *nm* (*Tech: dispositif*) corrector. **~ de tonalité** tone control.
correctif, -ive [kɔʀɛktif, iv] **1** *adj gymnastique,* (*Pharm*) *substance* corrective. **2** *nm* (*médicament*) corrective; (*mise au point*) rider, qualifying statement; (*fig: contrepartie*) antidote.
correction [kɔʀɛksjɔ̃] *nf* **(a)** (*U*) *[erreur, abus]* correction, putting right; *[manuscrit]* correction, emendation; *[mauvaise habitude]* correction; *[épreuves]*, correction, (proof)reading; *[compas]* correction; *[trajectoire]* correction; *[examen]* correcting, marking, correction. **apporter une ~ aux propos de qn** to amend what sb has said; *V* **maison.**
(b) (*châtiment*) (corporal) punishment, thrashing. **recevoir une bonne ~** to get a good hiding *ou* thrashing.
(c) (*surcharge, rature*) correction. (*Typ*) **~s d'auteur** author's emendations.
(d) (*U; V* **correct**) accuracy; correctness; propriety.
correctionnel, -elle [kɔʀɛksjɔnɛl] *adj* (*Jur*) **peine ~le** penalty (*imposed by courts*); **tribunal (de police) ~, ~le*** criminal *ou* police court.
corrélatif, -ive [kɔʀelatif, iv] *adj, nm* correlative.
corrélation [kɔʀelɑsjɔ̃] *nf* correlation; connection. **être en ~ étroite avec** to be closely related to *ou* connected with, be in close correlation with.
correspondance [kɔʀɛspɔ̃dɑ̃s] *nf* **(a)** (*conformité*) correspondence, conformity; (*Archit: symétrie*) balance. **~ de goûts/d'idées entre 2 personnes** conformity of 2 people's tastes/ideas; **être en parfaite ~ d'idées avec X** to have ideas that correspond perfectly to X's *ou* that are perfectly in tune with X's.
(b) (*Math*) relation. **~ biunivoque** one-to-one mapping, bijection.
(c) (*échange de lettres*) correspondence. **avoir** *ou* **entretenir une longue ~ avec qn** to engage in a lengthy correspondence with sb; **être en ~ commerciale avec qn** to have a business correspondence with sb; **nous avons été en ~** we have corresponded, we have been in correspondence; **être en ~ téléphonique avec qn** to be in touch by telephone with sb; **par ~** *cours* correspondence (*épith*); **il a appris le latin par ~** he learned Latin by *ou* through a correspondence course.
(d) (*ensemble de lettres*) mail, post (*Brit*), correspondence; (*Littérat*) *[auteur]* correspondence; (*Presse*) letters to the Editor. **il reçoit une volumineuse ~** he receives large quantities of mail *ou* a heavy post (*Brit*); **dépouiller/lire sa ~** to go through/read one's mail *ou* one's correspondence.
(e) (*transports*) connection. **~ ferroviaire/d'autobus** rail/bus connection; **attendre la ~** to wait for the connection; **l'autobus n'assure pas la ~ avec le train** the bus does not connect with the train.
correspondancier, -ière [kɔʀɛspɔ̃dɑ̃sje, jɛʀ] *nm,f* correspondence clerk.
correspondant, e [kɔʀɛspɔ̃dɑ̃, ɑ̃t] **1** *adj* (*gén: qui va avec, par paires*) corresponding; (*Géom*) *angles* corresponding. **ci-joint un chèque ~ à la facture** enclosed a cheque in respect of the invoice.
2 *nm,f* **(a)** (*gén, Presse*) correspondent; (*Scol*) penfriend, correspondent. **~ de guerre** war correspondent; **(membre) ~ de l'institut** corresponding member of the institute.
(b) (*Scol: responsable d'un interne*) friend acting in loco parentis (*for child at boarding school*).
correspondre [kɔʀɛspɔ̃dʀ(ə)] (41) **1 correspondre à** *vt indir* **(a)** (*s'accorder avec*) *goûts* to suit; *capacités* to fit; *description* to correspond to, fit. **sa version des faits ne correspond pas à la réalité** his version of the facts doesn't square *ou* tally with what happened in reality.
(b) (*être l'équivalent de*) *système, institutions, élément symétrique* to correspond to. **le yard correspond au mètre** the yard corresponds to the metre.
2 *vi* **(a)** (*écrire*) to correspond (*avec* with).
(b) (*communiquer*) *[mers]* to be linked; *[chambres]* to communicate (*avec* with).
(c) (*Transport*) **~ avec** to connect with.
3 se correspondre *vpr [chambres]* to communicate (with one another); *[éléments d'une symétrie]* to correspond.
corrida [kɔʀida] *nf* bullfight; (**fig: désordre*) carry-on* (*Brit*), to-do*. (*fig*) **ça va être la (vraie) ~!*** all hell will break loose*, there'll be a great carry-on*.
corridor [kɔʀidɔʀ] *nm* corridor, passage. (*Géog, Hist*) **le ~ polonais** the Polish Corridor.
corrigé [kɔʀiʒe] *nm* (*Scol*) *[exercice]* correct version; *[traduction]* fair copy. **recueil de ~s de problèmes** key to exercises, answer book.
corriger [kɔʀiʒe] (3) **1** *vt* **(a)** (*repérer les erreurs de*) *manuscrit* to correct, emend; (*Typ*) *épreuves* to correct, (proof)read; (*Scol*) *examen, dictée* to correct, mark.
(b) (*rectifier*) *erreur, défaut* to correct, put right; *théorie, jugement* to put right; *abus* to remedy, put right; *manières* to improve; (*Naut*) *compas* to correct, adjust; (*Aviat, Mil*) *trajectoire* to correct; (*Méd*) *vue, vision* to correct. **~ ses actions** to mend one's ways; (*frm*) **~ une remontrance par un sourire** to soften a remonstrance with a smile; (*frm*) **~ l'injustice du sort** to mitigate the injustice of fate, soften the blows of unjust Fate (*littér*).
(c) (*guérir*) **~ qn de** *défaut* to cure *ou* rid sb of.
(d) (*punir*) to thrash.
2 se corriger *vpr* (*devenir raisonnable*) to mend one's ways. **se ~ de** *défaut* to cure *ou* rid o.s. of.
corrigeur, -euse [kɔʀiʒœʀ, øz] *nm,f* (*Typ*) compositor.
corrigible [kɔʀiʒibl(ə)] *adj* rectifiable, which can be put right.
corroboration [kɔʀɔbɔʀɑsjɔ̃] *nf* corroboration.
corroborer [kɔʀɔbɔʀe] (1) *vt* to corroborate.
corrodant, e [kɔʀɔdɑ̃, ɑ̃t] *adj, nm* corrosive.
corroder [kɔʀɔde] (1) *vt* to corrode, eat into; (*fig littér*) to erode.
corroierie [kɔʀwaʀi] *nf* (*activité*) curriery, currying; (*atelier*) curriery.
corrompre [kɔʀɔ̃pʀ(ə)] (4) **1** *vt* **(a)** (*soudoyer*) *témoin, fonctionnaire* to bribe, corrupt.
(b) (*frm: altérer*) *mœurs, jugement, jeunesse, texte* to corrupt; *langage* to debase. **mots corrompus par l'usage** words corrupted *ou* debased by usage.
(c) *air, eau, aliments* to taint; (*Méd*) *sang* to contaminate.
2 se corrompre *vpr [mœurs, jeunesse]* to become corrupt; *[goût]* to become debased; *[aliments etc]* to go off, become tainted.
corrompu, e [kɔʀɔ̃py] (*ptp de* **corrompre**) *adj* corrupt.
corrosif, -ive [kɔʀozif, iv] **1** *adj acide, substance* corrosive; (*fig*) *ironie, œuvre, écrivain* caustic, scathing. **2** *nm* corrosive.
corrosion [kɔʀozjɔ̃] *nf* (*lit*) *[métaux]* corrosion; *[rochers]* erosion; (*fig*) *[volonté etc]* erosion.
corroyage [kɔʀwajaʒ] *nm [cuir]* currying; *[métal]* welding.
corroyer [kɔʀwaje] (8) *vt cuir* to curry; *métal* to weld; *bois* to trim.
corroyeur [kɔʀwajœʀ] *nm* currier.
corrupteur, -trice [kɔʀyptœʀ, tʀis] **1** *adj* (*littér*) *spectacle, journal* corrupting. **2** *nm,f* (*soudoyeur*) briber; (*littér: dépravateur*) corrupter.
corruptible [kɔʀyptibl(ə)] *adj* (*littér*) *juges etc* corruptible; (†) *matière* perishable.
corruption [kɔʀypsjɔ̃] *nf* **(a)** *[juge, témoin]* bribery, corruption. **~ de fonctionnaire** bribery of a public official.

(b) (*dépravation:* V **corrompre**) (*action*) corruption; debasing; (*résultat*) corruption; debasement.
(c) (*décomposition*) *[aliments etc]* decomposition; *[sang]* contamination.

corsage [kɔrsaʒ] *nm* (†: *chemisier*) blouse; *[robe]* bodice.

corsaire [kɔrsɛr] *nm* **(a)** (*Hist: marin, navire*) privateer. **(b)** (*pirate*) pirate, corsair. **(c)** **(pantalon)** ~ breeches.

Corse [kɔrs(ə)] *nf* Corsica.

corse [kɔrs(ə)] **1** *adj* Corsican. **2** *nm* (*Ling*) Corsican. **3** *nmf*: C~ Corsican.

corsé, e [kɔrse] (*ptp de* **corser**) *adj* **(a)** *vin* vigorous, lively; *mets, sauce* spicy. **(b)** (*scabreux*) *histoire* spicy. **(c)** (*: *intensif*) **une intrigue ~e** a really lively intrigue; **des ennuis ~s** some (really) nasty difficulties.

corselet [kɔrsəlɛ] *nm* **(a)** (*cuirasse*) cors(e)let; (*vêtement*) corselet. **(b)** (*Zool*) corselet.

corser [kɔrse] (1) *vt* **(a)** *repas* to make spicier, pep up*; *vin* to strengthen; *assaisonnement* to pep up*.
(b) *difficulté* to intensify, aggravate; *histoire, intrigue, récit* to liven up. **l'histoire** *ou* **l'affaire se corse** the plot thickens! (*hum*); **maintenant ça se corse** things are hotting up *ou* getting lively now.

corset [kɔrsɛ] *nm* (*sous-vêtement*) corset; (*pièce de costume*) bodice. ~ **orthopédique** *ou* **médical** surgical corset.

corseter [kɔrsəte] (5) *vt* (*lit*) to corset; (*fig: enserrer*) to constrain, constrict.

corsetier, -ière [kɔrsətje, jɛr] *nm,f* corset-maker.

corso [kɔrso] *nm*: ~ **(fleuri)** procession of floral floats.

cortège [kɔrtɛʒ] *nm [fête, célébration]* procession; *[prince etc]* cortège, retinue. ~ **nuptial** bridal procession; ~ **funèbre** funeral procession *ou* cortège; ~ **de manifestants/grévistes** procession of demonstrators/strikers; (*fig littér*) ~ **de malheurs/faillites** trail of misfortunes/bankruptcies; ~ **de visions/souvenirs** succession of visions/memories.

cortex [kɔrtɛks] *nm* cortex.

cortical, e, *mpl* **-aux** [kɔrtikal, o] *adj* (*Anat, Bot*) cortical.

corticosurrénale [kɔrtikɔsyrenal] *nf* adrenal cortex.

cortisone [kɔrtizɔn] *nf* cortisone.

corvéable [kɔrveabl(ə)] *adj* (*Hist*) liable to the corvée; *V* **taillable.**

corvée [kɔrve] *nf* **(a)** (*Mil*) (*travail*) fatigue (duty); (*rare: soldats*) fatigue party. **être de ~** to be on fatigue (duty); ~ **de vaisselle** ≈ cookhouse fatigue; ~ **de ravitaillement** supply duty.
(b) (*toute tâche pénible*) chore, drudgery (*U*). **quelle ~!** what drudgery!, what an awful chore!
(c) (*Hist*) corvée (*statute labour*).
(d) (*Can*) voluntary work, bee* (*US, Can*).

corvette [kɔrvɛt] *nf* corvette; *V* **capitaine.**

coryphée [kɔrife] *nm* (*Théât*) coryphaeus.

coryza [kɔriza] *nm* (*Méd*) coryza (*T*), cold in the head.

cosaque [kɔzak] *nm* cossack.

cosécante [kɔsekɑ̃t] *nf* cosecant.

cosignataire [kɔsiɲatɛr] *adj, nmf* cosignatory.

cosinus [kɔsinys] *nm* cosine.

cosmétique [kɔsmetik] **1** *adj* cosmetic. **2** *nm* hair oil.

cosmétologie [kɔsmetɔlɔʒi] *nf* beauty care.

cosmétologue [kɔsmetɔlɔg] *nmf* cosmetic expert.

cosmique [kɔsmik] *adj* cosmic; *V* **rayon.**

cosmogonie [kɔsmɔgɔni] *nf* cosmogony.

cosmographie [kɔsmɔgrafi] *nf* cosmography.

cosmographique [kɔsmɔgrafik] *adj* cosmographic.

cosmologie [kɔsmɔlɔʒi] *nf* cosmology.

cosmonaute [kɔsmɔnot] *nmf* cosmonaut, astronaut.

cosmopolite [kɔsmɔpɔlit] *adj* cosmopolitan.

cosmopolitisme [kɔsmɔpɔlitism(ə)] *nm* cosmopolitanism.

cosmos [kɔsmos] *nm* (*univers*) cosmos; (*Aviat: espace*) (outer) space.

cossard, e* [kɔsar, ard(ə)] **1** *adj* lazy. **2** *nm,f* lazybones.

cosse [kɔs] *nf* **(a)** *[pois, haricots]* pod, hull. **(b)** (*Élec*) terminal spade tag. **(c)** (*: *flemme*) lazy mood. **avoir la ~** to feel as lazy as anything, be in a lazy mood.

cossu, e [kɔsy] *adj personne* well-off, well-to-do; *maison* rich-looking, opulent(-looking).

costal, e, *mpl* **-aux** [kɔstal, o] *adj* (*Anat*) costal.

costard‡ [kɔstar] *nm* suit.

costaud, e [kɔsto, od] *adj personne* strong, sturdy; *chose* solid, strong, sturdy. **un (homme) ~** a strong *ou* sturdy man.

costume [kɔstym] **1** *nm* **(a)** (*régional, traditionnel etc*) costume, dress. ~ **national** national costume *ou* dress; (*hum*) **en ~ d'Adam/d'Ève** in his/her birthday suit (*hum*).
(b) (*Ciné, Théât*) costume.
(c) (*complet*) suit.
2: costume de bain bathing costume (*Brit*) *ou* suit; **costume de cérémonie** ceremonial dress (*U*); **costume de chasse** hunting gear (*U*).

costumer [kɔstyme] (1) **1** *vt*: ~ **qn en Indien** *etc* to dress sb up as a Red Indian *etc.* **2 se costumer** *vpr* (*porter un déguisement*) to wear fancy dress; *[acteur]* to get into costume; **se ~ en Indien** *etc* to dress up as a Red Indian *etc*; *V* **bal.**

costumier [kɔstymje] *nm* (*fabricant, loueur*) costumier, costumer; (*Théât: employé*) wardrobe master.

costumière [kɔstymjɛr] *nf* (*Théât*) wardrobe mistress.

cosy(-corner), *pl* **cosy(-corners)** [kozi(kɔrnœr)] *nm* corner divan (with shelves attached).

cotangente [kɔtɑ̃ʒɑ̃t] *nf* cotangent.

cotation [kɔtɑsjɔ̃] *nf [valeur boursière]* quotation; *[timbre, voiture]* valuation; *[devoir scolaire]* marking. **la ~ en Bourse de sa société** *ou* **des actions de sa société** the quoting of his firm *ou* his firm's shares on the stock exchange.

cote [kɔt] **1** *nf* **(a)** (*fixation du prix*) *[valeur boursière]* quotation; *[timbre, voiture d'occasion]* quoted value. (*Bourse*) **inscrit à la ~** quoted on the stock exchange list; *V* **hors.**
(b) (*évaluation*) *[devoir scolaire]* mark; (*Courses*) *[cheval]* odds (*de* on). ~ **(morale)** *[film]* rating.
(c) (*popularité*) rating, standing. **avoir une bonne** *ou* **grosse ~** to be (very) highly thought of, be highly rated (*auprès de* by), have a high standing (*auprès de* with); **avoir la ~*** to be very popular (*auprès de* with), be very well thought of *ou* highly rated (*auprès de* by); **sa ~ est en baisse** his popularity is on the decline *ou* wane.
(d) (*sur une carte: altitude*) spot height; (*sur un croquis: dimension*) dimensions. **il y a une ~ qui est effacée** one of the dimensions has got rubbed out; **l'ennemi a atteint la ~ 215** the enemy reached hill 215; **les explorateurs ont atteint la ~ 4.550/ –190** the explorers reached the 4,550-metre mark above sea level/190-metre mark below ground.
(e) (*marque de classement*) (*gén*) classification mark, serial number *ou* mark; *[livre de bibliothèque]* class(ification) mark, shelf mark, pressmark.
(f) (*part*) (*Fin*) ~ **mobilière/foncière** property/land assessment; *V* **quote-part.**
2: cote d'alerte (*lit*) *[rivière]* danger mark *ou* level, flood level; (*fig*) *[prix]* danger mark; (*fig*) *[situation]* crisis point; **cote d'amour: ce politicien a la cote d'amour** this politician stands highest in the public's affection; (*fig*) **cote mal taillée** rough-and-ready settlement.

côte [kot] *nf* **(a)** (*Anat*) rib. (*Anat*) **~s flottantes** floating ribs; **on peut lui compter les ~s** he's all skin and bone; (*fig*) **avoir les ~s en long†** to be a lazybones; (*fig*) **se tenir les ~s (de rire)** to split one's sides (with laughter); **~ à ~** side by side; *V* **caresser.**
(b) (*Boucherie*) *[bœuf]* rib; *[veau, agneau]* cutlet; *[mouton, porc]* chop. ~ **première** loin chop; *V* **faux**[2].
(c) (*nervure*) *[chou, tricot, coupole]* rib. **une veste à ~s** a ribbed jacket.
(d) (*pente*) *[colline]* slope, hillside; (*Aut*) *[route]* hill. **il a dû s'arrêter dans la ~** he had to stop on the hill; **ne pas dépasser au sommet d'une ~** do not overtake on the brow of a hill; (*Aut*) **en ~** on a hill; *V* **course, démarrage.**
(e) (*littoral*) coast; (*ligne du littoral*) coastline. **les ~s de France** the French coast(s) *ou* coastline; **la ~ d'Azur** the Riviera; **la ~-d'Ivoire** the Ivory Coast; **~ rocheuse/ découpée/basse** rocky/indented/low coastline; **sur la ~** *ou* **les ~s, il fait plus frais** it is cooler along *ou* on the coast; **la route qui longe la ~** the coast road; (*Naut*) **aller à la ~** to run ashore; (*fig*) **être à la ~†** to be down to *ou* have hit rock-bottom, be on one's beam-ends.

côté [kote] **1** *nm* **(a)** (*partie du corps*) side. **être blessé au ~** to be wounded in the side; **l'épée au ~** (with) his sword by his side; **être couché sur le ~** to be lying on one's side; **à son ~** at his side, beside him; **aux ~s de** by the side of; *V* **point**[1].
(b) (*face, partie latérale*) *[objet, route, feuille]* side. **de chaque ~** *ou* **des deux ~s de la cheminée** on each side *ou* on both sides of the fireplace; **il a sauté de l'autre ~ du mur/du ruisseau** he jumped over the wall/across the stream; **le bruit vient de l'autre ~ de la rivière/de la pièce** the sound comes from across *ou* over the river *ou* from the other side of the river/from the other side of the room; **de l'autre ~ de la forêt il y a des prés** on the other side of the forest *ou* beyond the forest there are meadows; (*fig*) **de l'autre ~ de la barricade** *ou* **de la barrière** on the other side of the fence; (*Naut*) **un navire sur le ~** a ship on her beam-ends.
(c) (*aspect*) side, point. **le ~ pratique/théorique** the practical/theoretical side; **les bons et les mauvais ~s de qn/de qch** the good and bad sides *ou* points of sb/sth; **il a un ~ sympathique** there's a likeable side to him; **prendre qch du bon/ mauvais ~** to look on the bright/black side (of things); **prendre qn par son ~ faible** to attack sb's weak spot; **par certains ~s** in some respects *ou* ways; **de ce ~(-là)** in that respect; **d'un ~ ... d'un autre ~ ...** (*alternative*) on (the) one hand ... on the other hand ...; (*hésitation*) in one respect *ou* way ... in another respect *ou* way ...; **(du) ~ santé tout va bien*** healthwise* *ou* as far as health is concerned everything is fine.
(d) (*parti, branche familiale*) side. **se ranger** *ou* **se mettre du ~ du plus fort** to side with the strongest; **du ~ paternel** on his father's side.
(e) (*précédé de 'de': direction*) way, direction, side. **de ce ~-ci/-là** this/that way; **de l'autre ~** the other way, in the other direction; **nous habitons du ~ de la poste** we live in the direction of the post office; **le vent vient du ~ de la mer/du ~ opposé** the wind is blowing from the sea/from the opposite direction; **ils se dirigeaient du ~ des prés/du ~ opposé** they were heading towards the meadows/in the opposite direction; **venir de tous ~s** to come from all directions; **assiégé de tous ~s** besieged on *ou* from all sides; **chercher qn de tous ~s** to look for sb everywhere *ou* all over the place, search high and low for sb; (*fig*) **je l'ai entendu dire de divers ~s** I've heard it from several quarters *ou* sources; **de ~ et d'autre** here and there; (*fig*) **de mon ~, je ferai tout pour l'aider** for my part, I'll do everything I can to help him; (*fig*) **voir de quel ~ vient le vent** to see which way the wind is blowing; **~ du vent** windward side; **~ sous le vent** leeward side; **ils ne sont pas partis du bon ~** they didn't go the right way *ou* in the right direction.
(f) (*Théât*) **~ cour** opposite prompt side, stage right; **~ jardin** prompt side, stage left; **un appartement ~ jardin/~ rue** a flat overlooking the garden/overlooking the street.
2 à côté *adv* **(a)** (*proximité*) nearby; (*pièce ou maison adjacente*) next door. **la maison/les gens (d')à ~** the house/the people next door; **nos voisins d'à ~** our next-door neighbours; **à**

~ **de** next to, beside; **l'hôtel est (tout) à** ~ the hotel is just close by.

(b) (*en dehors du but*) **ils ont mal visé, les bombes sont tombées à** ~ their aim was bad because the bombs went astray *ou* fell wide; **à** ~ **de la cible** off target, wide of the target; (*fig*) **il a répondu à** ~ **de la question** his answer was off the point; (*fig*) **passer à** ~ **de qch*** to miss sth (narrowly).

(c) (*en comparaison*) by comparison. **à** ~ **de** compared to, by comparison with, beside; **leur maison est grande à** ~ **de la nôtre** their house is big compared to ours.

(d) (*en plus*) besides. **à** ~ **de** besides, as well as; **il est paresseux, à** ~ **de ça il aime son travail*** he is lazy, but on the other hand he does like his work.

3 de côté *adv* **(a)** (*de travers*) *marcher, regarder, se tourner* sideways. **un regard de** ~ a sidelong look; **porter son chapeau de** ~ to wear one's hat (tilted) to *ou* on one side.

(b) (*en réserve*) *mettre, garder* aside. **mettre de l'argent de** ~ to put money by *ou* aside.

(c) (*à l'écart*) **se jeter de** ~ to leap aside *ou* to the *ou* one side; **laisser qn/qch de** ~ to leave sb/sth aside *ou* to one side *ou* out.

coté, e [kɔte] (*ptp de* **coter**) *adj*: **être bien** ~ to be highly thought of *ou* rated *ou* considered; **être mal** ~ not to be thought much of, not to be highly thought of *ou* rated *ou* considered; **historien (très)** ~ historian who is (very) highly thought of *ou* rated *ou* considered, historian who is held in high esteem; **vin (très)** ~ highly-rated wine.

coteau, *pl* ~**x** [kɔto] *nm* (*colline*) hill; (*versant*) slope, hillside. **à flanc de** ~ on the hillside.

côtelé, e [kotle] *adj* ribbed; *V* **velours.**

côtelette [kotlɛt] *nf* **(a)** (*Culin*) *[mouton, porc]* chop; *[veau]* cutlet. **(b)** (*favoris*) ~**s***† mutton chops.

coter [kɔte] (1) *vt* **(a)** *valeur boursière* to quote; *timbre-poste, voiture d'occasion* to quote the market price of; *cheval* to put odds on; (*Scol*) *devoir* to mark; *film, roman* to rate. **voiture trop vieille pour être cotée à l'Argus** car which is too old to be listed (*in the secondhand car book*).

(b) *carte* to put spot heights on; *croquis* to mark in the dimensions on.

(c) *pièce de dossier* to put a classification mark *ou* serial number *ou* serial mark on; *livre de bibliothèque* to put a class(ification) mark *ou* shelf-mark *ou* pressmark on.

coterie [kɔtʀi] *nf* (*gén péj*) set. ~ **littéraire** literary coterie *ou* clique *ou* set.

cothurne [kɔtyʀn(ə)] *nm* buskin.

côtier, -ière [kotje, jɛʀ] *adj pêche* inshore; *navigation, région, fleuve* coastal. **un (bateau)** ~ a coaster.

cotillon [kɔtijɔ̃] *nm* **(a)** (*serpentins etc*) **accessoires de** ~, ~**s** party novelties (*confetti, streamers, paper hats etc*). **(b)** (††: *jupon*) petticoat. **courir le** ~† to flirt with the girls. **(c)** (*danse*) cotillion, cotillon.

cotisant, e [kɔtizɑ̃, ɑ̃t] *nm,f* (*V* **cotisation**) subscriber; contributor. **seuls les** ~**s ont ce droit** only those who pay their subscriptions (*ou* dues *ou* contributions) have this right.

cotisation [kɔtizɑsjɔ̃] *nf* **(a)** (*quote-part*) *[club]* subscription; *[syndicat]* subscription, dues; *[sécurité sociale, pension]* contributions. **la** ~ **est obligatoire** one must pay one's subscription (*ou* dues *ou* contributions).

(b) (*collecte*) collection. **souscrire à une** ~ to contribute to a collection.

cotiser [kɔtize] (1) **1** *vi* (*V* **cotisation**) to subscribe, pay one's subscription; to pay one's contributions (*à* to). **2 se cotiser** *vpr* to club together.

côtoiement [kotwamɑ̃] *nm* **(a)** (*V* **côtoyer**) **ces** ~**s quotidiens avec les artistes l'avaient rendu plus sensible** this daily mixing *ou* these daily encounters with artists had made him more sensitive; **ces** ~**s quotidiens avec la mort/l'illégalité l'avaient rendu intrépide** these daily brushes with death/illegality had made him fearless.

(b) (*V* **se côtoyer**) **le** ~ **de la farce et du tragique** the meeting *ou* closeness of farce and tragedy.

coton [kɔtɔ̃] *nm* **(a)** (*plante, fil*) cotton. ~ **à broder** embroidery thread; ~ **à repriser** darning thread *ou* cotton; ~ **hydrophile** cotton wool (*Brit*), absorbent cotton (*US*).

(b) (*tampon*) (cotton-wool) swab. **mets un** ~ **dans ton nez** put some *ou* a bit of cotton wool in your nose.

(c) (*loc*) **avoir du** ~ **dans les oreilles*** to have cloth ears*; **j'ai les bras/jambes en** ~ my arms/legs feel like jelly *ou* cotton wool; **c'est** ~, **ce problème*** it's a tricky *ou* stiff one*; *V* **élever, filer.**

cotonnade [kɔtɔnad] *nf* cotton fabric.

cotonner (se) [kɔtɔne] (1) *vpr [lainage]* to fluff up.

cotonneux, -euse [kɔtɔnø, øz] *adj* **(a)** *fruit, feuille* downy. **(b)** (*fig*) *brouillard* wispy; *nuage* fluffy, fleecy, cotton-wool (*épith*); *bruit* muffled.

cotonnier, -ière [kɔtɔnje, jɛʀ] **1** *adj* cotton (*épith*). **2** *nm* (*Bot*) cotton plant.

côtoyer [kotwaje] (8) **1** *vt* **(a)** (*longer*) (*en voiture, à pied etc*) to drive (*ou* walk *etc*) along *ou* alongside; *[rivière]* to run *ou* flow alongside; *[route]* to skirt, run along *ou* alongside.

(b) (*coudoyer*) to mix with, rub shoulders with.

(c) (*fig: frôler*) *[personne]* to be close to; *[procédé, situation]* to be bordering *ou* verging on. **cela côtoie la malhonnêteté** that is bordering *ou* verging on dishonesty; **il aime à** ~ **l'illégalité** he likes to do things that verge on illegality *ou* that come close to being illegal.

2 se côtoyer *vpr [individus]* to mix, rub shoulders; *[genres, extrêmes]* to meet, come close.

cotre [kɔtʀ(ə)] *nm* (*Naut*) cutter.

cottage [kɔtaʒ] *nm* cottage.

cotte [kɔt] *nf* **(a)** (*Hist*) ~ **de mailles** coat of mail; ~ **d'armes** coat of arms (*surcoat*). **(b)** (*salopette*) (pair of) dungarees (*Brit*), overalls; (††: *jupe*) petticoat.

cotutelle [kɔtytɛl] *nf* joint guardianship.

cotuteur, -trice [kɔtytœʀ, tʀis] *nm,f* joint guardian.

cotylédon [kɔtiledɔ̃] *nm* (*Anat, Bot*) cotyledon.

cou [ku] **1** *nm* (*Anat, Couture, de bouteille*) neck. **porter qch au** ~ *ou* **autour du** ~ to wear sth round one's neck; **jusqu'au** ~ (*lit: enlisé*) up to one's neck; (*fig*) **endetté jusqu'au** ~ up to one's eyes in debt, in debt up to the hilt; **sauter** *ou* **se jeter au** ~ **de qn** to throw one's arms around sb's neck, fall on sb's neck; *V* **bride, casser** *etc.* **2**: **cou-de-pied** *nm, pl* **cous-de-pied** instep.

couac [kwak] *nm* (*Mus*) *[instrument]* false note, goose note; *[voix]* false note.

couard, e [kwaʀ, aʀd(ə)] **1** *adj* cowardly. **il est trop** ~ **pour cela** he's too cowardly *ou* too much of a coward for that. **2** *nm,f* coward.

couardise [kwaʀdiz] *nf* cowardice.

couchage [kuʃaʒ] *nm* **(a)** (*installation pour la nuit*) **il faudra organiser le** ~ **en route** we'll have to organize our sleeping arrangements on the way; **matériel de** ~ sleeping equipment; *V* **sac**[1]. **(b)** (*péj: gén pl*) = **coucherie.**

couchant [kuʃɑ̃] **1** *adj*: **soleil** ~ setting sun; **au soleil** ~ at sundown (*US*) *ou* sunset; *V* **chien. 2** *nm* (*ouest*) west; (*aspect du ciel, à l'ouest*) sunset.

couche [kuʃ] *nf* **(a)** (*épaisseur*) *[peinture]* coat; *[beurre, fard, bois, neige]* layer; (*Culin*) layer. **ils avaient une** ~ **épaisse de crasse** they were thickly covered in *ou* coated with dirt, they were covered in a thick layer of dirt; (*fig*) **en tenir** *ou* **avoir une** ~* to be really thick*.

(b) (*Horticulture*) hotbed; *V* **champignon.**

(c) (*zone superposée*) layer, stratum; (*catégories sociales*) level, stratum. ~**s de l'atmosphère** layers *ou* strata of the atmosphere; (*Bot*) ~**s ligneuses** woody *ou* ligneous layers; **dans toutes les** ~**s de la société** at all levels of society, in every social stratum.

(d) *[bébé]* napkin, nappy, diaper (*US*). ~**-culotte** shaped nappy *ou* diaper (*US*).

(e) (*Méd: accouchement*) ~**s** confinement; **mourir en** ~**s** to die in childbirth; **une femme en** ~**s** a woman in labour; **elle a eu des** ~**s pénibles** she had a difficult confinement; *V* **faux**[2].

(f) (*littér: lit*) bed. **une** ~ **de feuillage** a bed of leaves.

couche- [kuʃ] *préf V* **coucher.**

couché, e [kuʃe] (*ptp de* **coucher**) *adj* **(a)** (*étendu*) lying (down); (*au lit*) in bed. **Médor,** ~**!** lie down, Rover! **(b)** (*penché*) *écriture* sloping, slanting. **(c)** *V* **papier.**

coucher [kuʃe] (1) **1** *vt* **(a)** (*mettre au lit*) to put to bed; (*donner un lit*) to put up. **on peut vous** ~ we can put you up, we can offer you a bed; **nous pouvons** ~ **4 personnes** we can put up *ou* sleep 4 people; **être/rester couché** to be/stay in bed.

(b) (*étendre*) *blessé* to lay out; *échelle etc* to lay down; *bouteille* to lay on its side. **il y a un arbre couché en travers de la route** there's a tree (lying) across the road; **la rafale a couché le bateau** the gust of wind made the boat keel over *ou* keeled the boat over; **le vent a couché les blés** the wind has flattened the corn; *V* **joue.**

(c) (*frm: inscrire*) to inscribe. ~ **qn dans un testament** to name sb in a will; ~ **qn sur une liste** to inscribe *ou* include sb's name on a list; ~ **un article dans un contrat** to insert a clause into a contract.

2 *vi* **(a)** (*passer la nuit, séjourner*) to sleep. **nous avons couché à l'hôtel/chez des amis** we spent the night at a hotel/with friends, we slept (the night) *ou* put up at a hotel/at friends'; **nous couchions à l'hôtel/chez des amis** we were staying in a hotel/ with friends; **il faudra qu'il couche par terre** he'll have to sleep on the floor; *V* **beau.**

(b) (*: *se coucher*) to go to bed. **cela nous a fait** ~ **très tard** that kept us up very late.

(c) (*: *avoir des rapports sexuels*) ~ **avec qn** to sleep *ou* go to bed with sb; **ils couchent ensemble** they sleep together; **c'est une fille sérieuse, qui ne couche pas** she's a sensible girl and she doesn't sleep around.

3 se coucher *vpr* **(a)** to go to bed. **se** ~ **comme les poules** to go to bed early *ou* when the sun goes down; *V* **comme.**

(b) (*s'étendre*) to lie down. **va te** ~**!*** clear off!*; **il m'a envoyé (me)** ~* he sent me packing; **il se coucha sur l'enfant pour le protéger** he lay on top of the child to protect him; (*Sport*) **se** ~ **sur les avirons/le guidon** to bend over the oars/the handlebars.

(c) *[soleil, lune]* to set, go down.

(d) (*Naut*) *[bateau]* to keel over.

4 *nm* **(a)** (*moment*) **surveiller le** ~ **des enfants** to see the children into bed; **le** ~ **était toujours à 9 heures** bedtime was always at 9 o'clock.

(b) (†: *logement*) accommodation. **le** ~ **et la nourriture** board and lodging; (*Hist*) **le** ~ **du roi** the king's going-to-bed ceremony.

(c) (au) ~ **du soleil** (at) sunset *ou* sundown (*US*); **le soleil à son** ~ the setting sun.

5: **couche-tard*** *nmf inv* late-bedder*, night-owl; **couche-tôt*** *nmf inv* early-bedder*.

coucherie [kuʃʀi] *nf* (*gén pl: péj*) sleeping around (*U*).

couchette [kuʃɛt] *nf* (*Rail*) couchette, berth; (*Naut*) *[voyageur]* berth, couchette; *[marin]* bunk.

coucheur [kuʃœʀ] *nm V* **mauvais.**

coucheuse [kuʃøz] *nf* (*péj*) girl who sleeps around.

couci-couça* [kusikusa] *adv* so-so*.

coucou [kuku] **1** *nm* **(a)** (*oiseau*) cuckoo; (*pendule*) cuckoo clock; (*péj: avion*) (old) crate*. **(b)** (*fleur*) cowslip. **2** *excl*: ~ **(me voici)!** peek-a-boo!

coude [kud] *nm* **(a)** (*Anat, partie de la manche*) elbow. ~**s au corps** (with one's) elbows in; (*fig*) **se tenir** *ou* **serrer les** ~**s** to show great solidarity, stick together; ~ **à** ~ shoulder to shoulder, side by side; **ce ~ à ~ le réconfortait** this jostling companionship comforted him; *V* **coup, doigt, huile** *etc.*

(b) *[route, rivière]* bend; *[tuyau, barre]* bend.

coudé, e [kude] (*ptp de* **couder**) *adj tuyau, barre* angled, bent at an angle, with a bend in it.

coudée [kude] *nf* (††) cubit††. (*fig*) **avoir ses** *ou* **les ~s franches** to have elbow room; (*fig*) **dépasser qn de cent ~s**† to stand head and shoulders above sb, be worth a hundred times more than sb.

couder [kude] (1) *vt tuyau, barre de fer* to put a bend in, bend (at an angle).

coudoiement [kudwamɑ̃] *nm* (close) contact, rubbing shoulders, mixing.

coudoyer [kudwaje] (8) *vt gens* to rub shoulders with, mix with, come into contact with. (*fig*) **dans ce pamphlet, la stupidité coudoie la mesquinerie la plus révoltante** in this pamphlet, stupidity stands side by side with the most despicable pettiness.

coudre [kudʀ(ə)] (48) *vt pièces de tissu* to sew (together); *pièce, bouton* to sew on; *vêtement* to sew up, stitch up; (*Reliure*) *cahiers* to stitch; (*Méd*) *plaie* to sew up, stitch (up). ~ **un bouton/une pièce à une veste** to sew a button/patch on a jacket; ~ **une semelle (à l'empeigne)** to stitch a sole (to the upper); **apprendre à** ~ to learn sewing *ou* to sew; ~ **à la main/à la machine** to sew by hand/by machine; *V* **dé, machine**[3].

coudrier [kudʀije] *nm* hazel tree.

couenne [kwan] *nf* **(a)** *[lard]* rind. **(b)** (:) (*peau*) hide*; (*imbécile*) (silly) twit: (*Brit*), twerp:. **(c)** (*Méd*) *[sang]* buffy coat; *[peau]* membrane.

couenneux, -euse [kwanø, øz] *adj V* **angine.**

couette [kwɛt] *nf* **(a)** *[cheveux]* ~**s** bunches. **(b)** (*Tech*) bearing; (*Naut*) ways (*pl*).

couffe [kuf] *nf*, **couffin** [kufɛ̃] *nm [bébé]* Moses basket; (†: *cabas*) (straw) basket.

coug(o)uar [kugwaʀ] *nm* cougar.

couic [kwik] *excl* erk!, squeak!

couille‡ [kuj] *nf* (*gén pl*) ball‡. ~**s**‡ balls‡, bollocks‡; ~ **molle** gutless individual.

couillon: [kujɔ̃] *nm* bloody (*Brit*) *ou* damn idiot: *ou* cretin:.

couillonnade: [kujɔnad] *nf* (*action*) boob:; (*rare: propos*) bullshit‡ (*U*).

couillonner: [kujɔne] (1) *vt* to do*, swindle. **on t'a couillonné, tu t'es fait** ~ you've been had* *ou* done* *ou* swindled.

couinement [kwinmɑ̃] *nm* (*V* **couiner**) squealing (*U*), squeal; whining (*U*), whine.

couiner [kwine] (1) *vi [animal]* to squeal; (*péj*) *[enfant]* to whine.

coulage [kulaʒ] *nm* **(a)** *[cire, ciment]* pouring; *[statue, cloche]* casting. **(b)** (*: *négligence*) wastage (*U*).

coulant, e [kulɑ̃, ɑ̃t] **1** *adj* **(a)** *pâte* runny; (*fig*) *vin* smooth; (*fig*) *style* (free-)flowing, smooth; *V* **nœud. (b)** (*: *indulgent*) *personne* easy-going. **2** *nm* **(a)** *[ceinture]* sliding loop. **(b)** (*Bot*) runner.

coule [kul] *nf* **(a)** (:) **être à la** ~ to know the ropes, know the tricks of the trade; **elle l'avait à la** ~ she had it easy*. **(b)** (*capuchon*) cowl.

coulé, e [kule] (*ptp de* **couler**) **1** *adj V* **brasse. 2** *nm* (*Mus*) slur; (*Danse*) glide; (*Billard*) follow. **3 coulée** *nf [métal]* casting. ~**e de lave** lava flow; ~**e de boue/neige** mud/snowslide.

coulemelle [kulmɛl] *nf* parasol mushroom.

couler [kule] (1) **1** *vi* **(a)** *[liquide]* to run, flow; *[sang]* to flow; *[larmes]* to run down, flow; *[sueur]* to run down; *[fromage, bougie]* to run; *[rivière]* to flow. **la sueur coulait sur son visage** perspiration was running down *ou* (*plus fort*) pouring down his face; ~ **à flots** *[vin, champagne]* to be flowing freely; (*fig*) **le sang a coulé** blood has been shed.

(b) faire ~ *eau* to run; **faire ~ un bain** to run a bath, run water for a bath; (*fig*) **faire ~ le sang** to shed blood, cause bloodshed; (*fig*) **ça a fait ~ beaucoup d'encre** it caused much ink to flow; (*fig*) **ça fera ~ de la salive** that'll cause some tongue-wagging *ou* set (the) tongues wagging.

(c) *[robinet]* to run; (*fuir*) to leak; *[récipient, stylo]* to leak. **ne laissez pas ~ les robinets** don't leave the taps running *ou* the taps on; **il a le nez qui coule** his nose is running, he has a runny *ou* running nose.

(d) *[paroles]* to flow; *[roman, style]* to flow (along). ~ **de source** (*être clair*) to be obvious; (*s'enchaîner*) to follow naturally.

(e) *[vie, temps]* to slip by, slip past.

(f) *[bateau, personne]* to sink. ~ **à pic** to sink straight to the bottom.

2 *vt* **(a)** *cire, ciment* to pour; *métal* to cast; *statue, cloche* to cast. (*Aut*) ~ **une bielle** to run a big end.

(b) (*passer*) ~ **une existence paisible/des jours heureux** to enjoy a peaceful existence/happy days.

(c) *bateau* to sink, send to the bottom; (*fig*) (*discréditer*) *personne* to discredit; (*: *faire échouer*) *candidat* to bring down. **c'est son accent/l'épreuve de latin qui l'a coulé*** it was his accent/the Latin paper that brought him down; **il s'est coulé dans l'esprit des gens** he has lowered himself in people's estimation, he brought discredit upon himself.

(d) (*glisser*) *regard, sourire* to steal; *pièce de monnaie* to slip.

(e) (*filtrer*) *liquide* to pour. ~ **la lessive**† to boil the washing.

3 se couler *vpr* **(a)** (*se glisser*) **se ~ dans/à travers** to slip into/through.

(b) se la ~ douce* to have it easy*, have an easy time (of it)*.

couleur [kulœʀ] **1** *nf* **(a)** colour; (*nuance*) shade, tint, hue (*littér*). **les ~s fondamentales** the primary colours; **une robe de ~ claire/sombre/bleue** a light-/dark-coloured/blue dress; **une belle ~ rouge** a beautiful shade of red, a beautiful red tint; **aux ~s délicates** delicately coloured, with delicate colours; **film/cartes en ~s** colour film/postcards; **vêtements noirs ou de ~** dark or colourful clothes; **la ~, les ~s** (*linge de couleur*) coloureds; **je n'aime pas les ~s de son appartement** I don't like the colour scheme *ou* the colours in his flat; *V* **goût.**

(b) (*peinture*) paint. ~**s à l'eau/à l'huile** watercolours/oil colours, water/oil paint; **il y a un reste de ~ dans le tube** there is some paint left in the tube; **boîte de ~s** paintbox, box of paints; *V* **crayon, marchand.**

(c) (*carnation*) ~**s** colour; **perdre ses/reprendre des ~s** to lose/get back one's colour; *V* **changer, haut.**

(d) (*U: vigueur*) colour. **ce récit a de la** ~ this tale is colourful; **sans** ~ colourless.

(e) (*caractère*) colour, flavour. **le poème prend soudain une ~ tragique** the poem suddenly takes on a tragic colour *ou* note.

(f) (*Pol: étiquette*) colour. **on ne connaît guère la ~ de ses opinions** hardly anything is known about the colour of his opinions.

(g) (*Cartes*) suit; *V* **annoncer.**

(h) (*Sport*) *[club, écurie]* ~**s** colours; **les ~s** (*drapeau*) the colours.

(i) ~ **locale** local colour; **ces costumes font très ~ locale** these costumes give plenty of local colour.

(j) (*loc*) **homme/femme de** ~ coloured man/woman; **sous ~ de qch** under the guise of sth; **sous ~ de faire** while pretending to do; **montrer/présenter qch sous de fausses ~s** to show/present sth in a false light; **décrire** *ou* **peindre qch sous les plus sombres/vives ~s** to paint the darkest/rosiest picture of sth, paint sth in the darkest/rosiest colours; **l'avenir se présente sous les plus sombres ~s** the future looms very dark; **elle n'a jamais vu la ~ de son argent*** she's never seen the colour of his money*; *V* **voir.**

2 *adj inv*: **des yeux ~ d'azur** sky blue eyes; **tissu ~ cyclamen/mousse** cyclamen-coloured/moss-green material; ~ **chair** flesh-coloured, flesh (*épith*); ~ **paille** straw-coloured.

couleuvre [kulœvʀ(ə)] *nf*: ~ **(à collier)** grass snake; ~ **lisse** smooth snake; ~ **vipérine** viperine snake; *V* **avaler.**

couleuvrine [kulœvʀin] *nf* (*Hist*) culverin.

coulis [kuli] **1** *adj m V* **vent. 2** *nm* **(a)** (*Culin*) purée. ~ **de tomates** tomato purée; ~ **d'écrevisses** crayfish bisque. **(b)** (*Tech*) (*mortier*) grout; (*métal*) molten metal (*filler*).

coulissant, e [kulisɑ̃, ɑ̃t] *adj porte, panneau* sliding (*épith*).

coulisse [kulis] *nf* **(a)** (*Théât: gén pl*) wings. **en ~, dans les ~s** (*Théât*) in the wings; (*fig*) behind the scenes; (*fig*) **les ~s de la politique** what goes on behind the political scene(s); (*fig*) **rester dans la** ~ to work behind the scenes.

(b) *[porte, tiroir]* runner; *[rideau]* top hem; *[robe]* casing; (*panneau mobile*) sliding door; (*Tech: glissière*) slide. **porte à** ~ sliding door; (*fig*) **regard en** ~ sidelong glance *ou* look; *V* **pied, trombone.**

(c) (*Bourse*) unofficial Stock Market.

coulisseau, *pl* **~x** [kuliso] *nm [tiroir]* runner; (*Tech*) slide.

coulisser [kulise] (1) **1** *vt tiroir, porte* to provide with runners; *rideau* to hem (the top of). **jupe coulissée** skirt with a drawstring waist.

2 *vi [porte, rideau, tiroir]* to slide, run.

coulissier [kulisje] *nm* unofficial broker.

couloir [kulwaʀ] *nm [bâtiment]* corridor, passage; *[wagon]* corridor; *[appareil de projection]* channel, track; (*Athlétisme*) lane; (*Géog*) gully; (*Tennis*) alley, tramlines (*Brit*); (*Pol*) lobby. ~ **aérien** air (traffic) lane; ~ **de navigation** shipping lane; (*Géog*) ~ **d'avalanches** avalanche corridor; (*Pol*) **bruits de ~(s)** rumours; (*Pol*) **intrigues de ~(s)** backstage manoeuvring.

coulpe [kulp(ə)] *nf* (*littér, hum*) **battre sa** ~ to repent openly.

coup [ku] **1** *nm* **(a)** (*heurt, choc*) knock; (*affectif*) blow, shock. **se donner un ~ à la tête/au bras** to knock *ou* hit *ou* bang one's head/arm; **la voiture a reçu un** ~ the car has had a knock; **donner des ~s dans la porte** to bang *ou* hammer at the door; **donner un ~ sec pour dégager qch** to give sth a sharp rap *ou* knock to release it; **ça a porté un ~ sévère à leur moral** it dealt a severe blow to their morale; **en prendre un ~*** *[carosserie]* to have a bash*; *[personne, confiance]* to take a blow; **ça lui a fait un ~*** it's given him a (bit of a) shock, it was a bit of a blow (for him); *V* **accuser, marquer.**

(b) (*marquant l'agression*) blow. **il m'a donné un** ~ he hit me; ~ **de pied** kick; ~ **de poing** punch; **en venir aux ~s** to come to blows; **les ~s tombaient dru** *ou* **pleuvaient** blows rained down *ou* fell thick and fast; **donner/recevoir un ~ de bâton/de fouet** to strike/be struck with a stick/a whip; **d'un ~ de fouet il fit partir les chevaux** with a lash of his whip, he set the horses moving; **enfoncer un portail à ~s de bélier** to ram down a gate; **il a reçu** *ou* **pris un ~ de poing dans la figure** he was punched in the face; **il a reçu un ~ de pied** he was kicked; **il a reçu un ~ de griffe** he was clawed; **faire le ~ de poing avec qn** to fight alongside sb; **il a reçu un ~ de couteau** he was knifed; **tuer qn à ~s de couteau/pierres** to knife *ou* stab/stone sb to death; **blessé de plusieurs ~s de couteau** with several stab-wounds; **lancer un ~ de queue** to lash its tail; **le cheval lui lança un ~ de sabot** the horse kicked out at him; **donner un ~ de croc** to snap (*à* at); **donner un ~ de dents dans** to bite, take a bite at; **donner un ~ de bec** to (give a) peck; **donner un ~ de corne à qn** to butt sb; **donner un ~ de gueule*** to shout one's mouth off:; (*fig*) **un ~ d'épée dans l'eau** a futile act; (*fig*) **un ~ de pied au derrière*** a kick in the pants*.

(c) *[arme à feu]* shot. ~ **de feu** shot; ~ **de fusil** rifle shot; ~ **de revolver/de mousqueton** gun/musket shot; **tuer qn d'un ~ de fusil** to shoot sb dead (with a rifle); **touché d'un ~ de feu** shot; **faire le ~ de feu avec qn** to fight alongside sb; **tué de plusieurs**

~s de revolver gunned down; il jouait avec le fusil quand le ~ est parti he was playing with the rifle when it went off; *V* tirer.

(d) (*mouvement du corps*) jeter *ou* lancer un ~ d'œil à qn to glance at sb, look quickly at sb; jeter un ~ d'œil à *texte, exposition* to have a quick look at, glance at; allons jeter un ~ d'œil let's go and have a look; il y a un beau ~ d'œil d'ici there's a lovely view from here; un ~ d'œil lui suffit one glance *ou* one quick look was enough; ~ de coude nudge; d'un ~ de coude, il attira son attention he nudged him to attract his attention; donner un ~ de genou/d'épaule à qn to knee/shoulder sb; donner un ~ de genou/d'épaule dans la porte to strike (at) the door with one's knee/shoulder; il me donna un ~ de genou dans le ventre he thrust his knee into my stomach; il me donna un ~ de genou pour me réveiller he nudged me with his knee to waken me; l'oiseau donna un ~ d'aile the bird flapped its wings *ou* gave a flap with *ou* of its wings; il donna un ~ de reins pour se relever he heaved himself up; donner un ~ de reins pour soulever qch to heave sth up; le chat lapait son lait à petits ~s de langue the cat was lapping up its milk; un ~ d'ongle a scratch.

(e) (*habileté*) avoir le ~ to have the knack; avoir le ~ de main to have the touch; avoir le ~ d'œil to have a good eye; attraper le ~ to get the knack; avoir un bon ~ de crayon to be good at sketching.

(f) (*action de manier un instrument*) ~ de crayon/de plume/de pinceau stroke of a pencil/pen/brush; ~ de marteau blow of a hammer; d'un ~ de pinceau with a stroke of his brush; donner un ~ de lime à qch to run a file over sth, give sth a quick file; donner *ou* passer un ~ de chiffon/d'éponge à qch to give sth a wipe (with a cloth/sponge), wipe sth (with a cloth/sponge), go over sth with a cloth/sponge; donner un ~ de brosse/de balai à qch to give sth a brush/a sweep, brush/sweep sth; donner un ~ de fer à qch to run the iron over sth, give sth a press; donner un ~ de pinceau/de peinture à un mur to give a wall a touch/a coat of paint; donne un ~ d'aspirateur à la chambre go over the room with the hoover; donne-toi un ~ de peigne run a comb through your hair; donner *ou* passer un ~ de téléphone *ou* de fil* à qn to make a phone call to sb, give sb a ring (*Brit*) *ou* call *ou* buzz*, ring sb up (*Brit*), call sb up, phone sb; il faut que je donne un ~ de téléphone I must make a phone call, I've got to give somebody a ring (*Brit*) *ou* call; recevoir un ~ de téléphone *ou* de fil* (de qn) to have a (phone)call (from sb); un ~ de volant maladroit a causé l'accident a clumsy turn of the wheel caused the accident; ~ de frein (brutal) (sharp) braking (*U*); donner un brusque ~ de frein (*lit*) to brake suddenly *ou* sharply; (*fig*) to put on the brakes sharply; ~ d'archet (stroke of the) bow; ~ de cymbale clash of cymbals; avoir un bon ~ de fourchette to be a hearty *ou* big eater.

(g) (*Sport: geste*) (*Cricket, Golf, Tennis*) stroke; (*Tir*) shot; (*Boxe*) blow, punch; (*Échecs*) move. (*Tennis*) ~ droit drive; ~ par ~ blow by blow; (*Boxe, fig*) ~ bas blow *ou* punch below the belt; (*Ftbl, Rugby*) ~ d'envoi kick-off; (*Ftbl*) ~ franc free kick; (*Ftbl*) ~ de pied de réparation penalty kick; (*Rugby*) ~ de pied tombé drop kick; (*fig*) tous les ~s sont permis no holds barred; faire ~ double (*lit*) to do a right and left; (*fig*) to kill two birds with one stone; *V* discuter, marquer.

• (h) (*bruit*) ~ de tonnerre (*lit*) clap of thunder, thunderclap; (*fig*) bombshell, bolt from the blue, thunderbolt; ~ de sonnette ring; je n'ai pas entendu le ~ de sonnette I didn't hear the bell ring; ~ de fusil report, (gun)shot; ~s de fusil gunfire; ~ de feu shot; entendre des ~s de canon to hear guns firing; arrêtez au ~ de sifflet stop when the whistle blows; à son ~ de sifflet at a blow from his whistle; sonner 3 ~s to ring 3 times; les douze ~s de midi the twelve strokes of noon; sur le ~ de midi at the stroke of noon; (*Théât*) frapper les trois ~s to sound the three knocks (*in French theatres, before the curtain rises*); il y eut un ~ à la porte there was a knock at the door.

(i) (*produit par les éléments*) ~ de vent gust *ou* blast of wind; passer en ~ de vent to rush past like a whirlwind *ou* hurricane; (*visite*) to pay a flying visit (*Brit*); ~ de roulis roll; ~ de tangage pitch; ~ de mer heavy swell; ~ de chien squall; prendre un ~ de soleil to be *ou* get sunburnt; elle m'a montré son ~ *ou* ses ~s de soleil she showed me her sunburn; prendre un ~ d'air *ou* de froid to catch a chill; prendre un ~ de vieux: to put years on.

(j) (*événement fortuit*) ~ du sort *ou* du destin blow dealt by fate; ~ de chance *ou* de veine*, ~ de pot: stroke *ou* piece of luck; ~ de déveine* rotten luck (*U*); ~ dur hard blow; c'est un sale ~ it's a dreadful blow.

(k) (*action concertée, hasardeuse*) [*cambrioleurs*] job:. c'est un ~ à faire *ou* tenter it's worth (having) a go* *ou* a bash*; tenter le ~ to try one's luck, have a go*; réussir un beau ~ to pull it off; être dans le ~/hors du ~ to be/not to be in on it; *V* manquer, monter[2], valoir.

(l) (*contre qn*) trick. c'est bien un ~ à lui that's just like him *ou* typical of him; faire un sale ~ à qn to play a (dirty) trick on sb; il nous fait le ~ chaque fois he never fails to do that; un ~ de vache: *ou* de salaud: a dirty trick:; un ~ en traître a stab in the back; faire un ~ de vache à qn: to do the dirty on sb:.

(m) (*: *quantité bue*) boire un ~ to have a drink (*gen of wine*); je te paie un ~ (à boire) I'll buy you a drink; donner *ou* verser un ~ de cidre/de rouge à qn to pour sb a drink of cider/of red wine; vous boirez bien un ~ avec nous? (you'll) have a drink with us?; il a bu un ~ de trop he's had one too many*.

(n) (*: *fois*) time. à tous (les) ~s, à chaque *ou* tout ~ every time; du premier ~ first time *ou* go*; pour un ~ for once; du même ~ at the same time; pleurer/rire un bon ~ to have a good cry/laugh.

(o) (*moyen*) à ~(s) de: enfoncer des clous à ~s de marteau to hammer nails in; détruire qch à ~s de hache to hack sth to pieces; tuer un animal à ~s de bâton to beat an animal to death; traduire un texte à ~ de dictionnaire to translate a text relying heavily on a dictionary; réussir à ~ de publicité to succeed through repeated advertising *ou* through a massive publicity drive.

(p) (*effet*) sous le ~ de *surprise, émotion* under the influence of; sous le ~ d'une forte émotion in a highly emotional state, under the influence of a powerful emotion; (*Admin*) être sous le ~ d'une condamnation to have a current conviction; (*Admin*) être sous le ~ d'une mesure d'expulsion to be under an expulsion order; (*Admin*) tomber sous le ~ de la loi [*activité, acte*] to be a statutory offence.

(q) (*loc*) à ~ sûr definitely; après ~ afterwards, after the event; ~ sur ~ in quick succession, one after the other; du ~ suddenly; pour le ~: c'est pour le ~ qu'il se fâcherait then he'd really get angry, then he'd get all the angrier; sur le ~ (*instantanément*) outright; mourir sur le ~ (*assassinat*) to be killed outright; (*accident*) to die *ou* be killed instantly; sur le ~ je n'ai pas compris at the time I didn't understand; d'un seul ~ at one go; tout à ~, tout d'un ~ all of a sudden, suddenly, all at once; un ~ pour rien (*lit*) a go for nothing, a trial go; (*fig*) a waste of time; en mettre *ou* ficher* un ~ to really put one's back into it, pull out all the stops*; en prendre un (vieux) ~* to take a hammering*; tenir le ~ to hold out; c'est encore un ~ de 1.000 F* that'll be another 1,000 francs to fork out*; *V* cent[1], quatre.

2: (*fig*) coup d'arrêt sharp check; donner un coup d'arrêt à to check, put a brake on; (*fig*) coup de balai clean sweep; (*fig*) coup de bambou* = coup de pompe*; coup de barre (*fig, Pol*) sudden change of direction; donner un coup de barre to alter course, change direction; c'est le coup de barre* = c'est le coup de fusil; (*Jur*) coups et blessures assault and grievous bodily harm; coup de boutoir (*Mil, Sport, gén*) thrust; [*vent, vagues*] battering (*U*); coup de chapeau raising of one's hat; saluer qn d'un coup de chapeau to raise one's hat to sb; coup de collier: il faudra donner un coup de collier we'll have to put our backs into it; (*lit, fig*) coup de dés toss of the dice; coup d'éclat (glorious) feat; coup d'essai first attempt; coup d'État coup (d'état); le coup de l'étrier one for the road; (*fig*) coup de feu last-minute preparations (*in a restaurant etc*); (*fig*) coup de filet haul; coup de force bid for power; (*fig*) coup de foudre love at first sight; (*fig*) coup de fouet lift (*fig*); coup fourré stab in the back; (*fig*) coup de fusil: c'est le coup de fusil the prices are extortionate; coup de grâce (*lit*) coup de grâce; (*fig*) death-blow; coup de grisou firedamp explosion; coup de Jarnac stab in the back; coup du lapin* rabbit punch; (*dans un accident de route*) whiplash; coup de main (*aide*) helping hand, hand; (*raid*) raid; donne-moi un coup de main give me a hand; coup de maître master stroke; (*fig*) coup de massue crushing blow; le coup du père François* a stab in the back; coup-de-poing (américain) *nm, pl* coups-de-poing (américains) knuckle-duster; coup de pompe*: avoir le coup de pompe to be fagged out* *ou* shattered*; coup de pouce (*pour finir un travail*) final touch; (*pour aider qn*) (little) push in the right direction; coup de sang stroke; coup de sonde sounding (*U*); coup de tabac squall; coup de tête (sudden) impulse; coup de théâtre (*Théât*) coup de théâtre; (*gén*) dramatic turn of events; (*fig*) coup de torchon = coup de balai; coup de Trafalgar underhand trick.

coupable [kupabl(ə)] 1 *adj* (a) (*fautif*) *personne* guilty (*de* of); *V* non, plaider.

(b) (*blâmable*) *désirs, amour* guilty (*épith*); *action, négligence* culpable, reprehensible; *faiblesse* reprehensible.

2 *nmf* (*d'un méfait, d'une faute*) culprit, guilty party (*frm, hum*). le grand ~ c'est le jeu the real culprit is gambling, gambling is chiefly to be blamed.

coupage [kupaʒ] *nm* [*vin*] (*avec un autre vin*) blending (*U*); (*avec de l'eau*) dilution (*U*), diluting (*U*). ce sont des ~s, ce sont des vins de ~ these are blended wines.

coupant, e [kupɑ̃, ɑ̃t] *adj* (*lit*) *lame, brin d'herbe* sharp(-edged); (*fig*) *ton, réponse* sharp.

coupe[1] [kup] *nf* (a) (*à fruits, dessert*) dish; (*contenu*) dish(ful); (*à boire*) goblet. une ~ de champagne a goblet of champagne; *V* loin. (b) (*Sport: objet, épreuve*) cup.

coupe[2] [kup] *nf* (a) (*Couture*) (*action*) cutting(-out); (*pièce de tissu*) length; (*façon d'être coupé*) cut. leçon de ~ lesson in cutting out; robe de belle ~/de ~ sobre beautifully/simply cut dress; ~ nette *ou* franche clean cut.

(b) (*Sylviculture*) (*action*) cutting (down); (*étendue de forêt*) felling area; (*surface, tranche*) section. ~ sombre *ou* d'ensemencement thinning (out); ~ réglée periodic felling.

(c) [*cheveux*] cutting. ~ (de cheveux) (hair)cut; ~ au rasoir razor-cut.

(d) (*pour examen au microscope*) section. ~ histologique histological section.

(e) (*dessin, plan*) section. le navire vu en ~ a (cross) section of the ship; ~ transversale cross *ou* transversal section; ~ longitudinale longitudinal section.

(f) (*Littérat*) [*vers*] break, caesura.

(g) (*Cartes*) cut, cutting (*U*). jouer sous la ~ de qn to lead (after sb has cut).

(h) (*loc*) être sous la ~ de qn [*personne*] to be under sb's thumb; [*firme, organisation etc*] to be under sb's control; tomber sous la ~ de qn to fall prey to sb, fall into sb's clutches; faire des ~s sombres dans to make drastic cuts in; mettre en ~ réglée to bleed systematically (*fig*).

coupe- [kup] *préf V* couper.

coupé, e[1] [kupe] (*ptp de* couper) 1 *adj* (a) bien/mal ~ *vêtement* well/badly cut. (b) *communications, routes* cut off. (c) *vin* blended. 2 *nm* (*Aut, Danse*) coupé.

coupée² [kupe] *nf* (*Naut*) gangway (*opening, with ladder*); *V* **échelle.**

coupelle [kupɛl] *nf* **(a)** (*petite coupe*) (small) dish. **(b)** (*Chim*) cupel.

couper [kupe] (1) **1** *vt* **(a)** (*gén*) to cut; *bois* to chop; *arbre* to cut down, fell; (*séparer*) to cut off; (*découper*) *rôti* to carve, cut up; (*partager*) *gâteau* to cut, slice; (*entailler*) to slit; (*fig*) *[vent]* to sting. ~ **qch en (petits) morceaux** to cut sth up, cut sth into (little) pieces; ~ **en tranches** to slice, cut into slices; ~ **la gorge à qn** to slit *ou* cut sb's throat; ~ **la tête à qn** to cut *ou* chop sb's head off; ~ **(les pages d')un livre** to slit open *ou* cut the pages of a book; **livre non coupé** book with pages uncut; **il a coupé le ruban trop court** he has cut the ribbon too short; **coupez-lui une tranche de pain** cut him a slice of bread; **se** ~ **les cheveux/les ongles** to cut one's hair/nails; **se faire** ~ **les cheveux** to get one's hair cut, have a haircut; *V* **tête, vif.**

(b) (*Couture*) *vêtement* to cut out; *étoffe* to cut.

(c) (*raccourcir*) *émission* to cut (down); (*retrancher*) *passages inutiles* to cut (out), take out, delete.

(d) (*arrêter*) *eau, gaz* to cut off; (*au compteur*) to turn off; (*Élec*) *courant etc* to cut off; (*au compteur*) to switch off, turn off; *communications, route, pont* to cut off; *relations diplomatiques* to cut off, break off; (*Téléc*) to cut off; (*Ciné*) *prise de vues* to cut. (*Ciné*) **coupez!** cut!; (*Aut*) ~ **l'allumage** *ou* **le contact** to cut out *ou* switch off the ignition; ~ **le vent** to cut out the wind; ~ **la faim à qn** to take the edge off sb's hunger; ~ **la fièvre à qn** to bring down sb's fever; ~ **le chemin** *ou* **la route à qn** to cut sb off, cut in front of sb; ~ **la route d'un véhicule** to cut a vehicle off, cut a vehicle's path off; ~ **l'appétit à qn** to spoil sb's appetite, take away sb's appetite; ~ **la retraite à qn** to cut off sb's line of retreat; ~ **les vivres à qn** to cut off sb's means of subsistence; ~ **les ponts avec qn** to break off communications with sb.

(e) (*interrompre*) *voyage* to break; *journée* to break up. **nous nous arrêterons à X pour** ~ **le voyage** we'll stop at X to break the journey, we'll break the journey at X.

(f) (*fig: isoler*) ~ **qn de** to cut sb off from.

(g) (*traverser*) *[ligne]* to intersect, cut; *[route]* to cut across, cross. **le chemin de fer coupe la route en 2 endroits** the railway cuts across *ou* crosses the road at 2 points; **une cloison coupe la pièce** a partition cuts the room in two.

(h) (*Cartes*) *jeu* to cut; (*prendre avec l'atout*) to trump.

(i) (*Sport*) *balle* to cut.

(j) (*mélanger*) *lait etc, vin* (*à table*) to dilute, add water to; *vin* (*à la production*) to blend. **vin coupé d'eau** wine diluted with water.

(k) (*loc*) ~ **les bras** *ou* **bras et jambes à qn** to make sb feel weak; ~ **la poire en deux** to meet halfway; ~ **les cheveux en quatre** to split hairs, quibble; ~ **ses effets à qn** to steal sb's thunder; ~ **l'herbe sous le pied à qn** to cut the ground from under sb's feet; ~ **la parole à qn** *[personne]* to cut sb short; *[émotion]* to render sb speechless; ~ **le sifflet*** *ou* **la chique‡ à qn** to shut sb up*, take the wind out of sb's sails; **ça te la coupe!‡** that shuts you up!*; ~ **la respiration** *ou* **le souffle à qn** (*lit*) to wind sb; (*fig*) to take sb's breath away; (*fig*) **j'en ai eu le souffle coupé** it (quite) took my breath away; **un accent à** ~ **au couteau** an accent you could cut with a knife; **un brouillard à** ~ **au couteau** a real pea souper*, a fog you could cut with a knife; **une bêtise à** ~ **au couteau** crass stupidity (*U*).

2 couper à *vt indir* **(a)** (*échapper à*) *corvée* to get out of. **tu n'y couperas pas d'une amende** you won't get away with it without paying a fine, you won't get out of paying a fine; **tu n'y couperas pas** you won't get out of it.

(b) ~ **court à** to cut short.

3 *vi* **(a)** *[couteau, verre]* to cut; *[vent]* to be biting. **ce couteau coupe bien** this knife cuts well *ou* has a good cutting edge.

(b) (*prendre un raccourci*) ~ **à travers champs** to cut across country *ou* the fields; ~ **au plus court** to take the quickest way; ~ **par un sentier** to cut through by way of *ou* cut along a path.

(c) (*Cartes*) (*diviser le jeu*) to cut; (*jouer atout*) to trump.

4 se couper *vpr* **(a)** to cut o.s. **se** ~ **à la jambe** to cut one's leg; (*fig*) **se** ~ **en quatre pour (aider) qn** to bend over backwards to help sb.

(b) (*) to give o.s. away.

5: coupe-choux* *nm inv* short sword; **coupe-cigare(s)** *nm inv* cigar cutter; **coupe-circuit** *nm inv* cutout, circuit breaker; **coupe-coupe** *nm inv* machete; **coupe-feu** *nm inv* firebreak; **coupe-file** *nm inv* pass; **coupe-frites** *nm inv* chip-cutter *ou* -slicer (*Brit*), french-fry-cutter *ou* -slicer (*US*); **coupe-gorge** *nm inv* dangerous back alley; († *ou hum*) **coupe-jarret** *nm* cutthroat; **coupe-légumes** *nm inv* vegetable-cutter; **coupe-œufs** *nm inv* egg-slicer; **coupe-papier** *nm inv* paper knife; **coupe-pâte** *nm inv* pastry-cutter; **coupe-tomates** *nm inv* tomato-slicer; **coupe-vent** *nm inv* windbreak.

couperet [kupʀɛ] *nm [boucher]* chopper, cleaver; *[guillotine]* blade, knife.

couperose [kupʀoz] *nf* blotches (*on the face*), rosacea (*T*).

couperosé, e [kupʀoze] *adj* blotchy, affected by rosacea (*attrib*) (*T*).

coupeur, -euse [kupœʀ, øz] *nm,f* (*Couture*) cutter. **un** ~ **de cheveux en quatre** a hairsplitter, a quibbler.

couplage [kuplaʒ] *nm* (*Élec, Tech*) coupling.

couple [kupl(ə)] **1** *nm* **(a)** (*époux, danseurs*) couple; (*patineurs, animaux*) pair. (*Patinage*) **l'épreuve en** *ou* **par** ~**s** the pairs (event).

(b) (*Phys*) couple. ~ **moteur** torque; ~ **de torsion** torque.

(c) (*Naut*) (square) frame; (*Aviat*) frame.

2 *nf ou nm* (†: *deux*) **un** *ou* **une** ~ **de** a couple of.

3 *nf* (*Chasse*) couple.

coupler [kuple] (1) *vt* **(a)** (*Chasse*) to couple (together), leash together. **(b)** (*Tech*) to couple together *ou* up. (*Phot*) **télémètre couplé** coupled rangefinder; (*Rail*) **bielles couplées** coupling rods.

couplet [kuplɛ] *nm* (*strophe*) verse; (*péj*) little piece, tirade. (*chanson*) ~**s satiriques** satirical song.

coupole [kupɔl] *nf* **(a)** (*Archit*) dome. **petite** ~ cupola, small dome; **être reçu sous la C**~ to become *ou* be made a member of the Académie française. **(b)** (*Mil*) *[char d'assaut]* revolving gun turret.

coupon [kupɔ̃] **1** *nm* **(a)** (*Couture, Tex*) (*reste*) remnant; (*rouleau*) roll.

(b) (*Fin*) ~ **(de dividende)** coupon; **avec** ~ **attaché/détaché** cum-/ex-dividend; ~ **de rente** income coupon.

(c) (*billet, ticket*) coupon. ~ **de théâtre** theatre ticket.

2: coupon-réponse *nm, pl* **coupons-réponse** reply coupon; **coupon-réponse international** international reply coupon.

coupure [kupyʀ] *nf* (*blessure, brèche, Ciné*) cut; (*fig: fossé*) break, division; (*billet de banque*) note. ~ **(de presse** *ou* **de journal)** (newspaper) cutting, (newspaper) clipping; ~ **(de courant)** power cut; (*Banque*) **petites/grosses** ~**s** small/big notes, notes of small/big denomination; **il y aura des** ~**s ce soir** (*électricité*) there'll be power cuts tonight; (*eau, gaz*) the gas (*ou* water) will be cut off tonight.

cour [kuʀ] **1** *nf* **(a)** *[bâtiment]* yard, courtyard. **être sur (la)** ~ to look onto the (back)yard; **la** ~ **de la caserne** the barracks square; ~ **de cloître** cloister garth; **la** ~ **du collège** the college quadrangle *ou* quad (*arg Scol*); ~ **d'école** schoolyard, playground; ~ **de ferme** farmyard; **la** ~ **de la gare** the station forecourt; ~ **d'honneur** main courtyard; ~ **d'immeuble** (back)yard of a block of flats (*Brit*) *ou* an apartment building (*US*); ~ **de récréation** playground; *V* **côté.**

(b) (*Jur*) court. **Messieurs, la C**~**!** ≃ be upstanding in court! (*Brit*), all rise! (*US*); *V* **haut.**

(c) *[roi]* court; (*fig*) *[personnage puissant, célèbre]* following. **vivre à la** ~ to live at court; **faire sa** ~ **à** *roi* to pay court to; *supérieur, femme* to pay one's respects to; **être bien/mal en** ~ to be in/out of favour (*auprès de qn* with sb); **homme/noble de** ~ court gentleman/nobleman; **gens de** ~ courtiers, people at court; **c'est la** ~ **du roi Pétaud** it's absolute bedlam*.

(d) *[femme]* (*soupirants*) following; (*essai de conquête*) wooing (*U*), courting (*U*). **faire la** ~ **à une femme** to woo *ou* court a woman.

2: cour d'appel ≃ Court of Appeal; **cour d'assises** ≃ Crown Court, court of assizes; **cour de cassation** Court of Cassation, (*final*) Court of Appeal; **cour des comptes** revenue court; **cour de justice** court of justice; (*Mil*) **cour martiale** court-martial; (*Hist*) **la Cour des Miracles** *area of Paris famed for its disreputable population*; (*fig*) **chez eux c'est une vraie cour des miracles** their place is a real den of thieves; **cour de sûreté de l'état** state security court.

courage [kuʀaʒ] *nm* **(a)** (*bravoure*) courage, bravery, guts*. ~ **physique/moral** physical/moral courage; **se battre avec** ~ to fight courageously *ou* with courage *ou* bravely; **s'il y va, il a du** ~**!** if he goes, he'll have guts!*; **vous n'aurez pas le** ~ **de lui refuser** you won't have the heart to refuse him.

(b) (*ardeur*) will, spirit. **entreprendre une tâche/un travail avec** ~ to undertake a task/job with a will; **je voudrais finir ce travail, mais je ne m'en sens pas le** ~ I'd like to get this work finished, but I don't feel up to it; **un petit verre pour vous donner du** ~* just a small one to buck you up*.

(c) (*loc*) ~**! nous y sommes presque!** cheer up! *ou* take heart! (*littér*) we're almost there!; **avoir le** ~ **de ses opinions** to have the courage of one's convictions; **prendre son** ~ **à deux mains** to take one's courage in both hands; **perdre** ~ to lose heart, become discouraged; **reprendre** ~ to take fresh heart.

courageusement [kuʀaʒøzmɑ̃] *adv* bravely, courageously. **entreprendre** ~ **une tâche** to tackle a task with a will.

courageux, -euse [kuʀaʒø, øz] *adj* brave, courageous. **il n'est pas très** ~ **pour l'étude** he hasn't got much will for studying; **je ne suis pas très** ~ **aujourd'hui** I don't feel up to very much today.

courailler [kuʀɑje] (1) *vi* (*péj*) ~ **(après les femmes)** to chase after women.

couramment [kuʀamɑ̃] *adv* **(a)** (*aisément*) fluently. **parler le français** ~ to speak French fluently *ou* fluent French.

(b) (*souvent*) commonly. **ce mot s'emploie** ~ this word is in current usage; **ça se dit** ~ it's a common *ou* an everyday expression; **cela arrive** ~ it's a common occurrence; **cela se fait** ~ it's quite a common thing to do, it's quite common practice.

courant, e [kuʀɑ̃, ɑ̃t] **1** *adj* **(a)** (*normal, habituel*) *dépenses* everyday, standard, ordinary; (*Comm*) *modèle, taille, marque* standard. **l'usage** ~ everyday *ou* ordinary *ou* standard usage; **en utilisant les procédés** ~**s on gagne du temps** it saves time to use the normal *ou* ordinary *ou* standard procedures; **il nous suffit pour le travail** ~ he'll do us for the routine *ou* everyday business *ou* work; *V* **vie.**

(b) (*fréquent*) common. **ce procédé est** ~**, c'est un procédé** ~ it's quite common practice *ou* quite a common procedure; **ce genre d'incident est très** ~ **ici** this kind of incident is very common here, this kind of thing is a common occurrence here.

(c) (*en cours, actuel*) *année, semaine* current, present; (*Comm*) inst(ant). **dans la semaine** ~**e** by the end of this week; (*Comm*) **votre lettre du 5** ~ your letter of the 5th inst.; *V* **expédier, monnaie** *etc.*

(d) (*qui court*) *V* **chien, compte, eau** *etc.*

2 *nm* **(a)** *[cours d'eau, mer, atmosphère]* current. ~ **(atmosphérique)** airstream, current; *[cours d'eau]* **le** ~ the current; (*Mét*) ~ **d'air froid/chaud** cold/warm airstream; **il y a trop de** ~

the current's too strong; (*lit*) **suivre/remonter le ~** to go with/against the current; (*fig*) **suivre le ~** to go with the stream, follow the crowd; (*fig*) **remonter le ~** to get back on one's feet, climb back up.

(b) (*déplacement*) *[population, échanges commerciaux]* movement. **~s de population** movements *ou* shifts of (the) population; **établir une carte des ~s d'immigration et d'émigration** to draw up a map of migratory movement(s).

(c) (*mouvement*) *[opinion, pensée]* trend, current. **les ~s de l'opinion** the trends of public opinion; **un ~ de scepticisme/de sympathie** a wave of sceptism/sympathy; (*Littérat*) **le ~ romantique/surréaliste** the romantic/surrealist movement.

(d) (*Élec*) current, power. **~ continu/alternatif** direct/alternating current; **couper le ~** to cut off the power; **rétablir le ~** to put the power back on; (*fig*) **entre ce chanteur et le public le ~ passe** this singer really gets through to his audience; *V* **coupure, pris.**

(e) (*cours*) course. **dans le ~ de la semaine/du mois** in the course of the week/month; **je dois le voir dans le ~ de la semaine** I'm to see him some time during the week.

(f) au ~: être au ~ (*savoir la nouvelle*) to know (about it); (*bien connaître la question*) to be well-informed; **être au ~ de** *incident, accident, projets* to know about; *méthodes, théories nouvelles* to be well up on*, be up to date on; **mettre qn au ~ de** *faits, affaire* to tell sb (about), put sb in the picture about*; *méthodes, théories* to bring sb up to date on; **il s'est vite mis au ~ dans son nouvel emploi** he soon got the hang of things* in his new job; **tenir qn au ~ de** *faits, affaire* to keep sb informed of *ou* posted about*; *méthodes, théories* to keep sb up to date on; **s'abonner à une revue scientifique pour se tenir au ~** to subscribe to a science magazine to keep o.s. up to date (on things) *ou* abreast of things.

3 courante *nf* **(a)** (‡: *diarrhée*) **la ~e** the runs‡.

(b) (*Mus: danse, air*) courante, courant.

courbatu, e [kuʀbaty] *adj* (stiff and) aching, aching all over.

courbature [kuʀbatyʀ] *nf* ache. **ce match de tennis m'a donné des ~s** this tennis match has made me ache *ou* has given me aches and pains; **être plein de ~s** to be aching all over.

courbaturé, e [kuʀbatyʀe] *adj* aching (all over).

courbe [kuʀb(ə)] **1** *adj trajectoire, ligne, surface* curved; *branche* curved, curving.

2 *nf* (*gén, Géom*) curve. **le fleuve fait une ~** the river makes a curve, the river curves; (*Cartographie*) **~ de niveau** contour line; (*Méd*) **~ de température** temperature curve.

courber [kuʀbe] (1) **1** *vt* **(a)** (*plier*) *branche, tige, barre de fer* to bend. **branches courbées sous le poids de la neige** branches bowed down with *ou* bent under *ou* bent with the weight of the snow; **l'âge l'avait courbé** he was bowed *ou* bent with age; (*fig*) **~ qn sous sa loi** to make sb bow down before *ou* make sb submit to one's authority.

(b) (*pencher*) **~ la tête** to bow *ou* bend one's head; **courbant le front sur son livre** his head bent over *ou* his head down over a book; (*fig*) **~ la tête *ou* le front** to submit; *V* **échine.**

2 *vi* to bend. **~ sous le poids** to bend under the weight.

3 se courber *vpr* **(a)** *[arbre, branche, poutre]* to bend, curve.

(b) *[personne]* (*pour entrer, passer*) to bend (down), stoop; (*signe d'humiliation*) to bow down; (*signe de déférence*) to bow (down). **il se courba pour le saluer** he greeted him with a bow; **se ~ en deux** to bend (o.s.) double.

(c) (*littér: se soumettre*) to bow down (*devant* before).

courbette [kuʀbɛt] *nf* **(a)** (*salut*) low bow. (*fig*) **faire des ~s à *ou* devant qn** to bow and scrape to sb. **(b)** *[cheval]* curvet.

courbure [kuʀbyʀ] *nf [ligne, surface]* curvature. **~ rentrante/sortante/en S** inward/outward/S curve; **~ du nez/des reins** curve of the nose/the back.

courette [kuʀɛt] *nf* small (court)yard.

coureur, -euse [kuʀœʀ, øz] **1** *nm,f* (*Athlétisme*) runner; (*Cyclisme*) cyclist, competitor; (*Aut*) driver, competitor. **~ de fond/de demi-fond** long-/middle-distance runner; **~ de 110 mètres haies** 110 metres hurdler.

2 *nm* **(a)** (*Zool*) **(oiseaux) ~s** running birds.

(b) (*péj: amateur de*) **c'est un ~ de cafés/de bals** he hangs round cafés/dances; **c'est un ~ (de filles *ou* femmes)** he's a womanizer *ou* a woman-chaser; **il est assez ~** he's a bit of a womanizer.

3 coureuse *nf* (*péj: débauchée*) manhunter. **elle est un peu ~euse** she's a bit of a manhunter.

4: coureur automobile racing(-car) driver; (*Can Hist*) **coureur de *ou* des bois** trapper, coureur de bois (*US, Can*); **coureur cycliste** racing cyclist; (*péj*) **coureur de dot** fortune-hunter; **coureur motocycliste** motorcycle *ou* motorbike racer.

courge [kuʀʒ(ə)] *nf* **(a)** (*plante, fruit*) gourd, squash (*US, Can*); (*Culin*) marrow (*Brit*), squash (*US, Can*). **(b)** (‡) idiot, nincompoop*, berk‡ (*Brit*).

courgette [kuʀʒɛt] *nf* courgette (*Brit*), zucchini.

courir [kuʀiʀ] (11) **1** *vi* **(a)** (*gén, Athlétisme*) to run; (*Aut, Cyclisme*) to race; (*Courses*) to run, race. **entrer/sortir en courant** to run in/out; **~ à toutes jambes, ~ à perdre haleine** to run as fast as one's legs can carry one, run like the wind; **~ comme un dératé*** *ou* **ventre à terre** to run flat out; **elle court comme un lapin *ou* lièvre** she runs *ou* can run like a hare; **faire ~ un cheval** to race *ou* run a horse; **il ne fait plus ~** he doesn't race *ou* run horses any more; **un cheval trop vieux pour ~** a horse too old to race *ou* to be raced.

(b) (*se précipiter*) to rush. **~ chez le docteur/chercher le docteur** to rush *ou* run to the doctor's/for the doctor; **je cours l'appeler** I'll go *ou* run and call him straight away; **spectacle qui fait ~ tout Paris *ou* tous les Parisiens** show that all Paris is rushing *ou* running to see; **faire qch en courant** to do sth in a rush *ou* hurry; **elle m'a fait ~** she had me running all over the place; **un petit mot en courant** just a (rushed) note *ou* a few hurried lines; **~ partout pour trouver qch** to hunt everywhere for sth; **tu peux toujours ~!*** you can whistle for it!*.

(c) (*avec à, après, sur*) **~ à l'échec/à une déception/à sa perte** to be heading for failure/a disappointment/ruin; **~ après qch** to chase after sth; **gardez cet argent pour l'instant, il ne court pas après** keep this money for now as he's not in any hurry *ou* rush for it *ou* he's not desperate for it; (*lit, fig*) **~ après qn** to run after sb; **~ après les femmes** to be a woman-chaser, chase women; **~ sur ses 20/30 ans** to be approaching 20/30; **~ sur ses 60/70 ans** to be approaching *ou* pushing* 60/70; **~ sur le système *ou* le haricot à qn‡** to get on sb's nerves *ou* wick‡ (*Brit*).

(d) *[nuages etc]* to speed, scud (*littér*); *[ombres, reflets]* to speed, race; *[eau]* to rush; *[chemin]* to run. **une onde courait sur les blés** a wave passed through the corn; **un frisson lui courut par tout le corps** a shiver went *ou* ran through his body; **sa plume courait sur le papier** his pen was running across the paper; **faire *ou* laisser ~ sa plume** to let one's pen flow *ou* run (on *ou* freely).

(e) (*se répandre*) **faire ~ un bruit/une nouvelle** to spread a rumour/a piece of news; **le bruit court que ...** rumour has it that ..., there is a rumour that ..., the rumour is that ... ; **le bruit a récemment couru que ...** rumour recently had it that ..., the rumour has recently gone round that ...; **il court sur leur compte de curieuses histoires** there are some strange stories going round about them.

(f) (*se passer*) **l'année/le mois qui court** the current *ou* present year/month; **par le(s) temps qui cour(en)t** (with things as they are *ou* things being as they are) nowadays; **laisser ~*** to let things alone; **laisse ~*** forget it*, drop it*.

(g) (*Naut*) to sail.

(h) (*Fin*) *[intérêt]* to accrue; *[bail]* to run.

2 *vt* **(a)** (*Sport*) *épreuve* to compete in. **~ un 100 mètres** to run (in) *ou* compete in a 100 metres race; **~ le Grand Prix** to race in the Grand Prix.

(b) (*Chasse*) **~ le cerf/le sanglier** to hunt the stag/the boar, go staghunting/boarhunting; (*fig*) **~ deux lièvres à la fois** to have one's finger in more than one pie.

(c) (*rechercher*) *honneurs* to seek avidly; (*s'exposer à*) *danger* to face. **~ les aventures *ou* l'aventure** to seek adventure; **~ un (gros) risque** to run a (high *ou* serious) risk; **~ sa chance** to try one's luck; **il court le risque d'être accusé** he runs the risk *ou* chance *ou* is in danger of being accused; **c'est un risque à ~** it's a risk we'll have to take *ou* run; (*Théât*) **~ le cachet** to run after any sort of work.

(d) (*parcourir*) *les mers, le monde* to roam, rove; *la campagne, les bois* to roam *ou* rove (through); (*faire le tour de*) *les magasins, bureaux* to go round. **j'ai couru les agences toute la matinée** I've been going round the agencies all morning, I've been going from agency to agency all morning; **~ les rues** (*lit*) to wander *ou* roam the streets; (*fig*) to be run-of-the-mill; **le vrai courage ne court pas les rues** real courage is hard to find; **des gens comme lui, ça ne court pas les rues*** people like him are not thick on the ground* (*Brit*) *ou* are few and far between.

(e) (*fréquenter*) **~ les théâtres/les bals** to do the rounds of (all) the theatres/dances; **~ les filles** to chase the girls; **~ la gueuse†** to go wenching†; **~ le guilledou† *ou* la prétentaine†** to go gallivanting†, go wenching†.

(f) (‡) **~ qn** to get up sb's nose‡ (*Brit*) *ou* on sb's wick‡ (*Brit*), bug sb‡ (*US*).

couronne [kuʀɔn] *nf* **(a)** *[fleurs]* wreath, circlet. **~ funéraire *ou* mortuaire** (funeral) wreath; **~ de fleurs d'oranger** orange-blossom headdress, circlet of orange-blossom; **~ de lauriers** laurel wreath, crown of laurels; **~ d'épines** crown of thorns; **en ~** in a ring; *V* **fleur.**

(b) (*diadème*) *[roi, pape]* crown; *[noble]* coronet.

(c) (*autorité royale*) **la ~** the Crown; **la ~ d'Angleterre/de France** the crown of England/of France, the English/French crown; **aspirer/prétendre à la ~** to aspire to/lay claim to the throne *ou* the crown; **de la ~** *joyaux, colonie* crown (*épith*).

(d) (*objet circulaire*) crown; (*pain*) circular loaf; *[dent]* crown; (*Archit, Astron*) corona. (*Aut*) **~ dentée** crown wheel.

couronnement [kuʀɔnmɑ̃] *nm* **(a)** *[roi, empereur]* coronation, crowning. **(b)** *[édifice, colonne]* top, crown; *[mur]* coping; *[toit]* ridge. **(c)** (*fig*) *[carrière]* crowning achievement.

couronner [kuʀɔne] (1) **1** *vt* **(a)** *souverain* to crown. **on le couronna roi** he was crowned king, they crowned him king; *V* **tête.**

(b) *ouvrage, auteur* to award a prize to; (*Hist*) *lauréat, vainqueur* to crown with a laurel wreath.

(c) (*littér: orner, ceindre*) to crown; *[diadème] front* to encircle. **couronné de fleurs** wreathed *ou* encircled with flowers; **remparts qui couronnent la colline** ramparts which crown the hill; **un pic couronné de neige** a peak crowned with snow, a snow-capped peak.

(d) (*parachever*) to crown. **cela couronne son œuvre/sa carrière** that is the crowning achievement of his work/his career; (*iro*) **et pour ~ le tout** and to crown it all; **ses efforts ont été couronnés de succès** his efforts were crowned with success.

(e) *dent* to crown.

2 se couronner *vpr*: **se ~ (le genou)** *[cheval, personne]* to graze its (*ou* one's) knee.

courre [kuʀ] *vt V* **chasse**[1].

courrier [kuʀje] *nm* **(a)** (*lettres reçues*) mail, post (*Brit*), letters; (*lettres à écrire*) letters. **le ~ de 11 heures** the 11 o'clock post (*Brit*) *ou* mail; *V* **retour.**

(b) (†) (*avion, bateau*) mail; (*Mil: estafette*) courier; (*de diligence*) post. **l'arrivée du ~ de Bogota** the arrival of the Bogota mail; *V* **long, moyen.**

(c) (*Presse*) (*rubrique*) column; (*nom de journal*) ≃ Mail. ~

du cœur (women's) advice column, problem page; ~ **des lecteurs** letters to the Editor; ~ **littéraire** literary column; ~ **économique** financial page.

courriériste [kuʀjeʀist(ə)] *nmf* columnist.

courroie [kuʀwa] *nf* (*attache*) strap; (*Tech*) belt. (*Tech*) ~ **de transmission** driving belt; (*Aut*) ~ **de ventilateur** fan belt.

courroucé, e [kuʀuse] (*ptp de* **courroucer**) *adj* wrathful, incensed.

courroucer [kuʀuse] (3) (*littér*) **1** *vt* to anger, incense. **2 se courroucer** *vpr* to become incensed.

courroux [kuʀu] *nm* (*littér*) ire (*littér*), wrath.

cours [kuʀ] **1** *nm* **(a)** (*déroulement, Astron*) course; *[événements]* course, run; *[saisons]* course, progression; *[guerre, maladie]* progress, course; *[pensées, idées]* course; *V* **suivre.**

(b) *[rivière]* (*cheminement*) course; (*écoulement*) flow. **avoir un ~ rapide/régulier** to be fast-/smooth-flowing; **sur une partie de son ~** on *ou* along part of its course; **descendre le ~ de la Seine** to go down the Seine.

(c) (*Fin*) *[monnaie]* currency; *[valeurs, matières premières]* price; *[devises]* rate. ~ **légal** legal tender; (*Bourse*) ~ **d'ouverture/de clôture** opening/closing price; ~ **des devises** *ou* **du change** foreign exchange rate; **au ~ (du jour)** at the price of the day; **au ~ du marché** at (the) market price; **le ~ des voitures d'occasion** the (selling) price of secondhand cars.

(d) (*leçon*) class; (*Univ: conférence*) lecture; (*série de leçons*) course. (*manuel*) ~ **de chimie** chemistry coursebook; (*notes*) ~ **de droit** law (course) notes; **faire** *ou* **donner un ~ sur** to give a class *ou* lecture on; to give a course on; **il donne des ~ en fac** he lectures at university; ~ **du soir** (*pl*) evening classes; ~ **par correspondance** correspondence course; ~ **de vacances** holiday (*Brit*) *ou* vacation (*US*) course.

(e) (*Scol: établissement*) school. ~ **privé** private school; ~ **de jeunes filles** girls' school *ou* college; ~ **de danse** dancing school.

(f) (*Scol: enseignement primaire*) class. ~ **préparatoire** first-year infants (class); ~ **élémentaire/moyen** primary/intermediate classes (*of primary school*); ~ **supérieur**†† secondary school; ~ **complémentaire** ≈ secondary modern school.

(g) (*avenue*) walk.

(h) (*loc*) **avoir ~** *[monnaie]* to be legal tender; (*fig*) to be current, be in current use; **ne plus avoir ~** *[monnaie]* to be no longer legal tender *ou* currency, be out of circulation; *[expression]* to be obsolete, be no longer in use *ou* no longer current; **ces plaisanteries n'ont plus ~ ici** jokes like that are no longer appreciated here; **en ~** *année* current (*épith*); *affaires* in hand, in progress; *essais* in progress, under way; **en ~ de** in the process of; **en ~ de réparation/réfection** in the process of being repaired/rebuilt; **en ~ de route** on the way; **au ~ de** in the course of, during; **donner (libre) ~ à** *imagination* to give free rein to; *douleur* to give free expression to; *joie, sentiment* to give vent to, give free expression to; **il donna (libre) ~ à ses larmes** he let his tears flow freely.

2: cours d'eau *generic term for streams, rivers and waterways*; **le confluent de deux cours d'eau** the confluence of two rivers; **un petit cours d'eau traversait cette vallée** a stream ran across this valley.

course [kuʀs(ə)] **1** *nf* **(a)** (*action de courir*) run. **la ~ et la marche** running and walking; **prendre sa ~** to set off at speed; **le cheval, atteint d'une balle en pleine ~** the horse, hit by a bullet in mid gallop; **il le rattrapa à la ~** he ran after him and caught him (up); *V* **pas**[1].

(b) (*discipline*) (*Athlétisme*) running; (*Aut, Courses, Cyclisme*) racing. **faire de la ~ pour s'entraîner** to go running to keep in training; (*Aut, Cyclisme*) **tu fais de la ~?** do you race?; ~ **de fond/demi-fond** long-distance/middle-distance running; ~ **sur piste/route** track/road racing; (*fig*) **la ~ aux armements** the arms race; (*fig*) **la ~ au pouvoir** the race for power; **faire la ~ avec qn** to race with sb; **allez, on fait la ~** let's have a race, I'll give you a race, I'll race you; *V* **champ, écurie.**

(c) (*épreuve*) race. ~ **de fond/sur piste** long-distance/track race; (*Courses*) **les ~s** the races; **parier aux ~s** to bet on the races.

(d) (*voyage*) *[autocar]* trip, journey; *[taxi]* journey. **payer le prix de la ~, payer la ~** to pay the fare; *[taxi]* **il n'a fait que 3 ~s hier** he only picked up *ou* had 3 fares yesterday.

(e) (*fig*) *[projectile]* flight; *[navire]* rapid course; *[nuages, ombres]* racing, swift passage; *[temps]* swift passage, swift passing (*U*).

(f) (*excursion*) (*à pied*) hike; (*ascension*) climb.

(g) (*au magasin*) shopping (*U*); (*commission*) errand. **elle est sortie faire des ~s** she has gone out to do *ou* get some shopping; **j'ai quelques ~s à faire** I've a bit of shopping to do, I've one or two things to buy; **faire une ~** to (go and) get something from the shop(s) (*Brit*) *ou* store(s) (*US*); to run an errand.

(h) (*Tech*) *[pièce mobile]* movement; *[piston]* stroke. **à bout de ~** at full stroke; **à mi-~** at half-stroke.

(i) (*Naut*) privateering. **faire la ~** to privateer, go privateering; *V* **guerre.**

(j) (*loc*) **être à bout de ~** to be worn out; **être dans la ~*** to be with-it*; **être en fin de ~** to be on the blink*, be going west*.

2: course attelée harness race; **course automobile** motor race; **course de chevaux** horse-race; (*Sport Aut*) **course de côte** hill climb; **course contre la montre** (*Sport*) race against the clock, time-trial; (*fig*) race against the clock; **course par étapes** stage race; **course de relais** relay race; **course en sac** sack race; **course de taureaux** bullfight; **course de trot** trotting race; **course de vitesse** sprint.

coursier[1] [kuʀsje] *nm* (*littér: cheval*) charger (*littér*), steed (*littér*).

coursier[2]**, -ière** [kuʀsje, jɛʀ] *nm,f* messenger.

coursive [kuʀsiv] *nf* (*Naut*) gangway (*connecting cabins*).

court[1]**, e** [kuʀ, kuʀt(ə)] **1** *adj* **(a)** (*gén*) *objet, récit, durée, mémoire* short; *introduction, séjour* short, brief. **il a été très ~** he was very brief; **de ~e durée** *enthousiasme, ardeur* short-lived; **c'est plus ~ par le bois** it's quicker *ou* shorter through the wood; **il connaît un chemin plus ~** he knows a shorter way; **la journée m'a paru ~e** the day has passed *ou* seemed to pass quickly, it has been a short day; **avoir l'haleine** *ou* **la respiration ~e** *ou* **le souffle ~** to be quickly out of breath, be short-winded; *V* **idée, manche**[1]**, mémoire**[1] *etc.*

(b) (*insuffisant*) **il lui a donné 10 jours, c'est ~** he's given him 10 days, which is (a bit) on the short side *ou* which isn't very long; **100 F pour le faire, c'est ~*** 100 francs to do it — that's not very much.

(c) (*loc*) **tirer à la ~e paille** to draw lots; **à sa ~e honte** to his humiliation; **être à ~** to be short; **être à ~ d'argent/d'arguments** to be short of money/arguments; **prendre au plus ~** to go the shortest way; **prendre qn de ~** to catch sb unawares *ou* on the hop* (*Brit*).

2 *adv* **(a)** *coiffer, habiller* short. **les cheveux coupés ~** with short(-cut) hair, with hair cut short.

(b) s'arrêter ~ to stop short; **demeurer** *ou* **se trouver ~** to be at a loss; *V* **couper, pendre, tourner.**

3: (*Culin*) **court-bouillon** *nm, pl* **courts-bouillons** court-bouillon; (*Élec*) **court-circuit** *nm, pl* **courts-circuits** short (-circuit); **court-circuiter** *vt* (*lit*) to short(-circuit); (*fig*) to bypass, short-circuit; **courte échelle** leg up; **faire la courte échelle à qn** to give sb a leg up; **court-jus*** *nm inv* short-circuit; (*Ciné*) **court métrage** short film; **court-vêtu, e,** *mpl* **court-vêtus** *adj* short-skirted.

court[2] [kuʀ] *nm* (tennis) court.

courtage [kuʀtaʒ] *nm* brokerage.

courtaud, e [kuʀto, od] *adj* **(a)** *personne* dumpy, squat. **un ~** a dumpy *ou* squat little man. **(b) un (chien/cheval) ~** a docked and crop-eared dog/horse.

courtier, -ière [kuʀtje, jɛʀ] *nm,f* broker. ~ **en vins** wine-broker; ~ **maritime** ship-broker.

courtilière [kuʀtiljɛʀ] *nf* mole cricket.

courtine [kuʀtin] *nf* curtain.

courtisan [kuʀtizɑ̃] *nm* (*Hist*) courtier; (*fig*) sycophant. **des manières de ~** sycophantic manners.

courtisane [kuʀtizan] *nf* (*Hist, littér*) courtesan, courtezan.

courtiser [kuʀtize] (1) *vt* († *ou littér*) *femme* to woo, court, pay court to; (*flatter*) to pay court to, fawn on (*péj*).

courtois, e [kuʀtwa, waz] *adj* courteous; (*Littérat*) courtly.

courtoisement [kuʀtwazmɑ̃] *adv* courteously.

courtoisie [kuʀtwazi] *nf* courtesy, courteousness.

couru, e [kuʀy] (*ptp de* **courir**) *adj* **(a)** *restaurant, spectacle* popular. **(b) c'est ~*** it's a (dead) cert* (*Brit*), it's a sure thing*.

couscous [kuskus] *nm* (*Culin*) couscous.

cousette [kuzɛt] *nf* dressmaker's apprentice.

couseuse [kuzøz] *nf* stitcher, sewer.

cousin[1]**, e** [kuzɛ̃, in] *nm,f* cousin. ~ **germain** first *ou* full cousin; **~s issus de germains** second cousins; **ils sont un peu ~s** they are related (in some way); *V* **mode**[1]**, roi.**

cousin[2] [kuzɛ̃] *nm* gnat, midge.

cousinage† [kuzinaʒ] *nm* (*entre germains*) cousinhood, cousinship; (*vague parenté*) relationship.

cousiner† [kuzine] (1) *vi* to be on familiar terms (*avec* with).

coussin [kusɛ̃] *nm* *[siège]* cushion; (*Tech*) *[collier de cheval]* padding. ~ **d'air** air cushion.

coussinet [kusinɛ] *nm* **(a)** *[siège, genoux]* (small) cushion. **(b)** (*Tech*) bearing. ~ **de tête de bielle** *[arbre de transmission]* big end bearing; *[rail]* chair.

cousu, e [kuzy] (*ptp de* **coudre**) *adj* sewn, stitched. (*fig*) **être (tout) ~ d'or** to be rolling in riches; (*fig*) **c'est ~ de fil blanc** it's blatant, it sticks out a mile; ~ **main** (*lit*) handsewn, hand-stitched; (**fig*) **c'est du ~ main** it's top quality stuff; ~ **machine** machine-sewn; *V* **bouche, motus.**

coût [ku] *nm* (*lit, fig*) cost. **le ~ de la vie** the cost of living; *V* **indice.**

coûtant [kutɑ̃] *adj m*: **prix ~** cost price.

couteau, *pl* **~x** [kuto] **1** *nm* **(a)** (*pour couper*) knife; *[balance]* knife edge; (*coquillage*) razor-shell. ~ **à beurre/dessert/fromage/poisson** butter/dessert/cheese/fish knife; *V* **brouillard, lame.**

(b) (*loc*) **vous me mettez le ~ sous** *ou* **sur la gorge** you're holding a pistol at my head; **être à ~(x) tiré(s)** to be at daggers drawn (*avec* with); **remuer** *ou* **retourner le ~ dans la plaie** to twist the knife in the wound, rub it in*.

2: couteau de chasse hunting knife; **couteau à cran d'arrêt** flick-knife; **couteau de cuisine** kitchen knife; **couteau à découper** carving knife; **couteau à éplucher, couteau éplucheur, couteau à légumes** (potato) peeler; **couteau à pain** breadknife; (*Peinture*) **couteau à palette** *ou* **de peintre** palette knife; **couteau pliant** *ou* **de poche** pocket knife; **couteau-scie** *nm, pl* **couteaux-scies** serrated-edged knife; **couteau de table** table knife.

coutelas [kutlɑ] *nm* (*couteau*) large (kitchen) knife; (*épée*) cutlass.

coutelier, -ière [kutəlje, jɛʀ] *nmf* (*fabricant, marchand*) cutler.

coutellerie [kutɛlʀi] *nf* (*industrie*) cutlery industry; (*atelier*) cutlery works; (*magasin*) cutlery shop, cutler's (shop); (*produits*) cutlery.

coûter [kute] (1) **1** *vi* **(a)** *[achat]* to cost. **combien ça coûte?** how much is it?, how much does it cost?; **ça coûte cher?** is it expensive?, does it cost a lot?; **ça m'a coûté 10 F** it cost me 10 francs; **les vacances, ça coûte!** holidays are expensive *ou* cost a lot!; **ça coûte une fortune** *ou* **les yeux de la tête** it costs a fortune *ou* the earth*; **ça va lui ~ cher** (*lit*) it'll cost him a lot; (*fig: erreur, impertinence*) it will cost him dear(ly); **ça coûtera ce que ça coûtera*** never mind the expense *ou* cost, blow the expense*; **tu pourrais le faire, pour ce que ça te coûte!** you could easily do it — it wouldn't make any difference to you *ou* it wouldn't put you to any trouble; **ça ne coûte rien d'essayer** it costs nothing to try.

(b) (*fig*) **cet aveu/ce renoncement m'a coûté** this confession/renouncement cost me dear; **cette démarche me coûte** this is a painful step for me (to take); **il m'en coûte de refuser** it pains *ou* grieves me to have to refuse; *V* **premier.**

(c) coûte que coûte at all costs, no matter what; **il faut y arriver coûte que coûte** we must get there at all costs.

2 *vt fatigue, larmes* to cost. **ça m'a coûté bien des mois de travail** it cost me many months' work; **ça lui a coûté la tête/la vie** it cost him his head/life.

coûteusement [kutøzmɑ̃] *adv* expensively.

coûteux, -euse [kutø, øz] *adj* costly, expensive; (*fig*) *aveu, renoncement* painful. **ce fut une erreur ~euse** it was a costly mistake *ou* a mistake that cost him (*ou* us *etc*) dear.

coutil [kuti] *nm [vêtements]* drill, twill; *[matelas]* ticking.

coutre [kutʀ(ə)] *nm* coulter.

coutume [kutym] *nf* **(a)** (*usage: gén, Jur*) custom; (*Jur: recueil*) customary.

(b) (*habitude*) **avoir ~ de** to be in the habit of; **plus/moins que de ~** more/less than usual; **comme de ~** as usual; **selon sa ~** as is his custom *ou* wont (*littér*), following his usual custom; *V* **fois.**

coutumier, -ière [kutymje, jɛʀ] **1** *adj* customary, usual. (*gén péj*) **il est ~ du fait** that is what he usually does, that's his usual trick*; *V* **droit**³. **2** *nm* (*Jur*) customary.

couture [kutyʀ] *nf* **(a)** (*action, activité, ouvrage*) sewing; (*confection*) dressmaking; (*profession*) women's fashions. **faire de la ~** to sew; *V* **haut, maison, point**².

(b) (*suite de points*) seam. **sans ~(s)** seamless; **faire une ~ à grands points** to tack *ou* baste a seam; **~ apparente** *ou* **sellier** topstitching, overstitching; **~ anglaise/plate** *ou* **rabattue** French/flat seam; **examiner** *ou* **regarder qch sous toutes les ~s** to examine sth from every angle; *V* **battre.**

(c) (*cicatrice*) scar.

(d) (*suture*) stitches.

couturé, e [kutyʀe] *adj visage* scarred.

couturier [kutyʀje] *nm* couturier, fashion designer.

couturière [kutyʀjɛʀ] *nf* **(a)** (*personne*) dressmaker; (*en atelier etc*) dressmaker, seamstress†. **(b)** (*Théât*) dress rehearsal.

couvain [kuvɛ̃] *nm* (*œufs*) brood; (*rayon*) brood cells.

couvaison [kuvɛzɔ̃] *nf* (*période*) incubation; (*action*) brooding, sitting.

couvée [kuve] *nf [poussins]* brood, clutch; *[œufs]* clutch; (*fig*) (*enfants*) brood.

couvent [kuvɑ̃] *nm* **(a)** *[sœurs]* convent, nunnery†; *[moines]* monastery. **entrer au ~** to enter a convent. **(b)** (*internat*) convent (school).

couventine [kuvɑ̃tin] *nf* (*religieuse*) conventual; (*jeune fille élevée au couvent*) convent schoolgirl.

couver [kuve] (1) **1** *vi [feu, incendie]* to smoulder; *[haine, passion]* to smoulder, simmer; *[émeute]* to be brewing; *[complot]* to be hatching. **~ sous la cendre** (*lit*) to smoulder under the embers; (*fig*) *[passion]* to smoulder, simmer; *[émeute]* to be brewing.

2 *vt* **(a)** *œufs [poule]* to sit on; *[appareil]* to hatch. (*emploi absolu*) **la poule était en train de ~** the hen was sitting on her eggs *ou* was brooding.

(b) (*fig*) *enfant* to be overcareful with; *maladie* to be sickening for, be getting; *vengeance* to brew, plot; *révolte* to plot. **enfant couvé par sa mère** child brought up by an overcautious *ou* overprotective mother; **~ qn/qch des yeux** *ou* **du regard** (*complaisance*) to look lovingly at sb/sth; (*convoitise*) to look longingly at sb/sth.

couvercle [kuvɛʀkl(ə)] *nm [casserole, boîte à biscuits, bocal]* lid; *[bombe aérosol]* cap, top; (*qui se visse*) (screw-)cap, (screw-)top; (*Tech*) *[piston]* cover.

couvert, e¹ [kuvɛʀ, ɛʀt(ə)] (*ptp de* **couvrir**) **1** *adj* **(a)** (*habillé*) covered (up). **il est trop ~ pour la saison** he's too wrapped up *ou* he's wearing too many clothes for the time of year; **cet enfant ne reste jamais ~ au lit** this child will never keep himself covered up in bed *ou* will never keep his bedcovers *ou* bedclothes on (him); **il est resté ~ dans l'église** he kept his hat on inside the church.

(b) ~ de covered in *ou* with; **il a le visage ~ de boutons** his face is covered in *ou* with spots; **des pics ~s de neige** snow-covered *ou* snow-clad (*littér*) peaks; **~ de chaume** *toit* thatched; *maison* thatch-roofed, thatched; **le rosier est ~ de fleurs** the rosebush is a mass of *ou* is covered in flowers.

(c) (*voilé*) *ciel* overcast, clouded over (*attrib*); *voix* hoarse. **par temps ~** when the sky is overcast; *V* **mot.**

(d) *rue, allée, cour* covered; *V* **marché.**

(e) (*protégé par un supérieur*) covered.

2 *nm* **(a)** (*ustensiles*) place setting. **une ménagère de 12 ~s** a canteen of 12 place settings; **leurs ~s sont en argent** their cutlery is silver; **j'ai sorti les ~s en argent** I've brought out the silver cutlery.

(b) (*à table*) **mettre le ~** to lay *ou* set the table; **mettre 4 ~s** to lay *ou* set 4 places, lay *ou* set the table for 4; **table de 4 ~s** table laid *ou* set for 4; **mets un ~ de plus** lay *ou* set another *ou* an extra place; **il a toujours son ~ mis chez nous** he can come and eat with us at any time, there's always a place for him at our table; **le vivre** *ou* **gîte et le ~** board and lodging.

(c) (*au restaurant*) cover charge.

(d) (*abri*) (*littér*) **sous le ~ d'un chêne** under the shelter of an oak tree; **à ~ de la pluie** sheltered from the rain; (*Mil*) **(être) à ~** (to be) under cover; (*Mil*) **se mettre à ~** to get under *ou* take cover.

(e) (*loc*) **se mettre à ~ (contre des réclamations)** to cover *ou* safeguard o.s. (against claims); **être à ~ des soupçons** to be safe from suspicion; **sous (le) ~ de** *prétexte* under cover of; **ils l'ont fait sous le ~ de leurs supérieurs** they did it by hiding behind the authority of their superiors; **sous (le) ~ de la plaisanterie** while trying to appear to be joking.

couverte² [kuvɛʀt(ə)] *nf* (*Tech*) glaze.

couverture [kuvɛʀtyʀ] *nf* **(a)** (*literie*) blanket. **~ de laine/chauffante** wool *ou* woollen/electric blanket; **~ de voyage** travelling rug; (*fig*) **amener** *ou* **tirer la ~ à soi** to take (all) the credit, get unfair recognition.

(b) (*toiture*) roofing. **~ de chaume** thatched roofing; **~ en tuiles** tiled roofing.

(c) *[cahier, livre]* cover; (*jaquette*) dust cover.

(d) (*Mil*) cover; (*fig: prétexte, paravent*) cover. **troupes de ~** covering troops; **~ aérienne** aerial cover.

(e) (*Fin*) cover, margin.

couveuse [kuvøz] *nf* (*poule*) sitter, brooder. **~ (artificielle)** incubator.

couvrant, e [kuvʀɑ̃, ɑ̃t] **1** *adj peinture* that covers well. **2 couvrante*** *nf* blanket, cover.

couvre- [kuvʀ(ə)] *préf V* **couvrir.**

couvreur [kuvʀœʀ] *nm* roofer.

couvrir [kuvʀiʀ] (18) **1** *vt* **(a)** (*gén*) *livre, meuble, sol, chargement* to cover (*de, avec* with); *casserole, récipient* to cover (*de, avec* with), put the lid on. **~ un toit d'ardoises/de chaume/de tuiles** to slate/thatch/tile a roof; **des tableaux couvraient tout un mur** pictures covered a whole wall; **~ le feu** to bank up the fire.

(b) (*habiller*) to cover. **couvre bien les enfants** wrap the children up well, cover the children up well; **une cape lui couvrait tout le corps** *ou* **le couvrait tout entier** he was completely covered in a cape; **un châle lui couvrait les épaules** her shoulders were covered with *ou* by a shawl, she had a shawl around *ou* over her shoulders.

(c) (*recouvrir de, parsemer de*) **~ qch/qn de** (*gén*) to cover sth/sb with *ou* in; **la rougeole l'avait couverte de boutons** her bout of measles had her covered in spots; **son mari l'avait couverte de bleus** her husband had bruised her all over *ou* had covered her in *ou* with bruises; **~ une femme de cadeaux** to shower a woman with gifts, shower gifts upon a woman; **~ qn de caresses/baisers** to cover *ou* shower sb with caresses/kisses; **~ qn d'injures/d'éloges** to shower sb with insults/praises, heap insults/praise upon sb; **cette aventure l'a couvert de ridicule** this affair has covered him with ridicule.

(d) (*cacher, masquer*) *son, voix* to drown; *mystère, énigme* to conceal. **le bruit de la rue couvrait la voix du conférencier** the noise from the street drowned the lecturer's voice; (*lit, fig*) **~ son jeu** to hold *ou* keep one's cards close to one's chest; **sa frugalité couvre une grande avarice** his frugality conceals great avarice; **~ qch du nom de charité** to pass sth off as charity, label sth charity.

(e) (*protéger*) to cover. **~ qn de son corps** to cover *ou* shield sb with one's body; (*Mil*) **~ la retraite** to cover one's retreat; (*fig*) **~ qn/les fautes de qn** to screen sb/sb's mistakes; (*fig*) **pour se ~ il a invoqué ...** to cover *ou* shield himself he referred to ... .

(f) (*Fin*) *frais, dépenses* to cover; *[assurance]* to cover.

(g) (*parcourir*) *kilomètres, distance* to cover.

(h) (*Zool*) *jument etc* to cover.

2 se couvrir *vpr* **(a)** *[arbre etc]* **se ~ de fleurs/feuilles au printemps** to come into bloom/leaf in the spring; **les prés se couvrent de fleurs** the meadows are becoming a mass of flowers; *[personne]* **se ~ de taches** to cover o.s. in splashes; **se ~ de boutons** to become covered in *ou* with spots; **se ~ de gloire** to cover o.s. with glory; **se ~ de honte/ridicule** to bring shame/ridicule upon o.s., cover o.s. with shame/ridicule.

(b) (*s'habiller*) to cover up, wrap up; (*mettre son chapeau*) to put on one's hat. **il fait froid, couvrez-vous bien** it's cold so wrap *ou* cover (yourself) up well.

(c) *[ciel]* to become overcast, cloud over. **le temps se couvre** the sky is *ou* it's becoming very overcast.

(d) (*Boxe, Escrime*) to cover.

3: (*hum*) **couvre-chef** *nm, pl* **couvre-chefs** hat, headgear (*U: hum*); **couvre-feu** *nm, pl* **couvre-feux** curfew; **couvre-lit** *nm, pl* **couvre-lits** bedspread, coverlet; **couvre-livre** *nm, pl* **couvre-livres** book cover; **couvre-pied(s)** *nm, pl* **couvre-pieds** quilt; **couvre-radiateur** *nm, pl* **couvre-radiateurs** shelf (*over a radiator*).

coxalgie [kɔksalʒi] *nf* coxalgia.

coyote [kɔjɔt] *nm* coyote, prairie wolf.

crabe [kʀɑb] *nm* **(a)** (*Zool*) crab. **marcher en ~** to walk crabwise *ou* crabways; *V* **panier. (b)** (*véhicule*) caterpillar-tracked vehicle.

crac [kʀak] *excl [bois, glace etc]* crack; *[étoffe]* rip. **tout à coup ~! tout est à recommencer** suddenly bang! and we're right back where we started.

crachat [kʀaʃa] *nm* **(a)** spit (*U*), spittle (*U*). **trottoir couvert de ~s** pavement spattered with spittle; **il a reçu un ~ dans l'œil** someone has spat in his eye. **(b)** (*: *plaque, insigne*) decoration.

craché, e* [kʀaʃe] (*ptp de* **cracher**) *adj*: **c'est son père tout ~** he's the spitting image of his father; **c'est lui tout ~** that's just like him, that's him all over*.

crachement [kʀaʃmɑ̃] *nm* **(a)** (*expectoration*) spitting (*U*) **~ de sang** spitting of blood; **il eut des ~s de sang** he had spasms of spitting blood *ou* of blood-spitting.

(b) (*projection*) *[flammes, vapeur]* burst; *[étincelles]* shower.

(c) *(bruit) [radio, mitrailleuses]* crackling (*U*), crackle.
cracher [kʀaʃe] (1) **1** *vi* **(a)** *(avec la bouche)* to spit. **rincez-vous la bouche et crachez** rinse (out) your mouth and spit (it) out; ~ **sur qn** (*lit*) to spit at sb; (*fig*) to spit on sb; **il ne crache pas sur le caviar*** he doesn't turn his nose up at caviar; **c'est comme si je crachais en l'air*** I'm banging *ou* it's like banging my head against a brick wall.
(b) *[stylo, plume]* to splutter, splotch; *[micro]* to crackle.
2 *vt* **(a)** *[personne] sang etc* to spit; *bouchée* to spit out; (*fig*) *injures* to spit (out); (‡) *argent* to cough up‡, stump up‡. ~ **ses poumons‡** to cough up one's lungs‡.
(b) *[canon] flammes* to spit (out); *projectiles* to spit out; *[cheminée, volcan, dragon]* to belch (out). **le moteur crachait des étincelles** the engine was sending out showers of sparks; **le robinet crachait une eau brunâtre** the tap was spitting out dirty brown water.
crachin [kʀaʃɛ̃] *nm* drizzle.
crachiner [kʀaʃine] (1) *vt* to drizzle.
crachoir [kʀaʃwaʀ] *nm* spittoon, cuspidor (*US*). (*fig*) **tenir le ~*** to hold the floor; (*fig*) **j'ai tenu le ~ à ma vieille tante tout l'après-midi** I had to (sit and) listen to my old aunt spouting all afternoon*.
crachotement [kʀaʃɔtmɑ̃] *nm* crackling (*U*), crackle.
crachoter [kʀaʃɔte] (1) *vi [haut-parleur, téléphone]* to crackle.
crack [kʀak] *nm* **(a)** *(poulain)* crack *ou* star horse. **(b)** (*: *as*) wizard*; *(en sport)* ace. **c'est un ~ au saut en longeur** he's an ace long jumper.
cracking [kʀakiŋ] *nm* (*Chim*) cracking.
cracra‡ [kʀakʀa] *adj*, **cradingue‡** [kʀadɛ̃g] *adj*, **crado‡** [kʀado] *adj* grotty‡ (*Brit*), shabby.
craie [kʀɛ] *nf* (*substance, bâtonnet*) chalk. ~ **de tailleur** tailor's chalk, French chalk; **écrire qch à la ~ sur un mur** to chalk sth up on a wall.
craindre [kʀɛ̃dʀ(ə)] (52) *vt* **(a)** *[personne]* to fear, be afraid of. **je ne crains pas la mort/la douleur** I do not fear *ou* I'm not afraid of *ou* I have no fear of death/pain; **ne craignez rien** don't be afraid *ou* frightened; **oui, je le crains!** yes, I'm afraid so! *ou* I fear so!; **il sait se faire ~** he knows how to make himself feared, he knows how to make people fear him *ou* put people in fear of him.
(b) ~ **de faire qch** to be afraid of doing sth; **il craint de se faire mal** he's afraid of hurting himself; **je ne crains pas de dire que ...** I am not afraid of saying that ...; **je crains d'avoir bientôt à partir** I fear *ou* I'm afraid I may have to leave soon; **craignant de manquer le train, il se hâta** he hurried along, afraid of missing *ou* afraid (that) he might miss the train, he made haste lest he miss (*frm*) *ou* for fear of missing the train.
(c) ~ **que: je crains qu'il (n')attrape froid** I'm afraid that *ou* I fear that he might catch cold; **ne craignez-vous pas qu'il arrive?** aren't you afraid he'll come? *ou* he might come?; **je crains qu'il (ne) se soit perdu** I'm afraid that he might *ou* may have got lost; **il est à ~ que ...** it is to be feared that ...; (*iro*) **je crains que vous (ne) vous trompiez, ma chère** I fear you are mistaken, my dear; **elle craignait qu'il ne se blesse** she feared *ou* was afraid that he would *ou* might hurt himself.
(d) ~ **pour** *vie, réputation, personne* to fear for.
(e) *[aliment, produit]* ~ **le froid/l'eau bouillante** to be easily damaged by (the) cold/by boiling water; **'craint l'humidité/la chaleur'** 'keep *ou* store in a dry place/cool place', 'do not expose to a damp atmosphere/to heat'; **c'est un vêtement qui ne craint pas/qui craint** it's a hard-wearing *ou* sturdy/delicate garment; **ces animaux craignent la chaleur** these animals can't stand heat.
crainte [kʀɛ̃t] *nf* **(a)** fear. **la ~ de la maladie *ou* d'être malade l'arrête** fear of illness *ou* of being ill stops him; **il a la ~ du gendarme** he is in fear of the police, he is afraid of *ou* he fears the police; **soyez sans ~, n'ayez ~** have no fear, never fear; **j'ai des ~s à son sujet** I'm worried about him; **sans ~** (*adj*) without fear, fearless; (*adv*) without fear, fearlessly; **avec ~** fearfully, full of fear; **la ~ qu'on ne les entende** the fear that they might be overheard; (*Prov*) **la ~ est le commencement de la sagesse** only the fool knows no fear.
(b) (*loc*) **dans la ~ de, (par) ~ de** for fear of; **de ~ d'une erreur** for fear of there being a mistake, lest there be a mistake (*frm*); **(par) ~ d'être suivi, il courut** he ran for fear of being followed *ou* lest he should be followed (*frm*) *ou* fearing that he might be followed (*frm*); **de ~ que** for fear that, fearing that; **de ~ qu'on ne le suive, il courut** he ran for fear of being followed *ou* fearing that he might be followed *ou* lest he be followed (*frm*).
craintif, -ive [kʀɛ̃tif, iv] *adj personne, animal, caractère* timorous, timid; *regard, ton, geste* timid.
craintivement [kʀɛ̃tivmɑ̃] *adv agir, parler* timorously, timidly.
cramer‡ [kʀame] (1) *vi [maison]* to be burnt (up), go up in flames; *[mobilier]* to go up in flames *ou* smoke.
cramoisi, e [kʀamwazi] *adj* crimson.
crampe [kʀɑ̃p] *nf* cramp. **avoir une ~ au mollet** to have cramp (*Brit*) *ou* a cramp (*US*) in one's calf; ~ **d'estomac** stomach cramp; (*hum*) **la ~ de l'écrivain** writer's cramp (*hum*).
crampon [kʀɑ̃pɔ̃] *nm* **(a)** (*Tech*) cramp (iron), clamp. **(b)** *[chaussure de football]* stud; *[fer à cheval]* calk. *[alpiniste]* ~ **(à glace)** crampon. **(c)** (*Bot*) tendril. **(d)** (*: *personne*) clinging bore. **elle est ~** she clings like a leech, she's a clinging bore.
cramponner [kʀɑ̃pɔne] (1) **1** *vt* **(a)** (*Tech*) to cramp (together), clamp (together).
(b) (**fig*) to cling to.
2 se cramponner *vpr* (*pour ne pas tomber*) to hold on, hang on. (*fig*) **elle se cramponne** (*ne vous lâche pas*) she clings; (*ne veut pas mourir*) she's holding on (to life); **se ~ à** *branche, volant, bras* to cling (on) to, clutch, hold on to; *personne* (*lit*) to cling (on) to; (*fig*) *vie, espoir, personne* to cling to.
cran [kʀɑ̃] *nm* **(a)** (*pour accrocher, retenir*) *[pièce dentée, crémaillère]* notch; *[arme à feu]* catch; *[ceinture, courroie]* hole. **hausser un rayon de plusieurs ~s** to raise a shelf a few notches *ou* holes; ~ **de sûreté** safety catch; ~ **d'arrêt** *V* **couteau.**
(b) (*servant de repère*) (*Couture, Typ*) nick. ~ **de mire** bead.
(c) *[cheveux]* wave. **le coiffeur lui avait fait un ~ *ou* des ~s** the hairdresser had put her hair in waves.
(d) (*: *courage*) guts*.
(e) (*loc*) **monter/descendre d'un ~** (*dans la hiérarchie*) to move up/come down a rung *ou* peg; **il est monté/descendu d'un ~ dans mon estime** he has gone up/down a notch *ou* peg in my estimation; **être à ~** to be very edgy.
crâne[1] [kʀɑn] *nm* (*Anat*) skull, cranium (*T*); (*fig*) head. **avoir mal au ~*** to have an awful head*; (*fig*) **avoir le ~ étroit* *ou* dur*** to be thick(skulled)*; *V* **bourrage, bourrer, fracture.**
crâne[2]† [kʀɑn] *adj* gallant.
crânement† [kʀɑnmɑ̃] *adv* gallantly.
crâner* [kʀɑne] (1) *vi* to swank*, show off*. **ce n'est pas la peine de ~** it's nothing to swank* *ou* show off* about.
crânerie† [kʀɑnʀi] *nf* gallantry.
crâneur, -euse* [kʀɑnœʀ, øz] *nm,f* swank*, show-off*. **faire le ~** to swank* *ou* show off*; **elle est un peu ~euse** she's a bit of a show-off*.
crânien, -ienne [kʀɑnjɛ̃, jɛn] *adj* cranial; *V* **boîte.**
craniologie [kʀanjɔlɔʒi] *nf* craniology.
cranter [kʀɑ̃te] (1) *vt* (*Tech*) *pignon, roue* to put notches in. **tige crantée** notched stem.
crapaud [kʀapo] **1** *nm* **(a)** (*Zool*) toad; *V* **bave, fauteuil. (b)** (*: *gamin*) brat*. **2: crapaud de mer** angler(-fish).
crapouillot [kʀapujo] *nm* (*Hist Mil*) trench mortar.
crapule [kʀapyl] *nf* (*personne*) villain; (††: *racaille*) riffraff, scum*.
crapulerie [kʀapylʀi] *nf* **(a)** (*rare: caractère*) villainy, vile nature. **(b)** (*acte*) villainy.
crapuleusement [kʀapyløzmɑ̃] *adv agir* with villainy.
crapuleux, -euse [kʀapylø, øz] *adj action* villainous; *vie* dissolute; *V* **crime.**
craquage [kʀakaʒ] *nm* (*Chim*) cracking.
craque‡ [kʀak] *nf* whopper‡, whopping lie*.
craqueler [kʀakle] (4) **1** *vt vernis, faïence, terre [usure, âge]* to crack; (*Tech*) *[artisan]* to crackle. **2 se craqueler** *vpr [vernis, faïence, terre]* to crack.
craquellement [kʀakɛlmɑ̃] *nm* cracking.
craquelure [kʀaklyʀ] *nf [porcelaine]* crackle (*U*); *[tableau]* craquelure (*U*). **couvert de ~s** a mass of *ou* covered in cracks.
craquement [kʀakmɑ̃] *nm* (*bruit*) *[arbre, branche qui se rompt]* crack, cracking sound, snap; *[plancher, boiserie]* creak, creaking (*U*); *[feuilles sèches, neige]* crackling (*U*), crunching (*U*); *[chaussures]* squeaking (*U*). **le ~ continuel des arbres/de la banquise** the constant creaking of the trees/iceberg.
craquer [kʀake] (1) **1** *vi* **(a)** (*produire un bruit*) *[parquet]* to creak, squeak; *[feuilles mortes]* to crackle; *[neige]* to crunch; *[chaussures]* to squeak; *[biscuit]* to crunch. **faire ~ ses doigts** to crack one's fingers; **faire ~ une allumette** to strike a match.
(b) (*céder*) *[bas]* to rip, go* (*Brit*); *[bois, couche de glace etc]* to crack; *[branche]* to crack, snap. **veste qui craque aux coutures** jacket which is coming apart *ou* going* (*Brit*) at the seams; *V* **plein.**
(c) (*s'écrouler*) *[entreprise, gouvernement]* to be falling apart (at the seams), be on the verge of collapse.
2 *vt* **(a)** *pantalon* to rip, split. ~ **un bas*** to rip *ou* tear a stocking.
(b) ~ **une allumette** to strike a match.
craqueter [kʀakte] (4) *vi [parquet]* to creak; *[brindilles]* to crackle.
crasse [kʀas] **1** *nf* **(a)** (*saleté*) grime, filth. **(b)** (*: *sale tour*) dirty trick*. **faire une ~ à qn** to play a dirty trick on sb*. **(c)** (*Tech*) (*scorie*) dross, scum, slag; (*résidus*) scale. **2** *adj ignorance, bêtise* crass; *paresse* unashamed.
crasseux, -euse [kʀasø, øz] *adj* grimy, filthy.
crassier [kʀasje] *nm* slag heap.
cratère [kʀatɛʀ] *nm* crater.
cravache [kʀavaʃ] *nf* (riding) crop. (*fig*) **mener qn à la ~** to drive sb ruthlessly.
cravacher [kʀavaʃe] (1) **1** *vt cheval* to use the crop on. **2** *vi* (*) (*foncer*) to belt along*; (*pour finir un travail*) to work like mad*, pull out all the stops*.
cravate [kʀavat] *nf* **(a)** *[chemise]* tie. (*hum*) ~ **de chanvre** hangman's rope; ~ **de commandeur de la Légion d'honneur** ribbon of commander of the Legion of Honour; *V* **épingle, jeter. (b)** (*Lutte*) headlock. **(c)** (*Naut*) sling.
cravater [kʀavate] (1) *vt* **(a)** (*lit*) *personne* to put a tie on. **cravaté de neuf** wearing a new tie; **se ~** to put one's *ou* a tie on.
(b) (*prendre au collet*) (*gén*) to grab round the neck, put a stranglehold on; (*Lutte*) to put in a headlock.
(c) (‡: *duper*) ~ **qn** to take sb for a ride‡; **se faire ~** to be *ou* get taken for a ride‡.
crawl [kʀol] *nm* crawl (*swimming*). **nager le ~** to do *ou* swim the crawl.
crawler [kʀole] (1) *vi* to do *ou* swim the crawl. **dos crawlé** backstroke.
crayeux, -euse [kʀɛjø, øz] *adj terrain, substance* chalky; *teint* chalk-white.
crayon [kʀɛjɔ̃] **1** *nm* **(a)** (*pour écrire etc*) pencil. **écrire au ~** to write with a pencil; **écrivez cela au ~** write that in pencil; **notes au ~** pencilled notes; **avoir le ~ facile** to be a good drawer, be good at drawing; *V* **coup.**

(b) (*bâtonnet*) pencil.
(c) (*Art: dessin*) pencil drawing, pencil sketch.
2: crayon à bille ball-point pen, Biro ® (*Brit*); **crayon de couleur** crayon, colouring pencil; **crayon gras** soft lead pencil; **crayon hémostatique** styptic pencil; **crayon au nitrate d'argent** silver-nitrate pencil, caustic pencil; **crayon noir** lead pencil; **crayon de rouge à lèvres** lipstick; **crayon à sourcils** eyebrow pencil; **crayon pour les yeux** eyeliner pencil.

crayonnage [kʀɛjɔnaʒ] *nm* (*dessin*) (pencil) drawing, sketch.

crayonner [kʀɛjɔne] (1) *vt notes* to scribble, jot down (in pencil); *dessin* to sketch. **ayant crayonné rapidement quelques notes** having hastily scribbled *ou* jotted down a few pencil notes, having hastily pencilled a few notes; **il crayonna rapidement la silhouette de l'arbre** he made a rapid (pencil) sketch of the tree's outline, he rapidly sketched the outline of the tree.

créance [kʀeɑ̃s] *nf* **(a)** (*Fin, Jur*) (financial) claim, debt (*seen from the creditor's point of view*); (*titre*) letter of credit. ~ **hypothécaire** mortgage loan (*seen from the creditor's point of view*); *V* **lettre.**
(b) († *ou littér: crédit, foi*) credence. **donner ~ à qch** (*rendre croyable*) to lend credibility to sth; (*ajouter foi à*) to give *ou* attach credence to sth (*littér*).

créancier, -ière [kʀeɑ̃sje, jɛʀ] *nm,f* creditor.

créateur, -trice [kʀeatœʀ, tʀis] **1** *adj* creative. **2** *nm,f* (*gén, Rel*) creator. **le C~** the Creator.

création [kʀeɑsjɔ̃] *nf* **(a)** (*V* **créer**) creation, creating; first production.
(b) (*chose créée*) (*Théât: représentation*) first production; (*Comm*) product; (*Art, Haute Couture*) creation. (*Rel*) **la ~** the Creation; **cette ~ de Topaze par Jouvet est vraiment remarquable** Jouvet's creation of the role of Topaze is truly remarkable.

créativité [kʀeativite] *nf* creativeness, creativity; (*Ling*) creativity.

créature [kʀeatyʀ] *nf* (*gén*) creature.

crécelle [kʀesɛl] *nf* rattle; *V* **voix.**

crèche [kʀɛʃ] *nf* **(a)** (*Rel: de Noël*) crib. **(b)** (*établissement*) crèche, day nursery. **(c)** (‡: *chambre, logement*) pad‡.

crécher‡ [kʀeʃe] (6) *vi* to hang out‡. **je ne sais pas où ~ cette nuit** I don't know where I'm going to kip down‡ tonight.

crédence [kʀedɑ̃s] *nf* **(a)** (*desserte*) credence. **(b)** (*Rel*) credence (table), credenza.

crédibilité [kʀedibilite] *nf* credibility.

crédit [kʀedi] *nm* **(a)** (*paiement échelonné, différé*) credit. **12 mois de ~** 12 months' credit; **faire ~ à qn** to give sb credit; **faites-moi ~, je vous paierai la semaine prochaine** let me have (it on) credit — I'll pay you next week; **'la maison ne fait pas (de) ~'** 'we are unable to give credit to our customers', 'no credit is given here'; **acheter/vendre qch à ~** to buy/sell sth on credit *ou* on easy terms; **possibilités de ~** easy *ou* credit terms available; **ces gens qui achètent tout à ~** these people who buy everything on credit *ou* on H.P. (*Brit*) *ou* on tick* (*surtout Brit*) *ou* on time (*US*); **vente à ~** selling on easy terms *ou* on credit.
(b) (*prêt*) credit. **établissement de ~** credit institution; **l'ouverture d'un ~** the granting of credit; **~ bancaire** bank credit; **~ hypothécaire** mortgage; **~ bail** leasing; *V* **lettre.**
(c) (*dans une raison sociale*) bank. **C~ Agricole/Municipal** Agricultural/Municipal Savings Bank.
(d) (*excédent d'un compte*) credit. **porter une somme au ~ de qn** to credit sb *ou* sb's account with a sum, credit a sum to sb *ou* sb's account.
(e) (*Pol: gén pl: fonds*) **~s** funds. **~s budgétaires** budget allocation; **~s extraordinaires** extraordinary funds.
(f) (*Can Univ: unité de valeur*) credit (*US, Can*).
(g) (*frm*) **firme/client qui a du ~** creditworthy firm/client; **cette théorie connaît un grand ~** this theory is very widely accepted; **ça donne du ~ à ce qu'il affirme** that lends credit to what he says; **faire ~ à l'avenir** to put one's trust in the future, have faith in the future; **bonne action à mettre** *ou* **porter au ~ de qn** good deed which is to sb's credit *ou* which counts in sb's favour; **perdre tout ~ auprès de qn** to lose sb's confidence; **trouver ~ auprès de qn** *[racontars]* to find credence with sb (*frm*); *[personne]* to win sb's confidence; **il a utilisé son ~ auprès de lui (pour)** he used his credit with him (to).

créditer [kʀedite] (1) *vt* **(a)** (*Fin*) **~ qn/un compte de** *somme* to credit sb/an account with. **(b)** (*Sport*) **être crédité de** *temps* to be credited with.

créditeur, -trice [kʀeditœʀ, tʀis] **1** *adj* in credit (*attrib*). **compte/solde ~** credit account/balance. **2** *nm,f* customer in credit.

créditiste [kʀeditist(ə)] (*Can*) **1** *adj*: **le Parti ~** the Creditiste Party (*Can*). **2** *nmf* Creditiste (*Can*). **le Ralliement des ~s** Social Credit Rally (*Can*).

credo [kʀedo] *nm* **(a)** (*Rel*) **le C~** the (Apostle's) Creed. **(b)** (*principes*) credo, creed.

crédule [kʀedyl] *adj* credulous, gullible.

crédulité [kʀedylite] *nf* credulity, gullibility.

créer [kʀee] (1) *vt* **(a)** (*gén*) to create. **le pouvoir/la joie de ~** the power/joy of creation; **se ~ une clientèle** to build up a clientèle; **~ des ennuis/difficultés à qn** to create problems/difficulties for sb, cause sb problems/difficulties; *V* **fonction. (b)** (*Théât*) *rôle* to create; *pièce* to produce (for the first time).

crémaillère [kʀemajɛʀ] *nf* **(a)** *[cheminée]* trammel. (*fig*) **pendre la ~** to have a house-warming (party). **(b)** (*Rail, Tech*) rack. **chemin de fer à ~** rack railway, cog railway; **engrenage/direction à ~** rack-and-pinion gear/steering.

crémant [kʀemɑ̃] *adj, nm champagne* cremant.

crémation [kʀemɑsjɔ̃] *nf* cremation.

crématoire [kʀematwaʀ] **1** *adj* crematory; *V* **four. 2** *nm* crematorium, crematory (*furnace*).

crème [kʀɛm] **1** *nf* **(a)** (*Culin*) (*produit laitier*) cream; (*peau sur le lait*) skin; (*entremets*) cream dessert. (*liqueur*) **~ de bananes/cacao** crème de bananes/cacao; **fraises à la ~** strawberries and cream; **gâteau à la ~** cream cake; *V* **chou**[1], **fromage** *etc.*
(b) (*produit pour la toilette, le nettoyage*) cream. **~ de beauté** beauty cream; **~ pour les chaussures/pour le visage** shoe/face cream; **les ~s de (la maison) X** beauty creams from *ou* by X.
(c) (*fig: les meilleurs*) **la ~** the (real) cream, the crème de la crème; **c'est la ~ des pères** he's the best of (all) fathers; **ses amis ce n'est pas la ~** his friends aren't exactly the cream of society *ou* the crème de la crème.
2 *adj inv* cream(-coloured).
3 *nm* (*café crème*) white coffee (*surtout Brit*), coffee with milk *ou* cream.
4: crème anglaise (egg) custard; **crème anti-rides** anti-wrinkle cream; **crème au beurre** butter cream; **crème brûlée** crème brûlée; **crème au caramel** crème caramel, caramel cream *ou* custard; **crème Chantilly** = **crème fouettée; crème démaquillante** cleansing cream, make-up removing cream; **crème fond de teint** foundation cream; **crème fouettée** whipped cream; **crème glacée** ice cream; **crème grasse** dry-skin cream; **crème hydratante** moisturizing cream, moisturizer; **crème pâtissière** confectioner's custard; **crème à raser** shaving cream; **crème renversée** cream mould.

crémerie [kʀɛmʀi] *nf* (*magasin*) dairy; (*tearoom*) teashop. **changeons de ~*** let's push off* somewhere else, let's take our custom elsewhere! (*hum*).

crémeux, -euse [kʀemø, øz] *adj* creamy.

crémier [kʀemje] *nm* dairyman.

crémière [kʀemjɛʀ] *nf* dairywoman.

crémone [kʀemɔn] *nf* espagnolette bolt.

créneau, *pl* **~x** [kʀeno] *nm* **(a)** *[rempart]* crenel, crenelle; (*Mil*) *[tranchée]* slit.
(b) (*Aut*) **faire un ~** to reverse into a parking space (*between two cars*); **j'ai raté mon ~** I've parked badly.
(c) (*espace libre*) *[horaire, marché commercial]* gap; *[programmes radiophoniques]* slot.

crénelage [kʀɛnlaʒ] *nm* (*Tech*) milling.

crénelé, e [kʀɛnle] (*ptp de* **créneler**) *adj mur, arête* crenellated; *feuille, bordure* scalloped, crenate (*Bot*).

créneler [kʀɛnle] (4) *vt* **(a)** *muraille* to crenellate, crenel; *tranchée* to make a slit in. **(b)** *roue* to notch; *pièce de monnaie* to mill.

crénom [kʀenɔ̃] *excl*: **~ de nom!†** confound it!, dash it all! (*surtout Brit*).

créole [kʀeɔl] **1** *adj accent, parler* creole; *V* **riz. 2** *nm* (*Ling*) Creole. **3** *nmf* Creole.

créosote [kʀeozɔt] *nf* creosote.

crêpage [kʀɛpaʒ] *nm* **(a)** (*V* **crêper**) backcombing; crimping. **(b) ~ de chignon*** set-to*, shindy*.

crêpe[1] [kʀɛp] *nf* (*Culin*) pancake. **faire sauter une ~** to toss a pancake; **elle l'a retourné comme une ~*** she made him make an about-turn *ou* a volte-face.

crêpe[2] [kʀɛp] *nm* **(a)** (*Tex*) crepe, crêpe, crape. **~ de Chine** crepe de Chine.
(b) (*noir: de deuil*) black mourning crepe. **voile de ~** mourning veil; **porter un ~** (*au bras*) to wear a black armband; (*autour du chapeau*) to wear a black hatband; (*aux cheveux, au revers*) to wear a black ribbon.
(c) (*matière*) **semelles (de) ~** crepe (rubber) soles.

crêper [kʀepe] (1) **1** *vt* **(a)** *cheveux* to backcomb. **(b)** (*Tex*) to crimp. **2 se crêper** *vpr [cheveux]* to crimp, frizz. **se ~ le chignon*** to tear each other's hair out, have a set-to*.

crêperie [kʀɛpʀi] *nf* pancake shop.

crépi, e [kʀepi] (*ptp de* **crépir**) *adj, nm* roughcast.

crépir [kʀepiʀ] (2) *vt* to roughcast.

crépissage [kʀepisaʒ] *nm* roughcasting.

crépitation [kʀepitɑsjɔ̃] *nf [feu, électricité]* crackling. (*Méd*) **~ osseuse** crepitus; **~ pulmonaire** crepitations.

crépitement [kʀepitmɑ̃] *nm* (*V* **crépiter**) crackling; sputtering, spluttering; rattle; patter.

crépiter [kʀepite] (1) *vi [feu, électricité]* to crackle; *[chandelle, friture]* to sputter, splutter; *[mitrailleuse]* to rattle out; *[grésil]* to rattle, patter. **les applaudissements crépitèrent** a ripple of applause broke out.

crépon [kʀepɔ̃] *nm* seersucker.

crépu, e [kʀepy] *adj cheveux* frizzy, woolly, fuzzy.

crépusculaire [kʀepyskylɛʀ] *adj* (*littér, Zool*) crepuscular. **lumière ~** twilight glow.

crépuscule [kʀepyskyl] *nm* (*lit*) twilight, dusk; (*fig*) twilight.

crescendo [kʀeʃɛndo] **1** *adv* **(a)** (*Mus*) crescendo.
(b) aller ~ *[vacarme, acclamations]* to rise in a crescendo, grow louder and louder, crescendo; *[colère, émotion]* to grow *ou* become ever greater.
2 *nm* (*Mus*) crescendo. **le ~ de sa colère/de son émotion** the rising tide of his anger/emotion.

cresson [kʀesɔ̃] *nm*: **~ (de fontaine)** watercress.

cressonnière [kʀesɔnjɛʀ] *nf* watercress bed.

Crésus [kʀezys] *n* Croesus; *V* **riche.**

crétacé, e [kʀetase] **1** *adj* Cretaceous. **2** *nm*: **le ~** the Cretaceous period.

crête [kʀɛt] *nf* **(a)** (*Zool*) *[coq]* comb; *[oiseau]* crest; *[batracien]* horn. **~ de coq** cockscomb.
(b) (*arête*) *[mur]* top; *[toit]* ridge; *[montagne]* ridge, crest; *[vague]* crest; *[graphique]* peak. **la ~ du tibia** the edge *ou* crest (*T*) of the shin, the shin; (*Géog*) **(ligne de) ~** watershed.

Crète [kʀɛt] *nf* Crete.

crétin, e [kʀetɛ̃, in] **1** *adj* (*péj*) cretinous*, idiotic, moronic*. **2** *nm,f* (*péj*) idiot, moron*, cretin*; (*Méd*) cretin.

crétinerie [kʀetinʀi] *nf* **(a)** (*U*) idiocy, stupidity. **(b)** idiotic *ou* stupid thing, idiocy.
crétinisme [kʀetinism(ə)] *nm* (*Méd*) cretinism; (*péj*) idiocy, stupidity.
crétois, e [kʀetwa, waz] **1** *adj* Cretan. **2** *nm* (*Ling*) Cretan. **3** *nm,f*: **C~(e)** Cretan.
cretonne [kʀətɔn] *nf* cretonne.
creusage [kʀøzaʒ] *nm*, **creusement** [kʀøzmɑ̃] *nm* [*fondations*] digging; [*canal*] digging, cutting.
creuser [kʀøze] (1) **1** *vt* **(a)** (*évider*) *bois, falaise* to hollow (out); *sol, roc* to make *ou* dig a hole in, dig out; (*au marteau-piqueur*) to drill a hole in. **~ la neige de ses mains nues** to dig into the snow with one's bare hands; **il a fallu ~ beaucoup** *ou* **profond** we (*ou* he *etc*) had to dig deep.
(b) *puits* to sink, bore; *fondations, mine* to dig; *canal* to dig, cut; *tranchée, fosse* to dig (out); *sillon* to plough; *trou* (*gén*) to dig, make; (*au marteau-piqueur*) to drill, bore; *tunnel* to make, bore, dig. **~ un tunnel sous une montagne** to bore *ou* drive a tunnel under a mountain; (*fig*) **~ sa propre tombe** to dig one's own grave; (*fig*) **ça a creusé un abîme** *ou* **un fossé entre eux** that has created *ou* thrown a great gulf between them; (*fig*) **~ son sillon**† to plough one's own furrow.
(c) (*fig: approfondir*) *problème, sujet, idée* to go into (deeply *ou* thoroughly), look into (closely). **c'est une idée à ~** it's something to be gone into (more deeply *ou* thoroughly), it's an idea we (*ou* they *etc*) should pursue.
(d) (*fig*) **la mer se creuse** there's a swell coming on; **la fatigue lui creusait les joues** his face looked gaunt *ou* hollow with tiredness; **visage creusé de rides** face furrowed with wrinkles; **~ les reins** to draw o.s. up, throw out one's chest; **la promenade, ça creuse (l'estomac)*** walking gives you a real appetite; **se ~ (la cervelle** *ou* **la tête)*** to rack *ou* cudgel one's brains; **il ne s'est pas beaucoup creusé!*** he didn't overtax himself!, he hasn't knocked himself out!*
2 *vi*: **~ dans la terre/la neige** to dig *ou* burrow into the soil/snow.
creuset [kʀøzɛ] *nm* **(a)** (*Chim, Ind*) crucible. **le ~ d'un haut-fourneau** the heart *ou* crucible of a blast furnace; **~ de verrerie** glassmaker's crucible.
(b) (*fig*) (*lieu de brassage*) melting pot; (*littér: épreuve*) crucible (*littér*), test. **le ~ de la souffrance** the test of suffering.
creux, -euse [kʀø, øz] **1** *adj* **(a)** (*évidé*) *arbre, tige, dent* hollow; (*fig*) *toux, voix* hollow, deep; *son* hollow; *estomac* empty. (*fig*) **j'ai la tête** *ou* **la cervelle ~euse** my mind's a blank, I feel quite empty-headed; **travailler le ventre** *ou* **l'estomac ~** to work on an empty stomach; **avoir l'estomac** *ou* **le ventre ~** to feel empty *ou* ravenous; *V* **nez, sonner.**
(b) (*concave*) *surface* concave, hollow; *yeux* deep-set, sunken; *joue* gaunt, hollow; *visage* gaunt. **aux yeux ~** hollow-eyed; *V* **assiette, chemin.**
(c) (*vide de sens*) *paroles* empty, hollow, meaningless; *idées* barren, futile; *raisonnement* weak, flimsy.
(d) les jours ~ slack days; **les heures ~euses** (*gén*) slack periods; (*pour électricité, téléphone etc*) off-peak periods; *V* **classe.**
2 *nm* **(a)** (*cavité*) [*arbre*] hollow, hole; [*rocher, dent*] cavity, hole. (*fig*) **avoir un ~ dans l'estomac** to feel empty *ou* ravenous.
(b) (*dépression*) hollow. **un ~ boisé** a wooded hollow; **présenter des ~ et des bosses** to be full of bumps and holes *ou* hollows; **le ~ de la main** the hollow of one's hand; **des écureuils qui mangent dans le ~ de la main** squirrels which eat out of one's hand; **le ~ de l'aisselle** the armpit; **le ~ de l'estomac** the pit of the stomach; **le ~ de l'épaule** the hollow of one's shoulder; **au ~ des reins** in the small of one's back; *V* **gravure.**
(c) (*fig: activité réduite*) slack period. **après Noël, les ventes connaissent le ~ de janvier** after Christmas, there's a slackening-off in sales in January *ou* sales go through the January slack period.
(d) (*Naut*) [*voile*] belly; [*vague*] trough. **il y avait une mer de 2 mètres de ~** there were 2-metre high seas *ou* waves; (*fig*) **il est dans le ~ de la vague** his fortunes are at their lowest ebb.
crevaison [kʀəvɛzɔ̃] *nf* (*Aut*) puncture (*Brit*), flat.
crevant, e‡ [kʀəvɑ̃, ɑ̃t] *adj* (*fatigant*) killing*, gruelling; (*amusant*) priceless*, killing*. **ce travail est ~** this work is killing* *ou* really wears you out; **c'était ~!** it was priceless!* *ou* a scream!*
crevard, e‡ [kʀəvaʀ, aʀd(ə)] *nm,f* (*goinfre*) guzzler‡, greedy beggar*; (*crève-la-faim*) down-and-out. (*moribond*) **c'est un ~** he's a goner*.
crevasse [kʀəvas] *nf* [*mur, rocher*] crack, fissure, crevice; [*sol*] crack, fissure; [*glacier*] crevasse; [*peau*] break (in the skin), crack. **avoir des ~s aux mains** to have chapped hands.
crevassé, e [kʀəvase] (*ptp de* **crevasser**) *adj sol* fissured, with cracks; *peau* chapped. **glacier très ~** glacier with a lot of crevasses.
crevasser [kʀəvase] (1) **1** *vt sol* to cause cracks *ou* fissures in, crack; *mains* to chap. **2 se crevasser** *vpr* [*sol*] to crack, become cracked; [*mains*] to chap, become *ou* get chapped.
crève‡ [kʀɛv] *nf* (*rhume*) (bad) cold. **attraper la ~** to catch one's death* (of cold).
crève- [kʀɛv] *préf V* **crever.**
crevé, e [kʀəve] (*ptp de* **crever**) **1** *adj* **(a)** *pneu* burst, punctured (*Brit*). **(b)** (‡) (*mort*) dead; (*fatigué*) fagged out‡, dead*, dead-beat‡. **2** *nm* (*Couture*) slash. **des manches à ~s** slashed sleeves.
crever [kʀəve] (5) **1** *vt* **(a)** (*percer*) *pneu* to burst, puncture (*Brit*); *barrage, ballon* to burst. **~ les yeux à qn** (*intentionnellement*) to gouge (out) *ou* put out sb's eyes; (*accidentellement*) to blind sb (in both eyes); **des débris de verre lui ont crevé un œil** broken glass blinded him in one eye; **j'ai un pneu (de) crevé** I've got a flat (tyre) *ou* a puncture (*Brit*); (*fig*) **~ le cœur à qn** to break sb's heart; (*fig*) **cela crève les yeux** it's as plain as the nose on your face; (*fig*) **cela te crève les yeux!** it's staring you in the face!
(b) (*: *exténuer*) **~ qn** [*personne*] to wear sb out, work sb to death*; [*tâche, marche*] to wear sb out, fag sb out‡, kill sb*; **~ un cheval** to ride *ou* work a horse into the ground *ou* to death; **se ~ la santé** *ou* **la peau‡ (à faire)** to wear o.s. to a shadow (doing), ruin one's health (doing); **se ~ (au travail)** (*gén*) to work o.s. to death; [*ménagère etc*] to work one's fingers to the bone*.
(c) (‡) **~ la faim** to be starving* *ou* famished*; **on la crève ici!** they starve us here!
2 *vi* **(a)** (*éclater, s'ouvrir*) [*pneu*] to puncture (*Brit*), burst; [*sac, abcès*] to burst. **les nuages crevèrent** the clouds burst, the heavens opened; (*Culin*) **faire ~ du riz** to boil rice until the grains burst *ou* split.
(b) (*péj: être plein de*) **~ de santé** to be bursting with health; **~ de graisse** to be enormously fat; **~ d'orgueil** to be bursting *ou* bloated with pride; **~ de jalousie** to be full of jealousy, be bursting with jealousy; **il en crevait de dépit** he was full of resentment about it; *V* **rire.**
(c) (*mourir*) [*animal, plante*] to die (off); (‡) [*personne*] to die, kick the bucket‡, snuff it‡ (*Brit*). **un chien crevé** a dead dog; **~ de faim/froid‡** to starve/freeze to death; **~ de soif‡** to die of thirst; (*fig*) **~ de: on crève de froid ici*** we are freezing here, it's perishing cold here*; **on crève de chaud ici*** it's boiling in here*; **je crève de faim*** I'm starving* *ou* famished* *ou* ravenous; **je crève de soif*** I'm dying of thirst*, I'm parched*; **~ d'ennui*** to be bored to tears *ou* death, be bored out of one's mind*.
(d) (*Aut etc*) to have a puncture (*Brit*), have a burst *ou* flat tyre. **faire 100 km sans ~** to drive 100 km without a puncture (*Brit*) *ou* flat.
3: crève-cœur *nm inv* heartbreak; **crève-la-faim** *nmf inv* down-and-out.
crevette [kʀəvɛt] *nf*: **~ (rose)** prawn; **~ grise** shrimp; *V* **filet.**
crevettier [kʀəvetje] *nm* (*filet*) shrimp net; (*bateau*) shrimp boat.
cri [kʀi] **1** *nm* **(a)** (*éclat de voix*) (*d'horreur, d'effroi, d'acclamation*) cry, shout; (*de douleur*) cry, scream; (*pour terroriser*) shout, cry. **le ~ du nouveau-né** the cry of the newborn babe; **~ de surprise** cry *ou* exclamation of surprise; **~ aigu** *ou* **perçant** piercing cry *ou* scream, shrill cry; [*animal*] squeal; **~ sourd** *ou* **étouffé** muffled cry *ou* shout; **~ de colère** shout of anger, cry of rage; **jeter** *ou* **pousser des ~s** to shout (out), cry out; **elle jeta un ~ de douleur** she cried out in pain, she gave a cry of pain; **pousser des ~s de paon** to give *ou* make piercing screams, scream, shriek; *V* **étouffer.**
(b) (*exclamation*) cry. **~ d'alarme/d'approbation** cry of alarm/approval; **le ~ des marchands ambulants** the hawkers' cries; **marchant au ~ de 'liberté'** marching to shouts *ou* cries of 'freedom'; (*fig*) **le ~ des opprimés** the cries of the oppressed; (*fig*) **ce poème est un véritable ~ d'amour** this poem is a cry of love; (*fig*) **le ~ de la conscience** the voice of conscience; *V* **dernier, haut.**
(c) [*oiseau*] call, twitter; [*canard*] quack; [*cochon*] squeal, grunt (*pour autres cris V* **crier**). (*terme générique*) **le ~ du chien est l'aboiement** a dog's cry is its bark, the noise a dog makes is called barking *ou* a bark; **quel est le ~ de la grenouille?** what noise does a frog make?
(d) (*littér: crissement*) squeal, screech.
2: cri du cœur heartfelt cry, cry from the heart, cri de cœur; **cri de guerre** (*lit*) war cry; (*fig*) slogan, war cry.
criaillement [kʀiɑjmɑ̃] *nm* **(a)** (*gén pl*) [*oie*] squawking (*U*); [*paon*] squawking (*U*), screeching (*U*); [*bébé*] bawling (*U*), squalling (*U*). **(b)** = **criailleries.**
criailler [kʀiɑje] (1) *vi* **(a)** [*oie*] to squawk; [*paon*] to squawk, screech; [*bébé*] to bawl, squall. **(b)** (*rouspéter*) to grouse*, grumble; (*houspiller*) to nag.
criailleries [kʀiɑjʀi] *nfpl* (*rouspétance*) grousing* (*U*), grumbling (*U*); (*houspillage*) nagging (*U*).
criailleur, -euse [kʀiɑjœʀ, øz] **1** *adj* squawking, scolding. **2** *nm,f* (*rouspéteur*) grouser*.
criant, e [kʀijɑ̃, ɑ̃t] *adj erreur* glaring (*épith*); *injustice* rank (*épith*), gross (*épith*), glaring (*épith*); *preuve* striking (*épith*), glaring (*épith*); *contraste, vérité* striking (*épith*). **portrait ~ de vérité** portrait strikingly true to life.
criard, e [kʀijaʀ, aʀd(ə)] *adj* (*péj*) *enfant* yelling, squalling; *femme* scolding; *oiseau* squawking; *son, voix* piercing; (*fig*) *couleurs, vêtement* loud, garish. (*fig*) **dette ~e** pressing debt.
criblage [kʀiblaʒ] *nm* (*V* **cribler**) sifting; grading; riddling; screening; jigging.
crible [kʀibl(ə)] *nm* (*à main*) riddle; (*Ind, Min*) screen, jig, jigger. **~ mécanique** screening machine; **passer au ~** (*lit*) to riddle, put through a riddle; (*fig*) *idée, proposition* to examine closely; *déclaration, texte* to go through *ou* over with a fine-tooth comb.
criblé, e [kʀible] (*ptp de* **cribler**) *adj*: **~ de** *balles, flèches, trous* riddled with; *taches* covered in. **visage ~ de boutons** face covered in spots *ou* pimples, spotty face; **~ de dettes** crippled with debts, up to one's eyes in debt.
cribler [kʀible] (1) *vt* **(a)** (*tamiser*) *graines* to sift; *fruits* to grade; *sable* to riddle, sift; *charbon* to riddle, screen; *minerai* to screen, jig.
(b) (*percer*) **~ qch/qn de** *balles, flèches* to riddle sth/sb with; **~ qn de** *questions* to bombard sb with.
cribleur, -euse [kʀiblœʀ, øz] **1** *nm,f* (*V* **cribler**: *ouvrier*) sifter; grader; riddler; screener; jigger. **2 cribleuse** *nf* (*machine*) sifter, sifting machine.
cric [kʀik] *nm*: **~ (d'automobile)** (car) jack; **soulever qch au ~**

to jack sth up; ~ **hydraulique** hydraulic jack; ~ **à vis** screw jack.

cric-crac [kRikkRak] *excl, nm*: **le ~ du plancher qui grince** the noise of creaking *ou* squeaking floorboards; **~, fit la porte qui s'ouvrit lentement** creak went the door as it opened slowly.

cricket [kRikɛt] *nm* (*Sport*) cricket.

cricoïde [kRikɔid] **1** *adj* (*Anat*) cricoid. **2** *nm*: **le ~** the cricoid cartilage.

cri-cri [kRikRi] *nm* (*cri du grillon*) chirping; (*: *grillon*) cricket.

criée [kRije] *nf*: **(vente à la) ~** (sale by) auction; **vendre qch à la ~** to auction sth (off), sell sth by auction; **salle des ~s** auction room, salesroom.

crier [kRije] (7) **1** *vi* **(a)** *[personne]* to shout, cry (out); (*ton aigu*) to scream, screech, squeal, shriek; (*pleurer*) to cry, scream, squall; (*de joie*) to shout; (*de douleur, peur*) to cry out, scream, yell (out); (*hurler*) to yell, howl, roar. ~ **de douleur** to give a yell *ou* scream *ou* cry of pain, cry *ou* yell *ou* scream out in pain; ~ **à tue-tête** *ou* **comme un sourd** to shout one's head off, bellow away; ~ **comme un veau** to bawl one's head off; ~ **comme un beau diable** *ou* **un putois** to shout *ou* scream one's head off (in protest); **tu ne peux pas parler sans ~?** do you have to shout?, can't you talk without shouting?

(b) *[oiseau]* to call, twitter; *[canard]* to quack; *[cochon]* to squeal; (*grogner*) to grunt; *[dindon]* to gobble; *[hibou, singe]* to call, screech, hoot; *[mouette]* to cry; *[oie]* to honk; *[perroquet]* to squawk; *[souris]* to squeak.

(c) (*grincer*) *[porte, plancher, roue]* to creak, squeak; *[frein]* to squeal, screech; *[soulier, étoffe]* to squeak; (*fig*) *[couleur]* to scream, shriek. **faire ~ la craie sur le tableau** to make the chalk squeak on the blackboard.

(d) (*avec prép*) ~ **contre** *ou* **après* qn** to nag (at) *ou* scold sb, go on at sb*; **tes parents vont ~** your parents are going to make a fuss; ~ **contre qch** to shout about sth; **elle passe son temps à lui ~ après*** she's forever (going) on at him*; ~ **à la trahison/au scandale** to call it treason/a scandal, start bandying words like treason/scandal about; ~ **au miracle** to hail (it as) a miracle, call it a miracle; ~ **à l'assassin** *ou* **au meurtre** to shout 'murder'; ~ **au loup/au vol** to cry wolf/thief.

2 *vt* **(a)** *ordre, injures* to shout (out), yell (out); (*proclamer*) *mépris, indignation* to proclaim; *innocence* to protest. **elle cria qu'elle venait de voir un rat dans la cave** she shouted *ou* (*plus fort*) screamed (out) that she'd just seen a rat in the cellar; ~ **à qn de se taire** *ou* **qu'il se taise** to shout at sb to be quiet; ~ **qch sur les toits** to cry *ou* proclaim sth from the rooftops.

(b) (*pour vendre*) ~ **les journaux dans la rue** to sell newspapers in the street; **on entendait les marchandes ~ leurs légumes** you could hear the vegetable sellers crying *ou* shouting their wares, you could hear the shouts of the women selling their vegetables; **au coin de la rue, un gamin criait les éditions spéciales** at the street corner a kid was shouting out *ou* calling out the special editions.

(c) (*pour avertir, implorer*) ~ **casse-cou** to warn of (a) danger; **sans ~ gare** without a warning; ~ **grâce** (*lit*) to beg for mercy; (*fig*) to beg for peace *ou* mercy *ou* a respite; **quand j'ai parlé de me lancer tout seul dans l'entreprise, ils ont crié casse-cou** when I spoke of going into the venture on my own they were quick to point out the risks; ~ **famine** *ou* **misère** to complain that the wolf is at the door, cry famine; ~ **vengeance** to cry out for vengeance.

crieur, -euse [kRijœR, øz] *nm,f*: ~ **de journaux** newspaper seller; (*Hist*) ~ **public** town crier.

crime [kRim] *nm* **(a)** (*meurtre*) murder. **il s'agit bien d'un ~** it's definitely a case of murder; **retourner sur les lieux du ~** to go back to the scene of the crime; **la victime/l'arme du ~** the murder victim/weapon; ~ **crapuleux** foul crime; ~ **passionnel** crime passionnel; **~s de guerre** war crimes; ~ **de lèse-majesté** crime of lèse-majesté; **~ (à motif) sexuel** sex murder *ou* crime; **le ~ parfait** the perfect crime.

(b) (*Jur: délit grave*) crime, offence, felony (*Jur*). ~ **contre l'État** offence *ou* crime against the State; ~ **contre les mœurs** sexual offence, offence against public decency; ~ **contre un particulier** crime against a private individual; ~ **contre nature** unnatural act, crime against nature; (*Prov*) **le ~ ne paie pas** crime doesn't pay (*Prov*).

(c) (*sens affaibli*) crime. **c'est un ~ de faire** it's criminal *ou* a crime to do; **il est parti avant l'heure? ce n'est pas un ~!** he went off early? well, it's not a crime!

(d) († *ou littér: péché, faute*) sin, crime.

Crimée [kRime] *nf*: **la ~** the Crimea.

criminaliser [kRiminalize] (1) *vt* (*Jur*) *affaire* to refer to the criminal court.

criminaliste [kRiminalist(ə)] *nmf* specialist in criminal law.

criminalité [kRiminalite] *nf* **(a)** (*actes criminels*) criminality, crime. **la ~ juvénile** juvenile criminality. **(b)** (*rare*) *[acte]* criminal nature, criminality.

criminel, -elle [kRiminɛl] **1** *adj* (*gén, Jur*) *acte, personne, procès* criminal. (*sens affaibli*) **il serait ~ de laisser ces fruits se perdre** it would be criminal *ou* a crime to let this fruit go to waste; *V* **incendie**.

2 *nm,f* (*V* **crime**) murderer (*ou* murderess); criminal. ~ **de guerre** war criminal; (*hum: coupable*) **voilà le ~** there's the culprit *ou* the guilty party.

3 *nm* (*juridiction*) **avocat au ~** criminal lawyer; **poursuivre qn au ~** to take criminal proceedings against sb, prosecute sb in a criminal court.

criminellement [kRiminɛlmɑ̃] *adv agir* criminally. (*Jur*) **poursuivre qn ~** to take criminal proceedings against sb, prosecute sb in a criminal court.

criminologie [kRiminɔlɔʒi] *nf* criminology.

criminologiste [kRiminɔlɔʒist(ə)] *nmf* criminologist.

crin [kRɛ̃] *nm* **(a)** (*poil*) *[cheval]* hair (*U*); *[matelas, balai]* (horse)hair. ~ **végétal** vegetable (horse)hair. **(b) à tous ~s, à tout ~** *conservateur, républicain* diehard, dyed-in-the-wool; **révolutionnaire à tout ~** out-and-out revolutionary.

crincrin* [kRɛ̃kRɛ̃] *nm* (*péj*) (*violon*) squeaky fiddle; (*son*) squeaking, scraping.

crinière [kRinjɛR] *nf* **(a)** *[animal]* mane. **(b)** *[personne]* shock *ou* mop of hair, (flowing) mane. **il avait une ~ rousse** he had a mop of red hair. **(c)** *[casque]* plume.

crinoline [kRinɔlin] *nf* crinoline petticoat. **robe à ~** crinoline (dress).

crique [kRik] *nf* creek, inlet.

criquet [kRikɛ] *nm* (*Zool*) locust; (*gén: grillon, sauterelle*) grasshopper.

crise [kRiz] **1** *nf* **(a)** (*Méd*) *[rhumatisme, goutte, appendicite]* attack; *[épilepsie, apoplexie]* fit.

(b) (*accès*) outburst, fit; (*lubie*) fit, mood. ~ **de colère** *ou* **rage/de dégoût** fit of anger *ou* rage/of disgust; **elle est prise d'une ~ de nettoyage** she's felt *ou* got a sudden urge to do a spring-clean, she's in a spring-cleaning mood.

(c) (*: *colère*) rage, tantrum. **piquer une ~** to throw a tantrum *ou* a fit*, fly off the handle*.

(d) (*bouleversement*) (*moral, Pol*) crisis; (*Écon*) crisis, slump. **en période de ~, il faut ...** in time(s) of crisis *ou* times of trouble we must ...; **pays/économie en (état de) ~** country/economy in a (state of) crisis.

(e) (*pénurie*) shortage. ~ **de main d'œuvre** shortage of manpower.

2: **crise d'appendicite** appendicitis attack; **crise d'asthme** attack of asthma; **crise cardiaque** heart attack; **crise de confiance** crisis of confidence; **crise de conscience** crisis of conscience; **crise économique** economic crisis, slump; **crise d'épilepsie** epileptic fit; **crise de foi** = **crise religieuse**; **crise de foie** bilious *ou* liverish attack; **crise de larmes** fit of crying *ou* tears, crying fit; **crise du logement** housing shortage; **crise ministérielle** cabinet crisis; **crise de nerfs** attack of nerves, fit of hysterics; **crise du papier** paper shortage; **crise du pouvoir** leadership crisis; **crise religieuse** crisis of belief.

crispant, e [kRispɑ̃, ɑ̃t] *adj* (*énervant*) irritating, aggravating*, annoying. **ce qu'il est ~!*** he really gets on my nerves!*, he's a real pain in the neck!*

crispation [kRispɑsjɔ̃] *nf* **(a)** (*contraction*) *[traits, visage]* contortion, tensing; *[muscles]* contraction; *[cuir]* shrivelling-up.

(b) (*spasme*) twitch. **des ~s nerveuses** nervous twitches *ou* twitching; **une ~ douloureuse de la main** a painful twitching of the hand; (*fig*) **donner des ~s à qn** to get on sb's nerves*.

(c) (*nervosité*) state of tension.

crispé, e [kRispe] (*ptp de* **crisper**) *adj sourire* nervous, strained, tense; *personne* tense, on edge (*attrib*).

crisper [kRispe] (1) **1** *vt* **(a)** (*plisser, rider*) *cuir* to shrivel (up). **le froid crispe la peau** the cold makes one's skin feel taut *ou* tight.

(b) (*contracter*) *visage* to contort; *muscles, membres* to tense, flex; *poings* to clench. **la douleur crispait les visages** their faces were contorted *ou* tense with grief; **les mains crispées sur le volant** clutching the wheel tensely, with hands clenched on the wheel.

(c) (*: *agacer*) ~ **qn** to get on sb's nerves*.

2 se crisper *vpr [visage]* to tense; *[sourire]* to become strained *ou* tense; *[poing]* to clench; (*fig*) *[personne]* to get edgy* *ou* tense. **ses mains se crispèrent sur le manche de la pioche** his hands tightened on the pickaxe, he clutched the pickaxe tensely.

crispin [kRispɛ̃] *nm*: **gants à ~** gauntlets.

criss [kRis] *nm* kris, creese.

crissement [kRismɑ̃] *nm* (*V* **crisser**) crunch(ing); screech(ing), squeal(ing); whisper(ing), rustling, rustle. **s'arrêter dans un ~ de pneus** to screech to a halt.

crisser [kRise] (1) *vi [neige, gravier]* to crunch; *[pneus, freins]* to screech, squeal; *[soie, taffetas]* to whisper, rustle. ~ **des dents** to grind one's teeth.

cristal, *pl* **-aux** [kRistal, o] *nm* **(a)** (*Chim, Min*) crystal. ~ **(de roche)** rock crystal (*U*), quartz (*U*); **~ (de plomb)** (lead) crystal; **de** *ou* **en ~** crystal (*épith*); (*fig littér*) **le ~ de sa voix, sa voix de ~** his crystal-clear voice, the crystal-clear quality of his voice; ~ **de Bohème** Bohemian crystal; ~ **d'Islande** Iceland spar; *V* **boule**[1].

(b) (*objet: gén pl*) crystal(ware) (*U*), piece of crystal(ware), fine glassware (*U*). **les ~aux du lustre** the crystal droplets of the chandelier.

(c) (*pour le nettoyage*) **~aux (de soude)** washing soda.

cristallerie [kRistalRi] *nf* (*fabrication*) crystal (glass-)making; (*fabrique*) (crystal) glassworks; (*objets*) crystal(ware), fine glassware.

cristallier [kRistalje] *nm* (*Hist*) (*chercheur*) crystal seeker; (*ouvrier*) crystal engraver.

cristallin, e [kRistalɛ̃, in] **1** *adj* (*Min*) crystalline; *son, voix* crystal-clear; *eau* crystalline. **2** *nm* (*Anat*) crystalline lens.

cristallisation [kRistalizɑsjɔ̃] *nf* (*gén*) crystallization.

cristalliser *vti*, **se cristalliser** *vpr* [kRistalize] (1) to crystallize.

cristallisoir [kRistalizwaR] *nm* crystallizing dish.

cristallographie [kRistalɔgRafi] *nf* crystallography.

cristallomancie [kRistalɔmɑ̃si] *nf* crystal-gazing, crystallomancy.

critère [kRitɛR] *nm* (*preuve*) criterion; (*pierre de touche*) measure, criterion. **ceci n'est pas un ~ suffisant pour prouver l'authenticité du document** this is not a good enough criterion to prove the document's authenticity; **la richesse matérielle n'est**

pas un ~ de succès material wealth is not a criterion of success; **ceci constituera un ~ de sa bonne foi** this will be a test of his good faith; **le style n'est pas le seul ~ pour juger de la valeur d'un roman** style is not the only measure *ou* criterion by which one can judge the value of a novel; **son seul ~ est l'avis du parti** his only criterion is the opinion of the party.

critérium [kʀiteʀjɔm] *nm* **(a)** (*Cyclisme*) rally; (*Natation*) gala. **(b)** (†) = **critère.**

critiquable [kʀitikabl(ə)] *adj* open to criticism (*attrib*).

critique[1] [kʀitik] *adj* (*en crise, alarmant*) *situation, période* critical; (*décisif, crucial*) *moment, phase* crucial, decisive, critical; *situation, période* crucial, critical; (*Sci*) *pression, vitesse* critical. **dans les circonstances ~s, il perd la tête** in critical situations *ou* in emergencies *ou* in a crisis, he loses his head; **ils étaient dans une situation ~** they were in a critical situation *ou* a tight spot*; *V* **âge.**

critique[2] [kʀitik] **1** *adj* **(a)** (*qui juge ou fait un choix*) *jugement, notes, édition* critical. **avoir l'esprit ~** to have a critical mind; *V* **apparat.**

(b) (*défavorable*) critical, censorious (*frm*). **d'un œil ~** with a critical eye; **il s'est montré très ~ (au sujet de ...)** he was very critical (of ...); **esprit ~** criticizing *ou* critical mind.

2 *nf* **(a)** (*blâme*) criticism. **il ne supporte pas la ~ *ou* les ~s** he can't tolerate criticism; **les nombreuses ~s qui lui ont été adressées** the many criticisms that were levelled at him; **faire une ~ à (l'endroit de) qch/qn** to criticize sth/sb; **une ~ que je lui ferais est qu'il ...** one criticism I would make of him is that he ...; **la ~ est aisée** it's easy to criticize.

(b) (*analyse*) *[texte, œuvre]* appreciation, critique; *[livre, spectacle]* review. (*art de juger*) **la ~** criticism; **la ~ littéraire/musicale** literary/music criticism; **faire la ~ de** *livre sorti de presse, concert* to review, write a crit of*; *poème* to write an appreciation *ou* a critique of; **une ~ impartiale** an impartial *ou* unbiased review *ou* crit*; (*Littérat*) **la nouvelle ~** the new (French) criticism.

(c) (*personnes*) **la ~** the critics. **la ~ a bien accueilli sa pièce** his play was well received by the critics.

3 *nmf* (*commentateur*) critic. **un ~ de théâtre/de musique/d'art/de cinéma** a drama/music/art/cinema *ou* film critic; **un ~ littéraire** a literary critic.

critiquer [kʀitike] (1) *vt* **(a)** (*blâmer*) to criticize. **il critique tout/tout le monde** he finds fault with *ou* criticizes everything/everybody. **(b)** (*juger*) *livre, œuvre* to assess, make an appraisal of; (*examiner*) to examine (critically).

croassement [kʀɔasmɑ̃] *nm* caw, cawing (*U*).

croasser [kʀɔase] (1) *vi* to caw.

croate [kʀɔat] **1** *adj* Croatian. **2** *nm* (*Ling*) Croat, Croatian. **3** *nmf*: **C~** Croat, Croatian.

Croatie [kʀɔasi] *nf* Croatia.

croc [kʀo] *nm* **(a)** (*dent*) fang. **montrer les ~s** *[animal]* to bare its teeth, show its teeth *ou* fangs; (*fig: menacer*) to show one's teeth. **(b)** (*grappin*) hook; (*fourche*) hook. **~ de boucherie/de marinier** meat/boat hook; **~ à fumier** muck rake.

croc-en-jambe, *pl* **crocs-en-jambe** [kʀɔkɑ̃ʒɑ̃b] *nm*: **faire un ~ à qn** (*lit*) to trip sb (up); (*fig*) to trip sb up, pull a fast one on sb*; **un ~ me fit perdre l'équilibre** somebody tripped me (up) and I lost my balance, I was tripped (up) and lost my balance; (*fig*) **méfiez-vous des crocs-en-jambe de vos collaborateurs** mind your colleagues don't pull a fast one on you* *ou* don't try and do you down*.

croche [kʀɔʃ] *nf* (*Mus*) quaver (*Brit*), eighth (note) (*US*). **double ~** semiquaver (*Brit*), sixteenth (note) (*US*); **triple/quadruple ~** demisemi/hemidemisemiquaver (*Brit*), thirty-second/sixty-fourth note (*US*).

croche-pied, *pl* **croche-pieds** [kʀɔʃpje] *nm* = **croc-en-jambe.**

crochet [kʀɔʃɛ] **1** *nm* **(a)** (*fer recourbé*) (*gén*) hook; *[chiffonnier]* spiked stick; *[patte de pantalon etc]* fastener, clip, fastening; *[cambrioleur, serrurier]* picklock. (*Rail*) **~ d'attelage** coupling; **~ de boucherie *ou* de boucher** meat hook; (†) **~ à boutons *ou* bottines** buttonhook.

(b) (*aiguille*) crochet hook; (*technique*) crochet. **couverture au ~** a crocheted blanket; **faire du ~** to crochet; **faire qch au ~** to crochet sth.

(c) (*Boxe*) **~ du gauche/du droit** left/right hook.

(d) (*détour*) *[véhicule]* sudden swerve; *[route]* sudden turn; *[voyage, itinéraire]* detour. **il a fait un ~ pour éviter l'obstacle** he swerved to avoid the obstacle; **faire un ~ par une ville** to make a detour through a town.

(e) (*Typ*) **~s** square brackets; **entre ~s** in square brackets.

(f) *[serpent]* fang.

(g) (*Archit*) crocket.

(h) (*loc*) **vivre aux ~s de qn** to live off *ou* sponge on* sb.

2: crochet radiophonique talent show.

crochetage [kʀɔʃtaʒ] *nm [serrure]* picking.

crocheter [kʀɔʃte] (5) *vt* **(a)** *serrure* to pick; *porte* to pick the lock on. **(b)** *chiffons* to hook out.

crocheteur [kʀɔʃtœʀ] *nm* (*voleur*) picklock.

crochu, e [kʀɔʃy] *adj nez* hooked; *mains, doigts* claw-like. **au nez ~** hook-nosed; (*fig*) **avoir les doigts ~s*** (*être avare*) to be grasping *ou* tight-fisted; (*être voleur*) to be light-fingered*; *V* **atome.**

crocodile [kʀɔkɔdil] *nm* (*Zool, peau*) crocodile. **un sac en ~ *ou* croco*** a crocodile(-skin) handbag; *V* **larme.**

crocus [kʀɔkys] *nm* crocus.

croire [kʀwaʀ] (44) **1** *vt* **(a)** *personne, fait, histoire* to believe. **je n'arrive pas à ~ qu'il a réussi** I (just) can't believe he has succeeded; **auriez-vous cru cela de lui?** would you have believed it possible of him *ou* expected it of him?; **je te crois sur parole** I'll take your word for it; **le croira qui voudra, mais ...** believe it or not (but) ...; **je veux bien le ~** I can quite (well) believe it; **je n'en crois rien** I don't believe (a word of) it; **~ qch dur comme fer*** to believe sth firmly, be absolutely convinced of sth.

(b) (*avec infin ou que: penser, estimer*) to believe, think; (*déduire*) to believe, assume, think. **nous croyons qu'il a dit la vérité** we believe *ou* think that he told the truth; **elle croyait avoir perdu son sac** she thought she had lost her bag; **il a bien cru manquer son train** he really thought he would miss his train; **il n'y avait pas de lumière, j'ai cru qu'ils étaient couchés** there was no light so I thought *ou* assumed they had gone to *ou* were in bed; **il a cru bien faire** he meant well, he thought he was acting for the best; **je crois que oui** I think so; **je crois que non** I think not, I don't think so; **il n'est pas là? — je crois que si** isn't he in? — (yes) I think he is; **on ne croyait pas qu'il viendrait** we didn't think he'd come; **elle ne croit pas/elle ne peut pas ~ qu'il mente** she doesn't think/can't believe he is lying.

(c) (*avec adj, adv*) (*juger, estimer*) to think, believe, consider; (*supposer*) to think, believe. **croyez-vous cette réunion nécessaire?** do you think *ou* believe this meeting is necessary?, do you consider this meeting (to be) necessary?; **on l'a cru mort** he was believed *ou* presumed (to be) dead; **on les croyait en France** they were believed *ou* thought to be in France; **je la croyais ailleurs/avec vous** I thought she was somewhere else/with you; **il n'a pas cru utile *ou* nécessaire de me prévenir** he didn't think it necessary to warn me.

(d) en ~ (*s'en rapporter à*): **à l'en ~** to listen to *ou* hear him, if you (were to) go by *ou* listen to what he says; **s'il faut en ~ les journaux** if we (are to) go by what the papers say, if we are to believe the papers, if the papers are anything to go by; **vous pouvez m'en ~, croyez en mon expérience** (you can) take it from me, take it from one who knows; **si vous m'en croyez** if you want my opinion; **il n'en croyait pas ses oreilles/ses yeux** he couldn't believe his ears/his eyes.

(e) (*loc*) **c'est à ~ qu'il est sourd** you'd think he was deaf; **c'est à n'y pas ~!** it's beyond belief!, it's unbelievable!, it's hardly credible!; (*frm*) **il est à ~ que** it is to be supposed *ou* presumed that; **il faut ~ que** it would seem that, one must assume that, it must be assumed that; **~ de son devoir de faire** to think *ou* feel it one's duty to do; **il ne croyait pas si bien dire!** he didn't know how right he was!, he never spoke a truer word; **on croirait une hirondelle** it looks as though it could be *ou* it looks like a swallow; **on croirait (entendre) une clarinette** it sounds like *ou* it could be a clarinet (playing); **on croirait qu'il va gagner** he looks like winning, it looks as if he is going to win; **on croirait qu'elle ne comprend pas** she doesn't seem to understand, you might almost think she didn't understand; **tu ne peux pas ~ *ou* (*frm*) vous ne sauriez ~ combien il nous manque** you cannot (begin to) imagine how much we miss him; **non, mais qu'est-ce que vous croyez?*** what do you imagine?; **je vous *ou* te crois!*** you bet!*, rather!; **je ne suis pas celle que vous croyez!** I'm not THAT sort of person!; **faut pas ~!*** make no mistake (about it); **on croit rêver!*** I don't BELIEVE it!, whatever next!

2 *vi* (*Rel: avoir la foi*) to believe, be a believer.

3 croire à *vt indir innocence de qn, vie éternelle, Père Noël* to believe in; *justice, médecine* to have faith *ou* confidence in, believe in; *promesses* to believe (in), have faith in. **il ne croit plus à rien** he no longer believes in anything; **on a cru d'abord à un accident** at first they took it for an accident *ou* to be an accident, at first they believed it was *ou* it to be an accident; **pour faire ~ à un suicide** to make people think it was suicide, to give the impression *ou* appearance of (a) suicide; **il ne croit pas à la guerre** (*pense qu'elle n'aura pas lieu*) he doesn't think *ou* believe *ou* reckon there will be a war; (*pense qu'elle ne sert à rien*) he doesn't believe in war; **non, mais tu crois au Père Noël!** well, you really DO live in cloud-cuckoo land!; (*frm*) **veuillez ~ à mes sentiments dévoués** yours sincerely, I am, sir, your devoted servant (*frm*).

4 croire en *vt indir* to believe in; **~ en Dieu** to believe in God; **~ en qn** to have faith *ou* confidence in sb; **il croit trop en lui-même** he is too self-confident, he is overconfident, he has an over-inflated opinion of himself.

5 se croire *vpr* **(a)** (*avec attribut*) **se ~ fort/malin** to think one is strong/(very) clever; **il se croit un acteur** he thinks he's a good *ou* a great* actor.

(b) (*être prétentieux*) to have an inflated opinion of o.s.

croisade [kʀwazad] *nf* (*Hist, fig*) crusade. **la ~ des Albigeois** the Albigensian Crusade.

croisé[1], **e**[1] [kʀwaze] (*ptp de* **croiser**) **1** *adj veste* double-breasted; *rimes, vers* alternate. **race ~e** crossbreed; **tissu ~** twill; *V* **bras, feu**[1], **mot. 2** *nm* (*Tex*) twill.

croisé[2] [kʀwaze] *nm* (*Hist*) crusader.

croisée[2] [kʀwaze] *nf* **(a) ~ de chemins** crossroads, crossing; (*fig*) **à la ~ des chemins** at the crossroads, at the parting of the ways; (*Archit*) **~ d'ogives** intersecting ribs; (*Archit*) **~ du transept** transept crossing. **(b)** (*littér: fenêtre*) window, casement (*littér*).

croisement [kʀwazmɑ̃] *nm* **(a)** *[fils, brins]* crossing. **l'étroitesse de la route rendait impossible le ~ des véhicules** the narrowness of the road made it impossible for vehicles to pass (one another).

(b) (*Bio, Zool*) *[races, espèces, plantes]* crossing (*U*), crossbreeding (*U*), interbreeding (*U*) (*avec* with). **faire des ~s de race** to rear *ou* produce crossbreeds, cross(breed); **est-ce un ~? *ou* le produit d'un ~?** is it a cross(breed)?

(c) (*carrefour*) crossroads, junction. **au ~ de la route et de la voie ferrée, il y a un passage à niveau** where the road and the railway cross, there is a level crossing; **le ~ des deux voies ferrées se fait sur deux niveaux** the two railway lines cross at two levels; au ~ des chemins, il s'arrêtèrent they stopped where the paths crossed *ou* at the junction of the paths.

croiser [kRwaze] (1) **1** *vt* **(a)** *bras* to fold, cross; *jambes* to cross; *fourchettes, fils, lignes* to cross. **elle croisa son châle sur sa poitrine** she folded her shawl across *ou* over her chest; **les jambes croisées** cross-legged; (*lit, fig*) ~ **le fer** to cross swords (*avec* with); (*fig*) **se** ~ **les bras** to lounge around, sit around idly.

(b) (*intersecter, couper*) *route* to cross, cut across; *ligne* to cross, cut across, intersect (*T*).

(c) (*passer à côté de*) *véhicule, passant* to pass. **les autos se sont croisées** the cars passed each other; **notre train a croisé le rapide** our train passed the express going in the other direction; **son regard croisa le mien** his eyes met mine.

(d) (*accoupler, mâtiner*) *races, animaux, plantes* to cross(breed), interbreed (*avec* with). **l'âne peut se** ~ **avec le cheval** the ass can (inter)breed with the horse; (*croisement contrôlé*) the ass can be crossed with the horse.

2 *vi* **(a)** (*Habillement*) **cette veste croise bien** that jacket has got a nice *ou* good overlap; **cette saison les couturiers font** ~ **les vestes** this season fashion designers are making jackets double-breasted; **il avait tellement grossi qu'il ne pouvait plus (faire)** ~ **sa veste** he'd got so fat that he couldn't get his jacket to fasten over *ou* across *ou* that his jacket wouldn't fasten across any more.

(b) (*Naut*) to cruise.

3 se croiser *vpr* **(a)** *[chemins, lignes]* to cross, cut (across) each other, intersect. **deux chemins qui se croisent à angle droit** two roads which cross at right angles *ou* which cut (across) each other at right angles; (*fig*) **nos regards** *ou* **nos yeux se croisèrent un instant** our eyes met for a moment.

(b) *[personnes, véhicules]* to pass each other. (*fig*) **ma lettre s'est croisée avec la sienne, nos lettres se sont croisées** my letter crossed his (in the post), our letters crossed (in the post).

(c) (*Hist*) to take the cross, go on a crusade.

croiseur [kRwazœR] *nm* cruiser (*warship*).

croisière [kRwazjɛR] *nf* cruise. **partir en** ~, **faire une** ~ to go on a cruise; **ce voilier est idéal pour la** ~ this boat is ideal for cruising; *V* **vitesse**.

croisillon [kRwazijɔ̃] *nm [croix, charpente]* crosspiece, crossbar; *[église]* transept. ~**s** *[fenêtre]* lattice work; *V* **fenêtre**.

croissance [kRwasɑ̃s] *nf [enfant, embryon, ville, industrie]* growth, development; *[plante]* growth. ~ **économique** economic growth *ou* development; ~ **zéro** zero economic growth; **arrêté dans sa** ~ arrested in his growth *ou* development; **maladie de** ~ growth disease.

croissant[1] [kRwasɑ̃] *nm* **(a)** (*forme*) crescent. ~ **de lune** crescent of the moon; **en** ~ crescent-shaped. **(b)** (*Culin*) croissant.

croissant[2], **e** [kRwasɑ̃, ɑ̃t] *adj nombre, tension* growing, increasing, rising; *chaleur* rising; *froid* increasing. **le rythme** ~ **des accidents** the increasing rate of accidents, the rising accident rate.

croître [kRwatR(ə)] (55) *vi* **(a)** *[enfant, plante]* to grow; *[ville]* to grow, increase in size. ~ **en beauté/sagesse** to grow in beauty/wisdom; ~ **dans l'estime de qn** to rise *ou* grow in sb's esteem; **vallon où croissent de nombreuses espèces** valley where various species of plant grow.

(b) *[ambition, bruit, quantité]* to grow, increase. **les jours croissent** the days are getting longer *ou* are lengthening; ~ **en nombre/volume** to increase in number/size *ou* volume; **l'inquiétude sur son état de santé ne cessait de** ~ there was increasing anxiety over the state of his health; **son enthousiasme ne cessa de** ~ he grew more and more enthusiastic (about it); **la chaleur ne faisait que** ~ the heat got more and more intense, the temperature kept on rising.

(c) *[rivière]* to swell, rise; *[lune]* to wax; *[vent]* to rise. **les pluies ont fait** ~ **la rivière** the rains have swollen the river, the river waters have swollen *ou* risen after the rains.

(d) (*loc*) (*Bible*) **croissez et multipliez!** multiply and be fruitful!; (*iro*) **ça ne fait que** ~ **et embellir** (things are getting) better and better! (*iro*).

croix [kRwa] **1** *nf* **(a)** (*gén, Hér, Rel*) cross. ~ **celtique/grecque/latine** Celtic/Greek/Latin cross; ~ **de Malte/de Saint-André** Maltese/St Andrew's cross; (*Hér*) ~ **ancrée/fleuretée** cross moline/fleury *ou* flory; **en** ~ crosswise, in the form of a cross; **mettre des bâtons en** ~ to lay sticks crosswise, criss-cross sticks; **les pétales des crucifères sont disposés en** ~ the petals of the Cruciferae form a cross *ou* are arranged crosswise; **chemins qui se coupent en** ~ paths which cut each other at right angles *ou* crosswise; **mettre en** ~, **mettre à mort sur la** ~ to crucify; **mise en** ~ crucifixion; **mettre les bras en** ~ to stretch out one's arms at the sides; **pour le faire sortir, c'est** *ou* **il faut la** ~ **et la bannière** it's the devil's own job *ou* a devil of a job to get him to go out; *V* **chemin, grand, signe**.

(b) (*décoration*) cross; (*Scol: récompense*) prize, medal.

(c) (*marque*) cross. **faire** *ou* **mettre une** ~ **devant un nom** to put a cross in front of *ou* by a name; **(appeler) les noms marqués d'une** ~ (to call out) the names which have a cross against them *ou* with a cross against them; (*fig*) **tes vacances, tu peux faire une** ~ **dessus*** you might just as well forget all about your holidays *ou* write your holidays off*; (*fig*) **si tu lui prêtes ton livre, tu peux faire une** ~ **dessus!*** if you lend him your book, you can say goodbye to it!*; (*fig*) **faire une** ~ **à la cheminée** to mark sth in red letters.

(d) (*fig: souffrance, épreuve*) cross, burden. **chacun a sa** ~ each of us has his (own) cross to bear.

2: croix gammée swastika; (*Mil*) **Croix de guerre** Military Cross; **croix de Lorraine** cross of Lorraine; **Croix-Rouge** Red Cross; **Croix-du-Sud** Southern Cross.

croquant[1]† [kRɔkɑ̃] *nm* (*péj*) yokel, (country) bumpkin.

croquant[2], **e** [kRɔkɑ̃, ɑ̃t] *adj* crisp, crunchy.

croque au sel [kRɔkosɛl] *loc adv*: **à la** ~ with salt (and nothing else), with a sprinkling of salt.

croque-madame [kRɔkmadam] *nm inv toasted cheese sandwich with ham and fried egg.*

croque-mitaine, *pl* **croque-mitaines** [kRɔkmitɛn] *nm* bog(e)y man, ogre (*fig*). **ce maître est un vrai** ~ this schoolmaster is a real ogre.

croque-monsieur [kRɔkməsjø] *nm inv toasted cheese sandwich with ham.*

croque-mort, *pl* **croque-morts*** [kRɔkmɔR] *nm* (*péj*) pallbearer. **avoir un air de** ~ to have a funereal look *ou* a face like an undertaker.

croquenot* [kRɔkno] *nm* clodhopper*.

croquer [kRɔke] (1) **1** *vt* **(a)** (*manger*) *biscuits, noisettes, bonbons* to crunch; *fruits* to munch. **pastille à laisser fondre dans la bouche sans (la)** ~ pastille to be sucked slowly and not chewed *ou* crunched; ~ **le marmot***† to hang around (waiting)*, kick one's heels*.

(b) (*: *dépenser, gaspiller*) ~ **de l'argent** to squander money, go through money like water*; ~ **un héritage** to squander *ou* go through an inheritance.

(c) (*dessiner*) to sketch. **être (joli) à** ~ to be as pretty as a picture.

(d) (*camper*) *personnage* to sketch, outline, give a thumbnail sketch of.

2 *vi* **(a)** *[fruit]* to be crunchy, be crisp; *[salade]* to be crisp. **le sucre croque sous la dent** sugar is crunchy to eat *ou* when you eat it; **des pommes qui croquent** crunchy apples.

(b) ~ **dans une pomme** to bite into an apple.

croquet [kRɔkɛ] *nm* (*Sport*) croquet.

croquette [kRɔkɛt] *nf* (*Culin*) croquette. ~**s de chocolat** chocolate croquettes.

croqueuse [kRɔkøz] *nf*: ~ **de diamants** gold digger, fortune-hunter.

croquignolet, -ette* [kRɔkiɲɔlɛ, ɛt] *adj* (*mignon*) (rather) sweet, cute (*US*), dinky*.

croquis [kRɔki] *nm* (*dessin*) (rough) sketch; (*fig: description*) sketch. **faire un** ~ **de qch** to sketch sth, make a (rough) sketch of sth; (*fig*) **faire un rapide** ~ **de la situation** to give a rapid outline *ou* thumbnail sketch of the situation; (*fig*) ~ **d'audience** court-room sketches.

crosne [kRon] *nm* Chinese artichoke.

cross(-country) [kRɔs(kuntRi)] *nm* (*course*) cross-country race *ou* run; (*Sport*) cross-country racing *ou* running.

crosse [kRɔs] *nf* **(a)** (*poignée*) *[fusil]* butt; *[revolver]* grip. **frapper qn à coups de** ~ to hit sb with the butt of one's rifle; **mettre** *ou* **lever la** ~ **en l'air*** (*se rendre*) to show the white flag (*fig*), lay down one's arms; (*se mutiner*) to mutiny, refuse to fight.

(b) (*bâton*) (*Rel*) crook, crosier, crozier. (*Sport*) ~ **de golf** golf club; ~ **de hockey** hockey stick.

(c) (*partie recourbée*) *[violon]* head, scroll. ~ **de piston** crosshead; ~ **de l'aorte** arch of the aorta, aortic arch; ~ **de fougère** crosier (*fern*).

(d) chercher des ~**s à qn*** to pick a quarrel with sb; **s'il me cherche des** ~**s*** if he's looking for a chance to make trouble *ou* to pick a quarrel with me.

(e) (*Culin*) ~ **de bœuf** knuckle of beef.

crotale [kRɔtal] *nm* rattlesnake.

crotte [kRɔt] *nf* **(a)** (*excrément*) *[brebis, lapin]* droppings. ~ **de cheval** horse droppings *ou* manure (*U*) *ou* dung (*U*); **son chien a déposé une** ~ **sur le palier** his dog has messed *ou* done its business on the landing; ~**!***† blast (it)!* (*Brit*), oh heck!*; **c'est de la** ~ **de bique*** it's a load of (old) rubbish*; **c'est pas de la** ~* it's not cheap rubbish; **il ne se prend pas pour une** ~* he thinks he's a big shot*.

(b) (*bonbon*) **une** ~ **de chocolat** a chocolate whirl.

(c) (†: *boue*) mud.

crotter [kRɔte] (1) **1** *vt* to muddy, dirty, cover in mud. **souliers tout crottés** muddy shoes, shoes covered in mud. **2** *vi [chien]* to do its business, mess.

crottin [kRɔtɛ̃] *nm*: ~ **(de cheval/d'âne)** (horse/donkey) droppings *ou* dung (*U*) *ou* manure (*U*).

croulant, e [kRulɑ̃, ɑ̃t] **1** *adj mur* crumbling, tumbledown; *maison* ramshackle, tumbledown, crumbling; (*fig*) *autorité, empire* crumbling, tottering. **2** *nm* (‡) old fogey‡. **les** ~**s** the old folk, the old ones*, the old fogeys‡.

crouler [kRule] (1) *vi* **(a)** (*s'écrouler*) *[maison, mur]* to collapse, tumble down, fall down; *[masse de neige]* to collapse; *[terre]* to give (way), collapse; (*fig*) *[empire]* to collapse. **le mur a croulé sous la force du vent** the wall collapsed *ou* caved in under the force of the wind; **la terre croula sous ses pas the ground** gave (way) *ou* caved in *ou* collapsed under his feet; **le tremblement de terre a fait** ~ **les maisons** the earthquake has brought the houses down *ou* has demolished the houses; (*fig*) **la salle croulait sous les applaudissements** the room shook with the applause, the audience raised the roof with their applause; (*fig*) **se laisser** ~ **dans un fauteuil** to collapse into an armchair.

(b) (*menacer de s'écrouler, être délabré*) **une maison qui croule** a ramshackle *ou* tumbledown *ou* crumbling house, a house which is falling into ruin *ou* going to rack and ruin; **un mur qui croule** a crumbling *ou* tumbledown wall; (*fig*) ~ **sous le poids de qch** to collapse *ou* stagger under the weight of sth; (*fig*) **une civilisation qui croule** a tottering civilization.

croup [kRup] *nm* (*Méd*) croup. **faux** ~ spasmodic croup, child-crowing.

croupe [kRup] *nf* **(a)** *[cheval]* croup, crupper, rump, hindquarters. **en** ~: **monter en** ~ to ride pillion; **il monta en** ~ **et ils partirent** he got on behind and off they went; **il avait en** ~ **son ami** he had his friend behind him (on the pillion).

(b) (*) *[personne]* rump*.
(c) (*fig*) ~ **(d'une colline)** hilltop.
croupetons [kʀuptɔ̃] *adv*: **se tenir** *ou* **être à** ~ to be crouching, be squatting, be (down) on one's hunkers*; **se mettre à** ~ to crouch *ou* squat down, go down on one's hunkers*.
croupi, e [kʀupi] (*ptp de* **croupir**) *adj eau* stagnant.
croupier [kʀupje] *nm* croupier.
croupière [kʀupjɛʀ] *nf* crupper. **tailler des** ~**s à qn**† to put a spoke in sb's wheel.
croupion [kʀupjɔ̃] *nm* (*Orn*) rump; (*Culin*) parson's nose, pope's nose (*US*); (*‡hum*) *[personne]* rear (end)*, backside*.
croupir [kʀupiʀ] (2) *vi [eau]* to stagnate. (*fig*) *[personne]* ~ **dans son ignorance/dans l'oisiveté/dans le vice** to wallow *ou* remain sunk in (one's own) ignorance/in idleness/in vice.
croustade [kʀustad] *nf* croustade.
croustillant, e [kʀustijɑ̃, ɑ̃t] *adj* **(a)** (*V* **croustiller**) crusty; crisp; crunchy. **(b)** (*fig: grivois*) spicy.
croustiller [kʀustije] (1) *vi [pain, pâte]* to be crusty; *[croissant, galette, chips]* to be crisp *ou* crunchy.
croûte [kʀut] **1** *nf* **(a)** *[pain, pâte]* crust; *[fromage]* rind; *[vol-au-vent]* case. **à la** ~**!*** (*venez manger*) come and get it!*, grub's up!‡; (*allons manger*) let's go and get it!* *ou* eat!; *V* **casser, gagner, pâté.**
(b) (*à la surface d'un liquide*) ~ **de glace** layer of ice; ~ **de peinture** (*dans un pot*) skin of paint.
(c) (*sédiment, sécrétion durcie*) *[plaie]* scab. **couvert d'une** ~ **de glace** crusted with ice, covered with a crust of ice; ~ **calcaire** *ou* **de tartre** layer of scale *ou* fur; **une** ~ **de tartre s'était formée sur les parois de la chaudière** the sides of the boiler were covered in scale *ou* had furred up, a layer of scale had collected on the sides of the boiler; **gratter des** ~**s de peinture/cire sur une table** to scrape lumps of paint/wax off a table.
(d) (*fig: vernis*) ~ **de culture** veneer of culture; ~ **de bêtise** (thick) layer of stupidity.
(e) (*cuir*) undressed leather *ou* hide. **sac en** ~ hide bag.
(f) (*péj: tableau*) daub.
2: (*Culin*) **croûte aux champignons** mushrooms on toast; (*Culin*) **croûte au fromage** cheese on toast, toasted cheese, ≃ Welsh rarebit *ou* rabbit; **croûte de pain** crust of bread; (*péj*) **croûtes de pain** old crusts; (*Géol*) **la croûte terrestre** the earth's crust.
croûter‡ [kʀute] (1) *vi* to nosh‡, have some grub‡.
croûteux, -euse [kʀutø, øz] *adj* scabby, covered with scabs.
croûton [kʀutɔ̃] *nm* **(a)** (*bout du pain*) crust; (*Culin*) crouton. **(b)** (*péj: personne*) fuddy-duddy*, old fossil*.
croyable [kʀwajabl(ə)] *adj* credible. **ce n'est pas** ~! it's unbelievable!, it's incredible!
croyance [kʀwajɑ̃s] *nf* **(a)** (*U*) ~ **à** belief in, faith in; ~ **en** belief in. **(b)** (*opinion*) belief. ~**s religieuses** religious beliefs.
croyant, e [kʀwajɑ̃, ɑ̃t] **1** *adj*: **être** ~ to be a believer; **ne pas être** ~ to be a non-believer. **2** *nm,f* believer. **les** ~**s** the faithful (*esp Moslems*).
cru[1]**, e**[1] [kʀy] *adj* **(a)** (*non cuit*) *aliments* raw; *abricots, pruneaux* uncooked, raw. **lait** ~ milk straight from the cow.
(b) (*Tech: non apprêté*) *soie* raw; *chanvre, toile* raw, untreated; *métal* crude, raw. **cuir** ~ untreated *ou* raw leather, rawhide.
(c) *lumière, couleur* harsh, garish.
(d) (*franc, réaliste*) *description, mot* forthright, blunt. **une réponse** ~**e** a straight *ou* blunt *ou* forthright reply; **je vous le dis tout** ~ I'll tell you straight out*, I'll give it to you straight*.
(e) (*choquant*) *histoire, chanson, langage* crude, coarse. **parler** ~ to speak coarsely *ou* crudely, be coarse of speech.
(f) (*loc*) **à** ~: **construire à** ~ to build without foundations; (*Équitation*) **monter à** ~ to ride bareback; († *ou littér*) **être chaussé à** ~ to wear one's boots (*ou* shoes) without (any) socks.
cru[2] [kʀy] *nm* **(a)** (*terroir, vignoble*) vineyard. (*lit, fig*) **du** ~ local; **un vin d'un bon** ~ a good vintage. **(b)** (*vin*) wine. **un grand** ~ a famous *ou* great wine *ou* vintage; *V* **bouilleur. (c)** (*loc*) **de son (propre)** ~ of his own invention *ou* devising.
cruauté [kʀyote] *nf* **(a)** *[personne, destin]* cruelty; *[bête sauvage]* ferocity. **(b)** act of cruelty, cruel act, cruelty.
cruche [kʀyʃ] *nf* **(a)** (*récipient*) pitcher, (earthenware) jug; (*contenu*) jug(ful). **(b)** (‡: *imbécile*) ass*, twit‡ (*Brit*).
cruchon [kʀyʃɔ̃] *nm* small jug; (*contenu*) small jug(ful).
crucial, e, *mpl* **-aux** [kʀysjal, o] *adj question, année, problème* crucial.
crucifère [kʀysifɛʀ] *adj* cruciferous.
crucifiement [kʀysifimɑ̃] *nm* crucifixion. (*fig*) **le** ~ **de la chair** the crucifying of the flesh.
crucifier [kʀysifje] (7) *vt* (*lit, fig*) to crucify.
crucifix [kʀysifi] *nm* crucifix.
crucifixion [kʀysifiksjɔ̃] *nf* crucifixion.
cruciforme [kʀysifɔʀm(ə)] *adj* cruciform.
cruciverbiste [kʀysivɛʀbist(ə)] *nmf* crossword-puzzle enthusiast.
crudité [kʀydite] *nf* **(a)** (*U*) *[langage]* crudeness, coarseness; *[couleur]* harshness, garishness; *[lumière]* harshness. **(b)** (*propos*) ~**s** coarse remarks, coarseness (*U*); **dire des** ~**s** to make coarse remarks. **(c)** (*Culin*) ~**s** ≃ salads.
crue[2] [kʀy] *nf [rivière]* swelling, rising. **en** ~ in spate; **les** ~**s du Nil** the Nile floods; **la fonte des neiges provoque des** ~**s subites** the spring thaw produces a sudden rise in river levels.
cruel, -elle [kʀyɛl] *adj* **(a)** (*méchant*) *personne, acte, paroles* cruel; *animal* ferocious.
(b) (*douloureux*) *perte* cruel; *destin, sort* cruel, harsh; *remords, froid* cruel, bitter; *nécessité* cruel, bitter. **cette** ~**le épreuve, courageusement supportée** this cruel ordeal, borne with courage.
cruellement [kʀyɛlmɑ̃] *adv* (*V* **cruel**) cruelly; ferociously; harshly. **l'argent fait** ~ **défaut** the lack of money is sorely felt; ~ **éprouvé par ce deuil** sorely *ou* greviously distressed by this bereavement.
crûment [kʀymɑ̃] *adv dire, parler* bluntly, forthrightly, plainly. **éclairer** ~ to cast a harsh light over.
crustacé [kʀystase] *nm* (*Zool*) shellfish (*U*) (*crabs, lobsters and shrimps*), member of the lobster family, crustacean (*T*). (*Culin*) ~**s** seafood, shellfish.
crypte [kʀipt(ə)] *nf* crypt.
cryptocommuniste [kʀiptɔkɔmynist(ə)] *nmf* crypto-communist.
cryptogramme [kʀiptɔgʀam] *nm* cryptogram.
cryptographie [kʀiptɔgʀafi] *nf* cryptography.
cryptographique [kʀiptɔgʀafik] *adj* cryptographic.
crypton [kʀiptɔ̃] *nm* = **krypton.**
Cuba [kyba] *nf* Cuba.
cubage [kybaʒ] *nm* **(a)** (*action*) cubage. **(b)** (*volume*) cubage, cubature, cubic content. ~ **d'air** air space.
cubain, e [kybɛ̃, ɛn] **1** *adj* Cuban. **2** *nm,f*: **C**~**(e)** Cuban.
cube [kyb] **1** *nm* (*Géom, Math, gén*) cube; *[jeu]* building block, (wooden) brick. (*Math*) **le** ~ **de 2 est 8** 2 cubed is 8, the cube of 2 is 8; **élever au** ~ to cube. **2** *adj*: **centimètre/mètre** ~ cubic centimetre/metre; *V* **cylindrée.**
cuber [kybe] (1) **1** *vt nombre* to cube; *volume, solide* to cube, measure the volume of; *espace* to measure the cubic capacity of.
2 *vi [récipient]* ~ **20 litres** to have a cubic capacity of 20 litres; (*fig*) **avec l'inflation leurs dépenses vont** ~ with inflation their expenses are going to mount up.
cubique [kybik] **1** *adj* cubic; *V* **racine. 2** *nf* (*Math: courbe*) cubic.
cubisme [kybism(ə)] *nm* cubism.
cubiste [kybist(ə)] *adj, nmf* cubist.
cubital, e, *mpl* **-aux** [kybital, o] *adj* ulnar.
cubitus [kybitys] *nm* ulna.
cucul* [kyky] *adj*: ~ **(la praline)** silly, goofy*.
cueillette [kœjɛt] *nf* **(a)** (*V* **cueillir**) picking; gathering; (*Ethnologie*) gathering. **la** ~ **du houblon/des pommes** hop-/apple-picking; **cette tribu pratique la** ~ the people of this tribe are gatherers.
(b) (*fruits etc*) harvest (of fruit), crop (of fruit). **elle me montra sa** ~ she showed me the (bunch of) flowers she'd picked; **mûres, myrtilles en abondance: quelle** ~**!** brambles, bilberries galore: what a harvest! *ou* crop!
cueillir [kœjiʀ] (12) *vt* **(a)** *fleurs* to pick, gather; (*séparément*) to pick, pluck; *pommes, poires etc* to pick; *fraises, mûres* to gather, pick.
(b) (*fig: attraper*) *ballon* to catch; *baiser* to snatch *ou* steal; (*) *voleur* to nab*, pick up. ~ **les lauriers de la victoire** to win *ou* bring home the laurels (of victory); **il est venu nous** ~ **à la gare*** he came to collect *ou* get us *ou* pick us up at the station; **il m'a cueilli à froid** (*bagarre, débat*) he caught me off guard *ou* on the hop* (*Brit*).
cuiller, cuillère [kɥijɛʀ] **1** *nf* **(a)** (*ustensile*) spoon; (*contenu*) spoonful. **prenez une** ~ **à café de sirop** take a teaspoonful of cough mixture; **petite** ~ (*à thé, à dessert*) ≃ teaspoon; *V* **dos, ramasser, trois.**
(b) (‡: *main*) **serrer la** ~ **à qn** to shake sb's paw*.
(c) (*Pêche*) **pêche à la** ~ spoon-bait fishing, fishing with a spoon (bait).
(d) (*Tech*) *[grenade]* (safety) catch.
2: **cuiller à café** coffee spoon, ≃ teaspoon; **cuiller à dessert** dessertspoon; **cuiller à moutarde** mustard spoon; **cuiller à pot** ladle (*V* **coup**); **cuiller à soupe** soupspoon, ≃ tablespoon; **cuiller de verrier** (glassblower's) ladle.
cuillerée [kɥijʀe] *nf* spoonful. (*Culin*) ~ **à soupe** ≃ tablespoonful; (*Culin*) ~ **à café** ≃ teaspoonful.
cuir [kɥiʀ] **1** *nm* **(a)** (*peau apprêtée*) leather. **ceinture/semelles de** ~ leather belt/soles; **objets** *ou* **articles en** ~ leather articles *ou* goods; (*collectivement*) leathercraft, leatherwork.
(b) (*sur l'animal vivant, avant tannage*) hide.
(c) (*: *faute de liaison*) false liaison (*intrusive z- or t-sound*); *V* **relié, rond, tanner.**
2: **cuir artificiel** imitation leather; **cuir bouilli** cuir-bouilli; **cuir brut** rawhide; (*Anat*) **cuir chevelu** scalp; **cuir de crocodile** crocodile skin; **cuir en croûte** undressed leather; **cuir à rasoir** (barber's *ou* razor) strop; **cuir de serpent** snakeskin; **cuir suédé** suede, suède; **cuir de vache** cowhide; **cuir de veau** calfskin; **cuir verni** patent leather; **cuir vert** = **cuir brut.**
cuirasse [kɥiʀas] *nf* (*Hist*) *[chevalier]* cuirass, breastplate; (*Naut*) armour(-plate *ou* -plating); (*Zool*) cuirass; (*fig*) armour; *V* **défaut.**
cuirassé, e [kɥiʀase] (*ptp de* **cuirasser**) **1** *adj soldat* cuirassed, in cuirass, breastplated; *navire* armour-plated, armoured. (*fig*) **être** ~ **contre qch** to be hardened against sth, be proof against sth. **2** *nm* battleship.
cuirasser [kɥiʀase] (1) **1** *vt chevalier* to cuirass, put a cuirass *ou* breastplate on; *navire* to armour-plate; (*fig: endurcir*) to harden (*contre* against).
2 se cuirasser *vpr* **(a)** *[chevalier]* to put on a cuirass *ou* breastplate.
(b) (*fig: s'endurcir*) to harden o.s. (*contre* against). **se** ~ **contre la douleur/l'émotion** to harden o.s. against suffering/emotion.
cuirassier [kɥiʀasje] *nm* (*Hist*) cuirassier; (*Mil*) (*soldat*) (armoured) cavalryman. (*régiment*) **le 3e** ~ the 3rd (armoured) cavalry.
cuire [kɥiʀ] (38) **1** *vt* **(a)** (*aussi faire* ~) *plat, dîner* to cook. ~ **à feu doux** *ou* **doucement** to cook gently *ou* slowly; ~ **à petit feu** to simmer; **laisser** *ou* **faire** ~ **à feu doux** *ou* **à petit feu pendant 20**

minutes (allow to) simmer *ou* cook gently for 20 minutes; ~ **au bain-marie** ≈ to heat in a double saucepan, heat in a bain-marie; ~ **à la broche** to cook *ou* roast on the spit, spit-roast; ~ **au four** *pain, gâteau, pommes* to bake; *viande* to roast; *pommes de terre* to roast, bake; ~ **à la vapeur/au gril/à la poêle/à l'eau/à la casserole** to steam/grill/fry/boil/stew; ~ **au beurre** to cook in butter; ~ **au gaz/à l'électricité** to cook on *ou* with gas/by *ou* on electricity; **faire** *ou* **laisser** ~ **qch pendant 15 minutes** to cook (*ou* boil *ou* roast) sth for 15 minutes; **faites-le** ~ **dans son jus** cook *ou* stew it in its own juice; **faire bien/peu** ~ **qch** to cook sth thoroughly *ou* well/slightly *ou* lightly; **faire trop** ~ **qch** to overcook sth; **ne pas faire assez** ~ **qch** to undercook sth; **il l'a fait** ~ **à point** he cooked it to a turn; *V* **carotte, cuit, dur.**

(b) four qui cuit mal la viande oven which cooks *ou* does meat badly *ou* unevenly.

(c) (*Boulangerie*) *pain* to bake.

(d) *briques, porcelaine* to fire; *V* **terre.**

(e) à ~ *chocolat* cooking (*épith*); *prunes, poires* stewing (*épith*); **pommes à** ~ cooking apples, cookers* (*Brit*).

2 *vi* **(a)** *[aliment]* to cook. ~ **à gros bouillon(s)** to boil hard *ou* fast; **le dîner cuit à feu doux** *ou* **à petit feu** the dinner is cooking gently *ou* is simmering *ou* is on low; ~ **dans son jus** to cook in its own juice, stew.

(b) (*fig*) *[personne]* ~ **au soleil** to roast in the sun; ~ **dans son jus*** (*avoir très chaud*) to be boiling* *ou* roasting*; (*se morfondre*) to stew in one's own juice; **on cuit ici!*** it's boiling (hot)* *ou* roasting* in here!

(c) (*brûler, picoter*) **les mains/yeux me cuisaient** my hands/eyes were smarting *ou* stinging; **mon dos me cuit** my back is burning.

(d) (*frm*) **il lui en a cuit** he suffered for it, he had good reason to regret it; **il vous en cuira** you'll rue the day (you did it) (*frm*), you'll live to rue it (*frm*).

cuisant, e [kɥizɑ̃, ɑ̃t] *adj* **(a)** (*physiquement*) *douleur* smarting, sharp, burning; *blessure* burning, stinging; *froid* bitter, biting. **(b)** (*moralement*) *remarque* caustic, stinging; *échec, regret* bitter.

cuisine [kɥizin] **1** *nf* **(a)** (*pièce*) kitchen; (*Naut*) galley. **table/couteau de** ~ kitchen table/knife; *V* **batterie, latin, livre**[1] *etc.*

(b) (*art culinaire*) cookery, cooking; (*préparation*) cooking; (*nourriture apprêtée*) cooking, food. **apprendre la** ~ to learn cookery; **la** ~ **prend du temps** cooking takes time; **une** ~ **épicée** hot *ou* spicy dishes *ou* food; **une** ~ **soignée** carefully prepared dishes *ou* food; **aimer la bonne** ~ to like good cooking *ou* food; **il est en train de faire la** ~ he's busy cooking *ou* making the meal; **chez eux, c'est le mari qui fait la** ~ the husband does the cooking *ou* the husband is the cook in their house; **savoir faire la**~, **faire de la bonne** ~ to be a good cook, be good at cooking.

(c) (*personnel*) *[maison privée]* kitchen staff; *[cantine etc]* kitchen *ou* catering staff.

(d) (*fig péj*) ~ **électorale** electoral manoeuvres *ou* jiggery-pokery*; **je n'aime pas beaucoup sa petite** ~ I'm not very fond of his little fiddles *ou* his underhand tricks.

2: cuisine au beurre/à l'huile cooking with *ou* in butter/oil; **cuisine bourgeoise** (good) plain cooking *ou* fare; **faire une cuisine bourgeoise** to do (good) plain cooking; **cuisine de cantine** canteen food; **la cuisine française** French cooking *ou* cuisine; **cuisine de restaurant** restaurant meals *ou* food; (*Mil*) **cuisine roulante** field kitchen.

cuisiner [kɥizine] (1) *vt* **(a)** *plat* to cook. **il cuisine bien** he's a good cook; **ne la dérange pas quand elle cuisine** don't bother her when she's cooking. **(b)** (**fig*) *personne* to grill*, pump* for information *etc.*

cuisinier, -ière [kɥizinje, jɛʀ] **1** *nm,f* (*personne*) cook. **2 cuisinière** *nf* (*à gaz, électrique*) cooker; (*à bois*) (kitchen) range. ~**ière à gaz** gas cooker *ou* stove; ~**ière à charbon** solid fuel stove, coal-fired cooker; (*vieux modèle*) kitchen range.

cuissard [kɥisaʀ] *nm [armure]* cuisse; *[cycliste]* shorts (*pl*).

cuissardes [kɥisaʀd(ə)] *nfpl [pêcheur]* waders; (*mode féminine*) thigh boots.

cuisse [kɥis] **1** *nf* (*Anat*) thigh. (*Culin*) ~ **de mouton** leg of mutton *ou* lamb; ~ **de poulet** chicken leg, drumstick; (*fig*) **se croire sorti de la** ~ **de Jupiter*** to think a lot of o.s., think no small beer of o.s. (*Brit*); **tu te crois sorti de la** ~ **de Jupiter!*** you think you're God's gift to mankind!*

2: cuisse madame (*poire*) cuisse madam pear.

cuisseau, *pl* ~**x** [kɥiso] *nm* haunch (of veal).

cuisson [kɥisɔ̃] *nf [aliments]* cooking; *[pain, gâteau]* baking; *[briques]* firing. (*Culin*) **ceci demande une longue** ~ this needs to be cooked (*ou* baked) for a long time; (*Culin*) **temps de** ~ cooking time.

cuissot [kɥiso] *nm* haunch (of venison *ou* wild boar).

cuistance‡ [kɥistɑ̃s] *nf* (*préparation de nourriture*) cooking, preparing the grub‡; (*nourriture*) nosh‡, grub‡.

cuistot* [kɥisto] *nm* cook.

cuistre [kɥistʀ(ə)] *nm* prig, priggish pedant.

cuistrerie [kɥistʀəʀi] *nf* priggish pedantry.

cuit, e[1] [kɥi, kɥit] (*ptp de* **cuire**) *adj* **(a)** *aliment, plat* cooked, ready (*attrib*); *pain, viande* ready (*attrib*), done (*attrib*). **bien** ~ well cooked *ou* done; **trop** ~ overdone; **pas assez** ~ underdone; ~ **à point** done to a turn.

(b) (*loc*) **c'est du tout** ~* it's *ou* it'll be a cinch*, it's *ou* it'll be a walkover*; **il est** ~* (*il va se faire prendre*) he's done for, his goose is cooked*; (*il va perdre*) it's all up for him, he's had it*; **c'est** ~ **(pour ce soir)*** we've had it (for tonight)*.

cuite[2] [kɥit] *nf* **(a)** (‡) **prendre une** ~ to get plastered‡ *ou* canned‡; **il a pris une sacrée** ~ he got really plastered‡, he was really rolling drunk*. **(b)** (*Tech: cuisson*) firing.

cuiter (se)‡ [kɥite] *vpr* to get plastered‡ *ou* canned‡.

cuivre [kɥivʀ(ə)] *nm* **(a)** ~ **(rouge)** copper; ~ **jaune** brass; **objets** *ou* **articles en** ~ copperware; **casseroles à fond** ~ copper-bottomed pans; *V* **gravure.**

(b) (*Art*) copperplate.

(c) (*ustensiles*) ~**s** (*de cuivre*) copper; (*de cuivre et laiton*) brasses; **faire (briller) les** ~**s** to do the brass *ou* the brasses.

(d) (*Mus*) **les** ~**s** the brass; **orchestre de** ~**s** brass band.

cuivré, e [kɥivʀe] (*ptp de* **cuivrer**) *adj reflets* coppery; *peau, teint* bronzed. **voix** ~**e** (deep) resonant voice; **cheveux aux reflets** ~**s** hair with auburn glints *ou* copper lights in it.

cuivrer [kɥivʀe] (1) *vt* (*Tech*) to copper(plate), cover with copper; *peau, teint* to bronze.

cuivreux, -euse [kɥivʀø, øz] *adj* (*Chim*) *métal* cuprous. **oxyde** ~ cuprous oxide, cuprite.

cul [ky] **1** *nm* **(a)** (∵*Anat*) backside*, bum‡ (*Brit*), arse∵, ass∵ (*US*). **il est tombé le** ~ **dans l'eau** he fell arse first in the water∵; **un coup de pied au** ~ a kick *ou* boot up the arse∵ *ou* backside*; *V* **feu**[1], **tirer, trou** *etc.*

(b) (*Hist Habillement*) **(faux)** ~ bustle.

(c) (*fig: fond, arrière*) *[bouteille]* bottom. **faire un cendrier d'un** ~ **de bouteille** to make an ashtray with *ou* from the bottom of a bottle; ~ **de verre/de pot** glass-/jug-bottom; **pousser une voiture au** ~* to give a car a shove.

(d) (*loc*) **faire** ~ **sec** to down one's drink in a oner‡ (*Brit*) *ou* at one go*; **allez,** ~ **sec!** right, bottoms up!*; **renverser** ~ **par-dessus tête** to turn head over heels; **on l'a dans le** ~∵ that's really screwed us (up)∵; **en tomber** *ou* **rester sur le** ~* to be taken aback, be flabbergasted; **être comme** ~ **et chemise** to be as thick as thieves; **tu peux te le mettre** *ou* **foutre au** ~**!**∵ (you can) shove *ou* stick it up your arse!∵, go and stuff yourself!‡ (*Brit*) *ou* fuck yourself!∵; **mon** ~**!**∵ my arse!∵ (*Brit*), my ass!∵ (*US*).

2: cul d'artichaut artichoke bottom; **cul-de-basse-fosse** *nm, pl* **culs-de-basse-fosse** dungeon; (*Orn*) **cul-blanc** *nm, pl* **culs-blancs** wheatear; **cul-de-jatte** *nm, pl* **culs-de-jatte** legless cripple; **cul-de-lampe** *nm, pl* **culs-de-lampe** (*Archit*) cul-de-lampe; (*Typ*) tailpiece; (*péj*) **cul-de-poule: bouche/sourire en cul-de-poule** pouting mouth/smile; (*Orn*) **cul-rouge** *nm, pl* **culs-rouges** great spotted woodpecker; **cul-de-sac** *nm, pl* **culs-de-sac** (*rue*) cul-de-sac, dead end; (*fig*) blind alley; (*fig péj*) **cul-terreux** *nm, pl* **culs-terreux** yokel, country bumpkin.

3 *adj inv* (‡: *stupide*) silly. **quel** ~**, ce type!** he's a real twerp‡ *ou* he's wet‡, that chap!

culasse [kylas] *nf* **(a)** *[moteur]* cylinder head; *V* **joint. (b)** *[canon, fusil]* breech. ~ **(mobile)** breechblock; *V* **bloc.**

culbute [kylbyt] *nf* **(a)** (*cabriole*) somersault; (*chute*) tumble, fall. **faire une** ~ (*cabriole*) to (turn a) somersault; (*chute*) to (take a) tumble, fall (head over heels).

(b) (**fig*) *[ministère]* collapse, fall; *[banque]* collapse. **faire la** ~ *[spéculation, banque]* to collapse; *[entreprise]* to go bust*; **ce spéculateur a fait la** ~ this speculator has come a cropper*.

culbuter [kylbyte] (1) **1** *vi [personne]* to (take a) tumble, fall (head over heels); *[chose]* to topple (over), fall (over); *[voiture]* to somersault, turn a somersault, overturn. **il a culbuté dans l'étang** he tumbled *ou* fell into the pond.

2 *vt chaise etc* to upset, knock over; *personne* to knock over; (*fig*) *ennemi* to overwhelm; (*fig*) *ministère etc* to bring down, topple.

culbuteur [kylbytœʀ] *nm* **(a)** (*Tech*) *[moteur]* rocker arm. **(b)** *[benne]* tipper. **(c)** (*jouet*) tumbler.

culer [kyle] (1) *vi* (*Naut*) *[bateau]* to go astern; *[vent]* to veer astern. **brasser à** ~ to brace aback.

culinaire [kylinɛʀ] *adj* culinary. **l'art** ~ culinary art, the art of cooking.

culminant, e [kylminɑ̃, ɑ̃t] *adj V* **point**[1].

culminer [kylmine] (1) *vi* **(a)** *[sommet, massif]* to tower (*au-dessus de* above). ~ **à** to reach its highest point at; **le Massif central culmine à 1.886 mètres au Puy de Sancy** the Massif Central reaches its highest point of 1,886 metres at the Puy de Sancy; **le Mont-Blanc culmine à 4.807 mètres** Mont Blanc reaches 4,807 metres at its highest point.

(b) (*fig*) *[colère]* to reach a peak, come to a head.

(c) (*Astron*) to reach its highest point.

culot [kylo] *nm* **(a)** (*: *effronterie*) cheek*. **il a du** ~ he has a lot of cheek*; **tu ne manques pas de** ~**!** you've got a nerve!* *ou* a cheek!*

(b) *[ampoule]* cap; *[cartouche]* cap, base; *[bougie]* body; *[obus, bombe]* base.

(c) (*résidu*) *[pipe]* dottle; (*Ind*) *[creuset]* residue.

culottage [kylɔtaʒ] *nm [pipe]* seasoning.

culotte [kylɔt] **1** *nf* **(a)** *[enfant]* pants; *[femme]* (†) knickers. **bonbons de** ~ trouser buttons; *V* **couche, fond, gaine.**

(b) (*Boucherie*) rump.

(c) (*loc*) **baisser** *ou* **poser** ~‡ (*lit*) to pull *ou* take one's knickers (*Brit*) *ou* panties (*US*) down; (*fig*) to back down; **chez eux c'est elle qui porte la** ~ she wears the trousers in their house; **prendre une** ~* (*au jeu*) to come a cropper*, lose heavily; (*fig*) **trembler** *ou* **faire dans sa** ~‡, **mouiller sa** ~‡ to wet oneself‡ (*fig*), pee one's pants‡ (*fig*), shake in one's shoes.

2: culotte de bain† (swimming *ou* bathing) trunks; **culotte(s) bouffante(s)** jodhpurs; (†) bloomers; **culotte(s) de cheval** riding breeches; **culotte(s) courte(s)/longue(s)** short/long trousers; **culotte de golf** plus fours, knickerbockers; (*péj Mil*) **culotte de peau: une (vieille) culotte de peau** a colonel Blimp.

culotté, e [kylɔte] (*ptp de* **culotter**) *adj* **(a)** (*) cheeky*. **(b)** *pipe* seasoned; *cuir* mellowed.

culotter [kylɔte] (1) **1** *vt* **(a)** *pipe* to season. **(b)** (*rare*) *petit garçon* to put trousers on. **2 se culotter** *vpr* **(a)** *[pipe]* to season. **(b)** (*rare*) *[enfant]* to put one's trousers on.

culottier, -ière† [kylɔtje, jɛʀ] *nm,f* trouser maker, breeches maker†.

culpabilité [kylpabilite] *nf* guilt; *V* **sentiment.**

culte [kylt(ə)] *nm* **(a)** (*vénération*) cult, worship. **le ~ de Dieu** the worship of God; **le ~ du feu/du soleil** fire-/sun-worship; **avoir le ~ de** *justice* to make a cult *ou* religion of; *argent* to worship; **avoir un ~ pour qn** to (hero) worship sb; **rendre** *ou* **vouer un ~ à qn/la mémoire de qn** to worship sb/sb's memory.

(b) (*pratiques*) cult; (*religion*) religion. **abandonner le/changer de ~** to give up/change one's religion; **le ~ catholique** the Catholic form of worship; **les objets du ~** liturgical objects; *V* **denier, liberté, ministre.**

(c) (*office protestant*) (church) service. **assister au ~** to attend the (church) service.

cultivable [kyltivabl(ə)] *adj terrain* suitable for cultivation, cultivable.

cultivateur, -trice [kyltivatœʀ, tʀis] **1** *adj peuple* agricultural, farming (*épith*). **2** *nm,f* farmer. **3** *nm* (*machine*) cultivator.

cultivé, e [kyltive] (*ptp de* **cultiver**) *adj* (*instruit*) *homme, esprit* cultured, cultivated. **peu ~** with *ou* of little culture.

cultiver [kyltive] (1) **1** *vt* **(a)** *jardin, champ* to cultivate. **~ la terre** to cultivate the soil, till *ou* farm the land; **des terrains cultivés** cultivated lands, lands under cultivation.

(b) *céréales, légumes, vigne* to grow, cultivate.

(c) (*exercer*) *goût, mémoire, don* to cultivate. **~ son esprit** to improve *ou* cultivate one's mind.

(d) (*pratiquer*) *art, sciences* to cultivate. (*iro*) **il cultive la grossièreté** he makes a point of being rude, he goes out of his way to be rude.

(e) (*fréquenter*) *personne* to cultivate. **c'est une relation à ~** it's a connection which should be cultivated; **~ l'amitié de qn** to cultivate sb's friendship.

2 se cultiver *vpr* to improve *ou* cultivate one's mind.

cultuel, -elle [kyltɥɛl] *adj*: **édifices ~s** places of worship; **association ~le** *religious administrative organization.*

culture [kyltyʀ] *nf* **(a)** *[champ, jardin]* cultivation; *[légumes]* growing, cultivating, cultivation. **méthodes de ~** farming methods, methods of cultivation; **~ mécanique** mechanized farming; **~ intensive/extensive** intensive/extensive farming; **pays de moyenne/grande ~** country with a medium-scale/large-scale farming industry; **~ maraîchère/fruitière** vegetable/fruit farming.

(b) (*terres cultivées*) **~s** land(s) under cultivation, arable land.

(c) *[esprit]* improvement, cultivation. **la ~** culture; **la ~ occidentale** western culture; **~ scientifique/générale** scientific/general knowledge *ou* education; **~ classique** classical culture *ou* education; **~ de masse** mass culture.

(d) **~ physique** physical culture *ou* training, P.T.; **faire de la ~ physique** to do physical training.

(e) (*Bio*) **~ microbienne/de tissus** microbe/tissue culture; *V* **bouillon.**

culturel, -elle [kyltyʀɛl] *adj* cultural.

culturisme [kyltyʀism(ə)] *nm* body-building.

cumin [kymɛ̃] *nm* (*Culin*) caraway seeds, cumin.

cumul [kymyl] *nm* **(a)** *[fonctions, charges]* plurality; *[avantages]* amassing; *[traitements]* concurrent drawing. **le ~ de fonctions est interdit** it is forbidden to hold more than one office at the same time *ou* concurrently; **le ~ de la pension de retraite et de cette allocation est interdit** it is forbidden to draw the retirement pension and this allowance at the same time *ou* concurrently.

(b) (*Jur*) *[droits]* accumulation. **avec ~ de peines** sentences to run consecutively; **~ d'infractions** combination of offences.

cumulable [kymylabl(ə)] *adj fonctions* which may be held concurrently *ou* simultaneously; *traitements* which may be drawn concurrently *ou* simultaneously.

cumulard [kymylaʀ] *nm* (*péj*) *holder of several remunerative positions.*

cumulatif, -ive [kymylatif, iv] *adj* cumulative.

cumulativement [kymylativmɑ̃] *adv exercer des fonctions* simultaneously, concurrently; (*Jur*) *purger des peines* consecutively.

cumuler [kymyle] (1) *vt* **(a)** *fonctions* to hold concurrently *ou* simultaneously; *traitements* to draw concurrently *ou* simultaneously. **~ 2 traitements** to draw 2 separate salaries; **~ les fonctions de directeur et de comptable** to act simultaneously as manager and accountant, hold concurrently the positions of manager and accountant.

(b) (*Jur*) *droits* to accumulate.

cumulo-nimbus [kymylonɛ̃bys] *nm* cumulonimbus.

cumulus [kymylys] *nm* cumulus (*T*). **~ de beau temps** (*pl*) fine-weather clouds; **~ d'orage** (*pl*) storm clouds.

cunéiforme [kyneifɔʀm(ə)] *adj* **(a)** *écriture, caractère* wedge-shaped, cuneiform (*T*). **(b)** (*Anat*) **les (os) ~s** the cuneiform bones (*of the tarsus*).

cupide [kypid] *adj air* greedy, filled with greed (*attrib*); *personne* grasping, greedy, moneygrubbing.

cupidement [kypidmɑ̃] *adv* greedily.

cupidité [kypidite] *nf* (*caractère: V* **cupide**) grasping nature; greed. (*défaut*) **la ~** cupidity (*littér*), greed.

Cupidon [kypidɔ̃] *nm* Cupid.

cuprifère [kypʀifɛʀ] *adj* cupriferous (*T*), copper-bearing.

cupule [kypyl] *nf* (*Bot*) cupule; *[gland]* (acorn) cup.

curabilité [kyʀabilite] *nf* curability.

curable [kyʀabl(ə)] *adj* curable.

curaçao [kyʀaso] *nm* curaçao.

curage [kyʀaʒ] *nm [fossé, égout]* clearing- *ou* cleaning-out; *[puits]* cleaning-out.

curare [kyʀaʀ] *nm* curare.

curatelle [kyʀatɛl] *nf* (*V* **curateur**) guardianship; trusteeship.

curateur, -trice [kyʀatœʀ, tʀis] *nm,f [mineur, aliéné]* guardian; *[succession]* trustee.

curatif, -ive [kyʀatif, iv] *adj* curative.

cure[1] [kyʀ] *nf* **(a)** (*traitement*) course of treatment. **une ~ (thermale)** ≃ a course of treatment *ou* a cure at a spa; **faire une ~ (thermale) à Vichy** to take the waters at Vichy; **~ d'amaigrissement** slimming course; **~ de sommeil** hypnotherapy (*U*), sleep therapy (*U*).

(b) (*grande consommation de*) **~ de: une ~ de fruits/de légumes/de lait** a fruit/vegetable/milk cure, a fruit-/vegetable-/milk-only diet; **~ de repos** rest cure; **nous avons fait une ~ de théâtre, cet hiver** we had a positive orgy of theatregoing this winter.

cure[2] [kyʀ] *nf* (*littér, hum*) **n'avoir ~ de qch** to care little about sth, pay no attention to sth; **il n'en a ~** he's not worried about that, he pays no attention to that; **je n'ai ~ de ces formalités** I've no time for these formalities.

cure[3] [kyʀ] *nf* (*Rel*) (*fonction*) cure; (*paroisse*) cure, ≃ living; (*maison*) presbytery, ≃ vicarage. **~ de village** village living *ou* cure.

cure- [kyʀ] *préf V* **curer.**

curé [kyʀe] *nm* parish priest. **~ de campagne** country priest; **se faire ~*** to go in for the priesthood; (*péj*) **les ~s** clerics; **il n'aime pas les ~s** he hates clerics; **élevé chez les ~s** brought up by clerics; *V* **bouffer**[2]**, Monsieur.**

curée [kyʀe] *nf* **(a)** (*Chasse*) quarry. **donner la ~ aux chiens** to give the quarry to the hounds. **(b)** (*fig: ruée*) scramble (for the spoils). **se ruer** *ou* **aller à la ~** to scramble for the spoils.

curer [kyʀe] (1) **1** *vt* **(a)** *fossé, égout* to clear *ou* clean out; *puits* to clean out; *pipe* to clean out, scrape out.

(b) **se ~ les dents/le nez** to pick one's teeth/nose; **se ~ les ongles/oreilles** to clean one's nails/ears.

2: cure-dent *nm, pl* **cure-dents** toothpick; **cure-ongles** *nm inv* nail-cleaner; **cure-oreille** *nm, pl* **cure-oreilles** earpick; **cure-pipe** *nm, pl* **cure-pipes** pipe cleaner.

curetage [kyʀtaʒ] *nm* curetting, curettage.

cureter [kyʀte] (5) *vt* to curette.

cureton [kyʀtɔ̃] *nm* (*péj*) priestling.

curette [kyʀɛt] *nf* (*Tech*) scraper; (*Méd*) curette.

curie[1] [kyʀi] *nf* (*Hist romaine*) curia; (*Rel*) Curia.

curie[2] [kyʀi] *nm* (*Phys*) curie.

curieusement [kyʀjøzmɑ̃] *adv* strangely, curiously, oddly, peculiarly.

curieux, -euse [kyʀjø, øz] **1** *adj* **(a)** (*intéressé*) **esprit ~** inquiring mind; **~ de tout** curious about everything; **il est particulièrement ~ de mathématiques** he's especially interested in *ou* keen on mathematics; **~ d'apprendre** keen to learn; **je serais ~ de voir/savoir** I'd be interested *ou* curious to see/know.

(b) (*indiscret*) curious, inquisitive, nosey*. **lancer un regard ~ sur qch** to glance inquisitively *ou* nosily* *ou* curiously at sth.

(c) (*bizarre*) *coïncidence, individu, réaction* strange, curious, funny. **ce qui est ~, c'est que ...** the funny *ou* strange *ou* curious thing is that ...; *V* **bête, chose.**

2 *nm* (*U: étrangeté*) **le ~, dans cette affaire** the funny *ou* strange thing in *ou* about this business; **le plus ~ de la chose** the funniest *ou* strangest thing *ou* the most curious thing about it.

3 *nm,f* **(a)** (*indiscret*) inquisitive person, nosey-parker*, busybody*. **petite ~euse!** little nosey-parker!* (*Brit*) *ou* Nosy Parker* (*US*), nosey little thing!*

(b) (*gén mpl: badaud*) (inquisitive) onlooker, bystander. **éloigner les ~** to move the bystanders along; **venir en ~** to come (just) for a look *ou* to have a look.

curiosité [kyʀjozite] *nf* **(a)** (*U: intérêt*) curiosity. **~ intellectuelle** intellectual curiosity; **cette ~ de tout** this curiosity about (knowing) everything; **ayant eu la ~ d'essayer cette méthode ...** having been curious enough to try this method ... .

(b) (*U: indiscrétion*) curiosity, inquisitiveness, nosiness*. **des ~s malsaines** unhealthy curiosity; **par (pure) ~** out of (sheer) curiosity; **poussé par la ~** spurred on by curiosity; **la ~ est un vilain défaut** curiosity killed the cat.

(c) (*site, monument etc*) curious *ou* unusual sight *ou* feature; (*bibelot*) curio. **les ~s de la ville** the (interesting *ou* unusual) sights of the town; **un magasin de ~s** a curio *ou* curiosity shop; **cet objet n'a qu'une valeur de ~** this object has only a curiosity value; **ce timbre est une ~ pour les amateurs** this stamp has a curiosity value for collectors.

curiste [kyʀist(ə)] *nmf* person taking the waters (*at a spa*).

curling [kœʀliŋ] *nm* curling.

curriculum vitae [kyʀikylɔmvite] *nm inv* curriculum vitae.

curry [kyʀi] *nm* curry. **poulet au ~** curried chicken, chicken curry.

curseur [kyʀsœʀ] *nm [règle à calculer]* slide, cursor; *[fermeture éclair]* slider.

cursif, -ive [kyʀsif, iv] *adj* **(a)** (*lié*) *écriture, lettre* cursive. **écrire en ~** to write in cursive script. **(b)** (*rapide*) *lecture, style* cursory.

curule [kyʀyl] *adj*: **chaise ~** curule chair.

curviligne [kyʀviliɲ] *adj* curvilinear.

cutané, e [kytane] *adj* skin (*épith*), cutaneous (*T*). **affection ~e** skin trouble; *V* **sous.**

cuti* [kyti] *nf abrév de* **cuti-réaction.**

cuticule [kytikyl] *nf* (*Bot, Zool*) cuticle.

cuti-réaction [kytiʀeaksjɔ̃] *nf* skin test. **faire une ~** to take a skin test; *V* **virer.**

cuvage [kyvaʒ] *nm [raisins]* fermentation (*in a vat*).

cuve [kyv] *nf [fermentation, teinture]* vat; *[brasserie]* mash tun; *[mazout]* tank; *[eau]* cistern, tank; *[blanchissage]* laundry vat. (*Phot*) **~ de développement** developing tank.

cuvée [kyve] *nf* (*contenu*) vatful; (*produit de toute une vigne*) vintage. **tonneaux d'une même ~** barrels of the same vintage;

vin de la première ~ wine from the first vintage; **la ~ 1937** the 1937 vintage; *V* **tête.**

cuver [kyve] (1) **1** *vt*: **~ son vin** to sleep it off*; **~ sa colère** to sleep off *ou* work off one's anger. **2** *vi [vin, raisins]* to ferment.

cuvette [kyvɛt] *nf* **(a)** (*récipient portatif*) (*gén*) basin, bowl; (*pour la toilette*) washbowl. **~ de plastique** plastic bowl.
(b) (*partie creuse*) *[lavabo]* washbasin, basin; *[évier]* basin; *[W.-C.]* pan.
(c) (*Géog*) basin.
(d) *[baromètre]* cistern, cup.
(e) *[montre]* cap.

cyanose [sjanoz] *nf* (*Méd*) cyanosis.

cyanure [sjanyʀ] *nm* cyanide.

cybernéticien, -ienne [sibɛʀnetisjɛ̃, jɛn] *nm,f* cyberneticist.

cybernétique [sibɛʀnetik] *nf* cybernetics (*sg*).

cyclable [siklabl(ə)] *adj*: **piste ~** cycle track.

cyclamen [siklamɛn] *nm* cyclamen.

cycle[1] [sikl(ə)] *nm* **(a)** (*révolution, Astron, Bio, Élec*) cycle.
(b) (*Littérat*) cycle. **le ~ breton** the Breton cycle.
(c) (*Scol*) **~ (d'études)** academic cycle; (*Scol*) **premier/deuxième ~** middle/upper school; (*Univ*) **premier ~** first and second year; (*Univ*) **deuxième ~** Final Honours; **étudiant de troisième ~** ≃ postgraduate *ou* Ph.D. student; **~ d'orientation** ≃ middle school (*transition classes*).

cycle[2] [sikl(ə)] *nm* (*bicyclette*) cycle. **l'industrie du ~** the cycle industry; **magasin de ~s** cycle shop; **marchand de ~s** bicycle merchant *ou* seller; **tarif: ~s 10 F, automobiles 45 F** charge: cycles and motorcycles 10 francs, cars 45 francs.

cyclique [siklik] *adj* cyclic(al).

cyclisme [siklism(ə)] *nm* cycling.

cycliste [siklist(ə)] **1** *adj*: **course/champion ~** cycle race/champion; **coureur ~** racing cyclist. **2** *nmf* cyclist.

cyclo-cross [siklɔkʀɔs] *nm* (*Sport*) cyclo-cross; (*épreuve*) cyclo-cross race.

cycloïdal, e, *mpl* **-aux** [siklɔidal, o] *adj* cycloid(al).

cycloïde [siklɔid] *nf* cycloid.

cyclomoteur [siklɔmɔtœʀ] *nm* moped.

cyclomotoriste [siklɔmɔtɔʀist(ə)] *nmf* moped rider.

cyclonal, e, *mpl* **-aux** [siklɔnal, o] *adj* cyclonic.

cyclone [siklon] *nm* (*Mét: typhon*) cyclone; (*Mét: zone de basse pression*) zone of low pressure; (*vent violent*) hurricane; (*fig*) whirlwind. **entrer comme un ~** to sweep *ou* come in like a whirlwind; *V* **œil.**

cyclope [siklɔp] *nm* (*Myth*) **C~** Cyclops; **travail de ~** Herculean task.

cyclopéen, -éenne [siklɔpeɛ̃, eɛn] *adj* (*Myth*) cyclopean. **travail ~** Herculean task.

cyclotron [siklɔtʀɔ̃] *nm* cyclotron.

cygne [siɲ] *nm* swan. **jeune ~** cygnet; **~ mâle** cob; *V* **bec, chant**[1]**, col.**

cylindrage [silɛ̃dʀaʒ] *nm* (*V* **cylindrer**) rolling; rolling up; pressing.

cylindre [silɛ̃dʀ(ə)] *nm* **(a)** (*Géom*) cylinder. **~ droit/oblique** right (circular)/oblique (circular) cylinder; **~ de révolution** cylindrical solid of revolution.
(b) (*rouleau*) roller; *[rouleau-compresseur]* wheel, roller. **~ d'impression** printing cylinder; *V* **bureau, presse.**
(c) *[moteur]* cylinder. **moteur à 4 ~s en ligne** a straight-4 engine; **moteur à 6 ~s en V** a vee-six *ou* V6 engine; **moteur à 2 ~s opposés** a flat-2 engine; **une 6 ~s** a 6-cylinder (car).

cylindrée [silɛ̃dʀe] *nf [moteur, cylindres]* capacity. **avoir une ~ de 1600 cm³** to have a capacity of 1600 ccs; **une voiture de grosse/petite ~, une grosse/petite ~** a big-/small-engined car; **les petites ~s consomment peu** cars with small engines *ou* small-engined cars don't use much (petrol).

cylindrer [silɛ̃dʀe] (1) *vt* (*former en cylindre*) *métal* to roll; *papier* to roll (up); (*presser, aplatir*) *linge* to press; *route* to roll.

cylindrique [silɛ̃dʀik] *adj* cylindrical.

cymbale [sɛ̃bal] *nf* cymbal; *V* **coup.**

cymbalier [sɛ̃balje] *nm* cymbalist.

cynégétique [sineʒetik] **1** *adj* cynegetic. **2** *nf* cynegetics (*sg*).

cynique [sinik] **1** *adj* cynical; (*Philos*) Cynic. **2** *nm* cynic; (*Philos*) Cynic.

cyniquement [sinikmɑ̃] *adv* cynically.

cynisme [sinism(ə)] *nm* cynicism; (*Philos*) Cynicism.

cynocéphale [sinɔsefal] *nm* dog-faced baboon, cynocephalus (*T*).

cynodrome [sinɔdʀom] *nm* greyhound track.

cyprès [sipʀɛ] *nm* cypress.

cypriote [sipʀijɔt] **1** *adj* Cypriot. **2** *nmf*: **C~** Cypriot.

cyrillique [siʀilik] *adj* Cyrillic.

cystite [sistit] *nf* cystitis (*U*).

Cythère [sitɛʀ] *nf* Cythera.

cytise [sitiz] *nm* laburnum.

cytologie [sitɔlɔʒi] *nf* cytology.

cytoplasme [sitɔplasm(ə)] *nm* cytoplasm.

czar [tsaʀ] *nm* = **tsar.**

czarewitch [tsaʀevitʃ] *nm* = **tsarévitch.**

czariste [tsaʀist(ə)] *adj* = **tsariste.**

D

D, d [de] *nm* (*lettre*) D, d; *V* **système.**

d' [d(ə)] *V* **de**[1]**, de**[2]**.**

da [da] *V* **oui.**

dab: [dab] *nm* (*père*) old man*, father.

d'abord [dabɔʀ] *loc adv V* **abord.**

dacquois, e [dakwa, waz] **1** *adj* of *ou* from Dax. **2** *nm,f*: **D~(e)** inhabitant *ou* native of Dax.

dacron [dakʀɔ̃] *nm* ® Dacron ®.

dactyle [daktil] *nm* (*Poésie*) dactyl; (*Bot*) cocksfoot.

dactylique [daktilik] *adj* dactylic.

dactylo [daktilo] *nf abrév de* **dactylographe, dactylographie.**

dactylographe [daktilɔgʀaf] *nf* typist.

dactylographie [daktilɔgʀafi] *nf* typing, typewriting. **elle apprend la ~** she's learning to type, she's learning typing.

dactylographier [daktilɔgʀafje] (7) *vt* to type (out).

dactylographique [daktilɔgʀafik] *adj* typing (*épith*).

dada[1] [dada] *nm* **(a)** (*langage enfantin: cheval*) horsy, gee-gee (*Brit langage enfantin*). **viens faire du ~** *ou* **à ~** come and ride the gee-gee *ou* the horsy.
(b) (*fig: marotte*) hobby-horse (*fig*). **enfourcher son ~** to get on one's hobby-horse, launch o.s. on one's pet subject.

dada[2] [dada] *adj* (*Art, Littérat*) Dada, dada.

dadais [dadɛ] *nm*: **(grand) ~** awkward lump (of a youth) (*péj*); **espèce de grand ~!** you great lump! (*péj*).

dadaïsme [dadaism(ə)] *nm* dadaism.

dadaïste [dadaist(ə)] *adj, nmf* dadaist.

dague [dag] *nm* **(a)** dagger. **(b)** *[cerf]* spike.

daguerréotype [dageʀeɔtip] *nm* (*procédé*) daguerreotype; (*instrument*) daguerre photographic device.

daguet [dagɛ] *nm* young stag, brocket.

dahlia [dalja] *nm* dahlia.

dahoméen, -enne [daɔmeɛ̃, ɛn] **1** *adj* Dahomean. **2** *nm,f*: **D~(ne)** Dahomean.

Dahomey [daɔmɛ] *nm* Dahomey.

daigner [dɛɲe] (1) *vt* to deign, condescend. **il n'a même pas daigné nous regarder** he did not even deign to look at us; (*frm*) **daignez nous excuser** be so good as to excuse us.

daim [dɛ̃] *nm* (*gén*) (fallow) deer; (*mâle*) buck; (*peau*) buckskin, doeskin; (*cuir suédé*) suede. **chaussures en ~** suede shoes.

daine [dɛn] *nf* doe.

dais [dɛ] *nm* canopy.

dallage [dalaʒ] *nm* (*U: action*) paving, flagging; (*surface, revêtement*) paving, pavement.

dalle [dal] *nf* **(a)** *[trottoir]* paving stone, flag(stone). **une ~ de pierre** a stone slab; **~ funéraire** slab, ledger.
(b) *[paroi de rocher]* slab.
(c) (:) **que ~** damn all: (*Brit*); **je n'y pige** *ou* **n'entrave que ~** I don't get it*, I can understand damn all: (*Brit*); **je n'y vois que ~** I can't see a ruddy: (*Brit*) *ou* damn: thing; **avoir la ~ en pente** to be a bit of a boozer:; *V* **rincer.**

daller [dale] (1) *vt* to pave, flag.

dalleur [dalœʀ] *nm* flag layer, paviour.

dalmate [dalmat] **1** *adj* Dalmatian. **2** *nm* (*Ling*) Dalmatian. **3** *nmf*: **D~** Dalmatian.

Dalmatie [dalmasi] *nf* Dalmatia.

dalmatien, -ienne [dalmasjɛ̃, jɛn] *nm,f* (*chien*) Dalmatian.

daltonien, -ienne [daltɔnjɛ̃, jɛn] *adj* colour-blind.

daltonisme [daltɔnism(ə)] *nm* colour-blindness, daltonism (*T*).

dam [dɑ̃] *nm*: **au (grand) ~ de** (*au détriment de*) (much) to the detriment of; (*au déplaisir de*) to the (great) displeasure of.

damas [dama] *nm* (*tissu*) damask; (*acier*) Damascus steel, damask; (*prune*) damson.

Damas [dama] *n* Damascus.

damasquinage [damaskinaʒ] *nm* damascening.

damasquiner [damaskine] (1) *vt* to damascene.

damassé, e [damase] (*ptp de* **damasser**) **1** *adj tissu* damask. **2** *nm* damask cloth.

damasser [damase] (1) *vt* to damask.

damassure [damasyʀ] *nf* damask design, damask effect.

dame [dam] 1 *nf* **(a)** (*gén: femme*) lady; (*: *épouse*) wife, good lady†. **il y a une ~ qui vous attend** there is a lady waiting for you; **votre ~ m'a dit que*** ... your wife told me that ...; **alors ma petite ~!*** now then, my good lady!; **vous savez, ma bonne ~!*** you know, my dear!; (*Jur*) **la ~ X** Mrs X; **pour ~s** *coiffeur, liqueur* ladies'; **de ~** *sac, manteau* lady's.
(b) (*de haute naissance*) lady. **la première ~ de France** France's First Lady; **une grande ~** a highborn *ou* great lady; **jouer les grandes ~s** to play the fine lady; **les belles ~s des beaux quartiers** the fashionable *ou* fine ladies of the best districts; (*hum*) **la ~ de ses pensées** his lady-love (*hum*).
(c) (*Cartes, Échecs*) queen; (*Dames*) king; (*Jacquet*) piece, man; **le jeu de ~s, les ~s** draughts (*Brit*), checkers (*US*); **aller à ~** (*Dames*) to make a king; (*Échecs*) to queen; **la ~ de pique** the queen of spades.
(d) (*Tech: hie*) beetle, rammer; (*Naut*) rowlock.
2 *excl* (†) **~ oui/non!** why yes/no!, indeed yes/no!
3: **dame catéchiste** catechism mistress; **dame de charité** benefactress; **dame de compagnie** lady's companion; **dame d'honneur** lady-in-waiting; **dame-jeanne** *nf, pl* **dames-jeannes** demijohn; **dame patronnesse** patroness; **dame pipi**‡ lady toilet attendant.

damer [dame] (1) *vt* **(a)** *terre* to ram *ou* pack down; *neige* (*à ski*) to tread (down), pack (down); (*avec un rouleau*) to roll, pack (down). **(b)** *pion* (*Dames*) to crown; (*Échecs*) to queen. (*fig*) **~ le pion à qn** to get the better of sb, checkmate sb.

damier [damje] *nm* (*Dames*) draughtboard (*Brit*), checkerboard (*US*); (*dessin*) check (pattern). **en** *ou* **à ~** chequered; **les champs formaient un ~** the fields were laid out like a draughtboard *ou* like patchwork.

damnable [dɑnabl(ə)] *adj* (*Rel*) damnable; *passion, idée* despicable, abominable.

damnation [dɑnasjɔ̃] *nf* damnation. **~!**† damnation!; *V* **enfer.**

damné, e [dɑne] (*ptp de* **damner**) 1 *adj* (*: *maudit*) cursed*, confounded*†; *V* **âme.** 2 *nm,f* damned person. **les ~s** the damned; **mener une vie de ~** to live the life of the damned; *V* **souffrir.**

damner [dɑne] (1) 1 *vt* to damn. **faire ~ qn*** to drive sb mad*, drive sb to drink*. 2 **se damner** *vpr* to damn o.s. **se ~ pour qn** to risk damnation for sb.

Damoclès [damɔklɛs] *nm* Damocles; *V* **épée.**

damoiseau, *pl* **~x** [damwazo] *nm* (*Hist*) page, squire; (†, *hum*) young beau†.

damoiselle [damwazɛl] *nf* (*Hist*) damsel††.

dan [dan] *nm* (*Judo*) dan. **il est deuxième ~** he's a second dan.

Danaïdes [danaid] *nfpl V* **tonneau.**

dancing [dɑ̃siŋ] *nm* dance hall.

dandinement [dɑ̃dinmɑ̃] *nm* (*V* **dandiner**) waddle, waddling; lolloping about.

dandiner (se) [dɑ̃dine] (1) *vpr* [*canard*] to waddle; [*personne*] to lollop from side to side. **avancer** *ou* **marcher en se dandinant** to waddle along.

dandy† [dɑ̃di] *nm* dandy.

dandysme [dɑ̃dism(ə)] *nm* (*Hist*) dandyism.

Danemark [danmaʀk] *nm* Denmark.

danger [dɑ̃ʒe] *nm* **(a)** danger. **être en ~** to be in danger; **ses jours sont en ~** his life is in danger; **mettre en ~** to endanger, jeopardize; **en ~ de** in danger of; **il est en ~ de mort** he is in danger *ou* peril of his life; **courir un ~** to run a risk; **en cas de ~** in case of emergency; **ça n'offre aucun ~** it doesn't present any danger, it is quite safe; **il y a (du) ~ à faire cela** it is dangerous to do that, there is a danger in doing that; **il est hors de ~** he is out of danger; **cet automobiliste est un ~ public** that driver is a public menace; **les ~s de la route** road hazards; **sans ~** (*adj*) safe; (*adv*) safely; **attention ~!** look out!
(b) (*) **(il n'y a) pas de ~!** no way!*, no fear!*; **pas de ~ qu'il vienne!** there's no fear *ou* risk *ou* danger that he'll come *ou* of his coming.

dangereusement [dɑ̃ʒʀøzmɑ̃] *adv* dangerously.

dangereux, euse [dɑ̃ʒʀø, øz] *adj chemin, ennemi, doctrine, animal* dangerous; *entreprise* dangerous, hazardous, risky. **zone ~euse** danger zone.

danois, e [danwa, waz] 1 *adj* Danish. 2 *nm* (*Ling*) Danish. 3 *nm,f*: **D~(e)** Dane; (*chien*) **(grand) ~** Great Dane.

dans [dɑ̃] *prép* **(a)** (*lit, fig: lieu*) in; (*changement de lieu*) into, to; (*à l'intérieur de*) in, inside; (*dans des limites*) within. **il habite ~ l'Est/le Jura** he lives in the East/the Jura; **il n'habite pas ~ Londres même, mais en banlieue** he doesn't live in London itself, but in the suburbs; **le ministère est ~ la rue de Rivoli** the ministry is in the rue de Rivoli; **courir ~ l'herbe/les champs** to run around in *ou* run through the grass/fields; **s'enfoncer/pénétrer ~ la forêt** to make one's way deep into/go into *ou* enter the forest; **ils sont partis ~ la montagne** they have gone off to the mountains; **elle erra ~ la ville/les rues/la campagne** she wandered through *ou* round *ou* about the town/the streets/the countryside; **ne marche pas ~ l'eau** don't walk in *ou* through the water; **il est tombé ~ la rivière** he fell into *ou* in the river; **~ le périmètre/un rayon très restreint** within the perimeter/a very restricted radius; **vous êtes ~ la bonne direction** you are going the right way *ou* in the right direction; **ils ont voyagé ~ le même train/avion** they travelled on the same train/plane; **mettre qch ~ un tiroir** to put sth in a drawer; **cherche** *ou* **regarde ~ la boîte** look inside *ou* in the box; **verser du vin ~ les verres** to pour wine into the glasses; **jeter l'eau sale ~ l'évier** to pour the dirty water down the sink; **~ le fond/le bas/le haut de l'armoire** at *ou* in the back/the bottom/the top of the wardrobe; **elle fouilla ~ ses poches/son sac** she went through her pockets/bag; **il reconnut le voleur ~ la foule/l'assistance** he recognized the thief in *ou* among the crowd/among the spectators; **il a reçu un coup de poing ~ la figure/le dos** he was punched *ou* he got a punch in the face/back; **il l'a lu ~ le journal/(l'œuvre de) Gide** he read it in the newspaper/in (the works of) Gide; **l'idée était ~ l'air depuis un moment** the idea had been in the air for some time; **qu'est-ce qui a bien pu se passer ~ sa tête?** what can have got into his head?, what can he have been thinking of?; **ce n'est pas ~ ses projets** he's not planning to do *ou* on doing that, that's not one of his plans; **il avait ~ l'idée** *ou* **l'esprit** *ou* **la tête que** he had a feeling that, he had it in his mind that; **elle avait ~ l'idée** *ou* **~ la tête de faire** she had a mind to do; **il y a de la tristesse ~ son regard/sourire** there's a certain sadness in his eyes/smile.
(b) (*lieu: avec idée d'extraction*) out of, from. **prendre qch ~ un tiroir** to take sth out of *ou* from a drawer; **boire du café ~ une tasse/un verre** to drink coffee out of *ou* from a cup/glass; **la chèvre lui mangeait ~ la main** the goat ate out of his hand; **le chien a mangé ~ mon assiette** the dog ate off my plate; **il l'a appris/copié ~ un livre** he learnt/copied it from *ou* out of a book.
(c) (*temps: gén*) in. **il est ~ sa 6e année** he's in his 6th year; **~ ma jeunesse** *ou* **mon jeune temps** in my youth, in my younger days; **~ les siècles passés** in previous centuries; **~ les mois à venir** in the months to come *ou* the coming months; **un mois ~ l'autre/l'un ~ l'autre, il s'y retrouve** from one month to the next/all in all he manages to break even; **~ le cours** *ou* **le courant de l'année** in the course of the year; *V* **temps¹, vie.**
(d) (*temps futur*) in; (*dans des limites*) within, inside, in (the course of). **il part ~ 2 jours/une semaine** he leaves in 2 days *ou* 2 days' time/a week *ou* a week's time; **~ combien de temps serez-vous prêt?** how long will it be before you are ready?; **il arrive** *ou* **il sera là ~ une minute** *ou* **un instant** he'll be here in a minute; **cela pourrait se faire ~ le mois/la semaine** it could be done within the month/week *ou* inside a month/week; **je l'attends ~ la matinée/la nuit** I'm expecting him some time this morning/some time tonight *ou* (some time) in the course of the morning/night.
(e) (*état, condition, manière*) in. **être ~ les affaires/l'industrie/les textiles** to be in business/industry/textiles; **vivre ~ la misère/l'oisiveté/la peur** to live in poverty/idleness/fear; **être assis/couché ~ une mauvaise position** to be sitting/lying in an awkward position; **je l'aime beaucoup ~ cette robe/ce rôle** I really like her in that dress/part; **il était plongé ~ la tristesse/une profonde méditation** he was plunged in grief/plunged deep in thought; **ses idées sont ~ la plus grande confusion** his ideas are as confused as can be, his ideas are in a state of great confusion; **et ~ tout cela, qu'est-ce que vous devenez?** and with all this going on *ou* in the meantime how are things with you?; **il est difficile de travailler ~ ce bruit/ces conditions** it's difficult to work in this noise/these conditions; **~ le brouillard/l'obscurité** in fog/darkness, in the fog/the dark; **le camion passa ~ un bruit de ferraille** the lorry rattled past; **elles sortirent ~ un frou-frou de soie** they left in a rustle of silk; **il est ~ une mauvaise passe** he's going through a bad patch (*surtout Brit*); **il n'est pas ~ le complot/le secret** he's not in on the plot/secret; **elle n'est pas ~ un bon jour** it's not one of her good days, she's having *ou* it's one of her off days.
(f) (*situation, cause*) in, with. **~ sa peur, elle poussa un cri** she cried out in fright *ou* fear; **elle partit tôt, ~ l'espoir de trouver une place** she left early in the hope of finding *ou* hoping to find a seat; **~ ces conditions** *ou* **ce cas-là, je refuse** in that case *ou* if that's the way it is* I (shall) refuse; **il l'a fait ~ ce but** he did it with this aim in view.
(g) (*approximation*) **~ les** (*prix*) (round) about, (something) in the region of; (*temps, grandeur*) (round) about, something like, some; **cela vaut/coûte ~ les 50 F** it is worth/costs in the region of 50 francs *ou* (round) about 50 francs; **il faut compter ~ les 3 ou 4 mois (pour terminer)** we'll have to allow something like 3 or 4 months *ou* some 3 or 4 months (to finish off); **il vous faut ~ les 3 mètres de tissu** you'll need something like 3 metres of fabric *ou* about *ou* some 3 metres of fabric; **cette pièce fait ~ les 8 m²** this room is about *ou* some 8 m².
(h) (*introduisant un complément*) **mettre son espoir ~ qn/qch** to pin one's hopes on sb/sth; **avoir confiance ~ l'honnêteté de qn/le dollar** to have confidence in sb's honesty/the dollar; **c'est ~ votre intérêt de le faire** it's in your own interest to do it.

dansant, e [dɑ̃sɑ̃, ɑ̃t] *adj mouvement, lueur* dancing; *musique* lively. **thé ~** (early evening) dance; **soirée ~e** dance.

danse [dɑ̃s] *nf* **(a)** (*valse, tango etc*) dance. **la ~** (*art*) dancing, the dance; (*action*) dancing; **~ folklorique** folk dance; **~ du ventre** belly dance; **~ de guerre** war dance; **~ classique** ballet dancing; **ouvrir la ~** to open the dancing; **avoir la ~ de Saint Guy** (*Méd*) to have St Vitus's dance; (*fig*) to have the fidgets; **de ~** *professeur, leçon* dancing; *musique* dance; *V* **mener, piste.**
(b) (‡: *volée*) belting‡, (good) hiding.

danser [dɑ̃se] (1) 1 *vi* (*gén*) to dance; [*ombre, flamme*] to flicker, dance; [*flotteur*] to bob (up and down), dance; [*bateau*] to pitch, dance. **faire ~ qn** to (have a) dance with sb; **après dîner il nous a fait ~** after dinner he got us dancing; **voulez-vous ~ (avec moi)?, vous dansez?** shall we dance?, would you like to dance?; (*fig*) **~ devant le buffet*** to have to sing for one's supper (*fig*); **~ de joie** to dance for joy.
2 *vt* to dance.

danseur [dɑ̃sœʀ] *nm* (*gén*) dancer; (*partenaire*) partner. **~ (classique** *ou* **de ballet)** ballet dancer; **~ étoile** (*Opéra*) principal dancer; **~ de corde** tightrope walker; **~ de claquettes** tap dancer.

danseuse [dɑ̃søz] *nf* (*gén*) dancer; (*partenaire*) partner. **~ (classique** *ou* **de ballet)** ballet dancer; **~ étoile** (*Opéra*) prima ballerina; **~ de cabaret** cabaret dancer; (*à vélo*) **en ~** standing on the pedals.

dantesque [dɑ̃tɛsk(ə)] *adj* Dantesque, Dantean.
Danube [danyb] *nm* Danube.
danubien, -ienne [danybjɛ̃, jɛn] *adj* Danubian.
dard [daʀ] *nm [animal]* sting; (*Mil†*) javelin, spear.
Dardanelles [daʀdanɛl] *nfpl*: les ~ the Dardanelles.
darder [daʀde] (1) *vt* **(a)** (*lancer*) *flèche* to shoot. **le soleil dardait ses rayons sur la maison** the sun's rays beat down on the house; **il darda un regard haineux sur son rival** he shot a look full of hate at his rival.
(b) (*dresser*) *piquants, épines* to point. **le clocher dardait sa flèche vers le ciel** the church tower pointed its spire towards the sky.
dare-dare* [daʀdaʀ] *loc adv* double-quick*, like the clappers* (*Brit*). **accourir** ~ to come belting up*, come running up double-quick*.
darne [daʀn(ə)] *nf [poisson]* steak.
dartre [daʀtʀ(ə)] *nf* sore.
darwinien, -ienne [daʀwinjɛ̃, jɛn] *adj* Darwinian.
darwinisme [daʀwinism(ə)] *nm* Darwinism.
datable [databl(ə)] *adj* dat(e)able. **manuscrit facilement** ~ manuscript which can easily be dated.
datation [datɑsjɔ̃] *nf [contrat, manuscrit]* dating.
date [dat] *nf* date. ~ **de naissance/mariage/paiement** date of birth/marriage/payment; **à quelle** ~ **cela s'est-il produit?** on what date did that occur?; **à cette** ~**-là il était déjà mort** by that time *ou* by then he was already dead; **lettre en** ~ **du 23 mai** letter dated May 23rd; ~ **limite** deadline; **j'ai pris** ~ **avec lui pour le 18 mai** I have set *ou* fixed a date with him for May 18th; **cet événement fait** ~ **dans l'histoire** this event stands out in *ou* marks a milestone in history; **sans** ~ undated; **le premier en** ~ the first *ou* earliest; **le dernier en** ~ the latest *ou* most recent; **de longue** *ou* **vieille** ~ (*adj*) long-standing; **de fraîche** ~ (*adj*) recent; **connaître qn de longue** *ou* **vieille/fraîche** ~ to have known sb for a long/short time.
dater [date] (1) **1** *vt lettre, événement* to date. **lettre datée du 6/de Paris** letter dated the 6th/from Paris; **non daté** undated.
2 *vi* **(a)** (*remonter à*) ~ **de** to date back to, date from; **ça ne date pas d'hier** it has been going a long time; **à** ~ **de demain** as from tomorrow, from tomorrow onwards; **de quand date votre dernière rencontre?** when did you last meet?
(b) (*faire date*) **événement qui date dans l'histoire** event which stands out in *ou* marks a milestone in history.
(c) (*être démodé*) to be dated. **ça commence à** ~ it's beginning to date.
dateur [datœʀ] *nm [montre]* date indicator. (*tampon*) **(timbre)** ~ date stamp.
datif, -ive [datif, iv] *adj, nm* dative.
datte [dat] *nf* (*Bot, Culin*) date.
dattier [datje] *nm* date palm.
daube [dob] *nf* (*viande*) stew, casserole. **faire une** ~ *ou* **de la viande en** ~ to make a (meat) stew *ou* casserole; **bœuf en** ~ casserole of beef, beef stew.
dauber [dobe] (1) *vi* (*††, littér*) to jeer.
dauphin [dofɛ̃] *nm* **(a)** (*Zool*) dolphin. **(b)** (*Hist*) **le D**~ the Dauphin. **(c)** (*fig: successeur*) heir apparent.
Dauphine [dofin] *nf* Dauphine, Dauphiness.
dauphinois, e [dofinwa, waz] *adj* of *ou* from the Dauphiné; *V* **gratin.**
daurade [dɔʀad] *nf* gilt-head.
davantage [davɑ̃taʒ] *adv* **(a)** (*plus*) *gagner, acheter* more; (*négatif*) any more; (*interrogatif*) (any) more. **bien/encore/même** ~ much/still/even more; **je n'en sais pas** ~ I don't know any more (about it), I know no more *ou* nothing further (about it); **il s'approcha** ~ he drew closer *ou* nearer; **en veux-tu** ~? do you want (any *ou* some) more?
(b) (*plus longtemps*) longer; (*négatif, interrogatif*) any longer. **sans s'attarder/rester** ~ without lingering/staying any longer.
(c) (*de plus en plus*) more and more. **les prix augmentent chaque jour** ~ prices go up more and more every day.
(d) ~ **de** (some) more; (*négatif*) any more; **vouloir** ~ **de pain/temps** to want (some) more bread/time; **veux-tu** ~ **de viande?** do you want (any *ou* some) more meat?; **il n'en a pas voulu** ~ he didn't want any more (of it).
(e) ~ **que** (*plus*) more than; (*plus longtemps*) longer than; **tu te crois malin mais il l'est** ~ **(que toi)** you think you're sharp but he is more so than you *ou* but he is sharper (than you).
davier [davje] *nm* (*Chirurgie*) forceps; (*Menuiserie*) cramp.
de[1] [də] *prép* (*contraction avec le, les*: **du, des**) **(a)** (*copule introduisant compléments après vb, loc verbale, adj, n*) **décider** ~ **faire** to decide to do, decide on doing; **éviter** ~ **faire** to avoid doing; **empêcher qn** ~ **faire** to prevent sb (from) doing; **il est fier** ~ **parler 3 langues** he is proud of being able *ou* of his ability to speak 3 languages; **c'est l'occasion** ~ **protester** this is an opportunity for protesting *ou* to protest; **avoir l'habitude** ~ **qch/**~ **faire** to be used to sth/to doing; **je ne vois pas l'intérêt d'écrire** I don't see the point of *ou* in writing; **content** ~ **faire qch/**~ **qch** pleased to do sth/with sth; **il est pressé** ~ **partir** he is in a hurry to go; **se souvenir/se servir** ~ **qch** to remember/use *ou* make use of sth; **il est difficile/impossible/agréable** ~ **faire cela** it is difficult/impossible/pleasant to do that; **il est amoureux d'elle** he is in love with her; **le bombardement** ~ **Londres** the bombing of London; **et elle** ~ **se moquer de nos efforts!** and she made fun of our efforts!
(b) (*déplacement, provenance*) from, out of, of; (*localisation*) in, on. **être/provenir/s'échapper** ~ to be/come/escape from; **sauter du toit** to jump from *ou* off the roof; **en sortant** ~ **la maison** coming out of the house, on leaving the house; ~ **sa fenêtre elle voit la mer** she can see the sea from her window; **il arrive du Japon** he has just arrived from Japan; **il y a une lettre** ~ **Paul** there's a letter from Paul; **nous recevons des amis du Canada** we have friends from Canada staying (with us); **(ce sont) des gens** ~ **la campagne/la ville** (they are) country folk/townsfolk, (they are) people from the country/town; **on apprend** ~ **Londres que ...** we hear *ou* it is announced from London that ...; **les magasins** ~ **Londres/Paris** the London/Paris shops, the shops in London/Paris; **des pommes** ~ **notre jardin** apples from our garden; ~ **lui** *ou* ~ **sa part, rien ne m'étonne** nothing he does (ever) surprises me; **le train/l'avion** ~ **Londres** (*provenance*) the train/plane from London; (*destination*) the London train/plane, the train/plane for London; **les voisins du 2e (étage)** the neighbours on the 2nd floor; **né** ~ **parents pauvres** born of poor parents; ~ **6 qu'ils étaient (au départ) ils ne sont plus que 2** of *ou* out of the original 6 there are only 2 left; **le Baron** ~ **la Roche** Baron de la Roche; *V* **côté, près** *etc.*
(c) (*appartenance*) of, *souvent traduit par cas génitif.* **la maison** ~ **David/**~ **notre ami/**~ **nos amis/**~ **l'actrice** David's/our friend's/our friends'/the actress's house; **le mari** ~ **la reine d'Angleterre** the Queen of England's husband; **la patte du chien** the dog's paw; **le pied** ~ **la table** the leg of the table, the table leg; **le bouton** ~ **la porte** the door knob; **le pouvoir** ~ **l'argent** the power of money; **un** ~ **mes amis** a friend of mine, one of my friends; **un ami** ~ **mon père/des enfants** a friend of my father's/of the children's; **un ami** ~ **la famille** a friend of the family, a family friend; **il n'est pas** ~ **notre famille** he is no relation of ours; **le roi** ~ **France** the King of France; **l'attitude du Canada** Canada's attitude, the Canadian attitude; **un roman** ~ **Wells** a novel by Wells, a novel of Wells'; **la boutique du fleuriste/boulanger** the florist's/baker's shop; **quel est le nom** ~ **cette fleur/cette rue/cet enfant?** what is this flower/street/child called?, what's the name of this flower/street/child?; **il a la ruse du renard** he's as cunning as a fox, he's got the cunning of a fox; **c'est bien** ~ **lui de sortir sans manteau** it's just like him *ou* it's typical of him to go out without a coat (on).
(d) (*gén sans article: caractérisation*) *gén rendu par des composés.* **vase** ~ **cristal** crystal vase; **robe** ~ **soie** silk dress; **robe** ~ **soie pure** dress of pure silk; **sac** ~ **couchage** sleeping bag; **permis** ~ **conduire** driving licence; **une fourrure** ~ **prix** a costly *ou* an expensive fur; **la société** ~ **consommation** the consumer society; **un homme** ~ **goût/d'une grande bonté** a man of taste/great kindness; **un homme d'affaires** a businessman; **les journaux d'hier/du dimanche** yesterday's/the Sunday papers; **le professeur d'anglais** the English teacher, the teacher of English; **la route** ~ **Tours** the Tours road, the road for Tours; **un travail** ~ **3 jours** a 3-day job; **les romanciers du 20e siècle** 20th-century novelists; **il est d'une bêtise!** he's so stupid! *ou* incredibly stupid!; **il est** ~ **son temps** he's a man of his times, he moves with the times; **il est l'homme du moment** he's the man of the moment; **être** ~ **taille** *ou* ~ **force à faire qch** to be equal to doing sth, be up to doing sth*; **regard** ~ **haine/dégoût** look of hate/disgust; **3 jours** ~ **libres** 3 free days, 3 days free; **quelque chose** ~ **beau/cher** something lovely/expensive; **rien** ~ **neuf/d'intéressant** nothing new/interesting *ou* of interest; **le plus grand** ~ **sa classe** the biggest in his class; **le seul** ~ **mes collègues** the only one of my colleagues; **il y a 2 verres** ~ **cassés** there are 2 broken glasses *ou* glasses broken.
(e) (*gén sans article: contenu*) of. **une bouteille** ~ **vin/lait** a bottle of wine/milk; **une tasse** ~ **thé** a cup of tea; **une pincée/cuillerée** ~ **sel** a pinch/spoonful of salt; **une poignée** ~ **gens** a handful of people; **une collection** ~ **timbres** a stamp collection; **une boîte** ~ **bonbons** a box of sweets; **un car** ~ **touristes/d'enfants** a coachload *ou* coachful of tourists/children.
(f) (*temps*) **venez** ~ **bonne heure** come early; ~ **nos jours** nowadays, these days; **du temps où** in the days when, at a time when; **d'une minute/d'un jour à l'autre** (*incessamment*) any minute/day now; (*progressivement*) from one minute/day to the next; ~ **jour** by day, during the day; **elle reçoit** ~ **6 à 8** she's at home (to visitors) from 6 to 8; **3 heures du matin/**~ **l'après-midi** 3 (o'clock) in the morning/afternoon, 3 a.m./p.m.; **il n'a rien fait** ~ **la semaine/l'année** he hasn't done a thing all week/year; ~ **(toute) ma vie je n'ai entendu pareilles sottises** I've never heard such nonsense in (all) my life; ~ **mois en mois/jour en jour** from month to month/day to day; *V* **ici, suite.**
(g) (*mesure*) **une pièce** ~ **6 m²** a room (measuring) 6 m²; **un enfant** ~ **5 ans** a 5-year-old (child); **un bébé** ~ **6 mois** a 6-month(-old) baby, a baby of 6 months; **elle a acheté 2 kg** ~ **pommes** she bought 2 kg of apples; **une table** ~ **2 mètres** ~ **large** a table 2 metres wide *ou* in width, a 2 metres wide table; **un rôti** ~ **2 kg** a 2-kg joint, a joint weighing 2 kg; **une côtelette** ~ **4 F** a chop costing 4 francs; **ce poteau a 5 mètres** ~ **haut** *ou* ~ **hauteur/**~ **long** *ou* ~ **longueur** this post is 5 metres high *ou* in height/long *ou* in length; **elle est plus grande que lui** *ou* **elle le dépasse** ~ **5 cm** she is 5 cm taller than he is, she is taller than him by 5 cm; **une attente** ~ **2 heures** a 2-hour wait; **un voyage** ~ **3 jours** a 3-day journey, a 3 days' journey; **une promenade** ~ **3 km/3 heures** a 3-km/3-hour walk; **il gagne 9 F** ~ **l'heure** he earns 9 francs an hour *ou* per hour.
(h) (*moyen*) with, on, by. **frapper/faire signe** ~ **la main** to strike/make a sign with the hand; **s'aider des deux mains/**~ **sa canne pour se lever** to help o.s. up with (the aid of) both hands/one's stick, get up with the help of both hands/one's stick; **je l'ai fait** ~ **mes propres mains** I did it with my own two hands; **vivre** ~ **charité/**~ **rien** to live on charity/nothing at all; **se nourrir** ~ **racines/fromage** to live on roots/cheese; **il vit** ~ **sa peinture** he lives by (his) painting; **faire qch** ~ **rien/d'un bout de bois** to make sth out of nothing/a bit of wood; **il fit 'non'** ~ **la tête** he shook his head.
(i) (*manière*) with, in, *souvent traduit par adv.* **aller** *ou* **mar-**

cher d'une allure paisible/d'un bon pas to walk (along) unhurriedly/briskly; **connaître qn ~ vue/nom** to know sb by sight/name; **citer qch ~ mémoire** to quote sth from memory; **parler d'une voix émue/ferme** to speak emotionally/firmly *ou* in an emotional/firm voice; **regarder qn d'un air tendre** to look at sb tenderly, give sb a tender look; **il est pâle ~ teint** *ou* **visage** he has a pale complexion.

(j) (*cause, agent*) with, in, from. **mourir d'une pneumonie/~ vieillesse** to die of pneumonia/old age; **pleurer/rougir ~ dépit/~ honte** to weep/blush with vexation/with *ou* for shame; (*saisi*) **~ colère, il la gifla** he slapped her in anger; **~ crainte** *ou* **peur de faire** for fear of doing; **être surpris/étonné ~ qch/~ voir** to be surprised/astonished at sth/at seeing *ou* to see; **être fatigué du voyage/~ répéter** to be tired from the journey/of repeating; **s'écrouler ~ fatigue** to be dropping (with fatigue); **elle rit ~ le voir si maladroit** she laughed to see him *ou* on seeing him so clumsy; **heureux d'avoir réussi** happy to have succeeded; **contrarié ~ ce qu'il se montre si peu coopératif** annoyed at his being so uncooperative.

(k) (*copule: apposition*) of, *souvent non traduit.* **la ville ~ Paris** the town of Paris; **le jour ~ Pâques** Easter Sunday *ou* Day; **le jour ~ Noël** Christmas Day; **le mois ~ juin** the month of June; **le prénom ~ Paul n'est plus si populaire** the name Paul is not so popular these days; **le terme ~ 'franglais'** the word 'franglais'; **ton idiot ~ fils** that stupid son of yours, your clot of a son*; **ce cochon ~ temps nous gâche nos vacances** this rotten weather is spoiling our holiday; **un ~ plus/~ moins/~ trop** one more/less/too many.

de² [d(ə)], **du, de la, des,** (**du, de la = de l'** *devant voyelle et h muet*) **1** *art partitif* **(a)** (*dans affirmation*) some (*souvent omis*); (*dans interrogation, hypothèse*) any, some; (*avec nég*) any, no. **boire du vin/~ la bière/~ l'eau** to drink wine/beer/water; **il but ~ l'eau au robinet** he drank some water from the tap; **si on prenait ~ la bière/du vin?** what about some beer/wine?; **acheter des pommes/~ bonnes pommes** to buy some apples/some good apples; **il y a des gens qui aiment la poésie** some people like poetry; **cela demande du courage/~ la patience** this requires courage/patience; **il faut manger du pain avec du fromage** you should eat bread with cheese; **donnez-nous ~ vos nouvelles** let us have your news; **je n'ai pas ~ ses nouvelles depuis** I haven't had (any) news from *ou* of him *ou* I haven't heard from *ou* of him since; **au déjeuner, nous avons eu du poulet** we had chicken for lunch; **vous ne voulez vraiment pas ~ vin?** don't you really want any wine?; **voudriez-vous du thé?** would you like some tea?; **voulez-vous du thé ou du café?** would you like tea or coffee?; **voulez-vous du pain/des œufs/~ la farine?** do you need (any) bread/eggs/flour?; **avez-vous du pain/des œufs/~ la farine à me passer?** do you have any bread/eggs/flour you could let me have?, I wonder if you could let me have some bread/eggs/flour?; **on peut acheter ~ la laine chez Dupont** you can buy wool at Dupont's; **j'ai acheté ~ la laine** I bought some wool; **il n'y a plus d'espoir** there is no hope left; **il a joué du Chopin/des valses ~ Chopin** he played (some) Chopin/some Chopin waltzes; **si j'avais ~ l'argent, je prendrais des vacances** if I had any *ou* some money, I'd take a holiday; **ça, c'est du chantage/du vol!** that's blackmail/robbery!; **ça, c'est ~ la veine!*** what a piece *ou* stroke of luck!

(b) (*loc*) a, an. **faire du bruit/des histoires** to make a noise/a fuss; **avoir ~ l'humour** to have a sense of humour; **donnez-moi du feu** give me a light; **on va faire du feu** let's light the *ou* a fire; **il y a ~ la lumière, donc il est chez lui** there's a light on, so he must be in.

2 *art indéf pl* **(a) des, de** some (*souvent omis*); (*nég*) any, no. **des enfants ont cassé les carreaux** some children have broken the window panes; **elle élève des chats mais pas de chiens** she breeds cats but not dogs; **j'ai des voisins charmants** *ou* **de charmants voisins** I have charming neighbours; **je n'ai pas de voisins** I haven't (got) any neighbours, I have no neighbours; **avoir des doutes sur** to have doubts about.

(b) (*intensif*) **elle est restée des mois et des mois sans nouvelles** she was without (any) news for months and months, she went for months and months without (any) news; **j'ai attendu des heures** I waited (for) hours; **nous n'avons pas fait des kilomètres** we didn't exactly walk miles; **ils en ont cueilli des kilogrammes (et des kilogrammes)** they picked pounds (and pounds).

dé [de] *nm* **(a) ~ (à coudre)** thimble; (*fig: petit verre*) tiny glass; (*fig*) **ça tient dans un ~ à coudre** it will fit into a thimble.

(b) (*Jeux*) die, dice. **jouer aux ~s** to play dice; **les ~s sont jetés** the die is cast; (*Culin*) **couper des carottes en ~s** to dice carrots; *V* **coup.**

déambulatoire [deɑ̃bylatwaʀ] *nm* ambulatory.

déambuler [deɑ̃byle] (1) *vi* to stroll, wander, saunter (about *ou* along).

débâcle [debɑkl(ə)] *nf [armée]* rout; *[régime]* collapse; *[glaces]* breaking up, débâcle (*T*).

déballage [debalaʒ] *nm* **(a)** (*action*) *[objets]* unpacking. **(b)** *[marchandises]* display (*of loose goods*). **(c)** (*: *paroles, confession*) outpouring.

déballer [debale] (1) *vt affaires* to unpack; *marchandises* to display, lay out; (*) *vérité, paroles* to let out; (*) *sentiments* to pour out, give vent to; (**péj*) *savoir* to air (*péj*).

débandade [debɑ̃dad] *nf* (*déroute*) headlong flight; (*dispersion*) scattering. **en ~, à la ~** in disorder; **tout va à la ~** everything's going to rack and ruin *ou* to the dogs*.

débander [debɑ̃de] (1) **1** *vt* **(a)** (*Méd*) to unbandage, take the bandage(s) off. **~ les yeux de qn** to remove a blindfold from sb's eyes.

(b) *arc, ressort* to relax, slacken (off).

(c) (*rare: mettre en déroute*) to rout, scatter.

2 *vi* (✱) to go limp. **travailler 10 heures sans ~✱** to work 10 hours without letting up*.

3 se débander *vpr [armée, manifestants]* to scatter, break up; *[arc, ressort]* to relax, slacken.

débaptiser [debatize] (1) *vt* to change the name of, rename.

débarbouillage [debaʀbujaʒ] *nm [visage]* washing.

débarbouiller [debaʀbuje] (1) **1** *vt visage* to wash. **2 se débarbouiller** *vpr* to wash (one's face).

débarbouillette [debaʀbujɛt] *nf* (*Can*) face-cloth, flannel (*Brit*).

débarcadère [debaʀkadɛʀ] *nm* landing stage.

débardage [debaʀdaʒ] *nm* unloading, unlading.

débarder [debaʀde] (1) *vt* (*Naut*) to unload, unlade.

débardeur [debaʀdœʀ] *nm* (*ouvrier*) docker, stevedore; (*vêtement*) slipover, tank top.

débarquement [debaʀkəmɑ̃] *nm* (*V* **débarquer**) landing; unloading. **navire** *ou* **péniche de ~** landing craft (*inv*).

débarquer [debaʀke] (1) **1** *vt* **(a)** *marchandises* to land; unload; *passagers* to land; (*Mil*) to land.

(b) (*: *congédier*) to sack*, turf* *ou* kick out*. **se faire ~** to get the push*, get kicked out* *ou* turfed out*.

2 *vi [passagers]* to disembark, land; (*Mil*) to land. **il a débarqué chez mes parents hier soir*** he turned up at my parents' place last night; **tu débarques!*** where have you been?*

débarras [debaʀa] *nm* **(a)** (*pièce*) lumber room, junk room; (*placard, soupente*) junk hole*, glory hole, junk closet (*US*). **(b) bon ~!** good riddance!; **il est parti, quel ~!** thank goodness he has gone!

débarrasser [debaʀase] (1) **1** *vt* **(a)** *local* to clear (*de* of). **~ (la table)** to clear the table.

(b) ~ qn de *fardeau, manteau, chapeau* to relieve sb of; *habitude* to break *ou* rid sb of; *ennemi, mal* to rid sb of; *liens* to release sb from; **débarrasse le plancher*** hop it!* (*Brit*), make yourself scarce!*

2 se débarrasser *vpr*: **se ~ de** *objet, personne* to get rid of, rid o.s. of; *vêtement* to take off, remove; *sentiment* to rid o.s. of, get rid of, shake off; *idée* to rid o.s. of, put aside; *mauvaise habitude* to break o.s. of, rid o.s. of.

débat [deba] *nm* (*discussion*) discussion, debate; (*polémique*) debate. **~ intérieur** inner struggle; (*Jur, Pol: séance*) **~s** proceedings, debates.

débâter [debɑte] (1) *vt bête de somme* to unsaddle.

débâtir [debɑtiʀ] (2) *vt* (*Couture*) to take out *ou* remove the tacking *ou* basting in.

débattre [debatʀ(ə)] (41) **1** *vt problème, question* to discuss, debate; *prix, traité* to discuss. **le prix reste à ~** the price has still to be discussed.

2 se débattre *vpr* (*contre un adversaire*) to struggle (*contre* with); (*contre le courant*) to struggle (*contre* against); (*contre les difficultés*) to struggle (*contre* against, with), wrestle (*contre* with). **se ~ comme un beau diable** *ou* **comme un forcené** to struggle like the very devil *ou* like one possessed.

débauchage [deboʃaʒ] *nm* (*licenciement*) laying off, dismissal.

débauche [deboʃ] *nf* **(a)** (*vice*) debauchery. **mener une vie de ~** to lead a debauched life *ou* a life of debauchery; **scène de ~** scene of debauchery; **partie de ~** orgy; *V* **lieu.**

(b) (*abondance*) **~ de** profusion *ou* abundance *ou* wealth of; **~ de couleurs** riot of colour.

débauché, e [deboʃe] (*ptp de* **débaucher**) **1** *adj personne, vie* debauched. **2** *nm,f* (*viveur*) debauchee.

débaucher [deboʃe] (1) **1** *vt* **(a)** (†: *corrompre*) to debauch, corrupt; (*: *inviter à s'amuser*) to entice away, tempt away.

(b) (*inviter à la grève*) to incite to strike; (*licencier*) to lay off, dismiss, make redundant.

2 se débaucher *vpr* to turn to (a life of) debauchery, become debauched.

débaucheur [deboʃœʀ] *nm* (*V* **débaucher**) debaucher; tempter; strike agitator.

débaucheuse [deboʃøz] *nf* (*V* **débaucher**) debaucher; temptress; strike agitator.

débecter✱, débéqueter✱ [debɛkte] (1) *vt* (*dégoûter*) to disgust. **ça me débecte** it's disgusting, it makes me sick*.

débile [debil] *adj corps, membre* weak, feeble; *esprit* feeble; *santé* frail, poor; *enfant* sickly, weak. **c'est un ~ mental** (*lit*) he is mentally deficient, he is a mental defective; (*péj*) he's a moron (*péj*).

débilitant, e [debilitɑ̃, ɑ̃t] *adj* (*V* **débiliter**) debilitating; enervating; demoralizing.

débilité [debilite] *nf* (†: *faiblesse*) debility. **~ mentale** mental deficiency.

débiliter [debilite] (1) *vt [climat]* to debilitate, enervate; *[milieu]* to enervate; *[propos]* to demoralize.

débinage* [debinaʒ] *nm* knocking*, slamming*, running down.

débine* [debin] *nf*: **être dans la ~** to be on one's uppers*; **tomber dans la ~** to fall on hard times.

débiner* [debine] (1) **1** *vt* (*dénigrer*) *personne* to knock*, slam*, run down. **2 se débiner** *vpr* (*se sauver*) to do a bunk✱ (*Brit*), clear off*.

débineur* [debinœʀ] *nm* knocker*.

débit [debi] **1** *nm* **(a)** (*Fin*) debit; *[relevé de compte]* debit side. **mettre** *ou* **porter 100 F au ~ de qn** to debit sb *ou* sb's account with 100 francs, charge 100 francs to sb's account; **pouvez-vous me faire le** *ou* **mon ~?** can I pay for it please?

(b) (*Comm: vente*) turnover (of goods), sales. **article qui a un bon/faible ~** article which sells well/poorly; **n'achète pas ton fromage dans cette boutique, il n'y a pas assez de ~** don't buy your cheese in this shop, there isn't a big enough turnover; **cette boutique a du ~** this shop has a quick turnover (of goods).

(c) *[fleuve]* (rate of) flow; *[gaz, électricité]* output; *[pompe]* flow, outflow; *[tuyau]* discharge; *[machine]* output; *[moyen de transport: métro, téléphérique]* passenger flow. **il n'y a pas assez de ~ au robinet** there is not enough flow out of the tap *ou* pressure in the tap.

(d) (*élocution*) delivery. **un ~ rapide/monotone** a rapid/monotonous delivery.

(e) (*Menuiserie*) cutting up, sawing up. **~ d'un arbre en rondins** sawing up of a tree into logs.

2: débit de boissons (*petit bar ou café*) bar; (*Admin: terme générique*) drinking establishment; **débit de tabac** tobacconist's (shop).

débitable [debitabl(ə)] *adj bois* which can be sawn *ou* cut up.

débitage [debitaʒ] *nm [bois]* cutting up, sawing up.

débitant, e [debitɑ̃, ɑ̃t] *nm,f*: **~ (de boissons)** ≃ licensed grocer; **~ (de tabac)** tobacconist.

débiter [debite] (1) *vt* **(a)** (*Fin*) *personne, compte* to debit. **pouvez-vous me ~ cet article?** can I pay for this item?

(b) (*Comm*) *marchandises* to retail, sell.

(c) *[usine, machine]* to produce. **ce fleuve/tuyau débite tant de m³ par seconde** the flow of this river/through this pipe is so many m³ per second.

(d) (*péj: dire*) *âneries* to utter, mouth; *insultes* to pour forth; *sermon* to spout. **il me débita tout cela sans s'arrêter** he poured all that out to me without stopping.

(e) (*tailler*) *bois* to cut up, saw up; *viande* to cut up.

débiteur, -trice [debitœʀ, tʀis] **1** *adj* (*Fin*) *solde* debit (*épith*); *personne, organisme* debtor (*épith*). **mon compte est ~ (de 50 F)** my account has a debit balance (of 50 francs) *ou* is (50 francs) in the red*.

2 *nm,f* (*Fin, fig*) debtor. (*lit, fig*) **être le ~ de qn** to be indebted to sb, be in sb's debt.

déblai [deblɛ] *nm* **(a)** (*nettoyage*) clearing; (*Tech: terrassement*) earth-moving, excavations. **(b) ~s** (*gravats*) rubble, debris (*sg*); (*terre*) earth.

déblaiement [deblɛmɑ̃] *nm [chemin, espace]* clearing.

déblatérer* [deblateʀe] (6) *vi* **(a)** (*médire*) **~ contre** to go on about*, slam*. **(b)** (*dire des bêtises*) to drivel (on)*, talk twaddle*.

déblayage [deblɛjaʒ] *nm* **(a)** = **déblaiement. (b)** (*fig*) **le ~ d'une question** (doing) the spadework on a question.

déblayer [debleje] (8) *vt* **(a)** *décombres* to clear away, remove; *chemin, porte, espace* to clear; *pièce* to clear up, tidy up; (*Tech*) *terrain* to level off.

(b) *travail* to prepare. (*fig*) **~ le terrain** to clear the ground *ou* the way; **déblaye (le terrain)!*** push off!* (*Brit*), get lost!*

déblocage [deblɔkaʒ] *nm* (*V* **débloquer**) freeing; releasing; unjamming; unblocking.

débloquer [deblɔke] (1) **1** *vt* **(a)** (*Fin*) *compte* to free, release; (*Écon*) *stocks, marchandises, crédits* to release; *prix, salaires* to free.

(b) (*Tech*) *machine* to unjam; *écrou, freins* to release; *route* to unblock.

2 *vi* (**:**) (*dire des bêtises*) to talk twaddle* *ou* rot* *ou* drivel*; (*être fou*) to be off one's rocker**:**.

débobiner [debɔbine] (1) *vt* (*Couture*) to unwind, wind off; (*Élec*) to unwind, uncoil.

déboires [debwaʀ] *nmpl* (*déceptions*) disappointments, heartbreaks; (*échecs*) setbacks, reverses; (*ennuis*) trials, difficulties.

déboisement [debwazmɑ̃] *nm [montagne]* deforestation; *[endroit, forêt]* clearing.

déboiser [debwaze] (1) *vt montagne* to deforest; *endroit, forêt* to clear of trees.

déboîtement [debwatmɑ̃] *nm* (*Méd*) dislocation; (*Aut: V* **déboîter**) pulling out; changing lanes.

déboîter [debwate] (1) **1** *vt membre* to dislocate; *porte* to take off its hinges; *tuyaux* to disconnect; *objet* to dislodge, knock out of place. **se ~ l'épaule** to dislocate one's shoulder.

2 *vi* (*Aut*) (*du trottoir*) to pull out; (*d'une file*) to change lanes, pull out; (*Mil*) to break rank.

débonnaire [debɔnɛʀ] *adj* (*bon enfant*) easy-going, good-natured; (†: *trop bon, faible*) soft, weak. **air ~** kindly appearance.

débordant, e [debɔʀdɑ̃, ɑ̃t] *adj activité* exuberant; *enthousiasme, joie* overflowing, unbounded; (*Mil*) **mouvement ~** outflanking manoeuvre.

débordement [debɔʀdəmɑ̃] *nm* **(a)** *[rivière, liquide]* overflowing (*U*); *[liquide en ébullition]* boiling over (*U*); (*Mil, Sport*) outflanking (*U*).

(b) *[joie]* outburst; *[paroles, injures]* torrent, rush; *[activité]* explosion. **~ de vie** bubbling vitality.

(c) (*débauches*) **~s** excesses; **devant les ~s de son fils, il lui coupa les vivres** confronted with his son's excesses, he cut off his allowance.

déborder [debɔʀde] (1) **1** *vi* **(a)** *[récipient, liquide]* to overflow; *[fleuve, rivière]* to burst its banks, overflow; *[liquide bouillant]* to boil over. **les pluies ont fait ~ le réservoir** the rains caused the reservoir to overflow; **faire ~ le café** to let the coffee boil over; **tasse/boîte pleine à ~** cup/box full to the brim *ou* to overflowing (*de* with); **l'eau a débordé du vase/de la casserole** the water has overflowed the vase/has boiled over the saucepan; **les vêtements qui débordaient de la valise** the clothes spilling out of the suitcase; **la foule débordait sur la chaussée** the crowd was overflowing onto the roadway; (*fig*) **cela a fait ~ le vase, c'est la goutte qui a fait ~ le vase** that was the last straw, that was the straw that broke the camel's back; (*fig*) **son cœur débordait, il fallait qu'il parle** his heart was (full to) overflowing and he just had to speak.

(b) (*fig*) **~ de santé** to be bursting with health; **~ de vitalité/joie** to be bubbling *ou* brimming over with vitality/joy, be bursting with vitality/joy; **son cœur débordait de reconnaissance** his heart was overflowing *ou* bursting with gratitude; **~ de colère** to be bursting with anger; **~ de richesses** to be overflowing with riches.

2 *vt* **(a)** (*dépasser*) *enceinte, limites* to extend beyond; (*Mil, Pol, Sport*) *ennemi* to outflank. **leur maison déborde les autres** their house juts out from the others; **la nappe doit ~ la table** the tablecloth should hang over *ou* overhang the edge of the table; **le conférencier/cette remarque déborde le cadre du sujet** the lecturer/that remark goes beyond the bounds of the subject; **il a débordé (le temps imparti)** he has run over (the allotted time); (*Mil, Pol, Sport*) **se laisser ~ sur la droite** to allow o.s. to be outflanked on the right; **être débordé de travail** to be snowed under with work*, be up to one's eyes in work*.

(b) *couvertures, lit* to untuck. **~ qn** to untuck sb *ou* sb's bed; **il s'est débordé en dormant** he *ou* his bed came untucked in his sleep.

(c) (*Couture*) *jupe, rideau* to remove the border from.

débotté [debɔte] *nm* (*frm*) **au ~** unprepared.

débotter [debɔte] (1) **1** *vt*: **~ qn** to take off sb's boots. **2 se débotter** *vpr* to take one's boots off.

débouchage [debuʃaʒ] *nm [bouteille]* uncorking, opening; *[tuyau]* unblocking.

débouché [debuʃe] *nm* **(a)** (*gén pl*) (*Comm: marché*) outlet; (*carrière*) opening, prospect.

(b) *[défilé]* opening. **au ~ de la vallée (dans la plaine)** where the valley opens out (into the plain); **il s'arrêta au ~ de la rue** he stopped at the end of the street; **la Suisse n'a aucun ~ sur la mer** Switzerland has no outlet to the sea.

déboucher [debuʃe] (1) **1** *vt* **(a)** *lavabo, tuyau* to unblock.

(b) *bouteille de vin* to uncork, open; *carafe, flacon* to unstopper, take the stopper out of; *tube* to uncap, take the cap *ou* top off.

2 *vi* to emerge, come out. **~ de** *[personne, voiture]* to emerge from, come out of; **~ sur** *ou* **dans** *[rue]* to run into, open onto *ou* into; *[personne, voiture]* to come out onto *ou* into, emerge onto *ou* into; (*fig*) **cette discussion débouche sur une impasse** this discussion is approaching stalemate *ou* is leading up a blind alley.

3 se déboucher *vpr [bouteille]* to come uncorked; *[tuyau]* to unblock, come unblocked.

déboucheoir [debuʃwaʀ] *nm [lavabo]* plunger.

déboucler [debukle] (1) *vt ceinture* to unbuckle, undo. **je suis toute débouclée** my hair has all gone straight *ou* has gone quite straight, the curl has come out of my hair.

déboulé [debule] *nm* (*Danse*) déboulé; (*Courses*) charge. (*Chasse*) **au ~** on breaking cover.

débouler [debule] (1) **1** *vi* **(a)** (*Chasse*) *[lapin]* to bolt. **(b)** (*dégringoler*) to tumble down. **2** *vt* (*: *dévaler*) to belt down*. **~ l'escalier** to come belting down the stairs*.

déboulonnage [debulɔnaʒ] *nm*, **déboulonnement** [debulɔnmɑ̃] *nm* (*V* **déboulonner**) removal of bolts (*de* from); sacking*, firing; discrediting.

déboulonner [debulɔne] (1) *vt* **(a)** *machine* to remove the bolts from, take the bolts out of. **(b)** (*) *haut fonctionnaire* (*renvoyer*) to sack*, fire; (*discréditer*) to discredit, bring down.

débourber [debuʀbe] (1) *vt fossé* to clear of mud, clean out; *canal* to dredge; *véhicule* to pull out of the mud.

débours [debuʀ] *nm* (*dépense*) outlay. **pour rentrer dans ses ~** to recover one's outlay.

déboursement [debuʀsmɑ̃] *nm* (*rare*) laying out, disbursement (*frm*).

débourser [debuʀse] (1) *vt* to pay out, lay out, disburse (*frm*). **sans ~ un sou** without paying *ou* laying out a penny, without being a penny out of pocket.

debout [d(ə)bu] *adv, adj inv* **(a)** *personne* (*en position verticale*) standing (up); (*levé*) up. **être** *ou* **se tenir ~** to stand; **être ~** (*levé*) to be up; (*guéri*) to be up (and about); **se mettre ~** to stand up, get up; **il préfère être** *ou* **rester ~** he prefers to stand *ou* remain standing; **voulez-vous, je vous prie, rester ~** will you please remain standing; **hier, nous sommes restés ~ jusqu'à minuit** yesterday we stayed up till midnight; **leur enfant se tient ~ maintenant** their child can stand (up) now; **il l'aida à se (re)mettre ~** he helped him (back) up, he helped him (back) to his feet; **~, il paraît plus petit** he looks smaller standing (up); **la pièce est si petite qu'on ne peut pas se tenir ~** the room is so small that it's impossible to stand upright; **il est si fatigué, il tient à peine ~** he is so tired he can hardly stand; **elle est ~ toute la journée** she is on her feet all day; **ces gens ~ nous empêchent de voir** we can't see for *ou* because of the people standing in front of us; **~!** get up!, on your feet!; **~ là-dedans!*** get up, you lot!*; *V* **dormir, magistrature.**

(b) *bouteille, meuble* (*position habituelle*) standing up(right); (*position inhabituelle*) standing (up) on end. **mettre qch ~** to stand sth up(right); to stand sth (up) on end; **les tables, ~ le long du mur** the tables, standing (up) on end along the wall; **mets les bouteilles ~** stand the bottles up(right).

(c) *édifice, mur* standing (*attrib*). (*fig*) **ces institutions sont** *ou* **tiennent encore ~** these institutions are still going; **cette théorie/ce record est encore ~** this theory/record still stands *ou* is still valid; **cette théorie tient ~ après tout** this theory holds up after all; **ça ne tient pas ~ ce que tu dis** what you say doesn't stand up; **son histoire ne tient pas ~** his story doesn't hold water.

débouté [debute] *nm* (*Jur*) ≃ nonsuit.

déboutement [debutmɑ̃] *nm* (*Jur*) ≃ nonsuiting.

débouter [debute] (1) *vt* (*Jur*) ≃ to nonsuit. **~ qn de sa plainte** ≃ to nonsuit a plaintiff.

déboutonner [debutɔne] (1) **1** *vt* to unbutton, undo. **2 se**

déboutonner *vpr* **(a)** *[personne]* to unbutton *ou* undo one's jacket (*ou* coat *etc*), unbutton *ou* undo o.s.; *[habit]* to come unbuttoned *ou* undone. **(b)** (*: *se confier*) to open up*.

débraillé, e [debʀɑje] (*ptp de* **débrailler**) **1** *adj tenue, personne* untidy, slovenly-looking; *manières* slovenly; *style* sloppy, slipshod. **2** *nm [tenue, manières]* slovenliness; *[style]* sloppiness. **être en ~** to be half-dressed.

débrailler (se)* [debʀɑje] (1) *vpr* to loosen one's clothing.

débranchement [debʀɑ̃ʃmɑ̃] *nm* (*V* **débrancher**) disconnecting; unplugging; cutting (off); splitting up.

débrancher [debʀɑ̃ʃe] (1) *vt* (*gén*) to disconnect; *appareil électrique* to unplug, disconnect; *téléphone* to cut off, disconnect; *courant* to cut (off), disconnect; (*Rail*) *wagons* to split up.

débrayage [debʀɛjaʒ] *nm* **(a)** (*objet*) (*Aut*) clutch; *[appareil-photo]* release button. **(b)** (*action*) *[moteur]* declutching, disengagement of the clutch; *[appareil photo]* releasing. **(c)** (*grève*) stoppage.

débrayer [debʀeje] (8) **1** *vi* **(a)** (*Aut*) to declutch (*Brit*), disengage the clutch; (*Tech*) to operate the release mechanism. **(b)** (*faire grève*) to stop work, come out on strike. **le personnel a débrayé à 4 heures** the staff stopped work at 4 o'clock. **2** *vt* (*Tech*) to release.

débridé, e [debʀide] (*ptp de* **débrider**) *adj* unbridled, unrestrained.

débridement [debʀidmɑ̃] *nm [instincts]* unbridling, unleashing; *[plaie]* lancing, incising.

débrider [debʀide] (1) *vt cheval* to unbridle; *volaille* to untruss; *plaie* to lance, incise. (*fig*) **sans ~** non-stop.

débris [debʀi] *nm* **(a)** (*pl: morceaux*) fragments, pieces; (*décombres*) debris (*sg*); (*détritus*) rubbish (*U*). **des ~ de verre/de vase** fragments *ou* pieces of glass/of a vase; **des ~ de métal** scraps of metal.

(b) (*pl: fig littér: restes*) *[mort]* remains; *[plat, repas]* leftovers, scraps; *[armée, fortune]* remains, remnants; *[état]* ruins; *[édifice]* ruins, remains.

(c) (*éclat, fragment*) fragment.

(d) (*péj: personne*) (**vieux**) **~** old wreck, old dodderer.

débrouillage [debʀujaʒ] *nm* (*V* **débrouiller**) disentangling; untangling; sorting out; unravelling.

débrouillard, e* [debʀujaʀ, aʀd(ə)] *adj* (*malin*) smart*, resourceful.

débrouillardise* [debʀujaʀdiz] *nf* smartness*, resourcefulness.

débrouillement [debʀujmɑ̃] *nm* = **débrouillage.**

débrouiller [debʀuje] (1) **1** *vt* **(a)** (*démêler*) *fils* to disentangle, untangle; *papiers* to sort out; *problème* to sort out, untangle; *mystère* to unravel, disentangle.

(b) (*: *éduquer*) **~ qn** (*gén*) to teach sb how to look after himself (*ou* herself); (*à l'école*) to teach sb the basics.

2 se débrouiller *vpr* to manage. **débrouillez-vous** you'll have to manage on your own *ou* sort things out yourself; **il m'a laissé me ~ (tout seul) avec mes ennemis** he left me to cope (alone) with my enemies; **il s'est débrouillé pour obtenir la permission d'y aller** he somehow managed to get permission to go, he wangled* permission to go; **c'est toi qui as fait l'erreur, maintenant débrouille-toi pour la réparer** you made the mistake so now sort it out yourself*.

débroussaillement [debʀusajmɑ̃] *nm [terrain]* clearing (*de* of); *[problème]* spadework (*de* on).

débroussailler [debʀusaje] (1) *vt terrain* to clear (of brushwood); *problème* to do the spadework on.

débusquer [debyske] (1) *vt lièvre, cerf* to drive out (from cover); *personne* to drive out, chase out, flush out.

début [deby] *nm* **(a)** *[semaine, livre, action]* beginning, start; *[discours]* beginning, opening. **du ~ à la fin** from beginning to end; **les scènes du ~ sont très belles** the opening scenes are very beautiful; **salaire de ~** starting salary; **dès le ~** from the outset *ou* the start *ou* the (very) beginning; **au ~** at first, in the beginning; **au ~ du mois prochain** early next month, at the beginning of next month.

(b) ~s: ses ~s furent médiocres he made an indifferent start; **à mes ~s (dans ce métier)** when I started (in this job); **ce projet en est encore à ses ~s** the project is still in its early stages *ou* at the early stages; **faire ses ~s dans le monde** to make one's début in society; **faire ses ~s sur la scène** to make one's début *ou* one's first appearance on the stage.

débutant, e [debytɑ̃, ɑ̃t] **1** *adj* novice (*épith*). **2** *nm* (*gén*) beginner, novice; (*Théât*) debutant actor. **3 débutante** *nf* (*gén*) beginner, novice; (*Théât*) debutant actress; *[haute société]* debutante.

débuter [debyte] (1) **1** *vi* **(a)** *[personne]* to start (out). **~ bien/mal** to make a good/bad start, start well/badly; **il a débuté (dans la vie) comme livreur** he started (life) as a delivery boy; **elle a débuté dans 'Autant en emporte le vent'** she made her debut *ou* her first appearance in 'Gone with the Wind'; **il débute (dans le métier), soyez indulgent** he is just starting (in the business) so don't be too hard on him; **l'orateur a débuté par des excuses** the speaker started (off) *ou* began *ou* opened by apologizing; **~ dans le monde** to make one's début in society, come out; **pour ~** to start (off) with.

(b) *[livre, concert, manifestation]* to start, begin, open (*par*, *sur* with).

2 *vt* (*) *semaine, réunion, discours* to start, begin, open (*par*, *sur* with). **il a bien débuté l'année** he has begun *ou* started the year well.

deçà [dəsa] *adv* **(a) en ~ de** (on) this side of; (*fig*) short of; **en ~ du fleuve/de la montagne** this side of the river/of the mountain; **en ~ de ses moyens** within his means; **en ~ d'une certaine intensité, on ne peut plus rien entendre** below a certain intensity, one can no longer hear anything; **ce qu'il dit est très en ~ de la vérité** what he says is well short of the truth; **tu vois la rivière, sa maison se trouve en ~** you see the river — his house is this side of it; **au ~ de**†† (on) this side of.

(b) (*littér*) **~, delà** here and there, on this side and that.

décachetage [dekaʃtaʒ] *nm* unsealing, opening.

décacheter [dekaʃte] (4) *vt lettre* to unseal, open; *colis* to break open.

décade [dekad] *nf* (*décennie*) decade; (*dix jours*) period of ten days.

décadenasser [dekadnase] (1) *vt porte* to unpadlock, remove the padlock from.

décadence [dekadɑ̃s] *nf* (*processus*) decline, decadence, decay; (*état*) decadence. **la ~ de l'empire romain** the decline of the Roman empire; **tomber en ~** to fall into decline; *V* **grandeur.**

décadent, e [dekadɑ̃, ɑ̃t] **1** *adj* decadent, declining, decaying. **2** *nm,f* decadent.

décaèdre [dekaɛdʀ(ə)] **1** *adj* decahedral.

2 *nm* decahedron.

décaféiner [dekafeine] (1) *vt* to decaffeinate. **café décaféiné** decaffeinated coffee, caffeine-free coffee.

décagonal, e, *mpl* **-aux** [dekagɔnal, o] *adj* decagonal.

décagone [dekagɔn] *nm* decagon.

décagramme [dekagʀam] *nm* decagram(me).

décaissement [dekɛsmɑ̃] *nm* payment.

décaisser [dekese] (1) *vt objet* to uncrate, unpack; *argent* to pay out.

décalage [dekalaʒ] *nm* **(a)** (*écart*) gap, interval; (*entre deux concepts*) gap, discrepancy; (*entre deux actions successives*) interval, time-lag (*entre* between). **le ~ entre le rêve et la réalité** the gap between dream and reality; **il y a un ~ entre le coup de feu et le bruit de la détonation** there is an interval *ou* a time-lag between the shot and the sound of the detonation; **le ~ horaire entre l'est et l'ouest des USA** the time difference between the east and west of the USA.

(b) (*déplacement d'horaire*) move forward *ou* back. **il y a un ~ d'horaire/de date** (*avance*) the timetable/date is brought forward; (*retard*) the timetable/date is put back.

(c) (*dans l'espace*) (*avancée*) jutting out; (*retrait*) standing back; (*déplacement*) *[meuble, objet]* shifting forward *ou* back.

décalaminage [dekalaminaʒ] *nm* decarbonization, decoking (*Brit*), decoke* (*Brit*).

décalaminer [dekalamine] (1) *vt* to decarbonize, decoke (*Brit*).

décalcification [dekalsifikɑsjɔ̃] *nf* decalcification.

décalcifier [dekalsifje] (7) *vt* to decalcify.

décalcomanie [dekalkɔmani] *nf* (*procédé*) decalcomania, decal; (*image*) transfer, decal. **faire de la ~** to decal.

décaler [dekale] (1) *vt* **(a)** *horaire, départ, repas* (*avancer*) to bring *ou* move forward; (*retarder*) to put back. **décalé d'une heure** (*avancé*) brought *ou* moved forward an hour; (*retardé*) put back an hour.

(b) *pupitre, immeuble* (*avancer*) to move *ou* shift forward; (*reculer*) to move *ou* shift back. **décalez-vous d'un rang** move forward (*ou* back) a row; **une série d'immeubles décalés par rapport aux autres** a row of blocks out of line with *ou* jutting out from the others.

(c) (*déséquilibrer*) *meuble, objet* to unwedge.

décalitre [dekalitʀ(ə)] *nm* decalitre.

décalogue [dekalɔg] *nm* Decalogue.

décalotter [dekalɔte] (1) *vt* to take the top off.

décalquage [dekalkaʒ] *nm* (*V* **décalquer**) tracing; transferring.

décalque [dekalk(ə)] *nm* (*dessin: V* **décalquer**) tracing; transfer; (*fig: imitation*) reproduction, copy.

décalquer [dekalke] (1) *vt* (*avec papier transparent*) to trace; (*par pression*) to transfer.

décamètre [dekamɛtʀ(ə)] *nm* decametre.

décamper* [dekɑ̃pe] (1) *vi* (*déguerpir*) to clear out* *ou* off*, decamp*. **décampez d'ici!** clear off!*, scram!‡

décan [dekɑ̃] *nm* decan.

décanal, e, *mpl* **-aux** [dekanal, o] *adj* decanal.

décanat [dekana] *nm* (*dignité, durée*) deanship.

décaniller* [dekanije] (1) *vi* (*partir*) to clear out* *ou* off*, decamp*.

décantage [dekɑ̃taʒ] *nm,* **décantation** [dekɑ̃tɑsjɔ̃] *nf* (*V* **décanter, se décanter**) settling (and decanting); clarification.

décanter [dekɑ̃te] (1) **1** *vt liquide, vin* to settle, allow to settle (and decant). (*fig*) **~ ses idées** to allow the dust to settle around one's ideas; **il faut laisser ~ ce liquide pendant une nuit** this liquid must be allowed to settle overnight.

2 se décanter *vpr [liquide, vin]* to settle; (*fig*) *[idées]* to become clear. **il faut laisser les choses se ~, après on verra** we'll have to let things clarify themselves *ou* we'll have to allow the dust to settle and then we'll see.

décanteur [dekɑ̃tœʀ] *nm* decanter (*Tech: apparatus*).

décapage [dekapaʒ] *nm* (*V* **décaper**) cleaning, cleansing; scouring; pickling; scrubbing; sanding; burning off.

décapant [dekapɑ̃] *nm* (*acide*) pickle, acid solution; (*abrasif*) scouring agent, abrasive; (*pour peinture*) paint stripper.

décaper [dekape] (1) *vt* (*gén*) to clean, cleanse; (*à l'abrasif*) to scour; (*à l'acide*) to pickle; (*à la brosse*) to scrub; (*au papier de verre*) to sand; (*au chalumeau*) to burn off; (*enlever la peinture*) to strip. **d'abord il faut bien ~ la surface de toute rouille** first you must clean the surface of any rust.

décapitation [dekapitɑsjɔ̃] *nf [personne]* beheading.

décapiter [dekapite] (1) *vt personne* to behead; (*accidentellement*) to decapitate; *arbre* to top, cut the top off; (*fig*) *parti, complot* to remove the top men from.

décapode [dekapɔd] *nm* decapod. **~s** Decapoda.

décapotable [dekapɔtabl(ə)] *adj* (*Aut*) convertible.

décapoter [dekapɔte] (1) *vt*: ~ **une voiture** to put down the roof (*Brit*) *ou* top (*US*) of a car.
décapsuler [dekapsyle] (1) *vt* to take the cap *ou* top off.
décapsuleur [dekapsylœʀ] *nm* bottle-opener.
décarcasser (se)* [dekaʀkase] (1) *vpr* to flog o.s. to death*, slog one's guts out‡, go to a hell of a lot of trouble*.
décarreler [dekɑʀle] (4) *vt* to take the tiles up from.
décasyllabe [dekasilab] **1** *adj* decasyllabic. **2** *nf* decasyllable.
décasyllabique [dekasilabik] *adj* = **decasyllabe.**
décathlon [dekatlɔ̃] *nm* decathlon.
décati, e [dekati] *adj* (*péj*) *vieillard* decrepit, broken-down; *visage* aged; *beauté* faded.
décavé, e [dekave] *adj* **(a)** (*ruiné*) *joueur* ruined, cleaned out*; (*) *banquier* ruined. **(b)** (*: *hâve*) *visage* haggard, drawn.
décédé, e [desede] (*ptp de* **décéder**) *adj, nm,f* (*frm*) deceased.
décéder [desede] (6) *vi* (*frm*) to die. **M X, décédé le 14 mai** Mr X, who died on May 14th; **il est décédé depuis 20 ans** he died 20 years ago, he's been dead 20 years.
décelable [deslabl(ə)] *adj* detectable, discernible.
déceler [desle] (5) *vt* **(a)** (*trouver*) to discover, detect. **on a décelé des traces de poison** traces of poison have been detected; **on peut ~ dans ce poème l'influence germanique** the Germanic influence can be discerned *ou* detected in this poem.
(b) (*montrer*) to indicate, reveal.
décélération [deseleʀɑsjɔ̃] *nf* deceleration.
décembre [desɑ̃bʀ(ə)] *nm* December; *pour loc V* **septembre.**
décemment [desamɑ̃] *adv* (*convenablement*) decently, fittingly; (*raisonnablement*) reasonably, properly. **j'arrivais à jouer ~ (du piano)** I managed to play (the piano) reasonably well *ou* quite decently; **je ne peux pas ~ l'accepter** I cannot reasonably *ou* properly accept it.
décence [desɑ̃s] *nf* (*bienséance*) decency, propriety; (*réserve*) (sense of) decency. **il aurait pu avoir la ~ de ...** he could *ou* might have had the decency to ... .
décennal, e, *mpl* **-aux** [desenal, o] *adj* decennial.
décennie [deseni] *nf* decade.
décent, e [desɑ̃, ɑ̃t] *adj* (*bienséant*) decent, proper; (*discret, digne*) proper; (*acceptable*) reasonable, decent. **je vais changer de robe pour être un peu plus ~e** I am going to change my dress to look a bit more decent; **il eût été plus ~ de refuser** it would have been more proper to refuse.
décentrage [desɑ̃tʀaʒ] *nm* decentration.
décentralisateur, -trice [desɑ̃tʀalizatœʀ, tʀis] **1** *adj* decentralizing (*épith*), decentralization (*épith*). **2** *nm,f* advocate of decentralization.
décentralisation [desɑ̃tʀalizɑsjɔ̃] *nf* decentralization.
décentraliser [desɑ̃tʀalize] (1) *vt* to decentralize.
décentrement [desɑ̃tʀəmɑ̃] *nm,* **décentration** [desɑ̃tʀɑsjɔ̃] *nf* (*Opt*) decentration; (*action*) decentring, throwing off centre.
décentrer [desɑ̃tʀe] (1) **1** *vt* to decentre, throw off centre. **2 se décentrer** *vpr* to move off centre.
déception [desɛpsjɔ̃] *nf* disappointment, let-down*.
décérébrer [deseʀebʀe] (6) *vt* to decerebrate.
décernement [desɛʀnəmɑ̃] *nm* award.
décerner [desɛʀne] (1) *vt* **(a)** *prix* to award; *récompense* to give, award. **(b)** (*Jur*) to issue.
décès [desɛ] *nm* death, decease (*frm*). **'fermé pour cause de ~'** 'closed owing to bereavement'; *V* **acte.**
décevant, e [desvɑ̃, ɑ̃t] *adj* **(a)** disappointing. **(b)** (††: *trompeur*) deceptive, delusive.
décevoir [desvwaʀ] (28) *vt* **(a)** to disappoint. **(b)** (††: *tromper*) to deceive, delude.
déchaîné, e [deʃene] (*ptp de* **déchaîner**) *adj passions, flots, éléments* raging, unbridled, unleashed; *enthousiasme* wild, unbridled; *personne* wild; *foule* raging, wild; *opinion publique* furious. **il est ~ contre moi** he is furious *ou* violently angry with me.
déchaînement [deʃɛnmɑ̃] *nm* **(a)** (*V* **se déchaîner**) bursting out; explosion; breaking (out); eruption; flying into a rage.
(b) (*état agité, violent*) *[flots, éléments, passions]* fury, raging. **un ~ d'idées/d'injures** a torrent of ideas/of abuse.
(c) (*colère*) (raging) fury. **un tel ~ contre son fils** such an outburst of fury at his son.
déchaîner [deʃene] (1) **1** *vt* **(a)** *tempête, violence, passions, colère* to unleash; *enthousiasme* to arouse; *opinion publique* to rouse; *campagne* to give rise to. **~ l'hilarité générale** to give rise to general hilarity; **~ les huées/les cris/les rires** to raise a storm of booing/shouting/laughter.
(b) *chien* to unchain, let loose.
2 se déchaîner *vpr [fureur, passions]* to burst out, explode; *[rires]* to break out; *[tempête]* to break, erupt; *[personne]* to fly into a rage (*contre* against), loose one's fury (*contre* upon). **la tempête se déchaînait** the storm was raging furiously; **la presse se déchaîna contre lui** the press loosed its fury on him.
déchanter [deʃɑ̃te] (1) *vi* to become disillusioned. **maintenant, il commence à ~** he is now becoming (somewhat) disillusioned.
décharge [deʃaʀʒ(ə)] *nf* **(a)** (*Élec*) **~ (électrique)** electrical discharge; **il a pris une ~ (électrique) dans les doigts** he got an electric shock in his fingers.
(b) (*salve*) volley of shots, salvo. **on entendit le bruit de plusieurs ~s** a volley of shots was heard; **il a reçu une ~ de chevrotines dans le dos** he was hit in the back by a volley of buckshot.
(c) (*Jur*) discharge; (*Comm: reçu*) receipt. **il faut me signer la ~ pour ce colis** you have to sign the receipt for this parcel for me; (*fig*) **il faut dire à sa ~ que ...** it must be said in his defence that ...; *V* **témoin.**
(d) (*dépôt*) **~ (publique *ou* municipale)** rubbish tip *ou* dump (*Brit*), garbage dump (*US*).
(e) (*Typ*) offset sheet.
(f) (*Archit*) **voûte/arc de ~** relieving *ou* discharging vault/ arch.
déchargement [deʃaʀʒəmɑ̃] *nm [cargaison, véhicule, arme]* unloading. **commencer le ~ d'un véhicule** to start unloading a vehicle.
décharger [deʃaʀʒe] (3) **1** *vt* **(a)** *véhicule, animal* to unload; *bagages, marchandises* to unload (*de* from). **je vais vous ~: donnez-moi vos paquets/votre manteau** let me unload *ou* unburden you — give me your bags/your coat.
(b) (*soulager*) *conscience, cœur* to unburden, disburden (*auprès de* to). **~ sa colère *ou* bile** to vent one's anger *ou* spleen (*sur qn* (up)on sb).
(c) (*Jur*) **~ un accusé** to discharge an accused person.
(d) **~ qn de** *dette* to release sb from; *impôt* to exempt sb from; *responsabilité, travail, tâche* to relieve sb of, release sb from. **se ~ de ses responsabilités** to pass off one's responsibilities (*sur qn* onto sb); **il s'est déchargé sur moi du soin de prévenir sa mère** he loaded onto me *ou* handed over to me the job of telling his mother.
(e) *arme* (*enlever le chargeur*) to unload; (*tirer*) to discharge, fire. **il déchargea son pistolet sur la foule** he fired *ou* discharged his revolver into the crowd.
(f) (*Élec*) to discharge. **la batterie s'est déchargée pendant la nuit** the battery has run down *ou* gone flat *ou* lost its charge overnight.
(g) (*Tech*) *bassin* to drain off the excess of; *support, étai* to take the load *ou* weight off.
2 *vi [tissu]* to lose its colour.
décharné, e [deʃaʀne] (*ptp de* **décharner**) *adj corps, membre* all skin and bone (*attrib*), emaciated; *doigts* bony, fleshless; *visage* fleshless, emaciated; *squelette* fleshless; (*fig*) *paysage* bare.
décharner [deʃaʀne] (1) *vt* (*amaigrir*) to emaciate; (*rare: ôter la chair*) to remove the flesh from. **cette maladie l'a complètement décharné** this illness has left him mere skin and bone *ou* has left him completely emaciated.
déchaussé, e [deʃose] (*ptp de* **déchausser**) *adj personne* barefoot(ed); *pied* bare; *dent* loose; *mur* exposed.
déchaussement [deʃosmɑ̃] *nm [dent]* loosening.
déchausser [deʃose] (1) **1** *vt arbre* to expose *ou* lay bare the roots of; *mur* to lay bare the foundations of. **~ un enfant** to take a child's shoes off, take the shoes off a child.
2 se déchausser *vpr [personne]* to take one's shoes off; *[dents]* to come *ou* work loose.
dèche‡ [dɛʃ] *nf*: **dans la ~** (stony (*Brit*)*ou* flat) broke*, on one's uppers*.
déchéance [deʃeɑ̃s] *nf* **(a)** (*morale*) decay, decline, degeneration; (*physique*) degeneration; (*Rel*) fall; *[civilisation]* decline, decay. **(b)** (*Pol*) *[souverain]* deposition, dethronement. (*Jur*) **~ de la puissance paternelle** loss of parental rights.
déchet [deʃɛ] *nm* **(a)** (*restes, résidus*) **~s** *[viande, tissu]* scraps, waste (*U*); *[métal]* scrap (*U*), scraps; (*épluchures*) peelings; (*ordures*) refuse (*U*), rubbish (*U*). **~s de viande/de métal** scraps of meat/metal; **~s radio-actifs** nuclear *ou* radioactive waste; **va jeter les ~s à la poubelle** go and throw the rubbish in the dustbin.
(b) (*reste*) *[viande, tissu, métal]* scrap, bit.
(c) (*gén, Comm: perte*) waste, loss. **il y a du ~** (*dans une marchandise etc*) there is some waste *ou* wastage; (*fig: dans un examen*) there are (some) failures, there is (some) wastage (of students); **~ de route** loss in transit.
(d) (*péj*) (*raté*) failure, wash-out*, dead loss*; (*épave*) wreck, dead-beat*. **les ~s de l'humanité** the dregs *ou* scum of humanity.
déchiffonner [deʃifɔne] (1) *vt* to smooth out, uncrease. **sa robe s'est déchiffonnée toute seule** the creases have come out of her dress (on their own).
déchiffrable [deʃifʀabl(ə)] *adj message* decipherable; *code* decodable, decipherable; *écriture* decipherable, legible.
déchiffrage [deʃifʀaʒ] *nm,* **déchiffrement** [deʃifʀəmɑ̃] *nm* (*V* **déchiffrer**) deciphering; decoding; sight-reading; unravelling, fathoming; reading.
déchiffrer [deʃifʀe] (1) *vt message, hiéroglyphe* to decipher; *code* to decode; *écriture* to make out, decipher; (*Mus*) to sight-read; *énigme* to unravel, fathom; *sentiment* to read, make out.
déchiffreur, -euse [deʃifʀœʀ, øz] *nm,f [code]* decoder; *[inscriptions, message]* decipherer.
déchiqueté, e [deʃikte] (*ptp de* **déchiqueter**) *adj montagne, relief, côte* jagged, ragged; *feuille* jagged(-edged); *corps* mutilated.
déchiqueter [deʃikte] (4) *vt* (*lit*) to tear *ou* cut *ou* pull to pieces *ou* shreds, shred; (*fig*) to pull *ou* tear to pieces. **la malheureuse victime fut déchiquetée par le train/l'explosion** the unfortunate victim was cut to pieces *ou* crushed by the train/blown to pieces by the explosion.
déchiqueture [deʃiktyʀ] *nf [tissu]* slash; *[feuille]* notch. **~s** *[côte, montagne]* jagged *ou* ragged outline.
déchirant, e [deʃiʀɑ̃, ɑ̃t] *adj drame* heartbreaking, heartrending; *cri, spectacle* heartrending, harrowing; *douleur* agonizing, searing.
déchirement [deʃiʀmɑ̃] *nm* **(a)** *[tissu]* tearing, ripping; *[muscle]* tearing. **(b)** (*douleur*) wrench, heartbreak. **(c)** (*Pol: divisions*) **~s** rifts, splits.
déchirer [deʃiʀe] (1) **1** *vt* **(a)** (*mettre en morceaux*) *papier, lettre* to tear up, tear to pieces; (*faire un accroc à*) *vêtement* to tear, rip; (*arracher*) *page* to tear out (*de* from); (*ouvrir*) *sac, enveloppe* to tear open; *bande de protection* to tear off; (*mutiler*) *corps* to tear to pieces. **~ un papier/tissu en deux** to tear a piece of paper/cloth in two *ou* in half.
(b) (*fig*) **leurs cris déchirèrent l'air/le silence** their cries rent

the air/pierced the silence; **ce bruit me déchire les oreilles** that noise is splitting my ears; **cette toux lui déchirait la poitrine** his chest was racked by this cough; **un spectacle qui déchire (le cœur)** a heartrending *ou* harrowing sight; **elle est déchirée par le remords/la douleur** she is torn by remorse/racked by pain; **les dissensions continuent à ~ le pays** the country continues to be torn (apart) by dissension, dissension is still tearing the country apart; **~ qn à belles dents** to tear *ou* pull sb to pieces.

2 se déchirer *vpr [vêtement]* to tear, rip; *[sac]* to burst. (*fig*) **le brouillard s'est déchiré** the fog has broken up; **se ~ un muscle** to tear a muscle; **se ~ les mains** to graze *ou* skin one's hands; (*fig*) **son cœur se déchira** his heart broke; (*fig*) **ces deux êtres ne cessent de se ~** these two people are constantly tearing each other to pieces *ou* apart.

déchirure [deʃiʀyʀ] *nf [tissu]* tear, rip, rent; *[ciel]* break *ou* gap in the clouds. **~ musculaire** torn muscle; **se faire une ~ musculaire** to tear a muscle.

déchoir [deʃwaʀ] (25) *vi* (*frm*) **(a)** *[personne]* to lower o.s., demean o.s. **ce serait ~ que d'accepter** you would be lowering *ou* demeaning yourself if you accepted; **~ de son rang** to fall from rank. **(b)** *[réputation, influence]* to decline, wane.

déchristianisation [dekʀistjanizɑsjɔ̃] *nf* dechristianization.

déchristianiser [dekʀistjanize] (1) *vt* to dechristianize.

déchu, e [deʃy] (*ptp de* **déchoir**) *adj roi* deposed, dethroned; (*Rel*) *ange, humanité* fallen. (*Jur*) **être ~ de ses droits** to be deprived of one's rights, forfeit one's rights.

décibel [desibɛl] *nm* decibel.

décidé, e [deside] (*ptp de* **décider**) *adj* **(a)** (*résolu*) **maintenant je suis ~** now I have made up my mind; **il est ~ à agir** he is determined to act; **il est ~ à tout** he is prepared to do anything; **il était ~ à ce que je parte** he was determined that I should leave; **j'y suis tout à fait ~** I am quite determined (to do it).

(b) (*volontaire*) *air, ton* determined, decided; *personne* determined; (*net, marqué*) *goût* decided, definite.

(c) (*fixé*) *question* settled, decided. **bon, c'est ~** right, that's settled *ou* decided then; **c'est une chose ~e** the matter is settled.

décidément [desidemɑ̃] *adv* (*en fait*) certainly, undoubtedly, indeed. **oui, c'est ~ une question de chance** yes, it is certainly *ou* undoubtedly *ou* indeed a matter of luck; (*intensif*) **~, je perds toujours mes affaires!** I'm ALWAYS losing my things, I lose EVERYTHING!; **~, tu m'ennuies aujourd'hui** you're really annoying me today, you ARE annoying me today; **~, il est cinglé*** he's really crazy *ou* touched*, there's no doubt about it — he's crazy *ou* touched*.

décider [deside] (1) **1** *vt* **(a)** *[personne]* (*déterminer, établir*) to decide. **~ qch** to decide on sth; **il a décidé ce voyage au dernier moment** he decided on this trip at the last moment; **~ que** to decide that; **~ de faire qch** to decide to do sth; **comment ~ qui a raison?** how is one to decide who is right?; **c'est à lui de ~** it's up to him to decide; **elle décida qu'elle devait démissionner** she decided *ou* came to the decision that she must resign; **les ouvriers ont décidé la grève/de faire grève/de ne pas faire grève** the workers decided on a strike/to go on strike/against a strike *ou* not to go on strike.

(b) (*persuader*) *[personne]* to persuade; *[conseil, événement]* to decide, convince. **~ qn à faire** to persuade *ou* induce sb to do; **c'est moi qui l'ai décidé à ce voyage** I'm the one who persuaded *ou* induced him to go on this journey; **la bonne publicité décide les clients éventuels** good publicity convinces possible clients.

(c) *[chose]* (*provoquer*) to cause, bring about. **ces scandales ont finalement décidé le renvoi du directeur** these scandals finally brought about *ou* caused the manager's dismissal.

2 décider de *vt indir* (*être l'arbitre de*) to decide; (*déterminer*) to decide, determine. **~ de l'importance/de l'urgence de qch** to decide on the *ou* as to the importance/urgency of sth, decide how important/urgent sth is; **les résultats de son examen décideront de sa carrière** the results of his exam will decide *ou* determine his career; **le sort en a décidé autrement** fate has decided *ou* ordained *ou* decreed otherwise.

3 se décider *vpr* **(a)** *[personne]* to come to *ou* make a decision, make up one's mind. **se ~ à qch** to decide on sth; **se ~ à faire qch** to make up one's mind to do sth, make the decision to do sth; **je ne peux pas me ~ à lui mentir** I cannot bring myself to lie to him, I cannot make up my mind to lie to him; **se ~ pour qch** to decide on *ou* in favour of sth, plump for sth.

(b) *[problème, affaire]* to be decided *ou* settled *ou* resolved. **la question se décide aujourd'hui** the question is being decided *ou* settled *ou* resolved today; **leur départ s'est décidé très vite** they very quickly decided to leave.

(c) *[temps]* (*) **est-ce qu'il va se ~ à faire beau?** do you think it'll turn out fine after all?; **ça ne veut pas se ~** it won't make up its mind*.

décigramme [desigʀam] *nm* decigram(me).

décilitre [desilitʀ(ə)] *nm* decilitre.

décimal, e, *mpl* **-aux** [desimal, o] *adj, nf* decimal.

décimalisation [desimalizɑsjɔ̃] *nf* decimalization.

décimaliser [desimalize] (1) *vt* to decimalize.

décimation [desimɑsjɔ̃] *nf* decimation.

décimer [desime] (1) *vt* to decimate.

décimètre [desimɛtʀ(ə)] *nm* decimetre; *V* **double.**

décisif, -ive [desizif, iv] *adj argument, combat* decisive, conclusive; *intervention, influence* decisive; *moment* decisive, critical; *ton* decisive, authoritative. **le coup/facteur ~** the deciding move/factor.

décision [desizjɔ̃] *nf* **(a)** (*choix*) decision. **arriver à une ~** to come to *ou* reach a decision; **prendre la ~ de faire qch** to take the decision to do sth; **la ~ appartient à X** the decision is X's; **soumettre qch à la ~ de qn** to submit sth to sb for his decision; **l'architecte a soumis ses plans à la ~ de l'administration** the architect submitted his plans to the administration for its decision; *V* **pouvoir²**.

(b) (*verdict*) decision. **~ administrative/judiciaire/gouvernementale** administrative/judicial/government decision.

(c) (*qualité*) decision, decisiveness. **montrer de la ~** to show decision *ou* decisiveness; **avoir l'esprit de ~** to be decisive.

déclamateur, -trice [deklamatœʀ, tʀis] (*péj*) **1** *adj* ranting, declamatory. **2** *nm,f* ranter, declaimer.

déclamation [deklamɑsjɔ̃] *nf* (*art*) declamation (*U*); (*péj*) ranting (*U*), spouting (*U*). **toutes leurs belles ~s** all their grand ranting.

déclamatoire [deklamatwaʀ] *adj* **(a)** (*péj*) *ton* ranting, bombastic, declamatory; *style* bombastic, turgid. **(b)** (*littér*) *rythme* declamatory.

déclamer [deklame] (1) *vt* to declaim; (*péj*) to spout. (*littér*) **~ contre** to inveigh *ou* rail against.

déclarable [deklaʀabl(ə)] *adj* (*Douane*) *marchandise* declarable, dutiable; (*Impôts*) *revenus* declarable.

déclarant, e [deklaʀɑ̃, ɑ̃t] *nm,f* (*Jur*) informant.

déclaratif, -ive [deklaʀatif, iv] *adj* (*Jur*) declaratory; (*Ling*) declarative.

déclaration [deklaʀɑsjɔ̃] *nf* **(a)** (*manifeste, proclamation*) declaration; (*discours, commentaire*) statement; (*aveu*) admission; (*révélation*) revelation. **dans une ~ télévisée** in a televised statement; **le ministre n'a fait aucune ~** the minister did not make a statement; **selon sa propre ~, il était ivre** he himself admits that he was drunk, by his own admission he was drunk.

(b) (*amoureuse*) **~ (d'amour)** declaration of love; **faire une** *ou* **sa ~ à qn** to make a declaration of love to sb, declare one's love to sb.

(c) (*Jur*) *[naissance, décès]* registration, notification; *[vol, perte, changement de domicile]* notification. **envoyer une ~ de changement de domicile** to send notification of change of address; **~ en douane** customs declaration; **~ des droits de l'homme** declaration of the rights of man; **~ de faillite** declaration of bankruptcy; **~ de guerre** declaration of war; **~ d'impôts** tax declaration, statement of income; (*formulaire*) tax return; **faire sa ~ d'impôts** to make out one's statement of income *ou* one's tax return, fill in one's tax return; **~ de principe** statement *ou* declaration of principle; **~ publique** public statement; **~ de revenus** statement of income; **~ sous serment** statement under oath.

déclaratoire [deklaʀatwaʀ] *adj* (*Jur*) declaratory.

déclaré, e [deklaʀe] (*ptp de* **déclarer**) *adj opinion* professed; *athée, révolutionnaire* declared, self-confessed; *ennemi* sworn, avowed; *intention* avowed, declared.

déclarer [deklaʀe] (1) **1** *vt* **(a)** (*annoncer*) to announce, state, declare; (*proclamer*) to declare; (*avouer*) to admit, confess to. **~ son amour (à qn)** to declare one's love (to sb), make a declaration of one's love (to sb); **~ la guerre à une nation/à la pollution** to declare war on a nation/on pollution; **le président déclara la séance levée** the chairman declared the meeting closed; **~ qn coupable/innocent** to find sb guilty/innocent.

(b) ~ que ... to declare *ou* say that ...; **je vous déclare que je n'y crois pas** I tell you I don't believe it; **ils ont déclaré que nous avions menti** they claimed that we had lied.

(c) (*Admin*) *marchandises, revenus, employés* to declare; *naissance, décès* to register, notify. **le père doit aller ~ l'enfant à la mairie** the father has to go and register the child at the town hall; **~ qn en faillite** to declare sb bankrupt; **qu'avez-vous à ~?** have you anything to declare?

2 se déclarer *vpr* **(a)** (*se prononcer*) to declare *ou* state one's opinion. **se ~ en faveur de l'intégration raciale** to declare o.s. *ou* profess o.s. in favour of racial integration; **se ~ pour/contre qch** to come out in favour of/against sth; **il s'est déclaré l'auteur de ces poèmes/crimes** he stated that he had written the poems/committed the crimes; **se ~ satisfait** to declare o.s. satisfied; **se ~ offensé** to say one is offended.

(b) (*apparaître*) *[incendie, épidémie]* to break out.

(c) *[amoureux]* to make a declaration of one's love, declare *ou* avow (*littér*) one's love.

déclassé, e [deklɑse] (*ptp de* **déclasser**) **1** *adj* **(a)** *personne* déclassé; *coureur* relegated (*in the placing*); *billet, wagon* reclassed; *hôtel* downgraded. **il s'estimait ~ de jouer avec l'équipe B** he considered himself lowered in status *ou* downgraded to be playing with the B team.

(b) *fiche, livre* out of order (*attrib*).

2 *nm,f* déclassé.

déclassement [deklɑsmɑ̃] *nm* (*V* **déclasser**) fall *ou* drop in status; relegation (*in the placing*); change of class; downgrading.

déclasser [deklɑse] (1) *vt* **(a)** (*socialement, dans une hiérarchie*) to lower in status. **il se déclassait par de telles fréquentations** he was lowering himself socially *ou* demeaning himself by keeping such company; **il estimait qu'on l'avait déclassé en le mettant dans l'équipe B** he felt that he had suffered a drop in status *ou* that he had been downgraded by being put in the B team.

(b) (*rétrograder*) (*Sport: au classement*) *coureur* to relegate (*in the placing*); (*Rail*) *voyageur* to change the class of; (*Admin*) *hôtel* to downgrade.

(c) (*déranger*) *fiches, livres* to get out of order, put back in the wrong order.

déclenchement [deklɑ̃ʃmɑ̃] *nm* (*V* **déclencher**) release; setting off; triggering off; activating; launching; starting; opening.

déclencher [deklɑ̃ʃe] (1) **1** *vt* **(a)** (*actionner*) *ressort,*

mécanisme to release; *sonnerie* to set off, trigger off, activate; *appareil-photo* to release the shutter of. **ce bouton déclenche l'ouverture/la fermeture de la porte** this button activates the opening/closing of the door.
(b) (*provoquer*) *attaque, grève, insurrection* to launch, start; *catastrophe, guerre, crise politique, réaction nerveuse* to trigger off. **c'est ce mot qui a tout déclenché** this is the word which triggered everything off.
(c) (*Mil*) *tir* to open; *attaque* to launch. **~ l'offensive** to launch the offensive.
2 se déclencher *vpr [ressort, mécanisme]* to release itself; *[sonnerie]* to go off; *[attaque, grève]* to start, begin; *[catastrophe, crise, réaction nerveuse]* to be triggered off.

déclencheur [deklɑ̃ʃœʀ] *nm* (*Tech*) release mechanism.

déclic [deklik] *nm* (*bruit*) click; (*mécanisme*) trigger mechanism.

déclin [deklɛ̃] *nm* **(a)** (*affaiblissement: V* **décliner**) decline; deterioration; waning; fading; falling off. **le ~ du jour** the close of day; (*littér*) **au ~ de la vie** at the close of life, in the twilight of life (*littér*).
(b) (*loc*) **être à son ~** *[soleil]* to be setting; *[lune]* to be on the wane, be waning; **être sur le** *ou* **son ~** *[malade]* to be deteriorating *ou* on the decline; *[acteur, homme politique]* to be on the decline *ou* on the wane; **être en ~** *[talent, prestige]* to be on the decline *ou* on the wane; *[forces, intelligence, civilisation, art]* to be in decline *ou* on the wane.

déclinable [deklinabl(ə)] *adj* declinable.

déclinaison [deklinɛzɔ̃] *nf* (*Ling*) declension; (*Astron, Phys*) declination.

déclinant, e [deklinɑ̃, ɑ̃t] *adj* (*qui s'affaiblit: V* **décliner**) declining; deteriorating; waning; fading; falling off.

décliner [dekline] (1) **1** *vt* **(a)** (*frm: refuser*) *offre, invitation, honneur* to decline, refuse. **la direction décline toute responsabilité en cas de perte ou de vol** the management accepts no responsibility *ou* refuses to accept responsibility for loss or theft of articles; (*Jur*) **~ la compétence de qn** to refuse to recognize sb's competence.
(b) (*Ling*) to decline. **ce mot ne se décline pas** this word is indeclinable.
(c) (*frm: réciter*) **~ son identité** to give one's personal particulars; **déclinez vos nom, prénoms, titres et qualités** state your name, forenames, qualifications and status.
2 *vi* **(a)** (*s'affaiblir*) *[malade, santé]* to decline, deteriorate, go downhill; *[talent, ardeur, beauté, sentiment]* to wane, fade; *[vue]* to deteriorate; *[forces, facultés]* to wane, decline, fade; *[prestige, popularité]* to wane, fall off, decline; *[civilisation, empire]* to decline.
(b) (*baisser*) *[jour]* to draw to a close; *[soleil, lune]* to be setting, go down; (*Astron*) *[astre]* to set; (*Tech*) *[aiguille aimantée]* to deviate.

déclivité [deklivite] *nf* slope, incline, declivity (*frm*).

déclouer [deklue] (1) *vt caisse* to open; *planche* to remove.

décocher [dekɔʃe] (1) *vt* **(a)** *flèche* to shoot, fire; *coup de poing* to throw; *ruade* to let fly. **(b)** (*fig*) *œillade, regard* to shoot, flash, dart; *sourire* to flash; *remarque* to fire, let fly.

décoction [dekɔksjɔ̃] *nf* decoction.

décodage [dekɔdaʒ] *nm* (*V* **décoder**) decoding, cracking*; deciphering.

décoder [dekɔde] (1) *vt code* to decode, crack*; *message* to decipher.

décodeur [dekɔdœʀ] *nm* (*V* **décoder**) decoder; decipherer.

décoiffer [dekwafe] (1) *vt* **(a)** (*ébouriffer*) **~ qn** to disarrange sb's hair; **il s'est/le vent l'a décoiffé** he/the wind has disarranged *ou* messed up* his hair; **je suis toute décoiffée** my hair is in a mess *ou* is (all) messed up*.
(b) (*ôter le chapeau*) **~ qn** to take sb's hat off; **il se décoiffa** he took his hat off.
(c) (*Tech*) *obus* to uncap.

décoincement [dekwɛ̃smɑ̃] *nm* (*gén*) unjamming, loosening (*de* of); (*Tech*) removal of the wedge (*de* from).

décoincer [dekwɛ̃se] (3) *vt* (*gén*) to unjam, loosen. (*Tech*) **~ qch** to remove the wedge from sth.

décolérer [dekɔleʀe] (6) *vi*: **ne jamais ~** to be always in a temper; **il ne décolère pas depuis hier** he hasn't calmed down *ou* cooled off* since yesterday, he's still angry from yesterday.

décollage [dekɔlaʒ] *nm [timbre]* unsticking; (*Aviat*) takeoff.

décollation [dekɔlɑsjɔ̃] *nf* decapitation, beheading.

décollement [dekɔlmɑ̃] *nm [timbre]* unsticking; (*Méd*) *[rétine]* detachment.

décoller [dekɔle] (1) **1** *vt* (*gén*) to unstick; (*en trempant*) *timbre* to soak off; (*à la vapeur*) *timbre* to steam off; *lettre* to steam open; *V* **oreille**.
(b) (*: *se débarrasser de*) *créanciers, poursuivants* to shake off. **quel raseur, je ne suis pas arrivé à m'en ~!** *ou* **le ~!** what a bore — I couldn't manage to shake him off! *ou* get rid of him!
2 *vi* **(a)** (*Aviat*), (*fig*) *[industrie, pays]* to take off.
(b) (*: *maigrir*) to lose weight.
(c) (*: *partir*) *[gêneur]* to budge, shift; *[drogué]* to get off*. **ce casse-pieds n'a pas décollé (d'ici) pendant deux heures** that so-and-so sat *ou* stayed here for two solid hours without budging*; (*Sport*) **~ du peloton** (*en avant*) to pull away from *ou* ahead of the bunch; (*en arrière*) to fall *ou* drop behind the bunch.
3 se décoller *vpr [timbre]* to come unstuck; (*Méd*) *[rétine]* to become detached.

décolletage [dekɔltaʒ] *nm* **(a)** *[robe]* (*action*) cutting out of the neck; (*décolleté*) (low-cut) neckline, décolletage. **(b)** (*Agr*) topping; (*Tech*) cutting (from the bar).

décolleté, e [dekɔlte] (*ptp de* **décolleter**) **1** *adj robe* low-necked, low-cut, décolleté; *femme* wearing a low-cut dress, décolleté (*attrib*). **robe ~e dans le dos** dress cut low at the back.
2 *nm [robe]* low neck(line), décolletage; *[femme]* (bare) neck and shoulders; (*plongeant*) cleavage.
3: décolleté bateau bateau *ou* boat neck; **décolleté plongeant** plunging neckline; **décolleté en pointe** V-neck.

décolleter [dekɔlte] (4) **1** *vt* **(a)** *personne* to bare *ou* reveal the neck and shoulders of; *robe* to cut out the neck of. **(b)** (*Agr*) to top; (*Tech*) to cut (from the bar). **2 se décolleter** *vpr* to wear a low-cut dress.

décolonisateur, -trice [dekɔlɔnizatœʀ, tʀis] **1** *adj* decolonization (*épith*), decolonizing (*épith*). **2** *nm,f* decolonizer.

décolonisation [dekɔlɔnizɑsjɔ̃] *nf* decolonization.

décoloniser [dekɔlɔnize] (1) *vt* to decolonize.

décolorant, e [dekɔlɔʀɑ̃, ɑ̃t] **1** *adj* decolorizing (*épith*), bleaching (*épith*), decolorant (*épith*). **2** *nm* decolorant, bleaching agent, decolorizer.

décoloration [dekɔlɔʀɑsjɔ̃] *nf* (*V* **décolorer**) decoloration; bleaching, lightening; fading. **se faire faire une ~** to have one's hair bleached.

décoloré, e [dekɔlɔʀe] (*ptp de* **décolorer**) *adj vêtement* faded; *cheveux* bleached, lightened; *teint, lèvres* pale, colourless.

décolorer [dekɔlɔʀe] (1) **1** *vt liquide, couleur* to decolour, decolorize; *cheveux* to bleach, lighten; *tissu* (*au soleil*) to fade; (*au lavage*) to take the colour out of, fade.
2 se décolorer *vpr [liquide, couleur]* to lose its colour; *[tissu]* to fade, lose its colour. **elle s'est décolorée, elle s'est décoloré les cheveux** she has bleached *ou* lightened her hair.

décombres [dekɔ̃bʀ(ə)] *nmpl* rubble, debris (*sg*).

décommander [dekɔmɑ̃de] (1) **1** *vt marchandise* to cancel (an order for); *invités* to put off; *invitation* to cancel. **2 se décommander** *vpr* to cancel an appointment.

décomposable [dekɔ̃pozabl(ə)] *adj* (*V* **décomposer**) that can be split up; that can be broken up; that can be factorized; decomposable; resoluble; that can be analysed *ou* broken down.

décomposer [dekɔ̃poze] (1) **1** *vt* **(a)** (*analyser*) (*gén*) to split up *ou* break up into its component parts; (*Math*) *nombre* to factorize, express as a product of prime factors; (*Chim*) to decompose; (*Phys*) *lumière* to break up *ou* split up; (*Tech*) *forces* to resolve; (*Ling*) *phrase* to analyse, break down, split up; *problème, idée* to dissect, break down. **l'athlète décomposa le mouvement devant nous** the athlete broke the movement up for us *ou* went through the movement slowly for us; **la phrase se décompose en 3 propositions** the sentence can be broken down *ou* split up *ou* analysed into 3 clauses.
(b) (*défaire*) *visage* to contort, distort. **l'horreur décomposa son visage** his face contorted *ou* was distorted with horror; **il était décomposé** he was looking very drawn.
(c) (*altérer*) *viande* to cause to decompose *ou* rot. **la chaleur décomposait les cadavres** the heat was causing the corpses to decompose *ou* to decay.
2 se décomposer *vpr* **(a)** (*pourrir*) *[viande]* to decompose, rot; *[cadavre]* to decompose, decay.
(b) *[visage]* to change dramatically. **à cette nouvelle il se décomposa** when he heard this news his face *ou* expression changed dramatically.

décomposition [dekɔ̃pozisjɔ̃] *nf* **(a)** (*V* **décomposer**) splitting up into its component parts; factorization; decomposition; breaking up; splitting up; resolution; analysis; breaking down; dissection.
(b) (*bouleversement*) *[visage]* contortion.
(c) (*pourriture*) decomposition, decay. **cadavre en ~** corpse in a state of decomposition *ou* decay; **société/système en ~** society/system in decay.

décompresseur [dekɔ̃pʀesœʀ] *nm* decompression tap; (*Aut*) decompressor.

décompression [dekɔ̃pʀesjɔ̃] *nf* decompression.

décomprimer [dekɔ̃pʀime] (1) *vt* to decompress.

décompte [dekɔ̃t] *nm* (*compte*) detailed account, breakdown (of an account); (*déduction*) deduction. **faire le ~ des points** to count up *ou* tot up* (*surtout Brit*) the points; **vous voulez faire mon ~?** will you make out my bill (*Brit*) *ou* check (*US*)?

décompter [dekɔ̃te] (1) **1** *vt* (*défalquer*) to deduct. **2** *vi [horloge]* to strike *ou* chime at the wrong time.

déconcentration [dekɔ̃sɑ̃tʀɑsjɔ̃] *nf* (*Admin*) devolution, decentralization; (*Ind*) dispersal.

déconcentré, e [dekɔ̃sɑ̃tʀe] (*ptp de* **déconcentrer**) *adj* **(a)** (*Admin*) devolved, decentralized; (*Ind*) dispersed. **(b)** (*Sport*) who has lost concentration.

déconcentrer [dekɔ̃sɑ̃tʀe] (1) **1** *vt* (*Admin*) to devolve, decentralize; (*Ind*) to disperse. **2 se déconcentrer** *vpr* (*Sport*) *[athlète]* to lose (one's) concentration.

déconcertant, e [dekɔ̃sɛʀtɑ̃, ɑ̃t] *adj* disconcerting.

déconcerter [dekɔ̃sɛʀte] (1) *vt* (*décontenancer*) to disconcert, confound, throw (out)*; (††: *déjouer*) to thwart, frustrate.

déconfit, e [dekɔ̃fi, it] *adj* **(a)** (*dépité*) *personne, air, mine* crestfallen, downcast. **avoir la mine ~e** to look downcast *ou* crestfallen. **(b)** (††: *battu*) defeated, discomfited††.

déconfiture* [dekɔ̃fityʀ] *nf* (*déroute*) (*gén*) failure, collapse, defeat; *[parti, armée]* defeat; (*financière*) (financial) collapse, ruin.

décongélation [dekɔ̃ʒelɑsjɔ̃] *nf* thawing (out).

décongeler [dekɔ̃ʒle] (5) *vt* to thaw (out).

décongestionner [dekɔ̃ʒɛstjɔne] (1) *vt* (*Méd*) *poumons* to decongest, relieve congestion in; *malade* to relieve congestion in; (*fig*) *rue* to relieve congestion in; *services, aéroport, universités, administration* to relieve the pressure on.

déconnecter [dekɔnɛkte] (1) *vt* to disconnect.

déconner‡ [dekɔne] (1) *vi* (*dire des bêtises*) to talk twaddle* *ou* drivel* *ou* a load of rubbish‡, blather*; (*faire des erreurs*) *[per-*

sonne] to boob*, blunder; (*mal fonctionner*) *[machine]* to be on the blink*.

déconseiller [dekɔ̃seje] (1) *vt* to advise against. **~ qch à qn/à qn de faire qch** to advise sb against sth/sb against doing sth; **c'est déconseillé** it's not advisable, it's inadvisable.

déconsidération [dekɔ̃sideʀɑsjɔ̃] *nf* discredit, disrepute.

déconsidérer [dekɔ̃sideʀe] (6) *vt* to discredit. **il s'est déconsidéré en agissant ainsi** he has discredited himself *ou* brought discredit upon himself by acting thus.

déconsigner [dekɔ̃siɲe] (1) *vt valise* to collect (from the left luggage); *bouteille* to return the deposit on; *troupes* to release from 'confinement to barracks'.

décontenancer [dekɔ̃tnɑ̃se] (3) *vt* to disconcert, discountenance (*frm*).

décontracté, e [dekɔ̃tʀakte] (*ptp de* **décontracter**) *adj* (*détendu*) relaxed; (*: *insouciant*) relaxed, cool*.

décontracter *vt,* **se décontracter** *vpr* [dekɔ̃tʀakte] (1) to relax.

décontraction [dekɔ̃tʀaksjɔ̃] *nf* (*V* **décontracté**) relaxation; coolness, cool*.

déconvenue [dekɔ̃vny] *nf* (*déception*) disappointment.

décor [dekɔʀ] *nm* **(a)** (*Théât*) **le ~, les ~s** the scenery (*U*), the décor (*U*); **~ de cinéma** film set; **quel beau ~!** what a lovely set!, what lovely scenery! *ou* décor!; **on dirait un ~** *ou* **des ~s de théâtre** it looks like a stage setting *ou* a theatre set, it looks like scenery for a play; *[véhicule, conducteur]* **aller** *ou* **entrer dans le ~*** *ou* **les ~s*** to drive off the road, drive into a ditch (*ou* tree *ou* hedge *etc*); **envoyer qn dans le ~*** *ou* **les ~s*** to force sb off the road; *V* **changement.**

(b) (*paysage*) scenery; (*arrière-plan*) setting; (*intérieur de maison*) décor (*U*), decorations. **~ de montagnes** mountain scenery; **dans un ~ sordide de banlieue** in a sordid suburban setting; **dans un ~ de verdure** amid green scenery, in a setting of greenery; **photographié dans son ~ habituel** photographed in his usual setting.

décorateur, -trice [dekɔʀatœʀ, tʀis] *nm,f* **(a)** (*d'intérieurs*) (interior) decorator; *V* **ensemblier, peintre. (b)** (*Théât*) (*architecte*) stage *ou* set designer; (*exécutant, peintre*) set artist.

décoratif, -ive [dekɔʀatif, iv] *adj ornement* decorative, ornamental; *arts* decorative; (*) *personne* decorative.

décoration [dekɔʀɑsjɔ̃] *nf* **(a)** (*action*) decoration.

(b) (*gén pl: ornement*) decorations; (*ensemble des ornements*) decoration. **~s de Noël** Christmas decorations; **j'admirais la ~ de cette église** I was admiring the decoration of the church.

(c) (*médaille*) decoration.

décorer [dekɔʀe] (1) *vt* **(a)** (*embellir*) (*gén*) to decorate; *robe* to trim. **~ un appartement pour Noël** to decorate a flat for Christmas; **l'ensemblier qui a décoré leur appartement** the designer who did the (interior) decoration of their flat; (*fig*) **~ qch du nom de** to dignify sth with the name of.

(b) (*médailler*) to decorate (*de* with). **on va le ~** (*gén*) he is to be decorated; (*Légion d'honneur*) he is to be made a member of the Legion of Honour; **un monsieur décoré** a gentleman with *ou* wearing a decoration.

décorner [dekɔʀne] (1) *vt page* to smooth out; *animal* to dehorn; *V* **vent.**

décorticage [dekɔʀtikaʒ] *nm* (*V* **décortiquer**) shelling; hulling, husking; dissection.

décortication [dekɔʀtikɑsjɔ̃] *nf [arbre]* cleaning of the bark; (*Méd*) decortication.

décortiquer [dekɔʀtike] (1) *vt* **(a)** *crevettes, amandes* to shell; *riz* to hull, husk; (*fig*) *texte* to dissect (in minute detail). **(b)** (*Méd*) *cœur* to decorticate. **(c)** (*Sylviculture*) to remove the bark of.

décorum [dekɔʀɔm] *nm*: **le ~** (*convenances*) the proprieties, decorum; (*étiquette*) etiquette.

décote [dekɔt] *nf* (*Fin*) *[devises, valeur]* below par rating; *[impôts]* tax relief.

découcher [dekuʃe] (1) *vi* to stay out all night, spend the night away from home.

découdre [dekudʀ(ə)] (48) **1** *vt* **(a)** *vêtement* to unpick, take the stitches out of; *bouton* to take off; *couture* to unpick, take out.

(b) en ~ (*littér, hum: se battre*) to fight, do battle; (††: *se battre en duel*) to fight a duel.

2 se découdre *vpr [robe]* to come unstitched; *[bouton]* to come off; *[couture]* to come apart.

découler [dekule] (1) *vi* (*dériver*) to ensue, follow (*de* from). **il découle de cela que ...** it ensues *ou* follows from this that ... .

découpage [dekupaʒ] *nm* **(a)** *[papier, gâteau]* cutting up; *[viande]* carving; *[image, métal]* cutting out.

(b) (*image*) cut-out. **un cahier de ~s** a cut-out book; **faire des ~s** to make cut-out figures.

(c) (*Ciné*) cutting.

(d) (*Pol*) **~ électoral** division into constituencies, distribution of constituencies.

découpe [dekup] *nf* **(a)** (*Couture*) (*coupe*) cut; (*coupure*) cut-out. **(b)** *[bois]* cutting off (of upper part of tree).

découpé, e [dekupe] (*ptp de* **découper**) *adj relief, sommets, côte* jagged, indented; *feuille* jagged, serrate (*T*).

découper [dekupe] (1) *vt* **(a)** (*Culin*) *viande, volaille* to carve, cut (up); *gâteau* to cut (up). **couteau/fourchette à ~** carving knife/fork.

(b) *papier, tissu* to cut up; *bois* to jigsaw; *images, métal* to cut out. **~ un article dans un magazine** to cut an article out of a magazine; *V* **scie.**

(c) (*fig littér*) to indent. **les indentations qui découpent la côte** the indentations which cut into the coastline; **la montagne découpe ses aiguilles sur le ciel** the mountain's peaks stand out (sharp) against the sky; **sa silhouette se découpe dans la lumière** his figure stands out *ou* is outlined against the light.

découpeur, -euse [dekupœʀ, øz] **1** *nm,f* (*personne*) *[viande]* carver; *[métal]* cutter; *[bois]* jigsaw operator. **2 découpeuse** *nf* (*machine*) (*gén*) cutting machine; *[bois]* fretsaw, jigsaw.

découplé, e [dekuple] *adj*: **bien ~** *athlète etc* well-built, well-proportioned.

découpure [dekupyʀ] *nf* **(a)** (*forme, contour*) jagged *ou* indented outline. **la ~ de la côte est régulière** the coastline is evenly indented.

(b) (*gén pl: échancrure*) **~s** *[côte]* indentations; *[arête]* jagged *ou* indented edge *ou* outline; *[dentelle, guirlande]* scalloped edge.

(c) (*morceau*) bit *ou* piece cut out. **~s de papier** cut-out bits of paper.

décourageant, e [dekuʀaʒɑ̃, ɑ̃t] *adj nouvelle* disheartening, discouraging; *élève, travail, situation* disheartening.

découragement [dekuʀaʒmɑ̃] *nm* discouragement, despondency.

décourager [dekuʀaʒe] (3) **1** *vt* **(a)** (*démoraliser*) to discourage, dishearten. **il ne faut pas se laisser ~ par un échec** one must not be discouraged *ou* disheartened by a setback.

(b) (*dissuader*) to discourage, put off. **sa froideur décourage la familiarité** his coldness discourages familiarity; **pour ~ les malfaiteurs** to deter wrongdoers; **~ qn de qch/de faire qch** to discourage sb from sth/from doing sth, put sb off sth/doing sth; **~ qn d'une entreprise** to discourage *ou* deter sb from an undertaking, put sb off an undertaking.

2 se décourager *vpr* to lose heart, become disheartened *ou* discouraged.

découronner [dekuʀɔne] (1) *vt roi* to dethrone, depose. (*fig*) **arbre découronné par la tempête** tree that has had its top *ou* its topmost branches blown off by the storm.

décousu, e [dekuzy] (*ptp de* **découdre**) **1** *adj* (*Couture*) unstitched; (*fig*) *style* disjointed, rambling, desultory; (*fig*) *idées* disconnected, unconnected; *dissertation, travail* scrappy, disjointed; *paroles, conversation* disjointed, desultory. **couture ~e** seam that has come unstitched *ou* unsewn; **ourlet ~** hem that has come down *ou* come unstitched *ou* come unsewn.

2 *nm [style]* disjointedness, desultoriness; *[idées, raisonnement]* disconnectedness.

découvert, e [dekuvɛʀ, ɛʀt(ə)] (*ptp de* **découvrir**) **1** *adj* **(a)** (*mis à nu*) *corps, tête* bare, uncovered; *V* **visage.**

(b) (*sans protection*) *lieu* open, exposed. **en terrain ~** in open country *ou* terrain; **allée ~e** open avenue.

(c) (*loc*) **à ~: être à ~ dans un champ** to be exposed *ou* without cover in a field; **la plage laissée à ~ par la marée** the beach left exposed by the tide; (*fig*) **parler à ~** to speak frankly *ou* openly; **agir à ~** to act openly; **mettre qch à ~** to expose sth, bring sth into the open.

2 *nm* (*Fin*) *[firme, compte]* overdraft; *[caisse]* deficit; *[objet assuré]* uncovered amount *ou* sum. **~ du Trésor** Treasury deficit; **tirer de l'argent à ~** to overdraw one's account; **crédit à ~** unsecured credit; **vendre à ~** to sell short; **vente à ~** short sale.

3 découverte *nf* discovery. **aller** *ou* **partir à la ~e** to go off in a spirit of discovery; **aller à la ~e de** to go in search of.

découvreur, -euse [dekuvʀœʀ, øz] *nm,f* discoverer.

découvrir [dekuvʀiʀ] (18) **1** *vt* **(a)** (*trouver*) *trésor, loi scientifique, terre inconnue* to discover; *indices, complot* to discover, unearth; *cause, vérité* to discover, find out, unearth; *personne cachée* to discover, find. **~ que** to discover *ou* find out that; **il veut ~ comment/pourquoi c'est arrivé** he wants to find out *ou* discover how/why it happened; **je lui ai découvert des qualités insoupçonnées** I have discovered some unsuspected qualities in him; **elle s'est découvert un cousin en Amérique/un talent pour la peinture** she found out *ou* discovered she had a cousin in America/a gift for painting; **c'est dans les épreuves qu'on se découvre** one finds out about oneself *ou* one finds *ou* discovers one's true self in testing situations; **il craint d'être découvert** (*percé à jour*) he is afraid of being found out; (*trouvé*) he is afraid of being found *ou* discovered; **~ le pot aux roses*** to get to the bottom of it, find out about the fiddle*.

(b) (*enlever ce qui couvre, protège*) *plat, casserole* to take the lid *ou* cover off; *voiture* to open the roof of; *statue* to unveil; (*Échecs*) *roi* to uncover; (*Mil*) *frontière* to expose, uncover; *corps* to uncover; *membres, poitrine, épaules, tête* to bare, uncover; (*mettre à jour*) *ruines* to uncover. **elle enleva les housses et découvrit les meubles** she removed the dust sheets and uncovered the furniture; **il découvrit son torse/avant-bras** he bared *ou* uncovered his torso/forearm; **j'ai dû rester découvert toute la nuit** I must have been uncovered all night; **il resta découvert devant elle** he kept his hat off in her presence; (*Mil*) **ils découvrirent leur aile gauche** they exposed their left wing, they left their left wing open to attack.

(c) (*laisser voir*) to reveal. **une robe qui découvre le dos** a dress which reveals the back; **son sourire découvre des dents superbes** when he smiles he shows his beautiful teeth.

(d) (*voir*) to see, have a view of; (*Naut*) *terre* to sight. **du haut de la falaise on découvre toute la baie** from the top of the cliff you have a view of the whole bay.

(e) (*révéler, dévoiler*) to reveal, disclose. **~ ses projets/intentions/motifs** to reveal *ou* disclose one's plans/intentions/motives (*à qn* to sb); **se ~ à qn** to lay bare *ou* open one's heart to sb, confide in sb; **~ son cœur** to lay bare *ou* open one's heart; (*lit, fig*) **~ son jeu** to show one's hand.

2 se découvrir *vpr* **(a)** *[personne]* (*chapeau*) to take off one's hat; (*habits*) to undress, take off one's clothes; (*couvertures*) to throw off the bedclothes, uncover o.s. **en altitude on**

doit se ~ le moins possible at high altitudes you must keep covered up as much as possible; *V* **avril.**
(b) *(Boxe, Escrime)* to leave o.s. open; *(Mil)* to expose o.s., leave o.s. open to attack.
(c) *[ciel, temps]* to clear. **ça va se ~** it will soon clear.

décrassage [dekʀasaʒ] *nm,* **décrassement** [dekʀasmɑ̃] *nm* (*V* **décrasser**) cleaning; cleaning-out; cleaning-up. (*: *toilette*) **un bon ~** a good scrubbing-down *ou* clean-up.

décrasser [dekʀase] (1) *vt* **(a)** *objet boueux, graisseux* to clean, get the mud (*ou* grease *etc*) off; *linge* to soak the dirt out of; *chaudière* to clean out, clean; *(Aut) bougie* to clean (up). **se ~** to give o.s. a good scrubbing(-down) *ou* clean-up, get the muck off (o.s.) *(Brit)*; **se ~ le visage/les mains** to give one's face/hands a scrub, clean up one's face/hands; **le bon air, ça décrasse les poumons** fresh air cleans out the lungs; **rouler à 150 à l'heure, ça décrasse le moteur** driving at 100 mph gives the engine a good decoking *(Brit) ou* decarbonization *(US)*.
(b) *(fig: dégrossir) rustre* to take the rough edges off.

décrépir [dekʀepiʀ] (2) **1** *vt mur* to remove the roughcast from. **façade décrépie** peeling façade. **2 se décrépir** *vpr [mur]* to peel.

décrépit, e [dekʀepi, it] *adj personne* decrepit; *maison* dilapidated, decrepit.

décrépitude [dekʀepityd] *nf [personne]* decrepitude; *[nation, civilisation]* decay. **tomber en ~** *[personne]* to become decrepit; *[nation]* to decay.

decrescendo [dekʀeʃɛndo] **1** *adv (Mus)* decrescendo. *(fig)* **sa réputation va ~** his reputation is declining *ou* waning. **2** *nm (Mus)* decrescendo.

décret [dekʀɛ] *nm (Pol, Rel)* decree. *(Pol)* **~-loi** statutory order, ≃ Order in Council; *(fig littér)* **les ~s de la Providence** the decrees of Providence; *(fig)* **les ~s de la mode** the dictates of fashion.

décréter [dekʀete] (6) *vt (Pol) mobilisation* to order; *état d'urgence* to declare; *mesure* to decree. **le président a décrété la nomination d'un nouveau ministre** the president ordered the appointment of a new minister; **~ que** *(Pol), [patron, chef]* to decree *ou* order that; *(Rel)* to ordain *ou* decree that; **il a décrété qu'il ne mangerait plus de betteraves*** he announced that he wouldn't eat beetroot any more.

décrier [dekʀije] (7) *vt œuvre, mesure, principe* to decry *(littér)*, disparage, discredit. **la chasteté, une vertu si décriée de nos jours** chastity, a much disparaged *ou* discredited virtue nowadays; **ces auteurs maintenant si décriés par la critique** these authors now so disparaged by the critics; *(littér)* **il décria fort ma conduite** he (strongly) censured my behaviour.

décrire [dekʀiʀ] (39) *vt* **(a)** *(dépeindre)* to describe.
(b) *(parcourir) trajectoire* to follow. **l'oiseau/l'avion décrivait des cercles au-dessus de nos têtes** the bird/plane flew in circles overhead; **la route décrit une courbe prolongée** the road makes *ou* follows a wide curve; **le satellite décrit une ellipse** the satellite follows *ou* makes *ou* describes an elliptical orbit; **le bras de la machine décrivit une ellipse** the arm of the machine described an ellipse.

décrochage [dekʀɔʃaʒ] *nm* **(a)** *[rideaux, tableaux]* taking down; unhooking; *[wagon]* uncoupling. **(b)** (*: *abandon: V* **décrocher**) falling back; failure to make the grade *ou* to keep up; dropping out, opting out.

décroché [dekʀɔʃe] *nm (Constr)* recess. **dans le mur il y a un ~** the wall is recessed.

décrochement [dekʀɔʃmɑ̃] *nm* **(a)** *[wagon]* uncoupling. **(b)** *(Géol)* thrust fault, slide. **(c) = décroché.**

décrocher [dekʀɔʃe] (1) **1** *vt* **(a)** *(détacher) tableau* to take down; *rideau* to take down, unhook; *vêtement* to take down, take off the hook *ou* peg; *fermoir* to undo, unclasp; *poisson* to unhook; *wagon* to uncouple; *téléphone (pour répondre)* to pick up, lift; *(pour l'empêcher de sonner)* to take off the hook. **il n'a pas pu ~ son cerf-volant qui s'était pris dans l'arbre** he couldn't free *ou* unhook his kite which had got caught in the tree; **le téléphone est décroché** the telephone is off the hook; *V* **bâiller.**
(b) (*: *obtenir) prix, contrat, poste, récompense* to get, land*. **il a décroché une belle situation** he's landed (himself) a fine job*.
2 *vi* **(a)** *(Téléc)* to pick up *ou* lift the receiver.
(b) *(Mil)* to pull back, break off the action.
(c) (*: *abandonner*) *(on ne peut pas suivre)* to fall by the wayside *(fig)*, fail to keep up; *(on se désintéresse)* to drop out, opt out; *(on cesse d'écouter)* to switch off*.
3 se décrocher *vpr [tableau, vêtement]* to fall down *ou* off; *[rideau]* to fall down, come unhooked; *[fermoir]* to come undone; *[poisson]* to get unhooked; *[wagon]* to come uncoupled. **le cerf-volant pris dans l'arbre s'est finalement décroché** the kite which had been caught in the tree finally came free.

décroiser [dekʀwaze] (1) *vt jambes* to uncross; *bras* to unfold; *fils* to untwine, untwist.

décroissance [dekʀwasɑ̃s] *nf (gén: diminution)* decrease, decline *(de* in); *[popularité, natalité]* decline, drop, fall *(de* in); *[population]* decline, decrease, fall *(de* in).

décroissant, e [dekʀwasɑ̃, ɑ̃t] *adj intensité* decreasing; *vitesse* decreasing, falling; *(Math)* descending. **par ordre ~** in decreasing *ou* descending order.

décroissement [dekʀwasmɑ̃] *nm [jours]* shortening; *[lune]* waning.

décroît [dekʀwa] *nm [lune]* **dans** *ou* **sur son ~** in its last quarter.

décroître [dekʀwatʀ(ə)] (55) *vi [nombre, population]* to decrease, diminish, decline; *[intensité]* to decrease, diminish; *[eaux, crue]* to subside, go down; *[importance, pouvoir]* to decline; *[popularité]* to decline, drop; *[vitesse]* to drop, fall off; *[fièvre]* to go down, subside; *[force]* to decline, diminish, fail; *[revenus]* to get less, diminish; *[lune]* to wane; *[jour]* to get shorter; *[silhouette]* to get smaller and smaller; *[bruit]* to die away, fade; *[lumière]* to fade, grow fainter *ou* dimmer. **ses forces vont (en) décroissant** his strength is failing *ou* gradually diminishing *ou* declining; **cette ville a beaucoup décru en importance** this town has greatly declined in importance.

décrotter [dekʀɔte] (1) *vt chaussures* to get the mud off; *(fig) rustre* to take the rough edges off.

décrottoir [dekʀɔtwaʀ] *nm (lame)* mud-scraper, shoescraper; *(paillasson)* wire (door)mat.

décrue [dekʀy] *nf [eaux, rivière]* fall *ou* drop in level *(de* of); *(fig) [popularité]* decline, drop *(de* in); *[importance, pouvoir]* decline *(de* in). **la ~ des eaux atteint 2 mètres** the water level *ou* flood-level has fallen *ou* dropped by 2 metres.

décryptage [dekʀiptaʒ] *nm* deciphering.

décrypter [dekʀipte] (1) *vt (décoder)* to decipher.

déçu, e [desy] *(ptp de* **décevoir**) *adj* disappointed.

déculottée‡ [dekylɔte] *nf (défaite)* clobbering‡.

déculotter [dekylɔte] (1) **1** *vt*: **~ qn** to take off *ou* down sb's trousers. **2 se déculotter** *vpr (lit)* to take off *ou* down one's trousers; *(‡fig) (céder)* to grovel, lose face; *(reculer)* to funk it‡, lose one's nerve.

décuple [dekypl(ə)] **1** *adj (rare)* tenfold. **un revenu ~ du mien** an income ten times as large as mine.
2 *nm*: **vingt est le ~ de deux** twenty is ten times two; **il gagne le ~ de ce que je gagne** he earns ten times what I earn; **il me l'a rendu au ~** he paid me back tenfold.

décuplement [dekypləmɑ̃] *nm (lit)* tenfold increase. *(fig)* **grâce au ~ de nos forces** thanks to our greatly increased strength.

décupler [dekyple] (1) *vti* to increase tenfold. *(fig)* **la colère décuplait ses forces** anger gave him the strength of ten.

dédaignable [dedɛɲabl(ə)] *adj*: **pas ~** not to be despised.

dédaigner [dedeɲe] (1) *vt* **(a)** *(mépriser) personne* to despise, look down on, scorn; *honneurs, richesse* to scorn, despise, disdain. **il ne dédaigne pas de rire avec ses subordonnés** he doesn't consider it beneath him to joke with his subordinates; **il ne dédaigne pas un verre de vin de temps à autre** he's not averse to the occasional glass of wine.
(b) *(négliger) offre, adversaire* to spurn, think nothing of; *menaces, insultes* to disregard, discount. **ce n'est pas à ~** *(honneur, offre)* it's not to be sniffed at *ou* despised; *(danger, adversaire)* it can't just be shrugged off; *(littér)* **il dédaigna de répondre/d'y aller** he did not deign to reply/go.

dédaigneusement [dedɛɲøzmɑ̃] *adv* disdainfully, scornfully, contemptuously.

dédaigneux, -euse [dedɛɲø, øz] *adj personne, air* scornful, disdainful, contemptuous. **~ de** contemptuous *ou* scornful *ou* disdainful of; *(littér)* **il est ~ de plaire** he scorns to please.

dédain [dedɛ̃] *nm* contempt, scorn, disdain *(de* for). **sourire de ~** disdainful *ou* scornful smile.

dédale [dedal] *nm [rues, idées]* maze.

dedans [d(ə)dɑ̃] **1** *adv* **(a)** *(à l'intérieur)* inside; *(pas à l'air libre)* indoors, inside. **voulez-vous dîner dehors ou ~?** do you want to have dinner outside or inside? *ou* outdoors or indoors?; **la maison est laide, mais ~** *ou* **au-~ c'est très joli** it's an ugly-looking house but it's lovely inside; **nous sommes restés ~ toute la journée** we stayed in *ou* inside *ou* indoors all day; **elle cherche son sac, tout son argent est ~** she is looking for her bag — all her money is in it; **prenez ce fauteuil, on est bien ~** have this chair, you'll be comfortable in it *ou* you'll find it comfortable; **de** *ou* **du ~ on n'entend rien** you can't hear a sound from inside; **rentrons ~** *ou* **au -~, il fera plus chaud** let's go in *ou* inside *ou* indoors, it will be warmer; **passez par ~ pour aller au jardin** go through the house to get to the garden; *V* **là, pied.**
(b) *(loc)* **marcher les pieds en ~** to walk with one's toes *ou* feet turned in, walk pigeon-toed; **il n'en pense pas moins en** *ou* **au ~ (de lui)** he still has private reservations about it; **au ~** inside; **la situation au ~ (du pays)** the situation in the interior (of the country); **un bus lui est rentré ~*** a bus hit him *ou* ran into him; **il a dérapé, il y avait un arbre, il est rentré** *ou* **entré ~*** he skidded, there was a tree and he ran *ou* went *ou* crashed straight into it; **il s'est mis en colère et lui est rentré ~*** he got angry and laid into him‡ *ou* gave him what for‡; **il s'est fichu*** *ou* **foutu‡ ~** he got it all wrong*; **mettre*** *ou* **ficher*** *ou* **foutre‡ qn ~** to get sb confused, make sb get it wrong*; **il s'est fait mettre ~‡** he got himself put away‡ *ou* put inside‡.
2 *nm [objet, bâtiment etc]* inside. **le coup a été préparé du ~** it's an inside job; **c'est quelqu'un du ~ qui a fait cela** it's somebody from inside *ou* it's an insider who did it.

dédicace [dedikas] *nf* **(a)** *(imprimée)* dedication; *(manuscrite) [livre, photo]* dedication, inscription. **(b)** *[église]* consecration, dedication.

dédicacer [dedikase] (3) *vt livre, photo* to sign, autograph *(à qn* for sb), inscribe *(à qn* to sb).

dédicatoire [dedikatwaʀ] *adj* dedicatory, dedicative.

dédier [dedje] (7) *vt*: **~ à** *(Rel)* to consecrate to, dedicate to; **~ ses efforts à** to devote *ou* dedicate one's efforts to; **~ un livre à** to dedicate a book to.

dédire (se) [dediʀ] (37) *vpr* **(a)** *(manquer à ses engagements)* to go back on one's word. **se ~ d'une promesse** to go back on a promise. **(b)** *(se rétracter)* to retract, recant. **se ~ d'une affirmation** to withdraw a statement, retract (a statement); *V* **cochon**[1].

dédit [dedi] *nm* **(a)** *(Comm)* forfeit, penalty. **un ~ de 30.000 F** a 30,000-franc penalty. **(b)** *(rétraction)* retraction; *(manquement aux engagements)* failure to keep one's word.

dédommagement [dedɔmaʒmɑ̃] *nm* compensation. **en ~, je lui ai donné une bouteille de vin** in compensation *ou* to make up for it, I gave him a bottle of wine; **en ~ des dégâts** *ou* **à titre de ~ pour les dégâts, on va me donner 50 F** they will give me 50 francs in compensation for the damage; **en ~ du mal que je vous donne** to make up for the trouble I'm causing you.

dédommager [dedɔmaʒe] (3) *vt* (*indemniser*) **~ qn** to compensate sb (*de* for), give sb compensation (*de* for); **je l'ai dédommagé en lui donnant une bouteille de vin** I gave him a bottle of wine in compensation *ou* to make up for it; **~ qn d'une perte** to compensate sb for a loss, make good sb's loss; **comment vous ~ du dérangement que je vous cause?** how can I ever repay you *ou* make up for the trouble I'm causing?; **le succès le dédommage de toutes ses peines** his success is compensation *ou* compensates for all his troubles.

dédorer [dedɔʀe] (1) *vt* to remove the gilt from. **bijou dédoré** piece of jewellery that has lost its gilt.

dédouanement [dedwanmɑ̃] *nm* (*Comm*) clearing *ou* clearance through customs, customs clearance.

dédouaner [dedwane] (1) *vt* (*Comm*) to clear through customs; (**fig*) *personne* to clear (the name of), put in the clear*.

dédoublement [dedubləmɑ̃] *nm [classe]* dividing *ou* splitting in two. **le ~ d'un train** the running *ou* putting-on of a relief train; (*Psych*) **~ de la personnalité** split *ou* dual personality.

dédoubler [deduble] (1) **1** *vt* **(a)** *manteau* to remove the lining of.

(b) *classe* to split *ou* divide in two; *ficelle* to separate the strands of. **~ un train** to run *ou* put on a relief train; **pour Noël on a dû ~ tous les trains** at Christmas they had to run additional trains on all services.

(c) *couverture* to unfold, open out.

2 se dédoubler *vpr* (*se déplier*) to unfold, open out. (*Psych*) **sa personnalité se dédoublait** he suffered from a split *ou* dual personality; **je ne peux pas me ~*** I can't be in two places at once; **l'image se dédoublait dans l'eau** there was a double outline reflected in the water.

déductible [dedyktibl(ə)] *adj* (*Fin*) *frais, somme* deductible. **dépenses non ~s** non-deductible expenses.

déductif, -ive [dedyktif, iv] *adj* deductive.

déduction [dedyksjɔ̃] *nf* **(a)** (*Comm*) deduction. **~ faite de** after deducting, after deduction of; **ça entre en ~ de ce que vous nous devez** that's deductible from what you owe us, that'll be taken off what you owe us.

(b) (*forme de raisonnement*) deduction, inference; (*conclusion*) conclusion, inference.

déduire [dedɥiʀ] (38) *vt* (*Comm*) to deduct (*de* from); (*conclure*) to deduce, infer (*de* from). **tous frais déduits** after deduction of expenses.

déesse [deɛs] *nf* goddess.

de facto [defakto] *loc adv* de facto.

défaillance [defajɑ̃s] **1** *nf* **(a)** (*évanouissement*) blackout; (*faiblesse physique*) feeling of weakness *ou* faintness; (*faiblesse morale*) weakness, failing. **avoir une ~** (*évanouissement*) to faint, have a blackout; (*faiblesse*) to feel faint *ou* weak; **faire son devoir sans ~** to do one's duty without flinching.

(b) (*mauvais fonctionnement*) (mechanical) fault, (temporary) failure *ou* breakdown (*de* in). **l'accident était dû à une ~ de la machine** the accident was caused by a fault in the machine.

(c) (*insuffisance*) weakness. **élève qui a des ~s (en histoire et en maths)** pupil who has certain shortcomings *ou* weak points (in history and maths); **devant la ~ du gouvernement** faced with the weakness of the government *ou* the government's failure to act; **mémoire sans ~** faultless memory.

2: défaillance cardiaque heart failure; **défaillance mécanique** mechanical fault; **défaillance de mémoire** lapse of memory.

défaillant, e [defajɑ̃, ɑ̃t] *adj* **(a)** (*affaibli*) *forces* failing, declining; *santé, mémoire, raison* failing; *courage, volonté* faltering, weakening; *cœur* weak.

(b) (*tremblant*) *voix, pas* unsteady, faltering; *main* unsteady.

(c) (*près de s'évanouir*) *personne* weak, faint (*de* with).

(d) (*Jur*) *partie, témoin* defaulting. **candidat ~** candidate who fails to appear.

défaillir [defajiʀ] (13) *vi* **(a)** (*s'évanouir*) to faint. **elle défaillait de bonheur/de faim** she felt faint with happiness/hunger.

(b) *[forces]* to weaken, fail; *[courage, volonté]* to falter, weaken; *[mémoire]* to fail. **faire son devoir sans ~** to do one's duty without flinching.

défaire [defɛʀ] (60) **1** *vt* **(a)** *échafaudage etc* to take down, dismantle; *installation électrique etc* to dismantle.

(b) *couture, tricot* to undo, unpick; *écheveau* to undo, unravel, unwind; *corde, nœud, ruban* to undo, untie; *courroie, fermeture, robe* to undo, unfasten; *valise, bagages* to unpack; *cheveux, nattes* to undo. **~ ses bagages** to unpack (one's luggage).

(c) ~ le lit (*pour changer les draps*) to strip the bed; (*pour se coucher*) to untuck the bed *ou* sheets, pull back the sheets; (*mettre en désordre*) to unmake *ou* rumple the bed.

(d) *mariage* to break up; *contrat, traité* to break. **cela défit tous nos plans** it ruined all our plans; **il (faisait et) défaisait les rois** he (made and) unmade kings; **elle se plaît à ~ tout ce que j'essaie de faire pour elle** she takes pleasure in undoing everything I try to do for her.

(e) (*miner*) **la maladie l'avait défait** his illness had left him shattered; **la douleur défaisait ses traits** pain distorted his features.

(f) (*littér*) *ennemi, armée* to defeat.

(g) (*littér*) **~ qn de** *liens, gêneur* to rid sb of, relieve sb of, deliver sb from (*littér*); *habitude* to break sb of, cure sb of, rid sb of; *défaut* to cure sb of, rid sb of.

2 se défaire *vpr* **(a)** *[nœud, ficelle, coiffure]* to come undone; *[couture]* to come undone *ou* apart; *[légumes, viande]* (*à la cuisson*) to fall to pieces, disintegrate; *[mariage, amitié]* to break up.

(b) (*se déformer*) **ses traits se défirent, son visage se défit** his face crumpled, his face twisted with grief *ou* pain *etc.*

(c) se ~ de (*se débarrasser de*) *gêneur, vieillerie, odeur* to get rid of; *image, idée* to put *ou* get out of one's mind; *habitude* to break *ou* cure o.s. of, get rid of; *défaut* to cure o.s. of; (*se séparer de*) *souvenir, collaborateur* to part with.

défait, e[1] [defɛ, ɛt] (*ptp de* **défaire**) *adj* **(a)** *visage* ravaged, haggard; *cheveux* tousled, ruffled, dishevelled. **(b)** *lit* unmade, rumpled, disarranged. **(c)** *armée* defeated.

défaite[2] [defɛt] *nf* (*Mil*) defeat; (*fig*) defeat, failure. **~ électorale** defeat at the polls.

défaitisme [defetism(ə)] *nm* defeatism.

défaitiste [defetist(ə)] *adj, nmf* defeatist.

défalcation [defalkɑsjɔ̃] *nf* deduction. **~ faite des frais** after deduction of expenses.

défalquer [defalke] (1) *vt* to deduct.

défausser (se) [defose] (1) *vpr* (*Cartes*) to discard, throw out *ou* away. **se ~ (d'une carte)** to discard; **il s'est défaussé à trèfle** he discarded a club.

défaut [defo] **1** *nm* **(a)** *[pierre précieuse, métal]* flaw; *[étoffe, verre]* flaw, fault; *[machine]* defect, fault; *[bois]* blemish; *[roman, tableau, système]* flaw, defect. **sans ~** flawless, faultless.

(b) *[personne]* fault, failing; *[caractère]* defect, fault, failing (*de* in). **chacun a ses petits ~s** we've all got our little faults *ou* our shortcomings *ou* failings; **il n'a aucun ~** he's perfect, he hasn't a single failing; **la gourmandise n'est pas un gros ~** greediness isn't such a bad fault, it isn't a (great) sin to be greedy; *V* **curiosité.**

(c) (*désavantage*) drawback. **ce plan/cette voiture a ses ~s** this plan/car has its drawbacks; **le ~ de** *ou* **avec* cette voiture, c'est que ...** the trouble *ou* snag *ou* drawback with this car is that ... .

(d) (*manque*) **~ de** *raisonnement* lack of; *main-d'œuvre* shortage of.

(e) (*loc*) **faire ~** *[temps, argent]* to be lacking; (*Jur*) *[prévenu, témoin]* to default; *[débiteur]* to default (*à* on); **la patience/le temps lui fait ~** he lacks patience/time; **le courage lui a finalement fait ~** his courage failed him in the end; **ses amis lui ont finalement fait ~** his friends let him down in the end; **à ~ de** for lack *ou* want of; **à ~ de vin, il boira du cidre** if there's no wine *ou* for want of wine, he'll drink cider; **elle cherche une table ovale, ou, à ~, ronde** she is looking for an oval table, or, failing that, a round one (will do); **être en ~** to be at fault *ou* in the wrong; **se mettre en ~** to put o.s. in the wrong; **prendre qn en ~** to catch sb out; **c'est votre mémoire qui est en ~** it's your memory that's at fault; (*Jur*) **condamner/juger qn par ~** to sentence/judge sb in his absence; (*Math*) **calculer qch par ~** to calculate sth to the nearest decimal point; **il pèche par ~** he doesn't try hard enough.

2: (*Jur*) **défaut-congé** *nm, pl* **defaut-congés** *dismissal of case through non-appearance of plaintiff;* (*lit, fig*) **le défaut de la cuirasse** the chink in the armour; **le défaut de l'épaule** the hollow beneath the shoulder; **défaut de fabrication** manufacturing defect; (*Phys*) **défaut de masse** mass defect; (*Jur*) **défaut de paiement** default in payment, non-payment; **défaut de prononciation** speech impediment *ou* defect.

défaveur [defavœʀ] *nf* disfavour (*auprès de* with). **être en ~** to be out of favour, be in disfavour; **s'attirer la ~ de** to incur the disfavour of.

défavorable [defavɔʀabl(ə)] *adj* unfavourable (*à* to). **voir qch d'un œil ~** to view sth with disfavour.

défavorablement [defavɔʀabləmɑ̃] *adv* unfavourably.

défavoriser [defavɔʀize] (1) *vt* (*désavantager*) *[décision, loi]* to penalize; *[défaut, timidité]* to put at a disadvantage; *[examinateur, patron]* to put at an unfair disadvantage. **il a défavorisé l'aîné** he treated the eldest less fairly (than the others); **j'ai été défavorisé par rapport aux autres candidats** I was put at an unfair disadvantage with respect to *ou* compared with the other candidates; **aider les couches les plus défavorisées de la population** to help the most underprivileged *ou* disadvantaged sections of the population.

défécation [defekɑsjɔ̃] *nf* (*Physiol*) defecation; (*Chim*) defecation, purification.

défectif, -ive [defɛktif, iv] *adj verbe* defective.

défection [defɛksjɔ̃] *nf [amis]* desertion, failure to give support; *[alliés politiques]* defection, failure to support; *[troupes]* failure to give *ou* lend assistance *ou* to assist; *[candidats]* failure to attend *ou* appear; *[invités]* failure to appear. **faire ~** *[partisans]* to fail to lend support; *[invités]* to fail to appear *ou* turn up; **il y a eu plusieurs ~s** (*membres d'un parti*) a number of people have withdrawn their support, there has been a sharp drop in support; (*invités, candidats*) several people failed to appear, there were several non-appearances.

défectueux, -euse [defɛktɥø, øz] *adj* faulty, defective.

défectuosité [defɛktɥozite] *nf* (*état*) defectiveness, faultiness; (*défaut*) imperfection, (slight) defect *ou* fault (*de* in).

défendable [defɑ̃dabl(ə)] *adj* (*Mil*) *ville* defensible; (*soutenable*) *conduite* defensible, justifiable; *position* tenable, defensible.

défendant [defɑ̃dɑ̃] *V* **corps.**

défendeur, -deresse [defɑ̃dœʀ, dʀɛs] *nm,f* (*Jur*) defendant. **~ en appel** respondent.

défendre [defɑ̃dʀ(ə)] (41) **1** *vt* **(a)** (*protéger: gén, Jur, Mil*) to defend; (*soutenir*) *personne, opinion* to stand up for, defend (*contre* against); *cause* to champion, defend (*contre* against). **ville défendue par 2 forts** town defended *ou* protected by 2 forts; **manteau qui (vous) défend du froid** coat that protects you from *ou* against the cold; *V* **corps**.

(b) (*interdire*) ~ **qch à qn** to forbid sb sth; ~ **à qn de faire** *ou* **qu'il fasse** to forbid sb to do; **le médecin lui défend le tabac/la mer** the doctor has forbidden him *ou* won't allow him to smoke/to go to the seaside; ~ **sa porte à qn** to bar one's door to sb, refuse to allow sb in; **ne fais pas ça, c'est défendu** don't do that, it's not allowed *ou* it's forbidden; **il est défendu de fumer** smoking is prohibited *ou* not allowed; **il est défendu de parler** speaking is not allowed; *V* **fruit**[1].

2 se défendre *vpr* **(a)** (*se protéger: gén, Jur, Mil*) to defend o.s. (*contre* against); (*contre brimades, critiques*) to stand up for o.s., defend o.s. (*contre* against). **se ~ du froid/de la pluie** to protect o.s. from the cold/rain; (*fig*) **il se défend bien/mal en affaires** he gets on *ou* does quite well/he doesn't do very well in business; (*fig*) **il se défend** he gets along *ou* by, he can hold his own (quite well).

(b) (*se justifier*) **se ~ d'avoir fait qch** to deny doing *ou* having done sth; **il se défendit d'être vexé/jaloux** he denied being *ou* that he was annoyed/jealous; **sa position/son point de vue se défend** his position/point of view is quite defensible; **ça se défend!*** it holds *ou* hangs together (nicely).

(c) (*s'empêcher de*) **se ~ de** to refrain from; **il ne pouvait se ~ d'un sentiment de pitié/gêne** he couldn't help feeling pity/embarrassment; **elle ne put se ~ de sourire** she could not refrain from smiling, she couldn't suppress a smile.

défenestration [defənɛstʀɑsjɔ̃] *nf* defenestration.

défenestrer [defənɛstʀe] (1) *vt* to defenestrate.

défense[1] [defɑ̃s] *nf* **(a)** (*protection: gén, Mil*) defence. (*fortifications etc*) ~**s** defences; ~ **nationale/anti-aérienne** *ou* **contre avions/passive** national/anti-aircraft/civil defence; **les ~s d'une frontière** border defences; **la ~ du pays** the country's defence *ou* protection; **la ~ des opprimés est notre cause** our cause is the defence *ou* protection of the oppressed; **ligne de ~** line of defence; **ouvrage de ~** fortification; **aller à la ~ de qn** to go *ou* rally to sb's defence; **prendre la ~ de qn** to stand up for sb, defend sb.

(b) (*résistance*) defence. **opposer une ~ courageuse** to put up a courageous defence; (*Physiol, Psych*) **mécanisme/instinct de ~** defence mechanism/instinct; **moyens de ~** means of defence; **sans ~** (*trop faible*) defenceless; (*non protégé*) unprotected; **sans ~ contre les tentations** helpless *ou* defenceless against temptation; *V* **légitime**.

(c) (*Jur*) defence; (*avocat*) counsel for the defence. **assurer la ~ d'un accusé** to conduct the case for the defence; **la parole est à la ~** (the counsel for) the defence may now speak; **qu'avez vous à dire pour votre ~?** what have you to say in your defence?

(d) (*interdiction*) ~ **d'entrer** no entrance, no entry, no admittance; **propriété privée, ~ d'entrer** private property, no admittance *ou* keep out; **danger: ~ d'entrer** danger — keep out; ~ **de fumer/stationner** no smoking/parking, smoking/parking prohibited; ~ **d'afficher** (stick) no bills; **j'ai oublié la ~ qu'il m'a faite de faire cela**† I forgot that he forbade me to do that.

défense[2] [defɑ̃s] *nf [éléphant, morse, sanglier]* tusk.

défenseur [defɑ̃sœʀ] *nm* (*gén, Mil*) defender; *[cause]* champion, defender; *[doctrine]* advocate; (*Jur*) counsel for the defence. **l'accusé et son ~** the accused and his counsel.

défensif, -ive [defɑ̃sif, iv] **1** *adj* (*Mil, fig*) defensive. **2 défensive** *nf*: **la ~ive** the defensive; **être** *ou* **se tenir sur la ~ive** to be on the defensive.

déféquer [defeke] (6) **1** *vt* (*Chim*) to defecate, purify. **2** *vi* (*Physiol*) to defecate.

déférence [defeʀɑ̃s] *nf* deference. **par ~ pour** in deference to.

déférent, e [defeʀɑ̃, ɑ̃t] *adj* deferential, deferent; *V* **canal**.

déférer [defeʀe] (6) *vt* **(a)** (*Jur*) *affaire* to refer to the court. ~ **un coupable à la justice** to hand a guilty person over to the law. **(b)** (*céder*) to defer (*à* to). **(c)** (†: *conférer*) to confer (*à* on, upon).

déferlement [defɛʀləmɑ̃] *nm [vagues]* breaking; *[violence]* surge, spread; *[véhicules, touristes]* flood. **ils étaient impuissants devant le ~ des troupes** they were powerless before the advancing tide of the troops; **ce ~ d'enthousiasme le prit par surprise** this sudden wave of enthusiasm took him by surprise; **le ~ de haine/des sentiments anti-catholiques dans tout le pays** the hatred/anti-Catholic feeling which has engulfed the country *ou* swept through the country.

déferler [defɛʀle] (1) **1** *vi [vagues]* to break. (*fig*) **la violence/haine déferla sur le pays** violence/hatred swept *ou* surged through the country; (*fig*) **les voitures déferlaient sur les plages** cars were streaming towards the beaches; (*fig*) **la foule déferla dans la rue/sur la place** the crowd surged into the street/over the square.

2 *vt voile, pavillon* to unfurl.

défi [defi] *nm* (*frm*) challenge; (*fig: bravade*) defiance. **lancer un ~ à qn** to challenge sb; **relever un ~** to take up *ou* accept a challenge; **mettre qn au ~** to defy sb (*de faire* to do); **c'est un ~ au bon sens** it defies good sense, it goes against common sense; **d'un air/ton de ~** defiantly.

défiance [defjɑ̃s] *nf* mistrust, distrust. **avec ~** with mistrust *ou* distrust, distrustingly, mistrustingly; **sans ~** (*adj*) unsuspecting; (*adv*) unsuspectingly; **mettre qn en ~** to arouse sb's mistrust, make sb slightly suspicious.

défiant, e [defjɑ̃, ɑ̃t] *adj* mistrustful, distrustful.

déficeler [defisle] (4) **1** *vt* to untie. **2 se déficeler** *vpr [paquet]* to come untied *ou* undone.

déficience [defisjɑ̃s] *nf* (*Méd, fig*) deficiency. ~ **musculaire** muscular insufficiency; ~ **de mémoire** lapse of memory; ~ **mentale** mental deficiency.

déficient, e [defisjɑ̃, ɑ̃t] *adj* (*Méd*) *force, intelligence* deficient; (*fig*) *raisonnement* weak. **enfant ~** (*intellectuellement*) mentally deficient child; (*physiquement*) child with a physical disability, physically disabled *ou* handicapped child.

déficit [defisit] *nm* (*Fin*) deficit. **être en ~** to be in deficit; (*Pysch*) defect; **le ~ budgétaire** the budget deficit.

déficitaire [defisitɛʀ] *adj* (*Fin*) in deficit (*attrib*); *récolte* poor; *année* poor (*en* in), bad (*en* for).

défier [defje] (7) **1** *vt* **(a)** *adversaire* to challenge (*à* to). ~ **qn en combat singulier** to challenge sb to single combat.

(b) *mort, adversité* to defy, brave; *opinion publique* to fly in the face of, defy; *autorité* to defy, challenge. **à des prix qui défient toute concurrence** at absolutely unbeatable prices.

(c) ~ **qn de faire qch** to defy *ou* challenge sb to do sth; **je t'en défie!** I dare *ou* challenge you (to)!

2 se défier *vpr*: **se ~ de** to distrust, mistrust; **je me défie de moi-même** I don't trust myself; **défie-toi de ton caractère impulsif** be on your guard against *ou* beware of your impulsiveness; (††) **défie-toi de lui!** beware of him!, be on your guard against him!

défiguration [defigyʀɑsjɔ̃] *nf [vérité]* distortion; *[texte, tableau]* mutilation; *[visage]* disfigurement.

défigurer [defigyʀe] (1) *vt* **(a)** *[blessure, maladie]* to disfigure; *[bouton, larmes] visage* to spoil. **l'acné qui la défigurait** the acne which marred *ou* spoiled her looks.

(b) (*altérer*) *pensée, réalité, vérité* to distort; *texte, tableau* to mutilate, deface; *monument* to deface; *paysage* to disfigure, mar, spoil.

défilé [defile] *nm* **(a)** (*cortège*) procession; (*manifestation*) march; (*Mil*) march-past, parade. ~ **de mode** *ou* **de mannequins** fashion parade.

(b) (*succession*) *[visiteurs]* procession, stream; *[voitures]* stream; *[impressions, pensées]* stream, succession.

(c) (*Géog*) (narrow) gorge, narrow pass, defile.

défiler [defile] (1) **1** *vt* **(a)** *aiguille, perles* to unthread; *chiffons* to shred.

(b) (*Mil*) *troupes* to put under cover (*from the enemy's fire*).

2 *vi* (*Mil*) to march past, parade; *[manifestants]* to march (*devant* past). **les souvenirs défilaient** a constant stream of memories passed through his mind; **les visiteurs défilaient devant le mausolée** the visitors filed past the mausoleum; **la semaine suivante tous les voisins défilèrent chez nous** the following week we were visited by all the neighbours one after the other; **nous regardions le paysage qui défilait devant nos yeux** we watched the scenery pass by *ou* (*plus vite*) flash by.

3 se défiler *vpr* **(a)** *[aiguille]* to come unthreaded; *[perles]* to come unstrung *ou* unthreaded.

(b) (*Mil*) to take cover (*from the enemy's fire*).

(c) (**fig*) (*s'éclipser*) to slip away *ou* off; (*se dérober*) to sneak off.

défini, e [defini] (*ptp de* **définir**) *adj* **(a)** (*déterminé*) definite, precise. **terme bien ~** well-defined term. **(b)** (*Gram*) *article* definite. **passé ~** preterite.

définir [definiʀ] (2) *vt idée, sentiment, position* to define; (*Géom, Gram*) to define; *personne* to define, characterize; *conditions* to specify, define. **il se définit comme un humaniste** he describes *ou* defines himself as a humanist; **notre politique se définit comme étant avant tout pragmatiste** our policies can be defined *ou* described as being essentially pragmatic.

définissable [definisabl(ə)] *adj* definable.

définitif, -ive [definitif, iv] **1** *adj* **(a)** (*final*) *résultat, destination, résolution* final; *mesure, installation, victoire, fermeture* permanent, definitive; *solution* definitive, final, permanent; *étude, édition* definitive. **son départ était ~** he was leaving for good, his departure was final.

(b) (*sans appel*) *décision* final; *refus* definite, decisive; *argument* conclusive. **un jugement ~** a final judgment.

2 définitive *nf*: **en ~ive** (*à la fin*) eventually; (*somme toute*) when all is said and done.

définition [definisjɔ̃] *nf [concept, mot]* definition; *[mots croisés]* clue; (*TV*) (picture) resolution.

définitivement [definitivmɑ̃] *adv partir* for good; *résoudre* conclusively, definitively; *exclure, s'installer* for good, permanently, definitively; *refuser, décider, savoir* definitely, positively; *nommer* on a permanent basis, permanently.

déflagration [deflagʀɑsjɔ̃] *nf* (*Chim*) deflagration; (*gén*) explosion.

déflagrer [deflagʀe] (1) *vi* to deflagrate.

déflation [deflɑsjɔ̃] *nf* deflation.

déflationniste [deflɑsjɔnist(ə)] **1** *adj politique* deflationist; *mesures etc* deflationary. **2** *nmf* deflationist.

déflecteur [deflɛktœʀ] *nm* (*Aut*) quarter-light (*Brit*); (*Tech*) jet deflector; (*Naut*) deflector.

défleurir [deflœʀiʀ] (2) (*littér*) **1** *vt fleur* to remove the flower of; *buisson* to remove the blossom of. **2** *vi* to shed its flower, shed its blossom.

déflexion [deflɛksjɔ̃] *nf* deflection.

défloraison [deflɔʀɛzɔ̃] *nf* (*Bot, littér*) falling of blossoms.

défloration [deflɔʀɑsjɔ̃] *nf [jeune fille]* defloration.

déflorer [deflɔʀe] (1) *vt jeune fille* to deflower; (*littér*) *sujet, moments* to take the bloom off (*littér*), spoil the charm of.

défoliation [defɔljɑsjɔ̃] *nf* defoliation.

défonçage [defɔ̃saʒ] *nm*, **defoncement** [defɔ̃smɑ̃] *nm* (*V* **défoncer**) staving in; smashing in *ou* down; breaking in; ripping *ou* ploughing *ou* breaking up; deep-ploughing.

défoncer [defɔ̃se] (3) **1** *vt caisse, barque* to stave in, knock *ou* smash the bottom out of; *porte, clôture* to smash in *ou* down, stave in; *sommier, fauteuil* to break *ou* burst the springs of; *route, terrain [bulldozers, camions]* to rip *ou* plough *ou* break up; (*Agr*) to plough deeply, deep-plough. **un vieux fauteuil tout défoncé** an old sunken armchair; **la route défoncée par les pluies** the road broken up by the rains, the road full of potholes *ou* ruts after the rains.

2 se défoncer *vpr* (*arg Drogue*) to get high (*arg*).

déformant, e [defɔʀmɑ̃, ɑ̃t] *adj miroir* distorting.

déformation [defɔʀmɑsjɔ̃] *nf* **(a)** (*V* **déformer**) bending (out of shape); putting out of shape; deformation; distortion; misrepresentation; warping; corruption. **par une curieuse ~ d'esprit, il poussait tout au macabre** by a strange twist in his character, he would take everything to gruesome extremes; **~ professionnelle** job conditioning; **c'est de la ~ professionnelle** he's (*ou* you are *etc*) completely conditioned by his (*ou* your *etc*) job; **par ~ professionnelle** as a result of being so conditioned by one's job.
(b) (*V* **se déformer**) loss of shape.
(c) (*Méd*) deformation.

déformer [defɔʀme] (1) **1** *vt objet, bois, métal* to bend (out of shape); *chaussures, vêtements* to put out of shape; *corps* to deform; *visage, image, vision* to distort; *vérité, pensée* to distort, misrepresent; *esprit, goût* to warp, corrupt. **un vieillard au corps déformé** an old man with a deformed *ou* misshapen body; **veste déformée** jacket which has lost its shape *ou* has gone out of shape; **traits déformés par la douleur** features contorted *ou* distorted by pain; (*fig*) **il est déformé par son métier** he has been conditioned by his job; **chaussée déformée** uneven road surface.
2 se déformer *vpr [objet, bois, métal]* to be bent (out of shape), lose its shape; *[vêtement]* to lose its shape.

défoulement [defulmɑ̃] *nm [instincts, sentiments]* (psychological) release. **moyen de ~** (psychological) outlet *ou* means of release; **après les examens on a besoin de ~** after the exams you need some kind of (psychological) release *ou* you need to let off steam* *ou* to unwind.

défouler (se) [defule] (1) *vpr* to work off one's frustrations *ou* tensions, release one's pent-up feelings, let off steam*, unwind.

défourner [defuʀne] (1) *vt pain* to take out of the oven; *poteries* to take out of the kiln.

défraîchir [defʀeʃiʀ] (2) **1** *vt* (*rare*) to take the freshness from.
2 se défraîchir *vpr [fleur, couleur]* to fade; *[tissu]* (*passer*) to fade; (*s'user*) to become worn.

défrayer [defʀeje] (8) *vt* **(a)** (*payer*) **~ qn** to pay *ou* settle *ou* meet sb's expenses. **(b)** (*être en vedette*) **~ la conversation** to be the main topic of conversation; **~ la chronique** to be widely talked about, be in the news, be the talk of the town (*fig*).

défrichage [defʀiʃaʒ] *nm*, **défrichement** [defʀiʃmɑ̃] *nm [forêt, terrain]* clearing (*for cultivation*). (*fig*) **~ d'un sujet** spadework (done) on a subject.

défricher [defʀiʃe] (1) *vt forêt, terrain* to clear (*for cultivation*); (*fig*) *sujet, question* to open up (*fig*). (*fig*) **~ le terrain** to prepare the ground *ou* way (*fig*), clear the way (*fig*).

défricheur [defʀiʃœʀ] *nm* (*lit*) land-clearer, settler; (*fig*) pioneer.

défriper [defʀipe] (1) *vt* to smooth out.

défriser [defʀize] (1) *vt cheveux* to uncurl; (**‡**: *contrarier*) *personne* to annoy, madden*.

défroisser [defʀwase] (1) *vt* to smooth out.

défroque [defʀɔk] *nf* (*frusques*) old cast-offs; *[moine]* effects (*left by a dead monk*).

défroqué, e [defʀɔke] (*ptp de* **défroquer**) **1** *adj* unfrocked, defrocked. **2** *nm* unfrocked *ou* defrocked priest *ou* monk.

défroquer [defʀɔke] (1) **1** *vt* to defrock, unfrock. **2** *vi*, **se défroquer** *vpr* to give up the cloth, renounce one's vows.

défunt, e [defœ̃, œ̃t] **1** *adj* (*frm*) *personne* late (*épith*); (*littér fig*) *espoir, année* which is dead and gone; (*littér fig*) *assemblée, projet* defunct. **son ~ père**†, **~ son père** his late father. **2** *nm,f* deceased.

dégagé, e [degaʒe] (*ptp de* **dégager**) *adj* **(a)** *route* clear; *ciel* clear, cloudless; *espace, site* open, clear; *vue* wide, open; *front, nuque* bare. **(b)** *allure, ton, manières* casual, jaunty.

dégagement [degaʒmɑ̃] *nm* **(a)** (*action de libérer: V* **dégager**) freeing; extricating; relief; redemption; release; clearing. (*Aut*) **voie de ~** slip road; (*Aut*) **itinéraire de ~** alternative route (*to relieve traffic congestion*).
(b) *[obligation]* freeing *ou* releasing o.s. (*de* from). **le ~ d'une promesse** going back on a promise.
(c) (*émanation*) *[fumée, gaz, chaleur]* emission, emanation; *[parfum]* emanation. **un ~ de vapeurs toxiques** a discharge *ou* an emission of toxic fumes.
(d) (*Sport*) (*Escrime*) disengagement; (*Ftbl, Rugby*) clearance.
(e) (*espace libre*) *[forêt]* clearing; *[appartement]* passage; (*Tech*) *[camion]* clearance, headroom (*de* above).

dégager [degaʒe] (3) **1** *vt* **(a)** (*libérer*) *personne* to free, extricate; *objet, main* to free; (*Mil*) *troupe, ville* to relieve, bring relief to; (*Ftbl, Rugby*) *ballon* to clear, kick *ou* clear downfield; (*Escrime*) *épées* to disengage; (*Fin*) *crédits, titres* to release (*for a specific purpose*); *objet en gage* to redeem, take out of pawn. **cela devrait se ~ facilement** it should come free easily; **après l'accident on a dû ~ les blessés au chalumeau** after the accident the injured had to be cut loose *ou* free (from the wreckage); (*fig*) **~ qn de sa promesse/d'une obligation** to release *ou* free sb from his promise/an obligation; (*fig*) **~ sa responsabilité d'une affaire** to disclaim *ou* deny (all) responsibility in a matter; (*fig*) **~ sa parole** to go back on one's word; (*Sport*) **l'arrière dégagea en touche** the back cleared *ou* kicked the ball into touch; (*Habillement*) **col/robe qui dégage le cou/les épaules** collar/dress which leaves the neck/shoulders bare.
(b) *place, passage, table* to clear (*de* of); (*Méd*) *gorge, nez, poitrine* to clear. **~ la place des manifestants** to clear the demonstrators off the square, clear the square of demonstrators; (*fig*) **~ son esprit d'idées fausses** to free *ou* rid one's mind of false ideas; **allons, dégagez!*** move along!; **dégage!‡** clear off!‡, buzz off!‡ (*Brit*).
(c) (*exhaler*) *odeur, fumée, gaz, chaleur* to give off, emit; (*fig*) *enthousiasme* to radiate. **le paysage dégageait une impression de tristesse** the landscape had a sad look about it.
(d) (*extraire*) *conclusion* to draw; *idée, sens* to bring out. **quelles impressions as-tu dégagées de ton voyage?** what impressions have you gained *ou* can you single out from your trip?; (*Math*) **~ l'inconnue** to isolate the unknown quantity; **l'idée principale qu'on peut ~ de ce rapport** the main idea that can be drawn *ou* derived *ou* extracted from this report; **je vous laisse ~ la morale de cette histoire** I'll let you extract the moral from *ou* unearth the moral of this story; **~ la vérité de l'erreur** to separate truth from untruth.
2 se dégager *vpr* **(a)** *[personne]* to free *ou* extricate o.s., get free; (*Mil*) *[troupe]* to extricate itself (*de* from). (*fig*) **se ~ de** *dette* to free o.s. of; *obligation* to free *ou* release o.s. from; *affaire* to get *ou* back out of; *promesse* to go back on; (*fig*) **j'ai une réunion mais je vais essayer de me ~** I have a meeting but I'll try to get out of it; (*fig*) **il s'est dégagé d'une situation très délicate** he extricated himself from a very tricky situation.
(b) *[ciel, rue, nez]* to clear. (*fig*) **se ~ de préjugés** to free o.s. *ou* shake o.s. free of prejudice.
(c) *[odeur, fumée, gaz, chaleur]* to emanate, be given off; *[électricité]* to be given off; (*fig*) *[enthousiasme]* to emanate, radiate; *[impression d'ennui ou de tristesse]* to emanate (*de* from). **la rumeur qui se dégage de la foule** the murmur rising from the crowd.
(d) *[conclusion]* to be drawn; *[impression, idée, sens]* to emerge; *[morale]* to be drawn, emerge (*de* from). **il se dégage de tout cela que ...** from all this it emerges that ...; **le Mont-Blanc/la silhouette se dégagea du brouillard** Mont Blanc/the outline loomed up out of the fog.

dégaine* [degɛn] *nf* (*démarche*) gawky walk (*U*), gawkiness (*U*); (*air, accoutrement*) gawky look, gawkiness (*U*). **quelle ~!** what a gawky sight!, what a loon!* *ou* a gawk!*

dégainer [degene] (1) **1** *vt épée* to unsheathe, draw; *pistolet* to draw. **2** *vi* to draw one's sword *ou* gun.

déganter (se) [degɑ̃te] (1) *vpr* to take off one's gloves. **sa main dégantée** his ungloved hand.

dégarni, e [degaʀni] (*ptp de* **dégarnir**) *adj front, arbre, salle, rayon* bare; *compte en banque* low; *tête, personne* balding.

dégarnir [degaʀniʀ] (2) **1** *vt maison, salle, vitrine* to empty, clear; *arbre de Noël* to strip (of decorations); *compte en banque* to drain, draw heavily on; (*Mil*) *ville, place* to withdraw troops from.
2 se dégarnir *vpr [salle]* to empty; *[tête, personne]* to go bald; *[arbre]* to lose its leaves; *[bois]* to become sparse; (*Comm*) *[rayons]* to be cleaned out *ou* cleared; (*Comm*) *[stock]* to run out, be cleaned out, become depleted.

dégât [degɑ] *nm* damage (*U*). **la grêle a causé beaucoup de ~** *ou* **~s** the hail caused widespread damage *ou* a lot of damage; *V* **limiter.**

dégauchir [degoʃiʀ] (2) *vt bois* to surface; *pierre* to dress.

dégauchissement [degoʃismɑ̃] *nm*, **dégauchissage** [degoʃisaʒ] *nm* (*V* **dégauchir**) surfacing; dressing.

dégauchisseuse [degoʃisøz] *nf* surface-planing machine.

dégel [deʒɛl] *nm* (*lit, fig*) thaw; *V* **barrière.**

dégelée* [deʒle] *nf* (*coups*) thrashing, hiding, beating. **une ~ de coups** a hail *ou* shower of blows.

dégeler [deʒle] (5) **1** *vt* **(a)** *lac, terre* to thaw (out); *glace* to thaw, melt; (*) *pieds, mains* to warm up, get warmed up.
(b) (**fig*) *invité, réunion* to thaw (out); *atmosphère* to unfreeze.
(c) (*Fin*) to unfreeze.
2 *vi* **(a)** *[neige, lac]* to thaw (out).
(b) (*Culin*) **faire ~** to thaw, leave to thaw.
3 *vb impers*: **ça dégèle** it's thawing.
4 se dégeler *vpr [personne]* (*lit*) to warm up, get o.s. warmed up; (*fig*) to thaw (out).

dégénéré, e [deʒeneʀe] (*ptp de* **dégénérer**) **1** *adj* (*abâtardi*) degenerate; (*Psych*†) defective. **2** *nm,f* degenerate; (*Psych*†) defective.

dégénérer [deʒeneʀe] (6) *vi* **(a)** (*s'abâtardir*) *[race]* to degenerate; *[qualité]* to deteriorate.
(b) (*mal tourner*) to degenerate (*en* into). **leur dispute a dégénéré en rixe** their quarrel went from bad to worse and they came to blows, their quarrel degenerated into a brawl; **un coup de froid qui dégénère en grippe** a chill which develops into flu.

dégénérescence [deʒeneʀesɑ̃s] *nf* **(a)** *[personne]* (*morale*) degeneracy; (*physique, mentale*) degeneration. **(b)** *[moralité, race]* degeneration, degeneracy; *[qualité]* deterioration (*de* in). **(c)** (*Méd*) *[cellule]* degeneration.

dégermer [deʒɛʀme] (1) *vt* to degerm, remove the germ from.

dégingandé, e* [deʒɛ̃gɑ̃de] *adj* gangling, lanky.

dégivrage [deʒivʀaʒ] *nm* (*V* **dégivrer**) defrosting; de-icing.

dégivrer [deʒivʀe] (1) *vt réfrigérateur, pare-brise* to defrost; (*Aviat*) to de-ice.

dégivreur [deʒivʀœʀ] *nm* (*V* **dégivrer**) defroster; de-icer.

déglaçage [deglasaʒ] *nm*, **déglacement** [deglasmɑ̃] *nm* (*V* **déglacer**) deglazing; removal of the glaze (*de* from); removal of the ice (*de* from), melting of the ice (*de* on).

déglacer [deglase] (3) *vt* (*Culin*) to deglaze; *papier* to remove the glaze from; (*rare: dégeler*) *surface* to remove the ice from, melt the ice on.

déglinguer* [deglɛ̃ge] (1) **1** *vt objet, appareil* to knock to pieces. **ce fauteuil est tout déglingué** this armchair is falling *ou* coming apart *ou* is (all) falling to pieces. **2 se déglinguer** *vpr [objet, appareil]* to fall to pieces, fall *ou* come apart.

déglutir [deglytiʀ] (2) *vt* (*Méd*) to swallow.

déglutition [deglytisjɔ̃] *nf* (*Méd*) swallowing, deglutition (*T*).

dégobiller‡ [degɔbije] (1) *vti* (*vomir*) to throw up‡, spew (up)‡.

dégoiser* [degwaze] (1) **1** *vt boniments, discours* to spout*. **qu'est-ce qu'il dégoise?** what is he rattling on about?* **2** *vi* (*parler*) to rattle on*, go on (and on)*. (*médire*) **~ sur le compte de qn** to tittle-tattle about sb.

dégommage‡ [degɔmaʒ] *nm* (*V* **dégommer**) **le ~ de qn** the busting‡ *ou* demoting of sb; the unseating of sb; giving the push to sb*, the sacking of sb*.

dégommer‡ [degɔme] (1) *vt* (*dégrader*) to bust‡, demote; (*détrôner*) to unseat; (*renvoyer*) to give the push to*, sack*.

dégonflage‡ [degɔ̃flaʒ] *nm* chickening out*, backing out. **j'appelle ça du ~!** that's what I call being chicken* *ou* yellow (-bellied)‡, that's what I call chickening out*.

dégonflard, e‡ [degɔ̃flaʀ, aʀd(ə)] *nm,f* (*lâche*) yellow-belly‡.

dégonflé, e [degɔ̃fle] (*ptp de* **dégonfler**) *adj* **(a)** *pneu* flat. **(b)** (‡: *lâche*) chicken* (*attrib*), yellow(-bellied)‡. **c'est un ~** he's a yellow-belly‡, he's chicken* *ou* yellow*.

dégonflement [degɔ̃fləmɑ̃] *nm [ballon, pneu]* deflation; *[enflure]* reduction.

dégonfler [degɔ̃fle] (1) **1** *vt pneu* to let down, let the air out of, deflate; *ballon* to deflate, let the air out of; *enflure* to reduce, bring down. **2 se dégonfler** *vpr* **(a)** *[ballon, enflure, pneu]* to go down. **(b)** (*: *avoir peur*) to chicken out*, back out.

dégonfleur, -euse‡ [degɔ̃flœʀ, øz] *nm,f* = **dégonflard‡**.

dégorgement [degɔʀʒəmɑ̃] *nm* **(a)** (*débouchage*) *[évier, égout]* clearing out.

(b) (*évacuation*) *[eau, bile]* discharge.

(c) (*écoulement*) *[égout, rivière]* discharge; *[gouttière]* discharge, overflow.

(d) (*Tech: lavage*) *[cuir]* cleaning, cleansing; *[laine]* scouring.

dégorgeoir [degɔʀʒwaʀ] *nm* (*conduit d'évacuation*) overflow duct *ou* pipe; (*Pêche*) disgorger.

dégorger [degɔʀʒe] (3) **1** *vt* **(a)** *évier, égout* to clear out.

(b) *[tuyau] eau* to discharge, pour out; (*fig*) *[rue, train] voyageurs* to disgorge, pour forth *ou* out.

(c) (*Tech: laver*) *cuir, étoffe* to clean, cleanse; *laine* to scour.

2 *vi* **(a)** *[étoffe]* to soak (*to release impurities*); (*Culin*) *[viande]* to soak; *[escargots]* to be covered with salt; *[concombres]* to sweat. **faire ~** *étoffe* to soak; *viande* to soak; *escargots* to cover in salt; *concombres* to sweat.

(b) ~ dans *[égout, gouttière]* to discharge into; *[rivière]* to discharge itself into.

3 se dégorger *vpr [eau]* to be discharged, pour out; (*fig*) *[voyageurs]* to pour forth *ou* out.

dégot(t)er* [degɔte] (1) *vt* (*trouver*) to dig up*, unearth, find.

dégoulinade [degulinad] *nf* trickle.

dégoulinement [degulinmɑ̃] *nm* (*V* **dégouliner**) trickling; dripping.

dégouliner [deguline] (1) *vi* (*en filet*) to trickle; (*goutte à goutte*) to drip. **ça me dégouline dans le cou** it's dripping *ou* trickling down my neck.

dégoupiller [degupije] (1) *vt grenade* to take the pin out of.

dégourdi, e* [deguʀdi] (*ptp de* **dégourdir**) **1** *adj* (*malin*) smart, resourceful, bright. **il n'est pas très ~** he's not really on the ball*, he's not all that smart *ou* bright, he's pretty clueless* (*Brit*).

2 *nm,f*: **c'est un ~** he's a smart one *ou* a fly one*, he knows what's what*, he's on the ball*; (*iro*) **quel ~ tu fais!** you're a bright spark!* (*Brit*) *ou* a smart one! *ou* a bright one! (*iro*).

dégourdir [deguʀdiʀ] (2) **1** *vt eau* to warm (up); *membres* (*ankylosés*) to bring the circulation back to; (*gelés*) to warm up; (*fig*) *provincial* to teach a thing or two to*. **le service militaire/d'habiter à Paris le dégourdira** military service/living in Paris will shake him up a bit *ou* teach him a thing or two*.

2 se dégourdir *vpr*: **il est sorti pour se ~ un peu (les jambes)** he went out to stretch his legs a bit; (*fig*) **elle s'est un peu dégourdie depuis l'an dernier** she seems to have learnt a thing or two* *ou* got a bit livelier since last year.

dégoût [degu] *nm* **(a)** (*U: répugnance*) disgust (*U*), distaste (*U*) (*pour, de* for). **j'éprouve un certain ~ pour son comportement** I feel somewhat disgusted at his behaviour; **avoir du ~ pour** to feel (a sense of) disgust *ou* distaste for; **il fit une grimace de ~** he screwed up his face in disgust *ou* distaste; **ce ~ de la vie m'étonnait** such world-weariness *ou* such weariness of life surprised me.

(b) dislike. **nos goûts et nos ~s** our likes and dislikes.

dégoûtamment [degutamɑ̃] *adv* (*rare*) *manger, se conduire* disgustingly.

dégoûtant, e [degutɑ̃, ɑ̃t] *adj* disgusting, revolting. **espèce de (vieux) ~!*** you disgusting *ou* filthy (old) beast!*, you dirty old man!*

dégoûtation [degutɑsjɔ̃] *nf* (*: *saleté*) disgusting *ou* filthy mess; (*rare: dégoût*) disgust.

dégoûté, e [degute] (*ptp de* **dégoûter**) *adj*: **c'est un homme ~ maintenant que tous ses projets ont échoué** he is sick at heart *ou* fed up* now that all his plans have failed; **être ~ de** to be sick of; **il fait le ~** (*devant un mets, une offre*) he turns his nose up (at it) in distaste; **il mange des sauterelles/il sort avec cette femme, il n'est pas ~!** he eats grasshoppers/he goes out with that woman — he's not (too) fussy! *ou* choosy!*

dégoûter [degute] (1) **1** *vt* **(a)** (*répugner à*) to disgust. **cet homme me dégoûte** that man disgusts me *ou* fills me with disgust, I find that man disgusting *ou* revolting; **ce plat me dégoûte** I find this dish disgusting *ou* revolting; **la vie me dégoûte** I'm weary of life, I'm sick *ou* weary of living, I'm fed up with life*.

(b) ~ qn de qch (*ôter l'envie de*) to put sb (right) off sth; (*remplir de dégoût pour*) to make sb feel disgusted with; **c'est à vous ~ d'être honnête** it's enough to put you (right) off being honest; **si tu n'aimes pas ça, n'en dégoûte pas les autres** if you don't like it, don't put the others off; **dégoûté de la vie** weary *ou* sick of life *ou* living; **je suis dégoûté par ces procédés** I'm disgusted *ou* revolted by this behaviour.

2 se dégoûter *vpr*: **se ~ de qn/qch** to get sick of sb/sth*; **il se dégoûte dans cet appartement sale** he's sick of this dirty flat*, he dislikes it (intensely) in this dirty flat.

dégoutter [degute] (1) *vi* to drip. **dégouttant de sueur** dripping with sweat; **l'eau qui dégoutte du toit** the water dripping (down) from *ou* off the roof; **manteau dégouttant de pluie** dripping wet coat.

dégradant, e [degʀadɑ̃, ɑ̃t] *adj* degrading.

dégradation [degʀadɑsjɔ̃] *nf* **(a)** (*V* **dégrader**) degradation; debasement; defiling; damaging; erosion; defacing; shading-off. (*Jur*) **~ civique** loss of civil rights.

(b) (*V* **se dégrader**) degradation; debasement; loss of one's (physical) powers; deterioration; decline; weakening; worsening; shading-off. (*Phys*) **la ~ de l'énergie** the degradation *ou* dissipation of energy.

dégradé [degʀade] *nm [couleurs]* gradation; *[lumière]* (gradual) moderation; (*Ciné*) grading. **un ~ de couleurs** a gradation of colours, a colour gradation.

dégrader [degʀade] (1) **1** *vt* **(a)** (*Mil*) *officier* to degrade.

(b) *personne* to degrade, debase.

(c) *qualité* to debase; *beauté* to defile, debase.

(d) *mur, bâtiment [vandales]* to damage, cause damage to; *[pluie]* to erode, cause to deteriorate; *monument, façade* to deface, damage; (*Géol*) *roches* to erode, wear away. **les mauvais ouvriers dégradent le matériel** bad workers damage the equipment.

(e) (*Art*) *couleurs* to shade off; *lumière* to subdue. **couleurs dégradées** colours which shade into each other *ou* shade off gradually.

2 se dégrader *vpr* **(a)** *[personne]* (*s'avilir moralement*) to degrade o.s., debase o.s., become degraded *ou* debased; (*s'affaiblir physiquement*) to lose one's physical powers.

(b) *[situation, qualité, santé, bâtiment]* to deteriorate; *[valeurs morales, intérêt, forces]* to decline; *[monnaie]* to grow weaker. **le temps se dégrade** the weather is beginning to break, there's a change for the worse in the weather.

(c) (*Sci*) *[énergie]* to become dissipated *ou* degraded; (*Art*) *[couleurs]* to shade off; *[lumière]* to become subdued.

dégrafer [degʀafe] (1) **1** *vt vêtement* to unfasten, unhook, undo; *ceinture* to unbuckle, unfasten, undo; *personne* to unfasten *ou* unhook *ou* undo the dress *etc* of, unfasten, unhook, undo.

2 se dégrafer *vpr [robe, bracelet]* to come undone *ou* unfastened; *[personne]* to unfasten *ou* unhook *ou* undo one's dress *etc.*

dégraissage [degʀɛsaʒ] *nm*: **le ~ d'un vêtement** removal of the grease marks from a piece of clothing; **le ~ du bouillon** skimming the fat off the broth; **'~ et nettoyage à sec'** 'dry cleaning'.

dégraissant [degʀɛsɑ̃] *nm* (*produit*) spot remover.

dégraisser [degʀese] (1) *vt* **(a)** *vêtement* to take the grease marks out of. **(b)** (*Culin*) *bouillon* to skim (the fat off); *viande* to remove the fat from, cut the fat off. **(c)** (*Menuiserie*) *bois* to trim the edges of.

degré [dəgʀe] *nm* **(a)** (*gén: niveau*) degree; (*stade de développement*) stage, degree; (*Admin: échelon*) grade; (*littér: marche*) step. **haut ~ de civilisation** high degree *ou* level of civilization; **à un ~ avancé** de at an advanced stage of; (*Alpinisme*) **mur de 6e ~** grade 6 wall; (*fig*) **les ~s de l'échelle sociale** the rungs of the social ladder (*fig*); **avare au plus haut ~** miserly in the extreme, miserly to a degree; **jusqu'à un certain ~** to some *ou* a certain extent *ou* degree, to a degree; **par ~(s)** by degrees; *V* **dernier, troisième.**

(b) (*Gram, Mus, Sci*) degree. **équation du 1er/2e ~** equation of the 1st/2nd degree; **il fait 20 ~s dans la chambre** it's 20 degrees (centigrade) in the room; **la température a baissé/est montée de 2 ~s** there has been a 2-degree drop/rise in temperature, the temperature has gone down *ou* dropped/gone up *ou* risen 2 degrees; **~ d'alcool d'une boisson** proof of an alcoholic drink; **~ en alcool d'un liquide** percentage of alcohol in a liquid; **alcool à 90 ~s** 90% proof alcohol; **du cognac à 40 ~s** 70° proof brandy (*Brit*); **vin de 11 ~s** 11° wine (*on Gay-Lussac scale, = 19° Sykes (Brit) and 22° proof (US)*); **ce vin fait (du) 11 ~s** this wine is 11°; **~ centigrade/Fahrenheit/Baumé** degree centigrade/Fahrenheit/Baumé.

(c) (*Méd*) **~ de brûlure** degree of burns; **brûlure du premier/deuxième ~** first/second degree burn; (*Scol*) **enseignement du premier/second ~** primary/secondary education; **enseignant du premier/second ~** primary/secondary schoolteacher; (*Sociol*) **~ de parenté** degree of (family) relationship *ou* of kinship (*frm*); **cousins au premier ~** first cousins; **cousins au second ~** second cousins, first cousins once removed; **parents au premier/deuxième ~** relatives of the first/second degree.

dégressif, -ive [degʀesif, iv] *adj* degressive.

dégrèvement [degʀɛvmɑ̃] *nm* **(a)** = tax relief (*U*), reduction of tax (*de* on). **le ~ d'un produit** the reduction of the tax(es) on a product; **le ~ d'une industrie** the reduction of the tax burden on an industry; **le ~ d'un contribuable** the granting of tax relief to a taxpayer. **(b)** (*Jur: d'hypothèque*) disencumbrance.

dégrever [degʀəve] (5) *vt produit* to reduce the tax(es) on; *industrie* to reduce the tax burden on; *contribuable* to grant tax relief to; *immeuble* to disencumber.

dégringolade [degʀɛ̃gɔlad] *nf* (*V* **dégringoler**) tumbling (down); tumble.

dégringoler [degʀɛ̃gɔle] (1) **1** *vi [personne, objet]* to tumble (down); *[monnaie]* to take a tumble; *[prix, firme, réputation]* to tumble. **il a dégringolé jusqu'en bas** he tumbled all the way down, he came *ou* went tumbling *ou* crashing down; **elle a essayé de prendre un livre et elle a fait ~ toute la pile** she tried to get a book and toppled the whole pile over *ou* brought the whole pile (crashing) down.
2 *vt escalier, pente* to rush *ou* leap down.

dégrisement [degʀizmɑ̃] *nm* (*lit, fig*) sobering up.

dégriser [degʀize] (1) **1** *vt* (*lit*) to sober up; (*fig*) to sober up, bring back down to earth. **2 se dégriser** *vpr* (*rare*) to sober up; (*fig*) to sober up, come back down to earth.

dégrossir [degʀosiʀ] (2) *vt* **(a)** *bois, planche* to trim, cut down to size; *marbre* to rough-hew.
(b) (*fig*) *projet, travail* to rough out, work out roughly.
(c) (*) *personne* to knock the rough edges off, polish up. **individu mal dégrossi** coarse *ou* unpolished *ou* unrefined individual; **il s'est un peu dégrossi** he has lost some of his rough edges.

dégrossissage [degʀosisaʒ] *nm* (*V* **dégrossir**) trimming; rough-hewing; roughing-out. **le ~ d'une personne** knocking the rough edges off a person, polishing up *ou* refining a person.

dégrouiller (se)* [degʀuje] (1) *vpr* (*se dépêcher*) to hurry up, get a move on*. **allez, dégrouille(-toi)!** come on, hurry up! *ou* get a move on!*

déguenillé, e [degnije] **1** *adj* ragged, tattered. **2** *nm,f* ragamuffin.

déguerpir* [degɛʀpiʀ] (2) *vi* (*s'enfuir*) to clear off*, scarper‡ (*Brit*). **faire ~** *ennemi* to scatter; *voleur* to chase *ou* drive off.

dégueulasse‡ [degœlas] *adj* (*mauvais, injuste*) lousy‡, rotten‡; (*crasseux, vicieux*) filthy. **c'est ~ de faire ça** that's a lousy‡ *ou* rotten‡ thing to do; **c'est un ~** he's a lousy *ou* rotten swine‡, he's a filthy dog‡.

dégueuler‡ [degœle] (1) *vti* (*vomir*) to throw up‡, spew (up)‡, puke (up)‡.

déguisé, e [degize] (*ptp de* **déguiser**) *adj* **(a)** (*pour tromper*) in disguise (*attrib*), disguised; (*pour s'amuser*) in fancy dress, in costume (*US*), dressed up.
(b) (*fig*) *voix, écriture* disguised; *ambition, sentiment* disguised, masked, veiled. **non ~** unconcealed, undisguised.

déguisement [degizmɑ̃] *nm* (*pour tromper*) disguise; (*pour s'amuser*) fancy dress, costume (*US*), disguise. (*littér*) **sans ~** without disguise, openly.

déguiser [degize] (1) **1** *vt* (*gén*) *voix, écriture, visage* to disguise; *pensée, ambition, vérité* to disguise, mask, veil; *poupée, enfant* to dress up (*en* as a (*sg*), as (*pl*)). (*littér*) **je ne puis vous ~ ma surprise** I cannot conceal my surprise from you.
2 se déguiser *vpr* (*pour tromper*) to disguise o.s.; (*pour s'amuser*) to dress up. **se ~ en Peau-Rouge** to dress up as a Red Indian.

dégustateur [degystatœʀ] *nm* wine taster.

dégustation [degystɑsjɔ̃] *nf [coquillages, fromages]* sampling. **~ de vin(s)** wine-tasting session; **ici, ~ d'huîtres à toute heure** oysters available *ou* served at all times.

déguster [degyste] (1) **1** *vt vins* to taste; *coquillages, fromages* to sample; *repas, café* to enjoy, savour; (*fig*) *spectacle* to enjoy, savour. **as-tu fini ton café? non, je le déguste** have you finished your coffee? — no I'm still enjoying it.
2 *vi* (*: *souffrir*) **qu'est-ce qu'il a dégusté!** (*coups*) he didn't half catch it!* *ou* cop it!*; (*douleur*) he didn't half have a rough time!*

déhanché, e [deɑ̃ʃe] (*ptp de* **se déhancher**) *adj démarche [femme etc]* swaying; *[infirme]* lop-sided; *posture [femme etc]* leaning; *[infirme]* lop-sided; *cheval* hipshot.

déhanchement [deɑ̃ʃmɑ̃] *nm* (*V* **déhanché**) (*mouvement*) swaying; lop-sided walk; (*posture*) leaning position; lop-sidedness.

déhancher (se) [deɑ̃ʃe] (1) *vpr* **(a)** (*en marchant*) to sway one's hips. **(b)** (*immobile*) to stand with *ou* lean one's weight on one hip.

dehors [dəɔʀ] **1** *adv* **(a)** (*à l'extérieur*) outside; (*à l'air libre*) outside, outdoors, out of doors; (*pas chez soi*) out. **attendez-le ~** wait for him outside; **je serai ~ toute la journée** I shall be out all day; **par beau temps, les enfants passent la journée ~** when it's fine, the children spend the day outdoors *ou* out of doors *ou* outside; **il fait plus frais dedans que ~** it is cooler inside than out(side) *ou* indoors than out(doors); **cela ne se voit pas de ~** it can't be seen from (the) outside; **passez par ~ pour aller au jardin** go round the outside (of the house) to get to the garden; **dîner/déjeuner ~** to eat *ou* dine/eat *ou* lunch out; **jeter *ou* mettre* *ou* ficher* *ou* foutre‡ qn ~** to throw *ou* kick‡ *ou* chuck‡ sb out; (*renvoyer*) to sack* *ou* fire* sb, throw *ou* kick‡ *ou* chuck‡ sb out; **mettre le nez *ou* le pied ~** to set foot outside; **il fait un temps à ne pas mettre le nez ~** it's weather for staying indoors.
(b) (*loc*) **en ~ de** (*lit*) outside; (*fig*) (*sans rapport avec*) outside, irrelevant to; (*excepté*) apart from; **ne passez pas la tête en ~ de la fenêtre** don't put your head out of the window *ou* outside the window; **ce passage est en ~ du sujet** this passage is outside the subject *ou* is irrelevant (to the subject); **marcher les pieds en ~** to walk with one's feet *ou* toes turned out; **en ~ de cela, il n'y a rien de neuf** apart from that *ou* beyond that, there's nothing new; **cette question est en ~ de ses possibilités** this question is beyond his capabilities; (*fig*) **il a voulu rester en ~** he wanted to stay uninvolved; **au ~, elle paraît calme, mais c'est une nerveuse** outwardly she looks relaxed, but she is highly strung; **au ~, la situation est tendue** outside the country, the situation is tense.
2 *nm* **(a)** (*extérieur*) outside. **on n'entend pas les bruits du ~** you can't hear the noise from outside; **nos employés sont honnêtes, ce sont des gens du ~ qui ont commis ce vol** our employees are honest — it must be outsiders *ou* people from outside who are responsible for the theft; **les affaires du ~** foreign affairs.
(b) (*apparences: pl*) **les ~ sont trompeurs** apppearances are deceptive; **sous des ~ aimables, il est dur** under a friendly exterior, he is a hard man.
(c) (*Patinage*) **faire des ~** to skate on the outside edge.

déicide [deisid] **1** *adj* deicidal. **2** *nmf* deicide. **3** *nm* (*crime*) deicide.

déification [deifikɑsjɔ̃] *nf* deification.

déifier [deifje] (7) *vt* to deify.

déisme [deism(ə)] *nm* deism.

déiste [deist(ə)] **1** *adj* deistic, deist. **2** *nmf* deist.

déité [deite] *nf* (*littér*) (mythological) deity.

déjà [deʒa] *adv* **(a)** already. **il a ~ fini** he has finished already, he has already finished; **est-il ~ rentré?** has he come home yet?; (*surprise*) has he come home already?; **à 3 heures il avait ~ écrit 3 lettres** he'd already written 3 letters by 3 o'clock; **~ à cette époque** as far back as then, already *ou* even at that time; **j'aurais ~ fini si tu ne me dérangeais pas tout le temps** I would have finished by now *ou* already if you wouldn't keep bothering me all the time; **je l'aurais ~ dit, si je n'avais pas craint de le vexer** I would have said it before now *ou* by now *ou* already if I hadn't been afraid of offending him; **c'est ~ vieux tout ça!** all that's already out of date!, all that's old hat!*
(b) (*auparavant*) before, already. **je suis sûr de l'avoir ~ rencontré** I'm sure I've met him before, I'm sure I've already met him; **j'ai ~ fait ce genre de travail** I've done that sort of work before, I've already done that sort of work.
(c) (*intensif*) **1.000 F, c'est ~ pas mal*** 1,000 francs, that's not bad at all; **30 tonnes, c'est ~ un gros camion** 30 tons, that's quite a big truck *ou* that's a fair-sized truck; **il est ~ assez paresseux** he's lazy enough as it is; **enfin, c'est ~ quelque chose!** anyway, it's better than nothing! *ou* it's a start!; **~ que je ne suis pas riche*, s'il faut encore payer une amende ...** as it is I'm not rich *ou* I'm not rich as it is but if I (should) have to pay a fine as well ... .
(d) (*: *interrogatif*) **qu'est-ce qu'il a dit, ~?** what was it he said again?, what did he say again?; **c'est combien, ~?** how much is it again?, how much did you say it was again?; *V* **ores**.

déjanter (se) [deʒɑ̃te] (1) *vpr [pneu]* to come off its rim.

déjection [deʒɛksjɔ̃] *nf* **(a)** (*Méd*) evacuation. **~s** dejecta (*T*), faeces, excrement. **(b)** (*Géol*) **~s** ejecta, ejectamenta; *V* **cône**.

déjeté, e [deʒte] *adj position, mur, arbre, infirme* lop-sided, crooked; *colonne vertébrale* twisted. **il est tout ~** he's all lop-sided.

déjeuner [deʒœne] (1) **1** *vi* **(a)** (*gén: à midi*) to (have) lunch. **nous avons déjeuné de fromage et de pain** we had bread and cheese for lunch, we lunched on bread and cheese; **inviter qn à ~** to invite sb to lunch; **rester à ~ chez qn** to stay and have lunch with sb, stay to lunch at sb's; **viens ~ avec nous demain** come and have lunch with us tomorrow, come to lunch with us tomorrow; **nous avons déjeuné sur l'herbe** we had a picnic lunch; **ne pars pas sans ~** don't go before you've had your lunch.
(b) (††: *le matin*) to (have) breakfast; *V* **petit, pouce**.
2 *nm* **(a)** (*repas de midi*) (*gén*) lunch, luncheon (*frm*); (*repas cérémonieux*) dinner. **prendre son ~** to have lunch; **j'ai eu du poulet à ~** I had chicken for lunch; **demain j'ai ma mère à ~** I've got my mother coming for lunch tomorrow.
(b) (††: *du matin*) breakfast.
(c) (*tasse et soucoupe*) breakfast cup and saucer.
(d) ça a été un vrai ~ de soleil (*vêtement*) it didn't take long to fade; (*objet*) it soon gave up the ghost*, it didn't last long; (*résolution*) it was a flash in the pan, it didn't last long, it was short-lived.

déjouer [deʒwe] (1) *vt complot* to foil, thwart; *plan* to thwart, frustrate; *ruse* to outsmart; *surveillance* to elude. **~ les plans de l'ennemi** to frustrate the enemy in his plans, confound the enemy's plans.

déjuger (se) [deʒyʒe] (3) *vpr* to go back on *ou* reverse one's decision.

delà [dəla] **1** *adv* **(a) au-~** beyond; **au-~ il y a l'Italie** beyond (that) is Italy; **il a eu ce qu'il voulait et bien au-~** he had all he wanted and more (besides); **vous avez droit à 10 bouteilles et pas au-~/mais au-~ vous payez une taxe** you're entitled to 10 bottles and no more/but above that you pay duty; **n'allez pas au-~** don't go beyond *ou* over that figure (*ou* sum *etc*), don't exceed that figure; **mes connaissances ne vont pas au-~** that's as far as my knowledge goes, that's the extent of my knowledge; *V* **au-delà**.
(b) par ~, par-~ beyond; **devant eux il y a le pont et par(-)~ l'ennemi** in front of them is the bridge and beyond (that) the enemy *ou* and on the other *ou* far side (of it), the enemy.
(c) en ~ beyond, outside; **la clôture était à 20 mètres et il se tenait un peu en ~** the fence was 20 metres away and he was standing just beyond it *ou* outside it.
(d) (*littér*) **de ~ les mers** from beyond *ou* over the seas; *V* **deçà**.
2 *prép* **(a) au ~ de** *lieu, frontière* beyond, on the other side of; *somme, limite* over, above; (*littér*) **au ~ des mers** overseas, beyond *ou* over the seas; **ceci va au ~ de tout ce que nous espérions** this goes (far) beyond anything we hoped for; **au ~ de la conscience/douleur** beyond consciousness/pain; **aller au ~ de ses forces/moyens** to go beyond *ou* exceed one's strength/means.
(b) (*gén littér*) **par ~** beyond; **par ~ les mers** overseas, beyond *ou* over the seas; **par ~ les apparences** beneath appearances; **par ~ les siècles** across the centuries.

délabré, e [delabʀe] (*ptp de* **délabrer**) *adj maison* dilapidated, ramshackle (*épith*), tumbledown (*épith*); *mobilier, matériel* broken-down; *vêtements* ragged, tattered; *santé* impaired, broken (*épith*); *mur* falling down (*épith*), crumbling, in ruins (*attrib*); *affaires* in a poor *ou* sorry state (*attrib*); *fortune* depleted.

délabrement [delɑbʀəmɑ̃] *nm [maison]* dilapidation, decay, ruin; *[santé, affaires]* poor *ou* sorry state; *[vêtements]* raggedness; *[mobilier, matériel, mur]* decay, ruin; *[fortune]* depletion. **état de ~** dilapidated state, state of decay *ou* ruin.

délabrer [delɑbʀe] (1) **1** *vt maison* to ruin; *mobilier, matériel* to spoil, ruin; *santé* to ruin, impair. **2 se délabrer** *vpr [maison, mur, matériel]* to fall into decay; *[santé]* to break down; *[affaires]* to go to rack and ruin.

délacer [delase] (3) **1** *vt chaussures* to undo (the laces of); *corset* to unlace. **2 se délacer** *vpr* **(a)** *[chaussures]* to come undone; *[corset]* to come unlaced *ou* undone. **(b)** *[personne]* to undo one's shoes; to unlace one's corset.

délai [delɛ] **1** *nm* **(a)** (*temps accordé*) time limit. **c'est un ~ trop court pour ...** it's too short a time for ...; **je vous donne 3 mois, c'est un ~ impératif** I'll give you 3 months and that's an absolute deadline; **avant l'expiration du ~** before the deadline; **dans le ~ prescrit** within the allotted *ou* prescribed time, within the time laid down *ou* allotted; **dans un ~ de 6 jours** within (a period of) 6 days; **livrable dans un ~ de quinze jours** allow two weeks for delivery; **un ~ de 10 jours pour payer est insuffisant** (a period of) 10 days to pay is not enough; **prolonger un ~** to extend a time limit *ou* a deadline; **lundi prochain, c'est le dernier ~** next Monday is the absolute deadline.

(b) (*période d'attente*) waiting period. **il faut compter un ~ de huit jours** you'll have to allow a week, there'll be a week's delay.

(c) (*sursis*) extension of time. **un dernier ~ de 10 jours** a final extension of 10 days; **accorder des ~s successifs** to allow further extensions (of time); **il va demander un ~ pour achever le travail** he's going to ask for more time to finish off the job.

(d) (*loc*) **dans le(s) plus bref(s) ~(s)** as soon *ou* as quickly as possible; **ce sera fait dans les ~s** it'll be done within the time limit *ou* allotted time; **à bref ~** at short notice; (*très bientôt*) shortly, very soon; **sans ~** without delay, immediately.

2: délai-congé *nm, pl* **délais-congés** term *ou* period of notice; **délai de livraison** delivery time *ou* period; **délai de paiement** term of payment, time for payment; **délai de préavis = délai-congé**; **délai de rigueur** absolute deadline, strict time limit.

délainage [delɛnaʒ] *nm* fellmongering.

délainer [delene] (1) *vt* to remove the wool from, dewool.

délaissement [delɛsmɑ̃] *nm* (*action*) abandonment, desertion; (*état*) neglect, state of neglect *ou* abandonment; (*Jur*) relinquishment *ou* renunciation (*of a right*).

délaisser [delese] (1) *vt* **(a)** (*abandonner*) *famille, ami, travail* to quit, give up, abandon. **épouse délaissée** deserted wife; **enfant délaissé** abandoned child.

(b) (*négliger*) *famille, ami, travail* to neglect. **épouse/fillette délaissée** neglected wife/little girl.

(c) (*Jur*) *droit* to relinquish.

délassant, e [delɑsɑ̃, ɑ̃t] *adj bain* relaxing, refreshing; *lecture* diverting, entertaining.

délassement [delɑsmɑ̃] *nm* (*état*) relaxation, rest; (*distraction*) relaxation, diversion.

délasser [delɑse] (1) **1** *vt* (*reposer*) *membres* to refresh; (*divertir*) *personne, esprit* to divert, entertain. **un bon bain, ça délasse** a good bath is relaxing *ou* refreshing; **c'est un livre qui délasse** it's an entertaining *ou* a relaxing sort of book.

2 se délasser *vpr* (*se détendre*) to relax.

délateur, -trice [delatœʀ, tʀis] *nm,f* (*frm*) informer.

délation [delɑsjɔ̃] *nf* denouncement, informing. **une atmosphère de ~** an incriminatory atmosphere; **faire une ~** to inform.

délavage [delavaʒ] *nm* (*Tech: V* **délaver**) watering down; fading; waterlogging.

délavé, e [delave] (*ptp de* **délaver**) *adj* **(a)** *tissu, jeans* faded; *inscription* washed-out. **un ciel ~ après la pluie** a watery *ou* washed-out (blue) sky after rain. **(b)** *terre* waterlogged.

délaver [delave] (1) *vt* **(a)** *aquarelle* to water down; *tissu, inscription* to (cause to) fade (*by the action of water*). **(b)** *terre* to waterlog.

délayage [delɛjaʒ] *nm* (*V* **délayer**) thinning down; mixing; dragging-out, spinning-out; padding-out. (*péj*) **faire du ~** *[personne, écrivain]* to waffle* (*surtout Brit*); **son commentaire est un pur ~** his commentary is pure waffle* *ou* padding.

délayer [deleje] (8) *vt couleur* to thin down; (*Culin*) *farine, poudre* to mix (*to a certain consistency*) (*dans* with); (*fig péj*) *idée* to drag *ou* spin out; *texte* to pad out. **~ 100 grammes de farine dans un litre d'eau** mix 100 grammes of flour and *ou* with a litre of water; **quelques idées habilement délayées** a few ideas cleverly spun out.

delco [dɛlko] *nm* ® distributor; *V* **tête**.

délectable [delɛktabl(ə)] *adj* (*littér*) delectable.

délectation [delɛktɑsjɔ̃] *nf* delight, delectation (*littér*); (*Rel*) delight. **~ morose** delectatio morosa.

délecter [delɛkte] (1) **1** *vt* (*littér*) to delight. **2 se délecter** *vpr*: **se ~ de qch/à faire** to delight *ou* revel *ou* take delight in sth/in doing; **il se délectait** he was revelling in it, he took great delight in it, he was thoroughly enjoying it.

délégation [delegɑsjɔ̃] *nf* **(a)** (*groupe*) delegation; (*commission*) commission. **nous venons en ~ voir le patron** we have come as a delegation to see the boss.

(b) (*mandat*) delegation. **quand il est absent, sa secrétaire signe le courrier par ~** when he is away his secretary signs his letters on his authority; **il agit par ~** *ou* **en vertu d'une ~** he is acting on sb's authority; (*Jur*) **~ de créance** assignment *ou* delegation of debt; **~ de pouvoirs** delegation of powers; (*Mil*) **~ de solde** assignment of pay (*to relatives*).

(c) (*Admin: succursale*) branch, office(s).

délégué, e [delege] (*ptp de* **déléguer**) **1** *adj* delegated. **membre ~** delegate; (*Écon*) **administrateur ~** managing director; (*Ciné*) **producteur ~** associate producer; (*Pol*) **ministre ~** ministerial delegate. **2** *nm,f* (*représentant*) delegate, representative.

déléguer [delege] (6) *vt pouvoirs, personne* to delegate (*à* to); (*Jur*) *créance* to assign, delegate.

délestage [delɛstaʒ] *nm* (*Élec*) power cut; *[ballon, navire]* removal of ballast (*de* from), unballasting.

délester [delɛste] (1) **1** *vt navire, ballon* to remove ballast from, unballast; (*Élec*) to cut off power from. (*fig*) **~ qn d'un fardeau** to relieve sb of a burden; (*: *voler*) **~ qn de qch** to relieve sb of sth.

2 se délester *vpr [bateau, ballon]* to jettison ballast. (*Aviat*) **se ~ de ses bombes** (*en cas de panne*) to jettison its bombs; (*sur l'objectif*) to release its bombs; (*fig*) **elle se délesta de ses colis** she unloaded *ou* dropped her parcels.

délétère [deletɛʀ] *adj émanations, gaz* noxious, deleterious; (*fig*) *influence, propagande* pernicious, deleterious.

délibérante [delibeʀɑ̃t] *adj f*: **assemblée ~** deliberative assembly.

délibération [delibeʀɑsjɔ̃] *nf* **(a)** (*débat*) deliberation, debate. **~s** proceedings, deliberations; **mettre une question en ~** to debate *ou* deliberate (over *ou* upon) an issue; **après ~ du jury** after the jury's due deliberation.

(b) (*réflexion*) deliberation, consideration.

(c) (*décision*) decision, resolution. **~s** resolutions; **par ~ du jury** on the jury's recommendation.

délibérative [delibeʀativ] *adj f*: **avoir voix ~ive** to have voting rights.

délibéré, e [delibeʀe] (*ptp de* **délibérer**) **1** *adj* (*intentionnel*) deliberate; (*assuré*) resolute, determined; *V* **propos**. **2** *nm* (*Jur*) deliberation (*of court at end of trial*). **mettre une affaire en ~** to deliberate on a matter.

délibérément [delibeʀemɑ̃] *adv* (*volontairement*) deliberately, intentionally; (*après avoir réfléchi*) with due consideration; (*résolument*) resolutely.

délibérer [delibeʀe] (6) **1** *vi* (*débattre*) (*gén*) to deliberate, confer, debate; *[jury]* to confer, deliberate; (*réfléchir*) to deliberate, consider. **après avoir mûrement délibéré** after having pondered the matter, after duly considering the matter; **~ sur une question** to deliberate (over *ou* upon) an issue.

2 délibérer de *vt indir* (*décider*) **~ de qch** to deliberate sth; **~ de faire qch** to decide *ou* resolve to do sth (after deliberation).

délicat, e [delika, at] *adj* **(a)** (*fin*) *dentelle, parfum, forme, couleur* delicate; *fil, voile, facture, travail* fine; *mets* dainty. **un objet gravé de facture ~e** a finely engraved object.

(b) (*fragile*) *tissu, fleur, enfant, santé* delicate. **il a la peau très ~e** he has very tender *ou* delicate skin; **lotion pour peaux ~es** lotion for sensitive skins.

(c) (*difficile*) *situation, question,* (*Méd*) *opération* delicate, tricky. **c'est ~!** it's rather delicate! *ou* tricky!

(d) (*gén nég*) (*scrupuleux*) *personne, conscience* scrupulous. **des procédés peu ~s** unscrupulous *ou* dishonest methods; **il ne s'est pas montré très ~ envers vous** he hasn't behaved very fairly *ou* decently towards you.

(e) (*raffiné*) *sentiment, goût, esprit, style* refined, delicate; *attention* thoughtful; *geste* delicate, thoughtful. **ces propos conviennent peu à des oreilles ~es** this conversation isn't suitable for delicate *ou* sensitive ears.

(f) (*précis*) *nuance* subtle, fine, delicate; *oreille* sensitive, fine; *travail* fine, delicate.

(g) (*léger*) *toucher, touche* gentle, delicate. **prendre qch d'un geste ~** to take sth gently *ou* delicately.

(h) (*plein de tact*) tactful.

(i) (*exigeant*) fussy, particular. **cet enfant est ~ pour manger** this child is fussy *ou* particular about his food; **faire le ~** (*nourriture*) to be particular *ou* fussy; (*spectacle*) to be squeamish; (*propos*) to be easily shocked.

délicatement [delikatmɑ̃] *adv* **(a)** (*finement*) **tableau ~ coloré** finely *ou* delicately coloured painting; **dentelle ~ ouvragée** finely *ou* delicately worked lace; **mets ~ préparé** daintily *ou* delicately prepared dish.

(b) (*avec précision*) **exécuter un travail ~** to do a piece of work delicately *ou* finely; **nuance ~ exprimée** subtly *ou* finely *ou* delicately expressed shade of meaning.

(c) (*avec légèreté*) **prendre qch ~ entre ses mains** to take sth gently *ou* delicately in one's hands.

(d) (*avec raffinement*) **sentiment ~ exprimé** delicately expressed feeling.

délicatesse [delikatɛs] *nf* **(a)** (*finesse*) *[dentelle, parfum, couleur, forme]* delicacy; *[mets]* daintiness; *[fil, voile, facture, travail]* fineness.

(b) (*fragilité*) *[peau]* tenderness, delicacy; *[tissu]* delicacy.

(c) (*scrupules*) *[personne, procédés]* scrupulousness. **sa manière d'agir manque de ~** his behaviour shows a lack of thoughtfulness.

(d) (*raffinement*) *[sentiment, goût, esprit, style]* refinement, delicacy; *[attention]* thoughtfulness; *[geste]* delicacy, thoughtfulness.

(e) (*tact*) tact. **par ~ il se retira** he withdrew tactfully *ou* out of politeness.

(f) (*précision*) *[nuance]* subtlety, fineness, delicacy; *[oreille]* sensitivity, fineness; *[travail]* fineness, delicacy.

(g) (*légèreté*) gentleness. **il prit le vase avec ~** he picked up the vase gently *ou* delicately.

(h) (*rare: caractère complexe*) *[situation, question]*, (*Méd*) *[opération]* delicacy.

(i) (*prévenances: gén pl*) consideration (*U*), (kind) attentions. **avoir des ~s pour qn** to show attentions to sb, show consideration for sb.

délice [delis] *nm* (*plaisir*) delight. **quel ~ de s'allonger au soleil!** what a delight to lie in the sun!; **se plonger dans l'eau avec ~** to jump into the water with sheer delight; **ce dessert est un vrai ~** this dessert is quite delightful *ou* delicious.

délices [delis] *nfpl* (*plaisirs*) delights. **les ~ de l'étude** the delights of study; **toutes les ~ de la terre se trouvaient réunies là** every worldly delight was to be found there; **faire ses ~ de qch** to take delight in sth; **cette vie rustique ferait les ~ de mon père** this country life would be the delight of my father; **ce livre ferait les ~ de mon père** this book would be a delight to *ou* would delight my father, my father would revel in this book.

délicieusement [delisjøzmɑ̃] *adv* delightfully, exquisitely. **elle chante ~ (bien)** she sings delightfully (well); **c'est ~ beau** it's exquisitely beautiful; **une poire ~ parfumée** a deliciously *ou* delightfully scented pear; **s'enfoncer ~ dans les couvertures** to snuggle down into the covers with delight.

délicieux, -ieuse [delisjø, jøz] *adj fruit* delicious; *goût* delicious, delightful; *lieu, personne, sensation, anecdote* charming, delightful.

délictueux, -ueuse [deliktɥø, ɥøz] *adj* (*Jur*) criminal. **fait ~** criminal act.

délié, e [delje] (*ptp de* **délier**) **1** *adj* **(a)** (*agile*) *doigts* nimble, agile; *esprit* astute, penetrating. **avoir la langue ~e** to have a long tongue (*fig*). **(b)** (*fin*) *taille* slender; *fil, écriture* fine. **2** *nm* *[lettre]* (thin) upstroke. **les pleins et les ~s** the downstrokes and the upstrokes (*in handwriting*); (*Mus*) **avoir un bon ~** to have a flowing *ou* an even touch.

délier [delje] (7) **1** *vt* **(a)** *corde, paquet, prisonnier* to untie; *gerbe* to unbind. **déliez-lui les mains** untie his hands; (*fig*) **~ la langue de qn** to loosen sb's tongue; *V* **bourse.**

(b) **~ qn de** *obligation, serment* to free *ou* release sb from; (*Rel*) *péché* to absolve sb from.

2 se délier *vpr* **(a)** *[lien]* to come untied; *[prisonnier]* to untie o.s., get (o.s.) free; *[langue]* to loosen. **sous l'effet de l'alcool les langues se délient** as alcohol starts to take effect tongues are loosened.

(b) **se ~ d'un serment** to free *ou* release o.s. from an oath.

délimitation [delimitɑsjɔ̃] *nf* (*V* **délimiter**) demarcation; delimitation; definition; determination.

délimiter [delimite] (1) *vt terrain, frontière* to demarcate, delimit; *sujet, rôle* to define (the scope of), delimit; *responsabilités, attributions* to determine.

délinquance [delɛ̃kɑ̃s] *nf* criminality. **~ juvénile** juvenile delinquency.

délinquant, e [delɛ̃kɑ̃, ɑ̃t] **1** *adj* delinquent. **jeunesse ~e** juvenile delinquents *ou* offenders. **2** *nm,f* delinquent, offender. **~ primaire** first offender.

déliquescence [delikesɑ̃s] *nf* **(a)** (*Chim: action*) deliquescence. **(b)** (*fig*) decay. **tomber en ~** to fall into decay.

déliquescent, e [delikesɑ̃, ɑ̃t] *adj* **(a)** (*Chim*) deliquescent. **(b)** (*fig*) *personne* decrepit; *esprit* enfeebled; *régime, mœurs, société* decaying; *atmosphère* devitalizing.

délire [deliʀ] **1** *nm* **(a)** (*Méd*) delirium. **dans un accès de ~** in a fit of delirium; **avoir le** *ou* **du ~** to be delirious, rave; **c'est du ~!*** it's sheer madness! *ou* lunacy!

(b) (*frénésie*) frenzy. **sa passion allait jusqu'au ~** his passion was becoming frenzy (*littér*); **dans le ~ de son imagination** in his wild *ou* frenzied imagination; **acclamé par une foule en ~** acclaimed by a crowd gone wild *ou* berserk *ou* by a frenzied crowd; **quand l'acteur parut, ce fut le** *ou* **du ~*** when the actor appeared there was frenzied excitement.

2: délire alcoolique alcoholic mania; **délire de grandeur** delusions of grandeur; **délire hallucinatoire** hallucinatory delirium; **délire de persécution** persecution mania; (*Littérat*) **délire poétique** poetic frenzy.

délirer [deliʀe] (1) *vi* (*Méd*) to be delirious. **~ de joie** to be delirious with joy; **il délire!*** he's raving!*, he's out of his mind!*

délirium tremens [deliʀjɔmtʀemɛ̃s] *nm* delirium tremens.

délit [deli] *nm* (*gén*) crime, offence; (*Jur*) offence. **~ de fuite** failure to report an accident; **~ de presse** violation of the press laws; *V* **corps, flagrant.**

délivrance [delivʀɑ̃s] *nf* **(a)** *[prisonniers]* release; *[pays]* deliverance, liberation. **il attendait sa ~** he waited for his deliverance.

(b) (*fig: soulagement*) relief. **il est parti, quelle ~!** he's gone — what a relief!

(c) *[passeport, reçu]* issue, delivery; *[ordonnance]* issue; *[lettre, marchandise]* delivery.

(d) (*littér: accouchement*) delivery, confinement.

délivrer [delivʀe] (1) **1** *vt* **(a)** *prisonnier, esclave* to set free. **~ qn de** *rival* to relieve *ou* rid sb of; *liens, obligation* to free sb from, relieve sb of; *crainte* to relieve sb of; **être** *ou* **se sentir délivré d'un grand poids** to be *ou* feel relieved of a great weight.

(b) *passeport, reçu* to issue, deliver; *lettre, marchandise* to deliver; *ordonnance* to give, issue.

2 se délivrer *vpr* *[prisonnier etc]* to free o.s. (*de* from); (*fig*) to get relief (*de* from).

déloger [delɔʒe] (3) **1** *vt locataire* to turn *ou* throw out; *fugitif* to flush out; *lièvre* to start; *objet, ennemi* to dislodge (*de* from). **2** *vi* to move out (*in a hurry*). **délogez de là!** clear out of there!*

déloyal, e, *mpl* **-aux** [delwajal, o] *adj personne* disloyal (*envers* towards); *conduite* disloyal, underhand; *procédé* unfair; (*Sport*) *coup* foul (*épith*), dirty (*épith*). (*Comm*) **concurrence ~e** unfair competition.

déloyalement [delwajalmɑ̃] *adv* disloyally.

déloyauté [delwajote] *nf* **(a)** (*U: V* **déloyal**) disloyalty; unfairness. **(b)** (*action*) disloyal act.

Delphes [dɛlf] *n* Delphi.

delta [dɛlta] *nm* (*Géog, Ling*) delta. (*Aviat*) **à ailes (en) ~** delta-winged.

deltaïque [dɛltaik] *adj* deltaic, delta (*épith*).

deltoïde [dɛltɔid] *adj, nm* (*Méd*) deltoid.

déluge [delyʒ] *nm* (*pluie*) downpour, deluge; *[larmes, paroles, injures]* f ood; *[compliments, coups]* shower; *[sang]* sea. (*Bible*) **le ~** the Flood, the Deluge; **ça date du ~, ça remonte au ~** it's as old as the hills *ou* as Adam, it's out of the Ark; *V* **après.**

déluré, e [delyʀe] (*ptp de* **délurer**) *adj* (*éveillé*) smart, resourceful; (*péj*) forward, pert.

délurer [delyʀe] (1) **1** *vt* (*dégourdir*) to make smart *ou* resourceful; (*péj*) to make forward *ou* pert.

2 se délurer *vpr* (*se dégourdir*) to become smart *ou* resourceful; (*péj*) to become forward *ou* pert. **il s'est déluré au régiment** he became something of a smart lad *ou* he learnt a thing or two* in the army.

démagnétisation [demaɲetizɑsjɔ̃] *nf* demagnetization.

démagnétiser [demaɲetize] (1) *vt* to demagnetize.

démagogie [demagɔʒi] *nf* demagogy, demagoguery.

démagogique [demagɔʒik] *adj* popularity-seeking, demagogic.

démagogue [demagɔg] **1** *nm* demagogue. **2** *adj* calculated to arouse popular support, demagogic.

démaillage [demɑjaʒ] *nm* *[bas]* laddering (*surtout Brit*); *[tricot]* undoing, unravelling.

démailler [demɑje] (1) **1** *vt bas* to ladder (*surtout Brit*); *filet* to undo (the mesh of); *tricot* to undo (the stitches of), unravel; *chaîne* to unlink, separate the links of. **ses bas sont démaillés** her stockings are laddered (*surtout Brit*) *ou* have got ladders (*surtout Brit*) in them.

2 se démailler *vpr* *[bas]* to ladder (*surtout Brit*), run; *[tricot]* to unravel, come unravelled; *[filet]* to develop holes. **la chaîne s'est démaillée** the links of the chain have come apart.

démailloter [demajɔte] (1) *vt enfant* to take off the nappy of (*Brit*) *ou* diaper of (*US*).

demain [d(ə)mɛ̃] *adv* tomorrow. **~ matin** tomorrow morning; **~ soir** tomorrow evening *ou* night; **~ en huit/en quinze** a week/two weeks tomorrow; **à dater** *ou* **à partir de ~** (as) from tomorrow, from tomorrow on; **~ il fera jour** tomorrow is another day; **ce n'est pas ~ la veille*** it's not just around the corner, that won't happen just yet *ou* for a bit yet; **ce n'est pas pour ~*** it's not just around the corner, it's not going to happen in a hurry; **~ est jour férié** tomorrow is a holiday; **à ~** see you tomorrow; **d'ici (à) ~ tout peut changer** everything might be different by tomorrow; (*fig*) **le monde de ~** the world of tomorrow, tomorrow's world; *V* **après, remettre.**

démanché, e [demɑ̃ʃe] (*ptp de* **démancher**) **1** *adj bras* out of joint (*attrib*), dislocated; (*) *objet* loose; *meuble* rickety; *personne* gawky, awkward. **le marteau est ~** the hammer has no handle *ou* has lost its handle. **2** *nm* (*Mus*) shift.

démancher [demɑ̃ʃe] (1) **1** *vt outil* to take the handle off; (*: *disloquer*) *meuble* to knock a leg off; *bras* to put out of joint, dislocate.

2 *vi* (*Mus*) to shift.

3 se démancher *vpr* **(a)** *[outil]* to lose its handle; *[bras]* to be put out of joint, be dislocated; (*) *[meuble, objet]* to fall to bits. **se ~ le bras** to dislocate one's arm, put one's arm out of joint.

(b) (*: *se mettre en quatre*) to go out of one's way, move heaven and earth (*pour faire* to do).

demande [d(ə)mɑ̃d] *nf* **(a)** (*requête*) request (*de* for); (*revendication*) demand (*de* for); (*Admin*) *[emploi, autorisation, naturalisation]* application (*de* for); *[remboursement, dédommagement]* claim (*de* for); (*Écon: opposé à offre*) demand; (*Cartes*) bid. (*gén*) **faire une ~** to make a request; **faire une ~ d'emploi/de naturalisation** to apply for a post/for naturalization; (*annonces*) **'~s d'emploi'** 'situations wanted'; **faire une ~ d'argent/de remboursement** to put in *ou* make a request for money/reimbursement (*à qn* to sb), request money/reimbursement (*à qn* from sb); **et maintenant, à la ~ générale** ... and now, by popular request ...; (*Admin*) **adressez votre ~ au ministère** apply to the ministry; **~ (en mariage)** proposal (of marriage); **faire sa ~ (en mariage)** to propose; **à** *ou* **sur la ~ de qn** at sb's request; **sur ~** on request; (*Admin*) on application.

(b) (*Jur*) **~ en divorce** divorce petition; **~ en renvoi** request for remittal; **~ principale/accessoire/subsidiaire** chief/secondary/contingency petition.

(c) (†: *question*) question.

demandé, e [d(ə)mɑ̃de] (*ptp de* **demander**) *adj* (*Comm etc*) in demand. **cet article est très ~** this item is (very) much in demand, there is a great demand for this item.

demander [d(ə)mɑ̃de] (1) **1** *vt* **(a)** (*solliciter*) *chose, conseil, réponse, entrevue* to ask for, request (*frm*); *volontaire* to call for, ask for; (*Admin, Jur*) *délai, emploi, divorce* to apply for; *indemnité, dommages* to claim; *réunion, enquête* to call for, ask for. **~ qch à qn** to ask sb for sth; **~ un service** *ou* **une faveur à qn** to ask sb a favour; (*Mil*) **~ une permission** to ask for *ou* request (*frm*) leave; **~ la permission de** to ask *ou* request (*frm*) permission to; **~ à voir qn/à parler à qn** to ask to see sb/to speak to sb; **~ à qn de faire** *ou* **qu'il fasse qch** to ask *ou* request (*frm*) sb to do sth; **il a demandé à partir plus tôt** he has asked to leave early; **~ la paix** to sue for peace; **~ des nouvelles de qn, ~ après qn*** to inquire *ou* ask after sb; **puis-je vous ~ (de me passer) du pain?** may I trouble you for some bread?, would you mind passing me some bread?; **vous n'avez qu'à ~** you only have to ask.

(b) (*appeler*) *médecin, prêtre, plombier* to send for. **il va fal-**

loir ~ un médecin we'll have to send for *ou* call (out *ou* for) a doctor; **demande un médecin** send for a doctor; **le blessé demande un prêtre** the injured man is asking *ou* calling for a priest.

(c) (*au téléphone, au bureau etc*) *personne, numéro* to ask for. (*au téléphone*) **demandez-moi M X** get me Mr X; **on le demande au bureau/au téléphone** he is wanted at the office/on the phone, someone is asking for him at the office/on the phone; **le patron vous demande** the boss wants to see you *ou* speak to you *ou* is asking to see you.

(d) (*désirer*) to be asking for, want. **ils demandent 10 F de l'heure et une semaine de congé** they are asking (for) 10 francs an hour and a week's holiday; **il demande à partir plus tôt** he wants to *ou* is asking to leave early *ou* earlier; **il demande qu'on le laisse partir** he wants us to *ou* is asking us to let him go; **il ne demande qu'à apprendre/à se laisser convaincre** all he wants is to learn/to be convinced, he's only too willing to learn/be convinced; **le chat miaule, il demande son lait** the cat's mewing — he's asking for his milk; **je ne demande pas mieux!** *ou* **que ça!** that's exactly *ou* just what I'd like!, I'll be *ou* I'm only too pleased!; **il ne demandera pas mieux que de vous aider** he'll be only too pleased to help you; **je demande à voir!*** that I MUST see!; **tout ce que l'on demande c'est qu'il fasse beau** all (that) we ask is that we have good weather.

(e) (*s'enquérir de*) *heure, nom, chemin* to ask. **~ qch à qn** to ask sb sth; **~ quand/comment/pourquoi c'est arrivé** to ask when/how/why it happened; **va ~!** go and ask!; **je ne t'ai rien demandé, je ne te demande rien** I didn't ask you, I'm not asking you; (*excl*) **je vous le demande!, je vous demande un peu!*** honestly!* what do you think of that!

(f) (*nécessiter*) *[travail, décision etc]* to require, need. **cela demande un effort** it requires an effort; **ces plantes demandent beaucoup d'eau/à être arrosées** these plants need *ou* require a lot of water/watering; **ce travail va (lui) ~ 6 heures** this job will take (him) 6 hours *ou* will require 6 hours, he'll need 6 hours to do this job; **cette proposition demande réflexion** this proposal needs thinking over; **cette proposition demande toute votre attention** this proposal calls for *ou* requires your full attention.

(g) (*exiger*) **~ qch de** *ou* **à qn** to ask sth of sb; **il demande de ses employés qu'ils travaillent bien** he asks *ou* requires of his employees that they work well; **~ beaucoup à** *ou* **de la vie/de ses élèves** to ask a lot out of life *ou* of life/of one's pupils; **il ne faut pas trop lui en ~!** you mustn't ask too much of him!

(h) (*Comm*) **ils (en) demandent 50 F** they are asking *ou* want 50 francs (for it); **ils m'en ont demandé 50 F** they asked (me) for 50 francs for it; **'on demande une vendeuse'** 'shop assistant wanted'; **ils demandent 3 vendeuses** they are advertising for *ou* they want 3 shop assistants; **on demande beaucoup de vendeuses en ce moment** shop assistants are very much in demand *ou* are in great demand just now.

(i) (*loc*) **~ aide et assistance** to request aid; **~ audience** to request an audience; **~ l'aumône** *ou* **la charité** to ask *ou* beg for charity; **~ grâce** to ask for mercy; **~ l'impossible** to ask the impossible; **~ pardon à qn** to apologize to sb; **je vous demande pardon** I apologize, I'm sorry; **~ la lune** to ask for the moon; **~ la parole** to ask to be allowed to speak; **~ qn en mariage, ~ la main de qn** to ask for sb's hand (in marriage); **sans ~ son reste** without waiting for more.

2 se demander *vpr* (*hésiter, douter*) to wonder. **on peut vraiment se ~ s'il a perdu la tête** one may well wonder *ou* ask if he isn't out of his mind; **il se demande où aller/ce qu'il doit faire** he is wondering where to go/what to do; **il se demanda: suis-je vraiment aussi bête?** he asked himself *ou* wondered: am I really so stupid?; **ils se demandent bien pourquoi il a démissionné** they can't think why he resigned, they really wonder why he resigned; **cela ne se demande pas!** that's a stupid question!

demandeur[1], -deresse [d(ə)mɑ̃dœʀ, dʀɛs] *nm,f* (*Jur*) plaintiff; (*en divorce*) petitioner. **~ en appel** appellant.

demandeur[2], -euse [d(ə)mɑ̃dœʀ, øz] *nm,f* (*Téléc*) caller. **~ d'emploi** person looking for work, job-seeker.

démangeaison [demɑ̃ʒɛzɔ̃] *nf* itching (*U*), itching sensation. **avoir des ~s** to be itching; **j'ai des ~s dans le dos** my back is itching; **j'ai une ~** I've got an itch; (*fig rare*) **~ de faire** itch *ou* urge to do; (*fig rare*) **~ de qch** longing for sth.

démanger [demɑ̃ʒe] (3) *vt*: **son dos/son coup de soleil le** *ou* (*rare*) **lui démange** his back/sunburn itches *ou* is itching; **où est-ce que ça (vous) démange?** where does it *ou* do you itch?, where is it *ou* are you itching?; **ça démange** it itches, it's itching; (*fig*) **le poing le démange** he's itching for a fight; (*fig*) **la main me démange** I'm itching *ou* dying to hit him (*ou* her *etc*); (*fig*) **la langue me démange** I'm dying to speak; (*fig*) **ça me démange de faire ..., l'envie me démange de faire ...** I'm dying to do ... .

démantèlement [demɑ̃tɛlmɑ̃] *nm* (*V* **démanteler**) demolition, demolishing; breaking up; bringing down.

démanteler [demɑ̃tle] (5) *vt* (*Mil*) *forteresse, remparts* to demolish; *organisation, gang* to break up; (*fig*) *empire, monarchie* to bring down.

démantibuler [demɑ̃tibyle] (1) **1** *vt* (*) *objet* to demolish, break up. **2 se démantibuler** *vpr* (*) to fall apart.

démaquillage [demakijaʒ] *nm* removal of make-up. **le ~ d'un acteur** the removal of an actor's make-up; **l'acteur commença son ~** the actor started to take off *ou* remove his make-up; **crème pour le ~** make-up remover, make-up removing cream.

démaquillant, e [demakijɑ̃, ɑ̃t] **1** *adj* make-up removing (*épith*). **2** *nm* make-up remover.

démaquiller [demakije] (1) **1** *vt yeux, visage* to remove the make-up from, take the make-up off. **~ un acteur** to take off *ou* remove an actor's make-up. **2 se démaquiller** *vpr* to take one's make-up off, remove one's make-up.

démarcage [demaʀkaʒ] *nm* = **démarquage.**

démarcatif, -ive [demaʀkatif, iv] *adj* (*rare*) demarcating.

démarcation [demaʀkɑsjɔ̃] *nf* demarcation (*de, entre* between); *V* **ligne[1]**.

démarchage [demaʀʃaʒ] *nm* door-to-door selling.

démarche [demaʀʃ(ə)] *nf* **(a)** (*façon de marcher*) gait, walk. **avoir une ~ pesante/gauche** to have a heavy/an awkward gait *ou* walk, walk heavily/awkwardly.

(b) (*intervention*) step. **faire une ~ auprès de qn (pour obtenir qch)** to approach sb (to obtain sth); **toutes nos ~s se sont trouvées sans effet** none of the steps we took were effective; **les ~s nécessaires pour obtenir qch** the necessary *ou* required procedures *ou* steps to obtain sth; **l'idée de (faire) cette ~ m'effrayait** I was frightened at the idea of (taking) this step.

(c) (*cheminement*) *[raisonnement, pensée]* processes; (*façon de penser*) thought processes.

démarcheur [demaʀʃœʀ] *nm* (*vendeur*) door-to-door salesman; (*pour un parti etc*) (door-to-door) canvasser.

démarcheuse [demaʀʃøz] *nf* (*vendeuse*) door-to-door saleswoman; (*pour un parti etc*) (door-to-door) canvasser.

démarier [demaʀje] (7) *vt* (*Agr*) to thin out.

démarquage [demaʀkaʒ] *nm [linge, argenterie]* removal of the identifying mark(s) (*de* on); *[auteur, œuvre]* copying (*de* from). (*Sport*) **le ~ d'un joueur** the drawing away of a marker; **cet ouvrage est un ~ grossier** this work is a crude plagiarism *ou* copy.

démarque [demaʀk(ə)] *nf* (*Comm*) *[article]* markdown, marking-down.

démarqué, e [demaʀke] (*ptp de* **démarquer**) *adj* (*Sport*) *joueur* unmarked.

démarquer [demaʀke] (1) **1** *vt* **(a)** *linge, argenterie* to remove the (identifying) mark(s) from; (*Comm*) *article* to mark down. **(b)** *œuvre, auteur* to plagiarize, copy. **(c)** (*Sport*) *joueur* to stop marking. **2 se démarquer** *vpr* (*Sport*) to lose *ou* shake off one's marker. (*fig*) **se ~ de** to dissociate o.s. from.

démarrage [demaʀaʒ] **1** *nm* **(a)** (*départ*) *[véhicule]* moving off (*U*). **~ en trombe** shooting off (*U*); **il a calé au ~** he stalled as he moved off; **secoués à chaque ~ du bus** shaken about every time the bus moved off.

(b) (*fig*) *[affaire, campagne, élève, débutant]* start. **l'excellent/le difficile ~ de la campagne électorale** the excellent/difficult start to the electoral campaign.

(c) (*Sport: accélération*) *[coureur]* pulling away (*U*).

(d) (*Naut*) casting off, unmooring.

(e) (*rare: mise en marche*) *[véhicule]* starting. **le ~ d'une affaire/campagne** getting an affair/a campaign going.

2: démarrage en côte hill start; **démarrage à la manivelle** crank-starting.

démarrer [demaʀe] (1) **1** *vi* **(a)** *[moteur, conducteur]* to start (up); *[véhicule]* to move off; (*fig*) *[affaire, campagne]* to get moving, get off the ground; *[élève, débutant]* to start off. **l'affaire a bien démarré** the affair got off to a good start *ou* started off well; **~ en trombe** to shoot off; **faire ~** *affaire, campagne* to get moving, get off the ground; **l'économie va-t-elle enfin ~?** is the economy at last going to get moving? *ou* going to get off the ground?; **il a bien démarré en latin** he has got off to a good start in Latin, he started off well in Latin.

(b) (*Sport: accélérer*) *[coureur]* to pull away.

(c) (*Naut*) to cast off, unmoor.

2 démarrer de *vt indir* (*démordre de*) *idée, projet* to let go of; **il ne veut pas ~ de son idée** he just won't let go of his idea.

3 *vt* (*rare*) *véhicule* to start, get started; (*Naut*) *embarcation* to cast off, unmoor; (**fig*) *affaire, travail* to get going on*.

démarreur [demaʀœʀ] *nm* (*Aut*) starter.

démasquer [demaske] (1) **1** *vt* **(a)** (*dévoiler*) *imposteur, espion, hypocrisie* to unmask; *plan* to unveil, uncover. **~ ses batteries** (*Mil*) to unmask one's batteries; (*fig*) to show one's hand, lay one's cards on the table.

(b) (*rare lit*) to unmask.

2 se démasquer *vpr [imposteur]* to drop one's mask; (*rare lit*) to take off one's mask.

dématage [dematɑʒ] *nm* (*V* **démâter**) dismasting; losing its masts.

démâter [demɑte] (1) **1** *vt* to dismast. **2** *vi* to lose its masts, be dismasted.

d'emblée [dɑ̃ble] *loc adv V* **emblée.**

démêlage [demɛlaʒ] *nm* (*lit, fig*) disentangling, untangling.

démêlé [demele] *nm* (*dispute*) dispute, quarrel. (*ennuis*) **~s** problems; **il a eu des ~s avec la justice** he has fallen foul of the law *ou* has had some problems *ou* trouble with the law; **il risque d'avoir des ~s avec l'administration** he's likely to come up against the authorities.

démêler [demele] (1) **1** *vt* **(a)** *ficelle, écheveau* to disentangle, untangle; *cheveux* to untangle, comb out; (*fig*) *problème, situation* to untangle, sort out; (*fig*) *intentions, machinations* to unravel, get to the bottom of. († *ou littér*) **~ qch d'avec** *ou* **de** to distinguish *ou* tell sth from.

(b) (*littér: débattre*) **~ qch avec qn** to dispute sth with sb; **je ne veux rien avoir à ~ avec lui** I do not wish to have to contend with him.

2 se démêler *vpr* (†, *littér: se tirer de*) **se ~ de** *embarras, difficultés* to disentangle o.s. from, extricate o.s. from.

démêloir [demɛlwaʀ] *nm* (large-toothed) comb.

démêlures [demɛlyʀ] *nfpl* (*rare*) combings.

démembrement [demɑ̃bʀəmɑ̃] *nm* (*V* **démembrer**) dismemberment; slicing up.

démembrer [demɑ̃bʀe] (1) *vt animal* to dismember; *domaine, pays conquis* to slice up, carve up.

déménagement [demenaʒmɑ̃] *nm* **(a)** *[meubles]* removal; *[pièce]* emptying (of furniture) (*U*). **camion de ~** removal van; **le ~ du mobilier s'est bien passé** moving the furniture *ou* the removal of the furniture went off well; **le ~ du bureau/laboratoire a posé des problèmes** moving the furniture out of the office/laboratory *ou* emptying the office/laboratory of (its) furniture proved (to be) no easy matter; **ils ont fait 4 ~s en 3 jours** they made 4 removals in 3 days.
(b) (*changement de domicile*) move, moving (house) (*U*). **faire un ~** to move (house); **on a dû perdre ça pendant le ~** we must have lost that during the move; **3 ~s en une année, c'est trop** 3 moves in one year is too much, moving (house) 3 times in one year is too much.

déménager [demenaʒe] (3) **1** *vt meubles, affaires* to move, remove; *maison, pièce* to move the furniture out of, empty (of furniture).
2 *vi* **(a)** to move (house). **~ à la cloche de bois** to (do a moonlight) flit (*Brit*), shoot the moon.
(b) (‡) (*partir*) to clear off‡; (*aller très vite*) to shift*. **il déménage avec cette bagnole!** he doesn't half shift with that car!‡
(c) (‡: *être fou*) to be off one's rocker‡.

déménageur [demenaʒœʀ] *nm* (*entrepreneur*) furniture remover; (*ouvrier*) removal man (*Brit*), (furniture) mover (*US*).

démence [demɑ̃s] *nf* (*Méd*) dementia; (*Jur*) mental disorder; (*gén*) madness, insanity. **c'est de la ~** it's (sheer) madness, it's insane; (*Méd*) **~ précoce** dementia praecox.

démener (se) [dɛmne] (5) *vpr* (*se débattre*) to thrash about, struggle (violently); (*se dépenser*) to exert o.s. **se ~ comme un beau diable** to thrash about *ou* struggle violently; **si on se démène un peu on aura fini avant la nuit** if we put our back(s) into it a bit* *ou* if we exert ourselves a bit we'll finish before nightfall; **ils se démenèrent tant et si bien que ...** they exerted themselves to such an extent that ..., they made such a great effort that ... .

dément, e [demɑ̃, ɑ̃t] **1** *adj* mad, insane. **c'est ~!** it's incredible! *ou* unbelievable! **2** *nm,f* (*Méd*) demented person.

démenti [demɑ̃ti] *nm* (*déclaration*) denial, refutation; (*fig: apporté par les faits, les circonstances*) refutation. **opposer un ~ à** *nouvelle, allégations, rumeurs* to deny formally; **publier un ~** to publish a denial; **sa version des faits reste sans ~** his version of the facts remains uncontradicted *ou* unchallenged; (*fig*) **son expression opposait un ~ à ses paroles** his expression belied his words.

démentiel, -ielle [demɑ̃sjɛl] *adj* insane.

démentir [demɑ̃tiʀ] (16) **1** *vt* **(a)** *[personne] nouvelle, rumeur* to refute, deny; *personne* to contradict. **~ (formellement) que ...** to deny formally that ... ; **il dément ses principes par son attitude** he belies his principles by his (very) attitude.
(b) *[faits] témoignage* to refute; *apparences* to belie; *espoirs* to disappoint. **la douceur de son sourire est démentie par la dureté de son regard** the hardness in her eyes belies the sweetness of her smile; **les résultats ont démenti les pronostics des spécialistes** the results have not lived up to *ou* come up to the predictions of the specialists.
2 se démentir *vpr* (*nég: cesser*) **son amitié/sa fidélité ne s'est jamais démentie** his friendship/loyalty has never failed; **leur intérêt pour ces mystères, qui ne s'est jamais démenti** their unfailing *ou* never-failing interest in these mysteries.

démerdard‡ [demɛʀdaʀ] *adj m*: **il est ~, c'est un ~** he's a crafty bugger‡‡ (*Brit*) *ou* shrewd customer*, there are no flies on him (*Brit*); **il n'est pas ~ pour deux sous** he's bloody clueless‡ (*Brit*), he hasn't got a clue*.

démerder (se)‡ [demɛʀde] (1) *vpr* (*se dépêcher*) to get one's finger out‡ (*Brit*), get a move on. (*se débrouiller*) **il sait se ~ dans la vie** he knows how to look after himself all right*, he knows his way around all right*; (*se tirer d'affaire*) **il a voulu y aller, maintenant qu'il se démerde tout seul** he wanted to go so now he can get out of his own bloody (*Brit*) *ou* damn mess‡; **il s'est démerdé pour avoir une permission** the crafty bugger‡‡ (*Brit*) *ou* son-of-a-bitch‡ wangled himself some leave.

démerdeur‡ [demɛʀdœʀ] *adj m* (*rare*) = **démerdard‡**.

démérite [demeʀit] *nm* (*littér*) demerit (*littér*), fault. **où est son ~, dans ce cas?** what has he done to merit this disfavour? *ou* censure?, wherein lies his fault in this case? (*littér*); **une erreur qui entraîna le ~** an error that brought censure *ou* disfavour in its wake; **son ~ fut d'avoir ...** his fault *ou* demerit was to have ... .

démériter [demeʀite] (1) **1 démériter de** *vt indir patrie, institution* to show o.s. unworthy of.
2 *vi* (*Rel*) to deserve to fall from grace. (*gén*) **~ auprès de qn *ou* aux yeux de qn** to come down in sb's eyes *ou* regard (*frm*); **en quoi a-t-il démérité?** wherein lies his fault?, what has he done to deserve this censure?; **il n'a jamais démérité** he has never been guilty of an unworthy action.

démesure [deməzyʀ] *nf* *[personnage]* excessiveness, immoderation; *[propos, exigences, style]* outrageousness, immoderateness. **la ~, comme mode de vie** immoderation as a way of life.

démesuré, e [deməzyʀe] *adj orgueil, ambition, prétentions, taille* disproportionate, immoderate, inordinate; *territoire, distances* vast, enormous; (*hum*) *membres* enormous.

démesurément [deməzyʀemɑ̃] *adv exagérer, augmenter* disproportionately, immoderately, inordinately. **territoire qui s'étendait ~** territory of vast *ou* inordinate proportions; **~ long** excessively *ou* immoderately *ou* inordinately long.

démettre [demɛtʀ(ə)] (56) **1** *vt* **(a)** (*disloquer*) *articulation* to dislocate. **se ~ le poignet/la cheville** to dislocate one's wrist/ankle, put one's wrist/ankle out of joint.
(b) (*révoquer*) **~ qn de ses fonctions/son poste** to dismiss sb from his duties/post.
(c) (*Jur*) **~ qn de son appel** to dismiss sb's appeal.
2 se démettre *vpr* (*frm: démissionner*) to resign, hand in one's resignation. **se ~ de ses fonctions/son poste** to resign (from) one's duties/post, hand in one's resignation.

demeurant [dəmœʀɑ̃] *nm*: **au ~** for all that.

demeure [dəmœʀ] *nf* **(a)** (*maison*) residence; (*littér: domicile*) residence, dwelling place (*littér*); *V* **dernier**.
(b) (*loc*) **à ~** *installations* permanent; **s'installer à ~ dans la ville** to make one's permanent home *ou* set o.s. up permanently in the town; **il ne faudrait pas qu'ils y restent à ~** they mustn't stay there permanently; **mettre qn en ~ de faire qch** to instruct *ou* order sb to do sth; (*Jur*) **mettre qn en ~ (de payer)** to give sb notice to pay; *V* **mise**[2].

demeuré, e [dəmœʀe] **1** *ptp de* **demeurer**. **2** *adj* half-witted. **3** *nm,f* half-wit.

demeurer [dəmœʀe] (1) *vi* **(a)** (*avec aux avoir*) **~ quelque part** (*habiter*) to live somewhere; (*séjourner*) to stay somewhere; **il demeure rue d'Ulm** he lives in the rue d'Ulm.
(b) (*frm: avec aux être*) (*avec attrib, adv de lieu: rester*) to remain; (*subsister*) to remain, subsist. **~ fidèle/quelque part** to remain faithful/somewhere; **il lui faut ~ couché** he must remain in bed; **la conversation en est demeurée là** the conversation was taken no further *ou* was left at that.
(c) (*frm: être transmis*) **~ à qn** to be left to sb; **la maison leur est demeurée de leur mère** the house was left to them by their mother, they inherited the house from their mother.

demi[1] [d(ə)mi] *adv*: **~ plein/nu** half-full/-naked; **il n'était qu'à ~ rassuré** he was only half reassured; **il ne te croit qu'à ~** he only half believes you; **il a fait le travail à ~** he has (only) done half the work, he has (only) half done the work; **je ne fais pas les choses à ~** I don't do things by halves; **ouvrir la porte à ~** to half open the door, open the door halfway.

demi[2]**, e** [d(ə)mi] **1** *adj* **(a)** (*avant n: inv, avec trait d'union*) **une ~-livre/-douzaine/-journée** half a pound/dozen/day, a half-pound/half-dozen/half-day; **un ~-tour de clef** half a turn of the key, a half turn of the key; *V* **demi-**.
(b) (*après n: avec et, nominal*) **une livre/heure et ~e** one and a half pounds/hours, a pound/an hour and a half; **un centimètre/kilo et ~** one and a half centimetres/kilos, one centimetre/kilo and a half; **à midi/six heures et ~e** at half past twelve/six; **2 fois et ~e plus grand/autant** 2 and a half times greater/as much; *V* **malin**.
2 *nm,f* (*fonction pronominale*) **un ~, une ~e** (a) half; **un pain/une bouteille? — non un~/une ~e** one loaf/bottle? — no, (a) half *ou* no, half a loaf/bottle *ou* no, a half-loaf/half-bottle; **est-ce qu'un ~ suffira, ou faut-il deux tiers?** will (a) half do, or do we need two-thirds? **deux ~s font un entier** two halves make a whole.
3 demie *nf* (*à l'horloge*) **la ~e** the half-hour; **la ~e a sonné** the half-hour has struck; **c'est déjà la ~e** it's already half past; **sur la ~e de 6 heures** at half past 6; **on part à la ~e** we'll leave at half past; **le bus passe à la ~e** the bus comes by at half past (the hour), the bus comes by on the half-hour; **la pendule sonne les heures et les ~es** the clock strikes the hours and the halves *ou* the half-hours.
4 *nm* **(a)** (*bière*) ≈ half-pint, half*. **garçon, un ~** a half-pint *ou* a half, please.
(b) (*Sport*) half-back. (*Rugby*) **~ de mêlée** scrum half; (*Rugby*) **~ d'ouverture** stand-off half.

demi- [d(ə)mi] **1** *préf* half-; semi... .
2: **demi-bas** *nm inv* kneesock; **demi-bouteille** *nf, pl* **demi-bouteilles** half-bottle; **demi-cercle** *nm, pl* **demi-cercles** (*figure*) semicircle; (*instrument*) protractor; **en demi-cercle** semicircular; **demi-colonne** *nf, pl* **demi-colonnes** semi-column, demi-column, half-column; **demi-deuil** *nm* half-mourning (*V* **poularde**); **demi-dieu** *nm, pl* **demi-dieux** demigod; **demi-douzaine** *nf, pl* **demi-douzaines** half-a-dozen, half-dozen; **une demi-douzaine d'œufs** half-a-dozen eggs, a half-dozen eggs; **une demi-douzaine suffit** a half-dozen *ou* half-a-dozen will do; **cette demi-douzaine d'apéritifs m'a coupé les jambes** those half-a-dozen drinks knocked me off my feet; (*Géom*) **demi-droite** *nf, pl* **demi-droites** half-line, half-ray; **demi-fin, e** *adj petit pois* small; *aiguille* medium; *or* 12-carat; (*Sport*) **demi-finale** *nf, pl* **demi-finales** semifinal; (*Sport*) **demi-finaliste** *nmf, pl* **demi-finalistes** semifinalist; **demi-fond** *nm, pl* **demi-fonds** (*discipline*) medium-distance running; (*épreuve*) medium-distance race; **coureur de demi-fond** medium-distance runner; **demi-frère** *nm, pl* **demi-frères** half-brother; (*Comm*) **demi-gros** *nm* wholesale trade; **demi-heure** *nf, pl* **demi-heures**: **une demi-heure** half an hour, a half-hour; **la première demi-heure passe très lentement** the first half-hour goes very slowly; **demi-jour** *nm, pl* **demi-jour(s)** (*gén*) half-light; (*le soir*) twilight; **demi-journée** *nf, pl* **demi-journées**: **une demi-journée** half a day, a half-day; **faire des demi-journées de nettoyage/couture** to work half-days cleaning/sewing; **travailler à la demi-journée** to work half-days; **demi-litre** *nm, pl* **demi-litres**: **un demi-litre (de)** half a litre (of), a half-litre (of); **ce demi-litre de lait** this half-litre of milk; (*Sport*) **demi-longueur** *nf, pl* **demi-longueurs**: **une demi-longueur** half a length, a half-length; **la demi-longueur d'avance qui lui a valu le prix** the half-length lead that won him the prize; **demi-lune** *nf, pl* **demi-lunes** (*Mil*) demilune; (*Rail*) relief line; **en demi-lune** semicircular, half-moon (*epith*); **demi-mal** *nm*: **il n'y a que *ou* ce n'est que demi-mal** it could have been worse, there's no great harm done; **demi-mesure** *nf, pl* **demi-mesures** half-measure; (*Habillement*) **la demi-mesure** semifinished clothing; **s'habiller en demi-mesure** to buy semi-finished

clothing; **demi-mondaine** *nf, pl* **demi-mondaines** demi-mondaine; **demi-monde** *nm* demi-monde; **demi-mot** *nm*: **à demi-mot** without having to spell things out; **se faire comprendre à demi-mot** to make o.s. understood without having to spell it out; **ils se comprenaient à demi-mot** they didn't have to spell things out to each other; (*Mus*) **demi-pause** *nf, pl* **demi-pauses** minim rest; **demi-pension** *nf* (*à l'hôtel*) half-board, bed and breakfast with dinner (*Brit*); (*Scol*) half-board; **demi-pensionnaire** *nmf, pl* **demi-pensionnaires** half-boarder, school luncher; **demi-place** *nf, pl* **demi-places** (*Transport*) half-fare; (*Ciné, Théât etc*) half-price ticket *ou* seat; (*péj*) **demi-portion** *nf, pl* **demi-portions** weed* (*péj*), weedy* person (*péj*); **demi-queue** *nm inv*: **(piano) demi-queue** baby grand; **demi-reliure** *nf, pl* **demi-reliures** half-binding; **demi-saison** *nf* spring *ou* autumn, cool season; **un manteau de demi-saison** a spring *ou* an autumn coat; **demi-sel** (*adj inv*) *beurre* slightly salted; **(fromage) demi-sel** (slightly salted) cream cheese; (*nm: arg Crime: pl* **demi-sels**) small-time pimp; **demi-sœur** *nf, pl* **demi-sœurs** half-sister; (*Mil*) **demi-solde** *nf, pl* **demi-soldes** half-pay; **demi-sommeil** *nm* half-sleep; (*Mus*) **demi-soupir** *nm, pl* **demi-soupirs** quaver rest (*surtout Brit*); **demi-tarif** *nm* half-price; (*Transport*) half-fare; **billet** *etc* **(à) demi-tarif** half-price ticket *etc*; **voyager à demi-tarif** to travel at half-fare; (*Art, fig*) **demi-teinte** *nf, pl* **demi-teintes** half-tone; (*Mus*) **demi-ton** *nm, pl* **demi-tons** semitone, half-tone (*US*); (*Aviat*) **demi-tonneau** *nm, pl* **demi-tonneaux** half flick (*Brit*) *ou* snap (*US*) roll; (*lit*) **demi-tour** *nm, pl* **demi-tours** about-turn; (*Aut*) U-turn; (*lit*) **faire un demi-tour** to make an about-turn; (*fig*) **faire demi-tour** to (turn and) go back; **demi-vierge** *nf, pl* **demi-vierges** virgin in name only; (*Sport*) **demi-volée** *nf, pl* **demi-volées** half-volley.

demiard [dəmjaʀ] *nm* (*Can*) half-pint (*Brit*), 0,284 litre.

démilitarisation [demilitaʀizɑsjɔ̃] *nf* demilitarization.

démilitariser [demilitaʀize] (1) *vt* to demilitarize.

déminage [deminaʒ] *nm* *[terrain]* mine clearance; *[eaux]* minesweeping.

déminer [demine] (1) *vt* to clear of mines.

démineur [deminœʀ] *nm* bomb disposal expert.

démis, e [demi, iz] (*ptp de* **démettre**) *adj* dislocated.

démission [demisjɔ̃] *nf* (*lit*) resignation; (*fig*) abdication. **donner sa ~** to hand in *ou* tender (*frm*) one's resignation; **la ~ des parents modernes** the abdication of parental responsibilities on the part of modern parents.

démissionnaire [demisjɔnɛʀ] **1** *adj* resigning, who has resigned. **2** *nmf* person resigning.

démissionner [demisjɔne] (1) **1** *vi* to resign, hand in one's notice; (*fig*) *[parents, enseignants]* to give up. **2** *vt* (*iro*) **~ qn*** to give sb his cards* (*Brit*) *ou* his pink slip* (*US*); **on l'a démissionné** they persuaded him to resign (*iro*).

démiurge [demjyʀʒ(ə)] *nm* demiurge.

démobilisation [demɔbilizɑsjɔ̃] *nf* demobilization, demob*.

démobiliser [demɔbilize] (1) *vt* to demobilize, demob*.

démocrate [demɔkʀat] **1** *adj* democratic. **2** *nmf* democrat.

démocrate-chrétien, -ienne [demɔkʀatkʀetjɛ̃, jɛn] *adj, nm,f* Christian Democrat.

démocratie [demɔkʀasi] *nf* democracy. **~ directe/représentative** direct/representative democracy; **~ populaire** people's democracy.

démocratique [demɔkʀatik] *adj* democratic. (*Can*) **le Nouveau Parti Démocratique** the New Democratic Party.

démocratiquement [demɔkʀatikmɑ̃] *adv* democratically.

démocratisation [demɔkʀatizɑsjɔ̃] *nf* democratization.

démocratiser [demɔkʀatize] (1) **1** *vt* to democratize. **2 se démocratiser** *vpr* to democratize, become (more) democratic.

démodé, e [demɔde] (*ptp de* **se démoder**) *adj* *vêtement, manières, institution* old-fashioned, out-of-date; *procédé, théorie* outmoded, old-fashioned.

démoder (se) [demɔde] (1) *vpr* (*V* **démodé**) to become old-fashioned, go out of fashion; to become outmoded.

démographe [demɔgʀaf] *nmf* demographer, demographist.

démographie [demɔgʀafi] *nf* demography.

démographique [demɔgʀafik] *adj* demographic. **poussée ~** increase in population, population increase.

demoiselle [d(ə)mwazɛl] **1** *nf* **(a)** (*frm, hum: jeune*) young lady; (*d'un certain âge*) single lady, maiden lady. (*dial: fille*) **votre ~*** your daughter.

(b) (††: *noble*) damsel††.

(c) (†: *employée*) **la ~/les ~s du téléphone** the telephone lady/ladies; **~ de magasin** shop lady.

(d) (*Zool*) dragonfly.

(e) (*Tech*) rammer.

2: demoiselle de compagnie (lady's) companion; **demoiselle d'honneur** (*à un mariage*) bridesmaid; (*d'une reine*) maid of honour.

démolir [demɔliʀ] (2) *vt* **(a)** (*lit*) *maison, quartier* to demolish, pull down. **on démolit beaucoup dans le quartier** they are pulling down *ou* demolishing a lot of houses *ou* they are doing a lot of demolition in this area.

(b) (*abîmer*) *jouet, radio, voiture* to wreck, demolish, smash up*. **cet enfant démolit tout!** that child wrecks *ou* demolishes everything!; **ces boissons vous démolissent l'estomac/la santé*** these drinks play havoc with *ou* ruin your stomach//health.

(c) (*fig: détruire*) *autorité* to overthrow, shatter, bring down; *influence* to overthrow, destroy; *doctrine* to demolish, crush; *espoir* to crush, shatter; *foi* to shatter, destroy.

(d) (*fig*) *personne* (*: *abattre*) to do for*, do in*; (‡: *assommer*) to exterminate*, annihilate*; (*: *critiquer*) to slate* (*surtout Brit*), tear to pieces, demolish*. **ces excès/cette maladie l'avait démoli** these excesses/this illness had just about done for him*; **les critiques l'ont démoli/ont démoli sa pièce** the critics tore him/his play to pieces, he/his play was slated* (*surtout Brit*) *ou* demolished* by the critics; **je vais lui ~ le portrait‡** I'm going to smash his face in‡; **ces 40 kilomètres de marche m'ont démoli** that 40-kilometre walk has done for me* *ou* shattered me*, I'm whacked* (*Brit*) *ou* shattered* after that 40-kilometre walk.

démolissage* [demɔlisaʒ] *nm* (*critique*) slating* (*Brit*), panning*.

démolisseur, -euse [demɔlisœʀ, øz] *nm,f* (*ouvrier*) demolition worker; (*entrepreneur*) demolition contractor; (*fig*) *[doctrine]* demolisher.

démolition [demɔlisjɔ̃] *nf* **(a)** *[immeuble, quartier]* demolition, pulling down; (*fig*) *[doctrine etc]* demolition, crushing. **la ~, ça rapporte** there's money in the demolition business, demolition is a profitable business; **entreprise de ~** demolition contractor(s); **l'immeuble est en ~** the building is (in the course of) being demolished; *V* **chantier**.

(b) (*rare: décombres*) **~s** debris (*sg*), ruins.

démon [demɔ̃] *nm* **(a)** (*Rel*) demon, fiend; (*fig*) (*harpie*) harpy; (*séductrice*) evil woman; (*enfant*) devil, demon. **le ~** the Devil; **le ~ de midi** middle-aged lust; **le ~ du jeu** a passion for gambling; **le ~ de la luxure/de l'alcool/de la curiosité** the demon lechery/drink/curiosity; *V* **possédé**.

(b) (*Myth*) genius, daemon. **écoutant son ~ familier/son mauvais ~** listening to his familiar/evil spirit.

démonétisation [demɔnetizɑsjɔ̃] *nf* (*Fin*) demonetization.

démonétiser [demɔnetize] (1) *vt* (*Fin*) to demonetize.

démoniaque [demɔnjak] **1** *adj* demoniac(al), fiendish. **2** *nmf* person possessed by the devil *ou* by an evil spirit, demoniac.

démonologie [demɔnɔlɔʒi] *nf* demonology.

démonstrateur, -trice [demɔ̃stʀatœʀ, tʀis] *nm,f* demonstrator (*of commercial products*).

démonstratif, -ive [demɔ̃stʀatif, iv] *adj* **(a)** *personne, caractère* demonstrative. **peu ~** undemonstrative. **(b)** *argument, preuve* demonstrative, illustrative. **(c)** (*Gram*) demonstrative. **les ~s** the demonstratives.

démonstration [demɔ̃stʀɑsjɔ̃] *nf* **(a)** (*manifestation: gén pl*) **~ de joie/d'amitié** demonstration *ou* show of joy/friendship; **accueillir qn avec des ~s d'amitié** to welcome sb with a great show of friendship; (*Mil*) **~ de force** show of force; (*Mil*) **~ aérienne/navale** display of air/naval strength.

(b) (*gén, Math*) *[vérité, loi]* demonstration; *[théorème]* proof. **cette ~ est convaincante** this demonstration is convincing; **~ par l'absurde** reductio ad absurdum.

(c) (*Comm*) *[fonctionnement, appareil]* demonstration. **faire une ~** to give a demonstration; **faire la ~ d'un appareil** to demonstrate an appliance; **un appareil de ~** a demonstration model.

démontable [demɔ̃tabl(ə)] *adj* (*gén*) that can be dismantled. **armoire ~** knockdown cupboard, cupboard that can be dismantled *ou* taken to pieces.

démontage [demɔ̃taʒ] *nm* (*V* **démonter**) taking down; dismantling; taking to pieces; taking apart; taking off. **pièces perdues lors de ~s successifs** pieces lost during successive dismantling operations; **c'était un ~ difficile** it was a difficult dismantling job *ou* operation, the dismantling was a difficult job *ou* operation.

démonté, e [demɔ̃te] (*ptp de* **démonter**) *adj* (*houleux*) *mer* raging, wild.

démonte-pneu, *pl* **démonte-pneus** [demɔ̃tpnø] *nm* tyre lever (*Brit*), tire iron (*US*).

démonter [demɔ̃te] (1) **1** *vt* **(a)** (*démanteler*) *installation, échafaudage, étagères, tente* to take down, dismantle; *moteur* to strip down, dismantle; *armoire, appareil, horloge, arme* to dismantle, take to pieces, take apart; *circuit électrique* to dismantle.

(b) (*détacher*) *rideau* to take down; *pneu, porte* to take off.

(c) (*déconcerter*) to disconcert. **ça m'a complètement démonté** I was completely taken aback by that, that really disconcerted me; **il ne se laisse jamais ~** he never gets flustered, he's never flustered, he always remains unruffled.

(d) (*Équitation*) *cavalier* to throw, unseat.

2 se démonter *vpr* **(a)** *[assemblage, pièce]* to come apart.

(b) (*perdre son calme: gén nég*) to lose countenance. **répondre sans se ~** to reply without losing countenance; **il ne se démonte pas pour si peu** he's not that easily flustered, it takes more than that to make him lose countenance.

démontrable [demɔ̃tʀabl(ə)] *adj* demonstrable.

démontrer [demɔ̃tʀe] (1) *vt* (*prouver*) *loi, vérité* to demonstrate; *théorème* to prove; (*expliquer*) *fonctionnement* to demonstrate; (*faire ressortir*) *urgence, nécessité* to show, demonstrate. **~ l'égalité de 2 triangles** to demonstrate *ou* prove *ou* show that 2 triangles are equal; **~ qch (à qn) par A plus B** to prove sth conclusively (to sb); **sa hâte démontrait son inquiétude** his haste clearly indicated his anxiety; **tout cela démontre l'urgence de ces réformes** all this goes to show *ou* shows *ou* demonstrates the urgency of these reforms.

démoralisant, e [demɔʀalizɑ̃, ɑ̃t] *adj* demoralizing.

démoralisateur, -trice [demɔʀalizatœʀ, tʀis] *adj* demoralizing.

démoralisation [demɔʀalizɑsjɔ̃] *nf* demoralization.

démoraliser [demɔʀalize] (1) **1** *vt* to demoralize. **2 se démoraliser** *vpr* to lose heart, become demoralized.

démordre [demɔʀdʀ(ə)] (41) *vi*: **il ne démord pas de son avis/sa décision** he is sticking to his opinion/decision, he won't give up his opinion/decision; **il ne veut pas en ~** he won't budge an inch, he is sticking to his guns.

Démosthène [demɔstɛn] *nm* Demosthenes.

démoucheté, e [demuʃte] *adj* *fleuret* unbuttoned.

démoulage [demulaʒ] *nm* (*V* **démouler**) removal from the mould; turning out.

démouler [demule] (1) *vt statue* to remove from the mould; *flan, gâteau* to turn out.

démoustication [demustikɑsjɔ̃] *nf* clearing of mosquitoes (*de* from).

démoustiquer [demustike] (1) *vt* to clear of mosquitoes.

démultiplicateur, -trice [demyltiplikatœʀ, tʀis] **1** *adj* reduction (*épith*), reducing (*épith*). **2** *nm* reduction system.

démultiplication [demyltiplikɑsjɔ̃] *nf* (*procédé*) reduction; (*rapport*) reduction ratio.

démultiplier [demyltiplije] (7) *vt* to reduce, gear down.

démuni, e [demyni] (*ptp de* **démunir**) *adj* **(a)** (*sans ressources*) impoverished.
(b) (*privé de*) ~ **de** without, lacking in; ~ **d'ornements** unornamented, unadorned; ~ **de protection** unprotected; ~ **de défenses** undefended; ~ **de talents/d'attraits** without talent/attraction, untalented/unattractive; ~ **d'intérêt** lacking in interest, without interest, uninteresting; ~ **de tout** destitute; ~ **d'argent** penniless, without money; ~ **de papiers d'identité** without identity papers.

démunir [demyniʀ] (2) **1** *vt*: ~ **qn de** *vivres* to deprive sb of; *ressources, argent* to divest *ou* deprive sb of; ~ **qch de** to divest sth of. **2 se démunir** *vpr* (*se défaire de*) **se** ~ **de** to part with, give up.

démystification [demistifikɑsjɔ̃] *nf* enlightenment.

démystifier [demistifje] (7) *vt* to enlighten, disabuse.

démythifier [demitifje] (7) *vt* to demythologize.

dénasalisation [denazalizɑsjɔ̃] *nf* denasalization.

dénasaliser [denazalize] (1) *vt* to denasalize.

dénatalité [denatalite] *nf* fall *ou* decrease in the birth rate.

dénationalisation [denasjɔnalizɑsjɔ̃] *nf* denationalization.

dénationaliser [denasjɔnalize] (1) *vt* to denationalize.

dénaturation [denatyʀɑsjɔ̃] *nf* (*Tech*) denaturation.

dénaturé, e [denatyʀe] (*ptp de* **dénaturer**) *adj* **(a)** (*Tech*) *alcool, sel* denatured. **(b)** *goût, mœurs, parents* unnatural.

dénaturer [denatyʀe] (1) *vt* **(a)** to distort, misrepresent. **(b)** (*Tech*) *alcool, substance alimentaire* to denature; (*rare: altérer*) *goût, aliment* to alter completely, change the nature of.

dénazification [denazifikɑsjɔ̃] *nf* denazification.

dénégation [denegɑsjɔ̃] *nf* (*gén, Jur*) denial.

déneigement [denɛʒmɑ̃] *nm* snow-clearing (operation), snow removal.

déneiger [deneʒe] (3) *vt* to clear of snow, clear the snow from.

déni [deni] *nm* (*Jur*) ~ **de justice** denial of justice (*by judge in refusing to hear a case*).

déniaiser [denjeze] (1) *vt*: ~ **qn** (*dégourdir*) to teach sb about life; (*dépuceler*) to take away sb's innocence; **se** ~ to learn about life; to lose one's innocence.

dénicher [deniʃe] (1) **1** *vt* **(a)** (*: *trouver*) *objet* to unearth*; *bistro* to discover; *personne* to track *ou* hunt down, run to earth.
(b) (*débusquer*) *fugitif, animal* to drive out (of hiding).
(c) (*enlever du nid*) *œufs, oisillons* to take out of the nest.
2 *vi* (*rare*) *[oiseau]* to leave the nest.

dénicheur, -euse [deniʃœʀ, øz] *nm,f* **(a)** (*hum*) ~ **de** *antiquités, trouvailles* unearther of (*hum*). **(b)** (*d'oiseaux*) bird's-nester.

dénicotiniser [denikɔtinize] (1) *vt*: **cigarette dénicotinisée** nicotine-free cigarette.

denier [dənje] **1** *nm* **(a)** (*monnaie*) (*Hist romaine*) denarius; (*Hist française*) denier. **ça ne leur a pas coûté un** ~† it didn't cost them a farthing; **l'ayant payé de ses** ~**s**† having paid for it out of his own pocket.
(b) (*Tex: unité de poids*) denier. **bas de 30** ~**s** 30-denier stockings.
2: **le denier du culte** the collection for the clergy; **les 30 deniers de Judas** Judas's 30 pieces of silver; **les deniers publics** the public coffers, public monies.

dénier [denje] (7) *vt* **(a)** *responsabilité* to deny, disclaim; *faute* to deny. **(b)** (*refuser*) ~ **qch à qn** to deny *ou* refuse sb sth.

dénigrement [denigʀəmɑ̃] *nm* denigration, defamation.

dénigrer [denigʀe] (1) *vt* to denigrate, run down.

dénivelée [denivle] *nf* (*Tech*) difference in height (*between firearm and target*).

déniveler [denivle] (4) *vt* (*abaisser*) to make uneven; (*rendre inégal*) to lower, put on a lower level.

dénivellation [denivɛlɑsjɔ̃] *nf*, (*rare*) **dénivellement** [denivɛlmɑ̃] *nm* **(a)** (*U: V* **déniveler**) making uneven; lowering, putting on a lower level. **(b)** (*pente*) slope; (*cassis, creux*) unevenness (*U*), dip. **(c)** (*différence de niveau*) difference in level *ou* altitude. **la dénivellation** *ou* **le dénivellement entre deux points** the difference in level between two points.

dénombrable [denɔ̃bʀabl(ə)] *adj* countable.

dénombrement [denɔ̃bʀəmɑ̃] *nm* counting.

dénombrer [denɔ̃bʀe] (1) *vt* (*compter*) to count; (*énumérer*) to enumerate, list.

dénominateur [denɔminatœʀ] *nm* (*Math*) denominator. (*Math, fig*) ~ **commun** common denominator; **plus petit** ~ **commun** lowest common denominator.

dénominatif, -ive [denɔminatif, iv] *adj, nm* denominative.

dénomination [denɔminɑsjɔ̃] *nf* (*nom*) designation, appellation (*frm*), denomination (*frm*); (*rare: action*) denomination (*frm*), naming.

dénommé, e [denɔme] (*ptp de* **dénommer**) *adj* (*parfois péj*) **le** ~ **X** a certain X, the man called X; **on m'a présenté un** ~ **Dupont** I was introduced to someone *ou* a man by the name of Dupont *ou* who called himself Dupont.

dénommer [denɔme] (1) *vt* (*frm*) (*donner un nom à*) to denominate (*frm*), name; (*rare: désigner*) to designate, denote; (*Jur*) to name.

dénoncer [denɔ̃se] (3) **1** *vt* **(a)** (*révéler*) *coupable* to denounce; *forfait, abus* to expose. (*fig*) **sa hâte le dénonça** his haste gave him away *ou* betrayed him; ~ **qn à la police** to inform against sb, give sb away to the police.
(b) (*signaler publiquement*) *abus, danger, injustice* to denounce, declaim against.
(c) (*annuler*) *contrat, traité* to denounce.
(d) (*littér: dénoter*) to announce, indicate.
2 se dénoncer *vpr* to give o.s. up, come forward. **se** ~ **à la police** to give o.s. up to the police.

dénonciateur, -trice [denɔ̃sjatœʀ, tʀis] **1** *adj* denunciatory, accusatory. **2** *nm,f* **(a)** *[criminel]* denouncer, informer; *[forfait]* exposer. **(b)** ~ **de** *injustices etc* denouncer of.

dénonciation [denɔ̃sjɑsjɔ̃] *nf [criminel]* denunciation; *[forfait, abus]* exposure (*U*); *[traité]* denunciation, denouncement. **emprisonné sur la** ~ **de qn** imprisoned on the strength of a denunciation by sb.

dénotation [denɔtɑsjɔ̃] *nf* (*Ling*) denotation.

dénoter [denɔte] (1) *vt* (*révéler*) to indicate, denote; (*Ling*) to denote.

dénouement [denumɑ̃] *nm* (*Théât*) dénouement; *[affaire, aventure, intrigue]* outcome, conclusion.

dénouer [denwe] (1) **1** *vt* **(a)** *nœud, lien* to untie, undo; *cheveux* to let down, loose, undo. **les cheveux dénoués** with her hair (falling) loose.
(b) *situation* to untangle, resolve; *difficultés, intrigue* to untangle, clear up, resolve.
2 se dénouer *vpr* **(a)** *[lien, nœud]* to come untied, come undone; *[cheveux]* to come loose, come undone, come down; *V* **langue**.
(b) *[intrigue, situation]* to be resolved.

dénoûment [denumɑ̃] *nm* (*rare*) = **dénouement**.

dénoyauter [denwajote] (1) *vt fruit* to stone (*Brit*), pit (*US*). **appareil à** ~ = **dénoyauteur**.

dénoyauteur [denwajotœʀ] *nm* stoner (*Brit*), pitter (*US*).

denrée [dɑ̃ʀe] *nf* **(a)** food, foodstuff. ~**s alimentaires** foodstuffs; ~**s périssables** perishable foods *ou* foodstuffs; ~**s coloniales** colonial produce.
(b) (*fig: littér, hum*) commodity. **l'honnêteté devient une** ~ **rare** honesty is becoming a rare commodity.

dense [dɑ̃s] *adj foule*, (*Phys*) dense; *feuillage, brouillard* dense, thick; *style* compact, condensed.

densimètre [dɑ̃simɛtʀ(ə)] *nm* densimeter, hydrometer.

densité [dɑ̃site] *nf* (*Démographie, Phys*) density; *[brouillard]* denseness, thickness; (*rare*) *[foule]* denseness. **région à forte/faible** ~ **(de population)** densely/sparsely populated area, area with a high/low population density.

dent [dɑ̃] **1** *nf* **(a)** *[homme, animal]* tooth. ~**s du haut/du bas/de devant/du fond** upper/lower/front/back teeth; ~ **de lait/de sagesse** milk/wisdom tooth; ~ **de remplacement** permanent tooth; ~ **gâtée/creuse** bad/hollow tooth; **mal** *ou* **rage de** ~ toothache (*U*); *V* **arracher, brosse, faux**[2] *etc.*
(b) *[herse, fourche, fourchette]* prong; *[râteau]* tooth, prong; *[scie, peigne]* tooth; *[roue, engrenage]* tooth, cog; *[feuille]* serration; *[arête rocheuse]* jag. **en** ~**s de scie** *couteau* serrated; *montagne* jagged.
(c) (*loc*) **avoir la** ~* to be hungry; **avoir la** ~ **dure** to be scathing in one's comments (about others); **avoir/garder une** ~ **contre qn** to have/hold a grudge against sb; **avoir les** ~**s longues** (†:*faim*) to be ravenous *ou* starving; (*fig: être ambitieux*) to have one's sights fixed high; **être sur les** ~**s** (*épuisé*) to be worn out *ou* dog-tired*; (*très occupé*) to be under great pressure; **faire** *ou* **percer ses** ~**s** to teethe, cut (one's) teeth; **il vient de percer une** ~ he has just cut a tooth; **croquer/manger qch à belles** ~**s** to bite into sth/eat sth with gusto; **manger/rire du bout des** ~**s** to eat/laugh half-heartedly; **parler/marmotter entre ses** ~**s** to talk/mumble between one's teeth; **n'avoir rien à se mettre sous la** ~ not to have a bite to eat; **on voudrait bien quelque chose à se mettre sous la** ~ we wouldn't say no to a bite (to eat)* *ou* something to eat; **il mange tout ce qui lui tombe sous la** ~ he eats everything he comes across; *V* **armé, casser, coup** *etc.*
2: **dent-de-lion** *nf, pl* **dents-de-lion** dandelion.

dentaire [dɑ̃tɛʀ] *adj* dental; *V* **formule, prothèse**.

dental, e, *mpl* **-aux** [dɑ̃tal, o] *adj, nf* (*Ling*) dental.

denté, e [dɑ̃te] *adj* (*Tech*) toothed; (*Bot*) dentate; *V* **roue**.

dentelé, e [dɑ̃tle] (*ptp de* **denteler**) *adj arête* jagged; *contour, côte* indented, jagged; (*Bot*) dentate; (*Anat*) serrate.

denteler [dɑ̃tle] (4) *vt* (*Tech*) *timbre-poste* to perforate. (*fig: découper*) **l'érosion avait dentelé la côte** erosion had indented the coastline *ou* had given the coast a jagged outline; **les pics qui dentelaient l'horizon** the peaks that stood in a jagged line along the horizon.

dentelle [dɑ̃tɛl] *nf* lace (*U*). **col de** ~ lace collar; ~ **à l'aiguille** *ou* **au point** needle-point lace; ~ **de papier** lacy paper; **crêpe** ~ thin pancake, crêpe.

dentellerie [dɑ̃tɛlʀi] *nf* (*fabrication*) lacemaking; (*Comm*) lace manufacture.

dentellier, -ière [dɑ̃təlje, jɛʀ] **1** *adj industrie* lace (*épith*). **2** *nm,f* lacemaker. **3 dentellière** *nf* (*machine*) lacemaking machine.

dentelure [dɑ̃tlyʀ] *nf [timbre-poste]* perforations; *[feuille]* serration; *[côte, arête]* jagged outline. **les** ~**s d'une côte** the indentations *ou* jagged outline of a coastline.

dentier [dɑ̃tje] *nm* denture, dental plate.

dentifrice [dɑ̃tifʀis] **1** *nm* toothpaste, dentifrice. **2** *adj*: **eau** ~ mouthwash; **poudre** ~ tooth powder; **pâte** ~ toothpaste.

dentine [dɑ̃tin] *nf* dentine.

dentiste [dɑ̃tist(ə)] *nmf* dentist; *V* **chirurgien**.

dentition [dɑ̃tisjɔ̃] *nf* (*dents*) teeth (*pl*); (*croissance*) dentition. ~ **de lait** teething.

denture [dɑ̃tyʀ] *nf* (*humaine*) teeth (*pl*), set of teeth, dentition (*T*); (*Tech*) *[roue]* teeth (*pl*), cogs.

dénudé, e [denyde] (*ptp de* **dénuder**) *adj* (*gén*) bare; *crâne* bald; *colline* bare, bald.

dénuder [denyde] (1) **1** *vt* **(a)** (*Tech*) *fil* to bare, strip; (*Méd*) *os* to strip.
(b) *arbre, sol, colline* to bare, strip.
(c) *bras, dos [robe]* to leave bare; *[mouvement]* to bare.
2 se dénuder *vpr* **(a)** *[personne]* to strip (off).
(b) *[colline, arbre]* to become bare, be bared; (*rare*) *[crâne]* to be balding, be going bald.

dénué, e [denɥe] (*ptp de* **dénuer**) *adj*: ~ **de** devoid of; ~ **de bon sens** senseless, devoid of sense; ~ **d'intérêt** devoid of interest; ~ **de talent/d'imagination** lacking in *ou* without talent/imagination, untalented/unimaginative; ~ **de tout** destitute; ~ **de tout fondement** completely unfounded *ou* groundless.

dénuement [denymɑ̃] *nm [personne]* destitution, privation; (*littér*) *[logement]* bareness. (*fig littér*) ~ **moral** moral deprivation.

dénuer (se) [denɥe] (1) *vpr* (*littér*) to deprive o.s. (*de* of).

dénûment [denymɑ̃] *nm* = **dénuement.**

dénutrition [denytʀisjɔ̃] *nf* undernutrition.

déodorant [deɔdɔʀɑ̃] *adj m, nm*: **(produit)** ~ deodorant; ~ **(corporel)** deodorant.

déodoriser [deɔdɔʀize] (1) *vt* to deodorize.

déontologie [deɔ̃tɔlɔʒi] *nf* professional code of ethics, deontology (*T*).

déontologique [deɔ̃tɔlɔʒik] *adj* ethical, deontological (*T*).

dépailler [depɑje] (1) *vt chaise* to remove the straw seating from. **cette chaise se dépaille** the straw seating is coming off this chair.

dépannage [depanaʒ] *nm* (*V* **dépanner**) fixing; repairing; bailing out*, helping out. **voiture de** ~ breakdown lorry (*Brit*) *ou* truck (*US*); **service de** ~ breakdown service; **ils ont fait 3** ~**s aujourd'hui** they've fixed 3 breakdowns today; **partir pour un** ~ to go out on a repair *ou* breakdown job.

dépanner [depane] (1) *vt véhicule, poste de télévision* to get going (again), fix, repair; *automobiliste* to fix the car of; (*: *tirer d'embarras*) *personne* to bail out*, help out.

dépanneur [depanœʀ] *nm* (*Aut*) breakdown mechanic; (*TV*) television engineer, television repairman.

dépanneuse [depanøz] *nf* breakdown lorry (*Brit*), breakdown truck (*US*), wrecker (*US*).

dépaqueter [depakte] (4) *vt* to unpack.

dépareillé, e [depaʀeje] (*ptp de* **dépareiller**) *adj collection* incomplete; *objet* odd (*épith*). (*Comm*) **articles** ~**s** oddments; (*Comm*) **couverts** ~**s** odd cutlery.

dépareiller [depaʀeje] (1) *vt collection, service de table* to make incomplete, spoil. **en cassant cette assiette tu as dépareillé le service** you've spoilt the set now you've broken that plate.

déparer [depaʀe] (1) *vt paysage* to spoil, disfigure, mar; *beauté, qualité* to detract from, mar. **cette pièce ne déparerait pas ma collection** my collection certainly wouldn't be any the worse for this piece.

déparié, e [depaʀje] (*ptp de* **déparier**) *adj* (*rare*) *chaussures, gants* odd (*épith*).

déparier [depaʀje] (7) *vt* (*rare*) *gants, chassures* to split up.

départ¹ [depaʀ] *nm* **(a)** *[voyageur]* leaving (*U*), departure; *[train, véhicule]* (*sur horaire etc*) departure; *[excursion]* departure. **observer le** ~ **du train** to watch the train leave; **le** ~ **est à 8 heures** the train (*ou* coach *etc*) leaves at 8 o'clock; **arriver au** ~ (*excursion*) to arrive at the place of departure; **fixer l'heure/le jour de son** ~ to set a time/day for one's departure; (*Rail*) '~ **des grandes lignes**' 'main line departures'; **dès son** ~ **j'ai ...** as soon as he had left I ...; **mon** ~ **de l'hôtel** my departure from *ou* my leaving the hotel; **peu après mon** ~ **de l'hôtel** soon after I had left the hotel, soon after my departure from the hotel; **c'est bientôt le** ~ **en vacances** we'll soon be off on holiday (*Brit*) *ou* vacation (*US*), we'll soon be leaving on our holidays (*Brit*) *ou* on vacation (*US*); **alors, c'est pour bientôt le grand** ~? well then, how soon is the great departure?; **le** ~ **du train/bateau est imminent** the train/boat is leaving any time now *ou* is about to depart; **son** ~ **précipité** his hasty departure; **la levée du matin est à 7.30 heures et le** ~ **du courrier se fait à 9 heures** the morning collection is at 7.30 and the mail leaves town at 9 o'clock; *V* **tableau.**
(b) (*Sport*) start. **un bon** ~ a good start; (*lit, fig*) **un faux** ~ a false start; **donner le** ~ **aux coureurs** to give the runners the starting signal, start the race; **les coureurs se rassemblent au** ~ the runners are assembling at the start; ~ **lancé/arrêté** flying/standing start.
(c) *[employé, ministre]* leaving (*U*), quitting (*U*), departure. **le** ~ **du ministre a fait l'effet d'une bombe** the minister's leaving *ou* quitting *ou* departure was something of a bombshell; **le ministre annonça son** ~ the minister announced that he was going to quit *ou* that he was leaving; **demander le** ~ **d'un employé/fonctionnaire** to ask an employee/a civil servant to leave *ou* quit.
(d) (*origine*) *[processus, transformation]* start, starting (*U*). **la substance de** ~ the original substance; **de la langue de** ~ **à la langue d'arrivée** from the source language to the target language; *V* **point¹.**
(e) (*loc*) **être sur le** ~ to be about to leave *ou* go; **excursions au** ~ **de Chamonix** excursions (leaving *ou* departing) from Chamonix, (day) trips from Chamonix; (*fig*) **au** ~ at the start *ou* outset.

départ² [depaʀ] *nm* (†, *littér*) **faire le** ~ **entre deux concepts** to draw *ou* make a distinction between two concepts.

départager [depaʀtaʒe] (3) *vt concurrents* to decide between; *votes* to settle, decide; (*littér*) *opinions* to decide between; (*littér*) *camps opposés* to separate. ~ **l'assemblée** to settle the voting in the assembly.

département [depaʀtəmɑ̃] *nm* (*division du territoire*) department (*one of the 95 main administrative divisions of France*), ≃ region (*Brit*); (*ministère*) ministry, department.

départemental, e, *mpl* **-aux** [depaʀtəmɑ̃tal, o] *adj* (*V* **département**) departmental; ministerial. **(route)** ~**e** secondary road, ≃ B-road (*Brit*).

départir [depaʀtiʀ] (16) **1** *vt* (†, *littér: attribuer*) *tâche* to assign; *faveur* to accord (*frm*). **2 se départir** *vpr* (*gén nég: abandonner*) **se** ~ **de** *ton, attitude* to abandon, depart from; *sourire* to drop.

dépassé, e [depɑse] (*ptp de* **dépasser**) *adj* (*périmé*) outmoded, superseded; (*: *désorienté*) out of one's depth (*attrib*).

dépassement [depɑsmɑ̃] *nm* **(a)** (*Aut*) overtaking (*Brit*: *U*), passing (*U*). **tout** ~ **est dangereux** overtaking is always dangerous, it is always dangerous to overtake; '~ **interdit**' 'no overtaking'; **après plusieurs** ~**s dangereux ...** after perilously overtaking several vehicles ... .
(b) (*Fin*) ~ **(de crédit)** overspending (*U*); **un** ~ **de crédit de 5 millions** overspending by 5 million francs.
(c) ~ **(de soi-même)** surpassing of oneself.

dépasser [depɑse] (1) **1** *vt* **(a)** (*aller plus loin que*) *endroit* to pass, go past; (*Aviat*) *piste* to overshoot; (*distancer*) *véhicule, personne* to overtake (*Brit*), pass. **dépassez les feux et prenez la première rue à gauche** go through *ou* pass the lights and take the first left.
(b) (*déborder de*) *alignement* (*horizontalement*) to jut out over, overhang; (*verticalement*) to jut out above, stand higher than.
(c) (*excéder*) *limite, quantité mesurable* to exceed. ~ **qch en hauteur/largeur** to be higher *ou* taller/wider than sth, exceed sth in height/width; **il a dépassé son père (de 10 cm) maintenant** he's (10 cm) taller than his father now; **cette plante a dépassé l'autre** this plant has outgrown the other *ou* is now taller than the other; ~ **en nombre** to outnumber; **tout colis qui dépasse 20 kg/la limite (de poids)** all parcels in excess of *ou* exceeding *ou* over 20 kg/the (weight) limit; ~ **le nombre prévu** to be more than expected; **la réunion ne devrait pas** ~ **3 heures** the meeting shouldn't go on longer than *ou* last longer than 3 hours, the meeting shouldn't exceed 3 hours (in length); **il ne veut pas** ~ **100 F** he won't go above *ou* over 100 francs; **ça va** ~ **100 F** it'll be more than *ou* over 100 francs; ~ **en rendement** to be more productive than; **elle a dépassé la quarantaine** she is over forty, she has turned forty; (*Méd*) **'ne pas** ~ **la dose'** 'it is dangerous to exceed the stipulated dose'; **le prix de cet appartement dépasse nos moyens** this flat is beyond our means.
(d) (*surpasser*) *valeur, prévisions* to exceed; *réputation* to outshine; *rival* to outmatch, outstrip. ~ **qn en violence/intelligence** to surpass sb in violence/intelligence; **pour la paresse/l'appétit il dépasse tout le monde** he beats everybody for laziness/appetite; **il dépasse tous ses camarades** he is ahead of *ou* he surpasses all his friends; **sa réputation dépasse de loin celle de ses collègues** his reputation by far outshines that of his colleagues, he has a far greater reputation than his colleagues; **sa bêtise dépasse tout ce qu'on peut imaginer** his stupidity goes beyond all imagining *ou* goes beyond anything you could imagine *ou* beggars the imagination; **l'homme doit se** ~ man must try to transcend himself *ou* surpass himself; **les résultats ont dépassé notre attente** the results exceeded *ou* surpassed our expectations.
(e) (*outrepasser*) *moyens, instructions* to go beyond; *attributions* to go beyond, overstep; *crédits* to exceed. **cela dépasse les bornes** *ou* **les limites** *ou* **la mesure** that's the absolute limit, that's going too far; **il a dépassé les bornes** *ou* **la mesure** *ou* **la dose*** he has really gone too far *ou* overstepped the mark; **cela a dépassé le stade de la plaisanterie** it has gone beyond a joke; **les mots ont dû** ~ **sa pensée** he must have been carried away (to have said that); **cela dépasse mes forces/ma compétence** it's beyond my strength/capabilities; **cela me dépasse** it's beyond me; **il a dépassé ses forces** he has overtaxed himself *ou* overdone it.
(f) (*: *dérouter*) **cela/cet argument me dépasse!** it/this argument is beyond me!; **être dépassé (par les événements)** to be overtaken (by events); **il est complètement dépassé!** he is completely out of his depth!
2 *vi* **(a)** (*Aut*) to overtake (*Brit*), pass. **'défense de** ~**'** 'no overtaking'.
(b) (*faire saillie*) *[bâtiment, tour]* to stick out; *[planche, balcon, rocher]* to stick out, jut out, protrude; *[clou]* to stick out; *[jupon]* to show (*de, sous* below); *[chemise]* to be hanging out (*de* of), be untucked. **il y a quelque chose qui dépasse du tiroir** something's sticking *ou* hanging out of the drawer; **leur chien a toujours un bout de langue qui dépasse** their dog always has the end of his tongue hanging out.

dépassionner [depasjɔne] (1) *vt débat* to take the heat out of.

dépatouiller (se)* [depatuje] (1) *vpr*: **se** ~ **de** *situation difficile* to get out of; **laisse-le se** ~**!** leave him to *ou* let him get out of it on his own!

dépavage [depavaʒ] *nm* removal of the cobbles *ou* cobblestones (*de* from).

dépaver [depave] (1) *vt* to dig up the cobbles *ou* cobblestones from.

dépaysé, e [depeize] (*ptp de* **dépayser**) *adj* like a fish out of water (*attrib*). **je me sens très** ~ **ici** I feel very much like a fish out of water here, I feel very strange here, I don't feel at home at all here.

dépaysement [depeizmɑ̃] *nm* (*désorientation*) disorientation, feeling of strangeness; (*changement salutaire*) change of scenery. **aimer le ~** to like a change of scenery.

dépayser [depeize] (1) *vt* (*désorienter*) to disorientate; (*changer agréablement*) to give a change of scenery to, give a welcome change of surroundings to. **ce séjour me dépaysait** this stay gave me a change of scenery *ou* a welcome change of surroundings.

dépeçage [depəsaʒ] *nm*, (*rare*) **dépècement** [depɛsmɑ̃] *nm* (*V* **dépecer**) jointing, cutting up; dismembering; carving up.

dépecer [depəse] (5) *vt animal* *[boucher]* to joint, cut up; *[lion]* to dismember, tear limb from limb; (*fig*) *territoire, état* to carve up, dismember.

dépêche [depɛʃ] *nf* dispatch. **~ (télégraphique)** telegram, wire; **~ diplomatique** diplomatic dispatch.

dépêcher [depeʃe] (1) **1** *vt* to dispatch, send (*auprès de* to).

2 se dépêcher *vpr* to hurry. **il se dépêchait** (*il marchait etc*) he was hurrying (along); (*il travaillait*) he was hurrying; **dépêche-toi!** hurry (up)!, (be) quick!; **se ~ de faire qch** to hurry (in order) to do sth; **il se dépêchait de finir son travail** he was hurrying (in order) to get his work finished *ou* to finish his work; **dépêche-toi de les commander, il n'y en aura bientôt plus** hurry up and order them or there soon won't be any left.

dépeigner [depeɲe] (1) *vt*: **~ qn** to make sb's hair untidy, ruffle sb's hair; **dépeigné par le vent** with windswept hair; **elle entra toute dépeignée** she came in with uncombed *ou* dishevelled hair.

dépeindre [depɛ̃dʀ(ə)] (52) *vt* to depict.

dépenaillé, e [depənɑje] *adj personne, vêtements* (*débraillé*) messy; (*en haillons*) tattered, ragged; *drapeau, livre* tattered.

dépendance [depɑ̃dɑ̃s] *nf* **(a)** (*interdépendance*) dependence (*U*), dependency. **la ~ de qch vis-à-vis de qch d'autre** the dependence of sth (up)on sth else; **un réseau subtil de ~s** a subtle network of dependencies *ou* interdependencies.

(b) (*asservissement, subordination*) subordination. **la ~ de qn vis-à-vis de qn d'autre** the subordination of sb to sb else; **être dans la ~** to be subordinate *ou* in a position of subordination; **être sous** *ou* **dans la ~ de qn** to be subordinate to sb.

(c) (*bâtiment*) *[hôtel, château, ferme]* outbuilding.

(d) (*Hist Pol: territoire*) dependency.

(e) (*Psych*) *[drogué]* dependence, dependency.

dépendant, e [depɑ̃dɑ̃, ɑ̃t] *adj* (*V* **dépendre de**) **~ de** answerable to, responsible to; dependent (up)on.

dépendre [depɑ̃dʀ(ə)] (41) **1 dépendre de** *vt indir* **(a)** *[employé]* to be answerable to, be responsible to; *[organisation]* to be dependent (up)on; *[territoire]* to be dependent (up)on, be a dependency of. **~ (financièrement) de ses parents** to be financially dependent (up)on one's parents; **ce pays dépend économiquement de la France** this country is economically dependent (up)on France; **je ne veux ~ de personne** I don't wish to be dependent (up)on anyone *ou* to have to depend (up)on anyone; **ce terrain dépend de leur domaine** this piece of land is part of *ou* belongs to their property; **ne ~ que de soi-même** to be answerable only to oneself, be one's own boss*.

(b) *[décision, résultat, phénomène]* to depend (up)on, be dependent (up)on. **ça va ~ du temps** it'll (all) depend on the weather; — **ça dépend** — it (all) depends; **il dépend de vous/de ceci que ...** it depends *ou* rests (up)on you/this whether ...; **il ne dépend que de vous que ...** it depends *ou* rests entirely (up)on you whether ..., it's entirely up to you whether ...; **il dépend de toi de réussir** (your) success depends on you, it depends on you *ou* it's up to you whether you succeed (or not).

2 *vt lustre, guirlandes* to take down.

dépens [depɑ̃] *nmpl* **(a)** (*Jur*) costs. **être condamné aux ~** to be ordered to pay costs, have costs awarded against one. **(b) aux ~ de** at the expense of; **rire aux ~ de qn** to (have a) laugh at sb's expense; **je l'ai appris à mes ~** I learnt this to my cost.

dépense [depɑ̃s] *nf* **(a)** (*argent dépensé, frais*) spending (*U*), expense, expenditure (*U*); (*sortie*) outlay, expenditure (*U*). **une ~ de 1.000 F** an outlay *ou* expenditure of 1,000 francs; **les ~s du ménage** household expenses; **contrôler les ~s de qn** to control sb's expenditure *ou* spending; **je n'aurais pas dû faire cette ~** I should not have incurred that expense (*frm*) *ou* spent that money; **j'hésite, c'est une grosse ~** I'm hesitating, it's a large outlay *ou* it's a lot to lay out; **calculer ~s et recettes** to calculate expenditure and receipts; **~s publiques** public expenditure *ou* spending; **pousser qn à la ~** to make sb spend some money *ou* incur an expense (*frm*); **faire la ~ d'une voiture** to lay out money *ou* spend money on a car; **regarder à la ~** to watch one's spending *ou* what one spends.

(b) (*fig*) *[électricité, essence]* consumption. **~s d'imagination** expenditure of imagination; **~ physique** (physical) exercise; **~ de temps** spending of time (*U*), time spent (*U*).

dépenser [depɑ̃se] (1) **1** *vt* **(a)** *argent* to spend; (*fig*) *électricité, essence* to use. **~ sans compter** to spend without counting the cost, spend lavishly; **elle dépense peu pour la nourriture** she doesn't spend much on food, she spends little on food.

(b) (*fig*) *forces, énergie* to expend, use up; *temps, jeunesse* to spend, use up. **~ son trop-plein d'énergie** to use up one's surplus energy; **vous dépensez inutilement votre salive** you're wasting your breath.

2 se dépenser *vpr* to exert o.s. **se ~ en démarches inutiles** to waste one's energies in useless procedures; **pour ce projet il s'est dépensé sans compter** he has put all his energy *ou* energies into this project.

dépensier, -ière [depɑ̃sje, jɛʀ] **1** *adj* extravagant. **c'est une ~ière** she's a spendthrift. **2** *nm,f* (*trésorier de couvent*) bursar.

déperdition [depɛʀdisjɔ̃] *nf* (*Sci, gén*) loss.

dépérir [depeʀiʀ] (2) *vi* *[personne]* to fade away, waste away; *[santé, forces]* to fail, decline; *[plante]* to wither; *[commerce]* to (be on the) decline, fall off; *[affaire]* to (be on the) decline, go downhill.

dépérissement [depeʀismɑ̃] *nm* (*V* **dépérir**) fading away, wasting away; failing; decline; withering; falling off.

dépersonnalisation [depɛʀsɔnalizɑsjɔ̃] *nf* depersonalization.

dépersonnaliser [depɛʀsɔnalize] **1** *vt* to depersonalize. **2 se dépersonnaliser** *vpr* *[relations etc]* to become impersonal, become depersonalized; (*Psych*) to become depersonalized.

dépêtrer [depetʀe] (1) **1** *vt*: **~ qn de** (*lit*) *bourbier, ronces, harnachement* to extricate sb from, free sb from; (*fig*) *situation* to extricate sb from, get sb out of.

2 se dépêtrer *vpr* (*lit, fig*) to extricate o.s., free o.s. **se ~ de** *ronces, situation* to extricate *ou* free o.s. from, get out of; (*fig*) *liens* to free o.s. from; *gêneur* to get free of, get rid of.

dépeuplement [depœpləmɑ̃] *nm* (*V* **dépeupler**) depopulation; emptying of people (*ou* fish *ou* wildlife); clearing (of trees *etc*). **le ~ tragique de ces forêts** the tragic disappearance of wildlife from these forests.

dépeupler [depœple] (1) **1** *vt région, ville* to depopulate; (*temporairement*) *salle, place* to empty (of people); *rivière* to empty of fish; *forêt, région* to empty of wildlife; *écuries etc* to empty; *forêt* to clear (of trees, plants *etc*).

2 se dépeupler *vpr* (*V* **dépeupler**) to be depopulated; to be emptied of people (*ou* fish *ou* wildlife); to be emptied; to be cleared (of trees *etc*).

déphasage [defɑzaʒ] *nm* (*Phys*) phase difference; (**fig: perte de contact*) being out of touch.

déphasé, e [defɑze] (*ptp de* **déphaser**) *adj* (*Phys*) out of phase; (*: *désorienté*) out of touch (*attrib*), not with it* (*attrib*).

déphaser* [defɑze] (1) *vt* (*désorienter*) to put out of touch.

dépiauter* [depjote] (1) *vt* to skin.

dépilation [depilɑsjɔ̃] *nf* (*V* **dépiler**) hair loss.

dépilatoire [depilatwaʀ] *adj* depilatory.

dépiler [depile] (1) *vt* (*Méd*) to cause hair loss to; (*Tech*) *peaux* to grain.

dépiquer [depike] (1) *vt* (*Couture*) to unpick, unstitch; (*Agr*) *laitue etc* to transplant; *blé* to thresh; *riz* to hull.

dépistage [depistaʒ] *nm* (*V* **dépister**) tracking down; detection; unearthing. **centre de ~ anticancéreux** cancer screening unit.

dépister [depiste] (1) *vt* **(a)** *gibier, criminel* to track down; *maladie* to detect; *influence, cause* to unearth, detect. **(b)** (*semer*) **~ qn** to throw sb off the scent, give sb the slip*.

dépit [depi] *nm* **(a)** (great) vexation, (great) frustration. **causer du ~ à qn** to vex *ou* frustrate sb greatly, cause sb much heartache; **il en a conçu du ~** he was greatly vexed *ou* frustrated by it.

(b) en ~ de in spite of; **en ~ du bon sens** contrary to all good sense.

dépité, e [depite] (*ptp de* **dépiter**) *adj* greatly vexed, greatly frustrated. **un peu ~** vexed, frustrated.

dépiter [depite] (1) *vt* (*littér*) to vex greatly, frustrate greatly.

déplacé, e [deplase] (*ptp de* **déplacer**) *adj présence* uncalled-for; *intervention, scrupule* misplaced, out of place (*attrib*); *remarque, propos* uncalled-for, out of place (*attrib*); *V* **personne.**

déplacement [deplasmɑ̃] **1** *nm* **(a)** (*action*) (*V* **déplacer**) moving; shifting; displacement; transfer; (*V* **se déplacer**) movement; displacement. **ça vaut le ~** it's worth going (to).

(b) (*voyage*) travel (*U*), travelling (*U*). **les ~s coûtent cher** travelling *ou* travel is expensive; **être en ~ (pour affaires)** to be on a (business) trip; *V* **frais**[2].

(c) (*Naut*) displacement. **~ de 10.000 tonnes** 10,000 tons' displacement.

2: déplacement d'air displacement of air; **déplacement d'organe** organ displacement; **déplacement de troupes** movement of troops; **déplacement de vertèbre** slipped disc.

déplacer [deplase] (3) **1** *vt* **(a)** *objet, meuble, élève* to move, shift; (*Méd*) *articulation, os* to displace. **se ~ une articulation** to put a joint out, displace a joint; **se ~ une vertèbre** to slip a disc.

(b) *usine, fonctionnaire* to transfer, move; *collectivité* to move, shift.

(c) (*fig*) *problème, question* to shift the emphasis of.

(d) (*Naut*) to displace. **navire qui déplace 10.000 tonnes** ship with a 10,000-ton displacement.

2 se déplacer *vpr* **(a)** *[pièce mobile]* to move; *[air, substance]* to move, be displaced.

(b) *[animal]* to move (along); *[personne]* (*se mouvoir*) to move, walk; (*circuler*) to move (around); (*voyager*) to travel. **il ne se déplace qu'avec peine** he can get around *ou* about *ou* he can move only with difficulty; **il est interdit de se ~ pendant la classe** no moving around during class; **il ne se déplace qu'en avion** he travels only by air; **il se déplace fréquemment** he's a frequent traveller, he travels a lot.

déplaire [deplɛʀ] (54) **1** *vt* **(a)** (*n'être pas aimé de*) **il déplaît à tout le monde** he is disliked by everyone; **cette mode/ville/femme me déplaît** I dislike *ou* I don't like *ou* I don't care for this fashion/town/woman; **au bout d'un moment, cela risque de ~** after a while it can become disagreeable *ou* irksome; (*frm*) **il me déplaît de faire ...** I dislike doing ...; (*frm*) **il me déplairait d'avoir à vous renvoyer** I should not care to have to dismiss you.

(b) (*irriter*) **~ à qn** to displease sb; **il fait tout pour nous ~** he does all he can to displease us; **ceci a profondément déplu** this gave profound *ou* great displeasure; **il cherche à ~** he is trying to be disagreeable.

(c) (†, *hum*) **elle est, n'en déplaise à son mari, bien moins intelligente que sa sœur** with all due respect to her husband, she is far less intelligent than her sister; **j'irai la voir, n'en**

déplaise à votre père whatever your father may think, I shall go and see her.

2 se déplaire *vpr*: se ~ **quelque part** to dislike it somewhere; **elle se déplaît ici/à la campagne** she dislikes it *ou* doesn't like it here/in the country; se ~ **dans son nouvel emploi** to be unhappy in one's new job, dislike one's new job.

déplaisant, e [deplɛzɑ̃, ɑ̃t] *adj* disagreeable, unpleasant.

déplaisir [deplɛziʀ] *nm* (*contrariété*) displeasure, annoyance. **faire qch sans** ~ to do sth without showing any displeasure *ou* annoyance; **faire qch avec (le plus grand)** ~ to do sth with (the greatest) displeasure.

déplantage [deplɑ̃taʒ] *nm*, (*rare*) **déplantation** [deplɑ̃tɑsjɔ̃] *nf* (*V* **déplanter**) transplanting; digging up.

déplanter [deplɑ̃te] (1) *vt plante* to transplant; *plate-bande* to dig up.

déplantoir [deplɑ̃twaʀ] *nm* trowel.

déplâtrage [deplɑtʀaʒ] *nm* (*Constr*) **le** ~ **d'un mur** stripping the plaster off a wall, stripping a wall of its plaster; (*Méd*) **le** ~ **d'un membre** taking a limb out of plaster *ou* out of its plaster cast, taking a plaster cast off a limb.

déplâtrer [deplɑtʀe] (1) *vt* (*Constr*) to strip the plaster off; (*Méd*) to take out of plaster, take the plaster cast off.

dépliage [deplijaʒ] *nm* (*V* **déplier**) unfolding; opening out.

dépliant, e [deplijɑ̃, ɑ̃t] **1** *adj* extendible. **fauteuil** ~ armchair that converts into a bed. **2** *nm* (*prospectus*) leaflet, folder; (*grande page*) fold-out page.

dépliement [deplimɑ̃] *nm* = **dépliage**.

déplier [deplije] (7) **1** *vt* **(a)** *serviette, vêtement* to unfold; *carte, journal* to open out, unfold; (*fig*) *jambes* to stretch out.

(b) (*rare*, †: *déballer*) *paquet* to open out, open up. ~ **sa marchandise** to spread out one's wares.

2 se déplier *vpr [carte, journal]* to come unfolded, open out; *[vêtement, serviette]* to come unfolded; *[feuille d'arbre]* to open out, unfold.

déplissage [deplisaʒ] *nm* (*V* **déplisser**) *[étoffe]* taking the pleats out of; smoothing (out).

déplisser [deplise] (1) **1** *vt étoffe plissée* to take the pleats out of; *étoffe avec faux plis* to flatten (out), smooth (out); (*littér*) *front* to smooth. **2 se déplisser** *vpr [jupe]* to come unpleated, lose its pleats.

déploiement [deplwamɑ̃] *nm [voile, drapeau]* unfurling; *[ailes]* spreading; *[troupes]* deployment; *[richesses, forces, amabilité, talents]* display.

déplomber [deplɔ̃be] (1) *vt colis, compteur* to unseal; *dent* to remove the filling from, take the filling out of.

déplorable [deplɔʀabl(ə)] *adj* (*regrettable, exécrable*) deplorable; (*blâmable*) deplorable, disgraceful.

déplorablement [deplɔʀabləmɑ̃] *adv* (*V* **déplorable**) deplorably; disgracefully.

déplorer [deplɔʀe] (1) *vt* (*trouver fâcheux*) to regret (deeply), deplore; (*littér: s'affliger de*) to lament.

déployer [deplwaje] (8) **1** *vt* **(a)** *carte, tissu* to open out, spread out; *voile, drapeau* to unfurl; *ailes* to spread.

(b) *troupes* to deploy; *assortiment, échantillons* to spread out, lay out. ~ **en éventail** *troupes* to fan out; **il déploie tout un assortiment dans sa vitrine** he displays a wide variety of goods in his window.

(c) *richesses, fastes* to make a display of, display; *talents, ressources, forces* to display, exhibit.

(d) ~ **beaucoup d'activité** to engage in great activity; **ils ont déployé d'importantes forces de police** they put a large police force into action; *V* **rire**.

2 se déployer *vpr [voile, drapeau]* to unfurl; *[ailes]* to spread; *[troupes]* to deploy; *[cortège]* to spread out.

déplumer [deplyme] (1) **1** *vt* (†) to pluck. **2 se déplumer** *vpr [oiseau]* to moult, lose its feathers; (*: *perdre ses cheveux*) to go bald, lose one's hair.

dépoétiser [depɔetize] (1) *vt* to take the romance out of, make prosaic.

dépoitraillé, e [depwatʀɑje] *adj* (*péj*) **quelle tenue, il est tout** ~! how untidy he is — his shirt's all undone at the front showing his chest!

dépolarisant, e [depɔlaʀizɑ̃, ɑ̃t] **1** *adj* depolarizing. **2** *nm* depolarizer.

dépolarisation [depɔlaʀizɑsjɔ̃] *nf* depolarization.

dépolariser [depɔlaʀize] (1) *vt* to depolarize.

dépoli, e [depɔli] (*ptp de* **dépolir**) *adj V* **verre**.

dépolir [depɔliʀ] (2) **1** *vt argent, étain* to tarnish; *verre* to frost. **2 se dépolir** *vpr* to tarnish.

dépolitisation [depɔlitizɑsjɔ̃] *nf* (*V* **dépolitiser**) making politically neutral; making politically unaware; depoliticization.

dépolitiser [depɔlitize] (1) *vt débat* to remove the political aspect of, make politically neutral, depoliticize; *personne, groupe* to make politically unaware, depoliticize.

déponent, e [depɔnɑ̃, ɑ̃t] **1** *adj* (*Ling*) deponent. **2** *nm* deponent (verb).

dépopulation [depɔpylɑsjɔ̃] *nf* depopulation.

déportation [depɔʀtɑsjɔ̃] *nf* (*exil*) deportation, transportation; (*internement*) imprisonment (in a concentration camp).

déporté, e [depɔʀte] (*ptp de* **déporter**) *nm,f* (*exilé*) deportee; (*interné*) prisoner (in a concentration camp).

déportement [depɔʀtəmɑ̃] *nm* **(a)** (*embardée*) ~ **vers la gauche** swerve to the left. **(b)** (†: *écarts de conduite*) ~s misbehaviour, excesses.

déporter [depɔʀte] (1) *vt* **(a)** *personne* (*exiler*) to deport, transport; (*interner*) to send to a concentration camp. **(b)** (*faire dévier*) to carry off course. **le vent l'a déporté** the wind carried *ou* blew him off course.

déposant, e [depozɑ̃, ɑ̃t] *nm,f* (*épargnant*) depositor; (*Jur*) deponent.

dépose [depoz] *nf [tapis]* lifting, taking up; *[serrure, moteur]* taking out, removal; *[rideau]* taking down.

déposer [depoze] (1) **1** *vt* **(a)** (*poser*) to lay down, put down, set down; *ordures* to dump. ~ **une gerbe** (*sur une tombe etc*) to lay a wreath; **'défense de** ~ **des ordures'** 'dumping of rubbish is prohibited', 'no rubbish to be tipped' (*Brit*), 'no tipping'; (*fig*) ~ **les armes** to lay down (one's) arms; (*fig*) ~ **le masque** to drop one's mask; (*littér*) ~ **un baiser sur le front de qn** to plant a kiss on sb's forehead.

(b) (*laisser*) *chose* to leave; *personne* to drop, set down. ~ **sa carte** to leave one's card; **on a déposé une lettre/un paquet pour vous** somebody left a letter/parcel for you, somebody dropped a letter/parcel in for you*; ~ **une valise à la consigne** to deposit *ou* leave a suitcase at the left-luggage (office); **je te dépose à la gare** I'll drop you (off) at the station, I'll set you down at the station; **l'autobus le déposa à la gare** the bus dropped him at the station; **est-ce que je peux vous** ~ **quelque part?** can I give you a lift anywhere?, can I drop you anywhere?

(c) (*Fin*) *argent, valeur* to deposit.

(d) (*Admin, Jur etc*) *plainte* to lodge; *réclamation* to file; *marque de fabrique* to register; *projet de loi* to bring in, table; *rapport* to send in, file. ~ **son bilan** to file a statement of affairs (*in a bankruptcy petition*); *V* **marque**.

(e) (*destituer*) *souverain* to depose.

(f) *[eau, vin] sable, lie* to deposit.

(g) (*démonter*) *tenture* to take down; *tapis* to take up, lift; *serrure, moteur* to take out, remove.

2 *vi* **(a)** *[liquide]* to form a sediment, form a deposit. **laisser** ~ to leave to settle.

(b) (*Jur*) to testify.

3 se déposer *vpr [poussière, lie]* to settle.

dépositaire [depozitɛʀ] *nmf* **(a)** *[objet confié]* depository; (*fig*) *[secret, vérité]* possessor, guardian. (*Jur*) ~ **public** ≈ authorized depository. **(b)** (*Comm: agent*) agent (*de* for).

déposition [depozisjɔ̃] *nf* **(a)** (*Jur*) deposition. **(b)** *[souverain]* deposition, deposing. **(c)** (*Art*) ~ **de croix** Deposition.

déposséder [depɔsede] (6) *vt*: ~ **qn de** *terres* to dispossess sb of; *place, biens* to deprive sb of; *charge* to divest *ou* deprive sb of; **ils se sentaient dépossédés** they felt dispossessed.

dépossession [depɔsesjɔ̃] *nf* (*V* **déposséder**) dispossession; deprivation; divesting. **leur sentiment de** ~ their feeling of being dispossessed.

dépôt [depo] **1** *nm* **(a)** (*action de déposer*) *[argent, valeurs]* deposit(ing). **ils ont procédé au** ~ **d'une gerbe sur sa tombe** they laid a wreath on his grave; **le** ~ **des manteaux au vestiaire est obligatoire** (all) coats must be left *ou* deposited in the cloakroom; **le** ~ **d'une marque de fabrique** the registration of a trademark; (*Jur*) **le** ~ **légal** registration of copyright; *V* **mandat**.

(b) (*garde*) **avoir qch en** ~ to hold sth in trust; **confier qch en** ~ **à qn** to entrust sth to sb.

(c) (*chose confiée*) **restituer un** ~ to return what has been entrusted to one; ~ **sacré** sacred trust; (*Fin*) ~ **(bancaire)** (bank) deposit; (*Fin*) ~ **à vue** deposit on current account (*Brit*); ~ **à terme** fixed term deposit; *V* **banque, compte**.

(d) (*garantie*) deposit. **verser un** ~ to put down *ou* pay a deposit.

(e) (*sédiment*) *[liquide, lie]* sediment, deposit. ~ **de sable** silt (*U*); ~ **de tartre** fur (*U*); **l'eau a formé un** ~ **calcaire dans la bouilloire** the water has furred up the kettle.

(f) (*entrepôt*) warehouse, store; *[autobus]* depot, garage; *[trains]* depot, shed; (*Mil*) depot.

(g) (*Comm: point de vente*) **il n'y a pas de boulangerie/laiterie mais un** ~ **de pain/de lait à l'épicerie** there is no baker's/dairy but they sell bread/milk at the grocer's *ou* but the grocer supplies *ou* sells bread/milk.

(h) (*prison*) jail, prison. **il a passé la nuit au** ~ he spent the night in the cells *ou* in jail.

2: (*Aut*) **dépôt d'essence** petrol (*Brit*) *ou* gasoline (*US*) depot; **dépôt de marchandises** goods (*Brit*) *ou* freight (*US*) depot *ou* station; **dépôt de munitions** ammunition dump; **dépôt d'ordures** (rubbish) dump *ou* tip (*Brit*), garbage dump (*US*).

dépotage [depɔtaʒ] *nm*, **dépotement** [depɔtmɑ̃] *nm* (*V* **dépoter**) transplanting; decanting.

dépoter [depɔte] (1) *vt plante* to take out of the pot, transplant; *liquide* to decant.

dépotoir [depɔtwaʀ] *nm* **(a)** (*lit, fig: décharge*) dumping ground, rubbish dump, rubbish tip (*Brit*), garbage dump (*US*). **(b)** (*usine*) sewage works.

dépouille [depuj] *nf* **(a)** (*peau*) skin, hide; (*Zool: de mue*) cast; *[serpent]* slough. **(b)** (*littér: cadavre*) ~ **(mortelle)** (mortal) remains. **(c)** (*littér: butin*) ~s plunder, spoils.

dépouillé, e [depuje] (*ptp de* **dépouiller**) *adj style, décor* bare, bald. ~ **de** lacking in, without, stripped of.

dépouillement [depujmɑ̃] *nm* **(a)** (*V* **dépouiller**) perusal; going through; studying. **le** ~ **du courrier a pris 3 heures** going through the mail *ou* the perusal of the mail took 3 hours, it took 3 hours to go through *ou* peruse the mail; **le** ~ **du scrutin** counting the votes.

(b) (*ascèse, pauvreté*) voluntary deprivation; (*sobriété*) lack of ornamentation.

dépouiller [depuje] (1) *vt* **(a)** (*examiner en détail*) *comptes, journal, courrier, ouvrage* to go through, peruse; *auteur* to go through, study (in detail). ~ **un scrutin** to count the votes.

(b) (*écorcher*) to skin; (*écorcer*) to bark, strip the bark from.

(c) (*enlever à*) ~ **qn de** *vêtements* to strip *ou* divest (*littér*) sb of; *économies, fortune, honneur, dignité* to strip *ou* denude sb of; *emploi, droits* to divest *ou* deprive sb of.

(d) (*dégarnir*) ~ **qch de** *ornements* to strip *ou* divest *ou* denude sth of; *feuilles, fleurs* to strip *ou* denude sth of; **un livre**

qui dépouille l'amour de son mystère a book that strips *ou* divests love of its mystery, a book that removes the mystery from love.

(e) (*littér: dénuder*) to strip. le vent dépouille les arbres the wind strips *ou* denudes (*littér*) the trees of their leaves; l'hiver dépouille les champs winter strips *ou* denudes (*littér*) the fields; ~ un autel to remove the ornaments from an altar, strip an altar (of its ornaments); (*fig*) ~ son style to strip one's style of ornaments.

(f) (*littér: spolier*) ~ un voyageur to despoil (*littér*) *ou* strip a traveller of his possessions; ~ un héritier to deprive *ou* divest an heir of his inheritance; ce père avare a dépouillé ses enfants this tight-fisted father has deprived *ou* stripped his children of everything; ils ont dépouillé le pays they have plundered the country *ou* laid the country bare.

(g) (*littér: se défaire de*) *vêtement* to shed (*littér*), divest o.s. of (*littér*); (*Zool*) *peau* to cast off, shed; *prétention, orgueil* to cast off, cast aside.

2 se dépouiller *vpr* **(a)** (*littér*) se ~ de *vêtements* to shed (*littér*), divest o.s. of (*littér*); *possessions* to divest *ou* deprive o.s. of; (*fig*) *arrogance* to cast off *ou* aside, divest o.s. of; *[arbre] feuilles, fleurs* to shed; *[prés etc] verdure, fleurs* to become stripped *ou* denuded (*littér*) of. les arbres se dépouillent (de leurs feuilles) the trees are shedding their leaves; la campagne se dépouille (de son feuillage *ou* de sa verdure) the countryside is losing its greenery; son style s'était dépouillé de toute redondance his style had been stripped *ou* divested of all ornament.

(b) *[animal qui mue]* to cast off *ou* shed its skin; *[vin]* to settle.

dépourvu, e [depuʀvy] **1** *adj*: ~ de *élément essentiel* without, lacking in; *relations, ressources* lacking *ou* wanting in, without; *intérêt, qualités, bon sens* devoid of, lacking *ou* wanting in; *méchanceté, mauvaises intentions* devoid of, without; *confort, courage, talent* wanting *ou* lacking in; ~ d'ornements unornamented, without ornaments; ~ d'argent penniless, without money; ce récit n'est pas ~ d'intérêt/de qualités this story is not devoid of interest/qualities *ou* not without interest/its qualities; des gens ~s (de tout) destitute people.

2 *nm*: prendre qn au ~ to catch sb unprepared; il a été pris au ~ par cette question inattendue he was caught off his guard *ou* unprepared by this unexpected question.

dépoussiérage [depusjeʀaʒ] *nm* removal of dust (*de* from). techniques de ~ dust removal techniques.

dépoussiérer [depusjeʀe] (6) *vt* to remove dust from.

dépravation [depʀavɑsjɔ̃] *nf* (*état*) depravity.

dépravé, e [depʀave] (*ptp de* **dépraver**) **1** *adj* depraved. **2** *nm,f* degenerate.

dépraver [depʀave] (1) *vt* to deprave. les mœurs se dépravent morals are becoming depraved.

dépréciateur, -trice [depʀesjatœʀ, tʀis] *nm,f* disparager, belittler.

dépréciatif, -ive [depʀesjatif, iv] *adj propos, jugement* depreciatory, disparaging; *mot, sens* derogatory, disparaging.

dépréciation [depʀesjɑsjɔ̃] *nf* depreciation (*de* in).

déprécier [depʀesje] (7) **1** *vt* (*faire perdre de la valeur à*) to depreciate; (*dénigrer*) to belittle, disparage, depreciate. **2 se déprécier** *vpr [monnaie, objet]* to depreciate; *[personne]* to belittle *ou* disparage o.s., be self-depreciating.

déprédateur, -trice [depʀedatœʀ, tʀis] (*V* **déprédation**) **1** *adj* plundering (*épith*); depredatory (*frm*). **2** *nm,f* plunderer; depredator (*frm*); embezzler.

déprédation [depʀedɑsjɔ̃] *nf* **(a)** (*gén pl*) (*pillage*) plundering (*U*), depredation (*frm*); (*dégâts*) damage (*U*), depredation (*frm*). **(b)** (*Jur: détournement*) misappropriation, embezzlement.

déprendre (se) [depʀɑ̃dʀ(ə)] (58) *vpr* (*littér*) se ~ de to lose one's fondness for.

dépressif, -ive [depʀesif, iv] *adj* depressive.

dépression [depʀesjɔ̃] *nf* **(a)** ~ (de terrain) depression; le village était dans une ~ the village was in a depression *ou* was low-lying; la maison était dans une ~ the house stood in a dip.

(b) ~ (atmosphérique) (atmospheric) depression; ~ centrée sur le nord de la France a trough of low pressure over northern France.

(c) (*Psych*) (*état*) depression. ~ (nerveuse) (nervous) breakdown; elle fait de la ~ she is having a bad fit of depression.

(d) ~ (économique) (economic) depression *ou* slump.

déprimant, e [depʀimɑ̃, ɑ̃t] *adj* (*moralement*) depressing; (*physiquement*) enervating, debilitating.

déprime* [depʀim] *nf*: la ~ the blues*.

déprimé, e [depʀime] (*ptp de* **déprimer**) *adj* **(a)** (*moralement*) depressed, low (*attrib*); (*physiquement*) low (*attrib*). **(b)** *terrain* depressed, low-lying.

déprimer [depʀime] (1) *vt* **(a)** (*moralement*) to depress; (*physiquement*) to debilitate, enervate. **(b)** (*enfoncer*) to depress.

De profundis [depʀɔfɔ̃dis] *nm* de profundis.

dépucelage‡ [depyslaʒ] *nm*: ~ d'une fille taking of a girl's virginity.

dépuceler‡ [depysle] (4) *vt fille*, (*hum*) *garçon* to take the virginity of. elle s'est fait ~ à 13 ans she lost it when she was 13‡; c'est lui qui l'a dépucelée she lost it to him‡; c'est avec elle que je me suis dépucelé it was with her that I had it for the first time‡, she gave me my first experience.

depuis [dəpɥi] **1** *prép* **(a)** (*durée avec point de départ*) since, ever since (*intensif*). il attend ~ hier/ce matin he has been waiting (ever) since yesterday/this morning; il attendait ~ lundi/le 3 mars he had been waiting (ever) since Monday/since March 3rd; ~ leur dispute ils ne se parlent/parlaient plus they haven't/hadn't spoken to each other (ever) since their quarrel *ou* (ever) since they quarrelled; ils ont toujours habité la même maison ~ leur mariage they've lived in the same house ever since they were married, they've always lived in the same house since they were married; je ne l'ai pas vue ~ qu'elle/~ le jour où elle s'est cassé la jambe I haven't seen her since she/since the day she broke her leg; elle joue du violon ~ son plus jeune âge she has played the violin since *ou* from early childhood, she has been playing *ou* has played the violin (ever) since she was very small; ~ cette affaire il est très méfiant (ever) since that affair he has been very suspicious; ~ quand le connaissez-vous? (for) how long have you known him?, how long is it that you've known him?; ~ quelle date êtes-vous ici? since when have you been here?, when did you arrive here?; ~ cela, (*littér*) ~ lors since then *ou* that time, from that time forward (*littér*), ever since; (*iro*) ~ quand es-tu (devenu) expert sur la question? since when have you been an expert on the matter? (*iro*); ~ le matin jusqu'au soir from morning till night.

(b) (*durée*) for. il est malade ~ une semaine he has been ill for a week (now); ~ combien de temps êtes-vous/travaillez-vous ici? — je suis/travaille ici ~ 5 ans how long have you been here/been working here? — I've been here/been working here (for) 5 years *ou* for the last 5 years; il est parti/mort ~ 2 ans he has been gone/dead (for) 2 years; ~ ces derniers jours/mois il a bien changé he has changed a great deal in *ou* over the last few days/months; elle cherche du travail ~ plus d'un mois she's been looking for a job for over *ou* more than a month; il dormait ~ une heure quand le réveil sonna he had been sleeping *ou* asleep for an hour when the alarm went off; mort ~ longtemps long since dead; tu le connais ~ longtemps? — ~ toujours have you known him long? *ou* for a long time? — I've known him all my life *ou* I've always known him; je la connaissais ~ peu quand elle est partie I hadn't known her long *ou* I had known her (for) only a short time *ou* I had only known her a little while when she left; nous n'avons pas été au théâtre ~ des siècles we haven't been to the theatre for *ou* in ages; c'est ~ peu qu'elle/~ peu elle a recommencé à sortir it's only lately *ou* recently *ou* of late that/lately *ou* recently *ou* of late she has started going out again.

(c) (*lieu: à partir de*) since, from. nous roulons/roulions sous la pluie ~ Londres it's been raining/it rained all the way from London; ~ Nice il a fait le plein 3 fois he's filled up 3 times since Nice; le concert est retransmis ~ Paris/nos studios the concert is broadcast from Paris/our studios; il sera bientôt possible de téléphoner ~ la lune it'll soon be possible to telephone from the moon.

(d) (*rang, ordre, quantité*) from. ~ le simple soldat jusqu'au général from private (right up) to general; ~ le premier jusqu'au dernier from the first to the last; robes ~ 20 F jusqu'à ... dresses from 20 francs to ..., dresses starting at 20 francs (and) going up to ...; ~ 5 grammes jusqu'à ... from 5 grammes (up) to ...; ils ont toutes les tailles ~ le 36 they have all sizes from 36 upwards, they have all sizes starting at 36.

(e) ~ que, ~ le temps que: ~ qu'il habite ici, il n'a cessé de se plaindre he hasn't stopped complaining (ever) since he's lived here; ~ qu'il est ministre il ne nous parle plus now that he is *ou* since he became a minister he doesn't speak to us any more; ~ qu'il avait appris son succès il désirait *ou* il avait désiré la féliciter he had wanted to congratulate her ever since he had heard of her success; ~ le temps qu'il apprend le français, il devrait pouvoir le parler considering how long *ou* for all the time he's been learning French, he ought to be able to speak it; ~ le temps qu'il est ici, il ne nous a jamais dit un mot in all the time he has been here he has never said a word to us; ~ le temps que nous ne nous étions vus! it's ages since we (last) saw each other!, long time no see!*; ~ le temps que je voulais voir ce film! I had been wanting to see that film for ages! *ou* for such a long time!; ~ le temps que je dis que je vais lui écrire! I've been saying I'll write to him for ages!; ~ que le monde est monde since time immemorial.

2 *adv* ever since, since (then). ~, nous sommes sans nouvelles we have been without news ever since; nous étions en vacances ensemble, je ne l'ai pas revu ~ we were on holiday together and I haven't seen him since (then).

dépuratif, -ive [depyʀatif, iv] *adj, nm* depurative.

députation [depytɑsjɔ̃] *nf* (*envoi, groupe*) deputation, delegation; (*mandat de député*) position of deputy. candidat à la ~ parliamentary candidate; se présenter à la ~ to stand for parliament.

député [depyte] *nm* **(a)** (*au parlement*) deputy, ≃ member of Parliament (*Brit*), ≃ representative (*US*). elle a été élue ~ de Metz she has been elected (as) deputy *ou* member for Metz; le ~-maire de Rouen the deputy and mayor of Rouen.

(b) (*envoyé d'un prince*) envoy; (*envoyé d'une assemblée*) delegate.

députer [depyte] (1) *vt*: ~ qn pour faire/aller to delegate sb to do/go; ~ qn à *ou* auprès d'une assemblée/auprès de qn to send sb (as representative) to an assembly/to sb.

der* [dɛʀ] *nf*: la ~ des ~s the war to end all wars.

déracinable [deʀasinabl(ə)] *adj préjugé* eradicable. difficilement ~ difficult to eradicate.

déracinement [deʀasinmɑ̃] *nm* (*V* **déraciner**) uprooting; eradication.

déraciner [deʀasine] (1) *vt arbre, personne* to uproot; *erreur* to eradicate; *préjugé* to root out, eradicate.

déraillement [deʀɑjmɑ̃] *nm* derailment.

dérailler [deʀɑje] (1) *vi [train]* to be derailed, go off *ou* leave the rails; (*: *divaguer*) to rave*, talk twaddle*; (*: *mal fonctionner*) to be up the spout* (*Brit*), be on the blink*. faire ~ un train to derail a train.

dérailleur [deʀɑjœʀ] *nm [bicyclette]* dérailleur gears; (*Rail*) derailer, derailing stop.

déraison [deʀɛzɔ̃] *nf (littér)* folly.

déraisonnable [deʀɛzɔnabl(ə)] *adj* unreasonable.

déraisonnablement [deʀɛzɔnabləmɑ̃] *adv* unreasonably.

déraisonner [deʀɛzɔne] (1) *vi (littér) (dire des bêtises)* to talk nonsense; *(être fou)* to rave.

dérangement [deʀɑ̃ʒmɑ̃] *nm* **(a)** *(gêne)* trouble. **(toutes) mes excuses pour le ~** my apologies for the trouble I'm causing *ou* for the inconvenience.

(b) *(déplacement)* **pour vous éviter un autre ~** to save you another trip; **voilà 10 F pour votre ~** here's 10 francs for coming *ou* for taking the trouble to come.

(c) *(bouleversement) [affaires, papiers]* disorder *(de* in). **en ~** *machine, téléphone* out of order; **~ d'esprit**† mental disturbance.

déranger [deʀɑ̃ʒe] (3) **1** *vt* **(a)** *(déplacer) papiers* to disturb; *vêtements* to disarrange, ruffle; *coiffure* to disarrange, ruffle, mess up*.

(b) *(gêner, importuner)* to trouble, bother; *(surprendre) animal, cambrioleur* to disturb. **je ne vous dérange pas?** I trust I'm not disturbing you?; **les cambrioleurs ont été dérangés** the burglars were disturbed; **elle viendra vous voir demain, si cela ne vous dérange pas** she'll come and see you tomorrow, if that's all right by you* *ou* if that's no trouble to you; **elle ne veut pas ~ le docteur inutilement** she doesn't want to bother the doctor unnecessarily; **ne me dérangez pas toutes les cinq minutes** don't come bothering me every five minutes; **~ qn dans son sommeil** to disturb sb's sleep; **on le dérange toutes les nuits en ce moment** he is disturbed every night at the moment; **ça vous dérange si je fume?** do you mind *ou* will it bother you if I smoke?; *(pancarte)* **'ne pas ~'** 'do not disturb'.

(c) *(dérégler) projets, routine* to disrupt, upset; *machine* to put out of order. **les essais atomiques ont dérangé le temps** the nuclear tests have unsettled *ou* upset the weather; **ça lui a dérangé l'esprit** this has disturbed his mind; **il a le cerveau dérangé, il est dérangé** he *ou* his mind is deranged *ou* unhinged; **il a l'estomac dérangé, il est dérangé** his stomach is upset, he has an upset stomach *ou* a stomach upset.

2 se déranger *vpr* **(a)** *[médecin, réparateur]* to come out.

(b) *(pour une démarche, une visite)* to go along, come along. **sans vous ~, sur simple appel téléphonique, nous vous renseignons** without leaving your home, you can obtain information simply by telephoning us; **je me suis dérangé pour rien, c'était fermé** it was a waste of time going (along) *ou* it was a wasted journey *ou* trip because it was closed.

(c) *(changer de place)* to move. **il s'est dérangé pour me laisser passer** he moved *ou* stepped aside to let me pass; **surtout, ne vous dérangez pas pour moi** please don't put yourself out *ou* go to any inconvenience on my account.

dérapage [deʀapaʒ] *nm [véhicule]* skid. **faire un ~** to skid; **faire un ~ contrôlé** to do a controlled skid.

déraper [deʀape] (1) *vi* **(a)** *[véhicule]* to skid; *[piéton, semelles, échelle]* to slip. **(b)** *[ancre]* to be atrip *ou* aweigh; *[bateau]* to trip her anchor.

dératé, e [deʀate] *nm,f V* **courir.**

dératisation [deʀatizɑsjɔ̃] *nf* rat extermination.

dératiser [deʀatize] (1) *vt*: **~ un lieu** to exterminate the rats in a place, rid a place of rats.

derby [dɛʀbi] *nm (Ftbl, Rugby)* derby; *(Équitation)* Derby.

derechef [dəʀəʃɛf] *adv († ou littér)* once more, once again.

déréglé, e [deʀegle] *(ptp de* **dérégler***) adj (V* **dérégler***)* out of order *(attrib)*; upset; unsettled; dissolute. **les élucubrations de son imagination ~e** the ravings of his wild *ou* disordered imagination.

dérèglement [deʀɛgləmɑ̃] *nm [machine, mécanisme]* disturbance; *[pouls, estomac, temps]* upset; *[esprit]* unsettling *(U)*; *[mœurs]* dissoluteness *(U)*. *(littér, frm)* **~s** *(dépravations)* dissoluteness.

dérégler [deʀegle] (6) **1** *vt* **(a)** *mécanisme* to throw out (of order), disturb; *machine* to disturb the mechanism of, put out of order; *pouls* to upset; *esprit* to unsettle; *habitudes, temps* to upset, unsettle; *estomac, appétit* to upset.

(b) *vie, mœurs* to make dissolute.

2 se dérégler *vpr [mécanisme, machine, appareil]* to go wrong; *[pouls, estomac, temps]* to be upset; *[esprit]* to become unsettled; *[mœurs]* to become dissolute. **cette montre se dérègle tout le temps** this watch keeps going wrong.

dérider [deʀide] (1) **1** *vt personne* to brighten up; *front* to uncrease. **2 se dérider** *vpr [personne]* to brighten (up); *[front]* to uncrease.

dérision [deʀizjɔ̃] *nf* derision, mockery. **par ~** derisively, mockingly; **de ~** of derision, derisive; **c'est une ~!** it's derisory!

dérisoire [deʀizwaʀ] *adj somme, résultat* derisory, pathetic; *proposition, offre* derisory.

dérisoirement [deʀizwaʀmɑ̃] *adv* pathetically.

dérivatif, -ive [deʀivatif, iv] **1** *adj* derivative. **2** *nm* distraction. **il a son travail comme ~ à sa douleur** he has his work to take his mind off *ou* to distract him from his sorrow.

dérivation [deʀivɑsjɔ̃] *nf* **(a)** *[rivière]* diversion; *V* **canal. (b)** *(Ling, Math)* derivation. **(c)** *(Élec)* shunt. **(d)** *(Aviat, Naut)* drift, deviation.

dérive [deʀiv] *nf* **(a)** *(déviation)* drift, leeway. **~ sur bâbord** drift to port; **navire en ~** ship adrift; **~ des continents** continental drift; *(lit)* **à la ~** adrift; *(fig)* **aller à la ~** to drift; *(fig)* **tout va à la ~** everything has been left to drift (along); **partir à la ~** to go drifting off. **(b)** *(dispositif) (Aviat)* fin, vertical stabilizer *(US)*; *(Naut)* centre-board.

dérivé, e [deʀive] *(ptp de* **dériver***)* **1** *adj (gén, Chim, Math)* derived. **2** *nm (Chim, Ling, Math)* derivative; *(produit)* by-product. **3 dérivée** *nf (Math)* derivative.

dériver [deʀive] (1) **1** *vt* **(a)** *rivière* to divert; *(Chim, Ling, Math)* to derive; *(Élec)* to shunt. **(b)** *(Tech: dériveter)* to unrivet.

2 dériver de *vt indir* to derive *ou* stem from; *(Ling)* to derive from, be derived from, be a derivative of.

3 *vi (Aviat, Naut)* to drift; *(fig) [orateur]* to wander *ou* drift (away) from the subject.

dériveur [deʀivœʀ] *nm (voile)* storm sail; *(bateau)* sailing dinghy *(with centre-board)*.

dermatite [dɛʀmatit] *nf* = **dermite.**

dermatologie [dɛʀmatɔlɔʒi] *nf* dermatology.

dermatologique [dɛʀmatɔlɔʒik] *adj* dermatological.

dermatologiste [dɛʀmatɔlɔʒist(ə)] *nmf,* **dermatologue** [dɛʀmatɔlɔg] *nmf* dermatologist.

dermatose [dɛʀmatoz] *nf* dermatosis.

derme [dɛʀm(ə)] *nm* dermis, derm, derma.

dermique [dɛʀmik] *adj* dermic, dermal.

dermite [dɛʀmit] *nf* dermatitis.

dernier, -ière [dɛʀnje, jɛʀ] **1** *adj* **(a)** *(dans le temps, l'espace) (gén)* last; *étage* top *(épith)*; *rang* back *(épith)*; *branche* upper, highest. **arriver (bon) ~** to come in last (well behind the others); **la ~ière marche de l'escalier** *(en bas)* the bottom step; *(en haut)* the top step; **prends le ~ mouchoir de la pile** *(dessus)* take the top handkerchief in the pile; *(dessous)* take the bottom handkerchief in the pile; *(Presse)* **en ~ière page** on the back page; **les 100 ~ières pages** the last 100 pages; *(Sport)* **être en ~ière position** to be in (the) last place, bring up the rear; **durant les ~s jours du mois** in the last few days of the month, as the month was drawing to a close; **l'artiste, dans ses ~ières œuvres...** the artist, in his final *ou* last works...; **les ~ières années de sa vie** the last few years of his life; **il faut payer avant le 15, ~ délai** it must be paid by the 15th at the latest, the 15th is the deadline for payment; **15 octobre, ~ délai pour les inscriptions** 15th October is the closing *ou* final date for registration, registration must be completed by 15th October at the latest; *V* **jugement, premier.**

(b) *(en mérite) élève* bottom, last. **être reçu ~** to come last *ou* bottom *(à* in); **il est toujours ~ (en classe)** he's always bottom (of the class), he's always last (in the class); **c'est bien la ~ière personne à qui je demanderais!** he's the last person I'd ask!

(c) *(gén avant n: le plus récent)* last, latest. **le ~ roman de X** X's latest *ou* last novel; **ces ~s mois/jours** (during) the last couple of *ou* few months/days; **ces ~s incidents/événements** these latest *ou* most recent incidents/events; **ces ~s temps** lately, of late; **aux ~ières nouvelles, il était à Paris** the last I *(ou* we *etc)* heard (of him) he was in Paris, the latest news was that he was in Paris; **voici les ~ières nouvelles concernant l'accident** here is the latest news of the accident, here is an up-to-the-minute report on the accident; **nouvelles de ~ière heure** *ou* **minute** stop-press news; *(fig)* **collaborateur/combattant de la ~ière heure** last-minute helper/fighter; *(Presse)* **~ière édition** (late) final; **c'est le ~ cri** *ou* **la ~ière mode** it's the very latest thing *ou* fashion.

(d) *(extrême)* **il s'est montré grossier au ~ point** *ou* **degré** he was extremely rude; **il a protesté avec la ~ière énergie** he protested most vigorously *ou* with the utmost vigour; **examiner qch dans les ~s détails** to study sth in the most minute *ou* in the minutest detail; **le ~ degré de perfection** the height *ou* summit of perfection; **le ~ degré de la souffrance** the depths of suffering; **c'est du ~ ridicule** it's utterly ridiculous, it's ridiculous in the extreme; **c'est du ~ chic** it's the last word in elegance, it's ultra-smart; **c'est de la ~ière importance** it is of the utmost importance; **il est du ~ bien avec le patron** he's on the best of terms with his boss.

(e) *(pire) qualité* lowest, poorest. **de ~ ordre** very inferior; **vendre des morceaux de ~ choix** to sell the poorest quality *ou* most inferior cuts of meat; **c'était la ~ière chose à faire!** that was the last thing to do!; **faire subir les ~s outrages à une femme** to ravish *ou* violate a woman.

(f) *(évoquant la mort)* last. **ses ~s moments** *ou* **instants** his last *ou* dying moments; **être à sa ~ière heure** to be on one's deathbed; **jusqu'à mon ~ jour** until the day I die, until my dying day; **je croyais que ma ~ière heure était venue** I thought my last *ou* final hour had come; **dans les ~s temps il ne s'alimentait plus** towards the end he stopped eating; *(littér)* **rendre le ~ soupir** to breathe one's last *(littér)*; *(frm)* **rendre les ~s devoirs** to pay one's last respects; *(Rel)* **les ~s sacrements** the last sacraments *ou* rites.

(g) *(précédent)* last, previous. **les ~s propriétaires sont partis à l'étranger** the last *ou* previous owners went abroad; **le ~ détenteur du record était américain** the last *ou* previous holder of the record was an American; **l'an/le mois ~** last year/month.

(h) *(final, ultime) échelon, grade* top, highest. **après un ~ regard/effort** after one last *ou* final look/effort; **quel est votre ~ prix?** *(pour vendre)* what's the lowest you'll go?; *(pour acheter)* what's your final offer?; **en ~ière analyse** in the final *ou* last analysis; **en ~ lieu** finally; **mettre la ~ière main à qch** to put the finishing touches to sth; **avoir le ~ mot** to have the last word; **en ~ ressort** in the last instance; **en ~ recours** as a last resort; **les ~ières volontés de qn** the last wishes of sb; **les ~ières dispositions du défunt** the deceased's last will and testament; **accompagner qn à sa ~ière demeure** to accompany sb to his final resting place.

2 *nm,f* **(a)** last (one). **parler/sortir le ~** to speak/leave last; **les ~s arrivés n'auront rien** the last ones to arrive *ou* the last arrivals will get nothing; **le ~ venu** *(lit)* the last to come; *(fig péj)* just anybody; **tu seras servi le ~** you'll be served last, you'll be the last to get served; **il est le ~ de sa classe/de la liste** he's at the bottom of the class/list; **voilà le ~ de la classe** there's the one *ou* boy who's bottom of the class *ou* last in the class; **il a été reçu dans les ~s** his pass-mark was one of the lowest, he was nearly bottom in the exam; **elle a tendance à gâter son (petit) ~** she's inclined to spoil her youngest (child); **il est le ~ à pouvoir** *ou* **qui puisse faire cela** he's the last person to be able to do that; **c'est le ~ de mes soucis** it's the last of my worries; **ils ont été tués jusqu'au ~** they were all killed (right down) to the last man, every single one of them was killed; **c'est la ~ière à qui vous puissiez demander un service** she's the last person you can ask a favour of.

(b) (*péj*) **le ~ des imbéciles** an absolute imbecile, a complete and utter fool; **le ~ des filous** an out-and-out scoundrel; **c'est le ~ des ~s!** he's the lowest of the low.

(c) ce ~, cette ~ière (*de deux*) the latter; (*de plusieurs*) this last, the last-mentioned.

3 *nm* (*étage*) top floor *ou* storey (*Brit*) *ou* story (*US*). **acheter qch/arriver en ~** to buy sth/arrive last.

4 dernière *nf* (*Théât*) last performance. **vous connaissez la ~ière?*** have you heard the latest?

5: dernier-né, dernière-née *nm,f, mpl* **derniers-nés** last-born, youngest child; (*fig: œuvre*) latest *ou* most recent creation.

dernièrement [dɛʀnjɛʀmɑ̃] *adv* (*il y a peu de temps*) recently; (*ces derniers temps*) lately, recently.

dérobade [deʀɔbad] *nf* side-stepping (*U*); (*Équitation*) refusal.

dérobé, e [deʀɔbe] (*ptp de* **dérober**) **1** *adj escalier, porte* secret, hidden. **2 dérobée** *nf*: **à la ~e** secretly, surreptitiously.

dérober [deʀɔbe] (1) **1** *vt* **(a)** (*voler*) to steal. **~ qch à qn** to steal sth from sb; **~ un baiser (à qn)** to steal a kiss (from sb).

(b) (*cacher*) **~ qch à qn** to hide *ou* conceal sth from sb; **une haie dérobait la palissade aux regards** a hedge hid *ou* screened the fence from sight, a hedge concealed the fence; **~ qn à la justice/au danger/à la mort** to shield sb from justice/danger/death.

(c) (*littér: détourner*) *regard, front* to turn away.

2 se dérober *vpr* **(a)** (*refuser d'assumer*) to shy away. **se ~ à son devoir/à ses obligations** to shy away from *ou* shirk one's duty/obligations; **se ~ à une discussion** to shy away from a discussion; **je lui ai posé la question mais il s'est dérobé** I put the question to him but he evaded the issue *ou* shied away.

(b) (*se cacher de*) to hide (o.s.), conceal o.s. **se ~ aux regards** to hide (o.s.) from view; **se ~ à la justice** to hide from justice; **pour se ~ à la curiosité dont il était l'objet** in order to escape the curiosity surrounding him.

(c) (*se libérer*) to slip away. **se ~ à l'étreinte de qn** to slip out of sb's arms; **il voulut la prendre dans ses bras mais elle se déroba** he tried to take her in his arms but she shrank *ou* slipped away.

(d) (*s'effondrer*) *[sol]* to give way. **ses genous se dérobèrent (sous lui)** his knees gave way (beneath him).

(e) (*Équitation*) to refuse.

dérogation [deʀɔgasjɔ̃] *nf* (special) dispensation. **ceci constitue une ~ par rapport à la loi** this constitutes a departure from the law; **aucune ~ ne sera permise** no departure from this will be permitted, no special dispensation will be allowed; **certaines ~s sont prévues dans le règlement** certain special dispensations are allowed for in the rules; **il a obtenu ceci par ~** he obtained this by special dispensation.

dérogatoire [deʀɔgatwaʀ] *adj* dispensatory.

déroger [deʀɔʒe] (3) *vi* **(a)** (*déchoir*) (*gén*) to lower o.s., demean o.s.; (*Hist*) to lose rank and title. **(b)** (*enfreindre*) **~ à qch** to go against sth, depart from sth; **ce serait ~ à la règle établie** that would go against the established order *ou* procedure.

dérouillée: [deʀuje] *nf* thrashing, belting:.

dérouiller [deʀuje] (1) **1** *vt* **(a)** *métal* to remove the rust from. (*fig*) **je vais me ~ les jambes** I'm going to stretch my legs.

(b) (*:: battre*) to give a thrashing *ou* belting: to, thrash.

2 *vi* (*:*) (*souffrir*) to go through it* (*surtout Brit*), have a hard time of it; (*se faire battre*) to cop it:, catch it*.

déroulement [deʀulmɑ̃] *nm* **(a)** *[match, cérémonie]* progress; *[action, histoire]* development, unfolding, progress. **pendant le ~ des opérations** during the course of (the) operations, while the operations were in progress; **pendant le ~ du film** while the film was on, during the film; **rien n'est venu troubler le ~ de la manifestation** the demonstration went off *ou* passed without incident, nothing happened to disturb the course of the demonstration.

(b) (*V* **dérouler**) unwinding; uncoiling; unrolling.

dérouler [deʀule] (1) **1** *vt fil, bobine* to unwind; *cordage* to uncoil; *nappe, carte* to unroll; (*Tech*) *tronc d'arbre* to peel a veneer from. **le serpent déroule ses anneaux** the snake uncoils; **il déroula dans son esprit les événements de la veille** in his mind he went over *ou* through the events of the previous day; (*littér*) **la rivière déroule ses méandres** the river snakes *ou* winds along its tortuous course.

2 se dérouler *vpr* **(a)** (*lit*) *[fil, bobine]* to unwind, come unwound; *[ruban]* to unwind, uncoil, come unwound; *[carte, drapeau]* to unroll, come unrolled.

(b) (*se produire*) to take place, happen, occur; (*se situer*) to take place. **la ville où la cérémonie s'est déroulée** the town where the ceremony took place; **c'est là que toute ma vie s'est déroulée** it was there that my whole life was spent.

(c) (*se développer*) *[histoire, faits]* to progress, develop, unfold. **la manifestation s'est déroulée dans le calme** the demonstration went off peacefully; **comment s'est déroulé le match?** how did the match go (off)?; **à mesure que l'histoire se déroulait** as the story unfolded *ou* developed *ou* progressed; **son existence se déroulait, calme et morne** his life went on, calm and drab; **le paysage se déroulait devant nos yeux** the landscape unfolded before our eyes.

déroutant, e [deʀutɑ̃, ɑ̃t] *adj* disconcerting.

déroute [deʀut] *nf* rout. **armée en ~** routed army; **mettre en ~** to rout, put to rout *ou* flight.

déroutement [deʀutmɑ̃] *nm* (*Aviat, Naut*) rerouting, diversion.

dérouter [deʀute] (1) *vt avion, navire* to reroute, divert; *candidat, orateur* to disconcert, throw (out)*, put out; *poursuivants, police, recherches* to throw *ou* put off the scent.

derrick [dɛʀik] *nm* derrick.

derrière [dɛʀjɛʀ] **1** *prép* **(a)** (*à l'arrière de, à la suite de*) behind. **il se cache ~ le fauteuil** he's hiding behind the armchair; **il avait les mains ~ le dos** he had his hands behind his back; **sors de ~ le lit** come out from behind the bed; **passe (par) ~ la maison** go round the back of *ou* round behind the house; **marcher l'un ~ l'autre** to walk one behind the other; (*lit, fig*) **il a laissé les autres loin ~ lui** he left the others far *ou* a long way behind (him); **disparaître ~ une colline** to disappear behind a hill.

(b) (*fig*) behind. **il faut chercher ~ les apparences** one must look beneath (outward) appearances; **~ sa générosité se cache l'intérêt le plus sordide** behind his generosity lurks *ou* his generosity hides the most sordid self-interest; **faire qch ~ (le dos de) qn** to do sth behind sb's back; **dire du mal ~ le dos de qn** to say (unkind) things behind sb's back; **il a laissé 3 enfants ~ lui** he left 3 children; **le président avait tout le pays ~ lui** the president had the whole country behind him *ou* had the backing of the whole country; **ayez confiance, je suis ~ vous** take heart, I'll support you *ou* back you up *ou* I'm on your side; **il faut toujours être ~ lui** *ou* **son dos** you've always got to keep an eye *ou* a watch on him; **un vin de ~ les fagots** an extra-special (little) wine; **une bouteille de ~ les fagots** a bottle of the best; *V* **idée**.

(c) (*Naut*) (*dans le bateau*) abaft; (*sur la mer*) astern of.

2 *adv* **(a)** behind. **vous êtes juste ~** you're just *ou* right behind it (*ou* us *etc*); **on l'a laissé (loin) ~** we (have) left him (far *ou* a long way) behind; **il est assis 3 rangs ~** he's sitting 3 rows back *ou* 3 rows behind (us *ou* them *etc*); **il a pris des places ~** he has got seats at the back; (*Aut*) **il a préféré monter ~** he preferred to sit in the back; **chemisier qui se boutonne (par) ~** blouse which buttons up *ou* does up at the back; **passe le plateau ~** pass the tray back; **regarde ~, on nous suit** look behind (you) *ou* look back — we're being followed; **il est ~** he's behind (us *ou* them *etc*); **regarde ~** (*au fond de la voiture*) look in the back; (*derrière un objet*) look behind (it); **arrêtez de pousser, ~!** stop pushing back there!, you behind *ou* back there, stop pushing!; (*fig*) **tu peux être sûr qu'il y a quelqu'un ~** you can be sure that there's somebody at the back of it (all) *ou* behind it (all).

(b) par-~: c'est fermé, entre *ou* **passe par-~** it's locked, go in by the back *ou* go in (by) the back way; **attaquer par-~** *ennemi* to attack from behind *ou* from the rear; *adversaire* to attack from behind; **dire du mal de qn par-~** to say (unkind) things behind sb's back; **il fait tout par-~** he does everything behind people's backs *ou* in an underhand way.

(c) (*Naut*) (*dans le bateau*) aft, abaft; (*sur la mer*) astern.

3 *nm* **(a)** *[personne]* bottom, behind*; *[animal]* hindquarters, rump. **donner un coup de pied au ~** *ou* **dans le ~ de qn** to kick sb in the behind*, give sb a kick in *ou* on the behind* *ou* in the pants:; **quand j'ai eu 20 ans mon père m'a chassé à coups de pied dans le ~** when I was 20 my father sent me packing *ou* kicked me out*; *V* **botter**.

(b) *[objet]* back; *[maison]* back, rear. **le ~ de la tête** the back of the head; **habiter sur le ~** to live at the back (of the house); **roue/porte de ~** back *ou* rear wheel/door; *V* **patte**.

(c) (*rare*) **~s** *[édifice]* back, rear; *[armée]* rear.

derviche [dɛʀviʃ] *nm* dervish. **~ tourneur** dancing dervish.

des [de] *V* **de¹, de²**.

dès [dɛ] *prép* **(a)** (*dans le temps*) **dimanche il a commencé à pleuvoir ~ le matin** on Sunday it rained from the morning onwards, on Sunday it started raining (right) in the morning; **~ le 15 août nous ne travaillerons plus qu'à mi-temps** (as) from August 15th we will only be working half-time; **~ le début** from the (very) start *ou* beginning, right from the start *ou* beginning; **~ son retour il fera le nécessaire** as soon as he's back *ou* immediately upon his return he'll do what's necessary; **~ son retour il commença à se plaindre** as soon as he was back *ou* from the moment he was back he started complaining; **il se précipita vers la sortie ~ la fin du spectacle** as soon as *ou* immediately (*surtout Brit*) the performance was over he rushed towards the exit; **~ l'époque romaine on connaissait le chauffage central** as early as *ou* as far back as Roman times people used central heating; **~ son enfance il a collectionné les papillons** he has collected butterflies since (his) childhood *ou* ever since he was a child; **~ maintenant** *ou* **à présent** from now on, as from now, henceforth (*frm, littér*); **~ l'abord/ce moment** from the very beginning *ou* the outset/that moment.

(b) (*dans l'espace*) **~ Lyon il se mit à pleuvoir** we ran into rain *ou* it started to rain as *ou* when we got to Lyons; **~ Lyon il a plu sans arrêt** it never stopped raining from Lyons onwards *ou* after Lyons; **~ l'entrée vous êtes accueillis par des slogans publicitaires** advertising slogans hit you as soon as *ou* immediately (*surtout Brit*) you walk in the door; **~ le seuil je sentis qu'il se passait quelque chose** (even) standing in the doorway *ou* as I walked in at the door I sensed that something was going on.

(c) (*dans une gradation*) **~ sa première année il brilla en anglais** he was good at English right from the first year; **~ le premier verre il roula sous la table** after the (very) first glass he collapsed under the table; **~ la troisième chanson elle se mit à pleurer** at the third song she started to cry.

(d) (*loc*) **~ que** as soon as, immediately; **~ qu'il aura fini il viendra** as soon as *ou* immediately (*surtout Brit*) he's finished he'll come; ~ **lors** (*depuis lors*) from that moment (on), from that time on, from then on; (*conséquemment*) that being the case, consequently; ~ **lors il ne fuma plus** from that time *ou* moment on he stopped smoking; ~ **lors il décida de ne plus fumer** from that moment he decided he wouldn't smoke any more; **vous ne pouvez rien prouver contre lui,** ~ **lors vous devez le relâcher** you can prove nothing against him and that being the case *ou* and so you'll have to release him; ~ **lors que** (*temporel*) as soon as; (*relation de conséquence*) (*si*) from the moment that; (*puisque*) since, as; ~ **lors que vous décidez de faire cela, nous ne pouvons plus rien pour vous** from the moment (that) you choose to do that, we can do nothing more for you; ~ **lors qu'il a choisi de démissionner, il n'a plus droit à ceci** since *ou* as he has decided to hand in his notice he is no longer entitled to this; **peu m'importe ceci,** ~ **lors qu'ils sont heureux** this is not important to me since *ou* so long as they are happy.

désabusé, e [dezabyze] (*ptp de* **désabuser**) *adj personne, air* disenchanted; *ton* disenchanted, of disillusion; (††: *détrompé*) disabused, undeceived. **geste** ~ gesture of disillusion.

désabusement [dezabyzmɑ̃] *nm* disillusionment.

désabuser [dezabyze] (1) *vt* to disillusion (*de* about), disabuse (*de* of), undeceive (*de* of).

désacclimater [dezaklimate] (1) *vt* to disacclimatize.

désaccord [dezakɔʀ] *nm* **(a)** (*mésentente*) discord. **être en** ~ **avec sa famille/son temps** to be at odds *ou* at variance with one's family/time.

(b) (*divergence*) (*entre personnes, points de vue*) disagreement; (*entre idées, intérêts*) conflict, clash. **le** ~ **qui subsiste entre leurs intérêts** their unresolved conflict *ou* clash of interests; **leurs intérêts sont en** ~ **avec les nôtres** their interests conflict *ou* clash with ours.

(c) (*contradiction*) discrepancy. ~ **entre la théorie et la réalité** discrepancy between (the) theory and (the) reality; **les deux versions de l'accident sont en** ~ **sur bien des points** the two versions of the accident are at odds on *ou* diverge on many points; **ce qu'il dit est en** ~ **avec ce qu'il fait** what he says conflicts with what he does, there is a discrepancy between what he says and what he does.

désaccordé, e [dezakɔʀde] (*ptp de* **désaccorder**) *adj piano* out of tune.

désaccorder [dezakɔʀde] (1) **1** *vt piano* to put out of tune. **2 se désaccorder** *vpr* to go out of tune.

désaccoupler [dezakuple] (1) *vt wagons* to uncouple; (*Élec*) to disconnect.

désaccoutumer [dezakutyme] (1) **1** *vt*: ~ **qn de qch/de faire** to get sb out of the habit of sth/of doing, disaccustom sb from sth/from doing (*frm*). **2 se désaccoutumer** *vpr*: **se** ~ **de qch/de faire** to lose the habit of sth/of doing.

désacralisation [desakʀalizɑsjɔ̃] *nf*: **la** ~ **d'une institution/profession** the removal of an institution/a profession from its pedestal.

désacraliser [desakʀalize] (1) *vt institution, profession* to remove from its pedestal. **la médecine se trouve désacralisée** medicine has been removed from its pedestal.

désaffectation [dezafɛktɑsjɔ̃] *nf* closing down.

désaffecté, e [dezafɛkte] (*ptp de* **désaffecter**) *adj* disused.

désaffecter [dezafɛkte] (1) *vt* to close down. **le lycée a été désaffecté pour en faire une prison** the lycée was closed down and converted (in)to a prison.

désaffection [dezafɛksjɔ̃] *nf* loss of affection *ou* fondness (*pour* for).

désaffectionner (se)† [dezafɛksjɔne] (1) *vpr*: **se** ~ **de** to lose one's affection *ou* fondness for.

désagréable [dezagʀeabl(ə)] *adj* unpleasant, disagreeable.

désagréablement [dezagʀeabləmɑ̃] *adv* unpleasantly, disagreeably.

désagrégation [dezagʀegɑsjɔ̃] *nf* (*V* **désagréger, se désagréger**) disintegration; breaking up.

désagréger [dezagʀeʒe] (3 *et* 6) **1** *vt* (*lit*) to disintegrate, break up; (*fig*) to break up. **2 se désagréger** *vpr* to break up, disintegrate; (*fig*) *[société, groupe]* to break up, disintegrate; *[foule]* to break up; *[amitié]* to break up.

désagrément [dezagʀemɑ̃] *nm* **(a)** (*gén pl: inconvénient, déboire*) annoyance, trouble (*U*). **malgré tous les** ~**s que cela entraîne** despite all the annoyances *ou* trouble it involves; **c'est un des** ~**s de ce genre de métier** it's one of the annoyances of *ou* part of the trouble with this kind of job; **cette voiture m'a valu bien des** ~**s** this car has given me a great deal of trouble.

(b) (*frm: déplaisir*) displeasure. **causer du** ~ **à qn** to cause sb displeasure.

désaimantation [dezɛmɑ̃tɑsjɔ̃] *nf* demagnetization.

désaimanter [dezɛmɑ̃te] (1) *vt* to demagnetize.

désaltérant, e [dezalteʀɑ̃, ɑ̃t] *adj* thirst-quenching.

désaltérer [dezalteʀe] (6) **1** *vt* to quench *ou* slake (*frm*) the thirst of. **le vin ne désaltère pas** wine does not quench a thirst, wine is not a thirst-quenching drink. **2 se désaltérer** *vpr* to quench *ou* slake (*frm*) one's thirst.

désamorçage [dezamɔʀsaʒ] *nm* **(a)** *[fusée, pistolet]* removal of the primer (*de* from); (*fig*) *[situation, conflit]* defusing. **(b)** *[dynamo]* failure.

désamorcer [dezamɔʀse] (3) *vt fusée, pistolet* to remove the primer from; *pompe* to drain; (*fig*) *situation explosive* to defuse; *crise, mouvement de revendication* to forestall, nip in the bud.

désapparié, e [dezapaʀje] (*ptp de* **désapparier**) *adj* = **déparié.**

désapparier [dezapaʀje] (7) *vt* = **déparier.**

désappointement [dezapwɛ̃tmɑ̃] *nm* disappointment.

désappointer [dezapwɛ̃te] (1) *vt* to disappoint.

désapprendre [dezapʀɑ̃dʀ(ə)] (58) *vt* (*littér*) to forget; (*volontairement*) to unlearn.

désapprobateur, -trice [dezapʀɔbatœʀ, tʀis] *adj* disapproving.

désapprobation [dezapʀɔbɑsjɔ̃] *nf* disapproval, disapprobation (*frm*).

désapprouver [dezapʀuve] (1) *vt acte, conduite* to disapprove of. **je le désapprouve quand il refuse de les aider** I disapprove of him for refusing to help them, I disapprove of his refusing *ou* refusal to help them; **je le désapprouve de les inviter** I disagree with his inviting them, I disapprove of his inviting them; **le public désapprouva** the audience showed its disapproval; **elle désapprouve qu'il vienne** she disapproves of his coming.

désarçonner [dezaʀsɔne] (1) *vt [cheval]* to throw, unseat; *[adversaire]* to unseat, unhorse; (*fig*) *[argument]* to throw*, nonplus. **son calme/sa réponse me désarçonna** I was completely thrown* *ou* nonplussed by his calmness/reply.

désargenté, e [dezaʀʒɑ̃te] (*ptp de* **désargenter**) *adj* **(a) un métal** ~ a metal with the silver worn off. **(b)** (*: *sans un sou*) broke* (*attrib*).

désargenter [dezaʀʒɑ̃te] (1) *vt* **(a)** *métal* to rub *ou* wear the silver off. **cette fourchette se désargente** the silver is wearing off this fork. **(b)** ~ **qn*** to leave sb broke*, leave sb's coffers empty (*hum*).

désarmant, e [dezaʀmɑ̃, ɑ̃t] *adj* disarming.

désarmé, e [dezaʀme] (*ptp de* **désarmer**) *adj pays, personne* unarmed; (*fig: démuni*) helpless.

désarmement [dezaʀməmɑ̃] *nm [personne, forteresse]* disarming; *[pays]* disarmament; *[navire]* laying up.

désarmer [dezaʀme] (1) **1** *vt* **(a)** *adversaire, pays* to disarm.

(b) *mine* to disarm, defuse; *fusil* to unload; (*mettre le cran de sûreté*) to put the safety catch on.

(c) (*Naut*) to lay up.

(d) (*fig: émouvoir*) to disarm. **son sourire/sa réponse me désarma** his smile/answer disarmed me.

2 *vi [pays]* to disarm; (*fig*) *[haine]* to yield, abate. **il ne désarme pas contre son fils** he is unrelenting in his (venomous) attitude towards his son; **il ne désarme pas et veut intenter un nouveau procès** he will not yield and wants to start new proceedings.

désarrimage [dezaʀimaʒ] *nm* shifting (of the cargo).

désarrimer [dezaʀime] (1) *vt* to shift, cause to shift.

désarroi [dezaʀwa] *nm [personne]* (feeling of) helplessness, disarray (*littér*); *[armée, équipe]* confusion. **ceci l'avait plongé dans le** ~ **le plus profond** this had plunged him into a state of utter confusion; **être en plein** ~ to be in (a state of) utter confusion, feel quite helpless.

désarticulation [dezaʀtikylɑsjɔ̃] *nf [membre]* dislocation; (*Chirurgie*) disarticulation.

désarticuler [dezaʀtikyle] (1) **1** *vt membre* (*déboîter*) to dislocate; (*Chirurgie: amputer*) to disarticulate; *mécanisme* to upset; *horaire, prévisions* to upset, disrupt. **il s'est désarticulé l'épaule** he dislocated his shoulder.

2 se désarticuler *vpr [acrobate]* to contort o.s.

désassemblage [dezasɑ̃blaʒ] *nm* dismantling.

désassembler [dezasɑ̃ble] (1) *vt* to dismantle, take apart. **l'étagère s'est désassemblée** the shelves are coming to bits *ou* coming apart.

désassorti, e [dezasɔʀti] (*ptp de* **désassortir**) *adj service de table* unmatching, unmatched; *magasin, marchand* sold out (*attrib*).

désassortir [dezasɔʀtiʀ] (2) *vt service de table* to break up, spoil; *magasin* to clear out.

désastre [dezastʀ(ə)] *nm* (*lit, fig*) disaster. **courir au** ~ to head straight for disaster; **les** ~**s causés par la tempête** the damage caused by the storm.

désastreusement [dezastʀøzmɑ̃] *adv* disastrously.

désastreux, -euse [dezastʀø, øz] *adj erreur, décision, récolte, influence* disastrous; *bilan, conditions, temps* terrible, appalling.

désavantage [dezavɑ̃taʒ] *nm* (*handicap*) disadvantage, handicap; (*inconvénient*) disadvantage, drawback. **avoir un** ~ **sur qn** to be at a disadvantage *ou* be handicapped in comparison with sb; **cela présente bien des** ~**s** it has many disadvantages *ou* drawbacks; **être/tourner au** ~ **de qn** to be/turn to sb's disadvantage; **voir qn à son** ~ to see sb in an unfavourable *ou* in a disadvantageous light; **se montrer à son** ~ to show o.s. to one's disadvantage, show o.s. in an unfavourable light; **malgré le** ~ **du terrain, ils ont gagné** they won even though the ground put them at a disadvantage.

désavantager [dezavɑ̃taʒe] (3) *vt* to put at a disadvantage. **cette mesure nous désavantage par rapport aux autres** this measure puts us at a disadvantage by comparison with the others; **cela désavantage surtout les plus pauvres** this puts the very poor at the greatest disadvantage, this is particularly disadvantageous *ou* detrimental to the very poor, this penalizes the very poor in particular; **nous sommes désavantagés par rapport aux USA dans le domaine économique** in the economic field we are handicapped *ou* disadvantaged *ou* at a disadvantage by comparison with the USA; **se sentir désavantagé par rapport à son frère** to feel unfavourably treated by comparison with one's brother.

désavantageusement [dezavɑ̃taʒøzmɑ̃] *adv* unfavourably, disadvantageously.

désavantageux, -euse [dezavɑ̃taʒø, øz] *adj* unfavourable, disadvantageous.

désaveu [dezavø] *nm* (*rétractation*) retraction; (*reniement*) *[opinion, propos]* disowning, disavowal, repudiation; (*blâme*) repudiation, disowning (*U*); *[signature]* disclaiming, repudiation. **encourir le** ~ **de qn** to be disowned *ou* repudiated by sb;

(*Jur*) ~ **de paternité** repudiation of paternity, contestation of legitimacy.

désavouer [dezavwe] (1) **1** *vt* **(a)** (*renier*) *livre, opinion, propos* to disown, disavow, repudiate; *promesse* to disclaim, deny, repudiate; *signature* to disclaim, repudiate; *paternité* to disclaim, deny.

(b) (*blâmer*) *personne, action* to repudiate, disown.

2 se désavouer *vpr* (*revenir sur ses opinions*) to retract; (*revenir sur ses paroles*) to take back what one has said, retract, withdraw one's statement *etc*.

désaxé, e [dezakse] (*ptp de* **désaxer**) **1** *adj* unbalanced. **2** *nm,f* unbalanced person.

désaxer [dezakse] (1) *vt roue* to put out of true; *personne, esprit* to unbalance.

descellement [desɛlmɑ̃] *nm* (*V* **desceller**) freeing; unsealing, breaking the seal of.

desceller [desele] (1) *vt pierre* to (pull) free; *acte* to unseal, break the seal on.

descendance [desɑ̃dɑ̃s] *nf* (*enfants*) descendants, issue (*frm*); (*origine*) descent, lineage (*littér*).

descendant, e [desɑ̃dɑ̃, ɑ̃t] **1** *adj direction, chemin* downward, descending; *marée* ebb; (*Mus*) *gamme* falling, descending; (*Mil*) *garde* coming off duty (*attrib*); (*Rail*) *voie, train* down (*épith*); *bateau* sailing downstream. **2** *nm,f* descendant.

descendeur, -euse [desɑ̃dœʀ, øz] **1** *nm,f* (*Ski*) downhill specialist, downhiller. **2** *nm* (*Alpinisme*) descender.

descendre [desɑ̃dʀ(ə)] (41) **1** *vi* **(a)** (*aller*) to go down; (*venir*) to come down (*à, vers* to, *dans* into); *[fleuve]* to flow down; *[oiseau]* to fly down, descend; *[avion]* to climb *ou* come down, descend. **descends me voir** come down and *ou* to see me; **descends le prévenir** go down and warn him; ~ **à pied/à bicyclette/en voiture/en parachute** to walk/cycle/drive/parachute down; **on descend par un sentier étroit** the way down is by a narrow path, you go down a narrow path; ~ **en courant/en titubant** to run/stagger down; ~ **en train/par l'ascenseur** to go down by train/in the lift (*Brit*) *ou* elevator (*US*); ~ **par la fenêtre** to climb *ou* get *ou* come down through the window; **nous sommes descendus en 10 minutes** we got down in 10 minutes; (*fig Pol*) ~ **dans la rue** to take one's protest onto the streets; (*fig*) ~ **dans l'arène** to enter the arena; (*Alpinisme*) ~ **en rappel** to abseil, rope down; ~ **à Marseille** to go down to Marseilles; ~ **en ville** to go into town.

(b) ~ **de** *toit, rocher, arbre* to climb *ou* come down from; **il descendait de l'échelle** he was climbing *ou* coming down (from) the ladder; **il est descendu de sa chambre** he came down from his room; ~ **de la colline** to come *ou* climb *ou* walk down the hill; **fais** ~ **le chien du fauteuil** get the dog down off *ou* from the armchair, get the dog off the armchair.

(c) (*d'un moyen de transport*) ~ **de voiture/du train** to get out of the car/off *ou* out of the train, alight from the car/train (*frm*); **beaucoup de voyageurs sont descendus à Lyon** many people got off *ou* out at Lyons; ~ **à terre** to go ashore, get off the boat; ~ **de cheval** to dismount; ~ **de bicyclette** to get off one's bicycle, dismount from (*frm*) one's bicycle.

(d) (*atteindre*) *[habits, cheveux]* ~ **à** *ou* **jusqu'à** to come down to; **son manteau lui descendait jusqu'aux chevilles** his coat came down to his ankles; **ses cheveux lui descendent sur les épaules** his hair is down on his shoulders *ou* comes down to his shoulders.

(e) (*loger*) ~ **dans un hôtel** *ou* **à l'hôtel** to put up *ou* stay at a hotel; ~ **chez des amis** to stay with friends.

(f) *[colline, route]* ~ **en pente douce** to slope gently down; ~ **en pente raide** to drop *ou* fall away sharply; **la route descend en tournant** *ou* **en lacets** the road winds downwards; **le puits descend à 60 mètres** the well goes down 60 metres.

(g) *[obscurité, neige]* to fall; *[soleil]* to go down, sink. **le brouillard descend sur la vallée** the fog is coming down over the valley; **le soleil descend sur l'horizon** the sun is going down on the horizon; **le soir descendait** evening was falling; **les impuretés descendent au fond** the impurities fall *ou* drop to the bottom; **la neige descend en voltigeant** the snow is fluttering down; **ça descend bien!*** it's bucketing down!* *ou* tipping it down!*.

(h) (*baisser*) *[baromètre]* to fall; *[mer, marée]* to go out, ebb; *[prix]* to come down, fall, drop; *[valeurs boursières]* to fall. **le thermomètre** *ou* **la température descend** the temperature is dropping *ou* falling; **ma voix ne descend pas plus bas** my voice doesn't *ou* won't go any lower.

(i) (*s'abaisser*) ~ **dans l'estime de qn** to go down in sb's estimation; **il est descendu bien bas/jusqu'à mendier** he has stooped very low/to begging; (*iro*) **il est descendu jusqu'à nous parler** he deigned *ou* condescended to speak to us (*iro*).

(j) (*faire irruption*) **la police est descendue dans cette boîte de nuit** the police have raided the night club, there was a police raid on the night club; **des amis nous sont soudain descendus sur le dos*** some friends suddenly descended *ou* landed* on us.

(k) (**:**) *[vin, repas]* **ça descend bien** that goes down well, that goes down a treat* (*surtout Brit*); **mon déjeuner ne descend pas** my lunch won't go down; **se promener pour faire** ~ **son déjeuner** to help one's lunch down by taking a walk; **boire un verre pour faire** ~ **son déjeuner** to wash *ou* help one's lunch down with a drink.

2 descendre de *vt indir* (*avoir pour ancêtre*) to be descended from; **l'homme descend du singe** man is descended from the ape.

3 *vt* **(a)** *escalier, colline, pente* to go down, descend (*frm*). ~ **l'escalier/les marches précipitamment** to dash downstairs/down the steps; **la péniche descend le fleuve** the barge goes down the river; ~ **une rivière en canoë** to go down a river in a canoe, canoe down a river; ~ **la rue en courant** to run down the street; (*Mus*) ~ **la gamme** to go down the scale.

(b) (*porter, apporter*) *valise* to get down, take down, bring down; *meuble* to take down, bring down. **faire** ~ **ses bagages** to have one's luggage brought *ou* taken down; **si tu montes descends-moi mes lunettes** if you go upstairs *ou* if you're going upstairs bring *ou* fetch me my glasses down; **il faut** ~ **la poubelle tous les soirs** the dustbin (*Brit*) *ou* garbage can (*US*) must be taken down every night; ~ **des livres d'un rayon** to reach *ou* take books down from a shelf; **je te descends en ville** I'll take *ou* drive you into town, I'll give you a lift into town.

(c) (*baisser*) *étagère, rayon* to lower. **descends les stores** pull the blinds down, lower the blinds; ~ **une étagère d'un cran** to lower a shelf (by) a notch, take a shelf down a notch.

(d) (**:** *abattre*) *avion* to bring down, shoot down; (*tuer*) *personne* to knock off**:**; (*boire*) *bouteille* to down*. **il risquait de se faire** ~ he was liable to get himself *ou* be knocked off**:**; (*fig*) ~ **qn en flammes** to shoot sb down in flames, demolish sb.

descente [desɑ̃t] **1** *nf* **(a)** (*action*) going down (*U*), descent; (*Aviat*) descent. **la** ~ **dans le puits est dangereuse** going down the well is dangerous; **en montagne, la** ~ **est plus fatigante que la montée** in mountaineering, coming down *ou* the descent is more tiring than going up *ou* the climb; **le téléphérique est tombé en panne dans la** ~ the cable-car broke down on the *ou* its way down; (*Aviat*) **la** ~ **dure 20 minutes** the descent lasts 20 minutes; (*Aviat*) ~ **en vol plané** gliding descent; (*Aviat*) ~ **en feuille morte** falling leaf; (*Aviat*) ~ **en tire-bouchon** spiral dive; ~ **en parachute** parachute drop; (*Ski*) **(épreuve de)** ~ downhill (race *ou* run); (*Alpinisme*) ~ **en rappel** abseiling, roping down; **accueillir qn à la** ~ **du train/bateau** to meet sb off the train/boat; **il m'a accueilli à ma** ~ **de voiture** he met me as I got out of the car; *V* **tuyau**.

(b) (*raid, incursion*) raid. ~ **de police** police raid; **faire une** ~ **sur** *ou* **dans** to raid, make a raid on; **les enfants ont fait une** ~ **sur les provisions/dans le frigidaire*** the children have raided the larder/fridge.

(c) la ~ **des bagages prend du temps** it takes time to bring down the luggage; **s'occuper de la** ~ **d'un tonneau à la cave** to get on with taking a barrel down to the cellar.

(d) (*partie descendante*) (downward) slope, incline. **s'engager dans la** ~ to go off on the downward slope; **la** ~ **est rapide** it's a steep (downward) slope; **freiner dans les** ~**s** to break going downhill *ou* on the downhill; **le frein a lâché au milieu de la** ~ the brakes gave way halfway down (the slope *ou* incline); **la** ~ **de la cave/du garage** the entrance into the cellar/garage; **avoir une bonne** ~* to be fond of one's food (*ou* drink), be a big eater (*ou* drinker).

2: (*Art, Rel*) **descente de croix** Deposition; (*Rel*) **descente aux enfers** descent into Hell; **descente de lit** bedside rug; (*Méd*) **descente d'organe** prolapse of an organ.

descriptif, -ive [dɛskʀiptif, iv] **1** *adj* descriptive **2** *nm* descriptive brochure.

description [dɛskʀipsjɔ̃] *nf* description. **faire la** ~ **de** to describe.

désembourber [dezɑ̃buʀbe] (1) *vt* to get out of *ou* extricate from (*frm*) the mud.

désembourgeoiser (se) [dezɑ̃buʀʒwaze] (1) *vpr* to become less bourgeois, lose some of one's middle-class habits *ou* attitudes.

désembouteiller [dezɑ̃buteje] (1) *vt* (*Aut*) to unblock.

désembuer [dezɑ̃bye] (1) *vt vitre* to demist.

désemparé, e [dezɑ̃paʀe] (*ptp de* **désemparer**) *adj* **(a)** (*fig*) bewildered, distraught. **(b)** *navire* crippled, disabled; *avion* crippled.

désemparer [dezɑ̃paʀe] (1) **1** *vi*: **sans** ~ without stopping. **2** *vt* (*Naut*) to cripple, disable.

désemplir [dezɑ̃pliʀ] (2) **1** *vt* (*rare*) to empty. **2** *vi*: **ne pas** ~ to be never empty *ou* always full; **le magasin ne désemplit jamais** the shop is never empty *ou* is always full. **3 se désemplir** *vpr* to empty.

désenchaîner [dezɑ̃ʃene] (1) *vt* to unchain, unfetter (*littér*).

désenchantement [dezɑ̃ʃɑ̃tmɑ̃] *nm* **(a)** disenchantment, disillusion. **(b)** (†: *action*) disenchanting.

désenchanter [dezɑ̃ʃɑ̃te] (1) *vt* **(a)** *personne* to disenchant, disillusion. **(b)** (*littér*) *activité* to dispel the charm of; (††: *lever le charme*) to free from a *ou* the spell, disenchant.

désencombrement [dezɑ̃kɔ̃bʀəmɑ̃] *nm* clearing.

désencombrer [dezɑ̃kɔ̃bʀe] (1) *vt passage* to clear.

désencrasser [dezɑ̃kʀase] (1) *vt* to clean out.

désencroûter* [dezɑ̃kʀute] (1) *vt*: ~ **qn** to get sb out of the *ou* a rut, shake sb up*; se ~ to get (o.s.) out of the *ou* a rut, shake o.s. up*.

désenfiler [dezɑ̃file] (1) *vt aiguille* to unthread; *perles* to unstring. **mon aiguille s'est désenfilée** my needle has come unthreaded.

désenfler [dezɑ̃fle] (1) *vi* to go down, become less swollen. **l'eau salée fait** ~ **les entorses** salt water makes sprains go down.

désengagement [dezɑ̃gaʒmɑ̃] *nm* disengagement.

désengager [dezɑ̃gaʒe] (3) *vt troupes* to disengage. ~ **qn d'une obligation** to free sb from an obligation.

désengorger [dezɑ̃gɔʀʒe] (3) *vt* to unblock.

désenivrer [dezɑ̃nivʀe] (1) *vti* to sober up.

désennuyer [dezɑ̃nɥije] (8) **1** *vt*: ~ **qn** to relieve sb's boredom; **la lecture désennuie** reading relieves (one's) boredom. **2 se désennuyer** *vpr* to relieve the *ou* one's boredom.

désensabler [dezɑ̃sable] (1) *vt voiture* to dig out of the sand; *chenal* to dredge.

désensibilisation [desɑ̃sibilizasjɔ̃] *nf* (*Méd, Phot*) desensitization.

désensibiliser [desɑ̃sibilize] (1) *vt* (*Méd, Phot*) to desensitize.

désensorceler [dezɑ̃sɔʀsəle] (4) *vt* to free from a *ou* the spell, free from enchantment, disenchant.
désentortiller [dezɑ̃tɔʀtije] (1) *vt* to disentangle, unravel.
désentraver [dezɑ̃tʀave] (1) *vt* to unshackle.
désenvaser [dezɑ̃vɑze] (1) *vt* (*sortir*) to get out of *ou* extricate from (*frm*) the mud; (*nettoyer*) to clean the mud off; *port, chenal* to dredge.
désenvenimer [dezɑ̃vnime] (1) *vt plaie* to take the poison out of; (*fig*) *relations* to remove the venom *ou* bitterness from.
désépaissir [dezepesiʀ] (2) *vt cheveux* to thin (out).
déséquilibre [dezekilibʀ(ə)] *nm* (*dans un rapport de forces, de quantités*) imbalance, disequilibrium (*frm*); (*mental, nerveux*) unbalance, disequilibrium (*frm*); (*lit: manque d'assise*) unsteadiness. **l'armoire est en ~** the cupboard is unsteady.
déséquilibré, e [dezekilibʀe] (*ptp de* **déséquilibrer**) **1** *adj budget, esprit* unbalanced. **2** *nm,f* unbalanced person.
déséquilibrer [dezekilibʀe] (1) *vt* (*lit*) to throw off balance; (*fig*) *esprit, personne* to unbalance.
désert, e [dezɛʀ, ɛʀt(ə)] **1** *adj* deserted; *V* **île**. **2** *nm* (*Géog*) desert; (*fig*) desert, wilderness (*littér*); *V* **prêcher**.
déserter [dezɛʀte] (1) *vti* to desert.
déserteur [dezɛʀtœʀ] **1** *nm* deserter. **2** *adj m* deserting. **les soldats ~s** the deserters, the deserting soldiers.
désertification [dezɛʀtifikɑsjɔ̃] *nf* population drain.
désertion [dezɛʀsjɔ̃] *nf* desertion.
désertique [dezɛʀtik] *adj lieu* desert (*épith*), barren; *climat, plante* desert (*épith*).
désescalade [dezɛskalad] *nf* de-escalation.
désespérant, e [dezɛspeʀɑ̃, ɑ̃t] *adj lenteur, nouvelle, bêtise* appalling; *enfant* hopeless; *temps* maddening, sickening.
désespéré, e [dezɛspeʀe] (*ptp de* **désespérer**) **1** *adj personne* in despair (*attrib*), desperate; *situation* desperate, hopeless; *cas* hopeless; *tentative* desperate. **appel/regard ~** cry/look of despair, desperate cry/look; (*sens affaibli*) **je suis ~ d'avoir à le faire** I'm desperately sorry to have to do it.
2 *nm,f* desperate person, person in despair; (*suicidé*) suicide (*person*).
désespérément [dezɛspeʀemɑ̃] *adv* desperately; (*sens affaibli*) hopelessly. **salle ~ vide** hopelessly empty room.
désespérer [dezɛspeʀe] (6) **1** *vt* (*décourager*) to drive to despair. **il désespère ses parents** he drives his parents to despair, he is the despair of his parents.
2 *vi* (*se décourager*) to despair, lose hope, give up hope.
3 désespérer de *vt indir* to despair of; **je désespère de toi/de la situation** I despair of you/of the situation; **je désespère de son succès** I despair of his being successful; **~ de faire qch** to have lost (all) hope *ou* have given up (all) hope of doing sth, despair of doing sth; **il désespère de leur faire entendre raison** he has lost all hope of making them see reason, he despairs of making them see reason; **je ne désespère pas de les amener à signer** I haven't lost hope *ou* given up hope of getting them to sign.
4 se désespérer *vpr* to despair. **elle passe ses nuits à se ~** her nights are given over to despair.
désespoir [dezɛspwaʀ] **1** *nm* (*perte de l'espoir*) despair; (*chagrin*) despair, despondency. **il fait le ~ de ses parents** he is the despair of his parents; **sa paresse fait mon ~** his laziness drives me to despair *ou* to desperation; **sa supériorité fait le ~ des autres athlètes** his superiority is the despair of the other athletes; **être au ~** to be in despair; (*sens affaibli*) **je suis au ~ de ne pouvoir venir** I'm desperately sorry not to be able to come; **en ~ de cause, on fit appel au médecin** in desperation, we called in the doctor.
2: (*Bot*) **désespoir des peintres** London pride, saxifrage.
déshabillage [dezabijaʒ] *nm* undressing.
déshabillé [dezabije] *nm* négligée.
déshabiller [dezabije] (1) **1** *vt* to undress; (*fig*) to reveal. **2 se déshabiller** *vpr* to undress, take off one's clothes; (*: *ôter son manteau etc*) to take off one's coat *ou* things. **déshabillez-vous dans l'entrée** leave your coat *ou* things in the hall.
déshabituer [dezabitɥe] (1) **1** *vt*: **~ qn de (faire) qch** to get sb out of the habit of (doing) sth, break sb of the habit of (doing) sth.
2 se déshabituer *vpr*: **se ~ de qch/de faire qch** (*volontairement*) to break o.s. of the habit *ou* get (o.s.) out of the habit of sth/of doing sth; (*: *à force d'inaction etc*) to get out of *ou* lose the habit of sth/of doing sth.
désherbage [dezɛʀbaʒ] *nm* weeding.
désherbant [dezɛʀbɑ̃] *nm* weed-killer.
désherber [dezɛʀbe] (1) *vt* to weed.
déshérence [dezeʀɑ̃s] *nf* escheat. **tomber en ~** to escheat.
déshérité, e [dezeʀite] (*ptp de* **déshériter**) *adj* (*désavantagé*) deprived. **les ~s** the underprivileged, the have-nots*.
déshériter [dezeʀite] (1) *vt héritier* to disinherit; (*désavantager*) to deprive. **déshérité par la nature** ill-favoured by nature.
déshonnête [dezɔnɛt] *adj* (*littér*) unseemly (†, *littér*), immodest.
déshonnêtement [dezɔnɛtmɑ̃] *adv* (*littér*) immodestly.
déshonnêteté [dezɔnɛtte] *nf* (*littér*) unseemliness (†, *littér*), immodesty.
déshonneur [dezɔnœʀ] *nm* disgrace, dishonour.
déshonorant, e [dezɔnɔʀɑ̃, ɑ̃t] *adj* dishonourable, degrading.
déshonorer [dezɔnɔʀe] (1) **1** *vt* **(a)** (*discréditer*) *profession* to disgrace, dishonour; *personne* to dishonour, be a disgrace to, bring disgrace *ou* dishonour upon. **il se croirait déshonoré de travailler** he would think it beneath him to work.
(b) (†) *femme, jeune fille* to dishonour†.
2 se déshonorer *vpr* to bring disgrace *ou* dishonour on o.s.
déshydratation [dezidʀatɑsjɔ̃] *nf* dehydration.
déshydrater *vt*, **se déshydrater** *vpr* [dezidʀate] (1) to dehydrate.
déshydrogénation [dezidʀɔʒenɑsjɔ̃] *nf* dehydrogenation, dehydrogenization.
déshydrogéner [dezidʀɔʒene] (6) *vt* to dehydrogenate, dehydrogenize.
déshypothéquer [dezipɔteke] (6) *vt* to free from mortgage.
desiderata [dezideʀata] *nmpl* (*souhaits*) desiderata, wishes, requirements.
design [dizajn] **1** *nm* design. **2** *adj inv* ≈ Design Centre (*épith*).
désignation [deziɲɑsjɔ̃] *nf* (*appellation*) name, designation (*frm*); (*élection*) naming, appointment, designation.
designer [dizajnœʀ] *nm* designer.
désigner [deziɲe] (1) *vt* **(a)** (*montrer*) to point out, indicate. **~ qn du doigt** to point sb out (with one's finger); **ces indices le désignent clairement comme coupable** these signs point clearly to him *ou* make him out clearly as the guilty party; **~ qch à l'attention de qn** to draw *ou* call sth to sb's attention; **~ qch à l'admiration de qn** to point sth out for sb's admiration.
(b) (*nommer*) to name, appoint, designate. **le gouvernement a désigné un nouveau ministre** the government has named *ou* appointed *ou* designated a new minister; **~ qn pour remplir une mission** to designate sb to undertake a mission; **~ qn à un poste** to appoint sb to a post; **que des volontaires se désignent!** volunteers step forward!; **membre/successeur désigné** member/successor elect *ou* designate.
(c) (*qualifier*) to mark out. **sa hardiesse le désigne pour (faire) cette tentative** his boldness marks him out for this attempt; **c'était le coupable désigné/la victime désignée** he was the classic culprit/victim; **être tout désigné pour faire qch** to be cut out to do sth, be altogether suited to doing sth.
(d) (*dénommer*) to designate (*frm*). **~ qn par son nom** to refer to sb by his name; **on désigne sous ce nom toutes les substances toxiques** this name designates all toxic substances.
(e) (*représenter*) to refer to. **ces métaphores désignent toutes le héros** these metaphors all refer to the hero; **les mots qui désignent des objets concrets** the words which denote concrete objects.
désillusion [dezilyzjɔ̃] *nf* disillusion(ment).
désillusionner [dezilyzjɔne] (1) *vt* to disillusion.
désincarné, e [dezɛ̃kaʀne] *adj* (*lit*) disembodied; (*fig: gén péj*) rarefied.
désinence [dezinɑ̃s] *nf* (*Ling*) ending, inflexion.
désinentiel, -elle [dezinɑ̃sjɛl] *adj* inflexional.
désinfectant, e [dezɛ̃fɛktɑ̃, ɑ̃t] *adj, nm* disinfectant. **produit ~** disinfectant.
désinfecter [dezɛ̃fɛkte] (1) *vt* to disinfect.
désinfection [dezɛ̃fɛksjɔ̃] *nf* disinfection.
désintégration [dezɛ̃tegʀɑsjɔ̃] *nf* (*V* **désintégrer**) splitting-up; breaking-up; splitting; disintegration. **la ~ de la matière** the disintegration of matter.
désintégrer [dezɛ̃tegʀe] (6) **1** *vt groupe* to split up, break up; *roche* to break up; *atome* to split. **2 se désintégrer** *vpr* [*groupe*] to split up, break up, disintegrate; [*roche*] to disintegrate, break up.
désintéressé, e [dezɛ̃teʀese] (*ptp de* **désintéresser**) *adj* (*généreux*) disinterested, unselfish, selfless; (*impartial*) disinterested.
désintéressement [dezɛ̃teʀɛsmɑ̃] *nm* **(a)** (*générosité*) unselfishness, selflessness; (*impartialité*) disinterestedness. **avec ~** unselfishly. **(b)** (*Fin*) [*créancier*] paying off.
désintéresser [dezɛ̃teʀese] (1) **1** *vt créancier* to pay off. **2 se désintéresser** *vpr*: **se ~ de** to lose interest in.
désintérêt [dezɛ̃teʀɛ] *nm* disinterest, lack of interest.
désintoxication [dezɛ̃tɔksikɑsjɔ̃] *nf* (*V* **désintoxiquer**) treatment for alcoholism, detoxification (*T*); treatment for drug addiction, detoxification (*T*). **faire une cure de ~** to undergo (a spell of) treatment for alcoholism (*ou* drug addiction).
désintoxiquer [dezɛ̃tɔksike] (1) *vt alcoolique* to treat for alcoholism, dry out*; *drogué* to treat for drug addiction; (*fig: purifier l'organisme*) *citadin, gros mangeur* to cleanse the system of.
désinvolte [dezɛ̃vɔlt(ə)] *adj* (*sans gêne*) casual, offhand; (*à l'aise*) casual, relaxed.
désinvolture [dezɛ̃vɔltyʀ] *nf* casualness. **avec ~** casually, in an offhand way.
désir [deziʀ] *nm* **(a)** (*souhait*) wish, desire. **le ~ de qch** the wish *ou* desire for sth; **le ~ de faire qch** the desire to do sth; **vos ~s sont des ordres** your wish is my command; **selon le ~ de qn** in accordance with sb's wishes; **prendre ses ~s pour des réalités** to indulge in wishful thinking, wish o.s. into believing things.
(b) (*convoitise*) desire. **le ~ de qch** the desire for sth; **yeux brillants de ~** eyes shining with desire. **(c)** (*sensualité*) desire.
désirabilité [deziʀabilite] *nf* desirability.
désirable [deziʀabl(ə)] *adj* desirable. **peu ~** undesirable.
désirer [deziʀe] (1) *vt* **(a)** (*vouloir*) to want, desire (*frm*). **~ faire qch** to want *ou* wish to do sth; **que désirez-vous?** (*au magasin*) what would you like?, what can I do for you?; (*dans une agence, un bureau*) what can I do for you?; **Madame désire?** (*dans une boutique*) can I help you, madam?; [*maître d'hôtel etc*] you rang, madam?; **il désire que tu viennes tout de suite** he wishes *ou* wants you to come at once; **désirez-vous qu'on vous l'envoie?** would you like it sent to you?, do you wish to have it sent to you?
(b) (*sexuellement*) to desire.
(c) (*loc*) **se faire ~*** to play hard-to-get*; **la cuisine laisse à ~** the cooking leaves something to be desired *ou* is not (quite) up to the mark* (*surtout Brit*); **ça laisse beaucoup à ~** it leaves much to be desired; **la décoration ne laisse rien à ~** the decoration leaves nothing to be desired *ou* is all that one could wish.

désireux, -euse [deziʀø, øz] *adj*: **~ de** anxious to, desirous to (*frm*).
désistement [dezistəmɑ̃] *nm* (*Jur, Pol*) withdrawal.
désister (se) [deziste] (1) *vpr* **(a)** (*Pol*) to stand down (*surtout Brit*), withdraw (*en faveur de qn* in sb's favour). **(b)** (*Jur*) **se ~ de** *action, appel* to withdraw.
désobéir [dezɔbeiʀ] (2) *vi* to disobey. **~ à qn/à un ordre** to disobey sb/an order; **il désobéit sans cesse** he's always being disobedient.
désobéissance [dezɔbeisɑ̃s] *nf* disobedience (*U*) (*à* to).
désobéissant, e [dezɔbeisɑ̃, ɑ̃t] *adj* disobedient.
désobligeamment [dezɔbliʒamɑ̃] *adv* (*frm*) disagreeably, unpleasantly.
désobligeance [dezɔbliʒɑ̃s] *nf* (*frm*) disagreeableness, unpleasantness.
désobligeant, e [dezɔbliʒɑ̃, ɑ̃t] *adj* disagreeable, unpleasant, offensive.
désobliger [dezɔbliʒe] (3) *vt* (*frm*) to offend.
désodorisant, e [dezɔdɔʀizɑ̃, ɑ̃t] *adj, nm* deodorant.
désodoriser [dezɔdɔʀize] (1) *vt* to deodorize.
désœuvré, e [dezœvʀe] *adj* idle. **il restait ~ pendant des heures** he spent hours with nothing to do *ou* at a loose end (*Brit*) *ou* at loose ends (*US*); **les ~s qui se promenaient dans le parc** people with nothing to do walking in the park.
désœuvrement [dezœvʀəmɑ̃] *nm* idleness. **aller au cinéma par ~** to go to the pictures for something to do *ou* for want of anything better to do.
désolant, e [dezɔlɑ̃, ɑ̃t] *adj nouvelle, situation* distressing. **cet enfant/le temps est vraiment ~** this child/the weather is terribly disappointing; **il est ~ qu'elle ne puisse pas venir** it's a terrible shame *ou* such a pity that she can't come.
désolation [dezɔlɑsjɔ̃] *nf* **(a)** (*consternation*) distress, grief. **être plongé dans la ~** to be plunged in grief *ou* sadness; **il fait la ~ de sa mère** he causes his mother great distress, he breaks his mother's heart. **(b)** (*dévastation*) desolation, devastation.
désolé, e [dezɔle] (*ptp de* **désoler**) *adj* **(a)** *endroit* desolate. **(b)** *personne, air* (*affligé*) distressed; (*contrit*) sorry. **(je suis) ~ de vous avoir dérangé** (I'm) sorry to have disturbed you; **~, je dois partir** (very) sorry, I have to go.
désoler [dezɔle] (1) **1** *vt* **(a)** (*affliger*) to distress, grieve, sadden; (*contrarier*) to upset. **(b)** (*littér: dévaster*) to desolate, devastate. **2 se désoler** *vpr* to be upset. **inutile de vous ~** it's no use upsetting yourself.
désolidariser (se) [desɔlidaʀize] (1) *vpr*: **se ~ de** to dissociate o.s. from.
désopilant, e [dezɔpilɑ̃, ɑ̃t] *adj* screamingly funny*, hilarious.
désordonné, e [dezɔʀdɔne] *adj* **(a)** *pièce, personne* untidy, disorderly; *mouvements* uncoordinated; *combat, fuite* disorderly; *esprit* muddled, disorganized. **être ~ dans son travail** to be disorganized in one's work.
(b) (*littér*) *vie* disorderly; *dépenses, imagination* reckless, wild.
désordre [dezɔʀdʀ(ə)] *nm* **(a)** (*état*) *[pièce, vêtements, cheveux]* untidiness, disorderliness; *[affaires publiques, service]* disorderliness, disorder; *[esprits]* confusion. **il ne supporte pas le ~** he can't bear untidiness; **mettre une pièce en ~, mettre du ~ dans une pièce** to make a room untidy; **mettre du ~ dans sa coiffure** to make one's hair untidy, mess up one's hair*; **être en ~** *[pièce, affaires]* to be untidy *ou* in disorder *ou* in a mess*; *[cheveux, toilette]* to be untidy; *[service administratif]* to be in a state of disorder; **jeter quelques idées en ~ sur le papier** to jot down a few disordered *ou* random ideas; **quel ~!** what a muddle! *ou* mess!*; **il régnait dans la pièce un ~ indescriptible** the room was in an indescribable muddle *ou* mess*, the room was indescribably untidy.
(b) (*agitation*) disorder. **des agitateurs qui sèment le ~ dans l'armée** agitators who spread unrest in the army; **faire du ~ (dans la classe/dans un lieu public)** to cause a commotion *ou* a disturbance (in class/in a public place); **arrêté pour ~ sur la voie publique** arrested for disorderly conduct in the streets; **jeter le ~ dans les esprits** to throw people's minds into confusion; **c'est un facteur de ~** this is a disruptive influence.
(c) (*émeute*) **~s** disturbance, disorder (*U*); **de graves ~s ont éclaté** serious disturbances have broken out, there have been serious outbreaks of disorder.
(d) (*littér: débauche*) dissoluteness, licentiousness. **mener une vie de ~** to lead a dissolute *ou* licentious life; **regretter les ~s de sa jeunesse** to regret the dissolute *ou* licentious ways *ou* the licentiousness of one's youth.
(e) (*Méd*) **~ fonctionnel/hépatique** functional/liver disorder.
désorganisation [dezɔʀganizɑsjɔ̃] *nf* disorganization.
désorganiser [dezɔʀganize] (1) *vt* (*gén*) to disorganize; *projet, service* to disrupt, disorganize. **à cause de la grève, nos services sont désorganisés** owing to the strike our services are disrupted *ou* disorganized.
désorientation [dezɔʀjɑ̃tɑsjɔ̃] *nf* disorientation.
désorienté, e [dezɔʀjɑ̃te] (*ptp de* **désorienter**) *adj* (*égaré*) disorientated; (*déconcerté*) bewildered, confused.
désorienter [dezɔʀjɑ̃te] (1) *vt* (*égarer*) to disorientate; (*déconcerter*) to bewilder, confuse, disorientate.
désormais [dezɔʀmɛ] *adv* in future, henceforth (†, *littér*), from now on.
désossé, e [dezɔse] (*ptp de* **désosser**) *adj viande* boned; (*fig*) *personne* supple; *style* flaccid.
désossement [dezɔsmɑ̃] *nm [viande]* boning.
désosser [dezɔse] (1) *vt viande* to bone; (*fig*) *texte* to take to pieces. (*fig*) **acrobate qui se désosse** acrobat who can twist himself in every direction.
désoxydant, e [dezɔksidɑ̃, ɑ̃t] **1** *adj* deoxidizing. **2** *nm* deoxidizer.
désoxyder [dezɔkside] (1) *vt* to deoxidize.
despote [dɛspɔt] **1** *adj* despotic. **2** *nm* despot; (*fig*) tyrant.
despotique [dɛspɔtik] *adj* despotic.
despotiquement [dɛspɔtikmɑ̃] *adv* despotically.
despotisme [dɛspɔtism(ə)] *nm* (*lit*) despotism; (*fig*) tyranny.
desquamation [deskwamɑsjɔ̃] *nf* desquamation.
desquamer [dɛskwame] (1) **1** *vt* to remove (*in scales*). **2 se desquamer** *vpr* to flake off, desquamate (*T*).
desquels, desquelles [dekɛl] *V* **lequel.**
dessaisir [desezir] (2) **1** *vt* (*Jur*) **~ un tribunal d'une affaire** to remove a case from a court. **2 se dessaisir** *vpr*: **se ~ de** to give up, part with, relinquish.
dessaisissement [desezismɑ̃] *nm* **(a)** (*Jur*) **~ d'un tribunal/juge (d'une affaire)** removal of a case from a court/judge; **(b)** (*V* **se dessaisir**) giving up, relinquishment.
dessalage [desalaʒ] *nm*, **dessalaison** [desalɛzɔ̃] *nf [eau de mer]* desalination; *[poisson]* soaking.
dessalé, e* [desale] (*ptp de* **dessaler**) *adj* (*déluré*) **il est drôlement ~ depuis qu'il a fait son service militaire** he has really learnt a thing or two since he did his military service*.
dessalement [desalmɑ̃] *nm* = **dessalage.**
dessaler [desale] (1) *vt* **(a)** *eau de mer* to desalinate, desalinize; *poisson* to soak (*to remove the salt*). **faire ~** *ou* **mettre à ~ de la viande** to put meat to soak.
(b) (*: *délurer*) **~ qn** to teach sb a thing or two*, teach sb about life; **il s'était dessalé au contact de ses camarades** he had learnt a thing or two* *ou* learnt about life through contact with his friends.
dessangler [desɑ̃gle] (1) *vt cheval* to ungirth; *paquetage* to unstrap; (*détendre sans défaire*) to loosen the girths of; loosen the straps of.
dessaouler* [desule] (1) *vti* = **dessoûler*.**
desséchant, e [deseʃɑ̃, ɑ̃t] *adj vent* parching, drying; (*fig*) *études* mind-deadening.
dessèchement [desɛʃmɑ̃] *nm* (*action*) drying (out), parching; (*état*) dryness; (*fig: amaigrissement*) emaciation; (*fig: du cœur*) hardness.
dessécher [deseʃe] (6) **1** *vt* **(a)** *terre, végétation* to dry out, parch; *plante, feuille* to wither, dry out, parch. **le vent dessèche la peau** wind dries (out) the skin; **la soif me dessèche la bouche** my mouth is dry *ou* parched with thirst.
(b) (*volontairement*) *aliments etc* to dry, dehydrate, desiccate.
(c) (*fig: racornir*) *cœur* to harden. **l'amertume/la vie lui avait desséché le cœur** bitterness/life had left him stony-hearted; **desséché par l'étude** dried up through study; **il s'était desséché à force d'étudier** he had become as dry as dust as a result of too much studying.
(d) (*amaigrir*) to emaciate. **les maladies l'avaient desséché** illness had left him wizened *ou* emaciated; **les épreuves l'avaient desséché** his trials and tribulations had worn him to a shadow.
2 se dessécher *vpr [terre]* to dry out, become parched; *[plante, feuille]* to wither, dry out; *[aliments]* to dry out, go dry; *[bouche, lèvres]* to go dry, become parched; *[peau]* to dry out.
dessein [desɛ̃] *nm* (*littér*) (*intention*) intention, design; (*projet*) plan, design. **son ~ est** *ou* **il a le ~ de faire** he intends *ou* means to do; **former le ~ de faire qch** to make up one's mind to do sth, form a plan to do sth; **avoir des ~s sur qn** to have designs on sb; **c'est dans ce ~ que** it is with this in mind *ou* with this intention that; **il est parti dans le ~ de** *ou* **à ~ de faire fortune** he went off meaning *ou* intending to make his fortune *ou* with the intention of making his fortune; **faire qch à ~** to do sth intentionally *ou* deliberately.
desseller [desele] (1) *vt* to unsaddle.
desserrage [desɛʀaʒ] *nm [vis, écrou]* unscrewing, undoing, loosening; *[câble]* loosening, slackening; *[frein]* releasing.
desserré, e [deseʀe] (*ptp de* **desserrer**) *adj vis, écrou* undone (*attrib*), loose; *nœud, ficelle* loose, slack; *cravate, ceinture* loose; *frein* off (*attrib*).
desserrement [desɛʀmɑ̃] *nm* (*V* **se desserrer**) slackening; loosening; releasing; relaxation.
desserrer [deseʀe] (1) **1** *vt nœud, ceinture, ficelle* to loosen, slacken; *étau* to loosen, release; *étreinte* to relax, loosen; *poing, dents* to unclench; *écrou* to unscrew, undo, loosen; *frein* to release, take *ou* let off; *objets alignés, mots, lignes* to space out. **~ sa ceinture de 2 crans** to loosen *ou* slacken one's belt 2 notches; (*fig*) **il n'a pas desserré les dents** he hasn't opened his mouth *ou* lips.
2 se desserrer *vpr [ficelle, câble]* to slacken, come loose; *[nœud]* to come undone *ou* loose; *[écrou]* to work *ou* come loose *ou* undone; *[frein]* to release itself; *[étreinte]* to relax, loosen.
dessert [desɛʀ] *nm* dessert, pudding, sweet (*Brit*).
desserte [desɛʀt(ə)] *nf* **(a)** (*meuble*) sideboard table.
(b) (*service de transport*) **la ~ d'une localité par bateau** the servicing of an area by water transport; **la ~ de la ville est assurée par un car** there is a bus service to the town.
(c) *[prêtre]* cure.
dessertir [desɛʀtiʀ] (2) *vt* to unset, remove from its setting.
desservant [desɛʀvɑ̃] *nm* priest in charge.
desservir[1] [desɛʀviʀ] (14) *vt* **(a)** *repas, plat* to clear away. **vous pouvez ~ (la table)** you can clear away, you can clear the table.
(b) (*nuire à*) *personne* to go against, put at a disadvantage; *intérêts* to harm. **il est desservi par sa mauvaise humeur** his bad temper goes against him *ou* puts him at a disadvantage; **il m'a desservi auprès de mes amis** he did me a disservice with my friends.
desservir[2] [desɛʀviʀ] (14) *vt* **(a)** (*Transport*) to serve. **le village est desservi par 3 autobus chaque jour** there is a bus service from the village *ou* a bus runs from the village 3 times daily; **le**

village est desservi par 3 lignes d'autobus the village is served by *ou* has 3 bus services; **ville bien desservie** town well served by public transport.

(b) *[porte, couloir]* to lead into.

(c) *[prêtre]* to serve.

dessiccatif, -ive [desikatif, iv] **1** *adj* desiccative. **2** *nm* desiccant.

dessiccation [desikɑsjɔ̃] *nf* (*Chim*) desiccation; *[aliments]* drying, desiccation, dehydration.

dessiller [desije] (1) *vt* (*fig*) ~ **les yeux à qn** to open sb's eyes (*fig*); **mes yeux se dessillèrent** my eyes were opened, the scales fell from my eyes (*surtout Brit*).

dessin [desɛ̃] *nm* **(a)** (*représentation graphique*) drawing. **il a fait un (joli)** ~ he did a (nice) drawing; **il passe son temps à faire des** ~**s** he spends his time drawing; **il fait toujours des petits** ~**s sur son cahier** he's always doodling on his exercise book; ~ **à la plume/au fusain/au trait** pen-and-ink/charcoal/line drawing; ~ **animé** cartoon (film); ~ **humoristique** cartoon (*in a newspaper etc*); ~ **publicitaire/de mode** advertisement/fashion drawing; (*hum*) **il n'a rien compris, fais lui donc un** ~**!*** he hasn't understood a word — explain it in words of one syllable *ou* you'll have to spell it out for him; *V* **carton.**

(b) (*art*) **le** ~ drawing; **il est doué pour le** ~ he has a gift for drawing; **école de** ~ drawing school; ~ **technique/industriel** technical/industrial drawing; ~ **de mode** fashion design; **table/planche à** ~ drawing table/board.

(c) (*motif*) pattern, design. **un tissu avec des** ~**s jaunes** material with a yellow pattern on it; **le** ~ **des veines sur la peau** the pattern of the veins on the skin.

(d) (*contour*) outline, line. **la bouche a un joli** ~ the mouth has a good line *ou* is finely delineated.

dessinateur, -trice [desinatœʀ, tʀis] *nm,f* (*artiste*) drawer; (*technicien*) draughtsman. ~ **humoristique** cartoonist; ~ **industriel/de mode** industrial/fashion designer; ~ **de publicité** commercial artist.

dessiner [desine] (1) **1** *vt* **(a)** to draw. **il dessine bien** he's good at drawing, he draws well; ~ **à grands traits** to draw a broad outline of; ~ **au pochoir** to stencil; ~ **au crayon/à l'encre** to draw in pencil/ink.

(b) (*faire le plan, la maquette de*) *véhicule, meuble* to design; *plan d'une maison* to draw; *jardin* to lay out, landscape. (*fig*) **une bouche/oreille bien dessinée** a finely delineated mouth/ear.

(c) *[chose]* **les champs dessinent un damier** the fields are laid out like a checkerboard *ou* like (a) patchwork; **un vêtement qui dessine bien la taille** a garment that shows off the waist well.

2 se dessiner *vpr* **(a)** *[contour, forme]* to stand out, be outlined. **des collines se dessinaient à l'horizon** hills stood out on the horizon.

(b) (*se préciser*) *[tendance]* to become apparent; *[projet]* to take shape. **on voit se** ~ **une tendance à l'autoritarisme** an emergent tendency to authoritarianism may be noted, a tendency towards authoritarianism is becoming apparent; **un sourire se dessina sur ses lèvres** a smile formed on his lips.

dessouder [desude] (1) *vt* to unsolder. **le tuyau s'est dessoudé** the pipe has come unsoldered.

dessoûler* [desule] (1) *vti* to sober up.

dessous [d(ə)su] **1** *adv* **(a)** (*sous*) *placé, suspendre* under, underneath, beneath; *passer* under, underneath; (*plus bas*) below. **mettez votre valise** ~ put your suitcase underneath (it) *ou* under it; **soulevez ces dossiers: la liste est** ~ lift up those files — the list is underneath (them) *ou* under them; **passez (par)** ~ go under(neath) (it); **tu as mal lu, il y a une note** ~ you misread it — there is a note underneath; **retirer qch de** ~ **le lit/la table** to get sth from under(neath) the bed/table; **ils ont pris le buffet par (en)** ~ they took hold of the sideboard from underneath.

(b) au-~ below; **au-**~ **de** (*lit*) below, underneath; (*fig*) *possibilités, limite* below; (*fig: pas digne de*) beneath; **ils habitent au-**~ they live downstairs *ou* underneath; **sa jupe lui descend au-**~ **du genou** her skirt comes down to below her knees *ou* reaches below her knees; **les enfants au-**~ **de 7 ans ne paient pas** children under 7 *ou* the under-sevens don't pay; **20° au-**~ **(de zéro)** 20° below (zero); **des articles à 20 F et au-**~ items at 20 francs and less *ou* below; **être au-**~ **de sa tâche** (*incapable*) not to be up to one's task; (*indigne*) to be beneath one's task; **il est au-**~ **de tout!** he's the absolute limit!, he's the end!; **le service est au-**~ **de tout** the service is hopeless *ou* a disgrace.

(c) en ~ (*sous*) under(neath); (*plus bas*) below; (*hypocritement*) in an underhand (*Brit*) *ou* underhanded (*US*) manner; **en** ~ **de** below; **il s'est glissé en** ~ he slid under(neath); **les locataires d'en** ~ the people who rent the flat below *ou* downstairs; **jeter un coup d'œil en** ~ **à qn, regarder qn en** ~ to give sb a shifty look; **faire qch en** ~ to do sth in an underhand (*Brit*) *ou* underhanded (*US*) manner; **il est très en** ~ **de la moyenne** he's well below (the) average.

2 *nm* **(a)** *[objet]* bottom, underside; *[pied]* sole; *[main]* inside; *[avion, voiture, animal]* underside; *[tissu]* wrong side. **du** ~ *feuille, drap* bottom; **les gens/l'appartement du** ~ the people/the flat downstairs (from us *ou* them *etc*), the people/flat below (us *ou* them *etc*); **le** ~ **de la table est poussiéreux** the table is dusty underneath; **les fruits du** ~ **sont moisis** the fruit at the bottom *ou* the fruit underneath is mouldy; **avoir le** ~ to get the worst of it.

(b) (*côté secret*) **le** ~ **de l'affaire** *ou* **l'histoire** the hidden side of the affair; les ~ **de la politique** the unseen *ou* hidden side of politics; **connaître le** ~ **des cartes** to have inside information.

(c) (*Habillement*) undergarment. **les** ~ underwear, undies*.

3: dessous de bouteille bottle mat; **dessous de bras** dress shield; **dessous de plat** table mat, place mat; **dessous de robe** slip, petticoat; **dessous de table** under the counter payment; **dessous de verre** coaster.

dessus [d(ə)sy] **1** *adv* **(a)** (*sur*) *placé, poser, monter* on top (of it); *collé, écrit, fixer* on it; *passer, lancer* over (it); (*plus haut*) above. **mettez votre valise** ~ put your suitcase on top (of it); **regardez ces dossiers: la liste doit être** ~ have a look at those files — the list must be on top (of them); **il n'y a pas de timbre** ~ there's no stamp on it; **c'est écrit** ~ it's written on it; **montez** ~ (*tabouret, échelle*) get up on it; **passez (par)** ~ go over it; **il a sauté par** ~ he jumped over it; **ôter qch de** ~ **la table** to take sth (from) off the table; **il n'a même pas levé la tête de** ~ **son livre** he didn't even look up from his book, he didn't even take his eyes off his book; **il lui a tapé/tiré** ~ he hit him/shot at him; **il nous sont arrivés** *ou* **tombés** ~ **à l'improviste** they dropped in on us unexpectedly.

(b) au-~ above; (*à l'étage supérieur*) upstairs; (*posé sur*) on top; (*plus cher etc*) over, above; **au-**~ **de** (*plus haut que, plus au nord que*) above; (*sur*) on top of; (*fig*) *prix, limite* over, above; *possibilités* beyond; **la valise est au-**~ **de l'armoire** the suitcase is on top of the wardrobe; **les enfants au-**~ **de 7 ans paient** children over 7 *ou* the over-sevens pay; **20° au-**~ **(de zéro)** 20° above (zero); **il n'y a pas d'articles au-**~ **de 20 F** there are no articles over 20 francs; **cette tâche est au-**~ **de ses capacités** this task is beyond his capabilities; **il est au-**~ **de ces petites mesquineries** he is above this petty meanness; **être au-**~ **de tout soupçon/reproche** to be above all suspicion/beyond all reproach; **pour le confort, il n'y a rien au-**~ there's nothing to beat it for comfort.

2 *nm* **(a)** *[objet, pied, tête]* top; *[main]* back. **du** ~ *feuille, drap* top; **le** ~ **de la table est en marbre** the table-top *ou* the top of the table is marble; **les gens/l'appartement du** ~ the people/flat above (us *ou* them *etc*) *ou* upstairs (from us *ou* them *etc*); **les fraises du** ~ **sont plus belles (qu'en dessous)** the strawberries on top are nicer (than the ones underneath); (*fig*) **le** ~ **du panier** the pick of the bunch; (*élite sociale*) the upper crust; **elle portait 3 vestes de laine: celle du** ~ **était bleue** she was wearing 3 cardigans and the top one was blue.

(b) (*loc*) **avoir le** ~ to have the upper hand, be on top; **prendre le** ~ to get the upper hand; **reprendre le** ~ to get over it; **il a été très malade/déprimé mais il a repris le** ~ **rapidement** he was very ill/depressed but he soon got over it.

3: dessus de lit bedspread; **dessus de table** table runner.

destin [dɛstɛ̃] *nm* (*fatalité, sort*) fate; (*existence, avenir, vocation*) destiny.

destinataire [dɛstinatɛʀ] *nmf [lettre]* addressee (*frm*); *[marchandise]* consignee; *[mandat]* payee. **remettre une lettre à son** ~ to hand a letter to the person it is addressed to.

destination [dɛstinɑsjɔ̃] *nf* **(a)** (*direction*) destination. **à** ~ **de** *avion, train* to; *bateau* bound for; *voyageur* travelling to; *lettre* addressed to; **arriver à** ~ to reach one's destination, arrive (at one's destination); **train/vol 702 à** ~ **de Paris** train number 702/flight (number) 702 to *ou* for Paris.

(b) (*usage*) *[édifice, appareil, somme d'argent]* purpose. **quelle** ~ **comptez-vous donner à cette somme/pièce?** to what purpose do you intend to put this money/room?

destiné, e[1] [dɛstine] (*ptp de* **destiner**) *adj* **(a)** (*prévu pour*) ~ **à faire qch** intended *ou* meant to do sth; **ces mesures sont** ~**es à freiner l'inflation** these measures are intended *ou* meant to put a brake on inflation; **ce texte est** ~ **à être lu à haute voix** this text is intended *ou* meant to be read aloud; **cette pommade est** ~**e à guérir les brûlures** this ointment is intended for healing burns; **livre** ~ **aux enfants** book (intended *ou* meant) for children; **édifice** ~ **au culte** building intended for worship; **ce terrain est** ~ **à être construit** this ground is intended for construction *ou* to be built on.

(b) (*voué à*) ~ **à qch** destined for sth; ~ **à faire** destined to do; **ce livre était** ~ **au succès** this book was destined for success; **cette œuvre était** ~**e à l'échec** this work was destined to fail, it was fated that this work should be a failure; **il était** ~ **à une brillante carrière** he was destined for a brilliant career; **elle était** ~**e à mourir jeune** she was destined *ou* fated to die young.

destinée[2] [dɛstine] *nf* (*fatalité, sort*) fate; (*existence, avenir, vocation*) destiny. **unir sa** ~ **à celle de qn** to unite one's destiny with sb's; **promis à de hautes** ~**s** who promises great things.

destiner [dɛstine] (1) *vt* **(a)** (*attribuer*) ~ **sa fortune à qn** to intend *ou* mean sb to have one's fortune, intend that sb should have one's fortune; **il vous destine ce poste** he intends *ou* means you to have this post; ~ **une allusion/un coup à qn** to intend an allusion/a blow for sb; ~ **un accueil enthousiaste à qn** to reserve an enthusiastic welcome for sb; **nous destinons ce livre à tous ceux qui souffrent** this book is intended *ou* meant (by us) for all who are suffering, this book is aimed at all who are suffering; **il ne put attraper le ballon qui lui était destiné** he couldn't catch the ball meant for *ou* aimed at him; **sans deviner le sort qui lui était destiné** (*par le destin*) not knowing what fate he was destined for *ou* what fate lay *ou* was in store for him; (*par ses ennemis*) not knowing what fate lay *ou* was in store for him; **cette lettre t'était/ne t'était pas destinée** this letter was/was not meant *ou* intended for you.

(b) (*affecter*) ~ **qch à qch:** ~ **une somme à l'achat de qch** to intend to use a sum *ou* earmark a sum to buy sth, earmark a sum for sth; ~ **un local à un usage précis** to intend a place to have a specific use, have a specific use in mind for a place; **les fonds seront destinés à la recherche** the money will be assigned to *ou* used for research.

(c) (*vouer*) to destine. ~ **qn à une fonction** to destine sb for a post *ou* to fill a post; ~ **qn à être médecin** to destine sb to be a doctor; **sa bravoure le destinait à mourir de mort violente** his boldness marked him out *ou* destined him to die a violent death;

(*littér*) ~ **une jeune fille à qn** to intend a girl *ou* a girl's hand for sb; **il se destine à l'enseignement/à être ingénieur** he intends to go nto teaching/to be an engineer.

destituer [dɛstitɥe] (1) *vt ministre* to dismiss; *roi* to depose. ~ **un officier de son commandement** to relieve an officer of his command; ~ **qn de ses fonctions** to relieve sb of his duties.

destitution [dɛstitysjɔ̃] *nf [ministre]* dismissal; *[officier]* discharge; *[fonctionnaire]* dismissal, discharge; *[roi]* deposition.

destrier [dɛstʀije] *nm* (*Hist littér*) steed (*littér*), charger (*littér*).

destroyer [dɛstʀwaje] *nm* (*Naut*) destroyer.

destructeur, -trice [dɛstʀyktœʀ, tʀis] **1** *adj* destructive. **2** *nm,f* destroyer.

destructible [dɛstʀyktibl(ə)] *adj* destructible.

destructif, -ive [dɛstʀyktif, iv] *adj* destructive, destroying (*épith*).

destruction [dɛstʀyksjɔ̃] *nf* (*gén*) destruction (*U*); *[armée, flotte]* destroying (*U*), destruction (*U*); *[rats, insectes]* extermination (*U*). **les ~s causées par la guerre** the destruction caused by the war.

désuet, -ète [desɥɛ, ɛt] *adj méthode, théorie* outdated, antiquated; *genre* outmoded; *charme* old-fashioned; *mode, vêtement* outdated; *mot, expression, coutume* outdated, outmoded.

désuétude [desɥetyd] *nf* disuse, obsolescence, desuetude (*frm*). **tomber en** ~ *[loi]* to fall into abeyance; *[expression, coutume]* to become obsolete, fall into disuse.

désuni, e [dezyni] (*ptp de* **désunir**) *adj couple, famille* divided, disunited; *mouvements* uncoordinated; *coureur, cheval* off his stride (*attrib*).

désunion [dezynjɔ̃] *nf [couple, parti]* disunity, dissension (*de* in).

désunir [dezyniʀ] (2) **1** *vt famille* to divide, disunite; *pierres, planches* to separate. **2 se désunir** *vpr [athlète]* to lose one's stride.

détachable [detaʃabl(ə)] *adj* detachable.

détachage [detaʃaʒ] *nm* (*nettoyage*) stain removal.

détachant [detaʃɑ̃] *nm* stain remover.

détaché, e [detaʃe] (*ptp de* **détacher**) *adj* (*indifférent, aussi Mus*) detached; *V* **pièce**.

détachement [detaʃmɑ̃] *nm* **(a)** (*indifférence*) detachment. **regarder/dire qch avec** ~ to look at/say sth with (an air of) detachment; **le ~ qu'il montrait pour les biens matériels** the disregard he showed for material goods.

(b) (*Mil*) detachment.

(c) *[fonctionnaire]* secondment. **être en** ~ to be on secondment.

détacher[1] [detaʃe] (1) **1** *vt* **(a)** (*délier*) *chien, cheval* to untie, let loose; *prisonnier* to untie, (let) loose, unbind; *paquet, objet* to undo, untie; *wagon, remorque* to take off, detach. ~ **un wagon d'un convoi** to detach a coach from a train; **il détacha la barque/le prisonnier/le paquet de l'arbre** he untied the boat/the prisoner/the parcel from the tree.

(b) (*dénouer*) *vêtement, ceinture* to undo, unfasten, loose; *lacet, nœud* to undo, untie, loose; *soulier, chaîne* to unfasten, undo. **il détacha la corde du poteau** he untied *ou* removed the rope from the post.

(c) (*ôter*) *peau, écorce* to remove (*de* from), take off; *papier collé* to remove, unstick (*de* from); *rideau, tableau* to take down (*de* from); *épingle* to take out (*de* of), remove; *reçu, bon* to tear out (*de* of), detach (*de* from). **l'humidité avait détaché le papier** the damp had unstuck *ou* loosened the paper; ~ **des feuilles d'un bloc** to tear *ou* take some sheets out of a pad, detach some sheets from a pad; ~ **un morceau de plâtre du mur** to remove a piece of plaster from the wall, take a piece of plaster from *ou* off the wall; **il détacha une pomme de l'arbre** he took an apple (down) from the tree, he picked an apple off the tree; **détachez bien les bras du corps** keep your arms well away from your body; (*fig*) **il ne pouvait ~ son regard du spectacle** he could not take his eyes off the sight; (*sur coupon etc*) **'partie à ~'** 'tear off (this section)'; **'~ suivant le pointillé'** 'tear off along the dotted line'.

(d) (*envoyer*) *personne* to send, dispatch; (*Admin: affecter*) to second. **se faire ~ auprès de qn/à Londres** to be sent on secondment to sb/to London; (*Admin*) **être détaché** to be on secondment.

(e) (*mettre en relief*) *lettres* to separate; *syllabes, mots* to articulate, separate; (*Peinture*) *silhouette, contour* to bring out, make stand out; (*Mus*) *notes* to detach. ~ **une citation** to make a quotation stand out, bring out a quotation.

(f) (*éloigner*) ~ **qn de qch/qn** to turn sb away from sth/sb; **son cynisme a détaché de lui tous ses amis** his cynicism has turned his friends away from him.

2 se détacher *vpr* **(a)** (*se délier*) *[chien]* to free itself, get loose, loose itself (*de* from); *[prisonnier]* to free o.s., get loose (*de* from); *[paquet]* to come undone *ou* untied *ou* loose; *[barque]* to come untied, loose itself (*de* from); *[wagon]* to come off, detach itself (*de* from). **le paquet s'était détaché de l'arbre de Noël** the parcel had fallen off the Christmas tree.

(b) (*se dénouer*) *[ceinture, soulier]* to come undone *ou* unfastened *ou* loose; *[lacet, ficelle]* to come undone *ou* untied *ou* loose.

(c) (*se séparer*) *[fruit, ficelle]* to come off; *[page]* to come loose, come out; *[peau, écorce]* to come off; *[papier collé]* to come unstuck, come off; *[épingle]* to come out, fall out; *[rideau]* to come down. **le papier s'était détaché à cause de l'humidité** the paper had come loose *ou* come away because of the damp; **un bloc de pierre se détacha du rocher** a block of stone came off *ou* broke off the rock; **l'écorce se détachait de l'arbre** the bark was coming off the tree *ou* was coming away from the tree; **la capsule spatiale s'est détachée de la fusée** the space capsule has separated from *ou* come away from the rocket.

(d) (*Sport etc*) *[coureur]* to pull *ou* break away (*de* from). **un petit groupe se détacha du reste des manifestants** a small group broke away from the rest of the demonstrators.

(e) (*ressortir*) to stand out. **la forêt se détache sur le ciel clair** the forest stands out against the clear sky.

(f) se ~ de (*renoncer à*) to turn one's back on, renounce; (*se désintéresser de*) to grow away from; **se ~ des plaisirs de la vie** to turn one's back on *ou* renounce the pleasures of life; **ils se sont détachés l'un de l'autre** they have grown apart.

détacher[2] [detaʃe] (1) *vt* to remove the stains from, clean. **donner une robe à ~** to take a dress to be cleaned *ou* to the cleaner's; **~ au savon/à la benzine** to clean with soap/benzine.

détail [detaj] *nm* **(a)** (*particularité*) detail. **dans les (moindres) ~s** in (minute) detail; **se perdre dans les ~s** to lose o.s. in details; **entrer dans les ~s** to go into detail(s) *ou* particulars; **je n'ai pas remarqué ce ~** I didn't notice that detail *ou* point; **ce n'est qu'un ~!** (that's) a mere detail!; *V* **revue**.

(b) (*description précise*) *[facture, compte]* breakdown. **examiner le ~ d'un compte** to examine a breakdown of *ou* the particulars of an account; **pourriez-vous nous faire le ~ de la facture/de ce qu'on vous doit?** could you give us a breakdown of the invoice/of what we owe you?; **il nous a fait le ~ de ses aventures** he gave us a detailed account *ou* a rundown* of his adventures; **en** *ou* **dans le ~** in detail.

(c) (*Comm*) retail. **commerce/magasin/prix de ~** retail business/shop/price; **vendre au ~** *marchandise, vin* to (sell) retail; *articles, couverts* to sell separately; **marchand de ~** retailer, retail dealer; **il fait le gros et le ~** he deals in wholesale and retail.

détaillant, e [detajɑ̃, ɑ̃t] *nm,f* retailer, retail dealer.

détaillé, e [detaje] (*ptp de* **détailler**) *adj récit, plan, explications* detailed.

détailler [detaje] (1) *vt* **(a)** (*Comm*) *articles* to sell separately; *marchandise* to sell retail. **nous détaillons les services de table** we sell dinner services in separate pieces, we will split up dinner services; **est-ce que vous détaillez cette pièce de tissu?** do you sell lengths of this piece of material?

(b) (*passer en revue*) *plan* to detail, explain in detail; *récit* to tell in detail; *incidents, raisons* to detail, give details of. **il m'a détaillé (de la tête aux pieds)** he examined me *ou* looked me over (from head to foot).

détaler [detale] (1) *vi [lapin]* to bolt; (*) *[personne]* to take off*.

détartrage [detaʀtʀaʒ] *nm* (*V* **détartrer**) scaling; descaling.

détartrer [detaʀtʀe] (1) *vt dents* to scale, remove the tartar from; *chaudière etc* to descale, remove fur from.

détaxe [detaks(ə)] *nf* (*réduction*) reduction in tax; (*suppression*) removal of tax (*de* from); (*remboursement*) tax refund.

détaxer [detakse] (1) *vt* (*réduire*) to reduce the tax on; (*supprimer*) to remove the tax on, take the tax off.

détecter [detɛkte] (1) *vt* to detect. **appareil à ~ les mines** mine detector.

détecteur, -trice [detɛktœʀ, tʀis] **1** *adj dispositif* detecting (*épith*), detector (*épith*); *lampe, organe* detector (*épith*). **2** *nm* detector. **~ d'ondes/de mines** wave/mine detector; **~ de faux billets** forged banknote detector.

détection [detɛksjɔ̃] *nf* detection. **~ sous-marine/électromagnétique** underwater/electromagnetic detection.

détective [detɛktiv] *nm* detective. **~ privé** private detective *ou* investigator.

déteindre [detɛ̃dʀ(ə)] (52) **1** *vt [personne, produit]* to take the colour out of; *[soleil]* to fade, take the colour out of.

2 *vi* (*au lavage*) *[étoffe]* to run, lose its colour; *[couleur]* to run, come out; (*par l'humidité*) *[couleur]* to come off; (*au soleil*) *[étoffe]* to fade, lose its colour; *[couleur]* to fade. **~ sur** (*lit*) *[couleur]* to run into; (*fig: influencer*) *[trait de caractère]* to rub off on; **mon pantalon a déteint sur les rideaux** some of the colour has come out of my trousers on to the curtains.

dételage [detlaʒ] *nm* (*V* **dételer**) unyoking; unharnessing; unhitching; uncoupling.

dételer [detle] (4) **1** *vt bœufs* to unyoke; *chevaux* to unharness; *voiture* to unhitch; *wagon* to uncouple, unhitch.

2 *vi* (*) to leave off working*. **sans ~** *travailler, faire qch* without letting up*; **on dételle à 5 heures** we knock off* at 5 o'clock; **3 heures sans ~** 3 hours on end *ou* at a go* *ou* without a break.

détendeur [detɑ̃dœʀ] *nm [bouteille de gaz]* relief valve; *[installation frigorifique]* regulator.

détendre [detɑ̃dʀ(ə)] (41) **1** *vt ressort* to release; *corde* to slacken, loosen; (*Phys*) *gaz* to release the pressure of; *corps, esprit* to relax. **~ les jambes** to unbend *ou* straighten out one's legs; **ces vacances m'ont détendu** these holidays have made me more relaxed; **pour ~ un peu ses nerfs** to calm *ou* soothe his nerves a little; **pour ~ la situation/les relations internationales** to relieve *ou* ease the situation/the tension of international relations; **il n'arrivait pas à ~ l'atmosphère** he couldn't manage to ease the strained *ou* tense atmosphere.

2 se détendre *vpr* **(a)** *[ressort]* to lose its tension; *[corde]* to become slack, slacken; (*Phys*) *[gaz]* to be reduced in pressure.

(b) (*fig*) *[visage, esprit, corps]* to relax; *[nerfs]* to calm down; *[atmosphère]* to relax, become less tense. **aller à la campagne pour se ~** to go to the country for relaxation *ou* to unwind*; **détendez-vous!** relax!, let yourself unwind!*; **la situation internationale s'est détendue** the international situation has grown less tense *ou* has relaxed *ou* eased; **pour que leurs rapports se détendent** to make their relations less strained *ou* more relaxed.

détendu, e [detɑ̃dy] (*ptp de* **détendre**) *adj personne, visage, atmosphère* relaxed; *câble* slack; *ressort* unextended.

détenir [detniʀ] (22) *vt* **(a)** *record, grade, titres* to hold; *secret,* *objets volés* to be in possession of, have in one's possession; *moyen* to have (in one's possession). ~ **le pouvoir** to be in power, have *ou* hold the power.

(b) *prisonnier* to detain, hold (prisoner).

détente [detɑ̃t] *nf* **(a)** (*délassement*) relaxation. ~ **physique/intellectuelle** physical/intellectual relaxation; **avoir besoin de ~ nerveuse** to need to relax *ou* unwind*; **ce voyage a été une (bonne) ~** this trip has been (very) relaxing; **quelques instants/une semaine de ~** a few moments'/a week's relaxation.

(b) (*décrispation*) *[relations]* easing (*dans* of); *[atmosphère]* relaxation (*dans* in). (*Pol*) **la ~** détente.

(c) (*élan*) *[sauteur]* spring; *[lanceur]* thrust. **ce sauteur a de la ~ *ou* une bonne ~** this jumper has plenty of spring *ou* a powerful spring; **d'une ~ rapide, il bondit sur sa victime** with a swift bound he leaped upon his victim.

(d) (*relâchement*) *[ressort, arc]* release; *[corde]* slackening, loosening.

(e) (*lit, fig: gâchette*) trigger; *V* **dur.**

(f) (*Tech*) *[pendule]* catch; *[gaz]* reduction in pressure; *[moteur à explosion]* expansion.

détenteur, -trice [detɑ̃tœʀ, tʀis] *nm,f [secret]* possessor, keeper; *[record, titres, objet volé]* holder.

détention [detɑ̃sjɔ̃] *nf* **(a)** (*possession*) *[armes]* possession; *[titres]* holding; (*Jur*) *[bien]* holding. **(b)** (*captivité*) detention, holding. (*Jur*) ~ **préventive** (pre-trial) custody.

détenu, e [dɛtny] (*ptp de* **détenir**) *nm,f* prisoner. ~ **politique** political prisoner.

détergent, e [detɛʀʒɑ̃, ɑ̃t] *adj, nm* detergent.

détérioration [deteʀjɔʀɑsjɔ̃] *nf* (*V* **détériorer, se détériorer**) damaging (*de* of), damage (*de* to); deterioration (*de* in); worsening (*de* in).

détériorer [deteʀjɔʀe] (1) **1** *vt objet, relations* to damage, spoil; *santé, bâtiment* to damage. **2 se détériorer** *vpr [matériel, bâtiment]* to deteriorate; *[relations, situation]* to deteriorate, worsen.

déterminable [detɛʀminabl(ə)] *adj* determinable.

déterminant, e [detɛʀminɑ̃, ɑ̃t] **1** *adj* (*décisif*) determining (*épith*), deciding (*épith*). **2** *nm* (*Ling*) determiner; (*Math*) determinant.

déterminatif, -ive [detɛʀminatif, iv] **1** *adj* determinative; *proposition* defining (*épith*). **2** *nm* determiner, determinative.

détermination [detɛʀminɑsjɔ̃] *nf* **(a)** *[cause, sens]* determining, establishing; *[date, quantité]* determination, fixing.

(b) (*résolution*) decision, resolution. **il prit la ~ de ne plus recommencer** he made up his mind *ou* determined not to do it again.

(c) (*fermeté*) determination. **il le regarda avec ~** he looked at him with (an air of) determination *ou* determinedly.

(d) (*Philos*) determination.

déterminé, e [detɛʀmine] (*ptp de* **déterminer**) **1** *adj* **(a)** *personne, air* determined, resolute. **(b)** (*précis*) *but, intentions* specific, definite, well-defined; (*spécifique*) *quantité, distance, date* given (*épith*). **(c)** (*Philos*) *phénomènes* predetermined. **2** *nm* (*Gram*) determinatum.

déterminer [detɛʀmine] (1) *vt* **(a)** (*préciser*) *cause, distance, sens d'un mot* to determine, establish; *date, lieu, quantité* to determine, fix. ~ **par des calculs où les astronautes vont amerrir** to calculate *ou* work out where the astronauts will splash down.

(b) (*décider*) to decide, determine. ~ **qn à faire** to decide *ou* determine sb to do; **ils se sont déterminés à agir** they have made up their minds *ou* have determined to act.

(c) (*motiver*) *[chose]* to determine. **conditions qui déterminent nos actions** conditions which determine our actions; **c'est ce qui a déterminé mon choix** that is what fixed *ou* determined *ou* settled my choice; **ceci a déterminé d'importants retards** this caused *ou* brought about long delays.

(d) (*Gram*) to determine.

déterminisme [detɛʀminism(ə)] *nm* determinism.

déterministe [detɛʀminist(ə)] **1** *adj* determinist(ic). **2** *nmf* determinist.

déterré, e [deteʀe] (*ptp de* **déterrer**) *nm,f*: **avoir une tête *ou* une mine de ~** to look deathly pale *ou* like death warmed up*.

déterrer [deteʀe] (1) *vt objet enfoui* to dig up, unearth; *arbre* to uproot, dig up; *mort* to dig up, disinter; (*) *vieil objet, bouquin* to dig out*, unearth.

détersif, -ive [detɛʀsif, iv] *adj, nm* detergent, detersive.

détersion [detɛʀsjɔ̃] *nf* cleaning.

détestable [detɛstabl(ə)] *adj temps, humeur, conditions, repas* foul, ghastly; *habitude* odious, loathsome, foul; *personne, caractère* odious, detestable, hateful.

détestablement [detɛstabləmɑ̃] *adv jouer, chanter* appallingly (badly), dreadfully (badly).

détester [detɛste] (1) *vt* to hate, detest. **il déteste la peinture/les enfants/le fromage** he hates *ou* detests *ou* can't bear painting/children/cheese; **elle déteste attendre** she hates *ou* detests *ou* can't bear having to wait; **il ne déteste pas le chocolat** he is quite keen on *ou* is rather fond of *ou* is not averse to chocolate; **il ne déteste pas (de) faire parler de lui** he's not averse to having people talk about him.

détonant, e [detɔnɑ̃, ɑ̃t] *adj, nm* **(mélange)** ~ explosive (mixture).

détonateur [detɔnatœʀ] *nm* detonator.

détonation [detɔnɑsjɔ̃] *nf [bombe, obus]* detonation, explosion; *[fusil]* report, bang.

détoner [detɔne] (1) *vi* to detonate, explode.

détonner [detɔne] (1) *vi* **(a)** *[couleurs]* to clash (with each other); *[meuble]* to be out of place, be out of keeping; *[personne]* to be out of place, clash. **ses manières vulgaires détonnent dans ce milieu raffiné** his vulgar manners are out of place in this refined milieu.

(b) (*Mus*) (*sortir du ton*) to go out of tune; (*chanter faux*) to sing out of tune.

détordre [detɔʀdʀ(ə)] (41) *vt* to untwist, unwind. **le câble s'est détordu** the cable came untwisted *ou* unwound.

détortiller [detɔʀtije] (1) *vt* to unwind, untwist.

détour [detuʀ] *nm* **(a)** (*sinuosité*) bend, curve. **la rivière fait des ~s** the river meanders and winds about; **ce sentier est plein de ~s** this path is full of twists and turns *ou* is full of bends, this is a very winding path; **au ~ du chemin** at the bend of *ou* in the path.

(b) (*déviation*) detour. **en passant par Chartres vous évitez un ~ de 2 km** by going straight through Chartres you will avoid a 2-km detour; *V* **tour**[2].

(c) (*subterfuge*) roundabout means; (*circonlocution*) circumlocution. **explique-toi sans ~s** just say straight out what you mean, explain yourself without beating about the bush; **user de longs ~s *ou* prendre beaucoup de ~s pour demander qch** to ask for sth in a very roundabout way.

détourné, e [detuʀne] (*ptp de* **détourner**) *adj chemin* roundabout (*épith*); *moyen* roundabout (*épith*), indirect; *reproche* indirect, oblique. **je l'ai appris de façon ~e** I heard it in a roundabout way.

détournement [detuʀnəmɑ̃] *nm [rivière]* diversion, rerouting. ~ **d'avion** highjacking; ~ **de fonds** embezzlement *ou* misappropriation of funds; ~ **de mineur** (*perversion*) corruption of a minor; (*Jur: enlèvement*) abduction of a minor.

détourner [detuʀne] (1) **1** *vt* **(a)** (*dévier*) *route, ruisseau, circulation, convoi* to divert, reroute; *avion [pirate de l'air]* to hijack; *soupçon* to divert (*sur* on to); *coup* to parry, ward off. ~ **l'attention de qn** to divert *ou* distract sb's attention; ~ **la conversation** to turn *ou* divert the conversation, change the subject; **pour ~ leur colère** to ward off *ou* avert their anger.

(b) (*tourner d'un autre côté*) to turn away. ~ **les yeux *ou* le regard** to avert one's gaze, look away, turn one's eyes away; ~ **la tête** to turn one's head away.

(c) (*écarter*) to divert. ~ **qn de sa route/de son chemin** to divert sb from his road/from *ou* off his path, take *ou* lead sb off his road/path; ~ **qn d'un projet/de faire** to dissuade sb from a plan/from doing, put sb off a plan/doing; ~ **qn de qn** to put sb off sb, turn sb away from sb; ~ **qn du droit chemin** to lead sb astray, lead sb off the straight and narrow; ~ **qn de son devoir** to lead sb away *ou* divert sb from his duty; **pour le ~ de ses soucis** to divert him from his worries, to take his mind off his worries.

(d) (*voler*) *argent* to embezzle, misappropriate; *marchandises* to misappropriate.

2 se détourner *vpr* to turn away. **se ~ de sa route** (*pour aller ailleurs*) to make a detour *ou* diversion; (*par erreur*) to go off the right road; (*fig*) **il s'est détourné de tous ses amis** he has turned away *ou* aside from all his friends.

détracteur, -trice [detʀaktœʀ, tʀis] **1** *adj* disparaging. (*rare*) ~ **de** disparaging of. **2** *nm,f* detractor, disparager, belittler.

détraqué, e [detʀake] (*ptp de* **détraquer**) *adj machine* broken down; (*) *personne* unhinged*, cracked*; *temps* unsettled, upside-down* (*attrib*), crazy*; *nerfs, santé* shaky*; *imagination* unbalanced. **cette horloge est ~e** this clock has gone completely wrong *ou* is bust*; **il a l'estomac ~** his stomach is out of order *ou* out of sorts; **avoir le cerveau ~*** to be unhinged* *ou* cracked*, have a screw loose‡; **c'est un ~*** he's a headcase‡, he's off his head‡.

détraquement [detʀakmɑ̃] *nm [machine]* breakdown; *[santé, nerfs]* shakiness*. **à cause du ~ de mon estomac** because of my upset stomach.

détraquer [detʀake] (1) **1** *vt machine* to put out of order; *personne* (*physiquement*) to put out of sorts; *estomac* to put out of sorts, put out of order; *nerfs* to shake up*, upset. **ces orages ont détraqué le temps** these storms have unsettled the weather *ou* caused the weather to break; **cela lui a détraqué le cerveau*, ça l'a détraqué*** that has unhinged him* *ou* turned his brain*.

2 se détraquer *vpr [machine]* to go wrong, break down; *[estomac]* to get out of sorts *ou* out of order, be upset. **le temps se détraque** the weather is breaking *ou* is becoming unsettled.

détrempe [detʀɑ̃p] *nf* **(a)** (*Peinture*) (*substance*) tempera; (*tableau*) tempera painting. **peindre en *ou* à la ~** to paint in tempera. **(b)** (*Tech*) *[acier]* softening.

détremper [detʀɑ̃pe] (1) *vt* **(a)** (*délayer*) *terre, pain* to soak; *couleurs* to dilute, water down; *chaux* to mix with water, slake (*T*); *mortier* to mix with water, temper (*T*). **chemins détrempés** sodden *ou* waterlogged paths; **ma chemise est détrempée** my shirt is soaking (wet) *ou* soaked.

(b) (*Tech*) *acier* to soften.

détresse [detʀɛs] *nf* **(a)** (*sentiment*) distress. **son cœur en ~** his anguished heart.

(b) (*situation*) distress. **être dans la ~** to be in distress *ou* in dire straits; **bateau/avion en ~** boat/plane in distress; **entreprise en ~** business in difficulties; **envoyer un appel/un signal de ~** to send out a distress call/signal.

détriment [detʀimɑ̃] *nm*: **au ~ de** to the detriment of.

détritique [detʀitik] *adj roche* detrital.

détritus [detʀitys] *nmpl* rubbish (*U*), refuse (*U*).

détroit [detʀwa] *nm* (*Géog*) strait. **le ~ de Gibraltar/du Bosphore** the straits of Gibraltar/of the Bosphorus.

détromper [detʀɔ̃pe] (1) **1** *vt personne* to disabuse (*de* of). **2 se détromper** *vpr* to be disillusioned. **si tu crois que je vais accepter, détrompe-toi!** if you think I'm going to accept, (I'm afraid) I'll have to disillusion you! *ou* you'll have to think again!

détrôner [detʀone] (1) *vt souverain* to dethrone, depose; (*fig*) to oust, dethrone.

détrousser [detʀuse] (1) *vt* († *ou hum*) **~ qn** to relieve sb of his money *ou* luggage *etc* (*hum*), rob sb.

détrousseur [detʀusœʀ] *nm* († *ou hum*) bandit, footpad†. **~ de grand chemin** highwayman.

détruire [detʀɥiʀ] (38) *vt* **(a)** (*ravager*) *bâtiment, ville, document, déchets* to destroy; *avion, machines* to destroy, write off*. **un incendie a détruit l'hôtel** the hotel was burnt down, the hotel was destroyed by fire; **la ville a été complètement détruite** the town was wiped out *ou* razed to the ground *ou* completely destroyed; **cet enfant détruit tout** this child wrecks *ou* ruins everything *ou* smashes everything up*; **la tempête a détruit les récoltes** the storm has ruined the crops.

(b) (*tuer*) *population, armée* to wipe out; *animaux, insectes* to destroy, exterminate. **il a essayé de se ~** he tried to do away with himself.

(c) (*ruiner*) *empire* to destroy; *santé, réputation* to ruin, wreck; *sentiment* to destroy, kill; *espoir, théorie, projet* to ruin, wreck, put paid to* (*surtout Brit*). **les effets se détruisent** the effects cancel each other out; **cela détruit tous ses beaux arguments** that destroys *ou* puts paid to* (*surtout Brit*) all his fine arguments.

dette [dɛt] *nf* **(a)** (*Fin*) debt. **avoir des ~s** to be in debt, have debts; **faire des ~s** to get into debt, run up debts; **avoir 1.000 F de ~s** to be 1,000 francs in debt, be in debt to the tune of 1,000 francs*; **~ de jeu, ~ d'honneur** a gambling *ou* gaming debt is a debt of honour; **la ~ publique** *ou* **de l'État** the national debt; *V* **prison, reconnaissance. (b)** (*morale*) debt. **~ d'amitié/de reconnaissance** debt of friendship/gratitude; **je suis en ~ envers vous** I am indebted to you; **il a payé sa ~ envers la société** he has paid his debt to society; **je vous garde une ~ de reconnaissance** I shall remain gratefully indebted to you.

deuil [dœj] *nm* **(a)** (*perte*) bereavement. **il a eu un ~ récemment** he was recently bereaved, he recently suffered a bereavement (*frm*), there has recently been a death in his family.

(b) (*affliction*) mourning (*U*), grief. **cela nous a plongés dans le ~** it has plunged us into mourning *ou* grief; **si nous pouvons vous réconforter dans votre ~** if we can comfort you in your grief *ou* sorrow; **décréter un ~ national** to declare national mourning.

(c) (*vêtements*) mourning (clothes). **en grand ~** in deep mourning; **être/se mettre en ~** to be in/go into mourning; **quitter le ~** to come out of mourning; **prendre/porter le ~ d'un ami** to go into/be in mourning for a friend; (*fig*) **porter le ~ de ses espoirs/illusions** to grieve for one's lost hopes/illusions; (*littér*) **la forêt/nature est en ~** the forest/nature is in mourning; *V* **demi-, ongle.**

(d) (*durée*) mourning. **jour/semaine de ~** day/week of mourning; **le ~ du président dura un mois** the mourning for the president lasted a month.

(e) (*cortège*) funeral procession. **conduire** *ou* **mener le ~** to head the funeral procession, be (the) chief mourner.

(f) (*) **faire son ~ de qch** to kiss sth goodbye*, say goodbye to sth*; **les vacances sont annulées, j'en ai fait mon ~** the holidays have been cancelled but I am resigned to it *ou* it's no use crying about it.

deutérium [døteʀjɔm] *nm* deuterium.

deux [dø] **1** *adj inv* **(a)** two. **les ~ yeux/mains** *etc* both eyes/hands *etc*; **ses ~ jambes** both his legs, his two legs; **montrez-moi les ~** show me both (of them) *ou* the two of them; **~ fois** twice; **il ne peut être en ~ endroits/aux ~ endroits à la fois** he can't be in two places/in both places at once; **je les ai vus tous (les) ~** I saw them both, I saw both of them, I saw the two of them; (*lit, fig*) **à ~ tranchants** two-edged, double-edged; **des ~ côtés de la rue** on both sides *ou* on either side of the street; **tous les ~ jours/mois** every other day/month, every two days/months; **habiter** *ou* **vivre à ~** to live together *ou* as a couple; **il y a ~ t dans 'commettre'** there are two t's in 'commettre'; (*en épelant*) **~ t/l** double t/l, tt/ll.

(b) (*quelques*) a couple, a few. **c'est à ~ pas/à ~ minutes d'ici** it's only a short distance/just a few minutes from here, it's only a step/only a couple of minutes from here; **pouvez-vous attendre ~ (ou trois) minutes?** could you wait two (or three) minutes? *ou* a couple of minutes?; **vous y serez en ~ secondes** you'll be there in two ticks* (*surtout Brit*) *ou* in no time (at all); **j'ai ~ mots à vous dire** I want to have a word with you, I've a word to say to you.

(c) (*deuxième*) second. **volume/acte ~** volume/act two; **le ~ janvier** the second of January; **Jacques ~** James the Second; *pour autres loc V* **six.**

(d) (*Mus*) **mesure à ~-~/à ~-quatre/à ~-huit** two-two/two-four/two-eight time.

(e) (*loc*) **essayer et réussir, cela fait ~** to try and to succeed are two (entirely) different things, to try is one thing but to succeed is another thing altogether; **pris entre ~ feux** caught in the crossfire; **moi et les maths, ça fait ~!*** I haven't a clue about maths*, I don't get on with maths*; **il ne faut plus qu'il y ait ~ poids (et) ~ mesures** we must no longer have two sets of standards *ou* two different yardsticks; **être assis** *ou* **se trouver entre ~ chaises** to be *ou* fall between two stools; (*Prov*) **~ précautions valent mieux qu'une** better safe than sorry (*Prov*); **~ avis valent mieux qu'un** two heads are better than one (*Prov*); **en ~ temps, trois mouvements il l'a réparé*** he repaired it in two ticks* (*surtout Brit*) *ou* before you could say Jack Robinson* (*hum*).

2 *nm inv* (*chiffre*) two. (*Cartes, Dés*) **le ~** the two, the deuce; **couper en ~** to cut in two *ou* in half; **marcher ~ par ~** *ou* **~ à ~** to walk two by two *ou* in pairs *ou* two abreast; **à nous ~** (*à un ami*) let's get on then; (*à un ennemi*) now let's fight it out!; *pour autres loc V* **six** *et* **moins, pas**[1].

3: (*Aut*) **deux-chevaux** *nf inv* 2 CV (*car*); (*Naut*) **deux-mâts** *nm inv* two-master; **deux-pièces** *nm inv* (*ensemble*) two-piece suit; (*maillot*) two-piece (costume); (*appartement*) two-room flat (*Brit*) *ou* apartment (*US*); **deux-points** *nm inv* colon; **deux-ponts** *adj, nm inv* (*Naut*) two-decker; (*Aviat*) double-decker; (*Admin*) **deux-roues** *nm inv* two-wheeled vehicle; **deux-temps** (*adj*) (*Aut*) two-stroke; (*nm inv*) (*moteur*) two-stroke (engine); (*Mus*) half-common time.

deuxième [døzjɛm] **1** *adj, nmf* second; *pour loc V* **sixième. 2** (*Admin*) **le Deuxième Bureau** the intelligence branch *ou* service; (*Mil*) **deuxième classe** *nm inv V* **soldat.**

deuxièmement [døzjɛmmɑ̃] *adv* second(ly).

dévaler [devale] (1) **1** *vt* to tear down, hurtle down. **il dévala les escaliers quatre à quatre** he tore *ou* hurtled down the stairs, he came tearing *ou* hurtling down the stairs four at a time. **2** *vi [rochers]* to hurtle down; *[lave]* to rush down, gush down; *[terrain]* to fall away sharply. **il a dévalé dans les escaliers et s'est cassé le bras** he tumbled down the stairs and broke his arm.

dévaliser [devalize] (1) *vt maison* to strip, burgle; *banque* to rob. **~ qn** to strip sb of what he has on him; **~ un magasin** (*lit*) *[voleurs]* to strip *ou* burgle a shop; (*fig*) *[clients]* to buy up a shop.

dévalorisation [devalɔʀizɑsjɔ̃] *nf* depreciation.

dévaloriser [devalɔʀize] (1) **1** *vt marchandises, collection* to reduce the value of; *monnaie, talent* to depreciate. **2 se dévaloriser** *vpr [monnaie, marchandise]* to fall in value.

dévaluation [devalɥɑsjɔ̃] *nf* devaluation.

dévaluer [devalɥe] (1) *vt* to devalue, devaluate (*US*).

devancement [dəvɑ̃smɑ̃] *nm*: **~ d'une échéance** (making of a) payment in advance *ou* before time; (*Mil*) **~ d'appel** enlistment before call-up.

devancer [dəvɑ̃se] (3) *vt* **(a)** (*distancer*) *coureur* to get ahead of, get in front of; *concurrent, rival* to get ahead of, forestall.

(b) (*précéder*) to arrive before, arrive ahead of. **il m'a devancé au carrefour** he got to the crossroads before me; (*littér*) **~ son siècle** to be ahead of *ou* in advance of one's time.

(c) (*aller au devant de*) *question, objection, désir* to anticipate. **j'allais le faire mais il m'a devancé** I was going to do it but he did it first *ou* got there first.

(d) (*faire qch en avance*) (*Mil*) **~ l'appel** to enlist before call-up; (*Fin*) **~ la date d'un paiement** to make a payment before it is due.

devancier, -ière [dəvɑ̃sje, jɛʀ] *nm,f* precursor.

devant [d(ə)vɑ̃] **1** *prép* **(a)** (*position: en face de*) in front of, before (*littér*); (*mouvement: le long de*) past. **ma voiture est ~ la porte** my car is (just) outside *ou* at the door; **~ nous se dressait un vieux chêne** before us *ou* in front of us stood an old oak tree; **le bateau est ancré ~ le port** the boat is anchored outside the port; **il est passé ~ moi sans me voir** he walked past me *ou* he passed me *ou* he went right by me without seeing me; **elle était assise ~ la fenêtre** she was sitting at *ou* by the window; **il est passé** *ou* **a filé ~ nous comme une flèche** he shot past us (like an arrow), he flashed past us; **va-t-en de ~ la vitrine** move away from (in front of) the window; **va-t-en de ~ la lumière** get out of the *ou* my light; **de ~ mes yeux**† out of my sight!

(b) (*lit, fig: en avant de*) (*proximité*) in front of; (*distance*) ahead of. **il marchait ~ moi** he was walking in front of *ou* ahead of me; **il est loin ~ nous** he is a long way ahead of us; **regarde ~ toi** look in front of you *ou* straight ahead (of you); **il est ~ moi en classe** (*lit*) he sits in front of me at school; (*fig*) he is ahead of me at *ou* in school; **fuir ~ qn** to flee before *ou* from sb; **(droit) ~ nous se dressait la muraille** the wall rose up (straight) in front of *ou* ahead of us; (*fig*) **avoir du temps/de l'argent ~ soi** to have time/money in hand *ou* to spare; **il a tout l'avenir ~ lui** he has his whole future in front of *ou* before him, his whole future lies before him *ou* in front of him; **allez droit ~ vous, vous trouverez le village** go straight on *ou* ahead and you'll come to the village; (*fig*) **aller droit ~ soi (sans s'occuper des autres)** to go straight on (regardless of others); **passe ~ moi si tu es pressé** you go first *ou* in front of me if you're in a hurry; **elle est passée ~ moi chez le boucher** she pushed (in) in front of me at the butcher's.

(c) (*en présence de*) before, in front of. **s'incliner ~ qn** to bow before sb; **comparaître ~ ses juges** to appear before one's judges; **ne dis pas cela ~ les enfants/tout le monde** don't say that in front of the children/everyone; **cela s'est passé juste ~ nous** *ou* **nos yeux** it happened before *ou* in front of our very eyes; **imperturbable ~ le malheur d'autrui** unmoved by *ou* in the face of other people's misfortune; (*fig*) **reculer ~ ses responsabilités** to shrink from one's responsibilities; (*Jur*) **par-~ notaire/Maître X** in the presence of a notary/Maître X.

(d) (*fig*) (*face à*) faced with, in the face of; (*étant donné*) in view of, considering. **~ la gravité de la situation** in view of *ou* considering the gravity of the situation; **rester ferme ~ le danger** to stand fast in the face of danger; **il ne sut quelle attitude prendre ~ ces faits** he did not know what line to adopt when faced *ou* confronted with these facts; **tous égaux ~ la loi** everyone (is) equal in the eyes of the law.

2 *adv* **(a)** in front. **vous êtes juste ~** you are right in front of it; **vous êtes passé ~** you came past *ou* by it; **je suis garé juste ~** I am parked just out at the front *ou* just outside; **en passant ~, regarde si la boutique est ouverte** see if the shop is open as you go past; **corsage qui se boutonne (par-)~** blouse which buttons up *ou* does up at the front; **entre par-~, le jardin est fermé** go in (by) the front (way) because the garden is closed.

(b) (*en avant*) ahead, in front. **il est parti ~** he went on ahead *ou* in advance; **il est loin ~** he's a long way ahead; (*Naut*) **attention, obstacle (droit) ~** stand by! hazard ahead!; **il est assis 3 rangs ~** he's sitting 3 rows in front (of us); **passe ~, je te rejoindrai** (you) go on ahead and I'll catch you up; **fais passer le**

plateau ~ pass the tray forward; **il a pris des places ~** he has got front seats *ou* seats at the front *ou* up front*; (*Aut*) **il a préféré monter ~** he preferred to sit in (the) front; **marchez ~, les enfants** walk in front, children; **passe ~, il roule trop lentement** go past him *ou* overtake him *ou* get in front of him, he's going too slowly; **passez ~, je ne suis pas pressé** after you *ou* you go first *ou* you go in front of me, I'm in no hurry; *V* **pied.**

3 *nm* **(a)** *[maison, voiture, objet]* front; *[bateau]* fore, bow(s). **habiter sur le ~** to live at the front (of the house *etc*); **de ~** *roue, porte* front; *V* **patte, point².**

(b) prendre le(s) ~(s): voyant qu'il hésitait, j'ai pris les ~s pour lui parler seeing that he hesitated, I made the first move *ou* took the initiative and spoke to him; **nous étions plusieurs sur cette affaire, j'ai dû prendre les ~s en offrant un contrat plus intéressant** there were several of us after the job so I had to forestall the others and offer a more competitive contract.

(c) au-~ (de): je le vis de loin et j'allai au-~ (de lui) I saw him in the distance and went (out) to meet him; **aller au-~ des désirs de qn** to anticipate sb's wishes; **courir au-~ du danger** to court danger; **aller au-~ des ennuis** *ou* **difficultés** to anticipate problems *ou* trouble.

devanture [d(ə)vɑ̃tyʀ] *nf* **(a)** (*étalage*) display; (*vitrine*) (shop) window (*Brit*), (store) window (*US*). **à la ~** on display; (*dans la vitrine*) in the window. **(b)** (*façade*) (shop) front.

dévastateur, -trice [devastatœʀ, tʀis] *adj torrent, orage* devastating, ruinous; *passion* destructive.

dévastation [devastɑsjɔ̃] *nf* (*U: V* **dévaster**) devastation; destruction. **les ~s de la guerre/de la tempête** the ravages of war/the storm, the devastation *ou* havoc wreaked by war/the storm.

dévasté, e [devaste] (*ptp de* **dévaster**) *adj pays, ville, cultures* devastated; *maison* ruined.

dévaster [devaste] (1) *vt pays, ville* to devastate; *cultures, maison* to devastate, destroy; (*fig*) *âme* to devastate, ravage.

déveine* [devɛn] *nf* (piece of) rotten luck*. **être dans la ~** to be out of luck, be damned unlucky*; **avoir la ~ de** to have the rotten luck to*; **quelle ~!** what rotten luck!*

développable [devlɔpabl(ə)] *adj* (*gén, Géom*) developable.

développé [devlɔpe] *nm* (*Sport*) press.

développement [devlɔpmɑ̃] *nm* **(a)** *[intelligence, corps, science]* development; *[industrie, affaire, commerce]* development, expansion, growth. **une affaire en plein ~** a fast-expanding *ou* fast-developing business; **l'entreprise a pris un ~ important** the firm has expanded *ou* developed greatly *ou* has undergone a sizeable expansion; **la crise a pris un ~ inattendu** the crisis has taken an unexpected turn *ou* has developed in an unexpected way, there has been an unexpected development in the crisis.

(b) *[sujet]* exposition; (*Mus*) *[thème]* development. **entrer dans des ~s inutiles** to go into unnecessary details, develop the subject unnecessarily.

(c) (*Phot*) developing, development.

(d) (*Cyclisme*) *distance travelled in one revolution of the pedals, expressed in English in terms of gear ratio.*

(e) (*Géom*) *[solide]* development; (*Algèbre*) *[fonction]* development; *[expression algébrique]* simplification.

développer [devlɔpe] (1) **1** *vt* **(a)** *corps, muscle, intelligence* to develop; *commerce, industrie* to develop, expand. **~ le goût de l'aventure chez les enfants** to bring out *ou* develop adventurousness in children; **il faut ~ les échanges entre les pays** exchanges between countries should be developed; **elle a des bras peu développés** she has rather thin *ou* underdeveloped arms; **une poitrine bien/peu développée** a well-developed/an underdeveloped bust.

(b) *récit, argument, projet* to develop, enlarge (up)on, elaborate upon. **il faut ~ ce paragraphe** this paragraph needs developing *ou* expanding.

(c) (*Phot*) *film* to develop. **envoyer une pellicule à ~** to send (off) a film to be developed.

(d) (*déballer*) *paquet* to unwrap.

(e) (*déployer*) *parchemin* to unroll; *coupon de tissu* to unfold; *armée, troupes* to deploy.

(f) (*Géom*) *solide* to develop; (*Algèbre*) *fonction, série* to develop; *expression algébrique* to simplify.

(g) vélo qui développe 6 mètres bicycle which moves forward 6 metres for every complete revolution of the pedal.

2 se développer *vpr* **(a)** *[personne, esprit, plante]* to develop; *[affaire]* to expand, develop.

(b) *[armée]* to spread out; *[fleuve]* to spread out.

(c) *[habitude]* to spread.

devenir [dəvniʀ] (22) **1** *vi* **(a)** to become. **~ capitaine/médecin** to become a captain/a doctor; **que veux-tu ~ dans la vie?** what do you want to do *ou* be in life?; **cet enfant maladif est devenu un homme solide** that sickly child has turned out *ou* turned into *ou* has become a strong man; **il est devenu tout rouge** he turned *ou* went quite red; **il devient de plus en plus agressif** he's becoming *ou* growing *ou* getting more and more aggressive; **~ vieux/grand** to grow *ou* get old/tall; **arrête, tu deviens grossier** stop it, you're getting *ou* becoming rude *ou* starting to be rude; **c'est à ~ fou!** it's enough to drive you mad!

(b) (*advenir de*) **bonjour, que devenez-vous?*** hullo, how are you making out?* *ou* getting on? *ou* doing?*; **qu'étais-tu devenu? nous te cherchions partout** where *ou* wherever had you got to? we have been looking for you everywhere; **que sont devenues mes lunettes?** where *ou* wherever have my glasses got to? *ou* gone?; **que sont devenus tes grands projets?** what has become of your fine plans?; **que deviendrais-je sans toi?** what(ever) would I do *ou* what(ever) would become of me without you?; **qu'allons-nous ~?** what is going to happen to us?, what will become of us?

2 *nm* evolution. **quel est le ~ de l'homme?** what is man's destiny?; **nous sommes en ~** we are constantly evolving.

dévergondage [devɛʀgɔ̃daʒ] *nm* licentious *ou* loose living.

dévergondé, e [devɛʀgɔ̃de] (*ptp de* **se dévergonder**) *adj femme* shameless, bad; *homme* wild, bad; *conversation* licentious, shameless. **vie ~e** licentious *ou* loose living; **c'est une ~e** she's a shameless hussy; **c'est un ~** he leads a wild life.

dévergonder (se) [devɛʀgɔ̃de] (1) *vpr* to run wild, get into bad ways.

déverrouillage [devɛʀujaʒ] *nm* (*V* **déverrouiller**) unbolting; unlocking, opening.

déverrouiller [devɛʀuje] (1) *vt porte* to unbolt; *culasse* to unlock, open.

devers [dəvɛʀ] *prép V* **par-devers.**

déversement [devɛʀsəmɑ̃] *nm* (*V* **déverser**) pouring(-out); tipping(-out); unloading.

déverser [devɛʀse] (1) **1** *vt liquide* to pour (out); *sable, ordures* to tip (out); *bombes* to unload. **la rivière déverse ses eaux dans le lac** the river flows into *ou* pours its waters into the lake; **il déversa toute sa colère sur moi** he unloaded his anger upon me; (*fig*) **le train déversa des milliers de banlieusards** the train disgorged *ou* discharged thousands of commuters; (*fig*) **~ des produits sur le marché européen** to dump *ou* unload products onto the European market.

2 se déverser *vpr* to pour (out). **la rivière se déverse dans le lac** the river flows into *ou* pours its waters into the lake; **un orifice par où se déversaient des torrents d'eaux boueuses** an opening out of which poured torrents of muddy water.

déversoir [devɛʀswaʀ] *nm [canal]* overflow; *[réservoir]* spillway, overflow; (*fig*) outlet.

dévêtir [devetiʀ] (20) **1** *vt enfant, poupée* to undress. **~ un enfant** to take a child's clothes off (him), take the clothes off a child. **2 se dévêtir** *vpr* to undress, get undressed, take one's clothes off.

déviation [devjɑsjɔ̃] *nf* **(a)** *[projectile, navire, aiguille aimantée]* deviation; *[circulation]* diversion.

(b) (*Aut: détour obligatoire*) diversion.

(c) (*Méd*) *[organe]* inversion; *[utérus]* displacement; *[colonne vertébrale]* curvature.

(d) (*écart de conduite etc*) deviation.

déviationnisme [devjɑsjɔnism(ə)] *nm* deviationism.

déviationniste [devjɑsjɔnist(ə)] *adj, nmf* deviationist.

dévidage [devidaʒ] *nm* (*V* **dévider**) unwinding; winding.

dévider [devide] (1) *vt* **(a)** (*dérouler*) *pelote, bobine* to unwind. **elle m'a dévidé tout son chapelet*** she reeled off all her grievances to me*. **(b)** (*mettre en pelote*) *fil* to wind into a ball *ou* skein; *écheveau* to wind up.

dévidoir [devidwaʀ] *nm [fil, tuyau]* reel; *[câbles]* drum, reel.

dévier [devje] (7) **1** *vi* **(a)** *[aiguille magnétique]* to deviate; *[ballon, bateau, projectile]* to veer (off course), turn (off course). **le ballon a dévié vers la gauche** the ball veered to the left; **le poteau a fait ~ le ballon** the post deflected the ball; **le vent nous a fait ~ (de notre route)** the wind blew *ou* turned us off course *ou* made us veer off course; **nous avons dévié par rapport à notre route** we've gone off course, we're off course.

(b) (*fig*) *[doctrine]* to alter; *[conversation]* to turn, divert (*sur* (on)to). **voyant que la conversation déviait dangereusement** seeing that the conversation was taking a dangerous turn *ou* was turning onto dangerous ground; **nous avons dévié par rapport au projet initial** we have moved away *ou* diverged *ou* departed from the original plan; **on m'accuse de ~ de ma ligne politique** I'm accused of deviating *ou* departing from my political line; **rien ne me fera ~ de mes principes** nothing will turn me away from my principles, nothing will make me depart *ou* swerve from my principles; **il fit ~ la conversation vers des sujets plus neutres** he turned *ou* diverted the conversation onto more neutral subjects.

2 *vt route, circulation* to divert; *projectile, coup* to deflect, divert. **avoir la colonne vertébrale déviée** to have curvature of the spine.

devin, devineresse [dəvɛ̃, dəvinʀɛs] *nm,f* soothsayer, seer. **je ne suis pas ~*** I don't have second sight, I can't see into the future.

devinable [d(ə)vinabl(ə)] *adj résultat* foreseeable; *énigme* solvable; *secret, raison* that can be guessed, guessable.

deviner [d(ə)vine] (1) *vt secret, raison* to guess; *énigme* to solve. **~ l'avenir** to foretell the future; (*littér*) **~ qn** to see into sb; **devine pourquoi/qui** guess why/who; **vous ne devinez pas?** can't you guess?; **je ne devine pas** I give up, I don't know.

devineresse [dəvinʀɛs] *nf V* **devin.**

devinette [d(ə)vinɛt] *nf* riddle, conundrum. (*lit*) **jouer aux ~s** to play at (asking) riddles; **arrête de jouer aux ~s*** stop playing guessing games *ou* talking in riddles.

devis [d(ə)vi] *nm* estimate, quotation.

dévisager [devizaʒe] (3) *vt* to stare at, look hard at.

devise [d(ə)viz] *nf* **(a)** (*Hér*) (*formule*) motto, watchword; (*figure emblématique*) device. **(b)** *[maison de commerce]* slogan; *[parti]* motto, slogan. **simplicité est ma ~** simplicity is my motto. **(c)** (*Fin*) **~s** (foreign) currency; *V* **cours.**

deviser [dəvize] (1) *vi* (*littér*) to converse (*de* about, on).

dévissage [devisaʒ] *nm* (*V* **dévisser**) unscrewing, undoing; fall.

dévisser [devise] (1) **1** *vt* to unscrew, undo. (*fig*) **se ~ la tête/le cou** to screw one's head/neck round. **2** *vi [alpiniste]* to fall (off).

de visu [devizy] *loc adv*: **s'assurer/se rendre compte ~** to make sure/see for o.s.

dévitaliser [devitalize] (1) *vt dent* to devitalize.

dévoilement [devwalmɑ̃] *nm* (*V* **dévoiler**) unveiling; unmasking; disclosure; revelation. **le ~ d'un mystère** the unfolding of a mystery.

dévoiler [devwale] (1) *vt statue* to unveil; *intention, secret, vérité* to unveil, unmask; *avenir* to unveil, disclose; *nom, date* to reveal, disclose. **le mystère s'est dévoilé** the mystery has been unfolded.

devoir [d(ə)vwaʀ] (28) **1** *vt* **(a)** (*avoir à payer*) *chose, somme d'argent* to owe. ~ **qch à qn** to owe sb sth; **elle (lui) doit 200 F/2 jours de travail** she owes (him) 200 francs/2 days' work; **il réclame seulement ce qui lui est dû** he is asking only for what is owing *ou* due to him, he is only asking for his due(s).
(b) (*être redevable*) ~ **qch à qch** to owe sth to sth; ~ **qch à qn** to owe sth to sb, be indebted to sb for sth; **il ne veut rien ~ à personne** he doesn't want to be indebted to anyone *ou* to owe anyone anything; **c'est à son courage qu'elle doit la vie** to his courage she owes her life, it's thanks to his courage that she's alive; **je dois à mes parents d'avoir réussi** I have my parents to thank for my success, I owe my success to my parents; **c'est à Fleming que l'on doit la découverte de la pénicilline** we have Fleming to thank for the discovery of penicillin, it is to Fleming that we owe the discovery of penicillin.
(c) (*être tenu à*) to owe. ~ **le respect/l'obéissance à qn** to owe sb respect/obedience; **il lui doit bien cela!** it's the least he can do for him!; **avec les honneurs dûs à son rang** with honours befitting his rank.
2 *vb aux* **(a)** (*obligation*) to have to. **elle doit (absolument) partir ce soir** she (really) has to *ou* she (really) must go tonight; **il aurait dû la prévenir** he should have *ou* ought to have warned her; **il avait promis, il devait le faire** he had promised so he had to do it; **il devrait maintenant connaître le chemin** he ought to *ou* should know the way by now; **dois-je lui écrire tout de suite?** must I *ou* do I have to *ou* have I got to write to him straight away?; **vous ne devez pas entrer sans frapper** you are not to *ou* must not come in without knocking; **non, tu ne dois pas le rembourser** no, you need not *ou* don't have to pay it back.
(b) (*fatalité*) **cela devait arriver un jour** it (just) had to happen *ou* it was bound to happen some time; **elle ne devait pas apprendre la nouvelle avant le lendemain** she was not to hear the news until the next day; (*littér*) **dût-il** *ou* **même s'il devait être condamné, il refuserait de parler** even if he were (to be) found guilty he would refuse to talk, were he to be found guilty *ou* should he be found guilty he would still refuse to talk; **les choses semblent ~ s'arranger/empirer** it looks as though things are *ou* things seem to be sorting themselves out/getting worse.
(c) (*prévision*) **il devait acheter une moto mais c'était trop cher** he was (going) to buy *ou* he was to have bought a motorbike but it was too expensive; **il doit arriver ce soir** he is due (to arrive) tonight, he is to arrive tonight; **elle doit vous téléphoner demain** she is to ring you tomorrow; **tu ne devais pas venir avant 8 heures** you were not supposed to come *ou* you were not expected before 8; **vous deviez le lui cacher** you were (supposed) to hide it *ou* to have hidden it from him.
(d) (*probabilité*) **il doit faire froid ici en hiver** it must be cold here in winter; **vous devez vous tromper** you must be mistaken; **il a dû se tromper** *ou* **il doit s'être trompé de chemin** he must have lost his way; **il devait être 6 heures quand il est sorti** it must have been 6 when he went out; **elle ne doit pas être bête, vous savez** she can't be stupid, you know; **il ne devait pas être loin du sommet quand il a abandonné** he can't have been far from the top when he gave up; **cela devrait pouvoir s'arranger** it should be possible to put that right, we should be able to put that right.
3 se devoir *vpr*: **se ~ à qn/qch** to have to devote o.s. to sb/sth; **une mère se doit à sa famille** a mother has to *ou* must devote herself to her family; **nous nous devons de le lui dire** it is our duty *ou* we are duty bound to tell him; **comme il se doit** (*comme il faut*) as is proper *ou* right; (*comme prévu*) as expected.
4 *nm* **(a)** (*obligation morale*) duty. **agir par ~** to act from a sense of duty; **un homme de ~** a man of conscience *ou* with a sense of duty.
(b) (*ce que l'on doit faire*) duty. **accomplir** *ou* **faire** *ou* **remplir son ~** to carry out *ou* do one's duty; **les ~s du citoyen/d'une charge** the duties of a citizen/post; **se faire un ~ de faire** to make it one's duty to do; **il est de mon/ton/son** *etc* **~ de faire** it is my/your/his *etc* duty to do; **~s religieux** religious duties; (*frm*) **il se mit en ~ de répondre à la lettre** he prepared to reply to the letter.
(c) (*Scol*) (*à la maison*) homework; (*en classe*) exercise. **faire ses ~s** to do one's homework; **il n'a pas de ~ de français aujourd'hui** he has no French homework tonight; **~s de vacances** homework to be done over the holidays.
(d) (†, *hum: hommage*) **~s** respects; **présenter ses ~s à qn** to pay one's respects to sb; *V* **dernier**.

dévoltage [devɔltaʒ] *nm* reduction in voltage.

dévolter [devɔlte] (1) *vt* to reduce the voltage of.

dévolu, e [devɔly] **1** *adj*: **être ~ à qn** *[succession, droits]* to be devolved upon *ou* to sb; *[charge]* to be handed down *ou* passed on to sb; **le budget qui a été ~ à la recherche** the funds that have been allotted *ou* granted to research; **la part de gâteau qui m'avait été ~e*** the piece of cake that had been allotted to me; **c'est à moi qu'il a été ~ de commencer** it fell to my lot to start.
2 *nm V* **jeter**.

dévolution [devɔlysjɔ̃] *nf* devolution.

dévorant, e [devɔʀɑ̃, ɑ̃t] *adj faim* raging (*épith*); *curiosité, soif* burning (*épith*); *passion* devouring (*épith*), consuming (*épith*); (*littér*) *flammes* all-consuming (*littér*), ravaging (*épith*).

dévorer [devɔʀe] (1) *vt* **(a)** (*manger*) *[fauve]* to devour; *[personne]* to devour, wolf*. **des limaces ont dévoré mes laitues** slugs have eaten up *ou* devoured my lettuces; **cet enfant dévore!** this child has a huge appetite!; **on est dévoré par les moustiques!** we're being eaten alive by mosquitoes!; **~ un livre** to devour a book; **~ qn/qch du regard** *ou* **des yeux** to eye sb/sth greedily *ou* covetously; *V* **loup**.
(b) (*consumer*) to consume. **le feu dévore le bâtiment** the fire is consuming *ou* devouring the building; **il a dévoré sa fortune** he has consumed his (whole) fortune; **voiture qui dévore les kilomètres** *ou* **la route** car which eats up the miles; **c'est une tâche qui dévore tous mes loisirs** it's a task which swallows up all my free time.
(c) (*littér*) (*tourmenter*) *[jalousie, remords, soucis]* to consume, devour; *[maladie]* to consume. **la soif le dévore** he has a burning thirst, he is consumed with thirst; **être dévoré de remords/jalousie** to be eaten up with *ou* consumed with *ou* devoured by remorse/jealousy.
(d) (*frm: cacher*) **~ un affront** to swallow an affront; **~ ses larmes** to choke back *ou* gulp back one's tears.

dévoreur, -euse [devɔʀœʀ, øz] *nm,f* (*rare*) devourer (*rare*). (*fig*) **un ~ de livres** an avid reader; **ce projet est un gros ~ de crédits** this project takes a huge amount of money *ou* is a great drain on funds.

dévot, e [devo, ɔt] *adj* (*gén*) devout, pious; (*péj: bigot*) pi*, holier-than-thou. (*péj*) **une vieille ~e** a pi old woman*; *V* **faux**[2].

dévotement [devɔtmɑ̃] *adv* devoutly, piously.

dévotion [devosjɔ̃] *nf* **(a)** (*piété*) devoutness, religious devotion; *V* **faux**[2].
(b) **~s** devotions; **faire ses ~s** to perform one's devotions.
(c) (*culte*) devotion. (*fig*) **avoir une ~ pour qn** to worship sb; **être à la ~ de qn** to be totally devoted to sb; **il avait à sa ~ plusieurs employés** he had several totally devoted employees.

dévoué, e [devwe] (*ptp de* **se dévouer**) *adj infirmière* devoted, dedicated; *femme* devoted; *ami, serviteur* devoted, faithful. **être ~ à qn/qch** to be devoted to sb/sth; (††: *formule de lettre*) **votre ~ serviteur** your devoted servant; *V* **croire**.

dévouement [devumɑ̃] *nm [mère, ami, voisin]* devotion; *[infirmière, sauveteur, soldat]* devotion, dedication. **~ à un parti** devotion to a party; **avec ~** devotedly; **avoir un ~ aveugle pour qn** to be blindly devoted to sb.

dévouer (se) [devwe] (1) *vpr* **(a)** (*se sacrifier*) to sacrifice o.s. **il se dévoue pour les autres** he sacrifices himself *ou* makes a sacrifice of himself for others; **c'est toujours moi qui me dévoue!** it's always me who makes the sacrifices!; (*hum*) **personne ne veut y aller? bon, je me dévoue** so nobody wants to go? all right, I'll be a martyr (*hum*).
(b) (*se consacrer à*) **se ~ à** to devote *ou* dedicate o.s. to.

dévoyé, e [devwaje] (*ptp de* **dévoyer**) **1** *adj* delinquent. **2** *nm,f* reprobate, delinquent. **une bande de jeunes ~s** a gang of young delinquents.

dévoyer [devwaje] (8) **1** *vt* to lead astray. **2 se dévoyer** *vpr* to go astray.

dextérité [dɛksteʀite] *nf* skill, dexterity. **avec ~** skilfully, dextrously, with dexterity.

dextre [dɛkstʀ(ə)] *nf* (††, *hum*) right hand.

dey [dɛ] *nm* dey.

dia [dja] *excl V* **hue**.

diabète [djabɛt] *nm* diabetes (*sg*). **avoir du ~** to have diabetes.

diabétique [djabetik] *adj, nmf* diabetic.

diable [djɑbl(ə)] *nm* **(a)** (*Myth, Rel*) devil. **le ~** the Devil; **s'agiter comme un beau ~** to thrash about like the (very) devil; **protester comme un beau ~** to protest for all one is worth; **cet enfant a le ~ au corps** this child is the very devil; **faire le ~ à quatre** to create the devil of a rumpus; **que le ~ l'emporte!** the devil take him!; **le ~ m'emporte si j'y comprends quelque chose!** the devil take me† *ou* the deuce† if I understand any of it!, I'll be damned if I understand it!*; **c'est bien le ~ si on ne trouve pas à les loger** it would be most unusual if we couldn't find anywhere for them to stay; **ce n'est pas le ~** it's not the end of the world; **(fait) à la ~** (done) any old how; **tirer le ~ par la queue** to live from hand to mouth, be on one's uppers; **se démener comme un ~ dans un bénitier** to be like a cat on a hot tin roof; *V* **avocat**[1].
(b) (*excl*) **D~!**† **c'est difficile!** it's dashed *ou* deuced difficult!†; **~ oui/non!** good gracious yes/no!; **du ~ si je le sais!** the devil take me† *ou* the deuce† if I know!; **allons, du courage que ~!** cheer up, dash it!*; **où ~ a-t-elle mis son sac?** where the dickens *ou* devil has she put her bag?†; **pourquoi/quand ~ l'as-tu jeté?** why/when the dickens *ou* devil did you throw it out?†
(c) **au ~: être situé/habiter au ~ (vauvert)** to be situated/live miles from anywhere *ou* at the back of beyond (*Brit*); **envoyer qn au ~** *ou* **à tous les ~s** to tell sb to go to the devil; **il peut aller au ~, qu'il aille au ~!** he can go to the devil!; **au ~ l'avarice/le percepteur!** the devil take avarice/the tax collector!
(d) **du ~, de tous les ~s: il fait un froid du ~** *ou* **de tous les ~s** it's devilish cold†; **il faisait un vent du ~** *ou* **de tous les ~s** there was the *ou* a devil of a wind†, it was devilish windy†; **on a eu un mal du ~ à le faire avouer** we had the *ou* a devil of a job making him own up†.
(e) (†) **en ~** deuced†, dashed†; **il est menteur en ~** he is a deuced *ou* dashed liar†; **il est courageux/robuste en ~** he is devilishly *ou* dashed brave/strong†.
(f) (*enfant*) devil, rogue. (*personne*) **pauvre ~** poor devil *ou* wretch; **grand ~** tall fellow; **c'est un bon/ce n'est pas un mauvais ~** he's a nice/he's not a bad sort *ou* fellow; **leur enfant est très ~** their child is a real little devil.
(g) **~ de** wretched; **ce ~ d'homme** that wretched fellow; **cette ~ d'affaire** this wretched business; **avec ce ~ de temps on ne peut pas sortir** we can't go out in this wretched weather.
(h) (*jouet*) jack-in-the-box; (*chariot*) hand truck.

diablement* [djɑbləmɑ̃] *adv* devilish*†, dashed*, hellish(ly)*.

diablerie [djɑbləʀi] *nf* **(a)** (*espièglerie*) devilment, roguishness; (*acte*) mischief (*U*). **leurs ~s me feront devenir folle** their mischief will drive me mad. **(b)** (††: *machination*)

machination, evil intrigue. **(c)** (††: *sorcellerie*) devilry.
diablesse [djɑblɛs] *nf* (*diable femelle*) she-devil; (†: *mégère*) shrew, vixen; (*: *bonne femme*) wretched woman. **cette enfant est une vraie ~** that child is a little devil.
diablotin [djɑblɔtɛ̃] *nm* (*lit, fig*) imp; (*pétard*) (Christmas) cracker (*surtout Brit*), favor (*US*).
diabolique [djabɔlik] *adj* diabolic(al), devilish.
diaboliquement [djabɔlikmɑ̃] *adv* diabolically.
diabolo [djabɔlo] *nm* (*jouet*) diabolo. (*boisson*) **~ grenadine/menthe** grenadine/mint (cordial) and lemonade.
diachronie [djakʀɔni] *nf* diachrony.
diachronique [djakʀɔnik] *adj* diachronic.
diaconal, e, *mpl* **-aux** [djakɔnal, o] *adj* diaconal.
diaconat [djakɔna] *nm* diaconate.
diaconesse [djakɔnɛs] *nf* deaconess.
diacre [djakʀ(ə)] *nm* deacon.
diacritique [djakʀitik] *adj* diacritic(al). **un signe ~** a diacritic (mark).
diadème [djadɛm] *nm* (*lit, fig: couronne*) diadem; (*bijou féminin*) tiara.
diagnostic [djagnɔstik] *nm* diagnosis.
diagnostique [djagnɔstik] *adj* diagnostic.
diagnostiquer [djagnɔstike] (1) *vt* (*lit, fig*) to diagnose.
diagonal, e, *mpl* **-aux** [djagɔnal, o] **1** *adj* diagonal. **2 diagonale** *nf* diagonal. **couper un tissu dans la ~e** to cut a fabric on the cross (*Brit*) *ou* on the diagonal; **en ~e** diagonally; (*fig*) **lire en ~e** to skim through.
diagonalement [djagɔnalmɑ̃] *adv* diagonally.
diagramme [djagʀam] *nm* (*schéma*) diagram; (*courbe, graphique*) chart, graph.
dialectal, e, *mpl* **-aux** [djalɛktal, o] *adj* dialectal, dialectic(al).
dialecte [djalɛkt(ə)] *nm* dialect.
dialecticien, -ienne [djalɛktisjɛ̃, jɛn] *nm,f* dialectician.
dialectique [djalɛktik] **1** *adj* dialectic(al); *V* **matérialisme. 2** *nf* (*raisonnement*) dialectic; (*Sci*) dialectic.
dialectiquement [djalɛktikmɑ̃] *adv* dialectically.
dialectologie [djalɛktɔlɔʒi] *nf* dialectology.
dialogue [djalɔg] *nm* (*entre syndicats, ministres etc, Littérat*) dialogue; (*entre amis etc*) conversation, talk, dialogue. **c'est un ~ de sourds** it's a dialogue of the deaf.
dialoguer [djalɔge] (1) **1** *vt roman* to put into dialogue (form). **2** *vi [amis]* to have a conversation, converse; *[syndicats]* to have a dialogue.
dialoguiste [djalɔgist(ə)] *nmf* dialogue writer, screen writer.
dialyse [djaliz] *nf* dialysis.
diamant [djamɑ̃] *nm* (*gén*) diamond; *V* **croqueuse.**
diamantaire [djamɑ̃tɛʀ] *nm* (*tailleur*) diamond-cutter; (*vendeur*) diamond merchant.
diamantifère [djamɑ̃tifɛʀ] *adj* diamantiferous.
diamétral, e, *mpl* **-aux** [djametʀal, o] *adj* diametral, diametric(al).
diamétralement [djametʀalmɑ̃] *adv* (*Géom*) diametrally, diametrically. **points de vue ~ opposés** diametrically opposite *ou* opposed views.
diamètre [djamɛtʀ(ə)] *nm [arbre, cercle, courbe]* diameter.
diane [djan] *nf* (*Mil*†) reveille. **sonner/battre la ~** to sound/beat the reveille.
Diane [djan] *nf* Diane, Diana. **~ chasseresse** Diana the Huntress.
diantre [djɑ̃tʀ(ə)] *excl* (†, *hum*) by Jove! (†, *hum*), by gad! (†, *hum*). **qui/pourquoi/comment ~ ...?** who/why/how the deuce ...?† *ou* the devil ...?†
diantrement [djɑ̃tʀəmɑ̃] *adv* (†, *hum*) devilish†, deuced†.
diapason [djapazɔ̃] *nm* (*Mus*) (*registre*) compass, range, diapason; (*instrument*) tuning fork, diapason. **~ de Scheibler** tonometer; (*fig*) **être au ~ d'une situation** to be in tune with a situation; (*fig*) **se mettre au ~ de qn** to get in tune with sb *ou* on to sb's wavelength; **il s'est vite mis au ~** he soon fell *ou* got in tune with (the ideas of) the others.
diaphane [djafan] *adj tissu* diaphanous, filmy; *parchemin, porcelaine* translucent; *mains* diaphanous.
diaphanéité [djafaneite] *nf* (*littér: V* **diaphane**) diaphanousness; filminess; translucence.
diaphragme [djafʀagm(ə)] *nm* (*Anat, Bot, Tech*) diaphragm; (*contraceptif*) diaphragm, (Dutch) cap (*Brit*).
diaphragmer [djafʀagme] (1) *vi* (*Phot*) to stop down.
diapo* [djapo] *nf abrév de* **diapositive.**
diapositive [djapozitiv] *nf* transparency, slide.
diapré, e [djapʀe] (*ptp de* **diaprer**) *adj* mottled, variegated, many-coloured.
diaprer [djapʀe] (1) *vt* (*littér*) to mottle, variegate.
diaprure [djapʀyʀ] *nf* (*U: littér*) variegation, mottled effect.
diarrhée [djaʀe] *nf* diarrhoea.
diarrhéique [djaʀeik] *adj* diarrhoeal, diarrhoeic.
diastase [djastɑz] *nf* diastase.
diastasique [djastɑzik] *adj* diastatic, diastasic.
diastole [djastɔl] *nf* diastole.
diathermie [djatɛʀmi] *nf* diathermy, diathermia.
diatomique [diatɔmik] *adj* diatomic.
diatonique [djatɔnik] *adj* diatonic.
diatoniquement [djatɔnikmɑ̃] *adv* diatonically.
diatribe [djatʀib] *nf* diatribe.
dichotomie [dikɔtɔmi] *nf* (*Bot, littér*) dichotomy.
dichotomique [dikɔtɔmik] *adj* dichotomous, dichotomic.
dichromatique [dikʀɔmatik] *adj* dichromatic.
dico* [diko] *nm abrév de* **dictionnaire.**
dicotylédone [dikɔtiledɔn] **1** *adj* dicotyledonous. **2** *nf* dicotyledon.
dictaphone [diktafɔn] *nm* ® Dictaphone ®.
dictateur [diktatœʀ] *nm* dictator. (*fig*) **faire le ~** to play the dictator; **ton/allure de ~** dictatorial tone/manner.
dictatorial, e, *mpl* **-aux** [diktatɔʀjal, o] *adj* dictatorial.
dictature [diktatyʀ] *nf* dictatorship. **la ~ du prolétariat** dictatorship of the proletariat; (*fig*) **c'est de la ~!** this is tyranny!
dictée [dikte] *nf* (*action*) dictating, dictation; (*exercice*) dictation. **écrire sous la ~** to take down a dictation; **écrire sous la ~ de qn** to take down sb's dictation *ou* what sb dictates; **~ musicale** musical dictation; (*littér*) **les ~s de son cœur** the dictates of one's heart.
dicter [dikte] (1) *vt lettre, (fig) condition, action* to dictate. **ils nous ont dicté leurs conditions** they laid down *ou* dictated their conditions to us; **les mesures que nous dicte la situation** steps that the situation imposes upon us; **il m'a dicté sa volonté** he imposed his will upon me; **sa réponse (lui) est dictée par sa femme/par la peur** his wife/fear dictated his reply; **je n'aime pas qu'on me dicte ce que je dois faire!** I won't be dictated to!; **une paix dictée** peace on the enemy's terms.
diction [diksjɔ̃] *nf* (*débit*) diction, delivery; (*art*) speech production. **professeur/leçons de ~** speech production teacher/lessons.
dictionnaire [diksjɔnɛʀ] *nm* dictionary. **~ des synonymes** dictionary of synonyms; **~ de langue/de rimes** language/rhyme dictionary; **~ encyclopédique/étymologique** encyclopaedic/etymological dictionary; **~ géographique** gazetteer; **c'est un vrai ~** *ou* **un ~ vivant** he's a walking encyclopaedia.
dicton [diktɔ̃] *nm* saying, dictum.
didactique [didaktik] *adj poème, exposé* didactic; *mot, terme* technical.
didactiquement [didaktikmɑ̃] *adv* didactically.
dièdre [djɛdʀ(ə)] **1** *adj angle* dihedral. **2** *nm* dihedron, dihedral.
diérèse [djeʀɛz] *nf* (*Ling*) di(a)eresis.
dièse [djɛz] *adj, nm* (*Mus*) sharp. **fa/sol ~** F/G sharp.
diesel [djezɛl] *nm* diesel. **(moteur/camion) ~** diesel engine/lorry (*Brit*) *ou* truck (*US*).
diéser [djeze] (6) *vt* (*Mus*) to sharpen, make sharp.
diète[1] [djɛt] *nf* (*Méd*) (*jeûne*) starvation diet; (*régime*) diet. **~ lactée/végétale** milk/vegetarian diet; **mettre qn à la ~** to put sb on a starvation diet; **il est à la ~** he has been put on a starvation diet.
diète[2] [djɛt] *nf* (*Hist*) diet.
diététicien, -ienne [djetetisjɛ̃, jɛn] *nm,f* dietician, dietitian.
diététique [djetetik] **1** *adj* dietary, dietetic(al). **2** *nf* dietetics (*sg*).
dieu, *pl* **~x** [djø] *nm* **(a)** god. **les ~x de l'Antiquité** the gods of Antiquity; **le ~ Chronos** the god Chronos.
(b) (*dans le monothéisme*) **D~** God; **le D~ des chrétiens/musulmans** the God of the Christians/Muslims; **D~ le père** God the Father; **une société/génération sans D~** a godless society/generation; **le bon D~** the good *ou* dear Lord; **donner/recevoir le bon D~** to offer/receive the Lord (in Sacrament); **on lui donnerait le bon D~ sans confession** he looks as if butter wouldn't melt in his mouth; *V* **âme, homme.**
(c) (*fig: idole*) god.
(d) (*loc*) **mon D~!** my goodness!, goodness me!; **(grand) D~!, grands D~x!** great heavens!, goodness gracious (me)!; **mon D~ oui, on pourrait ...** well yes, we could ...; **D~ vous bénisse!** God bless you!; **que D~ vous assiste!** God be with you!; **à D~ ne plaise!, D~ m'en garde!** God forbid!; **D~ vous entende/aide!** may God hear/help you; **D~ seul le sait** God only *ou* alone knows; **D~ sait s'il est généreux/si nous avons essayé!** God knows he is generous/we have tried!; **D~ sait pourquoi elle a épousé un homme si stupide** heaven *ou* God (only) knows why she married such a stupid man; **D~ merci,** (*frm*) **D~ soit loué!** thank God!, praise God! *ou* the Lord!, God *ou* the Lord be praised!; **D~ merci, il n'a pas plu** it didn't rain, thank goodness *ou* thank God *ou* thank heaven(s); **c'est pas D~ possible!*** that's just not possible; **à-D~-vat!** (*entreprise risquée*) well, it's in God's hands; (*départ*) go in God's name, God be with you; **D~ m'est témoin que je n'ai jamais ...** as God is my witness I have never ...; **tu vas te taire bon D~!**: for Christ's sake: will you be quiet!; *V* **amour, grâce, plaire.**
diffamant, e [difamɑ̃, ɑ̃t] *adj* (*V* **diffamer**) slanderous; defamatory; libellous.
diffamateur, -trice [difamatœʀ, tʀis] (*V* **diffamer**) **1** *adj* slanderous; defamatory; libellous. **2** *nm,f* slanderer.
diffamation [difamɑsjɔ̃] *nf* **(a)** (*U: V* **diffamer**) slandering; defamation; libelling. (*Jur*) **la ~** slander; libel; (*Jur*) **un procès en ~** (*pour injures verbales*) an action for slander; (*pour injures écrites*) an action for libel.
(b) (*propos*) slander (*U*); (*pamphlet*) libel (*U*). **les ~s des journaux** the libellous reports in the newspapers.
diffamatoire [difamatwaʀ] *adj* (*V* **diffamer**) slanderous; defamatory; libellous.
diffamer [difame] (1) *vt* to slander, defame; (*Jur*) (*en paroles*) to slander; (*par écrit*) to libel.
différé, e [difeʀe] (*ptp de* **différer**) *adj* (*TV*) (pre-)recorded. **émission en ~** (pre-)recorded broadcast, recording.
différemment [difeʀamɑ̃] *adv* differently.
différence [difeʀɑ̃s] *nf* **(a)** (*gén*) difference. **~ d'opinion** difference of opinion; **~ d'âge/de prix** difference in age/price, age/price difference; **quelle ~ avec les autres!** what a difference from the others!; **ne pas faire de ~** to make no distinction (*entre* between); **faire la ~** to know the difference (*entre* between); **faire des ~s entre ses subordonnés** to discriminate between one's subordinates, treat one's subordinates differently; **tu auras à payer la ~** you will have to make up *ou* pay the difference.

(b) (*loc*) **à la ~ de** unlike; **à la ~** *ou* **à cette ~ que** except (for the fact) that.

différenciateur, -trice [difeʀɑ̃sjatœʀ, tʀis] *adj* differentiating, differential.

différenciation [difeʀɑ̃sjɑsjɔ̃] *nf* differentiation.

différencier [difeʀɑ̃sje] (7) **1** *vt* to differentiate. **2 se différencier** *vpr* (*être différent de*) to differ (*de* from); (*devenir différent*) to become differentiated (*de* from); (*se rendre différent*) to differentiate o.s. (*de* from).

différend [difeʀɑ̃] *nm* difference of opinion, disagreement. **avoir un ~ avec qn** to have a difference of opinion with sb.

différent, e [difeʀɑ̃, ɑ̃t] *adj* **(a)** (*dissemblable*) different (*de* from). **dans des circonstances ~es, je vous aurais aidé** if things had been different *ou* in other *ou* different circumstances, I would have helped you.

(b) (*pl, gén avant n: divers*) different, various. **à ~es reprises** on several different *ou* on various occasions; **à ~es heures de la journée** at different times of day; **pour ~es raisons** for various *ou* divers (*frm*) reasons.

différentiation [difeʀɑ̃sjɑsjɔ̃] *nf* (*Math*) differentiation.

différentiel, -elle [difeʀɑ̃sjɛl] *adj, nm, nf* (*gén*) differential.

différer [difeʀe] (6) **1** *vi* **(a)** (*être dissemblable*) to differ, be different (*de* from, *en, par* in). **cette maladie ne diffère en rien de la rougeole** this illness is no different *ou* is in no way different from measles.

(b) (*diverger*) to differ. **elle et moi différons sur** *ou* **en tout** she and I differ about everything.

(c) (*varier*) to differ, vary. **la mode diffère de pays à pays** fashions differ *ou* vary from one country to the next.

2 *vt travail* to postpone, put off; *jugement, paiement, départ* to defer, postpone. **~ une décision** to defer *ou* postpone making *ou* put off making a decision; **à quoi bon ~ plus longtemps?** why delay any longer?; (*frm*) **~ de** *ou* **à faire qch** to delay *ou* defer *ou* postpone doing sth; *V* **crédit.**

difficile [difisil] *adj* **(a)** (*ardu*) *travail, problème* difficult. **il nous est ~ de prendre une décision tout de suite** it is difficult *ou* hard for us *ou* we find it difficult *ou* hard to make a decision straight away; **il a eu un moment ~ lorsque sa femme est morte** he went through a difficult *ou* hard *ou* trying time when his wife died; **il a trouvé l'expédition ~** he found the expedition hard going *ou* heavy going; **~ à faire** difficult *ou* hard to do; **morceau ~ (à jouer)** *ou* **d'exécution ~** difficult *ou* hard piece to play.

(b) (*délicat*) *position, situation* difficult, awkward, tricky*. **ils ont des fins de mois ~s** they find things difficult at the end of the month.

(c) *personne* (*contrariant*) difficult, trying; (*exigeant*) hard *ou* difficult to please (*attrib*), fussy. **un enfant ~** a difficult child, a problem child; **elle est ~ pour ce qui est de** *ou* **en ce qui concerne la propreté** she's a stickler for cleanliness, she's very fussy *ou* particular about cleanliness; **être** *ou* **se montrer ~ sur la nourriture** to be difficult *ou* fussy *ou* finicky about one's food; **faire le** *ou* **la ~** to be hard to please *ou* (over-)fussy; **il ne faut pas être trop ~** *ou* **(trop) faire le ~** it's no good being too hard to please *ou* too fussy *ou* overfussy; **cette chambre ne vous plaît pas? vous êtes vraiment ~!** don't you like this room? you really are hard *ou* difficult to please!; *V* **vivre.**

difficilement [difisilmɑ̃] *adv marcher, s'exprimer* with difficulty. **c'est ~ visible/croyable** it's difficult *ou* hard to see/believe; **il gagne ~ sa vie** he has difficulty *ou* trouble earning a living, he finds it difficult *ou* hard to earn a living.

difficulté [difikylte] *nf* **(a)** (*U*) difficulty. **selon la ~ du travail** according to the difficulty of the work; **faire qch avec ~** to do sth with difficulty; **avoir/éprouver de la ~ à faire qch** to have difficulty (in) doing sth, find it difficult *ou* hard to do sth; **j'ai eu beaucoup de ~ à trouver des arguments** I had great difficulty finding *ou* I was hard put to it to find any arguments.

(b) (*embarras, obstacle*) difficulty, problem; *[texte, morceau de musique]* difficult passage, difficulty. **avoir des ~s financières** to be in financial difficulties *ou* straits; **il s'est heurté à de grosses ~s** he has come up against grave difficulties; **ils ont des ~s avec leurs enfants** they have problems *ou* trouble with their children; **cela ne fait** *ou* **ne présente aucune ~** this poses no problem, that is no problem; **il y a une ~** there's a problem *ou* hitch* *ou* snag*; **il a fait des ~s pour accepter nos conditions** he made *ou* raised difficulties about accepting our conditions; **il n'a pas fait de ~s pour nous suivre** he followed us without ado *ou* fuss; **c'est là la ~** that's where the trouble lies, that's the difficulty; **être en ~** to be in difficulties *ou* in trouble; **mettre qn en ~** to put sb in a difficult situation; **en cas de ~** in case of difficulty.

difficultueux, -euse [difikyltɥø, øz] *adj* difficult, awkward.

difforme [difɔʀm(ə)] *adj corps, membre* deformed, misshapen, twisted; *visage, arbre* twisted.

difformité [difɔʀmite] *nf* (*V* **difforme**) deformity, misshapenness; twistedness. (*Méd*) **présenter des ~s** to have deformities, be deformed.

diffracter [difʀakte] (1) *vt* to diffract.

diffraction [difʀaksjɔ̃] *nf* diffraction; *V* **réseau.**

diffus, e [dify, yz] *adj chaleur, lumière, douleur* diffuse; *pensée, rêverie* diffuse, vague; *style, récit, écrivain* diffuse, wordy.

diffusément [difyzemɑ̃] *adv parler, écrire* diffusely; *apercevoir* vaguely.

diffuser [difyze] (1) *vt lumière, chaleur* to diffuse; *bruit, idée* to spread (abroad), circulate, diffuse; *livres* to distribute; *émission* to broadcast. **programme diffusé en direct** live programme, programme broadcast live.

diffuseur [difyzœʀ] *nm* (*Aut, Tech: appareil*) diffuser; (*Presse: distributeur*) distributor; (*fig: propagateur*) diffuser, spreader.

diffusion [difyzjɔ̃] *nf* (*V* **diffuser**) diffusion; spreading, circulation; distribution; broadcasting.

digérer [diʒeʀe] (6) *vt* **(a)** *aliment, connaissance* to digest. **~ bien/mal** to have a good/bad digestion; (*fig*) **c'est du Marx mal digéré** it's ill-digested Marx.

(b) (*: *supporter*) *insulte, attitude* to stomach*, put up with. **si tu crois que je vais ~ ça sans protester!** if you think I'll put up with *ou* stand for that without protest!; **je ne peux plus ~ son insolence** I won't put up with *ou* stand for his insolence any longer, I can't stomach his insolence any longer*.

digeste* [diʒɛst(ə)] *adj aliment* easily digested, easily digestible.

digestibilité [diʒɛstibilite] *nf* digestibility.

digestible [diʒɛstibl(ə)] *adj* easily digested, easily digestible.

digestif, -ive [diʒɛstif, iv] **1** *adj* digestive; *V* **tube. 2** *nm* (*Méd*) digestive; (*liqueur*) liqueur.

digestion [diʒɛstjɔ̃] *nf* digestion. **j'ai une ~ difficile** I have trouble with my digestion, I have digestive problems.

digital, e[1], *mpl* **-aux** [diʒital, o] *adj* (*Anat*) digital; *V* **empreinte**[2].

digitale[2] [diʒital] *nf* digitalis. **~ pourprée** foxglove.

digitaline [diʒitalin] *nf* digitalin.

digne [diɲ] *adj* **(a)** (*auguste*) dignified. **il avait un air très ~** he had a very dignified air (about him).

(b) (*qui mérite*) **~ de** *admiration, intérêt* worthy of, deserving (of); **~ de ce nom** worthy of the name; **~ d'être remarqué** noteworthy; **~ d'éloges** praiseworthy; **~ de foi** trustworthy; **~ de pitié** pitiable; **~ d'envie** enviable; **vous devez vous montrer ~s de représenter la France** you must show that you are fit *ou* worthy to represent France; **livre à peine ~ d'être lu** book which is scarcely worth reading *ou* which scarcely deserves to be read; **il n'est pas ~ de vivre** he's not fit to live; (*littér*) **je ne suis pas ~ que vous m'offriez votre soutien** I am not worthy of your offering me your support (*littér*).

(c) (*à la hauteur*) worthy. **son ~ fils/père/représentant** his worthy son/father/representative; (*lit, péj*) **tu es le ~ fils** *ou* **tu es ~ de ton père!** you're fit to be your father's son, you take after your father; **avoir un adversaire ~ de soi** to have an opponent worthy of oneself; **œuvre ~ de son auteur** work worthy of its author; **avec une attitude peu ~ d'un juge** with an attitude little befitting a judge *ou* unworthy of a judge; **un dessert ~ d'un si fin repas** a fitting dessert for such a fine meal.

dignement [diɲmɑ̃] *adv* **(a)** (*noblement*) with dignity. **garder ~ le silence** to maintain a dignified silence. **(b)** (*justement*) fittingly, justly. **être ~ récompensé** to receive a fitting *ou* just reward, be fittingly *ou* justly rewarded.

dignitaire [diɲitɛʀ] *nm* dignitary.

dignité [diɲite] *nf* **(a)** (*noblesse*) dignity. **la ~ du travail** the dignity of labour; **la ~ de la personne humaine** human dignity; **avoir de la ~** to be dignified, have dignity; **manquer de ~** to be lacking in dignity, be undignified; (*hum*) **c'est contraire à sa ~** it is beneath his dignity; **elle entra, pleine de ~** she came in with great dignity.

(b) (*fonction*) dignity. **être élevé à la ~ de juge** to be promoted to the dignity of judge.

digramme [digʀam] *nm* digraph.

digression [digʀesjɔ̃] *nf* digression. **faire une ~** to digress, make a digression.

digue [dig] *nf* **(a)** (*lit*) (*gén*) dyke, dike; (*pour protéger la côte*) sea wall. **(b)** (*fig*) brake, barrier.

diktat [diktat] *nm* diktat.

dilapidateur, -trice [dilapidatœʀ, tʀis] **1** *adj* spendthrift, wasteful. **2** *nm,f* spendthrift, squanderer. **~ des fonds publics** embezzler of public funds.

dilapidation [dilapidɑsjɔ̃] *nf* (*V* **dilapider**) squandering, wasting; embezzlement, misappropriation.

dilapider [dilapide] (1) *vt* (*gaspiller*) *héritage, fortune* to squander, waste; (*détourner*) *biens, fonds publics* to embezzle, misappropriate.

dilatabilité [dilatabilite] *nf* dilatability.

dilatable [dilatabl(ə)] *adj corps* dilatable.

dilatant, e [dilatɑ̃, ɑ̃t], **dilatateur, -trice** [dilatatœʀ, tʀis] **1** *adj* dilative. **2** *nm* dilat(at)or, dilatant.

dilatation [dilatɑsjɔ̃] *nf* (*V* **dilater**) dila(ta)tion; distension; expansion; swelling. **avoir une ~ d'estomac** to have a distended stomach.

dilater [dilate] (1) **1** *vt pupille* to dilate; *narine, estomac* to distend, dilate; *métal, gaz, liquide* to cause to expand, cause the expansion of; *pneu* to cause to swell, distend. (*fig*) **~ le cœur** to swell the heart, cause the heart to swell.

2 se dilater *vpr* (*V* **dilater**) to dilate; to distend; to expand; to swell. **se ~ les poumons** to open *ou* swell one's lungs; (*fig*) **son cœur se dilate de joie** his heart is swelling with joy; **se ~ la rate*** to split one's sides (laughing)*; **ça me dilate (la rate)*** it's side-splitting*.

dilatoire [dilatwaʀ] *adj* dilatory. **manœuvres** *ou* **moyens ~s** delaying *ou* dilatory *ou* stalling tactics; **donner une réponse ~** to give a reply which allows one to gain time *ou* play for time.

dilemme [dilɛm] *nm* dilemma.

dilettante [diletɑ̃t] *nmf* (*en art*) dilettante, dabbler; (*péj: amateur*) amateur. **faire qch en ~** to dabble in sth; **faire un travail en ~** to do a piece of work in an amateurish way.

dilettantisme [diletɑ̃tism(ə)] *nm* amateurishness. **faire qch avec ~** to do sth in an amateurish way *ou* amateurishly.

diligemment [diliʒamɑ̃] *adv* (*littér*) (*avec soin*) diligently; (*avec célérité*) promptly, speedily.

diligence [diliʒɑ̃s] *nf* **(a)** (†, *littér: empressement*) haste, dispatch (*littér*). **faire ~** to make haste, hasten; **en ~** posthaste, speedily.

(b) (*littér: soin*) diligence, conscientiousness. (*Jur*) **à la ~ du ministre** at the minister's behest (*frm*) *ou* request.

(c) (*Hist: voiture*) diligence, stagecoach.

diligent, e [diliʒɑ̃, ɑ̃t] *adj* (*littér*) **(a)** (*actif*) *serviteur* speedy, prompt. **(b)** (*assidu*) *employé, travail* diligent, conscientious; *soins, attention* diligent, sedulous (*littér*).

diluer [dilɥe] (1) *vt liquide* to dilute; *peinture* to thin (down); (*fig*) *discours* to dilute; *force* to mitigate, dilute. **alcool dilué** alcohol diluted with water.

dilution [dilysjɔ̃] *nf* (*V* **diluer**) dilution; thinning (down); mitigation.

diluvien, -ienne [dilyvjɛ̃, jɛn] *adj pluie* torrential; (*Bible*) *époque* diluvian.

dimanche [dimɑ̃ʃ] *nm* Sunday. **le ~ des Rameaux/de Pâques** Palm/Easter Sunday; **le ~ de Noël** the Sunday after Christmas; **les ~s de l'Avent/de Carême** the Sundays in Advent/Lent; **mettre son costume** *ou* **ses habits du ~** to put on one's Sunday clothes *ou* one's Sunday best; **promenade du ~** Sunday walk; **peintre du ~** amateur *ou* spare-time painter; **chauffeur du ~** weekend driver; *pour autres loc V* **samedi.**

dîme [dim] *nf* (*Hist*) tithe. **lever une ~ sur qch** to tithe sth; **payer la ~ du vin/des blés** to pay tithes *ou* the tithe on wine/corn; (*fig*) **le grossiste/l'État prélève sa ~ (sur la marchandise)** the wholesaler takes his/the State takes its cut (on the goods).

dimension [dimɑ̃sjɔ̃] *nf* **(a)** (*taille*) *[pièce, terrain]* size. **avoir la même ~** to be the same size, have the same dimensions; **de grande/petite ~** large/small-sized, of large/small dimensions; **faire une étagère à la ~ d'un recoin** to make a shelf to fit (into) an alcove; (*fig*) **une faute de cette ~** a mistake of this magnitude; (*fig*) **un repas à la ~ de son appétit** a meal commensurate with one's appetite; (*fig*) **une tâche à la ~ de son talent** a task equal to *ou* commensurate with one's talent.

(b) (*mesures*) **~s** dimensions; **quelles sont les ~s de la pièce?** what are the dimensions *ou* measurements of the room?, what does the room measure?; **placard fait aux ~s du mur** cupboard built to the dimensions of the wall; **quelles sont vos ~s?** what are your statistics? *ou* measurements?; **mesurez-le dans la plus grande ~** measure it at the widest *ou* longest point; **à 2/3 ~s** 2-/3-dimensional.

(c) (*Philos*) dimension.

diminué, e [diminɥe] (*ptp de* **diminuer**) *adj* **(a) il est (très)** *ou* **c'est un homme (très) ~ depuis son accident** he has (really) gone downhill *ou* he's not (at all) the man he was since his accident.

(b) (*Mus*) diminished; (*Tricot*) *vêtement* fully-fashioned; *rang* decreased.

diminuer [diminɥe] (1) **1** *vt* **(a)** (*réduire*) *longueur, largeur* to reduce, decrease; *durée, volume, nombre, quantité* to reduce, cut down, decrease; *vitesse* to reduce, decrease; *frais* to reduce, cut (down); *prix, impôts, consommation* to reduce, bring down, cut; *son* to lower, turn down; *portion* to reduce, cut down; (*Tricot*) to decrease; *valeur* to reduce, bring down; *beauté, ardeur, courage* to lessen; *chances de succès, plaisir, intérêt* to lessen, reduce, diminish; *forces* to cut down, decrease. **ça l'a beaucoup diminué physiquement/moralement** this has greatly undermined him physically/mentally.

(b) (*dénigrer*) *personne* to belittle; *mérite, talent* to belittle, depreciate. **il veut toujours se ~** he's always trying to belittle himself.

(c) (*réduire le salaire de*) *employé* to cut *ou* reduce the salary of.

2 *vi* (*décroître*) **(a)** *[violence, intensité]* to diminish, lessen; *[lumière]* to fade, diminish; *[bruit]* to die down, diminish; *[circulation]* to decrease in volume; *[pluie]* to let up, diminish; *[orage]* to die down, die away, subside; *[intérêt, ardeur]* to die down, decrease, diminish. **l'attaque/le bruit diminue d'intensité** the attack/noise is decreasing in intensity *ou* is subsiding.

(b) *[effectifs, nombre]* to decrease, diminish, fall, drop; *[prix, consommation, valeur, pression]* to go down, come down, fall, drop; *[provisions]* to diminish; *[forces]* to decline, diminish. **~ de longueur/largeur** to grow shorter/narrower, decrease in length/breadth; **le (prix du) beurre a diminué** butter has gone *ou* come down (in price); **ça a diminué de volume** it has been reduced in volume; **les jours diminuent** the days are growing shorter *ou* drawing in (*Brit*).

diminutif, -ive [diminytif, iv] **1** *adj suffixe* diminutive. **2** *nm* (*Ling*) diminutive; (*petit nom*) pet name (*de* for), diminutive (*de* of).

diminution [diminysjɔ̃] *nf* **(a)** (*réduction: V* **diminuer**) reduction; decreasing; cutting-down; cutting-back; bringing-down; lowering; turning-down; lessening. **il nous a consenti une petite ~** he gave *ou* allowed us a small reduction; (*Tricot*) **commencer les ~s** to begin decreasing *ou* to decrease.

(b) (*décroissance: V* **diminuer**) diminishing; lessening; fading; dying-down; decrease in volume (*de* in); letting-up; dying-away; subsiding; decrease (*de* in). **une ~ très nette du nombre des accidents** a marked decrease *ou* drop in the number of accidents.

dimorphe [dimɔʀf(ə)] *adj* dimorphous, dimorphic.

dimorphisme [dimɔʀfism(ə)] *nm* dimorphism.

dinar [dinaʀ] *nm* dinar.

dinde [dɛ̃d] *nf* **(a)** turkey hen; (*Culin*) turkey. **~ rôtie/de Noël** roast/Christmas turkey. **(b)** (*péj: fille stupide*) stupid little goose.

dindon [dɛ̃dɔ̃] *nm* **(a)** (*gén*) turkey, (*mâle*) turkey cock. **(b)** (**: homme sot*) **être le ~ (de la farce)** to be made a fool of; *V* **pavaner.**

dindonneau, *pl* **~x** [dɛ̃dɔno] *nm* turkey poult.

dîner [dine] (1) **1** *vi* **(a)** to have dinner, dine (*frm*). **~ aux chandelles** to have dinner *ou* dine (*frm*) by candlelight; **~ d'une tranche de pain** to have a slice of bread for dinner; **avoir qn à ~** to have sb for *ou* to dinner; *V* **dormir.**

(b) (*Can, Suisse, Belgique*) to have lunch, lunch (*frm*).

2 *nm* **(a)** dinner. **ils donnent un ~ demain** they are having a dinner party tomorrow; **~ de famille/d'affaires** family/business dinner; **avant le ~** before dinner.

(b) (*Can, Suisse, Belgique*) lunch.

dînette [dinɛt] *nf* **(a)** (*jeu d'enfants*) doll's tea party. **jouer à la ~** to play at having a tea party; **venez à la maison, vous savez on fera la ~*** come home for a meal — it'll only be a snack you know. **(b)** (*jouet*) **~ de poupée** doll's tea set, toy tea set.

dîneur, -euse [dinœʀ, øz] *nm,f* diner.

dingue* [dɛ̃g], **dingo*†** [dɛ̃go] **1** *adj* nuts*, crazy*, barmy*. **il est ~ de cette fille/de ce chanteur** he's crazy* *ou* nuts* about *ou* over that girl/singer, he's mad about *ou* on that girl/singer*.

2 *nmf* nutcase*, loony‡. **on devrait l'envoyer chez les ~s** he ought to be locked up, he ought to be sent to the loony bin‡; **c'est un ~ de la voiture/de la guitare** he's crazy* *ou* nuts* *ou* mad* about cars/guitar-playing.

dinguer* [dɛ̃ge] (1) *vi*: **aller ~** *[personne]* to fall flat on one's face, go sprawling; *[chose]* to go crashing down, go flying*; **les boîtes ont failli ~ par terre** the tins nearly came crashing down; (*fig*) **envoyer ~ qn** to tell sb to clear *ou* buzz (*Brit*) *ou* push off*, send sb packing; **envoyer ~ qch** to send sth flying*.

dinosaure [dinozɔʀ] *nm* dinosaur.

diocésain, e [djɔsezɛ̃, ɛn] *adj, nm,f* diocesan.

diocèse [djɔsɛz] *nm* diocese.

diode [djɔd] *nf* diode.

dionysiaque [djɔnizjak] *adj* Dionysian, Dionysiac. **les ~s** the Dionysia.

Dionysos [djɔnizɔs] *nm* Dionysus, Dionysos.

dioptrie [djɔptʀi] *nf* dioptre.

dioptrique [djɔptʀik] **1** *adj* dioptric(al). **2** *nf* dioptrics (*sg*).

diorama [djɔʀama] *nm* diorama.

dioxyde [djɔksid] *nm* dioxide.

diphasé, e [difɑze] *adj* diphase, diphasic, two-phase.

diphtérie [difteʀi] *nf* diphtheria.

diphtérique [difteʀik] *adj* diphther(it)ic, diphtherial.

diphtongaison [diftɔ̃gɛzɔ̃] *nf* diphthongization.

diphtongue [diftɔ̃g] *nf* diphthong.

diphtonguer *vt*, **se diphtonguer** *vpr* [diftɔ̃ge] (1) to diphthongize.

diplodocus [diplɔdɔkys] *nm* diplodocus.

diplomate [diplɔmat] **1** *adj* diplomatic. **2** *nmf* (*ambassadeur*) diplomat; (*personne habile*) diplomatist. **3** *nm* (*Culin*) ≃ trifle.

diplomatie [diplɔmasi] *nf* (*Pol, fig*) diplomacy. **le personnel de la ~** the diplomatic staff.

diplomatique [diplɔmatik] *adj* (*gén*), (*fig*) *maladie* diplomatic; *V* **valise.**

diplomatiquement [diplɔmatikmɑ̃] *adv* (*Pol, fig*) diplomatically.

diplôme [diplom] *nm* (*titre*) diploma, certificate; (*examen*) examination, exam. **avoir des ~s** to have qualifications.

diplômé, e [diplome] (*ptp de* **diplômer**) **1** *adj* qualified. **2** *nm,f* holder of a diploma.

diplômer [diplome] (1) *vt* to award a diploma to.

diplopie [diplɔpi] *nf* double vision, diplopia (*T*).

dipsomane [dipsɔman] **1** *adj* dipsomaniacal. **2** *nmf* dipsomaniac.

dipsomanie [dipsɔmani] *nf* dipsomania.

diptère [diptɛʀ] **1** *adj temple* dipteral; *insecte* dipterous, dipteran. **2** *nm* (*Zool*) dipteran. **les ~s** the Diptera.

diptyque [diptik] *nm* (*Hist: tablette, Art*) diptych; (*fig: roman*) work in two parts.

dire [diʀ] (37) **1** *vt* **(a)** to say. **avez-vous quelque chose à ~?** have you got anything to say?; **'j'ai froid' dit-il** 'I'm cold' he said; **on peut commencer: elle a dit oui** we can start: she said yes *ou* she said we could; **~ bonjour/quelques mots à qn** to say hullo/a few words to sb; **il m'a dit, 'je comprends'** he said to me, 'I understand'; **comment dit-on ça en anglais?** what's the English for that?, how do you say that in English?; **~ qch carrément** *ou* **crûment** to put sth (quite) bluntly, state sth (quite) plainly *ou* frankly; **comme disent les Anglais** as the English put it *ou* say; **~ ce qu'on pense** to speak one's mind, say what one thinks; **ne plus savoir quoi ~** to be at a loss for words; **il dit n'importe quoi** he'll say anything *ou* any (old) thing, he says the first thing that enters his head; **il n'a pas dit un mot** he hasn't said *ou* spoken *ou* uttered a (single) word; **qu'est-ce que les gens vont ~!, qu'en dira-t-on?** whatever will people *ou* they say!; **il ne croyait pas si bien ~** he didn't know how right he was, he never spoke a truer word; **ce n'est pas une chose à ~, il est préférable de ne pas le ~** it is not the sort of thing one says, it's not the sort of thing to say, it is better left unsaid; (*aux enchères*) **qui dit mieux?** any advance?; **il a au moins 70 ans, que dis-je, plutôt 80** he must be at least 70 — what am I saying? — more like 80; **où va-t-il? — il ne l'a pas dit ou il n'a pas dit*** where is he going? — he didn't say; (*Cartes*) **c'est à vous de ~** your call; *V* **bien, mal, parler.**

(b) (*+ que*) to say that; **~ à qn que** to tell sb that, say to sb that; **il dit qu'il nous a écrit, il dit nous avoir écrit** he says that he wrote to us; **il a bien dit qu'il ne rentrerait pas** he did say that he would not be coming home; **doit-il venir? — elle dit que oui/que non** is he coming? — she says he is/he isn't *ou* she says so/not; **la radio et les journaux avaient dit qu'il pleuvrait** (both) the radio and the papers had said it would rain; **vous nous dites dans votre lettre que** you tell us in *ou* you say in your letter that; **votre lettre/la loi dit clairement que** your letter/the law says clearly that *ou* clearly states that; **l'espoir fait vivre, dit-on** you can live on hope, as the saying has it *ou* as the saying goes *ou* as they say; **on dit que ...** rumour has it that ..., they say that ..., it is said that ...; **on le dit malade/à Londres** he's rumoured to be ill/in London; **à** *ou* **d'après ce qu'il dit** according to him, according to what he says; **il sait ce qu'il dit** he knows what he's talking about; **il ne sait pas ce qu'il dit** he doesn't know what he is talking about! *ou* what he is saying!; **qu'est-ce qui me dit que c'est vrai?** how can I tell it's the truth?, how am I to know *ou* how do I know it's the truth?

(c) *mensonges, nouvelle, adresse, nom* to tell; *sentiment* to tell of, express. **~ qch à qn** to tell sb sth; **il m'a dit quelque chose qui m'a fait rire** he told me something that made me laugh; **j'ai quelque chose à vous ~** there's something I want to tell you; **~ des bêtises** to talk nonsense; **~ la bonne aventure/l'avenir** to tell fortunes/the future; **~ la bonne aventure à qn** to tell sb's fortune; **dis-nous-en la raison** give *ou* tell us the reason (for it); **il nous a dit toute sa joie/tout son soulagement** he told us of his great joy/relief, he told us how happy/how relieved he was; **ce nom, cela me dit quelque chose** this name rings a bell; **cela ne me dit rien du tout** that doesn't mean a thing to me; **qu'est-ce que ça dit, ton jardin?*** how is your garden doing?*

(d) (*ordonner, prévenir*) to tell. **dites-lui de partir/qu'il parte ce soir** tell him to go/that he must leave tonight; **il a dit de venir de bonne heure** he said we were to come *ou* he said to come* early, he told us to come early; **fais ce qu'on te dit!** do as *ou* what you are told!; **ça suffit, j'ai dit!** I said that's enough!; **on nous a dit de l'attendre** we were told to wait for him; **'méfie-toi' me dit-il** he told me *ou* he said to me, 'be cautious'; *V* **envoyer.**

(e) (*objecter*) to say (*à, contre* against). **que veux-tu que je dise à** *ou* **contre ça?** what can I say against that?, how can I object to that?; **tu n'as rien à ~, tu aurais fait la même chose** YOU can't say anything! *ou* YOU can talk! you would have done exactly the same thing!; **tais-toi, tu n'as rien à ~!** be quiet, it's nothing to do with you! *ou* you keep out of this!; **je n'ai rien à ~ sur son travail** I cannot complain about his work; **tu n'as rien à ~, tu es bien servi** you can't say anything *ou* you can't complain *ou* object, with what you've got.

(f) *poèmes* to say, recite; *prière* to say; *rôle* to speak. **~ son chapelet** to say the rosary, tell one's beads†; **~ la messe** to say mass; **l'acteur a très mal dit ce passage** the actor spoke these lines very badly.

(g) (*plaire*) **cela vous dit de sortir?** do you feel like going out?, do you fancy (*surtout Brit*) going out?; **cela ne me dit rien** I don't feel like it at all, it doesn't appeal to me at all, I don't fancy (*surtout Brit*) it at all; **rien ne me dit en ce moment** I am not in the mood for anything *ou* I don't feel like doing anything just now; **si le cœur vous en dit** if you feel like it, if you feel so inclined; **cela ne me dit rien qui vaille** I don't like the look of that, that looks suspicious to me; **pour l'instant, cette robe ne dit rien*, mais attendez qu'elle soit finie!** for the moment this dress doesn't look anything special *ou* doesn't look up to much*, but just wait until it's finished!

(h) *[chose]* (*indiquer*) to say, show. **ma montre dit 6 heures** my watch says 6 o'clock, it is 6 o'clock by my watch; **son visage disait sa déception** his face gave away his disappointment, disappointment was written all over his face; **son silence en dit long** his silence speaks for itself *ou* speaks volumes *ou* tells its own story.

(i) (*penser*) to think. **qu'est-ce que tu dis de ma robe?** what do you think of *ou* how do you like my dress?; **qu'est-ce que vous dites de la question?** what do you think *ou* how do you feel about the question?, what are your feelings on the subject?; **qu'est-ce que vous diriez d'une promenade?** what would you say to a walk?, how about a walk?; **et ~ qu'il aurait pu se tuer!** to think he might have killed himself!; **on dirait qu'il n'aime pas cette ville** one gets the impression he does not like this town, he doesn't seem to like this town; **qui aurait dit qu'elle allait gagner?** who would have thought (that) she would win?; **on dirait qu'il va pleuvoir** it looks like rain; **on dirait qu'il va pleurer** he looks as though he is going to cry; **on se dirait en France** you would think you were in France; **cette eau est noire, on dirait de l'encre** this water is black — it looks like ink; **on dirait du poulet** it tastes like *ou* it's like chicken; **on dirait du Brahms** it sounds like *ou* it's like Brahms; **qui l'eût dit!** who would have thought it!

(j) (*décider*) **venez bientôt, disons demain** come soon, let's make it tomorrow *ou* (let's) say tomorrow; **tout n'est pas dit** the last word has not been said, it isn't all over yet; **c'est plus facile à ~ qu'à faire** it's easier said than done; **il est dit** *ou* **il a été dit que je ne gagnerai jamais** I'm destined never to win; **bon, c'est dit** *ou* **voilà qui est dit** right, it's settled *ou* it's all arranged; **ce qui est dit est dit** what's said is said; **tenez-vous-le pour dit** mark my words; **à l'heure dite** at the appointed time *ou* hour; **au jour dit** on the appointed day; *V* **aussitôt.**

(k) (*appeler*) **X, dit le Chacal** X, known as the Jackal.

(l) (*admettre*) to say, admit. **il faut bien ~ que** I must say *ou* admit that; **disons-le, il nous ennuie** let's be frank *ou* to be frank *ou* let's face it*, he bores us.

(m) (*loc*) **je ne dis pas non** I won't say no; **qui dit argent dit problèmes** money means problems; **tu l'as dit!** how right you are!, you('ve) said it!; **ceci dit** (*à ces mots*) thereupon, having said this; (*avec restriction*) nevertheless, having said this; (*littér*) **ce disant** so saying; **pour ainsi ~** so to speak; **comme qui dirait*** as you might say; **ou pour mieux ~ ...** or, rather ..., or, to put it another way ...; **j'entends comme qui dirait des grognements** I can hear what sounds like groans *ou* something like groans; **dis donc!** (*à propos*) by the way; (*holà*) hey!; **tu me l'envoies, dis, cette lettre?** you will send me that letter, won't you?; **comme on dit, comme dit** *ou* **disait l'autre*** as they say, so to speak; **je suis sûr, je te dis*** I'm certain, I tell you; **pour tout ~** in fact; **~ que ...** to think that ...; **~ qu'il aurait pu rater ça** (and) to think he might have missed it; **je vous l'avais bien dit!** I told you so!, didn't I tell you?; **que tu dis** (*ou* **qu'il dit** *etc*)!: that's your (*ou* his *etc*) story!*, that's what you say (*ou* he says *etc*); **à qui le dites-vous!** *ou* **le dis-tu!** don't I know it!*, you're telling ME!*; **cela va sans ~** it goes without saying; **à vrai ~, à ~ vrai** to tell (you) the truth, in actual fact, to be (quite) truthful; **quand je vous le disais!** didn't I tell you?; **je ne veux pas avoir à le lui ~ deux fois** I don't want to have to tell him again; **il n'y a pas à ~** there's no doubt about it, there's no denying it, there's no getting away from it; **je ne vous dis que cela!** just let me tell you!; **on a beau ~** say what you like *ou* will; **comment dirais-je ...** how shall I put it?, what can I say?; **que dites-vous, qu'est-ce que tu dis?** *ou* **vous dites?** (I beg your) pardon?, what did you say?; **c'est ~ s'il est content** that just shows you how pleased he is; **c'est beaucoup ~** that's saying a lot; **c'est peu ~** that's an understatement; **c'est trop ~** that's saying too much; **c'est (tout) ~** that (just) shows you; **c'est moi qui vous le dis** you take my word for it; **c'est vous qui le dites** YOU say so, that's what YOU say; **ce n'est pas pour ~, mais** (*se vanter*) I don't mean *ou* wish to boast, but ...; (*se plaindre*) I don't mean *ou* wish to complain, but ...; **c'est-à-~** that is (to say); **c'est-à-~ que je ne le savais pas** well actually *ou* well the thing is *ou* I'm afraid I didn't know; **qu'est-ce à ~?** what does that mean?; **est-ce à ~ que ...?** does this mean that ...?, is that to say that ...?; **entre nous soit dit, il est un peu bête** (just) between the two of us *ou* confidentially he is a bit of an idiot; **soit dit en passant** let it be said in passing, incidentally.

(n) (*avec faire, laisser, vouloir*) **faire ~ qch à qn** to send word of sth to sb; **faire ~ à qn de venir** to send for sb; **faire ~ à qn qu'on a besoin de lui** to let sb know that he is needed; **faire ~ à qn des choses (qu'il n'a pas dites)** to put words in sb's mouth; **il ne se l'est pas fait ~ deux fois** he did not need *ou* have to be told twice; **elle partit sans se le faire ~ deux fois** she was off without a second bidding *ou* without having to be told twice; **par la torture on fait ~ aux gens ce qu'on veut** people can be made to say *ou* you can make people say anything under torture; **je ne lui ai pas fait ~** I didn't make him say it; **laisser ~** to let people talk; **laisse ~!** let them talk!, never mind what they say!; **je me suis laissé ~ que** I hear that, I was told that; **vouloir ~** (*signifier*) to mean; **que veut ~ ce mot/sa réponse?** what does this word/his answer mean?, what is the meaning of this word/his answer?; **cette phrase ne veut rien ~** this sentence does not mean a thing; **c'est bien cela que je veux ~** that is exactly *ou* just what I mean; **cela dit bien ce que cela veut ~** it means exactly *ou* just what it says; **cela ne veut pas ~ qu'il viendra** *ou* **qu'il vienne** that does not mean (to say) that *ou* it does not follow that he will come.

2 se dire *vpr* **(a)** to say to o.s. **il se dit qu'il était inutile de rester** he said to himself that there was no point in staying; **il faut bien se ~ que** one has to realize *ou* accept that.

(b) (*se prétendre*) **il se dit malade** he claims to be ill *ou* that he is ill; **elle se dit sa cousine** she claims to be his cousin, she says she is his cousin.

(c) elles se dirent au revoir they said goodbye (to each other).

(d) (*sens passif*) **cela ne se dit pas en société** this word is not in polite use, it's not the sort of thing one says in company; **cela ne se dit plus en français** this expression is no longer used *ou* in use in French; **cela se dit de la même façon en anglais et en français** it's the same in English and in French; **comment se dit ... en français?** what is the French for ...?, how do you say ... in French?

3 *nm* (*déclaration*) statement. **d'après ses ~s** according to him *ou* to what he says; **au ~ de** according to; **au ~ de** *ou* **selon le ~ de tous** by all accounts; **croire aux ~s de qn** to believe what sb says; (*Jur*) **leurs ~s ne concordent pas** their statements do not agree.

direct, e [diʀɛkt, ɛkt(ə)] **1** *adj* **(a)** (*sans détour*) *route* direct; *reproche, regard* direct; *question* direct, straight; *allusion* direct, pointed (*épith*). **c'est le chemin le plus ~** it's the most direct route; **il m'a parlé de manière très ~e, il a été très ~** he spoke to me in a very direct *ou* straightforward way *ou* very frankly, he didn't beat about the bush.

(b) (*sans intermédiaire*) *impôt, descendant, adversaire, responsabilité* direct; *cause* immediate, direct; (*Jur*) *action* direct. **ses chefs ~s** his immediate superiors; **ligne téléphonique ~e** (*privée*) private *ou* direct line; (*automatique*) automatic dialling system; **être en rapport** *ou* **contact ~** *ou* **en relations ~es avec** to deal directly *ou* be in direct contact with; **se mettre en rapport ~ avec qn** to contact sb *ou* make contact with sb directly; **il n'y a pas de rapport** *ou* **lien ~ entre les deux faits** there is no direct connection *ou* link between the two facts; **il a pris une part très ~e à cette affaire** he was directly involved in this business.

(c) (*absolu*) **en contradiction ~e** in direct *ou* complete contradiction.

(d) (*Astron*) direct; (*Ling*) *style, discours* direct; (*Logique*) *proposition* positive; *V* **complément.**

(e) (*Rail*) *train* fast (*épith*), non-stop (*épith*), express (*épith*); *voiture* through (*épith*). **ce train est ~ jusqu'à Lyon** this is a fast *ou* non-stop train to Lyons.

2 *nm* **(a)** (*Rail*) express (train), fast train. **le ~ Paris-Dijon** the Paris-Dijon express.

(b) (*Boxe*) jab. **~ du gauche/du droit** straight left/right.

(c) (*Rad, TV*) **c'est du ~** it's live; **émission en ~** live broadcast; **parler/faire un reportage en ~ de New York** to be speaking/reporting live from New York.

directement [diʀɛktəmɑ̃] *adv* **(a)** (*immédiatement*) straight, straight away. **il est ~ allé se coucher** he went straight *ou* directly to bed, he went to bed straight away; **en rentrant il est allé ~ au réfrigérateur pour voir ce qu'il y avait à manger** when he came home he went straight to the fridge *ou* he made a beeline for the fridge to see what there was to eat.

(b) (*sans détour*) straight, directly. **cette rue mène ~ à la gare** this street leads straight to the station; **cet escalier communique ~ avec la cave** this staircase leads straight *ou* directly to the cellar; **il est entré ~ dans le vif du sujet** he came straight to the point.

(c) (*personnellement*) directly. **il m'a très ~ accusé de ce crime** he accused me of this crime straight out *ou* to my face; **sa bonne foi est ~ mise en cause** it's a direct challenge to his good faith; **tout ceci ne me concerne pas ~ mais ...** none of this concerns me directly *ou* personally but ..., none of this is of any immediate concern to me but ...; **les secteurs de l'économie les plus ~ touchés par la crise** the sectors of the economy most directly *ou* immediately affected by the crisis.

(d) (*sans intermédiaire*) direct, straight. **adressez-vous ~ au patron** apply to the boss direct *ou* in person, go straight to the boss; **j'ai été ~ le trouver pour le lui demander** I went to find him myself *ou* in person to ask him about it; **~ du producteur au consommateur** direct *ou* straight from (the) producer to (the) consumer; **colis expédié ~ à l'acheteur** parcel sent direct to the buyer.

(e) (*diamétralement*) (*lit*) directly; (*fig*) completely, utterly, directly. **la maison ~ en face** the house directly opposite; **~ opposé** diametrically *ou* utterly opposed; **~ contraire/contradictoire** completely *ou* utterly contrary/contradictory.

directeur, -trice [diʀɛktœʀ, tʀis] **1** *adj* (*dirigeant*) directing; (*fig: principal*) *idée* leading, principal, main; *principe* guiding; *force* guiding, driving; (*Tech*) *bielle* driving; *roue* front; *V* **comité, ligne[1], plan[1].**

2 *nm* **(a)** (*responsable*) *[banque, usine]* manager; (*Admin*) head; (*Ciné, TV: technicien*) director. **~ commercial/général/du personnel** sales/general/personnel manager; (*Univ*) **le ~ de l'U.E.R. d'anglais** the head of the English department.

(b) (*administrateur*) director.

(c) ~ (d'école) headmaster (*Brit*), principal (*US*).

3 directrice *nf* **(a)** *[entreprise]* manageress; (*propriétaire*) director; (*Admin*) head.

(b) ~trice d'école/de lycée (primary/secondary school) headmistress (*Brit*), principal (*US*).

(c) (*Math*) directrix.

4: directeur artistique artistic director; **directeur de cabinet (d'un ministre)** principal private secretary; **directeur de conscience** director, spiritual adviser; **directeur gérant** managing director; **directeur de journal** newspaper editor; **directeur de la photographie** director of photography; **directeur de prison** prison governor; **directeur spirituel = directeur de conscience**; (*Univ*) **directeur de thèse** supervisor.

direction [diʀɛksjɔ̃] *nf* **(a)** (*lit, fig: sens*) direction; (*route, chemin*) direction, way. **vous n'êtes pas dans** *ou* **vous n'avez pas pris la bonne ~** you're not going the right way *ou* in the right direction, you're not on the right road; **dans quelle ~ est-il parti?** which way did he go? *ou* head?; **aller dans la ~ de** *ou* **en ~ de Paris, prendre la ~ de Paris** to go towards *ou* in the direction of Paris; **train/avion en ~ de ...** train/plane for *ou* going to ...; **bateau en ~ de ...** ship bound *ou* heading for ...; (*fig*) **nous devons chercher dans une autre ~** we must look in some other *ou* a different direction, we must direct our search elsewhere; (*fig*) **l'enquête a pris une nouvelle ~** the inquiry has taken a new turn; **dans toutes les ~s** in all directions.

(b) (*action d'administrer: V* **diriger**) management; running; editorship; leadership; directing; supervision; conducting. **il a été chargé de** *ou* **on lui a confié la ~ de l'enquête/des travaux** he has been put in charge of the inquiry/the work; **avoir la ~ de** (*gén, Admin, Ind*) to run, be at the head of, be in charge of (the running of); *recherches, travaux* to supervise, oversee, be in charge of; **prendre la ~ de** (*gén, Admin*) to take over the running of; *usine, entreprise* to take over the running *ou* management of; *équipe, travaux* to take charge of, take over the supervision of; *mouvement, pays* to take over the leadership of; *débats* to take control of; *journal* to take over *ou* take on the editorship of; **sous sa ~** under his leadership (*ou* management *etc*); **prendre la ~ des opérations** to take charge *ou* control (of the running of operations); **il a travaillé sous la ~ d'un spécialiste** he has worked under the supervision of an expert; **il a fait ses études sous la ~ de X** he studied under X; (*Mus*) **orchestre (placé) sous la ~ de X** orchestra conducted by X.

(c) (*fonction*) *[usine, entreprise, théâtre]* post of (factory *ou* theatre *etc*) manager, managership; *[école]* headship; *[journal]* editorship; (*Admin*) post of chief executive *ou* director general, director-generalship. **on lui a offert la ~ de l'usine/d'une équipe de chercheurs** he was offered the post of factory manager/of leader *ou* head of a research team.

(d) (*personnel dirigeant*) *[usine, service, équipe]* management; *[journal]* editorial board. **se plaindre à la ~** to make a complaint to the board *ou* the management; **la ~ décline toute responsabilité** the directors accept *ou* the management accepts no responsibility; *V* **changement.**

(e) (*bureau*) (*Admin*) director's office; *[usine]* manager's office; *[école]* headmaster's (*ou* headmistress's) office (*Brit*), principal's office (*US*); *[journal]* editor's office.

(f) (*service*) department. **adressez-vous à la ~ du personnel** apply to the personnel department.

(g) (*Aut: mécanisme*) steering. **~ assistée** power steering; *V* **rupture.**

directionnel, -elle [diʀɛksjɔnɛl] *adj* (*Tech*) directional.

directive [diʀɛktiv] *nf* (*gén pl*) directive, order, instruction.

Directoire [diʀɛktwaʀ] *nm* (*Hist*) **le ~** the Directory, the Directoire; **fauteuil/table ~** Directoire chair/table; *V* **style.**

directorial, e, *mpl* **-iaux** [diʀɛktɔʀjal, jo] *adj fonction, responsabilité* (*Comm, Ind*) managerial; (*Admin*) of directors; (*Scol*) of headmaster (*ou* headmistress) (*Brit*), of principal (*US*). **fauteuil/bureau ~** manager's *ou* director's *ou* headmaster's (*Brit*) *ou* principal's (*US*) *etc* chair/office.

directrice [diʀɛktʀis] *V* **directeur.**

dirigeable [diʀiʒabl(ə)] *adj, nm* dirigible, airship.

dirigeant, e [diʀiʒɑ̃, ɑ̃t] **1** *adj classe* ruling. **2** *nm,f [entreprise]* director, manager; *[parti, syndicat]* leader; *[pays]* leader, ruler.

diriger [diʀiʒe] (3) **1** *vt* **(a)** (*administrer*) (*gén, Admin*) to run, be head of, be in charge of; *entreprise, usine, théâtre* to manage, run; *journal* to run, edit; *pays, mouvement, parti* to lead, run; *opération, manœuvre* to direct, be in charge of; *recherches, travaux* to supervise, oversee, be in charge of; *enquête, procès* to conduct; *débat* to conduct, lead; *orchestre* to conduct. **~ la circulation** to control the traffic; (*Mil*) **~ le tir** to direct the firing; **mal ~ une entreprise** to mismanage a business, run a business badly; **équipe bien/mal dirigée** team under good/bad leadership *ou* management, well-/badly-run team; **savoir ~** to know how to command *ou* lead, be a good manager *ou* leader; **ils n'ont pas su ~ leurs enfants** they weren't able to guide their children; **a-t-il bien su ~ sa vie?** did he manage to run his life properly?; **cette idée dirige toute notre politique** this idea guides *ou* determines our whole policy; **l'ambition dirige tous ses actes** ambition rules *ou* guides his every act; *V* **économie, loisir.**

(b) (*guider*) *voiture* to steer; *avion* to pilot, fly; *bateau* to steer, navigate; *cheval* (*de trait*) to steer; (*de selle*) to guide. (*fig*) **bien/mal ~ sa barque** to run one's affairs well/badly; **bateau qui se dirige facilement** boat which is easy to steer.

(c) (*acheminer*) *marchandises, convoi* to send (*vers, sur* to); *personnes* to direct, send (*sur, vers* to). **on m'a mal dirigé** I was misdirected *ou* sent the wrong way.

(d) (*orienter*) **~ une arme sur** to point *ou* level *ou* aim a weapon at; **~ un canon/télescope sur** to train *ou* point a gun/telescope on; **~ une lampe de poche/lumière sur** to shine a torch/light on; **~ son attention sur qn/qch** to turn one's attention to *ou* on sb/to sth; **~ son regard** *ou* **ses yeux sur** *ou* **vers qch** to look towards *ou* in the direction of sth; **le pompier dirigea sa lance vers les flammes** the fireman aimed *ou* pointed his hose at *ou* trained his hose on the flames; **la flèche est dirigée vers la gauche** the arrow is pointing left *ou* to(wards) the left; **~ ses pas vers un lieu** to make for *ou* make one's way to *ou* head for a place; **on devrait ~ ce garçon vers les sciences** we should steer this boy towards the sciences; **nous dirigeons notre enquête/nos travaux dans une voie nouvelle** we are conducting our inquiry/carrying out our work along new lines; **son regard se dirigea vers elle** he turned his gaze towards *ou* on her; **~ un article/une allusion contre qn/qch** to aim *ou* direct an article/an allusion at sb/sth; **~ une critique contre qn/qch** to aim *ou* direct *ou* level a criticism at sb/sth; **les poursuites dirigées contre lui** the proceedings directed *ou* brought against him.

2 se diriger *vpr* **(a) se ~ vers** (*aller, avancer vers*) to make for, head for, make one's way towards; **il se dirigea vers la sortie** he made his way towards *ou* made for the exit; **le bateau/la voiture semblait se diriger vers le port** the boat/car seemed to be heading *ou* making for the harbour; **l'avion se dirigea vers le nord** the plane flew *ou* headed northwards; **se ~ droit sur qch/qn** to make a beeline *ou* make straight for sth/sb.

(b) (*se guider*) to find one's way. **se ~ sur les étoiles/le soleil** to navigate *ou* sail by the stars/the sun; **se ~ au radar** to navigate by radar; **il n'est pas facile de se ~ dans le brouillard** it isn't easy to find one's way in the fog.

dirigisme [diʀiʒism(ə)] *nm* planned economy.

dirigiste [diʀiʒist(ə)] **1** *adj méthode, système* of planned economy. **2** *nmf* economic planner.

disant [dizɑ̃] *V* **soi-disant.**

discal, e, *mpl* **-aux** [diskal, o] *adj* (*Méd*) of the intervertebral discs. **hernie ~e** slipped disc.

discernable [disɛʀnabl(ə)] *adj* discernible, detectable.

discernement [disɛʀnəmɑ̃] *nm* **(a)** (*sagesse*) discernment, judgment. **manquer de ~** to be lacking in judgment *ou* discernment; **agir sans ~** to act without proper judgment.

(b) (*action*) distinguishing, discriminating, distinction. **sans ~** without (making a) distinction; (*littér*) **le ~ de la vérité d'avec l'erreur** distinguishing truth from error, discriminating between truth and error.

discerner [disɛʀne] (1) *vt* **(a)** (*distinguer*) *forme* to discern, make out, perceive; *bruit* to detect, hear; *nuance* to discern, detect; *douleur* to feel.

(b) (*différencier*) to distinguish, discriminate (*entre* between). **~ une couleur d'une** *ou* **d'avec une autre/le vrai du faux** to distinguish *ou* tell one colour from another/truth from falsehood.

disciple [disipl(ə)] *nm* (*élève*) disciple; (*adepte*) follower, disciple.

disciplinable [disiplinabl(ə)] *adj* disciplinable.

disciplinaire [disiplinɛʀ] *adj* disciplinary.

disciplinairement [disiplinɛʀmɑ̃] *adv* in a disciplinary way.

discipline [disiplin] *nf* **(a)** (*règle*) discipline; *V* **compagnie, conseil. (b)** (*matière*) discipline, subject.

discipliné, e [disipline] (*ptp de* **discipliner**) *adj* (well-)disciplined.

discipliner [disipline] (1) *vt soldats, élèves* to discipline; *impulsions* to discipline, control; (*fig*) *cheveux* to control, keep tidy. **il faut apprendre à se ~** one must learn self-control *ou* self-discipline *ou* to discipline oneself.

discobole [diskɔbɔl] *nm* discus thrower; (*Antiq*) discobolus.
discoïde [diskɔid] *adj* discoid(al), disc- *ou* disk-shaped.
discontinu, e [diskɔ̃tiny] **1** *adj ligne, fonction* discontinuous; (*intermittent*) *bruit, effort* intermittent. **bande jaune** *ou* **blanche** ~**e** *[route]* broken yellow *ou* white line. **2** *nm* (*Philos*) discontinuity.
discontinuer [diskɔ̃tinɥe] (1) *vti* (*littér*) to discontinue, cease, stop, break off. **sans** ~ without stopping, without a break; **pendant 2 heures sans** ~ for 2 hours at a stretch *ou* without stopping *ou* without a break.
discontinuité [diskɔ̃tinɥite] *nf* discontinuity.
disconvenir [diskɔ̃vniʀ] (22) *vi* (*littér: nier*) **ne pas** ~ **de/que: je n'en disconviens pas** I don't deny it; **je ne puis** ~ **que ce soit vrai** I cannot deny the truth of it *ou* that it's true.
discophile [diskɔfil] *nmf* record enthusiast.
discordance [diskɔʀdɑ̃s] *nf* **(a)** *[caractères]* conflict, clash (*U*); *[opinions]* difference, conflict; *[sons]* discord (*U*), discordance, dissonance; *[couleurs]* clash (*U*), clashing (*U*). **leurs témoignages présentent des** ~**s graves** their evidence shows serious disagreements *ou* discrepancies, their evidence conflicts seriously.
(b) (*Géol*) unconformability, discordance.
discordant, e [diskɔʀdɑ̃, ɑ̃t] *adj* **(a)** *caractères, opinions, témoignages* conflicting, discordant; *sons, cris, bruits* discordant, harsh; *instruments* out of tune; *couleurs* clashing, discordant. **elle a une voix** ~**e** she has a harsh *ou* grating voice, her voice grates.
(b) (*Géol*) unconformable, discordant.
discorde [diskɔʀd(ə)] *nf* (*littér*) discord, dissension. **mettre** *ou* **semer la** ~ to sow discord, cause dissension; *V* **pomme.**
discorder [diskɔʀde] (1) *vi [sons]* to be discordant; *[couleurs]* to clash; *[témoignages]* to conflict.
discothèque [diskɔtɛk] *nf* (*collection*) record collection; (*meuble*) record cabinet; (*bâtiment*) record library; (*club*) disco(thèque).
discoureur, -euse [diskuʀœʀ, øz] *nm,f* (*péj*) speechifier, windbag* (*péj*).
discourir [diskuʀiʀ] (11) *vi* **(a)** (*faire un discours*) to discourse, expatiate (*sur, de* upon); (*péj*) to hold forth (*sur, de* upon), speechify. **elle le suivit sans** ~ she followed him without demur *ou* without a murmur. **(b)** (*bavarder*) to talk (away).
discours [diskuʀ] *nm* **(a)** (*allocution*) speech. ~ **d'ouverture/de clôture** opening/closing speech; ~ **du trône** Queen's (*ou* King's) speech, speech from the throne; **faire** *ou* **prononcer un** ~ to make *ou* deliver a speech; **prononcer un** ~ **sur la tombe de qn** to deliver a funeral oration for sb.
(b) (*péj*) talking (*U*), chatter (*U*). **tous ces beaux** ~ **n'y changeront rien** all these fine words *ou* all this fine talk won't make any difference; **suis-moi sans faire de** ~**!** follow me without argument *ou* any arguing; **que de** ~**!** what a lot of fuss (about nothing)!; **perdre son temps en** ~ to waste one's time talking *ou* in idle (chit)chat; **il m'a tenu un long** ~ **sur ce qui lui était arrivé** he spun me a long yarn *ou* he told me a long-drawn-out tale about what had happened to him; **elle m'a tenu des** ~ **à n'en plus finir** she went on and on as if she was never going to stop.
(c) le ~ (*expression verbale*) speech; (*Ling*) discourse; (*Philos: raisonnement*) discursive reasoning *ou* thinking; (*Rhétorique*) discourse; (*Ling*) **(au)** ~ **direct/indirect** (in) direct/indirect *ou* reported speech; **les parties du** ~ (*Ling*) the parts of speech; (*Rhétorique*) the parts of discourse.
(d) (*Philos: traité*) discourse, treatise. **le D**~ **de la Méthode** the Discourse on Method.
discourtois, e [diskuʀtwa, waz] *adj* discourteous.
discourtoisement [diskuʀtwazmɑ̃] *adv* discourteously.
discourtoisie [diskuʀtwazi] *nf* (*littér*) discourtesy.
discrédit [diskʀedi] *nm [personne]* discredit, disfavour; *[idée, théorie, œuvre]* discredit, disrepute. **tomber dans le** ~ to fall into disrepute; **être en** ~ to be discredited *ou* in disrepute; *V* **jeter.**
discréditer [diskʀedite] (1) **1** *vt personne* to discredit; *théorie, œuvre* to discredit, bring into disrepute. **c'est une opinion tout à fait discréditée de nos jours** it is an opinion which has gone right out of favour *ou* which is quite discredited nowadays.
2 se discréditer *vpr [idée, théorie]* to become discredited, fall into disrepute; *[personne]* to bring discredit upon o.s., discredit o.s. **se** ~ **aux yeux de** *ou* **auprès de qn** to discredit o.s. *ou* bring discredit upon o.s. in the eyes of sb.
discret, -ète [diskʀɛ, ɛt] *adj* **(a)** (*réservé, retenu*) *personne, attitude* discreet, reserved; *allusion, reproche, compliment* discreet. **soyez** ~**, ne lui parlez pas de sa défaite** be tactful *ou* discreet and don't mention his defeat to him.
(b) (*qui n'attire pas l'attention*) *personne, manière* unassuming; *parfum, maquillage* discreet, unobtrusive; *vêtement* sober, plain, simple; *couleur* quiet, restrained; *lumière* subdued; *endroit* quiet, secluded; *parole, regard* discreet. **il lui remit un paquet sous emballage** ~ he handed her a plainly wrapped parcel; **'envoi** ~**'** 'sent under plain cover'; **n'y a-t-il pas une façon plus** ~**ète de m'avertir?** isn't there a more discreet *ou* less conspicuous way of warning me?
(c) (*qui garde les secrets*) discreet.
(d) (*Math*) *quantité* discrete; (*Phys*) *fonction* discontinuous.
discrètement [diskʀɛtmɑ̃] *adv* **(a)** *se tenir à l'écart, parler* discreetly, quietly; *reprocher* discreetly, quietly. **il a** ~ **fait allusion à ...** he made a discreet allusion to *ou* gently hinted at ... .
(b) *se maquiller* discreetly, unobtrusively; *s'habiller* quietly, soberly, simply; (*pour ne pas être vu, entendu*) discreetly. **parler** ~ **à l'oreille de qn** to have a quiet *ou* discreet word in sb's ear.
discrétion [diskʀesjɔ̃] *nf* **(a)** (*art de garder un secret*) discretion. ~ **assurée** discretion assured.
(b) (*réserve*) *[personne, attitude]* discretion, tact. **sa** ~ **est exemplaire** he's a model of discretion *ou* tact.
(c) (*modération*) *[maquillage]* unobtrusiveness; *[vêtement]* sobriety, plainness, simpleness. **avec** ~ *s'habiller etc* discreetly, soberly, plainly, simply; *se conduire* discreetly, unobtrusively; *parler* discreetly.
(d) (*littér: discernement*) discretion.
(e) (*loc*) **vin** *etc* **à** ~ unlimited wine *etc*, as much wine *etc* as you want; (*littér*) **être à la** ~ **de qn** to be in sb's hands.
discrétionnaire [diskʀesjɔnɛʀ] *adj* discretionary.
discriminant [diskʀiminɑ̃] *nm* (*Math*) discriminant.
discrimination [diskʀiminɑsjɔ̃] *nf* discrimination.
discriminatoire [diskʀiminatwaʀ] *adj mesures* discriminatory, discriminating.
discriminer [diskʀimine] (1) *vt* (*littér*) to distinguish. **apprendre à** ~ **les méthodes** to learn how to discriminate *ou* distinguish between methods.
disculpation [diskylpɑsjɔ̃] *nf* exoneration, exculpation (*frm*).
disculper [diskylpe] (1) **1** *vt* to exonerate, exculpate (*frm*) (*de* from). **2 se disculper** *vpr* to exonerate o.s., vindicate o.s., exculpate o.s. (*frm*) (*auprès de qn* in sb's eyes).
discursif, -ive [diskyʀsif, iv] *adj* discursive.
discussion [diskysjɔ̃] *nf* **(a)** *[problème]* discussion, examination (*de* of); *[projet de loi]* debate (*de* on), discussion (*de* of). **mettre une question en** ~ to bring a matter up for discussion; **le projet de loi est en** ~ the bill is being debated *ou* is under discussion.
(b) (*débat*) discussion, debate; (*pourparlers, échanges de vues*) discussion(s), talks; (*conversation*) discussion, talk. **les délégués sont en** ~ the delegates are in conference.
(c) (*querelle*) argument, quarrel. **avoir une violente** ~ **avec qn** to have a violent disagreement *ou* quarrel *ou* argument with sb; **suis-moi et pas de** ~**s** follow me and no argument.
discutable [diskytabl(ə)] *adj solution, théorie* debatable, questionable, arguable; *goût* doubtful, questionable.
discutailler* [diskytɑje] (1) *vi* (*péj*) (*bavarder*) to chat (away)*, natter (away)* (*surtout Brit*); (*débattre sans fin*) to argue (*sur* over), go on* (*sur* about), discuss; (*ergoter*) to wrangle, quibble (*sur* over). ~ **dans le vide** to argue *ou* quibble over nothing.
discuter [diskyte] (1) **1** *vt* **(a)** (*débattre*) *problème* to discuss, examine; *projet de loi* to debate, discuss; *prix* to argue about, haggle over.
(b) (*contester*) *ordre* to question, dispute. ~ **les droits de qn** to question sb's rights; **ministre très discuté** much discussed *ou* very controversial minister; **question très discutée** vexed *ou* much disputed question; **théorie très discutée** very controversial theory; **ça se discute, ça peut se** ~ that's debatable *ou* disputable.
(c) ~ **le coup*** *ou* **le bout de gras**‡ (*parler*) to have a chat* *ou* natter* (*surtout Brit*) *ou* chinwag‡ (*Brit*); (*parlementer*) to argue away.
2 *vi* **(a)** (*être en conférence*) to have a discussion, confer (*avec* with); (*parler*) to talk (*avec* with); (*parlementer*) to argue (*avec* with). ~ **de** *ou* **sur qch** to discuss sth; ~ **(de) politique** *etc* to discuss *ou* talk politics *etc*; **on ne peut pas** ~ **avec lui!*** it's no good arguing with him!, you can't have a discussion with him.
(b) (*protester*) to argue. **suivez-moi sans** ~ follow me and no argument; **j'en ai décidé ainsi et il n'y a pas à** ~ my mind's made up about it and that's that *ou* that's final *ou* and there's nothing further to be said; **tu discutes?**‡ no ifs and buts!* (*Brit*), no ifs ands or buts!* (*US*), no arguments!
(c) (*débattre*) ~ **de** *ou* **sur** *question, problème* to discuss; **ensuite, nous avons discuté du prix** then we discussed the price; ~ **sur le cas de qn** to discuss sb's case; **j'en ai discuté avec lui et il est d'accord** I have discussed the matter *ou* talked the matter over with him and he agrees; **vous discutez sur des points sans importance** you are arguing about *ou* niggling over trifles.
disert, e [dizɛʀ, ɛʀt(ə)] *adj* (*frm, hum, péj*) loquacious, articulate, fluent.
disette [dizɛt] *nf* **(a)** (*manque*) *[vivres, idées]* scarcity, shortage, dearth. **(b)** (*famine*) food shortage, scarcity (of food).
diseur, -euse [dizœʀ, øz] *nm,f*: ~ **de bonne aventure** fortune-teller; ~ **de bons mots** wit, wag.
disgrâce [disgʀɑs] *nf* (*défaveur, déchéance*) disgrace. **encourir** *ou* **mériter la** ~ **de qn** to incur sb's disfavour *ou* displeasure; **tomber en** ~ to fall into disgrace; **la** ~ **du ministre** the minister's disgrace.
disgracié, e [disgʀasje] (*ptp de* **disgracier**) *adj* (*en disgrâce*) in disgrace, disgraced; (*laid*) ill-favoured, ugly.
disgracier [disgʀasje] (7) *vt* to disgrace, dismiss from favour.
disgracieux, -ieuse [disgʀasjø, jøz] *adj geste* inelegant, awkward; *démarche* inelegant, awkward, ungainly; *visage* ill-favoured; *forme, objet* unsightly.
disjoindre [disʒwɛ̃dʀ(ə)] (49) **1** *vt planches, tôles, tuiles* to take apart, separate; *tuyaux* to disconnect, take apart; *pierres* to break apart; (*fig*) *problèmes* to separate, split. **ces deux questions sont disjointes** these two matters are not connected.
2 se disjoindre *vpr [planches, tôles, tuiles]* to come apart *ou* loose, separate; *[tuyaux, pierres]* to come apart. **planches/tuiles disjointes** planks/tiles which are coming apart *ou* loose, loose planks/tiles; **tuyaux disjoints** pipes which have come apart *ou* undone.
disjoncteur [disʒɔ̃ktœʀ] *nm* (*Élec*) circuit breaker, cutout.
disjonctif, -ive [disʒɔ̃ktif, iv] *adj, nf* disjunctive.
disjonction [disʒɔ̃ksjɔ̃] *nf* disjunction, separation.
dislocation [dislɔkɑsjɔ̃] *nf* (*V* **disloquer**) dislocation; dis-

mantling; smashing; breaking up; dispersal; dismemberment; (*Géol*) fault.

disloquer [dislɔke] (1) **1** *vt* **(a)** *bras, épaule* to dislocate, put out of joint. **avoir l'épaule disloquée** to have a dislocated shoulder.
(b) *machine, meuble* (*démonter*) to dismantle, take apart *ou* to pieces; (*casser*) to smash, break up. **la chaise est toute disloquée** the chair is all smashed *ou* broken.
(c) *rassemblement, cortège* to disperse, break up; *troupes* to disperse, scatter.
(d) *empire* to dismantle, dismember, break up.
2 se disloquer *vpr* **(a) se ~ le bras** to dislocate one's arm, put one's arm out of joint; **son épaule s'est disloquée** his shoulder has been dislocated.
(b) *[meuble]* to come apart, fall to pieces.
(c) *[troupes]* to disperse, scatter; *[cortège]* to disperse, break *ou* split up.
(d) *[empire]* to break up, disintegrate.

disparaître [disparɛtʀ(ə)] (57) *vi* **(a)** (*lit: s'en aller, devenir invisible*) to disappear, vanish. **le fuyard disparut au coin de la rue/dans la foule** the fugitive disappeared *ou* vanished round the corner of the street/into the crowd; **~ discrètement** to slip away quietly; **~ furtivement** to sneak away *ou* out; **je ne veux pas le voir, je disparais** I don't want to see him so I'll just slip away *ou* disappear *ou* I'll be off; **~ aux regards** to vanish out of sight, disappear from view; **~ à l'horizon** *[soleil]* to disappear *ou* vanish *ou* sink below the horizon; *[bateau]* to vanish *ou* disappear over the horizon; **l'arbre disparut dans le brouillard** the tree vanished *ou* was swallowed up in the fog; **le bâtiment disparaît sous le lierre** the building is (half-)hidden under a cloak of ivy.
(b) (*être porté manquant*) *[personne]* to go missing, disappear; *[objet]* to disappear. **il a disparu de son domicile** he is missing *ou* has gone missing *ou* has disappeared from home; **trois camions ont disparu (du garage)** three lorries have disappeared *ou* are missing *ou* have gone (from the garage); **~ sans laisser de traces** to disappear without trace; **il a disparu de la circulation*** he seems to have vanished into thin air.
(c) (*passer, s'effacer*) *[joie, crainte etc]* to disappear, vanish, evaporate; *[sourire, rougeur, douleur, cicatrice]* to disappear, vanish, (*graduellement*) to fade; *[jeunesse]* to vanish, be lost; *[brouillard]* to disappear, vanish.
(d) (*mourir*) *[race, civilisation]* to die (out), vanish; *[coutume]* to die out, disappear; *[personne]* to die; (*se perdre*) *[navire]* to sink, be lost. **si je venais à ~, tu n'aurais pas de soucis matériels** if I were to die, you wouldn't have any financial worries; **tout le charme de la Belle Époque disparaît avec elle** all the charm of the Belle Époque dies *ou* vanishes with her; **~ en mer** to be lost at sea; (*Naut*) **~ corps et biens** to go down with all hands.
(e) faire ~ *objet* to remove, hide away *ou* out of sight; *document* to dispose of, get rid of; *tache, trace, obstacle, difficulté* to remove; *personne* to eliminate, get rid of, do away with*; *crainte* to dispel, eliminate; **cela a fait ~ la douleur/la rougeur** it made the pain/red mark go away, it got rid of the pain/all trace of the red mark; **faire ~ un objet** *[prestidigitateur]* to make an object vanish; **le voleur fit ~ le bijou dans sa poche** the thief concealed the jewel *ou* hid the jewel out of sight in his pocket; **il prenait de gros morceaux de pain qu'il faisait ~ dans sa bouche** he was taking large hunks of bread and cramming them into his mouth; **ils firent ~ toute trace de leur passage** they destroyed *ou* wiped out *ou* removed all trace of their visit; **faire ~ une inscription** *[temps]* to erase *ou* efface *ou* wear away an inscription; *[personne]* to erase *ou* wipe out *ou* remove an inscription.

disparate [disparat] *adj éléments* disparate; *objets, mobilier* disparate, ill-assorted; *couple, couleurs* ill-assorted, badly matched.

disparité [disparite] *nf [éléments, salaires]* disparity (*de* in); *[objets, couleurs]* ill-assortedness (*U*).

disparition [disparisjɔ̃] *nf* **(a)** *[personne]* disappearance; *[cicatrice, rougeur]* disappearance, (*graduelle*) fading; *[brouillard]* lifting, thinning; *[soleil]* sinking, setting; *[tache, obstacle]* disappearance, removal. **la ~ de la douleur sera immédiate** the pain will be relieved *ou* will diminish *ou* vanish immediately.
(b) (*mort, perte*) *[personne]* death; *[espèce]* disappearance, extinction; *[coutume, langue]* disappearance, dying out; *[objet, bateau]* loss, disappearance.

disparu, e [dispaʀy] (*ptp de* **disparaître**) **1** *adj* **(a)** (*révolu*) *monde, époque* bygone (*épith*), vanished; *bonheur, jeunesse* lost, departed.
(b) (*effacé*) **une lueur menaçante, aussitôt ~e, brilla dans ses yeux** a dangerous gleam flickered and died in his eyes, his eyes glinted dangerously for a brief moment; **un sentiment d'espoir, bientôt ~, l'anima un court instant** hope filled him for a brief moment only to fade again.
(c) (*mort*) *personne* dead, departed; *race, coutume, langue* vanished, dead, extinct; (*dont on est sans nouvelles*) *victime* missing. **il a été porté ~** (*Mil*) he has been reported missing; (*dans une catastrophe*) he is missing, believed dead; **marin ~ en mer** sailor lost at sea.
2 *nm,f* (*mort*) dead person; (*dont on a perdu la trace*) missing person. (*littér*) **le cher ~** the dear departed; **il y a 5 morts et 3 ~s dans ce naufrage** there are 5 (reported) dead and 3 missing in this shipwreck.

dispendieusement [dispɑ̃djøzmɑ̃] *adv* (*frm*) *vivre* extravagantly, expensively.

dispendieux, -ieuse [dispɑ̃djø, jøz] *adj* (*frm*) *goûts, luxe* extravagant, expensive.

dispensaire [dispɑ̃sɛʀ] *nm* community clinic; (†) people's dispensary.

dispensateur, -trice [dispɑ̃satœʀ, tʀis] (*littér*) **1** *adj* dispensing. **2** *nm,f* dispenser.

dispense [dispɑ̃s] *nf* (*exemption*) exemption (*de* from); (*permission*) special permission; (*Rel*) dispensation (*de* from). **~ du service militaire/d'un examen** exemption from military service/from an exam; **~ d'âge pour passer un examen** permission to sit an exam under the statutory age limit.

dispenser [dispɑ̃se] (1) **1** *vt* **(a)** (*exempter*) to exempt, excuse (*de faire* from doing, *de qch* from sth). (*Rel*) **~ qn d'un vœu** to release sb from a vow; **je vous dispense de vos réflexions** I can do without your comments, you can spare me your comments; (*frm, hum*) **dispensez-moi de sa vue** spare me the sight of him; (*frm*) **je me dispenserai** *ou* **dispensez-moi d'en dire plus** spare me the necessity of saying any more; **se faire ~** to get exempted.
(b) (*littér: distribuer*) *bienfaits* to dispense; *charme* to radiate; *lumière* to dispense, give out. **~ à qn son dévouement** to bestow *ou* lavish one's devotion on sb; (*Méd*) **~ des soins à un malade** to give medical care to a patient.
2 se dispenser *vpr*: **se ~ de** *corvée* to avoid, get out of; *remarque* to refrain from; **se ~ de faire qch** to get out of doing sth, not to bother doing sth; **il peut se ~ de travailler** he doesn't need to work, he has no need to bother working; **je me dispenserais bien d'y aller** I would (gladly) get out of *ou* save myself the bother of going if I could; (*iro*) **il s'est dispensé de s'excuser** he didn't see any necessity for excusing himself.

dispersé, e [dispɛʀse] (*ptp de* **disperser**) *adj habitat* scattered; *esprit* unselective, undisciplined; *travail* disorganized, bitty*.

disperser [dispɛʀse] (1) **1** *vt* **(a)** (*éparpiller*) *papiers, feuilles* to scatter, spread about; (*dissiper*) *brouillard* to disperse, break up; (*répartir*) *personnes* to disperse, spread out; *collection* to break up; (*faire partir*) *foule, ennemi* to scatter, disperse; (*Mil: congédier*) to dismiss. **tous nos amis sont maintenant dispersés** all our friends are now scattered.
(b) (*fig: déconcentrer*) *ses forces, ses efforts* to dissipate.
2 se disperser *vpr [foule]* to scatter, disperse, break up; *[élève, artiste]* to overdiversify, dissipate one's efforts. **ne vous dispersez pas trop!** don't overdiversify!, don't try to do too many different things at once!

dispersion [dispɛʀsjɔ̃] *nf* (*V* **disperser**) scattering; spreading about; dispersal; breaking up; dismissal; dissipation; (*Chim, Phys*) dispersion. **évitez la ~ dans votre travail** don't attempt to do too many things at once, don't overdiversify in your work.

disponibilité [dispɔnibilite] *nf* **(a)** *[choses]* availability. (*Jur*) **~ des biens** (*faculté du possesseur*) ability to transfer one's property; (*caractère des possessions*) transferability of property.
(b) (*Fin*) **~s** available funds, liquid assets.
(c) mettre en ~ *fonctionnaire* to free from duty temporarily, grant leave of absence to; *officier* to place on reserve; **mise en ~** *[fonctionnaire]* leave of absence; *[officier]* transfer to reserve duty.
(d) *[élève, esprit, auditoire]* alertness, receptiveness. **~ d'esprit** alertness *ou* receptiveness of mind.

disponible [dispɔnibl(ə)] *adj* **(a)** *livre, appartement, fonds* available. **avez-vous des places ~s pour ce soir?** are there any seats (available) for this evening?; **il n'y a plus une seule place ~** there's not a single seat left *ou* not one spare seat; **je ne suis pas ~ ce soir** I'm not free tonight; (*Jur*) **biens ~s** transferable property.
(b) fonctionnaire ~ civil servant on leave of absence *ou* temporarily freed from duty; **officier ~** officer on reserve.
(c) *élève, esprit, auditoire* alert, receptive.

dispos, e [dispo, oz] *adj personne* refreshed, in good form (*attrib*), full of energy (*attrib*). **avoir l'esprit ~** to have a fresh mind; *V* **frais**[1].

disposé, e [dispoze] (*ptp de* **disposer**) *adj* **(a) être ~ à faire** to be willing *ou* disposed *ou* prepared to do; **être peu ~ à faire** to be unwilling to do, not to be disposed *ou* prepared to do; **bien/mal ~** in a good/bad mood; **bien/mal ~ à l'égard de** *ou* **pour** *ou* **envers qn** well-/ill-disposed towards sb.
(b) *terrain* situated, sited. **comment le terrain est-il ~?** what is the site like?; **pièces bien/mal ~es** well-/badly-laid-out rooms.

disposer [dispoze] (1) **1** *vt* **(a)** (*arranger*) *personnes, meubles, fleurs* to arrange; *couverts* to set, lay. **~ des troupes sur le terrain** to draw up *ou* range *ou* dispose troops on the battlefield; **~ des objets en ligne/en cercle** to place *ou* lay *ou* arrange things in a row/in a circle; **on avait disposé le buffet dans le jardin** they had laid out *ou* set out the buffet in the garden.
(b) ~ qn à faire/à qch (*engager à*) to dispose *ou* incline sb to do/towards sth; (*frm: préparer à*) to prepare sb to do/for sth; **cela ne dispose pas à l'optimisme** it doesn't (exactly) incline one to optimism.
2 *vi* (*frm: partir*) to leave. **vous pouvez ~** you may leave (now), (now) you can go.
3 disposer de *vt indir* (*avoir l'usage de*) to have (at one's disposal). **~ d'une voiture** to have a car (at one's disposal), have the use of a car; **~ d'une somme d'argent** to have a sum of money at one's disposal *ou* available (for one's use); **il disposait de quelques heures pour visiter Lyon** he had a few hours free *ou* to spare in which to visit Lyons; **avec les moyens dont il dispose** with the means at his disposal *ou* available to him; **si vous voulez vous pouvez en ~** if you wish you can use it; (*Jur*) **~ d'un domaine (par testament)** to dispose of an estate (in one's will); **il dispose de ses employés/de ses amis de manière abusive** he takes advantage of his employees/friends; **droit des peuples à ~ d'eux-mêmes** right of nations to self-determination.
4 se disposer *vpr*: **se ~ à faire** (*se préparer à*) to prepare to

do, be about to do; **il se disposait à quitter le bureau** he was about to *ou* was preparing to *ou* was getting ready to leave the office.

dispositif [dispozitif] *nm* **(a)** (*mécanisme*) device, mechanism. ~ **d'alarme** alarm *ou* warning device; ~ **de sûreté** safety device.
(b) (*moyens prévus*) plan of action. (*Mil*) ~ **d'attaque** attack force; (*Mil*) ~ **de défense** defence system; ~ **de contrôle** control force; ~ **de combat** fighting plan; **tout un** ~ **a été établi pour enrayer l'inflation** a complete plan of action has been drawn up to curb inflation; **un important** ~ **(policier) a été mis en place pour disperser les manifestants** a large police operation was set up to disperse the demonstrators.
(c) (*Jur*) *[jugement]* pronouncement; *[loi]* purview.

disposition [dispozisjɔ̃] *nf* **(a)** (*arrangement*) (*action*) arrangement, arranging, placing; (*résultat*) arrangement, disposition, layout. **selon la** ~ **des pions/des joueurs** according to how the pawns/players are placed; **ils ont changé la** ~ **des objets dans la vitrine** they have changed the arrangement *ou* layout of the things in the window; **cela dépend de la** ~ **du terrain** that depends on the situation of the ground, it depends how the ground lies; **la** ~ **des lieux/pièces** the layout of the premises/rooms.
(b) (*usage*) disposal. (*Jur*) **avoir la libre** ~ **de qch** to have free disposal of sth, be free to dispose of sth; **mettre qch/être à la** ~ **de qn** to put sth/be at sb's disposal; **la maison/la bibliothèque est à votre** ~ the house/library is at your disposal, you can have the run of the house/library; **les moyens (mis) à notre** ~ **sont insuffisants** we have insufficient means at our disposal; **je me mets** *ou* **tiens à votre entière** ~ **pour de plus amples renseignements** I am entirely at your disposal *ou* service should you require further information; (*Jur*) **l'inculpé a été mis à la** ~ **de la justice** the accused was handed over to the law.
(c) (*mesures*) ~**s** (*préparatifs*) arrangements, preparations; (*précautions*) measures, precautions, steps; **prendre des** *ou* **ses** ~**s pour que qch soit fait** to make arrangements *ou* take steps to have sth done *ou* for sth to be done; **prendre ses** ~**s pour partir** to make arrangements for *ou* prepare for one's departure; **nous avons prévu des** ~**s spéciales** we have arranged for special steps *ou* measures *ou* precautions to be taken.
(d) (*manière d'être*) mood, humour, frame of mind. **être dans de bonnes/mauvaises** ~**s** to be in a good/bad mood *ou* humour; **être dans de bonnes** ~**s pour faire qch** to be in the right mood to do sth, be in the right frame of mind for doing sth; **être dans les meilleures** ~**s** to be in the best of moods; **être dans de bonnes/de mauvaises/les meilleures** ~**s à l'égard de qn** to feel well-disposed/ill-disposed/most kindly disposed towards sb; **est-il toujours dans les mêmes** ~**s à l'égard de ce projet/candidat?** does he still feel the same way *ou* have the same feelings about this plan/candidate?; ~ **d'esprit** mood, state *ou* frame of mind.
(e) (*inclination, aptitude*) ~**s** bent, aptitude, natural ability; **avoir des** ~**s pour la musique/les langues/le tennis** to have a (special) aptitude for *ou* a gift for music/languages/tennis.
(f) (*tendance*) *[personne]* predisposition, tendency; *[objet]* tendency (*à* to). **avoir une** ~ **au rhumatisme/à contracter une maladie** to have a tendency to rheumatism/to catch an illness; **ce bateau a une curieuse/fâcheuse** ~ **à ...** this boat has a strange/unfortunate tendency to ..., this boat is prone to ... .
(g) (*Jur*) clause. ~**s testamentaires** provisions of a will, testamentary provisions; ~**s entre vifs** donation inter vivos; *V* **dernier**.

disproportion [dispʀɔpɔʀsjɔ̃] *nf* disproportion (*de* in).

disproportionné, e [dispʀɔpɔʀsjɔne] *adj* disproportionate (*à, avec* to), out of (all) proportion (*à, avec* with). **il a une tête** ~**e** his head is disproportionately *ou* abnormally large; **un salaire** ~ **au travail** a salary which is disproportionate to *ou* out of (all) proportion with the work.

dispute [dispyt] *nf* **(a)** (*querelle*) argument, quarrel. ~ **d'amoureux** lovers' tiff *ou* quarrel. **(b)** (††: *débat polémique*) debate, dispute.

disputé, e [dispyte] (*ptp de* **disputer**) *adj match* close, closely fought.

disputer [dispyte] (1) **1** *vt* **(a)** (*contester*) ~ **qch/qn à qn** to fight with sb for *ou* over sth/sb; ~ **la victoire/la première place à son rival** to fight for victory/for first place with one's rival, fight one's rival for victory/first place; **elle essaya de lui** ~ **la gloire de son invention** she tried to rob him of the glory of his invention; (*littér*) **le** ~ **en beauté/en grandeur à qn** to vie with *ou* rival sb in beauty/greatness; ~ **le terrain** (*Mil*) to contest the ground inch by inch; (*fig*) to fight every inch of the way.
(b) (*livrer*) *combat* to fight; *match* to play. **le match a été disputé** *ou* **s'est disputé en Angleterre** the match was played *ou* took place in England.
(c) (*: *gronder*) to tell off*, tick off* (*Brit*). **se faire** ~ **par son père** to get a telling-off* *ou* ticking-off* (*Brit*) from one's father.
2 se disputer *vpr* **(a)** (*se quereller*) to quarrel, argue, have a quarrel *ou* an argument (*avec* with). **il s'est disputé avec son oncle** he quarrelled *ou* had a quarrel *ou* an argument with his uncle.
(b) (*se battre pour*) to fight over, contest. **deux chiens se disputent un os** two dogs are fighting over a bone; **deux candidats se disputent un siège à l'Académie** two candidates are contesting a seat at the Academy.

disquaire [diskɛʀ] *nm* (*commerçant*) record-dealer.

disqualification [diskalifikɑsjɔ̃] *nf* (*Sport*) disqualification.

disqualifier [diskalifje] (7) *vt* **(a)** (*Sport: exclure*) to disqualify. **(b)** (*fig: discréditer*) to dishonour, bring discredit on. **il s'est disqualifié aux yeux de l'opinion** he has destroyed people's trust in him *ou* people's good opinion of him.

disque [disk(ə)] *nm* **(a)** (*gén, Méd*) disc, disk. ~ **d'embrayage** clutch plate; *V* **freins**. **(b)** (*Sport*) discus. **(c)** (*Mus*) record, disc*. ~ **microsillon** *ou* **à longue durée** long-playing record, L.P.

dissection [disɛksjɔ̃] *nf* dissection. **de** ~ *instrument, table* dissecting, dissection.

dissemblable [disɑ̃blabl(ə)] *adj* dissimilar, different (*de* from, to).

dissemblance [disɑ̃blɑ̃s] *nf* dissimilarity, difference (*de* in).

dissémination [diseminɑsjɔ̃] *nf* **(a)** (*action*) *[graines]* scattering; *[troupes, maisons, usines]* scattering, spreading; *[idées]* dissemination. **(b)** (*état*) *[maisons, personnes]* dispersal, scattering; *[points de vente]* thin distribution, dispersal.

disséminer [disemine] (1) **1** *vt graines* to scatter; *troupes, maisons* to scatter, spread (out); *idées* to disseminate. **les points de vente sont très disséminés** the (sales) outlets are widely scattered *ou* thinly distributed.
2 se disséminer *vpr [graines]* to scatter; *[personnes]* to spread (out). **les pique-niqueurs se disséminèrent aux quatre coins de la forêt** the picnickers spread out *ou* scattered to the four corners of the forest.

dissension [disɑ̃sjɔ̃] *nf* dissension.

dissentiment [disɑ̃timɑ̃] *nm* disagreement, difference of opinion.

disséquer [diseke] (6) *vt* (*lit, fig*) to dissect.

dissertation [disɛʀtɑsjɔ̃] *nf* (*Scol, hum*) essay; (*péj*, ††: *traité*) dissertation.

disserter [disɛʀte] (1) *vi* **(a)** (*Scol*) ~ **sur** (*parler*) to speak on, discourse upon (*frm*); (*écrire*) to write an essay on. **(b)** (*péj*) to hold forth (*de, sur* about).

dissidence [disidɑ̃s] *nf* (*sécession*) (*Pol*) rebellion, dissidence; (*Rel*) dissent; (*dissidents*) rebels, dissidents; (*littér: divergence*) disagreement, dissidence. **entrer en** ~ to break away, rebel; **être en** ~ to have broken away; **rejoindre la** ~ to join the dissidents *ou* the rebels.

dissident, e [disidɑ̃, ɑ̃t] **1** *adj* (*Pol*) dissident; (*Rel*) dissenting. **2** *nm,f* (*Pol*) rebel, dissident; (*Rel*) dissenter. **un groupe** ~ a breakaway *ou* splinter group.

dissimilation [disimilɑsjɔ̃] *nf* (*Ling*) dissimilation.

dissimilitude [disimilityd] *nf* dissimilitude, dissimilarity.

dissimulateur, -trice [disimylatœʀ, tʀis] **1** *adj* dissembling. **2** *nm,f* dissembler.

dissimulation [disimylɑsjɔ̃] *nf* (*U: duplicité*) dissimulation, dissembling; (*cachotterie*) dissimulation (*U*), dissembling (*U*); (*action de cacher*) concealment. **agir avec** ~ to act in an underhand way; (*Jur*) ~ **d'actif** (fraudulent) concealment of assets.

dissimulé, e [disimyle] (*ptp de* **dissimuler**) *adj caractère, enfant* secretive.

dissimuler [disimyle] (1) **1** *vt* (*cacher*) *objet, personne, sentiment, difficulté* to conceal, hide (*à qn* from sb); (*Fin*) *bénéfices* to conceal; (*déguiser*) *sentiment, difficulté, défaut* to conceal, disguise. **il sait bien** ~ he's good at pretending *ou* dissembling (*frm*); **il parvenait mal à** ~ **son impatience/son envie de rire** he had great difficulty in covering up *ou* disguising *ou* hiding his annoyance/his urge to laugh; **je ne vous dissimulerai pas qu'il y a de gros problèmes** I won't disguise *ou* conceal the fact that there are serious problems.
2 se dissimuler *vpr* to conceal *ou* hide o.s. **il essaie de se** ~ **la vérité/qu'il a tort** he tries to close his eyes to the truth/to the fact that he's wrong, he tries to conceal the truth/the fact that he's wrong from himself.

dissipateur, -trice [disipatœʀ, tʀis] **1** *adj* wasteful, extravagant, prodigal. **2** *nm,f* spendthrift, squanderer, prodigal.

dissipation [disipɑsjɔ̃] *nf* **(a)** (*indiscipline*) misbehaviour, unruliness; (*littér: débauche*) dissipation. **une vie de** ~ a dissipated life, a life of dissipation.
(b) (*dilapidation*) *[fortune]* squandering, dissipation; (*folle dépense*) extravagance.
(c) *[fumée, nuage]* dissipation, dispersal; *[brouillard]* clearing, lifting, dispersal; *[craintes]* dispelling.

dissiper [disipe] (1) **1** *vt* **(a)** (*chasser*) *brouillard, fumée* to dispel, disperse; *nuage* to break up, disperse; *soupçon, crainte* to dissipate, dispel; *malentendu* to clear up.
(b) (*dilapider*) *fortune* to dissipate, squander, fritter away; *jeunesse* to waste, dissipate; (*littér*) *santé* to ruin, destroy.
(c) ~ **qn** to lead sb astray *ou* into bad ways; **il dissipe ses petits camarades en classe** he is a distracting influence on *ou* he distracts his little friends in class.
2 se dissiper *vpr* **(a)** (*disparaître*) *[fumée]* to drift away, disperse; *[nuages]* to break (up), disperse; *[brouillard]* to clear, lift, disperse; *[inquiétude]* to vanish, melt away; *[malaise, fatigue]* to disappear, go away, wear off.
(b) *[élève]* to become undisciplined *ou* unruly, misbehave. **mener une vie dissipée, se** ~ to lead a dissolute *ou* dissipated life.

dissociable [disɔsjabl(ə)] *adj molécules* dissociable, separable; *problèmes* separable.

dissociation [disɔsjɑsjɔ̃] *nf [molécules, problèmes]* dissociation, separation.

dissocier [disɔsje] (7) **1** *vt molécules, problèmes* to dissociate.
2 se dissocier *vpr [éléments, groupe, équipe]* to break up, split up. **nous tenons à nous** ~ **de ces groupes/vues** we are anxious to dissociate ourselves from these groups/views.

dissolu, e [disɔly] (*ptp de* **dissoudre**) *adj* dissolute.

dissolubilité [disɔlybilite] *nf* (*V* **dissoluble**) dissolubility; solubility.

dissoluble [disɔlybl(ə)] *adj assemblée* dissoluble; *substance* soluble.

dissolution [disɔlysjɔ̃] *nf* **(a)** (*Jur*) *[assemblée, mariage]* dissolution; *[groupe, parti]* dissolution, disbanding; *[com-*

pagnie] winding-up, dissolution. **prononcer la ~ de** to dissolve.
(b) (*désagrégation*) *[groupe, association]* breaking-up, splitting-up; *[empire]* crumbling, decay, dissolution. **l'unité nationale est en pleine ~** national unity is crumbling *ou* disintegrating *ou* falling apart.
(c) *[sucre etc]* dissolving. **tourner jusqu'à ~ complète du cachet** stir until the tablet has completely dissolved.
(d) (*colle*) rubber solution.
(e) (*littér: débauche*) dissoluteness, dissipation.
dissolvant, e [disɔlvɑ̃, ɑ̃t] **1** *adj* (*lit*) solvent, dissolvent; (*fig*) *doctrines* undermining (*épith*), demoralizing; *climat* debilitating. **2** *nm* (*produit*) solvent. (*pour les ongles*) **~ (gras)** nail varnish remover.
dissonance [disɔnɑ̃s] *nf* (*Mus*) (*intervalle*) dissonance; (*fig*) clash; (*manque d'harmonie*) discord, dissonance. (*fig*) **des ~s de tons dans un tableau** clashes of colour in a painting.
dissonant, e [disɔnɑ̃, ɑ̃t] *adj sons, accord* dissonant, discordant; *couleurs* clashing (*épith*).
dissoudre [disudʀ(ə)] (51) **1** *vt* **(a)** *sel* to dissolve. **faire ~ du sucre** to dissolve sugar.
(b) (*Jur, Pol*) *assemblée* to dissolve; *parti, groupement* to disband, break up; *mariage* to dissolve.
2 se dissoudre *vpr* **(a)** *[sel, sucre]* to dissolve, be dissolved.
(b) *[association]* to disband, break up.
dissuader [disɥade] (1) *vt* to dissuade (*de qch* from sth, *de faire* from doing). **il m'a dissuadé d'y aller** he talked me out of going, he persuaded me not to go.
dissuasion [disɥazjɔ̃] *nf* dissuasion; *V* **force**.
dissyllabe [disilab] **1** *adj* disyllabic. **2** *nm* disyllable.
dissyllabique [disilabik] *adj* disyllabic.
dissymétrie [disimetʀi] *nf* dissymmetry.
dissymétrique [disimetʀik] *adj* dissymmetric(al).
distance [distɑ̃s] *nf* **(a)** (*éloignement, intervalle, trajet*) distance. **à quelle ~ est la gare?** how far (away) is the station?, what's the distance to the station?; **parcourir de grandes/petites ~s** to cover great/small distances; (*Sport*) **il est meilleur sur les grandes ~s** he's better over long distances; **habiter à une grande ~/à quelques kilomètres de ~** to live a great distance away *ou* a long way away/a few kilometres away (*de* from); **rester à une ~ respectueuse derrière qn** to stay a respectful distance behind sb; **entendre un bruit/distinguer qch à une ~ de 30 mètres** to hear a noise/make out sth from a distance of 30 metres *ou* from 30 metres away; **à 2 ou 3 ans de ~ je m'en souviens encore** 2 or 3 years later I can still remember it; **nés à quelques années de ~** born within a few years of one another, born a few years apart; **quelle ~ parcourue depuis son dernier roman!** what a long way *ou* how far he has come since his last novel.
(b) (*écart*) gap. **la ~ qui sépare deux générations/points de vue** the gap between *ou* which separates two generations/points of view; **la guerre a mis une grande ~ entre ces deux peuples** the war has left a great gulf between these two nations.
(c) (*loc*) **garder ses ~s** to keep one's distance (*vis à vis de* from); **prendre ses ~s** (*Mil*) to form open order; (*Scol etc*) to space out; (*fig*) to stand aloof (*à l'égard de* from); **tenir qn à ~** to keep sb at a distance *ou* at arm's length; **se tenir à ~** to keep one's distance, stand aloof; **tenir la ~** *[coureur, conférencier]* to go *ou* do *ou* cover the distance, last the course; **de ~ en ~** at intervals, here and there; **à ~** (*dans l'espace*) at *ou* from a distance, from afar; (*dans le temps*) at *ou* from a distance; **le prestidigitateur fait bouger des objets à ~** the conjurer moves objects from a distance; **mettre en marche à ~** *appareil* to start up by remote control; (*Phot*) **~ focale** focal length; *V* **commande**.
distancer [distɑ̃se] (3) *vt* **(a)** *coureur* to outrun, outdistance, leave behind; *voiture* to outdistance, leave behind; *concurrent, élève* to outstrip, outclass, leave behind. **se laisser ~** to be left behind, be outdistanced (*par* by); **ne nous laissons pas ~** let's not fall behind *ou* be left behind.
(b) (*Sport: disqualifier*) to disqualify.
distant, e [distɑ̃, ɑ̃t] *adj* **(a)** *lieu* far-off, faraway, distant; *événement* distant, far-off. **~ d'un lieu** far away from a place; **une ville ~e de 10 km** a town 10 km away; **deux villes ~es de 10 km (l'une de l'autre)** two towns 10 km apart *ou* 10 km away from one another.
(b) *attitude* distant, aloof. **il s'est montré très ~** he was very stand-offish.
distendre [distɑ̃dʀ(ə)] (41) **1** *vt peau* to distend; *muscle, corde,* (*fig*) *lien* to strain. **2 se distendre** *vpr [lien]* to slacken, become looser; *[ventre, peau]* to distend, become distended.
distension [distɑ̃sjɔ̃] *nf [peau, estomac]* distension; *[corde]* slackening, loosening.
distillateur [distilatœʀ] *nm* distiller (*person*).
distillation [distilɑsjɔ̃] *nf* distillation, distilling.
distiller [distile] (1) *vt alcool* to distil; *suc* to elaborate; (*fig*) *ennui, venin* to exude. **eau distillée** distilled water.
distillerie [distilʀi] *nf* (*usine*) distillery; (*industrie*) distilling.
distinct, e [distɛ̃(kt), distɛ̃kt(ə)] *adj* **(a)** (*indépendant*) distinct, separate (*de* from). **(b)** (*net*) distinct, clear.
distinctement [distɛ̃ktəmɑ̃] *adv* distinctly, clearly.
distinctif, -ive [distɛ̃ktif, iv] *adj* distinctive.
distinction [distɛ̃ksjɔ̃] *nf* **(a)** (*différentiation*) distinction. **faire la ~ entre** to make a distinction between; **sans ~ (de race)** without distinction (of race).
(b) (*décoration, honneur*) distinction.
(c) (*raffinement*) distinction, refinement. **il a de la ~** he is very distinguished *ou* refined, he has great distinction.
(d) (*éminence*) distinction, eminence. (*frm*) **un pianiste de la plus haute ~** a pianist of the highest distinction.
distinguable [distɛ̃gabl(ə)] *adj* distinguishable.
distingué, e [distɛ̃ge] (*ptp de* **distinguer**) *adj* **(a)** (*élégant, bien élevé*) *personne* distinguished; *allure* elegant, refined, distinguished. **il a l'air très ~** he looks very distinguished, he has a very distinguished look about him; **ça fait très ~** it's very distinguished *ou* distingué.
(b) (*illustre*) distinguished, eminent. **notre ~ collègue, le professeur X** our distinguished *ou* eminent colleague, Professor X.
(c) (*formule épistolaire*) **agréez l'expression de mes sentiments ~s ou de ma considération ~e** yours faithfully (*surtout Brit*), yours truly, sincerely yours.
distinguer [distɛ̃ge] (1) **1** *vt* **(a)** (*percevoir*) *objet, bruit* to make out, distinguish, perceive; *ironie* to distinguish, perceive. **~ qn dans la foule** to pick out *ou* spot sb in the crowd; **on commença à ~ les collines à travers la brume** the hills began to be visible through the mist, you could begin to make out the hills through the mist; **il distingue mal sans lunettes** he can't see very well without his glasses.
(b) (*différencier*) to distinguish. **~ une chose d'une autre ou d'avec une autre** to distinguish *ou* tell one thing from another; **savoir ~ les oiseaux/plantes** to be able to distinguish birds/plants; **les deux sœurs sont difficiles à ~ (l'une de l'autre)** the two sisters are difficult to tell apart; **~ le bien du mal/un Picasso d'un ou d'avec un Braque** to tell good from evil/a Picasso from a Braque, distinguish between good and evil/between a Picasso and a Braque; **tu la distingueras à sa veste rouge** you will recognize her *ou* pick her out by her red jacket; **distinguons, il y a chanteur et chanteur** we must make a distinction, there are singers and singers *ou* good singers and bad singers.
(c) (*rendre différent*) to distinguish, set apart (*de* from), mark off. **c'est son accent qui le distingue des autres** it is his accent which distinguishes him from *ou* makes him different from the others *ou* which sets him apart.
(d) (*frm*) (*choisir*) to single out; (*honorer*) to honour. **on l'a distingué pour faire le discours d'adieu** he was singled out to make the farewell speech; **l'Académie Française a distingué X pour son œuvre poétique** the Académie Française has honoured X for his works of poetry.
2 se distinguer *vpr* **(a)** (*différer*) to distinguish o.s., be distinguished (*de* from). **ces objets se distinguent par** *ou* **grâce à leur couleur** these objects can be distinguished by their colour; **les deux frères se distinguent (l'un de l'autre) par leur taille** you can tell the two brothers apart by their (different) height; **il se distingue par son accent/sa démarche** his accent/his way of walking makes him stand out *ou* makes him seem quite different.
(b) (*se signaler, réussir*) to distinguish o.s. **se ~ (pendant une guerre) par son courage** to distinguish o.s. (in a war) by one's courage; **il s'est distingué par ses découvertes en physique** he has become famous for *ou* from his discoveries in physics, he's made a name for himself by his discoveries in physics; (*hum*) **il se distingue par son absence** he is noticeable *ou* conspicuous by his absence; **il s'est particulièrement distingué en latin** he has done particularly well *ou* he has particularly distinguished himself in Latin.
distinguo [distɛ̃go] *nm* (*nuance*) distinction.
distique [distik] *nm* distich.
distordre *vt,* **se distordre** *vpr* [distɔʀdʀ(ə)] (41) to twist.
distorsion [distɔʀsjɔ̃] *nf* (*gén, Anat, Téléc*) distortion; (*Écon*) imbalance, disequilibrium.
distraction [distʀaksjɔ̃] *nf* **(a)** (*inattention*) absent-mindedness, abstraction, lack of attention. **j'ai eu une ~** my concentration lapsed, my attention wandered; **cette ~ lui a coûté la vie** this one lapse in concentration cost him his life; **les ~s proverbiales des savants** the proverbial absent-mindedness of scientists.
(b) (*détente, dérivatifs*) diversion, recreation; (*passe-temps*) distraction, entertainment, amusement. **il a besoin de ~** he needs some diversions *ou* distractions.
(c) (*Jur: vol*) abstraction. **~ de fonds** misappropriation of funds.
distraire [distʀɛʀ] (50) **1** *vt* **(a)** (*divertir*) to entertain, divert, amuse.
(b) (*déranger*) to distract, divert (*de* from). **~ l'attention de qn** to distract sb's attention; (*Scol*) **il distrait ses camarades** he distracts his friends; **se laisser facilement ~ de son travail** to be easily distracted from one's work; **~ qn de son chagrin** to take sb's mind off his grief.
(c) (*frm: voler*) to abstract (*de* from). **~ des fonds** to misappropriate funds.
2 se distraire *vpr* to amuse o.s., enjoy o.s. **j'ai envie d'aller au cinéma pour me distraire** I feel like going to the cinema — it'll take my mind off things.
distrait, e [distʀɛ, ɛt] (*ptp de* **distraire**) *adj personne, caractère* absent-minded; *attitude* inattentive, abstracted. **d'un air ~** absent-mindedly, abstractedly; **d'une oreille ~e** with only half an ear, abstractedly.
distraitement [distʀɛtmɑ̃] *adv* absent-mindedly, abstractedly.
distrayant, e [distʀɛjɑ̃, ɑ̃t] *adj* entertaining, diverting. **les romans policiers sont d'une lecture ~e** detective novels make pleasant light reading.
distribanque [distʀibɑ̃k] *nm* cash dispenser.
distribuer [distʀibɥe] (1) *vt* **(a)** (*donner*) *objets* to distribute, give out, hand out; *vivres* to distribute, share out; *courrier* to deliver; *récompense* to distribute, present; (*Fin*) *actions* to allot; *dividendes* to distribute, pay; *travail* to allot, allocate, distribute; *argent* to distribute; *rôle* to assign, give out; *cartes* to deal (out); *ordres* to hand out, deal out; *saluts, sourires, enseignement* to dispense (*à* to).
(b) (*répartir*) to distribute, arrange; (*Typ*) *caractères* to

distribute. **on distribue ces plantes en 4 espèces** these plants are divided into 4 species; **savoir ~ son temps** to know how to allocate *ou* divide (up) one's time; **comment les pièces sont-elles distribuées?** how are the rooms set out? *ou* laid out?; **~ les masses dans un tableau** to arrange *ou* distribute the masses in a picture; **mon emploi du temps est mal distribué** my timetable is badly arranged.

(c) (*amener*) to distribute, carry. **~ l'eau dans les campagnes** to distribute *ou* carry *ou* convey water to country areas; **le sang est distribué dans tout le corps par le cœur** blood is pumped *ou* carried round the body by the heart.

(d) (*Comm*) *film, produit* to distribute.

distributeur, -trice [distʀibytœʀ, tʀis] **1** *nm,f* (*agent commercial*) distributor.

2 *nm* (*appareil*) machine; (*Aut*) distributor. **~ automatique** vending machine, slot machine; (*Rail*) **~ de billets** ticket machine; (*Agr*) **~ d'engrais** manure- *ou* muck-spreader; **~ d'essence**† petrol pump (*Brit*), gasoline pump (*US*).

distributif, -ive [distʀibytif, iv] *adj* distributive.

distribution [distʀibysjɔ̃] *nf* **(a)** *[objets]* distribution, giving out, handing out; *[vivres]* distribution, sharing out; *[argent]* distribution; *[cartes]* deal; *[courrier]* delivery; (*Fin*) *[actions]* allotment; *[dividendes]* distribution, payment. **la ~ du travail sera faite suivant l'âge** the work will be shared out *ou* allotted *ou* allocated according to age; **~ gratuite** free gifts; **~ des prix** (*gén*) prize giving; (*Scol*) prize day, speech day.

(b) (*répartition*) distribution, arrangement. **la ~ des mots dans une phrase** the distribution of words in a sentence; **la ~ des meubles dans une pièce** the arrangement of the furniture in a room; **cet appartement a une bonne/mauvaise ~ (des pièces)** the flat is well/badly laid out.

(c) (*Ciné, Théât: acteurs*) cast. **~ par ordre d'entrée en scène** cast *ou* characters in order of appearance; **qui est responsable de la ~ de cette pièce?** who's in charge of (the) casting (of) this play?

(d) (*acheminement*) *[eau, électricité]* supply. **la ~ du sang dans le corps** the circulation of blood in the body.

(e) (*Comm*) *[livres, films]* distribution. **nos réseaux de ~** our distribution network.

(f) (*Aut, Tech*) distribution.

distributionnel, -elle [distʀibysjɔnɛl] *adj* distributional.

distributivement [distʀibytivmɑ̃] *adv* distributively.

distributivité [distʀibytivite] *nf* distributiveness.

district [distʀik(t)] *nm* district.

dit [di] *nm* (*Littérat*) story, tale.

dithyrambe [ditiʀɑ̃b] *nm* (*poème*) dithyramb; (*éloge*) panegyric, eulogy.

dithyrambique [ditiʀɑ̃bik] *adj paroles* laudatory, eulogistic; *éloges* extravagant; (*Littérat*) dithyrambic. **une critique ~** a rave review.

dito [dito] *adv* (*Comm*) ditto.

diurétique [djyʀetik] *adj, nm* diuretic.

diurne [djyʀn(ə)] *adj* diurnal.

diva [diva] *nf* († *ou hum*) diva, prima donna.

divagation [divagɑsjɔ̃] *nf* (*gén pl*) *[malade]* wandering, rambling, divagation (*frm*); (*) raving.

divaguer [divage] (1) *vi* (*délirer*) to ramble, divagate (*frm*); (*: *dire des bêtises*) to rave. **il commence à ~** he is beginning to ramble, his mind is beginning to wander; **tu divagues!*** you're off your head!*

divan [divɑ̃] *nm* divan (*seat*); (*Hist*) divan. **~-lit** divan (bed).

divergence [divɛʀʒɑ̃s] *nf* (*V* **diverger**) divergence; difference.

divergent, e [divɛʀʒɑ̃, ɑ̃t] *adj* (*V* **diverger**) divergent; differing.

diverger [divɛʀʒe] (3) *vi [chemins, rayons]* to diverge; *[opinions]* to diverge, differ.

divers, e [divɛʀ, ɛʀs(ə)] *adj* **(a)** (*pl*) (*varié*) *couleurs, coutumes, opinions* diverse, varied; (*différent*) *sens d'un mot, moments, occupations* different, various. **frais ~, dépenses ~es** sundries, miscellaneous expenses; *V* **fait**[1].

(b) (*pl: plusieurs*) various, several. **~es personnes m'en ont parlé** various *ou* several people have spoken to me about it.

(c) (*littér: changeant*) *spectacle* varied, changing (*épith*).

diversement [divɛʀsəmɑ̃] *adv* in various ways, in diverse ways. **son livre a été ~ reçu** his book has had a varied reception.

diversifier [divɛʀsifje] (7) *vt méthodes, exercices* to vary; *production* to diversify. **avoir une économie/une gamme de produits diversifiée** to have a varied economy/range of products; **nous devons nous ~ davantage** we must diversify (our production) more.

diversion [divɛʀsjɔ̃] *nf* (*Mil, littér*) diversion. **faire ~** to create a diversion; **faire ~ au chagrin de qn** to take sb's mind off his sorrow.

diversité [divɛʀsite] *nf* (*grand nombre*) *[opinions, possibilités]* range, variety; (*variété*) *[sujet, spectacle]* variety, diversity; (*divergence: entre deux opinions etc*) diversity, difference, divergence.

divertir [divɛʀtiʀ] (2) **1** *vt* **(a)** (*amuser*) to amuse, entertain, divert.

(b) (*frm: voler*) to abstract, divert. **~ des fonds/une succession** to misappropriate funds/an inheritance.

(c) (††: *détourner*) to distract (*de* from). **~ qn d'un projet** to distract sb's mind from a plan.

2 se divertir *vpr* to amuse o.s., enjoy o.s. **se ~ l'esprit** to occupy one's mind, amuse *ou* entertain o.s.; (*littér*) **se ~ de qn** to make fun of sb, laugh at sb.

divertissant, e [divɛʀtisɑ̃, ɑ̃t] *adj* amusing, entertaining, diverting.

divertissement [divɛʀtismɑ̃] *nm* **(a)** (*U: amusement*) diversion, recreation, relaxation; (*passe-temps*) distraction, entertainment, amusement, diversion.

(b) (*Mus*) divertimento, divertissement.

(c) (*Jur: vol*) misappropriation.

(d) (*Philos ou* ††) distraction.

dividende [dividɑ̃d] *nm* (*Fin, Math*) dividend.

divin, e [divɛ̃, in] *adj* **(a)** *caractère, justice, service* divine. **le ~Achille** the divine Achilles; **la ~e Providence** divine Providence; **notre ~ Père/Sauveur** our Holy Father/Saviour; **l'amour ~** sacred *ou* holy *ou* divine love; **le sens du ~** the sense of the divine; *V* **bonté, droit**[3].

(b) (*: *excellent*) *poésie, beauté, mets, robe, temps* divine, heavenly.

divinateur, -trice [divinatœʀ, tʀis] **1** *adj* divining, foreseeing. **instinct ~** instinctive foresight. **2** *nm,f* (††) diviner, soothsayer.

divination [divinɑsjɔ̃] *nf* divination.

divinatoire [divinatwaʀ] *adj science* divinatory.

divinement [divinmɑ̃] *adv* divinely.

divinisation [divinizɑsjɔ̃] *nf* deification.

diviniser [divinize] (1) *vt* to deify.

divinité [divinite] *nf* (*essence divine*) divinity; (*lit, fig: dieu*) deity, divinity.

diviser [divize] (1) **1** *vt* **(a)** (*fractionner*) (*gén*) to divide; *tâche, ressources* to share out, split up; *gâteau* to cut up, divide up *ou* out. **~ une somme en 3/en 3 parties** to divide *ou* split a sum of money into 3/into 3 parts; **~ une somme entre plusieurs personnes** to share (out) *ou* divide (out) a sum among several people; **le pays est divisé en deux par des montagnes** the country is split *ou* divided in two by mountains; **~ un groupe en plusieurs équipes** to split a group up into several teams; **ce livre se divise en plusieurs chapitres** this book is divided into several chapters.

(b) (*désunir*) *famille, adversaires* to divide, set at variance. **~ pour régner** divide and rule; **les historiens sont très divisés à ce sujet** historians are divided on this subject; **l'opinion est divisée en deux par cette affaire** opinion is split over this affair.

(c) (†: *séparer*) to divide, separate. **un rideau divise la chambre d'avec le salon** *ou* **du salon** a curtain separates the bedroom (off) from the drawing room.

(d) (*Math*) to divide. **~ 4 par 2** to divide 4 by 2.

2 se diviser *vpr* **(a)** (*se scinder*) *[groupe, cellules]* to split up, divide (*en* into).

(b) (*se ramifier*) *[route]* to fork, divide; *[tronc d'arbre]* to fork.

diviseur [divizœʀ] *nm* **(a)** (*Math*) divisor. **nombre/fraction ~** divisor number/fraction; **plus grand commun ~** highest common factor. **(b)** (*personne*) divisive force *ou* influence.

divisibilité [divizibilite] *nf* divisibility.

divisible [divizibl(ə)] *adj* divisible.

division [divizjɔ̃] *nf* **(a)** (*fractionnement*) division; (*partage*) sharing out, division (*en* into). **~ du travail** division of labour; **~ cellulaire** cellular division.

(b) (*désaccord*) division. **il y a une ~ au sein du parti** there's a split *ou* rift within the party; **semer la ~** to sow discord (*entre* among).

(c) (*Math*) division. **faire une ~** to do a division (sum).

(d) (*section, service, circonscription*) division; (*Scol: classe*) group, section; (*Mil, Sport*) division; *V* **général.**

(e) (*graduation, compartiment*) division.

(f) (*chapitre*) *[livre, discours, exposé]* division; (*branche*) *[science]* division.

divisionnaire [divizjɔnɛʀ] **1** *adj* divisional. **2** *nm* (*Mil*) major-general; (*Police*) superintendent.

divorce [divɔʀs(ə)] *nm* (*lit, fig*) divorce (*avec, d'avec* from). **demander le ~** to sue for (a) divorce, ask for a divorce; **obtenir le ~** to obtain *ou* get a divorce.

divorcé, e [divɔʀse] (*ptp de* **divorcer**) **1** *adj* (*lit, fig*) divorced (*de* from). **2** *nm,f* divorcee.

divorcer [divɔʀse] (3) *vi* **(a)** (*Jur*) to get a divorce, be *ou* get divorced. **~ d'avec sa femme/son mari** to divorce one's wife/husband. **(b)** (*fig*) to break (*d'avec, de* with).

divulgateur, -trice [divylgatœʀ, tʀis] *nm,f* divulger.

divulgation [divylgɑsjɔ̃] *nf* disclosure, divulging, divulgence.

divulguer [divylge] (1) *vt* to divulge, disclose.

dix [dis] **1** *adj inv, nm* ten. **les ~ commandements** the Ten Commandments; *pour autres loc V* **six.**

2: dix-huit *adj inv, nm* eighteen; **dix-huitième** *adj, nmf* eighteenth; **dix-huitièmement** *adv* in (the) eighteenth place; **dix-neuf** *adj inv, nm* nineteen; **dix-neuvième** *adj, nmf* nineteenth; **dix-neuvièmement** *adv* in (the) nineteenth place; **dix-sept** *adj inv, nm* seventeen; **dix-septième** *adj, nmf* seventeenth; **dix-septièmement** *adv* in (the) seventeenth place.

dixième [dizjɛm] *adj, nmf* tenth. **~** *nm* **(de la Loterie nationale)** *tenth share in a ticket (in the National Lottery).*

dixièmement [dizjɛmmɑ̃] *adv* tenthly, in the (tenth) place.

dizain [dizɛ̃] *nm* ten-line poem.

dizaine [dizɛn] *nf* (*dix*) ten; (*quantité voisine de dix*) about ten, ten or so; *pour loc V* **soixantaine.**

djellaba [dʒɛlaba] *nf* jellaba.

djinn [dʒin] *nm* jinn, djinn.

do [do] *nm inv* (*Mus*) (*note*) C; (*en chantant la gamme*) doh.

docile [dɔsil] *adj personne, caractère* docile, meek, obedient; *animal* docile; *cheveux* manageable.

docilement [dɔsilmɑ̃] *adv* docilely, obediently.

docilité [dɔsilite] *nf* docility, obedience.

docimologie [dɔsimɔlɔʒi] *nf* (statistical) analysis of test *ou* exam results.

dock [dɔk] *nm* **(a)** (*bassin*) dock; (*cale de construction*) dockyard. **~ de carénage/flottant** dry/floating dock. **(b)** (*hangar, bâtiment*) warehouse.

docker [dɔkɛʀ] *nm* docker.

docte [dɔkt(ə)] *adj* (*littér, hum*) learned.

doctement [dɔktəmɑ̃] *adv* (*littér, hum*) learnedly.

docteur [dɔktœʀ] *nm* (*gén, Univ*) doctor (*ès, en* of); (*Méd*) doctor. ~ **en médecine** doctor of medicine; **le** ~ **Lebrun** Dr Lebrun; (*Rel*) **les** ~**s de l'Église** the Doctors of the Church.

doctoral, e, *mpl* **-aux** [dɔktɔʀal, o] *adj* (*péj: pédantesque*) *ton* pompous, bombastic.

doctoralement [dɔktɔʀalmɑ̃] *adv* (*péj*) pompously, bombastically.

doctorat [dɔktɔʀa] *nm* doctorate (*ès, en* in). ~ **de 3e cycle** ≃ Ph.D.

doctoresse [dɔktɔʀɛs] *nf* lady doctor.

doctrinaire [dɔktʀinɛʀ] **1** *adj* (*dogmatique*) doctrinaire; (*sentencieux*) pompous, sententious. **2** *nmf* doctrinaire, doctrinarian.

doctrinal, e, *mpl* **-aux** [dɔktʀinal, o] *adj* doctrinal.

doctrine [dɔktʀin] *nf* doctrine.

document [dɔkymɑ̃] *nm* document. **nous avons des** ~**s le prouvant** we have documentary evidence (of that), we have documents to prove it.

documentaire [dɔkymɑ̃tɛʀ] **1** *adj intérêt* documentary. **à titre** ~ for your (*ou* his *etc*) information. **2** *nm* (*film*) documentary (film).

documentaliste [dɔkymɑ̃talist(ə)] *nmf* archivist; (*Presse, TV*) researcher.

documentation [dɔkymɑ̃tɑsjɔ̃] *nf* documentation, literature, information; (*Presse, TV: service*) research.

documenter [dɔkymɑ̃te] (1) **1** *vt personne, livre* to document. **documenté** *personne* well-informed; *livre* well-documented, well-researched. **2 se documenter** *vpr* to gather information *ou* material (*sur* on, about).

dodécaèdre [dɔdekaɛdʀ(ə)] *nm* dodecahedron.

dodécagonal, e, *mpl* **-aux** [dɔdekagɔnal, o] *adj* dodecagonal.

dodécagone [dɔdekagɔn] *nm* dodecagon.

dodécaphonique [dɔdekafɔnik] *adj* dodecaphonic.

dodécaphonisme [dɔdekafɔnism(ə)] *nm* dodecaphony.

dodelinement [dɔdlinmɑ̃] *nm* [*tête*] nodding (*with sleep, age*).

dodeliner [dɔdline] (1) *vi*: **il dodelinait de la tête** his head kept nodding (gently) forward.

dodo [dodo] *nm* (*langage enfantin: sommeil*) bye-byes (*langage enfantin*), sleep; (*lit*) bye-byes (*langage enfantin*), bed. **faire** ~ to have gone to bye-byes (*langage enfantin*), be asleep; **il est temps d'aller au** ~ it's time to go to bye-byes (*langage enfantin*); **(fais)** ~! come on, sleepy-time!

dodu, e [dody] *adj personne, poule, bras* plump; *enfant, joue* chubby.

doge [dɔʒ] *nm* doge.

dogmatique [dɔgmatik] *adj* dogmatic.

dogmatiquement [dɔgmatikmɑ̃] *adv* dogmatically.

dogmatiser [dɔgmatize] (1) *vi* to dogmatize.

dogmatisme [dɔgmatism(ə)] *nm* dogmatism.

dogme [dɔgm(ə)] *nm* (*lit, fig*) dogma. (*Rel*) **le** ~ the dogma.

dogue [dɔg] *nm* (*Zool*) mastiff; *V* **humeur.**

doigt [dwa] *nm* **(a)** [*main, gant*] finger; [*animal*] digit. ~ **de pied** toe; **se mettre** *ou* **se fourrer les** ~**s dans le nez** to pick one's nose; *V* **bague, compter, petit** *etc.*

(b) (*mesure*) **raccourcir une jupe de 2/3** ~**s** to shorten a skirt by 1/2 inches; **un** ~ **de vin** a drop of wine; **il a été à deux** ~**s de se tuer/de la mort/de réussir** he was within an ace *ou* an inch of being killed/of death/of succeeding; **la balle est passée à un** ~ **de sa tête** the bullet passed within a hairsbreadth *ou* an inch of his head.

(c) (*loc*) **avoir des** ~**s de fée** [*ménagère*] to have nimble fingers; [*infirmière*] to have gentle hands; **il ne fait rien de ses dix** ~**s** he's an idle *ou* a lazy good-for-nothing, he is bone idle (*surtout Brit*); **il ne sait rien faire de ses dix** ~**s** he's a good-for-nothing; **faire marcher qn au** ~ **et à l'œil** to keep a tight rein on sb, make sb toe the line; **avec lui, ils obéissent au** ~ **et à l'œil** with him, they have to toe the line; **se mettre** *ou* **se fourrer le** ~ **dans l'œil (jusqu'au coude)*** to be kidding o.s.*; **là tu te mets** *ou* **te fourres le** ~ **dans l'œil*** you're completely up the pole*, you've got another think coming* (*Brit*); **il n'a pas levé** *ou* **bougé le petit** ~ **pour nous aider** he didn't lift a finger to help us; **son petit** ~ **le lui a dit** a little bird told him; **mettre le** ~ **sur le problème** to put one's finger on the problem; **mettre le** ~ **dans l'engrenage** to get involved *ou* mixed up *ou* caught up in something; **filer** *ou* **glisser entre les** ~**s de qn** to slip through sb's fingers; **ils sont (amis) comme les (deux)** ~**s de la main** they're very thick with one another*, they're as thick as thieves; **je le ferais les** ~**s dans le nez*** I can do it standing on my head *ou* with my eyes closed; **il a gagné les** ~**s dans le nez*** he romped home; **avoir un morceau de musique dans les** ~**s** to know a piece of music like the back of one's hand.

doigté [dwate] *nm* [*pianiste, dactylo, chirurgien*] touch; (*Mus*) (*jeu des doigts*) fingering technique; (*position des doigts*) fingering; (*fig: tact*) diplomacy, tact.

doigter [dwate] (1) *vti* (*Mus*) to finger.

doigtier [dwatje] *nm* fingerstall.

doit [dwa] *nm* debit. ~ **et avoir** debit and credit.

doléances [dɔleɑ̃s] *nfpl* (*plaintes*) complaints; (*réclamations*) grievances.

dolent, e [dɔlɑ̃, ɑ̃t] *adj* (*littér*) *personne* doleful, mournful; *air, voix* doleful, plaintive.

doline [dɔlin] *nf* doline.

dollar [dɔlaʀ] *nm* dollar.

dolman [dɔlmɑ̃] *nm* dolman (*hussar's jacket*).

dolmen [dɔlmɛn] *nm* dolmen.

dolomie [dɔlɔmi] *nf,* **dolomite** [dɔlɔmit] *nf* dolomite. **les Dolomites** the Dolomites.

dolomitique [dɔlɔmitik] *adj* dolomitic.

Dom [dɔ̃] *nm* Dom.

domaine [dɔmɛn] *nm* **(a)** (*propriété*) estate, domain, property. **le** ~ **de la couronne** the crown lands; (*Jur*) **le** ~ **(de l'État)** (*propriété*) *state administered property;* (*service*) *state property department*; **ses œuvres sont maintenant tombées dans le** ~ **public** his works are now out of copyright.

(b) (*sphère*) field, province, domain, sphere. **ce n'est pas de mon** ~ it's not my field *ou* sphere; **dans tous les** ~**s** in every domain *ou* field; (*fig Pol*) ~ **réservé** (head of state's) private domain.

domanial, e, *mpl* **-iaux** [dɔmanjal, jo] *adj* (*d'un domaine privé*) domanial; (*d'un domaine public*) national (*épith*), state (*épith*).

dôme [dom] *nm* (*voûte*) dome; (*cathédrale*) cathedral. (*littér*) **le** ~ **du ciel** the vault of heaven; (*fig*) **un** ~ **de verdure** a canopy of foliage *ou* greenery; (*Géog*) ~ **volcanique** volcanic dome.

domestication [dɔmɛstikɑsjɔ̃] *nf* (*action*) domestication, domesticating; (*résultat*) domestication.

domesticité [dɔmɛstisite] *nf* **(a)** (*condition de domestique*) domestic service. **(b)** (*personnel*) (domestic) staff, household. **une nombreuse** ~ a large staff of servants. **(c)** [*animal*] domesticity.

domestique [dɔmɛstik] **1** *nmf* servant, domestic. **les** ~**s** the servants, the staff (of servants); **je ne suis pas ton** ~! I'm not your servant!

2 *adj* **(a)** (*ménager*) *travaux* domestic, household (*épith*); *soucis, querelle* domestic, family (*épith*). **les dieux** ~**s** the household gods.

(b) (*Comm*) *marché, consommation* domestic.

(c) (*Zool*) domestic, domesticated. **le chien est un animal** ~ the dog is a domestic animal; **canards** ~**s et canards sauvages** tame *ou* domesticated ducks and wild ducks.

domestiquer [dɔmɛstike] (1) *vt animal* to domesticate; *peuple* to subjugate; *vent, marée* to harness.

domicile [dɔmisil] *nm* place of residence, home, domicile (*Admin*); (*Jur*) [*société*] registered address; (*sur formulaire*) address. ~ **légal** official domicile; **quitter le** ~ **conjugal** to leave the marital home; **sans** ~, (*Admin*) **sans** ~ **fixe** of no fixed abode *ou* address; **dernier** ~ **connu** last known address; **travailler à** ~ to work at home; **il cherche du travail (à faire) à** ~ he's looking for work (to do) at home; **je vous l'apporterai à** ~ I'll bring it to your home; **livrer à** ~ to deliver; **faire des livraisons à** ~ to carry out deliveries; **'livraisons à** ~**'** 'deliveries', 'we deliver'; **'réparations à** ~**'** 'home repairs carried out'; *V* **élire, violation.**

domiciliaire [dɔmisiljɛʀ] *adj* domiciliary.

domiciliation [dɔmisiljɑsjɔ̃] *nf* domiciliation.

domicilier [dɔmisilje] (7) *vt chèque* to domicile. **être domicilié** to be domiciled (*Admin*), have one's home (*à* in); **je me suis fait** ~ **à Lyon** I gave Lyons as my official address *ou* place of residence.

dominance [dɔminɑ̃s] *nf* (*Bio*) dominance.

dominant, e [dɔminɑ̃, ɑ̃t] **1** *adj pays, nation* dominant; *opinion, vent* prevailing; *idée, trait* dominant, main (*épith*); *rôle* dominant; *passion* ruling (*épith*); *problème, préoccupation* main (*épith*), chief (*épith*); *position* dominating (*épith*); (*Bio, Jur*) dominant.

2 dominante *nf* (*caractéristique*) dominant characteristic; (*couleur*) dominant *ou* predominant colour; (*Mus*) dominant. **tableau à** ~**e rouge** painting with red as the dominant *ou* predominant colour.

dominateur, -trice [dɔminatœʀ, tʀis] **1** *adj personne, caractère* domineering, overbearing; *voix, geste, regard* imperious; *pays* dominating (*épith*); *passion* ruling (*épith*). **2** *nm,f* (*littér*) ruler.

domination [dɔminɑsjɔ̃] *nf* (*Pol: autorité*) domination, dominion, rule; (*fig: emprise*) domination, influence. **la** ~ **de la Gaule (par Rome)** the domination of Gaul (by Rome); **la** ~ **de Rome (sur la Gaule)** Roman rule *ou* domination (over Gaul); **les pays sous la** ~ **britannique** countries under British rule *ou* domination *ou* dominion, countries under the sway of Britain; **exercer sa** ~**/une** ~ **morale sur qn** to exert one's influence/a moral influence on sb; **un besoin insatiable de** ~ an insatiable need to dominate; ~ **de soi-même** self-control, self-domination.

dominer [dɔmine] (1) **1** *vt* **(a)** (*être maître de*) *personne, pays* to dominate. **il voulait** ~ **le monde** he wanted to rule the world; **ces enfants sont dominés par leur père** these children are kept down *ou* dominated by their father; **il se laisse** ~ **par sa femme** he's dominated by his wife; **elle ne sait pas** ~ **ses élèves** she can't keep her pupils in order *ou* under control, she can't keep control over her pupils.

(b) (*surpasser*) *adversaire, concurrent* to outclass, tower above, surpass. **il domine de loin les autres étudiants** he is miles better than *ou* way above the other students*; **écrivain qui domine son siècle** writer who dominates his century; **se faire** ~ **par l'équipe adverse** to be dominated *ou* outclassed by the opposing team; **parler fort pour** ~ **le bruit de la rue** to speak loudly to be heard above the noise from the street; **chez lui cette passion domine toutes les autres** this passion dominates *ou* overshadows all others in him; **le problème de la pollution domine tous les autres** the problem of pollution overshadows all others.

(c) (*maîtriser*) *sentiment* to control, master, overcome; *problème* to overcome, master; *sujet* to master; *situation* to dominate, master. **elle ne put** ~ **son trouble** she couldn't overcome her confusion; **se** ~ to control o.s., keep o.s. under control; **il ne sait pas se** ~ he has no control over himself *ou* no self-control.

(d) (*diriger, gouverner*) to dominate, govern. **l'idée maîtresse/la préoccupation qui domine toute son œuvre** the key idea/the main concern which dominates *ou* governs his whole work.

(e) (*surplomber*) to tower above, dominate. **rocher/terrasse qui domine la mer** rock/terrace which overlooks the sea; **il dominait la foule de sa haute taille** he towered above the crowd with his great height; **de là-haut on domine la vallée** from up there you overlook the whole valley.

2 *vi* **(a)** (*être le meilleur*) *[nation]* to hold sway; *[orateur, concurrent]* to be in the dominant position; (*Sport*) *[équipe]* to be in the dominant position, be on top; *[coureur]* to be in a commanding position. **l'Angleterre a dominé sur les mers pendant des siècles** England ruled the seas *ou* held dominion over the seas for centuries; **dans les débats, il domine nettement** in debates, he's way above the rest* *ou* he's definitely the strongest speaker; **leur équipe a dominé pendant tout le match** their team was on top throughout the match; **ce coureur a dominé pendant les premiers kilomètres** this runner was on his own *ou* was out in front for the first few kilometres; (*fig*) **~ de la tête et des épaules** to be head and shoulders above the others.

(b) (*prédominer*) *[caractère, défaut, qualité]* to predominate; *[idée, théorie]* to prevail; *[préoccupation, intérêt]* to be dominant, predominate; *[parfum]* to predominate; *[couleur]* to stand out, predominate. **dans cette réunion, l'élément féminin dominait** at that meeting the female element predominated *ou* was predominant; **c'est l'ambition qui domine chez lui** ambition is his dominant characteristic; **c'est le jaune qui domine** it is yellow which stands out *ou* which is the predominant colour.

dominicain, e [dɔminikɛ̃, ɛn] *adj, nm,f* (*Pol, Rel*) Dominican.

dominical, e, *mpl* **-aux** [dɔminikal, o] *adj* Sunday (*épith*), dominical (*frm*); *V* **oraison, repos.**

dominion [dɔminjɔn] *nm* (*Brit: état*) dominion (*of the British Commonwealth*).

domino [dɔmino] *nm* (*Habillement, Jeu*) domino. (*jeu*) **les ~s** dominoes (*sg*).

dommage [dɔmaʒ] **1** *nm* **(a)** (*préjudice*) harm (*U*), injury. **causer un ~ à qn** to cause *ou* do sb harm; **pour réparer le ~ que je vous ai causé** to repair the harm I've caused you, to repair the injury I've done you; (*Jur*) **~ causé avec intention de nuire** malicious damage.

(b) (*ravages*) **~s** damage (*U*); **causer des ~s aux récoltes** to damage *ou* cause damage to the crops; **les ~s sont inestimables** there is incalculable damage.

(c) (*loc*) **c'est ~!, quel ~!** what a pity! *ou* shame!; **il est vraiment ~ que ...** it's such a great pity that ...; **(c'est** *ou* **quel) ~ que tu ne puisses pas venir** it's a *ou* what a pity *ou* shame (that) you can't come; (*iro*) **ça ne te plaît pas? c'est bien ~!** you don't like it? well, that really is a shame! (*iro*) *ou* pity isn't it?* (*iro*).

2: dommage(s) corporel(s) physical injury; **dommages de guerre** war damages; **dommages et intérêts, dommages-intérêts** *nmpl* damages; **dommage(s) matériel(s)** material damage.

dommageable [dɔmaʒabl(ə)] *adj* prejudicial, harmful, injurious (*à* to).

domptable [dɔ̃tabl(ə)] *adj* tam(e)able.

domptage [dɔ̃taʒ] *nm* taming.

dompter [dɔ̃te] (1) *vt animal* to tame; *cheval* to break in; *fauve* to train; *enfant insoumis* to subdue; *rebelles* to put down, subdue; *sentiments, passions* to master, control, overcome; *nature, fleuve* to tame.

dompteur, -euse [dɔ̃tœʀ, øz] *nm,f* (*gén*) trainer. **~ de lions** liontamer; **~ de chevaux** horsebreaker.

don [dɔ̃] *nm* **(a)** (*aptitude*) gift, talent. **~s littéraires** literary gifts *ou* talents; **avoir un ~ pour** to have a gift *ou* talent for; **avoir le ~ des maths** to have a gift for maths; **elle a le ~ de m'énerver** she has a knack of *ou* a genius for getting on my nerves; **cette proposition n'a pas eu le ~ de lui plaire** this proposal was not destined to *ou* didn't happen to please him.

(b) (*cadeau*) gift; (*offrande*) donation. **~ en argent** cash donation; **~ en nature** donation in kind; (*littér*) **les ~s de la terre** the gifts of the earth; **faire ~ de** *fortune, maison* to donate; **je lui ai fait ~ de ce livre** I made him a present *ou* gift of that book, I gave him that book as a gift; **cette tâche exige le ~ de soi** this task demands real self-sacrifice *ou* self-denial.

donataire [dɔnatɛʀ] *nmf* donee.

donateur, -trice [dɔnatœʀ, tʀis] *nm,f* donor.

donation [dɔnɑsjɔ̃] *nf* donation.

donc [dɔ̃k *en tête de proposition ou devant voyelle; ailleurs* dɔ̃] *conj* **(a)** (*par conséquent*) therefore, so, thus; (*après une digression*) so, then. **il partit ~ avec ses amis et ...** so he left with his friends and ..., he left with his friends then and ...; **si ce n'est pas la variole c'est ~ la rougeole** if it's not smallpox then it's measles.

(b) (*intensif: marque la surprise*) then, so. **c'était ~ un espion?** he was a spy then?, so he was a spy?; **voilà ~ ce dont il s'agissait** this is what it was (all) about then, so this is what it was (all) about.

(c) (*de renforcement*) **allons ~!** come on!, come now!; **écoute-moi ~** do listen to me; **demande-lui ~** go on, ask him; **tais-toi ~!** do be quiet!; **regardez ~ ça comme c'est joli** just look at that, isn't it pretty?; **pensez ~!** what do you expect?; (*iro*) that'll be the day!*; **comment ~?** how do you mean?; **quoi ~?** what was that?, what did you say?; **dis ~, dites ~** (*introduit une question*) tell me, I say; (*introduit un avertissement, une injonction*) look (here) ...; **non mais dis ~, ne te gêne pas!** look (here) don't put yourself out; **dites ~ Jacques, où avez-vous rangé l'aspirateur?** I say, Jacques, where did you put the vacuum cleaner?; **tiens ~!** well, well!, I say!

dondon* [dɔ̃dɔ̃] *nf* big *ou* fat woman. **une grosse ~** a big lump* of a woman *ou* girl.

donjon [dɔ̃ʒɔ̃] *nm* keep, donjon.

don Juan [dɔ̃ʒɥɑ̃] *nm* don Juan.

donjuanesque [dɔ̃ʒɥanɛsk(ə)] *adj* don Juan-like, donjuanesque.

donjuanisme [dɔ̃ʒɥanism(ə)] *nm* donjuanism.

donnant, e [dɔnɑ̃, ɑ̃t] *adj* **(a)** (†) generous, open-handed.

(b) (*loc: emploi participial*) **~, ~: avec lui, c'est ~, ~** with him, it's fifty-fifty *ou* everything's on a fifty-fifty basis; **~, ~ je te prête mon livre, tu me prêtes ton stylo** fair's fair — I lend you my book and you lend me your pen.

donne [dɔn] *nf* (*Cartes*) deal. **à vous la ~** your deal; **faire la ~** to deal (out) the cards; **il y a mauvaise** *ou* **fausse ~** it's a misdeal.

donné, e [dɔne] (*ptp de* **donner**) **1** *adj* **(a)** (*déterminé*) *lieu, date* given, fixed; *V* **moment.**

(b) étant ~ la situation in view of *ou* given *ou* considering the situation; **étant ~ que tu es parti** seeing *ou* given that you left.

(c) (*: *pas cher*) (dirt) cheap*.

2 donnée *nf* **(a)** (*Math, Sci*) *[problème]* datum; **~es** data.

(b) (*chose connue*) piece of information. **~es** facts, particulars; **manquer de ~es** to be short of facts.

(c) *[roman]* main theme, basic idea *ou* element.

donner [dɔne] (1) **1** *vt* **(a)** (*gén: offrir*) **~ qch à qn** to give sth to sb, give sb sth; **je le lui ai donné** I gave it (to) him; **donné c'est donné** a gift is a gift; **~ son cœur/son amitié (à qn)** to give one's heart/one's friendship (to sb); **~ à manger/boire à qn** to give sb something to eat/drink; **~ son sang pour un malade** to give one's blood for somebody who is ill; **~ son sang pour une cause** to shed one's blood for a cause; **~ sa vie/son temps pour une cause** to give up one's life/one's time for a cause; **~ qch à qn par testament** to bequeath sth to sb; **~ qch pour** *ou* **contre qch d'autre** to give sth in exchange for sth else, exchange sth for sth else; **en ~ à qn pour son argent** to give sb his money's worth; **on ne les vend pas, on les donne** we're not selling them, we're giving them away; **c'est donné*** it's dirt-cheap*; *V* **change, matière.**

(b) (*remettre, confier*) to give, hand; *copie d'examen* to hand in, give in. **~ quelque chose à faire à qn** to give sb something to do; **je donnerai la lettre au concierge** I shall hand the letter (in) to the caretaker; **donnez-moi les outils** give me *ou* hand me *ou* pass me the tools; **~ ses chaussures à ressemeler/au cordonnier** to take one's shoes (in) to be mended/to the cobbler's, put one's shoes in to be mended/at the mender's.

(c) (*céder*) *vieux vêtements* to give away. **~ sa place à une dame** to give up one's seat to a lady; **je donnerais beaucoup pour savoir** I would give a lot to know; *V* **langue.**

(d) (*distribuer*) to hand out, give out; *cartes* to deal (out). (*Cartes*) **c'est à vous de ~** it's your deal.

(e) (*communiquer, indiquer*) *description, détails, idée, avis* to give. **il lui a donné l'ordre de partir** he has ordered him to go; **pouvez-vous me ~ l'heure?** can you tell me the time?; *V* **alarme, alerte.**

(f) (*accorder*) *moyen, occasion* to give; *permission, interview* to grant, give; *prix, décoration* to award, give. **~ sa fille en mariage à qn** to give one's daughter to sb in marriage; **donnez-moi le temps d'y réfléchir** give me time to think about it; **on lui a donné 24 heures pour quitter le pays** he was given 24 hours to leave the country; **il n'est pas donné à tout le monde d'être bon en maths** not everyone is lucky enough *ou* it is not given to everyone to be good at maths; **l'intelligence n'est pas donnée à tout le monde** not everyone is gifted with intelligence; **je vous le donne en mille** you'll never guess; **se ~ un maître/un président** to choose a master/a president; (*Rel*) **~ la communion** *etc* **à** to give communion *etc* to; (*fig*) **on lui donnerait le bon Dieu sans confession** he looks as if butter wouldn't melt in his mouth.

(g) (*causer*) *plaisir, courage* to give (*à* to); *peine, mal* to cause, give (*à* to). **~ de l'appétit à qn** to give sb an appetite; **cela donne chaud/froid/soif/faim** this makes you (feel) hot/cold/thirsty/hungry; **~ le vertige/le mal de mer (à qn)** to make sb (feel) giddy/seasick; **cela donne des maux de tête** that causes headaches *ou* gives you headaches; **ça va vous ~ des forces** that'll give you strength; **se ~ du mal/de la peine** to take (great) trouble/pains; **se ~ du bon temps** to have a good time, live it up*; **s'en ~ à cœur joie, s'en ~*** to have a whale of a time*, have the time of one's life.

(h) (*avec à + infin: faire*) **il m'a donné à penser/à sentir que** he made me think/feel that; **ces événements nous ont donné (beaucoup) à réfléchir** these events have given us (much) food for thought; **c'est ce qu'on m'a donné à entendre** that is what I was given to understand *ou* led to believe; **~ à rire** to give cause for laughter.

(i) (*organiser*) *réception, bal* to give, hold (*à* for); *film* to show; *pièce* to perform, put on. **ça se donne encore?** *[film]* is it still on? *ou* showing?; *[pièce]* is it still on?

(j) (*indiquant une action sur qn/qch*) **~ un baiser/un coup de pied à qn** to give sb a kiss/a kick; **~ une gifle à qn** to slap sb's face; **~ une fessée à qn** to smack sb's bottom; **~ une caresse au chat** to stroke the cat; **donne-toi un coup de peigne** give your hair a quick comb; **~ un coup de balai à la pièce** to give the room a sweep; **~ un coup de chiffon à la pièce** to flick a duster over the room, give the room a quick dust; **ils se sont donné des coups** they exchanged blows; **je me donnerais des coups!** I could kick myself!

(k) (*conférer*) *poids, valeur* to add, give. **le brouillard donne un air triste à la ville** the fog makes the town look dismal; **il fumait pour se ~ une contenance** he was smoking to disguise his lack of composure; **elle se donne un air de jeune fille naïve** she gives herself the appearance of an innocent young thing, she likes to appear the innocent young thing.

(l) (*attribuer*) **quel âge lui donnez-vous?** how old do you take him to be? *ou* would you say he was?; **je lui donne 50 ans** I'd put his age at 50, I'd take him to be 50; **on lui donne des qualités qu'il n'a pas** he's said to have *ou* is credited with qualities which he hasn't got; *V* **raison, tort.**

(m) ~ **pour:** ~ **un fait pour certain** to present a fact as a certainty; **on le donne pour un homme habile** he is said *ou* made out to be a clever man; **il se donne pour un tireur d'élite** he makes himself out *ou* professes to be a crack shot.

(n) (*Mus*) *le la, la note, le ton* to give. (*fig*) ~ **le ton** *ou* **la note** to set the tone.

(o) (*produire*) *fruits, récolte* to yield; *résultat* to produce. **les pommiers ont bien donné cette année** the apple trees have produced a good crop *ou* given a good yield this year; **cette vigne donne un très bon vin** this vine produces a very good wine; **elle lui a donné un fils** she gave *ou* bore him a son; (*fig*) **cet écrivain donne un livre tous les ans** this writer produces a book every year.

(p) (‡: *dénoncer*) *complice* to squeal on‡, shop‡ (*Brit*), give away.

2 *vi* **(a)** (*frapper*) **aller** ~ **sur les rochers** to run onto *ou* strike the rocks; ~ **de la tête contre une porte** to knock *ou* bump one's head against a door; **le soleil donne en plein sur la voiture** the sun is beating down on *ou* shining right onto the car; **ne savoir où** ~ **de la tête*** not to know which way to turn.

(b) (*être la victime de*) ~ **dans** *piège* to fall into; *défaut* to lapse into; ~ **dans le snobisme** to be rather snobbish, have a tendency to be snobbish; *V* **panneau.**

(c) (*s'ouvrir sur*) ~ **sur** *[pièce, porte]* to give onto, open onto; *[fenêtre]* to overlook, open onto, look onto; **la maison donne sur la mer** the house faces *ou* looks onto the sea front.

(d) (*attaquer*) to attack. **l'artillerie va** ~ the artillery is going to fire; **faites** ~ **la garde** send in the guards!

(e) (*produire*) to yield. **cet arbre ne donnera pas avant 3 ans** this tree won't bear fruit for 3 years; (*fig*) **la radio donne à plein** the radio is turned right up; **mes tomates vont bientôt** ~ my tomatoes will soon be producing *ou* yielding fruit.

3 se donner *vpr*: **se** ~ **à** *cause, parti, travail* to devote o.s. to; **elle s'est donnée (à son amant)** she gave herself (to her lover); **il s'est donné à fond** he has given his all; *V* **main, rendez-vous.**

donneur, -euse [dɔnœʀ, øz] *nm,f* (*gén*) giver; (*Cartes*) dealer; (*arg Police: dénonciateur*) squealer‡, informer; (*Méd*) donor. (*Comm*) ~ **d'ordre** principal; ~ **de sang** blood donor.

Don Quichotte [dɔ̃kiʃɔt] *nm* Don Quixote.

don-quichottisme [dɔ̃kiʃɔtism(ə)] *nm* quixotism.

dont [dɔ̃] *pron rel* **(a)** (*provenant d'un complément de nom: indique la possession, la qualité etc*) whose, of which; (*antécédent humain*) whose. **la femme** ~ **vous apercevez le chapeau** the woman whose hat you can see; **c'est un pays** ~ **j'aime le climat** it's a country whose climate I like *ou* which has a climate I like *ou* the climate of which I like (*frm*); **un vagabond** ~ **les souliers laissaient voir les doigts de pied** a tramp whose shoes revealed his toes *ou* whose toes showed through his shoes; **les enfants** ~ **la mère travaille sont plus indépendants** children whose mothers go out to work are more independent; **l'histoire,** ~ **voici l'essentiel, est ...** the story, of which these are the main points, is ... .

(b) (*indiquant la partie d'un tout*) **il y a eu plusieurs blessés,** ~ **son frère** there were several casualties, among which *ou* among whom was his brother *ou* including his brother; **des livres dont j'ai lu une dizaine environ/dont une dizaine sont reliés** books of which I have read about ten/of which about ten are bound; **ils ont 3 filles** ~ **2 sont mariées** they have 3 daughters, 2 of whom are married *ou* of whom 2 are married *ou* 2 of them married; **il a écrit 2 romans** ~ **un est autobiographique** he has written 2 novels one of which is autobiographical; **l'histoire,** ~ **l'essentiel est ...** the story, the main point of which is ... .

(c) (*indique la manière, la provenance: V aussi* **de**) **la façon** ~ **elle marche/s'habille** the way she walks/(in which) she dresses, her way of walking/dressing; **la pièce** ~ **il sort** the room (which) he is coming out of *ou* out of which he is coming; **mines** ~ **on extrait de l'or** mines from which gold is extracted, mines (that) gold is extracted from; **la classe sociale** ~ **elle est sortie** the social class (which) she came from.

(d) (*provenant d'un complément prépositionnel d'adjectif, de verbe: V aussi les adjectifs et verbes en question*) **l'outil** ~ **il se sert** the tool (which) he is using; **la maladie** ~ **elle souffre** the illness she suffers from *ou* from which she suffers; **le vase** ~ **la maison m'a fait cadeau** the vase (which) the firm gave me *ou* presented me with, the vase with which the firm presented me; **le film/l'acteur** ~ **elle parle tant** the film/actor she talks so much about *ou* about which/whom she talks so much; **voilà ce** ~ **il faut vous assurer** that is what you must make sure of *ou* about; **l'accident** ~ **il a été responsable** the accident he was responsible for *ou* for which he was responsible; **le collier/l'enfant** ~ **elle est si fière** the necklace/child she is so proud of *ou* of which/whom she is so proud.

donzelle [dɔ̃zɛl] *nf* (*péj*) young miss (*péj*).

dopage [dɔpaʒ] *nm* doping.

dopant [dɔpɑ̃] *nm* dope (*U*).

doper [dɔpe] (1) **1** *vt* to dope. **2 se doper** *vpr* to take stimulants, dope o.s.

doping [dɔpiŋ] *nm* (*action*) doping; (*excitant*) dope (*U*).

dorade [dɔʀad] *nf* = **daurade.**

doré, e [dɔʀe] (*ptp de* **dorer**) **1** *adj* **(a)** (*couvert d'une dorure*) gilt, gilded. ~ **sur tranche** gilt-edged, with gilded edges; **le** ~ **de ce vase s'en va** the gilt is wearing off this vase.

(b) (*couleur d'or*) *peau* bronzed, tanned; *blé, cheveux* golden. (*fig*) **des rêves** ~**s** golden dreams; *V* **blouson, jeunesse.**

2 *nm* (*Can*) yellow pike, wall-eyed pike.

dorénavant [dɔʀenavɑ̃] *adv* from now on, henceforth (*frm*), henceforward (*frm*).

dorer [dɔʀe] (1) **1** *vt* **(a)** (*couvrir d'or*) *objet* to gild. **faire** ~ **un cadre** to have a frame gilded; (*fig*) ~ **la pilule à qn*** to gild *ou* sugar *ou* sweeten the pill for sb.

(b) (*Culin*) *gâteau* to glaze (*with egg yolk*). **le four dore bien la viande** the oven browns the meat well.

(c) *peau* to bronze, tan. (*littér*) **le soleil dore les blés** the sun turns the corn gold; **le soleil dore les dunes** the sun tinges the dunes with gold; **se** ~ **au soleil** to lie (and get brown) in the sun.

2 *vi* (*Culin*) *[rôti]* to brown. **faire** ~ **un poulet au four** to put a chicken in the oven to brown; **le poulet est bien doré cette fois** the chicken is well browned this time.

d'ores et déjà [dɔʀedeʒa] *adv V* **ores.**

doreur, -euse [dɔʀœʀ, øz] *nm,f* gilder.

dorien, -ienne [dɔʀjɛ̃, jɛn] **1** *adj* (*Géog*) Dorian, Doric; *dialecte* Doric; (*Mus*) *mode* Dorian. **2** *nm* (*Ling*) Doric (dialect).

dorique [dɔʀik] *adj, nm* Doric.

dorlotement [dɔʀlɔtmɑ̃] *nm* pampering, (molly)coddling, cosseting.

dorloter [dɔʀlɔte] (1) **1** *vt* to pamper, (molly)coddle, cosset. **il est trop dorloté** he's mollycoddled; **se faire** ~ to be pampered *ou* (molly)coddled *ou* cosseted. **2 se dorloter** *vpr* to coddle *ou* cosset o.s.

dormant, e [dɔʀmɑ̃, ɑ̃t] **1** *adj eau* still; (*Tech*) *châssis* fixed. **2** *nm [porte, châssis]* casing, frame.

dormeur, -euse [dɔʀmœʀ, øz] **1** *adj poupée* with shutting eyes. **2** *nm,f* sleeper; (*péj*) sleepyhead. **3** *nm* (*crabe*) crab. **4 dormeuse** *nf* (*boucle d'oreille*) stud earring.

dormir [dɔʀmiʀ] (16) *vi* **(a)** to sleep; (*être en train de dormir*) to be asleep, be sleeping. ~ **d'un sommeil léger/lourd** to sleep lightly/heavily; **il dormait d'un sommeil agité** he was tossing about in his sleep; **je n'ai pas dormi de la nuit/de 3 jours** I haven't slept a wink (all night)/for 3 days; **avoir envie de** ~ to feel sleepy; **essayez de** ~ **un peu** try to get some sleep; **ça m'empêche de** ~ *[café]* it keeps me awake; *[soucis]* I'm losing sleep over it; **ce n'est pas ça qui va m'empêcher de** ~ I'm not going to lose any sleep over that; **parler/chanter en dormant** to talk/sing in one's sleep.

(b) (*rester inactif*) *[eau]* to be still; *[argent, capital]* to lie idle; *[machines]* to be *ou* lie idle; *[nature, forêt]* to be still, be asleep. **tout dormait dans la maison/ville** everything was quiet *ou* still in the house/town; **investis ton capital plutôt que de le laisser** ~ invest your capital rather than leave it idle; **ce n'est pas le moment de** ~! this is no time for slacking *ou* idling; ~ **sur son travail** to be slack at one's work; *V* **pire.**

(c) (*loc*) **je dors debout** I'm asleep on my feet, I can't keep awake *ou* my eyes open; **une histoire à** ~ **debout** a cock-and-bull story; (*frm*) ~ **(de) son dernier sommeil** to sleep one's last sleep; ~ **comme un loir** *ou* **une marmotte** *ou* **une souche** to sleep like a log; **ne** ~ **que d'un œil** to sleep with one eye open; **il dort à poings fermés** he is sound *ou* fast asleep, he's dead to the world*; **cette nuit je vais** ~ **à poings fermés** tonight I'm going to sleep very soundly; ~ **du sommeil du juste** to sleep the sleep of the just; (*fig*) ~ **tranquille** *ou* **sur ses deux oreilles** (*sans soucis*) to sleep soundly; (*sans danger*) to sleep safely (in one's bed); **il n'en dort pas** *ou* **plus** he's losing sleep over it, he can't sleep for thinking of it; (*Prov*) **qui dort dîne** for the hungry man, to sleep is to dine.

dormitif, -ive [dɔʀmitif, iv] *adj* soporific.

dorsal, e, *mpl* **-aux** [dɔʀsal, o] **1** *adj* (*gén*) dorsal. (*Anat*) **la région** ~**e de la main** the back of the hand; *V* **épine, parachute.** **2 dorsale** *nf* **(a)** (*Ling*) dorsal consonant. **(b)** (*Géog*) ridge. (*Mét*) ~**e barométrique** ridge of high pressure.

dortoir [dɔʀtwaʀ] *nm* dormitory. **cité-** *ou* **ville-**~ dormitory town.

dorure [dɔʀyʀ] *nf* **(a)** (*couche d'or*) gilt, gilding; *[gâteau]* glaze (*of egg yolk*). **uniforme couvert de** ~**s** uniform covered in gold decorations. **(b)** (*action*) gilding.

doryphore [dɔʀifɔʀ] *nm* Colorado beetle.

dos [do] **1** *nm* **(a)** *[être animé, main, vêtement, siège, page]* back; *[livre]* spine; *[langue]* back, upper surface; *[lame, couteau]* blunt edge. **avoir le** ~ **rond** to be round-shouldered; **couché sur le** ~ lying on one's (*ou* its) back; **écrire au** ~ **d'une lettre/enveloppe** to write on the back of a letter/an envelope; **robe décolletée dans le** ~ low-backed dress; **'voir au** ~**'** 'see over'; **aller à** ~ **d'âne/de chameau** to ride on a donkey/a camel; **les vivres sont portés à** ~ **de chameau/d'homme** the supplies are carried by camel/men; **ils partirent, sac au** ~ they set off, (with) their rucksacks on their backs; **porter ses cheveux dans le** ~ to wear one's hair loose *ou* down one's back; **(vu) de** ~ **il a une allure jeune** (seen) from behind *ou* from the back he looks quite young; *V* **gros.**

(b) (*loc*) ~ **à** ~ back to back; (*fig*) **avoir bon** ~**: le train/ta mère a bon** ~ (that's right) blame the train/your mother (*iro*); **renvoyer 2 adversaires** ~ **à** ~ to send away *ou* dismiss 2 opponents unsatisfied; **se mettre qn à** ~ to turn sb against one; (*fig*) **avoir qn sur le** ~ to have sb breathing down one's neck *ou* standing over one; **on l'a dans le** ~‡ that's really messed *ou* mucked (*surtout Brit*) us up‡; **mettre qch sur le** ~ **de qn** (*responsabilité*) to saddle sb with sth, make sb shoulder the responsibility for sth; (*accusation*) to pin sth on sb; **il s'est mis une sale affaire sur le** ~ he has got himself mixed up in a nasty bit of business; **faire des affaires sur le** ~ **de qn** to do a bit of business at sb's expense; **il a tout pris sur le** ~* he bore the brunt of the whole thing; **n'avoir rien à se mettre sur le** ~ not to have a thing to wear; **tomber sur le** ~ **de qn** (*arriver à l'improviste*) to drop in on sb; (*attaquer*) (*lit*) to fall on sb, go for sb; (*fig*) to jump down sb's throat, go for sb; **faire qch dans** *ou* **der-**

rière le ~ de qn to do sth behind sb's back; **nous avions la mer/l'ennemi dans le ~** we had the sea/the enemy behind us *ou* at our back(s); **avoir le ~ tourné à la mer/à la porte** to have one's back to the sea/door; **dès qu'il a le ~ tourné** as soon as his back is turned; **il n'y va pas avec le ~ de la cuiller*** he certainly doesn't go in for half-measures*, there are no half-measures with him; *V* **froid.**

2: dos d'âne humpback (*Brit*), hogback, hogsback (*US*); **pont en dos d'âne** humpback bridge.

dosage [dozaʒ] *nm* (*action: V* **doser**) measuring out; correct proportioning; (*mélange*) mixture. (*fig*) **dans ce domaine, tout est question de ~** it's all a matter of striking a balance *ou* the right balance in this area; (*fig*) **un ~ très réussi de romanesque et de description historique** a most well-balanced mixture of romance and historical description, an excellent balance between romance and historical description.

dose [doz] *nf* **(a)** (*Pharm*) dose. **absorber une ~ excessive de barbituriques** to take an overdose of barbiturates; **s'en tenir à la ~ prescrite** to keep to the prescribed dose *ou* dosage.

(b) (*gén: proportion*) *[ingrédient, élément]* amount, quantity. (*hum*) **il a bu sa ~ quotidienne** he has drunk *ou* had his daily dose (*hum*); **en avoir sa ~*** to have one's share of it; (*fig*) **forcer la ~** to overstep the mark.

(c) (*fig*) **introduire une petite ~ d'ironie dans un récit** to introduce a touch of irony into a story; **il faut pour cela une ~ peu commune de courage/de mauvaise foi** for that you need an above-average amount of courage/bad faith; **affligé d'une forte ~ de stupidité** afflicted with more than one's fair share of stupidity; **j'aime bien la poésie/ce chanteur mais seulement par petites ~s *ou* à petites ~s** I like poetry/that singer all right but only in small doses.

doser [doze] (1) *vt* **(a)** (*Pharm*) *remède* to measure out a dose of; *ingrédient* to measure out; (*Chim, gén*) *ingrédient, élément* to measure out; *mélange* to proportion correctly, mix in the correct proportions.

(b) (*fig: mêler, combiner*) to strike a balance between. **savoir ~ compréhension et sévérité** to be good at striking a balance *ou* the right balance between understanding and severity.

(c) (*mesurer*) **savoir ~ ses efforts** to know how much effort to expend; **cet auteur sait ~ l'ironie** this author has a gift for using irony in just the right amounts.

doseur [dozœʀ] *nm* measure. **bouchon ~** measuring cap.

dossard [dosaʀ] *nm* (*Sport*) number (*worn by competitor*).

dossier [dosje] *nm* **(a)** *[siège]* back. **(b)** (*documents, Jur*) file, dossier. **constituer un ~ sur qn** to draw up a file on sb; (*Presse*) **'le ~ africain/du pétrole'** 'the Africa/oil file'. **(c)** (*classeur*) file, folder.

dot [dɔt] *nf [mariage]* dowry; (*Rel*) (spiritual) dowry. **apporter qch en ~** to bring a dowry of sth, bring sth as one's dowry; *V* **coureur.**

dotal, e, *mpl* **-aux** [dɔtal, o] *adj* dotal, dowry (*épith*).

dotation [dɔtɑsjɔ̃] *nf* (*Jur*) *[institution]* endowment; (*Hist*) *[fonctionnaire, dignitaire]* emolument.

doté, e [dɔte] (*ptp de* **doter**) *adj* (*pourvu*) **~ de** *équipement, matériel, dispositif* equipped with; *talent, courage, pouvoir* endowed with.

doter [dɔte] (1) *vt* **(a)** (*Jur*) *fille à marier* to provide with a dowry, dower; *institution* to endow; (*Hist*) *fonctionnaire, dignitaire* to endow with an emolument. **~ richement sa fille** to provide one's daughter with a large dowry.

(b) (*pourvoir de*) **~ de: ~ une armée d'un équipement moderne** to equip an army with modern equipment; **la nature l'avait doté d'un grand talent** nature had endowed him with *ou* had bestowed upon him a great talent.

douaire [dwɛʀ] *nm* dower.

douairière [dwɛʀjɛʀ] *nf* dowager.

douane [dwan] *nf* **(a)** (*service*) **~,** (*Admin*) **(service des) ~s** Customs; **il est employé aux ~s *ou* à la ~** he is employed by *ou* in the Customs (department); **marchandises (entreposées) en ~** bonded goods, goods in bond; *V* **bureau.**

(b) (*à la frontière*) **poste de ~,** ~ customs; **maison de la ~, ~** customs house, customs; (*à l'aéroport etc*) **passer à la ~** to go through (the) customs; (*dans le train*) **la visite de la ~** the customs check.

(c) (droits de) ~ customs dues *ou* duty, duty; **exempté de ~** duty-free, non-dutiable.

douanier, -ière [dwanje, jɛʀ] **1** *adj* custom(s) (*épith*); *V* **union.**

2 *nm,f* customs officer.

doublage [dublaʒ] *nm* **(a)** *[fil]* doubling; *[revêtement]* doubling, laying double; *[couverture]* doubling, folding (in half).

(b) *[film]* dubbing. **le ~ d'un acteur** standing in for an actor.

(c) *[vêtement, paroi, boîte, tableau]* lining; (*Naut*) *[coque]* sheathing.

(d) *[somme, quantité, lettre]* doubling.

double [dubl(ə)] **1** *adj* **(a)** *consonne, longueur, épaisseur* double; *inconvénient, avantage* double, twofold. **le prix est ~ de ce qu'il était** the price is double *ou* twice what it was; **faire qch en ~ exemplaire** to make two copies of sth, do sth in duplicate; **dispositif/machine à ~ effet** double-action *ou* dual-action device/machine; **ustensile à ~ usage** dual-purpose utensil; **faire ~ emploi** to be redundant; **cet appareil fait maintenant ~ emploi avec l'ancien** this apparatus now duplicates the old one *ou* makes the old one redundant; **fermer une porte à ~ tour** to double-lock a door; **enfermer qn à ~ tour** to put sb under lock and key; **à ~ tranchant** (*lit, fig*) double-edged; **boîte/valise à ~ fond** box/case with a false bottom; **mettre un fil (en) ~** to use a double thread, use a thread double(d); **mettre une couverture (en) ~** to put a blanket on double; *V* **bouchée, coup.**

(b) (*qui a des aspects opposés*) *vie, aspect* double. **à ~ face** *tissu* reversible; (*fig*) two-faced; **accusé de jouer un ~ jeu** accused of double-dealing *ou* of playing a double game (*Brit*); **phrase à ~ sens *ou* entente** sentence with a double meaning; *V* **agent.**

2 *nm* **(a)** (*quantité*) **manger/gagner le ~ (de qn)** to eat/earn twice as much (as sb) *ou* double the amount (that sb does); **il pèse le ~ de vous** he weighs *ou* is twice your weight, he weighs twice as much as you do; **4 est le ~ de 2** 4 is two times *ou* twice 2; **c'est le ~ du prix normal** it is twice *ou* double the normal price; **c'est le ~ de la distance Paris-Lyon** it's twice *ou* double the distance from Paris to Lyons; **hier il a mis le ~ de temps à faire ce travail** yesterday he took twice as long *ou* double the time to do this job; **nous attendons le ~ de gens** we expect twice as many people *ou* double the number of people; *V* **quitte.**

(b) (*copie, duplicata*) *[facture, acte]* copy; *[timbre]* duplicate, double, swap*; *[personne]* double; *[objet d'art]* replica, exact copy. **je viens de voir son ~** I've just seen his double; **il a tous les documents en ~** he has copies of all the documents; **on a tout en ~, pour plus de sûreté** we have two of everything to be on the safe side; **plier qch en ~** to fold sth in half *ou* in two.

(c) (*Tennis*) doubles. **le ~ dames/messieurs/mixte est renvoyé** the ladies'/men's/mixed doubles has been postponed; **faire un ~** to play a doubles match.

3 *adv payer, compter* double; *V* **voir.**

4: (*Tech*) **double allumage** *nm* dual ignition; (*Dominos*) **double-blanc** *nm, pl* **double-blancs** double blank; (*Tech*) **double commande** *nf* dual controls; **double-crème** *nm inv* cream cheese; (*Mus*) **double croche** *nf* semiquaver (*Brit*), sixteenth note (*US*); (*Aut*) **faire un double-débrayage** to double-declutch; **double-décimètre** *nm, pl* **double-décimètres** (20-cm) ruler; **double-fenêtre** *nf, pl* **double-fenêtres** double window; **double mètre** *nm* two-metre tape measure *ou* (measuring) tape; **double nœud** *nm* double knot; **doubles rideaux** *nmpl* double curtains; **double vue** *nf* second sight.

doublé, e [duble] (*ptp de* **doubler**) **1** *adj* **(a)** *vêtement* lined (*de* with). **~ de cuir/cuivre** *boîte, paroi* lined with leather/copper; **non ~** unlined; **~ de fourrure** fur-lined; **~ (de) coton/nylon** cotton-/nylon-lined, lined with cotton/nylon.

(b) *film* dubbed.

2 *nm* **(a)** (*victoire, réussite: Sport, fig*) double; (*coup double: Chasse*) right and left.

(b) (*Orfèvrerie*) rolled gold.

doublement [dubləmɑ̃] **1** *adv* (*pour deux raisons*) for a double reason, for two reasons; (*à un degré double*) doubly.

2 *nm* **(a)** *[somme, quantité, lettre]* doubling.

(b) *[feuille]* doubling, folding (in half); *[fil]* doubling.

(c) *[véhicule]* overtaking (*Brit*), passing.

doubler [duble] (1) **1** *vt* **(a)** (*augmenter*) *fortune, dose, longueur* to double. **~ le pas** to quicken one's pace, speed up; **~ (le salaire de) qn** to double sb's salary; **il a doublé son poids** he has doubled his weight.

(b) (*mettre en double*) *fil, ficelle* to use double, double; *revêtement* to double, lay double; *couverture* to double, fold (in half). **il faut ~ la ficelle pour que ce soit plus solide** you'll have to use the thread double *ou* double the thread to make it stronger.

(c) (*Scol*) *classe, année* to repeat.

(d) (*Ciné, Théât*) *acteur* to stand in for, double; *film* to dub.

(e) (*revêtir*) *boîte, paroi, tableau,* (*Habillement*) *veste, robe* to line (*de* with). **~ de fourrure une veste** to line a jacket with fur.

(f) (*dépasser*) *véhicule* to overtake (*Brit*), pass; (*Naut*) *cap* to double, round. (*fig*) **il a doublé ce cap important** he has got over this important hurdle *ou* turned this important corner; **~ le cap des 50 ans** to turn 50, pass the 50 mark.

2 *vi* **(a)** (*augmenter*) *[nombre, quantité, prix]* to double, increase twofold. **~ de poids/valeur** to double in weight/value; **le nombre des crimes a doublé** the number of crimes has doubled *ou* increased twofold.

(b) (*Aut*) to overtake (*Brit*), pass.

3 se doubler *vpr*: **se ~ de** to be coupled with; **chez lui le sens de l'honneur se double de courage** with him a sense of honour is coupled with *ou* goes hand in hand with courage; **ce dispositif se double d'un système d'alarme** this device works *ou* functions in conjunction with an alarm system; **c'est un savant doublé d'un pédagogue** he is a teacher as well as a scholar.

doublet [dublɛ] *nm* **(a)** (*Ling*) doublet. **(b)** (*Orfèvrerie*) doublet.

doublon [dublɔ̃] *nm* **(a)** (*monnaie*) doubloon. **(b)** (*Typ*) double.

doublure [dublyʀ] *nf* **(a)** (*étoffe*) lining. **(b)** (*Théât*) understudy; (*Ciné*) stand-in; (*pour scènes dangereuses*) stuntman (*ou* stuntwoman).

douce [dus] *V* **doux.**

douce-amère, *pl* **douces-amères** [dusamɛʀ] *nf* (*Bot*) woody nightshade, bittersweet.

douceâtre [dusɑtʀ(ə)] *adj saveur* sickly sweet; (*péj*) *air, sourire* sickly sweet, mawkish.

doucement [dusmɑ̃] **1** *adv* **(a)** (*légèrement*) *toucher, prendre, soulever* carefully, gently; *frapper* gently, softly; *éclairer* softly; *sourire, caresser* gently. **marcher ~** to tread carefully *ou* softly; **allez-y ~!*** easy *ou* gently does it!*, go easy!*

(b) (*à voix basse*) *parler, jouer* softly, quietly; (*sans colère*) *réprimander, parler* gently. **elle le gronda ~** she scolded him gently.

(c) (*graduellement*) *monter, progresser* gently, gradually; (*lentement*) *rouler, avancer* slowly; (*en douceur*) *démarrer* smoothly. **la route monte/descend ~** the road climbs/descends gradually *ou* goes gently up/down; **la température monte/descend ~** the temperature is slowly *ou* gradually rising/falling.

(d) (*: *tranquillement*) so-so*. **comment allez-vous? — (tout) ~** how are you? — so-so*.

(e) (*: *en cachette*) **s'amuser ~ de voir qn dans l'embarras** to have a quiet laugh* (to o.s.) at seeing sb in difficulties; **ça me fait ~ rigoler!** it doesn't half make me laugh!*

2 *excl*: ~! gently!, easy!; ~ **avec le whisky!** go easy on the whisky!*, careful with the whisky!; ~ **les basses!‡** take it easy!*, go easy!*

doucereux, -euse [dusʀø, øz] *adj goût, saveur* sickly sweet; (*péj*) *ton, paroles* sugary, honeyed; (*péj*) *personne, manières* suave, smooth*.

doucet, -ette [dusɛ, ɛt] **1** *adj* (†) meek, mild. **2 doucette** *nf* (*Bot*) corn-salad.

doucettement* [dusɛtmɑ̃] *adv commencer, avancer* gently; *vivre* quietly.

douceur [dusœʀ] *nf* **(a)** (*U: V* **doux**) softness; smoothness; mildness; gentleness; sweetness. ~ **angélique** angelic sweetness; **prendre qn par la ~** to deal gently with sb, use gentleness with sb; ~ **de vivre** gentle way of life; **les ~s de l'amitié** the (sweet) pleasures of friendship; *V* **plus.**

(b) (*gén pl*) (*sucrerie*) sweet; (*flatterie*) sweet talk (*U*).

(c) en ~ *démarrer* smoothly; *commencer, manœuvrer* gently; **il faut y aller en ~** we must go about it gently; **ça s'est passé en ~** it went off smoothly.

douche [duʃ] **1** *nf* **(a)** (*jet*) shower; (*système*) shower (bath). **prendre une ~** to have *ou* take a shower; **passer à la ~** to go for a shower. **(b)** (*salle*) ~s shower room. **(c)** (**fig*) (*déception*) let-down*; (*réprimande*) (good) telling-off* *ou* ticking-off* (*Brit*); (*averse, arrosage*) soaking, drenching. **ça nous a fait l'effet d'une ~ (froide) quand nous l'avons appris** it was a real let-down* when we found out.

2: douche écossaise (*rare: lit*) alternately hot and cold shower; (**fig*) series of ups and downs; **c'est vraiment la douche écossaise** it's all up one minute and down the next*, it's all ups and downs at the moment*.

doucher [duʃe] (1) **1** *vt* (*V* **douche**) ~ **qn** to give sb a shower; to let sb down (with a bump)*; to give sb a (good) telling-off* *ou* ticking-off* (*Brit*); to soak *ou* drench sb. **2 se doucher** *vpr* to have *ou* take a shower.

doué, e [dwe] (*ptp de* **douer**) *adj* **(a)** (*talentueux*) gifted, talented (*en* in). **être ~ pour** to have a gift for; (*iro*) **il n'est pas ~*** he's not exactly bright *ou* clever (*iro*).

(b) (*pourvu de*) ~ **de** *vie, raison* endowed with; *intelligence, talent, mémoire* blessed with, endowed with.

douer [dwe] (1) *vt*: ~ **qn de** *vie, raison* to endow sb with; *intelligence, talent, mémoire* to bless sb with, endow sb with.

douille [duj] *nf* [*cartouche*] (cartridge) case, cartridge; [*fil électrique*] (electric light) socket; [*manche*] socket.

douillet, -ette [dujɛ, ɛt] **1** *adj* **(a)** (*péj*) *personne* soft (*péj*). **(b)** *maison, atmosphère* cosy, snug; *nid, lit* soft, cosy; *vie* soft, cosy. **2 douillette** *nf* [*ecclésiastique*] (clerical) overcoat; [*bébé*] quilted coat.

douillettement [dujɛtmɑ̃] *adv* cosily, snugly. (*péj*) **élever un enfant ~** to (molly)coddle a child (*péj*).

douilletterie [dujɛtʀi] *nf* (*péj*) softness (*péj*).

douleur [dulœʀ] *nf* **(a)** (*physique*) pain. ~**s rhumatismales** rheumatic pains; ~**s dorsales** backache (*U*), back pains; **les ~s (de l'accouchement)** labour pains; *V* **accouchement.**

(b) (*morale*) grief, distress. **il a eu la ~ de perdre son frère** he had the distress of *ou* had to suffer the grief of losing his brother; **'nous avons la ~ de vous faire part du décès de'** 'it is our sad duty to tell you *ou* it is with great sorrow that we have to tell you of the death of'; **'nous avons la ~ d'apprendre que ...'** 'it was with great sorrow that we learned that ...'; *V* **grand.**

douloureusement [duluʀøzmɑ̃] *adv* (*V* **douloureux**) painfully; grievously; distressingly; distressfully.

douloureux, -euse [duluʀø, øz] **1** *adj* **(a)** *sensation, maladie, opération, membre* painful.

(b) *perte* grievous, distressing; *décision, spectacle* painful, distressing, harrowing; *séparation, circonstances, moment* painful, distressing; *regard, expression* distressed, pained.

2 douloureuse* *nf* (*hum: addition*) bill (*Brit*), check (*US*); **apportez-nous la ~euse** let's hear the worst* (*hum*), let's hear the extent of the damage* (*hum*), bring us the bad news* (*hum*); **la ~euse s'élevait à près de 1.000 F** the damage came to well-nigh 1,000 francs (*hum*).

doute [dut] *nm* **(a)** (*état d'incertitude*) doubt, uncertainty; (*Philos, Rel*) doubt. **être dans le ~** to be doubtful *ou* uncertain; **laisser qn dans le ~** to leave sb in (a state of) uncertainty; **être dans le ~ au sujet de qch** to be in doubt *ou* doubtful *ou* uncertain about sth; **le ~ l'envahit** he was invaded by doubt; **le ~ n'est plus permis quant à ...** there is no more room for doubt concerning ...; **le ~ subsiste quant à** there is still room for doubt concerning; **un air de ~** a doubtful air.

(b) (*soupçon, perplexité*) doubt. **je n'ai pas le moindre ~ à ce sujet** I haven't the slightest doubt about it; **avoir des ~s sur** *ou* **au sujet de qch/qn** to have misgivings *ou* (one's) doubts about sth/sb; **malgré tout, j'ai des ~s** nevertheless, I have my doubts; **il a émis des ~s à propos de ...** he expressed (his) doubts *ou* misgivings about ...; **un ~ plane sur l'affaire** a certain amount of *ou* an element of doubt hangs over the matter.

(c) (*loc*) (*Prov*) **dans le ~, abstiens-toi** when in doubt, don't!; **sans ~** (*vraisemblablement*) doubtless, no doubt; **sans (nul** *ou* **aucun) ~** (*incontestablement*) without (a) doubt; **sans ~ qu'il s'est trompé** he is doubtless *ou* no doubt mistaken; **il ne fait aucun ~ que ...** there is (absolutely) no doubt that ...; **ceci ne fait aucun ~** there is no doubt about it; **mettre en ~** *affirmation, honnêteté de qn* to question, challenge; **mettre en ~ que** to question whether; *V* **hors, ombre**[1].

douter [dute] (1) **1 douter de** *vt indir* **(a)** (*sentiment d'incertitude*) *identité, authenticité, existence de qch* to doubt, question, have doubts as to; *réussite* to be doubtful of. **je doute de l'authenticité de ce document** I doubt *ou* question the authenticity of this document, I have doubts as to the authenticity of this document; **il le dit mais j'en doute** he says so but I have my doubts *ou* but I doubt it; **il a dit la vérité, n'en doutez pas** he is telling the truth, you can be sure of that *ou* there's no doubt about that; **je doute d'avoir jamais fait/dit cela** I doubt that I ever did/said that; **je n'ai jamais douté du résultat** I never had any doubts about *ou* as to the result; ~ **que** + *subj*: **je doute qu'il vienne** I doubt if *ou* whether he'll come; **je ne doute pas qu'il le fera** *ou* **ne le fasse** I don't doubt *ou* I dare say that he'll do it; (*littér*) ~ **si** to doubt whether.

(b) (*Philos, Rel: esprit de réfutation*) ~ **de** *dogme philosophique ou religieux* to have *ou* entertain (*frm*) doubts about, doubt; **mieux vaut ~ que tout accepter** it is better to doubt than to accept everything.

(c) (*sentiment de méfiance*) ~ **de** *allié, sincérité de qn* to have (one's) doubts about, doubt; **je n'ai jamais douté de vous** I never doubted you, I never had any doubts about you; ~ **de la parole de qn** to doubt sb's word; **à n'en pas ~** undoubtedly, (there is) no doubt about it, without a doubt; **il ne doute de rien!*** he's got some nerve!*

2 se douter *vpr*: **se ~ de qch** to suspect sth; **je me doute de son inquiétude quand il apprendra la nouvelle** I can (just) imagine his anxiety when he learns the news; **je ne m'en suis jamais douté** I never guessed *ou* suspected for a moment; **ça, je m'en doutais depuis longtemps** I've thought so *ou* thought as much *ou* suspected as much for a long time; **j'étais (bien) loin de me douter que ...** little did I know that ...; **se ~ que** to suspect that, have an idea that; **il ne se doutait pas qu'elle serait là** he had no idea *ou* hadn't suspected (that) she would be there; **qu'il soit fâché, je m'en doute** I can well imagine that he's angry.

douteux, -euse [dutø, øz] *adj* **(a)** (*incertain*) *fait* doubtful, questionable, uncertain; *résultat, issue* doubtful, uncertain; *sens, date, réponse* doubtful. **il est ~ que** it is doubtful *ou* questionable that *ou* whether; **il n'est pas ~ que** there is no doubt that; **d'origine ~euse** of uncertain *ou* doubtful origin.

(b) (*péj*) (*médiocre*) *raisonnement, propreté, qualité* dubious, questionable; (*peu solide ou propre*) *vêtements, assiette, aliment* dubious-looking; *amarrage, passerelle* shaky, dubious-looking; *réputation, mœurs* dubious, doubtful, questionable; *individu* dubious, doubtful. **d'un goût ~** *décoration, cravate, plaisanterie* in questionable *ou* dubious taste.

douve [duv] *nf* **(a)** [*château*] moat; (*Agr*) drainage ditch; (*Équitation*) water jump. **(b)** [*tonneau*] stave. **(c)** (*Vét, Zool*) fluke. ~ **du foie** liver fluke.

Douvres [duvʀ(ə)] *n* Dover.

doux, douce [du, dus] **1** *adj* **(a)** (*lisse*) *peau, tissu* soft, smooth; (*souple, moelleux*) *matelas, suspension, brosse* soft; *V* **fer, lime.**

(b) (*non calcaire*) *eau* soft; *V aussi* **eau.**

(c) (*clément*) *temps, climat, température* mild; *brise, chaleur* gentle; (*Culin*) *feu* gentle, low. (*iro*) **il fait une douce chaleur** it's sweltering, it's not exactly cool (*iro*).

(d) (*au goût*) (*sucré*) *fruit, saveur, liqueur* sweet; (*pas fort*) *moutarde, fromage, tabac, piment* mild. ~ **comme le miel** as sweet as honey; *V* **orange.**

(e) (*à l'ouïe, la vue*) *son, musique, accents* sweet, gentle; *lumière, couleur* soft, mellow, subdued. **un nom aux consonances douces** a sweet-sounding name.

(f) (*modéré, peu brusque*) *pente, montée* gentle, gradual; *démarrage* smooth; *voiture, moteur* smooth-running. **en pente douce** gently sloping.

(g) (*patient, tolérant*) *personne, caractère, manières* mild, gentle; *sourire* gentle; (*non brutal*) *geste, personne, voix* gentle; *reproche* gentle, mild; *punition* mild. **il est ~ comme un agneau** he's as meek (*Brit*) *ou* gentle as a lamb; *V* **œil.**

(h) (*gén avant n: agréable*) *victoire, revanche, repos, tranquillité* sweet; *parfum, souvenirs, pensées* sweet, agreeable, pleasant. **se faire une douce violence** to inflict a pleasant burden upon o.s.; **cette pensée lui était douce** this thought gave him great pleasure; **qu'il m'était ~ de repenser à ces moments** what pleasure it gave me *ou* how pleasant *ou* agreeable for me to think over those moments; *V* **billet, couler.**

(i) (*loc*) **en douce** on the quiet.

2 *adv*: **ça va tout ~*** things are going so-so*; († *ou hum*) **tout ~!** gently (now)!, careful (now)!; *V* **filer.**

3 *nm,f* (*parfois péj: personne douce*) mild(-natured) person.

4 *nm*: **le ~** sweet tastes *ou* things; **préférer le ~ à l'amer** to prefer sweet tastes *ou* things to bitter.

5 douce *nf* († *ou hum: amoureuse*) sweetheart†.

douzain [duzɛ̃] *nm* (*Poésie*) twelve-line poem; (*Hist: monnaie*) douzain (*obsolete French coin*).

douzaine [duzɛn] *nf* (*douze*) dozen. (*environ douze*) **une ~** about *ou* roughly twelve, a dozen (or so); **une ~ d'huîtres/d'œufs** a dozen oysters/eggs; **une ~ d'années** roughly *ou* about twelve years, a dozen years (or so); **vendre qch à la ~** to sell sth by the dozen; (*fig*) **il y en a à la ~** there are dozens of them; *V* **treize.**

douze [duz] **1** *adj inv* twelve. (*Hist*) **les ~ tables** the Twelve Tables; (*Comm*) ~ **douzaines** a gross, twelve dozen; *pour loc V* **six. 2** *nm inv* twelve; *pour loc V* **six.**

douzième [duzjɛm] *adj, nmf* twelfth; *pour loc V* **sixième.**

douzièmement [duzjɛmmɑ̃] *adv* in (the) twelfth place, twelfthly.

doyen, -enne [dwajɛ̃, ɛn] *nm,f* (*Rel, Univ*) dean; [*équipe, groupe*] most senior member. [*assemblée, corps constitué*] ~ **(d'âge)** most senior member, doyen.

doyenné [dwajene] **1** *nm* (*Rel*) (*circonscription*) deanery; (*charge*) deanery, deanship. **2** *nf* (*poire*) ~ **(du comice)** comice (pear).

drachme [dʀakm(ə)] *nf* drachma.
draconien, -ienne [dʀakɔnjɛ̃, jɛn] *adj loi* excessively severe, draconian; *mesure* drastic, stringent, draconian.
dragage [dʀagaʒ] *nm* (*Tech: V* **draguer**) dredging; dragging. ~ **des mines** minesweeping.
dragée [dʀaʒe] *nf* **(a)** (*friandise*) sugared almond, dragée; (*Méd*) sugar-coated pill, dragée (*T*). **(b)** (*plomb de chasse*) small shot. **(c)** (*Agr*) dredge. **(d)** (*loc*) **tenir la ~ haute à qn** to make sb pay dearly (for sth).
dragéifier [dʀaʒeifje] (7) *vt* to sugar, coat with sugar. **comprimé dragéifié** sugared *ou* sugar-coated tablet.
dragon [dʀagɔ̃] *nm* **(a)** (*Myth, fig*) dragon. (*Zool*) ~ **volant** flying lizard *ou* dragon; (*fig*) **un ~ de vertu** a dragon of virtue. **(b)** (*Hist Mil*) dragoon. **~s (portés)**† motorcycle brigade.
dragonnade [dʀagɔnad] *nf* (*Hist*) dragonnade.
dragonne [dʀagɔn] *nf* *[épée]* sword-knot; *[parapluie]* loop (*for wrist*); *[bâton de ski]* wrist-strap.
dragonnier [dʀagɔnje] *nm* dragon tree.
drague [dʀag] *nf* **(a)** (*Pêche*) dragnet. **(b)** (*Tech*) (*machine*) dredge; (*navire, ponton*) dredger.
draguer [dʀage] (1) **1** *vt* **(a)** (*Pêche*) to fish with a dragnet.
(b) (*Tech*) (*pour nettoyer*) to dredge; (*pour trouver qch*) to drag; *mines* to sweep.
(c) (*Naut*) *[ancre]* ~ **(le fond)** to drag.
(d) (*:fig*) to chat up: (*Brit*), try and pick up: *ou* get off with: (*Brit*).
2 *vi* (:) to chat up girls: (*Brit*), try and pick up: birds* (*Brit*) *ou* girls.
dragueur [dʀagœʀ] *nm* (*pêcheur*) dragnet fisherman; (*ouvrier*) dredger; (*bateau*) dredger; (*:fig*) bloke* *ou* guy* who's always after the girls. ~ **de mines** minesweeper.
drain [dʀɛ̃] *nm* (*Agr*) (underground) drain; (*Méd*) drain.
drainage [dʀɛnaʒ] *nm* (*V* **drainer**) drainage; tapping, draining off.
drainer [dʀene] (1) *vt* (*Agr, Méd*) to drain; (*fig*) *main d'œuvre, capitaux* to drain (off), tap.
draisienne [dʀɛzjɛn] *nf* (*Hist*) dandy horse.
draisine [dʀezin] *nf* (*Rail*) track motorcar (*Brit*), gang car (*US*).
dramatique [dʀamatik] **1** *adj* **(a)** (*Théât*) *art, spectacle, artiste* dramatic. **(b)** (*passionnant, épique*) dramatic; (*tragique*) tragic. **2** *nf* (*TV*) **(émission)** ~ (television) play *ou* drama.
dramatiquement [dʀamatikmɑ̃] *adv* (*de façon épique*) dramatically; (*tragiquement*) tragically.
dramatisation [dʀamatizɑsjɔ̃] *nf* dramatization.
dramatiser [dʀamatize] (1) *vt* to dramatize.
dramaturge [dʀamatyʀʒ(ə)] *nmf* dramatist, playwright.
dramaturgie [dʀamatyʀʒi] *nf* (*art*) dramatic art, dramaturgy (*rare*); (*traité*) treatise on dramatic art.
drame [dʀam] *nm* **(a)** (*Théât*) drama. **l'histoire du ~** the history of (the) drama; ~ **lyrique** lyric drama.
(b) (*événement tragique*) drama, tragedy. ~ **de la jalousie** drama *ou* tragedy of jealousy; **la farce tournait au ~** the joke was going tragically wrong; **faire un ~ de qch** to make a drama out of sth; **n'en faites pas un ~** don't be so dramatic (about it), don't make (such) a drama out of it.
drap [dʀa] *nm* **(a)** (*tissu*) woollen cloth. **(b)** (*pièce de tissu*) ~ **(de lit)** sheet; **~s de soie/nylon** silk/nylon sheets; ~ **de dessus/dessous** top/bottom sheet; **être entre deux** *ou* **dans les ~s** to be between the sheets; (*fig*) **mettre qn dans de vilains ~s** *ou* (*iro*) **dans de beaux ~s** to land sb in a fine mess *ou* a nice pickle*.
drapé, e [dʀape] (*ptp de* **draper**) **1** *adj* draped. **tambours ~s** muffled drums. **2** *nm* draping (*U*).
drapeau, *pl* **~x** [dʀapo] *nm* **(a)** (*gén*) flag. **le ~ tricolore** the tricolour; **le ~ blanc/rouge** the white/red flag. **(b)** (*fig*) (*patrie*) flag; (*armée*) colours. **le respect du ~** respect for the flag; **être/combattre sous les ~x** to serve/fight with the colours. **(c)** (*fig: emblème*) flag. **le ~ de la liberté** the flag of liberty. **(d)** (*Naut*) **en ~** feathered; **mettre une hélice en ~** to feather a propeller.
draper [dʀape] (1) **1** *vt* to drape; (*Tex*) *laine* to process. **un foulard de soie drapait ses épaules** a silk scarf was draped over her shoulders, her shoulders were draped in a silk scarf.
2 se draper *vpr*: **se ~ dans** to drape o.s. in; (*fig péj*) **se ~ dans sa dignité** to stand on one's dignity; (*fig péj*) **se ~ dans sa vertu/son honnêteté** to cloak o.s. in one's virtue/honesty.
draperie [dʀapʀi] *nf* (*tenture*) drapery, hanging; (*Comm*) drapery, cloth; (*Art*) drapery.
drapier, -ière [dʀapje, jɛʀ] **1** *adj*: **industrie ~ière** clothing industry; **ouvrier ~** cloth-worker. **2** *nm* (*fabricant*) (woollen) cloth manufacturer. **(marchand) ~** draper (*Brit*), clothier.
drastique [dʀastik] *adj* (*Méd, gén*) drastic.
drave* [dʀav] *nf* (*Can Hist*) *[bois]* drive, rafting.
draver* [dʀave] (1) *vt* (*Can Hist*) *bois* to drive, raft.
draveur* [dʀavœʀ] *nm* (*Can Hist*) (log *ou* timber) driver, raftsman.
dravidien, -ienne [dʀavidjɛ̃, jɛn] *adj* Dravidian.
dressage [dʀɛsaʒ] *nm* **(a)** (*domptage: V* **dresser**) taming; breaking in; training; knocking *ou* licking into shape*. **(b)** (*rare*) *[tente]* pitching; *[échafaudage]* erection.
dresser [dʀese] (1) **1** *vt* **(a)** (*établir*) *inventaire, liste* to draw up, make out; *plan, carte* to draw up. (*Jur*) **~ un acte** to draw up an act; **~ (un) procès-verbal** *ou* **(une) contravention à qn** to report sb, book sb*; **il a dressé un bilan encourageant de la situation** he gave an encouraging review of the situation *ou* an encouraging run-down* on the situation.
(b) (*ériger*) *monument, statue, échafaudage* to put up, erect; *barrière, échelle* to put up, set up; *tente* to pitch, put up, erect; *mât* to raise, put up, erect; *lit* to put up. **nous avons dressé un buffet dans le jardin** we set *ou* laid out a buffet in the garden; **~ le couvert** *ou* **la table** to lay *ou* set the table.
(c) (*inciter*) **~ qn contre** to set sb against.
(d) *tête* to raise, lift; *menton* to stick out, jut out. (*fig*) **~ l'oreille** to prick up one's ears; *[chien]* **~ l'oreille** *ou* **ses oreilles** to prick up *ou* cock (up) its ears; **faire ~ les cheveux sur la tête à qn** to make sb's hair stand on end; **une histoire à faire ~ les cheveux sur la tête** a hair-raising story.
(e) (*dompter*) *animal sauvage* to tame; *cheval* to break (in); (*pour le cirque etc*) *chien, cheval* to train; (*) *recrue* to knock *ou* lick into shape*. **~ un chien à rapporter** to train a dog to retrieve; **animaux dressés** performing animals; **ça le dressera!*** that will knock *ou* lick him into shape*; **~ le poil à qn:** to rub sb up the wrong way*; **~ un enfant*** to teach a child his place; **les enfants/les élèves, ça se dresse!*** children/pupils should be taught their place.
2 se dresser *vpr* **(a)** *[personne]* to stand up (straight), draw o.s. up; (*assis*) to sit up (straight). **se ~ sur la pointe des pieds** to stand up on tiptoe; **se ~ de toute sa taille** to draw o.s. up to one's full height; **se ~ sur ses pattes de derrière** *[animal]* to rise (up) on(to) *ou* stand up on its hind legs; *[cheval]* to rear (up); *V* **ergot.**
(b) *[cheveux]* to stand on end; *[oreille]* to prick up.
(c) *[statue, bâtiment, obstacle]* to stand; (*avec grandeur, menace*) to tower (up). **un navire se dressa soudain dans le brouillard** a ship suddenly loomed (up) out of the fog.
(d) (*s'insurger*) to rise up (*contre, face à* against). **se ~ en justicier** to set o.s. up as dispenser of justice.
dresseur, -euse [dʀɛsœʀ, øz] *nm,f* trainer (*of animals*). **~ de lions/fauves** lion/wild animal tamer.
dressoir [dʀɛswaʀ] *nm* dresser.
dreyfusard, e [dʀɛfyzaʀ, aʀd(ə)] **1** *adj* (*Hist*) supporting *ou* defending Dreyfus. **2** *nm,f* supporter *ou* defender of Dreyfus.
dribble [dʀibl(ə)] *nm* (*Ftbl*) dribble.
dribbler [dʀible] (1) (*Ftbl*) **1** *vi* to dribble. **2** *vt* *ballon* to dribble; *joueur* to dribble past *ou* round.
drill [dʀij] *nm* (*Scol etc: exercices*) drill.
drille [dʀij] **1** *nm* (†) **bon** *ou* **joyeux ~** cheerful character*. **2** *nf* (*Tech*) hand-drill.
dring [dʀiŋ] *excl, nm* ding, ding-a-ling.
drisse [dʀis] *nf* (*Naut*) halyard.
drogue [dʀɔg] *nf* **(a)** (*Pharm*†) drug; (*péj*) patent medicine, quack remedy (*péj*). **(b)** (*stupéfiant*) drug; (*U*) drugs. **les ravages de la ~** the ravages of drugs; **une ~ dure/douce** a hard/soft drug; *V* **trafic.**
drogué, e [dʀɔge] (*ptp de* **droguer**) *nm,f* drug addict.
droguer [dʀɔge] (1) **1** *vt* **(a)** *malade* (*péj*) to dose up (*péj*); (*Méd*†) to give drugs to.
(b) *victime* to drug.
2 se droguer *vpr* **(a)** (*péj: de médicaments*) to dose o.s. (up) (*de* with).
(b) (*de stupéfiants*) to take drugs. **il se drogue** he's on drugs, he's taking drugs.
3 *vi* (*†: *attendre*) to kick *ou* cool one's heels*. **faire ~ qn** to leave sb kicking *ou* cooling his heels*.
droguerie [dʀɔgʀi] *nf* (*commerce*) drug trade; (*magasin*) hardware shop.
droguet [dʀɔgɛ] *nm* (*Tex*) drugget.
droguiste [dʀɔgist(ə)] *nmf* owner *ou* (*gérant*) keeper of hardware shop.
droit[1], **e**[1] [dʀwa, dʀwat] **1** *adj* (*après n: contraire de gauche*) *main, bras, jambe* right; *poche, soulier* right (-hand). **du côté ~** on the right-hand side; *V* **bras, centre, main.**
2 *nm* (*Boxe*) (*coup*) right. (*poing*) **direct du ~** straight right; **crochet du ~** right hook.
3 droite *nf* **(a) la ~e** the right (side), the right-hand side; **à ~e** on the right; (*direction*) to the right; **3e rue à ~e** 3rd street on the right; **à ma/sa ~e** on my/his right (hand), on my/his right (-hand) side; **le tiroir/chemin de ~e** the right-hand drawer/path; **il ne connaît pas sa ~e de sa gauche** he can't tell (his) left from (his) right; **à ~e de la fenêtre** to the right of the window; **de ~e à gauche** from right to left; **à ~e et à gauche,** (*frm, littér*) **de ~e et de gauche** (*de tous côtés*) this way and that; **il a couru à ~e et à gauche pour se renseigner** he tried everywhere *ou* all over the place to get some information; **c'est ce qu'on entend dire de ~e et de gauche** that's what one hears from all sides *ou* quarters.
(b) (*Aut*) **la ~e** the right; **rouler à ~e** to drive on the right; **garder** *ou* **tenir sa ~e** to keep to the right; **et votre ~e!** get *ou* move over!; *V* **conduite.**
(c) (*Pol*) **la ~e** the right (wing); **candidat/idées de ~e** right-wing candidate/ideas; **un homme de ~e** a man of the right; **elle est très à ~e** she's very right-wing *ou* very much on the right; **la ~e est divisée** the right wing is split; *V* **extrême.**
(d) (*Boxe*) (*coup*) right. (*main*) **crochet de la ~e** right hook.
droit[2], **e**[2] [dʀwa, dʀwat] **1** *adj* **(a)** (*sans déviation, non courbe*) *barre, ligne, route, nez* straight. **il va en ~e ligne à la ruine** he's making *ou* heading *ou* headed straight for disaster; **ça fait 4 km en ~e ligne** it's 4 km as the crow flies; (*fig*) **cela vient en ~e ligne de ...** that comes straight *ou* direct from ...; (*Rel*) **le ~ chemin** the straight and narrow (way); (*Couture*) **~ fil** straight grain; *V* **coup.**
(b) (*vertical, non penché*) *arbre, mur* upright, straight; (*Géom*) *prisme, cylindre, cône* right; *écriture* upright. **ce tableau n'est pas ~** this picture isn't (hanging) straight; **est-ce que mon chapeau est ~?** is my hat (on) straight?; **jupe ~e** straight skirt; **veston ~** single-breasted jacket; **tiens ta tasse ~e** hold your cup straight *ou* level; (*péj, hum*) **être ~ comme un pieu** *ou* **un piquet** to be as stiff as a poker *ou* ramrod (*péj*); **être ~ comme un i** to have a very upright posture, hold o.s. very erect; **se tenir ~ comme un i** to stand bolt upright *ou* very erect;

tiens-toi ~ (*debout*) stand up (straight); (*assis*) sit up (straight); *V* **angle.**

(c) (*honnête, loyal*) *personne* upright, straight(forward); *conscience* honest, straightforward.

(d) (*judicieux*) *jugement* sound, sane.

2 droite *nf* (*Géom*) **(ligne)** ~e straight line.

3 *adv viser, couper, marcher* straight. **aller/marcher ~ devant soi** to go/walk straight ahead; **écrire ~** to have (an) upright handwriting; **c'est ~ devant vous** it's straight ahead of you *ou* right in front of you; **aller ~ à la faillite** to be making *ou* heading *ou* headed straight for bankruptcy; (*fig*) **aller ~ au but** *ou* **au fait** to go straight to the point; (*fig*) **cela lui est allé ~ au cœur** it went straight to his heart; *V* **marcher.**

droit[3] [dʀwa] **1** *nm* **(a)** (*moral ou réglementaire: prérogative*) right. **avoir des ~s sur qn/qch** to have rights over sb/sth; **il n'a aucun ~ sur ce terrain** he has no right to this land; **~ de pêche/chasse** fishing/hunting rights; (*fig*) **les ~s du sang** rights of kinship; **c'est bien votre ~** you've every right to do so, you are perfectly entitled to do so, you're perfectly within your rights; **de quel ~ est-il entré?** what right had he *ou* what gave him the right to come in?; **avoir le ~ de vie ou de mort sur** to have (the) power of life and death over; **avoir ~ de regard sur** to have the rights to examine; *V* **ayant droit.**

(b) (*loc*) **avoir le ~ de faire** (*gén: simple permission, possibilité*) to be allowed to do; (*Admin, Jur: autorisation*) to have the right to do; **être en ~ de faire** to have a *ou* the right to do, be entitled to do; (*fig*) **on est en ~ de se demander pourquoi** ... one has every right *ou* one is entitled to wonder why ...; **avoir ~ à qch** to be entitled to sth; (*hum*) **il a eu ~ à une bonne râclée/réprimande*** he got *ou* earned himself a good hiding/telling-off*; **être dans son (bon) ~** to be (quite) within one's rights; **c'est à lui de (plein) ~** it's his by right(s) *ou* as of right, it is rightfully his; **le ~ du plus fort** the law of the jungle; **faire ~ à** *requête* to grant, accede to; *V* **bon**[1]**, force, qui.**

(c) (*droit subjectif*) right. **avoir le ~ pour soi** to have right on one's side; **de ~ comme de fait** both legitimately and effectively; **monarque de ~ divin** monarch by divine right.

(d) (*Jur: droit positif*) **le ~** law; (*Univ*) **faire son ~** *ou* **le ~** to study law; **~ civil/pénal** civil/criminal law; **~ constitutionnel/international** constitutional/international law; **~ canon** canon law; **~ romain** Roman law; **~ privé/public** private/public law; **~ coutumier/écrit** customary/statute law; **le ~ des gens** the law of nations; **étudier le ~ de la famille** to study family law.

(e) (*gén pl*) (*taxe*) duty, tax; (*d'inscription etc*) fee, fees. **~ d'entrée** entrance (fee); **~s d'inscription/d'enregistrement** enrolment/registration fee(s); **exempt de ~s** duty-free.

2: droit d'aînesse birthright; **droit d'asile** right of asylum; **droits d'auteur** royalties; **droit de cité:** (*fig*) **avoir droit de cité parmi/dans** to be established among/in; **droits civils** civil rights; **droits civiques** civic rights; **droit commun: un condamné/délit de droit commun** a common law criminal/crime; **droits de douane** customs duties; **droit de grâce** right of reprieve; **les droits de l'homme** human rights; (*Pol*) **droit d'initiative** *citizens' right to initiate legislation (in Switzerland etc)*; **les droits naturels** natural rights; (*Jur*) **droit réel** title; **droits de reproduction** reproduction rights; **'tous droits (de reproduction) réservés'** 'all rights reserved'; **droits de succession** death duties; **droit de timbre** stamp duty; (*Jur*) **droit de visite** (right of) access; **le droit de vote** the right to vote, the vote.

droitement [dʀwatmɑ̃] *adv agir, parler* uprightly, honestly; *juger* soundly.

droitier, -ière [dʀwatje, jɛʀ] **1** *adj* right-handed; (*rare: Pol*) right-wing. **2** *nm,f* right-handed person; (*rare: Pol*) right-winger. (*Tennis etc*) **c'est un ~** he's a right-handed player *ou* a right-hander.

droiture [dʀwatyʀ] *nf [personne]* uprightness, straightness, straightforwardness; *[conscience]* honesty. **~ de caractère** uprightness, rectitude (of character).

drolatique [dʀɔlatik] *adj* (*littér*) comical, droll.

drôle [dʀol] **1** *adj* **(a)** (*amusant*) *situation, accoutrement* funny, comical, amusing; (*spirituel*) *personne* funny, amusing. **je ne trouve pas ça ~** I don't find that funny *ou* amusing; **la vie n'est pas ~** life's no joke; *V* **histoire.**

(b) (*bizarre*) funny, peculiar, strange. **c'est ~, j'aurais juré l'avoir rangé** that's funny *ou* peculiar *ou* strange, I could have sworn I had put it away; **avoir un ~ d'air** to look funny *ou* peculiar *ou* strange; **un ~ de type** a strange *ou* peculiar fellow, a queer fish*, an oddbod*; **une ~ d'idée/d'odeur** a funny *ou* strange *ou* peculiar idea/smell; **il a fait une ~ de tête!** you should have seen his face!; **la ~ de guerre** the phoney war; **se sentir tout ~** to feel funny *ou* strange *ou* peculiar; **ça me fait (tout) ~ (de le voir)*** it gives me a funny *ou* strange *ou* odd feeling (to see him); **tu es ~, je ne pouvais pourtant pas l'insulter!*** you must be joking *ou* kidding* — I really couldn't insult him.

(c) (*: *intensif*) **un ~ d'orage** a fantastic* *ou* terrific* storm; **de ~s de muscles/progrès** fantastic *ou* terrific muscles/progress*.

2 *nm* (†*péj*) scamp, rascal.

drôlement [dʀolmɑ̃] *adv* **(a)** (*V* **drôle**) funnily; comically; amusingly; peculiarly; strangely.

(b) (*: *intensif*) **il fait ~ froid** it's terribly *ou* awfully *ou* dreadfully cold*, it isn't half cold*; **il est ~ musclé** he's awfully *ou* terribly muscular*, he's got an awful lot of muscle*; **il est ~ culotté** he's got some cheek*, he hasn't half got a cheek*; **il a ~ changé** he really has changed, he's changed an awful lot*.

drôlerie [dʀolʀi] *nf* **(a)** (*U*) funniness, comicalness, drollness. **(b)** (*propos, action*) funny *ou* comical *ou* amusing thing (to say *ou* do).

drôlesse† [dʀolɛs] *nf* (*péj*) hussy† (*péj*).

dromadaire [dʀɔmadɛʀ] *nm* dromedary.

drosophile [dʀozɔfil] *nf* (*Zool*) fruit fly, drosophila (*T*).

drosser [dʀɔse] (1) *vt* (*Naut*) *[vent, courant]* to drive.

dru, e [dʀy] **1** *adj herbe* thick, dense; *barbe* thick, bushy; *haie* thickset, dense; *pluie* heavy. **2** *adv pousser* thickly, densely; *tomber [pluie]* heavily, fast; *[coups]* thick and fast.

drug(-)store, *pl* **drug(-)stores** [dʀœgstɔʀ] *nm* drugstore.

druide [dʀɥid] *nm* druid.

druidique [dʀɥidik] *adj* druidic.

druidisme [dʀɥidism(ə)] *nm* druidism.

drupe [dʀyp] *nf* drupe.

dryade [dʀijad] *nf* (*Myth*) dryad, wood-nymph; (*Bot*) dryas.

du [dy] **1** *art partitif V* **de**[2]. **2** *prép + art déf* = **de**[1]**+le.**

dû, due [dy] (*ptp de* **devoir**) **1** *adj* **(a)** (*à restituer*) owing, owed; (*arrivé à échéance*) due. **la somme due** the sum owing *ou* owed, the sum due; **la somme qui lui est due** the sum owing *ou* owed *ou* due to him; *V* **chose, port**[2]**.**

(b) ~ à due to; **ces troubles sont ~s à ...** these troubles are due to ... .

(c) (*Admin, Jur*) **en (bonne et) due forme** in due form.

2 *nm* due; (*somme d'argent*) dues.

dualisme [dɥalism(ə)] *nm* dualism.

dualiste [dɥalist(ə)] **1** *adj* dualistic. **2** *nmf* dualist.

dualité [dɥalite] *nf* duality.

dubitatif, -ive [dybitatif, iv] *adj* doubtful, dubious, dubitative.

dubitativement [dybitativmɑ̃] *adv* doubtfully, dubiously, dubitatively.

duc [dyk] *nm* duke; *V* **grand.**

ducal, e, *mpl* **-aux** [dykal, o] *adj* ducal.

ducat [dyka] *nm* ducat.

duché [dyʃe] *nm* (*fonction*) dukedom; (*territoire*) dukedom, duchy.

duchesse [dyʃɛs] *nf* **(a)** duchess. (*péj*) **elle fait la** *ou* **sa ~** she's playing the grand lady *ou* putting on airs. **(b) (poire) ~** Duchesse pear.

ductile [dyktil] *adj* ductile.

ductilité [dyktilite] *nf* ductility.

duègne [dɥɛɲ] *nf* duenna.

duel[1] [dɥɛl] *nm* duel. **provoquer qn en ~** to challenge sb to a duel; **se battre en ~** to fight a duel (*avec* with); **~ oratoire** verbal duel *ou* battle; **~ d'artillerie** artillery battle.

duel[2] [dɥɛl] *nm* (*Ling*) dual (number).

duelliste [dɥelist(ə)] *nm* duellist.

duettiste [dɥetist(ə)] *nmf* duettist.

duffel-coat, *pl* **duffel-coats** [dœfœlkot] *nm* duffel coat.

dulcinée [dylsine] *nf* († *ou hum*) lady-love († *ou hum*).

dum-dum [dumdum] *nf inv*: **(balle) ~** dum-dum (bullet).

dûment [dymɑ̃] *adv* duly.

dumping [dœmpiŋ] *nm* (*Écon*) dumping. **faire du ~** to dump goods.

dune [dyn] *nf* dune.

dunette [dynɛt] *nf* (*Naut*) poop.

Dunkerque [dœ̃kɛʀk] *n* Dunkirk.

duo [dɥo] *nm* (*Mus*) duet; (*Théât*) duo; (*fig: plaisantins*) pair, duo; (*fig: dialogue*) exchange. **~ d'injures** slanging match* (*surtout Brit*), exchange of insults.

duodécimal, e, *mpl* **-aux** [dɥɔdesimal, o] *adj* duodecimal.

duodénal, e, *mpl* **-aux** [dɥɔdenal, o] *adj* duodenal.

duodénum [dɥɔdenɔm] *nm* duodenum.

dupe [dyp] **1** *nf* dupe. **prendre pour ~** to fool, take in, dupe; **être la ~ de qn** to be taken in *ou* fooled by sb; *V* **jeu, marché. 2** *adj*: **être ~ (de)** to be taken in (by), be fooled (by); **je ne** *ou* **n'en suis pas ~** I'm not taken in (by it), he (*ou* it *etc*) doesn't fool me.

duper [dype] (1) *vt* to dupe, deceive. **se ~ (soi-même)** to deceive o.s.

duperie [dypʀi] *nf* (*tromperie*) dupery (*U*), deception. **sentiment de ~** feeling one is being duped.

duplex [dyplɛks] **1** *adj inv* (*Téléc*) duplex, two-way; (*Rad, TV*) **émission ~** link-up. **2** *nm* (*appartement*) split-level apartment, duplex (*US*); (*Can*) duplex (house). (*Téléc: aussi* **émission en ~**) link-up.

duplicata [dyplikata] *nm inv* (*Admin, Jur*) duplicate.

duplicateur [dyplikatœʀ] *nm* duplicator, duplicating machine.

duplication [dyplikɑsjɔ̃] *nf* (*Math*) duplication; (*Bio*) doubling; (*Téléc*) installation of a duplex system.

duplicité [dyplisite] *nf* duplicity.

dur, e [dyʀ] **1** *adj* **(a)** (*ferme, résistant*) *roche, métal, lit, peau, crayon* hard; *carton, col, brosse* stiff; *viande* tough; *porte, serrure, levier* stiff. **être ~ d'oreille, être ~ de la feuille*, avoir l'oreille ~e** to be hard of hearing; **~ comme le roc** as hard as (a) rock; *V* **œuf.**

(b) (*difficile*) *problème* hard, stiff, tough; *sujet, travail, parcours* hard, tough, difficult. **~ à manier/digérer/croire** hard to handle/digest/believe; **être ~ à la détente*** to be tight-fisted*; **leur fils est un enfant très ~** their son is a very difficult child.

(c) (*pénible*) *climat, lumière, punition* harsh, hard, severe; *épreuve, solitude* hard; *combat* hard, fierce; (*âpre*) *vin, cidre* harsh, bitter. **il lui est ~ d'avoir à partir** it's hard for him to have to leave; **ce sont des vérités ~s à avaler** these are hard truths to take; (*souvent hum*) **la vie est ~e** it's a hard life, life's no bed of roses; (*souvent hum*) **les temps sont ~s** times are hard; *V* **coup.**

(d) (*sévère*) *personne* hard, harsh, severe; *traits, visage* hard; *voix, regard* hard, harsh, severe; *loi, critique* harsh, severe. **être ~ avec** *ou* **pour** *ou* **envers qn** to be tough *ou* harsh with sb, be hard on sb; *V* **école.**

(e) (*insensible, cruel*) *personne, regard* hard(-hearted). **c'est un cœur ~, il a le cœur ~** he's a hard-hearted man, he has a heart of stone.

(f) (*endurant*) **être ~ au mal** *ou* **à la douleur** to be tough in the face of *ou* be resilient to suffering; **être ~ à la peine** *ou* **à l'ouvrage** to be a tireless worker.

2 *adv* (*) *travailler, frapper* hard. **le soleil tape ~** the sun is beating down; **croire à qch ~ comme fer** to believe firmly in sth; **le vent souffle ~** the wind is blowing hard *ou* strongly.

3 *nm,f* (*: *résistant*) tough one; (*meneur, casseur*) tough nut*, tough guy*, hard one; (*gén Pol: intransigeant*) hard-liner. **un(e) ~(e) à cuire*** a hard nut to crack*.

4 *nm* **(a) construire en ~** to build a permanent structure; **une construction en ~** a permanent structure.

(b) (‡: *train*) train.

5 dure *nf* **(a) à la ~e** hard, roughly, rough; **être élevé à la ~e** to be brought up the hard way; **vivre à la ~e** to live rough; **coucher sur la ~e** to sleep rough (*surtout Brit*), sleep on the ground.

(b) (*) **en dire de ~es à qn** to give sb a good telling-off* *ou* ticking-off* (*Brit*); **en entendre de ~es** to get a good telling-off* *ou* ticking-off* (*Brit*); **en faire voir de ~es à qn** to give sb a hard *ou* tough time (of it)*; **en voir de ~es** to have a hard *ou* tough time (of it)*.

durabilité [dyʀabilite] *nf* durability.

durable [dyʀabl(ə)] *adj bonheur, monument, souvenir, lien* lasting; *étoffe* durable, long-lasting.

durablement [dyʀabləmɑ̃] *adv s'installer* on a long-term basis. **bâtir ~** to build something to last; **bâti ~** built to last.

duralumin [dyʀalymɛ̃] *nm* duralumin.

durant [dyʀɑ̃] *prép* (*au cours de*) during, in the course of; (*pendant*) for. **il a plu ~ la nuit** it rained in (the course of) *ou* during the night; **il peut rêvasser ~ des heures** *ou* **des heures ~** he can daydream for hours (on end); **2 heures ~** for (a full *ou* whole) 2 hours; **des années ~** for years (and years); **sa vie ~** throughout his life, for as long as he lived (*ou* lives).

duratif, -ive [dyʀatif, iv] *adj* durative.

durcir [dyʀsiʀ] (2) **1** *vt* (*lit, fig*) to harden. **cette coiffure la durcit** this hair style makes her look hard. **2** *vi*, **se durcir** *vpr* to harden.

durcissement [dyʀsismɑ̃] *nm* hardening.

durée [dyʀe] *nf* **(a)** (*relative*) *[spectacle, opération]* duration, length; *[bail]* term; *[matériau, pile, ampoule]* life; (*Mus*) *[note]* value, length, duration. **pour une ~ illimitée** for an unlimited length of time, for an unlimited period; **pendant une ~ d'un mois** for (the period of) one month; **pour la ~ des négociations** while negotiations continue, for the duration of the negotiations; **pendant la ~ des réparations** for the duration of repairs; **de courte ~** *séjour* short; *bonheur, répit* short-lived; **la ~ d'une mode/de cet effet dépend de ...** how long a fashion/this effect lasts depends on ...; **de longue ~** *effet* long-lasting; *pile* long-life (*épith*), long-lasting; *V* **disque**.

(b) (*absolue: grande durée*) *[événement, action]* length; *[matériau, pile]* long-life, life. **je m'étonne de la ~ de ce spectacle** I'm amazed at the length of this show.

(c) (*fait de subsister, se maintenir*) continuance. **il n'osait croire à la ~ de cette prospérité** he did not dare to believe that this prosperity would last *ou* to believe in the continuance of this prosperity.

(d) (*Philos*) duration.

durement [dyʀmɑ̃] *adv* (*V* **dur**) (*péniblement*) harshly; severely; fiercely; (*sévèrement*) harshly, severely; (*cruellement*) hard-heartedly. **~ éprouvé** sorely tried; **élever qn ~** to bring sb up harshly *ou* the hard way.

durer [dyʀe] (1) *vi* **(a)** to last. **combien de temps cela dure-t-il?** how long does it last?; **l'effet dure 2 minutes/mois** the effect lasts (for) 2 minutes/months; **le festival dure (pendant) 2 semaines** the festival lasts (for) 2 weeks.

(b) (*se prolonger*) *[mode, maladie, tempête]* to last. **la fête a duré toute la nuit/jusqu'au matin** the party went on *ou* lasted all night/until morning; **sa maladie dure depuis 2 mois** he has been ill for 2 months (now), his illness has lasted for 2 months (now); **ça fait 2 mois que ça dure** it has been going on *ou* it has lasted for 2 months (now); **ça n'a que trop duré** it's gone on too long already!; **ça va ~ longtemps, cette plaisanterie?** how much longer is this joke going to go on? *ou* continue?; **une semaine qui a duré des mois** a week that seemed to last for months; **ça durera ce que ça durera** I don't know if it'll last, it might last and it might not; **ça ne peut plus ~!** this can't go on (any longer)!; **faire ~ un travail/ses vacances** to spin out* (*Brit*) *ou* prolong a job/one's holiday; (*gén iro*) **faire ~ le plaisir** to prolong the agony; (*littér*) **le temps me dure** time hangs heavy on me *ou* on my hands; (*littér*) **l'inaction me dure** I am growing impatient at this inactivity.

(c) (*littér: subsister*) *[coutume]* to linger on; (*péj*) *[mourant]* to hang on (*péj*), linger on.

(d) (*se conserver*) *[matériau, vêtement, outil]* to last. **faire ~ des chaussures** to make shoes last; **cette somme doit te ~ un mois** the sum will have to last you a month.

dureté [dyʀte] *nf* (*V* **dur**) hardness; stiffness; toughness; harshness; severity; fierceness. **~ (de cœur)** hard-heartedness.

durillon [dyʀijɔ̃] *nm* (*aux mains*) callus, hard skin (*U*); (*aux pieds*) callus, corn.

durit, durite [dyʀit] *nf* ® (*Aut*) (radiator) hose.

duvet [dyvɛ] *nm* **(a)** *[oiseau, fruit, joues]* down. **(b)** (*sac de couchage*) (down-filled) sleeping bag.

duveter (se) [dyvte] (5) *vpr* to become downy.

duveteux, -euse [dyvtø, øz] *adj* downy.

dynamique [dinamik] **1** *adj* (*Phys, gén*) dynamic. **2** *nf* (*Phys*) dynamics (*sg*).

dynamiquement [dinamikmɑ̃] *adv* dynamically.

dynamisme [dinamism(ə)] *nm* (*Philos, gén*) dynamism.

dynamitage [dinamitaʒ] *nm* dynamiting.

dynamite [dinamit] *nf* (*lit, fig*) dynamite.

dynamiter [dinamite] (1) *vt* to dynamite, blow up with dynamite.

dynamiteur, -euse [dinamitœʀ, øz] *nm,f* dynamiter.

dynamo [dinamo] *nf* dynamo.

dynamo-électrique [dinamɔelɛktʀik] *adj* dynamoelectric.

dynamogène [dinamɔʒɛn] *adj*, **dynamogénique** [dinamɔʒenik] *adj* dynamogenic.

dynamographe [dinamɔgʀaf] *nm* dynamograph.

dynamomètre [dinamɔmɛtʀ(ə)] *nm* dynamometer.

dynastie [dinasti] *nf* dynasty.

dynastique [dinastik] *adj* dynastic, dynastical.

dyne [din] *nf* dyne.

dysenterie [disɑ̃tʀi] *nf* dysentery.

dysentérique [disɑ̃teʀik] *adj* dysenteric.

dyslexie [dislɛksi] *nf* dyslexia, word-blindness.

dyslexique [dislɛksik] *adj, nmf* dyslexic.

dyspepsie [dispɛpsi] *nf* (*Méd*) dyspepsia.

dyspepsique [dispɛpsik] *adj, nmf*, **dyspeptique** [dispɛptik] *adj, nmf* dyspeptic.

dyspnée [dispne] *nf* dyspnoea.

dystrophie [distʀɔfi] *nf*: **~ musculaire progressive** muscular dystrophy.

dytique [ditik] *nm* dytiscus.

E

E, e [ə] *nm* (*lettre*) E, e.

eau, *pl* **~x** [o] **1** *nf* **(a)** (*gén, Bijouterie, Méd*) water; (*pluie*) rain. **sans ~** *vin* neat, straight; **cuire à l'~** to boil; **se passer les mains à l'~** to rinse one's hands, give one's hands a quick wash; **diamant de la plus belle ~** diamond of the first water; **escroc de la plus belle ~** thoroughgoing thief; **la Compagnie** *ou* **le Service des E~x** ≈ the Water Board; *V* **bas, mort**[2], **ville** *etc*.

(b) (*loc*) **apporter de l'~ au moulin de qn** to strengthen *ou* back sb's case *ou* argument; (*Méd*) **aller aux ~x** to take the waters; (*Naut*) **aller sur l'~** (*flotter*) to be buoyant; (*naviguer*) to sail; **j'en avais l'~ à la bouche** my mouth was watering, it made my mouth water; (*Naut*) **être dans les ~x d'un navire** to be in the wake of a ship; **être en ~** to be bathed in perspiration *ou* sweat; (*Naut, Rail*) **faire de l'~** to take on (a supply of) water; **faire ~ (de toutes parts)** to leak (like a sieve); (*Naut*) **mettre à l'~** to launch; **se mettre à l'~** (*nager*) to get into the water; (*être sobre*) to go on the wagon*, keep off drink; **mettre de l'~ dans son vin** (*lit*) to water down one's wine; (*fig*) to climb down; (*Méd*) **elle a perdu les ~x** her waters have broken; **prendre les ~x** to take the waters; *[chaussures]* **prendre l'~** to leak, let in water; **il passera beaucoup d'~ sous les ponts** much water will have flowed under the bridge; (*Prov*) **porter de l'~ à la rivière** to carry coals to Newcastle (*Prov*); (*Prov*) **l'~ va à la rivière** money makes money, to him that has shall more be given; **s'en aller en ~ de boudin*** to flop; **il y a de l'~ dans le gaz*** things aren't running too smoothly.

2: eau bénite holy water; **eau céleste** methylated spirits; **eau de Cologne** eau de Cologne; **eau courante** running water; **eau douce** fresh water; (*Can*) **eau d'érable** maple sap; **les Eaux et Forêts** ≈ the National Forestry Commission; **eau forte** (*Art*) etching; (*Chim*) aqua fortis; **eau gazeuse** soda water; **eau de javel** bleach; **eau lourde** heavy water; **eaux ménagères** waste (household) water; **eau de mer** sea water; **eau minérale** mineral water; **eaux minérales** minerals; **eau oxygénée** hydrogen peroxide; **eau de pluie** rainwater; **eau potable** drinking water; **eau de rose** rose water; **roman/histoire à l'eau de rose** mawkish *ou* sentimental *ou* soppy* novel/story; **eau rougie** wine and water; **eau salée** salt water; **eau savonneuse** soapy water; **eau de Seltz** seltzer water; **eau de source** spring water; **eau sucrée** sugar water; **eaux territoriales** territorial waters; **dans les eaux territoriales françaises** in French waters; **eaux thermales** thermal springs *ou* waters; **eau de toilette** toilet water; **eaux usées** liquid waste; **eau de vaisselle** dish *ou* washing-up (*Brit*) water; **eau de vie (de prune/poire** *etc*) (plum/pear *etc*) brandy; **cerises à l'eau de vie** cherries in brandy.

ébahi, e [ebai] (*ptp de* **ébahir**) *adj* dumbfounded, flabbergasted, astounded.

ébahir [ebaiʀ] (2) *vt* to flabbergast, astound. **s'~** to gawp, wonder (*de voir* at seeing).

ébahissement [ebaismɑ̃] *nm* astonishment, amazement.

ébarbage [ebaʀbaʒ] *nm* (*V* **ébarber**) trimming; clipping.

ébarber [ebaʀbe] (1) *vt papier, métal* to trim; *plante* to clip, trim.

ébats [eba] *nmpl* frolics, gambols. **~ amoureux** love-making; **prendre ses ~ = s'ébattre.**

ébattre (s') [ebatʀ(ə)] (41) *vpr [animaux]* to frolic, frisk, gambol (about); *[enfants]* to play *ou* romp about, frolic.

ébaubir (s') [ebobiʀ] (2) *vpr* (†, *hum*) to gawp, wonder (*de voir* at seeing).

ébauche [eboʃ] *nf* **(a)** (*action: V* **ébaucher**) sketching out, roughing out; outlining; starting up; developing, opening up.

(b) (*résultat*) *[livre]* skeleton, outline; *[statue]* rough shape; *[projet]* (rough) outline. **l'~ d'une amitié** the beginnings of a friendship; **l'~ de relations futures** the first steps towards future relationships; **une ~ de sourire** the ghost *ou* flicker *ou* glimmer of a smile; **l'~ d'un geste** the hint of a gesture; **ce n'est que la première ~** this is just a rough draft; **c'est encore à l'état d'~** it's still in the early stages.

ébaucher [eboʃe] (1) **1** *vt livre* to sketch out, rough out; *plan* to outline; *tableau* to sketch out; *statue* to rough-hew; *amitié, conversation* to start up; *relations* to develop, open up. **~ un sourire** to give a faint smile, give a flicker *ou* glimmer *ou* ghost of a smile; **~ un geste** to give a hint of a movement, start to make a movement.

2 s'ébaucher *vpr [plan]* to form, take shape *ou* form; *[livre]* to take shape *ou* form; *[amitié]* to form, develop; *[conversation]* to start up; *[relations]* to open up. **une solution s'ébauche lentement** a solution is gradually evolving *ou* taking shape; **une idée à peine ébauchée** the bare bones *ou* the mere outline of an idea.

ébaudir *vt*, **s'ébaudir** *vpr* [ebodiʀ] (2) (††, *hum*) to rejoice (*de, à* over, at).

ébène [ebɛn] *nf* ebony. **cheveux/table d'~** ebony hair/table; *V* **bois.**

ébénier [ebenje] *nm* ebony (tree); *V* **faux[2]**.

ébéniste [ebenist(ə)] *nm* cabinetmaker.

ébénisterie [ebenist(ə)ʀi] *nf (métier)* cabinetmaking; (*façon, meuble*) cabinetwork.

éberluer [ebɛʀlɥe] (1) *vt* (*gén ptp*) to astound, flabbergast, dumbfound.

éblouir [ebluiʀ] (2) *vt (lit, fig)* to dazzle, bedazzle.

éblouissant, e [ebluisɑ̃, ɑ̃t] *adj (lit, fig)* dazzling.

éblouissement [ebluismɑ̃] *nm* **(a)** *[lampe]* dazzle. **(b)** (*émerveillement*) bedazzlement; (*spectacle*) dazzling sight. **(c)** (*Méd: étourdissement*) **avoir un ~** to take *ou* have a dizzy turn.

ébonite [ebɔnit] *nf* vulcanite, ebonite.

éborgner [ebɔʀɲe] (1) *vt*: **~ qn** to blind sb in one eye, put *ou* poke sb's eye out; **j'ai failli m'~ contre la cheminée*** I nearly put *ou* poked my eye out on the corner of the mantelpiece.

éboueur [ebwœʀ] *nm* dustman (*Brit*), garbage collector (*US*), refuse collector (*Brit Admin*).

ébouillanter [ebujɑ̃te] (1) *vt* (*gén*) to scald; *légumes* to scald, blanch; *théière* to warm.

éboulement [ebulmɑ̃] *nm* **(a)** (*action: V* **s'ébouler**) crumbling; collapsing; falling in, caving in; fall. **~ de rochers** rock fall; **~ de terre** fall of earth, landslip. **(b)** (*amas*) heap *ou* mass of rocks, earth *etc*.

ébouler [ebule] (1) **1** *vt* to cause to collapse *ou* crumble, bring down. **2 s'ébouler** *vpr [pente, falaise]* (*progressivement*) to crumble; (*soudainement*) to collapse; *[mur, toit]* to fall in, cave in, crumble; *[sable]* to fall; *[terre]* to fall, slip.

éboulis [ebuli] *nm* mass of fallen rocks, earth *etc*. **pente couverte d'~** scree-covered slope.

ébouriffant, e [ebuʀifɑ̃, ɑ̃t] *adj vitesse, prix* hair-raising.

ébouriffer [ebuʀife] (1) *vt* **(a)** *cheveux* to tousle, ruffle, dishevel; *plumes, poil* to ruffle. **le vent m'a ébouriffé** the wind tousled *ou* ruffled *ou* dishevelled my hair. **(b)** (*: *surprendre*) to amaze, astound.

ébranchage [ebʀɑ̃ʃaʒ] *nm*, **ébranchement** [ebʀɑ̃ʃmɑ̃] *nm* pruning, lopping.

ébrancher [ebʀɑ̃ʃe] (1) *vt* to prune, lop.

ébranchoir [ebʀɑ̃ʃwaʀ] *nm* billhook.

ébranlement [ebʀɑ̃lmɑ̃] *nm* (*V* **ébranler**) shaking; weakening; disturbance, unhinging. **l'~ provoqué par cette nouvelle** the shock caused by this news.

ébranler [ebʀɑ̃le] (1) **1** *vt vitres* to shake, rattle; *mur, sol* (*faire trembler*) to shake; (*affaiblir*) to weaken, make unsound; *nerfs* to shake; *santé* to weaken; *esprit* to disturb, unhinge; *résolution, confiance, gouvernement* to shake, weaken. **ça a fortement ébranlé ses nerfs/sa santé** it has shattered his nerves/health; **le monde entier a été ébranlé par cette nouvelle** the whole world was shaken *ou* shattered by the news; **ces paroles l'ont ébranlé** (*troublé, attendri*) these words shook him; **se laisser ~ par des prières** to allow o.s. to be swayed by pleas.

2 s'ébranler *vpr [véhicule, cortège]* to move off, set off.

ébrécher [ebʀeʃe] (6) *vt assiette* to chip; *lame* to nick; *fortune* to break into, make a hole in.

ébréchure [ebʀeʃyʀ] *nf [assiette]* chip; *[lame]* nick.

ébriété [ebʀijete] *nf* (*frm*) intoxication.

ébrouement [ebʀumɑ̃] *nm [cheval]* snort.

ébrouer (s') [ebʀue] (1) *vpr* **(a)** (*souffler*) *[cheval]* to snort. **(b)** (*s'ébattre*) *[personne, chien]* to shake o.s.

ébruitement [ebʀɥitmɑ̃] *nm* (*V* **ébruiter**) spreading; disclosing; divulging.

ébruiter [ebʀɥite] (1) *vt nouvelle, rumeur* to disclose, spread (about); *secret* to divulge, disclose. **pour que rien ne s'ébruite** so that nothing leaks out.

ébullition [ebylisjɔ̃] *nf [eau]* boiling point; (*fig: agitation*) turmoil, ferment. **porter à (l')~** to bring to the boil; **au moment de/avant l'~** as/before boiling point is reached, as/before it begins to boil; **être en ~** *[liquide]* to be boiling; *[ville, maison]* to be in an uproar; *[pays]* to be seething with unrest; *[personne]* (*par la chaleur*) to be boiling*; (*par la surexcitation*) to be bubbling over, be simmering with excitement; (*par la colère*) to be seething *ou* simmering with anger; *V* **point[1]**.

écaillage [ekɑjaʒ] *nm* (*V* **écailler**) scaling; opening; chipping; flaking, peeling.

écaille [ekɑj] *nf [poisson]* scale; *[tortue, huître]* shell; *[reptile]* scale; *[oignon]* scale; *[peinture sèche]* flake. **lunettes (à monture) d'~** horn-rimmed spectacles; **peigne en ~** tortoiseshell comb; **meuble en ~** piece of furniture in tortoiseshell.

écailler[1] [ekɑje] (1) **1** *vt poisson* to scale; *huîtres* to open; *peinture etc* to chip. **2 s'écailler** *vpr [peinture]* to flake (off), peel (off).

écailler[2], -ère [ekɑje, ɛʀ] *nm,f* oyster seller.

écailleux, -euse [ekɑjø, øz] *adj poisson, peau* scaly; *peinture* flaky, flaking.

écaillure [ekɑjyʀ] *nf* (*morceau de peinture*) chip, flake; (*surface écaillée*) chipped *ou* flaking patch.

écale [ekal] *nf [noix]* shell.

écaler [ekale] (1) *vt* to shell.

écarlate [ekaʀlat] *adj, nf* scarlet.

écarquiller [ekaʀkije] (1) *vt*: **~ les yeux** to stare wide-eyed (*devant* at).

écart [ekaʀ] **1** *nm* **(a)** *[objets]* distance, space, gap; *[dates]* interval, gap; *[chiffres, températures]* difference; *[opinions, points de vue]* difference, divergence; *[explications]* discrepancy, disparity (*entre* between). **~ par rapport à la règle** deviation *ou* departure from the rule; **il y a un ~ important de prix entre** there's a big difference in price between; (*lit, fig*) **réduire l'~ entre** to narrow *ou* close the gap between; (*Sport*) **réduire l'~ à la marque** to narrow *ou* close the gap between the scores.

(b) faire un ~ *[cheval apeuré]* to shy; *[voiture folle]* to swerve; *[personne surprise]* to jump out of the way, leap aside; **faire un ~ de régime** to allow o.s. an occasional break *ou* lapse in one's diet; (*Danse*) **faire le grand ~** to do the splits.

(c) à l'~: être à l'~ *[hameau]* to be out-of-the-way *ou* remote *ou* isolated; **tirer qn à l'~ pour lui dire qch** to take sb aside *ou* on one side to say sth to him; **mettre** *ou* **tenir qn à l'~** (*fig: empêcher de participer*) to keep sb in the background, keep sb out of things; (*lit: empêcher d'approcher*) to keep *ou* hold sb back; **se tenir** *ou* **rester à l'~** (*s'isoler*) to hold o.s. aloof, stand apart, keep (o.s.) to o.s.; (*ne pas approcher*) to stay in the background, keep out of the way; (*fig: ne pas participer*) to stay on the sidelines, keep out of things.

(d) à l'~ de: la maison est à l'~ de la route the house is (well) off the road *ou* is off the beaten track; **tenir qn à l'~ d'un lieu** to keep sb (well) away from a place; **tenir qn à l'~ d'une affaire** to keep sb out of an affair; **se tenir** *ou* **rester à l'~ des autres** to keep out of the way of *ou* well away from other people, hold (o.s.) aloof from others; **se tenir** *ou* **rester à l'~ d'une affaire/de la politique** to steer clear of *ou* keep out of an affair/out of politics.

(e) (*Cartes*) discard.

(f) (*Admin: hameau*) hamlet.

2: écart de conduite misdemeanour; **écart de jeunesse** youthful misdemeanour; **écart de langage** strong *ou* bad language (*U*); **écart de régime** break *ou* lapse in one's diet.

écarté, e [ekaʀte] (*ptp de* **écarter**) **1** *adj lieu, hameau* remote, isolated, out-of-the-way. **chemin ~** lonely road. **2** *nm* (*Cartes*) écarté.

écartèlement [ekaʀtɛlmɑ̃] *nm* (*supplice*) quartering; (*fig: tiraillement*) agonizing struggle.

écarteler [ekaʀtəle] (5) *vt* (*Hist: supplicier*) to quarter; (*fig: tirailler*) to tear apart. **il était écartelé entre ses obligations familiales et professionnelles** he was torn between family and professional obligations.

écartement [ekaʀtəmɑ̃] *nm* space, distance, gap (*de, entre* between). (*Rail*) **~ (des rails)** gauge; (*Aut*) **~ des essieux** wheelbase.

écarter [ekaʀte] (1) **1** *vt* **(a)** (*séparer*) *objets* to move apart, move away from each other, separate; *bras, jambes* to open, spread; *doigts* to spread (open), part; *rideaux* to draw (back). **il écarta la foule pour passer** he pushed his way through the crowd, he cut a path through the crowd; **il se tenait debout, les jambes écartées/les bras écartés** he stood with his legs *ou* feet wide apart/with his arms outspread *ou* with outspread arms.

(b) (*exclure*) *objection, solution* to dismiss, set *ou* brush aside; *idée* to dismiss, rule out; *candidature* to dismiss, turn down; *personne* (*d'une liste*) to remove, strike off; (*d'une équipe*) to remove, exclude (*de* from).

(c) (*éloigner*) *meuble* to move away, push away *ou* back; *foule, personne* to push back (*de* from), push aside. **tout danger est maintenant écarté** there is no further risk of danger; **ce**

chemin nous écarte du village this road takes *ou* leads us away from the village; **ça nous écarte de notre propos** this is taking *ou* leading us off the subject *ou* away from the issue; **ça l'écarte de l'étude** it distracts him from his studies.

(d) (*Cartes*) to discard.

2 s'écarter *vpr* **(a)** (*se séparer*) to draw aside, part. **la foule s'écarta pour le laisser passer** the crowd drew aside *ou* parted to let him through; **les nuages s'écartèrent pour montrer le soleil** the clouds parted and the sun shone through.

(b) (*s'éloigner*) to withdraw, move away, step back (*de* from). **le mur s'écarte dangereusement de la verticale** the wall is dangerously out of plumb; **la foule s'écarta du lieu de l'accident** the crowd moved away from the scene of the accident; **s'~ de sa route** to stray *ou* wander from one's path; **avec ce chemin nous nous écartons** this path is taking us out of our way; (*fig*) **s'~ du droit chemin** to wander from the straight and narrow; **s'~ de la norme** to deviate *ou* depart from the norm; **s'~ d'un sujet** to stray *ou* wander from a subject; **nous nous écartons!** we are getting away from the point!

écarteur [ekaʀtœʀ] *nm* (*Méd*) retractor.

ecchymose [ekimoz] *nf* bruise, ecchymosis (*T*).

Ecclésiaste [eklezjast] *nm*: **l'~** Ecclesiastes.

ecclésiastique [eklezjastik] **1** *adj vie, charge* ecclesiastical; *revenus* church (*épith*); *V* **habit. 2** *nm* ecclesiastic.

écervelé, e [esɛʀvəle] **1** *adj* (*étourdi*) scatterbrained, hare-brained, featherbrained. **2** *nm,f* scatterbrain, hare-brain, featherbrain.

échafaud [eʃafo] *nm* **(a)** scaffold. **monter à l'~** to mount the scaffold; (*lit*) **finir sur l'~** to die on the scaffold; (*fig*) **il finira sur l'~** he'll come to a sorry end; **il risque l'~** he's risking his neck. **(b)** (††: *estrade*) platform, stand.

échafaudage [eʃafodaʒ] *nm* **(a)** (*Constr*) scaffolding (U). **(b)** (*empilement*) *[objets]* heap, pile; *[idées]* frail structure. **(c)** (*élaboration*) *[fortune]* building up, amassing; *[théorie]* building up, construction.

échafauder [eʃafode] (1) **1** *vt* **(a)** *fortune* to build (up), amass; *projets* to construct, build; *théorie* to construct. **(b)** (*empiler*) to pile up, stack up. **2** *vi* (*Tech*) to put up *ou* erect scaffolding.

échalas [eʃala] *nm* (*perche*) stake, pole; (*: *personne*) spindle-shanks*, beanpole*.

échalier [eʃalje] *nm* (*échelle*) stile; (*clôture*) gate.

échalote [eʃalɔt] *nf* shallot.

échancré, e [eʃɑ̃kʀe] (*ptp de* **échancrer**) *adj robe* with a scooped neckline, with a V-neckline; *côte* indented; *feuille* serrated, jagged.

échancrer [eʃɑ̃kʀe] (1) *vt robe* to cut (out) a scoop neckline *ou* V neckline in; *côte* to indent.

échancrure [eʃɑ̃kʀyʀ] *nf [robe]* (*ronde*) low *ou* scoop neckline; (*en V*) V-neckline; *[côte]* indentation; *[feuille]* serration.

échange [eʃɑ̃ʒ] *nm* **(a)** (*gén, Échecs, Sci, Sport*) exchange; (*troc*) swap*. (*Écon*) **le volume des ~s** the volume of trade; **~s culturels** cultural exchanges; **~ de vues** exchange of views; **~ de bons procédés** exchange of friendly services; **~s commerciaux** trade, trading.

(b) en ~ (*par contre*) on the other hand; (*en guise de troc*) in exchange; (*pour compenser*) to make up for it; **en ~ de** in exchange for, in return for.

(c) faire (l')~ de qch to swap* *ou* exchange sth; **on a fait ~** we've done a swap* *ou* an exchange; **ils ont fait (l')~ de leur appartement** they've changed flats with each other, they've swapped* flats; (*Échecs*) **faire ~** to exchange pieces.

échangeabilité [eʃɑ̃ʒabilite] *nf* exchangeability.

échangeable [eʃɑ̃ʒabl(ə)] *adj* exchangeable.

échanger [eʃɑ̃ʒe] (3) *vt* **(a)** (*troquer*) to exchange, swap* (*contre* for, *avec* with). **~ son cheval borgne contre un aveugle** to make a bad bargain.

(b) *idées, regards, lettres* to exchange; *injures* to bandy. **ils ont échangé des remerciements** they thanked one another.

échangeur [eʃɑ̃ʒœʀ] *nm* **(a)** (*Aut: route*) interchange. **(b)** (*Tech*) *[chaleur]* heat exchanger.

échanson [eʃɑ̃sɔ̃] *nm* (*Hist*) cupbearer; (*hum*) wine waiter.

échantillon [eʃɑ̃tijɔ̃] *nm* (*lit*) sample; (*fig*) example, sample.

échantillonnage [eʃɑ̃tijɔnaʒ] *nm* (*action*) sampling; (*collection*) range *ou* selection of samples. **un ~ d'outils/de tissus** a selection of tools/fabrics.

échantillonner [eʃɑ̃tijɔne] (1) *vt* to sample.

échappatoire [eʃapatwaʀ] *nf* (*faux-fuyant*) evasion, way out.

échappé, e [eʃape] (*ptp de* **échapper**) **1** *nm,f* **(a)** (*Sport*) **le peloton a rejoint les ~s** the pack caught up with the breakaway group.

(b) (†† *ou hum*) **~ de l'asile** bedlamite ††.

2 échappée *nf* **(a)** (*Sport*) breakaway.

(b) (*vue*) vista; (*rayon de soleil*) gleam. **une ~e sur la plaine entre deux montagnes** a vista of the plain between two mountains.

échappement [eʃapmɑ̃] *nm* **(a)** (*Aut*) exhaust. **~ libre** cutout; **soupape/tuyau d'~** exhaust valve/pipe; *V* **pot. (b)** (*Horlogerie, Tech*) escapement.

échapper [eʃape] (1) **1** *vi* **(a) ~ à** *danger, destin, punition* to escape; *poursuivants* (*en fuyant*) to escape (from), get away from; (*par ruse*) to evade, elude; *obligation, responsabilité* to evade; **~ aux recherches** to elude investigation; **~ à la mort** to escape death; (*Écon*) **~ à l'impôt** (*par privilège*) to be exempt from taxation; (*illégalement*) to evade *ou* dodge* income tax, avoid paying income tax; **~ à la règle** to be an exception to the rule; **cela échappe à toute tentative de définition** it baffles *ou* eludes all definition; **il échappe à tout contrôle** he is beyond (any) control; (*Jur*) **cela échappe à notre juridiction** it is outside *ou* beyond our jurisdiction; **tu ne m'échapperas pas!** (*lit*) you won't get away from me!; (*fig*) you won't get off as easily as that!, I'll get you yet!; (*hum*) **nous n'échapperons pas à une tasse de thé** we won't get away without having (to have) a cup of tea; **essaie d'~ pour quelques jours à ton travail** try and escape *ou* get away from work for a few days; **rien n'échappe à sa vue** he notices everything, he doesn't miss a thing; **~ à la vue *ou* aux regards de qn** to escape sb's notice.

(b) ~ à l'esprit de qn to escape *ou* elude sb; **son nom m'échappe** his name escapes me *ou* has slipped my mind; **ce détail m'avait échappé** this detail had escaped me, I had overlooked this detail; **ce qu'il a dit m'a échappé** (*je n'ai pas entendu*) I did not catch what he said; (*je n'ai pas compris*) I did not understand *ou* get* *ou* grasp what he said; **l'opportunité d'une telle mesure m'échappe** I can't see *ou* I fail to see the point *ou* the use of such a measure; **rien ne lui échappe** (*il voit tout*) nothing escapes him, he doesn't miss a thing.

(c) ~ des mains de qn to slip out of *ou* slip from sb's hands; **~ des lèvres de qn** *[cri, parole]* to burst from sb's lips; **un cri de douleur lui échappa** he let out *ou* gave a cry of pain; **un gros mot lui a échappé** he let slip *ou* let out a swearword.

(d) il l'a échappé belle he had a narrow escape, that was a close shave (for him).

(e) laisser ~ *gros mot* to let out, let slip; *cri* to let out, utter; *objet* to let slip, drop; *secret* to let drop, let out; *occasion* to let slip, let go; *détail, faute* to overlook; **laisser ~ un prisonnier** to let a prisoner escape *ou* get away.

(f) faire ~ un prisonnier to help a prisoner (to) escape *ou* get out.

2 s'échapper *vpr* **(a)** *[prisonnier]* to escape (*de* from), break out (*de* of); *[cheval]* to escape (*de* from), get out (*de* of); *[oiseau]* to fly away; *[cri]* to escape, burst (*de* from). **la voiture réussit à s'~ malgré la foule** the car got away in spite of the crowd; (*fig*) **je m'échappe un instant pour préparer le dîner** I'll slip away for a moment *ou* I must leave you for a moment to get dinner ready; (*fig*) **j'ai pu m'~ du bureau de bonne heure** I managed to get away *ou* slip out early from the office; (*Sport*) **le coureur s'échappe dans la côte** the runner draws ahead *ou* pulls away on the uphill stretch.

(b) *[gaz]* to escape, leak; *[odeur, lumière etc]* to come, issue (*littér*) (*de* from). **la fumée s'échappe de la cheminée** smoke is coming from *ou* out of the chimney; **l'eau s'est échappée de la casserole** the water boiled over in the pan; **des flammes s'échappaient du toit** flames were darting *ou* coming out of the roof.

écharde [eʃaʀd(ə)] *nf* splinter (of wood).

écharpe [eʃaʀp(ə)] *nf [femme]* scarf; *[maire]* sash; (*bandage*) sling. **porter *ou* avoir le bras en ~** to have one's arm in a sling; **prendre en ~** *voiture* to hit sideways on.

écharper [eʃaʀpe] (1) *vt* (*lit, fig*) to tear to pieces. **se faire ~** to be torn to pieces.

échasse [eʃɑs] *nf* (*objet, Zool*) stilt. (*hum*) **être monté sur des ~s** to be long in the leg, have long legs.

échassier [eʃɑsje] *nm* wader (*bird*).

échauder [eʃode] (1) *vt* **(a)** (*fig: faire réfléchir*) **~ qn** to teach sb a lesson; **se faire ~** to burn one's fingers; *V* **chat. (b)** (*laver à l'eau chaude*) to wash in hot water; (*ébouillanter*) to scald. **~ la théière** to warm the teapot.

échauffant, e [eʃofɑ̃, ɑ̃t] *adj* (*constipant*) binding†, constipating.

échauffement [eʃofmɑ̃] *nm* **(a)** (*Sport*) warm-up. **(b)** *[terre]* heating; *[moteur]* overheating. **(c)** (*Méd*†) (*constipation*) constipation; (*inflammation*) inflammation; *[sang]* overheating.

échauffer [eʃofe] (1) **1** *vt* **(a)** *moteur, machine* to overheat, make hot; (*Sport*) *coureur* to make hot. **il était échauffé par la course, la course l'avait échauffé** *[coureur, cheval]* he was hot after the race.

(b) *imagination* to fire, excite. **cette intervention a échauffé le débat** the discussion became fiercer *ou* more heated after this speech; **après une heure de discussion les esprits étaient très échauffés** after arguing for an hour people were getting very heated *ou* worked up*; **tu commences à m'~* les oreilles *ou* la bile**† you're getting my goat*, you're putting me in a temper.

(c) (*Méd*†) **~ le sang** to overheat the blood; **~ la peau** to inflame the skin; **je suis un peu échauffé** I'm a bit constipated.

2 s'échauffer *vpr* **(a)** (*Sport*) to warm up.

(b) (*s'animer*) *[personne]* to become heated, get worked up*.

échauffourée [eʃofuʀe] *nf* (*avec la police*) brawl, clash; (*Mil*) skirmish.

échauguette [eʃogɛt] *nf* bartizan, watchtower.

èche [ɛʃ] *nf* (*Pêche*) bait.

échéance [eʃeɑ̃s] *nf* **(a)** (*date limite*) *[délai]* expiry date; *[bon, action]* maturity date; *[traite, emprunt]* redemption date; *[loyer]* date of payment; *[facture, dette]* settlement date; (*Bourse*) settling day. (*fig*) **~s politiques** political deadlines; (*fig*) **l'~ fatale** the day of reckoning, the fatal date.

(b) (*règlements à effectuer*) **l'~ de fin de mois** the end-of-month payments; **faire face à ses ~s** to meet one's financial obligations *ou* commitments; **avoir de lourdes ~s** to be heavily committed, have heavy financial commitments.

(c) (*laps de temps*) term. **à longue/courte ~** *traite* long-/short-term (*épith*); *bon* long-/short-dated; (*fig*) **à longue ~** in the long run; (*fig*) **à courte ~** before long.

échéancier [eʃeɑ̃sje] *nm* billbook.

échéant, e [eʃeɑ̃, ɑ̃t] *adj V* **cas.**

échec[1] [eʃɛk] *nm* **(a)** (*insuccès*) failure; (*revers*) setback. **subir un ~** (*gén*) to fail, suffer a setback; (*Mil*) to suffer a defeat *ou* setback; **l'~ des pourparlers** the breakdown in *ou* the failure of the talks; **sa tentative s'est soldée par un ~** his attempt has failed *ou* has ended in failure; **voué à l'~** bound to fail, doomed to failure.

(b) (*loc*) **tenir qn en ~** to hold sb in check; **faire ~ à qn** to foil *ou* frustrate *ou* thwart sb *ou* sb's plans.

échec[2] [eʃɛk] *nm* (*Jeux*) **les ~s** chess; **jeu d'~s** (*échiquier*) chessboard; (*pièces*) chessmen; **jouer aux ~s** to play chess; **être en ~** to be in check; **faire ~ au roi** to check the king; **~ au roi!** check!; **~ et mat** checkmate; **faire ~ et mat** to checkmate.

échelle [eʃɛl] **1** *nf* **(a)** (*objet*) ladder. (*fig*) **il n'y a plus qu'à tirer l'~** we may as well give it up, there's no point trying to take it further; *V* **court**[1].

(b) (*dimension*) scale. **carte à grande ~** large-scale map; **croquis à l'~** scale drawing; (*fig*) **sur une grande ~** on a large scale; **à l'~ nationale/mondiale** on a national/world scale; **un monde à l'~ de l'homme** a world fitted to man; **à l'~ de la firme** (*et non d'une seule usine*) at the level of the firm as a whole; (*en rapport avec son importance*) in proportion to the firm's size (*ou* requirements *etc*).

(c) *[bas, collant]* ladder (*Brit*), run.

(d) (*gradation, Mus*) scale.

2: **échelle de corde** rope ladder; **échelle des couleurs** range of colours; **échelle coulissante** extending *ou* extension ladder; **échelle de coupée** accommodation ladder; **échelle double** step-ladder; **les Échelles du Levant** the Ports of the Levant; **échelle mobile** sliding scale; **échelle mobile des pompiers** fireman's extending ladder; **échelle des salaires** salary scale; **échelle sociale** social scale *ou* ladder; **échelle des traitements** = **échelle des salaires; échelle des valeurs** scale of values.

échelon [eʃlɔ̃] *nm* **(a)** *[échelle]* rung; *[hiérarchie]* step, grade. (*Admin*) **fonctionnaire au 8e ~** official on grade 8 (of the salary scale); (*Admin*) **être au dernier/premier ~** to be on the highest *ou* top grade/on the lowest *ou* bottom grade; **monter d'un ~ dans la hiérarchie** to go up one step *ou* grade *ou* rung in the hierarchy; **grimper rapidement les ~s** to get ahead fast, get quick promotion.

(b) (*Admin: niveau*) level. **à l'~ national/du régiment** at the national/at regimental level; (*lit, fig*) **à tous les ~s** at every level.

(c) (*Mil: troupe*) echelon.

échelonnement [eʃlɔnmɑ̃] *nm* (*V* **échelonner**) spacing out, spreading out; spreading; staggering; grading; gradual introduction; disposing in echelons.

échelonner [eʃlɔne] (1) *vt* **(a)** *objets* to space out, spread out, place at intervals (*sur* over). **les bouées sont échelonnées à 50 mètres l'une de l'autre** the buoys are spaced *ou* placed 50 metres apart; **les membres du service d'ordre sont échelonnés tout au long du parcours** the police guard is stationed *ou* is lined up at intervals all along the route; **les bâtiments s'échelonnent sur 3 km** the buildings stretch over a distance of 3 km *ou* are spaced out over 3 km.

(b) *paiements* to spread (out) (*sur* over); *congés, vacances* to stagger (*sur* over).

(c) (*graduer*) *exercices, difficultés* (*dans la complexité*) to grade; (*dans le temps*) to introduce gradually.

(d) (*Mil*) to place in echelon, echelon.

échenilloir [eʃnijwaʀ] *nm* billhook, pruning hook.

écheveau, *pl* **~x** [eʃvo] *nm* skein, hank; (*fig*) tangle, web.

échevelé, e [eʃəvle] (*ptp de* **écheveler**) *adj personne* tousled, dishevelled; *course, danse, rythme* wild, frenzied.

écheveler [eʃəvle] (4) *vt* (*littér*) *personne* to ruffle *ou* tousle *ou* dishevel the hair of.

échevin [ɛʃvɛ̃] *nm* (*Hist*) alderman, principal county magistrate; (*Belgique*) deputy burgomaster; (*Can rare*) municipal councillor, alderman.

échiffer* [eʃife] (1) *vt* (*Can*) to tease, unravel.

échine [eʃin] *nf* **(a)** backbone, spine; (*Culin*) loin, chine. (*fig*) **il a l'~ souple** he kowtows to his superiors, he's a subservient sort of fellow; **plier** *ou* **courber l'~** to submit.

(b) (*Archit*) echinus.

échiner [eʃine] (1) **1** *vt* (††) to break the back of. **2 s'échiner** *vpr* (*fig*) to work o.s. to death *ou* into the ground, nearly kill o.s. (*à faire qch* doing sth). **s'~ à répéter/écrire qch** to wear o.s. out repeating/writing sth.

échiquier [eʃikje] *nm* (*Échecs*) chessboard. (*fig*) **notre place sur l'~ mondial** our place in the field *ou* on the scene of world affairs; **en ~** in a chequered pattern; (*Brit Pol*) **l'É~** the Exchequer.

écho [eko] *nm* **(a)** (*lit*) echo. **~ simple** echo; **~ multiple** reverberations.

(b) (*fig*) (*rumeur*) rumour, echo; (*témoignage*) account, report; (*réponse*) response. **avez-vous eu des ~s de la réunion?** did you get any inkling of what went on at the meeting?, did anything come back to you from the meeting?; **se faire l'~ de** *souhaits, opinions, inquiétudes* to echo, repeat; *rumeurs* to repeat, spread; **sa proposition est restée sans ~** his suggestion wasn't taken up, nothing further came of his suggestion.

(c) (*Presse*) miscellaneous news item, item of gossip. **(rubrique des) ~s** gossip column, news (items) in general.

échoir [eʃwaʀ] *vi* **(a)** (*littér*) **~ (en partage) à qn** to fall to sb's share *ou* lot; **il vous échoit de faire** it falls to you to do. **(b)** *[loyer, dettes]* to fall due; *[délai]* to expire.

échoppe†† [eʃɔp] *nf* (*boutique*) workshop; (*sur un marché*) stall, booth.

échotier† [ekɔtje] *nm* gossip columnist.

échouage [eʃwaʒ] *nm*, **échouement** [eʃumɑ̃] *nm* (*Naut*) (*état*) state of being aground; (*action*) grounding, running aground.

échouer [eʃwe] (1) **1** *vi* **(a)** *[personne]* to fail. **~ à un examen/dans une tentative** to fail an exam/in an attempt.

(b) *[tentative, plan]* to fail, miscarry, fall through.

(c) **faire ~** *complot* to foil; *projet* to wreck, ruin; **faire ~ les plans de l'ennemi** to foil the enemy's plans, frustrate *ou* thwart the enemy in his plans; **on a fait ~ leur tentative d'enlèvement du directeur** they were foiled in their attempt to kidnap the manager.

(d) (*aboutir*) to end up. **~ dans la misère** to end up in poverty; **nous avons finalement échoué dans un petit hôtel** we finally landed up *ou* ended up in a small hotel.

(e) (*Naut: aussi* **s'~**) *[bateau]* to run aground; *[débris d'épave]* to be washed up. **le bateau s'est échoué** *ou* **a échoué sur un écueil** the boat ran onto a reef; **le bateau s'est échoué** *ou* **a échoué sur un banc de sable** the boat ran aground on *ou* ran onto a sandbank; **bateau échoué** (*dans un port de marée*) boat lying high and dry; (*dans la vase*) boat sunk in(to) the mud.

2 *vt* (*Naut*) (*accidentellement*) to ground; (*volontairement*) to beach. **il a échoué sa barque sur un écueil** he ran his boat onto a reef.

3 s'échouer *vpr [bateau]* to run aground; *[débris d'épave]* to be washed up.

écimage [esimaʒ] *nm* pollarding, polling.

écimer [esime] (1) *vt arbre* to pollard, poll.

éclaboussement [eklabusmɑ̃] *nm* splash.

éclabousser [eklabuse] (1) *vt* to splash, spatter. **~ de sang** to spatter *ou* splash with blood; **ils ont été éclaboussés par le scandale** their good name has been smeared *ou* sullied by the scandal, the scandal has rather tarnished their image; **~ qn de son luxe** (*éblouir*) to dazzle sb with a show of wealth, show off one's wealth to sb; (*humilier*) to overwhelm sb with a show of wealth.

éclaboussure [eklabusyʀ] *nf [boue]* splash; *[sang]* spatter; (*fig: sur la réputation*) stain, smear, blot. **il y a des ~s sur la glace** there are smears *ou* spots on the mirror.

éclair [eklɛʀ] **1** *nm* **(a)** (*Mét*) flash of lightning; (*Phot*) flash. **il y a des ~s dans le lointain** it's lightning *ou* there's lightning in the distance; **~s de chaleur** summer lightning; **~ de magnésium** magnesium flash.

(b) **~ de colère** flash of anger; **~ d'intelligence/de génie** flash *ou* spark of intelligence/of genius; **~ de malice** mischievous glint.

(c) (*loc*) **passer comme un ~** *[coureur]* to dart *ou* flash past *ou* by; *[moment]* to fly *ou* flash past *ou* by; **comme un ~** like a flash, like greased lightning*; **en un ~** in a flash, in a split second; **un ~ dans sa vie** a ray of sunshine in his life.

(d) (*Culin*) éclair.

2 *adj inv attaque, visite* lightning (*épith*). **raid ~** (*Aviat*) blitz raid; (*Mil*) hit-and-run raid; *V* **guerre**.

éclairage [eklɛʀaʒ] *nm* (*intérieur*) lighting; (*luminosité extérieure*) light (level). **~ à l'électricité** electric lighting; **~ indirect** indirect *ou* concealed lighting; (*lit, fig*) **sous cet ~** in this light.

éclairagiste [eklɛʀaʒist(ə)] *nm* (*Théât*) electrician; (*Ciné*) lighting engineer.

éclairant, e [eklɛʀɑ̃, ɑ̃t] *adj* (*fig*) illuminating, enlightening; (*lit*) *pouvoir, propriétés* lighting (*épith*); *V* **fusée**.

éclaircie [eklɛʀsi] *nf* **(a)** bright interval, sunny spell. **une ~ dans les nuages** a break in the clouds.

(b) (*fig littér*) bright spot *ou* interval, ray of sunshine. **une vie monotone et sans ~** a life of cheerless monotony; **ce fut une ~ dans sa vie** it was a ray of sunshine in his life.

éclaircir [eklɛʀsiʀ] (2) **1** *vt* **(a)** *teinte* to lighten.

(b) *soupe* to make thinner, thin (down); *plantes* to thin (out); *arbres, cheveux* to thin.

(c) *mystère* to clear up, solve, explain; *question, pensée, situation* to clarify, make clear; (†) *doutes* to dispel. **pouvez-vous nous ~ sur ce point?** can you enlighten us on this point?

2 s'éclaircir *vpr* **(a)** *[ciel]* to clear; *[temps]* to clear up. **s'~ la voix** *ou* **la gorge** to clear one's throat.

(b) *[arbres, foule]* to thin out; *[cheveux]* to thin, get *ou* grow thin *ou* thinner.

(c) *[idées, situation]* to grow *ou* become clearer; *[mystère]* to be solved *ou* explained; (†) *[doutes]* to vanish.

éclaircissement [eklɛʀsismɑ̃] *nm [mystère]* solution, clearing up; *[texte obscur]* clarification. **j'exige des ~s sur votre attitude** I demand some explanation of your attitude.

éclairé, e [ekleʀe] (*ptp de* **éclairer**) *adj minorité* enlightened.

éclairement [eklɛʀmɑ̃] *nm* (*Phys*) illumination.

éclairer [ekleʀe] (1) **1** *vt* **(a)** *[lampe]* to light (up); *[soleil]* to shine (down) on. **une seule fenêtre était éclairée** there was a light in only one window, only one window was lit up; **une grande baie éclairait l'entrée** a large bay window gave light to the hall; (*littér*) **deux grands yeux éclairaient son visage** her large eyes seemed to light up her face; **un sourire éclaira son visage** his face lit up in a smile; **bien/mal éclairé** well-/badly-lit.

(b) *problème, situation* to throw *ou* shed light on, clarify, explain; *auteur, texte* to throw light on.

(c) **~ qn** (*lit: montrer le chemin*) to light the way for sb; (*fig: renseigner*) to enlighten sb (*sur* about); **~ la lanterne de qn** to put sb in the picture*.

(d) (*Mil*) **~ le terrain** to reconnoitre the area, scout out the ground; **~ un régiment** to reconnoitre for a regiment; **~ la route** (*Mil*) to scout out the route; (*Aut*) to show the way, go on ahead.

2 *vi*: **~ bien/mal** to give a good/poor light.

3 s'éclairer *vpr* **(a)** *[rue]* to be lit; (*fig*) *[visage]* to light up, brighten (up).

(b) *[situation]* to get clearer; *[question]* to be cleared up *ou* clarified. **tout s'éclaire!** I see it now!, the light is beginning to dawn!*

(c) **s'~ à l'électricité** to have electric light; **il a fallu s'~ à la bougie** we had to use candlelight; **prends une lampe pour t'~** take a lamp to light the way.

éclaireur [eklɛʀœʀ] *nm* **(a)** (*Mil*) scout. **avion ~** reconnaissance plane; (*lit, fig*) **partir en ~** to go off to have a scout around. **(b)** (*Scoutisme*) (boy) scout.

éclaireuse [eklɛʀøz] *nf* (girl) guide (*Brit*), girl scout (*US*).

éclat [ekla] *nm* **(a)** *[os, verre]* splinter, fragment; *[bois]* splinter; *[grenade, pierre]* fragment. **un ~ d'obus** a piece of shrapnel; **des ~s d'obus** shrapnel; *V* **voler.**

(b) *[lumière, métal, soleil]* brightness, brilliance, glare (*péj*); *[diamant, pierreries]* flash, brilliance; *[couleur]* brightness, vividness; *[braise]* glow; *[vernis]* shine, gloss; *[satin, bronze]* sheen; *[perle]* lustre. (*Aut*) **l'~ des phares** the glare of the headlights; (*Théât*) **l'~ (des lumières) de la rampe** the blaze *ou* glare of the footlights.

(c) *[yeux]* brightness, sparkle; *[teint, beauté]* radiance. **dans tout l'~ de sa jeunesse** in the full radiance *ou* bloom of her youth; **perdre son ~** to lose one's sparkle.

(d) *[gloire, cérémonie]* glamour, splendour; *[nom]* fame; *[richesse, époque]* brilliance, glamour; *[personnage]* glamour. **donner de l'~ à qch** to lend glamour to sth; **réception donnée avec ~** sumptuous *ou* dazzling reception; **ça s'est déroulé sans ~** it passed off quietly *ou* without fuss.

(e) (*scandale*) fuss, commotion. **faire un ~** to make *ou* cause a fuss, create a commotion.

(f) ~s de voix shouts; **sans ~ de voix** without voices being raised; **~ de colère** angry outburst; **avec un soudain ~ de colère** in a sudden blaze of anger; **~ de rire** roar *ou* burst of laughter; **on l'accueillit avec des ~s de rire** his arrival was greeted with roars *ou* shouts of laughter *ou* with a burst of laughter; **comme un ~ de tonnerre**† like a peal of thunder, like a thunderclap.

éclatant, e [eklatɑ̃, ɑ̃t] *adj* **(a)** *lumière* bright, brilliant, glaring (*péj*); *couleur* bright, vivid; *feu, soleil* blazing; *blancheur* dazzling.

(b) *teint* blooming, radiant; *beauté* radiant, dazzling. **~ de santé** radiant with health.

(c) *succès* dazzling, resounding; *revanche* shattering, devastating; *victoire* resounding; *gloire* shining; *vérité* manifest, self-evident; *exemple* striking, shining; *mensonge* blatant, flagrant, glaring. **il a des dons ~s** he is brilliantly gifted.

(d) *rire, bruit* loud; *voix* loud, ringing; *musique* blaring (*péj*), loud.

éclatement [eklatmɑ̃] *nm [bombe, mine]* explosion; *[obus]* bursting, explosion; *[pneu, ballon]* bursting; *[veine]* rupture (*de* of); *[parti]* break-up, split (*de* in). **à cause de l'~ d'un pneu** as a result of a burst tyre; **l'~ d'une bombe/d'un obus le couvrit de terre** an exploding bomb/shell covered him with earth.

éclater [eklate] (1) *vi* **(a)** *[mine, bombe]* to explode, blow up; *[obus]* to burst, explode; *[veine]* to rupture; *[bourgeon]* to burst open; *[pneu, chaudière]* to burst; *[verre]* to splinter, shatter; *[parti]* to break up; *[ville, services, structures familiales]* to break up. **j'ai cru que ma tête allait ~** I thought my head would burst.

(b) *[incendie, épidémie, guerre]* to break out; *[orage]* to break; *[scandale, nouvelle]* to break. **la nouvelle a éclaté comme un coup de tonnerre** the news came like a thunderclap *ou* burst like a bombshell.

(c) (*retentir*) **des cris ont éclaté** shouts were raised; **une détonation éclata** there was the blast of an explosion; **une fanfare éclata** there was a sudden flourish of trumpets, trumpet notes rang out; **un coup de fusil éclata** there was the crack of a rifle; **un coup de tonnerre éclata** there was a sudden peal of thunder; **des rires/des applaudissements ont éclaté** there was a roar of laughter/a burst of applause, laughter/applause broke out.

(d) (*se manifester*) *[vérité, bonne foi]* to shine out, shine forth (*littér*). **sa joie** *ou* **la joie éclate dans ses yeux/sur son visage** joy shines in his eyes/on his face.

(e) ~ de rire to burst out laughing; **il éclata (de rage)** he exploded (with rage); **~ en menaces** *ou* **en reproches** to inveigh (*contre* against), rail (*contre* at, against); **~ en sanglots** to burst into tears; **~ en applaudissements** to break *ou* burst into applause; **nous éclatâmes en protestations devant sa décision** we broke out in angry protest at his decision.

(f) faire ~ *mine* to detonate, blow up; *bombe, obus* to explode; *poudrière* to blow up; *pétard* to let off; *ballon* to burst; *tuyau* to burst, crack; *verre* to shatter, splinter; **cette remarque l'a fait ~ (de colère)** he blew up* at this remark; **faire** *ou* **laisser ~ sa joie** to give free rein to one's joy; **faire** *ou* **laisser ~ sa colère** to give vent *ou* give free rein to one's anger.

2 s'éclater‡ *vpr* (*se défouler*) to have a ball‡.

éclateur [eklatœʀ] *nm* (*Élec*) spark gap.

éclectique [eklɛktik] *adj* eclectic.

éclectisme [eklɛktism(ə)] *nm* eclecticism.

éclipse [eklips(ə)] *nf* (*Astron, fig*) eclipse. **carrière à ~s** career which goes by fits and starts; **personnalité à ~s** public figure who comes and goes, figure who is in and out of the public eye.

éclipser [eklipse] (1) **1** *vt* (*Astron*) to eclipse; *[événement, gloire]* to eclipse, overshadow; *[personne]* to eclipse, overshadow, outshine. **2 s'éclipser*** *vpr* to slip away, slip out.

écliptique [ekliptik] *adj, nm* ecliptic.

éclisse [eklis] *nf* (*Méd*) splint; (*Rail*) fishplate.

éclisser [eklise] (1) *vt* (*Méd*) to splint, put in splints; (*Rail*) to join with fishplates.

éclopé, e [eklɔpe] **1** *adj personne* limping, lame; *cheval* lame. **2** *nm,f* (*hum*) (*dans une bagarre*) (slightly) wounded person; (*dans un accident*) (slightly) injured person.

éclore [eklɔʀ] (45) *vi* **(a)** *[œuf]* to hatch; *[poussin]* to hatch (out); (*littér*) *[fleur]* to open out; *[amour, talent, jour]* to be born, dawn. (*littér*) **fleur à peine éclose/fraîche éclose** budding/fresh-blown flower. **(b) faire ~** *œuf* to hatch; (*littér*) *sentiment* to kindle; *qualités* to draw forth.

éclosion [eklozjɔ̃] *nf* (*V* **éclore**) hatching; opening; birth, dawn.

écluse [eklyz] *nf* (*Naut*) lock.

éclusée [eklyze] *nf* sluicing water.

écluser [eklyze] (1) *vt* **(a)** (‡: *boire*) to down*, knock back‡. **qu'est-ce qu'il a éclusé** what a hell of a lot he knocked back‡. **(b)** (*Tech*) *canal* to close the locks in.

éclusier, -ière [eklyzje, jɛʀ] *nm,f* lock keeper.

écœurant, e [ekœʀɑ̃, ɑ̃t] *adj conduite* disgusting, sickening; *personne* disgusting, loathsome; *gâteau, boisson* sickly (sweet); *chance, avantage* disgusting. **~ de banalité** painfully trivial.

écœurement [ekœʀmɑ̃] *nm* (*dégoût*) (*lit*) nausea; (*fig*) disgust; (*lassitude*) disillusionment, discouragement.

écœurer [ekœʀe] (1) *vt*: **~ qn** *[gâteau, boisson]* to make sb feel sick; *[conduite, personne]* to disgust sb, nauseate sb, make sb sick; *[avantage, chance]* to make sb sick, sicken sb; *[échec, déception]* to discourage sb, sicken sb.

école [ekɔl] **1** *nf* **(a)** (*établissement, secte*) school. **avion-/navire-~** training plane/ship; **elle fait l'~ depuis 15 ans** she has been teaching for 15 years; **l'~ reprend dans une semaine** school starts again in a week's time; **aller à l'~** (*en classe*) to go to school; (*dans le bâtiment*) to go to the school; **querelle d'~s** petty quarrel between factions; **son œuvre est une ~ de courage/de vertu** his work is an excellent schooling in courage/virtue.

(b) (*loc*) **être à bonne ~** to be in good hands; **il a été à dure** *ou* **rude ~** he learned about life the hard way; **à l'~ de qn** under sb's guidance; **apprendre la vie à l'~ de la pauvreté** to be schooled by poverty; **faire l'~ buissonnière** to play truant (*Brit*), play hooky (*US*); **faire ~** *[personne]* to collect a following; *[théorie]* to gain widespread acceptance.

2: école de l'air flying school; **école de danse** (*gén*) dancing school; (*classique*) ballet school; **école de dessin** art school; **école hôtelière** catering school, hotel management school; **école laïque** (*bâtiment*) state school; (*éducation*) state education; **école maternelle** nursery school; **école militaire** military academy; **École Nationale d'Administration** National Administration School; **école normale** ≃ teachers' training college; **École normale supérieure** *grande école for training of teachers*; **école de pensée** school of thought; **École polytechnique** École Polytechnique; **école de secrétariat** secretarial college; **école du soir** night school; *V* **haut, mixte** *etc.*

écolier [ekɔlje] *nm* schoolboy; (††) scholar ††; (*fig: novice*) novice. **papier format ~** exercise (book) paper; *V* **chemin.**

écolière [ekɔljɛʀ] *nf* schoolgirl.

écologie [ekɔlɔʒi] *nf* ecology.

écologique [ekɔlɔʒik] *adj* ecological.

écologiste [ekɔlɔʒist(ə)] *nmf* ecologist.

éconduire [ekɔ̃dɥiʀ] (38) *vt* **(a)** (*congédier*) *visiteur* to dismiss; *soupirant* to reject; *solliciteur* to put off.

(b) (*reconduire*) to usher out (*frm*).

économat [ekɔnɔma] *nm* (*fonction*) bursarship, stewardship; (*bureau*) bursar's office, steward's office; (*magasin*) staff cooperative *ou* store.

économe [ekɔnɔm] *adj* thrifty. **être ~ de son temps/ses efforts** *etc* to be sparing of one's time/efforts *etc.* **2** *nmf* bursar, steward.

économétrie [ekɔnɔmetʀi] *nf* econometrics (*sg*).

économétrique [ekɔnɔmetʀik] *adj* econometric.

économie [ekɔnɔmi] *nf* **(a)** (*science*) economics (*sg*); (*Pol: système*) economy. **~ politique** political economy; **~ de troc** barter economy; **~ dirigée** state-controlled economy.

(b) (*U: épargne*) economy, thrift. **par ~** for the sake of economy; **ménagère qui a le sens de l'~** careful *ou* thrifty housewife.

(c) (*gain*) saving. **faire une ~ de temps/d'argent** to save time/money; **représenter une ~ de temps** to represent a saving in time; **procédé permettant une ~ de temps/de main d'œuvre** time-saving/labour-saving process; **elle fait l'~ d'un repas par jour** she goes *ou* does without one meal a day; **avec une grande ~ de moyens** with very restricted *ou* limited means.

(d) (*gains*) **~s** savings; **avoir des ~s** to have (some) savings, have some money saved up; **faire des ~s** to save up, save money, put money by; **faire des ~s de chauffage** to economize on heating; **il n'y a pas de petites ~s** take care of the pennies and the pounds will take care of themselves, every little helps; (*fig péj*) **faire des ~s de bouts de chandelle** to make footling *ou* cheeseparing economies.

(e) *[livre]* arrangement; *[projet]* organization.

économique [ekɔnɔmik] **1** *adj* (*Écon*) economic; (*bon marché*) economical. **2** *nf* economics (*sg*).

économiquement [ekɔnɔmikmɑ̃] *adv* economically. (*Admin*) **les ~ faibles** the lower-income groups.

économiser [ekɔnɔmize] (1) *vt électricité* to economize on, save on; *temps* to save; *argent* to save up, put aside. **~ ses forces** to save one's strength; **~ sur le chauffage** to economize on *ou* cut down on heating.

économiste [ekɔnɔmist(ə)] *nmf* economist.

écope [ekɔp] *nf* (*Naut*) bale(r).

écoper [ekɔpe] (1) *vti* (*Naut*) to bale (out). **~ (d')une punition*** to cop it‡, catch it*; **c'est moi qui ai écopé** it was me *ou* I was the one who got it in the neck‡ *ou* who took the rap*.

écorce [ekɔʀs(ə)] *nf [arbre]* bark; *[orange]* peel, skin; (†: fig) *[personne]* appearance, exterior. (*Géol*) **l'~ terrestre** the earth's crust; (*Can*) **canot d'~** bark canoe.

écorcer [ekɔʀse] (3) *vt fruit* to peel; *arbre* to bark, strip the bark from.

écorché [ekɔʀʃe] *nm* (*Anat*) écorché; (*Tech*) cut-away (diagram).

écorchement [ekɔʀʃəmɑ̃] *nm [animal]* skinning.
écorcher [ekɔʀʃe] (1) *vt* **(a)** *(dépecer) animal* to skin; *criminel* to flay. **écorché vif** flayed alive.
(b) *(égratigner) peau, visage* to scratch, graze; *genoux* to graze, scrape. **il s'est écorché les mollets** he grazed *ou* barked his shins.
(c) *(par frottement)* to chafe, rub; *cheval* to gall.
(d) *(fig) mot, nom* to mispronounce. **il écorche l'allemand** he speaks broken German.
(e) *(*loc)* ~ **le client** to fleece* one's customers; ~ **les oreilles de qn** to grate on sb's ears.
écorcheur, -euse [ekɔʀʃœʀ, øz] *nm,f [animal]* skinner; *(*fig: hôtelier)* fleecer*, extortioner.
écorchure [ekɔʀʃyʀ] *nf (V* **écorcher***)* graze; scratch; scrape.
écorner [ekɔʀne] (1) *vt meuble* to chip the corner of; *livre* to turn down the corner of; *(fig) fortune* to make a hole in. **laisser une fortune bien écornée** to leave a greatly depleted fortune; **vieux livre tout écorné** old dog-eared book.
écornifler*† [ekɔʀnifle] (1) *vt* to cadge, scrounge *(chez qn* from sb).
écornifleur, -euse*† [ekɔʀniflœʀ, øz] *nm,f* cadger, scrounger.
écossais, e [ekɔsɛ, ɛz] **1** *adj temps, caractère* Scottish, Scots *(épith)*; *whisky, confiture* Scotch; *tissu* tartan, check; *V* **douche.**
2 *nm* **(a) É~** Scot, Scotsman; **les É~** the Scots.
(b) *(Ling) (dialecte anglais)* Scots; *(dialecte gaélique)* Gaelic.
(c) *(tissu)* tartan (cloth).
3 Écossaise *nf* Scot, Scotswoman.
Écosse [ekɔs] *nf* Scotland; *V* **nouveau.**
écosser [ekɔse] (1) *vt* to shell, pod. **petits pois/haricots à ~** peas/beans in the pod, unshelled peas/beans.
écosystème [ekɔsistɛm] *nm* ecosystem.
écot [eko] *nm* share (of a bill). **chacun a payé son ~** we *(ou* they *etc)* went Dutch*, we *(ou* they *etc)* all paid our *(ou* their *etc)* share.
écoulement [ekulmɑ̃] *nm* **(a)** *[eau]* flow. **tuyau/fossé d'~** drainage pipe/ditch.
(b) *(Méd)* discharge. **~ de sang** flow of blood, bleeding.
(c) *(fig) [foule]* dispersal; *[temps]* passage, passing. **l'~ des voitures** the flow of traffic.
(d) *(Comm)* selling, passing.
écouler [ekule] (1) **1** *vt* **(a)** *(Comm)* to sell, move. **~ des faux billets** to get rid of *ou* dispose of counterfeit money; **on n'arrive pas à ~ ce stock** this stock isn't moving *ou* selling; **nous avons écoulé tout notre stock** we've cleared all our stock.
(b) faire ~ *eau* to let out, run off.
2 s'écouler *vpr* **(a)** *[liquide] (suinter)* to seep *ou* ooze (out); *(fuir)* to leak (out); *(couler)* to flow (out); *(Méd) [pus]* to ooze out. **s'~ à grands flots** to pour out.
(b) *(fig) [temps]* to pass (by), go by; *[argent]* to disappear, melt away; *[foule]* to disperse, drift away. **en réfléchissant sur sa vie écoulée** thinking over his past life; **10 ans s'étaient écoulés** 10 years had passed *ou* had elapsed *ou* had gone by; **les fonds s'écoulent vite** (the) funds are soon spent *ou* exhausted.
(c) *(Comm)* to sell. **marchandise qui s'écoule bien** quick-selling item *ou* line; **nos produits se sont bien écoulés** our products have sold well.
écourter [ekuʀte] (1) *vt bâton* to shorten; *visite* to cut short, shorten, curtail; *texte, discours* to shorten, cut down; *queue* to dock.
écoute [ekut] *nf* **(a) être aux ~s** to be listening *(de* to); *(péj)* to listen in, eavesdrop *(de* on); *(fig: être aux aguets)* to be on the look-out *(de* for), keep one's ears open *(de* for).
(b) *(Rad)* listening *(de* to). *(Mil, Police)* **~ téléphonique** (phone) tapping *(U)*; **être à l'~ de** to be tuned in to, be listening to; **se mettre à** *ou* **prendre l'~** to tune in; **nous restons à l'~** we are staying tuned in; **heures de grande ~** *(Rad)* peak listening hours; *(TV)* peak viewing hours; *(Rad, TV)* **avoir une grande ~** to have a large audience; *V* **table.**
(c) *(Naut)* sheet.
(d) *[sanglier]* **~s** ears.
écouter [ekute] (1) **1** *vt* **(a)** *discours, chanteur* to listen to, hear; *radio, disque* to listen to. **j'ai été ~ sa conférence** I went to hear his lecture; **écoutons ce qu'il dit** let's listen to *ou* hear what he has to say; **~ qn jusqu'au bout** to hear sb out; **~ qn parler** to hear sb speak; **savoir ~** to be a good listener; **~ aux portes** to eavesdrop; **~ de toutes ses oreilles** to be all ears, listen with both ears; **n'~ que d'une oreille** to listen with (only) half an ear; **faire ~ un disque à qn** to play a record to sb.
(b) *justification, confidence* to listen to; *(Jur, Rel)* to hear. **écoute-moi au moins!** at least listen to *ou* hear what I have to say!
(c) *conseil* to listen to, take notice of. **écoute-moi** take my advice; **refuser d'~ un conseil** to turn a deaf ear to advice, disregard (a piece of) advice; **bon, écoute!** well, listen!; **ses conseils sont très écoutés** his advice is greatly valued; **il se fait ~ du ministre** he has the ear of the minister; **quelqu'un de très écouté** someone whose opinion is highly valued.
(d) *(obéir à)* to listen to, obey. **~ ses parents** to listen to *ou* obey one's parents; **vas-tu (m')~!** will you listen to me!; **faire ~ qn** to get sb to listen *ou* obey *ou* behave; **son père saura le faire ~** his father will teach him how to behave; **il sait se faire ~** *[père]* he knows how to make himself obeyed; *[professeur, officier]* he's good at commanding attention *ou* respect; **n'écoutant que son courage** letting (his) courage be his only guide.
2 s'écouter *vpr*: **elle s'écoute trop** she coddles herself; **si je m'écoutais je n'irais pas** I've a good mind not to go, if I had any sense I wouldn't go; **s'~ parler** to savour one's words; **il aime s'~ parler** he loves the sound of his own voice.
écouteur, -euse [ekutœʀ, øz] **1** *nm,f (personne) (attentif)* listener; *(indiscret)* eavesdropper. **2** *nm [téléphone]* receiver. *(Rad)* **~s** earphones, headphones.
écoutille [ekutij] *nf (Naut)* hatch(way).
écouvillon [ekuvijɔ̃] *nm [fusil]* swab; *[bouteilles]* (bottle-) brush; *[boulanger]* scuffle.
écouvillonnage [ekuvijɔnaʒ] *nm [fusil]* swabbing; *[bouteille, four]* cleaning.
écouvillonner [ekuvijɔne] (1) *vt fusil* to swab; *bouteille, four* to clean.
écrabouillage* [ekʀabujaʒ] *nm*, **écrabouillement*** [ekʀabujmɑ̃] *nm* squashing, crushing.
écrabouiller* [ekʀabuje] (1) *vt* to squash, crush. **se faire ~ par une voiture** to get flattened *ou* crushed by a car.
écran [ekʀɑ̃] *nm (gén)* screen; *(Phot)* filter. **mettre** *ou* **porter un roman à l'~** to film *ou* screen a novel; **ce mur fait ~ et nous isole du froid/du bruit** this wall screens *ou* shields us from the cold/noise, this wall acts as a screen *ou* shield (for us) against the cold/noise; **faire ~ à qn** *(abriter)* to screen *ou* shelter sb; *(gêner)* to get in the way of sb; *(éclipser)* to stand in the way of sb; **son renom me fait ~** his fame puts me in the shade; **~ de fumée/de protection** smoke/protective screen; **~ de verdure** screen of greenery; *V* **petit.**
écrasant, e [ekʀɑzɑ̃, ɑ̃t] *adj impôts, mépris, poids* crushing; *preuve, responsabilité, nombre* overwhelming; *travail* gruelling, back-breaking; *victoire, défaite* crushing, overwhelming; *chaleur* overpowering, overwhelming.
écrasé, e [ekʀɑze] *(ptp de* **écraser***) adj nez* flat, squashed; *perspective, relief* dwarfed.
écrasement [ekʀɑzmɑ̃] *nm (V* **écraser***)* crushing; swatting; stubbing out; mashing; grinding; pounding; squeezing; flattening; trampling down; running over; crushing; suppressing; overwhelming.
écraser [ekʀɑze] (1) **1** *vt* **(a)** *(gén)* to crush; *mouche* to swat; *mégot* to stub out; *(en purée)* to mash; *(en poudre)* to grind *(en* to); *(au pilon)* to pound; *(pour le jus)* to squeeze; *(en aplatissant)* to flatten out; *(en piétinant)* to trample down. **~ sous la dent** *biscuit* to crunch; *noix* to crush between one's teeth; **écrasé par la foule** squashed *ou* crushed in the crowd; **aïe, vous m'écrasez les pieds** ouch, you're standing *ou* treading on my feet; **~ le champignon*** to put one's foot hard down (on the accelerator), step on the gas*; **~ le frein** to stamp on *ou* slam on the brakes; *(fig)* **il écrase tout le monde par son savoir** he overshadows *ou* outshines everyone with his knowledge.
(b) *(tuer) [voiture]* to run over; *[avalanche]* to crush. **la voiture l'a écrasé** the car ran him over; **il s'est fait ~ par une voiture** he was run over by a car.
(c) *(fig: accabler)* to crush. **les impôts nous écrasent, nous sommes écrasés d'impôts** we are overburdened *ou* crushed by taxation; **il nous écrase de son mépris** he crushes *ou* withers us with his scorn; **écrasé de chaleur** overcome by the heat; **écrasé de sommeil/de douleur** overcome by sleep/with grief; **écrasé de travail** snowed under with* *ou* overloaded with work.
(d) *(vaincre) ennemi* to crush; *rébellion* to crush, suppress, put down. **notre équipe a été écrasée** *ou* **s'est fait écraser par les adversaires** we were beaten hollow by the opposing team; **il écrase tout le monde** he outstrips *ou* outdoes everyone; **en maths il écrase tout le monde** he outshines *ou* outdoes everyone at maths.
2 *vi*: **en ~**: to sleep like a log*.
3 s'écraser *vpr* **(a)** *[avion, auto]* to crash *(contre* into, against, *sur* on); *[objet, corps]* to be dashed *ou* smashed *ou* crushed *(contre* on, against).
(b) *[foule] (dans le métro)* to be *ou* get crushed *(dans* in). **on s'écrase pour en acheter** they're rushing to buy them; **on s'écrase devant les cinémas** there's a great crush to get into the cinemas.
(c) *(: se taire)* to pipe down*. **écrasons-nous, ça vaut mieux!** we'd better pipe down!*; **oh! écrase!** oh belt up!:
écraseur, -euse* [ekʀɑzœʀ, øz] *nm,f* roadhog*.
écrémage [ekʀemaʒ] *nm* skimming, creaming.
écrémer [ekʀeme] (6) *vt lait* to skim, cream; *(fig)* to cream off the best from. **lait écrémé** skimmed milk.
écrémeuse [ekʀemøz] *nf* creamer, (cream) separator.
écrevisse [ekʀəvis] *nf* (freshwater) crayfish, crawfish. **avancer** *ou* **marcher comme une ~** to take one step forward and two steps backward; *V* **rouge.**
écrier (s') [ekʀije] (7) *vpr* to exclaim, cry out.
écrin [ekʀɛ̃] *nm* case, box *(for silver, jewels)*, casket†.
écrire [ekʀiʀ] (39) *vt* **(a)** *(gén) mots, livres* to write; *(orthographier)* to spell; *(inscrire, marquer)* to write down. **je lui ai écrit que je viendrais** I wrote and told him I would be coming; **vous écrivez trop mal** your writing is too bad; **~ des commentaires au crayon** to pencil in comments, make notes *ou* comments in pencil; **~ gros/fin** to have large/small (hand)writing; **~ à la machine** to type, typewrite.
(b) *(loc)* **c'était écrit** it was bound to happen, it was inevitable; **il est écrit que je ne pourrai jamais y arriver!** I'm fated *ou* doomed never to succeed!; **c'est écrit sur sa figure** it's stamped *ou* written all over his face.
écrit [ekʀi] *nm (ouvrage)* piece of writing, written work; *(examen)* written paper; *(Jur)* document. **par ~** in writing; *(Scol)* **être bon à l'~** to be good *ou* do well at the written papers.
écriteau, *pl* **~x** [ekʀito] *nm* notice, sign.
écritoire [ekʀitwaʀ] *nf* writing case.
écriture [ekʀityʀ] *nf* **(a)** *(à la main)* (hand)writing *(U)*. **il a une belle ~** he has beautiful (hand)writing, he writes a good hand; **~ de chat** spidery (hand)writing.
(b) *(ensemble de signes)* writing *(U)*, script. **~ hiéroglyphique** hieroglyphic writing; **~ phonétique** phonetic script.

(c) (littér: style) writing (U), style.
(d) (Comm) ~s accounts, entries, books; employé aux ~s ledger clerk; tenir les ~s to do the book-keeping ou the accounts ou the books.
(e) (Fin) entry. passer une ~ to make an entry.
(f) (Rel) l'É~, les É~s, l'É~ Sainte Scripture, the Scriptures, (the) Holy Writ.

écrivailler [ekʀivɑje] (1) vi (péj) to scribble.

écrivailleur, -euse [ekʀivɑjœʀ, øz] nm,f, **écrivaillon** [ekʀivɑjɔ̃] nm (péj) scribbler.

écrivain [ekʀivɛ̃] nm (homme) writer. (femme-)~ woman writer; ~ public† (public) letter-writer.

écrivassier, -ière [ekʀivasje, jɛʀ] nm,f = écrivailleur.

écrou [ekʀu] nm (Tech) nut; V levée².

écrouelles†† [ekʀuɛl] nfpl scrofula.

écrouer [ekʀue] (1) vt (incarcérer) to imprison, lock away (in prison). ~ qn sous le numéro X to enter sb on the prison register under the number X.

écroulé, e [ekʀule] (ptp de s'écrouler) adj (a) à moitié ~ maison, mur half-ruined, tumbledown.
(b) être ~ (par le malheur) to be prostrate with grief; (par la fatigue) to be in a state of collapse; être ~ (de rire) to be doubled up ou rolling about with laughter.

écroulement [ekʀulmɑ̃] nm (V s'écrouler) fall; collapse; caving in; crumbling; crash.

écrouler (s') [ekʀule] (1) vpr (a) [mur] to fall (down), collapse; [rocher] to fall; [toit] to collapse, cave in, fall in; [empire] to collapse, crumble; [empire financier, entreprise] to fall, collapse, crash; [prix, cours] to collapse; [espoir, projet, théorie] to collapse, crumble; [personne] (tomber) to collapse ou crumble (to the ground); (*: s'endormir) to fall fast asleep. être près de s'~ to be on the verge of collapse; tous nos projets s'écroulent all our plans are crumbling ou falling apart, this is the collapse ou end of all our plans; s'~ de sommeil/de fatigue to be overcome ou collapse with sleepiness/weariness; il s'écroula dans un fauteuil* he flopped down ou slumped down ou collapsed into an armchair.
(b) (fig) [coureur, candidat] to collapse; [accusé] to break down.

écru, e [ekʀy] adj tissu raw, in its natural state; couleur ecru, natural-coloured. toile ~e unbleached linen; soie ~e raw silk (before dyeing).

ectoplasme [ɛktɔplasm(ə)] nm ectoplasm.

écu [eky] nm (Fin, papier) crown; (Hér, Hist) shield.

écubier [ekybje] nm hawse-hole.

écueil [ekœj] nm (lit) reef, shelf; (fig) (pierre d'achoppement) stumbling block. (pièges, dangers) ~(s) pitfall(s).

écuelle [ekɥɛl] nf (pour chien) bowl; (assiette creuse) bowl, porringer††; (Hist) platter; (contenu) bowlful.

écuellée [ekɥele] nf (dial) bowlful.

éculé, e [ekyle] (ptp de éculer) adj soulier down-at-heel; plaisanterie hackneyed, worn.

éculer [ekyle] (1) 1 vt souliers to wear down at the heel. 2 s'éculer vpr [plaisanterie] to become hackneyed, wear thin.

écumage [ekymaʒ] nm skimming.

écume [ekym] nf [mer] foam; [bouche] froth; [bière] foam, froth; [métal] dross; [confiture] scum; [savon, cheval] lather. pipe en ~ de mer meerschaum pipe; (fig) l'~ de la société the scum ou dregs of society.

écumer [ekyme] (1) 1 vt (a) bouillon to skim; métal to scum.
(b) (piller) to clean out, plunder. ~ les mers to buccaneer, pirate; ~ la ville à la recherche de to scour the town in search of.
2 vi [mer, confiture] to foam; [métal] to scum; [bouche, liquide] to froth; [cheval] to lather. (fig) ~ (de rage) to foam ou boil with rage.

écumeur [ekymœʀ] nm (Hist, hum) ~ des mers pirate, buccaneer.

écumeux, -euse [ekymø, øz] adj foamy, frothy.

écumoire [ekymwaʀ] nf skimmer. troué comme une ~ riddled with holes.

écureuil [ekyʀœj] nm squirrel.

écurie [ekyʀi] nf [chevaux, cyclistes etc] stable; (fig: endroit sale) pigsty. mettre un cheval à l'~ to stable a horse; ~ de course racing stable; ~s d'Augias Augean stables; V sentir.

écusson [ekysɔ̃] nm (insigne) badge; (Hér) [serrure] escutcheon; (Agr) shield-graft.

écuyer [ekɥije] nm (a) (cavalier) rider, horseman; (professeur d'équitation) riding master. ~ de cirque circus rider. (b) (Hist) (d'un chevalier) squire; (à la cour) equerry.

écuyère [ekɥijɛʀ] nf rider, horsewoman. ~ de cirque circus rider.

eczéma [ɛgzema] nm eczema.

eczémateux, -euse [ɛgzematø, øz] adj eczematous.

edelweiss [edɛlvajs] nm edelweiss.

Éden [edɛn] nm Eden.

édénique [edenik] adj Edenic.

édenté, e [edɑ̃te] (ptp de édenter) 1 adj (totalement) toothless; (partiellement) with (some) teeth missing. 2 nmpl: les E~s the Edentata, edentate mammals.

édenter [edɑ̃te] (1) vt to break the teeth of.

édicter [edikte] (1) vt loi to enact, decree; peine to decree.

édicule [edikyl] nm (hum: cabinets) public lavatory (surtout Brit) ou convenience (Brit), rest room (US); (kiosque) kiosk (surtout Brit).

édification [edifikɑsjɔ̃] nf [bâtiment] erection, construction; [esprit] edification, enlightenment.

édifice [edifis] nm edifice, building. ~ public public building; l'~ social the structure ou fabric of society.

édifier [edifje] (7) vt (a) maison to build, construct, erect; fortune, empire to build (up). (b) (moralement) to edify; (iro) to enlighten, edify.

édile [edil] nm (frm, hum) (town) councillor.

Édimbourg [edɛ̃buʀ] n Edinburgh.

édit [edi] nm (Hist) edict.

éditer [edite] (1) vt (publier) to publish; (annoter, commenter) to edit.

éditeur, -trice [editœʀ, tʀis] nm,f (V éditer) publisher; editor.

édition [edisjɔ̃] nf (a) (action de publier) publishing; [disques] record-making. travailler dans l'~ to be in publishing ou in the publishing business.
(b) (livre, journal) edition. ~ spéciale (journal) special edition; (magazine) special issue.
(c) (annotation) editing; (texte) edition. établir l'~ critique d'un texte to produce a critical edition of a text; ~ revue et corrigée/revue et augmentée revised and corrected/revised and enlarged edition.

éditorial, pl -iaux [editɔʀjal, jo] nm leading article, leader, editorial.

éditorialiste [editɔʀjalist(ə)] nmf leader ou editorial writer.

Édouard [edwaʀ] nm Edward.

édredon [edʀədɔ̃] nm eiderdown.

éducable [edykabl(ə)] adj educable, teachable.

éducateur, -trice [edykatœʀ, tʀis] 1 adj educational. 2 nm,f educator, instructor.

éducatif, -ive [edykatif, iv] adj educational, educative.

éducation [edykɑsjɔ̃] nf (a) (enseignement) education. les problèmes de l'~ educational problems; il faut faire l'~ politique des masses the masses must be educated politically; j'ai fait mon ~ à Paris I was educated ou I went to school in Paris; j'ai fait mon ~ musicale à Paris I studied music in Paris; il a reçu une bonne ~ he is well-educated ou well-read; ~ religieuse religious education; ~ professionnelle professional training; ~ physique physical training ou education; V maison, ministère.
(b) (discipline familiale) upbringing. une ~ spartiate a Spartan upbringing; avoir de l'~ (bonnes manières) to be well-mannered ou well-bred ou well brought up; manquer d'~ to be ill-mannered ou ill-bred, be badly brought up; sans ~ ill-bred, uncouth.
(c) [goût, volonté] training.

édulcorer [edylkɔʀe] (1) vt (a) (expurger) doctrine, propos to water down; texte osé to tone down, bowdlerize. (b) (Pharm) to sweeten.

éduquer [edyke] (1) vt enfant (à l'école) to educate; (à la maison) to bring up, rear; peuple to educate; goût, volonté to train. bien éduqué well-mannered, well-bred, well brought up; mal éduqué ill-mannered, ill-bred.

effaçable [efasabl(ə)] adj inscription erasable.

effacé, e [efase] (ptp de effacer) adj (a) teinte, couleur (qui a passé) faded; (sans éclat) subdued.
(b) personne, manières retiring, unassuming; vie retiring; rôle unobtrusive.
(c) menton receding; poitrine flat. (Escrime) en position ~e sideways (on).

effacement [efasmɑ̃] nm (a) (action d'effacer) [inscription] obliteration, wearing away; [bande magnétique] erasing; [mauvaise impression, faute] obliteration, blotting out; [craintes] dispelling. (Escrime) ~ du corps/des épaules drawing o.s./one's shoulders in.
(b) (fait d'être effacé) [inscription] obliteration; [couleur] fadedness; [souvenir] dimness.
(c) [personne] (par sa modestie) retiring ou self-effacing manner; (devant un rival) eclipse. vivre dans l'~ to live a retiring life; son ~ progressif au profit du jeune sous-directeur the gradual erosion of his position ou the way in which he was gradually being eclipsed by the young deputy director.

effacer [efase] (3) 1 vt (a) (lit: enlever) inscription, traces to obliterate, efface, erase; bande magnétique to erase; (à la gomme) to rub out, erase; (à l'éponge) to wipe off, sponge off; (en lavant) to wash off ou out; (au chiffon) to wipe off; (au grattoir) to scratch out. cette gomme efface bien this is a good rubber (Brit) ou eraser (US), this rubber (Brit) ou eraser (US) works well; prends un chiffon pour ~ use a cloth to rub it out ou wipe it off; efface le tableau clean the blackboard; un chemin à demi effacé a hardly distinguishable track.
(b) (fig: faire disparaître) mauvaise impression, souvenir to erase, efface; faute to erase, obliterate; craintes to dispel. la gloire n'efface pas le crime the glory cannot erase ou efface the crime; tenter d'~ son passé to try to live down ou blot out one's past; le temps efface tout everything fades with time.
(c) (éclipser) to outshine, eclipse.
(d) ~ le corps (Escrime) to stand sideways on; (gén) to draw o.s. in; effacez les épaules! shoulders back!; effacez le ventre! stomach in!
2 s'effacer vpr (a) [inscription] to wear away, wear off, become obliterated; [couleurs] to fade; [sourire] to fade, die. le crayon s'efface mieux que l'encre it is easier to rub out pencil than ink, pencil rubs out more easily than ink; tableau noir qui s'efface bien/mal blackboard which is easy/hard to clean.
(b) [crainte, impression, souvenir] to fade, diminish. tout s'efface avec le temps everything fades in ou with time; un mauvais souvenir qui s'efface difficilement an unpleasant memory which (it) is hard to forget ou which is slow to fade.
(c) (lit: s'écarter) to move aside, step back ou aside; (fig: se tenir en arrière) to keep in the background. l'auteur s'efface derrière ses personnages the author hides behind his charac-

ters; **elle s'efface le plus possible** she keeps (herself) in the background as much as possible.

effarant, e [efaʀɑ̃, ɑ̃t] *adj* (*effrayant*) alarming; (*intensif*) *vitesse, bêtise, prix* alarming, very worrying.

effaré, e [efaʀe] (*ptp de* **effarer**) *adj* alarmed (*de* by), aghast (*attrib*) (*de* at). **au visage** ~ with a look of alarm (on his face).

effarement [efaʀmɑ̃] *nm* alarm, trepidation.

effarer [efaʀe] (1) *vt* to alarm, fill with trepidation. (*sens affaibli: stupéfier*) **cette bêtise/hausse des prix m'effare** I find such stupidity/this rise in prices most alarming *ou* extremely worrying, I am aghast at *ou* appalled by such stupidity/this rise in prices.

effaroucher [efaʀuʃe] (1) **1** *vt* (*alarmer*) *animal* to frighten away *ou* off, scare away *ou* off; *personne timide etc* to frighten, scare; (*choquer*) to shock, alarm.

2 s'effaroucher *vpr* (*par timidité*) *[animal, personne]* to shy (*de* at), take fright (*de* at); (*par pudeur*) to be shocked *ou* alarmed (*de* by).

effectif, -ive [efɛktif, iv] **1** *adj aide* real (*épith*), positive (*épith*); *travail* effective, actual (*épith*), real (*épith*); (*Fin*) *capital* real (*épith*). **le couvre-feu sera ~ à partir de 22 heures** the curfew will take effect *ou* become effective as from 10 p.m.

2 *nm* (*nombre prévu*) *[armée, bataillon]* (projected) strength; *[classe, lycée]* (projected) total number of pupils; (*nombre réel*) *[armée, bataillon]* strength; *[classe, lycée]* size, (total) number of pupils; *[parti]* size, strength. (*fig: troupes: Mil, Pol*) **~s** numbers, strength (*U*); **le lycée n'a jamais atteint son ~ *ou* l'~ prévu** the (total) number of pupils in the school has never reached its projected level; **l'~ de la classe a triplé en 2 ans** the (total) number of pupils in the class has *ou* the (size of the) class has trebled in 2 years; (*Mil*) **l'~ est au complet** we are at full strength *ou* up to strength; **augmenter ses ~s** *[parti, lycée]* to boost its numbers.

effectivement [efɛktivmɑ̃] *adv* **(a)** *aider, travailler* effectively. **contribuer ~ à qch** to make a real *ou* positive contribution to sth.

(b) (*réellement*) actually, really. **je répète que cet incident s'est ~ produit** I repeat that this incident actually *ou* really happened *ou* did happen.

(c) (*en effet*) actually, in fact. **c'est ~ plus rapide** it's actually faster, it is in fact faster; **n'y-a-t-il pas risque de conflit? — ~!** is there not a risk of conflict? — quite (so)! *ou* there is indeed!; **~, quand ce phénomène se produit ...** indeed *ou* in fact, when this phenomenon occurs ... .

effectuer [efɛktɥe] (1) *vt manœuvre, opération, mission, réparation* to carry out; *expérience* to carry out, perform, make; *mouvement* to execute; *geste* to make, execute; *paiement* to make, effect; *trajet* to make, complete; *reprise économique etc* to undergo, stage. **le trajet s'effectue en 2 heures** the journey takes 2 hours (to complete); **le paiement peut s'~ de 2 façons** payment may be made in 2 ways; **le rapatriement des prisonniers s'est effectué sans incident** the repatriation of the prisoners went off without a hitch; **la rentrée scolaire s'est effectuée dans de bonnes conditions** the new school year got off to a good start.

efféminé, e [efemine] (*ptp de* **efféminer**) *adj* effeminate.

efféminer [efemine] (1) *vt* (*littér*) *personne* to make effeminate; *peuple, pensée* to emasculate.

effervescence [efɛʀvesɑ̃s] *nf* (*lit*) effervescence; (*fig*) agitation. **mettre la ville en ~** to set the town astir, put the town in a turmoil; **être en ~** to be in a turmoil (of excitement), be simmering with excitement; **l'~ révolutionnaire** the stirrings of revolution.

effervescent, e [efɛʀvesɑ̃, ɑ̃t] *adj* (*lit*) effervescent; (*fig*) agitated, in a turmoil (*attrib*).

effet [efɛ] *nm* **(a)** (*résultat*) *[action, médicament]* effect. **c'est un ~ de son inexpérience** it is because of *ou* a result of his inexperience; **c'est l'~ du hasard** it is quite by chance, it is the result of chance; **avoir *ou* produire beaucoup d'~/l'~ voulu** to have *ou* produce a considerable effect/the desired effect; **ces livres ont un ~ nocif sur la jeunesse** these books have a harmful effect on young people; **être *ou* rester sans ~** to be ineffective, have no effect; **créer un ~ de surprise** to create an effect of surprise; **en faisant cela il espérait créer un ~ de surprise** by doing this he was hoping to surprise them (*ou* us *etc*); **ces mesures sont demeurées sans ~** these measures had no effect *ou* were ineffective *ou* were of no avail; **avoir pour ~ de** to have the effect of, result in; **avoir pour ~ une augmentation/diminution de** to result in an increase/a decrease in; **ce médicament (me) fait de l'~/a fait son ~** this medicine is effective *ou* works (on me)/has taken effect *ou* has worked; *V* **relation.**

(b) (*impression*) impression. **faire *ou* produire un ~ considérable/déplorable (sur qn)** to make *ou* have a great/dreadful impression (on sb); **il a fait *ou* produit son petit ~** he managed to cause a bit of a stir *ou* a minor sensation; **il aime faire de l'~** he likes to create a stir; **c'est tout l'~ que ça te fait?** is that all it means to you?, is that all you feel about it?; **faire bon/mauvais ~ sur qn** to make a good/bad impression on sb; **il m'a fait bon ~** he made a good impression on me, I was favourably impressed by him; **ce tableau fait bon ~/beaucoup d'~ ici** this picture is quite/very effective here; **il me fait l'~ d'(être) une belle crapule** he strikes me as (being) a real crook, he seems like a real crook to me; **il me fait l'~ d'un renard** he puts me in mind of a fox, he reminds me of a fox; **cette déclaration a fait l'~ d'une bombe** this statement came as a bombshell; **cela m'a fait de l'~, de le voir dans cet état** it really affected me *ou* it gave me quite a turn to see him in that state; *V* **bœuf.**

(c) (*artifice, procédé*) effect. **~ de contraste/de style/comique** contrasting/stylistic/comic(al) effect; **~ de perspective/d'optique** 3-D *ou* 3-dimensional/visual effect; **~ facile** facile *ou* trite effect; **~ de lumière** (*au théâtre*) lighting effect; (*naturel, sur l'eau*) play of light (*U*), effects of light; **rechercher les ~s *ou* l'~** to strive for effect; **soigner ses ~s** to take great trouble over one's effects; **elle lui a coupé ses ~s** she stole his thunder; **manquer *ou* rater son ~** *[personne]* to spoil one's effect; *[plaisanterie]* to fall flat, misfire; **faire des ~s de voix** to use one's voice to dramatic effect, make dramatic use of one's voice; **cet avocat fait des ~s de manches** this barrister flourishes his arms *ou* waves his arms about in a most dramatic fashion.

(d) (*Tech*) **~ Doppler(-Fizeau)** Doppler effect; **machine à simple/double ~** single-/double-effect machine.

(e) (*Sport*) *[balle]* spin. **donner de l'~ à une balle** to spin a ball.

(f) (*Jur*) **avec ~ rétroactif** backdated; **prendre ~ à la date de** to take effect (as) from, be operative (as) from.

(g) (*Comm: valeur*) **~ de commerce, ~ bancaire** bill of exchange; **~ à vue** sight bill; **~ au porteur** bill payable to bearer; **~s publics** government securities.

(h) (*affaires, vêtements*) **~s** things, clothes.

(i) en ~: (*introduit une explication*) **cette voiture me plaît beaucoup, en ~, elle est rapide et confortable** I like this car very much because it's fast and comfortable; (*dans une réponse*) **étiez-vous absent, mardi dernier? — en ~, j'avais la grippe** were you absent last Tuesday? — yes (I was) *ou* that's right, I had flu; **cela me plaît beaucoup, en ~** yes (indeed), I like it very much; **c'est en ~ plus rapide** it's actually faster, it is in fact faster.

(j) (*loc*) **mettre à ~** to put into operation *ou* effect; **à cet ~** to that effect *ou* end; **sous l'~ de** *alcool* under the effect(s) *ou* influence of; *drogue* under the effect(s) of; **sous l'~ de la colère il me frappa** in his anger he hit me, he hit me in anger; **il était encore sous l'~ de la colère** his anger had not yet worn off, he was still angry.

effeuillage [efœjaʒ] *nm* **(a)** (*Agr*) thinning-out of leaves. **(b)** (*hum*) striptease.

effeuiller [efœje] (1) **1** *vt arbre, branche* *[arboriculteur]* to thin out the leaves of; *[vent]* to blow the leaves off. (*par jeu*) **~ une branche/une fleur** to pull *ou* pick the leaves off a branch/the petals off a flower; **~ la marguerite** to play 'she-loves-me, she-loves-me-not'. **2 s'effeuiller** *vpr* *[arbre]* to shed *ou* lose its leaves.

effeuilleuse [efœjøz] *nf* (*hum: femme*) stripper.

efficace [efikas] *adj remède, mesure* effective, efficacious, effectual; *personne, machine* efficient. **d'~s gardiens de la moralité** effective guardians of morality; *V* **grâce.**

efficacement [efikasmɑ̃] *adv* (*V* **efficace**) effectively, efficaciously, effectually; efficiently.

efficacité [efikasite] *nf* (*V* **efficace**) effectiveness, efficacy; efficiency.

efficience [efisjɑ̃s] *nf* efficiency.

efficient, e [efisjɑ̃, ɑ̃t] *adj* efficient.

effigie [efiʒi] *nf* effigy. **à l'~ de** bearing the effigy of; **en ~** in effigy.

effilé, e [efile] (*ptp de* **effiler**) **1** *adj doigt, silhouette* slender, tapering; *pointe, outil* highly-sharpened; *carrosserie* streamlined. **2** *nm [jupe, serviette]* fringe.

effiler [efile] (1) **1** *vt* **(a)** *objet* to taper; *lame* to sharpen; *lignes, forme* to streamline. **(b)** *étoffe* to fray; *cheveux* to thin (out). **2 s'effiler** *vpr [objet]* to taper; *[étoffe]* to fray.

effilochage [efilɔʃaʒ] *nm* fraying.

effilocher [efilɔʃe] (1) **1** *vt tissu* to fray. **2 s'effilocher** *vpr* to fray. **veste effilochée** frayed jacket.

efflanqué, e [eflɑ̃ke] *adj animal* raw-boned, mere skin and bones (*attrib*); *personne* emaciated, mere skin and bones (*attrib*). **c'était un cheval ~** the horse was mere skin and bones, the horse was a raw-boned creature.

effleurement [eflœʀmɑ̃] *nm* (*frôlement*) light touch. **elle sentit sur son bras l'~ d'une main** she felt the light touch of a hand on her arm, she felt a hand brush against her arm.

effleurer [eflœʀe] (1) *vt* (*frôler*) to touch lightly, brush (against); (*érafler*) to graze; (*fig*) *sujet* to touch (lightly) upon. **les oiseaux effleuraient l'eau** the birds skimmed (across) the water; **une idée lui effleura l'esprit** an idea crossed his mind; **ça ne m'a pas effleuré** it didn't cross my mind, it didn't occur to me; (*littér*) **ayant oublié le désir qui l'avait effleuré** having forgotten his fleeting desire.

effluve [eflyv] *nm* (*littér*) **~s** (*agréables*) fragrance, exhalation(s); (*désagréables*) effluvium (*pl* effluvia), exhalation(s); (*fig*) **les ~s du passé** the shadows of the past.

effondré, e [efɔ̃dʀe] (*ptp de* **s'effondrer**) *adj* (*abattu*) crushed (*de* by), prostrate (*de* with).

effondrement [efɔ̃dʀəmɑ̃] *nm* **(a)** (*V* **s'effondrer**) collapse; caving-in; falling-in; falling-down; falling-away; breaking-down. **(b)** (*abattement*) utter dejection.

effondrer (s') [efɔ̃dʀe] (1) *vpr* **(a)** *[toit, plancher]* to collapse, cave in, fall in; *[mur]* to collapse, fall down; *[terre]* to fall away, collapse; *[pont]* to collapse, cave in.

(b) (*fig*) *[empire, projets]* to collapse, fall in ruins; *[prix, marché]* to collapse; *[preuve, argument]* to collapse, fall down (completely).

(c) *[personne]* to collapse; (*fig*) *[accusé]* to break down. (*fig*) **elle s'est effondrée en larmes** she dissolved *ou* collapsed into tears, she broke down and wept.

efforcer (s') [efɔʀse] (3) *vpr*: **s'~ de faire** to try hard *ou* endeavour to do, do one's best to do; (*littér*) **s'~ à: il s'efforçait à une politesse dont personne n'était dupe** he was striving to remain polite but he convinced nobody *ou* but nobody was taken in; (†, *littér*) **ils s'efforçaient en vain** they were striving in vain.

effort [efɔʀ] *nm* **(a)** (*physique, intellectuel*) effort. **après bien des ~s** after much exertion *ou* effort; **la récompense de nos ~s** the reward for our efforts; **un (gros) ~ financier** a (large) financial outlay; **~ de volonté** effort of will; **cela demande un ~ de réflexion** that requires careful thought; **faire un ~ de mémoire** to make an effort *ou* try hard to remember; **cela demande un ~ d'attention** you have to make an effort to concentrate (on that); **tu dois faire un ~ d'imagination** you should (make an effort and) try to use your imagination.

(b) (*Tech*) stress, strain. **~ de torsion** torsional stress; **~ de traction** traction, pull; **l'~ que subissent les fondations** the strain on the foundations.

(c) (*loc*) **faire un ~** to make an effort; **faire de gros ~s pour réussir** to make a great effort to succeed, try very hard to succeed; **faire tous ses ~s** to do one's utmost *ou* all one can, make every effort; **faire un ~ sur soi-même pour rester calme** to make an effort to stay calm, try to keep calm; **faire l'~ de** to make the effort to; **plier sous l'~** to bend with the effort; (*Sport*) **rester en deçà de son ~** not to go all out, not to stretch o.s. (to one's limit); **encore un ~** just one more go, just a little more effort; **sans ~** effortlessly, easily; **avec ~** with an effort; *V* **moindre.**

effraction [efʀaksjɔ̃] *nf* (*Jur*) breaking and entering (*Jur*), breaking(-in). **entrer par ~** to break in; **ils sont entrés par ~ dans la maison** they broke into the house; *V* **vol²**.

effraie [efʀɛ] *nf*: **(chouette) ~** barn-owl.

effrangé, e [efʀɑ̃ʒe] (*ptp de* **effranger**) *adj* fringed; (*effiloché*) frayed.

effranger [efʀɑ̃ʒe] (3) **1** *vt* to fringe (*by fraying*). **2 s'effranger** *vpr* to fray. **ces manches s'effrangent** these sleeves are fraying (at the edges).

effrayant, e [efʀɛjɑ̃, ɑ̃t] *adj* frightening, fearsome; (*sens affaibli*) frightful, dreadful.

effrayer [efʀeje] (8) **1** *vt* to frighten, scare. **2 s'effrayer** *vpr* to be frightened *ou* scared (*de* by), take fright (*de* at).

effréné, e [efʀene] *adj course* wild, frantic; *passion, luxe* unbridled, unrestrained, wild.

effritement [efʀitmɑ̃] *nm [roche, mur]* crumbling(-away); *[valeurs morales]* crumbling(-away), disintegration. (*Pol*) **~ de la majorité** erosion *ou* crumbling-away of the majority; (*Fin*) **~ d'une monnaie** erosion of a currency, gradual decline in a currency.

effriter [efʀite] (1) **1** *vt biscuit, sucre* to crumble; *roche, falaise* to cause to crumble.

2 s'effriter *vpr [roche]* to crumble (away); *[valeurs morales]* to crumble (away), disintegrate; *[majorité électorale]* to crumble; *[monnaie]* to be eroded, decline in value.

effroi [efʀwa] *nm* (*littér*) terror, dread.

effronté, e [efʀɔ̃te] *adj personne, air, réponse* insolent, impudent; *mensonge, menteur* barefaced (*épith*), brazen, shameless. **l'~** (*enfant*) (the) impudent *ou* insolent child!; (*adulte*) (the) insolent fellow!

effrontément [efʀɔ̃temɑ̃] *adv* (*V* **effronté**) insolently, impudently; barefacedly, brazenly, shamelessly.

effronterie [efʀɔ̃tʀi] *nf [réponse, personne]* insolence, impudence, effrontery; *[mensonge]* shamelessness, effrontery.

effroyable [efʀwajabl(ə)] *adj* horrifying, appalling.

effroyablement [efʀwajabləmɑ̃] *adv* appallingly, horrifyingly. **~ mutilé** with appalling injuries.

effusion [efyzjɔ̃] *nf [tendresse, sentiment]* burst. **après ces ~s** after these effusions *ou* emotional demonstrations; **remercier qn avec ~** to thank sb effusively; **~ de sang** bloodshed.

égaiement [egɛmɑ̃] *nm* (*rare: V* **égayer**) cheering-up; brightening-up; amusement; enlivenment; merrymaking.

égailler (s') [egaje] (1) *vpr* to scatter, disperse.

égal, e, *mpl* **-aux** [egal, o] **1** *adj* **(a)** (*de même valeur*) equal (*à* to). **de poids ~** of equal weight; **à poids ~** weight for weight; **égaux en nombre** of equal numbers, equal in numbers; **à ~e distance de deux points** equidistant *ou* exactly halfway between two points; **d'adresse/d'audace ~e** of equal skill/boldness, equally skilful/bold.

(b) (*sans variation*) *justice* even, unvarying; *climat* equable, unchanging; *terrain* even, level; *bruit, rumeur* steady, even; *vent* steady. **de caractère ~** even-tempered, equable(-tempered); **marcher d'un pas ~** to walk with a regular *ou* an even step.

(c) (*loc*) **ça m'est ~** (*je n'y attache pas d'importance*) I don't mind, I don't feel strongly (about it); (*je m'en fiche*) I don't care; **tout lui est ~** he doesn't feel strongly about anything; **c'est ~, il aurait pu m'écrire** all the same *ou* be that as it may, he might have written (to me); **la partie n'est pas ~e (entre eux)** they are not evenly matched; **sa probité n'a d'~e que sa générosité** his integrity is matched *ou* equalled only by his generosity; **rester ~ à soi-même** to remain true to form, be still one's old self; *V* **arme, jeu.**

2 *nm,f* **(a)** (*personne*) equal. **il ne fréquente que ses égaux** he only associates with his equals.

(b) (*loc*) **d'~ à ~: il a traité d'~ à ~ avec moi** he treated me as his *ou* an equal; **nous parlions d'~ à ~** we talked to each other as equals; **à l'~ de** (*égal à*): **sa probité est à l'~ de sa générosité** his generosity is equalled *ou* matched by his integrity; (*comme*) **c'est une vraie mégère à l'~ de sa mère** she's a real shrew just like her mother; **sans ~** *beauté, courage* matchless, unequalled, peerless.

égalable [egalabl(ə)] *adj*: **difficilement ~** difficult to equal *ou* match.

également [egalmɑ̃] *adv* (*sans préférence*) equally; (*aussi*) also, too, as well. **elle lui a ~ parlé** (*elle aussi*) she also *ou* too spoke to him, she spoke to him too *ou* as well; (*à lui aussi*) she spoke to him as well *ou* too.

égaler [egale] (1) **1** *vt* **(a)** *personne, record* to equal (*en* in). (*Math*) **2 plus 2 égalent 4** 2 plus 2 equals 4; **personne ne l'a encore égalé en adresse** so far there has been no one to equal *ou* match his skill, so far no one has equalled him in skill *ou* matched him for skill; **son intégrité égale sa générosité** his generosity is matched *ou* equalled by his integrity, his integrity matches *ou* equals his generosity.

(b) (*comparer*) **~ qn à** to rank sb with; **c'est un bon compositeur mais je ne l'égalerais pas à Ravel** he's a good composer but I wouldn't rank him with *ou* put him beside Ravel.

(c) (†: *rendre égal*) **la mort égale tous les êtres** death makes all men equal *ou* levels all men.

2 s'égaler *vpr*: **s'~ à** (*se montrer l'égal de*) to equal, be equal to; (*se comparer à*) to liken o.s. to, compare o.s. to.

égalisateur, -trice [egalizatœʀ, tʀis] *adj* equalizing. (*Sport*) **le but ~** the equalizer.

égalisation [egalizɑsjɔ̃] *nf* (*Sport*) equalization; *[sol, revenus]* levelling. (*Sport*) **c'est l'~** they've scored the equalizer (*Brit*) *ou* the equalizing (*Brit*) *ou* tying (*US*) goal, they've equalized (*Brit*) *ou* tied (*US*).

égaliser [egalize] (1) **1** *vt chances* to equalize, make equal; *cheveux* to straighten up; *sol, revenus* to level (out). **2** *vi* (*Sport*) to equalize. **3 s'égaliser** *vpr [chances]* to become (more) equal; *[sol]* to level (out), become (more) level.

égalitaire [egalitɛʀ] *adj* egalitarian.

égalitarisme [egalitaʀism(ə)] *nm* egalitarianism.

égalitariste [egalitaʀist(ə)] *adj, nmf* egalitarian.

égalité [egalite] *nf [chances, hommes]* equality; (*Math*) identity; *[climat]* equableness, equability; *[pouls]* regularity; *[surface]* evenness, levelness. **~ d'humeur** evenness of temper, equableness, equanimity; **~ d'âme** equanimity; **à ~ de qualification on prend le plus âgé** in the case of equal qualifications we take the oldest; (*Sport*) **être à ~** (*après un but*) to be equal; (*fin du match*) to draw; *V* **pied.**

égard [egaʀ] *nm* **(a)** (*respect*) **~s** consideration; **il la reçut avec de grands ~s** he welcomed her with every *ou* great consideration; **il a beaucoup d'~s pour sa femme** he shows great consideration for his wife, he's very considerate to(wards) his wife; **manquer d'~s envers qn** to be inconsiderate to(wards) sb, show a lack of consideration for sb; **vous n'avez aucun ~ pour votre matériel** you have no respect for your equipment.

(b) à l'~ de (*envers*): **aimable à l'~ des enfants** friendly towards children; (*contre*) **des mesures ont été prises à son ~** measures have been taken concerning him *ou* with regard to him; (*en ce qui concerne*) **à l'~ de ce que vous me dites ...** concerning *ou* regarding *ou* with regard to what you tell me ...; (†: *en comparaison de*) **il est médiocre à l'~ de l'autre** he is mediocre in comparison with *ou* compared with the other.

(c) (*loc*) **par ~ pour** out of consideration for; **sans ~ pour** without regard for, without considering; **à tous ~s** in all respects; **à certains ~s** in certain respects; **à cet/aucun ~** in this/no respect; (*frm*) **eu ~ à** in view of, considering; **avoir ~ à** to take into account *ou* consideration.

égaré, e [egaʀe] (*ptp de* **égarer**) *adj* **(a)** *voyageur* lost; *animal* stray (*épith*), lost; *obus* stray (*épith*); *V* **brebis. (b)** *chemin, village* remote, out-of-the-way. **(c)** *air, regard* distraught, wild.

égarement [egaʀmɑ̃] *nm* **(a)** (*littér: trouble affectif*) distraction. **un ~ de l'esprit** mental distraction. **(b)** (*littér: dérèglements*) **~s** aberrations; **revenir de ses ~s** to return to the straight and narrow.

égarer [egaʀe] (1) **1** *vt* **(a)** *voyageur* to lead out of his way; *enquêteurs* to mislead; (*moralement*) *jeunes, esprits* to lead astray. (*frm*) **la douleur vous égare** you are distraught *ou* distracted with grief; **égaré par la douleur** distraught *ou* distracted with grief.

(b) *objet* to mislay.

2 s'égarer *vpr* **(a)** *[voyageur]* to lose one's way, get lost, lose o.s.; *[colis, lettre]* to get lost, go astray; *[discussion, auteur]* to wander from the point. **ne nous égarons pas!** let's stick to the point!, let's not wander from the point!; **il s'égare dans des détails** he loses himself *ou* he gets lost in details; **une espèce d'original égaré dans notre siècle** an eccentric sort of fellow who seems lost *ou* who seems out of place in the age we live in; (*fig, Rel*) **s'~ hors du droit chemin** to wander *ou* stray from the straight and narrow; **quelques votes socialistes se sont égarés sur ce candidat d'extrême droite** a few socialist votes have been lost to the candidate of the far right.

(b) mon esprit s'égare à cette pensée the thought of it makes me feel quite distraught.

égayement [egɛjmɑ̃] *nm* = **égaiement.**

égayer [egeje] (8) **1** *vt personne* (*remonter*) to cheer up*, brighten up; (*divertir*) to amuse, cheer up*; *pièce* to brighten up; *conversation* to enliven, liven up, brighten up.

2 s'égayer *vpr* to make merry. **s'~ aux dépens de qn** to make merry at sb's expense, make sb an object of fun; **s'~ à voir ...** to be highly amused *ou* entertained at seeing ... .

Égée [eʒe] *adj*: **la mer ~** the Aegean Sea.

égéen, -enne [eʒeɛ̃, ɛn] *adj peuples* Aegean.

Égérie [eʒeʀi] *nf* (*Hist*) Egeria. **é~** (*fig*) *[poète]* oracle; *[voleurs]* mastermind; **la police a arrêté l'é~ de la bande** the police have arrested the woman (*ou* girl) who masterminded the gang *ou* who was the brains *ou* driving force behind the gang.

égide [eʒid] *nf*: **sous l'~ de** under the aegis of.

églantier [eglɑ̃tje] *nm* wild *ou* dog rose(-bush).

églantine [eglɑ̃tin] *nf* wild *ou* dog rose, eglantine.

églefin [egləfɛ̃] *nm* = **aiglefin.**

église [egliz] *nf* **(a)** (*bâtiment*) church. **~ abbatiale** abbey church; **~ paroissiale** parish church; **aller à l'~** to go to church; **il est à l'~** (*pour l'office*) he's at *ou* in church; (*en curieux*) he's in the church; **se marier à l'~** to get married in church, have a church wedding.

(b) (*secte, clergé*) **l'É~** the Church; **l'É~ militante/triomphante** the Church militant/triumphant; **l'É~ anglicane** the Church of England, the Anglican Church; **l'É~ réformée** the Reformed Church; **l'É~ orthodoxe** the Greek Orthodox Church.

églogue [eglɔg] *nf* eclogue.

égocentrique [egɔsɑ̃tʀik] **1** *adj* egocentric, self-centred. **2** *nmf* egocentric, self-centred person.

égocentrisme [egɔsɑ̃tʀism(ə)] *nm* (*gén*) egocentricity, self-centredness; (*Psych*) egocentricity.

égoïne [egɔin] *nf*: **(scie-)~** hand-saw.

égoïsme [egɔism(ə)] *nm* selfishness, egoism.

égoïste [egɔist(ə)] **1** *adj* selfish, egoistic. **2** *nmf* selfish person, egoist.

égoïstement [egɔistəmɑ̃] *adv* selfishly, egoistically.

égorgement [egɔʀʒəmɑ̃] *nm*: **~ d'un mouton/prisonnier** slitting *ou* cutting of a sheep's/prisoner's throat.

égorger [egɔʀʒe] (3) *vt* (*lit*) to slit *ou* cut the throat of; (**fig*) *débiteur, client* to bleed white.

égorgeur [egɔʀʒœʀ] *nm* cut-throat.

égosiller (s') [egozije] (1) *vpr* (*crier*) to shout o.s. hoarse; (*chanter fort*) to sing at the top of one's voice.

égotisme [egɔtism(ə)] *nm* egotism.

égotiste [egɔtist(ə)] **1** *adj* (*littér*) egotistic(al). **2** *nmf* egotist.

égout [egu] *nm* sewer. **réseau** *ou* **système d'~s** sewerage system; **eaux d'~** sewage; *V* **tout.**

égoutier [egutje] *nm* sewer worker.

égouttage [egutaʒ] *nm*, **égouttement** [egutmɑ̃] *nm* (*V* **égoutter**) straining; wringing-out; draining; dripping.

égoutter [egute] (1) **1** *vt légumes* (*avec une passoire*) to strain; *linge* (*en le tordant*) to wring out; *fromage* to drain.

2 *vi [vaisselle]* to drain; *[linge, eau]* to drip. **faire ~ l'eau** to drain off the water; **mettre le linge à ~** to hang up the washing to drip; **'laver à la main et laisser ~'** 'wash by hand and drip dry'.

3 s'égoutter *vpr [arbre, linge, eau]* to drip; *[vaisselle]* to drain, drip.

égouttoir [egutwaʀ] *nm [vaisselle]* (*intégré dans l'évier*) draining board; (*mobile*) draining rack; *[légumes]* strainer, colander.

égratigner [egʀatiɲe] (1) *vt* (*lit*) to scratch; (*fig*) *adversaire* to have a dig at. **ces critiques l'ont quelque peu égratigné** this criticism piqued him somewhat.

égratignure [egʀatiɲyʀ] *nf* scratch; (*fig*) dig. **il s'en est sorti sans une ~** he came out of it without a scratch *ou* unscathed; **ce n'était qu'une ~ faite à son amour-propre** it was only a dig at his self-esteem.

égrenage [egʀənaʒ] *nm* (*V* **égrener**) shelling; podding; ginning. **l'~ du raisin** picking grapes off the bunch.

égrènement [egʀɛnmɑ̃] *nm*: **l'~ des heures/minutes** marking out the hours/minutes; **l'~ des hameaux le long de la vallée** the hamlets dotted along the valley; **l'~ du chapelet** telling one's beads (†, *littér*).

égrener [egʀəne] (5) **1** *vt* **(a)** (*lit*) *pois* to shell, pod; *blé, maïs, épi* to shell; *coton* to gin; *grappe* to pick grapes off. **~ des raisins** to pick grapes off the bunch.

(b) (*fig*) **~ son chapelet** to tell one's beads (†, *littér*), say the rosary; **la pendule égrène les heures** the clock marks out the hours.

2 s'égrener *vpr [raisins]* to drop off the bunch; *[blé]* to drop off the stalk; (*fig*) *[rire]* to ripple out. **les maisons s'égrenaient le long de la route** the houses were dotted along the road; **les notes cristallines du piano s'égrenaient dans le silence** the crystal notes of the piano fell one by one on the silence.

égreneuse [egʀənøz] *nf [céréales]* corn-sheller; *[coton]* gin.

égrillard, e [egʀijaʀ, aʀd(ə)] *adj* ribald, bawdy.

Égypte [eʒipt] *nf* Egypt.

égyptien, -ienne [eʒipsjɛ̃, jɛn] **1** *adj* Egyptian. **2** *nm,f*: **É~(ne)** Egyptian.

égyptologie [eʒiptɔlɔʒi] *nf* Egyptology.

égyptologue [eʒiptɔlɔg] *nmf* Egyptologist.

eh [e] *excl* hey! **~ oui!** I'm afraid so!; **~ bien** well.

éhonté, e [eɔ̃te] *adj action* shameless, brazen; *menteur, mensonge* shameless, barefaced, brazen.

eider [ɛdɛʀ] *nm* eider.

éjaculation [eʒakylɑsjɔ̃] *nf* (*Physiol*) ejaculation.

éjaculatoire [eʒakylatwaʀ] *adj* (*Physiol*) ejaculatory.

éjaculer [eʒakyle] (1) *vi* (*Physiol*) to ejaculate.

éjectable [eʒɛktabl(ə)] *adj V* **siège**[1].

éjecter [eʒɛkte] (1) *vt* (*Tech*) to eject; (*:*) to kick out*:*, chuck out*:*. **se faire ~*:*** to get o.s. kicked*:* *ou* chucked*:* out.

éjection [eʒɛksjɔ̃] *nf* (*Tech*) ejection; (*:*) kicking-out*:*, chucking-out*:*.

élaboration [elabɔʀɑsjɔ̃] *nf* (*V* **élaborer**) (careful) working-out; elaboration; development.

élaborer [elabɔʀe] (1) *vt plan, système* to work out (carefully), elaborate, develop; (*Bio, Physiol*) *bile, sève, aliments* to elaborate.

élagage [elagaʒ] *nm* (*lit, fig*) pruning.

élaguer [elage] (1) *vt* (*lit, fig*) to prune.

élagueur [elagœʀ] *nm* pruner.

élan[1] [elɑ̃] *nm* (*Zool*) elk, moose.

élan[2] [elɑ̃] *nm* **(a)** (*début de course*) run up. **prendre son ~** to take a run up; **mal calculer son ~** to misjudge one's run up; **saut avec/sans ~** running/standing jump; **ils ont couru jusque chez eux d'un seul ~** they dashed home without stopping (once); (*fig*) **l'~ du clocher vers le ciel** the soaring of the steeple into the sky, the thrust of the steeple towards the sky.

(b) (*vitesse acquise*) momentum. **prendre de l'~** *[coureur]* to gather speed; **perdre son ~** to lose one's momentum; **il a continué dans** *ou* **sur son ~** he continued to run at the same pace *ou* speed; **rien ne peut arrêter son ~** nothing can check *ou* stop his pace *ou* momentum; **emporté par son propre ~** (*lit*) carried along by his own impetus *ou* momentum; (*fig*) carried away on *ou* by the tide of his own enthusiasm.

(c) (*poussée, transport*) *[enthousiasme, colère]* surge, rush, burst. **les ~s de l'imagination** flights of fancy; **les rares ~s qu'il avait vers elle** the few surges *ou* rushes of affection he felt for her; **les ~s lyriques de l'orateur** the lyrical outbursts of the speaker.

(d) (*ardeur*) vigour, spirit, élan. **~ patriotique** patriotic fervour; **l'~ des troupes** the vigour *ou* spirit *ou* élan of the troops.

élancé, e [elɑ̃se] (*ptp de* **élancer**) *adj clocher, colonne, taille* slender.

élancement [elɑ̃smɑ̃] *nm* (*Méd*) shooting *ou* sharp pain. (*littér*) **~ de l'âme** yearning of the soul.

élancer[1] [elɑ̃se] (3) *vi [blessure]* to give shooting *ou* sharp pains. **mon doigt m'élance** I get shooting *ou* sharp pains in my finger.

élancer[2] [elɑ̃se] (3) **1** *vt* (*littér*) **le clocher élance sa flèche vers le ciel** the church steeple soars up *ou* thrusts upwards into the sky.

2 s'élancer *vpr* **(a)** (*se précipiter*) to hurl o.s., dash. **s'~ audehors** to rush *ou* dash outside; **s'~ comme une flèche vers** to dart towards; **s'~ d'un bond sur** to leap onto; **s'~ au secours de qn** to rush *ou* dash to help sb; **s'~ à la poursuite de qn** to hurl o.s. in pursuit of sb, hurl o.s. *ou* dash after sb; **s'~ vers qn** to leap *ou* dash towards sb; **s'~ sur qn** to hurl *ou* throw o.s. at sb, rush at sb; **s'~ à l'assaut d'une montagne/forteresse** to launch an attack on a mountain/fortress.

(b) (*littér: se dresser*) to soar *ou* thrust (upwards). **la tour s'élance vers le ciel** the tower soars *ou* thrusts up into the sky.

élargir [elaʀʒiʀ] (2) **1** *vt* **(a)** *rue* to widen; *robe* to let out; *souliers* to stretch, widen; (*fig*) *débat, connaissances* to broaden, widen. (*Pol*) **majorité élargie** increased majority; **ça lui élargit la taille** that makes her waist look fatter; **une veste qui élargit les épaules** a jacket that makes the shoulders look broader *ou* wider.

(b) (*Jur: libérer*) to release, free.

2 s'élargir *vpr [vêtement]* to stretch, get wider *ou* broader; *[route]* to widen, get wider; (*fig*) *[esprit, débat]* to broaden; *[idées]* to broaden, widen.

élargissement [elaʀʒismɑ̃] *nm* (*V* **élargir**) widening; letting-out; stretching; broadening; release, freeing.

élasticité [elastisite] *nf* (*V* **élastique**) elasticity; spring, buoyancy; flexibility; accommodating nature.

élastique [elastik] **1** *adj objet* elastic; *démarche* springy, buoyant; *sens, esprit* flexible; (*péj*) *conscience* accommodating; *règlement* elastic, flexible; (*Écon*) *offre, demande* elastic. **poignets en tissu ~** elasticated cuffs.

2 *nm* (*de bureau*) elastic *ou* rubber band; (*pour couture etc*) elastic (*U*). **en ~** elasticated, elastic; *V* **lâcher.**

Elbe [ɛlb] *nf*: **l'île d'~** (the isle of) Elba; (*fleuve*) the Elbe.

électeur, -trice [elɛktœʀ, tʀis] *nm,f* **(a)** (*Pol*) voter, elector. **le député et ses ~s** ≃ the member of parliament and his constituents; (*corps électoral*) **les ~s** the electorate, the voters.

(b) (*Hist*) **É~** Elector; **É~trice** Electress.

électif, -ive [elɛktif, iv] *adj* (*Pol*) elective.

élection [elɛksjɔ̃] *nf* **(a)** (*Pol, gén*) election. **jour des ~s** polling *ou* election day; **se présenter aux ~s** to stand as a candidate (in the election); **~ partielle** ≃ by-election; **~s législatives** ≃ general election; **~s municipales** ≃ local elections.

(b) (*choix*) **lieu/patrie d'~** place/country of one's (own) choosing *ou* choice; (*Jur*) **~ de domicile** choice of residence.

électoral, e, *mpl* **-aux** [elɛktɔʀal, o] *adj affiche, réunion* election (*épith*). **campagne ~e** election *ou* electoral campaign; **période ~e** election time; **il m'a promis son soutien ~** he promised me his backing in the election; *V* **agent, circonscription, corps** *etc.*

électoralisme [elɛktɔʀalism(ə)] *nm* electioneering.

électorat [elɛktɔʀa] *nm* **(a)** (*électeurs*) electorate; (*droit de vote*) franchise. **l'~ socialiste** the voters for the socialist party, the socialist vote. **(b)** (*Hist: principauté*) electorate.

électricien [elɛktʀisjɛ̃] *nm* electrician.

électricité [elɛktʀisite] *nf* electricity. **allumer l'~** to turn *ou* switch *ou* put the light on; **ça marche à l'~** it runs on electricity, it's electrically operated; (*fig*) **il y a de l'~ dans l'air*** the atmosphere is electric; *V* **panne.**

électrification [elɛktʀifikɑsjɔ̃] *nf* electrification.

électrifier [elɛktʀifje] (7) *vt* to electrify. **~ un village** to bring electricity *ou* electric power to a village.

électrique [elɛktʀik] *adj* electric(al); (*fig*) electrifying, electric.

électriquement [elɛktʀikmɑ̃] *adv* electrically.

électrisable [elɛktʀizabl(ə)] *adj foule* easily roused; *substance* chargeable, electrifiable.

électrisant, e [elɛktʀizɑ̃, ɑ̃t] *adj* (*fig*) *discours, contact* electrifying.

électrisation [elɛktʀizɑsjɔ̃] *nf [substance]* charging, electrifying.

électriser [elɛktʀize] (1) *vt substance* to charge, electrify; *audience* to electrify, rouse.

électro-aimant, *pl* **électro-aimants** [elɛktʀoɛmɑ̃] *nm* electromagnet.

électrocardiogramme [elɛktʀokaʀdjɔgʀam] *nm* electrocardiogram.

électrocardiographe [elɛktʀokaʀdjɔgʀaf] *nm* electrocardiograph.

électrocardiographie [elɛktʀɔkaʀdjɔgʀafi] *nf* electrocardiography.
électrochimie [elɛktʀɔʃimi] *nf* electrochemistry.
électrochimique [elɛktʀɔʃimik] *adj* electrochemical.
électrochoc [elɛktʀɔʃɔk] *nm* electric shock treatment, electroconvulsive therapy (*T*).
électrocuter [elɛktʀɔkyte] (1) *vt* to electrocute.
électrocution [elɛktʀɔkysjɔ̃] *nf* electrocution.
électrode [elɛktʀɔd] *nf* electrode.
électrodynamique [elɛktʀɔdinamik] **1** *adj* electrodynamic. **2** *nf* electrodynamics (*sg*).
électro-encéphalogramme, *pl* **électro-encéphalogrammes** [elɛktʀɔɑ̃sefalɔgʀam] *nm* electroencephalogram.
électro-encéphalographie [elɛktʀɔɑ̃sefalɔgʀafi] *nf* electroencephalography.
électrogène [elɛktʀɔʒɛn] *adj* (*Zool*) electric; *V* **groupe**.
électrolyse [elɛktʀɔliz] *nf* electrolysis.
électrolyser [elɛktʀɔlize] (1) *vt* to electrolyse.
électrolyseur [elɛktʀɔlizœʀ] *nm* electrolyser.
électrolyte [elɛktʀɔlit] *nm* electrolyte.
électrolytique [elɛktʀɔlitik] *adj* electrolytic(al).
électromagnétique [elɛktʀɔmaɲetik] *adj* electromagnetic.
électromagnétisme [elɛktʀɔmaɲetism(ə)] *nm* electromagnetism.
électromécanique [elɛktʀɔmekanik] **1** *adj* electromechanical. **2** *nf* electromechanical engineering.
électroménager [elɛktʀɔmenaʒe] **1** *adj appareil* (household *ou* domestic) electrical. **2** *nm* household *ou* domestic (electrical) appliances.
électrométallurgie [elɛktʀɔmetalyʀʒi] *nf* electrometallurgy.
électrométallurgique [elɛktʀɔmetalyʀʒik] *adj* electrometallurgical.
électromètre [elɛktʀɔmɛtʀ(ə)] *nm* electrometer.
électromoteur, -trice [elɛktʀɔmɔtœʀ, tʀis] **1** *adj* electromotive. **2** *nm* electric motor, electromotor.
électron [elɛktʀɔ̃] *nm* electron.
électronégatif, -ive [elɛktʀɔnegatif, iv] *adj* electronegative.
électronicien, -ienne [elɛktʀɔnisjɛ̃, jɛn] *nm,f* electronics engineer.
électronique [elɛktʀɔnik] *adj* (*gén*) electronic; *optique, télescope, microscope* electron (*épith*). **2** *nf* electronics (*sg*).
électrophone [elɛktʀɔfɔn] *nm* record player.
électropositif, -ive [elɛktʀɔpozitif, iv] *adj* electropositive.
électrostatique [elɛktʀɔstatik] **1** *adj* electrostatic. **2** *nf* electrostatics (*sg*).
électrotechnique [elɛktʀɔtɛknik] *nf* electrotechnics (*sg*).
électrothérapie [elɛktʀɔteʀapi] *nf* electrotherapy.
élégamment [elegamɑ̃] *adv* elegantly.
élégance [elegɑ̃s] *nf* (*V* **élégant**) elegance; generosity, handsomeness; neatness. ~**s (de style)** ornaments (of style); **perdre avec** ~ to be a graceful loser; **l'**~ **féminine** feminine elegance.
élégant, e [elegɑ̃, ɑ̃t] **1** *adj personne, toilette, style* elegant; *procédé, conduite* generous, handsome; *solution* elegant, neat. **2** *nm* (†) elegant man, man of fashion. **3 élégante** *nf* (†) elegant woman, woman of fashion.
élégiaque [eleʒjak] *adj* elegiac.
élégie [eleʒi] *nf* elegy.
élément [elemɑ̃] *nm* **(a)** (*composante*) *[structure, ensemble]* element, component; *[problème]* element; *[mélange]* ingredient, element; *[réussite]* factor, element; *[machine, appareil]* part, component. ~ **comique (d'un roman)** comic element (of a novel); **l'**~ **révolutionnaire était bien représenté** the revolutionary element was well represented; ~**s préfabriqués de cuisine/de bibliothèque** ready-made kitchen/shelf units; (*Mil*) ~**s blindés/aéroportés** armoured/airborne units.
(b) (*Chim*) element. (*Chim*) **l'**~ **hydrogène** the element hydrogen.
(c) (*Tech*) *[pile]* cell.
(d) (*fait*) fact. **nous manquons d'**~**s** we lack facts; **aucun** ~ **nouveau n'est survenu** there have been no new developments, no new facts have come to light; (*Mil*) ~**s de tir** range data.
(e) (*individu*) **c'est le meilleur** ~ **de ma classe** he's the best pupil in my class; **bons et mauvais** ~**s** good and bad elements; ~**s subversifs/ennemis** subversive/hostile elements.
(f) (*rudiments*) ~**s** basic principles, rudiments, elements; **il a quelques** ~**s de chimie** he has some elementary knowledge of chemistry; (*titre d'ouvrage*) '**É**~**s de Mécanique**' 'Elements of *ou* Elementary Mechanics'.
(g) (*milieu*) element. **les quatre** ~**s** the four elements; (*littér*) **les** ~**s (naturels)** the elements (*littér*); (*littér*) **l'**~ **liquide** the liquid element (*littér*); **quand on parle d'électronique il est dans son** ~* when you talk about electronics he's in his element; **parmi ces artistes il ne se sentait pas dans son** ~* he didn't feel at home *ou* he felt like a fish out of water among those artists.
élémentaire [elemɑ̃tɛʀ] *adj* **(a)** (*facile*) *problème* elementary; (*de base*) *notion* elementary, basic; *forme* rudimentary, basic; (*Scol*) *cours, niveau* elementary; (*évident*) *précaution* elementary, basic. **c'est** ~! it's elementary!; **la plus** ~ **courtoisie/discrétion veut que** ... elementary *ou* basic *ou* simple courtesy/discretion demands that ... . **(b)** (*Chim*) elemental.
Éléonore [eleɔnɔʀ] *nf* Eleanor.
éléphant [elefɑ̃] *nm* elephant. ~ **d'Asie/d'Afrique** Indian/African elephant; ~ **de mer** sea elephant, elephant seal; **comme un** ~ **dans un magasin de porcelaine** like a bull in a china shop.
éléphanteau, *pl* ~**x** [elefɑ̃to] *nm* baby elephant.
éléphantesque [elefɑ̃tɛsk(ə)] *adj* (*énorme*) elephantine, gigantic.
éléphantiasis [elefɑ̃tjazis] *nm* elephantiasis.
élevage [ɛlvaʒ] *nm* **(a)** *[bétail]* rearing, breeding; *[porcs, chevaux, vers à soie]* breeding; *[abeilles]* keeping. **l'**~ **(du bétail)** cattle breeding *ou* rearing; **l'**~ **des abeilles** beekeeping; **faire l'**~ **de** to rear; to breed; to keep; **région** *ou* **pays d'**~ cattle-rearing *ou* -breeding area.
(b) (*ferme*) cattle farm. ~ **de poulets** poultry farm.
élévateur, -trice [elevatœʀ, tʀis] *adj, nm,f*: **(muscle)** ~ elevator; **(appareil)** ~ elevator; (*Élec*) **(appareil** *ou* **transformateur)** ~ **de tension** step-up transformer; *V* **chariot.**
élévation [elevɑsjɔ̃] *nf* **(a)** (*action d'élever*) *[rempart, statue]* putting up, erection; *[objet, niveau]* raising; *[fonctionnaire]* raising, elevation; (*fig*) *[pensée, âme]* elevation. (*Math*) ~ **d'un nombre au carré** squaring of a number; (*Math*) ~ **d'un nombre à une puissance** raising of a number to a power; **son** ~ **au rang de** his being raised *ou* elevated to the rank of, his elevation to the rank of.
(b) (*action de s'élever*) *[température, niveau]* rise (*de* in).
(c) (*Rel*) **l'**~ the Elevation.
(d) (*tertre*) elevation, mound. ~ **de terrain** rise (in the ground).
(e) (*Archit, Géom: coupe, plan*) elevation.
(f) (*noblesse*) *[pensée, style]* elevation, loftiness.
élève [elɛv] *nmf* pupil, student; (*Mil*) cadet. ~ **professeur** student teacher, trainee teacher, ~ **infirmière** student nurse; ~ **officier** officer cadet.
élevé, e [ɛlve] (*ptp de* **élever**) *adj* **(a)** *prix, niveau* high; *pertes* heavy. **peu** ~ *prix, niveau* low; *pertes* slight.
(b) *cime, arbre* tall, lofty; *colline* high, lofty.
(c) *rang, grade* high, elevated. (*frm*) **être de condition** ~**e** to be of high birth; **occuper une position** ~**e** to hold a high position, be high-ranking.
(d) (*noble*) *pensée, style* elevated, lofty; *conception* exalted, lofty; *principes* high (*épith*).
(e) bien ~ well-mannered; **mal** ~ (*rustre*) bad-mannered, ill-mannered; (*impoli*) rude, impolite; **espèce de mal** ~! you rude creature!; **c'est mal** ~ **de parler en mangeant** it's bad manners *ou* it's rude to talk with your mouth full.
élever [ɛlve] (5) **1** *vt* **(a)** (*éduquer*) *enfant* to bring up, raise (*surtout US*). **il a été élevé dans du coton/selon des principes vertueux** he was given a sheltered/very moral upbringing; **son fils est élevé maintenant** his son is grown up now.
(b) (*faire l'élevage de*) *bétail* to rear, breed; *porcs, chevaux, vers à soie* to breed; *abeilles* to keep.
(c) (*dresser*) *rempart, mur, statue* to put up, erect, raise. (*littér*) **la maison élevait sa masse sombre** the dark mass of the house rose up *ou* reared up (*littér*); (*fig*) ~ **des objections/des protestations** to raise objections/a protest; (*fig*) ~ **des critiques** to make criticisms.
(d) (*hausser*) *édifice* to raise, make higher. ~ **la maison d'un étage** to raise the house by one storey, make the house one storey higher.
(e) (*lever, mettre plus haut*) *poids, objet* to lift (up), raise; *niveau, taux, prix* to raise; *voix* to raise; (*littér*) *yeux, bras* to raise, lift (up). **pompe qui élève l'eau** pump which raises water.
(f) ~ **sa pensée jusqu'aux grandes idées** to raise one's thoughts to *ou* set one's thoughts on higher things; **musique qui élève l'âme** elevating *ou* uplifting music; (*Rel*) **élevons nos cœurs vers le Seigneur** let us lift up our hearts unto the Lord.
(g) (*promouvoir*) to raise, elevate. **il a été élevé au grade de** he was raised *ou* elevated to the rank of; **chez eux l'abstinence est élevée à la hauteur d'une institution** for them abstinence is a way of life, they have made abstinence a way of life.
(h) (*Math*) ~ **une perpendiculaire** to raise a perpendicular; ~ **un nombre à la puissance 5** to raise a number to the power of 5; ~ **un nombre au carré** to square a number.
2 s'élever *vpr* **(a)** (*augmenter*) *[température, niveau, prix]* to rise, go up. **le niveau des élèves/de vie s'est élevé** the standard of the pupils/of living has risen *ou* improved.
(b) (*se dresser*) *[montagne, tour]* to rise. **la tour s'élève à 50 mètres au-dessus du sol** the tower rises *ou* stands 50 metres above the ground; **un mur s'élevait entre ces deux jardins** a wall stood between these two gardens; **la cime s'élève majestueusement au-dessus des forêts** the peak rises (up) *ou* towers majestically above the forests.
(c) (*monter*) *[avion]* to go up, ascend; *[oiseau]* to fly up, ascend. **l'avion s'élevait régulièrement** the plane was climbing *ou* ascending regularly; **la pensée s'élève vers l'absolu** thought soars *ou* ascends towards the Absolute; **l'âme s'élève vers Dieu** the soul ascends to(wards) God; **le ton s'élève, les voix s'élèvent** voices are beginning to rise.
(d) *[discussions]* to arise; *[objections, doutes]* to be raised, arise. **sa voix s'éleva dans le silence** his voice broke the silence; **aucune voix ne s'éleva en sa faveur** not a (single) voice was raised in his favour.
(e) (*dans la société*) to rise. **s'**~ **jusqu'au sommet de l'échelle** to climb to the top of the ladder; **s'**~ **à la force du poignet/par son seul travail** to work one's way up unaided/by the sweat of one's (own) brow; **s'**~ **au-dessus des querelles** to rise above (petty) quarrels.
(f) (*protester*) **s'**~ **contre** to rise up against.
(g) (*se bâtir*) to go up, be put up *ou* erected. **l'immeuble s'élève peu à peu** the block of flats is going up bit by bit *ou* is gradually going up.
(h) (*se monter*) **s'**~ **à** *[prix, pertes]* to total, add up to, amount to.
éleveur, -euse [ɛlvœʀ, øz] **1** *nm,f*: ~ **(de bétail)** cattle breeder *ou* rearer; ~ **de chevaux/porcs** horse/pig breeder; ~ **de vers à soie** silkworm breeder, sericulturist (*T*); ~ **d'abeilles** beekeeper; *V* **propriétaire. 2 éleveuse** *nf* (*pour poussins*) brooder.

elfe [ɛlf(ə)] *nm* elf.
élider *vt*, **s'élider** *vpr* [elide] (1) to elide.
éligibilité [eliʒibilite] *nf* (*Pol*) eligibility.
éligible [eliʒibl(ə)] *adj* (*Pol*) eligible.
élimer [elime] (1) **1** *vt vêtement, tissu* to wear thin. **2 s'élimer** *vpr [vêtement, tissu]* to wear thin, become threadbare. **chemise élimée au col/aux coudes** shirt worn (thin) *ou* wearing thin *ou* (which is) threadbare at the collar/elbows.
élimination [eliminɑsjɔ̃] *nf* (*gén*) elimination.
éliminatoire [eliminatwaʀ] **1** *adj épreuve* eliminatory (*épith*); *note, (Sport) temps* disqualifying (*épith*). **2** *nf* (*Sport*) (eliminating *ou* preliminary) heat.
éliminer [elimine] (1) *vt* **(a)** *candidat, élément indésirable* to eliminate; *concurrent* to eliminate, knock out. (*Pol*) **éliminé au second tour** eliminated in the second ballot; (*Scol*) **être éliminé à l'oral** to be eliminated *ou* fail in the oral; (*Sport*) **éliminé!** you're out!
(b) *possibilité* to rule out, eliminate; *données secondaires* to discard, eliminate; (*euph*) *témoin gênant* to dispose of, eliminate.
(c) (*Math, Méd*) to eliminate.
élire [eliʀ] (43) *vt* to elect. **~ domicile** to take up residence (*à* in).
Élisabeth [elizabɛt] *nf* = **Élizabeth.**
élisabéthain, e [elizabetɛ̃, ɛn] **1** *adj* Elizabethan. **2** *nm,f*: **É~(e)** Elizabethan.
élision [elizjɔ̃] *nf* elision.
élite [elit] *nf* élite. **l'~ (de)** the cream *ou* élite (of); **d'~: nature *ou* âme d'~** noble soul; (*Scol*) **sujet d'~** top-ranking student; (*Mil*) **corps/cavalerie d'~** crack corps/cavalry; **les ~s (de la nation)** the élite (of the nation); *V* **tireur.**
élitisme [elitism(ə)] *nm* élitism.
élitiste [elitist(ə)] *nmf* élitist.
élixir [eliksiʀ] *nm* elixir. **~ de longue vie** elixir of life; **~ parégorique** paregoric (elixir).
Élizabeth [elizabɛt] *nf* Elizabeth.
elle [ɛl] *pron pers f* **(a)** (*fonction sujet*) (*personne, nation*) she; (*chose*) it; (*animal, bébé*) she, it. **~s** they; **~ est couturière** she is a dressmaker; **prends cette chaise, ~ est plus confortable** have this chair — it is more comfortable; **je me méfie de sa chienne, ~ mord** I don't trust his dog because she *ou* it bites; **la fourmi emmagasine ce qu'~ trouve** the ant stores what it finds; **~, furieuse, a refusé** furious, she refused; **la Suisse a décidé qu'~ resterait neutre** Switzerland decided that she would remain neutral; **qu'est-ce qu'ils ont dit? — ~, rien** what did they say? — SHE said nothing; **il est venu mais pas ~/~s** he came but she/they didn't, he came but not her*/them*; **~ partie, j'ai pu travailler** with her gone *ou* after she had gone I was able to work; **~, ~ n'aurait jamais fait ça** SHE would never have done that; **~ renoncer? ce n'est pas son genre** HER give up? it wouldn't be like her; *V aussi* **même.**
(b) (*fonction objet, souvent emphatique*) (*personne, nation*) her; (*animal*) her, it; (*chose*) it. **il n'admire qu'~** he only admires her, she's the only one he admires; **je l'ai bien vue ~** I saw HER all right, I definitely saw HER; **je les ai bien vus, ~ et lui** I definitely saw both *ou* the two of them; **la revoir ~? jamais!** see HER again? never!
(c) (*emphatique avec qui, que*) **c'est ~ qui me l'a dit** she told me herself, it's she who told me; (*iro*) **c'est ~s qui le disent** that's THEIR story!, that's what THEY say!; (*frm*) **ce fut ~ qui lança le mouvement des suffragettes** it was she *ou* she it was (*frm*) who launched the suffragette movement; **voilà la pluie, et ~ qui est sortie sans manteau!** here comes the rain and to think she has gone out without a coat! *ou* and there she is out without a coat!; **chasse cette chienne, c'est ~ qui m'a mordu** chase that dog away, it's the one that bit me; **c'est ~/~s que j'avais invitée(s)** it's *ou* it was her/them I had invited; **c'est à ~ que je veux parler** it's HER I want to speak to, I want to speak to HER; **il y a une chouette dans le bois, c'est ~ que j'ai entendue cette nuit** there's a screech owl in the wood and that's what I heard last night.
(d) (*avec prép*) (*personne*) her; (*animal*) her, it; (*chose*) it. **ce livre est à ~** this book belongs to her *ou* is hers; **c'est à ~ de décider** it's up to her to decide, it's her decision; **c'est gentil à ~ d'avoir écrit** it was kind of her to write; **un ami à ~** a friend of hers, one of HER friends; **elle ne pense qu'à ~** she only thinks of herself; **elle a un appartement à ~** she has a flat of her own; **ses enfants à ~** HER children; **qu'est-ce qu'il ferait sans ~** what (on earth) would he do without her; **ce poème n'est pas d'~** this poem is not one of hers *ou* not one that she wrote; **il veut une photo d'~** he wants a photo of her; **vous pouvez avoir confiance en ~** (*femme*) she is thoroughly reliable, you can have complete confidence in her; (*machine*) it is thoroughly reliable.
(e) (*dans comparaisons*) (*sujet*) she; (*objet*) her. **il est plus grand qu'~/~s** he is taller than she is/they are *ou* than her/them; **je le connais aussi bien qu'~** (*aussi bien que je la connais*) I know him as well as (I know) her; (*aussi bien qu'elle le connaît*) I know him as well as she does *ou* as well as her*; **ne faites pas comme ~** don't do as *ou* what she does, don't do like her*.
(f) (*interrog, emphatique: gén non traduit*) **Alice est-~ rentrée?** is Alice back?; **sa lettre est-~ arrivée?** has his letter come?; **les infirmières sont-~s bien payées?** are nurses well paid?; **~ est loin, notre jeunesse!** it's so long since we were young!; **tu sais, ta tante, ~ n'est pas très aimable!** you know your aunt *ou* that aunt of yours isn't very nice!
ellébore [elebɔʀ] *nm* hellebore.
elle-même, *pl* **elles-mêmes** [ɛlmɛm] *pron V* **même.**
ellipse [elips(ə)] *nf* (*Géom*) ellipse; (*Ling*) ellipsis.
ellipsoïdal, e, *mpl* **-aux** [elipsɔidal, o] *adj* ellipsoidal.
ellipsoïde [elipsɔid] **1** *nm* ellipsoid. **2** *adj* (*Géom*) elliptical.
elliptique [eliptik] *adj* (*Géom*) elliptic(al); (*Ling*) elliptical.
elliptiquement [eliptikmɑ̃] *adv* (*Ling*) elliptically.
élocution [elɔkysjɔ̃] *nf* (*débit*) delivery; (*clarté*) diction. **défaut d'~** speech impediment; **professeur d'~** speech production teacher.
éloge [elɔʒ] *nm* **(a)** (*louange*) praise. **couvert *ou* comblé d'~s** showered with praise(s); **digne d'~** praiseworthy, commendable; **faire des ~s à qn** to praise sb (to his face); *V* **tarir.**
(b) faire l'~ de to praise, speak (very) highly of; **son ~ n'est plus à faire** I do not need to add to his praise; **c'est le plus bel ~ à lui faire** it's the highest praise one can give him; **faire son propre ~** to sing one's own praises, blow one's own trumpet* (*Brit*) *ou* horn* (*US*); **l'~ que vous avez fait de cette œuvre** your praise *ou* commendation of this work.
(c) (*littér: panégyrique*) eulogy. **prononcer l'~ funèbre de qn** to deliver a funeral oration in praise of sb.
élogieusement [elɔʒjøzmɑ̃] *adv* very highly, most favourably. **parler de qn ~** to speak very highly *ou* most favourably of sb.
élogieux, -ieuse [elɔʒjø, jøz] *adj* laudatory, eulogistic(al). **parler de qn en termes ~** to speak very highly *ou* most favourably of sb.
éloigné, e [elwaɲe] (*ptp de* **éloigner**) *adj* **(a)** (*dans l'espace*) *lieu, son* distant, far-off, faraway. **est-ce très ~ de la gare? — oui, c'est très ~** is it very far *ou* a long way (away) from the station? — yes, it's a long way; **~ de 3 km** 3 km away; **le village est trop ~ pour qu'on puisse y aller à pied** the village is too far away *ou* too far off for one to be able to walk there.
(b) (*dans le temps*) *époque, événement, échéance* distant (*de* from), remote (*de* from). **le passé ~** the distant *ou* remote past; **l'avenir ~** the distant *ou* far-off *ou* remote future; **dans un avenir peu ~** in the not-too-distant future, in the near future.
(c) *parent* distant; *ancêtre* remote. **la famille ~e** distant relatives; **je le connais de façon très ~e** he's only a distant acquaintance of mine.
(d) (*fig*) **être ~ de** to be far from, be a long way from; **sa version est très ~e de la vérité** his version is very far from (being) the truth; **un sentiment pas très ~ de la haine** an emotion not far removed from hatred; **rien n'est plus ~ de mes pensées** nothing is *ou* could be farther from my thoughts; **je ne suis pas très ~ de le croire** I almost believe him, I'm not far from believing him; **je suis fort ~ de ses positions** my point of view is very far removed from his.
(e) tenir ~ de to keep away from; **cette conférence m'a tenu ~ de chez moi** the conference kept me away from home; **se tenir ~ du feu** to keep away from *ou* clear of the fire; **se tenir ~ du danger/des querelles** to steer *ou* keep clear of danger/of quarrels, keep *ou* stay out of the way of danger/quarrels.
éloignement [elwaɲmɑ̃] *nm* **(a)** (*action d'éloigner*) *[personne indésirable]* taking away, removal; *[soupçons]* removal, averting; *[échéance]* putting off, postponement. **l'~ des objets obtenu au moyen d'une lentille spéciale** the distancing of objects by means of a special lens; **leur ~ de la cour, ordonné par le roi** their having been ordered away *ou* their banishment from the court by the king.
(b) (*action de s'éloigner*) *[être aimé]* (progressive) estrangement. **son ~ des affaires** his progressive disinvolvement with business.
(c) (*état: spatial, temporel*) distance. **l'~ rapetisse les objets** distance makes objects (look) smaller; **notre ~ de Paris complique le travail** our being so far from Paris *ou* our distance from Paris complicates the work; **en amour, l'~ rapproche** absence makes the heart grow fonder (*Prov*); **bruit étouffé par l'~** noise muffled by distance; **avec l'~, on juge mieux les événements** one can judge events better after a lapse of time *ou* from a distance.
éloigner [elwaɲe] (1) **1** *vt* **(a)** *objet* to move away, take away (*de* from). **éloigne ce coussin du radiateur** move *ou* take that cushion away from the radiator; **une lentille qui éloigne les objets** a lens that distances objects *ou* that makes objects look distant; **cette brume éloigne les collines** this mist makes the hills look further away.
(b) *personne* (*lit*) to take away, remove (*de* from); (*fig: exiler, écarter*) to send away (*de* from). (*fig*) **~ qn de** *être aimé, compagnons* to estrange sb from; *activité* to take sb away from; *tentations, carrière* to take sb away from, remove sb from; **son penchant pour la boisson éloigna de lui ses amis** his inclination for drink lost him his friends *ou* made his friends drift away from him; **ce chemin nous éloigne du village** this path takes *ou* leads us away from the village.
(c) *souvenir, idée* to banish, put away; *crainte* to remove, put away; *danger* to ward off, remove; *soupçons* to remove, avert (*de* from).
(d) *chose à faire, échéance, visite* to put off, postpone.
(e) (*espacer*) *visites* to make less frequent, space out.
2 s'éloigner *vpr* **(a)** *[tout objet en mouvement]* to move away; *[orage]* to go away, pass; *[bruit]* to go away, grow fainter. **le village s'éloignait et finit par disparaître dans la brume** the village got further (and further) away *ou* grew more and more distant and finally disappeared in the mist.
(b) *[personne]* (*par prudence etc*) to go away (*de* from); (*par pudeur, discrétion*) to go away, withdraw (*de* from). **s'~ en courant/en hâte** to run/hurry away *ou* off; **éloignez-vous, les enfants, ça risque d'éclater!** move away *ou* back, children, *ou* stand *ou* get back, children, it might explode!; **ne t'éloigne pas (trop) (de la voiture)** don't go (too) far *ou* don't go (too) far away (from the car); (*fig*) **s'~ de** *être aimé, compagnons* to become estranged from, grow away from; *sujet traité* to wander from; *position prise* to move away from; *devoir* to swerve *ou* deviate from; **là vous vous éloignez (du sujet)** you're wandering from *ou* getting off the point *ou* subject; **je**

la sentais s'~ (de moi) I felt her becoming estranged *ou* growing away from me, I felt her becoming more (and more) distant; **s'~ du droit chemin** to stray *ou* wander from the straight and narrow; **s'~ de la vérité** to wander from the truth.

(c) *[souvenir, échéance]* to grow more (and more) distant *ou* remote; *[danger]* to pass, go away; *[craintes]* to go away, retreat.

élongation [elɔ̃gɑsjɔ̃] *nf* **(a)** (*Méd*) strained *ou* pulled muscle. **les ~s font très mal** straining *ou* pulling a muscle is very painful; **se faire une ~** to strain *ou* pull a muscle. **(b)** (*Astron*) elongation; (*Phys*) displacement.

éloquemment [elɔkamɑ̃] *adv* eloquently.

éloquence [elɔkɑ̃s] *nf* eloquence. **il m'a fallu toute mon ~ pour la convaincre** I needed all the eloquence I could summon up *ou* muster to convince her; (*fig*) **l'~ de ces chiffres rend tout commentaire superflu** these figures speak for themselves *ou* need no comment.

éloquent, e [elɔkɑ̃, ɑ̃t] *adj orateur, discours, geste* eloquent. (*fig*) **ces chiffres sont ~s** these figures speak for themselves; **une étreinte plus ~e que toute parole** an embrace that spoke louder than any word(s), an embrace more eloquent *ou* meaningful than any word(s).

élu, e [ely] (*ptp de* **élire**) **1** *adj* (*Rel*) chosen; (*Pol*) elected.

2 *nm,f* **(a)** (*Pol*) (*député*) elected member, ≃ member of parliament, M.P.; (*conseiller*) elected representative, councillor. **les nouveaux ~s** the newly elected members; the newly elected councillors; **les citoyens et leurs ~s** the citizens and their elected representatives.

(b) (*hum: fiancé*) **l'~ de son cœur** her heart's desire (*hum*), her beloved; **quelle est l'heureuse ~e?** who's the lucky girl?

(c) (*Rel*) **les É~s** the Chosen ones, the Elect; **être l'~ de Dieu** to be chosen by God.

élucidation [elysidɑsjɔ̃] *nf* elucidation.

élucider [elyside] (1) *vt* to clear up, elucidate.

élucubrations [elykybʀɑsjɔ̃] *nfpl* (*péj*) wild imaginings.

élucubrer [elykybʀe] (1) *vti* (*péj*) **~ des théories fumeuses** to expound woolly theories; **je le laissai ~ à son aise** I let him indulge in his wild imaginings.

éluder [elyde] (1) *vt difficulté* to evade, elude; *loi, problème* to evade, dodge.

Élysée [elize] *nm* (*Myth*) **l'~** the Elysium; **(le palais de) l'~** the Elysée palace; **les Champs ~s** (*Myth*) the Elysian Fields; (*à Paris*) the Champs Élysées.

élyséen, -enne [elizeɛ̃, ɛn] *adj* Elysian.

élytre [elitʀ(ə)] *nm* (hard) outer wing, elytron (*T*).

émaciation [emasjɑsjɔ̃] *nf* emaciation.

émacier [emasje] (7) **1** *vt* to emaciate. **2 s'émacier** *vpr* to become emaciated *ou* wasted. **visage émacié** emaciated *ou* wasted face.

émail, *pl* **-aux** [emaj, o] *nm* (*substance, objet d'art*) enamel. **en** *ou* **d'~** enamel(led); **des ~aux décoraient la pièce** the room was decorated with enamels *ou* pieces of enamel work.

émaillage [emajaʒ] *nm* enamelling.

émaillé, e [emaje] (*ptp de* **émailler**) *adj* **(a)** (*lit*) enamelled. **(b)** (*fig: parsemé de*) **~ de** *étoiles* spangled *ou* studded with; *fautes, citations* peppered *ou* dotted with.

émailler [emaje] (1) *vt* **(a)** (*lit*) to enamel. **(b)** (*fig littér*) *[étoiles]* to stud, spangle. **des étoiles émaillaient le ciel** stars studded the sky, the sky was spangled *ou* studded with stars; **~ un texte de citations/d'erreurs** to pepper a text with quotations/errors.

émanation [emanɑsjɔ̃] *nf* **(a)** (*odeurs*) **~s** exhalations, emanations; **~s fétides** fetid emanations; **~s volcaniques** volatiles.

(b) (*fig*) product. **le pouvoir, ~ du peuple** power issues from the people, power is a product of the will of the people.

(c) (*Phys*) emanation; (*Rel*) procession.

émancipateur, -trice [emɑ̃sipatœʀ, tʀis] **1** *adj* liberating, emancipative. **2** *nm,f* liberator, emancipator.

émancipation [emɑ̃sipɑsjɔ̃] *nf* (*Jur*) emancipation; *[colonie, femme]* liberation, emancipation.

émanciper [emɑ̃sipe] (1) **1** *vt* (*Jur*) to emancipate; *femme* to emancipate, liberate; *esprit* to liberate, (set) free.

2 s'émanciper *vpr [femme]* to become emancipated *ou* liberated, liberate o.s.; *[esprit, art]* to become liberated, liberate *ou* free itself. (†*péj, hum*) **elle s'émancipe** she's becoming very independent.

émaner [emane] (1) **émaner de** *vt indir* (*Pol, Rel*) *[pouvoir etc]* to proceed from; *[ordres, note]* to come from, be issued by; *[chaleur, lumière, odeur]* to emanate *ou* issue *ou* come from; (*fig*) *[charme]* to emanate from, be radiated by.

émargement [emaʀʒəmɑ̃] *nm* **(a)** (*U: V* **émarger**) signing; annotating. **feuille d'~** (*feuille de paye*) paysheet; (*feuille de présence*) attendance sheet. **(b)** (*signature*) signature; (*annotation*) annotation.

émarger [emaʀʒe] (3) **1** *vt* **(a)** (*frm*) (*signer*) to sign; (*annoter*) to annotate.

(b) (*Typ*) to trim.

2 *vi* **(a)** (†: *toucher son salaire*) to draw one's salary. **à combien émarge-t-il par mois?** what is his monthly salary?

(b) ~ d'une certaine somme à un budget to receive a certain sum out of a budget.

émasculation [emaskylɑsjɔ̃] *nf* emasculation.

émasculer [emaskyle] (1) *vt* to emasculate.

emballage [ɑ̃balaʒ] *nm* **(a)** (*U*) (*dans un carton etc*) packing (-up); (*dans du papier*) wrapping(-up), doing-up. **papier d'~** packing paper; wrapping paper.

(b) (*Comm*) (*boîte, carton etc*) packet, package, packaging (*U*); (*papier*) wrapping (*U*). (*Comm*) **~ perdu/consigné** non-returnable/returnable bottle (*ou* can *etc*).

emballement [ɑ̃balmɑ̃] *nm* **(a)** (*) *[personne]* (*enthousiasme*) getting carried away* (*U*), getting worked up* (*U*); (*colère*) flying off the handle* (*U*), going off at the deep end* (*U*). **méfiez-vous de ses ~s** beware of his (sudden) crazes*.

(b) *[moteur]* racing; *[cheval]* bolting.

emballer [ɑ̃bale] (1) **1** *vt* **(a)** (*empaqueter*) (*dans un carton, de la toile etc*) to pack (up); (*dans du papier*) to wrap (up), do up.

(b) (‡: *emprisonner*) to run in‡, put in the clink‡.

(c) *moteur* to race.

(d) (*: *enthousiasmer*) *[idée, film]* to thrill to bits*. **je n'ai pas été très emballé par ce film** I wasn't exactly carried away* by that film, that film didn't exactly thrill me to bits*.

2 s'emballer *vpr* **(a)** (*) *[personne]* (*enthousiasme*) to get *ou* be carried away*, get worked up*; (*colère*) to fly off the handle*, go off (at) the deep end*.

(b) *[moteur]* to race; *[cheval]* to bolt. **cheval emballé** runaway *ou* bolting horse.

emballeur, -euse [ɑ̃balœʀ, øz] *nm,f* packer.

embarcadère [ɑ̃baʀkadɛʀ] *nm* landing stage, pier.

embarcation [ɑ̃baʀkɑsjɔ̃] *nf* (small) boat, (small) craft.

embardée [ɑ̃baʀde] *nf* (*Aut*) swerve; (*Naut*) yaw. **faire une ~** (*Aut*) to swerve; (*Naut*) to yaw.

embargo [ɑ̃baʀgo] *nm* embargo. **mettre l'~ sur** to impose *ou* put an embargo on, embargo; **lever l'~ (mis sur)** to lift *ou* raise the embargo (on).

embarquement [ɑ̃baʀkəmɑ̃] *nm [marchandises]* loading; *[passagers]* (*en bateau*) embarkation, boarding; (*en avion*) boarding.

embarquer [ɑ̃baʀke] (1) **1** *vt* **(a)** *passagers* to embark, take on board. **je l'ai embarqué dans le train*** I saw him onto the train, I put him on the train.

(b) *cargaison* (*en train, gén*) to load; (*en bateau*) to load, ship. (*Naut*) **le navire embarque des paquets d'eau** the boat is taking in *ou* shipping water.

(c) (‡) (*emporter*) to cart off*, lug off*; (*voler*) to pinch*, nick‡ (*Brit*); (*pour emprisonner*) to cart off* *ou* away*.

(d) (*: *entraîner*) **~ qn dans** to get sb mixed up in* *ou* involved in, involve sb in; **il s'est laissé ~ dans une sale histoire** he has got (himself) mixed up in* *ou* involved in a nasty bit of business; **une affaire bien/mal embarquée** an affair that has got off to a good/bad start.

2 *vi* **(a)** (*aussi* **s'~**) (*en bateau*) to embark, board, go aboard *ou* on board; (*en train*) to get on board, board; (*en avion*) to go on board, board. **il a embarqué hier pour le Maroc** he sailed for Morocco yesterday.

(b) (*Naut*) **le navire embarque, la mer embarque** we are *ou* the boat is shipping water.

3 s'embarquer *vpr* **(a) = 2a.**

(b) s'~ dans *aventure, affaire* to embark (up)on, launch (o.s.) into.

embarras [ɑ̃baʀa] *nm* **(a)** (*ennui*) hindrance, obstacle. **cela constitue un ~ supplémentaire** that's another hindrance *ou* obstacle; **je ne veux pas être un ~ pour vous** I don't want to be a hindrance to you, I don't want to hinder you *ou* get in your way; **causer** *ou* **faire toutes sortes d'~ à qn** to give *ou* cause sb no end of trouble*.

(b) (*gêne*) confusion, embarrassment. **dit-il avec ~** he said in some confusion *ou* with (some) embarrassment; **il remarqua mon ~ pour répondre** he noticed that I was at a loss for a reply *ou* at a loss how to reply *ou* that I was stuck* for a reply.

(c) (*situation délicate*) predicament, awkward position. **mettre** *ou* **plonger qn dans l'~** to put sb in an awkward position *ou* on the spot*; **tirer qn d'~** to get *ou* help sb out of an awkward position *ou* out of a predicament. **être dans l'~** (*en mauvaise position*) to be in a predicament *ou* an awkward position; (*dans un dilemme*) to be in a quandary *ou* in a dilemma; **ne vous mettez pas dans l'~ pour moi** don't put yourself out *ou* go to any trouble for me.

(d) (*gêne financière*) **~ (d'argent** *ou* **financier** *ou* **pécuniaire)** financial straits (*frm*) *ou* difficulties, money worries; **être dans l'~** to be in financial straits (*frm*) *ou* difficulties, be short of money.

(e) (*Méd*) **~ gastrique** upset stomach, stomach upset.

(f) (†: *encombrement*) **~ de circulation** *ou* **de voitures**† (road) congestion (*U*), traffic holdup; **les ~ de Paris** the congestion of the Paris streets.

(g) (*chichis, façons*) **faire des ~** to (make a) fuss, make a to-do; **c'est un faiseur d'~** he's a fusspot*, he's always making a fuss.

(h) l'~ du choix: elle a l'~ du choix, elle n'a que l'~ du choix her only problem is that she has too great a choice, her only difficulty is that of choosing *ou* deciding; **~ de richesses**† embarrassment of riches.

embarrassant, e [ɑ̃baʀasɑ̃, ɑ̃t] *adj* **(a)** *situation* embarrassing, uncomfortable; *problème* awkward, thorny. **(b)** *paquets* cumbersome, awkward. **ce que cet enfant peut être ~!** what a hindrance this child is!, this child is always in the way!

embarrassé, e [ɑ̃baʀase] (*ptp de* **embarrasser**) *adj* **(a)** (*gêné*) *personne* embarrassed, ill-at-ease (*attrib*); *sourire* embarrassed, uneasy. **être ~ de sa personne** to be awkward *ou* ill-at-ease; **il était tout timide et ~** he was very shy and ill-at-ease *ou* embarrassed; **je serais bien ~ de choisir entre les deux** I should really be at a loss (if I had) to choose between the two.

(b) (*peu clair*) *explication, phrase* muddled, confused.

(c) (*Méd*) **avoir l'estomac ~** to have an upset stomach; **j'ai la langue ~e** my tongue is furred (up) *ou* coated.

(d) (*encombré*) *table, corridor* cluttered (up). **j'ai les mains ~es** my hands are full.

embarrasser [ɑ̃baʀase] (1) **1** *vt* **(a)** (*encombrer*) *[paquets]* to clutter (up); *[vêtements]* to hinder, hamper. **enlève ce manteau qui t'embarrasse** take that coat off — it's in your way *ou* it's

hindering *ou* hampering you; **je ne t'embarrasse pas au moins?*** are you sure I'm not hindering you? *ou* I'm not in your way?
(b) (*désorienter*) ~ **qn** to put sb in a predicament *ou* an awkward position; **sa demande m'embarrasse** his request puts me in a predicament *ou* an awkward position *ou* on the spot*; **ça m'embarrasse de te le dire mais** ... I don't like to tell you this but ...; **il y a quelque chose qui m'embarrasse là-dedans** there's something about it that bothers *ou* worries me.
(c) (*Méd*) ~ **l'estomac** to lie heavy on the stomach.
2 s'embarrasser *vpr* **(a)** (*s'encombrer*) **s'~ de** *paquets, compagnon* to burden o.s. with.
(b) (*fig: se soucier*) to trouble o.s. (*de* about), be troubled (*de* by). **sans s'~ des détails** without troubling *ou* worrying about the details; **en voilà un qui ne s'embarrasse pas de scrupules** there's one person for you who doesn't burden *ou* trouble himself with scruples.
(c) (*s'emmêler: dans un vêtement etc*) to get tangled *ou* caught up (*dans* in). (*fig*) **il s'embarrasse dans ses explications** he gets in a muddle with his explanations, he ties himself in knots with his explanations*.
embastillement [ɑ̃bastijmɑ̃] *nm* (††, *hum*) imprisonment.
embastiller [ɑ̃bastije] (1) *vt* (††,*hum*) to imprison.
embauchage [ɑ̃boʃaʒ] *nm* taking-on, hiring.
embauche [ɑ̃boʃ] *nf* (*action d'embaucher*) taking-on, hiring; (*travail disponible*) vacancy. **est-ce qu'il y a de l'~?** are there any vacancies?, are you taking anyone on? *ou* hiring anyone?; **bureau d'~** labour office.
embaucher [ɑ̃boʃe] (1) **1** *vt* to take on, hire. **2 s'embaucher** *vpr* to get o.s. taken on *ou* hired (*comme* as a (*sg*), as (*pl*)).
embaucheur, -euse [ɑ̃boʃœʀ, øz] *nm,f* hirer, labour contractor.
embaumé, e [ɑ̃bome] (*ptp de* **embaumer**) *adj air* fragrant, balmy (*littér*).
embaumement [ɑ̃bommɑ̃] *nm* embalming.
embaumer [ɑ̃bome] (1) **1** *vt cadavre* to embalm. **le lilas embaumait l'air** the scent of lilac hung heavy in the air; **l'air embaumait le lilas** the air was fragrant *ou* balmy (*littér*) with the scent of lilac. **2** *vi* to give out a fragrance, be fragrant.
embaumeur, -euse [ɑ̃bomœʀ, øz] *nm,f* embalmer.
embellir [ɑ̃beliʀ] (2) **1** *vt personne, jardin* to make (more) attractive; *ville* to smarten up, give a face lift to*; *vérité, récit* to embellish. **2** *vi [personne]* to grow lovelier *ou* more attractive, grow in beauty (*littér*).
embellissement [ɑ̃belismɑ̃] *nm [récit, vérité]* embellishment. **ce nouveau luminaire dans l'entrée est un ~** this new light fitting in the hall is a nice decorative touch *ou* is an improvement; **les récents ~s de la ville** the recent smartening-up of the town, the recent face lift the town has been given*.
emberlificoter* [ɑ̃bɛʀlifikɔte] (1) **1** *vt* (*enjôler*) to get round*; (*embrouiller*) to mix up*, muddle (up); (*duper*) to hoodwink*, bamboozle*.
2 s'emberlificoter *vpr (dans un vêtement)* to get tangled *ou* caught up (*dans* in). **il s'emberlificote dans ses explications** he gets in a terrible muddle *ou* he gets himself tied up in knots with his explanations*.
embêtant, e* [ɑ̃bɛtɑ̃, ɑ̃t] *adj* aggravating*, annoying; *situation* awkward, tricky. **que c'est ~!** what a nuisance!, how annoying! *ou* aggravating!*
embêtement* [ɑ̃bɛtmɑ̃] *nm* aggravation*, annoyance, nuisance (*U*).
embêter* [ɑ̃bete] (1) **1** *vt* (*gêner, préoccuper*) to bother, worry; (*importuner*) to pester, bother; (*irriter*) to aggravate*, annoy, get on one's nerves*; (*lasser*) to bore.
2 s'embêter *vpr* (*se morfondre*) to be bored, be fed up*. **qu'est-ce qu'on s'embête ici!** what a drag it is here!*, it's so boring here!; **il ne s'embête pas!** he does all right for himself!*
emblaver [ɑ̃blave] (1) *vt* to sow (with a cereal crop).
emblavure [ɑ̃blavyʀ] *nf* field (sown with a cereal crop).
emblée [ɑ̃ble] *adv*: **d'~** straightaway, right away, at once.
emblématique [ɑ̃blematik] *adj* (*lit*) emblematic; (*fig*) symbolic.
emblème [ɑ̃blɛm] *nm* (*lit*) emblem; (*fig*) symbol, emblem.
embobiner* [ɑ̃bɔbine] (1) *vt* (*enjôler*) to get round*; (*embrouiller*) to mix up*, muddle (up); (*duper*) to hoodwink*, bamboozle*.
emboîtage [ɑ̃bwataʒ] *nm* (*action*) fitting-together; *[livre]* casing-in.
emboîtement [ɑ̃bwatmɑ̃] *nm* fitting, interlocking.
emboîter [ɑ̃bwate] (1) **1** *vt* **(a)** *pièces, parties* to fit together, fit into each other. ~ **qch dans** to fit sth into.
(b) ~ **le pas à qn** (*lit*) to follow *ou* walk in sb's footsteps; (*fig*) to follow suit.
2 s'emboîter *vpr [pièces]* to fit together, fit into each other. **ces 2 pièces s'emboîtent exactement** these 2 parts fit together exactly; **des chaises qui peuvent s'~ pour le rangement** chairs that can be stacked (together) when not in use.
embolie [ɑ̃bɔli] *nf* embolism.
embonpoint [ɑ̃bɔ̃pwɛ̃] *nm* stoutness, portliness. **prendre de l'~** to grow stout.
embossage [ɑ̃bɔsaʒ] *nm* fore and aft mooring.
embosser [ɑ̃bɔse] (1) *vt* to moor fore and aft.
emboucher [ɑ̃buʃe] (1) *vt instrument* to raise to one's lips; *V* **mal.**
embouchure [ɑ̃buʃyʀ] *nf [fleuve]* mouth; *[mors]* mouthpiece; (*Mus*) mouthpiece, embouchure.
embourber [ɑ̃buʀbe] (1) **1** *vt voiture* to get stuck in the mud.
2 s'embourber *vpr [voiture]* to get stuck in the mud, get bogged down (in the mud). **notre voiture s'est embourbée dans le marais** our car got stuck in *ou* got bogged down in the marsh; (*fig*) **s'~ dans** *détails* to get bogged down in; *monotonie* to sink into.
embourgeoisement [ɑ̃buʀʒwazmɑ̃] *nm [personne, parti]* trend towards a middle-class outlook.
embourgeoiser [ɑ̃buʀʒwaze] (1) **1 s'embourgeoiser** *vpr [parti, personne]* to become middle-class, adopt a middle-class outlook; *[idée]* to become middle-class. **2** *vt* to make middle-class (in outlook).
embout [ɑ̃bu] *nm [canne]* tip, ferrule; *[tuyau]* nozzle.
embouteillage [ɑ̃butɛjaʒ] *nm* (*Aut*) traffic jam, (traffic) holdup; (†: *mise en bouteilles*) bottling.
embouteiller [ɑ̃buteje] (1) *vt* (*Aut*) to jam, block; (*Téléc*) *lignes* to block; (†) *vin, lait* to bottle.
emboutir [ɑ̃butiʀ] (2) *vt métal* to stamp; (*Aut fig*) to crash *ou* run into.
emboutissage [ɑ̃butisaʒ] *nm* stamping.
embranchement [ɑ̃bʀɑ̃ʃmɑ̃] *nm* **(a)** *[voies, routes, tuyaux]* junction. **(b)** (*route*) side road, branch road; (*Rail: voie*) branch line; (*tuyau*) branch pipe; (*rivière*) embranchment. **(c)** (*Bot, Zool: catégorie*) branch.
embrancher [ɑ̃bʀɑ̃ʃe] (1) **1** *vt tuyaux, voies* to join (up). ~ **qch sur** to join sth (up) to. **2 s'embrancher** *vpr [tuyaux, voies]* to join (up). **s'~ sur** to join (up) to.
embrasement [ɑ̃bʀɑzmɑ̃] *nm*: **l'~ du ciel au couchant** (*état*) the blazing *ou* fiery sky at sunset; (*action*) the flaring-up *ou* blazing-up of the sky at sunset; (*lueurs*) **des ~s soudains** sudden blazes of light.
embraser [ɑ̃bʀɑze] (1) **1** *vt* (*littér*) *maison, forêt etc* to set ablaze, set fire to; (*fig*) *ciel* to inflame, set aglow *ou* ablaze; *cœur* to kindle (a fire in), fire.
2 s'embraser *vpr [maison]* to blaze up, flare up; *[ciel]* to flare up, be set ablaze (*de* with); *[cœur]* to become inflamed, be fired (*de* with).
embrassade [ɑ̃bʀasad] *nf* (*gén pl*) hugging and kissing (*U*).
embrasse [ɑ̃bʀas] *nf* curtain loop, tieback (*US*). **rideaux à ~s** looped curtains.
embrassement [ɑ̃bʀasmɑ̃] *nm* (*littér*) = **embrassade.**
embrasser [ɑ̃bʀase] (1) **1** *vt* **(a)** (*donner un baiser*) to kiss. ~ **qn à pleine bouche** to kiss sb (full) on the lips; (*en fin de lettre*) **je t'embrasse (affectueusement)** with love.
(b) (*frm ou* †: *étreindre*) to embrace; *V* **rime.**
(c) (*frm: choisir*) *doctrine, cause* to embrace (*frm*), espouse (*frm*); *carrière* to take up, enter upon.
(d) (*couvrir*) *problèmes, sujets* to encompass, embrace. (*littér*) **il embrassa la plaine du regard** his eyes took in the plain, he took in the plain at a glance.
2 s'embrasser *vpr* to kiss (each other).
embrasure [ɑ̃bʀɑzyʀ] *nf* (*Constr, créneau*) embrasure. **il se tenait dans l'~ de la porte/la fenêtre** he stood in the doorway/the window.
embrayage [ɑ̃bʀɛjaʒ] *nm* **(a)** (*mécanisme*) clutch. **(b)** (*action*) (*Aut, Tech*) letting in *ou* engaging the clutch.
embrayer [ɑ̃bʀeje] (8) **1** *vt* **(a)** (*Aut, Tech*) to put into gear. **(b)** (*fig*) *affaire* to set rolling, set in motion. **2** *vi* (*Aut*) to let in the clutch.
embrigadement [ɑ̃bʀigadmɑ̃] *nm* recruitment.
embrigader [ɑ̃bʀigade] (1) *vt* to recruit.
embringuer: [ɑ̃bʀɛ̃ge] (1) *vt* to mix up*, involve. **il s'est laissé ~ dans une sale histoire** he got (himself) mixed up* *ou* involved in some nasty business.
embrocation [ɑ̃bʀɔkasjɔ̃] *nf* embrocation.
embrocher [ɑ̃bʀɔʃe] (1) *vt* (*Culin*) (*sur broche*) to spit, put on a spit; (*brochette*) to skewer. (*fig*) ~ **qn** to run sb through.
embrouillage [ɑ̃bʀujaʒ] *nm* = **embrouillement.**
embrouillamini* [ɑ̃bʀujamini] *nm* muddle, jumble.
embrouillé, e [ɑ̃bʀuje] (*ptp de* **embrouiller**) *adj style, problème* muddled, confused; *idées, souvenirs* muddled, confused, mixed-up; *papiers* muddled, mixed-up.
embrouillement [ɑ̃bʀujmɑ̃] *nm* (*V* **embrouiller**) (*action*) tangling; muddling up, mixing up; confusion; (*état*) tangle; muddle; confusion. **essayant de démêler l'~ de ses explications** trying to sort out his muddled explanations *ou* the confusion of his explanations.
embrouiller [ɑ̃bʀuje] (1) **1** *vt* **(a)** *ficelle* to tangle (up), snarl up; *objets, papiers* to muddle up, mix up; *affaire* to muddle (up), tangle up, confuse; *problème* to muddle (up), confuse.
(b) *personne* to muddle (up), confuse, mix up; *V* **ni.**
2 s'embrouiller *vpr* **(a)** *[idées, style, situation]* to become muddled *ou* confused.
(b) *[personne]* to get in a muddle, become confused *ou* muddled. **s'~ dans un discours/ses explications** to get in a muddle with *ou* tie o.s. up in knots* in a speech/with one's explanations; **s'~ dans ses dates** to get one's dates muddled (up) *ou* mixed up.
embroussaillé, e [ɑ̃bʀusaje] *adj chemin* overgrown; *barbe, sourcils, cheveux* bushy, shaggy.
embrumer [ɑ̃bʀyme] (1) *vt* (*littér*) to mist over, cloud over (*de* with); (*fig*) to cloud (*de* with). **à l'horizon embrumé** on the misty *ou* hazy horizon.
embruns [ɑ̃bʀœ̃] *nmpl* sea spray (*U*), spindrift (*U*).
embryologie [ɑ̃bʀijɔlɔʒi] *nf* embryology.
embryologique [ɑ̃bʀijɔlɔʒik] *adj* embryologic(al).
embryologiste [ɑ̃bʀijɔlɔʒist(ə)] *nmf* embryologist.
embryon [ɑ̃bʀijɔ̃] *nm* embryo.
embryonnaire [ɑ̃bʀijɔnɛʀ] *adj* (*Méd*) embryonic, embryonal; (*fig*) embryonic. (*fig*) **à l'état ~** in embryo, in an embryonic state.
embûche [ɑ̃byʃ] *nf* pitfall, trap. **semé d'~s** treacherous, full of pitfalls *ou* traps.
embuer [ɑ̃bɥe] (1) *vt* to mist (up), mist over. **vitre embuée**

misted(-up) window pane; **yeux embués de larmes** eyes misted (over) *ou* clouded with tears.

embuscade [ɑ̃byskad] *nf* ambush. **être *ou* se tenir en ~** to lie in ambush; **tendre une ~ à qn** to set (up) *ou* lay an ambush for sb; **tomber dans une ~** (*Mil*) to fall into an ambush; (*tendue par des brigands*) to fall into an ambush, be waylaid.

embusqué, e [ɑ̃byske] (*ptp de* **embusquer**) **1** *adj*: **être ~** *[soldats]* to lie *ou* wait in ambush. **2** *nm* (*arg Mil*) shirker.

embusquer [ɑ̃byske] (1) **1** *vt*: **~ qn** to put sb in ambush. **2 s'embusquer** *vpr* to take up one's position (for an ambush).

émécher [emeʃe] (6) *vt* (*gén ptp*) to make merry *ou* tipsy. **éméché** tipsy, merry.

émeraude [ɛmʀod] *nf, adj inv* emerald.

émergence [emɛʀʒɑ̃s] *nf* (*gén*) emergence. **(point d')~ d'une source** source of a spring.

émergent, e [emɛʀʒɑ̃, ɑ̃t] *adj rocher,* (*Phys*) emergent.

émerger [emɛʀʒe] (3) *vi* **(a)** (*apparaître*) *[rocher, cime]* to emerge, rise up; *[vérité, astre]* to emerge, come out; *[fait, artiste]* to emerge. **le sommet émergea du brouillard** the summit rose out of *ou* emerged from the fog.

(b) (*faire saillie*) *[rocher, fait, artiste]* to stand out. **des rochers qui émergent** salient rocks, rocks that stand out.

émeri [ɛmʀi] *nm* emery. **toile *ou* papier ~** emery paper; *V* **bouché.**

émerillon [ɛmʀijɔ̃] *nm* (*Zool*) merlin; (*Tech*) swivel.

émérite [emeʀit] *adj* highly skilled.

émersion [emɛʀsjɔ̃] *nf* emersion.

émerveillement [emɛʀvɛjmɑ̃] *nm* (*sentiment*) wonder; (*vision, sons etc*) wonderful thing, marvel.

émerveiller [emɛʀveje] (1) **1** *vt* to fill with wonder. **2 s'émerveiller** *vpr* to be filled with wonder. **s'~ de** to marvel at, be filled with wonder at.

émétique [emetik] *adj, nm* emetic.

émetteur, -trice [emɛtœʀ, tʀis] **1** *adj* **(a)** (*Rad*) transmitting; *V* **poste²**, **station. (b)** (*Fin*) issuing (*épith*). **2** *nm* transmitter. **~-récepteur** transmitter-receiver, transceiver.

émettre [emɛtʀ(ə)] (56) *vt* **(a)** *lumière [lampe]* to give (out), send out; (*Phys*) to emit; *son, radiation, liquide* to give out, send out, emit; *odeur* to give off, emit.

(b) (*Rad, TV*) to transmit. (*Rad*) **~ sur ondes courtes** to broadcast on shortwave.

(c) (*Fin*) *monnaie, actions, emprunt* to issue; *chèque* to draw; (*fig*) *idée, hypothèse* to voice, put forward; *vœux* to express.

émeu [emø] *nm* emu.

émeute [emøt] *nf* riot. **~s** riots, rioting.

émeutier, -ière [emøtje, jɛʀ] *nm,f* rioter.

émiettement [emjɛtmɑ̃] *nm* (*V* **émietter**) crumbling; breaking up, splitting up; dispersion; dissipation. **un ~ de petites parcelles de terre** a scattering of little plots of land.

émietter [emjete] (1) **1** *vt pain, terre* to crumble; *territoire* to break up, split up; *pouvoir, responsabilités* to disperse; *énergie, effort,* (*littér*) *temps* to dissipate.

2 s'émietter *vpr [pain, terre]* to crumble; *[pouvoir]* to disperse; *[énergie, existence]* to dissipate.

émigrant, e [emigʀɑ̃, ɑ̃t] *nm,f* emigrant.

émigration [emigʀɑsjɔ̃] *nf* emigration.

émigré, e [emigʀe] (*ptp de* **émigrer**) *nm,f* (*Hist*) émigré; (*Pol*) expatriate, émigré.

émigrer [emigʀe] (1) *vi* to emigrate; (*Zool*) to migrate.

émincé [emɛ̃se] *nm* (*plat*) émincé; (*tranche*) sliver, thin slice. **un ~ de veau/de foie de veau** émincé of veal/calves' liver.

émincer [emɛ̃se] (3) *vt* to slice thinly, cut into slivers *ou* thin slices.

éminemment [eminamɑ̃] *adv* eminently.

éminence [eminɑ̃s] *nf* **(a)** *[terrain]* knoll, hill; (*Méd*) protuberance. **(b)** (†) *[qualité, rang]* distinction, eminence. **Son/Votre É~** his/your Eminence. **(c)** (*cardinal*) Eminence. (*fig*) **~ grise** éminence grise.

éminent, e [eminɑ̃, ɑ̃t] *adj* distinguished, eminent. (*frm*) **mon ~ collègue** my learned *ou* distinguished colleague.

éminentissime [eminɑ̃tisim] *adj* (*hum*) most distinguished *ou* eminent; (*Rel*) most eminent.

émir [emiʀ] *nm* emir.

émirat [emiʀa] *nm* emirate.

émissaire [emisɛʀ] *nm* (*gén*) emissary; *V* **bouc.**

émission [emisjɔ̃] *nf* **(a)** (*action: V* **émettre**) giving out, sending out; emission; giving off; transmission; broadcast(ing); issue; drawing; voicing, putting forward; expression. (*Physiol*) **~ d'urine/de sperme** emission of urine/semen; (*Fin*) **monopole d'~** monopoly of issue; (*Fin*) **cours d'~** issue par; (*Phys*) **source d'~ (de lumière/chaleur)** (emitting) source (of light/heat); (*Phonétique*) **~ de voix** emission of sound (by the voice); *V* **banque.**

(b) (*Rad, TV: spectacle*) programme, broadcast. **dans une ~ télévisée/radiophonique** in a television/radio programme *ou* broadcast; **~ en direct/différé** live/(pre-)recorded programme *ou* broadcast; **as-tu le programme des ~s de la semaine?** have you got (the list of) this week's programmes?; **'nos ~s sont terminées'** 'that's the end of today's broadcasts *ou* programmes *ou* broadcasting'.

emmagasinage [ɑ̃magazinaʒ] *nm* (*V* **emmagasiner**) storing up, accumulation; storage, warehousing.

emmagasiner [ɑ̃magazine] (1) *vt* (*lit, fig: amasser*) to store up, accumulate; (*Comm*) to store, put into store, warehouse.

emmaillotement [ɑ̃majɔtmɑ̃] *nm* (*V* **emmailloter**) binding up, bandaging; wrapping up.

emmailloter [ɑ̃majɔte] (1) *vt doigt, pied* to bind (up), bandage, wrap up; *enfant* to wrap up.

emmanchement [ɑ̃mɑ̃ʃmɑ̃] *nm [outil]* fitting of a handle (*de* to, on, onto).

emmanché, e: [ɑ̃mɑ̃ʃe] (*ptp de* **emmancher**) *adj* (*crétin*) twit:, berk:.

emmancher [ɑ̃mɑ̃ʃe] (1) *vt pelle* to fix *ou* put a handle on. **~ une affaire*** to get a piece of business going*, get going on* *ou* make a start on a piece of business; **l'affaire s'emmanche mal*** things are getting off to a bad start; **une affaire bien/mal emmanchée*** a piece of business which has got off to a good/bad start.

emmanchure [ɑ̃mɑ̃ʃyʀ] *nf* armhole.

emmêlement [ɑ̃mɛlmɑ̃] *nm* (*action*) tangling; (*état*) tangle, muddle. **un ~ de tuyaux** a tangle of pipes.

emmêler [ɑ̃mele] (1) **1** *vt cheveux* to tangle (up), knot; *fil* to tangle (up), entangle, muddle up; (*fig*) *affaire* to confuse, muddle. (*fig*) **tu emmêles tout** you're confusing everything, you're getting everything mixed up *ou* muddled (up) *ou* confused.

2 s'emmêler *vpr* to tangle, get in a tangle.

emménagement [ɑ̃menaʒmɑ̃] *nm* moving in (*U*).

emménager [ɑ̃menaʒe] (3) *vi* to move in. **~ dans** to move into.

emmener [ɑ̃mne] (5) *vt* **(a)** *personne* (*comme otage*) to take away; (*comme invité, compagnon*) to take. **~ qn au cinéma** to take sb to the cinema; **~ qn en prison** to take sb (away *ou* off) to prison; **~ qn faire une balade en voiture** to take sb for a run in the *ou* one's car; **~ promener qn *ou* ~ qn faire une promenade** to take sb (off) for a walk; **~ déjeuner qn** to take sb out to *ou* for lunch; **voulez-vous que je vous emmène?** shall I give you a lift?, would you like a lift?

(b) (*: *emporter*) *chose* to take; (*comme bagages*) to take (with one). **tu vas ~ cette grosse valise?** are you going to take that great suitcase (with you)?

(c) (*Mil, Sport: guider*) *équipe, troupe* to lead.

emment(h)al [emɛ̃tal] *nm* Emmenthal (cheese).

emmerdant, e: [ɑ̃mɛʀdɑ̃, ɑ̃t] *adj* (*irritant*) bloody (*Brit*) *ou* damned annoying:; (*lassant*) bloody (*Brit*) *ou* damned boring:. **qu'est-ce qu'il est ~ avec ses histoires** what a bloody (*Brit*) *ou* damned nuisance: *ou* pain (in the neck): he is with his stories; **c'est vraiment ~ qu'il ne puisse pas venir** it's bloody (*Brit*) *ou* damned annoying: *ou* a hell of a nuisance: that he can't come.

emmerdement: [ɑ̃mɛʀdəmɑ̃] *nm*: **quel ~!** what a bloody: (*Brit*) *ou* damned nuisance!:; **avoir des ~s: j'ai eu tellement d'~s avec cette voiture** that car gave me so much bloody (*Brit*) *ou* damned trouble:, I had so many bloody (*Brit*) *ou* damned problems with that car:.

emmerder: [ɑ̃mɛʀde] (1) **1** *vt*: **~ qn** (*irriter*) to get on sb's wick: (*Brit*), give sb a pain in the neck*; (*volontairement*) to bug sb*, pester sb; (*préoccuper, contrarier*) to bug sb*, bother sb; (*lasser*) to bore the pants off sb:, bore sb stiff* *ou* to death*; **arrête de nous ~ avec tes histoires!** stop being such a bloody (*Brit*) *ou* damned nuisance: *ou* pain (in the neck): with your stories; **il m'emmerde à la fin, avec ses questions** he's really getting on my wick: *ou* up my nose: with his questions; **ça m'emmerde qu'il ne puisse pas venir** it's a damned nuisance: *ou* a hell of a nuisance: that he can't come; **je les emmerde!** to hell with them!:, bugger them!∵ (*Brit*).

2 s'emmerder *vpr* (*être ennuyé*) to be bored stiff* *ou* to death*, be pissed off∵. **je me suis emmerdé à réparer ce poste, et maintenant voilà qu'il ne le veut plus!** I really put myself out repairing this damned radio and now he doesn't even want it!:

emmerdeur, -euse: [ɑ̃mɛʀdœʀ, øz] *nm,f* damned nuisance:, pain in the neck:.

emmitoufler [ɑ̃mitufle] (1) *vt* to wrap up (warmly), muffle up. **s'~ (dans un manteau)** to wrap o.s. up (warmly) *ou* get muffled up (in a coat).

emmurer [ɑ̃myʀe] (1) *vt* to wall up, immure.

émoi [emwa] *nm* (*littér*) (*trouble*) agitation, emotion; (*de joie*) excitement; (*tumulte*) commotion. **doux ~** pleasant agitation; **dit-elle non sans ~** she said with some confusion *ou* a little flustered; **en ~** *cœur* in a flutter (*attrib*); *sens* agitated, excited; **la rue était en ~** the street was astir (*littér*) *ou* in a commotion.

émollient, e [emɔljɑ̃, ɑ̃t] *adj, nm* emollient.

émoluments [emɔlymɑ̃] *nmpl* (*Admin*) remuneration, emolument (*frm*), fee.

émondage [emɔ̃daʒ] *nm* pruning, trimming.

émonder [emɔ̃de] (1) *vt* to prune, trim.

émondeur, -euse [emɔ̃dœʀ, øz] *nm,f* pruner (*person*).

émondoir [emɔ̃dwaʀ] *nm* pruning hook.

émotif, -ive [emɔtif, iv] **1** *adj* emotional. **2** *nm,f* emotional person.

émotion [emosjɔ̃] *nf* (*vif sentiment*) emotion; (*peur*) fright; (*sensibilité*) emotion, feeling; (†: *tumulte*) commotion. **ils ont évité l'accident mais l'~ a été grande** they avoided the accident but it really gave them a bad fright; **donner des ~s à qn*** to give sb a (nasty) turn* *ou* fright.

émotionnel, -elle [emosjɔnɛl] *adj choc, réaction* emotional.

émotionner* [emosjɔne] (1) **1** *vt* to upset. **j'en suis encore tout émotionné** it gave me quite a turn*, I'm still all upset about it. **2 s'émotionner** *vpr* to get worked up*, get upset.

émotivité [emɔtivite] *nf* emotionalism.

émoulu, e [emuly] *adj*: **frais ~ (de l'école)** fresh from school, just out of school; **frais ~ de l'École polytechnique** fresh from *ou* just out of the École Polytechnique.

émoussé, e [emuse] (*ptp de* **émousser**) *adj couteau, tranchant* blunt; *goût, sensibilité* blunted, dulled.

émousser [emuse] (1) *vt lame, couteau, appétit* to blunt, take the edge off; *sentiment, souvenir, désir* to dull. **son talent s'est émoussé** his talent has lost its fine edge.

émoustillant, e* [emustijɑ̃, ɑ̃t] *adj présence* tantalizing, titillating; *propos* titillating.

émoustiller* [emustije] (1) *vt* to titillate, tantalize.

émouvant, e [emuvɑ̃, ɑ̃t] *adj* (*nuance de compassion*) moving, touching; (*nuance d'admiration*) stirring.

émouvoir [emuvwaʀ] (27) **1** *vt* **(a)** *personne (frapper)* to affect, disturb; (*troubler*) to (a)rouse, stir, affect; (*toucher*) to move; (*indigner*) to rouse (the indignation of); (*effrayer*) to disturb, worry, upset. **leur attitude ne l'émut/leurs menaces ne l'émurent pas le moins du monde** their attitude/threats didn't disturb *ou* worry *ou* upset him in the slightest; **plus ému qu'il ne voulait l'admettre par ce baiser/ces caresses** more affected *ou* (a)roused than he wished to admit by this kiss/these caresses; **le spectacle/leur misère l'émouvait profondément** the sight/their wretchedness moved *ou* disturbed him deeply *ou* upset him greatly; **~ qn jusqu'aux larmes** to move sb to tears; **cet auteur s'attache à ~ le lecteur** this author sets out to move *ou* stir the reader; **se laisser ~ par des prières** to be moved by entreaties, let o.s. be swayed by entreaties; **encore tout ému d'avoir frôlé l'accident/de cette rencontre** still very shaken *ou* greatly upset at having been so close to an accident/over that encounter.

(b) (*littér*) *pitié, colère* to (a)rouse. **~ la pitié de qn** to move sb to pity, (a)rouse sb's pity.

2 s'émouvoir *vpr* (*V* **émouvoir**) to be affected; to be disturbed; to be *ou* become (a)roused; to be stirred; to be moved; to be *ou* get worried, be *ou* get upset. **il ne s'émeut de rien** nothing upsets *ou* disturbs him; **dit-il sans s'~** he said calmly *ou* impassively *ou* quite unruffled; **s'~ à la vue de** to be moved at the sight of; **le pays entier s'est ému de l'affaire** the whole country was roused by the affair, the affair (a)roused the indignation of the whole country.

empaillage [ɑ̃pajaʒ] *nm* (*V* **empailler**) stuffing; bottoming.

empailler [ɑ̃paje] (1) *vt animal* to stuff; *chaise* to bottom (with straw).

empailleur, -euse [ɑ̃pajœʀ, øz] *nm,f [chaise]* upholsterer, (chair) bottomer; *[animal]* taxidermist.

empalement [ɑ̃palmɑ̃] *nm* impalement.

empaler [ɑ̃pale] (1) *vt* to impale.

empan [ɑ̃pɑ̃] *nm* (*Hist: mesure*) span.

empanaché, e [ɑ̃panaʃe] *adj* plumed.

empaquetage [ɑ̃paktaʒ] *nm* (*V* **empaqueter**) packing, packaging; parcelling up, wrapping up.

empaqueter [ɑ̃pakte] (4) *vt marchandises* to pack(age); *linge, colis* to parcel up, wrap up.

emparer (s') [ɑ̃paʀe] (1) *vpr* **(a)** *[personne]* **s'~ de** *objet, ballon* to seize *ou* grab (hold of), snatch up; *butin* to seize, grab; *personne* (*comme otage etc*) to seize; (*fig*) *conversation, sujet* to take over; (*fig*) *prétexte* to seize (up)on; (*Mil*) *ville, territoire, ennemi* to seize; **s'~ des moyens de production/de l'information** to take over *ou* seize the means of production/the information networks; **ils se sont emparés de la ville par surprise** they seized *ou* took the town by surprise; **ils se sont emparés du caissier et l'ont assommé** they grabbed (hold of) *ou* laid hold of the cashier and knocked him out; (*fig*) **son confesseur s'est emparé de son esprit** her confessor has gained *ou* got quite a hold over her way of thinking.

(b) s'~ de *[jalousie, colère, remords]* to take possession of; *[peur, désir, doute]* to take *ou* lay hold of; **cette obsession s'empara de son esprit** this obsession took possession of his mind, his mind was taken over by this obsession; **une grande peur/le remords s'empara d'elle** she was seized with a great fear/remorse.

empâtement [ɑ̃pɑtmɑ̃] *nm* (*V* **s'empâter**) thickening-out, fattening-out; thickening.

empâter [ɑ̃pɑte] (1) **1** *vt langue, bouche* to coat, fur (up); *traits* to thicken, coarsen. **ce régime l'a empâté** this diet has made him thicken *ou* fatten out.

2 s'empâter *vpr [personne, silhouette, visage]* to thicken out, fatten out; *[traits]* to thicken, grow fleshy; *[voix]* to become thick.

empattement [ɑ̃patmɑ̃] *nm* (*Constr*) footing; (*Aut*) wheelbase; (*Typ*) serif.

empêché, e [ɑ̃peʃe] (*ptp de* **empêcher**) *adj* **(a)** (*retenu*) detained, held up. **le professeur, ~, ne peut pas faire son cours** the teacher has been detained *ou* held up and is unable to give the class; **~ par ses obligations, il n'a pas pu venir** his commitments prevented him from coming, he was prevented from coming by his commitments.

(b) (*embarrassé*) **avoir l'air ~** to look *ou* seem embarrassed *ou* ill-at-ease.

(c) être bien ~ de: tu es bien ~ de me le dire you seem at a loss to know what to say.

empêchement [ɑ̃pɛʃmɑ̃] *nm* (*obstacle*) (unexpected) obstacle *ou* difficulty, hitch, holdup; (*Jur*) impediment. **il n'est pas venu, il a eu un ~** something unforeseen cropped up which prevented him from coming; **en cas d'~** if there's a hitch, should you be prevented from coming.

empêcher [ɑ̃peʃe] (1) **1** *vt* **(a)** *chose, action* to prevent, stop. **~ que qch (ne) se produise, ~ qch de se produire** to prevent sth from happening, stop sth happening; **~ que qn (ne) fasse** to prevent sb from doing, stop sb (from) doing.

(b) ~ qn de faire to prevent sb from doing, stop sb (from) doing; **rien ne nous empêche de partir** there's nothing stopping us (from) going *ou* preventing us from going *ou* preventing our going; **~ qn de sortir/d'entrer** to prevent sb from going out/coming in, keep sb in/out; **s'il veut le faire, on ne peut pas l'en ~** *ou* **l'~** if he wants to do it, we can't prevent him (from doing it) *ou* stop him (doing it); **ça ne m'empêche pas de dormir** (*lit*) it doesn't prevent me from sleeping *ou* stop me sleeping *ou* keep me awake; (*fig*) I don't lose any sleep over it.

(c) (*loc*) **qu'est-ce qui empêche (qu'on le fasse)?** what's there to stop us (doing it)? *ou* to prevent us (from doing it)?, what's stopping us (doing it)?*; **qu'est-ce que ça empêche?*** what odds* *ou* difference does that make?; **ça n'empêche rien*** it makes no odds* *ou* no difference; **ça n'empêche qu'il vienne*** that won't stop him coming, he's still coming anyway*; **il n'empêche qu'il a tort** nevertheless *ou* be that as it may, he is wrong; **n'empêche qu'il a tort** all the same *ou* it makes no odds*, he's wrong; **j'ai peut-être tort, n'empêche, il a un certain culot de dire ça!*** maybe I'm wrong, but all the same, he has got some cheek *ou* nerve saying that!*; *V* **empêcheur**.

2 s'empêcher *vpr* **(a)** (*littér*) **s'~ de faire** to stop o.s. (from) doing; **par politesse, il s'empêcha de bâiller** out of politeness he stifled a yawn *ou* he stopped himself yawning.

(b) ne pas pouvoir s'~ de faire: il n'a pas pu s'~ de rire he couldn't help laughing, he couldn't stop himself (from) laughing; **je ne peux m'~ de penser que** I cannot help thinking that; **je n'ai pu m'en ~** I could not help it, I couldn't stop myself.

empêcheur, -euse [ɑ̃pɛʃœʀ, øz] *nm,f*: **~ de danser en rond** spoilsport, killjoy; (*hum*) **un ~ de travailler/de s'amuser en rond** a spoilsport as far as work/enjoyment is concerned.

empeigne [ɑ̃pɛɲ] *nf [soulier]* upper.

empennage [ɑ̃pɛnaʒ] *nm* (*Aviat*) empennage; *[flèche]* feathering.

empenner [ɑ̃pene] (1) *vt flèche* to feather.

empereur [ɑ̃pʀœʀ] *nm* emperor.

empesage [ɑ̃pəzaʒ] *nm* starching.

empesé, e [ɑ̃pəze] (*ptp de* **empeser**) *adj col* starched; (*fig*) stiff, starchy.

empeser [ɑ̃pəze] (5) *vt* to starch.

empester [ɑ̃pɛste] (1) *vt* (*sentir*) *odeur, fumée* to stink of, reek of; (*empuantir*) *pièce* to stink out (*de* with), make stink (*de* of); (*fig littér: empoisonner*) to poison, taint (*de* with). **ça empeste ici** it stinks in here, there's a stink in here.

empêtrer (s') [ɑ̃petʀe] (1) *vpr* **(a)** (*lit*) **s'~ dans** to get tangled up in, get entangled in, get caught up in.

(b) (*fig*) **s'~ dans** *mensonges* to get o.s. tangled up in; *affaire* to get (o.s.) involved in, get (o.s.) mixed up in; **s'~ dans des explications** to tie o.s. up in knots trying to explain*, get tangled up in one's explanations; **s'~ de qn** to get (o.s.) landed with sb*, get tied up with sb*.

emphase [ɑ̃fɑz] *nf* **(a)** (*pomposité*) bombast, pomposity, grandiloquence. **avec ~** bombastically, pompously, grandiloquently; **sans ~** in a straightforward manner, simply. **(b)** (†: *force d'expression*) vigour.

emphatique [ɑ̃fatik] *adj* **(a)** (*grandiloquent*) bombastic, pompous, grandiloquent. **(b)** (*Ling*) emphatic.

emphatiquement [ɑ̃fatikmɑ̃] *adv* bombastically, pompously, grandiloquently.

emphysémateux, -euse [ɑ̃fizematø, øz] *adj* emphysematous.

emphysème [ɑ̃fizɛm] *nm* emphysema.

empiècement [ɑ̃pjɛsmɑ̃] *nm [corsage]* yoke.

empierrement [ɑ̃pjɛʀmɑ̃] *nm* **(a)** (*action: V* **empierrer**) metalling; ballasting; lining with stones. **(b)** (*couche de pierres*) road metal.

empierrer [ɑ̃pjeʀe] (1) *vt route* to metal; *voie de chemin de fer* to ballast; *bassin, cour, fossé* to line with stones.

empiètement [ɑ̃pjɛtmɑ̃] *nm* (*V* **empiéter**) **~ (sur)** encroachment (upon); trespassing on.

empiéter [ɑ̃pjete] (6) *vi*: **~ sur** *[territoire, état]* to encroach (up)on; *[mer]* to cut into, encroach (up)on; *[terrain]* to overlap into *ou* onto, encroach (up)on; *[route]* to run into *ou* onto, encroach (up)on; *[personne] droit, liberté* to encroach (up)on; *attributions* to trespass on; *[activité] attributions, activité* to encroach (up)on; *temps* to encroach (up)on, cut into.

empiffrer (s')ː [ɑ̃pifʀe] (1) *vpr* to stuff one's faceː, stuff o.s.* (*de* with).

empilage [ɑ̃pilaʒ] *nm*, **empilement** [ɑ̃pilmɑ̃] *nm* (*action*) piling-up, stacking-up; (*pile*) pile, stack.

empiler [ɑ̃pile] (1) **1** *vt* **(a)** to pile (up), stack (up). **(b)** (ː: *voler*) to doː, rookː. **se faire ~** to be had* *ou* doneː (*de* out of). **2 s'empiler** *vpr* **(a)** (*s'amonceler*) to be piled up (*sur* on). **(b)** (*s'entasser*) **s'~ dans** *local, véhicule* to squeeze *ou* pack into.

empileur, -euse [ɑ̃pilœʀ, øz] *nm,f* (*ouvrier*) stacker; (ː: *escroc*) swindler.

empire [ɑ̃piʀ] **1** *nm* **(a)** (*Pol*) empire. **pas pour un ~!** not for all the tea in China!, not for (all) the world!

(b) (*emprise*) influence, authority. **avoir de l'~ sur** to have influence *ou* a hold over, hold sway over; **prendre de l'~ sur** to gain influence *ou* a hold over; **exercer son ~ sur** to exert one's authority over, use one's influence over; **sous l'~ de** *peur, colère* in the grip of; *jalousie* possessed by; **sous l'~ de la boisson** under the influence of drink, the worse for drink; **~ sur soi-même** self-control, self-command.

2: l'Empire d'Occident the Western Empire; **l'Empire d'Orient** the Byzantine Empire.

empirer [ɑ̃piʀe] (1) **1** *vi* to get worse, deteriorate. **2** *vt* to make worse, worsen.

empirique [ɑ̃piʀik] **1** *adj* (*Philos, Phys*) empirical; (*Méd* ††) empiric. **2** *nm* (*Méd* ††) empiric.

empiriquement [ɑ̃piʀikmɑ̃] *adv* empirically.

empirisme [ɑ̃piʀism(ə)] *nm* empiricism.

empiriste [ɑ̃piʀist(ə)] *adj, nmf* (*Philos, Phys*) empiricist; (*Méd* ††) empiric.

emplacement [ɑ̃plasmɑ̃] *nm* (*gén*) site; (*pour construire*) site, location. **à** *ou* **sur l'~ d'une ancienne cité romaine** on the site of an ancient Roman city; **quelques pieux qui dépassaient de la neige indiquaient l'~ du chemin** a few posts sticking up above the snow showed the location of the path *ou* showed where the path was.

emplâtre [ɑ̃plɑtʀ(ə)] *nm* (*Méd*) plaster; (*Aut*) patch; (*: *personne*) (great) lump*, clot*. **ce plat vous fait un ~ sur l'estomac*** this dish lies heavy on *ou* lies like a (solid) lump in your stomach.

emplette† [ɑ̃plɛt] *nf* purchase. **faire l'~ de** to purchase; **faire des** *ou* **quelques ~s** to do some shopping, make some purchases.
emplir [ɑ̃pliʀ] (2) **1** *vt* (†, *littér*) **(a)** *verre, récipient* to fill (up) (*de* with). **(b)** *[foule, meubles]* to fill. **2 s'emplir** *vpr*: **s'~ de** to fill with; **la pièce s'emplissait de lumière/de gens** the room was filling with light/people.
emploi [ɑ̃plwa] *nm* **(a)** (*U: usage*) use. **je n'en ai pas l'~** I have no use for it; **l'~ qu'il fait de son argent/temps** the use he makes of his money/time, the use to which he puts his money/time; **sans ~** unused; **son ~ du temps** his timetable, his schedule; **un ~ du temps chargé** a heavy *ou* busy timetable, a busy schedule; *V* **double, mode[2]**.
(b) (*mode d'utilisation*) *[appareil, produit]* use; *[mot, expression]* use, usage. **un ~ nouveau de cet appareil** a new use for this piece of equipment; **divers ~s d'un mot** different uses of a word; **c'est un ~ très rare de cette expression** it's a very rare use *ou* usage of this expression.
(c) (*poste, travail*) job, employment (*U*). (*Écon*) **l'~** employment; **créer de nouveaux ~s** to create new jobs; **être sans ~** to be unemployed; **chercher de l'~** to look for a job *ou* for employment; (*Écon*) **la situation de l'~** the employment situation; (*Écon*) **plein-~** full employment; **avoir le physique/la tête de l'~*** to look the part; *V* **demande, offre.**
(d) (*rare Théât: rôle*) role, part.
employé, e [ɑ̃plwaje] (*ptp de* **employer**) *nm,f* employee. **~ de banque** bank employee *ou* clerk; **~ de commerce** commercial employee; **~ de bureau** office worker *ou* clerk; **~ des postes/des chemins de fer/du gaz** postal/railway (*Brit*) *ou* railroad (*US*)/gas worker; **on a sonné: c'est l'~ du gaz** there's someone at the door — it's the gas man; **~ de maison** domestic employee; **les ~s de cette firme** the staff *ou* employees of this firm.
employer [ɑ̃plwaje] (8) **1** *vt* **(a)** (*utiliser*) *appareil, système* to use, utilize; *outil, produit, mot, expression* to use; *force, moyen* to use, employ; *temps* to spend, use, employ. **~ toute son énergie à faire qch** to apply *ou* devote all one's energies to doing sth; **~ son temps à faire qch/à qch** to spend one's time doing sth/on sth; **~ son argent à faire qch/à qch** to spend *ou* use one's money doing sth/on sth; **bien ~** *temps, argent* to put to good use, make good use of, use properly; *mot, expression* to use properly *ou* correctly; **mal ~** *temps, argent* to misuse; *mot, expression* to misuse, use wrongly *ou* incorrectly; **ce procédé emploie énormément de matières premières** this process uses (up) huge amounts of raw materials.
(b) (*faire travailler*) *main d'œuvre, ouvrier* to employ. **ils l'emploient comme vendeur/à trier le courrier** they employ him as a salesman/to sort the mail; **cet ouvrier est mal employé à ce poste** this workman has been given the wrong sort of job *ou* is not suited to the post; **il est employé par cette société** he is employed by that firm, he works for that firm, he is on the staff of that firm.
2 s'employer *vpr*: **s'~ à faire qch/à qch** to apply *ou* devote o.s. to doing sth/to sth; **s'~ pour**† *ou* **en faveur de**† to go to great lengths *ou* exert o.s. on behalf of.
employeur, -euse [ɑ̃plwajœʀ, øz] *nm,f* employer.
emplumé, e [ɑ̃plyme] *adj* feathered, plumed.
empocher* [ɑ̃pɔʃe] (1) *vt* to pocket.
empoignade [ɑ̃pwaɲad] *nf* row*, set-to*.
empoigne [ɑ̃pwaɲ] *nf V* **foire.**
empoigner [ɑ̃pwaɲe] (1) **1** *vt* **(a)** to grasp, grab (hold of). **(b)** (*émouvoir*) to grip. **2 s'empoigner*** *vpr* (*se colleter*) to have a set-to*, have a go at one another*.
empois [ɑ̃pwa] *nm* starch (*for linen etc*).
empoisonnant, e* [ɑ̃pwazɔnɑ̃, ɑ̃t] *adj* (*irritant*) irritating; (*contrariant*) annoying, aggravating*. **oh, il est ~ avec ses questions** he's so irritating *ou* he's a darned nuisance* *ou* such a pain* with his questions.
empoisonnement [ɑ̃pwazɔnmɑ̃] *nm* **(a)** (*lit*) poisoning. **(b)** (*: *ennui*) darned nuisance* (*U*), bother (*U*). **tous ces ~s** all this bother.
empoisonner [ɑ̃pwazɔne] (1) **1** *vt* **(a)** (*lit*) **~ qn** to poison sb; *[aliments avariés]* to give sb food poisoning; **flèches empoisonnées** poisoned arrows; (*fig*) **des propos empoisonnés** poisonous words.
(b) (*fig: empuantir*) to stink out.
(c) (*) **~ qn** *[gêneur, casse-pieds]* to get on sb's nerves*, drive sb up the wall*; *[contretemps]* to annoy sb, aggravate sb*; *[corvée, travail]* to drive sb mad*, drive sb up the wall*; **ça m'empoisonne d'avoir à le dire mais ...** I hate to have to say this but ..., I don't like saying this but ...; **il m'empoisonne avec ses jérémiades** he gets on my nerves* *ou* drives me up the wall* with his complaints.
2 s'empoisonner *vpr* **(a)** (*lit*) to poison o.s.; (*par intoxication alimentaire*) to get food poisoning.
(b) (*: *s'ennuyer*) **qu'est-ce qu'on s'empoisonne** what a drag this is*, this is driving us mad* *ou* up the wall*.
empoisonneur, -euse [ɑ̃pwazɔnœʀ, øz] *nm,f* **(a)** (*lit*) poisoner. **(b)** (*) pain in the neck* (*U*), nuisance, bore.
empoissonner [ɑ̃pwasɔne] (1) *vt* to stock with fish.
emporté, e [ɑ̃pɔʀte] (*ptp de* **emporter**) *adj caractère, personne* quick-tempered, hot-tempered; *ton, air* angry.
emportement [ɑ̃pɔʀtəmɑ̃] *nm* fit of anger, rage, anger (*U*). **avec ~** angrily; (*littér*) **aimer qn avec ~** to love sb passionately, be wildly in love with sb.
emporte-pièce [ɑ̃pɔʀtəpjɛs] *nm inv* **(a)** (*Tech*) punch. **(b) à l'~** *caractère* incisive; *formule, phrase* incisive, sharp.
emporter [ɑ̃pɔʀte] (1) **1** *vt* **(a)** (*prendre comme bagage*) *vivres, vêtements etc* to take (with one). **emporter des vêtements chauds** to take warm clothes (with one); **j'emporte de quoi écrire** I'm taking something to write with; **si vous gagnez, vous pouvez l'~ (avec vous)** if you win, you can take it away (with you); **plats chauds/boissons à ~** take-away hot meals/drinks (*Brit*), hot meals/drinks to go (*US*); (*fig*) **~ un bon souvenir de qch** to take *ou* bring away a pleasant memory of sth; (*fig*) **~ un secret dans la tombe** to take a secret (with one) *ou* carry a secret to the grave; (*fig*) **il ne l'emportera pas en Paradis!** he'll soon be smiling on the other side of his face!
(b) (*enlever*) *objet inutile* to take away, remove; *prisonniers* to take away; *blessés* to carry *ou* take away; (*: *dérober*) to take. **emportez ces papiers/vêtements, nous n'en avons plus besoin** take those papers/clothes away *ou* remove those papers/clothes because we don't need them any more; **ils ont emporté l'argenterie!** they've made off with* *ou* taken the silver!; *V* **diable.**
(c) (*entraîner*) *[courant, vent]* to sweep along, carry along; *[navire, train]* to carry along; (*fig*) *[imagination]* to carry away *ou* along; *[colère]* to carry away; *[enthousiasme]* to carry away *ou* along, sweep along. **le courant emportait leur embarcation** the current swept *ou* carried their boat along; **emporté par son élan** carried *ou* borne along by his own momentum *ou* impetus; **emporté par son imagination/enthousiasme** carried along *ou* away by his imagination/enthusiasm; **se laisser ~ par la colère** to (let o.s.) give way to one's anger, let o.s. be carried away by one's anger; **le train qui m'emportait vers de nouveaux horizons** the train which carried *ou* swept me along towards new horizons; **le train qui allait m'~ vers de nouveaux horizons** the train which was going to carry *ou* bear me away towards new horizons.
(d) (*arracher*) *jambe, bras* to take off; *cheminée, toit* to blow away *ou* off; *pont, berge* to wash away, carry away; (*euph: tuer*) *[maladie]* to carry off. **l'obus lui a emporté le bras gauche** the shell blew off *ou* took off his left arm; **pont emporté par le torrent** bridge swept *ou* carried away by the flood; **la vague a emporté 3 passagers** the wave washed *ou* swept 3 passengers overboard; (*fig*) **plat qui emporte la bouche** *ou* **la gueule*** dish that takes the roof off your mouth*; (*fig*) **cette maladie l'a emporté à l'âge de 30 ans** this illness carried him off at the age of 30.
(e) (*gagner*) *prix* to carry off; (*Mil*) *position* to take, win. **~ la décision** to carry *ou* win the day.
(f) l'~ (sur) *[personne]* to gain *ou* get the upper hand (of); *[solution, méthode]* to prevail (over); **il a fini par l'~** he finally gained *ou* got the upper hand; **il va l'~ sur son adversaire** he's going to gain *ou* get the better of *ou* the upper hand of his opponent; **la modération/cette solution finit par l'~** moderation/this solution prevailed in the end, moderation/this solution finally won the day; **cette méthode l'emporte sur l'autre** this method is more satisfactory than the other one; **il l'emporte sur ses concurrents en adresse** he certainly outmatches his opponents in skill, his opponents can't match *ou* rival him for skill; **il l'emporte de justesse (sur l'autre) en force** he has the edge (on the other one) as far as strength goes.
2 s'emporter *vpr* **(a)** (*de colère*) to lose one's temper (*contre* with), flare up (*contre* at), blow up* (*contre* at).
(b) (*s'emballer*) *[cheval]* to bolt. **faire (s')~ son cheval** to make one's horse bolt.
empoté, e* [ɑ̃pɔte] **1** *adj* awkward, clumsy. **2** *nm,f* (*péj*) awkward lump*.
empourprer [ɑ̃puʀpʀe] (1) **1** *vt visage* to flush, (turn) crimson; *ciel* to (turn) crimson. **2 s'empourprer** *vpr [visage]* to flush, turn crimson; *[ciel]* to turn crimson.
empoussiérer [ɑ̃pusjeʀe] (6) *vt* to cover with dust, make dusty.
empreindre [ɑ̃pʀɛ̃dʀ(ə)] (52) (*littér*) **1** *vt* (*imprimer*) to imprint; (*fig*) (*marquer*) to stamp; (*nuancer*) to tinge (*de* with). **2 s'empreindre** *vpr*: **s'~ de** to be imprinted with; to be stamped with; to be tinged with.
empreint, e[1] [ɑ̃pʀɛ̃, ɛ̃t] (*ptp de* **empreindre**) *adj*: **~ de** *regret, jalousie* tinged with; *bonté, autorité* marked *ou* stamped with; *menaces* fraught *ou* heavy with.
empreinte[2] [ɑ̃pʀɛ̃t] *nf* **(a)** (*lit*) (*gén*) imprint, impression; *[animal]* track. **~ (de pas)** footprint; **~s (digitales)** (finger)-prints. **(b)** (*fig*) stamp, mark.
empressé, e [ɑ̃pʀese] (*ptp de* **s'empresser**) *adj* **(a)** (*prévenant*) *infirmière* attentive; *serveur* attentive, willing; *aide* willing; (*souvent péj*) *admirateur* assiduous, overzealous; *prétendant* assiduous, overattentive; *subordonné* overanxious to please (*attrib*), overzealous. (*péj*) **faire l'~ (auprès d'une femme)** to be overattentive (towards a woman), fuss around (a woman) (trying to please).
(b) (*littér: marquant de la hâte*) eager. **~ à faire** eager *ou* anxious to do.
empressement [ɑ̃pʀɛsmɑ̃] *nm* **(a)** (*V* **empressé**) attentiveness; willingness; overzealousness; assiduity; overattentiveness. **son ~ auprès des femmes** his fussing around women, his overattentiveness towards women; **elle me servait avec ~** she waited upon me attentively.
(b) (*hâte*) eagerness, anxiousness. **son ~ à partir me paraît suspect** his eagerness *ou* anxiousness to leave seems suspicious to me; **il montrait peu d'~ à ...** he showed little desire to ..., he was obviously not anxious to ...; **il s'exécuta avec ~** he complied eagerly.
empresser (s') [ɑ̃pʀese] (1) *vpr* **(a)** (*s'affairer*) to bustle about; (*péj*) to fuss about *ou* around (*péj*), bustle about *ou* around. **s'~ auprès** *ou* **autour de** *blessé* to surround with attentions; *nouveau venu, invité* to be attentive toward(s), surround with attentions; *femme courtisée* to dance attendance upon, fuss round; **ils s'empressèrent autour de la victime** they rushed to help *ou* assist the victim; **ils s'empressaient auprès de l'actrice** they surrounded the actress with attentions.
(b) (*se hâter*) **s'~ de faire** to hasten to do.

emprise [ɑ̃pʀiz] *nf* hold, ascendancy (*sur* over). **avoir beaucoup d'~ sur qn** to have a great hold *ou* have great ascendancy over sb; **sous l'~ de** under the influence of.

emprisonnement [ɑ̃pʀizɔnmɑ̃] *nm* imprisonment. **condamné à l'~ à perpétuité** sentenced to life imprisonment; **condamné à 10 ans d'~** sentenced to 10 years in prison, given a 10-year prison sentence.

emprisonner [ɑ̃pʀizɔne] (1) *vt* **(a)** (*en prison*) to imprison, put in prison *ou* jail, jail; (*fig: dans une chambre, un couvent*) to shut up, imprison.

(b) (*fig*) *[vêtement]* to confine; *[doctrine, milieu]* to trap. **ce corset lui emprisonne la taille** this corset grips her (too) tightly around the waist *ou* really confines her waist; **~ qn dans un système/un raisonnement** to trap sb within a system/by a piece of reasoning; **emprisonné dans ses habitudes/la routine** imprisoned within *ou* a prisoner of his habits/routine.

emprunt [ɑ̃pʀœ̃] *nm* **(a)** (*action d'emprunter*) *[argent, objet]* borrowing. **l'~ de sa voiture était la seule solution** (my) borrowing his car was the only solution; **ce n'était pas un vol, mais seulement un ~** it (*ou* I *ou* he *etc*) wasn't really stealing, only borrowing, I (*ou* he *etc*) was really just borrowing it, not stealing; (*Fin*) **recourir à l'~** to resort to borrowing *ou* to a loan.

(b) (*demande, somme*) loan. **ses ~s successifs l'ont mis en difficulté** successive borrowing has *ou* his successive loans have put him in difficulty; (*Fin*) **~ d'État/public** Government/ public loan (*with government etc as borrower*); (*Fin*) **~ à 5%** loan at 5% (interest); (*Fin*) **faire un ~ (d'un million à une banque)** to raise a loan (of a million from a bank).

(c) (*littéraire etc*) borrowing; (*terme*) loanword, borrowed word, borrowing. **c'est un ~ à l'anglais** it's a borrowing from English, it's a loanword from English.

(d) (*loc*) **d'~** *nom, autorité* assumed; *matériel* borrowed.

emprunté, e [ɑ̃pʀœ̃te] (*ptp de* **emprunter**) *adj* **(a)** (*gauche*) *air, personne* ill-at-ease (*attrib*), self-conscious, awkward. **(b)** (*artificiel*) *gloire, éclat,* sham, feigned.

emprunter [ɑ̃pʀœ̃te] (1) *vt* **(a)** *argent, objet* to borrow (*à* from); *idée* to borrow, take (*à* from); *chaleur* to derive, take (*à* from); (*Ling*) (*directement*) to borrow, take (*à* from); (*par dérivation*) to derive, take (*à* from). **~ un langage noble** to use *ou* adopt a noble style (of language); **cette pièce emprunte son intérêt à l'actualité de son sujet** this play derives its interest from the topicality of its subject.

(b) *nom, autorité* to assume, take on.

(c) *route* to take; *itinéraire* to follow.

emprunteur, -euse [ɑ̃pʀœ̃tœʀ, øz] *nm,f* borrower.

empuantir [ɑ̃pɥɑ̃tiʀ] (2) *vt* to stink out (*de* with).

ému, e [emy] (*ptp de* **émouvoir**) *adj personne* (*compassion*) moved; (*gratitude*) touched; (*joie*) excited; (*timidité, peur*) nervous, agitated; *air* filled with emotion; *voix* emotional, trembling with emotion; *souvenirs* tender, touching. **~ jusqu'aux larmes devant leur misère** moved to tears by their wretchedness; **très ~ lors de son premier rendez-vous amoureux/la remise des prix** very excited *ou* agitated on his first date/at the prize giving; **encore tout ~, il la remercia** still quite overcome *ou* still (feeling) very touched, he thanked her; **dit-il d'une voix ~e** he said with (some) emotion, he said in a voice trembling with emotion; **trop ~ pour les remercier/leur annoncer la nouvelle** too overcome to thank them/announce the news to them.

émulation [emylɑsjɔ̃] *nf* emulation. **esprit d'~** spirit of competition, competitive spirit.

émule [emyl] *nmf* (*littér*) (*concurrent*) imitator, emulator; (*égal*) equal. **il fut bientôt l'~ de cet escroc** he was soon no better than this crook; (*péj*) **ce fripon et ses ~s** this scoundrel and his like.

émulsif, -ive [emylsif, iv] *adj* (*Pharm*) emulsive; (*Chim*) emulsifying.

émulsion [emylsjɔ̃] *nf* emulsion.

en[1] [ɑ̃] *prép* **(a)** (*lieu*) in; (*changement de lieu*) to. **vivre ~ France/Normandie** to live in France/Normandy; **aller ~ Angleterre/Normandie** to go to England/Normandy; **aller de pays ~ pays/ville ~ ville** to go from country to country/town to town; **il voyage ~ Grèce/Corse** he's travelling around Greece/Corsica; **il habite ~ province/banlieue/ville** he lives in the provinces/the suburbs/the town; **aller ~ ville** to go (in)to town; **avoir des projets ~ tête** to have plans, have something in mind; **les objets ~ vitrine** the items in the window; **~ lui-même, il n'y croit pas** deep down *ou* in his heart of hearts he doesn't believe it; **je n'aime pas ~ lui cette obstination** I don't like this stubbornness of his, what I don't like about him is his stubbornness; *V* **âme, tête** *etc.*

(b) (*temps: date, durée*) in; (*progression, périodicité*) to. **~ semaine** in *ou* during the week; **~ automne/été/mars/1976** in autumn/summer/March/1976; **il peut le faire ~ 3 jours** he can do it in 3 days; **~ 6 ans je lui ai parlé deux fois** in (all of) 6 years I've spoken to him twice; **de jour ~ jour** from day to day, daily; **d'année ~ année** from year to year, yearly; **son inquiétude grandissait d'heure ~ heure** hour by hour *ou* as the hours went by he grew more (and more) anxious, he grew hourly more anxious.

(c) (*moyen de transport*) by. **~ taxi/train/avion** *etc* by taxi/ train *ou* rail/air *etc*; **aller à Londres ~ avion** to fly to London; **faire une promenade ~ barque/voiture** to go for a ride *ou* trip in a boat/car, go for a boat-/car-trip; **ils y sont allés ~ voiture** they went by car *ou* in a car; **ils sont arrivés ~ voiture** they arrived in a car *ou* by car; **ils ont remonté le fleuve ~ pirogue** they canoed up the river, they rowed up the river in a canoe.

(d) (*état, manière*) in, on; (*disposition*) in. **~ bonne santé** in good health; **il était ~ sang** he was covered in *ou* with blood; **partir ~ vacances/voyage** to go on holiday/on a journey; **faire qch ~ hâte/~ vitesse*** to do sth in a hurry *ou* hurriedly/quick* *ou* right away*; **elle est ~ rage** she is furious *ou* in a rage; **le toit est ~ flammes** the roof is on fire *ou* in flames *ou* ablaze; **il a laissé le bureau ~ désordre** he left the office untidy *ou* in (a state of) disorder *ou* in a mess; **être ~ noir/blanc** to be (dressed) in black/white, be wearing black/white; **elle est arrivée ~ manteau de fourrure** she arrived wearing *ou* in a fur coat *ou* with a fur coat on; **il était ~ chemise/pyjama** he was in his *ou* wearing his shirt/pyjamas; **elle était ~ bigoudis** she was in her rollers; **~ guerre** at war; **télévision/carte ~ couleur** colour television/postcard; **ils y vont ~ groupe/bande*** they are going in a group/bunch*; **~ cercle/rang** in a circle/row; *V* **état, haillon** *etc.*

(e) (*transformation*) into, to. **se changer ~** to change into; **se déguiser ~** to disguise o.s. as, dress up as; **traduire ~ italien** to translate into Italian; **convertir/transformer qch ~** to convert/transform sth into; **casser qch ~ morceaux** to break sth in(to) pieces; **couper/casser ~ deux** to cut/break in two; **partir ~ fumée** to end *ou* go up in smoke, fizzle out; **entrer *ou* tomber ~ disgrâce** to fall into disgrace; *V* **éclater, larmes.**

(f) (*copule avec comp, adv etc*) in. **c'est son père ~ plus jeune/petit** he's just like his father only younger/smaller, he's a younger/smaller version of his father; **je veux la même valise ~ plus grand** I want the same suitcase only bigger *ou* only in a bigger size, I want a bigger version of the same suitcase; **nous avons le même article ~ vert** we have *ou* do the same item in green; *V* **général, grand, gros** *etc.*

(g) (*conformité*) as. **~ tant que** as; **~ tant qu'ami *ou* ~ (ma) qualité d'ami de la famille, j'estime que/de mon devoir de ...** as a family friend, I feel that/it is my duty to...; **agir ~ tyran/lâche** to act like a tyrant/coward; **~ bon politicien/~ bon commerçant (qu'il est), il est très rusé** good politician/tradesman that he is *ou* like all good politicians/tradesmen, he's very cunning; **je le lui ai donné ~ cadeau/souvenir** I gave it to him as a present/ souvenir; *V* **qualité.**

(h) (*composition*) made of; (*présentation*) in. **le plat est ~ or/argent** the dish is made of gold/silver; **une bague ~ or/argent** a gold/silver ring; **une table ~ acajou** a mahogany table; **l'escalier sera ~ marbre** the staircase will be (in) marble; **une jupe ~ soie imprimée** a printed silk skirt, a skirt made (out) of printed silk; **~ quoi est-ce (que c'est) fait?, c'est ~ quoi?*** what's it made of? *ou* out of?; **l'œuvre de Proust ~ 6 volumes** Proust's works in 6 volumes; **une pièce ~ 3 actes** a 3-act play; **c'est écrit ~ anglais/vers/prose/lettres d'or** it is written in English/verse/prose/gold lettering.

(i) (*matière*) in, at, of. **~ politique/peinture/musique** in politics/art/music; **être bon *ou* fort ~ géographie** to be good at geography; **~ affaires, il faut de l'audace** you have to be bold in business; **licencié/docteur ~ droit** bachelor/doctor of law; *V* **expert, matière.**

(j) (*mesure*) in. **mesurer ~ mètres** to measure in metres; **compter ~ francs** to reckon in francs; **ce tissu se fait ~ 140 (cm)** this material comes in 140-cm widths *ou* is 140 cm wide; **~ long** lengthways, lengthwise; **~ large** widthways, widthwise; **~ hauteur/profondeur** in height/depth; **nous avons ce manteau ~ 3 tailles** we have *ou* do this coat in 3 sizes; **cela se vend ~ boîtes de 12** this is sold in boxes of 12; *V* **long, saut.**

(k) (*avec gérondif: manière, moyen etc*) **monter/entrer ~ courant** to run up/in; **sortir ~ rampant/boitant** to crawl/limp out; **se frayer un chemin/avancer ~ jouant des coudes** to elbow one's way through/forward; **endormir un enfant ~ le berçant** to rock a child to sleep; **vous ne le ferez obéir qu'~ le punissant** you'll only get him to obey by punishing him; **il s'est coupé ~ essayant d'ouvrir une boîte** he cut himself trying to open a tin; **il a fait une folie ~ achetant cette bague** it was very extravagant of him to buy this ring; **je suis allé jusqu'à la poste ~ me promenant** I went for *ou* took a walk as far as the post office; **ils ont réussi à le faire signer la lettre ~ lui racontant des histoires** they talked him into signing the letter, they got him to sign the letter by spinning him some yarn.

(l) (*avec gérondif: simultanéité, durée*) **~ apprenant la nouvelle, elle s'est évanouie** she fainted at the news *ou* when she heard the news *ou* on hearing the news; **il a buté ~ montant dans l'autobus** he tripped getting into *ou* as he got into the bus; **j'ai écrit une lettre (tout) ~ vous attendant** I wrote a letter while I was waiting for you; **il s'est endormi ~ lisant le journal** he fell asleep (while) reading the newspaper, he fell asleep over the newspaper; **fermez la porte ~ sortant** shut the door as you go out; **il est sorti ~ haussant les épaules/~ criant au secours** he left shrugging his shoulders/shouting for help *ou* with a shrug of his shoulders/a cry for help.

(m) (*introduisant compléments*) in. **croire ~ Dieu** to believe in God; **avoir confiance/foi ~ qn** to have confidence/faith in sb.

en[2] [ɑ̃] *pron* **(a)** (*lieu*) **quand va-t-il à Nice? — il ~ revient** when is he off to Nice? — he's just (come) back (from there); **elle était tombée dans une crevasse, on a eu du mal à l'~ sortir** she had fallen into a crevasse and they had difficulty *ou* trouble (in) getting her out (of it); **le bénéfice qu'il ~ a tiré** the profit he got out of it *ou* from it; **il faut ~ tirer une conclusion** we must draw a conclusion from it; (*fig*) **où ~ sommes-nous?** (*livre, leçon*) where have we got (up) to?, where are we now?; (*situation*) where do we stand?

(b) (*cause, agent, instrument*) **je suis si inquiet que je n'~ dors pas** I can't sleep for worrying, I am so worried that I can't sleep; **il saisit sa canne et l'~ frappa** he seized his stick and struck her with it; **ce n'est pas moi qui ~ perdrai le sommeil** I won't lose any sleep over it; **quelle histoire! nous ~ avons beaucoup ri** what a business! we had a good laugh over *ou* about it; **il a été gravement blessé, il pourrait ~ rester infirme** he has been seriously injured and could remain crippled (as a result *ou* because of it); ~ **mourir** (*maladie*) to die of it; (*blessure*) to die because of it *ou* as a result of it; **elle ~ est aimée/très blessée** she is loved by him/very hurt by it.

(c) (*complément de vb, d'adj, de n*) **rendez-moi mon projecteur, j'~ ai besoin** give me back my projector — I need it; **qu'est-ce que tu ~ feras?** what will you do with it (*ou* them)?; **on lui apprend des mots faciles pour qu'il s'~ souvienne** he is taught easy words so that he will remember *ou* retain them; **c'est une bonne classe, les professeurs ~ sont contents** they are a good class and the teachers are pleased with them; **elle, mentir? elle ~ est incapable** she couldn't lie if she tried; **elle a réussi et elle n'~ est pas peu fière** she has been successful and she is more than a little proud of herself *ou* of it; **il ne fume plus, il ~ a perdu l'habitude** he doesn't smoke any more — he has got out of *ou* has lost the habit; **sa décision m'inquiète car j'~ connais tous les dangers** her decision worries me because I am aware of all the dangers (of it) *ou* of all its possible dangers; **je t'~ donne/offre 10 F** I'll give/offer you 10 francs for it.

(d) (*quantitatif, indéf*) of it, of them (*souvent omis*). **si vous aimez les pommes, prenez-~ plusieurs** if you like apples, take several; **il avait bien des lettres à écrire mais il n'~ a pas écrit la moitié/beaucoup** he had a lot of letters to write but he hasn't written half of them/many (of them); **le vin est bon mais il n'y ~ a pas beaucoup** the wine is good but there isn't much (of it); **si j'~ avais** if I had any; **voulez-vous du pain/des pommes? il y ~ a encore** would you like some bread/some apples? we have still got some (left); **il n'y ~ a plus** there isn't (*ou* aren't) any left, there's (*ou* there are) none left; **si vous cherchez un crayon, vous ~ trouverez des douzaines/un dans le tiroir** if you are looking for a pencil you will find dozens (of them)/one in the drawer; **élevé dans le village, j'~ connaissais tous les habitants** (having been) brought up in the village I knew all its inhabitants; **a-t-elle des poupées? — oui, elle ~ a 2/trop/de belles** has she any dolls? — yes, she has 2/too many/some lovely ones; **nous avons du vin, j'~ ai acheté une bouteille hier** we have some wine because I bought a bottle yesterday; **j'~ ai assez/ras le bol:** I've had enough (of it)/a bellyful: (of it); **des souris ici? nous n'~ avons jamais vu(es)** mice here? we've never seen any; **il ~ aime une autre** he loves another (*littér*), he loves somebody else; ~ **voilà/voici un** there/here is one (of them) now.

(e) (*renforcement*) *non traduit.* **il s'~ souviendra de cette réception** he'll certainly remember that party; **je n'~ vois pas, moi, de places libres** well (I must say), I don't see any empty seats; **tu ~ as eu de beaux jouets à Noël!** well you did get some lovely toys *ou* what lovely toys you got for Christmas!

(f) (*loc verbales*) *non traduit.* ~ **être quitte pour la peur** to get off with a fright; ~ **venir aux mains** to come to blows; **ne pas ~ croire ses yeux/ses oreilles** not to believe one's eyes/ears; ~ **être réduit à faire** to be reduced to doing; **il ~ est** *ou* **il ~ arrive à penser que** he has come to think that; **je ne m'~ fais pas** I don't worry *ou* care, I don't take any notice; **ne vous ~ faites pas** don't worry, never mind; **il ~ est** *ou* **il ~ va de même pour** the same goes for, the same may be said for; *V* **accroire, assez, entendre** *etc.*

enamourer (s')†† [ɑ̃namuʀe] (1) *vpr*: **s' ~ de** to become enamoured of†.

énarque [enaʀk] *nmf* énarque (*student or former student of the École Nationale d'Administration*).

en-avant [ɑ̃navɑ̃] *nm inv* (*Sport*) forward pass.

encablure [ɑ̃kablyʀ] *nf* cable's length.

encadrement [ɑ̃kadʀəmɑ̃] *nm* **(a)** (*U: V* **encadrer**) framing; training (and supervision). **'tous travaux d'~'** 'all framing (work) undertaken'.

(b) (*embrasure*) *[porte, fenêtre]* frame. **il se tenait dans l'~ de la porte** he stood in the doorway.

(c) (*cadre*) frame. **cet ~ conviendrait mieux au sujet** this frame would be more appropriate to the subject.

(d) (*Admin etc: cadres, instructeurs*) training personnel.

encadrer [ɑ̃kadʀe] (1) *vt* **(a)** *tableau* to frame. (*iro*) **c'est à ~!*** that's priceless!*, that's one to remember!*

(b) (*instruire*) *étudiants, débutants, recrues* to train (and supervise).

(c) (*fig: entourer*) *cour, plaine, visage* to frame, surround; *prisonnier* to surround; (*par 2 personnes*) to flank. **les collines qui encadraient la plaine** the hills that framed *ou* surrounded the plain; **encadré de ses gardes du corps** surrounded by his bodyguards; **l'accusé, encadré de 2 gendarmes** the accused, flanked by 2 policemen.

(d) (*:* *gén nég: supporter*) to stick*, stand*. **je ne peux pas l'~** I can't stick* *ou* stand* *ou* abide him.

(e) (*Mil*) *objectif* to straddle.

encadreur [ɑ̃kadʀœʀ] *nm* (picture) framer.

encager [ɑ̃kaʒe] (3) *vt animal, oiseau* to cage (up); (*fig*) *personne* to cage in, cage up.

encaissable [ɑ̃kɛsabl(ə)] *adj* encashable (*Brit*), cashable.

encaisse [ɑ̃kɛs] *nf* cash in hand. ~ **métallique** gold and silver reserves; ~ **or** gold reserves.

encaissé, e [ɑ̃kese] (*ptp de* **encaisser**) *adj vallée* deep, steep-sided; *rivière* hemmed in by steep banks *ou* hills; *route* sunken, hemmed in by steep hills.

encaissement [ɑ̃kɛsmɑ̃] *nm* **(a)** (*V* **encaisser**) collection; receipt; receipt of payment for; cashing.

(b) *[vallée]* depth, steep-sidedness. **l'~ de la route/rivière faisait que le pont ne voyait jamais le soleil** the steep hills hemming in the road/river *ou* which reared up from the road/river stopped the sun from ever reaching the bridge.

encaisser [ɑ̃kese] (1) *vt* **(a)** *argent, loyer* to collect, receive; *facture* to receive payment for; *chèque* to cash; *effet de commerce* to collect.

(b) (*) *coups, affront, défaite* to take. **savoir ~** *[boxeur]* to be able to take a lot of beating *ou* punishment (*fig*); (*fig: dans la vie*) to be able to stand up to *ou* take a lot of beating *ou* buffeting; **qu'est-ce qu'il a encaissé!** (*coups*) what a hammering he got!*, what a beating he took!; (*injures, réprimande*) what a hammering he got!*, he certainly got what for!*; **qu'est-ce qu'on encaisse avec ces cahots** we're taking a real hammering on these bumps*.

(c) (*:* *gén nég: supporter*) **je ne peux pas ~ ce type** I can't stick* *ou* stand* *ou* abide that bloke; **il n'a pas encaissé cette décision** he couldn't stomach* that decision; **il n'a pas encaissé cette remarque** he didn't appreciate that remark one little bit*.

(d) (*Tech*) *route, fleuve, voie ferrée* to embank. **les montagnes qui encaissent la vallée** the mountains which enclose the valley; **la route s'encaisse entre les collines** the road is hemmed in by the hills.

(e) *objets* to pack in(to) boxes; *plantes* to plant in boxes *ou* tubs.

encaisseur [ɑ̃kɛsœʀ] *nm* collector (*of debts etc*).

encanaillement [ɑ̃kanɑjmɑ̃] *nm* (*V* **s'encanailler**) lowering in tone; cheapening of o.s.; mixing with the riffraff, slumming it*.

encanailler (s') [ɑ̃kanɑje] (1) *vpr* (*par snobisme*) to lower one's tone; (†: *sans intention*) to cheapen o.s.; (*par des fréquentations douteuses etc*) to mix with the riffraff, slum it*. **son style/langage s'encanaille** his style/language is taking a turn for the worse *ou* is becoming vulgar.

encapuchonner [ɑ̃kapyʃɔne] (1) *vt*: ~ **un enfant** to put a child's hood up; **la tête encapuchonnée** hooded; **un groupe de bambins encapuchonnés** a group of toddlers snug in their hoods.

encart [ɑ̃kaʀ] *nm* (*Typ*) insert, inset.

encarter [ɑ̃kaʀte] (1) *vt* (*Typ*) to insert, inset.

en-cas [ɑ̃kɑ] *nm* (*nourriture*) snack.

encastrement [ɑ̃kastʀəmɑ̃] *nm [interrupteur]* flush fitting; *[armoire, rayonnage]* recessed fitting.

encastrer [ɑ̃kastʀe] (1) *vt* (*dans un mur*) to embed (*dans* in(to)), sink (*dans* into); *interrupteur* to fit flush (*dans* with); *rayonnages, armoire* to recess (*dans* into), embed (*dans* into); (*dans un boîtier, une pièce de mécanisme*) *pièce* to fit (*dans* into). **tous les boutons sont encastrés dans le mur** all the switches are flush with the wall *ou* are embedded in *ou* sunk in the wall; **salle de bains avec armoire à pharmacie encastrée (dans le mur)** bathroom with medicine cabinet recessed into the wall; **de gros blocs encastrés dans la neige/le sol** great blocks sunk in *ou* embedded in the snow/ground; (*fig*) **la voiture s'est encastrée sous l'avant du camion*** the car jammed itself underneath the front of the lorry; **cette pièce s'encastre exactement dans le boîtier** this part fits exactly into the case; **ces pièces s'encastrent exactement l'une dans l'autre** these parts fit exactly into each other.

encaustiquage [ɑ̃kɔstikaʒ] *nm* polishing, waxing.

encaustique [ɑ̃kɔstik] *nf* polish, wax.

encaustiquer [ɑ̃kɔstike] (1) *vt* to polish, wax.

enceindre [ɑ̃sɛ̃dʀ(ə)] (52) *vt* (*gén ptp*) to encircle, surround (*de* with). **enceint de** encircled *ou* surrounded by.

enceinte[1] [ɑ̃sɛ̃t] *adj f* pregnant (*de qn* by sb), expecting* (*attrib*). **femme ~** pregnant woman, expectant mother; ~ **de cinq mois** five months pregnant, five months gone*.

enceinte[2] [ɑ̃sɛ̃t] *nf* **(a)** (*mur*) wall; (*palissade*) enclosure, fence. **une ~ de fossés défendait la place** the position was surrounded by defensive ditches *ou* was defended by surrounding ditches; **une ~ de pieux protégeait le camp** the camp was protected by an enclosure made of stakes; **mur d'~** surrounding wall.

(b) (*espace clos*) enclosure; *[couvent]* precinct. **dans l'~ de la ville** within *ou* inside the town; **dans l'~ du tribunal** in(side) the court room; **dans l'~ de cet établissement** within *ou* in(side) this establishment.

(c) (*Élec*) ~ **(acoustique)** speaker system, speakers.

encens [ɑ̃sɑ̃] *nm* incense. (*fig*) **l'~ des louanges/de leur flatterie** the heady wine of praise/of their flattery.

encensement [ɑ̃sɑ̃smɑ̃] *nm* (*V* **encenser**) (in)censing; praising (*U*) to the skies.

encenser [ɑ̃sɑ̃se] (1) *vt* to (in)cense; (*fig*) to heap *ou* shower praise(s) upon, praise to the skies.

encenseur [ɑ̃sɑ̃sœʀ] *nm* (*Rel*) thurifer, censer-bearer; (*fig*†) flatterer.

encensoir [ɑ̃sɑ̃swaʀ] *nm* censer, thurible. (*fig péj*) **manier l'~** to pour out (inordinate) flattery.

encéphale [ɑ̃sefal] *nm* encephalon.

encéphalique [ɑ̃sefalik] *adj* encephalic.

encéphalogramme [ɑ̃sefalɔgʀam] *nm* encephalogram.

encerclement [ɑ̃sɛʀkləmɑ̃] *nm* (*V* **encercler**) surrounding; encircling.

encercler [ɑ̃sɛʀkle] (1) *vt [murs]* to surround, encircle; *[armée, police]* to surround. (*littér*) **il encercla sa taille de ses bras puissants** he encircled her waist with his powerful arms.

enchaîné [ɑ̃ʃene] *nm* (*Ciné*) change; *V* **fondu.**

enchaînement [ɑ̃ʃɛnmɑ̃] *nm* **(a)** (*suite logique*) *[épisodes, preuves]* linking.

(b) (*Ciné, Théât: liaisons*) *[scènes, séquences]* linking.

(c) (*série*) ~ **de circonstances** sequence *ou* series *ou* string of circumstances; ~ **d'événements** chain *ou* series *ou* string of events; **des ~s de circonstances absolument imprévisibles** an absolutely unforeseeable series of circumstances.

(d) (*Danse*) enchaînement. (*Mus*) ~ **des accords** chord progression.

enchaîner [ɑ̃ʃene] (1) **1** *vt* **(a)** (*lier*) *animal* to chain up; *prisonnier* to put in chains, chain up. ~ **un animal/prisonnier à un arbre** to chain an animal/a prisoner (up) to a tree; ~ **2 prisonniers l'un à l'autre** to chain 2 prisoners together.

(b) (*fig littér*) *[secret, souvenir, sentiment]* to bind. **l'amour**

enchaîne les cœurs love binds hearts (together); **ses souvenirs l'enchaînaient à ce lieu** his memories tied *ou* bound *ou* chained him to this place.

(c) (*fig: asservir*) *peuple* to enslave; *presse* to muzzle, gag. ~ **la liberté** to put freedom in chains.

(d) (*assembler*) *faits, épisodes* to link together, connect up; *séquences, scènes* to forge links between, link (together *ou* up); *paragraphes, pensées, mots* to link (together *ou* up), put together, string together. **incapable d'~ deux pensées/paragraphes** incapable of linking *ou* putting *ou* stringing two thoughts/paragraphs together; (*Ciné*) ~ **(la scène suivante)** to change to *ou* move on to the next scene; (*Ciné*) **on va ~ les dernières scènes** we'll carry on with the last scenes.

2 *vi* (*Ciné, Théât*) to carry *ou* move on (to the next scene). **sans laisser à Jean le temps de répondre, Paul enchaîna: 'd'abord ...** without giving Jean the time to reply, Paul went on *ou* continued: 'first ...; **on enchaîne, enchaînons** (*Ciné, Théât*) let's carry on *ou* keep going; (*: *dans un débat etc*) let's go on *ou* carry on, let's continue.

3 s'enchaîner *vpr [épisodes, séquences]* to follow on from each other, be linked (together); *[preuves, faits]* to be linked (together). **tout s'enchaîne** it's all linked up *ou* connected, it all ties up; **des paragraphes/raisonnements qui s'enchaînent bien** well-linked paragraphs/pieces of reasoning, paragraphs/pieces of reasoning that are well strung *ou* put together.

enchanté, e [ɑ̃ʃɑ̃te] (*ptp de* **enchanter**) *adj* **(a)** (*ravi*) enchanted (*de* by), delighted (*de* with), enraptured (*de* by). (*frm*) ~ **(de vous connaître)** how do you do?, (I'm) very pleased to meet you. **(b)** (*magique*) *forêt, demeure* enchanted.

enchantement [ɑ̃ʃɑ̃tmɑ̃] *nm* **(a)** (*action*) enchantment; (*effet*) (magic) spell, enchantment. **comme par ~** as if by magic.

(b) (*ravissement*) delight, enchantment. **ce spectacle fut un ~** the sight of this was an absolute delight *ou* was enchanting *ou* delightful; **être dans l'~** to be enchanted *ou* delighted *ou* enraptured.

enchanter [ɑ̃ʃɑ̃te] (1) **1** *vt* **(a)** (*ensorceler*) to enchant, bewitch. **(b)** (*ravir*) to enchant, delight, enrapture. **ça ne m'enchante pas beaucoup** I'm not exactly taken with it, it doesn't exactly appeal to me *ou* fill me with delight.

2 s'enchanter *vpr* (*littér*) to rejoice (*de* at).

enchanteur, -teresse [ɑ̃ʃɑ̃tœʀ, tʀɛs] **1** *adj* enchanting, bewitching. **2** *nm* (*sorcier*) enchanter; (*fig*) charmer. **3 enchanteresse** *nf* enchantress.

enchâssement [ɑ̃ʃɑsmɑ̃] *nm* **(a)** setting (*dans* in). **(b)** (*Ling*) embedding.

enchâsser [ɑ̃ʃɑse] (1) **1** *vt* to set (*dans* in). (*littér*) **~ une citation dans un texte** to insert a quotation into a text. **2 s'enchâsser** *vpr*: **s'~ (l'un dans l'autre)** to fit exactly together; **s'~ dans** to fit exactly into.

enchère [ɑ̃ʃɛʀ] *nf* **(a)** (*Comm: offre*) bid. **faire une ~** to bid, make a bid; **faire monter les ~s** to raise the bidding; *V* **vente.**

(b) (*Comm: vente*) **~s: mettre aux ~s** to put up for auction; **vendre aux ~s** to sell by auction; **acheté aux ~s** bought at an auction (sale).

(c) (*Cartes*) bid. **le système des ~s** the bidding system.

enchérir [ɑ̃ʃeʀiʀ] (2) *vi* **(a)** (*Comm*) **~ sur une offre** to make a higher bid; **il a enchéri sur mon offre** he bid higher than I did, he made a bid higher than mine; **~ sur qn** to bid higher than sb, make a higher bid than sb; **~ sur une somme** to go higher than *ou* above *ou* over an amount.

(b) (*fig*) **~ sur** to go further than, go beyond, go one better than.

(c) (†: *augmenter*) to become more expensive.

enchérissement† [ɑ̃ʃeʀismɑ̃] *nm* = **renchérissement.**

enchérisseur, -euse [ɑ̃ʃeʀisœʀ, øz] *nm,f* bidder.

enchevêtrement [ɑ̃ʃ(ə)vɛtʀəmɑ̃] *nm [ficelles, branches]* entanglement; (*fig*) *[idées, situation]* confusion. **l'~ de ses idées** the confusion *ou* muddle his ideas were in; **un ~ de branches barrait la route** a tangle of branches blocked the way.

enchevêtrer [ɑ̃ʃ(ə)vɛtʀe] (1) **1** *vt ficelle* to tangle (up), entangle, muddle up; (*fig*) *idées, intrigue* to confuse, muddle.

2 s'enchevêtrer *vpr* **(a)** *[ficelles]* to get in a tangle, become entangled, tangle; *[branches]* to become entangled. **s'~ dans des cordes** to get caught up *ou* tangled up in ropes.

(b) *[situations, paroles]* to become confused *ou* muddled. **mots qui s'enchevêtrent les uns dans les autres** words that get confused together *ou* that run into each other; **s'~ dans ses explications** to tie o.s. up in knots* explaining (something).

enclave [ɑ̃klav] *nf* (*lit, fig*) enclave.

enclavement [ɑ̃klavmɑ̃] *nm* (*action*) enclosing, hemming in. (*état*) **l'~ d'un département dans un autre** one department's being enclosed by another.

enclaver [ɑ̃klave] (1) *vt* **(a)** (*entourer*) to enclose, hem in. **terrain complètement enclavé dans un grand domaine** piece of land completely enclosed within *ou* hemmed in by a large property. **(b)** (*encastrer*) **~ (l'un dans l'autre)** to fit together, interlock; **~ dans** to fit into. **(c)** (*insérer*) **~ entre** to insert between.

enclenchement [ɑ̃klɑ̃ʃmɑ̃] *nm* (*action*) engaging; (*état*) engagement; (*dispositif*) interlock.

enclencher [ɑ̃klɑ̃ʃe] (1) **1** *vt mécanisme* to engage; (*fig*) *affaire* to set in motion, get under way. **l'affaire est enclenchée** the business is under way. **2 s'enclencher** *vpr [mécanisme]* to engage.

enclin, e [ɑ̃klɛ̃, in] *adj*: **~ à qch/à faire qch** inclined *ou* prone to sth/to do sth.

enclore [ɑ̃klɔʀ] (45) *vt* to enclose, shut in. **~ qch d'une haie/d'une palissade/d'un mur** to hedge/fence/wall sth in.

enclos [ɑ̃klo] *nm* (*gén: terrain, clôture*) enclosure; *[chevaux]* paddock; *[moutons]* pen, fold.

enclume [ɑ̃klym] *nf* anvil; (*Anat*) anvil (bone), incus (*T*). (*fig*) **entre l'~ et le marteau** between the devil and the deep blue sea.

encoche [ɑ̃kɔʃ] *nf* (*gén*) notch; *[flèche]* nock. **faire une ~ à** *ou* **sur qch** to notch sth, make a notch in sth.

encocher [ɑ̃kɔʃe] (1) *vt* (*Tech*) to notch; *flèche* to nock.

encoignure [ɑ̃kɔɲyʀ] *nf* **(a)** (*coin*) corner. **(b)** (*meuble*) corner cupboard.

encollage [ɑ̃kɔlaʒ] *nm* pasting.

encoller [ɑ̃kɔle] (1) *vt* to paste.

encolure [ɑ̃kɔlyʀ] *nf [cheval, personne, robe]* neck; (*Comm: tour de cou*) collar size. (*Équitation*) **battre d'une ~** to beat by a neck.

encombrant, e [ɑ̃kɔ̃bʀɑ̃, ɑ̃t] *adj* (*lit*) *paquet* cumbersome, unwieldy, bulky; (*fig*) *présence* onerous, inhibiting. **cet enfant est très ~** (*agaçant*) this child is a real nuisance *ou* pest*; (*indésirable*) this child is in the way *ou* is a nuisance.

encombre [ɑ̃kɔ̃bʀ(ə)] *nm*: **sans ~** without mishap *ou* incident.

encombré, e [ɑ̃kɔ̃bʀe] (*ptp de* **encombrer**) *adj couloir* cluttered (up), obstructed; *passage* obstructed; *lignes téléphoniques* blocked; *profession, marché* saturated. **table ~e de papiers** table cluttered *ou* littered with papers.

encombrement [ɑ̃kɔ̃bʀəmɑ̃] *nm* **(a)** (*obstruction*) *[lieu]* congestion. **à cause de l'~ des lignes téléphoniques** because of the telephone lines being blocked; **l'~ du couloir rendait le passage malaisé** the corridor being (so) cluttered (up) *ou* congested *ou* all the clutter in the corridor made it difficult to get through; **un ~ de vieux meubles** a clutter of old furniture; **les ~s qui ralentissent la circulation** the obstructions *ou* holdups that slow down the traffic.

(b) (*volume*) *[meuble, véhicule]* bulk.

encombrer [ɑ̃kɔ̃bʀe] (1) **1** *vt pièce* to clutter (up); *couloir* to clutter (up), obstruct, congest; (*fig*) *mémoire* to clutter (up), encumber; *profession* to saturate; (*Téléc*) *lignes* to block; (*Comm*) *marché* to glut. **ces paquets encombrent le passage** these packages block the way *ou* are an obstruction; **ces boîtes m'encombrent** (*je les porte*) I'm loaded down with these boxes; (*elles gênent le passage*) these boxes are in my way *ou* are obstructing me; (*Téléc*) **les lignes sont encombrées** the lines are blocked.

2 s'encombrer *vpr*: **s'~ de** *paquets* to load o.s. with; *enfants* to burden *ou* saddle* o.s. with; **il ne s'encombre pas de scrupules** he's not overburdened with scruples, he's not overscrupulous.

encontre [ɑ̃kɔ̃tʀ(ə)] **1** *prép*: **à l'~ de** (*contre*) against, counter to; (*au contraire de*) contrary to; **aller à l'~ de** *[décision, faits]* to go against, run counter to; **je n'irai pas à l'~ de ce qu'il veut/fait** I shan't go against his wishes/what he does; **à l'~ de ce qu'il dit, mon opinion est que ...** contrary to what he says, my opinion is that ... .

2 *adv* (*rare*) **à l'~** in opposition, against it; **je n'irai pas à l'~** I shan't go against it, I shan't act in opposition.

encor [ɑ̃kɔʀ] *adv* (††, *Poésie*) = **encore.**

encorbellement [ɑ̃kɔʀbɛlmɑ̃] *nm* (*Archit*) corbelled construction. **fenêtre en ~** oriel window; **balcon en ~** corbelled balcony.

encorder [ɑ̃kɔʀde] (1) **1** *vt* to rope up. **2 s'encorder** *vpr* to rope up. **les alpinistes s'encordent** the climbers rope themselves together *ou* rope up.

encore [ɑ̃kɔʀ] *adv* **(a)** (*toujours*) still. **il restait ~ quelques personnes** there were still a few people left; **il en était ~ au brouillon** he was still working on the draft; (*péj*) **il en est ~ au stade de la règle à calculer/du complet cravate** he hasn't got past the slide rule/the collar and tie stage yet, he's still at the slide rule/the collar and tie stage; (*péj*) **tu en es ~ là!** haven't you got beyond *ou* past that yet!; **n'être ~ que: il n'est ~ qu'en première année/que caporal** he's only in first year/a corporal as yet, he's still only in first year/a corporal; **il n'est ~ que 8 heures** it's (still) only 8 o'clock; **ce malfaiteur court ~** the criminal is still at large.

(b) pas ~ not yet; **il n'est pas ~ prêt** he's not ready yet, he's not yet ready; **ça ne s'était pas ~ vu, ça ne s'était ~ jamais vu** that had never been seen before.

(c) (*pas plus tard que*) only. **~ ce matin** *ou* **ce matin ~, il semblait bien portant** only this morning he seemed quite well; **il me le disait ~ hier** *ou* **hier ~** he was saying that to me only yesterday.

(d) (*de nouveau*) again. **~ une fois** (once) again, once more; **ça s'est ~ défait** it has come undone (yet) again *ou* once more; **il a ~ laissé la porte ouverte** he has left the door open (yet) again; **elle a ~ acheté un nouveau chapeau** she has bought yet another new hat; **~ vous!** (not) you again!; **~ une fois non!** how many times do I have to tell you — no!; **quoi ~?, qu'y a-t-il ~?, que te faut-il ~?** what's the matter with you this time?, what is it THIS time?

(e) (*de plus, en plus*) more. **~ un!** yet another!, not another!; **~ un rhume** (yet) another cold; **~ une tasse?** another cup?; **vous prendrez bien ~ quelque chose?** *ou* **quelque chose ~?** surely you'll have something more? *ou* something else?; **~ un peu de thé?** a little more tea?, (any) more tea?; **~ quelques gâteaux?** (some *ou* any) more cakes?; **j'en veux ~** I want some more; **~ un mot, avant de terminer** (just) one more word before I finish; **que te faut-il ~?** what else *ou* more do you want?; **qu'est-ce que j'oublie ~?** what else have I forgotten?; **qui y avait-il ~?** who else was there?; **pendant ~ 2 jours** for another 2 days, for 2 more days, for 2 days more; **il y a ~ quelques jours avant de partir** there are a few (more) days to go before we leave; **~ un fou du volant!** (yet) another roadhog!; **en voilà ~ 2** here are 2 more *ou* another 2; **mais ~?** is that all?, what else?; *V* **non.**

(f) (*avec comp*) even, still, yet (*littér*). **il fait ~ plus froid qu'hier** it's even *ou* still colder than yesterday; **il fait ~ moins**

chaud qu'hier it's even less warm than it was yesterday; **il est ~ plus grand que moi** he is even taller than I am; **ils veulent l'agrandir ~ (plus)** they want to make it even *ou* still larger, they want to enlarge it even further; **~ pire, pire ~** even *ou* still worse, worse and worse; **~ autant** as much again.

(g) (*aussi*) too, also, as well. **tu le bats non seulement en force, mais ~ en intelligence** you beat him not only in strength but also in intelligence, not only are you stronger than he is but you are more intelligent too *ou* also *ou* as well.

(h) (*valeur restrictive*) even then, even at that. **~ ne sait-il pas tout** even then he doesn't know everything, and he doesn't even know everything (at that); **~ faut-il le faire** you still have to do it, you have to do it even so; **~ heureux que, ~ une chance que** (still) at least, let's think ourselves lucky that; (*iro*) **~ heureux qu'il ne se soit pas plaint au patron** (still) at least he didn't *ou* let's think ourselves lucky that he didn't complain to the boss; **on t'en donnera peut-être 10 F, et ~** they'll give you perhaps 10 francs for it, if that *ou* and perhaps not even that; **c'est passable, et ~!** it's (just about) passable, if that!; **et ~, ça n'a pas été sans mal** and even that wasn't easy; **si ~** if only; **si ~ je savais où ça se trouve, j'irais bien,** (*frm*) **~ irais-je bien si je savais où ça se trouve** if only I knew where it was, I would willingly go.

(i) (*littér*) **~ que** (*quoique*) even though; **~ qu'il eût mal, il voulut y aller** even though he felt ill he wanted to go.

encorner [ɑ̃kɔʀne] (1) *vt* to gore.

encornet [ɑ̃kɔʀnɛ] *nm* squid.

encourageant, e [ɑ̃kuʀaʒɑ̃, ɑ̃t] *adj* encouraging.

encouragement [ɑ̃kuʀaʒmɑ̃] *nm* encouragement.

encourager [ɑ̃kuʀaʒe] (3) *vt* (*gén*) to encourage (*à faire* to do). **~ qn au meurtre** to encourage sb to commit murder, incite sb to murder; **~ qn à l'effort** to encourage sb to make an effort; **~ qn du geste et de la voix** to cheer sb on; **encouragé par ses camarades, il a joué un vilain tour au professeur** egged on *ou* encouraged by his classmates, he played a nasty trick on the teacher.

encourir [ɑ̃kuʀiʀ] (11) *vt* (*littér*) *amende, frais* to incur; *mépris, reproche* to incur, bring upon o.s.; *punition* to bring upon o.s.

encrassement [ɑ̃kʀasmɑ̃] *nm* (*V* **encrasser**) fouling (up); sooting up; clogging (up), choking (up).

encrasser [ɑ̃kʀase] (1) **1** *vt* **(a)** *arme* to foul (up); *cheminée,* (*Aut*) *bougie* to soot up; *piston, poêle, tuyau, machine* to clog (up), choke (up), foul up.

(b) (*salir*) to make filthy, (make) dirty. **ongles encrassés de cambouis** nails encrusted *ou* filthy with engine grease.

2 s'encrasser *vpr* (*V* **encrasser**) to foul (up); to soot up; to clog (up), get choked (up).

encre [ɑ̃kʀ(ə)] **1** *nf* ink. **écrire à l'~** to write in ink; (*fig*) **de sa plus belle ~** in his best style. **2: encre de Chine** Indian ink; **encre d'imprimerie** printing ink; **encre sympathique** invisible ink.

encrer [ɑ̃kʀe] (1) *vt* to ink.

encreur [ɑ̃kʀœʀ] **1** *adj m rouleau, tampon* inking. **2** *nm* inker.

encrier [ɑ̃kʀije] *nm* inkwell, inkpot (*Brit*).

encroûté, e* [ɑ̃kʀute] (*ptp de* **encroûter**) *adj*: **être ~** to stagnate, be in a rut; **quel ~ tu fais!** you're really stagnating!, you're really in a rut!

encroûtement [ɑ̃kʀutmɑ̃] *nm* **(a)** *[personne]* getting into a rut. **essayons de le tirer de son ~** let's try and get him out of his rut; **l'~ dans certaines habitudes** gradually becoming entrenched in certain habits. **(b)** *[objet]* encrusting, crusting over.

encroûter [ɑ̃kʀute] (1) **1** *vt* (*entartrer*) to encrust, crust over.

2 s'encroûter *vpr* **(a)** (*) *[personne]* to stagnate, get into a rut. **s'~ dans** *habitudes, préjugés* to become entrenched in; **s'~ dans la vie de province** to get into the rut of provincial life.

(b) *[objet]* to crust over, form a crust.

enculé∵ [ɑ̃kyle] *nm* sod∵, bugger∵.

enculer∵ [ɑ̃kyle] (1) *vt* to bugger∵. (*fig*) **ils enculent les mouches** they are nit-picking*.

encyclique [ɑ̃siklik] *adj, nf*: **(lettre) ~** encyclical.

encyclopédie [ɑ̃siklɔpedi] *nf* encyclopaedia.

encyclopédique [ɑ̃siklɔpedik] *adj* encyclopaedic.

encyclopédiste [ɑ̃siklɔpedist(ə)] *nmf* (*Hist*) encyclopaedist.

endémie [ɑ̃demi] *nf* endemic (disease).

endémique [ɑ̃demik] *adj* (*Méd, fig*) endemic.

endetté, e [ɑ̃dete] (*ptp de* **endetter**) *adj* in debt (*attrib*). **très ~** deep in debt; (*fig*) **(très) ~ envers qn** (greatly) indebted to sb.

endettement [ɑ̃dɛtmɑ̃] *nm* getting into debt.

endetter *vt,* **s'endetter** *vpr* [ɑ̃dete] (1) to get into debt.

endeuiller [ɑ̃dœje] (1) *vt personne, pays* (*toucher par une mort*) to plunge into mourning; (*attrister*) to plunge into grief; *épreuve sportive, manifestation* to cast a (tragic) shadow over; (*littér*) *paysage* to make *ou* render dismal, give a dismal aspect to. **course endeuillée par la mort d'un pilote** race over which a tragic shadow was cast by the death of a driver.

endiablé, e [ɑ̃djɑble] *adj danse, rythme* boisterous, furious; *course* furious, wild; *personne* boisterous, turbulent.

endiamanté, e [ɑ̃djamɑ̃te] *adj mains, femme* bedecked with diamonds.

endiguage [ɑ̃digaʒ] *nm,* **endiguement** [ɑ̃digmɑ̃] *nm* (*V* **endiguer**) dyking (up); holding back; containing; checking.

endiguer [ɑ̃dige] (1) *vt* **(a)** *fleuve* to dyke (up). **(b)** (*fig*) *foule, invasion* to hold back, contain; *révolte* to check, contain; *sentiments, progrès* to check, hold back.

endimanché, e [ɑ̃dimɑ̃ʃe] (*ptp de* **s'endimancher**) *adj* (all done up) in one's Sunday best; (*fig*) *style* fancy, florid. (*péj*) **il a l'air ~** he looks terribly stiff in his Sunday best.

endimancher (s') [ɑ̃dimɑ̃ʃe] (1) *vpr* to put on one's Sunday best.

endive [ɑ̃div] *nf* chicory (*U*).

endocrine [ɑ̃dɔkʀin] *adj*: **glande ~** endocrine (gland).

endocrinien, -ienne [ɑ̃dɔkʀinjɛ̃, jɛn] *adj* endocrinal, endocrinous.

endoctrinement [ɑ̃dɔktʀinmɑ̃] *nm* indoctrination.

endoctriner [ɑ̃dɔktʀine] (1) *vt* to indoctrinate.

endoderme [ɑ̃dɔdɛʀm(ə)] *nm* endoderm.

endogène [ɑ̃dɔʒɛn] *adj* endogenous.

endolori, e [ɑ̃dɔlɔʀi] (*ptp de* **endolorir**) *adj* painful, aching. **~ par un coup** made tender by a blow.

endolorir [ɑ̃dɔlɔʀiʀ] (2) *vt* (*gén ptp*) to make painful.

endommagement [ɑ̃dɔmaʒmɑ̃] *nm* damaging.

endommager [ɑ̃dɔmaʒe] (3) *vt* to damage.

endormant, e [ɑ̃dɔʀmɑ̃, ɑ̃t] *adj* (deadly) boring, deadly dull, deadly*.

endormeur, -euse [ɑ̃dɔʀmœʀ, øz] *nm,f* (*péj: rare*) beguiler.

endormi, e [ɑ̃dɔʀmi] (*ptp de* **endormir**) *adj* **(a)** (*lit*) *personne* sleeping, asleep (*attrib*).

(b) (*fig*) (*: *apathique*) sluggish, languid; (*engourdi*) numb; (*assoupi*) *passion, facultés* dormant, quiescent; *ville, rue* sleepy, drowsy. **j'ai la main tout ~e** my hand has gone to sleep* *ou* is completely numb *ou* dead*; **à moitié ~** half asleep; **quel ~*** what a sleepyhead (he is).

endormir [ɑ̃dɔʀmiʀ] (16) **1** *vt* **(a)** *[somnifère, discours]* to put *ou* send to sleep; *[personne]* (*en berçant etc*) to send *ou* lull to sleep. **elle chantait pour l'~** she used to sing him to sleep.

(b) (**fig: ennuyer*) to send to sleep*, bore stiff*. **tu nous endors avec tes histoires!** you're sending us to sleep* *ou* boring us stiff* with your stories.

(c) (*anesthésier*) **~ qn** to put sb to sleep*, put sb under*, anaesthetize sb; (*hypnotiser*) to hypnotise sb, put sb under*.

(d) (*dissiper*) *douleur* to deaden; *soupçons* to allay, lull.

(e) (*tromper*) to beguile. **se laisser ~ par des promesses** to let o.s. be beguiled by promises, (let o.s.) be lulled into a false sense of security by promises.

2 s'endormir *vpr* **(a)** *[personne]* to go to sleep, fall asleep, drop off to sleep.

(b) (*fig; se relâcher*) to let up, slack off. **ce n'est pas le moment de nous ~** we can't (afford to) let up *ou* slack off now; **allons, ne vous endormez pas!** come on, don't go to sleep on the job!*; **s'~ sur ses lauriers** to rest on one's laurels.

(c) *[rue, ville]* to grow calm, fall asleep; *[passion, douleur]* to subside, die down; *[facultés]* to go to sleep*.

(d) (*euph: mourir*) to pass away.

endos [ɑ̃do] *nm* endorsement.

endosmose [ɑ̃dɔsmoz] *nf* endosmosis.

endossataire [ɑ̃dosatɛʀ] *nmf* endorsee.

endossement [ɑ̃dosmɑ̃] *nm* endorsement.

endosser [ɑ̃dose] (1) *vt* **(a)** (*revêtir*) *vêtement* to put on. (*fig*) **~ l'uniforme/la soutane** to enter the army/the Church.

(b) (*assumer*) *responsabilité* to take, shoulder (*de* for). **il a voulu me faire ~ son erreur** he wanted to load *ou* palm his mistake off onto me*, he wanted me to take *ou* shoulder the responsibility for his mistake.

(c) (*Comm, Fin*) to endorse.

endosseur [ɑ̃dosœʀ] *nm* endorser.

endothermique [ɑ̃dɔtɛʀmik] *adj* endothermic.

endroit [ɑ̃dʀwa] *nm* **(a)** (*localité, partie du corps*) place, spot; (*lieu de rangement, partie d'un objet*) place. **un ~ idéal pour le pique-nique/une usine** an ideal spot *ou* place for a picnic/a factory; **je l'ai mis au même ~** I put it in the same place; **manteau usé à plusieurs ~s** coat worn in several places, coat with several worn patches; **les gens de l'~** the local people, the locals*.

(b) *[livre, récit]* passage, part. **le plus bel ~ du film** the finest point in *ou* part of the film; **il arrêta sa lecture à cet ~** he stopped reading at that point.

(c) à l'~ où (at the place) where; **de/vers l'~ où** from/to (the place) where; **en** *ou* **à quel ~?** where(abouts)?, where exactly?; **en quelque ~ que ce soit** wherever it may be.

(d) (*loc*) **en plusieurs ~s** in several places; **par ~s** in places; **au bon ~** in *ou* at the right place; **à l'~ de** (*à l'égard de*) regarding, with regard to.

(e) (*bon côté*) right side. **à l'~** *vêtement* right side out, the right way out; *objet posé* the right way round; **remets tes chaussettes à l'~** turn your socks right side out *ou* the right way out; (*Tricot*) **une maille à l'~, une maille à l'envers** knit one – purl one, one plain – one purl; **tout à l'~** knit every row.

enduire [ɑ̃dɥiʀ] (38) *vt* **(a)** *[personne, appareil]* **~ une surface de** *peinture, vernis* to coat a surface with; *huile, boue* to coat *ou* smear a surface with; *colle* to coat a surface with; **ces émanations enduisaient de graisse les vitres** these fumes coated the panes with grease; **~ ses cheveux de brillantine** to grease one's hair with brilliantine, smear brilliantine on one's hair; **surface enduite d'une substance visqueuse** surface coated *ou* smeared with a sticky substance.

(b) *[substance]* to coat. **la colle qui enduit le papier** the glue coating the paper.

enduit [ɑ̃dɥi] *nm* coating.

endurable [ɑ̃dyʀabl(ə)] *adj* endurable, bearable.

endurance [ɑ̃dyʀɑ̃s] *nf* (*moral*) endurance; (*physique*) stamina, endurance.

endurant, e [ɑ̃dyʀɑ̃, ɑ̃t] *adj* tough, hardy. (*†: *patient*) **peu** *ou* **pas très ~ (avec)** not very patient (with).

endurci, e [ɑ̃dyʀsi] (*ptp de* **endurcir**) *adj cœur* hardened; *personne* hardened, hard-hearted. **un criminel ~** a hardened criminal; **un célibataire ~** a confirmed bachelor.

endurcir [ɑ̃dyʀsiʀ] (2) **1** *vt corps* to toughen; *âme* to harden. **2 s'endurcir** *vpr* (*physiquement*) to become tough; (*moralement*) to harden, become hardened. **il faut t'~ à la douleur** you must become hardened to pain.

endurcissement [ɑ̃dyʀsismɑ̃] *nm* (*V* **s'endurcir**) (*action*) becoming tough; becoming hardened; (*état*) toughness; hardness. ~ **à la douleur** being hardened to pain.

endurer [ɑ̃dyʀe] (1) *vt* to endure, bear.

Énéide [eneid] *nf*: **l'**~ the Aeneid.

énergétique [enɛʀʒetik] **1** *adj ressources, théorie* energy (*épith*), of energy; *aliment* energy-giving, energizing. **dépense** ~ expenditure of energy. **2** *nf* energetics (*sg*).

énergie [enɛʀʒi] *nf* **(a)** (*force physique*) energy. **dépenser beaucoup d'**~ **à faire qch** to expend a great deal of energy doing sth; **un effort pour lequel il avait besoin de toute son** ~ an effort for which he needed all his energy *ou* energies; **nettoyer/frotter avec** ~ to clean/rub energetically; **être** *ou* **se sentir sans** ~ to be *ou* feel lacking in energy, be *ou* feel unenergetic.

(b) (*fermeté, ressort moral*) spirit, vigour. **protester/refuser avec** ~ to protest/refuse vigorously *ou* forcefully *ou* with spirit; **cet individu sans** ~ **leur a cédé** this feeble *ou* sapless *ou* spiritless individual has given in to them; (*littér*) **l'**~ **du style/d'un terme** the vigour *ou* energy of style/of a term.

(c) (*Phys*) energy; (*Tech*) power. (*Tech*) ~ **électrique/mécanique/nucléaire** electrical/mechanical/nuclear power; (*Phys*) ~ **cinétique/potentielle** kinetic/potential energy; **réaction qui libère de l'**~ reaction that releases energy; **l'**~ **fournie par le moteur** the power supplied by the motor; **dépense** *ou* **consommation d'**~ power consumption; **la consommation d'**~ **est moindre si l'on utilise ce modèle de radiateur électrique** power consumption is reduced by the use of this type of electric radiator; **les diverses sources d'**~ the different sources of energy; **transport/source d'**~ conveying/source of power.

énergique [enɛʀʒik] *adj* **(a)** (*physiquement*) *personne* energetic; *mouvement, geste, effort* vigorous, energetic.

(b) (*moralement*) *personne* spirited, vigorous; *style* vigorous, energetic; *ton, voix* spirited, forceful; *refus, protestation, intervention* forceful, vigorous; *résistance* vigorous, powerful; *mesures* drastic, stringent; *punition* severe, harsh; *médicament* powerful, strong.

énergiquement [enɛʀʒikmɑ̃] *adv* (*V* **énergique**) energetically; vigorously; spiritedly; forcefully; powerfully; drastically; severely, harshly; strongly.

énergumène [enɛʀgymɛn] *nmf* rowdy character.

énervant, e [enɛʀvɑ̃, ɑ̃t] *adj* (*V* **énerver**) irritating; annoying; enervating.

énervé, e [enɛʀve] (*ptp de* **énerver**) *adj* (*agacé*) irritated, annoyed; (*agité*) nervous, nervy*, edgy*.

énervement [enɛʀvəmɑ̃] *nm* (*V* **énervé**) irritation, annoyance; nervousness, nerviness*, edginess*. **après les** ~**s du départ** after the upsets of the departure.

énerver [enɛʀve] (1) **1** *vt* **(a)** ~ **qn** (*agiter*) to set sb's nerves on edge; (*agacer*) to irritate sb, annoy sb, get on sb's nerves*; (*exprès*) to irritate sb, annoy sb.

(b) (*littér: débiliter*) to enervate.

2 s'énerver *vpr* to get excited*, get worked up*. **ne t'énerve pas!** don't get excited!*, don't get (all) worked up* *ou* edgy*.

enfance [ɑ̃fɑ̃s] *nf* **(a)** (*jeunesse*) childhood; *[garçon]* boyhood; *[fille]* girlhood; (*petite enfance*) infancy; (*fig: début*) infancy. **science encore dans son** ~ science still in its infancy; **c'est l'**~ **de l'art** it's child's play *ou* kid's stuff*; *V* **retomber.**

(b) (*enfants*) children (*pl*). **la naïveté de l'**~ the naïvety of children *ou* of childhood; ~ **déshéritée** deprived children.

enfant [ɑ̃fɑ̃] **1** *nmf* **(a)** (*gén*) child; (*garçon*) (little) boy; (*fille*) (little) girl. **quand il était** ~**, il aimait grimper aux arbres** when he was a child *ou* a (little) boy *ou* as a child he liked climbing trees; **quand il était** ~**, ses parents l'emmenaient souvent à la campagne** when he was a child *ou* a (little) boy, his parents often took him to the country; **il se souvenait que, tout** ~**, il avait une fois ...** he remembered that, while still *ou* only a child, he had once ...; **c'est un grand** ~ he's such a child; **il est resté très** ~ he has stayed very childlike, he never really grew up; **faire l'**~ to behave childishly, behave like a child; **ne faites pas l'**~ don't be (so) childish, stop behaving like a child; *V* **bon**[1], **bonne**[2], **jardin** *etc.*

(b) (*descendant*) child. **sans** ~ childless; **des couples sans** ~ childless couples; **M X, décédé sans** ~ Mr X who died childless *ou* without issue (*Jur*); **faire un** ~ **à une femme*** to get a woman pregnant; (*fig*) **ce livre est son** ~ this book is his brain-child; *V* **attendre, marier, petit.**

(c) (*originaire*) **c'est un** ~ **du pays/de la ville** he's a native of these parts/of the town; ~ **de l'Auvergne/de Paris** child of the Auvergne/of Paris; **un** ~ **du peuple** a (true) child of the people.

(d) (*) **les** ~**s!** folks*, kids*; **bonne nouvelle, les** ~**s!** good news, folks!* *ou* kids!*

2: **enfant de l'amour** love child; **enfant de la balle** child of the theatre; (*Méd*) **enfant bleu** blue baby; (*Rel*) **enfant de chœur** altar boy; (*ingénu*) **il me prend pour un enfant de chœur!*** he thinks I'm still wet behind the ears!*; (*ange*) **ce n'est pas un enfant de chœur!*** he's no angel*; **enfant gâté** spoilt child, brat (*péj*); (*Rel*) **enfants de Marie** children of Mary; **c'est une enfant de Marie** (*lit*) she's in the children of Mary; (*: *ingénue*) she's a real innocent; **ce n'est pas une enfant de Marie!** she's no cherub!*, she's no innocent!; **enfant naturel** natural child; **enfant prodige** child prodigy; (*Bible, fig*) **enfant prodigue** prodigal son; **enfant terrible** (*lit*) unruly child; (*fig*) enfant terrible; **enfant de troupe** child reared by the army; **enfant trouvé** foundling; **enfant unique** only child; **famille à enfant unique** one-child family, family with one child.

enfantement [ɑ̃fɑ̃tmɑ̃] *nm* (†, *Bible: accouchement*) childbirth; (*littér, fig*) *[œuvre]* giving birth (*de* to).

enfanter [ɑ̃fɑ̃te] (1) **1** *vt* (†, *Bible: mettre au monde*) to give birth to, bear (*littér, Bible*); (*littér, fig: élaborer*) to give birth to (*littér*). **2** *vi* to give birth, be delivered (*littér, Bible*).

enfantillage [ɑ̃fɑ̃tijaʒ] *nm* (*conduite*) childishness (*U*); (*acte, futilité*) childishness (*U*), childish pursuit. **se livrer à des** ~**s** to indulge in childish pursuits, do childish things; **c'est de l'**~**, arrête ces** ~**s!** do grow up!, don't be so childish!, you're just being childish.

enfantin, e [ɑ̃fɑ̃tɛ̃, in] *adj* (*typique de l'enfance*) *joie, naïveté, confiance* childlike; (*puéril*) *attitude, réaction* childish, infantile. (*facile*) **c'est un travail** ~ it's simple *ou* dead easy*, it's child's play*; (*propre à l'enfant*) *rire/jeu* ~ child's laugh/game; *V* **classe, langage.**

enfariné, e [ɑ̃faʀine] *adj* (*lit*) dredged with flour; (*fig: poudré*) powdered. **arriver la gueule** ~**e‡** *ou* **le bec** ~* to turn up breezily, turn up all bright and unsuspecting*.

enfer [ɑ̃fɛʀ] **1** *nm* **(a)** (*Rel*) **l'**~ hell, Hell; (*Myth*) **les** ~**s** Hell; (*Prov*) **l'**~ **est pavé de bonnes intentions** the road to hell is paved with good intentions (*Prov*).

(b) (*fig*) **cette vie/usine est un** ~ this life/factory is (absolute) hell *ou* is (a) hell; **l'**~ **de la guerre/de l'alcoolisme** the purgatory of war/alcoholism.

(c) *[bibliothèque]* forbidden books department.

(d) d'~: **bruit/vision d'**~ hellish *ou* infernal noise/vision; **feu d'**~ raging fire; (*Jeu*) **jouer un jeu d'**~ to play for high stakes; **à un train d'**~ hell for leather (*Brit*) *ou* hellbent (*US*) for leather*.

2 *excl*: ~ **et damnation!*** hell and damnation!*

enfermer [ɑ̃fɛʀme] (1) **1** *vt* **(a)** (*mettre sous clef*) *enfant puni, témoin gênant* to shut up, lock up; *prisonnier* to shut up *ou* away, lock up; (*) *aliéné* to lock up*; *objet précieux* to lock away *ou* up; *animaux* to shut up (*dans* in). ~ **qch dans** *coffre* to lock sth away *ou* up in; *boîte, sac* to shut sth up *ou* away in; **il est bon à** ~ **(à l'asile)*** he ought to be locked up* *ou* certified*, he's certifiable*; **il était dans un tel état qu'ils ont dû l'**~ **à clef dans sa chambre** he was in such a state that they had to lock him (up) in his room; **il faudra l'**~ **à clef (pour qu'il ne puisse pas sortir)** you'll (*ou* we'll *etc*) have to lock him in (so that he can't get out).

(b) (*fig littér*) ~ **la culture dans une définition trop rigide** to confine *ou* imprison culture within an over-rigid definition; ~ **qn dans un dilemme/un cercle vicieux/ses contradictions** to trap sb in a dilemma/in a vicious circle/in his (self-)contradictions; **l'école enferme la créativité dans un carcan de conventions** school traps *ou* imprisons *ou* confines creativity in the strait jacket of conventions; ~ **le savoir dans des livres inaccessibles** to shut *ou* lock knowledge away in inaccessible books.

(c) (*littér: contenir, entourer*) to enclose, shut in. **les collines qui enfermaient le vallon** the hills that shut in *ou* enclosed the valley; (*littér*, †) **cette remarque enferme une certaine ironie** this remark contains an element of irony.

(d) (*Sport*) *concurrent* to hem *ou* box in.

2 s'enfermer *vpr* **(a)** (*lit*) to shut o.s. up *ou* in. **il s'est enfermé dans sa chambre** he shut himself away *ou* up in his room; **s'**~ **à clef** to lock o.s. away *ou* up *ou* in; **il s'est enfermé à clef dans son bureau** he has locked himself (away *ou* up) in his office; **ils se sont enfermés dans le salon pour discuter** they have closeted themselves in the lounge *ou* shut themselves away in the lounge to have a discussion; **elle s'enferme toute la journée** she stays shut up (indoors) all day long.

(b) (*fig*) **s'**~ **dans un mutisme absolu** to retreat into absolute silence; **s'**~ **dans un rôle/une attitude** to stick to a role/attitude; **s'**~ **dans sa décision/position** to keep *ou* stick stubbornly *ou* rigidly to one's decision/position; **s'**~ **dans un système** to lock o.s. into a rigid code of ethics.

enferrer (s') [ɑ̃feʀe] (1) *vpr* **(a)** (*s'embrouiller*) to tie o.s. up in knots*. **s'**~ **dans ses contradictions/ses mensonges** to tie *ou* tangle o.s. up in one's (self-)contradictions/one's lies, ensnare o.s. in the mesh of one's own contradictions/lies; **s'**~ **dans une analyse/une explication** to tie o.s. up in knots* trying to make an analysis/trying to explain.

(b) (*rare*) **s'**~ **sur** to spike o.s. on.

enfiévré, e [ɑ̃fjevʀe] (*ptp de* **enfiévrer**) *adj* feverish.

enfiévrer [ɑ̃fjevʀe] (6) *vt* **(a)** *imagination* to fire, stir up; *esprits* to rouse; *assistance* to inflame, rouse. **(b)** *malade* to make feverish; *visage, joues* to inflame.

enfilade [ɑ̃filad] *nf* (*série*) **une** ~ **de maisons** a row *ou* string of houses; **une** ~ **de colonnes/couloirs** a row *ou* series of columns/corridors; (*fig littér*) **une** ~ **de phrases/lieux communs** a string of sentences/commonplaces; **en** ~: **pièces/couloirs en** ~ series of linked rooms/corridors; **prendre en** ~ *boulevards* to go from one to the next; (*Mil*) *objectif* to rake, enfilade.

enfiler [ɑ̃file] (1) **1** *vt* **(a)** *aiguille* to thread; *perles* to string, thread. **on n'est pas là pour** ~ **des perles*** let's get on with it*, let's get down to it* *ou* to business; ~ **des anneaux sur une tringle** o slip rings onto a rod.

(b)(*: *passer*) *vêtement* to slip on, put on.

(c) (*: *fourrer*) ~ **un objet dans** to stick* *ou* shove* an object into.

(d) (*s'engager dans*) *ruelle, chemin* to take; *corridor* to enter, take. **au carrefour il tourna à gauche et enfila la rue de la Gare** at the crossroads he turned left into Rue de la Gare.

2 s'enfiler *vpr* **(a)** (*s'engager dans*) **s'**~ **dans** *escalier, couloir, ruelle* to disappear into.

(b) (‡: *s'envoyer*) *verre de vin* to knock back‡, down*; *nourriture* to guzzle‡, down*; *corvée* to land o.s. with*, get lumbered with* *ou* landed with*.

enfin [ɑ̃fɛ̃] *adv* **(a)** (*à la fin, finalement*) at last, finally. **il y est** ~ **arrivé** he has at last *ou* finally succeeded, he has succeeded at last; **quand va-t-il** ~ **y arriver?** when is he finally going to *ou* when on earth is he going to manage it?; ~**, après bien des efforts, ils y arrivèrent** at (long) last *ou* at length, after much effort, they managed it, after much effort they finally managed it; ~ **seuls!** alone at last!; ~, **ils se sont décidés!** they've made up their minds at last!

(b) (*en dernier lieu*) lastly, finally. **on y trouvait des fougères, des noisetiers, des framboisiers, ~ des champignons de toutes sortes** there were ferns, hazel trees, raspberry bushes and lastly *ou* finally all kinds of fungi; **... ensuite des manuels et des ouvrages de référence, ~ et surtout, des dictionnaires ...** and next manuals and reference works, and last but not least *ou* and last but by no means least, dictionaries.

(c) (*en conclusion*) in short, in a word. **rien n'était prêt, tous les invités se bousculaient, ~ (bref), la vraie pagaïe!** nothing was ready, the guests were all jostling each other — in short *ou* in a word, it was absolute chaos! *ou* it was absolute chaos, in fact!

(d) (*restrictif: disons, ou plutôt*) well. **elle était assez grosse, ~, potelée** she was rather fat, well (let's say *ou* at least), chubby; **pas exactement, ~, dans un sens, oui** not exactly, well — in a way, yes.

(e) (*somme toute*) after all. **c'est un élève qui, ~, n'est pas bête et pourrait ...** this pupil is not stupid, after all, and could ...; **c'est une méthode qui, ~, a fait ses preuves, et j'estime que ...** it is, after all, a well-tried method, and I believe that ... .

(f) (*toutefois*) still. **~, si ça vous plaît/si vous le voulez, prenez-le** still, if you like it/if you want it, take it.

(g) (*valeur exclamative*) **~! que veux-tu y faire!** anyway *ou* still, what can you do!; **~, tu aurais pu le faire!** all the same *ou* even so, you could have done it!; **(mais) ~! je viens de te le dire!** but I've just TOLD you!, (but) for goodness sake*, I've just TOLD you!; **~! un grand garçon comme toi!** come now *ou* come, come, a big boy like you!; **c'est son père, ~!** he IS his father, after all!

(h) mais ~ but; **j'irai, mais ~ ce ne sera pas de gaieté de cœur** I'll go, but not willingly; **car ~** because; **je ne pense pas qu'il voudra sortir ce soir, car ~ il vient juste d'arriver** I don't think he'll want to go out tonight, since *ou* as he has only just arrived.

enflammé, e [ɑ̃flame] (*ptp de* **enflammer**) *adj* **(a)** *allumette* burning; *torche, paille* blazing, ablaze (*attrib*); *ciel* ablaze (*attrib*), blazing, flaming.

(b) *visage, yeux* blazing, ablaze (*attrib*); *caractère* fiery, ardent, passionate; *esprit* afire (*attrib*), burning, on fire (*attrib*); *paroles* inflamed, fiery, ardent; *déclaration* impassioned, passionate, ardent.

(c) *plaie* inflamed.

enflammer [ɑ̃flame] (1) **1** *vt* **(a)** (*mettre le feu à*) *bois* to set on fire, set fire to, ignite; *allumette* to strike; (*fig littér*) *ciel* to set ablaze.

(b) (*exciter*) *visage, regard* to set ablaze; *colère, désir, foule* to inflame; *imagination* to fire, kindle; *esprit* to set on fire.

(c) *plaie* to inflame.

2 s'enflammer *vpr* **(a)** (*prendre feu*) *[bois]* to catch fire, ignite. **le bois sec s'enflamme bien** dry wood catches fire *ou* ignites *ou* kindles easily.

(b) (*fig*) *[visage, regard]* to blaze; *[sentiment, désir]* to flare up; *[imagination]* to be fired; *[orateur]* to become inflamed *ou* impassioned. **s'~ (de colère)** to flare up (in anger).

enflé, e [ɑ̃fle] (*ptp de* **enfler**) **1** *adj* **(a)** (*lit*) swollen. **(b)** (*fig*) *style* bombastic, turgid. **(c)** (†*fig*) **~ d'orgueil** puffed up *ou* swollen with pride. **2** *nm,f* (*: *imbécile*) twit*, clot*.

enfler [ɑ̃fle] (1) **1** *vt membre* to cause to swell (up), make swell (up); (*littér*) *voiles* to fill, swell; (*littér*) *fleuve* to (cause to) swell; *voix* to raise; *addition, facture* to inflate. **~ son style** to adopt a bombastic *ou* turgid style; **se faire ~ de 10 F*** to be done out of 10 francs*.

2 *vi* (*lit*) *[membre]* to become swollen, swell (up); (*: *prendre du poids*) to fill out.

3 s'enfler *vpr* **(a)** *[voix]* to rise; *[style]* to become bombastic *ou* turgid; *[son]* to swell.

(b) (*littér*) *[fleuve]* to swell, become swollen; *[vagues]* to surge, swell; *[voiles]* to fill (out), swell (out).

enflure [ɑ̃flyʀ] *nf* **(a)** (*Méd*) swelling. **(b)** *[style]* turgidity. **(c)** (*: *imbécile*) twit*, jerk* (*US*), clot*.

enfoncé, e [ɑ̃fɔ̃se] (*ptp de* **enfoncer**) *adj yeux* deep-set; *recoin* deep. **il avait la tête ~e dans les épaules** his head was sunk between his shoulders.

enfoncement [ɑ̃fɔ̃smɑ̃] *nm* **(a)** (*action d'enfoncer*) *[pieu]* driving in; *[porte]* breaking down *ou* open; *[lignes ennemies]* breaking through. (*Méd*) **il souffre d'un ~ de la cage thoracique/de la boîte crânienne** he has crushed ribs/a fractured skull.

(b) (*action de s'enfoncer*) *[sol]* giving way; *[fondations]* sinking. **cet ~ progressif dans le vice/la misère** this gradual sinking into vice/poverty.

(c) (*recoin*) *[mur]* recess, nook. **dissimulé dans un ~ de la muraille** hidden in a recess *ou* nook in the wall; **chalet enfoui dans un ~ du vallon** chalet tucked away in a corner of the valley.

enfoncer [ɑ̃fɔ̃se] (3) **1** *vt* **(a)** (*faire pénétrer*) *pieu, clou* to drive (well) in; *épingle, punaise* to stick (well) in, push (well) in. **~ un pieu dans** to drive a stake in(to); **~ une épingle dans** to stick *ou* push a pin in(to); **~ un couteau/une épée dans** to thrust *ou* plunge a knife/a sword into; **~ qch à coups de marteau** to hammer sth in, knock sth in with a hammer; (*fig*) **~ le clou** to hammer *ou* din it in*, drive the point home.

(b) (*mettre*) **~ les mains dans ses poches** to thrust *ou* dig one's hands (deep) into one's pockets; **~ son chapeau jusqu'aux yeux** to ram *ou* pull one's hat (right) down over one's eyes; **il lui enfonça sa canne dans les côtes** he prodded *ou* poked *ou* stuck him in the ribs with his walking stick; (*fig*) **qui a bien pu lui ~ ça dans le crâne?** *ou* **la tête?** who on earth put *ou* got that into his head?; **~ qn dans la misère/le désespoir** to plunge sb into poverty/despair; **ça les a enfoncés davantage dans les frais** that involved them in *ou* plunged them into even greater expense.

(c) (*défoncer*) *porte* to break open *ou* down; *devant, arrière d'un véhicule* to smash in; (*fig*) *lignes ennemies* to break through. **~ le plancher** to make the floor give way *ou* cave in, cause the floor to give way *ou* cave in; **le choc lui a enfoncé la cage thoracique/les côtes** the impact made his rib cage/his ribs cave in; **il a eu les côtes enfoncées** he had his ribs broken, his ribs were broken *ou* smashed; **le devant de sa voiture a été enfoncé** the front of his car has been smashed *ou* bashed* in; (*fig*) **~ une porte ouverte** *ou* **des portes ouvertes** to labour an obvious point.

(d) (*) (*battre*) to beat hollow*, hammer*; (*surpasser*) to lick*. **ils se sont fait ~!** they got beaten hollow!*, they got hammered!*; **il les enfonce tous** he has got them all licked*.

2 *vi* **(a)** (*pénétrer*) to sink in. **attention, on enfonce ici** careful, you'll sink in here; **on enfonçait dans la neige jusqu'aux cuisses** we sank up to our thighs in *ou* sank thigh-deep in(to) the snow.

(b) (*céder*) *[sol]* to give way, cave in. **ça enfonce sous le poids du corps** it gives way *ou* caves in beneath the weight of the body.

3 s'enfoncer *vpr* **(a)** *[lame, projectile]* **s'~ dans** to plunge *ou* sink into; **la lame s'enfonça dans sa poitrine** the blade plunged *ou* sank into his chest; **l'éclat d'obus s'enfonça dans le mur** the shell fragment embedded itself in the wall.

(b) (*disparaître*) (*dans l'eau, la vase etc*) to sink (*dans* into, in). (*fig*) **s'~ dans** *forêt, rue, l'ombre* to disappear into; *fauteuil, coussins* to sink deep into, sink back in(to); *misère* to sink into, be plunged into; *vice, rêverie* to plunge into, sink into; **il s'enfonça dans la brume** he disappeared into the mist; **chemin qui s'enfonce dans les bois** path which disappears into the woods; **je le regardais s'~, impuissant à le secourir** I watched him sinking (in), powerless to help him; **s'~ sous les édredons*** to bury o.s. under *ou* snuggle down under the eiderdown; **il s'est enfoncé jusqu'au cou dans une sale histoire** he's up to his neck in a nasty bit of business; **à mentir, tu ne fais que t'~ davantage** by lying, you're just getting yourself into deeper and deeper water *ou* into more and more of a mess.

(c) (*céder*) to give way. **le sol s'enfonce sous nos pas** the ground is giving way *ou* caving in beneath us; **les coussins s'enfoncent sous son poids** the cushions sink under his weight.

(d) (*faire pénétrer*) **s'~ une arête dans la gorge** to get a bone stuck in one's throat; **s'~ une aiguille dans la main** to stick *ou* run a needle into one's hand; **enfoncez-vous bien ça dans le crâne*** now get this into your (thick) head*, get this stuck in your (thick) head*.

enfonceur, -euse [ɑ̃fɔ̃sœʀ, øz] *nm,f* (*hum*) **c'est un ~ de porte(s) ouverte(s)** he's always labouring the obvious.

enfouir [ɑ̃fwiʀ] (2) **1** *vt* to bury (*dans* in). **il l'a enfoui dans sa poche** he tucked it (away) in his pocket; **chalet enfoui dans la neige** chalet buried away in the snow. **2 s'enfouir** *vpr*: **s'~ dans/sous** to bury o.s. (*ou* itself) in/under; **s'~ sous les draps** to bury o.s. *ou* burrow beneath the covers.

enfouissement [ɑ̃fwismɑ̃] *nm* burying.

enfourcher [ɑ̃fuʀʃe] (1) *vt cheval* to mount; *bicyclette* to mount, get astride. (*fig*) **~ son dada** to get on one's hobby-horse.

enfourner [ɑ̃fuʀne] (1) **1** *vt* **(a)** *aliment* to put in(to) the oven; *poterie* to put in(to) the kiln.

(b) (*: *avaler*) to put away* (*Brit*), down*. **qu'est-ce qu'il peut ~!** it's amazing what he manages to put away* *ou* stuff into himself*.

(c) (*: *enfoncer*) **~ qch dans** to shove* *ou* stuff* sth into.

2 s'enfourner *vpr*: **s'~ dans** *[personne]* to dive into; *[foule]* to rush into.

enfreindre [ɑ̃fʀɛ̃dʀ(ə)] (52) *vt* (*frm*) to infringe, break.

enfuir (s') [ɑ̃fɥiʀ] (17) *vpr* (*se sauver*) to run away, run off, flee (*littér*) (*chez, dans* to); (*s'échapper*) to run away, escape (*de* from); (*littér*) *[temps, souffrance]* to fly away (*littér*), flee (*littér*).

enfumer [ɑ̃fyme] (1) *vt pièce* to fill with smoke; *personne, renard, ruche* to smoke out. **atmosphère/pièce enfumée** smoky atmosphere/room.

engagé, e [ɑ̃gaʒe] (*ptp de* **engager**) **1** *adj* **(a)** *écrivain, littérature* engagé, committed. (*Pol*) **non ~** uncommitted.

(b) (*Archit*) *colonne* engaged.

2 *nm* **(a)** (*Mil*) (*soldat*) enlisted man. **~ volontaire** volunteer.

(b) (*Sport*) (*coureur*) competitor; (*cheval*) runner.

engageant, e [ɑ̃gaʒɑ̃, ɑ̃t] *adj mine* prepossessing, attractive; *air, sourire* engaging, winning, prepossessing; *proposition* attractive, tempting; *repas, gâteau* tempting, inviting. **il eut des paroles ~es** he spoke winningly.

engagement [ɑ̃gaʒmɑ̃] *nm* **(a)** (*promesse*) agreement, promise. **sans ~ de votre part** without obligation on your part; **signer un ~** to sign an agreement; **prendre l'~ de** to undertake to; **manquer à ses ~s** to fail to honour one's agreements, fail to keep one's promises.

(b) (*Théât: contrat*) engagement. **artiste sans ~** out of work artist(e).

(c) (*embauche*) *[ouvrier]* taking on, engaging.

(d) (*Fin*) *[capitaux]* investing; *[dépenses]* incurring. **~s financiers** financial commitments *ou* liabilities; **cela a nécessité l'~ de nouveaux frais** this meant committing further funds.

(e) (*amorce*) *[débat, négociations]* opening, start.

(f) (*Sport*) (*inscription*) entry; (*coup d'envoi*) kick-off; (*Boxe*) attack; (*Escrime*) engagement.

(g) (*Mil*) *[recrues]* enlistment; *[combat]* engaging; *[troupes fraîches]* throwing in, engaging. **tué dans un ~** killed in an engagement.

(h) (*Littérat, Pol: prise de position*) commitment. **politique de non ~** policy of non-commitment.
(i) (*mise en gage*) *[montre etc]* pawning.
(j) (*encouragement*) encouragement. **c'est un ~ à persévérer** it encourages one to persevere.
(k) (*introduction*) *[clef]* introduction, insertion; *[voiture]* entry.
(l) (*Méd*) *[fœtus]* engagement.

engager [ɑ̃gaʒe] (3) **1** *vt* **(a)** (*lier*) to bind, commit. **nos promesses nous engagent** we are bound to honour our promises, our promises are binding on us; **ça l'engagerait trop** that would commit him too far; **ça n'engage à rien** it doesn't commit you to anything; **~ sa parole** *ou* **son honneur** to give *ou* pledge (*frm*, †) one's word (of honour).
(b) (*embaucher*) *ouvrier* to take on, engage; *artiste* to engage. **je vous engage (à mon service)** you've got the job, I'm taking you on, you're hired.
(c) (*entraîner*) to involve. **ça l'a engagé dans de gros frais** that involved him in great expense; **ils l'ont engagé dans une affaire douteuse** they got him involved in a (rather) shady deal; **le pays est engagé dans une politique d'inflation** the country is pursuing an inflationary policy.
(d) (*encourager*) **~ qn à faire qch** to urge *ou* encourage sb to do sth; **je vous engage à la circonspection** I advise you to be (very) cautious.
(e) (*introduire*) to insert (*dans* in(to)); (*Naut*) *ancre* to foul. **il engagea sa clef dans la serrure** he fitted *ou* inserted his key in(to) the lock; **~ sa voiture dans une ruelle** to enter a lane, drive into a lane; (*Aut*) **c'était à lui de passer puisqu'il était engagé** it was up to him to go since he had already pulled out.
(f) (*amorcer*) *discussion* to open, start (up), get under way; *négociations* to enter into *ou* upon; (*Jur*) *procédure, poursuites* to institute (*contre* against). **~ la conversation** to engage in conversation, start up a conversation (*avec* with).
(g) (*Fin*) (*mettre en gage*) to pawn, put in pawn; (*investir*) to invest, lay out.
(h) (*Sport*) *concurrents* to enter. **15 chevaux sont engagés dans cette course** 15 horses are running in this race; **~ la partie** to kick off; **la partie est bien engagée** the match is well under way; **~ le fer** to cross swords.
(i) (*Mil*) *recrues* to enlist; *troupes fraîches* to throw in, engage; **~ le combat contre l'ennemi** to engage the enemy, join battle with the enemy†; **~ toutes ses forces dans la bataille** to throw all one's troops into the battle.
2 s'engager *vpr* **(a)** (*promettre*) to commit o.s. **s'~ à faire** to undertake *ou* promise to do; **il n'a pas voulu s'~ trop** he didn't want to commit himself (too far); **sais-tu à quoi tu t'engages?** do you know what you're letting yourself in for?, do you know what you're committing yourself to?
(b) (*s'embaucher*) to take a job (*chez* with). **il s'est engagé comme garçon de courses** he took a job as an errand boy, he got himself taken on as an errand boy.
(c) s'~ dans *frais* to incur; *discussion, pourparlers* to enter into; *affaire, entreprise* to become involved in; **le pays s'engage dans une politique dangereuse** the country is embarking on a dangerous policy.
(d) (*s'emboîter*) **s'~ dans** to engage into, fit into; (*pénétrer*) **s'~ dans** *[véhicule]* to enter, turn into; *[piéton]* to take, turn into; **s'~ sur la chaussée** to step onto the road; **j'avais la priorité puisque j'étais engagé (dans la rue)** I had (the) right of way since I had already pulled out *ou* drawn out (into the main street).
(e) (*s'amorcer*) *[pourparlers]* to begin, start (up), get under way. **une conversation s'engagea entre eux** they started up a conversation.
(f) (*Sport*) to enter (one's name) (*dans* for).
(g) (*Mil*) *[recrues]* to enlist. **s'~ dans l'armée de l'air** to join the air force; **le combat s'engagea avec vigueur** the fight began briskly; **des troupes fraîches s'engagèrent dans la bataille** fresh troops were thrown into the battle *ou* were brought in.
(h) (*Littérat, Pol: prendre position*) to commit o.s.

engeance† [ɑ̃ʒɑ̃s] *nf* (*péj*) mob, crew.
engelure [ɑ̃ʒlyʀ] *nf* chilblain.
engendrement [ɑ̃ʒɑ̃dʀəmɑ̃] *nm* *[enfant]* begetting†, fathering.
engendrer [ɑ̃ʒɑ̃dʀe] (1) *vt* **(a)** (*frm*) *enfant* to beget†, father. **(b)** (*Ling, Math, Phys*) to generate. **(c)** *colère, dispute* to breed, create; *malheurs* to breed, create, engender (*frm*). **il n'engendre pas la mélancolie** he's (always) good for a laugh*.
engin [ɑ̃ʒɛ̃] **1** *nm* (*machine*) machine; (*outil*) instrument, tool; (*Aut*) (large) vehicle; (*Aviat*) aircraft; (*) contraption*, gadget.
2: engin balistique ballistic missile; **engin blindé** armoured vehicle; **engin explosif** explosive device; **engins de guerre**† engines of war († *ou littér*); **engin non identifié** unidentified flying object; **engins (spéciaux)** missiles.
englober [ɑ̃glɔbe] (1) *vt* (*inclure*) to include (*dans* in); (*comprendre*) to embrace, include; (*annexer*) to take in, annexe, incorporate.
engloutir [ɑ̃glutiʀ] (2) **1** *vt nourriture* to gobble up, gulp *ou* wolf down; *navire* to engulf, swallow up; *fortune* to devour, run through. **qu'est-ce qu'il peut ~!*** it's amazing what he puts away!* (*Brit*), the amount of food he stuffs in is quite incredible!*; **la ville a été engloutie par un tremblement de terre** the town was swallowed up *ou* engulfed in *ou* by an earthquake.
2 s'engloutir *vpr [navire]* to be engulfed.
engloutissement [ɑ̃glutismɑ̃] *nm* (*V* **engloutir**) gobbling up; engulfing; devouring.
engluer [ɑ̃glye] (1) **1** *vt arbre, oiseau* to lime. **2 s'engluer** *vpr [oiseau]* to get caught *ou* stuck in (bird) lime. **s'~ les doigts** to get one's fingers sticky.
engoncer [ɑ̃gɔ̃se] (3) *vt* (*gén ptp*) to restrict, cramp. **ce manteau l'engonce** he looks cramped in that coat, that coat restricts his movements; **engoncé dans ses vêtements** (looking) cramped in his clothes; **le cou engoncé dans un gros col** his neck (stiffly) encased in a big collar.
engorgement [ɑ̃gɔʀʒəmɑ̃] *nm [tuyau]* obstruction, clogging, blocking; (*Méd*) engorgement; (*Comm*) glut.
engorger [ɑ̃gɔʀʒe] (3) *vt tuyau* to obstruct, clog, block; (*Méd*) to engorge; (*Comm*) to glut.
engouement [ɑ̃gumɑ̃] *nm* (*pour qn*) infatuation (*pour* for); (*pour qch*) passion (*pour* for).
engouer (s') [ɑ̃gwe] (1) *vpr*: **s'~ de** *ou* **pour qch** to develop a passion for sth; **s'~ de qn** to become infatuated with sb.
engouffrer [ɑ̃gufʀe] (1) **1** *vt charbon* to shoot (*dans* into); (*) *fortune* to swallow up, devour; (*) *nourriture* to gobble up, gulp down, wolf down; *navire* to swallow up, engulf. **qu'est-ce qu'il peut ~!*** it's amazing what he puts away!* (*Brit*).
2 s'engouffrer *vpr [vent]* to rush, sweep; *[flot, foule]* to surge, rush; *[personne]* to rush, dive; *[navire]* to sink (*dans* into).
engoulevent [ɑ̃gulvɑ̃] *nm* nightjar.
engourdir [ɑ̃guʀdiʀ] (2) **1** *vt* **(a)** *membres* to numb, make numb. **être engourdi par le froid** to be numb with cold; **j'ai la main engourdie** my hand is numb *ou* has gone to sleep* *ou* gone dead*.
(b) *esprit* to dull, blunt; *douleur* to deaden, dull. **la chaleur et le vin l'engourdissaient** the heat and the wine were making him sleepy *ou* drowsy.
2 s'engourdir *vpr [corps]* to become *ou* go numb; *[bras, jambe]* to become *ou* go numb, go to sleep*, go dead*; *[esprit]* to grow dull *ou* sluggish.
engourdissement [ɑ̃guʀdismɑ̃] *nm* **(a)** (*état*) *[membre, corps]* numbness; *[esprit]* (*torpeur*) sleepiness, drowsiness; (*affaiblissement*) dullness. **(b)** (*action: V* **s'engourdir**) numbing; dulling.
engrais [ɑ̃gʀɛ] *nm* **(a)** (*chimique*) fertilizer; (*animal*) manure. **~ vert** green manure; **~ azoté** nitrate fertilizer, nitrate. **(b)** (*engraissement*) **mettre un animal à l'~** to fatten up an animal.
engraissement [ɑ̃gʀɛsmɑ̃] *nm*, **engraissage** [ɑ̃gʀɛsaʒ] *nm [bœufs]* fattening (up); *[volailles]* cramming.
engraisser [ɑ̃gʀese] (1) **1** *vt volailles* to cram; *bétail* to fatten (up); *terre* to manure, fertilize; (‡) *personne* to fatten up. **quel pique-assiette, c'est nous qui devons l'~‡** we seem to be expected to feed up this scrounger* *ou* provide for this scrounger*; **l'État s'engraisse sur le dos du contribuable** the state grows fat at the taxpayer's expense; (*fig*) **~ l'État*** to enrich the state.
2 *vi* (*) *[personne]* to get fat(ter), put on weight.
engrangement [ɑ̃gʀɑ̃ʒmɑ̃] *nm [foin]* gathering in, garnering (*littér*).
engranger [ɑ̃gʀɑ̃ʒe] (3) *vt foin, moisson* to gather *ou* get in, garner (*littér*); (*fig littér*) to store (up).
engrenage [ɑ̃gʀənaʒ] *nm* gears, gearing; (*fig: d'événements*) chain. **~ à chevrons** double helical gearing; (*fig*) **quand on est pris dans l'~** when one is caught up in the system; *V* **doigt.**
engrener [ɑ̃gʀəne] (5) **1** *vt* **(a)** *roues dentées* to engage; (*fig*) *personne* to catch up (*dans* in), draw (*dans* into). (*fig*) **~ l'affaire** to set the thing going *ou* in motion.
(b) (*remplir de grain*) to feed *ou* fill with grain.
2 s'engrener *vpr [roues dentées]* to mesh (*dans* with), gear (*dans* into).
engrosser‡ [ɑ̃gʀose] (1) *vt*: **~ qn** to knock sb up***, get sb pregnant; **se faire ~** to get (o.s.) knocked up***, get (o.s.) pregnant (*par* by).
engueulade‡ [ɑ̃gœlad] *nf* (*dispute*) row*, slanging match*; (*réprimande*) bawling out‡, rocket‡ (*Brit*). **passer une ~ à qn** to bawl sb out‡, give sb a rocket‡ (*Brit*) *ou* hell‡; **avoir une ~ avec qn** to have a row* *ou* slanging match* with sb; **lettre d'~** stinking letter‡.
engueuler‡ [ɑ̃gœle] (1) **1** *vt*: **~ qn** to give sb a rocket‡ (*Brit*) *ou* hell‡, bawl sb out‡; **se faire ~** to get bawled out‡, get a rocket‡ (*Brit*) *ou* hell‡; *V* **poisson. 2 s'engueuler** *vpr* to have a slanging match* (*avec* with).
enguirlander [ɑ̃giʀlɑ̃de] (1) *vt* **(a)** (*) **~ qn** to give sb a telling-off*, tear sb off a strip‡ (*Brit*); **se faire ~** to get a telling-off*, get torn off a strip‡ (*Brit*). **(b)** (*orner*) to garland.
enhardir [ɑ̃aʀdiʀ] (2) **1** *vt* to make bolder. **enhardi par** emboldened by. **2 s'enhardir** *vpr* to become *ou* get bolder. **s'~ (jusqu')à dire** to make so bold as to say, be bold enough to say.
énième [ɛnjɛm] *adj* = **nième.**
énigmatique [enigmatik] *adj* enigmatic.
énigmatiquement [enigmatikmɑ̃] *adv* enigmatically.
énigme [enigm(ə)] *nf* (*mystère*) enigma, riddle; (*jeu*) riddle, puzzle. **trouver la clef** *ou* **le mot de l'~** to find the key *ou* clue to the puzzle *ou* riddle; **parler par ~s** to speak in riddles.
enivrant, e [ɑ̃nivʀɑ̃, ɑ̃t] *adj* (*lit, fig*) heady, intoxicating.
enivrement [ɑ̃nivʀəmɑ̃] *nm* (*fig*) *[personne]* elation, exhilaration. **l'~ du succès** the intoxication of success.
enivrer [ɑ̃nivʀe] (1) **1** *vt* (*lit*) to intoxicate, make drunk; (*fig*) to intoxicate. **le parfum m'enivrait** I was intoxicated by the perfume.
2 s'enivrer *vpr* (*lit*) to get drunk (*de* on), become intoxicated (*de* with); (*fig*) to become intoxicated (*de* with). **il passe son temps à s'~** he spends all his time getting drunk; **s'~ de mots** to get drunk on words; **enivré de succès** intoxicated with *ou* by success.
enjambée [ɑ̃ʒɑ̃be] *nf* stride. **d'une ~** in a stride; **faire de grandes ~s** to stride out, take big *ou* long strides; **il allait à grandes ~s vers...** he was striding (along) towards ... .
enjambement [ɑ̃ʒɑ̃bmɑ̃] *nm* (*Littérat*) enjambement.
enjamber [ɑ̃ʒɑ̃be] (1) *vt obstacle* to stride *ou* step over; *fossé* to

step *ou* stride across; *[pont]* to span, straddle, stretch across. **il enjamba la rampe et s'assit dessus** he sat down astride the banister.

enjeu, *pl* **~x** [ɑ̃ʒø] *nm [pari, guerre]* stake, stakes (*de* in). **quel est l'~ de la bataille?** what is at stake in the battle?, what are the battle stakes?

enjoindre [ɑ̃ʒwɛ̃dʀ(ə)] (49) *vt* (*frm*) **~ à qn de faire** to enjoin *ou* charge sb to do (*frm*).

enjôlement [ɑ̃ʒolmɑ̃] *nm* coaxing, wheedling, cajoling.

enjôler [ɑ̃ʒole] (1) *vt* to coax, wheedle, cajole. **elle a si bien su l'~ qu'il a accepté** she coaxed *ou* wheedled *ou* cajoled him into accepting it.

enjôleur, -euse [ɑ̃ʒolœʀ, øz] **1** *adj sourire, paroles* coaxing, wheedling, persuasive. **2** *nm,f* (*charmeur*) coaxer, wheedler; (*escroc*) twister. **3 enjôleuse** *nf* (*séductrice*) wily woman.

enjolivement [ɑ̃ʒɔlivmɑ̃] *nm* (*V* **enjoliver**) (*action*) ornamenting, embellishment, adornment; embroidering; (*détail*) ornament, embellishment, adornment; piece of embroidery.

enjoliver [ɑ̃ʒɔlive] (1) *vt objet* to ornament, embellish, adorn; *récit* to embroider, dress up.

enjoliveur [ɑ̃ʒɔlivœʀ] *nm* (*Aut*) hub cap.

enjolivure [ɑ̃ʒɔlivyʀ] *nf* = **enjolivement.**

enjoué, e [ɑ̃ʒwe] *adj* playful.

enjouement [ɑ̃ʒumɑ̃] *nm* playfulness.

enkystement [ɑ̃kistəmɑ̃] *nm* encystment.

enkyster (s') [ɑ̃kiste] (1) *vpr* to encyst.

enlacement [ɑ̃lasmɑ̃] *nm* (*étreinte*) embrace; (*enchevêtrement*) intertwining, interlacing.

enlacer [ɑ̃lase] (3) **1** *vt* **(a)** (*étreindre*) to embrace, clasp, hug. **le danseur enlaça sa cavalière** the dancer put his arm round his partner's waist.

(b) (*enchevêtrer*) *fils* to intertwine, interlace.

(c) (*entourer*) *[lianes]* to wind round, enlace, entwine.

2 s'enlacer *vpr* **(a)** *[amants]* to embrace, hug each other; *[lutteurs, guerriers]* to take hold of each other, clasp each other. **amoureux enlacés** lovers clasped in each other's arms *ou* clasped in a fond embrace.

(b) (*s'entrecroiser*) to intertwine, interlace. **fils inextricablement enlacés** hopelessly tangled threads; **des petites rues qui s'enlacent** side streets which twine *ou* wind in and out of each other.

(c) s'~ autour de *[lianes]* to twine round, wind round.

enlaidir [ɑ̃ledɪʀ] (2) **1** *vt* to make ugly. **cette coiffure l'enlaidit** that hair style makes her look very plain *ou* rather ugly. **2** *vi* *[personne]* to become ugly.

enlevé, e [ɑ̃lve] (*ptp de* **enlever**) *adj récit* spirited; *morceau de musique* executed with spirit *ou* brio.

enlèvement [ɑ̃lɛvmɑ̃] *nm* **(a)** *[personne]* kidnapping, abduction. **~ de bébé** babysnatching; **l'~ des Sabines** the Rape of the Sabine Women.

(b) *[objet]* taking *ou* carrying away; *[ordures]* collection, clearing (away); *[bagages, marchandises]* collection.

(c) (*Mil*) *[position]* capture, taking.

(d) *[meuble, objet]* removal, taking *ou* carrying away; (*Méd*) *[organe]* removal; *[couvercle]* lifting, removal.

enlever [ɑ̃lve] (5) **1** *vt* **(a)** (*gén*) to remove; *objet, couvercle* to remove, lift (off); *meuble* to remove, take away; *étiquette* to remove, take off; *tache* to remove, take off, take out; (*en brossant ou lavant etc*) to brush *ou* wash *etc* out *ou* off; *tapis* to take up, remove; *lustre, tableau* to take down; *peau de fruit* to take off, peel off, remove; (*Méd*) *organe* to remove, take out. **enlève tes mains de tes poches/de là** take your hands out of your pockets/off there, remove your hands from your pockets/from there; **~ le couvert** to clear the table; **enlève tes coudes de la table** take your elbows off the table.

(b) *vêtements* to take off, remove. **il enleva son chapeau pour dire bonjour** he took his hat off *ou* raised his hat in greeting; **j'enlève ma robe pour mettre quelque chose de plus confortable** I'll just slip out of this dress into something more comfortable, I'll just take off this dress and put on something more comfortable.

(c) ~ à qn *courage* to rob sb of; *espoir* to deprive sb of; *objet, argent* to take (away) from sb; **on lui a enlevé son commandement** he was relieved of his command; **on lui a enlevé la garde de l'enfant** the child was taken from his care; **ça lui enlèvera peut-être le goût de recommencer** perhaps that'll cure him of trying that again; **ça n'enlève rien à son mérite** that doesn't detract from his worth; **pour vous ~ tout scrupule** in order to allay your scruples, in order to dispel your misgivings.

(d) (*emporter*) *objet, meuble* to take away, carry away, remove; *ordures* to collect, clear (away). **il a fait ~ ses vieux meubles** he had his old furniture taken away; **il fut enlevé dans les airs** he was borne (up) *ou* lifted (up) into the air; (*frm*) **il a été enlevé par un mal foudroyant** he was borne off by a sudden illness; (*littér*) **la mort nous l'a enlevé** death has snatched *ou* taken him from us.

(e) (*kidnapper*) to kidnap, abduct. **se faire ~ par son amant** to elope with one's lover, be carried off by one's lover; (*hum*) **je vous enlève votre femme pour quelques instants** I'll just steal *ou* borrow your wife for a moment (if I may) (*hum*).

(f) (*remporter*) *victoire* to win; (*Mil*) *position* to capture, take. **il a facilement enlevé la course** he won the race easily, the race was a walkover* for him; **il l'a enlevé de haute lutte** he won it in a worthy fight; **elle enlève tous les suffrages** she wins everyone's sympathies, she wins everyone over; **~ la décision** to carry the day; **~ une affaire** (*tractation*) to pull off a deal; (*commande*) to get *ou* secure an order; (*marchandise*) to carry off *ou* get away with a bargain; **ça a été vite enlevé** (*marchandise*) it sold *ou* went quickly, it was snapped up*; (*: *travail*) it was done in no time.

(g) (*Art, Mus*) *morceau, mouvement* to execute with spirit *ou* brio.

(h) (*Sport*) *cheval* to urge on.

2 s'enlever *vpr* **(a)** *[tache]* to come out, come off; (*en brossant ou lavant etc*) to brush *ou* wash *etc* out *ou* off; *[peinture, peau, écorce]* to peel off, come off. **enlève-toi de là*** get out of the way*, mind out of the way!*

(b) (*Comm*) to sell. **ça s'enlève comme des petits pains*** it's selling like hot cakes*.

(c) (*Sport: sauter*) *[cheval]* to take off. **le cheval s'enlève sur l'obstacle** the horse takes off to clear the obstacle.

enlisement [ɑ̃lizmɑ̃] *nm* sinking.

enliser [ɑ̃lize] (1) **1** *vt*: **~ sa voiture** to get one's car stuck in the mud (*ou* sand *etc*).

2 s'enliser *vpr* **(a)** (*dans le sable etc*) *[personne]* to sink (*dans* into), be sucked down (*dans* into); *[bateau, voiture]* to sink (*dans* into), get stuck (*dans* in).

(b) (*fig*) (*dans les détails*) to get bogged down (*dans* in). **s'~ (dans la monotonie)** to sink into monotony.

enluminer [ɑ̃lymine] (1) *vt manuscrit* to illuminate; *visage* to flush.

enlumineur, -euse [ɑ̃lyminœʀ, øz] *nm,f* illuminator.

enluminure [ɑ̃lyminyʀ] *nf* illumination.

enneigé, e [ɑ̃neʒe] *adj pente, montagne* snowy, snow-covered; *maison* snowed up (*attrib*); *col, route* blocked by snow, snowed up (*attrib*), snowbound.

enneigement [ɑ̃nɛʒmɑ̃] *nm* (*hauteur de neige*) depth of snow, snowfall. **bulletin d'~** snow report.

ennemi, e [ɛnmi] **1** *adj* (*Mil*) enemy (*épith*); (*hostile*) hostile. **en pays ~** in enemy territory.

2 *nm,f* **(a)** enemy, foe († *ou littér*). **se faire des ~s** to make enemies (for o.s.); **se faire un ~ de qn** to make an enemy of sb; **passer à l'~** to go over to the enemy; **~ public numéro un** public enemy number one.

(b) être ~ de qch *[personne]* to be opposed to sth; **être ~ de la poésie/de la musique** to be strongly averse to poetry/music; **la hâte est l'~e de la précision** speed and accuracy don't mix *ou* don't go together; *V* **mieux.**

ennième [ɛnjɛm] *adj* = **nième.**

ennoblir [ɑ̃nɔbliʀ] (2) *vt* (*moralement*) to ennoble.

ennoblissement [ɑ̃nɔblismɑ̃] *nm* (*moral*) ennoblement.

ennuager (s') [ɑ̃nɥaʒe] (3) *vpr* (*littér*) *[ciel]* to cloud over. **ennuagé** cloudy, clouded.

ennui [ɑ̃nɥi] *nm* **(a)** (*désœuvrement*) boredom; (*littér: spleen*) ennui (*littér*), world-weariness (*littér*); (*monotonie*) tedium, tediousness. **écouter avec ~** to listen wearily; **c'est à mourir d'~** it's enough to bore you to tears *ou* death *ou* to bore you stiff*.

(b) (*tracas*) trouble, worry. **avoir des ~s de santé** to be troubled with bad health; **avoir des ~s d'argent** to have money worries; **elle a des tas d'~s** she has a great many worries, she has more than her share of troubles; **faire** *ou* **créer** *ou* **causer des ~s à qn** to make trouble for sb; **se préparer des ~s** to be looking for *ou* asking for trouble; **ça peut lui attirer des ~s** that could get him into trouble *ou* hot water*; **j'ai eu un ~ avec mon électrophone** I had some trouble *ou* bother with my record player, something went wrong with my record player; **si ça vous cause le moindre ~** if it is in any way inconvenient to you; **l'~, c'est que ...** the trouble is that ...; **quel ~!** what a nuisance!, bother it!* (*surtout Brit*).

(c) (*littér*, ††: *peine*) grief.

ennuyé, e [ɑ̃nɥije] (*ptp de* **ennuyer**) *adj* (*préoccupé*) worried, bothered (*de* about); (*contrarié*) annoyed (*de* at, about).

ennuyer [ɑ̃nɥije] (8) **1** *vt* **(a)** (*lasser*) to bore, weary (†, *littér*). **ce spectacle m'a profondément ennuyé** I was thoroughly bored by the show; **cela (vous) ennuie à force** it palls (on you) *ou* it becomes boring in the long run.

(b) (*préoccuper*) to worry; (*importuner*) to bother, put out*. **il y a quelque chose qui m'ennuie là-dedans** there's something that worries *ou* bothers me about it; **ça m'ennuierait beaucoup de te voir fâché** I should be really upset to see you cross; **ça m'ennuierait beaucoup d'y aller** it would really put me out* *ou* annoy me to go; **si cela ne vous ennuie pas trop** if it wouldn't put you to any trouble *ou* inconvenience, if you wouldn't mind; **je ne voudrais pas vous ~** I don't want to put you to any trouble *ou* inconvenience, I don't want to bother you *ou* put you out*; **ça m'ennuie, ce que tu me demandes de faire** what you're asking me to do is rather awkward *ou* a nuisance.

(c) (*irriter*) **~ qn** to annoy sb, get on sb's nerves*; **tu m'ennuies avec tes jérémiades** I'm getting fed up with* *ou* tired of your constant complaints, you're getting on my nerves with your constant complaints*.

2 s'ennuyer *vpr* **(a)** (*se morfondre*) to be bored (*de, à* with). **il s'ennuie à faire un travail monotone** he's getting bored doing a humdrum job; **s'~ à mourir** to be bored to tears *ou* to death, be bored stiff*; **on ne s'ennuie jamais avec lui** you're never bored when you're with him.

(b) s'~ de qn to miss sb.

ennuyeusement [ɑ̃nɥijøzmɑ̃] *adv* boringly, tediously.

ennuyeux, -euse [ɑ̃nɥijø, øz] *adj* **(a)** (*lassant*) *personne, spectacle, livre* boring, tedious; *travail* boring, tedious, wearisome. **~ comme la pluie** dull as ditchwater (*surtout Brit*), deadly dull.

(b) (*qui importune*) annoying, tiresome; (*préoccupant*) worrying. **ce qui t'arrive est bien ~** this is a very annoying *ou* tiresome thing to happen to you.

énoncé [enɔ̃se] *nm* **(a)** (*termes*) (*Scol*) *[sujet]* exposition; *[problème]* terms; (*Jur*) *[loi]* terms, wording. **(b)** (*Ling*) utterance. **(c)** *[faits, décision]* statement. (*Scol*) **pendant l'~ du sujet** while the subject is being read out.

énoncer [enɔ̃se] (3) *vt* (*gén*) to say, read; *idée* to express; *faits,* *conditions* to state, set out, set forth. (*littér*) **pour m'~ plus clairement†** to express myself more clearly, to put it more clearly; *V* **concevoir.**

énonciation [enɔ̃sjɑsjɔ̃] *nf [faits]* statement.

enorgueillir [ɑ̃nɔʀgœjiʀ] (2) **1** *vt* to make proud. **2 s'enorgueillir** *vpr*: s'~ **de** (*être fier de*) to pride o.s. on, boast about; (*avoir*) to boast; **la ville s'enorgueillit de 2 opéras et un théâtre** the town boasts 2 opera houses and a theatre.

énorme [enɔʀm(ə)] *adj* enormous, tremendous, huge. **mensonge ~** enormous *ou* whopping* lie, whopper*; **ça lui a fait un bien ~** it's done him a world* *ou* a power* *ou* a great deal of good; **il a accepté, c'est déjà ~** he has accepted and that's quite something; **c'est un type ~!*** he's a terrific* *ou* a tremendous* *ou* a great* bloke!

énormément [enɔʀmemɑ̃] *adv* **(a)** enormously, tremendously, terrifically*. **ça m'a ~ amusé** I was greatly *ou* hugely amused by it; **ça m'a ~ déçu** it greatly disappointed me, I was tremendously *ou* greatly disappointed by it; **il boit ~** he drinks a tremendous *ou* an enormous *ou* a terrific* amount.

(b) ~ d'argent/d'eau/de bruit a tremendous *ou* an enormous *ou* a terrific* amount of money/water/noise, a great deal of money/water/noise; **~ de gens/de voitures** a tremendous *ou* an enormous *ou* a terrific* number of people/cars, a great many people/cars.

énormité [enɔʀmite] *nf* **(a)** (*U*) *[poids, somme]* hugeness; *[demande, injustice]* enormity. **(b)** (*propos*) outrageous remark.

enquérir (s') [ɑ̃keʀiʀ] (21) *vpr* to inquire, ask (*de* about). **s'~ (de la santé) de qn** to ask *ou* inquire after sb *ou* after sb's health.

enquête [ɑ̃kɛt] *nf* (*gén, Jur*) inquiry; (*après un décès*) inquest; (*Police*) investigation; (*Comm, Sociol: sondage*) survey. (*Jur*) **ouvrir une ~** to set up *ou* open an inquiry; **faire une ~** (*Police*) to make an investigation, investigate; (*Comm, Sociol*) to do *ou* conduct a survey (*sur* on); (*Police*) **mener** *ou* **conduire une ~** to be in charge of *ou* lead an investigation; **~ administrative** public inquiry (*into planning proposals etc*); **~ parlementaire** parliamentary inquiry (*by parliamentary committee*); **~ statistique** statistical survey; (*Presse*) **'notre grande ~: les jeunes et la drogue'** 'our big investigation *ou* survey: youth and drugs'.

enquêter [ɑ̃kete] (1) *vi* (*Jur*) to hold an inquiry; (*Police*) to investigate; (*Comm, Sociol*) to conduct a survey. **ils vont ~ sur l'origine de ces fonds** they'll investigate the origin of these funds *ou* carry out an investigation into the origin of these funds.

enquêteur [ɑ̃kɛtœʀ] *nm* **(a)** (*Police*) officer in charge of *ou* (who is) leading the investigation. **les ~s poursuivent leurs recherches** the police are continuing their investigations; **les ~s sont aidés par la population du village** the police are being helped in their investigations by the people of the village; **un des ~s a été abattu** one of the officers involved in the investigation was shot dead.

(b) (*Comm, Sociol etc*) investigator. **des ~s sont venus à la porte poser toutes sortes de questions sur l'emploi de nos loisirs** some people doing *ou* conducting a survey came to the door asking all sorts of questions about what we do in our spare time; **il travaille comme ~ pour un institut de sondages** he works as an investigator *ou* he does *ou* conducts surveys for a poll organization.

enquêteuse [ɑ̃kɛtøz] *nf* (*Police etc*) officer in charge of *ou* leading an investigation; (*Sociol etc*) *V* **enquêtrice.**

enquêtrice [ɑ̃kɛtʀis] *nf* (*Comm, Sociol etc*) investigator; *V aussi* **enquêteur.**

enquiquinant, e* [ɑ̃kikinɑ̃, ɑ̃t] *adj* (*qui importune*) aggravating*, irritating; (*préoccupant*) worrying; (*lassant*) boring.

enquiquinement* [ɑ̃kikinmɑ̃] *nm*: **quel ~!** what a flipping nuisance!*; **avoir des ~s: j'ai eu tellement d'~s avec cette voiture** that car gave me so much flipping trouble*, I had so many flipping problems with that car*.

enquiquiner* [ɑ̃kikine] (1) **1** *vt* (*importuner*) to aggravate*, bother; (*préoccuper*) to bother, worry; (*lasser*) to bore.

2 s'enquiquiner *vpr* (*se morfondre*) to be fed up*, be bored. **s'~ à faire** to go to a heck of a lot of trouble to do*, put o.s. out to do.

enquiquineur, -euse* [ɑ̃kikinœʀ, øz] *nm,f* pest*, darned nuisance*. **c'est un ~** he's a pest* *ou* a darned nuisance*, he's a pain in the neck*.

enracinement [ɑ̃ʀasinmɑ̃] *nm* (*V* **enraciner, s'enraciner**) implanting, entrenchment; taking root; settling.

enraciner [ɑ̃ʀasine] (1) **1** *vt idée* to implant, entrench, root; *arbre* to root. **solidement enraciné** *préjugé* deep-rooted, firmly entrenched, deeply implanted; *famille* firmly rooted *ou* fixed; *bavard* firmly entrenched; *arbre* strongly rooted.

2 s'enraciner *vpr [arbre, préjugé]* to take root; *[bavard]* to settle o.s. down; *[immigrant]* to put down roots, settle.

enragé, e [ɑ̃ʀaʒe] (*ptp de* **enrager**) *adj* **(a)** (*: *passionné*) *chasseur, joueur* keen. **être ~ de** to be mad keen on* (*surtout Brit*), be mad* *ou* crazy about*; **c'est un ~ de la voiture** he's mad keen on cars* (*surtout Brit*), he's mad* *ou* crazy about cars*, he's a car fanatic.

(b) (*en colère*) furious.

(c) (*Vét*) rabid; *V* **vache.**

enrager [ɑ̃ʀaʒe] (3) *vi* **(a) faire ~ qn*** (*taquiner*) to tease sb; (*importuner*) to pester sb.

(b) (*frm*) to be furious, be in a rage. **j'enrage d'avoir fait cette erreur** I'm furious at having made this mistake; **il enrageait dans son coin** he was fretting and fuming; **être/sembler enragé** to be/look furious.

enrayage [ɑ̃ʀɛjaʒ] *nm [machine, arme]* jamming.

enrayer [ɑ̃ʀeje] (8) **1** *vt maladie, évolution* to check, stop; *machine, arme* to jam. **2 s'enrayer** *vpr [machine, arme]* to jam.

enrégimenter [ɑ̃ʀeʒimɑ̃te] (1) *vt* **(a)** (*péj: dans un parti*) to enlist, enrol. **se laisser ~ dans** *parti* to let o.s. be dragged into. **(b)** (*Mil†*) to enlist.

enregistrable [ɑ̃ʀʒistʀabl(ə)] *adj* recordable.

enregistrement [ɑ̃ʀʒistʀəmɑ̃] *nm* **(a)** *[fait, son, souvenir]* recording.

(b) (*disque, bande*) recording. **~ magnétique** tape recording.

(c) (*Jur*) *[acte]* registration. **l'E~** the Registration Department (*for legal transactions*); **droits** *ou* **frais d'~** registration fees.

(d) ~ des bagages registration of luggage.

enregistrer [ɑ̃ʀʒistʀe] (1) *vt souvenir, voix, musique* to record; (*sur bande*) to tape(-record); (*Jur*) *acte, demande, réclamation* to register; (*Comm*) *commande* to enter, record; *constatation* to note. **d'accord, j'enregistre*** *ou* **c'est enregistré*** all right, I'll make *ou* I've made a mental note of it, all right, I'll bear it in mind; **cet enfant enregistre tout ce qu'on dit** this child takes in *ou* retains *ou* registers everything one says; **(faire) ~ ses bagages** to register one's luggage.

enregistreur, -euse [ɑ̃ʀʒistʀœʀ, øz] **1** *adj appareil* recording. **2** *nm [température etc]* recorder, recording machine *ou* device.

enrhumer [ɑ̃ʀyme] (1) *vt* **1** to give a cold to. **être enrhumé** to have a cold. **2 s'enrhumer** *vpr* to catch (a) cold.

enrichi, e [ɑ̃ʀiʃi] (*ptp de* **enrichir**) *adj* **(a)** (*péj*) nouveau riche. **(b)** *pain* enriched; *lessive* improved (*de* with); *V* **uranium.**

enrichir [ɑ̃ʀiʃiʀ] (2) **1** *vt œuvre, esprit, langue, collection* to enrich; *[argent]* to make rich.

2 s'enrichir *vpr [commerçant]* to get *ou* grow rich; *[esprit]* to grow richer (*de* in); *[collection]* to be enriched (*de* with). **leur collection s'enrichit d'année en année** their collection is becoming richer from year to year.

enrichissant, e [ɑ̃ʀiʃisɑ̃, ɑ̃t] *adj* enriching.

enrichissement [ɑ̃ʀiʃismɑ̃] *nm* enrichment.

enrobage [ɑ̃ʀɔbaʒ] *nm,* **enrobement** [ɑ̃ʀɔbmɑ̃] *nm* coating.

enrober [ɑ̃ʀɔbe] (1) *vt bonbon* to coat (*de* with); *paroles* to wrap up (*de* in).

enrochement [ɑ̃ʀɔʃmɑ̃] *nm* rocks (*protecting a jetty etc*).

enrôlé [ɑ̃ʀole] *nm* recruit.

enrôlement [ɑ̃ʀolmɑ̃] *nm* (*V* **enrôler**) enlistment; signing on; enrolement.

enrôler *vt,* **s'enrôler** *vpr* [ɑ̃ʀole] (1) (*Mil*) to enlist, sign on, enrol; (*dans un parti*) to enrol, sign on.

enroué, e [ɑ̃ʀwe] (*ptp de* **enrouer**) *adj*: **être ~** to be hoarse, have a hoarse *ou* husky voice; **j'ai la voix ~e** my voice is hoarse *ou* husky.

enrouement [ɑ̃ʀumɑ̃] *nm* hoarseness, huskiness.

enrouer [ɑ̃ʀwe] (1) **1** *vt [froid, cris]* to make hoarse. **2 s'enrouer** *vpr* (*par le froid etc*) to go hoarse *ou* husky; (*en criant*) to make o.s. hoarse. **s'~ à force de chanter** to sing o.s. hoarse.

enroulement [ɑ̃ʀulmɑ̃] *nm* **(a)** (*U: V* **enrouler**) rolling-up; coiling-up; winding(-up). **(b)** (*Archit, Art*) volute, scroll, whorl; (*Élec*) coil.

enrouler [ɑ̃ʀule] (1) **1** *vt tapis* to roll up; *cheveux* to coil up; *corde, ruban* to wind up, coil up, roll up; *fil* to wind (*sur, autour de* round); *bobine* to wind. **~ une feuille autour de/dans** to roll a sheet of paper round/up in.

2 s'enrouler *vpr [serpent]* to coil up; *[film, fil]* to wind. **s'~ dans une couverture** to wrap *ou* roll o.s. up in a blanket.

enrubanner [ɑ̃ʀybane] (1) *vt* to decorate *ou* trim with ribbon(s) *ou* a ribbon; (*en attachant*) to tie up *ou* do up with (a) ribbon.

ensablement [ɑ̃sɑbləmɑ̃] *nm* **(a)** (*V* **ensabler**) silting-up; choking *ou* blocking (with sand); stranding; sinking into the sand. **(b)** (*tas de sable*) (*formé par le vent*) (sand) dune; (*formé par l'eau*) sandbank.

ensabler [ɑ̃sɑble] (1) **1** *vt port* to silt up, sand up; *tuyau* to choke *ou* block with sand; *bateau* to strand (on a sandbank); *voiture* to get stuck in the sand.

2 s'ensabler *vpr [port]* to silt up; *[bateau, voiture]* to get stuck in the sand. **je m'étais ensablé jusqu'aux essieux** my car had sunk in the sand up to the axles.

ensachage [ɑ̃saʃaʒ] *nm* bagging, packing (into bags).

ensacher [ɑ̃saʃe] (1) *vt* to bag, pack (into bags).

ensanglanter [ɑ̃sɑ̃glɑ̃te] (1) *vt visage* to cover with blood; *vêtement* to soak with blood. **manche ensanglantée** blood-soaked sleeve; **~ un pays** to bathe a country in blood.

enseignant, e [ɑ̃sɛɲɑ̃, ɑ̃t] **1** *adj* teaching; *V* **corps. 2** *nm,f* teacher.

enseigne [ɑ̃sɛɲ] **1** *nf* **(a)** (*Comm*) (shop) sign. **~ lumineuse** neon sign; **(restaurant) à l'~ du Lion Noir** the Black Lion (restaurant); **loger à l'~ du Lion Noir††** to put up at (the sign of) the Black Lion††; (*fig*) **être logés à la même ~** to be in the same boat.

(b) (*Mil, Naut*) ensign. **(défiler) ~s déployées** (to march) with colours flying.

(c) (*littér*) **à telle(s) ~(s) que** so much so that.

2 *nm* **(a)** (*Hist*) ensign.

(b) ~ de vaisseau (*de 1ère classe*) lieutenant; (*de 2e classe*) sub-lieutenant (*Brit*), ensign (*US*).

enseignement [ɑ̃sɛɲmɑ̃] *nm* **(a)** (*Admin*) education. **~ général** general education; **~ libre** denominational education; **~ ménager** home economics; **~ mixte** coeducation; **~ par correspondance** postal tuition; **~ primaire** *ou* **du premier degré** primary education; **~ secondaire** *ou* **du second degré/supérieur** *ou* **universitaire** secondary/higher *ou* university education; **~ privé/public** private/state education; **~ professionnel** professional *ou* vocational training; **~ pro-**

grammé programmed learning; ~ **technique** technical education.

(b) (*art d'enseigner*) teaching. ~ **moderne** modern (methods of) teaching.

(c) (*carrière*) teaching profession. **être dans l'**~ to be a teacher, be a member of the teaching profession.

(d) (*leçon donnée par l'expérience*) teaching, lesson. **on peut en tirer plusieurs** ~**s** it has taught us several things, we can draw many lessons from it; **les** ~**s du Christ** the teachings of Christ.

enseigner [ɑ̃seɲe] (1) *vt* to teach. ~ **qch à qn** to teach sb sth; ~ **à qn à faire qch** to teach sb (how) to do sth.

ensemble [ɑ̃sɑ̃bl(ə)] **1** *adv* **(a)** (*l'un avec l'autre*) together. **ils sont partis** ~ they left together; **tous** ~ all together.

(b) (*simultanément*) (*deux personnes*) together, both at once; (*plusieurs*) together, at the same time. **ils ont répondu** ~ (*deux*) they both answered together *ou* at once; (*plusieurs*) they all answered together *ou* at the same time, they answered all together.

(c) (*littér: à la fois*) **tout** ~ (*deux*) both, at once; (*plus de deux*) at (one and) the same time; **il était tout** ~ **triste et joyeux** he was both *ou* at once sad and happy.

(d) aller ~ (*être assorti*): **les deux serre-livres vont** ~ the two book ends are sold together; **ces deux idées vont** ~ these two ideas go together *ou* go hand in hand; **je trouve qu'ils vont bien** ~ I think they make a good couple *ou* that they go together well; **ces crapules vont bien** ~ (*deux*) they make a pretty *ou* fine pair (of rascals); (*plus de deux*) they make a fine bunch of rascals; **l'armoire et la table ne vont pas (bien)** ~ *ou* **vont mal** ~ the wardrobe and the table don't go (very well) together, the wardrobe doesn't go (very well) with the table.

(e) être bien ~ (*être en harmonie*) to be on good terms; (*être bien assorti*) to get on well (together), hit it off*; **ils sont mal** ~ (*brouillés*) they are on bad terms; (*mal assortis*) they don't get on (well) (together), they don't hit it off*.

2 *nm* **(a)** (*unité*) unity. **œuvre qui manque d'**~ work which lacks unity; **avec** ~, **avec un parfait** ~ simultaneously, as one man, with one accord; **ils répondirent avec un** ~ **touchant** it was positively touching to hear them all answer alike *ou* with one accord.

(b) (*totalité*) whole. **former un** ~ **harmonieux** to form a harmonious whole; **l'**~ **du personnel** the entire *ou* whole staff; **on reconnaît cette substance à l'**~ **de ses propriétés** you can identify this substance from all its various properties; **dans l'**~ on the whole, in the main, by and large; **les spectateurs dans leur** ~ the audience as a whole; **examiner la question dans son** ~ to examine the question in its entirety *ou* as a whole.

(c) d'~ *vue* overall, comprehensive, general; *étude* comprehensive, overall; *impression* overall, general; **mouvement d'**~ ensemble movement.

(d) (*groupement*) *[personnes]* set, group, body; *[objets, poèmes]* set, collection; *[faits]* set, series; *[meubles]* suite; *[lois]* body, corpus; (*Mus*) ensemble.

(e) (*zone résidentielle*) (housing) scheme *ou* development; *V* **grand.**

(f) (*Math*) set. ~ **vide** empty set; **théorie des** ~**s** set theory.

(g) (*Couture*) ensemble, outfit, suit. ~ **de ville** town suit; ~ **de voyage** travelling outfit; ~ **de plage** beach ensemble *ou* suit *ou* outfit.

ensemblier [ɑ̃sɑ̃blije] *nm* (*décorateur*) interior designer; (*Ciné*) set designer.

ensemencement [ɑ̃smɑ̃smɑ̃] *nm* sowing.

ensemencer [ɑ̃smɑ̃se] (3) *vt* (*Agr*) to sow; (*Bio*) to culture.

enserrer [ɑ̃seʀe] (1) *vt [vêtement]* to hug tightly. **son col lui enserre le cou** his collar is too tight; **il l'enserre dans ses bras** he holds *ou* clasps her in his arms; **vallée enserrée par des montagnes** valley shut in *ou* hemmed in by mountains.

ensevelir [ɑ̃səvliʀ] (2) *vt* (*frm: enterrer*) to bury; (*d'un linceul*) to shroud (*de* in); (*fig*) *peine, honte* to hide, bury; *[avalanche, décombres]* to bury. **enseveli sous la neige/la lave** buried beneath the snow/lava; **il est allé s'**~ **dans sa province** he has gone to hide himself away *ou* to bury himself in his province; **la nuit l'a enseveli** he was swallowed up in the darkness.

ensevelissement [ɑ̃səvlismɑ̃] *nm* (*dans la terre, sous une avalanche*) burying; (*dans un linceul*) shrouding.

ensilage [ɑ̃silaʒ] *nm* ensilage.

ensiler [ɑ̃sile] (1) *vt* to ensilage, ensile.

en-soi [ɑ̃swa] *nm* (*Philos*) en-soi.

ensoleillé, e [ɑ̃sɔleje] (*ptp de* **ensoleiller**) *adj* sunny.

ensoleillement [ɑ̃sɔlɛjmɑ̃] *nm* (*durée*) period *ou* hours of sunshine. **la région reçoit un** ~ **de 10 heures par jour** the region gets 10 hours of sunshine per day; **l'**~ **est meilleur sur le versant est de la montagne** there is more sun(shine) on the eastern side of the mountain, the eastern side of the mountain gets more sun(shine).

ensoleiller [ɑ̃sɔleje] (1) *vt* (*lit*) to fill with *ou* bathe in sunshine *ou* sunlight; (*fig*) to brighten, light up.

ensommeillé, e [ɑ̃sɔmeje] *adj* sleepy, drowsy. **aux yeux** ~**s** heavy-eyed with sleep, drowsy- *ou* sleepy-eyed, his eyes (still) heavy with sleep.

ensorceler [ɑ̃sɔʀsəle] (4) *vt* (*lit, fig*) to bewitch, put *ou* cast a spell on *ou* over.

ensorceleur, -euse [ɑ̃sɔʀsəlœʀ, øz] **1** *adj* (*rare*) bewitching, spellbinding. **2** *nm* (*lit*) sorcerer, enchanter; (*fig*) charmer. **3 ensorceleuse** *nf* (*lit*) witch, enchantress, sorceress; (*fig*) (*femme*) enchantress; (*hum: enfant*) charmer.

ensorcellement [ɑ̃sɔʀsɛlmɑ̃] *nm* (*action*) bewitching, bewitchment; (*charme*) charm, enchantment.

ensuite [ɑ̃sɥit] *adv* (*puis*) then, next; (*par la suite*) afterwards, later; (*en fin de compte*) in the end. **il nous dit** ~ **que** then *ou* next he said that; **d'accord mais** ~? all right but what now? *ou* what next? *ou* then what?; **il se mit à crier,** ~ **de quoi il claqua la porte** he started shouting, after which *ou* and after that he slammed the door.

ensuivre (s') [ɑ̃sɥivʀ(ə)] (40) *vpr* to follow, ensue. **il s'ensuit que** it follows that; **et tout ce qui s'ensuit** and all that that entails, and all that goes with it; **torturé jusqu'à ce que mort s'ensuive** tortured to death.

entablement [ɑ̃tabləmɑ̃] *nm* entablature.

entacher [ɑ̃taʃe] (1) *vt honneur* to soil, sully, taint; *joie* to taint, blemish. (*Jur*) **entaché de nullité** null and void; **entaché d'erreurs** spoilt *ou* marred by mistakes.

entaille [ɑ̃taj] *nf* **(a)** (*sur le corps*) (*gén*) cut, (*profonde*) gash, (*petite*) nick. **se faire une** ~ to cut o.s. **(b)** (*sur un objet*) notch; (*allongée*) groove; (*dans une falaise*) gash.

entailler [ɑ̃taje] (1) *vt* (*V* **entaille**) to cut; to gash; to nick; to notch. **carrière qui entaille la colline** quarry which cuts a gash in the hill; **s'**~ **la main** to cut *ou* gash one's hand.

entame [ɑ̃tam] *nf* first slice.

entamer [ɑ̃tame] (1) *vt* **(a)** *pain, jambon* to start (upon); *tonneau* to broach, tap; *bouteille, boîte, sac* to start, open; *tissu* to cut into; *patrimoine* to make a hole in, dip into.

(b) (*inciser*) *chair, tissu* to cut (into); *métal* to cut *ou* bite into.

(c) (*amorcer*) *journée, livre* to start; *travail* to start on; *négociations, discussion* to open; *poursuites* to institute, initiate. **la journée est déjà bien entamée** we are already well into the day.

(d) (*ébranler*) *résistance* to wear down, break down; *conviction* to shake, weaken.

(e) (*porter atteinte à*) *réputation, honneur* to damage, harm, cast a slur on.

(f) (*Cartes: commencer*) ~ **la partie** to open the game; **c'est à toi d'**~ it's you to open.

entartrage [ɑ̃taʀtʀaʒ] *nm* (*V* **entartrer**) furring-up; scaling.

entartrer [ɑ̃taʀtʀe] (1) **1** *vt chaudière, tuyau* to fur up, scale; *dents* to scale. **2 s'entartrer** *vpr* to fur up; to scale.

entassement [ɑ̃tasmɑ̃] *nm* **(a)** (*action*) *[objets]* piling up, heaping up; *[personnes]* cramming in, packing together. **(b)** (*tas*) pile, heap.

entasser [ɑ̃tase] (1) **1** *vt* **(a)** (*amonceler*) *objets, arguments* to pile up, heap up (*sur* onto); *argent* to hoard up, amass.

(b) (*tasser*) ~ **des objets/personnes dans** to cram *ou* pack objects/people into; **entassons-les là** let's cram *ou* pack them in there.

2 s'entasser *vpr* (*s'amonceler*) *[déchets, erreurs]* to pile up. **s'**~ **dans** *[voyageurs]* to cram *ou* pack into; **ils s'entassent à 10 dans cette pièce** there are 10 of them crammed *ou* packed into that room.

ente [ɑ̃t] *nf* (*Agr*) graft.

entendement [ɑ̃tɑ̃dmɑ̃] *nm* (*Philos*) understanding. **cela dépasse l'**~ that's beyond all understanding *ou* comprehension; **perdre l'**~ to lose one's reason.

entendeur [ɑ̃tɑ̃dœʀ] *nm*: **à bon** ~, **salut** a word to the wise is enough.

entendre [ɑ̃tɑ̃dʀ(ə)] (41) **1** *vt* **(a)** *voix etc* to hear. **il entendit du bruit** he heard a noise; **il entendit parler qn** he heard sb speak(ing); **j'entendais qn parler** *ou* **parler qn, j'entendais qu'on parlait** I heard *ou* could hear sb speaking; **il entend mal de l'oreille droite** he can't hear very well with his right ear; (*fig*) **il ne l'entend pas de cette oreille** he doesn't see it like that; **qu'est-ce que j'entends?** what did you say?, am I hearing right?; **tu vas être sage, tu entends!** you're to be good, do you hear (me)!; **ce qu'il faut** ~ **tout de même!*** really — the things you hear! *ou* the things people say!

(b) (*écouter*) to hear, listen to. **le patron a entendu les syndicats pendant une heure** the boss listened to *ou* heard the unions for an hour; **j'ai entendu son discours jusqu'au bout** I listened right to the end of his speech; **à l'**~ **c'est lui qui a tout fait** to hear him talk *ou* to listen to him you'd think he had done everything; **il ne veut rien** ~ he doesn't want to hear *ou* know about it, he just won't listen; (*Jur*) ~ **les témoins** to hear the witnesses; (*Rel*) ~ **la messe** to hear *ou* attend mass; ~ **raison** to listen to *ou* see reason; **comment lui faire** ~ **raison?** how do we make him see sense? *ou* reason?

(c) (*frm: comprendre*) to understand. **oui, j'entends bien, mais ...** yes, I fully *ou* quite understand but ...; **je vous entends** I see what you mean, now I understand (you); **en peinture, il n'y entend strictement rien** he doesn't know the first thing *ou* he doesn't have the first idea about painting; **il n'entend pas la plaisanterie** he can't take a joke, he doesn't know how to take a joke; **laisser** ~ **à qn que, donner à** ~ **à qn que** (*faire comprendre à qn que*) to give sb to understand that; (*donner l'impression que*) to let it be understood that, give sb the impression that; *V* **pire.**

(d) (*frm: avec infin: vouloir*) to intend, mean. **j'entends bien y aller** I certainly intend *ou* mean to go (there); **faites comme vous l'entendez** do as you see fit *ou* think best; **j'entends être obéi** *ou* **qu'on m'obéisse** I intend *ou* mean to be obeyed, I WILL be obeyed; **j'entends n'être pas commandé, je n'entends pas être commandé** I will not take orders from anyone, I will not be ordered about.

(e) (*vouloir dire*) to mean. **qu'entendez-vous par là?** what do you mean by that?; *V* **malice.**

(f) (*loc*) ~ **parler de** to hear of *ou* about; **j'en ai vaguement entendu parler** I did vaguely hear something about *ou* of it; **on n'entend plus parler de lui** you don't hear anything of him these days, you never hear of him any more; (*fig*) **il ne veut pas en** ~ **parler** he won't hear of it; ~ **dire que** to hear it said that; **d'après ce que j'ai entendu dire** from what I have heard, by all accounts; **on entend dire que** it is said *ou* rumoured that, rumour has it that; **on entend dire des choses étranges** there are strange rumours going about; **je l'ai entendu dire que** I heard him say that; **faire ~: elle fit ~ sa voix mélodieuse, sa voix mélodieuse se fit ~** her sweet voice was heard; **il a pu faire ~ sa voix dans le débat, sa voix a pu se faire ~ dans le débat** he was able to make himself heard in the debate; **on entendrait voler une mouche** you could hear a pin drop.

2 s'entendre *vpr* **(a)** (*être d'accord*) to agree; (*s'accorder*) to get on. **ils se sont entendus sur plusieurs points** they have agreed on several points; **ces collègues ne s'entendent pas** these colleagues don't get on (together *ou* with each other); **s'~ comme larrons en foire** to be as thick as thieves; **ils s'entendent à merveille** they get on extremely well (together *ou* with each other).

(b) (*s'y connaître*) **il s'y entend pour le faire** he's very good at it, he knows how to do it, he knows all about it; **il s'y entend!** he knows what he's doing!, he knows his onions!* (*Brit*) *ou* stuff!*

(c) (*comprendre*) **quand je dis magnifique, je m'entends, disons que c'est très joli** when I say it's magnificent, what I'm really saying *ou* what I really mean *ou* what I mean to say is that it's very attractive; **il le fera, moyennant finances, (cela) s'entend** he will do it, for a fee it's understood *ou* of course *ou* naturally; **entendons-nous bien!** let's be quite clear about *ou* on this, let's make quite sure we understand one another.

(d) (*être entendu*) **on ne s'entend plus ici** you can't hear yourself think in here; **le bruit s'entendait depuis la route** the noise could be heard from the road; **tu ne t'entends pas!, tu n'entends pas ce que tu racontes!** you don't know what you are saying!; **ça peut s'~ différemment suivant les contextes** that can be taken to mean different things depending on the context; (*fig*) **cette expression ne s'entend plus guère** that phrase is hardly ever used *ou* heard nowadays, you hardly ever hear that phrase nowadays.

entendu, e [ɑ̃tɑ̃dy] (*ptp de* **entendre**) *adj* **(a)** (*convenu*) agreed. **étant ~ que** it being understood *ou* agreed that, since; **il est bien ~ que vous n'en dites rien** of course it's understood *ou* it must be understood that you make no mention of it; **c'est (bien) ~, n'est-ce pas?** that's (all) agreed, isn't it?; **(c'est) ~!** right!, agreed!, right-oh!* (*Brit*).

(b) (*évidemment*) **bien ~!** of course!; **bien ~** *ou* **comme de bien ~* tu dormais!** as I might have known *ou* expected (you to be), you were asleep!

(c) (*concessif*) all right, granted, so we all agree. **c'est ~** *ou* **c'est une affaire ~e, il t'a poussé** all right, so he pushed you.

(d) (*complice*) *sourire, air* knowing. **oui, fit-il d'un air ~** yes, he said with a knowing look *ou* knowingly.

(e) (††: *habile*) competent.

entente [ɑ̃tɑ̃t] *nf* **(a)** (*amitié*) harmony, understanding; (*alliance*) understanding. **politique d'~ avec un pays** policy of friendship with a country; **l'E~ cordiale** the Entente Cordiale; **l'E~** *ou* **la Triple E~** the Triple Alliance; **vivre en bonne ~** to live in harmony *ou* harmoniously.

(b) (*accord*) agreement, understanding; (*Écon: cartel*) combine.

(c) (*rare: connaissance*) grasp, understanding; (*habileté*) skill; *V* **double.**

enter [ɑ̃te] (1) *vt* (*Agr*) to graft.

entérinement [ɑ̃teʀinmɑ̃] *nm* ratification, confirmation.

entériner [ɑ̃teʀine] (1) *vt* to ratify, confirm.

entérite [ɑ̃teʀit] *nf* enteritis.

enterrement [ɑ̃tɛʀmɑ̃] *nm* **(a)** (*action*) *[mort]* burial; *[projet]* laying aside, forgetting about; *[espoir]* end, death.

(b) (*cérémonie*) funeral, burial (service); (*convoi*) funeral procession. **faire** *ou* **avoir une tête** *ou* **mine d'~** to look down in the mouth*, look gloomy *ou* glum.

enterrer [ɑ̃teʀe] (1) *vt* **(a)** (*inhumer*) to bury, inter (*frm*). **hier il a enterré sa mère** yesterday he attended his mother's burial *ou* funeral; **on l'enterre ce matin** he is being buried this morning; **tu nous enterreras tous!** you'll outlive us all!; (*fig*) **s'~ dans un trou perdu** to bury o.s. in the back of beyond.

(b) (*enfouir*) *os, trésor* to bury; *plante* to plant.

(c) (*oublier*) *projet* to lay aside, forget about; *scandale* to hush up; *espoir* to forget about. **c'est une querelle enterrée depuis longtemps** that quarrel has long since been buried and forgotten (about) *ou* dead and buried; **~ sa vie de garçon** to have *ou* throw a stag party.

entêtant, e [ɑ̃tɛtɑ̃, ɑ̃t] *adj vin, parfum* heady (*épith*), which goes to the head.

en-tête, *pl* **en-têtes** [ɑ̃tɛt] *nm* heading. **papier à lettres à ~** headed notepaper.

entêté, e [ɑ̃tete] (*ptp de* **entêter**) *adj* stubborn, pigheaded*.

entêtement [ɑ̃tɛtmɑ̃] *nm* stubbornness, pigheadedness*.

entêter [ɑ̃tete] (1) **1** *vt [vin, parfum]* to go to the head of. **ce parfum entête** this perfume goes to your head. **2 s'entêter** *vpr* to persist (*dans qch* in sth, *à faire qch* in doing sth).

enthousiasmant, e [ɑ̃tuzjasmɑ̃, ɑ̃t] *adj spectacle, livre, idée* exciting, exhilarating.

enthousiasme [ɑ̃tuzjasm(ə)] *nm* enthusiasm. **avec ~** enthusiastically, with enthusiasm; **avoir des ~s soudains** to have sudden fits of enthusiasm *ou* sudden crazes.

enthousiasmer [ɑ̃tuzjasme] (1) **1** *vt* to fill with enthusiasm.

2 s'enthousiasmer *vpr* to be enthusiastic (*pour* about, over). **il s'enthousiasma tout de suite pour ...** he was immediately enthusiastic about *ou* over ..., he enthused straight away over ...; **c'est quelqu'un qui s'enthousiasme facilement** he's easily carried away (*pour* by).

enthousiaste [ɑ̃tuzjast(ə)] **1** *adj* enthusiastic (*de* about, over). **2** *nmf* enthusiast.

entichement [ɑ̃tiʃmɑ̃] *nm* (*pour une femme*) infatuation (*pour, de* for, with); (*pour une activité, théorie*) obsession (*de, pour* with).

enticher (s') [ɑ̃tiʃe] (1) *vpr* (*frm, péj*) **s'~ de** *femme* to become besotted *ou* infatuated with; *activité, théorie* to become excessively keen on; **il est entiché de vieux livres** he has a passion for old books.

entier, -ière [ɑ̃tje, jɛʀ] **1** *adj* **(a)** (*dans sa totalité*) *quantité, prix, année* whole, full; *surface, endroit* whole, entire. **boire une bouteille ~ière** to drink a whole *ou* full bottle; **payer place ~ière** (*Théât*) to pay the full price; (*Rail*) to pay the full fare *ou* price; **une heure ~ière** a whole *ou* full hour; **des heures ~ières** for hours (on end *ou* together); **dans le monde ~** in the whole *ou* entire world, in the whole of the world, throughout the world; **dans la France ~ière** throughout France, in the whole of France; *V* **nombre.**

(b) tout ~ entirely, completely; **se donner tout ~ à une tâche** to devote o.s. wholeheartedly *ou* entirely *ou* wholly to a task; **il était tout ~ à son travail** he was completely wrapped up in *ou* engrossed in his work.

(c) (*intact*) *objet, vertu* intact; (*Vét: non châtré*) entire. **aucune assiette n'était ~ière** there wasn't ONE unbroken plate; **la question reste ~ière** the question still remains unsolved.

(d) (*absolu*) *liberté, confiance* absolute, complete. **mon accord plein et ~** my full *ou* entire (and) wholehearted agreement; **donner ~ière satisfaction** to give complete satisfaction.

(e) (*sans demi-mesure*) *personne, caractère* unyielding, unbending; *opinion* strong, positive.

(f) (*Culin*) **pain ~** wholemeal bread; **lait ~** full-cream milk.

2 *nm* **(a)** (*Math*) whole. **deux demis font un ~** two halves make a whole.

(b) en ~ totally, in its entirety; **occupé en ~ par des bureaux** totally occupied by offices, occupied in its entirety by offices; **boire une bouteille en ~** to drink a whole *ou* full bottle; **lire/voir qch en ~** to read/see the whole of sth, read/watch sth right through; **la nation dans son ~** the nation as a whole.

entièrement [ɑ̃tjɛʀmɑ̃] *adv* entirely, completely, wholly. **je suis ~ d'accord avec vous** I fully *ou* entirely agree with you; **la ville a été ~ détruite** the town was wholly *ou* entirely destroyed.

entité [ɑ̃tite] *nf* entity.

entôler‡ [ɑ̃tole] (1) *vt* to do‡, con‡ (*de* out of), fleece‡ (*de* of).

entomologie [ɑ̃tɔmɔlɔʒi] *nf* entomology.

entomologique [ɑ̃tɔmɔlɔʒik] *adj* entomological.

entomologiste [ɑ̃tɔmɔlɔʒist(ə)] *nmf* entomologist.

entonner [ɑ̃tɔne] (1) *vt*: **~ une chanson** to break into song, strike up a song, start singing; **~ des louanges** to start singing sb's praises; **~ un psaume** to strike up a psalm, start singing a psalm.

entonnoir [ɑ̃tɔnwaʀ] *nm* (*Culin*) funnel; (*Géog*) swallow-hole, doline; (*trou*) *[obus]* shell-hole; *[bombe]* crater.

entorse [ɑ̃tɔʀs(ə)] *nf* **(a)** (*Méd*) sprain. **se faire une ~ au poignet** to sprain one's wrist.

(b) *[loi]* infringement (*à* of). **faire une ~ à la vérité** to twist the truth; **faire une ~ à ses habitudes** to break one's habits; **faire une ~ au règlement** to bend *ou* stretch the rules.

entortillement [ɑ̃tɔʀtijmɑ̃] *nm* (*action*) twisting, winding, twining; (*état*) entwinement.

entortiller [ɑ̃tɔʀtije] (1) **1** *vt* **(a)** *ruban* to twist, twine, wind; *bonbons* to wrap (up); (*fig*) *paroles* to make long and involved, complicate.

(b) (*) (*enjôler*) to get round*, wheedle, coax; (*embrouiller*) to mix up, muddle (up); (*duper*) to hoodwink*.

2 s'entortiller *vpr [liane]* to twist, wind, twine. (*fig*) **s'~ dans ses réponses** to get (all) mixed up in one's answers, get in a muddle with one's answers; **s'~ dans les couvertures** (*volontairement*) to wrap *ou* roll o.s. up in the blankets; (*involontairement*) to get caught up *ou* tangled up *ou* entangled in the blankets.

entour [ɑ̃tuʀ] *nm* (*littér*) **les ~s de qch** the surroundings of sth; **à l'~ de qch** around sth.

entourage [ɑ̃tuʀaʒ] *nm* **(a)** (*famille*) family circle; (*compagnie, familiers*) (*gén*) set, circle; *[roi, président]* entourage.

(b) (*bordure, cadre*) *[sculpture, fenêtre]* surround, surroundings; *[massif floral]* border, surround.

entouré, e [ɑ̃tuʀe] (*ptp de* **entourer**) *adj* **(a)** (*admiré*) popular. **une jeune femme très ~e** a very popular young woman; (*soutenu*) **pendant cette épreuve il était très ~** during this difficult time many people rallied round (him).

(b) ~ de surrounded with *ou* by.

entourer [ɑ̃tuʀe] (1) **1** *vt* **(a)** (*mettre autour*) **~ qch de** *clôture, arbres* to surround sth with; *cadre* to frame sth with, surround sth with; (*fig*) *mystère* to surround sth with, wrap sth in; **~ qn de** *gardes du corps, cordon de police,* (*fig*) *soins, prévenances* to surround sb with; **~ un champ d'une clôture** to put an enclosure round a field, surround a field with an enclosure; **il entoura ses épaules d'une couverture/d'un châle** he put *ou* wrapped a blanket/shawl (a)round her shoulders; **~ qn de ses bras** to put one's arms (a)round sb; **~ ses pieds d'une couverture** to put *ou* wrap a blanket round one's feet, wrap on

(b) (*être autour*) *[arbres, foule, clôture]* to surround; *[cadre]* to frame, surround; *[couverture, écharpe]* to be round; *[soldats]* to surround, encircle; *[admirateurs, cour,* (*fig*) *dangers, mystères]* to surround. **tout ce qui nous entoure** everything around us *ou* round about us; **le monde qui nous entoure** the world around *ou* about us, the world that surrounds us.

(c) (*cerner*) *[soldats, assiégeants]* to surround, encircle. **ils entourèrent les manifestants** they surrounded the demonstrators.

(d) (*soutenir*) *personne souffrante* to rally round. **ils ont su**

admirablement l'~ après la mort de sa mère they really rallied round him after his mother's death.

2 s'entourer *vpr*: **s'~ de** *amis, gardes du corps, luxe* to surround o.s. with; **s'~ de mystère** to surround o.s. with *ou* shroud o.s. in mystery; **s'~ de précautions** to take elaborate precautions.

entourloupette* [ɑ̃tuʀlupɛt] *nf* mean trick, rotten trick*. **faire une ~ à qn** to play a (rotten* *ou* mean) trick on sb.

entournure [ɑ̃tuʀnyʀ] *nf* armhole. **il est gêné aux ~s** (*lit*) his armholes are too tight; (*fig: il se sent gêné*) he's ill-at-ease, he feels awkward; (*fig: financièrement*) he is in (financial) difficulties, he is feeling the pinch*.

entracte [ɑ̃tʀakt(ə)] *nm* (*au théâtre, au concert*) interval, interlude; (*Ciné*) interval, intermission; (*Théât: divertissement*) entr'acte, interlude; (*fig: interruption*) interlude, break.

entraide [ɑ̃tʀɛd] *nf* mutual aid.

entraider (s') [ɑ̃tʀede] (1) *vpr* to help one another *ou* each other.

entrailles [ɑ̃tʀɑj] *nfpl* **(a)** *[animaux]* entrails, guts.

(b) (*littér*) *[personne]* entrails; (*ventre maternel*) womb. (*fig*) **sans ~** heartless, unfeeling; **la faim le mordait aux ~** hunger gnawed at him; **spectacle qui vous prend aux ~** *ou* **qui vous remue les ~** sight that grips *ou* shakes your very soul.

(c) (*littér*) *[édifice, terre]* bowels, depths.

entrain [ɑ̃tʀɛ̃] *nm [personne]* spirit, drive; *[réunion]* spirit, liveliness, go*. **avec ~** *répondre* with gusto; *travailler* spiritedly, with spirit *ou* plenty of drive; *manger* with gusto, heartily; **faire qch sans ~** to do sth half-heartedly *ou* unenthusiastically; **être plein d'~, avoir de l'~** to have plenty of *ou* be full of drive *ou* go*; **ça manque d'~** *[soirée]* it's dragging, it's not exactly lively.

entraînant, e [ɑ̃tʀɛnɑ̃, ɑ̃t] *adj paroles, musique* stirring, rousing.

entraînement [ɑ̃tʀɛnmɑ̃] *nm* **(a)** (*action d'entraîner*) *[roue, bielle etc]* driving; *[athlète]* training, coaching; *[cheval]* training. **~ à chaîne** chain drive.

(b) (*impulsion, force*) *[passions]* (driving) force, impetus; *[habitude]* force. **des ~s dangereux** dangerous impulses; **dans l'~ du débat** in the heat of the debate.

(c) (*Sport: préparation, exercice*) training (*U*). **2 heures d'~ chaque matin** 2 hours of training every morning; **course/terrain d'~** training course/ground; **manquer d'~** to be out of training; **il a de l'~** he's in training; **il est à l'~** he's in a training session, he's training.

entraîner [ɑ̃tʀene] (1) **1** *vt* **(a)** (*lit*) (*charrier*) *épave, objets arrachés* to carry *ou* drag along; (*Tech: mouvoir*) *bielle, roue, machine* to drive; (*tirer*) *wagons* to pull. **le courant les entraîna vers les rapides** the current carried *ou* dragged *ou* swept them along towards the rapids; **la locomotive entraîne une vingtaine de wagons** the locomotive pulls *ou* hauls twenty or so wagons; **le poids de ses habits l'entraîna vers le fond** the weight of his clothes dragged him (down) towards the bottom; **il entraîna son camarade dans sa chute** he pulled *ou* dragged his friend down in his fall; **danseur qui entraîne sa cavalière** dancer who carries his partner along (with him); (*fig*) **~ qn avec soi dans la ruine** to drag sb down with one in one's downfall.

(b) (*emmener*) *personne* to take (off) (*vers* towards). **il m'entraîna vers la sortie/dans un coin** he took me (off) towards the exit/into a corner; **il les entraîna à sa suite vers ...** he took them (along *ou* off) with him towards ... .

(c) (*fig: influencer*) to lead. **~ qn à voler qch** to get sb to steal sth; **~ ses camarades à boire/dans la débauche** to lead one's friends into drinking/debauchery; **se laisser ~ par ses camarades** to let o.s. be led by one's friends; **cela l'a entraîné à de grosses dépenses** that meant great expense for him, that led him to incur great expense.

(d) (*causer*) to bring about, lead to; (*impliquer*) to entail, mean. **ceci a entraîné des compressions budgétaires/dépenses imprévues** this has brought about *ou* led to budgetary restraints/unexpected expense; **si je vous comprends bien, ceci entraîne la perte de nos avantages** if I understand you, this means *ou* will mean *ou* will entail the loss of our advantages.

(e) (*emporter*) *[rythme]* to carry along; *[passion, enthousiasme, éloquence]* to carry away. **musique qui entraîne les danseurs** music which carries the dancers along; **son éloquence entraîna les foules** his eloquence carried the crowds along (with him); **son enthousiasme l'a entraîné trop loin/au-delà de ses intentions** his enthusiasm carried him too far/further than he intended; (*fig*) **se laisser ~ (par l'enthousiasme/ses passions/un rythme)** to (let o.s.) get *ou* be carried away (by enthusiasm/one's passions/a rhythm); (*fig*) **le rythme endiablé qui entraînait les danseurs** the wild rhythm which was carrying the dancers along.

(f) (*préparer*) *athlète* to train, coach; *cheval* to train (*à* for).

2 s'entraîner *vpr* **(a)** (*Sport*) to train. **il est indispensable de s'~ régulièrement** one must train regularly; **où est-il? — il s'entraîne au stade** where is he? — he's (doing some) training at the stadium; **s'~ à la course/au lancer du poids/pour le championnat** to get in training *ou* to train for running/for the shot put *ou* for putting the shot/for the championship; **s'~ à faire un certain mouvement** to practise a certain movement, work on a certain movement.

(b) (*gén*) **s'~ à faire qch** to train o.s. to do sth; **s'~ à la discussion/à l'art de la discussion** to train o.s. for discussion/in the art of discussion; **il s'entraîne à parler en public** he is training himself to speak in public.

entraîneur [ɑ̃tʀɛnœʀ] *nm [cheval]* trainer; *[équipe, coureur, boxeur]* coach, trainer. (*fig littér*) **un ~ d'hommes** a leader of men.

entraîneuse [ɑ̃tʀɛnøz] *nf [bar]* hostess; (*Sport*) coach, trainer.

entrapercevoir [ɑ̃tʀapɛʀsəvwaʀ] (28) *vt* to catch a (brief) glimpse of.

entrave [ɑ̃tʀav] *nf* **(a)** (*fig: obstacle*) hindrance (*à* to). **~ à la circulation** hindrance to traffic; **~ à la liberté d'expression** constraint upon *ou* obstacle to freedom of expression.

(b) *[animal]* hobble, fetter, shackle. *[prisonnier]* **~s** chains, fetters (*littér*); (*fig littér*) **se débarrasser des ~s de la rime** to free o.s. from the shackles *ou* fetters of rhyme (*littér*).

entraver [ɑ̃tʀave] (1) *vt* **(a)** (*gêner*) *circulation* to hold up; *action, plans* to hinder, hamper, get in the way of. **~ la carrière de qn** to hinder sb in his career.

(b) *animal* to hobble, shackle, fetter; *prisonnier* to chain (up), fetter (*littér*).

(c) (*‡: comprendre*) to get‡. **je n'y entrave que couic** *ou* **que dalle** I just don't get it‡, I don't twig (it) at all‡ (*Brit*).

entre [ɑ̃tʀ(ə)] *prép* **(a)** (*à mi-chemin de, dans l'intervalle de*) *objets, dates, opinions* between. **~ guillemets/parenthèses** in inverted commas/brackets; **~ le vert et le jaune** between green and yellow; **~ la vie et la mort** between life and death; **~ ciel et terre** between heaven and earth; **vous l'aimez saignant, à point ou ~ les deux?** do you like it rare, medium or between the two? *ou* or in-between?; **la vérité est ~ les deux** the truth is somewhere *ou* something between the two, the truth is somewhere *ou* something in-between; **c'était bien? — ~ les deux*** was it good? — yes and no *ou* — so-so*; *V* **asseoir, lire**[1].

(b) (*entouré par*) *murs* within, between; *montagnes* among, between. (*fig*) **enfermé ~ quatre murs** shut in; **encaissé ~ les hautes parois** enclosed between the high walls.

(c) (*au milieu de, parmi*) *pierres, objets épars, personnes* among, amongst. **il aperçut un objet brillant ~ les pierres** he saw an object shining among(st) the stones; **choisir ~ plusieurs choses** to choose from among several things, choose between several things; **il hésita ~ plusieurs routes** he wavered between several roads; **brave ~ les braves**† bravest of the brave†; (*frm*) **je le compte ~ mes amis** I number him among my friends; **lui, ~ autres, n'est pas d'accord** he, for one *ou* among others, doesn't agree; **~ autres (choses)** among other things; **~ autres (personnes)** among others; **l'un d'~ eux** one of them; **plusieurs d'~ nous** several of us, several of our number (*frm*); **il est intelligent ~ tous** he is supremely intelligent; **problème difficile ~ tous** inordinately *ou* particularly difficult problem; **cette heure ~ toutes** this (hour) of all hours; **je le reconnaîtrais ~ tous** I would know *ou* recognize him anywhere; **c'est le meilleur ~ tous mes amis** he's the best friend I have; **il l'a partagé ~ tous ses amis** he shared it out among all his friends.

(d) (*dans*) in, into. (*fig*) **ma vie est ~ vos mains** my life is *ou* lies in your hands; **j'ai eu ce livre ~ les mains** I had that book in my (very) hands; **prendre ~ ses bras** to take in(to) one's arms; **tomber ~ les mains de l'ennemi/d'escrocs** to fall into the hands of the enemy/of crooks.

(e) (*à travers*) through, between. **le poisson/le prisonnier m'a filé ~ les doigts** the fish/the prisoner slipped through my fingers; (*lit, fig*) **passer ~ les mailles du filet** to slip through the net; **je l'ai aperçu ~ les branches** I saw it through *ou* between the branches.

(f) (*indiquant une relation: deux choses*) between; (*plus de deux*) among. **rapports ~ deux personnes/choses** relationship between two people/things; **nous sommes ~ nous** *ou* **~ amis** we're all friends here, we're among friends; **~ nous** between you and me, between ourselves; **~ nous c'est à la vie, à la mort** we are *ou* shall be friends for life; **~ eux 4** among the 4 of them; **qu'y a-t-il exactement ~ eux?** what exactly is there between them?; **il n'y a rien de commun ~ eux** they have nothing in common *ou* no common ground; **ils se marient ~ eux** they intermarry; **ils préfèrent rester ~ eux** they prefer to keep (themselves) to themselves *ou* to be on their own; (*fig*) **ils se dévorent ~ eux** they are (constantly) at each other's throats; **ils se sont entendus ~ eux** they reached a mutual understanding, they understood each other *ou* one another; **ils se sont disputés ~ eux** they have quarrelled (with each other *ou* with one another); **laissons-les se battre ~ eux** let's leave them to fight it out (between *ou* among themselves); **on ne va pas se battre ~ nous** we're not going to fight (among ourselves).

(g) (*loc*) **~ chien et loup** when the shadows are falling; **~ deux âges** middle-aged; (*fig*) **~ deux portes** briefly, quickly; (*lit*) **~ deux eaux** just below the surface; (*fig*) **nager ~ deux eaux** to keep a foot in both camps; **pris ~ deux feux** caught in the crossfire; **~ quatre-z-yeux*** in private; **parler ~ ses dents** to mumble.

entrebâillement [ɑ̃tʀəbɑjmɑ̃] *nm*: **l'~ de la porte le fit hésiter** the door's being half-open *ou* ajar made him hesitate, he hesitated on seeing the door half-open *ou* ajar; **dans/par l'~ de la porte** in/through the half-open door.

entrebâiller [ɑ̃tʀəbɑje] (1) *vt* to half-open. **la porte est entrebâillée** the door is ajar *ou* half-open.

entrebâilleur [ɑ̃tʀəbɑjœʀ] *nm* door chain.

entrechat [ɑ̃tʀəʃa] *nm* (*Danse*) entrechat; (*hum: saut*) leap, spring. **faire des ~s** to leap about.

entrechoquement [ɑ̃tʀəʃɔkmɑ̃] *nm* (*V* **entrechoquer, s'entrechoquer**) knocking, banging; clinking; chattering; clashing.

entrechoquer [ɑ̃tʀəʃɔke] (1) **1** *vt* (*gén*) to knock *ou* bang together; *verres* to clink *ou* chink (together).

2 s'entrechoquer *vpr* (*gén*) to knock *ou* bang together; *[verres]* to clink *ou* chink (together); *[dents]* to chatter; *[épées]* to clash *ou* clang together; (*fig*) *[idées, mots]* to jostle together.

entrecôte [ɑ̃tʀəkot] *nf* entrecôte steak, rib steak.

entrecouper [ɑ̃tʀəkupe] (1) **1** *vt*: **~ de** *citations* to intersperse with; *rires, sarcasmes* to interrupt with; *haltes* to interrupt with, break with. **voix entrecoupée de sanglots** voice broken with sobs; **parler d'une voix entrecoupée** to speak in a broken voice, have a catch in one's voice as one speaks.

2 s'entrecouper *vpr [lignes]* to intersect, cut across each other.

entrecroisement [ɑ̃tʀəkʀwazmɑ̃] *nm* (*V* **entrecroiser**) intertwining; intersecting.

entrecroiser *vt*, **s'entrecroiser** *vpr* [ɑ̃tʀəkʀwaze] (1) *fils* to intertwine; *lignes, routes* to intersect.

entre-déchirer (s') [ɑ̃tʀədeʃiʀe] (1) *vpr* (*littér*) to tear one another *ou* each other to pieces.

entre-deux [ɑ̃tʀədø] *nm inv* **(a)** (*intervalle*) intervening period, period in between. **(b)** (*Sport*) jump ball. **(c)** (*Couture*) insertion.

entre-deux-guerres [ɑ̃tʀədøgɛʀ] *nm*: **l'~** the interwar years *ou* period; **pendant l'~** between the wars, in *ou* during the interwar years *ou* period.

entre-dévorer (s') [ɑ̃tʀədevɔʀe] (1) *vpr* (*littér*) to tear one another *ou* each other to pieces.

entrée [ɑ̃tʀe] **1** *nf* **(a)** (*arrivée*) *[personne]* entry, entrance; *[véhicule, bateau, armée occupante]* entry; (*Théât*) entrance. **à son ~, tous se sont tus** as he entered, everybody fell silent; **à son ~ dans le salon** as he entered (*ou* enters) the lounge; **faire une ~ remarquée** to be noticed as one enters; **faire une ~ discrète** to enter discreetly; **faire son ~ dans le salon** to enter the lounge; **l'~ en gare du train/au port du navire** the train's/ship's entry into the station/port; (*Théât*) **faire son ~** to make one's entrance; (*Théât*) **rater son ~** (*sur scène*) to fluff one's entrance; (*première réplique*) to fluff one's cue.

(b) (*accès*) entry, admission (*de, dans* to). **l'~ est gratuite/payante** there is no charge/there is a charge for admission; **'~ libre'** 'admission free'; **'~ interdite'** 'no admittance'; **'~ interdite à tout véhicule'** 'vehicles prohibited'; **on lui a refusé l'~ de la salle** he was refused admission *ou* entrance *ou* admittance to the hall; **billet d'~** (entrance) ticket; **cette porte donne ~ dans le salon** this door leads into the lounge.

(c) (*Comm*) *[marchandises]* entry. **droits d'~** import duties.

(d) (*Tech: pénétration*) *[pièce, clou]* insertion; *[fluide, air]* entry.

(e) (*fig: fait d'adhérer etc*) **~ dans un club** joining a club; **~ dans une famille** becoming part of a family; **~ au couvent/à l'hôpital** going into a convent/into hospital; **depuis son ~ à l'université** since he went to university; **se voir refuser son ~ dans un club/une école** to be refused admission *ou* admittance to a club/school, be rejected by a club/school; **faire son ~ dans le monde** to enter society, make one's début in society.

(f) (*fig*) **~ en fusion/ébullition** *etc* arrival at melting/boiling *etc* point.

(g) (*billet*) ticket. **j'ai pris 2 ~s** I got 2 tickets; **les ~s couvriront tous les frais** the receipts *ou* takings will cover all expenses.

(h) (*porte, portail etc*) entrance; *[tunnel, port]* entrance, mouth; *[trou, grotte]* mouth. (*Théât*) **~ des artistes** stage door; **~ de service** service entrance; *[villa]* tradesmen's entrance; **~ principale** main entrance.

(i) (*vestibule*) entrance (hall).

(j) (*fig littér: début*) outset; (*Mus: motif*) entry. **à l'~ de l'hiver/de la belle saison** as winter/the warm weather set (*ou* sets *etc*) in, at the very beginning of winter/the warm weather; **à l'~ de la vie** at life's outset.

(k) (*Culin: mets*) first course.

(l) (*Comm, Statistique*) entry; (*Lexicographie*) headword. **tableau à double ~** double entry table.

(m) (*loc*) **d'~, d'~ de jeu** from the outset.

2 entrées *fpl*: **avoir ses ~s chez qn** to come and go as one likes *ou* informally in sb's house; **avoir ses ~s auprès de qn** to have free *ou* easy access to sb; **il a ses ~s au ministère** he comes and goes freely in the ministry.

3: **entrée en action** activating; (*Tech*) **entrée d'air** air inlet; (*Théât*) **entrée de ballet** entrée de ballet; **entrée en fonctions** taking up office; **entrée en matière** introduction; **entrée en vigueur** coming into force *ou* application; **entrée en scène** entrance.

entre-égorger (s') [ɑ̃tʀegɔʀʒe] (3) *vpr* to cut each other's *ou* one another's throats.

entrefaites [ɑ̃tʀəfɛt] *nfpl*: **sur ces ~** (*à ce moment-là*) at that moment, at this juncture.

entrefer [ɑ̃tʀəfɛʀ] *nm* air-gap.

entrefilet [ɑ̃tʀəfilɛ] *nm* (*petit article*) paragraph, item.

entre-jambes [ɑ̃tʀəʒɑ̃b] *nm inv* (*Couture*) crotch.

entrelacement [ɑ̃tʀəlasmɑ̃] *nm* (*action, état*) intertwining, interlacing. **un ~ de ...** a network of ... .

entrelacer *vt*, **s'entrelacer** *vpr* [ɑ̃tʀəlase] (3) to intertwine, interlace.

entrelacs [ɑ̃tʀəla] *nm* (*Archit*) interlacing (*U*); (*Peinture*) interlace (*U*).

entrelardé, e [ɑ̃tʀəlaʀde] (*ptp de* **entrelarder**) *adj* larded (*de* with).

entrelarder [ɑ̃tʀəlaʀde] (1) *vt* (*Culin*) to lard. (*fig*) **~ de citations** to interlard *ou* intersperse with quotations.

entremêler [ɑ̃tʀəmele] (1) **1** *vt* **(a)** *choses* to (inter)mingle, intermix. **~ des scènes tragiques et des scènes comiques** to (inter)mingle *ou* intermix tragic and comic scenes.

(b) (*truffer de*) **~ un récit de** to intersperse *ou* pepper a tale with.

2 s'entremêler *vpr [branches, cheveux]* to become entangled (*à* with); *[idées]* to become intermingled.

entremets [ɑ̃tʀəmɛ] *nm* (cream) sweet *ou* dessert.

entremetteur [ɑ̃tʀəmɛtœʀ] *nm* **(a)** (*péj*) (*gén*) go-between; (*proxénète*) procurer, go-between. **(b)** (*intermédiaire*) go-between.

entremetteuse [ɑ̃tʀəmɛtøz] *nf* (*péj*) (*gén*) go-between; (*proxénète*) procuress, go-between.

entremettre (s') [ɑ̃tʀəmɛtʀ(ə)] (56) *vpr* **(a)** (*dans une querelle*) to act as mediator, mediate, intervene (*dans* in); (*péj*) to interfere (*dans* in). **(b)** (*intercéder*) to intercede (*auprès de* with).

entremise [ɑ̃tʀəmiz] *nf* intervention. **offrir son ~** to offer to act as mediator *ou* to mediate; **grâce à son ~** thanks to his intervention; **apprendre qch par l'~ de qn** to hear about sth through sb.

entrepont [ɑ̃tʀəpɔ̃] *nm* (*Naut*) steerage. **dans l'~** in steerage.

entreposage [ɑ̃tʀəpozaʒ] *nm* storing, storage.

entreposer [ɑ̃tʀəpoze] (1) *vt* (*gén*) to store, put into storage; (*en douane*) to put in a bonded warehouse.

entrepôt [ɑ̃tʀəpo] *nm* (*gén*) warehouse; (*Douane*) bonded warehouse; (*ville, port*) entrepot.

entreprenant, e [ɑ̃tʀəpʀənɑ̃, ɑ̃t] *adj* (*gén*) enterprising; (*avec les femmes*) forward.

entreprendre [ɑ̃tʀəpʀɑ̃dʀ(ə)] (58) *vt* **(a)** (*commencer*) *études etc* to begin *ou* start (upon), embark upon; *travail, démarche* to set about, begin *ou* start (upon), embark upon; *voyage* to set out (up)on, begin *ou* start (upon), embark upon; *procès* to start up; (*se lancer dans*) *voyage, travail* to undertake, embark upon, launch upon. **~ de faire qch** to undertake to do sth; **la peur d'~** the fear of undertaking things.

(b) *personne* (†: *courtiser*) to woo†, court†; (*pour raconter une histoire etc*) to buttonhole, collar*; (*pour poser des questions*) to tackle. **il m'entreprit sur le sujet de ...** he tackled me on the question of ... .

entrepreneur, -euse [ɑ̃tʀəpʀənœʀ, øz] *nm,f* (*en menuiserie etc*) contractor. **~ (en bâtiment)** building contractor; **~ de transports** haulage contractor; **~ de peinture** painter (and decorator); **~ de pompes funèbres** undertaker.

entreprise [ɑ̃tʀəpʀiz] *nf* **(a)** (*firme*) firm. **petite/grosse ~** small/big firm *ou* concern; **~ de déménagement/construction/camionnage** removal/building/haulage firm; **~ de travaux publics** civil engineering firm; *V* **chef**[1], **concentration**.

(b) (*dessein*) undertaking, venture, enterprise; *V* **esprit, libre**.

(c) (*hum: envers une femme*) **~s** advances.

entrer [ɑ̃tʀe] (1) **1** *vi* **(a)** (*lit*) (*gén*) (*aller*) to go in, enter; (*venir*) to come in, enter; (*à pied*) to walk in; (*en voiture*) to drive in; *[véhicule]* to drive in, go *ou* come in, enter. **~ dans** *pièce, jardin* to go *ou* come into, enter; *voiture* to get in(to); *région, pays [voyageurs]* to go *ou* come into, enter; *[armée]* to enter; **~ chez qn** to call in at sb's house, drop in on sb; **~ en gare/au port** to come into *ou* enter the station/harbour; **~ en courant** to run in, come running in; **~ en boitant** to limp in, come limping in, come in limping; **il entra discrètement** he came in *ou* entered discreetly, he slipped in; **~ en coup de vent** to burst in, come bursting in, come in like a whirlwind; **~ sans payer** to get in without paying; **entrez sans frapper** come *ou* go *ou* walk straight in (without knocking); **frappez avant d'~** knock before you go in *ou* enter; **entrez!** come in!; **entre donc!** come on in!; **qu'il entre!** tell him to come in, show him in; **entrons voir** let's go in and see; **je ne fais qu'~ et sortir** I'm only stopping for a moment; **les gens entraient et sortaient** people were going *ou* coming in and out; (*Théât*) **'entre la servante'** 'enter the maid'; (*Théât*) **'entrent 3 gardes'** 'enter 3 guards'; **~ par la porte de la cave/par la fenêtre** to go *ou* get in *ou* enter by the cellar door/the window; **je suis entré chez eux/le boucher** I called in at their house/the butcher's; **on y entre comme dans un moulin** you can just walk in.

(b) (*Comm*) *[marchandises, devises]* to enter. **tout ce qui entre (dans le pays) est soumis à une taxe** everything entering (the country) is subject to duty.

(c) (*s'enfoncer*) **la boule est entrée dans le trou** the ball went into the hole; **l'objet n'entre pas dans la boîte** the object doesn't *ou* won't go into *ou* fit (into) the box; **le tenon entre dans la mortaise** the tenon fits into the mortice; **ça n'entre pas** it doesn't fit, it won't go *ou* fit in; **la balle est entrée dans le poumon gauche/le montant de la porte** the bullet went into *ou* lodged itself in the left lung/the door frame; **son coude m'entrait dans les côtes** his elbow was digging into my ribs; **l'eau entre (à l'intérieur)/par le toit** the water gets inside/gets *ou* comes in through the roof; **l'air/la lumière entre dans la pièce** air/light comes into *ou* enters the room; **pour que l'air/la lumière puisse ~** to allow air/light to enter *ou* get in; **le vent entre de partout** the wind comes *ou* gets in from all sides *ou* blows in everywhere; **~ dans l'eau** *[baigneur]* to get into the water; (*en marchant*) to wade into the water; *[embarcation]* to enter the water; **~ dans le bain** to get into the bath; **~ dans le brouillard** *[randonneurs, avion]* to enter *ou* hit* fog; **la rage/jalousie est entrée dans son cœur** rage/jealousy filled his heart; **l'argent entre dans les caisses** money is coming in; **à force d'explications ça finira par ~*** explain it for long enough and it'll sink in*; **alors ces maths, ça entre?*** are you getting the hang of maths then?*; **c'est entré comme dans du beurre*** it went like a (hot) knife through butter.

(d) **laisser ~** *visiteur, intrus* to let in; *lumière, air* to let in, allow in; (*involontairement*) *eau, air, poussière* to let in; **ne laisse ~ personne** don't let anybody in; **laisser ~ qn dans** *pièce* to let sb into; *pays* to let sb into *ou* enter, allow sb into *ou* to enter; **on t'a laissé ~ au parti/club/dans l'armée** they've let you into *ou* let you join the party/club/army.

(e) (*fig: devenir membre*) **~ dans** *club, parti, firme* to join; *groupe, famille* to go *ou* come into; *métier* to go into; **~ dans la magistrature** to become a magistrate, enter the magistracy; **~ à l'hôpital/à l'asile** to go into hospital/an asylum; **~ dans l'armée** to join the army; **~ dans les affaires** to go into business; **~ dans la profession médicale** to enter the medical profession; **~ en religion/au couvent** to enter the religious life/a convent; **~ dans**

les ordres to take orders; **on l'a fait ~ comme serveur/sous-chef** he's been found a job as *ou* they got him taken on as a waiter/deputy chief clerk; **~ au service de qn** to enter sb's service; **~ dans l'histoire** to go down in history; **~ dans la légende** to become a legend; **~ dans l'usage courant** *[mot]* to come into *ou* enter common use; *V* **jeu, scène.**

(f) (*devenir*) **~ en convalescence** to begin convalescence; **~ en effervescence** to reach a state of effervescence (*frm*), begin to effervesce; **~ en ébullition** to reach boiling point, begin to boil; **~ en fureur** *ou* **rage** to fly into a fury *ou* rage; **~ en guerre** to enter the war; *V* **contact, fonction, vigueur** *etc.*

(g) faire ~ (*introduire*) *invité, visiteur, client* to show in; *pièce, tenon, objet à emballer* to fit in; (*en fraude*) *marchandises, immigrants* to smuggle in, take *ou* bring in; **faire ~ la voiture dans le garage** to get the car into the garage; **faire ~ une clef dans la serrure** to insert *ou* fit a key in the lock; **il m'a fait ~ dans leur club/au jury** (*m'a persuadé*) he had me join *ou* got me to join their club/the panel; (*a fait jouer son influence*) he got me into their club/onto the panel; (*m'a contraint*) he made me join their club/the panel; **il me fit ~ dans la cellule** he showed me into the cell; **faire ~ qch de force dans un emballage** to force *ou* stuff sth into a package.

2 entrer dans *vt indir* **(a)** (*heurter*) *arbre, poteau* to go into. (*Aut*) **quelqu'un lui est entré dedans*** someone banged into him*.

(b) (*partager*) *vues, peines de qn* to share. (*frm*) **~ dans les sentiments de qn** to share sb's *ou* enter into sb's feelings.

(c) (*être une composante de*) *catégorie* to fall into, come into; *mélange* to go into. **les substances qui entrent dans ce mélange** the substances which go into *ou* make up this mixture; **on pourrait faire ~ ceci dans la catégorie suivante** one might put this into the following category; **il y entre un peu de jalousie** there's a bit of jealousy comes into it; **votre avis est entré pour beaucoup dans sa décision** your opinion counted for a good deal in his decision; **il n'entre pas dans mes intentions de le faire** I don't have any intention of doing so; *V* **ligne**[1].

(d) (*fig: commencer*) **~ dans** *phase, période* to enter into *ou* (up)on; **~ dans une profonde rêverie/une colère noire** to go (off) into a deep daydream/a towering rage; **~ dans la vie active** to embark on *ou* enter active life; **~ dans la cinquantaine** to turn fifty; **~ dans la danse** (*lit*) to join in the dancing; (**fig*) to join up.

(e) (*fig: aborder*) **~ dans** *sujet, discussion* to enter into; **~ dans le vif du sujet** to get to *ou* reach the heart of the subject; **il s'agit d'~ véritablement dans la discussion** one must enter into the discussion properly; **sans ~ dans les détails/ces considérations** without going into details/these considerations; **il entra dans des considérations futiles** he went off into some futile considerations.

3 *vt* (*plus gén* **faire ~**) **(a)** *marchandises* (*par la douane*) to take *ou* bring in, import; (*en contrebande*) to take *ou* bring in, smuggle in.

(b) (*faire pénétrer*) **~ les bras dans les manches/les jambes dans les canons des pantalons** to put one's arms into the sleeves/one's legs into the trouser legs; **ne m'entre pas ta canne dans les côtes** stop digging your stick into my ribs.

(c) (*faire s'ajuster*) *pièce* to make fit (*dans qch* in sth). **comment allez-vous ~ cette armoire dans la chambre?** how are you going to get that wardrobe into the bedroom?

entresol [ɑ̃tʀəsɔl] *nm* entresol, mezzanine (*between ground and first floor*).

entre-temps [ɑ̃tʀətɑ̃] *adv* (*aussi* **dans l'~** †) meanwhile, (in the) meantime.

entretenir [ɑ̃tʀətniʀ] (22) **1** *vt* **(a)** (*conserver en bon état*) *propriété, bâtiment* to maintain, see to the upkeep of, look after; *vêtement* to look after; *route, machine* to maintain. **~ un jardin** to look after *ou* see to the upkeep of a garden; **ce meuble s'entretient facilement** it is easy to keep this piece of furniture in good condition *ou* to look after this piece of furniture.

(b) (*faire vivre*) *famille* to support, keep, maintain; *maîtresse* to keep, support; *armée* to keep, maintain; *troupe de théâtre etc* to support.

(c) (*faire durer*) *souvenir, sentiments* to keep alive; *haine, amitié* to keep alive, keep going, foster; *espoir* to cherish, keep alive. **~ l'inquiétude de qn** to keep sb feeling uneasy, keep sb in a state of anxiety; **~ des rapports suivis avec qn** to be in constant contact with sb; **~ une correspondance suivie avec qn** to keep up a regular correspondence with sb, correspond regularly with sb; **l'air marin entretient une perpétuelle humidité** the sea air maintains a constant state of humidity; **~ le feu** to keep the fire going *ou* burning; **~ qn dans l'erreur** to perpetuate sb's delusions, keep sb in ignorance; **j'entretiens des craintes à son sujet** I entertain grave fears for his safety (*frm*), I am afraid for him; **~ sa forme, s'~ (en bonne forme)** to keep o.s. in (good) shape, keep (o.s.) fit.

(d) (*frm: converser*) **~ qn** to converse with (*frm*) *ou* speak to sb; **il m'a entretenu pendant une heure** we conversed for an hour, he conversed with me for an hour; **il a entretenu l'auditoire de ses voyages** he addressed the audience (*frm*) *ou* spoke to the audience about his travels.

2 s'entretenir *vpr* **(a)** (*converser*) **s'~ avec qn** to converse with (*frm*) *ou* speak to sb; **ils s'entretenaient à voix basse** they were conversing in hushed tones.

(b) (*pourvoir à ses besoins*) to support o.s., be self-supporting. **il s'entretient tout seul maintenant** he is completely self-supporting now, he supports himself entirely on his own now.

entretenu, e [ɑ̃tʀətny] (*ptp de* **entretenir**) *adj femme* kept (*épith*). **jardin bien/mal ~** well-/badly-kept garden, well-/badly-tended garden.

entretien [ɑ̃tʀətjɛ̃] *nm* **(a)** (*conservation*) *[jardin, maison]* upkeep; *[route]* maintenance, upkeep; *[machine]* maintenance.

(b) (*aide à la subsistance*) *[famille, étudiant]* keep; *[armée, corps de ballet]* maintenance, keep. **pourvoir à l'~ de** *famille* to keep, support; *armée* to maintain.

(c) (*discussion privée*) discussion, conversation; (*accordé à qn*) interview; (*débat publique*) discussion. (*Pol*) **~(s)** talks, discussions; **demander un ~ à son patron** to ask one's boss for an interview; **nous aurons un ~ à Francfort avec nos collègues allemands** we shall be having a meeting *ou* having discussions in Frankfurt with our German colleagues.

entre-tuer (s') [ɑ̃tʀətɥe] (1) *vpr* to kill one another *ou* each other.

entrevoir [ɑ̃tʀəvwaʀ] (30) *vt* **(a)** (*voir indistinctement*) to make out; (*fig: pressentir*) to have a glimpse of, glimpse. **je commence à ~ la vérité** I have an inkling of the truth, I'm beginning to see the truth.

(b) (*apercevoir brièvement: lit, fig*) to catch a glimpse of, catch sight of; (*rare: recevoir à la sauvette*) to see briefly. **vous n'avez fait qu'~ les difficultés** you have only half seen the difficulties.

entrevue [ɑ̃tʀəvy] *nf* (*discussion*) meeting; (*audience*) interview; (*Pol*) talks (*pl*), discussions (*pl*), meeting.

entrouvert, e [ɑ̃tʀuvɛʀ, ɛʀt(ə)] (*ptp de* **entrouvrir**) *adj* (*gén*) half-open; *fenêtre, porte* ajar (*attrib*), half-open; *abîme* gaping. **ses lèvres ~es** her parted lips.

entrouvrir [ɑ̃tʀuvʀiʀ] (18) **1** *vt* to half-open. **2 s'entrouvrir** *vpr* (*gén*) to half-open; *[abîme]* to gape; *[lèvres]* to part.

entuber: [ɑ̃tybe] (1) *vt* to do:, con:. **se faire ~** to be done: *ou* conned:.

enturbanné, e [ɑ̃tyʀbane] *adj* turbaned.

énucléation [enykleɑsjɔ̃] *nf* (*Méd*) enucleation.

énucléer [enyklee] (1) *vt* (*Méd*) to enucleate.

énumératif, -ive [enymeʀatif, iv] *adj* enumerative.

énumération [enymeʀɑsjɔ̃] *nf* enumeration, listing.

énumérer [enymeʀe] (6) *vt* to enumerate, list.

énurésie [enyʀezi] *nf* (*Méd*) enuresis.

envahir [ɑ̃vaiʀ] (2) *vt* **(a)** (*Mil, gén*) to invade, overrun; *[douleur, sentiment]* to overcome, sweep through. **le sommeil l'envahissait** he was overcome by sleep, sleep was creeping *ou* stealing over him; **le jardin est envahi par les orties** the garden is overrun *ou* overgrown with nettles; **la foule envahit la place** the crowd swarmed *ou* swept into the square.

(b) (*gén hum: déranger*) **~ qn** to invade sb's privacy, intrude on sb's privacy.

envahissant, e [ɑ̃vaisɑ̃, ɑ̃t] *adj personne* interfering, intrusive; *passion* invading (*épith*), invasive (*épith*).

envahissement [ɑ̃vaismɑ̃] *nm* invasion.

envahisseur, -euse [ɑ̃vaisœʀ, øz] **1** *adj* invading. **2** *nm,f* invader.

envasement [ɑ̃vɑzmɑ̃] *nm [port]* silting up.

envaser [ɑ̃vɑze] (1) **1** *vt port* to silt up. **2 s'envaser** *vpr [port]* to silt up; *[bateau]* to stick in the mud; *[épave]* to sink in(to) the mud.

enveloppe [ɑ̃vlɔp] *nf* **(a)** (*pli postal*) envelope. **~ gommée/auto-adhésive** stick-down/self-seal envelope; **sous ~** *envoyer* under cover; **mettre une lettre sous ~** to put a letter in an envelope.

(b) (*emballage*) (*gén*) covering; (*en papier, toile*) wrapping; (*en métal*) casing; (*gaine*) *[graine]* husk; *[organe]* covering membrane; *[pneu]* cover, casing; *[dirigeable]* envelope; *[chaudière]* lagging, jacket. **dans une ~ de métal** in a metal casing.

(c) (*apparence*) outward appearance, exterior. **un cœur d'or sous une rude ~** a heart of gold beneath a rough exterior; (*fig*) **ça sert d'~ à des causes moins nobles** that serves to dress up *ou* cover over less worthy causes.

(d) (*littér: corps*) **il a quitté son ~ mortelle** he has cast off his earthly *ou* mortal frame (*littér*) *ou* shroud (*littér*).

(e) (*Math*) envelope.

enveloppement [ɑ̃vlɔpmɑ̃] *nm* **(a)** (*Méd*) pack. **(b)** (*Mil*) *[ennemi]* surrounding, encirclement. **manœuvre d'~** pincer movement.

envelopper [ɑ̃vlɔpe] (1) *vt* **(a)** *objet, enfant* to wrap (up). **l'emballage qui enveloppe le colis** the wrapping *ou* packaging round the parcel *ou* that the parcel is in, the paper in which the parcel is wrapped; **~ un membre de bandages** to swathe a limb in bandages; **il s'enveloppa dans une cape** he wrapped *ou* swathed himself in a cape, he wrapped a cape around him; (*fig hum*) **il s'enveloppa dans sa dignité** he donned an air of dignity; (*fig*) **~ qn de son affection** to envelop sb in one's affection, surround sb with one's affection; (*hum*) **elle est assez enveloppée*** she's well-padded* (*hum*).

(b) (*voiler*) *pensée, parole* to veil.

(c) (*gén littér: entourer*) *[brume]* to envelop, shroud. **le silence enveloppe la ville** the town is steeped *ou* wrapped *ou* shrouded in silence; **la lumière enveloppe la campagne** the countryside is bathed in light; **événement enveloppé de mystère** event shrouded *ou* veiled in mystery; **~ qn du regard** to envelop sb with one's gaze; **il l'enveloppa d'un regard haineux** he looked at him with total hatred; **il enveloppa la plaine du regard** he took in the plain with his gaze; **~ dans sa réprobation**† to include as the object of one's disapproval.

(d) (*Mil*) *ennemi* to surround, encircle.

envenimement [ɑ̃vnimmɑ̃] *nm [plaie]* poisoning; *[querelle]* embittering; *[situation]* worsening.

envenimer [ɑ̃vnime] (1) **1** *vt plaie* to make septic, poison; *querelle* to inflame, fan the flame of; *situation* to inflame, aggravate. **2 s'envenimer** *vpr [plaie]* to go septic, fester; *[querelle, situation]* to grow more bitter *ou* acrimonious.

envergure [ɑ̃vɛʀgyʀ] *nf* **(a)** *[oiseau, avion]* wingspan; *[voile]* breadth. **(b)** *[personne]* calibre; *[entreprise]* scale, scope; *[intelligence]* scope, range. **esprit de large ~** wide-ranging mind; **entreprise de grande ~** large-scale enterprise.

envers[1] [ɑ̃vɛʀ] *prép* towards, to. **cruel/traître ~ qn** cruel/a traitor to sb; **~ et contre tous** in the face of *ou* despite all opposition.

envers[2] [ɑ̃vɛʀ] *nm* **(a)** *[étoffe]* wrong side; *[vêtement]* wrong side, inside; *[papier]* back; *[médaille]* reverse (side); *[feuille d'arbre]* underside; *[peau d'animal]* inside. **l'~ et l'endroit** the wrong (side) and the right side; *(fig)* **quand on connaît l'~ du décor** when you know what is going on underneath it all, when you know the other side of the picture.

(b) à l'~ *vêtement* inside out; *objet* (*à la verticale*) upside down, wrong side up; (*à l'horizontale*) the wrong way round, back to front; (*mouvement*) in the wrong way; **il a mis la maison à l'~*** he turned the house upside down *ou* inside out; *(fig)* **tout marche** *ou* **va à l'~** everything is haywire *ou* is upside down, things are all wrong; *(fig)* **faire qch à l'~** (*à rebours*) to do sth the wrong way round; (*mal*) to do sth all wrong; *(fig)* **elle avait la tête à l'~** her mind was in a whirl; *V* **monde.**

envi [ɑ̃vi] *adv*: **à l'~** (*littér*) enviously (*rare*); **imiter qn à l'~** to vie with one another in imitating sb; **plats appétissants à l'~** dishes each more appetizing *ou* mouth-watering than the last.

enviable [ɑ̃vjabl(ə)] *adj* enviable.

envie [ɑ̃vi] *nf* **(a) ~ de qch/de faire** (*désir de*) desire for sth/to do; (*grand désir de*) craving *ou* longing for sth/to do; (*besoin de*) need for sth/to do; **avoir ~ de** *objet, changement, ami* to want; (*sexuellement*) *personne* to desire, want; **avoir ~ de faire qch** to want to do sth, feel like doing sth; **j'ai ~ de ce livre, ce livre me fait ~** I want *ou* should like *ou* I fancy* that book; **avoir une ~ de chocolat** to have a craving *ou* longing for chocolate; **cette ~ de changement lui passa vite** he soon lost this desire *ou* craving *ou* longing for change; **j'ai ~ d'y aller** I feel like going, I should like to go; **il lui a pris l'~ d'y aller** he suddenly felt like *ou* fancied going there, he suddenly felt the urge to go there; **je vais lui faire passer l'~ de recommencer*** I'll make sure he won't feel like doing that again in a hurry*; **avoir bien/presque ~ de faire qch** to have a good *ou* great mind/half a mind to do sth; **j'ai ~ qu'il s'en aille** I would like him to go away, I wish he would go away; **avoir ~ de rire** to feel like laughing; **avoir ~ de vomir** to feel sick (*surtout Brit*) *ou* like vomiting; **cela lui a donné (l')~ de rire** it made him want to laugh; **avoir ~*** (*d'aller aux toilettes*) to want to go*; *V* **mourir.**

(b) (*convoitise*) envy. **mon bonheur lui fait ~** he envies my happiness, my happiness makes him envious (of me); **ça fait ~** it makes you envious; **regarder qch avec (un œil d')~, jeter des regards d'~ sur qch** to look enviously at sth, cast envious eyes on sth; **digne d'~** enviable.

(c) (*Anat*) (*sur la peau*) birthmark; (*autour des ongles*) hangnail.

envier [ɑ̃vje] (7) *vt personne, bonheur etc* to envy, be envious of. **je vous envie votre maison** I wish I had your house *ou* a house like yours, I'm envious of your house; **je vous envie (de pouvoir le faire)** I envy you *ou* I'm envious of you (being able to do it); **ce pays n'a rien à ~ au nôtre** (*il est plus riche, grand etc*) that country has no cause to be jealous of us; (*il est aussi retardé, pauvre etc*) that country is just as badly off as we are, there's nothing to choose between that country and ours.

envieusement [ɑ̃vjøzmɑ̃] *adv* enviously.

envieux, -euse [ɑ̃vjø, øz] *adj* envious. **faire des ~** to excite *ou* arouse envy.

environ [ɑ̃viʀɔ̃] **1** *adv* about, or thereabouts, or so. **c'est à 100 km ~ d'ici** it's about 100 km from here, it's 100 km or so from here; **il était ~ 3 heures** it was about 3 o'clock, it was 3 o'clock or thereabouts.

2 *nmpl*: **les ~s** the surroundings; **aux ~s de 3 heures** (round) about 3 o'clock, 3 o'clock or thereabouts; **aux ~s de 10 F** (round) about *ou* in the region of 10 francs, 10 francs or thereabouts *ou* or so; **aux ~s** *ou* **dans les ~s du château** in the vicinity of *ou* near (to) the castle.

environnant, e [ɑ̃viʀɔnɑ̃, ɑ̃t] *adj* surrounding.

environnement [ɑ̃viʀɔnmɑ̃] *nm* environment.

environner [ɑ̃viʀɔne] (1) *vt* to surround, encircle. **s'~ d'experts** to surround o.s. with experts.

envisager [ɑ̃vizaʒe] (3) *vt* **(a)** (*considérer*) to view, consider, contemplate. **il envisage l'avenir de manière pessimiste** he views *ou* considers *ou* contemplates the future with pessimism, he has a pessimistic view of the future.

(b) (*prévoir*) to envisage. **nous envisageons des transformations** we are thinking of *ou* envisaging changes; **nous n'avions pas envisagé cela** we hadn't counted on *ou* envisaged that.

(c) (*projeter*) **~ de faire** to be thinking of doing, consider *ou* contemplate doing.

envoi [ɑ̃vwa] *nm* **(a)** (*U: V* **envoyer**) sending (off); dispatching; shipment; remittance. **faire un ~ de vivres** to send (a consignment of) supplies; **faire un ~ de fonds** to remit cash; **~ contre remboursement** cash on delivery.

(b) (*colis*) parcel. **~ de bouteilles** consignment of bottles; **~ en nombre** large consignment.

(c) (*Littérat*) envoi.

envol [ɑ̃vɔl] *nm [oiseau]* taking flight *ou* wing; *[avion]* takeoff, taking off; *[âme, pensée]* soaring, flight. **prendre son ~** *[oiseau]* to take flight *ou* wing; *[pensée]* to soar, take off.

envolée [ɑ̃vɔle] *nf*: **~ oratoire/poétique** flight of oratory/poetry.

envoler (s') [ɑ̃vɔle] (1) *vpr [oiseau]* to fly away; *[avion]* to take off; *[chapeau]* to blow off, be blown off; *[feuille]* to blow *ou* float away; *[temps]* to fly (past *ou* by); *[espoirs]* to vanish (into thin air); (*: *disparaître*) *[portefeuille, personne]* to disappear *ou* vanish (into thin air).

envoûtement [ɑ̃vutmɑ̃] *nm* bewitchment.

envoûter [ɑ̃vute] (1) *vt* to bewitch, cast a spell on. **être envoûté par qn** to be under sb's spell.

envoyé, e [ɑ̃vwaje] (*ptp de* **envoyer**) **1** *adj remarque, réponse* well-aimed, sharp. **ça, c'est ~!** well said!, well done! **2** *nm,f* (*gén*) messenger; (*Pol*) envoy; (*Presse*) correspondent. (*Presse*) **notre ~ spécial** our special correspondent.

envoyer [ɑ̃vwaje] (8) **1** *vt* **(a)** (*expédier*) *colis, lettre* to send (off); *vœux, amitiés* to send; (*Comm*) *marchandises* to dispatch, send off; (*par bateau*) to ship; *argent* to send, remit (*Admin*). **~ sa démission** to send in *ou* give in one's resignation; **~ sa candidature** to send in one's *ou* an application; **n'envoyez pas d'argent par la poste** do not send money by post; **envoie-moi un mot** drop me a line*.

(b) *personne* (*gén*) to send; (*en vacances*) to send off; (*en commissions*) to send (off) (*chez, auprès de* to); (*en mission*) *émissaire, troupes* to dispatch, send out. **envoie le petit à l'épicerie/aux nouvelles** send the child to the grocer's/to see if there's any news; **ils l'avaient envoyé chez sa grand-mère pour les vacances** they had sent him (off) *ou* packed him off* to his grandmother's for the holidays; *(fig)* **~ qn à la mort** to send sb to his death; **~ qn dans l'autre monde** to dispatch sb, dispose of sb.

(c) (*lancer*) *pierre* to throw, fling; (*avec force*) to hurl; *obus* to fire; *signaux* to send (out); (*Sport*) *ballon* to send. **~ des baisers à qn** to blow sb kisses; **~ des sourires à qn** to smile at sb, give sb smiles; **~ des œillades à qn** to ogle (at) sb, make eyes at sb; **~ des coups de pied/poing à qn** to kick/punch sb; **ne m'envoie pas ta fumée dans les yeux** don't blow (your) smoke in(to) my eyes; **il le lui a envoyé dans les dents‡** *ou* **les gencives‡** he really let him have it!*; **~ balader une balle sous le buffet*** to send a ball flying under the sideboard; (*Ftbl*) **~ le ballon au fond des filets** to put *ou* send the ball into the back of the net; **~ qn à terre** *ou* **au tapis** to knock sb down, knock sb to the ground; **~ un homme sur la lune** to send a man to the moon; (*Naut*) **~ par le fond** to send down *ou* to the bottom.

(d) (*Mil*) **~ les couleurs** to run up *ou* hoist the colours.

(e) (*loc*) **~ chercher qn/qch** to send for sb/sth; **~ promener qn*** *ou* **balader qn*, ~ qn coucher*, ~ qn sur les roses*** to send sb packing*, send sb about his business; **~ valser** *ou* **dinguer qch*** to send sth flying*; **il a tout envoyé promener*** he has chucked (up) everything‡, he has chucked the whole thing up‡; **il ne le lui a pas envoyé dire*** he gave it to him straight*, he told him straight to his face.

2 s'envoyer‡ *vpr* (*subir, prendre*) *corvée* to get stuck* *ou* landed* with; *bouteille* to knock back*; *nourriture* to scoff*. **je m'enverrais des gifles*** I could kick myself*; **s'~ une fille**✱ to have it off with a girl‡ (*Brit*), make it with a girl‡; **s'~ en l'air**✱ to have it off‡ (*Brit*), have it‡.

envoyeur, -euse [ɑ̃vwajœʀ, øz] *nm,f* sender; *V* **retour.**

enzyme [ɑ̃zim] *nm* enzyme.

éolien, -ienne [eɔljɛ̃, jɛn] **1** *adj* wind (*épith*), aeolian (*rare*); *V* **harpe. 2 éolienne** *nf* windmill, windpump.

épagneul, e [epaɲœl] *nm,f* spaniel.

épais, -aisse [epɛ, ɛs] **1** *adj* **(a)** (*gén*) *chevelure, peinture* thick; *neige* thick, deep; *barbe* bushy, thick; *silence* deep; *personne, corps* thickset; *nuit* pitch-black. **cloison ~se de 5 cm** partition 5 cm thick; **j'ai la langue ~se** my tongue is furred up *ou* coated; **au plus ~ de la forêt** in the thick *ou* the depths of the forest.

(b) (*péj: inhabile*) *esprit* dull; *personne* dense, thick(headed); *mensonge, plaisanterie* clumsy.

2 *adv*: **semer ~** to sow thick *ou* thickly; **il n'y en a pas ~!‡** there's not much of it!

épaisseur [epɛsœʀ] *nf* (*gén*) thickness; *[neige, silence]* depth; (*péj*) *[esprit]* dullness. **la neige a un mètre d'~** there is a metre of snow, the snow is a metre deep; **prenez deux ~s de tissu** take two thicknesses *ou* a double thickness of material; **dans l'~ de la nuit** in the depths of the night.

épaissir [epesiʀ] (2) **1** *vt substance* to thicken; *mystère* to deepen. **l'air était épaissi par les fumées** the air was thick with smoke; **l'âge lui épaissit les traits** his features are becoming coarse with age; **ce manteau m'épaissit beaucoup** this coat makes me look much broader *ou* fatter.

2 *vi* to get thicker, thicken. **il a beaucoup épaissi** he has thickened out a lot.

3 s'épaissir *vpr [substance]* to thicken, get thicker; *[chevelure, feuillage]* to get thicker; *[brouillard]* to thicken; *[ténèbres]* to deepen. **sa taille s'épaissit** his waist is getting thicker, he's getting stouter around the waist; **le mystère s'épaissit** the mystery deepens, the plot thickens.

épaississement [epesismɑ̃] *nm* thickening.

épanchement [epɑ̃ʃmɑ̃] *nm [sang]* effusion; *[sentiments]* outpouring. (*Méd*) **~ de synovie** water on the knee.

épancher [epɑ̃ʃe] (1) **1** *vt sentiments* (*irrités*) to give vent to, vent; (*tendres*) to pour forth. **2 s'épancher** *vpr [personne]* to open one's heart, pour out one's feelings; *[sang]* to pour out.

épandage [epɑ̃daʒ] *nm* (*Agr*) manure spreading, manuring.

épandre [epɑ̃dʀ(ə)] (41) **1** *vt* (†, *littér*) *liquide, tendresse* to pour forth (*littér*); (*Agr*) *fumier* to spread. **2 s'épandre** *vpr* (*littér*) to spread.

épanoui, e [epanwi] (*ptp de* **épanouir**) *adj fleur* in full bloom (*attrib*), full *ou* right out (*attrib*); *visage, sourire* radiant, beaming (*épith*); *corps, femme* in full bloom (*attrib*).

épanouir [epanwiʀ] (2) **1** *vt* (*littér*) *fleur* to open out; *branches, pétales* to open *ou* spread out; *visage* to light up.

2 s'épanouir *vpr [fleur]* to bloom, come out, open up *ou* out; *[visage]* to light up; *[personne]* (*physiquement*) to blossom (out), bloom; (*moralement*) to come out, open up; *[vase etc]* to open out, curve outwards. **à cette nouvelle il s'épanouit** his face lit up at the news.

épanouissement [epanwismɑ̃] *nm* (*V* **s'épanouir**) blooming; opening out; lighting up; blossoming (out); coming out; opening up.

épargnant, e [epaʀɲɑ̃, ɑ̃t] *nm,f* saver, investor.

épargne [epaʀɲ(ə)] *nf* (*somme*) savings. (*vertu*) **l'~** saving; **~ de temps/d'argent** saving of time/money; *V* **caisse.**

épargner [epaʀɲe] (1) *vt* **(a)** (*économiser*) *argent, nourriture, temps* to save. **~ 10 F sur une somme** to save 10 francs out of a sum; **~ sur la nourriture** to save *ou* make a saving on food; **ils n'ont pas épargné le poivre!*** they haven't stinted on *ou* spared the pepper!; **~ pour ses vieux jours** to save (up) for one's old age, put something aside for one's old age; **je n'épargnerai rien pour le faire** I'll spare nothing to get it done.

(b) (*éviter*) **~ qch à qn** to spare sb sth; **pour t'~ des explications inutiles** to save giving you *ou* to spare you useless explanations; **~ à qn la honte/le spectacle de** to spare sb the shame/the sight of; **pour m'~ la peine de venir** to save *ou* spare myself the bother of coming.

(c) (*ménager*) *ennemi etc* to spare. **l'épidémie a épargné cette région** that region was spared the epidemic.

éparpillement [epaʀpijmɑ̃] *nm* (*action: V* **éparpiller**) scattering; dispersal; distribution; dissipation; (*état*) *[troupes, succursales]* dispersal. **l'~ des maisons rendait les communications très difficiles** the houses being so scattered made communications difficult.

éparpiller [epaʀpije] (1) **1** *vt objets* to scatter; *troupes* to disperse; *points de vente* to distribute, scatter; *efforts, talent* to dissipate.

2 s'éparpiller *vpr* (*gén*) to scatter. **maisons qui s'éparpillent dans la campagne** houses that are dotted about the countryside; **c'est un homme qui s'éparpille beaucoup trop** he's a man who dissipates his efforts too much, he's a man who has too many strings to his bow (*Brit*), he spreads himself too thin (*US*).

épars, e [epaʀ, aʀs(ə)] *adj* (*littér*) scattered.

épatamment*† [epatamɑ̃] *adv* capitally*† (*Brit*), splendidly*.

épatant, e*† [epatɑ̃, ɑ̃t] *adj* splendid*, capital*† (*Brit*).

épate [epat] *nf*: **l'~** showing off*; **faire de l'~** to show off*.

épaté, e [epate] (*ptp de* **épater**) *adj vase etc* flat-bottomed; *nez* flat.

épatement [epatmɑ̃] *nm* **(a)** *[nez]* flatness. **(b)** (*) amazement.

épater [epate] (1) **1** *vt* (*) (*étonner*) to amaze, stagger*; (*impressionner*) to impress. **pour ~ le bourgeois** to shake *ou* shock middle-class attitudes; **pour ~ la galerie** to impress people, create a sensation; **ça t'épate, hein!** how about that!*, what do you think of that!

2 s'épater *vpr [objet, colonne]* to spread out.

épaule [epol] *nf* (*Anat, Culin*) shoulder. **large d'~s** broad-shouldered; **~ d'agneau** shoulder of lamb; *V* **changer, hausser, tête.**

épaulé-jeté, *pl* **épaulés-jetés** [epoleʒ(ə)te] *nm* clean and jerk.

épaulement [epolmɑ̃] *nm* (*mur*) retaining wall; (*rempart*) breastwork, epaulement; (*Géol*) escarpment.

épauler [epole] (1) *vt* **(a)** *personne* to back up, support. **il faut s'~ dans la vie** people must help *ou* support each other in life. **(b)** *fusil* to raise (to the shoulder). **il épaula puis tira** he took aim and fired. **(c)** (*Tech*) *mur* to support, retain.

épaulette [epolɛt] *nf* (*Mil*) epaulette; (*bretelle*) shoulder strap; (*rembourrage d'un vêtement*) shoulder pad.

épave [epav] *nf* **(a)** (*navire*) wreck; (*débris*) piece of wreckage, wreckage (*U*); (*déchets*) flotsam (and jetsam) (*U*).

(b) (*Jur: objet perdu*) derelict.

(c) (*fig*) (*restes*) ruin; (*loque humaine*) human wreck. **des ~s d'une civilisation autrefois florissante** ruins of a once-flourishing civilization.

épée [epe] *nf* **(a)** sword. **~ de Damoclès** sword of Damocles; **l'~ nue** *ou* **à la main** with drawn sword; *V* **cape, noblesse** *etc.* **(b)** (†: *escrimeur*) swordsman. **bonne ~** good swordsman.

épéiste [epeist(ə)] *nm* swordsman.

épeler [eple] (4 *ou* 5) *vt mot* to spell; *texte* to spell out.

éperdu, e [epɛʀdy] *adj* **(a)** *personne* distraught, overcome. **~ (de douleur/de terreur)** distraught *ou* frantic *ou* out of one's mind with grief/terror; **~ (de joie)** overcome *ou* beside o.s. with joy. **(b)** *gratitude* boundless; *regard* wild, distraught; *amour* passionate; *fuite* headlong, frantic. **désir/besoin ~ de bonheur** frantic desire for/need of happiness.

éperdument [epɛʀdymɑ̃] *adv crier, travailler* frantically, desperately; *aimer* passionately, madly. **je m'en moque ~** I couldn't care less.

éperlan [epɛʀlɑ̃] *nm* (*Zool*) smelt.

éperon [epʀɔ̃] *nm [cavalier, coq, montagne]* spur; (*Naut*) *[galère]* ram; *[pont]* cutwater.

éperonner [epʀɔne] (1) *vt cheval* to spur (on); *navire* to ram; (*fig*) *personne* to spur on. **botté et éperonné** booted and spurred, wearing boots and spurs.

épervier [epɛʀvje] *nm* **(a)** (*Orn*) sparrowhawk. **(b)** (*filet*) cast(ing) net.

éphèbe [efɛb] *nm* (*Hist*) ephebe; (*iro, péj*) beautiful young man.

éphémère [efemɛʀ] **1** *adj bonheur, succès* ephemeral, fleeting, short-lived; *moment* fleeting, short-lived; *publication* short-lived. **2** *nm* mayfly, ephemera (*T*).

éphéméride [efemeʀid] *nf* **(a)** (*calendrier*) block calendar, tear-off calendar. **(b)** (*Astron: tables*) **~s** ephemeris (*sg*).

Éphèse [efɛz] *n* Ephesus.

épi [epi] **1** *nm* **(a)** *[blé, maïs]* ear; *[fleur]* spike; *[cheveux]* tuft. **les blés sont en ~s** the corn is in the ear. **(b)** (*jetée*) groin, groyne.

2: épi de faîtage finial.

épice [epis] *nf* spice; *V* **pain.**

épicé, e [epise] (*ptp de* **épicer**) *adj viande, plat* highly spiced, spicy; *goût* spicy; (*fig*) *histoire* spicy, juicy*.

épicéa [episea] *nm* spruce.

épicentre [episɑ̃tʀ(ə)] *nm* epicentre.

épicer [epise] (3) *vt* to spice; (*fig*) to add spice to.

épicerie [episʀi] *nf* (*V* **épicier**) (*magasin*) grocer's (shop), greengrocer's (shop) (*Brit*); (*nourriture*) groceries, greengroceries (*Brit*); (*métier*) grocery trade, greengrocery trade (*Brit*). **aller à l'~** to go to the grocer's *ou* grocery; **~ fine** ≈ delicatessen.

épicier, -ière [episje, jɛʀ] *nm,f* (*Comm*) (*gén*) grocer; (*en fruits et légumes*) greengrocer (*Brit*). (*fig, péj*) **d'~** *idées, mentalité* small-town, parochial.

Épicure [epikyʀ] *nm* Epicurus.

épicurien, -ienne [epikyʀjɛ̃, jɛn] *adj, nm,f* epicurean.

épicurisme [epikyʀism(ə)] *nm* epicureanism.

épidémie [epidemi] *nf* epidemic.

épidémiologie [epidemjɔlɔʒi] *nf* epidemiology.

épidémiologique [epidemjɔlɔʒik] *adj* epidemiological.

épidémique [epidemik] *adj* (*lit*) epidemic; (*fig*) contagious, catching (*attrib*).

épiderme [epidɛʀm(ə)] *nm* epidermis (*T*), skin. **elle a l'~ délicat** she has a delicate skin.

épidermique [epidɛʀmik] *adj* **(a)** (*Anat*) skin (*épith*), epidermal (*T*), epidermic (*T*). **blessure ~** (surface) scratch. **(b)** (*fig*) **ce sujet provoque en lui une réaction ~** he always has the same immediate reaction to that subject.

épier [epje] (7) *vt personne* to spy on; *geste* to watch closely; *bruit* to listen out for; *occasion* to be on the look-out for, look (out) for, watch for.

épieu††, *pl* **~x** [epjø] *nm* (*Mil*) pike; (*Chasse*) hunting-spear.

épigastre [epigastʀ(ə)] *nm* epigastrium.

épiglotte [epiglɔt] *nf* epiglottis.

épigone [epigɔn] *nm* (*Littérat*) epigone.

épigramme [epigʀam] *nf* epigram.

épigraphe [epigʀaf] *nf* epigraph. **mettre un vers en ~** to use a line as an epigraph.

épigraphique [epigʀafik] *adj* epigraphic.

épilation [epilɑsjɔ̃] *nf* removal of (unwanted) hair.

épilatoire [epilatwaʀ] *adj* depilatory, hair-removing (*épith*).

épilepsie [epilɛpsi] *nf* epilepsy.

épileptique [epilɛptik] *adj* epileptic.

épiler [epile] (1) *vt jambes* to remove the hair from; *sourcils* to pluck. **elle s'épilait les jambes** she was removing the hair(s) from her legs; **crème à ~** hair-removing *ou* depilatory cream.

épilogue [epilɔg] *nm* (*littér*) epilogue; (*fig*) conclusion, dénouement.

épiloguer [epilɔge] (1) *vi* (*parfois péj*) to hold forth (*sur* on), go on* (*sur* about), expatiate (*frm, hum*) (*sur* upon).

épinard [epinaʀ] *nm* (*Bot*) spinach. (*Culin*) **~s** spinach (*U*); *V* **beurre.**

épine [epin] *nf* **(a)** *[buisson]* thorn, prickle; *[hérisson, oursin]* spine, prickle; *[porc-épic]* quill. **~ dorsale** backbone; **vous m'enlevez une belle ~ du pied** you have got me out of a spot*.

(b) (*arbre*) thorn bush. **~ blanche** hawthorn; **~ noire** blackthorn.

épinette [epinɛt] *nf* **(a)** (*Mus*) spinet. **(b)** (*Can*) spruce. **~ blanche** white spruce; **~ noire** black spruce; **~ rouge** tamarack, hackmatack.

épinettière [epinɛtjɛʀ] *nf* (*Can*) spruce *ou* tamarack grove.

épineux, -euse [epinø, øz] *adj plante* thorny, prickly; *problème* thorny, tricky, ticklish; *situation* tricky, ticklish; *caractère* prickly, touchy.

épinglage [epɛ̃glaʒ] *nm* pinning.

épingle [epɛ̃gl(ə)] *nf* pin. **~ à chapeau** hatpin; **~ à cheveux** hairpin; **virage en ~ à cheveux** hairpin bend; **~ de cravate** tie-clip, tie-pin; **~ à linge** clothes peg (*Brit*) *ou* pin (*US*); **~ de nourrice** *ou* **de sûreté** safety pin, (*grand modèle*) nappy (*Brit*) *ou* diaper (*US*) pin; **tirer son ~ du jeu** to withdraw, pull out, extricate o.s.

épingler [epɛ̃gle] (1) *vt* **(a)** (*attacher*) to pin (on) (*à, sur* to). **~ ses cheveux** to pin up one's hair; (*Couture*) **~ une robe** to pin up a dress. **(b)** (**:** *arrêter*) to nick**:** (*Brit*), nab*. **se faire ~** to get nicked**:** (*Brit*) *ou* nabbed*.

épinoche [epinɔʃ] *nf* stickleback.

Épiphanie [epifani] *nf* Epiphany, Twelfth Night. **à l'~** at Epiphany, on *ou* at Twelfth Night.

épiphénomène [epifenɔmɛn] *nm* epiphenomenon.

épiphyse [epifiz] *nf* epiphysis.

épique [epik] *adj* (*lit, fig*) epic; (*hum*) epic, dramatic.

épiscopal, e, *mpl* **-aux** [episkɔpal, o] *adj* episcopal.

épiscopat [episkɔpa] *nm* bishopric, episcopate, episcopacy.

épisode [epizɔd] *nm* episode. **roman/film à ~s** serial, serialized novel/film.

épisodique [epizɔdik] *adj* **(a)** (*occasionnel*) *événement* occasional; *rôle* fleeting, transitory. **(b)** (*secondaire*) *événement* minor, of secondary importance; *personnage* minor, secondary.

épisodiquement [epizɔdikmɑ̃] *adv* (*V* **épisodique**) occasionally; fleetingly.

épissure [episyʀ] *nf* splice.

épistémologie [epistemɔlɔʒi] *nf* (*Philos*) epistemology; (*Sci*) epistemics (*sg*).

épistémologique [epistemɔlɔʒik] *adj* epistemological.

épistolaire [epistɔlɛʀ] *adj style* epistolary. **être en relations ~s avec qn** to correspond with sb, exchange letters *ou* correspondence with sb.

épistolier, -ière [epistɔlje, jɛʀ] *nm,f* (*littér*) letter writer.

épitaphe [epitaf] *nf* epitaph.
épithélial, e, *mpl* **-aux** [epiteljal, o] *adj* epithelial.
épithélium [epiteljɔm] *nm* epithelium.
épithète [epitɛt] *nf* **(a)** (*Gram*) attribute. **adjectif** ~ attributive adjective. **(b)** (*qualificatif*) epithet.
épître [epitʀ(ə)] *nf* epistle.
éploré, e [eplɔʀe] *adj* (*littér*) *visage* bathed in tears; *personne* tearful, weeping, in tears (*attrib*); *voix* tearful.
éployé, e [eplwaje] *adj* (*littér, Hér*) spread (out).
épluchage [eplyʃaʒ] *nm* (*V* **éplucher**) cleaning; peeling; unwrapping; dissection.
épluche-légume, *pl* **épluche-légumes** [eplyʃlegym] *nm* potato peeler.
éplucher [eplyʃe] (1) *vt* **(a)** *salade, radis* to clean; *fruits, légumes, crevettes* to peel; *bonbon* to unwrap. **(b)** *texte, comptes* to go over with a fine-tooth comb, dissect.
épluchette [eplyʃɛt] *nf* (*Can*) corn-husking bee *ou* party.
éplucheur, -euse [eplyʃœʀ, øz] *nm,f* (automatic potato) peeler; (*péj*) faultfinder.
épluchure [eplyʃyʀ] *nf*: ~ **de pomme de terre** *etc* (piece of) potato *etc* peeling; ~s peelings.
épointer [epwɛ̃te] (1) *vt aiguille etc* to blunt. **crayon épointé** blunt pencil.
éponge [epɔ̃ʒ] *nf* sponge. **passons l'~!** let's let bygones be bygones!, let's forget all about it!; **passons l'~ sur cette vieille querelle!** let's draw a veil over *ou* forget all about that old quarrel!; **boire comme une** ~ to drink like a fish; ~ **métallique** scouring pad, scourer.
éponger [epɔ̃ʒe] (3) *vt liquide* to mop *ou* sponge up; *plancher, visage, front* to mop; (*Fin*) *dette etc* to soak up, absorb.
épopée [epɔpe] *nf* (*lit, fig*) epic; (*Littérat*) epic.
époque [epɔk] *nf* **(a)** (*gén*) time. **j'étais jeune à l'~** I was young at the time.
(b) (*Hist*) age, era, epoch. **l'~ révolutionnaire** the revolutionary era *ou* age; **à l'~ des Grecs** at the time of *ou* in the age of the Greeks; **la Belle É~** the Belle Époque, ≃ the Edwardian Age *ou* Era; **meuble d'~** genuine antique, piece of period furniture.
(c) faire ~: **cette invention a fait** ~ it was an epoch-making invention.
(d) (*Géol*) period.
époumoner (s') [epumɔne] (1) *vpr* (*lit, fig*) to shout *etc* o.s. hoarse. **il s'époumonait à chanter** he was singing himself hoarse.
épousailles [epuzaj] *nfpl* († *ou hum*) nuptials († *ou hum*).
épouse [epuz] *nf* wife, spouse († *ou hum*).
épousée [epuze] *nf* († *ou dial*) bride.
épouser [epuze] (1) *vt* **(a)** *personne* to marry, wed†; *idée* to embrace, espouse (*frm*); *cause* to espouse (*frm*). ~ **une grosse fortune** to marry into money, marry a large fortune (*hum*); **il a épousé sa cousine** he was married to his cousin, he married his cousin.
(b) *[robe]* to fit; *[route, tracé]* to follow; (*étroitement*) to hug.
épouseur† [epuzœʀ] *nm* suitor†, wooer†.
époussetage [epustaʒ] *nm* dusting.
épousseter [epuste] (4) *vt* (*nettoyer*) to dust; (*enlever*) to dust *ou* flick off.
époustouflant, e* [epustuflɑ̃, ɑ̃t] *adj* staggering*, amazing.
époustoufler* [epustufle] (1) *vt* to stagger*, flabbergast.
épouvantable [epuvɑ̃tabl(ə)] *adj* terrible, appalling, dreadful.
épouvantablement [epuvɑ̃tabləmɑ̃] *adv* terribly, appallingly, dreadfully.
épouvantail [epuvɑ̃taj] *nm* **(a)** (*à oiseaux*) scarecrow. **(b)** (*fig: croquemitaine*) (*personne*) bog(e)y; (*chose*) bugbear. **(c)** (*laideron*) fright.
épouvante [epuvɑ̃t] *nf* terror, (great) fear. **saisi d'~** terror-stricken; **il voyait arriver ce moment avec** ~ with dread he saw the moment approaching; **roman/film d'~** horror story/film.
épouvanter [epuvɑ̃te] (1) *vt* to terrify, appal; (*sens affaibli*) to appal.
époux [epu] *nm* husband, spouse († *ou hum*). **les** ~ the (married) couple, the husband and wife.
éprendre (s') [epʀɑ̃dʀ(ə)] (58) *vpr* (*littér*) **s'~ de** to fall in love with, become enamoured of (*littér*).
épreuve [epʀœv] *nf* **(a)** (*essai*) test. ~ **de résistance** resistance test; **résister à l'~ (du temps)** to stand the test (of time); (*fig*) ~ **de force** test of strength; **mettre à l'~** to put to the test; (*Tech*) **faire l'~ d'un métal** to test a metal; *V* **rude.**
(b) (*malheur*) ordeal, trial, hardship. **subir de rudes** ~s to pass through terrible ordeals, suffer great hardships, undergo great trials.
(c) (*Scol*) test. **corriger les** ~**s d'un examen** to mark the examination papers.
(d) (*Sport*) event. ~ **de sélection** heat; ~ **contre la montre** time-trial.
(e) (*Typ*) proof. **première** ~ galley proof; **dernière** ~ final proof; **corriger les** ~**s d'un livre** to proofread a book, correct the proofs of a book.
(f) (*Phot*) print; (*gravure*) proof.
(g) (*Hist, initiatique*) ordeal. ~**s d'initiation** initiation ordeals *ou* rites; ~ **du feu** ordeal by fire.
(h) à l'~ de: gilet à l'~ des balles bulletproof vest; **il a un courage à toute** ~ he has unfailing courage, his courage is equal to anything.
épris, e [epʀi, iz] (*ptp de* **éprendre**) *adj* (*frm*) (*d'une femme*) smitten† (*de* with), enamoured (*de* of) (*littér*), in love (*de* with). ~ **de** *travail, idée* in love with, enamoured of (*littér*).
éprouvant, e [epʀuvɑ̃, ɑ̃t] *adj travail, climat* testing.
éprouvé, e [epʀuve] (*ptp de* **éprouver**) *adj* (*sûr*) *moyen, remède* well-tried, proven; *spécialiste, qualités* (well-)proven; *ami* staunch, tried, steadfast.
éprouver [epʀuve] (1) *vt* **(a)** (*ressentir*) *sensation, sentiment* to feel, experience.
(b) (*subir*) *perte* to suffer, sustain (*frm*); *difficultés* to meet with, experience.
(c) (*tester*) *métal* to test; *personne* to put to the test, test.
(d) (*frm: affliger*) to afflict, distress. **très éprouvé par la maladie** sorely afflicted by illness (*frm*).
éprouvette [epʀuvɛt] *nf* test tube; *V* **bébé.**
epsilon [ɛpsilɔn] *nm* epsilon.
épuisant, e [epɥizɑ̃, ɑ̃t] *adj* exhausting.
épuisé, e [epɥize] (*ptp de* **épuiser**) *adj personne, cheval, corps* exhausted, worn-out (*attrib*); *énergie* spent; (*Comm*) *article* sold out (*attrib*); *stocks* exhausted (*attrib*); *livre* out of print. ~ **de fatigue** exhausted, tired out, worn-out.
épuisement [epɥizmɑ̃] *nm* (*gén*) exhaustion. **devant l'~ de ses finances** seeing that his money was exhausted *ou* had run out; (*Comm*) **jusqu'à ~ des stocks** while stocks last; **jusqu'à l'~ du filon** until the vein is (*ou* was) worked out; **faire marcher qn jusqu'à (l')~** to make sb walk till he drops (with exhaustion); **dans un grand état d'~** in a completely *ou* an utterly exhausted state, in a state of complete *ou* utter exhaustion.
épuiser [epɥize] (1) **1** *vt personne* to exhaust, tire out, wear out; *terre, sujet* to exhaust; *réserves, munitions* to use up, exhaust; *filon* to work out; *patience* to wear out, exhaust.
2 s'épuiser *vpr [réserves]* to run out; *[source]* to dry up; *[personne]* to exhaust o.s., wear o.s. out, tire o.s. out (*à faire qch* doing sth). **les stocks s'étaient épuisés** the stocks had run out; **ses forces s'épuisent peu à peu** his strength is gradually failing; **je m'épuise à vous le répéter** I'm wearing myself out repeating this (to you).
épuisette [epɥizɛt] *nf* (*Pêche*) landing net; (*à crevettes*) shrimping net.
épurateur [epyʀatœʀ] *nm* (*Tech*) purifier.
épuration [epyʀɑsjɔ̃] *nf* (*V* **épurer**) purification; refinement, refining; purge, weeding out.
épure [epyʀ] *nf* working drawing.
épurer [epyʀe] (1) *vt eau, huile* to purify; *langue, goût* to refine; (*Pol: éliminer*) to purge, weed out.
équarrir [ekaʀiʀ] (2) *vt* **(a)** *pierre, tronc* to square (off). **poutre mal équarrie** rough-hewn beam. **(b)** *animal* to quarter.
équarrissage [ekaʀisaʒ] *nm* (*V* **équarrir**) squaring (off); quartering.
équarrisseur [ekaʀisœʀ] *nm* knacker (*Brit*).
équateur [ekwatœʀ] *nm* equator. **république de l'É~** Ecuador.
équation [ekwɑsjɔ̃] *nf* equation. ~ **du second degré** quadratic equation.
équatorial, e, *mpl* **-aux** [ekwatɔʀjal, o] *adj* equatorial.
équatorien, -ienne [ekwatɔʀjɛ̃, jɛn] **1** *adj* Ecuadorian. **2** *nm,f*: **É~(ne)** Ecuadorian.
équerre [ekɛʀ] *nf* (*pour tracer*) (set) square; (*de soutien*) brace. **double** ~ T-square; **en** ~ at right angles; **ce tableau n'est pas d'~** this picture isn't straight *ou* level.
équestre [ekɛstʀ(ə)] *adj* equestrian. **centre** ~ riding school.
équeuter [ekøte] (1) *vt cerises* to remove the stalk from, pull the stalk off; *fraises* to hull.
équidé [ekide] *nm* member of the horse family. **les** ~**s** the Equidae (*T*).
équidistance [ekɥidistɑ̃s] *nf* equidistance.
équidistant, e [ekɥidistɑ̃, ɑ̃t] *adj* equidistant.
équilatéral, e, *mpl* **-aux** [ekɥilateʀal, o] *adj* equilateral.
équilibrage [ekilibʀaʒ] *nm* (*Aut*) *[roues]* balancing.
équilibre [ekilibʀ(ə)] *nm* **(a)** (*gén*) *[corps, objet]* balance, equilibrium. **perdre/garder l'~** to lose/keep one's balance; **avoir le sens de l'~** to have a (good) sense of balance; **se tenir** *ou* être **en** ~ **(sur)** *[personne]* to balance (on); *[objet]* to be balanced (on); **mettre qch en** ~ to balance sth (*sur* on); **en** ~ **instable sur le bord du verre** precariously balanced on the edge of the glass; **exercice/tour d'~** balancing exercise/act.
(b) ~ **(mental)** (mental) equilibrium, (mental) stability; **il a su garder (tout) son** ~ he managed to remain quite level-headed; **il manque d'~** he is rather unstable.
(c) (*harmonie*) *[couple]* harmony; *[activités]* balance, equilibrium.
(d) (*Écon, Pol*) ~ **budgétaire/économique** balance in the budget/economy; **budget en** ~ balanced budget; ~ **des pouvoirs** balance of power; ~ **politique** political balance; **l'~ du monde** the world balance of power.
(e) (*Sci*) equilibrium.
(f) (*Archit, Mus, Peinture*) balance.
équilibré, e [ekilibʀe] (*ptp de* **équilibrer**) *adj personne* stable, well-balanced, level-headed; *esprit* well-balanced; *vie* well-regulated, regular. **mal** ~ unstable, unbalanced.
équilibrer [ekilibʀe] (1) *vt* **(a)** (*contrebalancer*) *forces, poids, poussée* to counterbalance. **les avantages et les inconvénients s'équilibrent** the advantages and the disadvantages are evenly balanced *ou* counterbalance each other.
(b) (*mettre en équilibre*) *balance* to equilibrate, balance; *charge, embarcation, avion* to balance; (*Archit, Art*) to balance.
(c) (*harmoniser*) *emploi du temps, budget, pouvoirs* to balance.
equilibriste [ekilibʀist(ə)] *nmf* (*funambule*) tightrope walker; (*fig: jongleur*) juggler.
équinoxe [ekinɔks(ə)] *nm* equinox. **marée d'~** equinoctial tide; ~ **de printemps/d'automne** spring/autumn equinox.
équipage [ekipaʒ] *nm* **(a)** (*Aviat*) (air)crew; (*Naut*) crew; *V* **homme, rôle.**
(b) (*: *attirail*) gear* (*U*).
(c) (†) *[seigneur, chevaux]* equipage†. ~ **à deux chevaux** car-

riage and pair; ~ **à quatre chevaux** carriage and four; **en grand** ~ in state, in great array.

(d) (*Tech*) equipment (*U*), gear (*U*).

équipe [ekip] *nf* **(a)** (*Sport, gén*) team; *[rameurs]* crew. **jeu** *ou* **sport d'**~ team game; **jouer en** *ou* **par** ~**s** to play in teams; **l'**~ **de France a donné le coup d'envoi** the French team *ou* side kicked off; *V* **esprit.**

(b) (*groupe*) team. ~ **de chercheurs** research team, team of researchers; ~ **de sauveteurs** *ou* **de secours** rescue party *ou* squad *ou* team; (*Ind*) **l'**~ **de jour/de 8 heures** the day/8 o'clock shift; **travailler en** *ou* **par** ~**s** to work in teams; (*sur un chantier*) to work in gangs; (*Ind*) to work in shifts; **travailler en** ~ to work as a team; **faire** ~ **avec** to team up with; *V* **chef**[1].

(c) (*, *parfois péj*) bunch*, crew*.

équipée [ekipe] *nf [prisonnier]* escape, flight; *[aventurier]* undertaking, venture; *[promeneur, écolier]* escapade, jaunt.

équipement [ekipmɑ̃] *nm* **(a)** (*U: V* **équiper**) equipment; fitting out; kitting out (*de* with).

(b) (*matériel*) equipment, kit. **l'**~ **complet du skieur** all skiing equipment, the complete skier's kit, 'everything for the skier'.

(c) (*aménagement*) equipment. **l'**~ **électrique d'une maison** the electrical fittings of a house; **l'**~ **hôtelier d'une région** the hotel facilities *ou* amenities of a region; **l'**~ **industriel d'une région** the industrial plant of a region.

équiper [ekipe] (1) *vt troupe* to equip; *local* to equip, fit out; *sportif* to equip, kit out, fit out (*de* with). ~ **industriellement une région** to bring industry into a region; ~ **une machine d'un dispositif de sécurité** to fit a machine out with a safety device; **s'**~ *[sportif]* to equip o.s., kit o.s. out, get o.s. kitted out.

équipier, -ière [ekipje, jɛʀ] *nm,f (Sport)* team member.

équitable [ekitabl(ə)] *adj partage, jugement* equitable, fair; *personne* impartial, fair(-minded).

équitablement [ekitabləmɑ̃] *adv* equitably, fairly.

équitation [ekitɑsjɔ̃] *nf* (horse-)riding, equitation (*frm*).

équité [ekite] *nf* equity.

équivalence [ekivalɑ̃s] *nf* equivalence. **à** ~ **de prix, ce produit est meilleur** for the equivalent *ou* same price this is the better product; (*Univ*) **diplômes admis en** ~ recognized foreign diplomas.

équivalent, e [ekivalɑ̃, ɑ̃t] **1** *adj* equivalent (*à* to). **ces solutions sont** ~**es** these solutions are equivalent; **à prix** ~**, ce produit est meilleur** for the same *ou* equivalent price this is the better product.

2 *nm* equivalent (*de* of). **vous ne trouverez l'**~ **nulle part** you won't find the *ou* its like anywhere.

équivaloir [ekivalwaʀ] (29) *vi* (*lit*) *[quantité etc]* to be equivalent (*à* to); (*fig*) *[effet etc]* to be equivalent (*à* to), amount (*à* to).

équivoque [ekivɔk] **1** *adj* (*ambigu*) equivocal, ambiguous; (*louche*) dubious, questionable. **2** *nf* (*ambiguïté*) equivocation, ambiguity; (*incertitude*) doubt; (*malentendu*) misunderstanding. **conduite sans** ~ unequivocal *ou* unambiguous behaviour.

érable [eʀabl(ə)] *nm* maple.

érablière [eʀablijɛʀ] *nf* maple grove.

éraflement [eʀɑfləmɑ̃] *nm* scratching.

érafler [eʀɑfle] (1) *vt* to scratch, graze.

éraflure [eʀɑflyʀ] *nf* scratch, graze.

éraillé, e [eʀɑje] (*ptp de* **érailler**) *adj voix* rasping, hoarse, croaking (*épith*).

éraillement [eʀɑjmɑ̃] *nm [voix]* hoarseness.

érailler [eʀɑje] (1) *vt voix* to make hoarse; (*rayer*) *surface* to scratch. **s'**~ **la voix** to make o.s. hoarse.

Érasme [eʀasm(ə)] *nm* Erasmus.

ère [ɛʀ] *nf* era. **avant notre** ~ B.C.; **en l'an 1600 de notre** ~ in the year of our Lord 1600, in the year 1600 A.D.

érectile [eʀɛktil] *adj* erectile.

érection [eʀɛksjɔ̃] *nf [monument]* erection, raising; (*Physiol*) erection; (*fig*) establishment, setting-up.

éreintant, e* [eʀɛ̃tɑ̃, ɑ̃t] *adj travail* exhausting, back-breaking.

éreintement* [eʀɛ̃tmɑ̃] *nm* (*épuisement*) exhaustion; (*critique*) savage attack (*de* on), slating* (*surtout Brit*), panning*.

éreinter [eʀɛ̃te] (1) *vt* **(a)** (*épuiser*) *animal* to exhaust; (*) *personne* to shatter*, wear out. **être éreinté*** to be shattered* *ou* all in* *ou* worn out; **s'**~ **à faire qch** to wear o.s. out doing sth.

(b) (*critiquer*) *auteur, œuvre* to pull to pieces, slate* (*Brit*), pan*.

érésipèle [eʀezipɛl] *nm* = **érysipèle.**

erg [ɛʀg] *nm* (*Géog, Phys*) erg.

ergot [ɛʀgo] *nm* **(a)** *[coq]* spur; *[chien]* dew-claw. (*fig*) **monter** *ou* **se dresser sur ses** ~**s** to get one's hackles up. **(b)** *[blé etc]* ergot. **(c)** (*Tech*) lug.

ergotage [ɛʀgɔtaʒ] *nm* quibbling (*U*), cavilling (*U*), petty argument.

ergoter [ɛʀgɔte] (1) *vi* to quibble (*sur* about), cavil (*sur* at).

ergoteur, -euse [ɛʀgɔtœʀ, øz] *nm,f* quibbler, hair-splitter*.

ériger [eʀiʒe] (3) *vt* (*frm*) *monument, bâtiment* to erect; *société etc* to set up, establish. ~ **ses habitudes en doctrine** to raise one's habits to the status of a doctrine; ~ **un criminel en héros** to set a criminal up as a hero; **il s'érige en maître** he sets himself up as a master.

ermitage [ɛʀmitaʒ] *nm* (*d'ermite*) hermitage; (*fig*) retreat.

ermite [ɛʀmit] *nm* hermit.

éroder [eʀɔde] (1) *vt* to erode.

érosif, -ive [eʀozif, iv] *adj* erosive.

érosion [eʀozjɔ̃] *nf* (*lit, fig*) erosion.

érotique [eʀɔtik] *adj* erotic.

érotiquement [eʀɔtikmɑ̃] *adv* erotically.

érotisme [eʀɔtism(ə)] *nm* eroticism.

errance [ɛʀɑ̃s] *nf* (*littér*) wandering, roaming.

errant, e [ɛʀɑ̃, ɑ̃t] **1** *adj* (*gén*) wandering. **chien** ~ stray dog; *V* **chevalier, juif. 2** *nm,f* (*littér*) wanderer, rover.

erratique [ɛʀatik] *adj* (*Géol, Méd*) erratic.

errements [ɛʀmɑ̃] *nmpl* (*littér*) erring ways, bad habits.

errer [ɛʀe] (1) *vi* (*littér*) **(a)** *[voyageur]* to wander, roam; *[regard]* to rove, roam, wander (*sur* over); *[pensée]* to wander, stray. **un sourire errait sur ses lèvres** a smile hovered on *ou* flitted across his lips. **(b)** (*rare: se tromper*) to err.

erreur [ɛʀœʀ] *nf* **(a)** (*gén*) mistake, error; (*Statistique*) error. ~ **matérielle** *ou* **d'écriture** clerical error; ~ **de calcul** mistake in calculation, miscalculation; ~ **de date** mistake in the date; **faire une** ~ **de date** to make a mistake in *ou* be mistaken about the date; ~ **d'impression,** ~ **typographique** misprint, typographical error; ~ **de sens** wrong meaning; ~ **de traduction** mistranslation; ~ **(de) tactique** tactical error; ~ **de fait/de jugement** error of fact/of judgment.

(b) (*loc*) **par suite d'une** ~ due to an error *ou* a mistake; **sauf** ~ unless I'm (very much) mistaken; **par** ~ by mistake; ~ **profonde!, grave** ~! that's (just) where you're (*ou* he's *etc*) wrong!, you are (*ou* he is *etc*) very much mistaken (there)!; **commettre** *ou* **faire une** ~ to make a mistake *ou* an error; **faire** ~**, tomber dans l'**~ to be wrong *ou* mistaken; **être dans l'**~ to be mistaken, be under a misapprehension *ou* delusion; **il y a** ~**, ce n'est pas lui** there's been a mistake *ou* there's some mistake — it isn't him; **ce serait une** ~ **de croire que ...** it would be a mistake *ou* be wrong to think that ..., you would be mistaken in thinking that ...; **l'**~ **est humaine** to err is human.

(c) (*dérèglements*) ~**s** errors, lapses; ~**s de jeunesse** errors of youth; **retomber dans les** ~**s du passé** to lapse (back) into bad habits.

(d) (*Jur*) ~ **judiciaire** miscarriage of justice.

erroné, e [ɛʀɔne] *adj* erroneous.

erronément [ɛʀɔnemɑ̃] *adv* erroneously.

ersatz [ɛʀzats] *nm* (*lit, fig*) ersatz, substitute. ~ **de café** ersatz coffee.

erse [ɛʀs(ə)] *nm* (*Ling*) Erse.

éructation [eʀyktɑsjɔ̃] *nf* (*frm*) eructation (*frm*).

éructer [eʀykte] (1) *vi* (*frm*) to eructate (*frm*).

érudit, e [eʀydi, it] **1** *adj* erudite, learned, scholarly. **2** *nm,f* erudite *ou* learned person, scholar.

érudition [eʀydisjɔ̃] *nf* erudition, scholarship.

éruptif, -ive [eʀyptif, iv] *adj* eruptive.

éruption [eʀypsjɔ̃] *nf* eruption. **entrer en** ~ to erupt.

érysipèle [eʀizipɛl] *nm* erysipelas.

ès [ɛs] *prép*: **licencié** ~ **lettres/sciences** ≈ Bachelor of Arts/Science; **docteur** ~ **lettres** ≈ Ph.D.

esbigner (s')‡† [ɛsbiɲe] (1) *vpr* to skedaddle*, clear off*.

esbroufe‡ [ɛsbʀuf] *nf*: **faire de l'**~ to shoot a line‡; **il essaie de nous la faire à l'**~ he's shooting us a line‡, he's bluffing.

esbroufeur, -euse‡ [ɛsbʀufœʀ, øz] *nm,f* hot air merchant‡.

escabeau, *pl* ~**x** [ɛskabo] *nm* (*tabouret*) (wooden) stool; (*échelle*) stepladder, pair of steps (*Brit*). **tu me prêtes ton** ~? may I borrow your steps (*Brit*)? *ou* your stepladder?

escadre [ɛskadʀ(ə)] *nf* (*Naut*) squadron; (*Aviat*) wing.

escadrille [ɛskadʀij] *nf* (*Aviat*) flight.

escadron [ɛskadʀɔ̃] *nm* (*Mil*) squadron; (*fig: bande*) bunch*, crowd.

escalade [ɛskalad] *nf* **(a)** (*action: V* **escalader**) climbing; scaling. **partir faire l'**~ **d'une montagne** to set off to climb a mountain. **(b)** (*sport*) **l'**~ (rock) climbing; **une belle** ~ a beautiful (rock-)climb. **(c)** (*Pol, gén: aggravation*) escalation.

escalader [ɛskalade] (1) *vt montagne* to climb; *mur* to climb, scale; (*Hist*) *forteresse* to scale.

escale [ɛskal] *nf* **(a)** (*endroit*) (*Naut*) port of call; (*Aviat*) stop. **faire** ~ **à** (*Naut*) to call at, put in at; (*Aviat*) to stop over at.

(b) (*temps d'arrêt*) (*Naut*) call; (*Aviat*) stop(over). **vol sans** ~ non-stop flight; **faire une** ~ **de 5 heures à Marseille** (*Naut*) to put in at Marseilles for 5 hours; (*Aviat*) to stop (over) at Marseilles for 5 hours; (*Aviat*) ~ **technique** refuelling stop.

escalier [ɛskalje] *nm* (*marches*) stairs; (*cage*) staircase, stairway. **dans l'**~ *ou* **les** ~**s** on the stairs; ~ **d'honneur** main staircase *ou* stairway, main stairs; ~ **de service** backstairs; ~ **mécanique** *ou* **roulant** escalator, moving staircase; ~ **en colimaçon** spiral staircase; ~ **de secours** emergency stairs, fire escape; *V* **dérobé, esprit.**

escalope [ɛskalɔp] *nf* escalope.

escamotable [ɛskamɔtabl(ə)] *adj train d'atterrissage, antenne* retractable; *lit, siège* collapsible, fold-away (*épith*); *escalier* fold-away (*épith*).

escamotage [ɛskamɔtaʒ] *nm* (*V* **escamoter**) conjuring away; evading; getting *ou* skirting round; dodging; skipping; filching*, pinching*; retraction.

escamoter [ɛskamɔte] (1) *vt* **(a)** (*faire disparaître*) *cartes etc* to conjure away.

(b) (*fig*) *difficulté* to evade, get round, skirt round; *question* to dodge, evade; *mot* to skip.

(c) (*: *voler*) *portefeuille* to filch*, pinch*.

(d) *train d'atterrissage* to retract.

escamoteur, -euse [ɛskamɔtœʀ, øz] *nm,f* (*prestidigitateur*) conjurer.

escampette* [ɛskɑ̃pɛt] *nf V* **poudre.**

escapade [ɛskapad] *nf [écolier]* **faire une** ~ to run away *ou* off, do a bunk‡ (*Brit*); **on a fait une petite** ~ **pour le week-end** we went off on a jaunt for the weekend.

escarbille [ɛskaʀbij] *nf* smut.

escarboucle [ɛskaʀbukl(ə)] *nf* (*pierre*) carbuncle.

escarcelle†† [ɛskaʀsɛl] *nf* moneybag.

escargot [ɛskaʀgo] *nm* snail. **avancer comme un** ~ *ou* **à une allure d'**~ to go at a snail's pace.

escargotière [ɛskaʀgɔtjɛʀ] *nf* (*parc*) snailery; (*plat*) snail-dish.
escarmouche [ɛskaʀmuʃ] *nf* (*lit, fig*) skirmish.
escarpé, e [ɛskaʀpe] *adj* steep.
escarpement [ɛskaʀpəmɑ̃] *nm* (*côte*) steep slope, escarpment (*T*); (*rare: raideur*) steepness. (*Géol*) ~ **de faille** fault scarp.
escarpin [ɛskaʀpɛ̃] *nm* flat(-heeled) shoe.
escarpolette† [ɛskaʀpɔlɛt] *nf* swing.
Escaut [ɛsko] *nm*: l'~ the Scheldt.
escient [esjɑ̃] *nm*: **à bon** ~ advisedly; **à mauvais** ~ ill-advisedly.
esclaffer (s') [ɛsklafe] (1) *vpr* (*frm, hum*) to burst out laughing, guffaw.
esclandre [ɛsklɑ̃dʀ(ə)] *nm* scene. **faire** *ou* **causer un** ~ to make a scene.
esclavage [ɛsklavaʒ] *nm* (*lit*) (*état*) slavery, bondage (*littér*); (*système, fig*) slavery. **réduire en** ~ to enslave.
esclavagisme [ɛsklavaʒism(ə)] *nm* proslavery.
esclavagiste [ɛsklavaʒist(ə)] **1** *adj* proslavery (*épith*). **états** ~**s** slave states. **2** *nmf* proslaver.
esclave [ɛsklav] *nm* slave (*de qn/qch* to sb/sth). ~ **de la mode** slave of fashion; **vie d'**~ slave's life, life of slavery; **être l'**~ **d'une habitude** to be a slave to habit; **devenir l'**~ **d'une femme** to become enslaved to a woman.
escogriffe [ɛskɔgʀif] *nm*: **(grand)** ~ (great) bean-pole*.
escomptable [ɛskɔ̃tabl(ə)] *adj* discountable.
escompte [ɛskɔ̃t] *nm* discount.
escompter [ɛskɔ̃te] (1) *vt* to discount; (*fig*) to expect, reckon upon, count on.
escopette† [ɛskɔpɛt] *nf* blunderbuss.
escorte [ɛskɔʀt(ə)] *nf* (*gén, Mil, Naut*) escort; (*suite*) escort, retinue. (*fig*) **(toute) une** ~ **de** a whole train *ou* suite of; **sous bonne** ~ under escort; **faire** ~ **à** to escort.
escorter [ɛskɔʀte] (1) *vt* to escort.
escorteur [ɛskɔʀtœʀ] *nm* escort (ship).
escouade [ɛskwad] *nf* (*Mil*) squad; *[ouvriers]* gang, squad; (*fig: groupe de gens*) group, squad.
escrime [ɛskʀim] *nf* fencing. **faire de l'**~ to fence.
escrimer (s')* [ɛskʀime] (1) *vpr*: **s'**~ **à faire qch** to wear *ou* knock* o.s. out doing sth; **s'**~ **sur qch** to struggle away at sth.
escrimeur, -euse [ɛskʀimœʀ, øz] *nm,f* (*Sport*) fencer.
escroc [ɛskʀo] *nm* swindler, con man:.
escroquer [ɛskʀɔke] (1) *vt* to swindle, con:. ~ **qch à qn** to swindle sb out of sth, swindle *ou* con: sth out of sb.
escroquerie [ɛskʀɔkʀi] *nf* (*gén*) swindle, swindling (*U*); (*Jur*) fraud.
Ésope [ezɔp] *nm* Aesop.
ésotérique [ezɔteʀik] *adj* esoteric.
ésotérisme [ezɔteʀism(ə)] *nm* esotericism.
espace [ɛspas] *nm* (*Art, Philos, Phys, Typ, gén*) space. (*Phys*) ~**-temps** space time; ~ **de temps** space of time, interval (of time); **avoir assez d'**~ **pour bouger/vivre** to have enough room to move/live; **manquer d'**~ to lack space, be short of space *ou* room, be cramped for space; **laisser de l'**~ **(entre)** to leave some space (between); **laisser un** ~ **(entre)** to leave a space *ou* gap (between); **en l'**~ **de 3 minutes** within the space of 3 minutes; ~ **parcouru** distance covered; ~**s verts** green spaces *ou* areas; ~ **vital** living space.
espacement [ɛspasmɑ̃] *nm* (*action*) spacing out; (*résultat*) spacing. **devant l'**~ **de ses visites** since his visits were (*ou* are *etc*) becoming more infrequent *ou* spaced out, in view of the increasing infrequency of his visits.
espacer [ɛspase] (3) **1** *vt objets* to space out; *visites* to space out, make less frequent. **2 s'espacer** *vpr [visites, symptômes]* to become less frequent.
espadon [ɛspadɔ̃] *nm* swordfish.
espadrille [ɛspadʀij] *nf* rope-soled sandal, espadrille.
Espagne [ɛspaɲ] *nf* Spain; *V* **château.**
espagnol, e [ɛspaɲɔl] **1** *adj* Spanish. **2** *nm* (*Ling*) Spanish. **3** *nm,f*: **E**~**(e)** Spaniard.
espagnolette [ɛspaɲɔlɛt] *nf* (window) catch (*as on a continental casement window*). **fenêtre fermée à l'**~ window half-shut (resting on the catch).
espalier [ɛspalje] *nm* espalier. **arbre en** ~ espalier (tree).
espar [ɛspaʀ] *nm* (*Naut*) spar.
espèce [ɛspɛs] *nf* **(a)** (*Bio*) species. ~**s** species; ~ **humaine** human race; *V* **propagation.**
(b) (*sorte*) sort, kind, type. **de toute** ~ of all kinds *ou* sorts *ou* types; **ça n'a aucune** ~ **d'importance** that is of absolutely no importance *ou* not of the slightest importance; **c'était une** ~ **d'église** it was a kind *ou* sort of church; **formant des** ~**s de guirlandes** making (up) sort of* *ou* kind of* festoons, making (up) something resembling *ou* like festoons; **un voyou de la plus belle** ~ *ou* **de la pire** ~ a hoodlum of the worst kind *ou* sort.
(c) (*péj*) ~ **de: c'était une** ~ **d'église** it was some sort of church; **une** *ou* **un** ~ **d'excentrique est venu*** some eccentric turned up; **qu'est-ce que c'est que cette** *ou* **cet** ~ **de crétin?*** who's this stupid twit?: (*Brit*) *ou* idiot?; ~ **de maladroit!** you clumsy clot!* *ou* oaf!*
(d) (*Fin*) ~**s** cash; **versement en** ~**s** payment in cash *ou* in specie (*T*); (†, *hum*) **en** ~**s sonnantes et trébuchantes** in coin of the realm (*hum*).
(e) (*Philos, Rel*) species. **les Saintes** ~**s** the Eucharistic *ou* sacred species.
(f) (*frm, littér*) **en l'**~ in the case in point; *V* **cas.**
espérance [ɛspeʀɑ̃s] *nf* **(a)** (*espoir*) hope, expectation(s). (*Rel, gén*) **l'**~ hope; **dans** *ou* **avec l'**~ **de vous voir bientôt** hoping to see you soon, in the hope of seeing you soon; **contre toute** ~ against all expectations *ou* hope, contrary to expectation(s); ~**s trompeuses** false hopes; **donner de grandes** ~**s** to be very promising, show great promise; **avoir de grandes** ~**s** to have great prospects; **les plus belles** ~**s lui sont ouvertes** he has excellent prospects; **bâtir** *ou* **fonder des** ~**s sur** to build *ou* found one's hopes on; **mettre son** ~ *ou* **ses** ~**s en** *ou* **dans** to put one's hopes in, pin one's hopes on; **avoir l'**~ **de pouvoir ...** to be hopeful that one will be able to ... *ou* of being able to ...; **garder l'**~ **de pouvoir ...** to remain hopeful of being able to ... *ou* that one will be able to ..., hold on to the hope of being able to ... .
(b) (*sujet d'espoir*) hope. **c'est là toute mon** ~ that is my greatest hope, it's what I hope for most; **vous êtes toute mon** ~ you are my only hope.
(c) (*Sociol*) ~ **de vie** life expectancy, expectation of life.
(d) († *ou hum: financières*) ~**s** expectations; **il a de belles** ~**s du côté de sa tante** he has great expectations of an inheritance from his aunt († *ou hum*).
espérantiste [ɛspeʀɑ̃tist(ə)] *adj, nmf* Esperantist.
espéranto [ɛspeʀɑ̃to] *nm* Esperanto.
espérer [ɛspeʀe] (6) **1** *vt* (*souhaiter*) *succès, récompense, aide* to hope for. ~ **réussir** to hope to succeed; ~ **que** to hope that; **nous ne vous espérions plus** we'd given up (all) hope of seeing you *ou* of your coming; **je n'en espérais pas tant** I wasn't hoping *ou* I hadn't dared to hope for as much; **viendra-t-il? — je l'espère (bien)** *ou* **j'espère (bien)** will he come? — I (certainly) hope so; **ceci (nous) laisse** *ou* **fait** ~ **un succès rapide** this gives us hope of quick success *ou* allows us to hope for quick success; **n'espérez pas qu'il change d'avis** there is no point in hoping he'll change his mind; **j'espère bien n'avoir rien oublié** I hope I haven't forgotten anything.
2 *vi* (*avoir confiance*) to have faith. **il faut** ~ you must have faith; ~ **en** *Dieu, honnêteté de qn, bienfaiteur* to trust in.
espiègle [ɛspjɛgl(ə)] **1** *adj enfant* mischievous, impish; *air* roguish, mischievous. **2** *nmf* imp, monkey.
espièglerie [ɛspjɛgləʀi] *nf* **(a)** (*U: V* **espiègle**) mischievousness; impishness; roguishness. **(b)** (*tour*) piece of mischief, prank, monkey trick (*surtout Brit*).
espion, -onne [ɛspjɔ̃, ɔn] *nm,f* spy.
espionnage [ɛspjɔnaʒ] *nm* espionage, spying. **film/roman d'**~ spy film/novel *ou* thriller.
espionner [ɛspjɔne] (1) *vt personne, actions* to spy (up)on, keep a close watch on.
esplanade [ɛsplanad] *nf* esplanade.
espoir [ɛspwaʀ] *nm* **(a)** (*espérance*) hope. ~**s chimériques** wild hopes; **dans l'**~ **de vous voir bientôt** hoping to see *ou* in the hope of seeing you soon; **avoir l'**~**/le ferme** ~ **que** to be hopeful/very hopeful that; **il n'y a plus d'**~ **(de faire)** all hope is lost *ou* there's no longer any hope (of doing); **avoir bon** ~ **de faire/que** to have great hopes of doing/that, be confident of doing/that; **reprendre** ~ to (begin to) feel hopeful again, take heart once more; **sans** ~ *amour, situation* hopeless; **aimer sans** ~ to love without hope; *V* **lueur, rayon.**
(b) (*sujet d'espérance*) hope. **vous êtes mon dernier** ~ you are my last hope; **les jeunes** ~**s du ski/de la chanson** the young hopefuls of the skiing/singing world; **un des grands** ~**s de la boxe française** one of the great hopes in French boxing, one of France's great boxing hopes.
esprit [ɛspʀi] **1** *nm* **(a)** (*gén: pensée*) mind. **l'**~ **humain** the mind of man, the human mind *ou* intellect; **se reporter en** ~ *ou* **par l'**~ **à** to cast one's mind back to; **avoir l'**~ **libre** to have an open mind, be open-minded; **avoir l'**~ **large/étroit** to be broad-/narrow-minded; **avoir l'**~ **vif** to be quick-witted, have a lively mind; **à l'**~ **lent** slow-witted, slow-minded; **vivacité/lenteur d'**~ quickness/slowness of mind; **avoir l'**~ **clair** to have a clear head *ou* mind; **avoir l'**~ **mal tourné** to have a dirty mind; **il a l'**~ **ailleurs** his mind is elsewhere; **où ai-je l'**~? I'm miles away!, what am I thinking of?; **il n'a pas l'**~ **à ce qu'il fait** his mind is not on what he's doing; **dans mon** ~ **ça voulait dire** to my mind it meant; (*hum*) **l'**~ **est fort, mais la chair est faible** the spirit is willing but the flesh is weak; **il m'est venu à l'**~ **que** it crossed my mind that, it occurred to me that; (*Prov*) **un** ~ **sain dans un corps sain** mens sana in corpore sano, a sound mind in a healthy body; *V* **disposition, état, faible** *etc.*
(b) (*humour*) wit. **avoir de l'**~ to be witty; **faire de l'**~ to try to be witty *ou* funny; **manquer d'**~ to lack sparkle *ou* wit; *V* **femme, mot, trait** *etc.*
(c) (*être humain*) **son pouvoir sur les** ~**s/jeunes** ~**s** his power over people's minds/young minds *ou* people/young people; **c'est un** ~ **subtil** he is a shrewd man, he has a shrewd mind; **un de nos plus grands** ~**s** one of our greatest minds; *V* **beau, mauvais.**
(d) (*Rel, Spiritisme*) spirit. ~**, es-tu là?** is (there) anybody there?
(e) *[loi, époque, texte]* spirit.
(f) (*aptitude*) **avoir l'**~ **mathématique/d'analyse/d'entreprise** to have a mathematical/an analytical/an enterprising mind; **avoir l'**~ **des affaires** to have a good head for business; **avoir l'**~ **critique** to be critical, take a critical attitude; **avoir l'**~ **de critique** to like criticizing for its own sake; **avoir le bon** ~ **de** to have enough sense to, have the (good) sense to.
(g) (*attitude*) spirit. **l'**~ **de cette classe** *ou* **qui règne dans cette classe me déplaît** I do not like the (general) attitude of this class; ~ **de clan** clannishness; ~ **de chapelle** cliquishness; ~ **de révolte/sacrifice** spirit of rebellion/sacrifice; ~ **de compétition** competitive spirit; **dans un** ~ **de conciliation** in a spirit of conciliation; **faire preuve de mauvais** ~ to be a disruptive *ou* disturbing influence; **sans** ~ **de retour** wholeheartedly.
2: (*Méd*) **esprits animaux**† animal spirits; **esprit d'à-propos** ready wit; **esprit de caste** class consciousness; (*péj*) **esprits chagrins** faultfinders; **esprit de clocher** parochialism; **esprit de contradiction** argumentativeness; **esprit de corps** esprit de corps; **esprit d'équipe** team spirit; **esprit d'escalier: avoir l'es-**

prit d'escalier to be slow on the repartee, have a plodding mind; **esprit de famille** family feeling; (*péj*) clannishness; (*péj*) **esprit fort** dogmatic crank (*péj*); **esprit frappeur** spirit-rapper; **l'esprit malin** *ou* **du mal** the Evil spirit, the Evil one; (*Rel*) **l'Esprit Saint** the Holy Spirit *ou* Ghost; **esprit-de-sel** spirits of salt; **esprit de suite** consistency (*of thought*); **esprit de système** methodical *ou* systematic mind; **esprit-de-vin** spirits of wine.

esquif [ɛskif] *nm* (*littér*) skiff. **frêle ~** frail barque (*littér*).

esquille [ɛskij] *nf* splinter (of bone).

esquimau, -aude, *mpl* **~x** [ɛskimo, od] **1** *adj* Eskimo. **chien ~** husky. **2** *nm* (*Ling*) Eskimo; (*glace*) choc-ice; (*chien*) husky. **3** *nm,f*: **E~(de)** Eskimo.

esquintant, e: [ɛskɛ̃tɑ̃, ɑ̃t] *adj* exhausting. **un travail ~** an exhausting job, a job that (really) takes it out of you*.

esquinter* [ɛskɛ̃te] (1) **1** *vt* **(a)** (*abîmer*) *objet* to mess up*; *yeux, santé* to do in*, ruin; *adversaire* to beat up, bash up*; *voiture* to smash up. **se faire ~ par une voiture** *[automobiliste]* to have *ou* get one's car bashed* *ou* smashed into by another; *[cycliste, piéton]* to get badly bashed up* by a car.

(b) (*critiquer*) *film, livre* to pull to pieces, slate* (*Brit*), pan*.

2 s'esquinter *vpr* to tire *ou* knock* o.s. out. **s'~ à travailler** to work o.s. to death, work o.s. into the ground; **s'~ à étudier** to beat one's brains out* (studying), work o.s. into the ground studying.

esquisse [ɛskis] *nf* (*Peinture*) sketch; (*fig*) *[projet, atmosphère]* outline, sketch; *[geste, sourire]* beginnings, suggestion.

esquisser [ɛskise] (1) *vt* (*Peinture*) to sketch (out); (*fig*) *atmosphère* to sketch out, outline. **~ un geste** to make the merest suggestion of a gesture, half-make a gesture; **un certain progrès commence à s'~** one can begin to detect some progress.

esquive [ɛskiv] *nf* (*Boxe*) dodge; (*fig: en politique etc*) side-stepping (*U*). (*fig*) **passé maître dans l'art de l'~** past master in the art of sidestepping *ou* dodging his opponents *ou* the issue.

esquiver [ɛskive] (1) **1** *vt coup* to dodge; *obligation* to shirk, dodge; *question* to dodge, evade; *difficulté* to evade, get round, skirt round; *personne* to evade, elude, dodge. **2 s'esquiver** *vpr* to slip *ou* sneak away

essai [esɛ] *nm* **(a)** (*mise à l'épreuve*) *[produit]* testing; *[voiture]* trying out; testing. (*Aut*) **~s** trials; **~s de résistance** resistance tests; **venez faire l'~ de notre nouveau modèle** come and test drive *ou* try (out) our new model; **prendre qn à l'~** to take sb on for a trial period *ou* on a trial basis; **mettre à l'~** to test (out), put to the test; *V* **balance, banc, bout** *etc.*

(b) (*première utilisation*) **l'~ de ce produit n'a pas été convaincant** this product didn't prove very satisfactory when it was tried out; **faire l'~ d'un produit** to try out a product.

(c) (*tentative*) attempt, try; (*Sport*) attempt. **~ raté** failed attempt; **faire plusieurs ~s** to have several tries, make *ou* have several attempts; **faire des ~s infructueux** to make fruitless attempts; **où en sont tes ~s de plantations?** how are your efforts at growing things *ou* your attempts in the garden progressing?; **ce n'est pas mal pour un premier ~** that's not bad for a first try *ou* attempt *ou* go* *ou* shot*.

(d) (*Rugby*) try.

(e) (*Littérat*) essay.

essaim [esɛ̃] *nm* (*lit, fig*) swarm. (*fig*) **~ de jeunes filles/de vieilles femmes** bevy *ou* gaggle of girls/of old women.

essaimer [eseme] *vi* (*lit*) to swarm; (*fig*) *[famille]* to scatter; *[firme]* to spread, expand.

essayage [esɛjaʒ] *nm* (*Couture*) fitting, trying on; *V* **cabine, salon.**

essayer [eseje] (8) **1** *vt* **(a)** (*mettre à l'épreuve*) *produit* to test (out), try (out); *voiture* to test; *[client]* to test drive, try (out). **venez ~ notre nouveau modèle** come and test drive *ou* try (out) our new model; (*fig*) **~ sa force/son talent** to try *ou* test one's strength/skill.

(b) (*utiliser pour la première fois*) *voiture, produit* to try (out). **avez-vous essayé le nouveau boucher?*** have you tried the new butcher('s)?

(c) *vêtement* to try on. **il faut que je vous l'essaie** I must try it on you.

(d) (*tenter*) *méthode* to try. **~ de faire** to try *ou* attempt to do; **as-tu essayé les petites annonces?** have you tried the classified ads?, have you tried putting something in the classified ads?; **essaie de le faire** try to do it, try and do it; **il a essayé de s'échapper** he attempted *ou* tried to run away; **je vais ~** I'll try, I'll have a go* *ou* a try *ou* a shot* (at it); **essaie un peu pour voir** (*si tu y arrives*) have a try *ou* a go* and see; (**:** *si tu l'oses*) just you try!*, just let me see you try it!; **n'essaie pas de ruser avec moi** don't try being clever with me, don't try it on with me*.

2 s'essayer *vpr*: **s'~ à qch/à faire** to try one's hand at sth/at doing.

essayeur, -euse [esɛjœʀ, øz] *nm,f* (*Couture*) fitter.

essayiste [esejist(ə)] *nmf* essayist.

essence[1] [esɑ̃s] **1** *nf* **(a)** (*carburant*) petrol (*Brit*), gas(oline) (*US*); (*solvant*) spirit; *V* **distributeur, panne.**

(b) (*extrait*) *[plantes]* essential oil, essence; *[aliments]* essence. **~ de violette/de café** violet/coffee essence, essence of violet/coffee.

2: **essence de citron** lemon oil; **essence de lavande** oil of lavender; **essence minérale** mineral oil; **essence de rose** rose oil; **essence de térébenthine** oil of turpentine.

essence[2] [esɑ̃s] *nf* (*fondement*) *[conversation, question, doctrine]* gist, essence; *[livre, ouvrage]* gist; (*Philos*) essence. (*littér*) **par ~** in essence, essentially.

essence[3] [esɑ̃s] *nf* (*espèce*) *[arbres]* species. **~ à feuilles persistantes** evergreen species; (*fig littér*) **se croire d'une ~ supérieure** to think of o.s. as a superior being *ou* as of a superior species.

essentiel, -elle [esɑ̃sjɛl] **1** *adj* **(a)** (*indispensable*) essential. **ces formalités sont ~les** these formalities are essential (*à, pour* for).

(b) (*de base*) essential, basic, main (*épith*). **~ à** essential to.

2 *nm* **(a) l'~** the main thing; (*objets nécessaires*) the basic essentials; (*points principaux*) the essentials, the essential *ou* basic points; **tant qu'on a la santé, c'est l'~** as long as you have your health, that's the main thing; **l'~ est de ...** the main *ou* important thing is to ... .

(b) l'~ de *conversation* the main part of; *fortune* the best *ou* main part of, the bulk of; **l'~ de ce qu'il dit** most of what he says; **ils passaient l'~ de leur temps à faire ...** they spent the best part of their time doing ... .

essentiellement [esɑ̃sjɛlmɑ̃] *adv* (*par essence: frm*) essentially; (*surtout*) basically, essentially. **nous tenons ~ à ...** we are essentially concerned with ... .

esseulé, e [esœle] *adj* (*littér*) forsaken (*littér*), forlorn (*littér*).

essieu, *pl* **~x** [esjø] *nm* axle(-tree).

essor [esɔʀ] *nm* (*frm: envol*) *[oiseau, imagination]* flight; (*croissance*) *[entreprise, pays]* rapid development *ou* expansion; *[art, civilisation]* blossoming. **entreprise en plein ~** firm in full expansion; **prendre son ~** *[oiseau]* to fly up *ou* off; *[société]* to develop *ou* expand rapidly; **le cinéma connaît un nouvel ~** the cinema is enjoying a new boom.

essorage [esɔʀaʒ] *nm* (*V* **essorer**) wringing, mangling; wringing out; spin-drying.

essorer [esɔʀe] (1) *vt* (*avec essoreuse à rouleaux*) to wring, mangle; (*à la main*) to wring out; (*par la force centrifuge*) to spin-dry.

essoreuse [esɔʀøz] *nf* (*à rouleaux*) wringer, mangle; (*à tambour*) spin-dryer.

essoufflement [esufləmɑ̃] *nm* breathlessness (*U*), shortness of breath (*U*).

essouffler [esufle] (1) **1** *vt* to make breathless, wind. **il était essoufflé** he was out of breath *ou* winded *ou* puffed* (*Brit*).

2 s'essouffler *vpr* *[coureur]* to get out of breath, get puffed* (*Brit*); (*fig*) *[roman, travail]* to tail off, fall off; *[romancier]* to exhaust o.s. *ou* one's talent, dry up*.

essuie- [esɥi] *préf V* **essuyer.**

essuyage [esɥijaʒ] *nm* (*V* **essuyer**) (*gén*) wiping; drying; mopping; cleaning; dusting; wiping up, mopping up.

essuyer [esɥije] (8) **1** *vt* **(a)** (*nettoyer*) *objet mouillé, assiettes* to wipe, dry; *sol, surface mouillée* to wipe, mop; *tableau noir* to clean, wipe; *surface poussiéreuse* to dust; *eau* to wipe up, mop up. **s'~ les mains** to wipe one's hands (dry), dry one's hands; **essuie-toi les pieds** *ou* **essuie tes pieds avant d'entrer** wipe your feet before you come *ou* go in; **s'~ le torse/les pieds après un bain** to dry one's body/feet after a bath; **~ la vaisselle** to wipe *ou* dry up, do the drying-up (*Brit*), dry the dishes; **le tableau noir est mal essuyé** the blackboard has been badly cleaned *ou* hasn't been cleaned *ou* wiped properly; **nous avons essuyé les plâtres*** we had a lot of problems with settling in; (*fig*) we had a lot of teething troubles.

(b) (*subir*) *pertes, reproches, échec* to suffer; *insultes* to endure, suffer; *refus* to meet with; *tempête* to weather, ride out. **~ le feu de l'ennemi** to come under enemy fire; **~ un coup de feu** to be shot at.

2 s'essuyer *vpr* *[baigneur]* to dry o.s.

3: **essuie-glace** *nm inv* windscreen (*Brit*) *ou* windshield (*US*) wiper; **essuie-mains** *nm inv* hand towel; **essuie-verres** *nm inv* glass cloth.

est[1] [ɛ] *V* **être.**

est[2] [ɛst] **1** *nm* **(a)** (*point cardinal*) east. **le vent d'~** the east wind; **un vent d'~** an east(erly) wind, an easterly (*Naut*); **le vent tourne/est à l'~** the wind is veering east(wards) *ou* towards the east/is blowing from the east; **regarder vers l'~** *ou* **dans la direction de l'~** to look east(wards) *ou* towards the east; **à l'~** (*situation*) in the east; (*direction*) to the east, east(wards); **le soleil se lève à l'~** the sun rises in the east; **à l'~ de** east of, to the east of; **l'appartement est (exposé) à l'~/exposé plein ~** the flat faces (the) east *ou* eastwards/due east, the flat looks east(wards)/due east; **l'Europe/la France/la Bourgogne de l'~** Eastern Europe/France/Burgundy.

(b) (*régions orientales*) east. (*Pol*) **l'E~** the East; **la France de l'E~, l'E~** the East (of France); **les pays de l'E~** the eastern countries, the eastern world.

2 *adj inv région, partie* eastern; *entrée, paroi* east; *versant, côte* east(ern); *côté* east(ward); *direction* eastward, easterly; *V* **longitude.**

3: **est-allemand, e** *adj* East German; **Est-allemand, e** *nm,f, mpl* **Est-allemands** East German; **est-nord-est** *nm, adj inv* east-north-east; **est-sud-est** *nm, adj inv* east-south-east.

estafilade [ɛstafilad] *nf* gash, slash.

estaminet† [ɛstaminɛ] *nm* tavern; (*péj*) pothouse† (*péj*), (low) dive (*péj*).

estampage [ɛstɑ̃paʒ] *nm* (*V* **estamper**) fleecing**:**, swindling, diddling*; stamping. **c'est de l'~**: it's a plain swindle.

estampe [ɛstɑ̃p] *nf* (*image*) engraving, print; (*outil*) stamp. (*euph*) **venez voir mes ~s japonaises** you must let me show you my etchings.

estamper [ɛstɑ̃pe] (1) *vt* (**:** *voler*) to fleece**:**, swindle, diddle*; (*Tech*) to stamp.

estampeur, -euse [ɛstɑ̃pœʀ, øz] *nm,f* (**:**) swindler, shark*; (*Tech*) stamper.

estampillage [ɛstɑ̃pijaʒ] *nm* stamping, marking.

estampille [ɛstɑ̃pij] *nf* stamp.

estampiller [ɛstɑ̃pije] (1) *vt* to stamp.

este [ɛst(ə)] *adj V* **estonien.**

ester[1] [ɛste] *vi* (*Jur*) **~ en justice** to go to court (*as plaintiff or defendant*).

ester[2] [ɛstɛʀ] *nm* (*Chim*) ester.
esthète [ɛstɛt] *nmf* aesthete.
esthéticien, -ienne [ɛstetisjɛ̃, jɛn] *nm,f* (*Méd*) beautician; (*Art*) aesthetician.
esthétique [ɛstetik] **1** *adj jugement, sentiment* aesthetic; *pose, carrosserie* attractive, aesthetically pleasing; *V* **chirurgie. 2** *nf [visage, pose]* aesthetic quality, attractiveness. (*discipline*) **l'~** aesthetics (*sg*); **l'~ industrielle** industrial design.
esthétiquement [ɛstetikmɑ̃] *adv* aesthetically.
esthétisme [ɛstetism(ə)] *nm* aestheticism.
estimable [ɛstimabl(ə)] *adj* **(a)** (*frm: digne d'estime*) estimable (*frm*), highly considered *ou* respected; (*assez bon*) honest, sound.
(b) (*déterminable*) assessable, calculable. **dégâts difficilement ~s** damage which it is difficult to assess the extent of.
estimatif, -ive [ɛstimatif, iv] *adj*: **devis ~** estimate; **état ~** estimated statement.
estimation [ɛstimɑsjɔ̃] *nf* **(a)** (*U*) *[objet]* appraisal, valuation; *[dégâts, prix]* assessment, estimation; *[distance, quantité]* estimation, reckoning; *[propriété]* valuation, assessment. **(b)** (*chiffre donné*) estimate, estimation. **d'après mes ~s** according to my estimations *ou* reckonings; **~ injuste** unfair estimate.
estime [ɛstim] *nf* **(a)** (*considération*) esteem, respect, regard. **jouir d'une grande ~** to be highly respected *ou* regarded, be held in high esteem *ou* regard; **ce succès mérite l'~ de tous** this success deserves the respect of everyone; **avoir de l'~ pour** to have great esteem *ou* respect *ou* a great regard for; **tenir en piètre ~** to have little regard *ou* respect for; *V* **succès.**
(b) à l'~ by guesswork.
estimer [ɛstime] (1) *vt* **(a)** (*évaluer*) *objet* to appraise, value; *dégâts, prix* to assess, estimate; *distance, quantité* to estimate, reckon; *propriété* to value, assess. **faire ~ un bijou** to have a piece of jewellery appraised *ou* valued; **cette bague est estimée à 3.000 F** this ring is valued at 3,000 francs; **les pertes sont estimées à 2.000 morts** 2,000 people are estimated to have died, an estimated 2,000 people have died, the number of those dead is estimated at *ou* put at 2,000; **j'estime sa vitesse à 80 km/h** I reckon his speed to be 80 km/h, I would put his speed at 80 km/h.
(b) (*respecter*) *personne* to esteem, hold in esteem *ou* high esteem *ou* regard, respect. **estimé de tous** respected *ou* esteemed *ou* highly regarded by everyone; **savoir se faire ~** to know how to win people's respect *ou* regard *ou* esteem.
(c) (*faire cas de*) *qualité* to value highly *ou* greatly, prize, rate highly, appreciate. **il faut savoir ~ un service rendu** one must know how to appreciate a favour; **j'estime beaucoup sa loyauté** I greatly value his loyalty, I set great store by his loyalty; **c'est un plat très estimé** this dish is considered a great delicacy.
(d) (*considérer*) **~ que ...** to consider *ou* deem† that ...; **j'estime qu'il est de mon devoir de** I consider it *ou* deem it† (to be) my duty to; **il estime que vous avez tort de faire cela** he considers it wrong for you to do that; **il estime avoir raison** he considers he is right *ou* in the right; **nous estimons nécessaire de dire/que** we consider it *ou* deem it† necessary to say/that; **~ inutile de faire** to see no point in doing, consider it pointless to do; **s'~ heureux d'avoir/d'un résultat/que** to consider o.s. fortunate to have/with a result *ou* to have a result/that.
estivage [ɛstivaʒ] *nm* summering of cattle on mountain pastures.
estival, e, *mpl* **-aux** [ɛstival, o] *adj* summer (*épith*).
estivant, e [ɛstivɑ̃, ɑ̃t] *nm,f* holiday-maker, summer visitor.
estoc [ɛstɔk] *nm V* **frapper.**
estocade [ɛstɔkad] *nf* (*Tauromachie*) death-blow, final thrust. **donner l'~ à un taureau** to deal a bull the death-blow; (*fig*) **donner l'~ à une personne/un projet** to give *ou* deal the finishing blow to a person/a plan.
estomac [ɛstɔma] *nm* **(a)** stomach. **avoir mal à l'~** to have (a) stomach ache *ou* tummy ache*; **partir l'~ creux** to set off on an empty stomach; **avoir l'~ creux** *ou* **vide/bien rempli** *ou* **garni** to feel *ou* be empty/full (up); **j'ai l'~ dans les talons** my stomach thinks my throat's cut‡ (*surtout Brit*); **avoir un ~ d'autruche** to have a castiron digestive system *ou* a stomach of castiron; **prendre de l'~*** to develop a paunch; *V* **aigreur, creux, rester.**
(b) (‡) **avoir de l'~** (*du culot*) to have a nerve; (*du courage*) to have guts*; **il la lui a fait à l'~** he bluffed *ou* hoodwinked him.
estomaquer* [ɛstɔmake] (1) *vt* to flabbergast, stagger*.
estompe [ɛstɔ̃p] *nf* stump (*Art*).
estompé, e [ɛstɔ̃pe] (*ptp de* **estomper**) *adj couleurs, image* blurred, soft.
estomper [ɛstɔ̃pe] (1) *vt* (*Art*) *dessin* to stump, shade off (*with a stump*); (*fig: voiler*) *contours, souvenir* to blur, dim, soften. **la côte s'estompait dans la brume du soir** the coastline became blurred *ou* hazy *ou* indistinct in the evening mist.
Estonie [ɛstɔni] *nf* Estonia.
estonien, -ienne [ɛstɔnjɛ̃, jɛn] **1** *adj* Estonian. **2** *nm* (*Ling*) Estonian. **3** *nm,f*: **E~(ne)** Estonian.
estourbir‡ [ɛstuʀbiʀ] (2) *vt* (*assommer*) to stun; (*tuer*) to do in‡.
estrade [ɛstʀad] *nf* platform, rostrum, dais.
estragon [ɛstʀagɔ̃] *nm* tarragon.
estrapade [ɛstʀapad] *nf* strappado (torture).
estropié, e [ɛstʀɔpje] (*ptp de* **estropier**) *nm,f* cripple, maimed person.
estropier [ɛstʀɔpje] (7) *vt personne* to cripple, disable, maim; (*fig*) *texte, citation* to twist, distort; *langue étrangère, morceau de musique* to mangle, murder.
estuaire [ɛstɥɛʀ] *nm* estuary.
estudiantin, e [ɛstydjɑ̃tɛ̃, in] *adj* student (*épith*).
esturgeon [ɛstyʀʒɔ̃] *nm* sturgeon.
et [e] *conj* **(a)** (*lie des termes, des subordonnées*) and. **c'est vert ~ rouge** it's green and red; **la clarinette ~ le trombone sont des instruments de musique** the clarinet and the trombone are musical instruments; **il est travailleur ~ ne boit pas** he works hard and he doesn't drink; (*Mus*) **pour piano ~ orchestre** for piano and orchestra; **lui ~ moi nous nous entendons bien** he and I get along well; **~ lui ~ vous l'avez dit** he and you have both said so, both he and you have said so; **2 ~ 2 font 4** 2 and 2 make 4; **j'aime beaucoup ça, ~ vous?** I'm very fond of that, aren't you? *ou* what about you?, I like that very much – do you?; **je n'aime pas ça ~ lui non plus** I don't like that and nor does he *ou* and he doesn't either; **je n'ai rien vu, ~ toi?** I didn't see anything, did you? *ou* what about you?; **il ne peut ~ ne doit pas y aller** he cannot and must not go; (*répétition*) **il a ri ~ ri/pleuré ~ pleuré** he laughed and laughed/cried and cried; (*littér*) **Charles y alla, ~ Jules** Charles went, as did Jules; (*littér*) **un homme noble ~ pur ~ généreux** a noble, pure and generous man; **il y a mensonge ~ mensonge** there are lies and lies, there's lying and lying; **il y a erreur ~ erreur** there are mistakes and mistakes; **il y a vin ~ vin** there's wine and wine, there are wines and wines; **je ne l'approuve pas ~ ne l'approuverai jamais** I don't approve of it and (I) never shall *ou* will; **plus j'en mange ~ plus j'en ai envie** the more of it I eat the more I want.
(b) (*lie des principales: simultanéité, succession, conséquence*) and. **je suis né à Genève ~ mes parents aussi** I was born in Geneva and so were my parents, I was born in Geneva, as were my parents; **j'ai payé ~ je suis parti** I paid and left.
(c) (*valeur emphatique*) **~ alors/ensuite/après?** and so/then/afterwards?; **~ alors?** (*peu importe*) so (what)?*; **~ moi alors?** (and) what about me then?; **~ puis** and then; **~ puis?, ~ puis après?*** so (what)?*; **~ moi, je peux venir?** can I come too?; **~ vous osez revenir?** (*indignation*) and you dare (to) come back?; **~ lui alors qu'est-ce qu'il va dire?** what's HE going to have to say?; **~ ces livres que tu devais me prêter?** what about these books (then) that you were supposed to lend me?; **~ vous, vous y allez?** and what about you, are you going?; **~ si nous y allions aussi?** what about (us) going as well?, why don't we go too?; **~ voilà!** and there you are!; **~ voilà que le voisin revient ...** and then the next-door neighbour comes back ...; **~ voici que s'amène notre ami** (and) along comes our friend; **~ alors eux, voyant cela, ils sont partis** (and) so, seeing that, they left; (*littér*) **~ lui de sourire/se fâcher** whereupon he smiles/grows angry; **~ d'un ... ~ de deux** for one thing ... and for another; **il est bête, ~ d'un, ~ il est méchant, ~ de deux** he's stupid for one thing and for another he's a nasty character.
(d) vingt/trente *etc* **~ un** twenty-/thirty- *etc* one; **à midi/deux heures ~ quart** at (a) quarter past twelve/two; **le vingt/cent ~ unième** the twenty-first/hundred and first; *V* **mille**[1].
êta [ɛta] *nm* eta.
étable [etabl(ə)] *nf* cowshed.
établi [etabli] *nm* (work)bench.
établir [etabliʀ] (2) **1** *vt* **(a)** (*installer dans un lieu*) *immeuble* to put up; *usine* to set up, establish; *liaisons, communications* to establish, set up; *empire* to build, found. **~ son domicile** *ou* **sa demeure à** to set up house in, make one's home in; **l'ennemi a établi son camp/son quartier général dans le village** the enemy has pitched camp/has set up its headquarters in the village.
(b) (*instaurer*) to establish, institute; *gouvernement* to form, set up; *usage* to establish, institute; *impôt* to introduce, bring in; *règlement* to lay down, establish, institute.
(c) (*donner un emploi*) to set up, establish. **~ un fonctionnaire dans une charge** to set a civil servant up in a position; **il a cinq enfants à ~** he has five children to settle; **il lui reste deux filles à ~** he has still two daughters to marry off *ou* get established; **il a établi son fils médecin** he has set his son up *ou* established his son in medical practice.
(d) (*asseoir*) *démonstration* to base; *réputation* to found, base; *droits* to establish; *fortune* to found (*sur* on). **~ son pouvoir sur la force** to found *ou* base one's power on force.
(e) (*faire régner*) *autorité, paix* to establish (*sur* over). **~ son pouvoir sur le pays** to get control of the country, establish control over the country.
(f) (*dresser*) *liste* to draw up, make out; *programme* to arrange; *facture, chèque* to make out; *plans* to draw up, draft; *prix* to fix, work out.
(g) (*montrer*) *fait, comparaison* to establish. **~ l'innocence de qn** to establish sb's innocence; **il est établi que** it's an established fact that.
(h) (*nouer*) *relations* to establish. **ils ont établi une amitié solide** they have established a firm friendship.
(i) (*Sport*) **~ un record** to set (up) *ou* establish a record.
2 s'établir *vpr* **(a)** (*s'installer dans un lieu*) *[commerçant, jeune couple]* to settle. **une nouvelle usine s'est établie dans le village** a new factory has been set up *ou* they've set up a new factory in the village; **l'ennemi s'est établi sur la colline** the enemy has taken up position on the hill; **les Anglais se sont solidement établis dans leurs colonies** the English established *ou* settled themselves firmly in their colonies.
(b) (*s'instaurer*) *[usage]* to become customary *ou* common practice. **l'usage s'est établi de faire ...** it has become customary to do ..., it has become established custom to do ... .
(c) (*prendre un emploi*) **s'~ boulanger** to set o.s. up as a baker; **il s'est établi médecin** he has established himself *ou* set himself up in medical practice; **s'~ à son compte** to set up in business on one's own account.
(d) (*régner*) *[pouvoir, régime]* to become established. **son pouvoir s'est établi sur le pays** his rule has become (firmly) established throughout the country; **un grand silence s'établit, il s'établit un grand silence** there was a great silence, a great silence fell.
(e) (*se nouer*) *[amitié, contacts]* to develop, be established.

une amitié solide s'est établie entre eux, il s'est établi entre eux une solide amitié a firm friendship has developed *ou* has been established between them.

établissement [etablismɑ̃] *nm* **(a)** (*U: V* **établir**) putting-up; setting-up; establishment; building, founding; institution; forming; introduction, bringing-in; laying-down; basing; drawing-up; making-out; arranging; drafting; fixing, working-out.

(b) (*U: V* **s'établir**) settling; setting-up; establishment; development.

(c) (*bâtiment*) establishment. ~ **scolaire** school, educational establishment (*frm*); ~ **hospitalier** hospital; ~ **thermal** hydropathic establishment; ~ **religieux** religious institution; ~ **commercial** commercial establishment; ~ **industriel** industrial plant, factory; **avec les compliments des ~s X** with the compliments of X and Co. *ou* of the firm of X.

(d) (*colonie*) settlement.

étage [etaʒ] *nm* **(a)** *[bâtiment]* floor, storey (*Brit*), story (*US*). **au premier** ~ on the first floor; (*Can*) on the ground *ou* main floor; **maison à** *ou* **de deux ~s** three-storeyed (*Brit*) *ou* -storied (*US*) house, house with three floors; **grimper les ~s** to go up *ou* climb several storeys *ou* flights; **il grimpa 3 ~s** he went up *ou* walked up 3 floors *ou* flights; **les 3 ~s de la tour Eiffel** the 3 levels of the Eiffel Tower; *V* **bas**[1].

(b) *[fusée]* stage; *[mine]* level; *[jardin]* terrace, level; *[gâteau]* tier. (*Géog*) **~s de végétation** levels of vegetation; (*Tech*) ~ **de pression** pressure stage.

étagement [etaʒmɑ̃] *nm [vignobles]* terracing.

étager [etaʒe] (3) **1** *vt objets* to set out in tiered rows, lay out in tiers. **2 s'étager** *vpr [jardins, maisons]* to rise in tiers *ou* terraces. **la foule s'étage sur les gradins** the crowd is gathered on the terracing *ou* the steps; **vignobles étagés sur la colline** vines in terraced rows on the hillside.

étagère [etaʒɛʀ] *nf* (*tablette, rayon*) shelf; (*meuble*) shelves.

étai [etɛ] *nm* stay, prop, strut; (*Naut*) stay.

étaiement [etɛmɑ̃] *nm V* **étayage.**

étain [etɛ̃] *nm* (*Min*) tin; (*Orfèvrerie*) (*matière*) pewter; (*objet*) piece of pewterware, pewterware (*U*). **pot en** *ou* **d'~** pewter pot; *V* **papier.**

étal [etal] *nm [boucherie, marché]* stall.

étalage [etalaʒ] *nm* **(a)** (*Comm*) (*action*) display, displaying; (*devanture*) shop window, show window, display window; (*tréteaux*) stall, stand; (*articles exposés*) display. **présentation de l'~** window dressing; **disposer l'~** to dress the window; **chemise qui a fait l'~** shop-soiled shirt; **droit d'~** stallage.

(b) (*déploiement*) *[luxe, connaissances]* display, show. **faire ~ de** to make a show of, show off, parade.

(c) (*Métal*) **~s** bosh.

étalagiste [etalaʒist(ə)] *nmf* (*décorateur*) window dresser; (†: *marchand*) stallkeeper.

étale [etal] **1** *adj mer, situation* slack; *vent* steady. **navire ~** ship which makes no headway, becalmed ship. **2** *nm [mer]* slack (water).

étalement [etalmɑ̃] *nm* (*V* **étaler**) spreading; strewing; spreading-out; displaying; laying-out; application; staggering.

étaler [etale] (1) **1** *vt* **(a)** (*déployer*) *papiers, objets* to spread, strew (*sur* over); *journal, tissu* to spread out (*sur* on); (*Comm*) *marchandise* to display, lay out, spread out (*sur* on). (*Cartes*) ~ **son jeu** *ou* **ses cartes** to display *ou* lay down one's hand *ou* one's cards.

(b) (*étendre*) *beurre, peinture* to spread (*sur* on); *crème solaire* to apply, smooth on.

(c) (*répartir*) *paiements* to spread, stagger (*sur* over); *vacances* to stagger (*sur* over); *travaux, opération* to spread (*sur* over). (*Poste*) **étalez vos envois** space out your consignments; **les vacances/paiements s'étalent sur 4 mois** holidays/payments are staggered *ou* spread over a period of 4 months.

(d) (*fig*) *luxe, savoir* to parade, flaunt; *malheurs* to make a show of; *secrets* to give away, disclose. **il aime à en ~** he likes to cause a stir; **son ignominie s'étale au grand jour** his ignominy is plain for all to see.

2 s'étaler *vpr* **(a)** *[plaine, cultures]* to stretch out, spread out.

(b) *[richesse, vanité]* to be flaunted, flaunt itself; *[vaniteux]* to flaunt o.s.

(c) (*se vautrer*) **s'~ dans un fauteuil/sur un divan** to sprawl *ou* lounge in an armchair/on a divan; **étalé sur le tapis** sprawling on *ou* stretched out on the carpet.

(d) (*: *tomber*) **s'~ (par terre)** to come a cropper*, fall flat on the ground; **attention, tu vas t'~!** look out, you're going to fall flat on your face!*

étalon[1] [etalɔ̃] *nm* (*cheval*) stallion.

étalon[2] [etalɔ̃] *nm* (*mesure: Comm, Fin*) standard; (*fig*) yardstick. **kilogramme/balance ~** standard kilogram/scales; (*Écon*) **~-or** gold standard; (*Écon*) ~ **de change-or** gold exchange standard; **c'est devenu l'~ de la beauté** it has become the yardstick by which we measure beauty; *V* **mètre.**

étalonnage [etalɔnaʒ] *nm*, **étalonnement** [etalɔnmɑ̃] *nm* (*V* **étalonner**) calibration; standardization.

étalonner [etalɔne] (1) *vt* (*graduer*) *instrument* to calibrate; (*vérifier*) to standardize.

étamage [etamaʒ] *nm* (*V* **étamer**) tinning, tinplating; silvering.

étambot [etɑ̃bo] *nm* stern-post.

étamer [etame] (1) *vt* (*gén*) to tin, tinplate; *glace* to silver.

étameur [etamœʀ] *nm* tinsmith.

étamine [etamin] *nf* (*Bot*) stamen; (*tissu*) muslin; (*pour égoutter, cribler*) cheesecloth, butter muslin.

étanche [etɑ̃ʃ] *adj vêtements, chaussures, montre* waterproof; *chaussures, bateau, compartiment* watertight; (*fig*) watertight. **~ à l'air** airtight; *V* **cloison.**

étanchéité [etɑ̃ʃeite] *nf* (*V* **étanche**) waterproofness; watertightness; airtightness.

étanchement [etɑ̃ʃmɑ̃] *nm* (*littér: V* **étancher**) staunching; stemming; drying; quenching, slaking; stopping up; damming.

étancher [etɑ̃ʃe] (1) *vt* **(a)** *sang* to staunch, stem; (*littér*) *larmes* to dry, stem; (*littér*) *soif* to quench, slake; (*Naut*) *voie d'eau* to stop (up). **(b)** (*rendre étanche*) to make watertight; *écoulement, source* to dam up, stem.

étançon [etɑ̃sɔ̃] *nm* (*Tech*) stanchion, shore, prop.

étançonner [etɑ̃sɔne] (1) *vt* to shore up, prop up.

étang [etɑ̃] *nm* pond.

étant [etɑ̃] *prp de* **être.**

étape [etap] *nf* **(a)** (*trajet*: *gén, Sport*) stage; (*lieu d'arrêt*) (*gén*) stop, stopping place; (*Sport*) stopover point, staging point. **faire ~ à** to break the journey at, stop off at; **par petites ~s** in easy stages. **(b)** (*fig*) (*phase*) stage; (*palier*) stage, step.

état [eta] **1** *nm* **(a)** (*condition physique*) *[personne]* state, condition. **dans un tel ~ d'épuisement** in such a state of exhaustion; **bon ~ général** good general state of health; **~ (de santé)** health; **il n'est pas en ~ de le faire** he's in no condition *ou* (fit) state to do it; **dans quel ~ es-tu! tu saignes!** what a state you're in! you're bleeding!

(b) (*condition psychique*) state. **dans un grand ~ d'énervement** in a considerable state of nervous irritation; **il ne faut pas te mettre dans un ~ pareil** *ou* **des ~s pareils** you mustn't get yourself into such a state; **il était dans tous ses ~s** he was all worked up* *ou* in a terrible state; **il n'était pas dans son ~ normal** he wasn't his usual *ou* normal self.

(c) *[chose abstraite]* state; (*Chim*) *[corps]* state. **dans l'~ actuel de nos connaissances** in the present state of our knowledge, as our knowledge stands at (the) present; **réduit à l'~ de cendres** reduced to cinders; **quel est l'~ de la question?** where *ou* how do things stand in the matter?, what stage have things reached?

(d) *[objet, article d'occasion]* condition, state. **en bon/mauvais ~** in good/poor *ou* bad condition; **en ~** in (working) order; (*Naut*) **en ~ de naviguer** sea-worthy; **en ~ de marche** in working order; **remettre en ~** *voiture* to repair, renovate, do up*; *maison* to renovate, do up*; **tenir en ~** *voiture* to maintain in good order, keep in good repair; *maison* to keep in good repair, look after; **hors d'~** out of order; **sucre/pétrole à l'~ brut** sugar/oil in its raw *ou* unrefined *ou* crude state; **à l'~ (de) neuf** as good as new; **remettre qch en l'~** to put sth back *ou* leave sth as it was *ou* in the state it was when one found it.

(e) (*nation*) state. **être un É~ dans l'É~** to be a law unto itself; **l'É~-patron** the state as an employer; **l'É~-providence** the welfare state; *V* **affaire, chef**[1], **coup** *etc.*

(f) (†: *métier*) profession, trade; (*statut social*) station. **l'~ militaire** the military profession; **boucher/tailleur de son ~** butcher/tailor by trade; **donner un ~ à qn** to find sb a post *ou* trade; **honteux de son ~** ashamed of his station in life†.

(g) (*registre, comptes*) statement, account; (*inventaire*) inventory. **faire un ~ des recettes** *etc* to draw up a statement of the takings *etc*; **~ appréciatif** evaluation, estimation.

(h) (*loc*) **faire ~ de** *ses services etc* to instance, put forward; **(mettre) en ~ d'arrestation** (to put) under arrest; **en tout ~ de cause** in any case, whatever the case; **c'est un ~ de fait** it is an established *ou* irrefutable fact; (*hum*) **dans un ~ intéressant** in an interesting condition, in the family way*; **en ~ d'ivresse** in a drunken state, under the influence (of drink); (*gén, Bio, Psych*) **à l'~ latent** in a latent state; **mettre qn hors d'~ de nuire** to make sb harmless, draw sb's teeth (*fig*); (*Rel*) **en ~ de péché (mortel)** in a state of (mortal) sin.

2: (*Mil*) **état d'alerte** state of alert; **état d'âme** mood, vein of feeling; **état de choc** state of shock; **état de choses** state of affairs, situation; (*Admin*) **état civil** civil status; (*Psych*) **état de conscience** state of consciousness; **état de crise** state of crisis; **état d'esprit** frame *ou* state of mind; (*Hist*) **les états** *ou* **États généraux** the States General; (*Rel*) **état de grâce** state of grace; (*fig*) **en état de grâce** inspired; (*Pol*) **état de guerre** state of war; **en état de guerre** on a war footing; (*Jur*) **état des lieux** inventory of fixtures; (*Philos*) **l'état de nature** the natural state; (*Mil*) **états de service** service record; **état de siège** state of siege; (*Pol*) **état tampon** buffer state; (*Pol*) **état d'urgence** state of emergency; (*Psych*) **état de veille** waking state.

étatique [etatik] *adj système, doctrine* of state control.

étatisation [etatizɑsjɔ̃] *nf* (*doctrine*) state control. **~ d'une entreprise** placing of a concern under direct state control, takeover of a concern by the state.

étatiser [etatize] (1) *vt* to establish state control over, put *ou* bring under state control. **économie étatisée** state-controlled economy.

étatisme [etatism(ə)] *nm* state socialism, state control.

étatiste [etatist(ə)] **1** *adj système, doctrine* of state control. **2** *nmf* partisan of state control, state socialist.

état-major, *pl* **états-majors** [etamaʒɔʀ] *nm* **(a)** (*Mil*) (*officiers*) staff (*inv*); (*bureaux*) staff headquarters. **(b)** (*fig*) *[parti politique]* administrative staff (*inv*); *[entreprise]* top *ou* senior management.

États barbaresques [etabaʀbaʀɛsk(ə)] *nmpl*: **les ~** the Barbary States.

États-Unis [etazyni] *nmpl*: **les ~ (d'Amérique)** the United States (of America).

étau, *pl* **~x** [eto] *nm* (*Tech*) vice. **~ limeur** shaper; (*fig*) **l'~ se resserre (autour des coupables)** the noose is tightening (round the guilty men); **se trouver pris comme dans un ~** to find o.s. caught in a stranglehold.

étayage [etɛjaʒ] *nm*, **étayement** [etɛjmɑ̃] *nm* (*V* **étayer**) propping-up; shoring-up; support(ing); backing-up.

étayer [eteje] (8) *vt mur* to prop up, shore up; (*fig*) *théorie* to support, back up; régime, société to support, prop up.

et caetera, et cetera [ɛtsetera] loc etcetera, and so on (and so forth).

été [ete] nm summer(time). ~ de la Saint-Martin Indian summer; (Can) ~ des Indiens Indian summer; ~ comme hiver summer and winter alike; en ~ in (the) summer, in (the) summertime.

éteignoir [etɛɲwaʀ] nm (a) [bougie] extinguisher. (b) (personne) wet blanket, killjoy.

éteindre [etɛ̃dʀ(ə)] (52) 1 vt (a) incendie, poêle to put out, extinguish; bougie to blow out, snuff out, extinguish; cigarette to stub out, put out, extinguish. laisse ~ le feu let the fire go out; laisse le feu éteint leave the fire out.

(b) gaz, lampe to switch off, put out, turn off; électricité, chauffage, radio to turn off, switch off. éteins dans la cuisine put the kitchen light(s) out, switch out ou off the light in the kitchen; tous feux éteints without lights.

(c) pièce, endroit to put out the lights in. sa fenêtre était éteinte his window was dark, there was no light at ou in his window.

(d) colère to subdue; amour, envie to kill; soif to quench, slake.

(e) (Jur) dette to extinguish.

2 s'éteindre vpr (a) [agonisant] to pass away, die. famille qui s'est éteinte family which has died out.

(b) [colère] to abate, evaporate; [amour, envie] to die, fade.

(c) [cigarette, feu, gaz etc] to go out. la fenêtre s'est éteinte the light at the window went out, the window went dark.

éteint, e [etɛ̃, ɛ̃t] (ptp de éteindre) adj couleur faded; race, volcan extinct; regard dull, lacklustre; voix feeble, dying. chaux ~e slaked lime; c'est un homme ~ maintenant his spirit is broken now, he's a broken man now.

étendard [etɑ̃daʀ] nm (lit, fig) standard.

étendre [etɑ̃dʀ(ə)] (41) 1 vt (a) (déployer) journal, tissu to spread out, open out; (étaler) beurre to spread; (Culin) pâte to roll out; bras, jambes to stretch out; ailes to spread. ~ du linge (sur un fil) to hang out ou hang up the washing; veux-tu ~ le bras pour me passer ... would you mind stretching (your arm) and passing me ...; ~ un blessé to stretch out a wounded man; le cadavre, étendu sur le sol the corpse, stretched (out) ou spreadeagled on the ground; cette peinture s'étend facilement this paint goes on ou spreads easily.

(b) (‡) adversaire to floor*, lay out*; candidat (Scol) to fail, clobber‡; (Pol) to hammer*. se faire ~ [adversaire] to be laid out cold*, be flattened*; [candidat] to be failed, be clobbered‡; (Pol) to be hammered*.

(c) (agrandir) pouvoirs to extend (sur over); domaine to extend, expand; affaires, fortune to extend, increase, expand; cercle d'amis to widen, extend, expand; recherches to extend ou broaden (the field of), increase the scope of; connaissances, vocabulaire to widen, extend, increase. ~ son action à d'autres domaines to extend one's action to other fields; ~ une idée à une autre to extend one idea to (cover) another, apply one idea to another; sa bonté s'étend à tous his kindness extends to everyone; cette mesure s'étend à tous les citoyens this measure applies ou is applicable to ou covers all citizens.

(d) (diluer) vin to dilute, let down; sauce to thin, let down (de with).

(e) (Ling) sens to stretch, extend.

2 s'étendre vpr (a) [personne] (s'allonger) to stretch out (sur on); (se reposer) to have a lie down (surtout Brit), lie down; (fig: en expliquant) to elaborate. s'~ sur to elaborate on, enlarge on.

(b) (occuper un espace, une période) [côte, forêt] to stretch (out), extend; [cortège] to stretch (out) (jusqu'à as far as, to); (fig) [vacances, travaux] to stretch, extend (sur over). la plaine s'étendait à perte de vue the plain stretched (away) as far as the eye could see.

(c) (fig: augmenter) [brouillard, épidémie] to spread; [parti politique] to expand; [ville] to spread, expand; [pouvoirs, domaine, fortune] to increase, expand; [cercle d'amis] to expand, widen; [recherches] to broaden in scope; [connaissances, vocabulaire] to increase, widen.

étendu, e [etɑ̃dy] (ptp de étendre) 1 adj (a) (vaste) ville sprawling (épith), spread out (attrib); domaine extensive, large; connaissances, pouvoirs extensive, wide; vue wide, extensive; vocabulaire wide, large, extensive; sens d'un mot broad (épith), wide; dégâts extensive.

(b) (allongé) personne, jambes stretched out. ~ sur l'herbe lying ou stretched out on the grass.

2 étendue nf (a) (surface) [plaine] area, expanse. pays d'une grande ~e country with a large area ou which covers a large area; sur une ~e de 16 km over an expanse ou area of 16 km; sur toute l'~e de la province throughout the whole province, throughout the length and breadth of the province; grande ~e de sable large stretch ou expanse of sand; surpris par l'~e de ce territoire amazed at the sheer size ou extent of the territory.

(b) (durée) [vie] duration, length. sur une ~e de trois ans over a period of three years.

(c) (importance) [pouvoir, dégâts] extent; [affaires, connaissances, recherches] range, scope, extent. pouvoir/culture d'une grande ~e wide ou extensive power/culture, wide-ranging power/culture.

(d) (Mus) compass, range.

(e) (Philos) [matière] extension, extent.

éternel, -elle [etɛʀnɛl] 1 adj (a) (Philos, Rel) eternal.

(b) (sans fin) eternal, everlasting, endless, unending. ma reconnaissance sera ~e I shall be grateful (to you) for evermore, I'll be eternally grateful; soucis ~s never-ending ou endless worries.

(c) (perpétuel) perpetual. c'est un ~ insatisfait he is never happy with anything, he is perpetually dissatisfied.

(d) (*: inamovible: avant n) inevitable. son ~ chapeau sur la tête the inevitable hat on his head.

2 nm (a) (Rel) l'É~ the Eternal, the Everlasting; (hum) grand joueur devant l'É~ great gambler.

(b) l'~ féminin the eternal feminine ou woman.

éternellement [etɛʀnɛlmɑ̃] adv (V éternel) eternally; everlastingly; endlessly; perpetually.

éterniser [etɛʀnize] (1) 1 vt (a) débats, supplice, situation to drag out, draw out.

(b) (littér) nom, mémoire to immortalize, perpetuate.

2 s'éterniser vpr [situation, débat, attente] to drag on, go on and on; [visiteur] to stay ou linger too long. le jury s'éternise the jury is taking ages; on ne peut pas s'~ ici we can't stay here for ever.

éternité [etɛʀnite] nf eternity. (fig) cela fait une ~ ou des ~s que je ne l'avais rencontré it's ages since I'd met him, I hadn't met him in ages; il y a des ~s que tu m'as promis cela you promised me that ages ago, it's ages since you promised me that; ça a duré une ~ it lasted for ages; de toute ~ from the beginning of time, from time immemorial; pour l'~ to all eternity, eternally.

éternuement [etɛʀnymɑ̃] nm sneeze.

éternuer [etɛʀnɥe] (1) vi to sneeze.

étêtage [etɛtaʒ] nm, **étêtement** [etɛtmɑ̃] nm pollarding, polling.

étêter [etete] (1) vt arbre to pollard, poll; clou, poisson to cut the head off.

éthane [etan] nm ethane.

éther [etɛʀ] nm (Chim, Poésie) ether.

éthéré, e [eteʀe] adj (Chim, littér) ethereal.

éthéromane [eteʀɔman] nm ether addict.

éthéromanie [eteʀɔmani] nf addiction to ether.

Éthiopie [etjɔpi] nf Ethiopia.

éthiopien, -ienne [etjɔpjɛ̃, jɛn] 1 adj Ethiopian. 2 nm,f: E~(ne) Ethiopian.

éthique [etik] 1 adj ethical. 2 nf (Philos) ethics (sg); (code moral) moral code, code of ethics.

ethnie [ɛtni] nf ethnic group.

ethnique [ɛtnik] adj ethnic(al).

ethnographe [ɛtnɔgʀaf] nmf ethnographer.

ethnographie [ɛtnɔgʀafi] nf ethnography.

ethnographique [ɛtnɔgʀafik] adj ethnographic(al).

ethnologie [ɛtnɔlɔʒi] nf ethnology.

ethnologique [ɛtnɔlɔʒik] adj ethnologic(al).

ethnologue [ɛtnɔlɔg] nmf ethnologist.

éthyle [etil] nm ethyl.

éthylène [etilɛn] nm ethylene.

éthylique [etilik] nmf alcoholic.

éthylisme [etilism(ə)] nm alcoholism.

étiage [etjaʒ] nm (débit) low water (U) (of a river); (marque) low-water mark.

étincelant, e [etɛ̃slɑ̃, ɑ̃t] adj (V étinceler) sparkling; glittering; gleaming, twinkling; flashing; shining. conversation ~e scintillating ou brilliant conversation.

étinceler [etɛ̃sle] (4) vi (a) [diamant, lame] to sparkle, glitter; [étoile] to glitter, gleam, twinkle. la mer étincelle au soleil the sea sparkles ou glitters in the sun.

(b) [yeux, regard] ~ de colère to glitter ou flash with anger; ~ de joie to sparkle ou shine with joy.

(c) [conversation, esprit, intelligence] to sparkle; [beauté] to sparkle, shine.

(d) (littér) ~ de mille feux [soleil, nuit] to glitter with a myriad lights (littér).

étincelle [etɛ̃sɛl] nf (a) (parcelle incandescente) spark. ~ électrique electric spark; jeter des ~s to throw out sparks; (fig) c'est l'~ qui a mis le feu aux poudres it was this which touched off ou sparked off the incident; (fig) faire des ~s* to scintillate, shine.

(b) [lame, regard] flash, glitter. jeter des ~s [diamant, regard] to flash fire.

(c) [raison, intelligence] flicker, glimmer. ~ de génie spark ou flash of genius.

étincellement [etɛ̃sɛlmɑ̃] nm (V étinceler) sparkle (U); glitter (U); gleam (U), twinkling (U); flash (U); shining (U).

étiolement [etjɔlmɑ̃] nm (V étioler, s'étioler) blanching, etiolation (T); weakening; wilting; decline; withering.

étioler [etjɔle] (1) 1 vt (a) plante to blanch, etiolate (T). (b) personne to weaken, make sickly. 2 s'étioler vpr [plante] to wilt, grow weak; [personne] to languish, decline; [intelligence] to wither, become dull.

étique [etik] adj skinny, bony.

étiquetage [etiktaʒ] nm [paquet] labelling; [prix] marking, labelling.

étiqueter [etikte] (4) vt paquet to label; prix to mark, label; (fig) personne to label, classify (comme as).

étiquette [etikɛt] nf (a) (sur paquet) label; (de prix) ticket, label. ~ auto-collante/collante self-stick ou self-adhesive/stick-on label; ~ politique political label. (b) (protocole) l'~ etiquette.

étirage [etiʀaʒ] nm (V étirer) stretching; drawing.

étirer [etiʀe] (1) 1 vt peaux to stretch; métal, verre to draw (out). ~ ses membres to stretch one's limbs. 2 s'étirer vpr [personne] to stretch; [vêtement] to stretch; [convoi] to stretch out; [route] to stretch out ou away.

étoffe [etɔf] nf (a) (de laine etc) material, fabric; (fig: d'un livre) material, stuff.

(b) (fig) avoir l'~ de to have the makings of, be cut out to be; avoir l'~ d'un héros to be of the stuff heros are made of, have the makings of a hero; avoir de l'~ to have a strong personality.

étoffer [etɔfe] (1) **1** *vt style* to enrich; *discours, personnage* to fill out. **voix étoffée** rich *ou* deep voice; **discours étoffé** meaty speech. **2 s'étoffer** *vpr [personne]* to fill out.

étoile [etwal] *nf* **(a)** (*Astron*) star. ~ **filante** shooting star; ~ **polaire** pole star, north star; ~ **du berger** *ou* **du soir** evening star; **semé d'**~**s** starry, star-studded; **sans** ~ starless; **à la clarté des** ~**s** by starlight; **dormir** *ou* **coucher à la belle** ~ to sleep out (in the open), sleep under the stars.

(b) (*dessin, objet*) star. **général à deux** ~**s** two-star general; **(hôtel) trois** ~**s** three-star hotel; **moteur en** ~ radial engine.

(c) (*Ciné, Danse*) star. ~ **du cinéma** film star (*Brit*), movie star (*US*); ~ **de la danse** dancing star; ~ **montante** rising *ou* up-and-coming star.

(d) (*destinée*) **avoir foi en son** ~ to trust one's lucky star, trust to one's luck; **être né sous une bonne/mauvaise** ~ to be born under a lucky/an unlucky star; **son** ~ **a pâli** his star has set.

(e) ~ **de mer** starfish.

étoiler [etwale] (1) *vt* **(a)** (*parsemer*) to stud (*de* with). **nuit étoilée** starry *ou* starlit night; **ciel étoilé** starry *ou* star-studded sky. **(b)** (*fêler*) to make a star-shaped crack in.

étole [etɔl] *nf* (*Rel, gén*) stole.

étonnamment [etɔnamɑ̃] *adv* surprisingly, amazingly, astonishingly.

étonnant, e [etɔnɑ̃, ɑ̃t] **1** *adj* **(a)** (*surprenant*) surprising, amazing, astonishing. **rien d'**~ **à cela, cela n'a rien d'**~ there's nothing (so) surprising about that; **vous êtes** ~ you're incredible *ou* amazing, you're the absolute limit*.

(b) (*remarquable*) *personne* amazing, fantastic*, incredible.

2 *nm*: **l'**~ **est que** the astonishing *ou* amazing thing *ou* fact is that, what is astonishing *ou* amazing is that.

étonnement [etɔnmɑ̃] *nm* surprise, amazement, astonishment.

étonner [etɔne] (1) **1** *vt* to surprise, amaze, astonish. **ça m'étonne que** I am surprised that, it surprises me that; **ça ne m'étonne pas (que)** I'm not surprised (that), I don't wonder (that), it doesn't surprise me that; **ça m'étonnerait** I should be very surprised.

2 s'étonner *vpr* to be amazed, wonder, marvel (*de qch* at sth, *de voir* at seeing, *que + subj* that).

étouffant, e [etufɑ̃, ɑ̃t] *adj* stifling.

étouffée [etufe] *nf*: **à l'**~ *poisson, légumes* steamed; *viande* braised; **cuire à l'**~ to steam; to braise.

étouffement [etufmɑ̃] *nm* **(a)** (*mort*) suffocation. **tuer qn par** ~ to kill sb by suffocating *ou* smothering him; **mourir d'**~ to die of suffocation.

(b) (*Méd*) **sensation d'**~ feeling of suffocation *ou* breathlessness; **avoir des** ~**s** to have fits of breathlessness.

(c) (*action: U*) *[scandale]* hushing-up; *[rumeurs]* suppression, stifling; *[révolte]* quelling, suppression; *[scrupules]* stifling, overcoming.

(d) *[pas]* muffling.

étouffer [etufe] (1) **1** *vt* **(a)** *[assassin]* to suffocate, smother; *[chaleur, atmosphère]* to stifle, suffocate; *[sanglots, colère, aliment]* to choke. **le bébé s'est étouffé dans ses draps** the baby suffocated in its sheets; **s'**~ **en mangeant** to choke whilst eating; ~ **qn de baisers** to smother sb with kisses; **les scrupules ne l'étouffent pas** he isn't hampered by scruples, he doesn't let scruples cramp his style; **ça l'étoufferait de dire merci** it would kill him to say thank you; (*Agr*) **plantes qui étouffent les autres** plants which choke *ou* smother others.

(b) *bruit* to muffle, deaden; *bâillement* to stifle, smother, suppress; *sanglots, cris* to smother, choke back, stifle. **rires étouffés** suppressed *ou* smothered laughter; **voix étouffées** (*discrètes*) subdued voices; (*confuses*) muffled voices.

(c) *scandale* to hush up, keep quiet; *rumeurs, sentiments* to suppress, stifle; *révolte* to put down, quell, suppress; *scrupules* to stifle, overcome.

(d) *flammes* to extinguish, quench (*littér*). ~ **un feu** to put out *ou* smother a fire.

(e) (*: *voler*) to pinch*.

2 *vi* (*mourir étouffé*) to die of suffocation, suffocate to death; (*fig: être mal à l'aise*) to feel stifled, suffocate. ~ **de colère/de rire** to choke with anger/with laughter; ~ **de chaleur** to be stifling, be overcome with the heat; **on étouffe dans cette pièce** it's stifling in here, the heat is suffocating *ou* overpowering in here.

étouffoir [etufwaʀ] *nm* (*Mus*) damper.

étoupe [etup] *nf* (*de lin, chanvre*) tow; (*de cordages*) oakum.

étourderie [etuʀdəʀi] *nf* (*U*) thoughtlessness, heedlessness; (*faute*) thoughtless blunder. **agir par** *ou* **avec** ~ to act thoughtlessly *ou* without thinking.

étourdi, e [etuʀdi] (*ptp de* **étourdir**) **1** *adj personne, action* scatterbrained, thoughtless, heedless. **2** *nm,f* scatterbrain. **agir en** ~ to act irresponsibly *ou* thoughtlessly.

étourdiment [etuʀdimɑ̃] *adv* thoughtlessly, rashly.

étourdir [etuʀdiʀ] (2) **1** *vt* **(a)** (*assommer*) to stun, daze; (*fatiguer*) (*lit*) to deafen; (*fig*) to bemuse. **ce vacarme m'étourdit** this row is deafening; **ce mouvement m'étourdit** this movement makes my head spin *ou* makes me feel quite dizzy.

(b) ~ **qn** *[altitude, vin]* to make sb dizzy *ou* giddy; *[succès, parfum, vin]* to go to sb's head. **l'altitude m'étourdit** heights make me dizzy *ou* giddy, I've no head for heights.

(c) ~ **une douleur** to deaden *ou* numb a pain.

2 s'étourdir *vpr*: **il s'étourdit par la boisson** he drowns his sorrows in drink; **il s'étourdit par les plaisirs** he tries to forget *ou* to deaden his sorrows by living a life of pleasure; **il s'étourdit pour oublier** he keeps up a whirl of activity to forget; **s'**~ **de paroles** to get drunk on words, be carried away by the sound of one's own voice.

étourdissant, e [etuʀdisɑ̃, ɑ̃t] *adj bruit* deafening, stunning; *succès, beauté* staggering, stunning. **rythme** ~ intoxicating *ou* heady rhythm; ~ **de beauté** stunningly beautiful.

étourdissement [etuʀdismɑ̃] *nm* **(a)** (*syncope*) blackout; (*vertige*) dizzy spell, fit of giddiness. **ça me donne des** ~**s** it makes me feel dizzy, it makes my head swim*. **(b)** (*littér: surprise*) surprise. **(c)** (*littér: griserie*) exhilaration, intoxication.

étourneau, *pl* ~**x** [etuʀno] *nm* **(a)** (*Orn*) starling. **(b)** (*: *distrait*) scatterbrain, featherbrain.

étrange [etʀɑ̃ʒ] *adj* strange; (*bizarre*) odd, queer. **et chose** ~ (and) strange to say, strangely enough, the odd thing is; **aussi** ~ **que cela puisse paraître** strange as it may seem; **cela n'a rien d'**~ there is nothing strange about *ou* in that.

étrangement [etʀɑ̃ʒmɑ̃] *adv* (*bizarrement*) strangely, oddly, peculiarly; (*étonnamment*) surprisingly, amazingly. **ressembler** ~ **à** to be surprisingly *ou* amazingly *ou* suspiciously like.

étranger, -ère [etʀɑ̃ʒe, ɛʀ] **1** *adj* **(a)** (*d'un autre pays*) foreign; (*Pol*) *politique, affaires* foreign. **être** ~ **au pays** to be a foreigner; **visiteurs** ~**s** foreign visitors, visitors from abroad.

(b) (*d'un autre groupe*) strange, unknown (*à* to). **être** ~ **à un groupe** not to belong to a group, be an outsider; **il est** ~ **à notre famille** he is not a relative of ours, he is not a member of our family; **entrée interdite à toute personne** ~**ère (à l'établissement** *ou* **au service)** no entry for unauthorized persons, no unauthorized entry.

(c) (*inconnu*) *nom, usage, milieu* strange, unfamiliar (*à* to); *idée* strange, odd. **son nom/son visage ne m'est pas** ~ his name/face is not unknown *ou* not unfamiliar to me; **être** ~ **à** *[personne]* to be unfamiliar *ou* unacquainted with, have no knowledge of; *[chose]* to be unknown to; **la chimie lui est** ~**ère** chemistry is a closed book to him, he has no knowledge of chemistry; **cette personne/technique lui est** ~**ère** this person/technique is unfamiliar *ou* unknown to him, he is unfamiliar *ou* unacquainted with this person/technique; **ce sentiment ne lui est pas** ~ this feeling is not unknown to him, it is not unknown for him to feel this way.

(d) (*extérieur*) *donnée, fait* extraneous (*à* to). ~ **au sujet** irrelevant (to the subject), beside the point; **être** ~ **à un complot** not to be involved *ou* mixed up in a plot, have nothing to do with a plot.

(e) (*Méd, fig*) **corps** ~ foreign body.

2 *nm,f* **(a)** (*d'un autre pays*) foreigner; (*péj, Admin*) alien. **une** ~**ère** a foreign lady *ou* woman; **c'est une** ~**ère** she's a foreigner.

(b) (*inconnu*) stranger; (*à un groupe*) outsider, stranger.

3 *nm* (*pays*) foreign country, foreign parts. **vivre/voyager à l'**~ to live/travel abroad; **rédacteur pour l'**~ foreign editor.

étrangeté [etʀɑ̃ʒte] *nf* (*U*) *[conduite]* strangeness, oddness, queerness; (*fait ou événement etc bizarre*) odd *ou* strange fact *ou* event *etc*.

étranglement [etʀɑ̃gləmɑ̃] *nm* **(a)** *[victime]* strangulation; (*Hist: supplice*) garotting; (*fig*) *[presse, libertés]* stifling. **(b)** *[vallée]* neck; *[rue]* bottleneck, narrowing; *[taille]* constriction. **(c)** *[voix]* strain, tightness. **(d)** (*Méd*) strangulation.

étrangler [etʀɑ̃gle] (1) **1** *vt* **(a)** (*tuer*) *personne* to strangle, throttle; *poulet* to wring the neck of; (*Hist: supplicier*) to garotte. **mourir étranglé (par son écharpe)** to be strangled (by one's scarf); **elle s'est étranglée accidentellement** she was strangled accidentally, she accidentally strangled herself; **cette cravate m'étrangle** this tie is throttling me.

(b) *[rage etc]* to choke. **la fureur l'étranglait** he was choking with rage; **voix étranglée par l'émotion** voice choking *ou* strained *ou* tight with emotion.

(c) *presse, libertés* to strangle, stifle. **taxes qui étranglent les commerçants** taxes which cripple the traders.

(d) (*resserrer*) to squeeze (tightly). **taille étranglée** tightly constricted *ou* tightly corseted waist.

2 s'étrangler *vpr* **(a) s'**~ **de rire/colère** to choke with laughter/anger; **s'**~ **en pleurant** to choke with tears; **s'**~ **en mangeant** to choke whilst eating.

(b) *[voix, sanglots]* to catch in one's throat. **un cri s'étrangla dans sa gorge** a cry caught *ou* died in his throat.

(c) *[rue, couloir]* to narrow (down), make a bottleneck.

(d) (*Méd*) **hernie étranglée** strangulated hernia.

étrangleur, -euse [etʀɑ̃glœʀ, øz] *nm,f* strangler.

étrave [etʀav] *nf* stem.

être [ɛtʀ(ə)] (61) **1** *vb copule* **(a)** (*gén*) to be. **le ciel est bleu** the sky is blue; **elle veut** ~ **médecin** she wants to be a doctor; **soyez sages!** be good!; **tu n'es qu'un enfant** you are only a child; **si j'étais vous, je lui parlerais** if I were you I should *ou* would speak to her; **nous sommes 10 à vouloir partir** there are 10 of us wanting *ou* who want to go; *V* **ailleurs, ce, que** *etc*.

(b) (*pour indiquer la date*) **nous sommes** *ou* **on est le 12 janvier** it is January 12th; **on était en juillet** it was (in) July; **quel jour sommes-nous?** what day is it?, what's the date today?, what's today's date?

(c) (*avec à, de: appartenir*) **à qui est ce livre? — il est à moi** whose book is this? — it's mine *ou* it belongs to me; **je suis à vous** I'll be with you; **c'était à elle de protester** it was up to her to protest, it was her job to protest*; **nous sommes de la même religion** we are of the same faith; ~ **de la fête/de l'expédition** to take part in the celebration/expedition; **vous en êtes?** are you taking part?, are you in on this?*; (*péj*) **il en est*, c'en est une*** (*un homosexuel*) he's one of them* (*péj*); **je ne pourrai pas** ~ **des vôtres jeudi** I shan't be able to join you on Thursday.

(d) (*avec complément introduit par préposition: indiquant l'état, le fait, l'opinion etc; V aussi prép et noms en question*) to be. ~ **en colère/de bonne humeur** to be angry/in a good mood; ~ **pour la paix/contre la violence** to be for *ou* in favour of peace/against *ou* opposed to violence; **il est/n'est pas à son travail** his attention *ou* mind is/is not on his work; **il est au**

travail he is working; **le livre est à la reliure** the book is (away) being bound; **elle était en robe de chambre** she was in her dressing gown; **il est pour beaucoup dans sa nomination** he is largely responsible for his appointment, he had a lot to do with his being appointed; **elle n'y est pour rien** it's not her responsibility, it's not her fault, it has nothing to do with her; **je suis pour dormir ici** I am for sleeping here*, I am in favour of sleeping here; **au bal, elle sera en Bretonne** she will be dressed as a Breton girl at the dance.

2 *vb aux* **(a)** (*formant les temps composés actifs*) **il est passé hier** he came yesterday; **nous étions montés** we had gone upstairs; **elle serait tombée** she would *ou* might have fallen; **il n'est pas passé** he hasn't been; **nous nous sommes promenés** we had a walk, we went for a walk; **vous vous seriez bien trompés** you would have been greatly mistaken; **il s'est assis** he sat down; **elle s'est laissée aller** she has let herself go.

(b) (*formant le passif*) ~ **donné/fabriqué par ...** to be given/made by ...; **il est soutenu par son patron** he is backed up by his boss, he has the support *ou* the backing of his boss; **il a été blessé dans un accident** he was injured in an accident.

(c) (*avec à + infin: indiquant une obligation*) **ce livre est à lire/relier** this book must be read/bound; **le poisson est à manger tout de suite** the fish is to be eaten *ou* must be eaten at once; **cet enfant est à tuer!** I could kill *ou* murder that child!; **tout est à refaire** it's all got to be done again.

(d) (*avec à + infin: indiquant un état en cours*) **il est à travailler** he is (busy) working; **ma robe est à nettoyer*** my dress is being cleaned *ou* is at the cleaners'; **elle est toujours à le taquiner** she keeps teasing him, she's forever teasing him.

3 *vi* **(a)** (*exister*) to be. **je pense donc je suis** I think, therefore I am; **le meilleur homme qui soit** the kindest man that ever was, the kindest man living; **elle n'est plus** she is no more; **le temps n'est plus où ...** the time is past when ...; **que la lumière soit** let there be light; **un menteur s'il en est** a liar if ever there was one.

(b) (*se trouver, habiter*) **il est maintenant à Lille** he now lives *ou* he is now in Lille; **le village est à 10 km d'ici** the village is 10 km away from here; **j'y suis j'y reste** here I am and here I stay; **elle n'y est pour personne** she is not at home to anyone, she is not available (to anyone).

(c) (*: *avoir été* = *être allé*) **il n'avait jamais été à Londres** he'd never been to London; **avez-vous jamais été à l'étranger?** — **oui j'ai été en Italie l'an dernier** have you ever been abroad? — yes I went to Italy *ou* I was in Italy* last year.

(d) (*littér*) **il s'en fut la voir** he went (forth) to see her.

4 *vb impers* **(a)** **il est** + *adj* it is + *adj*; **il serait très agréable de voyager** it would be very pleasant to travel; **il n'est pas nécessaire qu'il vienne** it is not necessary for him to come, it is not necessary that he should come, he need not come.

(b) (*pour dire l'heure*) **il est 10 heures** it is 10 o'clock; **il serait temps de partir** it is time (for us) to go, it's time we went.

(c) (*littér: il y a*) **il est des gens qui** there are people who; **il était une fois ...** once upon a time there was ... .

(d) (*avoir atteint*) **en ~ à/dans: en ~ à la page 9** to be at page 9, have reached page 9; **où en est-il de** *ou* **dans ses études?** how far has he got with his studies?; **il en est à sa première année de médecine** he has reached his first year in medicine; **l'affaire en est là** that's how the matter stands, that's as far as it's got; (*fig*) **je ne sais plus où j'en suis** I don't know whether I am coming or going.

(e) (*se voir réduit à*) **en ~ à** + *infin*: **j'en suis à me demander** si I've come to wonder if, I've got to wondering if*; **il en est à mendier** he has come down to *ou* stooped to begging, he has been reduced to begging.

(f) (*loc*) **il en est de sa poche** he is out of pocket; **en ~ pour ses frais** *ou* **sa peine/son argent** to get nothing for one's trouble *ou* pains/money; **il n'en est rien** it's nothing of the sort, that's not it at all; **tu y es?*** (*tu es prêt*) are you ready?; (*comprends-tu*) do you follow me?, do you get it?*; **tu n'y es pas du tout!** you just don't get it!*

(g) (*avec ce: pour présenter un être, une chose*) **ce sera une belle cérémonie** it will be a beautiful ceremony; **c'est un docteur, il est docteur** he is a doctor.

(h) (*pour mettre en relief*) **c'est lui qui me l'a dit/qui vous le dira** he (is the one who) told me/(is the one who) will tell you; **c'est à qui dira son mot** they all want to have their say; **c'est moi qu'on attendait** I was the one they were waiting for, it was me they were waiting for; **c'est pour eux que je l'ai fait** I did it for their sake; **c'est que je le connais bien!** I know him so well!; **c'est qu'elle n'a pas d'argent** it's because *ou* just that she has no money; (*exclamatif*) but she has no money!; **ce n'est pas qu'il soit beau!** it's not that he's good-looking!

(i) (*est-ce que: forme interrogative*) **est-ce que vous saviez?** did you know?; **est-ce que c'est toi qui l'as battu?** was it you who beat him?

(j) **n'est-ce pas: il fait beau, n'est-ce pas?** isn't it a lovely day?, it's a lovely day isn't it?; **vous viendrez, n'est-ce pas?** you will come, won't you?, you are coming, aren't you?; **n'est-ce pas qu'il a promis?** he did promise, didn't he?

(k) (*pour exprimer la supposition*) **si ce n'était** were it not for, if it were not for, but for; (*littér*) **n'était son orgueil** were it not for his pride, if it were not for his pride; **ne serait-ce que pour quelques jours** if (it were) only for a few days; **ne serait-ce que pour nous ennuyer** if only to annoy us; **comme si de rien n'était** as if nothing had happened; (*Math*) **soit une droite XY** let XY be a straight line, take a straight line XY.

5 *nm* **(a)** (*gén, Sci*) being. ~ **humain/animé/vivant** human/animate/living being.

(b) (*individu*) being, person. **les ~s qui nous sont chers** our loved ones; **un ~ cher** a loved one; **c'était un ~ merveilleux** he was a wonderful person; (*péj*) **quel ~!** what a character!

(c) (*âme*) heart, soul, being. **il l'aimait de tout son ~** he loved her with all his heart; **au plus profond de notre ~** deep down in our souls; **tout son ~ se révoltait** his whole being rebelled.

(d) (*Philos*) being. **l'~ et le néant** being and nothingness.

étreindre [etʀɛ̃dʀ(ə)] (52) *vt* **(a)** (*frm*) (*dans ses bras*) *ami* to embrace, clasp in one's arms; *ennemi* to seize, grasp; (*avec les mains*) to clutch, grip, grasp. **les deux amis s'étreignirent** the two friends embraced each other.

(b) (*fig*) *[douleur]* to grip; *V* **qui.**

étreinte [etʀɛ̃t] *nf* (*frm*) *[ami]* embrace; *[ennemi]* stranglehold, grip; *[main]* clutch, grip, grasp; *[douleur]* grip. (*Mil*) **l'armée resserre son ~ autour de ...** the army is tightening its grip round ... .

étrenne [etʀɛn] *nf* (*gén pl*) (*à un enfant*) New Year's gift; (*au facteur etc*) ≈ Christmas box.

étrenner [etʀene] (1) **1** *vt* to use *ou* wear *etc* for the first time. **2** *vi* (*: *écoper*) to catch it*, cop it* (*Brit*), get it*.

étrier [etʀije] *nm* stirrup.

étrille [etʀij] *nf* (*brosse*) currycomb; (*crabe*) swimming-crab.

étriller [etʀije] (1) *vt cheval* to curry; (†, *hum: rosser*) to trounce†.

étripage [etʀipaʒ] *nm* gutting.

étriper [etʀipe] (1) **1** *vt lapin* to disembowel, gut; *volaille* to draw; *poisson* to gut; (*fig*) *adversaire* to cut open, hack about. **2 s'étriper*** *vpr* to make mincemeat of each other*, tear each other's guts out*.

étriqué, e [etʀike] (*ptp de* **étriquer**) *adj habit* skimpy, tight; *esprit* narrow; *vie* narrow, cramped. **il fait tout ~ dans son manteau** he looks cramped in his coat, he looks as though he's bursting out of his coat.

étriquer [etʀike] (1) *vt*: **ce vêtement l'étrique** this garment is too tight-fitting for him.

étrivière [etʀivjɛʀ] *nf* stirrup leather.

étroit, e [etʀwa, wat] *adj* **(a)** (*lit*) (*gén*) *rue, fenêtre, ruban* narrow; *espace* restricted, cramped, confined; *vêtement, chaussure* tight.

(b) (*littér: serré*) *nœud, étreinte* tight.

(c) (*fig: borné*) *vues* narrow, limited. **à l'esprit ~** narrow-minded.

(d) (*fig: intime*) *amitié* close (*épith*); *liens* close (*épith*), intimate (*épith*). **en collaboration ~e avec** in close collaboration with.

(e) (*fig: strict*) *surveillance* close (*épith*), strict (*épith*); (*littér*) *obligations* strong (*épith*), strict (*épith*); *coordination* close (*épith*); *soumission, subordination* strict (*épith*).

(f) (*Ling*) *acception* narrow (*épith*), strict (*épith*), restricted. **au sens ~ du terme** in the narrow *ou* strict sense of the term.

(g) **à l'~** cramped; **vivre** *ou* **être logé à l'~** to live in cramped *ou* confined conditions; **être à l'~ dans ses vêtements** to wear clothes which are too small, be cramped in one's clothes, be bursting out of one's clothes.

étroitement [etʀwatmɑ̃] *adv lier, unir* closely; *obéir* strictly; *surveiller* closely, strictly; *tenir* tightly. **être ~ logé** to live in cramped *ou* confined conditions.

étroitesse [etʀwatɛs] *nf* (*V* **étroit**) narrowness; crampedness; tightness; closeness. **l'~ de ce logement** the cramped accommodation; **~ (d'esprit)** narrow-mindedness.

étron [etʀɔ̃] *nm* (†, *hum*) turd*.

Étrurie [etʀyʀi] *nf* Etruria.

étrusque [etʀysk(ə)] **1** *adj* Etruscan. **2** *nm* (*Ling*) Etruscan. **3** *nmf*: **É~** Etruscan.

étude [etyd] *nf* **(a)** (*action*) (*gén*) study. (*Mus*) **l'~ d'un instrument** the study of an instrument, learning to play an instrument; **ce projet est à l'~** this project is under consideration *ou* is being studied; **mettre un projet à l'~, procéder à l'~ d'un projet** to investigate *ou* go into *ou* study a project; **avoir le goût de l'~** to like study *ou* studying; (*Écon*) **~ de marché** market research (*U*); *V* **bureau, voyage.**

(b) (*Scol, Univ*) **~s** studies; **faire ses ~s à Paris** to study in Paris, be educated in Paris; **travailler pour payer ses ~s** to work to pay for one's education; **faire des ~s de droit** to study law; **a-t-il fait des ~s?** has he studied at all?, has he been to university?

(c) (*ouvrage*) study; (*Écon, Sci*) paper, study; (*Littérat*) study, essay. (*Art*) **~s de fleurs** studies of flowers; (*Mus*) **~s pour piano** studies for (the) piano.

(d) (*Scol*) **(salle d')~** study *ou* prep room; **l'~ (du soir)** preparation, prep*.

(e) (*Jur*) (*bureau*) office; (*charge, clientèle*) practice.

étudiant, e [etydjɑ̃, ɑ̃t] **1** *adj vie, problèmes, allures* student (*épith*). **2** *nm,f* student. **~ en médecine/en lettres** medical/arts student; **~ de première année** first-year student.

étudié, e [etydje] (*ptp de* **étudier**) *adj* **(a)** (*calculé*) *jeu de scène* studied; *coupe, conception* carefully designed; (*Comm*) *prix* keen (*épith*) (*Brit*). **à des prix très ~s** at absolutely rock-bottom prices, at the keenest (*Brit*) *ou* the lowest possible prices; **studio d'une conception très ~e** very carefully *ou* thoughtfully designed flatlet.

(b) (*affecté*) *allure* studied; *sentiments* affected, assumed.

étudier [etydje] (7) **1** *vt* **(a)** (*apprendre*) *matière* (*gén*) to study; (*Univ*) to read, study; *instrument* to study, learn to play; (*Scol*) *leçon* to learn; *texte, auteur* to study. **s'amuser au lieu d'~** to have a good time instead of studying.

(b) (*examiner*) *projet* to study, examine, go into; *dossier, cas* to study, examine, scrutinize (*frm*). **~ les prix** to do a study of prices, compare prices; **~ les possibilités** to study *ou* examine *ou* go into the possibilities; **~ qch de près** to make a close study of sth, go into sth in detail, take a close look at sth.

(c) (*observer*) *terrain, adversaire* to study, observe closely;

visage to study, examine. **au début, je sentais qu'il m'étudiait constamment** at the start I sensed that he was observing me all the time.

(d) (*concevoir*) *procédé, dispositif* to devise; *machine, coupe* to design.

(e) (*calculer*) *gestes, ton, effets* to study, calculate.

2 s'étudier *vpr* **(a)** (*s'analyser*) to analyse o.s., be introspective; (*s'examiner*) to study o.s. *ou* one's appearance. **les deux adversaires s'étudiaient** the two opponents were studying *ou* observing each other closely.

(b) (†) **s'~ à faire** to strive *ou* try to do.

étui [etɥi] *nm [lunettes, violon, cigares]* case; *[revolver]* holster.

étuve [etyv] *nf* (*bains*) steamroom; (*de désinfection*) sterilizer; (*incubateur*) incubator; (*fig*) oven.

étuvée [etyve] *nf* (*Culin*) **à l'~** braised.

étymologie [etimɔlɔʒi] *nf* etymology.

étymologique [etimɔlɔʒik] *adj* etymological.

étymologiquement [etimɔlɔʒikmɑ̃] *adv* etymologically.

étymologiste [etimɔlɔʒist(ə)] *nmf* etymologist.

étymon [etimɔ̃] *nm* etymon.

eu, e [y] *ptp de* **avoir.**

eucalyptus [økaliptys] *nm* eucalyptus.

eucharistie [økaʀisti] *nf*: **l'E~** the Eucharist.

eucharistique [økaʀistik] *adj* eucharistic.

Euclide [øklid] *nm* Euclid.

euclidien, -ienne [øklidjɛ̃, jɛn] *adj* Euclidean.

eudiomètre [ødjɔmɛtʀ(ə)] *nm* eudiometer.

Eugène [øʒɛn] *nm* Eugene.

eugénique [øʒenik] **1** *nf* eugenics (*sg*). **2** *adj* eugenic.

eugénisme [øʒenism(ə)] *nm* eugenics (*sg*).

euh [ø] *excl* er! ...

eunuque [ønyk] *nm* eunuch.

euphémique [øfemik] *adj* euphemistic(al).

euphémiquement [øfemikmɑ̃] *adv* euphemistically.

euphémisme [øfemism(ə)] *nm* euphemism.

euphonie [øfɔni] *nf* euphony.

euphonique [øfɔnik] *adj* euphonious, euphonic.

euphoniquement [øfɔnikmɑ̃] *adv* euphoniously, euphonically.

euphorbe [øfɔʀb(ə)] *nf* euphorbia, spurge.

euphorie [øfɔʀi] *nf* euphoria.

euphorique [øfɔʀik] *adj* euphoric.

euphorisant [øfɔʀizɑ̃] *nm* pep pill.

euphoriser [øfɔʀize] (1) *vt* to set at ease, relax, reassure.

Euphrate [øfʀat] *nm*: **l'~** the Euphrates.

eurafricain, e [øʀafʀikɛ̃, ɛn] **1** *adj* Eurafrican. **2** *nm,f*: **E~(e)** Eurafrican.

eurasiatique [øʀazjatik] *adj* Eurasiatic.

Eurasie [øʀazi] *nf* Eurasia.

eurasien, -ienne [øʀazjɛ̃, jɛn] **1** *adj* Eurasian. **2** *nm,f*: **E~(ne)** Eurasian.

eurêka [øʀeka] *excl* eureka!

eurent [yʀ] *V* **avoir.**

Euripide [øʀipid] *nm* Euripides.

euristique [øʀistik] = **heuristique.**

eurochèque [øʀɔʃɛk] *nm* Eurocheque.

eurodollar [øʀɔdɔlaʀ] *nm* Eurodollar.

Europe [øʀɔp] *nf* Europe. **l' ~ des six** the Six (*Common Market countries*); **~ Centrale** Central Europe; **l' ~ verte** European *ou* Community agriculture.

européaniser [øʀɔpeanize] (1) *vt* to europeanize.

européen, -éenne [øʀɔpeɛ̃, eɛn] **1** *adj* European. **2** *nm,f*: **E~(ne)** European.

Eurovision [øʀɔvizjɔ̃] *nf* Eurovision.

eurythmie [øʀitmi] *nf* eurhythmics (*sg*).

eut [y] *V* **avoir.**

euthanasie [øtanazi] *nf* euthanasia.

eutrophisation [øtʀɔfizɑsjɔ̃] *nf* eutrophation.

eux [ø] *pron pers* **(a)** (*sujet*) they, THEY; (*objet*) them. **~ et toi, vous ne manquez pas d'aplomb** they and you are certainly sure of yourselves; **si j'étais ~** if I were *ou* was them *ou* they (*frm*); **il n'obéit qu'à ~** they are the only ones he obeys, he'll only obey them; **nous y allons, ~ non** *ou* **pas ~** we are going but they aren't *ou* they're not *ou* not them; **~ mentir? ce n'est pas possible** them tell a lie? I can't believe it; **ce sont ~ qui répondront** they are the ones who will reply, they'll reply; **~ ils n'ont rien à dire** THEY've got nothing to say; **ils l'ont bien fait, ~** THEY did it all right; **les aider, ~? jamais!** help THEM? never!; **~, pauvres innocents, ne l'ont jamais su** they, poor fools, never knew.

(b) (*avec prép*) **à ~ tout seuls, ils ont tout acheté** they bought everything all on their own; **cette maison est-elle à ~?** does this house belong to them?, is this house theirs?; **ils ont cette grande maison à ~ seuls** they have this big house all to themselves; **ils ne pensent qu'à ~, ces égoïstes** these selfish people only think of themselves; *V* **aussi, moi, toi.**

évacuateur, -trice [evakɥatœʀ, tʀis] **1** *adj* evacuation (*épith*). **2** *nm* sluice.

évacuation [evakɥɑsjɔ̃] *nf [pays, personnes]* evacuation; *[liquide]* draining, emptying; (*Méd*) evacuation.

évacué, e [evakɥe] (*ptp de* **évacuer**) *nm,f* evacuee.

évacuer [evakɥe] (1) *vt pays, ville, population* to evacuate; *salle, maison* to evacuate, clear; (*Méd*) to evacuate, discharge; *liquide* to drain (off). **faire ~** *salle, bâtiment* to clear.

évadé, e [evade] (*ptp de* **s'évader**) *nm,f* escaped man (*ou* woman), escapee.

évader (s') [evade] (1) *vpr* (*lit, fig*) to escape (*de* from). **faire ~ qn** to help sb (to) escape.

évaluable [evalɥabl(ə)] *adj* assessable. **difficilement ~** difficult to assess *ou* evaluate.

évaluation [evalɥɑsjɔ̃] *nf* (*V* **évaluer**) evaluation; assessment; valuation; estimation.

évaluer [evalɥe] (1) *vt* **(a)** (*expertiser*) *maison, bijou* to evaluate, assess, value (*à* at); *dégâts, prix* to assess, evaluate (*à* at). **faire ~ qch par un expert** to have sth valued *ou* appraised by an expert. **(b)** (*juger approximativement*) *fortune, nombre, distance* to estimate, assess (*à* at).

évanescent, e [evanesɑ̃, ɑ̃t] *adj* evanescent.

évangélique [evɑ̃ʒelik] *adj* evangelic(al).

évangélisateur, -trice [evɑ̃ʒelizatœʀ, tʀis] **1** *adj* evangelistic. **2** *nm,f* evangelist.

évangélisation [evɑ̃ʒelizɑsjɔ̃] *nf* evangelization.

évangéliser [evɑ̃ʒelize] (1) *vt* to evangelize.

évangélisme [evɑ̃ʒelism(ə)] *nm* evangelicalism, evangelism.

évangéliste [evɑ̃ʒelist(ə)] *nm* evangelist; (*Bible*) Evangelist.

évangile [evɑ̃ʒil] *nm* **(a)** (*Rel*) **É~** gospel; (*Rel*) **l'~ du jour** the day's gospel (reading), the day's reading from the gospel; **les É~s synoptiques** the synoptic Gospels. **(b)** (*fig*) gospel. **ce n'est pas l'~, ce n'est pas parole d'~** it's not gospel.

évanoui, e [evanwi] (*ptp de* **s'évanouir**) *adj blessé* unconscious. **tomber ~** to fall down in a faint.

évanouir (s') [evanwiʀ] (2) *vpr* (*lit*) *[personne]* (*syncope*) to faint (*de* from), pass out (*de* with); (*à la suite d'un accident, choc*) to lose consciousness, faint; (*fig*) *[rêves, apparition, craintes]* to vanish, disappear.

évanouissement [evanwismɑ̃] *nm* **(a)** (*syncope*) fainting fit; (*perte de conscience: accident etc*) loss of consciousness. **(b)** (*fig*) *[rêves, apparition, craintes]* disappearance, fading.

évaporation [evapɔʀɑsjɔ̃] *nf* evaporation.

évaporé, e [evapɔʀe] (*ptp de* **évaporer**) **1** *adj* (*péj*) *personne* giddy, scatterbrained. **2** *nm,f* scatterbrain.

évaporer [evapɔʀe] (1) **1** *vt* (*gén* **faire ~**) to evaporate. **2 s'évaporer** *vpr* (*lit*) to evaporate; (*: *disparaître*) to vanish *ou* disappear (into thin air).

évasé, e [evɑze] (*ptp de* **évaser, s'évaser**) *adj vallée, conduit* which widens *ou* opens out; *jambes, manches, jupe* flared. **verre à bords ~s** glass with a curving *ou* bell-shaped rim.

évasement [evɑzmɑ̃] *nm* **(a)** (*V* **évaser**) widening- *ou* opening-out; flaring. **(b)** (*V* **s'évaser**) opening-out; flare.

évaser [evɑze] (1) **1** *vt tuyau, ouverture* to widen, open out; (*Couture*) *jupe, poignets* to flare. **2 s'évaser** *vpr [passage, tuyau]* to open out; *[manches]* to flare.

évasif, -ive [evazif, iv] *adj* evasive.

évasion [evazjɔ̃] *nf* (*lit, fig: fuite*) escape. (*fig: tendance*) **l'~** escapism; (*fig*) **littérature d'~** escapist literature; (*fig*) **besoin d'~** need to escape; (*Écon*) **~ des capitaux** flight of capital; (*Admin*) **~ fiscale** tax evasion.

évasivement [evazivmɑ̃] *adv* evasively.

Ève [ɛv] *nf* Eve; *V* **connaître.**

évêché [eveʃe] *nm* (*région*) bishopric; (*palais*) bishop's palace; (*ville*) cathedral town.

éveil [evɛj] *nm* (*littér*) *[dormeur, intelligence]* awakening; *[amour]* awakening, dawning; *[soupçons, jalousie]* arousing. **être en ~** *[personne]* to be on the alert *ou* on the qui vive; *[sens]* to be alert *ou* wide awake, be aroused; **donner l'~** to give the alarm *ou* alert; **mettre qn en ~, donner l'~ à qn** to alert *ou* arouse sb's suspicions, put sb on his guard.

éveillé, e [eveje] (*ptp de* **éveiller**) *adj* (*alerte*) *enfant, esprit, air* alert, sharp, bright; (*à l'état de veille*) (wide-)awake.

éveiller [eveje] (1) **1** *vt* **(a)** (*littér: réveiller*) to awaken, waken. **tenir qn éveillé** to keep sb awake; *V* **rêve.**

(b) (*fig: faire naître*) *curiosité, sentiment, soupçons* to arouse, awaken; *passion* to kindle, arouse; *souvenirs* to awaken. **pour ne pas ~ l'attention** so as not to arouse attention.

(c) (*développer*) *esprit, intelligence* to stimulate.

2 s'éveiller *vpr* **(a)** (*littér: se réveiller*) (*lit*) to awaken, waken; (*fig*) *[ville, nature]* to come to life, wake (up).

(b) (*fig: naître*) *[sentiment, curiosité, soupçons]* to be aroused; *[amour]* to dawn, be aroused *ou* born.

(c) (*se développer*) *[intelligence, esprit]* to develop.

(d) (*littér: ressentir*) **s'~ à** *amour* to awaken to.

événement [evɛnmɑ̃] *nm* event, occurrence (*frm*). (*Pol*) **~s** events, incidents; **c'est un véritable ~ quand il dit merci** it's quite an event *ou* occasion when he says thank you; **semaine chargée en ~s** eventful week, action-packed week; *V* **dépasser, heureux, tournure.**

événementiel, -ielle [evɛnmɑ̃sjɛl] *adj*: **histoire ~le** factual history.

évent [evɑ̃] *nm* (*Zool*) *[baleine]* blowhole, spout (hole), spiracle (*T*).

éventail [evɑ̃taj] *nm* (*instrument*) fan; (*fig: gamme*) range. **en ~** fan-shaped; **en (forme d')~** *objet* fan-shaped; **en ~** *plusieurs objets* fanned out, splayed out; **doigts de pieds en ~:** splayed toes; *V* **déployer, voûte.**

éventaire [evɑ̃tɛʀ] *nm* (*corbeille*) tray, basket; (*étalage*) stall, stand.

éventé, e [evɑ̃te] (*ptp de* **éventer, s'éventer**) *adj parfum, vin* stale, musty; *bière* stale, flat.

éventer [evɑ̃te] (1) **1** *vt* **(a)** (*rafraîchir*) to air; (*avec un éventail*) to fan. **s'~ avec un journal** to fan o.s. with a newspaper; **rue très éventée** very windy *ou* exposed street. **(b)** (*fig: découvrir*) *secret, complot* to discover, lay open. **le secret est éventé** the secret is out; **c'est un truc éventé** it's a well-known *ou* a rather obvious *ou* a pretty well-worn trick. **2 s'éventer** *vpr [bière]* to go flat; *[vin, parfum]* to go stale *ou* musty.

éventration [evɑ̃tʀɑsjɔ̃] *nf* (*Méd*) rupture.

éventrer [evɑ̃tʀe] (1) *vt* **(a)** (*avec un couteau*) to disembowel; (*d'un coup de corne*) to gore. **il s'est éventré sur son volant** he ripped himself open *ou* eviscerated himself on his steering wheel.

(b) *boîte, sac* to tear open; *muraille, coffre* to smash open; *matelas* to rip open.

éventualité [evɑ̃tɥalite] *nf* **(a)** (*U*) possibility. **(b)** eventuality, contingency, possibility. **pour parer à toute ~** to guard against all eventualities *ou* possibilities *ou* contingencies; **dans l'~ d'un refus de sa part** should he refuse, in the event of his refusal.
éventuel, -elle [evɑ̃tɥɛl] *adj* possible.
éventuellement [evɑ̃tɥɛlmɑ̃] *adv* possibly. **~, nous pourrions** ... we could possibly *ou* perhaps ... .
évêque [evɛk] *nm* bishop.
évertuer (s') [evɛʀtɥe] (1) *vpr* **(a)** (*s'efforcer de*) **s'~ à faire** to strive *ou* do one's utmost *ou* struggle hard to do. **(b)** (*frm*, †: *se dépenser*) to strive, struggle. **s'~ contre qch** to struggle against sth.
éviction [eviksjɔ̃] *nf* (*Jur*) eviction; *[rival]* ousting, supplanting. **procéder à l'~ de** *locataires* to evict.
évidage [evidaʒ] *nm*, **évidement** [evidmɑ̃] *nm* hollowing-out, scooping-out.
évidemment [evidamɑ̃] *adv* (*bien sûr*) of course, obviously; (*frm: d'une manière certaine*) obviously.
évidence [evidɑ̃s] *nf* **(a)** (*caractère*) obviousness, evidence. **c'est l'~ même!** it's quite *ou* perfectly evident *ou* patently obvious; **se rendre à l'~** to bow *ou* yield to facts *ou* the evidence, face facts *ou* the evidence; **nier l'~** to deny the obvious *ou* the facts.
(b) (*fait*) obvious fact. **trois ~s se dégagent de ce discours** this speech brings three obvious facts to light; **c'est une ~ que de dire** it's a statement of the obvious *ou* it's stating the obvious to say.
(c) (*loc*) **(être) en ~** *[personne]* (to be) conspicuous *ou* in evidence; *[objet]* (to be) conspicuous *ou* in evidence, (be) in a prominent position; **mettre en ~** *personne* to bring to the fore; *fait* to bring to the fore, give prominence to; *objet* to put in a prominent *ou* conspicuous position; **se mettre en ~** to make o.s. conspicuous, make one's presence felt; **la lettre était bien en ~ sur la table** the letter was (lying) there for all to see *ou* was lying conspicuously on the table; **de toute ~, à l'~**† quite obviously *ou* evidently.
évident, e [evidɑ̃, ɑ̃t] *adj* obvious, evident. **il est ~ que** it is obvious *ou* evident that, it is plain for all to see that.
évider [evide] (1) *vt* to hollow out, scoop out.
évier [evje] *nm* sink.
évincement [evɛ̃smɑ̃] *nm [rival]* ousting, supplanting.
évincer [evɛ̃se] (3) *vt concurrent* to oust, supplant; (*rare Jur*) *locataire* to evict.
évitable [evitabl(ə)] *adj* avoidable.
évitage [evitaʒ] *nm* (*Naut: mouvement*) swinging; (*espace*) swinging room.
évitement [evitmɑ̃] *nm* (*Transport*) **voie d'~** loop line; **gare d'~** station with a loop line; (*Aut, Aviat*) **manœuvre d'~** avoidance action.
éviter [evite] (1) **1** *vt* **(a)** *coup, projectile* to avoid, dodge; *obstacle, danger, maladie, situation* to avoid, steer clear of; *gêneur, créancier* to avoid, keep clear of, evade; *regard* to avoid, evade, duck. **ils s'évitaient depuis quelque temps** they had been avoiding each other *ou* keeping clear of each other for some time; **~ qu'une situation n'empire** to avoid *ou* prevent the worsening of a situation.
(b) *erreur, mensonge, méthode* to avoid. **~ de faire qch** to avoid doing sth; **on lui a conseillé d'~ le sel** he has been advised to avoid *ou* keep off salt; **on lui a conseillé d'~ la mer/la marche** he has been advised to avoid the sea/walking; **évite le mensonge** *ou* **de mentir** avoid lying, shun lies (*littér*).
(c) ~ qch à qn to spare sb sth; **ça lui a évité d'avoir à se déplacer** that spared *ou* saved him the bother *ou* trouble of going; **s'~ toute fatigue** to spare o.s. any fatigue, save o.s. from getting at all tired.
2 *vi* (*Naut*) to swing.
évocateur, -trice [evɔkatœʀ, tʀis] *adj* evocative, suggestive (*de* of).
évocation [evɔkɑsjɔ̃] *nf* **(a)** *[souvenirs, faits]* evocation, recalling; *[scène, idée]* conjuring-up, evocation. **ces ~s la faisaient s'attendrir** she became more tender as she recalled these memories; **pouvoir d'~ d'un mot** evocative *ou* suggestive power of a word.
(b) (*littér*) *[démons]* evocation, calling-up, conjuring-up.
évolué, e [evɔlɥe] (*ptp de* **évoluer**) *adj peuple, civilisation* (highly) developed, advanced; *personne* broad-minded, enlightened. **une jeune fille très ~e** a girl with very progressive *ou* liberated views *ou* a very independent attitude.
évoluer [evɔlɥe] (1) *vi* **(a)** (*changer*) *[idées, civilisation, science]* to evolve, develop, advance; *[personne, goûts, maladie, tumeur]* to develop; *[situation]* to develop, evolve. **il a beaucoup évolué** his ideas have *ou* he has developed a great deal, he has come on a long way (in his ideas).
(b) (*se mouvoir*) *[danseur]* to move about; *[avion]* to circle; *[troupes]* to manoeuvre, wheel about.
évolutif, -ive [evɔlytif, iv] *adj* (*gén, Bio*) evolutive, evolutionary; (*Méd*) progressive; *V* ski.
évolution [evɔlysjɔ̃] *nf* **(a)** (*changement*) *[idées, civilisation, science]* evolution, development, advancement; *[personne, goûts, maladie, situation]* development. (*Bio*) **théorie de l'~** theory of evolution.
(b) (*mouvement*) movement. **il regardait les ~s du danseur/de l'avion** he watched the dancer as he moved about gracefully/the plane as it wheeled *ou* circled overhead; **suivre à la jumelle les ~s des troupes** to watch troop manoeuvres through field glasses.
évolutionnisme [evɔlysjɔnism(ə)] *nm* evolutionism.
évolutionniste [evɔlysjɔnist(ə)] **1** *adj* evolutionary. **2** *nmf* evolutionist.

évoquer [evɔke] (1) *vt* **(a)** (*remémorer*) *souvenirs* to recall, call up, evoke; *fait, événement* to evoke, recall.
(b) (*faire penser à*) *scène, idée* to call to mind, evoke, conjure up.
(c) (*effleurer*) *problème, sujet* to touch on, mention.
(d) (*littér: invoquer*) *démons* to evoke, call up, conjure up.
ex- [ɛks] *préf* ex-.
exacerbation [ɛgzasɛʀbɑsjɔ̃] *nf* exacerbation.
exacerber [ɛgzasɛʀbe] (1) *vt* to exacerbate, aggravate.
exact, e [ɛgza, akt(ə)] *adj* **(a)** (*fidèle*) *reproduction, compte rendu* exact, accurate, true. **est-il ~ que?** is it right *ou* correct that?; **c'est l'~e vérité** that's the absolute *ou* exact truth; **ce n'est pas tout à fait ~** that's not quite right *ou* accurate, that's not altogether correct; **~!*** quite right!, absolutely!, exactly!
(b) (*correct*) *définition, raisonnement* correct, exact; *réponse* correct, right; *calcul* correct, right.
(c) (*précis*) *dimension, nombre, valeur* exact, precise; *donnée* accurate, precise, correct. **l'heure ~e** the right *ou* exact time.
(d) (*ponctuel*) punctual, on time. **être ~ à un rendez-vous** to arrive at an appointment on time, arrive punctually for an appointment; **~ à payer ses dettes** punctual in paying one's debts.
(e) (*littér*) *discipline* exact, rigorous, strict; *obéissance* rigorous, strict, scrupulous.
exactement [ɛgzaktəmɑ̃] *adv* (*V* **exact**) exactly; accurately; correctly; precisely; rigorously; strictly; scrupulously. **c'est ~ ce que je pensais** it's just *ou* precisely what I was thinking.
exaction [ɛgzaksjɔ̃] *nf* exaction.
exactitude [ɛgzaktityd] *nf* **(a)** (*U: V* **exact**) exactness, exactitude (*frm*); accuracy; correctness; precision. **calculer qch avec ~** to calculate sth exactly *ou* accurately.
(b) (*ponctualité*) punctuality. **l'~ est la politesse des rois** punctuality is the politeness of kings.
(c) (*littér: minutie*) exactitude.
ex æquo [ɛgzeko] **1** *adj inv* (*Scol, Sport*) equally placed. **avoir le premier prix ~, être classé premier ~** to be placed first equal *ou* joint first; **les ~** the pupils who are placed equal. **2** *adv* **classer** equal.
exagération [ɛgzaʒeʀɑsjɔ̃] *nf* (*gén*) exaggeration. **on peut dire sans ~ que ...** one can say without any exaggeration *ou* without exaggerating that ...; **il est sévère sans ~** he's severe without taking it to extremes.
exagéré, e [ɛgzaʒeʀe] (*ptp de* **exagérer**) *adj* (*amplifié*) exaggerated; (*excessif*) excessive. **venir se plaindre après ça, c'est un peu ~** to come and complain after all that, it's a bit much* (*Brit*) *ou* too much (*US*); **il n'est pas ~ de dire** it is not an exaggeration *ou* not going too far to say.
exagérément [ɛgzaʒeʀemɑ̃] *adv* excessively, exaggeratedly.
exagérer [ɛgzaʒeʀe] (6) **1** *vt* (*gén*) to exaggerate; *attitude* to exaggerate, take too far; *qualités* to overdo, overemphasize. **sans ~, ça a duré 3 heures** without any exaggeration *ou* I'm not exaggerating *ou* kidding* it lasted 3 hours; **quand même il exagère** really he goes too far *ou* oversteps the mark.
2 s'exagérer *vpr difficultés* to exaggerate; *plaisirs, avantages* to overrate.
exaltant, e [ɛgzaltɑ̃, ɑ̃t] *adj* exalting, elating, exhilarating.
exaltation [ɛgzaltɑsjɔ̃] *nf* **(a)** (*surexcitation: gén*) intense excitement. **~ joyeuse** elation, rapturous joy; **~ mystique** exaltation. **(b)** (*glorification*) extolling, praising, exalting.
exalté, e [ɛgzalte] (*ptp de* **exalter**) *adj sentiments* elated; *imagination* wild, vivid; *esprit* excited. (*péj*) **ce sont des ~s** they are fanatics.
exalter [ɛgzalte] (1) *vt* **(a)** (*surexciter*) *imagination, esprit, courage* to fire, excite. **exalté par cette nouvelle** (*très excité*) excited by *ou* keyed up with excitement over this piece of news; (*euphorique*) elated *ou* overjoyed by *ou* at this piece of news; **il s'exalte facilement en lisant des romans** he is easily carried away when he reads novels.
(b) (*glorifier*) to exalt, glorify, praise.
examen [ɛgzamɛ̃] **1** *nm* **(a)** (*U: action d'étudier, d'analyser*) (*gén*) examination; *[situation]* examination, survey; *[question, demande, cas]* examination, consideration, investigation; *[appartement]* looking-round *ou* -over. **~ détaillé** scrutiny, close examination; **la question est à l'~** the matter is under consideration; (*Comm*) **à l'~** on approval.
(b) (*Méd*) **~ (médical)** (medical) examination *ou* test; **se faire faire des ~s** to have some tests done *ou* taken; **subir un ~ médical complet** to undergo *ou* have a complete *ou* thorough checkup, have a thorough medical examination.
(c) (*Scol*) exam, examination. **~ d'entrée/oral** entrance/oral examination.
2: (*Scol*) **examen blanc** mock exam; **examen de conscience** self-examination; (*Rel*) examination of conscience; **faire son examen de conscience** to examine one's conscience, take stock of o.s.; (*Univ*) **examen partiel** class exam; (*Scol*) **examen de passage** end-of-year exam; (*Méd*) **examen prénuptial** premarital examination; (*Méd*) **examen du sang** blood test; (*Sci*) **examen spectroscopique** spectroscopic examination; (*Méd*) **examen de la vue** sight test; **passer un examen de la vue** to have one's eyes tested.
examinateur, -trice [ɛgzaminatœʀ, tʀis] *nm,f* examiner.
examiner [ɛgzamine] (1) *vt* **(a)** (*analyser*) (*gén*) to examine; *situation* to examine, survey; *possibilité, faits* to examine, go into; *question, demande, cas* to examine, consider, investigate, look into; *comptes, dossier* to examine, go through; *notes, documents* to examine, have a close look at. **~ dans le** *ou* **en détail** to scrutinize, examine closely; **~ une question de près** to go closely into a question, take a close look at a question; (*fig*) **~ à la loupe** to look into *ou* examine in the greatest detail.

(b) (*regarder*) *objet, personne, visage* to examine, study; *ciel, horizon* to scan; *appartement, pièce* to have a (close) look round, look over. **~ les lieux** to have a look round, look round the place; **~ qch au microscope/à la loupe** to examine *ou* look at sth under a microscope/with a magnifying glass; **~ qn de la tête aux pieds** to look sb up and down (contemptuously); **s'~ devant la glace** to look at o.s. *ou* examine o.s. in the mirror.

(c) (*Méd*) *malade* to examine. **se faire ~ par un spécialiste** to be examined by a specialist, have o.s. examined by a specialist.

(d) (*Scol*) *étudiant* to examine.

exaspérant, e [ɛgzaspeʀɑ̃, ɑ̃t] *adj* exasperating, aggravating*.

exaspération [ɛgzaspeʀɑsjɔ̃] *nf* exasperation.

exaspérer [ɛgzaspeʀe] (6) *vt* **(a)** (*irriter*) to exasperate, aggravate*. **(b)** (*littér: aviver*) to exacerbate, aggravate.

exaucement [ɛgzosmɑ̃] *nm* fulfilment, granting.

exaucer [ɛgzose] (3) *vt vœu* to fulfil, grant; (*Rel*) *prière* to grant, answer. **~ qn** to grant sb's wish, answer sb's prayer.

ex cathedra [ɛkskatedʀa] *adv* ex cathedra.

excavateur [ɛkskavatœʀ] *nm* (*machine*) excavator, mechanical digger.

excavation [ɛkskavɑsjɔ̃] *nf* (*trou*) excavation. **~ naturelle** natural hollow *ou* cave *etc*; (*creusement*) excavation.

excavatrice [ɛkskavatʀis] *nf* = **excavateur.**

excaver [ɛkskave] (1) *vt* to excavate.

excédant, e [ɛksedɑ̃, ɑ̃t] *adj* (*énervant*) exasperating.

excédent [ɛksedɑ̃] *nm* surplus (*sur* over). **~ de poids/bagages** excess weight/luggage *ou* baggage; **budget en ~** surplus budget; **payer 3 F d'~** to pay 3 francs excess charge.

excédentaire [ɛksedɑ̃tɛʀ] *adj production* excess (*épith*), surplus (*épith*).

excéder [ɛksede] (6) *vt* **(a)** (*dépasser*) *longueur, temps, prix* to exceed, be greater than. **le prix excédait (de beaucoup) ses moyens** the price was (way *ou* far) beyond *ou* far exceeded his means; **les avantages excèdent les inconvénients** the advantages outweigh the disadvantages; **l'apprentissage n'excède pas 3 ans** the apprenticeship doesn't last more than 3 years *ou* lasts no more than *ou* does not exceed 3 years.

(b) (*outrepasser*) *pouvoir, droits* to overstep, exceed, go beyond; *forces* to overtax.

(c) (*accabler: gén pass*) to exhaust, weigh down, weary. **excédé de fatigue** overcome by tiredness, exhausted, tired out; **excédé de travail** overworked.

(d) (*agacer: gén pass*) to exasperate, irritate. **je suis excédé** I'm furious; **tu m'excèdes avec tes jérémiades!** your whining irritates me!, you exasperate me with your moaning!

excellemment [ɛksɛlamɑ̃] *adv* (*littér*) excellently.

excellence [ɛksɛlɑ̃s] *nf* **(a)** excellence. **il est le poète surréaliste par ~** he is the surrealist poet par excellence; **il aime la musique par ~** he loves music above all else. **(b) Son E~** his Excellency; **merci (Votre) E~** thank you, your Excellency.

excellent, e [ɛksɛlɑ̃, ɑ̃t] *adj* excellent.

exceller [ɛksele] (1) *vi* to excel (*dans ou en qch* in sth, *à faire* in doing).

excentricité [ɛksɑ̃tʀisite] *nf* eccentricity.

excentrique [ɛksɑ̃tʀik] **1** *adj personne, (Math) cercle* eccentric; *quartier* outlying. **2** *nmf* eccentric, crank (*péj*).

excentriquement [ɛksɑ̃tʀikmɑ̃] *adv* (*gén*) eccentrically.

excepté, e [ɛksɛpte] (*ptp de* **excepter**) **1** *adj*: **il n'a plus de famille sa mère ~e** he has no family left apart from *ou* except his mother, excluding his mother he has no family left.

2 *prép* except, but for, apart from. **~ quand** except *ou* apart from when; **~ que** except that.

excepter [ɛksɛpte] (1) *vt* to except (*de* from), make an exception of. **sans ~ personne** without excluding anyone, no one excepted.

exception [ɛksɛpsjɔ̃] *nf* **(a)** (*dérogation*) exception. **à quelques (rares) ~s près** with a (very) few exceptions; **c'est l'~ qui confirme la règle** it's the exception which proves the rule; **d'~** *tribunal, régime, mesure* special, exceptional.

(b) (*loc*) **faire une ~ à** *règle* to make an exception to; **faire ~ (à la règle)** to be an exception (to the rule); **faire ~ de** to make an exception of; **~ faite de, à l'~ de** except for, apart from, with the exception of; **sauf ~** allowing for exceptions; *V* **titre.**

exceptionnel, -elle [ɛksɛpsjɔnɛl] *adj* exceptional.

exceptionnellement [ɛksɛpsjɔnɛlmɑ̃] *adv* (*à titre d'exception*) in this particular instance, in particular instances; (*très: avec adj*) exceptionally. **ils se sont réunis ~ un dimanche** contrary to their general practice *ou* in this particular instance they met on a Sunday.

excès [ɛksɛ] **1** *nm* **(a)** (*surplus*) *[argent]* excess, surplus; *[marchandises, produits]* glut, surplus. **il y a un ~ d'acide** (*il en reste*) there is some acid left over *ou* some excess acid; (*il y en a trop*) there is too much acid; **~ de précautions** excessive care *ou* precautions; **~ de zèle** overzealousness; *V* **pécher.**

(b) (*gén, Méd, Pol: abus*) excess. **des ~ de langage** extreme *ou* immoderate language; **tomber dans l'~ inverse** to go to the opposite extreme; **~ (*pl*) de boisson** overindulgence in drink, intemperance; **~ (*pl*) de table** overindulgence at (the) table, surfeit of (good) food.

(c) (*loc*) (*littér*) **à l'~, jusqu'à l'~** to excess, excessively, inordinately; **généreux à l'~** overgenerous, generous to a fault; **avec ~** to excess, excessively; **il fait tout avec ~** he does everything to excess, he is excessive in everything he does; **boire avec ~** to drink to excess; **dépenser avec ~** to be excessive in one's spending.

2: (*Jur*) **excès de pouvoir** actions ultra vires; (*Aut*) **excès de vitesse** breaking *ou* exceeding the speed limit, speeding*; **coupable de plusieurs excès de vitesse** guilty of having broken *ou* exceeded the speed limit on several occasions.

excessif, -ive [ɛksesif, iv] *adj* excessive. **c'est une femme ~ive (en tout)** she takes everything to extremes *ou* too far; **30 F c'est ~!** 30 francs, that's far too much! *ou* that's excessive!

excessivement [ɛksesivmɑ̃] *adv* excessively.

exciper [ɛksipe] (1) **exciper de** *vt indir* (*frm*) *bonne foi, précédent* to plead.

excipient [ɛksipjɑ̃] *nm* excipient.

exciser [ɛksize] (1) *vt* to excise.

excision [ɛksizjɔ̃] *nf* excision.

excitabilité [ɛksitabilite] *nf* (*Bio*) excitability.

excitable [ɛksitabl(ə)] *adj* excitable, easily excited.

excitant, e [ɛksitɑ̃, ɑ̃t] **1** *adj* (*gén*) exciting. **2** *nm* stimulant.

excitation [ɛksitɑsjɔ̃] *nf* **(a)** (*Méd*) *[nerf, muscle]* excitation, stimulation; (*Élec*) *[électro-aimant]* excitation.

(b) (*incitation*) **~ à** incitement to.

(c) (*enthousiasme*) excitement, exhilaration; (*désir sexuel*) (sexual) excitement. **dans un état de grande ~** in a state of great excitement.

excité, e [ɛksite] (*ptp de* **exciter**) *nm,f* hothead*. **une poignée d'~s** a bunch of hotheads*; **ne fais pas attention, c'est un ~** don't take any notice — he gets carried away.

exciter [ɛksite] (1) **1** *vt* **(a)** (*provoquer*) *ardent désir* to arouse, waken, excite; *rire* to cause; *pitié* to rouse; *curiosité* to rouse, excite, whet; *imagination* to stimulate, fire, stir; *appétit* to whet, excite.

(b) (*aviver*) *colère, douleur* to intensify, increase; *ardeur* to increase. **cela ne fit qu'~ sa colère** that only increased his anger, that only made him even more angry.

(c) (*enthousiasmer*) *personne* to thrill, excite, exhilarate. **il était tout excité** he was all excited; **il ne semble pas très excité par son nouveau travail*** he doesn't seem very thrilled about *ou* by *ou* wild* about his new job; **excitant pour l'esprit** mentally stimulating.

(d) (*rendre nerveux*) *personne* to arouse, make tense; *chien, cheval* to pester, tease, excite; (*sexuellement*) to arouse *ou* excite (sexually). **le café m'exciterait trop** coffee would just act as a stimulant on me *ou* would make me too wakeful; **tous ses sens étaient excités** all his senses were aroused; **il est arrivé tout excité** he was all wound up* *ou* in quite a state when he arrived.

(e) (*: *irriter*) to irritate, exasperate, annoy. **il commence à m'~** he's getting on my nerves.

(f) (*encourager*) to urge on, spur on. **excitant ses chiens de la voix** urging on *ou* spurring on his dogs with shouts, shouting to urge on his dogs; **~ qn contre qn** to set sb against sb.

(g) (*inciter*) **~ à** to exhort to, incite to, urge to; **~ qn à faire qch** to push sb into doing sth, provoke *ou* urge sb to do sth; **~ des soldats au combat** to incite *ou* exhort soldiers to combat *ou* battle.

(h) (*Méd*) *nerf, muscle* to stimulate, excite; (*Élec*) *électro-aimant* to excite.

2 s'exciter *vpr* (*: *s'enthousiasmer*) to get excited *ou* wound up* (*sur, à propos de* about, over); (*devenir nerveux*) to get worked up*, get in a flap*; (*sexuellement*) to become (sexually) excited, be (sexually) aroused; (*: *se fâcher*) to get angry *ou* annoyed, fly off the handle*, get hot under the collar*.

exclamatif, -ive [ɛksklamatif, iv] *adj* exclamatory.

exclamation [ɛksklamɑsjɔ̃] *nf* exclamation; *V* **point**[1].

exclamer (s') [ɛksklame] (1) *vpr* to exclaim. **'dommage!' s'exclama-t-il** 'what a pity!' he exclaimed; (*littér*) **s'~ de colère/d'admiration** to cry out in anger/admiration; (*littér: protester*) **s'~ sur qch** to shout *ou* make a fuss about sth.

exclure [ɛksklyʀ] (35) *vt* **(a)** (*chasser*) (*d'une salle*) to turn *ou* put out; (*d'un parti politique*) to expel, oust; (*d'une école*) to expel, exclude; (*d'une université*) to send down (*de* from). **se faire ~ de** to get o.s. put out *ou* expelled *ou* sent down from.

(b) (*écarter*) *solution* to exclude, rule out; *hypothèse* to dismiss, turn down. **~ qch de son régime** to cut sth out of one's diet; **~ qch d'une somme** to exclude sth from a sum, leave sth out of a sum; **je tiens à être exclu de cette affaire** count me out of this business; **c'est tout à fait exclu** it's quite out of the question, it's just not on*; **idées qui s'excluent mutuellement** ideas which are mutually exclusive.

exclusif, -ive[1] [ɛksklyzif, iv] *adj* **(a)** *sentiment* exclusive. **il a un caractère (trop) ~** he's (too) exclusive in his relationships; **très ~ dans ses amitiés** very selective *ou* exclusive in his friendships; **très ~ dans ses goûts** very selective in his tastes.

(b) *droit* exclusive (*de qch* of sth, *de faire* to do). **dans le but ~ d'une amélioration/de faire ...** with the sole *ou* exclusive aim of making an improvement/of doing ... .

(c) (*Comm*) *droits* sole (*épith*), exclusive (*épith*); *représentant* sole (*épith*); *fabrication* exclusive (*epith*).

exclusion [ɛksklyzjɔ̃] *nf* **(a)** (*expulsion*) (*d'une salle*) exclusion; (*d'un parti politique*) expulsion; (*d'une école*) exclusion, expulsion (*de* from). **~ temporaire** *[étudiant]* rustication, suspension.

(b) à l'~ de (*sauf*) with the exclusion *ou* exception of; (*en écartant, rejetant*) to the exclusion of; **aimer les pommes à l'~ de tous les autres fruits** to love apples to the exclusion of all other fruit; **il peut manger de tous les fruits à l'~ des pommes** he can eat any fruit excluding apples *ou* with the exclusion *ou* exception of apples.

exclusive[2] [ɛksklyziv] *nf* (*frm*) bar, debarment. **tous sans ~** with none debarred; **frapper qn d'~, prononcer l'~ contre qn** to debar sb.

exclusivement [ɛksklyzivmɑ̃] *adv* **(a)** (*seulement*) exclusively, solely. **~ réservé au personnel** reserved for staff only. **(b)** (*non inclus*) **du 10 au 15 du mois ~** from the 10th to the 15th exclusive. **(c)** (*littér: de manière entière ou absolue*) exclusively.

exclusivité [ɛksklyzivite] *nf* **(a)** (*Comm*) exclusive rights. **(b)** (*Ciné*) **ce film passe en ~ à** this film is showing only *ou* exclusively at; **cinéma d'~** cinema with exclusive showing rights on new releases. **(c)** *[sentiment]* exclusiveness.

excommunication [ɛkskɔmynikɑsjɔ̃] *nf* excommunication.

excommunier [ɛkskɔmynje] (7) *vt* to excommunicate.

excrément [ɛkskʀemɑ̃] *nm* excrement (*U*), faeces (*pl*).

excrémenteux, -euse [ɛkskʀemɑ̃tø, øz] *adj*, **excrémentiel, -elle** [ɛkskʀemɑ̃sjɛl] *adj* excremental.

excréter [ɛkskʀete] (6) *vt* to excrete.

excrétion [ɛkskʀesjɔ̃] *nf* excretion. **~s** excreta.

excroissance [ɛkskʀwasɑ̃s] *nf* (*surtout Méd*) excrescence, outgrowth; (*fig*) outgrowth, development.

excursion [ɛkskyʀsjɔ̃] *nf* (*en car etc*) excursion, (sightseeing) trip; (*à pied*) walk, hike. **~ botanique** (*Scol*) nature walk; (*Sci*) field-study trip; **~ de 3 jours à travers le pays** 3-day tour *ou* (sightseeing) trip around the country; **~s d'un jour en autocar** day trips by coach.

excursionner [ɛkskyʀsjɔne] (1) *vi* (*V* **excursion**) to go on excursions *ou* trips; to go on walks, go hiking; to go touring. **station idéale pour ~** resort ideal for walks *ou* hiking, resort ideal as a base for touring.

excursionniste [ɛkskyʀsjɔnist(ə)] *nmf* (*en car etc*) (day) tripper; (*à pied*) hiker, walker.

excusable [ɛkskyzabl(ə)] *adj* excusable, forgivable.

excuse [ɛkskyz] *nf* **(a)** (*prétexte*) excuse. **bonne ~** good excuse; **mauvaises ~s** poor excuses; **sans ~** inexcusable; **il a pris pour ~ qu'il avait à travailler** he made *ou* gave the excuse that he had work to do, he used his work as an excuse; *V* **mot**.

(b) (*regret*) **~s** apology; **faire des ~s, présenter ses ~s** to apologize, offer one's apologies; **je vous dois des ~s** I owe you an apology; **exiger des ~s** to demand an apology; **mille ~s** do forgive me, I'm so sorry.

(c) faites ~: excuse me, 'scuse me*.

excuser [ɛkskyze] (1) **1** *vt* **(a)** (*pardonner*) *personne, faute* to excuse, forgive. **veuillez ~ mon retard** please excuse my being late *ou* my lateness, I do apologize for being late; **je vous prie de l'~** please excuse *ou* forgive him; (*frm*) **veuillez m'~, je vous prie de m'~** I beg your pardon, please forgive me (*pour avoir fait* for having done); **excusez-moi** excuse me, I'm sorry; **je m'excuse*** I'm sorry, sorry; **excusez-moi de vous le dire mais ...** excuse *ou* forgive *ou* pardon my saying so but ...; **excusez-moi de ne pas venir** excuse my not coming, I'm sorry I can't come; **vous êtes tout excusé** please don't apologize, you are quite forgiven.

(b) (*justifier*) to excuse. **cette explication n'excuse rien** this explanation is no excuse.

(c) (*dispenser*) to excuse. **il a demandé à être excusé pour la réunion de demain** he asked to be excused from tomorrow's meeting; **se faire ~** to ask to be excused; **'M Dupont: (absent) excusé'** 'Mr Dupont has sent an apology', 'apologies for absence received from Mr Dupont'.

2 s'excuser *vpr*: **s'~ de qch** to apologize for sth; **(aller) s'~ auprès de qn** to apologize to sb.

exécrable [ɛgzekʀabl(ə)] *adj* atrocious, execrable.

exécrablement [ɛgzekʀabləmɑ̃] *adv* atrociously, execrably.

exécration [ɛgzekʀɑsjɔ̃] *nf* **(a)** (*littér: haine*) execration, loathing. **avoir qch en ~** to hold sth in abhorrence. **(b)** (††: *imprécation*) curse.

exécrer [ɛgzekʀe] (6) *vt* to loathe, abhor, execrate.

exécutable [ɛgzekytabl(ə)] *adj tâche* possible, manageable; *projet* workable, feasible.

exécutant, e [ɛgzekytɑ̃, ɑ̃t] *nm,f* (*Mus*) performer, executant. (*fig péj: agent*) **il n'est qu'un ~** he just carries out (his) orders.

exécuter [ɛgzekyte] (1) **1** *vt* **(a)** (*accomplir*) *plan, ordre, mouvements* to execute, carry out; *projet, mission* to carry out, accomplish; *promesse* to fulfil, carry out; *travail* to do, execute; *tâche* to discharge, perform. **il a fait ~ des travaux dans sa maison** he had some work done on his house.

(b) (*confectionner*) *objet* to produce, make; *tableau* to paint, execute†.

(c) *commande, ordonnance* to make up. **il a fait ~ l'ordonnance par le pharmacien** he had the prescription made up by the chemist.

(d) (*Mus*) *morceau* to perform, execute. **brillamment exécuté** brilliantly executed *ou* played.

(e) (*tuer*) to execute, put to death; (*fig*) *[boxeur etc]* to dispose of, eliminate, wipe out.

(f) (*Jur*) *traité, loi, décret* to enforce.

2 s'exécuter *vpr* (*en s'excusant etc*) to comply; (*en payant*) to pay up. **je lui demandai de s'excuser — à contrecœur il finit par s'~** I asked him to apologize and finally he reluctantly complied *ou* did so; **vint le moment de l'addition, il s'exécuta de mauvaise grâce et nous partîmes** when the time came to settle the bill he paid up with bad *ou* ill grace and we left.

exécuteur, -trice [ɛgzekytœʀ, tʀis] **1** *nm,f [arrêt, décret]* enforcer. **2** *nm* (*Hist*) **~ (des hautes œuvres)** executioner; (*Jur*) **~ (testamentaire)** executor.

exécutif, -ive [ɛgzekytif, iv] *adj, nm*: **pouvoir ~** executive power; **l'~** the executive.

exécution [ɛgzekysjɔ̃] *nf* **(a)** (*V* **exécuter**) execution; carrying out; accomplishment; fulfilment; discharge; performance; production; making; painting; making up; enforcement. **mettre à ~** *projet, idées* to put into operation, execute, carry out; *loi* to enforce; **'~!'** '(get) on with it!*'; **l'~ des travaux a été ralentie** the work has been slowed down, there have been delays *ou* hold-ups with the work; (*Mus*) **d'une ~ difficile** difficult to play; (*Jur*) **en ~ de la loi** in compliance *ou* accordance with the law; *V* **voie**.

(b) *[condamné]* execution. **~ capitale** capital execution.

(c) (*Jur*) *[débiteur]* execution of a writ (*de* against). **~ forcée** execution of a writ.

exécutoire [ɛgzekytwaʀ] *adj* (*Jur*) executory.

exégèse [ɛgzeʒɛz] *nf* exegesis.

exégète [ɛgzeʒɛt] *nm* exegete.

exemplaire [ɛgzɑ̃plɛʀ] **1** *adj mère, punition* exemplary. **infliger une punition ~ à qn** to make an example of sb (by punishing him).

2 *nm* **(a)** *[livre, formulaire]* copy. **en deux ~s** in duplicate; **en trois ~s** in triplicate.

(b) (*échantillon*) specimen, example.

exemplairement [ɛgzɑ̃plɛʀmɑ̃] *adv* exemplarily.

exemple [ɛgzɑ̃pl(ə)] *nm* **(a)** (*modèle*) example. **l'~ de leur faillite/de sa sœur lui sera bien utile** their failure/his sister will be a useful example for him; **il est l'~ de la vertu/l'honnêteté** he sets an example of virtue/honesty, he is a model of virtue/honesty; **citer qn/qch en ~** to quote sb/sth as an example; **donner l'~ de l'honnêteté/de ce qu'il faut faire** to give *ou* set an example of honesty/of what to do; **donner l'~** to set an example; **suivre l'~ de qn** to follow sb's example; **prendre ~ sur qn** to take sb as a model; **à l'~ de son père** just like one's father, following in one's father's footsteps; **faire un ~ de qn** (*punir*) to make an example of sb; **il faut absolument faire un ~** we must make an example of somebody; **il faut les punir, pour l'~** they must be punished, as an example; *V* **prêcher**.

(b) (*cas, spécimen*) example. **voici un ~ de leur avarice** here is an example *ou* instance of their meanness; **voici un bel ~ du gothique flamboyant** this is a fine example of flamboyant gothic; **ce pays fournit un ~ typique de monarchie constitutionnelle** this country provides a typical example of a constitutional monarchy; **le seul ~ que je connaisse** the only example *ou* instance I know of *ou* am aware of; **être d'une bêtise/avarice sans ~** to be of unparalleled stupidity/meanness; **il en existe plusieurs: ~, le rat musqué** there are several, for example the muskrat.

(c) (*Lexicographie*) example, illustrative phrase.

(d) par ~ (*explicatif*) for example *ou* instance; **(ça) par ~!** (*surprise*) my word!; (*indignation*) oh really!; (*: *par contre*) **c'est assez cher, par ~ on y mange bien** it's pretty dear, but there again the food is good*.

exempt, e [ɛgzɑ̃, ɑ̃t] **1** *adj* **(a)** (*dispensé de*) **~ de** *service militaire, corvée, impôts* exempt from; **~ de taxes** tax-free, duty-free.

(b) (*dépourvu de*) **~ de** *vent, dangers, arrogance, erreurs* free from; **entreprise ~e de dangers** danger-free undertaking, undertaking free from all danger.

2 *nm* (*Hist: Mil, Police*) exempt.

exempter [ɛgzɑ̃te] (1) *vt* **(a)** (*dispenser*) to exempt (*de* from). **(b)** (*préserver de*) **~ qn de** *soucis* to save sb from.

exemption [ɛgzɑ̃psjɔ̃] *nf* exemption.

exerçant, e [ɛgzɛʀsɑ̃, ɑ̃t] *adj*: **médecin ~** practising doctor.

exercé, e [ɛgzɛʀse] (*ptp de* **exercer**) *adj yeux, oreilles* keen, trained.

exercer [ɛgzɛʀse] (3) **1** *vt* **(a)** (*pratiquer*) *métier* to carry on, be in; *profession* to practise, exercise; *fonction* to fulfil, exercise; *talents* to exercise; (*littér*) *charité, hospitalité* to exercise, practise. *[médecin, avocat]* **il exerce encore** he's still practising *ou* in practice.

(b) *droit, pouvoir* to exercise (*sur* over); *contrôle, influence* to exert, exercise (*sur* over); *représailles* to take (*sur* on); *poussée, pression* to exert (*sur* on). **~ des pressions sur qn** to bring pressure to bear on sb; **~ ses sarcasmes contre qn** to use one's sarcasm on sb, make sb the butt of one's sarcasm; **ses sarcasmes s'exerçaient impitoyablement contre elle** she was the butt of his pitiless sarcasm; **les forces qui s'exercent sur le levier** the force exerted on *ou* brought to bear on the lever; (*Jur*) **~ des poursuites contre qn** to bring an action against sb.

(c) (*aguerrir*) *corps, esprit* to train, exercise (*à* to, for); *mémoire, jugement, facultés* to exercise. **~ des élèves à lire** *ou* **à la lecture** to exercise pupils in reading, get pupils to practise their reading; **~ un chien à rapporter le journal** to train a dog to bring back the morning paper.

(d) (*éprouver*) *sagacité, habileté* to tax; *patience* to try, tax.

2 s'exercer *vpr [pianiste, sportif]* to practise. **s'~ à** *technique, mouvement* to practise; **s'~ à la patience** to train o.s. to be patient; **s'~ à faire qch** to train o.s. to do sth.

exercice [ɛgzɛʀsis] **1** *nm* **(a)** (*V* **exercer**) *[métier, profession]* practice; *[droit]* exercising; *[facultés]* exercise; (*Rel*) *[culte]* exercise. **l'~ du pouvoir** the exercise of power; **après 40 ans d'~** after 40 years in practice; **dans l'~ de ses fonctions** in the execution *ou* discharge of his duties; **être en ~** *[médecin]* to be in practice; *[juge, fonctionnaire]* to be in *ou* hold office; **entrer en ~** to take up *ou* assume one's duties.

(b) (*V* **s'exercer**) practice, practising.

(c) (*activité physique*) **l'~** exercise; **prendre** *ou* **faire de l'~** to take some exercise.

(d) (*Mil*) **l'~** exercises, drill; **aller à l'~** to go on exercises; **faire l'~** to drill, be at drill.

(e) (*Mus, Scol, Sport: petit travail d'entraînement*) exercise. **~ pour piano** piano exercise; *V* **cahier**.

(f) (*Admin, Fin: période*) accounting period.

2: exercices d'assouplissement keep fit exercises; (*Fin*) **exercice budgétaire** budgetary year; **exercices phonétiques** phonetic drills; (*Rel*) **exercices spirituels** spiritual exercises; **exercices structuraux** structure drills; (*Littérat*) **exercice de style** stylistic composition; (*Mil*) **exercices de tir** shooting drill *ou* practice.

exerciseur [ɛgzɛʀsizœʀ] *nm* chest expander.

exergue [ɛgzɛʀg(ə)] *nm*: **en ~**: (*lit*) **cette médaille porte en ~ l'inscription ...** this medal is inscribed below ...; **le chapitre**

portait en ~ une citation de X the chapter bore in epigraph a quotation from X, a quotation from X provided the epigraph to the chapter *ou* headed the chapter; **mettre une citation en ~ à un chapitre** to head a chapter with a quotation, put in a quotation as (an) epigraph to a chapter; **mettre un proverbe en ~ à un tableau** to inscribe a painting with a proverb; (*fig: en évidence*) **mettre une idée/une phrase en ~** to bring out *ou* underline an idea/a sentence.
exhalaison [ɛgzalɛzɔ̃] *nf* (*littér*) (*désagréable*) exhalation; (*agréable*) fragrance (*U*), exhalation.
exhaler [ɛgzale] (1) *vt* (*littér*) **(a)** *odeur, vapeur* to exhale. **une odeur délicieuse s'exhalait de ...** a delicious smell was rising (up) from ...
(b) *soupir* to breathe; *plainte* to utter, give forth (*littér*); *joie, douleur* to give vent *ou* expression to. **un soupir s'exhala de ses lèvres** a sigh rose from his lips.
exhaussement [ɛgzosmɑ̃] *nm* raising.
exhausser [ɛgzose] (1) *vt construction* to raise (up). **~ une maison d'un étage** to add a floor to a house.
exhaustif, -ive [ɛgzostif, iv] *adj* exhaustive.
exhaustivement [ɛgzostivmɑ̃] *adv* exhaustively.
exhiber [ɛgzibe] (1) **1** *vt* (*péj*) *savoir, richesse* to display, flaunt; *chiens savants etc* to show, exhibit; (*frm*) *document, passeport* to present, show, produce; *seins, corps,* (*hum*) *mollets etc* to show off, display.
2 s'exhiber *vpr* **(a)** (*péj*) to show o.s. off (in public), parade.
(b) (*outrage à la pudeur*) to expose o.s.
exhibition [ɛgzibisjɔ̃] *nf* **(a)** (*V* **exhiber**) display; flaunting; show, exhibition; presentation, production. **que signifient ces ~s?** what do you mean by this exhibitionism? **(b)** (*rare: spectacle forain*) show, display.
exhibitionnisme [ɛgzibisjɔnism(ə)] *nm* exhibitionism.
exhibitionniste [ɛgzibisjɔnist(ə)] *nmf* exhibitionist. **il est un peu ~** he's a bit of an exhibitionist.
exhortation [ɛgzɔʀtɑsjɔ̃] *nf* exhortation.
exhorter [ɛgzɔʀte] (1) *vt* to exhort (*à faire* to do, *à qch* to sth), urge (*à faire* to do).
exhumation [ɛgzymɑsjɔ̃] *nf* (*V* **exhumer**) exhumation; excavation; unearthing, digging up *ou* out, disinterring; recollection, recalling.
exhumer [ɛgzyme] (1) *vt corps* to exhume; *ruines, vestiges* to excavate; (*fig*) *faits, vieux livres* to unearth, dig up *ou* out, disinter; *souvenirs* to recollect, recall.
exigeant, e [ɛgziʒɑ̃, ɑ̃t] *adj client, hôte* particular (*attrib*), demanding, hard to please (*attrib*); *enfant, amant* demanding, hard to please (*attrib*); *parents, patron, travail, amour* demanding, exacting. **je ne suis pas ~*, donnez-moi 100 F** I'm not asking for much — give me 100 francs.
exigence [ɛgziʒɑ̃s] *nf* **(a)** (*U*) *[client]* particularity; *[maître]* strictness. **il est d'une ~ insupportable** he's impossibly demanding *ou* particular.
(b) (*gén pl: revendication, condition*) demand, requirement. **produit satisfaisant à toutes les ~s** product which meets all requirements.
exiger [ɛgziʒe] (3) *vt* **(a)** (*réclamer*) to demand, require (*qch de qn* sth of *ou* from sb), insist on (*qch de qn* sth from sb). **j'exige de le faire** I insist on doing it, I demand to do it; **j'exige que vous le fassiez** I insist on your doing it, I demand *ou* insist that you do it; **j'exige (de vous) des excuses** I demand an apology (from you), I insist on an apology (from you); **la loi l'exige** the law requires *ou* demands it; **des titres universitaires sont exigés pour ce poste** university degrees are required *ou* needed *ou* are a requirement for this post; **trop ~ de ses forces** to ask *ou* demand too much of one's strength.
(b) (*nécessiter*) to require, call for, demand. **cette plante exige beaucoup d'eau** this plant needs *ou* requires a lot of water.
exigibilité [ɛgziʒibilite] *nf* payability.
exigible [ɛgziʒibl(ə)] *adj* (*Comm, Jur*) payable, due for payment.
exigu, -uë [ɛgzigy] *adj lieu* cramped, exiguous (*littér*); *ressources* scanty, meagre; *délais* short.
exiguïté [ɛgzigɥite] *nf* (*V* **exigu**) crampedness, exiguity (*littér*); scantiness, meagreness; shortness.
exil [ɛgzil] *nm* exile.
exilé, e [ɛgzile] (*ptp de* **exiler**) *nm,f* exile.
exiler [ɛgzile] (1) **1** *vt* (*Pol*) to exile; (*fig littér*) to banish. **se sentir exilé (loin de)** to feel like an outcast *ou* exile (far from); (*fig*) **une note importante exilée en bas de page** an important note tucked away at the bottom of the page.
2 s'exiler *vpr* (*Pol*) to go into exile. (*fig*) **s'~ à la campagne** to bury o.s. in the country; (*fig*) **s'~ en Australie** to exile o.s. to Australia, take o.s. off to Australia; (*fig*) **s'~ loin du monde** to cut o.s. off from the world.
existant, e [ɛgzistɑ̃, ɑ̃t] *adj coutume, loi, prix* existing, in existence.
existence [ɛgzistɑ̃s] *nf* **(a)** (*Philos, Rel: présence*) existence.
(b) (*vie quotidienne*) existence, life. **dans l'~** in life; *V* **moyen.**
existentialisme [ɛgzistɑ̃sjalism(ə)] *nm* existentialism.
existentialiste [ɛgzistɑ̃sjalist(ə)] *adj, nmf* existentialist.
existentiel, -ielle [ɛgzistɑ̃sjɛl] *adj* existential.
exister [ɛgziste] (1) *vi* **(a)** (*vivre*) to exist. (*péj*) **il se contente d'~** he is content with just getting by *ou* just existing.
(b) (*être réel*) to exist, be. **pour lui, la peur n'existe pas** there is no such thing as fear *ou* fear doesn't exist as far as he is concerned; **quoi que vous pensiez, le bonheur ça existe** whatever you may say, there is such a thing as happiness.
(c) (*se trouver*) to be, be found. **la vie existe-t-elle sur Mars?** is there life on Mars?; **produit qui existe en pharmacie** product (to be) found in chemists' shops; **le costume régional n'existe plus guère** regional dress is scarcely ever (to be) found *ou* seen these days; **les dinosaures n'existent plus/existent encore** dinosaurs are extinct/are still in existence; **les bateaux à aubes n'existent plus/existent encore** paddle steamers no longer/still exist; **il existe encore une copie** there is still one copy extant; **pourquoi monter à pied? les ascenseurs ça existe!** why walk up? there are lifts, you know! *ou* lifts have been invented!
(d) (*il y a*) **il existe** there is, there are; **il n'existe pas de ...** there is no ..., there are no ...; **il existe des bégonias de plusieurs couleurs** begonias come* *ou* are found in several colours.
exode [ɛgzɔd] *nm* (*lit, fig*) exodus. (*Bible*) **l'E~** the Exodus; **~ rural** drift from the land.
exonération [ɛgzɔneʀɑsjɔ̃] *nf* (*Fin*) exemption (*de* from).
exonérer [ɛgzɔneʀe] (6) *vt* (*Fin*) to exempt (*de* from).
exorbitant, e [ɛgzɔʀbitɑ̃, ɑ̃t] *adj prix* exorbitant; *demande, prétention* exorbitant, inordinate, outrageous.
exorbité, e [ɛgzɔʀbite] *adj yeux* bulging (*de* with).
exorcisation [ɛgzɔʀsizɑsjɔ̃] *nf* exorcizing.
exorciser [ɛgzɔʀsize] (1) *vt* to exorcize.
exorciseur [ɛgzɔʀsizœʀ] *nm* exorcizer.
exorcisme [ɛgzɔʀsism(ə)] *nm* exorcism.
exorciste [ɛgzɔʀsist(ə)] *nm* exorcist.
exorde [ɛgzɔʀd(ə)] *nm* introduction, exordium (*T*).
exosmose [ɛgzɔsmoz] *nf* exosmosis.
exotique [ɛgzɔtik] *adj pays, plante* exotic.
exotisme [ɛgzɔtism(ə)] *nm* exoticism. **aimer l'~** to love all that is exotic.
expansibilité [ɛkspɑ̃sibilite] *nf* expansibility.
expansible [ɛkspɑ̃sibl(ə)] *adj* expansible.
expansif, -ive [ɛkspɑ̃sif, iv] *adj* expansive. **il s'est montré peu ~** he was not very forthcoming *ou* communicative.
expansion [ɛkspɑ̃sjɔ̃] *nf* **(a)** (*extension*) expansion. **l'~ d'une doctrine** the spreading of a doctrine; **notre économie est en pleine ~** our economy is booming, we have a booming *ou* fast-expanding economy; **univers** *etc* **en ~** expanding universe *etc.*
(b) (*effusion*) expansiveness (*U*), effusiveness (*U*). **avec de grandes ~s** expansively, effusively.
expansionnisme [ɛkspɑ̃sjɔnism(ə)] *nm* expansionism.
expansionniste [ɛkspɑ̃sjɔnist(ə)] *adj, nmf* expansionist.
expansivité [ɛkspɑ̃sivite] *nf* expansiveness.
expatriation [ɛkspatʀijɑsjɔ̃] *nf* expatriation.
expatrié, e [ɛkspatʀije] (*ptp de* **expatrier**) *nm,f* expatriate.
expatrier [ɛkspatʀije] (7) **1** *vt* to expatriate. **2 s'expatrier** *vpr* to expatriate o.s., leave one's country.
expectative [ɛkspɛktativ] *nf* (*incertitude*) state of uncertainty; (*attente prudente*) cautious approach. **être *ou* rester dans l'~** (*incertitude*) to be still waiting *ou* hanging on (to hear *ou* see *etc*); (*attente prudente*) to hold back, wait and see.
expectorant, e [ɛkspɛktɔʀɑ̃, ɑ̃t] *adj, nm* expectorant.
expectoration [ɛkspɛktɔʀɑsjɔ̃] *nf* expectoration.
expectorer [ɛkspɛktɔʀe] (1) *vti* to expectorate.
expédient, e [ɛkspedjɑ̃, ɑ̃t] **1** *adj* (*frm*) expedient. **2** *nm* expedient, makeshift. **vivre d'~s** *[personne]* to live by one's wits; *[état]* to resort to short-term measures.
expédier [ɛkspedje] (7) *vt* **(a)** *lettre, paquet* to send, dispatch. **~ par la poste** to send through the post; **~ par le train** to send by rail *ou* train; **~ par bateau** *lettres, colis* to send surface mail; *matières premières* to ship, send by sea; (*fig*) **je l'ai expédié en vacances chez sa grand-mère*** I sent *ou* packed* him off to his grandmother's for the holidays; (*fig hum*) **~ qn dans l'autre monde** to bump sb off*.
(b) (*) *client, visiteur* to dispose of. **~ une affaire** to dispose of *ou* dispatch a matter, get a matter over with; **~ son déjeuner en 5 minutes** to polish off* one's lunch in 5 minutes.
(c) (*Admin*) **~ les affaires courantes** to deal with *ou* dispose of day-to-day matters.
expéditeur, -trice [ɛkspeditœʀ, tʀis] **1** *adj* dispatching, forwarding. **2** *nm,f* sender; *V* **retour.**
expéditif, -ive [ɛkspeditif, iv] *adj* quick, expeditious.
expédition [ɛkspedisjɔ̃] *nf* **(a)** (*action*) *[lettre, vivres, renforts]* dispatch; (*par bateau*) shipping.
(b) (*paquet*) consignment; (*par bateau*) shipment.
(c) (*Mil, Sci*) expedition. **~ de police** police raid; (*fig*) **quelle ~!** what an expedition!, what an upheaval!
(d) (*Admin*) **l'~ des affaires courantes** the dispatching of day-to-day matters.
expéditionnaire [ɛkspedisjɔnɛʀ] **1** *adj* (*Mil*) expeditionary. **2** *nmf* (*Comm*) forwarding agent; (*Admin*) copyist.
expéditivement [ɛkspeditivmɑ̃] *adv* expeditiously.
expérience [ɛkspeʀjɑ̃s] *nf* **(a)** (*pratique*) experience. **avoir de l'~** to have experience, be experienced; (*frm*) **avoir l'~ du monde** to have experience of the world, know the ways of the world; **sans ~** inexperienced; **il est sans ~ de la vie** he has no experience of life; **savoir par ~** to know by *ou* from experience; **il a une longue ~ de l'enseignement** he has a lot of teaching experience.
(b) (*aventure humaine*) experience. **~ amoureuse** love affair; **tente l'~, tu verras bien** try it and see; **faire l'~ de qch** to experience sth; **ils ont fait une ~ de vie communautaire** they experimented with communal living.
(c) (*essai scientifique*) experiment. **vérité *ou* fait d'~** experimental truth *ou* fact; **faire une ~ sur un cobaye** to do *ou* carry out an experiment on a guinea-pig.
expérimental, e, *mpl* **-aux** [ɛkspeʀimɑ̃tal, o] *adj* experimental.
expérimentalement [ɛkspeʀimɑ̃talmɑ̃] *adv* experimentally.
expérimentateur, -trice [ɛkspeʀimɑ̃tatœʀ, tʀis] *nm,f* experimenter.
expérimentation [ɛkspeʀimɑ̃tɑsjɔ̃] *nf* experimentation.

expérimenté, e [ɛkspeʀimɑ̃te] (*ptp de* **expérimenter**) *adj* experienced.
expérimenter [ɛkspeʀimɑ̃te] (1) *vt appareil* to test; *remède* to experiment with, try out; *méthode* to test out, try out. **~ en laboratoire** to experiment *ou* do experiments in a laboratory.
expert, e [ɛkspɛʀ, ɛʀt(ə)] **1** *adj* expert, skilled (*en* in, *à* at). **être ~ en la matière** to be expert *ou* skilled in the subject.
2 *nm* (*connaisseur*) expert (*en* in, at), connoisseur (*en* in, of); (*spécialiste*) expert; (*d'assurances*) valuer; (*Naut*) surveyor. **médecin** *etc* **~** medical *etc* expert.
3: expert-comptable *nm, pl* **experts-comptables** ≃ chartered accountant (*Brit*), ≃ certified public accountant (*US*).
expertement [ɛkspɛʀtəmɑ̃] *adv* expertly.
expertise [ɛkspɛʀtiz] *nf* (*évaluation*) expert evaluation *ou* appraisal; (*rapport*) valuer's *ou* expert's report.
expertiser [ɛkspɛʀtize] (1) *vt bijou* to value, appraise; *dégâts* to appraise, evaluate. **faire ~ un diamant** to have a diamond valued.
expiable [ɛkspjabl(ə)] *adj* expiable.
expiation [ɛkspjɑsjɔ̃] *nf* expiation (*de* of), atonement (*de* for). **en ~ de ses crimes** in expiation of *ou* atonement for his crimes.
expiatoire [ɛkspjatwaʀ] *adj* expiatory.
expier [ɛkspje] (7) *vt péchés, crime* to expiate, atone for. (*fig*) **~ une imprudence** to pay for an imprudent act.
expirant, e [ɛkspiʀɑ̃, ɑ̃t] *adj* dying.
expiration [ɛkspiʀɑsjɔ̃] *nf* (*gén*) expiration, expiry. **venir à ~** to expire; **à l'~ du délai** at the expiry of the deadline, when the deadline expires.
expirer [ɛkspiʀe] (1) **1** *vt air* to breathe out, expire (*T*). **expirez lentement!** breathe out slowly! **2** *vi* (*mourir, prendre fin*) to expire.
explétif, -ive [ɛkspletif, iv] **1** *adj* expletive, expletory. **2** *nm* expletive.
explicable [ɛksplikabl(ə)] *adj* explicable, explainable.
explicatif, -ive [ɛksplikatif, iv] *adj* explanatory, explicative. (*Gram*) **proposition relative ~ive** non-restrictive relative clause.
explication [ɛksplikɑsjɔ̃] *nf* **(a)** *[phénomène]* explanation (*de* for); *[méthode]* explanation (*de* of). **les ~s sont écrites au dos** the explanations *ou* instructions are written on the back.
(b) (*justification*) explanation (*de qch* for sth). **votre conduite demande des ~s** your conduct requires some explanation; **j'exige des ~s** I demand an explanation.
(c) (*discussion*) discussion; (*dispute*) argument.
(d) (*Scol*) *[auteur, passage]* commentary (*de* on), analysis (*de* of). **~ de texte** critical analysis *ou* appreciation of a text, interpretation (of a text).
explicite [ɛksplisit] *adj* explicit.
explicitement [ɛksplisitmɑ̃] *adv* explicitly.
expliciter [ɛksplisite] (1) *vt* to make (more *ou* quite) explicit, explain, clarify.
expliquer [ɛksplike] (1) **1** *vt* **(a)** (*faire comprendre*) to explain. **il m'a expliqué comment faire** he told me *ou* explained to me how to do it; **je lui ai expliqué qu'il avait tort** I pointed out to him *ou* explained to him that he was wrong.
(b) (*rendre compte de*) to account for, explain. **cela explique qu'il ne soit pas venu** that explains why he didn't come, that accounts for his not coming.
(c) (*Scol*) *texte* to comment on, criticize, analyse. **~ un passage de Flaubert** to give a critical analysis *ou* a critical appreciation *ou* a critical interpretation of a passage from Flaubert.
2 s'expliquer *vpr* **(a)** (*donner des précisions*) to explain o.s., make o.s. clear. **je m'explique** let me explain, let me make myself clear; **s'~ sur ses projets** to talk about *ou* explain one's plans; **s'~ devant qn** to justify o.s. to sb, explain one's actions to sb.
(b) (*comprendre*) to understand. **je ne m'explique pas bien qu'il soit parti** I can't see *ou* understand *ou* it isn't at all clear to me why he should have left.
(c) (*être compréhensible*) **son retard s'explique par le mauvais temps** his lateness is explained by the bad weather, the bad weather accounts for *ou* explains his lateness; **leur attitude s'explique: ils n'ont pas reçu notre lettre** that explains their attitude: they didn't get our letter; **tout s'explique!** it's all clear now!, I see it all now!
(d) (*parler clairement*) **s'~ bien/mal** to express *ou* explain o.s. well/badly; **je me suis peut-être mal expliqué** perhaps I have explained *ou* expressed myself badly, perhaps I didn't make myself (quite) clear.
(e) (*discuter*) **s'~ avec qn** to explain o.s. to sb, have it out with sb*; **va t'~ avec lui** go and sort it out with him, go and explain yourself to him; **après s'être longuement expliqués ils sont tombés d'accord** after having discussed the matter for a long time they finally reached an agreement; **ils sont allés s'~ dehors*** they went to fight it out outside *ou* to finish it off outside.
exploit [ɛksplwa] *nm* exploit, feat. (*Jur*) **~ d'huissier** writ.
exploitable [ɛksplwatabl(ə)] *adj* (*gén*) exploitable.
exploitant, e [ɛksplwatɑ̃, ɑ̃t] *nm,f* farmer. **le petit ~ (agricole)** the smallholder (*Brit*), the small farmer.
exploitation [ɛksplwatɑsjɔ̃] *nf* **(a)** (*action: V* **exploiter**) working; exploitation; running, operating. **mettre en ~** *domaine, ressources* to exploit, develop; **frais/méthodes d'~** running *ou* operating costs/methods.
(b) (*entreprise*) concern. **~ agricole/commerciale/industrielle** farming/business/industrial concern; **~ minière/forestière** mining/forestry development.
exploiter [ɛksplwate] (1) *vt mine, sol* to work, exploit; *entreprise* to run, operate; *ressources* to exploit; *idée, situation* to exploit, make the most of; *personne, bonté* to exploit.
exploiteur, -euse [ɛksplwatœʀ, øz] *nm,f* exploiter.
explorateur, -trice [ɛksplɔʀatœʀ, tʀis] *nm,f* (*personne*) explorer.
exploration [ɛksplɔʀɑsjɔ̃] *nf* exploration.
explorer [ɛksplɔʀe] (1) *vt* (*gén*) *pays* to explore; *possibilité, problème* to investigate, examine, explore.
exploser [ɛksploze] (1) *vi [bombe, chaudière]* to explode, blow up; *[gaz]* to explode; *[colère]* to burst out, explode. **il explosa (de colère)** he flared up, he exploded with *ou* in anger; **faire ~** *bombe* to explode, detonate; *bâtiment* to blow up; (*fig*) **cette remarque le fit ~** he blew up *ou* flared up at that remark.
explosible [ɛksplozibl(ə)] *adj mélange* explosive.
explosif, -ive [ɛksplozif, iv] *adj, nm* explosive.
explosion [ɛksplozjɔ̃] *nf [bombe, gaz, chaudière]* explosion; *[colère]* outburst, explosion; *[joie]* outburst. **faire ~** *[bombe, poudrière]* to explode, blow up; *V* **moteur**[1].
exponentiel, -ielle [ɛkspɔnɑ̃sjɛl] *adj* exponential.
exportable [ɛkspɔʀtabl(ə)] *adj* exportable.
exportateur, -trice [ɛkspɔʀtatœʀ, tʀis] **1** *adj* export (*épith*), exporting. **pays ~** exporting country; **être ~ de** to export, be an exporter of. **2** *nm,f* exporter.
exportation [ɛkspɔʀtɑsjɔ̃] *nf* (*action*) export, exportation; (*produit*) export.
exporter [ɛkspɔʀte] (1) *vt* to export.
exposant, e [ɛkspozɑ̃, ɑ̃t] **1** *nm,f [foire, salon]* exhibitor. **2** *nm* (*Math*) exponent.
exposé [ɛkspoze] *nm* (*action*) account, statement, exposition (*frm*); (*conférence: gén, Scol*) talk. **faire un ~ sur** to give a talk on; (*Jur*) **~ des motifs** preamble (*in bill, stating grounds for it adoption*).
exposer [ɛkspoze] (1) **1** *vt* **(a)** (*exhiber*) *marchandises* to put on display, display; *tableaux* to exhibit, show. **ce peintre expose dans cette galerie** that painter shows *ou* exhibits at that gallery; **c'est resté exposé pendant 3 mois** it has been on display *ou* on show for 3 months; (*frm*) **son corps est exposé dans l'église** he is lying in state in the church.
(b) (*expliquer*) (*gén*) to explain; *faits, raisons* to expound, set out, make known; *griefs* to air, make known; *théories, idées* to expound, explain, set out, put forward. **il nous exposa la situation** he explained the situation to us.
(c) (*mettre en danger*) (*gén*) *personne, objet* to expose (*à* to); (*Hist*) *condamné, enfant* to expose; *vie, réputation* to risk. **c'est une personnalité très exposée** because of his position he is very vulnerable to criticism *ou* very much exposed to criticism, his position makes him an easy target for criticism; **sa conduite l'expose à des reproches** his conduct lays him open to censure; **c'est exposé à être découvert** it is liable to be discovered.
(d) (*orienter, présenter*) to expose; (*Phot*) to expose. **~ au soleil/aux regards** to expose to sunlight/to view; **maison exposée au sud** house facing (due) south, house with a southern aspect; **maison bien exposée** well-situated house; **endroit très exposé** (*au vent, à l'ennemi*) very exposed place.
(e) (*Littérat*) *action* to set out; (*Mus*) *thème* to introduce.
2 s'exposer *vpr* to expose o.s. **s'~ à** *danger, reproches* to expose o.s. to, lay o.s. open to; **s'~ à des poursuites** to run the risk of prosecution, lay o.s. open to *ou* expose o.s. to prosecution.
exposition [ɛkspozisjɔ̃] *nf* **(a)** *[marchandises]* display; *[faits, raisons, situation, idées]* exposition; *[condamné, enfant]* exposure; (*au danger, à la chaleur*) exposure (*à* to).
(b) (*foire, salon*) exhibition, show. **l'E~ Universelle** the World Fair.
(c) (*Phot*) exposure.
(d) (*Littérat, Mus*) exposition. **scène d'~** expository *ou* introductory scene.
(e) (*orientation*) *[maison]* aspect.
exprès[1] [ɛkspʀɛ] *adv* (*spécialement*) specially; (*intentionnellement*) on purpose, deliberately, intentionally. **venir (tout) ~ pour** to come specially to; **il l'a fait ~** he did it on purpose *ou* deliberately *ou* intentionally; **il ne l'a pas fait ~** he didn't do it on purpose, he didn't mean to do it; **et par** *ou* **comme un fait ~ il l'avait perdu** by some (almost) deliberate coincidence he had lost it, it would have to happen that he had lost it.
exprès[2], **-esse** [ɛkspʀɛs] *adj* **(a)** *interdiction, ordre* formal, express; (*Jur*) *clause* express.
(b) (*inv*) **(lettre/colis) ~** express letter/parcel; **(messager) ~†** express messenger; **envoyer qch en ~** to send sth by express post, send sth express.
express [ɛkspʀɛs] *adj, nm inv* **(train) ~** fast train; **(café) ~** espresso (coffee).
expressément [ɛkspʀesemɑ̃] *adv* (*formellement*) expressly; (*spécialement*) specially.
expressif, -ive [ɛkspʀesif, iv] *adj geste, regard, physionomie* expressive; *langage* expressive, vivid.
expression [ɛkspʀɛsjɔ̃] *nf* **(a)** (*gén*) expression. **au-delà de toute ~** beyond (all) expression, inexpressible; **veuillez agréer l'~ de mes sentiments les meilleurs** yours faithfully (*Brit*), yours truly; **visage plein d'~/sans ~** expressive/expressionless face; **jouer avec beaucoup d'~** to play with great feeling *ou* expression; *V* **liberté, moyen.**
(b) (*Math: formule*) expression; (*Gram: locution*) phrase, expression. **~ figée** set *ou* fixed expression, set phrase; **~ toute faite** cliché, hack phrase; (*fig*) **réduit à sa plus simple ~** reduced to its simplest terms *ou* expression.
expressionnisme [ɛkspʀɛsjɔnism(ə)] *nm* expressionism.
expressionniste [ɛkspʀɛsjɔnist(ə)] **1** *adj* expressionist (*épith*), expressionistic. **2** *nmf* expressionist.
expressivement [ɛkspʀesivmɑ̃] *adv* expressively.

expressivité [ɛkspʀesivite] *nf* expressiveness.
exprimable [ɛkspʀimabl(ə)] *adj* expressible.
exprimer [ɛkspʀime] (1) **1** *vt* **(a)** (*signifier*) to express; *pensée* to express, give utterance to (*frm*); *opinion* to voice, express. **mots qui expriment un sens** words which express *ou* convey a meaning; **regards qui expriment la colère** looks which express *ou* indicate anger; **œuvre qui exprime parfaitement l'artiste** work which expresses the artist completely.
(b) (*Écon, Math*) to express. **somme exprimée en francs** sum expressed in francs; **le signe + exprime l'addition** the sign + indicates *ou* stands for addition.
(c) (*littér*) *jus* to press out.
2 **s'exprimer** *vpr* to express o.s. **s'~ par gestes** to use gestures to express o.s.; **je me suis peut-être mal exprimé** perhaps I have expressed myself badly, perhaps I have put it badly; **si je peux m'~ ainsi** if I may put it like that; (*fig*) **il faut permettre au talent de s'~** talent must be allowed free expression *ou* to express itself; **la joie s'exprima sur son visage** (his) joy showed in his expression, his face expressed his joy.
expropriation [ɛkspʀɔpʀijɑsjɔ̃] *nf* (*action*) compulsory purchase; (*arrêté*) compulsory purchase order.
exproprier [ɛkspʀɔpʀije] (7) *vt propriété* to place a compulsory purchase order on.
expulser [ɛkspylse] (1) *vt* (*gén*) *élève* to expel (*de* from); *étranger* to deport, expel (*de* from); *locataire* to evict (*de* from), throw out (*de* of); (*Ftbl*) *joueur* to send off; *manifestant* to eject (*de* from), throw out, turn out (*de* of); (*Anat*) *déchets* to evacuate, excrete.
expulsion [ɛkspylsjɔ̃] *nf* (*V* **expulser**) expulsion; deportation; eviction; throwing out; ejection; turning out; sending off; evacuation, excretion (*de* from).
expurger [ɛkspyʀʒe] (3) *vt* to expurgate, bowdlerize.
exquis, -ise [ɛkski, iz] *adj plat, choix, politesse* exquisite; *personne, temps* delightful.
exsangue [ɛksɑ̃g] *adj visage, lèvres* bloodless; (*fig*) *littérature* anaemic. **les guerres/impôts ont laissé le pays ~** wars/taxes have left the country weak and drained.
exsudation [ɛksydɑsjɔ̃] *nf* (*frm*) exudation (*frm*).
exsuder [ɛksyde] *vti* (*frm*) (*lit*) to exude. (*fig*) **son visage exsude la joie** his face radiates joy.
extase [ɛkstɑz] *nf* (*Rel*) ecstasy; (*sexuelle*) climax; (*fig*) ecstasy, rapture. **il est en ~ devant sa fille** he is rapturous about his daughter, he goes into raptures over his daughter; **tomber/rester en ~ devant un tableau** to go into ecstasies at/stand in ecstasy before a painting.
extasié, e [ɛkstɑzje] (*ptp de* **s'extasier**) *adj* ecstatic, enraptured.
extasier (s') [ɛkstɑzje] (7) *vpr* to go into ecstasies *ou* raptures (*devant, sur* over).
extatique [ɛkstatik] *adj* ecstatic, enraptured.
extenseur [ɛkstɑ̃sœʀ] **1** *adj*: **(muscle) ~** extensor. **2** *nm* (*Sport*) chest expander.
extensibilité [ɛkstɑ̃sibilite] *nf* extensibility.
extensible [ɛkstɑ̃sibl(ə)] *adj matière* extensible; *définition* extendable.
extensif, -ive [ɛkstɑ̃sif, iv] *adj* (*Agr*) *culture* extensive; *sens* wide, extensive.
extension [ɛkstɑ̃sjɔ̃] *nf* **(a)** (*étirement*) *[membre, ressort]* stretching; (*Méd*) *[membre]* traction. **le ressort atteint son ~ maximum** the spring is fully stretched *ou* is stretched to its maximum.
(b) (*augmentation*) *[épidémie, grève, incendie]* extension, spreading; *[commerce, domaine]* expansion; *[pouvoirs]* extension, expansion. **prendre de l'~** *[entreprise, épidémie]* to spread, extend, develop.
(c) (*élargissement*) *[loi, mesure]* extension (*à* to); (*Ling*) *[sens]* extension (*à* to); (*Logique*) extension. **par ~ (de sens)** by extension.
exténuant, e [ɛkstenɥɑ̃, ɑ̃t] *adj* exhausting.
exténuer [ɛkstenɥe] (1) **1** *vt* to exhaust, tire out. **2 s'exténuer** *vpr* to exhaust o.s., tire o.s. out (*à faire qch* doing sth).
extérieur, e [ɛksteʀjœʀ] **1** *adj* **(a)** (*à un lieu*) *paroi* outer, outside, exterior; *escalier, W.-C.* outside; *quartier, cour* outer; *bruit* external, outside; *décoration* exterior, outside. **apparence ~e** *[personne]* outward appearance; *[maison]* outside.
(b) (*à l'individu*) *monde, influences* external, outside; *activité, intérêt* outside; *réalité* external. **signes ~s de richesse** outward signs of wealth; **manifestation ~e de colère** outward show *ou* display of anger.
(c) (*étranger*) *commerce, vente* external, foreign; *politique, nouvelles* foreign.
(d) (*superficiel*) *amabilité* surface (*épith*), superficial. **sa gaieté est toute ~e** his gaiety is all on the surface *ou* all an outward display.
(e) (*sans relation avec*) **être ~ à une question/un sujet** to be external to *ou* outside a question/a subject, be beyond the scope of a question/a subject; **c'est tout à fait ~ à moi** it has nothing to do with me, it doesn't concern me in the least; **interdit à toute personne ~e à l'usine/au chantier** factory employees/site workers only.
(f) (*Géom*) *angle* exterior.
2 *nm* **(a)** *[objet, maison]* outside, exterior.
(b) à l'~ (*au dehors*) outside; **c'est à l'~ (de la ville)** it's outside (the town); (*fig*) **juger qch de l'~** (*d'après son apparence*) to judge sth by appearances; (*en tant que profane*) to judge sth from the outside.
(c) (*pays etc*) foreign countries. **entretenir de bonnes relations avec l'~** to have good foreign relations; **vendre beaucoup à l'~** to sell a lot abroad *ou* to foreign countries; **recevoir des nouvelles de l'~** to have news from abroad; **cellule sans communication avec l'~** cell without communication with the outside world.
(d) (*Ciné*) location shots. **prises de vue en ~** shots taken on location; **les ~s ont été tournés à Paris** the shots on location were taken in Paris.
(e) (*frm: apparence*) exterior, (outward) appearance. **avoir un ~ agréable** to have a pleasant appearance *ou* exterior.
extérieurement [ɛksteʀjœʀmɑ̃] *adv* **(a)** (*du dehors*) on the outside, externally. **(b)** (*en apparence*) on the surface, outwardly.
extériorisation [ɛksteʀjɔʀizɑsjɔ̃] *nf [joie etc]* display, outward expression; (*Psych*) externalization, exteriorization.
extérioriser [ɛksteʀjɔʀize] (1) *vt joie etc* to show, express; (*Psych*) to exteriorize, externalize. **les enfants ont besoin de s'~** (*personnalité*) children need to express themselves; (*énergie*) children need an outlet for their energy, children need to let off steam*.
extériorité [ɛksteʀjɔʀite] *nf* (*Philos*) exteriority.
exterminateur, -trice [ɛkstɛʀminatœʀ, tʀis] **1** *adj* exterminating; *V* **ange**. **2** *nm,f* exterminator.
extermination [ɛkstɛʀminɑsjɔ̃] *nf* extermination; *V* **camp**.
exterminer [ɛkstɛʀmine] (1) *vt* (*lit, fig*) to exterminate, wipe out.
externat [ɛkstɛʀna] *nm* (*Scol*) day school. (*Méd*) **faire son ~ à** to be a non-resident student *ou* an extern (*US*) at.
externe [ɛkstɛʀn(ə)] **1** *adj surface etc* external, outer; *angle* exterior. **à usage ~** for external use only. **2** *nmf* (*Scol*) day pupil; (*Méd*) non-resident student at a teaching hospital, extern (*US*).
exterritorialité [ɛkstɛʀitɔʀjalite] *nf* exterritoriality.
extincteur, -trice [ɛkstɛ̃ktœʀ, tʀis] **1** *adj* extinguishing. **2** *nm* (fire) extinguisher.
extinction [ɛkstɛ̃ksjɔ̃] *nf [incendie, lumières]* extinction, extinguishing, putting out; (*fig*) *[peuple]* extinction, dying out; (*Jur*) *[dette, droit]* extinguishment. **~ de voix** loss of voice, aphonia (*T*); **avoir une ~ de voix** to lose one's voice; (*Mil, fig*) **avant l'~ des feux** before lights out.
extirpable [ɛkstiʀpabl(ə)] *adj* eradicable.
extirpation [ɛkstiʀpɑsjɔ̃] *nf* (*V* **extirper**) eradication; extirpation; rooting out; pulling up, pulling out.
extirper [ɛkstiʀpe] (1) *vt* (*littér*) *abus, vice* to eradicate, extirpate (*littér*), root out; (*Chirurgie*) to extirpate; (*rare*) *herbes* to root out, pull up, pull out. **impossible de lui ~ une parole!*** it's impossible to drag *ou* get a word out of him!; **~ qn de son lit*** to drag *ou* haul sb out of bed; **s'~ de son manteau** to extricate o.s. from one's coat.
extorquer [ɛkstɔʀke] (1) *vt* to extort (*à qn* from sb).
extorqueur, -euse [ɛkstɔʀkœʀ, øz] *nm,f* extortioner.
extorsion [ɛkstɔʀsjɔ̃] *nf* extortion.
extra [ɛkstʀa] **1** *nm inv* (*domestique*) extra servant *ou* help; (*gâterie*) (special) treat. **se faire un ~** to give o.s. a treat, treat o.s. to something special.
2 *adj inv* (*Comm: supérieur*) *fromage, vin* first-rate, extra-special; *tissu* top-quality; (*: *excellent*) *film, week-end, personne* fantastic*, terrific*, great*. (*Comm*) **de qualité ~** of the finest *ou* best quality.
3: extra-fin, e *adj bonbons* superfine, extra fine; *haricots, petits pois, aiguille* extra fine; **extra-fort, e** (*adj*) *carton, moutarde* extra strong; (*nm*) (*Couture*) bias binding; **extra-légal, e** *adj* extra-legal; **extra-muros** *adj, adv* outside the town; **extra-parlementaire** *adj* extra-parliamentary; **extra-sensible** *adj* extra-sensible; **extra-sensoriel, -elle** *adj* extrasensory; **extra-terrestre** *adj* extra-terrestrial; **extra-territorialité** *nf* extraterritoriality; **extra-utérin, e** *adj* extra-uterine; *V* **voyant**.
extracteur [ɛkstʀaktœʀ] *nm* extractor.
extractif, -ive [ɛkstʀaktif, iv] *adj industrie etc* extractive, mining.
extraction [ɛkstʀaksjɔ̃] *nf* **(a)** *[pétrole]* extraction; *[charbon]* mining; *[marbre]* quarrying. **(b)** (*Math, Méd*) extraction. **(c)** (††: *origine*) **de haute/basse ~** of noble/mean extraction *ou* descent, of high/low birth.
extrader [ɛkstʀade] (1) *vt* to extradite.
extradition [ɛkstʀadisjɔ̃] *nf* extradition.
extraire [ɛkstʀɛʀ] (50) *vt* **(a)** *minerai, pétrole* to extract; *charbon* to mine; *marbre* to quarry.
(b) *gaz, jus* to extract. **~ un liquide en pressant/en tordant** *etc* to squeeze out/wring out *etc* a liquid.
(c) *dent* to extract, pull out; *clou* to pull out; (*Math*) *racine* to extract; *balle* to extract, remove.
(d) ~ de *poche, placard* to take *ou* bring *ou* dig* out of; *prison, avalanche* to rescue from, get out of; **passage extrait d'un livre** extract from a book, passage taken from a book; **s'~ de son manteau*** to extricate o.s. from one's coat; **s' ~ de sa voiture** to climb out of one's car.
extrait [ɛkstʀɛ] *nm [discours, journal]* extract; *[livre, auteur]* extract, excerpt; (*Admin*) extract (*de* from). **~ de lavande** *etc* essence *ou* extract of lavender *etc*; **~ de viande** beef extract; **~ de naissance** *etc* birth *etc* certificate.
extraordinaire [ɛkstʀaɔʀdinɛʀ] *adj* **(a)** (*étrange*) *événement, costume, opinions* extraordinary. **l'~ est que** the extraordinary thing is that.
(b) (*exceptionnel*) *beauté* exceptional; *succès, force* extraordinary, exceptional. **c'est un acteur ~** he's an extraordinary *ou* a remarkable actor; **ce roman n'est pas ~** this novel isn't up to much*, there's nothing particularly good *ou* very special about this novel.
(c) (*Pol*) *moyens, mesures, assemblée* special; *V* **ambassadeur**.
(d) si par ~ if by some unlikely chance; **quand par ~** on those rare occasions when.

extraordinairement [ɛkstʀaɔʀdinɛʀmɑ̃] *adv* (*exceptionnellement*) extraordinarily, exceptionally; (*d'une manière étrange*) extraordinarily.
extrapolation [ɛkstʀapɔlɑsjɔ̃] *nf* extrapolation.
extrapoler [ɛkstʀapɔle] (1) *vti* to extrapolate (*à partir de* from).
extravagance [ɛkstʀavagɑ̃s] *nf* **(a)** (*caractère*) *[costume, conduite]* eccentricity, extravagance. **(b)** (*acte*) eccentric *ou* extravagant behaviour (*U*). **dire des ~s** to talk wildly *ou* extravagantly.
extravagant, e [ɛkstʀavagɑ̃, ɑ̃t] *adj idée, théorie* extravagant, wild, crazy; *prix* excessive, extravagant.
extravaguer† [ɛkstʀavage] (1) *vi* to rave, talk wildly.
extraverti, e [ɛkstʀavɛʀti] = **extroverti.**
extrême [ɛkstʀɛm] **1** *adj* **(a)** (*le plus éloigné*) extreme, far. **à l'~ bout de la table** at the far end of the table, at the very end of the table; **dans son ~ jeunesse** in his very young days, in his earliest youth; **à l'~ opposé** at the opposite extreme (*de* of).
(b) (*le plus intense*) extreme, utmost. **dans la misère ~** in extreme *ou* the utmost poverty; **c'est avec un plaisir ~ que** it is with the greatest *ou* the utmost pleasure that; **il m'a reçu avec une ~ amabilité** he received me in the friendliest possible way *ou* with the utmost kindness; **il fait une chaleur ~** it is extremely hot; **d'une pâleur/difficulté ~** extremely pale/difficult; *V* **rigueur, urgence.**
(c) (*après n: excessif, radical*) *théories, moyens* extreme. **ça l'a conduit à des mesures ~s** that drove him into taking drastic *ou* extreme steps; **il a un caractère ~** he tends to go to extremes, he is an extremist by nature.
2 *nm* **(a)** (*opposé*) extreme. **les ~s se touchent** extremes meet; **passer d'un ~ à l'autre** to go from one extreme to the other *ou* to another.
(b) (*Math*) **~s** extremes.
(c) à l'~, jusqu'à l'~ in the extreme, to a degree; **cela lui répugnait à l'~** he was extremely loath to do it; **noircir une situation à l'~** to paint the blackest possible picture of a situation; **scrupuleux à l'~** scrupulous to a fault.
3: extrême droite/gauche extreme right/left (wing), far right/left; **extrême-onction** *nf* Extreme Unction; **Extrême-Orient** *nm* Far East; **extrême-oriental, e,** *mpl* **extrême-orientaux** *adj* far eastern, oriental.
extrêmement [ɛkstʀɛmmɑ̃] *adv* extremely, exceedingly.
extrémisme [ɛkstʀemism(ə)] *nm* extremism.
extrémiste [ɛkstʀemist(ə)] *adj, nmf* extremist.
extrémité [ɛkstʀemite] *nf* **(a)** (*bout*) (*gén*) end; *[aiguille]* point; *[objet mince]* tip; *[village, île]* extremity, limit; *[lac, péninsule]* head.
(b) (*frm: situation critique*) plight, straits. **être dans la pénible ~ de devoir** to be in the unfortunate necessity of having to; **réduit à la dernière ~** in the most dire plight *ou* straits; **être à toute ~, être à la dernière ~** to be on the point of death.
(c) (*frm: action excessive*) extremes, extreme lengths. **se porter à une ~ *ou* à des ~s** to go to extremes; **pousser qn à une ~ *ou* à des ~s** to push *ou* drive sb to extremes *ou* into taking extreme action; **se livrer à des ~s (sur qn)** to assault sb; **d'une ~ dans l'autre** from one extreme to another.
(d) (*Anat: pieds et mains*) **~s** extremities.
extroverti, e [ɛkstʀɔvɛʀti] *adj, nm,f* extrovert.
exubérance [ɛgzybeʀɑ̃s] *nf* (*caractère*) exuberance (*U*); (*action*) exuberant behaviour (*U*) (*ou* talk (*U*) *etc*). **parler avec ~** to speak exuberantly.
exubérant, e [ɛgzybeʀɑ̃, ɑ̃t] *adj* (*gén*) exuberant.
exultation [ɛgzyltɑsjɔ̃] *nf* exultation.
exulter [ɛgzylte] (1) *vi* to exult.
exutoire [ɛgzytwaʀ] *nm* outlet, release.
ex-voto [ɛksvɔto] *nm inv* ex-voto.
eye-liner [ajlajnœʀ] *nm* eyeliner.

F

F, f [ɛf] *nm ou nf* (*lettre*) F, f.
fa [fɑ] *nm inv* (*Mus*) F; (*en chantant la gamme*) fa; *V* **clef.**
fable [fɑbl(ə)] *nf* (*genre*) fable; (*légende*) fable, legend; (*mensonge*) tale, story, fable. **quelle ~ va-t-il inventer?** what yarn *ou* tale will he spin?; **être la ~ de toute la ville** to be the laughing stock of the whole town.
fabliau, *pl* **~x** [fɑblijo] *nm* fabliau.
fablier [fɑblije] *nm* book of fables.
fabricant [fabʀikɑ̃] *nm* manufacturer. **~ de papier** paper manufacturer *ou* maker; **~ d'automobiles** car manufacturer.
fabricateur, -trice [fabʀikatœʀ, tʀis] *nm,f*: **~ (de fausse monnaie)** counterfeiter, forger; **~ (de fausses nouvelles)** fabricator, spinner of yarns; **~ (de faux papiers)** forger (of documents), counterfeiter.
fabrication [fabʀikɑsjɔ̃] *nf* **(a)** (*industrielle*) manufacture, manufacturing; (*artisanale, personnelle*) making. **la ~ industrielle/en série** factory *ou* industrial/mass production; **de ~ française** made in France, French-made, of French make; **de bonne ~** well-made, of good *ou* high-quality workmanship; **un romancier réduit à la ~ en série** a novelist reduced to churning out novels by the dozen *ou* to mass-producing his works; **une robe de sa ~** a dress of her own making, a dress she has (*ou* had *etc*) made herself; *V* **défaut, secret.**
(b) *[faux]* forging; *[fausses nouvelles]* fabricating. **~ de fausse monnaie** counterfeiting *ou* forging money.
fabrique [fabʀik] *nf* **(a)** (*établissement*) factory. **~ de gants** glove factory; **~ de papier** paper mill; *V* **marque, prix. (b)** (*littér: fabrication, facture*) workmanship. **de bonne ~** well-made, of good *ou* high quality workmanship. **(c)** (*Rel*) **la ~** the fabric.
fabriquer [fabʀike] (1) *vt* **(a)** *meuble, outil, chaussures* (*industriellement*) to manufacture; (*de façon artisanale, chez soi*) to make; *faux* to forge; *fausses nouvelles* to fabricate; *incident, histoire* to fabricate, invent, make up. **~ de la fausse monnaie** to counterfeit *ou* forge money; **~ en série** to mass-produce; **~ industriellement** to manufacture, produce industrially; **~ de façon artisanale** to make *ou* produce on a small scale; **c'est une histoire fabriquée de toutes pièces** this story is all made up *ou* is a complete fabrication from start to finish; **il s'est fabriqué un personnage de prophète** he created *ou* invented a prophetic character for himself; **il s'est fabriqué un poste de radio/une cabane** he built *ou* made himself a radio set/a shed.
(b) (**: faire*) **qu'est-ce qu'il fabrique?** what (on earth) is he doing? *ou* is he up to?*; **des fois, je me demande ce que je fabrique ici!** sometimes I really wonder what the heck I'm doing here!*
fabulateur, -trice [fabylatœʀ, tʀis] *adj* (*d'imagination*) **faculté ~trice** faculty for fantasizing; (*de mythomanie*) **tendance ~trice** tendency to fabricate stories *ou* to fantasize.
fabulation [fabylɑsjɔ̃] *nf* (*V* **fabulateur**) fantasizing; fabrication.
fabuleusement [fabyløzmɑ̃] *adv* fabulously, fantastically.
fabuleux, -euse [fabylø, øz] *adj* **(a)** (*littér*) (*des temps anciens, de la mythologie*) mythical, legendary; (*de la légende, du merveilleux*) fabulous. **(b)** (*intensif: prodigieux*) *richesse, exploits, vitesse* fabulous, fantastic.
fabuliste [fabylist(ə)] *nm* fabulist, writer of fables.
fac [fak] *nf* (*arg Univ*) *abrév de* **faculté.**
façade [fasad] *nf* **(a)** (*devant de maison*) (*gén*) façade, front; (*Archéol*) façade; (*Comm*) frontage; (*côté de maison*) side; *[magasin]* front. **~ latérale** side wall; **~ ouest** west side *ou* wall; **la ~ arrière de la maison** the back of the house; **les ~s des magasins** the shop fronts; **3 pièces en ~** 3 rooms at *ou* facing the front.
(b) (*fig: apparence*) façade. **~ d'honnêteté/de vertu** façade *ou* outward show *ou* pretence of honesty/virtue; **ce n'est qu'une ~** it's just a front *ou* façade, it's a mere pretence; **de ~** *luxe, vertu, foi* sham.
(c) (*‡: figure*) **se refaire la ~** to redo one's face; **il va te démolir la ~** he's going to smash your mug *ou* face in‡.
face [fas] **1** *nf* **(a)** (*frm, Méd: visage*) face. **les blessés de la ~** people with facial injuries; **tomber ~ contre terre** to fall flat on the ground *ou* flat on one's face; **se prosterner ~ contre terre** to prostrate o.s. with one's face to the ground; (*Rel*) **la ~ de Dieu** the Holy face; **~ de rat/de singe‡** rat/monkey face‡; **sauver/perdre la ~** to save/lose face; **opération destinée à sauver la ~** face-saving move; *V* **voiler¹.**
(b) (*côté*) *[disque, objet]* side; *[médaille, pièce de monnaie]* front, obverse; (*Math*) *[cube, figure]* side, face. **la ~ cachée de la lune** the hidden face *ou* side of the moon; **mets l'autre ~ (du disque)** put on *ou* play the other side (of the record), turn the record over; (*fig*) **question à double ~** two-sided question; (*lit, fig*) **examiner un objet/une question sous *ou* sur toutes ses ~s** to examine an object/a problem from all sides; **la pièce est tombée sur ~ *ou* côté ~** the coin fell face up; (*jeu de pile ou face*) **~!** heads!; *V* **pile.**
(c) (*aspect*) face. **la ~ changeante des choses** the changing face of things; **le monde a changé de ~** (the face of) the world has changed.
(d) (*littér: surface*) **la ~ de la terre *ou* du globe** the face of the

earth; **la ~ de l'océan** the surface of the ocean.

(e) (*loc*) **faire ~** to face (up to) things; **faire ~ à** *lieu, objet, personne* to face, be opposite; *ennemi, difficulté, obligation* to face; *épreuve, adversaire, obligation* to face up to, face; *dette, engagement* to meet; **leurs maisons se font ~** their houses are facing *ou* opposite each other; **il a dû faire ~ à des dépenses élevées** he has been faced with *ou* he has had to face considerable expense.

(f) à la ~ de: il éclata de rire à la ~ de son professeur he burst out laughing in his teacher's face; **proclamer à la ~ de l'univers** *ou* **du monde** to proclaim to the universe *ou* to the whole world.

(g) en ~ de (*en vis à vis de*) opposite; (*en présence de*) in front of; **au banquet, on les a mis l'un en ~ de l'autre** *ou* **en ~ l'un de l'autre** at the banquet, they were placed opposite each other *ou* facing each other; **les deux ennemis étaient maintenant l'un en ~ de l'autre** the two enemies now stood facing each other *ou* face to face *ou* were now face to face; **il n'ose rien dire en ~ de son patron** he daren't say anything in front of his boss; **ne te mets pas en ~ de moi/de ma lumière** don't stand in my way/in my light; (*fig*) **se trouver en ~ d'un danger/problème** to be confronted *ou* faced with a danger/problem; (*fig*) **en ~ de cela** on the other hand.

(h) en ~ (*directement, ouvertement*): **regarder qn (bien) en ~** to look sb (straight) in the face; **il lui a dit en ~ ce qu'il pensait de lui** he told him to his face what he thought of him; **regarder la mort en ~** to look death in the face; **il faut voir les choses en ~** one must see things as they are, one must face facts; **avoir le soleil en ~** to have the sun in one's eyes.

(i) en ~ (*de l'autre côté de la rue*) across the street, opposite, over the road; **j'habite en ~** I live across the street *ou* over the road *ou* opposite; **la maison d'en ~** the house across the street *ou* over the road *ou* opposite; **le trottoir d'en ~** the opposite pavement, the pavement on the other *ou* opposite side; **la dame d'en ~** the lady (from) across the street *ou* (from) over the road, the lady opposite.

(j) de ~ *portrait* full-face; *nu, portrait en pied* frontal; *attaque* frontal; *place* (*au théâtre*) in the centre, facing the front of the stage; (*dans le train etc*) facing the engine; **voir qn de ~** to see sb face on; **attaquer de ~** to make a frontal attack (on), attack from the front; **un personnage/cheval de ~** the front view of a person/horse; **avoir une vue de ~ sur qch** to have a front view of sth; **assis de ~ dans l'autobus** sitting facing the front of the bus, sitting facing forward in the bus; **avoir le vent de ~** to have the wind in one's face.

(k) ~ à facing; **il se dressa ~ à l'ennemi** he positioned himself facing the enemy; **~ à ces problèmes, il se sentait impuissant** faced with *ou* in the face of such problems, he felt helpless; **~ à ~** *lieux, objets* opposite *ou* facing each other; *personnes, animaux* face to face, facing each other; **~ à ~ avec** *lieu, objet* opposite, facing; *personne, animal* face to face with; **~ à ~ avec une difficulté** faced with *ou* up against a difficulty.

2: face à face *nm inv* (*rencontre, gén, TV*) encounter; **face-à-main** *nm, pl* **faces-à-main** lorgnette.

facétie [fasesi] *nf* (*drôlerie*) joke; (*farce*) prank, trick. **faire des ~s** to play pranks *ou* tricks; **dire des ~s** to crack jokes.

facétieusement [fasesjøzmɑ̃] *adv* (*V* **facétieux**) impishly, mischievously; humorously.

facétieux, -euse [fasesjø, øz] *adj* (*espiègle*) impish, mischievous; (*comique*) humorous.

facette [fasɛt] *nf* (*lit, fig*) facet. **à ~s** *pierre* faceted; *caractère, personnage* many-faceted, many-sided; (*Bio*) **yeux à ~s** compound eyes.

facetter [fasete] (1) *vt* to facet.

fâché, e [fɑʃe] (*ptp de* **fâcher**) *adj* **(a)** (*en colère, mécontent*) angry, cross (*contre* with). **elle a l'air ~(e)** she looks cross *ou* angry; **tu n'es pas ~, au moins?** you're not angry *ou* cross with me, are you?

(b) (*brouillé*) **ils sont ~s** they have fallen out, they are on bad terms; **elle est ~e avec moi** she has fallen out with me.

(c) (*contrarié*) sorry (*de qch* about sth). (*frm*) **je suis ~ de ne pas pouvoir vous aider** I am sorry that I cannot help you; **je ne suis pas ~ d'avoir fini ce travail** I'm not sorry to have finished this job; (*hum*) **je ne serais pas ~ que vous me laissiez tranquille** I wouldn't mind being left alone *ou* in peace, I wouldn't object to a bit of peace and quiet.

fâcher [fɑʃe] (1) **1** *vt* **(a)** (*mettre en colère*) to anger, make angry, vex. **tu ne réussiras qu'à le ~ davantage** you will only make him more angry *ou* angrier.

(b) (*frm: contrarier*) to grieve (*frm*), distress. **cette triste nouvelle me fâche beaucoup** this sad news grieves me (*frm*) *ou* greatly distresses me.

2 se fâcher *vpr* **(a)** (*se mettre en colère*) to get angry, lose one's temper. **se ~ contre qn/pour** *ou* **au sujet de qch** to get angry *ou* annoyed with sb/about *ou* over sth; (*hum*) **se ~ tout rouge*** to blow one's top* (*hum*) (*contre qn* at sb), flare up; (*hum*) **si tu continues, je vais me ~ tout rouge*** if you go on like that, I'll blow my top* *ou* go through the roof*.

(b) (*se brouiller*) to fall out (*avec* with). **ils se sont fâchés à mort à propos d'une femme** they have fallen out for good *ou* have quarrelled bitterly over a woman.

fâcherie [fɑʃʀi] *nf* (*brouille*) quarrel.

fâcheusement [fɑʃøzmɑ̃] *adv* *survenir* (most) unfortunately *ou* awkwardly. **~ surpris** (most) unpleasantly surprised.

fâcheux, -euse [fɑʃø, øz] **1** *adj* (*blâmable*) *exemple, influence, décision* deplorable, regrettable, unfortunate; (*ennuyeux*) *coïncidence, incident, situation* unfortunate, awkward, regrettable. **il est ~ qu'il ait cru devoir s'abstenir** it's unfortunate *ou* a pity that he felt it necessary to abstain; **le ~ dans tout ça c'est que ...** the unfortunate *ou* annoying thing about it (all) is that ... .

2 *nm,f* (*littér: importun*) bore.

facial, e, *mpl* **~s** *ou* **-aux** [fasjal, o] *adj* facial; *V* **angle**.

faciès [fasjɛs] *nm* (*visage*) features, facies (*Ethnologie, Méd*); (*Bot, Géog*) facies.

facile [fasil] **1** *adj* **(a)** (*aisé*) *travail, problème* easy (*à faire* to do). **~ d'accès, d'accès ~** easy to reach, of easy access; **avoir la vie ~** to live *ou* have an easy life; **ils ne lui rendent pas la vie ~** they don't make life easy for him; **plus ~ à dire qu'à faire** easier said than done; **c'est trop ~ de s'indigner** it's too easy to get indignant; **~ comme tout*** dead easy*.

(b) (*spontané*) **avoir la parole ~** (*parler aisément*) to be an articulate speaker, have a fluent tongue; (*parler volontiers*) to have a ready tongue *ou* the gift of the gab*; **il a la plume ~** (*écrire aisément*) he has an eloquent pen; (*être toujours prêt à écrire*) he finds it easy to write, writing comes easy to him; **avoir la larme ~** to be quick to shed a tear, be easily moved to tears; **il a l'argent ~*** he's very casual about money, money just slips through his fingers; **avoir la gachette ~** to be trigger-happy; **il a le couteau ~** he's all too quick to use his knife, he's very ready with his knife.

(c) (*péj*) (*superficiel*) **effet/ironie ~** facile effect/irony; **littérature ~** cheap literature.

(d) *caractère* easy-going. **il est d'humeur ~** he is easy-going; **il est ~ à vivre/contenter** he's easy to get on with *ou* along with/to please; **il n'est pas ~ tous les jours** he's not always easy to get on with *ou* along with.

(e) (*péj*) *femme* loose (*épith*), of easy virtue. **une fille ~** a woman of easy virtue.

2 *adv* (:) at least. **elle a 50 ans ~** she's easily 50, she's 50 anyway*.

facilement [fasilmɑ̃] *adv* (*gén*) easily. **médicament ~ toléré par l'organisme** medicine easily *ou* readily tolerated by the body; **il se fâche ~** he loses his temper *ou* gets cross easily, he's quick-tempered; **on met ~ 10 jours*** it takes 10 days easily *ou* anyway*, it takes at least 10 days.

facilité [fasilite] *nf* **(a)** *[devoir, problème, travail]* easiness.

(b) *[succès, victoire]* ease; *[expression, style]* fluency. **il travaille avec ~** he works with ease; **il s'exprime avec ~** *ou* **avec une grande ~ de parole** he expresses himself with (great) fluency *ou* ease *ou* (very) articulately *ou* fluently; *V* **solution**.

(c) (*aptitude*) ability, aptitude. **cet élève a beaucoup de ~** this pupil has great ability *ou* aptitude; **il a beaucoup de ~ pour les langues** he has a great aptitude *ou* talent for languages; **la ~ n'est pas tout: il faut aussi travailler** ability *ou* aptitude is not enough — you also have to work.

(d) (*gén pl: possibilité*) facility. **avoir la ~/toutes (les) ~s de** *ou* **pour faire qch** to have the/every opportunity to do sth *ou* of doing sth; **~s de transport** transport facilities; (*Comm*) **~s de crédit** credit facilities; (*Comm*) **~s de paiement** easy terms.

(e) (*tendance*) tendency. **il a une certaine ~ à se mettre en colère** he has a certain tendency to lose his temper; **la ~ avec laquelle il se met en colère m'inquiète** his quick-temperedness worries me.

(f) (*littér: complaisance*) readiness. **il a une grande ~ à croire ce qu'on raconte/à se plier à une règle** he has a great readiness *ou* is very ready to believe what people tell him/to comply with a rule.

faciliter [fasilite] (1) *vt* (*gén*) to make easier, facilitate. **ça ne va pas ~ les choses** that's not going to make matters *ou* things (any) easier, that's not going to ease matters; **pour lui ~ sa mission/tâche** to make his mission/work easier, make the mission/work easier for him.

façon [fasɔ̃] *nf* **(a)** (*manière*) way. **voilà la ~ dont il procède** this is how *ou* the way he does it; **il s'y prend de** *ou* **d'une ~ curieuse** he sets about things in a peculiar way *ou* fashion (*frm*); **de quelle ~ est-ce arrivé?** how did it happen?; **il faut le faire de la ~ suivante** you must do it in the following way *ou* as follows; **je le ferai à ma ~** I shall do it my own way; **à la ~ d'un enfant** like a child, as a child would do; **sa ~ d'agir/de répondre** *etc* the way he behaves/answers *etc*, his way of behaving/answering *etc*; **(c'est une) ~ de parler** it's a way of saying *ou* putting it; **je vais lui dire ma ~ de penser** I'll tell him what I think about it; **c'est une ~ de voir (les choses)** it's one way of seeing things *ou* of looking at things; (*Prov*) **la ~ de donner vaut mieux que ce qu'on donne** it's the thought that counts.

(b) (*loc*) **rosser qn de (la) belle ~**†† to give sb a sound thrashing; **d'une certaine ~, c'est vrai** it is true in a way *ou* in some ways; **d'une ~ générale** generally speaking, as a general rule; **de toute(s) ~(s)** in any case, at any rate, anyway; **de cette ~** (in) this way; **d'une ~ ou d'une autre** somehow or other, one way or another; **en aucune ~** in no way; **de quelque ~ qu'il s'y prenne** however *ou* no matter how he goes about it; **je vais lui jouer un tour de ma ~** I'm going to play a trick of my own on him; **un poème de ma ~** a poem written by me; **un plat de ma ~** a dish of my own making *ou* made by me; **de ~ à ne pas le déranger** so as not to disturb him; **de ~ à ce qu'il puisse regarder, de (telle) ~ qu'il puisse regarder** so that he can see.

(c) sans ~: accepter sans ~ to accept without fuss; **il est sans ~** he is unaffected; **merci, sans ~** no thanks really *ou* honestly; **repas sans ~** simple *ou* unpretentious meal; **et sans plus de ~s** and without further ado.

(d) ~s manners, behaviour; **ses ~s me déplaisent profondément** I find his manners extremely unpleasant, I don't like his behaviour at all; **en voilà des ~s!** what sort of behaviour is this!, that's no way to behave!; **faire des ~s** (*minauderies*) to be affected; (*chichis*) to make a fuss.

(e) (*Couture*) *[robe]* cut, making-up. **robe d'une bonne ~**† well-cut dress; **payer la ~** to pay for the tailoring *ou* making-up; **travailler à ~** to make up customers' own material.

(f) (*imitation*) **veste ~ daim/cuir** jacket in imitation suede/leather; **bijoux ~ antique** old-fashioned *ou* antique style jewellery.

(g) (†: *genre*) **une ~ de maître d'hôtel** a head waiter of sorts; **une ~ de roman** a novel of sorts.

(h) (*Agr*) **donner une ~ à la terre** to till the land.

faconde [fakɔ̃d] *nf* (*littér*) (*facilité d'élocution*) volubility; (*bagout*) loquaciousness. **avoir de la ~** to be very voluble *ou* loquacious.

façonnage [fasɔnaʒ] *nm* (*V* **façonner**) shaping; fashioning; modelling; hewing; tilling; manufacturing; making; moulding; forming.

façonnement [fasɔnmɑ̃] *nm [esprits, caractère]* moulding, shaping, forming.

façonner [fasɔne] (1) *vt* **(a)** (*travailler*) to shape, fashion; *argile* to model, shape, fashion; *tronc d'arbre, bloc de pierre* to hew, shape; *terre, sol* to till.

(b) (*fabriquer*) *pièce, clef* (*industriellement*) to manufacture; (*artisanalement*) to make; *chapeau, robe, statuette* to fashion, make.

(c) (*former*) *caractère, personne* to mould, shape, form. (*littér*) **~ qn à** *travail, discipline, violence* to train sb for.

façonnier, -ière [fasɔnje, jɛʀ] *adj* (*maniéré*) over-refined. **elle est ~ière** she puts on airs and graces, she's over-refined.

fac-similé, *pl* **fac-similés** [faksimile] *nm* facsimile.

facteur [faktœʀ] *nm* **(a)** (*Poste*) postman; *V* **factrice. (b)** (*élément, Math*) factor. **le ~ chance/prix** the chance/price factor; (*Math*) **mise en ~s** factorization; (*Méd*) **~ Rhésus** Rhesus *ou* Rh factor. **(c)** (*fabricant*) **~ de pianos** piano maker; **~ d'orgues** organ builder.

factice [faktis] *adj marbre, beauté* artificial; *cuir, bijou* imitation (*épith*), artificial; *barbe* false; *bouteilles, articles exposés* dummy (*épith*); *enthousiasme, amabilité* false, artificial, feigned. **tout semblait ~, le marbre du sol et la civilité des employés** everything seemed phoney* *ou* artificial, from the marble floor to the politeness of the employees.

facticement [faktismɑ̃] *adv* artificially.

factieux, -euse [faksjø, øz] **1** *adj* factious, seditious. **2** *nm,f* seditionary.

faction [faksjɔ̃] *nf* **(a)** (*groupe factieux*) faction.

(b) (*garde*) *[sentinelle]* sentry (duty), guard (duty); *[soldat, guetteur]* guard (duty); (*fig*) *[personne qui attend]* long watch. **être de** *ou* **en ~** *[soldat, guetteur]* to be on guard (duty), stand guard; *[sentinelle]* to be on guard (duty) *ou* (sentry) duty, stand guard; (*fig*) *[personne qui attend]* to keep *ou* stand watch; **mettre qn de ~** to put sb on guard (duty).

factionnaire [faksjɔnɛʀ] *nm* (*sentinelle, garde*) sentry *ou* guard (on duty).

factitif, -ive [faktitif, iv] *adj* (*Ling*) factitive, causative.

factoriel, -ielle [faktɔʀjɛl] **1** *adj* (*Math*) factorial. **analyse ~le** factor analysis. **2 factorielle** *nf* (*Math*) factorial.

factotum [faktɔtɔm] *nm* (*homme à tout faire*) odd-job man, general handyman, (general) factotum (*hum*); (*péj: larbin*) (general) dogsbody (*péj*).

factrice [faktʀis] *nf* (*Poste*) postwoman.

facturation [faktyʀasjɔ̃] *nf* (*opération*) invoicing; (*bureau*) invoice office.

facture [faktyʀ] *nf* **(a)** (*note*) (*gén*) bill; (*Comm*) invoice.

(b) (*manière, style*) *[œuvre d'art]* construction; *[artiste]* technique. **poème de ~ délicate/gauche** sensitively/awkwardly constructed poem; **meubles de bonne ~** well-made furniture, furniture of good workmanship.

(c) (*Tech*) *[piano, orgue etc]* making.

facturer [faktyʀe] (1) *vt* (*établir une facture pour*) to invoice; (*compter*) to charge (for), put on the bill, include in the bill. **~ qch 20 F (à qn)** to charge *ou* bill (sb) 20 francs for sth; **ils ont oublié de ~ l'emballage** they've forgotten to charge for the packing, they've forgotten to include the packing in the bill.

facturier [faktyʀje] *nm* invoice clerk.

facturière [faktyʀjɛʀ] *nf* invoice clerkess *ou* clerk.

facultatif, -ive [fakyltatif, iv] *adj travail, examen, cours* optional; *halte, arrêt* request (*épith*).

faculté [fakylte] *nf* **(a)** (*Univ*) faculty. **la ~ des Lettres/de Médecine** the faculty of Arts/Medicine, the Arts/Medical faculty; (*Can*) **F~ des Arts/Sciences** faculty of Arts/Science; (*Québec*) **F~ des études supérieures** graduate and post-graduate studies; (*arg Univ: université*) **quand j'étais en ~** *ou* **à la ~** when I was at university *ou* college (*Brit*) *ou* school (*US*); **professeur de ~** university lecturer; (*hum*) **la ~ me défend le tabac** I'm not allowed to smoke on doctor's orders; **il osait s'attaquer à la F~** he dared to attack the medical profession.

(b) (*don*) faculty; (*pouvoir*) power; (*propriété*) property. **avoir une grande ~ de concentration** to have great powers of concentration *ou* a great faculty for concentration; **avoir une grande ~ de mémoire** to have great powers of memory; **avoir la ~ de marcher/de la préhension** to have the power of walking/of grasping; (*pl: aptitudes intellectuelles*) **~s** faculties; **ce problème dépasse mes ~s** this problem is beyond my powers; **jouir de** *ou* **avoir toutes ses ~s** to be in (full) possession of all one's faculties.

(c) (*droit*) right, option; (*possibilité*) power, freedom, possibility. **le propriétaire a la ~ de vendre son bien** the owner has the right to sell *ou* the option of selling his property; **je te laisse la ~ de choisir** I'll give you the freedom to choose *ou* the possibility *ou* option of choosing; (*frm*) **le Premier ministre a la ~ de révoquer certains fonctionnaires** the Prime Minister has the faculty *ou* power of dismissing certain civil servants.

fada [fada] **1** *adj* (*dial: fou*) cracked*, crackers* (*attrib*), barmy* (*Brit*). **2** *nm* crackpot*.

fadaise [fadɛz] *nf* (*littér: gén pl*) (*bagatelle*) trifle; (*platitude*) twaddle (*U*), balderdash (*U*), nonsense (*U*).

fadasse [fadas] *adj* (*péj*) wishy-washy, insipid.

fade [fad] *adj soupe, cuisine* tasteless, insipid; *goût* insipid, flat, bland; *lumière, teinte* dull; *compliment, plaisanterie* tame, insipid; *décor, visage, individu* insipid, dull; *conversation, style* dull, insipid, vapid; *politesses, amabilité* insipid, conventional. **l'odeur ~ du sang** the sickly smell of blood; **la beauté ~ de certaines blondes** the insipid beauty of some blondes.

fadé, e‡ [fade] *adj* (*iro*) first-class, sensational (*iro*). **il est drôlement ~** he's a prize specimen*.

fadeur [fadœʀ] *nf* **(a)** (*V* **fade**) tastelessness; insipidness; flatness, blandness; dullness; tameness; vapidness, vapidity; conventionality; sickliness.

(b) (*platitudes*) **~s** sweet nothings, insipid *ou* bland compliments; **dire des ~s à une dame** to say sweet nothings to *ou* pay insipid *ou* bland compliments to a lady.

fading [fadiŋ] *nm* (*Rad*) fading.

fafiots‡† [fafjo] *nmpl* (*billets*) (bank)notes.

fagot [fago] *nm* bundle of sticks *ou* firewood; *V* **derrière, sentir.**

fagoter [fagɔte] (1) **1** *vt* (*péj: accoutrer*) *enfant* to dress up, rig out*. **il est drolement fagoté** he's wearing a peculiar getup* *ou* rig-out*, he's peculiarly rigged out* *ou* dressed. **2 se fagoter** *vpr* to rig o.s. out*, dress o.s.

faiblard, e [fɛblaʀ, aʀd(ə)] *adj* (*péj*) (*gén*) weak; *élève, personne* (*en classe*) weak, on the slow *ou* weak side (*attrib*); (*physiquement*) (rather) weakly; *argument, démonstration* feeble, weak, on the weak side (*attrib*).

faible [fɛbl(ə)] **1** *adj* **(a)** (*gén*) *personne, esprit, support, pays* weak. **je me sens encore très ~ (des jambes)** I still feel very weak *ou* shaky (on my legs); **être ~ du cœur/des jambes** to have a weak heart/weak legs; **avoir la vue ~** *ou* **les yeux ~s** to have weak *ou* poor eyesight, have weak eyes; (*hum, iro*) **une ~ femme** one of the weaker sex; **il est trop ~ avec elle/ses élèves** he is too soft with her/with his pupils; **il est ~ de caractère** he has a weak character; *V* **économiquement, sexe.**

(b) (*maigre*) (*Écon*) *rendement, revenu* low, poor; *demande* light, slack, low, poor; *intensité* low; *résistance, protestation* mild, weak; *somme* low, small; *quantité* small, slight; *écart, différence* slight, small; *espoir* faint, slight, slender; *avantage* slight. **il a une ~ attirance pour le travail** he has very little urge to work; **il a de ~s chances de s'en tirer** (*optimiste*) he has a slight chance of pulling through; (*pessimiste*) his chances of pulling through are slight *ou* slim, he has a poor chance of pulling through; **vous n'avez qu'une ~ idée de sa puissance** you have only a slight *ou* faint idea *ou* the merest inkling of his power; **à une ~ hauteur** at low height, not very high up; **à une ~ profondeur** not far below the surface, (at) a slight distance beneath the surface; (*Pol*) **une ~ majorité** a narrow *ou* slight majority; (*Naut*) **de ~ tirant d'eau** shallow draught.

(c) *voix, pouls* weak, faint, feeble; *lumière* dim, weak, faint; *bruit, odeur* faint, slight; *vent* light, faint; *café* weak. (*Mét*) **vent ~ à modéré** wind light to moderate; **~ en alcool** low in alcoholic content *ou* in alcohol; **de ~ teneur en sucre/cuivre** of low sugar/copper content.

(d) (*médiocre*) *élève* weak, slow; *expression, devoir, style* weak, poor; *raisonnement, argument* weak, poor, feeble, lame. **il est ~ en français** he's weak *ou* poor at *ou* in French; **c'est un escroc, et le terme est ~** he's a crook, and that's putting it mildly; **le côté ~ de ce raisonnement** the weak side of this argument; *V* **esprit, point¹, temps¹.**

2 *nm* **(a)** (*sans défense*) **les ~s et les opprimés** the weak *ou* feeble and the oppressed.

(b) (*sans volonté*) weakling. **c'est un ~, elle en fait ce qu'elle veut** he's a weakling — she does what she wants with him.

(c) (*littér*) (*déficience*) weak point. **le ~ de ce livre, ce sont les dialogues** the dialogues are the weak point in this book; **le ~ chez moi, c'est la mémoire** my weak point is my memory.

(d) (*penchant*) weakness. **il a un ~ pour le chocolat** he has a weakness for chocolate; **il a un ~ pour sa fille** he has a soft spot for his daughter.

3: faible d'esprit (*adj*) feeble-minded; (*nmf*) feeble-minded person.

faiblement [fɛbləmɑ̃] *adv* (*V* **faible**) weakly; mildly; faintly; feebly; dimly; slightly; lightly. **le vent soufflait ~ vers la terre** the wind blew lightly landwards, a light wind blew landwards; (*Écon*) **la demande reprend ~** demand is picking up slowly; **~ alcoolisé/gazéifié** slightly alcoholic/gaseous.

faiblesse [fɛblɛs] *nf* **(a)** (*U: V* **faible**) weakness; mildness; faintness; feebleness; dimness; lightness. **la ~ de la demande** the light *ou* slack *ou* low *ou* poor demand; **la ~ du revenu** the low *ou* poor revenue, the smallness of the revenue; **~ à l'égard de qn** softness *ou* weakness towards sb; **sa ~ de constitution** his weak *ou* frail constitution, the weakness *ou* frailty of his constitution; **sa ~ de caractère** his weak character, his weakness of character; **~ d'esprit** feeble-mindedness; **avoir la ~ d'accepter** to be weak enough to accept.

(b) (*syncope*) sudden weakness, dizzy spell; (*défaillance coupable*) (moment's) weakness; (*insuffisance, préférence*) weakness. **il a une ~ dans le bras gauche** he has a weakness in his left arm; **chacun a ses petites ~s** we all have our little foibles *ou* weaknesses.

faiblir [fɛbliʀ] (2) *vi* **(a)** *[malade, branche]* to get weaker, weaken; *[cœur, vue, intelligence]* to fail; *[forces, courage]* to fail, flag, give out; *[influence]* to wane, fall off; *[résolution, autorité]* to weaken. **elle a faibli à la vue du sang/à sa vue** she felt weak *ou* faint when she saw the blood/at the sight of him; **il a faibli devant leurs prières** he weakened in the face of their pleas; **pièce qui faiblit au 3e acte** play that falls off *ou* weakens in the 3rd act; (*Mil*) **la première ligne a faibli sous le choc** the front line weakened under the impact.

(b) *[voix]* to weaken, get weaker *ou* fainter; *[bruit, protesta-*

tion] to die out *ou* down; *[lumière]* to dim, get dimmer *ou* fainter; *[pouls]* to weaken, fail; *[vent]* to slacken, abate, drop; *[rendement]* to slacken (off); *[intensité, espoir]* to diminish; *[résistance]* to weaken, slacken; *[chances]* to weaken, run out. **l'écart faiblit entre eux** the gap is closing *ou* narrowing between them.

faïence [fajɑ̃s] *nf* (*substance*) (glazed) earthenware; (*objets*) crockery (*U*), earthenware (*U*); (*vase, objet*) piece of earthenware, earthenware (*U*). **assiette en/carreau de ~** earthenware plate/tile; **~ de Delft** delft, delftware; *V* **chien.**

faïencerie [fajɑ̃sʀi] *nf* earthenware factory.

faignant, e [fɛɲɑ̃, ɑ̃t] = **fainéant.**

faille[1] [faj] *nf* (*Géol*) fault; (*fig*) (*point faible*) flaw, weakness; (*cassure*) rift. **il y a une ~ dans votre raisonnement** there's a flaw in your argument; *V* **ligne**[1].

faille[2] [faj] *V* **falloir.**

failli[1] [faji] *ptp de* **faillir.**

failli[2], **e** [faji] *adj, nm,f* (*Comm*) bankrupt.

faillibilité [fajibilite] *nf* fallibility.

faillible [fajibl(ə)] *adj* fallible.

faillir [fajiʀ] *vi* **(a)** (*manquer*) **avoir failli: j'ai failli tomber/réussir** I almost *ou* very nearly fell/succeeded, I all but fell/succeeded; **j'ai bien failli me laisser tenter** I almost *ou* very nearly let myself be tempted; **il a failli se faire écraser** he almost *ou* very nearly got run over, he narrowly missed getting run over.

(b) (*frm: manquer à*) **~ à** *engagement, devoir* to fail in; *promesse, parole* to fail to keep; **son cœur/courage lui faillit**† his heart/courage failed him; **il résista jusqu'au bout sans ~** he resisted unfailingly *ou* unflinchingly to the end.

(c) (†: *fauter*) to lapse.

faillite [fajit] **1** *nf* **(a)** (*Comm*) bankruptcy.

(b) (*fig: échec*) *[espoir, tentative, méthode]* collapse, failure; *[gouvernement]* collapse, downfall.

(c) (*loc*) **être en ~** (*Comm*) to be bankrupt *ou* in a state of bankruptcy; (*fig*) to be in a state of collapse; **faire ~** (*Comm*) to go bankrupt; (*fig*) to collapse; **déclarer/mettre qn en ~** to declare/make sb bankrupt.

2: (*Comm*) **faillite frauduleuse** fraudulent bankruptcy; (*Comm*) **faillite simple** bankruptcy.

faim [fɛ̃] *nf* hunger. **avoir (très) ~** to be (very) hungry; **manger sans ~** (*sans besoin réel*) to eat for the sake of eating; (*sans appétit*) to pick at one's food; **ça m'a donné ~** it made me hungry; **manger à sa ~** to eat one's fill; (*fig*) **avoir ~ de** *honneur, tendresse, justice* to hunger for, crave (for); **sa ~ de richesses/d'absolu** his yearning for wealth/the absolute; **j'ai une ~ de loup** *ou* **une ~ canine** I'm ravenous *ou* famished, I could eat a horse; (*Prov*) **la ~ fait sortir** *ou* **chasse le loup du bois** hunger will drive him out; *V* **crever, mourir, rester** *etc.*

faîne [fɛn] *nf* beechnut.

fainéant, e [feneɑ̃, ɑ̃t] **1** *adj* lazy, idle; *V* **roi. 2** *nm,f* idler, loafer.

fainéanter [feneɑ̃te] (1) *vi* to idle *ou* loaf about.

fainéantise [feneɑ̃tiz] *nf* laziness, idleness.

faire [fɛʀ] (60) **1** *vt* **(a)** (*fabriquer*) *meuble, voiture, confiture, vin* to make; *mur, maison, nid* to build; *pain, gâteau* to make, bake. **cette école fait de bons ingénieurs*** this school turns out* *ou* produces good engineers.

(b) (*être l'auteur de*) *faute, déclaration, promesse, offre* to make; *discours, film* to make; *liste* to make, draw up; *chèque* to make out, write; *conférence, cours, réception* to give; *livre, dissertation* to write, produce; *tableau* to paint; *dessin, carte* to draw; *compliment, visite* to pay; *faveur* to do; *farce, tour* to play. **il lui a fait 3 enfants*** he got her pregnant 3 times*, she had 3 children by him.

(c) (*avoir une activité, une occupation*) *bonne action, travail, jardinage, service militaire* to do; *tennis, rugby* to play. **que faites-vous dans la vie?, quel métier faites-vous?** what do you do (for a living)?, what is your job?, what job do you do?; **qu'est-ce que tu fais ce soir?** what are you doing tonight?; **j'ai beaucoup/je n'ai rien à ~** I have a lot/nothing to do; **ils sont en retard, qu'est-ce qu'ils peuvent bien ~?** they are late – what on earth are they doing? *ou* are they up to?*; **~ du théâtre** (*professionnel*) to be on the stage, be an actor; (*amateur*) to do a bit of acting; **il ne fait pas de sport** he doesn't play any games, he doesn't take part in any sport; **~ de la voiture** to drive, go driving; **il fait beaucoup de voiture/de bicyclette** he does a lot of driving/cycling; **~ du tricot** to knit; **~ un peu de tricot/de couture** to do a bit of knitting/sewing; **~ de la photographie** to go in for photography; **~ du bricolage** to do odd jobs.

(d) (*étudier*) *examen* to do, take; (*Scol**) *roman, comédie* to do. **~ des études** to study; **~ du** *ou* **son droit/sa médecine** to do *ou* study law/medicine; **~ de la recherche** to do research; **~ du français** to study *ou* do *ou* take French, be learning French; **~ du piano/du violon** to play *ou* learn the piano/violin; **va ~ ton piano*** go and practise your piano, go and do your piano practice; **~ l'école hôtelière/navale** to be *ou* study at catering school/naval college.

(e) (*préparer*) *repas* to make, cook, prepare; *soupe, sauce, dessert* to make; *salade* to prepare. **~ du thé/du café** to make (some) tea/(some) coffee; **elle fait un rôti/du lapin** she is doing *ou* cooking a roast/a rabbit.

(f) (*mettre en ordre, nettoyer*) *lit* to make; *ménage, pièce* to do; *argenterie* to polish, clean, do; *chaussures* to clean, do, polish; *valise* to pack. **~ les carreaux** to clean the windows; **~ le jardin** to do the gardening; **~ la vaisselle** to do the dishes, do the washing-up (*Brit*), wash up (*Brit*).

(g) (*accomplir une action*) *match* to play; *compte, problème* to do; *projet* to make; *rêve, chute, sieste* to have; *geste* to make; *pas, bond* to take; *sourire, sursaut, secousse* to give. **~ un voyage** to go on a journey, take a trip; **~ une promenade** to go for *ou* take a walk; **~ une réparation** to do a repair (job); **~ un tournoi** *[participant]* to go in for *ou* enter *ou* play in a tournament; *[organisateur]* to organize a tournament; **~ une coupe/un shampooing à qn** to cut/shampoo sb's hair; **~ de l'essence** to fill up with petrol; **~ de l'eau** *[train, bateau]* to take on water; **~ la vidange** to change the oil; **~ de l'herbe pour (nourrir) les lapins** to cut grass for the rabbits.

(h) (*Méd*) *diabète, tension* to have, suffer from; *grippe* to get, go down with. **~ de la fièvre** to have *ou* run a temperature; **~ des complexes** to have a complex, have hang-ups*; **~ une dépression nerveuse** to have a nervous breakdown.

(i) (*besoins naturels*) **~ ses (petits) besoins** *[personne]* to go to the toilet; *[animal]* to make a mess; **le chat a fait (ses ordures** *ou* **ses saletés** *ou* **sa crotte) dans la cuisine** the cat has made a mess in the kitchen; (*langage enfantin*) **~ pipi** to go and spend a penny* (*Brit*), go to the john* (*US*), do a wee-wee* (*Brit*); **~ caca** to do a pooh (*langage enfantin*).

(j) (*parcourir, visiter*) to do. **~ un long trajet** to travel a long way, have a long journey; **~ 10 km** to do *ou* cover 10 km; **~ (une moyenne de) 100 km/h, ~ du cent** to do *ou* average 100 km/h; **~ Rome/la Grèce en 2 jours** to do Rome/Greece in 2 days; **~ Lyon-Paris en 5 heures** to get from Lyons to Paris in 5 hours; **~ tous les magasins pour trouver qch** to do all *ou* comb the stores *ou* try every store in search of sth; **il a fait toute la ville pour trouver ...** he has been all over *ou* he has combed the town looking for ...; **~ les bistros/les boîtes de nuit** to do the round of the cafés/night clubs; **commerçant qui fait les foires** tradesman who does *ou* goes the round of the markets.

(k) (*Comm*) *l'épicerie, les légumes* to sell, deal in; (*Agr*) *blé, betteraves* to grow, produce. **~ le gros/le détail** to be a wholesale dealer/a retailer, be in the wholesale/retail trade; **nous ne faisons pas les boutons/cette marque** we do not stock *ou* carry *ou* keep buttons/this make; **cet hôtel fait aussi restaurant** this hotel is also run as a restaurant.

(l) (*mesurer, peser, coûter: langue familière*) **cette cuisine fait 6 mètres de large sur 3 de long** this kitchen is 6 metres wide by 3 metres long; **ce rôti fait bien 3 kg** this joint weighs a good 3 kg; **ça fait encore loin jusqu'à Paris** it is still quite a long way *ou* quite far to Paris; **combien fait cette chaise?** how much is this chair?; **cette table fera un bon prix** this table will go for *ou* will fetch a high price; **je vous fais ce fauteuil 100 F** I'll let you have *ou* I'll give you this armchair for 100 francs.

(m) (*imiter l'apparence de*) **~ le malade/le mort** to sham ill(ness)/dead; **~ le sourd** *ou* **la sourde oreille** to feign deafness, pretend to be deaf; **~ l'innocent/la bête/le timide** to play *ou* act the innocent/the fool/shy; **~ le dictateur** to act the dictator; **~ l'imbécile** *ou* **le pitre** to play *ou* act the fool; **ne fais pas l'enfant/l'idiot** don't be so childish/so stupid, don't behave so childishly/so stupidly.

(n) (*tenir un rôle, faire fonction de*) (*Théât*) to play the part of, be. **il fait le fantôme dans 'Hamlet'** he plays (the part of) the ghost in 'Hamlet'; **~ le Père Noël** to be Father Christmas (*Brit*) *ou* Santa Claus; **leur fils fait le jardinier pendant les vacances** their son's being the gardener *ou* acting as gardener during the holidays; **quel idiot je fais!** what a fool I am! *ou* I look!; **ils font un beau couple** they make a fine couple.

(o) (*transformer*) to make. **la vie a fait de lui un aigri** life has made him *ou* turned him into a bitter man, life has embittered him; **il a fait d'une grange une demeure agréable** he has transformed *ou* turned *ou* made a barn into a comfortable home; **elle a fait de son neveu son héritier** she made her nephew her heir; **il veut en ~ un avocat** he wants to make a lawyer of him, he wants him to be a lawyer; **se ~ moine/marin** to become a monk/a sailor.

(p) (*représenter*) **on le fait plus riche qu'il n'est** he's made out *ou* people make him out to be richer than he is; **ne faites pas les choses plus sombres qu'elles ne sont** don't paint things blacker *ou* don't make things out to be worse than they are.

(q) (*avoir un effet sur*) **~ du bien/du mal à ...** to do good/harm to ...; **~ du chagrin** *ou* **de la peine à qn** to cause grief to sb, make sb unhappy; **~ le malheur/le bonheur de qn** to make sb very unhappy/happy; **~ la joie de qn** to delight sb; **cela fait la richesse du pays** that's what makes the country rich; **qu'est-ce que cela peut bien te ~?** what does it matter to you?, what difference can it possibly make to you?; **qu'est-ce que ça fait?*** so what?*; **la mort de son père ne lui a rien fait** his father's death didn't affect him, he was unaffected by his father's death; **cela ne vous ferait rien de sortir?** would you mind going out?; **~ des piqûres/rayons à qn** to give sb injections/X-rays; **qu'est-ce qu'on lui fait à l'hôpital?** what are they doing to him in hospital?; **qu'est-ce qu'on t'a donc fait!** whatever have they done to you!; **ils ne peuvent rien me faire** they can't do anything to me, they can't hurt me; **ça ne fait rien** it doesn't matter, it's of no importance.

(r) (*servir de*) to serve as, be used as, do duty as. **la cuisine fait salle à manger** the kitchen serves as *ou* is used as a dining room.

(s) qu'avez-vous fait de votre sac/de vos enfants? what have you done with *ou* where have you left your bag/your children?; **qu'ai-je bien pu ~ de mes lunettes?** where on earth have I put *ou* left my glasses?

(t) (*dans un calcul*) **24 en tout, ce qui en fait 2 chacun** 24 altogether, which gives *ou* makes 2 each; (*addition*) **deux et deux font quatre** two and two make *ou* are four; **cela fait combien en tout?** how much does that make altogether?

(u) (*loc*) **pour ce qu'on en fait!** for all that we (*ou* you *etc*) do with it!, for all the good it is to us (*ou* you *etc*)!; **n'en faites rien** do nothing of the sort; **n'avoir que ~ de** to have no need of; **~ tant (et si bien) que** to finish *ou* end up by; **ne ~ que** (*faire constamment*): **ne ~ que de protester** to keep on and on *ou* be constantly protesting; **il ne fait que bavarder** he won't stop chattering, he does nothing but chatter; (*faire seulement*) **je ne fais que d'arriver** I've only just come; **je ne fais que dire la vérité** I'm only telling the truth *ou* saying what's true; **je ne fais que passer** I am just passing by; **la ~ à qn au sentiment*** to take sb in by appealing to his emotions.

2 *vi* **(a)** (*agir, procéder*) to act, do. **~ vite** to act quickly; **faites vite!** be quick about it!, make it quick!; **il a bien fait** he did the right thing; **il a bien fait de partir** he was quite right *ou* he did right to go; **tu as mal fait** you behaved badly, you did the wrong thing; **~ de son mieux** to do one's best; **on ferait bien/mieux de le prévenir** it would be a good/better idea *ou* safer/much safer to warn him; **ça commence à bien ~!*** this has gone on quite long enough!, this is getting beyond a joke!; **faites comme vous voulez** do as you please, please yourself; **faites comme chez vous** make yourself at home; **que voulez-vous qu'on y fasse?** what do you expect us to do (about it)?; **il n'y a rien à faire** (*lit*) there's nothing we can do; (*fig*) there's nothing doing, it's useless *ou* hopeless; **il sait y ~** he's good at getting things his own way; **pour bien ~** ... the best is to ... .

(b) (*dire*) to say. **vraiment? fit-il** really? he said; **il fit un 'ah' de surprise** he gave a surprised 'ah'; **le chat fait miaou** the cat goes *ou* says miaow.

(c) (*durer*) **ce chapeau (me) fera encore un hiver** this hat will last me *ou* will do me another winter.

(d) (*paraître*) to look. **ce vase fait bien sur la table** the vase looks nice on the table; (*fig*) **cela fait mal dans le tableau!*** it looks pretty bad*, it doesn't quite fit the picture; **~ vieux/jeune** to look old/young (for one's age); **elle fait très femme** she's very womanly(-looking) *ou* grown-up looking for her age.

(e) (*gén au futur: devenir*) to make; *[personne]* to make, have the makings of. **cette branche fera une belle canne** this branch will make a fine walking stick; **cet enfant fera un bon musicien** this child has the makings of *ou* will make a good musician; **il veut ~ médecin**‡ he wants to be a doctor.

(f) (*besoins naturels*) to go. **as-tu fait ce matin?** have you been this morning?

3 *vb impers* **(a) il fait jour/nuit/clair/sombre** it is daylight/dark/light/dull; **il fera beau demain** it *ou* the weather will be fine tomorrow, tomorrow will be fine; **il fait du soleil** the sun is shining, it is sunny; **il fait lourd** it *ou* the weather is close; **il fait faim/soif*** we are hungry/thirsty.

(b) (*exprimant le temps écoulé*) **cela fait 2 ans/très longtemps que je ne l'ai pas vu** it is 2 years/a very long time since I last saw him, I haven't seen him for 2 years/for a very long time.

(c) il fait bon + *infin* it is nice *ou* pleasant; **il fait bon se promener** it is nice *ou* pleasant to go for a walk; **il ne fait pas bon le contredire** it is unwise *ou* it's better not to contradict him.

(d) (*) **cela fait que nous devons partir** the result is that we must leave, as a result *ou* so we must leave.

4 *vb substitut* to do. **ne manquez pas le train comme nous l'avons fait** don't miss the train as we did; **il travaille mieux que je ne fais** he works better than I do; **as-tu payé la note? — non, c'est lui qui l'a fait** did you pay the bill? — no, he did; **puis-je téléphoner? — faites, je vous en prie** may I phone? — (yes) please do *ou* (yes) by all means.

5 se faire *vpr* **(a) se ~ les ongles** to do one's nails; **se ~ une robe** to make o.s. a dress; **il se fait sa cuisine** he does his own cooking; **il se fait 4.000 F par mois** he earns *ou* gets *ou* makes 4,000 francs a month; **il s'est fait beaucoup d'amis/d'ennemis** he has made himself a great many friends/enemies.

(b) se ~ une idée to get some idea; **se ~ des idées** to imagine things, have illusions; **s'en ~** to worry; **il ne s'en fait pas** he does not worry, he is not the worrying type; (*excl*) he's got a nerve!; *V* **bile, raison** *etc.*

(c) (*se former*) *[fromage]* to ripen, mature; *[vin]* to mature. (*fig*) **il s'est fait tout seul** he is a self-made man.

(d) (+ *attribut: devenir*) to become, get. **se ~ vieux** to be getting old; **il se faisait tard** it was getting late; (*littér*) **il se fit violent sous l'insulte** he turned *ou* became violently angry at the insult.

(e) (+ *adj: devenir volontairement*) **se ~ beau** to make o.s. beautiful; **se ~ tout petit** to make o.s. small.

(f) se ~ à to become used to, get used to; **il ne peut pas se ~ au climat** he can't get used to the climate; **il faut se le ~!**‡ (*travail*) it's a hell of a fag!‡ (*Brit*), it's hellish heavy-going!‡; (*personne*) he's a real pain in the neck*.

(g) cela ne se fait pas it's not done; **les jupes longues se font beaucoup cette année** long skirts are in* this year *ou* are being worn a lot this year.

(h) (*impers*) **il peut/il pourrait se ~ qu'il pleuve** it may/it might (well) rain; **comment se fait-il qu'il soit absent?** how is it (that) he is absent?, how does he happen to be absent?, how come he's absent?*

(i) se ~ mal to hurt o.s.; **se ~ peur** to give o.s. a fright.

(j) se ~ + *infin*: **elle s'est fait opérer** she was operated on, she had an operation; **tu vas te ~ gronder** you'll get yourself into trouble *ou* told off*; **il s'est fait remettre le document** he had the document handed over to him; **il s'est fait ouvrir par le voisin** he got the neighbour to let him in; **fais-toi vite vomir: c'est du poison** quick, make yourself vomit *ou* be sick — it's poisonous; **elle s'en est fait montrer le fonctionnement** she had a demonstration of how it worked.

6 *vb aux* + *infin* **(a)** (*être la cause de*) **la pluie fait pousser l'herbe** the rain makes the grass grow; **mon voisin fait pousser des dahlias** my neighbour grows dahlias; **j'ai fait démarrer la voiture** I made the car start, I got the car going *ou* started; **elle a fait lire les enfants** she made the children read; **elle a fait opérer sa fille** she had her daughter operated on; **il lui a fait lire Stendhal** he made him read Stendhal; **il lui a fait boire un grog** he gave her some grog to drink.

(b) (*aider à*) **~ traverser la rue à un aveugle** to help a blind man across the road; **~ faire ses devoirs à un enfant** to help a child with his homework, see that a child does his homework; **~ manger un invalide** to (help to) feed an invalid; **on a dû les ~ sortir par la fenêtre** they had to help *ou* get them out through the window.

(c) (*inviter à*) **~ entrer/monter qn** to show *ou* ask sb in/up(stairs); **~ venir le docteur/un employé** to send for the doctor/an employee.

(d) (*donner une tâche à exécuter*) **~ faire qch par qn** to have sth done *ou* made by sb; **~ faire qch à qn** to have sb do *ou* make sth; **(se) ~ faire une robe** to have a dress made; **~ réparer une voiture/une montre** to have a car/a watch repaired; **~ faire la vaisselle à qn** to have sb do *ou* get sb to do the dishes.

(e) (*laisser*) **~ entrer/sortir le chien** to let the dog in/out; **faites entrer le public** let the public in; **elle a fait tomber une tasse** she dropped a cup.

(f) (*forcer*) to make. **il lui a fait ouvrir le coffre-fort** he made him open *ou* forced him to open the safe.

7: faire-part *nm inv* announcement (of a birth *ou* marriage *ou* death *etc*); **faire-part de mariage** ≈ wedding invitation; **faire-valoir** *nm inv* (*Agr*) development (of land); (*personne*) foil.

fair-play [fɛʀplɛ] *nm inv* fair play. **c'est un joueur ~** he plays fair.

faisable [fəzabl(ə)] *adj* feasible. **est-ce ~ en 2 jours?** can it be done in 2 days?; **est-ce ~ à pied?** can it be done on foot?, is it quite feasible on foot?

faisan [fəzɑ̃] *nm* **(a)** (*oiseau*) (*gén*) pheasant; (*mâle*) cock pheasant; *V* **faisane.**

(b) (†: *escroc*) shark.

faisandé, e [fəzɑ̃de] (*ptp de* **faisander**) *adj* **(a)** (*Culin*) *gibier, goût* high. **je n'aime pas le ~** I don't like high game; **viande trop ~e** meat which has gone off (*Brit*) *ou* gone bad.

(b) (*péj*) *littérature, société* unwholesome and corrupt, decadent; *milieux* crooked.

faisandeau, *pl* **~x** [fəzɑ̃do] *nm* young pheasant.

faisander [fəzɑ̃de] (1) *vt* (*Culin*) **(faire** *ou* **laisser) ~** to hang.

faisanderie [fəzɑ̃dʀi] *nf* pheasantry.

faisandier [fəzɑ̃dje] *nm* pheasant breeder.

faisane [fəzan] *nf, adj f*: **(poule) ~** hen pheasant.

faisceau, *pl* **~x** [fɛso] **1** *nm* **(a)** (*fagot*) bundle. (*réseau*) **~ de preuves/faits** body *ou* network of proofs/facts; **nouer en ~** to tie in a bundle; **nouer en ~x** to tie into bundles.

(b) (*Mil*) **~x (d'armes)** stack (of arms); **mettre en ~x** *fusils* to stack; **former/rompre les ~x** to stack/unstack arms.

(c) (*rayons*) beam. **le ~ de sa lampe** the beam of his torch; **~ convergent/divergent** convergent/divergent beam.

(d) (*Antiq, Hist*) **~x** fasces.

2: (*Phys*) **faisceau d'électrons** electron beam; (*Élec*) **faisceau hertzien** radio wave; **faisceau lumineux** beam of light; (*Anat*) **faisceau musculaire/nerveux** fasciculus *ou* fascicule of muscle/nerve fibres.

faiseur, -euse [fəzœʀ, øz] **1** *nm,f*: **~ de**† *monuments, meubles* maker of; (†*hum, péj*) *romans, tableaux, opéras* producer of.

2 *nm* (†) (*péj: hâbleur*) show-off; (*escroc*) shark. (*frm: tailleur*) **(bon) ~** good tailor.

3: faiseuse d'anges backstreet abortionist; (*péj*) **faiseur de bons mots** punster, wag; **faiseur d'embarras** fusspot; (*péj*) **faiseur d'intrigues** schemer; (*péj*) **faiseur de littérature** scribbler; (*péj*) **faiseur** *m*, **-euse** *f* **de mariages** matchmaker; (*péj*) **faiseur de miracles** miracle-worker; (*péj*) **faiseur de phrases** speechifier; (*péj*) **faiseur de projets** schemer; (*péj*) **faiseur de vers** poetaster (*péj*), versifier.

fait[1] [fɛ] **1** *nm* **(a)** (*événement*) event, occurrence; (*donnée*) fact. **il s'agit d'un ~ courant/rare** this is a common/rare occurrence *ou* event; **aucun ~ nouveau n'est survenu** no new development has taken place; *V* **erreur, point**[1].

(b) (*acte*) **le ~ de manger/bouger** the fact of eating/moving, eating/moving; (*Jur, Mil*) **être puni pour ~ d'insoumission** to be punished for (an act of) insubordination; *V* **haut.**

(c) (*loc*) **au ~** (*à propos*) by the way; **au ~!** (*à l'essentiel*) come to the point!; **aller droit/en venir au ~** to go straight/get to the point; **au ~ de** (*au courant*) conversant *ou* acquainted with, informed of; **être au ~ (de)** to be informed (of); **est-il au ~?** does he know?, is he informed?; **mettre qn au ~ (d'une affaire)** to acquaint *ou* familiarize sb with (the facts of) a matter, inform sb of (the facts of) a matter; **de ~** (*de facto*) *gouvernement, dictature* de facto; (*en fait*) in fact; **il est de ~ que** it is a fact that; **de ce ~** therefore, for this reason; **du ~ de qch** on account *ou* as a result of sth; **du ~ qu'il a démissionné** on account of *ou* as a result of his having resigned; **en ~** in (actual) fact, in point of fact; **en ~ de** (*en guise de*) by way of a; (*en matière de*) as regards, in the way of; **en ~ de repas on a eu droit à un sandwich** we were allowed a sandwich by way of a meal; **le ~ est que** the fact is that; **le ~ que** the fact that; **le ~ est là** that's the fact of the matter; **être le ~ de** (*être typique de*) to be typical *ou* characteristic of; (*être causé par*) to be the work of; **par le ~** in fact; **par ce ~** by this very fact; **par le ~ même** by this very or selfsame fact; **par le ~ même que/de** by the very fact that/of; **par le (simple) ~ de** by the simple fact of; **par le ~ même de son obstination** because of *ou* by his very obstinacy, by the very fact of his obstinacy; **par son (propre) ~** through *ou* by his (own) doing; **c'est un ~** that's a fact; **c'est un ~ que** it's a fact that; **dire son ~ à qn** to tell sb what's what, talk straight to sb; **prendre ~ et cause pour qn** to fight for sb's cause, take up the cudgels for sb; **comme par un ~ exprès** almost as if on purpose; *V* **sur, sûr, tout, voie.**

2: **fait accompli** fait accompli; **mettre qn devant le fait accompli** to present sb with a fait accompli; **fait d'armes** feat of arms; **fait divers** (*nouvelle*) (short) news item; (*événement insignifiant*) trivial event; (*rubrique*) **'faits divers'** '(news) in brief'; **faits et gestes** actions, doings; **épier les moindres faits et gestes de qn** to spy on sb's slightest actions *ou* movements; **faits de guerre** exploits in war, heroic exploits; (*Ling*) **fait de langue** fait de langue, language event; (*Ling*) **fait de parole** fait de parole, speech event; **le fait du prince** the imperial fiat; **faits de résistance** acts of resistance.

fait[2], e [fɛ, fɛt] (*ptp de* **faire**) *adj* **(a) être ~ pour** to be suitable *ou* made *ou* meant for; **voitures ~es pour la course** cars (specially) made *ou* designed *ou* conceived for racing; **ces souliers ne sont pas ~s pour la marche** these are not proper walking shoes, these shoes are not suitable *ou* designed for walking in; **ceci n'est pas ~ pour lui plaire** this is not going to *ou* is not calculated to *ou* likely to please him; **ce discours n'est pas ~ pour le rassurer** this is not the kind of speech to reassure him, this sort of speech isn't likely to reassure him; **il est ~ pour être médecin** he's cut out to be a doctor.

(b) (*fini*) **c'en est ~ de notre vie calme** that's the end of our quiet life, it's goodbye to peace and quiet in our life!*; **c'en est ~ de moi** I am done for, it's all up with me!*; **c'est toujours ça de ~** that's one job done, that's one thing out of the way.

(c) avoir la jambe/main bien ~e to have shapely *ou* nice legs/pretty *ou* nice hands.

(d) (*mûr*) *personne* mature; *fromage* ripe.

(e) (*loc*) **comment est-il ~?** what is he like?, what does he look like?; **regarde comme tu es ~!** look at the way you're dressed!, look what a sight you are!; **il est ~ (comme un rat)*** he's in for it now!*, he's cornered!; **c'est bien ~ pour toi** you asked for it!*, you got what you deserved!; **c'est bien ~!** it serves them (*ou* him *etc*) right!

faîtage [fɛtaʒ] *nm* (*poutre*) ridgepole; (*couverture*) roofing; (*littér: toit*) roof.

faîte [fɛt] *nm* **(a)** (*poutre*) ridgepole.

(b) (*sommet*) *[montagne]* summit; *[arbre]* top; *[maison]* rooftop. **~ du toit** rooftop; *V* **ligne[1]**.

(c) (*fig: summum*) **~ de la gloire** pinnacle *ou* height of glory; **parvenu au ~ des honneurs** having attained the highest honours.

faitout *nm*, **fait-tout** *nm inv* [fɛtu] stewpot.

faix [fɛ] *nm* (*littér: lit, fig*) burden. **sous le ~ (de)** under the weight *ou* burden (of).

fakir [fakiʀ] *nm* (*Rel*) fakir; (*Music-Hall*) wizard.

fakirisme [fakiʀism(ə)] *nm* (*Rel*) practice of a fakir. (*fig*) **c'est du ~!** (*divination*) it's prophesy!; (*pouvoir magique*) it's wizardry!

falaise [falɛz] *nf* cliff.

falbalas [falbala] *nmpl* frills and flounces *ou* furbelows; (*péj*) frippery (*U*) (*péj*), furbelows (*péj*).

fallacieusement [falasjøzmɑ̃] *adv promettre* deceptively.

fallacieux, -euse [falasjø, øz] *adj promesse, apparence, appellation* deceptive; *arguments, raisonnement* fallacious; *espoir* illusory, delusive.

falloir [falwaʀ] (29) **1** *vb impers* **(a)** (*besoin*) **il va ~ 10.000 F** we're going to need 10,000 francs, it's going to take 10,000 francs; **il doit ~ du temps/de l'argent pour faire cela** it must take time/money *ou* you must need time/money to do that; **il me le faut à tout prix** I must have it at all costs, I desperately need it; **il lui faut quelqu'un pour l'aider** he needs *ou* wants somebody to help him; **il vous faut tourner à gauche** you have *ou* need to turn left; **faut-il aussi de l'ail?** do we need *ou* want garlic as well?; **c'est juste ce qu'il faut** (*outil etc*) that's just what we need *ou* want, that's exactly what's required; (*assaisonnement*) there's *ou* that's just the right amount; (*au magasin*) **qu'est-ce qu'il vous faut?** what are you looking for?; **il n'en faut pas beaucoup pour qu'il se mette à pleurer** it doesn't take much to make him cry; **c'est plus qu'il n'en faut** that's more than we need *ou* is needed; **il faudrait avoir plus de temps** we'd have to have more time, we'd need more time.

(b) (*obligation*) **~ faire: il va ~ le faire** it'll have to be done, we'll have to do it; **il va ~ y aller** we'll have to go; **il ne fallait pas faire ça, c'est tout** you shouldn't have done that and that's all there is to it; **que vous fallait-il faire?** what did you have to do?; **il faudrait qu'il parte** he ought to *ou* should go; **il m'a fallu obéir** I had to comply; **s'il le faut** (*besoin*) if need be; (*obligation*) if I (*ou* we *etc*) have to; **que faut-il leur dire?** what shall I (*ou* we *etc*) tell them?; **le faut-il? — il le faut** do I (*ou* we *etc*) have to? — yes you do; **il a bien fallu!** I (*ou* we *etc*) HAD to!

(c) (*obligation*) **~ que: il va ~ qu'il parte** he'll have to *ou* he has got to go; **il faut qu'il le fasse** he'll have to *ou* he has got to do it; **il faut qu'il soit malade pour qu'il s'arrête de travailler** he has to be ill before he stops working.

(d) (*intensif*) **il fallait me le dire** you should have told me; **il faut voir ce spectacle** this show is a must, you must see this show; **faut voir ça, quel luxe!*** you should see the luxury of it!; — **il ne fallait pas!** — you shouldn't have!; **va pas ~ traîner*** we can't afford to mess about*; **faudrait pas qu'il essaie!*** he'd better not try!*; **fallait-il vraiment le dire?** did you really have to say it?; **il ne faudrait surtout pas lui en parler** don't speak to him about it whatever you do; **(il) faut dire qu'il est culotté*** you've got to admit he's got a cheek*.

(e) (*probabilité*) **il faut que tu te sois trompé** you must have made a mistake; **s'il est absent, il faut qu'il soit malade** if he's absent he must be ill *ou* it must be because he's ill; **il faut être fou pour parler comme ça** you must be mad to talk like that; **faut-il donc être bête!** some people are so *ou* really stupid; **faut-il qu'il soit bête!** he must be so *ou* really stupid; **faut (pas) être gonflé!*** it takes some nerve!*

(f) (*fatalité*) **il a fallu qu'elle l'apprenne** she would have to hear about it; **faut-il donc abandonner si près du but?** do we have to give up when we're so near to the goal?; **il faut toujours qu'elle se trouve des excuses** she always has to find some excuse.

(g) (*loc*) (*hum*) **elle a ce qu'il faut*** she's got what it takes*; **il faut ce qu'il faut*** you've got to do things properly *ou* in style; **(il) faut le faire!** (*admiratif*) that takes some doing!; (**: péjoratif*) that takes some beating!; **(il) faut se le faire!‡** (*personne*) he's a real pain in the neck*; (*travail*) it's a hell of a fag!‡ (*Brit*), it's really heavy-going; **(il) faut voir** (*réserve*) we'll have to see; (*admiration*) you should see!; **faudrait voir à voir*** just (you) take it easy*; **(il) faudrait voir à faire/ne pas faire*** you'd better mind *ou* make sure you do/don't do ...; **il ne faut pas y songer** it's out of the question; **il faut bien vivre/manger** you have to live/eat; **il faut vous dire que ...** I must *ou* I have to tell you (confidentially) that ...; **il faut de tout pour faire un monde** it takes all sorts to make a world; **il ne faut jamais remettre au lendemain ce qu'on peut faire le jour même** never put off till tomorrow what you can do today, procrastination is the thief of time (*Prov*); **(il) faut le voir pour le croire** it needs *ou* has to be seen to be believed; **ce qu'il faut entendre!** the things you hear!; *V* **comme**.

2 s'en falloir *vpr* (*frm*) **s'en ~ de: tu n'es pas à l'heure, il s'en faut de 5 minutes** you're not on time, by a matter of 5 minutes; **il ne s'en fallait que de 100 F pour qu'il ait la somme** he was only *ou* just 100 francs short of the full amount; **il s'en faut de beaucoup qu'il soit heureux** he is far from being happy, he is by no means happy; **il s'en est fallu d'un cheveu qu'il ne soit pris** he was within a hair's breadth *ou* an ace of being caught; **il a fini, ou peu s'en faut** he has as good as finished, he has just about finished; **peu s'en fallut (pour) que** *ou* **il ne s'en est guère fallu pour que** *ou* **il s'en est fallu de peu (pour) que ça n'arrive** this came very close to happening, this very nearly happened, it wouldn't have taken much for this to happen; **et il s'en faut!, tant s'en faut!** far from it!, not by a long way! *ou* chalk! (*Brit*); **ça m'a coûté 50 F ou peu s'en faut** that cost me the best part of 50 francs, that cost me very nearly 50 francs; **peu s'en est fallu qu'il pleure** he all but *ou* he almost wept; *V* **entendre, se fier, voir**.

falot[1] [falo] *nm* lantern.

falot[2], e [falo, ɔt] *adj personne* dreary, colourless; *lueur, lumière* wan, pale.

falsificateur, -trice [falsifikatœʀ, tʀis] *nm,f* falsifier.

falsification [falsifikɑsjɔ̃] *nf* (*V* **falsifier**) falsification; doctoring; alteration; adulteration.

falsifier [falsifje] (7) *vt comptes, faits* to falsify, doctor, alter; *document, signature* to falsify, alter; *aliment* to doctor, adulterate.

falzar‡ [falzaʀ] *nm* pants*, trousers.

famé, e [fame] *adj V* **mal**.

famélique [famelik] *adj* half-starved.

fameusement [faməzmɑ̃] *adv* (**: très*) remarkably, really. **c'est ~ bon** it's remarkably *ou* really good.

fameux, -euse [famø, øz] *adj* **(a)** (**: après n: bon*) *mets, vin* first-rate, first-class.

(b) pas ~ *mets, travail, temps* not too good, not so great*; *roman, auteur* not up to much*; **et le temps pour demain? — pas ~** and tomorrow's weather? — not all that good *ou* not all that fine *ou* not up to much*; **il n'est pas ~ en latin/en maths** he's not too good *ou* not all that good at Latin/maths.

(c) (*avant n: intensif*) **c'est un ~ trajet/problème/travail** it's a real *ou* it's quite a *ou* some journey/problem/piece of work; **c'est une ~euse erreur/migraine/raclée** it's quite a *ou* it's a real mistake/headache/thrashing; **c'est un ~ salaud‡** he's a downright *ou* an out-and-out *ou* a real bastard‡; **c'est une ~euse vaisselle** that's an awful lot of *ou* a stupendous washing-up; **c'est un ~ gaillard** (*bien bâti*) he's a strapping fellow; (*chaud lapin*) he's a bit of a lad *ou* a randy fellow*.

(d) (*avant n: bon*) *mets, idée, voiture* first-rate, great*, fine. **c'est une ~euse aubaine** it's a real *ou* great stroke of luck; **il a fait un ~ travail** he's done a first-class *ou* first-rate *ou* fine job; (*iro*) **elle était ~euse, ton idée!** what a bright *ou* great* idea you had! (*iro*).

(e) (**: fonction de référence*) **quel est le nom de cette ~euse rue?** what's the name of that (famous) street?; **ah, c'est ce ~ Paul dont tu m'as tant parlé** so this is the famous Paul you've told me so much about; **c'est ça, sa ~euse honnêteté** so this is his much-vaunted honesty.

(f) (*après n: célèbre*) famous (*pour* for).

familial, e, *mpl* **-aux** [familjal, o] **1** *adj ennui, problème* family (*épith*), domestic (*épith*); *liens, vie, entreprise* family (*épith*); *V* **aide, allocation. 2 familiale** *nf* estate car (*Brit*), station wagon (*US*).

familiariser [familjaʀize] (1) **1** *vt*: **~ qn avec** to familiarize sb with, get sb used to.

2 se familiariser *vpr* to become familiarized. **se ~ avec** *lieu* to familiarize o.s. with; *personne* to become acquainted with; *langue, faits, méthode* to familiarize o.s. with, get to know, become acquainted with; *bruit, danger* to get used *ou* accustomed to; **peu familiarisé avec cette maison** unfamiliar with this house; **ses pieds, peu familiarisés avec le sol rocailleux** his feet, unused *ou* unaccustomed to the stony ground.

familiarité [familjaʀite] *nf* **(a)** (*bonhomie*) familiarity; (*désinvolture*) offhandedness, (over)familiarity.

(b) (*privautés*) **~s** familiarities; **cessez ces ~s** stop these familiarities, stop taking liberties.

(c) (*habitude de*) **~ avec** *langue, auteur, méthode* familiarity with.

(d) (*atmosphère amicale*) informality. (*littér*) **dans la ~ de**

on familiar terms *ou* terms of familiarity with.

familier, -ière [familje, jɛʀ] **1** *adj* **(a)** (*bien connu*) *technique, problème, spectacle, objet, voix* familiar. **sa voix/cette technique m'est ~ière** I'm familiar with his voice/this technique, his voice/this technique is familiar *ou* well-known to me; **la langue anglaise lui est devenue ~ière** he has become (thoroughly) familiar with *ou* at home with the English language.

(b) (*routinier*) *tâche* familiar. **cette attitude lui est ~ière** this is a familiar *ou* customary attitude of his; **le mensonge lui était devenu ~** lying had become quite a habit of his *ou* had become almost second nature to him.

(c) (*amical*) *entretien, atmosphère* informal, friendly, casual.

(d) (*désinvolte*) *personne, surnom* (over)familiar; *ton, remarque* (over)familiar, offhand; *attitude, manières* offhand. **il devient vite ~** he soon gets (too) familiar; **(trop) ~ avec ses supérieurs/clients** overfamiliar with his superiors/customers; **être ~ avec les femmes** to be overfamiliar with women.

(e) (*non recherché*) *mot, expression* familiar, colloquial; *style, registre* familiar, conversational, colloquial. **expression ~ière** colloquialism, colloquial phrase *ou* expression.

(f) *divinités* household (*épith*); *V* **démon.**

2 *nm [club, théâtre]* regular visitor (*de* to). **le crime a été commis par un ~ (de la maison)** the crime was committed by a very good friend of the household *ou* by a regular visitor to the house.

familièrement [familjɛʀmɑ̃] *adv* (*amicalement*) *s'entretenir* informally; (*cavalièrement*) *se conduire, s'adresser à qn* familiarly; (*sans recherche*) *parler, s'exprimer* familiarly, colloquially. **comme on dit ~** as you say familiarly *ou* colloquially *ou* in conversation; **il te parle un peu (trop) ~** he's speaking to you a bit too familiarly.

famille [famij] *nf* **(a)** (*gén*) family. **~ éloignée/proche** distant/close family *ou* relations *ou* relatives; **avez-vous de la ~?** have you any family?; **~ nombreuse** large family; **avez-vous de la ~ à Londres?** have you any family *ou* relations *ou* relatives in London?; **on a prévenu la ~** the relatives *ou* the next of kin (*frm*) have been informed; **elle promenait (toute) sa petite ~*** she was taking her (entire) brood* for a walk; **elle fait partie de la ~, elle est de la ~** she is part *ou* one of the family; *V* **beau.**

(b) (*fig*) *[plantes, langues]* family. (*Mus*) **la ~ des cuivres** the brass family; (*Ling*) **~ de mots** word family.

(c) (*loc*) **de ~** *possessions, réunion, dîner* family (*épith*); **c'est un tableau de ~** this painting is a family heirloom; *V* **air**[2], **caveau, chef**[1] *etc.*

(d) c'est de ~, ça tient de ~ it runs in the family; **en ~** (*avec la famille*) with the family; (*comme une famille*) as a family; **tout se passe en ~** it's all in the family; **passer ses vacances en ~** to spend one's holidays with the family; **il est sans ~** he has no family; **des ~s*: un (petit) bridge des ~s*** a quiet *ou* cosy little game of bridge.

famine [famin] *nf* (*épidémie*) famine; (*littér: privation*) starvation. **nous allons à la ~** we are heading for starvation, we are going to starve; *V* **crier, salaire.**

fan* [fan] *nm* (*admirateur*) fan.

fana* [fana] *adj, nmf* (*mordu de*) **il est ~ *ou* c'est un ~ de la voile/de Bach** he's a sailing/Bach fanatic.

fanage [fanaʒ] *nm* tossing, turning, tedding.

fanal, *pl* -aux [fanal, o] *nm* (*feu*) *[train]* headlight, headlamp; *[mât]* lantern; (*phare*) beacon, lantern; (*lanterne à main*) lantern, lamp.

fanatique [fanatik] **1** *adj* fanatical (*de* about). **2** *nmf* (*gén, Sport*) fanatic; (*Pol, Rel*) fanatic, zealot. **~ du ski/du football/des échecs** skiing/football/chess fanatic.

fanatiquement [fanatikmɑ̃] *adv* fanatically.

fanatiser [fanatize] (1) *vt* to rouse to fanaticism, fanaticize (*frm*).

fanatisme [fanatism(ə)] *nm* fanaticism.

faner [fane] (1) **1** *vi* (*littér*) to make hay.

2 *vt* **(a)** *herbe* to toss, turn, ted. **on fane (l'herbe) après la fauchaison** the tossing *ou* turning of the hay *ou* the tedding is done after the mowing.

(b) (*littér*) *fleur, couleur, beauté* to fade. **femme (que l'âge a) fanée** woman whose looks have faded.

3 se faner *vpr [plante]* to fade, wither, wilt; *[peau]* to wither; *[teint, beauté, couleur]* to fade.

faneur, -euse [fanœʀ, øz] **1** *nm,f* (*ouvrier*) haymaker. **2 faneuse** *nf* (*machine*) tedder.

fanfare [fɑ̃faʀ] *nf* **(a)** (*orchestre*) brass band. **la ~ du régiment** the regimental band.

(b) (*musique*) fanfare. **~ de clairons** fanfare of bugles; **~ de trompettes** flourish *ou* fanfare of trumpets; **des ~s éclatèrent** brassy music rang forth (from every side); (*fig*) **cette alliance a été annoncée par les ~s de la presse** this alliance was blazoned *ou* trumpeted forth by the press.

(c) (*fig*) **en ~** *réveil, départ* clamorous, tumultuous; *réveiller, partir* noisily, with great commotion; **il est arrivé en ~** (*avec bruit*) he came in noisily *ou* with great commotion; (*fièrement*) he came in triumphantly; **annoncer en ~** *réforme etc* to blazon *ou* trumpet forth, publicize widely.

fanfaron, -onne [fɑ̃faʀɔ̃, ɔn] **1** *adj personne, attitude* boastful; *air, propos* bragging, boastful. **il avait un petit air ~** he was quite full of himself, he looked very pleased with himself. **2** *nm,f* braggart. **faire le ~** to brag, boast, go around bragging *ou* boasting.

fanfaronnade [fɑ̃faʀɔnad] *nf* bragging (*U*), boasting (*U*), boast.

fanfaronner [fɑ̃faʀɔne] (1) *vi* to brag, boast.

fanfreluche [fɑ̃fʀəlyʃ] *nf* (*sur rideau etc*) trimming. **robe ornée de ~s** dress trimmed with frills and flounces.

fange [fɑ̃ʒ] *nf* (*littér*) mire (*littér*); *V* **traîner, vautrer.**

fangeux, -euse [fɑ̃ʒø, øz] *adj* (*littér*) miry (*littér*).

fanion [fanjɔ̃] *nm [vélo, club, bateau]* pennant. (*Mil*) **~ de commandement** commanding officer's pennant.

fanon [fanɔ̃] *nm* **(a)** *[baleine]* plate of baleen; (*matière*) whalebone (*U*). **(b)** *[cheval]* fetlock. **(c)** *[bœuf]* dewlap; *[dindon]* wattle.

fantaisie [fɑ̃tezi] *nf* **(a)** (*caprice*) whim. **elle se plie à toutes ses ~s, elle lui passe toutes ses ~s** she gives in to his every whim; **s'offrir une ~ en allant *ou* s'offrir la ~ d'aller au restaurant** to give o.s. a treat by having a meal out *ou* by eating out; **je me suis payé une petite ~** (*bijou etc*) I bought myself a little present.

(b) (*extravagance*) extravagance. **cette guerre est une ~ coûteuse** this war is a wasteful extravagance; **ces ~s vestimentaires** such extravagance *ou* extravagances of dress.

(c) (*littér: bon plaisir*) **agir selon sa ~/vivre à sa ~/n'en faire qu'à sa ~** to behave/live/do as the fancy takes one; **il lui a pris la ~ de faire** he took it into his head to do; **à votre ~** as it may please you.

(d) (*imagination*) fancy, imagination. **être plein de ~** to be full of imagination *ou* very fanciful *ou* imaginative; **manquer de ~** *[vie]* to be monotonous *ou* uneventful; *[personne]* to be lacking in imagination; **c'est de la ~ pure** that is sheer *ou* pure fantasy *ou* fancy *ou* imagination.

(e) boucles d'oreille (de) ~ fancy earrings; **rideaux ~** fancy curtains; **boutons ~** fancy *ou* novelty buttons.

(f) (*œuvre*) (*Littérat*) fantasy; (*Mus*) fantasia.

fantaisiste [fɑ̃tezist(ə)] **1** *adj* **(a)** *nouvelle, explication* fanciful, whimsical.

(b) (*péj: fumiste*) shallow. **c'est un ~** he's shallow, he's a bit of a phoney*.

(c) (*bizarre*) eccentric, unorthodox; (*farceur*) whimsical, clownish, comical.

2 *nmf* **(a)** (*Théât*) variety artist *ou* entertainer.

(b) (*original*) eccentric.

fantasmagorie [fɑ̃tasmagɔʀi] *nf* phantasmagoria.

fantasmagorique [fɑ̃tasmagɔʀik] *adj* phantasmagorical.

fantasme [fɑ̃tasm(ə)] *nm* fantasy.

fantasque [fɑ̃task(ə)] *adj* (*littér*) *personne, humeur* whimsical, capricious; *chose* weird, fantastic.

fantassin [fɑ̃tasɛ̃] *nm* foot soldier, infantryman. **2.000 ~s** 2,000 foot.

fantastique [fɑ̃tastik] **1** *adj* **(a)** *atmosphère* uncanny, weird, eerie; *événement* uncanny, fantastic; *rêve* weird, fantastic. **conte ~** tale of fantasy *ou* of the supernatural; **roman ~** novel of the fantastic, gothic novel; **le cinéma ~** the cinema of the fantastic.

(b) (*) (*excellent*) fantastic*, terrific*, great*; (*énorme, incroyable*) fantastic*, incredible.

2 *nm*: **le ~** the fantastic, the uncanny; (*Littérat*) (*gén*) the literature of fantasy *ou* of the fantastic, (*de l'âge romantique*) gothic literature; (*Ciné*) the fantastic.

fantastiquement [fɑ̃tastikmɑ̃] *adv* (*V* **fantastique**) uncannily; weirdly; eerily; fantastically*; terrifically*; incredibly.

fantoche [fɑ̃tɔʃ] *nm, adj* puppet.

fantomatique [fɑ̃tɔmatik] *adj* ghostly.

fantôme [fɑ̃tom] **1** *nm* (*spectre*) ghost, phantom. (*fig*) **c'est un ~ de ministre** he is minister in name only. **2** *adj firme, administrateur* bogus. **bateau ~** ghost *ou* phantom ship; (*Pol*) **cabinet ~** shadow cabinet; *V* **vaisseau.**

faon [fɑ̃] *nm* (*Zool*) fawn.

faquin†† [fakɛ̃] *nm* wretch, cad†.

faramineux, -euse* [faʀaminø, øz] *adj bêtise etc* staggering*, fantastic*, mind-boggling*; *prix* colossal, astronomical*, sky-high* (*attrib*). **toi et tes idées ~euses!** you and your brilliant ideas!

faraud, e† [faʀo, od] **1** *adj* boastful. **tu n'es plus si ~** you are no longer quite so boastful *ou* full of yourself *ou* pleased with yourself. **2** *nm,f* braggart. **faire le ~** to brag, boast.

farce[1] [faʀs(ə)] *nf* **(a)** (*tour*) (practical) joke, prank, hoax. **faire une ~ à qn** to play a (practical) joke *ou* a prank *ou* a hoax on sb; **~s (et) attrapes** (*objets*) (assorted) tricks; **magasin de ~s-attrapes** joke (and novelty) shop.

(b) (*Théât*) farce. **grosse ~** slapstick comedy.

(c) (*fig*) farce; *V* **dindon.**

farce[2] [faʀs(ə)] *nf* (*gén*) stuffing; (*à la viande*) forcemeat.

farceur, -euse [faʀsœʀ, øz] *nm,f* (*espiègle*) (practical) joker; (*blagueur*) joker, wag; (*péj: fumiste*) clown (*péj*). **il est très ~** (*espiègle*) he's quite a (practical) joker, he likes playing tricks *ou* (practical) jokes; (*blagueur*) he's quite a wag *ou* joker, he likes joking.

farcir [faʀsiʀ] (2) **1** *vt* **(a)** (*Culin*) to stuff. **tomates farcies** stuffed tomatoes.

(b) (*fig péj: surtout ptp*) **~ de** to stuff *ou* cram *ou* pack with; **c'est farci de fautes** it's crammed *ou* packed with mistakes; **j'en ai la tête farcie** I've as much as I can take, I've got a headful of it*.

2 se farcir *vpr* **(a)** (*péj*) **se ~ la mémoire de** to cram *ou* pack one's memory with.

(b) (‡) (*subir*) *lessive, travail, personne* to get stuck *ou* landed with*; (*déguster*) **mets** to have o.s.‡, knock back‡; (*avaler*) *bouteille* to polish off*; *gateaux* to scoff*, gobble down*, guzzle*; (‡‡) *fille* to have it off with‡. **il faudra se ~ la belle-mère pendant 3 jours** we'll have to put up with the mother-in-law for 3 days; **il faut se le ~!** (*importun, bavard*) he's a bit of a pain (in the neck)*; (*livre*) it's hellish heavy-going!‡, it's a hell of a fag!‡ (*Brit*).

fard [faʀ] *nm* (*maquillage*) make-up; (†: *poudre*) rouge†, paint;

[acteur] greasepaint. (*fig*) **sans ~** *parler* openly; *élégance* unpretentious, simple; *V* **piquer.**

fardeau, *pl* **~x** [faʀdo] *nm* (*lit*) load, burden (*littér*); (*fig*) burden. **sous le ~ de** under the weight *ou* burden of; **souhaitons que ceci ne lui soit pas un ~ toute sa vie** let this not be a millstone round his neck *ou* a burden to him all his life.

farder [faʀde] (1) **1** *vt* (*Théât*) *acteur* to make up; (††) *visage* to rouge†, paint; (*littér*) *vérité* to disguise, mask, veil.

2 se farder *vpr* (*se maquiller*) to make (o.s.) up; (†: *se poudrer*) to rouge *ou* paint one's face†; *[acteur]* to make up. **femme outrageusement fardée** woman wearing heavy make-up, heavily made-up woman.

farfadet [faʀfadɛ] *nm* sprite, elf.

farfelu, e [faʀfəly] **1** *adj idée, projet* cranky, scatty*, hare-brained; *personne, conduite* cranky, scatty*, eccentric. **2** *nm,f* eccentric.

farfouiller* [faʀfuje] (1) *vi* to rummage about (*dans* in).

faribole [faʀibɔl] *nf* (*littér*) (piece of) nonsense. **conter des ~s** to talk nonsense *ou* twaddle; **~s (que tout cela)!** (stuff and) nonsense!, fiddlesticks!†

farine [faʀin] **1** *nf [blé]* flour. **de même ~**† of the same ilk.

2: farine d'avoine oatmeal; **farine lactée** (cornflour) gruel; **farine de lin** linseed meal; **farine de maïs** cornflour (*Brit*), cornstarch (*US*); **farine de moutarde** mustard powder; *V* **fleur.**

fariner [faʀine] (1) *vt* to flour.

farineux, -euse [faʀinø, øz] **1** *adj consistance, aspect, goût* floury, chalky; *chocolat* powdery, chalky; *fromage* chalky; *pomme de terre* floury; *pomme* dry. **2** *nm*: **(aliment) ~** starchy *ou* farinaceous (*T*) food.

farniente [faʀnjɛnte] *nm* idle life, idleness. **faire du ~ sur la plage** to lounge *ou* idle about on the beach.

farouche [faʀuʃ] *adj* **(a)** (*timide*) *personne, animal* shy, timid; (*peu sociable*) *voisin etc* unsociable. **ces daims ne sont pas ~s** these deer are not a bit shy *ou* timid *ou* are quite tame; (*iro*) **c'est une femme peu ~** she doesn't exactly keep you at arm's length (*iro*).

(b) (*hostile*) fierce. **ennemi ~** bitter enemy *ou* foe.

(c) (*opiniâtre*) *volonté* unshakeable, inflexible; *résistance* unflinching, fierce; *énergie* irrepressible.

(d) (*indompté*) savage, wild.

farouchement [faʀuʃmɑ̃] *adv* fiercely.

fart [faʀ(t)] *nm* (ski) wax. **~ de montée** climbing wax.

fartage [faʀtaʒ] *nm* waxing (*of skis*).

farter [faʀte] (1) *vt* to wax (*skis*).

fascicule [fasikyl] *nm* volume; (*livraison*) part, volume, fascicle (*T*).

fascinant, e [fasinɑ̃, ɑ̃t] *adj* (*gén*) fascinating; *beauté* bewitching, fascinating.

fascination [fasinɑsjɔ̃] *nf* fascination. **exercer une grande ~** to exert (a) great fascination (*sur* on, over), have (a) great fascination (*sur* for).

fasciner [fasine] (1) *vt* (*gén*) to fascinate; (*soumettre à son charme*) to bewitch. **se laisser ~ par des promesses** to allow o.s. to be bewitched by promises.

fascisant, e [faʃizɑ̃, ɑ̃t] *adj* fascistic.

fascisme [fasism(ə)] *nm* fascism.

fasciste [fasist(ə)] *adj, nmf* fascist.

fast back [fastbak] *nm* fastback.

faste[1] [fast(ə)] *nm* splendour.

faste[2] [fast(ə)] *adj* (*littér*) *année* (*de chance*) lucky; (*prospère*) good. **jour ~** lucky day.

fastidieusement [fastidjøzmɑ̃] *adv* tediously, tiresomely, boringly.

fastidieux, -euse [fastidjø, øz] *adj* tedious, tiresome, boring.

fastueusement [fastɥøzmɑ̃] *adv* sumptuously, luxuriously. **recevoir qn ~** (*pour dîner*) to entertain sb lavishly; (*à son arrivée*) to give sb a lavish reception.

fastueux, -euse [fastɥø, øz] *adj* sumptuous, luxurious. **mener une vie ~euse** to lead a sumptuous *ou* luxurious existence, live a life of great luxury.

fat† [fa(t)] **1** *adj* conceited, smug. **2** *nm* conceited *ou* smug person.

fatal, e, *mpl* **~s** [fatal] *adj* **(a)** (*funeste*) *accident, issue* fatal; *coup* fatal, deadly. **erreur ~e!** grievous *ou* fatal error!; **être ~ à qn/qch** to be *ou* prove fatal *ou* disastrous to *ou* for sb/sth; **le tabac/la boisson lui fut ~(e)** smoking/drink was *ou* proved fatal to *ou* for him.

(b) (*inévitable*) inevitable. **c'était ~!** it was inevitable, it was fated *ou* bound to happen; **il était ~ qu'elle le fasse** she was bound *ou* fated to do it, it was inevitable that she should do it.

(c) (*marqué par le destin*) *instant* fatal, fateful; *air, ton* fateful, fated; *V* **femme.**

fatalement [fatalmɑ̃] *adv* (*inévitablement*) **~, il est tombé!** inevitably, he fell!; **au début, ce fut ~ mauvais** at the beginning, it was inevitably *ou* unavoidably bad; **ça devait ~ arriver** it was bound *ou* fated to happen.

fatalisme [fatalism(ə)] *nm* fatalism.

fataliste [fatalist(ə)] **1** *adj* fatalistic. **2** *nmf* fatalist.

fatalité [fatalite] *nf* **(a)** (*destin*) fate, fatality (*littér*). **être poursuivi par la ~** to be pursued by fate.

(b) (*coïncidence*) fateful coincidence. **par quelle ~ se sont-ils rencontrés?** by what fateful coincidence did they meet?; **ce serait vraiment une ~ si je ne le vois pas** it would really be an extraordinary coincidence if I don't see him.

(c) (*inévitabilité*) inevitability. **la ~ de la mort/de cet événement** the inevitability of death/this event.

fatidique [fatidik] *adj* (*lourd de conséquences*) *décision, paroles, date* fateful; (*crucial*) *moment* fatal, fateful.

fatigant, e [fatigɑ̃, ɑ̃t] *adj* (*épuisant*) tiring; (*agaçant*) *personne* annoying, tiresome, tedious; *conversation* tiresome, tedious. **c'est ~ pour la vue** it's tiring *ou* a strain on the eyes; **c'est ~ pour le cœur** it's a strain on the heart; **tu es vraiment ~ avec tes questions** you really are annoying *ou* tiresome *ou* a nuisance with your questions; **c'est ~ de devoir toujours tout répéter** it's annoying *ou* tiresome *ou* a nuisance to have to repeat everything all the time.

fatigue [fatig] *nf* (*gén*) tiredness (*U*), fatigue (*U*); (*Méd, Tech*) fatigue. **tomber *ou* être mort de ~** to be dead tired, be dead beat*, be all in*; **il a voulu nous épargner cette ~** he wanted to save *ou* spare us the strain; **elle avait de soudaines ~s** she had sudden bouts of fatigue *ou* periods of tiredness; **se remettre des ~s du voyage** to get over the wear and tear *ou* the strain *ou* the tiring effects of the journey; **pour se reposer de la ~ du voyage** to rest after the tiring journey *ou* the weary journey; **cette ~ dans le bras gauche** this weakness in the left arm; **~ des yeux** eyestrain; *V* **recru.**

fatigué, e [fatige] (*ptp de* **fatiguer**) *adj* **(a)** *personne* tired, weary, fatigued (*frm*); *voix, traits, membres* tired, weary; *yeux* strained; *cœur* strained, overworked; *cerveau* overtaxed, overworked; *estomac, foie* upset. **il a les bras ~s** his arms are tired *ou* weary; **avoir les yeux ~s** to have eyestrain *ou* strained eyes; **à trente ans, ils ont déjà l'organisme ~** by thirty their bodies are already tired *ou* overworked; **~ par le voyage** travel-worn *ou* -weary, tired *ou* weary through *ou* after travelling; **(*péj*) il est né ~** he's bone-lazy *ou* bone-idle.

(b) ~ de *jérémiades, voiture, femme* tired of; **~ de vivre** tired of living.

(c) *poutre, joint, moteur, habits* worn.

fatiguer [fatige] (1) **1** *vt* **(a)** (*physiquement*) **~ qn** *[maladie, effort, études]* to make sb tired *ou* weary, tire sb; *[professeur, patron]* to overwork sb; **ces efforts fatiguent, à la longue** all this effort tires *ou* wears you out in the end; **ça fatigue les yeux/le cœur/les bras/l'organisme** it is *ou* puts a strain on the eyes/heart/arms/whole body; **se ~ les yeux/le cœur/les bras** to strain one's eyes/heart/arms.

(b) *bête de somme [effort, montée]* to tire, put a strain on; *[propriétaire]* to overwork; *moteur, véhicule [effort, montée]* to put (a) strain on, strain; *[propriétaire]* to overwork, strain; *poutre, pièce, joint* to put strain on; *outil, chaussures, vêtement* to wear out; *terre, sol* to exhaust, impoverish; *arbre* to impoverish.

(c) (*fig: agacer*) to annoy; (*lasser*) to wear out. **tu commences à me ~** you're beginning to annoy me; **avec ses sermons il fatigue, à la longue** in the end he wears you out with all his sermons.

(d) vt ~ la salade to mix *ou* toss the salad.

2 *vi [moteur]* to labour, strain; *[poutre, pièce, joint]* to become strained, show (signs of) strain; *[personne]* to tire, grow tired *ou* weary.

3 se fatiguer *vpr* **(a)** to get tired. **se ~ à faire qch** to tire o.s. out doing sth; (*iro*) **il ne s'est pas trop fatigué** he didn't overdo it *ou* overwork (*iro*), he didn't kill himself*.

(b) (*se lasser de*) **se ~ de qch/de faire** to get tired *ou* weary of sth/of doing.

(c) (*s'évertuer à*) **se ~ à répéter/expliquer** to take the trouble to repeat/explain; **ne te fatigue pas* *ou* pas la peine de te ~*, il est borné** he's just dim so don't bother to *ou* there's no need to wear yourself out *ou* no point wearing yourself out, he's just dim so don't waste your time *ou* your breath.

fatras [fatʀa] *nm [choses]* jumble; *[idées]* hotchpotch, jumble.

fatuité [fatɥite] *nf* self-complacency, self-conceit.

faubourg [fobuʀ] *nm* (inner) suburb. **avoir l'accent des ~s** to have a working-class accent (*only applied to residents of Paris suburbs*).

faubourien, -ienne [fobuʀjɛ̃, jɛn] *adj accent, manières* working-class (*only applied to residents of Paris suburbs*).

fauchage [foʃaʒ] *nm* (*V* **faucher**) reaping; mowing; scything; cutting.

fauchaison [foʃɛzɔ̃] *nf* **(a)** (*époque*) *[pré]* mowing (time), reaping (time); *[blés]* reaping (time). **(b)** (*action*) = **fauchage.**

fauche [foʃ] *nf* **(a)** (**:** *vol*) pinching*, swiping*, nicking**:** (*Brit*). **(b)** (††) = **fauchaison.**

fauché, e* [foʃe] (*ptp de* **faucher**) *adj* (*sans argent*) (stony-)broke*, flat *ou* dead broke* (*attrib*), hard up*. **il est ~ comme les blés** he hasn't got a bean* *ou* a brass farthing (*Brit*), he hasn't a penny to his name.

faucher [foʃe] (1) **1** *vt* **(a)** *blé* to reap; *champs, prés* to mow, reap; *herbe* (*avec une faux*) to scythe, mow, cut; (*mécaniquement*) to mow, cut. **on va ~ demain** we're mowing *ou* reaping tomorrow.

(b) (*fig: abattre*) *[vent]* to flatten; *[véhicule]* to knock over *ou* down, mow down; *[tir]* to mow down; *[explosion]* to flatten, blow over. **la mort l'a fauché en pleine jeunesse** death cut him down in the prime of (his) youth; **avoir un bras fauché par l'explosion** to have an arm blown off by the explosion; **avoir une jambe fauchée par le train** to have a leg cut off *ou* taken off by the train.

(c) (**:** *voler*) *portefeuille, femme* to pinch*, swipe*, nick**:** (*Brit*).

2 *vi [cheval]* to dish.

faucheur, -euse [foʃœʀ, øz] **1** *nm,f* (*personne*) mower, reaper. **2** *nm* = **faucheux. 3 faucheuse** *nf* (*machine*) reaper, mower.

faucheux [foʃø] *nm* harvestman (*Brit*), harvest-spider, daddy-long-legs (*US*).

faucille [fosij] *nf* sickle. **la ~ et le marteau** the hammer and sickle.

faucon [fokɔ̃] *nm* falcon, hawk. **chasser au ~** to hawk.

fauconneau, *pl* **~x** [fokɔno] *nm* young falcon *ou* hawk.

fauconnerie [fokɔnʀi] *nf* (*art*) falconry; (*chasse*) hawking, falconry; (*lieu*) hawk house.

fauconnier [fokɔnje] *nm* falconer, hawker.
faufil [fofil] *nm* tacking *ou* basting thread.
faufilage [fofilaʒ] *nm* tacking, basting.
faufiler [fofile] (1) **1** *vt* to tack, baste.
2 se faufiler *vpr* (*dans un passage étroit*) to worm *ou* inch *ou* edge one's way into; (*entre des obstacles, des personnes*) to dodge in and out of, thread one's way through. **se ~ par un sentier étroit** to thread *ou* edge one's way along a narrow path; **se ~ parmi la foule** to worm *ou* inch *ou* thread one's way through the crowd, slip through the crowd; **se ~ entre les** *ou* **au milieu des voitures** to nip *ou* dodge in and out of the traffic, thread one's way through the traffic; **il se faufila à l'intérieur/au dehors** he wormed *ou* inched *ou* edged his way in/out.
faufilure [fofilyʀ] *nf* (*Couture*) tacked *ou* basted seam; (*action*) tacking, basting.
faune[1] [fon] *nm* (*Myth*) faun.
faune[2] [fon] *nf* (*Zool*) wildlife, fauna (*T*); (*péj: personnes*) set, mob. **~ marine** marine animal-life; **~ des Alpes** Alpine wildlife *ou* fauna (*T*).
faunesque [fonɛsk(ə)] *adj* faunlike.
faussaire [fosɛʀ] *nmf* forger.
fausse [fos] *adj f V* **faux**[2].
faussement [fosmɑ̃] *adv accuser* wrongly, wrongfully; *croire* erroneously, falsely. **~ modeste** falsely modest; **~ intéressé** superficially *ou* falsely interested; **d'un ton ~ indifférent** in a tone of feigned indifference, in a deceptively detached tone of voice.
fausser [fose] (1) *vt* **(a)** *calcul, statistique, fait* to distort, alter; *réalité, pensée* to distort, pervert; *sens d'un mot* to distort; *esprit* to unsettle, disturb; *jugement* to distort, disturb.
(b) *clef* to bend; *serrure* to break; *poulie, manivelle, charnière* to buckle, bend; *essieu, volant, hélice* to warp, buckle, bend; *lame* to warp, bend. **soudain il se troubla, sa voix se faussa** suddenly he became flustered and his voice became strained.
(c) (*loc*) **~ compagnie à qn** to give sb the slip, slip *ou* sneak away from sb; **vous nous avez de nouveau faussé compagnie hier soir** you gave us the slip again last night, you sneaked *ou* slipped off again last night.
fausset[1] [fosɛ] *nm* falsetto (voice). **d'une voix de ~** in a falsetto voice.
fausset[2] [fosɛ] *nm [tonneau]* spigot, spile.
fausseté [foste] *nf* **(a)** *[idée, accusation, dogme]* falseness, falsity. **(b)** *[caractère, personne]* duplicity, deceitfulness. **(c)** (†: *propos mensonger*) falsity†, falsehood.
faustien, -ienne [fostjɛ̃, jɛn] *adj* Faustian.
faut [fo] *V* **falloir.**
faute [fot] **1** *nf* **(a)** (*erreur*) mistake, error. **faire** *ou* **commettre une ~** to make a mistake *ou* an error; **~ de grammaire** grammatical mistake *ou* error; **~ de ponctuation** mistake in punctuation, error of punctuation.
(b) (*mauvaise action*) misdeed; (*Jur*) offence; (†: *péché de chair*) lapse (from virtue), sin (of the flesh). **commettre une ~** (*gén*) to commit a misdeed *ou* misdemeanour; (†: *péché de chair*) to sin; **une ~ contre** *ou* **envers la religion** a sin *ou* transgression against religion; **commettre une ~ professionnelle grave** to commit a serious professional misdemeanour.
(c) (*Sport*) (*Ftbl etc*) offence; (*Tennis*) fault. **le joueur a fait une ~** the player committed an offence; **faire une ~ de main** to handle the ball; **faire une ~ de pied** to foot fault; **faire une double ~ (de service)** to serve a double fault, double-fault; **~!** (*pour un joueur*) foul!; (*Tennis: pour la balle*) fault!
(d) (*responsabilité*) fault. **par la ~ de Richard/sa ~** because of Richard/him; **c'est de la ~ de Richard/de sa ~** it's Richard's fault/his fault; **c'est la ~ à Richard/sa ~*** it's because of Richard/him, it's through Richard/him*; **la ~ lui en revient** the fault lies with him; **à qui la ~?** whose fault is it?, who's to blame?
(e) (*loc*) **être/se sentir en ~** to be/feel at fault *ou* in the wrong; **prendre qn en ~** to catch sb out; **il ne se fait pas ~ de faire** he doesn't shy from *ou* at doing, he doesn't fail to do; **ce livre perdu lui fait bien ~**† he really misses that lost book; **~ de** for *ou* through lack of; **~ d'argent** for want of *ou* through lack of money; **~ de temps** for *ou* through lack of time; **~ de mieux** for lack *ou* want of anything better, failing anything better; **~ de quoi** failing which, otherwise; **le combat cessa ~ de combattants** the battle died down, there being nobody left to carry on the fight; (*Prov*) **~ de grives, on mange des merles** you have to cut your coat according to your cloth (*Prov*), beggars can't be choosers (*Prov*); (*Prov*) **~ avouée est à demi pardonnée** a sin confessed is a sin half pardoned; *V* **sans.**
2: (*Ling*) **faute d'accord** mistake in (the) agreement; **faute de calcul** miscalculation, error in calculation; (*Ski*) **faute de carres** edging mistake; (*Jur*) **faute civile** civil wrong; (*Aut*) **faute de conduite** (*erreur*) driving error; (*infraction*) driving offence; **faute d'étourderie** = **faute d'inattention**; **faute de français** grammatical mistake (*in French*); **faute de frappe** typing error; **faute de goût** error of taste; **faute d'impression** misprint; **faute d'inattention** careless *ou* thoughtless mistake; **faute d'orthographe** spelling mistake; (*Jur*) **faute pénale** criminal offence; (*Admin*) **faute de service** act of (administrative) negligence.
fauter† [fote] (1) *vi [jeune fille]* to sin.
fauteuil [fotœj] **1** *nm* (*gén*) armchair; (*avec dos rembourré, moderne*) easy chair, armchair; *[président]* chair; *[théâtre, académicien]* seat. **occuper le ~** (*siéger comme président*) to be in the chair; (*fig*) **il est arrivé dans un ~*** he walked it*, he romped home*.
2: (*Théât*) **fauteuil de balcon** balcony seat; seat in the dress circle; (*région de la salle*) **fauteuils de balcon** dress circle; **fauteuil à bascule** rocking chair; **fauteuil club** (big) leather easy chair; **fauteuil crapaud** squat armchair; **fauteuil dentaire** dentist's chair; **fauteuil de jardin** garden chair; (*Théât*) **fauteuil d'orchestre** seat in the front *ou* orchestra stalls (*Brit*) *ou* the orchestra (*US*); (*région de la salle*) **fauteuils d'orchestre** front *ou* orchestra stalls (*Brit*); **fauteuil pivotant** swivel chair; **fauteuil pliant** folding chair; **fauteuil roulant** wheelchair; **fauteuil tournant** = **fauteuil pivotant.**
fauteur [fotœʀ] *nm*: **~ de troubles** *ou* **de désordre** trouble-maker, mischief-maker, agitator; **~ de guerre** warmonger.
fautif, -ive [fotif, iv] **1** *adj* **(a)** *conducteur* at fault (*attrib*); *élève, enfant* naughty, guilty. **il se sentait ~** he felt (he was) at fault *ou* in the wrong *ou* guilty.
(b) *texte, liste, calcul* faulty, incorrect; *citation* incorrect; (*littér*) *mémoire* poor, faulty.
2 *nm,f*: **c'est moi le ~** I'm the one to blame *ou* the guilty one *ou* the culprit.
fautivement [fotivmɑ̃] *adv* by mistake, in error.
fauve [fov] **1** *adj* **(a)** *tissu, couleur* tawny, fawn(-coloured); (*littér*) *odeur* musky; *V* **bête.**
(b) (*Art*) **période ~** Fauvist period.
2 *nm* **(a)** (*animal*) wildcat. **ça sent le ~ ici*** it doesn't half stink (of sweat) here*.
(b) (*couleur*) fawn.
(c) (*Art*) Fauvist, painter of the Fauvist school. **les F~s** the Fauvists *ou* Fauves.
faux[1] [fo] *nf* scythe.
faux[2], **fausse** [fo, fos] **1** *adj* **(a)** (*imité*) *argent, billet* forged, fake; *marbre, bijoux, meuble* (*en toc*) imitation; (*pour duper*) false, fake; *documents, signature* false, fake; *tableau* fake. **fausse pièce** forged *ou* fake coin, dud*; **une fausse carte** a trick card; **~ papiers** forged identity papers; **fausse monnaie** forged currency.
(b) (*postiche*) *dent, nez* false.
(c) (*simulé*) *bonhomie, colère, désespoir, modestie* feigned. **un ~ air de prude/de bonhomie** an air of false prudery/good-naturedness; **fausse dévotion** false piety.
(d) (*mensonger*) *déclaration, promesse, prétexte* false, spurious (*frm*). **c'est ~** it's wrong *ou* untrue.
(e) (*pseudo*) *savant, écrivain* bogus, sham (*épith*).
(f) (*fourbe*) *personne, attitude* false, deceitful; *regard* deceitful.
(g) (*inexact*) *calcul, numéro, rue* wrong; *idée* mistaken, wrong; *affirmation, faits* wrong, untrue; *instrument de mesure, raisonnement* wrong, inaccurate, faulty; *instrument de musique, voix* out of tune; *vers* faulty. **c'est ~** *[résultat]* that's wrong; *[fait]* that's wrong *ou* untrue; **il est ~ (de dire) qu'il y soit allé** it's wrong *ou* incorrect to say that he went, it's not true (to say) that he went; **dire quelque chose de ~** to say something (that's) wrong *ou* untrue; **faire fausse route** (*lit*) to go the wrong way, take the wrong road; (*fig*) to be on the wrong track; **faire un ~ pas** (*lit*) to trip, stumble; (*fig*) to make a foolish mistake.
(h) (*non fondé*) *espoir, rumeur, soupçons, principe* false. **avoir de fausses craintes** to have groundless *ou* ill-founded fears.
(i) (*gênant, ambigu*) *position, situation, atmosphère* awkward, false.
2 *nm* **(a)** (*mensonge, Philos*) **le ~** falsehood; *V* **vrai.**
(b) (*contrefaçon*) forgery; (*tableau, meuble, document*) fake, forgery. **faire un ~** to commit a forgery; (*Jur*) **pour ~ et usage de ~** for forgery and the use of forgeries; *V* **inscrire.**
3 *adv* **(a)** *chanter, jouer* out of tune, off key. **sonner ~** *[rire, paroles]* to have a false *ou* hollow ring, sound false.
(b) **à ~: porter à ~** to jut out, overhang; (*fig*) **tomber à ~** to come at the wrong moment; **accuser qn à ~** to accuse sb unjustly *ou* wrongly.
4: **fausse alerte** false alarm; **faux ami** (*traître*) false friend; (*Ling*) false friend, faux ami, deceptive cognate; **faux bond: faire un faux bond à qn** to stand sb up*; **faux-bourdon** *nm, pl* **faux-bourdons** (*Mus*) faux bourdon; (*Entomologie*) faux bourdon, drone; **faux bruit** false rumour; **faux chignon** hair-piece; **fausse clef** skeleton key; **faux col** *[chemise]* detachable collar; *[bière]* head; **fausses côtes** floating ribs (*part of the brisket*); **fausse couche** miscarriage; **faire une fausse couche** to have a miscarriage; (*lit, fig*) **faux départ** false start; **faux dévôt, fausse dévote** *nm,f* pharisee; **faux ébénier** laburnum; **fausse fenêtre** blind window; **faux-filet** *nm* sirloin; **faux frais** (*pl*) extras, incidental expenses; **faux frère** false friend; **faux-fuyant** *nm, pl* **faux-fuyants** evasion, equivocation, dodge*; **assez de faux-fuyants** stop dodging* *ou* evading the issue, stop hedging; **user de faux-fuyants** to equivocate, prevaricate, evade the issue; **faux jeton*** devious character*; **fausse joie** vain joy; **faux jour** (*lit*) deceptive light; **sous un faux jour** (*fig*) in a false light; **fausse manœuvre** (*lit*) wrong movement; (*fig*) wrong move; **faux-monnayeur** *nm, pl* **faux-monnayeurs** forger, counterfeiter; **faux mouvement** clumsy *ou* awkward movement; **faux nom** false *ou* assumed name; **fausse note** (*Mus*) wrong note; (*fig*) sour note; (*fig*) **sans une fausse note** without a sour note, smoothly; **fausse nouvelle** false report; **faux ourlet** false hem; (*lit, fig*) **fausse piste** wrong track; **faux plafond** false ceiling; **faux pli** crease; (*Naut*) **faux(-)pont** orlop deck; **fausse porte** false door; **faux problème** non-problem, non-issue; **fausse pudeur** false modesty; **faux seins** falsies*; **faux semblant** sham, pretence; **user de faux semblants** to put up a pretence; **faux sens** mistranslation; **faux serment** false oath; (*Théât*) **fausse sortie** sham exit; (*fig*) **il a fait une fausse sortie** he made a pretence of leaving; **faux témoignage** (*déposition mensongère*) false evidence (*U*); (*délit*) perjury; **faux témoin** lying witness.
faveur[1] [favœʀ] *nf* **(a)** (*frm: gentillesse*) favour. **faites-moi la ~**

de ... would you be so kind as to ...; **fais-moi une ~** do me a favour; **obtenir qch par ~** to get sth as a favour; **par ~ spéciale (de la direction)** by special favour (of the management).

(b) (*considération*) (*littér, hum*) **avoir la ~ du ministre** to be in favour with the minister; **gagner/perdre la ~ du public** to win/lose public favour, find favour/fall out of favour with the public; (*littér*) **être en ~** to be in favour (*auprès de qn* with sb).

(c) (*littér, hum*) **~s** favours; **elle lui a refusé ses ~s** she refused him her favours; **elle lui a accordé ses dernières ~s** she bestowed her (ultimate) favours upon him (*littér, hum*).

(d) de ~ preferential, special; **billet de ~** complimentary ticket; **régime de ~** preferential treatment.

(e) en ~ de (*à cause de*) in consideration of, on account of; (*au profit de*) in favour of, for; (*dans un but charitable*) in aid of, on behalf of, for; **en ma/sa ~** in my/his favour.

(f) à la ~ de thanks to, owing to; **à la ~ de la nuit** under cover of darkness.

faveur² [favœʀ] *nf* (*ruban*) ribbon, favour.

favorable [favɔʀabl(ə)] *adj* **(a)** *moment, occasion* right, favourable; *terrain, position* favourable. **par temps ~** in favourable weather; **avoir un préjugé ~ envers** to be biased in favour of; **jouir d'un préjugé ~** to be favourably considered; **recevoir un accueil ~** to meet with a favourable reception; **se montrer sous un jour ~** to show o.s. in a favourable light; **prêter une oreille ~ à** to lend a sympathetic *ou* kindly ear to; **voir qch d'un œil ~** to view sth favourably *ou* with a favourable eye.

(b) *[personne]* **être ~ à** to be favourable to.

favorablement [favɔʀabləmɑ̃] *adv* favourably.

favori, -ite [favɔʀi, it] **1** *adj* favourite.

2 *nm* **(a)** (*préféré, gagnant probable*) favourite. **cet acteur est un ~ du public** this actor is a favourite with the public; **le ~ des jeunes** the favourite with *ou* of young people; (*Sport*) **ils sont partis ~s** they started off favourites.

(b) (*Hist*) king's favourite.

3 favorite *nf* favourite; (*Hist*) king's favourite *ou* mistress.

favoris [favɔʀi] *nmpl* side whiskers, sideboards*, sideburns*.

favoriser [favɔʀize] (1) *vt* **(a)** (*avantager, encourager*) *candidat, ambitions, commerce, parti* to favour. **les événements l'ont favorisé** events favoured him *ou* were to his advantage; **la fortune le favorise** fortune favours him. **(b)** (*faciliter*) to further, favour. **ceci a favorisé la rébellion/sa fuite** this furthered *ou* favoured the rebellion/his escape.

favorite [favɔʀit] *V* **favori.**

favoritisme [favɔʀitism(ə)] *nm* favouritism.

fayot [fajo] *nm* **(a)** (*: *Culin*) bean. **(b)** (‡*péj: lèche-bottes*) bootlicker.

fayotter‡ [fajɔte] (1) *vi* (*faire du zèle*) to suck up‡.

féal, e, *mpl* **-aux** [feal, o] **1** *adj* (††) loyal, trusty. **2** *nm,f* (*littér, hum*) loyal supporter.

fébrifuge [febʀifyʒ] **1** *adj* febrifuge (*T*), which brings down one's temperature. **2** *nm* febrifuge, antipyretic.

fébrile [febʀil] *adj* (*lit, fig*) feverish, febrile (*frm*).

fébrilement [febʀilmɑ̃] *adv* feverishly.

fébrilité [febʀilite] *nf* feverishness.

fécal, e, *mpl* **-aux** [fekal, o] *adj* faecal. **matières ~es** faeces.

fèces [fɛs] *nfpl* faeces.

fécond, e [fekɔ̃, ɔ̃d] *adj* **(a)** (*non stérile*) *femelle, fleur* fertile.

(b) (*prolifique*) prolific.

(c) (*fertile*) *sujet, idée* fruitful; *esprit* creative, fertile; (*littér*) *terre* fruitful, rich, fecund (*littér*). **journées/vacances ~es en mésaventures/événements** days/holidays abounding in mishaps/events.

fécondateur, -trice [fekɔ̃datœʀ, tʀis] *adj* (*littér*) fertilizing.

fécondation [fekɔ̃dasjɔ̃] *nf* **(a)** (*U: V* **féconder**) impregnation; insemination; fertilization. **(b)** (*acte, moment*) **la ~** fertilization; **la ~ artificielle** artificial insemination; **le mystère de la ~** the mystery of fertilization.

féconder [fekɔ̃de] (1) *vt femme* to make pregnant, impregnate (*frm*); *animal* to inseminate, fertilize; *fleur* to pollinate, fertilize; (*littér*) *terre* to make fruitful; (*fig*) *esprit* to enrich.

fécondité [fekɔ̃dite] *nf* fertility, fecundity (*littér*); (*fig*) *[terre, sujet, idée]* fruitfulness, richness, fecundity (*littér*).

fécule [fekyl] *nf* starch. **~ (de pommes de terre)** potato flour.

féculent, e [fekylɑ̃, ɑ̃t] *adj* starchy. **~s** starchy food(s).

fédéral, e, *mpl* **-aux** [fedeʀal, o] *adj* federal.

fédéraliser [fedeʀalize] (1) *vt* to federalize.

fédéralisme [fedeʀalism(ə)] *nm* federalism.

fédéraliste [fedeʀalist(ə)] *adj, nmf* federalist.

fédératif, -ive [fedeʀatif, iv] *adj* federative.

fédération [fedeʀasjɔ̃] *nf* federation.

fédéré, e [fedeʀe] (*ptp de* **fédérer**) *adj* federate.

fédérer [fedeʀe] (6) *vt* to federate.

fée [fe] *nf* fairy. **la ~ du logis** the perfect home-maker; **la ~ Carabosse** the (wicked) fairy Carabossa; *V* **conte, doigt.**

feed-back [fidbak] *nm inv* feedback.

feeder [fidœʀ] *nm* (*Tech*) feeder.

féerie [fe(e)ʀi] *nf* **(a)** (*Ciné, Théât*) extravaganza, spectacular (*incorporating features from pantomime*). **(b)** (*littér: vision enchanteresse*) **~ des soirées d'été/d'un ballet** enchantment of summer evenings/of a ballet; **la ~ à jamais perdue de l'enfance** the irretrievable fairytale world of childhood.

féerique [fe(e)ʀik] *adj* magical, fairy (*épith*).

feignant, e [fɛɲɑ̃, ɑ̃t] = **fainéant.**

feindre [fɛ̃dʀ(ə)] (52) **1** *vt* (*simuler*) *enthousiasme, ignorance, innocence* to feign. **la colère** to pretend to be angry, feign anger; **~ d'être/de faire** to pretend to be/do; **il feint de ne pas comprendre** he pretends not to understand; **~ de dormir** to feign sleep, pretend to be asleep.

2 *vi* (*frm*) to dissemble, dissimulate. **inutile de ~ (avec moi)** no use pretending (with me).

feint, e¹ [fɛ̃, fɛ̃t] (*ptp de* **feindre**) *adj* **(a)** *émotion, maladie* feigned, affected. **(b)** (*Archit*) *fenêtre etc* false.

feinte² [fɛ̃t] *nf* **(a)** (*manœuvre*) (*gén*) dummy move; (*Ftbl, Rugby*) dummy (*Brit*), fake (*US*); (*Boxe, Escrime*) feint. **(b)** (*littér: ruse*) sham (*U*), pretence. **agir/parler sans ~** to act/speak without dissimulation.

feinter [fɛ̃te] (1) **1** *vt* **(a)** (*Ftbl, Rugby*) to dummy (*Brit*) *ou* fake (*US*) (one's way past); (*Boxe, Escrime*) to feint at. **(b)** (‡: *rouler, avoir*) to trick, have*, take in. **j'ai été feinté** I've been had* *ou* taken in. **2** *vi* (*Escrime*) to feint.

feldspath [fɛldspat] *nm* fel(d)spar.

fêler [fele] (1) **1** *vt* to crack. **avoir le cerveau fêlé*** *ou* **la tête fêlée*** to be a bit cracked*. **2 se fêler** *vpr* to crack.

félicitations [felisitɑsjɔ̃] *nfpl* congratulations (*pour* on). **~!** congratulations!; **faire ses ~ à qn de** *ou* **sur qch** to congratulate sb on sth; (*Scol, Univ*) **avec les ~ du jury** highly commended, summa cum laude.

félicité [felisite] *nf* (*littér, Rel*) bliss (*U*).

féliciter [felisite] (1) **1** *vt* to congratulate (*qn de ou sur qch* sb on sth). (*iro*) **je vous félicite!** congratulations! (*iro*), well done! (*iro*); **eh bien je ne vous félicite pas** you don't get any praise for that.

2 se féliciter *vpr* to congratulate o.s. (*de* on), be very glad *ou* pleased (*de* about). **je n'y suis pas allé et je m'en félicite** I didn't go and I'm glad *ou* very pleased I didn't; **il se félicitait d'avoir refusé d'y aller** he was congratulating himself on having *ou* patting himself on the back* for having refused to go.

félidés [felide] *nmpl* (*Zool*) **les ~** the Felidae (*T*), the cat family.

félin, e [felɛ̃, in] *adj race* feline; *allure, grâce* feline, catlike. (*Zool*) **les ~s** the (big) cats.

fellah [fela] *nm* fellah.

félon, -onne [felɔ̃, ɔn] (*frm*) **1** *adj* perfidious (*frm*), disloyal, treacherous. **2** *nm* (*aussi hum*) traitor. **3 félonne** *nf* (*aussi hum*) traitress.

félonie [felɔni] *nf* (*frm*) (*U*) perfidy (*frm*), disloyalty; (*acte*) act of treachery, perfidy.

felouque [f(ə)luk] *nf* felucca.

fêlure [felyʀ] *nf* (*lit, fig*) crack.

femelle [fəmɛl] **1** *adj* (*Bot, Tech, Zool*) female; *animal* (*gén*) she-, female; *oiseau* hen-, female; *baleine, éléphant* cow-, female. **2** *nf* (*Zool*) female; (‡*péj: femme*) female‡ (*péj*).

féminin, e [feminɛ̃, in] **1** *adj* (*gén, Ling*) feminine; *hormone, population, sexe* female; *mode, revendications, vêtements,* (*Sport*) *épreuve, équipe* women's, female. **problèmes ~s** (*affectifs, intimes*) feminine *ou* women's problems; (*relatifs au statut de la femme*) female *ou* women's problems; **elle est très peu ~e** she's not very feminine; **elle est déjà très ~e** she's already quite a young lady; **il a des traits assez ~s** he has rather feminine *ou* womanish features; *V* **éternel, intuition, rime** *etc.*

2 *nm* (*Ling*) feminine. **au ~** in the feminine.

féminisant, e [feminizɑ̃, ɑ̃t] *adj* feminizing.

féminisation [feminizɑsjɔ̃] *nf* feminization.

féminiser [feminize] (1) **1** *vt* (*Bio*) to feminize; (*Ling*) to make feminine, put in the feminine; (*rendre efféminé*) to make effeminate. **2 se féminiser** *vpr* (*Bio*) to feminize; (*devenir efféminé*) to become effeminate.

féminisme [feminism(ə)] *nm* feminism.

féministe [feminist(ə)] *adj, nmf* feminist.

féminité [feminite] *nf* femininity.

femme [fam] **1** *nf* **(a)** (*individu*) woman. (*espèce*) **la ~** woman; **une jeune ~** a young woman *ou* lady; **les droits de la ~ mariée** the rights of married women *ou* a married woman; **la ~ au foyer** the woman in the home *ou* at home; (*slogan*) a woman's place is in the home; **la ~ de sa vie** the only woman for him; **elle n'est pas ~ à faire ceci** she's not the type (of woman) to do that; **ce que ~ veut ...** what a woman wants ...; *V* **bon¹, bout, chercher** *etc.*

(b) (*épouse*) wife. **demander qn pour ~**† to ask (for) sb's hand (in marriage)†; **prendre qn pour ~**† to take sb as one's wife (†, *hum*), take sb to wife (*littér*); **chercher/prendre ~** to seek/take a wife (*littér*).

(c) (*profession*) **~ médecin/professeur** (lady *ou* woman) doctor/teacher.

2 *adj inv* **(a) être/devenir ~** (*nubile*) to have reached *ou* attained/reach *ou* attain womanhood; (*n'être plus vierge*) to be/become a woman; **être très ~** (*féminine*) to be very much a woman, be very womanly.

(b) professeur/médecin ~ woman *ou* lady teacher/doctor.

3: femme d'affaires businesswoman; **femme auteur** authoress; **femme de chambre** chambermaid; **femme de charge** housekeeper; (*péj*) **femme entretenue**† kept woman; **femme d'esprit** woman of wit and learning; **femme fatale** femme fatale; **femme d'intérieur** domesticated woman; **être femme d'intérieur** to be homely (*surtout Brit*) *ou* houseproud; **femme de lettres** woman of letters; **femme de mauvaise vie**† loose woman; **femme de ménage** domestic help, cleaning lady; **femme du monde** society woman; **femme de petite vertu**† woman of easy virtue; **femme de tête** intellectual woman, bluestocking.

femmelette [famlɛt] *nf* (*péj*) (*homme*) weakling; (*femme*) frail female.

fémoral, e, *mpl* **-aux** [femɔʀal, o] *adj* femoral.

fémur [femyʀ] *nm* thighbone, femur (*T*); *V* **col.**

fenaison [fənɛzɔ̃] *nf* (*époque*) haymaking time; (*action*) haymaking.

fendant [fɑ̃dɑ̃] *nm* Swiss white wine (*from the Valais region*).

fendillé, e [fɑ̃dije] (*ptp de* **fendiller**) *adj* (*V* **fendiller**) crazed; sprung; chapped.

fendillement [fɑ̃dijmɑ̃] *nm* (*V* **fendiller**) crazing; springing; chapping.

fendiller [fɑ̃dije] (1) 1 *vt glace, plâtre, porcelaine, terre, vernis* to craze; *bois* to spring; *lèvres, peau* to chap. 2 **se fendiller** *vpr* to craze (over); to spring; to chap.

fendoir [fɑ̃dwaʀ] *nm* chopper, cleaver.

fendre [fɑ̃dʀ(ə)] (41) 1 *vt* (a) *[personne]* (*couper en deux*) *bûche, ardoise* to split; *tissu* to slit, slash. ~ **du bois** to chop wood; **il lui fendit le crâne d'un seul coup de son arme** he cleft open *ou* he split his skull with a single blow of his weapon.

(b) *[éléments, cataclysme, accident] rochers* to cleave; *mur, plâtre, meuble* to crack. **cette chute lui a fendu le crâne** this fall cracked *ou* split his skull open; **le séisme fendit la colline dans le sens de la longueur** the earthquake cleft the hill lengthwise *ou* along its length; *V* **geler.**

(c) (*pénétrer*) to cut through, cleave through (*littér*). ~ **les flots/l'air** to cleave through (*littér*) the waves/air; **le soc fend la terre** the ploughshare cuts through the earth; (*fig*) ~ **la foule** to push *ou* cleave (*littér*) one's way through the crowd.

(d) (*Habillement*) (*prévoir une fente*) *jupe* to put a slit in; *veste* to put a vent in; *manche* to put a slash in.

(e) (*loc*) **ce récit me fend le cœur** *ou* **l'âme** this story breaks my heart *ou* makes my heart bleed; **des soupirs à ~ l'âme** heart-rending *ou* heartbreaking sighs.

2 **se fendre** *vpr* (a) (*se fissurer*) to crack.

(b) **il s'est fendu le crâne** he has cracked his skull; **se ~ la lèvre** to cut one's lip; **se ~ la pipe**: *ou* **la pêche**: to laugh one's head off, split one's sides*; **se ~ la gueule**: to crease o.s.: (*Brit*).

(c) (*Escrime*) to lunge.

(d) (:) **se ~ de** *somme* to shell out:; *bouteille, cadeau* to lash out on*; **il ne s'est pas fendu!** he didn't exactly break himself!*

fendu, e [fɑ̃dy] (*ptp de* **fendre**) *adj crâne* cracked; *lèvre* cut; *manche* slashed; *veste* with a vent; *jupe* slit. **la bouche ~e jusqu'aux oreilles** with a grin (stretching) from ear to ear.

fenestrage [f(ə)nɛstʀaʒ] *nm* = **fenêtrage.**

fenestration [f(ə)nɛstʀɑsjɔ̃] *nf* (*Archit, Méd*) fenestration.

fenêtrage [f(ə)nɛtʀaʒ] *nm* (*Archit*) windows, fenestration.

fenêtre [f(ə)nɛtʀ(ə)] *nf* (a) window. **regarder/sauter par la ~** to look out of *ou* through/jump out of the window; (*dans un train*) **coin** *ou* **place côté ~** window seat, seat by the window; **~ à guillotine** sash window; **~ à battants/à meneaux** casement/mullioned window; **~ treillisée, ~ à croisillons** lattice window; **~ mansardée** dormer window; **~ en saillie** bow window, bay window; **~ à tabatière** skylight; **~ borgne** dim and viewless window; (*Ciné*) **~ d'observation** port, (projectionist's) window; *V* **faux**[2], **porte** *etc.*

(b) *[enveloppe]* window. **laisser une ~ sur un formulaire** to leave a space on a form.

(c) (*Anat: dans l'oreille*) fenestra.

fenêtrer [f(ə)nɛtʀe] (1) *vt* (*Archit*) to make windows in.

fenil [fəni(l)] *nm* hayloft.

fennec [fenɛk] *nm* fennec.

fenouil [fənuj] *nm* fennel.

fente [fɑ̃t] *nf* (a) (*fissure*) *[mur, terre]* crack, fissure; *[bois]* crack, split; *[rocher]* cleft, fissure.

(b) (*interstice*) (*dans un volet, une palissade*) slit; (*dans une boîte à lettres*) slot, opening; (*dans une tirelire etc*) slit, slot; (*dans la tête d'une vis*) slot; (*dans une jupe*) slit; (*dans un veston*) vent; (*dans une pèlerine etc*) slit, armhole.

fenugrec [f(ə)nygʀɛk] *nm* fenugreek.

féodal, e, *mpl* **-aux** [feɔdal, o] 1 *adj* feudal. 2 *nm* feudal lord.

féodaliser [feɔdalize] (1) *vt* to feudalize.

féodalisme [feɔdalism(ə)] *nm* feudalism.

féodalité [feɔdalite] *nf* (*Hist*) feudal system, feudalism, feudality.

fer [fɛʀ] 1 *nm* (a) (*métal*) iron. (*lit, fig*) **de ~** iron (*épith*); **volonté de ~** will of iron, iron will; *V* **âge, chemin, fil** *etc.*

(b) (*barre, poutre*) iron girder. **~ en T/U** T/U girder.

(c) (*embout*) *[cheval]* shoe; *[soulier]* steel tip; *[club de golf]* head; *[flèche, lance]* head, point; *[rabot]* blade, iron; *V* **plaie, quatre.**

(d) (*outil*) *[relieur]* blocking stamp; *[tailleur]* iron.

(e) (*fig: arme*) (*Escrime*) **engager/croiser le ~** to engage/cross swords; **par le ~ et par le feu** by fire and by sword.

(f) (††: *chaînes*) **~s** chains, fetters, irons; **mettre un prisonnier aux ~s** to clap a prisoner in irons; (*fig littér*) **être dans les ~s** to be in chains *ou* irons.

(g) (*Méd* ††) **~s** forceps.

2: **fer-blanc** *nm, pl* **fers-blancs** tin(plate); **fer doux** soft iron; **fer forgé** wrought iron; **fer à friser** curling tongs; **fer à gaufrer** goffering iron; (*fig*) **fer de lance** spearhead; **fer à repasser** (*ancien modèle*) (flat)iron; (*électrique*) (electric) iron; **donner un coup de fer (à repasser) à qch** to run the iron over sth, press sth; **fer rouge** red-hot iron; **marquer au fer rouge** to brand; **fer à souder** soldering iron.

ferblanterie [fɛʀblɑ̃tʀi] *nf* (*métier*) tinplate making; (*produit*) tinware; (*commerce*) tin trade; (*rare: boutique*) ironmonger's (shop) (*Brit*), hardware store (*US*).

ferblantier [fɛʀblɑ̃tje] *nm* tinsmith. **ouvrier ~** tinplate worker.

Ferdinand [fɛʀdinɑ̃] *nm* Ferdinand.

férié, e [feʀje] *adj*: **jour ~** public holiday, official holiday; **le lundi suivant est ~** the following Monday is a holiday.

férir [feʀiʀ] *vt*: **sans coup ~** without meeting *ou* encountering any opposition.

ferler [fɛʀle] (1) *vt* (*Naut*) to furl.

fermage [fɛʀmaʒ] *nm* (*procédé*) tenant farming; (*loyer*) (farm) rent.

fermail, *pl* **-aux**†† [fɛʀmaj, o] *nm* (metal) clasp.

ferme[1] [fɛʀm(ə)] 1 *adj* (a) (*lit*) *chair, fruit* firm; *sol* firm, solid. **cette viande est un peu ~** this meat is a bit tough; *V* **terre.**

(b) (*assuré*) *main, écriture* steady, firm; *voix* firm; *style, exécution, trait* confident, assured. **être ~ sur ses jambes** to be steady on one's legs *ou* feet; **marcher d'un pas ~** to walk with a firm stride *ou* step; **rester ~ dans l'adversité** to remain steadfast in adversity; *V* **attendre.**

(c) (*déterminé*) *personne, ton* firm; *décision, résolution* firm, definite. **avec la ~ intention de faire** with the firm intention of doing.

(d) (*Comm*) *achat, vente* firm; *acheteur, vendeur* firm, definite; (*Bourse*) *marché, cours* steady. **prix ~s et définitifs** firm prices, no extras to pay, no hidden extras.

2 *adv* (a) (*intensif*) *travailler, cogner* hard. **boire ~** to drink hard; **discuter ~** to discuss vigorously; *V* **tenir.**

(b) (*Comm*) *acheter, vendre* definitely.

ferme[2] [fɛʀm(ə)] *nf* (a) (*domaine*) farm; (*habitation*) farmhouse. **~ collective** collective farm; **~ d'élevage** cattle(-breeding) farm; *V* **cour, fille, valet.** (b) (*Jur: contrat*) farm lease; (*Hist: perception*) farming (*of taxes*). **donner à ~** *terres* to let, farm out; **prendre à ~** *terres* to farm (on lease).

ferme[3] [fɛʀm(ə)] *nf* (*Constr*) roof timbers, truss.

ferme[4] [fɛʀm(ə)] *excl*: **la ~!**: shut up!:, pipe down!*; *V aussi* **fermer.**

fermé, e [fɛʀme] (*ptp de* **fermer**) *adj* (a) *porte, magasin, valise, chambre* shut; *col, route* closed; *espace* closed-in; *voiture* shut (up), locked; *angle* narrow; *voyelle* close(d); *syllabe* closed; *série, ensemble* closed; *robinet* off (*attrib*); *chemise* fastened (*attrib*), done up (*attrib*). **attendez, la porte est ~e** wait, the door's locked; (*Ftbl*) **pratiquer un jeu ~** to play a tight game.

(b) *milieu, club* exclusive, select. **cette carrière lui est ~e** this career is not open to him *ou* is closed to him.

(c) *visage, air* inscrutable, impassive, impenetrable; *caractère* impassive, uncommunicative; *personne* uncommunicative.

(d) **être ~ à** *sentiment, qualité* to be impervious to *ou* untouched by *ou* closed to; *science, art* to have no appreciation of, have no feeling for.

fermement [fɛʀməmɑ̃] *adv* (*lit, fig*) firmly.

ferment [fɛʀmɑ̃] *nm* (*lit*) ferment, fermenting agent, leaven (*U*); (*fig*) ferment (*U*).

fermentation [fɛʀmɑ̃tɑsjɔ̃] *nf* fermentation. (*fig*) **~ (des esprits)** excitement of people's minds; **en ~** (*lit*) fermenting; (*fig*) in a ferment.

fermenter [fɛʀmɑ̃te] (1) *vi* (*lit*) to ferment, work; (*fig littér*) *[esprits]* to be in a ferment.

fermer [fɛʀme] (1) 1 *vt* (a) *porte, fenêtre, tiroir, paquet* to close, shut; *rideaux* to draw (to), close, shut; *store* to pull down, draw (down), close, shut; *magasin, café, musée* (*le soir*) to shut, close; (*pour cause de vacances*) to shut (up), close. **~ à clef** *porte* to lock; *chambre* to lock (up); **~ au verrou** to bolt; **il ferma violemment la porte** he slammed the door shut; **~ (la porte) à double tour** to double-lock (the door); **~ la porte au nez de qn** to shut *ou* slam the door in sb's face; (*fig*) **~ sa porte** *ou* **sa maison à qn** to close one's door to sb; (*fig*) **maintenant, toutes les portes lui sont fermées** all doors are closed to him now; (*fig*) **~ la porte aux abus** to close the door to abuses; **va ~** go and close *ou* shut the door; **on ferme!** (it's) closing time!, the shop (*ou* pub *etc*) is closing (now); **on ferme en juillet** we close *ou* shut down in July, we're closed *ou* shut in July; **on ferme un jour par semaine** we close *ou* shut one day a week, we are closed *ou* shut one day a week; *V* **parenthèse.**

(b) *yeux, bouche, paupières* to close, shut. **ferme ta gueule**∵ shut your gob∵ *ou* trap: *ou* face:; **la ferme**:, **ferme-la**: shut *ou* belt up:, wrap up: (*Brit*), shut your mouth:, pipe down*; **je n'ai pas fermé l'œil de la nuit** I didn't get a wink of sleep *ou* I didn't sleep a wink all night; **~ les yeux sur** *misère, scandale* to close *ou* shut one's eyes to; *abus, fraude, défaut* to turn a blind eye to; **s'ils sont d'accord pour ~ les yeux, bon** if they don't mind turning a blind eye, all well and good; (*fig*) **~ son cœur à la pitié** to close one's heart to pity.

(c) *couteau, livre, éventail* to close, shut; *lettre* to close; *parapluie* to put down, close, shut; *main, poing* to close; *manteau, gilet* to do up, fasten.

(d) (*boucher*) *chemin, passage* to block, bar; *accès* to shut off, close off. **des montagnes ferment l'horizon** mountains form the horizon; **le champ/jardin était fermé par une haie** the field/garden was closed in *ou* enclosed by a hedge; (*Sport*) **~ le jeu** to tighten up play.

(e) (*interdire l'accès de*) *frontière, col, route* to close; *aéroport* to close (down), shut (down).

(f) (*cesser l'exploitation de*) *magasin, restaurant, école* to close (down), shut (down). **~ boutique** to shut up shop, close down; **ils ont dû ~ pour des raisons financières** they had to close down because of *ou* shut up shop because of financial difficulties.

(g) (*arrêter*) *liste, souscription, compte en banque, débat* to close. **~ la marche** to bring up the rear; **~ le cortège** to bring up the rear of the procession.

(h) *gaz, électricité, radio* to turn off, switch off, put off; *eau, robinet* to turn off; *lumière* to turn off *ou* out, switch off, put off; *vanne* to close.

2 *vi* (a) *[fenêtre, porte, boîte]* to close, shut. **cette porte/boîte ferme mal** this door/box doesn't close *ou* shut properly.

(b) *[magasin]* (*le soir*) to close, shut; (*définitivement, pour les vacances*) to close down, shut down. **ça ferme à 7 heures** they close *ou* shut at 7 o'clock, closing time is 7 o'clock.

(c) *[vêtement]* to do up, fasten. **ça ferme par devant** it does up *ou* fastens at the front.

3 **se fermer** *vpr* (a) *[porte, fenêtre, livre]* to close, shut; *[fleur, coquillage]* to close (up); *[blessure]* to close (up); *[paupières, yeux]* to close, shut. **cela se ferme par devant** it does

up *ou* fastens at the front; **l'avenir se fermait devant lui** the future was closing before him; **quand on essaie de lui expliquer cela, son esprit se ferme** when you try to explain that to him his mind closes up *ou* he closes his mind to it; **son cœur se fermait à la vue de cette misère** he refused to be moved *ou* touched by *ou* to let his heart *ou* feelings be touched by the sight of this poverty.

(b) *[personne]* **se ~ à la pitié/l'amour** to close one's heart *ou* mind to pity/love; **il se ferme tout de suite, dès qu'on le questionne d'un peu près** he clams up *ou* closes up immediately one tries to question him closely.

fermeté [fɛʀmәte] *nf* (*V* **ferme**[1]) firmness; solidness; steadiness; confidence; assurance; steadfastness. **avec ~** firmly, resolutely.

fermette [fɛʀmɛt] *nf* (small) farmhouse.

fermeture [fɛʀmәtyʀ] *nf* **(a)** (*action: V* **fermer**) closing; shutting; drawing; pulling down; locking; bolting; blocking; shutting off; closing off; closing down; shutting down; turning off; switching off; switching out. (*Comm*) **~ annuelle** annual closure; (*Comm*) **~ définitive** permanent closure; **à (l'heure de) la ~** at closing time; **'ne pas gêner la ~ des portes'** 'do not obstruct the doors (when closing)'.

(b) (*mécanisme*) *[coffre-fort]* catch, latch; *[vêtement]* fastener, fastening; *[sac]* fastener, catch, clasp. **~ à glissière, ~ éclair** ® zip (fastener) (*Brit*), zipper.

fermier, -ière [fɛʀmje, jɛʀ] **1** *adj*: **poulet/beurre ~** farm chicken/butter. **2** *nm* **(a)** (*cultivateur*) farmer. **(b)** (*Hist*) **~ général** farmer general. **3 fermière** *nf* farmer's wife; (*indépendante*) (woman) farmer.

fermoir [fɛʀmwaʀ] *nm [livre, collier, sac]* clasp.

féroce [feʀɔs] *adj animal, regard, personne* ferocious, fierce, savage; *répression, critique* fierce, savage; *envie* savage, raging; *appétit* ferocious, ravenous. **avec une joie ~** with (a) savage joy; *V* **bête**.

férocement [feʀɔsmɑ̃] *adv* (*V* **féroce**) ferociously, fiercely, savagely.

férocité [feʀɔsite] *nf* (*V* **féroce**) ferocity, ferociousness, fierceness, savagery.

Féroé [feʀɔe] *nm*: **les îles ~** the Faroe Islands.

ferrage [fɛʀaʒ] *nm [cheval]* shoeing.

ferraillage [fɛʀɑjaʒ] *nm* (*Constr*) (iron) framework.

ferraille [fɛʀɑj] *nf* **(a)** (*déchets de fer*) scrap (iron), old iron. **tas de ~** scrap heap; **bruit de ~** clanking *ou* rattling noise; **mettre une voiture à la ~** to scrap a car, send a car for scrap. **(b)** (*: *monnaie*) small *ou* loose change.

ferrailler†† [fɛʀɑje] (1) *vi* (*péj*) to clash swords.

ferrailleur [fɛʀɑjœʀ] *nm* **(a)** scrap merchant. **(b)** (††*péj*) swashbuckler.

Ferrare [fɛʀaʀ] *nf* Ferrara.

ferrate [fɛʀat] *nm* ferrate.

ferré, e [fɛʀe] (*ptp de* **ferrer**) *adj* **(a)** *canne, bâton* steel-tipped; *soulier* hobnailed; *lacet* tagged; *cheval* shod; *roue* steel-rimmed. (*Rail*) **voie ~e** (*rails*) track, permanent way (*T*); (*route*) line; **par voie ~e** by rail, by train.

(b) (*: *calé*) well up* (*sur, en* in). **être ~ sur un sujet** to be well up* in a subject *ou* hot* at a subject, know a subject inside out.

ferrement [fɛʀmɑ̃] *nm* **(a)** (*garniture*) iron fitment. **(b)** = **ferrage**.

ferrer [fɛʀe] (1) *vt* **(a)** *cheval* to shoe; *roue* to rim with steel; *soulier* to nail; *lacet* to tag; *bâton* to tip, fit a metal tip to; *porte* to fit with iron corners. **(b)** *poisson* to strike.

ferret [fɛʀɛ] *nm* **(a)** *[lacet]* (metal) tag. **(b)** (*Minér*) **~ d'Espagne** red haematite.

ferreux [fɛʀø] *adj m* ferrous.

ferrique [fɛʀik] *adj* ferric.

ferrite [fɛʀit] *nf* ferrite.

ferro- [fɛʀɔ] *préf* (*Chim, Phys*) ferro-.

ferro-alliage, *pl* **ferro-alliages** [fɛʀɔaljaʒ] *nm* iron alloy.

ferronnerie [fɛʀɔnʀi] *nf* (*atelier*) ironworks; (*métier*) ironwork; (*objets*) ironwork, ironware. **faire de la ~ d'art** to be a craftsman in wrought iron; **une grille entièrement en ~** a gate made entirely in wrought iron; **c'est un beau travail de ~** that's a fine piece of wrought iron work.

ferronnier [fɛʀɔnje] *nm* (*artisan*) craftsman in (wrought) iron; (*commerçant*) ironware merchant. **~ d'art** craftsman in wrought iron.

ferroviaire [fɛʀɔvjɛʀ] *adj réseau, trafic* railway (*épith*) (*Brit*), railroad (*épith*) (*US*), rail (*épith*).

ferrugineux, -euse [fɛʀyʒinø, øz] *adj* ferruginous.

ferrure [fɛʀyʀ] *nf* **(a)** *[porte]* (ornamental) hinge. **(b)** *[cheval]* shoeing.

ferry-boat, *pl* **ferry-boats** [fɛʀebot] *nm [voitures]* (car) ferry; *[trains]* (train) ferry.

fertile [fɛʀtil] *adj sol, région* fertile, fruitful, productive; *esprit, imagination* fertile. **affaire ~ en rebondissements** affair which triggers off *ou* which spawns a whole series of new developments; **journée ~ en événements/en émotions** eventful/emotion-packed day.

fertilisable [fɛʀtilizabl(ә)] *adj* fertilizable.

fertilisant, e [fɛʀtilizɑ̃, ɑ̃t] *adj* fertilizing.

fertilisation [fɛʀtilizɑsjɔ̃] *nf* fertilization.

fertiliser [fɛʀtilize] (1) *vt* to fertilize.

fertilité [fɛʀtilite] *nf* (*lit, fig*) fertility. **d'une grande ~ d'esprit** with a highly fertile mind.

féru, e [feʀy] *adj* (*frm*) **être ~ de** to be keen on *ou* passionately interested in.

férule [feʀyl] *nf* (*Hist Scol*) ferula. (*fig*) **être sous la ~ de qn** to be under sb's (firm *ou* iron) rule.

fervent, e [fɛʀvɑ̃, ɑ̃t] **1** *adj* fervent, ardent. **2** *nm,f* devotee. **~ de musique** music lover.

ferveur [fɛʀvœʀ] *nf* fervour, ardour. **avec ~** fervently, ardently.

fesse [fɛs] *nf* **(a)** (*Anat*) buttock. **les ~s** the buttocks, the bottom, the bum: (*Brit hum*), the backside*; **coup de pied aux ~s*** kick in the backside* *ou* in the pants*; *V* **pousser, serrer** *etc*.

(b) (∵: *femmes*) **de la ~: film où il y a de la ~** film with lots of (bare) bums (*Brit*) *ou* ass (*US*) and tits in it∵; **il y avait de la ~ à ce bal** there were some really smart *ou* sexy pieces: *ou* there was some lovely crumpet: (*Brit*) at that dance.

fessée [fese] *nf* spanking.

fesse-mathieu, *pl* **fesse-mathieux**†† [fɛsmatjø] *nm* skinflint.

fesser [fese] (1) *vt* to give a spanking to, spank.

fessier, -ière [fesje, jɛʀ] **1** *adj muscles* buttock (*épith*), gluteal (*T*). **2** *nm*(:) behind, backside*, ass: (*US*).

fessu, e* [fesy] *adj* with a big bottom (*attrib*).

festif, -ive [fɛstif, iv] *adj* festive.

festin [fɛstɛ̃] *nm* feast. **c'était un vrai ~** it was a real feast.

festival, *pl* **~s** [fɛstival] *nm* (*Mus, Théât*) festival. (*fig*) **ce fut un vrai ~ (de talent)!** what a brilliant display (of talent) it was!

festivités [fɛstivite] *nfpl* (*gén*) festivities; (*: *repas joyeux*) festivities, merrymaking.

festoiement [fɛstwamɑ̃] *nm* feasting.

feston [fɛstɔ̃] *nm* (*guirlande, Archit*) festoon; (*Couture*) scallop; *V* **point**[2].

festonner [fɛstɔne] (1) *vt façade* to festoon; *robe* to scallop.

festoyer [fɛstwaje] (8) *vi* to feast.

fêtard, e* [fɛtaʀ, aʀd(ә)] *nm,f* (*péj*) high liver, roisterer. **réveillé par une bande de ~s** woken up by a band of merrymakers *ou* roisterers.

fête [fɛt] **1** *nf* **(a)** (*commémoration*) (*religieuse*) feast; (*civile*) holiday. **la Toussaint est la ~ de tous les saints** All Saints' Day is the feast of all the saints; **le 11 novembre est la ~ de la Victoire** November 11th is the day we celebrate *ou* for celebrating the Victory (in the First World War); **Noël est la ~ des enfants** Christmas is the festival for children.

(b) (*jour du prénom*) feast day, name day. **la ~ de la Saint-Jean** Saint John's day; **souhaiter sa *ou* bonne ~ à qn** to wish sb a happy feast day.

(c) (*congé*) holiday. **nous avons 3 jours de ~ au 15 août** we have 3 days off around August 15th; **les ~s (de fin d'année)** the (Christmas and New Year) holidays.

(d) (*foire*) fair; (*kermesse*) fête, fair; (*exposition, salon*) festival, show. **~ paroissiale/communale** parish/local fête *ou* fair; **~ de la bière/du jambon** beer/ham festival; **~ de l'aviation** air show; **la ~ de la moisson** the harvest festival; **~ de la vendange** festival of the grape harvest; **c'est la ~ au village** the fair is on in the village; **la ~ de la ville a lieu le premier dimanche de mai** the town festival takes place on the first Sunday in May; **la foule en ~** the festive crowd; **air/atmosphère de ~** festive air/atmosphere; *V* **comité, jour** *etc*.

(e) (*réception*) **donner une ~ dans son château/parc** to put on a lavish entertainment in one's château/grounds; **donner une petite ~ pour célébrer sa nomination** to hold a little party to celebrate one's appointment; **les ~s en l'honneur d'un souverain étranger** the celebrations in honour of a foreign monarch; **c'est la ~ chez nos voisins** our neighbours are celebrating.

(f) (*allégresse collective*) **la ~** celebration.

(g) (*loc*) **hier il était à la ~** he had a field day yesterday, it was his day yesterday; **je n'étais pas à la ~** it was no picnic (for me)*, I was feeling pretty uncomfortable; **il n'avait jamais été à pareille ~** he'd never had such a fine time; **être de la ~** to be one of the party; **ça va être ta ~:** you've got it coming to you*, you're going to get it in the neck:; **faire sa ~ à qn:** to bash sb up:; **faire la ~*** to live it up*, have a wild time; **faire ~ à qn** to give sb a warm welcome *ou* reception; **le chien fit ~ à son maître** the dog fawned on *ou* made up to its master; **elle se faisait une ~ d'y aller/de cette rencontre** she was really looking forward to going/to this meeting.

2: **fête carillonnée** great feast day; **fête de charité** charity bazaar *ou* fair; **Fête-Dieu** *nf, pl* **Fêtes-Dieu** Corpus Christi; **fête de famille** family celebration; **fête foraine** fun fair; **fête légale** public holiday; **la fête des Mères** Mother's Day, Mothering Sunday; **fête mobile** movable feast; **la fête des morts** All Souls' Day; **fête nationale** national holiday *ou* festival; (*Can*) **le jour de la Fête nationale** Confederation Day; **fête de village** village fête.

fêter [fete] (1) *vt anniversaire, victoire* to celebrate; *personne* to fête. **~ un ami qui revient d'un long voyage** to have a celebration for a friend who is back from a long journey.

fétiche [fetiʃ] *nm* (*lit*) fetish; (*fig: mascotte*) mascot.

fétichisme [fetiʃism(ә)] *nm* fetishism.

fétichiste [fetiʃist(ә)] *adj, nmf* fetishist.

fétide [fetid] *adj* fetid.

fétidité [fetidite] *nf* fetidness.

fétu [fety] *nm*: **~ (de paille)** wisp of straw.

feu[1] [fø] **1** *nm* **(a)** (*source de chaleur*) fire. **~ de bois/tourbe** wood/peat fire; **allumer/faire un ~** to light/make a fire; **faire du ~** to make fire; **jeter qch au ~** to throw sth on the fire; **un ~ d'enfer brûlait dans la cheminée** a fire blazed brightly *ou* a hot fire blazed in the fireplace; (*pour une cigarette*) **avez-vous du ~?** do you have a light?; **condamné au (supplice du) ~** condemned to be burnt at the stake; (*Hist*) **juger par le ~** to try by fire (*Hist*); **sur un ~ de braises** on glowing embers.

(b) (*incendie*) fire. **prendre ~** to catch fire; **mettre le ~ à qch** to set fire to sth, set sth on fire; **le ~ a pris dans la grange** fire has broken out in the barn; **en ~** on fire; **il y a le ~** there's a fire; (*fig*) **il n'y a pas le ~!*** there's no panic!*, take your time!; **au ~!** fire!

(c) (*signal lumineux*) (*Aut, Aviat, Naut*) light. **le ~ était (au) rouge** the lights were at red; **s'arrêter au(x) feu(x)** to stop at the lights; **naviguer tous ~x éteints** to sail without lights; **les ~x de la côte** the lights of the shore.

(d) (*Culin*) (*brûleur*) ring, burner; (*plaque électrique*) ring (*Brit*). **cuisinière à 3 ~x** cooker with 3 rings (*Brit*) *ou* burners; **mettre qch/être sur le ~** to put sth/be on the stove; **plat qui va sur le ~** *ou* **au ~** ovenproof *ou* fireproof dish; **faire cuire à ~ doux/vif** to cook over a slow/fast *ou* brisk heat; (*au four*) to cook in a slow/fast *ou* hot oven; **faire cuire à petit ~** to cook gently; (*fig*) **faire mourir qn à petit ~** to kill sb by inches.

(e) (*Mil*) (*combat*) action; (*tir*) fire. **aller au ~** to go to the firing line; **tué au ~** killed in action; **faire ~** to fire; **~!** fire!; **~ à volonté!** fire at will!; **sous le ~ de l'ennemi** under enemy fire; **~ nourri/rasant/roulant** sustained/grazing/running fire; (*fig*) **un ~ roulant de questions** a running fire of questions; **des ~x croisés** crossfire; **~ en rafales** firing in bursts.

(f) (*arg Crime: revolver*) gun, gat‡, rod‡.

(g) (††: *maison*) hearth†, homestead. **un hameau de 15 ~x** a hamlet of 15 homesteads; **sans ~ ni lieu**† with neither hearth nor home†.

(h) (*ardeur*) fire. **plein de ~** full of fire; **parler avec ~** to speak with fire; **dans le ~ de l'action/de la discussion** in the heat of (the) action/the discussion; **le ~ de son éloquence** the fire of his eloquence; **il prend facilement ~ dans la discussion** he easily gets heated in discussion; **un tempérament de ~** a fiery temperament; **avoir du ~ dans les veines** to have fire in one's blood.

(i) (*sensation de brûlure, de chaleur*) **j'ai le ~ au visage** my face is burning; **j'ai la gorge/les joues en ~** my throat is/my cheeks are burning; **le poivre met la bouche en ~** pepper makes your mouth burn; **le ~ lui monta au visage** the blood rushed to his face; **le ~ du rasoir** shaving rash; **le ~ d'un whisky** the fire *ou* the fiery taste of a whisky; **le ~ de la fièvre** the heat of fever.

(j) (*éclairage*) light. **être sous le ~ des projecteurs** (*lit*) to be in the glare of the spotlights; (*fig*) to be in the limelight; **mettre pleins ~x sur qn/qch** to put the spotlight on sb/sth; **pleins ~x sur** spotlight on; **les ~x de la rampe** the footlights.

(k) (*littér: éclat*) **les ~x d'une pierre précieuse** the fire of a precious stone; **ce diamant jette mille ~x** this diamond flashes *ou* sparkles brilliantly; **le ~ de son regard** the fire in his gaze, his fiery gaze.

(l) (*littér: lumière*) **les ~x de la nuit** the lights in the night; **les ~x du couchant** the fiery glow of sunset; **le ~ du ciel** the fire of heaven; **les ~x de la ville** the lights of the town; (*chaleur*) **les ~x de l'été** the summer heat.

(m) (*loc*) **avoir le ~ sacré** to burn with zeal; **faire ~ de tout bois** to make the most of what one has, turn everything to account; **mettre le ~ aux poudres** to light the powder keg; **avoir le ~ au derrière*** *ou* **au cul‡** to be in a devil of a hurry*; **mettre une ville à ~ et à sang** to put a town to fire and the sword; **mettre à ~ une fusée** to fire off a rocket; **au moment de la mise à ~** at the moment of blast-off; **jeter** *ou* **lancer ~ et flammes** to breathe fire and fury, be in a towering rage; *V* **arme, baptême, coin** *etc.*

2 *adj inv*: **rouge ~** flame red; **de couleur ~** flame-coloured; **chien noir et ~** black and tan dog.

3: **feu arrière** rear light; **feu d'artifice** (*fusée*) firework; (*spectacle*) firework display, fireworks; **feu de Bengale** Bengal light; **feu de brousse** bush fire; **feu de camp** campfire; **feu de cheminée** chimney fire; **ils ont eu un feu de cheminée** their chimney went on fire; (*Aut*) **feux de croisement** dipped headlights (*Brit*), low beams (*US*); (*Aut*) **feu de dépassement** indicator; **feu follet** will-o'-the-wisp; **feu grégeois** Greek fire; **feu de joie** bonfire; (*Aut*) **feu orange** orange light, amber (light); (*fig*) **feu de paille** flash in the pan; **feu de pinède** (pine) forest fire; (*Aut*) **feu de position** sidelight; **feu rouge** (*couleur*) red light; (*objet*) traffic light; **tournez au prochain feu rouge** turn at the next set of traffic lights; **feux de route** headlamps, headlights; **feu vert** green light; (*fig*) **donner le feu vert à qch/qn** to give sth/sb the green light *ou* the go-ahead.

feu[2], e [fø] *adj* (*inv devant art ou adj poss*) (*frm*) **~ ma tante, ma ~e tante** my late aunt.

feuillage [fœjaʒ] *nm* (*sur l'arbre*) foliage (*U*); (*coupé*) greenery (*U*). **les oiseaux gazouillaient dans le ~** *ou* **les ~s** the birds were twittering among the leaves.

feuillaison [fœjɛzɔ̃] *nf* leafing, foliation (*T*). **à l'époque de la ~** when the trees come into leaf.

feuille [fœj] **1** *nf* **(a)** [*arbre, plante*] leaf; (*littér: pétale*) petal. **à ~s caduques** deciduous; *V* **trèfle, trembler.**

(b) [*papier, bois, ardoise, acier*] sheet. **les ~s d'un cahier** the leaves of an exercise book; **doré à la ~ d'or** gilded with gold leaf.

(c) (*bulletin*) slip; (*formulaire*) form; (*journal*) paper; (*: *oreille*) ear, lug*. **dur de la ~*** hard of hearing.

2: **feuille de chêne** (*Bot*) oak-leaf; (*Mil fig*) general's insignia; **feuille de chou** (*péj: journal*) rag; **oreilles en feuille de chou*** cauliflower ears*; **feuille de garde** endpaper; **feuille d'impôt** tax form *ou* slip; **feuille morte** dead leaf; (*Aviat*) **descendre en feuille morte** to do the falling leaf; (*couleur*) **feuille-morte** *adj inv* russet; **feuille de paye** pay slip; **feuille de présence** attendance sheet; (*Mil*) **feuille de route** travel warrant; **feuille de température** temperature chart; **feuilles de thé** tea leaves; **feuille de vigne** (*Bot, Culin*) vine leaf; (*Sculp*) fig leaf; **feuille volante** loose sheet.

feuillet [fœjɛ] *nm* **(a)** [*cahier, livre*] leaf, page; [*bois*] layer. **(b)** [*ruminants*] omasum, manyplies.

feuilleté, e [fœjte] (*ptp de* **feuilleter**) **1** *adj roche* foliated. **pâte ~e** puff pastry, flaky pastry. **2** *nm* (*pâtisserie*) pastry. **~ au jambon/aux amandes** ham/almond pastry.

feuilleter [fœjte] (4) *vt* **(a)** *pages, livre* to leaf through; (*fig: lire rapidement*) to leaf *ou* skim *ou* glance through.

(b) (*Culin*) **~ de la pâte** to turn and roll (puff *ou* flaky) pastry; **cette pâte n'est pas assez feuilletée** this pastry hasn't been turned and rolled enough.

feuilleton [fœjtɔ̃] *nm* (*Presse, Rad, TV*) (*histoire à suivre*) serial; (*histoire complète*) series (*sg*). **publié en ~** serialized; *V* **roman[1]**.

feuilletoniste [fœjtɔnist(ə)] *nmf* serial writer.

feuillette [fœjɛt] *nf* cask, barrel (*containing 114-140 litres*).

feuillu, e [fœjy] **1** *adj* leafy. **2** *nm* broad-leaved tree.

feuillure [fœjyʀ] *nf* rebate, rabbet.

feulement [følmɑ̃] *nm* growl.

feuler [føle] (1) *vi* to growl.

feutrage [føtʀaʒ] *nm* felting.

feutre [føtʀ(ə)] *nm* (*Tex*) felt; (*chapeau*) felt hat; (*stylo*) felt-tip (pen), felt pen.

feutré, e [føtʀe] (*ptp de* **feutrer**) *adj* **(a)** *étoffe, surface* felt-like, felt (*épith*). **(b)** (*fig*) *atmosphère, bruit* muffled. **marcher à pas ~s** to walk with a muffled tread, pad along *ou* about.

feutrer [føtʀe] (1) **1** *vt* to line with felt, felt; (*fig: amortir*) to muffle. **2** *vi* to felt. **3 se feutrer** *vpr* to felt.

feutrine [føtʀin] *nf* (lightweight) felt.

fève [fɛv] *nf* **(a)** (*Bot*) broad bean. **(b)** charm (*hidden in cake for Twelfth Night*). **(c)** (*Can**) bean. **~s jaunes** wax beans; **~s vertes** string *ou* French beans; **~s au lard** pork and beans, (baked) beans.

février [fevʀije] *nm* February; *pour loc V* **septembre.**

fi [fi] *excl* (††, *hum*) bah!, pooh! **faire ~ de** to snap one's fingers at.

fiabilité [fjabilite] *nf* reliability.

fiable [fjabl(ə)] *adj* reliable.

fiacre [fjakʀ(e)] *nm* (hackney) cab *ou* carriage, hackney.

fiançailles [fjɑ̃saj] *nfpl* engagement.

fiancé, e [fjɑ̃se] (*ptp de* **fiancer**) **1** *adj* engaged. **être ~** to be engaged. **2** *nm* (*homme*) fiancé. (*couple*) **les ~s** the engaged couple. **3 fiancée** *nf* fiancée.

fiancer [fjɑ̃se] (3) **1** *vt* to betroth (*frm*) (*avec, à* to). **2 se fiancer** *vpr* to become *ou* get engaged (*avec, à* to).

fiasco [fjasko] *nm* fiasco. **faire ~** to be *ou* turn out a fiasco.

fiasque [fjask(ə)] *nf* wine flask.

fibranne [fibʀan] *nf* bonded fibre.

fibre [fibʀ(ə)] *nf* **(a)** (*lit: gén*) fibre. **~ de bois/verre** wood/glass fibre; **dans le sens des ~s** with the grain.

(b) (*fig: âme*) **avoir la ~ maternelle/militaire** to be a born mother/soldier, have a strong maternal/military streak in one; **faire jouer la ~ patriotique** to play on *ou* stir patriotic feelings; **toutes ses ~s se révoltèrent** everything within him rebelled.

fibreux, -euse [fibʀø, øz] *adj texture* fibrous; *viande* stringy.

fibrine [fibʀin] *nf* fibrin.

fibrinogène [fibʀinɔʒɛn] *nm* fibrinogen.

fibrociment [fibʀɔsimɑ̃] *nm* fibrocement.

fibrome [fibʀom] *nm* fibroma.

ficelage [fislaʒ] *nm* (*action*) tying (up); (*liens*) string.

ficeler [fisle] (4) *vt* **(a)** *paquet, rôti* to tie up; *prisonnier* to tie up. **ficelé comme un saucisson** tied up like a parcel *ou* in a bundle. **(b)** (*: *habiller*) to rig out*, get up*. **ta mère t'a drôlement ficelé!** that's some rig-out* *ou* get-up* your mother has put you in!; **être bien/mal ficelé** to be well/badly rigged out* *ou* got up*.

ficelle [fisɛl] *nf* **(a)** (*matière*) string; (*morceau*) piece *ou* length of string; (*pain*) stick (of French bread); (*arg Mil*) stripe (*of officer*).

(b) (*loc*) **tirer les ~s** to pull the strings; **connaître les ~s du métier** to know the tricks of the trade, know the ropes; **la ~ est un peu grosse** you can see right through it.

fiche[1] [fiʃ] *nf* **(a)** (*carte*) (index) card; (*feuille*) sheet, slip; (*formulaire*) form. **~ perforée** perforated card; **~ de paye** pay slip; (*Police*) **~ signalétique** identification sheet; **mettre en ~** to index. **(b)** (*cheville*) pin, peg; (*Élec*) (*broche*) pin; (*prise*) plug.

fiche[2]* [fiʃ] *vb V* **ficher[2]***.

ficher[1] [fiʃe] (1) **1** *vt* **(a)** (*mettre en fiche*) *renseignements* to file; *suspects* to put on file. **tous les meneurs sont fichés à la police** the police have files on all subversives.

(b) (*enfoncer*) to stick in, drive in. **~ qch en terre** to drive sth into the ground.

2 se ficher *vpr* to stick. **la flèche s'est fichée dans la cible** the arrow embedded itself in the target; **j'ai une arête fichée dans le gosier** I've got a fishbone stuck in my throat, a fishbone has got stuck in my throat.

ficher[2]* [fiʃe] (1) **1** *vt* **(a)** (*faire*) to do. **qu'est-ce qu'il fiche, il est déjà 8 heures** what on earth *ou* what the heck* is he doing *ou* is he up to* — it's already 8 o'clock; **qu'est-ce que tu as fichu aujourd'hui?** what have you been up to* *ou* what have you done today?; **il n'a rien fichu de la journée** he hasn't done a darned* *ou* blinking* (*Brit*) thing all day, he hasn't done a stroke all day*; **(pour) ce que j'en ai à fiche, de leurs histoires** what's it to me, all this carry-on* of theirs?

(b) (*donner*) **~ une trempe** *ou* **raclée à qn** to give sb a walloping*; **ça me fiche la trouille** it gives me the jitters* *ou* the willies*; **ce truc me fiche la migraine** this darned* *ou* blinking* (*Brit*) thing gives me a headache; **fiche-moi la paix!** leave me alone!; **eux, faire ça? je t'en fiche!** you think they'd do that? not a hope!* *ou* you'll be lucky!*; **ça va nous ~ la poisse** that'll bring us bad luck *ou* put a jinx on us; **je vous fiche mon billet que ...** I bet you anything (you like) *ou* my bottom dollar* that ...; **qui est-ce qui m'a fichu un idiot pareil!** of all the blinking (*Brit*) idiots!*, how stupid can you get!*

(c) (*mettre*) to put. **fiche-le dans le tiroir** bung* *ou* stick* it in the drawer; **~ qn à la porte** to chuck* *ou* kick* *ou* boot* sb out; **se faire ~ *ou* fiche à la porte** to get o.s. chucked* *ou* kicked* out, get the push* *ou* the sack*; **~ qch par la fenêtre/à la corbeille** to chuck* sth out of the window/in the bin; **ce médicament me fiche à plat** this medicine knocks me right out*; **~ qch par terre** to send sth flying; (*fig*) **ça fiche tout par terre** that mucks* *ou* messes* everything up; **~ qch en l'air** to mess sth up*, get sth in a mess; **tout ~ en l'air** (*envoyer promener*) to chuck everything up*; **~ qn dedans** (*emprisonner*) to put sb inside*; (*faire se tromper*) to drop sb in it*, mess sb up*; **ça m'a fichu en colère** that really made me (hopping) mad*.

(d) ~ le camp to clear off*, shove off‡, push off*; **fiche-moi le camp!** clear off*, shove off‡, push off!*, beat it!*, scram!‡

2 se ficher *vpr* **(a)** (*se mettre*) **attention, tu vas te ~ ce truc dans l'œil** careful, you're going to stick that thing in your eye; (*fig*) **se ~ qch dans le crâne** to get sth into one's head *ou* noddle*; (*fig*) **je me suis fichu dedans** I (really) boobed‡; **se ~ par terre** to go sprawling, come a cropper; **il s'est fichu en l'air avec sa bagnole de sport** he smashed himself up* in his sports car.

(b) (*se gausser*) **se ~ de qn** to pull sb's leg; **se ~ de qch** to make fun of sth; (*être indifférent*) **se ~ de qn/qch** not to give a darn about sb/sth*, not to care two hoots about sb/sth*; (*dépasser les bornes*) **se ~ de qn** to mess sb about* (*Brit*); **laisse-le tomber, tu vois bien qu'il se fiche de toi** drop him — it's perfectly obvious that he's leading you on* *ou* he couldn't care less about you; **il s'en fiche pas mal** he couldn't care less *ou* give a darn* (about it); **ah ça ils se fichent de nous, 10 F pour une bière!** what (on earth) do they take us for! *ou* they really must think we're idiots, 10 francs for a pint!; **il se fiche de nous, c'est la 3e fois qu'il se décommande** he's really messing us about* (*Brit*) *ou* he's giving us the runaround* — that's the third time he has cried off; **ce garagiste se fiche du monde!** that garage man is the absolute limit!* *ou* has got a flipping (*Brit*) *ou* darned nerve!*, who the heck* does that garage man think he is!; **là, ils ne se sont vraiment pas fichus de nous** they really did us proud!; **il s'en fiche comme de sa première chemise *ou* comme de l'an quarante** he couldn't care two hoots* *ou* tuppence* (*Brit*) (about it), what the heck does HE care!*

(c) (‡) **va te faire fiche!** get lost!*, go to blazes!*, take a running jump!*; **j'ai essayé, mais va te faire ~!** **ça n'a pas marché** I did try but blow me* (*surtout Brit*), it didn't work.

fichier [fiʃje] *nm* file.

fichtre* [fiʃtʀ(ə)] *excl* gosh!*

fichtrement* [fiʃtʀəmɑ̃] *adv* dashed* (*Brit*), darned*. **ça a coûté ~ cher** it was dashed (*Brit*) *ou* darned expensive*.

fichu[1] [fiʃy] *nm* (head)scarf; (*Hist: couvrant le corsage*) fichu.

fichu[2], e* [fiʃy] (*ptp de* **ficher[2]**) *adj* **(a)** (*avant n*) (*sale*) *temps, métier, idée* darned*, wretched*; (*mauvais*) rotten*, lousy*, foul*; (*sacré*) one heck of a*, a heck of a*. **avec ce ~ temps on ne peut rien faire** with this darned* *ou* wretched* weather we can't do a thing; **il fait un ~ temps** the weather's rotten* *ou* lousy* *ou* foul*, what rotten* *ou* lousy* *ou* foul* weather; **il a un ~ caractère** he's got a rotten* *ou* lousy* temper, he's a nasty piece of work*; **il y a une ~e différence** there's one heck of a *ou* a heck of a difference*.

(b) (*après n: perdu, détruit*) *malade, vêtement* done for*; *appareil* done for*, bust*. **il/ce veston est ~** he/this jacket has had it* *ou* is done for*; **avec ce temps, le pique-nique est ~** with weather like this, we've had it for the picnic* *ou* the picnic has had it*.

(c) (*habillé*) rigged out*, got up*. **regarde comme il est ~!** look at the way he's rigged out* *ou* got up*; **~ comme l'as de pique** looking like a scarecrow.

(d) (*bâti, conçu*) **elle est bien ~e** she's a smart piece‡ *ou* a bit of all right‡ (*surtout Brit*); **cet appareil/ce livre est bien ~** this is a clever little job/book*; **cet appareil/ce livre est mal ~** this gadget/book is badly put together *ou* is hopeless; **il est tout mal ~** he's a fright; **comment c'est ~ ce truc?** how does this thing work?

(e) [*malade*] **être mal ~ *ou* pas bien ~** to feel rotten*, be under the weather* *ou* out of sorts.

(f) (*capable*) **il est ~ d'y aller, tel que je le connais** knowing him, he's quite likely *ou* liable to go *ou* it's quite on the cards that he'll go; **il n'est (même) pas ~ de réparer ça** he hasn't even got the gumption to mend the thing*, he can't even mend the blinking (*Brit*) *ou* darned thing*.

fictif, -ive [fiktif, iv] *adj* **(a)** (*imaginaire*) *personnage, exemple* imaginary. **reconstitution ~ive d'un crime** staged reconstruction of a crime; **naturellement tout ceci est ~** of course this is all imagined *ou* imaginary.

(b) (*faux*) *nom* false, assumed, fictitious; *adresse* fictitious, false; *promesse, sentiment* false. **créer une concurrence ~ive en lançant une sous-marque** to stimulate artificial competition by launching a sub-brand.

(c) (*Écon*) fictitious.

fiction [fiksjɔ̃] *nf* **(a)** (*imagination*) fiction, imagination. **cette perspective est encore du domaine de la ~** this prospect still belongs in the realms of fiction; **livre de ~** work of fiction.

(b) (*fait imaginé*) invention; (*situation imaginaire*) fiction; (*roman*) (work of) fiction; (*mythe*) illusion, myth. **c'est une ~ de son esprit** it's a figment of his imagination; **heureusement, ce que je vous décris est une ~** fortunately all that I've been telling you is imaginary.

fictivement [fiktivmɑ̃] *adv* in fiction.

fidèle [fidɛl] **1** *adj* **(a)** (*loyal*) faithful, loyal; *époux* faithful. (*littér*) **~ serviteur/épée** trusty *ou* loyal servant/sword; (*lit, fig*) **demeurer ~ au poste** to be loyal *ou* faithful to one's post, stay at one's post; **rester ~ à** *ami, femme* to remain faithful *ou* true to; *promesse* to be *ou* remain faithful to, keep; *principe, idée* to remain true *ou* faithful to, stand by; *habitude, mode* to keep to; **être ~ à soi-même** to be true to o.s.; **~ à lui-même *ou* à son habitude, il est arrivé en retard** true to form *ou* true to character he arrived late.

(b) (*habituel*) *lecteur, client* regular, faithful. **nous informons nos ~s clients que ...** we wish to inform our customers that ...; **être ~ à un produit/une marque** always to buy a product/brand.

(c) (*exact*) *historien, narrateur* faithful; *souvenir, récit, portrait, traduction* faithful, accurate; *mémoire, appareil, montre* accurate, reliable; *son, reproduction* faithful. **sa description est ~ à la réalité** his description is a true *ou* an accurate picture of the situation.

2 *nmf* **(a)** (*Rel*) believer. **les ~s** (*croyants*) the faithful; (*assemblée*) the congregation.

(b) (*client*) regular (customer); (*lecteur*) regular (reader). **je suis un ~ de votre émission depuis 10 ans** I have been a regular listener to your programme for 10 years.

(c) (*adepte*) [*doctrine, mode, écrivain*] follower, devotee.

fidèlement [fidɛlmɑ̃] *adv* **(a)** (*loyalement*) faithfully, loyally.

(b) (*régulièrement*) faithfully, regularly. **j'écoute ~ vos émissions depuis 10 ans** I have been listening to your programmes regularly *ou* I have been a regular listener to your programmes for the past 10 years.

(c) (*scrupuleusement*) faithfully.

(d) (*conformément à la réalité*) faithfully, accurately. **combat ~ décrit dans un livre** fight which is accurately described in a book.

fidélité [fidelite] *nf* (*V* **fidèle**) faithfulness; loyalty; accuracy; reliability; (*Comm: à un produit*) fidelity. **la ~ (conjugale)** marital fidelity; *V* **haut, jurer.**

fiduciaire [fidysjɛʀ] *adj* fiduciary.

fief [fjɛf] *nm* (*Hist*) fief; (*fig: zone d'influence*) [*firme, organisation*] preserve; [*parti, secte*] stronghold; (*hum: domaine*) private kindom. **~ (électoral)** electoral stronghold; (*hum*) **ce bureau est son ~** this office is his kingdom.

fieffé, e [fjefe] *adj* arrant.

fiel [fjɛl] *nm* (*lit, fig*) gall. **propos pleins de ~** words filled with gall.

fielleux, -euse [fjɛlø, øz] *adj* venomous, rancorous, spiteful.

fiente [fjɑ̃t] *nm* [*oiseau*] droppings.

fienter [fjɑ̃te] (1) *vi* to excrete.

fier, fière [fjɛʀ] *adj* **(a)** (*arrogant*) proud, haughty (*frm*). **~ comme Artaban** (as) proud as a peacock; **trop ~ pour accepter** too proud to accept; **faire le ~** (*être méprisant*) to be aloof, give o.s. airs; (*faire le brave*) to be full of o.s.; **c'est quelqu'un de pas ~*** he's not stand-offish *ou* stuck-up*; **devant le danger, il n'était plus si ~** when he found himself faced with danger, he wasn't so full of himself any more; *V* **fier-à-bras.**

(b) (*littér: noble*) *âme, démarche* proud, noble. **avoir fière allure** to cut a fine figure, cut a dash.

(c) ~ de qch/de faire qch proud of sth/to do sth; **elle est fière de sa beauté** she's proud of her beauty; **toute fière de sortir avec son papa** as proud as can *ou* could be to be going out with her daddy; **il n'y a pas de quoi être ~** there's nothing to feel proud about *ou* to be proud of *ou* to boast about; **je n'étais pas ~ de moi** I didn't feel very proud of myself, I felt pretty small*.

(d) (*intensif: avant n*) **~ imbécile** first-class *ou* prize* *ou* egregious idiot; **fière canaille** out-and-out *ou* downright scoundrel; **il a un ~ toupet** he has the devil of a cheek*; **je te dois une fière chandelle** I'm terribly indebted to you.

(e) (*littér: fougueux*) *cheval* mettlesome. **le ~ Aquilon** the harsh *ou* chill north wind.

fier (se) [fje] (7) *vpr* **(a)** (*question de loyauté*) **se ~ à** *allié, promesses, discrétion* to trust; **on ne peut pas se ~ à lui** one cannot trust him, he's not to be trusted, he can't be trusted; **ne vous fiez pas aux apparences/à ce qu'il dit** don't go by *ou* trust appearances/what he says; **il a l'air calme mais il ne faut pas s'y ~** he looks calm but you can't trust that *ou* go by that.

(b) (*question de fiabilité*) **se ~ à** *appareil, collaborateur, instinct, mémoire* to trust, rely on; *destin, hasard* to trust to. **ne te fie pas à ta mémoire, prends-en note** don't trust to memory, make a note of it.

fier-à-bras, *pl* fiers-à-bras [fjɛʀabʀa] *nm* braggart.

fièrement [fjɛʀmɑ̃] *adv* (*dignement*) proudly; (*†: *extrêmement*) devilishly*†.

fiérot, e* [fjeʀo, ɔt] *adj* cocky*. **faire le ~** to show off; **tout ~ (d'avoir gagné/de son succès)** as pleased as Punch (about winning/about *ou* at his success).

fierté [fjɛʀte] *nf* (*gén*) pride; (*péj: arrogance*) pride, haughtiness (*frm*). **tirer ~ de** to get a sense of pride from; **sa ~ est d'avoir réussi tout seul** he takes pride in having succeeded all on his own; **son jardin est sa ~** his garden is his pride and joy.

fieu [fjø] *nm* (*† ou dial*) son, lad.

fièvre [fjɛvʀ(ə)] *nf* **(a)** (*température*) fever, temperature. **avoir un accès de ~** to have a bout of fever; **avoir (de) la ~/beaucoup de ~** to have *ou* run a temperature/a high temperature; **avoir 39 de ~** to have a temperature of 104(°F) *ou* 39 (°C); **une ~ de cheval** a raging fever; **il a les yeux brillants de ~** his eyes are bright with fever.

(b) (*maladie*) fever. **~ jaune/typhoïde** yellow/typhoid fever; **~ aphteuse** foot-and-mouth disease; **~ quarte** quartan fever *ou* ague; **avoir les ~s** to have marsh fever.

(c) (*fig: agitation*) fever, excitement. **parler avec ~** to speak excitedly; **dans la ~ du départ** in the heat of departure, in the excitement of going away; **la ~ de l'or/des élections** gold/election fever.

(d) (*fig: envie*) fever. **être pris d'une ~ d'écrire** to be seized with a frenzied *ou* feverish urge to write.

fiévreusement [fjevʀøzmɑ̃] *adv* feverishly, excitedly.
fiévreux, -euse [fjevʀø, øz] *adj* (*Méd, fig*) feverish.
fifille [fifij] *nf* (*langage enfantin*) daughter. (*péj*) **~ à sa maman** mummy's (*Brit*) *ou* mommy's (*US*) little girl.
fifre [fifʀ(ə)] *nm* (*instrument*) fife; (*joueur*) fife player.
fifrelin† [fifʀəlɛ̃] *nm*: **ça ne vaut pas un ~** that's not worth a farthing (*Brit*) *ou* nickel (*US*).
figaro [figaʀo] *nm* (*hum*) barber.
figé, e [fiʒe] (*ptp de* **figer**) *adj style* stilted, fixed; *manières* stiff, constrained; *société, mœurs* rigid, ossified; *attitude, sourire* set, fixed. **être ~ dans des structures anciennes** to be set rigidly in outdated structures; (*Ling*) **expression ~e** set expression.
figement [fiʒmɑ̃] *nm* (*V* **figer**) congelation; clotting, coagulation.
figer [fiʒe] (3) **1** *vt huile, sauce* to congeal; *sang* to clot, coagulate. **le cri le figea sur place** the cry froze *ou* rooted him to the spot; **figé par la peur** terror-stricken; **histoire à vous ~ le sang** bloodcurdling story, story to make one's blood run cold; **figé par la mort** stiffened by death.
2 *vi [huile]* to congeal; *[sang]* to clot, coagulate.
3 se figer *vpr [sauce, huile]* to congeal; *[sang]* (*lit*) to clot, coagulate; (*fig*) to freeze; *[sourire, regard]* to freeze; *[visage]* to stiffen, freeze. **il se figea au garde-à-vous** he stood rigidly *ou* he froze to attention.
fignolage* [fiɲɔlaʒ] *nm* touching up*, polishing up.
fignoler* [fiɲɔle] (1) *vt* (*soigner*) to touch up*, polish up, put the finishing touches to. **ça c'est du travail fignolé** that's a really neat job*; **c'est une voiture fignolée** this car is nicely finished off.
figue [fig] *nf* (*Bot*) fig. **~ de Barbarie** prickly pear; *V* **mi-**.
figuier [figje] *nm* fig tree. **~ de Barbarie** prickly pear.
figurant, e [figyʀɑ̃, ɑ̃t] *nm,f* (*Ciné*) extra; (*Théât*) walk-on, supernumerary; (*fig*) (*pantin*) puppet, cipher; (*complice*) stooge. **avoir un rôle de ~** (*dans un comité, une conférence*) to be a puppet *ou* cipher, play a minor part, be a mere onlooker; (*dans un crime etc*) to be a stooge; (*Théât*) to have a walk-on part.
figuratif, -ive [figyʀatif, iv] **1** *adj* **(a)** *art, peinture* representational, figurative; *peintre, tableau* representational. **(b)** *plan, écriture* figurative. **2** *nm,f* representational artist.
figuration [figyʀɑsjɔ̃] *nf* **(a)** (*Théât*) (*métier*) playing walk-on parts; (*rôle*) walk-on (part); (*figurants*) walk-on actors; (*Ciné*) (*métier*) working as an extra; (*rôle*) extra part; (*figurants*) extras. **faire de la ~** (*Théât*) to do walk-on parts; (*Ciné*) to work as an extra.
(b) (*rare: représentation*) representation.
figurativement [figyʀativmɑ̃] *adv* diagrammatically.
figure [figyʀ] **1** *nf* **(a)** (*visage*) face; (*mine*) face, countenance (*frm*). **sa ~ s'allongea** his face fell; *V* **casser, chevalier**.
(b) (*personnage*) figure. **~ équestre** equestrian figure; **les grandes ~s de l'histoire** the great figures of history; (*Cartes*) **les ~s** the court *ou* face cards.
(c) (*image*) illustration, picture; (*Danse, Ling, Patinage*) figure; (*Math: tracé*) diagram, figure. **~ géométrique** geometrical figure; **faire une ~** to draw a diagram.
(d) (*loc*) **faire ~ de favori** to be generally thought of as the favourite, be looked on as the favourite; **faire ~ d'idiot** to look a fool; **faire ~ dans le monde**†† to cut a figure in society†; **faire bonne ~** to put up a good show; **faire (une) triste ~** to look downcast, look sorry for o.s.; **faire triste ~ à** to give a cool reception to, greet unenthusiastically; **faire triste *ou* piètre ~** to cut a sorry figure, look a sorry sight; **il n'a plus ~ humaine** he is disfigured beyond recognition.
2: **figure de ballet** balletic figure; **figure chorégraphique** choreographic figure; **figures imposées** compulsory figures; **figures libres** freestyle (skating); **figure de proue** (*Naut*) figurehead; (*fig: chef*) key figure; **figure de rhétorique** rhetorical figure; **figure de style** stylistic device.
figuré, e [figyʀe] (*ptp de* **figurer**) *adj langage, style, sens* figurative; *prononciation* symbolized; *plan, représentation* diagrammatic. **mot employé au ~** word used figuratively; **au propre comme au ~** in the literal as well as the metaphorical *ou* figurative sense.
figurément [figyʀemɑ̃] *adv* figuratively, metaphorically.
figurer [figyʀe] (1) **1** *vt* to represent. **le peintre l'avait figuré sous les traits de Zeus** the painter had shown *ou* represented him in the guise of Zeus; **la scène figure un palais** the scene is a palace; **la balance figure la justice** scales are the symbol of justice.
2 *vi* **(a)** (*être mentionné*) to appear. **son nom figure en bonne place/ne figure pas parmi les gagnants** his name is high up amongst/does not appear amongst the winners; **~ sur une liste/dans l'annuaire** to appear on a list/in the directory.
(b) (*Théât*) to have a walk-on part; (*Ciné*) to be an extra.
3 se figurer *vpr* to imagine. **figurez-vous une grande maison** picture *ou* imagine a big house; **si tu te figures que tu vas gagner** if you fancy *ou* imagine you're going to win; **figurez-vous que j'allais justement vous téléphoner** would you believe it *ou* it so happens I was just about to phone you; **je ne tiens pas à y aller, figure-toi!** I'm not particularly keen on going, believe you me*, believe it or not, I've no particular desire to go.
figurine [figyʀin] *nf* figurine.
fil [fil] **1** *nm* **(a)** (*brin*) *[coton, nylon]* thread; *[laine]* yarn; *[cuivre, acier]* wire; *[haricots, marionnette]* string; *[araignée]* thread; *[appareil électrique]* wire. (*fig*) **les ~s d'une affaire** the ins and outs of an affair, the threads of an affair; **il tient dans sa main tous les ~s de l'affaire** he has his hands on all the strings; (*Tex*) **~ de trame/de chaîne** weft/warp yarn; **tu as tiré un ~ à ton manteau** you have pulled a thread in your coat; **ramasser un ~** to pick up a thread; (*fig: téléphone*) **j'ai ta mère au bout du ~** I have your mother on the line *ou* phone; **haricots pleins de ~s/sans ~s** stringy/stringless beans; *V* **coup, inventer** *etc.*
(b) (*Tex: matière*) linen. **chemise de ~** linen shirt; **chaussettes pur ~ (d'Écosse)** lisle socks.
(c) (*sens*) *[bois, viande]* grain. **couper dans le sens du ~** to cut with the grain; **dans le sens contraire du ~** against the grain; *V* **droit**[2].
(d) (*tranchant*) edge. **donner du ~ à un rasoir** to give an edge to a razor; **passer un prisonnier au ~ de l'épée** to put a prisoner to the sword.
(e) (*cours*) *[discours, pensée]* thread. **suivre/interrompre le ~ d'un discours/de ses pensées** to follow/interrupt the thread of a speech/one's thoughts; **tu m'as interrompu et j'ai perdu le ~** you've interrupted me and I've lost the thread; **au ~ des jours/des ans** with the passing days/years; **raconter sa vie au ~ de ses souvenirs** to tell one's life story as the memories drift back; **suivre le ~ de l'eau** to follow the current; **le bateau/papier s'en allait au ~ de l'eau** the boat/paper was drifting away with *ou* on the stream *ou* current.
(f) (*loc*) **maigre *ou* mince comme un ~** as thin as a rake; **donner du ~ à retordre à qn** to give sb a headache, make life difficult for sb; **avoir un ~ à la patte*** to be tied down; **ne tenir qu'à un ~** to hang by a thread; **de ~ en aiguille** one thing leading to another, gradually.
2: **fil d'Ariane** (*Myth*) Ariadne's clew; (*fig*) vital lead; **fil conducteur** *[enquête]* vital lead; *[récit]* main theme, leading strand; **fil à coudre** (sewing) thread; **fil à couper le beurre** cheesewire (*Brit*); **fil électrique** electric wire; **fil de fer** wire; (*fig*) **avoir les jambes comme des fils de fer** to have legs like matchsticks; **fil de fer barbelé** barbed wire; **fil-de-fériste** *nmf, pl* **fil-de-féristes** high-wire artiste; (*Tex*) **fil-à-fil** *nm inv* pepper and salt; **fil (à linge)** (washing *ou* clothes) line; **fil (à pêche)** (fishing) line; **fil à plomb** plumbline; **fil à souder** soldering wire; **fil de terre** earth wire (*Brit*), ground wire (*US*); **fils de la vierge** gossamer (*U*), gossamer threads.
filage [filaʒ] *nm [laine]* spinning.
filament [filamɑ̃] *nm* (*Bio, Élec*) filament; *[glu, bave]* strand, thread.
filamenteux, -euse [filamɑ̃tø, øz] *adj* filamentous.
filandreux, -euse [filɑ̃dʀø, øz] *adj viande* stringy; *discours, explication* long-winded.
filant, e [filɑ̃, ɑ̃t] *adj liquide* free-running; *V* **étoile**.
filasse [filas] **1** *nf* tow. **2** *adj inv*: **cheveux (blonds) ~** tow-coloured hair.
filateur [filatœʀ] *nm* mill owner.
filature [filatyʀ] *nf* **(a)** (*Tex*) (*action*) spinning; (*usine*) mill.
(b) (*surveillance*) shadowing (*U*), tailing* (*U*). **prendre qn en ~** to shadow sb, put a tail on sb*.
file [fil] *nf [personnes, objets]* line. **~ (d'attente)** queue; **~ de voitures** (*en stationnement*) line of cars; (*roulant*) line *ou* stream of cars; (*Aut*) **se mettre sur *ou* prendre la ~ de gauche/droite** to move into the left-hand/right-hand lane; **se garer en double ~** to double-park; **se mettre en ~** to line up; **se mettre à la ~, prendre la ~** to join the queue; **marcher à la ~ *ou* en ~** to walk in line; **entrer/sortir en ~ *ou* à la ~** to file in/out; **en ~ indienne** in single *ou* Indian file; **chanter plusieurs chansons à la ~** to sing several songs in succession *ou* one after the other; *V* **chef**[1].
filer [file] (1) **1** *vt* **(a)** *laine, coton, acier, verre* to spin. *[araignée, chenille]* to spin. (*fig*) **~ un mauvais coton** (*au physique*) to be in a bad way; (*au moral*) to get into bad ways; **verre filé** spun glass.
(b) (*prolonger*) *image, comparaison* to spin out; *son, note* to draw out. (*fig*) **~ le parfait amour** to spin out love's sweet dream; **métaphore filée** long-drawn-out metaphor.
(c) (*Police etc: suivre*) to shadow, tail*.
(d) (*Naut*) *amarre* to veer out. **navire qui file 20 nœuds** ship which does 20 knots.
(e) (*: *donner*) **~ à qn de l'argent/un objet** to slip sb some money/an object*; **~ à qn une maladie** to land sb with an illness*; **~ à qn un coup de poing** to land sb a blow*; **file-toi un coup de peigne** run a comb through your hair.
(f) (*démailler*) *bas* to ladder.
2 *vi* **(a)** *[liquide, fromage]* to run; *[lampe, flamme]* to smoke. **il faisait ~ du sable entre ses doigts** he was running sand through his fingers.
(b) (*: *courir, passer*) *[personne]* to fly* by *ou* past, dash by *ou* past; *[train, voiture]* to fly by; *[cheval, temps]* to fly (by). **~ bon train/comme le vent/à toute allure** to go at a fair speed/like the wind/at top speed; **il fila comme une flèche devant nous** he darted *ou* zoomed* straight past us; **~ à la poste/voir qn** to dash to the post office/to see sb.
(c) (*: *s'en aller*) to go off. **le voleur avait déjà filé** the thief had already made off*; **il faut que je file** I must dash *ou* fly*; **file dans ta chambre** off to your room with you; **allez, file, garnement!** clear off, pest!*; **~ à l'anglaise** to take French leave, run off; **~ entre les doigts de qn** *[poisson, (fig) argent]* to slip between sb's fingers; *[voleur]* to slip through sb's grasp; **~ doux** to behave (o.s. nicely), keep a low profile*.
(d) (*se démailler*) *[maille]* to run; *[collant]* to ladder.
filet [filɛ] *nm* **(a)** (*petite quantité*) *[eau, sang]* dribble, trickle; *[fumée]* wisp; *[lumière]* (thin) shaft *ou* streak. **il avait un ~ de voix** his voice was very thin; **mettez un ~ de vinaigre** add a drop *ou* a dash of vinegar.
(b) *[poisson]* fillet; *[viande]* fillet steak. **un rôti dans le ~** a roasting joint (from rump and sirloin); **~ mignon** fillet mignon.

(**c**) (*nervure*) *[langue]* frenum; *[pas de vis]* thread; (*Typ*) rule. **~s nerveux** nerve endings.

(**d**) (*Pêche, Sport*) net. **~ (à provisions)** string bag; **~ (à bagages)** (luggage) rack; **~ à crevettes/à papillons/à cheveux/à poissons** *ou* **de pêche** shrimping/butterfly/hair/fishing net; (*Ftbl*) **envoyer la balle au fond des ~s** to send the ball into the back of the net; **travailler sans ~** *[acrobates]* to perform without a safety net; (*fig*) to be out on one's own; **tendre un ~** *[chasseur]* to set a snare; *[police]* to set a trap; **le ~ se resserre** the net is closing in *ou* tightening; (*fig*) **attirer qn dans ses ~s** to ensnare sb; *V* **coup.**

filetage [filtaʒ] *nm* (*action*) threading; *[pas de vis]* thread.

fileter [filte] (5) *vt vis, tuyau* to thread.

fileur, -euse [filœʀ, øz] *nm,f* spinner.

filial, e, *mpl* **-aux** [filjal, o] **1** *adj* filial. **2 filiale** *nf* (*Comm*) subsidiary (company).

filialement [filjalmɑ̃] *adv* with filial devotion.

filiation [filjɑsjɔ̃] *nf [personnes]* filiation; *[idées, mots]* relation. **être issu de qn par ~ directe** to be a direct descendant of sb.

filière [filjɛʀ] *nf* (**a**) *[carrière]* path(way); *[administration]* channels, procedures; *[recel, drogue]* network. **la ~ administrative** the administrative procedures *ou* channels; **passer par** *ou* **suivre la ~ pour devenir directeur** to work one's way up to become a director; **de nouvelles ~s sont offertes aux jeunes ingénieurs** new paths are open to young engineers; **les policiers ont réussi à remonter toute la ~** the police have managed to trace the network right through to the man at the top; **on a découvert de nouvelles ~s pour le passage de la drogue** new channels for drug trafficking have been discovered.

(**b**) (*Tech*) (*pour étirer*) drawplate; (*pour fileter*) screwing die.

filiforme [filifɔʀm(ə)] *adj antenne, patte* threadlike, filiform (*T*); (*) *jambes* spindly; (*) *corps* spindly, lanky; (*Méd*) *pouls* thready.

filigrane [filigʀan] *nm [papier, billet]* watermark; *[objet]* filigree. **en ~** (*lit*) as a watermark; filigree (*épith*); (*fig*) just beneath the surface; **sa haine apparaissait en ~ dans ses paroles** there was veiled hatred in his words.

filigraner [filigʀane] (1) *vt papier, billet* to watermark; *objet* to filigree.

filin [filɛ̃] *nm* rope.

fille [fij] **1** *nf* (**a**) (*opp de* **fils**) daughter. **la ~ de la maison** the daughter of the house; (*, *souvent péj*) **la ~ Martin** the Martin girl*; (*littér*) **la peur, ~ de la lâcheté** fear, the daughter of cowardice; (*Rel*) **oui, ma ~** yes, my child; *V* **jouer, petit.**

(**b**) (*opp de* **garçon**) (*enfant*) girl; (*femme*) woman; (†: *vierge*) maid†. **c'est une grande/petite ~** she's a big/little girl; **elle est belle ~** she's a good-looking girl; **c'est une bonne** *ou* **brave ~** she's a nice girl *ou* a good sort; **elle n'est pas ~ à se laisser faire** she's not one to let herself be messed about (*surtout Brit*); **être encore/rester ~**† to be still/stay unmarried; **mourir ~** to die an old maid; *V* **beau, jeune, vieux.**

(**c**) (*servante*) **~ de ferme** farm girl; **~ d'auberge** serving maid; **ma ~**†† my girl.

(**d**) (†*péj: prostituée*) whore†.

2: fille d'Ève* daughter of Eve; (*Hist*) **fille d'honneur** maid of honour; **fille de joie** loose woman, woman of easy virtue; **fille à marier** girl of marriageable age; (*péj*) **fille-mère** *nf, pl* **filles-mères** unmarried mother; **fille publique** streetwalker; **fille des rues** woman of the streets, streetwalker; **fille de salle** (*restaurant*) waitress; (*hôpital*) orderly; (*péj*†) **fille à soldats** loose woman, trollop†; **fille soumise**† registered prostitute.

fillette [fijɛt] *nf* (**a**) (little) girl. **rayon ~s** girls' department. (**b**) (*bouteille*) (half-)bottle.

filleul [fijœl] *nm* godson, godchild. **~ de guerre** adoptive son (*in wartime*).

filleule [fijœl] *nf* goddaughter.

film [film] *nm* (**a**) (*Ciné*) (*pellicule*) film; (*œuvre*) film, picture*, movie* (*surtout US*). **le grand ~** the feature film, the big picture*; (*fig*) **retracer le ~ des événements (de la journée)** to go over the day's events. (**b**) (*mince couche*) film.

filmage [filmaʒ] *nm* (*Ciné*) filming, shooting.

filmer [filme] (1) *vt personne, paysage* to film; *film, scène* to film, shoot. **théâtre filmé** drama on film.

filmique [filmik] *adj* film (*épith*), cinematic. **l'œuvre ~ de Renoir** Renoir's (film) work.

filmographie [filmɔgʀafi] *nf* filmography.

filmologie [filmɔlɔʒi] *nf* film studies.

filon [filɔ̃] *nm* (*Minér*) vein, lode; (*: *combine*) cushy number*. (*fig: mine d'or*) **trouver le ~** to strike it lucky *ou* rich; **on n'a pas fait de recherches sur ce sujet, c'est un ~ qu'il faudrait exploiter** no research has been done on that subject – it's a line worth developing; **il exploite ce ~ depuis des années** that (theme *ou* line) has been a lucrative source of income to him *ou* a real money-spinner for him for years now; **être dans l'immobilier c'est un bon ~** it's a cushy number* *ou* a soft option* dealing in property *ou* real estate.

filou [filu] *nm* (*escroc*) rogue, swindler; (*enfant espiègle*) rogue.

filouter* [filute] (1) **1** *vt personne* to cheat, do*, diddle* (*hum*); *argent, objets* to snaffle*, filch*. **il m'a filouté (de) 10 F** he has diddled me out of 10 francs*.

2 *vi* (*tricher*) to cheat; (*voler*) to diddle*. **il est difficile de ~ avec le fisc** it's hard to diddle the tax man*.

filouterie [filutʀi] *nf* fraud (*U*), swindling (*U*).

fils [fis] **1** *nm* son. **le ~ de la maison** the son of the house; **M Martin ~** young Mr Martin; (*Comm*) **Martin ~** Mr Martin junior; (*Comm*) **Martin et F~** Martin and Son (*ou* Sons); **le ~ Martin** the Martin boy; **elle est venue avec ses 2 ~** she came with her 2 sons *ou* boys; **c'est bien le ~ de son père** he's very much his father's son *ou* a chip off the old block; (*frm*) **les ~ de la France/de Charlemagne** the sons of France/of Charlemagne; (*frm*) **être le ~ de ses œuvres** to be a self-made man; (*Rel*) **oui, mon ~** yes, my son; (*Rel*) **le F~ de l'homme/de Dieu** the son of man/of God; **~ de garce!**‡† son of a bitch!‡

2: fils de famille young man with money; (*péj*) **fils à papa** daddy's boy.

filtrage [filtʀaʒ] *nm [liquide]* filtering; *[nouvelles, spectateurs]* screening.

filtrant, e [filtʀɑ̃, ɑ̃t] *adj substance* filtering (*épith*); *pouvoir* of filtration; *verre* filter (*épith*). **virus ~** filterable virus.

filtrat [filtʀa] *nm* filtrate.

filtration [filtʀɑsjɔ̃] *nf [liquide]* filtering, filtration.

filtre [filtʀ(ə)] *nm* (*gén, Chim, Élec, Opt*) filter; *[cafetière]* filter; *[cigarette]* filter tip. **papier-~** filter paper; **(café-)~** (filter) coffee; **cigarette avec ~** filter tip cigarette; **'avec ou sans ~?'** 'tipped or plain?'

filtrer [filtʀe] (1) **1** *vt liquide, lumière, son* to filter; *nouvelles, spectateurs* to screen. **2** *vi [liquide]* to filter (through), seep through; *[lumière, son, nouvelles]* to filter through.

fin[1], fine[1] [fɛ̃, fin] **1** *adj* (**a**) (*mince*) *tranche, couche, papier, tissu* thin; *cheveux, sable, poudre, papier de verre* fine; *pointe, pinceau* fine; *bec d'oiseau* thin, pointed; *lame* sharp, keen; *écriture* small, fine; *taille, doigt, jambe* slender, slim. **plume fine** fine pen; **sel ~** table salt; **petits pois ~s/très ~s/extra ~s** high-quality/top-quality/superfine (graded) garden peas; **une petite pluie fine** a fine drizzle; *V* **peigne.**

(**b**) (*raffiné, supérieur*) *lingerie* fine; *porcelaine, travail* fine, delicate; *traits, visage* fine; *silhouette, membres* neat, shapely; *produits, aliments* high-class; *mets* choice, exquisite; *or, pierres* fine. **faire un repas ~** to have a superb *ou* an exquisite meal; **vins ~s** fine wines; **perles fines** real pearls; **fine fleur de froment** finest wheat flour; **la fine fleur de l'armée française** the pride *ou* flower of the French army; **le ~ du ~** the last word (*de* in); *V* **épicerie, partie[2].**

(**c**) (*très sensible*) *vue, ouïe* sharp, keen; *goût, odorat* fine, discriminating. **avoir l'oreille** *ou* **l'ouïe fine** to have a keen ear, have keen hearing; *V* **nez.**

(**d**) (*subtil*) *personne* subtle, astute; *esprit, observation* shrewd, sharp; *allusion, nuance* subtle; *sourire* wise, shrewd. **faire des plaisanteries fines sur qch** to joke wittily about sth; **il n'est pas très ~** he's not very bright; **ce n'est pas très ~ de sa part** it's not very clever of him; (*iro*) **comme c'est ~!** that really is clever! (*iro*); (*iro*) **c'est ~ ce que tu as fait!** that was clever of you! (*iro*); **il se croit plus ~ que les autres** he thinks he's smarter than everybody else; **bien ~ qui pourrait le dire** it would take a shrewd man to say that; **tu as l'air ~!** you look a fine sight!; **jouer au plus ~ avec qn** to try to outsmart sb.

(**e**) (*avant n: très habile, connaisseur*) expert. **~ connaisseur** connoisseur; **~ gourmet, fine gueule** gourmet, epicure; **fine lame** expert swordsman; **~ tireur** crack shot; **~ voilier** fast yacht; *V* **bec.**

(**f**) (*avant n: intensif*) **au ~ fond de la campagne** in the depths of the country; **au ~ fond du tiroir** right at the back of the drawer; **savoir le ~ mot de l'histoire** to know the real story (behind it all).

2 *adv moudre, tailler* finely. **écrire ~** to write small; **~ prêt** quite *ou* all ready; **~ soûl** dead *ou* blind drunk*.

3: fines herbes mixed herbs, fines herbes; **fin limier** (keen) sleuth; **fine mouche, fin renard** sharp customer.

fin[2] [fɛ̃] **1** *nf* (**a**) (*gén*) end; *[année, réunion]* end, close; *[compétition]* end, finish, close. **vers** *ou* **sur la ~** towards the end; **le quatrième en partant de** *ou* **en commençant par la ~** the fourth from the end, the last but three; **~ juin, à la ~ (de) juin** at the end of June; (*Comm*) **~ courant** at the end of the current month; **jusqu'à la ~** to the very end; **jusqu'à la ~ des temps** *ou* **des siècles** until the end of time; **la ~ du monde** the end of the world; **avoir des ~s de mois difficiles** to have difficulty making ends meet at the end of the month, run short of money at the end of the month; **en ~ de semaine** towards *ou* at the end of the week; **on n'en verra jamais la ~** we'll never see the end of this; **à la ~ il a réussi à se décider** he eventually managed *ou* in the end he managed to make up his mind; **tu m'ennuies, à la ~!*** you're getting on my nerves now!*, you're beginning to get on my nerves!*; **en ~ d'après-midi** towards the end of the afternoon, in the late afternoon; **en ~ de liste** at the end of the list; **en ~ de compte** (*après tout*) really, when it comes down to it*; (*en dernière analyse*) in the last analysis; **sans ~** (*adj*) endless; (*adv*) endlessly; **arriver en ~ de course** *[vis]* to screw home; *[piston]* to complete its stroke; *[batterie]* to wear out; (*) *[personne]* to be worn out, come to the end of the road*; **prendre ~** to come to an end; **être sur sa ~, toucher à** *ou* **tirer à sa ~** to be coming to an end, be drawing to a close (*frm*); **on arrive à la ~ du spectacle** it's getting near the end of the show, the show is coming to an end; **mettre ~ à** to put an end to, end; **mettre ~ à ses jours** to put an end to one's life; **mener qch à bonne ~** to bring sth to a successful conclusion, deal successfully with sth, carry sth off successfully; **faire une ~** to settle down; *V* **début, mot** *etc.*

(**b**) (*ruine*) end. **c'est la ~ de tous mes espoirs** that's the end of all my hopes; **c'est la ~ de tout*** *ou* **des haricots*** that's the last straw!*, that's all we needed! (*iro*).

(**c**) (*mort*) end, death. **avoir une ~ tragique** to die a tragic death, meet a tragic end; **il a eu une belle ~** he had a fine end.

(**d**) (*but*) end, aim, purpose; (*Philos*) end. **~ en soi** end in itself; (*Prov*) **la ~ justifie les moyens** the end justifies the means; **il est arrivé** *ou* **parvenu à ses ~s** he got his way in the end, he achieved his ends; **à cette ~** to this end, with this end in view; **à quelle ~ faites-vous cela?** what is your purpose in doing that?; **c'est à plusieurs ~s** it has a variety of purposes; **à seule ~ de faire** for the sole purpose of doing; (*frm*) **à toutes ~s utiles** for your information, on a point of information; *V* **qui.**

2: fin de non-recevoir (*Jur*) demurrer, objection; (*fig*) blunt refusal; (*péj*) **fin de race** *adj inv* degenerate; **fin de section** *[autobus]* stage limit; (*Can*) **fin de semaine** weekend; (*Comm*) **fin de série** oddment; (*péj*) **fin de siècle** *adj inv* decadent, fin de siècle.

final, e[1], *mpl* **~s** [final] **1** *adj* **(a)** (*terminal*) final; *V* **point**[1].

(b) (*marquant la finalité: Ling, Philos*) final. (*Ling*) **proposition ~e** purpose *ou* final clause.

2 *nm* (*Mus*) finale.

3 finale *nf* **(a)** (*Sport*) final. **quart de ~e** quarter final; **demi-~e** semifinal.

(b) (*syllabe*) final *ou* last syllable; (*voyelle*) final *ou* last vowel.

finale[2] [final] *nm* (*Mus*) finale.

finalement [finalmɑ̃] *adv* (*à la fin*) in the end, finally; (*en conclusion*) finally; (*après tout*) really, when it comes down to it*.

finalisme [finalism(ə)] *nm* finalism.

finaliste [finalist(ə)] **1** *adj* (*Philos*) finalist. **2** *nmf* (*Philos, Sport*) finalist.

finalité [finalite] *nf* finality.

finance [finɑ̃s] *nf* **(a)** (*Pol*) (*recettes et dépenses*) **~s** finances; (*administration*) **les F~s** ≈ the Treasury, the Exchequer (*Brit*), the Treasury Department (*US*); **il est aux F~s** *[employé]* he works at the Treasury; *[ministre]* he has the Exchequer; **l'état de mes ~s*** the state of my finances, my financial state; **les** *ou* **mes ~s sont à sec*** (my) funds are exhausted; *V* **loi, ministre.**

(b) (*Fin*) finance. **la (haute) ~** (*activité*) (high) finance; (*personne*) (top) financiers; *V* **moyennant.**

financement [finɑ̃smɑ̃] *nm* financing.

financer [finɑ̃se] (3) **1** *vt* to finance, back (*with money*), put up the money for. **2** *vi* (*) to fork out*.

financier, -ière [finɑ̃sje, jɛʀ] **1** *adj* **(a)** (*Fin*) financial. **soucis ~s** money *ou* financial worries; *V* **marché, place. (b)** (*Culin*) **(sauce) ~ière** sauce financière; **quenelles (sauce) ~ière** quenelles sauce financière. **2** *nm* financier.

financièrement [finɑ̃sjɛʀmɑ̃] *adv* financially.

finasser* [finase] (1) *vi* to use trickery. **inutile de ~ avec moi!** there's no point trying to use your tricks on me!

finasserie* [finasʀi] *nf* trick, dodge, ruse.

finassier, -ière [finasje, jɛʀ] *nm,f* trickster, dodger.

finaud, e [fino, od] **1** *adj* wily. **2** *nm* wily bird. **c'est un petit ~*** he's as crafty as they come*, there are no flies on him*, he's nobody's fool. **3 finaude** *nf* crafty minx.

finauderie [finodʀi] *nf* (*U*) wiliness, guile; (*action*) wile, dodge.

fine[2] [fin] *nf* **(a)** (*alcool*) liqueur brandy, fine. **~ Champagne** fine champagne; *V* **fin**[1]. **(b)** (*huître*) **~ de claire** green oyster.

finement [finmɑ̃] *adv ciselé, brodé* finely, delicately; *faire remarquer* subtly; *agir, manœuvrer* cleverly, shrewdly.

finesse [finɛs] *nf* **(a)** (*minceur*) *[cheveux, poudre]* fineness; *[pointe]* fineness, sharpness; *[lame]* keenness, sharpness; *[écriture]* smallness, neatness; *[taille]* slenderness, slimness; *[couche, papier]* thinness.

(b) (*raffinement*) *[broderie, porcelaine, travail, traits]* delicacy, fineness; *[aliments, mets]* delicacy, choiceness. **son visage est d'une grande ~** he has very refined *ou* delicate features.

(c) (*sensibilité*) *[sens]* sharpness, sensitivity; *[vue, odorat, goût]* sharpness, keenness; *[ouïe]* sharpness, acuteness, keenness.

(d) (*subtilité*) *[personne]* sensitivity; *[esprit, observation, allusion]* subtlety.

(e) ~s *[langue, art]* niceties, finer points; *[affaire]* ins and outs; **il connaît toutes les ~s** he knows all the tricks *ou* the ins and outs.

fini, e [fini] (*ptp de* **finir**) **1** *adj* **(a)** (*terminé*) finished, over. **tout est ~ entre nous** it's all over between us, we're finished, we're through*; **~e la rigolade!*** the party* *ou* the fun is over!; **(c'est) ~ de rire maintenant** the fun *ou* joke is over now.

(b) (*) *acteur, homme politique* finished; *chose* finished, done (*attrib*). **il est ~** he is finished, he is a has-been*.

(c) (*usiné, raffiné*) finished. **produits ~s** finished goods *ou* articles; **costume bien/mal ~** well-/badly-finished suit.

(d) (*péj: complet*) *menteur, escroc, ivrogne* utter, out-and-out.

(e) (*Math, Philos*) finite.

2 *nm [ouvrage]* finish. **ça manque de ~** it needs a few finishing touches.

finir [finiʀ] (2) **1** *vt* **(a)** (*achever*) *travail, études, parcours* to finish, complete; (*clôturer*) *discours, affaire* to end, conclude. **finis ton travail** *ou* **de travailler avant de partir** finish your work before you leave; **il a fini ses jours à Paris** he ended his days in Paris; **finis ton pain!** finish your bread!, eat up your bread!; **il finira (d'user) sa veste en jardinant** he can wear out his old jacket (doing the) gardening; **il a fini son temps** *[soldat, prisonnier]* he has done *ou* served his time.

(b) (*arrêter*) to stop (*de faire* doing). **finissez donc!** do stop it!; **finissez de vous plaindre!** stop complaining!; **vous n'avez pas fini de vous chamailler!** haven't you done enough squabbling!, can't you stop your squabbling!

(c) (*parachever*) *œuvre d'art, meuble, mécanisme* to put the finishing touches to.

2 *vi* **(a)** (*se terminer*) to finish, end. **le cours finit à deux heures** the class finishes *ou* ends at two; **les vacances finissent demain** the holidays are over tomorrow; **la réunion/le jour finissait** the meeting/the day was drawing to a close; **le sentier finit ici** the path ends *ou* comes to an end here *ou* tails off here; **il est temps que cela finisse** it's time it (was) stopped; **ce film finit bien** this film has a happy ending; **tout cela va mal ~** it will all have a sorry end, it will all end in disaster.

(b) *[personne]* to finish up, end up. **il finira mal** he will come to a bad end; **il finira en prison** he will end up in prison; **~ dans la misère** to end one's days *ou* end up in poverty.

(c) (*mourir*) to die. **il a fini dans un accident de voiture** he died in a car accident.

(d) ~ en qch to end in sth; **ça finit en pointe/en chemin de terre** it ends in a point/in a path.

(e) ~ par se décider/remarquer/trouver to make up one's mind/notice/find in the end *ou* eventually; **~ par une dispute/un concert** to end in an argument/with a concert; **il a fini par se décider** he finally *ou* eventually made up his mind, he made up his mind in the end; **tu finis par m'ennuyer** you're beginning to annoy me; *V* **queue.**

(f) en ~ avec qch/qn to have *ou* be done with sth/sb; **il faut en ~ avec cette situation** we'll have to put an end to this situation; **nous en aurons bientôt fini** we'll soon be finished with it, we'll soon have it over and done with; **quand en auras-tu fini avec tes jérémiades?** when will you ever stop moaning?; **je vais lui parler pour qu'on en finisse** I'll talk to him so that we can get the matter settled; **pour vous en ~** to cut the story short; **qui n'en finit pas, à n'en plus ~** *route, discours, discussions* never-ending, endless; **elle n'en finit pas de se préparer** she takes an age to get ready, her preparations are a lengthy business; **on n'en aurait jamais fini de raconter ses bêtises** you could go on for ever recounting the stupid things he has done; **il a des jambes qui n'en finissent pas** he's all legs*.

finish [finiʃ] *nm* (*Sport*) finish. **combat au ~** fight to the finish.

finissage [finisaʒ] *nm* (*Couture, Tech*) finishing.

finisseur, -euse [finisœʀ, øz] *nm,f* **(a)** (*Couture, Tech*) finisher. **(b)** (*Sport*) good *ou* strong finisher.

finition [finisjɔ̃] *nf* (*action*) finishing; (*résultat*) finish. **la ~ est parfaite** the finish is perfect; (*Couture*) **faire les ~s** to put the finishing touches; (*Constr*) **travaux de ~** finishing off.

finlandais, e [fɛ̃lɑ̃dɛ, ɛz] **1** *adj* Finnish. **2** *nm* (*Ling*) Finnish. **3** *nm,f*: **F~(e)** Finn.

Finlande [fɛ̃lɑ̃d] *nf* Finland.

finnois, e [finwa, waz] **1** *adj* Finnish. **2** *nm* (*Ling*) Finnish. **3** *nm,f*: **F~(e)** Finn.

finno-ougrien, -ienne [finɔugʀijɛ̃, ijɛn] *adj, nm* (*Ling*) Finno-Ugric, Finno-Ugrian.

fiole [fjɔl] *nf* phial, flask; (*: *tête*) face, mug*.

fiord [fjɔʀ(d)] *nm* = **fjord.**

fioriture [fjɔrityʀ] *nf [dessin]* flourish; (*Mus*) fioritura. **~s de style** flourishes *ou* embellishments of style, frills.

firmament [fiʀmamɑ̃] *nm* (*littér*) firmament (*littér*). (*fig*) **au ~ de** at the height of.

firme [fiʀm(ə)] *nf* firm.

fisc [fisk] *nm* ≈ Inland Revenue (*Brit*), ≈ Internal Revenue (*US*). **agent du ~** ≈ Inland Revenue official (*Brit*), ≈ Collector of Internal Revenue (*US*).

fiscal, e, *pl* **-aux** [fiskal, o] *adj* fiscal, tax (*épith*). **l'année ~e** the tax *ou* fiscal year; **timbre ~** revenue *ou* fiscal stamp; **politique ~e** tax *ou* fiscal policy; *V* **fraude.**

fiscalisation [fiskalizɑsjɔ̃] *nf [revenus]* making subject to tax; *[prestation sociale]* funding by taxation.

fiscaliser [fiskalize] (1) *vt revenus* to make subject to tax; *prestation sociale* to fund by taxation.

fiscalité [fiskalite] *nf* (*système*) tax system; (*impôts*) taxation.

fissible [fisibl(ə)] *adj* fissile, fissionable.

fissile [fisil] *adj* (*Géol*) tending to split; (*Phys*) fissile, fissionable.

fission [fisjɔ̃] *nf* fission. **~ de l'atome** atomic fission.

fissuration [fisyʀɑsjɔ̃] *nf* fissuring, cracking, splitting.

fissure [fisyʀ] *nf* (*lit*) crack, fissure; (*fig*) crack; (*Anat*) fissure.

fissurer [fisyʀe] (1) **1** *vt* to crack, fissure; (*fig*) to split. **2 se fissurer** *vpr* to crack, fissure.

fiston* [fistɔ̃] *nm* son, lad, junior (*US*). **dis-moi, ~** tell me, son *ou* sonny* *ou* laddie*.

fistulaire [fistylɛʀ] *adj* fistular, fistulous.

fistule [fistyl] *nf* fistula.

fistuleux, -euse [fistylø, øz] *adj* fistulous.

five o'clock [fajvɔklɔk] *nm* (†, *hum*) (afternoon) tea.

fixage [fiksaʒ] *nm* (*Art, Phot, Tex*) fixing.

fixateur [fiksatœʀ] *nm* (*Art*) fixative spray; (*Coiffure*) hair cream; (*avant la mise en plis*) setting lotion; (*Phot*) fixer. **bain ~** fixing bath.

fixatif [fiksatif] *nm* fixative.

fixation [fiksɑsjɔ̃] *nf* **(a)** (*Chim, Psych, Zool*) fixation; (*Phot*) fixing. **(b)** (*attache*) fastening. (*Ski*) **~ (de sécurité)** (safety) binding. **(c)** *[peuple]* settling. **(d)** *[salaires, date]* fixing.

fixe [fiks(ə)] **1** *adj* **(a)** (*immobile*) *point, panneau* fixed; *emploi* permanent, steady; *regard* vacant, fixed. **regarder qn les yeux ~s** to gaze *ou* look fixedly *ou* intently at sb, fix an unblinking gaze *ou* stare on sb; *V* **barre, domicile** *etc.*

(b) (*prédéterminé*) *revenu* fixed; *jour, date* fixed, set. **à heure ~** at a set time, at set times; *V* **prix.**

(c) (*inaltérable*) *couleur* fast, permanent. **encre bleu ~** permanent blue ink; *V* **idée.**

2 *nm* basic *ou* fixed salary.

fixe-chaussettes [fiksʃosɛt] *nm inv* garter.

fixer [fikse] (1) **1** *vt* **(a)** (*attacher*) to fix, fasten (*à, sur* to). (*fig*) **~ qch dans sa mémoire** to fix sth firmly in one's memory.

(b) (*décider*) *date* to fix, arrange, set. **~ la date/l'heure d'un rendez-vous** to arrange *ou* set *ou* fix the date/the time for a meeting; (*fig*) **~ son choix sur qch** to decide *ou* settle on sth; **mon choix s'est fixé sur cet article** I settled *ou* decided on this article; (*fig*) **je ne suis pas encore fixé sur ce que je ferai I**

haven't made up my mind what to do yet, I haven't got any fixed plans in mind yet; **avez-vous fixé le jour de votre départ?** have you decided what day you are leaving (on)?; **à l'heure fixée** at the agreed *ou* appointed time; **au jour fixé** on the appointed day.

(c) *regard, attention* to fix. ~ **les yeux sur qn/qch,** ~ **qn/qch du regard** to stare at sb/sth; **il le fixa longuement** he looked hard *ou* stared at him; ~ **son attention sur** to focus one's attention on; **mon regard se fixa sur lui** I fixed my gaze on him, my gaze fastened on him.

(d) (*déterminer*) *prix, impôt, délai* to fix, set; *règle, principe* to lay down, determine; *idées* to clarify, sort out; *conditions* to lay down, set. **les droits et les devoirs fixés par la loi** the rights and responsibilities laid down *ou* determined by law; ~ **ses idées sur le papier** to set one's ideas down on paper; (*Ling*) **mot fixé par l'usage** word fixed by usage; (*Ling*) **l'orthographe s'est fixée** the spelling has become fixed.

(e) (*renseigner*) ~ **qn sur qch*** to put sb in the picture about sth*, enlighten sb as to sth; **être fixé sur le compte de qn** to be wise to sb*, have sb weighed up* (*Brit*) *ou* sized up* *ou* taped* (*Brit*); **alors, es-tu fixé maintenant?*** have you got the picture now?*

(f) ~ **qn** to make sb settle (down); **seul le mariage pourra le** ~ marriage is the only thing that will make him settle down.

(g) (*Phot*) to fix.

2 se fixer *vpr* (*s'installer*) to settle. **il s'est fixé à Lyon** he settled in Lyons.

fixité [fiksite] *nf [opinions]* fixity, fixedness; *[regard]* steadiness.

fjord [fjɔʀ(d)] *nm* fiord, fjord.

flac [flak] *excl* splash!

flaccidité [flaksidite] *nf* flabbiness, flaccidity.

flacon [flakɔ̃] *nm* (small, stoppered) bottle; (*Chim*) flask.

flafla* [flafla] *nm*: **faire des** ~**s** to show off.

flagellateur [flaʒɛlatœʀ] *nm* flogger, scourger, flagellator (*frm*).

flagellation [flaʒɛlɑsjɔ̃] *nf* flogging, flagellation (*frm*); (*Rel*) scourging.

flagelle [flaʒɛl] *nm* flagellum.

flagellé, e [flaʒele] (*ptp de* **flageller**) *adj, nm* (*Zool*) flagellate.

flageller [flaʒele] (1) *vt* to flog, scourge, flagellate (*frm*); (*Rel*) to scourge; (*fig*) to flay. ~ **le vice** to castigate vice.

flageoler [flaʒɔle] (1) *vi*: ~ **(sur ses jambes)** (*de faiblesse*) to be sagging at the knees; (*de peur*) to quake at the knees.

flageolet [flaʒɔlɛ] *nm* **(a)** (*Mus*) flageolet. **(b)** (*Bot*) flageolet, dwarf kidney bean.

flagorner [flagɔʀne] (1) *vt* (*frm*) to toady to, fawn upon.

flagornerie [flagɔʀnəʀi] *nf* (*frm, hum*) toadying (*U*), fawning (*U*), sycophancy (*U*).

flagorneur, -euse [flagɔʀnœʀ, øz] (*frm*) **1** *adj* toadying, fawning, sycophantic. **2** *nm,f* toady, fawner, sycophant.

flagrant, e [flagʀɑ̃, ɑ̃t] *adj mensonge* blatant; *erreur* flagrant, blatant, glaring; *injustice* glaring, blatant. **prendre qn en** ~ **délit** to catch sb red-handed *ou* in the act *ou* in flagrante delicto (*T*); **pris en** ~ **délit de mensonge** caught out blatantly lying.

flair [flɛʀ] *nm [chien]* sense of smell, nose; (*fig*) sixth sense, intuition.

flairer [fleʀe] (1) *vt* **(a)** to smell (at), sniff (at); (*Chasse*) to scent. **(b)** (*fig*) to scent, sense, smell. ~ **quelque chose de louche** to smell *ou* scent something fishy, smell a rat; ~ **le danger** to sense *ou* scent danger.

flamand, e [flamɑ̃, ɑ̃d] **1** *adj* Flemish. **2** *nm* **(a) F**~ Fleming; les **F**~s the Flemish. **(b)** (*Ling*) Flemish. **3 F**~**e** *nf* Flemish woman.

flamant [flamɑ̃] *nm* flamingo. ~ **rose** (pink) flamingo.

flambage [flɑ̃baʒ] *nm* **(a)** *[volaille]* singeing; *[instrument]* sterilizing (*with flame*). **(b)** (*Tech*) buckling.

flambant [flɑ̃bɑ̃] *adv*: ~ **neuf** brand new.

flambart*†, **flambard***† [flɑ̃baʀ] *nm* swankpot*. **faire le** *ou* **son** ~ to swank*.

flambé, e[1]‡ [flɑ̃be] (*ptp de* **flamber**) *adj personne* finished. **il est** ~! he's had it!*; **l'affaire est** ~**e!** that's torn it!* (*Brit*).

flambeau, *pl* ~**x** [flɑ̃bo] *nm* **(a)** (flaming) torch; *V* **retraite**. **(b)** (*fig, frm*) torch. **passer le** ~ **à qn** to pass on *ou* hand on the torch to sb. **(c)** (*chandelier*) candlestick.

flambée[2] [flɑ̃be] *nf* **(a)** (*feu*) (quick) blaze. **(b)** (*fig*) *[violence]* outburst; *[prix]* explosion. ~ **de colère** angry outburst, flare-up.

flambement [flɑ̃bmɑ̃] *nm* (*Tech*) buckling.

flamber [flɑ̃be] (1) **1** *vi [bois]* to burn; *[feu]* to blaze, flame; *[incendie]* to blaze. **la maison a flambé en quelques minutes** in a few minutes the house was ablaze *ou* blazing.

2 *vt* **(a)** *crêpe* to flambé.

(b) *volaille, cheveux* to singe; (*Méd*) *aiguille, instrument de chirurgie* to sterilize (*in a flame*).

flamboiement [flɑ̃bwamɑ̃] *nm [flammes]* blaze, blazing; *[lumière]* blaze; *[yeux]* flash, gleam. **dans un** ~ **de couleurs** in a blaze of colour.

flamboyant, e [flɑ̃bwajɑ̃, ɑ̃t] **1** *adj* **(a)** *feu, lumière* blazing; *yeux* flashing, blazing; *couleur* flaming; *regard* fiery; *ciel, soleil* blazing; *épée, armure* gleaming, flashing. **(b)** (*Archit*) flamboyant. **2** *nm* (*Archit*) flamboyant style.

flamboyer [flɑ̃bwaje] (8) *vi [flamme]* to blaze (up), flame (up); *[yeux]* to flash, blaze; *[soleil, ciel]* to blaze; *[couleur]* to flame; *[épée, armure]* to gleam, flash.

flamingant, e [flamɛ̃gɑ̃, ɑ̃t] **1** *adj* Flemish-speaking. **2** *nm,f*: **F**~**(e)** Flemish speaker; (*Pol*) Flemish nationalist.

flamme [flam] *nf* **(a)** (*lit*) flame. **être en** ~**s, être la proie des** ~**s** to be on fire *ou* ablaze; (*Aviat, fig*) **descendre (qch/qn) en** ~**s** to shoot (sth/sb) down in flames; **dévoré par les** ~**s** consumed by fire *ou* the flames.

(b) (*fig: ardeur*) fire, fervour. **discours plein de** ~ passionate *ou* fiery speech; **jeune homme plein de** ~ young man full of fire.

(c) (*fig: éclat*) fire, brilliance. **la** ~ **de ses yeux** *ou* **de son regard** his flashing eyes.

(d) (*littér: amour*) love, ardour (*littér*).

(e) (*drapeau*) pennant, pennon.

flammé, e [flame] *adj céramique* flambé.

flammèche [flamɛʃ] *nf* (flying) spark.

flan [flɑ̃] *nm* **(a)** (*Culin*) custard tart. **(b)** (*Tech*) *[imprimeur]* flong; *[monnaie]* blank, flan; *[disque]* mould. **(c)** (*) **il en est resté comme deux ronds de** ~ you could have knocked him down with a feather*; **c'est du** ~ it's a load of waffle!* (*surtout Brit*) *ou* hooey*.

flanc [flɑ̃] *nm* **(a)** *[personne]* side; *[animal]* side, flank. (†, *littér*) **l'enfant qu'elle portait dans son** ~ the child she was carrying in her womb; **être couché sur le** ~ to lie *ou* be lying on one's side; **tirer au** ~* to skive‡ (*Brit*), swing the lead*; **être sur le** ~ to be laid up; (‡*fig*) to be all in*; **cette grippe m'a mis sur le** ~ that bout of flu has knocked me out*; *V* **battre**.

(b) *[navire]* side; *[armée]* flank; *[montagne]* slope, side. **à** ~ **de coteau** *ou* **de colline** on the hillside; **prendre de** ~ (*Naut, fig*) to catch broadside on; (*Mil*) to attack on the flank; *V* **prêter**.

flancher* [flɑ̃ʃe] (1) *vi* *[cœur]* to pack up* (*surtout Brit*); *[troupes]* to quit. **sa mémoire a flanché** his memory failed him; **c'est le moral qui a flanché** he lost his nerve; **il a flanché en math** he fell down *ou* came down in maths; **sans** ~ without flinching; **ce n'est pas le moment de** ~ this is no time for weakening *ou* weakness.

flanchet [flɑ̃ʃɛ] *nm* (*Boucherie*) flank.

Flandre(s) [flɑ̃dʀ(ə)] *nf(pl)* Flanders.

flandrin [flɑ̃dʀɛ̃] *nm* (††, *péj*) **grand** ~ great gangling fellow.

flanelle [flanɛl] *nf* (*Tex*) flannel.

flâner [flɑne] (1) *vi* to stroll, saunter; (*péj*) to hang about, lounge about. **va chercher du pain, et sans** ~! go and get some bread, and get a move on!*

flânerie [flɑnʀi] *nf* stroll, saunter; (*péj*) idling *ou* lounging about (*U*). **perdre son temps en** ~**s** to idle one's time away.

flâneur, -euse [flɑnœʀ, øz] **1** *adj* idle. **2** *nm,f* stroller; (*péj*) idler, lounger, loafer.

flanquer[1] [flɑ̃ke] (1) *vt* to flank. **la boutique qui flanque la maison** the shop adjoining *ou* flanking the house; **flanqué de ses gardes du corps** flanked by his bodyguards; (*péj*) **il est toujours flanqué de sa mère** he always has his mother in tow* *ou* at his side.

flanquer[2]* [flɑ̃ke] (1) **1** *vt* **(a)** (*jeter*) ~ **qch par terre** (*lit*) to fling sth to the ground; (*fig*) to put paid to sth, knock sth on the head*; ~ **qn par terre** to fling sb to the ground; ~ **qn à la porte** to chuck sb out‡; (*licencier*) to sack sb*, give sb the sack*, fire sb; ~ **tout en l'air** to pack it all in* (*Brit*), chuck it all up‡.

(b) (*donner*) ~ **une gifle à qn** to cuff sb round the ear, give sb a clout*; ~ **la trouille à qn** to give sb a scare, put the wind up sb*; ~ **2 ans de prison à qn** to send sb down (*Brit*) *ou* put sb inside for 2 years.

2 se flanquer‡ *vpr*: **se** ~ **par terre** to fall flat on one's face, measure one's length.

flapi, e [flapi] *adj* dog-tired*, dead-beat*.

flaque [flak] *nf*: ~ **de sang/d'eau** *etc* pool of blood/water *etc*; (*petite flaque*) ~ **d'eau** puddle.

flash [flaʃ] *nm* **(a)** (*Phot*) flash(light). **au** ~ by flash(light). **(b)** (*Rad, TV*) newsflash; (*Ciné*) flash.

flasque[1] [flask(ə)] *adj peau* flaccid, flabby; (*fig*) *personne* spineless, spiritless; *style* limp.

flasque[2] [flask(ə)] *nf* flask.

flasque[3] [flask(ə)] *nm* **(a)** (*Aut*) hub cap; *[tracteur]* wheel disc. **(b)** (*Mil*) cheek.

flatté, e [flate] (*ptp de* **flatter**) *adj portrait* flattering.

flatter [flate] (1) **1** *vt* **(a)** (*flagorner*) to flatter. ~ **servilement qn** to fawn upon sb; (*fig*) **cette photo la flatte** this photo flatters her.

(b) (*faire plaisir*) *[compliment, décoration]* to flatter, gratify. **je suis très flatté de cet honneur** I am most flattered by this honour; **cela le flatte dans son orgueil** it flatters his vanity.

(c) (*frm: favoriser*) *manie, goûts* to pander to; *vice, passion* to encourage.

(d) (*littér: tromper*) ~ **qn d'un espoir** to hold out false hopes to sb; ~ **qn d'une illusion** to delude sb.

(e) (*frm: charmer*) *oreille, regard* to delight, charm, be pleasing to; *goût* to flatter. ~ **le palais** to delight the taste buds.

(f) (*frm: caresser*) to stroke, pat.

2 se flatter *vpr* (*frm*) **(a)** (*prétendre*) **se** ~ **de faire** to claim *ou* profess to be able to do; **il se flatte de tout comprendre** he professes to understand everything; **je me flatte de le persuader en 10 minutes** I flatter myself that I can persuade him in 10 minutes.

(b) (*s'enorgueillir*) **se** ~ **de qch** to pride o.s. on sth; **elle se flatte de son succès** she prides herself on her success; **et je m'en flatte!** and I'm proud of it!

(c) (*se leurrer*) to delude o.s. **se** ~ **d'un vain espoir** to cherish a forlorn hope; **s'il croit réussir, il se flatte!** if he thinks he can succeed, he is deluding himself!

flatterie [flatʀi] *nf* flattery (*U*). (*littér, hum*) **vile** ~ base flattery.

flatteur, -euse [flatœʀ, øz] **1** *adj* flattering. **comparaison** ~**euse** flattering comparison; **faire un tableau** ~ **de la situation** to paint a rosy picture of the situation; **ce n'est pas** ~! it's not very flattering. **2** *nm,f* flatterer. (*littér, hum*) **c'est un vil** ~ he's a base flatterer.

flatteusement [flatøzmɑ̃] *adv* flatteringly.
flatulence [flatylɑ̃s] *nf* wind, flatulence.
flatulent, e [flatylɑ̃, ɑ̃t] *adj* flatulent.
fléau, *pl* **~x** [fleo] *nm* **(a)** (*calamité*) scourge, curse; (**fig*) plague, bane. **(b)** *[balance]* beam; (*Agr*) flail.
fléchage [fleʃaʒ] *nm* arrowing, signposting (with arrows).
flèche[1] [flɛʃ] **1** *nf* **(a)** arrow, shaft (*littér*). **~ en caoutchouc** rubber-tipped dart; (*fig*) **les ~s de l'Amour** *ou* **de Cupidon** Cupid's darts *ou* arrows; **monter en ~** (*lit*) to rise like an arrow; (*fig*) to soar, rocket; **c'est un acteur qui monte en ~** this actor is shooting to the top *ou* rocketing to fame; **les prix sont montés en ~** prices have shot up *ou* rocketed; **partir comme une ~** to set off like a shot; **il est passé devant nous comme une ~** he shot past us.
(b) (*fig: critique*) **diriger ses ~s contre qn** to direct one's shafts against sb; **la ~ du Parthe** the Parthian shot; **faire ~ de tout bois** to use all means available to one; **il fait ~ de tout bois** it's all grist to his mill, he'll use any means he can.
(c) (*direction*) (direction) arrow, pointer.
(d) *[église]* spire; *[grue]* jib; *[mât]* pole; *[affût, canon]* trail; *[balance]* pointer; *[charrue]* beam; *[attelage]* pole. **atteler en ~** to drive tandem; **cheval de ~** lead horse.
2: flèche lumineuse (*sur l'écran*) arrow; (*torche*) arrow pointer.
flèche[2] [flɛʃ] *nf* (*Culin*) flitch.
flécher [fleʃe] (1) *vt* to arrow, mark (with arrows). **parcours fléché** arrowed course, course marked *ou* signposted with arrows.
fléchette [fleʃɛt] *nf* dart. **jouer aux ~s** to play darts.
fléchir [fleʃiʀ] (2) **1** *vt* **(a)** (*plier*) to bend; (*Méd*) *articulation* to flex; (*fig*) to bend. **~ le genou devant qn** to bend *ou* bow the knee to *ou* before sb.
(b) (*fig: apaiser*) *personne* to sway; *colère* to soothe.
2 *vi* **(a)** (*gén*) to bend; *[planches]* to sag, bend; *[armées]* to give ground, yield; *[genoux]* to sag; *[volonté]* to weaken; *[attention]* to flag; *[recettes, talent, nombre]* to fall off; (*Bourse*) *[prix]* to ease, drop. **ses jambes** *ou* **ses genoux fléchirent** his knees sagged.
(b) (*s'apaiser*) to yield, soften, be moved. **il fléchit devant leurs prières** he yielded to *ou* was moved by their entreaties; **il s'est laissé ~** he allowed himself to be won round *ou* persuaded *ou* swayed.
fléchissement [fleʃismɑ̃] *nm* (*V* **fléchir**) bending; flexing; bowing; soothing; sagging; yielding; weakening; flagging; falling off; easing off, drop; softening; swaying.
fléchisseur [fleʃisœʀ] *adj m, nm* (*Anat*) **(muscle) ~** flexor.
flegmatique [flɛgmatik] *adj* phlegmatic.
flegmatiquement [flɛgmatikmɑ̃] *adv* phlegmatically.
flegme [flɛgm(ə)] *nm* composure, phlegm. **il perdit son ~** he lost his composure *ou* cool*.
flemmard, e* [flemaʀ, aʀd(ə)] **1** *adj* bone-idle*, workshy. **2** *nm,f* idler, loafer, slacker.
flemmarder* [flemaʀde] (1) *vi* to loaf about, lounge about.
flemme* [flɛm] *nf* laziness. **j'ai la ~ de le faire** I can't be bothered doing it; **tirer sa ~** to idle around, loaf about.
flet [flɛ] *nm* flounder.
flétan [fletɑ̃] *nm* halibut.
flétrir[1] [fletʀiʀ] (2) **1** *vt* (*faner*) to wither, fade. **l'âge a flétri son visage** age has withered his face. **2 se flétrir** *vpr [fleur]* to wither, wilt; *[beauté]* to fade; *[peau]* to wither; (*fig*) *[cœur]* to wither.
flétrir[2] [fletʀiʀ] (2) *vt* **(a)** (*stigmatiser*) *personne, conduite* to condemn; *réputation* to blacken. **(b)** (*Hist*) to brand.
flétrissure[1] [fletʀisyʀ] *nf [fleur, peau]* withered state; *[teint]* fading.
flétrissure[2] [fletʀisyʀ] *nf* **(a)** *[réputation, honneur]* stain, blemish (*à* on). **(b)** (*Hist*) brand.
fleur [flœʀ] **1** *nf* **(a)** flower; *[arbre]* blossom, bloom. **en ~(s)** in bloom, in blossom, in flower; **papier à ~s** flowered *ou* flower-patterned *ou* flowery paper; **assiette à ~s** flower-patterned *ou* flowery plate; **ni ~s ni couronnes** no flowers by request; (*fig*) **couvrir qn de ~s** to shower praise on sb.
(b) (*le meilleur*) **la ~ de** the flower of; **à** *ou* **dans la ~ de l'âge** in the prime of life, in one's prime; **il est dans la ~ de sa jeunesse** he is in the full bloom *ou* blush (*littér*) of youth; (†, *hum*) **perdre sa ~** to lose one's honour (†, *hum*); *V* **fin**[1].
(c) (*loc*) **comme une ~*** hands down*, without trying; **il est arrivé le premier comme une ~** he won hands down*, he romped home (to win); **à ~ de terre** just above the ground; **un écueil à ~ d'eau** a reef just above the water *ou* which just breaks the surface of the water; **j'ai les nerfs à ~ de peau** I'm all on edge, my nerves are all on edge; **sensibilité à ~ de peau** superficial sensitivity; **faire une ~ à qn*** to do sb an unexpected good turn *ou* an unexpected favour; **s'envoyer des ~s** (*réfléchi*) to pat o.s. on the back*; (*réciproque*) to pat each other on the back*; (*hum*) **~ bleue** naïvely sentimental; **il est resté ~ bleue en vieillissant** even in his old age he is still a bit of a romantic.
2: fleur de farine fine wheaten flour; **fleurs de givre** frost patterns; (*Hér*) **fleur de lis** fleur-de-lis; **fleurs d'oranger** orange blossom; **fleurs de rhétorique/de soufre/de vin** flowers of rhetoric/sulphur/wine.
fleuraison [flœʀɛzɔ̃] *nf* = **floraison.**
fleurdelisé, e [flœʀdəlize] *adj* decorated with fleurs-de-lis.
fleurer [flœʀe] (1) *vt* (*littér*) to have the scent of, smell sweetly of. **ça fleure bon le pain grillé** there's a lovely smell of toast; **~ bon la lavande** to smell (sweetly) of *ou* have the scent of lavender.
fleuret [flœʀɛ] *nm* (*épée*) foil.
fleurette [flœʀɛt] *nf* (†, *hum*) floweret; *V* **conter.**
fleuri, e [flœʀi] (*ptp de* **fleurir**) *adj* **(a)** *fleur* in bloom; *branche* in blossom; *jardin, pré* in flower *ou* bloom; *tissu, papier* flowered, flowery; *appartement* decorated *ou* decked out with flowers; *table* decorated *ou* decked with flowers. **à la boutonnière ~e** (*avec une fleur*) wearing *ou* sporting a flower in his buttonhole; (*avec une décoration*) wearing a decoration in his buttonhole.
(b) *nez d'ivrogne* red; *teint* florid; (*fig*) *style* flowery, florid. (*hum*) **une barbe ~e** a flowing white beard.
fleurir [flœʀiʀ] (2) **1** *vi* **(a)** *[arbre]* to blossom, (come into) flower; *[fleur]* to flower, (come into) bloom; (*hum*) *[menton d'adolescent]* to grow downy, begin to sprout a beard; *[visage]* to come out in spots *ou* pimples; (*littér*) *[qualité, sentiment]* to blossom (*littér*). **un sourire fleurit sur ses lèvres** his lips broke into a smile.
(b) (*imparfait* **florissait,** *prp* **florissant**) *[commerce, arts]* to flourish, prosper, thrive.
2 *vt salon* to decorate with *ou* deck out with flowers. **~ une tombe/un mort** to put flowers on a grave/on sb's grave; (*frm*) **~ une femme** to offer a flower to a lady; **~ sa boutonnière** to put a flower in one's buttonhole; **un ruban fleurissait (à) sa boutonnière** he was wearing a decoration on his lapel; **fleurissez-vous, mesdames, fleurissez-vous!** treat yourselves to some flowers, ladies!, buy yourselves a buttonhole (*Brit*) *ou* boutonnière (*US*), ladies!
fleuriste [flœʀist(ə)] *nmf* (*personne*) florist; (*boutique*) florist's (shop).
fleuron [flœʀɔ̃] *nm [couronne]* floweret; *[bâtiment]* finial; (*fig*) *[collection]* jewel. (*fig*) **c'est le plus beau ~ de ma collection** it's the finest jewel *ou* piece in my collection.
fleuve [flœv] **1** *nm* (*lit*) river. **~ de boue/de lave** river of mud/of lava; **~ de larmes** flood of tears; **~ de sang** river of blood. **2** *adj inv* marathon (*épith*), interminable; *V* **roman**[1].
flexibilité [flɛksibilite] *nf* flexibility.
flexible [flɛksibl(ə)] **1** *adj métal* flexible, pliable, pliant; *branche, roseau* pliable, pliant; *caractère* (*accommodant*) flexible, adaptable; (*malléable*) pliant, pliable. **2** *nm* (*câble*) flexible coupling; (*tuyau*) flexible tubing *ou* hose.
flexion [flɛksjɔ̃] *nf* **(a)** (*courbure*) *[ressort, lame d'acier]* flexion, bending; *[poutre, pièce]* bending, sagging. **résistance à la ~** bending strength.
(b) *[membre, articulation]* flexing, bending. **faire plusieurs ~s du bras/du corps** to flex the arm/bend the body several times.
(c) (*Ling*) inflection, inflexion. **langue à ~** inflected language.
flexionnel, -elle [flɛksjɔnɛl] *adj langue, désinence* inflexional, inflectional, inflected.
flexueux, -euse [flɛksɥø, øz] *adj* flexuous, flexuose.
flexuosité [flɛksɥozite] *nf* flexuosity.
flexure [flɛksyʀ] *nf* flexure.
flibuste [flibyst(ə)] *nf* (*piraterie*) freebooting, buccaneering; (*pirates*) freebooters, buccaneers.
flibustier [flibystje] *nm* (*pirate*) freebooter, buccaneer; (*†: *escroc*) swindler, crook.
flic* [flik] *nm* cop*, copper*, policeman. **les ~s** the cops*, the police.
flicaille: [flikaj] *nf*: **la ~** the cops*, the fuzz:, the bulls: (*US*).
flic flac [flikflak] *excl* splash! **ses chaussures font ~ dans la boue** his shoes slop in the mud *ou* go splash splash through the mud.
flingot: [flɛ̃go] *nm*, **flingue:** [flɛ̃g] *nm* gun, rod:, gat:.
flinguer: [flɛ̃ge] (1) *vt* to gun down, put a bullet in. (*fig*) **il y a de quoi se ~!** it's enough to make you want to end it all! *ou* make you shoot yourself!
flint(-glass) [flint(glas)] *nm* flint glass.
flipper[1] [flipœʀ] *nm* (*billard électrique*) pin-ball machine.
flipper[2]: [flipe] (1) *vi* (*être déprimé*) to sag*; (*être exalté*) to flip:, be high:.
flirt [flœʀt] *nm* **(a)** (*U: action*) flirting (*U*); (*amourette*) brief romance. **avoir un ~ avec qn** to have a brief romance with sb. **(b)** (*amoureux*) boyfriend.
flirter [flœʀte] (1) *vi* to flirt. (*fréquenter*) **~ avec qn** to go about with sb; (*fig*) **~ avec** *idée, parti* to flirt with.
flirteur, -euse [flœʀtœʀ, øz] *nm,f* flirt.
floc [flɔk] *nm, excl* plop, splash.
flocon [flɔkɔ̃] *nm [neige]* flake; *[écume]* fleck; *[laine]* flock. **~s d'avoine** oat flakes, rolled oats; **~s de maïs** cornflakes; **la neige tombe à gros ~s** the snow is falling in big flakes; **purée en ~s** dehydrated potato flakes.
floconneux, -euse [flɔkɔnø, øz] *adj nuage, étoffe* fluffy; *écume, substance, liquide* frothy.
flonflons [flɔ̃flɔ̃] *nmpl* blare. **les ~ de la musique foraine** the blaring music of the fairground.
flopée* [flɔpe] *nf*: **une ~ de** loads of*, masses of; **il y a une** *ou* **des ~(s) de touristes** there are masses of tourists.
floraison [flɔʀɛzɔ̃] *nf* **(a)** (*lit*) (*épanouissement*) flowering, blossoming; (*époque*) flowering time. **rosiers qui ont plusieurs ~s** rosebushes which have several flowerings. **(b)** (*fig*) *[talents]* flowering, blossoming; *[affiches, articles]* rash, crop.
floral, e, *mpl* **-aux** [flɔʀal, o] *adj* **(a)** *art, composition* floral; *exposition* flower (*épith*). **(b)** (*Bot*) *enveloppe, organes* floral.
floralies [flɔʀali] *nfpl* flower show.
flore [flɔʀ] *nf* (*plantes*) flora; (*livre*) plant guide. **~ intestinale** intestinal flora.
floréal [flɔʀeal] *nm* Floreal (eighth month in the French Republican calendar).
Florence [flɔʀɑ̃s] *n* (*ville*) Florence.
florentin, e [flɔʀɑ̃tɛ̃, in] **1** *adj* Florentine. **2** *nm* (*Ling*) Florentine dialect. **2** *nm,f*: **F~(e)** Florentine.

florès [flɔʀɛs] *nm* (*littér, hum*) **faire ~** *[personne]* to shine, enjoy (great) success; *[théorie]* to enjoy (great) success, be in vogue.
floriculture [flɔʀikyltyʀ] *nf* flower-growing, floriculture (*T*).
florifère [flɔʀifɛʀ] *adj* (*qui a des fleurs*) flower-bearing; (*qui porte beaucoup de fleurs*) which is a prolific flowerer.
florilège [flɔʀilɛʒ] *nm* anthology.
florin [flɔʀɛ̃] *nm* florin.
florissant, e [flɔʀisɑ̃, ɑ̃t] *adj pays, économie, théorie* flourishing; *santé, teint* blooming.
flot [flo] *nm* **(a)** (*littér*) *[lac, mer]* **~s** waves; **les ~s** the waves; **voguer sur les ~s bleus** to sail the ocean blue; (*fig*) **les ~s de sa chevelure** her flowing locks *ou* mane (*littér*).
(b) (*fig: grande quantité*) *[boue]* stream; *[véhicules, visiteurs, insultes]* flood, stream; *[larmes, lettres]* flood, spate. **un** *ou* **des ~(s) de rubans/dentelle** a cascade of ribbons/lace.
(c) (*marée*) **le ~** the floodtide, the incoming tide.
(d) (*loc*) **à (grands) ~s** in streams *ou* torrents; **l'argent coule à ~s** money flows like water; **la lumière entre à ~s** light is streaming in *ou* flooding in *ou* pouring in; **être à ~** (*lit*) *[bateau]* to be afloat; (*fig*) *[personne, entreprise]* to be on an even keel; *[personne]* to have one's head above water; **remettre à ~** *bateau* to refloat; *entreprise* to bring back onto an even keel; (*lit, fig*) **mettre à ~** to launch; **la mise à ~ d'un bateau** the launching of a ship.
flottabilité [flɔtabilite] *nf* buoyancy.
flottable [flɔtabl(ə)] *adj bois, objet* buoyant; *rivière* floatable.
flottage [flɔtaʒ] *nm* floating (of logs down a river).
flottaison [flɔtɛzɔ̃] *nf*: **ligne de ~** waterline.
flottant, e [flɔtɑ̃, ɑ̃t] **1** *adj* **(a)** *bois, glace, mine* floating; *brume* drifting; *V* **île, virgule.**
(b) *cheveux, cape* (loose and) flowing; *vêtement* loose.
(c) (*Fin, Pol*) floating; *effectifs* fluctuating. **dette ~e** floating debt.
(d) *caractère, esprit* irresolute, vacillating. **rester ~** to be unable to make up one's mind (*devant* when faced with).
(e) (*Méd*) *rein* floating.
2 *nm* (*short*) shorts.
flotte [flɔt] *nf* **(a)** (*Aviat, Naut*) fleet. **(b)** (*) (*pluie*) rain; (*eau*) water. **(c)** (*flotteur*) float.
flottement [flɔtmɑ̃] *nm* **(a)** (*hésitation*) wavering, hesitation. **on observa un certain ~ dans la foule** certain parts of the crowd were seen to waver *ou* hesitate; **il y a eu un ~ électoral important** there was strong evidence *ou* a strong element of indecision among voters.
(b) (*Mil: dans les rangs*) swaying, sway.
(c) (*relâchement*) (*dans une œuvre, copie*) vagueness, imprecision; (*dans le travail*) unevenness (*dans* in). **le ~ de son esprit/imagination** his wandering mind/roving imagination.
(d) (*ondulation*) *[fanion]* fluttering. **le ~ du drapeau dans le vent** the fluttering *ou* flapping of the flag in the wind.
(e) (*Fin*) floating.
flotter [flɔte] (1) **1** *vi* **(a)** (*lit: sur l'eau*) to float. **faire ~ qch sur l'eau** to float sth on the water.
(b) (*fig: au vent*) *[brume]* to drift, hang; *[parfum]* to hang; *[cheveux]* to stream (out); *[drapeau]* to fly, flap; *[fanion]* to flutter. *[cape, écharpe]* **~ au vent** to flap *ou* flutter in the wind.
(c) (*être trop grand*) *[vêtement]* to hang loose. **il flotte dans ses vêtements** his clothes hang baggily *ou* loosely about him, his clothes are too big for him.
(d) (*littér: errer*) *[pensée, imagination]* to wander, rove. **un sourire flottait sur ses lèvres** a smile hovered on *ou* played about his lips.
(e) (*fig: hésiter*) to waver, hesitate.
(f) (*Fin*) *[devise]* to float. **faire ~** to float.
2 *vb impers* (*: *pleuvoir*) to rain.
3 *vt bois* to float (down a waterway).
flotteur [flɔtœʀ] *nm* *[filet, hydravion, carburateur]* float; *[chasse d'eau]* ballcock.
flottille [flɔtij] *nf* *[bateaux, bateaux de guerre]* flotilla; *[avions]* squadron.
flou, e [flu] **1** *adj* **(a)** *dessin, trait, contour* blurred; *image* hazy, vague; *photo* blurred, fuzzy; *couleur* soft.
(b) *robe* loose(-fitting); *coiffure* soft, loosely waving.
(c) *idée, pensée, théorie* woolly, vague.
2 *nm* *[photo, tableau]* fuzziness; *[couleur]* softness; *[robe]* looseness. **le ~ de son esprit** the vagueness *ou* woolliness (*péj*) of his mind.
flouer*† [flue] (1) *vt* (*duper*) to diddle*, swindle. **se faire ~** to be taken in, be had*.
fluctuation [flyktɥasjɔ̃] *nf* *[prix]* fluctuation; *[opinion publique]* swing, fluctuation (*de* in).
fluctuer [flyktɥe] (1) *vi* to fluctuate.
fluet, -ette [flyɛ, ɛt] *adj corps* slight, slender; *personne* slightly built, slender; *taille, membre, doigt* slender, slim; *voix* thin, reedy, piping.
fluide [flɥid] **1** *adj liquide, substance* fluid; *style* fluid, flowing; *ligne, silhouette* flowing; (*Écon*) *main d'œuvre* flexible. **la circulation est ~** traffic flows freely; **la situation politique reste ~** the political situation remains fluid.
2 *nm* (*gaz, liquide*) fluid; (*fig: pouvoir*) (mysterious) power. **il a du ~, il a un ~ magnétique** he has mysterious powers.
fluidification [flɥidifikɑsjɔ̃] *nf* fluidification, fluxing.
fluidifier [flɥidifje] (7) *vt* to fluidify, flux.
fluidité [flɥidite] *nf* *[liquide, style]* fluidity; *[ligne, silhouette]* flow; *[circulation]* free flow; (*Écon*) *[main d'œuvre]* flexibility.
fluor [flyɔʀ] *nm* fluorine.
fluorescéine [flyɔʀesein] *nf* fluorescein.
fluorescence [flyɔʀesɑ̃s] *nf* fluorescence.
fluorescent, e [flyɔʀesɑ̃, ɑ̃t] *adj* fluorescent.
fluorine [flyɔʀin] *nf* fluorspar, fluorite, calcium fluoride.
fluorure [flyɔʀyʀ] *nm* fluoride.
flush [flœʃ] *nm* (*Cartes*) flush.
flûte [flyt] **1** *nf* **(a)** (*instrument*) flute; (*verre*) flute, flute glass; (*pain*) long French loaf. (*Mus*) **petite ~** piccolo; (*jambes*) **~s*** pins*; **se tirer les ~s**‡ to skip off*, do a bunk‡; *V* **bois, jouer.**
(b) (*Hist: navire*) store ship.
2 *excl* (*) drat it!*, dash it!* (*Brit*).
3: **flûte à bec** recorder; **La Flûte enchantée** The Magic Flute; **flûte de Pan** panpipes, Pan's pipes; **flûte traversière** transverse flute.
flûté, e [flyte] *adj voix* flute-like, fluty.
flûteau, *pl* **~x** [flyto] *nm*, **flutiau**, *pl* **~x** [flytjo] *nm* (*flûte*) reed pipe, (simple) flute; (*mirliton*) mirliton.
flûtiste [flytist(ə)] *nmf* flautist, flutist.
fluvial, e, *mpl* **-aux** [flyvjal, o] *adj eaux, pêche, navigation* river (*épith*); *érosion* fluvial (*epith*).
fluvio-glaciaire [flyvjɔglasjɛʀ] *adj* fluvioglacial.
flux [fly] *nm* **(a)** (*grande quantité*) *[argent]* flood; *[paroles, récriminations]* flood, spate.
(b) (*marée*) floodtide, incoming tide. **le ~ et le reflux** the ebb and flow.
(c) (*Phys*) flux, flow. **~ électrique/magnétique/lumineux** electric/magnetic/luminous flux.
(d) (*Méd*) **~ de sang** flow of blood; **~ menstruel** menstrual flow.
fluxion [flyksjɔ̃] *nf* (*Méd*) swelling, inflammation; (*dentaire*) gumboil. **~ de poitrine** pneumonia.
foc [fɔk] *nm* jib. **grand/petit ~** outer/inner jib; **~ d'artimon** mizzen-topmast staysail.
focal, e, *mpl* **-aux** [fɔkal, o] **1** *adj* focal. **2 focale** *nf* (*Géom, Opt*) focal distance *ou* length.
focaliser [fɔkalize] (1) **1** *vt* (*Phys, fig*) to focus (*sur* on). **2 se focaliser** *vpr* to be focused (*sur* on).
Foehn [føn] *nm* foehn.
foène, foëne [fwɛn] *nf* pronged harpoon, fish gig.
fœtal, e, *mpl* **-aux** [fetal, o] *adj* foetal, fetal.
fœtus [fetys] *nm* foetus, fetus.
fofolle [fɔfɔl] *adj f V* **fou-fou.**
foi [fwa] *nf* **(a)** (*croyance*) faith. **avoir la ~** to have (a religious) faith; **perdre la ~** to lose one's faith; **il faut avoir la ~!*** you've got to be (really) dedicated!; **il n'y a que la ~ qui sauve!** faith is a marvellous thing!; **la ~ du charbonnier** blind (and simple) faith; **sans ~ ni loi** fearing neither God nor man; *V* **article, profession.**
(b) (*confiance*) faith, trust. **avoir ~ en Dieu** to have faith *ou* trust in God; **avoir ~ en qn/qch/l'avenir** to have faith in sb/sth/the future; **digne de ~** *témoin* reliable, trustworthy; *témoignage* reliable; *V* **ajouter.**
(c) (*assurance*) (pledged) word. **respecter la ~ jurée** to honour one's (sworn *ou* pledged) word; **~ d'honnête homme!** on my word as a gentleman!, on my word of honour!; **cette lettre en fait ~** this letter proves *ou* attests it; **les réponses doivent être envoyées avant le 10 janvier à minuit, la date de la poste faisant ~** replies must be postmarked no later than midnight January 10th; **sous la ~ du serment** under *ou* on oath; **sur la ~ de vagues rumeurs** on the strength of vague rumours; **sur la ~ des témoins** on the word *ou* testimony of witnesses; **en ~ de quoi j'ai décidé ...** (*gén*) on the strength of which I have decided ...; (*Jur*) in witness whereof I have decided ...; **(être) de bonne/mauvaise ~** (to be) sincere/insincere, (be) honest/dishonest.
(d) ma ~ ... well ...; **ma ~, c'est comme ça, mon vieux** well, that's how it is, old chap; **ça, ma ~, je n'en sais rien** well, I don't know anything about that; **c'est ma ~ vrai que ...** well it's certainly *ou* undeniably true that ...
foie [fwa] *nm* **(a)** liver. **~ de veau/de volaille** calf's/chicken liver; **~ gras** foie gras. **(b) avoir les ~s**‡ to be scared to death*.
foin[1] [fwɛ̃] *nm* hay. **faire les ~s** to make hay; **à l'époque des ~s** in the haymaking season; **~ d'artichaut** choke; **faire du ~*** to kick up* a fuss *ou* row *ou* shindy* (*surtout Brit*); *V* **rhume.**
foin[2] [fwɛ̃] *excl* (††, *hum*) **~ des soucis d'argent/des créanciers!** a plague on money worries/creditors!, the devil take money worries/creditors!
foire [fwaʀ] *nf* **(a)** (*marché*) fair; (*exposition commerciale*) trade fair; (*fête foraine*) fun fair. **~ aux bestiaux** cattle fair *ou* market; *V* **larron.**
(b) (*loc*) **avoir la ~**†‡ to have the runs* *ou* skitters‡ (*Brit*); **faire la ~*** to whoop it up*, go on a spree; **c'est la ~ ici!, c'est une vraie ~!*** it's bedlam in here!, it's a proper madhouse!*; **c'est une ~ d'empoigne** it's a free-for-all.
foirer [fwaʀe] (1) *vi* (*) *[vis]* to slip; *[obus]* to hang fire; (‡) *[projet]* to fall through.
foireux, -euse‡ [fwaʀø, øz] *adj* (*peureux*) yellow(-bellied)‡.
fois [fwa] *nf* **(a)** time. **une ~** once; **deux ~** twice; **trois ~** three times; (*aux enchères*) **une ~, deux ~, trois ~ adjugé** going, going, gone!; **pour la toute première ~** for the very first time; **quand je l'ai vu pour la première/dernière ~** when I first/last saw him, the first/last time I saw him; **c'est bon** *ou* **ça va pour cette ~** I'll let you off this time *ou* (just) this once; **de ~ à autre**† from time to time, now and again; **plusieurs ~** several times, a number of times; **peu de ~** on few occasions; **bien des ~, maintes (et maintes) ~** many a time, many times; **autant de ~ que** as often as, as many times as; **y regarder à deux** *ou* **à plusieurs ~ avant d'acheter qch** to think twice *ou* very hard before buying sth; **s'y prendre à** *ou* **en 2/plusieurs ~ pour faire qch** to take 2/several attempts *ou* goes to do sth; **payer en plusieurs ~** to pay in several instalments; **frapper qn par deux/trois ~** to hit sb twice/three times; *V* **autre, encore, merci** *etc.*
(b) (*dans un calcul*) **une ~** once; **deux ~** twice; **trois/quatre** *etc* **~** three/four *etc* times; **une ~ tous les deux jours** once

every two days, once every other *ou* second day; **3 ~ par an, 3 ~ l'an†** 3 times a year; **9 ~ sur 10** 9 times out of 10; **4 ~ plus d'eau/de voitures** 4 times as much water/as many cars; **quatre ~ moins d'eau** four times less water, a quarter as much water; **quatre ~ moins de voitures** a quarter as many cars; (*Math*) **3 ~ 5 (font 15)** 3 times 5 (is *ou* makes 15); **il avait deux ~ rien** *ou* **trois ~ rien** (*argent*) he had absolutely nothing, he hadn't a bean*; (*blessure*) he had the merest scratch, he had nothing at all wrong with him; **et encore merci! — oh, c'est deux ~ rien** *ou* **trois ~ rien** and thanks again! — oh, please don't mention it!

(c) une ~ once; **il était une ~, il y avait une ~** once upon a time there was; (*Prov*) **une ~ n'est pas coutume** just the once will not hurt, once (in a while) does no harm; **pour une ~!** for once!; **en une ~** at *ou* in one go; **une (bonne) ~ pour toutes** once and for all; **une ~ (qu'il sera) parti** once he has left; **une ~ qu'il n'était pas là** once *ou* on one occasion when he wasn't there.

(d) (*) **des ~** (*parfois*) sometimes; **des ~, il est très méchant** he can be very nasty at times *ou* on occasion, sometimes he's pretty nasty; **si des ~ vous le rencontrez** if you should happen *ou* chance to meet him; **non mais, des ~!** (*scandalisé*) do you MIND!; (*en plaisantant*) you must be joking!; **des ~ que** (just) in case; **attendons, des ~ qu'il viendrait** let's wait in case he comes; **allons-y, des ~ qu'il resterait des places** let's go — there may be some seats left, let's go in case there are some seats left.

(e) à la ~ at once, at the same time; **ne répondez pas tous à la ~** don't all answer at once; **il était à la ~ grand et gros** he was both tall and fat; **il était à la ~ grand, gros et fort** he was tall, fat and strong as well; **faire deux choses à la ~** to do two things at once *ou* at the same time.

foison [fwazɔ̃] *nf*: **il y a du poisson/des légumes à ~** there is an abundance of fish/vegetables, there is fish/are vegetables in plenty; **il y en avait à ~ au marché** there was plenty of it *ou* there were plenty of them at the market.

foisonnement [fwazɔnmɑ̃] *nm* **(a)** (*épanouissement*) burgeoning; (*abondance*) profusion, abundance, proliferation. **(b)** *[chaux]* expansion.

foisonner [fwazɔne] (1) *vi* **(a)** *[idées, erreurs]* to abound. proliferate; *[gibier]* to abound. **pays qui foisonne de** *ou* **en matières premières** country which abounds in raw materials; **pays qui foisonne de** *ou* **en talents** country which has a profusion *ou* an abundance of talented people *ou* is teeming with talented people; **texte foisonnant d'idées/de fautes** text teeming with ideas/mistakes.

(b) *[chaux]* to expand.

fol [fɔl] *V* **fou.**

folâtre [fɔlɑtʀ(ə)] *adj enfant* playful, frisky, frolicsome; *gaieté, jeux* lively, jolly; *caractère* lively, sprightly. (*frm, hum*) **il n'est pas d'humeur ~** he's not in a playful mood.

folâtrer [fɔlɑtʀe] (1) *vi [enfants]* to frolic, romp; *[chiots, poulains]* to gambol, frolic, frisk. **au lieu de ~ tu ferais mieux de travailler** instead of playing about you would do better to work.

folâtrerie [fɔlɑtʀəʀi] *nf* (*littér*) (*U: caractère*) playfulness, sprightliness; (*action*) frolicking (*U*), romping (*U*), gambolling (*U*).

foliacé, e [fɔljase] *adj* foliated, foliaceous.

foliation [fɔljɑsjɔ̃] *nf* (*développement*) foliation, leafing; (*disposition*) leaf arrangement.

folichon, -onne* [fɔliʃɔ̃, ɔn] *adj* (*gén nég*) pleasant, interesting, exciting. **aller à ce dîner, ça n'a rien de ~** going to this dinner won't be much fun *ou* won't be very exciting; **la vie n'est pas toujours ~ne avec ma belle-mère** life's not always fun with my mother-in-law.

folie [fɔli] *nf* **(a)** (*U*) (*Méd*) madness, lunacy, insanity; (*gén*) madness, lunacy, folly. **il a un petit grain de ~*** there's a streak of eccentricity in his character; (*Méd*) **~ furieuse** raving madness; (*fig*) **c'est de la ~ douce** *ou* **pure** *ou* **furieuse** it's utter madness *ou* lunacy, it's sheer folly *ou* lunacy; **avoir la ~ des grandeurs** to have delusions of grandeur; **il a la ~ des timbres-poste** he is mad about stamps, he is stamp-mad*; **aimer qn à la ~** to be madly in love with sb, love sb to distraction; **il a eu la ~ de refuser** he was mad enough to refuse, he had the folly *ou* madness to refuse.

(b) (*bêtise, erreur, dépense*) extravagance. **il a fait des ~s dans sa jeunesse** he had his fling *ou* a really wild time in his youth; **des ~s de jeunesse** follies of youth, youthful indiscretions *ou* extravagances; **ils ont fait une ~ en achetant cette voiture** (*erreur*) they were mad *ou* crazy to buy that car; (*dépense importante*) it was wildly extravagant of them to buy that car; **vous avez fait des ~s en achetant ce cadeau** you have been far too extravagant in buying this present; **il ferait des ~s pour elle/pour la revoir** he would give *ou* do anything for her/to see her again; (*hum*) **je ferais des ~s pour un morceau de fromage** I would give *ou* do anything for a piece of cheese; **une nouvelle ~ de sa part** (*dépense*) another of his extravagances; (*projet*) another of his hare-brained schemes.

(c) (*Hist: maison*) pleasure house.

(d) les F~s Bergères the Folies Bergères.

folié, e [fɔlje] *adj* foliate.

folio [fɔljo] *nm* folio.

folklore [fɔlklɔʀ] *nm* folklore.

folklorique [fɔlklɔʀik] *adj* **(a)** *chant, costume* folk. **(b)** (*: *excentrique*) *personne, tenue, ambiance* outlandish. **la réunion a été assez ~** the meeting was a rather rum* (*surtout Brit*) *ou* weird *ou* quaint affair.

folk song [fɔlksɔ̃g] *nm* folk music.

folle [fɔl] *V* **fou.**

follement [fɔlmɑ̃] *adv* **(a)** *espérer, dépenser* madly. **~ amoureux** madly *ou* wildly in love, head over heels in love; **il se lança ~ à leur poursuite** he dashed after them in mad pursuit; **avant de te lancer ~ dans cette aventure** before rushing headlong into *ou* jumping feet first into this business.

(b) (*énormément*) *drôle, intéressant* madly, wildly. **on s'est ~ amusé** we had a fantastic* time; **il désire ~ lui parler** he is dying* to speak to her, he wants desperately to speak to her.

follet, -ette [fɔlɛ, ɛt] *adj* (*étourdi*) scatterbrained; *V* **feu¹, poil.**

follicule [fɔlikyl] *nm* follicle.

folliculine [fɔlikylin] *nf* folliculin.

fomentateur, -trice [fɔmɑ̃tatœʀ, tʀis] *nm,f* troublemaker, agitator, fomenter.

fomentation [fɔmɑ̃tɑsjɔ̃] *nf* fomenting, fomentation.

fomenter [fɔmɑ̃te] (1) *vt* (*lit, fig*) to foment, stir up.

fonçage [fɔ̃saʒ] *nm* (*V* **foncer³**) bottoming; sinking, boring; lining.

foncé, e [fɔ̃se] (*ptp de* **foncer**) *adj couleur* (*gén*) dark; (*tons pastels*) deep. **à la peau ~e** dark-skinned.

foncer¹ [fɔ̃se] (3) *vi* **(a)** (*: *aller à vive allure*) *[conducteur, voiture]* to tear* *ou* belt* *ou* hammer* along; *[coureur]* to charge* *ou* tear* along. **maintenant, il faut que je fonce** I must dash *ou* fly* now.

(b) (*se précipiter*) to charge (*vers* at, *dans* into). **~ sur** *ou* **vers l'ennemi/l'obstacle** to charge at *ou* make a rush at the enemy/obstacle; **le camion a foncé sur moi** the truck came charging straight at me; (*lit, fig*) **~ sur un objet** to make straight for *ou* make a beeline for an object; **~ dans la foule** *[camion, taureau, police]* to charge into the crowd; **~ (tête baissée) dans la porte/dans le piège** to walk straight into the door/straight *ou* headlong into the trap; (*fig*) **~ dans le brouillard** to forge ahead regardless, forge ahead in the dark; **la police a foncé dans le tas** the police charged in.

foncer² [fɔ̃se] (3) **1** *vt couleur* to make darker. **2** *vi [liquide, couleur]* to turn *ou* go darker.

foncer³ [fɔ̃se] (3) *vt tonneau* to bottom; *puits* to sink, bore; (*Culin*) *moule* to line.

fonceur, -euse [fɔ̃sœʀ, øz] *nm,f* man (*ou* woman) of tremendous drive *ou* of driving ambition.

foncier, -ière [fɔ̃sje, jɛʀ] *adj* **(a)** *impôt, revenu* land (*épith*); *noblesse, propriété* landed (*épith*). **propriétaire ~** landowner.

(b) *qualité, différence* fundamental, basic. **la malhonnêteté ~ière de ces pratiques** the fundamental *ou* basic dishonesty of these practices; **être d'une ~ière malhonnêteté** to have an innate streak of dishonesty.

foncièrement [fɔ̃sjɛʀmɑ̃] *adv* fundamentally, basically.

fonction [fɔ̃ksjɔ̃] *nf* **(a)** (*métier*) post, office. (*tâches*) **~s** office, duties; **entrer en ~s** *[employé]* to take up one's post; *[maire, président]* to come into *ou* take office, take up one's post; **de par ses ~s** by virtue of his office; **être en ~** to be in office; **la ~ publique** the public *ou* state service; **voiture/logement de ~** car/accommodation which goes with a post; *V* **démettre, exercice.**

(b) (*gén, Gram: rôle*) function. **~ biologique** biological function; **cet organe a pour ~ de, la ~ de cet organe est de** the function of this organ is to; (*Gram*) **avoir** *ou* **faire ~ de sujet** to function *ou* act as a subject; (*fig, hum*) **c'est la ~ qui crée l'organe** the organ is shaped by its function.

(c) (*Math*) **~ (algébrique)** (algebraic) function; (*Chim*) **~ acide** acid(ic) function; (*Math*) **être ~ de** to be a function of.

(d) (*loc*) **faire ~ de directeur/d'ambassadeur** to act as a manager/as an ambassador; **il n'y a pas de porte, ce rideau en fait ~** there is no door but this curtain serves the purpose *ou* does instead; **sa réussite est ~ de son travail** his success depends on how well he works; **en ~ de** according to.

fonctionnaire [fɔ̃ksjɔnɛʀ] *nmf* (*gén*) state servant *ou* employee; (*dans l'administration*) *[ministère]* ≃ civil servant; *[municipalité]* local authority employee. **haut ~** high-ranking *ou* top civil servant; **petit ~** minor (public) official; **les ~s de l'enseignement** state-employed teachers.

fonctionnarisation [fɔ̃ksjɔnaʀizɑsjɔ̃] *nf*: **la ~ de la médecine** the state takeover of medicine; **le gouvernement propose la ~ des médecins** the government proposes taking doctors into the public service.

fonctionnariser [fɔ̃ksjɔnaʀize] (1) *vt*: **~ qn** to make sb an employee of the state; (*dans l'administration*) to take sb into the public service; **~ un service** to take over a service (to be run by the state).

fonctionnarisme [fɔ̃ksjɔnaʀism(ə)] *nm* (*péj*) officialdom. **c'est le règne du ~** officialdom is taking over.

fonctionnel, -elle [fɔ̃ksjɔnɛl] *adj* functional.

fonctionnellement [fɔ̃ksjɔnɛlmɑ̃] *adv* functionally.

fonctionnement [fɔ̃ksjɔnmɑ̃] *nm [appareil, entreprise, institution]* working, functioning, operation; (*Méd*) *[organisme]* functioning. **en état de bon ~** in good working order; **pour assurer le (bon) ~ de l'appareil** to keep the machine in (good) working order; **pour assurer le (bon) ~ du service** to ensure the smooth running of the service; **panne due au mauvais ~ du carburateur** breakdown due to a fault *ou* a malfunction in the carburettor; **pendant le ~ de l'appareil** while the machine is in operation *ou* is functioning.

fonctionner [fɔ̃ksjɔne] (1) *vi [mécanisme, machine]* to work, function; *[entreprise]* to function, operate. **faire ~** *machine* to operate; **notre téléphone/télévision fonctionne mal** there's something wrong with our phone/television, our phone/television isn't working properly; **ça ne fonctionne pas** it's out of order, it's not working; **sais-tu faire ~ la machine à laver?** can you operate *ou* do you know how to work the washing machine?

fond [fɔ̃] **1** *nm* **(a)** *[récipient, vallée etc]* bottom; *[armoire]* back; *[jardin]* bottom, far end; *[pièce]* far end, back. (*Min*) **le ~** the (coal) face; **être/tomber au ~ de l'eau** to be at/fall to the bottom of the water; (*Min*) **travailler au ~** to work at *ou* on the (coal) face; (*Naut*) **envoyer par le ~** to send to the bottom; **y a-t-**

il beaucoup de ~? is it very deep?; **l'épave repose par 10 mètres de** ~ the wreck is lying 10 metres down; (*Naut*) **à** ~ **de cale** (down) in the hold; **le** ~ **de la gorge/l'œil** the back of the throat/eye; **au** ~ **du couloir** down the corridor, at the far end of the corridor; **au** ~ **de la boutique** at the back of the shop; **ancré au** ~ **de la baie** anchored at the (far) end of the bay; **village perdu au** ~ **de la province** village in the depths *ou* heart *ou* wilds of the country; **sans** ~ (*lit, fig*) bottomless; *V* **bas**[1], **double, fin**[1] *etc.*

(b) (*fig: tréfonds*) **le** ~ **de son cœur est pur** deep down his heart is pure; **savoir lire au** ~ **des cœurs** to be able to see deep (down) into people's hearts; **merci du** ~ **du cœur** I thank you from the bottom of my heart; **il pensait au** ~ **de son cœur** *ou* **de lui(-même) que** deep down he thought that, in his heart of hearts he thought that; **vous avez deviné/je vais vous dire le** ~ **de ma pensée** you have guessed/I shall tell you what I really think *ou* what my feelings really are; **regarder qn au** ~ **des yeux** to look deep into sb's eyes; **il a un bon** ~, **il n'a pas un mauvais** ~ he's basically a good person, he's a good person at heart *ou* bottom; **il y a chez lui un** ~ **d'honnêteté/de méchanceté** there's an ingrained honesty/maliciousness about him; **il y a un** ~ **de vérité dans ce qu'il dit** there's an element *ou* a grain of truth in what he says; **toucher le** ~ **de la douleur/misère** to plumb the depths of sorrow/misery.

(c) (*essentiel*) *[affaire, question, débat]* heart. **c'est là le** ~ **du problème** that's the heart *ou* core of the problem; **ce qui compose le** ~ **de son discours/de sa nourriture** what forms the basis of his speech/diet; **il faut aller jusqu'au** ~ **de cette histoire** we must get to the root of this business; **débat de** ~ background discussion; **ouvrage de** ~ basic work; (*Presse*) **article de** ~ leading article, leader.

(d) (*Littérat, gén: contenu*) content; (*Jur*) substance. **le** ~ **et la forme** content and form.

(e) (*arrière-plan*) *[tableau, situation]* background. **avec** ~ **musical** with background music, with music in the background; **blanc sur** ~ **noir** white on a black background; **ceci tranchait sur le** ~ **assez sombre de la conversation** this contrasted with the general gloom of the conversation; **avec cette sombre perspective pour** ~ with this gloomy prospect in the background; *V* **bruit, toile.**

(f) (*petite quantité*) drop. **versez-m'en juste un** ~ **(de verre)** pour me just a drop; **ils ont vidé les** ~**s de bouteilles** they emptied what was left in the bottles *ou* the dregs from the bottles; **il va falloir racler les** ~**s de tiroirs** we'll have to fish around* *ou* scrape around for pennies.

(g) (*lie*) sediment, deposit.

(h) (*Sport*) **de** ~ *épreuves, course, coureur* long-distance (*épith*); *V* **demi-, ski.**

(i) *[chapeau]* crown; *[pantalon]* seat. (*fig*) **c'est là que j'ai usé mes** ~**s de culotte** that's where I spent my early school years.

(j) (*loc*) **le** ~ **de l'air est frais*** it's a bit chilly, there's a nip in the air; **au** ~, **dans le** ~ (*sous les apparences*) at bottom; (*en fait*) basically, really; **il n'est pas méchant au** ~ he's not a bad sort basically *ou* at heart; **il fait semblant d'être désolé, mais dans le** ~ **il est bien content** he makes out he's upset but he's quite pleased really *ou* but deep down he's quite pleased; **dans le** ~ *ou* **au** ~, **ça ne change pas grand'chose** basically *ou* really, that makes no great difference; **étudier une question à** ~ to study a question thoroughly *ou* in depth; **il est soutenu à** ~ **par ses amis** he is backed up to the hilt by his friends; **visser un boulon à** ~ to screw a bolt (right) home; **à** ~ **de train** hell for leather*, full tilt; **de** ~ **en comble** *fouiller, détruire* from top to bottom; **ce retard bouleverse mes plans de** ~ **en comble** this delay throws my plans right out, this delay completely overturns my plans.

2: fond d'artichaut artichoke heart; **les fonds marins** the seabed; **fond de robe** (full-length) slip *ou* petticoat; **fond de teint** (make-up) foundation.

fondamental, e, *mpl* **-aux** [fɔ̃damɑ̃tal, o] *adj* (*essentiel*) *question, recherche, changement* fundamental, basic; (*foncier*) *égoïsme, incompréhension* basic, inherent, fundamental. **son** *ou* **note** ~**(e)** fundamental (note); **c'est** ~ it's a basic necessity *ou* truth.

fondamentalement [fɔ̃damɑ̃talmɑ̃] *adv vrai, faux* inherently, fundamentally; *modifier, opposer* radically, fundamentally. ~ **méchant/généreux** basically *ou* fundamentally malicious/generous; **cela vient** ~ **d'un manque d'organisation** that arises from a basic *ou* an underlying lack of organization, basically that arises from a lack of organization.

fondant, e [fɔ̃dɑ̃, ɑ̃t] **1** *adj neige* thawing, melting; *fruit* that melts in the mouth. **2** *nm* (*Culin*) fondant; (*Chim*) flux.

fondateur, -trice [fɔ̃datœʀ, tʀis] *nm,f* founder. **membre** ~ founder member.

fondation [fɔ̃dɑsjɔ̃] *nf* (*action*) foundation; (*institut*) foundation. (*Constr*) ~**s** foundations.

fondé, e [fɔ̃de] (*ptp de* **fonder**) **1** *adj* **(a)** *crainte, réclamation* well-founded, justified. **bien** ~ well-founded, fully justified; **mal** ~ ill-founded, groundless; **ce qu'il dit n'est pas** ~ what he says has no foundation, there are no grounds for what he says; ~ **sur des ouï-dire** based on hearsay.

(b) être ~ **à faire/croire/dire** to have good reason to do/believe/say, have (good) grounds for doing/believing/saying.

2: *nm* ~ **(de pouvoir)** (*Jur*) authorized representative; (*cadre bancaire*) senior banking executive.

fondement [fɔ̃dmɑ̃] *nm* **(a)** foundation. **sans** ~ without foundation, unfounded, groundless; **jeter les** ~**s de** to lay the foundations of. **(b)** (*hum: derrière*) fundament† (*hum*).

fonder [fɔ̃de] (1) **1** *vt* **(a)** (*créer*) *ville, parti, prix littéraire* to found; *commerce* to set up, found (*frm*); *famille* to start. ~ **un foyer** to start a home and family.

(b) (*baser*) to base, found (*sur* on). ~ **sa richesse sur** to build one's wealth on; ~ **une théorie sur** to base a theory on; ~ **tous ses espoirs sur** to place *ou* pin all one's hopes on.

(c) (*justifier*) *réclamation* to justify; *V* **fondé.**

2 se fonder *vpr*: **se** ~ **sur** *[personne]* to go by, go on, base o.s. on (*frm*); *[théorie, décision]* to be based on; **sur quoi vous fondez-vous pour l'affirmer?** what grounds do you have for maintaining this?

fonderie [fɔ̃dʀi] *nf* **(a)** (*usine d'extraction*) smelting works; (*atelier de moulage*) foundry. **(b)** (*action*) founding, casting.

fondeur [fɔ̃dœʀ] *nm* (*Métal*) caster.

fondre [fɔ̃dʀ(ə)] (41) **1** *vt* **(a)** (*liquéfier*) *substance* to melt; *argenterie, objet de bronze* to melt down; *minerai* to smelt; *neige* to melt, thaw; (*fig*) *dureté, résolution* to melt.

(b) (*couler*) *cloche, statue* to cast, found.

(c) (*réunir*) to combine, fuse together (*en* into).

(d) (*Peinture*) *couleur, ton* to merge, blend.

2 *vi* **(a)** (*à la chaleur*) (*gén*) to melt; *[neige]* to melt, thaw; (*dans l'eau*) to dissolve. **faire** ~ *beurre* to melt; *sel, sucre* to dissolve; *neige* to melt, thaw; **ce fruit/bonbon fond dans la bouche** this fruit/sweet melts in your mouth.

(b) (*fig*) *[colère, résolution]* to melt away; *[provisions, réserves]* to vanish; (*Culin: réduire*) to shrink. ~ **comme neige au soleil** to melt away *ou* vanish like the snow; **l'argent fond entre ses mains** money runs through his fingers; **cela fit** ~ **sa colère** at that his anger melted (away); **elle fondait sous ses caresses** she melted beneath his caresses; **j'ai fondu*** I've thinned down; **j'ai fondu de 5 kg** I've lost 5 kg; ~ **en larmes** to dissolve *ou* burst into tears.

(c) (*s'abattre*) ~ **sur qn** *[vautour, ennemi]* to swoop down on sb; *[malheurs]* to sweep down on sb.

3 se fondre *vpr* **(a)** *[cortèges, courants]* to merge (*en* into).

(b) se ~ **dans la nuit/brume** to fade (away) *ou* merge into the night/mist.

fondrière [fɔ̃dʀijɛʀ] *nf* pothole, rut, hole.

fonds [fɔ̃] *nm* **(a)** ~ **(de commerce)** business; **il possède le** ~ **mais pas les murs** he owns the business but not the property; ~ **de terre** land (*U*).

(b) (*ressources*) *[musée, bibliothèque]* collection; *[œuvre d'entraide]* fund. ~ **de secours/de solidarité/d'amortissement** relief/solidarity/sinking fund; ~ **de garantie** guarantee fund; **le F**~ **Monétaire International** the International Monetary Fund; (*fig*) **ce pays a un** ~ **folklorique très riche** this country has a rich fund of folklore *ou* a rich folk heritage.

(c) (*Fin: pl*) (*argent*) sums of money, money; (*capital*) funds, capital; (*pour une dépense précise*) funds. **pour transporter les** ~ to transport the money; **investir des** ~ **importants dans** to invest large sums of money *ou* a large amount of capital in; **réunir les** ~ **nécessaires à un achat** to raise the necessary funds for a purchase; ~ **publics/secrets** public/secret funds; **mise de** ~ **initiale** initial (capital) outlay; **ne pas être/être en** ~ to be out of/be in funds; **je lui ai prêté de l'argent, ça a été à** ~ **perdus** I lent him money, but I had to kiss it goodbye* *ou* say goodbye to it*; ~ **de roulement** working capital; *V* **appel, bailleur, détournement** *etc.*

fondu, e [fɔ̃dy] (*ptp de* **fondre**) **1** *adj* **(a)** (*liquide*) *beurre* melted; *métal* molten. **neige** ~**e** slush.

(b) (*Métal: moulé*) **statue de bronze** ~ cast bronze statue.

(c) (*fig*) *contours* blurred, hazy; *couleurs* blending.

2 *nm* **(a)** (*Peinture*) *[couleurs]* blend. **le** ~ **de ce tableau me plaît** I like the way the colours blend in this picture.

(b) (*Ciné*) ~ **(enchaîné)** dissolve; **fermeture en** ~ fade-out; **ouverture en** ~ fade-in.

3 fondue *nf* (*Culin*) (cheese) fondue. ~**e bourguignonne** fondue bourguignonne, meat fondue.

fongible [fɔ̃ʒibl(ə)] *adj* fungible.

fongicide [fɔ̃ʒisid] **1** *adj* fungicidal. **2** *nm* fungicide.

fontaine [fɔ̃tɛn] *nf* (*ornementale*) fountain; (*naturelle*) spring; (*murale*) fountain. (*fig*) ~ **de** fountain of; (*hum*) **cette petite, c'est une vraie** ~* this child turns on the taps at anything; (*Prov*) **il ne faut pas dire** ~ **je ne boirai pas de ton eau** don't burn your bridges *ou* your boats.

fontanelle [fɔ̃tanɛl] *nf* fontanelle.

fonte [fɔ̃t] *nf* **(a)** (*action*) *[substance]* melting; *[argenterie, objet de bronze]* melting down; *[minerai]* smelting; *[neige]* melting, thawing; *[cloche, statue]* casting, founding. **à la** ~ **des neiges** when the thaw comes, when the snow melts *ou* thaws.

(b) (*métal*) cast iron. ~ **brute** pig-iron; **en** ~ *tuyau, radiateur* cast-iron (*épith*).

(c) (*Typ*) fount.

fontes [fɔ̃t] *nfpl* holsters (*on saddle*).

fonts [fɔ̃] *nmpl*: ~ **baptismaux** (baptismal) font.

foot* [fut] *nm abrév de* **football.**

football [futbol] *nm* football, soccer. **jouer au** ~ to play football; *V* **ballon.**

footballeur [futbolœʀ] *nm* footballer, football *ou* soccer player.

footing [futiŋ] *nm* jogging (*U*). **faire du** ~ to go jogging; **faire un (petit)** ~ to go for a (little) jog.

for [fɔʀ] *nm*: **dans** *ou* **en son** ~ **intérieur** in one's heart of hearts, deep down inside.

forage [fɔʀaʒ] *nm [roche, paroi]* drilling, boring; *[puits]* sinking, boring.

forain, e [fɔʀɛ̃, ɛn] **1** *adj* fairground (*épith*); *V* **baraque, fête. 2** *nm* (*acteur*) (fairground) entertainer. **(marchand)** ~ stallholder.

forban [fɔʀbɑ̃] *nm* (*Hist: pirate*) pirate; (*fig: escroc*) shark, crook.

forçage [fɔʀsaʒ] *nm* (*Agr*) forcing.

forçat [fɔʀsa] *nm* (*bagnard*) convict; (*galérien, fig*) galley slave. **travailler comme un ~** to work like a (galley) slave; **c'est une vie de ~** it's (sheer) slavery.

force [fɔʀs(ə)] **1** *nf* **(a)** *[personne] (vigueur)* strength. **avoir de la ~** to have strength, be strong; **avoir de la ~ dans les bras** to be strong in the arm; **je n'ai plus la ~ de parler** I've no strength left to talk; **il ne connaît pas sa ~** he doesn't know his own strength; **à la ~ des bras** by the strength of one's arms; **à la ~ du poignet** (*lit*) (*grimper*) by the strength of one's arms; (*fig*) (*obtenir qch, réussir*) by the sweat of one's brow; **cet effort l'avait laissé sans ~** the effort had left him drained (of strength); **c'est une ~ de la nature** he's a mighty figure; **dans la ~ de l'âge** in the prime of life; **~ morale/intellectuelle** moral/intellectual strength; (*fig*) **c'est ce qui fait sa ~** that is where his great strength lies; *V* **bout, union.**

(b) (*violence*) force. **recourir/céder à la ~** to resort to/give in to force; **employer la ~ brutale** *ou* **brute** to use brute force; **la ~ prime le droit** might is right.

(c) (*ressources physiques*) **~s** strength; **reprendre des ~s** to get one's strength back, regain one's strength; **ses ~s l'ont trahi** his strength failed *ou* deserted him; **au-dessus de mes ~s** too much for me, beyond me; **frapper de toutes ses ~s** to hit as hard as one can *ou* with all one's might; **désirer qch de toutes ses ~s** to want sth with all one's heart.

(d) *[coup, vent, habitude]* force; *[argument]* strength, force; *[sentiment]* strength; *[alcool, médicament]* strength. **vent de ~ 4** force 4 wind; **dans toute la ~ du terme** in the fullest *ou* strongest sense of the word; **la ~ de l'évidence** the weight of evidence; **par la ~ des choses** by force of circumstance(s); **les ~s naturelles** *ou* **de la nature** the forces of nature; **les ~s aveugles du destin** the blind forces of fate; **les ~s vives du pays** the living strength of a country; **~ nous est/lui est d'accepter** we have/he has no choice but to accept, we are/he is forced to accept; **avoir ~ de loi** to have force of law; *V* **cas, idée, ligne**[1].

(e) (*Mil*) strength. **~s** forces; **notre ~ navale** our naval strength; (*Pol*) **les ~s de l'opposition** the opposition forces; **d'importantes ~s de police** large contingents of police; **armée d'une ~ de 10.000 hommes** army with a strength of 10,000 men; **être dans une position de ~** to be in a position of strength.

(f) (*valeur*) **les 2 joueurs sont de la même ~** the 2 players are evenly *ou* well matched; **ces 2 cartes sont de la même ~** these 2 cards have the same value; **il est de première ~ au bridge** he's a first-class bridge player, he's first-rate at bridge; **il est de ~ à le faire** he's equal to it, he's up to (doing) it*; **tu n'es pas de ~ à lutter avec lui** you're no match for him; **à ~s égales, à égalité de ~s** on equal terms.

(g) (*Phys*) force. (*Élec*) **la ~** 30-amp circuit; **~ de gravité** force of gravity; **~ centripète/centrifuge** centripetal/centrifugal force; (*Élec*) **faire installer la ~** to have a 30-amp *ou* cooker (*ou* immerser *etc*) circuit put in.

(h) (*loc*) **attaquer/arriver en ~** to attack/arrive in force; **ils étaient venus en ~** they had come in strength; (*Sport*) **passer un obstacle en ~** to get past an obstacle by sheer effort; **faire entrer qch de ~ dans** to cram *ou* force sth into; **faire entrer qn de ~** *ou* **par la ~ dans** to force sb to enter; **enlever qch de ~ à qn** to remove sth forcibly from sb, take sth from sb by force; **entrer de ~ chez qn** to force one's way into *ou* force an entry into sb's house; **affirmer avec ~** to insist, state firmly; **insister avec ~ sur un point** to insist strongly on a point; **vouloir à toute ~** to want absolutely *ou* at all costs; **obtenir qch par ~** to get sth by *ou* through force; **à ~ d'essayer, il a réussi** by dint of trying he succeeded; **à ~ de gentillesse** by dint of kindness; **à ~, tu vas le casser*** you'll end up breaking it; (*Naut*) **faire ~ de rames** to ply the oars; (*Naut*) **faire ~ de voiles** to cram on sail.

2 *adv* (†*hum*) many, a goodly number of (*hum*). **boire ~ bouteilles** to drink a goodly number of bottles; **avec ~ remerciements** with profuse thanks.

3: **force d'âme** fortitude, moral strength; **la force armée** the army, the military; **les forces armées** the armed forces; **force de caractère** strength of character; (*Élec*) **force contre-électromotrice** back electromotive force; **force de dissuasion** deterrent power; **les Forces Françaises Libres** the Free French (Forces); **force de frappe** strike force; **force d'inertie** force of inertia; (*Mil, Police*) **forces d'intervention** peace-keeping forces; **les forces de l'ordre** the police (*esp in cases of civil disorder*); **la force publique** the authorities charged with public order.

forcé, e [fɔʀse] (*ptp de* **forcer**) *adj* **(a)** (*imposé*) *cours, mariage* forced; (*poussé*) *comparaison* forced. **atterrissage ~** forced *ou* emergency landing; **prendre un bain ~** to take an unintended dip; **conséquence ~e** inevitable consequence; *V* **marche**[1], **travail**[1].

(b) (*feint*) *rire, sourire* forced; *amabilité* affected, put-on.

(c) (*) **c'est ~** there's no way round it*, it's inevitable; **c'est ~ que tu sois en retard** it's obvious you're going to be late.

forcement [fɔʀsəmɑ̃] *nm* forcing.

forcément [fɔʀsemɑ̃] *adv* inevitably. **ça devait ~ arriver** it was bound to happen, it was inevitable; **il le savait ~ puisqu'on le lui a dit** he must have known since he was told; **il est enrhumé — ~, il ne se couvre pas** he's got a cold — of course (he has), he doesn't wear warm clothes; **c'est voué à l'échec — pas ~** it's bound to fail — not necessarily.

forcené, e [fɔʀsəne] **1** *adj* (*fou*) deranged, out of one's wits (*attrib*) *ou* mind (*attrib*); (*acharné*) *ardeur, travail* frenzied; (*fanatique*) *joueur, travailleur* frenzied; *partisan, critique* fanatical.

2 *nm,f* maniac. (*hum*) **~ du travail** demon for work; (*hum*) **les ~s du vélo/de la canne à pêche** cycling/angling fanatics.

forceps [fɔʀsɛps] *nm* pair of forceps, forceps (*pl*).

forcer [fɔʀse] (3) **1** *vt* **(a)** (*contraindre*) to force, compel (*frm*). **~ qn à faire qch** to force sb to do sth, make sb do sth; **il est forcé de garder le lit** he is forced to stay in bed; **il a essayé de me ~ la main** he tried to force my hand; **~ qn au silence/à des démarches/à la démission** to force sb to keep silent/to take action/to resign.

(b) (*faire céder*) *coffre, serrure* to force; *porte, tiroir* to force (open); *blocus* to run; *barrage* to force; *ville* to take by force. **~ le passage** to force one's way through; (*fig*) **~ la porte de qn** to force one's way in; **~ la consigne** to bypass orders; **sa conduite force le respect/l'admiration** his behaviour commands respect/admiration; (*Sport*) **il a réussi à ~ la décision** he managed to settle *ou* decide the outcome.

(c) (*traquer*) *cerf, lièvre* to run *ou* hunt down; *ennemi* to track down. **la police a forcé les bandits dans leur repaire** the police tracked the gangsters down to their hideout.

(d) (*pousser*) *cheval* to override; *fruits, plantes* to force; *talent, voix* to strain; *allure* to increase; (*fig*) *destin* to tempt, brave. **votre interprétation force le sens du texte** your interpretation stretches *ou* twists the meaning of the text; (*fig*) **il a forcé la dose*** *ou* **la note*** he overdid it.

2 *vi* to overdo it, force it. **j'ai voulu ~, et je me suis claqué un muscle** I overdid it and pulled a muscle; **il a gagné sans ~*** he had no trouble winning*, he won easily; **ne force pas, tu vas casser la corde** don't force it or you'll break the rope; **arrête de tirer, tu vois bien que ça force** stop pulling – can't you see it's jammed?; **~ sur ses rames** to strain at one's oars; **il force un peu trop sur l'alcool*** he overdoes the drink a bit*.

3 se forcer *vpr* to force o.s., make an effort (*pour faire* to do). **il se force à travailler** he forces himself to work, he makes himself work.

forcing [fɔʀsiŋ] *nm* (*Boxe*) pressure. **faire le ~** to pile on the pressure; **négociations menées au ~** negotiations conducted under pressure.

forcir [fɔʀsiʀ] (2) *vi* to broaden out.

forclore [fɔʀklɔʀ] (45) *vt* (*Jur*) to debar.

forclusion [fɔʀklyzjɔ̃] *nf* (*Jur*) debarment.

forer [fɔʀe] (1) *vt roche, paroi* to drill, bore; *puits* to sink, bore.

forestier, -ière [fɔʀɛstje, jɛʀ] **1** *adj région, végétation, chemin* forest (*épith*). **exploitation ~ière** (*activité*) forestry, lumbering; (*lieu*) forestry site; *V* **garde**[2]. **2** *nm* forester.

foret [fɔʀɛ] *nm* drill.

forêt [fɔʀɛ] *nf* (*lit, fig*) forest. **~-galerie** gallery forest; **~ vierge** virgin forest; *V* **arbre, eau.**

foreuse [fɔʀøz] *nf* drill.

forfaire [fɔʀfɛʀ] (60) *vi* (*frm*) **~ à qch** to be false to sth, betray sth; **~ à l'honneur** to forsake honour.

forfait [fɔʀfɛ] *nm* **(a)** (*Comm*) fixed *ou* set price. **travailler au ~** to work for a flat rate *ou* fixed sum; **notre nouveau ~-vacances** our new holiday package; **à ~** for a fixed sum; **nous payons un ~ qui comprend la location et les réparations éventuelles** we pay a set price which includes the hire and any repairs.

(b) (*Sport: abandon*) withdrawal, scratching. **gagner par ~** to win by default, win by a walkover*; **déclarer ~** to withdraw.

(c) (*littér: crime*) infamy (*littér*).

forfaitaire [fɔʀfɛtɛʀ] *adj* inclusive. **indemnité ~** inclusive payment, lump sum payment; **voyage à prix ~** package *ou* (all-)inclusive holiday *ou* tour.

forfaitairement [fɔʀfɛtɛʀmɑ̃] *adv payer, évaluer* on an inclusive basis.

forfaiture [fɔʀfetyʀ] *nf* (*Jur*) abuse of authority; (*Hist*) felony; (*littér: crime*) act of treachery.

forfanterie [fɔʀfɑ̃tʀi] *nf* (*caractère*) boastfulness; (*acte*) bragging (*U*).

forge [fɔʀʒ(ə)] *nf* (*atelier*) forge, smithy; (*fourneau*) forge; (†: *fonderie*) ironworks; *V* **maître.**

forger [fɔʀʒe] (3) *vt* **(a)** *métal* to forge; (*fig*) *caractère* to form, mould. (*littér*) **~ des liens** to forge bonds; (*Prov*) **c'est en forgeant qu'on devient forgeron** practice makes perfect (*Prov*); **il s'est forgé une réputation d'homme sévère** he has won *ou* earned himself the reputation of being a stern man; **se ~ un idéal** to create an ideal for o.s.; **se ~ des illusions** to build up illusions; *V* **fer.**

(b) (*inventer*) *mot* to coin; *exemple, prétexte* to contrive, make up; *histoire, mensonge, plan* to concoct. **cette histoire est forgée de toutes pièces** this story is a complete fabrication.

forgeron [fɔʀʒəʀɔ̃] *nm* blacksmith, smith; *V* **forger.**

formalisation [fɔʀmalizɑsjɔ̃] *nf* formalization.

formaliser [fɔʀmalize] (1) **1** *vt* to formalize. **2 se formaliser** *vpr* to take offence (*de* at).

formalisme [fɔʀmalism(ə)] *nm* **(a)** (*péj*) formality. **pas de ~ ici** we don't stand on ceremony here; **s'encombrer de ~** to weigh o.s. down with formalities. **(b)** (*Art, Philos*) formalism.

formaliste [fɔʀmalist(ə)] **1** *adj* **(a)** (*péj*) formalistic. **(b)** (*Art, Philos*) formalist. **2** *nmf* formalist.

formalité [fɔʀmalite] *nf* (*Admin*) formality. (*fig*) **ce n'est qu'une ~** it's a mere formality; (*fig*) **sans autre ~** without any more *ou* further ado.

formant [fɔʀmɑ̃] *nm* **(a)** (*Ling, Phonétique*) formant. **(b)** = **formatif.**

format [fɔʀma] *nm [livre]* format, size; *[papier, objet]* size. **en ~ de poche** in pocket format; **papier ~ international** A4 paper (*Brit*).

formateur, -trice [fɔʀmatœʀ, tʀis] *adj élément, expérience* formative.

formatif, -ive [fɔʀmatif, iv] **1** *adj langue* inflected, flexional; *préfixe* formative. **2 formative** *nf* (*Ling*) formative.

formation [fɔʀmɑsjɔ̃] *nf* **(a)** (*U: développement*) *[gouvernement, croûte, fruits]* formation, forming. **à (l'époque de) la ~** *[adolescent]* at puberty; *[fruit]* when forming; **parti en voie** *ou* **en cours de ~** party in the process of formation.

(b) (*apprentissage*) training. **la ~ du caractère** the forming *ou* moulding of character; **~ d'ingénieur** training as an engineer; **il a reçu une ~ littéraire** he received a literary education; **~ des maîtres/professionnelle** teacher/professional training.

(c) (*Aviat, Bio, Géol, Ling, Mil, Pol*) formation. (*Aviat*) **voler en ~** to fly in formation; **~ musicale** music group.

forme [fɔʀm(ə)] *nf* **(a)** (*contour, apparence*) form, shape. **cet objet est de ~ ronde/carrée** this object is round/square, this object has a round/square shape; **en ~ de poire/cloche** pear-/bell-shaped; **elle a des ~s gracieuses** she has a graceful form *ou* figure; **vêtement qui moule les ~s** clinging *ou* figure-hugging garment; **une ~ apparut dans la nuit** a form *ou* figure appeared out of the darkness; **n'avoir plus ~ humaine** to be unrecognizable; **sans ~** *chapeau* shapeless; *pensée* formless; **prendre la ~ d'un rectangle** to take the form *ou* shape of a rectangle; **prendre la ~ d'un entretien** to take the form of a talk; **prendre ~** *[statue, projet]* to take shape; **sous ~ de comprimés** in tablet form; **sous la ~ d'un vieillard** in the guise of *ou* as an old man; **sous toutes ses ~s** in all its forms.

(b) (*genre*) *[civilisation, gouvernement]* form. **les ~s d'énergie** the forms of energy; **~ de vie** (*présence effective*) form of life, life-form; (*coutumes*) way of life; **une ~ de pensée différente de la nôtre** a different way of thinking from our own; **les animaux ont-ils une ~ d'intelligence?** do animals have a form of intelligence?

(c) (*Art, Jur, Littérat, Philos*) form. **soigner la ~** to be careful about form; **poème à ~ fixe** fixed-form poem; **poème en ~ d'acrostiche** poem forming an acrostic; **remarques de pure ~** purely formal remarks; **pour la ~** as a matter of form, for form's sake; **en bonne (et due) ~** in due form; (*fig*) **sans autre ~ de procès** without further ado; **faites une réclamation en ~** put in a formal request; *V* **fond, vice.**

(d) (*convenances*) **~s** proprieties, conventions; **respecter les ~s** to respect the proprieties *ou* conventions; **refuser en y mettant des ~s** to decline as tactfully as possible; **faire une demande dans les ~s** to make a request in the correct form.

(e) (*Ling*) form. **mettre à la ~ passive** to put in the passive.

(f) (*Tech, Typ*) forme; *[cordonnier]* last; *[modiste]* (dress) form; (*partie de chapeau*) crown; *V* **haut.**

(g) (*Sport, gén: condition physique*) form. **être en ~** to be on form, be fit; **hors de ~** off form, out of form; **en grande ~** in top *ou* peak form; **retour de ~** return to form; **baisse de ~** loss of form; **la ~ revient** his form's coming back; **être en pleine ~** to be right on form*.

(h) (*Mus*) **~ sonate** sonata form.

formel, -elle [fɔʀmɛl] *adj* **(a)** (*catégorique*) definite, positive. **dans l'intention ~le de refuser** with the definite intention of refusing; **je suis ~!** I'm definite! **(b)** (*Art, Philos*) formal. **(c)** (*extérieur*) *politesse* formal.

formellement [fɔʀmɛlmɑ̃] *adv* **(a)** (*catégoriquement*) positively. **(b)** (*Art, Philos*) formally.

former [fɔʀme] (1) **1** *vt* **(a)** *gouvernement* to form; *compagnie* to form, establish; *liens d'amitié* to form, create; *croûte, dépôt* to form. **il s'est formé des liens entre nous** bonds have formed *ou* been created between us; **le cône que forme la révolution d'un triangle** the cone formed by the revolution of a triangle.

(b) *collection* to form, build up; *convoi* to form; *forme verbale, phrase* to form, make up. **~ correctement ses phrases** to form *ou* make up correct sentences; **le train n'est pas encore formé** they haven't made up the train yet.

(c) (*être le composant de*) to make up, form. **article formé de 3 paragraphes** article made up of *ou* consisting of 3 paragraphs; **ceci forme un tout** this forms a whole.

(d) (*dessiner*) to make, form. **ça forme un rond** it makes *ou* forms a circle; **la route forme des lacets** the road winds; **il forme bien/mal ses lettres** he forms his letters well/badly.

(e) (*éduquer*) *soldats, ingénieurs* to train; *intelligence, caractère, goût* to form, develop. **les voyages forment la jeunesse** travel broadens the mind of the young.

(f) **~ l'idée *ou* le projet de faire qch** to form *ou* have the idea of doing sth; **nous formons des vœux pour votre réussite** we wish you every success.

2 se former *vpr* **(a)** (*se rassembler*) to form, gather. **des nuages se forment à l'horizon** clouds are forming *ou* gathering on the horizon; **se ~ en cortège** to form a procession; **l'armée se forma en carré *ou* forma le carré** the army took up a square formation.

(b) *[dépôt, croûte]* to form.

(c) (*apprendre un métier etc*) to train o.s.; (*éduquer son goût, son caractère*) to educate o.s.

(d) (*se développer*) *[goût, caractère, intelligence]* to form, develop; *[fruit]* to form. **les fruits commencent à se ~ sur l'arbre** fruit begins to form on the tree; **une jeune fille qui se forme** a girl who is maturing; **son jugement n'est pas encore formé** his judgment is as yet unformed; **cette jeune fille est formée maintenant** this girl has become a woman now.

Formica [fɔʀmika] *nm* ® Formica ®.

formidable [fɔʀmidabl(ə)] *adj* **(a)** (*très important*) *coup, obstacle, bruit* tremendous.

(b) (*: *très bien*) fantastic*, great*, tremendous*.

(c) (*: *incroyable*) incredible. **c'est tout de même ~ qu'on ne me dise jamais rien!** all the same it's a bit much* that nobody ever tells me anything!; **il est ~: il convoque une réunion et il est en retard!** he's marvellous (*iro*) *ou* incredible — he calls a meeting and then he's late!

(d) (*littér: effrayant*) fearsome.

formidablement [fɔʀmidabləmɑ̃] *adv* (*V* **formidable**) tremendously*; fantastically*. **on s'est ~ amusé** we had a fantastic time*; **comment ça a marché? — ~!** how did it go? — great!* *ou* fantastic!*

formique [fɔʀmik] *adj* formic.

formol [fɔʀmɔl] *nm* formol, formalin.

formosan, e [fɔʀmozɑ̃, an] **1** *adj* Formosan. **2** *nm,f*: **F~(e)** Formosan.

Formose [fɔʀmoz] *nf* Formosa.

formulable [fɔʀmylabl(ə)] *adj* which can be formulated.

formulaire [fɔʀmylɛʀ] *nm* **(a)** (*à remplir*) form. **(b)** *[pharmaciens, notaires]* formulary.

formulation [fɔʀmylɑsjɔ̃] *nf* (*V* **formuler**) formulation; expression; drawing up. **il faudrait changer la ~ de votre demande** you should change the way your request is formulated.

formule [fɔʀmyl] *nf* **(a)** (*Chim, Math*) formula. **~ dentaire** dentition, dental formula.

(b) (*expression*) phrase, expression; (*magique, prescrite par l'étiquette*) formula. **~ heureuse** happy turn of phrase; **~ de politesse** polite phrase; (*en fin de lettre*) letter ending; **~ publicitaire** advertising slogan; **~ toute faite** ready-made phrase; **~ incantatoire** incantation.

(c) (*méthode*) system, way. **~ de paiement** method of payment; **~ de vacances** holiday programme *ou* schedule; **trouver la bonne ~** to hit on *ou* find the right system.

(d) (*formulaire*) form. **~ de chèque/de télégramme** cheque/telegram form.

formuler [fɔʀmyle] (1) *vt plainte, requête* to formulate, set out; *sentiment* to formulate, express; *ordonnance, acte notarié* to draw up; (*Chim, Math*) to formulate.

fornicateur, -trice [fɔʀnikatœʀ, tʀis] *nm,f* fornicator.

fornication [fɔʀnikɑsjɔ̃] *nf* fornication.

forniquer [fɔʀnike] (1) *vi* to fornicate.

fors†† [fɔʀ] *prép* save, except.

forsythia [fɔʀsitja] *nm* forsythia.

fort, e [fɔʀ, fɔʀt(ə)] **1** *adj* **(a)** (*puissant*) *personne, état, motif, lunettes* strong. **il est ~ comme un bœuf *ou* un Turc** he's as strong as an ox *ou* a horse; **il est de ~e constitution** he has a strong constitution; **le dollar est une monnaie ~e** the dollar is a strong currency; (*Mil*) **une armée ~e de 20.000 hommes** an army 20,000 strong; (*Cartes*) **la dame est plus ~e que le valet** the queen is higher than the jack; **avoir affaire à ~e partie** to have a strong *ou* tough opponent; **user de la manière ~e** to use strong-arm methods; *V* **homme, main.**

(b) (*euph: gros*) *personne* stout, large; *hanche* broad, wide, large; *jambe* heavy, large; *poitrine* large, ample. **elle s'habille au rayon (pour) femmes ~es** she gets her clothes from the outsize department; **elle est un peu ~e des hanches** she has rather wide *ou* broad *ou* large hips, she is rather wide- *ou* large-hipped.

(c) (*solide, résistant*) *carton* strong, stout; *colle, métal* strong; *V* **château, coffre, place.**

(d) (*intense*) *vent* strong, high; *bruit* loud; *lumière, rythme, battements* strong; *colère, douleur, chaleur* great, intense; *houle, pluie* heavy; *sentiments* strong, great, intense. **j'ai une ~e envie de le lui dire** I'm very *ou* strongly tempted to tell him; **il avait une ~e envie de rire/de pleurer** he very much wanted to laugh/cry; **aimer les sensations ~es** to enjoy sensational experiences *ou* big thrills.

(e) (*corsé*) *remède, café, thé, mélange* strong; *rhume* heavy; *fièvre* high.

(f) (*marqué*) *pente* pronounced, steep; *accent* marked, pronounced, strong; *dégoût, crainte* great; *impression* great, strong. **il y a de ~es chances pour qu'il vienne** there's a (very) good chance he'll come, he's very likely to come; **une œuvre ~e** a work that has impact.

(g) (*violent*) *secousse, coup* hard.

(h) (*quantitativement*) *somme* large, great; *hausse, baisse, différence* great, big; *dose* large, big; *consommation, augmentation* high. **faire payer le prix ~** to charge the full *ou* the list price; **il est ~ en gueule*** he's loud-mouthed* *ou* a loud-mouth‡; *V* **temps**[1].

(i) (*courageux, obstiné*) *personne* strong. **être ~ dans l'adversité** to be strong *ou* to stand firm in (the face of) adversity; **âme ~e** steadfast soul; **esprit ~**† freethinker; **~e tête** rebel.

(j) (*doué*) good (*en, à* at), able. **il est ~ en histoire/aux échecs** he's good at history/at chess; **il est très ~!** he's very good (at it)!; **être ~ sur un sujet** to be well up on* *ou* good at a subject; **il a trouvé plus ~ que lui** he has found *ou* met (more than) his match *ou* someone to outmatch him; **ce n'est pas très ~ (de sa part)*** that's not very clever *ou* bright of him; **cette remarque n'était pas très ~e*** that wasn't a very intelligent *ou* clever *ou* bright thing to say; (*iro*) **quand il s'agit de critiquer, il est ~** (oh yes) he can criticize all right! *ou* he's very good at criticizing!; *V* **point**[1].

(k) (*de goût prononcé*) *tabac, moutarde, café* strong (-flavoured); *goût, odeur* strong. **vin ~ en alcool** strong wine, wine with a high alcoholic content; **avoir l'haleine ~e** to have bad breath.

(l) (*loc*) **~ de leur assentiment/de cette garantie** in a strong position because of their approval/of this guarantee; **être ~ de son bon droit** to be confident of one's rights; **nos champions se font ~ de gagner** our champions are confident they will win *ou* confident of winning; **je me fais ~ de le réparer** I'm (quite) sure I can mend it, I can mend it, don't worry *ou* you'll see; **se porter ~ pour qn** to answer for sb; **au sens ~ du terme** in the strongest sense of the term; **à plus ~e raison, tu aurais dû venir** all the more reason for you to have come; **à plus ~e raison, parce que ...** the more so because ...; **c'est plus ~ que moi** I can't help it; (*hum*) **c'est plus ~ que de jouer au bouchon!** it's a real puzzle!, it's beyond me!; **c'est trop ~!** that's too much!, that's going too far!; (*hum*) **c'est trop ~ pour moi** it's above *ou* beyond me; **elle est ~e celle-là!*** that takes the biscuit!* (*surtout Brit*), that beats everything!*; **c'est un peu ~*** that's a bit much* *ou* steep*, that's going a bit (too) far*; **et le plus ~** *ou* **et ce qu'il y a de plus ~, c'est que ...** and the best (part) of it is that ...; *V* **verbe.**

2 *adv* **(a)** (*intensément*) *parler, crier* loudly, loud; *lancer, serrer, souffler* hard. **frapper ~** (*bruit*) to knock loudly; (*force*) to hit hard; **sentir ~** to have a strong smell; **parlez plus ~** speak up *ou* louder; **respirez bien ~** breathe deeply, take a deep breath; **son cœur battait très ~** his heart was pounding *ou* was beating hard; **le feu marche trop ~** the fire is (up) too high *ou* is burning too fast; **tu y vas un peu ~ tout de même*** even so, you're overdoing it a bit* *ou* going a bit far*; **c'est de plus en plus ~!*** it's better and better.

(b) (*littér: beaucoup*) greatly. **cela me déplaît ~** that displeases me greatly *ou* a great deal; **j'en doute ~** I very much doubt it; **il y tient ~** he is very keen on it; **j'ai ~ à faire avec lui** I have a hard job with him, I've got my work cut out with him.

(c) (*littér: très*) *aimable* most; *mécontent, intéressant* most, highly. **il est ~ inquiet** he is very *ou* most anxious; **c'est ~ bon** it is very *ou* exceedingly good, it is most excellent (*frm*); **j'en suis ~ aise** I am most pleased; **j'ai ~ envie de faire ceci** I am most desirous to do *ou* of doing this (*littér*); **il y avait ~ peu de monde** there were very few people; **~ bien!** very good!, excellent!; **tu refuses? ~ bien tu l'auras voulu** you refuse? very well, be it on your own head; **c'est ~ bien dit** very well said; **tu le sais ~ bien** you know very well.

3 *nm* **(a)** (*forteresse*) fort.

(b) (*personne*) **le ~ l'emporte toujours contre le faible** the strong will always win against the weak; (*Scol péj*) **un ~ en thème** a swot*, an egghead*; *V* **raison.**

(c) (*spécialité*) strong point, forte. **l'amabilité n'est pas son ~** kindness is not his strong point *ou* his forte.

(d) (*littér: milieu*) **au ~ de** *été* at the height of; *hiver* in the depths *ou* dead of; **au plus ~ du combat** (*lieu*) in the thick of the battle; (*intensité*) when the battle was at its most intense, at the height of the battle.

4: fort des Halles market porter.

fortement [fɔʀtəmɑ̃] *adv conseiller* strongly; *tenir* fast, tight(ly); *frapper* hard; *serrer* hard, tight(ly). **il est ~ probable** it is highly *ou* most probable; **~ marqué/attiré** strongly marked/attracted; **il en est ~ question** it is being (very) seriously considered; **j'espère ~ que vous le pourrez** I very much hope that you will be able to; **boiter ~** to have a pronounced limp, limp badly; **il est ~ intéressé par l'affaire** he is highly *ou* most interested in the matter.

forteresse [fɔʀtəʀɛs] *nf* (*lit*) fortress, stronghold; (*fig*) stronghold. **~ volante** flying fortress.

fortifiant, e [fɔʀtifjɑ̃, ɑ̃t] **1** *adj médicament, boisson* fortifying; *air* invigorating, bracing; (*littér*) *exemple, lecture* uplifting.

2 *nm* (*Pharm*) tonic.

fortification [fɔʀtifikɑsjɔ̃] *nf* fortification.

fortifier [fɔʀtifje] (7) **1** *vt corps, âme* to strengthen, fortify; *position, opinion, impression* to strengthen; *ville* to fortify. **l'air marin fortifie** (the) sea air is fortifying.

2 se fortifier *vpr* (*Mil*) to fortify itself; *[opinion, amitié, position]* to grow stronger, be strengthened; *[santé]* to grow more robust.

fortin [fɔʀtɛ̃] *nm* (small) fort.

fortiori [fɔʀsjɔʀi] *loc adv*: **à ~** all the more so, a fortiori.

fortran [fɔʀtʀɑ̃] *nm* Fortran.

fortuit, e [fɔʀtɥi, ɥit] *adj événement, circonstance, remarque, rencontre* fortuitous, chance (*épith*); *coïncidence* fortuitous; *découverte* fortuitous, chance (*épith*), accidental.

fortuitement [fɔʀtɥitmɑ̃] *adv* (*V* **fortuit**) fortuitously; by chance; accidentally.

fortune [fɔʀtyn] *nf* **(a)** (*richesse*) fortune. **situation de ~** financial situation; **ça vaut une ~** it's worth a fortune; **cet homme est l'une des plus grosses ~s de la région** that man has one of the largest fortunes *ou* that man is one of the wealthiest in the area; **avoir de la ~** to have private means; **faire ~** to make one's fortune; (*fig*) **le mot a fait ~** the word has really become popular, the word has really caught on*; *V* **impôt, revers.**

(b) (*chance*) luck (*U*), fortune (*U*); (*destinée*) fortune. **quelle a été la ~ de ce roman?** what were the fortunes of this novel?; **tenter** *ou* **chercher ~** to seek one's fortune; **connaître des ~s diverses** (*sujet pluriel*) to enjoy varying fortunes; (*sujet singulier*) to have varying luck; **il a eu la (bonne) ~ de le rencontrer** he was fortunate enough to meet him, he had the good fortune to meet him; **ayant eu la mauvaise ~ de le rencontrer** having had the misfortune *ou* the ill-fortune to meet him; **venez dîner à la ~ du pot** come to dinner and take pot luck with us; (*Jur, Naut*) **~s de mer** sea risks, perils of the sea; (*Prov*) **la ~ sourit aux audacieux** fortune favours the brave.

(c) de ~ *réparations, moyens* makeshift; *installation* makeshift, rough-and-ready; *compagnon* chance (*épith*); (*Naut*) **mât/gouvernail de ~** jury mast/rudder.

fortuné, e [fɔʀtyne] *adj* (*riche*) wealthy, well-off; (*littér: heureux*) fortunate.

forum [fɔʀɔm] *nm* (*place, colloque*) forum.

fosse [fos] *nf* (*trou*) pit; (*tombe*) grave; (*Sport*) (*pour le saut*) (sand)pit; (*Anat*) fossa. **~ d'aisances** cesspool; **~ commune** common *ou* communal grave; **~ à fumier** manure pit; (*lit, fig*) **~ aux lions** lions' den; **~ marine** deep; **~s nasales** nasal fossae; **~ d'orchestre** orchestra pit; **~ aux ours** bear pit; **~ à purin = ~ à fumier**; **~ septique** septic tank.

fossé [fose] *nm* (*gén*) ditch; (*fig: écart*) gulf, gap. (*fig*) **un ~ les sépare** a gulf lies between them; **~ d'irrigation** irrigation channel *ou* ditch; **~ anti-char** anti-tank ditch.

fossette [fosɛt] *nf* dimple.

fossile [fosil] (*lit, fig*) **1** *nm* fossil. **2** *adj* fossil (*épith*), fossilized.

fossilifère [fosilifɛʀ] *adj* fossiliferous.

fossilisation [fosilizɑsjɔ̃] *nf* fossilization.

fossiliser [fosilize] (1) (*lit, fig*) **1** *vt* to fossilize. **2 se fossiliser** *vpr* to fossilize, become fossilized.

fossoyeur [foswajœʀ] *nm* gravedigger; (*fig*) destroyer.

fou [fu], **fol** *devant n commençant par une voyelle ou h muet*, **folle** [fɔl] *f* **(a)** (*Méd, gén*, *: *sot*) mad, crazy. **~ à lier, ~ furieux** raving mad; **il est devenu subitement ~** he suddenly went mad *ou* crazy *ou* insane; (*lit, fig*) **ça l'a rendu ~** it drove him mad *ou* crazy; **c'est à devenir ~** it's enough to drive you mad *ou* crazy, it's enough to drive you to distraction; **~ de colère/de désir/de chagrin** out of one's mind* *ou* crazed with anger/desire/grief; **~ de joie** delirious *ou* out of one's mind* with joy; **~ d'amour** madly *ou* wildly in love (*pour* with); **elle est folle de lui/de ce musicien** she's mad* *ou* crazy* about *ou* she's mad keen* (*surtout Brit*) on him/that musician; **tu es complètement ~ de refuser*** you're completely mad *ou* absolutely crazy to refuse*; **y aller? (je ne suis) pas si ~!*** go there?, I'm not that crazy!*; **pas folle, la guêpe*** he's (*ou* she's) not stupid *ou* daft* you know!; *V* **fou-fou.**

(b) (*insensé*) *terreur, rage, course* mad, wild; *amour, joie, espoir* mad, insane; *idée, désir, tentative, dépense* mad, insane, crazy; *audace* insane; *imagination* wild, insane; *regard, gestes* wild, crazed. **avoir le ~ rire** to have the giggles; (†, *hum*) **folle jeunesse** wild youth.

(c) (*: *énorme*) *courage, énergie, succès* fantastic*, terrific, tremendous; *peur* terrific, tremendous. **j'ai un mal de tête ~** I've got a splitting headache*, my head's killing me*; **j'ai une envie folle de chocolat/d'y aller** I've got a mad desire for some chocolate/to go*; **j'ai eu un mal ~ pour venir** I had a terrific *ou* terrible job* to get here; **tu as mis un temps ~** you've taken absolutely ages* *ou* an absolute age*; **gagner/dépenser un argent ~** to earn/spend loads *ou* pots of money*; **payer un prix ~** to pay a ridiculous *ou* an astronomical price; **rouler à une vitesse folle** to go at a fantastic* *ou* terrific *ou* tremendous speed; **il y a un monde ~** there are masses of people, there's a fantastic crowd* *ou* a huge great crowd*; **c'est ~ ce qu'il y a comme monde** it's incredible how many people there are, what a fantastic crowd*; **c'est ~ ce qu'on s'amuse** what a great *ou* fantastic time we're having!*; **c'est ~ ce qu'il a changé** it's incredible *ou* unbelievable how he has changed.

(d) (*déréglé*) *boussole, aiguille* erratic, wobbling all over the place (*attrib*); *camion, moteur, cheval* runaway (*épith*), out-of-control (*épith*); *mèche de cheveux* stray, unruly. **avoir les cheveux ~s** to have one's hair in a mess *ou* all over the place.

2 *nm* **(a)** (†, *hum*: **fol**) (*Méd, fig*) madman, lunatic. **courir comme un ~** to run like a madman *ou* lunatic; **arrête de faire le ~** stop playing *ou* acting the fool; **ce jeune ~** this young lunatic *ou* fool; **espèce de vieux ~** you silly old fool, you old lunatic; *V* **histoire, maison, plus.**

(b) (*Échecs*) bishop.

(c) (*Hist: bouffon*) jester, fool.

(d) (*Zool*) gannet.

3 folle *nf* madwoman, lunatic; (*péj: homosexuel*) **(grande) folle** queen‡; **cette vieille folle** that old madwoman, that mad old woman.

4: folle avoine wild oats.

foucade [fukad] *nf* (*littér*) whim, passing fancy.

foudre[1] [fudʀ(ə)] *nf* **(a)** lightning; (*Myth: attribut*) thunderbolt. **frappé par la ~** struck by lightning; **la ~ est tombée sur la maison** the house was struck by lightning; **comme la ~, avec la rapidité de la ~** like lightning, as quick as a flash; *V* **coup.**

(b) (*colère*) (*Rel*) **~s** anathema (*sg*); (*fig*) **s'attirer les ~s de qn** to bring down sb's wrath upon o.s.

foudre[2] [fudʀ(ə)] *nm* (†, *hum*) **~ de guerre** outstanding *ou* great leader (in war); **ce n'est pas un ~ de guerre** he has no flair for leadership.

foudre[3] [fudʀ(ə)] *nm* (*tonneau*) tun; *V* **wagon.**

foudroiement [fudʀwamɑ̃] *nm* striking (by lightning).

foudroyant, e [fudʀwajɑ̃, ɑ̃t] *adj progrès, vitesse, attaque* lightning (*épith*); *poison, maladie* violent (*épith*); *succès* thundering (*épith*), stunning (*épith*). **une nouvelle ~e** a bolt from the blue, a thunderbolt; **il lui lança un regard ~** he looked daggers at him.

foudroyer [fudʀwaje] (8) *vt [foudre]* to strike; *[coup de feu, maladie, malheur]* to strike down. **la décharge électrique la foudroya** she received a severe electric shock; **cette nouvelle le foudroya** he was thunderstruck *ou* floored* by the news; **~ qn du regard** to look daggers at sb, glare at sb; **dans le champ il y avait un arbre foudroyé** in the field lay *ou* stood a tree that had been struck by lightning.

fouet [fwɛ] *nm* (*cravache*) whip; (*Culin: batteur*) whisk. **donner le ~ à qn** to give sb a whipping *ou* flogging; *V* **coup, plein.**

fouettard [fwɛtaʀ] *adj V* **père.**

fouettement [fwɛtmɑ̃] *nm [pluie]* lashing.

fouetter [fwete] (1) **1** *vt personne* to whip, flog; *cheval* to whip; (*Culin*) *crème, blanc d'œuf* to whip, whisk; (*fig*) *imagination* to fire; *désir* to whip up. **la pluie fouette les vitres** the rain lashes *ou* whips the window panes; **le vent le fouettait au visage** the wind whipped his face; **l'air frais fouette le sang** fresh air whips up the blood; (*fig*) **il n'y a pas de quoi ~ un chat** it's nothing to make a fuss about; (*hum*) **fouette cocher!** don't spare the horses! (*hum*); *V* **autre.**

2 *vi* **(a) ~ contre: la pluie fouette contre les vitres** the rain lashes *ou* whips against the window panes.

(b) (‡: *avoir peur*) to be scared stiff* *ou* to death*.

(c) (*: *puer*) to reek, stink. **ça fouette ici!** there's one hell of a stench *ou* stink in here!*
fou-fou, fofolle* [fufu, fɔfɔl] *adj* scatty* (*Brit*), crazy.
fougère [fuʒɛʀ] *nf* fern. **ces plantes sont des** ~**s** these plants are ferns; **clairière envahie de** ~**(s)** clearing overgrown with bracken.
fougue [fug] *nf [personne, discours, attaque]* ardour, spirit. **plein de** ~ *orateur, réponse* ardent, fiery; *cheval* mettlesome, fiery; **la** ~ **de la jeunesse** the hotheadedness of youth; **avec** ~ with spirit, ardently.
fougueusement [fugøzmɑ̃] *adv* with spirit, ardently. **se ruer** ~ **sur qn** to hurl o.s. impetuously at sb.
fougueux, -euse [fugø, øz] *adj réponse, tempérament, orateur* fiery, ardent; *jeunesse* hotheaded, fiery; *cheval* mettlesome, fiery; *attaque* spirited.
fouille [fuj] *nf* **(a)** *[personne]* searching, frisking; *[maison, bagages]* searching. **(b)** (*Archéol*) ~**s** excavation(s), dig*; **faire des** ~**s dans une région** to carry out excavations in an area, excavate an area. **(c)** (*Constr*) (*action*) excavation; (*lieu*) excavation (site).
fouiller [fuje] (1) **1** *vt pièce, mémoire* to search; *personne* to search, frisk; *bagages, poches* to search, go through; *région, bois* to search, scour, comb; *question* to go (deeply) into; *sol* to dig; *terrain* to excavate, dig up; *bas-relief* to undercut. **il fouillait l'horizon avec ses jumelles** he scanned *ou* searched the horizon with his binoculars; **il fouilla l'obscurité des yeux** he peered into the darkness; **il le fouilla du regard** he gave him a searching look; **étude/analyse très fouillée** very detailed study/analysis; **rinceaux très fouillés** finely detailed (plaster-) mouldings.
2 *vi* to rummage. ~ **dans** *tiroir, armoire* to rummage in, dig about in; *poches* to go through, grope in; *bagages* to go through; *mémoire* to delve into, search; **qui a fouillé dans mes affaires?** who has been through *ou* who has been rummaging *ou* digging about in my things?
3 se fouiller *vpr* to go through one's pockets. **tu peux toujours te** ~**!*** you haven't a hope in hell!*, nothing doing!*
fouillis [fuji] *nm [papiers, objets]* jumble, muddle; *[branchages]* tangle; *[idées]* jumble, hotchpotch. **faire du** ~ (*dans une pièce*) *[personne]* to make a mess; *[objets]* to look a mess, look messy; **sa chambre est en** ~ his room is in a dreadful muddle, his room is a jumble of bits and pieces; **il régnait un** ~ **indescriptible** everything was in an indescribable muddle *ou* mess.
fouinard, e [fwinaʀ, aʀd(ə)] = **fouineur.**
fouine [fwin] *nf* (*Zool*) stone marten. (*fig*) **c'est une vraie** ~ he's a real snoop(er)* (*péj*); **visage de** ~ weasel-faced.
fouiner [fwine] (1) *vi* (*péj*) to nose around *ou* about. **je n'aime pas qu'on fouine dans mes affaires** I don't like people nosing *ou* ferreting about in my things; **être toujours à** ~ **partout** to be always poking one's nose into things.
fouineur, -euse [fwinœʀ, øz] (*pej*) **1** *adj* prying, nosey*. **2** *nm,f* nosey parker* (*Brit*), Nosey Parker* (*US*), snoop(er)*.
fouir [fwiʀ] (2) *vt* to dig.
fouisseur, -euse [fwisœʀ, øz] **1** *adj* burrowing, fossorial (*T*). **2** *nm* burrower, fossorial animal (*T*).
foulage [fulaʒ] *nm [raisin]* pressing; *[drap]* fulling; *[cuir]* tanning.
foulant, e* [fulɑ̃, ɑ̃t] *adj travail* killing*, back-breaking. **ce n'est pas trop** ~ it won't kill you*; *V* **pompe**[1].
foulard [fulaʀ] *nm* **(a)** (*écharpe*) (*carré*) (head)scarf; (*long*) scarf. **(b)** (*U: tissu*) foulard.
foule [ful] *nf* **(a)** (*gén*) crowd, throng (*littér*); (*péj: populace*) mob. (*le peuple*) **la** ~ the masses; **une** ~ **hurlante** a howling mob; **la** ~ **et l'élite** the masses and the élite; *V* **psychologie.**
(b) (*loc*) **il y avait** ~ **à la réunion** there were crowds at the meeting; **il n'y avait pas** ~**!** there was hardly anyone there!; **il y avait une** ~ **de gens** there was a crowd *ou* host of people, there were crowds of people; **j'ai une** ~ **de choses à te dire** I've got loads* *ou* masses (of things) to tell you; **elle m'a posé une** ~ **de questions** she asked me heaps* *ou* loads* of questions; **il y avait une** ~ **de livres** there were masses *ou* loads* *ou* heaps* of books; **ils vinrent en** ~ **à l'exposition** they came in crowds *ou* they flocked to the exhibition; **les idées me venaient en** ~ ideas were crowding into my head, I had a host *ou* a multitude of ideas.
foulée [fule] *nf [cheval, coureur]* stride. (*Sport*) **suivre qn dans la** ~**, être dans la** ~ **de qn** to follow (close) on sb's heels; (*fig*) **il travailla encore 3 heures dans la** ~ he worked on for another 3 hours while he was at it *ou* for another 3 hours without a break.
fouler [fule] (1) **1** *vt raisins* to press; *drap* to full; *cuir* to tan. (*littér*) ~ **le sol de sa patrie** to walk upon *ou* tread (upon) native soil; ~ **aux pieds quelque chose de sacré** to trample something sacred underfoot, trample on something sacred.
2 se fouler *vpr* **(a) se** ~ **la cheville/le poignet** to sprain one's ankle/wrist.
(b) (*: *travailler dur*) to flog o.s. to death*. **il ne se foule pas beaucoup, il ne se foule pas la rate** he doesn't exactly flog himself to death* *ou* overtax himself.
fouleur, -euse [fulœʀ, øz] *nm,f [drap]* fuller; *[cuir]* tanner.
fouloir [fulwaʀ] *nm [drap]* fulling mill; *[cuir]* tanning drum.
foulon [fulɔ̃] *nm V* **terre.**
foulque [fulk(ə)] *nf* coot.
foulure [fulyʀ] *nf* sprain.
four [fuʀ] **1** *nm* **(a)** *[boulangerie, cuisinière]* oven; *[potier]* kiln; *[usine]* furnace. **cuire au** ~ *gâteau* to bake; *viande* to roast; **plat allant au** ~ ovenproof *ou* fireproof dish; **il a ouvert la bouche comme un** ~* he opened his great cavern of a mouth; **je ne peux pas être au** ~ **et au moulin** I can't do two things at once; *V* **banal**[2]**, noir, petit.**
(b) (*arg Théât*) flop, fiasco. **cette pièce est** *ou* **a fait un** ~ this play is a flop *ou* has fallen flat.
2: four à chaux lime kiln; **four crématoire** crematorium furnace; (*Ind*) **four électrique** electric furnace; **four solaire** solar furnace.
fourbe [fuʀb(ə)] *adj personne, caractère* deceitful, false-hearted, treacherous; *air, regard* deceitful, treacherous. **c'est un** ~ he is a deceitful *ou* false-hearted *ou* treacherous rogue.
fourberie [fuʀbəʀi] *nf* (*littér*) (*U*) deceitfulness, treachery; (*acte, geste*) deceit, piece of treachery. **à cause de ses** ~**s** because of his treachery *ou* deceits.
fourbi* [fuʀbi] *nm* (*attirail*) gear* (*U*), clobber* (*U*); (*fouillis*) mess. **canne à pêche, hameçons et tout le** ~ fishing rod, hooks, you name it!*, fishing rod, hooks and goodness knows what else!*; **partir en vacances avec le bébé, ça va en faire du** *ou* **un** ~ going on holiday with the baby, that'll mean a whole heap of gear* *ou* clobber*.
fourbir [fuʀbiʀ] (2) *vt arme* to furbish. (*fig*) ~ **ses armes** to prepare for battle, get ready for the fray.
fourbissage [fuʀbisaʒ] *nm* furbishing.
fourbu, e [fuʀby] *adj* exhausted.
fourche [fuʀʃ(ə)] *nf* **(a)** (*pour le foin*) pitchfork; (*pour bêcher*) fork. **(b)** *[arbre, chemin, bicyclette]* fork; *[pantalon, jambes]* crotch. **la route faisait une** ~ the road forked.
fourcher [fuʀʃe] (1) *vi [arbre, chemin]* (†) to fork; *[cheveux]* to split (at the ends). **ma langue a fourché** I made *ou* it was a slip of the tongue.
fourchette [fuʀʃɛt] *nf* **(a)** (*pour manger*) fork. ~ **à gâteaux/à huîtres** pastry/oyster fork; **il a une bonne** ~ *ou* **un bon coup de** ~ he has a hearty appetite, he's a good *ou* hearty eater. **(b)** *[oiseau]* wishbone; *[cheval]* frog; (*Aut*) selector fork (*Brit*); (*Tech*) fork. **(c)** (*Statistique*) **la** ~ **s'agrandit/se rétrécit** the margin is widening/narrowing.
fourchu, e [fuʀʃy] *adj arbre, chemin* forked; *menton* jutting (*épith*). **animal au pied** ~ cloven-hoofed animal; *V* **langue.**
fourgon [fuʀgɔ̃] *nm* (*wagon*) coach, wag(g)on; (*camion*) (large) van, lorry; (*diligence*) coach, carriage. ~ **à bagages** luggage van; ~ **à bestiaux** cattle truck; ~ **de déménagement** removal *ou* furniture van; ~ **funéraire** hearse; (*Mil*) ~ **de munitions** munitions wagon; ~ **mortuaire** = ~ **funéraire**; ~ **postal** mail van; ~ **de queue** rear brake van; (*Mil*) ~ **de vivres** supply wagon.
fourgonner [fuʀgɔne] (1) **1** *vt poêle, feu* to poke, rake. **2** *vi* (*parmi des objets*) to poke about, rake about. **je l'entendais qui fourgonnait dans la cuisine/dans le placard** I heard him clattering *ou* poking about in the kitchen/cupboard.
fourgonnette [fuʀgɔnɛt] *nf* (small) van, delivery van.
fourguer* [fuʀge] (1) *vt* (*vendre*) to flog* (*à* to), unload* (*à* onto). (*donner*) ~ **qch à qn** to unload sth onto sb*, palm sth off onto sb*.
fourmi [fuʀmi] *nf* ant; (*fig: personne*) beaver. ~ **maçonne** builder *ou* worker ant; **avoir des** ~**s dans les jambes** to have pins and needles in one's legs.
fourmilier [fuʀmilje] *nm* anteater.
fourmilière [fuʀmiljɛʀ] *nf* (*monticule*) ant-hill; (*intérieur*) ants' nest; (*fig*) hive of activity. **cette ville/ce bureau est une (vraie)** ~ this town/office is a hive of activity.
fourmillant, e [fuʀmijɑ̃, ɑ̃t] *adj foule* milling, swarming; *cité* teeming.
fourmillement [fuʀmijmɑ̃] *nm* **(a)** *[insectes, personnes]* swarming; *[idées]* teeming. **le** ~ **de la rue** the swarming *ou* milling crowds in the street; **un** ~ **d'insectes** a mass of swarming insects; **un** ~ **d'idées** a welter of ideas.
(b) (*gén pl: picotement*) ~**s** pins and needles (*dans* in).
fourmiller [fuʀmije] (1) *vi [insectes, personnes]* to swarm. **dissertation où fourmillent les erreurs** essay teeming with mistakes; ~ **de** *insectes, personnes* to be swarming *ou* crawling *ou* teeming with; *idées, erreurs* to be teeming with; **forêt qui fourmille de lapins, forêt où les lapins fourmillent** forest which is overrun with *ou* that teems with rabbits; (*fig*) **les pieds me fourmillent** I've got pins and needles in my feet.
fournaise [fuʀnɛz] *nf* (*feu*) blaze, blazing fire; (*fig: endroit surchauffé*) furnace, oven.
fourneau, *pl* ~**x** [fuʀno] *nm* **(a)** (†: *cuisinière, poêle*) stove†. **(b)** *[forge, chaufferie]* furnace; *[pipe]* bowl; *V* **haut.**
fournée [fuʀne] *nf* (*lit, fig*) batch.
fourni, e [fuʀni] (*ptp de* **fournir**) *adj herbe* luxuriant, lush; *cheveux* thick, abundant; *barbe, sourcils* bushy, thick. **chevelure peu** ~**e** sparse *ou* thin head of hair; **table bien** ~**e** well-stocked *ou* well-supplied table; **boutique bien** ~**e** well-stocked shop.
fournil [fuʀni] *nm* bakery, bakehouse.
fourniment* [fuʀnimɑ̃] *nm* gear* (*U*). **il va falloir emporter tout un** ~ we'll have to take a whole heap of gear* *ou* stuff* *ou* clobber*.
fournir [fuʀniʀ] (2) **1** *vt* **(a)** (*approvisionner*) *client, restaurant* to supply. ~ **qn en viande/légumes** to supply sb with meat/vegetables.
(b) (*procurer*) *matériel, main d'œuvre* to supply, provide; *preuves, secours* to supply, furnish; *renseignements* to supply, provide, furnish; *pièce d'identité* to produce; *prétexte, exemple* to give, supply. ~ **qch à qn** to supply sb with sth, supply sth to sb, provide sb with sth, furnish sb with sth, produce sth for sb; ~ **à qn l'occasion/les moyens** to provide sb with the opportunity/the means, give sb *ou* afford sb the opportunity/the means (*de faire* of doing); ~ **du travail à qn** to provide sb with work; ~ **le vivre et le couvert** to provide board and lodging.
(c) (*produire*) *effort* to put in; *prestation* to give; *récolte* to supply. ~ **un gros effort** to put in a lot of effort, make a great (deal of) effort.

(d) (*Cartes*) ~ **(une carte)** to follow suit; ~ **à cœur** to follow suit in hearts.

2 fournir à *vt indir besoins* to provide for; *dépense, frais* to defray. **ses parents fournissent à son entretien** his parents give him his keep *ou* provide (for) his maintenance.

3 se fournir *vpr* to provide o.s. (*de* with). **se ~ en** *ou* **de charbon** to get (in) supplies of coal; **je me fournis toujours chez le même épicier** I always buy *ou* get my groceries from the same place, I always shop at the same grocer's.

fournisseur [fuʀnisœʀ] *nm* (*commerçant*) tradesman (*surtout Brit*), purveyor (*frm*); (*détaillant*) stockist (*Brit*), retailer; (*Comm, Ind*) supplier. **~ de viande/papier** supplier *ou* purveyor (*frm*) of meat/paper, meat/paper supplier; **les pays ~s de la France** countries that supply France (with goods *ou* imports); **les ~s de l'armée** army contractors; **chez votre ~ habituel** at your local stockist('s) (*Brit*) *ou* retailer('s); **nos ~s manquent de matière première** our suppliers are out of raw materials.

fourniture [fuʀnityʀ] *nf [matériel, marchandises]* supply(ing). **~s (de bureau)** office supplies, stationery; **~s scolaires** school stationery.

fourrage [fuʀaʒ] *nm* (*Agr*) fodder, forage. **~ vert** herbage.

fourrager [fuʀaʒe] (3) *vi*: **~ dans** *papiers, tiroir* to rummage through, dig about in.

fourragère[1] [fuʀaʒɛʀ] *adj f*: **plante/betterave ~** fodder plant/beet.

fourragère[2] [fuʀaʒɛʀ] *nf* (*Mil*) fourragère.

fourré[1] [fuʀe] *nm* thicket. **se cacher dans les ~s** to hide in the bushes.

fourré[2]**, e** [fuʀe] (*ptp de* **fourrer**) *adj bonbon, chocolat* filled; *manteau, gants* fur-lined; (*molletonné*) fleecy-lined. **~ d'hermine** ermine-lined; **chocolats ~s** chocolate creams, chocolates; **gâteau ~ à la crème** cream(-filled) cake; **tablette de chocolat ~ à la crème** bar of cream-filled chocolate; *V* **coup.**

fourreau, *pl* **~x** [fuʀo] *nm* **(a)** *[épée]* sheath, scabbard; *[parapluie]* cover. **mettre au/tirer du ~ son épée** to sheathe/unsheathe one's sword. **(b) une robe/jupe ~** a sheath (dress/skirt).

fourrer [fuʀe] (1) **1** *vt* **(a)** (*) (*enfoncer*) to stick*, shove*, stuff; (*mettre*) to stick*. **où ai-je bien pu le ~?** where the heck did I stick *ou* put it?*; **~ ses mains dans ses poches** to stuff *ou* stick* *ou* shove* one's hands in one's pockets; **~ qch dans un sac** to stuff *ou* shove* sth into a bag; **qui t'a fourré ça dans le crâne?** who put that (idea) into your head?; **~ son nez partout/dans les affaires des autres** to poke *ou* stick* one's nose into everything/into other people's business; **~ qn dans le pétrin** to land sb in the soup* *ou* in it* (*surtout Brit*); **~ qn en prison** to stick sb in prison*; *V* **doigt.**

(b) *volaille* to stuff; *manteau* to line (with fur).

2 se fourrer* *vpr* **(a) se ~ une idée dans la tête** to get an idea into one's head; **il s'est fourré dans la tête que ...** he has got it into his head that ... .

(b) se ~ dans un coin/sous la table to get in a corner/under the table; **où a-t-il encore été se ~?** where has he got to now?; **il ne savait plus où se ~** he didn't know where to put himself; **être toujours fourré chez qn** to be never off sb's doorstep; **son ballon est allé se ~ dans la niche du chien** his ball ended up in *ou* landed in the dog's kennel; **se ~ dans un guêpier** to land o.s. in the soup* *ou* in it* (*surtout Brit*).

fourre-tout [fuʀtu] *nm inv* (*pièce*) lumber room, junk room, glory-hole; (*placard*) junk cupboard, glory-hole; (*sac*) holdall. **sa chambre est un vrai ~*** his bedroom is an absolute tip*; (*péj*) **sa dissertation/son livre est un vrai ~** his essay/book is a real jumble of ideas; **un discours/une loi ~** a rag-bag of a speech/law.

fourreur [fuʀœʀ] *nm* furrier.

fourrier [fuʀje] *nm* (*Hist Mil*) (*pour le logement*) harbinger; (*pour les vivres*) quartermaster; (*fig littér*) forerunner, harbinger (*littér*); *V* **sergent**[1].

fourrière [fuʀjɛʀ] *nf* pound. **emmener une voiture à la ~** to tow away a car.

fourrure [fuʀyʀ] *nf* (*pelage*) coat; (*matériau, manteau etc*) fur.

fourvoiement [fuʀvwamɑ̃] *nm* (*littér*: *V* **se fourvoyer**) losing one's way; going off the track.

fourvoyer [fuʀvwaje] (8) **1** *vt*: **~ qn** *[guide]* to get sb lost, mislead sb; *[mauvais renseignement]* to mislead sb; *[mauvais exemple]* to lead sb astray.

2 se fourvoyer *vpr* (*lit: s'égarer*) to lose one's way; (*fig: se tromper*) to go off the track. **se ~ dans un quartier inconnu** to stray into an unknown district (by mistake); **dans quelle aventure s'est-il encore fourvoyé?** what has he got involved in now?; **il s'est complètement fourvoyé en faisant son problème** he has gone completely wrong *ou* completely off the track with his problem.

foutaise‡ [futɛz] *nf* a load of old rubbish‡ (*U*). **dire des ~s** to talk rot* *ou* a load of old rubbish‡; **se disputer pour une ~** *ou* **des ~s** to quarrel over damn all‡.

foutoir‡ [futwaʀ] *nm* bloody (*Brit*) *ou* damned shambles‡ (*sg*).

foutre‡ [futʀ(ə)] **1** *vt* **(a)** (*faire*) to do. **qu'est-ce qu'il fout, il est déjà 8 heures** what the hell‡ is he doing *ou* up to* — it's already 8 o'clock; **il n'a rien foutu de la journée** he hasn't done a bloody∵ (*Brit*) *ou* ruddy‡ (*Brit*) *ou* damned‡ thing all day, he's done damn all‡ *ou* bugger all∵ (*Brit*) today; **j'en ai rien à ~, de leurs histoires** I don't bloody (*Brit*) care∵ *ou* give a damn‡ about their carry-on.

(b) (*donner*) **~ une trempe** *ou* **raclée à qn** to give sb a belting‡ *ou* thumping‡, beat the hell out of sb‡; **~ une gifle à qn** to fetch (*Brit*) *ou* give sb a clout‡; **ça me fout la trouille** it gives me the bloody (*Brit*) willies∵ *ou* creeps∵; **fous-moi la paix!** lay off!‡, bugger off!∵; **je t'en fous!** not a bloody (*Brit*) hope!∵, you'll be bloody (*Brit*) lucky!∵; **qu'est-ce qui m'a foutu un idiot pareil!** of all the flaming idiots!‡, how bloody (*Brit*) stupid can you get!∵

(c) (*mettre*) **fous-le là/dans ta poche*** shove* it in here/in your pocket; **~ qn à la porte** to give sb the boot*, kick sb out*; **il a tout foutu en l'air** he chucked the whole flaming lot away‡; **il a foutu le vase par terre** he knocked the flaming vase off‡, he sent the bloody (*Brit*) vase flying‡; **ça fout tout par terre** *ou* **en l'air** that buggers (*Brit*) *ou* screws everything up∵; **ça l'a foutu en rogne** that really made him bloody (*Brit*) mad∵.

(d) ~ le camp to bugger off∵ (*Brit*), sod off∵ (*Brit*), screw off∵ (*US*); **fous-moi le camp!** bugger off!∵, sod off!∵

2 se foutre *vpr* **(a)** (*se mettre*) (*fig*) **je me suis foutu dedans** I really boobed‡; **tu vas te ~ par terre** you're going to fall flat on your face *ou* go sprawling.

(b) (*se gausser*) **se ~ de qn/qch** to take the mickey out of sb/sth‡; (*être indifférent*) not to give a damn about sb/sth‡; (*dépasser les bornes*) **se ~ de qn** to mess* *ou* bugger∵ (*Brit*) sb about; **100 F pour ça, ils se foutent de nous** *ou* **du monde** 100 francs for that! — they must take us for bloody idiots∵ (*Brit*) *ou* assholes∵ (*US*) *ou* what the hell do they take us for!‡; **ça, je m'en fous pas mal** I couldn't give a damn‡ about that.

(c) (∵) **va te faire ~!** (go and) get knotted!‡ (*Brit*) *ou* stuffed!‡ (*Brit*), fuck you!∵; **je lui ai bien demandé, mais va te faire ~: il n'a jamais voulu** I did ask him but bugger me∵, he wouldn't do it.

foutriquet [futʀikɛ] *nm* (*péj*) (little) nobody, little runt*.

foutu, e‡ [futy] (*ptp de* **foutre**) *adj* **(a)** (*avant n*) (*intensif: sale*) bloody∵ (*Brit*), ruddy‡ (*Brit*), damned‡; (*mauvais*) bloody awful∵, ruddy awful‡ (*Brit*), damned awful‡; (*sacré*) one *ou* a hell of a‡.

(b) (*après n*) *malade, vêtement* done for* (*attrib*); *appareil* buggered‡ (*Brit*), screwed up‡, bust*.

(c) (*habillé*) got up*, rigged out*.

(d) (*bâti, conçu*) **cet appareil est bien ~** this device is bloody (*Brit*) *ou* damned clever‡; **ce manuel est mal ~** this textbook's bloody (*Brit*) *ou* damned hopeless‡.

(e) (*malade*) **être mal ~** *ou* **pas bien ~** to feel bloody (*Brit*) awful‡ *ou* lousy‡.

(f) (*capable*) **il est ~ de le faire** he's quite likely *ou* liable to go and do it; **il est même pas ~ de réparer ça** he can't even mend the bloody (*Brit*) thing‡.

fox-hound, *pl* **fox-hounds** [fɔksawnd] *nm* foxhound.

fox(-terrier), *pl* **fox(-terriers)** [fɔks(tɛʀje)] *nm* fox terrier.

fox(-trot) [fɔks(tʀɔt)] *nm inv* foxtrot.

foyer [fwaje] *nm* **(a)** (*frm*) (*maison*) home; (*famille*) family. **~ conjugal/paternel** conjugal/paternal home; **~ uni** close *ou* united family; **les joies du ~** the joys of family life; **quand il revint au ~** *ou* **à son ~** when he came back home; **un jeune ~** a young couple; *V* **femme, fonder, renvoyer.**

(b) *[locomotive, chaudière]* firebox; (*âtre*) hearth, fireplace; (*dalle*) hearth(stone).

(c) (*résidence*) *[vieillards, soldats]* home; *[jeunes]* hostel; *[étudiants]* hostel, hall. **~ éducatif** special (residential) school; **~ d'étudiants** students' hall (of residence) *ou* hostel.

(d) (*lieu de réunion*) *[jeunes, retraités]* club; (*Théât*) foyer. **~ des artistes** greenroom; **~ des jeunes** youth club.

(e) (*Math, Opt, Phys*) focus. **à ~ variable** variable-focus (*épith*).

(f) ~ de *incendie, infection* seat of, centre of; *lumière* source of; *agitation* centre of; **~ d'extrémistes** centre of extremist activities.

frac [fʀak] *nm* tails, tail coat. **être en ~** to be in tails, be wearing a tail coat.

fracas [fʀaka] *nm [objet qui tombe]* crash; *[train, tonnerre, vagues]* roar; *[ville, bataille]* din. **tomber avec ~** to fall with a crash, come crashing down; **annoncer une nouvelle à grand ~** to create a sensation with a piece of news; *V* **perte.**

fracassant, e [fʀakasɑ̃, ɑ̃t] *adj bruit* thunderous, deafening; *nouvelle, déclaration* shattering, staggering, sensational; *succès* thundering (*épith*), sensational.

fracasser [fʀakase] (1) **1** *vt objet* to smash, shatter; *porte* to smash (down), shatter; *mâchoire, épaule* to shatter, smash.

2 se fracasser *vpr*: **se ~ contre** *ou* **sur** *[vagues]* to crash against; *[bateau, véhicule]* to be shattered *ou* be smashed (to pieces) against; **la voiture est allée se ~ contre l'arbre** the car crashed into the tree.

fraction [fʀaksjɔ̃] *nf* (*Math*) fraction; *[groupe, somme, terrain]* part. **une ~ de seconde** a fraction of a second, a split second; **par ~ de 3 jours/de 10 unités** for every 3-day period/10 units; **une ~ importante du groupe** a large proportion of the group.

fractionnaire [fʀaksjɔnɛʀ] *adj* (*Math*) fractional.

fractionnel, -elle [fʀaksjɔnɛl] *adj attitude, menées* divisive.

fractionnement [fʀaksjɔnmɑ̃] *nm* splitting up, division.

fractionner [fʀaksjɔne] (1) **1** *vt groupe, somme, travail* to divide (up), split up. **mon emploi du temps est trop fractionné** my timetable is too disjointed *ou* bitty (*Brit*). **2 se fractionner** *vpr [groupe]* to split up, divide.

fracture [fʀaktyʀ] *nf* (*Géol, Méd*) fracture. **~ du crâne** fractured skull, fracture of the skull; **~ ouverte** open fracture.

fracturer [fʀaktyʀe] (1) *vt* (*Géol, Méd*) to fracture; *serrure* to break (open); *coffre-fort, porte* to break open.

fragile [fʀaʒil] *adj corps, vase* fragile, delicate; *organe, peau* delicate; *cheveux* brittle; *santé* fragile, delicate, shaky; *construction, économie, preuve* flimsy, shaky; *équilibre* delicate, shaky; *bonheur, paix* frail, flimsy, fragile; *gloire* fragile; *pouvoir, prospérité* fragile, flimsy; *argument, hypothèse* flimsy, frail. (*sur étiquette*) **'attention ~'** 'fragile, with care'; (*physiquement, affectivement*) **ne soyez pas trop brusque, elle est encore ~** don't be too rough with her — she is still (feeling) rather fragile *ou* frail; ~ **comme du verre** as delicate as porcelain *ou* china.

fragilement [fʀaʒilmɑ̃] *adv*: **pouvoir ~ établi** power established on a flimsy *ou* shaky foundation; **argument ~ étayé** flimsily upheld argument.

fragilité [fʀaʒilite] *nf* (*V* **fragile**) fragility; delicacy; brittleness; shakiness; flimsiness; frailty.

fragment [fʀagmɑ̃] *nm* **(a)** *[vase, roche, papier]* fragment, bit, piece; *[os, vitre]* fragment, splinter, bit; *[meuble]* piece; *[cheveux]* snippet, bit.

(b) *[conversation]* bit, snatch; *[chanson]* snatch; *[lettre]* bit, part; *[roman]* (*bribe*) fragment; (*extrait*) passage, extract. **je vais vous en lire un ~** I'll read you a bit *ou* part of it, I'll read you a passage *ou* an extract from it.

fragmentaire [fʀagmɑ̃tɛʀ] *adj connaissances* sketchy, patchy, fragmentary; *étude, exposé* sketchy, fragmentary; *effort, travail* sketchy, fragmented. **nous avons une vue très ~ des choses** we have only a sketchy *ou* an incomplete picture of the situation.

fragmentairement [fʀagmɑ̃tɛʀmɑ̃] *adv* in a sketchy way, sketchily.

fragmentation [fʀagmɑ̃tasjɔ̃] *nf* (*V* **fragmenter**) fragmentation; splitting up; breaking up; division.

fragmenter [fʀagmɑ̃te] (1) **1** *vt matière* to break up, fragment; *état, terrain* to fragment, split up, break up; *étude, travail, livre, somme* to split up, divide (up). ~ **la publication d'un livre** to divide up the publication of a book; **avoir une vision fragmentée du monde** to have a fragmented view of life; **ce travail est trop fragmenté** this piece of work is too fragmented *ou* has too many subdivisions.

2 se fragmenter *vpr [roches]* to fragment, break up.

frai [fʀɛ] *nm* (*œufs*) spawn; (*alevins*) fry; (*époque*) spawning season; (*ponte*) spawning.

fraîche [fʀɛʃ] *V* **frais**[1].

fraîchement [fʀɛʃmɑ̃] *adv* **(a)** (*récemment*) freshly, newly. ~ **arrivé** freshly *ou* newly *ou* just arrived; **fruit ~ cueilli** freshly picked fruit; **amitié ~ nouée** newly-formed friendship.

(b) (*froidement*) *accueillir* coolly. **comment ça va? — ~!*** how are you? — a bit chilly!*

fraîcheur [fʀɛʃœʀ] *nf [boisson]* coolness; *[aliment, sentiment, jeunesse]* freshness; *[pièce]* (*agréable*) coolness; (*froid*) chilliness; *[âme]* purity; *[accueil]* coolness, chilliness; *[couleurs]* freshness, crispness. **la ~ du soir/de la nuit** the cool of the evening/of the night.

fraîchir [fʀeʃiʀ] (2) *vi [temps, température]* to get cooler; (*Naut*) *[brise, vent]* to freshen.

frais[1], **fraîche** [fʀɛ, fʀɛʃ] **1** *adj* **(a)** (*lit*) *vent* cool, fresh; *eau, endroit* cool; (*fig*) *accueil* chilly, cool. **il fait un peu ~ ici** it's a bit chilly *ou* cool here; *V* **fond.**

(b) (*fig*) *couleur* fresh, clear, crisp; *joues, teint* fresh; *parfum* fresh; *haleine* fresh, sweet; *voix* clear; *joie, âme* unsullied, pure.

(c) (*récent*) *plaie* fresh; *traces, souvenir* recent, fresh; *peinture* wet, fresh; *nouvelles* recent. **l'encre est encore fraîche** the ink is still wet; *V* **date.**

(d) (*inaltéré, pas en conserve*) *poisson, légumes, lait* fresh; *œuf* fresh, new-laid; *pain* new, fresh. **un peu d'air ~** a breath of *ou* a little fresh air; **ses vêtements ne sont plus très ~** his clothes don't look very fresh; *V* **chair.**

(e) (*jeune, reposé*) *troupes* fresh. ~ **et dispos** fresh (as a daisy); ~ **comme un gardon** bright as a button; **fraîche comme une rose** as fresh as a daisy; **elle est encore très fraîche pour son âge** she's still very fresh-faced *ou* fresh-looking for her age.

(f) (*Comm*) **argent ~** ready cash.

(g) (*) **être ~** to be in a fix* *ou* a nice mess*.

2 *adv* **(a) il fait ~** (*bon*) it's cool; (*froid*) it's chilly; **en été, il faut boire ~** in summer you need cool *ou* cold drinks; **servir ~** serve cold *ou* chilled.

(b) (*récemment*) newly. **herbe ~** *ou* **fraîche coupée** newly *ou* freshly cut grass; ~ **émoulu de l'université** fresh *ou* newly down (*surtout Brit*) *ou* graduated from university; ~ **débarqué de sa province** fresh *ou* newly up from the country; **habillé/rasé de ~** freshly changed/shaven.

3 *nm*: **prendre le ~** to take a breath of cool air; **mettre (qch) au ~** to put (sth) in a cool place.

4 fraîche *nf* (**sortir**) **à la ~** (to go out) in the cool of evening.

frais[2] [fʀɛ] *nmpl* **(a)** (*gén: débours*) expenses; (*facturés*) charges; (*à comptabiliser: Comm, Écon: charges*) costs; (*Admin: droits*) charges, fee(s). ~ **de déplacement/de logement** travelling/accommodation expenses; ~ **d'entretien** *[jardin, maison]* (cost of) upkeep; *[machine, équipement]* maintenance costs; ~ **d'expédition/de timbre** forwarding/stamp charges; ~ **d'enregistrement** registration fee(s); (*Comm*) ~ **généraux** overheads; ~ **divers** sundry *ou* miscellaneous expenses, sundries; (*Jur*) ~ **de justice** (legal) costs; ~ **de main d'œuvre** labour costs; ~ **de scolarité** school fees; **séjour tous ~ compris** holiday inclusive of all costs; **voyage d'affaires tous ~ payés** business trip with all expenses paid; (*Comm*) **tous ~ payés** after costs; **faire de grands ~** to go to great expense; **ça m'a fait beaucoup de ~** it cost me a great deal of money; *V* **faux**[2].

(b) (*loc*) **se mettre en ~** (*lit*) to go to great expense; (*fig*) to put o.s. out, go to great lengths; **se mettre en ~ pour qn/pour recevoir qn** to put o.s. out for sb/to entertain sb; **faire les ~ de la conversation** (*parler*) to keep the conversation going; (*en être le sujet*) to be the (main) topic of conversation; **nous ne voulons pas faire les ~ de cette erreur** we do not want to have to bear the brunt of this mistake; **rentrer dans** *ou* **faire ses ~** to recover one's expenses; **j'ai essayé d'être aimable mais j'en ai été pour mes ~** I tried to be friendly but I might just as well have spared myself the trouble *ou* but I was wasting my time; **aux ~ de la maison** at the firm's expense; **à ses ~** at one's own expense; **aux ~ de la princesse*** at the firm's (*ou* the taxpayer's *etc*) expense; **il l'a acheté à moindre/à grands ~** it didn't cost/it cost him a lot, he paid very little/a great deal for it; **à peu de ~** cheaply, at little cost; **il s'en est tiré à peu de ~** he got off lightly.

fraisage [fʀɛzaʒ] *nm* (*V* **fraiser**) countersinking; milling.

fraise [fʀɛz] **1** *nf* **(a)** (*fruit*) strawberry. ~ **des bois** wild strawberry; *V* **ramener, sucrer.**

(b) (*Tech*) (*pour trou de vis*) countersink (bit); *[métallurgiste]* milling-cutter; *[dentiste]* drill.

(c) (*Boucherie*) ~ **de veau** calf's caul.

(d) (*Hist: col*) ruff, fraise; (*Zool: caroncule*) wattle.

2 *adj inv couleur* strawberry pink.

fraiser [fʀeze] (1) *vt* (*Tech*) *trou* to countersink; *pièce* to mill. **à tête fraisée** countersunk.

fraiseur [fʀɛzœʀ] *nm* milling machine operator.

fraiseuse [fʀɛzøz] *nf* milling machine.

fraisier [fʀezje] *nm* strawberry plant.

fraisure [fʀezyʀ] *nf* countersink, countersunk hole.

framboise [fʀɑ̃bwaz] *nf* (*fruit*) raspberry; (*liqueur*) raspberry liqueur.

framboisier [fʀɑ̃bwazje] *nm* raspberry bush.

franc[1], **franche** [fʀɑ̃, fʀɑ̃ʃ] **1** *adj* **(a)** (*loyal*) *personne* frank, straightforward; *réponse* frank, straight(forward), plain; *regard* candid, open; *gaieté* open; *entrevue* frank, candid. **pour être ~ avec vous** to be frank *ou* plain *ou* candid with you; ~ **comme l'or** perfectly frank; *V* **jouer.**

(b) (*net*) *situation* clear-cut, unequivocal; *différence, réaction* clear(-cut); *cassure* clean; *hostilité, répugnance* clear, definite; *couleur* clear, pure. (*Jur*) **5 jours ~s** 5 clear days.

(c) (*péj: entier*) *imbécile* utter, downright, absolute; *canaille* downright, out-and-out, absolute; *ingratitude* downright, sheer. **c'est une franche comédie/grossièreté** it's downright *ou* utterly hilarious/rude, it's sheer comedy/rudeness.

(d) (*libre*) *zone, ville* free. (*Comm*) ~ **de** free of; **(livré) ~ de port** *marchandises* carriage-paid; *paquet* post-free, postage paid; (*fig*) ~ **du collier**† hard-working; *V* **corps, coudée, coup.**

(e) (*Agr*) **(arbre) ~** cultivar; **greffer sur ~** to graft onto a cultivar.

2 *adv*: **à vous parler ~** to be frank *ou* plain *ou* candid with you; **je vous le dis tout ~** I'm being frank *ou* candid with you.

3: (*Naut*) **franc-bord** *nm, pl* **francs-bords** freeboard; **franc-maçon** *nm, pl* **francs-maçons** freemason; **franc-maçonnerie** *nf inv* freemasonry; **franc-parler** *nm inv* outspokenness; **avoir son franc-parler** to speak one's mind, be outspoken; **franc-tireur** *nm, pl* **francs-tireurs** (*Mil*) irregular, franc tireur; (*fig*) independent, freelance; **faire qch/agir en franc-tireur** to do sth/act off one's own bat (*Brit*) *ou* independently.

franc[2] [fʀɑ̃] *nm* (*monnaie*) franc. **ancien/nouveau ~** old/new franc; ~ **lourd/léger** revalued/pre-revaluation franc.

franc[3], **franque** [fʀɑ̃, fʀɑ̃k] **1** *adj* Frankish. **2** *nm*: **F~** Frank. **3** *nf*: **Franque** Frank.

français, e [fʀɑ̃sɛ, ɛz] **1** *adj* French; *V* **jardin.**

2 *nm* **(a) F~** Frenchman; **les F~** (*gens*) the French, French people; (*hommes*) Frenchmen; **le F~ moyen** the average Frenchman, the man in the street.

(b) (*Ling*) French. **tu ne comprends pas le ~?*** ≃ don't you understand (plain) English?; **c'est une faute de ~** ≃ it's a grammatical mistake.

3 Française *nf* Frenchwoman.

franc-comtois, e, *mpl* **francs-comtois** [fʀɑ̃kɔ̃twa, waz] **1** *adj* of *ou* from (the) Franche-Comté. **2** *nm,f*: **F~(e)** inhabitant *ou* native of Franche-Comté.

France [fʀɑ̃s] *nf* France; *V* **vieux.**

Francfort [fʀɑ̃kfɔʀ] *n* Frankfurt; *V* **saucisse.**

franchement [fʀɑ̃ʃmɑ̃] *adv* **(a)** (*honnêtement*) *parler, répondre* frankly, plainly, candidly; *agir* openly. **pour vous parler ~** to be frank *ou* plain *ou* candid with you, to speak plainly to you; **avouez ~ que vous exagérez** admit frankly *ou* openly that you are going too far; ~ **qu'en penses-tu?** what do you honestly think?; ~**! j'en ai assez!** really! *ou* honestly! I've had enough!; **il y a des gens, ~!** really! *ou* honestly! some people!; ~ **non** frankly no.

(b) (*sans hésiter*) *entrer, frapper* boldly. **il entra ~** he walked straight *ou* boldly in; **appuyez-vous ~ sur moi** don't be afraid to lean on me, lean hard on me; **allez-y ~** (*explication etc*) go straight to the point, say it straight out; (*opération, manœuvre etc*) go right ahead!, go right at it!*

(c) (*sans ambiguïté*) clearly. **je lui ai posé la question ~** I put the question to him straight; **dis-moi ~ ce que tu veux** tell me straight out *ou* clearly what you want; **c'est ~ rouge** it's a clear red, it's clearly red; **c'est ~ au-dessous de la moyenne** it's clearly *ou* well below average.

(d) (*intensif: tout à fait*) *mauvais, laid* utterly, downright, really; *bon* really; *impossible* downright, utterly; *irréparable* utterly, absolutely. **ça m'a ~ dégoûté** it really *ou* utterly disgusted me; **ça s'est ~ mal passé** it went really badly; **on s'est ~ bien amusé** we really *ou* thoroughly enjoyed ourselves; **c'est ~ trop (cher)** it's much *ou* far too dear.

franchir [fʀɑ̃ʃiʀ] (2) *vt obstacle* to clear, get over; *fossé* to clear, jump over; *rue, rivière, ligne d'arrivée* to cross; *seuil* to cross, step across; *porte* to go through; *distance* to cover; *mur du son* to break (through); *difficulté* to get over, surmount; *borne, limite* to overstep, go beyond. (*littér*) ~ **les mers** to cross the sea; ~ **le Rubicon** to cross the Rubicon; **il lui reste 10 mètres à ~** he still has 10 metres to go; ~ **le cap de la soixantaine** to turn sixty, pass the sixty mark; **le pays vient de ~ un cap important** the country has just passed a major turning point; **sa renommée a franchi les frontières** his fame has crossed frontiers; **l'historien, franchissant quelques siècles ...** the historian, passing over a few centuries ... .

franchise [fʀɑ̃ʃiz] *nf* **(a)** *[personne, réponse]* frankness, straightforwardness; *[regard]* candour, openness. **en toute ~** quite frankly.

(b) (*exemption*) (*gén*) exemption; (*Hist*) *[ville]* franchise. **~ (douanière)** exemption from (customs) duties; **colis en ~** duty-free parcel; '**~ postale**' ≃ 'official paid'; **~ de bagages** baggage allowance.

(c) (*Assurance*) excess.

franchissable [fʀɑ̃ʃisabl(ə)] *adj obstacle* surmountable. **limite facilement ~** limit that can easily be overstepped.

franchissement [fʀɑ̃ʃismɑ̃] *nm [obstacle]* clearing; *[rivière, seuil]* crossing; *[limite]* overstepping.

francisation [fʀɑ̃sizɑsjɔ̃] *nf* (*Ling*) gallicizing, Frenchifying.

franciscain, e [fʀɑ̃siskɛ̃, ɛn] *adj, nm,f* Franciscan.

franciser [fʀɑ̃size] (1) *vt* (*Ling*) to gallicize, Frenchify.

franco [fʀɑ̃ko] *adv* (*Comm*) **~ (de port)** *marchandise* carriage-paid; *colis* post-free, postage-paid; **y aller ~*** (*explication etc*) to go straight to the point, come straight out with it*; (*opération, manœuvre etc*) to go right at it*, go right ahead.

franco- [fʀɑ̃ko] *préf* franco-.

franco-canadien [fʀɑ̃kɔkanadjɛ̃] *nm* Canadian French.

francophile [fʀɑ̃kɔfil] *adj, nmf* francophile.

francophilie [fʀɑ̃kɔfili] *nf* francomania.

francophobe [fʀɑ̃kɔfɔb] *adj, nmf* francophobe.

francophobie [fʀɑ̃kɔfɔbi] *nf* francophobia.

francophone [fʀɑ̃kɔfɔn] **1** *adj* French-speaking; (*Can*) primarily French-speaking. **2** *nmf* (native) French speaker; (*Can*) Francophone (*Can*).

francophonie [fʀɑ̃kɔfɔni] *nf* French-speaking communities.

franco-québécois [fʀɑ̃kɔkebekwa] *nm* Quebec French.

frange [fʀɑ̃ʒ] *nf [tissu, cheveux]* fringe; (*fig*) *[conscience, sommeil]* threshold. **une ~ de lumière** a band of light; (*Opt*) **~s d'interférence** interference fringes.

franger [fʀɑ̃ʒe] (3) *vt* (*gén ptp*) to fringe (*de* with).

frangin* [fʀɑ̃ʒɛ̃] *nm* brother.

frangine* [fʀɑ̃ʒin] *nf* sister.

frangipane [fʀɑ̃ʒipan] *nf* (*Culin*) almond paste, frangipane. **gâteau fourré à la ~** frangipane (pastry).

franglais [fʀɑ̃glɛ] *nm* Franglais.

franque [fʀɑ̃k] *V* **franc³**.

franquette* [fʀɑ̃kɛt] *nf*: **à la bonne ~** *recevoir, manger* simply, without any fuss; **venez manger, ce sera à la bonne ~** come and eat with us — it'll be a pretty simple meal *ou* we won't go to any special trouble (for you).

franquisme [fʀɑ̃kism(ə)] *nm* Francoism.

franquiste [fʀɑ̃kist(ə)] **1** *adj* pro-Franco. **2** *nmf* Franco supporter.

frappant, e [fʀapɑ̃, ɑ̃t] *adj* striking; *V* **argument**.

frappe [fʀap] *nf* **(a)** *[monnaie, médaille]* (*action*) stamping, striking; (*empreinte*) stamp, impression.

(b) *[dactylo, pianiste]* touch; *[machine à écrire]* (*souplesse*) touch; (*impression*) typeface. **la lettre est à la ~** the letter is being typed (out); **c'est la première ~** it's the top copy; *V* **faute**.

(c) (*péj: voyou*) tough guy.

(d) (*Sport*) *[boxeur]* punch; *[footballeur]* kick. **il a une bonne ~ de la balle** he kicks the ball well, he has a good kick; *V* **force**.

frappé, e [fʀape] (*ptp de* **frapper**) *adj* **(a)** (*saisi*) struck. **~ de panique** panic-stricken; **~ de stupeur** thunderstruck; **(très) ~ de voir que ...** (very) struck to see that ... .

(b) *velours* embossed. (*fig*) **vers bien ~s** neatly turned lines (of verse); *V* **coin**.

(c) *champagne, café* iced. **boire un vin bien ~** to drink a wine well chilled.

frappement [fʀapmɑ̃] *nm* striking.

frapper [fʀape] (1) **1** *vt* **(a)** (*cogner*) *personne, surface [poing, projectile]* to hit, strike; *[couteau]* to stab, strike; *cordes, clavier* to strike; *coups* to strike, deal. **~ le sol du pied** to stamp (one's foot) on the ground; **~ sec*** to hit hard; (*Hist*) **~ d'estoc et de taille** to cut and thrust; (*Théât*) **~ les trois coups** to give the three knocks (*to annouce start of performance*); **la pluie/la lumière frappait le mur** the rain lashed (against)/the light fell on the wall; (*fig*) **ce qui a frappé mon regard/mon oreille** what caught my eye/reached my ears; (*fig*) **~ un grand coup** to strike a decisive blow; **frappé à mort** fatally *ou* mortally wounded.

(b) (*fig*) *[malheur, maladie]* to strike (down); *[coïncidence, détail]* to strike. **frappé de paralysie/par le malheur** stricken with paralysis/by misfortune; **ce deuil le frappe cruellement** this bereavement is a cruel blow to him; **cela l'a frappé de stupeur** he was thunderstruck *ou* dumbfounded at this; **cette découverte le frappa de panique/d'horreur** he was panic-/horror-stricken at this discovery, this discovery filled him with panic/horror; **~ l'imagination** to catch *ou* fire the imagination; **ce qui (me) frappe** what strikes me.

(c) (*fig*) *[mesures, impôts]* to hit. **ces impôts/amendes frappent les plus pauvres** these taxes/fines hit the very poor; **ces impôts frappent lourdement les petits commerçants** these taxes are hitting small businesses hard; **l'amende qui frappe les contrevenants à ce règlement** the fine imposed upon those who infringe this regulation; **~ qn d'une amende/d'un impôt** to impose a fine/a tax upon sb; **la loi doit ~ les coupables** the law must punish the guilty; **ils ont frappé la vente du tabac d'un impôt supplémentaire** they have put *ou* slammed* an extra tax on tobacco sales.

(d) *monnaie, médaille* to strike, stamp.

(e) (*glacer*) *champagne, vin* to put on ice; *café* to ice.

2 *vi* to strike (*sur* on, *contre* against). **~ du poing sur la table** to bang one's fist on the table; **~ sur la table avec une règle** to tap the table *ou* (*plus fort*) to knock the table *ou* bang on the table with a ruler; **~ dans ses mains** to clap one's hands; **~ du pied** to stamp (one's foot); (*lit, fig*) **~ à la porte** to knock on *ou* at the door; **on a frappé** there's someone at the door, there was a knock at the door; **entrez sans ~** come in without knocking, come straight in; (*fig*) **~ à toutes les portes** to try every door; (*fig*) **~ à la bonne/mauvaise porte** to go to the right/wrong person *ou* place; (*fig*) **il faut d'abord ~ à la tête** we must aim at the top first.

3 se frapper *vpr* **(a) se ~ la poitrine** to beat one's breast; **se ~ le front** to tap one's forehead.

(b) (*: *se tracasser*) to get (o.s.) worked up*, get (o.s.) into a state*.

frappeur [fʀapœʀ] *adj m V* **esprit**.

frasil [fʀasi *ou* fʀazil] *nm* (*Can*) frazil (*Can*).

frasque [fʀask(ə)] *nf* (*gén pl*) prank, escapade. **faire des ~s** to get up to mischief *ou* high jinks*.

fraternel, -elle [fʀatɛʀnɛl] *adj* brotherly, fraternal. **se montrer ~ envers qn** to behave in a brotherly manner towards sb.

fraternellement [fʀatɛʀnɛlmɑ̃] *adv* in a brotherly way, fraternally.

fraternisation [fʀatɛʀnizɑsjɔ̃] *nf* fraternization, fraternizing. **élan de ~** surge of brotherly feeling.

fraterniser [fʀatɛʀnize] (1) *vi [pays, personnes]* to fraternize (*avec* with).

fraternité [fʀatɛʀnite] *nf* **(a)** (*amitié*) brotherhood (*U*), fraternity (*U*). **il y a une ~ d'esprit entre eux** there is a kinship *ou* brotherhood of spirit between them; *V* **liberté**. **(b)** (*Rel*) fraternity, brotherhood.

fratricide [fʀatʀisid] **1** *adj* fratricidal. **2** *nmf* fratricide. **3** *nm* (*crime*) fratricide.

fraude [fʀod] *nf* (*gén*) fraud (*U*); (*à un examen*) cheating; (*envers le fisc*) tax evasion. **en ~** *fabriquer, vendre* fraudulently; *lire, fumer* secretly; **passer qch/faire passer qn en ~** to smuggle sth/sb in; **~ électorale** electoral fraud; **~ fiscale** tax evasion.

frauder [fʀode] (1) **1** *vt* to defraud, cheat. **~ le fisc** to evade taxation. **2** *vi* (*gén*) to cheat; **~ sur la quantité/qualité** to cheat over the quantity/quality.

fraudeur, -euse [fʀodœʀ, øz] *nm,f* (*gén*) person guilty of fraud; (*à la douane*) smuggler; (*envers le fisc*) tax evader. (*à un examen*) **les ~s seront lourdement sanctionnés** cheating will be *ou* candidates who cheat will be severely punished; **il a un tempérament ~, il est ~** he has a tendency towards cheating.

frauduleusement [fʀodyløzmɑ̃] *adv* fraudulently.

frauduleux, -euse [fʀodylø, øz] *adj trafic, pratiques, concurrence* fraudulent. **sans intention ~euse de ma part** with no intention of cheating on my part.

frayer [fʀeje] (8) **1** *vt chemin* to open up, clear. **~ le passage à qn** to clear the way for sb; (*fig*) **~ la voie** to pave the way.

2 se frayer *vpr* (*lit*) **se ~ un passage (dans la foule)** to force *ou* plough *ou* elbow one's way through (the crowd); (*fig*) **se ~ un chemin vers les honneurs** to work one's way up to fame.

3 *vi* **(a)** *[poisson]* to spawn.

(b) (*fig*) **~ avec** to mix *ou* associate with.

frayeur [fʀɛjœʀ] *nf* fright. **tu m'as fait une de ces ~s!** you gave me a dreadful fright!; **cri/geste de ~** cry/gesture of fear, startled cry/gesture.

fredaine [fʀədɛn] *nf* mischief (*U*), escapade. **faire des ~s** to be up to mischief.

fredonnement [fʀədɔnmɑ̃] *nm* humming.

fredonner [fʀədɔne] (1) *vt* to hum. **elle fredonnait dans la cuisine** she was humming (away) (to herself) in the kitchen.

freezer [fʀizœʀ] *nm* freezing compartment, freezer (*of refrigerator*).

frégate [fʀegat] *nf* (*Hist, Mil, Naut*) frigate; (*Zool*) frigate bird; *V* **capitaine**.

frein [fʀɛ̃] **1** *nm [voiture]*, (*aussi fig*) brake; *[cheval]* bit. **c'est un ~ à l'expansion** it acts as a brake upon expansion; **mets le ~** put the brake on; **mettre un ~ à** *inflation, colère, ambitions* to put a brake on, curb, check; **sans ~** *imagination, curiosité* unbridled, unchecked; *V* **bloquer, coup, ronger**.

2: **frein aérodynamique** air brake; **frein à disques** disc brake; **frein à main** handbrake; **frein moteur** engine breaking; **frein à pied** footbrake; **frein à tambours** drum brake.

freinage [fʀɛnaʒ] *nm* (*action*) braking. **dispositif de ~** braking system; **traces de ~** tyre marks (*caused by braking*); **un bon ~** good braking.

freiner [fʀene] (1) **1** *vt véhicule* to pull up, slow down; *progression, coureur* to slow up *ou* down, hold up; *progrès, évolution* to put a brake on, check; *enthousiasme, joie, personne* to check.

2 *vi* (*Aut*) to brake; (*à ski, en patins etc*) to slow down. **~ à bloc** to jam on the brakes; **il freina brusquement** he braked suddenly, he suddenly jammed on the brakes.

frelater [fʀəlate] (1) *vt vin, aliment* to adulterate. (*fig*) **un milieu frelaté** a tainted *ou* slightly corrupt milieu.

frêle [fʀɛl] *adj tige, charpente* flimsy, frail, fragile; *enfant, femme, corps* frail, fragile; *voix* thin, frail. (*littér*) **de ~s espérances** frail *ou* flimsy hopes.

frelon [fʀəlɔ̃] *nm* hornet.

freluquet [fʀəlykɛ] *nm* (*péj*) whippersnapper.

frémir [fʀemiʀ] (2) *vi* **(a)** *[personne, corps]* (*de peur*) to quake, tremble, shudder; (*d'horreur*) to shudder, shiver; (*de fièvre, froid*) to shiver; (*de colère*) to shake, tremble, quiver; (*d'impatience, de plaisir, d'espoir*) to quiver, tremble (*de* with). **ça me fait ~** it makes me shudder; **il frémit de tout son être** his whole being quivered *ou* trembled; **histoire à vous faire ~** story that gives you the shivers* *ou* that makes you shudder *ou* shiver; **aux moments de suspense toute la salle frémissait** at the moments of suspense the whole audience trembled.

(b) *[lèvres, feuillage]* to tremble, quiver; *[narine, aile, corde]* to quiver; *[eau chaude]* to simmer, quiver. **sensibilité frémissante** quivering sensitivity.
frémissement [fʀemismɑ̃] *nm* **(a)** (*humain: V* **frémir**) shudder; shiver; quiver. **un ~ de plaisir** a thrill *ou* quiver of pleasure; **un long ~ parcourut son corps** a shiver ran all the way through him *ou* ran the length of his body; **le ~ de son être** his quivering *ou* shivering *ou* shuddering being; **un ~ parcourut la salle** a quiver ran through the room.
(b) *[lèvres, feuillage]* trembling (*U*), quivering (*U*); *[narine, aile, corde]* quivering (*U*); *[eau chaude]* simmering, quivering.
frêne [fʀɛn] *nm* ash (tree); (*bois*) ash.
frénésie [fʀenezi] *nf* frenzy. **avec ~** *travailler, applaudir* frenetically, furiously; **aimer qn avec ~** to be wildly *ou* desperately in love with sb.
frénétique [fʀenetik] *adj applaudissements, passion, rythme* frenzied, frenetic.
frénétiquement [fʀenetikmɑ̃] *adv aimer* wildly, desperately; *travailler, applaudir* frenetically, furiously.
fréquemment [fʀekamɑ̃] *adv* frequently, often.
fréquence [fʀekɑ̃s] *nf* (*gén*) frequency; *V* **modulation.**
fréquent, e [fʀekɑ̃, ɑ̃t] *adj* frequent.
fréquentable [fʀekɑ̃tabl(ə)] *adj*: **sont-ils ~s?** are they the sort of people one can associate with?; **ils ne sont pas ~s** they aren't the sort of people one associates with, they aren't nice to know*.
fréquentatif, -ive [fʀekɑ̃tatif, iv] *adj* frequentative.
fréquentation [fʀekɑ̃tasjɔ̃] *nf* **(a)** (*action*) *[établissement]* frequenting. **la ~ de ces gens** seeing these people frequently *ou* often. **(b)** (*gén pl: relation*) company (*U*), associate. **des ~s douteuses** dubious company *ou* associates; **ce n'est pas une ~ pour une jeune fille bien élevée** that isn't the sort of company for a well-brought-up young lady to keep.
fréquenté, e [fʀekɑ̃te] (*ptp de* **fréquenter**) *adj lieu, établissement* busy. **très ~** very busy, much frequented; **établissement bien/mal ~** establishment of good/ill repute.
fréquenter [fʀekɑ̃te] (1) *vt lieu* to frequent; *voisins* to see frequently *ou* often; *jeune fille* to go around with; (*littér*) *auteurs classiques* to keep company with. **~ la bonne société** to move in fashionable circles; **il fréquente plus les cafés que la faculté** he's in cafés more often than at lectures; **il les fréquente peu** he seldom sees them; **nous nous fréquentons beaucoup** we see quite a lot of each other, we see each other quite often *ou* frequently; **ces jeunes gens se fréquentent depuis un an** those young people have been going around together for a year now.
frère [fʀɛʀ] *nm* **(a)** (*gén, fig*) brother. **partager en ~s** to share like brothers; **alors, vieux ~!*** well, old pal!* *ou* mate!* (*Brit*) *ou* buddy!* (*US*); (*fig*) **j'ai trouvé le ~ de ce vase chez un antiquaire*** I found the partner to this vase in an antique shop; (*Mil*) **~s d'armes** brothers in arms; (*Pol*) **partis/peuples ~s** sister parties/countries; *V* **demi-, faux**[2].
(b) (*Rel*) (*égal*) brother; (*paroissien*) brother; (*moine*) brother, friar. **les hommes sont tous ~s** all men are brothers; (*Rel*) **mes (bien chers) ~s** (dearly beloved) brethren; **~ lai** lay brother; **~ mendiant** mendicant friar; **~ Antoine** Brother Antoine, Friar Antoine; **on l'a mis en pension chez les ~s** he has been sent to a Catholic boarding school.
frérot* [fʀeʀo] *nm* kid brother*.
fresque [fʀɛsk(ə)] *nf* (*Art*) fresco; (*Littérat*) portrait.
fret [fʀɛ] *nm* (*prix*) (*Aviat, Naut*) freight(age); (*Aut*) carriage; (*cargaison*) (*Aviat, Naut*) freight, cargo; (*Aut*) load. (*Comm: affréter*) **prendre à ~** to charter.
fréter [fʀete] (6) *vt* (*gén: prendre à fret*) to charter; (*Naut: donner à fret*) to freight.
fréteur [fʀetœʀ] *nm* (*Naut*) owner.
frétillant, e [fʀetijɑ̃, ɑ̃t] *adj poisson* wriggling; *personne* frisky, lively. **~ d'impatience** fidgeting *ou* quivering with impatience.
frétillement [fʀetijmɑ̃] *nm [poisson]* wriggling (*U*). **un ~ d'impatience** a quiver of impatience.
frétiller [fʀetije] (1) *vi [poisson]* to wriggle; *[chien]* to wag its tail; *[personne]* to wriggle, fidget. **~ d'impatience** to fidget *ou* quiver with impatience; **~ de joie** to be quivering *ou* quiver with joy; **le chien frétillait de la queue** the dog was wagging its tail; (*hum, péj*) **elle frétille de l'arrière-train** she's wiggling her bottom (*hum*).
fretin [fʀətɛ̃] *nm* (*poissons*) fry; (*fig rare*) small fry; *V* **menu**[2].
freudien, -ienne [fʀødjɛ̃, jɛn] *adj* Freudian.
freudisme [fʀødism(ə)] *nm* Freudianism.
friabilité [fʀijabilite] *nf [roche, sol]* crumbly nature, flakiness, friability (*T*).
friable [fʀijabl(ə)] *adj roche, sol* crumbly, flaky, friable (*T*); (*Culin*) *pâte* crumbly.
friand, e [fʀijɑ̃, ɑ̃d] **1** *adj*: **~ de** *lait, miel, bonbons* partial to, fond of; (*fig*) *compliments, chatteries* fond of. **2** *nm* (*pâté*) (minced) meat pie; (*sucré*) small almond-flavoured cake.
friandise [fʀijɑ̃diz] *nf* sweet, candy, sweetmeat†. **c'est une ~** it's a delicacy.
fric: [fʀik] *nm* (*argent*) dough:, cash*, lolly:. **il a du ~** he's loaded (with cash):.
fricandeau, *pl* **~x** [fʀikɑ̃do] *nm* fricandeau.
fricassée [fʀikase] *nf* fricassee.
fricative [fʀikativ] *adj f, nf* fricative.
fric-frac*, *pl* **fric-frac(s)** [fʀikfʀak] *nm* break-in.
friche [fʀiʃ] *nf* fallow land (*U*). (*lit, fig*) **en ~** (lying) fallow; (*lit, fig*) **être/laisser en ~** to lie/let lie fallow.
frichti* [fʀiʃti] *nm,* **fricot*** [fʀiko] *nm* nosh: (*U*), grub* (*U*). **préparer son ~** to cook up one's nosh:.
fricoter* [fʀikɔte] (1) **1** *vt plat* to cook up. (*fig*) **qu'est-ce qu'il fricote?** what's he cooking up?*, what's he up to?* **2** *vi*: **~ avec qn** to knock about with sb*.
friction [fʀiksjɔ̃] *nf* (*Phys, Tech*) friction; (*massage*) rub, rubdown; (*chez le coiffeur*) scalp massage; (*fig: conflits*) friction.
frictionner [fʀiksjɔne] (1) *vt* to rub. **se ~ après un bain** to rub o.s. down after a bath.
fridolin [fʀidɔlɛ̃] *nm* (*péj: Allemand*) Kraut, Fritz.
frigidaire [fʀiʒidɛʀ] *nm* ® refrigerator, fridge (*Brit*).
frigide [fʀiʒid] *adj* frigid.
frigidité [fʀiʒidite] *nf* frigidity.
frigo* [fʀigo] *nm* fridge (*Brit*), refrigerator.
frigorifier [fʀigɔʀifje] (7) *vt* (*lit*) to refrigerate; (*fig: pétrifier*) to petrify, freeze to the spot. **être frigorifié*** (*avoir froid*) to be frozen stiff.
frigorifique [fʀigɔʀifik] *adj mélange* refrigerating (*épith*); *camion, wagon* refrigerator (*épith*); *V* **armoire.**
frileusement [fʀiløzmɑ̃] *adv* with a shiver.
frileux, -euse [fʀilø, øz] *adj personne* sensitive to (the) cold; *geste, posture* shivery. **il est très ~** he feels the cold easily, he is very sensitive to (the) cold; **elle se couvrit de son châle d'un geste ~** with a shiver she pulled her shawl around her.
frimaire [fʀimɛʀ] *nm* (*Hist*) Frimaire (*third month in the French Republican calendar*).
frimas [fʀimɑ] *nmpl* (*littér*) wintry weather.
frime* [fʀim] *nf*: **c'est de la ~** that's a lot of eyewash*, it's all put on*; **c'est pour la ~** it's all *ou* just for show.
frimousse [fʀimus] *nf* (sweet) little face.
fringale* [fʀɛ̃gal] *nf* (*faim*) raging hunger. (*désir*) **une ~ de** a craving for; **j'ai la ~** I'm ravenous* *ou* famished* *ou* starving*.
fringant, e [fʀɛ̃gɑ̃, ɑ̃t] *adj cheval* frisky, high-spirited; *personne, allure* dashing.
fringué, e: [fʀɛ̃ge] (*ptp de* **(se) fringuer**) *adj* dressed, done up*. **bien/mal ~** well-/badly-dressed; **vise un peu comme elle est ~e!** look what she's got on!, look what she's done up in!*
fringuer: [fʀɛ̃ge] (1) **1 se fringuer** *vpr* (*s'habiller*) to get dressed; (*s'habiller élégamment*) to doll (o.s.) up*, do o.s. up*. **2** *vt* to dress.
fringues: [fʀɛ̃g] *nfpl* clobber: (*U*) (*Brit*), togs:.
friper [fʀipe] (1) *vt* to crumple (up), crush. **ça se fripe facilement** it crumples *ou* crushes easily; **des habits tout fripés** badly crumpled *ou* rumpled clothes; (*fig*) **visage tout fripé** crumpled(-up) face.
friperie† [fʀipʀi] *nf* (*boutique*) secondhand clothes shop (*Brit*) *ou* store (*US*).
fripier, -ière [fʀipje, jɛʀ] *nm,f* secondhand clothes dealer.
fripon, onne [fʀipɔ̃, ɔn] **1** *adj air, allure, visage, yeux* roguish, mischievous, cheeky; *nez* cheeky, saucy. **2** *nm,f* (†: *gredin*) knave†, rascally fellow†; (*: *nuance affectueuse*) rascal, rogue. **petit ~!** you little rascal! *ou* rogue!
friponnerie [fʀipɔnʀi] *nf* (*acte*) piece of mischief, prank. **les ~s de ce gamin** the mischief this little imp gets up to, the pranks of the little imp.
fripouille [fʀipuj] *nf* (*péj*) rogue, scoundrel. (*nuance affectueuse*) **petite ~!*** you little devil!* *ou* rogue!
frire [fʀiʀ] *vt* (*aussi* **faire ~**) to fry; *V* **pâte, poêle**[1].
frise [fʀiz] *nf* (*Archit, Art*) frieze; (*Théât*) border; *V* **cheval.**
frisé, e [fʀize] (*ptp de* **friser**) **1** *adj cheveux* (very) curly; *personne, animal* curly-haired. **il est tout ~** he has very curly hair; **~ comme un mouton** curly-headed *ou* -haired, frizzy-haired; *V* **chou**[1]. **2** *nm* (*péj: Allemand*) Jerry. **3 frisée** *nf* (*chicorée*) endive.
friser [fʀize] (1) **1** *vt* **(a)** *cheveux* to curl; *moustache* to twirl. **~ qn** to curl sb's hair; *V* **fer.**
(b) (*frôler*) *surface* to graze, skim; *catastrophe, mort* to be within a hair's breadth of, be within an ace of; *insolence* to border on, verge on. **~ la soixantaine** to be getting on towards sixty, be close to sixty, be pushing sixty*.
2 *vi [cheveux]* to curl, be curly; *[personne]* to have curly hair. **faire ~ ses cheveux** to make one's hair go curly; (*chez le coiffeur*) to have one's hair curled.
3 se friser *vpr* to curl one's hair. **se faire ~** (*par un coiffeur*) to have one's hair curled.
frisette [fʀizɛt] *nf* little curl, little ringlet.
frison[1] [fʀizɔ̃] *nm* little curl *ou* ringlet (*around face or neck*).
frison[2]**, -onne** [fʀizɔ̃, ɔn] **1** *adj* Frisian *ou* Friesian. **2** *nm* (*Ling*) Frisian *ou* Friesian. **3** *nm,f*: **F~(ne)** Frisian *ou* Friesian. **4 frisonne** *nf*: **(vache) ~ne** Frisian *ou* Friesian (cow).
frisotter [fʀizɔte] (1) **1** *vt* to crimp, curl tightly. **2** *vi* to curl tightly.
frisquet [fʀiskɛ] *adj m vent* chilly. **il fait ~** it's chilly, there's a chill *ou* nip in the air.
frisson [fʀisɔ̃] *nm [froid, fièvre]* shiver; *[répulsion, peur]* shudder, shiver; *[volupté]* thrill, shiver, quiver. **elle fut prise** *ou* **saisie d'un ~** a sudden shiver ran through her; **la fièvre me donne des ~s** this fever is making me shiver *ou* is giving me the shivers*; **ça me donne le ~** it gives me the creeps* *ou* the shivers*, it makes me shudder *ou* shiver.
frissonnement [fʀisɔnmɑ̃] *nm* **(a)** (*action: V* **frissonner**) quaking; trembling; shuddering; shivering; quivering; rustling; rippling. **(b)** (*frisson*) shiver, shudder. **~ de volupté** thrill *ou* shiver *ou* quiver of sensual delight.
frissonner [fʀisɔne] (1) *vi* **(a)** *[personne, corps]* (*de peur*) to quake, tremble, shudder; (*d'horreur*) to shudder, shiver; (*de fièvre, froid*) to shiver; (*de volupté, désir*) to quiver, tremble (*de* with). **le vent le fit ~** the wind made him shiver *ou* shudder.
(b) *[feuillage]* to quiver, rustle; *[lac]* to ripple. **la lumière frissonnait sur l'eau** the light shimmered on *ou* over the water.
frisure† [fʀizyʀ] *nf* curls. **ses cheveux tenaient bien la ~** her hair held curls *ou* a curl well; **faire une ~ à qn** to curl sb's hair.
frit, e [fʀi, fʀit] (*ptp de* **frire**) **1** *adj* (*Culin*) fried. (*:: *fichu, perdu*) **ils sont ~s** they've had it*, their goose is cooked*, their number's up*; *V* **pomme.**

2 frite *nf* (*gén pl*) chip. ~s chips, French fried potatoes, French fries (*surtout US*); **un steak *ou* bifteck** ~s a steak and chips (*Brit*) *ou* French fries *ou* French fried potatoes.
friterie [fʀitʀi] *nf* (*boutique*) chip shop (*Brit*).
friteuse [fʀitøz] *nf* chip pan (*Brit*), deep fryer.
friture [fʀityʀ] *nf* **(a)** (*Culin*) (*méthode*) frying; (*graisse*) (deep) fat (*for frying*); (*mets*) fried fish (*U ou pl*). **le docteur me déconseille les** ~s the doctor advises me against fried food; **(petite)** ~ small fish (*U ou pl*); **une** ~ **de goujons** (a dish of) fried gudgeon.
(b) (*Rad**) crackle, crackling (*U*).
fritz [fʀits] *nm* (*péj: Allemand*) Kraut, Fritz; (*soldat*) Jerry.
frivole [fʀivɔl] *adj personne* frivolous, shallow; *occupation, argument* frivolous, trivial.
frivolement [fʀivɔlmɑ̃] *adv* frivolously.
frivolité [fʀivɔlite] *nf* (*V* **frivole**) frivolity, frivolousness; shallowness; triviality; (*gén pl: bagatelle*) frivolities. (*Comm: articles*) ~s fancy goods.
froc [fʀɔk] *nm* **(a)** (*Rel*) frock, habit. **porter le** ~ to be a monk, wear the habit of a monk; (*fig*) **jeter le** ~ **aux orties** to unfrock o.s., leave the priesthood. **(b)** (*‡: pantalon*) bags*, breeches*.
froid, e [fʀwa, fʀwad] **1** *adj* **(a)** *personne, nature, boisson, couleur* cold; *manières, accueil* cold, chilly; *auteur, style* cold, frigid; *détermination, calcul* cold, cool. **colère** ~**e** controlled anger; **il fait un temps assez** ~ the weather is rather cold; **d'un ton** ~ coldly; **ça me laisse** ~ it leaves me cold; **garder la tête** ~**e** to keep cool, keep a cool head; ~ **comme le marbre** as cold as marble; *V* **battre, sang, sueur** *etc.*
(b) à ~**: laminer/souder à** ~ to cold-roll/-weld; **démarrer à** ~ to start (from) cold; **coller à** ~ to glue without preheating; **opérer à** ~ (*Méd*) to perform cold surgery; (*fig*) to let things cool down before acting; (*fig*) **parler à** ~ **de qch** to speak coldly *ou* coolly of sth; (*fig*) **prendre *ou* cueillir qn à** ~* to catch sb unawares *ou* off guard; *V* **ciseau.**
2 *nm* **(a) le** ~ (*gén*) the cold; (*industrie*) refrigeration; **j'ai** ~ I am cold; **j'ai** ~ **aux pieds** my feet are cold; **il fait** ~**/un** ~ **de canard*** it's cold/freezing cold *ou* perishing*; **ça me donne *ou* fait** ~ it makes me (feel) cold; **ça me fait** ~ **dans le dos** (*lit*) it gives me a cold back, it makes my back cold; (*fig*) it sends shivers down my spine; **prendre *ou* attraper (un coup de)** ~ to catch cold *ou* a chill; **vague *ou* coup de** ~ cold spell; **les grands** ~**s** the cold of winter; **n'avoir pas** ~ **aux yeux** *[homme d'affaires, aventurier]* to be venturesome *ou* adventurous; *[enfant]* to have plenty of pluck; *V* **craindre, jeter, mourir.**
(b) (*brouille*) coolness (*U*). **malgré le** ~ **qu'il y avait entre eux** despite the coolness that existed between them; **être en** ~ **avec qn** to be on bad terms *ou* not to be on good terms with sb.
froidement [fʀwadmɑ̃] *adv accueillir, remercier* coldly; *calculer, réfléchir* coolly; *tuer* cold-bloodedly, in cold blood. **il me reçut** ~ I got a cold *ou* chilly reception (from him), he greeted me coldly; **meurtre accompli** ~ cold-blooded murder; (*hum*) **comment vas-tu? —** ~**!** how are you? — cold! (*hum*).
froideur [fʀwadœʀ] *nf [personne, sentiments]* coldness; *[manières, accueil]* coldness, chilliness; *[style, auteur]* coldness, frigidity. **recevoir qn avec** ~ to give sb a cold *ou* chilly *ou* cool reception, greet sb coldly; **contempler qch avec** ~ to contemplate sth coldly *ou* coolly; (*littér*) **la** ~ **de son cœur** her coldness of heart.
froidure†† [fʀwadyʀ] *nf* cold (*U*), cold season.
froissement [fʀwasmɑ̃] *nm* **(a)** *[tissu]* crumpling, creasing.
(b) (*bruit*) rustle, rustling (*U*). **des** ~**s soyeux** the sound of rustling silk.
(c) (*Méd*) ~ **(d'un muscle)** (muscular) strain.
(d) (*fig littér*) **évitez tout** ~ **d'amour-propre** try to avoid hurting anyone's feelings.
froisser [fʀwase] (1) **1** *vt tissu* to crumple, crease; *habit* to crumple, rumple, crease; *herbe* to crush; (*fig*) *personne* to hurt, offend. **ça l'a froissé dans son orgueil** that ruffled his pride; **il froissa la lettre et la jeta** he screwed up the letter and threw it away.
2 se froisser *vpr [tissu]* to crease, crumple; *[personne]* to take offence, take umbrage (*de* at). (*Méd*) **se** ~ **un muscle** to strain a muscle.
frôlement [fʀolmɑ̃] *nm* (*contact*) light touch, light contact (*U*); (*bruit*) rustle, rustling (*U*). **le** ~ **des corps dans l'obscurité** the light contact of bodies brushing against each other in the darkness.
frôler [fʀole] (1) *vt* (*lit*) (*toucher*) to brush against; (*passer près de*) to skim. **le projectile le frôla** the projectile skimmed past him; **l'automobiliste frôla le trottoir/le poteau** the driver just missed the pavement (*Brit*) *ou* sidewalk (*US*)/post; (*fig*) ~ **la mort/catastrophe** to come within a hair's breadth *ou* an ace of death/a catastrophe.
fromage [fʀɔmaʒ] **1** *nm* cheese. **biscuit/omelette/soufflé au** ~ cheese biscuit/omelette/soufflé; **nouilles au** ~ pasta with cheese (sauce), ≃ macaroni cheese; **plat au** ~ cheese dish; (*fig*) **trouver un (bon)** ~* to find a cushy job* *ou* cushy number*; *V* **cloche, plateau, poire.**
2: fromage blanc soft white cheese; **fromage de chèvre** goat's milk cheese; **fromage à la crème** cream cheese; **fromage fondu** cheese spread; **fromage frais** soft white cheese; **fromage gras** full-fat cheese; **fromage maigre** low-fat cheese; **fromage à pâte dure/molle** hard/soft cheese; **fromage à tartiner** cheese spread; **fromage de tête** pork brawn.
fromager, -ère [fʀɔmaʒe, ɛʀ] **1** *adj industrie, commerce, production* cheese (*épith*). **association** ~**ère** cheese producers' association. **2** *nm* **(a)** (*fabricant*) cheese maker; (*marchand*) cheesemonger (*surtout Brit*). **(b)** (*Bot*) kapok tree.
fromagerie [fʀɔmaʒʀi] *nf* cheese dairy.
froment [fʀɔmɑ̃] *nm* wheat.
from(e)ton‡ [fʀɔmtɔ̃] *nm* cheese.
fronce [fʀɔ̃s] *nf* gather. ~**s** gathers, gathering (*U*); **faire des** ~**s** to gather; **jupe à** ~**s** gathered skirt.
froncement [fʀɔ̃smɑ̃] *nm*: ~ **de sourcils** frown.
froncer [fʀɔ̃se] (3) *vt* (*Couture*) to gather. ~ **les sourcils** to frown, knit one's brows.
frondaison [fʀɔ̃dɛzɔ̃] *nf* (*feuillage*) foliage (*U*).
fronde[1] [fʀɔ̃d] *nf* (*arme*) sling; (*jouet*) catapult.
fronde[2] [fʀɔ̃d] *nf* (*révolte*) **esprit/vent de** ~ spirit/wind of revolt *ou* insurrection; (*Hist*) **la F**~ the Fronde.
fronder [fʀɔ̃de] (1) *vt* (*railler*) to lampoon, satirize.
frondeur, -euse [fʀɔ̃dœʀ, øz] *adj attitude, mentalité* recalcitrant, anti-authority; *propos* anti-authority.
front [fʀɔ̃] *nm* **(a)** (*Anat*) forehead, brow (*littér*); (*fig: tête*) head; (*littér: visage*) brow (*littér*), face; (*littér*) *[bâtiment]* façade, front. **il peut marcher le** ~ **haut** he can hold his head (up) high; (*littér*) **la honte sur son** ~ the shame on his brow (*littér*) *ou* face; ~ **de mer** (sea) front; ~ **de taille** coal face; *V* **courber, frapper.**
(b) (*Mét, Mil, Pol*) front. **aller *ou* monter au** ~ to go up to the front, go into action; **tué au** ~ killed in action; **le** ~ **ennemi** the enemy front; **le F**~ **populaire** the Popular Front.
(c) (*loc*) **attaque de** ~ frontal attack; **choc de** ~ head-on crash; **attaquer qn de** ~ (*lit*) to attack sb head-on; (*fig*) to attack sb head-on *ou* face to face; **se heurter de** ~ (*lit*) to collide head-on; (*fig*) to clash head-on; **marcher (à) trois de** ~ to walk three abreast; **mener plusieurs tâches de** ~ to have several tasks in hand *ou* on the go (at one time); **aborder de** ~ **un problème** to tackle a problem face to face; **il va falloir faire** ~ you'll (*ou* we'll *etc*) have to face up to it *ou* to things; **faire** ~ **à l'ennemi/aux difficultés** to face up *ou* stand up to the enemy/difficulties; **faire** ~ **commun contre qn/qch** to join forces against sb/sth, take a (united) stand against sb/sth; (*littér*) **avoir le** ~ **de faire** to have the effrontery *ou* front to do.
frontal, e, *mpl* **-aux** [fʀɔ̃tal, o] **1** *adj collision* head-on; (*Mil*) *attaque* frontal, head-on; (*Anat, Géom*) frontal. **2** *nm*: **(os)** ~ frontal (bone).
frontalier, -ière [fʀɔ̃talje, jɛʀ] **1** *adj ville, zone* border (*épith*), frontier (*épith*). **travailleurs** ~**s** workers who live near *ou* on the frontier *ou* border. **2** *nm,f* inhabitant of the border *ou* frontier zone.
frontière [fʀɔ̃tjɛʀ] **1** *nf* (*Géog, Pol*) frontier, border. **à l'intérieur et au-delà de nos** ~**s** at home and abroad; ~ **naturelle** natural boundary; ~ **linguistique** linguistic boundary; (*fig*) **faire reculer les** ~**s du savoir/d'une science** to push back the frontiers of knowledge/of a science; (*fig*) **à la** ~ **du rêve et de la réalité** on the borders of dream and reality, on the borderline between dream and reality; *V* **incident.**
2 *adj inv*: **ville/zone** ~ frontier *ou* border town/zone; *V* **garde**[1], **poste**[2].
frontispice [fʀɔ̃tispis] *nm* frontispiece.
fronton [fʀɔ̃tɔ̃] *nm* (*Archit*) pediment; (*pelote basque*) (front) wall.
frottement [fʀɔtmɑ̃] *nm* (*action*) rubbing; (*bruit*) rubbing (*U*), rubbing noise, scraping (*U*), scraping noise; (*Tech: contact qui freine*) friction. (*fig*) ~**s** friction (*U*).
frotter [fʀɔte] (1) **1** *vt* **(a)** (*gén*) *peau, membre* to rub; *cheval* to rub down. **frotte tes mains avec du savon** rub your hands with soap; ~ **son doigt sur la table** to rub one's finger on the table; ~ **une allumette** to strike a match.
(b) (*pour nettoyer*) *cuivres, meubles* to rub (up), shine; *plancher, casserole, pomme de terre* to scrub; *linge* to rub; *chaussures* (*pour cirer*) to rub (up), shine; (*pour enlever la terre*) to scrape.
(c) (†, *hum*) ~ **les oreilles à qn** to box sb's ears; **je vais te** ~ **l'échine** I'm going to beat you black and blue.
2 *vi* to rub, scrape. **la porte frotte (contre le plancher)** the door is rubbing *ou* scraping (against the floor).
3 se frotter *vpr* **(a)** (*en se lavant*) to rub o.s. (*lit, fig*) **se** ~ **les mains** to rub one's hands.
(b) se ~ **à la bonne société** to rub shoulders with high society; **se** ~ **à qn** to cross swords with sb; **il vaut mieux ne pas s'y** ~ I wouldn't cross swords with him!; *V* **qui.**
frottis [fʀɔti] *nm* (*Méd*) smear; (*Art*) scumble.
frottoir [fʀɔtwaʀ] *nm* (*à allumettes*) friction strip; (*pour le parquet*) (long-handled) brush.
froufrou [fʀufʀu] *nm* rustle, rustling, swish (*U*). **faire** ~ to rustle, swish.
froufroutant, e [fʀufʀutɑ̃, ɑ̃t] *adj* rustling, swishing.
froufrouter [fʀufʀute] (1) *vi* to rustle, swish.
froussard, e* [fʀusaʀ, aʀd(ə)] (*péj*) **1** *adj* chicken* (*attrib*), yellow-bellied‡ (*épith*). **2** *nm,f* coward.
frousse* [fʀus] *nf* fright. **avoir la** ~ to be scared (to death) *ou* scared stiff*; **quand il a sonné j'ai eu la** ~ when he rang I really got a fright *ou* the wind up*; **ça lui a fichu la** ~ that really put the wind up him* *ou* gave him a fright, that really scared him (to death) *ou* scared him stiff*; **tu te rappelles la** ~ **que j'avais avant les examens** you remember how scared I was *ou* the funk‡ I was in before the exams.
fructidor [fʀyktidɔʀ] *nm* Fructidor (*twelfth month in the French Republican calendar*).
fructifier [fʀyktifje] (7) *vi [arbre]* to bear fruit; *[terre]* to be productive; *[idée]* to bear fruit; *[capital, investissement]* to yield a profit.
fructueusement [fʀyktɥøzmɑ̃] *adv* fruitfully, profitably.
fructueux, -euse [fʀyktɥø, øz] *adj lectures, spéculation* fruitful, profitable; *collaboration, recherches* fruitful; *commerce* profitable.
frugal, e, *mpl* **-aux** [fʀygal, o] *adj* frugal.
frugalement [fʀygalmɑ̃] *adv* frugally.

frugalité [fʀygalite] *nf* frugality.

fruit[1] [fʀɥi] **1** *nm* **(a)** fruit (*gén U*). **il y a des ~s/3 ~s dans la coupe** there is some fruit/there are 3 pieces of fruit in the bowl; **passez-moi un ~** pass me some fruit *ou* a piece of fruit; (*espèce*) **l'orange et la banane sont des ~s** the orange and the banana are kinds of fruit *ou* are fruits; *V* **pâte, salade.**

(b) (*littér: produit*) fruit(s). **les ~s de la terre/de son travail** the fruits of the earth/of one's work; (*le résultat de*) **c'est le ~ de l'expérience/beaucoup de travail** it is the fruit of experience/of much work; (*littér*) **ils ont perdu le ~ de leur(s) travail/recherches** they lost the fruits of their work/research; **cet enfant est le ~ de leur union** this child is the fruit of their union (*littér*); **porter ses ~s** to bear fruit; **avec ~** fruitfully, profitably, with profit; **sans ~** fruitlessly, to no avail.

2: fruits confits candied *ou* glacé fruits; (*Bible, fig*) **fruit défendu** forbidden fruit; **fruits de mer** seafood(s); **fruit sec** (*séché*) dried fruit (*U*); (*fig: raté*) failure; **pour quelques étudiants qui trouvent leur voie combien de fruits secs ou d'indifférents!** for the few students who find the right path, how many fall by the wayside or show no interest!

fruit[2] [fʀɥi] *nm [mur]* batter.

fruité, e [fʀɥite] *adj* fruity.

fruiterie [fʀɥitʀi] *nf* fruiterer's (shop), greengrocery (*Brit*).

fruitier, -ière [fʀɥitje, jɛʀ] **1** *adj* fruit (*épith*). **2** *nm,f* fruiterer, greengrocer (*Brit*). **3 fruitière** *nf* (*fromagerie*) cheese dairy (*in Savoy, Jura*).

frusques [fʀysk(ə)] *nfpl* (*péj*) (*vêtements*) togs*, clobber‡ (*U*) (*Brit*); (*vieux vêtements*) rags.

fruste [fʀyst(ə)] *adj art, style* crude, unpolished; *manières* unpolished, crude, uncultivated; *personne* unpolished, uncultivated.

frustration [fʀystʀɑsjɔ̃] *nf* (*Psych*) frustration.

frustré, e [fʀystʀe] (*ptp de* **frustrer**) *adj* (*Psych*) frustrated.

frustrer [fʀystʀe] (1) *vt* **(a)** (*priver*) **~** *qn de satisfaction* to frustrate *ou* deprive sb of, do sb out of*; (*Jur*) *biens* to defraud sb of; **~ qn dans ses espoirs/efforts** to thwart *ou* frustrate sb's hopes/efforts, thwart sb in his hopes/efforts; (*Jur*) **~ qn au profit d'un autre** to defraud one party by favouring another.

(b) (*Psych*) to frustrate.

fuchsia [fyʃja] *nm* fuchsia.

fuel(-oil) [fjul(ɔjl)] *nm* (*combustible*) heating oil; (*carburant*) fuel oil.

fugace [fygas] *adj parfum, impression, lueur* fleeting; *beauté, fraîcheur* fleeting, transient.

fugacité [fygasite] *nf* (*V* **fugace**) fleetingness; transience.

fugitif, -ive [fyʒitif, iv] **1** *adj* (*en fuite*) *esclave, épouse* fugitive (*épith*), runaway (*épith*); (*fugace*) *vision, forme, émotion, impression* fleeting (*épith*); *calme* momentary (*épith*); *beauté, bonheur* fleeting, (*épith*), transient, short-lived; (*littér*) *jours, années* fleeting (*épith*).

2 *nm,f* fugitive.

fugitivement [fyʒitivmɑ̃] *adv entrevoir* fleetingly. **il pensa ~ à son doux sourire** he thought fleetingly *ou* briefly *ou* momentarily of her sweet smile.

fugue [fyg] *nf* **(a)** (*fuite*) running away (*U*). **faire une ~** to run away, abscond; **il a fait plusieurs ~s** he ran away *ou* absconded several times; **surveillez-le, il fait des ~s** keep an eye on him — he tends to run away *ou* he runs away (a lot); **~ amoureuse** elopement.

(b) (*Mus*) fugue.

fugueur, -euse [fygœʀ, øz] *nm,f* absconder. **surveillez-les, ce sont des ~s** keep an eye on them, they're (habitual) absconders; **un élève ~** an absconding pupil.

fuir [fɥiʀ] (17) **1** *vt* **(a)** (*éviter*) *personne, coterie, danger* to shun, avoid, fight shy of, flee (*littér*); *mauvais exemple* to avoid, shun; *obligation, responsabilité* to evade, shirk. **on le fuit comme la peste** we avoid him like the plague; (*fig*) **le sommeil/la tranquillité me fuit** sleep/quiet eludes me; (*littér*) **~ le monde** to flee society, withdraw from the world; (*littér*) **l'homme se fuit** man flees from his inner self.

(b) (*s'enfuir de*) *patrie, bourreaux, persécuteurs* to flee from, run away from, fly from (*littér*).

2 *vi* **(a)** (*s'enfuir*) *[prisonnier]* to run away, escape; *[troupes]* to take flight, flee (*devant* from); *[femme]* (*avec un amant*) to run off; (*pour se marier*) to elope (*avec* with). **faire ~** (*mettre en fuite*) to put to flight; (*chasser*) to chase off *ou* away; **laid à faire ~** repulsively ugly; **~ devant** *danger, obligations* to run away from.

(b) (*littér: passer rapidement*) *[esquif]* to speed along, glide swiftly along; *[heures, saison]* to fly *ou* slip by; *[temps]* to fly (by), slip by; *[horizon, paysage]* to recede. **l'été a fui si rapidement** summer flew *ou* slipped *ou* shot by so quickly; **les arbres semblaient ~ de part et d'autre de la route** the trees were whizzing *ou* flashing *ou* shooting past *ou* by on both sides of the road.

(c) (*s'échapper*) *[gaz]* to leak, escape; *[liquide]* to leak; (*n'être pas étanche*) *[récipient, robinet]* to leak.

fuite [fɥit] *nf* **(a)** *[fugitif]* flight, escape; *[prisonnier]* escape; *[amants]* flight; (*pour se marier*) elopement. (*Écon*) **la ~ des capitaux** the flight of capital; **dans sa ~ il perdit son portefeuille** he lost his wallet as he ran away *ou* in his flight; (*fig*) **sa ~ devant toute responsabilité est révoltante** his shirking *ou* evasion of all responsibility is disgusting; **prendre la ~** to take (to) flight *ou* to one's heels; **mettre qn en fuite** to put sb to flight; **les prisonniers sont en ~** the prisoners are on the run; **les voleurs en ~ n'ont pas été retrouvés** the runaway thieves haven't been found; **renversé par une voiture qui a pris la ~** knocked down by a hit-and-run driver; *V* **délit.**

(b) (*littér: passage rapide*) *[esquif]* swift passage; *[temps, heures, saisons]* (swift) passage *ou* passing.

(c) (*perte de liquide*) leak, leakage; (*fig: d'information*) leak. **~ de gaz/d'huile** gas/oil leak; **avaries dues à des ~s** damage due to *ou* caused by leakage; **il y a eu des ~s à l'examen** there have been leaks in the exam paper, questions have been leaked in the exam.

(d) (*trou*) *[récipient, tuyau]* leak.

(e) (*Art*) **point de ~** vanishing point.

fulgurant, e [fylgyʀɑ̃, ɑ̃t] *adj vitesse, progrès* lightning (*épith*), dazzling; *réplique* lightning (*épith*); *regard* blazing (*épith*), flashing (*épith*). **une douleur ~e me traversa le corps** an acute pain flashed *ou* shot through my body; **une clarté ~e illumina le ciel** a lightning *ou* blinding flash lit up the sky.

fulguration [fylgyʀɑsjɔ̃] *nf* (*lit*) flash (of lightning); (*fig*) flash.

fulgurer [fylgyʀe] (1) *vi* to flash.

fuligineux, -euse [fyliʒinø, øz] *adj* (*littér*) *couleur, flamme* sooty.

fulminant, e [fylminɑ̃, ɑ̃t] *adj* **(a)** (*en colère*) *patron* enraged, livid; (*menaçant*) *lettre, réponse, regard* angry and threatening. **~ de colère** enraged, livid (with anger).

(b) (*détonant*) *mélange* explosive. **poudre ~e** fulminating powder; **capsule ~e** percussion cap; **sels ~s** explosive salts (*of fulminic acid*).

fulminate [fylminat] *nm* fulminate.

fulmination [fylminɑsjɔ̃] *nf* **(a)** (*malédictions*) **~s** denunciations, fulminations. **(b)** (*Rel*) fulmination.

fulminer [fylmine] (1) **1** *vt reproches, insultes* to thunder forth; (*Rel*) to fulminate. **2** *vi* **(a)** (*pester*) to thunder forth. **~ contre** to fulminate *ou* thunder forth against. **(b)** (*Chim*) to fulminate, detonate.

fulminique [fylminik] *adj*: **acide ~** fulminic acid.

fumage [fymaʒ] *nm* (*Culin*) *[saucissons etc]* smoking, curing (*by smoking*); (*Agr*) *[terre]* manuring, dunging.

fumant, e [fymɑ̃, ɑ̃t] *adj* **(a)** (*chaud*) *cendres, cratère* smoking; *soupe, corps, naseaux* steaming; (*Chim*) fuming. (*fig*) **un coup ~** a master stroke. **(b)** (*en colère*) *patron* fuming. **~ de colère** fuming with anger.

fume- [fym] *préf V* **fumer.**

fumé, e[1] [fyme] (*ptp de* **fumer**) *adj jambon, saumon, verre* smoked. **verres ~s** tinted lenses; **aimer le ~** to like smoked food.

fumée[2] [fyme] *nf* **(a)** *[combustion]* smoke. **~ de tabac/de cigarettes** tobacco/cigarette smoke; **la ~ ne vous gêne pas?** do you mind my smoking?; **sans ~** *combustible* smokeless; *V* **avaler, noir, rideau.**

(b) (*vapeur*) *[soupe, étang, corps, naseaux]* steam. (*fig*) **les ~s de l'alcool** *ou* **de l'ivresse** the vapours of alcohol.

(c) (*loc*) **partir** *ou* **s'en aller en ~** to go up in smoke; (*Prov*) **il n'y a pas de ~ sans feu** there's no smoke without fire (*Prov*).

fumer [fyme] (1) **1** *vi* **(a)** *[volcan, cheminée, cendres, lampe]* to smoke; *[soupe, étang, corps]* to steam; *[produit chimique]* to emit *ou* give off fumes, fume.

(b) (*: *être en colère*) to be fuming. **il fumait de rage** he was fuming with rage.

(c) *[fumeur]* to smoke. **~ comme un sapeur** *ou* **pompier** to smoke like a chimney; *V* **défense**[1].

2 *vt* **(a)** *cigarettes, tabac* to smoke. **~ la cigarette/le cigare/la pipe** to smoke cigarettes/cigars/a pipe.

(b) (*Culin*) *aliments* to smoke, cure (*by smoking*).

(c) (*Agr*) *sol, terre* to manure.

3: fume-cigare *nm inv* cigar holder; **fume-cigarette** *nm inv* cigarette holder.

fumerie [fymʀi] *nf*: **~ (d'opium)** opium den.

fumerolle [fymʀɔl] *nf* (*gén pl*) (*gaz*) smoke and gas (*emanating from a volcano*); (*fumée*) wisp of smoke.

fumet [fymɛ] *nm [plat, viande]* aroma; *[vin]* bouquet, aroma.

fumeur, -euse [fymœʀ, øz] *nm,f* smoker. (*Rail*) **(compartiment) ~s** smoking compartment (*Brit*) *ou* car (*US*), smoker; **~ d'opium** opium smoker; **non-~** non-smoker.

fumeux, -euse [fymø, øz] *adj* **(a)** (*confus*) *idées, explication* hazy, woolly; *esprit* woolly; *théoricien* woolly-minded. **(b)** (*avec de la fumée*) *flamme, clarté* smoky; (*avec de la vapeur*) *horizon, plaine* hazy, misty.

fumier [fymje] *nf* **(a)** (*engrais*) dung, manure. **du ~ de cheval** horse-dung *ou* -manure *ou* -muck; **tas de ~** dunghill, dung *ou* muck *ou* manure heap. **(b)** (*‡péj: salaud*) bastard‡, shit‡‡.

fumigateur [fymigatœʀ] *nm* (*appareil: Agr, Méd*) fumigator.

fumigation [fymigɑsjɔ̃] *nf* fumigation.

fumigatoire [fymigatwaʀ] *adj* fumigating, fumigatory.

fumigène [fymiʒɛn] *adj engin, grenade* smoke (*épith*). (*Agr*) **(appareil) ~** smoke apparatus.

fumiste [fymist(ə)] **1** *nm* (*réparateur-installateur*) heating mechanic; (*ramoneur*) chimney sweep.

2 *nmf* (*péj*) (*paresseux*) (*étudiant, employé*) shirker, skiver‡ (*Brit*); (*plaisantin*) (*philosophe, politicien*) phoney*, fake.

3 *adj attitude* (*de paresseux*) shirking; (*de plaisantin*) phoney*. **il est un peu ~ (sur les bords)** he's a bit of a shirker *ou* skiver‡ (*Brit*); he's a bit of a phoney* *ou* fake.

fumisterie [fymistəʀi] *nf* **(a)** (*péj*) **c'est une ~** it's a fraud *ou* a con‡; **ce projet est une vaste ~** this project is a massive fraud *ou* a complete con‡; **c'est de la ~** (*tromperie*) it's a fraud *ou* a con‡, it's just eyewash*.

(b) (*établissement*) (heating mechanic's) workshop; (*métier*) stove-building.

fumoir [fymwaʀ] *nm* (*salon*) smoking room; (*Ind*) smokehouse.

fumure [fymyʀ] *nf* manuring; (*substance*) manure (*U*).

funambule [fynɑ̃byl] *nmf* tightrope walker, funambulist (*T*). **artiste ~** tightrope artiste.

funambulesque [fynɑ̃bylɛsk(ə)] *adj* (*lit*) *prouesse, art* of tightrope walking; (*fig: bizarre*) *idée, organisation* fantastic, bizarre.

funèbre [fynɛbʀ(ə)] *adj* **(a)** (*de l'enterrement*) *service,*

marche, décoration, oraison funeral (*épith*); *cérémonie, éloge, discours* funeral (*épith*), funerary (*épith*). **air ~** dirge; **veillée ~** deathwatch; *V* **entrepreneur, pompe**[2].
(b) (*lugubre*) *mélodie, ton* mournful, doleful; *silence, air, allure* lugubrious, funereal; *atmosphère, couleur, décor* gloomy, dismal.
funèbrement [fynɛbʀəmɑ̃] *adv* (*littér*) funereally, lugubriously.
funérailles [fyneʀɑj] *nfpl* (*frm: enterrement*) funeral, obsequies (*littér*).
funéraire [fyneʀɛʀ] *adj dalle, monument, urne* funeral (*épith*), funerary (*épith*). **pierre ~** gravestone; (*Can*) **salon ~** funeral home (*US, Can*) *ou* parlor (*US, Can*).
funeste [fynɛst(ə)] *adj* **(a)** (*désastreux*) *erreur* disastrous, grievous; *conseil, décision* disastrous, harmful; *influence* baneful, harmful; *suite, conséquence* dire, disastrous. **loin d'imaginer les suites ~s de cet accident** far from imagining the dire *ou* disastrous *ou* tragic consequences of that accident; **le jour ~ où je l'ai rencontrée** the fateful *ou* ill-fated day upon which I met her.
(b) (*de mort*) *pressentiment, vision* deathly (*épith*), of death.
(c) (*littér: mortel*) *accident* fatal; *coup* fatal, lethal, deadly, mortal; *projet* lethal, deadly. **politique ~ aux intérêts du pays** policy harmful *ou* lethal to the country's interests; **son ambition lui a été ~** his ambition had dire *ou* disastrous *ou* tragic consequences for him.
funiculaire [fynikylɛʀ] *nm* funicular (railway).
fur [fyʀ] *nm* **(a) au ~ et à mesure: classer/nettoyer qch au ~ et à mesure** to file/clean sth as one goes along; **dépenser au ~ et à mesure** to spend as fast *ou* as soon as one earns; **il vaut mieux leur donner leur argent de poche au ~ et à mesure qu'en une fois** it's better to give them their pocket money in dribs and drabs* *ou* as they need it rather than all in one go; **le frigidaire se vidait au ~ et à mesure** the fridge was emptied as fast as it was stocked up; **passe-moi les assiettes au ~ et à mesure** pass the plates to me as you go along.
(b) au ~ et à mesure que (*bonne organisation*) as, as soon as; (*manque d'économie*) as fast as, as soon as; **donnez-les nous au ~ et à mesure que vous les recevez** give them to us as (soon as) you receive them; **nous dépensions tout notre argent au ~ et à mesure que nous le gagnions** we spent all our money as fast as *ou* as soon as we earned it.
(c) au ~ et à mesure de: au ~ et à mesure de leur progression as they advanced, the further they advanced; **prenez-en au ~ et à mesure de vos besoins** take some as and when you need them, help yourselves as you find you need them.
furax‡ [fyʀaks] *adj inv* (*furieux*) livid (*attrib*), hopping mad* (*attrib*).
furet [fyʀɛ] *nm* (*animal*) ferret; (*jeu*) pass-the-slipper; (†: *curieux*) pry.
furetage [fyʀtaʒ] *nm* (*V* **fureter**) nosing *ou* ferreting *ou* prying about; rummaging (about).
fureter [fyʀte] (5) *vi* (*regarder partout*) to nose *ou* ferret *ou* pry about; (*fouiller partout: dans un tiroir etc*) to rummage (about).
fureteur, -euse [fyʀtœʀ, øz] **1** *adj regard, enfant* prying, inquisitive. **2** *nm,f* pry.
fureur [fyʀœʀ] *nf* **(a)** (*U: colère*) fury; (*accès de colère*) fit of rage. **crise** *ou* **accès de ~** fit of rage, furious outburst; **(être) pris de ~** to be seized with anger, fly into a rage (*contre qn* at sb); **être/entrer en ~** to be/become infuriated *ou* enraged; **être/entrer dans une ~ noire** to be in/go *ou* fly into a towering rage; **mettre en ~** to infuriate, enrage; **se mettre dans des ~s folles** to have mad fits of rage, fly into wild fits of anger.
(b) (*violence*) *[passion]* violence, fury; *[combat, attaque]* fury, furiousness; *[tempête, flots, vents]* fury.
(c) (*passion*) **la ~ du jeu** a passion *ou* mania for gambling; **il a la ~ de la vitesse/de lire** he has a mania for speed/reading; **la ~ de vivre** the lust *ou* passion for life.
(d) (*littér: transe*) **~ prophétique** prophetic frenzy; **~ poétique** poetic ecstasy *ou* frenzy.
(e) (*loc*) **avec ~** (*avec rage*) with rage, furiously; (*à la folie*) wildly, madly, passionately; **aimer qch/qn à la ~** to love sth/sb wildly *ou* madly *ou* passionately; **faire ~** to be all the rage.
furibard, e* [fyʀibaʀ, aʀd(ə)] *adj* (*furibond*) hopping mad* (*attrib*), livid (*attrib*), mad* (*attrib*).
furibond, e [fyʀibɔ̃, ɔ̃d] *adj personne* hopping mad* (*attrib*), livid (*attrib*), mad* (*attrib*); *colère* wild, furious; *ton, voix, yeux* enraged, furious.
furie [fyʀi] *nf* **(a)** (*péj: mégère*) shrew, termagant; (*Myth*) Fury.
(b) (*violence*) *[attaque, combat]* fury, furiousness; *[tempête, flots]* fury; *[passions]* violence, fury.
(c) (*passion*) **la ~ du jeu** a passion *ou* mania for gambling.
(d) (*colère*) fury.
(e) (*loc*) **en ~** *personne* infuriated, enraged, in a rage (*attrib*); *mer* raging; *tigre* enraged; **mettre qn en ~** to infuriate sb, enrage sb.
furieusement [fyʀjøzmɑ̃] *adv* (*avec fureur*) *attaquer* furiously; *répondre* angrily; (*gén hum: extrêmement*) *ressembler* amazingly, tremendously. **j'ai ~ envie d'une glace à la fraise** I'm simply dying for* *ou* I've got a terrible hankering for a strawberry ice cream.
furieux, -euse [fyʀjø, øz] *adj* **(a)** (*violent*) *combat, résistance* furious, violent; *tempête* raging, furious, violent; *V* **folie, fou. (b)** (*en colère*) *personne, animal* furious (*contre* with, at); *ton, geste* furious. **(c)** (*gén hum: fort*) *envie, coup* almighty* (*épith*), tremendous. **avoir un ~ appétit** to have an almighty* *ou* a prodigious appetite.
furoncle [fyʀɔ̃kl(ə)] *nm* boil, furuncle (*T*).
furonculose [fyʀɔ̃kyloz] *nf* (recurrent) boils, furunculosis (*T*).
furtif, -ive [fyʀtif, iv] *adj coup d'œil, geste* furtive, stealthy; *joie* secret.
furtivement [fyʀtivmɑ̃] *adv* furtively, stealthily.
fusain [fyzɛ̃] *nm* (*crayon*) charcoal (crayon); (*croquis*) charcoal (drawing); (*arbrisseau*) spindle-tree. **dessiner au ~** to draw in charcoal; **tracé au ~** charcoal(-drawn), (drawn) in charcoal.
fuseau, *pl* **~x** [fyzo] **1** *nm* **(a)** *[fileuse]* spindle; *[dentelière]* bobbin. **(b) (pantalon) ~, ~x** stretch ski pants. **(c)** (*loc*) **en (forme de) ~** *colonne* with a swelling; *cuisses, jambes* slender; **arbuste taillé en ~** shrub shaped into a cone. **2: fuseau horaire** time zone.
fusée [fyze] **1** *nf* **(a)** (*spatiale*) rocket; *[feu d'artifice]* rocket; *[obus, mine]* fuse. **partir comme une ~** to shoot *ou* whizz off like a rocket; *V* **avion.**
(b) (*Tech*) *[essieu]* spindle; (*Aut*) stub axle; *[montre]* fusee.
2: fusée antichar anti-tank rocket; **fusée éclairante** flare; **fusée-engin** *nf, pl* **fusée-engins** rocket shell; **fusée gigogne** *ou* **à étages** multi-stage rocket; **fusée interplanétaire** (interplanetary) space rocket.
fuselage [fyzlaʒ] *nm [avion]* fuselage.
fuselé, e [fyzle] *adj colonne* swelled; *doigts* tapering, slender; *cuisses, jambes* slender.
fuser [fyze] (1) *vi* **(a)** *[cris, rires]* to burst forth; *[liquide]* to gush *ou* spurt out; *[étincelles]* to fly (out); *[lumière]* to stream out *ou* forth. **(b)** *[bougie]* to run; *[pile]* to sweat; *[poudre]* to burn out.
fusibilité [fyzibilite] *nf* fusibility.
fusible [fyzibl(ə)] **1** *adj* fusible. **2** *nm* (*fil*) fuse(-wire); (*fiche*) fuse.
fusiforme [fyzifɔʀm(ə)] *adj* spindle-shaped, fusiform (*T*).
fusil [fyzi] **1** *nm* **(a)** (*arme*) (*de guerre, à canon rayé*) rifle, gun; (*de chasse, à canon lisse*) shotgun, gun. (*fig*) **c'est un bon ~** he's a good shot; (*Mil*†) **un groupe de 30 ~s** a group of 30 riflemen *ou* rifles; (*fig*) **changer son ~ d'épaule** to change one's allegiance.
(b) (*allume-gaz*) gas lighter; (*instrument à aiguiser*) steel.
2: fusil à canon rayé rifle, rifled gun; **fusil de chasse** shotgun, hunting gun; **fusil à deux coups** double-barrelled *ou* twin-barrel rifle; **fusil de guerre** army rifle; **fusil mitrailleur** machine gun; **fusil à répétition** repeating rifle; **fusil sous-marin** (underwater) speargun.
fusilier [fyzilje] *nm* rifleman; (*Hist*) fusilier. **les ~s** (*régiment*) rifles; (*Hist*) fusiliers; **~ marin** marine.
fusillade [fyzijad] *nf* (*bruit*) fusillade (*frm*), gunfire (*U*), shooting (*U*); (*combat*) shooting battle; (*exécution*) shooting.
fusiller [fyzije] (1) *vt* **(a)** (*exécuter*) to shoot. **~ qn du regard** to look daggers at sb. **(b)** (‡: *casser*) to mess* *ou* smash up.
fusion [fyzjɔ̃] *nf* **(a)** *[métal etc]* melting, fusion; *[glace]* melting, thawing. **en ~** *métal* molten.
(b) (*Bio, Phys*) fusion; *[atomes]* (nuclear) fusion.
(c) (*union*) *[cœurs, esprits]* uniting, fusion; *[partis]* merging, combining; *[systèmes, philosophies]* blending, merging, uniting; *[races]* assimilation; (*Comm*) *[sociétés]* merger, amalgamation. **la ~ de l'individu en Dieu/dans la nature** the union of the individual with God/nature.
fusionnement [fyzjɔnmɑ̃] *nm* (*Comm*) merging, amalgamating, amalgamation; (*Pol*) merging, combining.
fusionner [fyzjɔne] (1) *vti* (*Comm*) to merge, amalgamate; (*Pol*) to merge, combine.
fustigation [fystigɑsjɔ̃] *nf* (*littér: V* **fustiger**) flaying; censuring, denouncing, denunciation; birching, thrashing.
fustiger [fystiʒe] (3) *vt* **(a)** (*littér: critiquer*) *adversaire* to flay; *pratiques, mœurs* to censure, denounce. **(b)** (††: *fouetter*) to birch, thrash.
fût [fy] *nm* **(a)** *[arbre]* bole, trunk; *[colonne]* shaft; *[fusil]* stock. **(b)** (*tonneau*) barrel, cask.
futaie [fytɛ] *nf* (*groupe d'arbres*) cluster of (tall) trees; (*forêt*) forest (*of tall trees*); (*Sylviculture*) plantation of trees (*for timber*). **haute ~** mature (standing) timber.
futaille [fytɑj] *nf* (*barrique*) barrel, cask.
futaine [fytɛn] *nf* (*Tex*) fustian.
futé, e [fyte] *adj* wily, crafty, cunning, sly. **c'est une petite ~e** she's a crafty *ou* sly little minx.
futile [fytil] *adj* (*inutile*) *entreprise, tentative* futile, pointless; (*frivole*) *raison, souci, occupation, propos* trifling, trivial, futile; *personne, esprit* trivial, frivolous.
futilement [fytilmɑ̃] *adv* (*frivolement*) frivolously.
futilité [fytilite] *nf* **(a)** (*U: V* **futile**) futility; pointlessness; triviality; frivolousness. **(b) ~s** trivialities.
futur, e [fytyʀ] **1** *adj* (*prochain*) *génération, désastres, besoins* future (*épith*). (*Rel*) **dans la vie ~e** in the life to come, in the afterlife, in the hereafter; **~ mari** husband-to-be; **les ~s époux** the bride and groom-to-be; **tout pour la ~e maman** everything for the mother-to-be; **~ collègue/directeur/soldat** future colleague/director/soldier; **~ client** intending *ou* prospective customer; (*en herbe*) **un ~ président/champion** a budding *ou* future president/champion.
2 *nm* **(a)** (*conjoint*) fiancé, husband-to-be, intended†.
(b) (*avenir*) future.
(c) (*Ling*) **le ~** the future (tense); (*fig*) **parlez-en au ~** don't count your chickens (before they hatch); **le ~ proche** the immediate future; **le ~ simple** the future (tense); **le ~ antérieur** the future perfect *ou* anterior.
3 future *nf* (*conjointe*) fiancée, wife-to-be, intended†.
futurisme [fytyʀism(ə)] *nm* futurism.
futuriste [fytyʀist(ə)] **1** *nmf* futurist. **2** *adj décor* futuristic.
fuyant, e [fɥijɑ̃, ɑ̃t] *adj* **(a)** (*insaisissable*) *regard, air* evasive; *personne, caractère* elusive, evasive. **(b)** (*en retrait*) *menton, front* receding (*épith*). **(c)** (*littér: fugitif*) *ombre, vision* fleeting (*épith*). **(d)** (*Art*) *vues, lignes* receding (*épith*), vanishing (*épith*); *perspective* vanishing (*épith*).
fuyard, e [fɥijaʀ, aʀd(ə)] *nm,f* runaway.

G

G, g [ʒe] *nm (lettre)* G, g.

gabardine [gabaʀdin] *nf (tissu)* gabardine; (†: *manteau*) gabardine (raincoat).

gabarit [gabaʀi] *nm* **(a)** *(dimension) [objet, véhicule]* size. **(b)** (*) *[personne] (taille)* size; *(valeur)* calibre. **ce n'est pas le petit ~!** he's not exactly small!, he's rather on the large side! **(c)** *(Tech) (appareil de mesure)* gauge; *(maquette)* template.

gabegie [gabʒi] *nf (péj)* chaos, muddle, mess. **c'est une vraie ~!** it's a real mess!, it's total chaos!

gabelle [gabɛl] *nf (Hist: impôt)* salt tax, gabelle.

gabelou [gablu] *nm (Hist)* salt-tax collector; *(péj)* customs officer.

gabier [gabje] *nm (Naut)* topman.

Gabon [gabɔ̃] *nm* Gabon.

gâchage [gɑʃaʒ] *nm (V* **gâcher***)* tempering; mixing; wasting; botching.

gâche [gɑʃ] *nf [maçon]* (plasterer's) trowel; *[serrure]* striking plate, strike (plate).

gâcher [gɑʃe] (1) *vt* **(a)** *plâtre* to temper; *mortier* to mix.

(b) *(gaspiller) argent, talent, temps* to waste; *(rater) occasion* to waste, lose; *vie* to waste; *(bâcler) travail* to botch. **~ sa vie** to waste one's life.

(c) *(gâter)* to spoil. **il nous a gâché le** *ou* **notre plaisir** he spoiled our pleasure (for us); **il gâche le métier** he spoils it for others (*by selling cheap or working for a low salary*).

gâchette [gɑʃɛt] *nf [arme]* trigger; *[serrure]* tumbler. **il a la ~ facile** he's trigger-happy.

gâcheur, -euse [gɑʃœʀ, øz] **1** *adj* wasteful.

2 *nm,f* **(a)** *(de matériel)* wasteful person; *(d'argent)* spendthrift; *(de travail)* bungler, botcher.

(b) *(péj: snob, délicat)* fusspot*, fussy person. **quel ~, il ne supporte que les cravates en soie!** what a fussy dresser — he'll only wear silk ties!

3 *nm (ouvrier)* builder's mate (*who mixes cement or tempers plaster*).

gâchis [gɑʃi] *nm* **(a)** *(désordre)* mess. **tu as fait un beau ~!** you've made a fine mess of it! **(b)** *(gaspillage)* waste (*U*). **(c)** *(Tech)* mortar.

gadget [gadʒɛt] *nm (gén: machin)* thingummy* (*surtout Brit*), gizmo* (*US*); *(jouet, ustensile)* gadget; *(procédé, trouvaille)* gimmick.

gadin* [gadɛ̃] *nm*: **prendre** *ou* **ramasser un ~** to come a cropper*, fall flat on one's face.

gadoue [gadu] *nf (boue)* mud, sludge; *(neige)* slush; *(engrais)* night soil.

gaélique [gaelik] **1** *adj* Gaelic. **2** *nm (Ling)* Gaelic.

gaffe [gaf] *nf* **(a)** *(bévue)* blunder, boob*. **faire une ~** *(action)* to make a blunder *ou* a boob*; *(parole)* to drop a clanger* (*Brit*). **(b)** *(perche) (Naut)* boat hook; *(Pêche)* gaff. **(c)** (*) **faire ~** to be careful (*à* of); **fais ~!** watch out!, be careful!

gaffer [gafe] (1) **1** *vi (bévue)* to blunder, boob*; *(paroles)* to drop a clanger* (*Brit*). **il a gaffé lourdement** he made a terrible blunder *ou* boob*. **2** *vt (Naut)* to hook; *(Pêche)* to gaff.

gaffeur, -euse [gafœʀ, øz] *nm,f* blunderer, blundering fool. **il est drôlement ~!** he's always putting his foot in it!, he's a blundering fool!

gag [gag] *nm (Ciné, Théât)* gag.

gaga* [gaga] *adj* gaga*, senile.

gage [gaʒ] *nm* **(a)** *(à un créancier, arbitre)* security; *(à un prêteur)* pledge. **mettre qch en ~ (chez le prêteur)** to pawn sth (at the pawnbroker's); **laisser qch en ~** to leave sth as (a) security.

(b) *(garantie)* guarantee. **sa bonne forme physique est un ~ de succès** his fitness will guarantee him success *ou* assure him of success.

(c) *(témoignage)* proof, evidence (*U*). **donner des ~s de sa sincérité/son talent** to give proof *ou* evidence of one's sincerity/talent; **donner à qn un ~ d'amour/de fidélité** to give sb a token of one's love/faithfulness; **en ~ de notre amitié/de ma bonne foi** as a token *ou* in token of our friendship/of my good faith.

(d) *(Jeux)* forfeit.

(e) *(salaire)* **~s** wages; **assassin/tueur à ~s** hired assassin/killer; **être aux ~s de qn** *(gén)* to be employed by sb; *(péj)* to be in the pay of sb.

gager [gaʒe] (3) *vt* **(a)** *(frm: parier)* **~ que** to wager that, bet that; **gageons que ..., je gage que ...** I bet (you) that ... . **(b)** *emprunt* to guarantee.

gageure [gaʒyʀ] *nf* **(a)** *(entreprise difficile)* **c'est une véritable ~ que de vouloir tenter seul cette ascension** it's attempting the impossible to try to do this climb alone; **il a réussi la ~ de faire cette ascension tout seul** he achieved the impossible — he managed to do the climb on his own, despite the odds he managed to do the climb on his own.

(b) (††: *pari*) wager.

gagnant, e [gaɲɑ̃, ɑ̃t] **1** *adj numéro etc* winning (*épith*). **on donne ce concurrent ~** this competitor is the favourite to win *ou* is expected to win. **2** *nm,f* winner.

gagne- [gaɲ] *préf V* **gagner.**

gagner [gaɲe] (1) **1** *vt* **(a)** *(acquérir par le travail)* to earn. **~ sa vie** to earn one's living; **~ son pain** to earn one's daily bread; **~ de l'argent** *(par le travail)* to earn *ou* make money; *(dans une affaire)* to make money; **~ de quoi vivre** to earn a living; **~ des mille et des cents*** to earn *ou* make a packet*; **~ sa croûte*** *ou* **son bifteck*** to earn one's bread and butter.

(b) *(mériter)* to earn. **il a bien gagné ses vacances** he's really earned his holiday.

(c) *(acquérir par le hasard)* to win. **~ le gros lot** *(lit, fig)* to hit *ou* win the jackpot.

(d) *(obtenir) réputation etc* to gain. **vous n'y gagnerez rien** you'll gain nothing by it; **vous n'y gagnerez rien de bon** you'll get nothing out of it; **~ du temps** *(temporiser)* to gain time; *(économiser)* to save time; **~ du poids** to put on *ou* gain weight; **~ de la place** to save space; **~ du terrain** *(lit, fig)* to gain ground; **à sortir par ce temps, vous y gagnerez un bon rhume** you'll get nothing but a bad cold going out in this weather.

(e) *(être vainqueur de) bataille, procès, course* to win. (†) **~ qn aux échecs** to beat sb at chess; **~ qn de vitesse** to beat sb to it*.

(f) *(se concilier) gardiens, témoins* to win over. **~ l'estime/le cœur de qn** to win sb's esteem *ou* regard/heart; **~ la confiance de qn** to win *ou* gain sb's confidence; **savoir se ~ des amis** to know how to win friends; **se laisser ~ par les prières de qn** to be won over by sb's prayers; **~ qn à une cause** to win sb over to a cause; **~ qn à sa cause** to win sb over.

(g) *(envahir)* **le sommeil les gagnait** sleep was creeping over them *ou* was gradually overcoming them; **la gangrène gagne la jambe** the gangrene is spreading to his leg; **le froid les gagnait** they were beginning to feel the cold; **le feu gagna rapidement les rues voisines** the fire quickly spread to the neighbouring streets.

(h) *(atteindre) lieu, frontière, refuge* to reach. **~ le port** to reach port; **~ le large** *(Naut)* to get out into the open sea.

2 *vi* **(a)** *(être vainqueur)* to win. **~ aux courses** to win on the horses *ou* at the races; **il a gagné aux courses hier** he had a win at the races yesterday; **il gagne sur tous les tableaux** he's winning all the way *ou* on all fronts; **eh bien, tu as gagné!*** well, you got what you asked for!*

(b) *(trouver un avantage)* **vous y gagnez** it's in your interest, it's to your advantage; **vous gagnerez à ce que personne ne le sache** it'll be to your advantage *ou* it will be better for you if nobody knows about it; **qu'est-ce que j'y gagne?** what do I get out of it? *ou* gain from it?; **vous gagneriez à partir en groupe** you'd be better off going in a group; **~ au change** to make on the deal.

(c) *(s'améliorer)* **~ en hauteur** to increase in height; **son style gagne en force ce qu'il perd en élégance** his style gains in vigour what it loses in elegance; **ce vin gagnera à vieillir** this wine will improve with age; **il gagne à être connu** he improves on acquaintance; **ce roman gagne à être relu** this novel gains by a second reading, this novel is better at a second reading.

(d) *(s'étendre) [incendie, épidémie]* to spread, gain ground.

3: **gagne-pain*** *nm inv* job; **gagne-petit** *nm inv* low wage earner; **c'est un gagne-petit** he doesn't earn much (money).

gagneur [gaɲœʀ] *nm* winner.

gai, e [ge] *adj* **(a)** *(joyeux) personne, vie* cheerful, gay, happy; *voix, visage* cheery, cheerful, happy; *roman, conversation* cheerful, gay; *caractère* cheerful, merry. **c'est un ~ luron** he's a cheery *ou* happy fellow; **~ comme un pinson** happy as a lark; **tu n'as pas l'air (bien) ~** you don't look too happy.

(b) *(euph: ivre)* merry, tipsy.

(c) *(riant) couleur, robe* bright, gay; *pièce* bright, cheerful. **on va peindre la chambre en jaune pour faire ~** we're going to paint the bedroom yellow to brighten it up.

(d) *(iro: amusant)* **j'ai oublié mon parapluie, c'est ~!** that's great*, I've forgotten my umbrella! *(iro)*; **ça ne va pas être ~** *ou* **ça va être ~ la rentrée sur Paris, dimanche!** it's going to be great fun, going back to Paris this Sunday! *(iro)*; **ça va être ~, les vacances avec lui!** I can see we're going to have a good holiday *ou* the holidays are going to be great fun with him around! *(iro)*.

gaiement [gemɑ̃] *adv (V* **gai***)* cheerfully; gaily; happily; cheerily; merrily. *(iro)* **allons-y ~!** come on then, let's get on with it!; *(iro)* **il va recommencer ~ à faire les mêmes bêtises** he'll blithely *ou* gaily start the same old tricks again.

gaieté [gete] *nf [personne, caractère]* cheerfulness, gaiety; *[couleur]* brightness, gaiety; *[conversation, pièce, roman]* cheerfulness, gaiety. **ce n'est pas de ~ de cœur qu'il accepta** it was with no light heart that he accepted; *(iro)* **les ~s de la vie d'écolier!** the delights *ou* joys of school life! *(iro)*.

gaillard, e [gajaʀ, aʀd(ə)] **1** *adj* **(a)** *(alerte) personne* strong; *allure* lively, springy, sprightly. **vieillard encore ~** sprightly *ou* spry old man.

(b) *(grivois) propos* bawdy, ribald.

2 *nm* **(a)** *(costaud)* **(robuste** *ou* **grand** *ou* **beau) ~** strapping *ou* hale and hearty *ou* robust fellow.

(b) (*: *type*) fellow, chap* (*Brit*). **toi, mon ~ je t'ai à l'œil!** I've got my eye on you, mate!* (*Brit*) *ou* chum!*

3 gaillarde *nf* **(a)** (*) (*femme forte*) strapping wench* *ou* woman*; (*femme hardie*) bold lass. **c'est une sacrée ~e** she's quite a woman!* *ou* lass!*

(b) (*Mus*) galliard.

4: gaillard (d'avant) forecastle (head), fo'c'sle; (*Hist*) **gaillard d'arrière** quarter-deck.

gaillardement [gajaʀdəmɑ̃] *adv* (*avec bonne humeur*) cheerfully; (*sans faiblir*) bravely, gallantly. **ils attaquèrent la côte ~** they set off energetically *ou* cheerfully up the hill; **il porte ~ sa soixantaine** he's a sprightly *ou* vigorous sixty-year-old.

gaillardise [gajaʀdiz] *nf* bawdy *ou* ribald remark.

gaîment [gemɑ̃] *adv* = **gaiement.**

gain [gɛ̃] *nm* **(a)** (*salaire*) (*gén*) earnings; *[ouvrier]* earnings, wages, wage. **pour un ~ modeste** for a modest wage.

(b) (*lucre*) **le ~** gain; **pousser qn au ~** to push *ou* urge sb to make money; **l'amour du ~** the love of gain.

(c) (*bénéfices*) **~s** *[société]* profits; (*au jeu*) winnings; (*à la Bourse*) profits; **se retirer sur son ~** (*jeu*) to pull out with one's winnings intact; (*spéculation*) to retire on the proceeds *ou* with what one has made; **~s illicites** illicit gains; **compensation des ~s et des pertes** compensation of gains and losses.

(d) (*avantage matériel*) *[élections, guerre de conquête]* gains. **ce ~ de 3 sièges leur donne la majorité** winning *ou* gaining these 3 seats has given them a majority.

(e) (*avantage spirituel*) benefit. **tirer un ~ (énorme) de qch** to gain *ou* draw (great) benefit from sth.

(f) (*économie*) saving. **~ de temps/d'argent/de place** saving of time/of money/of space; **ce procédé permet un ~ de 50 minutes/d'électricité** this procedure saves 50 minutes/electricity; **ça nous permet un ~ de temps** it's time-saving, it saves us time.

(g) (*littér: obtention*) *[bataille, procès]* winning; *[fortune, voix d'électeurs]* gaining.

(h) ~ de cause: avoir *ou* **obtenir ~ de cause** (*lit*) to win the case; (*fig*) to be proved *ou* pronounced right; **donner ~ de cause à qn** (*Jur*) to decide the case in favour of sb; (*fig*) to pronounce sb right.

gaine [gɛn] *nf* (*Habillement*) girdle; (*Bot, fourreau*) sheath; (*piédestal*) plinth; (*enveloppe*) *[obus]* priming tube. **~ d'aération** ventilation shaft; **~ culotte** pantie girdle.

gainer [gene] (1) *vt* to cover. **jambes gainées de soie** legs sheathed in silk; **objet gainé de cuir** leather-covered *ou* -cased object.

gaîté [gete] *nf* = **gaieté.**

gala [gala] *nm* official reception. **de ~** *soirée, représentation* gala; **~ de bienfaisance** reception for charity.

Galaad [galaad] *nm* Galahad.

galactique [galaktik] *adj* galactic.

galactogène [galaktɔʒɛn] *adj* galactagogue.

galactomètre [galaktɔmɛtʀ(ə)] *nm* lactometer.

galactose [galaktoz] *nm* galactose.

galalithe [galalit] *nf* ® Galalith ®.

galamment [galamɑ̃] *adv* courteously, gallantly. **se conduire ~** to behave courteously *ou* gallantly *ou* in a gentlemanly fashion.

galandage [galɑ̃daʒ] *nm* (brick) partition.

galant, e [galɑ̃, ɑ̃t] **1** *adj* **(a)** (*courtois*) gallant, courteous, gentlemanly. **soyez ~, ouvrez-lui la porte** be a gentleman and open the door for her; **c'est un ~ homme** he is a gentleman.

(b) *ton, humeur, propos* flirtatious, gallant; *scène, tableau* amorous, romantic; *conte* racy, spicy; *rendez-vous* romantic; *poésie* amorous, courtly. **en ~e compagnie** *homme* with a lady friend (*hum*); *femme* with a gentleman friend (*hum*).

2 *nm* (†† *ou hum: soupirant*) gallant††, suitor††, admirer († *ou hum*).

galanterie [galɑ̃tʀi] *nf* (*courtoisie*) gallantry, chivalry; (*propos*) gallant remark; (*intrigue*) love affair.

galantine [galɑ̃tin] *nf* galantine.

galapiat† [galapja] *nm* (*polisson*) rapscallion†, scamp.

Galatée [galate] *nf* Galatea.

galaxie [galaksi] *nf* galaxy.

galbe [galb(ə)] *nm [meuble, visage, cuisse]* curve. **des cuisses d'un ~ parfait** shapely thighs.

galbé, e [galbe] (*ptp de* **galber**) *adj* with curved outlines. **bien ~** *corps* curvaceous, shapely; *objet* beautifully shaped.

galber [galbe] (1) *vt* to shape (*into curves*), curve.

gale [gal] *nf* **(a)** (*Méd*) scabies, itch; (*Vét*) *[chien, chat]* mange; *[mouton]* scab; (*Bot*) scab. (*hum*) **tu peux boire dans mon verre, je n'ai pas la ~!‡** you can drink out of my glass — you won't catch anything from me!*

(b) (*fig: personne*) nasty character, nasty piece of work*. **il est mauvais** *ou* **méchant comme la ~** he's a really nasty piece of work*.

galéjade [galeʒad] *nf* (*dial*) tall story.

galéjer [galeʒe] (6) *vi* (*dial*) to spin a yarn. **oh, tu galèjes!** that's a tall story!

galène [galɛn] *nf* galena, galenite.

galère [galɛʀ] *nf* **(a)** (*Hist: bateau*) galley. **on l'a envoyé aux ~s** they sent him to the galleys.

(b) (*loc*) **qu'est-il allé faire dans cette ~?** why did he have to get involved in this business?; **dans quelle ~ me suis-je embarqué!** whatever have I let myself in for?

galerie [galʀi] **1** *nf* **(a)** (*couloir*) (*gén*) gallery; *[mine]* gallery, level; *[fourmilière]* gallery; *[taupinière]* tunnel.

(b) (*Art*) (*magasin*) gallery; (*salle de musée*) room, gallery; (*rare: collection*) collection.

(c) (*Théât: balcon*) circle. **premières/deuxièmes ~s** dress/upper circle; **les troisièmes ~s** the gods* (*Brit*), the gallery.

(d) (*public, spectateurs*) gallery, audience. **faire le pitre pour amuser la ~** to act the fool to amuse the audience; **il a dit cela pour la ~** he said that for appearances' sake.

(e) (*Aut*) roof rack; (*Archit: balustrade*) gallery.

2: galerie d'art art gallery; **galerie marchande** shopping arcade; **galerie de peinture** *ou* **de tableaux** picture gallery; (*Littérat*) **galerie de portraits** collection of pen portraits.

galérien [galeʀjɛ̃] *nm* (*Hist*) galley slave. (*fig*) **travailler comme un ~** to work like a (galley) slave.

galet [galɛ] *nm* **(a)** (*pierre*) pebble. **~s** shingle. **(b)** (*Tech*) wheel, roller.

galetas [galtɑ] *nm* (*mansarde*) garret; (*taudis*) hovel.

galette [galɛt] *nf* **(a)** (*Culin*) (*gâteau*) *round, flat cake made of puff pastry*; (*crêpe*) pancake; (*Naut*) ship's biscuit. **~ des Rois** *cake eaten in France on Twelfth Night.* **(b)** (‡: *argent*) dough‡, lolly‡ (*Brit*).

galeux, -euse [galø, øz] **1** *adj* **(a)** *personne* affected with scabies, scabious (*T*); *chien* mangy; *mouton* scabby; *plante, arbre* scabby; *plaie* caused by scabies *ou* the itch; *éruption* scabious. **il m'a traité comme un chien ~** he treated me like dirt *ou* as if I was the scum of the earth; *V* **brebis.**

(b) (*fig: sordide*) *murs* peeling, flaking; *pièce, quartier* squalid, dingy, seedy.

2 *nm,f* (*personne méprisable*) scabby *ou* scruffy individual. **pour lui je suis un ~, il ne veux pas me fréquenter** as far as he's concerned I'm the lowest of the low *ou* the scum of the earth and he wants nothing to do with me.

galhauban [galobɑ̃] *nm* (*Naut*) back-stay.

Galice [galis] *nf* Galicia (*in Spain*).

Galicie [galisi] *nf* Galicia (*in central Europe*).

Galien [galjɛ̃] *nm* Galen.

Galilée[1] [galile] *nm* Galileo.

Galilée[2] [galile] *nf* Galilee.

galiléen, -enne [galileɛ̃, ɛn] (*Géog*) **1** *adj* Galilean. **2** *nm,f*: **G~(ne)** Galilean.

galimatias [galimatja] *nm* (*propos*) gibberish (*U*); (*écrit*) tedious nonsense (*U*), twaddle (*U*).

galion [galjɔ̃] *nm* galleon.

galipette* [galipɛt] *nf* somersault. **faire la ~** to somersault.

galle [gal] *nf* gall.

Galles [gal] *nfpl V* **pays, prince.**

gallican, e [galikɑ̃, an] *adj, nm,f* Gallican.

gallicanisme [galikanism(ə)] *nm* Gallicanism.

gallicisme [galisism(ə)] *nm* (*idiotisme*) French idiom; (*dans une langue étrangère: calque*) gallicism.

gallinacé, e [galinase] **1** *adj* gallinaceous. **2** *nm* gallinacean.

gallique [galik] *adj* gallic.

gallium [galjɔm] *nm* gallium.

gallo- [galo] *préf* Gallo-.

gallois, e [galwa, waz] **1** *adj* Welsh. **2** *nm* **(a) G~** Welshman; **les G~** the Welsh. **(b)** (*Ling*) Welsh. **3 Galloise** *nf* Welshwoman.

gallon [galɔ̃] *nm* gallon. (*Can*) **gallon canadien** *ou* **impérial** Imperial gallon (*4.545 litres*); **gallon américain** US gallon (*3.785 litres*).

gallo-romain, e [galoʀɔmɛ̃, ɛn] **1** *adj* Gallo-Roman. **2** *nm,f*: **Gallo-Romain(e)** Gallo-Roman.

galoche [galɔʃ] *nf* (*sabot*) clog; (*chaussure*) *wooden-soled shoe*; *V* **menton.**

galon [galɔ̃] *nm* **(a)** (*Couture*) braid (*U*), piece of braid; (*Mil*) stripe. (*fig Mil*) **il a gagné ses ~s au combat** he got his stripes in battle; (*fig Mil*) **prendre du ~** to get promotion. **(b)** (*Can*) measuring tape, tape measure.

galonné, e [galɔne] (*ptp de* **galonner**) *adj* (*Mil*) *manche, uniforme* with stripes on. **un ~*** a brass hat*.

galonner [galɔne] (1) *vt* (*Couture*) to trim with braid.

galop [galo] *nm* **(a)** gallop. **petit ~** canter; **grand ~** (full) gallop; **~ d'essai** (*lit*) trial gallop; (*fig*) trial run; **nous avons fait un ~ de quelques minutes** we galloped for a few minutes; **cheval au ~** galloping horse; **prendre le ~, se mettre au ~** to break into a gallop; **mettre son cheval au ~** to put one's horse into a gallop; **partir au ~** *[cheval]* to set off at a gallop; *[personne]* to take off like a shot, rush off *ou* away; **nous avons dîné au ~** we ate our dinner in a great rush; **va chercher tes affaires au ~!** go and get your things, at the double! *ou* and look smart (about it)!; (*Mil*) **au ~! chargez!** charge!

(b) (*danse*) gallopade.

galopade [galɔpad] *nf* (*Équitation*) hand gallop; (*fig: course précipitée*) stampede. (*fig*) **~ effrénée** mad rush.

galopant, e [galɔpɑ̃, ɑ̃t] *adj* (*qui progresse rapidement*) *inflation* galloping; *V* **phtisie.**

galoper [galɔpe] (1) *vi [cheval]* to gallop; *[imagination]* to run wild, run riot; *[enfant]* to run. **les enfants galopent dans les couloirs** the children charge *ou* hare* (*Brit*) along the corridors; **j'ai galopé toute la journée!*** I've been haring* (*Brit*) *ou* rushing around all day!

galopin* [galɔpɛ̃] *nm* (*polisson*) urchin, ragamuffin. **espèce de petit ~!** you little rascal! *ou* ragamuffin!

galure‡ [galyʀ] *nm*, **galurin‡** [galyʀɛ̃] *nm* (*chapeau*) hat, headgear* (*U*).

galvanique [galvanik] *adj* galvanic.

galvanisation [galvanizɑsjɔ̃] *nf* galvanization.

galvaniser [galvanize] (1) *vt* (*lit, Tech*) to galvanize; (*fig: stimuler*) to galvanize (into action).

galvanisme [galvanism(ə)] *nm* (*Méd*) galvanism.

galvanomètre [galvanɔmɛtʀ(ə)] *nm* galvanometer.

galvanoplastie [galvanɔplasti] *nf* (*reproduction*) electrotyping, galvanoplasty; (*dépôt*) electroplating.

galvanoplastique [galvanɔplastik] *adj* galvanoplastic.

galvanotype [galvanɔtip] *nm* electrotype.

galvanotypie [galvanɔtipi] *nf* electrotyping.

galvaudage [galvodaʒ] *nm* (a) *[nom, réputation]* tarnishing, bringing into disrepute, sullying; *[talent]* prostituting, debasing. (b) (*vagabondage*) loafing about, idling around.
galvaudé, e [galvode] (*ptp de* **galvauder**) *adj expression* trite, hackneyed.
galvauder [galvode] (1) 1 *vt réputation, nom* to tarnish, sully, bring into disrepute; *talent* to prostitute, debase; *expression* to make trite *ou* hackneyed.
2 *vi* (†: *vagabonder*) to loaf about, idle around.
3 **se galvauder** *vpr* (*s'avilir*) to demean o.s., lower o.s., compromise o.s.
galvaudeux, -euse† [galvodø, øz] *nm,f* (*vagabond*) tramp; (*bon à rien*) good-for-nothing.
gambade [gɑ̃bad] *nf* leap, caper. **faire des ~s** *[personne, enfant]* to leap (about), caper (about), prance about; *[animal]* to gambol, leap (about), frisk about.
gambader [gɑ̃bade] (1) *vi [animal]* to gambol, leap (about), frisk about; *[personne, enfant]* to leap (about), caper (about), prance about; *[esprit]* to flit *ou* jump (from one idea to another). **~ de joie** to jump for joy.
gambe [gɑ̃b] *nf V* **viole.**
gamberger‡ [gɑ̃bɛʀʒe] (3) *vi* to think.
gambette* [gɑ̃bɛt] *nf* leg.
Gambie [gɑ̃bi] *nf*: **la ~** (*pays*) (the) Gambia; (*fleuve*) the Gambia.
gambiller‡† [gɑ̃bije] (1) *vi* to dance, jig*.
gambit [gɑ̃bi] *nm* (*Échecs*) gambit.
gamelle [gamɛl] *nf [soldat]* mess tin; *[ouvrier]* billy-can, billy. (*lit, fig*) **ramasser** *ou* **prendre une ~*** to come a cropper*.
gamète [gamɛt] *nm* gamete.
gamin, e [gamɛ̃, in] 1 *adj* (*espiègle*) mischievous, playful; (*puéril*) childish. 2 *nm,f* (*: *enfant*) kid*. **quand j'étais ~** when I was a kid* *ou* a nipper*; **~ des rues** street urchin.
gaminerie [gaminʀi] *nf* (*espièglerie*) playfulness (*U*); (*puérilité*) childishness (*U*). **faire des ~s** to play (mischievous) pranks; to be childish.
gamma [gama] *nm* gamma; *V* **rayon.**
gamme [gam] *nf* (a) (*Mus*) scale. **faire des ~s** to practise scales; **~ ascendante/descendante** rising/falling scale. (b) (*série*) *[couleurs, articles]* range; *[sentiments]* gamut, range. **toute la ~*** the whole lot.
gammée [game] *adj f V* **croix.**
ganache [ganaʃ] *nf* (a) (*†: *imbécile*) **(vieille) ~** (old) fool, (old) duffer*. (b) *[cheval]* lower jaw.
Gand [gɑ̃] *n* Ghent.
gandin [gɑ̃dɛ̃] *nm* (*péj*) dandy.
gang [gɑ̃g] *nm* gang (*of crooks*).
Gange [gɑ̃ʒ] *nm*: **le ~** the Ganges.
ganglion [gɑ̃glijɔ̃] *nm* ganglion.
ganglionnaire [gɑ̃glijɔnɛʀ] *adj* ganglionic.
gangrène [gɑ̃gʀɛn] *nf* (*Méd*) gangrene; (*fig*) corruption, canker (*fig*).
gangrener [gɑ̃gʀəne] (5) *vt* (a) (*Méd*) to gangrene. **membre gangrené** gangrenous limb. (b) (*fig*) to corrupt. **société gangrenée** society in decay.
gangreneux, -euse [gɑ̃gʀənø, øz] *adj* gangrenous.
gangster [gɑ̃gstɛʀ] *nm* gangster; (*fig*) shark, swindler, crook.
gangstérisme [gɑ̃gsteʀism(ə)] *nm* gangsterism.
gangue [gɑ̃g] *nf [minerai, pierre]* gangue. **~ de boue** coating *ou* layer of mud; (*fig: carcan*) strait jacket (*fig*).
ganse [gɑ̃s] *nf* (*Habillement*) braid.
gant [gɑ̃] 1 *nm* (a) glove. **~s de caoutchouc/de boxe** rubber/boxing gloves.
(b) (*loc*) **remettre les ~s*** to take up boxing again; **cette robe lui va comme un ~** this dress fits her like a glove; **ton idée me va comme un ~** your idea suits me down to the ground; **il ne s'agit pas de prendre** *ou* **mettre des ~s** there's no point using kid-glove methods *ou* trying to be as gentle as possible; **je ne vais pas prendre des ~s avec lui** I'm not going to pull my punches with him; **tu ferais mieux de prendre des ~s avec lui** you'd better handle him with kid gloves; **il va falloir prendre des ~s pour lui annoncer la nouvelle** we'll have to break the news to him gently; (*lit, fig*) **jeter/relever le ~** to throw down/take up the gauntlet; *V* **main, retourner** *etc.*
2: **gant de crin** massage glove; **gant de toilette** (face) flannel (*Brit*), wash glove.
gantelet [gɑ̃tlɛ] *nm* (*Mil, Sport*) gauntlet; (*Tech*) hand leather.
ganter [gɑ̃te] (1) 1 *vt main, personne* to fit with gloves, glove (*rare*), put gloves on. **tu es bien ganté** these gloves look nice on you *ou* suit your hand well; **ganté de cuir** wearing *ou* with leather gloves; **main gantée de cuir** leather-gloved hand.
2 *vi*: **~ du 7** to take (a) size 7 in gloves.
3 **se ganter** *vpr* to put on one's gloves.
ganterie [gɑ̃tʀi] *nf* (*usine*) glove factory; (*magasin*) glove shop; (*commerce*) glove trade; (*industrie*) glove-making industry.
gantier, -ière [gɑ̃tje, jɛʀ] *nm,f* glover.
garage [gaʀaʒ] 1 *nm* (*Aut*) garage. **as-tu mis la voiture au ~?** have you put the car in the garage? *ou* away?
2: **garage d'autobus** bus depot *ou* garage; **garage d'avions** hangar; **garage de** *ou* **à bicyclettes** bicycle shed; **garage de canots** boathouse; *V* **voie.**
garagiste [gaʀaʒist(ə)] *nm* (*propriétaire*) garage owner; (*mécanicien*) garage mechanic. **le ~ m'a dit que ...** the man at the garage *ou* the mechanic told me that ... .
garance [gaʀɑ̃s] 1 *nf* (*Bot: teinture*) madder. 2 *adj inv* madder(-coloured).
garant, e [gaʀɑ̃, ɑ̃t] *nm,f* (*gén, personne, état*) guarantor (*de* for); (*chose: garantie*) guarantee (*de* of). **servir de ~ à qn** *[personne]* to stand surety for sb, act as guarantor for sb; *[honneur, parole]* to be sb's guarantee; **être** *ou* **se porter ~ de qch** (*Jur*) to be answerable *ou* responsible for sth; (*gén: assurer*) to vouch for sth, guarantee sth; **ils vont échouer, ça je m'en porte ~** they'll come to grief — I can absolutely guarantee it.
garanti, e [gaʀɑ̃ti] (*ptp de* **garantir**) 1 *adj* (*Comm*) guaranteed. **~ étanche/3 ans** guaranteed waterproof/for 3 years; **~ à l'usage** guaranteed for normal use; **~ pure laine** warranted *ou* guaranteed pure wool; (*fig*) **~ sur facture*** sure as anything, sure as heck*; **il va refuser, c'est ~*** he'll refuse — it's a cert* (*Brit*) *ou* it's for sure, he is sure to refuse.
2 **garantie** *nf* (a) (*Comm*) guarantee. **sous ~e** under guarantee; *V* **bon**[2].
(b) (*assurance*) guarantee, guaranty (*T*); (*gage*) security, surety; (*fig: protection*) safeguard. **ils nous ont donné leur ~e que ...** they gave us their guarantee that ...; **si on a la ~e qu'ils se conduiront bien ...** if we have a firm undertaking *ou* a guarantee that they'll behave ...; **servir de ~e** *[bijoux]* to act as a surety *ou* security *ou* guarantee; *[otages]* to be used as a security; *[honneur]* to be a guarantee; **donner des ~es** to give guarantees; **il faut prendre des ~es** we have to find sureties; **cette entreprise présente toutes les ~es de sérieux** there is every indication that this firm is a reliable concern; **c'est une ~e de succès** it's a guarantee of success; **c'est une ~e contre le chômage/l'inflation** it's a safeguard against unemployment/inflation.
(c) (*caution*) **donner sa ~e à** to guarantee, stand security *ou* surety for, be guarantor for.
(d) *[police d'assurance]* cover (*U*).
(e) (*loc*) **sans ~e: je vous dis ça, mais c'est sans ~e** I can't vouch for what I'm telling you, I can't guarantee that what I'm telling you is right; **j'essaierai de le faire pour jeudi mais sans ~e** I'll try and get it done for Thursday but I can't guarantee it *ou* I'm not making any promises; **ils ont bien voulu essayer de le faire, sans ~e de succès** they were quite willing to try and do it, but they couldn't guarantee success.
3: **garantie constitutionnelle** constitutional guarantee; **garantie d'intérêt** guaranteed interest; **garantie de paiement** guarantee of payment; **garanties parlementaires** guarantee in law.
garantir [gaʀɑ̃tiʀ] (2) *vt* (a) (*gén, Comm: assurer*) to guarantee. **~ que** to assure *ou* guarantee that; **je te garantis que ça ne se passera pas comme ça!*** I can assure you *ou* believe you me* things won't turn out like that!; **le poulet sera tendre, le boucher me l'a garanti** the chicken will be tender — the butcher assured me it would be; **je te garantis le fait** I can vouch for the fact; **il m'a garanti le succès** he guaranteed me success, he assured me I would be successful; *V* **garanti.**
(b) (*protéger*) **~ qch de** to protect sth from; **se ~ les yeux (du soleil)** to protect one's eyes (from the sun).
garce‡ [gaʀs(ə)] *nf* (*péj*) (*méchante*) bitch‡; (*dévergondée*) tart‡. **c'est une ~ de vie‡†** what a bloody (*Brit*) *ou* damned awful life‡.
garçon [gaʀsɔ̃] 1 *nm* (a) (*enfant, fils*) boy. **tu es un grand ~ maintenant** you're a big boy now; **traiter qn comme un petit ~** to treat sb like a child *ou* a little boy; **à côté d'eux, on est des petits ~s** compared with them we're only beginners; **cette fille est un ~ manqué** *ou* **un vrai ~** this girl is a real tomboy.
(b) (*jeune homme*) young man. (*hum*) **eh bien mon ~ ...** well my boy ...; **c'est un brave ~** he's a good sort *ou* a nice fellow; **ce ~ ira loin** that young man will go far.
(c) (*commis*) (shop) assistant. **~ boulanger/boucher** baker's/butcher's assistant; (*jeune homme*) baker's/butcher's boy; **~ coiffeur** hairdresser's assistant.
(d) (*serveur*) waiter.
(e) (*célibataire*) bachelor. **être/rester ~** to be/remain single *ou* a bachelor; **vivre en ~** to lead a bachelor's life; *V* **enterrer, vie, vieux.**
2: **garçon d'ascenseur** lift attendant; (*jeune homme*) lift boy; **garçon de bureau** office assistant; (*jeune homme*) office boy; **garçon de cabine** cabin boy; **garçon de café** waiter; **garçon de courses** messenger; (*jeune homme*) errand boy; **garçon d'écurie** stable lad; **garçon d'étage** boots (*sg*); **garçon de ferme** farm hand; **garçon d'honneur** best man, groomsman; **garçon de laboratoire** laboratory assistant; **garçon livreur** delivery man; (*jeune homme*) delivery boy; **garçon de recettes** bank messenger; **garçon de salle** waiter.
garçonne [gaʀsɔn] *nf*: **à la ~** *coiffure* urchin cut; **être coiffée à la ~** to have an urchin cut.
garçonnet [gaʀsɔnɛ] *nm* small boy. **taille ~** boy's size.
garçonnière [gaʀsɔnjɛʀ] *nf* bachelor flat (*Brit*) *ou* apartment (*US*).
garde[1] [gaʀd(ə)] 1 *nf* (a) (*surveillance*) **on lui avait confié la ~ des bagages/prisonniers** he had been put in charge of the luggage/the prisoners, he had been given the job of looking after *ou* of guarding the luggage/the prisoners; **il s'est chargé de la ~ des bagages/prisonniers** he undertook to look after *ou* to guard *ou* to keep an eye on the luggage/the prisoners; **la ~ des frontières est assurée par ...** the task *ou* job of guarding the frontiers is carried out by ...; **confier qch/qn à la ~ de qn** to entrust sth/sb to sb's care, leave sth/sb in sb's care; **prendre en ~** *enfant, animal* to take into one's care, look after; **il nous ont laissé leur enfant en ~** they left their child in our care; **Dieu vous ait en sa (sainte) ~** (may) God be with you; **être sous la ~ de la police** to be under police guard; **être/mettre qn sous bonne ~** to be/put sb under guard.
(b) (*Jur: après divorce*) custody. **l'enfant a été laissé à la ~ de la mère** the child was left in the custody of the mother; **c'est elle qui a eu la ~ des enfants** she had *ou* got *ou* was given (the) custody of the children.
(c) (*veille*) *[soldat]* guard duty; *[infirmière etc]* ward duty. **cette ~ a duré 2 heures** he (*ou* we *etc*) stood *ou* was (*ou* were) on watch for 2 hours; **(être) de ~** *[infirmière, sentinelle]* (to be) on

duty; **pharmacie de ~** chemist on duty, duty chemist; **quel est le médecin de ~?** who is the doctor on duty?; *V* **chien, monter[1], poste[2].**

(d) (*groupe, escorte*) guard. (*Mil*) **~ descendante/montante** old/relief guard; *V* **arrière, avant, corps** *etc.*

(e) (*personne*) *[salle d'hôpital]* nurse. **~ de jour/de nuit** day/night nurse.

(f) (*position, Boxe, Escrime*) guard. (*Escrime*) **~s** positions; **en ~!** on guard!; **se mettre en ~** to take one's guard; **avoir/tenir la ~ haute** to have/keep one's guard up; **fermer/ouvrir sa ~** to close/open one's guard.

(g) *[épée]* hilt. **jusqu'à la ~** (*lit*) (up) to the hilt; **il s'est enferré jusqu'à la ~** (*fig*) he's in it up to his neck*.

(h) (*Typ*) **(page de) ~** flyleaf.

(i) (*Tech*) *[serrure]* **~s** wards.

(j) (*Aut*) **~ au toit** headroom; **laisser une ~ suffisante à la pédale** to allow enough play on the pedal.

(k) (*Cartes*) **avoir la ~ à cœur** to have a stop in hearts.

(l) (*loc*) (*littér*) **n'avoir ~ de faire** to take good care not to do, make sure one doesn't do; **mettre qn en ~** to put sb on his guard, warn sb (*contre* against); **mise en ~** warning; **faire bonne ~** to keep a close watch; **prendre ~ de ne pas faire, prendre ~ à ne pas faire†** to be careful *ou* take care not to do; **prenez ~ de (ne pas) tomber** mind you don't fall, be careful *ou* take care you don't fall *ou* not to fall; **prenez ~ qu'il ne prenne pas froid** mind *ou* watch *ou* be careful he doesn't catch cold; **prends ~!** (*exhortation*) watch out!; (*menace*) watch it!*; **prends ~ à toi** watch yourself*, take care; **prends ~ aux voitures** be careful of the cars, watch out for *ou* mind the cars; **sans prendre ~ au danger** without considering *ou* heeding the danger; **sans y prendre ~** without realizing it; **être/se mettre/se tenir sur ses ~s** to be/put o.s./stay on one's guard; (*Mil*) **~-à-vous** *nm inv* (*action*) standing to attention (*U*); (*cri*) order to stand to attention; **~-à-vous (fixe)!** attention!; **ils exécutèrent des ~-à-vous impeccables** they stood to attention faultlessly; **rester/se mettre au ~-à-vous** to stand at/stand to attention.

2: garde d'enfants child minder; (*à domicile*) baby-sitter; **garde impériale** imperial guard; **garde judiciaire** legal surveillance (*of impounded property*); (*Jur*) **garde juridique** legal liability; **garde mobile** *mobile guard*; **garde municipale** *municipal guard*; **garde pontificale** papal guard; **garde républicaine** *republican guard*; (*Jur*) **garde à vue** ≃ police custody.

garde[2] [gaʀd(ə)] **1** *nm* **(a)** *[prisonnier]* guard; *[domaine, propriété, château]* warden; *[jardin public]* keeper.

(b) (*Mil: soldat*) guardsman; (*Hist*) guard, guardsman; (*sentinelle*) guard.

2: garde champêtre rural policeman; **garde du corps** bodyguard; **garde forestier** forest warden, forester; **garde impérial** imperial guard *ou* guardsman; **garde mobile** *mobile guard ou guardsman*; **garde municipal** *municipal guard ou guardsman*; **garde pontifical** papal guard *ou* guardsman; **garde républicain** *republican guard ou guardsman*; **garde des Sceaux** ≃ Lord Chancellor; (*Hist*) ≃ Keeper of the Seals; *V aussi* **garder.**

garde- [gaʀd(ə)] *préf V* **garder.**

gardé, e [gaʀde] (*ptp de* **garder**) *adj*: **passage à niveau ~/non ~** manned/unmanned level crossing; (*Alpinisme, Ski*) **cabane ~e/non ~e** hut with/without resident warden; *V* **chasse[1], proportion.**

gardénal [gaʀdenal] *nm* phenobarbitone (*Brit*), phenobarbital (*US*), Luminal ®.

gardénia [gaʀdenja] *nm* gardenia.

garder [gaʀde] (1) **1** *vt* **(a)** (*surveiller*) *enfants, magasin* to look after, mind; *bestiaux* to look after, guard; *bagages, trésor, prisonnier* to look after, guard, watch over; (*défendre*) *frontière, passage, porte* to guard. **le chien garde la maison** the dog guards the house; (*Jur*) **~ qn à vue** ≃ to keep sb in custody; **~ des enfants (à domicile)** to baby-sit; **garde ma valise pendant que j'achète un livre** look after *ou* keep an eye on my suitcase while I buy a book; **on n'a pas gardé les cochons ensemble!*** you've a nerve to take liberties like that!*; **toutes les issues sont gardées** all the exits are guarded, a watch is being kept on all the exits; **une statue gardait l'entrée** a statue stood at the entrance *ou* guarded the entrance.

(b) (*ne pas quitter*) **~ la chambre** to stay in one's room; **~ le lit** to stay in bed; **un rhume lui a fait ~ la chambre** he stayed in his room because of his cold, his cold kept him at home *ou* in his room.

(c) (*conserver*) *denrées, marchandises, papiers* to keep. **ces fleurs ne gardent pas leur parfum** these flowers lose their scent; **il ne peut rien ~** he can't keep anything; (*: *vomir*) he can't keep anything down.

(d) (*conserver sur soi*) *vêtement* to keep on. **gardez donc votre chapeau** do keep your hat on.

(e) (*retenir*) *personne, employé, clients* to keep; *[police]* to detain. **~ qn à déjeuner** to have sb stay for lunch; **~ un élève en retenue** to keep a pupil in, keep a pupil in detention.

(f) (*mettre de côté*) to keep, put aside *ou* to one side; (*réserver*) *place* (*pendant absence*) to keep (*à, pour* for); (*avant l'arrivée d'une personne*) to save, keep (*à, pour* for). **je lui ai gardé une côtelette pour ce soir** I've kept *ou* saved a chop for him for tonight; **j'ai gardé de la soupe pour demain** I've kept *ou* saved *ou* I've put aside some soup for tomorrow; **~ le meilleur pour la fin** to keep the best till the end; **~ qch pour la bonne bouche** to keep the best till last; **je lui garde un chien de ma chienne*** he's got it coming to him from me*; **~ une poire pour la soif** to keep something in hand. *V* **dent.**

(g) (*maintenir*) to keep. **~ les yeux baissés/la tête haute** to keep one's eyes down/one's head up; **~ un chien enfermé/en laisse** to keep a dog shut in/on a leash.

(h) (*ne pas révéler*) to keep. **~ le secret** to keep the secret; **~ ses pensées pour soi** to keep one's thoughts to oneself; **gardez cela pour vous** keep this to yourself, keep it under your hat*.

(i) (*conserver*) *souplesse, élasticité, fraîcheur* to keep, retain; *jeunesse, droits, facultés* to retain; *habitudes* to keep up. **il a gardé toutes ses facultés** he still has all his faculties, he's still in possession of all his faculties; **~ les apparences** to keep up appearances; **~ son calme** to keep calm; **~ sa raison** to stay sane; **~ le silence** to keep silent *ou* silence; **~ l'anonymat** to remain anonymous; **~ la ligne** to keep one's figure; **~ rancune à qn** to bear sb a grudge; **j'ai eu du mal à ~ mon sérieux** I had a job keeping *ou* to keep a straight face.

(j) (*protéger*) **~ qn de l'erreur/de ses amis** to save sb from error/from his friends; **ça vous gardera du froid** it'll protect you from the cold; **Dieu** *ou* **le Ciel vous garde** God be with you; **la châsse qui garde ces reliques** the shrine which houses these relics.

2 se garder *vpr* **(a)** *[denrées]* to keep. **ça se garde bien** it keeps well.

(b) se ~ de qch (*se défier de*) to beware of *ou* be wary of sth; (*se protéger de*) to protect o.s. from sth, guard against sth; **gardez-vous de décisions trop promptes/de vos amis** beware *ou* be wary of hasty decisions/of your own friends; **se ~ de faire qch** to be careful not to do sth; **elle s'est bien gardée de le prévenir** she was very careful not to warn him, she carefully avoided warning him; **vous allez lui parler? — je m'en garderai bien!** are you going to speak to him? — that's one thing I won't do! *ou* that's the last thing I'd do!

3: garde-barrière *nmf, pl* **gardes-barrière(s)** level-crossing keeper; **garde-boue** *nm inv* mudguard; **garde-chasse** *nm, pl* **gardes-chasse(s)** gamekeeper; **garde-chiourme** *nm, pl* **garde(s)-chiourme(s)** (*Hist*) warder (*of galley slaves*); (*fig*) martinet; **garde-corps** *nm inv* (*Naut*) lifeline, manrope; **garde-côte** *nm, pl* **garde-côte(s)** coastguard ship; **garde-feu** *nm inv* fireguard; **garde-fou** *nm, pl* **garde-fous** (*en fer*) railing; (*en pierre*) parapet; **garde-frein** *nm, pl* **gardes-frein(s)** guard, brakeman; (*Mil*) **garde-magasin** *nm, pl* **gardes-magasin(s)** ≃ quartermaster; **garde-malade** *nmf, pl* **gardes-malades** home nurse; **garde-manger** *nm inv* (*armoire*) meat safe; (*pièce*) pantry, larder; **garde-meuble** *nm, pl* **garde-meuble** furniture depository; **mettre une armoire au garde-meuble(s)** to put a wardrobe in store; **garde-nappe** *nm, pl* **garde-nappe(s)** tablemat; **garde-pêche** *nm inv* (*personne*) water bailiff; (*frégate*) fisheries protection ship; **une vedette garde-pêche** fisheries protection launch; **garde-place** *nm, pl* **garde-place(s)** holder *ou* slot (for reservation ticket) (*in a railway compartment*); **garde-port** *nm, pl* **gardes-port(s)** wharf *ou* harbour master; **garde-robe** *nf, pl* **garde-robes** (*habits*) wardrobe; (*Rail*) **garde-voie** *nm, pl* **gardes-voie(s)** line guard; *V aussi* **garde[1], garde[2].**

garderie [gaʀdəʀi] *nf*: **~ (d'enfants)** day nursery, crèche (*in a school, factory etc where children are looked after outside school hours while their parents are working*).

gardeur [gaʀdœʀ] *nm*: **~ de troupeaux** herdsman; **~ de vaches** cowherd; **~ de chèvres** goatherd; **~ de cochons** pig-keeper, swineherd†; **~ d'oies** gooseherd; **~ de dindons** turkey-keeper.

gardeuse [gaʀdøz] *nf* (*V* **gardeur**) herdswoman; cowherd†; swineherd; goose girl; turkey-keeper.

gardian [gaʀdjɑ̃] *nm* herdsman (*in the Camargue*).

gardien, -ienne [gaʀdjɛ̃, jɛn] **1** *nm,f* *[prisonnier]* guard; *[prison]* officer, warder, guard; *[propriété, château]* warden; *[usine, locaux]* guard; *[musée, hôtel]* attendant; *[cimetière]* caretaker, keeper; *[jardin public, phare, zoo]* keeper; *[réserve naturelle]* warden; (*fig: défenseur*) guardian, protector. **le ~ du troupeau** the herdsman; (*fig*) **la constitution, ~ne des libertés** the constitution, protector *ou* guardian of freedom; **les ~s de l'ordre public** the keepers of public order; *V* **ange.**

2: gardien de but (goal)keeper; **gardien d'immeuble** caretaker (*of a block of flats*); **gardien de musée** museum attendant; **gardien de nuit** night watchman; **gardien de la paix** policeman (*in a town*); **gardien de phare** lighthouse keeper; **gardien de prison** prison warder.

gardiennage [gaʀdjɛnaʒ] *nm* *[immeuble]* caretaking; *[locaux]* guarding; *[port]* security.

gardon [gaʀdɔ̃] *nm* roach; *V* **frais[1].**

gare[1] [gaʀ] **1** *nf* (*Rail*) station. **~ d'arrivée/de départ** station of arrival/departure; **~ de marchandises/de voyageurs** goods/passenger station; **le train entre/est en ~** the train is coming in/is in; **l'express de Dijon entre en ~ sur voie 6** the train now approaching platform 6 is the express from Dijon, the express from Dijon is now approaching platform 6; *V* **chef[1].**

2: gare maritime harbour station; **gare routière** (*camions*) haulage depot; (*autocars*) coach (*Brit*) *ou* bus (*US*) station; **gare de triage** marshalling yard.

gare[2]* [gaʀ] *excl* (*attention*) **~ à toi!, ~ à tes fesses!‡** (just) watch it!*; **~ à toi** *ou* **à tes fesses si tu recommences!** you'll be for it if you start that again!*; **~ au premier qui bouge!** whoever makes the first move will be in trouble!, the first one to move will be for it!*; **et fais ce que je dis, sinon ~!** and do what I say, or else!*; **~ à ne pas recommencer** just make sure you don't do it again!; **la porte est basse, ~ à ta tête** it's a low door so mind your head; **~ aux conséquences/à ce type** beware of the consequences/this fellow; *V* **crier.**

garenne [gaʀɛn] *nf* rabbit warren; *V* **lapin.**

garer [gaʀe] (1) **1** *vt* *véhicule* to park; *train* to put into a siding; *embarcation* to dock; *récolte* to (put into) store. (*fig*) **~ son argent** *ou* **sa fortune** to put one's money *ou* fortune in a safe place; **d'habitude, je gare devant la porte** I usually park at the door.

2 se garer *vpr* **(a)** *[automobiliste]* to park.

(b) (*se ranger de côté*) *[véhicule, automobiliste]* to draw into the side; *[piéton]* to move aside, get out of the way.

(c) (*: *éviter*) **se ~ de qch/qn** to avoid sth/sb, steer clear of sth/sb.

Gargantua [gaʀgɑ̃tɥa] *nm* Gargantua. **appétit de ~** gargantuan *ou* gigantic appetite; **c'est un ~** he has a gargantuan *ou* gigantic appetite.

gargantuesque [gaʀgɑ̃tɥɛsk(ə)] *adj appétit* gargantuan.

gargariser (se) [gaʀgaʀize] (1) *vpr* to gargle. (*fig péj*) **se ~ de grands mots** to revel in big words.

gargarisme [gaʀgaʀism(ə)] *nm* gargle.

gargote [gaʀgɔt] *nf* cheap restaurant *ou* eating-house.

gargouille [gaʀguj] *nf* (*Archit*) gargoyle; (*Constr*) waterspout.

gargouillement [gaʀgujmɑ̃] *nm* = **gargouillis.**

gargouiller [gaʀguje] (1) *vi [eau]* to gurgle; *[intestin]* to rumble.

gargouillis [gaʀguji] *nm* (*gén pl*) *[eau]* gurgling (*U*); *[intestin]* rumbling (*U*). **faire des ~s** *[eau]* to gurgle; *[intestin]* to rumble.

garnement [gaʀnəmɑ̃] *nm* (*gamin*) (young) imp; (*adolescent*) tearaway.

garni, e [gaʀni] (*ptp de* **garnir**) **1** *adj* **(a)** (*rempli*) **bien ~** *bourse* well-lined; **un portefeuille bien ~** a wallet full of notes, a well-filled wallet; **un réfrigérateur bien ~** a well-stocked fridge; **il a encore une chevelure bien ~e** he has still got a good head of hair.

(b) (*Culin*) *plat, viande* served with vegetables and (*gén*) chips (*Brit*) *ou* French fries (*US*). **cette entrecôte est bien ~e** this steak has a generous helping of chips (*Brit*) *ou* French fries (*US*) with it; *V* **bouquet**[1], **choucroute.**

(c) (†: *meublé*) *chambre* furnished.

2 *nm* furnished accommodation (*for letting*). (†) **il vivait en ~** he lived in furnished accommodation *ou* rooms.

garnir [gaʀniʀ] (2) **1** *vt* **(a)** *[personne]* (*protéger, équiper*) **~ de** to fit out with; **~ une porte d'acier** to fit a door with steel plate; **~ une canne d'un embout** to put a tip on the end of a walking stick; **~ une muraille de canons** to range cannons along a wall; **~ une boîte de tissu** to line a box with material; **~ un mur de pointes** to arm a wall with spikes, set spikes along a wall; **mur garni de canons/pointes** wall bristling with cannons/spikes.

(b) *[chose]* (*couvrir*) **l'acier qui garnit la porte** the steel plate covering the door; **les canons qui garnissent la muraille** the cannons lining the wall *ou* ranged along the wall; **des pointes garnissent le mur** spikes are set in the wall; **le cuir qui garnit la poignée** the leather covering the handle; **coffret garni de velours** casket lined with velvet, velvet-lined casket.

(c) (*approvisionner*) *bibliothèque* to fill; *boîte, caisse* to fill; *réfrigérateur* to stock; *chaudière* to stoke; *hameçon* to bait (*de* with). **le cuisinier garnissait les plats de charcuterie** the cook was setting out *ou* putting cold meats on the plates; **~ de livres une bibliothèque** to fill (the shelves of) a library with books; (*Mil*) **~ les remparts** to garrison the ramparts; **les boîtes, garnies de chocolats, partaient à l'emballage** the boxes filled with chocolates were going to be packed.

(d) (*remplir*) *boîte* to fill; (*recouvrir*) *surface, rayon* to cover, fill. **une foule dense garnissait les trottoirs** a dense crowd covered *ou* packed the pavements; **les chocolats qui garnissaient la boîte** the chocolates which filled the box; **boîte garnie de chocolats** box full of chocolates; **plats garnis de tranches de viande** plates filled with *ou* full of slices of meat.

(e) (*enjoliver*) *vêtement* to trim; *étagère* to decorate; *aliment* to garnish (*de* with). **~ une jupe d'un volant** to trim a skirt with a frill; **~ une table de fleurs** to decorate a table with flowers; **les bibelots qui garnissent la cheminée** the trinkets which decorate the mantelpiece; **des plats joliment garnis de charcuterie** plates artistically decorated with cold meats; **des côtelettes garnies de cresson/de mayonnaise** chops garnished with cress/with mayonnaise.

2 se garnir *vpr [salle, pièce]* to fill up (*de* with). **la salle commençait à se ~** the room was beginning to fill up.

garnison [gaʀnizɔ̃] *nf* (*troupes*) garrison. (**ville de**) **~** garrison town; **vie de ~** garrison life; **être en ~ à, tenir ~ à** to be stationed *ou* garrisoned at.

garniture [gaʀnityʀ] **1** *nf* **(a)** (*décoration*) *[robe, chapeau]* trimming (*U*); *[table]* set of table linen, place mats *etc*; *[coffret]* lining; *[aliment, plat]* garnish. (*Aut*) **la ~ intérieure de cette voiture est très soignée** the upholstery in this car *ou* the interior trim in this car is well-finished.

(b) (*Culin*) (*légumes*) vegetables (*accompanying the meat course*); (*sauce à vol-au-vent*) filling. **servi avec ~** served with vegetables, vegetables included; **~ non comprise** vegetables extra *ou* not included.

(c) (*Typ*) furniture.

(d) (*Tech: protection*) *[chaudière]* lagging (*U*); *[boîte]* covering (*U*). **avec ~ de caoutchouc/cuir** with rubber/leather fittings *ou* fitments; **~ d'embrayage/de frein** clutch/brake lining.

2: garniture de cheminée mantelpiece ornaments; **garniture de foyer** (set of) fire irons; **garniture de lit** (set of) bed linen; **garniture périodique** sanitary towel (*Brit*) *ou* napkin (*US*); **garniture de toilette** toilet set.

garou [gaʀu] *nm V* **loup.**

garrigue [gaʀig] *nf* garrigue, scrubland.

garrot [gaʀo] *nm [cheval]* withers; (*Méd*) tourniquet; (*supplice*) garrotte.

garrotter [gaʀɔte] (1) *vt* to tie up; (*fig*) to muzzle. **~ qn sur** to tie *ou* strap sb down to.

gars* [gɑ] *nm* (*enfant, jeune homme*) lad; (*fils*) lad, boy; (*type*) bloke* (*Brit*), guy*. **mon petit ~** my lad; **dis-moi mon ~** tell me son *ou* sonny* *ou* laddie*; **au revoir les ~!** cheerio boys!* *ou* fellows!*; **un ~ du milieu** a bloke* (*Brit*) *ou* fellow in the underworld.

Gascogne [gaskɔɲ] *nf* Gascony; *V* **golfe.**

gascon, -onne [gaskɔ̃, ɔn] **1** *adj* Gascon. **2** *nm* (*Ling*) Gascon. **3** *nm,f*: **G~(ne)** Gascon; *V* **promesse.**

gasconnade [gaskɔnad] *nf* (*littér: vantardise*) boasting (*U*), bragging (*U*).

gas-oil [gazɔjl] *nm* diesel oil.

Gaspard [gaspaʀ] *nm* Gaspar.

gaspillage [gaspijaʒ] *nm* (*V* **gaspiller**) wasting; squandering.

gaspiller [gaspije] (1) *vt eau, nourriture, temps, dons* to waste; *fortune* to waste, squander. **qu'est-ce que tu gaspilles!** how you waste things!, how w7steful you are!

gaspilleur, -euse [gaspijœʀ, øz] **1** *adj* wasteful. **2** *nm,f [eau, nourriture, temps, dons]* waster; *[fortune]* squanderer.

gastéropode [gasteʀɔpɔd] *nm* gastropod, gasteropod. **~s** Gastropoda.

gastralgie [gastʀalʒi] *nf* stomach pains, gastralgia (*T*).

gastralgique [gastʀalʒik] *adj* gastralgic.

gastrique [gastʀik] *adj* gastric; *V* **embarras.**

gastrite [gastʀit] *nf* gastritis.

gastro-entérite, *pl* **gastro-entérites** [gastʀoɑ̃teʀit] *nf* gastro-enteritis (*U*).

gastro-entérologie [gastʀoɑ̃teʀɔlɔʒi] *nf* gastroenterology.

gastro-entérologue, *pl* **gastro-entérologues** [gastʀoɑ̃teʀɔlɔg] *nmf* gastroenterologist.

gastro-intestinal, e, *mpl* **-aux** [gastʀoɛ̃tɛstinal, o] *adj* gastro-intestinal.

gastronome [gastʀɔnɔm] *nmf* gourmet, gastronome.

gastronomie [gastʀɔnɔmi] *nf* gastronomy.

gastronomique [gastʀɔnɔmik] *adj* gastronomic; *V* **menu**[1].

gastropode [gastʀɔpɔd] *nm* = **gastéropode.**

gâte- [gɑt] *préf V* **gâter.**

gâteau, *pl* **~x** [gɑto] *nm* **(a)** (*pâtisserie*) cake; (*au restaurant*) gateau. **~ d'anniversaire/aux amandes** birthday/almond cake; **~ de semoule/de riz** semolina/rice pudding; **manger des ~x secs** to eat biscuits; *V* **papa, petit.**

(b) (*fig: butin, héritage*) loot. **se partager le ~** to share the loot; **vouloir sa part du ~** to want one's share of the loot *ou* one's slice of the cake.

(c) c'est du ~* it's a piece of cake* (*Brit*), it's a walkover*.

(d) (*de plâtre etc*) cake. (*Agr*) **~ de miel** *ou* **de cire** honeycomb.

gâter [gɑte] (1) **1** *vt* **(a)** (*abîmer*) *viande, fruit* to make go bad; *paysage, mur, papier, visage* to ruin, spoil; *plaisir, goût* to ruin, spoil; *esprit, jugement* to have a harmful effect on. **avoir les dents gâtées** to have bad teeth; **tu vas te ~ les dents avec ces sucreries** you'll ruin your teeth with these sweets; **et, ce qui ne gâte rien, elle est jolie** and she's pretty, which is all to the good *ou* is even better.

(b) (*choyer*) *enfant etc* to spoil. **nous avons été gâtés cette année, il a fait très beau** we've been really lucky this year — the weather has been lovely; (*iro*) **il pleut, on est gâté!** our luck's in! (*iro*) *ou* just our luck! (*iro*) — it's raining!; **la malheureuse n'est pas gâtée par la nature** nature hasn't been very kind to the poor girl; *V* **enfant.**

2 se gâter *vpr [viande]* to go bad, go off; *[fruit]* to go bad; *[temps]* to change (for the worse), take a turn for the worse; (*) *[ambiance, relations]* to take a turn for the worse. **le temps va se ~** the weather's going to change for the worse *ou* going to break; **ça commence** *ou* **les choses commencent à se ~ (entre eux)** things are beginning to go badly *ou* wrong (between them); **mon père vient de rentrer, ça va se ~!** my father has just come in and there's going to be trouble! *ou* things are going to turn nasty!

3: gâte-sauce *nm inv* kitchen boy; (*péj*) bad cook.

gâterie [gɑtʀi] *nf* little treat. **je me suis payé une petite ~** (*objet*) I've treated myself to a little something, I've bought myself a little present; (*sucrerie*) I've bought myself a little treat.

gâteux, -euse* [gɑtø, øz] **1** *adj* (*sénile*) *vieillard* senile, gaga*, doddering (*épith*). **il l'aime tellement qu'il en est ~** he loves her so much (that) it has made him *ou* he has gone a bit soft in the head*.

2 *nm*: (**vieux**) **~** (*sénile*) dotard, doddering old man; (*péj: radoteur, imbécile*) silly old duffer*.

3 gâteuse *nf*: (**vieille**) **~euse** doddering old woman; silly old woman.

gâtisme [gɑtism(ə)] *nm [vieillard]* senility; *[personne stupide]* idiocy, stupidity.

gauche[1] [goʃ] **1** *adj* (*après n*) *bras, soulier, côté, rive* left. **du côté ~** on the left(-hand) side; *V* **arme, main, marier.**

2 *nm* (*Boxe*) (*coup*) left. (*poing*) **direct du ~** straight left; **crochet du ~** left hook.

3 *nf* **(a) la ~** the left (side), the left-hand side; **à ~** on the left; (*direction*) to the left; **à ma/sa ~** on my/his left, on my/his left-hand side; **le tiroir/chemin de ~** the left-hand drawer/path; **rouler à ~** *ou* **sur la ~** to drive on the left; **mettre de l'argent à ~*** to put money aside (on the quiet); *V* **conduite, jusque** *et pour autres exemples V* **droite**[1].

(b) (*Pol*) **la ~** the left (wing); **les ~s** the parties of the left; **un homme de ~** a man of the left; *V* **extrême** *et pour autres exemples V* **droite**[1].

(c) (*Boxe*) (*coup*) left. (*main*) **crochet de la ~** left hook.

gauche[2] [goʃ] *adj* **(a)** (*maladroit*) *personne, style, geste* awkward, clumsy; (*emprunté*) *air, manière* awkward, gauche. **(b)** (*tordu*) *planche, règle* warped; (*Math*) *courbe, surface* skew.

gauchement [goʃmɑ̃] *adv* clumsily, awkwardly.

gaucher, -ère [goʃe, ɛʀ] **1** *adj* left-handed. **2** *nm,f* left-handed person; (*Sport*) left-hander.

gaucherie [goʃʀi] *nf [allure]* awkwardness (*U*); *[action, expression]* clumsiness (*U*); (*acte*) awkward *ou* clumsy behaviour (*U*). **une ~ de style** a clumsy turn of phrase.

gauchir [goʃiʀ] (2) **1** *vt* (*Aviat, Menuiserie*) to warp; (*fig*) *idée, fait* to distort, misrepresent; *esprit* to warp. **2** *vi* to warp. **3 se gauchir** *vpr* to warp.
gauchisant, e [goʃizɑ̃, ɑ̃t] *adj auteur* with left-wing *ou* leftist tendencies; *théorie* with a left-wing *ou* leftish bias.
gauchisme [goʃism(ə)] *nm* leftism.
gauchissement [goʃismɑ̃] *nm* (*V* **gauchir**) warping; distortion, misrepresentation.
gauchiste [goʃist(ə)] **1** *adj* leftist (*épith*). **2** *nmf* leftist.
gaudriole* [godʀijɔl] *nf* **(a)** (*U*) womanizing. **celui-là, pour la ~, il est toujours prêt!** he's always game for a spot of womanizing!*, he's a great one for the women!* **(b)** (*propos*) broad joke.
gaufrage [gofʀaʒ] *nm* (*V* **gaufrer**) embossing; figuring; goffering.
gaufre [gofʀ(ə)] *nf* (*Culin*) waffle; *V* **moule**[1].
gaufrer [gofʀe] (1) *vt papier, cuir* (*en relief*) to emboss; (*en creux*) to figure; *tissu* to goffer. **sur papier gaufré** on embossed paper; *V* **fer**.
gaufrette [gofʀɛt] *nf* wafer.
gaufrier [gofʀije] *nm* waffle iron.
gaufrure [gofʀyʀ] *nf* (*V* **gaufrer**) embossing (*U*); embossed design; figuring (*U*); goffering (*U*).
gaulage [golaʒ] *nm* (*V* **gauler**) beating; shaking down.
Gaule [gol] *nf* Gaul.
gaule [gol] *nf* (*perche*) (long) pole (*used for beating trees or goading animals*); (*Pêche*) fishing rod.
gauler [gole] (1) *vt arbre* to beat (*using long pole to bring down the fruit or nuts*); *fruits, noix* to bring down, shake down (*with a 'gaule'*).
gaullien, -ienne [goljɛ̃, jɛn] *adj* de Gaullian.
gaullisme [golism(ə)] *nm* Gaullism.
gaulliste [golist(ə)] *adj, nmf* Gaullist.
gaulois, e [golwa, waz] **1** *adj* **(a)** (*de Gaule*) Gallic. **(b)** (*grivois*) bawdy. **esprit ~** (broad *ou* bawdy) Gallic humour. **2** *nm* (*Ling*) Gaulish. **3** *nm,f*: **G~(e)** Gaul. **4 gauloise** *nf* (®: *cigarette*) Gauloise (*cigarette*).
gauloisement [golwazmɑ̃] *adv* bawdily.
gauloiserie [golwazʀi] *nf* (*propos*) bawdy story (*ou* joke *etc*); (*caractère grivois*) bawdiness.
gauss [gos] *nm* (*Phys*) gauss.
gausser (se) [gose] (1) *vpr* (*littér: se moquer*) to laugh (and make fun), mock. **vous vous gaussez!** you joke!; **se ~ de** to deride, make mock of (*littér*), poke fun at.
gavage [gavaʒ] *nm* (*Élevage*) force-feeding.
gave [gav] *nm* mountain stream (*in the Pyrenees*).
gaver [gave] (1) **1** *vt animal* to force-feed; *personne* to fill up (*de* with). **je suis gavé!** I'm full (up)!, I'm full to bursting!*; (*fig*) **on les gave de connaissances inutiles** they cram them with useless knowledge.
2 se gaver *vpr*: **se ~ de** *nourriture* to stuff o.s. with; *romans* to devour; **il se gave de films** he's a glutton for films, he's a real film addict; **si tu te gaves maintenant, tu ne pourras plus rien manger au moment du dîner** if you go stuffing yourself* *ou* filling yourself up now, you won't be able to eat anything at dinner time.
gavotte [gavɔt] *nf* gavotte.
gavroche [gavʀɔʃ] *nm* street urchin (*in Paris*).
gaz [gɑz] **1** *nm inv* **(a)** (*Chim*) gas. **le ~ (domestique)** (domestic) gas (*U*); (*Mil*) **les ~** gas; **l'employé du ~** the gasman; **à ~** gas (*épith*); **vous avez le ~?** are you on gas?, do you have gas?; **il s'est suicidé au ~** he gassed himself; **suicide au ~** (suicide by) gassing; (*Aut*) **mettre les ~*** to step on the gas*, put one's foot down*; *V* **bec, chambre, eau** *etc*.
(b) (*euph: pet*) wind (*U*). **avoir des ~** to have wind.
2: (*Aut*) **gaz d'admission** air-fuel mixture; **gaz asphyxiant** poison gas; **gaz carbonique** carbon dioxide; **gaz de combat** poison gas (*for use in warfare*); (*Aut*) **gaz d'échappement** exhaust gas; **gaz d'éclairage**† = **gaz de ville**; **gaz hilarant** laughing gas; **gaz des houillères** firedamp (*U*); **gaz lacrymogène** teargas; **gaz des marais** marsh gas; (*Mil*) **gaz moutarde** mustard gas; **gaz parfait** perfect *ou* ideal gas; **gaz rare** rare gas; **gaz sulfureux** sulphur dioxide; **gaz de ville** town gas.
gaze [gɑz] *nf* gauze.
gazé, e [gɑze] (*ptp de* **gazer**) *adj* (*Mil*) gassed. **les ~s de 14-18** the (poison) gas victims of the 1914-18 war.
gazéification [gazeifikɑsjɔ̃] *nf* (*V* **gazéifier**) gasification; aeration.
gazéifier [gazeifje] (7) *vt* (*Chim*) to gasify; *eau minérale* to aerate.
gazelle [gazɛl] *nf* gazelle.
gazer [gɑze] (1) **1** *vi* (*: *aller, marcher*) **ça gaze?** (*affaires, santé*) how's things?*, how goes it?*; (*travail*) how goes it?*, how's it going?*; (*c'est arrangé?*) is it O.K.?*; **ça gaze avec ta belle-mère?** how's it going with your *ou* are you getting on O.K. with your ma-in-law?*; **ça a/ça n'a pas gazé?** did it/didn't it go O.K.?*; **ça ne gaze pas fort** (*santé*) I'm not feeling so *ou* too great*; (*affaires*) things aren't going too well*; **il y a quelque chose qui ne gaze pas** there's something slightly fishy about it, there's something wrong somewhere.
2 *vt* (*Mil*) to gas.
gazetier [gaztje] *nm* (†† *ou hum*) journalist.
gazette [gazɛt] *nf* (††, *hum, littér*) newspaper. (*hum*) **c'est dans la ~ locale** it's in the local rag; **c'est une vraie ~** he's a mine of information about the latest (local) gossip; **faire la ~** to give a rundown* (*de* on).
gazeux, -euse [gɑzø, øz] *adj* (*Chim*) gaseous; *boisson* fizzy; *V* **eau**.
gazier, -ière [gɑzje, jɛʀ] **1** *adj* (*rare*) gas (*épith*). **2** *nm* gasman.
gazoduc [gɑzɔdyk] *nm* gas main, gas pipeline.
gazogène [gɑzɔʒɛn] *nm* gas producer (*plant*).
gazoline [gɑzɔlin] *nf* gasoline, gasolene.
gazomètre [gɑzɔmɛtʀ(ə)] *nm* gasometer.
gazon [gɑzɔ̃] *nm* (*pelouse*) lawn. (*herbe*) **le ~** turf (*U*), grass (*U*); **une motte de ~** a turf, a sod; **~ anglais** (*pelouse*) well-kept *ou* smooth lawn.
gazonnage [gɑzɔnaʒ] *nm*, **gazonnement** [gɑzɔnmɑ̃] *nm* planting with grass.
gazonner [gɑzɔne] (1) *vt talus, terrain* to plant with grass.
gazouillement [gazujmɑ̃] *nm* (*V* **gazouiller**) chirping (*U*), warbling (*U*); babbling (*U*); gurgling (*U*), gurgle.
gazouiller [gazuje] (1) *vi [oiseau]* to chirp, warble; *[ruisseau]* to babble; *[bébé]* to gurgle, babble.
gazouilleur, -euse [gazujœʀ, øz] *adj* (*V* **gazouiller**) chirping, warbling; babbling; gurgling.
gazouillis [gazuji] *nm [oiseau]* chirping, warbling; *[ruisseau]* babbling.
geai [ʒɛ] *nm* jay.
géant, e [ʒeɑ̃, ɑ̃t] **1** *adj* gigantic; *animal, plante* gigantic, giant (*épith*); *paquet, carton* giant-size (*épith*), giant (*épith*). **2** *nm* (*lit, fig*) giant; (*Écon, Pol*) giant power; *V* **pas**[1]. **3 géante** *nf* giantess.
Gédéon [ʒedeɔ̃] *nm* Gideon.
géhenne [ʒeɛn] *nf* (*Bible: enfer*) Gehenna.
geignant, e [ʒɛɲɑ̃, ɑ̃t] *adj* (*V* **geindre**) groaning; moaning; whining; complaining.
geignard, e* [ʒɛɲaʀ, aʀd(ə)] **1** *adj personne* moaning; *voix* whining. **2** *nm,f* moaner.
geignement [ʒɛɲmɑ̃] *nm* moaning (*U*).
geindre [ʒɛ̃dʀ(ə)] (52) *vi* (*gémir*) to groan, moan (*de* with); (*péj: pleurnicher*) to moan; *[vent]* to whine, moan. **il geint tout le temps*** he never stops *ou* he's always moaning *ou* complaining *ou* griping*; (*littér*) **le vent faisait ~ les peupliers/le gréement** the wind made the poplars/the rigging groan.
geisha [gɛʃa] *nf* geisha (girl).
gel [ʒɛl] *nm* **(a)** (*temps*) frost. **un jour de ~** one frosty day; **plantes tuées par le ~** plants killed by (the) frost. **(b)** (*glace*) frost. **'craint le ~'** 'keep away from extreme cold'. **(c)** (*Écon*) *[crédits]* freezing. **(d)** (*substance*) gel.
gélatine [ʒelatin] *nf* gelatine.
gélatineux, -euse [ʒelatinø, øz] *adj* jelly-like, gelatinous.
gelé, e[1] [ʒ(ə)le] (*ptp de* **geler**) *adj* (*Théât*) *public* cold (*fig*), unresponsive; (*: *soûl*) tight*, canned‡.
gelée[2] [ʒ(ə)le] *nf* **(a)** (*gel*) frost. **~ blanche** white frost, hoarfrost. **(b)** (*Culin*) *[viande, volaille, fruits]* jelly. **poulet en ~** chicken in aspic *ou* jelly; **~ de framboises** raspberry jelly.
geler [ʒ(ə)le] (5) **1** *vt* **(a)** *eau, rivière* to (make) freeze *ou* ice over; *buée* to turn to ice; *sol* to freeze.
(b) *membre* to cause frostbite to. **les nuits printanières ont gelé les bourgeons** the buds were blighted by frost during the spring nights; **le skieur a eu les pieds gelés** the skier's feet were frostbitten, the skier had frostbite on both feet; **ils sont morts gelés** they froze to death, they died of exposure.
(c) (*: *refroidir*) **tu nous gèles, avec la fenêtre ouverte** you're making us freeze with that window open; **j'ai les mains gelées** my hands are frozen (stiff); **je suis gelé** I'm frozen (stiff).
(d) (*Fin*) *prix, crédits* to freeze.
2 se geler* *vpr* (*avoir froid*) to freeze. **on se gèle ici** we're *ou* it's freezing here; **on se les gèle‡** it's bloody (*Brit*) *ou* damned freezing‡, it's brass monkey weather‡; **vous allez vous ~, à l'attendre** you'll get frozen stiff waiting for him.
3 *vi* **(a)** *[eau, lac]* to freeze (over), ice over; *[sol, linge]* to freeze; *[récoltes]* to be attacked *ou* be blighted by frost; *[doigt, membre]* to be freezing, be frozen. **les salades ont gelé sur pied** the lettuces have frozen on their stalks.
(b) (*avoir froid*) to be frozen, freeze. **on gèle ici** we're *ou* it's freezing here.
4 *vb impers*: **il gèle** it's freezing; **il a gelé dur** *ou* (*littér*) **à pierre fendre** it froze hard, there was a hard frost.
gélifier [ʒelifje] (7) **1** *vt* to make gel. **2 se gélifier** *vpr* to gel.
gélinotte [ʒelinɔt] *nf* hazel hen.
gélose [ʒeloz] *nf* agar-agar.
gélule [ʒelyl] *nf* (*Méd*) capsule.
gelure [ʒ(ə)lyʀ] *nf* (*Méd*) frostbite (*U*).
Gémeaux [ʒemo] *nmpl* (*Astron*) Gemini. **être (des) ~** to be (a) Gemini.
gémellaire [ʒemelɛʀ] *adj* twin (*épith*).
gémination [ʒeminɑsjɔ̃] *nf* gemination.
géminé, e [ʒemine] **1** *adj* (*Ling*) *consonne* geminate; (*Archit*) gemeled, gemel; (*Bio*) geminate. **2 géminée** *nf* (*Ling*) geminate.
gémir [ʒemiʀ] (2) *vi* **(a)** (*geindre*) to groan, moan (*de* with). **~ sur son sort** to bemoan one's fate; (*littér*) **~ sous l'oppression** to groan under oppression.
(b) (*fig: grincer*) *[ressort, plancher]* to creak; *[vent]* to moan, whine. **les gonds de la porte gémissaient horriblement** the door hinges made a horrible creaking noise.
(c) *[colombe]* to cry plaintively, moan.
gémissement [ʒemismɑ̃] *nm* (*V* **gémir**) groaning (*U*); moaning (*U*); creaking (*U*); whining (*U*).
gemmage [ʒɛmaʒ] *nm* tapping (*of pine trees*).
gemme [ʒɛm] *nf* **(a)** (*Minér*) gem(stone). **(b)** (*résine de pin*) (pine) resin; *V* **sel**.
gemmé, e [ʒeme] (*ptp de* **gemmer**) *adj* (*littér*) gemmed, studded with precious stones.
gemmer [ʒeme] (1) *vt* to tap (*pine trees*).
gémonies [ʒemɔni] *nfpl* (*littér*) **vouer** *ou* **traîner qn aux ~** to subject sb to *ou* hold sb up to public obloquy.
gênant, e [ʒɛnɑ̃, ɑ̃t] *adj* **(a)** (*irritant*) **l'eau est coupée, c'est vraiment ~** they've cut the water off — it's a real nuisance; **il**

est ~ avec sa fumée he's a nuisance with his smoke; *V* **gêner.**

(b) *(embarrassant)* *situation, moment, témoin* awkward, embarrassing; *révélations, regard, présence* embarrassing.

gencive [ʒɑ̃siv] *nf (Anat)* gum. **il a pris un coup dans les ~s*** he got a sock on the jaw* *ou* kick in the teeth*.

gendarme [ʒɑ̃daʀm(ə)] *nm (policier)* gendarme, policeman *(in countryside and small towns)*; *(Hist Mil) (cavalier)* horseman; *(soldat)* soldier, man-at-arms; (*†: *hareng*) bloater. *(fig)* **faire le** ~ to put one's foot down; *(hum)* **sa femme est un vrai** ~ his wife's a real battle-axe*; **jouer aux ~s et aux voleurs** to play cops and robbers; *V* **chapeau, peur.**

gendarmer (se) [ʒɑ̃daʀme] (1) *vpr* to kick up a fuss* *(contre* about). **il faut se ~ pour qu'elle aille se coucher/pour la faire manger** you really have to take quite a strong line (with her) *ou* you really have to lay down the law to get her to go to bed/to get her to eat.

gendarmerie [ʒɑ̃daʀməʀi] *nf (corps militaire)* gendarmerie, police force *(in countryside and small towns)*; *(bureaux)* police station *(in countryside and small towns)*; *(caserne)* gendarmes' barracks, police barracks; *(Hist Mil) (cavalerie)* heavy cavalry *ou* horse; *(garde royale)* royal guard.

gendre [ʒɑ̃dʀ(ə)] *nm* son-in-law.

gène [ʒɛn] *nm* gene.

gêne [ʒɛn] *nf* **(a)** *(malaise physique)* discomfort. **il ressentait une certaine ~ à respirer** he experienced some *ou* a certain difficulty in breathing.

(b) *(désagrément, dérangement)* trouble, bother. **je ne voudrais vous causer aucune** ~ I wouldn't like to put you to any trouble *ou* bother, I wouldn't want to be a nuisance; *(Prov)* **où il y a de la ~, il n'y a pas de plaisir** comfort comes first, there's no sense in being uncomfortable; *(péj)* some people only think of their own comfort.

(c) *(manque d'argent)* financial difficulties *ou* straits. **vivre dans la ~/dans une grande ~** to be in financial difficulties *ou* straits/in great financial difficulties *ou* straits.

(d) *(confusion, trouble)* embarrassment. **un moment de ~** a moment of embarrassment; **j'éprouve de la ~ devant lui** I feel embarrassed *ou* ill-at-ease in his presence; **il éprouva de la ~ à lui avouer cela** he felt embarrassed to admit that to her; *V* **sans.**

gêné, e [ʒene] *(ptp de* **gêner***)* *adj* **(a)** *(à court d'argent)* short (of money) *(attrib)*, hard up* *(attrib)*. **être ~ aux entournures** to be short of money *ou* hard up*.

(b) *(embarrassé)* *personne, sourire, air* embarrassed, self-conscious; *silence* uncomfortable, embarrassed, awkward. **j'étais ~!** I was (so) embarrassed!, I felt (so) awkward *ou* uncomfortable.

généalogie [ʒenealɔʒi] *nf [famille]* ancestry, genealogy; *[animaux]* pedigree; *(Bio) [espèces]* genealogy; *(sujet d'études)* genealogy. **faire** *ou* **dresser la ~ de qn** to trace sb's ancestry *ou* genealogy.

généalogique [ʒenealɔʒik] *adj* genealogical; *V* **arbre.**

généalogiste [ʒenealɔʒist(ə)] *nmf* genealogist.

gêner [ʒene] (1) **1** *vt* **(a)** *(physiquement) [fumée, bruit]* to bother; *[vêtement étroit, obstacle]* to hamper. ~ **le passage** to be in the way; **ça me gêne** *ou* **c'est gênant pour respirer/pour écrire** it hampers my breathing/hampers me when I write; **le bruit me gêne pour travailler** noise bothers me *ou* disturbs me when I'm trying to work; **son complet le gêne (aux entournures)** his suit is uncomfortable; **ces papiers me gênent** *ou* **sont gênants** these papers are in my way.

(b) *(déranger)* *personne* to bother, put out; *projet* to hamper, hinder. **je crains de** ~ I am afraid to bother people *ou* put people out; **je ne voudrais pas (vous)** ~ I don't want to bother you *ou* put you out *ou* be in the way; **j'espère que ça ne vous gêne pas d'y aller** I hope it won't inconvenience you *ou* put you out to go; **cela vous gênerait de faire mes courses/de ne pas fumer?** would you mind doing my shopping/not smoking?; **et alors, ça te gêne?*** so what?*, what's it to you?

(c) *(financièrement)* to put in financial difficulties. **ces dépenses vont les ~ considérablement** *ou* **vont les ~ aux entournures*** these expenses are really going to put them in financial difficulties *ou* make things tight for them *ou* make them hard up*.

(d) *(mettre mal à l'aise)* to make feel ill-at-ease *ou* uncomfortable. **ça me gêne de vous dire ça mais ...** I hate to tell you but ...; **ça me gêne de me déshabiller chez le médecin** I find it embarrassing to get undressed at the doctor's; **sa présence me gêne** his presence *ou* he makes me feel uncomfortable, he cramps my style; **son regard la gênait** his glance made her feel ill-at-ease *ou* uncomfortable; **cela le gêne qu'on fasse tout le travail pour lui** it embarrasses him to have *ou* he feels awkward about having all the work done for him.

2 se gêner *vpr* **(a)** *(se contraindre)* to put o.s. out. **ne vous gênez pas pour moi** don't mind me, don't put yourself out for me; **il ne faut pas vous ~ avec moi** don't stand on ceremony with me; **non mais! je vais me ~!** why shouldn't I!; **il y en a qui ne se gênent pas!** some people just don't care!; **il ne s'est pas gêné pour le lui dire** he told him straight out, he didn't mind telling him.

(b) *(économiser)* to tighten one's belt.

général, e, *mpl* **-aux** [ʒeneʀal, o] **1** *adj* **(a)** *(d'ensemble)* *vue, tableau* general; *(vague)* general. **un tableau ~ de la situation** a general *ou* an overall picture of the situation; **avoir le goût des idées ~es** to have a preference for broad *ou* general ideas; **remarques d'ordre très ~** comments of a very general nature; **se lancer dans des considérations ~es sur le temps** to venture some general remarks about the weather; **d'une façon** *ou* **manière ~e** in a general way, generally; *(précédant une affirmation)* generally *ou* broadly speaking.

(b) *(total, global)* *assemblée, grève etc* general. *(commun)* **dans l'intérêt ~** in the general *ou* common interest; **cette opinion est devenue ~e** this is now a widely shared *ou* generally held opinion; **la mêlée devint ~e** the fight turned into a general free-for-all; **à l'indignation/la surprise ~e** to the indignation/surprise of most *ou* many people; **à la demande ~e** in response to popular *ou* general demand; *V* **concours, état, médecine** *etc.*

(c) en ~ *(habituellement)* usually, generally, in general; *(de façon générale)* generally, in general. **je parle en ~** I'm speaking in general terms *ou* generally.

(d) *(Admin: principal)* general *(épith)*. **conseil ~** general council; **secrétaire ~** *(gén)* general secretary; *[organisation internationale]* secretary-general; *V* **directeur, fermier, président** *etc.*

2 *nm* **(a)** *(Mil)* general; *V* **mon.**

(b) *(Philos)* **le ~** the general; **aller du ~ au particulier** to go from the general to the particular.

3 générale *nf* **(a)** *(épouse du général)* general's wife; *V* **Madame.**

(b) *(Théât)* **(répétition) ~e** (final) dress rehearsal.

(c) *(Mil)* **battre** *ou* **sonner la ~e** to call to arms.

4: général d'armée general; *(Aviat)* air chief marshal; **général de brigade** brigadier; *(Aviat)* air commodore; **général en chef** general-in-chief, general-in-command; **général de corps d'armée** lieutenant-general; *(Aviat)* air marshal; **général de division** major-general; *(Aviat)* air vice-marshal.

généralat [ʒeneʀala] *nm (fonction)* generalship. **pendant son ~** during his time as a general.

généralement [ʒeneʀalmɑ̃] *adv* generally. **il est ~ chez lui après 8 heures** he's generally *ou* usually at home after 8 o'clock; ~ **parlant** generally speaking; **coutume assez ~ répandue** fairly widespread custom.

généralisable [ʒeneʀalizabl(ə)] *adj* *mesure, observation* which can be applied generally.

généralisateur, -trice [ʒeneʀalizatœʀ, tʀis] *adj*: **tendance ~trice** tendency to generalize *ou* towards generalization; **il a un esprit ~** he is given to generalizing.

généralisation [ʒeneʀalizɑsjɔ̃] *nf* *(extension, énoncé)* generalization.

généraliser [ʒeneʀalize] (1) **1** *vt* **(a)** *(étendre)* to generalize; *méthode* to put *ou* bring into general *ou* widespread use. *(Méd)* **cancer généralisé** general cancer; **la semaine de 5 jours se généralise en France** the 5-day (working) week is becoming general in France.

(b) *(raisonner)* to generalize. **il aime beaucoup ~** he loves to generalize.

2 se généraliser *vpr [infection]* to become widespread; *[procédé]* to become widespread, come into general use.

généralissime [ʒeneʀalisim] *nm* generalissimo.

généraliste [ʒeneʀalist(ə)] *nm* *(Méd)* G.P., general practitioner.

généralité [ʒeneʀalite] *nf* **(a)** *(presque totalité)* majority. **dans la ~ des cas** in the majority of cases, in most cases. **(b)** *(caractère général) [affirmation]* general nature. **(c) ~s** *(introduction)* general points; *(péj: banalités)* generalities.

générateur, -trice [ʒeneʀatœʀ, tʀis] **1** *adj* *force* generating; *fonction* generative, generating. ~ **de** *(gén)* which causes, productive of; *(Math)* which generates, generating; ~ **de désordres** *ou* **de troubles** which causes trouble; **usine ~trice** generator.

2 *nm* *(Tech)* ~ **(de vapeur)** steam boiler.

3 génératrice *nf* **(a)** *(Tech)* **~trice (d'électricité)** generator.

(b) *(Math)* **(ligne) ~trice** generating line.

génératif, -ive [ʒeneʀatif, iv] *adj* *(Ling)* generative. **grammaire ~ive** generative grammar.

génération [ʒeneʀɑsjɔ̃] *nf* *(gén)* generation. ~ **spontanée** spontaneous generation.

générer [ʒeneʀe] (6) *vt* *(Ling)* to generate.

généreusement [ʒeneʀøzmɑ̃] *adv* *(V* **généreux***)* generously; nobly; magnanimously.

généreux, -euse [ʒeneʀø, øz] **1** *adj* **(a)** *(libéral)* generous. **être ~ de son temps** to be generous with one's time.

(b) *(noble, désintéressé)* *acte, caractère* generous; *âme, sentiment* generous, noble; *adversaire* generous, magnanimous.

(c) *(riche)* *sol* productive, fertile, generous; *vin* generous, full-bodied. **femmes aux formes ~euses** women with generous curves.

2 *nm,f*: **faire le ~** to act generous*.

générique [ʒeneʀik] **1** *adj* generic. *(Ling)* **terme ~** generic term. **2** *nm* *(Ciné)* credit titles, credits.

générosité [ʒeneʀozite] *nf* **(a)** *(libéralité)* *[pourboire]* generosity.

(b) *(noblesse)* *[acte, caractère]* generosity; *[âme, sentiment]* nobility; *[adversaire]* generosity, magnanimity. **avoir la ~ de** to be generous enough to, have the generosity to.

(c) *(largesses)* **~s** kindnesses.

Gênes [ʒɛn] *n* Genoa.

genèse [ʒənɛz] *nf (Bible)* **la G~** Genesis; *(élaboration)* genesis.

genet [ʒ(ə)nɛ] *nm* jennet.

genêt [ʒ(ə)nɛ] *nm* broom *(Bot)*.

généticien, -ienne [ʒenetisjɛ̃, jɛn] *nm,f* geneticist.

génétique [ʒenetik] **1** *adj* genetic. **2** *nf* genetics *(sg)*.

génétiquement [ʒenetikmɑ̃] *adv* genetically.

gêneur, -euse [ʒɛnœʀ, øz] *nm,f (importun)* intruder. *(représentant un obstacle)* **supprimer un ~/les ~s** to do away with a person who is *ou* stands/people who are *ou* stand in one's way.

Genève [ʒ(ə)nɛv] *n* Geneva.

genevois, e [ʒən(ə)vwa, waz] **1** *adj* Genevan. **2** *nm,f*: **G~(e)** Genevan.

genévrier [ʒənevʀije] *nm* juniper.

génial, e, *mpl* **-aux** [ʒenjal, o] *adj* **(a)** (*inspiré*) *écrivain, invention* of genius; *plan, idée* inspired (*gén épith*). **savant ~/découverte ~e** scientist/discovery of genius; **un plan d'une conception ~e** an inspired idea, a brilliantly thought out idea.
(b) (*: *formidable*) fantastic*. **c'est ~!** that's fantastic!*; **c'est un type ~!** he's a tremendous *ou* fantastic bloke* (*Brit*) *ou* guy*; **elle est ~e ton idée** that's a brilliant *ou* an inspired idea.

génialement [ʒenjalmɑ̃] *adv* **(a)** (*magistralement*) with genius, brilliantly. **(b)** (*rare: magnifiquement*) brilliantly.

génie [ʒeni] **1** *nm* **(a)** (*aptitude supérieure*) genius. **avoir du ~** to have genius; **éclair** *ou* **trait de ~** stroke of genius; **homme de ~** man of genius; **compositeur/idée/découverte de ~** composer/idea/discovery of genius.
(b) (*personne*) genius. **ce n'est pas un ~!** he's no genius!
(c) (*talent*) **(avoir) le ~ des maths/des affaires** (to have) a genius for maths/for business; **avoir le ~ du mal** to have an evil bent; **il a le ~ de** *ou* **pour dire ce qu'il ne faut pas** he has a genius for saying the wrong thing.
(d) (*caractère inné*) **le ~ latin** the Latin genius; **le ~ de la langue française** the genius of the French language.
(e) (*Myth*) (*gén*) spirit; *[histoires arabes]* genie. **~ des airs/des eaux** spirit of the air/waters; **être le bon/mauvais ~ de qn** to be sb's good/evil genius.
(f) (*Mil*) **le ~** ≃ the Engineers; **soldat du ~** sapper, engineer; **faire son service dans le ~** to do one's service in the Engineers.
2: génie civil (*branche*) civil engineering; (*corps*) civil engineers; **génie maritime** (*branche*) marine engineering; (*corps*) marine engineers (*under State command*); **génie militaire** (*branche*) military engineering; (*corps*) ≃ Engineers; *V* **ingénieur.**

genièvre [ʒənjɛvʀ(ə)] *nm* (*boisson*) Hollands, geneva; (*arbre*) juniper; (*fruit*) juniper berry. **grains de ~** juniper berries.

génisse [ʒenis] *nf* heifer.

génital, e, *mpl* **-aux** [ʒenital, o] *adj* genital. **organes ~aux, parties ~es** genitals, genital organs.

géniteur, -trice [ʒenitœʀ, tʀis] **1** *nm,f* (*hum: parent*) parent. **2** *nm* (*Zool: reproducteur*) sire.

génitif [ʒenitif] *nm* genitive (case).

génito-urinaire [ʒenitɔyʀinɛʀ] *adj* genito-urinary.

génocide [ʒenɔsid] *nm* genocide.

génois, e [ʒenwa, waz] **1** *adj* Genoese. **2** *nm,f*: **G~(e)** Genoese. **3 génoise** *nf* (*Culin*) Genoese sponge.

genou, *pl* **~x** [ʒ(ə)nu] *nm* **(a)** (*Anat, Habillement, Zool*) knee. **avoir les ~x cagneux** *ou* **rentrants** to be knock-kneed; **mes ~x se dérobèrent sous moi** my legs gave way under me; **avoir de la vase jusqu'aux ~x, être dans la vase jusqu'aux ~x** to be up to one's knees *ou* be knee-deep in mud.
(b) à ~x: il était à ~x he was kneeling, he was on his knees; **se mettre à ~x** to kneel down, go down on one's knees; (*fig*) **se mettre à ~x devant qn** to go down on one's knees to sb; **c'est à se mettre à ~x!*** it's out of this world!*; **tomber/se jeter à ~x** to fall/ throw o.s. on *ou* to one's knees; **j'en suis tombé à ~x!*** I just about dropped!*; **demander qch à (deux) ~x** to ask for sth on bended knee; **je te demande pardon à ~x** I beg you to forgive me.
(c) (*Tech*) ball and socket joint.
(d) (*loc*) **avoir/prendre qn sur ses ~x** to have/take sb on one's knee; **faire du ~ à qn*** to play footsie with sb*; **tomber aux ~x de qn** to fall at sb's feet, go down on one's knees to sb; **être aux ~x de qn** to idolize *ou* worship sb; (*littér*) **fléchir** *ou* **plier** *ou* **ployer le ~ devant qn** to bend the knee to sb; (*littér*) **mettre (un) ~ à terre devant qn** to go down on one knee before sb; **être sur les ~x*** to be on one's knees*, be tired out; **ça m'a mis sur les ~x de courir à droite et à gauche** I was run off my feet dashing here, there and everywhere.

genouillère [ʒ(ə)nujɛʀ] *nf* (*Méd*) knee support; (*Sport*) kneepad, kneecap.

genre [ʒɑ̃ʀ] *nm* **(a)** (*espèce*) kind, type, sort. **~ de vie** lifestyle, way of life; **c'est le ~ de femme qui** she is the type *ou* the kind *ou* the sort of woman who; **les rousses, ce n'est pas mon ~** redheads aren't my type; **lui c'est le ~ grognon*** he's the grumpy sort*; **ce type n'est pas mal en son ~** that fellow isn't bad in his own way *ou* isn't bad of his type; **cette maison n'est pas mauvaise en son ~** that house isn't bad of its type; **ce qui se fait le mieux dans le ~** the best of its kind; **réparations en tout ~** *ou* **en tous ~s** all kinds of repairs *ou* repair work undertaken; **chaussures en tout ~** all kinds of shoes; **quelque chose de ce ~** *ou* **du même ~** something of the kind, that sort of thing; **il a écrit un ~ de roman** he wrote a novel of sorts *ou* a sort of novel; **plaisanterie d'un ~ douteux** doubtful joke; *V* **unique.**
(b) (*allure*) **avoir bon ~** to look a nice sort; **avoir mauvais ~** to be coarse-looking; **je n'aime pas son ~** I don't like the way he carries on; **il a un drôle de ~** he's a bit weird; **avoir le ~ bohème/artiste** to be a bohemian/an arty type; **avoir un ~ prétentieux** to have a pretentious manner; **faire du ~** to stand on ceremony; **c'est un ~ qu'il se donne** it's (just) something *ou* an air he puts on; **ce n'est pas son ~ de ne pas répondre** it's not like him not to answer.
(c) (*Art, Littérat, Mus*) genre. (*Peinture*) **tableau de ~** genre painting; **œuvre dans le ~ ancien/italien** work in the old/Italian style *ou* genre.
(d) (*Gram*) gender.
(e) (*Philos, Sci*) genus. **le ~ humain** mankind, the human race.

gens[1] [ʒɑ̃] **1** *nmpl* **(a)** people, folk*. **connais-tu ces ~?** do you know these people? *ou* folk?*; **ce sont des ~ compétents** they are competent people *ou* folk*; **il faut savoir prendre les ~** you've got to know how to handle people; **les ~ sont fous!** some people are mad!, people are mad (at times)!; **les ~ de la ville** townspeople, townsfolk; **les ~ du pays** *ou* **du coin*** the local people, the locals*; *V* **droit[3], jeune, monde** *etc.*
(b) (*loc, avec accord féminin de l'adjectif antéposé*) **ce sont de petites/de braves ~** they are people of modest means/good people *ou* folk*; **les vieilles ~ sont souvent crédules** old people *ou* folk* are often gullible; **c'est une insulte aux honnêtes ~** it's an insult to honest people; (*hum*) **écoutez bonnes ~** harken, ye people (*hum*).
(c) (†, *hum: serviteurs*) servants. **il appela ses ~** he called his servants.
2: gens d'affaires† business people; (*Hist*) **gens d'armes** men-at-arms†; **les gens d'Église** the clergy; (*Hist*) **gens d'épée** soldiers (*of the aristocracy*); **gens de lettres** men of letters; **les gens de loi**† the legal profession; **gens de maison** people in service; **gens de mer** sailors, seafarers; (*Hist*) **les gens de robe** the legal profession; **gens de service = gens de maison; les gens de théâtre** the acting profession, theatrical people; **les gens du voyage** travelling entertainers.

gens[2] [ʒɛ̃s] *nf* (*Hist*) gens.

gent [ʒɑ̃] *nf* (†† *ou hum*) race, tribe. **la ~ canine** the canine race; **la ~ féminine** the fair sex.

gentiane [ʒɑ̃sjan] *nf* gentian.

gentil, -ille [ʒɑ̃ti, ij] **1** *adj* **(a)** (*aimable*) kind (*avec, pour* to). **il a toujours un mot ~ pour chacun** he always has a kind word for everyone *ou* to say to everyone; **tu seras ~ de me le rendre** would you mind giving it back to me, would you be so kind as to give it back to me (*frm*); **c'est ~ à toi de ...** it's very kind *ou* nice *ou* good of you to ...; **tu es ~ tout plein*** you're so sweet; **tout ça, c'est bien ~ mais ...** that's (all) very nice *ou* well but ...; **ça n'est pas très ~** that's not very nice *ou* kind; **il n'est pas très ~** he's not very nice; **il a une ~le petite femme/fille** he has a nice little wife/daughter; **sois ~, va me le chercher** be a dear and go and get it for me; **va me le chercher, tu seras ~** would you mind going to get it for me.
(b) (*sage*) good. **il n'a pas été ~** he hasn't been a good boy; **sois ~, je reviens bientôt** be good, I'll be back soon.
(c) (*gracieux*) *visage, endroit* nice, pleasant. **c'est ~ mais ça ne casse rien*** it's quite nice but it's nothing special.
(d) (*rondelet*) *somme* tidy, fair.
2 *nm* (*Hist, Rel*) gentile.

gentilhomme [ʒɑ̃tijɔm], *pl* **gentilshommes** [ʒɑ̃tizɔm] *nm* (*Hist, fig*) gentleman. **~ campagnard** country squire.

gentilhommière [ʒɑ̃tijɔmjɛʀ] *nf* (small) country seat, (small) manor house.

gentillesse [ʒɑ̃tijɛs] *nf* **(a)** (*U: amabilité*) kindness. **être d'une grande ~** to be very kind; **me ferez-vous la ~ de faire ...** would you be so kind as to do ..., would you do me the kindness of doing ....
(b) (*faveur*) favour, kindness. **remercier qn de toutes ses ~s** to thank sb for all his kindness(es); **avoir des ~s pour qn** to be kind to sb; **une ~ en vaut une autre** one good turn deserves another; **il lui disait des ~s** he said kind *ou* nice things to him.

gentillet, -ette [ʒɑ̃tijɛ, ɛt] *adj* nice little (*épith*); (*péj*) nice enough.

gentiment [ʒɑ̃timɑ̃] *adv* (*aimablement*) kindly; (*gracieusement*) nicely. **ils jouaient ~** they were playing nicely *ou* like good children; (*iro*) **on m'a ~ fait comprendre que ...** they told me in the nicest *ou* kindest possible way that ... (*iro*).

gentleman [dʒɛntləman], *pl* **gentlemen** [dʒɛntləmɛn] *nm* gentleman.

génuflexion [ʒenyflɛksjɔ̃] *nf* (*Rel*) genuflexion. **faire une ~** to make a genuflexion, genuflect.

géo [ʒeo] *nf* (*arg Scol*) *abrév de* **géographie.**

géocentrique [ʒeɔsɑ̃tʀik] *adj* geocentric.

géodésie [ʒeɔdezi] *nf* geodesy.

géodésique [ʒeɔdezik] *adj* geodesic. **point ~** triangulation point.

géodynamique [ʒeɔdinamik] **1** *adj* geodynamic. **2** *nf* geodynamics (*sg*).

géographe [ʒeɔgʀaf] *nmf* geographer.

géographie [ʒeɔgʀafi] *nf* geography. **~ humaine** human geography.

géographique [ʒeɔgʀafik] *adj* geographic(al); *V* **dictionnaire.**

géographiquement [ʒeɔgʀafikmɑ̃] *adv* geographically.

geôle [ʒol] *nf* (*littér*) gaol (*Brit*), jail.

geôlier, -ière [ʒolje, jɛʀ] *nm,f* (*littér*) gaoler (*Brit*), jailer.

géologie [ʒeɔlɔʒi] *nf* geology.

géologique [ʒeɔlɔʒik] *adj* geological.

géologiquement [ʒeɔlɔʒikmɑ̃] *adv* geologically.

géologue [ʒeɔlɔg] *nmf* geologist.

géomagnétique [ʒeɔmaɲetik] *adj* geomagnetic.

géomagnétisme [ʒeɔmaɲetism(ə)] *nm* geomagnetism.

géométral, e, *mpl* **-aux** [ʒeɔmetʀal, o] *adj* plane (*not in perspective*).

géomètre [ʒeɔmɛtʀ(ə)] *nm* (*arpenteur*) surveyor; (††: *mathématicien*) geometer.

géométrie [ʒeɔmetʀi] *nf* (*science*) geometry; (*livre*) geometry book. **~ descriptive** descriptive geometry; **~ plane** plane geometry; **~ analytique** analytical geometry; **~ dans l'espace** solid geometry; (*Aviat*) **à ~ variable** swing-wing.

géométrique [ʒeɔmetʀik] *adj* geometric(al); (††: *mathématique*) mathematical; *V* **lieu, progression.**

géométriquement [ʒeɔmetʀikmɑ̃] *adv* (*V* **géométrique**) geometrically; with mathematical precision.

géomorphologie [ʒeɔmɔʀfɔlɔʒi] *nf* geomorphology.

géophysique [ʒeɔfizik] **1** *adj* geophysical. **2** *nf* geophysics (*sg*).

géopolitique [ʒeɔpɔlitik] **1** *adj* geopolitical. **2** *nf* geopolitics (*sg*).

Georges [ʒɔʀʒ] *nm* George.
Géorgie [ʒeɔʀʒi] *nf* (*URSS, USA*) Georgia.
géorgien, -ienne [ʒeɔʀʒjɛ̃, jɛn] **1** *adj* Georgian. **2** *nm* (*Ling*) Georgian. **3** *nm,f*: **G~(ne)** Georgian.
géorgique [ʒeɔʀʒik] *adj* (*Hist Littérat*) georgic.
géosynclinal, *pl* **-aux** [ʒeosɛ̃klinal, o] *nm* geosyncline.
géothermie [ʒeɔtɛʀmi] *nf* geothermal science.
géothermique [ʒeɔtɛʀmik] *adj* geothermal.
gérance [ʒeʀɑ̃s] *nf* [*commerce, immeuble, appartement*] management. **il assure la ~ d'une usine** he manages a factory; **au cours de sa ~** while he was manager; **prendre un commerce en ~** to take over the management of a business; **il a mis son commerce en ~** he has appointed a manager for his business.
géranium [ʒeʀanjɔm] *nm* geranium.
gérant [ʒeʀɑ̃] *nm* [*usine, café, banque*] manager; [*immeuble, appartement*] managing agent; [*journal*] editing manager.
gérante [ʒeʀɑ̃t] *nf* manageress.
gerbage [ʒɛʀbaʒ] *nm* (*V* **gerber**) binding, sheaving; stacking, piling.
gerbe [ʒɛʀb(ə)] *nf* [*blé*] sheaf; [*osier*] bundle; [*fleurs*] spray; (*fig*) [*souvenirs, preuves*] collection. **déposer une ~ sur une tombe** to place a spray of flowers on a grave; **le choc provoqua une ~ d'étincelles/d'écume** the impact sent up a shower *ou* burst of sparks/a shower *ou* flurry of foam; **~ d'eau** spray *ou* shower of water; **éclater/retomber en ~** to go up/fall in a shower *ou* burst of sparks.
gerber [ʒɛʀbe] (1) *vt* (*Agr*) to bind into sheaves, sheave; (*Tech*) *tonneaux* to stack, pile.
gerboise [ʒɛʀbwaz] *nf* jerboa.
gercement [ʒɛʀsmɑ̃] *nm* (*V* **gercer**) chapping; cracking.
gercer [ʒɛʀse] (3) **1** *vt peau, lèvres* to chap, crack; *sol* to crack. **avoir les lèvres toutes gercées** to have badly chapped lips.
2 *vi, se gercer vpr* (*V* **gercer**) to chap; to crack.
gerçure [ʒɛʀsyʀ] *nf* (small) crack. **pour éviter les ~s, achetez la crème X** to avoid chapped hands *etc ou* to avoid chapping, buy X cream.
gérer [ʒeʀe] (6) *vt société, commerce* to manage; *fortune, biens* to administer, manage. **il gère bien ses affaires** he manages his affairs well; **il a mal géré son affaire** he has mismanaged his business, he has managed his business badly.
gerfaut [ʒɛʀfo] *nm* (*Orn*) gyrfalcon.
gériatrie [ʒeʀjatʀi] *nf* geriatrics (*sg*).
gériatrique [ʒeʀjatʀik] *adj* geriatric.
germain, e [ʒɛʀmɛ̃, ɛn] **1** *adj* **(a)** *V* **cousin[1]**. **(b)** (*Hist*) German. **2** *nm,f* (*Hist*) **G~(e)** German.
Germanie [ʒɛʀmani] *nf* (*Hist*) Germania.
germanique [ʒɛʀmanik] **1** *adj* Germanic. **2** *nm* (*Ling*) Germanic. **3** *nmf*: **G~** Germanic.
germanisant, e [ʒɛʀmanizɑ̃, ɑ̃t] *nm,f* = **germaniste.**
germanisation [ʒɛʀmanizɑsjɔ̃] *nf* germanization.
germaniser [ʒɛʀmanize] (1) *vt* to germanize.
germanisme [ʒɛʀmanism(ə)] *nm* (*Ling*) germanism.
germaniste [ʒɛʀmanist(ə)] *nmf* German scholar, germanist.
germanium [ʒɛʀmanjɔm] *nm* germanium.
germanophile [ʒɛʀmanɔfil] *adj, nmf* germanophil(e).
germanophilie [ʒɛʀmanɔfili] *nf* germanophilia.
germanophobe [ʒɛʀmanɔfɔb] **1** *adj* germanophobic. **2** *nmf* germanophobe.
germanophobie [ʒɛʀmanɔfɔbi] *nf* germanophobia.
germe [ʒɛʀm(ə)] *nm* **(a)** (*Bio*) [*embryon*] germ; [*œuf*] germinal disc; [*pomme de terre*] eye; (*Méd: microbe*) germ. **~ de dent** tooth bud; *V* **porteur.**
(b) (*fig: source*) [*maladie, erreur, vie*] seed. **~ d'une idée** germ of an idea; **avoir** *ou* **contenir en ~** to contain in embryo, contain the seeds of.
germer [ʒɛʀme] (1) *vi* to sprout, shoot, germinate; (*fig*) [*idée, sentiment*] to germinate. **pommes de terre germées** sprouting potatoes.
germicide [ʒɛʀmisid] **1** *adj* germicidal. **2** *nm* germicide.
germinal[1], e, *mpl* **-aux** [ʒɛʀminal, o] *adj* germinal.
germinal[2] [ʒɛʀminal] *nm* Germinal (*seventh month in the French Republican calendar*).
germinateur, -trice [ʒɛʀminatœʀ, tʀis] *adj* germinative.
germinatif, -ive [ʒɛʀminatif, iv] *adj* germinal.
germination [ʒɛʀminɑsjɔ̃] *nf* (*Bot, fig*) germination.
germoir [ʒɛʀmwaʀ] *nm* (*Agr*) seed tray.
gérondif [ʒeʀɔ̃dif] *nm* (*Ling*) (*latin*) (*avec être*) gerundive; (*complément de nom*) gerund; (*français*) gerund.
gérontocratie [ʒeʀɔ̃tɔkʀasi] *nf* gerontocracy.
gérontocratique [ʒeʀɔ̃tɔkʀatik] *adj* gerontocratic.
gérontologie [ʒeʀɔ̃tɔlɔʒi] *nf* gerontology.
gérontologique [ʒeʀɔ̃tɔlɔʒik] *adj* gerontological.
gésier [ʒezje] *nm* gizzard.
gésir [ʒeziʀ] *vi* (*être étendu*) to be lying (down), lie (down). **il gît/gisait sur le sol** he is lying/was lying *ou* lay on the ground; (*fig*) **là gît le problème** there lies the problem; *V* **ci.**
gestation [ʒɛstasjɔ̃] *nf* gestation. **en ~** in gestation.
geste[1] [ʒɛst(ə)] *nm* **(a)** (*mouvement*) gesture. **~ d'approbation/d'effroi** gesture of approval/of terror; **~ maladroit** *ou* **malheureux** clumsy gesture *ou* movement; **pas un ~ ou je tire!** one move and I'll shoot!; **faire un ~ de la main** to gesture with one's hand, give a wave (of one's hand); **faire un ~ de la tête** (*affirmatif*) to nod (one's head), give a nod; (*négatif*) to shake one's head; **il refusa d'un ~** he made a gesture of refusal, he gestured his refusal; **il le fit entrer d'un ~ de la tête/main** he nodded/waved him in, he nodded/waved to him to come in; **il le fit entrer d'un ~** he motioned *ou* gestured to him to come in; **il lui indiqua la porte d'un ~** with a gesture he showed him the door; (*fig*) **il ne fit pas un ~ pour l'aider** he didn't lift a finger *ou* make a move to help him; (*fig*) **tu n'as qu'un ~ à faire pour qu'il revienne** you only have to say the word *ou* just say the word and he'll come back; *V* **encourager, fait[1], joindre.**
(b) (*action*) act, deed; (*action généreuse*) gesture, act, deed. **~ lâche/méprisable** cowardly/despicable act *ou* deed; **~ de réconciliation** gesture of reconciliation; **c'était un beau ~** it was a noble gesture *ou* deed; **faites un ~** make a gesture.
geste[2] [ʒɛst(ə)] *nf* (*Littérat*) *collection of epic poems centred around the same hero*; *V* **chanson.**
gesticulation [ʒɛstikylɑsjɔ̃] *nf* gesticulation, gesticulating (*U*).
gesticuler [ʒɛstikyle] (1) *vi* to gesticulate.
gestion [ʒɛstjɔ̃] *nf* [*entreprise*] management; [*biens*] administration, management. **mauvaise ~** mismanagement, bad management.
gestionnaire [ʒɛstjɔnɛʀ] **1** *adj* administrative, management (*épith*). **2** *nmf* administrator.
gestuel, -elle [ʒɛstɥɛl] *adj* gestural.
geyser [ʒɛzɛʀ] *nm* geyser.
Ghana [gana] *nm* Ghana.
ghanéen, -enne [ganeɛ̃, ɛn] **1** *adj* Ghanaian. **2** *nm,f*: **G~(ne)** Ghanaian.
ghetto [gɛto] *nm* ghetto.
gibbeux, -euse [ʒibø, øz] *adj* (*Astron, littér*) gibbous, gibbose.
gibbon [ʒibɔ̃] *nm* gibbon.
gibbosité [ʒibozite] *nf* (*Astron, littér*) hump, gibbosity (*T*).
gibecière [ʒibsjɛʀ] *nf* (*gén*) (leather) shoulder bag; [*chasseur*] gamebag; [*écolier*] (†) satchel.
gibelin [ʒiblɛ̃] *nm* (*Hist*) Ghibelline.
gibelotte [ʒiblɔt] *nf fricassee of rabbit in wine.*
giberne [ʒibɛʀn(ə)] *nf* cartridge pouch.
gibet [ʒibɛ] *nm* gibbet, gallows. (*Hist*) **condamner au ~** to condemn to death by hanging, condemn to the gallows.
gibier [ʒibje] *nm* **(a)** game. **gros/menu ~** big/small game; **~ d'eau** waterfowl; **~ à poil** game animals; **~ à plume** game birds.
(b) (*fig: personne*) prey. **les policiers attendaient leur ~** the policemen awaited their prey; **~ de potence** gallows bird; **le gros ~** big game (*fig*).
giboulée [ʒibule] *nf* (sudden) shower, sudden downpour. **~ de mars** ≃ April shower.
giboyeux, -euse [ʒibwajø, øz] *adj pays, forêt* abounding in game, well-stocked with game.
gibus [ʒibys] *nm* opera hat.
giclée [ʒikle] *nf* spurt, squirt.
giclement [ʒikləmɑ̃] *nm* (*V* **gicler**) spurting, squirting.
gicler [ʒikle] (1) *vi* (*jaillir*) to spurt, squirt. **faire ~ de l'eau d'un robinet** to squirt water from a tap; **le véhicule a fait ~ de l'eau à son passage** the passing vehicle sent up a spray of water.
gicleur [ʒiklœʀ] *nm* (*Aut*) jet. **~ de ralenti** slow-running jet.
gifle [ʒifl(ə)] *nf* (*lit*) slap (in the face), smack (on the face); (*fig*) slap in the face. **donner une ~ à qn** to slap sb in the face, give sb a slap in the face; *V* **paire[2], tête.**
gifler [ʒifle] (1) *vt* to slap (in the face). **~ qn** to slap *ou* smack sb's face, slap sb in the face; **visage giflé par la grêle** face lashed by the hail.
gigantesque [ʒigɑ̃tɛsk(ə)] *adj taille* gigantic, immense; *objet, entreprise* gigantic, giant* (*épith*); *bêtise* immense.
gigantisme [ʒigɑ̃tism(ə)] *nm* (*Méd*) gigantism; (*fig: grandeur*) gigantic size *ou* proportions. **ville/entreprise atteinte de ~** city/firm that suffers from overexpansion on a gigantic scale.
gigogne [ʒigɔɲ] *nf V* **fusée, lit, poupée, table.**
gigolo [ʒigɔlo] *nm* gigolo.
gigot [ʒigo] *nm* (*Culin*) **~ (de mouton)/(d'agneau)** leg of mutton/lamb; **~ (de chevreuil)** haunch of venison; **une tranche de ~** a slice off the leg of mutton *ou* lamb *etc*, a slice off the joint; (*fig*) **elle a de bons ~s*** she has nice sturdy legs; *V* **manche[1].**
gigoter* [ʒigɔte] (1) *vi* to wriggle (about).
gigue [ʒig] *nf* (*Mus*) gigue; (*danse*) jig. (*jambes*) **~s*** legs; (*péj: fille*) **une grande ~** a bean-pole (of a girl)*; (*Culin*) **~ de chevreuil** haunch of venison.
gilde [gild(ə)] *nf* = **guilde.**
gilet [ʒilɛ] *nm* (*de complet*) waistcoat (*Brit*), vest (*US*); (*cardigan*) cardigan. **~ (de corps** *ou* **de peau)** vest (*Brit*), undershirt (*US*); **~ pare-balles** bulletproof jacket; **~ de sauvetage** life jacket; *V* **pleurer.**
giletier, -ière [ʒiltje, jɛʀ] *nm,f* waistcoat (*Brit*) *ou* vest (*US*) maker.
gin [dʒin] *nm* gin.
gingembre [ʒɛ̃ʒɑ̃bʀ(ə)] *nm* ginger.
gingival, e, *mpl* **-aux** [ʒɛ̃ʒival, o] *adj* gingival. **pâte ~e** gum ointment.
gingivite [ʒɛ̃ʒivit] *nf* inflammation of the gums, gingivitis (*T*).
girafe [ʒiʀaf] *nf* (*Zool*) giraffe; (*péj: personne*) beanpole*; (*Ciné*) boom; *V* **peigner.**
girandole [ʒiʀɑ̃dɔl] *nf* (*chandelier*) candelabra, girandole; (*feu d'artifice*) girandole.
girasol [ʒiʀasɔl] *nm* girasol.
giration [ʒiʀɑsjɔ̃] *nf* gyration.
giratoire [ʒiʀatwaʀ] *adj* gyrating, gyratory; *V* **sens.**
girl [gœʀl] *nf* chorus girl.
girofle [ʒiʀɔfl(ə)] *nm* cloves; *V* **clou.**
giroflée [ʒiʀɔfle] *nf* stock.
giroflier [ʒiʀɔflije] *nm* clove tree.
girolle [ʒiʀɔl] *nf* chanterelle.
giron [ʒiʀɔ̃] *nm* (*Anat: genoux*) lap; (*fig: sein*) bosom. (*fig*) **rentrer dans le ~ de l'église** to return to the fold, return to the bosom of the Church.
girond, e* [ʒiʀɔ̃, ɔ̃d] *adj* well-padded*, plump.
Gironde [ʒiʀɔ̃d] *nf*: **la ~** the Gironde.
girouette [ʒiʀwɛt] *nf* weather vane *ou* cock. (*fig*) **c'est une vraie**

~ he changes (his mind) with the weather (*fig*), he changes his mind depending on which way the wind is blowing.
gisait, gisaient [ʒizɛ] *V* **gésir.**
gisant [ʒizɑ̃] *nm* (*Art*) recumbent statue (*on tomb*).
gisement [ʒizmɑ̃] *nm* **(a)** (*Minér*) deposit. **(b)** (*Naut*) bearing.
gisent [ʒiz], **gît** [ʒi] *V* **ci, gésir.**
gitan, e [ʒitɑ̃, an] **1** *adj* gipsy (*épith*). **2** *nm,f*: G~(e) gipsy. **3 gitane** *nf* (®: *cigarette*) Gitane (*cigarette*).
gîte[1] [ʒit] *nm* **(a)** (*abri*) shelter; (†: *maison*) home. **rentrer au ~** to return home; **ils lui donnent le ~ et le couvert** they give him board and lodging.
(b) (*Chasse*) *[lièvre]* form.
(c) (*Boucherie*) ~ **(à la noix)** topside; **gîte-gîte** shin.
(d) (*Minér*) deposit.
gîte[2] [ʒit] *nf* (*Naut*) (*emplacement d'épave*) bed (*of a sunken ship*). **donner de la ~** to list, heel.
gîter [ʒite] (1) *vi* (*littér*) to lodge; (*Naut*) (*pencher*) to list, heel; (*être échoué*) to be aground.
givrage [ʒivʀaʒ] *nm* (*Aviat*) icing.
givre [ʒivʀ(ə)] *nm* **(a)** (hoar)frost, rime (*T*); *V* **fleur. (b)** (*Chim*) crystallization.
givré, e [ʒivʀe] (*ptp de* **givrer**) *adj* **(a)** *arbre* covered in frost; *fenêtre, hélice* frosted-up, iced-up, covered in frost. **orange** *etc* ~**e** orange *etc* sorbet served in the (orange) skin. **(b)** (*) (*ivre*) plastered‡; (*fou*) cracked‡, bonkers‡ (*Brit*), nuts‡.
givrer *vt*, **se givrer** *vpr* [ʒivʀe] (1) to frost up, ice up.
glabre [glabʀ(ə)] *adj* (*imberbe*) hairless; (*rasé*) clean-shaven; (*Bot*) glabrous.
glaçage [glasaʒ] *nm* *[viande, papier, étoffe]* glazing; *[gâteau]* (*au sucre*) icing; (*au blanc d'œuf*) glazing.
glace[1] [glas] *nf* **(a)** (*eau congelée*) ice (*U*). **cube de ~** ice cube; **seau/pince à ~** ice bucket/tongs; **le thermomètre est à la ~** the thermometer is at freezing (point); (*lit, fig*) **briser** *ou* **rompre la ~** to break the ice; *V* **crampon, hockey.**
(b) (*Géog*) ~**s** ice sheets, ice fields; ~**s flottantes** drift ice, ice floes; **canal bloqué par les ~s** canal blocked with ice *ou* with ice floes; **bateau pris dans les ~s** icebound ship.
(c) (*fig*) **de ~** *accueil* icy, frosty, ice-cold; *expression, visage* stony, frosty; **rester de ~** to remain unmoved.
(d) (*Culin*) (*crème*) ice cream; (*jus de viande*) glaze; (*pour pâtisserie: glaçage*) royal icing. **~ à l'eau/à la crème** water/dairy ice; **~ à la vanille/au café** vanilla/coffee ice cream; *V* **sucre.**
glace[2] [glas] *nf* **(a)** (*miroir*) mirror. **~ à main** hand mirror; *V* **armoire. (b)** (*plaque de verre*) sheet of (plate) glass; plate glass (*U*). **la ~ d'une vitrine** the glass of a shop window. **(c)** *[véhicule]* (*vitre*) window; *V* **essuyer, laver.**
glacé, e [glase] (*ptp de* **glacer**) *adj* *neige, lac* frozen; *vent, eau, chambre* icy, freezing; *boisson* icy, ice-cold; *cuir, tissu* glazed; *fruit* glacé; *accueil, attitude, sourire* stiff, chilly. **je suis ~** I'm frozen (stiff), I'm chilled to the bone; **j'ai les mains ~es** my hands are frozen; **à servir ~** to be served iced *ou* ice-cold; **café/chocolat ~** iced coffee/chocolate; *V* **crème, marron**[1], **papier** *etc.*
glacer [glase] (3) **1** *vt* **(a)** *liquide* (*geler*) to freeze; (*rafraîchir*) to chill, ice. **mettre des boissons à ~** to put some drinks to chill.
(b) *personne, membres* to make freezing, freeze. **ce vent glace les oreilles** this wind is freezing to the ears *ou* freezes your ears; **ce vent vous glace** it's a freezing *ou* perishing (cold) wind, this wind chills you to the bone.
(c) (*fig*) **~ qn** (*réfrigérer*) to turn sb cold, chill sb; (*paralyser*) to make sb's blood run cold; **cela l'a glacé d'horreur** *ou* **d'épouvante** he was frozen with terror at this; **~ le sang de qn** to make sb's blood run cold, chill sb's blood; (*littér*) **cette réponse lui glaça le cœur** this reply turned his heart to ice; **son attitude vous glace** he has a chilling way about him, his attitude turns you cold.
(d) *viande, papier, étoffe* to glaze; *gâteau* (*au sucre*) to ice; (*au blanc d'œuf*) to glaze.
2 se glacer *vpr* *[eau]* to freeze. **mon sang se glaça dans mes veines** my blood ran cold *ou* my blood froze in my veins; **son sourire/son expression se glaça** his smile/expression froze.
glaciaire [glasjɛʀ] *adj* *période, calotte* ice (*épith*); *relief, régime, vallée, érosion* glacial.
glacial, e, *mpl* **~s** *ou* **-aux** [glasjal, o] *adj* **(a)** *froid* icy, freezing (*épith*); *nuit, pluie, vent* icy, freezing (cold); *V* **océan. (b)** (*fig*) *accueil* icy, frosty, ice-cold; *silence* frosty, icy. **c'est quelqu'un de ~** he's as cold as ice, he's a real iceberg.
glaciation [glasjɑsjɔ̃] *nf* glaciation.
glacier [glasje] *nm* **(a)** (*Géog*) glacier. **(b)** (*fabricant*) ice-cream maker; (*vendeur*) ice-cream man; *V* **pâtissier.**
glacière [glasjɛʀ] *nf* icebox. (*fig*) **c'est une vraie ~ ici!** it's like a fridge *ou* an icebox here!
glacis [glasi] *nm* **(a)** (*Art*) glaze. **(b)** (*Archit*) weathering; (*Géog, Mil*) glacis.
glaçon [glasɔ̃] *nm* *[rivière]* block of ice; *[toit]* icicle; *[boisson]* ice cube; (*péj: personne*) iceberg. **un whisky avec des ~s** a whisky on the rocks; **mes pieds sont comme des ~s** my feet are like blocks of ice.
gladiateur [gladjatœʀ] *nm* gladiator.
glaïeul [glajœl] *nm* gladiola, gladiolus.
glaire [glɛʀ] *nf* *[œuf]* white; (*Méd*) phlegm.
glaireux, -euse [glɛʀø, øz] *adj* slimy.
glaise [glɛz] *nf* clay; *V* **terre.**
glaiseux, -euse [glɛzø, øz] *adj* clayey.
glaisière [glɛzjɛʀ] *nf* clay pit.
glaive [glɛv] *nm* two-edged sword. (*littér*) **le ~ de la justice** the sword of justice.
glanage [glanaʒ] *nm* gleaning.
gland [glɑ̃] *nm* (*Bot*) acorn; (*Anat*) glans; (*ornement*) tassel.
glande [glɑ̃d] *nf* gland. **avoir des ~s** to have swollen glands.
glander‡ [glɑ̃de] (1) *vi*, **glandouiller‡** [glɑ̃duje] (1) *vi* (*traînailler*) to footle around*; (*attendre*) to hang about*, kick one's heels*.
glandulaire [glɑ̃dylɛʀ] *adj* glandular.
glaner [glane] (1) *vt* (*lit, fig*) to glean.
glaneur, -euse [glanœʀ, øz] *nm,f* gleaner.
glapir [glapiʀ] (2) *vi* *[renard, chien]* to yap, yelp; (*péj*) *[personne]* to yelp, squeal.
glapissement [glapismɑ̃] *nm* (*V* **glapir**) yapping; yelping; squealing.
glas [glɑ] *nm* knell (*U*), toll (*U*). **on sonne le ~** the bell is tolling, they are tolling the knell *ou* bell; (*fig*) **sonner le ~ de** to toll *ou* sound the knell of.
glaucome [glokom] *nm* glaucoma.
glauque [glok] *adj* *yeux, eau* dull blue-green.
glèbe [glɛb] *nf* (*Hist, littér*) glebe.
glissade [glisad] *nf* **(a)** (*par jeu*) slide; (*chute*) slip; (*dérapage*) skid. (*Aviat*) **~ sur l'aile** sideslip; **il fit une ~ mortelle** he slipped and was fatally injured; **faire des ~s sur la glace** to slide on the ice. **(b)** (*Danse*) glissade.
glissant, e [glisɑ̃, ɑ̃t] *adj* *sol, savon* slippery; *V* **terrain.**
glissé, e [glise] (*ptp de* **glisser**) *adj, nm*: **(pas) ~** glissé.
glissement [glismɑ̃] *nm* *[porte, rideau, pièce]* sliding; *[bateau]* gliding. **~ électoral (à gauche)** electoral swing (to the left); **~ de sens** shift in meaning; **~ de terrain** landslide.
glisser [glise] (1) **1** *vi* **(a)** (*avancer*) to slide along; *[voilier, nuages, patineurs]* to glide along. **le bateau glissait sur les eaux** the boat glided over the water; (*Ski*) **avec ce fart, on glisse bien** you slide easily with this wax, this wax slides easily; **il fit ~ le fauteuil (sur le sol)** he slid the armchair (along the floor).
(b) (*tomber*) to slide. **ils glissèrent le long de la pente dans le ravin** they slid down the slope into the gully; **il se laissa ~ le long du mur** he slid down the wall; **une larme glissa le long de sa joue** a tear trickled *ou* slid down his cheek; **d'un geste maladroit il fit ~ le paquet dans le ravin** with a clumsy gesture he sent the parcel sliding down into the gully; **il fit ~ l'argent dans sa poche** he slipped the money into his pocket.
(c) (*fig: aller*) to slip. **le pays glisse vers l'anarchie** the country is slipping *ou* sliding towards anarchy; **le pays glisse vers la droite** the country is swinging towards the right; **il glisse dans la délinquance** he's slipping into crime; **ça glisse vers la pornographie** that's heading towards *ou* verging on pornography.
(d) (*déraper*) *[personne]* to slip; *[véhicule, pneus]* to skid. **il a glissé sur la glace et il est tombé** he slipped on the ice and fell; **son pied a glissé** his foot slipped; **le couteau a glissé (sur le bois) et je me suis coupé** the knife slipped (on the wood) and I cut myself; **il m'a fait ~** he made me slip.
(e) (*être glissant*) *[parquet]* to be slippery. **attention, ça glisse** be careful, it's slippery (underfoot).
(f) (*coulisser*) *[tiroir, rideau]* to slide; *[curseur, anneau]* to slide (along). **ces tiroirs ne glissent pas bien** these drawers don't slide (in and out) easily.
(g) (*échapper de*) **~ de la table** to slip *ou* slide off the table; **~ de la poêle/des mains** to slip *ou* slide out of the frying pan/one's hands; (*fig*) **le voleur leur a glissé entre les mains** the thief slipped (right) through their fingers.
(h) (*effleurer*) **~ sur: ses doigts glissaient sur les touches** his fingers slipped over the keys; **les reproches glissent sur lui (comme l'eau sur les plumes d'un canard)** reproaches roll off him like water off a duck's back; **~ sur un sujet** to skate over a subject; **glissons!** let's not dwell on it, let's skate over that, let that pass; (*Prov*) **glissez, mortels, n'appuyez pas!** enough said!; **la balle glissa sur le blindage** the bullet glanced off the armour plating; **son regard glissa d'un objet à l'autre** he glanced from one object to another, his eyes slipped from one object to another.
2 *vt* (*introduire*) **~ qch sous/dans qch** to slip sth under/into sth; **~ une lettre sous la porte** to slip *ou* slide a letter under the door; **il me glissa un billet dans la main** he slipped a note into my hand; (*fig*) **~ un mot à l'oreille de qn** to slip *ou* drop a word in sb's ear; (*fig*) **il glisse toujours des proverbes dans sa conversation** he's always slipping proverbs into his conversation; **il me glissa un regard en coulisse** he gave me a sidelong glance; **il me glissa que ...** he whispered to me that ....
3 se glisser *vpr* **(a)** *[personne, animal]* **se ~ quelque part** to slip somewhere; **le chien s'est glissé sous le lit/derrière l'armoire** the dog has slipped under the bed/behind the cupboard; **se ~ dans les draps** to slip *ou* slide between the sheets; **le voleur a réussi à se ~ dans la maison** the thief managed to steal *ou* slip into the house; **il a réussi à se ~ jusqu'au premier rang** he managed to edge *ou* worm his way to the front *ou* to slip through to the front.
(b) *[erreur, sentiment]* **se ~ dans** to creep into; **l'inquiétude/le soupçon se glissa en lui/dans son cœur** anxiety/suspicion crept *ou* stole into him/into his heart; **une erreur s'est glissée dans le texte** a mistake has slipped *ou* crept into the text.
glissière [glisjɛʀ] *nf* slide *ou* sliding channel. **porte/panneau/système à ~** sliding door/panel/device; (*Aut*) **~ de sécurité** crash barrier; *V* **fermeture.**
glissoire [gliswaʀ] *nf* slide (*on ice or snow*).
global, e, *mpl* **-aux** [glɔbal, o] *adj* *somme* total (*épith*), overall (*épith*), aggregate (*épith*); *résultat, résumé* overall (*épith*); *perspective, vue* global (*épith*), overall (*épith*).
globalement [glɔbalmɑ̃] *adv* (*en bloc*) globally; (*pris dans son ensemble*) taken as a whole.
globe [glɔb] *nm* **(a)** (*sphère, monde*) globe. **~ oculaire** eyeball; **le ~ terrestre** the globe, the earth. **(b)** (*pour recouvrir*) glass

cover, globe. (*fig*) **mettre qch sous ~** to keep sth under glass.
globe-trotter, *pl* **globe-trotters** [glɔbtʀɔtœʀ] *nm* globe-trotter.
globulaire [glɔbylɛʀ] *adj* (*sphérique*) global; (*Physiol*) corpuscular; *V* **numération.**
globule [glɔbyl] *nm* (*gén, Chim*) globule; (*Physiol*) corpuscle. **~s rouges/blancs** red/white corpuscles.
globuleux, -euse [glɔbylø, øz] *adj forme* globular; *œil* protruding.
glockenspiel [glɔkɛnʃpil] *nm* glockenspiel.
gloire [glwaʀ] *nf* **(a)** (*renommée*) glory. **trouver la ~ sur le champ de bataille** to win glory on the battlefield; **la ~ littéraire** literary fame; **être au sommet de la ~ ou en pleine ~** to be at the height of one's fame; **il s'est couvert de ~ à l'examen** he covered himself in glory at the exam; **elle a eu son heure de ~** she has had her hour of glory; **(faire qch) pour la ~** (to do sth) for the glory of it *ou* for love*.
(b) (*distinction*) **sa plus grande ~ a été de faire** his greatest distinction *ou* his greatest claim to fame was to do; **s'attribuer toute la ~ de qch** to give o.s. all the credit for sth, take all the glory for sth; **tirer ~ de qch** to vaunt sth; **il s'en fait ~!** he glories in it! *ou* prides himself on it!
(c) (*littér, Rel: éclat*) glory. **la ~ de Rome/de Dieu** the glory of Rome/God; **le trône/le séjour de ~** the throne/the Kingdom of Glory.
(d) (*louange*) glory, praise. **~ à Dieu** glory to God, praise be to God; **~ à tous ceux qui ont donné leur vie** glory to all those who gave their lives; **disons-le à sa ~** it must be said in praise of him; **poème/chant à la ~ de** poem/song in praise of; **célébrer** *ou* **chanter la ~ de** to sing the praises of; *V* **rendre.**
(e) (*personne: célébrité*) celebrity. (*hum*) **toutes les ~s de la région étaient là** all the worthies (*hum*) *ou* notables of the region were there.
(f) (*Art: auréole*) glory. **Christ en ~** Christ in majesty.
glorieusement [glɔʀjøzmɑ̃] *adv* gloriously.
glorieux, -euse [glɔʀjø, øz] *adj exploit, mort, personne* glorious; *air, ton* self-important. (*littér, péj*) **tout ~ de sa richesse/de pouvoir dire ...** glorying in *ou* priding himself on his wealth/being able to say ... .
glorification [glɔʀifikasjɔ̃] *nf* glorification.
glorifier [glɔʀifje] (7) **1** *vt* to glorify, extol. **~ Dieu** to glorify God. **2 se glorifier** *vpr*: **se ~ de** to glory in, take great pride in.
gloriole [glɔʀjɔl] *nf* misplaced vanity, vainglory. **faire qch par ~** to do sth out of (misplaced) vanity *ou* vainglory.
glose [gloz] *nf* (*annotation*) gloss.
gloser [gloze] (1) **1** *vt* to annotate, gloss. **2** *vi* to ramble on (*sur* about).
glossaire [glɔsɛʀ] *nm* glossary.
glossine [glɔsin] *nf* glossina.
glottal, e, *mpl* **-aux** [glɔtal, o] *adj* glottal.
glotte [glɔt] *nf* glottis. **coup de ~** glottal stop.
glouglou [gluglu] *nm* **(a)** *[eau]* gurgling, glug-glug*. **faire ~** to gurgle, go glug-glug*. **(b)** *[dindon]* gobbling, gobble-gobble. **faire ~** to gobble, go gobble-gobble.
glouglouter [gluglute] (1) *vi [eau]* to gurgle; *[dindon]* to gobble.
gloussement [glusmɑ̃] *nm* (*V* **glousser**) chuckle; cluck.
glousser [gluse] (1) *vi [personne]* to chuckle; *[poule]* to cluck.
glouton, -onne [glutɔ̃, ɔn] **1** *adj personne* gluttonous, greedy; *appétit* voracious. **2** *nm,f* glutton. **3** *nm* (*Zool*) glutton.
gloutonnement [glutɔnmɑ̃] *adv manger* gluttonously, greedily; *lire* voraciously. **avalant ~ son repas** gulping his meal down gluttonously *ou* greedily, guzzling (down) his meal*.
gloutonnerie [glutɔnʀi] *nf* gluttony, greed.
glu [gly] *nf* (*pour prendre les oiseaux*) birdlime. **prendre les oiseaux à la ~** to lime birds; **on dirait de la ~, c'est comme de la ~** it's like glue.
gluant, e [glyɑ̃, ɑ̃t] *adj* sticky, gummy.
glucide [glysid] *nm* glucide.
glucose [glykoz] *nm* glucose.
gluten [glytɛn] *nm* gluten.
glycémie [glisemi] *nf* glycaemia.
glycérine [gliseʀin] *nf* glycerin(e), glycerol (*T*).
glycine [glisin] *nf* wisteria, wistaria.
glycogène [glikɔʒɛn] *nm* glycogen.
glycol [glikɔl] *nm* glycol.
gnangnan* [ɲɑ̃ɲɑ̃] *nmf* whining lump*, drip*. **qu'est-ce qu'il est ~!** what a drip* *ou* a whining lump* he is!
gneiss [gnes] *nm* gneiss.
gniole* [ɲol] *nf* = **gnôle*.**
gnocchi [ɲɔki] *nmpl* gnocchi.
gnognote* [ɲɔɲɔt] *nf*: **c'est de la ~!** it's rubbish!; **c'est pas de la ~!** that's really something!*
gnôle* [ɲol] *nf* (*eau de vie*) firewater*, hooch*.
gnome [gnom] *nm* gnome.
gnomique [gnɔmik] *adj* gnomic.
gnon* [ɲɔ̃] *nm* bash*. **prendre un ~** to get bashed*.
gnose [gnoz] *nf* gnosis.
gnosticisme [gnɔstisism(ə)] *nm* gnosticism.
gnostique [gnɔstik] *adj, nmf* gnostic.
gnou [gnu] *nm* gnu, wildebeest.
go [go] *V* **tout.**
goal [gol] *nm* goalkeeper, goalie*.
gobelet [gɔblɛ] *nm [enfant, pique-nique]* beaker; (*étain, verre, argent*) tumbler; *[dés]* cup. **un ~ en plastique/papier** a plastic/paper cup.
gobe-mouches [gɔbmuʃ] *nm inv* (*Orn*) flycatcher.
gober [gɔbe] (1) *vt huître, œuf* to swallow (whole); (*fig*) *mensonge, histoire* to swallow. **je ne le gobe pas tellement*** I'm not terribly keen on him.
goberger (se)* [gɔbɛʀʒe] (3) *vpr* (*faire bonne chère*) to indulge o.s.; (*prendre ses aises*) to pamper o.s.
godailler [gɔdaje] (1) *vi* = **goder.**
godasse* [gɔdas] *nf* shoe.
godelureau, *pl* **~x** [gɔdlyʀo] *nm* (young) dandy.
goder [gɔde] (1) *vi* to pucker, be puckered. **sa jupe godait de partout** her skirt was all puckered.
godet [gɔdɛ] *nm* **(a)** (*gén: récipient*) jar, pot; (*à peinture*) pot. **viens boire un ~ avec nous*** come and have a jar* (*Brit*) *ou* a drink with us. **(b)** (*Couture*) flare. **(c)** (*Tech*) bucket.
godiche [gɔdiʃ] *adj* lumpish, oafish. **quelle ~, ce garçon!** what an awkward lump *ou* what a clumsy oaf that boy is!
godille [gɔdij] *nf* **(a)** (*Sport*) scull; (*Ski*) wedeln. **(b) à la ~** *système* dicky* (*Brit*), ropey* (*Brit*), cheesy* (*US*); *jambe, bras* dicky* (*Brit*). **télévision qui marche à la ~** television which goes erratically, ropey (*Brit*) *ou* cheesy (*US*) television*.
godiller [gɔdije] (1) *vi* (*Sport*) to scull; (*Ski*) to wedel, use the wedeln technique.
godillot* [gɔdijo] *nm* boot.
goéland [gɔelɑ̃] *nm* seagull, gull.
goélette [gɔelɛt] *nf* schooner.
goémon [gɔemɔ̃] *nm* wrack.
goglu [gɔgly] *nm* (*Can*) bobolink, ricebird.
gogo[1]* [gɔgo] *nm* (*personne crédule*) sucker*, mug‡. **c'est bon pour les ~s** it's a con‡, it's a mug's game‡.
gogo[2]* [gɔgo] *adv* (*en abondance*) **à ~** galore; **on avait du vin à ~** we had wine galore.
goguenard, e [gɔgnaʀ, aʀd(ə)] *adj* mocking.
goguenardise [gɔgnaʀdiz] *nf* mocking.
goguenot‡ [gɔgno] *nm,* **gogues‡** [gɔg] *nmpl* (*toilettes*) bog‡ (*Brit*), loo*, john‡ (*US*).
goguette* [gɔgɛt] *nf*: **être en ~** to be on the binge*.
goinfre* [gwɛ̃fʀ(ə)] (*glouton*) **1** *adj* piggish*. **2** *nm* pig*.
goinfrer (se) [gwɛ̃fʀe] (1) *vpr* to make a pig of o.s.*, make a beast of o.s.* **se ~ de gâteaux** to guzzle cakes*.
goinfrerie [gwɛ̃fʀəʀi] *nf* piggery*, piggishness*.
goitre [gwatʀ(ə)] *nm* goitre.
goitreux, -euse [gwatʀø, øz] **1** *adj* goitrous. **2** *nm,f* person suffering from goitre.
golden [gɔldɛn] *nf inv* Golden Delicious.
golf [gɔlf] *nm* (*Sport*) golf; (*terrain*) golf course *ou* links. **~ miniature** miniature golf; **culottes** *ou* **pantalon de ~** plus fours; *V* **joueur.**
golfe [gɔlf(ə)] *nm* gulf; (*petit*) bay. **le ~ de Gascogne** the Bay of Biscay; **le ~ du Lion** the Gulf of Lions; **le ~ Persique** the Persian Gulf.
golfeur, -euse [gɔlfœʀ, øz] *nm,f* golfer.
gomina [gɔmina] *nf* ® hair cream, Brylcreem ®.
gominer (se) [gɔmine] (1) *vpr* to put hair cream on, Brylcreem ®. **cheveux gominés** plastered- *ou* smarmed-down hair, hair plastered *ou* smarmed down with Brylcreem ®.
gommage [gɔmaʒ] *nm* (*V* **gommer**) rubbing-out; erasing; gumming.
gomme [gɔm] **1** *nf* (*U: substance*) gum; (*Méd*) gumma; (*pour effacer*) rubber (*Brit*), eraser (*US*). **mettre** *ou* **donner toute la ~*** to put one's foot right down*, give it full throttle; **à la ~*** *personne, outil, système, idée* pathetic*, useless; *renseignement* useless, hopeless; *V* **boule[1].**
2: gomme adragante tragacanth; **gomme arabique** gum arabic; **gomme-gutte** *nf, pl* **gommes-guttes** gambage, cambogia; **gomme laque** lac; **gomme-résine** *nf, pl* **gommes-résines** gum resin.
gommer [gɔme] (1) *vt* **(a)** (*effacer*) *mot, trait* to rub out, erase; (*fig*) *ride, souvenir, différence* to erase. **(b)** (*enduire*) to gum. **papier gommé** gummed paper.
gommeux, -euse [gɔmø, øz] **1** *adj arbre* gum-yielding; *substance* sticky, gummy. **2** *nm* (*†: jeune prétentieux*) pretentious (young) toff*† (*Brit*).
gommier [gɔmje] *nm* gum tree.
gonade [gɔnad] *nf* gonad.
gond [gɔ̃] *nm* hinge; *V* **sortir.**
gondolage [gɔ̃dɔlaʒ] *nm* (*V* **gondoler**) crinkling; warping; buckling.
gondolant, e* [gɔ̃dɔlɑ̃, ɑ̃t] *adj* (*amusant*) side-splitting*.
gondole [gɔ̃dɔl] *nf* gondola.
gondolement [gɔ̃dɔlmɑ̃] *nm* = **gondolage.**
gondoler [gɔ̃dɔle] (1) **1** *vi [papier]* to crinkle; *[planche]* to warp; *[tôle]* to buckle. **2 se gondoler** *vpr* **(a)** *[papier]* to crinkle; *[planche]* to warp; *[tôle]* to buckle. **(b)** (*: *rire*) to split one's sides laughing*, be doubled up with laughter.
gondolier, -ière [gɔ̃dɔlje, jɛʀ] *nm,f* gondolier.
gonfalon [gɔ̃falɔ̃] *nm* gonfalon.
gonfalonier [gɔ̃falɔnje] *nm,f* gonfalonier.
gonfanon [gɔ̃fanɔ̃] *nm* = **gonfalon.**
gonfanonier [gɔ̃fanɔnje] *nm* = **gonfalonier.**
gonflage [gɔ̃flaʒ] *nm* inflating (*U*), inflation (*U*).
gonflé, e [gɔ̃fle] (*ptp de* **gonfler**) *adj* **(a)** *yeux, visage* puffy, swollen; *ventre* (*par la maladie*) distended, swollen; (*par un repas*) blown-out, bloated. **il a les joues bien ~es** he has chubby *ou* plump cheeks; **je me sens un peu ~** I feel a bit bloated.
(b) (*fig*) **il est ~!** (*courageux*) he's got some nerve!*; (*impertinent*) he's got a nerve!* *ou* some cheek!*; **être ~ à bloc** to be raring to go*.
gonflement [gɔ̃fləmɑ̃] *nm [ballon, pneu]* inflation; *[visage, ventre]* swelling; *[prix, résultats]* inflation; *[effectifs]* (*augmentation*) swelling; (*exagération*) exaggeration. **le ~ de son estomac m'inquiétait** his swollen stomach worried me.
gonfler [gɔ̃fle] (1) **1** *vt* **(a)** *pneu, ballon* (*avec une pompe*) to pump up, inflate; (*en soufflant*) to blow up, inflate; *aérostat* to inflate; *poitrine, joues, narines* to puff out. **les pluies ont gonflé**

la rivière the rain has swollen the river *ou* caused the river to swell; **le vent gonfle les voiles** the wind fills (out) *ou* swells the sails; **un paquet gonflait sa poche** his pocket was bulging with a package; **un soupir gonflait sa poitrine** a sigh swelled his chest; **éponge gonflée d'eau** sponge swollen with water; **la bière me gonfle** *ou* **me fait ~ l'estomac** beer blows out my stomach, beer makes me feel bloated *ou* makes my stomach bloated; **il avait les yeux gonflés par le manque de sommeil** his eyes were puffy *ou* swollen with lack of sleep.

(b) (*fig: dilater*) to swell. **ses succès l'ont gonflé d'orgueil** his successes have made his head swell *ou* made him puffed up (with pride); **l'orgueil gonfle son cœur** his heart is swollen with pride; **l'espoir lui gonflait le cœur** his heart was swelling *ou* bursting with hope; **le chagrin lui gonflait le cœur** his heart was heavy with sorrow; **cœur gonflé de joie/d'indignation** heart bursting with joy/indignation.

(c) (*fig: grossir*) *prix, résultat* to inflate; *effectif* (*augmenter*) to swell; (*exagérer*) to exaggerate. **on a gonflé l'importance de l'incident** the incident has been blown up out of (all) proportion, they have exaggerated the importance of the incident.

2 *vi* (*enfler*) *[genou, cheville]* to swell (up); *[bois]* to swell; (*Culin*) *[pâte]* to rise. **faire ~ le riz/les lentilles** to leave the rice/lentils to swell (up) (in water).

3 se gonfler *vpr* **(a)** *[rivière]* to swell; *[poitrine]* to swell, expand; *[voiles]* to swell, fill (out).

(b) (*fig*) **se ~ (d'orgueil)** to be puffed up (with pride), be bloated with pride; **son cœur se gonfle (de tristesse)** his heart is heavy (with sorrow); **son cœur se gonfle d'espoir** his heart is bursting with hope.

gonfleur [gɔ̃flœʀ] *nm* air pump.
gong [gɔ̃(g)] *nm* (*Mus*) gong; (*Boxe*) bell.
goniomètre [gɔnjɔmɛtʀ(ə)] *nm* goniometer.
goniométrie [gɔnjɔmetʀi] *nf* goniometry.
goniométrique [gɔnjɔmetʀik] *adj* goniometric(al).
gonocoque [gɔnɔkɔk] *nm* gonococcus.
gonsesse‡, gonzesse‡ [gɔ̃zɛs] *nf* (*péj*) bird‡ (*Brit*), chick‡ (*US*).
gordien [gɔʀdjɛ̃] *adj m V* **nœud.**
goret [gɔʀɛ] *nm* piglet. (*à un enfant*) **petit ~!** you mucky (little) pup!*
gorge [gɔʀʒ(ə)] **1** *nf* **(a)** *[personne]* (*cou, gosier*) throat; (*littér: seins*) breast, bosom (*littér*); *[oiseau]* (*poitrine*) breast; (*gosier*) throat. **avoir la ~ sèche** to have a dry throat; **avoir la ~ serrée** to have a lump in one's throat; **rire à pleine ~** *ou* **à ~ déployée** to roar with laughter, laugh heartily; **chanter à pleine ~** *ou* **à ~ déployée** to sing at the top of one's voice; *V* **chat, couper, couteau** *etc.*

(b) (*vallée, défilé*) gorge.
(c) (*rainure*) *[moulure, poulie]* groove; *[serrure]* tumbler.
(d) (*loc*) **prendre qn à la ~** *[créancier]* to put a gun to sb's head (*fig*); *[agresseur]* to grab sb by the throat; *[fumée, odeur]* to get in sb's throat; *[peur]* to grip sb by the throat; **tenir qn à la ~** (*lit*) to hold sb by the throat; (*fig: avoir à sa merci*) to have a stranglehold on sb, have sb by the throat; **l'os lui est resté dans la** *ou* **en travers de la ~** the bone (got) stuck in his throat; (*fig*) **ça lui est resté dans la** *ou* **en travers de la ~** (*il n'a pas aimé*) he found it hard to take, he couldn't swallow it; (*il n'a pas osé le dire*) it *ou* the words stuck in his throat; **faire des ~s chaudes de qch** to laugh sth to scorn; **je lui enfoncerai** *ou* **ferai rentrer ses mots dans la ~** I'll make him eat his words; *V* **tendre**[1].

2: gorge-de-pigeon *adj inv* dapple-grey; **des (cerises) gorge-de-pigeon** *type of cherry.*

gorgée [gɔʀʒe] *nf* mouthful. **boire à petites ~s** to sip, take little sips; **boire à grandes ~s** to drink in gulps, gulp; **vider un verre d'une seule ~** to empty a glass in one gulp, down a glass in one.
gorger [gɔʀʒe] (3) **1** *vt* to fill (*de* with). **~ qn de pâtisseries** to fill sb up *ou* stuff* sb with cakes; **terre/éponge gorgée d'eau** earth/sponge saturated with *ou* full of water; **fruits gorgés de soleil** fruit bursting with sunshine.

2 se gorger *vpr*: **se ~ (de nourriture)** to gorge o.s., stuff o.s.* (with food); **se ~ de bananes** to gorge o.s. on *ou* with bananas; **se ~ de bon air** to drink in fresh air; **éponge qui se gorge d'eau** sponge which soaks up water.

Gorgone [gɔʀgɔn] *nf* (*Myth*) Gorgon. (*Zool*) **g~** gorgonia.
gorille [gɔʀij] *nm* (*Zool*) gorilla; (*: *garde du corps*) bodyguard.
gosier [gozje] *nm* (*Anat*) throat; (*: *gorge*) throat, gullet. **ça m'est resté en travers du ~*** (*lit*) it (got) stuck in my throat; (*fig*) I couldn't swallow it, I found it hard to take.
gosse* [gɔs] *nmf* kid*. **sale ~** little brat*; **elle est restée très ~** she's still a kid at heart*; (*péj*) **~ de riches** spoilt rich brat*; *V* **beau.**
Goth [gɔt] *nmf* Goth.
gothique [gɔtik] *adj* Gothic.
gotique [gɔtik] *nm* (*Ling*) Gothic.
gouache [gwaʃ] *nf* gouache.
gouaille [gwɑj] *nf* cheeky *ou* cocky* humour.
gouailler [gwɑje] (1) *vi* to have a cheeky *ou* cocky* sense of humour. **en gouaillant** with cheeky *ou* cocky* humour.
gouailleur, -euse [gwɑjœʀ, øz] *adj* cheeky, cocky*.
goualante*†† [gwalɑ̃t] *nf* popular song.
gouape [gwap] *nf* thug.
goudron [gudʀɔ̃] *nm* tar. **~ de houille** coal tar.
goudronnage [gudʀɔnaʒ] *nm* tarring.
goudronner [gudʀɔne] (1) *vt route* to tar.
goudronneux, -euse [gudʀɔnø, øz] *adj* tarry.
gouffre [gufʀ(ə)] *nm* **(a)** (*Géog*) abyss, gulf, chasm.

(b) (*fig*) **le ~ de l'oubli** the depths of oblivion; **c'est un ~ d'ignorance/de bêtise** he's abysmally ignorant/utterly stupid; **cette entreprise est un vrai ~** this business just swallows up money; **cette femme est un ~** this woman is a bottomless pit where money is concerned; **nous sommes au bord du ~** we are on the brink of the abyss.

gouge [guʒ] *nf* gouge.
gouine‡ [gwin] *nf* dyke‡.
goujat [guʒa] *nm* boor, churl.
goujaterie [guʒatʀi] *nf* boorishness.
goujon [guʒɔ̃] *nm* (*poisson*) gudgeon; (*Tech: cheville*) pin, bolt.
goulache, goulasch [gulaʃ] *nf* goulash.
goulée [gule] *nf [liquide]* gulp; *[solide]* big mouthful. **prendre une ~ d'air frais** (*gorgée*) to take in a lungful of air; (*: *bol d'air*) to get some fresh air.
goulet [gulɛ] *nm* (*Naut*) narrows, bottleneck (*at entrance of harbour*); (*Géog*) gully.
goulot [gulo] *nm [bouteille]* neck. **boire au ~** to drink straight from the bottle; **~ d'étranglement** bottleneck (*fig*).
goulu, e [guly] **1** *adj personne* greedy, gluttonous; *regards* greedy. **2** *nm,f* glutton.
goulûment [gulymɑ̃] *adv* greedily, gluttonously.
goupil†† [gupi(l)] *nm* fox.
goupille [gupij] *nf* (*Tech*) pin.
goupillé, e* [gupije] (*ptp de* **goupiller**) *adj* (*arrangé*) **bien/mal ~** *machine, plan, procédé* well/badly thought out; **comment est-ce ~, ce mécanisme?** how does this thing work?
goupiller [gupije] (1) **1** *vt* **(a)** (*: *combiner*) to fix*. **il a bien goupillé son affaire** he fixed things nicely for himself*.
(b) (*Tech*) to pin.

2 se goupiller* *vpr* (*s'arranger*) **comment est-ce que ça se goupille pour demain?** what's the gen (*Brit*) *ou* dope (*US*) for tomorrow?*; **ça s'est bien/mal goupillé, notre plan** our plan came off (all right)/didn't come off*.

goupillon [gupijɔ̃] *nm* (*Rel*) (holy water) sprinkler, aspergillum; (*à bouteille*) bottle brush.
gourance‡ [guʀɑ̃s] *nf* boob‡, bloomer*.
gourbi [guʀbi] *nm* (*arabe*) shack; (*: *taudis*) slum.
gourd, e[1] [guʀ, guʀd(ə)] *adj* numb (*with cold*).
gourde[2] [guʀd(ə)] **1** *nf* (*Bot: récipient*) gourd; (*à eau, alcool*) flask; (*: *empoté*) clot*, dumbbell* (*US*). **2** *adj* (*) thick*.
gourdin [guʀdɛ̃] *nm* club, bludgeon.
gourer (se)‡ [guʀe] (1) *vpr* to boob‡, make a boob‡. **je me suis gouré de numéro** I've boobed‡ over the number, I got the wrong number; **je me suis gouré dans mes calculs** I boobed in my calculations‡.
gourgandine*†† [guʀgɑ̃din] *nf* hussy*†.
gourmand, e [guʀmɑ̃, ɑ̃d] **1** *adj* (*lit, fig*) greedy. **~ comme un chat** greedy but fussy *ou* choos(e)y; **être ~ de** to be avid for. **2** *nm,f* gourmand. **3** *nm* (*Agr*) sucker.
gourmander [guʀmɑ̃de] (1) *vt* (*littér*) to rebuke, berate (*littér*).
gourmandise [guʀmɑ̃diz] *nf* **(a)** greed, greediness. **elle regardait le gâteau avec ~** she looked greedily at the cake. **(b) ~s** delicacies, sweetmeats†.
gourme [guʀm(ə)] *nf* (*Méd*) impetigo; (*Zool*) strangles (*sg*); *V* **jeter.**
gourmé, e [guʀme] *adj* starchy, stiff.
gourmet [guʀmɛ] *nm* gourmet, epicure.
gourmette [guʀmɛt] *nf [cheval]* curb chain; *[poignet]* chain bracelet.
gourou [guʀu] *nm* guru.
gousse [gus] *nf [vanille, petits pois]* pod. **~ d'ail** clove of garlic.
gousset [gusɛ] *nm [gilet, pantalon]* fob; *[slip]* gusset.
goût [gu] *nm* **(a)** (*sens*) taste. **amer au ~** bitter to the taste; **avoir le ~ fin** to have a fine palate.

(b) (*saveur*) taste. **cela a un ~ de moisi** it tastes mouldy; **ça a bon ~** it tastes good, it has a nice taste; **ça a mauvais ~** it has a bad taste, it tastes nasty; **cette glace n'a pas vraiment un ~ de fraise** this ice cream doesn't really taste like strawberry *ou* hasn't really got a strawberry taste *ou* flavour; **la soupe a un ~** the soup tastes funny *ou* has a funny taste; **un plat sans ~** a tasteless *ou* flavourless dish; (*fig*) **la vie n'a plus de ~ pour lui** he has no longer any taste for life, he has lost his taste for life; (*fig*) **ses souvenirs ont un ~ amer** he has bitter memories; **ça a un ~ de revenez-y*** it's very more-ish*; *V* **arrière, avant.**

(c) (*jugement*) taste. **(bon) ~** (good) taste; **avoir du/manquer de ~** to have/lack taste; **avoir un ~ vulgaire** to have vulgar tastes; **le ~ ne s'apprend pas** taste can't be learned; **faire qch sans/avec ~** to do something tastelessly/tastefully; **elle s'habille avec beaucoup de ~** she has very good *ou* a lot of taste in dress, she has very good dress sense; **à mon/son ~** for my/his liking, for my/his taste(s); **un homme/une femme de ~** a man/woman of taste; *V* **faute.**

(d) de bon ~ *vêtement, ameublement* tasteful, in good taste (*attrib*); **de mauvais ~** *bijoux, plaisanterie, meubles* tasteless, in bad *ou* poor taste (*attrib*); **garni d'un ameublement de bon/mauvais ~** furnished in good/bad taste, with tasteful/tasteless furnishings; **c'est une plaisanterie de mauvais ~** this joke is in bad taste *ou* is bad form; **il serait de mauvais ~/d'un ~ douteux de faire** it would be in bad *ou* poor/doubtful taste to do; (*iro*) **il serait de bon ~ d'y aller/qu'il se mette à travailler** it would be as well to go/if he started doing some work.

(e) (*penchant*) taste, liking (*de, pour* for). **il a peu de ~ pour ce genre de travail** this sort of work is not to his taste *ou* liking, he is not keen on this sort of work; **il n'a aucun ~ pour les sciences** the sciences don't appeal to him, he has no taste for the sciences; **il a le ~ de l'ordre** he has a taste for order; **il a le ~ du risque** he likes taking risks; **faire qch par ~** to do sth from inclination *ou* because one has a taste for it; **prendre ~ à qch** to get *ou* acquire a taste *ou* liking for sth, get to like sth; **il n'avait ~ à rien** he didn't feel like (doing) anything; **ce n'est pas du ~ de chacun** it's not to everybody's taste; **cela m'a mis en ~** that gave me a taste for it; **c'est tout à fait à mon ~** this is very much to my taste; **il la trouve à son ~** she is to his taste, she suits his taste; **faire passer le ~ du pain à qn*** to do sb in‡; *V* **chacun.**

(f) (*tendances, penchants*) **~s** tastes; **avoir des ~s dispendieux/modestes** to have expensive/simple tastes; **avoir des ~s communs** to have (some) tastes in common; (*Prov*) **des ~s et des couleurs (on ne discute pas)** there's no accounting for taste(s); (*Prov*) **tous les ~s sont dans la nature** it takes all sorts to make a world.

(g) (*style*) style. **dans le ~ classique/de X** in the classical style/the style of X; **ou quelque chose dans ce ~-là*** or something of that sort; **au ~ du jour** in keeping with the style of the day *ou* with current tastes; **il s'est mis au ~ du jour** he has brought himself into line with current tastes.

goûter [gute] (1) **1** *vt* **(a)** *aliment* to taste. **goûte-le, pour voir si c'est assez salé** taste it and see if there's enough salt.

(b) *repos, spectacle* to enjoy, savour.

(c) (*littér*) *écrivain, œuvre, plaisanterie* to appreciate. **il ne goûte pas l'art abstrait** he doesn't appreciate abstract art, abstract art isn't to his taste.

2 goûter à *vt indir aliment, plaisir* to taste, sample; **il y a à peine goûté** he's hardly touched it; **voulez-vous ~ à mon gâteau?** would you like to try *ou* sample my cake?; **goûtez-y** (*vin*) have a sip *ou* taste, taste it; (*plat*) have a taste, taste it.

3 goûter de *vt indir* (*faire l'expérience de*) to have a taste of, taste; **il a goûté de la vie militaire/de la prison** he has had a taste of army/prison life, he has tasted army/prison life.

4 *vi* (*faire une collation*) to have tea. **inviter des enfants à ~** to ask children to tea.

5 *nm* tea. **donner un ~ d'enfants** to give *ou* have a children's (tea) party.

goutte [gut] **1** *nf* **(a)** (*lit, fig*) drop. **~ de rosée** dewdrop; **~ de sueur** bead of sweat; **suer à grosses ~s** to be streaming with sweat; **pleuvoir à grosses ~s** to rain heavily; **il est tombé quelques ~s** a few spots *ou* drops of rain have fallen; **du lait? — une ~** milk? — just a drop; **savourer qch ~ à ~** to savour sth drop by drop; **tomber ~ à ~** to drip.

(b) (*Pharm*) **~s** drops; **~s pour les yeux/le nez** eye/nose drops.

(c) (*: *eau-de-vie*) **on va prendre la ~** *ou* **un verre de ~** we'll have a dram* *ou* a nip*.

(d) (††, *hum: rien*) **je n'y vois/entends ~** I see/hear not a thing (††, *hum*).

(e) (*Méd*) gout.

(f) (*loc*) **avoir la ~ au nez** to have a dripping *ou* running nose; **c'est une ~ d'eau dans la mer** it's a drop in the ocean; **c'est la ~ (d'eau) qui fait déborder le vase** it's the last straw (that breaks the camel's back); *V* **ressembler.**

2: (*Bijouterie*) **goutte d'eau** drop, droplet; (*Méd*) **goutte-à-goutte** *nm inv* drip; **alimenter qn au goutte-à-goutte** to put sb on a drip, drip-feed sb.

gouttelette [gutlɛt] *nf* droplet.

goutter [gute] (1) *vi* to drip (*de* from).

goutteux, -euse [gutø, øz] *adj* gouty.

gouttière [gutjɛʀ] *nf* (*horizontale*) gutter; (*verticale*) drainpipe; (*Méd*) (plaster) cast; (*Anat: sur os*) groove; *V* **chat.**

gouvernable [guvɛʀnabl(ə)] *adj* governable.

gouvernail [guvɛʀnaj] *nm* (*pale*) rudder; (*barre*) helm, tiller. **~ de direction** rudder; **~ de profondeur** elevator; (*fig*) **tenir le ~** to be at the helm.

gouvernant, e [guvɛʀnɑ̃, ɑ̃t] **1** *adj parti, classe* ruling (*épith*), governing (*épith*). (*Pol*) **les ~s** the government. **2 gouvernante** *nf* (*institutrice*) governess; (*dame de compagnie*) housekeeper.

gouverne [guvɛʀn(ə)] *nf* **(a) pour ta ~** for your guidance. **(b)** (*Naut*) steering; (*Aviat*) control surface.

gouverné [guvɛʀne] *nm* (*gén pl*) citizen. **les ~s et les gouvernants** the governed and the governing.

gouvernement [guvɛʀnəmɑ̃] *nm* (*administration, régime*) government; (*cabinet*) Cabinet, Government. **former le ~** to form a government; **soutenir le ~** to back the government; **il est au ~** he's a member of the Cabinet; **sous un ~ socialiste** under socialist rule *ou* government.

gouvernemental, e, *mpl* **-aux** [guvɛʀnəmɑ̃tal, o] *adj député* of the governing party; *organe, politique* government (*épith*), governmental (*épith*); *journal* pro-government. **le parti ~** the governing *ou* ruling party, the party in office; **l'équipe ~e** the Cabinet.

gouverner [guvɛʀne] (1) *vt* **(a)** (*Pol*) to govern, rule. **le parti qui gouverne** the party in power *ou* in office, the governing *ou* ruling party; **peuple capable de se ~ lui-même** nation capable of governing its own affairs *ou* of self-government.

(b) (*fig littér*) to control. **savoir ~ son cœur** to have control over one's heart; **se laisser ~ par l'ambition/par qn** to let o.s. be ruled *ou* governed by ambition/by sb; **il sait fort bien se ~** he is well able to control himself.

(c) (*Naut*) to steer, helm. **~ vers tribord** to steer to(wards) starboard.

(d) (*Gram*) to govern, take.

gouverneur [guvɛʀnœʀ] *nm* (*Admin, Pol*) governor. **~ (militaire)** commanding officer; (*Can*) **~ général** governor general; (*Can*) **lieutenant-~** lieutenant-governor.

goyave [gɔjav] *nf* guava.

Graal [gʀɑl] *nm* Grail.

grabat [gʀaba] *nm* pallet, mean bed.

grabataire [gʀabatɛʀ] **1** *adj* bedridden. **2** *nmf* bedridden invalid.

grabuge* [gʀabyʒ] *nm*: **il va y avoir du ~** there'll be ructions* *ou* a rumpus*; **faire du ~** to create havoc *ou* mayhem.

grâce [gʀɑs] *nf* **(a)** (*charme*) [*personne, geste*] grace; [*chose, paysage*] charm. **plein de ~** graceful; **un visage sans ~** a plain face; **avec ~** *danser* gracefully; *s'exprimer* elegantly; **faire des ~s** to put on airs (and graces).

(b) (*faveur*) favour. **demander une ~ à qn** to ask a favour of sb; **accorder une ~ à qn** to grant sb a favour; (*frm, hum*) **il nous a fait la ~ d'accepter** he did us the honour of accepting (*frm, hum*); **elle nous a fait la ~ de sa présence** *ou* **d'être présente** she graced *ou* honoured us with her presence; **être dans les bonnes ~s de qn** to be in favour with sb, be in sb's good graces *ou* good books*; **être en ~** to be in favour; **rentrer en ~** to come back into favour; **chercher/gagner les bonnes ~s de qn** to seek/gain sb's favour; **délai de ~** days of grace; **donner à qn une semaine de ~** to give sb a week's grace; *V* **coup, trouver.**

(c) bonne ~ (*bonne volonté, affabilité*) good grace; **mauvaise ~** (*mauvaise volonté*) bad grace; **faire qch de** *ou* **avec bonne/mauvaise ~** to do sth with (a) good/bad grace; **il y a mis de la mauvaise ~** he did it with (a) bad grace; **il a eu la bonne ~ de reconnaître ...** he had the grace to recognize ...; **il aurait mauvaise ~ à refuser** it would be bad form *ou* in bad taste for him to refuse.

(d) (*miséricorde*) mercy; (*Jur*) pardon. **la ~ royale/présidentielle** the royal/presidential pardon; **demander** *ou* **crier ~** to beg *ou* cry for mercy; **~!** (have) mercy!; **de ~, laissez-le dormir** for pity's sake *ou* for goodness' sake let him sleep; **je vous fais ~ des détails/du reste** I'll spare you the details/the rest; *V* **droit³, recours, trouver.**

(e) (*reconnaissance*) **dire les ~s** to say grace (*after a meal*), give thanks; **~ à qn/qch** thanks to sb/sth; **~ à Dieu!** thank God!, thank goodness!; (*Can*) **(Jour d')Action de ~** Thanksgiving (Day) (*US, Can*); *V* **action, rendre.**

(f) (*Rel*) grace; (*fig: don*) gift. (*Rel*) **Marie, pleine de ~** Mary, full of grace; **avoir la ~** to have a gift; (*fig*) **il a été touché par la ~** he has been inspired; (*fig*) **c'est la ~ que nous lui souhaitons** that is what we wish for him; **à la ~ de Dieu!** it's in God's hands!; **~ efficace/suffisante/vivifiante** efficacious/sufficient/life-giving grace; *V* **an, état.**

(g) (*déesse*) **les trois G~s** the three Graces.

(h) (*titre, gén Brit*) **Sa G~ ...** His *ou* Her Grace ... .

gracier [gʀasje] (7) *vt* to pardon.

gracieusement [gʀasjøzmɑ̃] *adv* (*élégamment*) gracefully; (*aimablement*) amiably, kindly; (*gratuitement*) free of charge.

gracieuseté [gʀasjøzte] *nf* (*frm*) (*amabilité*) amiability; (*geste élégant*) graceful gesture; (*cadeau*) free gift. (*iro*) **je vous remercie de vos ~s** so kind of you to say so (*iro*).

gracieux, -ieuse [gʀasjø, jøz] *adj* **(a)** (*élégant*) *gestes, silhouette, personne* graceful.

(b) (*aimable*) *sourire, abord, personne* amiable, kindly; *enfant* amiable. (*frm*) **notre ~euse souveraine** our gracious sovereign (*frm*).

(c) (*frm: gratuit*) *aide, service* gratuitous (*frm*); *V* **titre.**

gracile [gʀasil] *adj personne* slender; *cou* slender, swanlike.

gracilité [gʀasilite] *nf* slenderness.

Gracques [gʀak] *nmpl*: **les ~** the Gracchi.

gradation [gʀadɑsjɔ̃] *nf* gradation.

grade [gʀad] *nm* **(a)** (*dans la hiérarchie: Admin, Mil*) rank. **monter en ~** to be promoted; **en prendre pour son ~*** to get a proper dressing-down*. **(b)** (*titre: Univ*) degree. **le ~ de licencié** the (first) degree. **(c)** (*Math*) grade. **(d)** (*Tech*) [*huile*] grade.

gradé [gʀade] *nm* (*Mil*) (*gén*) officer; (*subalterne*) = N.C.O., non-commissioned officer; (*Pol*) officer.

gradient [gʀadjɑ̃] *nm* pressure gradient.

gradin [gʀadɛ̃] *nm* (*Théât*) tier; [*stade*] step (of the terracing); (*Agr*) terrace. **en ~s** terraced; **la colline s'élevait/descendait en ~s** the hill went up/down in steps *ou* terraces.

graduation [gʀadɥɑsjɔ̃] *nf* [*instrument*] graduation.

gradué, e [gʀadɥe] (*ptp de* **graduer**) *adj exercices* graded; *règle, thermomètre* graduated.

graduel, -elle [gʀadɥɛl] **1** *adj progression* gradual; *difficultés* progressive. **2** *nm* (*Rel*) gradual.

graduellement [gʀadɥɛlmɑ̃] *adv* gradually.

graduer [gʀadɥe] (1) *vt exercices* to increase in difficulty; *difficultés, efforts* to step up *ou* increase gradually; *règle, thermomètre* to graduate.

graffiti [gʀafiti] *nmpl* graffiti.

grailler [gʀɑje] (1) *vi* **(a)** (‡: *manger*) to nosh‡. **(b)** [*corneille*] to caw.

graillon [gʀɑjɔ̃] *nm* (*péj: déchet*) bit of burnt fat. **ça sent le ~ ici** there's a smell of burnt fat here.

grain [gʀɛ̃] **1** *nm* **(a)** [*blé, riz, maïs*] grain. (*céréales*) **le ~** (the) grain; **donner du ~ aux poules** to give grain to chickens; **alcool** *ou* **eau-de-vie de ~(s)** grain alcohol; **le commerce des ~s** the grain trade; (*Rel*) **le bon ~** the good seed; *V* **poulet.**

(b) [*café*] bean; [*moutarde*] seed. **~ de café** coffee bean; **~ de raisin** grape; **~ de poivre** peppercorn; **~ de groseille/cassis** red currant/blackcurrant (berry); **poivre en ~s** whole pepper *ou* peppercorns; **acheter du café en ~s** to buy unground coffee, buy coffee beans; **mettre son ~ de sel*** to put one's oar in*.

(c) [*collier, chapelet*] bead; (*Méd: petite pilule*) pellet.

(d) (*particule*) [*sable, farine, pollen*] grain; [*poussière*] speck. (*fig*) **un ~ de fantaisie** a touch of fantasy; **un ~ de bon sens** a grain *ou* an ounce of common sense; **il n'y a pas un ~ de vérité dans ce qu'il dit** there's not a grain *ou* scrap of truth in what he says; **il a un (petit) ~** he's a bit touched*, he's not quite all there*; **il faut parfois un petit ~ de folie** it sometimes helps to have a touch of madness *ou* to be a bit eccentric.

(e) (*texture*) grain. **à gros ~s** coarse-grained; **travailler dans le sens du ~** to work with the grain; *V* **gros.**

(f) (*averse brusque*) heavy shower; (*Naut: bourrasque*) squall; *V* **veiller.**

(g) (††: *poids*) grain; (*Can*) grain (*0,0647 gramme*).

2: **grain de beauté** mole, beauty spot.

graine [gʀɛn] *nf* (*Agr*) seed. **~s de radis** radish seeds; **tu vois ce**

qu'a fait ton frère, prends-en de la ~* you've seen what your brother has done so take a leaf out of his book*; **c'est de la ~ de voleur** he has the makings of a thief; *V* **mauvais, monter.**

grainer [gʀene] (1) = **grener.**

graineterie [gʀɛnt(ə)ʀi] *nf* (*commerce*) seed trade; (*magasin*) seed shop.

grainetier, -ière [gʀɛntje, jɛʀ] *nm,f* seed merchant.

graissage [gʀɛsaʒ] *nm* [*machine*] greasing, lubricating. **faire faire un ~ complet de sa voiture** to take one's car in for a complete lubricating job.

graisse [gʀɛs] **1** *nf* [*personne, animal*] fat; (*Culin*) fat; (*lubrifiant*) grease. **prendre de la ~** to put on fat; *V* **bourrelet, paquet.**

2: graisse de baleine whale blubber; **graisse de phoque** seal blubber; **graisse de porc** lard; **graisse de viande** dripping.

graisser [gʀese] (1) *vt* (*lubrifier*) (*gén*) to grease, lubricate; *bottes* to wax; (*salir*) to get grease on, make greasy. (*fig*) **~ la patte à qn*** to grease *ou* oil sb's palm*.

graisseur [gʀesœʀ] *nm* lubricator. **dispositif ~** lubricating *ou* greasing device.

graisseux, -euse [gʀɛsø, øz] *adj main, objet* greasy; *nourriture* greasy, fatty; *bourrelet* fatty, of fat; *tissu, tumeur* fatty.

graminacée [gʀaminase] *nf* = **graminée.**

graminée [gʀamine] *adj f, nf*: **une (plante) ~** a grass; **les (plantes) ~s** (the) grasses, the graminae (*T*).

grammaire [gʀamɛʀ] *nf* (*science, livre*) grammar. **faute de ~** grammatical mistake; **règle de ~** grammatical rule, rule of grammar; **exercice/livre de ~** grammar exercise/book.

grammairien, -ienne [gʀamɛʀjɛ̃, jɛn] *nm,f* grammarian.

grammatical, e, *mpl* **-aux** [gʀamatikal, o] *adj* (*gén*) grammatical. **exercice ~** grammar *ou* grammatical exercise; *V* **analyse.**

grammaticalement [gʀamatikalmɑ̃] *adv* grammatically.

grammaticalisation [gʀamatikalizasjɔ̃] *nf* (*Ling*) grammaticalization.

gramme [gʀam] *nm* gramme. **il n'a pas un ~ de jugeote** he hasn't an ounce of gumption*.

gramophone† [gʀamɔfɔn] *nm* gramophone†.

grand, e [gʀɑ̃, gʀɑ̃d] **1** *adj* **(a)** (*de haute taille*) *personne, verre* tall; *arbre, échelle* high, big, tall.

(b) (*plus âgé, adulte*) **son ~ frère** his big *ou* older brother; **il a un petit garçon et deux ~es filles** he has a little boy and two older *ou* grown-up daughters; **ils ont 2 ~s enfants** they have 2 grown-up children; **quand il sera ~** [*enfant*] when he's grown-up; [*chiot*] when it's big, when it's fully grown; **il est assez ~ pour savoir** he's big enough *ou* old enough to know; **tu es ~/~e maintenant** you're a big boy/girl now; **les ~es classes** the senior forms.

(c) (*en dimensions*) (*gén*) big, large; *hauteur, largeur* great; *bras, distance, voyage* long; *pas, enjambées* big, long; (*lit, fig*) *marge* wide. **aussi/plus ~ que nature** as large as/larger than life; **ouvrir de ~s yeux** to open one's eyes wide; **ouvrir la fenêtre/la bouche toute ~e** to open the window/one's mouth wide.

(d) (*en nombre, quantité*) *vitesse, poids, valeur, puissance* great; *nombre, quantité* large, great; *famille* large, big; *foule* large, great, big; *dépense* great; *fortune* great, large. **la ~e majorité des gens** the great *ou* vast majority of people; **une ~e partie de ce qu'il a** a great *ou* large proportion of what he has.

(e) (*intense, violent*) *bruit, cri* great, loud; *froid* severe, intense; *chaleur* intense; *vent* strong, high; *effort, danger, plaisir, déception* great; *pauvreté* great, dire (*épith*); *soupir* deep, big. **il fait une ~e chaleur/un ~ froid** it's extremely *ou* intensely hot/cold, we're having a particularly hot/cold spell, the heat/cold is intense; **pendant les ~s froids** during the cold season, in the depth of winter; **pendant les ~es chaleurs** during the hot season, at the height of summer; **l'incendie a causé de ~s dégâts** the fire has caused extensive *ou* enormous damage *ou* a great deal of damage; **avec un ~ rire** with a loud *ou* great laugh; **~ chagrin** deep *ou* great sorrow; **les ~es douleurs sont muettes** great sorrow is often silent; *V* **frapper.**

(f) (*riche, puissant*) *pays, firme, banquier, industriel* leading, big. **les ~s trusts** the big trusts; **le ~ capital** big money; **un ~ personnage** an important person; (*lit*) **un ~ seigneur** a great *ou* powerful lord; (*fig*) **faire le ~ seigneur** to play *ou* act the grand *ou* fine gentleman; **faire le ~ seigneur avec qn** to lord it over sb; **~e dame** great lady.

(g) (*important*) *aventure, nouvelle, progrès, intelligence* great; *difficulté, différence, appétit* great, big; *ville, travail* big. **c'est un ~ jour/honneur pour nous** this is a great day/honour for us; **son mérite est ~** it's greatly to his credit.

(h) (*principal*) **la ~e nouvelle/question/difficulté** the great *ou* main news/question/difficulty; **il a eu le ~ mérite d'avoir ...** to his great credit he has ..., his great merit was to have ...; **le ~ moment approche** the great moment is coming; **le ~ jour approche** the great day *ou* D. day is coming; **le ~ soir** the great evening; **les ~s points/les ~es lignes de son discours** the main points/lines of his speech; **les ~s fleuves du globe** the major *ou* main *ou* great rivers of the globe; **c'est la ~e question** (*problème*) it's the main *ou* major issue; (*interrogation*) it's the big question *ou* the $64,000 question*.

(i) (*intensif*) *travailleur* great, hard; *collectionneur* great, keen; *buveur* heavy, hard; *mangeur* big; *fumeur* heavy; *ami, rêveur, menteur* great. **c'est un ~ ennemi du bruit** he cannot abide noise; **un ~ amateur de musique** a great music lover; **~ lâche/sot!** you great coward/fool!; **~e jeunesse** extreme youth; **~ âge** great age, old age; **~e vieillesse** extreme *ou* great age; **un ~ mois/quart d'heure** a good month/quarter of an hour; **rester un ~ moment** to stay a good while; **un ~ kilomètre** a good kilometre; **un ~ verre d'eau** a nice big *ou* long glass of water; **un ~ panier de champignons** a full basket of mushrooms; **les ~s blessés** the seriously wounded; **les ~s malades** the very ill *ou* sick; **un ~ invalide/brûlé** a badly *ou* seriously disabled/burned person; **à ~ ahan**†† with much striving.

(j) (*remarquable*) *champion, œuvre, savant, civilisation* great. **un ~ vin/homme** a great wine/man; **une ~e année** a vintage *ou* great year; **le ~ Molière** the great Molière; **c'est du (tout) ~ art** it's (very) great art; **c'est du (tout) ~ Mozart*** it's Mozart at his best *ou* greatest; **les ~s esprits se rencontrent** great minds think alike; *V* **couture, maison.**

(k) (*de gala*) *réception, dîner* grand. **en ~e cérémonie/pompe** with great ceremony/pomp; **en ~e tenue** in full dress; **en ~e toilette** in finest array, in one's most elegant attire; **en ~ uniforme** in full regimentals; **en ~ apparat** in full regalia; **de ~ apparat** *habit* full-dress (*épith*).

(l) (*noble*) *âme* noble, great; *pensée* high, lofty; *cœur* noble, big. **se montrer ~ (et généreux)** to be big-hearted *ou* magnanimous.

(m) (*exagéré*) **de ~s mots** high-flown *ou* fancy words; **tout de suite les ~s mots!** you go off the deep end straight away!, you start using these high-sounding words straight away!; **voilà le ~ mot lâché!** now you've come out with it at last!, that's the word I've (*ou* we've *etc*) been waiting for!; **faire de ~es phrases** to trot out high-flown sentences; **prendre de ~s airs** to put on airs, give oneself airs; **faire de ~s gestes** to wave one's arms about; *V* **cheval.**

(n) (*loc adv, adj*) **à ma ~e surprise/honte** much to my surprise/embarrassment, to my great surprise/shame; **de ~e classe** *produit* high-class; *œuvre, exploit* admirable; **de ~ cœur** wholeheartedly; **le groupe/bureau (était) au ~ complet** the whole group/office (was there); **à ~s cris** vociferously; **à ~e distance** *détection* long-range (*épith*), at long range; *apercevoir* from a long way off *ou* away; **à ~e eau: laver à ~e eau** *sol* to wash *ou* sluice down; *légumes* to wash thoroughly; **de ~e envergure** *opération* large-scale (*épith*); *auteur* of great stature; *réforme* far-reaching; **à ~s frais** at great expense; **au ~ galop** at full gallop; **au ~ jamais** never ever; **au ~ jour** (*lit*) in broad daylight; (*fig*) in the open; **employer les ~s moyens** to use drastic *ou* extreme measures; **de ~ matin** very early in the morning; **en ~e partie** largely, in the main; **marcher** *ou* **avancer à ~s pas** to stride along; **à ~-peine** with great difficulty; **à ~ renfort de** *publicité* with the help of much, having recourse to much; *arguments* with the help *ou* support of many; **à ~ spectacle** *revue* spectacular; **boire qch à ~s traits** to take big *ou* large gulps of sth; **à ~e vitesse** at great speed; *V* **bandit.**

(o) (*loc verbales: beaucoup de*) **avoir ~ air, avoir ~e allure** to look very impressive; **~ bien: cela te fera (le plus) ~ bien** that'll do you a great deal of *ou* the world of good; **j'en pense le plus ~ bien** I think most highly of it; **faire ~ bruit** to cause quite a stir; **faire ~ cas de** to attach great importance to, set great store by; **il n'y a pas ~ danger** there's no great danger; **il n'y a pas ~ mal** (*après accident*) (there's) no harm done; **il n'y a pas ~ mal à ce qu'il fasse** there's not much harm *ou* wrong in him doing; **il n'y a pas ~ monde** there aren't very many (people) here; **avoir ~-peine à faire qch** to have great difficulty in doing sth; **cela lui fera ~ tort** it'll do him a lot of harm; *V* **train.**

(p) (*loc verbales: bien, très*) **avoir ~ avantage à** to be well advised to; **il aurait ~ avantage à** it would be very much to his advantage to, he would be well advised to; **il a ~ besoin d'un bain/de se reposer** he is in great need of a bath/a rest, he badly needs a bath/a rest; **elle avait ~e envie d'un bain/de faire** she very much wanted a bath/to do, she was longing for a bath/to do; **avoir ~ faim** to be very hungry; **il aurait ~ intérêt à ...** it would be very much in his (own) interest to ..., he would be well advised to ...; **prendre ~ intérêt à qch** to take great interest in sth; **il fait ~ jour** it's broad daylight; **avoir ~ peur** to be very frightened *ou* very much afraid; **avoir ~ peur que** to be very much afraid that; **avoir ~ soif** to be very thirsty; **prendre ~ soin de qch/faire** to take great care of sth/to do; **il est ~ temps de faire ceci** it's high time this was done *ou* we did this.

2 *adv*: **voir ~** to think big*, envisage things on a large scale; **faire ~** to do things on a large scale *ou* in a big way; **ces souliers chaussent ~** these shoes are big-fitting; **faire qch en ~** to do sth on a large *ou* big scale *ou* in a big way; **ouvrir ~ la fenêtre** to open the window wide.

3 *nm* **(a)** (*Scol*) older *ou* bigger boy, senior boy *ou* pupil (*frm*). **jeu pour petits et ~s** game for old and young alike *ou* for the young and the not-so-young.

(b) (*terme d'affection*) **mon ~** son, my lad.

(c) les ~s de ce monde men in high places; (*Pol*) **les quatre G~s** the Big Four.

(d) Pierre/Alexandre/Frédéric le G~ Peter/Alexander/Frederick the Great.

4 grande *nf* **(a)** (*Scol*) older *ou* bigger girl, senior girl *ou* pupil (*frm*).

(b) (*terme d'affection*) **ma ~e** (my) dear.

5: le grand air the open air; **grand angle** (*Phot*) (*adj inv*) wide-angle (*épith*); (*nm inv*) wide-angle lens; **grand-angulaire** (*Phot*) (*adj*) wide-angle (*épith*); (*nm, pl* **grand-angulaires**) wide-angle lens; (*Hist*) **la Grande Armée** the Grande Armée (*army of Napoleon*); (*Aut*) **grands axes** (main) trunk roads; **la grande banlieue** the outer suburbs; (*Can*) **grand-bois*** *nm* virgin forest; **la Grande-Bretagne** Great Britain; **grand chantre** precentor; **grand chef** big boss; **grand-chose: on ne sait pas grand-chose à son sujet** we don't know (very) much about him; **cela ne vaut pas grand-chose** it's not worth much, it's not up to much*; **es-tu blessé? — ce n'est pas grand-chose** are you hurt? — it's nothing much; **il n'y a pas grand-chose dans ce magasin** there isn't much *ou* there's nothing much in this shop; **il n'y a pas grand-chose à dire** there's not a lot to say, there's nothing much to say; **il n'en sortira pas grand-chose de bon** not much good will come out of this, I can't see much good coming out of this; **tu y connais grand-chose?*** do you know much about it? (*V* **pas**[2]); **un grand commis de l'État** a top-ranking *ou* senior civil servant; **les grands corps de l'État** senior branches of the civil service; **grand-croix** (*nf inv*) Grand Cross (*of the Légion d'honneur*); (*nm, pl* **grands-croix**) *holder of the Grand Cross*; **grand-duc** *nm, pl* **grands-ducs** (*prince*) grand duke; (*Orn*) eagle owl (*V* **tournée**[2]); **grand-duché** *nm, pl* **grands-duchés** grand duchy; **grande-duchesse** *nf, pl* **grandes-duchesses** grand duchess; **grandes eaux: les grandes eaux de Versailles** the fountains of Versailles; **regarde-le pleurer, c'est les grandes eaux!** look at him crying, he's really turned on the waterworks!; (*Danse, Gym*) **le grand écart** the splits; **faire le grand écart** to do the splits; **la grande échelle (des pompiers)** the (firemen's) big (turntable) ladder; (*Univ*) **grande école** grande école, *prestigious state-run school of university level with competitive entrance examination, eg École Polytechnique*; (*Scol*) **être à la grande école*** to be at the big school*; **grand ensemble** housing scheme; **grand escalier** grand staircase; **grand d'Espagne** (Spanish) grandee; **les grands fauves** the big cats; **le grand film*** the feature *ou* main film, the big picture*; (*Naut*) **les grands fonds** the ocean deeps; (*Hist*) **la Grande Guerre** the Great War; **Grand-Guignol** *nm*: **c'est du Grand-Guignol** it's all blood and thunder; **grand-guignolesque** *adj situation, événement, pièce de théâtre* gruesome, bloodcurdling; (*Géog*) **les Grands Lacs** the Great Lakes; (*Naut*) **le grand large** the high seas; (*Rail, fig*) **les grandes lignes** the main lines; (*Comm*†) **grand-livre** *nm, pl* **grands-livres** ledger; **le Grand Londres** Greater London; **grand magasin** department store; **grand maître** (*Échecs, Franc-Maçonnerie*) Grand Master; **grand manitou*** big boss*; **grand-maman** *nf, pl* **grands-mamans** granny*, grandma; **grand mât** mainmast; **grand-mère** *nf, pl* **grands-mères** grandmother; (*: *vieille dame*) (old) granny*; **grand-messe** *nf, pl* **grand-messes** high mass; **le grand monde** high society; **le grand nord** the far North; **grand officier** Grand Officer; **grand-oncle** *nm, pl* **grands-oncles** great-uncle; **le Grand Orient** the Grand Lodge of France; **grand ouvert** wide open; **grand-papa** *nm, pl* **grands-papas** grandpa, grandad*; **grands-parents** *nmpl* grandparents; **les grands patrons** (*gén*) the big bosses; (*Méd*) ≃ the top consultants; **grand-père** *nm, pl* **grands-pères** grandfather; (*: *vieux monsieur*) old man; (*péj*) **avance, grand-père!‡** get a move on, grandad!*; **grande personne** grown-up; **grand prêtre** high priest; **le grand public** the general public; (*Pol*) **grande puissance** major power; **la grande roue** *[fête foraine]* the big wheel; **grand-route** *nf, pl* **grand-routes** main road; **la grand-rue** *nf* the high *ou* main street; **le grand siècle** the 17th century (*in France*), the grand siècle; **les grands singes** the great apes; **grande surface** hypermarket; **grand-tante** *nf, pl* **grands-tantes** great-aunt; **grand teint** *adj inv* colourfast, fastcolour (*épith*); **grand tourisme: voiture de grand tourisme** G.T. saloon car; **le Grand Turc** the Sultan; **les grandes vacances** the summer holidays (*Brit*) *ou* vacation (*US*); (*Univ*) the long vacation; **grand veneur** master of the royal hounds; **grand-vergue** *nf, pl* **grands-vergues** main yard; **la grande vie** the good life; **mener la grande vie** to live in style, live the good life; **grand-voile** *nf, pl* **grands-voiles** mainsail; (*littér*) **le grand voyage** the last great journey (*littér*).

grandelet, -ette*† [gʀɑ̃dlɛ, ɛt] *adj*: **Louise est ~te maintenant** Louise is a big girl now.

grandement [gʀɑ̃dmɑ̃] *adv* **(a)** (*tout à fait*) **se tromper ~** to be greatly mistaken; **avoir ~ raison/tort** to be absolutely right/wrong.

(b) (*largement*) *aider* a great deal. **il a ~ le temps** he easily has time, he has plenty of time *ou* easily enough time; **il y en a ~ assez** there's plenty of it *ou* easily enough (of it); **être ~ logé** to have plenty of room *ou* ample room (in one's house); **nous ne sommes pas ~ logés** we haven't (very) much room; **je lui suis ~ reconnaissant** I'm deeply *ou* extremely grateful to him; **il est ~ temps de partir** it's high time we went.

(c) (*généreusement*) *agir* nobly. **faire les choses ~** to do things lavishly *ou* in grand style.

grandet, -ette* [gʀɑ̃dɛ, ɛt] *adj* = **grandelet***.

grandeur [gʀɑ̃dœʀ] *nf* **(a)** (*dimension*) size. **c'est de la ~ d'un crayon** it's the size of *ou* as big as a pencil; **ils sont de la même ~** they are the same size; **~ nature** life-size; *V* **haut, ordre.**

(b) (*importance*) *[œuvre, sacrifice, amour]* greatness.

(c) (*dignité*) greatness; (*magnanimité*) magnanimity. **faire preuve de ~** to show magnanimity; **la ~ humaine** the greatness of man; **~ d'âme** nobility of soul.

(d) (*gloire*) greatness. **~ et décadence de** rise and fall of; **politique de ~** politics of grandeur.

(e) (*Astron, Math*) magnitude. (*Math*) **~ variable** variable magnitude; (*fig*) **gaffe de première ~** blunder of the first order.

(f) (†: *titre*) **Sa G~ l'évêque de X** (the) Lord Bishop of X; **oui, Votre G~** yes, my Lord.

(g) (*honneurs*) **~s** glory; *V* **folie.**

grandiloquence [gʀɑ̃dilɔkɑ̃s] *nf* grandiloquence, bombast.

grandiloquent, e [gʀɑ̃dilɔkɑ̃, ɑ̃t] *adj* grandiloquent, bombastic.

grandiose [gʀɑ̃djoz] *adj œuvre, spectacle, paysage* imposing, grandiose.

grandir [gʀɑ̃diʀ] (2) **1** *vi* **(a)** *[plante, enfant]* to grow; *[ombre portée]* to grow (bigger). **il a grandi de 10 cm** he has grown 10 cm; **je le trouve grandi** he has grown *ou* he's bigger since I last saw him; **en grandissant tu verras que** as you grow up you'll see that; (*fig*) **il a grandi dans mon estime** he's gone up in my estimation; **enfant grandi trop vite** lanky *ou* gangling child.

(b) *[sentiment, influence, foule]* to increase, grow; *[bruit]* to grow (louder), increase; *[firme]* to grow, expand. **l'obscurité grandissait** (the) darkness thickened; **son pouvoir va grandissant** his power grows ever greater *ou* constantly increases; **~ en sagesse** to grow *ou* increase in wisdom.

2 *vt* **(a)** (*faire paraître grand*) *[microscope]* to magnify. **~ les dangers/difficultés** to exaggerate the dangers/difficulties; **ces chaussures te grandissent** those shoes make you (look) taller; **il se grandit en se mettant sur la pointe des pieds** he made himself taller by standing on tiptoe.

(b) (*rendre prestigieux*) **cette épreuve l'a grandi** this trial has made him grow in stature.

grandissant, e [gʀɑ̃disɑ̃, ɑ̃t] *adj foule, bruit, sentiment* growing. **nombre/pouvoir (sans cesse) ~** (ever-)growing *ou* increasing number/power.

grandissement† [gʀɑ̃dismɑ̃] *nm* (*Opt*) magnification.

grandissime [gʀɑ̃disim] *adj* (*hum: très grand*) tremendous.

grange [gʀɑ̃ʒ] *nf* barn.

granit(e) [gʀanit] *nm* granite.

granité, e [gʀanite] **1** *adj* granitelike. **2** *nm* (*tissu*) (rough) linen; (*glace*) granita (*Italian ice cream*).

graniteux, -euse [gʀanitø, øz] *adj* (*Minér*) granitic.

granitique [gʀanitik] *adj* granite (*épith*), granitic.

granivore [gʀanivɔʀ] **1** *adj* granivorous. **2** *nm* granivore.

granulaire [gʀanylɛʀ] *adj* (*Sci*) granular.

granulation [gʀanylɑsjɔ̃] *nf* **(a)** (*grain*) grainy effect. **~s** granular *ou* grainy surface. **(b)** (*action: Tech*) granulation.

granule [gʀanyl] *nm* granule; (*Pharm*) small pill.

granulé, e [gʀanyle] (*ptp de* **granuler**) **1** *adj surface* granular. **2** *nm* granule.

granuler [gʀanyle] (1) *vt métal, poudre* to granulate.

granuleux, -euse [gʀanylø, øz] *adj* granular.

grape(-)fruit [gʀɛpfʀut] *nm* grapefruit.

graphe [gʀaf] *nm* (*Écon, Math*) graph.

graphie [gʀafi] *nf* (*Ling*) written form.

graphique [gʀafik] **1** *adj* graphic. **2** *nm* (*courbe*) graph.

graphiquement [gʀafikmɑ̃] *adv* graphically.

graphisme [gʀafism(ə)] *nm* **(a)** (*technique*) (*Design*) graphics (*sg*); (*Art*) graphic arts. **(b)** (*style*) *[peintre, dessinateur]* style of drawing. **(c)** (*écriture individuelle*) hand, handwriting; (*alphabet*) script.

graphitage [gʀafitaʒ] *nm* (*Tech*) graphitization.

graphite [gʀafit] *nm* graphite.

graphiter [gʀafite] (1) *vt* to graphitize. **lubrifiant graphité** graphitic lubricant.

graphiteux, -euse [gʀafitø, øz] *adj* graphitic.

graphologie [gʀafɔlɔʒi] *nf* graphology.

graphologique [gʀafɔlɔʒik] *adj* of handwriting.

graphologue [gʀafɔlɔg] *nmf* graphologist.

grappe [gʀap] *nf [fleurs]* cluster. **~ de raisin** bunch of grapes; **en** *ou* **par ~s** in clusters; **~s humaines** clusters of people.

grappillage [gʀapijaʒ] *nm* (*V* **grappiller**) gleaning; fiddling*; picking up; gathering; lifting. **ses ~s se montaient à quelques centaines de francs** his pickings amounted to several hundred francs.

grappiller [gʀapije] (1) **1** *vi* (*après la vendange*) to glean (*in vineyards*); (*faire de petits profits*) to fiddle (a few pounds)*. **arrête de ~, prends la grappe** stop picking (at it) and take the whole bunch; **il a beaucoup grappillé chez d'autres auteurs** he has lifted a lot from other authors.

2 *vt connaissances, nouvelles* to pick up; *grains, fruits* to gather; *idées* to lift. **~ quelques sous** to fiddle a few pounds*.

grappin [gʀapɛ̃] *nm [bateau]* grapnel; *[grue]* grab. **mettre le ~ sur qn*** to grab sb, collar sb*; **mettre le ~ sur qch*** to get one's claws on *ou* into sth*.

gras, grasse [gʀɑ, gʀɑs] **1** *adj* **(a)** *substance, aliment, bouillon* fatty. **fromage ~** full fat cheese; **crème grasse pour la peau** rich moisturizing cream; *V* **chou**[1], **corps** *etc.*

(b) (*gros*) *personne, animal, visage, main* fat; *bébé* podgy; *volaille* plump. **être ~ comme un chanoine, être ~ à lard** to be as round as a barrel; *V* **tuer, vache.**

(c) (*graisseux, huileux*) *mains, cheveux, surface* greasy; *peinture* oily; *pavé, rocher* slimy; *boue, sol* sticky, slimy; *V* **houille.**

(d) (*épais*) *trait, contour* thick; *V* **caractère, crayon, plante**[1].

(e) *toux* loose, phlegmy; *voix, rire* throaty.

(f) (*vulgaire*) *mot, plaisanterie* coarse, crude.

(g) (*abondant*) *pâturage* rich, luxuriant; *récompense* fat* (*épith*). **la paye n'est pas grasse** the pay is rather meagre, it's not much of a salary; **j'ai touché 200 F, ce n'est pas ~*** I earned 200 francs, which is hardly a fortune; **il n'y a pas ~ à manger*** there's not much to eat.

(h) (*loc*) **faire la grasse matinée** to have a lie in *ou* a long lie.

2 *nm* **(a)** (*Culin*) fat; *[baleine]* blubber; (*Théât*) greasepaint. **~-double** tripe; **j'ai les mains couvertes de ~** my hands are covered in grease.

(b) (*partie charnue*) *[jambe, bras]* **le ~ de** the fleshy part of.

3 *adv* **(a) manger ~** to eat fatty foods; (*Rel*) **faire ~** to eat meat.

(b) il tousse ~ he has a loose *ou* phlegmy cough; **parler/rire ~*** to speak/laugh coarsely.

grassement [gʀɑsmɑ̃] *adv* **(a)** *rétribuer* generously, handsomely. (*péj*) **vivre ~** to live off the fat of the land; **c'est ~ payé** it's highly paid, it's well paid. **(b)** *parler, rire* coarsely.

grasseyement [gʀasɛjmɑ̃] *nm* guttural pronunciation.

grasseyer [gʀaseje] (1) *vi* to have a guttural pronunciation; (*Ling*) to use a fricative (Parisian) R.

grassouillet, -ette* [gʀɑsujɛ, ɛt] *adj* podgy, plump.

gratification [gʀatifikɑsjɔ̃] *nf* (*Admin*) bonus. **~ de fin d'année** Christmas box *ou* bonus.

gratifier [gʀatifje] (7) *vt*: **~ qn de** *récompense, avantage,* (*iro*) *amende* to present sb with; *sourire, bonjour* to favour *ou* grace sb with; (*iro*) *punition* to reward sb with (*iro*); **il nous gratifia d'un long sermon sur l'obéissance** he favoured *ou* honoured us with a long sermon on obedience.

gratin [gʀatɛ̃] *nm* **(a)** (*Culin*) (*plat*) cheese(-topped) dish, gratin (*T*); (*croûte*) cheese topping, gratin (*T*). **au ~** au gratin; **~ de pommes de terre** potatoes au gratin; **~ dauphinois** gratin Dauphinois.

(b) (*: *haute société*) **le ~** the upper crust*, the nobs* (*Brit*), the swells* (*US*); **tout le ~ de la ville était à sa réception** all the nobs* (*Brit*) *ou* swells* (*US*) of the town were at his reception.

gratiné, e [gʀatine] (*ptp de* **gratiner**) **1** *adj* **(a)** (*Culin*) au gratin.

(b) (*: *intensif*) *épreuve, amende* (really) stiff*; *aventures, plaisanterie* (really) wild*. **il m'a passé une engueulade ~e** he didn't half give me a telling-off*, he gave me a heck of a telling-off*; **c'est un examen ~** it's a heck of an exam (to get through)*, it's a really stiff exam; **c'est un type ~** (*en mal, en bien*) he's absolutely incredible*.

2 gratinée *nf* onion soup au gratin.

gratiner [gʀatine] (1) **1** *vt* (*Culin*) *pommes de terre* to cook au gratin.

2 *vi* (*attacher*) *[sauce]* to stick. **la sauce a gratiné dans le/au fond du plat** the sauce has stuck to the dish/to the bottom of the dish; **le plat est tout gratiné** there's sauce (*ou* pudding *etc*) stuck all over the dish.

gratis [gʀatis] **1** *adj* free. **2** *adv* free, for nothing.

gratitude [gʀatityd] *nf* gratitude, gratefulness.

grattage [gʀataʒ] *nm* (*V* **gratter**) scratching; scraping; scratching off; scratching out; scraping off.

gratte* [gʀat] *nf* (*petit bénéfice illicite*) pickings. **faire de la ~** to make a bit on the side*.

gratte- [gʀat] *préf V* **gratter.**

grattement [gʀatmɑ̃] *nm* scratching.

gratter [gʀate] (1) **1** *vt* **(a)** *surface* (*avec un ongle, une pointe*) to scratch; (*avec un outil*) to scrape. **gratte-moi le dos** scratch my back for me.

(b) (*enlever*) *tache* to scratch off; *inscription* to scratch out; *boue, papier peint* to scrape off.

(c) (*irriter*) **ce drap me gratte** this sheet is making me itch; **ça (me) gratte** I've got an itch; (*fig*) **vin qui gratte la gorge** wine which catches in one's throat.

(d) (*) **~ quelques francs** to fiddle a few pounds*; **~ (de l'argent) sur la dépense** to scrimp on one's spending; **~ les fonds de tiroir** to raid the piggy bank (*fig*), scrape around to find enough money; **il n'y a pas grand-chose à ~** there's not much to be made on that.

(e) (*arg Sport: dépasser*) to overtake.

2 *vi* **(a)** *[plume]* to scratch. **j'entends quelque chose qui gratte** I can hear something scratching.

(b) *[drap]* (*irriter*) to be scratchy; (*démanger*) to itch, be itchy.

(c) (*: *économiser*) to save.

(d) (*: *travailler*) to slog (away)*.

(e) (*: *écrire*) to scribble.

(f) (†: *frapper*) **~ à la porte** to tap at the door.

(g) (*: *jouer de*) **~ du violon** to scrape (away at) one's violin; **~ de la guitare** to strum (away on) one's guitar.

3 se gratter *vpr* to scratch (o.s.). (*fig*) **tu peux toujours te ~!**‡ you can whistle for it!*

4: gratte-ciel *nm inv* skyscraper; (*Bot*) **gratte-cul** *nm inv* rose hip; **gratte-dos** *nm inv* back-scratcher; (*péj*) **gratte-papier** *nm inv* penpusher (*péj*); **gratte-pieds** *nm inv* shoe-scraper.

grattoir [gʀatwaʀ] *nm* scraper.

grattures [gʀatyʀ] *nfpl* scrapings.

gratuit, e [gʀatɥi, ɥit] *adj* **(a)** (*lit: sans payer*) free. **entrée ~e** admission free; (*frm*) **à titre ~** free of charge. **(b)** (*non-motivé*) *supposition, affirmation* unwarranted; *cruauté, insulte* wanton, gratuitous; *geste* gratuitous, unmotivated. **(c)** (*littér: désintéressé*) *bienveillance* disinterested.

gratuité [gʀatɥite] *nf* **(a)** (*lit: V* **gratuit**) **la ~ de l'éducation/des soins médicaux a permis le progrès** free education/medical care has allowed progress.

(b) (*non-motivation: V* **gratuit**) unwarranted nature; wantonness; gratuitousness; unmotivated nature.

gratuitement [gʀatɥitmɑ̃] *adv* **(a)** (*gratis*) *entrer, participer, soigner* free (of charge). **(b)** (*sans raison*) *détruire* wantonly, gratuitously; *agir* gratuitously, without motivation. **supposer ~ que** to make the unwarranted supposition that.

gravats [gʀavɑ] *nmpl* (*Constr*) rubble.

grave [gʀav] **1** *adj* **(a)** (*posé*) *air, ton, personne* grave, solemn; (*digne*) *assemblée* solemn.

(b) (*important*) *raison, opération* serious; *faute, avertissement* serious, grave. **c'est une ~ question que vous me posez là** that is a serious question you are putting to me.

(c) (*alarmant*) *maladie, nouvelle, situation, danger* grave, serious; *blessure, menace, résultat* serious. **blessé ~** seriously injured man, serious casualty; **l'heure est ~** it is a serious *ou* grave moment; **ne vous en faites pas, ce n'est pas (bien) ~** never mind — there's no harm done *ou* it's not serious.

(d) *note* low; *son, voix* deep, low-pitched.

2 *nm* (*Ling*) grave (accent); (*Mus*) low register. (*Rad*) '**~-aigu**' 'bass-treble'; (*Rad*) **appareil qui vibre dans les ~s** set that vibrates at the bass tones; (*Mus*) **les ~s et les aigus** (the) low and high notes, the low and high registers.

graveleux, -euse [gʀavlø, øz] *adj* **(a)** (*grivois*) smutty. **(b)** *terre* gravelly; *fruit* gritty.

gravelle [gʀavɛl] *nf* (*Méd* ††) gravel††.

gravelure [gʀavlyʀ] *nf* (*rare*) smut (*U*).

gravement [gʀavmɑ̃] *adv* **(a)** *parler, marcher* gravely, solemnly.

(b) (*de manière alarmante*) *blesser, offenser* seriously. **être ~ compromis** to be seriously compromised; **être ~ menacé** to be under a serious threat; **être ~ coupable** to be guilty of a serious offence *ou* crime; **être ~ malade** to be gravely *ou* seriously ill.

graver [gʀave] (1) *vt signe, inscription* (*sur pierre, métal, papier*) to engrave; (*sur bois*) to carve, engrave; (*fig: dans la mémoire*) to engrave, imprint (*dans* on); *médaille, monnaie* to engrave; *disque* to cut. **~ à l'eau-forte** to etch; **faire ~ des cartes de visite** to get some visiting cards printed; (*fig*) **c'est gravé sur son front** it's written all over his face; (*fig*) **c'est gravé dans sa mémoire** it's imprinted *ou* engraved on his memory.

graveur [gʀavœʀ] *nm* (*sur pierre, métal, papier*) engraver; (*sur bois*) (wood) engraver, woodcutter. **~ à l'eau-forte** etcher.

gravide [gʀavid] *adj animal, utérus* gravid. **truie ~** sow in pig.

gravier [gʀavje] *nm* **(a)** (*caillou*) (little) stone, bit of gravel. **(b)** (*Géol, revêtement*) gravel (*U*). **allée de** *ou* **en ~** gravel *ou* gravelled path.

gravillon [gʀavijɔ̃] *nm* **(a)** (*petit caillou*) bit of grit *ou* gravel. **(b)** (*revêtement*) *[route]* (loose) chippings; *[jardin etc]* (fine) gravel (*U*). **du ~, des ~s** loose chippings.

gravillonner [gʀavijɔne] (1) *vt* to gravel. **~ une route** to gravel a road, put loose chippings on a road.

gravimétrie [gʀavimetʀi] *nf* gravimetry.

gravir [gʀaviʀ] (2) *vt montagne* to climb (up). **~ péniblement une côte** to struggle up a slope; **~ les échelons de la hiérarchie** to climb the rungs of the hierarchical ladder.

gravitation [gʀavitɑsjɔ̃] *nf* gravitation.

gravité [gʀavite] *nf* **(a)** (*U: V* **grave**) gravity, graveness; solemnity; seriousness. **c'est un accident sans ~** it wasn't a serious accident. **(b)** (*Phys, Rail*) gravity; *V* **centre, force.**

graviter [gʀavite] (1) *vi* **(a)** (*tourner*) *[astre]* to revolve (*autour de* round, about); *[politicien]* to hover, revolve (*autour de* round). **il gravite dans les milieux diplomatiques** he moves in diplomatic circles; **pays satellite qui gravite dans l'orbite d'une grande puissance** country that is the satellite of a major power; **cette planète gravite autour du soleil** this planet revolves around *ou* orbits the sun.

(b) (*tendre vers*) *[astre]* **~ vers** to gravitate towards.

gravois† [gʀavwa] *nmpl* = **gravats.**

gravure [gʀavyʀ] **1** *nf* **(a)** (*V* **graver**) engraving; carving; imprinting; cutting.

(b) (*reproduction*) (*dans une revue*) plate; (*au mur*) print.

2: gravure sur bois (*technique*) woodcutting, wood engraving; (*dessin*) woodcut, wood engraving; **gravure en creux** intaglio engraving; **gravure sur cuivre** copperplate (engraving); **gravure directe** hand-cutting; **gravure à l'eau-forte** etching; **gravure de mode** fashion plate.

gré [gʀe] *nm* **(a)** *[personnes]* **à mon/votre ~** (*goût*) to my/your liking *ou* taste; (*désir*) as I/you like *ou* please *ou* wish; (*choix*) as I/you like *ou* prefer *ou* please; (*rare: avis*) **c'est trop moderne, à mon ~** it's too modern for my liking *ou* to my mind; **c'est à votre ~?** is it to your liking? *ou* taste?; **agir** *ou* **(en) faire à son ~** to do as one likes *ou* pleases *ou* wishes; **venez à votre ~ ce soir ou demain** come tonight or tomorrow, as you like *ou* prefer *ou* please; **on a fait pour le mieux, au ~ des uns et des autres** we did our best to take everyone's wishes into account; **contre le ~ de qn** against sb's will.

(b) (*loc*) **de ~ à ~** by mutual agreement; **il le fera de ~ ou de force** he'll do it whether he likes it or not, he'll do it willy-nilly; **de son plein ~** of one's own free will, of one's own accord; **de bon ~** willingly; **de mauvais ~** reluctantly, grudgingly; *V* **bon**[1], **savoir.**

(c) *[choses]* **au ~ de: flottant au ~ de l'eau** drifting wherever the water carries (*ou* carried) it, drifting (along) on *ou* with the current; **volant au ~ du vent** *chevelure* flying in the wind; *plume, feuille* carried along by the wind; *planeur* gliding wherever the wind carries (*ou* carried) it; **au ~ des événements** *décider, agir* according to how *ou* the way things go; **balloté au ~ des événements** tossed about by events; **il décorait sa chambre au ~ de sa fantaisie** he decorated his room as the fancy took him.

grèbe [gʀɛb] *nm* grebe.

grec, grecque [gʀɛk] **1** *adj île, personne, langue* Greek; *habit, architecture, vase* Grecian, Greek; *profil, traits* Grecian. **2** *nm* (*Ling*) Greek. **3** *nm,f*: **G~(que)** Greek. **4 grecque** *nf* (*décoration*) (Greek) fret.

Grèce [gʀɛs] *nf* Greece.

gréco-latin, e [gʀekɔlatɛ̃, in] *adj* Gr(a)eco-Latin.

gréco-romain, e [gʀekɔʀɔmɛ̃, ɛn] *adj* Gr(a)eco-Roman.

gredin† [gʀədɛ̃] *nm* (*coquin*) knave††, blackguard††.

gredinerie†† [gʀədinʀi] *nf* (*caractère*) knavishness††; (*action*) knavery††.

gréement [gʀemɑ̃] *nm* (*Naut*) rigging.

gréer [gʀee] (1) *vt* (*Naut*) to rig.

greffage [gʀɛfaʒ] *nm* (*Bot*) grafting.

greffe[1] [gʀɛf] *nf* **(a)** (*U: V* **greffer**) transplanting; grafting. **(b)** (*opération*) (*Méd*) *[organe]* transplant; *[tissu]* graft; (*Bot*) graft. **une ~ du cœur/rein** a heart/kidney transplant.

greffe[2] [gʀɛf] *nm* Clerk's Office (*of courts*).

greffer [gʀefe] (1) *vt* (*Méd*) *organe* to transplant; *tissu* to graft; (*Bot*) to graft. **là-dessus se sont greffées d'autres difficultés** further difficulties have cropped up (in connection with it).

greffier [gʀefje] *nm* clerk (of the court).

greffon [gʀɛfɔ̃] *nm* (*V* **greffer**) transplant, transplanted organ; graft.

grégaire [gʀegɛʀ] *adj* gregarious.

grégarisme [gʀegaʀism(ə)] *nm* gregariousness.

grège [gʀɛʒ] *adj V* **soie**[1].

grégeois [gʀeʒwa] *adj m V* **feu**[1].
Grégoire [gʀegwaʀ] *nm* Gregory.
grégorien, -ienne [gʀegɔʀjɛ̃, jɛn] **1** *adj* Gregorian. **2** *nm*: **(chant)** ~ Gregorian chant, plainsong.
grêle[1] [gʀɛl] *adj jambes, silhouette* spindly; *personne* lanky; *son* shrill; *V* **intestin**[1].
grêle[2] [gʀɛl] *nf* hail. **averse de** ~ hail storm; *(fig)* ~ **de coups/de pierres** hail *ou* shower of blows/stones; *V* **canon**[1].
grêlé, e [gʀele] *(ptp de* **grêler***) adj* pockmarked.
grêler [gʀele] (1) **1** *vb impers*: **il grèle** it is hailing. **2** *vt*: **la tempête a grêlé les vignes** the storm has left the vines damaged by (the) hail; **région qui a été grêlée** region where crops have been damaged by hail.
grêlon [gʀɛlɔ̃] *nm* hailstone.
grelot [gʀəlo] *nm* (little spherical) bell.
grelottement [gʀəlɔtmɑ̃] *nm (V* **grelotter***)* shivering; jingling.
grelotter [gʀəlɔte] (1) *vi* **(a)** *(trembler)* to shiver *(de* with). ~ **de fièvre** to be shivery with fever, shiver with fever. **(b)** *(tinter)* to jingle.
greluche: [gʀəlyʃ] *nf* bird: *(Brit)*, chick: *(US)*.
grenade [gʀənad] *nf* **(a)** *(Bot)* pomegranate. **(b)** *(explosif)* grenade. ~ **à fusil/main** rifle/hand grenade; ~ **lacrymogène/fumigène** teargas/smoke grenade; ~ **sous-marine** depth charge. **(c)** *(insigne)* badge *(on soldier's uniform etc)*.
Grenade [gʀənad] *n* Granada.
grenadier [gʀənadje] *nm* **(a)** *(Bot)* pomegranate tree. **(b)** *(Mil)* grenadier.
grenadine [gʀənadin] *nf* grenadine.
grenaille [gʀənɑj] *nf*: **de la** ~ *(projectiles)* shot; *(pour poules)* middlings; ~ **de plomb** lead shot; ~ **de fer** iron filings.
grenaison [gʀənɛzɔ̃] *nf* seeding.
grenat [gʀəna] **1** *nm* garnet. **2** *adj inv* dark red, garnet-coloured.
grené, e [gʀəne] *(ptp de* **grener***) adj cuir, peau* grainy; *dessin* stippled.
greneler [gʀənle] (4) *vt (Tech) cuir, papier* to grain.
grener [gʀəne] (5) **1** *vt (Tech) sel, sucre* to granulate, grain. **2** *vi (Agr) [plante]* to seed.
grenier [gʀənje] *nm* attic, garret; *(pour conserver le grain etc)* loft. ~ **à blé** *(lit)* corn loft; *(fig)* granary; ~ **à foin** hayloft.
grenouillage [gʀənujaʒ] *nm (Pol péj)* jiggery-pokery *(péj)*.
grenouille [gʀənuj] *nf* frog. *(péj)* ~ **de bénitier** Holy Joe* *(Brit péj)*; **c'est une vraie** ~ **de bénitier** he *ou* she is very pi* *(Brit péj) ou* a proper Holy Joe* *(Brit péj)*; *V* **homme.**
grenu, e [gʀəny] *adj (épith)* grainy; *cuir, papier* grained; *(Géol) roche* granular.
grenure [gʀənyʀ] *nf* graining.
grès [gʀɛ] *nm* **(a)** *(Géol)* sandstone. **(b)** *(Poterie)* stoneware. **cruche/pot de** ~ stoneware pitcher/pot.
gréseux, -euse [gʀezø, øz] *adj* sandstone *(épith)*.
grésil [gʀezi(l)] *nm (Mét)* (fine) hail.
grésillement [gʀezijmɑ̃] *nm (V* **grésiller**[1]*)* sizzling, sputtering; crackling.
grésiller[1] [gʀezije] (1) *vi (crépiter) [huile, friture]* to sizzle, sputter; *[poste de radio, téléphone]* to crackle.
grésiller[2] [gʀezije] (1) *vb impers*: **il grésille** fine hail is falling, it's hailing.
gressin [gʀesɛ̃] *nm* bread stick.
grève [gʀɛv] **1** *nf* **(a)** *(arrêt du travail)* strike. **se mettre en** ~ to go on strike, strike; **être en** ~, **faire** ~ to be on strike, be striking; **entreprendre une** ~ to take strike action, go on strike; *V* **briseur, piquet.**
(b) *(rivage) [mer]* shore, strand *(littér)*; *[rivière]* bank, strand *(littér)*.
2: grève bouchon disruptive strike *(leading to lay-offs etc)*; **grève de la faim** hunger strike; **grève perlée** ≃ go-slow; **grève sauvage** wildcat strike; **grève de solidarité** sympathy strike; **grève surprise** lightning strike; **grève sur le tas** sit-down strike; **grève tournante** strike by rota; **grève du zèle** ≃ work-to-rule.
grever [gʀəve] (5) *vt budget* to put a strain on; *économie, pays* to burden. **la hausse des prix grève sérieusement le budget des ménagères** the rise in prices puts a serious strain on the housewife's budget; **être grevé d'impôts** to be weighed down with *ou* crippled by taxes; **une maison grevée d'hypothèques** a house mortgaged down to the last brick.
gréviste [gʀevist(ə)] *nmf* striker. **les employés** ~**s** the striking employees.
gribouillage [gʀibujaʒ] *nm (écriture)* scrawl *(U)*, scribble; *(dessin)* doodle, doodling *(U)*.
gribouille [gʀibuj] *nm* short-sighted idiot *(fig)*, rash fool.
gribouiller [gʀibuje] (1) **1** *vt (écrire)* to scribble, scrawl; *(dessiner)* to scrawl. **2** *vi (dessiner)* to doodle.
gribouilleur, -euse [gʀibujœʀ, øz] *nm,f (écrivain)* scribbler.
gribouillis [gʀibuji] *nm* = **gribouillage.**
grièche [gʀijɛʃ] *adj V* **pie-grièche.**
grief [gʀijɛf] *nm* grievance. **faire** ~ **à qn de qch** to hold sth against sb; **ils me font** ~ **d'être parti** they reproach me *ou* they hold it against me for having left.
grièvement [gʀijɛvmɑ̃] *adv*: ~ **blessé** (very) seriously injured.
griffe [gʀif] *nf* **(a)** *(Zool) [mammifère, oiseau]* claw. **le chat fait ses** ~**s** the cat is sharpening its claws; *(lit, fig)* **sortir** *ou* **montrer/rentrer ses** ~**s** to show/draw in one's claws; *(fig)* **tomber sous la** ~**/arracher qn des** ~**s d'un ennemi** to fall into/snatch sb from the clutches of an enemy; *(fig)* **les** ~**s de la mort** the jaws of death; *V* **coup.**
(b) *(marque) [couturier]* maker's label *(inside garment)*; *(signature) [couturier]* signature; *[fonctionnaire]* signature stamp; *(fig: empreinte) [auteur, peintre]* stamp *(fig)*. **l'employé a mis sa** ~ **sur le document** the clerk stamped his signature on the document.
(c) *(Bijouterie)* claw.
(d) *(Bot)* tendril.
griffer [gʀife] (1) *vt* **(a)** *[chat]* to scratch; *(avec force)* to claw; *[ronces]* to scratch. **attention, il griffe!** be careful — he scratches!; **dans sa rage, elle lui griffa le visage** in her rage she clawed *ou* scratched his face.
(b) *(Haute Couture) chaussures* to put one's name to. **un manteau griffé** a coat with a famous name *ou* label.
griffon [gʀifɔ̃] *nm (chien)* griffon; *(vautour)* griffon vulture; *(Myth)* griffin.
griffonnage [gʀifɔnaʒ] *nm (écriture)* scribble; *(dessin)* hasty sketch.
griffonner [gʀifɔne] (1) **1** *vt (écrire)* to scribble, jot down; *(dessiner)* to sketch hastily. **2** *vi (écrire)* to scribble; *(dessiner)* to sketch hastily.
griffu, e [gʀify] *adj (lit, péj)* **pattes** *ou* **mains** ~**es** claws.
griffure [gʀifyʀ] *nf* scratch, claw mark.
grignotage [gʀiɲɔtaʒ] *nm [salaires, espaces verts, majorité]* (gradual) erosion, eroding.
grignotement [gʀiɲɔtmɑ̃] *nm [souris]* nibbling, gnawing.
grignoter [gʀiɲɔte] (1) **1** *vt* **(a)** *[personne]* to nibble (at); *[souris]* to nibble (at), gnaw (at).
(b) *(fig) (réduire) salaires, espaces verts, libertés* to eat away (at), erode gradually; *(obtenir) avantage, droits* to win gradually. ~ **du terrain** to gradually gain ground; **il a grignoté son adversaire*** he gradually made up *ou* gained ground on his opponent.
2 *vi (manger peu)* to nibble (at one's food), pick at one's food.
grigou* [gʀigu] *nm (avare)* penny-pincher*, skinflint.
gri-gri [gʀigʀi] *nm* = **gris-gris.**
gril [gʀi(l)] *nm (Culin)* steak pan, grill pan. *(fig)* **être sur le** ~* to be on tenterhooks, be like a cat on hot bricks.
grillade [gʀijad] *nf (viande)* grill.
grillage[1] [gʀijaʒ] *nm (action: V* **griller**[1]*)* toasting; grilling; roasting; singeing.
grillage[2] [gʀijaʒ] *nm (treillis métallique) (gén)* wire netting *(U)*; *(très fin)* wire mesh *(U)*; *[clôture]* wire fencing *(U)*.
grillager [gʀijaʒe] (3) *vt (V* **grillage**[2]*)* to put wire netting on; to put wire mesh on; to put wire fencing on. **à travers la fenêtre grillagée on voyait le jardin** through the wire mesh covering the window we could see the garden; **on va** ~ **le jardin** we're going to put wire fencing around the garden.
grille [gʀij] *nf* **(a)** *(clôture)* railings; *(portail)* (metal) gate.
(b) *(claire-voie) [cellule, fenêtre]* bars; *[comptoir, parloir]* grille; *[château-fort]* portcullis; *[égout, trou]* (metal) grate, (metal) grating; *[radiateur de voiture]* grille, grid; *[poêle à charbon]* grate.
(c) *(répartition) [salaires, tarifs]* scale; *[programmes de radio]* schedule; *[horaires]* grid, schedule.
(d) *(codage)* (cipher *ou* code) grid. ~ **de mots croisés** crossword puzzle (grid).
(e) *(Élec)* grid.
grille- [gʀij] *préf V* **griller**[1].
grillé, e [gʀije] *(ptp de* **griller***) adj (arg Crime)* **il est** ~ his cover's been blown *(arg)*.
griller[1] [gʀije] (1) **1** *vt* **(a)** *(Culin: aussi* **faire** ~*) pain, amandes* to toast; *poisson, viande* to grill; *café, châtaignes* to roast.
(b) *(brûler) visage, corps* to burn. **se** ~ **les pieds devant le feu** to toast one's feet in front of the fire; **se** ~ **au soleil** to roast in the sun.
(c) *[chaleur]* to scorch. *[froid]* ~ **les bourgeons/plantes** to make the buds/plants shrivel up.
(d) *(mettre hors d'usage) fusible, lampe (court-circuit)* to blow; *(trop de courant)* to burn out; *moteur* to burn out.
(e) *(*loc)* ~ **une cigarette** to have a smoke*; ~ **un feu rouge** to jump the lights*; ~ **une étape** to cut out a stop; ~ **qn à l'arrivée** to pip sb at the post* *(Brit)*.
(f) *(Tech) minerai* to roast; *coton* to singe.
2 *vi* **(a)** *(Culin)* **faire** ~ *pain* to toast; *viande* to grill; *café* to roast; **on a mis les steaks à** ~ we've put the steaks on to grill *ou* on the grill.
(b) *(fig)* ~ **(d'impatience** *ou* **d'envie) de faire** to be itching to do.
(c) *(*: brûler)* **on grille ici!** we're *ou* it's roasting *ou* boiling in here!*; **ils ont grillé dans l'incendie** they were roasted in the fire.
3: grille-pain *nm inv* toaster.
griller[2] [gʀije] (1) *vt fenêtre, porte* to put bars on. **fenêtre grillée** barred window.
grilloir [gʀijwaʀ] *nm* grill.
grillon [gʀijɔ̃] *nm* cricket.
grimaçant, e [gʀimasɑ̃, ɑ̃t] *adj visage, bouche (de douleur, de colère etc)* twisted; *(sourire figé)* grinning unpleasantly.
grimace [gʀimas] *nf* **(a)** *(de douleur etc)* grimace; *(pour faire rire, effrayer)* grimace, (funny) face. **l'enfant me fit une** ~ the child made a face at me; **s'amuser à faire des** ~**s** to play at making *ou* pulling (funny) faces *ou* at making grimaces; **il eut** *ou* **fit une** ~ **de dégoût/de douleur** he grimaced with disgust/pain, his face twisted with disgust/pain; **avec une** ~ **de dégoût/de douleur** with a disgusted/pained expression; **il eut** *ou* **fit une** ~ he pulled a wry face, he grimaced; **il fit la** ~ **quand il connut la décision** he pulled a long face when he learned of the decision; *V* **apprendre, soupe.**
(b) *(hypocrisies)* ~**s** hypocritical façade; **toutes leurs** ~**s me dégoûtent** I find their hypocritical façade quite sickening.
(c) *(pli de vêtement)* pucker.
grimacer [gʀimase] (3) **1** *vi* **(a)** *(par contorsion)* ~ **(de douleur)** to grimace with pain; ~ **(de dégoût)** to pull a wry face (in dis-

gust); ~ **(sous l'effort)** to grimace *ou* screw one's face up (with the effort); **le soleil le faisait ~** the sun made him screw his face up; **à l'annonce de la nouvelle il grimaça** he pulled a wry face *ou* he grimaced when he heard the news.

(b) (*par sourire figé*) *[personne]* to grin unpleasantly; *[portrait]* to wear a fixed grin.

(c) (*faire des plis*) to pucker.

2 *vt* (*littér*) ~ **un sourire** to pull a sardonic smile; **il grimaça des remerciements** he expressed his thanks with a sardonic smile.

grimacier, -ière [gʀimasje, jɛʀ] *adj* (*affecté*) affected; (*hypocrite*) hypocritical. **cet enfant est (un) ~** this child pulls *ou* makes such faces, this child is always pulling *ou* making faces.

grimage [gʀimaʒ] *nm* (*Théât*) (*action*) making up; (*résultat*) (stage) make-up.

grimer [gʀime] (1) **1** *vt* (*Théât: maquiller*) to make up. **on l'a grimé en vieille dame** he was made up as an old lady. **2 se grimer** *vpr* to make up.

grimoire [gʀimwaʀ] *nm* **(a)** (*écrit inintelligible*) piece of mumbo jumbo; (*illisible*) illegible scrawl (*U*), unreadable scribble. **(b)** (*livre de magie*) **un (vieux) ~** (magician's) book of magic spells.

grimpant, e [gʀɛ̃pɑ̃, ɑ̃t] *adj*: **plante ~e** climbing plant, climber; **rosier ~** climbing rose.

grimpée [gʀɛ̃pe] *nf* (*montée*) (steep) climb.

grimper [gʀɛ̃pe] (1) **1** *vi* **(a)** *[personne, animal]* to climb (up); (*avec difficulté*) to clamber up. **~ aux arbres** to climb trees; **~ à l'échelle** to climb (up) the ladder; **~ sur *ou* dans un arbre** to climb onto *ou* into a tree; **~ le long de la gouttière** to climb up the drain pipe; **grimpé sur la table/le toit** having climbed *ou* clambered onto the table/roof.

(b) *[route, plante]* to climb. **ça grimpe dur!** it's a hard *ou* stiff *ou* steep climb!

(c) (*) *[fièvre]* to soar (up); *[prix]* to rocket, soar (up).

2 *vt montagne, côte* to climb (up), go up. **~ l'escalier** to climb (up) the stairs; **~ un étage** to climb up a *ou* one floor.

3 *nm* (*Athlétisme*) (rope-)climbing (*U*).

grimpette* [gʀɛ̃pɛt] *nf* (steep little) climb.

grimpeur, -euse [gʀɛ̃pœʀ, øz] **1** *adj, nm*: **(oiseaux) ~s** scansores (*T*). **2** *nm,f* (*varappeur*) climber; (*cycliste*) hill-specialist.

grinçant, e [gʀɛ̃sɑ̃, ɑ̃t] *adj ironie* grating; *ton, musique* grating, jarring.

grincement [gʀɛ̃smɑ̃] *nm* (*V* **grincer**) grating; creaking; scratching. (*fig*) **il ne l'a pas accepté sans ~s de dents** he accepted it only with much gnashing of teeth; *V* **pleur.**

grincer [gʀɛ̃se] (3) *vi [objet métallique]* to grate; *[plancher]* to creak; *[plume]* to scratch. **~ des dents (de colère)** to grind *ou* gnash one's teeth (in anger); (*fig*) **ce bruit vous fait ~ des dents** this noise sets your teeth on edge.

grincheux, -euse [gʀɛ̃ʃø, øz] **1** *adj* (*acariâtre*) grumpy. **humeur ~euse** grumpiness. **2** *nm,f* misery.

gringalet [gʀɛ̃galɛ] **1** *adj m* (*péj: chétif*) puny. **2** *nm* (*péj*) **(petit) ~** puny little chap (*Brit*), (little) runt.

griotte [gʀijɔt] *nf* Morello cherry.

grippage [gʀipaʒ] *nm* (*Tech: V* **gripper**) jamming; seizing up.

grippal, e, *mpl* **-aux** [gʀipal, o] *adj* flu-like, influenzal (*T*).

grippe [gʀip] *nf* flu, influenza (*T*). **avoir la ~** to have (the) flu, have influenza; **il a une petite ~** he's got a slight touch of flu; **~ intestinale** gastric flu; (*fig*) **prendre qn/qch en ~** to take a sudden dislike to sb/sth.

grippé, e [gʀipe] (*ptp de* **gripper**) *adj*: **il est ~** he's got (the) flu; **rentrer ~** to go home with (the) flu; **les ~s** people with *ou* suffering from flu.

grippement [gʀipmɑ̃] *nm* = **grippage.**

gripper [gʀipe] (1) *vti* (*Tech*) to jam. **le moteur a *ou* s'est grippé** the engine has seized up.

grippe-sou*, *pl* **grippe-sous** [gʀipsu] *nm* (*avare*) penny-pincher*, skinflint.

gris, e [gʀi, gʀiz] **1** *adj* **(a)** *couleur, temps* grey (*Brit*), gray (*US*). **~ acier/ardoise/fer/perle/souris** steel/slate/iron/pearl/squirrel grey; **~-bleu/-vert** blue-/green-grey; **cheval ~ pommelé** dapple-grey horse; **aux cheveux ~** grey-haired; **il fait ~** it's a grey *ou* dull day; *V* **ambre, éminence, matière** *etc.*

(b) (*morne*) *vie* colourless, dull; *pensées* grey.

(c) (*éméché*) tipsy*.

(d) faire ~e mine à qn to give sb a cool reception; **faire ~e mine** to look rather surly *ou* grumpy.

2 *nm* **(a)** (*couleur*) grey.

(b) (*tabac*) shag.

(c) (*Équitation*) grey (horse).

grisaille [gʀizɑj] *nf* **(a)** *[vie]* colourlessness, dullness; *[ciel, temps, paysage]* greyness. **(b)** (*Art*) grisaille. **peindre qch en ~** to paint sth in grisaille.

grisant, e [gʀizɑ̃, ɑ̃t] *adj* (*stimulant*) exhilarating; (*enivrant*) intoxicating.

grisâtre [gʀizɑtʀ(ə)] *adj* greyish.

grisbi [gʀizbi] *nm* (*arg Crime*) dough‡, lolly‡ (*Brit*), loot‡.

grisé [gʀize] *nm* grey tint.

griser [gʀize] (1) **1** *vt [alcool]* to make tipsy*; (*fig*) *[air, vitesse, parfum]* to intoxicate. **ce vin l'avait grisé** the wine had gone to his head *ou* made him tipsy*; **l'air de la montagne grise** the mountain air goes to your head (like wine); **se laisser ~ par le succès/des promesses** to let success/promises go to one's head; **se laisser ~ par l'ambition** to be carried away by ambition.

2 se griser *vpr [buveur]* to get tipsy* (*avec, de* on). **se ~ de** *air, vitesse* to get drunk on; *émotion, paroles* to allow o.s. to be intoxicated by *ou* carried away by.

griserie [gʀizʀi] *nf* intoxication.

grisette [gʀizɛt] *nf* (*Hist*) grisette.

gris-gris [gʀigʀi] *nm [indigène]* grigri; (*gén*) charm.

grison†† [gʀizɔ̃] *nm* ass.

grisonnant, e [gʀizɔnɑ̃, ɑ̃t] *adj* greying (*attrib*). **il avait les tempes ~es** he was greying *ou* going grey round *ou* at the temples.

grisonnement [gʀizɔnmɑ̃] *nm* greying.

grisonner [gʀizɔne] (1) *vi* to be greying, be going grey.

grisou [gʀizu] *nm* firedamp; *V* **coup.**

grive [gʀiv] *nf* (*Orn*) thrush; *V* **faute.**

grivèlerie [gʀivɛlʀi] *nf* (*Jur*) *offence of ordering food or drink in a restaurant and being unable to pay for it.*

grivois, e [gʀivwa, waz] *adj* saucy.

grivoiserie [gʀivwazʀi] *nf* (*mot*) saucy expression; (*attitude*) sauciness; (*histoire*) saucy story.

grizzli, grizzly [gʀizli] *nm* grizzly bear.

grœnendael [gʀɔ(n)ɛndal] *nm* Groenendael (sheepdog).

Groënland [gʀɔɛnlɑ̃d] *nm* Greenland.

groënlandais, e [gʀɔɛnlɑ̃dɛ, ɛz] **1** *adj* of *ou* from Greenland, Greenland (*épith*). **2** *nm,f*: **G~(e)** Greenlander.

grog [gʀɔg] *nm* grog.

groggy* [gʀɔgi] *adj inv* dazed; (*Boxe*) groggy.

grognard [gʀɔɲaʀ] *nm* (*Hist*) *soldier of the old guard of Napoleon I.*

grognement [gʀɔɲmɑ̃] *nm [personne]* growl, grunt; *[cochon]* grunting (*U*), grunt; *[sanglier]* snorting (*U*), snort; *[ours, chien]* growling (*U*), growl.

grogner [gʀɔɲe] (1) **1** *vi [personne]* to grumble, moan*; *[cochon]* to grunt, snort; *[sanglier]* to snort; *[ours, chien]* to growl. **2** *vt insultes* to growl (out), grunt (out).

grognon [gʀɔɲɔ̃] *adj air, expression, vieillard* grumpy, gruff (*épith*); *attitude* surly; *enfant* grouchy. **elle est ~, quelle ~!** what a grumbler! *ou* moaner!*

groin [gʀwɛ̃] *nm [animal]* snout; (*péj*) *[personne]* ugly *ou* hideous face.

grol(l)e‡ [gʀɔl] *nf* shoe.

grommeler [gʀɔmle] (4) **1** *vi [personne]* to mutter (to o.s.), grumble to o.s.; *[sanglier]* to snort. **2** *vt insultes* to mutter.

grommellement [gʀɔmɛlmɑ̃] *nm* muttering, indistinct grumbling.

grondement [gʀɔ̃dmɑ̃] *nm* (*V* **gronder**) rumbling; growling; (angry) muttering. **le ~ de la colère/de l'émeute** the rumbling of mounting anger/of the threatening riot; **le train passa devant nous dans un ~ de tonnerre** the train thundered past us.

gronder [gʀɔ̃de] (1) **1** *vt enfant* to scold. **il faut que je vous gronde* d'avoir fait ce cadeau** you're very naughty to have bought this present, I'll really have to tell you off* for buying this present.

2 *vi* **(a)** *[canon, train, orage, torrent]* to rumble; *[chien]* to growl; *[foule]* to mutter (angrily).

(b) (*fig*) *[colère, émeute]* to be brewing (up).

(c) (*littér: grommeler*) to mutter.

gronderie [gʀɔ̃dʀi] *nf* scolding.

grondeur, -euse [gʀɔ̃dœʀ, øz] *adj ton, humeur, personne* grumbling; *vent, torrent* rumbling. **d'une voix ~euse** in a grumbling voice.

grondin [gʀɔ̃dɛ̃] *nm* gurnard.

groom [gʀum] *nm* bellboy.

gros, grosse[1] [gʀo, gʀos] **1** *adj* **(a)** (*dimension*) (*gén*) big, large; *peau, lèvres, corde* thick; *chaussures* big, heavy; *personne, ventre, bébé* fat, big; *pull, manteau* thick, heavy. **le ~ bout** the thick end; **il pleut à grosses gouttes** heavy *ou* great drops of rain are falling; **c'est ~ comme une tête d'épingle/mon petit doigt** it's the size of *ou* it's no bigger than a pinhead/my little finger.

(b) (*important*) *travail* big; *problème, ennui, erreur* serious, great, big; *somme* large, substantial; *firme* big, large; *soulagement, progrès* great; *dégâts* extensive, serious; (*violent*) *rhume, averse* heavy; *fièvre* high. **une grosse affaire** a large business, a big concern; **les grosses chaleurs** the height of summer, the hot season; **un ~ mensonge** a terrible lie, a whopper*; (*fig*) **c'est un ~ morceau*** (*travail*) it's a big job; (*obstacle*) it's a big hurdle (to clear) *ou* a big obstacle (to get over); **il a un ~ appétit** he has a big appetite; **la grosse industrie** heavy industry.

(c) (*houleux*) *mer* heavy. (*gonflé*) **la rivière est grosse** the river is swollen.

(d) (*sonore*) *voix* booming (*épith*); *soupir* deep, big. **~ rire** guffaw.

(e) (*riche et important*) big. **un ~ industriel/banquier** a big industrialist/banker.

(f) (*intensif*) **un ~ buveur** a heavy drinker; **un ~ mangeur** a big eater; **un ~ kilo/quart d'heure** a good kilo/quarter of an hour; **tu es un ~ fainéant/nigaud*** you're a big *ou* great lazybones/silly*.

(g) (*rude*) *drap, laine, vêtement* coarse; *traits du visage* thick, heavy. **le ~ travail, les ~ travaux** the heavy work; **son ~ bon sens est réconfortant** his down-to-earth common sense *ou* plain common sense is a comfort; **il aime la grosse plaisanterie** he likes obvious *ou* unsubtle *ou* inane jokes; **oser nous dire cela, c'est vraiment un peu ~** it's a bit thick* *ou* he's really pushing his luck*, daring to say that to us; **une grosse vérité** an obvious truth.

(h) ~ de: avoir les yeux ~ de larmes to have eyes filled *ou* brimming with tears; **cœur ~ de chagrin** heart heavy with sorrow; **regard ~ de menaces** threatening look, look charged with threats; **l'incident est ~ de conséquences** the incident is loaded with consequences.

(i) (†: *enceinte*) pregnant. **grosse de 6 mois** 6 months pregnant.

(j) (*loc*) **jouer ~ jeu** to play for big *ou* high stakes; **avoir le**

cœur ~ to have a heavy heart; **le chat fait le ~ dos** the cat is arching its back; **faire les ~ yeux (à un enfant)** to glower (at a child); **faire la grosse voix*** to speak gruffly *ou* sternly; (*fig*) **avoir une grosse tête:** to feel thick-headed; **faire une grosse tête à qn:** to bash sb up*, smash sb's face in:; **un mensonge ~ comme une maison** a blatant lie, a lie that sticks out like a sore thumb; (*péj*) **c'est une histoire de ~ sous** there's big money involved; **je la voyais venir, avec ses ~ sabots*** you could tell what she was getting at a mile off*, it was pretty obvious what her little game was*; **il me disait des 'Monsieur' ~ comme le bras** he was falling over himself to be polite to me and kept addressing me as 'sir' *ou* kept calling me 'sir' (at two second intervals).

2 *nm* **(a)** (*personne*) (*corpulent*) fat man; (*riche*) rich man. **un petit ~*** a fat little man *ou* bloke* (*Brit*) *ou* guy*; **mon ~*** old man*, old boy*; (*péj*) **un ~ plein de soupe:** a big fat lump: (*péj*); **les ~** the big bugs*, the big shots*.

(b) (*principal*) **le ~ de: le ~ du travail est fait** the bulk of *ou* the main part of the work is done; **le ~ de l'armée/de l'assistance** the main body of the army/the audience; **le ~ de l'orage est passé** the worst of the storm is past; **faites le plus ~ d'abord** do the main things *ou* the essentials first; **une évaluation en ~** a rough *ou* broad estimate; **dites-moi, en ~, ce qui s'est passé** tell me roughly *ou* broadly what happened.

(c) (*milieu*) **au ~ de l'hiver** in the depth of winter; **au ~ de l'été/de la saison** at the height of summer/of the season.

(d) (*Comm*) **le (commerce de) ~** the wholesale business; **il fait le ~ et le détail** he deals in *ou* trades in both wholesale and retail; **maison/prix de ~** wholesale firm/prices; **papetier en ~** wholesale stationer; **acheter/vendre en ~** to buy/sell wholesale; *V* **demi-, marchand.**

3 grosse *nf* (*personne*) fat woman. **ma grosse*** old girl*, old thing*; (*péj*) **c'est une bonne grosse:** she's a good-natured lump of a girl*; *V aussi* **grosse**².

4 *adv*: **écrire ~** to write big, write in large letters; **c'est écrit en ~** it's written in big *ou* large letters; **il risque ~** he's risking a lot *ou* a great deal; **ça peut nous coûter ~** it could cost us a lot *ou* a great deal; **je donnerais ~ pour ...** I'd give a lot *ou* a great deal to ...; **il y a ~ à parier que ...** it's a safe bet that ...; **en avoir ~ sur le cœur** *ou* **sur la patate:** to be upset *ou* peeved*.

5: (*Orn*) **gros-bec** *nm, pl* **gros-becs** hawfinch; **gros bétail** cattle; **gros bonnet*** bigwig*, big shot*; (*Mus*) **grosse caisse** (big *ou* bass) drum; **grosse cavalerie*** heavy stuff*; **gros gibier** big game; (*Can*) **grosse-gorge:** *nf* goitre; (*Tex*) **gros-grain** *nm, pl* **gros-grains** grosgrain; **gros intestin** large intestine; **Gros-jean*** *nm*: **il s'est retrouvé Gros-jean comme devant** he found himself back at square one (*Brit*); **grosse légume* = gros bonnet***; (*lit, fig*) **gros lot** jackpot; **gros mot** vulgarity, coarse word; **gros mots** bad language; (*Archit*) **gros œuvre** shell (*of a building*); **gros orteil** big toe; **gros pain** large (crusty) loaf; (*Phot*) **gros plan** close-up; **en gros plan** in close-up; **gros rouge*** (red) plonk*, rough (red) wine; **gros sel** cooking salt; **gros temps** rough weather; **par gros temps** in rough weather *ou* conditions; (*Presse*) **gros titre** headline.

groseille [gʀozɛj] **1** *nf*: **~ (rouge)** red currant; **~ (blanche)** white currant; **~ à maquereau** gooseberry. **2** *adj inv* (cherry-) red.

groseillier [gʀozɛje] *nm* currant bush. **~ rouge/blanc** red/ white currant bush; **~ à maquereau** gooseberry bush.

grosse² [gʀos] *nf* (*Jur*) engrossment; (*Comm*) gross.

grossesse [gʀosɛs] *nf* pregnancy. **~ nerveuse** nervous pregnancy; *V* **robe.**

grosseur [gʀosœʀ] *nf* **(a)** [*objet*] size; [*fil, bâton*] thickness; [*personne*] weight, fatness. **être d'une ~ maladive** to be unhealthily fat; **as-tu remarqué sa ~?** have you noticed how fat he is? **(b)** (*tumeur*) lump.

grossier, -ière [gʀosje, jɛʀ] *adj* **(a)** *matière, tissu* coarse; *vin* rough; *aliment* unrefined; *ornement, instrument* crude.

(b) (*sommaire*) *travail* superficially done, roughly done; *imitation* crude, poor; *dessin* rough; *solution, réparation* rough-and-ready; *estimation* rough. **avoir une idée ~ière des faits** to have a rough idea of the facts.

(c) (*lourd*) *manières* unrefined, crude; *esprit, être* unrefined; *traits du visage* coarse, thick; *ruse* crude; *plaisanterie* unsubtle, inane; *erreur* stupid, gross (*épith*); *ignorance* crass (*épith*).

(d) (*bas, matériel*) *plaisirs, jouissances* base.

(e) (*insolent*) *personne* rude; (*vulgaire*) *plaisanterie, geste* coarse; *personne* coarse, uncouth. **il s'est montré très ~ envers eux** he was very rude to them; **~ personnage!** uncouth individual!; **il est ~ avec les femmes** he is coarse *ou* uncouth in his dealings with women.

grossièrement [gʀosjɛʀmɑ̃] *adv* **(a)** (*de manière sommaire*) *exécuter, réparer* roughly, superficially; *façonner* crudely; *dessiner, tisser* roughly; *imiter* crudely. **pouvez-vous me dire ~ combien ça va coûter?** can you tell me roughly how much that will cost?

(b) (*de manière vulgaire*) coarsely; (*insolemment*) rudely.

(c) (*lourdement*) **se tromper ~** to make a gross error.

grossièreté [gʀosjɛʀte] *nf* **(a)** (*U*) (*insolence*) rudeness; (*vulgarité*) [*personne*] coarseness, uncouthness; [*plaisanterie, geste*] coarseness. **dire des ~s** to use coarse language *ou* expressions.

(b) (*rusticité*) [*fabrication*] crudeness; [*travail, exécution*] superficiality; [*étoffe*] coarseness.

(c) (*littér: manque de finesse*) [*personne*] lack of refinement; [*traits*] coarseness. **la ~ de ses manières** his unrefined *ou* crude manners.

grossir [gʀosiʀ] (2) **1** *vi* [*personne*] (*signe de déficience*) to get fat(ter), put on weight; (*signe de santé*) to put on weight; [*fruit*] to swell, grow; [*rivière*] to swell; [*tumeur*] to swell, get bigger; [*foule*] to grow (larger), swell; [*somme, économies*] to grow, get bigger; [*bruit*] to get louder, grow (louder), swell. **l'avion grossissait dans le ciel** the plane grew larger *ou* bigger in the sky.

2 *vt* **(a)** (*faire paraître plus gros*) *personne* to make look fatter. **ce genre de vêtement (vous) grossit** clothing of this sort *ou* kind makes one look fatter.

(b) [*microscope*] to magnify; [*lentille, lunettes*] to enlarge, magnify; (*fig*) [*imagination*] *dangers, importance* to magnify, exaggerate.

(c) (*exagérer volontairement*) *fait, événement* to exaggerate, blow up*.

(d) *cours d'eau* to swell; *voix* to raise.

(e) *somme* to increase, add to; *foule* to swell. **~ les rangs/le nombre de** to swell the ranks/the numbers of.

grossissant, e [gʀosisɑ̃, ɑ̃t] *adj* **(a)** *lentille, verre* magnifying, enlarging. **(b)** *foule, bruit* swelling, growing.

grossissement [gʀosismɑ̃] *nm* **(a)** [*tumeur*] swelling, enlarging. [*personne*] **pour empêcher un ~ excessif** to prevent excessive weight-gain.

(b) [*objet*] magnification, magnifying; (*fig*) [*dangers etc*] magnification, exaggeration; (*fig*) [*faits*] exaggeration, blowing up*; (*pouvoir grossissant*) [*microscope*] magnification, (magnifying) power; [*imagination*] magnification; (*aspect grossi*) [*objet, dangers*] magnification.

grossiste [gʀosist(ə)] **1** *adj* wholesale (*épith*). **2** *nmf* wholesaler, wholesale dealer.

grosso modo [gʀosomodo] *adv* **(a)** (*sans entrer dans les détails*) more or less, roughly. **je vous explique ça ~** I'll explain the broad *ou* rough outlines of it to you. **(b)** (*tant bien que mal*) after a fashion.

grotesque [gʀotɛsk(ə)] **1** *adj* (*risible*) ludicrous; (*difforme*) grotesque. **il est d'un ~ incroyable** he's absolutely ridiculous; (*Littérat*) **le ~** the grotesque. **2** *nf* (*Art*) grotesque.

grotesquement [gʀotɛskəmɑ̃] *adv* (*V* **grotesque**) ludicrously; grotesquely.

grotte [gʀot] *nf* (*naturelle*) cave; (*artificielle*) grotto.

grouillant, e [gʀujɑ̃, ɑ̃t] *adj foule, masse* milling, swarming. **~ de** *touristes, insectes* swarming *ou* teeming *ou* crawling with; **boulevard/café ~ (de monde)** street/café swarming *ou* teeming *ou* crawling with people.

grouillement [gʀujmɑ̃] *nm* [*foule, touristes*] milling, swarming; [*vers, insectes*] swarming.

grouiller [gʀuje] (1) **1** *vi* [*foule, touristes*] to mill about; [*café, rue*] to be swarming *ou* teeming with people. **~ de** *touristes, insectes* to be swarming *ou* teeming *ou* crawling with. **2 se grouiller** *vpr* (*) to get a move on*, stir one's stumps*.

grouillot [gʀujo] *nm* messenger (boy).

groupage [gʀupaʒ] *nm* (*Comm*) [*colis*] bulking.

groupe [gʀup] **1** *nm* **(a)** (*Art, Écon, Pol, Sociol*) group. **le ~ de la majorité** the M.P.s of the majority party; **psychologie de ~** group psychology.

(b) [*personnes*] group, knot; [*touristes*] party, group. **des ~s se formaient dans la rue** groups (of people) *ou* knots of people were forming in the street; **~ de manifestants/de curieux** group of demonstrators/onlookers; **par ~s de 3 ou 4** in groups of 3 or 4, in threes or fours; **travailler/marcher en ~** to work/ walk in *ou* as a group.

(c) [*objets*] **~ de maisons** cluster *ou* group of houses; **~ d'arbres** clump *ou* cluster *ou* group of trees.

2: groupe de combat fighter group; **groupe électrogène** generating set; **groupe hospitalier** hospital complex; **groupe de mots** word group, phrase; **groupe parlementaire** parliamentary group (*M.P.s of the same party*); **groupe de pression** pressure group; **groupe sanguin** blood group; **groupe scolaire** school complex; **groupe de tête** (*Sport*) group of leaders; (*Scol*) top pupils (in the class); (*Écon*) (group of) leading firms; **groupe de travail** working party.

groupement [gʀupmɑ̃] *nm* **(a)** (*action*) [*personnes, objets, faits*] grouping. **~ de mots par catégories** grouping words by categories. **(b)** (*groupe*) group. **~ révolutionnaire** band of revolutionaries, revolutionary band.

grouper [gʀupe] (1) **1** *vt personnes, objets, faits* to group; (*Comm*) *colis* to bulk; *efforts, ressources, moyens* to pool. **savoir ~ ses idées** to know how to put one's ideas together; **~ des colis par destination** to bulk parcels according to their destination.

2 se grouper *vpr* [*foule*] to gather. **les consommateurs doivent se ~ pour se défendre** consumers must band together to defend their interests; (*fig*) **se ~ autour d'un chef** to rally round a leader; **le village groupé autour de l'église** the village clustered round the church; *V* **habitat.**

groupuscule [gʀupyskyl] *nm* (*Pol péj*) small group.

gruau [gʀyo] *nm* (*graine*) hulled grain, groats. **farine de ~** fine wheat flour; **pain de ~** fine wheaten bread.

grue [gʀy] *nf* **(a)** (*Tech, TV*) crane. **(b)** (*Orn*) crane; *V* **pied. (c)** (*:péj: prostituée*) tart: (*péj*).

gruger [gʀyʒe] (3) *vt* (*littér: duper*) to dupe.

grumeau, *pl* **~x** [gʀymo] *nm* [*sel, sauce*] lump. **la sauce fait des ~x** the sauce is going lumpy.

grumeler (se) [gʀymle] (5) *vpr* [*sauce*] to go lumpy; [*lait*] to curdle.

grumeleux, -euse [gʀymlø, øz] *adj sauce* lumpy; *lait* curdled; *fruit* gritty; *peau* bumpy, lumpy.

gruppetto [gʀupeto], *pl* **gruppetti** [gʀupeti] *nm* (*Mus*) gruppetto, turn.

grutier [gʀytje] *nm* crane driver.

gruyère [gʀyjɛʀ] *nm* gruyère (cheese).

Guadeloupe [gwadlup] *nf* Guadeloupe.

guadeloupéen, -enne [gwadlupeɛ̃, ɛn] 1 *adj* Guadelupian. 2 *nm,f*: G~(ne) inhabitant *ou* native of Guadeloupe.
guano [gwano] *nm [oiseau]* guano; *[poisson]* manure.
Guatémala [gwatemala] *nm* Guatemala.
guatémalien, -ienne [gwatemaljɛ̃, jɛn] 1 *adj* Guatemalan. 2 *nm,f*: G~(ne) Guatemalan.
guatémaltèque [gwatemaltɛk] 1 *adj* Guatemalan. 2 *nmf*: G~ Guatemalan.
gué [ge] *nm* ford. passer (une rivière) à ~ to ford a river.
guéable [geabl(ə)] *adj* fordable.
guéer [gee] (1) *vt* to ford.
guelfe [gɛlf(ə)] 1 *adj* Guelphic. 2 *nmf* Guelph.
guelte [gɛlt(ə)] *nf (Comm)* commission.
guenille [gənij] *nf* (piece of) rag. ~s (old) rags; en ~s in rags (and tatters).
guenon [gənɔ̃] *nf (Zool)* female monkey; *(péj: laideron)* fright, (ugly) hag.
guépard [gepaʀ] *nm* cheetah.
guêpe [gɛp] *nf* wasp; *V* fou, taille[1].
guêpier [gepje] *nm (piège)* trap; *(nid)* wasp's nest.
guêpière [gɛpjɛʀ] *nf (Hist)* waspie.
guère [gɛʀ] *adv* (a) *(avec adj ou adv: pas très, pas beaucoup)* hardly, scarcely. elle ne va ~ mieux she's hardly *ou* scarcely any better; il n'est ~ poli he's not very polite, he's hardly *ou* scarcely polite; le chef, ~ satisfait de cela, ... the boss, little *ou* hardly satisfied with that, ...; il n'y a ~ plus de 2 km there is barely *ou* scarcely 2 km to go; ça ne fera ~ moins de 100 F that won't be (very) much less than 100 francs.
(b) *(avec vb)* ne ... ~ *(pas beaucoup)* not much *ou* really; *(pas souvent)* hardly *ou* scarcely ever; *(pas longtemps)* not (very) long; je n'aime ~ qu'on me questionne I don't much like *ou* really care for being questioned; cela ne te va ~ that doesn't really suit you; ce n'est plus ~ à la mode that's hardly *ou* scarcely fashionable at all nowadays; il ne vient ~ nous voir he hardly *ou* scarcely ever comes to see us; cela ne durera ~ that won't last (for) very long; il ne tardera ~ he won't be (very) long now; *(frm)* l'aimez-vous? — ~ do you like it? — not (very) much *ou* not really *ou* not particularly.
(c) *(avec de, que)* il n'y a ~ de monde there's hardly *ou* scarcely anybody there; il n'y a ~ que lui qui ... he's about the only one who ..., there's hardly *ou* scarcely anyone but he who ...; il n'y a ~ que ceci que ... there's hardly *ou* scarcely anything but this that ... .
guéret [geʀɛ] *nm* fallow land *(U)*.
guéridon [geʀidɔ̃] *nm* pedestal table.
guérilla [geʀija] *nf* guerrilla warfare *(U)*. ~ urbaine urban guerrilla warfare.
guérillero [geʀijeʀo] *nm* guerrilla.
guérir [geʀiʀ] (2) 1 *vt (Méd: soigner) malade, maladie* to cure, make better; *membre, blessure* to heal. *(fig)* je ne peux pas le ~ de ses mauvaises habitudes I can't cure *ou* break him of his bad habits.
2 *vi* (a) *(Méd: aller mieux) [malade, maladie]* to get better, be cured; *[blessure]* to heal, mend. sa main guérie était encore faible his hand although healed was still weak; il est guéri (de son angine) he is cured (of his throat infection).
(b) *(fig) [chagrin, passion]* to heal.
3 se guérir *vpr [malade, maladie]* to get better, be cured. se ~ d'une habitude to cure *ou* break o.s. of a habit; se ~ par les plantes to cure o.s. by taking herbs, cure o.s. with herbs; se ~ d'un amour malheureux to get over *ou* recover from an unhappy love affair.
guérison [geʀizɔ̃] *nf [malade]* recovery; *[maladie]* curing *(U)*; *[membre, plaie]* healing *(U)*. sa ~ a été rapide he made a rapid recovery; *V* voie.
guérissable [geʀisabl(ə)] *adj malade, maladie* curable. sa jambe/blessure est ~ his leg/injury can be healed.
guérisseur, -euse [geʀisœʀ, øz] *nm,f* healer; *(péj)* quack (doctor) *(péj)*.
guérite [geʀit] *nf* (a) *(Mil)* sentry box. (b) *(sur chantier etc)* workman's hut; *(servant de bureau)* site office.
Guernesey [gɛʀn(ə)zɛ] *nf* Guernsey.
guernesiais, e [gɛʀnəzjɛ, ɛz] 1 *adj* of *ou* from Guernsey, Guernsey *(épith)*. 2 *nm,f*: G~(e) inhabitant *ou* native of Guernsey.
guerre [gɛʀ] 1 *nf* (a) *(conflit)* war. de ~ *correspondant, criminel* war *(épith)*; ~ civile/sainte/atomique civil/holy/atomic war; ~ de religion/de libération war of religion/of liberation; entre eux c'est la ~ ouverte there's open war(fare) between them.
(b) *(technique)* warfare; la ~ atomique/psychologique/de tranchées atomic/psychological/trench warfare.
(c) *(loc)* en ~ *(lit, fig)* at war *(avec, contre* with, against); dans les pays en ~ in the warring countries, in the countries at war; *(Mil)* faire la ~ à to wage war on *ou* against; soldat qui a fait la ~ soldier who was in the war; ton chapeau a fait la ~* your hat has been in the wars*; *(fig)* elle lui fait la ~ pour qu'il s'habille mieux she is constantly battling with him to get him to dress better; faire la ~ aux abus/à l'injustice to wage war against *ou* on abuses/injustice; de ~ lasse elle finit par accepter she grew tired of resisting and finally accepted; *(Prov)* à la ~ comme à la ~ we'll just have to make the best of things, you must take things as you find them *ou* as they come; *V* entrer, partir[1].
2: guerre éclair blitzkrieg; guerre d'embuscade guerrilla warfare; guerre d'extermination war of extermination; guerre froide cold war; guerre mondiale world war; guerre de mouvement war of movement; guerre des nerfs war of nerves; guerre à outrance all-out war; guerre de position war of position; la guerre de quatorze the 1914–18 war; la guerre de Sécession the American Civil War; guerre de succession war of succession; guerre totale total warfare; guerre d'usure war of attrition.
guerrier, -ière [gɛʀje, jɛʀ] 1 *adj nation, air* warlike; *danse, chants, exploits* war *(épith)*. 2 *nm,f* warrior.
guerroyer [gɛʀwaje] (8) *vi (littér)* to wage war *(contre* against, on).
guet [gɛ] 1 *nm* (a) faire le ~ to be on the watch *ou* look-out; avoir l'œil au ~ to keep one's eyes open *ou* skinned*; avoir l'oreille au ~ to keep one's ears open.
(b) *(Hist: patrouille)* watch.
2: guet-apens *nm, pl* guets-apens *(lit)* ambush, ambuscade; *(fig)* trap, ambush.
guêtre [gɛtʀ(ə)] *nf* gaiter.
guêtré, e [getʀe] *adj (Hist, hum)* wearing gaiters *ou* spats.
guetter [gete] (1) *vt* (a) *(épier) victime, ennemi* to watch (intently).
(b) *(attendre) signal, personne* to watch (out) for, be on the look-out for; *(hostilement)* to lie in wait for. ~ le passage/l'arrivée de qn to watch (out) for sb (to pass)/(to come); *(fig)* ~ l'occasion to watch out for the opportunity, be on the look-out for the opportunity; *(fig)* la crise cardiaque le guette there's a heart attack lying in wait for him; *(fig)* la faillite le guette he is threatened by bankruptcy.
guetteur [gɛtœʀ] *nm (Mil)* look-out; *(Hist)* watch.
gueulante: [gœlɑ̃t] *nf*: pousser une *ou* sa ~ *(protestation)* to shout one's mouth off:; *(acclamation)* to give an almighty cheer *ou* yell*; *(douleur)* to give an almighty yell*.
gueulard, e [gœlaʀ, aʀd(ə)] 1 *adj (:)* (a) *(braillard) personne* loud-mouthed; *air, musique* noisy. bébé ~ bawling brat; ce qu'il est ~! isn't he a loud-mouth!* (b) *(criard) couleur, vêtement* gaudy, garish. 2 *nm (Tech)* throat.
gueule [gœl] 1 *nf* (a) (*: *bouche*) mouth. (ferme) ta ~! shut your trap!: *ou* face!:; ça vous emporte *ou* brûle la ~ it takes the roof off your mouth; il dépense beaucoup d'argent pour la ~ he spends a lot on feeding his face*; tu peux crever la ~ ouverte you can go to hell for all I care:; il nous laisserait bien crever la ~ ouverte he wouldn't give a damn what happened to us:; *V* coup.
(b) (*: *figure*) face. il a une bonne/sale ~ I like/I don't like the look of him; faire la ~ to look sulky; faire une ~ d'enterrement to look a real misery; il a fait une sale ~ quand il a appris la nouvelle: he didn't half pull a face when he heard the news*; cette bagnole a de la ~ that's a great-looking car!*, that's some car!*; cette maison a une drôle de ~ that's a weird-looking house; ~ de raie: fish-face:; *V* casser, soûler.
(c) *[animal]* mouth. *(fig)* se jeter *ou* se mettre dans la ~ du loup to throw o.s. into the lion's jaws.
(d) *(ouverture) [four]* mouth; *[canon]* muzzle.
2: gueule de bois* hangover; avoir la gueule de bois* to have a hangover, be feeling the effects of the night before*; gueule cassée *war veteran with severe facial injuries*; *(Bot)* gueule-de-loup *nf, pl* gueules-de-loup snapdragon; gueule noire miner.
gueulement: [gœlmɑ̃] *nm (cri)* bawl. pousser des ~s *(douleur)* to yell one's head off*; *(colère)* to shout one's mouth off:.
gueuler: [gœle] (1) 1 *vi* (a) *(parler fort)* to bawl, bellow; *(chanter fort)* to bawl; *(hurler de douleur)* to yell (one's head off) *(de* with); *(protester)* to bellyache: *(contre* about). ça va le faire ~ *(de douleur)* that'll make him yell*; *(de mécontentement)* that'll have him shouting his mouth off:; ça va ~ there'll be all hell let loose:, there'll be one hell of a row:.
(b) *[poste de radio]* to blast out, blare out. faire ~ sa télé to turn one's telly up full blast*.
2 *vt ordres* to bawl (out), bellow (out); *chanson* to bawl.
gueules [gœl] *nm (Hér)* gules.
gueuleton* [gœltɔ̃] *nm* blow-out*, nosh-up*.
gueuletonner* [gœltɔne] (1) *vi* to have a blow-out*, have a nosh-up*.
gueuse [gøz] *nf* (a) (†, *littér*) *(mendiante)* beggarwoman; *(coquine)* rascally wench; *V* courir. (b) *[fonte]* pig.
gueuserie [gøzʀi] *nf (littér) (action)* villainous act; *(condition)* beggary.
gueux [gø] *nm* (†, *littér*) *(mendiant)* beggar; *(coquin)* rogue, villain.
Gugusse [gygys] *nm (clown)* ≈ Coco the clown; (*: *type, personne*) bloke* *(Brit)*, guy*; (*: *personne ridicule*) twit* *(Brit)*, nincompoop.
gui [gi] *nm* (a) *(Bot)* mistletoe. (b) *(Naut)* boom.
guibol(l)e* [gibɔl] *nf (jambe)* leg. *[ivrogne, convalescent]* ~s pins*.
guiches [giʃ] *nfpl* kiss curls.
guichet [giʃɛ] *nm* (a) *(comptoir individuel)* window. *(bureau)* ~(s) *[banque, poste]* counter; *[théâtre]* box office, ticket office; *[gare]* ticket office, booking office *(Brit)*; adressez-vous au ~ d'à côté inquire at the next window; renseignez-vous au(x) ~(s) *(banque, poste)* go and ask at the counter; *(théâtre, gare)* go and ask at the ticket office; *(à la poste)* '~ fermé' 'position closed'; *V* jouer.
(b) *[porte, mur]* wicket, hatch; *(grillagé)* grille.
guichetier, -ière [giʃtje, jɛʀ] *nm,f [banque]* teller, counter clerk.
guidage [gidaʒ] *nm (Min, Tech)* guides; *(Aviat)* guidance; *V* radio-guidage.
guide [gid] 1 *nm* (a) *(personne)* guide; *(livre)* guide(book); *(fig: idée, sentiment)* guide. l'ambition est son seul ~ ambition is his only guide; ~ de montagne mountain guide.
(b) *(Tech: glissière)* guide. ~ de courroie belt-guide.
2 *nfpl (rênes)* ~s reins.
3 *nf (éclaireuse)* (Catholic) girl guide *(Brit)* *ou* girl scout *(US)*.

guide- [gid] *préf V* **guider.**
guider [gide] (1) **1** *vt* (*conduire*) *voyageur, embarcation, cheval* to guide; (*fig: moralement etc*) to guide. **l'ambition le guide** he is guided by (his) ambition, ambition is his guide; **organisme qui guide les étudiants durant leur première année** organization that provides guidance for first-year students; **il m'a guidé dans mes recherches** he guided me through *ou* in my research; **se laissant ~ par son instinct** letting himself be guided by (his) instinct, letting (his) instinct be his guide; **se guidant sur les étoiles/leur exemple** using the stars/their example as a guide; *V* **visite.**
2: guide-âne *nm, pl* **guide-ânes** (*livre*) basic handbook.
guidon [gidɔ̃] *nm* **(a)** *[vélo]* handlebars. **(b)** (*drapeau*) guidon. **(c)** *[mire]* foresight, bead.
guigne[1] [giɲ] *nf*: **il s'en soucie comme d'une ~** he doesn't care a fig about it.
guigne[2]* [giɲ] *nf* (*malchance*) rotten luck*. **avoir la ~** to be jinxed*; **porter la ~ à qn** to put a jinx *ou* hoodoo on sb*; **quelle ~!** what rotten luck!*
guigner [giɲe] (1) *vt femme* to eye surreptitiously; *héritage, place* to have one's eye on, eye. **il guignait du coin de l'œil** he was casting surreptitious *ou* sidelong glances.
guignol [giɲɔl] *nm* **(a)** (*Théât*) (*marionnette*) puppet (*name of popular French glove puppet*); (*spectacle*) puppet show (≃ *Punch and Judy show*). **aller au ~** to go to the puppet show; **c'est du ~!** it's a real farce!, it's burlesque!
(b) (*péj: personne*) clown. **arrête de faire le ~!** stop clowning about!, stop acting the clown!
guignolet [giɲɔlɛ] *nm* cherry liqueur.
guignon [giɲɔ̃] *nm* = **guigne**[2].
guilde [gild(ə)] *nf* (*Hist*) guild.
Guillaume [gijom] *nm* William.
guillaume [gijom] *nm* rabbet plane.
guilledou [gijdu] *nm V* **courir.**
guillemet [gijmɛ] *nm* inverted comma (*Brit*), quotation mark. **ouvrez les ~s** open (the) inverted commas; **fermez les ~s** close (the) inverted commas; (*iro*) **sa digne épouse, entre ~s** his noble wife, quote unquote *ou* in inverted commas (*Brit*); **mettre un mot entre ~s** to put a word in quotation marks *ou* inverted commas (*Brit*) *ou* quotes.
guilleret, -ette [gijʀɛ, ɛt] *adj* **(a)** (*enjoué*) *personne, air* perky, bright. **être tout ~** to be full of beans*. **(b)** (*leste*) *propos* saucy.
guillochage [gijɔʃaʒ] *nm* ornamentation with guilloche.
guillocher [gijɔʃe] (1) *vt* to ornament with guilloche.
guillochis [gijɔʃi] *nm* guilloche.
guillochure [gijɔʃyʀ] *nf* guilloche pattern.
guillotine [gijɔtin] *nf* guillotine; *V* **fenêtre.**
guillotiner [gijɔtine] (1) *vt* to guillotine.
guimauve [gimov] *nf* (*Bot*) marsh mallow; (*Culin*) marshmallow. (*fig péj*) **c'est de la ~** (*mou*) it's jelly; (*sentimental*) it's mush*; **chanson (à la) ~** sloppy* *ou* mushy* song.
guimbarde [gɛ̃baʀd(ə)] *nf* (*Mus*) Jew's harp. (*: *voiture*) **(vieille) ~** old banger* (*Brit*), old crock*.
guimpe [gɛ̃p] *nf* (*Rel*) wimple; (*corsage*) chemisette.
guincher* [gɛ̃ʃe] (1) *vi* (*danser*) to dance.
guindé, e [gɛ̃de] (*ptp de* **guinder**) *adj personne, air* stiff, starchy; *style* stilted.
guinder [gɛ̃de] (1) **1** *vt style* to make stilted. **des vêtements qui le guindent** *ou* **qui guindent son allure** clothes that make him look stiff (and starchy). **2 se guinder** *vpr [personne]* to become starchy; *[style]* to become stilted.
Guinée [gine] *nf* Guinea.
guinée [gine] *nf* guinea.
guinéen, -enne [gineɛ̃, ɛn] **1** *adj* Guinean. **2** *nm,f*: **G~(ne)** native of Guinea, Guinean.
guingois* [gɛ̃gwa] *adv* (*de travers*) **de ~** skew-whiff*; **le tableau est (tout) de ~** the picture is skew-whiff* *ou* wonky* *ou* lop-sided; **il se tient tout de ~ sur sa chaise** he's sitting lop-sidedly *ou* skew-whiff* in his chair.
guinguette [gɛ̃gɛt] *nf open-air café or dance hall.*
guipure [gipyʀ] *nf* guipure.
guirlande [giʀlɑ̃d] *nf [fleurs]* garland. **~ de Noël** tinsel garland; **~ de papier** paper chain; **~ lumineuse** string of fairy lights (*Brit*) *ou* Christmas tree lights.
guise [giz] *nf* **(a) n'en faire qu'à sa ~** to do as one pleases *ou* likes; **à ta ~!** as you wish! *ou* please! *ou* like!
(b) (*loc*) **en ~ de** by way of; **en ~ de remerciement il m'a offert un livre/il m'a flanqué une gifle** by way of thanks he gave me a book/he slapped me in the face; **en ~ de chapeau il portait un pot de fleurs** he was wearing a flowerpot by way of a hat.
guitare [gitaʀ] *nf* guitar. **~ hawaïenne** Hawaian guitar.
guitariste [gitaʀist(ə)] *nmf* guitarist, guitar player.
guitoune [gitun] *nf* (*arg Mil*) tent.
gus* [gys] *nm* (*personne, type*) guy*, bloke* (*Brit*).
gustatif, -ive [gystatif, iv] *adj* (*Bio*) gustative, gustatory; *V* **nerf, papille.**
gustation [gystɑsjɔ̃] *nf* (*Bio*) gustation.
guttural, e, *mpl* **-aux** [gytyʀal, o] **1** *adj langue, son, consonne* guttural; *voix* guttural, throaty. **2 gutturale** *nf* (*Phonétique*) guttural.
Guyane [gɥijan] *nf* Guiana.
gym [ʒim] *nf* (*abrév de* **gymnastique**) gym, P.E.
gymkhana [ʒimkana] *nm* rally. **~ motocycliste** motorcycle scramble.
gymnase [ʒimnɑz] *nm* (*Sport*) gymnasium, gym; (*Suisse: lycée*) secondary school (*Brit*), high school (*US*).
gymnaste [ʒimnast(ə)] *nmf* gymnast.
gymnastique [ʒimnastik] **1** *nf* **(a)** (*Sport*) gymnastics (*sg*); (*Scol*) physical education, gymnastics (*sg*). **de ~** *professeur, instrument* physical education (*épith*), P.E. (*épith*); **~ corrective** *ou* **médicale** remedial gymnastics (*sg*); **~ rythmique** eurhythmics (*sg*); **~ acrobatique** acrobatics (*sg*); **~ respiratoire** breathing exercises; **~ suédoise** Swedish movements; **faire de la ~** (*Sport*) to do gymnastics; (*au réveil etc*) to do exercises; *V* **pas**[1].
(b) (*fig*) gymnastics (*sg*). **~ intellectuelle** *ou* **de l'esprit** mental gymnastics (*sg*); **j'ai dû me livrer à toute une ~ pour faire coïncider nos dates de vacances** I had to tie myself in knots *ou* stand on my head to get our holiday dates to coincide; **quelle ~ il faut faire pour aller d'une banlieue à une autre** what a palaver* *ou* a performance to get from one suburb to another.
2 *adj* (*rare*) gymnastic.
gymnique [ʒimnik] **1** *adj* gymnastic. **2** *nf* (*rare*) gymnastics (*sg*).
gynécée [ʒinese] *nm* (*Hist*) gynaeceum; (*fig*) den of females.
gynécologie [ʒinekɔlɔʒi] *nf* gynaecology.
gynécologique [ʒinekɔlɔʒik] *adj* gynaecological.
gynécologiste [ʒinekɔlɔʒist(ə)] *nmf,* **gynécologue** [ʒinekɔlɔg] *nmf* gynaecologist.
gypaète [ʒipaɛt] *nm* bearded vulture, lammergeyer.
gypse [ʒips(ə)] *nm* gypsum.
gypseux, -euse [ʒipsø, øz] *adj* gypseous.
gyrocompas [ʒiʀɔkɔ̃pɑ] *nm* gyrocompass.
gyroscope [ʒiʀɔskɔp] *nm* gyroscope.
gyroscopique [ʒiʀɔskɔpik] *adj* gyroscopic.

H

H, h [aʃ] *nm ou nf* (*lettre*) H, h. **H aspiré** aspirate h; **H muet** silent *ou* mute h; *V* **bombe, heure.**
ha ['ɑ, hɑ] *excl [surprise, colère etc]* oh! ho!; *[rire]* ha-ha!
habile [abil] *adj* **(a)** (*adroit*) *mains* skilful, skilled, clever; *ouvrier, chirurgien* skilful, skilled; *diplomate, tactique, démarche* clever, smart; *film, pièce de théâtre* clever. **être ~ à (faire) qch** to be clever *ou* skilful at (doing) sth; **façonné d'une main ~** fashioned by a skilful *ou* skilled *ou* cunning hand.
(b) (*Jur*) fit (*à* to).
habilement [abilmɑ̃] *adv* (*V* **habile**) skilfully; cleverly. **~ façonné** skilfully *ou* cunningly made.
habileté [abilte] *nf* **(a)** (*adresse: V* **habile**) skill, skilfulness; cleverness; smartness. **(b)** (*artifice, truc*) clever move, skilful move. **(c)** (*Jur*) = **habilité.**
habilitation [abilitɑsjɔ̃] *nf* (*Jur*) capacitation.
habilité [abilite] *nf* (*Jur*) fitness.
habiliter [abilite] (1) *vt* (*Jur*) to capacitate. **être habilité à faire qch** (*Jur, Pol*) to be empowered to do sth; (*gén*) to be entitled to do sth.
habillage [abijaʒ] *nm* **(a)** *[acteur, poupée]* dressing. **(b)** (*Tech*) *[montre]* assembly; *[bouteille]* labelling and sealing; *[marchandise]* packaging and presentation; *[machine]* casing; *[chaudière]* lagging; *[viande, volaille]* dressing.
habillé, e [abije] (*ptp de* **habiller**) *adj* **(a)** *robe* smart, dressy; *soirée* dressy. **trop ~** *costume* too dressy, over-dressy, over-smart; *personne* overdressed, too dressed up; **ça fait très ~** it looks very smart *ou* dressy *ou* posh*.
(b) *personne* dressed. **être bien/mal ~** to be well/badly dressed; **être ~ de noir/d'un complet** to be dressed in *ou* wearing black/a suit; **se coucher tout ~** to go to bed fully dressed *ou* with all one's clothes on.
habillement [abijmɑ̃] *nm* (*action*) clothing; (*toilette, costume*) clothes, dress (*U*), outfit; (*Mil: uniforme*) outfit; (*profession*) clothing trade, rag trade* (*Brit*), garment industry (*US*).

habiller [abije] (1) **1** *vt* **(a)** *poupée, enfant* (*vêtir*) to dress (*de* in); (*déguiser*) to dress up (*en* as). **cette robe vous habille bien** that dress really suits you *ou* looks good on you; **un rien l'habille** she looks good in the simplest thing; **~ un enfant en Peau-Rouge** to dress a child up as a Red Indian.

(b) (*fournir en vêtements*) *enfant, miséreux* to clothe; (*Mil*) *recrues* to provide with uniforms. **elle habille entièrement ses enfants** she makes all her children's clothes; (*Couture*) **elle se fait ~ par X, c'est X qui l'habille** she buys *ou* gets all her clothes from X's, X makes all her clothes; **ce tissu habille bien** this is good dress material (*ou* suit *etc* material).

(c) (*recouvrir, envelopper*) *mur, fauteuil, livre* to cover (*de* with); *bouteille* to label and seal; *marchandise* to package; *machine, radiateur* to encase (*de* in); *chaudière* to lag (*de* with). **~ un fauteuil d'une housse** to put a loose cover on a chair; (*fig*) **il faut ~ ce coin de la pièce qui est un peu nu** we must put something in *ou* do something with this rather bare corner of the room.

(d) (*Culin*) *viande, volaille* to dress; (*Horticulture*) *arbre* to trim (for planting); (*Typ*) *gravure* to set the text around.

(e) (*Tech*) *montre* to assemble.

2 s'habiller *vpr* **(a)** (*mettre ses habits*) to dress (o.s.), get dressed; (*se déguiser*) to dress up (*en* as). **aider qn à s'~** to help sb on with his clothes, help sb get dressed; **elle s'habille trop jeune/vieux** she wears clothes that are too young/old for her; **s'~ en Arlequin/Peau-Rouge** to dress up as Harlequin/a Red Indian; **elle s'habille long/court** she wears long/short skirts, she wears her skirts long/short; **faut-il s'~ pour la réception?** must we dress (up) for the reception?; **comment t'habilles-tu ce soir?** what are you wearing tonight?; **ne vous habillez pas, c'est en famille** don't (bother to) dress up — it's a family party; **elle ne sait pas s'~** she has no clothes sense *ou* dress sense.

(b) (*Couture*) **s'~ chez un tailleur/au Prisunic** to buy *ou* get one's clothes from a tailor/at Prisunic; **s'~ sur mesure** to have one's clothes made (to measure).

habilleur, -euse [abijœʀ, øz] *nm,f* (*Théât*) dresser.

habit [abi] **1** *nm* **(a)** **~s** clothes; **mettre/ôter ses ~s** to put on/take off one's clothes *ou* things; **~s de travail/du dimanche/de deuil** working/Sunday/mourning clothes; **il portait ses ~s du dimanche** he was wearing his Sunday best *ou* Sunday clothes; **il était encore en ~ de voyage** he was still in his travelling clothes *ou* in the clothes he'd worn for the journey; *V* **brosse.**

(b) (*costume*) dress (*U*), outfit. **~ d'arlequin** Harlequin suit *ou* costume; (*Prov*) **l'~ ne fait pas le moine** appearances are (sometimes) deceptive, do not judge by appearances.

(c) (*vêtement de soirée*) tails. **en ~** wearing tails, in evening dress; **l'~ est de rigueur** formal *ou* evening dress must be worn; (*sur carte d'invitation*) 'white tie', 'dress: formal'.

(d) (*Rel*) **prendre l'~** *[homme]* to take (holy) orders; *[femme]* to take the veil.

2: habit de cheval† riding habit; (*Hist*) **habit de cour** court dress (*U*); **habit ecclésiastique** clerical dress (*U*); (*fig*) **porter l'habit ecclésiastique** to be a cleric; **habit de gala** formal *ou* evening dress (*U*); **habit militaire** military dress (*U*); **habit religieux** (monk's) habit; **habit de soirée** = **habit de gala**; **habit vert** (*green coat of*) *member of the Académie Française*.

habitabilité [abitabilite] *nf [maison]* habitability; *[voiture, ascenseur]* capacity.

habitable [abitabl(ə)] *adj* (in)habitable.

habitacle [abitakl(ə)] *nm* **(a)** (*Naut*) binnacle; (*Aviat*) cockpit. **(b)** (*Rel, littér*) dwelling place (*littér*), abode (*littér*).

habitant, e [abitɑ̃, ɑ̃t] **1** *nm,f [maison]* occupant, occupier; *[ville, pays]* inhabitant. **pays/ville de 3 millions d'~s** country/town of 3 million inhabitants; **les ~s de la maison** the people who live in the house, the occupants of the houseu **les ~s du village/du pays** the people who live in the village/country, the inhabitants of the village/country; **être** *ou* **loger chez l'~** *[touristes]* to stay with the locals; *[soldats]* to be billeted on the locals *ou* local people; **~s des cavernes** cave dwellers.

2 (*Can**) farmer; (*French Canadian*) habitant (*Can*).

habitat [abita] *nm* (*Bot, Zool*) habitat; (*conditions de logement*) housing *ou* living conditions; (*Géog: mode de peuplement*) settlement. (*Géog*) **~ rural/nomade/dispersé/groupé** rural/nomadic/scattered/grouped settlement.

habitation [abitɑsjɔ̃] *nf* **(a)** (*fait de résider*) living, dwelling (*littér*). **locaux à usage d'~** dwelling houses; **conditions d'~** housing *ou* living conditions; **impropre à l'~** unfit for human habitation, uninhabitable.

(b) (*domicile*) residence, home, dwelling place (*littér*). **l'appentis qui lui sert d'~** the outhouse that serves as his home; **changer d'~** to change one's (place of) residence.

(c) (*logement, bâtiment*) house. **des ~s modernes** modern housing *ou* houses; **groupe d'~s** (*immeuble*) block of flats (*Brit*), apartment building (*US*); (*lotissement*) housing estate (*Brit*) *ou* development; **~ à loyer modéré** (*Admin: appartement*) ≃ council flat (*Brit*), public housing unit (*US*); **~s à loyer modéré** (*Admin: immeuble*) ≃ (block of) council flats (*Brit*), public housing (*US*).

habiter [abite] (1) **1** *vt maison, appartement* to live in, occupy; *zone, planète, région* to inhabit; (*fig*) *[idée, sentiment]* to dwell in. **~ la banlieue** to live in the suburbs; **la maison n'a pas l'air habitée** the house doesn't look lived-in *ou* occupied; **est-ce que cette maison est habitée?** does anyone live in this house?, is this house occupied?

2 *vi* to live (*en, dans* in). **~ à la campagne/chez des amis** to live in the country/with friends.

habituation [abitɥasjɔ̃] *nf* (*accoutumance*) habituation (*à* to).

habitude [abityd] *nf* **(a)** (*accoutumance*) habit. **avoir/prendre l'~ de faire** to be/get used to doing; **avoir pour ~** *ou* **l'~ de faire** to be in the habit of doing; **prendre de mauvaises ~s** to pick up *ou* get into bad habits; **perdre une ~** to break a habit, get out of a habit; **faire perdre une ~ à qn** to break sb of a habit; **avoir une longue ~ de** to have long experience of; **ce n'est pas dans ses ~s de faire cela** he doesn't usually do that, he doesn't make a habit of (doing) that; **j'ai l'~!** I'm used to it; **je n'ai pas l'~ de me répéter** I'm not in the habit of repeating myself; (*Prov*) **l'~ est une seconde nature** habit is second nature; **il a ses petites ~s** he has his (pet) ways *ou* habits; *V* **esclave.**

(b) (*coutume*) **~s** customs; **les ~s d'un pays** the customs of a country.

(c) (*loc*) **d'~** usually; **par ~** out of habit, from force of habit; **comme d'~** as usual; **selon** *ou* **suivant** *ou* **comme à son ~** as he usually does, as is his wont (*frm*).

habitué, e [abitɥe] (*ptp de* **habituer**) *nm,f [maison]* regular visitor, habitué(e); *[café]* regular (customer), habitué(e).

habituel, -elle [abitɥɛl] *adj* usual, customary, habitual. **d'un geste qui lui était ~** with his usual gesture, with that typical gesture of his.

habituellement [abitɥɛlmɑ̃] *adv* usually, generally.

habituer [abitɥe] (1) **1** *vt*: **~ qn à qch/à faire** (*accoutumer, endurcir*) to accustom sb to sth/to doing, get sb used to sth/to doing; (*apprendre, entraîner*) to teach sb sth/to do; **on m'a habitué à obéir** I've been taught to obey; **être habitué à qch/à faire** to be used *ou* accustomed to sth/to doing.

2 s'habituer *vpr*: **s'~ à qch/à faire** to get *ou* grow used *ou* accustomed to sth/to doing, accustom o.s. to sth/to doing.

hâblerie ['ɑbləʀi] *nf* (*manière d'être*) bragging, boasting; (*propos*) boast, big talk* (*U*).

hâbleur, -euse ['ɑblœʀ, øz] **1** *adj* bragging, boasting, boastful. **2** *nm,f* braggart, boaster.

Habsbourg ['apsbuʀ] *nmf* Hapsburg.

hachage ['aʃaʒ] *nm* (*V* **hacher**) chopping; mincing.

hache ['aʃ] *nf* axe. **~ d'armes** battle-axe; (*lit*) **~ de guerre** hatchet, axe; (*fig*) **déterrer/enterrer la ~ de guerre** to take up/bury the hatchet; (*fig*) **visage taillé à la ~** *ou* **à coups de ~** angular *ou* roughly-hewn face.

hache- ['aʃ] *préf V* **hacher.**

haché, e ['aʃe] (*ptp de* **hacher**) **1** *adj* **(a)** *viande* minced. **bifteck ~** minced beef *ou* steak (*Brit*), (beef *ou* steak) mince (*Brit*), ground beef *ou* hamburger (*US*). **(b)** *style* jerky; *phrases* jerky, broken. **2** *nm* mince (*Brit*), minced meat (*Brit*), ground beef (*US*).

hachement ['aʃmɑ̃] *nm* = **hachage.**

hacher ['aʃe] (1) **1** *vt* **(a)** (*couper*) (*au couteau etc*) to chop; (*avec un appareil*) to mince. **~ menu** to mince, chop finely; **~ menu comme chair à pâté** to make mincemeat of.

(b) (*déchiqueter*) *récolte* to slash to pieces; *soldats* to cut to pieces. **je me ferais plutôt ~ que d'accepter** I'd go through fire rather than accept; **il se ferait ~ pour vous** he'd go through fire for you.

(c) (*interrompre*) *discours, phrases* to break up; *V* **haché.**

2: hache-légumes *nm inv* vegetable-chopper; **hache-paille** *nm inv* chaff-cutter; **hache-viande** *nm inv* (meat-)mincer.

hachette ['aʃɛt] *nf* hatchet.

hachis ['aʃi] *nm [légumes]* chopped vegetables; *[viande]* mince (*Brit*) (*U*), minced meat (*farce*) forcemeat (*U*). **~ de porc** pork mince; **~ Parmentier** ≃ shepherd's *ou* cottage pie (*Brit*).

hachisch ['aʃiʃ] *nm* hashish.

hachoir ['aʃwaʀ] *nm* (*couteau*) *[viande]* chopper, cleaver; *[légumes]* chopper; (*planche*) chopping board; (*appareil*) (meat-)mincer.

hachurer ['aʃyʀe] (1) *vt* (*Art*) to hatch; (*Cartographie*) to hachure.

hachures ['aʃyʀ] *nfpl* (*Art*) hatching (*U*), hachures; (*Cartographie*) hachures.

haddock ['adɔk] *nm* haddock.

hagard, e ['agaʀ, aʀd(ə)] *adj yeux* wild; *visage, air, gestes* distraught, frantic, wild.

haie ['ɛ] *nf* **(a)** (*clôture*) hedge. **~ d'aubépines** hawthorn hedge; **~ vive** quickset hedge.

(b) (*Sport: obstacle*) *[coureur]* hurdle; *[chevaux]* fence. **course de ~s** *[coureur]* hurdles (race): *[chevaux]* steeplechase; **110 mètres ~s** 110 metres hurdles.

(c) (*fig: rangée*) *[spectateurs, policiers]* line, row. **faire une ~ d'honneur** to form a guard of honour; **faire la ~** to form a line.

haillon ['ɑjɔ̃] *nm* rag. **en ~s** in rags, in tatters.

haillonneux, -euse ['ɑjɔnø, øz] *adj* (*littér*) in rags, in tatters, tattered and torn.

haine ['ɛn] *nf* hatred (*de, pour* of, for). **des ~s mesquines** petty hatreds *ou* dislikes; **prendre qn en ~** to take a violent dislike *ou* a strong aversion to sb; **avoir de la ~ pour** to feel hatred for, be filled with hate *ou* hatred for; **par ~ de** out of *ou* through hatred of.

haineusement ['ɛnøzmɑ̃] *adv dire, regarder* with hatred; *saisir* malevolently.

haineux, -euse ['ɛnø, øz] *adj parole* full of hatred; *caractère, joie* malevolent. **regard ~** look of hate *ou* hatred, look full of hate *ou* hatred.

haïr ['aiʀ] (10) *vt* to detest, abhor, hate. **elle me hait de l'avoir trompée** she hates me for having deceived her; **je hais ses manières affectées** I can't stand *ou* I hate *ou* I loathe her affected ways.

haire ['ɛʀ] *nf* hair shirt.

haïssable ['aisabl(ə)] *adj* detestable, hateful.

Haïti [aiti] *nf* Haiti.

haïtien, -ienne [aisjɛ̃, jɛn] **1** *adj* Haitian. **2** *nm,f*: **H~(ne)** Haitian.

halage ['alaʒ] *nm* (*Naut*) towing. **(chemin de) ~** towpath; **cheval de ~** towhorse.

hâle ['ɑl] *nm* (sun)tan, sunburn.

hâlé, e ['ɑle] (*ptp de* **hâler**) *adj* (sun)tanned, sunburnt.

haleine [alɛn] *nf* **(a)** (*souffle*) breath; (*respiration*) breathing (*U*). **avoir l'~ courte** to be short of breath *ou* short-winded; **retenir son ~** to hold one's breath; **être hors d'~** to be out of breath, be breathless; **perdre ~** to lose one's breath, get out of breath; **reprendre ~** (*lit*) to get one's breath *ou* wind back, regain one's breath; (*fig*) to take a breather; **d'une seule ~** *dire* in one breath, in the same breath; *faire* (all) at one go; **il respirait d'une ~ régulière** his breathing was regular.
(b) (*air expiré*) breath. **avoir mauvaise ~** *ou* **l'~ forte** to have bad breath; **j'ai senti à son ~ qu'il avait bu** I smelt *ou* could smell drink on his breath, I could tell from his breath that he'd been drinking; (*fig*) **l'~ glaciale de la crevasse/rivière** the icy breath of the crevasse/river.
(c) (*loc*) **tenir qn en ~** (*attention*) to hold sb spellbound *ou* breathless; (*incertitude*) to keep sb in suspense *ou* on tenterhooks; **travail de longue ~** long-term job, long and exacting job; **à perdre ~**: **rire à perdre ~** to laugh until one's sides ache *ou* until one is out of breath; **courir à perdre ~** to run until one is out of breath *ou* gasping for breath.

haler ['ale] (1) *vt corde, ancre* to haul in; *bateau* to tow.

hâler ['ɑle] (1) *vt* to (sun)tan, sunburn.

haletant, e ['altɑ̃, ɑ̃t] *adj personne* (*essoufflé*) panting, gasping for breath (*attrib*), out of breath (*attrib*); (*assoiffé, effrayé*) panting (*de* with); (*curieux*) breathless (*de* with); *animal* panting; *poitrine* heaving; *voix* breathless, gasping. **sa respiration était ~e** he was panting, his breath came in gasps.

halètement ['alɛtmɑ̃] *nm* (*V* **haleter**) panting; gasping for breath; puffing; heaving.

haleter ['alte] (5) *vi* **(a)** (*manquer d'air*) to pant, gasp for breath, puff; (*de soif, d'émotion*) to pant (*de* with). **son auditoire haletait** his audience listened with bated breath. **(b)** *[poitrine]* to heave; *[moteur]* to puff.

haleur ['alœʀ] *nm* (boat)hauler.

Haligonien, -ienne [aligɔnjɛ̃, jɛn] **1** *adj* Haligonian. **2** *nm,f*: **~(ne)** Haligonian.

hall ['ol] *nm [hôtel, immeuble]* hall, foyer; *[gare]* arrival (*ou* departure) hall.

hallali [alali] *nm* (*Chasse*) (*mise à mort*) kill; (*sonnerie*) mort.

halle ['al] *nf* (*marché*) (covered) market, (*grande pièce*) hall. (*alimentation en gros*) **~s** central food market; **les H~s (de Paris)** *the central food market of Paris* ≃ Covent Garden (*Brit*); *V* **fort.**

hallebarde ['albaʀd(ə)] *nf* halberd; *V* **pleuvoir.**

hallebardier ['albaʀdje] *nm* halberdier.

hallier ['alje] *nm* thicket, brush (*U*), brushwood (*U*).

Halloween [alɔwin] *nf* (*Can*) Hallowe'en.

hallucinant, e [alysinɑ̃, ɑ̃t] *adj spectacle, ressemblance* staggering*, incredible.

hallucination [alysinɑsjɔ̃] *nf* hallucination. **tu as des ~s!*** you must be seeing things!

hallucinatoire [alysinatwaʀ] *adj* hallucinatory.

halluciné, e [alysine] (*ptp de* **halluciner**) **1** *adj malade* suffering from hallucinations. **avoir un air ~** to look wild-eyed *ou* distracted. **2** *nm,f* (*Méd: malade, fou*) hallucinated person; (*: *fou, exalté*) raving lunatic*, crackpot*.

halluciner [alysine] (1) *vt* to hallucinate.

hallucinogène [alysinɔʒɛn] **1** *adj* hallucinogenic. **2** *nm* hallucinogen.

halo ['alo] *nm* (*Astron, Tech: auréole*) halo. (*fig*) **~ de gloire** cloud of glory.

halogène [alɔʒɛn] (*Chim*) **1** *adj* halogenous. **2** *nm* halogen.

halte ['alt(ə)] *nf* **(a)** (*pause, repos*) stop, break; (*fig: répit*) pause. **faire ~** to (make a) stop.
(b) (*endroit*) stopping place; (*Rail*) halt.
(c) (*loc*) **~!** (*gén: arrêtez-vous*) stop!; (*Mil*) halt!; **~ aux essais nucléaires!** an end to *ou* no more atomic tests!; **dire ~ à un conflit** to call a halt to a conflict, put a stop *ou* an end to a conflict; **~-là!** (*Mil*) halt!, who goes there?; (*fig*) just a moment!, hold on!; **~-là! vous exagérez** hold on, you're going too far.

haltère [altɛʀ] *nm* (*à boules*) dumbbell; (*à disques*) barbell. **faire des ~s** to do weight lifting; *V* **poids.**

haltérophile [alteʀɔfil] *nmf* weight lifter.

haltérophilie [alteʀɔfili] *nf* weight lifting.

hamac ['amak] *nm* hammock.

Hambourg ['ɑ̃buʀ] *n* Hamburg.

hamburger ['ɑ̃buʀgœʀ] *nm* hamburger.

hameau, *pl* **~x** ['amo] *nm* hamlet.

hameçon [amsɔ̃] *nm* (fish) hook; *V* **mordre.**

hammam ['amam] *nm* hammam.

hampe[1] ['ɑ̃p] *nf [drapeau]* pole; *[lance]* shaft; *[lettre]* downstroke, upstroke; (*Bot*) scape.

hampe[2] ['ɑ̃p] *nf [cerf]* breast; *[bœuf]* flank.

hamster ['amstɛʀ] *nm* hamster.

han ['ɑ̃, hɑ̃] *excl* oof! **il poussa un ~ et souleva la malle** he gave a grunt as he lifted the trunk.

hanap ['anap] *nm* (*Hist*) (lidded) goblet.

hanche ['ɑ̃ʃ] *nf [personne]* hip; *[cheval]* haunch; *V* **tour**[2].

hand-ball ['ɑ̃dbal] *nm* handball.

handicap ['ɑ̃dikap] *nm* (*lit, fig*) handicap.

handicapé, e ['ɑ̃dikape] (*ptp de* **handicaper**) **1** *adj* handicapped. **2** *nm,f* handicapped person. **~ mental/physique** mentally/physically handicapped person; **~ moteur** spastic.

handicaper ['ɑ̃dikape] (1) *vt* (*lit, fig*) to handicap.

hangar ['ɑ̃gaʀ] *nm [matériel, machines]* shed; *[fourrage]* barn; *[marchandises]* warehouse, shed; *[avions]* hangar. **~ de locomotives** engine shed.

hanneton ['antɔ̃] *nm* cockchafer, maybug; *V* **piqué.**

Hanovre ['anɔvʀ(ə)] *n* Hanover.

hanovrien, -ienne ['anɔvʀjɛ̃, jɛn] **1** *adj* Hanoverian. **2** *nm,f*: **H~(ne)** Hanoverian.

hanse ['ɑ̃s] *nf* (*Hist*) Hanse.

hanséatique ['ɑ̃seatik] *adj* Hanseatic.

hanter ['ɑ̃te] (1) *vt [fantôme, personne, souvenir]* to haunt. (*fig*) **~ les mauvais lieux** to haunt places of ill repute; **maison hantée** haunted house.

hantise ['ɑ̃tiz] *nf* obsessive fear. **avoir la ~ de la maladie** to be haunted by the fear of illness, have an obsessive fear of illness.

happement ['apmɑ̃] *nm* (*V* **happer**) snapping (up); snatching (up); grabbing.

happer ['ape] (1) *vt* (*avec la gueule, le bec*) to snap up, snatch; (*avec la main*) to snatch (up), grab. **se faire ~ par une voiture** to be hit by a car; **happé par l'abîme** dragged down into the abyss.

haquenée†† ['akne] *nf* palfrey††.

hara-kiri ['aʀakiʀi] *nm* hara-kiri, hari-kiri. **(se) faire ~** to commit hara-kiri.

harangue ['aʀɑ̃g] *nf* harangue.

haranguer ['aʀɑ̃ge] (1) *vt* to harangue, hold forth to *ou* at.

haras ['aʀɑ] *nm* stud farm.

harassant, e ['aʀasɑ̃, ɑ̃t] *adj* exhausting, wearing.

harassé, e ['aʀase] (*ptp de* **harasser**) *adj* exhausted, tired out, worn out. **~ de travail** overwhelmed with work.

harassement ['aʀasmɑ̃] *nm* exhaustion.

harasser ['aʀase] (1) *vt* (*rare*) to exhaust.

harcèlement ['aʀsɛlmɑ̃] *nm* (*V* **harceler**) harassing; plaguing; pestering; badgering; harrying; worrying.

harceler ['aʀsəle] (5) *vt personne* (*de critiques, d'attaques*) to harass, plague (*de* with); (*de questions, de réclamations*) to plague, pester, badger (*de* with); (*Mil*) *ennemi* to harass, harry; *animal* to worry, harass; *gibier* to hunt down, harry. **~ qn pour obtenir qch** to pester sth out of sb, get sth by pestering *ou* plaguing *ou* badgering sb.

harde ['aʀd(ə)] *nf [cerfs]* herd.

hardes ['aʀd(ə)] *nfpl* (*péj: vieux habits*) old clothes, rags.

hardi, e ['aʀdi] *adj* **(a)** (*audacieux*) bold, daring.
(b) (*effronté*) *décolleté* daring, bold; *plaisanterie* daring, audacious; *fille* bold, brazen; (†) *mensonge* brazen, barefaced (*épith*).
(c) (*original*) *talent, imagination* bold (*épith*).
(d) (*loc excl*) **~ les gars!** go to it, lads!, come on, lads!; **et ~ petit! les voilà qui poussent la voiture*** and heave-ho! there they are pushing the car.

hardiesse ['aʀdjɛs] *nf* **(a)** (*littér: audace*) boldness, daring. **avoir la ~ de** to be bold *ou* daring enough to; **montrer une grande ~** to show great boldness *ou* daring.
(b) (*effronterie*) *[personne]* audacity, effrontery, impudence; *[livre, plaisanterie]* audacity; *[costume]* boldness. **la ~ de son décolleté choqua tout le monde** everyone was shocked by her daring neckline, the boldness of her neckline shocked everyone.
(c) (*originalité*) *[style, tableau]* boldness. **des ~s de style** bold turns of phrase.
(d) (*libertés*) **~s** *[livre, pamphlet]* bold statements; *[domestique, soupirant]* liberties; **~s de langage** bold language (*U*).

hardiment ['aʀdimɑ̃] *adv* (*V* **hardi**) boldly; daringly; audaciously; brazenly. **ne vous engagez pas trop ~** don't commit yourself rashly.

harem ['aʀɛm] *nm* harem.

hareng ['aʀɑ̃] *nm* herring. **~ saur** smoked *ou* red herring, kipper; *V* **sec, serré.**

harengère ['aʀɑ̃ʒɛʀ] *nf* (*péj*) fishwife (*péj*).

hargne ['aʀɲ(ə)] *nf* aggressiveness, belligerence.

hargneusement ['aʀɲøzmɑ̃] *adv* (*V* **hargneux**) aggressively; belligerently; fiercely.

hargneux, -euse ['aʀɲø, øz] *adj personne, caractère, ton* aggressive, belligerent; *chien* aggressive, fierce.

haricot ['aʀiko] *nm* **(a)** bean. **des ~s!‡** nuts to that (*ou* him *ou* you *etc.*)!‡; **~ beurre** butter bean; **~ blanc** haricot bean; **~ grimpant** *ou* **rampant** *ou* **à rame** runner bean; **~ rouge** kidney bean; **~ vert** French bean; *V* **courir, fin**[1].
(b) (*Culin*) **~ de mouton** haricot of mutton, mutton stew.

haridelle ['aʀidɛl] *nf* (*péj: cheval*) nag, jade.

harmonica [aʀmɔnika] *nm* harmonica, mouth organ.

harmonie [aʀmɔni] *nf* (*Littérat, Mus, gén*) harmony; (*section de l'orchestre*) wind section; (*fanfare*) wind band. (*Mus*) **~s** harmonies; (*Littérat*) **~ imitative** onomatopoeia; **être en ~ avec** to be in harmony *ou* in keeping with; **vivre en bonne ~** to live together harmoniously *ou* in harmony; *V* **table.**

harmonieusement [aʀmɔnjøzmɑ̃] *adv* harmoniously.

harmonieux, -euse [aʀmɔnjø, øz] *adj* (*gén*) harmonious. **couleurs ~euses** well-matched *ou* harmonizing colours.

harmonique [aʀmɔnik] **1** *adj* harmonic. **2** *nm* (*Mus*) harmonic.

harmoniquement [aʀmɔnikmɑ̃] *adv* harmonically.

harmonisation [aʀmɔnizɑsjɔ̃] *nf* harmonization. (*Ling*) **~ vocalique** vowel harmony.

harmoniser [aʀmɔnize] (1) **1** *vt* to harmonize. **2 s'harmoniser** *vpr* to harmonize. **s'~ avec** to be in harmony with, harmonize with.

harmonium [aʀmɔnjɔm] *nm* harmonium.

harnachement ['aʀnaʃmɑ̃] *nm [cheval]* (*action*) harnessing; (*objet*) harness; [*personne*] rig-out*.

harnacher ['aʀnaʃe] (1) **1** *vt cheval* to harness. (*fig péj*) **il était drôlement harnaché** he had the strangest rig-out*. **2 se harnacher** *vpr [personne]* to rig o.s. out*.

harnais ['aʀnɛ] *nm*, **harnois**†† ['aʀnwa] *nm [cheval]* harness; (††: *armure, équipement*) equipment. (*Tech*) **~ d'engrenage** train of gear wheels.

haro ['aʀo] *excl* (*Jur* ††) harrow!, haro! (††, *Jur*). (*fig*) **crier ~ sur** to inveigh *ou* rail against.

harpagon [aʀpagɔ̃] *nm* Scrooge.

harpe ['aʀp(ə)] *nf* (*Mus*) harp. **~ éolienne** aeolian *ou* wind harp.

harpie ['aʀpi] *nf* (*Myth, péj*) harpy; (*Zool*) harpy eagle.

harpiste ['aʀpist(ə)] *nmf* harpist.

harpon ['aʀpɔ̃] *nm* (*Pêche*) harpoon; (*Constr*) toothing stone.

harponnage ['aʀpɔnaʒ] *nm*, **harponnement** ['aʀpɔnmɑ̃] *nm* harpooning.

harponner ['aʀpɔne] (1) *vt baleine* to harpoon; (*:) *malfaiteur* to collar*; (*:) *passant, voisin* to waylay, corner.

harponneur ['aʀpɔnœʀ] *nm* harpooner.

hasard ['azaʀ] *nm* **(a)** (*événement fortuit*) **un ~ heureux/malheureux** a stroke *ou* piece of luck/bad luck, a stroke of good fortune/misfortune; **quel ~ de vous rencontrer ici!** what a coincidence meeting you here!, fancy meeting you here!*; **c'est un vrai *ou* pur ~ que je sois libre** it's quite by chance *ou* coincidence that I'm free; **par un curieux ~** by a curious coincidence; **on l'a retrouvé par le plus grand des ~s** it was quite by chance *ou* it was a piece of sheer luck that they found him; **les ~s de la vie/de la carrière** the fortunes of life/one's career.

(b) (*destin*) chance, fate, luck; (*Statistique*) chance; **les caprices du ~** the whims of fate; **le ~ fait bien les choses: nous étions dans le même hôtel** as luck would have it *ou* by a stroke of good fortune we were *ou* we happened to be in the same hotel; **faire confiance *ou* s'en remettre au ~** to trust to luck; **il ne laisse jamais rien au ~** he never leaves anything to chance; **faire la part du ~** (*événements futurs*) to allow for chance (to play its part); (*événements passés*) to admit that chance had a hand in it; **le ~ a voulu qu'il soit *ou* (*littér*) fût absent** as luck would have it he was not there, fate willed that he should be absent (*littér*); **c'est ça le ~!*** that's the luck of the draw!*; **c'est un fait du ~** it's a matter of chance; *V* **jeu.**

(c) (*risques*) **~s** hazards; **les ~s de la guerre** the hazards of war.

(d) (*loc*) **au ~** *aller* aimlessly; *agir* haphazardly, in a haphazard way; *dire* without thinking; *tirer, bombarder* at random; **voici des exemples au ~** here are some random examples *ou* some examples taken at random; **il a acheté ces livres au ~ des ventes/de ses voyages** he bought these books just as he came across them in the sales/on his trips; **à tout ~** (*en cas de besoin*) just in case; (*espérant trouver ce qu'on cherche*) on the off chance; **on avait emporté une tente à tout ~** we had taken a tent just in case; **je suis entré à tout ~** I looked in on the off chance; **par ~** by chance, by accident; **nous nous sommes rencontrés tout à fait par ~** we met quite by chance *ou* by accident; **je passais par ~** I happened to be passing by; **tu n'aurais pas par ~ 100 F à me prêter?** you wouldn't by any chance have *ou* you wouldn't happen to have 100 francs to lend me?; **voudrais-tu par ~ m'apprendre mon métier?** you wouldn't be trying to teach me my job by any chance?; **comme par ~!** what a coincidence!; **il est arrivé comme par ~ au moment où on débouchait les bouteilles** he turned up as if by chance as we were opening the bottles; **si par ~ tu le vois** if you happen to see him, if by chance you should see him; **par le plus grand des ~s** by the most extraordinary coincidence.

hasardé, e ['azaʀde] (*ptp de* **hasarder**) *adj* = **hasardeux.**

hasarder ['azaʀde] (1) **1** *vt vie, réputation* to risk; *remarque, hypothèse, démarche* to hazard, venture; *argent* to gamble, risk. **2 se hasarder** *vpr*: **se ~ dans un endroit dangereux** to venture into a dangerous place; **se ~ à faire** to risk doing, venture to do.

hasardeux, -euse ['azaʀdø, øz] *adj entreprise* hazardous, risky; *hypothèse* dangerous, rash. **il serait bien ~ de** it would be dangerous *ou* risky to.

hasch ['aʃ] *nm* (*arg Drogue*) hash (*arg*), pot (*arg*), grass (*arg*).

haschisch ['aʃiʃ] *nm* = **hachisch.**

hase ['ɑz] *nf* doe (*female hare*).

hâte ['ɑt] *nf* (*empressement*) haste; (*impatience*) impatience. **à la ~** hurriedly, hastily; **en (grande *ou* toute) ~** posthaste, with all possible speed; **mettre de la ~ à faire qch** to do sth speedily *ou* in a hurry *ou* hurriedly; **avoir ~ de faire** to be eager *ou* anxious to do; **je n'ai qu'une ~, c'est d'avoir terminé ce travail** all I'm anxious to do is get this work finished; **sans ~** unhurriedly.

hâté, e ['ɑte] (*ptp de* **hâter**) *adj travail* hastily *ou* hurriedly done.

hâter ['ɑte] (1) **1** *vt fin, développement* to hasten; *départ* to bring forward, hasten; *fruit* to bring on, force. **~ le pas** to quicken *ou* hasten one's pace *ou* step.

2 se hâter *vpr* to hurry, hasten. **se ~ de faire** to hurry *ou* hasten *ou* make haste to do; **hâtez-vous** hurry up; **je me hâte de dire que** I hasten to say that; **hâte-toi lentement** more haste, less speed (*Prov*); **ne nous hâtons pas de juger** let's not be in a hurry to judge *ou* too hasty in our judgments.

hâtif, -ive ['ɑtif, iv] *adj développement* precocious; *fruit, saison* early; *travail* hurried; *décision, conclusion* hasty.

hâtivement ['ɑtivmɑ̃] *adv* hurriedly, hastily.

hauban ['obɑ̃] *nm* (*Naut*) shroud.

haubert ['obɛʀ] *nm* (*Hist*) coat of mail, hauberk.

hausse ['os] *nf* **(a)** [*prix, niveau, température*] rise, increase (*de* in); (*Bourse*) rise (*de* in). **une ~ inattendue de la température/des prix** an unexpected increase *ou* rise in temperature/prices; **~ de salaire** (pay) rise; **la ~ du coût de la vie** the rise in the cost of living; **être en ~** [*prix*] to be going up *ou* rising; [*marchandises*] to be going up (in price); (*Bourse*) **à la ~: marché/tendance à la ~** rising market/trend; (*fig*) **sa cote est *ou* ses actions sont en ~** things are looking up for him, his popularity is increasing; *V* **jouer.**

(b) [*fusil*] backsight adjuster.

haussement ['osmɑ̃] *nm*: **~ d'épaules** shrug; **il eut un ~ d'épaules** he shrugged (his shoulders).

hausser ['ose] (1) **1** *vt* **(a)** (*élever*) to raise. **~ les épaules** to shrug (one's shoulders); **~ la voix *ou* le ton** to raise one's voice; **ça ne le hausse pas dans mon estime** that doesn't raise him (up) in my esteem.

(b) *mur* to heighten, raise; *maison* to heighten, make higher.

2 se hausser *vpr*: **se ~ sur la pointe des pieds** to stand up on tiptoe; **se ~ au niveau de qn** to raise o.s. up to sb's level.

haussier ['osje] *nm* (*Bourse*) bull.

haut, e ['o, 'ot] **1** *adj* **(a)** *mur, montagne* high; *herbe, arbre, édifice* tall, high. **un mur ~ de 3 mètres** a wall 3 metres high; **~ de plafond** with a high ceiling, high-ceilinged; **une ~e silhouette** a tall figure; **de ~e taille** tall; **des chaussures à ~s talons** high-heeled shoes; **un chien ~ sur pattes** a long-legged dog; **il a le front ~** he has a high forehead.

(b) *plafond, branche, nuage* high. **le plus ~ étage** the top floor; **dans les plus ~es branches de l'arbre** in the topmost branches of the tree; (*lit, fig*) **marcher la tête ~e *ou* le front ~** to walk with one's head held high; (*Naut*) **les ~es voiles** the (flying) kites; *V* **montagne, ville.**

(c) *rivière, température, prix* high; (*Élec*) *fréquence, voltage* high; *note, ton* high, high-pitched. **c'est (la) marée ~e, la mer est ~e** it is high tide, the tide is in; **à marée ~e** at high tide; **en ~e mer** on the open sea, on the high seas; **pendant les ~es eaux du fleuve** while the river is high, during high water; **n'avoir jamais une parole plus ~e que l'autre** to be even-spoken; **pousser les ~s cris** to exclaim in horror *ou* indignation, raise one's hands in horror; **à voix ~e, à ~e voix** aloud, out loud; **le prix de l'or est au plus ~** the price of gold has reached a peak *ou* maximum; *V* **verbe.**

(d) (*gén avant n*) (*fig: élevé, supérieur*) *qualité, rang* high; *âme, pensée* lofty, noble. **avoir une ~e idée *ou* opinion de soi-même** to have a high *ou* an exalted opinion of o.s.; **c'est du plus ~ comique** it's highly amusing *ou* comical, it's excruciatingly funny; **~ en couleur** (*rougeaud*) with a high colour *ou* a ruddy complexion; (*coloré, pittoresque*) colourful; **avoir la ~e main sur qch** to have supreme control of sth; (*hum*) **~s faits** heroic deeds; **de ~ rang** high-ranking; **de ~e naissance** of noble *ou* high birth; **les ~es cartes** the high cards, the picture cards; **la ~e cuisine/couture/coiffure** haute cuisine/couture/coiffure; **les ~es mathématiques** higher mathematics; **la ~e finance** high finance; (*Mil*) **~ commandement** high command; **~ fonctionnaire** high- *ou* top-ranking civil servant; **~ personnage** high-ranking person; (*lit, fig*) **de ~e voltige** acrobatic; **la ~e bourgeoisie** the upper middle classes.

(e) (*ancien*) **dans la plus ~e antiquité** in earliest antiquity; **le ~ moyen âge** the Early Middle Ages; **le ~ Empire** the Early (Roman) Empire; (*Ling*) **le ~ allemand** Old High German.

(f) (*Géog*) **le H~ Rhin** the Upper Rhine; **la H~e Normandie** Upper Normandy; **les H~es-Terres** the highlands; (*Can Hist*) **le H~ Canada** Upper Canada.

2 *nm* **(a)** [*arbre, colline, robe, armoire*] top. **dans le ~** at the top, high up; **le mur a 3 mètres de ~** the wall is 3 metres high; **au *ou* en ~ de l'arbre** at the top of the tree, high up in the tree; **le ~ du visage** the top part of the face; **les pièces du ~** the rooms upstairs, the upstairs rooms; **les voisins du ~** the neighbours upstairs; **l'étagère du ~** the top shelf; **en ~ de l'échelle sociale** high up the social ladder; **combien fait-il de ~?** how high is it?; (*fig*) **des ~s et des bas** ups and downs; **tenir le ~ du pavé** to take pride of place.

(b) du ~ de: du ~ d'un arbre from the top of a tree; **tomber du ~ du 5e étage** to fall from the 5th floor; **parler du ~ d'une tribune/d'un balcon** to speak from a platform/a balcony; (*fig*) **regarder qn du ~ de sa grandeur** to look down at sb from one's lofty height (*fig*).

(c) (*Géog*) **les H~s de Meuse/de Seine** the upper reaches of the Meuse/Seine.

(d) (*loc*) **voir les choses de ~** to take a detached view of things; **tomber de ~** (*lit*) to fall from a height; (*fig*) to have one's hopes dashed, come down with a crash; **prendre qch de (très) ~** to take sth in a (very) high and mighty way, react (most) indignantly; **traiter qn de ~** to look down on sb; **regarder qn de ~ en bas** to look sb up and down; **frapper de ~ en bas** to strike downwards; **en ~** at the top; **il habite en ~/tout en ~** he lives upstairs/right at the top; **manteau boutonné jusqu'en ~** coat buttoned right up *ou* (right) up to the top; **regarder par en ~** to look from upstairs *ou* above; **en ~ de** at the top of; **les voleurs sont passés par en ~** the burglars came (in) from upstairs *ou* from above; (*lit, fig*) **d'en ~** from above; *V* **bas**[1], **là.**

3 haute *nf*: **(les gens de) la ~e**: the upper crust*, the toffs: (*Brit*), the swells:.

4 *adv* **(a)** *monter, sauter, voler* high. **mettez vos livres plus ~** put your books higher up; **il a sauté le plus ~** he jumped the highest.

(b) *parler* loudly. **lire/penser tout ~** to read/think aloud *ou* out loud; **mettez la radio plus ~** turn up the radio; **j'ose le dire bien ~** I'm not afraid of saying it out loud; **parle plus ~!** speak up!; (*Mus*) **monter ~** to hit the top notes; **chanter trop ~** to sing sharp.

(c) (*sur un colis*) 'this side up'.

(d) (*sur le plan social*) **des gens ~ placés** people in high places; **arriver ~** to reach a high position; **viser ~** to aim high.

(e) (*en arrière*) **aussi ~ qu'on peut remonter** as far back as we can go; **'voir plus ~'** 'see above'; **comme je l'ai dit plus ~** as I said above *ou* previously.

(f) ~ les mains! hands up!, stick 'em up!:; **gagner ~ la main** to win hands down.

5: (*Hist*) **haut-de-chausse(s)** *nm, pl* **hauts-de-chausse(s)**

(knee) breeches, trunk-hose; **haut-le-cœur** *nm inv* retch, heave; **avoir un haut-le-cœur** to retch, heave; **haut commissaire** high commissioner; **haut commissariat** high commissionership; (*Mus*) **haute-contre**, *pl* **hautes-contre** (*adj, nm: chanteur*) counter tenor; (*nf: voix*) counter tenor; **haut-le-corps** *nm inv* (sudden) start, jump; **avoir un haut-le-corps** to start, jump; (*Jur*) **Haute Cour** high court (*for impeachment of French President or Ministers*); (*Équitation*) **haute école** haute école; (*fig*) **c'est de la haute école** it's very advanced (stuff*); (*Rad*) **haute fidélité** hi-fi, high fidelity; (*Naut*) **haut-fond** *nm, pl* **hauts-fonds** shallow, shoal; **haut-de-forme** *nm, pl* **hauts-de-forme** top hat; **haut-fourneau** *nm, pl* **hauts-fourneaux** blast *ou* smelting furnace; **haut lieu: le haut lieu de la culture/musique** the Mecca of culture/music; **en haut lieu** in high places; **haut-mal††** *nm inv* falling sickness††; **haut-parleur** *nm, pl* **haut-parleurs** (loud)speaker; (*Art*) **haut-relief** *nm, pl* **hauts-reliefs** high relief; **haute trahison** high treason; **haut vol, haute volée: de haut vol, de haute volée** *personne* high-flying; *projet* far-reaching; *V* **lutte, montagne.**

hautain, e ['otɛ̃, ɛn] *adj personne* haughty; *air, manière* haughty, lofty.

hautainement ['otɛnmɑ̃] *adv* haughtily, loftily.

hautbois ['obwɑ] *nm* oboe.

hautboïste ['obɔist(ə)] *nmf* oboist, oboe player.

hautement ['otmɑ̃] *adv* (*extrêmement*) highly; (*ouvertement*) openly.

hauteur ['otœʀ] *nf* **(a)** (*élévation verticale*) *[tour, montagne, arche, personne]* height; *[son]* pitch; (*Auto*) *[châssis]* ground clearance. **il se redressa de toute sa ~** he drew himself up to his full height; (*Aut*) **~ maximum 3 mètres** headroom 3 metres; **tomber de toute sa ~** *[personne]* to measure one's length, fall flat; *[armoire]* to come crashing down; **perdre de la ~** to lose height; **prendre de la ~** to climb, gain height; **à ~ d'appui** at leaning height; **à ~ des yeux** at eye level; **à ~ d'homme** at the right height *ou* level for a man; (*fig*) **élever l'épargne à la ~ d'une institution** to make saving a way of life; *V* **saut.**

(b) (*Géom*) perpendicular height; (*ligne*) perpendicular; (*Astron*) altitude.

(c) (*plan horizontal*) **à la ~ de: arriver à la ~ de qn** to draw level with sb; **la procession arrivait à sa ~** the procession was drawing level with him; **nous habitons à la ~ de la mairie** we live up by the town hall; (*Naut*) **arriver à la ~ d'un cap** to come abreast of a cape.

(d) (*fig: digne de*) **être à la ~ de la situation** to be equal to the situation; **il s'est vraiment montré à la ~*** he proved he was up to it*; **ne pas se sentir à la ~*** not to feel up to it*, not to feel equal to the task.

(e) (*colline*) height, hill. **gagner les ~s** to make for the heights *ou* hills.

(f) (*fig: noblesse*) loftiness, nobility. **la ~ de ses sentiments** his noble *ou* lofty sentiments, the loftiness *ou* nobility of his sentiments.

(g) (*fig: arrogance*) haughtiness, loftiness. **parler avec ~** to speak haughtily *ou* loftily.

hauturier, -ière ['otyʀje, jɛʀ] *adj*: **navigation ~ière** ocean navigation; **pilote ~** deep-sea pilot.

havage ['avaʒ] *nm* (mechanical) cutting.

havanais, -e ['avanɛ, ɛz] **1** *adj* of *ou* from Havana. **2** *nm,f*: **H~(e)** inhabitant *ou* native of Havana.

Havane ['avan] **1** *nf*: **la ~** Havana. **2** *nm* **h~** (*cigare*) Havana. **3** *adj inv* **h~** (*couleur*) tobacco (brown).

hâve ['ɑv] *adj* (*émacié*) gaunt, haggard; (*pâle*) wan.

haveneau, *pl* **~x** ['avno] *nm* shrimping net.

haver ['ave] (1) *vt* (*Tech*) to cut (*mechanically*).

haveuse ['avøz] *nf* cutting machine.

havrais, e ['ɑvʀɛ, ɛz] **1** *adj* from *ou* of Le Havre. **2** *nm,f*: **H~(e)** inhabitant *ou* native of Le Havre.

havre ['ɑvʀ(ə)] *nm* (*littér: lit, fig*) haven. **~ de paix** haven of peace.

havresac ['ɑvʀəsak] *nm* haversack, knapsack.

Hawaï [awai] *n* Hawaii.

hawaïen, -ïenne [awajɛ̃, jɛn] **1** *adj* Hawaiian. **2** *nm* (*Ling*) Hawaiian. **3** *nm,f*: **H~(ne)** Hawaiian.

Haye ['ɛ] *nf*: **La ~** the Hague.

hé ['e, he] *excl* (*pour appeler*) hey!; (*pour renforcer*) well. **~! ~!** well, well!, ha-ha!; **~ non!** I should think not!

heaume ['om] *nm* (*Hist*) helmet.

hebdomadaire [ɛbdɔmadɛʀ] *adj, nm* weekly.

hebdomadairement [ɛbdɔmadɛʀmɑ̃] *adv* weekly.

hébergement [ebɛʀʒəmɑ̃] *nm* (*V* **héberger**) putting up, lodging; taking in; harbouring.

héberger [ebɛʀʒe] (3) *vt visiteurs* to put up, lodge; *réfugiés* to take in; *évadé* to harbour, take in. **les sinistrés ont été hébergés chez des voisins** the victims were taken in *ou* given shelter by neighbours; **pouvez-vous nous ~?** can you put us up? *ou* accommodate us?

hébété, e [ebete] (*ptp de* **hébéter**) *adj regard, air, personne* dazed. **être ~ de fatigue/de douleur** to be numbed with fatigue/pain; **~ par l'alcool** stupefied by *ou* besotted with drink.

hébétement [ebɛtmɑ̃] *nm* stupor.

hébéter [ebete] (6) *vt [alcool]* to besot, stupefy; *[lecture, télévision]* to daze, numb; *[fatigue, douleur]* to numb.

hébétude [ebetyd] *nf* (*littér*) stupor; (*Méd*) hebetude.

hébraïque [ebʀaik] *adj* Hebrew (*épith*), Hebraic.

hébraïsant, e [ebʀaizɑ̃, ɑ̃t] *nm,f* Hebraist, Hebrew scholar.

hébraïser [ebʀaize] (1) *vt* to assimilate into Jewish culture.

hébraïsme [ebʀaism(ə)] *nm* Hebraism.

hébraïste [ebʀaist(ə)] *nmf* = **hébraïsant.**

hébreu, *pl* **~x** [ebʀø] **1** *adj m* Hebrew. **2** *nm* (*Ling*) Hebrew. **pour moi, c'est de l'~*** it's all Greek *ou* double Dutch to me!* **3** *nm*: **H~** Hebrew.

Hébrides [ebʀid] *nfpl*: **les ~** the Hebrides.

hécatombe [ekatɔ̃b] *nf* (*tuerie*) slaughter, hecatomb; (*fig: à un examen etc*) (wholesale) slaughter *ou* massacre. **faire une ~ de** to slaughter.

hectare [ɛktaʀ] *nm* hectare.

hectique [ɛktik] *adj* (*Méd*) hectic.

hecto [ɛkto] *nm abrév de* **hectogramme, hectolitre.**

hecto ... [ɛkto] *préf* hecto ... .

hectogramme [ɛktɔgʀam] *nm* hectogram(me).

hectolitre [ɛktɔlitʀ(ə)] *nm* hectolitre.

hectomètre [ɛktɔmɛtʀ(ə)] *nm* hectometre.

hectométrique [ɛktɔmetʀik] *adj* hectometre (*épith*).

hectowatt [ɛktɔwat] *nm* hectowatt, 100 watts (*pl*).

hédonisme [edɔnism(ə)] *nm* hedonism.

hédoniste [edɔnist(ə)] **1** *adj* hedonist(ic). **2** *nmf* hedonist.

hégélianisme [egeljanism(ə)] *nm* Hegelianism.

hégélien, -ienne [egeljɛ̃, jɛn] *adj, nm,f* Hegelian.

hégémonie [eʒemɔni] *nf* hegemony.

hégire [eʒiʀ] *nf*: **l'~** the Hegira.

hein* ['ɛ̃, hɛ̃] *excl* (*de surprise, pour faire répéter*) eh?*. **qu'est-ce que tu feras, ~?** what are you going to do (then), eh?*; **ça suffit, ~!** that's enough, O.K.?* *ou* all right?*

hélas ['elɑs] *excl* alas! **~ non!** I'm afraid not!, unfortunately not; **~ oui!** I'm afraid so!, yes unfortunately; **mais ~, ils n'ont pas pu en profiter** but unfortunately *ou* sadly they were not able to reap the benefits of it.

Hélène [elɛn] *nf* Helen, Helena, Ellen.

héler ['ele] (6) *vt navire, taxi* to hail; *personne* to call, hail.

hélianthe [eljɑ̃t] *nm* helianthus, sunflower.

hélianthine [eljɑ̃tin] *nf* (*Chim*) helianthine, methyl orange.

hélice [elis] *nf* (*Tech*) propeller, screw(-propeller); (*Archit, Géom*) helix. **escalier en ~** spiral staircase.

hélicoïdal, e, *mpl* **-aux** [elikɔidal, o] *adj* (*gén*) helical; (*Bot, Math*) helicoid.

hélicoïde [elikɔid] *adj, nm, nf* helicoid.

hélicon [elikɔ̃] *nm* helicon.

hélicoptère [elikɔptɛʀ] *nm* helicopter.

héligare [eligaʀ] *nf* heliport.

héliographe [eljɔgʀaf] *nm* heliograph.

héliographie [eljɔgʀafi] *nf* (*Typ*) heliography.

héliogravure [eljɔgʀavyʀ] *nf* heliogravure.

héliomarin, e [eljɔmaʀɛ̃, in] *adj cure* of sun and sea-air. **établissement ~** seaside sanatorium specializing in heliotherapy.

héliport [elipɔʀ] *nm* heliport.

héliporté, e [elipɔʀte] *adj* transported by helicopter.

hélium [eljɔm] *nm* helium.

hellène [elɛn] **1** *adj* Hellenic. **2** *nmf*: **H~** Hellene.

hellénique [elenik] *adj* Hellenic.

hellénisant, e [elenizɑ̃, ɑ̃t] *adj, nm,f*: **(juif) ~** hellenistic Jew; **(savant) ~** hellenist, Hellenic scholar.

hellénisation [elenizɑsjɔ̃] *nf* hellenization.

helléniser [elenize] (1) *vt* to hellenize.

hellénisme [elenism(ə)] *nm* hellenism.

helléniste [elenist(ə)] *nmf* = **hellénisant.**

helvète [ɛlvɛt] **1** *adj* Helvetian. **2** *nmf*: **H~** Helvetian.

Helvétie [ɛlvesi] *nf* Helvetia.

helvétique [ɛlvetik] *adj* Swiss, Helvetian (*rare*).

helvétisme [ɛlvetism(ə)] *nm* (*Ling*) Swiss idiom.

hem ['ɛm, hɛm] *excl* (*gén*) hem!, h'm!; (*pour appeler*) hey!

hématie [emati] *nf* red (blood) corpuscle.

hématologie [ematɔlɔʒi] *nf* haematology.

hématome [ematom] *nm* haematoma (*T*).

hémicycle [emisikl(ə)] *nm* semicircle, hemicycle. **l'~ (de l'Assemblée nationale)** ≃ the benches of the Commons (*Brit*) *ou* House of Representatives (*US*).

hémiplégie [emipleʒi] *nf* paralysis of one side, hemiplegia (*T*).

hémiplégique [emipleʒik] **1** *adj* paralyzed on one side, hemiplegic (*T*). **2** *nmf* person paralyzed on one side, hemiplegic (*T*).

hémisphère [emisfɛʀ] *nm* (*gén*) hemisphere. **~ sud/nord** southern/northern hemisphere.

hémisphérique [emisfeʀik] *adj* hemispheric(al).

hémistiche [emistiʃ] *nm* hemistich.

hémoglobine [emɔglɔbin] *nf* haemoglobin.

hémophile [emɔfil] **1** *adj* haemophilic. **2** *nmf* haemophiliac.

hémophilie [emɔfili] *nf* haemophilia.

hémorragie [emɔʀaʒi] *nf* bleeding (*U*), haemorrhage. **~ interne** internal bleeding (*U*) *ou* haemorrhage; (*fig*) **l'~ due à la guerre** the dramatic loss of manpower through war, the sapping of a country's resources through war; (*fig*) **~ de capitaux** massive outflow of capital; (*fig*) **l' ~ des cerveaux** the brain-drain.

hémorragique [emɔʀaʒik] *adj* haemorrhagic.

hémorroïdaire [emɔʀɔidɛʀ] *adj malade* with haemorrhoids. **remède ~** medicament for haemorrhoids.

hémorroïdal, e, *mpl* **-aux** [emɔʀɔidal, o] *adj* haemorrhoidal.

hémorroïde [emɔʀɔid] *nf* (*gén pl*) haemorrhoid, pile.

hémostatique [emɔstatik] *adj, nm* haemostatic.

hendécagone [ɛ̃dekagɔn] *nm* (*Géom*) hendecagon.

henné ['ene] *nm* henna.

hennin ['enɛ̃] *nm* (*Hist: bonnet*) hennin.

hennir ['eniʀ] (2) *vi* to neigh, whinny; (*fig péj*) to bray.

hennissement ['enismɑ̃] *nm* neigh, whinny; (*fig péj*) braying (*U*).

Henri [ɑ̃ʀi] *nm* Henry.

hep ['ɛp, hɛp] *excl* hey!

hépatique [epatik] **1** *adj* (*Méd*) hepatic. **2** *nmf* person who suffers from a liver complaint. **3** *nf* (*Bot*) liverwort, hepatic (*T*).

hépatisme [epatism(ə)] *nm* hepatic symptoms (*pl*).

hépatite [epatit] *nf* hepatitis.
heptaèdre [ɛptaɛdʀ(ə)] *nm* heptahedron.
heptagonal, e, *mpl* **-aux** [ɛptagɔnal, o] *adj* heptagonal.
heptagone [ɛptagɔn] *nm* heptagon.
heptasyllabe [ɛptasilab] **1** *adj* heptasyllabic. **2** *nm* heptasyllable.
héraldique [eʀaldik] **1** *adj* heraldic. **2** *nf* heraldry.
héraldiste [eʀaldist(ə)] *nmf* heraldist, expert on heraldry.
héraut [ˈeʀo] *nm* **(a)** (*Hist*) ~ **(d'armes)** herald. **(b)** (*fig littér*) herald, harbinger (*littér*).
herbacé, e [ɛʀbase] *adj* herbaceous.
herbage [ɛʀbaʒ] *nm* (*herbe*) pasture, pasturage; (*pré*) pasture.
herbager, -ère [ɛʀbaʒe, ɛʀ] *nm,f* grazier.
herbe [ɛʀb(ə)] *nf* **(a)** (*plante*) grass (*U*); (*Bot: espèce*) grass; (*arg Drogue*) grass (*arg*), pot (*arg*). **dans les hautes ~s** in the long *ou* tall grass; **la moitié de leurs terres est en ~** half their estate is under grass; **arracher une ~** to pull up a blade of grass; **~s folles** wild grasses; *V* **déjeuner, mauvais** *etc.*
(b) (*Culin, Méd*) herb. **~s médicinales/aromatiques/potagères** medicinal/aromatic/kitchen herbs; *V* **fin[1], omelette.**
(c) (*loc*) **en ~** *blé* green, unripe; (*fig*) *avocat, mécanicien* budding (*épith*); **ce gamin est un avocat/un mécanicien en ~** this lad is a budding lawyer/mechanic *ou* has the makings of a lawyer/mechanic; **couper** *ou* **faucher l'~ sous les pieds de qn** to cut the ground from under sb's feet; *V* **manger.**
herbeux, -euse [ɛʀbø, øz] *adj* grassy.
herbicide [ɛʀbisid] **1** *adj* herbicidal. **2** *nm* weed-killer.
herbier [ɛʀbje] *nm* (*collection, planches*) herbarium.
herbivore [ɛʀbivɔʀ] **1** *adj* herbivorous. **2** *nm* herbivore.
herborisation [ɛʀbɔʀizɑsjɔ̃] *nf* (*action*) collection of plants.
herboriser [ɛʀbɔʀize] (1) *vi* to collect plants, botanize.
herboriste [ɛʀbɔʀist(ə)] *nmf* herbalist.
herboristerie [ɛʀbɔʀist(ə)ʀi] *nf* (*commerce*) herb trade; (*magasin*) herbalist's shop.
herbu, e [ɛʀby] *adj* grassy.
Hercule [ɛʀkyl] *nm* (*Myth*) Hercules. (*fig*) **c'est un h~** he's a real Hercules; **h~ de foire** strong man.
herculéen, -éenne [ɛʀkyleɛ̃, eɛn] *adj* Herculean.
hercynien, -enne [ɛʀsinjɛ̃, ɛn] *adj* Armorican, Hercynian.
hère [ˈɛʀ] *nm*: **pauvre ~** poor *ou* miserable wretch.
héréditaire [ereditɛʀ] *adj* hereditary.
héréditairement [ereditɛʀmɑ̃] *adv* hereditarily.
hérédité [eredite] *nf* **(a)** (*Bio*) heredity (*U*). **une lourde ~** an ominous heredity; (*fig: culturelle etc*) **une ~ catholique/royaliste** a Catholic/Royalist heritage.
(b) (*Jur*) (*droit*) right of inheritance; (*caractère héréditaire*) hereditary nature.
hérésie [erezi] *nf* (*Rel*) heresy; (*fig*) sacrilege, heresy. (*hum*) **servir du vin rouge avec le poisson est une véritable ~!** it's absolute sacrilege to serve red wine with fish!
hérétique [eretik] **1** *adj* heretical. **2** *nmf* heretic.
hérissé, e [ˈerise] (*ptp de* **hérisser**) *adj* **(a)** (*dressé*) *poils, cheveux* standing on end, bristling; *barbe* bristly.
(b) (*garni*) **~ de poils** bristling with hairs; **~ d'épines/de clous** spiked with thorns/nails; **~ d'obstacles/de fusils** bristling with obstacles/rifles.
(c) (*garni de pointes*) *cactus, tige* prickly.
hérisser [ˈerise] (1) **1** *vt* **(a)** *[animal]* **le chat hérisse ses poils** the cat bristles its coat *ou* makes its coat bristle (up); **le porc-épic hérisse ses piquants** the porcupine bristles its spines *ou* makes its spines bristle (up); **l'oiseau hérisse ses plumes** the bird ruffles its feathers.
(b) *[vent, froid]* **le vent hérisse ses cheveux** the wind makes his hair stand on end.
(c) (*armer*) **~ une planche de clous** to spike a plank with nails; **~ une muraille de créneaux** to top *ou* crown a wall with battlements; **il avait hérissé la dictée de pièges** he had put a good sprinkling of tricky points into the dictation.
(d) (*garnir*) **des clous hérissent la planche** the plank is spiked with nails; **les créneaux qui hérissent la muraille** the battlements crowning the wall; **de nombreuses difficultés hérissent le texte** numerous difficulties are scattered through the text.
(e) (*mettre en colère*) **~ qn** to put *ou* get sb's back up*, ruffle sb; **faites attention de ne pas le ~** be careful not to put his back up* *ou* to ruffle him; **il y a une chose qui me hérisse, c'est le mensonge** there's one thing that gets my back up* *ou* that makes me bristle and that's lying.
2 se hérisser *vpr* **(a)** *[poils, cheveux]* to stand on end, bristle (up).
(b) *[animal]* to bristle (up). **le chat se hérissa** the cat's fur stood on end *ou* bristled (up), the cat bristled (up).
(c) (*se fâcher*) to bristle, get one's back up*.
hérisson [ˈeʀisɔ̃] *nm* (*Zool*) hedgehog; (*Tech*) (*brosse*) (chimney sweep's) brush; (*fig: personne insociable*) prickly type, hedgehog. (*mal coiffé*) **c'est un vrai ~** his hair sticks out all over the place.
héritage [eʀitaʒ] *nm* **(a)** (*action*) inheritance.
(b) (*argent, biens*) inheritance; (*coutumes, système*) heritage, legacy. **faire un ~** to come into an inheritance; **laisser qch en ~ à qn** to leave sth to sb, bequeath sth to sb; **avoir une maison par ~** to have inherited a house; (*péj*) **tante/oncle à ~** wealthy *ou* rich aunt/uncle; (*fig*) **l'~ du passé** the heritage *ou* legacy of the past.
hériter [eʀite] (1) *vti* to inherit. **~ (de) qch de qn** to inherit sth from sb; **~ de son oncle** to inherit *ou* come into one's uncle's property; **~ d'une maison** to inherit a house; **impatient d'~** eager to gain his inheritance; **il a hérité d'un vieux chapeau*** he has inherited *ou* acquired an old hat; **il a hérité d'un rhume*** he's picked up a cold.
héritier [eʀitje] *nm* heir. **~ naturel** heir-at-law; **il est l'~ d'une grande fortune** he is heir to a large fortune; (*hum*) **elle lui a donné un ~** she produced him an heir *ou* a son and heir; **~ présomptif de la couronne** heir apparent (to the throne).
héritière [eʀitjɛʀ] *nf* heiress.
hermaphrodisme [ɛʀmafʀɔdism(ə)] *nm* hermaphroditism.
hermaphrodite [ɛʀmafʀɔdit] **1** *adj* hermaphrodite, hermaphroditic(al). **2** *nm* hermaphrodite.
herméneutique [ɛʀmenøtik] **1** *adj* hermeneutic. **2** *nf* hermeneutics (*sg*).
hermétique [ɛʀmetik] *adj* **(a)** (*étanche*) *boîte, joint* airtight, watertight, hermetic. **cela assure une fermeture ~ de la porte** this makes sure that the door closes tightly *ou* that the door is a tight fit.
(b) (*fig: impénétrable*) *barrage, secret* impenetrable; *mystère* sealed, impenetrable. **visage ~** closed *ou* impenetrable expression.
(c) (*obscur*) *écrivain, livre* abstruse, obscure. (*Littérat*) **poésie/poète ~** hermetic poetry/poet.
(d) (*Alchimie*) hermetic.
hermétiquement [ɛʀmetikmɑ̃] *adv fermer, joindre* tightly, hermetically; (*fig*) *s'exprimer* abstrusely, obscurely. **joint ~ soudé** hermetically soldered joint; **emballage ~ fermé** hermetically sealed package; **local ~ clos** sealed(-up) premises; **secret ~ gardé** closely guarded secret.
hermétisme [ɛʀmetism(ə)] *nm* (*péj: obscurité*) abstruseness, obscurity; (*Alchimie, Littérat*) hermetism.
hermine [ɛʀmin] *nf* (*animal, fourrure*) ermine; (*avec pelage d'été*) stoat, ermine (*rare*).
herminette [ɛʀminɛt] *nf* adze.
herniaire [ˈɛʀnjɛʀ] *adj* hernial; *V* **bandage.**
hernie [ˈɛʀni] *nf* hernia, rupture. **~ discale** slipped disc; **~ étranglée** strangulated hernia.
hernié, e [ˈɛʀnje] *adj organe* herniated.
Hérode [eʀɔd] *nm* Herod.
Hérodiade [eʀɔdjad] *nf* Herodiad.
Hérodote [eʀɔdɔt] *nm* Herodotus.
héroï-comique [eʀɔikɔmik] *adj* mock-heroic.
héroïne [eʀɔin] *nf* (*femme*) heroine; (*drogue*) heroin.
héroïque [eʀɔik] *adj* heroic. **l'époque ~** the pioneering days.
héroïquement [eʀɔikmɑ̃] *adv* heroically.
héroïsme [eʀɔism(ə)] *nm* heroism. **boire ces médicaments si mauvais, c'est de l'~!*** taking such nasty medicines is nothing short of heroic! *ou* is nothing short of heroism!
héron [ˈeʀɔ̃] *nm* heron.
héros [ˈeʀo] *nm* hero. **mourir en ~** to die the death of a hero *ou* a hero's death; **le ~ du jour** the hero of the day.
herpès [ɛʀpɛs] *nm* herpes.
herpétique [ɛʀpetik] *adj* herpetic.
hersage [ˈɛʀsaʒ] *nm* (*Agr*) harrowing.
herse [ˈɛʀs(ə)] *nf* (*Agr*) harrow; *[château]* portcullis; (*Théât*) batten.
hertz [ɛʀts] *nm* hertz.
hertzien, -ienne [ɛʀtsjɛ̃, jɛn] *adj* Hertzian.
hésitant, e [ezitɑ̃, ɑ̃t] **1** *adj personne, début* hesitant; *caractère* wavering, hesitant; *voix, pas* hesitant, faltering. **2** *nm,f* (*votant*) 'don't-know'.
hésitation [ezitɑsjɔ̃] *nf* hesitation. **sans ~** without hesitation, unhesitatingly; **j'accepte sans ~** I accept without hesitation *ou* unhesitatingly; **après bien des ~s** after much hesitation; **il eut un moment d'~ et répondit ...** he hesitated for a moment and replied ..., after a moment's hesitation he replied ...; **je n'ai plus d'~s** I shall hesitate no longer; **ses ~s continuelles** his continual hesitations *ou* dithering.
hésiter [ezite] (1) *vi* **(a)** (*balancer*) to hesitate. **il n'y a pas à ~** there are no two ways about it; **sans ~** without hesitating, unhesitatingly; **~ à faire** to hesitate to do, be unsure whether to do; **j'hésite à vous déranger** I don't like to disturb you, I hesitate to disturb you; **il hésitait sur la route à suivre** he hesitated as to *ou* dithered over which road to take; **~ sur une date** to hesitate over a date; **~ entre plusieurs possibilités** to waver between several possibilities.
(b) (*s'arrêter*) to hesitate. **~ dans ses réponses** to be hesitant in one's replies; **~ en récitant sa leçon** to falter in reciting one's lesson, recite one's lesson falteringly *ou* hesitantly; **~ devant l'obstacle** to falter *ou* hesitate before an obstacle.
hétéroclite [eteʀɔklit] *adj* (*disparate*) *ensemble, roman, bâtiment* heterogeneous; *objets* sundry, assorted; (*bizarre*) *personne* eccentric.
hétérodoxe [eteʀɔdɔks(ə)] *adj* heterodox.
hétérodoxie [eteʀɔdɔksi] *nf* heterodoxy.
hétérogène [eteʀɔʒɛn] *adj* heterogeneous.
hétérogénéité [eteʀɔʒeneite] *nf* heterogeneousness.
hétérosexualité [eteʀɔsɛksɥalite] *nf* heterosexuality.
hétérosexuel, -elle [eteʀɔsɛksɥɛl] *adj* heterosexual.
hêtraie [ˈɛtʀɛ] *nf* beech grove.
hêtre [ˈɛtʀ(ə)] *nm* (*arbre*) beech (tree); (*bois*) beech (wood).
heu [ˈø] *excl* (*doute*) h'm!, hem!; (*hésitation*) um!, er!
heur†† [œʀ] *nm* good fortune. (*littér, iro*) **je n'ai pas eu l'~ de lui plaire** I did not have the good fortune to please him, I was not fortunate enough to please him.
heure [œʀ] *nf* **(a)** (*mesure de durée*) hour; (*Scol*) period, class. **j'ai attendu une bonne ~/une petite ~** I waited (for) a good hour/just under an hour; **j'ai attendu 2 ~s d'horloge** I waited 2 solid hours*; **il a parlé des ~s** he spoke for hours; **pendant les ~s de classe/de bureau** during school/office hours; **gagner/coûter 20 F (de) l'~** to earn/cost 20 francs an hour *ou* per hour; (*Aut*) **faire du 100 (km) à l'~** to do 60 miles *ou* 100 km an hour *ou* per hour; **1 ~/3 ~s de travail** 1 hour's/3 hours' work; **lutter pour la semaine de 30 ~s (de travail)** to fight for a 30-hour (working) week; **faire des/10 ~s supplémentaires** to work *ou* do

overtime/10 hours' overtime; **les ~s supplémentaires sont bien payées** you get well paid for (doing) overtime, overtime hours are well-paid; **fait dans les 24 ~s** done within 24 hours.

(b) (*divisions de la journée*) **savoir l'~** to know what time it is, know the time; **avez-vous l'~?** have you got the time?; **quelle ~ avez-vous?** what time do you make it?; **il est 6 ~s/6 ~s 10/6 ~s moins 10/6 ~s et demie** it is 6 (o'clock)/10 past 6/10 to 6/half past 6; **10 ~s du matin/du soir** 10 (o'clock) in the morning/at night, 10 a.m./p.m.; (*frm*) **à 16 ~s 30** at 4.30 p.m., at 16.30 (*frm*); **il est 8 ~s passées** *ou* **sonnées** it's gone 8; **à 4 ~s pile** *ou* **sonnant(es)** *ou* **tapant(es)*** *ou* **pétant(es)*** at exactly 4 (o'clock), at dead on 4 (o'clock)*, at 4 (o'clock) on the dot*; **à 4 ~s juste(s)** at 4 sharp; **les bus passent à l'~** the buses come on the hour; **à une heure avancée (de la nuit)** at a late hour (of the night), late on (in the night); **à une ~ indue** at an *ou* some ungodly hour; (*Can*) **~ avancée** daylight saving time; *V* **demander.**

(c) (*l'heure fixée*) time. **c'est l'~** it's time; **avant l'~** before time, ahead of time, early; **à l'~ (juste)** (right *ou* exactly) on time; **après l'~** late; **il n'a pas d'~** he has no fixed timetable *ou* schedule; **~ de Greenwich** Greenwich mean time; **~ légale/locale/d'été** standard/local/summer time; **l'~ militaire** the right *ou* exact time; **votre ~ sera la mienne** name *ou* say a time; **mettre sa montre à l'~** to set *ou* put one's watch right; **ma montre/l'horloge est toujours à l'~** my watch/the clock is always right *ou* keeps good time; **l'~ c'est l'~** on time is on time.

(d) (*moment*) time, moment. **je n'ai pas une ~ à moi** I haven't a moment to myself; (*frm*) **l'~ est venue** *ou* **a sonné** the time has come; **nous avons passé ensemble des ~s heureuses** we spent many happy hours together; **l'~ du déjeuner** lunchtime, time for lunch; **l'~ d'aller se coucher** bedtime, time for bed; **l'~ du biberon** (baby's) feeding time; **à l'~** *ou* **aux ~s des repas** at mealtime(s); **~ d'affluence** *ou* **de pointe** (*trains, circulation*) rush hour, peak hour; (*magasin*) peak shopping period, busy period; **~ de pointe** (*téléphone*) peak period; **les ~s creuses** (*gén*) the slack periods; (*pour électricité, téléphone etc*) off-peak periods; **les problèmes de l'~** the problems of the moment; **à l'~ H** at zero hour; **l'~ est grave** it is a grave moment; **à l'~ dite** at the appointed *ou* prearranged time; **à l'~ du danger** at the time of danger; **l'~ de vérité** the hour of truth; **l'~ est à la concertation** the present mood is one of *ou* it is now time for consultation and dialogue; *V* **bon¹, dernier, premier.**

(e) (*avec adj poss*) **il est poète/aimable à ses ~s** he writes poetry/he can be quite pleasant when the fancy takes him *ou* when he feels like it; **ce doit être Paul, c'est son ~** it must be Paul — it's his (usual) time; **elle a eu son ~ de gloire/de célébrité** she has had her hour of glory/fame; **il aura son ~** (*de gloire etc*) his hour *ou* time will come; **il attend son ~** he is biding his time *ou* waiting for the right moment; **son ~ viendra/est venue** (*de mourir*) his time will come/has come.

(f) (*mesure de distance*) hour. **Chartres est à plus d'une ~ de Paris** Chartres is more than an hour from Paris *ou* more than an hour's run from Paris; **c'est à 2 ~s de route** it's 2 hours away by road; **il y a 2 ~s de route/train** it's a 2-hour drive/train journey, it takes 2 hours by car/train (to get there).

(g) (*Rel*) **~s canoniales** canonical hours; (*Rel*) **Grandes/Petites ~s** night/daylight offices; **Livre d'H~s** Book of Hours.

(h) (*loc*) **à l'~ qu'il est il doit être arrivé** he must have arrived by now; (*fig: de nos jours*) **à l'~ qu'il est** *ou* **à cette ~** at this moment in time; **à toute ~** at any time (of the day); **repas chaud à toute ~** hot meals all day; **24 ~s sur 24** round the clock, 24 hours a day; **d'~ en ~** hourly, hour by hour; (*lit*) **d'une ~ à l'autre: cela varie d'une ~ à l'autre** it varies from one hour to the next; **nous l'attendons d'une ~ à l'autre** we are expecting him any time now; **'Paris à l'~ écossaise'** 'Paris goes Scottish'; **la France à l'~ de l'ordinateur** France in the computer age; **pour l'~**† for the time being; (*littér*) **sur l'~** at once; **tout à l'~** (*passé récent*) a short while ago, just now; (*futur proche*) in a little while, shortly.

heureusement [œʀøzmɑ̃] *adv* **(a)** (*par bonheur*) fortunately, luckily. **~, il n'y avait personne** fortunately there was no one there.

(b) (*tant mieux*) **il est parti, ~!** he has gone, thank goodness!; **~ pour lui!** fortunately *ou* luckily for him!; **~ qu'il est parti*** thank goodness he has gone.

(c) (*judicieusement*) happily. **mot ~ choisi** happily chosen word; **phrase ~ tournée** judiciously formed sentence.

(d) (*favorablement*) successfully. **l'entreprise fut ~ menée à bien** the task was successfully completed.

heureux, -euse [œʀø, øz] *adj* **(a)** (*gén après n*) (*rempli de bonheur*) *personne, souvenir, vie* happy. **il a tout pour être ~** he has everything he needs to be happy *ou* to make him happy; **ils vécurent ~** they lived happily ever after; **~ comme un poisson dans l'eau** happy as a sandboy; **ces jouets vont faire des ~!** these toys will make some children very happy; *V* **bon¹, ménage.**

(b) (*satisfait*) **être ~ de: je suis très ~ d'apprendre la nouvelle** I am very glad *ou* happy *ou* pleased to hear the news; **M et Mme X sont ~ de vous annoncer ...** Mr and Mrs X are happy *ou* pleased to announce ...; **je suis ~ de ce résultat** I am pleased *ou* happy with this result; **je suis ~ de cette rencontre** I am pleased *ou* glad about this meeting; **il sera trop ~ de vous aider** he'll be only too glad *ou* happy *ou* pleased to help you; **~ de vous revoir** nice *ou* good *ou* pleased to see you again.

(c) (*gén avant n*) (*qui a de la chance*) *personne* fortunate, lucky. **~ au jeu/en amour** lucky at cards/in love; **tu peux t'estimer ~ que** you can think yourself lucky *ou* fortunate that; **c'est ~ (pour lui) que** it is fortunate *ou* lucky (for him) that; **il accepte de venir** — (*iro*) **c'est encore ~!** he's willing to come — it's just as well *ou* I should think so too!; **encore ~ que je m'en sois souvenu!** it's just as well *ou* it's lucky *ou* it's a good thing that I remembered!; *V* **élu, main.**

(d) (*gén avant n: optimiste, agréable*) *disposition, caractère* happy, cheerful. **il a** *ou* **c'est une ~euse nature** he has a happy *ou* cheerful nature.

(e) (*judicieux*) *décision, choix* fortunate, happy; *formule, expression, effet, mélange* happy, felicitous (*frm*).

(f) (*favorable*) *présage* propitious, happy; *résultat, issue* happy. **par un ~ hasard** by a fortunate coincidence; **attendre un ~ événement** to be expecting a happy event.

heuristique [øʀistik] **1** *adj* heuristic. **2** *nf* heurism.

heurt ['œʀ] *nm* (*lit: choc*) collision; (*fig: conflit*) clash. **sans ~s** (*adj*) smooth; (*adv*) smoothly; **leur amitié ne va pas sans quelques ~s** their friendship has its ups and downs, their friendship goes through occasional rough patches.

heurté, e ['œʀte] (*ptp de* **heurter**) *adj couleurs* clashing; *style, jeu* jerky, uneven; *discours* jerky, halting.

heurter ['œʀte] (1) **1** *vt* **(a)** (*lit: cogner*) *objet* to strike, hit; *personne* to collide with; (*bousculer*) to jostle; (*entrechoquer*) *verres* to knock together. **sa tête heurta la table** his head struck the table; **la voiture heurta un arbre** the car ran into *ou* struck a tree.

(b) (*fig: choquer*) *personne, préjugés* to come up against; *théorie, bon goût, bon sens, tradition* to go against, run counter to; *amour-propre* to upset; *opinions* to conflict *ou* clash with. **~ qn de front** to clash head-on with sb.

2 *vi*: **~ à** to knock at *ou* on; **~ contre** *pierre, marche* to stumble against; *récif* to strike.

3 se heurter *vpr* **(a)** (*s'entrechoquer*) [*passants, voitures*] to collide (with each other). **ses idées se heurtaient dans sa tête** his head was a jumble of ideas, ideas jostled about in his head.

(b) (*s'opposer*) [*personnes, opinions, couleurs*] to clash (with each other).

(c) se ~ à *ou* **contre qn/qch** to collide with sb/sth; **se ~ à un refus** to come up against a refusal, meet with a refusal; **se ~ à un problème** to come up against a problem.

heurtoir ['œʀtwaʀ] *nm* [*porte*] (door) knocker; (*Tech: butoir*) stop; (*Rail*) buffer.

hévéa [evea] *nm* hevea.

hexaèdre [ɛgzaɛdʀ(ə)] **1** *adj* hexahedral. **2** *nm* hexahedron.

hexagonal, e, *mpl* **-aux** [ɛgzagɔnal, o] *adj* hexagonal.

hexagone [ɛgzagɔn] *nm* (*Géom*) hexagon. (*fig*) **l'~ (national)** France.

hexamètre [ɛgzamɛtʀ(ə)] **1** *adj* hexameter (*épith*), hexametric(al). **2** *nm* hexameter.

hiatus [jatys] *nm* (*Ling*) hiatus; (*fig*) break, hiatus.

hibernal, e, *mpl* **-aux** [ibɛʀnal, o] *adj* winter (*épith*), hibernal.

hibernation [ibɛʀnɑsjɔ̃] *nf* hibernation. (*Méd*) **~ artificielle** induced hypothermia.

hiberner [ibɛʀne] (1) *vi* to hibernate.

hibiscus [ibiskys] *nm* hibiscus.

hibou, *pl* **~x** ['ibu] *nm* owl.

hic* ['ik] *nm*: **c'est là le ~** that's the snag* *ou* the trouble, there's the rub.

hickory ['ikɔʀi] *nm* hickory.

hideur ['idœʀ] *nf* (*littér*) hideousness (*U*).

hideusement ['idøzmɑ̃] *adv* hideously.

hideux, -euse ['idø, øz] *adj* hideous.

hie ['i] *nf* rammer.

hier [jɛʀ] *adv* yesterday. **~ (au) soir** yesterday evening, last night *ou* evening; **toute la matinée d'~** all yesterday morning; **toute la journée d'~** all day yesterday; **je ne suis pas né d'~** I wasn't born yesterday; **il avait tout ~ pour se décider** he had all (day) yesterday to make up his mind.

hiérarchie ['jeʀaʀʃi] *nf* hierarchy.

hiérarchique ['jeʀaʀʃik] *adj* hierarchic(al). **chef** *ou* **supérieur ~** senior in rank *ou* in the hierarchy. *V* **voie.**

hiérarchiquement ['jeʀaʀʃikmɑ̃] *adv* hierarchically.

hiérarchisation ['jeʀaʀʃizɑsjɔ̃] *nf* (*action*) organization into a hierarchy; (*organisation*) hierarchical organization.

hiérarchiser ['jeʀaʀʃize] (1) *vt* to organize into a hierarchy.

hiératique [jeʀatik] *adj* hieratic.

hiéroglyphe ['jeʀɔglif] *nm* (*Ling*) hieroglyph(ic). **~s** (*plusieurs symboles*) hieroglyph(ic)s; (*système d'écriture*) hieroglyphics; (*fig péj*) hieroglyphics (*fig*).

hiéroglyphique ['jeʀɔglifik] *adj* hieroglyphic(al).

hi-han ['iɑ̃] *excl* heehaw!

hi-hi [hihi] *excl* (*rire*) tee-hee!, hee-hee!; (*pleurs*) sniff-sniff!

hilarant, e [ilaʀɑ̃, ɑ̃t] *adj aventure* hilarious, side-splitting; *V* **gaz.**

hilare [ilaʀ] *adj personne* mirthful, hilarious (*épith*).

hilarité [ilaʀite] *nf* hilarity, mirth.

hile ['il] *nm* (*Anat, Bot*) hilum.

himalayen, -enne [imalajɛ̃, ɛn] *adj* Himalayan.

hindi ['indi] *nm* (*Ling*) Hindi.

hindou, e [ɛ̃du] **1** *adj nationalité* Indian; *coutumes, dialecte* Hindu, Hindoo. **2** *nm,f*: **H~(e)** (*citoyen*) Indian; (*croyant*) Hindu, Hindoo.

hindouisme [ɛ̃duism(ə)] *nm* Hinduism, Hindooism.

hindouiste [ɛ̃duist(ə)] *adj, nmf* Hindu, Hindoo.

Hindoustan [ɛ̃dustɑ̃] *nm* Hindustan.

hindoustani [ɛ̃dustani] *nm* (*Ling*) Hindustani.

hippie ['ipi] *adj, nmf* hippy.

hippique [ipik] *adj* horse (*épith*), equestrian. **concours ~** show-jumping event, horse show; **course ~** horse-race; **le sport ~** equestrian sport.

hippisme [ipism(ə)] *nm* (horse) riding.

hippocampe [ipɔkɑ̃p] *nm* (*Myth*) hippocampus; (*poisson*) sea horse.

Hippocrate [ipɔkʀat] *nm* Hippocrates.

hippodrome [ipɔdʀom] *nm* racecourse; (*Antiq*) hippodrome.

hippogriffe [ipɔgʀif] *nm* hippogriff, hippogryph.

Hippolyte [ipɔlit] *nm* Hippolytus.

hippomobile [ipɔmɔbil] *adj* horse-drawn.

hippophagique [ipɔfaʒik] *adj*: **boucherie ~** horsemeat butcher's.

hippopotame [ipɔpɔtam] *nm* hippopotamus, hippo*.

hippy, *pl* **hippies** ['ipi] = **hippie.**

hirondelle [iʀɔ̃dɛl] *nf* **(a)** (*Zool*) swallow. (*Prov*) **une ~ ne fait pas le printemps** one swallow doesn't make a summer (*Prov*); *V* **nid. (b)** (*†: *policier*) bicycle bobby* (*Brit*).

hirsute [iʀsyt] *adj* **(a)** (*ébouriffé*) *tête* tousled; *gamin* shaggy-haired; *barbe* shaggy. **un individu ~** a hairy *ou* hirsute individual. **(b)** (*Bio*) hirsute.

hispanique [ispanik] *adj* Hispanic.

hispanisant, e [ispanizɑ̃, ɑ̃t] *nm, f* hispanist, Spanish scholar.

hispanisme [ispanism(ə)] *nm* hispanicism.

hispaniste [ispanist(ə)] *nmf* = **hispanisant.**

hispano-américain, e [ispanɔameʀikɛ̃, ɛn] **1** *adj* Spanish-American. **2** *nm,f*: **Hispano-Américain(e)** Spanish-American.

hispano-arabe [ispanɔaʀab] *adj* Hispano-Moresque.

hisse: oh hisse ['ois] *excl* heave (ho)!

hisser ['ise] (1) **1** *vt* (*Naut*) to hoist; (*soulever*) *objet* to hoist, haul up, heave up; *personne* to haul up, heave up. **~ les couleurs** to run up *ou* hoist the colours; **hissez les voiles!** up sails!; (*fig*) **~ qn au pouvoir** to hoist sb into a position of power.

2 se hisser *vpr* to heave o.s. up, haul o.s. up. **se ~ sur un toit** to heave *ou* haul o.s. (up) onto a roof; (*fig*) **se ~ à la première place/au pouvoir** to pull o.s. up to first place/a position of power.

histoire [istwaʀ] *nf* **(a)** (*science, événements*) **l'~** history; **l'~ jugera** posterity will be the judge; **l'~ est un continuel recommencement** history is constantly being remade; **laisser son nom dans l'~** to find one's place in history; **l'~ ancienne/naturelle/du moyen âge** ancient/natural/medieval history; **l'~ de France** French history, the history of France; **l'H~ sainte** Biblical history; **la petite ~** the footnotes of history; **pour la petite ~** for the record; **~ romancée** anecdotal *ou* fictionalized history; (*fig*) **tout cela, c'est de l'~ ancienne*** all that's ancient history*.

(b) (*déroulement de faits*) history, story. **l'~ du château de Windsor** the history of Windsor Castle; **raconter l'~ de sa vie** to tell one's life story *ou* the story of one's life.

(c) (*Scol**) (*livre*) history book; (*leçon*) history (lesson). **on a (l')~ à 2 heures** we have history at 2 o'clock.

(d) (*récit, conte*) story; (*: *mensonge*) story*, fib*. **une ~ vraie** a true story; **~s de pêche/de chasse** fishing/hunting stories; **~s de revenant** ghost stories; **~ drôle** funny story, joke; **~ de fous** shaggy-dog story; **c'est une ~ à dormir debout** it's a cock-and-bull story *ou* a tall story; **qu'est-ce que c'est que cette ~?** what on earth is all this about?, just what is all this about?; **tout ça, ce sont des ~s** that's just a lot of fibs*, you've made all that up; **tu me racontes des ~s** you're pulling my leg, come off it!*; **le plus beau** *ou* **curieux de l'~ c'est que** the best part *ou* strangest part of it is that; **c'est toute une ~** it's a long story; **l'~ veut qu'il ait dit** the story goes that he said.

(e) (*: *affaire, incident*) business. **c'est une drôle d'~** it's a funny business; **il vient de lui arriver une curieuse ~/une drôle d'~** something odd/funny has just happened to him; **pour une ~ d'argent/de femme** because of something to do with money/a woman; **se mettre dans une sale ~, se mettre une sale ~ sur le dos** to get mixed up in some nasty business; **sa nomination va faire toute une ~** his appointment will cause a lot of fuss *ou* a great to-do, there will be quite a fuss *ou* to-do over his appointment; **c'est toujours la même ~!** it's always the same old story; **ça, c'est une autre ~!** that's (quite) another story!

(f) (*: *ennui*) **~s** trouble; **faire des ~s à qn** to make trouble for sb; **cela ne peut lui attirer** *ou* **lui valoir que des ~s** that's bound to get him into trouble, that will cause him nothing but trouble.

(g) (*: *chichis*) fuss, to-do, carry-on*. **faire un tas d'~s** to make a whole lot of fuss *ou* a great to-do; **quelle ~ pour si peu!** what a to-do *ou* fuss *ou* carry-on* over so little; **allez, au lit, et pas d'~s!** come along now, off to bed, and I don't want any fuss!

(h) (*) **~ de faire** just to do; **~ de prendre l'air** just for a breath of (fresh) air; **~ de rire** just for a laugh*, just for fun; **il a essayé, ~ de voir/de faire quelque chose** he had a go just to see what it was like/just for something to do *ou* just to be doing something.

(i) (*: *machin*) thingummyjig*, whatsit*.

histologie [istɔlɔʒi] *nf* histology.

histologique [istɔlɔʒik] *adj* histological.

historié, e [istɔʀje] *adj* (*Art*) historiated.

historien, -ienne [istɔʀjɛ̃, jɛn] *nm,f* (*savant*) historian; (*étudiant*) history student, historian.

historiette [istɔʀjɛt] *nf* little story, anecdote.

historiographe [istɔʀjɔgʀaf] *nm* historiographer.

historique [istɔʀik] **1** *adj étude, vérité* historical; *personnage, événement, monument* historic. **2** *nm*: **faire l'~ de** *problème, affaire* to review, make a review of; *institution, mot* to examine the history of.

historiquement [istɔʀikmɑ̃] *adv* historically.

hitlérien, -ienne [itleʀjɛ̃, jɛn] *adj, nm,f* Hitlerite, Nazi.

hittite ['itit] **1** *adj* Hittite. **2** *nmf*: **H~** Hittite.

hiver [ivɛʀ] *nm* winter. **il fait un temps d'~** it's like winter, it's wintry weather; **jardin d'~** wintergarden; **sports d'~** winter sports.

hivernal, e, *mpl* **-aux** [ivɛʀnal, o] *adj* (*lit: de l'hiver*) *brouillard, pluies* winter (*épith*), hibernal (*littér*); (*fig: comme en hiver*) *atmosphère, température, temps* wintry (*épith*). **il faisait une température ~e** it was as cold as (in) winter, it was like winter.

hiverner [ivɛʀne] (1) *vi* to winter.

ho ['o, ho] *excl* (*appel*) hey (there)!; (*surprise, indignation*) oh!

hobereau, *pl* **~x** ['ɔbʀo] *nm* (*Orn*) hobby; (*péj: seigneur*) local (country) squire.

hochement ['ɔʃmɑ̃] *nm*: **~ de tête** (*affirmatif*) nod (of the head); (*négatif*) shake (of the head).

hochequeue ['ɔʃkø] *nm* wagtail.

hocher ['ɔʃe] (1) *vt*: **~ la tête** (*affirmativement*) to nod (one's head); (*négativement*) to shake one's head.

hochet ['ɔʃɛ] *nm* [*bébé*] rattle; (*fig*) toy.

hockey ['ɔkɛ] *nm* hockey. **~ sur glace** ice hockey; **~ sur gazon** field hockey.

hockeyeur, -euse ['ɔkɛjœʀ, øz] *nm,f* hockey player.

hoirie [waʀi] *nf* (††) inheritance; *V* **avancement.**

holà ['ɔla, hɔla] **1** *excl* hold! **2** *nm*: **mettre le ~ à qch** to put a stop *ou* an end to sth.

holding ['ɔldiŋ] *nm* holding company.

hold-up ['ɔldœp] *nm inv* hold-up. **condamné pour le ~ d'une banque** sentenced for having held up a bank *ou* for a bank hold-up.

hollandais, e ['ɔlɑ̃dɛ, ɛz] **1** *adj* Dutch. **2** *nm* **(a) H~** Dutchman. **(b)** (*Ling*) Dutch. **3 Hollandaise** *nf* Dutchwoman.

Hollande ['ɔlɑ̃d] *nf* Holland.

hollande ['ɔlɑ̃d] **1** *nf* (*toile*) holland; (*pomme de terre*) holland potato. **2** *nm* (*fromage*) Dutch cheese; (*papier*) Holland.

holocauste [ɔlɔkost(ə)] *nm* **(a)** (*Rel, fig: sacrifice*) sacrifice; (*Rel juive*) holocaust. **offrir qch en ~** to offer sth up in sacrifice; (*littér*) **se donner en ~** to make a total sacrifice of one's life. **(b)** (*victime*) sacrifice.

homard ['ɔmaʀ] *nm* lobster. (*Culin*) **~ à la nage** lobster cooked in a court-bouillon.

homélie [ɔmeli] *nf* homily.

homéopathe [ɔmeɔpat] *nmf* homoeopath(ist). **médecin ~** homoeopathic doctor.

homéopathie [ɔmeɔpati] *nf* homoeopathy.

homéopathique [ɔmeɔpatik] *adj* homoeopathic.

Homère [ɔmɛʀ] *nm* Homer.

homérique [ɔmeʀik] *adj* Homeric.

homicide [ɔmisid] **1** *adj* (†, *littér*) homicidal. **2** *nmf* (*littér: criminel*) homicide (*littér*), murderer (*ou* murderess). **3** *nm* (*Jur: crime*) homicide (*US*), murder. **~ volontaire** murder; **~ involontaire, ~ par imprudence** manslaughter.

hommage [ɔmaʒ] *nm* **(a)** (*marque d'estime*) tribute. **rendre ~ à qn/au talent de qn** to pay homage *ou* (a) tribute to sb/to sb's talent; **rendre ~ à Dieu** to pay homage to God; **recevoir l'~ d'un admirateur** to accept the tribute paid by an admirer.

(b) (*frm: civilités*) **~s** respects; **présenter ses ~s à une dame** to pay one's respects to a lady; **présentez mes ~s à votre femme** give my respects to your wife; **daignez agréer mes respectueux ~s** yours faithfully (*Brit*), yours truly.

(c) (*don*) **acceptez ceci comme un ~** *ou* **en ~ de ma gratitude** please accept this as a mark *ou* token of my gratitude; **faire ~ d'un livre** to give a presentation copy of a book; **~ de l'auteur/de l'éditeur** with the author's/publisher's compliments.

(d) (*Hist*) homage.

hommasse [ɔmas] *adj* mannish.

homme [ɔm] **1** *nm* **(a)** (*individu*) man. (*espèce*) **l'~** man, mankind; **un ~ fait** a grown man; **l'enfant devient ~** the child grows into *ou* becomes a man; **des vêtements d'~** men's clothes; **voilà mon ~** (*que je cherche*) there's my man; (*qu'il me faut*) that's the man for me; (*: *mon mari*) here comes that man of mine*; (*fig*) **l'~ fort du régime** the muscleman of the régime; *V* **abominable, âge,** *etc.*

(b) (*loc*) **parler d'~ à ~** to speak man to man, have a man-to-man talk; **il n'est pas ~ à mentir** he's not one to lie *ou* a man to lie; **comme un seul ~** as one man; **il a trouvé son ~** (*un égal*) he has found his match; (*Prov*) **un ~ averti en vaut deux** forewarned is forearmed; (*Prov*) **l'~ propose, Dieu dispose** man proposes, God disposes (*Prov*); (*Naut*) **un ~ à la mer!** man overboard!

2: homme d'action man of action; **homme d'affaires** businessman; **homme d'armes††** man-at-arms††; **homme de barre** helmsman; **homme à bonnes fortunes** ladykiller, ladies' man; **homme des cavernes** cave man; **homme de confiance** right-hand man; **homme d'église** man of the Church; **homme d'équipage** member of a ship's crew; **navire avec 30 hommes d'équipage** ship with a crew of 30 (men); **homme d'esprit** man of wit and learning; **homme d'État** statesman; **homme à femmes** womanizer; **homme-grenouille** *nm, pl* **hommes-grenouilles** frogman; **l'homme de la rue** the man in the street; **homme de lettres** man of letters; **homme lige** liege man; **homme de loi** man of law; **homme de main** hired man; **homme du monde** society man; **homme-orchestre** *nm, pl* **hommes-orchestres** one-man band; **homme de paille** stooge, puppet; **homme de peine** workhand; **homme de plume** man of letters, writer; **homme de robe††** legal man, lawyer; **homme-sandwich** *nm, pl* **hommes-sandwiches** sandwich man; **homme de science** man of science; **homme à tout faire** odd-job man; (*Mil*) **homme de troupe** private.

homocentre [ɔmɔsɑ̃tʀ(ə)] *nm* common centre.

homocentrique [ɔmɔsɑ̃tʀik] *adj* homocentric.

homogène [ɔmɔʒɛn] *adj* homogeneous. (*Pol: en France*) **ministère ~** *government where all ministers are of the same party.*

homogénéisation [ɔmɔʒeneizɑsjɔ̃] *nf* homogenization.

homogénéiser [ɔmɔʒeneize] (1) *vt* to homogenize.

homogénéité [ɔmɔʒeneite] *nf* homogeneity, homogeneousness.

homographe [ɔmɔgʀaf] **1** *adj* homographic. **2** *nm* homograph.

homologation [ɔmɔlɔgasjɔ̃] *nf* (*Sport*) ratification; (*Jur*) approval, sanction.

homologie [ɔmɔlɔʒi] *nf* (*Sci*) homology; (*gén*) equivalence.

homologue [ɔmɔlɔg] **1** *adj* (*Sci*) homologous; (*gén*) equivalent, homologous (*de* to). **2** *nm* (*Chim*) homologue; (*personne*) equivalent, counterpart, opposite number.

homologuer [ɔmɔlɔge] (1) *vt* (*Sport*) to ratify; (*Jur*) to approve, sanction.

homonyme [ɔmɔnim] **1** *adj* homonymous. **2** *nm* (*Ling*) homonym; (*personne*) namesake.

homonymie [ɔmɔnimi] *nf* homonymy.

homonymique [ɔmɔnimik] *adj* homonymic.

homophone [ɔmɔfɔn] **1** *adj* (*Ling*) homophonous; (*Mus*) homophonic. **2** *nm* homophone.

homophonie [ɔmɔfɔni] *nf* homophony.

homosexualité [ɔmɔsɛksɥalite] *nf* homosexuality.

homosexuel, -elle [ɔmɔsɛksɥɛl] *adj, nm,f* homosexual.

Honduras ['ɔ̃dyʀas] *nm*: **le ~** the Honduras.

hondurien, -ienne ['ɔ̃dyʀjɛ̃, jɛn] **1** *adj* Honduran. **2** *nm,f*: **H~(ne)** Honduran.

hongre ['ɔ̃gʀ(ə)] **1** *adj* gelded. **2** *nm* gelding.

Hongrie ['ɔ̃gʀi] *nf* Hungary.

hongrois, e ['ɔ̃gʀwa, waz] **1** *adj* Hungarian. **2** *nm* (*Ling*) Hungarian. **3** *nm,f*: **H~(e)** Hungarian.

honnête [ɔnɛt] **1** *adj* **(a)** (*intègre*) *personne* honest, decent; *juge* honest; *conduite* decent; *procédés, intentions* honest, honourable. **ce sont d'~s gens** they are decent people *ou* folk*; **un vin ~** an honest little wine.
(b) (*vertueux*) *femme* honest, decent.
(c) (*juste*) *marché* fair; *prix* fair, reasonable.
(d) (*satisfaisant*) *résultats* reasonable, fair; *repas* reasonable. **ce livre est ~** this book isn't bad *ou* is reasonable *ou* is fair; **rester dans une ~ moyenne** to maintain a fair average.
(e) (†, *hum: poli*) courteous. **vous êtes trop ~!** you're too kind!
2: (*Hist*) **honnête homme** gentleman, man of breeding.

honnêtement [ɔnɛtmɑ̃] *adv* (*V* **honnête**) honestly; decently; honourably; fairly; reasonably; courteously. **c'est ~ payé** it's reasonably paid, you get a fair *ou* reasonable wage for it; **~, vous le saviez bien!** come now, you knew!

honnêteté [ɔnɛtte] *nf* (*V* **honnête**) honesty; decency; fairness; courtesy.

honneur [ɔnœʀ] *nm* **(a)** (*dignité morale, réputation*) honour. **l'~ m'oblige à le faire** I am in honour bound to do it; **mettre son** *ou* **un (point d')~ à faire qch** to make it a point of honour to do sth; **jurer/promettre sur l'~** to swear/promise on one's honour; **homme/femme d'~** man/woman of honour, man/woman with a sense of honour; **bandit d'~** outlaw (because of a blood feud); *V* **dette, manquer** *etc.*
(b) (*mérite*) credit. **avec ~** creditably; **cette action est toute à son ~** this act does him (great) credit *ou* is much to his credit; **c'est à lui que revient l'~ d'avoir inventé ...** the credit is his for having invented ...; **faire ~ à** *ou* **être l'~ de sa famille/sa profession** to be a credit *ou* an honour to one's family/one's profession; *V* **tour**[2].
(c) (*privilège, faveur*) honour. **faire (à qn) l'~ de** to do sb the honour of; **avoir l'~ de** to have the honour of; **j'ai eu l'~ de recevoir sa visite** he honoured me with a visit; (*Admin: formule épistolaire*) **j'ai l'~ de solliciter ...** I am writing to ask ...; **j'ai l'~ de vous informer que** I am writing to inform you that, I beg to inform you that (*frm*); **garde/invité d'~** guard/guest of honour; **président/membre d'~** honorary president/member; *V* **baroud, champ, citoyen** *etc.*
(d) (*marques de distinction*) **~s** honours; **aimer/mépriser les ~s** to be fond of/despise honours; **couvert d'~s** covered in honours; **avec tous les ~s dus à son rang** with all the honour due to his rank; **les derniers ~s (funèbres)** the last tribute; **~s militaires** military honours; **se rendre avec** *ou* **obtenir les ~s de la guerre** (*Mil*) to be granted the honours of war; (*fig*) to suffer an honourable defeat; (*fig*) **faire les ~s de la maison** *etc* **à qn** to do the honours and show sb round the house *etc*; **avoir les ~s de la première page** to get a mention on the first page; **avoir les ~s de la cimaise** to have one's works exhibited; *V* **rendre.**
(e) (*Cartes*) honour.
(f) (*titre*) **votre H~** Your Honour.
(g) (*loc*) **~ aux vainqueurs!** honour to the conquerors!; **~ aux dames** ladies first; **à vous l'~** after you; **être à l'~** to be in *ou* have the place of honour; **être en ~** *[coutume etc]* to be the done thing; *[style, mode]* to be in favour; **en l'~ de nos hôtes** in honour of our guests; **en l'~ de cet événement** on the occasion of this event; **à qui ai-je l'~?** to whom do I have the honour of speaking?; **que me vaut l'~ de votre visite?** to what do I owe the honour of your visit?; (*iro*) **en quel ~ toutes ces fleurs?*** what are all those flowers in aid of?*; (*iro*) **peux-tu me dire en quel ~ tu entres sans frapper?** just who do you think you are coming in like that without knocking?; **faire ~ à ses engagements/sa signature** to honour one's commitments/signature; **faire ~ à un repas** to do justice to a meal; **il a fini la partie pour l'~** he gallantly finished the game (for its own sake); **faire un bras d'~ à qn** ≃ to give sb the V sign; *V* **à, rendre.**

honnir ['ɔniʀ] (2) *vt* (*frm*) to hold in contempt. **honni soit qui mal y pense** evil be to him who evil thinks.

honorabilité [ɔnɔʀabilite] *nf [personne, sentiments]* worthiness. **soucieux d'~** anxious to be thought honourable.

honorable [ɔnɔʀabl(ə)] *adj* (*lit: estimable*) *personne, buts* honourable, worthy; *sentiments* creditable, worthy; (*: *suffisant*) *salaire, résultats* decent. (*frm, hum*) **l'~ compagnie** this worthy company (*frm, hum*); (*frm, iro*) **mon ~ collègue** my honourable *ou* esteemed colleague (*frm, iro*); *V* **amende.**

honorablement [ɔnɔʀabləmɑ̃] *adv* (*V* **honorable**) honourably; worthily; creditably; decently. **~ connu dans le quartier** known and respected in the district.

honoraire [ɔnɔʀɛʀ] **1** *adj* honorary. **professeur ~** professor emeritus. **2** *nmpl*: **~s** fee, fees.

honorer [ɔnɔʀe] (1) **1** *vt* **(a)** (*glorifier*) *savant, Dieu* to honour. **~ la mémoire de qn** to honour the memory of sb.
(b) (*littér: estimer*) to hold in high regard *ou* esteem. **je l'honore à l'égal de ...** I have the same regard *ou* esteem for him as I do for ...; **mon honoré collègue** my esteemed *ou* respected colleague.
(c) (*gratifier*) **~ qn de qch** to honour sb with sth; **il m'honorait de son amitié/de sa présence** he honoured me with his friendship/his presence; (*iro*) **il ne m'a pas honoré d'un regard** he did not honour me with so much as a glance (*iro*), he did not (even) deign to look at me; **je suis très honoré** I am highly *ou* greatly honoured.
(d) (*faire honneur à*) to do credit to, be a credit to. **cette franchise l'honore** this frankness does him credit; **il honore sa profession/son pays** he's a credit *ou* an honour to his profession/country.
(e) (*Comm*) *chèque, signature* to honour; (*rare*) *médecin, notaire* to settle one's account with. **votre honorée du ...** yours of the ... .
2 s'honorer *vpr*: **s'~ de** to pride o.s. upon; **pays qui s'honore de ses artistes** country which prides itself upon its artists.

honorifique [ɔnɔʀifik] *adj* honorary. **à titre ~** honorary; **fonction accordée à titre ~** honorary post; **il a été nommé à titre ~** his appointment was an honorary one, he was appointed on an honorary basis.

honte ['ɔ̃t] *nf* **(a)** (*déshonneur, humiliation*) disgrace, shame. **couvrir qn de ~** to bring disgrace *ou* shame on sb, disgrace sb; **quelle ~** *ou* **c'est une ~ pour la famille!** what a disgrace to the family!, he brings shame upon the family!; **faire la ~** *ou* **être la ~ de la famille/profession** to be the disgrace of one's family/profession; (*littér*) **~ à celui qui ...** shame upon him who ... (*littér*); **il n'y a aucune ~ à être ...** there's no shame *ou* disgrace in being ...; **c'est une ~!** that's disgraceful! *ou* a disgrace!
(b) (*sentiment de confusion, gêne*) shame. **à ma (grande) ~** to my (great) shame; **sans ~** shamelessly; **sans fausse ~** quite naturally; **avoir ~ (de qch/de faire)** to be *ou* feel ashamed (of sth/of doing); **faire ~ à qn** to make sb (feel) ashamed; **elle n'a aucune ~†** she is utterly shameless, she has no shame; **toute ~ bue** dead to *ou* lost to shame; **faire ~ à qn de sa lenteur** to make sb (feel) ashamed of his slowness; **il leur fait ~ par sa rapidité** he puts them to shame with his speed; *V* **court**[1].

honteusement ['ɔ̃tøzmɑ̃] *adv* (*V* **honteux**) shamefully; ashamedly; disgracefully.

honteux, -euse ['ɔ̃tø, øz] *adj* **(a)** (*déshonorant*) shameful; (*confus*) ashamed (*de* of). **c'est ~!** it's a disgrace!, it's disgraceful! *ou* shameful!; *V* **maladie, partie**[2]. **(b)** (*cachant ses opinions*) **bourgeois/communiste ~** apologetic bourgeois/communist.

hop ['ɔp, hɔp] *excl*: **~ (là)!** (*pour faire sauter*) hup!; (*pour faire partir*) off you go!

hôpital, *pl* **-aux** [ɔpital, o] *nm* hospital. **c'est l'~ qui se moque de la charité!** ≃ it's the pot calling the kettle black.

hoquet ['ɔkɛ] *nm* hiccough. **avoir le ~** to have (the) hiccoughs; **il a eu un ~ de dégoût/peur** he gulped with distaste/fear.

hoqueter ['ɔkte] (4) *vi* to hiccough.

Horace [ɔʀas] *nm* Horatio; (*le poète*) Horace.

horaire [ɔʀɛʀ] **1** *adj* **(a)** *salaire, moyenne* hourly. **débit/vitesse ~** rate/speed per hour. **(b)** (*Astron*) horary; *V* **fuseau. 2** *nm* timetable, schedule. **3** *nmf* employee paid by the hour.

horde ['ɔʀd(ə)] *nf* horde.

horion ['ɔʀjɔ̃] *nm* (†*hum, gén pl*) blow, punch. **échanger des ~s avec la police** to exchange blows with the police.

horizon [ɔʀizɔ̃] *nm* **(a)** (*limite, ligne, Art*) horizon. **la ligne d'~** (*gén, Art*) the horizon; **un bateau sur l'~** a boat on the horizon *ou* skyline; **on voyait à l'~ ...** one could see on the horizon ...; **s'enfoncer/disparaître à l'~** to sink/disappear below the horizon.
(b) (*Astron*) horizon.
(c) (*paysage*) landscape, view. **un des plus beaux ~s qui soit** one of the most beautiful landscapes *ou* views; **on découvre un vaste ~/un ~ de collines** you come upon a vast panorama/a hilly landscape; **changer d'~** to have a change of scenery *ou* scene; **ce fond de vallon humide était tout son ~** the bottom of this damp valley was all he ever saw; **voyager vers de nouveaux ~s** to make for new horizons.
(d) (*fig: perspective*) horizon. **ça lui ouvert de nouveaux ~s** it opened (out) new horizons for him; **l'~ politique/international** the political/international scene; *V* **tour**[2].

horizontal, e *mpl* **-aux** [ɔʀizɔ̃tal, o] **1** *adj* horizontal. **2 horizontale** *nf* horizontal. **placer qch à l'~e** to put sth horizontal *ou* in a horizontal position.

horizontalement [ɔʀizɔ̃talmɑ̃] *adv* horizontally.

horizontalité [ɔʀizɔ̃talite] *nf* horizontality, horizontalness.

horloge [ɔʀlɔʒ] *nf* clock. **il a la régularité d'une ~** he's as regular as clockwork; **il est 2 heures à l'~ de la chambre** it's 2 o'clock by *ou* according to the bedroom clock; **l'~ parlante** the speaking clock (*Brit*); **~ normande** grandfather clock; *V* **heure.**

horloger, -ère [ɔʀlɔʒe, ɛʀ] **1** *adj* *industrie* watch-making (*épith*), clock-making (*épith*). **2** *nm,f* watchmaker; (*horloges en particulier*) clockmaker. **~ bijoutier** jeweller (specializing in clocks and watches).

horlogerie [ɔʀlɔʒʀi] *nf* (*fabrication*) watch-making; (*horloges en particulier*) clock-making; (*objets*) time-pieces; (*magasin*) watchmaker's (shop); clockmaker's (shop). ~ **bijouterie** jeweller's shop (specializing in clocks and watches); **pièces d'~** clock components; *V* **mouvement.**

hormis ['ɔʀmi] *prép* (*frm*) but, save.

hormonal, e, *mpl* **-aux** [ɔʀmɔnal, o] *adj* hormonal, hormone (*épith*).

hormone [ɔʀmɔn] *nf* hormone.

horoscope [ɔʀɔskɔp] *nm* horoscope. **tirer l'~ à qn** to cast sb's horoscope.

horreur [ɔʀœʀ] *nf* **(a)** (*effroi, répulsion*) horror. **il était devenu pour elle un objet d'~** he had become a source of horror to her; **frappé** *ou* **saisi d'~** horror-stricken, horror-struck; **une vision d'~** a horrific *ou* horrendous *ou* horrifying sight; **l'~ d'agir/du risque qui le caractérise** the horror of acting/taking risks which is typical of him.

(b) (*laideur*) *[crime, guerre]* horror. **l'esclavage dans toute son ~** slavery in all its horror.

(c) (*chose horrible, dégoûtante*) **les ~s de la guerre** the horrors of war; **ce film/travail est une ~*** this film/piece of work is terrible *ou* awful *ou* dreadful; **ce chapeau est une ~*** this hat is a fright *ou* is hideous *ou* ghastly*; **c'est une ~*** (*femme*) she's a fright, she is hideous *ou* ghastly*; (*tableau etc*) it's hideous *ou* ghastly*; **quelle ~!** how dreadful! *ou* awful!; *V* **musée.**

(d) (*: *actes ou propos dégoûtants*) **~s** dreadful *ou* terrible things; **débiter des ~s sur qn** to say dreadful *ou* terrible things about sb.

(e) (*loc*) **faire ~ à qn: cet individu me fait ~** that individual disgusts me; **le mensonge me fait ~** I loathe *ou* detest lying, I have a horror of lying; **la viande me fait ~** I can't stand *ou* bear meat, I loathe *ou* detest meat; **avoir qch/qn en ~** to loathe *ou* detest sth/sb; **j'ai ce genre de livre en ~** I loathe *ou* detest this type of book, I have a horror of this type of book; **prendre qch/qn en ~** to come to loathe *ou* detest sth/sb; **avoir ~ de** to loathe, detest.

horrible [ɔʀibl(ə)] *adj* (*effrayant*) *crime, accident, blessure* horrible; (*extrême*) *chaleur, peur* terrible, dreadful; (*très laid*) *chapeau, tableau* horrible, hideous, ghastly*; (*très mauvais*) *temps* terrible, ghastly*, dreadful; *travail* terrible, dreadful.

horriblement [ɔʀibləmɑ̃] *adv* (*de façon effrayante*) horribly; (*extrêmement*) horribly, terribly, dreadfully.

horrifier [ɔʀifje] (7) *vt* to horrify. **elle était horrifiée par la dépense** she was horrified at the expense.

horripiler [ɔʀipile] (1) *vt*: **~ qn** to try sb's patience, exasperate sb.

hors ['ɔʀ] **1** *prép* **(a)** (*excepté*) except (for), apart from, save (*littér*), but (*seulement avec no one, nothing etc*). (*littér*) **~ que** save that (*littér*).

(b) (*dans loc*) **mettre qn ~ la loi** to outlaw sb; **St Paul ~ les murs** St Paul's without *ou* outside the walls; **théâtre ~ les murs** suburban theatre.

(c) (*espace, temps*) **~ de** (*position*) outside, out of, away from; (*changement de lieu*) out of; **vivre ~ de la ville** to live out of town *ou* outside the town; **vivre ~ de son pays** to live away from *ou* outside one's own country; **le choc l'a projeté ~ de la pièce/de la voiture** the impact threw him out of the room/car; **il est plus agréable d'habiter ~ du centre** it is pleasanter to live away from *ou* outside the centre; **~ de chez lui/son milieu, il est malheureux comme un poisson ~ de l'eau** he's like a fish out of water when he's away from (his) home/his familiar surroundings; **vivre ~ de son temps/la réalité** to live in a different age/in a dream world; **~ de saison** (*lit*) out of season; (*fig*, †: *inopportun*) untimely, out of place; **~ d'ici!** get out of here!; (*Prov*) **~ de l'Église, point de salut** without the Church there is no salvation.

(d) (*fig*) **~ de: il est ~ d'affaire** he is out of the wood (*fig*), he's over the worst; **~ d'atteinte** (*lit*) out of reach; (*fig*) beyond reach; **~ d'atteinte de** *projectiles* out of range *ou* reach of; **mettre ~ de combat** to put out of the fight *ou* contest (*Sport*); **être ~ de danger** to be out of danger, be safe; **il est ~ de doute qu'il a raison** he is undoubtedly right, it is beyond doubt that he is right; **mettre qn/être ~ d'état de nuire** to render sb/be harmless; **~ d'haleine** out of breath; **~ de là** apart from that; **~ de mesure** *ou* **proportion** out of proportion (*avec* with); **~ de portée** (*lit*) out of reach; (*fig*) beyond reach; **ce tableau est ~ de prix** the price of this picture is exorbitant *ou* prohibitive; **~ de propos** untimely, inopportune; **c'est ~ de question** it is out of the question; **être ~ de soi** to be beside o.s. (with anger, excitement *etc*); **cette remarque l'a mise ~ d'elle** she was beside herself at this remark, this remark infuriated her; **~ d'usage** out of service *ou* action; **mettre ~ d'usage** to put out of action.

2: hors-bord *nm inv* speedboat (*with outboard motor*); (*Mil*) **hors cadre** *adj inv* detached, seconded; **hors commerce** *adj inv* for restricted sale only (*attrib*); **hors classe** *adj inv* exceptional; **hors-concours** *adj inv* ineligible to compete; (*fig*) in a class of one's own; (*Bourse*) **hors-cote** *adj inv* not quoted on the Stock Exchange; **hors-d'œuvre** *nm inv* (*lit*) hors d'œuvre, starter*; (*Sport*) **hors jeu** *adj inv* offside; **hors-jeu** *nm inv* offside; **hors-la-loi** *nm inv* outlaw; **hors ligne, hors pair** *adj inv* outstanding, unparalleled, matchless; **hors série** *adj inv talent, don* incomparable, outstanding; **une table/machine hors série** a table/machine made to order, a custom-built table/machine; **hors-taxe** *adj inv, adv* duty-free; **hors-texte** *nm inv* plate.

hortensia [ɔʀtɑ̃sja] *nm* hydrangea.

horticole [ɔʀtikɔl] *adj* horticultural.

horticulteur, -trice [ɔʀtikyltœʀ, tʀis] *nm,f* horticulturist.

horticulture [ɔʀtikyltyʀ] *nf* horticulture.

hospice [ɔspis] *nm* **(a)** (*hôpital*) home. **~ de vieillards** old people's home; (*péj*) **mourir à l'~** to die in the poorhouse. **(b)** *[monastère]* hospice.

hospitalier, -ière [ɔspitalje, jɛʀ] **1** *adj* **(a)** *services, personnel* hospital (*épith*). **établissement ~** hospital. **(b)** (*accueillant*) hospitable. **2** *nm,f* **(a)** (*religieux*) **(frère) ~, (sœur) ~ière** hospitaller. **(b)** (*infirmier*) nurse.

hospitalisation [ɔspitalizɑsjɔ̃] *nf* hospitalization.

hospitaliser [ɔspitalize] (1) *vt* to hospitalize, send to hospital.

hospitalité [ɔspitalite] *nf* hospitality. **donner l'~ à qn** to give *ou* offer sb hospitality.

hostellerie† [ɔstɛlʀi] *nf* hostelry†.

hostie [ɔsti] *nf* (*Rel*) host; (††: *victime*) sacrificial victim.

hostile [ɔstil] *adj foule, forces, accueil* hostile (*à* to, towards). **~ à** *projet etc* opposed *ou* hostile to.

hostilement [ɔstilmɑ̃] *adv* hostilely.

hostilité [ɔstilite] *nf* hostility. (*Mil*) **les ~s** hostilities.

hôte [ot] **1** *nm* (*maître de maison*) host; (†: *aubergiste*) landlord, host. (†, *littér: animal*) **~ d'un bois/d'un marais** inhabitant of a wood/marsh; *V* **table. 2** *nmf* (*invité*) guest; (*client*) patron; (*locataire*) occupant. **~ payant** paying guest.

hôtel [otɛl] **1** *nm* hotel. **vivre/coucher à l'~** to live/sleep in a hotel; **aller à l'~** to put up at a hotel; *V* **maître, rat.**

2: hôtel-Dieu *nm, pl* **hôtels-Dieu** general hospital; **hôtel-meublé** *nm, pl* **hôtels-meublés** lodging house, residential hotel; **l'hôtel de la Monnaie** ≈ the Mint; **hôtel (particulier)** (private) mansion; **hôtel de passe** *hotel used by prostitutes and the like*; **hôtel-restaurant** *nm, pl* **hôtels-restaurant** hotel (with public restaurant); **hôtel des ventes** salerooms; **hôtel de ville** town hall.

hôtelier, -ière [otəlje, jɛʀ] **1** *adj industrie, profession* hotel (*épith*); *V* **école. 2** *nm,f* hotelier, hotel-keeper.

hôtellerie [otɛlʀi] *nf* (*auberge*) inn, hostelry†; (*profession*) hotel business.

hôtesse [otɛs] *nf* (*maîtresse de maison*) hostess; (†: *aubergiste*) landlady. **~ (de l'air)** air hostess; **~ (d'accueil)** receptionist, hostess.

hotte ['ɔt] *nf* (*panier*) basket (*carried on the back*); *[cheminée]* hood. *[cuisine]* **~ aspirante** cooker hood; **la ~ du Père Noël** Father Christmas's sack.

hou ['u, hu] *excl [peur]* boo!; *[honte]* tut-tut!

houblon ['ublɔ̃] *nm* (*plante*) hop; (*comme ingrédient de la bière*) hops.

houe ['u] *nf* hoe.

houille ['uj] *nf* coal. **~ blanche** hydroelectric power; **~ verte** marine power, wave energy; **~ grasse/maigre** bituminous/lean coal.

houiller, -ère ['uje, ɛʀ] **1** *adj bassin, industrie* coal (*épith*); *terrain* coal-bearing. **2 houillère** *nf* coalmine.

houle ['ul] *nf* swell (*U*).

houlette ['ulɛt] *nf [pâtre, évêque]* crook; *[jardinier]* trowel, spud. **sous la ~ de** under the leadership of.

houleux, -euse ['ulø, øz] *adj mer* undulating, swelling; *séance* stormy, turbulent; *salle, foule* tumultuous, turbulent.

houp ['up, hup] *excl* = **hop.**

houppe ['up] *nf [plumes, cheveux]* tuft; *[fils]* tassel. **~ à poudrer** powder puff.

houppelande ['uplɑ̃d] *nf* (loose-fitting) greatcoat.

houppette ['upɛt] *nf* powder puff.

hourra ['uʀa, huʀa] *excl* hurrah! **pousser des ~s** to cheer, shout hurrah; **hip, hip, hip ~!** hip hip hurrah!

houspiller ['uspije] (1) *vt* (*réprimander*) to scold, tell off, tick off*; (†: *malmener*) to hustle.

housse ['us] *nf* (*gén*) cover; *[meubles]* (*pour protéger temporairement*) dust cover; (*pour recouvrir à neuf*) loose cover; (*en tissu élastique*) stretch cover. *[habits]* **~ (penderie)** hanging wardrobe.

houx ['u] *nm* holly.

huard* ['yaʀ] *nm* (*Can*) loon.

hublot ['yblo] *nm* porthole.

huche ['yʃ] *nf* (*coffre*) chest; (*pétrin*) dough trough. **~ à pain** bread bin.

hue ['y, hy] *excl* gee up! (*fig*) **ils tirent tous à ~ et à dia** they aren't all pulling together.

huées ['ɥe] *nfpl* boos, hoots. **sous les ~ de la foule** to the boos of the crowd.

huer ['ɥe] (1) **1** *vt* to boo. **2** *vi [chouette]* to hoot.

huguenot, e ['ygno, ɔt] *adj, nm,f* Huguenot.

Hugues ['yg] *nm* Hugh.

huilage [ɥilaʒ] *nm* oiling, lubrication.

huile [ɥil] *nf* **(a)** (*liquide*) oil. (*Culin*) **fait à l'~** cooked in oil; **~ vierge** unrefined olive oil; **~ de ricin** castor oil; **~ de table/de graissage/solaire** salad/lubricating/sun(tan) oil; **~ d'arachide/d'olive/de tournesol** groundnut/olive/sunflower oil; **~ de foie de morue** cod-liver oil; **~ de lin** linseed oil; **~ de paraffine** paraffin oil; **~ de coude*** elbow grease; (*fig*) **jeter** *ou* **verser de l'~ sur le feu** to add fuel to the flames; (*fig*) **une mer d'~** a glassy sea; *V* **lampe, saint, tache.**

(b) (*: *notabilité*) bigwig*, big noise*, big shot*; (*Mil*) brass hat*. **les ~s** the top brass*, the big shots*.

(c) (*Peinture*) (*tableau*) oil painting; (*technique*) oil painting, oils. **fait à l'~** done in oils; *V* **peinture.**

huiler [ɥile] (1) *vt machine* to oil, lubricate. **papier huilé** oil-paper; **salade trop huilée** oily salad.

huilerie [ɥilʀi] *nf* (*usine*) oil-works; (*commerce*) oil-trade; (*moulin*) oil-mill.

huileux, -euse [ɥilø, øz] *adj liquide, matière* oily; *aspect, surface* oily, greasy.

huilier [ɥilje] *nm* (oil and vinegar) cruet, oil and vinegar bottle.

huis [ɥi] *nm* (††) door. (*Jur*) **à ~ clos** in camera; (*Jur*) **ordonner le ~ clos** to order proceedings to be held in camera.

huissier [ɥisje] *nm* (*appariteur*) usher; (*Jur*) ≈ bailiff.

huit ['ɥi(t)] **1** *adj inv* eight; *pour loc V* **six.**

2 *nm inv* (*chiffre, nombre, Cartes*) eight; (*figure*) figure of eight. **lundi/samedi en** ~ a week (on) Monday/Saturday, Monday/Saturday week*.

3: huit jours *nmpl* (*une semaine*) a week; **dans huit jours** in a week; **donner à qn ses huit jours** to give sb his (week's) notice, give sb his cards* (*Brit*) *ou* his pink slip* (*US*); **huit reflets** *nm* top hat.

huitain ['ɥitɛ̃] *nm* octet, octave.

huitaine ['ɥitɛn] *nf* eight or so, about eight. **dans une** ~ **(de jours)** in a week or so; (*Jur*) **son cas a été remis à** ~ the hearing is postponed for one week.

huitante ['ɥitɑ̃t] *adj inv* (*Suisse*) eighty.

huitième ['ɥitjɛm] **1** *adj, nmf* eighth. **le** ~ **art** the cinema; **la** ~ **merveille du monde** the eighth wonder of the world; *pour autres loc V* **sixième**. **2** *nf* (*Scol*) class 8 (*penultimate class of primary school*) (*Brit*), eighth grade (*US*). **3** *nmpl* (*Sport*) ~**s de finale** second round in a five-round knock-out competition.

huitièmement ['ɥitjɛmmɑ̃] *adv* eighthly.

huître [ɥitʀ(ə)] *nf* oyster.

hulotte ['ylɔt] *nf* tawny owl.

hululement [ylylmɑ̃] *nm* hooting, screeching.

hululer [ylyle] (1) *vi* to hoot, screech.

hum ['œm, hœm] *excl* hem!, h'm!

humain, e [ymɛ̃, ɛn] **1** *adj* (*gén*) human; (*compatissant, compréhensif*) humane. **justice/espèce** ~**e** human justice/race; **il n'avait plus figure** ~**e** he was disfigured beyond recognition; **se montrer** ~ to show humanity, act humanely (*envers* towards); **il s'est sauvé, c'est** ~ he ran away — it's only human; *V* **géographie, respect, voix** *etc*.

2 *nm* **(a)** (*Philos*) **l'**~ the human element.

(b) (*être humain*) human (being). **les** ~**s** humans, human beings.

humainement [ymɛnmɑ̃] *adv* (*avec bonté*) humanely; (*par l'homme*) humanly. **ce n'est pas** ~ **possible** it is not humanly possible.

humanisation [ymanizɑsjɔ̃] *nf* humanization.

humaniser [ymanize] (1) *vt doctrine* to humanize; *conditions* to make more humane, humanize. **misanthrope qui s'humanise** misanthropist who is becoming more human.

humanisme [ymanism(ə)] *nm* humanism.

humaniste [ymanist(ə)] **1** *adj* humanistic. **2** *nmf* humanist.

humanitaire [ymanitɛʀ] *adj* humanitarian.

humanitarisme [ymanitaʀism(ə)] *nm* (*péj*) unrealistic humanitarianism.

humanitariste [ymanitaʀist(ə)] **1** *adj* (*péj*) unrealistically humanitarian. **2** *nmf* unrealistic humanitarian.

humanité [ymanite] *nf* **(a)** (*le genre humain*) **l'**~ humanity, mankind. **(b)** (*bonté*) humaneness, humanity. **geste d'**~ humane gesture. **(c)** (*Philos, Rel*) humanity. **(d)** (*Scol*) **les** ~**s** the classics, the humanities.

humanoïde [ymanɔid] *nm* humanoid.

humble [œ̃bl(ə)] *adj* (*modeste, pauvre*) humble; (*obscur*) humble, lowly. **d'**~ **naissance** of humble *ou* lowly birth *ou* origins; **à mon** ~ **avis** in my humble opinion.

humblement [œ̃bləmɑ̃] *adv* humbly.

humectage [ymɛktaʒ] *nm* (*V* **humecter**) dampening; moistening.

humecter [ymɛkte] (1) *vt linge, herbe* to dampen; *front* to moisten, dampen. **s'**~ **le gosier*** to wet one's whistle*; **s'**~ **les lèvres** to moisten one's lips.

humer ['yme] (1) *vt plat* to smell; *air* to inhale, breathe in.

humérus [ymeʀys] *nm* humerus.

humeur [ymœʀ] *nf* **(a)** (*disposition momentanée*) mood, humour. **être de bonne** ~ to be in a good mood *ou* humour, be in good spirits; **être de mauvaise** ~ to be in a bad mood, be out of humour; **se sentir d'**~ **à travailler** to feel in the mood *ou* humour for working *ou* for work *ou* in the mood to work; **cela l'a mis de bonne** ~ that put him in a good mood *ou* humour *ou* in good spirits; **il est d'**~ **massacrante, il est d'une** ~ **de dogue** *ou* **de chien** he's in a rotten* *ou* foul temper *ou* mood; ~ **noire** black mood; **roman/film plein de bonne** ~ good-humoured novel/film, novel/film full of good humour; *V* **saute**.

(b) (*tempérament*) temper, temperament. **être d'**~ *ou* **avoir l'**~ **batailleuse** to be fiery-tempered; **être d'**~ **maussade** to be sullen, be a sullen type; **il est d'**~ **inégale/égale** he is moody/even-tempered, he has an uneven/even temper; **il y a incompatibilité d'**~ **entre eux** they are temperamentally unsuited *ou* incompatible; **un enfant plein de bonne** ~ a sunny-natured child, a child with a cheerful *ou* sunny nature.

(c) (*irritation*) bad temper, ill humour. **passer son** ~ **sur qn** to take out *ou* vent one's bad temper *ou* ill humour on sb; **accès** *ou* **mouvement d'**~ fit of (bad) temper *ou* ill humour; **geste d'**~ bad-tempered gesture; **agir par** ~ to act in a fit of (bad) temper *ou* ill humour; **dire qch avec** ~ to say sth ill-humouredly *ou* testily (*littér*); (*littér*) **cela lui donne de l'**~ that makes him ill-humoured *ou* bad-tempered.

(d) (*Méd*) secretion. ~ **aqueuse/vitreuse de l'œil** aqueous/vitreous humour of the eye; **les** ~**s**†† the humours††.

humide [ymid] *adj mains, front* moist, damp; *torchon, habits, mur, poudre, herbe* damp; *local, climat, région, chaleur* humid, (*plutôt froid*) damp; *tunnel, cave* dank, damp; *saison, route* wet. **yeux** ~**s d'émotion** eyes moist with emotion; **elle lui lança un regard** ~ she looked at him with moist eyes; **temps lourd et** ~ muggy weather; **mains** ~**s et collantes** clammy hands.

humidificateur [ymidifikatœʀ] *nm* humidifier.

humidification [ymidifikɑsjɔ̃] *nf* humidification.

humidifier [ymidifje] (7) *vt* to humidify.

humidité [ymidite] *nf* [*air*] humidity, (*plutôt froide*) dampness; [*sol, mur*] dampness; [*tunnel, cave*] dankness, dampness. ~ **(atmosphérique)** humidity (of the atmosphere); **air saturé d'**~ air saturated with moisture; **dégâts causés par l'**~ damage caused by (the) damp; **traces d'**~ **sur le mur** traces of moisture *ou* of damp on the wall; **taches d'**~ damp patches, patches of damp; (*sur emballage*) **'craint l'**~**', 'à protéger de l'**~**'** 'to be kept dry', 'keep in a dry place'.

humiliant, e [ymiljɑ̃, ɑ̃t] *adj* humiliating.

humiliation [ymiljɑsjɔ̃] *nf* (*gén*) humiliation; (*Rel*) humbling (*U*).

humilier [ymilje] (7) *vt* (*rabaisser*) to humiliate; (††, *Rel: rendre humble*) to humble. **s'**~ **devant** to humiliate *ou* humble o.s. before.

humilité [ymilite] *nf* (*modestie*) humility, humbleness. **ton d'**~ humble tone.

humoral, e, *mpl* **-aux** [ymɔʀal, o] *adj* humoral.

humoriste [ymɔʀist(ə)] *nmf* humorist.

humoristique [ymɔʀistik] *adj ton, histoire* humorous; *genre, écrivain* humoristic; *V* **dessin**.

humour [ymuʀ] *nm* humour. ~ **noir** sick *ou* morbid humour; **manquer d'**~ to have no sense of humour; **avoir beaucoup d'**~ to have a good *ou* great sense of humour.

humus [ymys] *nm* humus.

Hun ['œ̃] *nm* (*Hist*) Hun.

hune ['yn] *nf* top. **mât de** ~ topmast; **grande** ~ maintop.

hunier ['ynje] *nm* topsail.

huppe ['yp] *nf* (*oiseau*) hoopoe; (*crête*) crest.

huppé, e ['ype] *adj* (*Orn*) crested; (*: *riche*) posh* (*Brit*), classy*.

hure ['yʀ] *nf* head. (*Culin*) ~ **de sanglier** boar's head.

hurlement ['yʀləmɑ̃] *nm* (*V* **hurler**) roaring (*U*), roar; yelling (*U*), yell; howling (*U*), howl; bellowing (*U*), bellow; squealing (*U*), squeal; wailing (*U*), wail.

hurler ['yʀle] (1) **1** *vi* **(a)** [*personne*] (*de douleur*) to roar, yell (out), bellow; (*de peur*) to scream, yell; [*foule*] to roar (*de* with, in). ~ **de colère** to roar *ou* bellow with anger.

(b) [*chien*] to howl; [*vent*] to howl, roar; [*freins*] to squeal; [*sirène*] to wail. **chien qui hurle à la lune** *ou* **à la mort** dog baying at the moon; ~ **avec les loups** to follow the pack *ou* crowd (*fig*).

(c) (*jurer*) [*couleurs*] to clash. **ce tableau bleu sur le mur vert, ça hurle!** that blue picture really clashes with the green wall.

2 *vt* to yell, roar, bellow.

hurluberlu [yʀlybɛʀly] *nm* crank.

hurrah ['uʀa, huʀa] *excl* = **hourra**.

hussard ['ysaʀ] *nm* hussar.

hussarde [ysaʀd(ə)] *nf*: **à la** ~ roughly.

hutte ['yt] *nf* hut.

hyacinthe [jasɛ̃t] *nf* (*pierre*) hyacinth, jacinth; (†: *fleur*) hyacinth.

hybridation [ibʀidɑsjɔ̃] *nf* hybridization.

hybride [ibʀid] *adj, nm* hybrid.

hybrider [ibʀide] (1) *vt* to hybridize.

hybridisme [ibʀidism(ə)] *nm*, **hybridité** [ibʀidite] *nf* hybridism, hybridity.

hydracide [idʀasid] *nm* hydracid.

hydratant, e [idʀatɑ̃, ɑ̃t] **1** *adj* moisturizing. **2** *nm* moisturizer.

hydratation [idʀatɑsjɔ̃] *nf* (*Chim, Méd*) hydration.

hydrate [idʀat] *nm* hydrate. ~ **de carbone** carbohydrate.

hydrater [idʀate] (1) **1** *vt* to hydrate. **2 s'hydrater** *vpr* to become hydrated.

hydraulique [idʀolik] **1** *adj* hydraulic. **2** *nf* hydraulics (*sg*).

hydravion [idʀavjɔ̃] *nm* seaplane, hydroplane.

hydre [idʀ(ə)] *nf* hydra.

hydrocarbure [idʀɔkaʀbyʀ] *nm* hydrocarbon.

hydrocéphale [idʀɔsefal] **1** *adj* hydrocephalic, hydrocephalous. **2** *nmf* person suffering from hydrocephalus.

hydrocéphalie [idʀɔsefali] *nf* hydrocephalus.

hydrocortisone [idʀɔkɔʀtizɔn] *nf* hydrocortisone.

hydrocution [idʀɔkysjɔ̃] *nf* (*Méd*) immersion syncope.

hydrodynamique [idʀɔdinamik] **1** *adj* hydrodynamic. **2** *nf* hydrodynamics (*sg*).

hydroélectricité [idʀɔelɛktʀisite] *nf* hydroelectricity.

hydro-électrique [idʀɔelɛktʀik] *adj* hydroelectric.

hydrofoil [idʀɔfɔjl] *nm* hydrofoil (*boat*).

hydrogénation [idʀɔʒenɑsjɔ̃] *nf* hydrogenation.

hydrogène [idʀɔʒɛn] *nm* hydrogen. ~ **lourd** heavy hydrogen.

hydrogéner [idʀɔʒene] (6) *vt* to hydrogenate, hydrogenize.

hydroglisseur [idʀɔglisœʀ] *nm* hydroplane (*boat*).

hydrographe [idʀɔgʀaf] *nm* hydrographer.

hydrographie [idʀɔgʀafi] *nf* hydrography.

hydrographique [idʀɔgʀafik] *adj* hydrographic(al).

hydrologie [idʀɔlɔʒi] *nf* hydrology.

hydrologique [idʀɔlɔʒik] *adj* hydrologic(al).

hydrologiste [idʀɔlɔʒist(ə)] *nmf*, **hydrologue** [idʀɔlɔg] *nmf* hydrologist.

hydrolyse [idʀɔliz] *nf* hydrolysis.

hydrolyser [idʀɔlize] (1) *vt* to hydrolyse.

hydromel [idʀɔmɛl] *nm* mead.

hydromètre [idʀɔmɛtʀ(ə)] *nm* (*Tech*) hydrometer.

hydrométrie [idʀɔmetʀi] *nf* hydrometry.

hydrophile [idʀɔfil] *adj V* **coton**.

hydropique [idʀɔpik] **1** *adj* dropsical, hydropic(al). **2** *nmf* person suffering from dropsy.

hydropisie [idʀɔpizi] *nf* dropsy.

hydroptère [idʀɔptɛʀ] *nm* hydrofoil.

hydrosphère [idʀɔsfɛʀ] *nf* hydrosphere.

hydrostatique [idʀɔstatik] **1** *adj* hydrostatic. **2** *nf* hydrostatics (*sg*).

hydrothérapie [idʀɔteʀapi] *nf* (*traitement*) hydrotherapy; (*science*) hydrotherapeutics (*sg*).

hydrothérapique [idʀɔteʀapik] *adj* (*V* **hydrothérapie**) hydrotherapic; hydrotherapeutic.

hydroxyde [idʀɔksid] *nm* hydroxide.

hyène [jɛn] *nf* hyena.

hygiène [iʒjɛn] *nf* hygiene; (*science*) hygienics (*sg*), hygiene. **ça manque d'~** it's unhygienic; **~ corporelle** personal hygiene; **avoir de l'~** to be fastidious about one's personal hygiene.

hygiénique [iʒjenik] *adj* hygienic. **promenade ~** constitutional (walk); *V* **papier, seau, serviette.**

hygiéniste [iʒjenist(ə)] *nmf* hygienist.

hygromètre [igʀɔmɛtʀ(ə)] *nm* hygrometer.

hygrométrie [igʀɔmetʀi] *nf* hygrometry.

hygrométrique [igʀɔmetʀik] *adj* hygrometric.

hygroscope [igʀɔskɔp] *nm* hygroscope.

hymen [imɛn] *nm* (*littér: mariage*) marriage; (*Anat*) hymen.

hyménée [imene] *nm* marriage.

hymne [imn(ə)] *nm* (*Littérat, Rel*) hymn. (*fig*) **son discours était un ~ à la liberté** his speech was a hymn to liberty; **~ national** national anthem.

hyper ... [ipɛʀ] *préf* hyper ... .

hyperacidité [ipɛʀasidite] *nf* hyperacidity.

hyperbole [ipɛʀbɔl] *nf* (*Math*) hyperbola; (*Littérat*) hyperbole.

hyperbolique [ipɛʀbɔlik] *adj* (*Math, Littérat*) hyperbolic.

hypercorrect, e [ipɛʀkɔʀɛkt, ɛkt(ə)] *adj* (*Ling*) hypercorrect.

hypercorrection [ipɛʀkɔʀɛksjɔ̃] *nf* (*Ling*) hypercorrection.

hyperémotivité [ipɛʀemɔtivite] *nf* excess emotionality.

hyperglycémie [ipɛʀglisemi] *nf* hyperglycaemia.

hypermétrope [ipɛʀmetʀɔp] *adj* long-sighted, hypermetropic (*T*).

hypermétropie [ipɛʀmetʀɔpi] *nf* long-sightedness, hypermetropia (*T*).

hypernerveux, -euse [ipɛʀnɛʀvø, øz] *adj* over-excitable.

hypernervosité [ipɛʀnɛʀvozite] *nf* over-excitability.

hypersensibilité [ipɛʀsɑ̃sibilite] *nf* hypersensitivity, hypersensitiveness.

hypersensible [ipɛʀsɑ̃sibl(ə)] *adj* hypersensitive.

hypersexué, e [ipɛʀsɛksɥe] *adj* oversexed.

hypertendu, e [ipɛʀtɑ̃dy] *adj* suffering from high blood pressure, suffering from hypertension (*T*).

hypertension [ipɛʀtɑ̃sjɔ̃] *nf* high blood pressure, hypertension (*T*).

hypertrophie [ipɛʀtʀɔfi] *nf* hypertrophy.

hypertrophier [ipɛʀtʀɔfje] (7) *vt* to hypertrophy.

hypertrophique [ipɛʀtʀɔfik] *adj* hypertrophic.

hypnose [ipnoz] *nf* hypnosis.

hypnotique [ipnɔtik] *adj* (*lit*) hypnotic; (*fig*) hypnotic, mesmeric, mesmerizing.

hypnotiser [ipnɔtize] (1) *vt* (*lit*) to hypnotize; (*fig*) to hypnotize, mesmerize. (*fig*) **être hypnotisé par la peur de se tromper** to be transfixed by the fear of making an error; **s'~ sur un problème** to be mesmerized by a problem.

hypnotiseur [ipnɔtizœʀ] *nm* hypnotist.

hypnotisme [ipnɔtism(ə)] *nm* hypnotism.

hypo ... [ipɔ] *préf* hypo ... .

hypocondriaque [ipɔkɔ̃dʀijak] **1** *adj* (*Méd*) hypochondriac; (*mélancolique*) gloomy. **2** *nmf* hypochondriac; gloomy type.

hypocondrie [ipɔkɔ̃dʀi] *nf* hypochondria.

hypocrisie [ipɔkʀizi] *nf* hypocrisy.

hypocrite [ipɔkʀit] **1** *adj* hypocritical. **2** *nmf* hypocrite.

hypocritement [ipɔkʀitmɑ̃] *adv* hypocritically.

hypodermique [ipɔdɛʀmik] *adj* hypodermic.

hypoglycémie [ipɔglisemi] *nf* hypoglycaemia.

hypophyse [ipɔfiz] *nf* pituitary gland, hypophysis (*T*).

hypotension [ipɔtɑ̃sjɔ̃] *nf* low blood pressure, hypotension (*T*).

hypoténuse [ipɔtenyz] *nf* hypotenuse.

hypothécable [ipɔtekabl(ə)] *adj* mortgageable.

hypothécaire [ipɔtekɛʀ] *adj* hypothecary. **garantie ~** mortgage security; **prêt ~** mortgage loan.

hypothèque [ipɔtɛk] *nf* mortgage.

hypothéquer [ipɔteke] (6) *vt maison* to mortgage; *créance* to secure (by mortgage); (*fig*) *avenir* to sign away.

hypothermie [ipɔtɛʀmi] *nf* hypothermia.

hypothèse [ipɔtɛz] *nf* hypothesis.

hypothétique [ipɔtetik] *adj* hypothetical.

hypothétiquement [ipɔtetikmɑ̃] *adv* hypothetically.

hystérectomie [isteʀɛktɔmi] *nf* hysterectomy.

hystérie [isteʀi] *nf* hysteria. **~ collective** mob hysteria.

hystérique [isteʀik] **1** *adj* hysterical. **2** *nmf* (*Méd*) hysteric; (*péj*) hysterical sort.

I

I, i [i] *nm* (*lettre*) I, i; *V* **droit[2], point[1].**

iambe [jɑ̃b] *nm* (*Littérat*) (*pied*) iambus, iambic; (*vers, poème*) iambic.

iambique [jɑ̃bik] *adj* iambic.

ibère [ibɛʀ] **1** *adj* Iberian. **2** *nmf*: **I~** Iberian.

ibérique [ibeʀik] *adj* Iberian.

ibid [ibid] *adv*, **ibidem** [ibidɛm] *adv* ibid, ibidem.

ibis [ibis] *nm* ibis.

Icare [ikaʀ] *nm* Icarus.

iceberg [ajsbɛʀg] *nm* iceberg.

icelui [isəlɥi], **icelle** [isɛl], *pl* **iceux** [isø], **icelles** [isɛl] *pron* (††, *Jur, hum*) = **celui-ci, celle-ci, ceux-ci, celles-ci.**

ichtyologie [iktjɔlɔʒi] *nf* ichthyology.

ichtyologique [iktjɔlɔʒik] *adj* ichthyologic(al).

ichtyologiste [iktjɔlɔʒist(ə)] *nmf* ichthyologist.

ici [isi] *adv* **(a)** here. **~!** (*à un chien*) here!; **loin/près d'~** far from/near here; **il y a 10 km d'~ à Paris** it's 10 km from here to Paris; **passez par ~** come this way; **par ~ s'il vous plaît** this way please; **c'est ~ que** this is the place where, it is (*ou* was *etc*) here that; **~ on est un peu isolé** we're a bit cut off (out) here; **le bus vient jusqu'~ *ou* s'arrête ~** the bus comes as far as this *ou* this far.

(b) (*temporel*) **d'~ demain/la fin de la semaine** by tomorrow/the end of the week; **d'~ peu** before (very) long, shortly; **d'~ là** between now and then, before then, in the meantime; **jusqu'~** (up) until now; (*dans le passé*) (up) until then; **d'~ à ce qu'il se retrouve en prison, ça ne va pas être long** it won't be long before he lands up in jail (again); **d'~ à ce qu'il accepte, ça risque de faire long** it might be (quite) some time before he says yes; **le projet lui plaît, mais d'~ à ce qu'il accepte!** he likes the plan, but there's a difference between just liking it and actually agreeing to it!

(c) (*loc*) **ils sont d'~/ne sont pas d'~** they are/aren't local *ou* from around here *ou* from this area; **les gens d'~** the local people; **je vois ça d'~!*** I can just see that!; **tu vois d'~ la situation/sa tête!*** you can (just) imagine the situation/the look on his face!; **vous êtes ~ chez vous** please make yourself (quite) at home; **~ présent** here present; **'~ Alain Proviste'** (*au téléphone*) 'Alain Proviste speaking *ou* here'; (*à la radio*) 'this is Alain Proviste'; **'~ Radio Luxembourg'** 'this is Radio Luxembourg'; **~ et là** here and there; (*Rel, hum*) **~-bas** here below; **les choses d'~-bas** things of this world *ou* of this life; **la vie d'~-bas** life here below; (*au marché*) **par ~ Mesdames, par ~ les belles laitues!** this way, ladies, lovely lettuces this way! *ou* over here!; **par ~** (*dans le coin*) around here.

icône [ikon] *nf* icon.

iconoclasme [ikɔnɔklasm(ə)] *nm* iconoclasm.

iconoclaste [ikɔnɔklast(ə)] **1** *nmf* iconoclast. **2** *adj* iconoclastic.

iconographe [ikɔnɔgʀaf] *nmf* iconographer.

iconographie [ikɔnɔgʀafi] *nf* (*étude*) iconography; (*images*) (collection of) illustrations.

iconographique [ikɔnɔgʀafik] *adj* iconographic(al).

ictère [iktɛʀ] *nm* icterus.

idéal, e, *mpl* -aux [ideal, o] **1** *adj* (*imaginaire*) ideal; (*rêvé, parfait*) *maison, vacances* ideal; *perfection* absolute.

2 *nm* **(a)** (*modèle, aspiration*) ideal; (*valeurs morales*) ideals. **il n'a pas d'~** he has no ideal in life, he hasn't any ideals.

(b) (*le mieux*) **l'~ serait qu'elle l'épouse** the ideal thing *ou* solution would be for her to marry him, it would be ideal if she were to marry him *ou* if she married him.

idéalement [idealmɑ̃] *adv* ideally.

idéalisation [idealizasjɔ̃] *nf* idealization.

idéaliser [idealize] (1) *vt* to idealize.

idéalisme [idealism(ə)] *nm* idealism.

idéaliste [idealist(ə)] **1** *adj* (*gén*) idealistic; (*Philos*) idealist. **2** *nmf* idealist.

idée [ide] **1** *nf* **(a)** (*concept*) idea. **l'~ de nombre/de beauté** the idea of number/of beauty; **l'~ que les enfants se font du monde** the idea *ou* concept children have of the world; **c'est lui qui a eu le premier l'~ d'un moteur à réaction** it was he who first thought of *ou* conceived the idea of the jet engine, he was the first to hit upon the idea of the jet engine.

(b) (*pensée*) idea. **il a eu l'~ *ou* l'~ lui est venue de faire** he had the idea *ou* hit upon the idea of doing, the idea occurred to him to do; **l'~ ne lui viendrait jamais de nous aider** it would never occur to him to help us, he would never think of helping us; **ça m'a donné l'~ qu'il ne viendrait pas** that made me think that he wouldn't come; **à l'~ de faire qch/de qch** at the idea *ou* thought of doing sth/of sth; **tout est dans l'~ qu'on s'en fait** it's all in the mind; **avoir une ~ derrière la tête** to have something at the back of one's mind; *V* **changer, haut, ordre[1]** *etc.*

(c) (*illusion*) idea. **tu te fais des ~s** you're imagining things; **ne te fais pas des ~s** don't get ideas into your head; **ça pourrait**

lui donner des ~s it might give him ideas *ou* put ideas into his head; **quelle ~!** the (very) idea!, what an idea!; **il a de ces ~s!** the ideas he has!, the things he thinks up!; **on n'a pas ~ (de faire des choses pareilles)!*** it's incredible (doing things like that)!

(d) (*suggestion*) idea. **son ~ est meilleure** his idea is better; **quelques ~s pour votre jardin/vos menus** a few ideas *ou* suggestions for your garden/for meals to make; **de nouvelles ~s-vacances/~s-rangement** some new holiday/storage tips *ou* hints.

(e) (*vague notion*) idea. **donner à qn/se faire une ~ des difficultés** to give sb/get an *ou* some idea of the difficulties; **avez-vous une ~ *ou* la moindre ~ de l'heure/de son âge?** have you got any idea of the time/of his age?; **je n'en ai pas la moindre ~** I haven't the faintest *ou* least *ou* slightest idea; **vous n'avez pas ~ de sa bêtise** you have no idea how stupid he is, you have no conception of his stupidity; **j'ai (comme une) ~ qu'il n'acceptera pas** I (somehow) have an idea *ou* a feeling *ou* I have a sort of feeling that he won't accept.

(f) (*opinion*) **~s** ideas, views; **~s politiques/religieuses** political/religious ideas *ou* views; **ce n'est pas dans ses ~s** he doesn't hold with that; **avoir des ~s larges/étroites** to be broad-minded/narrow-minded; (*péj*) **avoir les ~s courtes** to have limited ideas, not to think very deeply.

(g) (*goût, conception personnelle*) ideas. **juger selon son ~** to judge in accordance with one's own ideas; **agir selon son ~** to act *ou* do as one sees fit; **il n'en fait qu'à son ~** he does just as he likes; **pour être décorateur il faut de l'~ *ou* un peu d'~** to be a decorator you have to have some imagination *ou* a few ideas; **il y a de l'~*** (*projet*) there's something in it; (*décoration intérieure*) it's got (a certain) something.

(h) (*esprit*) **avoir dans l'~ que** to have an idea that, have it in one's mind that; **il a dans l'~ de partir au Mexique** he's thinking of going to Mexico; **ça m'est sorti de l'~** it went clean* *ou* right out of my mind *ou* head; **cela ne lui viendrait jamais à l'~** it would never occur to him *ou* enter his head; **on ne m'ôtera pas de l'~ qu'il a menti** you won't get me to believe that he didn't lie; **il s'est mis dans l'~ de faire** he took *ou* got it into his head to do.

2: **idée fixe** idée fixe, obsession; **idée-force** *nf, pl* **idées-forces** strong point, key idea; **idée de génie, idée lumineuse** brilliant idea, brainwave; **idée noire** black *ou* gloomy thought; **idée reçue** generally accepted idea.

idem [idɛm] *adv* ditto, idem. **il a mauvais caractère et son frère ~*** he's bad-tempered and so is his brother *ou* and his brother's the same.

identifiable [idɑ̃tifjabl(ə)] *adj* identifiable.

identification [idɑ̃tifikɑsjɔ̃] *nf* identification (*à, avec* with).

identifier [idɑ̃tifje] (7) **1** *vt* (*reconnaître*) to identify. (*assimiler à*) **~ qch/qn à *ou* avec *ou* et** to identify sth/sb with.

2 s'identifier *vpr*: **s'~ à** (*se mettre dans la peau de*) *personnage, héros* to identify with; (*être l'équivalent de*) to identify o.s. with, become identified with.

identique [idɑ̃tik] *adj* identical (*à* to). **elle reste toujours ~ à elle-même** she never changes, she's always the same.

identiquement [idɑ̃tikmɑ̃] *adv* identically.

identité [idɑ̃tite] *nf* **(a)** (*similarité*) identity, similarity; (*Math, Psych: égalité*) identity. **une ~ de goûts les rapprocha** (their) similar tastes brought them together.

(b) (*Admin*) identity. **~ d'emprunt** assumed *ou* borrowed identity; **vérification/papiers d'~** identity check/papers; **l'~ judiciaire** ≈ the Criminal Records Office; *V* **carte, pièce.**

idéogramme [ideɔgʀam] *nm* ideogram.

idéographie [ideɔgʀafi] *nf* ideography.

idéographique [ideɔgʀafik] *adj* ideographic(al).

idéologie [ideɔlɔʒi] *nf* ideology.

idéologique [ideɔlɔʒik] *adj* ideological.

idéologue [ideɔlɔg] *nmf* ideologist.

idiolecte [idjɔlɛkt(ə)] *nm* idiolect.

idiomatique [idjɔmatik] *adj* idiomatic. **expression ~** idiom, idiomatic expression.

idiome [idjom] *nm* idiom (*language*).

idiosyncrasie [idjɔsɛ̃kʀazi] *nf* idiosyncrasy.

idiot, e [idjo, idjɔt] **1** *adj action, personne, histoire* idiotic, stupid; (*Méd*) idiotic. **2** *nm,f* (*gén, Méd*) idiot. **ne fais pas l'~*** (*n'agis pas bêtement*) don't be an idiot; (*ne simule pas la bêtise*) stop acting stupid*; **l'~ du village** the village idiot.

idiotement [idjɔtmɑ̃] *adv* idiotically, stupidly.

idiotie [idjɔsi] *nf* **(a)** (*U*) *[action, personne]* idiocy, stupidity; (*Méd*) idiocy.

(b) (*action*) idiotic *ou* stupid thing to do; (*parole*) idiotic *ou* stupid thing to say; (*livre, film*) rubbish (*U*). **ne va pas voir de telles ~s** don't go and see such rubbish *ou* such an idiotic *ou* such a stupid film (*ou* play *etc*); **et ne dis/fais pas d'~s** and don't say/do anything stupid *ou* idiotic.

idiotisme [idjɔtism(ə)] *nm* idiom, idiomatic phrase.

idoine [idwan] *adj* (*Jur, hum: approprié*) appropriate, fitting.

idolâtre [idɔlɑtʀ(ə)] **1** *adj* (*Rel, fig*) idolatrous (*de* of). **2** *nm* (*Rel*) idolater. **3** *nf* (*Rel*) idolatress.

idolâtrer [idɔlɑtʀe] (1) *vt* to idolize.

idolâtrie [idɔlɑtʀi] *nf* (*Rel, fig*) idolatry.

idole [idɔl] *nf* (*Rel, fig*) idol.

idylle [idil] *nf* (*poème*) idyll; (*amour*) romance.

idyllique [idilik] *adj* idyllic.

if [if] *nm* (*arbre*) yew (tree); (*bois*) yew.

igloo, iglou [iglu] *nm* igloo.

Ignace [iɲas] *nm* Ignatius.

igname [iɲam] *nf* yam.

ignare [iɲaʀ] (*péj*) **1** *adj* ignorant. **2** *nmf* ignoramus.

ignifugation [ignifygɑsjɔ̃] *nf* fireproofing.

ignifuge [ignifyʒ] **1** *adj produit* fireproofing (*épith*). **2** *nm* fireproofing substance.

ignifugé, e [ignifyʒe] (*ptp de* **ignifuger**) *adj* fireproofed.

ignifuger [ignifyʒe] (3) *vt* to fireproof.

ignoble [iɲɔbl(ə)] *adj* (*abject*) ignoble, vile, base; (*sens affaibli: dégoûtant*) vile, revolting.

ignoblement [iɲɔbləmɑ̃] *adv* ignobly, vilely, basely.

ignominie [iɲɔmini] *nf* **(a)** (*caractère*) ignominy; (*acte*) ignominious *ou* disgraceful act; (*conduite*) ignominious *ou* disgraceful behaviour (*U*). **(b)** (*déshonneur*) ignominy, disgrace.

ignominieusement [iɲɔminjøzmɑ̃] *adv* ignominiously.

ignominieux, -euse [iɲɔminjø, øz] *adj* ignominious.

ignorance [iɲɔʀɑ̃s] *nf* **(a)** (*U*) (*inculture*) ignorance. (*méconnaissance*) **~ de** ignorance of; **tenir qn/être dans l'~ de qch** to keep sb/be in ignorance *ou* in the dark about sth; **dans l'~ des résultats** not knowing the results.

(b) (*manque*) **de graves ~s en maths/en matière juridique** serious gaps in his knowledge of maths/legal matters; *V* **pécher.**

ignorant, e [iɲɔʀɑ̃, ɑ̃t] **1** *adj* (*ne sachant rien*) ignorant (*en* about). (*ne connaissant pas*) **~ de** ignorant *ou* unaware of; **~ des usages, il ...** ignorant *ou* unaware of the customs, he ..., not knowing the customs, he ... .

2 *nm,f* ignoramus. **ne fais pas l'~** stop pretending you don't know what I mean (*ou* what he said *etc*); **parler en ~** to speak from ignorance.

ignoré, e [iɲɔʀe] (*ptp de* **ignorer**) *adj travaux, chercheurs, événement* unknown. **~ de tous** (*inconnu*) unknown to anybody; (*boudé*) ignored by all; **vivre ~** to live in obscurity.

ignorer [iɲɔʀe] (1) **1** *vt* **(a)** (*ne pas connaître*) *affaire, incident* to be unaware of, not to know about *ou* of; *fait, artiste, écrivain* not to know. **~ que** not to know that, be unaware that; **~ comment/si** not to know how/if; **vous n'ignorez certainement pas que/comment** you (will) doubtless know that/how; **j'ignore tout de cette affaire** I don't know anything *ou* I know nothing about this business; **je n'ignorais pas ces problèmes** I was (fully) aware of these problems, I was not unaware of these problems; **j'ignore avoir dit cela** I am not aware of having said that; *V* **nul.**

(b) (*bouder*) *personne* to ignore.

(c) (*être sans expérience de*) *plaisir, guerre, souffrance* not to know, to have had no experience of. (*hum*) **des gosses qui ignorent le savon** kids who have never seen (a cake of) soap *ou* who are unaware of the existence of soap; **des joues qui ignorent le rasoir** cheeks that never see a razor.

2 s'ignorer *vpr* (*se méconnaître*) **une tendresse qui s'ignore** an unconscious tenderness; **c'est un poète qui s'ignore** he's an unconscious poet.

iguane [igwan] *nm* iguana.

il [il] *pron pers m* **(a)** (*personne*) he; (*bébé, animal*) it, he; (*chose*) it; (*bateau, nation*) she, it. **~s** they; **~ était journaliste** he was a journalist; **prends ce fauteuil, ~ est plus confortable** have this chair — it's more comfortable; **je me méfie de son chien, ~ mord** I don't trust his dog — it bites; **l'insecte emmagasine la nourriture qu'~ trouve** the insect stores the food it finds; **le Japon/le Canada a décidé qu'~ n'accepterait pas** Japan/Canada decided she *ou* they* wouldn't accept; *V* **avoir, fumée, jeunesse** *etc.*

(b) (*impers*) it. **~ fait beau** it's a fine day; **~ y a un enfant/3 enfants** there is a child/are 3 children; **~ est vrai que** it is true that; **~ faut que j'y aille** I've got to go (there).

(c) (*interrog, emphatique,* *: *non traduit*) **Paul est-~ rentré?** is Paul back?; **le courrier est-~ arrivé?** has the mail come?; **les enfants sont-~s bien couverts?** are the children warmly wrapped up?; **~ est si beau cet enfant/cet arbre** this child/tree is so beautiful; **tu sais, ton oncle, ~ est arrivé*** your uncle has arrived you know.

île [il] **1** *nf* island, isle (*littér*). **les Î~s** the (French) West Indies.

2: **les îles anglo-normandes** the Channel Islands; **l'île de Beauté** Corsica; **les îles Britanniques** the British Isles; (*Culin*) **île flottante** floating island; **l'île Maurice** Mauritius; **les îles Scilly** the Scilly Isles, the Scillies; **les îles Shetland** the Shetland Islands, Shetland; **les îles Sorlingues = les îles Scilly**; **les îles Vierges** the Virgin Islands.

Iliade [iljad] *nf*: **l'~** the Iliad.

iliaque [iljak] *adj* iliac.

îlien, îlienne [iljɛ̃, iljɛn] *nm,f* (Breton) islander.

illégal, e, *mpl* **-aux** [ilegal, o] *adj* illegal, unlawful (*Admin*).

illégalement [ilegalmɑ̃] *adv* illegally, unlawfully (*Admin*).

illégalité [ilegalite] *nf* illegality; *[action]* illegality, unlawfulness (*Admin*); (*acte illégal*) illegality.

illégitime [ileʒitim] *adj* **(a)** (*illégal*) *acte, enfant* illegitimate. **(b)** (*non fondé*) *optimisme, cruauté* unwarranted, unwarrantable; *prétention, revendication* illegitimate.

illégitimement [ileʒitimmɑ̃] *adv* (*V* **illégitime**) illegitimately; unwarrantedly, unwarrantably.

illégitimité [ileʒitimite] *nf* (*V* **illégitime**) illegitimacy; unwarrantableness.

illettré, e [iletʀe] *adj, nm,f* illiterate.

illicite [ilisit] *adj* illicit.

illicitement [ilisitmɑ̃] *adv* illicitly.

illico* [iliko] *adv* (*tout de suite*) straightaway, right away, at once, pronto*.

illimité, e [ilimite] *adj moyen, domaine, ressource* unlimited, limitless; *confiance* boundless, unbounded; *congé, durée* indefinite, unlimited.

illisibilité [ilizibilite] *nf* illegibility.

illisible [ilizibl(ə)] *adj* (*indéchiffrable*) illegible, unreadable; (*mauvais*) unreadable.

illisiblement [ilizibləmɑ̃] *adv* (*V* **illisible**) **écrire ~** to write illegibly; to write unreadable stuff.

illogique [ilɔʒik] *adj* illogical.

illogiquement [ilɔʒikmɑ̃] *adv* illogically.

illogisme [ilɔʒism(ə)] *nm* illogicality.
illumination [ilyminɑsjɔ̃] *nf* **(a)** (*U: V* **illuminer**) lighting; illumination; floodlighting.
(b) (*lumières*) ~s illuminations, lights; **les ~s de Noël** the Christmas lights *ou* illuminations.
(c) (*inspiration*) flash of inspiration.
illuminé, e [ilymine] (*ptp de* **illuminer**) **1** *adj* (*V* **illuminer**) lit up (*attrib*); illuminated; floodlit. **2** *nm,f* (*péj: visionnaire*) visionary, crank (*péj*).
illuminer [ilymine] (1) **1** *vt* **(a)** (*éclairer*) to light up, illuminate. ~ **au moyen de projecteurs** to floodlight.
(b) (*fig*) *[joie, foi, colère]* to light up; (*Rel*) *prophète, âme* to enlighten, illuminate. **le bonheur illuminait son visage** his face shone *ou* was illuminated *ou* was aglow with happiness, happiness lit up his face.
2 s'illuminer *vpr [visage, ciel]* to light up (*de* with); *[rue, vitrine]* to be lit up.
illusion [ilyzjɔ̃] *nf* illusion. ~ **d'optique** optical illusion; **ne te fais aucune** ~ don't be under any illusion, don't delude *ou* kid* yourself; **tu te fais des ~s** you're deluding *ou* kidding* yourself; **ça donne l'~ de grandeur** it gives an illusion of size; **ça lui donne l'~ de servir à quelque chose** *ou* **qu'il sert à quelque chose** it gives him the illusion *ou* it makes him feel that he's doing something useful; **cet imposteur/ce stratagème ne fera pas ~ longtemps** this impostor/tactic won't delude *ou* fool people for long; *V* **bercer, jouet.**
illusionner [ilyzjɔne] (1) **1 s'illusionner** *vpr*: to delude o.s. (*sur qch* about sth); **s'~ sur qn** to delude o.s. *ou* be mistaken about sb. **2** *vt* (*induire en erreur*) to delude.
illusionnisme [ilyzjɔnism(ə)] *nm* conjuring.
illusionniste [ilyzjɔnist(ə)] *nmf* conjurer, illusionist.
illusoire [ilyzwaʀ] *adj* (*trompeur*) illusory, illusive.
illusoirement [ilyzwaʀmɑ̃] *adv* deceptively, illusorily.
illustrateur, -trice [ilystʀatœʀ, tʀis] *nm,f* illustrator.
illustratif, -ive [ilystʀatif, iv] *adj* illustrative.
illustration [ilystʀɑsjɔ̃] *nf* **(a)** (*gravure*) illustration; (*exemple*) illustration; (*iconographie*) illustrations. **à l'~ abondante** copiously illustrated. **(b)** (*action, technique*) illustration; **l'~ par l'exemple** illustration by example.
illustre [ilystʀ(ə)] *adj* illustrious, renowned. (*frm, iro*) **l'~ M X** the illustrious Mr X; (*hum*) **un ~ inconnu** a distinguished person of whom no one has (ever) heard (*hum*), a person of obscure repute (*hum*).
illustré, e [ilystʀe] **1** *adj* illustrated. **2** *nm* (*journal*) comic.
illustrer [ilystʀe] (1) **1** *vt* **(a)** (*avec images, notes*) to illustrate (*de* with). **(b)** (*littér: rendre fameux*) to bring fame to, render illustrious (*littér*).
2 s'illustrer *vpr [personne]* to win fame *ou* renown, become famous (*par, dans* through).
illustrissime [ilystʀisim] *adj* (*hum ou* ††) most illustrious.
îlot [ilo] *nm* (*île*) small island, islet; (*bloc de maisons*) block; (*fig: petite zone*) island. ~ **de fraîcheur/de verdure** oasis *ou* island of coolness/of greenery; ~ **de résistance** pocket of resistance.
îlotage [ilɔtaʒ] *nm* patrolling the block.
ilote [ilɔt] *nmf* (*Hist*) Helot; (*fig*) slave, serf.
image [imaʒ] **1** *nf* **(a)** (*dessin*) picture. **les ~s d'un film** the frames of a film; (*Ciné, TV*) **l'~ est nette/floue** the picture is clear/fuzzy; **popularisé par l'~** popularized by the camera; *V* **chasseur, livre¹, sage.**
(b) ~ **de** (*représentation*) picture of; (*ressemblance*) image of; **une ~ fidèle de la France** a faithful picture of France; **ils présentent l'~ du bonheur** they are the picture of happiness; **fait à l'~ de** made in the image of; **Dieu créa l'homme à son ~** God created man in his own image.
(c) (*comparaison, métaphore*) image. **les ~s chez Blake** Blake's imagery; **s'exprimer par ~s** to express o.s. in images.
(d) (*reflet*) (*gén*) reflection, image; (*Phys*) image. **regarder son ~ dans l'eau** to gaze at one's reflection in the water; **~ réelle/virtuelle** real/virtual image.
(e) (*vision mentale*) image, picture. ~ **visuelle/auditive** visual/auditory image; **se faire une ~ fausse/idéalisée de qch** to have a false/an idealized picture of sth.
2: **image d'Épinal** (*lit*) *popular 18th/19th century print depicting traditional scenes of French life*; (*fig*) **cette réunion familiale était une touchante image d'Épinal** the family reunion was a touching scene of traditional family life; **image de marque** *[produit]* brand image; *[parti, firme, politicien]* public image; **image pieuse** holy picture.
imagé, e [imaʒe] (*ptp de* **imager**) *adj* full of imagery (*attrib*).
imager [imaʒe] (3) *vt style, langage* to embellish with images.
imagerie [imaʒʀi] *nf* (*Hist: commerce*) coloured-print trade; (*images, gravures*) prints; (*Littérat: images*) imagery.
imagier [imaʒje] *nm* (*Hist*) (*peintre*) painter of popular pictures; (*sculpteur*) sculptor of figurines; (*imprimeur*) coloured-print maker; (*vendeur*) print seller.
imaginable [imaʒinabl(ə)] *adj* conceivable, imaginable. **difficilement ~** hard to imagine; **un tel comportement n'était pas ~ il y a 50 ans** such behaviour was inconceivable 50 years ago; *V* **possible.**
imaginaire [imaʒinɛʀ] *adj* (*fictif*) imaginary; *monde* make-believe, imaginary. **ces persécutés/incompris ~s** these people who (falsely) believe they are *ou* believe themselves persecuted/misunderstood; *V* **malade, nombre.**
imaginairement [imaʒinɛʀmɑ̃] *adv* in (one's) imagination.
imaginatif, -ive [imaʒinatif, iv] *adj* imaginative.
imagination [imaʒinɑsjɔ̃] *nf* (*faculté*) imagination; (*chimère, rêve*) imagination (*U*), fancy. **tout ce qu'il avait vécu en ~** everything he had experienced in his imagination; **ce sont de pures ~s** that's sheer imagination, those are pure fancies; **en proie à ses ~s** a prey to his fancies *ou* imaginings.
imaginer [imaʒine] (1) **1** *vt* **(a)** (*se représenter, supposer*) to imagine. ~ **que** to imagine that; **tu imagines la scène!** you can imagine *ou* picture the scene!; **je l'imaginais plus vieux** I imagined him to be older, I pictured him as being older; **qu'allez-vous ~ là?** what on earth are you thinking of?; (*ton de défi*) **et tu vas t'y opposer, j'imagine?** and I imagine *ou* suppose you're going to oppose it?
(b) (*inventer*) *système, plan* to devise, think up. **qu'est-il encore allé ~?*** now what has he dreamed up? *ou* thought up?; **il a imaginé d'ouvrir un magasin** he has taken it into his head to open up a shop, he has dreamed up the idea of opening a shop.
2 s'imaginer *vpr* **(a)** (*se figurer*) to imagine. **imagine-toi une île paradisiaque** imagine *ou* picture an island paradise; **comme on peut se l'~ ...** as you can (well) imagine ... .
(b) (*se voir*) to imagine o.s., picture o.s. **s'~ à 60 ans/en vacances** to imagine *ou* picture o.s. at 60/on holiday.
(c) (*croire que*) **s'~ que** to imagine *ou* think that; **il s'imaginait pouvoir faire cela** he imagined *ou* thought he could do that.
imbattable [ɛ̃batabl(ə)] *adj prix, personne, record* unbeatable.
imbécile [ɛ̃besil] **1** *adj* (*stupide*) stupid, idiotic; (*Méd*) imbecilic.
2 *nmf* **(a)** (*idiot*) idiot, imbecile. **faire l'~*** to act the fool; **ne fais pas l'~*** (*n'agis pas bêtement*) don't be an idiot*; (*ne simule pas la bêtise*) stop acting stupid*; **le premier ~ venu te le dira** any fool will tell you; **c'est un ~ heureux** he's living in a fool's paradise.
(b) (*Méd*) imbecile.
imbécilement [ɛ̃besilmɑ̃] *adv* stupidly, idiotically.
imbécillité [ɛ̃besilite] *nf* **(a)** (*U*) *[action, personne]* idiocy, imbecility; (*Méd*) imbecility.
(b) (*action*) idiotic *ou* stupid *ou* imbecile thing to do; (*propos*) idiotic *ou* stupid *ou* imbecilic thing to say; (*film, livre*) rubbish (*U*). **ne va pas voir de telles ~s** don't go and see such rubbish *ou* such an idiotic *ou* such a stupid film (*ou play etc*).
imberbe [ɛ̃bɛʀb(ə)] *adj personne* beardless, smooth-cheeked; *visage* beardless.
imbiber [ɛ̃bibe] (1) **1** *vt* (*imprégner*) ~ **un tampon/une compresse** *etc* **de** to moisten *ou* impregnate a pad/compress *etc* with; **imbibé d'eau** *chaussures, étoffe* saturated (with water); *terre* saturated, waterlogged.
2 s'imbiber *vpr*: **s'~ de** to become saturated with; (*fig*) **s'~ de vin*** to soak up wine; **être imbibé*** to be tipsy.
imbrication [ɛ̃bʀikɑsjɔ̃] *nf [problèmes, souvenirs, parcelles]* interweaving; *[plaques, tuiles]* overlapping.
imbriquer [ɛ̃bʀike] (1) **1 s'imbriquer** *vpr [problèmes, affaires]* to be linked *ou* interwoven; *[plaques]* to overlap (each other). **ça s'imbrique l'un dans l'autre** *[cubes]* they fit into each other; *[problèmes]* they are linked *ou* interwoven; **cette nouvelle question est venue s'~ dans une situation déjà compliquée** this new issue has arisen to complicate an already complex situation.
2 *vt cubes* to fit into each other; *plaques* to overlap.
imbroglio [ɛ̃bʀɔljo] *nm* imbroglio; (*Théât*) theatrical imbroglio.
imbu, e [ɛ̃by] *adj* (*plein de*) ~ **de** *soi-même, sentiments* full of; *préjugés* full of, steeped in.
imbuvable [ɛ̃byvabl(ə)] *adj* (*lit*) undrinkable; (*: *mauvais*) *personne* unbearable, insufferable; *film* unbearably awful*.
imitable [imitabl(ə)] *adj* which can be imitated, imitable. **facilement ~** easy to imitate, easily imitated.
imitateur, -trice [imitatœʀ, tʀis] **1** *adj* imitative. **2** *nm,f* imitator; (*Théât*) *[voix, personne]* impersonator; *[bruits etc]* imitator.
imitatif, -ive [imitatif, iv] *adj* imitative.
imitation [imitɑsjɔ̃] *nf* **(a)** (*U: V* **imiter**) imitation; impersonation; mimicry; copying; forgery. **avoir le don d'~** to have a gift for imitating people *ou* for mimicry, be good at taking people off*.
(b) (*pastiche*) imitation; (*sketch*) impression, imitation, impersonation; (*tableau, bijou, fourrure*) imitation.
(c) (*loc*) **à l'~ de** in imitation of; **d'~, en ~** imitation (*épith*); **c'est en ~ cuir** it's imitation leather; **un portefeuille ~ cuir** an imitation leather wallet.
imiter [imite] (1) *vt* **(a)** *bruit* to imitate; *personnage célèbre* to imitate, impersonate, take off*; *voix, geste* to imitate, mimic; *modèle, héros, style* to imitate, copy; *document, signature* to forge. **il se leva et tout le monde l'imita** he got up and everybody did likewise *ou* followed suit.
(b) (*avoir l'aspect de*) *[matière, revêtement]* to look like. **un lino qui imite le marbre** an imitation marble lino.
immaculé, e [imakyle] *adj linge, surface* spotless, immaculate; *blancheur* immaculate; *réputation* spotless, unsullied, immaculate; *honneur* unsullied. **d'un blanc ~** spotlessly white; (*Rel*) **l'I~e Conception** the Immaculate Conception.
immanence [imanɑ̃s] *nf* immanence.
immanent, e [imanɑ̃, ɑ̃t] *adj* immanent (*à* in); *V* **justice.**
immangeable [ɛ̃mɑ̃ʒabl(ə)] *adj* uneatable, inedible.
immanquable [ɛ̃mɑ̃kabl(ə)] *adj cible, but* impossible to miss (*attrib*). **c'était ~!** it had to happen!, it was bound to happen!, it was inevitable!
immanquablement [ɛ̃mɑ̃kabləmɑ̃] *adv* inevitably.
immatérialité [imateʀjalite] *nf* immateriality.
immatériel, -elle [imateʀjɛl] *adj légèreté, minceur* ethereal; (*Philos*) immaterial.
immatriculation [imatʀikylɑsjɔ̃] *nf* registration. **numéro d'~** registration (*Brit*) *ou* license (*US*) number; *V* **carte, plaque.**
immatriculer [imatʀikyle] (1) *vt véhicule, personne* to register. **faire ~** *véhicule* to register; **se faire ~** to register; **une voiture immatriculée dans le Vaucluse/CX 175** a car with a

Vaucluse registration (number)/with (the) registration (*Brit*) *ou* license (*US*) number CX 175.

immaturité [imatyʀite] *nf* (*littér*) immaturity.

immédiat, e [imedja, at] **1** *adj* (*gén*) immediate; *soulagement* immediate, instant (*épith*). **c'est en contact ~ avec le mur** it is in direct contact with the wall. **2** *nm*: **dans l'~** for the time being, for the moment.

immédiatement [imedjatmɑ̃] *adv* (*sur-le-champ*) immediately, at once, directly; (*sans intermédiaire*) immediately, directly.

immédiateté [imedjatte] *nf* (*Philos*) immediacy.

immémorial, e, *mpl* **-aux** [imemɔʀjal, o] *adj* age-old. (*littér*) **de temps ~** from time immemorial.

immense [imɑ̃s] *adj* (*gén*) immense; *mer, espace, horizon* boundless, vast, immense; *foule, fortune, pays* vast, immense, huge; *avenir* boundless; *influence, avantage* immense, tremendous; *succès* huge, immense, tremendous.

immensément [imɑ̃semɑ̃] *adv* immensely, tremendously.

immensité [imɑ̃site] *nf* (*V* **immense**) immensity, immenseness; vastness; hugeness. (*littér*) **le regard perdu dans l'~** gazing into infinity.

immergé, e [imɛʀʒe] (*ptp de* **immerger**) *adj terres* submerged. **~ par 100 mètres de fond** lying under 100 metres of water; **rochers ~s** submerged *ou* underwater rocks, rocks under water; **la partie ~e de la balise** the part of the buoy which is under water *ou* which is submerged.

immerger [imɛʀʒe] (3) **1** *vt objet* to immerse, submerge; *fondations* to build under water; *déchets* to dump at sea, dispose of at sea; *câble* to lay under water; *corps* to bury at sea; (*Rel*) *catéchumène* to immerse.

2 s'immerger *vpr [sous-marin]* to dive, submerge.

immérité, e [imeʀite] *adj* undeserved, unmerited.

immersion [imɛʀsjɔ̃] *nf* (*V* **immerger**) immersion; submersion; underwater building; dumping *ou* disposal at sea; underwater laying; burying at sea; diving.

immettable [ɛ̃mɛtabl(ə)] *adj vêtement* unwearable.

immeuble [imœbl(ə)] **1** *nm* **(a)** (*bâtiment*) building; (*à usage d'habitation*) block of flats (*Brit*), apartment building (*US*); *V* **gérant.**

(b) (*Jur*) real estate (*U*).

2 *adj* (*Jur*) real, immovable.

3: immeuble de bureaux office block; **immeuble de rapport** residential property (for renting), investment property; **immeuble tour** tower block; **immeuble à usage locatif** block of rented flats.

immigrant, e [imigʀɑ̃, ɑ̃t] *adj, nm,f* immigrant.

immigration [imigʀɑsjɔ̃] *nf* immigration.

immigré, e [imigʀe] (*ptp de* **immigrer**) *adj, nm,f* immigrant.

immigrer [imigʀe] (1) *vi* to immigrate (*à, dans* into).

imminence [iminɑ̃s] *nf* imminence.

imminent, e [iminɑ̃, ɑ̃t] *adj danger, crise, départ* imminent, impending (*épith*).

immiscer (s') [imise] (3) *vpr*: **s'~ dans** to interfere in *ou* with.

immixtion [imikstjɔ̃] *nf*: **~ dans** interference in *ou* with.

immobile [imɔbil] *adj personne, eau, air, arbre* motionless, still; *visage* immobile; *pièce de machine* fixed; (*littér, fig*) *dogme* immovable; *institutions* unchanging, permanent. **rester ~** to stay *ou* keep still.

immobilier, -ière [imɔbilje, jɛʀ] **1** *adj* (*Comm*) *vente, crise* property (*épith*); (*Jur*) *biens, succession* in real property (*attrib*). **la situation ~ière est satisfaisante** the property situation is satisfactory, the situation of the property market is satisfactory.

2 *nm*: **l'~** (*Comm*) the property business, the real-estate business; (*Jur*) the real property, the immovables.

immobilisation [imɔbilizɑsjɔ̃] *nf* **(a)** *[membre blessé, circulation, capitaux]* immobilization. **cela a entraîné l'~ totale de la circulation/des affaires** that brought the traffic/brought business to a complete standstill, that brought about the complete immobilization of traffic/of business; **attendez l'~ totale du train/de l'avion** wait until the train is completely stationary/the aircraft has come to a complete standstill *ou* stop; **l'~ de la machine** (*elle s'immobilise*) the stopping of the machine; (*on la stoppe*) bringing the machine to a halt *ou* standstill, the stopping of the machine; (*on l'empêche de fonctionner*) the immobilization of the machine.

(b) (*Jur*) *[bien]* conversion into an immovable.

(c) (*Fin*) *[capitaux]* immobilization, tying up. **~s** fixed assets.

immobiliser [imɔbilize] (1) **1** *vt troupes, membre blessé* to immobilize; *file, circulation, affaires* to bring to a standstill, immobilize; *machine, véhicule* (*stopper*) to stop, bring to a halt *ou* standstill; (*empêcher de fonctionner*) to immobilize; (*Jur*) *biens* to convert into immovables; (*Fin*) to immobilize, tie up. **ça l'immobilise à son domicile** it keeps him housebound; **la peur l'immobilisait** he was paralyzed with fear, he was rooted to the spot with fear.

2 s'immobiliser *vpr [personne]* to stop, stand still; *[machine, véhicule, échanges commerciaux]* to come to a halt *ou* a standstill.

immobilisme [imɔbilism(ə)] *nm [gouvernement, firme]* opposition to progress *ou* change. **faire de/être partisan de l'~** to try to maintain/support the status quo.

immobiliste [imɔbilist(ə)] *adj politique* designed to maintain the status quo. **c'est un ~** he is a supporter of the status quo, he is opposed to progress.

immobilité [imɔbilite] **1** *nf [personne, foule, eau, arbre]* stillness, motionlessness; *[visage]* immobility; *[institutions]* unchanging nature, permanence. **le médecin lui ordonna l'~ complète** the doctor ordered him not to move (at all).

2: immobilité forcée forced immobility; **immobilité politique** lack of political change, political inertia.

immodération [imɔdeʀɑsjɔ̃] *nf* immoderation.

immodéré, e [imɔdeʀe] *adj* immoderate, inordinate.

immodérément [imɔdeʀemɑ̃] *adv* immoderately.

immodeste [imɔdɛst(ə)] *adj* (*rare*) immodest.

immodestement [imɔdɛstəmɑ̃] *adv* immodestly.

immodestie [imɔdɛsti] *nf* (*rare*) immodesty.

immolateur†† [imɔlatœʀ] *nm* immolator.

immolation [imɔlɑsjɔ̃] *nf* (*V* **immoler**) (*Hist, Rel*) immolation; sacrifice; sacrificing; self-sacrifice.

immoler [imɔle] (1) **1** *vt* (*Hist, Rel*) to immolate, sacrifice (*à* to); (*gén*) to sacrifice (*à* to); (*littér: massacrer*) to slay (*littér*). **2 s'immoler** *vpr* to sacrifice o.s. (*à* to).

immonde [imɔ̃d] *adj taudis* squalid, foul; *langage, action, personne* base, vile; (*Rel*) unclean.

immondice [imɔ̃dis] *nf* **(a)** (*ordures*) **~s** refuse (*U*); (*littér*) **commettre/proférer des ~s** to do/say unspeakable things. **(b)** (*littér ou* †: *saleté*) filth (*U*).

immoral, e, *mpl* **-aux** [imɔʀal, o] *adj* immoral.

immoralement [imɔʀalmɑ̃] *adv* immorally.

immoralisme [imɔʀalism(ə)] *nm* immoralism.

immoraliste [imɔʀalist(ə)] *adj, nmf* immoralist.

immoralité [imɔʀalite] *nf* immorality.

immortaliser [imɔʀtalize] (1) **1** *vt* to immortalize. **2 s'immortaliser** *vpr* to win immortality, win eternal fame.

immortalité [imɔʀtalite] *nf* immortality.

immortel, -elle [imɔʀtɛl] **1** *adj* immortal. **2** *nm*: **I~** *member of the Académie Française.* **3 immortelle** *nf* (*fleur*) everlasting flower.

immotivé, e [imɔtive] *adj action, crime* unmotivated; *réclamation, crainte* groundless.

immuabilité [imɥabilite] *nf* = **immutabilité.**

immuable [imɥabl(ə)] *adj lois, passion* unchanging, immutable; *paysage, routine* unchanging; *sourire* unchanging, perpetual. **il est resté ~ dans ses convictions** he remained unchanged in his convictions; **vêtu de son ~ complet à carreaux** wearing that eternal checked suit of his.

immuablement [imɥabləmɑ̃] *adv fonctionner, se passer* immutably; *triste, grognon* perpetually.

immunisation [imynizɑsjɔ̃] *nf* immunization.

immuniser [imynize] (1) *vt* (*Méd*) to immunize. (*fig*) **être immunisé contre les tentations** to be immune to temptation; (*fig*) **ça l'immunisera contre le désir de recommencer** this'll stop him ever *ou* this'll cure him of ever wanting to do it again.

immunité [imynite] *nf* (*Bio, Jur*) immunity. **~ diplomatique** diplomatic immunity; **~ parlementaire** ≃ parliamentary privilege.

immunologie [imynɔlɔʒi] *nf* immunology.

immutabilité [imytabilite] *nf* immutability.

impact [ɛ̃pakt] *nm* (*lit, fig*) impact. **l'argument a de l'~** the argument has some impact; *V* **point**[1].

impair, e [ɛ̃pɛʀ] **1** *adj nombre* odd, uneven; *jour* odd; *vers* irregular (*with uneven number of syllables*); *organe* unpaired.

2 *nm* **(a)** (*gaffe*) blunder, faux pas. **commettre un ~** to (make a) blunder, make a faux pas.

(b) (*Casino*) **miser sur l'~** to put one's money on the odd numbers.

impalpable [ɛ̃palpabl(ə)] *adj* impalpable.

imparable [ɛ̃paʀabl(ə)] *adj coup, tir* unstoppable. (*fig*) **une riposte ~** an unanswerable riposte.

impardonnable [ɛ̃paʀdɔnabl(ə)] *adj faute* unforgivable, unpardonable. **vous êtes ~ (d'avoir fait cela)** you cannot be forgiven (for doing that), it is unforgivable of you (to have done that).

imparfait, e [ɛ̃paʀfɛ, ɛt] **1** *adj* (*gén*) imperfect. **2** *nm* (*Ling*) **l'~** the imperfect (tense).

imparfaitement [ɛ̃paʀfɛtmɑ̃] *adv* imperfectly.

impartial, e, *mpl* **-aux** [ɛ̃paʀsjal, o] *adj* impartial, unbiased, unprejudiced.

impartialement [ɛ̃paʀsjalmɑ̃] *adv* impartially, without bias *ou* prejudice.

impartialité [ɛ̃paʀsjalite] *nf* impartiality. **en toute ~** from a completely impartial standpoint.

impartir [ɛ̃paʀtiʀ] (2) *vt* (*littér: attribuer à*) **~ des devoirs à** to assign duties to; **~ des pouvoirs à** to invest powers in; **~ des dons à** to bestow gifts upon, impart gifts to; (*Jur: accorder à*) **~ un délai à** to grant an extension to; **dans les délais impartis** within the time allowed; **les dons que Dieu nous a impartis** the gifts God has bestowed upon us *ou* has endowed us with *ou* has imparted to us.

impasse [ɛ̃pas] **1** *nf* **(a)** (*cul-de-sac*) dead end, cul-de-sac; (*sur panneau*) 'no through road'.

(b) (*fig*) impasse. **être dans l'~** *[négociations]* to be at deadlock, have reached deadlock.

(c) (*Scol, Univ*) **j'ai fait 3 ~s en géographie** I missed out 3 topics in my geography revision.

(d) (*Cartes*) finesse. **faire une ~** to (make a) finesse.

2: (*Fin*) **impasse budgétaire** budget deficit.

impassibilité [ɛ̃pasibilite] *nf* impassiveness, impassivity, impassibility.

impassible [ɛ̃pasibl(ə)] *adj* impassive, impassible.

impassiblement [ɛ̃pasibləmɑ̃] *adv* impassively, impassibly.

impatiemment [ɛ̃pasjamɑ̃] *adv* impatiently.

impatience [ɛ̃pasjɑ̃s] *nf* impatience. **il était dans l'~ de la revoir** he was impatient to see her again, he couldn't wait to see her again; **il répliqua avec ~ que** he replied impatiently that; (*littér*) **se rappelant leurs ~s d'adolescents** remembering their impatient attitudes as teenagers *ou* the impatient moments of

their adolescence; **avoir des ~s dans les jambes**† to have fidgety legs, have the fidgets*.
impatiens [ɛ̃pasjɛ̃s] *nf inv* = **impatiente.**
impatient, e [ɛ̃pasjɑ̃, ɑ̃t] **1** *adj personne, geste, attente* impatient. **~ de faire** impatient *ou* eager to do; **je suis si ~ de vous revoir** I am longing to see you again, I am so impatient to see you again, I just can't wait to see you again*; **quel ~!** what an impatient character!
2 impatiente *nf (Bot)* busy-lizzy, impatiens *(T)*.
impatientant, e [ɛ̃pasjɑ̃tɑ̃, ɑ̃t] *adj* irritating, annoying.
impatienter [ɛ̃pasjɑ̃te] (1) **1** *vt* to irritate, annoy. **2 s'impatienter** *vpr* to grow *ou* get impatient, lose patience *(contre ou de qn* with sb, *contre ou de qch* at sth).
impavide [ɛ̃pavid] *adj (littér)* undaunted *(littér)*.
impayable* [ɛ̃pɛjabl(ə)] *adj (drôle)* priceless*. **il est ~!** he's priceless!*, he's a scream!*
impayé, e [ɛ̃peje] **1** *adj* unpaid. **2** *nm*: **~s** outstanding payments.
impeccable [ɛ̃pekabl(ə)] *adj* **(a)** *(parfait) travail, style* perfect, faultless, impeccable; *employé* perfect. **(c'est) ~!*** great!*, smashing!*
(b) *(propre) personne* impeccable, impeccably dressed; *appartement, voiture* spotless, spotlessly clean, impeccable.
impeccablement [ɛ̃pekabləmɑ̃] *adv* (*V* **impeccable**) perfectly; faultlessly; impeccably; spotlessly.
impécunieux, -euse [ɛ̃pekynjø, øz] *adj (littér)* impecunious *(littér)*.
impécuniosité [ɛ̃pekynjozite] *nf (littér)* impecuniousness *(littér)*.
impédance [ɛ̃pedɑ̃s] *nf (Élec)* impedance.
impedimenta [ɛ̃pedimɛ̃ta] *nmpl (Mil, fig)* impedimenta.
impénétrabilité [ɛ̃penetʀabilite] *nf* (*V* **impénétrable**) impenetrability; unfathomableness; inscrutability.
impénétrable [ɛ̃penetʀabl(ə)] *adj forêt* impenetrable (*à* to, by); *mystère, desseins* unfathomable, impenetrable; *personnage, caractère* inscrutable, impenetrable, unfathomable; *visage* inscrutable, impenetrable.
impénitence [ɛ̃penitɑ̃s] *nf* unrepentance, impenitence.
impénitent, e [ɛ̃penitɑ̃, ɑ̃t] *adj* unrepentant, impenitent.
impensable [ɛ̃pɑ̃sabl(ə)] *adj événement hypothétique* unthinkable; *événement arrivé* unbelievable.
imper* [ɛ̃pɛʀ] *nm (abrév de* **imperméable**) mac.
impératif, -ive [ɛ̃peʀatif, iv] **1** *adj (obligatoire, urgent) besoin, consigne* urgent, imperative; *(impérieux) geste, ton* imperative, commanding; *(Jur) loi* mandatory; *V* **mandat. 2** *nm* **(a)** *(Ling)* **l'~** the imperative (mood). **(b)** *(prescription) [fonction, charge]* requirement; *[mode]* demand; *(nécessité) [situation]* necessity; *(Mil)* imperative. **des ~s d'horaire nous obligent à ...** we are obliged by the demands of our timetable to ....
impérativement [ɛ̃peʀativmɑ̃] *adv* imperatively. **je le veux ~ pour demain** it is imperative that I have it for tomorrow, I absolutely must have it for tomorrow.
impératrice [ɛ̃peʀatʀis] *nf* empress.
imperceptibilité [ɛ̃pɛʀsɛptibilite] *nf* imperceptibility.
imperceptible [ɛ̃pɛʀsɛptibl(ə)] *adj* **(a)** *(non perceptible) son, détail, nuance* imperceptible (*à* to). **(b)** *(à peine perceptible) son, sourire* faint, imperceptible; *détail, changement, nuance* minute, imperceptible.
imperceptiblement [ɛ̃pɛʀsɛptibləmɑ̃] *adv* imperceptibly.
imperdable [ɛ̃pɛʀdabl(ə)] *adj partie, match* that cannot be lost.
imperfectible [ɛ̃pɛʀfɛktibl(ə)] *adj* which cannot be perfected, unperfectible.
imperfectif, -ive [ɛ̃pɛʀfɛktif, iv] *adj, nm* imperfective.
imperfection [ɛ̃pɛʀfɛksjɔ̃] *nf* (*U: caractère imparfait*) imperfection; *(défaut) [personne, caractère]* shortcoming, imperfection, defect; *[ouvrage, dispositif, mécanisme]* imperfection, defect, fault.
impérial, e, *mpl* **-aux** [ɛ̃peʀjal, o] **1** *adj* imperial. **2 impériale** *nf* **(a)** *[autobus]* top *ou* upper deck. **autobus à ~e** ≈ double-decker (bus); **monter à l'~e** to go upstairs *ou* on top. **(b)** *(barbe)* imperial.
impérialement [ɛ̃peʀjalmɑ̃] *adv* imperially.
impérialisme [ɛ̃peʀjalism(ə)] *nm* imperialism.
impérialiste [ɛ̃peʀjalist(ə)] **1** *adj* imperialist(ic). **2** *nmf* imperialist.
impérieusement [ɛ̃peʀjøzmɑ̃] *adv* imperiously. **avoir ~ besoin de qch** to need sth urgently, have urgent need of sth.
impérieux, -euse [ɛ̃peʀjø, øz] *adj (autoritaire) personne, ton, caractère* imperious; *(pressant) besoin, nécessité* urgent, pressing; *obligation* pressing.
impérissable [ɛ̃peʀisabl(ə)] *adj œuvre* imperishable; *souvenir, gloire* undying *(épith)*, imperishable; *monument, valeur* undying *(épith)*.
impéritie [ɛ̃peʀisi] *nf (littér: incompétence)* incompetence.
imperméabilisation [ɛ̃pɛʀmeabilizɑsjɔ̃] *nf* waterproofing.
imperméabiliser [ɛ̃pɛʀmeabilize] (1) *vt* to waterproof.
imperméabilité [ɛ̃pɛʀmeabilite] *nf (lit) [terrain]* impermeability; *[tissu]* waterproof qualities, impermeability. *(fig littér: insensibilité)* **~ à** imperviousness to.
imperméable [ɛ̃pɛʀmeabl(ə)] **1** *adj (lit) terrain, roches* impermeable; *revêtement, tissu* waterproof. **~ à l'eau** waterproof; **~ à l'air** airtight; *(fig: insensible)* **~ à** impervious to. **2** *nm (manteau)* raincoat, mackintosh†.
impersonnalité [ɛ̃pɛʀsɔnalite] *nf* impersonality; *(Ling)* impersonal form.
impersonnel, -elle [ɛ̃pɛʀsɔnɛl] *adj* impersonal.
impersonnellement [ɛ̃pɛʀsɔnɛlmɑ̃] *adv* impersonally.
impertinemment [ɛ̃pɛʀtinamɑ̃] *adv* impertinently.
impertinence [ɛ̃pɛʀtinɑ̃s] *nf (U)* impertinence; *(propos)* impertinent remark, impertinence.
impertinent, e [ɛ̃pɛʀtinɑ̃, ɑ̃t] *adj* impertinent. **c'est un petit ~!** he's an impertinent child!
imperturbabilité [ɛ̃pɛʀtyʀbabilite] *nf* imperturbability.
imperturbable [ɛ̃pɛʀtyʀbabl(ə)] *adj sang-froid, gaieté, sérieux* unshakeable; *personne, caractère* imperturbable. **rester ~** to remain unruffled.
imperturbablement [ɛ̃pɛʀtyʀbabləmɑ̃] *adv* imperturbably. **il écouta ~** he listened imperturbably *ou* unperturbed *ou* unruffled.
impétigo [ɛ̃petigo] *nm* impetigo.
impétrant, e [ɛ̃petʀɑ̃, ɑ̃t] *nm,f (Jur)* applicant.
impétueusement [ɛ̃petɥøzmɑ̃] *adv (littér)* impetuously.
impétueux, -euse [ɛ̃petɥø, øz] *adj (littér: fougueux) caractère, jeunesse* impetuous, hotheaded; *orateur* fiery; *rythme* impetuous; *torrent, vent* raging.
impétuosité [ɛ̃petɥozite] *nf (littér) [rythme, personne]* impetuousness, impetuosity. **il faut se méfier de l'~ des torrents de montagne** one must beware of raging mountain streams.
impie [ɛ̃pi] **1** *adj acte, parole* impious, ungodly, irreligious. **2** *nmf* ungodly *ou* irreligious person.
impiété [ɛ̃pjete] *nf (U)* impiety, ungodliness, irreligiousness; *(parole, acte)* impiety.
impitoyable [ɛ̃pitwajabl(ə)] *adj (gén)* merciless, pitiless, ruthless.
impitoyablement [ɛ̃pitwajabləmɑ̃] *adv* mercilessly, pitilessly, ruthlessly.
implacabilité [ɛ̃plakabilite] *nf* implacability.
implacable [ɛ̃plakabl(ə)] *adj (impitoyable)* implacable.
implacablement [ɛ̃plakabləmɑ̃] *adv* implacably.
implant [ɛ̃plɑ̃] *nm (Méd)* implant.
implantation [ɛ̃plɑ̃tɑsjɔ̃] *nf* (*V* **implanter**) *(action)* introduction; settling; setting up; implanting; *(résultat)* introduction; settlement; establishment; implantation.
implanter [ɛ̃plɑ̃te] (1) **1** *vt (introduire) usage, mode* to introduce; *race, immigrants* to settle; *usine, industrie* to set up, establish; *idée, préjugé* to implant; *(Méd)* to implant.
2 s'implanter *vpr [établissements, usines]* to be set up *ou* established; *[immigrants, race]* to settle; *[idées]* to become implanted; *[parti politique]* to establish itself, become established. **des traditions solidement implantées** deeply-rooted *ou* deeply-entrenched traditions.
implication [ɛ̃plikɑsjɔ̃] *nf* **(a)** *(conséquences, répercussions)* **~s** implications. **(b)** *(relation logique)* implication. **(c) ~ dans** *(mise en cause)* implication in; *(participation à)* implication *ou* involvement in.
implicite [ɛ̃plisit] *adj condition, foi, volonté* implicit.
implicitement [ɛ̃plisitmɑ̃] *adv* implicitly.
impliquer [ɛ̃plike] (1) *vt* **(a)** *(supposer)* to imply *(que* that). **(b) ~ qn dans** *(mettre en cause)* to implicate sb in; *(mêler à)* to implicate *ou* involve sb in.
implorant, e [ɛ̃plɔʀɑ̃, ɑ̃t] *adj* imploring, beseeching. **me regardant d'un air ~** looking at me imploringly *ou* beseechingly, giving me a beseeching *ou* an imploring look.
imploration [ɛ̃plɔʀɑsjɔ̃] *nf* entreaty.
implorer [ɛ̃plɔʀe] (1) *vt (supplier) personne, Dieu* to implore, beseech; *(demander) faveur, aide* to implore. **~ qn de faire** to implore *ou* beseech *ou* entreat sb to do.
imploser [ɛ̃ploze] (1) *vi* to implode.
implosif, -ive [ɛ̃plozif, iv] *adj* implosive.
implosion [ɛ̃plozjɔ̃] *nf* implosion.
impoli, e [ɛ̃pɔli] *adj* impolite, rude *(envers* to).
impoliment [ɛ̃pɔlimɑ̃] *adv* impolitely, rudely.
impolitesse [ɛ̃pɔlitɛs] *nf (U: attitude)* impoliteness, rudeness; *(remarque)* impolite *ou* rude remark; *(acte)* impolite thing to do, impolite action. **répondre avec ~** to answer impolitely *ou* rudely; **c'est une ~ que de faire** it is impolite *ou* rude to do.
impolitique [ɛ̃pɔlitik] *adj* impolitic.
impondérabilité [ɛ̃pɔ̃deʀabilite] *nf* imponderability.
impondérable [ɛ̃pɔ̃deʀabl(ə)] **1** *adj* imponderable. **2** *nm*: **~s** imponderables.
impopulaire [ɛ̃pɔpylɛʀ] *adj* unpopular.
impopularité [ɛ̃pɔpylaʀite] *nf* unpopularity.
importable [ɛ̃pɔʀtabl(ə)] *adj (Écon)* importable; *vêtement* unwearable.
importance [ɛ̃pɔʀtɑ̃s] *nf* **(a)** *[problème, affaire, personne]* importance; *[événement, fait]* importance, significance. **avoir de l'~** *[question]* to be important, be of importance; *[personne]* to be important; **ça a beaucoup d'~ pour moi** it is very important to me, it matters a great deal to me; **sans ~** *personne* unimportant; *problème, incident, détail* unimportant, insignificant; **c'est sans ~, ça n'a pas d'~** it doesn't matter, it's of no importance *ou* consequence; **d'une certaine ~** *problème, événement* fairly *ou* rather important; **de la plus haute ~, de la première ~** *problème, affaire* of paramount importance; *événement* momentous, of paramount *ou* of the highest importance.
(b) *(taille) [somme, effectifs, firme]* size; *(ampleur) [dégâts, désastre, retard]* extent. **d'une certaine ~** *firme* sizeable; *dégâts* considerable.
(c) *(loc)* **prendre de l'~** *[question]* to gain in importance, become more important; *[firme]* to increase in size; *[personne]* to become more important; *(péj)* **se donner de l'~, prendre des airs d'~** to act important; *(frm)* **l'affaire est d'~** this is no trivial matter; *(littér)* **tancer/rosser qn d'~** to give sb a thorough dressing-down/trouncing *(littér)*.
important, e [ɛ̃pɔʀtɑ̃, ɑ̃t] *adj* **(a)** *personnage, question, rôle* important; *événement, fait* important, significant. **peu ~** of little *ou* of no great importance, of little significance; **rien d'~**

nothing important *ou* of importance; **l'~ est de** the important thing is to.

(b) (*quantitativement*) *somme* considerable, sizeable; *retard* considerable; *dégâts* extensive, considerable. **la présence d'un ~ service d'ordre** the presence of a considerable number *ou* a large contingent of police.

(c) (*péj*) *airs* (self-)important; *personnage* self-important. **faire l'~** to act important.

importateur, -trice [ɛ̃pɔʀtatœʀ, tʀis] **1** *adj* importing. **pays ~ de blé** wheat-importing country. **2** *nm,f* importer.

importation [ɛ̃pɔʀtɑsjɔ̃] *nf* **(a)** (*Comm*) *[marchandises]* importation. **articles d'~** imported articles. **(b)** *[animal, plante, maladie]* introduction. **le tabac est d'~ récente** tobacco is a recent import. **(c)** (*produit: lit, fig*) import.

importer[1] [ɛ̃pɔʀte] (1) *vt marchandises* to import; *coutumes, danses* to import, introduce (*de* from).

importer[2] [ɛ̃pɔʀte] (1) *vi* **(a)** (*être important*) to matter. **les conventions importent peu aux jeunes** conventions don't matter much *ou* aren't very important *ou* matter little to young people; **ce qui importe, c'est d'agir vite** the important thing is *ou* what matters is to act quickly; **que lui importe le malheur des autres!** what does he care about other people's unhappiness?, what does other people's unhappiness matter to him?; (*frm*) **il importe de faire** it is important to do; (*frm*) **il importe qu'elle connaisse les risques** it is important that she knows *ou* should know the risks.

(b) peu importe *ou* (*littér*) **qu'importe qu'il soit absent** what does it matter if *ou* it matters little (*frm*) that he is absent; **peu importe le temps, nous sortirons** we'll go out whatever the weather *ou* no matter what the weather is like; **peu m'importe** (*je n'ai pas de préférence*) I don't mind; (*je m'en moque*) I don't care; **achetez des pêches ou des poires, peu importe** buy peaches or pears — it doesn't matter which; **quel fauteuil veux-tu? — oh, n'importe** which chair will you have? — it doesn't matter *ou* I don't mind; **il ne veut pas? qu'importe!** doesn't he want to? what does it matter! *ou* it doesn't matter!; **les appartements sont chers, n'importe, ils se vendent!** flats are expensive, but no matter *ou* but never mind, they still sell.

(c) n'importe qui anybody, anyone; **n'importe quoi** anything; **n'importe comment** anyhow; **n'importe où** anywhere; **n'importe quand** anytime; **il a fait cela n'importe comment!** he did that anyhow *ou* any old how* (*Brit*); **n'importe lequel** *ou* **laquelle d'entre nous/vous** *etc* any (one) of us/you *etc*; **entrez dans n'importe quelle boutique** go into any shop; **n'importe quel docteur vous dira la même chose** any doctor will tell you the same (thing); **venez à n'importe quelle heure** come (at) any time; **n'importe comment, il part ce soir** he leaves tonight in any case *ou* anyhow; **ce n'est pas n'importe qui** he is not just anybody.

import-export [ɛ̃pɔʀɛkspɔʀ] *nm* import-export business.

importun, e [ɛ̃pɔʀtœ̃, yn] **1** *adj* (*frm*) *curiosité, présence, pensée, plainte* troublesome, importunate (*frm*); *arrivée, visite* inopportune, ill-timed; *personne* importunate (*frm*), irksome. **je ne veux pas être ~** (*déranger*) I don't wish to disturb you *ou* to intrude; (*irriter*) I don't wish to be importunate (*frm*) *ou* irksome; **se rendre ~ par** to make o.s. objectionable by.

2 *nm,f* (*gêneur*) irksome individual; (*visiteur*) intruder.

importunément [ɛ̃pɔʀtynemɑ̃] *adv* (*frm*) (*de façon irritante*) importunately (*frm*); (*à un mauvais moment*) inopportunely.

importuner [ɛ̃pɔʀtyne] (1) *vt* (*frm*) *[représentant, mendiant]* to importune (*frm*), bother; *[insecte, bruit]* to trouble, bother; *[interruptions, remarques]* to bother. **je ne veux pas vous ~** I don't wish to put you to any trouble *ou* to bother you.

importunité [ɛ̃pɔʀtynite] *nf* (*frm*) *[démarche, demande]* importunity (*frm*). (*sollicitations*) **~s** importunities.

imposable [ɛ̃pozabl(ə)] *adj personne, revenu* taxable; *V* **matière.**

imposant, e [ɛ̃pozɑ̃, ɑ̃t] *adj* (*majestueux*) *personnage, stature* imposing; *allure* stately; (*considérable*) *majorité, mise en scène* impressive; *nombre, foule* imposing, impressive. **~e paysanne** (*iro: gros*) peasant woman with an imposing figure; **la présence d'un ~ service d'ordre** the presence of an imposing number *ou* a large contingent of police.

imposer [ɛ̃poze] (1) **1** *vt* **(a)** (*prescrire*) *tâche, travail, date* to set; *règle, conditions* to impose, lay down; *punition, taxe* to impose (*à* on); *prix* to set, fix. **~ ses idées/sa présence à qn** to impose *ou* force one's ideas/one's company on sb; **~ des conditions à qch** to impose *ou* place conditions on sth; **~ un travail/une date à qn** to set sb a piece of work/a date; **~ un régime à qn** to put sb on a diet; **la décision leur a été imposée par les événements** the decision was forced *ou* imposed (up)on them by events; **il nous a imposé son candidat** he has imposed his candidate on us; **on lui a imposé le silence** silence has been imposed upon him; *V* **prix.**

(b) (*faire connaître*) **~ son nom** *[candidat]* to come to the fore; *[artiste]* to make o.s. known, compel recognition; *[firme]* to establish itself, become an established name; **il m'impose/sa conduite impose le respect** he commands/his behaviour compels my respect.

(c) (*Fin: taxer*) *marchandise, revenu, salariés* to tax.

(d) (*Rel*) **~ les mains** to lay on hands.

(e) en ~ à qn to impress sb; **il en impose** he's an imposing individual; **sa présence/son intelligence en impose** his presence/his intelligence is imposing; **ne vous en laissez pas ~ par ses grands airs** don't let yourself be impressed by his haughty manner.

2 s'imposer *vpr* **(a)** (*être nécessaire*) *[décision, action]* to be essential *ou* vital *ou* imperative. **dans ce cas, le repos s'impose** in this case rest is essential *ou* vital *ou* imperative; **ces mesures ne s'imposaient pas** these measures were unnecessary; **quand on est à Paris une visite au Louvre s'impose** when in Paris, a visit to the Louvre is imperative *ou* is a must*.

(b) (*se contraindre à*) **s'~ une tâche** to set o.s. a task; **s'~ de faire** to make it a rule to do.

(c) (*montrer sa prominence*) **s'~ par ses qualités** to compel recognition because of one's qualities; **il s'est imposé dans sa branche** he has made a name for himself in his branch; **il s'est imposé comme le seul susceptible d'avoir le prix** he emerged as the only one likely to get the prize.

(d) (*imposer sa présence à*) **s'~ à qn** to impose (o.s.) upon sb; **je ne voudrais pas m'~** I do not want to impose.

imposition [ɛ̃pozisjɔ̃] *nf* (*Fin*) taxation. (*Rel*) **l'~ des mains** the laying on of hands.

impossibilité [ɛ̃pɔsibilite] *nf* impossibility. **l'~ de réaliser ce plan** the impossibility of carrying out this plan; **y a-t-il ~ à cela?** is that impossible?; **y a-t-il ~ à ce que je vienne?** is it impossible for me to come?; **être dans l'~ de faire qch** to be unable *ou* find it impossible to do sth; **l'~ dans laquelle il se trouvait de ...** the fact that he was unable to ..., the fact that he found it impossible to ...; **se heurter à des ~s** to come up against insuperable obstacles.

impossible [ɛ̃pɔsibl(ə)] **1** *adj* **(a)** (*irréalisable, improbable*) impossible. **~ à faire** impossible to do; **il est ~ de/que** it is impossible to/that; **il est ~ qu'il soit déjà arrivé** he cannot possibly have arrived yet; **il m'est ~ de le faire** it's impossible for me to do it, I can't possibly do it; **pouvez-vous venir lundi? — non, cela m'est ~** can you come on Monday? — no, I can't *ou* no, it's impossible; (*Prov*) **~ n'est pas français** there's no such word as 'impossible'.

(b) (*pénible, difficile*) *enfant, situation* impossible. **rendre l'existence ~ à qn** to make sb's life impossible *ou* a misery; **elle a des horaires ~s** she has impossible *ou* terrible hours.

(c) (*invraisemblable*) *nom, titre* ridiculous, impossible. **se lever à des heures ~s** to get up at an impossible *ou* a ridiculous time *ou* hour; **il lui arrive toujours des histoires ~s** impossible things are always happening to him.

2 *nm* **(a) l'~** the impossible; **tenter l'~** to attempt the impossible; **je ferai l'~ (pour venir)** I'll do my utmost (to come).

(b) par ~ by some miracle, by some remote chance; **si par ~ je terminais premier ...** if by some miracle *ou* some remote chance I were to finish first ....

imposte [ɛ̃pɔst(ə)] *nf* (*fenêtre*) transom (window).

imposteur [ɛ̃pɔstœʀ] *nm* impostor.

imposture [ɛ̃pɔstyʀ] *nf* imposture, deception.

impôt [ɛ̃po] **1** *nm* (*taxe*) tax; (*U: taxes*) taxes, taxation; (*gén: contributions*) (income) tax. **payer des ~s** to pay tax; **je paye plus de 1.000 F d'~s** I pay more than 1,000 francs in tax *ou* 1,000 francs tax; **frapper d'un ~** to put a tax on; **~ direct/indirect** direct/indirect tax; *V* **assiette, déclaration, feuille** *etc.*

2: impôt sur les bénéfices tax on profits; **impôt sur le chiffre d'affaires** tax on turnover, ≃ corporation tax; **impôt foncier** ≃ land tax; **impôt sur la fortune** wealth tax; **impôt sur les plus-values** ≃ capital gains tax; (*littér*, †) **impôt de sang** blood tribute.

impotence [ɛ̃pɔtɑ̃s] *nf* disability.

impotent, e [ɛ̃pɔtɑ̃, ɑ̃t] **1** *adj* disabled, crippled. **l'accident l'a rendu ~** the accident has disabled *ou* crippled him. **2** *nm,f* disabled person, cripple.

impraticable [ɛ̃pʀatikabl(ə)] *adj idée* impracticable, unworkable; *tâche* impracticable; (*Sport*) *terrain* unfit *ou* unsuitable for play; *route, piste* impassable. **~ pour les** *ou* **aux véhicules à moteur** unfit *ou* unsuitable for motor vehicles, impassable to motor vehicles.

imprécation [ɛ̃pʀekɑsjɔ̃] *nf* imprecation (*littér*), curse.

imprécatoire [ɛ̃pʀekatwaʀ] *adj* (*littér*) imprecatory (*littér*).

imprécis, e [ɛ̃pʀesi, iz] *adj* (*gén*) imprecise; *tir* inaccurate.

imprécision [ɛ̃pʀesizjɔ̃] *nf* (*V* **imprécis**) imprecision; inaccuracy.

imprégnation [ɛ̃pʀeɲɑsjɔ̃] *nf* (*V* **imprégner**) (*gén*) impregnation; permeation; imbuing. **taux d'~ alcoolique** level of alcohol in the blood; **pour apprendre une langue, rien ne vaut une lente ~** to learn a language, nothing can beat slow immersion in it, to learn a language nothing can beat gradually immersing oneself in it.

imprégner [ɛ̃pʀeɲe] (6) **1** *vt tissu, matière* to impregnate (*de* with); *pièce, air* to permeate, fill (*de* with); *esprit* to imbue, impregnate (*de* with). **cette odeur imprégnait toute la rue** the smell filled *ou* pervaded the whole street; **l'amertume qui imprégnait ses paroles** the bitterness which pervaded his words; **maison imprégnée de lumière** house flooded with light; **imprégné des préjugés de sa caste** imbued with *ou* impregnated with the prejudices of his class.

2 s'imprégner *vpr*: **s'~ de** *[tissu, substance]* to become impregnated with; *[local, air]* to become permeated *ou* filled with; *[esprits, élèves]* to become imbued with, absorb; **séjourner à l'étranger pour s'~ de la langue étrangère** to live abroad to immerse o.s in *ou* to absorb the foreign language; (*fig*) **s'~ d'alcool** to soak up alcohol.

imprenable [ɛ̃pʀənabl(ə)] *adj forteresse* impregnable. **vue ~ sur la vallée** open *ou* unimpeded *ou* unrestricted outlook over the valley (*no future building plans*).

impréparation [ɛ̃pʀepaʀɑsjɔ̃] *nf* lack of preparation.

imprésario [ɛ̃pʀesaʀjo] *nm* manager, impresario.

imprescriptibilité [ɛ̃pʀɛskʀiptibilite] *nf* (*Jur*) imprescriptibility.

imprescriptible [ɛ̃pʀɛskʀiptibl(ə)] *adj* (*Jur*) imprescriptible; *V* **droit.**

impression [ɛ̃pʀesjɔ̃] *nf* **(a)** (*sensation physique*) feeling, impression; (*sentiment, réaction*) impression. **ils échangèrent leurs ~s (de voyage)** they exchanged their impressions (of the journey); **l'~ que j'ai de lui** the impression I have of him, my impression of him; **ça m'a fait peu d'~/une grosse ~** that made little/a great impression upon me; **faire bonne/mauvaise ~** to create a good/bad impression; **avoir l'~ que** to have a feeling that, get *ou* have the impression that; **il ne me donne *ou* fait pas l'~ d'(être) un menteur** I don't get the impression that he is a liar, he doesn't give me the impression of being a liar; **faire ~** *[film, orateur]* to make an impression, have an impact.

(b) *[livre, tissu, motif]* printing. **~ en couleur** colour printing; **ce livre en est à sa 3e ~** this book is at its 3rd impression; **le livre est à l'~** the book is with the printers; **l'~ de ce livre est soignée** this book is beautifully printed; *V* **faute.**

(c) (*motif*) pattern. **tissu à ~s florales** floral pattern(ed) fabric, fabric with a floral pattern.

(d) (*Phot*) *[image]* exposure. **temps d'~** exposure (time); **technique de double ~** technique of double exposure.

(e) (*Peinture*) undercoat.

(f) (†: *empreinte, pas*) imprint.

impressionnabilité [ɛ̃pʀesjɔnabilite] *nf* (*émotivité*) impressionability, impressionableness.

impressionnable [ɛ̃pʀesjɔnabl(ə)] *adj personne* impressionable.

impressionnant, e [ɛ̃pʀesjɔnɑ̃, ɑ̃t] *adj* (*imposant*) *somme, spectacle, monument* impressive; (*bouleversant*) *scène, accident* upsetting.

impressionner [ɛ̃pʀesjɔne] (1) *vt* **(a)** (*frapper*) to impress; (*bouleverser*) to upset. **cela risque d'~ les enfants** this may upset children; **ne te laisse pas ~** don't let yourself be impressed.

(b) (*Opt, Phot*) *rétine* to show up on. **~ la pellicule** *[image, sujet]* to show up on; *[photographe]* to expose; **la pellicule n'a pas été impressionnée** the film hasn't been exposed.

impressionnisme [ɛ̃pʀesjɔnism(ə)] *nm* impressionism.

impressionniste [ɛ̃pʀesjɔnist(ə)] **1** *adj* impressionistic. **2** *nmf* impressionist.

imprévisibilité [ɛ̃pʀevizibilite] *nf* unpredictability.

imprévisible [ɛ̃pʀevizibl(ə)] *adj* unforeseeable, unpredictable.

imprévision [ɛ̃pʀevizjɔ̃] *nf* (*littér*) **l'~ d'un événement** the failure to foresee an event.

imprévoyance [ɛ̃pʀevwajɑ̃s] *nf* (*négligence*) lack of foresight; (*en matière d'argent*) improvidence.

imprévoyant, e [ɛ̃pʀevwajɑ̃, ɑ̃t] *adj* (*V* **imprévoyance**) lacking (in) foresight; improvident.

imprévu, e [ɛ̃pʀevy] **1** *adj événement, succès, réaction* unforeseen, unexpected; *courage, geste* unexpected; *dépense(s)* unforeseen. **de manière ~e** unexpectedly.

2 *nm* **(a) l'~** the unexpected, the unforeseen; **j'aime l'~** I like not to foresee everything in advance, I like not knowing what's going to happen; **un peu d'~** an element of surprise *ou* of the unexpected *ou* of the unforeseen; **vacances pleines d'~** holidays full of surprises; **en cas d'~** if anything unexpected *ou* unforeseen crops up; **sauf ~** barring any unexpected *ou* unforeseen circumstances, unless anything unexpected *ou* unforeseen crops up.

(b) (*incident, ennui*) something unexpected *ou* unforeseen, unexpected *ou* unforeseen event. **il y a un ~** something unexpected *ou* unforeseen has cropped up; **tous ces ~s nous ont retardés** all these unexpected *ou* unforeseen events have delayed us.

imprimable [ɛ̃pʀimabl(ə)] *adj* printable.

imprimé, e [ɛ̃pʀime] (*ptp de* **imprimer**) **1** *adj tissu, feuille* printed.

2 *nm* **(a)** (*formulaire*) printed form; (*Poste*) printed matter (*U*). **catalogue/section des ~s** catalogue/department of printed books.

(b) (*tissu*) **l'~** printed material *ou* fabrics, prints; **~ à fleur** floral print (fabric *ou* material); **l'~ et l'uni** printed and plain fabrics *ou* material.

imprimer [ɛ̃pʀime] (1) *vt* **(a)** *livre, foulard, billets de banque, dessin* to print.

(b) (*apposer*) *visa, cachet* to stamp (*dans* on, in).

(c) (*marquer*) *rides, traces, marque* to imprint (*dans* in, on). **une scène imprimée dans sa mémoire** a scene imprinted on his memory.

(d) (*publier*) *texte, ouvrage* to publish; *auteur* to publish the work of. **la joie de se voir imprimé** the joy of seeing o.s. *ou* one's work in print.

(e) (*communiquer*) **~ un mouvement/une impulsion à** to impart *ou* transmit a movement/an impulse to; **~ une direction à** to give a direction to.

imprimerie [ɛ̃pʀimʀi] *nf* (*firme, usine*) printing works; (*atelier*) printing house; (*section*) printery; (*pour enfants*) printing outfit *ou* kit. (*technique*) **l'~** printing; *V* **caractère.**

imprimeur [ɛ̃pʀimœʀ] *nm* (*directeur*) printer. **(ouvrier-)~** printer; **~-éditeur** printer and publisher; **~-libraire** printer and bookseller.

improbabilité [ɛ̃pʀɔbabilite] *nf* unlikelihood, improbability.

improbable [ɛ̃pʀɔbabl(ə)] *adj* unlikely, improbable.

improbité [ɛ̃pʀɔbite] *nf* (*littér*) lack of integrity.

improductif, -ive [ɛ̃pʀɔdyktif, iv] *adj* unproductive.

improductivité [ɛ̃pʀɔdyktivite] *nf* unproductiveness, lack of productivity.

impromptu, e [ɛ̃pʀɔ̃pty] **1** *adj* (*improvisé*) *départ* sudden (*épith*); *visite* surprise (*épith*); *repas, exposé* impromptu (*épith*). **faire un discours ~ sur un sujet** to speak off the cuff *ou* make an impromptu speech on a subject, extemporize on a subject.

2 *nm* (*Littérat, Mus*) impromptu.

3 *adv* (*à l'improviste*) *arriver* impromptu; (*de chic*) *répondre* off the cuff, impromptu. **il arriva ~, un soir de juin** he arrived impromptu *ou* (quite) out of the blue one evening in June.

imprononçable [ɛ̃pʀɔnɔ̃sabl(ə)] *adj* unpronounceable.

impropre [ɛ̃pʀɔpʀ(ə)] *adj* **(a)** *terme* inappropriate. **(b) ~ à** *outil, personne* unsuitable for, unsuited to; **eau ~ à la consommation** water unfit for (human) consumption.

improprement [ɛ̃pʀɔpʀəmɑ̃] *adv* improperly. **s'exprimer ~** not to express o.s. properly.

impropriété [ɛ̃pʀɔpʀijete] *nf [forme]* incorrectness, inaccuracy. **~ (de langage)** (language) error, mistake.

improuvable [ɛ̃pʀuvabl(ə)] *adj* unprovable.

improvisateur, -trice [ɛ̃pʀɔvizatœʀ, tʀis] *nm,f* improviser.

improvisation [ɛ̃pʀɔvizɑsjɔ̃] *nf* improvisation. **faire une ~** to improvise; (*Jazz*) **~ collective** jam session.

improvisé, e [ɛ̃pʀɔvize] (*ptp de* **improviser**) *adj* (*de fortune*) *équipe* scratch (*épith*); *réforme, table* improvised, makeshift; (*impromptu*) *pique-nique, discours, leçon* improvised; (*fait tel pour la circonstance*) *cuisinier, infirmier* acting (*épith*). **avec des moyens ~s** with whatever means are available *ou* to hand.

improviser [ɛ̃pʀɔvize] (1) **1** *vt* **(a)** *discours, réunion, table, pique-nique*, (*Mus*) to improvise. **il a dû ~** *[musicien, organisateur]* he had to improvise; *[acteur, orateur]* he had to improvise *ou* ad-lib*.

(b) ~ qn cuisinier/infirmier to get sb to act as cook/nurse.

2 s'improviser *vpr* **(a)** *[secours, réunion]* to be improvised.

(b) s'~ cuisinier/infirmier to act as cook/nurse; **on ne s'improvise pas menuisier** you don't just suddenly become a joiner, you don't become a joiner just like that.

improviste [ɛ̃pʀɔvist(ə)] *nm*: **à l'~** unexpectedly, without warning; **je lui ai fait une visite à l'~** I dropped in (up)on him unexpectedly *ou* without warning; **prendre qn à l'~** to catch sb unawares.

imprudemment [ɛ̃pʀydamɑ̃] *adv circuler, naviguer* carelessly; *parler* unwisely, imprudently. **un inconnu qu'il avait ~ suivi** a stranger whom he had foolishly *ou* imprudently *ou* unwisely followed; **s'engager ~ sur la chaussée** to step out carelessly onto the road.

imprudence [ɛ̃pʀydɑ̃s] *nf* **(a)** (*U: V* **imprudent**) carelessness; imprudence; foolishness. **il a eu l'~ de mentionner ce projet** he was foolish *ou* unwise *ou* imprudent enough to mention the project; (*Jur*) **blessures par ~** injuries through negligence; *V* **homicide.**

(b) (*action imprudente*) **commettre une ~** to do something foolish *ou* imprudent; **ne faites pas d'~s** don't do anything foolish *ou* silly, do be careful.

imprudent, e [ɛ̃pʀydɑ̃, ɑ̃t] **1** *adj conducteur, geste, action* careless; *alpiniste* careless, imprudent; *remarque* imprudent, unwise, foolish; *projet* foolish, foolhardy. **il est ~ de se baigner tout de suite après un repas** it's unwise *ou* not wise to bathe immediately after a meal; **il se montra ~ en refusant de porter un gilet de sauvetage** he was unwise *ou* silly *ou* foolish to refuse to wear a life jacket.

2 *nm,f* imprudent *ou* careless person. **il faut punir ces ~s** (*conducteurs*) these careless drivers must be punished.

impubère [ɛ̃pybɛʀ] **1** *adj* below the age of puberty. **2** *nmf* (*Jur*) *child under the legal age for marriage.*

impubliable [ɛ̃publijabl(ə)] *adj* unpublishable.

impudemment [ɛ̃pydamɑ̃] *adv* (*frm: V* **impudent**) impudently; brazenly, shamelessly.

impudence [ɛ̃pydɑ̃s] *nf* (*frm*) **(a)** (*U: V* **impudent**) impudence; brazenness, shamelessness. **quelle ~!** what impudence!

(b) (*acte*) impudent action; (*parole*) impudent remark. **je ne tolèrerai pas ses ~s** I won't put up with *ou* tolerate his impudent behaviour *ou* his impudence.

impudent, e [ɛ̃pydɑ̃, ɑ̃t] *adj* (*frm*) (*insolent*) impudent; (*cynique*) brazen, shameless.

impudeur [ɛ̃pydœʀ] *nf* (*V* **impudique**) immodesty; shamelessness.

impudicité [ɛ̃pydisite] *nf* (*U*) immodesty, shamelessness.

impudique [ɛ̃pydik] *adj* (*indécent*) immodest, shameless; (*impudent*) shameless.

impudiquement [ɛ̃pydikmɑ̃] *adv* (*V* **impudique**) immodestly; shamelessly.

impuissance [ɛ̃pɥisɑ̃s] *nf* **(a)** (*faiblesse*) powerlessness, helplessness; (*inutilité*) *[efforts]* ineffectiveness. **~ à faire** powerlessness *ou* incapacity to do; **je suis dans l'~ de le faire** it is beyond my power to do it, I am incapable of doing it.

(b) (*sexuelle*) impotence.

impuissant, e [ɛ̃pɥisɑ̃, ɑ̃t] **1** *adj* **(a)** *personne* powerless, helpless; *effort* ineffectual, unavailing. **~ à faire** powerless to do, incapable of doing. **(b)** (*sexuellement*) impotent. **2** *nm* impotent man.

impulsif, -ive [ɛ̃pylsif, iv] *adj* impulsive.

impulsion [ɛ̃pylsjɔ̃] *nf* **(a)** (*mécanique, électrique*) impulse.

(b) (*fig: élan*) impetus. **l'~ donnée à l'économie** the boost *ou* impetus given to the economy; **sous l'~ de leurs chefs/des circonstances** through the impetus given by their leaders/by circumstances; **sous l'~ de la vengeance/de la colère** driven *ou* impelled by a spirit of revenge/by anger, under the impulse of revenge/anger.

(c) (*mouvement, instinct*) impulse. **cédant à des ~s morbides** yielding to morbid impulses.

impulsivité [ɛ̃pylsivite] *nf* impulsiveness.

impunément [ɛ̃pynemɑ̃] *adv* with impunity. **on ne se moque pas ~ de lui** one can't make fun of him with impunity, you can't make fun of him and (expect to) get away with it*.

impuni, e [ɛ̃pyni] *adj* unpunished.

impunité [ɛ̃pynite] *nf* impunity. **en toute ~** with complete impunity.

impur, e [ɛ̃pyʀ] *adj* **(a)** (*altéré*) *liquide, air* impure; *race* mixed; (*Rel*) *animal* unclean. **(b)** (*immoral*) *geste, pensée, femme* impure.
impurement [ɛ̃pyʀmɑ̃] *adv* impurely.
impureté [ɛ̃pyʀte] *nf* (*gén*) impurity. **vivre dans l'~** to live in a state of impurity; **~s** impurities.
imputabilité [ɛ̃pytabilite] *nf* (*Jur*) imputability.
imputable [ɛ̃pytabl(ə)] *adj* **(a) ~ à** *faute, accident* imputable to, ascribable to, attributable to. **(b)** (*Fin*) **~ sur** chargeable to.
imputation [ɛ̃pytɑsjɔ̃] *nf* **(a)** (*accusation*) imputation (*frm*), charge. **(b)** (*Fin*) *[somme]* **~ à** charging to.
imputer [ɛ̃pyte] (1) *vt* **(a)** (*attribuer à*) **~ à** to impute to, attribute to, ascribe to. **(b)** (*Fin*) **~ à ou sur** to charge to.
imputrescibilité [ɛ̃pytʀesibilite] *nf* rotproofness, imputrescibility (*T*).
imputrescible [ɛ̃pytʀesibl(ə)] *adj* that does not rot, imputrescible (*T*).
inabordable [inabɔʀdabl(ə)] *adj personne* unapproachable; *lieu* inaccessible; *prix* prohibitive. **maintenant, le beurre est ~** butter is a prohibitive price these days.
inabrité, e [inabʀite] *adj* unsheltered, unprotected.
inabrogeable [inabʀɔʒabl(ə)] *adj* (*Jur*) unrepealable.
inaccentué, e [inaksɑ̃tɥe] *adj* unstressed, unaccented, unaccentuated.
inacceptable [inaksɛptabl(ə)] *adj* (*non recevable*) *offre, plan* unacceptable; (*inadmissible*) *propos* inadmissible.
inaccessibilité [inaksesibilite] *nf* inaccessibility.
inaccessible [inaksesibl(ə)] *adj* **(a)** *montagne, personne, but* inaccessible; *objet* inaccessible, out of reach (*attrib*). **(b) ~ à** (*insensible à*) impervious to.
inaccompli, e [inakɔ̃pli] *adj* (*littér*) *vœux* unfulfilled; *tâche* unaccomplished.
inaccomplissement [inakɔ̃plismɑ̃] *nm* (*littér*) *[vœux]* nonfulfilment; *[tâche]* non-execution.
inaccoutumé, e [inakutyme] *adj* unusual. (*littér*) **~ à** unaccustomed to, unused to.
inachevé, e [inaʃve] *adj* unfinished, uncompleted. **une impression d'~** a feeling of incompleteness *ou* incompletion.
inachèvement [inaʃɛvmɑ̃] *nm* incompletion.
inactif, -ive [inaktif, iv] *adj* **(a)** *vie, personne* (*oisif, non employé*) idle, inactive; *capitaux, exploitation, machine* inactive, idle; (*Bourse*) *marché* slack; *population* non-working. **(b)** (*inefficace*) *remède* ineffective, ineffectual.
inaction [inaksjɔ̃] *nf* (*oisiveté*) inactivity, idleness.
inactivité [inaktivite] *nf* (*non-activité*) inactivity. (*Admin, Mil*) **être en ~** to be out of active service.
inadaptation [inadaptɑsjɔ̃] *nf* maladjustment. **~ à** failure to adjust to *ou* adapt to.
inadapté, e [inadapte] **1** *adj personne, enfance* maladjusted. **~ à** not adapted *ou* adjusted to; **un genre de vie complètement ~ à ses ressources** a way of life not at all adapted to his resources.
2 *nm,f* (*péj: adulte*) misfit; (*Admin, Psych*) maladjusted person.
inadéquat, e [inadekwa, at] *adj* inadequate.
inadéquation [inadekwɑsjɔ̃] *nf* inadequacy.
inadmissibilité [inadmisibilite] *nf* (*Jur*) inadmissibility.
inadmissible [inadmisibl(ə)] *adj* **(a)** *conduite, négligence* inadmissible, intolerable. **(b)** (*Jur*) *témoignage, preuve* inadmissible.
inadvertance [inadvɛʀtɑ̃s] *nf* oversight. **par ~** inadvertently, by mistake.
inaliénabilité [inaljenabilite] *nf* inalienability.
inaliénable [inaljenabl(ə)] *adj* inalienable.
inaltérabilité [inalteʀabilite] *nf* (*V* **inaltérable**) **(a)** stability; fastness; fade-resistance; permanence. **~ à l'air** stability in air, ability to resist exposure to the atmosphere; **~ à la chaleur** heat-resistance, ability to withstand heat; (*littér*) **l'~ du ciel** the unvarying blueness of the sky. **(b)** unchanging nature; unfailing nature; unshakeable nature; steadfastness. **l'~ de son calme** his unchanging *ou* unshakeable calmness.
inaltérable [inalteʀabl(ə)] *adj* **(a)** *métal, substance* stable; *couleur* (*au lavage*) fast; (*à la lumière*) fade-resistant; *vernis, encre* permanent; (*littér*) *ciel, cycle* unchanging. **~ à l'air/à la chaleur** unaffected by air/heat.
(b) *humeur, sentiments* unchanging, unfailing, unshakeable; *santé* unfailing; *principes, espoir* steadfast, unshakeable, unfailing. **leur amitié est restée ~** their friendship remained unaltered *ou* steadfast.
inaltéré, e [inalteʀe] *adj* unchanged, unaltered.
inamical, e, *mpl* **-aux** [inamikal, o] *adj* unfriendly.
inamovibilité [inamɔvibilite] *nf* (*Jur*) *[fonction]* permanence; *[juge, fonctionnaire]* irremovability.
inamovible [inamɔvibl(ə)] *adj* **(a)** (*Jur*) *juge, fonctionnaire* irremovable; *fonction, emploi* from which one is irremovable.
(b) (*fixe*) *plaque, panneau* fixed. **cette partie est ~** this part is fixed *ou* cannot be removed.
(c) (*hum*) *casquette, sourire* eternal. **il travaille toujours chez X? il est vraiment ~** is he still with X? — he's a permanent fixture *ou* he's built in with the bricks (*hum, surtout Brit*).
inanimé, e [inanime] *adj matière* inanimate; *personne, corps* (*évanoui*) unconscious, senseless; (*mort*) lifeless. **tomber ~** to fall senseless to the ground, fall to the ground unconscious.
inanité [inanite] *nf [conversation]* inanity; *[querelle, efforts]* futility, pointlessness; *[espoirs]* vanity, futility.
inanition [inanisjɔ̃] *nf* exhaustion through lack of nourishment. **tomber/mourir d'~** to faint with/die of hunger.
inapaisable [inapɛzabl(ə)] *adj colère, chagrin, besoin* unappeasable; *soif* unquenchable.
inapaisé, e [inapeze] *adj* (*V* **inapaisable**) unappeased; unquenched.
inaperçu, e [inapɛʀsy] *adj* unnoticed. **passer ~** to pass *ou* go unnoticed; **le geste ne passa pas ~** the gesture did not go unnoticed *ou* unremarked.
inappétence [inapetɑ̃s] *nf* (*manque d'appétit*) lack of appetite.
inapplicable [inaplikabl(ə)] *adj* inapplicable (*à* to). **dans ce cas, la règle est ~** in this case, the rule cannot be applied *ou* is inapplicable.
inapplication [inaplikɑsjɔ̃] *nf* **(a)** *[élève]* lack of application. **(b)** *[loi]* non-application.
inappliqué, e [inaplike] *adj* **(a)** *écolier* lacking in application (*attrib*). **cet écolier est ~** this pupil lacks application, this pupil does not apply himself. **(b)** *méthode* not applied (*attrib*); *loi, règlement* not enforced (*attrib*).
inappréciable [inapʀesjabl(ə)] *adj* **(a)** (*précieux*) *aide, service* invaluable; *avantage, bonheur* inestimable. **(b)** (*difficilement décelable*) *nuance, différence* inappreciable, imperceptible.
inapte [inapt(ə)] *adj* (*incapable*) incapable. **~ aux affaires/à certains travaux** unsuited to *ou* unfitted for business/certain kinds of work; **un accident l'a rendu ~ au travail** an accident has made him unfit for work; **~ à faire** incapable of doing; (*Mil*) **~ (au service)** unfit (for military service).
inaptitude [inaptityd] *nf* (*mentale*) inaptitude, incapacity; (*physique*) unfitness (*à qch* for sth, *à faire qch* for doing sth). (*Mil*) **~ (au service)** unfitness (for military service).
inarrangeable [inaʀɑ̃ʒabl(ə)] *adj querelle* beyond reconciliation (*attrib*); *appareil, outil* beyond repair (*attrib*).
inarticulé, e [inaʀtikyle] *adj mots, cris* inarticulate.
inassimilable [inasimilabl(ə)] *adj notions, substance, immigrants* that cannot be assimilated.
inassimilé, e [inasimile] *adj notions, immigrants, substance* unassimilated.
inassouvi, e [inasuvi] *adj haine, colère, désir* unappeased; *faim* unsatisfied, unappeased; *soif* (*lit, fig*) unquenched; *personne* unfulfilled. **vengeance ~e** unappeased desire for revenge, unsated lust for revenge (*littér*); **soif ~e de puissance** unappeased *ou* unquenched lust for power.
inassouvissable [inasuvisabl(ə)] *adj* insatiable.
inattaquable [inatakabl(ə)] *adj poste, position* unassailable; *preuve* irrefutable; *argument* unassailable, irrefutable; *conduite, réputation* irreproachable, unimpeachable; *personne* beyond reproach (*attrib*).
inattendu, e [inatɑ̃dy] **1** *adj* unexpected, unforeseen. **2** *nm*: **l'~** the unexpected; **l'~ d'une remarque** the unexpectedness of a remark.
inattentif, -ive [inatɑ̃tif, iv] *adj* inattentive. **~ à** (*ne prêtant pas attention à*) inattentive to; (*se souciant peu de*) *dangers, détails matériels* heedless of, unmindful of.
inattention [inatɑ̃sjɔ̃] *nf* **(a)** (*U*) inattention. **(b) (instant d')~** moment of inattention, moment's inattention; **(faute d')~** careless mistake. **(c)** (*littér: manque d'intérêt pour*) **~ à** *convenances, détails matériels* lack of concern for.
inaudible [inodibl(ə)] *adj* (*non ou peu audible*) inaudible; (*péj: mauvais*) unbearable.
inaugural, e, *mpl* **-aux** [inɔgyʀal, o] *adj séance, cérémonie* inaugural; *vol, voyage* maiden (*épith*). **discours ~** *[député]* maiden *ou* inaugural speech; (*lors d'une inauguration*) inaugural speech; (*lors d'un congrès*) opening *ou* inaugural speech.
inauguration [inɔgyʀɑsjɔ̃] *nf* (*V* **inaugurer**) **(a)** (*U*) unveiling; inauguration; opening. **cérémonie/discours d'~** inaugural ceremony/lecture *ou* speech. **(b)** (*cérémonie*) opening ceremony; inauguration; unveiling ceremony.
inaugurer [inɔgyʀe] (1) *vt* **(a)** *monument, plaque* to unveil; *route, bâtiment* to inaugurate, open; *manifestation, exposition* to open. **(b)** (*fig: commencer*) *politique, période* to inaugurate. **nous inaugurions une période de paix** we were entering a time of peace. **(c)** (*fig: utiliser pour la première fois*) *raquette, bureau, chapeau* to christen*.
inauthenticité [inotɑ̃tisite] *nf* inauthenticity.
inauthentique [inotɑ̃tik] *adj document, fait* not authentic (*attrib*); (*Philos*) *existence* unauthentic.
inavouable [inavwabl(ə)] *adj procédé, motifs, mœurs* shameful, too shameful to mention (*attrib*); *bénéfices* undisclosable.
inavoué, e [inavwe] *adj crime* unconfessed; *sentiments* unconfessed, unavowed.
inca [ɛ̃ka] **1** *adj* Inca. **2** *nmf*: **I~** Inca.
incalculable [ɛ̃kalkylabl(ə)] *adj* (*gén*) incalculable. **un nombre ~ de** countless numbers of, an incalculable number of.
incandescence [ɛ̃kɑ̃desɑ̃s] *nf* incandescence. **en ~** white-hot, incandescent; **porter qch à ~** to heat sth white-hot *ou* to incandescence; *V* **lampe, manchon.**
incandescent, e [ɛ̃kɑ̃desɑ̃, ɑ̃t] *adj substance, filament* incandescent, white-hot; (*fig*) *imagination* burning.
incantation [ɛ̃kɑ̃tɑsjɔ̃] *nf* incantation.
incantatoire [ɛ̃kɑ̃tatwaʀ] *adj* incantatory; *V* **formule.**
incapable [ɛ̃kapabl(ə)] **1** *adj* **(a)** (*inapte*) incapable, incompetent, useless*.
(b) ~ de faire (*par incompétence, impossibilité morale*) incapable of doing; (*impossibilité physique, physiologique*) unable to do, incapable of doing; **j'étais ~ de bouger** I was unable to move, I was incapable of movement; **elle est ~ de mentir** she's incapable of lying, she can't tell a lie.
(c) ~ d'amour incapable of loving, unable to love; **~ de malhonnêteté** incapable of dishonesty *ou* of being dishonest; **~ du moindre effort** unable to make the least effort, incapable of making the least effort.
(d) (*Jur*) incapable.
2 *nmf* **(a)** (*incompétent*) incompetent. **c'est un ~** he's useless* *ou* incapable, he's an incompetent.

(b) (*Jur*) incapable person.

incapacité [ɛ̃kapasite] **1** *nf* **(a)** (*incompétence*) incompetence, incapability.

(b) (*impossibilité*) **~ de faire** incapacity *ou* inability to do; **être dans l'~ de faire** to be unable to do, be incapable of doing.

(c) (*invalidité*) disablement, disability. **~ totale/partielle/permanente** total/partial/permanent disablement *ou* disability.

(d) (*Jur*) incapacity. **~ de jouissance** incapacity (*by exclusion from a right*); **~ d'exercice** incapacity (*by restriction of a right*).

2: (*Jur*) **incapacité civile** civil incapacity; **incapacité de travail** industrial disablement *ou* disability.

incarcération [ɛ̃kaʀseʀɑsjɔ̃] *nf* incarceration, imprisonment.

incarcérer [ɛ̃kaʀseʀe] (6) *vt* to incarcerate, imprison.

incarnat, e [ɛ̃kaʀna, at] **1** *adj teint* rosy, pink; *teinture* crimson. **2** *nm* rosy hue, rosiness, crimson tint.

incarnation [ɛ̃kaʀnɑsjɔ̃] *nf* (*Myth, Rel*) incarnation. (*fig: image*) **être l'~ de** to be the incarnation *ou* embodiment of.

incarné, e [ɛ̃kaʀne] (*ptp de* **incarner**) *adj* **(a)** (*Rel*) incarnate; (*fig: personnifié*) incarnate, personified. **cette femme est la méchanceté ~e** this woman is wickedness incarnate *ou* personified, this woman is the embodiment of wickedness.

(b) *ongle* ingrown.

incarner [ɛ̃kaʀne] (1) **1** *vt* (*représenter*) *[personne]* to embody, personify, incarnate; *[œuvre]* to embody; (*Théât*) *[acteur]* to play; (*Rel*) to incarnate.

2 s'incarner *vpr* **(a)** (*être représenté par*) **s'~ dans** *ou* **en** to be embodied in; **tous nos espoirs s'incarnent en vous** you embody all our hopes, you are the embodiment of all our hopes.

(b) (*Rel*) **s'~ dans** to become *ou* be incarnate in.

(c) *[ongle]* to become ingrown.

incartade [ɛ̃kaʀtad] *nf* **(a)** (*écart de conduite*) prank, escapade. **ils étaient punis à la moindre ~** they were punished for the slightest prank; **faire une ~** to go on an escapade. **(b)** (*Équitation: écart*) swerve. **faire une ~** to shy.

incassable [ɛ̃kɑsabl(ə)] *adj* unbreakable.

incendiaire [ɛ̃sɑ̃djɛʀ] **1** *nmf* fire-raiser, arsonist. **2** *adj balle, bombe* incendiary; *discours, propos* inflammatory, incendiary; *lettre d'amour, œillade* passionate; *V* **blond.**

incendie [ɛ̃sɑ̃di] **1** *nm* **(a)** (*sinistre*) fire, blaze, conflagration (*littér*). **un ~ s'est déclaré dans ...** a fire broke out in ...; *V* **assurance, foyer, pompe**[1].

(b) (*fig littér*) **l'~ du couchant** the blaze of the sunset, the fiery glow of the sunset; **l'~ de la révolte/de la passion** the fire of revolt/of passion.

2: **incendie criminel** arson (*U*), case of arson; **incendie de forêt** forest fire.

incendié, e [ɛ̃sɑ̃dje] (*ptp de* **incendier**) *adj*: **les fermiers ~s ont tout perdu** the farmers who were the victims of the fire have lost everything.

incendier [ɛ̃sɑ̃dje] (7) *vt* **(a)** (*mettre le feu à*) to set fire to, set on fire, set alight; (*brûler complètement*) *bâtiment* to burn down; *voiture* to burn; *ville, récolte, forêt* to burn (to ashes).

(b) (*fig*) *désir, passion* to kindle, inflame; *imagination* to fire; *bouche, gorge* to burn, set on fire. **la fièvre lui incendiait le visage** (*sensation*) fever made his face burn; (*apparence*) his cheeks were burning *ou* glowing with fever; (*littér*) **le soleil incendie le couchant** the setting sun sets the sky ablaze.

(c) (*: *réprimander*) **~ qn** to give sb a rocket* (*Brit*) *ou* a telling-off*; **tu vas te faire ~** you'll catch it*, you'll get a rocket* (*Brit*).

incertain, e [ɛ̃sɛʀtɛ̃, ɛn] *adj* **(a)** *personne* uncertain, unsure (*de qch* about *ou* as to sth). **~ de savoir la vérité, il ...** uncertain *ou* unsure as to whether he knew the truth, he ...; **encore ~ sur la conduite à suivre** still undecided *ou* uncertain about which course to follow.

(b) *démarche* uncertain, hesitant.

(c) *temps* uncertain, unsettled; *contour* indistinct, blurred; *allusion* vague; *lumière* dim, vague.

(d) *succès, entreprise* uncertain, doubtful; *date, durée* uncertain, unspecified; *origine* uncertain; *fait* uncertain, doubtful.

incertitude [ɛ̃sɛʀtityd] *nf* **(a)** (*U*) *[personne, résultat, fait]* uncertainty. **être dans l'~** to be in a state of uncertainty, feel uncertain. **(b)** **~s** (*hésitations*) doubts, uncertainties; (*impondérables*) *[avenir, entreprise]* uncertainties.

incessamment [ɛ̃sesamɑ̃] *adv* (*sans délai*) (very) shortly. **il doit arriver ~** he'll be here any minute now *ou* very shortly.

incessant, e [ɛ̃sesɑ̃, ɑ̃t] *adj pluie* incessant, unceasing; *efforts, activité* ceaseless, incessant, unremitting; *bruit, réclamations, coups de téléphone* incessant, unceasing, continual.

incessibilité [ɛ̃sesibilite] *nf* non-transferability.

incessible [ɛ̃sesibl(ə)] *adj* non-transferable.

inceste [ɛ̃sɛst(ə)] *nm* incest.

incestueusement [ɛ̃sɛstɥøzmɑ̃] *adv* incestuously.

incestueux, -euse [ɛ̃sɛstɥø, øz] **1** *adj relations, personne* incestuous; *enfant* born of incest. **2** *nm,f* (*Jur*) person guilty of incest.

inchangé, e [ɛ̃ʃɑ̃ʒe] *adj* unchanged, unaltered. **la situation/son expression reste ~e** the situation/his expression remains unchanged *ou* the same *ou* unaltered.

inchangeable [ɛ̃ʃɑ̃ʒabl(ə)] *adj* unchangeable.

inchantable [ɛ̃ʃɑ̃tabl(ə)] *adj* unsingable.

inchauffable [ɛ̃ʃofabl(ə)] *adj* impossible to heat (*attrib*).

inchavirable [ɛ̃ʃaviʀabl(ə)] *adj* uncapsizable, self-righting.

inchoatif, -ive [ɛ̃kɔatif, iv] *adj* inchoative, inceptive.

incidemment [ɛ̃sidamɑ̃] *adv* incidentally, in passing.

incidence [ɛ̃sidɑ̃s] *nf* (*conséquence*) effect; (*Écon, Phys*) incidence; *V* **angle.**

incident, e [ɛ̃sidɑ̃, ɑ̃t] **1** *adj* (*frm, Jur: accessoire*) incidental; (*Phys*) incident. **puis-je vous demander, de manière toute ~e?** may I ask you, quite incidentally?; **je désirerais poser une question ~e** I'd like to ask a question in connection with this matter, I'd like to interpose a question.

2 *nm* (*gén*) incident; (*Jur*) point of law. **la vie n'est qu'une succession d'~s** life is just a series of minor incidents; **~ imprévu** unexpected incident, unforeseen event; **l'~ est clos** that's an end of the matter.

3 incidente *nf* (*Ling*) **(proposition) ~e** parenthesis, parenthetical clause.

4: **incident diplomatique** diplomatic incident; **incident de frontière** border incident; **incident de parcours** (*gén*) (minor *ou* slight) setback, hitch; (*santé*) (minor *ou* slight) setback; (*lit, hum fig*) **incident technique** technical hitch.

incinérateur [ɛ̃sineʀatœʀ] *nm* incinerator.

incinération [ɛ̃sineʀɑsjɔ̃] *nf* (*V* **incinérer**) incineration; cremation.

incinérer [ɛ̃sineʀe] (6) *vt ordures, cadavre* to incinerate; (*au crématorium*) to cremate.

incise [ɛ̃siz] *nf* (*Mus*) phrase. (*Ling*) **(proposition) ~** interpolated clause; **il m'a dit, en ~, que** he told me in passing *ou* in parenthesis that.

inciser [ɛ̃size] (1) *vt écorce, arbre* to incise, make an incision in; *peau* to incise; *abcès* to lance. **~ un arbre pour en extraire la résine** to tap a tree.

incisif, -ive [ɛ̃sizif, iv] **1** *adj ton, style, réponse* cutting, incisive; *regard* piercing. **2 incisive** *nf* (*dent*) incisor.

incision [ɛ̃sizjɔ̃] *nf* **(a)** (*U: V* **inciser**) incising; incision; lancing.

(b) (*entaille*) incision. **faire une ~ dans** to make an incision in, incise.

incisive [ɛ̃siziv] *V* **incisif.**

incitation [ɛ̃sitɑsjɔ̃] *nf* incitement (*à* to). (*Jur*) **~ à la débauche/au meurtre** incitement to immoral behaviour/to murder.

inciter [ɛ̃site] (1) *vt*: **~ qn à faire** to prompt *ou* incite *ou* encourage sb to do; **cela m'incite à la méfiance** that prompts me to be on my guard, that puts me on my guard; **cela les incite à la violence/la révolte** that incites them to violence/revolt; **ça n'incite pas au travail** it doesn't (exactly) encourage one to work, it's no incentive to work; **ça vous incite au découragement** it makes you feel (positively) discouraged; **ça vous incite à la paresse** it encourages laziness (in one), it encourages one to be lazy.

incivil, e [ɛ̃sivil] *adj* uncivil, rude.

incivilement [ɛ̃sivilmɑ̃] *adv* uncivilly, rudely.

incivilité [ɛ̃sivilite] *nf [attitude, ton]* incivility, rudeness; (*propos impoli*) uncivil *ou* rude remark. **ce serait commettre une ~ que de ...** it would be uncivil to ... .

inclassable [ɛ̃klɑsabl(ə)] *adj* which cannot be categorized, unclassifiable.

inclémence [ɛ̃klemɑ̃s] *nf* inclemency.

inclément, e [ɛ̃klemɑ̃, ɑ̃t] *adj* inclement.

inclinaison [ɛ̃klinɛzɔ̃] **1** *nf* **(a)** (*déclivité*) *[plan, pente]* incline; *[route, voie ferrée]* incline, gradient; *[toit]* slope, slant, pitch; *[barre, tuyau]* slope, slant. **l'~ exceptionnelle de la route** the exceptionally steep gradient of the road, the exceptional steepness of the road.

(b) (*état penché*) *[mur]* lean; *[mât, tour]* lean, tilt; *[chapeau]* slant, tilt; *[appareil, tête]* tilt; *[navire]* list. **l'~ comique de son chapeau sur l'oreille gauche** the comic way in which his hat was cocked *ou* tilted over his left ear; **accentuez l'~ de la tête** tilt your head forward more.

(c) (*Géom*) *[droite, surface]* angle; *V* **angle.**

2: (*Phys*) **inclinaison magnétique** magnetic declination.

inclination [ɛ̃klinɑsjɔ̃] *nf* **(a)** (*penchant*) inclination. **suivre son ~** to follow one's (own) inclination; **son ~ naturelle au bonheur** his natural inclination *ou* tendency towards happiness; **~s altruistes** altruistic tendencies; **une certaine ~ à mentir** a certain inclination *ou* tendency to tell lies; **avoir de l'~ pour la littérature** to have a strong liking *ou* a penchant for literature; **~ pour qn**† liking for sb.

(b) **~ de (la) tête** (*acquiescement*) nod; (*salut*) inclination of the head; **~ (du buste)** bow.

incliné, e [ɛ̃kline] (*ptp de* **incliner**) *adj* **(a)** (*raide*) *pente, toit* steep, (steeply) sloping.

(b) (*penché*) *tour, mur* leaning; *récipient* tilted; *V* **plan**[1].

(c) **être ~ à penser que ...** to be inclined to think that ...; **être ~ au mal** to have a leaning *ou* a tendency towards what is bad.

incliner [ɛ̃kline] (1) **1** *vt* **(a)** (*pencher*) *appareil, mât, bouteille* to tilt; (*littér: courber*) *arbre* to bend (over); *[architecte] toit, surface* to slope. **le vent incline le navire** the wind heels the boat over; **~ la tête** *ou* **le front** (*pour saluer*) to give a slight bow, incline one's head; (*pour acquiescer*) to nod (one's head), incline one's head; **~ la tête de côté** to tilt *ou* incline one's head on one side; **~ le buste** *ou* **le corps** (*saluer*) to bow, give a bow; **inclinez le corps plus en avant** lean *ou* bend forward more; *V* **plan**[1].

(b) (*littér*) **~ qn à l'indulgence** to encourage sb to be indulgent; **ceci m'incline à penser que** that makes me inclined to think that, that leads me to believe that.

2 *vi* **(a)** **~ à** (*tendre à*) to tend towards; (*pencher pour*) to be *ou* feel inclined towards; **il incline à l'autoritarisme/à l'indulgence** he tends towards authoritarianism/indulgence, he tends *ou* is inclined to be authoritarian/indulgent; **dans ce cas, il inclinait à la clémence/sévérité** in this instance he felt inclined to be merciful/severe *ou* he inclined towards clemency/severity; **le ministre inclinait vers des mesures très sévères** the minister inclined towards (taking) strong measures; **~ à penser/croire que** to be inclined to think/believe that; **j'incline**

à accepter cette offre/rejeter cette solution I'm inclined to accept this offer/reject this solution.

(b) (*littér*) *[mur]* to lean; *[arbre]* to bend. **la colline inclinait doucement vers la mer** the hill sloped gently (down) towards the sea.

(c) (*bifurquer*) ~ **vers** to veer (over) towards *ou* to.

3 s'incliner *vpr* **(a)** (*se courber*) to bow (*devant* before). **s'~ jusqu'à terre** to bow to the ground.

(b) (*rendre hommage à*) **s'~ devant qn** *ou* **devant la supériorité de qn** to bow before sb's superiority; **devant tant de talent/de noblesse, je m'incline** I bow before such a wealth of talent/such nobleness; **devant un tel homme, on ne peut que s'~** one can only bow (down) before such a man; **il est venu s'~ devant la dépouille mortelle du président** he came to pay his last respects at the coffin of the president.

(c) (*céder*) **s'~ devant l'autorité de qn** to yield *ou* bow to sb's authority; **s'~ devant un ordre** to accept an order; **puisque vous me le commandez, je n'ai plus qu'à m'~ et obéir** since you order me to do it, I can only accept it and obey.

(d) (*s'avouer battu*) to admit defeat. **le boxeur s'inclina (devant son adversaire) à la 3e reprise** the boxer admitted defeat in the 3rd round; **il dut s'~ devant un adversaire plus fort que lui** faced with an opponent stronger than himself, he was forced to give in *ou* to admit defeat, he had to bow to his opponent who was stronger than him; (*Sport*) **Marseille s'est incliné devant Saint-Étienne 2 buts à 3** Marseilles went down to *ou* lost to Saint-Étienne by 2 goals to 3.

(e) *[arbre]* to bend over; *[mur]* to lean; *[navire]* to heel (over); *[chemin, colline]* to slope; *[toit]* to be sloping. **le soleil s'incline à l'horizon** the sun is sinking (down) towards the horizon.

inclure [ɛ̃klyʀ] (35) *vt* **(a)** (*insérer*) *clause* to insert (*dans* in); *nom* to include (*dans* in); (*joindre à un envoi*) *billet, chèque* to enclose (*dans* in).

(b) (*contenir*) to include. **ce récit en inclut un autre** this is a story within a story.

inclus, e [ɛ̃kly, yz] (*ptp de* **inclure**) *adj* **(a)** (*joint à un envoi*) enclosed.

(b) (*compris*) *frais* included. **eux ~** including them; **jusqu'au 10 mars ~** until March 10th inclusive, up to and including March 10th; **jusqu'au 3e chapitre ~** up to and including the 3rd chapter; **les frais sont ~ dans la note** the bill is inclusive of expenses, expenses are included in the bill; *V* **ci.**

(c) (*Math*) (*ensemble*) ~ **dans** included in; **A est ~ dans B** A is the subset of B.

inclusif, -ive [ɛ̃klyzif, iv] *adj* (*Gram, Logique*) inclusive.

inclusion [ɛ̃klyzjɔ̃] *nf* (*insertion*) insertion, inclusion; (*présence*) inclusion; (*Math*) inclusion.

inclusivement [ɛ̃klyzivmɑ̃] *adv* inclusively. **jusqu'au 16e siècle ~** up to and including the 16th century; **jusqu'au 1er janvier ~** until January 1st inclusive, up to and including January 1st.

incoercible [ɛ̃kɔɛʀsibl(ə)] *adj toux* uncontrollable; *besoin, désir, rire* uncontrollable, irrepressible.

incognito [ɛ̃kɔɲito] **1** *adv* incognito. **2** *nm*: **garder l'~, rester dans l'~** to remain incognito; **laisser l'~ à qn** to allow sb to remain incognito; **l'~ lui plaisait** he liked being incognito; **l'~ dont il s'entourait** the secrecy with which he surrounded himself.

incohérence [ɛ̃kɔeʀɑ̃s] *nf* **(a)** (*U: V* **incohérent**) incoherency, incoherence; inconsistency. **l'~ entre les différentes parties du discours** the inconsistency of the different parts of the speech.

(b) (*dans un texte etc*) inconsistency, discrepancy; (*propos, acte etc*) inconsistency. **les ~s de sa conduite** the inconsistency of his behaviour, the inconsistencies in his behaviour.

incohérent, e [ɛ̃kɔeʀɑ̃, ɑ̃t] *adj geste, langage, texte* incoherent; *comportement* inconsistent.

incollable* [ɛ̃kɔlabl(ə)] *adj*: **il est ~ (en histoire)** you can't catch him out* *ou* he's got all the answers (on history).

incolore [ɛ̃kɔlɔʀ] *adj ciel, liquide, style* colourless; *verre, vernis* clear; (*littér*) *sourire* wan.

incomber [ɛ̃kɔ̃be] (1) **incomber à** *vt indir* (*frm*) *[devoirs, responsabilité]* to be incumbent (up)on; *[frais, réparations, travail]* to be sb's responsibility; **il m'incombe de faire** it is my responsibility to do, it is incumbent upon me to do, the onus is on me to do; **ces frais leur incombent entièrement** these costs are to be paid by them in full *ou* are entirely their responsibility.

incombustible [ɛ̃kɔ̃bystibl(ə)] *adj* incombustible.

incommensurabilité [ɛ̃kɔmɑ̃syʀabilite] *nf* incommensurability.

incommensurable [ɛ̃kɔmɑ̃syʀabl(ə)] *adj* **(a)** (*immense*) immeasurable. **(b)** (*sans commune mesure: Math, littér*) incommensurable (*avec* with).

incommodant, e [ɛ̃kɔmɔdɑ̃, ɑ̃t] *adj odeur* unpleasant, offensive; *bruit* annoying, unpleasant; *chaleur* uncomfortable.

incommode [ɛ̃kɔmɔd] *adj* **(a)** *pièce, appartement* inconvenient; *heure* awkward, inconvenient; *armoire, outil* impractical, awkward. **(b)** *siège* uncomfortable; (*fig*) *position, situation* awkward, uncomfortable.

incommodé, e [ɛ̃kɔmɔde] (*ptp de* **incommoder**) *adj* indisposed, unwell.

incommodément [ɛ̃kɔmɔdemɑ̃] *adv installé, assis* awkwardly, uncomfortably; *logé* inconveniently; *situé* inconveniently, awkwardly.

incommoder [ɛ̃kɔmɔde] (1) *vt*: **~ qn** *[bruit]* to disturb *ou* bother sb; *[odeur, chaleur]* to bother sb; *[comportement]* to make sb feel ill-at-ease *ou* uncomfortable.

incommodité [ɛ̃kɔmɔdite] *nf* (*V* **incommode**) inconvenience; awkwardness; impracticality; lack of comfort.

incommunicabilité [ɛ̃kɔmynikabilite] *nf* incommunicability.

incommunicable [ɛ̃kɔmynikabl(ə)] *adj* incommunicable.

incommutabilité [ɛ̃kɔmytabilite] *nf* inalienability.

incommutable [ɛ̃kɔmytabl(ə)] *adj* inalienable.

incomparable [ɛ̃kɔ̃paʀabl(ə)] *adj* (*sans pareil*) incomparable, matchless; (*dissemblable*) not comparable.

incomparablement [ɛ̃kɔ̃paʀabləmɑ̃] *adv*: ~ **plus/mieux** incomparably more/better.

incompatibilité [ɛ̃kɔ̃patibilite] *nf* (*gén, Sci*) incompatibility. (*Jur*) ~ **d'humeur** (mutual) incompatibility; **il y a ~ d'humeur entre les membres de cette équipe** the members of this team are (temperamentally) incompatible.

incompatible [ɛ̃kɔ̃patibl(ə)] *adj* incompatible (*avec* with).

incompétence [ɛ̃kɔ̃petɑ̃s] *nf* (*gén*) lack of knowledge; (*Jur*) incompetence. **il reconnaît volontiers son ~ en musique** he freely admits to his lack of knowledge of music *ou* that he knows nothing about music.

incompétent, e [ɛ̃kɔ̃petɑ̃, ɑ̃t] *adj* (*gén*) inexpert; (*Jur*) incompetent. **en ce qui concerne la musique/les maths je suis ~** as far as music goes/maths go I'm not competent *ou* I'm incompetent to judge.

incomplet, -ète [ɛ̃kɔ̃plɛ, ɛt] *adj* incomplete.

incomplètement [ɛ̃kɔ̃plɛtmɑ̃] *adv renseigné* incompletely; *rétabli, guéri* not completely.

incomplétude [ɛ̃kɔ̃pletyd] *nf* (*littér: insatisfaction*) nonfulfilment.

incompréhensibilité [ɛ̃kɔ̃pʀeɑ̃sibilite] *nf* incomprehensibility.

incompréhensible [ɛ̃kɔ̃pʀeɑ̃sibl(ə)] *adj* (*gén*) incomprehensible.

incompréhensif, -ive [ɛ̃kɔ̃pʀeɑ̃sif, iv] *adj* (*peu tolérant*) *parents etc* lacking in understanding; (*peu coopératif*) *interlocuteur* unsympathetic, unwilling to understand. **il s'est montré totalement ~** he (just) refused to understand, he was totally unsympathetic; **ses parents se montrent totalement ~s** his parents show a total lack of understanding.

incompréhension [ɛ̃kɔ̃pʀeɑ̃sjɔ̃] *nf* **(a)** (*V* **incompréhensif**) lack of understanding (*envers* of); unwillingness to understand. **(b) l'~ d'un texte** the failure to understand a text, the lack of understanding *ou* comprehension of a text.

incompressibilité [ɛ̃kɔ̃pʀesibilite] *nf* (*Phys*) incompressibility. **l'~ du budget** the irreducibility of the budget.

incompressible [ɛ̃kɔ̃pʀesibl(ə)] *adj* (*Phys*) incompressible. **nos dépenses sont ~s** our expenses cannot be reduced *ou* cut down.

incompris, e [ɛ̃kɔ̃pʀi, iz] *adj* misunderstood. **X fut un grand ~ à son époque** X was never understood by his contemporaries.

inconcevable [ɛ̃kɔ̃svabl(ə)] *adj* (*gén*) inconceivable. **avec un toupet ~** with unbelievable *ou* incredible cheek.

inconcevablement [ɛ̃kɔ̃svabləmɑ̃] *adv* inconceivably, incredibly.

inconciliabilité [ɛ̃kɔ̃siljabilite] *nf* irreconcilability.

inconciliable [ɛ̃kɔ̃siljabl(ə)] *adj* irreconcilable.

inconditionnel, -elle [ɛ̃kɔ̃disjɔnɛl] **1** *adj acceptation, ordre, soumission* unconditional; *appui* wholehearted, unconditional, unreserved; *partisan, foi* unquestioning.

2 *nm,f [homme politique, doctrine]* unquestioning supporter. **les ~s des sports d'hiver** winter sports enthusiasts *ou* fanatics.

inconditionnellement [ɛ̃kɔ̃disjɔnɛlmɑ̃] *adv* (*V* **inconditionnel**) unconditionally; wholeheartedly; unreservedly; unquestioningly.

inconduite [ɛ̃kɔ̃dɥit] *nf* (*débauche*) wild *ou* loose *ou* shocking behaviour (*U*).

inconfort [ɛ̃kɔ̃fɔʀ] *nm [logement]* lack of comfort, discomfort. **l'~ lui importait peu** discomfort didn't matter to him in the least.

inconfortable [ɛ̃kɔ̃fɔʀtabl(ə)] *adj maison, meuble* uncomfortable; (*lit, fig*) *position* uncomfortable, awkward.

inconfortablement [ɛ̃kɔ̃fɔʀtabləmɑ̃] *adv* (*V* **inconfortable**) uncomfortably; awkwardly.

incongru, e [ɛ̃kɔ̃gʀy] *adj attitude, bruit* unseemly; *remarque* incongruous, ill-placed, ill-chosen; (†, *littér*) *personne* uncouth.

incongruité [ɛ̃kɔ̃gʀɥite] *nf* **(a)** (*U*) incongruity, unseemliness. **(b** (*propos*) unseemly *ou* ill-chosen *ou* ill-placed remark; (*acte*) unseemly action, unseemly behaviour (*U*).

incongrûment [ɛ̃kɔ̃gʀymɑ̃] *adv agir, parler* in an unseemly way.

inconnu, e [ɛ̃kɔny] **1** *adj destination, fait* unknown; *odeur, sensation* new, unknown; *ville, personne* unknown, strange (*à, de* to). **son visage m'était ~** his face was new *ou* unknown to me, I didn't know his face; **une joie ~e l'envahit** he was seized with a strange joy *ou* a joy that was (quite) new to him; **on se sent très seul en pays ~** one feels very lonely in a strange country *ou* in a foreign country *ou* in strange surroundings; **s'en aller vers des contrées ~es** to set off in search of unknown *ou* unexplored *ou* uncharted lands; **~ à cette adresse** not known at this address; *V* **soldat.**

2 *nm,f* stranger, unknown person. **pour moi, ce peintre-là, c'est un ~** I don't know this painter, this painter is unknown to me; **ce roman, écrit par un illustre ~** this novel, written by some eminent author of whom no one has ever heard; **le malfaiteur n'était pas un ~ pour la police** the culprit was known *ou* was not unknown *ou* was no stranger to the police; **ne parle pas à des ~s** don't talk to strangers.

3 *nm* (*ce qu'on ignore*) **l'~** the unknown.

4 inconnue *nf* (*élément inconnu*) unknown factor *ou* quantity; (*Math*) unknown. **dans cette entreprise, il y a beaucoup d'~es** there are lots of unknowns *ou* unknown factors in this venture.

inconsciemment [ɛ̃kɔ̃sjamɑ̃] *adv* (*involontairement*) unconsciously, unwittingly; (*à la légère*) thoughtlessly, recklessly, rashly.

inconscience [ɛ̃kɔ̃sjɑ̃s] *nf* **(a)** (*physique*) unconsciousness. **sombrer dans l'~** to lose consciousness, sink into unconsciousness. **(b)** (*morale*) thoughtlessness, recklessness, rashness. **mais c'est de l'~!** that's sheer madness! *ou* stupidity!

inconscient, e [ɛ̃kɔ̃sjɑ̃, ɑ̃t] **1** *adj* (*évanoui*) unconscious; (*échappant à la conscience*) *sentiment* subconscious; (*machinal*) *mouvement* unconscious, automatic; (*irréfléchi*) *décision, action, personne* thoughtless, reckless, rash; (*: *fou*) mad*. **~ de** *événements extérieurs* unaware of, not aware of; *conséquence* unaware of, not aware of, oblivious to; **c'est un ~*** he's mad*, he's a madman*.
2 *nm* (*Psych*) **l'~** the subconscious, the unconscious.

inconséquence [ɛ̃kɔ̃sekɑ̃s] *nf* (*manque de logique*) inconsistency, inconsequence; (*légèreté*) thoughtlessness (*U*), fecklessness (*U*).

inconséquent, e [ɛ̃kɔ̃sekɑ̃, ɑ̃t] *adj* (*illogique*) *comportement, personne* inconsistent, inconsequent; (*irréfléchi*) *démarche, décision, personne* thoughtless.

inconsidéré, e [ɛ̃kɔ̃sideʀe] *adj* ill-considered, thoughtless, rash.

inconsidérément [ɛ̃kɔ̃sideʀemɑ̃] *adv* thoughtlessly, rashly, without thinking.

inconsistance [ɛ̃kɔ̃sistɑ̃s] *nf* (*V* **inconsistant**) flimsiness; weakness; colourlessness; runniness; watery *ou* thin consistency.

inconsistant, e [ɛ̃kɔ̃sistɑ̃, ɑ̃t] *adj* **(a)** *preuve, idée, espoir* flimsy; *intrigue de roman* flimsy, weak; *personne* colourless; *caractère* colourless, weak. **(b)** *crème* runny; *bouillie, soupe* watery, thin.

inconsolable [ɛ̃kɔ̃sɔlabl(ə)] *adj personne* disconsolate, inconsolable; *chagrin* inconsolable.

inconsolé, e [ɛ̃kɔ̃sɔle] *adj personne* disconsolate; *chagrin* unconsoled.

inconsommable [ɛ̃kɔ̃sɔmabl(ə)] *adj* unfit for consumption (*attrib*).

inconstance [ɛ̃kɔ̃stɑ̃s] *nf* (*U*) *[conduite, temps, fortune]* fickleness; *[amour]* inconstancy, fickleness. (*littér*) **~s** (*dans le comportement*) inconsistencies; (*en amour*) infidelities, inconstancies.

inconstant, e [ɛ̃kɔ̃stɑ̃, ɑ̃t] *adj* (*V* **inconstance**) fickle; inconstant.

inconstatable [ɛ̃kɔ̃statabl(ə)] *adj* impossible to ascertain (*attrib*), unascertainable.

inconstitutionnalité [ɛ̃kɔ̃stitysjɔnalite] *nf* unconstitutionality.

inconstitutionnel, -elle [ɛ̃kɔ̃stitysjɔnɛl] *adj* unconstitutional.

inconstitutionnellement [ɛ̃kɔ̃stitysjɔnɛlmɑ̃] *adv* unconstitutionally.

incontestabilité [ɛ̃kɔ̃testabilite] *nf* incontestability.

incontestable [ɛ̃kɔ̃tɛstabl(ə)] *adj* (*indiscutable*) incontestable, unquestionable, indisputable. **il a réussi, c'est ~** he's succeeded, there is no doubt about that, it's undeniable that he has succeeded.

incontestablement [ɛ̃kɔ̃tɛstabləmɑ̃] *adv* incontestably, unquestionably, indisputably. **c'est prouvé? — ~** is it proved? — beyond any shadow of doubt.

incontesté, e [ɛ̃kɔ̃tɛste] *adj autorité, principe, fait* uncontested, undisputed. **le chef/maître ~** the undisputed chief/master; **le gagnant ~** the undisputed *ou* outright winner.

incontinence [ɛ̃kɔ̃tinɑ̃s] **1** *nf* **(a)** (*Méd*) incontinence. **~ (d'urine)** incontinence, enuresis (*T*); **~ nocturne** bedwetting, enuresis (*T*).
(b) (†, *littér: luxure*) incontinence.
2: incontinence de langage lack of restraint in speech; **incontinence verbale** garrulousness, verbal diarrhoea*.

incontinent[1], **e** [ɛ̃kɔ̃tinɑ̃, ɑ̃t] *adj* **(a)** (*Méd*) *personne* incontinent, enuretic (*T*); *vessie* weak. **(b)** (†, *littér: débauché*) incontinent (†, *littér*).

incontinent[2] [ɛ̃kɔ̃tinɑ̃] *adv* (†, *littér: sur-le-champ*) forthwith (†, *littér*).

incontrôlable [ɛ̃kɔ̃tʀolabl(ə)] *adj* (*non vérifiable*) unverifiable; (*irrépressible*) uncontrollable.

incontrôlé, e [ɛ̃kɔ̃tʀole] *adj* (*V* **incontrôlable**) unverified; uncontrolled.

inconvenance [ɛ̃kɔ̃vnɑ̃s] *nf* **(a)** (*U*) impropriety, unseemliness. **(b)** (*acte*) impropriety, indecorous *ou* unseemly behaviour (*U*); (*remarque*) impropriety, indecorous *ou* unseemly language (*U*).

inconvenant, e [ɛ̃kɔ̃vnɑ̃, ɑ̃t] *adj comportement, parole* improper, indecorous, unseemly; *question* improper; *personne* ill-mannered.

inconvénient [ɛ̃kɔ̃venjɑ̃] *nm* **(a)** (*désavantage*) *[situation, plan]* disadvantage, drawback, inconvenience.
(b) (*conséquences fâcheuses*) **~s** (unpleasant) consequences, drawbacks; **il subit maintenant les ~s d'une situation qu'il a lui-même créée** he now has to put up with the consequences *ou* drawbacks of a situation which he himself created; **tu feras ce que tu voudras mais nous ne voulons pas en supporter les ~s** you can do what you like but we don't want to have to suffer the consequences.
(c) (*risque*) **n'y a-t-il pas d'~ à mettre ce plat en faïence au four?** isn't there a risk in putting this earthenware plate in the oven?; **peut-on sans ~ prendre ces deux médicaments ensemble?** can one safely take these two medicines together?, is there any danger in taking these two medicines together?; **on peut modifier sans ~ notre itinéraire** we can easily change our route, we can change our route without any inconvenience.
(d) (*obstacle, objection*) **l'~ c'est que je ne serai pas là** the annoying thing is *ou* the one drawback is that I won't be there; **pouvez-vous sans ~ vous libérer jeudi?** would it be convenient for you to get away on Thursday?, will you be able to get away on Thursday without any difficulty?; **voyez-vous un ~** *ou* **y a-t-il un ~ à ce que je parte ce soir?** have you *ou* is there any objection to my leaving this evening?; **si vous n'y voyez pas d'~ ...** if you have no objections... .

inconvertibilité [ɛ̃kɔ̃vɛʀtibilite] *nf* inconvertibility.

inconvertible [ɛ̃kɔ̃vɛʀtibl(ə)] *adj* (*Fin*) inconvertible.

incoordination [ɛ̃kɔɔʀdinɑsjɔ̃] *nf [idées, opération]* lack of coordination; (*Méd*) incoordination, lack of coordination.

incorporable [ɛ̃kɔʀpɔʀabl(ə)] *adj* incorporable.

incorporalité [ɛ̃kɔʀpɔʀalite] *nf* incorporeality.

incorporation [ɛ̃kɔʀpɔʀɑsjɔ̃] *nf* **(a)** (*U: V* **incorporer**) mixing; blending; incorporation; insertion; integration. **(b)** (*Mil*) (*appel*) enlistment (*à* into); (*affectation*) posting; *V* **sursis**.

incorporéité [ɛ̃kɔʀpɔʀeite] *nf* = **incorporalité**.

incorporel, -elle [ɛ̃kɔʀpɔʀɛl] *adj* (*immatériel*) incorporeal.

incorporer [ɛ̃kɔʀpɔʀe] (1) *vt* **(a)** *substance, aliment* to mix (*à, avec* with, into), blend (*à, avec* with).
(b) *territoire* to incorporate (*dans, à* into); *chapitre* to incorporate (*dans* in, into), insert (*dans* in).
(c) *personne* to incorporate, integrate (*dans, à* into). **il a très bien su s'~ à notre groupe** he was very easily incorporated into our group, he fitted very easily into our group.
(d) (*Mil*) (*appeler*) to recruit. (*affecter*) **~ qn dans** to enrol *ou* enlist sb into; **on l'a incorporé dans l'infanterie** he was recruited *ou* drafted into the infantry.

incorrect, e [ɛ̃kɔʀɛkt, ɛkt(ə)] *adj* **(a)** (*fautif*) *réglage, interprétation* faulty; *solution* incorrect, wrong.
(b) (*inconvenant*) *terme, langage* improper, impolite; *tenue* incorrect, indecent.
(c) (*mal élevé*) *personne* discourteous, impolite.
(d) (*déloyal*) *personne, procédé* underhand. **être ~ avec qn** to treat sb in an underhand way, behave in an underhand way towards sb.

incorrectement [ɛ̃kɔʀɛktəmɑ̃] *adv* (*V* **incorrect**) faultily; incorrectly; wrongly; improperly; impolitely; indecently; discourteously; in an underhand way.

incorrection [ɛ̃kɔʀɛksjɔ̃] *nf* **(a)** (*U*) (*impropriété*) *[terme]* impropriety; (*inconvenance*) *[tenue, personne, langage]* impropriety, incorrectness; (*déloyauté*) *[procédés, concurrent]* dishonesty, underhand nature.
(b) (*terme impropre*) impropriety; (*action inconvenante*) incorrect *ou* improper *ou* impolite behaviour (*U*); (*remarque inconvenante*) impolite *ou* improper remark.

incorrigible [ɛ̃kɔʀiʒibl(ə)] *adj enfant, distraction* incorrigible. **cet enfant est ~!** this child is incorrigible!, this child will never learn!

incorruptibilité [ɛ̃kɔʀyptibilite] *nf* incorruptibility.

incorruptible [ɛ̃kɔʀyptibl(ə)] *adj* incorruptible.

incrédibilité [ɛ̃kʀedibilite] *nf* incredibility.

incrédule [ɛ̃kʀedyl] **1** *adj* (*sceptique*) incredulous; (*Rel*) unbelieving. **2** *nmf* (*Rel*) unbeliever, non-believer.

incrédulité [ɛ̃kʀedylite] *nf* (*V* **incrédule**) incredulity; unbelief, lack of belief. **avec ~** incredulously, with incredulity.

increvable [ɛ̃kʀəvabl(ə)] *adj ballon* which cannot be burst, unburstable; *pneu* unpuncturable, puncture-proof; (*: *infatigable*) *animal, travailleur* tireless; *moteur* which will never wear out *ou* pack in* (*Brit*).

incriminer [ɛ̃kʀimine] (1) *vt* (*mettre en cause*) *personne* to incriminate, accuse; *action, conduite* to bring under attack; (*mettre en doute*) *honnêteté, bonne foi* to call into question. **après avoir analysé la clause incriminée du contrat ...** after having analysed the offending clause *ou* the clause in question *ou* at issue in the contract... .

incrochetable [ɛ̃kʀɔʃtabl(ə)] *adj serrure* burglar-proof, which cannot be picked.

incroyable [ɛ̃kʀwajabl(ə)] *adj* (*invraisemblable*) incredible, unbelievable; (*inouï*) incredible, amazing.

incroyablement [ɛ̃kʀwajabləmɑ̃] *adv* (*étonnamment*) incredibly, unbelievably, amazingly.

incroyance [ɛ̃kʀwajɑ̃s] *nf* (*Rel*) unbelief. **être dans l'~** to be in a state of unbelief, be a non-believer.

incroyant, e [ɛ̃kʀwajɑ̃, ɑ̃t] **1** *adj* unbelieving. **2** *nm,f* unbeliever, non-believer.

incrustation [ɛ̃kʀystɑsjɔ̃] *nf* **(a)** (*Art*) (*technique*) inlaying; (*ornement*) inlay. **des ~s d'ivoire** inlaid ivory work, ivory inlays; **table à ~s d'ivoire** table inlaid with ivory; **~s de dentelle** lace panels.
(b) (*croûte*) (*dans un récipient*) fur; (*dans une chaudière*) scale; (*sur une roche*) incrustation. **pour empêcher l'~** to prevent furring, to prevent the formation of scale.

incruster [ɛ̃kʀyste] (1) **1** *vt* **(a)** (*Art*) (*insérer*) **~ qch dans** to inlay sth into; (*décorer*) **~ qch de** to inlay sth with; **incrusté de** inlaid with.
(b) *chaudière* to coat with scale, scale up; *récipient* to fur up.
2 s'incruster *vpr* **(a)** *[corps étranger, caillou]* **s'~ dans** to become embedded in.
(b) (*fig*) *[invité]* to take root (*fig*). **il va s'~ chez nous** he'll get himself settled down in our house and we'll never move him.
(c) *[radiateur, conduite]* to become incrusted (*de* with), fur up.

incubateur, -trice [ɛ̃kybatœʀ, tʀis] **1** *adj* incubating. **2** *nm* incubator.

incubation [ɛ̃kybɑsjɔ̃] *nf* (*Méd*) incubation; *[œuf]* incubation; (*fig*) *[révolte]* incubation, hatching. **période d'~** incubation period.

incuber [ɛ̃kybe] (1) *vt* to hatch, incubate.

inculcation [ɛ̃kylkɑsjɔ̃] *nf* inculcation, instilling.

inculpation [ɛ̃kylpɑsjɔ̃] *nf* (*chef d'accusation*) charge (*de* of); (*action*) charging. **sous l'~ de** on a charge of.

inculpé, e [ɛ̃kylpe] (*ptp de* **inculper**) *nm,f* person charged.
inculper [ɛ̃kylpe] (1) *vt* to charge (*de* with).
inculquer [ɛ̃kylke] (1) *vt*: ~ **à qn** *principes, politesse, notions* to inculcate in sb, instil into sb.
inculte [ɛ̃kylt(ə)] *adj terre* uncultivated; *chevelure, barbe* unkempt; *esprit, personne* uneducated.
incultivable [ɛ̃kyltivabl(ə)] *adj* unfarmable, unworkable.
inculture [ɛ̃kyltyʀ] *nf [personne]* lack of education; (*rare*) *[terre]* lack of cultivation.
incunable [ɛ̃kynabl(ə)] *nm* early printed book, incunabulum.
incurabilité [ɛ̃kyʀabilite] *nf* incurability, incurableness.
incurable [ɛ̃kyʀabl(ə)] **1** *adj* (*Méd*) incurable; (*fig*) *bêtise, ignorance* incurable (*épith*), hopeless (*épith*). **2** *nmf* (*Méd*) incurable.
incurablement [ɛ̃kyʀabləmɑ̃] *adv* incurably; (*fig*) hopelessly, incurably.
incurie [ɛ̃kyʀi] *nf* (*frm: négligence*) carelessness, negligence.
incursion [ɛ̃kyʀsjɔ̃] *nf* (*lit, fig*) incursion, foray (*en, dans* into). **faire une ~ dans** to make an incursion *ou* a foray into.
incurvé, e [ɛ̃kyʀve] (*ptp de* **incurver**) *adj* curved.
incurver [ɛ̃kyʀve] (1) **1** *vt pied de chaise, fer forgé* to form *ou* bend into a curve, curve. **2 s'incurver** *vpr* **(a)** *[barre]* to bend, curve; *[poutre]* to sag. **(b)** *[ligne, profil, route]* to curve.
indatable [ɛ̃databl(ə)] *adj* undatable.
Inde [ɛ̃d] *nf* India. **les ~s** the Indies; (†† *Pol: Antilles*) **les ~s occidentales** the West Indies; (††: *Indonésie*) **les ~s orientales** the East Indies; *V* **cochon**[1].
indébrouillable [ɛ̃debʀujabl(ə)] *adj affaire* almost impossible *ou* difficult to sort out (*attrib*).
indécemment [ɛ̃desamɑ̃] *adv* indecently.
indécence [ɛ̃desɑ̃s] *nf* **(a)** (*U: V* **indécent**) indecency; obscenity; impropriety. **(b)** (*action*) act of indecency, indecency; (*propos*) obscenity, indecency. **se livrer à des ~s** to indulge in indecent behaviour *ou* acts of indecency.
indécent, e [ɛ̃desɑ̃, ɑ̃t] *adj* (*impudique*) indecent; (*grivois*) *chanson* obscene, dirty*; (*déplacé*) improper, indecent; (*insolent*) *chance* disgusting. **il a une chance ~e** he's disgustingly lucky; **habille-toi, tu es ~!** get dressed, you're indecent! *ou* you're not decent!
indéchiffrable [ɛ̃deʃifʀabl(ə)] *adj* (*illisible*) *texte, partition* indecipherable; (*incompréhensible*) *traité, pensée* incomprehensible; (*impénétrable*) *personne, regard* inscrutable.
indéchirable [ɛ̃deʃiʀabl(ə)] *adj* tear-proof.
indécis, e [ɛ̃desi, iz] *adj* **(a)** *personne* (*par nature*) indecisive; (*temporairement*) undecided. **~ sur** *ou* **devant** undecided *ou* uncertain about; **c'est un ~** he's indecisive, he can never make up his mind.
(b) (*douteux*) *temps, paix* unsettled; *bataille* indecisive; *problème* undecided, unsettled; *victoire* undecided. **le résultat est encore ~** the result is as yet undecided.
(c) (*vague*) *réponse, sourire* vague; *pensée* undefined, vague; *forme, contour* indecisive, indistinct.
indécision [ɛ̃desizjɔ̃] *nf* (*irrésolution chronique*) indecisiveness; (*temporaire*) indecision, uncertainty (*sur* about). **je suis dans l'~ quant à nos projets pour l'été** I'm uncertain *ou* undecided about our plans for the summer.
indéclinable [ɛ̃deklinabl(ə)] *adj* indeclinable.
indécollable [ɛ̃dekɔlabl(ə)] *adj objet* that won't come unstuck *ou* come off, that cannot be unstuck. **ces invités sont ~s*** you can't get rid of these guests.
indécomposable [ɛ̃dekɔ̃pozabl(ə)] *adj* (*gén*) that cannot be broken down (*en* into).
indécrochable [ɛ̃dekʀɔʃabl(ə)] *adj* (*lit*) that won't come unhooked *ou* come off; (**fig*) *diplôme* which it's impossible to get.
indécrottable* [ɛ̃dekʀɔtabl(ə)] *adj* (*borné*) hopelessly thick*. (*incorrigible*) **c'est un paresseux ~** he's hopelessly lazy.
indéfectibilité [ɛ̃defɛktibilite] *nf* (*frm*) indestructibility.
indéfectible [ɛ̃defɛktibl(ə)] *adj* indestructible.
indéfectiblement [ɛ̃defɛktibləmɑ̃] *adv* unfailingly.
indéfendable [ɛ̃defɑ̃dabl(ə)] *adj* (*lit, fig*) indefensible.
indéfini, e [ɛ̃defini] *adj* (*vague*) *sentiment* undefined; (*indéterminé*) *quantité, durée* indeterminate, indefinite; (*Ling*) indefinite.
indéfiniment [ɛ̃definimɑ̃] *adv* indefinitely.
indéfinissable [ɛ̃definisabl(ə)] *adj* indefinable.
indéformable [ɛ̃defɔʀmabl(ə)] *adj* that will keep its shape.
indéfrisable† [ɛ̃defʀizabl(ə)] *nf* perm.
indélébile [ɛ̃delebil] *adj* (*lit, fig*) indelible.
indélébilité [ɛ̃delebilite] *nf* indelibility.
indélicat, e [ɛ̃delika, at] *adj* **(a)** (*mufle*) indelicate, tactless. **(b)** (*malhonnête*) *employé* dishonest; *procédé* dishonest, underhand.
indélicatement [ɛ̃delikatmɑ̃] *adv* (*V* **indélicat**) indelicately, tactlessly; dishonestly.
indélicatesse [ɛ̃delikatɛs] *nf* (*V* **indélicat**) indelicacy, tactlessness (*U*); dishonesty (*U*).
indémaillable [ɛ̃demajabl(ə)] *adj* ladderproof, run-resist. **en ~** in run-resist material; *jersey, bas* run-resist.
indemne [ɛ̃dɛmn(ə)] *adj* (*sain et sauf*) unharmed, unhurt, unscathed.
indemnisable [ɛ̃dɛmnizabl(ə)] *adj* entitled to compensation (*attrib*).
indemnisation [ɛ̃dɛmnizɑsjɔ̃] *nf* (*action*) indemnification; (*somme*) indemnity, compensation. **l'~ a été fixée à 10 F** the indemnity *ou* compensation was fixed at 10 francs; **10 F d'~** 10 francs compensation.
indemniser [ɛ̃dɛmnize] (1) *vt* (*dédommager*) to indemnify (*de* for); (*d'une perte*) to compensate (*de* for); (*de frais*) to indemnify, reimburse (*de* for). **se faire ~** to get indemnification *ou* compensation, get reimbursed; **~ qn en argent** to pay sb compensation in cash.
indemnité [ɛ̃dɛmnite] *nf* (*dédommagement*) *[perte]* compensation (*U*), indemnity; *[frais]* allowance. **~ de guerre** war indemnity; **~ de logement/de transport/de résidence** housing/travel/weighting allowance; **~ parlementaire** M.P.'s salary.
indémontable [ɛ̃demɔ̃tabl(ə)] *adj* which cannot be taken apart *ou* dismantled; (*fixé à une paroi etc*) which cannot be taken down.
indémontrable [ɛ̃demɔ̃tʀabl(ə)] *adj* indemonstrable, unprovable.
indéniable [ɛ̃denjabl(ə)] *adj* undeniable, indisputable, unquestionable. **vous avez grossi, c'est ~** there's no doubt that *ou* it's undeniable that you have put on weight.
indéniablement [ɛ̃denjabləmɑ̃] *adv* undeniably, indisputably, unquestionably.
indentation [ɛ̃dɑ̃tɑsjɔ̃] *nf* indentation.
indépassable [ɛ̃depɑsabl(ə)] *adj limite* impassable. **en plongée sous-marine, 800 mètres est la limite ~** in deep-sea diving 800 metres is the very deepest one can go; **au 100 mètres, 9 secondes est la limite ~** in the 100 metres race, 9 seconds cannot be bettered *ou* is unbeatable.
indépendamment [ɛ̃depɑ̃damɑ̃] *adv* **(a)** (*abstraction faite de*) **~ de** irrespective *ou* regardless of. **(b)** (*outre*) **~ de** apart from, over and above. **(c)** (†: *de façon indépendante*) independently.
indépendance [ɛ̃depɑ̃dɑ̃s] *nf* (*gén*) independence.
indépendant, e [ɛ̃depɑ̃dɑ̃, ɑ̃t] *adj* (*gén*) independent (*de* of). **pour des causes** *ou* **raisons ~es de notre volonté** for reasons beyond *ou* outside our control; **'à louer: chambre ~e'** 'to let: flatlet *ou* room with private *ou* separate entrance'.
indéracinable [ɛ̃deʀasinabl(ə)] *adj* ineradicable.
indéréglable [ɛ̃deʀeglabl(ə)] *adj* which will not break down.
Indes [ɛ̃d] *nfpl V* **Inde.**
indescriptible [ɛ̃dɛskʀiptibl(ə)] *adj* indescribable.
indésirable [ɛ̃deziʀabl(ə)] *adj, nmf* undesirable.
indestructibilité [ɛ̃dɛstʀyktibilite] *nf* indestructibility.
indestructible [ɛ̃dɛstʀyktibl(ə)] *adj objet, sentiment, matériau* indestructible; (*fig*) *marque, impression* indelible.
indéterminable [ɛ̃detɛʀminabl(ə)] *adj* indeterminable.
indétermination [ɛ̃detɛʀminɑsjɔ̃] *nf* **(a)** (*imprécision*) vagueness. **(b)** (*irrésolution*) (*chronique*) indecisiveness; (*temporaire*) indecision, uncertainty.
indéterminé, e [ɛ̃detɛʀmine] *adj* **(a)** (*non précisé*) *date, cause, nature* unspecified; *forme, longueur, quantité* indeterminate. **pour des raisons ~es** for reasons which were not determined; **à une date encore ~e** at a date to be specified *ou* as yet unspecified *ou* as yet undecided.
(b) (*imprécis*) *impression, sentiment* vague; *contours, goût* indeterminable, vague.
(c) (*rare: irrésolu*) **je suis encore ~ sur ce que je vais faire** I'm still undecided *ou* uncertain about what I'm going to do.
index [ɛ̃dɛks] *nm* **(a)** (*doigt*) forefinger, index finger; (*repère*) *[instrument]* pointer; (*aiguille*) *[cadran]* needle, pointer; (*liste alphabétique*) index; (*indice*) index.
(b) (*Rel*) **l'I ~** the Index; (*fig*) **mettre qn/qch à l'I ~** to blacklist sb/sth.
indexation [ɛ̃dɛksɑsjɔ̃] *nf* (*Écon*) indexing.
indexé, e [ɛ̃dɛkse] (*ptp de* **indexer**) *adj* indexed.
indexer [ɛ̃dɛkse] (1) *vt* (*Écon*) to index (*sur* to).
indic [ɛ̃dik] *nm* (*arg Police: abrév de* **indicateur**) (copper's) nark (*Brit arg*), grass (*arg*).
indicateur, -trice [ɛ̃dikatœʀ, tʀis] **1** *adj V* **panneau, poteau.**
2 *nm,f*: **~ (de police)** (police) informer.
3 *nm* **(a)** (*guide*) guide; (*horaire*) timetable.
(b) (*Tech: compteur, cadran*) gauge, indicator.
(c) (*Chim: substance*) **~ (coloré)** indicator.
4: indicateur d'altitude altimeter; **indicateur des chemins de fer** railway timetable; (*Naut*) **indicateur de direction** direction finder; *[voitures]* (direction) indicator; **indicateur immobilier** property gazette; **indicateur de niveau d'eau** water(-level) gauge; **indicateur de pression** pressure gauge; **indicateur des rues** street directory; **indicateur de vitesse** (*Aut*) speedometer; (*Aviat*) airspeed indicator.
indicatif, -ive [ɛ̃dikatif, iv] **1** *adj* indicative (*de* of); (*Ling*) indicative; *V* **titre.**
2 *nm* **(a)** (*Rad: mélodie*) theme *ou* signature tune.
(b) *[poste émetteur]* **~ (d'appel)** call sign; (*Téléc*) **~ téléphonique** (dialling) code.
(c) (*Ling*) **l'~** the indicative.
indication [ɛ̃dikɑsjɔ̃] **1** *nf* **(a)** (*renseignement*) piece of information, information (*U*). **qui vous a donné cette ~?** who gave you that (piece of) information?, who told you that?
(b) (*mention*) **quelle ~ porte la pancarte?** what does the notice say?, what has the notice got on it?; **sans ~ de date/de prix** with no indication of the date/price, without a date stamp/price label; **les ~s du compteur** the reading on the meter; **l'annuaire portait l'~ du téléphone** the directory gave the phone number.
(c) (*U: notification*) *[prix, danger, mode d'emploi]* indication. **l'~ du virage dangereux a permis d'éviter les accidents** signposting the dangerous bend has prevented accidents; **l'~ d'une date est impérative** a date stamp must be shown, the date must be indicated; **l'~ de l'heure vous sera fournie ultérieurement** you will be given the time *ou* informed of the time later; **rendre obligatoire l'~ des prix** to make it compulsory to mark *ou* show prices.
(d) (*indice*) indication (*de* of). **c'est une ~ suffisante de sa culpabilité** that's a good enough indication of his guilt.

(e) (*directive*) instruction, direction. **sauf ~ contraire** unless otherwise stated; **sur son ~** on his instruction.

2: (*Comm*) **indication d'origine** place of origin; **on doit faire figurer l'indication d'origine** one must show the place of origin; (*Théât*) **indications scéniques** stage directions; (*Méd*) **indication (thérapeutique)** *[remède, traitement]* indication.

indice [ɛ̃dis] *nm* **(a)** (*signe*) indication, sign. **être l'~ de** to be an indication *ou* a sign of; **il n'y avait pas le moindre ~ de leur passage** there was no sign *ou* evidence *ou* indication that they had been there.

(b) (*élément d'information*) clue; (*Jur: preuve*) piece of evidence. **rechercher des ~s du crime** to look for clues about the crime.

(c) (*Math*) suffix; (*degré de racine*) index; *[fonctionnaire]* rating, grading. (*Math*) **'a' ~ 2** a (suffix) two; **~ des prix/du coût de la vie** price/cost of living index; (*Aut*) **~ d'octane** rating; (*Admin*) **~ de traitement** salary grading.

indiciaire [ɛ̃disjɛʀ] *adj traitement* grade-related. **classement ~ d'un fonctionnaire** grading of a civil servant.

indicible [ɛ̃disibl(ə)] *adj* inexpressible, unspeakable.

indiciblement [ɛ̃disibləmɑ̃] *adv* inexpressibly, unspeakably.

indien, -ienne [ɛ̃djɛ̃, jɛn] **1** *adj* Indian; *V* **chanvre, file, océan.**

2 *nm,f*: **I~(ne)** *[Inde]* Indian; *[Amérique]* (Red *ou* American) Indian.

3 indienne *nf* **(a)** (*Hist: tissu*) printed calico.

(b) overarm sidestroke. **nager** *ou* **faire l'~ne** to swim with an overarm stroke.

indifféremment [ɛ̃difeʀamɑ̃] *adv* **(a)** (*indistinctement*) **supporter ~ le froid et le chaud** to stand heat and cold equally well, stand either heat or cold; **fonctionner ~ au gaz ou à l'électricité** to run equally well *ou* just as well on gas or electricity; **manger de tout ~** to eat indiscriminately, eat (just) anything; **il est impoli ~ avec ses chefs et ses subordonnés** he is equally impolite to those above him and to those below him; **sa haine se portait ~ sur les blancs et les noirs** his hatred was directed indiscriminately at blacks and whites *ou* was directed at blacks and whites alike.

(b) (*littér: avec indifférence*) indifferently.

indifférence [ɛ̃difeʀɑ̃s] *nf* **(a)** (*désintérêt*) indifference (*à l'égard de* to, towards), lack of concern (*à l'égard de* for). **(b)** (*froideur*) indifference (*envers* to, towards).

indifférenciable [ɛ̃difeʀɑ̃sjabl(ə)] *adj* which cannot be differentiated.

indifférenciation [ɛ̃difeʀɑ̃sjɑsjɔ̃] *nf* lack of differentiation.

indifférencié, e [ɛ̃difeʀɑ̃sje] *adj* (*Bio, Sci*) undifferentiated; (*littér*) indistinguishable.

indifférent, e [ɛ̃difeʀɑ̃, ɑ̃t] **1** *adj* **(a)** (*sans importance*) **il est ~ de faire ceci ou cela** it doesn't matter *ou* it's immaterial whether one does this or that; **elle m'est/ne m'est pas ~e** I am/am not indifferent to her; **il m'est ~ de partir ou de rester** it is indifferent *ou* immaterial to me *ou* it doesn't matter to me whether I go or stay; **parler de choses ~es** to talk of this and that.

(b) (*peu intéressé*) *spectateur* indifferent (*à* to, towards), unconcerned (*à* about). **il était ~ à tout ce qui ne concernait pas sa spécialité** he was indifferent to *ou* unconcerned about everything outside his own speciality.

2 *nm,f* indifferent *ou* unconcerned person.

indifférer [ɛ̃difeʀe] (6) *vt*: **ceci/mon opinion l'indiffère (profondément)** he's (quite) indifferent to this/my opinion, he couldn't care less about this/my opinion.

indigence [ɛ̃diʒɑ̃s] *nf* (*misère*) poverty, destitution, indigence (*frm*); (*fig*) *[style]* poverty. **tomber/être dans l'~** to become/be destitute; **~ intellectuelle** intellectual penury, poverty of intellect; **~ d'idées** poverty *ou* paucity of ideas.

indigène [ɛ̃diʒɛn] **1** *nmf* (*aux colonies*) native; (*personne du pays*) local.

2 *adj* **(a)** (*des non-colons*) *coutume* native; *population* native, indigenous; (*Bot, Zool: non importé*) indigenous, native. **visitez la ville ~** visit the old town.

(b) (*des gens du pays*) *main d'œuvre, population* local.

indigent, e [ɛ̃diʒɑ̃, ɑ̃t] **1** *adj personne* destitute, poverty-stricken, indigent (*frm*); *imagination* poor; *végétation* poor, sparse. **2** *nm,f* pauper. **les ~s** the destitute, the poor.

indigeste [ɛ̃diʒɛst(ə)] *adj* (*lit, fig*) indigestible, difficult to digest (*attrib*).

indigestion [ɛ̃diʒɛstjɔ̃] *nf* attack of indigestion, indigestion (*U*). **il s'est donné une ~ de pâtisseries** (*lit*) he gave himself *ou* he got indigestion from eating too many cakes; (*fig: manger à satiété*) he sickened himself of cakes, he had a surfeit of cakes; (*fig*) **avoir/se donner une ~ de romans policiers** to be sick of/sicken o.s. of detective stories; **j'en ai une ~, de toutes ces histoires*** I'm sick (and tired) of all these complications*, I'm fed up with all these complications*.

indignation [ɛ̃diɲɑsjɔ̃] *nf* indignation. **avec ~** indignantly.

indigne [ɛ̃diɲ] *adj* **(a)** (*pas digne de*) **~ de** *amitié, confiance, personne* unworthy of, not worthy of; **il est ~ de ton amitié** he is unworthy of *ou* does not deserve your friendship; **il est ~ de vivre** he doesn't deserve to live, he's not fit to live; **ce livre est ~ de figurer dans ma bibliothèque** this book is not worthy of a place in my library; **c'est ~ de vous** (*travail, emploi*) it is beneath you; (*conduite, attitude*) it is unworthy of you.

(b) (*abject*) *acte* shameful; (*lit, fig*) *personne* unworthy. **mère/époux ~** unworthy mother/husband; **c'est un père ~** he's not fit to be a father.

indigné, e [ɛ̃diɲe] (*ptp de* **indigner**) *adj* indignant (*par* at).

indignement [ɛ̃diɲmɑ̃] *adv* shamefully.

indigner [ɛ̃diɲe] (1) **1** *vt*: **~ qn** to make sb indignant.

2 s'indigner *vpr* (*se fâcher*) to become *ou* get indignant *ou* annoyed (*de* about, at, *contre* with, about, at). (*être écœuré*) **s'~ que/de, être indigné que/de** to be indignant that/about *ou* at; **je l'écoutais s'~ contre les spéculateurs** I listened to him going on* *ou* sounding off* indignantly about speculators; **je m'indigne de penser/voir que** it makes me indignant *ou* it fills me with indignation *ou* it annoys me to think/see that.

indignité [ɛ̃diɲite] *nf* **(a)** (*U*) *[personne]* unworthiness; *[conduite]* baseness, shamefulness. **(b)** (*acte*) shameful act. **c'est une ~!** it's a disgrace!, it's shameful!

indigo [ɛ̃digo] **1** *nm* (*matière, couleur*) indigo. **2** *adj inv* indigo (blue).

indigotier [ɛ̃digɔtje] *nm* (*Bot*) indigo-plant.

indiqué, e [ɛ̃dike] (*ptp de* **indiquer**) *adj* **(a)** (*conseillé*) advisable. **ce n'est pas très ~** it's not really advisable, it's really not the best thing to do.

(b) (*adéquat*) **prenons ça, c'est tout ~** let's take that — it's just what we need; **pour ce travail M X est tout ~** Mr X is the obvious choice *ou* is just the man we need for that job; **c'est le moyen ~** it's the best *ou* right way to do it; **c'était un sujet tout ~** it was obviously an appropriate *ou* a suitable subject.

(c) (*prescrit*) *médicament, traitement* appropriate. **le traitement ~ dans ce cas est ...** the appropriate *ou* normal treatment in this case is ...; **ce remède est particulièrement ~ dans les cas graves** this drug is particularly appropriate *ou* suitable for serious cases.

indiquer [ɛ̃dike] (1) *vt* **(a)** (*désigner*) to point out, indicate. **~ qch/qn du doigt** to point sth/sb out (*à qn* to sb), point to sth/sb, indicate sth/sb; **~ qch de la main/tête** to indicate sth with one's hand/with a nod; **il m'indiqua du regard le coupable** his glance *ou* look directed me towards the culprit; **~ la réception/les toilettes à qn** to direct sb to *ou* show sb the way to the reception desk/the toilets.

(b) (*montrer*) *[flèche, aiguille, voyant, écriteau]* to show, indicate. **~ l'heure** *[montre]* to give *ou* show *ou* tell the time; **la petite aiguille indique les heures** the small hand shows *ou* marks the hours; **l'horloge indiquait 2 heures** the clock said *ou* showed it was 2 o'clock; **qu'indique la pancarte?** what does the sign say?

(c) (*recommander*) **~ à qn** *livre, hôtel, médecin* to tell sb of, suggest to sb.

(d) (*dire*) *[personne] heure, solution* to tell; *dangers, désavantages* to point out, show. **il m'indiqua comment le réparer** he told me how to mend it; **il m'en indiqua le mode d'emploi** he told me how to use it.

(e) (*fixer*) *heure, date, rendez-vous* to give, name. **à l'heure indiquée, je ...** at the time indicated *ou* stated, I ...; at the agreed *ou* appointed time, I ...; **à la date indiquée** on the given *ou* agreed day.

(f) (*faire figurer*) *[étiquette, plan, cartographe]* to show; *[table, index]* to give, show. **est-ce indiqué sur la facture/dans l'annuaire?** is it given *ou* mentioned on the invoice/in the directory?; **il a sommairement indiqué les fenêtres sur le plan** he quickly marked *ou* drew in the windows on the plan; **quelques traits pour ~ les spectateurs/ombres** a few strokes to give an impression of spectators/shadows; **quelques rapides croquis pour ~ le jeu de scène** a few rapid sketches to give a rough idea of the action.

(g) (*dénoter*) to indicate, point to. **tout indique que les prix vont augmenter** everything indicates that prices are going to rise, everything points to a forthcoming rise in prices; **cela indique une certaine négligence/hésitation de sa part** that shows *ou* points to a certain carelessness/hesitation on his part.

indirect, e [ɛ̃diʀɛkt, ɛkt(ə)] *adj* (*gén*) indirect; (*Jur*) *ligne, héritier* collateral. **d'une manière ~e** in a roundabout *ou* an indirect way; **apprendre qch de manière ~e** to hear of sth in a roundabout way; *V* **discours, éclairage, impôt.**

indirectement [ɛ̃diʀɛktəmɑ̃] *adv* (*gén*) indirectly; (*de façon détournée*) *faire savoir, apprendre* in a roundabout way.

indiscernable [ɛ̃disɛʀnabl(ə)] *adj* indiscernible, imperceptible.

indiscipline [ɛ̃disiplin] *nf* (*insubordination*) indiscipline, lack of discipline. **faire preuve d'~** to behave in an undisciplined *ou* unruly manner.

indiscipliné, e [ɛ̃disipline] *adj troupes, écolier* undisciplined; *cheveux* unmanageable.

indiscret, -ète [ɛ̃diskʀɛ, ɛt] *adj* **(a)** (*trop curieux*) *personne* indiscreet, inquisitive; *question, curiosité* indiscreet; *regard, yeux* inquisitive, prying. **à l'abri des regards ~s/des oreilles ~ètes** out of the reach of *ou* away from prying *ou* inquisitive eyes/of inquisitive eavesdroppers; **mettre des documents à l'abri des ~s** to put documents out of the reach of inquisitive people. **(b)** (*qui divulgue*) *personne, bavardage* indiscreet. **secret révélé par des langues ~ètes** secret revealed by wagging tongues *ou* indiscreet prattlers; **ne confiez rien aux ~s** don't entrust anything to people who can't keep quiet.

indiscrètement [ɛ̃diskʀɛtmɑ̃] *adv* (*V* **indiscret**) indiscreetly; inquisitively.

indiscrétion [ɛ̃diskʀesjɔ̃] *nf* **(a)** (*curiosité: V* **indiscret**) indiscreetness, indiscretion; inquisitiveness. **excusez mon ~** forgive my indiscretion; (*suivi d'une question*) forgive me for asking; **sans ~, peut-on savoir si ...** without wanting to be *ou* without being indiscreet, may we ask whether ... .

(b) (*tendance à divulguer*) indiscretion. **il est d'une telle ~!** he's so indiscreet!

(c) (*action ou parole indiscrète*) indiscreet word *ou* act, indiscretion. **son sort dépend d'une ~** it needs only one indiscreet remark to seal his fate; **la moindre ~ vous perdrait** the slightest indiscretion would finish you.

indiscutable [ɛ̃diskytabl(ə)] *adj* indisputable, unquestionable.

indiscutablement [ɛ̃diskytabləmɑ̃] *adv* indisputably, unquestionably.

indiscuté, e [ɛ̃diskyte] *adj* undisputed.

indispensable [ɛ̃dispɑ̃sabl(ə)] **1** *adj* essential. **ces outils/précautions sont ~s** these tools/precautions are essential; **ce collaborateur m'est ~** this collaborator is indispensable to me, I cannot do without this collaborator; **il est ~ que/de faire** it is essential *ou* absolutely necessary *ou* vital that/to do; **je crois qu'il est ~ qu'ils y aillent** I think it's vital *ou* essential that they (should) go; **emporter les vêtements ~s (pour le voyage)** to take the clothes which are essential *ou* indispensable (for the journey); **prendre les précautions ~s** to take the necessary precautions; **crédits/travaux ~s à la construction d'un bâtiment** funds/work essential *ou* vital for the construction of a building; **l'eau est un élément ~ à la vie** water is an essential element for life; **savoir se rendre ~** to make o.s. indispensable.

2 *nm*: **nous n'avions que l'~** we only had what was absolutely essential *ou* necessary *ou* indispensable; **faire l'~ d'abord** to do what is essential *ou* absolutely necessary first; **l'~ est de ...** it is absolutely necessary *ou* essential to ... .

indisponibilité [ɛ̃dispɔnibilite] *nf* unavailability.

indisponible [ɛ̃dispɔnibl(ə)] *adj* (*gén*) not available (*attrib*), unavailable; (*Jur*) unavailable.

indisposé, e [ɛ̃dispoze] (*ptp de* **indisposer**) *adj* (*fatigué, malade*) indisposed, unwell, out of sorts*; (*euph*) *femme* indisposed.

indisposer [ɛ̃dispoze] (1) *vt* (*rendre malade*) *[aliment, chaleur]* to upset; (*mécontenter*) *[personne, remarque]* to antagonize. **il a des allures qui m'indisposent** his way of behaving irritates me *ou* puts me off him*; **~ qn contre soi** to antagonize sb, set sb against one, alienate sb; **tout l'indispose!** anything annoys hims, he takes a dislike to everything; **cette scène trop violente risque d'~ les spectateurs** this very violent scene is likely to alienate *ou* antagonize the audience.

indisposition [ɛ̃dispozisjɔ̃] *nf* (*malaise*) (slight) indisposition, upset; (*euph: règles*) period.

indissociable [ɛ̃disɔsjabl(ə)] *adj* *problèmes* indissociable.

indissolubilité [ɛ̃disɔlybilite] *nf* indissolubility.

indissoluble [ɛ̃disɔlybl(ə)] *adj* indissoluble.

indissolublement [ɛ̃disɔlybləmɑ̃] *adv* indissolubly. **~ liés** *problèmes* indissolubly linked (*à* to).

indistinct, e [ɛ̃distɛ̃(kt), ɛ̃kt(ə)] *adj* *forme, idée, souvenir* indistinct, vague; *rumeur, murmure* indistinct, confused; *couleurs* vague. **des voix ~es** a confused murmur of voices.

indistinctement [ɛ̃distɛ̃ktəmɑ̃] *adv* **(a)** (*confusément: V* **indistinct**) indistinctly; vaguely; confusedly. **des bruits qui me provenaient ~ du salon** confused noises which reached my ears from the lounge.

(b) (*ensemble*) indiscriminately. **confondus ~ dans la réprobation générale** indiscriminately included in the general criticism; **tuant ~ femmes et enfants** killing women and children indiscriminately *ou* without distinction.

(c) (*indifféremment*) **cette cuisinière marche ~ au gaz ou à l'électricité** this cooker runs either on gas or on electricity *ou* runs equally well *ou* just as well on gas or on electricity; **sa haine se portait ~ sur les blancs et les noirs** his hatred was directed indiscriminately at blacks and whites *ou* was directed at blacks and whites alike.

individu [ɛ̃dividy] *nm* **(a)** (*gén, Bio: unité*) individual.

(b) (*hum: anatomie*) **fort occupé de son ~** very taken up with himself, very preoccupied with his own little self; **dans la partie la plus charnue de son ~** in the fleshiest part of his anatomy.

(c) (*péj: homme*) fellow, individual, character. **un ~ l'aborda** a fellow came up to him; **il aperçut un drôle d'~/un ~ chevelu** he noticed an odd-looking/a long-haired character *ou* individual.

individualisation [ɛ̃dividɥalizɑsjɔ̃] *nf* **(a)** (*V* **individualiser**) individualization; personalization; tailoring to (suit) individual *ou* particular requirements. (*Jur*) **l'~ d'une peine** sentencing according to the needs of the offender.

(b) (*V* **s'individualiser**) individualization.

individualisé, e [ɛ̃dividɥalize] (*ptp de* **individualiser**) *adj* *caractères, groupe* distinctive; *objet personnel, voiture* personalized. **groupe fortement ~** highly distinctive group, group with a distinctive identity; **des solutions ~es selon les différents besoins** solutions which are tailored to suit individual *ou* particular requirements.

individualiser [ɛ̃dividɥalize] (1) **1** *vt* (*caractériser*) to individualize; (*personnaliser*) *objet personnel, voiture* to personalize; *solutions, horaire* to tailor to (suit) individual *ou* particular requirements; (*Jur*) *peine* to suit to the needs of the offender.

2 s'individualiser *vpr [personne, groupe, région]* to acquire an identity of one's *ou* its own, become more individual.

individualisme [ɛ̃dividɥalism(ə)] *nm* individualism.

individualiste [ɛ̃dividɥalist(ə)] **1** *adj* individualistic. **2** *nmf* individualist.

individualité [ɛ̃dividɥalite] *nf* (*caractère individuel*) individuality; (*personne*) individual; (*personnalité*) personality.

individuel, -elle [ɛ̃dividɥɛl] *adj* **(a)** (*propre à l'individu*) (*gén*) individual; *responsabilité, défaut, contrôle, livret* personal, individual; *caractères* distinctive, individual. **propriété ~le** personal *ou* private property; **liberté ~le** personal freedom, freedom of the individual.

(b) (*isolé*) *fait* individual, isolated; *sachet* individual. **les cas ~s seront examinés** individual cases *ou* each individual case will beexamined.

(c) (*Sport*) **épreuve ~le** individual event.

individuellement [ɛ̃dividɥɛlmɑ̃] *adv* individually.

indivis, e [ɛ̃divi, iz] *adj* (*Jur*) *propriété, succession* undivided, joint (*épith*); *propriétaires* joint (*épith*). **par ~** *posséder* jointly; *transmettre* to be held in common.

indivisibilité [ɛ̃divizibilite] *nf* indivisibility.

indivisible [ɛ̃divizibl(ə)] *adj* indivisible.

indivisiblement [ɛ̃divizibləmɑ̃] *adv* indivisibly.

indivision [ɛ̃divizjɔ̃] *nf* (*Jur*) joint possession *ou* ownership.

Indochine [ɛ̃dɔʃin] *nf* Indochina.

indochinois, e [ɛ̃dɔʃinwa, waz] **1** *adj* Indochinese. **2** *nm,f*: **I~(e)** Indochinese.

indocile [ɛ̃dɔsil] *adj* *enfant* unruly, recalcitrant, intractable; *mémoire* intractable.

indocilité [ɛ̃dɔsilite] *nf* (*V* **indocile**) unruliness; recalcitrance; intractability.

indo-européen, -éenne [ɛ̃dɔœʀɔpeɛ̃, eɛn] **1** *adj* Indo-European. **2** *nm* (*Ling*) Indo-European. **3** *nm,f*: **Indo-Européen(ne)** Indo-European.

indolemment [ɛ̃dɔlamɑ̃] *adv* indolently.

indolence [ɛ̃dɔlɑ̃s] *nf [élève]* idleness, indolence; *[pouvoirs publics]* apathy, lethargy; *[air, geste, regard]* indolence, languidness.

indolent, e [ɛ̃dɔlɑ̃, ɑ̃t] *adj* (*V* **indolence**) idle; indolent; apathetic; lethargic; languid.

indolore [ɛ̃dɔlɔʀ] *adj* painless.

indomptable [ɛ̃dɔ̃tabl(ə)] *adj* *animal, adversaire, peuple, (hum) femme* untameable, which *ou* who cannot be tamed; *cheval* untameable, which cannot be broken *ou* mastered; *enfant* unmanageable, uncontrollable; *caractère, courage, volonté* indomitable, invincible; *passion, haine* ungovernable, invincible, uncontrollable.

indompté, e [ɛ̃dɔ̃te] *adj* *enfant, animal, peuple* untamed, wild; *cheval* unbroken, untamed; *courage* undaunted; *énergie* unharnessed, untamed; *passion* ungoverned, unsuppressed.

Indonésie [ɛ̃dɔnezi] *nf* Indonesia.

indonésien, -enne [ɛ̃dɔnezjɛ̃, ɛn] **1** *adj* Indonesian. **2** *nm,f*: **I~(ne)** Indonesian.

indou, e [ɛ̃du] = **hindou.**

indu, e [ɛ̃dy] *adj* (*hum, littér: déplacé*) *joie* unseemly; *dépenses* unwarranted. **sans optimisme ~** without undue optimism; *V* **heure.**

indubitable [ɛ̃dybitabl(ə)] *adj* *preuve* indubitable, undoubted. **c'est ~** there is no doubt about it, it's beyond doubt, it's indubitable.

indubitablement [ɛ̃dybitabləmɑ̃] *adv* (*assurément*) undoubtedly, indubitably. **vous vous êtes ~ trompé** you have undoubtedly made a mistake.

inducteur, -trice [ɛ̃dyktœʀ, tʀis] **1** *adj* (*gén*) inductive. **2** *nm* (*aimant*) inductor.

inductif, -ive [ɛ̃dyktif, iv] *adj* (*gén*) inductive.

induction [ɛ̃dyksjɔ̃] *nf* (*gén*) induction.

induire [ɛ̃dɥiʀ] (38) *vt* **(a) ~ qn en erreur** to mislead sb, lead sb astray.

(b) (†: *inciter*) **~ qn à péché, gourmandise** to lead sb into; **~ qn à faire** to induce sb to do.

(c) (*inférer*) to infer, induce (*de* from). **j'en induis que** I infer from it that.

induit, e [ɛ̃dɥi, it] (*Élec*) **1** *adj* induced. **2** *nm* armature.

indulgence [ɛ̃dylʒɑ̃s] *nf* **(a)** (*U: V* **indulgent**) indulgence; leniency. **une erreur qui a rencontré l'~ du jury** a mistake for which the jury made allowances *ou* which the jury was prepared to overlook; **il a demandé l'~ du jury pour son client** he asked the jury to make allowances for *ou* to show leniency towards his client; **avec ~** leniently, with leniency, indulgently; **sans ~** (*adj*) unsympathetic; (*adv*) unsympathetically; **regard plein d'~** indulgent look.

(b) (*Rel*) indulgence.

indulgent, e [ɛ̃dylʒɑ̃, ɑ̃t] *adj* *parent* indulgent (*avec* with); *juge, examinateur* lenient (*envers* towards); *critique, commentaire* indulgent; *regard* indulgent. **15, c'est une note trop ~e** 15 is (far) too lenient *ou* kind a mark; **se montrer ~** *[juge]* to show leniency; *[examinateur]* to be lenient.

indûment [ɛ̃dymɑ̃] *adv* *protester* unduly; *détenir* without due cause *ou* reason, wrongfully. **s'ingérer ~ dans les affaires de qn** to interfere unnecessarily in sb's business.

industrialisation [ɛ̃dystʀijalizɑsjɔ̃] *nf* industrialization.

industrialiser [ɛ̃dystʀijalize] (1) **1** *vt* to industrialize. **2 s'industrialiser** *vpr* to become industrialized.

industrie [ɛ̃dystʀi] **1** *nf* **(a)** (*activité, secteur, branche*) industry. **~ légère/lourde** light/heavy industry; **~ alimentaire/chimique/automobile** food/chemical/car *ou* automobile (*US*) industry; **doter un pays d'une ~** to provide a country with an industrial structure; *V* **pointe.**

(b) (*entreprise*) industry, industrial concern; *V* **capitaine.**

(c) (*littér*, †) (*ingéniosité*) ingenuity; (*ruse*) cunning.

(d) (*activité*) **exerçant sa coupable ~** practising his disreputable business *ou* trade; *V* **chevalier.**

2: industries du livre book-related industries; **industrie de luxe** luxury goods industry; **industrie de précision** precision tool industry; **l'industrie du spectacle** the entertainment business, show business; **industrie de transformation** processing industry.

industriel, -elle [ɛ̃dystʀijɛl] **1** *adj* industrial. **fer ~** wrought iron; **bronze ~** gun-metal; *V* **quantité. 2** *nm* (*chef d'industrie*) industrialist, manufacturer. **les ~s du textile/de l'automobile** textile/car *ou* automobile (*US*) manufacturers.

industriellement [ɛ̃dystʀijɛlmɑ̃] *adv* industrially. **géré ~** run on *ou* along industrial lines.

industrieux, -euse [ɛ̃dystʀijø, øz] *adj* (*littér: besogneux*) industrious.

inébranlable [inebʀɑ̃labl(ə)] *adj* **(a)** *adversaire, interlocuteur* steadfast, unwavering; *personne, foi, résolution* unshakeable, steadfast, unwavering; *certitude* unshakeable, unwavering. **il était ~ dans sa conviction que ...** he was steadfast *ou* unshakeable *ou* unwavering in his belief that ...

(b) *objet massif, monumental* solid; *objet fixé ou encastré* immovable, solidly *ou* firmly fixed. **il avait si bien enfoncé le pieu qu'il était maintenant ~** he had hammered the post in so hard that it was now as firm *ou* solid as a rock *ou* that it was now quite immovable.

inébranlablement [inebʀɑ̃lablәmɑ̃] *adv* unshakeably.

inéchangeable [ineʃɑ̃ʒabl(ә)] *adj* (*Comm*) *article* not exchangeable (*attrib*).

inécoutable [inekutabl(ә)] *adj musique* unbearable, unbearable to listen to (*attrib*).

inécouté, e [inekute] *adj avis* unheeded; *prophète, expert* unlistened to (*attrib*), unheeded.

inédit, e [inedi, it] **1** *adj* **(a)** (*non publié*) *texte, auteur* (previously *ou* hitherto) unpublished.

(b) (*nouveau*) *méthode, trouvaille* novel, new, original.

2 *nm* **(a)** (*texte inédit*) (previously *ou* hitherto) unpublished material (*U*) *ou* work.

(b) (*le neuf*) **l'~** novelty (*U*); **c'est de l'~** that's novel.

inéducable [inedykabl(ә)] *adj* ineducable.

ineffable [inefabl(ә)] *adj* ineffable.

ineffablement [inefablәmɑ̃] *adv* ineffably.

ineffaçable [inefasabl(ә)] *adj* indelible, ineffaceable.

inefficace [inefikas] *adj remède, mesure* ineffective, ineffectual, inefficacious; *machine, employé* inefficient.

inefficacement [inefikasmɑ̃] *adv* (*V* **inefficace**) ineffectively, ineffectually, inefficaciously; inefficiently.

inefficacité [inefikasite] *nf* (*V* **inefficace**) ineffectiveness, ineffectualness, inefficacy; inefficiency.

inégal, e, *mpl* **-aux** [inegal, o] *adj* **(a)** (*différent*) unequal. **d'~e grosseur** of unequal size; **de force ~e** of unequal strength; **les hommes sont ~aux** men are not equal.

(b) (*irrégulier*) *sol, pas, rythme, mouvement* uneven; *pouls* irregular, uneven; *artiste, sportif* erratic; *œuvre, jeu* uneven; *étalement, répartition* uneven; *humeur, caractère* uneven, changeable; *conduite* changeable. **d'intérêt ~** of varying *ou* mixed interest.

(c) (*disproportionné*) *lutte, partage* unequal.

inégalable [inegalabl(ә)] *adj* incomparable, matchless.

inégalé, e [inegale] *adj* unequalled, unrivalled, unmatched.

inégalement [inegalmɑ̃] *adv* (*différemment, injustement*) unequally; (*irrégulièrement*) unevenly. **livre ~ apprécié** book which met (*ou* meets) with varying approval.

inégalité [inegalite] *nf* **(a)** (*différence*) *[hauteurs, volumes]* difference (*de* between); *[sommes, parts]* difference, disparity (*de* between). **cette ~ d'âge ne les gênait pas** this difference *ou* disparity in their ages didn't worry them; **l'~ de l'offre et de la demande** the difference *ou* disparity between supply and demand.

(b) (*Math*) inequality.

(c) (*injustice*) inequality.

(d) (*irrégularité*) *[sol, pas, rythme, répartition]* unevenness; *[humeur, caractère]* unevenness, changeability; *[conduite]* changeability. **dans ce livre il y a des ~s** there are weak parts in this book, the book is a bit patchy; **~s de terrain** unevenness of the ground, bumps in the ground; **~s d'humeur** unevenness of temper.

inélégamment [inelegamɑ̃] *adv* inelegantly.

inélégance [inelegɑ̃s] *nf* (*V* **inélégant**) inelegance; ungainliness; discourtesy.

inélégant, e [inelegɑ̃, ɑ̃t] *adj* **(a)** (*sans grâce*) *geste, toilette, femme* inelegant; *allure* inelegant, ungainly. **(b)** (*indélicat*) *procédés* discourteous. **c'était très ~ de sa part d'agir ainsi** it was very poor taste on his part to behave like this.

inéligibilité [ineliʒibilite] *nf* (*Pol*) ineligibility.

inéligible [ineliʒibl(ә)] *adj* (*Pol*) ineligible.

inéluctabilité [inelyktabilite] *nf* inescapability, ineluctability (*frm*).

inéluctable [inelyktabl(ә)] *adj, nm* inescapable, ineluctable (*frm*).

inéluctablement [inelyktablәmɑ̃] *adv* inescapably, ineluctably (*frm*).

inemployable [inɑ̃plwajabl(ә)] *adj procédé* unusable.

inemployé, e [inɑ̃plwaje] *adj* (*sans utilisation présente*) *méthode, outil, argent, talent* unused; (*gâché*) *dévouement, énergie* unchannelled, unused.

inénarrable [inenaʀabl(ә)] *adj* **(a)** (*désopilant*) *incident, scène* hilarious, priceless*, too funny for words (*attrib*); *vêtement, démarche* incredibly funny, priceless*. **son ~ mari** her incredible husband*. **(b)** (*incroyable*) *péripéties, aventure* incredible.

inentamé, e [inɑ̃tame] *adj réserve d'essence, d'argent* intact (*attrib*); *victuailles* intact (*attrib*), untouched; *bouteille* unopened; *énergie, moral* (as yet) intact (*attrib*).

inéprouvé, e [inepʀuve] *adj méthode, vertu, procédé* untested, untried, not yet put to the test (*attrib*); *émotion* not yet experienced (*attrib*).

inepte [inɛpt(ә)] *adj personne* inept, useless*, hopeless*; *histoire, raisonnement* inept.

ineptie [inɛpsi] *nf* **(a)** (*U*) (*gén*) ineptitude. **(b)** (*acte, propos*) ineptitude; (*idée, œuvre*) nonsense (*U*), rubbish (*U*). **dire des ~s** to talk nonsense; **ce qu'il a fait est une ~** what he did was utterly stupid.

inépuisable [inepɥizabl(ә)] *adj* inexhaustible. **il est ~ sur ce sujet** he could talk for ever on that subject.

inéquation [inekwasjɔ̃] *nf* (*Math*) inequation.

inéquitable [inekitabl(ә)] *adj* inequitable.

inerte [inɛʀt(ә)] *adj* (*immobile*) *corps, membre* lifeless; *visage* expressionless; (*sans réaction*) *personne* passive, inert; *esprit, élève* apathetic; (*Sci*) inert. **réagis, ne reste pas ~ sur ta chaise, à ne rien faire** do something — don't just sit there passively as if there's nothing to do.

inertie [inɛʀsi] *nf [personne]* inertia, passivity, apathy; *[service administratif]* apathy, inertia; *[élève]* apathy; (*Phys*) inertia; *V* **force**.

inescompté, e [inɛskɔ̃te] *adj* unexpected, unhoped-for.

inespéré, e [inɛspeʀe] *adj* unexpected, unhoped-for.

inesthétique [inɛstetik] *adj pylône, usine, cicatrice* unsightly; *démarche, posture* ungainly.

inestimable [inɛstimabl(ә)] *adj aide* inestimable, invaluable; *valeur* priceless, incalculable.

inévitable [inevitabl(ә)] *adj obstacle, accident* unavoidable; (*fatal*) *résultat* inevitable, inescapable; (*hum*) *chapeau, cigare* inevitable. **c'était ~!** it was inevitable!, it was bound to happen!, it HAD to happen!; **l'~** the inevitable.

inévitablement [inevitablәmɑ̃] *adv* inevitably.

inexact, e [inɛgza(kt), akt(ә)] *adj* **(a)** *renseignement, calcul, traduction, historien* inaccurate, inexact. **non, c'est ~** no, that's not correct *ou* that's wrong. **(b)** (*sans ponctualité*) unpunctual. **être ~ à un rendez-vous** to be late for an appointment.

inexactement [inɛgzaktәmɑ̃] *adv traduire, relater* inaccurately, incorrectly.

inexactitude [inɛgzaktityd] *nf* **(a)** (*U: manque de précision*) inaccuracy. **(b)** (*erreur*) inaccuracy. **(c)** (*manque de ponctualité*) unpunctuality (*U*).

inexaucé, e [inɛgzose] *adj prière* (as yet) unanswered; *vœu* (as yet) unfulfilled.

inexcusable [inɛkskyzabl(ә)] *adj faute, action* inexcusable, unforgivable. **vous êtes ~ (d'avoir fait cela)** you had no excuse (for doing that), it was inexcusable *ou* unforgivable of you (to have done that).

inexécutable [inɛgzekytabl(ә)] *adj projet* impractical, impracticable, unworkable, not feasible (*attrib*); *travail* which cannot be carried out, impractical, impracticable; *musique* unplayable; *ordre* which cannot be carried out *ou* executed.

inexécution [inɛgzekysjɔ̃] *nf [contrat, obligation]* nonfulfilment.

inexercé, e [inɛgzɛʀse] *adj soldats* inexperienced, untrained; *oreille* unpractised.

inexistant, e [inɛgzistɑ̃, ɑ̃t] *adj* (*absent*) *service d'ordre, réseau téléphonique, aide* non-existent; (*imaginaire*) *difficultés* imaginary, non-existent. (*péj*) **quant à son mari, il est ~** as for her husband, he's a (complete) nonentity.

inexistence [inɛgzistɑ̃s] *nf* non-existence.

inexorabilité [inɛgzɔʀabilite] *nf* (*V* **inexorable**) inexorability; inflexibility.

inexorable [inɛgzɔʀabl(ә)] *adj destin, vieillesse* inexorable; *juge* unyielding, inflexible, inexorable (*littér*). **il fut ~ à leurs prières** he was unmoved by their entreaties.

inexorablement [inɛgzɔʀablәmɑ̃] *adv* inexorably.

inexpérience [inɛkspeʀjɑ̃s] *nf* inexperience, lack of experience.

inexpérimenté, e [inɛkspeʀimɑ̃te] *adj personne* inexperienced; *mouvements, gestes* inexpert; *arme, produit* untested.

inexpiable [inɛkspjabl(ә)] *adj* inexpiable.

inexpié, e [inɛkspje] *adj* inexpiated.

inexplicable [inɛksplikabl(ә)] *adj* unexplainable, inexplicable; (*déconcertant*) inexplicable.

inexplicablement [inɛksplikablәmɑ̃] *adv* inexplicably, unexplainably.

inexpliqué, e [inɛksplike] *adj* unexplained.

inexploitable [inɛksplwatabl(ә)] *adj* unexploitable.

inexploité, e [inɛksplwate] *adj* unexploited.

inexplorable [inɛksplɔʀabl(ә)] *adj* unexplorable.

inexploré, e [inɛksplɔʀe] *adj* unexplored.

inexplosible [inɛksplozibl(ә)] *adj* non-explosive.

inexpressif, -ive [inɛkspʀesif, iv] *adj visage* expressionless, inexpressive, blank; *style, mots* inexpressive.

inexprimable [inɛkspʀimabl(ә)] *adj, nm* inexpressible.

inexprimé, e [inɛkspʀime] *adj sentiment* unexpressed; *reproches* unspoken.

inexpugnable [inɛkspygnabl(ә)] *adj citadelle* impregnable, unexpugnable (*T*).

inextensible [inɛkstɑ̃sibl(ә)] *adj matériau* that does not stretch, unstretchable; *étoffe* non-stretch; (*fig*) inextensible.

in extenso [inɛkstɛ̃so] **1** *loc adv publier, lire* in full. **2** *loc adj texte, discours* full (*épith*).

inextinguible [inɛkstɛ̃gibl(ә)] *adj* (*littér*) *passion* inextinguishable; *haine, besoin, soif* unquenchable; *rire* uncontrollable.

in extremis [inɛkstʀemis] **1** *loc adv sauver, arriver* at the last minute. **2** *loc adj sauvetage, succès* last-minute (*épith*); *mariage, testament* deathbed (*épith*).

inextricable [inɛkstʀikabl(ә)] *adj* inextricable.

inextricablement [inɛkstʀikablәmɑ̃] *adv* inextricably.

infaillibilité [ɛ̃fajibilite] *nf* infallibility.

infaillible [ɛ̃fajibl(ә)] *adj méthode, remède, personne* infallible; *instinct* unerring, infallible.

infailliblement [ɛ̃fajiblәmɑ̃] *adv* (*à coup sûr*) inevitably, without fail; (*sans erreur*) infallibly.

infaisable [ɛ̃fәzabl(ә)] *adj* impossible, impracticable, not feasible (*attrib*). **ce n'est pas ~** it's not impossible, it's (just about) feasible.

infamant, e [ɛ̃famɑ̃, ɑ̃t] *adj acte* infamous, ignominious; *accusation* libellous; *propos* defamatory; *terme* derogatory; (*Jur*) *peine* infamous (*involving exile or deprivation of civil rights*).

infâme [ɛ̃fɑm] *adj métier, action, trahison* unspeakable, vile, loathsome; *traître* infamous, vile; *complaisance, servilité* shameful, vile; *entremetteur, spéculateur* despicable; *odeur, taudis* revolting, vile, disgusting.
infamie [ɛ̃fami] *nf* **(a)** (*honte*) infamy. **couvert d'~** covered with infamy.
(b) (*caractère infâme*) *[personne, acte]* infamy.
(c) (*insulte*) vile abuse (*U*); (*action infâme*) infamous *ou* vile deed; (*ragot*) slanderous gossip (*U*). **c'est une ~** it's absolutely scandalous, it's an absolute scandal; **dire des ~s sur le compte de qn** to make slanderous remarks about sb.
infant [ɛ̃fɑ̃] *nm* infante.
infante [ɛ̃fɑ̃t] *nf* infanta.
infanterie [ɛ̃fɑ̃tʀi] *nf* infantry. **avec une ~ de 2.000 hommes** with 2,000 foot, with an infantry of 2,000 men; **~ de marine** marines; **d'~** *bataillon etc* infantry (*épith*).
infanticide [ɛ̃fɑ̃tisid] **1** *adj* infanticidal. **2** *nmf* (*personne*) infanticide, child-killer. **3** *nm* (*acte*) infanticide.
infantile [ɛ̃fɑ̃til] *adj* (*Méd, Psych*) *maladie* infantile; *médecine, clinique* child (*épith*); (*puéril*) infantile, childish, babyish.
infantilisme [ɛ̃fɑ̃tilism(ə)] *nm* (*Méd, Psych*) infantilism; (*puérilité*) infantile *ou* childish *ou* babyish behaviour. **c'est de l'~!** how childish!
infarctus [ɛ̃faʀktys] *nm* (*Méd*) infarction (*T*), infarct (*T*). **~ du myocarde** coronary thrombosis, myocardial infarction (*T*); **il a eu ou fait trois ~** he has had three coronaries.
infatigable [ɛ̃fatigabl(ə)] *adj* indefatigable, tireless, untiring.
infatigablement [ɛ̃fatigabləmɑ̃] *adv* indefatigably, tirelessly, untiringly.
infatuation [ɛ̃fatɥɑsjɔ̃] *nf* (*frm: vanité*) self-conceit, self-importance.
infatué, e [ɛ̃fatɥe] (*ptp de* **s'infatuer**) *adj air, personne* conceited, vain. **être ~ de son importance** to be full of one's own importance; **être ~ de son physique** to be vain *ou* conceited about one's looks; **~ de sa personne** *ou* **de lui-même** full of himself *ou* of self-conceit, self-important.
infatuer (s') [ɛ̃fatɥe] (1) *vpr* **(a)** (*s'engouer de*) **s'~ de** *personne, choses* to become infatuated with.
(b) (*tirer vanité de*) **s'~ de son importance** to become full of one's own importance; **s'~ de son physique** to become vain *ou* conceited about one's looks; **s'~ (de soi-même)** to become full of o.s. *ou* of self-conceit.
infécond, e [ɛ̃fekɔ̃, ɔ̃d] *adj terre, animal* barren, sterile, infertile; *esprit* infertile, sterile.
infécondité [ɛ̃fekɔ̃dite] *nf* (*V* **infécond**) barrenness; sterility; infertility.
infect, e [ɛ̃fɛkt, ɛkt(ə)] *adj goût, nourriture, vin, attitude*, vile, revolting; *temps* vile, filthy, foul; *taudis, chambre* vile, filthy; *travail, personne* vile; *livre, film* (*très mauvais*) rotten*, appalling; (*scandaleux*) revolting, vile. **odeur ~e** stench, vile *ou* foul smell.
infecter [ɛ̃fɛkte] (1) **1** *vt* (*gén*) *atmosphère, eau* to contaminate; (*Méd*) *personne, plaie* to infect; (*fig littér*) to poison, infect. **2 s'infecter** *vpr [plaie]* to become infected, turn septic.
infectieux, -euse [ɛ̃fɛksjø, øz] *adj* (*Méd*) infectious.
infection [ɛ̃fɛksjɔ̃] *nf* (*Méd*) infection; (*puanteur*) stench. **quelle ~!, c'est une ~!** what a stench!
inféodation [ɛ̃feɔdɑsjɔ̃] *nf* (*Pol*) allegiance (*à* to); (*Hist*) infeudation, enfeoffment.
inféoder [ɛ̃feɔde] (1) **1** *vt* (*Hist*) to enfeoff. **2 s'inféoder** *vpr*: **s'~ à** to give one's allegiance to, pledge allegiance *ou* o.s. to; **être inféodé à** to be pledged to.
inférence [ɛ̃feʀɑ̃s] *nf* inference.
inférer [ɛ̃feʀe] (6) *vt* to infer, gather (*de* from). **j'infère de ceci que ..., j'en infère que ...** I infer *ou* gather from this that ..., this leads me to conclude that ... .
inférieur, e [ɛ̃feʀjœʀ] **1** *adj* **(a)** (*dans l'espace*) (*gén*) lower; *mâchoire, lèvre* lower, bottom; *planètes* inferior. **la partie ~e de l'objet** the bottom part of the object; **le feu a pris dans les étages ~s** fire broke out on the lower floors; **descendez à l'étage ~** go down to the next floor *ou* the floor below, go to the next floor down.
(b) (*dans une hiérarchie*) *classes sociales, animaux, végétaux* lower. **à l'échelon ~** on the next rung down; **d'un rang ~** of a lower rank, lower in rank.
(c) *qualité* inferior, poorer; *vitesse* lower; *nombre* smaller, lower; *quantité* smaller; *intelligence, esprit* inferior. **forces ~es en nombre** forces inferior *ou* smaller in number(s).
(d) ~ à *nombre* less *ou* lower *ou* smaller than, below; *somme* smaller *ou* less than; *production* inferior to, less *ou* lower than; **note ~e à 20** mark below 20 *ou* less than 20; **intelligence/qualité ~e à la moyenne** below average *ou* lower than average intelligence/quality; **travail d'un niveau ~ à ...** work of a lower standard than ... *ou* below the standard of ...; **roman/auteur ~ à un autre** novel/author inferior to another; **être hiérarchiquement ~ à qn** to be lower (down) than sb *ou* be below sb in the hierarchy; (*fig*) **il est ~ à sa tâche** he isn't equal to his task, he isn't up to his task*.
2 *nm,f* inferior.
inférieurement [ɛ̃feʀjœʀmɑ̃] *adv* (*moins bien*) less well. **~ équipé** *armée, laboratoire, bateau* less well-equipped.
infériorité [ɛ̃feʀjɔʀite] *nf* inferiority. **~ en nombre** numerical inferiority, inferiority in numbers; **en état** *ou* **position d'~** in an inferior position, in a position of inferiority; *V* **comparatif, complexe.**
infernal, e, *mpl* **-aux** [ɛ̃fɛʀnal, o] *adj* **(a)** (*intolérable*) *bruit, allure, chaleur* infernal. **cet enfant est ~** this child is absolutely poisonous *ou* a little fiend.
(b) (*satanique*) *caractère, personne, complot* diabolical, infernal, devilish.
(c) (*effrayant*) *vision, supplice* diabolical; *V* **machine**³.
(d) (*Myth*) *divinité* infernal.
infertile [ɛ̃fɛʀtil] *adj* (*lit, fig*) infertile.
infertilité [ɛ̃fɛʀtilite] *nf* (*littér: lit, fig*) infertility.
infestation [ɛ̃fɛstɑsjɔ̃] *nf* (*Méd*) infestation.
infester [ɛ̃fɛste] (1) *vt* (*gén*) to infest, overrun; (*Méd*) to infest. **infesté de moustiques** infested with mosquitoes, mosquito-infested *ou* -ridden; **infesté de souris/pirates** infested with *ou* overrun with *ou* by mice/pirates.
infidèle [ɛ̃fidɛl] **1** *adj* **(a)** *ami* unfaithful, disloyal (*à qn* to sb); *époux* unfaithful (*à qn* to sb). (*littér*) **être ~ à une promesse** to be untrue *ou* faithless (*littér*) to one's promise.
(b) *récit, traduction, traducteur* unfaithful, inaccurate; *mémoire* unreliable.
(c) (*Rel*) infidel.
2 *nmf* (*Rel*) infidel.
infidèlement [ɛ̃fidɛlmɑ̃] *adv traduire, raconter* unfaithfully, inaccurately.
infidélité [ɛ̃fidelite] *nf* **(a)** (*U: inconstance*) *[ami]* disloyalty, unfaithfulness; *[époux]* infidelity, unfaithfulness (*à* to). (*littér*) **~ à une promesse** faithlessness (*littér*) to a promise.
(b) (*acte déloyal*) *[époux]* **elle lui pardonna ses ~s** she forgave his infidelities; **faire une ~ à qn** to be unfaithful to sb; **il a fait bien des ~s à sa femme** he has been unfaithful (to his wife) on many occasions, he has been guilty of infidelity (to his wife) on many occasions; (*hum*) **faire des ~s à son boucher/éditeur** to be unfaithful to *ou* forsake one's butcher/publisher (*hum*).
(c) (*U: manque d'exactitude*) *[description, historien]* inaccuracy; *[mémoire]* unreliability.
(d) (*erreur*) *[description, traducteur]* inaccuracy. **on trouve beaucoup d'~s dans cette traduction** we find many inaccuracies in this translation.
infiltration [ɛ̃filtʀɑsjɔ̃] *nf [hommes, idées]* infiltration; *[liquide]* percolation, infiltration; (*Méd*) infiltration. (*Méd*) **se faire faire des ~s** to have injections.
infiltrer (s') [ɛ̃filtʀe] (1) *vpr [hommes, idées]* to infiltrate; *[liquide]* to percolate (through), infiltrate; *[lumière]* to filter through. **s'~ dans** *[personne]* to infiltrate; *[idées]* to filter into, infiltrate (into); *[liquide]* to percolate (through), infiltrate; *[lumière]* to filter into; **s'~ dans un groupe/chez l'ennemi** to infiltrate a group/the enemy.
infime [ɛ̃fim] *adj* (*minuscule*) tiny, minute, minuscule; (*inférieur*) lowly, inferior.
infini, e [ɛ̃fini] **1** *adj* **(a)** (*Math, Philos, Rel*) infinite.
(b) (*sans limites*) *espace* infinite, boundless; *patience, bonté* infinite, unlimited, boundless; *douleur* immense; *prudence, soin* infinite, immeasurable; *quantité* infinite, unlimited; *bêtise* infinite, immeasurable.
(c) (*interminable*) *luttes, propos* interminable, never-ending. **un temps ~ me parut s'écouler** an eternity seemed to pass.
2 *nm*: **l'~** (*Philos*) the infinite; (*Math, Phot*) infinity; (*Phot*) **faire la mise au point à** *ou* **sur l'~** to focus to infinity; **l'~ des cieux** heaven's immensity, the infinity of heaven; **à l'~** *discourir* ad infinitum; *multiplier* to infinity; *se diversifier, faire varier* infinitely; **les blés s'étendaient à l'~** the corn stretched away endlessly into the distance.
infiniment [ɛ̃finimɑ̃] *adv* **(a)** (*immensément*) infinitely.
(b) (*sens affaibli: beaucoup*) infinitely. **~ long/grand** immensely *ou* infinitely long/large; **je vous suis ~ reconnaissant** I am immensely *ou* extremely *ou* infinitely grateful (to you); **je regrette ~** I'm extremely sorry; **ça me plaît ~** I like it immensely; **~ meilleur/plus intelligent** infinitely better/more intelligent; **avec ~ de soin/de tendresse** with infinite care/tenderness.
(c) l'~ grand the infinitely great; **l'~ petit** the infinitesimal.
infinité [ɛ̃finite] *nf* (*littér*) infinity. (*quantité infinie*) **une ~ de** an infinite number of.
infinitésimal, e, *mpl* **-aux** [ɛ̃finitezimal, o] *adj* (*Math, gén*) infinitesimal.
infinitif, -ive [ɛ̃finitif, iv] *adj, nm* infinitive. **~ de narration** historic infinitive.
infirmatif, -ive [ɛ̃fiʀmatif, iv] *adj* (*Jur*) invalidating. **~ de** invalidating, annulling, quashing.
infirmation [ɛ̃fiʀmɑsjɔ̃] *nf* (*Jur*) invalidation, annulment, quashing.
infirme [ɛ̃fiʀm(ə)] **1** *adj personne* crippled, disabled; (*avec l'âge*) infirm. **l'accident l'avait rendu ~** the accident had left him crippled *ou* disabled; **il est ~ du bras droit** he's crippled in his right arm, he has a crippled *ou* disabled right arm.
2 *nmf* cripple, disabled person. **les ~s** the crippled *ou* disabled; **~ du travail** industrially disabled person; **~ de guerre** war cripple.
infirmer [ɛ̃fiʀme] (1) *vt* (*démentir*) to invalidate; (*Jur*), *décision, jugement* to invalidate, annul, quash.
infirmerie [ɛ̃fiʀməʀi] *nf* (*gén*) infirmary; *[école]* sick bay, infirmary; *[navire]* sick bay.
infirmier [ɛ̃fiʀmje] *nm* (male) nurse.
infirmière [ɛ̃fiʀmjɛʀ] *nf* nurse. **~ chef** sister (*Brit*); **~ diplômée** registered nurse; **~-major** matron; **~ visiteuse** visiting nurse, ≃ district nurse; *V* **élève.**
infirmité [ɛ̃fiʀmite] *nf* **(a)** (*invalidité*) disability. **les ~s de la vieillesse** the infirmities of old age. **(b)** (†: *imperfection*) weakness, failing.
infixe [ɛ̃fiks(ə)] *nm* (*Ling*) infix.
inflammable [ɛ̃flamabl(ə)] *adj* inflammable, flammable.
inflammation [ɛ̃flamɑsjɔ̃] *nf* (*Méd*) inflammation.
inflammatoire [ɛ̃flamatwaʀ] *adj* (*Méd*) inflammatory.
inflation [ɛ̃flɑsjɔ̃] *nf* (*Écon*) inflation; (*fig*) (excessive) growth *ou* increase (*de* in).

inflationniste [ɛ̃flɑsjɔnist(ə)] **1** *adj tendance, danger* inflationary; *politique, économiste* inflationist. **2** *nmf* inflationist.
infléchi, e [ɛ̃fleʃi] (*ptp de* **infléchir**) *adj voyelle* inflected.
infléchir [ɛ̃fleʃiʀ] (2) **1** *vt* (*lit*) *rayon* to inflect, bend; (*fig*) *politique* to reorientate, bend. **2 s'infléchir** *vpr [route]* to bend, curve round; *[poutre]* to sag; (*fig*) *[politique]* to shift, move.
infléchissement [ɛ̃fleʃismɑ̃] *nm* (*V* **infléchir** (*fig*)) reorientation; (*V* **s'infléchir** (*fig*)) (slight) shift (*de* in).
inflexibilité [ɛ̃flɛksibilite] *nf* (*V* **inflexible**) inflexibility; rigidity.
inflexible [ɛ̃flɛksibl(ə)] *adj caractère, personne* inflexible, unyielding; *volonté* inflexible; *règle* inflexible, rigid. **il demeura ~ dans sa résolution** he remained inflexible *ou* unyielding *ou* unbending in his resolution.
inflexiblement [ɛ̃flɛksibləmɑ̃] *adv* (*V* **inflexible**) inflexibly; rigidly.
inflexion [ɛ̃flɛksjɔ̃] *nf* **(a)** (*inclinaison*) bend. **d'une légère ~ de la tête/du corps** with a slight nod/bow.
(b) *[voix]* inflexion, modulation.
(c) (*Ling*) **~ vocalique** vowel inflexion.
(d) (*déviation*) *[route, direction]* bend, curve (*de* in); (*Phys*) *[rayon]* deflection; (*Math*) *[courbe]* inflexion.
(e) (*fig*) *[politique]* reorientation (*de* of), shift (*de* in).
infliger [ɛ̃fliʒe] (3) *vt punition, tâche* to inflict (*à* on); *amende* to impose (*à* on); *affront* to deliver (*à* to). **~ sa présence à qn** to inflict one's presence *ou* o.s. on sb.
inflorescence [ɛ̃flɔʀesɑ̃s] *nf* inflorescence.
influençable [ɛ̃flyɑ̃sabl(ə)] *adj* easily influenced.
influence [ɛ̃flyɑ̃s] *nf* influence (*sur* on, upon). **c'est quelqu'un qui a de l'~** he's a person of influence, he's an influential person; **avoir une ~ bénéfique/néfaste sur** *[climat, médicament]* to have a beneficial/harmful effect on; **être sous l'~ de l'alcool** to be under the influence of alcohol; **être sous l'~ de la colère** to be in the grip of anger; **zone/sphère d'~** zone/sphere of influence; *V* **trafic.**
influencer [ɛ̃flyɑ̃se] (3) *vt* (*gén*) to influence; (*agir sur*) to act upon. **il ne faut pas se laisser ~ par lui** you mustn't let yourself be influenced by him, you mustn't let him influence you.
influent, e [ɛ̃flyɑ̃, ɑ̃t] *adj* influential.
influenza [ɛ̃flyɑ̃za] *nf* (*rare*) influenza.
influer [ɛ̃flye] (1) *vi*: **~ sur** to influence, have an influence on.
influx [ɛ̃fly] *nm* **(a)** (*Méd*) **~ nerveux** (nerve) impulse; **il manque d'~ nerveux** he lacks go *ou* drive. **(b)** (*fig: fluide*) influx††, inflow††.
in-folio, *pl* **in-folio(s)** [infɔljo] *nm, adj* folio.
informateur, -trice [ɛ̃fɔʀmatœʀ, tʀis] *nm,f* informant.
informaticien, -ienne [ɛ̃fɔʀmatisjɛ̃, jɛn] *nm,f* computer scientist.
informatif, -ive [ɛ̃fɔʀmatif, iv] *adj brochure* informative. **compagne de publicité ~ive pour un produit/une chaîne d'hôtels** advertising campaign giving information on a product/a hotel chain.
information [ɛ̃fɔʀmɑsjɔ̃] *nf* **(a)** (*renseignement*) piece of information; (*Presse, TV: nouvelle*) piece of news, news (*sg*). **voilà une ~ intéressante** here's an interesting piece of information *ou* some interesting information; **recueillir des ~s sur** to gather information on; **voilà nos ~s** here *ou* this is the news; **~s politiques** political news; **nous recevons une ~ de dernière minute** we've just received some last-minute *ou* late news.
(b) (*U: diffusion de renseignements*) information. **pour votre ~, sachez que** for your (own) information you should know that; **pour l'~ des voyageurs** for the information of travellers; **assurer l'~ du public en matière d'impôts** to ensure that the public is informed *ou* has information on the subject of taxation; **l'opposition a la main sur l'~** the opposition has got hold of the information network; **journal/presse d'~** serious newspaper/press.
(c) (*connaissances*) information, knowledge. **c'est un homme qui a une grande ~** he is a mine of information, he's a man with a great fund of information *ou* knowledge.
(d) (*Ordinateurs, Sci*) **l'~** information; **traitement de l'~** data processing, processing of information; **théorie de l'~** information theory.
(e) (*Jur*) **~ officielle** (judicial) inquiry; **ouvrir une ~** to start an initial *ou* a preliminary investigation.
informatique [ɛ̃fɔʀmatik] **1** *nf* (*science*) computer science; (*techniques*) data processing. **il est dans l'~** he's in computers; **l'ère de l'~** the age of the computer. **2** *adj* computer (*épith*).
informatisation [ɛ̃fɔʀmatizɑsjɔ̃] *nf* computerization.
informatiser [ɛ̃fɔʀmatize] (1) *vt* to computerize.
informe [ɛ̃fɔʀm(ə)] *adj masse, tas* shapeless, formless; *vêtement* shapeless; *visage, être* misshapen, ill-shaped, ill-formed; (*inachevé*) *projet* rough, undefined.
informé [ɛ̃fɔʀme] *nm V* **jusque.**
informer [ɛ̃fɔʀme] (1) **1** *vt* **(a)** (*d'un fait*) to inform, tell (*de* of, about); (*au sujet d'un problème*) to inform (*sur* about). **m'ayant informé de ce fait** having informed *ou* told me of this fact, having acquainted me with this fact; **s'il vient, vous voudrez bien m'en ~** if he comes, please let me know *ou* inform me *ou* tell me; **on vous a mal informé** (*faussement*) you've been misinformed *ou* wrongly informed; (*imparfaitement*) you've been badly informed *ou* ill-informed; **journaux/milieux bien informés** well-informed *ou* authoritative newspapers/circles.
(b) (*Philos*) **les concepts informent la matière** concepts impart *ou* give form to matter.
2 *vi* (*Jur*) **~ sur un crime** to inquire into *ou* investigate a crime; **~ contre X** to start inquiries concerning X.
3 s'informer *vpr* (*d'un fait*) to inquire, find out, ask (*de* about); (*dans une matière*) to inform o.s. (*sur le sujet de* about). **où puis-je m'~ de l'heure/à ce sujet/si?** where can I inquire *ou* find out *ou* ask about the time/about this matter/whether?; **s'~ de la santé de qn** to ask after *ou* inquire after *ou* about sb's health; **la nécessité pour l'homme moderne de s'~ (sur certains sujets)** the necessity for modern man to inform himself (about certain topics).
informulé, e [ɛ̃fɔʀmyle] *adj* unformulated.
infortune [ɛ̃fɔʀtyn] *nf* (*revers*) misfortune; (*U: adversité*) ill fortune, misfortune. **~s conjugales** marital misfortunes; **le récit de ses ~s** the tale of his woes *ou* misfortunes; *V* **compagnon.**
infortuné, e [ɛ̃fɔʀtyne] **1** *adj personne* hapless (*épith*), ill-fated, luckless, wretched; *démarche, décision* ill-fated, wretched. **2** *nm,f* (poor) wretch.
infraction [ɛ̃fʀaksjɔ̃] *nf* (*délit*) offence. (*Aut*) **être en ~** to be committing an offence, be in breach of the law; **~ à la loi** breach *ou* violation *ou* infraction of the law; **~ à la coutume** breach *ou* violation of custom; **règle qui ne souffre aucune ~** rule which suffers *ou* allows no infringement.
infranchissable [ɛ̃fʀɑ̃ʃisabl(ə)] *adj* (*lit*) impassable; (*fig*) insurmountable, insuperable.
infrangible [ɛ̃fʀɑ̃ʒibl(ə)] *adj* (*littér*) infrangible (*littér*).
infrarouge [ɛ̃fʀaʀuʒ] *adj, nm* infrared.
infra-son, *pl* **infra-sons** [ɛ̃fʀasɔ̃] *nm* infrasonic vibration.
infrastructure [ɛ̃fʀastʀyktyʀ] *nf* (*Constr*) substructure, understructure; (*Écon, fig*) infrastructure; (*Aviat*) ground installations.
infréquentable [ɛ̃fʀekɑ̃tabl(ə)] *adj* not to be associated with. **ce sont des gens ~s** they're people you just don't associate with *ou* mix with.
infroissable [ɛ̃fʀwasabl(ə)] *adj* uncrushable, crease-resistant.
infructueux, -euse [ɛ̃fʀyktɥø, øz] *adj* fruitless, unfruitful, unsuccessful.
infumable [ɛ̃fymabl(ə)] *adj* unsmokable.
infus, e [ɛ̃fy, yz] *adj* (*littér*) innate, inborn (*à* in); *V* **science.**
infuser [ɛ̃fyze] (1) *vt* **(a)** (*plus gén* **faire ~**) *tisane* to infuse; *thé* to brew, infuse. **laisser ~ le thé quelques minutes** leave the tea to brew *ou* infuse *ou* draw a few minutes; **le thé est-il assez infusé?** has the tea brewed *ou* infused (long) enough?
(b) (*fig*) to infuse (*à* into). **~ un sang nouveau à qch/à qn** to infuse *ou* inject *ou* instil new life into sth/sb.
infusion [ɛ̃fyzjɔ̃] *nf* **(a)** (*tisane*) infusion, herb tea. **~ de tilleul** lime (blossom) tea; **boire une ~** to drink some herb tea *ou* an infusion. **(b)** (*action*) infusion. **préparé par ~** prepared by infusion.
ingambe [ɛ̃gɑ̃b] *adj* spry, nimble.
ingénier (s') [ɛ̃ʒenje] (7) *vpr*: **s'~ à faire** to strive (hard) to do, try hard to do; (*iro*) **chaque fois qu'on range ses affaires, il s'ingénie à les remettre en désordre** every time you tidy up his belongings, he goes out of his way *ou* he contrives to mess them up again.
ingénieur [ɛ̃ʒenjœʀ] *nm* engineer. **~ chimiste/des mines/agronome** chemical/mining/agricultural engineer; **~ électricien/en génie civil** electrical/civil engineer; **~ du son** sound engineer; **~ des eaux et forêts** forestry expert.
ingénieusement [ɛ̃ʒenjøzmɑ̃] *adv* ingeniously, cleverly.
ingénieux, -euse [ɛ̃ʒenjø, øz] *adj* ingenious, clever.
ingéniosité [ɛ̃ʒenjozite] *nf* ingenuity, cleverness.
ingénu, e [ɛ̃ʒeny] **1** *adj* ingenuous, artless, naïve. **2** *nm,f* ingenuous *ou* artless *ou* naïve person. **3 ingénue** *nf* (*Théât*) ingénue. **jouer les ~es** to play ingénue roles.
ingénuité [ɛ̃ʒenɥite] *nf* ingenuousness, artlessness, naïvety.
ingénument [ɛ̃ʒenymɑ̃] *adv* ingenuously, artlessly, naïvely.
ingérence [ɛ̃ʒeʀɑ̃s] *nf* interference, interfering (*U*), meddling (*U*) (*dans* in).
ingérer [ɛ̃ʒeʀe] (6) **1** *vt* to ingest. **2 s'ingérer** *vpr*: **s'~ dans** to interfere in, meddle in.
ingestion [ɛ̃ʒɛstjɔ̃] *nf* ingestion.
ingouvernable [ɛ̃guvɛʀnabl(ə)] *adj* (*Pol*) ungovernable.
ingrat, e [ɛ̃gʀa, at] *adj personne* ungrateful (*envers* to, towards); *tâche, métier, sujet* thankless (*épith*), unrewarding; *sol* stubborn, barren, sterile; *visage* unprepossessing, unattractive; *contrée* bleak, hostile; *mémoire* unreliable, treacherous. **tu es un ~** you're an ungrateful person *ou* so-and-so*; *V* **âge.**
ingratement [ɛ̃gʀatmɑ̃] *adv* (*littér*) ungratefully.
ingratitude [ɛ̃gʀatityd] *nf* ingratitude, ungratefulness (*envers* to, towards). **avec ~** ungratefully.
ingrédient [ɛ̃gʀedjɑ̃] *nm* ingredient; (*fig*) ingredient, component.
inguérissable [ɛ̃geʀisabl(ə)] *adj* (*lit*) incurable; (*fig*) *habitude, paresse* incurable; *chagrin, amour* inconsolable.
ingurgitation [ɛ̃gyʀʒitɑsjɔ̃] *nf* ingurgitation.
ingurgiter [ɛ̃gyʀʒite] (1) *vt nourriture* to swallow, ingurgitate (*frm*); *vin* to gulp (down), swill (*péj*); (*fig*) to ingest, ingurgitate. **faire ~ de la nourriture/une boisson à qn** to make sb swallow food/a drink, force food/a drink down sb; **faire ~ des connaissances à qn** to force sb to take in facts, force *ou* stuff knowledge into sb.
inhabile [inabil] *adj* **(a)** *politicien, discours* inept; *manœuvre* inept, clumsy. **se montrer ~ dans la conduite des négociations** to mishandle the conduct of the negotiations, show a certain ineptitude in the handling of the negotiations.
(b) (*manuellement*) *ouvrier* unskilful, clumsy; *gestes, mains, dessin, travail* clumsy.
(c) (*Jur*) incapable. **~ à tester** incapable of making a will.
inhabilement [inabilmɑ̃] *adv* ineptly.
inhabileté [inabilte] *nf* (*littér: V* **inhabile**) ineptitude; clumsiness; unskilfulness.

inhabilité [inabilite] *nf* (*Jur*) incapacity (*à* to).
inhabitable [inabitabl(ə)] *adj* uninhabitable. **cette appartement est ~** it's impossible to live in this flat, this flat is uninhabitable.
inhabité, e [inabite] *adj région* uninhabited; *maison* uninhabited, unoccupied. **la maison a l'air ~e** the house looks uninhabited *ou* unoccupied *ou* unlived-in.
inhabituel, -elle [inabitɥɛl] *adj* unusual.
inhalateur, -trice [inalatœʀ, tʀis] **1** *nm* inhaler. (*Aviat*) **~ d'oxygène** oxygen mask. **2** *adj* inhaling.
inhalation [inalɑsjɔ̃] *nf* (*Méd*) inhalation. **faire *ou* prendre une *ou* des ~(s)** to have *ou* use an inhalation bath.
inhaler [inale] (1) *vt* (*Méd*) to inhale; (*littér*) to inhale, breathe (in).
inharmonieux, -euse [inaʀmɔnjø, øz] *adj* (*littér*) inharmonious.
inhérence [ineʀɑ̃s] *nf* (*Philos*) inherence.
inhérent, e [ineʀɑ̃, ɑ̃t] *adj* inherent (*à* in).
inhiber [inibe] (1) *vt* (*Physiol, Psych*) to inhibit.
inhibiteur, -trice [inibitœʀ, tʀis] *adj* inhibitory, inhibitive.
inhibition [inibisjɔ̃] *nf* (*Physiol, Psych*) inhibition.
inhospitalier, -ière [inɔspitalje, jɛʀ] *adj* inhospitable.
inhumain, e [inymɛ̃, ɛn] *adj* inhuman.
inhumainement [inymɛnmɑ̃] *adv* (*littér*) inhumanly.
inhumanité [inymanite] *nf* (*littér*) inhumanity.
inhumation [inymɑsjɔ̃] *nf* burial, interment, inhumation.
inhumer [inyme] (1) *vt* to bury, inter; *V* **permis**.
inimaginable [inimaʒinabl(ə)] *adj* unimaginable.
inimitable [inimitabl(ə)] *adj* inimitable.
inimitié [inimitje] *nf* enmity.
ininflammable [inɛ̃flamabl(ə)] *adj* non-flammable, non-inflammable.
inintelligemment [inɛ̃teliʒamɑ̃] *adv* unintelligently.
inintelligence [inɛ̃teliʒɑ̃s] *nf [personne, esprit]* lack of intelligence, unintelligence. (*incompréhension*) **l'~ du problème** the failure to understand the problem, the lack of understanding of the problem.
inintelligent, e [inɛ̃teliʒɑ̃, ɑ̃t] *adj* unintelligent.
inintelligibilité [inɛ̃teliʒibilite] *nf* unintelligibility.
inintelligible [inɛ̃teli ʒibl(ə)] *adj* unintelligible.
inintelligiblement [inɛ̃teliʒibləmɑ̃] *adv* unintelligibly.
inintéressant, e [inɛ̃teʀɛsɑ̃, ɑ̃t] *adj* uninteresting.
ininterrompu, e [inɛ̃tɛʀɔ̃py] *adj suite, ligne* unbroken; *file de voitures* unbroken, steady (*épith*), uninterrupted; *flot, vacarme* steady (*épith*), uninterrupted, non-stop; *effort, travail* unremitting, continuous, steady (*épith*). **12 heures de sommeil ~** 12 hours' uninterrupted *ou* unbroken sleep; **programme de musique ~e** programme of continuous music.
inique [inik] *adj* iniquitous.
iniquement [inikmɑ̃] *adv* iniquitously.
iniquité [inikite] *nf* (*gén, Rel*) iniquity.
initial, e, *mpl* **-aux** [inisjal, o] **1** *adj* initial. **2 initiale** *nf* initial. **mettre ses ~es sur qch** to put one's initials on sth, initial sth; *V* **vitesse**.
initialement [inisjalmɑ̃] *adv* initially.
initiateur, -trice [inisjatœʀ, tʀis] **1** *adj* innovatory. **2** *nm,f* (*maître, précurseur*) initiator; *[mode, technique]* innovator, pioneer; *[idée]* initiator, originator.
initiation [inisjɑsjɔ̃] *nf* initiation (*à* into). (*titre d'ouvrage*) **~ à la linguistique/philosophie** introduction to linguistics/philosophy.
initiatique [inisjatik] *adj rite* initiatory.
initiative [inisjativ] *nf* (*gén, Pol*) initiative. **prendre l'~ d'une action/de faire** to take the initiative for an action/of *ou* in doing; **garder l'~** to keep the initiative; **avoir de l'~** to have *ou* show initiative *ou* enterprise; **à *ou* sur l'~ de qn** on sb's initiative; **de sa propre ~** on one's own initiative; **elle manque d'~** she lacks initiative *ou* enterprise; *V* **droit³, syndicat**.
initié, e [inisje] (*ptp de* **initier**) **1** *adj* initiated. u4le lecteur **~/non ~** the initiated/uninitiated reader.
2 *nm,f* initiated person, initiate (*frm*). **les ~s** the initiated *ou* initiates (*frm*); **les non ~s** the uninitiated; **art réservé aux ~s** art accessible only to the initiated.
initier [inisje] (7) **1** *vt* to initiate (*à* into). **~ qn aux joies de la voile** to introduce sb to the joys of sailing. **2 s'initier** *vpr* to become initiated, initiate o.s. (*à* into).
injectable [ɛ̃ʒɛktabl(ə)] *adj* injectable.
injecté, e [ɛ̃ʒɛkte] (*ptp de* **injecter**) *adj* (*Méd, Tech*) injected (*de* with); *visage* congested. **(yeux) ~s de sang** bloodshot (eyes).
injecter [ɛ̃ʒɛkte] (1) *vt* (*Méd, Tech*) to inject.
injecteur, -trice [ɛ̃ʒɛktœʀ, tʀis] **1** *adj* injection (*épith*). **2** *nm* injector.
injection [ɛ̃ʒɛksjɔ̃] *nf* (*action, produit, piqûre*) injection; (*avec une poire etc*) douche; (*Géol, Tech*) injection. **à ~s** *seringue, tube* injection (*épith*); **à ~** *moteur, système* fuel injection (*épith*).
injonction [ɛ̃ʒɔ̃ksjɔ̃] *nf* injunction, command, order.
injouable [ɛ̃jwabl(ə)] *adj musique* unplayable; *pièce* unperformable.
injure [ɛ̃ʒyʀ] *nf* **(a)** (*insulte*) abuse (*U*), insult. **'espèce de salaud' est une ~** 'bastard' is a swearword *ou* an insult; **bordée d'~s** string of abuse *ou* insults; (*Jur*) **l'~ et la diffamation** abuse and slander.
(b) (*littér: affront*) **faire ~ à qn** to wrong sb, affront sb (*littér*); **il m'a fait l'~ de ne pas venir** he insulted *ou* affronted me by not coming.
(c) (*littér: dommage*) **l'~ des ans/du sort** the injury *ou* assault of years/of fate (*littér*).
injurier [ɛ̃ʒyʀje] (7) *vt* to abuse, insult, revile (*frm*).
injurieusement [ɛ̃ʒyʀjøzmɑ̃] *adv* (*V* **injurieux**) abusively; offensively; insultingly.
injurieux, -euse [ɛ̃ʒyʀjø, øz] *adj termes, propos* abusive, offensive; (*littér*) *attitude, article* insulting, offensive (*pour, à l'égard de* to).
injuste [ɛ̃ʒyst(ə)] *adj* (*contraire à la justice, manquant d'équité*) unjust; (*partial, tendancieux*) unfair (*avec, envers* to, towards).
injustement [ɛ̃ʒystəmɑ̃] *adv* (*V* **injuste**) unjustly; unfairly.
injustice [ɛ̃ʒystis] *nf* **(a)** (*U: V* **injuste**) injustice; unfairness. **(b)** (*acte*) injustice.
injustifiable [ɛ̃ʒystifjabl(ə)] *adj* unjustifiable.
injustifié, e [ɛ̃ʒystifje] *adj* unjustified, unwarranted.
inlassable [ɛ̃lɑsabl(ə)] *adj personne* tireless, untiring; *zèle* unflagging, tireless.
inlassablement [ɛ̃lasabləmɑ̃] *adv* (*V* **inlassable**) tirelessly; untiringly; unflaggingly.
inné, e [ine] *adj* innate, inborn. **idées ~es** innate ideas.
innervation [inɛʀvɑsjɔ̃] *nf* innervation.
innerver [inɛʀve] (1) *vt* to innervate.
innocemment [inɔsamɑ̃] *adv* innocently.
innocence [inɔsɑ̃s] *nf* (*gén*) innocence. **l'~ de ces farces** the innocence *ou* harmlessness of these pranks; **il l'a fait en toute ~** he did it in all innocence, he meant no harm (by it).
innocent, e [inɔsɑ̃, ɑ̃t] **1** *adj* (*Jur, Rel, gén*) innocent. **être ~ de qch** to be innocent of sth; **remarque/petite farce bien ~e** quite innocent *ou* harmless remark/little prank; **il est vraiment ~!** he is a real innocent!; **~ comme l'enfant *ou* l'agneau qui vient de naître** as innocent as a new-born babe.
2 *nm,f* **(a)** (*Jur*) innocent person; *V* **massacre**.
(b) (*candide*) innocent (person); (*niais*) simpleton. **ne fais pas l'~** don't act *ou* play the innocent, don't come the innocent with me* (*Brit*), don't put on an air of innocence; **quel ~ tu fais!** how innocent can you be?*, how innocent you are!; **l'~ du village** the village simpleton *ou* idiot; (*Prov*) **aux ~s les mains pleines** fortune favours the innocent.
innocenter [inɔsɑ̃te] (1) *vt* (*Jur: disculper*) to clear, prove innocent (*de* of); (*fig: excuser*) to excuse, justify.
innocuité [inɔkɥite] *nf* (*frm*) innocuousness (*frm*), harmlessness.
innombrable [inɔ̃bʀabl(ə)] *adj détails, péripéties, variétés* innumerable, countless; *foule* vast.
innomé, e [inɔme] *adj* = **innommé**.
innommable [inɔmabl(ə)] *adj conduite, action* unspeakable, unmentionable; *ordures* unspeakably foul.
innommé, e [inɔme] *adj* (*non dénommé*) unnamed; (*obscur, vague*) nameless.
innovateur, -trice [inɔvatœʀ, tʀis] **1** *adj* innovatory, innovative. **2** *nm,f* innovator.
innovation [inɔvɑsjɔ̃] *nf* innovation.
innover [inɔve] (1) **1** *vi* to innovate. **~ en matière de mode/d'art** *etc* to break new ground *ou* innovate in the field of fashion/art *etc*; **ce peintre innove par rapport à ses prédécesseurs** this painter is breaking new ground compared with his predecessors. **2** *vt* to create, invent.
inobservable [inɔpsɛʀvabl(ə)] *adj* unobservable.
inobservance [inɔpsɛʀvɑ̃s] *nf* (*littér*) inobservance, non-observance.
inobservation [inɔpsɛʀvɑsjɔ̃] *nf* (*littér, Jur*) non-observance, inobservance.
inobservé, e [inɔpsɛʀve] *adj* (*littér, Jur*) unobserved.
inoccupation [inɔkypɑsjɔ̃] *nf* (*littér*) inoccupation (*littér*), inactivity.
inoccupé, e [inɔkype] *adj* **(a)** (*vide*) *appartement* unoccupied, empty; *siège, emplacement* vacant, unoccupied, empty. **(b)** (*oisif*) unoccupied, idle.
inoculable [inɔkylabl(ə)] *adj* inoculable.
inoculation [inɔkylɑsjɔ̃] *nf* (*Méd: volontaire*) (preventive) inoculation; (*accidentelle*) infection. **l'~ (accidentelle) d'un virus/d'une maladie dans l'organisme par blessure** the (accidental) infection of the organism by a virus/by disease as a result of an injury.
inoculer [inɔkyle] (1) *vt* **(a) ~ un virus/une maladie à qn** (*Méd: volontairement*) to inoculate sb with a virus/a disease; (*accidentellement*) to infect sb with a virus/a disease; **~ un malade** to inoculate a patient (*contre* against).
(b) (*fig: communiquer*) **~ une passion** *etc* **à qn** to infect *ou* imbue sb with a passion *etc*; **~ un vice/des opinions à qn** to inoculate sb with a vice/ideas.
inodore [inɔdɔʀ] *adj gaz* odourless; *fleur* scentless.
inoffensif, -ive [inɔfɑ̃sif, iv] *adj personne, plaisanterie* inoffensive, harmless, innocuous; *piqûre, animal, remède* harmless, innocuous.
inondable [inɔ̃dabl(ə)] *adj* liable to flooding.
inondation [inɔ̃dɑsjɔ̃] *nf* **(a)** (*V* **inonder**) flooding; swamping; inundation. **(b)** (*lit*) flood; (*fig*) flood, deluge (*U*).
inonder [inɔ̃de] (1) *vt* **(a)** (*lit: d'eau*) to flood; (*fig: de produits*) to flood, swamp, inundate (*de* with). **tu as inondé toute la cuisine*** you've flooded the whole kitchen, you've literally swamped the kitchen; **les populations inondées** the flood victims; **inondé de soleil** bathed in sunlight; **inondé de lumière** suffused *ou* flooded with light; **la joie inonda son cœur** joy flooded into his heart.
(b) (*tremper*) to soak, drench. **se faire ~ (par la pluie)** to get soaked *ou* drenched (by the rain); **je suis inondé** I'm soaked (through) *ou* drenched *ou* saturated*; **~ ses cheveux de parfum** to saturate one's hair with scent; **la sueur inondait son visage** sweat was streaming down his face, his face was bathed in sweat; **inondé de larmes** *joues* streaming with tears; *yeux* full of tears.

inopérable [inɔpeʀabl(ə)] *adj* inoperable.
inopérant, e [inɔpeʀɑ̃, ɑ̃t] *adj* ineffectual, ineffective, inoperative.
inopiné, e [inɔpine] *adj rencontre* unexpected. **mort ~e** sudden death.
inopinément [inɔpinemɑ̃] *adv* unexpectedly.
inopportun, e [inɔpɔʀtœ̃, yn] *adj demande, remarque* ill-timed, inopportune, untimely. **le moment est ~** it is not the right *ou* best moment, it's not the most opportune moment.
inopportunément [inɔpɔʀtynemɑ̃] *adv* inopportunely.
inopportunité [inɔpɔʀtynite] *nf* (*littér*) inopportuneness, untimeliness.
inopposabilité [inɔpozabilite] *nf* (*Jur*) non-invocability.
inopposable [inɔpozabl(ə)] *adj* (*Jur*) non-invocable.
inorganique [inɔʀganik] *adj* inorganic.
inorganisé, e [inɔʀganize] *adj compagnie, industrie* unorganized; *personne* disorganized, unorganized; (*Sci*) unorganized.
inoubliable [inublijabl(ə)] *adj* unforgettable, never-to-be-forgotten (*épith*), never to be forgotten (*attrib*).
inouï, e [inwi] *adj événement, circonstances* unprecedented, unheard-of; *nouvelle* extraordinary, incredible; *vitesse, audace, force* incredible, unbelievable. **c'est/il est ~!*** it's/he's incredible! *ou* unbelievable!
inox [inɔks] *abrév de* **inoxydable.**
inoxydable [inɔksidabl(ə)] **1** *adj acier, alliage* stainless; *couteau* stainless steel (*épith*). **2** *nm* stainless steel.
inqualifiable [ɛ̃kalifjabl(ə)] *adj conduite, propos* unspeakable. **d'une ~ bassesse** unspeakably low.
inquiet, -ète [ɛ̃kjɛ, ɛt] *adj personne* (*momentanément*) worried, anxious; (*par nature*) anxious; *gestes* uneasy; *attente, regards* uneasy, anxious; *sommeil* uneasy, troubled; (*littér*) *curiosité, amour* restless. **je suis ~ de son absence** I'm worried at his absence, I'm worried *ou* anxious that he's not here; **je suis ~ de ne pas le voir** I'm worried *ou* anxious at not seeing him, I'm worried not to be able to see him; **c'est un (éternel) ~** he's a (perpetual) worrier.
inquiétant, e [ɛ̃kjetɑ̃, ɑ̃t] *adj* (*gén*) disturbing, worrying, disquieting; *personne* disturbing.
inquiéter [ɛ̃kjete] (6) **1** *vt* **(a)** (*alarmer*) to worry, disturb. **la santé de mon fils m'inquiète** my son's health worries *ou* disturbs me, I'm worried *ou* bothered about my son's health.
(b) (*harceler*) *ville, pays* to harass. **l'amant de la victime ne fut pas inquiété (par la police)** the victim's lover wasn't troubled *ou* bothered by the police.
2 s'inquiéter *vpr* **(a)** (*s'alarmer*) to worry. **ne t'inquiète pas** don't worry; **il n'y a pas de quoi s'~** there's nothing to worry about *ou* get worried about.
(b) (*s'enquérir*) **s'~ de** to inquire about; **s'~ de l'heure/de la santé de qn** to inquire what time it is/about sb's health.
(c) (*se soucier*) **s'~ de** to worry about, trouble (o.s.) about, bother about; **ne t'inquiète pas de ça, je m'en occupe** don't (you) trouble yourself *ou* worry *ou* bother about that — I'll see to it; **sans s'~ des circonstances/conséquences** without worrying *ou* bothering about the circumstances/consequences; **sans s'~ de savoir si ...** without troubling *ou* bothering to find out if ... .
inquiétude [ɛ̃kjetyd] *nf* anxiety; (*littér: agitation*) restlessness. **donner de l'~ *ou* des ~s à qn** to worry sb, give sb cause for worry *ou* anxiety; **éprouver des ~s au sujet de** to feel anxious *ou* worried about, feel some anxiety about; **soyez sans ~** have no fear; **fou d'~** mad with worry.
inquisiteur, -trice [ɛ̃kizitœʀ, tʀis] **1** *adj* inquisitive, prying. **2** *nm* inquisitor.
inquisition [ɛ̃kizisjɔ̃] *nf* **(a)** (*Hist*) **la (Sainte) I~** the Inquisition, the Holy Office. **(b)** (*péj: enquête*) inquisition.
inquisitorial, e, *mpl* **-aux** [ɛ̃kizitɔʀjal, o] *adj* inquisitorial.
inracontable [ɛ̃ʀakɔ̃tabl(ə)] *adj* (*trop osé*) unrepeatable; (*trop compliqué*) unrecountable.
insaisissabilité [ɛ̃sezisabilite] *nf* (*Jur*) non-seizability.
insaisissable [ɛ̃sezisabl(ə)] *adj fugitif, ennemi* elusive; *nuance, différence* imperceptible, indiscernible; (*Jur*) *biens* non-seizable.
insalissable [ɛ̃salisabl(ə)] *adj* dirt-proof.
insalubre [ɛ̃salybʀ(ə)] *adj climat* insalubrious, unhealthy; *bâtiment* insalubrious.
insalubrité [ɛ̃salybʀite] *nf* (*V* **insalubre**) insalubrity; unhealthiness.
insanité [ɛ̃sanite] *nf* (*U*) insanity, madness; (*acte*) insane act; (*propos*) insane talk (*U*). **proférer des ~s** to talk insanely.
insatiabilité [ɛ̃sasjabilite] *nf* insatiability.
insatiable [ɛ̃sasjabl(ə)] *adj* insatiable.
insatiablement [ɛ̃sasjabləmɑ̃] *adv* insatiably.
insatisfaction [ɛ̃satisfaksjɔ̃] *nf* dissatisfaction.
insatisfait, e [ɛ̃satisfɛ, ɛt] *adj personne* (*non comblé*) unsatisfied; (*mécontent*) dissatisfied; *désir, passion* unsatisfied. **c'est un éternel ~** he's never satisfied.
inscriptible [ɛ̃skʀiptibl(ə)] *adj* inscribable.
inscription [ɛ̃skʀipsjɔ̃] **1** *nf* **(a)** (*écrit*) (*gravée, imprimée, officielle*) inscription; (*manuscrite*) writing (*U*), inscription. **mur couvert d'~s** wall covered in writing *ou* inscriptions.
(b) (*action*) **l'~ du texte n'est pas comprise dans le prix** the inscription *ou* engraving of the text is not included in the price; **l'~ d'une question à l'ordre du jour** putting *ou* placing a question on the agenda; **cela a nécessité l'~ de nouvelles dépenses au budget** this necessitated adding further expenditure to the budget.
(c) (*immatriculation*) enrolment, registration; (*à l'université*) matriculation (*à* at); (*à un concours*) enrolment (*à* in), entering (*à* for). **l'~ à un parti/club** joining a party/club; **l'~ des enfants à l'école est obligatoire** it is compulsory to enrol *ou* register children for school; **il y a déjà 20 ~s pour la sortie de jeudi** 20 people have already signed on *ou* enrolled for Thursday's outing; **les ~s (en faculté) seront closes le 30 octobre** the closing date for enrolment *ou* matriculation (at the university) is October 30th; **votre ~ sur la liste dépend de ...** the inclusion of your name on the list depends on ...; **faire son ~ *ou* prendre ses ~s en faculté** to register (o.s.) *ou* enrol (o.s.) at the university; **droits d'~** enrolment fee.
2: (*Jur*) **inscription en faux** challenge (*to validity of document*); (*Jur*) **inscription hypothécaire** mortgage registration; **inscription maritime** registration of sailors; (*service*) **l'Inscription maritime** the Register of Sailors.
inscrire [ɛ̃skʀiʀ] (39) **1** *vt* **(a)** (*marquer*) *nom, date* to note down, write down. **~ des dépenses au budget** to list expenses in the budget; **~ une question à l'ordre du jour** to put *ou* place a question on the agenda; **ce n'est pas inscrit à l'ordre du jour** it isn't (down) on the agenda; **~ qch dans la pierre/le marbre** to inscribe *ou* engrave sth on stone/marble; (*fig*) **c'est demeuré inscrit dans ma mémoire** it has remained inscribed *ou* etched on my memory; (*fig*) **sa culpabilité est inscrite sur son visage** his guilt is written all over his face *ou* on his face; **greffier, inscrivez (sous ma dictée)** clerk, take *ou* note this down; **son nom est *ou* il est inscrit sur la liste des gagnants** his name is (written) on the list of winners.
(b) (*enrôler*) (*gén*) to put down; *soldat* to enlist; *étudiant* to register, enrol. **~ qn sur une liste d'attente/pour un rendez-vous** to put sb down *ou* put sb's name down on a waiting list/for an appointment; **je ne peux pas vous ~ avant le 3 août, le docteur est en vacances** I can't put you down for an appointment *ou* I can't give you an appointment before August 3rd as the doctor is on holiday.
(c) (*aussi* **faire ~**: *affilier*) **~ qn** to put sb down; **(faire) ~ un enfant à l'école** to put a child *ou* child's name down for school, enrol *ou* register a child for school; **(faire) ~ qn à la cantine/pour une vaccination** to register sb at the canteen/for a vaccination; **(faire) ~ qn à un concours** to enter *ou* enrol sb for *ou* put sb down for an exam.
(d) (*Math*) to inscribe.
2 s'inscrire *vpr* **(a)** (*s'enrôler*) (*à un parti ou club*) to join (*à* non traduit); (*sur la liste électorale*) to put one's name down (*sur* on); (*à l'université*) to register, enrol (*à* at); (*à un examen*) to register, enrol, enter (*à* for); (*à une épreuve sportive*) to put o.s. down, put one's name down, enter (*à* for). **je me suis inscrit pour des cours du soir** I've enrolled in *ou* for some evening classes; **s'~ avant le 9 octobre** to enrol *ou* register before October 9th.
(b) (*s'insérer dans*) **ces réformes s'inscrivent dans le cadre de notre nouvelle politique** these reforms lie *ou* come within the scope *ou* framework of our new policy; **cette décision s'inscrit dans la lutte contre le chômage** this decision fits in with *ou* is in keeping with the general struggle against unemployment.
(c) (*Math*) to be inscribed. (*fig*) **l'avion ennemi s'inscrivit dans le viseur** the enemy aircraft came up on the viewfinder; **la tour Eiffel s'inscrivait tout entière dans la fenêtre** the Eiffel Tower was framed in its entirety by the window.
(d) (*Jur*) **s'~ en faux** to lodge a challenge; **je m'inscris en faux contre de telles assertions** I strongly deny such assertions.
inscrit, e [ɛ̃skʀi, it] (*ptp de* **inscrire**) **1** *adj* **(a)** *étudiant* registered, enrolled; *candidat, électeur* registered; *V* **non.**
(b) (*Math*) inscribed.
2 *nm,f* (*membre d'un parti etc*) registered member; (*étudiant*) registered student; (*concurrent*) (registered) entrant; (*candidat*) registered candidate; (*électeur*) registered elector. **~ maritime** registered sailor.
insécable [ɛ̃sekabl(ə)] *adj* indivisible, undividable.
insecte [ɛ̃sɛkt(ə)] *nm* insect.
insecticide [ɛ̃sɛktisid] **1** *nm* insecticide. **2** *adj* insecticide (*épith*), insecticidal.
insectivore [ɛ̃sɛktivɔʀ] **1** *nm* insectivore. **~s** insectivores, Insectivora (*T*). **2** *adj* insectivorous.
insécurité [ɛ̃sekyʀite] *nf* insecurity.
insémination [ɛ̃seminɑsjɔ̃] *nf* insemination.
inséminer [ɛ̃semine] (1) *vt* to inseminate.
insensé, e [ɛ̃sɑ̃se] *adj* **(a)** (*fou*) *projet, action, espoir* insane; *personne, propos* insane, demented. **vouloir y aller seul, c'est ~!** it's insane *ou* crazy to want to go alone!; **c'est un ~!** he's demented! *ou* insane!, he's a madman!
(b) (*bizarre*) *architecture, arabesques* weird, extravagant.
insensibilisation [ɛ̃sɑ̃sibilizɑsjɔ̃] *nf* anaesthesia.
insensibiliser [ɛ̃sɑ̃sibilize] (1) *vt* to anaesthetize. (*fig*) **nous sommes insensibilisés aux atrocités de la guerre** we've become insensitive to the atrocities of war.
insensibilité [ɛ̃sɑ̃sibilite] *nf* (*morale*) insensitivity, insensibility; (*physique*) numbness. **~ au froid/à la douleur/aux reproches** insensitivity *ou* insensibility to cold/pain/blame.
insensible [ɛ̃sɑ̃sibl(ə)] *adj* **(a)** (*moralement*) insensible, insensitive (*à* to); (*physiquement*) numb. **~ au froid/à la douleur** insensible *ou* insensitive to cold/pain. **(b)** (*imperceptible*) imperceptible, insensible.
insensiblement [ɛ̃sɑ̃sibləmɑ̃] *adv* imperceptibly, insensibly.
inséparable [ɛ̃sepaʀabl(ə)] *adj* inseparable (*de* from). **ce sont des ~s** they are inseparable; (*chez l'oiselier*) **acheter des ~s** to buy a pair of lovebirds.
inséparablement [ɛ̃sepaʀabləmɑ̃] *adv* inseparably.
insérable [ɛ̃seʀabl(ə)] *adj* insertable.
insérer [ɛ̃seʀe] (6) **1** *vt feuillet* to insert (*dans* into); *annonce* to put, insert (*dans* in).
2 s'insérer *vpr* **(a)** (*faire partie de*) **s'~ dans** to fit into; **ces**

changements s'insèrent dans le cadre d'une restructuration de notre entreprise these changes come *ou* lie within *ou* fit into our overall plan for restructuring the firm.

(b) (*s'introduire dans*) **s'~ dans** to filter into; **le rêve s'insère parfois dans la réalité** sometimes the dreamworld invades reality.

insertion [ɛ̃sɛʀsjɔ̃] *nf* (*action*) insertion, inserting; (*résultat*) insertion.

insidieusement [ɛ̃sidjøzmɑ̃] *adv* insidiously.

insidieux, -euse [ɛ̃sidjø, øz] *adj* insidious.

insigne[1] [ɛ̃siɲ] *adj* (*éminent*) *honneur* distinguished; *services* notable, distinguished; *faveur* signal (*épith*), notable; (*iro*) *maladresse, mauvais goût* remarkable.

insigne[2] [ɛ̃siɲ] *nm* (*cocarde*) badge. (*frm: emblème*) **l'~ de, les ~s de** the insignia of; **portant les ~s de sa fonction** wearing the insignia of his office.

insignifiance [ɛ̃siɲifjɑ̃s] *nf* (*V* **insignifiant**) insignificance; triviality.

insignifiant, e [ɛ̃siɲifjɑ̃, ɑ̃t] *adj personne, visage, œuvre* insignificant; *affaire, somme* insignificant, trivial, trifling; *paroles* insignificant, trivial.

insinuant, e [ɛ̃sinɥɑ̃, ɑ̃t] *adj façons, ton, personne* ingratiating.

insinuation [ɛ̃sinɥasjɔ̃] *nf* insinuation, innuendo.

insinuer [ɛ̃sinɥe] (1) **1** *vt* to insinuate, imply. **que voulez-vous ~?** what are you insinuating? *ou* implying? *ou* suggesting?

2 s'insinuer *vpr*: **s'~ dans** *[personne]* to worm one's way into, insinuate o.s. into; *[eau, odeur]* to seep *ou* creep into; **l'humidité s'insinuait partout** the dampness was creeping in everywhere; **les idées qui s'insinuent dans mon esprit** the ideas that steal *ou* creep into my mind; **ces arrivistes s'insinuent partout** these opportunists worm their way in everywhere; **s'~ dans les bonnes grâces de qn** to worm one's way into *ou* insinuate o.s. into sb's favour.

insipide [ɛ̃sipid] *adj plat, boisson* insipid, tasteless; *goût* insipid; *conversation, style* insipid, wishy-washy, vapid; *écrivain, film, œuvre* insipid, wishy-washy.

insipidité [ɛ̃sipidite] *nf* (*V* **insipide**) insipidness, insipidity; tastelessness; vapidity.

insistance [ɛ̃sistɑ̃s] *nf* insistence (*à faire* on doing). **avec ~** *répéter, regarder* insistently.

insistant, e [ɛ̃sistɑ̃, ɑ̃t] *adj* insistent.

insister [ɛ̃siste] (1) *vi* **(a) ~ sur** *sujet, détail* to stress, lay stress on; *syllabe, note* to accentuate, emphasize, stress; **j'insiste beaucoup sur la ponctualité** I lay great stress upon punctuality; **frottez en insistant (bien) sur les taches** rub hard, paying particular attention to stains; **c'est une affaire louche, enfin n'insistons pas!** it's a shady business — however let us not dwell on it *ou* don't let us keep on about it*; **je préfère ne pas ~ là-dessus!** I'd rather not dwell on it, I'd rather let the matter drop.

(b) (*s'obstiner*) to be insistent (*auprès de* with), insist. **il insiste pour vous parler** he is insistent about wanting to talk to you; **comme ça ne l'intéressait pas, je n'ai pas insisté** since it didn't interest him I didn't push the matter *ou* I didn't insist; **sonnez encore, insistez, elle est un peu sourde** ring again and keep (on) trying because she's a little deaf; **bon, je n'insiste pas, je m'en vais*** O.K., I won't push it* — I'll go.

insociable [ɛ̃sɔsjabl(ə)] *adj* unsociable.

insolation [ɛ̃sɔlasjɔ̃] *nf* **(a)** (*malaise*) sunstroke (*U*), insolation (*T*). **j'ai eu une ~** I had a touch of sunstroke.

(b) (*ensoleillement*) (period of) sunshine. **ces stations ont malheureusement une ~ très faible** unfortunately these resorts have very little sun(shine); **cette région reçoit habituellement une ~ de 1.000 heures par an** this region regularly has 1,000 hours of sunshine a year.

(c) (*exposition au soleil*) *[personne]* exposure to the sun; *[pellicule]* exposure.

insolemment [ɛ̃sɔlamɑ̃] *adv* (*V* **insolent**) insolently; arrogantly; unashamedly; blatantly; brazenly.

insolence [ɛ̃sɔlɑ̃s] *nf* (*U: impertinence*) insolence; (*littér: morgue*) arrogance; (*remarque*) insolent remark. **encore une ~ comme celle-ci et je te renvoie** one more insolent remark like that *ou* any more of your insolence and I'll send you out.

insolent, e [ɛ̃sɔlɑ̃, ɑ̃t] *adj* **(a)** (*impoli*) *personne, attitude, réponse* insolent; (*littér*) *parvenu, vainqueur* arrogant. **tu es un ~** you're an insolent fellow.

(b) (*inouï*) *luxe, succès* unashamed, blatant; *joie* brazen, unashamed. **il a une chance ~e!** he has the luck of the devil!

insolite [ɛ̃sɔlit] *adj* unusual, strange.

insolubilité [ɛ̃sɔlybilite] *nf* (*V* **insoluble**) insolubility; insolvability.

insoluble [ɛ̃sɔlybl(ə)] *adj problème* insoluble, insolvable. **~ (dans l'eau)** *substance* insoluble (in water).

insolvabilité [ɛ̃sɔlvabilite] *nf* insolvency.

insolvable [ɛ̃sɔlvabl(ə)] *adj* insolvent.

insomniaque [ɛ̃sɔmnjak] *nmf* insomniac. **c'est un ~, il est ~** he's an insomniac.

insomnie [ɛ̃sɔmni] *nf* insomnia (*U*). **ses nuits d'~** his sleepless nights; **ses ~s** his (periods of) insomnia.

insondable [ɛ̃sɔ̃dabl(ə)] *adj gouffre, mystère, douleur* unfathomable; *stupidité* immense, unimaginable.

insonore [ɛ̃sɔnɔʀ] *adj* soundproof.

insonorisation [ɛ̃sɔnɔʀizasjɔ̃] *nf* soundproofing.

insonoriser [ɛ̃sɔnɔʀize] (1) *vt* to soundproof.

insouciance [ɛ̃susjɑ̃s] *nf* (*nonchalance*) inconcern, lack of concern; (*manque de prévoyance*) heedless *ou* happy-go-lucky attitude. **vivre dans l' ~** to live a carefree life.

insouciant, e [ɛ̃susjɑ̃, ɑ̃t] *adj* (*sans-souci*) *personne, vie, humeur* carefree, happy-go-lucky; *rire, paroles* carefree; (*imprévoyant*) heedless, happy-go-lucky. **quel ~ (tu fais)!** what a heedless *ou* happy-go-lucky person you are!

insoucieux, -euse [ɛ̃susjø, øz] *adj* carefree. **~ du lendemain** unconcerned about the future.

insoumis, e [ɛ̃sumi, iz] **1** *adj caractère, enfant* refractory, rebellious, insubordinate; *tribu, peuple, région* undefeated, unsubdued; (*Mil*) *soldat* absent without leave (*failing to report as instructed*). **2** *nm* (*Mil*) absentee.

insoumission [ɛ̃sumisjɔ̃] *nf* insubordination, rebelliousness; (*Mil*) absence without leave.

insoupçonnable [ɛ̃supsɔnabl(ə)] *adj* above *ou* beyond suspicion (*attrib*).

insoupçonné, e [ɛ̃supsɔne] *adj* unsuspected, undreamt-of (*de* by).

insoutenable [ɛ̃sutnabl(ə)] *adj spectacle, douleur, chaleur* unbearable; *théorie* untenable.

inspecter [ɛ̃spɛkte] (1) *vt* (*contrôler*) to inspect; (*scruter*) to inspect, examine.

inspecteur, -trice [ɛ̃spɛktœʀ, tʀis] *nm,f* (*gén*) inspector. **~ des finances** ≃ Treasury Inspector; **~ de police** police inspector; **~ du travail** ≃ Employee Welfare Officer; **~ des travaux finis*** skiver* (*who returns to work when there is nothing left to do*); **~ primaire** primary school inspector; **~ d'Académie** ≃ Chief Education Officer; **~ général de l'Instruction publique** ≃ School Inspector.

inspection [ɛ̃spɛksjɔ̃] *nf* **(a)** (*examen*) inspection. **faire l'~ de** to inspect. **(b)** (*inspectorat*) inspectorship; (*inspecteurs*) inspectorate. **~ académique** school inspection; (*service*) school inspectorate.

inspectorat [ɛ̃spɛktɔʀa] *nm* inspectorship.

inspirateur, -trice [ɛ̃spiʀatœʀ, tʀis] **1** *adj idée, force* inspiring; (*Anat*) inspiratory. **2** *nm,f* (*animateur*) inspirer; (*instigateur*) instigator. **le poète et son ~trice** the poet and the woman who inspires him.

inspiration [ɛ̃spiʀasjɔ̃] *nf* **(a)** (*U*) (*divine, poétique etc*) inspiration. **avoir de l'~** to have inspiration, be inspired; **selon l'~ du moment** according to the mood of the moment, as the mood takes me (*ou* you *etc*).

(b) (*idée*) inspiration, brainwave*. **par une heureuse ~** thanks to a flash of inspiration; **j'eus la bonne/mauvaise ~ de refuser** I had the bright idea/bad idea of refusing.

(c) (*instigation*) instigation; (*influence*) inspiration. **sous l'~ de qn** at sb's instigation, prompted by sb; **style/tableau d'~ romantique** style/picture of romantic inspiration.

(d) (*respiration*) inspiration.

inspiré, e [ɛ̃spiʀe] (*ptp de* **inspirer**) *adj* **(a)** *poète, œuvre, air* inspired. (*iro*) **qu'est-ce que c'est que cet ~!** whoever's this cranky fellow? *ou* this weirdy?* (*péj*).

(b) (*: *avisé*) **j'ai été bien/mal ~ de refuser son chèque** *ou* **quand j'ai refusé son chèque** I was truly inspired/ill inspired when I refused his cheque.

(c) ~ de inspired by; **une tragédie ~e des poèmes antiques** a tragedy inspired by the ancient poems.

inspirer [ɛ̃spiʀe] (1) **1** *vt* **(a)** *poète, prophète* to inspire. **sa passion lui a inspiré ce poème** his passion inspired him to write this poem; **cette idée ne m'inspire pas beaucoup*** this idea doesn't do much for me*, I'm not all that keen on this idea*.

(b) (*susciter*) *acte, personne* to inspire. **~ un sentiment à qn** to inspire sb with a feeling; **il ne m'inspire pas confiance** he doesn't inspire confidence in me, he doesn't inspire me with confidence, I don't really trust him; **toute l'opération était inspirée par un seul homme** the whole operation was inspired by one man; **l'horreur qu'il m'inspire** the horror he fills me with.

(c) (*rare: insuffler*) **~ de l'air dans qch** to breathe air into sth.

2 *vi* (*respirer*) to breathe in, inspire (*T*).

3 s'inspirer *vpr*: **s'~ d'un modèle** *[artiste]* to draw one's inspiration from a model, be inspired by a model; *[mode, tableau, loi]* to be inspired by a model.

instabilité [ɛ̃stabilite] *nf* (*V* **instable**) instability; (emotional) instability; unsteadiness. **l'~ du temps** the unsettled *ou* unstable (nature of the) weather; **l'~ d'une population nomade** the unsettled pattern of life of a nomadic population.

instable [ɛ̃stabl(ə)] *adj* (*Chim, Phys*) unstable; *opinions, situation, régime politique, prix* unstable; *personne, caractère* (emotionally) unstable; *temps* unsettled, unstable; *population nomade* unsettled; *meuble, échafaudage* unsteady; *V* **équilibre**.

installateur [ɛ̃stalatœʀ] *nm* fitter.

installation [ɛ̃stalasjɔ̃] *nf* **(a)** (*U: V* **installer**) installation, installing; putting in; putting up; pitching; fitting out. **il lui fallait maintenant songer à l'~ de son fils** he now had to think about setting his son up; **l'~ du téléphone devrait être gratuite pour les retraités** the telephone should be put in *ou* installed free for pensioners; **ils s'occupent aussi de l'~ du mobilier** they also take care of moving the furniture in.

(b) (*U: V* **s'installer**) setting up, setting up shop; settling; settling in. **il voulait fêter son ~** he wanted to celebrate moving in; **leur ~ terminée** when they had finally settled in.

(c) (*appareils etc: gén pl*) fittings, installations; *[usine]* plant (*U*). **l'~ électrique est défectueuse** the wiring is faulty; **~(s) sanitaire(s)/électrique(s)** sanitary/electrical fittings *ou* installations; **les ~s industrielles d'une région** the industrial installations *ou* plant of a region; **~s portuaires** port installations; **le camping est doté de toutes les ~s nécessaires** the camping site is equipped with all the necessary facilities.

(d) (*ameublement etc*) living arrangements, setup*. **ils ont une ~ provisoire** they have temporary living arrangements *ou* a temporary setup*; **qu'est-ce que vous avez comme ~?** what kind of a setup* do you have?

installé, e [ɛ̃stale] (*ptp de* **installer**) *adj* (*aménagé*) **bien/mal ~** *appartement* well/badly fitted out; *atelier, cuisine* well/

badly equipped *ou* fitted out; **ils sont très bien ~s** they have a comfortable *ou* nice home; **c'est un homme ~†** he is well-established.

installer [ɛ̃stale] (1) **1** *vt* **(a)** (*poser*) *électricité, chauffage central, téléphone, eau courante* to install, put in. **faire ~ le gaz/le téléphone** to have (the) gas/the telephone put in *ou* installed.

(b) (*accrocher*) *rideaux, étagère* to put up; (*placer, fixer*) *applique* to put in; *meuble* to put in, install; (*monter*) *tente* to put up, pitch. **où va-t-on ~ le lit?** where shall we put the bed?

(c) (*aménager*) *pièce, appartement* to fit out. **ils ont très bien installé leur petit appartement** they've got their flat well fitted out; **ils ont installé leur bureau dans le grenier, ils ont installé le grenier en bureau** they've turned the attic into a study, they've set up a study in the attic; **comment la cuisine est-elle installée?** how is the kitchen laid out? *ou* fitted out?

(d) *malade, jeune couple etc* to get settled, settle. **ils installèrent leurs hôtes dans une aile du château** they installed their guests in a wing of the château, they got their guests settled in a wing of the château; **il a installé son fils dentiste/à son compte** he set his son up as a dentist/in his own business.

(e) (*Admin: nommer*) *fonctionnaire, évêque* to install. **il a été officiellement installé dans ses fonctions** he has been officially installed in his post.

(f) (**: faire de l'épate*) **en ~** to make *ou* cause a stir, show off.

2 s'installer *vpr* **(a)** *[artisan, commerçant, médecin]* to set o.s up (*comme* as), set up shop (*comme* as). **s'~ à son compte** to set up on one's own, set up one's own business; **un dentiste s'est installé dans l'immeuble** a dentist has set himself up *ou* set up shop* in the building.

(b) (*se loger*) to settle; (*emménager*) to settle in. **laisse-leur le temps de s'~** give them time to settle in; **ils se sont installés à la campagne/à Lyon** they've settled *ou* set up house in the country/in Lyons; **pendant la guerre ils s'étaient installés chez des amis** during the war they moved in *ou* lived with friends; **s'~ dans une maison abandonnée** to set up home *ou* make one's home in an empty house; **ils sont bien installés dans leur nouvelle maison** they have made themselves a very comfortable home in their new house.

(c) (*sur un siège, à un emplacement*) to settle down. **s'~ commodément** to settle (down) comfortably; **s'~ par terre/dans un fauteuil** to settle down on the floor/in an armchair; **installe-toi comme il faut** (*confortablement*) make yourself comfortable; (*tiens-toi bien*) sit properly; **installons-nous près de cet arbre** let's sit down near this tree; **partout où il va il s'installe comme chez lui** wherever he goes he doesn't hesitate to make himself at home; **les forains se sont installés sur un terrain vague** the fairground people have set themselves up on a piece of wasteland.

(d) (*fig*) *[grève, maladie]* to take a firm hold, become firmly established; *[personne]* **s'~ dans** *inertie* to sink into, be sunk in; *malhonnêteté* to entangle o.s. in, get entangled in; **s'~ dans la guerre** to settle into *ou* become accustomed to the state of war.

instamment [ɛ̃stamɑ̃] *adv* insistently, earnestly.

instance [ɛ̃stɑ̃s] *nf* **(a)** (*autorité*) authority. **les ~s internationales** the international authorities.

(b) (*Jur*) (legal) proceedings. **introduire une ~** to institute (legal) proceedings; **en seconde ~** on appeal; **tribunal de première ~** court of first instance; **tribunal d'~** ≃ magistrates' court; **tribunal de grande ~** Departmental court, ≃ High court.

(c) (*prière, insistance*) **demander qch avec ~** to ask for something with insistence *ou* earnestness; **~s** entreaties; **sur *ou* devant les ~s de ses parents** in the face of his parents' entreaties.

(d) (*en cours*) **en ~: l'affaire est en ~** the matter is pending; **être en ~ de divorce** to be waiting for a divorce; **le train est en ~ de départ** the train is on the point of departure.

instant[1] [ɛ̃stɑ̃] *nm* **(a)** (*moment*) moment, instant. **des ~s de tendresse** tender moments, moments of tenderness; **j'ai cru (pendant) un ~ que** I thought for a moment *ou* a second *ou* one instant that; **(attendez) un ~!** wait *ou* just a moment!, wait one instant!

(b) (*le présent*) **il faut vivre dans l'~** you must live in the present (moment).

(c) (*loc*) **je l'ai vu à l'~** I've just this instant *ou* minute *ou* second seen him; **il faut le faire à l'~** we must do it this instant *ou* minute; **à l'~ (présent)** at this very instant *ou* moment *ou* minute; **à l'~ où je vous parle** as I'm speaking to you now; **à l'~ (même) où il sortit** just as he went out, (just) at the very moment *ou* instant he went out; **à chaque ~, à tout ~** (*d'un moment à l'autre*) at any moment *ou* minute; (*tout le temps*) all the time, every minute; **au même ~** at the (very) same moment *ou* instant; **d'~ en ~** from moment to moment, every moment; **dans l'~ (même)** the next instant, in (next to) no time (at all); **dans un ~** in a moment *ou* minute; **en un ~** in an instant, in no time (at all); **de tous les ~s** perpetual, constant; **par ~s** at times; **pour l'~** for the moment, for the time being; **je n'en doute pas un (seul) ~** I don't doubt it for a (single) moment.

instant[2], **e** [ɛ̃stɑ̃, ɑ̃t] *adj* (*littér: pressant*) insistent, pressing, earnest.

instantané, e [ɛ̃stɑ̃tane] **1** *adj lait, café* instant; *mort, réponse, effet* instantaneous; (*littér: bref*) *vision* momentary. **2** *nm* (*Phot*) snapshot, snap*.

instantanément [ɛ̃stɑ̃tanemɑ̃] *adv* instantaneously. **dissoudre dans de l'eau pour préparer ~ un bon café** dissolve in water to make good coffee instantly.

instar [ɛ̃staʀ] *nm*: **à l'~ de** following the example of, after the fashion of.

instauration [ɛ̃stɔʀɑsjɔ̃] *nf* institution.

instaurer [ɛ̃stɔʀe] (1) *vt* to institute.

instigateur, -trice [ɛ̃stigatœʀ, tʀis] *nm,f* instigator.

instigation [ɛ̃stigɑsjɔ̃] *nf* instigation. **à l'~ de qn** at sb's instigation.

instillation [ɛ̃stilɑsjɔ̃] *nf* instillation.

instiller [ɛ̃stile] (1) *vt* (*Méd, littér*) to instil (*dans* in, into). **il m'a instillé la passion du jeu** he instilled the love of gambling in *ou* into me.

instinct [ɛ̃stɛ̃] *nm* (*gén*) instinct. **~ grégaire** gregarious *ou* herd instinct; **~ de conservation** instinct of self-preservation; **il a l'~ des affaires** he has an instinct for business; **faire qch d'~** to do sth instinctively; **d'~, il comprit la situation** intuitively *ou* instinctively he understood the situation.

instinctif, -ive [ɛ̃stɛ̃ktif, iv] *adj* (*gén*) instinctive, instinctual.

instinctivement [ɛ̃stɛ̃ktivmɑ̃] *adv* instinctively.

instituer [ɛ̃stitɥe] (1) *vt règle, pratique* to institute; (*Rel*) *évêque* to institute; (*Jur*) *héritier* to appoint, institute.

institut [ɛ̃stity] *nm* institute. **l'I ~** the Institute (*the five French Academies*, ≃ Royal Society); **membre de l'I ~** ≃ Fellow of the Royal Society; **M X, de l'I~** ≃ Mr X, FRS; **~ de beauté** beauty salon *ou* parlor (*US*); **I~ Universitaire de Technologie** Technical College; **~ médico-légal** mortuary.

instituteur, -trice [ɛ̃stitytœʀ, tʀis] **1** *nm,f* (primary school) teacher. **2 institutrice** *nf* (*Hist: gouvernante*) governess.

institution [ɛ̃stitysjɔ̃] **1** *nf* (*gén*) institution; (*école*) private school.

2: institution canonique institution (*Rel*); (*Jur*) **institution d'héritier** appointment of an heir; **institution religieuse** (*pour filles*) convent school; (*pour garçons*) Catholic boys' school.

institutionnalisation [ɛ̃stitysjɔnalizɑsjɔ̃] *nf* institutionalization.

institutionnaliser [ɛ̃stitysjɔnalize] (1) *vt* to institutionalize.

institutionnel, -elle [ɛ̃stitysjɔnɛl] *adj* institutional.

institutrice [ɛ̃stitytʀis] *nf V* **instituteur.**

instructeur [ɛ̃stʀyktœʀ] **1** *nm* (*gén: moniteur*) instructor; (*Mil*) instructor. **2** *adj* (*Jur*) **juge *ou* magistrat ~** examining magistrate; **capitaine/sergent ~** drill captain/sergeant.

instructif, -ive [ɛ̃stʀyktif, iv] *adj* instructive.

instruction [ɛ̃stʀyksjɔ̃] *nf* **(a)** (*enseignement*) education. **l'~ que j'ai reçue** the teaching *ou* eduation I received; **~ civique** civics (*sg*); **~ militaire** army training; **~ religieuse** religious instruction; (*Scol*) R.I.

(b) (*culture*) education. **avoir de l'~** to be well educated; **être sans ~** to have no education.

(c) (*Jur*) *investigation and hearing of a case*. **~ (préparatoire)** investigation (*by juge d'instruction*); **~ définitive** hearing (*of a case*); *V* **juge.**

(d) (*Admin: circulaire*) directive. **~ ministérielle/préfectorale** ministerial/prefectural directive.

(e) (*ordres*) **~s** instructions; (*mode d'emploi*) instructions, directions; (*Informatique*) instruction; **suivre les ~s données sur le paquet** to follow the instructions *ou* directions given on the packet; **conformément/contrairement à vos ~s** in accordance with/contrary to your instructions.

instruire [ɛ̃stʀɥiʀ] (38) **1** *vt* **(a)** (*former*) (*gén*) to teach, educate; *recrue* to train. **l'école où elle instruit ces enfants** the school where she teaches those children; **~ qn dans l'art oratoire** to educate *ou* instruct sb in the art of oratory; **c'est la vie qui m'a instruit** life has educated me, life has been my teacher; **~ qn par l'exemple** to teach *ou* educate sb by example; **instruit par son exemple** having learnt from his example; **ces émissions ne visent pas à ~ mais à divertir** these broadcasts are not intended to teach *ou* educate *ou* instruct but to entertain.

(b) (*informer*) **~ qn de qch** to inform *ou* advise sb of sth; **on ne nous a pas instruits des décisions à prendre** we haven't been informed *ou* advised of the decisions to be taken.

(c) (*Jur*) *affaire* to conduct the investigation for. **~ contre qn** to conduct investigations concerning sb.

2 s'instruire *vpr* (*apprendre*) to educate o.s. (*hum*) **c'est comme ça qu'on s'instruit!** THAT'S how you improve your knowledge!; **s'~ de qch** (*frm: se renseigner*) to obtain information about sth, find out about sth; **s'~ auprès de qn des heures d'arrivée** to obtain information *ou* find out from sb about the times of arrival.

instruit, e [ɛ̃stʀɥi, it] (*ptp de* **instruire**) *adj* educated. **peu ~** uneducated.

instrument [ɛ̃stʀymɑ̃] *nm* (*lit, fig*) instrument. **~ de musique/de chirurgie/de mesure/à vent** musical/surgical/measuring/wind instrument; **~s aratoires** ploughing implements; **~s de travail** tools; (*fig*) **être l'~ de qn** to be sb's tool; **le président fut l'~ de/servit d'~ à la répression** the president was the instrument *ou* tool of/served as an *ou* the instrument of repression.

instrumental, e, *mpl* **-aux** [ɛ̃stʀymɑ̃tal, o] **1** *adj* (*Ling, Mus*) instrumental. **2** *nm* (*Ling*) instrumental.

instrumentation [ɛ̃stʀymɑ̃tɑsjɔ̃] *nf* instrumentation, orchestration.

instrumenter [ɛ̃stʀymɑ̃te] (1) **1** *vi* (*Jur*) to draw up a formal document (*deed, contract etc*). **2** *vt* (*Mus*) to orchestrate.

instrumentiste [ɛ̃stʀymɑ̃tist(ə)] *nmf* instrumentalist.

insu [ɛ̃sy] *nm* **(a)** (*en cachette de*) **à l'~ de qn** without sb's knowledge, without sb's knowing. **(b)** (*inconsciemment*) **à mon** (*ou* **ton** *etc*) **~** without my *ou* me (*ou* you *ou* your *etc*) knowing it; **je souriais à mon ~** I was smiling without knowing it.

insubmersible [ɛ̃sybmɛʀsibl(ə)] *adj* unsinkable.

insubordination [ɛ̃sybɔʀdinɑsjɔ̃] *nf* (*gén*) insubordination, rebelliousness; (*Mil*) insubordination.

insubordonné, e [ɛ̃sybɔʀdɔne] *adj* (*gén*) insubordinate, rebellious; (*Mil*) insubordinate.

insuccès [ɛ̃syksɛ] *nm* failure.

insuffisamment [ɛ̃syfizamɑ̃] *adv* (*V* **insuffisant**) insufficiently; inadequately. **tu dors ~** you're not getting adequate *ou* sufficient sleep.

insuffisance [ɛ̃syfizɑ̃s] *nf* **(a)** (*médiocrité*) inadequacy; (*manque*) insufficiency, inadequacy. **l'~ de nos ressources** the inadequacy of our resources, our inadequate *ou* insufficient resources; **nous souffrons d'une (grande) ~ de moyens** we are suffering from a (great) inadequacy *ou* insufficiency *ou* shortage of means; **une ~ de personnel** a shortage of staff.
(b) (*faiblesses*) **~s** inadequacies; **avoir des ~s en math** to be inadequate in *ou* at maths; **il y a des ~s dans son travail** there are inadequacies in his work.
(c) (*Méd*) **~(s) cardiaque(s)/thyroïdienne(s)** cardiac/thyroid insufficiency (*U*).

insuffisant, e [ɛ̃syfizɑ̃, ɑ̃t] *adj* (*en quantité*) insufficient; (*en qualité, intensité, degré*) inadequate. **ce qu'il nous donne est ~** what he gives us is insufficient *ou* inadequate *ou* not enough; **il est ~ en math** he's inadequate in *ou* at maths, he's not up to standard in maths; **nous travaillons avec un personnel ~** we're working with inadequate staffing *ou* with insufficient staff; **nous sommes en nombre ~** we are insufficient in number.

insufflation [ɛ̃syflɑsjɔ̃] *nf* (*Méd*) insufflation.

insuffler [ɛ̃syfle] (1) *vt* **(a) ~ le courage/le désir à qn** to inspire sb with courage/desire, breathe courage/desire into sb; (*Rel*) **~ la vie à** to breathe life into. **(b)** (*Méd*) *air* to blow, insufflate (*T*) (*dans* into).

insulaire [ɛ̃sylɛʀ] **1** *adj administration, population* island (*épith*); *attitude* insular. **2** *nmf* islander.

insularité [ɛ̃sylaʀite] *nf* insularity.

insuline [ɛ̃sylin] *nf* insulin.

insultant, e [ɛ̃syltɑ̃, ɑ̃t] *adj* insulting (*pour* to).

insulte [ɛ̃sylt(ə)] *nf* (*grossièreté*) abuse (*U*), insult; (*affront*) insult. (*frm*) **c'est me faire ~ que de ne pas me croire** you insult me by not believing me; (*fig*) **c'est une ~ *ou* c'est faire ~ à son intelligence** it's an insult *ou* affront to his intelligence.

insulté, e [ɛ̃sylte] (*ptp de* **insulter**) **1** *adj* insulted. **2** *nm* (*en duel*) injured party.

insulter [ɛ̃sylte] (1) *vt* (*faire affront à*) to insult; (*injurier*) to abuse, insult. (*fig littér*) **~ à** to be an insult to.

insulteur [ɛ̃syltœʀ] *nm* insulter.

insupportable [ɛ̃sypɔʀtabl(ə)] *adj douleur, bruit, personne, spectacle* unbearable, intolerable, insufferable.

insupportablement [ɛ̃sypɔʀtabləmɑ̃] *adv* unbearably, intolerably, insufferably.

insurgé, e [ɛ̃syʀʒe] (*ptp de* **s'insurger**) *adj, nm,f* rebel, insurgent.

insurger (s') [ɛ̃syʀʒe] (3) *vpr* (*lit, fig*) to rebel, rise up, revolt (*contre* against).

insurmontable [ɛ̃syʀmɔ̃tabl(ə)] *adj difficulté, obstacle* insurmountable, insuperable; *peur, dégoût* unconquerable.

insurmontablement [ɛ̃syʀmɔ̃tabləmɑ̃] *adv* (*V* **insurmontable**) insurmountably, insuperably; unconquerably.

insurpassable [ɛ̃syʀpɑsabl(ə)] *adj* unsurpassable, unsurpassed.

insurrection [ɛ̃syʀɛksjɔ̃] *nf* (*lit*) insurrection, revolt, uprising; (*fig*) revolt. **mouvement/foyer d'~** movement/nucleus of revolt.

insurrectionnel, -elle [ɛ̃syʀɛksjɔnɛl] *adj mouvement, gouvernement, force* insurrectionary.

intact, e [ɛ̃takt, akt(ə)] *adj objet, réputation, argent* intact (*attrib*).

intangibilité [ɛ̃tɑ̃ʒibilite] *nf* inviolability.

intangible [ɛ̃tɑ̃ʒibl(ə)] *adj* (*impalpable*) intangible; (*sacré*) inviolable.

intarissable [ɛ̃taʀisabl(ə)] *adj* (*lit, fig*) inexhaustible. **il est ~** he could talk for ever (*sur* about).

intarissablement [ɛ̃taʀisabləmɑ̃] *adv* inexhaustibly.

intégrable [ɛ̃tegʀabl(ə)] *adj* integrable.

intégral, e, *mpl* **-aux** [ɛ̃tegʀal, o] **1** *adj* complete. **le remboursement ~ de qch** the repayment in full of sth, the full *ou* complete repayment of sth; **publier le texte ~ d'un discours** to publish the text of a speech in full *ou* the complete text of a speech; (*Ciné*) **version ~e** uncut version; (*Presse*) **texte ~** unabridged version; **'texte ~'** 'unabridged'; **le nu ~** complete *ou* total nudity; *V* **calcul.**
2 intégrale *nf* (*Math*) integral; (*Mus*) (*série*) complete series; (*œuvre*) complete works. **l'~e des symphonies de Sibelius** the complete set of the symphonies of Sibelius.

intégralement [ɛ̃tegʀalmɑ̃] *adv* in full, fully.

intégralité [ɛ̃tegʀalite] *nf* whole. **l'~ de la somme vous sera remboursée** the whole of the sum will be repaid to you, the whole *ou* entire *ou* full sum *ou* amount will be repaid to you; **la somme vous sera remboursée dans son ~** the sum will be repaid to you in its entirety *ou* in toto *ou* in full; **l'~ de mon salaire** the whole of my salary, my whole *ou* entire salary; **votre salaire vous sera versé en ~ en francs français** you will be paid the whole of your salary *ou* your entire salary in French francs.

intégrant, e [ɛ̃tegʀɑ̃, ɑ̃t] *adj V* **partie**[2].

intégration [ɛ̃tegʀɑsjɔ̃] *nf* (*V* **intégrer**) (*gén*) integration (*à, dans* into). (*arg Univ*) **après son ~ à Polytechnique** after getting into the École Polytechnique.

intègre [ɛ̃tɛgʀ(ə)] *adj* upright, honest.

intégrer [ɛ̃tegʀe] (6) **1** *vt* (*Math*) to integrate; (*incorporer*) *idées, personne* to integrate (*à, dans* into). **2** *vi* (*arg Univ*) **~ à Polytechnique** *etc* to get into the École Polytechnique *etc.* **3 s'intégrer** *vpr* to become integrated (*à, dans* into).

intégrité [ɛ̃tegʀite] *nf* (*totalité*) integrity; (*honnêteté*) integrity, honesty, uprightness.

intellect [ɛ̃telɛkt] *nm* intellect.

intellectualisation [ɛ̃telɛktɥalizɑsjɔ̃] *nf* intellectualization.

intellectualiser [ɛ̃telɛktɥalize] (1) *vt* to intellectualize.

intellectualisme [ɛ̃telɛktɥalism(ə)] *nm* intellectualism.

intellectualiste [ɛ̃telɛktɥalist(ə)] *adj, nmf* intellectualist.

intellectualité [ɛ̃telɛktɥalite] *nf* (*littér*) intellectuality.

intellectuel, -elle [ɛ̃telɛktɥɛl] **1** *adj facultés, effort, supériorité* mental, intellectual; *fatigue* mental; *personne, mouvement, œuvre, vie* intellectual; (*péj*) highbrow (*péj*), intellectual. **activité ~le** mental *ou* intellectual activity, brainwork*; **les travailleurs ~s** those who work with their intellects.
2 *nm,f* intellectual; (*péj*) highbrow (*péj*), intellectual.

intellectuellement [ɛ̃telɛktɥɛlmɑ̃] *adv* (*V* **intellectuel**) mentally; intellectually.

intelligemment [ɛ̃teliʒamɑ̃] *adv* (*V* **intelligent**) intelligently; cleverly.

intelligence [ɛ̃teliʒɑ̃s] *nf* **(a)** (*aptitude, ensemble des facultés mentales*) intelligence. **avoir l'~ vive** to have a sharp *ou* quick mind, be sharp *ou* quick; **faire preuve d'~** to show intelligence; **avoir l'~ de faire** to have the intelligence *ou* the wit to do, be intelligent enough to do; **travailler avec ~/sans ~** to work intelligently/unintelligently; **il met beaucoup d'~ dans ce qu'il fait** he applies great intelligence to what he does; **c'est une ~ exceptionnelle** he has a great intellect *ou* mind *ou* brain, he is a person of exceptional intelligence; **les grandes ~s** the great minds *ou* intellects.
(b) (*compréhension*) **~ de** understanding of; **pour l'~ du texte** for a clear understanding of the text, in order to understand the text; **avoir l'~ des affaires** to have a good grasp *ou* understanding of business matters, have a good head for business.
(c) (*complicité*) secret agreement. **agir d'~ avec qn** to act in (secret) agreement with sb; **signe/sourire d'~** sign/smile of complicity; **être d'~ avec qn** to have a (secret) understanding *ou* agreement with sb; **vivre en bonne/mauvaise ~ avec qn** to be on good/bad terms with sb.
(d) (*relations secrètes*) **~s** secret relations; **avoir des ~s dans la place** to have secret relations *ou* contacts in the place; **entretenir des ~s avec l'ennemi** to have secret dealings with the enemy.

intelligent, e [ɛ̃teliʒɑ̃, ɑ̃t] *adj* (*doué d'intellect*) intelligent; (*à l'esprit vif, perspicace*) intelligent, clever, bright. **peu ~** unintelligent; **ce chien est (très) ~** this dog is (very) clever; **son livre est ~** his book shows intelligence.

intelligibilité [ɛ̃teliʒibilite] *nf* intelligibility.

intelligible [ɛ̃teliʒibl(ə)] *adj* intelligible. **à haute et ~ voix** loudly and clearly; **s'exprimer de façon peu ~** to express o.s. unintelligibly *ou* in an unintelligible manner.

intelligiblement [ɛ̃teliʒibləmɑ̃] *adv* intelligibly.

intempérance [ɛ̃tɑ̃peʀɑ̃s] *nf* (*V* **intempérant**) intemperance; overindulgence. **~s** excesses; **une telle ~ de langage** such excessive language; **de telles ~s de langage** such excesses of language.

intempérant, e [ɛ̃tɑ̃peʀɑ̃, ɑ̃t] *adj* (*immodéré*) intemperate; (*sensuel*) overindulgent, intemperate.

intempéries [ɛ̃tɑ̃peʀi] *nfpl* bad weather. **nous allons affronter les ~** we're going to brave the (bad) weather.

intempestif, -ive [ɛ̃tɑ̃pɛstif, iv] *adj* untimely. **pas de zèle ~!** no excessive zeal!

intempestivement [ɛ̃tɑ̃pɛstivmɑ̃] *adv* at an untimely moment.

intemporalité [ɛ̃tɑ̃pɔʀalite] *nf* (*V* **intemporel**: *littér*) timelessness; immateriality.

intemporel, -elle [ɛ̃tɑ̃pɔʀɛl] *adj* (*littér*) (*sans durée*) timeless; (*immatériel*) immaterial.

intenable [ɛ̃tnabl(ə)] *adj* (*intolérable*) *chaleur, situation* intolerable, unbearable; *personne* unruly; (*indéfendable*) *position, théorie* untenable.

intendance [ɛ̃tɑ̃dɑ̃s] *nf* (*Mil*) (*service*) Supply Corps; (*bureau*) Supplies office; (*Scol*) (*métier*) school management; (*bureau*) bursar's office, bursary; (*Hist: province*) intendancy.

intendant [ɛ̃tɑ̃dɑ̃] *nm* (*Mil*) quartermaster; (*Scol*) bursar; (*Hist*) intendant; (*régisseur*) steward.

intendante [ɛ̃tɑ̃dɑ̃t] *nf* **(a)** (*épouse*) intendant's wife. **(b)** (*Scol*) bursar; (*régisseur*) stewardess. **(c)** (*Rel*) Superior.

intense [ɛ̃tɑ̃s] *adj* (*gén*) intense; *froid* severe, intense; *circulation* dense, heavy.

intensément [ɛ̃tɑ̃semɑ̃] *adv* intensely.

intensif, -ive [ɛ̃tɑ̃sif, iv] **1** *adj* (*gén, Agr, Ling*) intensive; *V* **culture.** **2** *nm* (*Ling*) intensive.

intensification [ɛ̃tɑ̃sifikɑsjɔ̃] *nf* intensification.

intensifier *vt,* **s'intensifier** *vpr* [ɛ̃tɑ̃sifje] (7) to intensify.

intensité [ɛ̃tɑ̃site] *nf* **(a)** (*force: V* **intense**) intensity; severity; density, heaviness. **l'~ de la lumière me força à fermer les yeux** the intensity of the light forced me to shut my eyes; **mesurer l'~ d'une source lumineuse** to measure the intensity of a light source.
(b) (*Ling*) **accent d'~** stress accent.

intensivement [ɛ̃tɑ̃sivmɑ̃] *adv* intensively.

intenter [ɛ̃tɑ̃te] (1) *vt*: **~ un procès contre *ou* à qn** to start *ou* institute proceedings against sb; **~ une action contre *ou* à qn** to bring an action against sb.

intention [ɛ̃tɑ̃sjɔ̃] *nf* **(a)** intention. **agir dans une bonne ~** to act with good intentions; **c'est l'~ qui compte** it's the thought that counts; **il n'entre *ou* n'est pas dans ses ~s de démissionner** it's not his intention to resign, he has no intention of resigning; **à cette ~** with this intention, to this end; **avoir l'~ de faire** to intend *ou* mean to do, have the intention of doing; **je n'ai pas l'~ de le faire** I don't intend to do it, I have no intention of doing it; **avec *ou* dans l'~ de faire** with the intention of doing, with a view to doing; **avec *ou* dans l'~ de tuer** with intent to kill; *V* **enfer, procès.**
(b) à l'~ de qn *collecte* for the benefit of sb, in aid of sb;

renseignement for the benefit of sb, for the information of sb; *cadeau, prières, messe* for sb; *fête* in sb's honour; **livre/film à l'~ des enfants/du grand public** book/film aimed at children/the general public; **je l'ai acheté à votre ~** I bought it just *ou* specially for you.

intentionné, e [ɛ̃tɑ̃sjɔne] *adj*: **bien ~** well-meaning, well-intentioned; **mal ~** ill-intentioned.

intentionnel, -elle [ɛ̃tɑ̃sjɔnɛl] *adj* intentional, deliberate.

intentionnellement [ɛ̃tɑ̃sjɔnɛlmɑ̃] *adv* intentionally, deliberately.

inter [ɛ̃tɛʀ] *nm* (*Téléc*) = **interurbain**; (*Sport*) **~ gauche/droit** inside-left/-right.

inter ... [ɛ̃tɛʀ] *préf* inter... .

interaction [ɛ̃tɛʀaksjɔ̃] *nf* interaction.

interallié, e [ɛ̃tɛʀalje] *adj* inter-Allied.

interarmes [ɛ̃tɛʀaʀm(ə)] *adj inv opération* combined arms (*épith*).

intercalaire [ɛ̃tɛʀkalɛʀ] *adj*: **feuillet ~** inset, insert; **fiche ~** divider; **jour ~** intercalary day.

intercalation [ɛ̃tɛʀkalɑsjɔ̃] *nf* (*V* **intercaler**) insertion; interpolation; intercalation.

intercaler [ɛ̃tɛʀkale] (1) **1** *vt mot, exemple* to insert, interpolate; *feuillet* to inset, insert; *jour d'année bissextile* to intercalate. **~ quelques jours de repos dans un mois de stage** to fit a few days' rest into a training month; **on a intercalé dans le stage des visites d'usines** the training course was interspersed with *ou* broken by visits to factories.

2 s'intercaler *vpr*: **s'~ entre** *[coureur, voiture, candidat]* to come in between.

intercéder [ɛ̃tɛʀsede] (6) *vi* to intercede (*en faveur de* on behalf of, *auprès de* with).

intercellulaire [ɛ̃tɛʀselylɛʀ] *adj* intercellular.

intercepter [ɛ̃tɛʀsɛpte] (1) *vt ballon, message, ennemi* to intercept; *lumière, chaleur* to cut *ou* block off.

interception [ɛ̃tɛʀsɛpsjɔ̃] *nf* (*V* **intercepter**) interception; cutting *ou* blocking off. (*Mil*) **avion** *ou* **chasseur d'~** interceptor.

intercesseur [ɛ̃tɛʀsesœʀ] *nm* (*Rel, littér*) intercessor.

intercession [ɛ̃tɛʀsesjɔ̃] *nf* (*Rel, littér*) intercession.

interchangeabilité [ɛ̃tɛʀʃɑ̃ʒabilite] *nf* interchangeability.

interchangeable [ɛ̃tɛʀʃɑ̃ʒabl(ə)] *adj* interchangeable.

interclasse [ɛ̃tɛʀklɑs] *nm* (*Scol*) break (*between classes*).

intercommunal, e, *mpl* **-aux** [ɛ̃tɛʀkɔmynal, o] *adj décision, stade* ≃ intervillage, ≃ intermunicipal (*shared by several French communes*).

intercommunication [ɛ̃tɛʀkɔmynikɑsjɔ̃] *nf* intercommunication.

interconnecter [ɛ̃tɛʀkɔnɛkte] (1) *vt* (*Élec*) to interconnect.

interconnexion [ɛ̃tɛʀkɔnɛksjɔ̃] *nf* (*Élec*) interconnection.

intercontinental, e, *mpl* **-aux** [ɛ̃tɛʀkɔ̃tinɑ̃tal, o] *adj* ≃ interregional. intercontinental.

intercostal, e, *mpl* **-aux** [ɛ̃tɛʀkɔstal, o] **1** *adj* intercostal. **2** *nmpl* intercostal muscles, intercostals.

interdépartemental, e, *mpl* **-aux** [ɛ̃tɛʀdepaʀtəmɑ̃tal, o] *adj shared by several French departments.*

interdépendance [ɛ̃tɛʀdepɑ̃dɑ̃s] *nf* interdependence.

interdépendant, e [ɛ̃tɛʀdepɑ̃dɑ̃, ɑ̃t] *adj* interdependent.

interdiction [ɛ̃tɛʀdiksjɔ̃] *nf* **(a) ~ de** banning of, ban on; **l'~ du col roulé/des cheveux longs dans cette profession** the ban on polo necks/long hair in this profession; **l'~ de coller des affiches/de servir de l'alcool** the ban on the sticking of bills/the serving of alcohol, the ban on sticking bills/serving alcohol; **'~ de coller des affiches'** '(stick *ou* post) no bills', 'bill-sticking *ou* bill-posting prohibited'; **'~ formelle** *ou* **absolue de fumer'** 'strictly no smoking', 'smoking strictly prohibited'; **'~ de tourner à droite'** 'no right turn'; **~ d'en parler à quiconque/de modifier quoi que ce soit** it is (strictly) forbidden to talk to anyone/to alter anything; **malgré l'~ d'entrer** despite the fact that it was forbidden to enter *ou* that there was a 'no entry' sign; **renouveler à qn l'~ de faire** to reimpose a ban on sb's doing; **~ lui a été faite de sortir** he has been forbidden to go out; **l'~ faite aux fonctionnaires de cumuler plusieurs emplois** the banning of civil servants from holding several offices.

(b) (*interdit*) ban. **enfreindre/lever une ~** to break/lift a ban; **écriteau portant une ~** notice banning *ou* forbidding something; **un jardin public plein d'~s** a park full of notices *ou* signs forbidding this and that.

(c) (*suspension*) *[livre, film]* banning (*de* of), ban (*de* on); *[fonctionnaire]* bannningafrom office; *[prêtre]* interdiction. (*Jur*) **~ de séjour** *order denying former prisoner access to specified places.*

interdigital, e, *mpl* **-aux** [ɛ̃tɛʀdiʒital, o] *adj* interdigital.

interdire [ɛ̃tɛʀdiʀ] (37) **1** *vt* **(a)** (*prohiber*) to forbid; (*Admin*) *stationnement, circulation* to prohibit, ban. **~ l'alcool/le tabac à qn** to forbid sb alcohol/tobacco, forbid sb to drink/smoke; **~ à qn de faire qch** to tell sb not to do sth, forbid sb to do sth, prohibit (*frm*) sb from doing sth; **on a interdit les camions dans le centre de la ville** lorries have been barred *ou* banned from *ou* prohibited in the centre of the town.

(b) (*empêcher*) *[contretemps, difficulté]* to preclude, prevent; *[obstacle physique]* to block. **son état de santé lui interdit tout travail/effort** his state of health does not allow *ou* permit him to do any work/to make any effort; **sa maladie ne lui interdit pas le travail** his illness does not prevent him from working; **la gravité de la crise (nous) interdit tout espoir** the gravity of the crisis leaves us no hope, the gravity of the crisis precludes all hope; **leur attitude interdit toute négociation** their attitude precludes *ou* prevents any possibility of negotiation; **une porte blindée interdisait le passage** an armoured door blocked *ou* barred the way.

(c) (*frapper d'interdiction*) *fonctionnaire, prêtre* to ban from office; *film, réunion, journal* to ban. (*fig*) **on lui a interdit le club** he has been barred *ou* banned from the club; **~ sa porte aux intrus** to bar one's door to intruders.

2 s'interdire *vpr*: **s'~ toute remarque** to refrain *ou* abstain from making any remark; **nous nous sommes interdit d'intervenir** we have not allowed ourselves to intervene, we have refrained from intervening; **s'~ la boisson/les cigarettes** to abstain from drink *ou* drinking/smoking; **il s'interdit d'y penser** he doesn't let himself think about it *ou* allow himself to think about it; **il s'est interdit toute possibilité de revenir en arrière** he has (deliberately) denied himself *ou* not allowed himself any chance of going back on his decision.

interdisciplinaire [ɛ̃tɛʀdisiplinɛʀ] *adj* interdisciplinary.

interdit, e[1] [ɛ̃tɛʀdi, it] (*ptp de* **interdire**) **1** *adj film, livre* banned. **film ~ aux moins de dix-huit ans** ≃ X film; **film ~ aux moins de treize ans** ≃ A film; **passage/stationnement ~** no entry/parking; **il est strictement ~ de faire** it is strictly forbidden *ou* prohibited to do; **(il est) ~ de fumer** no smoking, smoking (is) prohibited.

2 *nm,f, adj*: **~ de séjour** (*person*) *under interdiction de séjour.*

3 *nm* (*interdiction*) (*Rel*) interdict; (*social*) prohibition. (*fig*) **jeter l'~ sur** *ou* **contre qn** to bar sb.

interdit, e[2] [ɛ̃tɛʀdi, it] *adj* dumbfounded, taken aback (*attrib*). **la réponse le laissa ~** the answer took him aback, he was dumbfounded by *ou* at the answer.

intéressant, e [ɛ̃teʀɛsɑ̃, ɑ̃t] *adj* **(a)** (*captivant*) *livre, détail, visage* interesting. **peu ~** (*ennuyeux*) *conférencier* uninteresting, dull; (*négligeable*) *personne* not worth bothering about (*attrib*); (*péj*) **un personnage peu ~** a worthless individual, an individual of little consequence; (*péj*) **il faut toujours qu'il cherche à se rendre ~** *ou* **qu'il fasse son ~** he always has to be the centre of attraction *ou* focus of attention; *V* **position**.

(b) (*avantageux*) *offre, affaire* attractive, worthwhile; *prix* favourable, attractive. **ce n'est pas très ~ pour nous** it's not really worth our while, it's not really worth it for us.

intéressé, e [ɛ̃teʀese] (*ptp de* **intéresser**) *adj* **(a)** (*qui est en cause*) concerned, involved. **les ~s, les parties ~es** the interested parties, the parties involved *ou* concerned; **dans cette affaire, c'est lui le principal ~** in this matter, he is the person *ou* party principally involved *ou* concerned.

(b) (*qui cherche son intérêt personnel*) *personne* self-seeking, self-interested; *motif* interested. **une visite ~e** a visit motivated by self-interest; **rendre un service ~** to do a good turn out of self-interest; **ce que je vous propose, c'est très ~** my suggestion to you is strongly motivated by self-interest.

intéressement [ɛ̃teʀɛsmɑ̃] *nm* (*Écon: système*) profit-sharing (scheme). **l'~ des travailleurs aux bénéfices de l'entreprise** (*action*) the workers' participation in *ou* sharing of the firm's profits.

intéresser [ɛ̃teʀese] (1) **1** *vt* **(a)** (*captiver*) to interest. **~ qn à qch** to interest sb in sth; **cela m'intéresserait de faire** I would be interested to do *ou* in doing, it would interest me to do; **ça ne m'intéresse pas** I'm not interested, it doesn't interest me; **rien ne l'intéresse** he is not interested *ou* takes no interest in anything; **le film l'a intéressé** he found the film interesting, the film interested him; **ça pourrait vous ~** this might interest you *ou* be of interest to you; **cette question n'intéresse pas (beaucoup) les jeunes** this matter is of no (great) interest to *ou* doesn't (greatly) interest young people; **il ne sait pas ~ son public** he doesn't know how to interest his audience; (*iro*) **continue, tu m'intéresses** do go on — I find that very interesting *ou* I'm all ears!*

(b) (*concerner*) to affect, concern. **la nouvelle loi intéresse les petits commerçants** the new law affects *ou* concerns the small shopkeeper.

(c) (*Comm, Fin*) **~ le personnel de l'usine aux bénéfices** to give the factory employees a share *ou* an interest in the profits, operate a profit-sharing scheme in the factory; **être intéressé dans une affaire** to have an interest *ou* a stake *ou* a financial interest in a business.

2 s'intéresser *vpr*: **s'~ à qch/qn** to be interested in sth/sb, take an interest in sth/sb; **il s'intéresse vivement/activement à cette affaire** he is taking a keen/an active interest in this matter; **il ne s'intéresse pas à nos activités** he is not interested in our activities, he doesn't concern himself with our activities; **il mérite qu'on s'intéresse à lui** he deserves one's *ou* people's interest; **il s'intéresse beaucoup à cette jeune fille** he is very interested in *ou* he is taking *ou* showing a great deal of interest in that girl.

intérêt [ɛ̃teʀɛ] *nm* **(a)** (*attention*) interest. **écouter avec ~/(un) grand ~** to listen with interest/with great interest; **prendre ~ à qch** to take an interest in sth; **il a perdu tout ~ à son travail** he has lost all interest in his work.

(b) (*bienveillance*) interest. **porter/témoigner de l'~ à qn** to take/show an interest in sb.

(c) (*originalité*) interest. **film dénué d'~** *ou* **sans aucun ~** film devoid of interest; **tout l'~ réside dans le dénouement** the interest is all in the ending.

(d) (*importance*) significance, importance, relevance. **l'~ des recherches spatiales** the significance *ou* importance *ou* relevance of space research; **après quelques considérations sans ~** after a few unimportant *ou* minor considerations *ou* considerations of minor interest *ou* importance; **c'est sans ~ pour la suite de l'histoire** it's of no relevance *ou* consequence *ou* importance for the rest of the story; **une découverte du plus haut ~** a discovery of the greatest *ou* utmost importance *ou* significance *ou* relevance; **la nouvelle a perdu beaucoup de son ~** the news has lost much of its significance *ou* interest.

(e) (*avantage*) interest. **ce n'est pas (dans) leur ~ de le faire** it is not in their interest to do it; **agir dans/contre son ~** to act in/against one's own interests; **dans l'~ général** in the general interest; **il y trouve son ~** he finds it to his (own) advantage, he finds it worth his while; **il sait où est son ~** he knows where his interest lies, he knows which side his bread is buttered; **il a (tout) ~ à accepter** it's in his interest to accept; (*sens affaibli*) he'd do well to accept, it would be a good thing if he accepted; **tu aurais plutôt ~ à te taire!*** you'd be well advised *ou* you'd do very well to shut up!*; **y a-t-il (un) ~ quelconque à se réunir?** is there any point at all in getting together?

(f) (*Fin*) interest. **7% d'~** 7% interest; **prêt à ~ élevé** high-interest loan; **prêter à** *ou* **avec ~** to lend at *ou* with interest; **~s composés** compound interest; *V* **taux.**

(g) (*recherche d'avantage personnel*) self-interest. **agir par ~** to act out of self-interest; *V* **mariage.**

(h) ~s interest(s); **la défense de nos ~s** the defence of our interests; (*Écon, Fin*) **il a des ~s dans l'affaire** he has a stake *ou* an interest *ou* a financial interest in the business.

interférence [ɛ̃tɛʀfeʀɑ̃s] *nf* (*Phys*) interference; (*fig*) (*conjonction*) conjunction; (*immixtion*) *[problème]* intrusion (*dans* into); *[personne, pays]* interference (*U*) (*dans* in). **l'~ des problèmes économiques et politiques** the conjunction of economic and political problems; **l'~ des problèmes économiques dans la vie politique** the intrusion of economic problems into political life; **il se produit des ~s entre les deux services gouvernementaux** there's interference between the two government services.

interférent, e [ɛ̃tɛʀfeʀɑ̃, ɑ̃t] *adj* (*Phys*) interfering.

interférer [ɛ̃tɛʀfeʀe] (6) *vi* (*Phys*) to interfere; (*fig*) to interact (adversely), interfere (*avec* with, *dans* in). **les deux procédures interfèrent** the two procedures interfere with each other.

interfluve [ɛ̃tɛʀflyv] *nm* interfluve.

intergouvernemental, e, *mpl* **-aux** [ɛ̃tɛʀguvɛʀnəmɑ̃tal, o] *adj* intergovernmental. (*Québec*) **Affaires ~es** Intergovernmental Affairs.

intérieur, e [ɛ̃teʀjœʀ] **1** *adj paroi, escalier* inner, interior, inside; *cour* inner; (*fig*) *vie, monde, voix* inner; *sentiment* inner, inward; (*Écon, Pol*) *politique, dette* domestic, internal; *marché* home (*épith*), domestic, internal; (*Transport*) *communication, réseau, navigation* inland. **le commerce ~** domestic trade; **mer ~e** inland sea; **la poche ~e de son manteau** the inside pocket of his coat; (*Géom*) **angle/point ~ à un cercle** angle/point interior to a circle; *V* **conduite, for.**

2 *nm* **(a)** *[tiroir]* inside; *[maison]* inside, interior. **l'~ de la maison était lugubre** the house was gloomy inside, the inside *ou* the interior of the house was gloomy; **l'~ de la ville** the inner town; **écrin avec un ~ de satin** case with a satin lining; **fermé de l'~** locked from the inside; **à l'~** (*lit*) inside; (*fig*) within; **à l'~ de la ville** inside the town; (*fig*) **à l'~ de lui-même, il pensait que** he thought inwardly *ou* within himself that; **rester à l'~** (*gén*) to stay inside; (*de la maison*) to stay inside *ou* indoors; **vêtement/veste d'~** indoor garment/jacket; **chaussures d'~** house shoes; *V* **femme.**

(b) *[pays]* interior. **l'~ (du pays) est montagneux** the interior (of the country) is mountainous, the inland part of the country is mountainous; **les villes de l'~** the inland cities *ou* towns, the cities *ou* towns of the interior; **la côte est riante mais l'~ est sauvage** the coast is pleasant, but it's wild further inland *ou* the hinterland is wild; **en allant vers l'~** going inland; **les ennemis de l'~** the enemies within (the country); **le moral de l'~** the morale at home, the country's morale, the morale within the country; **à l'~ de nos frontières** within *ou* inside our frontiers; *V* **ministère, ministre.**

(c) (*décor, mobilier*) interior. **un ~ bourgeois/douillet** a comfortable middle-class/cosy interior.

(d) (*Ftbl*) **~ gauche/droit** inside-left/-right.

intérieurement [ɛ̃teʀjœʀmɑ̃] *adv* inwardly. **rire ~** to laugh inwardly *ou* to o.s.

intérim [ɛ̃teʀim] *nm* (*période*) interim period. **il prendra toutes les décisions dans** *ou* **pendant l'~** he will make all the decisions in the interim; **il assure l'~ en l'absence du directeur** he deputizes for the manager in his absence *ou* in the interim; **diriger une firme par ~** to run a firm temporarily *ou* in a temporary capacity; **président/ministre par ~** acting *ou* interim president/minister.

intérimaire [ɛ̃teʀimɛʀ] **1** *adj directeur, ministre* acting (*épith*), interim (*épith*); *secrétaire, personnel, fonctions* temporary; *mesure, solution* interim (*épith*), temporary; (*Pol*) *gouvernement, chef de parti* caretaker (*épith*).

2 *nmf* (*secrétaire*) temporary secretary, temp*; (*fonctionnaire*) deputy; (*médecin, prêtre*) locum (tenens).

interindividuel, -elle [ɛ̃tɛʀɛ̃dividɥɛl] *adj* interpersonal. **psychologie ~le** psychology of interpersonal relationships.

intériorisation [ɛ̃teʀjɔʀizɑsjɔ̃] *nf* (*V* **intérioriser**) internalization; interiorization.

intérioriser [ɛ̃teʀjɔʀize] (1) *vt conflit, émotion* to internalize, interiorize; (*Ling*) *règles* to internalize.

intériorité [ɛ̃teʀjɔʀite] *nf* interiority.

interjectif, -ive [ɛ̃tɛʀʒɛktif, iv] *adj* interjectional.

interjection [ɛ̃tɛʀʒɛksjɔ̃] *nf* (*Ling*) interjection; (*Jur*) lodging of an appeal.

interjeter [ɛ̃tɛʀʒəte] (4) *vt* (*Jur*) **~ appel** to lodge an appeal.

interligne [ɛ̃tɛʀliɲ] **1** *nm* (*espace*) space between the lines; (*annotation*) insertion between the lines. **double ~** double spacing; **écrire qch dans l'~** to write *ou* insert sth between the lines *ou* in the space between the lines. **2** *nf* (*Typ*) lead.

interlocuteur, -trice [ɛ̃tɛʀlɔkytœʀ, tʀis] *nm,f* speaker, interlocutor (*frm*). **son/mon ~** the person he/I was speaking to; (*Pol*) **~ valable** valid representative (*in a negotiating capacity*).

interlope [ɛ̃tɛʀlɔp] *adj* **(a)** (*équivoque*) shady. **(b)** (*illégal*) illicit, unlawful. **navire ~** *ship carrying illicit merchandise.*

interloquer [ɛ̃tɛʀlɔke] (1) *vt* to take aback, dumbfound.

interlude [ɛ̃tɛʀlyd] *nm* (*Mus, TV*) interlude.

intermède [ɛ̃tɛʀmɛd] *nm* (*Théât, interruption*) interlude.

intermédiaire [ɛ̃tɛʀmedjɛʀ] **1** *adj niveau, choix, position* intermediate, middle (*épith*), intermediary. **une solution/couleur ~ entre** a solution/colour halfway between; **une date ~ entre le 25 juillet et le 3 août** a date midway between 25th July and 3rd August.

2 *nm*: **sans ~** *vendre, négocier* directly; **par l'~ de qn** through (the intermediary *ou* agency of) sb; **par l'~ de la presse** through the medium of the press.

3 *nmf* (*médiateur*) intermediary, mediator, go-between; (*Comm, Écon*) middleman.

interminable [ɛ̃tɛʀminabl(ə)] *adj conversation, série* endless, interminable, never-ending; (*hum*) *jambes, mains* extremely long.

interminablement [ɛ̃tɛʀminabləmɑ̃] *adv* endlessly, interminably.

interministériel, -elle [ɛ̃tɛʀministeʀjɛl] *adj* interdepartmental.

intermission [ɛ̃tɛʀmisjɔ̃] *nf* (*Méd*) intermission.

intermittence [ɛ̃tɛʀmitɑ̃s] *nf* **(a) par ~** *travailler* in fits and starts, sporadically, intermittently; *pleuvoir* on and off*, sporadically, intermittently; **le bruit nous parvenait par ~** the noise reached our ears at (sporadic) intervals.

(b) (*Méd*) (*entre deux accès*) remission; *[pouls, cœur]* irregularity.

(c) (*littér*) intermittence, intermittency.

intermittent, e [ɛ̃tɛʀmitɑ̃, ɑ̃t] *adj fièvre, lumière* intermittent; *douleur* sporadic, intermittent; *travail, bruit* sporadic, periodic; *pouls* irregular, intermittent.

intermoléculaire [ɛ̃tɛʀmɔlekylɛʀ] *adj* intermolecular.

internat [ɛ̃tɛʀna] *nm* **(a)** (*Scol*) (*établissement*) boarding school; (*système*) boarding; (*élèves*) boarders; *V* **maître.**

(b) (*Univ Méd*) (*stage obligatoire*) ≃ period *ou* time as a houseman (*Brit*) *ou* an intern (*US*); (*concours*) entrance examination (for hospital work); (*stage après concours*) hospital training (*as a doctor*).

international, e, *mpl* **-aux** [ɛ̃tɛʀnasjɔnal, o] **1** *adj* international. **2** *nm,f* (*Ftbl, Tennis etc*) international player; (*Athlétisme*) international athlete. **3 Internationale** *nf* (*association*) International; (*hymne*) Internationale.

internationalement [ɛ̃tɛʀnasjɔnalmɑ̃] *adv* internationally.

internationalisation [ɛ̃tɛʀnasjɔnalizɑsjɔ̃] *nf* internationalization.

internationaliser [ɛ̃tɛʀnasjɔnalize] (1) *vt* to internationalize.

internationalisme [ɛ̃tɛʀnasjɔnalism(ə)] *nm* internationalism.

internationaliste [ɛ̃tɛʀnasjɔnalist(ə)] *nmf* internationalist.

internationalité [ɛ̃tɛʀnasjɔnalite] *nf* internationality.

interne [ɛ̃tɛʀn(ə)] **1** *adj partie, politique, organe, hémorragie* internal; *oreille* inner; *angle* interior. **2** *nmf* (*Scol*) boarder. (*Univ Méd*) **~ (des hôpitaux)** house doctor (*Brit*), houseman (*Brit*), intern (*US*).

interné, e [ɛ̃tɛʀne] (*ptp de* **interner**) *nm,f* (*Pol*) internee; (*Méd*) inmate (of a mental hospital).

internement [ɛ̃tɛʀnəmɑ̃] *nm* (*Pol*) internment; (*Méd*) confinement (to a mental hospital).

interner [ɛ̃tɛʀne] (1) *vt* (*Pol*) to intern. (*Méd*) **~ qn (dans un hôpital psychiatrique)** to confine sb to a mental hospital; **on devrait l'~** he ought to be certified*, he should be put away*.

interocéanique [ɛ̃tɛʀɔseanik] *adj* interoceanic.

interosseux, -euse [ɛ̃tɛʀɔsø, øz] *adj* interosseous.

interparlementaire [ɛ̃tɛʀpaʀləmɑ̃tɛʀ] *adj* interparliamentary.

interpellateur, -trice [ɛ̃tɛʀpelatœʀ, tʀis] *nm,f* (*V* **interpeller**) interpellator; questioner; heckler.

interpellation [ɛ̃tɛʀpelɑsjɔ̃] *nf* (*V* **interpeller**) hailing (*U*); interpellation; questioning (*U*); heckling (*U*). (*Police*) **il y a eu une dizaine d'~s** about ten people were taken in for questioning.

interpeller [ɛ̃tɛʀpele] (1) *vt* (*appeler*) to call out to, shout out to, hail; (*apostropher*) to shout at; (*à la Chambre*) to interpellate, question; (*dans une réunion*) to question; (*avec insistence*) to heckle; (*Police*) to question. **les automobilistes se sont interpellés grossièrement** the motorists shouted insults at each other.

interpénétration [ɛ̃tɛʀpenetʀɑsjɔ̃] *nf* interpenetration.

interpénétrer (s') [ɛ̃tɛʀpenetʀe] (6) *vpr* to interpenetrate.

interphone [ɛ̃tɛʀfɔn] *nm* intercom.

interplanétaire [ɛ̃tɛʀplanetɛʀ] *adj* interplanetary.

interpolation [ɛ̃tɛʀpɔlɑsjɔ̃] *nf* interpolation.

interpoler [ɛ̃tɛʀpɔle] (1) *vt* to interpolate.

interposer [ɛ̃tɛʀpoze] (1) **1** *vt* (*lit, fig*) to interpose (*entre* between); *V* **personne.**

2 s'interposer *vpr* to intervene, interpose (o.s.) (*frm*). **elle s'interposa entre le père et le fils** she intervened *ou* came between *ou* interposed herself (*frm*) between father and son.

interposition [ɛ̃tɛʀpozisjɔ̃] *nf* (*V* **interposer**) interposition (*rare*); intervention; (*Jur*) fraudulent representation of one's identity (*by use of a third party's identity*).

interprétable [ɛ̃tɛʀpʀetabl(ə)] *adj* interpretable.

interprétariat [ɛ̃tɛʀpʀetaʀja] *nm* interpreting. **école d'~** interpreting school.

interprétation [ɛ̃tɛʀpʀetɑsjɔ̃] *nf* (*V* **interpréter**) rendering, interpretation, rendition. **donner de qch une ~ fausse** to give a false interpretation of sth, misinterpret sth; *V* **prix.**

interprète [ɛ̃tɛʀpʀɛt] *nmf* **(a)** (*Mus, Théât*) performer, interpreter; (*gén*) player (*ou* singer *etc*). (*Théât*) **les ~s par ordre d'entrée en scène ...** the cast in order of appearance ...; **un ~ de Molière/Bach** a performer *ou* an interpreter of Molière/Bach;

un ~ de Macbeth a performer *ou* an interpreter of Macbeth, a Macbeth; **Paul était l'~ de cette sonate** Paul played this sonata; **Paul était l'~ de cette chanson** Paul was the singer of *ou* sang this song.
(b) (*traducteur*) interpreter. **faire l'~** to interpret; **servir d'~** to act as an interpreter.
(c) (*porte-parole*) **servir d'~ à qn/aux idées de qn** to act *ou* serve as a spokesman for sb/for sb's ideas; **je me ferai votre ~ auprès du ministre** I'll speak to the minister on your behalf; (*fig*) **les gestes et les yeux sont les ~s de la pensée** gestures and the look in one's eyes express *ou* interpret one's thoughts.
(d) (*exégète*) *[texte]* interpreter, exponent; *[rêves, signes]* interpreter.
interpréter [ɛ̃tɛʀpʀete] (6) *vt* **(a)** (*Mus, Théât*) to perform, render, interpret. **il va (vous) ~ Hamlet/une sonate** he's going to play Hamlet/a sonata (for you); **il va (vous) ~ une chanson** he's going to sing (you) a song.
(b) (*expliquer*) to interpret. **il a mal interprété mes paroles** he misinterpreted my words; **~ qch en bien/mal** to take sth the right/wrong way.
interprofessionnel, -elle [ɛ̃tɛʀpʀɔfesjɔnɛl] *adj réunion* interprofessional; *V* **salaire.**
interrègne [ɛ̃tɛʀʀɛɲ] *nm* interregnum.
interrogateur, -trice [ɛ̃tɛʀɔgatœʀ, tʀis] **1** *adj air, regard, ton* questioning (*épith*), inquiring (*épith*). **d'un air** *ou* **ton ~** questioningly, inquiringly. **2** *nm,f* (oral) examiner.
interrogatif, -ive [ɛ̃tɛʀɔgatif, iv] **1** *adj air, regard* questioning (*épith*), inquiring (*épith*); (*Ling*) interrogative. **2** *nm* interrogative (word). **mettre à l'~** to put into the interrogative. **3 interrogative** *nf* interrogative clause.
interrogation [ɛ̃tɛʀɔgɑsjɔ̃] *nf* **(a)** (*V* **interroger**) questioning; interrogation; examination; consultation; testing.
(b) (*question*) question. (*Scol*) **~ (écrite)** (written) test; (*Scol*) **il y a 15 minutes d'~ (orale)** there's a 15-minute oral (test); (*Gram*) **~ directe/indirecte** direct/indirect question; **les sourcils levés, en signe d'~** his eyebrows raised questioningly *ou* inquiringly; **les yeux pleins d'une ~ muette** his eyes silently questioning; *V* **point**[1].
(c) (*réflexions*) **~s** questioning; **ces ~s continuelles sur la destinée humaine** this continual questioning about human destiny.
interrogatoire [ɛ̃tɛʀɔgatwaʀ] *nm* (*Police*) questioning; (*au tribunal*) cross-examination, cross-questioning (*U*); (*compte-rendu*) statement; (*fig: série de questions*) cross-examination, interrogation. **il a signé son ~** he signed his statement.
interroger [ɛ̃tɛʀɔʒe] (3) **1** *vt* (*gén*) to question (*sur* about); (*de manière serrée, prolongée*) to interrogate; *données, ciel, conscience* to examine; *mémoire* to consult, search. **~ un élève** to test *ou* examine a pupil (orally); **~ par écrit les élèves** to give a written test to the pupils; **~ qn du regard** to give sb a questioning *ou* an inquiring look, look questioningly *ou* inquiringly at sb.
2 s'interroger *vpr* (*sur un problème*) to question o.s. (*sur* about). **s'~ sur la conduite à tenir** to ponder over *ou* ask o.s. (about) what course to follow.
interrompre [ɛ̃tɛʀɔ̃pʀ(ə)] (41) **1** *vt* **(a)** (*arrêter*) *voyage, circuit électrique* to break, interrupt; *conversation* (*gén*) to interrupt, break off; (*pour s'interposer*) to break into, cut into; *études* to break off, interrupt. **il a interrompu la conversation pour téléphoner** he broke off *ou* interrupted his conversation to telephone; (*Méd*) **~ une grossesse** to terminate a pregnancy.
(b) (*couper la parole à, déranger*) **~ qn** to interrupt sb; **je ne veux pas qu'on m'interrompe (dans mon travail)** I don't want to be interrupted (in my work); **je ne veux pas ~ mais ...** I don't want to cut in *ou* interrupt but ... .
2 s'interrompre *vpr [personne, conversation]* to break off.
interrupteur, -trice [ɛ̃tɛʀyptœʀ, tʀis] **1** *nm* switch (*Élec*). **2** *nm,f* interrupter.
interruption [ɛ̃tɛʀypsjɔ̃] *nf* (*action*) interruption (*de* of); (*état*) break (*de* in), interruption (*de* of, in); (*Jur*) interruption of prescription. **une ~ de deux heures/trois mois** a break *ou* an interruption of two hours/three months; (*Méd*) **~ de grossesse** termination of pregnancy; **sans ~** *parler* without a break *ou* an interruption, uninterruptedly; *pleuvoir* without stopping, without a break; **un moment d'~** a moment's break.
interscolaire [ɛ̃tɛʀskɔlɛʀ] *adj* inter-schools.
intersection [ɛ̃tɛʀsɛksjɔ̃] *nf* intersection; *V* **point**[1].
intersidéral, e, *mpl* **-aux** [ɛ̃tɛʀsideʀal, o] *adj* intersidereal.
interstellaire [ɛ̃tɛʀstelɛʀ] *adj* interstellar.
interstice [ɛ̃tɛʀstis] *nm* crack, chink, interstice. **à travers les ~s des rideaux** through the slits in the curtains.
intersyndical, e, *mpl* **-aux** [ɛ̃tɛʀsɛ̃dikal, o] *adj* interunion.
intertropical, e, *mpl* **-aux** [ɛ̃tɛʀtʀɔpikal, o] *adj* intertropical.
interurbain, e [ɛ̃tɛʀyʀbɛ̃, ɛn] **1** *adj* **(a)** *relations* interurban.
(b) (*Téléc*) *communication* trunk (*Brit, épith*), long-distance; *téléphone* long-distance (*épith*). **2** *nm*: **l'~** the trunk call service (*Brit*), the long-distance telephone service.
intervalle [ɛ̃tɛʀval] *nm* **(a)** (*espace*) space, distance; (*entre 2 mots, 2 lignes*) space; (*temps*) interval; (*Mus*) interval.
(b) (*loc*) **c'est arrivé à 2 jours/mois d'~** it happened after a space *ou* an interval of two days/months; **à ~s réguliers/rapprochés** at regular/close intervals; **par ~s** at intervals; **dans l'~** (*temporel*) in the meantime, meanwhile; (*spatial*) in between.
intervenir [ɛ̃tɛʀvəniʀ] (22) *vi* **(a)** (*entrer en action*) to intervene. **il est intervenu en notre faveur** he interceded *ou* intervened on our behalf; **~ militairement dans un pays** to intervene militarily in the affairs of a country; **on a dû faire ~ l'armée** the army had to be brought in *ou* called in.
(b) (*Méd*) to operate.
(c) (*survenir*) *[fait, événement]* to take place, occur; *[accord]* to be reached, be entered into; *[décision, mesure]* to be taken; *[élément nouveau]* to arise, come up. **cette mesure intervient au moment où ...** this measure is being taken *ou* comes at a time when ... .
(d) (*Jur*) to intervene. (*gén*) **un accord est intervenu entre ...** an agreement was reached *ou* was entered into between ... .
intervention [ɛ̃tɛʀvɑ̃sjɔ̃] *nf* (*gén, Jur*) intervention; (*Méd*) operation. **son ~ en notre faveur** his intercession *ou* intervention on our behalf; **~ chirurgicale** surgical operation; **~ armée** armed intervention; **~ de l'État** state intervention; (*Écon*) **prix d'~** intervention price; *V* **force.**
interventionnisme [ɛ̃tɛʀvɑ̃sjɔnism(ə)] *nm* interventionism.
interventionniste [ɛ̃tɛʀvɑ̃sjɔnist(ə)] *adj, nmf* interventionist.
interversion [ɛ̃tɛʀvɛʀsjɔ̃] *nf* inversion. **~ des rôles** reversal *ou* inversion of roles.
intervertir [ɛ̃tɛʀvɛʀtiʀ] (2) *vt* to invert *ou* reverse the order of, invert. **~ les rôles** to reverse *ou* invert roles.
interview [ɛ̃tɛʀvju] *nf* (*Presse, TV*) interview.
interviewé, e [ɛ̃tɛʀvjuve] (*ptp de* **interviewer**) *nm,f* (*Presse, TV*) interviewee.
interviewer[1] [ɛ̃tɛʀvjuve] (1) *vt* (*Presse, TV*) to interview.
interviewer[2] [ɛ̃tɛʀvjuvœʀ] *nm* (*journaliste*) interviewer.
intervocalique [ɛ̃tɛʀvɔkalik] *adj* intervocalic.
intestat [ɛ̃tɛsta] **1** *adj* (*Jur*) **mourir ~** to die intestate. **2** *nmpl* intestates.
intestin[1] [ɛ̃tɛstɛ̃] *nm* intestine. **~s** intestines, bowels; **~ grêle** small intestine; **gros ~** large intestine.
intestin[2]**, e** [ɛ̃tɛstɛ̃, in] *adj* (*fig*) *querelle, guerre* internal.
intestinal, e, *mpl* **-aux** [ɛ̃tɛstinal, o] *adj* intestinal.
intimation [ɛ̃timɑsjɔ̃] *nf* (*Jur*) (*assignation*) summons (*sg*) (*before an appeal court*); (*signification*) notification.
intime [ɛ̃tim] **1** *adj* **(a)** (*privé*) *hygiène* personal; *vie* private; *chagrin, confidences* intimate; *secret* close, intimate; *cérémonie, mariage* quiet; *salon, atmosphère* intimate, cosy. **carnet** *ou* **journal ~** intimate *ou* private diary; **un dîner ~** (*entre amis*) a dinner with (old) friends; (*entre amoureux*) a romantic dinner.
(b) (*étroit*) *mélange, relation* intimate; *union* close; *ami* close, intimate, bosom (*épith*). **être ~ avec qn** to be intimate with *ou* close to sb.
(c) (*profond*) *nature, structure* intimate, innermost; *sens, sentiment, conviction* inner(most), inmost, intimate.
2 *nmf* close friend. **seuls les ~s sont restés dîner** only those who were close friends stayed to dinner; (*hum*) **Jo pour les ~s*** Jo to his friends *ou* buddies* (*hum*).
intimé, e [ɛ̃time] (*ptp de* **intimer**) *nm,f* (*Jur*) respondent, appellee.
intimement [ɛ̃timmɑ̃] *adj* intimately. **~ persuadé** deeply *ou* firmly convinced.
intimer [ɛ̃time] (1) *vt* **(a) ~ à qn l'ordre de faire** to order sb to do. **(b)** (*Jur*) (*assigner*) to summon (*before an appeal court*); (*signifier*) to notify.
intimidable [ɛ̃timidabl(ə)] *adj* easily intimidated.
intimidant, e [ɛ̃timidɑ̃, ɑ̃t] *adj* intimidating.
intimidateur, -trice [ɛ̃timidatœʀ, tʀis] *adj* intimidating.
intimidation [ɛ̃timidɑsjɔ̃] *nf* intimidation. **manœuvre/moyens d'~** device/means of intimidation; **on l'a fait parler en usant d'~** they scared *ou* frightened him into talking.
intimider [ɛ̃timide] (1) *vt* to intimidate. **ne te laisse pas ~ par lui** don't let him intimidate you, don't let yourself be intimidated by him.
intimisme [ɛ̃timism(ə)] *nm* (*Art, Littérat*) intimism.
intimiste [ɛ̃timist(ə)] *adj, nmf* (*Art, Littérat*) intimist.
intimité [ɛ̃timite] *nf* **(a)** (*vie privée*) privacy. **dans l'~ c'est un homme très simple** in private life, he's a man of simple tastes; **nous serons dans l'~** there will only be a few of us *ou* a few close friends or relatives; **se marier dans l'~** to have a private *ou* quiet wedding; **la cérémonie a eu lieu dans la plus stricte ~** the ceremony took place in the strictest privacy; **pénétrer dans l'~ de qn** to be admitted into sb's private life; **vivre dans l'~ de qn** to be in close contact with sb.
(b) (*familiarité*) intimacy. **dans l'~ conjugale** in the intimacy of one's married life; **vivre dans la plus grande ~ avec qn** to live on very intimate terms with sb.
(c) (*confort*) *[atmosphère, salon]* cosiness, intimacy.
(d) (*littér: profondeur*) depths. **dans l'~ de sa conscience** in the depths of *ou* innermost recesses of one's conscience.
intitulé [ɛ̃tityle] *nm [livre, loi, jugement]* title; *[chapitre]* heading, title.
intituler [ɛ̃tityle] (1) **1** *vt* to entitle, call. **2 s'intituler** *vpr [livre, chapitre]* to be entitled *ou* called; *[personne]* to call o.s., give o.s. the title of.
intolérable [ɛ̃tɔleʀabl(ə)] *adj* intolerable.
intolérablement [ɛ̃tɔleʀabləmɑ̃] *adv* intolerably.
intolérance [ɛ̃tɔleʀɑ̃s] *nf* intolerance.
intolérant, e [ɛ̃tɔleʀɑ̃, ɑ̃t] *adj* intolerant.
intonation [ɛ̃tɔnɑsjɔ̃] *nf* (*Ling, Mus*) intonation. **voix aux ~s douces** soft-toned voice.
intouchable [ɛ̃tuʃabl(ə)] *adj, nmf* untouchable.
intox(e)* [ɛ̃tɔks] *nf* (*Pol: abrév de* **intoxication**) brainwashing.
intoxication [ɛ̃tɔksikɑsjɔ̃] *nf* (*V* **intoxiquer**) poisoning (*U*); brainwashing, indoctrination. **~ alimentaire** food poisoning (*U*).
intoxiqué, e [ɛ̃tɔksike] (*ptp de* **intoxiquer**) *nm,f* (*par la drogue*) drug addict; (*par le tabac*) smoking addict; (*par l'alcool*) alcoholic.
intoxiquer [ɛ̃tɔksike] (1) **1** *vt* (*lit*) to poison; (*fig*) (*Pol*) to brainwash, indoctrinate; (*corrompre*) to poison the mind of. **être**

intoxiqué par le tabac/l'alcool/la drogue to be poisoned by the effects of tobacco/alcohol/drugs.

2 s'intoxiquer *vpr* to poison o.s.

intracellulaire [ɛ̃tʀaselylɛʀ] *adj* intracellular.

intradermique [ɛ̃tʀadɛʀmik] *adj* intradermal, intradermic.

intradermo(-réaction) [ɛ̃tʀadɛʀmɔ(ʀeaksjɔ̃)] *nf* skin reaction.

intraduisible [ɛ̃tʀadɥizibl(ə)] *adj texte* untranslatable; *sentiment, idée* inexpressible. **il eut une intonation ~** his intonation was impossible to interpret *ou* was quite unfathomable.

intraitable [ɛ̃tʀɛtabl(ə)] *adj* uncompromising, inflexible. **il est ~ sur la discipline** he's a stickler for discipline, he's uncompromising *ou* inflexible in matters of discipline.

intramusculaire [ɛ̃tʀamyskylɛʀ] *adj* intramuscular.

intransigeance [ɛ̃tʀɑ̃ziʒɑ̃s] *nf* intransigence.

intransigeant, e [ɛ̃tʀɑ̃ziʒɑ̃, ɑ̃t] *adj personne* uncompromising, intransigent; *morale* uncompromising. **les ~s** the intransigents.

intransitif, -ive [ɛ̃tʀɑ̃zitif, iv] *adj, nm* intransitive.

intransitivement [ɛ̃tʀɑ̃zitivmɑ̃] *adv* intransitively.

intransitivité [ɛ̃tʀɑ̃zitivite] *nf* intransitivity, intransitiveness.

intransmissibilité [ɛ̃tʀɑ̃smisibilite] *nf* intransmissibility; (*Jur*) untransferability, non-transferability.

intransmissible [ɛ̃tʀɑ̃smisibl(ə)] *adj* intransmissible; (*Jur*) untransferable, non-transferable.

intransportable [ɛ̃tʀɑ̃spɔʀtabl(ə)] *adj objet* untransportable; *malade* who is unfit *ou* unable to travel.

intra-utérin, e [ɛ̃tʀayteʀɛ̃, in] *adj* intra-uterine.

intraveineux, -euse [ɛ̃tʀavɛnø, øz] **1** *adj* intravenous. **2 intraveineuse** *nf* intravenous injection.

intrépide [ɛ̃tʀepid] *adj* (*courageux*) intrepid, dauntless, bold; (*résolu*) dauntless; *bavard* unashamed; *menteur* barefaced (*épith*), unashamed.

intrépidement [ɛ̃tʀepidmɑ̃] *adv* intrepidly, dauntlessly, boldly.

intrépidité [ɛ̃tʀepidite] *nf* intrepidity, dauntlessness, boldness. **avec ~** intrepidly, dauntlessly, boldly.

intrigant, e [ɛ̃tʀigɑ̃, ɑ̃t] **1** *adj* scheming. **2** *nm,f* schemer, intriguer.

intrigue [ɛ̃tʀig] *nf* (*manœuvre*) intrigue, scheme; (*liaison*) (love) affair, intrigue; (*Ciné, Littérat, Théât*) plot.

intriguer [ɛ̃tʀige] (1) **1** *vt* to intrigue, puzzle. **2** *vi* to scheme, intrigue.

intrinsèque [ɛ̃tʀɛ̃sɛk] *adj* intrinsic.

intrinsèquement [ɛ̃tʀɛ̃sɛkmɑ̃] *adv* intrinsically.

introduction [ɛ̃tʀɔdyksjɔ̃] *nf* **(a)** introduction (*à, auprès de* to). **paroles/chapitre d'~** introductory words/chapter; **lettre/mot d'~** letter/note of introduction.

(b) (*V* **introduire**) insertion; introduction; launching; smuggling; institution.

(c) (*V* **s'introduire**) admission, introduction.

introduire [ɛ̃tʀɔdɥiʀ] (38) **1** *vt* **(a)** (*faire entrer*) *objet* to place (*dans* in), insert, introduce (*dans* into); *liquide* to introduce (*dans* into); *visiteur* to show in; *mode* to launch, introduce; *idées nouvelles* to bring in, introduce; (*Ling*) *mot* to introduce (*dans* into). **il introduisit sa clef dans la serrure** he placed his key in the lock, he introduced *ou* inserted his key into the lock; **on m'introduisit dans le salon/auprès de la maîtresse de maison** I was shown into *ou* ushered into the lounge/shown in *ou* ushered in to see the mistress of the house; **~ des marchandises en contrebande** to smuggle in goods.

(b) (*présenter*) *ami, protégé* to introduce. **il m'introduisit auprès du directeur/dans le groupe** he put me in contact with *ou* introduced me to the manager/the group.

(c) (*Jur*) *instance* to institute.

2 s'introduire *vpr* **(a)** (*lit*) **s'~ dans un groupe** to work one's way into a group, be *ou* get o.s. admitted *ou* accepted into a group; **s'~ chez qn par effraction** to break into sb's home; **s'~ dans une pièce** to get into *ou* enter a room; **les prisonniers s'introduisaient un à un dans le tunnel** one by one the prisoners worked *ou* wriggled their way into the tunnel; **l'eau/la fumée s'introduisait partout** the water/smoke was getting in *ou* penetrating everywhere.

(b) (*fig*) *[usage, mode, idée]* to be introduced (*dans* into).

introduit, e [ɛ̃tʀɔdɥi, it] (*ptp de* **introduire**) *adj* (*frm*) **être bien ~ dans un milieu** to be well received in a certain milieu.

intromission [ɛ̃tʀɔmisjɔ̃] *nf* intromission.

intronisation [ɛ̃tʀɔnizɑsjɔ̃] *nf* (*V* **introniser**) enthronement; establishment.

introniser [ɛ̃tʀɔnize] (1) *vt* (*lit*) to enthrone; (*fig*) to establish.

introspectif, -ive [ɛ̃tʀɔspɛktif, iv] *adj* introspective.

introspection [ɛ̃tʀɔspɛksjɔ̃] *nf* introspection.

introuvable [ɛ̃tʀuvabl(ə)] *adj* which (*ou* who) cannot be found. **ma clef est ~** I can't find my key anywhere, my key is nowhere to be found; **l'évadé demeure toujours ~** the escaped prisoner has still not been found *ou* discovered, the escaped prisoner remains undiscovered; **ces meubles sont ~s aujourd'hui** furniture like this is unobtainable *ou* just cannot be found these days.

introversion [ɛ̃tʀɔvɛʀsjɔ̃] *nf* introversion.

introverti, e [ɛ̃tʀɔvɛʀti] **1** *adj* introverted. **2** *nm,f* introvert.

intrus, e [ɛ̃tʀy, yz] **1** *adj* intruding, intrusive. **2** *nm,f* intruder.

intrusion [ɛ̃tʀyzjɔ̃] *nf* (*gén, Géol*) intrusion. **~ dans les affaires de qn** interference *ou* intrusion in sb's affairs; (*Géol*) **roches d'~** intrusive rocks.

intuitif, -ive [ɛ̃tɥitif, iv] *adj* intuitive.

intuition [ɛ̃tɥisjɔ̃] *nf* intuition. **avoir de l'~** to have intuition; **l'~ féminine** feminine intuition. **elle eut l'~ que/de** she had an intuition that/of.

intuitivement [ɛ̃tɥitivmɑ̃] *adv* intuitively.

intumescence [ɛ̃tymesɑ̃s] *nf* (*Anat*) intumescence.

intumescent, e [ɛ̃tymesɑ̃, ɑ̃t] *adj* intumescent.

inusable [inyzabl(ə)] *adj vêtement* hard-wearing.

inusité, e [inyzite] *adj mot* uncommon, not in (common) use (*attrib*). **ce mot est pratiquement ~** this word is practically never used.

inusuel, -elle [inyzɥɛl] *adj* (*littér*) unusual.

inutile [inytil] *adj* **(a)** (*qui ne sert pas*) *objet* useless; *effort, parole* pointless. **amasser des connaissances ~s** to gather a lot of useless knowledge; **sa voiture lui est ~ maintenant** his car is (of) no use *ou* is no good *ou* is useless to him now; **c'est ~ (d'insister)!** it's useless *ou* no use *ou* no good (insisting)!, there's no point *ou* it's pointless (insisting)!; **c'est un ~** he's a useless character, he's useless *ou* no use.

(b) (*superflu*) *paroles, crainte, travail, effort* needless, unnecessary. **~ de vous dire que je ne suis pas resté** needless to say I didn't stay, I hardly need tell you I didn't stay; *V* **bouche**.

inutilement [inytilmɑ̃] *adv* needlessly, unnecessarily.

inutilisable [inytilizabl(ə)] *adj* unusable.

inutilisé, e [inytilize] *adj* unused.

inutilité [inytilite] *nf* (*V* **inutile**) uselessness; pointlessness; needlessness.

invaincu, e [ɛ̃vɛ̃ky] *adj* unconquered, unvanquished; (*Sport*) unbeaten.

invalidation [ɛ̃validɑsjɔ̃] *nf [contrat, élection]* invalidation; *[député]* removal (from office).

invalide [ɛ̃valid] **1** *nmf* disabled person. **~ de guerre** disabled ex-serviceman, invalid soldier; **~ du travail** industrially disabled person. **2** *adj* (*Méd*) disabled.

invalider [ɛ̃valide] (1) *vt* (*Jur*) to invalidate; (*Pol*) *député* to remove from office; *élection* to invalidate.

invalidité [ɛ̃validite] *nf* disablement, disability.

invariabilité [ɛ̃vaʀjabilite] *nf* invariability.

invariable [ɛ̃vaʀjabl(ə)] *adj* invariable; (*littér*) unvarying.

invariablement [ɛ̃vaʀjabləmɑ̃] *adv* invariably.

invariant, e [ɛ̃vaʀjɑ̃, ɑ̃t] *adj, nm* invariant.

invasion [ɛ̃vɑzjɔ̃] *nf* invasion.

invective [ɛ̃vɛktiv] *nf* invective. **~s** abuse, invectives.

invectiver [ɛ̃vɛktive] (1) **1** *vt* to hurl *ou* shout abuse at. **ils se sont violemment invectivés** they hurled *ou* shouted violent abuse at each other. **2** *vi* to inveigh, rail (*contre* against).

invendable [ɛ̃vɑ̃dabl(ə)] *adj* (*gén*) unsaleable; (*Comm*) unmarketable.

invendu, e [ɛ̃vɑ̃dy] **1** *adj* unsold. **2** *nm* unsold article. **retourner les ~s** (*magazines etc*) to return (the) unsold copies.

inventaire [ɛ̃vɑ̃tɛʀ] *nm* (*gén, Jur*) inventory; (*Comm*) (*liste*) stocklist; (*opération*) stocktaking; (*fig: recensement*) *[monuments, souvenirs]* survey. (*gén, Jur*) **faire un ~** to make an inventory; (*Comm*) to take stock, do the stocktaking; (*fig*) **faire l'~ de** to assess, make an assessment of, take stock of; *V* **bénéfice**.

inventer [ɛ̃vɑ̃te] (1) *vt* (*créer, découvrir*) (*gén*) to invent; *moyen* to devise; *mot* to coin; (*imaginer, trouver*) *moyen* to think up; *jeu* to think up, make up; *mot* to make up; *excuse, histoire fausse* to invent, make *ou* think up; (*Jur*) *trésor* to find. **il ne sait plus quoi ~ pour échapper à l'école** he doesn't know what to think up *ou* dream up next to get out of school; **il n'a pas inventé la poudre *ou* le fil à couper le beurre** he'll never set the Thames on fire, he's no bright spark; **ils avaient inventé de faire entrer les lapins dans le salon** they hit upon the idea *ou* they had the bright idea of bringing the rabbits into the drawing room; **je n'invente rien** I'm not making anything up, I'm not inventing a thing; **ce sont des choses qui ne s'inventent pas** those are things people just don't make up; *V* **pièce**.

inventeur, -trice [ɛ̃vɑ̃tœʀ, tʀis] *nm,f* inventor; (*Jur*) finder.

inventif, -ive [ɛ̃vɑ̃tif, iv] *adj* *esprit* inventive; *personne* resourceful, inventive.

invention [ɛ̃vɑ̃sjɔ̃] *nf* (*gén, péj*) invention; (*ingéniosité*) inventiveness, spirit of invention; (*Jur*) *[trésor]* finding. **cette excuse est une pure *ou* de la pure ~** that excuse is a pure invention *ou* fabrication; **l'histoire est de son ~** the story was made up *ou* invented by him *ou* was his own invention; **un cocktail de mon ~** a cocktail of my own creation; *V* **brevet**.

inventorier [ɛ̃vɑ̃tɔʀje] (7) *vt* (*gén, Jur*) to make an inventory of; (*Comm*) to make a stocklist of.

invérifiable [ɛ̃veʀifjabl(ə)] *adj* unverifiable.

inverse [ɛ̃vɛʀs(ə)] **1** *adj* (*gén*) opposite; (*Logique, Math*) inverse. **arriver en sens ~** to arrive from the opposite direction; **l'image apparaît en sens ~ dans le miroir** the image is reversed in the mirror; **dans l'ordre ~** in (the) reverse order.

2 *nm*: **l'~** (*gén*) the opposite, the reverse; (*Philos*) the converse; **tu as fait l'~ de ce que je t'ai dit** you did the opposite to *ou* of what I told you; **t'a-t-il attaqué ou l'~?** did he attack you or vice versa?, did he attack you or was it the other way round?; **à l'~** conversely; **cela va à l'~ de nos prévisions** that goes contrary to our plans.

inversé, e [ɛ̃vɛʀse] (*ptp de* **inverser**) *adj image* reversed; *relief* inverted.

inversement [ɛ̃vɛʀsəmɑ̃] *adv* (*gén*) conversely; (*Math*) inversely. **...et ~** ...and vice versa.

inverser [ɛ̃vɛʀse] (1) *vt ordre* to reverse, invert; *courant électrique* to reverse.

inverseur [ɛ̃vɛʀsœʀ] *nm* (*Élec, Tech*) reverser.

inversion [ɛ̃vɛʀsjɔ̃] *nf* (*gén, Anat*) inversion; (*Élec*) reversal. (*Mét*) **~ thermique** temperature inversion.

invertébré, e [ɛ̃vɛʀtebʀe] *adj, nm* invertebrate. **~s** invertebrates, Invertebrata (*T*).

inverti, e [ɛ̃vɛʀti] (*ptp de* **invertir**) *nm,f* homosexual, invert (*T*).

invertir† [ɛ̃vɛʀtiʀ] (2) *vt* to invert.

investigateur, -trice [ɛ̃vɛstigatœʀ, tʀis] **1** *adj technique* investigative; *esprit* inquiring (*épith*); *regard* searching (*épith*), scrutinizing (*épith*). **2** *nm,f* investigator.

investigation [ɛ̃vɛstigɑsjɔ̃] *nf* investigation, inquiry. **après une minutieuse ~ *ou* de minutieuses ~s le médecin diagnostiqua du diabète** after (a) thorough inspection the doctor diagnosed diabetes; **au cours de ses ~s le savant découvrit que ...** in the course of his research *ou* investigations the scientist discovered that ... .

investir [ɛ̃vɛstiʀ] (2) *vt* **(a)** (*Fin*) *capital* to invest.
(b) *fonctionnaire* to induct; *évêque* to invest. **~ qn de pouvoirs/droits** to invest *ou* vest sb with powers/rights, vest powers/rights in sb; **~ qn de sa confiance** to place one's trust in sb.
(c) (*Mil*) *ville, forteresse* to invest.

investissement [ɛ̃vɛstismɑ̃] *nm* (*Écon*) investment; (*Mil*) investing.

investiture [ɛ̃vɛstityʀ] *nf [candidat]* nomination; *[président du Conseil]* appointment; *[évêché]* investiture.

invétéré, e [ɛ̃veteʀe] *adj fumeur, joueur, menteur* inveterate; *habitude* inveterate, deep-rooted; *voleur, ivrogne* confirmed.

invincibilité [ɛ̃vɛ̃sibilite] *nf [adversaire, nation]* invincibility.

invincible [ɛ̃vɛ̃sibl(ə)] *adj adversaire, nation* invincible, unconquerable; *courage* indomitable; *charme* irresistible; *timidité, gêne* insurmountable; *difficultés* insurmountable, insuperable; *argument* unassailable.

invinciblement [ɛ̃vɛ̃sibləmɑ̃] *adv* invincibly.

inviolabilité [ɛ̃vjɔlabilite] *nf [droit]* inviolability; *[serrure]* impregnability. **~ parlementaire** parliamentary immunity.

inviolable [ɛ̃vjɔlabl(ə)] *adj droit* inviolable; *serrure* impregnable; *parlementaire, diplomate* immune.

inviolablement [ɛ̃vjɔlabləmɑ̃] *adv* inviolably.

inviolé, e [ɛ̃vjɔle] *adj* inviolate, unviolated.

invisibilité [ɛ̃vizibilite] *nf* invisibility.

invisible [ɛ̃vizibl(ə)] **1** *adj* (*impossible à voir*) invisible; (*minuscule*) barely visible (*à* to); (*Écon*) invisible. **la maison était ~ derrière les arbres** the house was invisible *ou* couldn't be seen behind the trees; **danger ~** unseen *ou* hidden danger; **il est ~ pour l'instant** he can't be seen *ou* he's unavailable at the moment; **il est ~ depuis 2 mois** he hasn't been seen (around) for 2 months.
2 *nm*: **l'~** the invisible.

invisiblement [ɛ̃vizibləmɑ̃] *adv* invisibly.

invitation [ɛ̃vitɑsjɔ̃] *nf* invitation, invite* (*à* to). **carte *ou* carton d'~** invitation card; **lettre d'~** letter of invitation; **faire une ~ à qn** to invite sb, extend an invitation to sb; **venir sans ~** to come uninvited *ou* without (an) invitation; **à *ou* sur son ~** at his invitation; (*fig*) **une ~ à déserter** *etc* an (open) invitation to desert *etc*.

invite [ɛ̃vit] *nf* (*littér*) invitation.

invité, e [ɛ̃vite] (*ptp de* **inviter**) *nm,f* guest.

inviter [ɛ̃vite] (1) *vt* **(a)** (*convier*) to invite, ask (*à* to). **~ qn chez soi/à dîner** to invite *ou* ask sb to one's house/to *ou* for dinner; **elle ne l'a pas invité à entrer/monter** she didn't invite *ou* ask him (to come) in/up; **il s'est invité** he invited himself.
(b) (*engager*) **~ à** to invite to; **~ qn à démissionner** to invite sb to resign; **il l'invita de la main à s'approcher** he beckoned *ou* motioned (to) her to come nearer; **ceci invite à croire que ...** this induces *ou* leads us to believe that ...; **la chaleur invitait au repos** the heat tempted one to rest.

invivable [ɛ̃vivabl(ə)] *adj* unbearable.

invocation [ɛ̃vɔkɑsjɔ̃] *nf* invocation (*à* to).

invocatoire [ɛ̃vɔkatwaʀ] *adj* (*littér*) invocatory (*littér*).

involontaire [ɛ̃vɔlɔ̃tɛʀ] *adj sourire, mouvement* involuntary; *peine, insulte* unintentional; *témoin, complice* unwitting.

involontairement [ɛ̃vɔlɔ̃tɛʀmɑ̃] *adv sourire* involuntarily; *bousculer qn* unintentionally, unwittingly. **l'accident dont je fus (bien) ~ le témoin** the accident to *ou* of which I was an *ou* the unwitting witness.

invoquer [ɛ̃vɔke] (1) *vt* **(a)** (*alléguer*) *excuse, argument* to put forward; *témoignage* to call upon; *jeunesse, ignorance* to plead; *loi, texte* to cite, refer to.
(b) (*appeler à l'aide*) *Dieu* to invoke, call upon. **~ le secours de qn** to call upon sb for help; **~ la clémence de qn** to beg sb *ou* appeal to sb for clemency.

invraisemblable [ɛ̃vʀɛsɑ̃blabl(ə)] *adj* (*improbable*) *fait, nouvelle* unlikely, improbable; *argument* implausible; (*extravagant*) *insolence, habit* incredible.

invraisemblablement [ɛ̃vʀɛsɑ̃blabləmɑ̃] *adv* (*V* **invraisemblable**) improbably; implausibly; incredibly.

invraisemblance [ɛ̃vʀɛsɑ̃blɑ̃s] *nf* (*V* **invraisemblable**) unlikelihood (*U*), unlikeliness (*U*), improbability; implausibility. **plein d'~s** full of improbabilities *ou* implausibilities.

invulnérabilité [ɛ̃vylneʀabilite] *nf* invulnerability.

invulnérable [ɛ̃vylneʀabl(ə)] *adj* (*lit*) invulnerable. (*fig*) **~ à** not vulnerable to, immune to.

iode [jɔd] *nm* iodine; *V* **phare, teinture.**

ioder [jɔde] (1) *vt* to iodize.

iodler [jɔdle] (1) *vt* = **jodler.**

iodoforme [jɔdɔfɔʀm(ə)] *nm* iodoform.

ion [jɔ̃] *nm* ion.

ionien, -ienne [jɔnjɛ̃, jɛn] **1** *adj* Ionian. **2** *nm* (*Ling*) Ionic.

ionique [jɔnik] **1** *adj* (*Archit*) Ionic; (*Sci*) ionic. **2** *nm* (*Archit*) **l'~** the Ionic.

ionisation [jɔnizɑsjɔ̃] *nf* ionization.

ioniser [jɔnize] (1) *vt* to ionize.

ionosphère [jɔnɔsfɛʀ] *nf* ionosphere.

iota [jɔta] *nm* iota. **je n'y ai pas changé un ~** I didn't change it one iota, I didn't change one *ou* an iota of it.

iourte [juʀt(ə)] *nf* = **yourte.**

ipéca [ipeka] *nm* ipecacuanha, ipecac (*US*).

Irak [iʀak] *nm* Iraq, Irak.

irakien, -ienne [iʀakjɛ̃, jɛn] **1** *adj* Iraqi. **2** *nm* (*Ling*) Iraqi. **3** *nm,f*: **I~(ne)** Iraqi.

Iran [iʀɑ̃] *nm* Iran.

iranien, -ienne [iʀanjɛ̃, jɛn] **1** *adj* Iranian. **2** *nm* (*Ling*) Iranian. **3** *nm,f*: **I~(ne)** Iranian.

Iraq [iʀak] *nm* = **Irak.**

iraquien, -ienne [iʀakjɛ̃, jɛn] = **irakien.**

irascibilité [iʀasibilite] *nf* short- *ou* quick-temperedness, irascibility.

irascible [iʀasibl(ə)] *adj*: **(d'humeur) ~** short- *ou* quick-tempered, irascible.

ire [iʀ] *nf* (*littér*) ire (*littér*).

iridié, e [iʀidje] *adj V* **platine.**

iridium [iʀidjɔm] *nm* iridium.

iris [iʀis] *nm* (*Anat, Phot*) iris; (*Bot*) iris, flag (*T*).

irisation [iʀizɑsjɔ̃] *nf* iridescence, irisation.

irisé, e [iʀize] (*ptp de* **iriser**) *adj* iridescent.

iriser [iʀize] (1) **1** *vt* to make iridescent. **2 s'iriser** *vpr* to become iridescent.

irlandais, e [iʀlɑ̃dɛ, ɛz] **1** *adj* Irish. **2** *nm* **(a)** (*Ling*) Irish. **(b)** **I~** Irishman; **les I~** the Irish. **3 Irlandaise** *nf* Irishwoman.

Irlande [iʀlɑ̃d] *nf* (*pays*) Ireland; (*État*) Irish Republic, Republic of Ireland. **~ du Nord** Northern Ireland, Ulster.

ironie [iʀɔni] *nf* (*lit, fig*) irony. **par une curieuse ~ du sort** by a strange irony of fate.

ironique [iʀɔnik] *adj* ironic(al).

ironiquement [iʀɔnikmɑ̃] *adv* ironically.

ironiser [iʀɔnize] (1) *vi* to be ironic(al) (*sur* about). **ce n'est pas la peine d'~** there's no need to be ironic(al) (about it).

ironiste [iʀɔnist(ə)] *nmf* ironist.

iroquois, e [iʀɔkwa, waz] **1** *adj peuplade* Iroquoian; (*Hist*) Iroquois. **2** *nm* (*Ling*) Iroquoian. **3** *nm,f*: **I~(e)** Iroquoian; Iroquois.

irradiation [iʀadjɑsjɔ̃] *nf* (*action*) irradiation; (*halo*) irradiation; (*rayons*) radiation, irradiation; (*Méd*) radiation.

irradier [iʀadje] (7) **1** *vt* to irradiate. **2** *vi [lumière etc]* to radiate, irradiate; *[douleur]* to radiate; (*fig*) to radiate.

irraisonné, e [iʀɛzɔne] *adj mouvement* irrational, unreasoned; *crainte* irrational, unreasoning.

irrationalisme [iʀasjɔnalism(ə)] *nm* irrationalism.

irrationalité [iʀasjɔnalite] *nf* irrationality.

irrationnel, -elle [iʀasjɔnɛl] *adj* (*gén, Math*) irrational.

irrationnellement [iʀasjɔnɛlmɑ̃] *adv* irrationally.

irréalisable [iʀealizabl(ə)] *adj* (*gén*) unrealizable, unachievable; *projet* impracticable, unworkable. **c'est ~** it's unfeasible *ou* unworkable.

irréalisé, e [iʀealize] *adj* (*littér*) unrealized, unachieved.

irréalisme [iʀealism(ə)] *nm* lack of realism, unrealism.

irréalité [iʀealite] *nf* unreality.

irrecevabilité [iʀəsvabilite] *nf* (*V* **irrecevable**) inadmissibility; unacceptability.

irrecevable [iʀəsvabl(ə)] *adj témoignage* inadmissible; *demande* unacceptable.

irréconciliable [iʀekɔ̃siljabl(ə)] *adj* irreconcilable, unreconcilable.

irréconciliablement [iʀekɔ̃siljabləmɑ̃] *adv* irreconcilably, unreconcilably.

irrécouvrable [iʀekuvʀabl(ə)] *adj* irrecoverable.

irrécupérable [iʀekypeʀabl(ə)] *adj* (*gén*) irretrievable; *ferraille, meubles* unreclaimable; *voiture* beyond repair (*attrib*). **il est ~** he has gone beyond *ou* is beyond rehabilitation; (*hum*) he's beyond recall.

irrécusable [iʀekyzabl(ə)] *adj témoin, juge* unimpeachable; *témoignage, preuve* incontestable, indisputable.

irréductibilité [iʀedyktibilite] *nf* (*V* **irréductible**) irreducibility; insurmountability, invincibility; indomitability; implacability.

irréductible [iʀedyktibl(ə)] *adj fait, élément,* (*Chim, Math, Méd*) irreducible; (*invincible*) *obstacle* insurmountable, invincible; *volonté* indomitable; (*farouche*) *opposition, ennemi* out-and-out (*épith*), unmitigated, implacable.

irréductiblement [iʀedyktibləmɑ̃] *adv* implacably. **être ~ opposé à une politique** *etc* to be in out-and-out opposition to *ou* implacably opposed to a policy *etc*.

irréel, -elle [iʀeɛl] *adj* unreal. (*Ling*) **(mode) ~** *mood expressing unreal condition.*

irréfléchi, e [iʀefleʃi] *adj geste, paroles, action* thoughtless, unconsidered; *personne* unthinking, hasty; *enfant* impulsive, hasty; *courage, audace* reckless, impetuous.

irréflexion [iʀeflɛksjɔ̃] *nf* thoughtlessness.

irréfutabilité [iʀefytabilite] *nf* irrefutability.

irréfutable [iʀefytabl(ə)] *adj* irrefutable.

irréfutablement [iʀefytabləmɑ̃] *adv* irrefutably.

irréfuté, e [iʀefyte] *adj* unrefuted.

irrégularité [iʀegylaʀite] *nf* **(a)** (*V* **irrégulier**) irregularity; unevenness; variation; fitfulness; erratic performance; dubiousness.
(b) (*action, caractéristique: gén pl*) irregularity. **les ~s du terrain/de ses traits** the irregularities of the land/in his features.

irrégulier, -ière [iʀegylje, jɛʀ] **1** *adj* **(a)** (*non symétrique etc*) *polygone, façade, traits* irregular; *écriture, terrain* irregular, uneven.

(b) (*non constant*) *développement, accélération* irregular; *rythme, courant, vitesse* irregular, varying (*épith*); *sommeil, pouls, respiration* irregular, fitful; *vent* fitful; *travail, effort, qualité* uneven; *élève, athlète* erratic.
(c) (*en fréquence*) *horaire, service, visites, intervalles* irregular.
(d) (*peu honnête ou légal*) *tribunal, troupes, opération, situation* irregular; *vie* unorthodox, irregular; *agent, homme d'affaires* dubious.
(e) (*Ling*) *verbe, construction* irregular.
2 *nm* (*Mil: gén pl*) irregular.

irrégulièrement [iʀegyljɛʀmɑ̃] *adv* (*V* **irrégulier**) irregularly; unevenly; fitfully; erratically; dubiously.
irréligieusement [iʀeliʒjøzmɑ̃] *adv* irreligiously.
irréligieux, -euse [iʀeliʒjø, øz] *adj* irreligious.
irréligion [iʀeliʒjɔ̃] *nf* irreligiousness, irreligion.
irrémédiable [iʀemedjabl(ə)] *adj dommage, perte* irreparable; *mal, vice* incurable, irremediable, beyond remedy (*attrib*). **essayer d'éviter l'**~ to try to avoid reaching the point of no return.
irrémédiablement [iʀemedjabləmɑ̃] *adv* (*V* **irrémédiable**) irreparably; incurably, irremediably.
irrémissible [iʀemisibl(ə)] *adj* (*littér*) irremissible.
irrémissiblement [iʀemisibləmɑ̃] *adv* (*littér*) irremissibly.
irremplaçable [iʀɑ̃plasabl(ə)] *adj* irreplaceable.
irréparable [iʀeparabl(ə)] *adj objet* irreparable, unmendable, beyond repair (*attrib*); *dommage, perte, gaffe* irreparable; *désastre* irretrievable. **la voiture est** ~ the car is beyond repair *ou* is a write-off.
irréparablement [iʀeparabləmɑ̃] *adv* (*V* **irréparable**) irreparably; irretrievably.
irrépréhensible [iʀepʀeɑ̃sibl(ə)] *adj* (*littér*) irreprehensible.
irrépressible [iʀepʀesibl(ə)] *adj* irrepressible.
irrépressiblement [iʀepʀesibləmɑ̃] *adv* irrepressibly.
irréprochable [iʀepʀɔʃabl(ə)] *adj personne, conduite, vie* irreproachable, beyond reproach (*attrib*); *tenue* impeccable, faultless.
irréprochablement [iʀepʀɔʃabləmɑ̃] *adv* (*V* **irréprochable**) (*littér*) irreproachably; impeccably, faultlessly.
irrésistible [iʀezistibl(ə)] *adj femme, charme, plaisir, force* irresistible; *besoin, désir, preuve, logique* compelling. **il est** ~! (*amusant*) he's hilarious!
irrésistiblement [iʀezistibləmɑ̃] *adv* irresistibly.
irrésolu, e [iʀezɔly] *adj personne* irresolute, indecisive; *problème* unresolved, unsolved.
irrésolution [iʀezɔlysjɔ̃] *nf* irresolution, irresoluteness, indecisiveness.
irrespect [iʀɛspɛ] *nm* disrespect.
irrespectueusement [iʀɛspɛktɥøzmɑ̃] *adv* disrespectfully.
irrespectueux, -euse [iʀɛspɛktɥø, øz] *adj* disrespectful (*envers* to, towards).
irrespirable [iʀɛspiʀabl(ə)] *adj air* unbreathable; (*fig: étouffant*) oppressive, stifling; (*dangereux*) unsafe, unhealthy. (*fig*) **l'atmosphère était** ~ you could have cut the atmosphere with a knife*, the atmosphere was oppressive *ou* stifling.
irresponsabilité [iʀɛspɔ̃sabilite] *nf* irresponsibility.
irresponsable [iʀɛspɔ̃sabl(ə)] *adj* irresponsible (*de* for).
irrétrécissable [iʀetʀesisabl(ə)] *adj* (*sur étiquette, publicité*) unshrinkable, non-shrink.
irrévérence [iʀeveʀɑ̃s] *nf* (*caractère*) irreverence; (*propos*) irreverent word; (*acte*) irreverent act.
irrévérencieusement [iʀeveʀɑ̃sjøzmɑ̃] *adv* irreverently.
irrévérencieux, -euse [iʀeveʀɑ̃sjø, øz] *adj* irreverent.
irréversibilité [iʀevɛʀsibilite] *nf* irreversibility.
irréversible [iʀevɛʀsibl(ə)] *adj* irreversible.
irrévocabilité [iʀevɔkabilite] *nf* (*Jur, littér*) irrevocability.
irrévocable [iʀevɔkabl(ə)] *adj* (*gén*) irrevocable; *temps, passé* beyond *ou* past recall (*attrib*), irrevocable. **l'**~ the irrevocable.
irrévocablement [iʀevɔkabləmɑ̃] *adv* irrevocably.
irrigable [iʀigabl(ə)] *adj* irrigable.
irrigateur [iʀigatœʀ] *nm* (*Agr, Méd*) irrigator (*machine*).
irrigation [iʀigɑsjɔ̃] *nf* (*Agr, Méd*) irrigation.
irriguer [iʀige] (1) *vt* (*Agr, Méd*) to irrigate.
irritabilité [iʀitabilite] *nf* irritability.
irritable [iʀitabl(ə)] *adj* irritable.
irritant, e [iʀitɑ̃, ɑ̃t] **1** *adj attitude, propos* irritating, annoying; *difficultés, délais* annoying, irksome; (*Méd*) irritant. **2** *nm* irritant.
irritation [iʀitɑsjɔ̃] *nf* (*colère*) irritation, annoyance; (*Méd*) irritation.
irrité, e [iʀite] (*ptp de* **irriter**) *adj gorge* irritated, inflamed; *geste, regard* irritated, annoyed, angry. **être** ~ **contre qn** to be annoyed *ou* angry with sb.
irriter [iʀite] (1) **1** *vt* **(a)** (*agacer*) to irritate, annoy, irk.
(b) (*enflammer*) *œil, peau, blessure* to make inflamed, irritate. **il avait la gorge irritée par la fumée** the smoke irritated his throat.
(c) (*littér: aviver*) *intérêt, curiosité* to arouse.
2 s'irriter *vpr* **(a)** (*s'agacer*) **s'**~ **de qch/contre qn** to get annoyed *ou* angry at sth/with sb, feel irritated at sth/with sb.
(b) *[œil, peau, blessure]* to become inflamed *ou* irritated.
irruption [iʀypsjɔ̃] *nf* (*entrée subite ou hostile*) irruption (*U*). ~ **des eaux** flooding (*U*) (*dans* into); **faire** ~ **(chez qn)** to burst in (on sb); **les eaux firent** ~ **dans les bas quartiers** the waters swept *ou* swirled into the low-lying parts of the town.
Isabelle [izabɛl] *nf* Isabel.
isabelle [izabɛl] **1** *adj* light-tan. **2** *nm* light-tan horse.
isard [izaʀ] *nm* izard.
isba [izba] *nf* isba.
Islam [islam] *nm* Islam.
islamique [islamik] *adj* Islamic.
islamisation [islamizɑsjɔ̃] *nf* Islamization.
islamiser [islamize] (1) *vt* to Islamize.
islamisme [islamism(ə)] *nm* Islamism.
islandais, e [islɑ̃dɛ, ɛz] **1** *adj* Icelandic. **2** *nm* (*Ling*) Icelandic. **3** *nm,f*: **I**~**(e)** Icelander.
Islande [islɑ̃d] *nf* Iceland.
isobare [izɔbaʀ] **1** *adj* isobaric. **2** *nf* isobar.
isocèle [izɔsɛl] *adj* isoceles.
isochrone [izɔkʀɔn] *adj* isochronal, isochronous.
isolable [izɔlabl(ə)] *adj* isolable.
isolant, e [izɔlɑ̃, ɑ̃t] **1** *adj* (*Constr, Élec*) insulating; (*insonorisant*) soundproofing, sound-insulating; (*Ling*) isolating. **2** *nm* insulator, insulating material.
isolateur [izɔlatœʀ] *nm* (*support*) insulator.
isolation [izɔlɑsjɔ̃] *nf* (*Élec*) insulation. ~ **phonique** *ou* **acoustique** soundproofing, sound insulation; ~ **thermique** thermal insulation.
isolationnisme [izɔlɑsjɔnism(ə)] *nm* isolationism.
isolationniste [izɔlɑsjɔnist(ə)] *adj, nmf* isolationist.
isolé, e [izɔle] (*ptp de* **isoler**) **1** *adj cas, personne, protestation* isolated; *lieu* isolated, lonely, remote; *philosophe, tireur, anarchiste* lone (*épith*); (*Élec*) insulated. **se sentir** ~ to feel isolated; **vivre** ~ to live in isolation.
2 *nm,f* (*théoricien*) loner; (*personne délaissée*) lonely person. **le problème des** ~**s** the problem of the lonely *ou* isolated; **on a rencontré quelques** ~**s** we met a few isolated people.
isoler [izɔle] (1) **1** *vt* **(a)** *prisonnier* to place in solitary confinement; *malade, citation, fait, mot* to isolate; *ville* to cut off, isolate. **ville isolée du reste du monde** town cut off from the rest of the world; **ses opinions l'isolent** his opinions isolate him *ou* set him apart.
(b) (*Élec*) to insulate; (*contre le bruit*) to soundproof, insulate; (*Bio, Chim*) to isolate.
2 s'isoler *vpr* (*dans un coin, pour travailler*) to isolate o.s. **s'**~ **du reste du monde** to cut o.s. off *ou* isolate o.s. from the rest of the world; **ils s'isolèrent quelques instants** they stood aside for a few seconds.
isolement [izɔlmɑ̃] *nm [personne délaissée, maison]* loneliness, isolation; *[théoricien, prisonnier, malade]* isolation; (*Pol*) *[pays]* isolation; (*Élec*) *[câble]* insulation. **sortir de son** ~ to come out of one's isolation.
isolément [izɔlemɑ̃] *adv* in isolation, individually. **chaque élément pris** ~ each element considered separately *ou* individually *ou* in isolation.
isoloir [izɔlwaʀ] *nm* polling booth.
isomère [izɔmɛʀ] **1** *adj* isomeric. **2** *nm* isomer.
isométrique [izɔmetʀik] *adj* (*Math, Sci*) isometric.
isomorphe [izɔmɔʀf(ə)] *adj* (*Chim*) isomorphic, isomorphous; (*Math*) isomorphic.
isomorphisme [izɔmɔʀfism(ə)] *nm* isomorphism.
isorel [izɔʀɛl] *nm* ® hardboard.
isotherme [izɔtɛʀm(ə)] **1** *adj* isothermal. **2** *nf* isotherm.
isotope [izɔtɔp] **1** *adj* isotopic. **2** *nm* isotope.
Israël [isʀaɛl] *nm* Israel.
israélien, -ienne [isʀaeljɛ̃, jɛn] **1** *adj* Israeli. **2** *nm,f*: **I**~**(ne)** Israeli.
israélite [isʀaelit] **1** *adj* Jewish. **2** *nm* (*gén*) Jew; (*Hist*) Israelite. **3** *nf* Jewess; Israelite.
issu, e[1] [isy] *adj*: ~ **de** (*résultant de*) stemming from; (*né de*) descended from, born of; **être** ~ **de** (*résulter de*) to stem from; (*être né de*) to be descended from *ou* born of.
issue[2] [isy] *nf* **(a)** (*sortie*) exit; *[eau, vapeur]* outlet. **voie sans** ~ (*lit, fig*) dead end; (*panneau*) 'no through road'; ~ **de secours** emergency exit; (*fig*) **il a su se ménager une** ~ he has managed to leave himself a way out.
(b) (*solution*) way out, solution. **la situation est sans** ~ there is no way out of *ou* no solution to the situation; **un avenir sans** ~ a future which has no prospect *ou* which leads nowhere *ou* without prospects.
(c) (*fin*) outcome. **heureuse** ~ happy outcome *ou* issue; ~ **fatale** fatal outcome; **à l'**~ **de** at the conclusion *ou* close of.
Istamboul [istɑ̃bul] *n* Istanbul.
isthme [ism(ə)] *nm* (*Anat, Géog*) isthmus.
isthmique [ismik] *adj* isthmian.
italianisant, e [italjanizɑ̃, ɑ̃t] *nm,f* (*Univ*) italianist; (*artiste*) italianizer.
italianisme [italjanism(ə)] *nm* (*Ling*) italianism.
Italie [itali] *nf* Italy.
italien, -ienne [italjɛ̃, jɛn] **1** *adj* Italian. **2** *nm* (*Ling*) Italian. **3** *nm,f*: **I**~**(ne)** Italian.
italique [italik] **1** *nm* **(a)** (*Typ*) italics. **mettre un mot en** ~**(s)** to put a word in italics, italicize a word. **(b)** (*Hist, Ling*) Italic. **2** *adj* (*Typ*) italic; (*Hist, Ling*) Italic.
item [itɛm] **1** *adv* (*Comm*) ditto. **2** *nm* (*Ling, Psych*) item.
itératif, -ive [iteʀatif, iv] *adj* (*gén, Gram*) iterative; (*Jur*) reiterated, repeated.
Ithaque [itak] *nf* Ithaca.
itinéraire [itineʀɛʀ] *nm* (*chemin*) route, itinerary; *[livre, pensée]* itinerary. (*fig*) **son** ~ **philosophique/religieux** his philosophical/religious path *ou* itinerary; **faire** *ou* **tracer un** ~ to map out a route *ou* an itinerary.
itinérant, e [itineʀɑ̃, ɑ̃t] *adj* itinerant, travelling. **ambassadeur** ~ roving ambassador; **troupe** ~**e** strolling players.
itou*† [itu] *adv* likewise. **et moi** ~! (and) me too!*
ivoire [ivwaʀ] *nm* ivory. **en** *ou* **d'**~ ivory (*épith*); *V* **côte, tour**[1].
ivoirien, -ienne [ivwaʀjɛ̃, jɛn] **1** *adj* of *ou* from the Ivory Coast Republic. **2** *nm,f*: **I**~**(ne)** inhabitant *ou* native of the Ivory Coast Republic.
ivraie [ivʀɛ] *nf* (*Bot*) rye grass; *V* **séparer.**

ivre [ivʀ(ə)] *adj* drunk, intoxicated. **~ de colère/de vengeance/d'espoir** wild with anger/vengeance/hope; **~ de joie** wild with joy, beside o.s. with joy; **~ de sang** thirsting for blood; **~ mort** dead *ou* blind drunk; **légèrement ~** slightly drunk, tipsy.
ivresse [ivʀɛs] *nf* (*ébriété*) drunkenness, intoxication. **dans l'~ du combat/de la victoire** in the exhilaration of the fight/of victory; **l'~ du plaisir** the (wild) ecstasy of pleasure; **avec ~** rapturously, ecstatically; **instants/heures d'~** moments/hours of rapture *ou* (wild) ecstasy; **~ chimique** drug dependence; *V* **état.**
ivrogne [ivʀɔɲ] **1** *nmf* drunkard; *V* **serment. 2** *adj* drunken (*épith*).
ivrognerie [ivʀɔɲʀi] *nf* drunkenness.

J

J, j [ʒi] *nm* (*lettre*) J, j; *V* **jour.**
j' [ʒ(ə)] *V* **je.**
jabot [ʒabo] *nm* **(a)** (*Zool*) crop. **(b)** (*Habillement*) jabot.
jacasse [ʒakas] *nf* (*Zool*) magpie.
jacassement [ʒakasmɑ̃] *nm* [*pie*] chatter (*U*); (*péj*) [*personnes*] jabber(ing) (*U*), chatter(ing) (*U*).
jacasser [ʒakase] (1) *vi* [*pie*] to chatter; (*péj*) [*personne*] to jabber, chatter.
jacasserie [ʒakasʀi] *nf* = **jacassement.**
jacasseur, -euse [ʒakasœʀ, øz] **1** *adj* jabbering, prattling. **2** *nm,f* chatterbox, prattler.
jachère [ʒaʃɛʀ] *nf* fallow; (*procédé*) practice of fallowing land. **laisser une terre en ~** to leave a piece of land fallow, let a piece of land lie fallow; **rester en ~** to lie fallow.
jacinthe [ʒasɛ̃t] *nf* hyacinth. **~ des bois** bluebell.
jack [ʒak] *nm* (*Téléc, Tex*) jack.
Jacob [ʒakɔb] *nm* Jacob.
jacobin, e [ʒakɔbɛ̃, in] **1** *adj* Jacobinic(al). **2** *nm* (*Hist*) **J~** Jacobin.
jacobinisme [ʒakɔbinism(ə)] *nm* Jacobinism.
jacobite [ʒakɔbit] *nm* Jacobite.
Jacot [ʒako] *nm* = **Jacquot.**
jacquard [ʒakaʀ] **1** *adj pull, tissu* Jacquard (weave). **2** *nm* (*métier*) Jacquard loom; (*tissu*) Jacquard (weave).
Jacqueline [ʒaklin] *nf* Jacqueline.
jacquerie [ʒakʀi] *nf* jacquerie. (*Hist*) **J~** Jacquerie.
Jacques [ʒak] *nm* James. **faire le ~*** to play *ou* act the fool, fool about.
jacquet [ʒakɛ] *nm* backgammon.
Jacquot [ʒako] *nm* (*personne*) Jimmy; (*perroquet*) Polly.
jactance [ʒaktɑ̃s] *nf* **(a)** (*: *bavardage*) chat*. **(b)** (*littér: vanité*) conceit.
jacter‡ [ʒakte] (1) *vi* to jabber, gas*; (*arg Police*) to talk, give‡, come clean‡.
jade [ʒad] *nm* (*pierre*) jade; (*objet*) jade object *ou* ornament. **de ~** jade.
jadis [ʒadis] **1** *adv* in times past, formerly, long ago. **mes amis de ~** my friends of long ago *ou* of old; **~ on se promenait dans ces jardins** in olden days *ou* long ago they used to walk in these gardens.
2 *adj*: **dans le temps ~, au temps ~** in days of old, in days gone by, once upon a time; **du temps ~** of times gone by, of olden days.
jaguar [ʒagwaʀ] *nm* jaguar.
jaillir [ʒajiʀ] (2) *vi* **(a)** [*liquide, sang*] to spurt out, gush forth; [*larmes*] to flow; [*geyser*] to spout up, gush forth; [*vapeur, source*] to gush forth; [*flammes*] to shoot up, spurt out; [*étincelles*] to fly out; [*lumière*] to flash on (*de* from, out of). **faire ~ des étincelles** to make sparks fly; **un éclair jaillit dans l'obscurité** a flash of lightning split the darkness.
(b) (*apparaître*) **des soldats jaillirent de tous côtés** soldiers sprang out *ou* leapt out from all directions; **le train jaillit du tunnel** the train shot *ou* burst out of the tunnel; **des montagnes jaillissaient au-dessus de la plaine** mountains reared up over the plain *ou* reared their peaks above the plain.
(c) [*cris, rires, réponses*] to burst forth *ou* out.
(d) [*idée*] to spring up; [*vérité, solution*] to spring (*de* from).
jaillissement [ʒajismɑ̃] *nm* [*liquide, vapeur*] spurt, gush; [*idées*] springing up, outpouring.
jais [ʒɛ] *nm* (*Minér*) jet. **perles de ~** jet beads; **des cheveux de ~** jet-black hair; *V* **noir.**
jalon [ʒalɔ̃] *nm* (*lit*) ranging-pole; [*arpenteur*] surveyor's staff; (*fig*) step, milestone. (*fig*) **planter** *ou* **poser les premiers ~s de qch** to prepare the ground for sth, pave the way for sth.
jalonnement [ʒalɔnmɑ̃] *nm* [*route*] marking out.
jalonner [ʒalɔne] (1) *vt* **(a)** (*déterminer un tracé*) *route, chemin de fer* to mark out *ou* off. **il faut d'abord ~** first the ground must be marked out.
(b) (*border, s'espacer sur*) to line, stretch along. **des champs de fleurs jalonnent la route** fields of flowers line the road; (*fig*) **carrière jalonnée de succès/d'obstacles** career marked by *ou* punctuated with successes/obstacles.
jalousement [ʒaluzmɑ̃] *adv* jealously.
jalouser [ʒaluze] (1) *vt* to be jealous of.
jalousie [ʒaluzi] *nf* **(a)** (*sentiment*) jealousy. **des petites ~s mesquines entres femmes** petty jealousies between women; **être malade de ~, crever de ~*** to be green with envy. **(b)** (*persienne*) venetian blind, jalousie.
jaloux, -ouse [ʒalu, uz] *adj* **(a)** (*gén*) jealous. **~ de qn/de la réussite de qn** jealous of sb/of sb's success; **~ de son autorité** jealous of his authority; **~ comme un tigre** madly jealous; **observer qn d'un œil ~** to keep a jealous eye on sb, watch sb jealously; **faire des ~** to make people jealous.
(b) (*littér: désireux*) **~ de** intent upon, eager for; **~ de perfection** eager for perfection.
jamaïquain, e [ʒamaikɛ̃, ɛn] **1** *adj* Jamaican. **2** *nm,f*: **J~(e)** Jamaican.
Jamaïque [ʒamaik] *nf* Jamaica.
jamais [ʒamɛ] *adv* **(a)** (*avec ou sans ne: négatif*) never, not ever. **il n'a ~ avoué** he never confessed; **n'a-t-il ~ avoué?** did he never confess?, didn't he ever confess?; **il travaille comme ~ il n'a travaillé** he's working as he's never worked before; **il n'a ~ autant travaillé** he has never worked as hard (before), he has never done so much work (before); **~ je n'ai vu un homme si égoïste** I have never met *ou* seen such a selfish man (before), never (before) have I met *ou* seen such a selfish man; **~ mère ne fut plus heureuse** there was never a happier mother; **il n'est ~ trop tard** it's never too late; **il ne lui a ~ plus écrit** he never wrote to her again, he has never *ou* he hasn't ever written to her since; **on ne l'a ~ encore entendu se plaindre** he's never yet been heard to complain; **ne dites ~ plus cela!** never say that again!, don't you ever say that again!; **il partit pour ne ~ plus revenir** he departed never (more) to return; **~ plus** *ou* **~ au grand ~ on ne me prendra à le faire** you'll never *ou* you won't ever catch me doing it again; **nous sommes restés 2 ans sans ~ recevoir de nouvelles** we were *ou* went 2 years without ever hearing any news, for 2 years we never (once) heard any news; **elle sort souvent mais ~ sans son chien** she often goes out but never without her dog; **il n'a ~ fait que critiquer (les autres)** he's never done anything but criticize (others); **ça ne fait ~ que 2 heures qu'il est parti** it's no more than 2 hours since he left; **ce n'est ~ qu'un enfant** he is only *ou* but a child (after all); **je n'ai ~ de ma vie vu un chien aussi laid** never in my life have I *ou* I have never in my life seen such an ugly dog; **accepterez-vous? — ~ de la vie!** will you accept? — never!, not on your life!*; **le referez-vous encore? — ~ plus!** *ou* **plus ~!** will you do it again? — never (again)!; **c'est ce que vous avez dit — ~!** that's what you said — never! *ou* I never did!* *ou* I never said that!; **presque ~** hardly *ou* scarcely ever, practically never; **c'est maintenant ou ~, c'est le moment ou ~** it's now or never; **c'est le moment ou ~ d'acheter** now is the time to buy, if ever there was a time to buy it's now; **une symphonie ~ jouée/terminée** an unplayed/unfinished symphony; **~ deux sans trois!** there's always a third time!; (*iro*) **alors, ~ on ne dit 'merci'?*** did nobody ever teach you to say 'thank you'? (*iro*); *V* **mieux, savoir.**
(b) (*sans ne: temps indéfini*) ever. **a-t-il ~ avoué?** did he ever confess?; **si ~ vous passez par Londres venez nous voir** if ever you're passing *ou* if ever you should pass *ou* should you ever pass through London come and see us; **si ~ j'avais un poste pour vous je vous préviendrais** if ever I had *ou* if I ever had a job for you I'd let you know; **si ~ tu rates le train, reviens** if by (any) chance you *ou* if you (should) happen to miss the train come back; **si ~ tu recommences, gare!** watch out if you ever start that again!; **les œufs sont plus chers que ~** eggs are dearer than ever (before); **c'est pire que ~** it's worse than ever; **avez-vous ~ vu ça?** have you ever seen *ou* did you ever see such a thing?; **c'est le plus grand que j'aie ~ vu** it's the biggest I've ever seen; **il désespère d'avoir ~ de l'avancement** he despairs of ever getting promotion *ou* of ever being promoted; **à ~** for good, for ever; **à tout ~, pour ~** for ever (and ever), for good and all*, for evermore (*littér*); **je renonce à tout ~ à le lui faire comprendre** I've given up ever trying to make him understand it; **leur amitié est à ~ compromise** their friendship will never be the same again.
jambage [ʒɑ̃baʒ] *nm* **(a)** [*lettre*] downstroke. **(b)** (*Archit*) jamb.

jambe [ʒɑ̃b] *nf* **(a)** (*Anat, Habillement, Zool*) leg. **remonte ta ~ (de pantalon)** roll up your trouser leg; (*Méd*) **~ de bois/artificielle/articulée** wooden/artificial/articulated leg; *V* **mi-.**

(b) (*loc*) **avoir les ~s comme du coton** to have legs like *ou* of jelly *ou* cotton wool; **avoir les ~s brisées, n'avoir plus de ~s, en avoir plein les ~s*** to be worn out *ou* on one's last legs* *ou* on one's knees*; **avoir 20 km dans les ~s** to have walked 20 km; **la peur/l'impatience lui donnait des ~s** fear/impatience lent new strength to his legs *ou* lent him speed; **tirer *ou* traîner la ~** to drag one's steps; (*boiter*) to limp along; **elle ne peut plus (se) tenir sur ses ~s** her legs are giving way under her, she can hardly stand; **tomber les ~s en l'air** to fall over backwards; **prendre ses ~s à son cou** to take to one's heels; **traiter qn par dessous *ou* par dessus la ~*** to treat sb offhandedly; **faire qch par dessous *ou* par dessus la ~*** to do sth carelessly *ou* in a slipshod way; **tenir la ~ à qn*** to buttonhole sb; **tirer dans les ~s de qn*** to make life difficult for sb; **il s'est jeté dans nos ~s*** he got under our feet*; **elle est toujours dans mes ~s*** she's always getting in my way *ou* under my feet*; *V* **beau, dégourdir** *etc.*

(c) (*Tech*) *[compas]* leg; (*étai*) prop, stay. **~ de force** (*Constr*) strut; (*Aut*) torque rod.

jambier, -ière[1] [ʒɑ̃bje, jɛʀ] *adj, nm*: **(muscle) ~** leg muscle.

jambière[2] [ʒɑ̃bjɛʀ] *nf* (*gén*) legging, gaiter; (*Sport*) pad; (*armure*) greave.

jambon [ʒɑ̃bɔ̃] *nm* **(a)** (*Culin*) ham. **~ cru** smoked (raw) ham; **~ blanc *ou* de Paris** boiled *ou* cooked ham; **~ de Parme** Parma ham. **(b)** (‡: *cuisse*) thigh.

jambonneau, *pl* **~x** [ʒɑ̃bɔno] *nm* knuckle of ham.

jamboree [ʒɑ̃bɔʀe] *nm* (*Scoutisme*) jamboree.

janissaire [ʒanisɛʀ] *nm* janissary.

jansénisme [ʒɑ̃senism(ə)] *nm* Jansenism; (*fig*) austere code of morals.

janséniste [ʒɑ̃senist(ə)] *adj, nmf* Jansenist.

jante [ʒɑ̃t] *nf [charrette]* felly; *[bicyclette, voiture]* rim.

janvier [ʒɑ̃vje] *nm* January; *pour loc V* **septembre.**

Japon [ʒapɔ̃] *nm* Japan.

japonais, e [ʒapɔnɛ, ɛz] **1** *adj* Japanese. **2** *nm* (*Ling*) Japanese. **3** *nm,f*: **J~(e)** Japanese.

japonaiserie [ʒapɔnɛzʀi] *nf,* **japonerie** [ʒapɔnʀi] *nf* Japanese curio.

jappement [ʒapmɑ̃] *nm* yap, yelp.

japper [ʒape] (1) *vi* to yap, yelp.

jaquette [ʒakɛt] *nf [homme]* morning coat; *[femme]* jacket; *[livre]* (dust) jacket, (dust) cover; *[dent]* crown.

jardin [ʒaʀdɛ̃] *nm* garden. **rester au ~** to stay in the garden; **siège/table de ~** garden seat/table; **~ d'acclimatation** zoological garden(s); **~ d'agrément** pleasure garden; **~ anglais *ou* à l'anglaise** landscape garden; **~ botanique** botanical garden(s); **~ d'enfants** nursery school, kindergarten; **~ à la française** formal garden; **~ d'hiver** winter garden; **~ japonais** Japanese garden; (*Bible*) **le ~ des Oliviers** the Mount of Olives, the Garden of Gethsemane; **~ potager** vegetable garden; **~ public** (public) park, public gardens; **~ de rapport** market garden; **~s suspendus** terraced gardens, hanging gardens; **~ zoologique = ~ d'acclimatation**; *V* **côté, cultiver, pierre.**

jardinage [ʒaʀdinaʒ] *nm* gardening.

jardiner [ʒaʀdine] (1) *vi* to garden, do some gardening.

jardinet [ʒaʀdinɛ] *nm* small garden.

jardinier, -ière [ʒaʀdinje, jɛʀ] **1** *adj* garden (*épith*). **culture ~ière** horticulture; **plantes ~ières** garden plants.

2 *nm,f* gardener.

3 jardinière *nf* **(a)** (*caisse à fleurs*) window box; (*d'intérieur*) jardiniere. **(b)** (*Culin*) **~ière (de légumes)** mixed vegetables, jardiniere. **(c)** (*Scol*) **~ière d'enfants** nursery school teacher, kindergarten teacher.

jargon [ʒaʀgɔ̃] *nm* **(a)** (*baragouin*) gibberish (*U*), double Dutch* (*U*).

(b) (*langue professionnelle*) jargon, lingo*†. **il ne connaît pas encore le ~** he doesn't know the jargon *ou* lingo*† yet; **~ administratif** officialese, official jargon; **~ de la médecine** medical jargon; **~ de métier** trade jargon *ou* slang.

jargonner [ʒaʀgɔne] (1) *vi* to jabber; (*utiliser un jargon*) to talk (professional *etc*) jargon.

Jarnac [ʒaʀnak] *n V* **coup.**

jarre [ʒaʀ] *nf* (earthenware) jar.

jarret [ʒaʀɛ] *nm* **(a)** (*Anat*) *[homme]* back of the knee, ham; *[animal]* hock. **avoir des ~s d'acier** to have strong legs. **(b)** (*Culin*) **~ de veau** knuckle *ou* shin of veal.

jarretelle [ʒaʀtɛl] *nf* suspender (*Brit*), garter (*US*).

jarretière [ʒaʀtjɛʀ] *nf* garter; *V* **ordre**[1].

jars [ʒaʀ] *nm* gander.

jaser [ʒaze] (1) *vi* **(a)** *[enfant]* to chatter, prattle; *[personne]* to chat away, chat on*; *[oiseau]* to twitter; *[jet d'eau, ruisseau]* to babble, sing. **on entend ~ la pie/le geai** you can hear the magpie/jay chattering. **(b)** (*arg Police*) to talk, give the game away*. **essayer de faire ~ qn** to try to make sb talk. **(c)** (*médire*) to gossip. **cela va faire ~ les gens** that'll set tongues wagging, that'll set people talking *ou* gossiping.

jaseur, -euse [ʒazœʀ, øz] **1** *adj enfant* chattering (*épith*), prattling (*épith*); *oiseau* chattering (*épith*), twittering (*épith*); *ruisseau, jet d'eau* singing (*épith*), babbling (*épith*); *personne* (*médisant*) tittle-tattling (*épith*), gossipy.

2 *nm* (*bavard*) gasbag, chatterbox; (*médisant*) gossip, tittle-tattle; (*Zool*) waxwing.

jasmin [ʒasmɛ̃] *nm* (*arbuste*) jasmine. (*parfum*) **(essence de) ~** jasmine (perfume).

jaspe [ʒasp(ə)] *nm* (*matière*) jasper; (*objet*) jasper ornament. **~ sanguin** bloodstone.

jaspé, e [ʒaspe] *adj* mottled, marbled.

jatte [ʒat] *nf* (shallow) bowl, basin.

jauge [ʒoʒ] *nf* **(a)** (*instrument*) gauge. **~ d'essence** petrol gauge; **~ (de niveau) d'huile** (oil) dipstick. **(b)** (*capacité*) *[réservoir]* capacity; *[navire]* tonnage, burden; (*Tex*) tension.

jaugeage [ʒoʒaʒ] *nm [navire, réservoir]* gauging.

jauger [ʒoʒe] (3) **1** *vt* **(a)** (*lit*) *réservoir* to gauge the capacity of; *navire* to measure the tonnage of.

(b) (*fig*) *personne* to size up. **il le jaugea du regard** he gave him an appraising look; **~ qn d'un coup d'œil** to size sb up at a glance.

2 *vi* to have a capacity of. **navire qui jauge 500 tonneaux** ship with a tonnage of 500, ship of 500 tonnes *ou* tons burden.

jaunâtre [ʒonɑtʀ(ə)] *adj lumière couleur* yellowish; *teint* sallow, yellowish.

jaune [ʒon] **1** *adj couleur, race* yellow; (*littér*) *blés* golden. **il a le teint ~** (*mauvaise mine*) he looks yellow *ou* sallow; (*basané*) he has a sallow complexion; **~ comme un citron *ou* un coing** as yellow as a lemon; *V* **corps, fièvre, nain** *etc.*

2 *nm* **(a) J~** Asiatic *ou* Asian (man); **les J~s** the yellow races; *V* **péril.**

(b) (*couleur*) yellow. **~ citron** lemon, lemon yellow; **~ d'or** golden yellow; **~ paille** straw colour; **~ serin** canary yellow.

(c) ~ (d'œuf) (egg) yolk, yellow of an egg.

(d) (*péj: non gréviste*) blackleg, scab‡.

3 *nf* **(a) J~** Asiatic *ou* Asian woman.

(b) (*péj: non gréviste*) blackleg, scab‡.

jaunet, -ette [ʒonɛ, ɛt] **1** *adj* slightly yellow, yellowish. **2** *nm* (††) gold coin.

jaunir [ʒoniʀ] (2) **1** *vt feuillage, doigts, vêtements* to turn yellow. **2** *vi* to yellow, turn *ou* become yellow.

jaunissant, e [ʒonisɑ̃, ɑ̃t] *adj* (*littér*) *papier, feuillage* yellowing; *blé* ripening, yellowing (*littér*).

jaunisse [ʒonis] *nf* (*Méd*) jaundice. **en faire une ~*** (*de dépit*) to have one's nose put out of joint, be pretty miffed*; (*de jalousie*) to be *ou* turn green with envy.

jaunissement [ʒonismɑ̃] *nm* yellowing.

Java [ʒava] *nf* Java.

java [ʒava] *nf* (*danse*) popular waltz. (*fig*) **faire la ~‡** to live it up*, have a rave-up‡.

javanais, e [ʒavanɛ, ɛz] **1** *adj* Javanese. **2** *nm* (*Ling*) Javanese; (*argot*) 'av' slang; (*charabia*) double Dutch*. **3** *nm,f*: **J~(e)** Javanese.

javel [ʒavɛl] *nf V* **eau.**

javeline [ʒavlin] *nf* (*Hist*) javelin.

javelle [ʒavɛl] *nf [céréales]* swath. **mettre en ~s** to lay in swathes.

javellisation [ʒavelizɑsjɔ̃] *nf* chlorination.

javelliser [ʒavelize] (1) *vt* to chlorinate. **cette eau est trop javellisée** there's too much chlorine in this water; **eau très javellisée** heavily chlorinated water.

javelot [ʒavlo] *nm* (*Mil, Sport*) javelin; *V* **lancement.**

jazz [dʒɑz] *nm* jazz. **la musique de ~** jazz (music).

je [ʒ(ə)] **1** *pron pers* I.

2 *nm*: **le ~** (*Ling*) the I-form, the 1st person; (*Philos*) the I.

3: je-m'en-fichisme* *nm* (I-)couldn't-care-less attitude*; **je-m'en-fichiste*** (*adj*) (I-)couldn't-care-less* (*épith*); (*nmf*) couldn't-care-less type*; **je-m'en-foutisme‡** *nm* (I-)couldn't-give-a-damn attitude‡; **je-m'en-foutiste‡** (*adj*) (I-)couldn't-give-a-damn‡ (*épith*); (*nmf*) couldn't-give-a-damn type‡; **je ne sais quoi** *nm inv* (certain) something; **elle a un je ne sais quoi qui attire** there's (a certain) something about her that is very attractive.

Jean [ʒɑ̃] *nm* John.

jean [dʒin] *nm* (pair of) jeans.

Jeanne [ʒan] *nf* Jane, Joan, Jean. **~ d'Arc** Joan of Arc; **coiffure à la ~ d'Arc** bobbed hair with a fringe.

jeannette [ʒanɛt] *nf* **(a) (croix à la) ~** gold cross (*worn around neck*). **(b)** (*planche à repasser*) sleeve-board. **(c)** (*prénom*) **J~** Janet, Jenny.

Jeannot [ʒano] *nm* Johnny. **~ lapin** bunny (rabbit), Mr Rabbit.

jeep [ʒip] *nf* jeep.

Jéhovah [ʒeɔva] *nm* Jehovah.

jennérien, -ienne [ʒeneʀjɛ̃, jɛn] *adj* Jennerian.

jenny [ʒeni] *nf* spinning jenny.

jérémiades* [ʒeʀemjad] *nfpl* moaning, whining.

Jérémie [ʒeʀemi] *nm* Jeremy; (*prophète*) Jeremiah.

Jéricho [ʒeʀiko] *n* Jericho.

Jéroboam [ʒeʀɔbɔam] *nm* Jeroboam. **j~** (*bouteille*) jeroboam (*bottle containing 3 litres*).

Jérôme [ʒeʀom] *nm* Jerome.

jerrycan [ʒeʀikan] *nm* jerry can.

Jersey [ʒɛʀzɛ] *nf* Jersey.

jersey [ʒɛʀzɛ] *nm* **(a)** (*chandail*) jersey, jumper (*Brit*), sweater. **(b)** (*tissu*) jersey (cloth). **~ de laine/de soie** jersey wool/silk; **point de ~** stocking stitch.

jersiais, e [ʒɛʀzjɛ, ɛz] **1** *adj* Jersey (*épith*), of *ou* from Jersey. (*Agr*) **race ~e** Jersey breed; **(vache) ~e** Jersey, Jersey cow. **2** *nm,f*: **J~(e)** inhabitant *ou* native of Jersey.

Jérusalem [ʒeʀyzalɛm] *n* Jerusalem.

jésuite [ʒezɥit] **1** *nm* (*Rel*) Jesuit. **2** *adj air, parti* Jesuit.

jésuitique [ʒezɥitik] *adj* Jesuitical.

jésuitiquement [ʒezɥitikmɑ̃] *adv* Jesuitically.

jésuitisme [ʒezɥitism(ə)] *nm* Jesuitism, Jesuitry.

jésus [ʒezy] *nm* **(a) J~** Jesus; **J~ Christ** Jesus Christ; **en 300 avant/après J~ Christ** in 300 B.C./A.D. **(b) (papier) ~** super royal (printing paper); **(papier) petit ~** super royal (writing paper). **(c)** (*statue*) statue of the infant Jesus. **(d)** (*terme d'affection*) **mon ~** (my) darling.

jet[1] [ʒɛ] **1** *nm* **(a)** (*jaillissement*) *[eau, gaz, flamme]* jet; *[sang]*

spurt, gush; *[salive]* stream; *[pompe]* flow. ~ **de lumière** beam of light.

(b) *[pierre, grenade] (action)* throwing; *(résultat)* throw. **à un ~ de pierre** at a stone's throw, a stone's throw away; **un ~ de 60 mètres au disque** a 60-metre discus throw; *V* **arme.**

(c) *(loc)* **premier ~** first sketch, rough outline; **du premier ~** at the first attempt *ou* shot* *ou* go*; **écrire d'un (seul) ~** to write in one go*; **à ~ continu** in a continuous *ou* an endless stream.

(d) *(Tech) (coulage)* casting; *(masselotte)* head. **couler une pièce d'un seul ~** to produce a piece in a single casting.

(e) *(Bot) (pousse)* main shoot; *(rameau)* branch.

2: jet d'eau *(fontaine)* fountain; *(gerbe)* spray; *(au bout d'un tuyau)* nozzle; *(Archit)* weathering; *(Naut)* **jet à la mer** jettison(ing).

jet[2] [dʒɛt] *nm (Aviat)* jet.

jeté [ʒ(ə)te] **1** *nm* **(a)** *(Danse)* **~ (simple)** jeté; **~ battu** grand jeté. **(b)** *(Sport)* snatch; *V* **épaulé. (c)** *(tricot)* **~ (simple)** make one. **2: jeté de table** table runner; **jeté de lit** bedspread.

jetée [ʒ(ə)te] *nf* jetty; *(grande)* pier. **~ flottante** floating bridge.

jeter [ʒ(ə)te] (4) **1** *vt* **(a)** *(lancer)* to throw; *(avec force)* to fling, hurl, sling*. **~ qch à qn** *(pour qu'il l'attrape)* to throw sth to sb; *(agressivement)* to throw *ou* fling *ou* hurl sth at sb; **~ qch par terre/par la fenêtre** to throw sth on the ground *ou* down/out of the window; **~ dehors** *ou* **à la porte** *visiteur* to throw out, chuck out‡; *employé* to sack, give the push to* *(Brit)*; **~ qn en prison** to throw *ou* sling* sb into prison; **il a jeté son agresseur à terre** he threw his opponent to the ground; **~ bas qch** to throw sth down; *[cheval]* **~ qn à terre** *ou* **à bas** to throw sb; *(Naut)* **~ à la mer** *personne* to throw overboard; *objet* to throw overboard, jettison; *(Naut)* **le navire a été jeté à la côte** the ship was flung towards the coast; *V* **ancre.**

(b) *(mettre au rebut) papiers, objets* to throw away *ou* out; *(Cartes)* to discard. **~ qch au panier/à la poubelle/au feu** to throw sth into the wastepaper basket/in the dustbin/in *ou* on the fire; **jette l'eau sale dans l'évier** pour *ou* tip *(surtout Brit)* (away) the dirty water down the sink; *V* **bon**[1].

(c) *(construire) pont* to throw *(sur* over, across); *fondations* to lay. **~ un pont sur une rivière** to bridge a river, throw a bridge over a river; *(fig)* **~ les bases d'une nouvelle Europe** to lay the foundations of a new Europe; *(Naut)* **jetez la passerelle!** set up the gangway!

(d) *(émettre) lueur* to give, give out, cast, shed; *cri* to give, utter, let out; *son* to let out, give out. **le diamant jette mille feux** the diamond flashes *ou* sparkles brilliantly; **ce nouveau tapis dans le salon, ça jette du jus‡** this new carpet really does something for the sitting room*, the new carpet in the sitting room is really quite something*.

(e) (*: *mettre rapidement*) **~ des vêtements dans un sac** to sling* *ou* throw some clothes into a bag; **va ~ cette carte à la boîte** go and slip *ou* pop* this card into the letterbox; **~ une veste sur ses épaules** to slip a jacket over *ou* round one's shoulders; **~ une idée sur le papier** to jot down an idea.

(f) *(fig: mettre, plonger)* to plunge, throw. **~ qn dans le désespoir** to plunge sb into despair; **~ qn dans les frais** to plunge sb into *ou* involve sb in a lot of expense; **~ qn dans l'embarras** to throw sb into confusion; **son obstination me jette hors de moi** his stubbornness drives me frantic *ou* wild.

(g) *(répandre)* to cast. **~ l'effroi chez/parmi** to sow alarm and confusion in/among; **~ le trouble chez qn** to disturb *ou* trouble sb; **~ le discrédit sur qn/qch** to cast discredit on sb/sth; **~ un sort à qn** to cast a spell on sb; **sa remarque a jeté un froid** his remark cast a chill.

(h) *(dire)* to say *(à* to). **il me jeta en passant que c'était commencé** he mentioned to me in passing that it had begun; **~ des remarques dans la conversation** to throw in *ou* toss in remarks; **~ des insultes/menaces** to hurl insults/threats; **je lui ai jeté la vérité/l'accusation à la figure** *ou* **à la tête** I flung the truth/accusation at him; **il lui jeta à la tête qu'il n'était qu'un imbécile** he burst out at him that he was nothing but a fool; **ils se jetèrent des injures à la tête** they hurled insults at each other.

(i) *(prendre une attitude)* **~ les épaules/la tête en avant** to throw *ou* thrust one's shoulders/head forward; **~ les bras autour du cou de qn** to throw *ou* fling one's arms round sb's neck; **elle lui jeta un regard plein de mépris** she cast a withering look at him, she looked *ou* glanced witheringly at him; **elle lui jeta un coup d'œil ironique** she flashed *ou* threw him an ironical glance, she glanced at him ironically.

(j) *(loc)* **~ les yeux sur qn** *(frm: regarder)* to cast a glance at sb; *(fig: vouloir épouser)* to have one's eye on sb; **~ un coup d'œil sur un livre** to glance at a book, take a quick look at a book; **~ un coup d'œil sur les enfants** to take a look at *ou* check up on the children; **~ un œil (sur qch)*** to take a look (at sth); **~ son bonnet par-dessus les moulins** to kick over the traces, have one's fling; **~ la première pierre** to cast the first stone; **~ son dévolu sur qch/qn** to set one's heart on sth/sb; **~ du lest** *(lit)* to dump ballast; *(fig)* to ditch *ou* sacrifice sth, make concessions; **on va s'en ~ un derrière la cravate‡** we'll have a quick one*; **n'en jetez plus!*** cut it out!*, pack it in!* *(Brit)*; **~ l'argent par les fenêtres** to spend money like water, throw money down the drain; **~ la soutane** *ou* **le froc aux orties** to unfrock o.s., leave the priesthood; **~ sa gourme** to sow one's wild oats; **~ le manche après la cognée** to throw in one's hand; **~ de la poudre aux yeux de qn** to impress sb; *V* **huile, masque.**

2 se jeter *vpr* **(a)** *(s'élancer)* **se ~ par la fenêtre** to throw o.s. out of the window; **se ~ dans les bras/aux pieds de qn** to throw o.s. into sb's arms/at sb's feet; **se ~ à genoux** to throw o.s. down on one's knees; **se ~ sur qn** to launch o.s. at sb, rush at sb; **se ~ sur sa proie** to swoop down *ou* pounce on one's prey; **il se jette sur la nourriture comme un affamé** he falls (up)on *ou* goes at the food like a starving man; **un chien s'est jeté sous les roues de notre voiture** a dog rushed out under the wheels of our car; **sa voiture s'est jetée contre un arbre** his car crashed into a tree; **se ~ à l'eau** *(lit)* to launch o.s. *ou* plunge into the water; *(fig)* to take the plunge; *(fig)* **se ~ à corps perdu dans une entreprise/dans la mêlée** to throw o.s. wholeheartedly into an enterprise/into the fray; *(fig)* **se ~ dans la politique/les affaires** to launch out into politics/business.

(b) *[rivière]* to flow *(dans* into). **le Rhône se jette dans la Méditerranée** the Rhone flows into the Mediterranean.

jeteur [ʒ(ə)tœʀ] *nm*: **~ de sort** wizard.

jeteuse [ʒ(ə)tøz] *nf*: **~ de sort** witch.

jeton [ʒ(ə)tɔ̃] *nm* **(a)** *(pièce) (gén)* token; *(Jeu)* counter; *(Roulette)* chip. **~ de téléphone** telephone token; **~ (de présence)** *(argent)* director's fees; *(objet)* token; *(somme)* **toucher ses ~s** to draw one's fees; *V* **faux**[2].

(b) (‡) *(coup)* biff*, bang. **recevoir un ~** to get a biff* *ou* bang; **avoir les ~s** to have the jitters* *ou* the willies‡; **ça lui a fichu les ~s** he got the wind up‡, it gave him the jitters* *ou* the willies‡.

jeu, *pl* **~x** [ʒø] **1** *nm* **(a)** *(U: amusement, divertissement)* play. **le ~ fait partie de l'éducation du jeune enfant** play forms part of the young child's education; **elle ne prend jamais part au ~ de ses camarades** she never joins in her friends' play; *(fig)* **le ~ du soleil sur l'eau** the play of the sun on the water.

(b) *(gén avec règles)* game. **~ d'intérieur/de plein air** indoor/outdoor game; **~ d'adresse** game of skill; **~ de cartes** card game; **le ~ d'échecs/de boules/de quilles** the game of chess/bowls/skittles; *V* **règle.**

(c) *(Sport: partie)* game. *(Tennis)* **il mène par 5 ~x à 2** he leads by 5 games to 2; **la pluie a ralenti le ~** the rain slowed down play (in the game).

(d) *(Sport: limites du terrain)* **en ~** in play; **hors ~** *(Tennis)* out (of play); *(Ftbl)* offside; **la balle est sortie du ~** the ball has gone out of play; **mettre** *ou* **remettre en ~** to throw in; **remise en ~** throw-in.

(e) *(U: Casino)* gambling. **il a perdu toute sa fortune au ~** he has gambled away his entire fortune, he lost his fortune (at) gambling; *V* **heureux, jouer.**

(f) *(ensemble des pions, boîte)* game, set. **~ d'échecs/de boules/de quilles** chess/bowls/skittle set; **~ de cartes** pack of cards.

(g) *(lieu)* **~ de boules** bowling ground; **~ de quilles** skittle alley.

(h) *(série complète) [clefs, aiguilles]* set. **~ d'orgue(s)** organ stop.

(i) *(Cartes)* hand. **il laisse voir son ~** he shows his hand; **je n'ai jamais de ~** I never have a good hand; *(fig)* **cacher/dévoiler son ~** to conceal/show one's hand.

(j) *(U: façon de jouer) (Sport)* game; *(Mus)* (manner of) playing; *(Ciné, Théât)* acting. *(Sport)* **il a un ~ rapide/lent/efficace** he plays a swift/a slow/an effective game; *(Mus)* **elle a un ~ saccadé/dur** she plays jerkily/harshly, her playing is jerky/harsh.

(k) *(U: Admin, Pol: fonctionnement)* working, interaction, interplay. **le ~ des alliances/des institutions** the interplay of alliances/of institutions; **mettre en ~** to bring into play, involve; *V* **mise.**

(l) *(manège)* **j'observais le ~ de l'enfant** I watched the child's little game; **c'est un ~ de dupes** it's a fool's *ou* mug's* game; **le ~ muet de deux complices** the silent exchanges of two accomplices.

(m) *(U: Tech)* play. **le ~ des pistons** the play of the pistons; **donner du ~ à qch** to loosen sth up a bit; **la vis a pris du ~** the screw has worked loose; **la porte ne ferme pas bien, il y a du ~** the door doesn't shut tight — there's a bit of play.

(n) *(loc)* **le ~ n'en vaut pas la chandelle** the game is not worth the candle; **il a beau ~ de protester maintenant** it's easy for him to complain now; **les forces en ~** the forces at work; **être en ~** to be at stake; **entrer/mettre en ~** to bring/come into play; **faire le ~ de qn** to play into sb's hands; **faire ~ égal avec qn** to be evenly matched; **il s'est fait un ~ de résoudre la difficulté** he made light work *ou* easy work of the problem; **c'est le ~** it's fair (play); **ce n'est pas de ~*** that's not (playing) fair; **c'est un ~ d'enfant** it's child's play; **par ~** for fun; **se piquer/se prendre au ~** to get excited over/get caught up in *ou* involved in the game; **être pris à son propre ~** to be caught out at one's own game, be hoist with one's own petard; **il mettra tout en ~ pour nous aider** he'll risk everything to help us; *V* **beau, double, entrée** *etc.*

2: *(Hist)* **jeux du cirque** circus games; *(Presse, Rad, TV)* **jeu-concours** *nm, pl* **jeux-concours** competition; **jeu de construction** building *ou* construction set; **jeux d'eau** dancing waters, fountains; *(Comm)* **jeu d'écritures** dummy entry; **jeu de hasard** game of chance; *(Sport)* **jeu de jambes** leg movement; **jeux de lumière** *(artificiels)* lighting effects; *(naturels)* play of light *(U)*; **jeu de massacre** *(à la foire)* Aunt Sally; *(fig)* wholesale massacre *ou* slaughter; **jeu de mots** play on words *(U)*, pun; **jeu de l'oie** ≈ snakes and ladders; **Jeux Olympiques** Olympic games; **Jeux Olympiques d'hiver** Winter Olympics; **jeu de patience** puzzle; **jeu de physionomie** facial expressions; *(Théât)* **jeu de scène** stage business *(U)*; **jeu de société** parlour game; *(Hist)* **jeux du stade** (ancient) Olympic games; *(TV)* **jeu télévisé** television game; *(questions)* (television) quiz.

jeudi [ʒødi] *nm* Thursday. **le ~ de l'Ascension** Ascension Day; **~ saint** Maundy Thursday. *pour autres loc V* **samedi.**

jeun [ʒœ̃] *adv*: **à ~** with *ou* on an empty stomach; **être à ~** *(n'avoir rien mangé/bu)* to have eaten/drunk nothing, have let nothing pass one's lips; *(ne pas être ivre)* to be sober; **rester à ~** to remain without eating anything, not to eat anything; **boire à ~** to drink on an empty stomach; *(Méd)* **à prendre à ~** to be taken on an empty stomach.

jeune [ʒœn] **1** *adj* **(a)** *(âge)* young. **c'est un homme ~** he's a young man; **mes ~s années** my youth, the years of my youth; **dans mon ~ âge** *ou* **temps** in my younger days, when I was younger; **vu son ~ âge** in view of his youth; **il n'est plus tout** *ou* **très ~** he's not as young as he was, he's not the young man he was, he's not in his first youth; **il est plus ~ que moi de 5 ans** he's 5 years younger than me, he's 5 years my junior; **~ chien** puppy (dog).

(b) (*qualité*) (*après n*) new, young; *industrie* new; (*dynamique*) forward-looking; *vin* young; *apparence, visage* youthful; *couleur, vêtement* young, which makes one look young. **soyez/restez ~s!** be/stay young! *ou* youthful!; **s'habiller ~** to dress young for one's age, dress in a young *ou* with-it* style.

(c) être ~ d'allure to be young-looking, be youthful in appearance, have a youthful look about one; **être ~ de caractère** *ou* **d'esprit** (*puéril*) to have a childish outlook, be immature; (*dynamique*) to have a youthful *ou* fresh outlook; **être ~ de cœur** to be young at heart; **être ~ de corps** to have a youthful figure.

(d) (*avoir l'air jeune*) **ils font ~** *ou* **~s** they look young; **il fait plus ~ que son âge** he looks younger than his age, he doesn't look his age; **qu'est-ce que ça le fait ~, ce costume!** how youthful *ou* young that suit makes him look!

(e) (*inexpérimenté*) raw, inexperienced, green*. **il est encore bien ~** he's still very inexperienced; **être ~ dans le métier** to be new *ou* a newcomer to the trade.

(f) (*cadet*) junior. **mon ~ frère** my younger brother; **mon plus ~ frère** my youngest brother; **Durand ~** Durand junior.

(g) (*: *insuffisant*) short, skimpy. **ça fait ~, c'est un peu ~** *[temps]* it's cutting it a bit short *ou* fine; *[argent]* it's a bit on the short side, it's pretty tight*.

2 *nm* young boy, youngster, youth. **~ (homme)** young man; **les ~s de maintenant** young people *ou* the young *ou* the youth of today; **club** *ou* **maison de ~s** youth club.

3 *nf* girl.

4: jeune femme young woman; **jeune fille** girl; **jeune garçon** boy, lad, young fellow; **jeune génération** younger generation; **jeunes gens** young people; **jeune homme** young man; (*fig*) **jeune loup** young Turk; **jeune marié** bridegroom; **jeune mariée** bride; **les jeunes mariés** the newly-weds; **ils sont jeunes mariés** they are young marrieds *ou* newly-weds; **un couple de jeunes mariés** a couple of newly-weds; (*Ciné, Théât*) **jeune premier** leading man; **jeune première** leading lady.

jeûne [ʒøn] *nm* fast. **rompre le ~** to break one's fast; **jour de ~** fast day.

jeûner [ʒøne] (1) *vi* (*gén*) to go without food; (*Rel*) to fast. **faire ~ un malade** to make an invalid go without food; **laisser ~ ses enfants** to let one's children go hungry.

jeunesse [ʒœnɛs] *nf* **(a)** (*période*) youth. (*littér*) **la ~ du monde** the dawn of the world; **en pleine ~** in the prime of youth; **dans ma ~** in my youth, in my younger days; **folie/erreur/péché de ~** youthful prank/mistake/indiscretion; **en raison de son extrême ~** owing to his extreme youth; (*Prov*) **il faut que ~ se passe** youth must have its fling; *V* **fou, œuvre, premier** *etc.*

(b) (*qualité*) youngness, youthfulness. **~ de cœur** youngness of heart; **la ~ de son visage/de son corps peut vous tromper** his youthful face/figure may mislead you; **la ~ de ce vin** the youngness of this wine; **avoir un air de ~** to have a youthful look (about one); **sa ~ d'esprit** his youthfulness of mind.

(c) (*personnes jeunes*) youth, young people. **la ~ dorée** the young jet set; **la ~ ouvrière** (the) young workers; **la ~ étudiante/des écoles** young people at university/at school; **livres pour la ~** books for the young *ou* for young people; **la ~ est partie devant** the young ones *ou* the young people have gone on ahead; (*Prov*) **si ~ savait, si vieillesse pouvait** if youth but knew, if old age but could; *V* **auberge, voyage.**

(d) (*†: *jeune fille*) (young) girl.

(e) (*gén pl: groupe*) youth. **les ~s communistes** the Communist Youth Movement.

jeunet, -ette* [ʒœnɛ, ɛt] *adj* (*péj*) rather young. **il est un peu ~ pour lire ce roman** he's rather young *ou* he's a bit on the young side to be reading this novel.

jeûneur, -euse [ʒønœʀ, øz] *nm,f* person who fasts *ou* is fasting.

jeunot, -otte* [ʒœno, ɔt] **1** *adj* = **jeunet*.** **2** *nm* (*péj*) young fellow*.

joaillerie [ʒɔajʀi] *nf* **(a)** (*travail*) jewelling; (*commerce*) jewel trade. **travailler dans la ~** to work in jewellery *ou* in the jewel trade. **(b)** (*marchandise*) jewellery. **(c)** (*magasin*) jeweller's (shop).

joaillier, -ière [ʒɔaje, jɛʀ] *nm,f* jeweller.

Job [ʒɔb] *nm* (*Rel*) Job.

job* [dʒɔb] *nm* (*travail*) (temporary) job.

jobard, e‡ [ʒɔbaʀ, aʀd(ə)] **1** *adj* gullible. **2** *nm,f* (*dupe*) sucker*, mug*.

jobarderie‡ [ʒɔbaʀdʀi] *nf*, **jobardise‡** [ʒɔbaʀdiz] *nf* gullibility.

jockey [ʒɔkɛ] *nm* jockey.

Joconde [ʒɔkɔ̃d] *nf*: **la ~** the Mona Lisa.

jocrisse† [ʒɔkʀis] *nm* (*niais*) simpleton.

jodler [ʒɔdle] (1) *vt* to yodel.

joie [ʒwa] *nf* **(a)** (*U*) joy; (*sens diminué*) pleasure. **à ma grande ~** to my great joy *ou* delight; **fou** *ou* **ivre de ~** wild with joy *ou* delight; **la nouvelle le mit au comble de la ~** he was overjoyed at hearing the news *ou* to hear the news; **accueillir une nouvelle avec une ~ bruyante** to greet the news with great shouts of joy; **ses enfants sont sa plus grande ~** his children are his greatest delight *ou* joy; **c'était une ~ de le regarder** it was a joy *ou* delight to look at him, he was a joy to look at; **quand aurons-nous la ~ de vous revoir?** when shall we have the pleasure of seeing you again?; **il accepta avec ~** he accepted with delight; **sauter** *ou* **bondir de ~** to jump for joy; *V* **cœur, feu[1], fille.**

(b) les ~s de la vie the joys of life; (*Rel*) **les ~s du monde** *ou* **de la terre** worldly *ou* earthly pleasures *ou* joys; **les ~s du mariage** the joys of marriage.

(c) (*loc*) **~ de vivre** joy in life, joie de vivre; **être plein de ~ de vivre** to be full of joie de vivre *ou* the joys of life; **cela le mit en ~** he was overjoyed at this; **ce livre a fait la ~ de tous** this book has delighted *ou* has given great pleasure to everyone; **il se faisait une telle ~ d'y aller** he was so looking forward to going; **je me ferai une ~ de le faire** I shall be delighted *ou* only too pleased to do it.

joindre [ʒwɛ̃dʀ(ə)] (49) **1** *vt* **(a)** (*mettre ensemble*) to join, put together. **~ 2 tables/planches** to put 2 tables/planks together; **~ 2 bouts de ficelle** to join 2 pieces of string; **~ un bout de ficelle à un autre** to join one piece of string to another; **~ les mains** to put *ou* bring one's hands together; **~ les talons/les pieds** to put one's heels/feet together; **il se tenait debout les talons joints** he was standing with his heels together.

(b) (*relier*) to join, link. **une digue/un câble joint l'île au continent** a dyke/a cable joins the island to *ou* links the island with the mainland.

(c) (*unir*) *efforts etc* to combine, join; *personnes* (*en mariage*) to join. **~ l'utile à l'agréable** to combine business with pleasure; **elle joint l'intelligence à la beauté** she combines intelligence and beauty; **~ le geste à la parole** to suit the action to the word; (*fig*) **~ les deux bouts*** to make (both) ends meet.

(d) (*ajouter*) to add, attach (*à* to); (*inclure*) *timbre, chèque etc* to enclose (*à* with). **les avantages joints à ce poste** the advantages attached to this post, the fringe benefits of this post; **carte jointe à un bouquet/cadeau** card attached to a bouquet/a gift.

(e) (*communiquer avec*) *personne* to get in touch with, contact. **essayez de le ~ par téléphone** try to get in touch with *ou* try to get hold of *ou* try to contact him by telephone.

2 *vi [fenêtre, porte]* to shut, close. **ces fenêtres joignent mal** these windows don't shut *ou* close properly; *[planches etc]* **est-ce que ça joint bien?** does it make a good join?, does it join well?

3 se joindre *vpr* **(a)** (*s'unir à*) **se ~ à** to join; **se ~ à la procession** to join the procession; **se ~ à la foule** to mingle *ou* mix with the crowd; **voulez-vous vous joindre à nous?** would you like to join us?; **se ~ à la discussion** to join in the discussion; **mon mari se joint à moi pour vous exprimer notre sympathie** my husband and I wish to express our sympathy, my husband joins me in offering our sympathy (*frm*).

(b) *[mains]* to join; *V* **ci.**

joint [ʒwɛ̃] *nm* **(a)** (*Anat, Géol, Tech: assemblage, articulation*) joint; (*ligne de jonction*) join; (*en ciment, mastic*) jointing. **~ de robinet** washer; **~ de cardan** cardan joint; **~ de culasse** cylinder head gasket.

(b) (*arg Drogue*) joint (*arg*).

(c) (*loc*) **faire le ~** to last *ou* hold out; *[argent]* to bridge the gap; **chercher/trouver le ~** to look (around) for/come up with the answer.

jointé, e [ʒwɛ̃te] *adj*: **cheval court-~/long-~** short-/long-pasterned horse, horse with short/long pasterns.

jointif, -ive [ʒwɛ̃tif, iv] *adj* joined, contiguous; *planches* butt-jointed. **(cloison) ~ive** butt-jointed partition.

jointure [ʒwɛ̃tyʀ] *nf* **(a)** (*Anat*) joint. **~ du genou** knee joint; **à la ~ du poignet** at the wrist (joint); **faire craquer ses ~s** to crack one's knuckles; **à la ~ de 2 os** at the joint between 2 bones; **les ~s du cheval** fetlock (joint), pastern. **(b)** (*Tech*) (*assemblage*) joint; (*ligne de jonction*) join.

joker [ʒɔkɛʀ] *nm* (*Cartes*) joker.

joli, e [ʒɔli] *adj* **(a)** *enfant, femme* pretty, attractive; *chanson, objet* pretty, nice; *pensée, promenade, appartement* nice. **d'ici la vue est très ~e** you get a very nice *ou* attractive view from here; **~ comme un cœur** pretty as a picture; **il est ~ garçon** he is (quite) good-looking; **le ~ et le beau sont deux choses bien différentes** prettiness and beauty are two very different things.

(b) (*: *non négligeable*) *revenu, profit* nice (*épith*), good, handsome (*épith*); *résultat* nice (*épith*), good. **ça fait une ~e somme** it's quite a tidy sum of money, it's a handsome sum of money, it's a good bit of money; **il a une ~e situation** he has a good position.

(c) (*iro: déplaisant*) nasty, unpleasant, fine (*iro*), nice (*iro*). **embarquez tout ce ~ monde!** take the whole nasty bunch *ou* crew* away!; **un ~ gâchis** a fine mess (*iro*); **un ~ coco*** *ou* **monsieur** a nasty character *ou* piece of work*; **être dans un ~ pétrin** *ou* **de ~s draps** to be in a fine mess (*iro*).

(d) (*loc*) **tout ça c'est bien ~ mais** that's all very well but; **le plus ~ (de l'histoire) c'est que** the best bit of it all *ou* about it all is that; **vous avez fait du ~!** you've made a fine mess of things!; **faire le ~ cœur** to play the ladykiller; **ce n'est pas ~ de mentir** it's not nice to tell lies; **ce n'était pas ~ à voir** it wasn't a pleasant *ou* pretty sight; (*iro*) **elle est ~e, votre idée!** that's a nice *ou* great* idea! (*iro*).

joliesse [ʒɔljɛs] *nf* (*littér*) *[personne]* prettiness; *[gestes]* grace.

joliment [ʒɔlimɑ̃] *adv* **(a)** (*d'une manière jolie*) nicely. **pièce ~ décorée** attractively *ou* nicely decorated room; **enfant ~ habillé** prettily *ou* attractively dressed child; (*iro*) **il l'a ~ arrangé** he sorted him out nicely *ou* good and proper*.

(b) (*: *très, beaucoup*) pretty*, jolly* (*Brit*). **il a ~ raison** he's quite right, he's dead right*; **il était ~ content/en retard** he was pretty* *ou* jolly* (*Brit*) glad/late.

jonc [ʒɔ̃] *nm* **(a)** (*plante*) rush, bulrush; (*canne*) cane, rattan. **corbeille** *ou* **panier de ~** rush basket. **(b)** (*Aut*) trim. **(c)** (*bijou*) (plain gold) bangle *ou* ring.

jonché, e [ʒɔ̃ʃe] (*ptp de* **joncher**) **1** *adj*: **~ de** littered *ou* strewn with. **2 jonchée** *nf* swath of flowers *ou* leafy branches (*for strewing*). des ~es de feuilles mortes couvraient la pelouse dead leaves lay in drifts on the lawn.

joncher [ʒɔ̃ʃe] (1) *vt*: ~ qch de to strew sth with.

jonchets [ʒɔ̃ʃɛ] *nmpl* spillikins.

jonction [ʒɔ̃ksjɔ̃] *nf* (*action*) joining, junction; (*état*) junction. à la ~ des 2 routes at the junction of the 2 roads, where the 2 roads meet; (*Mil*) opérer une ~ to effect a junction, link up; point de ~ junction, meeting point.

jongler [ʒɔ̃gle] (1) *vi* (*lit*) to juggle (*avec* with). (*fig*) ~ avec *chiffres* to juggle with, play with; *difficultés* to juggle with.

jonglerie [ʒɔ̃gləʀi] *nf* jugglery, juggling.

jongleur, -euse [ʒɔ̃glœʀ, øz] *nm,f* (a) (*gén*) juggler. (b) (*Hist*) (wandering) minstrel, jongleur.

jonque [ʒɔ̃k] *nf* (*Naut*) junk.

jonquille [ʒɔ̃kij] 1 *nf* daffodil, jonquil. 2 *adj inv* (bright) yellow.

Jordanie [ʒɔʀdani] *nf* Jordan.

jordanien, -ienne [ʒɔʀdanjɛ̃, jɛn] 1 *adj* Jordanian. 2 *nm,f*: J~(ne) Jordanian.

Joseph [ʒozɛf] *nm* Joseph.

Joséphine [ʒozefin] *nf* Josephine.

Josué [ʒozɥe] *nm* Joshua.

jouable [ʒwabl(ə)] *adj* playable.

joual [ʒwal] *nm* (*Can Ling*) joual (*Can*).

joue [ʒu] *nf* (a) (*Anat*) cheek. ~ contre ~ cheek to cheek; tendre la ~ to offer one's cheek; présenter *ou* tendre l'autre ~ to turn the other cheek.

(b) (*Mil*) en ~! take aim!; coucher *ou* mettre une cible/une personne en ~ to aim at *ou* take aim at a target/a person; coucher *ou* mettre en ~ un fusil to take aim with a rifle, aim a rifle.

(c) (*Naut*) ~s d'un navire bows of a ship.

jouer [ʒwe] (1) 1 *vi* (a) (*s'amuser*) to play (*avec* with). arrête, je ne joue plus stop it, I'm not playing any more; elle jouait avec son crayon/son collier she was toying with her pencil/necklace; (*fig*) ~ avec une idée to toy with an idea; (*fig*) ~ avec les sentiments de qn to play *ou* trifle with sb's feelings; (*fig*) ~ avec sa vie/sa santé to gamble with one's life/health; (*fig*) on ne joue pas avec ces choses-là matters like these are not to be treated lightly.

(b) ~ à la poupée to play with one's dolls; ~ aux soldats/aux Indiens to play (at) soldiers/(at) Red Indians; ~ à qui sautera le plus loin to play at seeing who can jump the furthest; ~ à faire des bulles de savon to play at making *ou* blowing soap bubbles; ~ aux cartes/aux échecs to play cards/chess; ~ au chat et à la souris (avec qn) to play cat and mouse with sb; il joue bien (au tennis) he is a good (tennis) player, he plays (tennis) well, he plays a good game (of tennis); il a demandé à ~ avec *ou* contre X aux échecs he asked to play X at chess; (*fig*) ~ au héros/à l'aristocrate to play the hero/the aristocrat; *V* bille *etc*.

(c) (*Mus*) to play. ~ du piano/de la guitare to play the piano/the guitar; l'orchestre joue ce soir à l'opéra the orchestra is playing at the opera this evening; ce pianiste joue bien/mal this pianist plays well/badly.

(d) (*Casino*) to gamble. et en plus, il joue and on top of that, he gambles; ~ à la Bourse to speculate *ou* gamble on the Stock Exchange; ~ sur les valeurs minières to speculate in mining stock; ~ sur la hausse/la baisse d'un produit to gamble on the rise/the fall of a product; ~ à la roulette to play roulette; ~ pair/impair to play (on) the even/odd numbers; ~ aux courses to bet on the horses; ils ont joué sur la faiblesse/la pauvreté des paysans they reckoned on *ou* were banking *ou* relying on the peasants' weakness/poverty.

(e) (*Ciné, Théât, TV*) to act. il joue dans 'Hamlet' he is acting *ou* he is in 'Hamlet'; il joue au théâtre X he is playing *ou* acting at the X theatre; elle joue très bien she is a very good actress, she acts very well; on joue à guichets fermés the performance is fully booked *ou* is booked out.

(f) (*fonctionner*) to work. la clef joue mal dans la serrure the key doesn't fit (in) the lock very well; faire ~ un ressort to activate *ou* trigger a spring; la barque jouait sur son ancre the boat bobbed about at anchor.

(g) (*joindre mal*) to fit loosely, be loose; [*bois*] (*travailler*) to warp. la clef joue dans la serrure the key fits loosely in the lock.

(h) [*soleil, lumière etc*] to play. la lumière jouait au plafond the light played *ou* danced on the ceiling.

(i) (*intervenir*) l'âge ne joue pas age doesn't come into it *ou* is of no consequence; cette augmentation joue pour tout le monde this rise applies to *ou* covers everybody; l'augmentation joue depuis le début de l'année the rise has been operative from *ou* since the beginning of the year; les préférences des uns et des autres jouent finalement different people's preferences are what matter *ou* what count in the end; cet élément a joué en ma faveur this factor worked in my favour; il a fait ~ ses appuis politiques pour obtenir ce poste he made use of his political connections to get this post.

(j) (*loc*) ~ sur les mots to play with words; faire qch pour ~ to do sth for fun; ~ serré to play (it) tight, play a close game; ~ perdant/gagnant to play a losing/winning game; ~ au plus fin *ou* malin to try to outsmart sb, see who can be the smartest; faire ~ la corde sensible to appeal to the emotions; ~ de malheur *ou* de malchance to be dogged by ill luck; (*lit, fig*) à vous (*ou* moi *etc*) de ~! your (*ou* my *etc*) go! *ou* turn!; (*Échecs*) your (*ou* my *etc*) move!; bien joué! (*lit*) well played!; (*lit, fig*) well done!; ~ avec le feu to play with fire.

2 *vt* (a) (*Ciné, Théât*) *rôle* to play, act; (*représenter*) *pièce, film* to put on, show. on joue 'Macbeth' ce soir 'Macbeth' is on *ou* being played this evening; elle joue toujours les soubrettes she always has the maid's part; (*fig*) ~ un rôle to play a part, put on an act; (*fig*) ~ la comédie to put on an act, put it on*; il a joué un rôle ridicule dans cette affaire he acted like a fool *ou* he made himself look ridiculous in that business; la pièce se joue au théâtre X the play is on at the X theatre; (*fig*) le drame s'est joué très rapidement the tragedy happened very quickly.

(b) (*simuler*) ~ les héros/les victimes to play the hero/the victim; ~ la surprise/le désespoir to affect *ou* feign surprise/despair.

(c) (*Mus*) *concerto, valse* to play. il va ~ du Bach he is going to play (some) Bach; il joue très mal Chopin he plays Chopin very badly.

(d) (*Jeux, Sport*) *partie d'échecs, de tennis* to play; *carte* to play; *pion* to play, move. ~ atout to play trumps; ~ un coup facile/difficile (*Sport*) to play an easy/a difficult shot; (*Échecs*) to make an easy/a difficult move.

(e) (*Casino*) *argent* to stake, wager; (*Courses*) *argent* to bet, stake (*sur* on); *cheval* to back, bet on; (*fig*) *fortune, possessions, réputation* to wager. ~ les consommations to play for drinks; ~ gros jeu *ou* un jeu d'enfer to play for high stakes; il ne joue que des petites sommes he only places small bets *ou* plays for small stakes; il a joué et perdu une fortune he gambled away a fortune; ~ sa réputation sur qch to stake *ou* wager one's reputation on sth.

(f) (*frm: tromper*) *personne* to deceive, dupe.

(g) (*loc*) il faut ~ le jeu you've got to play the game; ~ franc jeu to play fair; ~ double jeu to play a double game; ~ son va-tout *ou* le tout pour le tout to stake one's all; ~ un (mauvais) tour/une farce à qn to play a (dirty) trick/a joke on sb; ~ sa dernière carte to play one's last card, ~ la fille de l'air to vanish into thin air.

3 jouer de *vt indir* (a) (*manier*) to make use of, use. ils durent ~ du couteau/du revolver pour s'enfuir they had to use knives/revolvers to get away; les jeunes jouent trop facilement du couteau the young use knives *ou* the knife too readily; (*hum*) ~ de la fourchette to tuck in*; ~ des jambes* *ou* des flûtes: to run away, take to one's heels; (*hum*) ~ de l'œil to wink; ~ des coudes pour parvenir au bar/pour entrer to elbow one's way to the bar/one's way in.

(b) (*utiliser*) to make use of. il joue de sa maladie pour ne rien faire he plays on his illness to get out of doing anything; ~ de son influence pour obtenir qch to use *ou* make use of one's influence to get sth.

4 se jouer *vpr* (*frm*) se ~ de: (*tromper*) se ~ de qn to deceive sb, dupe sb; (*moquer*) se ~ des lois/de la justice to scoff at the law/at justice; (*triompher facilement de*) se ~ des difficultés to make light of the difficulties; il fait tout cela en se jouant he does it all without trying; il a réussi cet examen comme en se jouant he waltzed through that exam*, that exam was a walkover for him*.

jouet [ʒwɛ] *nm* (a) (*lit*) toy, plaything. (b) (*fig*) navire qui est le ~ des vagues ship which is the plaything of the waves; être le ~ d'une illusion/hallucination to be the victim of an illusion/a hallucination.

joueur, -euse [ʒwœʀ, øz] *nm,f* (*Échecs, Mus, Sport*) player; (*Jeu*) gambler. ~ de golf golfer; ~ de cornemuse (bag)piper; ~ de cartes card player; être beau/mauvais ~ to be a good/bad loser; il a un tempérament ~, il est très ~ [*enfant, animal*] he loves to play, he's very playful; [*parieur*] he's very keen on gambling, he's a keen gambler.

joufflu, e [ʒufly] *adj enfant* chubby-cheeked, round-faced; *visage* chubby. une paysanne ~e a chubby-faced *ou* round-faced countrywoman.

joug [ʒu] *nm* (a) (*Agr, fig*) yoke. tomber sous le ~ de to come under the yoke of; mettre sous le ~ to yoke, put under the yoke. (b) [*balance*] beam. (c) (*Antiq*) yoke.

jouir [ʒwiʀ] (2) 1 jouir de *vt indir* (*frm: savourer, posséder*) to enjoy. il jouissait de leur embarras évident he delighted at *ou* enjoyed their evident embarrassment; ~ de toutes ses facultés to be in full possession of one's faculties; cette pièce jouit d'une vue sur le jardin this room commands a view of the garden.

2 *vi* (:) (*plaisir sexuel*) to come*:. on va ~! we're going to have a hell of a time!:, we aren't half going to have fun!*; ça me fait ~ de les voir s'empoigner I get a great kick out of seeing them at each other's throats:.

jouissance [ʒwisɑ̃s] *nf* (a) (*volupté*) pleasure, enjoyment, delight; (*sensuelle*) sensual pleasure; (*: *orgasme*) climax. (*frm*) cela lui a procuré une vive ~ this afforded him intense pleasure.

(b) (*Jur: usage*) use, possession; [*propriété, bien*] use, enjoyment. avoir la ~ de certains droits to enjoy certain rights.

jouisseur, -euse [ʒwisœʀ, øz] 1 *adj* sensual. 2 *nm,f* sensualist.

joujou, *pl* ~x [ʒuʒu] *nm* (*langage enfantin*) toy. faire ~ avec une poupée to play with a doll.

joule [ʒul] *nm* joule.

jour [ʒuʀ] 1 *nm* (a) (*U: lumière*) day(light); (*période*) day(time). il fait ~ it is daylight; je fais ça le ~ I do it during the day *ou* in the daytime; voyager de ~ to travel by day; service de ~ day service; (*Mil*) être de ~ to be on day duty; ~ et nuit day and night; se lever avant le ~ to get up *ou* rise before dawn *ou* daybreak; un faible ~ filtrait à travers les volets a faint light filtered through the shutters; le ~ entra à flots daylight streamed *ou* flooded in; avoir le ~ dans les yeux to have the light in one's eyes; (*fig*) ces enfants sont le ~ et la nuit these children are as different as chalk and cheese (*Brit*) *ou* night and day; (*fig*) ça va mieux avec le nouveau produit? — c'est le ~ et la nuit! is it better with this new product? — there's absolutely no comparison!; *V* demain, grand, lumière *etc*.

(b) (*espace de temps*) day. quinze ~s a fortnight (*surtout Brit*), two weeks; dans huit ~s in a week, in a week's time; tous les ~s every day; tous les deux ~s every other day, every two days; tous les ~s que (le bon) Dieu fait every blessed day, day in day out; **c'était il y a 2 ~s** it was 2 days ago; **des poussins d'un ~** day-old chicks; (*fig*) **d'un ~** *célébrité, joie* short-lived, fleeting; **c'est à 2 ~s de marche/de voiture de ...** it is a 2 days' walk/drive from ...; **faire 30 ~s (de prison)** to do 30 days (in jail *ou* inside*); **dans 2 ~s** in 2 days' time, in 2 days; (*Prov*) **les ~s se suivent et ne se ressemblent pas** time goes by and every day is different, the days go by and each is different from the last.

(c) (*époque précise*) day. **un ~ viendra où ...** a day will come when ...; **le ~ n'est pas loin où ...** the day is not far off when ...; **un de ces ~s** one of these (fine) days; **à un de ces ~s!** see you again sometime!, be seeing you!*; **un ~ il lui écrivit** one day he wrote to her; **par un ~ de pluie/de vent** on a rainy/windy day; **le ~ d'avant** the day before, the previous day; **le ~ d'après** the day after, the next day, the following day; **le ~ de Noël/de Pâques** Christmas/Easter Day; **le ~ du marché** market day; **prendre ~ avec qn** to fix a day with sb, make a date with sb; (*iro*) **décidément c'est mon ~!** I'm having a real day of it today!, really it's just not my day today!; **ce n'est vraiment pas le ~!** you (*ou* we *etc*) have picked the wrong day! (*de ou pour faire* to do); **le goût/la mode du ~** the style/the fashion of the day; **l'homme du ~** the man of the moment; **nouvelles du ~** news of the day, the day's news; **un œuf du ~** a today's egg, an egg laid today; *V* **cours, grand, plat^2.**

(d) ~s (*époque indéterminée, vie*) time, days, life. **la fuite des ~s** the swift passage of time; **finir ses ~s à l'hôpital** to end one's days in hospital; **attenter à/mettre fin à ses ~s** to make an attempt on/put an end to one's life; **nous gardons cela pour nos vieux ~s/pour les mauvais ~s** we're keeping that for our old age/for a rainy day *ou* for hard times; **il faut attendre des ~s meilleurs** we must wait for better times *ou* days; **nous connaissons des ~s bien anxieux** this is an anxious time for us, we're going through an anxious time; **il est dans (un de) ses bons ~s/ses mauvais ~s** he's having a good spell/a bad spell, it's one of his good/bad days; *V* **beau, couler.**

(e) (*éclairage: lit, fig*) light. **le tableau est dans un mauvais ~** the picture is in a bad light; **montrer/présenter/voir qch sous un ~ favorable/flatteur** to show/present/see sth in a favourable/flattering light; **jeter un ~ nouveau sur** to throw (a) new light on; **se présenter sous un ~ favorable** *[projet]* to look promising *ou* hopeful; *[personne]* to show o.s. to advantage *ou* in a favourable light; **nous le voyons maintenant sous son véritable ~** now we see him in his true colours *ou* see what he is really like.

(f) (*ouverture*) *[mur]* gap, chink; *[haie]* gap. **clôture à ~** openwork fence.

(g) (*Couture*) **~ simple** openwork, drawn-threadwork; **drap à ~** sheets with an openwork border; **faire des ~s dans un drap/dans un mouchoir** to hemstitch a sheet/handkerchief.

(h) (*loc*) **donner le ~ à** to give birth to, bring into the world; **voir le ~** *[enfant]* to be born, come into the world; *[projet]* to be born, come into being; **venir au ~** *[enfant]* to be born, come into the world; **mettre au ~** (*révéler*) to bring to light; **se faire ~** to become clear, come out*; **il se fit ~ dans mon esprit** it all became clear to me, the light dawned on me; **vivre au ~ le ~** (*sans soucis*) to live from day to day; (*pauvrement*) to live from hand to mouth; **(être/mettre/tenir) à ~** (to be/bring/keep) up to date; **la mise à ~ d'un compte/dossier** the updating of an account/a file; **de ~ en ~** day by day, from day to day; **on l'attend d'un ~ à l'autre** he is expected any day (now); **~ après ~** day after day; **(il change d'avis) d'un ~ à l'autre** (he changes his mind) from one day to the next; **un ~ ou l'autre** sometime or other, sooner or later; **du ~ au lendemain** overnight; **cela arrive tous les ~s** it happens every day, it's an everyday occurrence; **de tous les ~s** everyday (*épith*), ordinary; **de nos ~s** these days, nowadays, in this day and age; (†, *hum*) **au ~ d'aujourd'hui** in this day and age; **(à prendre) 3 fois par ~** (to be taken) 3 times a day; **il y a 2 ans ~ pour ~** 2 years ago to the day.

2: le jour de l'An New Year's day; (*Mil*) **jour d'arrêt** day of detention; **donner 8 jours d'arrêt** to give a week's detention; **jour de congé** day off, holiday; **jour férié** public *ou* Bank holiday; **jour de fête** feastday, holiday; **le jour J** D-day; **le jour des Morts** All Souls' Day; **jour ouvrable** weekday; **le jour de la Pentecôte** Whitsunday; (*Scol*) **jour des prix** prize (giving) day; **jour de réception** (*Admin*) day of opening (to the public); *[dame du monde]* 'at home' day; **le jour de réception du directeur est le lundi** the director is available to see people on Mondays; **jour de repos** *[ouvrier]* day off; **le jour des Rois** Epiphany, Twelfth Night; **le jour du Seigneur** Sunday, the Sabbath†; **jour de sortie** *[domestique]* day off, day out; *[élève]* day out; **jour de travail** working day.

journal, *pl* **-aux** [ʒuʀnal, o] **1** *nm* **(a)** (*Presse*) (news)paper; (*magazine*) magazine; (*bulletin*) journal. **dans** *ou* **sur le ~** in the (news)paper; **un grand ~** a big *ou* national (*Brit*) paper *ou* daily*.

(b) (*intime*) diary, journal. **tenir son ~ intime** to keep a private *ou* personal diary.

2: (*Naut*) **journal de bord** (ship's) log; **journal d'enfants** *ou* **pour enfants** children's comic *ou* paper; **journal littéraire** literary journal; **journal de mode** fashion magazine; (*Rad*) **journal parlé** radio news; **journal sportif** sporting magazine; (*TV*) **journal télévisé** television news.

journalier, -ière [ʒuʀnalje, jɛʀ] **1** *adj* **(a)** (*de chaque jour*) *travail, trajet* daily (*épith*); (*banal*) *existence* everyday (*épith*), humdrum (*épith*). **c'est ~** it happens every day. **(b)** (†: *changeant*) changing, changeable. **2** *nm* (*Agr*) day labourer.

journalisme [ʒuʀnalism(ə)] *nm* (*métier, style*) journalism. **faire du ~** to be in journalism, be a journalist.

journaliste [ʒuʀnalist(ə)] *nmf* journalist. **~ sportif/parlementaire** sports/parliamentary correspondent; **~ à la radio** radio reporter.

journalistique [ʒuʀnalistik] *adj* journalistic. **style ~** journalistic style; (*péj*) journalese (*U*).

journée [ʒuʀne] *nf* **(a)** (*jour*) day. **dans** *ou* **pendant la ~** during the day; **(dans) la ~ d'hier** yesterday, in the course of yesterday; **passer sa ~/toute sa ~ à faire qch** to spend the day/one's entire day doing sth; **passer des ~s entières à rêver** to daydream for whole days on end.

(b) *[ouvrier]* **~ (de travail)** day's work; **~ (de salaire)** day's wages *ou* pay; **faire de dures ~s** to put in a heavy day's work, work long hours; **faire des ~s** *ou* **aller en ~ chez les autres** to work as a domestic help *ou* daily help; **il se fait de bonnes ~s** he gets a good daily wage, he makes good money (every day); **travailler/être payé à la ~** to work/be paid by the day; **faire la ~ continue** *[bureau, magasin]* to remain open over lunch *ou* all day; *[personne]* to work over lunch; **la ~ de 8 heures** the 8-hour day; **~ de repos** day off, rest day.

(c) (*événement*) day. **~s historiques** historic days; **~s d'émeute** days of rioting; (*Mil*) **la ~ a été chaude, ce fut une chaude ~** it was a hard struggle *ou* a stiff fight.

(d) (*distance*) **à 3 ~s de voyage/de marche** 3 days' journey/walk away; **voyager à petites ~s†** to travel in short *ou* easy stages.

journellement [ʒuʀnɛlmɑ̃] *adv* (*quotidiennement*) daily; (*souvent*) every day.

joute [ʒut] *nf* **(a)** (*Hist, Naut*) joust, tilt. **(b)** (*fig*) duel, joust, tilt. **~s oratoires** oratorical encounter *ou* contest, verbal sparring; **~s d'esprit** battle of wits; **~s nautiques** water tournament.

jouter [ʒute] (1) *vi* (*Hist*) to joust, tilt; (*fig*) to joust (*contre* against), spar (*contre* with).

jouteur [ʒutœʀ] *nm* (*rare*) jouster, tilter.

jouvence [ʒuvɑ̃s] *nf*: **Fontaine de J~** Fountain of Youth; **eau de ~** waters of youth; *V* **bain.**

jouvenceau, *pl* **~x** [ʒuvɑ̃so] *nm* (††, *hum*) stripling††, youth.

jouvencelle [ʒuvɑ̃sɛl] *nf* (††, *hum*) damsel (††, *hum*).

jouxter [ʒukste] (1) *vt* to adjoin, be next to, abut on.

jovial, e, *mpl* **-aux** *ou* **~s** [ʒɔvjal, o] *adj* jovial, jolly. **d'humeur ~e** in a jovial mood; **avoir la mine ~e** to look jolly *ou* jovial.

jovialement [ʒɔvjalmɑ̃] *adv* jovially.

jovialité [ʒɔvjalite] *nf* joviality, jollity.

joyau, *pl* **~x** [ʒwajo] *nm* (*lit, fig*) gem, jewel. **les ~x de la couronne** the crown jewels.

joyeusement [ʒwajøzmɑ̃] *adv* *célébrer* merrily, joyfully; *accepter* gladly, gaily.

joyeux, -euse [ʒwajø, øz] *adj* **(a)** *personne, groupe* merry, joyful, joyous; *repas* cheerful; *cris* joyful, merry; *musique* joyful, joyous; *visage* joyful. **c'est un ~ luron** *ou* **drille** he's a great one for laughs*, he is a jolly fellow; **être en ~euse compagnie** to be in merry company *ou* with a merry group; **être d'humeur ~euse** to be in a joyful mood; **ils étaient partis ~** they had set out merrily *ou* in a merry group; **il était tout ~ à l'idée de partir** he was overjoyed *ou* (quite) delighted at the idea of going.

(b) *nouvelle* joyful. **~ Noël!** merry *ou* happy Christmas!; **~euse fête!** many happy returns!

jubé [ʒybe] *nm* jube, rood-loft.

jubilaire [ʒybilɛʀ] *adj* (*Rel*) jubilee (*épith*).

jubilation [ʒybilɑsjɔ̃] *nf* jubilation, exultation.

jubilé [ʒybile] *nm* jubilee.

jubiler* [ʒybile] (1) *vi* to be jubilant, exult, gloat (*péj*).

jucher *vt*, **se jucher** *vpr* [ʒyʃe] (1) to perch (*sur* on, upon).

judaïque [ʒydaik] *adj* (*loi*) Judaic; (*religion*) Jewish.

judaïsme [ʒydaism(ə)] *nm* Judaism.

judas [ʒyda] *nm* (*fourbe*) Judas; (*Archit*) judas hole. (*Bible*) **J~** Judas.

Judée [ʒyde] *nf* Judaea, Judea.

judéo- [ʒydeɔ] *préf*: **judéo-allemand, e** *adj, nm* Yiddish; **judéo-christianisme** *nm* Judeo-Christianity; **judéo-espagnol, e** *adj, nm* Judeo-Spanish.

judiciaire [ʒydisjɛʀ] *adj* judicial. **pouvoir ~** judicial power; **poursuites ~s** judicial *ou* legal proceedings; **vente ~** sale by order of the court; **enquête ~** judicial inquiry, legal examination.

judiciairement [ʒydisjɛʀmɑ̃] *adv* judicially.

judicieusement [ʒydisjøzmɑ̃] *adv* judiciously.

judicieux, -euse [ʒydisjø, øz] *adj* judicious. **faire un emploi ~ de son temps** to use one's time judiciously, make judicious use of one's time.

judo [ʒydo] *nm* judo.

judoka [ʒydɔka] *nmf* judoka.

juge [ʒyʒ] **1** *nm* (*Jur, Rel, Sport, fig*) judge. **oui, Monsieur le J~** yes, your Honour; **(monsieur) le ~ X** Mr Justice X; **prendre qn pour ~** to appeal to sb's judgment, ask sb to be (the) judge; **être bon/mauvais ~** to be a good/bad judge; **être à la fois ~ et partie** to be both judge and judged; **je vous fais ~ (de tout ceci)** I'll let you be the judge (of it all); **se faire ~ de ses propres actes/de qch** to be the judge of one's own actions/of sth; **il est seul ~ en la matière** he is the only one who can judge.

2: (*Tennis*) **juge-arbitre** referee; (*Sport*) **juge d'arrivée** finishing judge; **juge d'instruction** examining judge *ou* magistrate; (*Tennis*) **juge de ligne** line judge; **juge de paix** justice of the peace, magistrate; **juge de touche** (*Rugby*) touch judge, linesman; (*Ftbl*) linesman.

jugé [ʒyʒe] *nm*: **au ~** (*lit, fig*) by guesswork; **tirer au ~** to fire blind; **faire qch au ~** to do sth by guesswork.

jugeable [ʒyʒabl(ə)] *adj* (*évaluable*) **difficilement ~** difficult to judge; (*Jur*) subject to judgment in court.

jugement [ʒyʒmɑ̃] *nm* **(a)** (*Jur: décision, verdict*) *[affaire criminelle]* sentence; *[affaire civile]* decision, award. **prononcer** *ou* **rendre un ~** to pass sentence; **passer en ~** to be brought for *ou* stand trial; **poursuivre qn en ~** to sue sb, take legal proceedings against sb; **on attend le ~ du procès** we (*ou* they) are awaiting the verdict; **~ par défaut** judgment by default.

(b) (*opinion*) judgment, opinion. **~ de valeur** value judgment; **exprimer/formuler un ~** to express/formulate an opinion; **porter un ~ (sur)** to pass judgment (on); **s'en remettre au ~ de qn** to defer to sb's judgment; **~ préconçu** prejudgment, preconception.

(c) (*discernement*) judgment. **avoir du/manquer de ~** to have/lack (good) judgment; **on peut faire confiance à son ~** you can trust his judgment; **il a une grande sûreté de ~** he has very sound judgment.

(d) (*Rel*) judgment. **le ~ de Dieu** the will of the Lord; (*Hist*) the Ordeal; **le J~ dernier** the Last Judgment, Doomsday.

jugeote* [ʒyʒɔt] *nf* gumption*. **ne pas avoir deux sous de ~** to have no gumption*.

juger [ʒyʒe] (3) **1** *vt* **(a)** (*Jur*) *affaire* to judge, try; *accusé* to pass judgment *ou* sentence on. **le tribunal jugera** the court will decide; **être jugé pour meurtre** to be tried for murder; **le jury a jugé qu'il n'était pas coupable** the jury found him not guilty; **l'affaire doit se ~ à l'automne** the case is to come before the court *ou* is to be heard in the autumn.

(b) (*décider, statuer*) to judge, decide. **à vous de ~ (ce qu'il faut faire/si c'est nécessaire)** it's up to you to decide *ou* to judge (what must be done/whether *ou* if it is necessary); **~ un différend** to arbitrate in a dispute.

(c) (*apprécier*) *livre, film, personne, situation* to judge. **~ qn sur la mine/d'après les résultats** to judge sb by his appearance/by *ou* on his results; **il ne faut pas ~ d'après les apparences** you must not judge from *ou* go by appearances; **~ qch/qn à sa juste valeur** to judge sth/sb at its/his real value; **jugez combien j'étais surpris** *ou* **si ma surprise était grande** imagine how surprised I was *ou* what a surprise I got.

(d) (*estimer*) **~ qch/qn ridicule** to consider *ou* find *ou* think sth/sb ridiculous; **~ que** to think *ou* consider that; **nous la jugeons stupide** we consider her stupid, we think she's stupid; **pourquoi est-ce que vous me jugez mal?** why do you think badly of me?, why do you have a low opinion of me?; **si vous le jugez bon** if you think it's a good idea *ou* it's advisable; **~ bon/malhonnête de faire** to consider it a good thing *ou* advisable/dishonest to do; **il se jugea perdu** he thought *ou* considered himself lost; **il se juge capable de le faire** he thinks *ou* reckons he is capable of doing it.

2 juger de *vt indir* to appreciate, judge. **si j'en juge par mon expérience/mes sentiments** judging by *ou* if I (can) judge by my experience/my feelings; **lui seul peut ~ de l'urgence** only he can appreciate the urgency, only he can tell how urgent it is; **autant que je puisse en ~** as far as I can judge; **jugez de ma surprise!** imagine my surprise!

3 *nm*: **au ~ = au jugé**; *V* **jugé**.

jugulaire [ʒygylɛʀ] **1** *adj veines, glandes* jugular. **2** *nf* **(a)** (*Mil*) chin strap. **(b)** (*Anat*) jugular vein.

juguler [ʒygyle] (1) *vt maladie* to arrest, halt; *envie, désirs* to suppress, repress; *inflation* to curb, stamp out; *révolte* to put down, quell, repress; *personne* to stifle, sit upon*.

juif, juive [ʒɥif, ʒɥiv] **1** *adj* Jewish. **2** *nm*: **J~** Jew; **le J~ errant** the Wandering Jew. **3 Juive** *nf* Jew, Jewess, Jewish woman.

juillet [ʒɥijɛ] *nm* July. **la révolution/monarchie de J~** the July revolution/monarchy; *pour autres loc V* **septembre** *et* **quatorze**.

juin [ʒɥɛ̃] *nm* June; *pour loc V* **septembre**.

juive [ʒɥiv] *V* **juif**.

juiverie [ʒɥivʀi] *nf* (*péj*) **la ~** the Jews, the Jewish people.

jujube [ʒyʒyb] *nm* (*fruit, pâte*) jujube.

juke-box, *pl* **juke-boxes** [ʒykbɔks] *nm* jukebox.

jules [ʒyl] *nm* **(a)** (*nom*) Julius; (*: *amoureux*) man, bloke* (*Brit*), guy*; (*arg Crime*) underworld spiv (*Brit*). **(b)** (*: *vase de nuit*) chamberpot, jerry* (*Brit*).

julien, -ienne [ʒyljɛ̃, jɛn] **1** *adj* (*Astron*) Julian. **2** *nm*: **J~** Julian. **3 julienne** *nf* **(a) J~ne** Juliana, Gillian. **(b)** (*Culin*) julienne. **(c)** (*Bot*) rocket.

Juliette [ʒyljɛt] *nf* Juliet.

jumeau, -elle, *mpl* **~x** [ʒymo, ɛl] **1** *adj lit, frère, sœur* twin. **c'est mon frère ~** he is my twin (brother); **fruits ~x** double fruits; **maisons ~elles** semidetatched houses; **muscles ~x** gastrocnemius (*sg*).

2 *nm,f* **(a)** (*personne*) twin. **vrais/faux ~x, vraies/fausses ~elles** identical/fraternal twin brothers, identical/fraternal twin sisters.

(b) (*sosie*) double.

3 *nm* (*Culin*) clod of beef.

4 jumelle *nf* (*gén pl*) **(a)** (*gén*) binoculars. **~elles de spectacle** *ou* **théâtre/de campagne** opera/field glasses; **~elle marine** binoculars.

(b) *[mât]* fish. (*Aut*) **~elle de ressort** shackle.

jumelage [ʒymlaʒ] *nm* twinning.

jumelé, e [ʒymle] (*ptp de* **jumeler**) *adj*: **colonnes ~es** twin pillars; **roues ~es** double wheels; (*loterie*) **billets ~s** double series ticket; **vergue ~e** twin yard; **mât ~** twin mast.

jumeler [ʒymle] (4) *vt villes* to twin; *efforts* to join; *mâts, poutres* to double up, fish (*T*).

jument [ʒymɑ̃] *nf* mare.

jungle [ʒɔ̃gl(ə)] *nf* (*lit, fig*) jungle. **la ~ des affaires** the jungle of the business world, the rat race of business.

junior [ʒynjɔʀ] **1** *adj* (*Comm, Sport, hum*) junior. **Dupont ~** Dupont junior; **équipe ~** junior team.

2 *nmf* (*Sport*) junior.

Junon [ʒynɔ̃] *nf* Juno.

junte [ʒœ̃t] *nf* junta.

jupe [ʒyp] **1** *nf* (*Habillement, Tech*) skirt. **~ plissée/droite** pleated/straight skirt; **~s** skirts; (*fig*) **être toujours dans les ~s de sa mère** to cling to one's mother's apron strings. **2: jupe-culotte** *nf, pl* **jupes-culottes** culotte, divided skirt.

jupette [ʒypɛt] *nf* (short) skirt.

Jupiter [ʒypitɛʀ] *nm* (*Astron*) Jupiter; (*Myth*) Jove, Jupiter.

jupon [ʒypɔ̃] *nm* **(a)** (*Habillement*) waist petticoat *ou* slip. **(b)** (*fig†: femme*) bit of skirt*. **aimer le ~** to love anything in a skirt.

Jura [ʒyʀɑ] *nm*: **le ~** the Jura (Mountains).

jurassien, -ienne [ʒyʀasjɛ̃, jɛn] **1** *adj* of the Jura Mountains, Jura (*épith*). **2** *nm,f*: **J~(ne)** inhabitant *ou* native of the Jura Mountains.

jurassique [ʒyʀasik] *adj, nm* Jurassic.

juré, e [ʒyʀe] (*ptp de* **jurer**) **1** *adj* (*qui a prêté serment*) sworn. (*fig*) **ennemi ~** sworn enemy.

2 *nm* juror, juryman. **Messieurs les ~s apprécieront** the members of the jury will bear that in mind.

3 jurée *nf* juror, jurywoman.

jurer [ʒyʀe] (1) **1** *vt* **(a)** (*promettre, prêter serment*) to swear, vow. **~ fidélité/obéissance/amitié à qn** to swear *ou* pledge loyalty/obedience/friendship to sb; **~ la perte de qn** to swear to ruin sb *ou* bring about sb's downfall; **je jure que je me vengerai** I swear *ou* vow I'll get *ou* have my revenge; **faire ~ à qn de garder le secret** to swear *ou* pledge sb to secrecy; **jure-moi que tu reviendras** swear (to me) you'll come back; **~ sur la Bible/sur la croix/(devant) Dieu** to swear on the Bible/on the cross/to God; **~ sur la tête de ses enfants** *ou* **de sa mère** to swear by all that one holds dearest *ou* with one's hand on one's heart; **il jurait ses grands dieux qu'il n'avait rien fait** he swore blind* *ou* by all the gods† *ou* to heaven that he hadn't done anything; **ah! je vous jure!** honestly!; **il faut de la patience, je vous jure, pour la supporter!** it takes *ou* you need patience, I can assure you, to put up with her.

(b) (*) **on ne jure plus que par lui** everyone swears by him; **on ne jure plus que par ce nouveau remède** everyone swears by this new medicine.

2 jurer de *vt indir* to swear to. **j'en jurerais** I could swear to it, I'd swear to it; **je suis prêt à ~ de son innocence** I'm willing to swear to his innocence; (*Prov*) **il ne faut ~ de rien** you never can tell.

3 *vi* **(a)** (*pester*) to swear, curse. **~ après** *ou* **contre qch/qn** to swear *ou* curse at sth/sb; **~ comme un charretier** to swear like a trooper.

(b) *[couleurs]* to clash, jar; *[propos]* to jar.

4 se jurer *vpr* **(a)** (*à soi-même*) to vow to o.s., promise o.s. **il se jura bien que c'était la dernière fois** he vowed it was the last time.

(b) (*réciproquement*) to pledge (to) each other, swear, vow. **ils se sont juré un amour éternel** they pledged *ou* vowed *ou* swore each other eternal love.

juridiction [ʒyʀidiksjɔ̃] *nf* **(a)** (*compétence*) jurisdiction. **hors de/sous sa ~** beyond/within his jurisdiction; **exercer sa ~** to exercise one's jurisdiction; **tombant sous la ~ de** falling *ou* coming within the jurisdiction of. **(b)** (*tribunal*) court(s) of law.

juridique [ʒyʀidik] *adj* legal, juridical (*T*). **études ~s** law *ou* legal studies.

juridiquement [ʒyʀidikmɑ̃] *adv* juridically, legally.

jurisconsulte [ʒyʀiskɔ̃sylt(ə)] *nm* jurisconsult.

jurisprudence [ʒyʀispʀydɑ̃s] *nf* **la ~** (*source de droit*) ≃ case law, jurisprudence; (*décisions*) precedents, judicial precedent. **faire ~** to set a precedent.

juriste [ʒyʀist(ə)] *nm [compagnie]* lawyer; (*auteur, légiste*) jurist. **un esprit de ~** a legal turn of mind.

juron [ʒyʀɔ̃] *nm* oath, curse, swearword. **dire des ~s** to swear, curse.

jury [ʒyʀi] *nm* (*Jur*) jury; (*Art, Sport*) panel of judges; (*Scol*) board of examiners, jury. (*Jur*) **président du ~** foreman of the jury; (*Jur*) **membre du ~** juryman, juror.

jus [ʒy] *nm* **(a)** (*liquide*) juice. **~ de fruit** fruit juice; **~ de raisin** grape juice; **~ de viande** gravy, juice from the meat; **plein de ~** juicy; **~ de la treille*** wine; *V* **cuire, jeter, mijoter** *etc.*

(b) (*) (*café*) coffee; (*courant*) juice*; (*discours, article*) talk. **c'est un ~ infâme** it's a foul brew*; **au ~!** coffee's ready!, coffee's up!*

(c) (*loc) **jeter/tomber au ~** *ou* **dans le ~** to throw/fall into the water *ou* drink*; **au ~!** into the water with him!, in he goes!

(d) (*arg Mil*) **soldat de 1er ~** ≃ lance corporal (*Brit*); **soldat de 2e ~** ≃ private; **c'est du 8 au ~** only a week to go (to the end of military service).

jusant [ʒyzɑ̃] *nm* ebb, ebb tide.

jusque [ʒysk(ə)] **1** *prép* **(a)** (*lieu*) **jusqu'à la, jusqu'au** to, as far as, (right) up to, all the way to; **j'ai couru jusqu'à la maison/l'école** I ran all the *ou* right the way home/to school; **j'ai marché jusqu'au village puis j'ai pris le car** I walked to *ou* as far as the village then I took the bus; **ils sont montés jusqu'à 2.000 mètres** they climbed up to 2,000 metres; **il s'est avancé jusqu'au bord du précipice** he walked (right) up to the edge of the precipice; **il a rampé jusqu'à nous** he crawled up to us; **il avait de la neige jusqu'aux genoux** he had snow up to his knees, he was knee-deep in snow; **la nouvelle est venue jusqu'à moi** the news has reached me; (*fig*) **il menace d'aller jusqu'au ministre** he's threatening to go right to the minister.

(b) (*temps*) **jusqu'à, jusqu'en** until, till, up to; **jusqu'en mai** until May; **jusqu'à samedi** until Saturday; **du matin jusqu'au soir** from morning till night; **jusqu'à 5 ans il vécut à la campagne** he lived in the country until *ou* up to the age of 5; **les enfants restent dans cette école jusqu'à (l'âge de) 10 ans** (the) children stay at this school until they are 10 *ou* until the age of 10; **marchez jusqu'à ce que vous arriviez à la mairie** walk until you reach the town hall, walk as far as the town hall; **rester jusqu'au bout** *ou* **à la fin** to stay till *ou* to the end; **de la Révolu-**

tion jusqu'à nos jours from the Revolution (up) to the present day.

(c) (*limite*) **jusqu'à 20 kg** up to 20 kg, not exceeding 20 kg; **véhicule transportant jusqu'à 15 personnes** vehicle which can carry up to *ou* as many as 15 people; **pousser l'indulgence jusqu'à la faiblesse** to carry indulgence to the point of weakness; **aller jusqu'à dire/faire** to go so far as to say/do; **j'irai bien jusqu'à lui prêter 50 F** I am prepared to lend him *ou* I'll go as far as to lend him 50 francs; **j'irai jusqu'à 100** I'll lend you up to 100.

(d) (*y compris*) even. **il a mangé jusqu'aux arêtes** he ate everything including *ou* even the bones, he ate the lot — bones and all*; **ils ont regardé ~ sous le lit** they even looked under the bed; **tous jusqu'au dernier l'ont critiqué** they all criticized him to a man, every single one of them criticized him.

(e) (*avec prép ou adv*) **accompagner qn ~ chez lui** to take *ou* accompany sb (right) home; **veux-tu aller ~ chez le boucher pour moi?** would you go (along) to the butcher's for me?; **jusqu'où?** how far?; **jusqu'à quand?** until when?, how long?; **jusqu'à quand restez-vous?** how long *ou* till when are you staying?; **jusqu'ici** (*temps présent*) so far, until now; (*au passé*) until then; (*lieu*) up to *ou* as far as here; **~-là** (*temps*) until then; (*lieu*) up to there; **jusqu'alors, ~s alors** until then; **en avoir ~-là*** to be fed up to the (back) teeth* (*de* with) (*Brit*); **s'en mettre ~-là*** to stuff o.s. to the gills*; **jusqu'à maintenant, jusqu'à présent** until now, so far; **~ (très) tard** until (very) late; **~ vers 9 heures** until about 9 o'clock.

(f) (*loc*) **jusqu'au bout** to the (very) end; **jusqu'à concurrence de 100 F** to the amount of 100 francs; **vrai jusqu'à un certain point** true up to a certain point; **jusqu'au fond** to the (very) bottom; **elle a été touchée jusqu'au fond du cœur** she was most deeply touched; **rougir jusqu'aux oreilles** to blush to the roots of one's hair; **il avait un sourire jusqu'aux oreilles** he was smiling *ou* beaming from ear to ear; (*Admin*) **jusqu'à nouvel ordre** until further notice; **jusqu'à plus ample informé** until further information is available, pending further information; **tu vois jusqu'à quel point tu t'es trompé** you see how wrong you were; **jusqu'au moment où** until, till; **faire qch jusqu'à plus soif*** to do sth until one has had more than enough; **jusqu'à la gauche*** to the (bitter) end.

2 *adv*: **~ et y compris** up to and including; **jusqu'à** (*même*) even; **j'ai vu jusqu'à des enfants tirer sur des soldats** I even saw children shooting at soldiers; **il n'est pas jusqu'au paysage qui n'ait changé** the very landscape *ou* even the landscape has changed.

3 *conj*: **jusqu'à ce que, jusqu'à tant que** until; **sonnez jusqu'à ce qu'on vienne ouvrir** ring until someone answers the door; **il faudra le lui répéter jusqu'à ce** *ou* **jusqu'à tant qu'il ait compris** you'll have to keep on telling him until he's understood.

4: **jusqu'au-boutisme** *nm* (*politique*) hard-line policy; (*attitude*) extremist attitude; **jusqu'au-boutiste** *nmf, pl* **jusqu'au-boutistes** whole-hogger*, hard-liner; **c'est un jusqu'au-boutiste** he takes things to the bitter end, he always goes the whole hog*.

jusques [ʒysk(ə)] (†, *littér*) = **jusque.**

justaucorps [ʒystokɔʀ] *nm* (*Hist*) jerkin.

juste [ʒyst(ə)] **1** *adj* **(a)** (*équitable*) *personne, notation* just, fair; *sentence, guerre, cause* just. **être ~ pour** *ou* **envers** *ou* **à l'égard de qn** to be fair to sb; **c'est un homme ~** he is a just man; **il faut être ~** one must be fair; **pour être ~ envers lui** in fairness to him, to be fair to him; **il n'est pas ~ de l'accuser** it is unfair to accuse him; **la conscience du ~** a clear *ou* an untroubled conscience; **les ~s** (*gén*) the just; (*Rel*) the righteous; **par un ~ retour des choses** by a fair *ou* just twist of fate.

(b) (*légitime*) *revendication, vengeance, fierté* just; *colère* righteous, justifiable. **à ~ titre** with just cause *ou* reason, justly *ou* rightly (so); **la ~ récompense de son travail** the just reward for his work.

(c) (*exact*) *addition, réponse, heure* right, exact. **à l'heure ~** right *ou* dead* on time; **à 6 heures ~s** on the stroke of 6, dead on 6 o'clock*; **apprécier qch à son ~ prix/sa ~ valeur** to appreciate the true price/the true worth of sth; **le ~ milieu** the happy medium, the golden mean; (*Pol*) the middle course.

(d) (*pertinent, vrai*) *idée, raisonnement* sound; *remarque, expression* apt. **il a dit des choses très ~s** he said some very sound things; **très ~!** good point!, quite right!

(e) (*qui apprécie avec exactitude*) *appareil, montre* accurate, right (*attrib*); *esprit* sound; *balance* accurate, true; *coup d'œil* appraising; *oreille* good.

(f) (*Mus*) *note* right, true; *voix* true; *instrument* in tune (*attrib*), well-tuned. **il a une voix ~** he sings in tune; **quinte ~** perfect fifth.

(g) (*trop court, étroit*) *vêtement, chaussure* tight; (*longueur, hauteur*) on the short side. (*quantité*) **1 kg pour 6, c'est un peu ~** 1 kg for 6 people — it's barely enough *ou* it's a bit on the short *ou* skimpy side; **3 heures pour faire cette traduction, c'est ~** 3 hours to do that translation — it's barely (allowing) enough; **elle n'a pas raté son train mais c'était ~** she didn't miss her train but it was a close thing.

(h) (*excl*) **~ ciel!†** heavens (above)!; **~ Dieu!†** almighty God!, ye Gods!

2 *adv* **(a)** (*avec exactitude*) *compter, viser* accurately; *raisonner* soundly; *deviner* rightly; *chanter* in tune. **tomber ~** (*deviner*) to say just the right thing, hit the nail on the head; **la pendule va ~** the clock is keeping good time.

(b) (*exactement*) just, exactly. **~ au-dessus** just above; **~ au coin** just on *ou* round the corner; **il a dit ~ ce qu'il fallait** he said exactly *ou* just what was needed; **~ au moment où j'entrais, il sortait** (just) at the very moment when I was coming in, he was going out; **j'ai ~ assez** I have just enough; **3 kg ~** 3 kg exactly.

(c) (*seulement*) only, just. **j'ai ~ à passer un coup de téléphone** I only *ou* just have to make a telephone call; **il est parti il y a ~ un moment** he left just *ou* only a moment ago.

(d) **(un peu) ~** *compter, prévoir* not quite enough, too little; **il est arrivé un peu ~** *ou* **bien ~** he cut it a bit too fine* (*Brit*) *ou* close, he arrived at the last minute; **il a mesuré trop ~** he didn't allow quite enough, he cut it a bit too fine* (*Brit*).

(e) (*loc*) **que veut-il au ~?** what exactly does he want? *ou* is he after?*, what does he actually want?; **au plus ~ prix** at the lowest *ou* minimum price; **calculer au plus ~** to work things out to the minimum; **comme de ~** as usual, of course, naturally; **comme de ~ il pleuvait!** and of course it was raining!; **tout ~** (*seulement*) only just; (*à peine*) hardly, barely; (*exactement*) exactly; **c'est tout ~ si je ne me suis pas fait insulter!** what I got was little more than a string of insults flung at me, I was practically insulted; **son livre vaut tout ~ la peine qu'on le lise** his book is barely worth reading.

justement [ʒystəmɑ̃] *adv* **(a)** (*précisément*) exactly, just, precisely. **il ne sera pas long, ~, il arrive** he won't be long, in fact he's just coming; **on parlait ~ de vous** we were just talking about you.

(b) (*à plus forte raison*) **puisque vous me l'interdisez ... eh bien, ~ je le lui dirai** since you forbid me to ... just for that I'll tell him.

(c) (*avec justesse, justice*) *raisonner, remarquer* rightly, justly, soundly. **~ puni** justly punished; **~ inquiet/fier** justifiably anxious/proud; **on peut dire ~ que ...** one would be right in saying that ..., one could justifiably say that ... .

justesse [ʒystɛs] *nf* **(a)** (*exactitude*) *[appareil, montre, balance]* accuracy, precision; *[calcul]* accuracy, correctness; *[réponse, comparaison, observation]* exactness; *[coup d'œil, oreille]* accuracy.

(b) *[note, voix, instrument]* accuracy.

(c) (*pertinence*) *[idée, raisonnement]* soundness; *[remarque, expression]* aptness, appropriateness. **on est frappé par la ~ de son esprit** one is struck by the soundess of his judgment *ou* by how sound his judgment is.

(d) (*loc*) **de ~** just, barely; **gagner de ~** to win by a narrow margin; **j'ai évité l'accident de ~** I avoided the accident by a hair's breadth, I had a narrow escape; **il s'en est tiré de ~** he got out of it by the skin of his teeth.

justice [ʒystis] *nf* **(a)** (*bon droit*) fairness, justice. **en bonne** *ou* **toute ~** in all fairness; **on lui doit cette ~ que ...** it must be said in fairness to him that ...; **ce n'est que ~ qu'il soit récompensé** it's only fair *ou* just that he should have his reward; **il a la ~ pour lui** justice is on his side.

(b) (*Admin, Jur*) justice; (*Pol*) law. **traiter qn avec ~** to treat sb justly; **exercer la ~** to exercise justice; **passer en ~** to stand trial; **les décisions de la ~** juridical decisions; **la ~ recherche le meurtrier** the murderer is wanted by the law; **il a eu des démêlés avec la ~** he's had a brush *ou* he's had dealings with the law, he's come up against the law; **aller en ~** to take a case to the courts *ou* to court; **demander/obtenir ~** to demand/obtain justice; **être traduit en ~** to be brought before the court(s); **la ~ de notre pays** the law of our country; **~ administrative/maritime/militaire** administrative/maritime/military law; **~ de paix** court of first instance. **V déni, palais, repris** *etc.*

(c) **rendre ~ à qn** to do sb justice; **rendre la ~** to dispense justice; **faire ~ de qch** (*récuser*) to refute sth; (*réfuter*) to disprove sth; **il a pu faire ~ des accusations** he was able to refute the accusations; **se faire ~** (*se venger*) to take the law into one's own hands, take (one's) revenge; (*se suicider*) to take one's life; **il faut lui rendre cette ~ qu'il n'a jamais cherché à nier** we must do him justice in one respect and that is that he's never tried to deny it, in fairness to him it must be said that he's never tried to deny it; **on n'a jamais rendu ~ à son talent** his talent has never had fair *ou* due recognition.

justiciable [ʒystisjabl(ə)] **1** *adj* (*passible de*) **~ de** justiciable, subject to court action; **criminel ~ de la cour d'assises** criminal subject to the criminal court *ou* to trial in the assizes; (*fig*) **situation ~ de mesures énergiques** situation where strong measures are indicated *ou* required, situation requiring strong measures.

2 *nmf* (*Jur*) *person subject to trial.* **les ~s** those to be tried; **les ministres sont ~s de la Haute cour** ministers are subject to trial by the High Court; (*fig*) **l'homme politique est ~ de l'opinion publique** politicians are answerable to public opinion.

justicier, -ière [ʒystisje, jɛʀ] *nm,f* **(a)** (*gén*) dispenser of justice, judge. **(b)** (*Jur††*) dispenser of justice.

justifiable [ʒystifjabl(ə)] *adj* justifiable. **cela n'est pas ~** that is unjustifiable, that can't be justified.

justificateur, -trice [ʒystifikatœʀ, tʀis] *adj raison, action* justificatory, justifying.

justificatif, -ive [ʒystifikatif, iv] *adj démarche, document* supporting, justificatory. **pièce ~ive** written proof *ou* evidence.

justification [ʒystifikɑsjɔ̃] *nf* **(a)** (*explication*) justification. **~ de la guerre** justification of war; **fournir des ~s** to give some justification. **(b)** (*preuve*) proof. **(c)** (*Typ*) justification.

justifier [ʒystifje] (7) **1** *vt* **(a)** (*légitimer*) *personne, attitude, action* to justify. **rien ne justifie cette colère** such anger is quite unjustified. **(b)** (*donner raison*) *opinion* to justify, bear out, vindicate; *espoir* to justify. **ça justifie mon point de vue** it bears out *ou* vindicates my opinion.

(c) (*prouver*) to prove, justify. **pouvez-vous ~ ce que vous affirmez?** can you justify *ou* prove your assertions?

(d) (*Typ*) to justify.

2 justifier de *vt indir* to prove. **~ de son identité** to prove one's identity.

3 se justifier *vpr* to justify o.s. **se ~ d'une accusation** to clear o.s. of an accusation.

jute [ʒyt] *nm* jute; *V* **toile.**
juter [ʒyte] (1) *vi* **(a)** *[fruit]* to be juicy, drip with juice. **pipe qui jute*** dribbling pipe. **(b)** (*: *faire un discours etc*) to spout*, hold forth.
juteux, -euse [ʒytø, øz] **1** *adj fruit* juicy. **2** *nm* (*arg Mil: adjudant*) adjutant.
juvénile [ʒyvenil] *adj allure* young, youthful. **plein de fougue ~** full of youthful enthusiasm.
juvénilité [ʒyvenilite] *nf* (*littér*) youthfulness.
juxtalinéaire [ʒykstalineɛʀ] *adj* (*littér*) **traduction ~** line by line translation.
juxtaposer [ʒykstapoze] (1) *vt* to juxtapose, place side by side. **propositions juxtaposées** juxtaposed clauses; **son français se réduit à des mots juxtaposés** his French is little more than a string of unconnected words.
juxtaposition [ʒykstapozisjɔ̃] *nf* juxtaposition.

K

K, k [ka] *nm* (*lettre*) K, k.
kabbale [kabal] *nf* = **cabale.**
kabyle [kabil] **1** *adj* Kabyle. **2** *nm* (*Ling*) Kabyle. **3** *nmf*: **K~** Kabyle.
Kabylie [kabili] *nf* Kabylia.
kafkaïen, -ïenne [kafkajɛ̃, jɛn] *adj* Kafkaesque.
kakatoès [kakatɔɛs] *nm* = **cacatoès.**
kaki [kaki] **1** *adj* khaki. **2** *nm* **(a)** (*couleur*) khaki. **(b)** (*Agr*) kaki.
kaléidoscope [kaleidɔskɔp] *nm* kaleidoscope.
kaléidoscopique [kaleidɔskɔpik] *adj* kaleidoscopic.
kamikaze [kamikaze] *nm* kamikaze.
kangourou [kɑ̃guʀu] *nm* kangaroo.
kantien, -ienne [kɑ̃tjɛ̃, jɛn] *adj* Kantian.
kantisme [kɑ̃tism(ə)] *nm* Kantianism.
kaolin [kaɔlɛ̃] *nm* kaolin.
kapok [kapɔk] *nm* kapok.
karaté [kaʀate] *nm* karate.
karstique [kaʀstik] *adj* karstic.
kart [kaʀt] *nm* go-cart, kart.
karting [kaʀtiŋ] *nm* go-carting, karting. **faire du ~** to go-cart, go karting.
kasbah [kazba] *nf* = **casbah.**
kayak [kajak] *nm* (*eskimo*) kayak; (*Sport*) canoe, kayak. **faire du ~** to go canoeing.
képi [kepi] *nm* kepi.
kermesse [kɛʀmɛs] *nf* (*fête populaire*) fair; (*fête de charité*) bazaar, charity fête. (*fig*) **c'est une vraie ~ là-dedans*** it's absolute bedlam in there; **~ paroissiale** church fête *ou* bazaar.
kérosène [keʀozɛn] *nm [avion, jet]* jet A1 fuel; *[fusée]* rocket fuel.
khâgne [kaɲ] *nf* = **cagne.**
khâgneux, -euse [kaɲø] *nm,f* = **cagneux[2].**
khalife [kalif] *nm* = **calife.**
khan [kɑ̃] *nm* khan.
khédive [kediv] *nm* khedive.
khmer, -ère [kmɛʀ] **1** *adj* Khmer. **2** *nmpl*: **les K~s** the Khmers.
khôl [kol] *nm* khol, kajal.
kibboutz [kibuts] *nm* kibbutz.
kidnappage [kidnapaʒ] *nm* (*rare*) = **kidnapping.**
kidnapper [kidnape] (1) *vt* to kidnap.
kidnapping [kidnapiŋ] *nm* (*rare*) kidnapping.
kidnappeur, -euse [kidnapœʀ, øz] *nm,f* kidnapper.
kief [kjɛf] *nm*, **kif[1]** [kif] *nm* kef, kif.
kif[2]* [kif] *nm*: **c'est du ~** it's all the same, it's all one, it makes no odds* (*Brit*).
kif-kif* [kifkif] *adj inv*: **c'est ~** it's all the same, it's all one, it makes no odds* (*Brit*).
kiki* [kiki] *nm*: **serrer le ~ à qn** to throttle sb, grab sb by the throat; *V* **partir.**
kil‡ [kil] *nm*: **~ de rouge** bottle of plonk* (*Brit*) *ou* cheap wine.
kilo [kilo] *nm* kilo.
kilo ... [kilo] *préf* kilo ... .
kilocycle [kilɔsikl(ə)] *nm* kilocycle.
kilogramme [kilɔgʀam] *nm* kilogramme.
kilométrage [kilɔmetʀaʒ] *nm* ≈ *[voiture, distance]* mileage; (*route*) marking with milestones.
kilomètre [kilɔmɛtʀ(ə)] *nm* kilometre.
kilométrer [kilɔmetʀe] (6) *vt route* ≈ to mark with milestones.
kilométrique [kilɔmetʀik] *adj*: **distance ~** distance in kilometres; **borne ~** ≈ milestone.
kilotonne [kilɔtɔn] *nf* kiloton.
kilowatt [kilɔwat] *nm* kilowatt.
kilowatt-heure, *pl* **kilowatts-heures** [kilɔwatœʀ] *nm* kilowatt-hour.
kimono [kimɔno] *nm* kimono.
kinase [kinaz] *nf* kinase.
kinésithérapeute [kineziteʀapøt] *nmf* physiotherapist.
kinésithérapie [kineziteʀapi] *nf* physiotherapy.
kiosque [kjɔsk(ə)] *nm [journaux etc]* kiosk, stall; *[jardin]* pavilion, summerhouse; *[sous-marin]* conning tower; *[bateau]* wheelhouse. **~ à musique** bandstand.
kirsch [kiʀʃ] *nm* kirsch.
kitchenette [kitʃənɛt] *nf* kitchenette.
kiwi [kiwi] *nm* kiwi.
klaxon, Klaxon [klaksɔn] *nm* ® (*Aut*) horn.
klaxonner [klaksɔne] (1) *vt* (*fort*) to hoot (one's horn), sound one's horn, (*doucement*) to toot (the horn). **klaxonne, il ne t'a pas vu** give a hoot *ou* toot on your horn *ou* give him a toot*, he hasn't seen you.
kleb(s)* [klɛp(s)] *nm* = **clebs*.**
kleptomane [klɛptɔman] *adj, nmf* kleptomaniac.
kleptomanie [klɛptɔmani] *nf* kleptomania.
knock-out [nɔkawt] (*Boxe*, ‡) **1** *adj* (knocked) out, out for the count*. **mettre qn ~** to knock sb out; **il est complètement ~** he's out cold*.
2 *nm* knock-out.
knout [knut] *nm* knout.
koala [kɔala] *nm* koala (bear).
kola [kɔla] *nm* = **cola.**
kolkhoze [kɔlkoz] *nm* kolkhoz.
kopeck [kɔpɛk] *nm* kopeck. **je n'ai plus un ~*** I haven't got a sou.
koran [kɔʀɑ̃] *nm* = **coran.**
krach [kʀak] *nm* (*Bourse*) crash.
Kremlin [kʀɛmlɛ̃] *nm*: **le ~** the Kremlin.
krypton [kʀiptɔ̃] *nm* krypton.
kummel [kymɛl] *nm* kümmel.
kurde [kyʀd(ə)] **1** *adj* Kurdish. **2** *nm* (*Ling*) Kurdish. **3** *nmf*: **K~** Kurd.
Kurdistan [kyʀdistɑ̃] *nm* Kurdistan.
kyrielle [kiʀjɛl] *nf [injures, réclamations]* string, stream; *[personnes]* crowd, stream; *[objets]* pile.
kyste [kist(ə)] *nm* cyst.
kystique [kistik] *adj* cystic.

L

L, l [ɛl] *nm ou nf* (*lettre*) L, l.

l' [l(ə)] *V* **le¹, le².**

la¹ [la] *V* **le¹, le².**

la² [la] *nm inv* (*Mus*) A; (*en chantant la gamme*) la. **donner le ~** (*lit*) to give an A; (*fig*) to set the tone *ou* the fashion.

là [la] **1** *adv* **(a)** (*par opposition à ici*) there; (*là-bas*) over there. **~, on s'occupera bien de vous** you will be well looked after there; **je le vois ~, sur la table** I can see it (over) there, on the table; **c'est ~ où *ou* que je suis né** that's where I was born; **il est allé à Paris, et de ~ à Londres** he went to Paris, and from there to London *ou* and then (from there) on to London; **c'est à 3 km de ~** it's 3 km away (from there); **quelque part par ~** somewhere around there *ou* near there; **passez par ~** go that way; *V* **çà.**

(b) (*ici*) here, there. **ne restez pas ~ au froid** don't stand here *ou* there in the cold; **M X n'est pas ~** Mr X isn't here *ou* in; **c'est ~ qu'il est tombé** that's *ou* this is where he fell; **déjà ~!** (are) you here already?; **qu'est-ce que tu fais ~?** (*lit*) what are you doing here?; (*fig: manigancer*) what are you up to?*; **les faits sont ~** there's no getting away from the facts.

(c) (*dans le temps*) then, (at) this *ou* that moment. **c'est ~ qu'il comprit qu'il était en danger** that was when *ou* it was then that he realized he was in danger; **à partir de ~** from then on, after that; **jusque-~** until then, until that moment *ou* time; **à quelques jours de ~** a few days later *ou* after(wards); *V* **ici.**

(d) (*dans cette situation*) **tout cela pour en arriver *ou* en venir ~!** all that effort just for this!; **il faut s'en tenir *ou* en rester ~** we'll have to leave it at that *ou* stop there; **la situation en est ~** that's how the situation stands at the moment, that's the state of play at present; **ils en sont ~** (*lit*) that's how far they've got up to, that's the stage they've reached; (*péj*) that's how low they've sunk; **ils n'en sont pas encore ~** they haven't got that far yet *ou* reached that stage yet; (*péj*) they haven't reached that stage yet *ou* come to that yet; **~ est *ou* c'est ~ qu'est la difficulté** that's where the difficulty lies; **il a bien fallu en passer par ~** it had to come (to that) in the end; **c'est bien ~ qu'on voit les paresseux!** that's where *ou* when you see who the lazy ones are!; **c'est ~ où *ou* que nous ne sommes plus d'accord** that's where I take issue *ou* start to disagree with you.

(e) (*intensif*) that. **ce jour-~** that day; **en ce temps-~** in those days; **cet homme-~ est détesté par tout le monde** everybody hates that man; **je veux celui-~** I want that one; **celui-/celle-~ alors!** (*irritation*) oh, that one!, oh him/her!; (*surprise*) how does he/she manage!, he/she is a wonder!; **c'est à ce point-~?** it's as bad as that, is it?; **ce qu'il dit ~ n'est pas bête** what he has just said isn't a bad idea; **la question n'est pas ~** that's not the point; **ne croyez pas ~ qu'on ne veuille pas de vous** don't get the idea that you're not wanted; **il y a ~ une contradiction** there's a contradiction in that; **il est entré dans une rage, mais ~, une de ces rages!** he flew into a rage, and what a rage!

(f) (*loc*) **de ~ son désespoir** hence his despair; **de ~ vient que nous ne le voyons plus** that's why he doesn't come any more; **de ~ à croire qu'il ment, il n'y a qu'un pas** there isn't much difference between saying that and thinking he's lying, that's tantamount to saying he's a liar; **de ~ à prétendre qu'il a tout fait seul, il y a loin** there's a big difference between saying that and claiming that he did it all himself; **qu'entendez-vous par ~?** what do you mean by that?; **loin de ~** far from it; **tout est ~** that's what matters *ou* counts; **il est (~ et) un peu ~*** you can't miss him, he makes his presence felt; **comme menteur, il est *ou* se pose ~ et un peu ~** he isn't half a liar*; **oh ~ *ou* alors ~, ça ne me surprend pas** (oh) now, that doesn't surprise me; **hé ~!** (*appel*) hey!; (*surprise*) good grief!; **~, ~ du calme** now, now calm down, there, there calm down; **oh ~ ~ (~ ~)** dear! dear!, dear *ou* dearie me!

2: **là-bas** (over) there, yonder (†, *littér*); **là-bas aux USA** over in the USA; **là-bas dans le nord** up (there) in the north; **là-dedans** (*lit*) inside, in there; (*fig*) in it, in that; **là-dessous** underneath, under there, under that; (*fig*) **il y a quelque chose là-dessous** there's something odd about it *ou* that, there's more to it than meets the eye; **là-dessus** (*lieu*) on that, on there; (*sur ces mots*) at that point, thereupon (*frm*); (*à ce sujet*) about that, on that point; **vous pouvez compter là-dessus** you can count on that; **là-haut** up there; (*dessus*) up on top; (*à l'étage*) upstairs; (*fig: au ciel*) on high, in heaven above.

label [labɛl] *nm* (*Comm*) stamp, seal. **~ d'origine/de qualité** stamp *ou* seal of origin/quality.

labeur [labœʀ] *nm* (*littér*) labour, toil (*U*).

labial, e, *mpl* **-aux** [labjal, o] **1** *adj consonne* labial; *muscle* lip (*épith*), labial (*T*). **2 labiale** *nf* labial.

labialisation [labjalizasjɔ̃] *nf* (*V* **labialiser**) labialization; rounding.

labialiser [labjalize] (1) *vt consonne* to labialize; *voyelle* to labialize, round.

labié, e [labje] *adj* (*Bot*) labiate.

labiodental, e *mpl* **-aux** [labjɔdɑ̃tal, o] *adj, nf* labiodental.

labo* [labo] *nm* (*abrév de* **laboratoire**) lab*.

laborantin, e [labɔʀɑ̃tɛ̃, in] *nm,f* laboratory *ou* lab* assistant.

laboratoire [labɔʀatwaʀ] *nm* laboratory. **~ de langues/de recherches** language/research laboratory; **~ d'analyses (médicales)** (medical) analysis laboratory.

laborieusement [labɔʀjøzmɑ̃] *adv* laboriously, with much effort. **gagner ~ sa vie** to earn a *ou* one's living by the sweat of one's brow.

laborieux, -euse [labɔʀjø, øz] *adj* **(a)** (*pénible*) laborious, painstaking; *entreprise, recherches* laborious; *style, récit* laboured, laborious; *digestion* heavy. **il a enfin fini, ça a été ~!*** he has finished at long last, it has been heavy going *ou* he made heavy weather of it.

(b) (*travailleur*) hard-working, industrious. **les classes ~euses** the working classes; **les masses ~euses** the toiling masses; **une vie ~euse** a life of toil *ou* hard work.

labour [labuʀ] *nm* (*avec une charrue*) ploughing (*Brit*), plowing (*US*); (*avec une bêche*) digging (over). **cheval de ~** plough-horse, cart-horse; **bœuf de ~** ox; **champ en ~** ploughed field; **marcher dans les ~s** to walk in the ploughed fields.

labourable [labuʀabl(ə)] *adj* (*V* **labour**) ploughable (*Brit*), plowable (*US*), which can be ploughed; which can be dug.

labourage [labuʀaʒ] *nm* (*V* **labour**) ploughing (*Brit*), plowing (*US*); digging.

labourer [labuʀe] (1) *vt* **(a)** (*avec une charrue*) to plough (*Brit*), plow (*US*); (*avec une bêche*) to dig (over). **terre qui se laboure bien** land which ploughs well *ou* is easy to plough; (*Naut*) **~ le fond** *[navire]* to scrape *ou* graze the bottom; *[ancre]* to drag; **terrain labouré par les sabots des chevaux** ground churned *ou* ploughed up by the horses' hooves.

(b) *visage* to make deep gashes in, rip *ou* slash into. **la balle lui avait labouré la jambe** the bullet had ripped into *ou* gashed his leg; **labouré de rides** lined *ou* furrowed with wrinkles; **ce corset me laboure les côtes** this corset is digging into my sides; **se ~ le visage/les mains** to gash *ou* lacerate one's face/hands.

laboureur [labuʀœʀ] *nm* ploughman (*Brit*), plowman (*US*); (*Hist*) husbandman.

Labrador [labʀadɔʀ] *nm* (*Géog, chien*) Labrador.

labyrinthe [labiʀɛ̃t] *nm* (*lit, fig*) maze, labyrinth; (*Méd*) labyrinth.

labyrinthique [labiʀɛ̃tik] *adj* labyrinthine.

lac [lak] *nm* lake. **le ~ Léman** Lake Geneva; **les ~s écossais** the Scottish lochs; (*fig*) **être (tombé) dans le ~*** to have fallen through, have come to nothing.

laçage [lɑsaʒ] *nm* lacing(-up).

Lacédémone [lasedemɔn] *n* Lacedaemonia.

lacédémonien, -ienne [lasedemɔnjɛ̃, jɛn] *adj, nm,f* Lacedaemonian.

lacement [lɑsmɑ̃] *nm* = **laçage.**

lacer [lɑse] (3) *vt chaussure* to tie (up); *corset* to lace up; (*Naut*) *voile* to lace. **lace tes chaussures *ou* tes lacets** do up *ou* tie your shoelaces; **ça se lace (par) devant** it laces up at the front.

lacération [laseʀɑsjɔ̃] *nf* (*V* **lacérer**) ripping up, tearing up; ripping *ou* tearing to shreds; laceration.

lacérer [laseʀe] (6) *vt papier, vêtement* to tear *ou* rip up, tear to shreds; *corps, visage* to lacerate.

lacet [lɑsɛ] *nm* **(a)** *[chaussure]* (shoe)lace; *[corset]* lace. **chaussures à ~s** lace-up shoes, shoes with laces.

(b) *[route]* (sharp) bend, twist. **en ~** winding, twisty; **la route fait des ~s *ou* monte en ~s** the road twists *ou* winds steeply up(wards).

(c) (*piège*) snare.

(d) (*Couture*) braid.

lâchage* [lɑʃaʒ] *nm* (*abandon*) desertion. **écœuré par le ~ de ses amis** disgusted at the way his friends had deserted him *ou* run out on him.

lâche [lɑʃ] **1** *adj* **(a)** (*détendu*) *corde, ressort* slack; *nœud* loose; *vêtement* loose(-fitting); *tissu* loosely-woven; *discipline, morale* lax; *règlement, canevas* loose; *style, expression* loose, woolly. **dans ce roman, l'intrigue est ~** the plot is loose *ou* rather diffuse in this novel.

(b) (*couard*) *personne, attentat, fuite* cowardly; *attitude, procédé* cowardly, low, craven (*frm*). **se montrer ~** to show o.s. a coward; **c'est assez ~ de sa part d'avoir fait ça** it was pretty cowardly *ou* low* of him to do that.

(c) (*littér: faible*) weak, feeble.

2 *nmf* coward.

lâchement [lɑʃmɑ̃] *adv* (*V* **lâche**) loosely; in a cowardly way. **il a ~ refusé** like a coward, he refused.

lâcher [lɑʃe] (1) **1** *vt* **(a)** *ceinture* to loosen, let out, slacken. **~ la taille d'une jupe** to let a skirt out at the waist; (*Pêche*) **~ du fil** to let out some line.

(b) *main, proie* to let go of; *bombes* to drop; *pigeon, ballon* to release; *chien de garde* to unleash, set loose; *frein* to release; (*Naut*) *amarres* to cast off; (*Chasse*) *chien, faucon* to slip. **lâche-moi!** let *ou* leave go (of me)!; **attention! tu vas ~ le verre** careful, you're going to drop the glass; **~ un chien sur qn** to set a dog on sb; **s'il veut acheter ce tableau, il va falloir qu'il les lâche* *ou* qu'il lâche ses sous*** if he wants this picture, he'll have to part with the cash*.

(c) *bêtise, juron* to come out with; *pet* to let out; (†) *coup de* *fusil* to fire. **voilà le grand mot lâché!** there's the fatal word!; ~ **un coup de poing/pied à qn**† to deal *ou* fetch sb a blow with one's fist/foot, let fly at sb with one's fist/foot.

(d) (*: *abandonner*) *époux* to walk out on, throw over*; *amant* to throw over*, jilt, drop*; *copain* to chuck up‡, throw over*, drop*; *études, métier* to give up, throw up*, chuck up‡ *ou* in‡; *avantage* to give up. (*Sport*) ~ **le peloton** to leave the rest of the field behind, build up a good lead (over the rest of the pack); **ne pas ~ qn** *[poursuivant, créancier]* to stick to sb; *[raseur, représentant]* not to leave sb alone; *[mal de tête]* not to let up on* *ou* leave sb; **il ne m'a pas lâché d'une semelle** he stuck close all the time, he stuck (to me) like a leech; **une bonne occasion, ça ne se lâche pas** *ou* **il ne faut pas la ~** you don't pass up an opportunity like that*.

(e) (*loc*) ~ **prise** (*lit*) to let go; (*fig*) to loosen one's grip; ~ **pied** to fall back, give way; ~ **la proie pour l'ombre** to give up what one has (already) for some uncertain *ou* fanciful alternative; ~ **du lest** (*Naut*) to throw out ballast; (* *fig*) to climb down; ~ **le morceau*** *ou* **le paquet*** to come clean*, sing‡; ~ **la bride** *ou* **les rênes à un cheval** to give a horse its head; (*fig*) ~ **la bride à qn** to give *ou* let sb have his head; **il les lâche avec des élastiques‡** he's as stingy as hell‡, he's a tight-fisted so-and-so*.

2 *vi [corde]* to break, give way; *[frein]* to fail. (*fig*) **ses nerfs ont lâché** he broke down, he couldn't take the strain.

3 *nm*: ~ **de ballons** release of balloons; ~ **de pigeons** release of pigeons.

lâcheté [lɑʃte] *nf* **(a)** (*U*) (*couardise*) cowardice, cowardliness; (*bassesse*) lowness. **par ~** through *ou* out of cowardice. **(b)** (*acte*) cowardly act, act of cowardice; low deed. **(c)** (*littér: faiblesse*) weakness, feebleness.

lâcheur, -euse* [lɑʃœʀ, øz] *nm,f* unreliable *ou* fickle so-and-so*. **alors, tu n'es pas venu, ~!** so you didn't come then — you're a dead loss!*, so you deserted us *ou* you let us down, you old so-and-so!*; **c'est une ~euse, ta sœur** your sister's a right one (*surtout Brit*) for letting people down*, your sister's a so-and-so the way she lets people down*.

lacis [lasi] *nm [ruelles]* maze; *[veines]* network; *[soie]* web.

laconique [lakɔnik] *adj personne, réponse, style* laconic, terse.

laconiquement [lakɔnikmɑ̃] *adv* laconically, tersely.

laconisme [lakɔnism(ə)] *nm* terseness.

lacrymal, e, *mpl* **-aux** [lakʀimal, o] *adj* lachrymal (*T*), tear (*épith*).

lacrymogène [lakʀimɔʒɛn] *adj V* **gaz, grenade.**

lacs [lɑ] *nm* (††, *littér*) snare.

lactaire [laktɛʀ] **1** *adj* (*Anat*) lacteal. **2** *nm* (*Bot*) (lacteous) mushroom.

lactalbumine [laktalbymin] *nf* lactalbumin.

lactase [laktɑz] *nf* lactase.

lactation [laktɑsjɔ̃] *nf* lactation.

lacté, e [lakte] *adj sécrétion* milky, lacteal (*T*); *couleur, suc* milky; *régime, farine* milk (*épith*); *V* **voie.**

lactique [laktik] *adj* lactic.

lactose [laktoz] *nm* lactose.

lacunaire [lakynɛʀ] *adj* (*Bio*) *tissu* lacunary, lacunal; *documentation* incomplete, deficient.

lacune [lakyn] *nf* **(a)** *[texte, mémoire]* gap, blank; *[manuscrit]* lacuna; *[connaissances]* gap, deficiency. **il y a de sérieuses ~s dans ce livre** this book has some serious deficiencies *ou* misses out *ou* overlooks some serious points *ou* things.

(b) (*Anat, Bot*) lacuna.

lacuneux, -euse [lakynø, øz] *adj* = **lacunaire.**

lacustre [lakystʀ(ə)] *adj* lake (*épith*), lakeside (*épith*).

lad [lad] *nm* (*Équitation*) stable-lad.

ladite [ladit] *adj V* **ledit.**

ladre [lɑdʀ(ə)] **1** *adj* (*littér: avare*) mean, miserly. **2** *nmf* (*littér*) miser.

ladrerie [lɑdʀəʀi] *nf* **(a)** (*littér: avarice*) meanness, miserliness. **(b)** (*Hist: hôpital*) leper-house.

lagon [lagɔ̃] *nm* lagoon.

lagunaire [lagynɛʀ] *adj* lagoon (*épith*), of a lagoon.

lagune [lagyn] *nf* lagoon.

lai[1] [lɛ] *nm* (*Poésie*) lay.

lai[2]**, e** [lɛ] *adj* (*Rel*) lay. **frère ~** lay brother.

laïc [laik] = **laïque.**

laîche [lɛʃ] *nf* sedge.

laïcisation [laisizɑsjɔ̃] *nf* secularization.

laïciser [laisize] *vt institutions* to secularize. **l'enseignement est aujourd'hui laïcisé** education is now under secular control.

laïcisme [laisism(ə)] *nm* secularism.

laïcité [laisite] *nf* (*caractère*) secularity; (*Pol: système*) secularism.

laid, e [lɛ, lɛd] *adj* **(a)** (*physiquement*) *personne, visage, animal* ugly(-looking); *ville, région* ugly, unattractive; *bâtiment* ugly, unsightly; *meubles, dessin* unattractive, ugly, awful*. ~ **comme un singe** *ou* **un pou** *ou* **à faire peur** ugly as sin; **il est très ~ de visage** he's got a terribly ugly face.

(b) (*frm: moralement*) *action* wretched, low, mean; *vice* ugly, loathsome. **c'est ~ de montrer du doigt** it's rude *ou* not nice to point; **c'est ~, ce que tu as fait** that wasn't a very nice thing to do, that was a nasty thing to do.

laidement [lɛdmɑ̃] *adv* (*sans beauté*) in an ugly way; (*littér: bassement*) wretchedly, meanly.

laideron [lɛdʀɔ̃] *nm* ugly girl *ou* woman. **c'est un vrai ~** she's a real ugly duckling.

laideur [lɛdœʀ] *nf* (*V* **laid**) **(a)** (*U*) ugliness; unattractiveness; unsightliness; wretchedness; lowness; meanness. **la guerre/l'égoïsme dans toute sa ~** the full horror of war/selfishness.

(b) les ~s de la vie the ugly side of life, the ugly things in life; **les ~s de la guerre** the ugliness of war.

laie[1] [lɛ] *adj f V* **lai**[2].

laie[2] [lɛ] *nf* (*Zool*) wild sow.

laie[3] [lɛ] *nf* (*sentier*) forest track *ou* path.

lainage [lɛnaʒ] *nm* **(a)** (*vêtement*) woollen (garment), woolly*. **la production des ~s** the manufacture of woollens *ou* of woollen goods.

(b) (*étoffe*) woollen material *ou* fabric. **un beau ~** fine quality woollen material.

laine [lɛn] **1** *nf* wool. **de ~** *vêtement, moquette* wool, woollen; **tapis de haute ~** deep *ou* thick pile wool carpet; *V* **bas**[2].

2: laine à matelas flock; **laine peignée** *[pantalon, veston]* worsted wool; *[pull]* combed wool; **laine à tricoter** knitting wool; **laine de verre** glass wool; **laine vierge** new wool.

laineux, -euse [lɛnø, øz] *adj tissu, plante* woolly.

lainier, -ière [lɛnje, jɛʀ] **1** *adj industrie* woollen (*épith*); *région* wool-producing. **2** *nm,f* (*marchand*) wool merchant; (*ouvrier*) wool worker.

laïque [laik] **1** *adj tribunal* lay, civil; *vie* secular; *habit* ordinary; *collège* non-religious. **l'enseignement** *ou* **l'école ~** state education (*in France*). **2** *nm* layman. **les ~s** laymen, the laity. **3** *nf* laywoman.

laisse [lɛs] *nf* **(a)** (*attache*) leash, lead. **tenir en ~** *chien* to keep on a leash *ou* lead; (*fig*) *personne* to keep on a lead *ou* in check. **(b)** (*Géog*) foreshore. ~ **de haute/basse mer** high-/low-water mark. **(c)** (*Poésie*) laisse.

laissé-pour-compte, *pl* **laissés-pour-compte** [lesepuʀkɔ̃t] **1** *adj* **(a)** (*Comm*) (*refusé*) rejected, returned; (*invendu*) unsold, left over.

(b) (*fig*) *personne* rejected; *chose* rejected, discarded.

2 *nm* (*Comm*) (*refusé*) reject; (*invendu*) unsold article. **vendre à bas prix les laissés-pour-compte** to sell off old *ou* leftover stock cheaply; (*fig*) **les laissés-pour-compte de la société** society's rejects; (*fig*) **les ouvriers ne veulent pas être des laissés-pour-compte maintenant que la mécanisation supprime de la main-d'œuvre** workers don't want to find themselves left on the scrap heap *ou* cast to one side now that mechanization is replacing manual labour; (*fig*) **ce sont les laissés-pour-compte du progrès** these people are the casualties of progress, progress has left these people out in the cold *ou* on the scrap heap.

laisser [lese] (1) **1** *vt* **(a)** (*abandonner*) *place, fortune, femme, objet* to leave. ~ **sa clef au voisin** to leave one's key with the neighbour, leave the neighbour one's key; **laisse-lui du gâteau** leave *ou* save him some cake, leave *ou* save some cake for him; **il m'a laissé ce vase pour 10 F** he let me have this vase for 10 francs; **laisse-moi le soin de le lui dire** leave it to me to tell him; **laissez, je vais le faire/c'est moi qui paie** leave that, I'll do it/I'm paying; **laisse-moi le temps d'y réfléchir** give me time to think about it; **il a laissé un bras/la vue dans l'accident** he lost an arm/his sight in the accident; **l'expédition était dangereuse: il y a laissé sa vie** it was a dangerous expedition: it cost him his life; **elle l'a laissé de meilleure humeur** she left him in a better mood; **au revoir, je vous laisse** bye-bye, I must leave you; **je l'ai laissé à son travail** I left him to get on with his work.

(b) (*faire demeurer*) *trace, regrets, goût* to leave. ~ **qn indifférent/dans le doute** to leave sb unmoved/in doubt; ~ **qn debout** to keep sb standing (up); **on lui a laissé ses illusions, on l'a laissé à ses illusions** we didn't disillusion him; **on l'a laissé dans l'erreur** we didn't tell him that he was mistaken; **il vaut mieux le ~ dans l'ignorance de nos projets** it is best to leave him in the dark *ou* not to tell him about our plans; ~ **un enfant à ses parents** (*gén*) to leave a child with his parents; (*Jur*) to leave a child in the custody of his parents; **vous laissez le village sur votre droite** you go past the village on your right; ~ **la vie à qn** to spare sb's life; ~ **qn en liberté** to allow sb to stay free.

(c) (*loc*) ~ **la porte ouverte** (*lit, fig*) to leave the door open; **il ne laisse jamais rien au hasard** he never leaves anything to chance; **c'était à prendre ou à ~** it was a case of take it or leave it; **avec lui il faut en prendre et en ~** you can only believe half of what he says, you must take what he tells you with a pinch of salt; **on l'a laissé pour mort** he was left for dead; **il laisse tout le monde derrière lui pour le** *ou* **par son talent/courage** he puts everyone else in the shade with his talent/courage; **il laisse tout le monde derrière en math** he is head and shoulders above *ou* streets* ahead of the others in maths; (*littér*) **il n'a pas laissé de me le dire** he didn't fail to tell me, he could not refrain from telling me; (*littér*) **cela n'a pas laissé de me surprendre** I couldn't fail to be surprised by *ou* at that; (*littér*) **ça ne laisse pas d'être vrai** it is true nonetheless; *V* **champ, désirer, plan**[1] *etc.*

2 *vb aux*: ~ **(qn) faire qch** to let sb do sth; **laisse-le entrer/partir** let him in/go; **laisse-le monter/descendre** let him come *ou* go up/down; **laissez-moi rire** don't make me laugh; ~ **voir ses sentiments** to let one's feelings show; **il n'en a rien laissé voir** he showed no sign of it; **laisse-le faire** (*sans l'aider*) let him alone, let him do it himself; (*à sa manière*) let him do it his own way; (*ce qui lui plaît*) let him do (it) as he likes *ou* wants; **il faut ~ faire le temps** we must let things take their course; **laisse faire!** oh, never mind!, don't bother; **j'ai été attaqué dans la rue et les gens ont laissé faire** I was attacked in the street and people did nothing; *V* **courir, penser, tomber.**

3 se laisser *vpr*: **se ~ persuader/exploiter/duper** to let o.s. be persuaded/exploited/fooled; **il s'est laissé attendrir par leur pauvreté** he was moved by their poverty; **il ne faut pas se ~ décourager/abattre** you mustn't let yourself become discouraged/downhearted; **je me suis laissé surprendre par la pluie** I got caught by the rain; **ce petit vin se laisse boire*** this wine goes down well *ou* nicely; **se ~ aller** to let o.s. go; **se ~ aller à mentir** to stoop to telling lies; **je me suis laissé faire*** I let myself be persuaded, I let myself be talked into it*; **je n'ai pas l'intention de me ~ faire** I'm not going to let myself be pushed around; **laisse-toi faire!** (*à qn qu'on soigne, habille etc*) oh come on, it won't hurt (you)! *ou* let me do it!; (*en offrant une liqueur etc*) oh come on, it won't do you any harm! *ou* be a devil!*; **laisse-toi faire, je vais te peigner** just let me comb your hair, keep still while I comb your hair; *V* **conter, dire, vivre** *etc*.

4: laisser-aller *nm inv* (*gén*) casualness, carelessness; *[travail, langage, vêtements]* slovenliness, carelessness; **laisser-faire** *nm* (*Écon*) laissez-faire (policy *ou* attitude); **laissez-passer** *nm inv* pass; (*Comm*) transire.

lait [lɛ] **1** *nm* milk. ~ **de vache/de chèvre/d'ânesse** cow's/goat's/ass's milk; ~ **concentré/condensé non sucré/entier/écrémé** evaporated/unsweetened condensed/unskimmed/skimmed milk; **mettre qn au** ~ to put sb on a milk diet; (*fig*) **boire du (petit)** ~ to lap it up (*fig*); **cela se boit comme du petit** ~ you don't notice you're drinking it; **frère/sœur de** ~ foster brother/sister; **chocolat au** ~ milk chocolate; *V* **café, cochon**[1], **dent**.

2: lait d'amande almond oil; **lait de beauté** beauty lotion; **lait caillé** curds; **lait de chaux** lime water; **lait de coco** coconut milk; **lait démaquillant** cleansing milk; **lait maternel** mother's milk, breast milk; (*Culin*) **lait de poule** eggflip.

laitage [lɛtaʒ] *nm* (*lait*) milk; (*produit laitier*) milk food *ou* product.

laitance [lɛtɑ̃s] *nf* soft roe.

laiterie [lɛtʀi] *nf* (*usine, magasin*) dairy; (*industrie*) dairy industry.

laiteux, -euse [lɛtø, øz] *adj* milky; *chair* creamy.

laitier, -ière [letje, lɛtjɛʀ] **1** *adj industrie, produit* dairy (*épith*); *production, vache* milk (*épith*).

2 *nm* **(a)** (*livreur*) milkman; (*vendeur*) dairyman.

(b) (*Ind*) slag.

3 laitière *nf* (*vendeuse*) dairywoman. (*vache*) **une (bonne)** ~**ière** a (good) milker.

laiton [lɛtɔ̃] *nm* (*alliage*) brass; (*fil*) brass wire.

laitue [lety] *nf* lettuce. ~ **romaine** cos lettuce.

laïus* [lajys] *nm inv* (*discours*) long-winded speech; (*verbiage*) verbiage (*U*), padding (*U*). **faire un** ~ to hold forth at great length, give a long-winded speech.

lama [lama] *nm* (*Zool*) llama; (*Rel*) lama.

lamaserie [lamazʀi] *nf* lamasery.

lambda [lɑ̃bda] *nm* lambda.

lambeau, *pl* ~**x** [lɑ̃bo] *nm* scrap. **en** ~**x** *vêtements* in tatters *ou* rags, tattered; *affiche* in tatters, tattered; **mettre en** ~**x** to tear to shreds *ou* bits; **tomber en** ~**x** to fall to pieces *ou* bits; (*fig*) ~**x de conversation/du passé** scraps of conversation/of the past.

lambin, e* [lɑ̃bɛ̃, in] **1** *adj* slow. **que tu es** ~ what a dawdler *ou* slowcoach* (*Brit*) *ou* slowpoke* (*US*) you are. **2** *nm,f* dawdler*, slowcoach* (*Brit*), slowpoke* (*US*).

lambiner* [lɑ̃bine] (1) *vi* to dawdle, dillydally*.

lambourde [lɑ̃buʀd(ə)] *nf* (*pour parquet*) backing strip (*on joists*); (*pour solive*) wall-plate.

lambris [lɑ̃bʀi] *nm* (*gén*) panelling (*U*); (*bois*) panelling (*U*), wainscoting (*U*).

lambrisser [lɑ̃bʀise] (1) *vt* (*V* **lambris**) to panel; to wainscot.

lame [lam] **1** *nf* **(a)** *[métal, verre]* strip; *[bois]* strip, lath; (*Aut*) *[ressort]* leaf; (*pour microscope*) slide.

(b) *[poignard, tondeuse]* blade. (*fig*) **visage en** ~ **de couteau** hatchet face.

(c) (*fig*) (*épée*) sword; (*escrimeur*) swordsman.

(d) (*vague*) wave.

2: lame de fond ground swell (*U*); **lame de parquet** floorboard, strip of parquet flooring; **lame de rasoir** razor blade.

lamé, e [lame] **1** *adj* lamé (*épith*). **robe** ~**e (d')or** gold lamé dress. **2** *nm* lamé.

lamelle [lamɛl] *nf* (*gén: de métal, plastique*) (small) plate; *[persiennes]* slat; *[champignon]* gill; (*pour microscope*) coverglass. ~ **de mica** mica flake; **couper en** ~**s** to cut into thin strips.

lamellibranches [lamɛlibʀɑ̃ʃ] *nmpl* lamellibranchia.

lamentable [lamɑ̃tabl(ə)] *adj résultat, état* lamentable, appalling, awful; *concurrent* appalling, awful; *sort, spectacle* miserable, pitiful; *cri* pitiful, woeful.

lamentablement [lamɑ̃tabləmɑ̃] *adv échouer* miserably, lamentably.

lamentation [lamɑ̃tɑsjɔ̃] *nf* (*cri de désolation*) lamentation, wailing (*U*); (*péj: jérémiade*) moaning (*U*); *V* **mur**.

lamenter (se) [lamɑ̃te] (1) *vpr* to moan, lament. **se** ~ **sur qch** to moan over sth, bemoan sth; **se** ~ **sur son sort** to bemoan *ou* lament one's fate; **arrête de te** ~ **sur ton propre sort** stop feeling sorry for yourself; **il se lamente d'avoir échoué** he is moaning over his failure.

lamento [lamɛnto] *nm* lament.

laminage [laminaʒ] *nm* lamination.

laminer [lamine] (1) *vt métal* to laminate. (*fig*) **ses marges bénéficiaires ont été laminées par les hausses** his profit margins have been eaten away *ou* eroded by price rises.

lamineur [laminœʀ] **1** *adj m*: **cylindre** ~ roller. **2** *nm* rolling mill operator.

laminoir [laminwaʀ] *nm* rolling mill. (*fig*) **passer/passer qn au** ~ to go/put sb through the mill *ou* through it*.

lampadaire [lɑ̃padɛʀ] *nm [intérieur]* standard lamp; *[rue]* street lamp. **(pied du)** ~ *[intérieur]* lamp standard; *[rue]* lamppost.

lampant [lɑ̃pɑ̃] *adj m V* **pétrole**.

lamparo [lɑ̃paʀo] *nm* lamp. **pêche au** ~ fishing by lamplight (*in Mediterranean*).

lampe [lɑ̃p(ə)] **1** *nf* lamp, light; (*ampoule*) bulb; (*Rad*) valve. **éclairé par une** ~ lit by lamplight *ou* by the light of a lamp.

2: lampe à acétylène acetylene lamp; **lampe à alcool** spirit lamp; **lampe à arc** arc light *ou* lamp; **lampe de bureau** desk lamp *ou* light; **lampe à carbure** carbide lamp; **lampe de chevet** bedside lamp *ou* light; **lampe-éclair** *nf, pl* **lampes-éclair, lampe-flash** *nf, pl* **lampes-flash** flashlight; **lampe à huile** oil lamp; **lampe à incandescence** incandescent lamp; **lampe de mineur** (miner's) safety lamp; **lampe à pétrole** paraffin (*Brit*) *ou* kerosene (*US*) *ou* oil lamp; **lampe de poche** torch (*Brit*), flashlight (*US*); **lampe à souder** (*lit*) blowlamp (*Brit*), blowtorch; (*arg Mil*) machine gun; **lampe-témoin** *nf, pl* **lampes-témoin** warning light; **lampe-tempête** *nf, pl* **lampes-tempête** storm lantern.

lampée* [lɑ̃pe] *nf* gulp, swig*. **boire qch à grandes** ~**s** to gulp *ou* swig* sth down.

lamper*† [lɑ̃pe] (1) *vt* to gulp down, swig (down)*.

lampion [lɑ̃pjɔ̃] *nm* Chinese lantern; *V* **air**[3].

lampiste [lɑ̃pist(ə)] *nm* (*lit*) light (maintenance) man; (**hum: subalterne*) underling, dogsbody* (*Brit*), toady* (*US*).

lampisterie [lɑ̃pistəʀi] *nf* lamp store.

lamproie [lɑ̃pʀwa] *nf* lamprey.

lance [lɑ̃s] *nf* **(a)** (*arme*) spear; *[tournoi]* lance. **donner un coup de** ~ **à qn, frapper qn d'un coup de** ~ to hit sb with one's lance; *V* **fer, rompre. (b)** (*tuyau*) hose; (*embout*) nozzle. ~ **d'arrosage** garden hose; ~ **d'incendie** fire hose.

lance- [lɑ̃s] *préf V* **lancer**.

lancée [lɑ̃se] *nf*: **être sur sa** ~ to be *ou* have got under way; **continuer sur sa** ~ to keep going, forge ahead; **il a encore travaillé 3 heures sur sa** ~ once he was under way *ou* once he'd got going* he worked for another 3 hours; **je peux encore courir 2 km sur ma** ~ now I'm in my stride I can run another 2 km.

lancement [lɑ̃smɑ̃] *nm* **(a)** (*V* **lancer**) launching; sending up; starting up; issuing; floating. **(b)** (*Sport*) throwing. ~ **du disque/du javelot/du marteau** throwing the discus/javelin/hammer; ~ **du poids** putting the shot.

lancer [lɑ̃se] (3) **1** *vt* **(a)** (*jeter*) (*gén*) to throw (*à* to); *bombes* to drop (*sur* on); (*Sport*) *disque, marteau, javelot* to throw; *poids* to put. ~ **une balle/son chapeau en l'air** to throw *ou* toss a ball/one's hat into the air *ou* up in the air; **lance-moi mes clefs** throw me my keys; (*Pêche*) ~ **sa ligne** to cast one's line; (*agressivement*) ~ **une pierre à qn** to hurl *ou* fling a stone at sb; **il lança sa voiture dans la foule** he launched *ou* hurled his car into the crowd; ~ **son chien contre qn** to set one's dog on sb; (*Mil*) ~ **ses hommes contre l'ennemi/à l'assaut** to launch one's men against the enemy/into the assault; ~ **les jambes en avant** to fling one's legs forward; ~ **son poing dans la figure de qn** to thump sb in the face*; ~ **un coup de poing** to lash out with one's fist, throw a punch; ~ **un coup de pied** to kick out, lash out with one's foot; ~ **une ruade** to buck; (*Sport*) **il lance à 15 mètres** he can throw 15 metres; (*fig*) ~ **un pont sur une rivière** to throw a bridge across a river; **la tour lance ses flèches de béton vers le ciel** the concrete spires of the tower thrust up into the sky.

(b) (*projeter*) *fumée* to send up *ou* out; *flammes, lave* to throw out. *[yeux, bijoux]* ~ **des éclairs** to flash (fire).

(c) (*émettre*) *accusations, menaces, injures* to hurl, fling; *avertissement, proclamation, mandat d'arrêt* to issue; *S.O.S.* to send out; *fausse nouvelle* to put out; *hurlement* to give out. ~ **un cri** to cry out; **elle lui lança un coup d'œil furieux** she flashed *ou* darted a furious glance at him; **'je refuse' lança-t-il fièrement** 'I refuse' he retorted proudly; **'salut' me lança-t-il du fond de la salle** 'hello' he called out to me from the far end of the room.

(d) (*faire démarrer*) *fusée* to launch, send up; *obus* to launch; *navire, attaque, campagne électorale* to launch; *souscription, idée* to launch; *affaire, entreprise* to launch, start up; *emprunt* to issue, float. ~ **une idée en l'air** to toss out an idea; **il a lancé son parti dans une aventure dangereuse** he has launched his party into *ou* set his party off on a dangerous venture; **ne le lancez pas sur son sujet favori** don't set him off on *ou* don't let him get launched on his pet subject; **une fois lancé, on ne peut plus l'arrêter!** once he gets the bit between his teeth *ou* once he gets warmed up *ou* launched there's no stopping him!

(e) (*mettre en renom*) *vedette, mode* to launch; *produit* to launch, bring out. ~ **qn dans la politique/les affaires/le monde** to launch sb into politics/in business/in society; **ce chanteur est lancé maintenant** this singer has made a name for himself *ou* has made his mark now.

(f) (*donner de l'élan*) *moteur* to open up; *voiture* to get up to full speed; *balançoire* to set going. ~ **un cheval** to give a horse its head; **lance le balancier de l'horloge** set the pendulum in the clock going; **la voiture lancée à fond, dévala la pente** the car roared away at top speed and hurtled down the slope; **la voiture une fois lancée** once the car gets up speed *ou* builds up speed.

2 se lancer *vpr* **(a)** (*prendre de l'élan*) to build up *ou* get up momentum *ou* speed. **il recula pour se** ~ he moved back to get up speed *ou* momentum; **pour faire de la balançoire il faut bien se** ~ to get a swing going you have to give yourself a good push forward.

(b) (*sauter*) to leap, jump; (*se précipiter*) to dash, rush. **se** ~ **dans le vide** to leap *ou* jump into space; **se** ~ **contre un obstacle** to dash *ou* rush at an obstacle; **se** ~ **en avant** to dash *ou* rush *ou* run forward; **se** ~ **à l'assaut d'une forteresse** to launch an assault on a fortress; **se** ~ **à l'assaut** to leap to the attack; **se** ~ **dans la bagarre** to pitch into the fight; **n'hésite pas, lance-toi** don't hesitate, off you go *ou* let yourself go.

(c) (*s'engager*) **se** ~ **dans** *discussion* to launch (forth) into, embark on; *aventure* to embark on, set off on; *dépenses* to embark on, take on; *passe-temps* to take up; **se** ~ **dans la politique/les affaires** (*essayer*) to launch out into politics/business; (*comme métier*) to take up politics/business; **se** ~ **dans la lecture d'un roman** to set about reading a novel; **il construit un bateau, il se lance*** he's building a boat — he's aiming high! *ou* he's thinking big!*

(d) (*: *se faire une réputation*) **il cherche à se ~** he's trying to make a name for himself.

3 *nm* **(a)** (*Sport*) (*gén*) throw. **il a droit à 3 ~s** he is allowed 3 attempts *ou* throws; **le ~ du poids etc** *V* **lancement.**

(b) (*Pêche*) (*attirail*) rod and reel. **(pêche au) ~** rod and reel fishing.

4: lance-flammes *nm inv* flamethrower; **lance-fusées** *nm inv* rocket launcher; **lance-grenades** *nm inv* grenade launcher; **lance-missiles** *nm inv* missile launcher; **lance-pierre(s)** *nm inv* catapult; **lance-roquettes** *nm inv* rocket launcher; **lance-satellites** *nm inv* satellite launcher; **lance-torpilles** *nm inv* torpedo tube.

lancette [lɑ̃sɛt] *nf* (*Archit, Méd*) lancet.

lanceur, -euse [lɑ̃sœʀ, øz] **1** *nm,f* (*Sport*) thrower; *[entreprise, actrice]* promoter. **2** *nm* (*Espace*) launcher.

lancier [lɑ̃sje] *nm* (*Mil*) lancer. (*danse*) **les ~s** the lancers.

lancinant, e [lɑ̃sinɑ̃, ɑ̃t] *adj* **(a)** *douleur* shooting (*épith*), throbbing (*épith*).

(b) (*obsédant*) *souvenir* haunting; *musique* insistent, monotonous. **ce que tu peux être ~ à toujours réclamer*** you are a real pain* *ou* you get on my nerves the way you're always asking for things.

lanciner [lɑ̃sine] (1) **1** *vi* to throb.

2 *vt [pensée]* to obsess, trouble; (*) *[enfant]* to torment. **il nous a lancinés pendant 3 jours pour aller au cirque** he tormented us *ou* he went on at us* for 3 days about going to the circus.

lançon [lɑ̃sɔ̃] *nm* sand-eel.

landais, e [lɑ̃dɛ, ɛz] *adj* from the Landes (region) (*south-west France*).

landau [lɑ̃do] *nm* (*voiture d'enfant*) pram, baby carriage (*US*); (*carrosse*) landau.

lande [lɑ̃d] *nf* moor. **les L~s** (*Géog*) the Landes (region) (*south-west France*); (*Admin*) the Landes department.

landgrave [lɑ̃dgʀav] *nm* (*Hist*) landgrave.

langage [lɑ̃gaʒ] **1** *nm* (*Ling, style*) language. **le ~ de l'amour/des fleurs** the language of love/of flowers; **en ~ administratif/technique** in administrative/technical jargon *ou* language; **quel ~!** what language!; **son ~ est incompréhensible** what he says *ou* the language he uses is incomprehensible; **je n'aime pas qu'on me tienne ce ~** I don't like being spoken to like that; **il m'a tenu un drôle de ~** he said some odd things to me; **quel ~ me tenez-vous là?** what do you mean by saying that?; **changer de ~** to change one's tune.

2: le langage des animaux animal language; **langage argotique** slang speech; **langage chiffré** cipher, code (language); **le langage enfantin** childish *ou* children's language; (*Philos*) **langage intérieur** inner language; **langage populaire** popular speech.

langagier, -ière [lɑ̃gaʒje, jɛʀ] *adj* linguistic, of language (*épith*).

lange [lɑ̃ʒ] *nm* small flannel blanket (for baby). **~s††** swaddling clothes††; **il faut lui mettre un ~** we must put an extra cover round him *ou* wrap him up (in an extra cover); (*fig*) **dans les ~s** in (its) infancy.

langer [lɑ̃ʒe] (3) *vt bébé* to change (the nappy of); (††) to wrap an extra blanket round. **table/matelas à ~** changing table/mat.

langoureusement [lɑ̃guʀøzmɑ̃] *adv* languorously, languishingly.

langoureux, -euse [lɑ̃guʀø, øz] *adj* languorous.

langouste [lɑ̃gust(ə)] *nf* crawfish, crayfish.

langoustier [lɑ̃gustje] *nm* (*filet*) crawfish net; (*bateau*) fishing boat (*for crawfish*).

langoustine [lɑ̃gustin] *nf* Dublin bay prawn. (*Culin*) **~s (frites)** (fried) scampi.

langue [lɑ̃g] **1** *nf* **(a)** (*Anat*) tongue. **~ de bœuf/veau** ox/veal tongue; **avoir la ~ blanche/pâteuse** to have a coated/furred tongue; **tirer la ~** (*au médecin*) to stick out *ou* put out one's tongue (*à qn* for sb); (*par impolitesse*) to stick out *ou* put out one's tongue (*à qn* at sb); (*: *être dans le besoin*) to have a rough time of it*; (*: *être frustré*) to be green with envy; (*: *avoir soif*) **il tirait la ~** his tongue was hanging out*; *V* **coup.**

(b) (*organe de la parole*) tongue. **avoir la ~ bien pendue** to have a ready tongue in one's head; **avoir la ~ bien affilée** to have a quick *ou* sharp tongue in one's head; (*hum*) **avoir la ~ fourchue** to speak with a forked tongue; **il a la ~ trop longue** he talks too much, he doesn't know how to keep his mouth shut; **il n'a pas la ~ dans sa poche** he's never at a loss for words; **perdre/retrouver sa ~** to lose/find one's tongue; **délier** *ou* (*rare*) **dénouer la ~ à qn** to loosen sb's tongue; **donner sa ~ au chat** to give in *ou* up; **j'ai le mot sur (le bout de) la ~** the word is on the tip of my tongue; **prendre ~ avec qn†** to make contact with sb; (*hum*) **les ~s vont aller bon train** tongues will start *ou* be set wagging.

(c) (*personne*) **mauvaise** *ou* **méchante ~** spiteful *ou* malicious gossip; (*iro*) **les bonnes ~s diront que ...** worthy *ou* upright folk will remark earnestly that ... .

(d) (*Ling*) language, tongue (*frm*). **la ~ française/anglaise** the French/English language; **les gens de ~ anglaise/française** English-speaking/French-speaking people; **~ maternelle** mother tongue; **une ~ vivante/morte/étrangère** a living/dead/foreign language; **la ~ écrite/parlée** the written/spoken language; (*Ling: en traduction*) **~ source** *ou* **de départ/cible** *ou* **d'arrivée** source/target language; **la ~ de Blake** the language of Blake; **il parle une ~ très pure** his use of the language is very pure, his spoken language is very pure; (*lit, fig*) **nous ne parlons pas la même ~** we don't speak the same language.

2: la langue du barreau legal parlance, the language of the courts; **langue-de-chat** *nf, pl* **langues-de-chat** finger biscuit, langue de chat; **la langue diplomatique** the language of diplomacy; **langue de feu** tongue of fire; **la langue journalistique** journalistic language, journalese (*péj*); **langue d'oc** langue d'oc, southern French; **langue d'oïl** langue d'oïl, northern French; **langue populaire** (*idiome*) popular language; (*usage*) popular speech; **langue de terre** strip *ou* spit of land; **langue de travail** working language; **langue verte** underworld slang; **langue de vipère** spiteful gossip.

languedocien, -ienne [lɑ̃gdɔsjɛ̃, jɛn] **1** *adj* of *ou* from Languedoc. **2** *nm,f*: **L~(ne)** inhabitant *ou* native of Languedoc.

languette [lɑ̃gɛt] *nf [bois, cuir]* tongue.

langueur [lɑ̃gœʀ] *nf* languidness, languor; (*fig*) *[style]* languidness. **regard plein de ~** languid *ou* languishing look.

languir [lɑ̃giʀ] (2) *vi* **(a)** (*dépérir*) to languish. **~ dans l'oisiveté/d'ennui** to languish in idleness/in boredom; **(se) ~ d'amour pour qn** to be languishing with love for sb.

(b) (*fig*) *[conversation, affaires, intrigue]* to flag.

(c) (*littér: désirer*) **~ après qn/qch** to languish for *ou* pine for *ou* long for sb/sth.

(d) (*: *attendre*) to wait, hang around*. **je ne languirai pas longtemps ici** I'm not going to hang around here for long*; **faire ~ qn** to keep sb waiting; **ne nous fais pas ~, raconte!** don't keep us in suspense, tell us about it!

languissamment [lɑ̃gisamɑ̃] *adv* (*littér*) languidly.

languissant, e [lɑ̃gisɑ̃, ɑ̃t] *adj personne* languid (*littér*), listless; *regard* languishing (*épith*); *conversation, industrie* flagging (*épith*); *récit, action* dull; *affaires* slack, flat.

lanière [lanjɛʀ] *nf [cuir]* thong, strap; *[étoffe]* strip; *[fouet]* lash; *[appareil photo]* strap.

lanoline [lanɔlin] *nf* lanolin.

lansquenet [lɑ̃skənɛ] *nm* (*Cartes, Hist*) lansquenet.

lanterne [lɑ̃tɛʀn(ə)] **1** *nf* lantern; (*électrique*) lamp, light; (*Hist: réverbère*) street lamp; (*Archit*) lantern. (*Aut*) **se mettre en ~s, allumer ses ~s** to switch on one's (side)lights; **les aristocrates à la ~!** string up the aristocracy!; *V* **vessie.**

2: lanterne de bicyclette bicycle lamp; **lanterne magique** magic lantern; **lanterne de projection** slide projector; **lanterne rouge** *[convoi]* rear *ou* tail light; *[maison close]* red light; (*fig: dernier*) tail-ender; **lanterne sourde** dark lantern; **lanterne vénitienne** Chinese lantern.

lanterneau, *pl* **~x** [lɑ̃tɛʀno] *nm [coupole]* lantern; *[escalier, atelier]* skylight.

lanterner [lɑ̃tɛʀne] (1) *vi* (*traîner*) to dawdle. **sans ~!** be quick about it!; **(faire) ~ qn** to let sb cool his heels, keep sb hanging about.

Laos [laɔs] *nm* Laos.

laotien, -ienne [laɔsjɛ̃, jɛn] **1** *adj* Laotian. **2** *nm,f*: **L~(ne)** Laotian.

lapalissade [lapalisad] *nf* statement of the obvious.

lapement [lapmɑ̃] *nm* lapping (*U*); (*gorgée*) lap.

laper [lape] (1) **1** *vt* to lap up. **2** *vi* to lap.

lapereau, *pl* **~x** [lapʀo] *nm* young rabbit.

lapidaire [lapidɛʀ] **1** *adj* (*lit*) lapidary; (*fig: concis*) *style, formule* succinct, terse. **2** *nm* (*artisan*) lapidary.

lapidation [lapidɑsjɔ̃] *nf* stoning.

lapider [lapide] (1) *vt* (*Hist: tuer*) to stone; (*attaquer*) to stone, throw *ou* hurl stones at.

lapin [lapɛ̃] *nm* (buck) rabbit. **~ domestique/de garenne** domestic/wild rabbit; **c'est un fameux ~*** he's quite a lad!*; (*terme d'affection*) **mon petit ~** my lamb, my sweetheart; *V* **chaud, courir, poser.**

lapine [lapin] *nf* (doe) rabbit.

lapiner [lapine] (1) *vi* to litter, give birth.

lapinière [lapinjɛʀ] *nf* rabbit hutch.

lapis(-lazuli) [lapis(lazyli)] *nm inv* lapis lazuli.

lapon, e [lapɔ̃, ɔn] **1** *adj* Lapp, Lappish. **2** *nm* (*Ling*) Lapp, Lappish. **3** *nm,f*: **L~(e)** Lapp, Laplander.

Laponie [lapɔni] *nf* Lapland.

laps [laps] *nm*: **~ de temps** lapse of time.

lapsus [lapsys] *nm* (*parlé*) slip (of the tongue); (*écrit*) slip (of the pen); (*révélateur*) Freudian slip. **faire un ~** to make a slip (of the tongue *ou* of the pen).

laquage [lakaʒ] *nm* lacquering.

laquais [lakɛ] *nm* lackey, footman; (*fig, péj*) lackey (*péj*), flunkey (*péj*).

laque [lak] **1** *nf* (*produit brut*) lac, shellac; (*vernis, peinture*) lacquer; (*pour les cheveux*) (hair) lacquer, hair spray. **2** *nm ou f* (*de Chine*) lacquer. **3** *nm* (*objet d'art*) piece of lacquer ware.

laqué, e [lake] (*ptp de* **laquer**) *adj* lacquered. **meuble (en) ~ blanc** piece of furniture with a white lacquer finish.

laquelle [lakɛl] *V* **lequel.**

laquer [lake] (1) *vt* to lacquer.

larbin [laʀbɛ̃] *nm* (*péj*) servant, flunkey (*péj*).

larcin [laʀsɛ̃] *nm* (*littér*) (*vol*) theft; (*butin*) spoils (*pl*). **dissimuler son ~** to hide one's spoils *ou* what one has stolen.

lard [laʀ] *nm* (*gras*) fat (of pig); (*viande*) bacon. **~ fumé** ≈ smoked bacon; **~ (maigre)** ≈ streaky bacon (*usually diced or in strips*); (*fig*) **se faire du ~‡** to lie back *ou* sit around and grow fat; (*fig*) **un gros ~‡** a fat lump‡; **on ne sait jamais avec lui si c'est du ~ ou du cochon*** you never know where you are with him* *ou* whether or not he's being serious; *V* **rentrer, tête.**

larder [laʀde] (1) *vt* (*Culin*) *viande* to lard. (*fig*) **~ qn de coups de couteau** to hack at sb with a knife; (*fig*) **texte lardé de citations** text larded *ou* loaded with quotations.

lardoire [laʀdwaʀ] *nm* (*Culin*) larding-needle, larding-pin; (*: *épée*) sword, steel.

lardon [laʀdɔ̃] *nm* (*Culin*) (*pour larder*) lardon, lardoon; (*: *enfant*) kid*.

lares [laʀ] *nmpl, adj pl*: **(dieux) ~** lares.

largable [laʀgabl(ə)] *adj* releasable.

large [laʀʒ(ə)] **1** *adj* **(a)** (*gén, dans la mensuration*) wide; (*impression visuelle d'étendue*) broad; *pantalon, meuble* wide;

dos, lame broad, wide; *visage, main* broad. **à cet endroit, le fleuve est le plus ~** here the river is at its widest; **le ~ ruban d'argent du Rhône** the broad silver ribbon of the Rhône; **trop ~ de 3 mètres** 3 metres too wide; **chapeau à ~s bords** broad-brimmed *ou* wide-brimmed hat; **décrire un ~ cercle** to describe a big *ou* wide circle; **ouvrir une ~ bouche** to open one's mouth wide; **d'un geste ~** with a broad *ou* sweeping gesture; **avec un ~ sourire** with a broad smile, smiling broadly; **ce veston est trop ~** this jacket is too big *ou* wide; **cette robe est trop juste, avez-vous quelque chose d'un peu plus ~?** this dress is too tight, do you have anything slightly looser? *ou* fuller?; **être ~ d'épaules** *[personne]* to be broad-shouldered; *[vêtements]* to be wide *ou* broad at the shoulders; **être ~ de dos/de hanches** *[personne]* to have a broad back/wide hips; *[vêtement]* to be wide at the back/the hips.

(b) (*important*) *concession, amnistie* broad, wide; *pouvoirs, diffusion* wide, extensive. **retransmettre de ~s extraits d'un match** to show extensive (recorded) extracts of a match; **faire une ~ part à qch** to give great weight to sth; **dans une ~ mesure** to a great *ou* large extent; **il a une ~ part de responsabilité dans l'affaire** he must take a large share of the responsibility *ou* blame in this matter.

(c) (*généreux*) *personne* generous. **1 kg de viande pour 4, c'est ~** 1 kg of meat for 4 is ample *ou* plenty; **une vie ~** a life of ease.

(d) (*non borné*) *opinion, esprit* broad (*épith*); *conscience* accommodating. **il est ~ d'idées** he is broad-minded; **dans son acception** *ou* **sens ~** in the broad sense of the term.

2 *adv*: **voir ~** to think big; **prends un peu plus d'argent, il vaut mieux prévoir ~** take a bit more money, it's better to be on the generous side *ou* to allow a bit extra *ou* too much (than too little); **calculer/mesurer ~** to be generous *ou* allow a bit extra in one's calculations/measurements; **cette marque taille** *ou* **habille ~** the sizes in this brand tend to be on the large side.

3 *nm* **(a)** (*largeur*) width. **une avenue de 8 mètres de ~** an avenue 8 metres wide *ou* 8 metres in width; **être au ~** (*avoir de la place*) to have plenty of room *ou* space; (*avoir de l'argent*) to have plenty of money; **acheter une moquette en 2 mètres de ~** to buy a carpet 2 metres wide; **cela se fait en 2 mètres et 4 mètres de ~** that comes in 2-metre and 4-metre widths; *V* **long, mener.**

(b) (*Naut*) **le ~** the open sea; **se diriger vers le/gagner le ~** to head for/reach the open sea; **au ~ de Calais** off Calais; **l'appel du ~** the call of the sea; (*fig*) **prendre le ~*** to clear off*, hop it*.

largement [laʀʒəmɑ̃] *adv* **(a)** (*lit*) *écarter* widely. **~ espacés** *arbres, maisons* widely spaced, wide apart; **fenêtre ~ ouverte** wide open window; **robe ~ décolletée** dress with a very open *ou* very scooped neckline.

(b) (*sur une grande échelle*) *répandre, diffuser* widely. **amnistie ~ accordée** wide *ou* widely-extended amnesty; **idée ~ répandue** widespread *ou* widely held view; **bénéficier de pouvoirs ~ étendus** to hold greatly increased powers.

(c) (*de loin*) considerably, greatly. **succès qui dépasse ~ nos prévisions** success which greatly exceeds our expectations *ou* is far beyond our expectations; **ce problème dépasse ~ ses compétences** this problem is altogether beyond *ou* is way beyond* his capabilities; **vous débordez ~ le sujet** you are greatly overstepping the subject, you are going well beyond the limits of the subject; **elle vaut ~ son frère** she's every bit as *ou* at least as good as her brother.

(d) (*amplement*) **vous avez ~ le temps** you have ample time *ou* plenty of time; **il y en a ~ (assez)** there's more than enough; **c'est ~ suffisant** that's plenty, that's more than enough; **cela me suffit ~** that's plenty *ou* ample *ou* more than enough for me; **il est ~ temps de commencer** its high time we started; **j'ai été ~ récompensé de ma patience** my patience has been amply rewarded; **ça vaut ~ la peine/la visite** it's well worth the trouble/the visit.

(e) (*généreusement*) *payer, donner* generously. **ils nous ont servis/indemnisés ~** they gave us generous helpings/compensation; **vivre ~** to live handsomely.

(f) (*au moins*) easily, at least. **il gagne ~ 3.000 F par mois** he earns easily *ou* at least 3,000 francs a month; **il est ~ 2 heures** it's well past 2 o'clock; **il a ~ 50 ans** he is well past 50, he is well into his fifties; **c'est à 5 minutes/5 km d'ici, ~** it's easily *ou* a good 5 minutes/5 km from here.

largesse [laʀʒɛs] *nf* **(a)** (*U*) generosity. **avec ~** generously. **(b)** (*dons*) **~s** liberalities. **faire des ~s** to make generous gifts.

largeur [laʀʒœʀ] *nf* **(a)** (*gén*: *V* **large**) width; breadth; *[voie ferrée]* gauge. **sur toute la ~** right across, all the way across; **dans le sens de la ~** widthways, widthwise; **quelle est la ~ de la fenêtre?** what is the width of the window?, how wide is the window?; **tissu en grande/petite ~** double width/single width material.

(b) *[idées]* broadness. **~ d'esprit** broad-mindedness; **~ de vues** broadness of outlook.

(c) (*: loc*) **dans les grandes ~s** with a vengeance, well and truly; **il s'est trompé dans les grandes ~s** he has slipped up with a vengeance, he has boobed this time, and how!‡; **cette fois on les a eus dans les grandes ~s** we didn't half put one over on them this time‡, we had them well and truly this time*.

largué, e [laʀge] (*ptp de* **larguer**) *adj*: **être ~*** to be all at sea.

larguer [laʀge] (1) *vt* **(a)** (*Naut*) *cordage* to loose, release; *voile* to let out, unfurl; *amarres* to cast off, slip.

(b) *parachutiste, bombe* to drop; *cabine spatiale* to release.

(c) (**: se débarrasser de*) *personne, emploi* to drop, throw over*, chuck‡; *objet* to chuck out‡, get rid of; *principes* to jettison, chuck (out)‡.

larigot [laʀigo] *nm V* **tirer.**

larme [laʀm(ə)] **1** *nf* **(a)** tear. **en ~s** in tears; **au bord des ~s** on the verge of tears; **~s de joie/de colère** tears of joy/rage; **verser toutes les ~s de son corps** to cry one's eyes out; **avec des ~s dans la voix** with tears in his voice, with a tearful voice; **avoir les ~s aux yeux** to have tears in one's eyes; **ça lui a fait venir les ~s aux yeux** it brought tears to his eyes; **elle a la ~ facile** she is easily moved to tears, tears come easily to her; **y aller de sa ~*** to have a good weep*, shed a (little) tear; **avoir toujours la ~ à l'œil** to be a real weeper; *V* **fondre, rire, vallée** *etc.*

(b) (**: goutte*) *[vin]* drop.

2: larmes de crocodile crocodile tears; **larmes de sang** tears of blood.

larmier [laʀmje] *nm* (*Archit*) dripstone.

larmoiement [laʀmwamɑ̃] *nm* (*V* **larmoyer**) watering (of the eyes); whimpering (*U*), snivelling (*U*).

larmoyant, e [laʀmwajɑ̃, ɑ̃t] *adj yeux* tearful, watery; *voix* tearful, whimpering; *récit* maudlin.

larmoyer [laʀmwaje] (8) *vi* **(a)** (*involontairement*) *[yeux]* to water, run. **(b)** (*pleurnicher*) to whimper, snivel.

larron [laʀɔ̃] *nm* (††, *Bible*) thief. **s'entendre comme ~s en foire** to be as thick as thieves; *V* **occasion, troisième.**

larvaire [laʀvɛʀ] *adj* (*Zool*) larval; (*fig*) embryonic.

larve [laʀv(ə)] *nf* (*Zool*) larva; (*asticot*) grub. (*péj*) **~ (humaine)** worm (*péj*), creature.

larvé, e [laʀve] *adj guerre, dictature* latent, (lurking) below the surface (*attrib*); (*Méd*) *fièvre, maladie* larvate.

laryngé, e [laʀɛ̃ʒe] *adj*, **laryngien, -ienne** [laʀɛ̃ʒjɛ̃, jɛn] *adj* laryngeal.

laryngite [laʀɛ̃ʒit] *nf* laryngitis.

laryngologie [laʀɛ̃gɔlɔʒi] *nf* laryngology.

laryngologiste [laʀɛ̃gɔlɔʒist(ə)] *nmf*, **laryngologue** [laʀɛ̃gɔlɔg] *nmf* throat specialist, laryngologist.

laryngoscope [laʀɛ̃gɔskɔp] *nm* laryngoscope.

laryngotomie [laʀɛ̃gɔtɔmi] *nf* laryngotomy.

larynx [laʀɛ̃ks] *nm* larynx, voice-box*.

las[1], lasse [lɑ, lɑs] *adj* (*frm*) weary, tired. **~ de qn/de faire qch/de vivre** tired *ou* weary of sb/of doing sth/of life; *V* **guerre.**

las[2]†† [lɑs] *excl* alas!

lasagne [lazaɲ] *nf* lasagne.

lascar* [laskaʀ] *nm* (*type louche*) character; (*malin*) rogue; (*hum: enfant*) terror. **drôle de ~** (*louche*) doubtful character *ou* customer*; (*malin*) real rogue, smart customer*; **je vous aurai, mes ~s!** I'll have you yet, you old rogues!

lascif, -ive [lasif, iv] *adj* lascivious, lustful.

lascivement [lasivmɑ̃] *adv* lasciviously, lustfully.

lascivité [lasivite] *nf* lasciviousness, lustfulness.

laser [lazɛʀ] *nm* laser.

lassant, e [lɑsɑ̃, ɑ̃t] *adj* (*frm*) wearisome, tiresome.

lasser [lɑse] (1) **1** *vt* (*frm*) *auditeur, lecteur* to weary, tire. **~ la patience/bonté de qn** to try *ou* tax sb's patience/goodness; **sourire lassé** weary smile; **lassé de tout** weary of everything.

2 se lasser *vpr*: **se ~ de qch/de faire qch** to (grow) weary of sth/of doing sth, tire *ou* grow tired of sth/of doing sth; **parler sans se ~** to speak without tiring *ou* flagging.

lassitude [lɑsityd] *nf* (*frm*) weariness (*U*), lassitude (*U*).

lasso [laso] *nm* lasso. **prendre au ~** to lasso.

latence [latɑ̃s] *nf* latency. **temps de ~** latent period; **période de ~** latency period.

latent, e [latɑ̃, ɑ̃t] *adj* (*gén*) latent. **à l'état ~** latent, in the latent state.

latéral, e, *mpl* -aux [lateʀal, o] **1** *adj* side (*épith*), lateral (*frm*).

2 latérale *nf* lateral (consonant).

latéralement [lateʀalmɑ̃] *adv* (*gén*) laterally; *être situé* on the side; *arriver, souffler* from the side; *diviser* sideways.

latérite [lateʀit] *nf* laterite.

latéritique [lateʀitik] *adj* lateritic.

latex [latɛks] *nm inv* latex.

latin, e [latɛ̃, in] **1** *adj* (*gén*) Latin; (*Rel*) *croix, église, rite* Latin. (*Ling*) **les langues ~es** the romance *ou* latin languages; *V* **Amérique, quartier, voile[1].**

2 *nm* (*Ling*) Latin. **~ vulgaire** vulgar Latin; (*péj*) **~ de cuisine** dog Latin; *V* **bas[1], perdre.**

3 *nm,f*: **L~(e)** Latin. **les L~s** the Latin people, the Latins.

latinisation [latinizɑsjɔ̃] *nf* latinization.

latiniser [latinize] (1) *vti* to latinize.

latinisme [latinism(ə)] *nm* latinism.

latiniste [latinist(ə)] *nmf* (*spécialiste*) latinist, Latin scholar; (*enseignant*) Latin teacher; (*étudiant*) Latin student.

latinité [latinite] *nf* (*Ling: caractère*) latinity; (*civilisation*) Latin world.

latino-américain, e [latinoameʀikɛ̃, ɛn] *adj* Latin-American.

latitude [latityd] *nf* **(a)** (*Astron, Géog*) latitude. **Paris est à 48° de ~ Nord** Paris is situated at latitude 48° north.

(b) (*région: gén pl*) latitude. **sous toutes les ~s** in all latitudes, in all parts of the world.

(c) (*fig*) latitude, scope. **avoir toute ~ de faire qch** to be quite free *ou* at liberty to do sth; **laisser/donner toute ~ à qn** to allow/give sb full scope; **on a une certaine ~** we have some latitude *ou* some freedom of movement.

latitudinaire [latitydinɛʀ] *adj, nmf* (*littér*) latitudinarian.

latrines [latʀin] *nfpl* latrines.

lattage [lataʒ] *nm* lathing.

latte [lat] *nf* (*gén*) lath; *[plancher]* board.

latter [late] (1) *vt* to lath.

lattis [lati] *nm* lathing (*U*), lathwork (*U*).

laudanum [lodanɔm] *nm* laudanum.

laudateur, -trice [lodatœʀ, tʀis] *nm,f* (*littér*) adulator, laudator (*frm*).

laudatif, -ive [lodatif, iv] *adj* laudatory. **parler de qn en termes ~s** to speak highly of sb, be full of praise for sb.

lauréat, e [lɔʀea, at] 1 *adj* (prize-)winning. 2 *nm,f* (prize) winner. **les ~s du prix Nobel** the Nobel prize-winners.

Laurent [lɔʀɑ̃] *nm* Lawrence.

laurier [lɔʀje] 1 *nm* (*Bot*) laurel; (*Culin*) bay leaves (*pl*). (*Culin*) **feuille de ~** bay leaf; (*Culin*) **mettre du ~** to put in some bay leaves; (*fig*) **~s** laurels; **s'endormir** *ou* **se reposer sur ses ~s** to rest on one's laurels.

2: **laurier-cerise** *nm, pl* **lauriers-cerises** cherry laurel; **laurier-rose** *nm, pl* **lauriers-roses** oleander; **laurier-sauce** *nm, pl* **lauriers-sauce** bay.

lavable [lavabl(ə)] *adj* washable.

lavabo [lavabo] *nm* washbasin. (*euph*) **~s** toilets, loo* (*Brit*).

lavage [lavaʒ] 1 *nm* **(a)** *[plaie]* bathing; *[corps, cheveux]* washing. (*Méd*) **~ d'estomac/d'intestin** stomach/intestinal wash.

(b) *[murs, vêtement, voiture]* washing (*U*); *[tache]* washing off *ou* out (*U*). **après le ~ vient le rinçage** after the wash comes the rinse; **pour un meilleur ~, utilisez ...** for a better wash, use ...; **le ~ des sols à la brosse/à l'éponge** scrubbing/sponging (down) floors; **on a dû faire 3 ~s: c'était si sale!** it had to be washed 3 times, it was so dirty!; **le ~ de la vaisselle** dishwashing, washing-up (*Brit*).

(c) (*Tech*) *[gaz, charbon, laine]* washing.

2: **lavage de cerveau** brainwashing; **on lui a fait subir un lavage de cerveau** he was brainwashed.

lavallière [lavaljɛʀ] *nf*: **(cravate) ~** lavallière.

lavande [lavɑ̃d] *nf* lavender. **(eau de) ~** lavender water; **bleu ~** lavender blue.

lavandière [lavɑ̃djɛʀ] *nf* (*laveuse*) washerwoman.

lavasse* [lavas] *nf* dishwater* (*fig*). **ce café, c'est de la ~** *ou* **une vraie ~** this coffee is like dishwater*.

lave [lav] *nf* lava (*U*).

lave- [lav] *préf V* **laver.**

lavé, e [lave] (*ptp de* **laver**) *adj couleur* washy, washed-out; (*Art*) wash (*épith*); (*fig*) *ciel, yeux* pale.

lavement [lavmɑ̃] *nm* (*Méd*) enema, rectal injection.

laver [lave] (1) 1 *vt* **(a)** (*gén*) to wash; *mur* to wash (down); *plaie* to bathe, cleanse; *tache* to wash out *ou* off; (*Méd*) *intestin* to wash out. **~ avec une brosse** to scrub (down); **~ avec une éponge** to (wash with a) sponge; **~ à grande eau** to swill down; **~ la vaisselle** to wash the dishes, wash up (*Brit*), do the washing up (*Brit*); (*fig*) **il faut ~ son linge sale en famille** it doesn't do to wash one's dirty linen in public; (*fig*) **~ la tête à qn** to haul sb over the coals, give sb a dressing down; *V* **machine**³.

(b) (*emploi absolu*) *[savon]* to wash; *[personne]* to do the washing.

(c) (*fig*) *affront, injure* to avenge; *péchés, honte* to cleanse, wash away. **~ qn d'une accusation/d'un soupçon** to clear sb of an accusation/of suspicion.

(d) (*Art*) *couleur* to dilute; *dessin* to wash.

2 se laver *vpr* **(a)** to have a wash. **se ~ la figure/les mains** to wash one's face/hands; **se ~ les dents** to clean *ou* brush one's teeth; **se ~ dans un lavabo/une baignoire** to have a stand-up wash/a bath, wash (o.s.) at the basin/in the bath; **ce tissu se lave bien** this material washes well; **le cuir ne se lave pas** leather isn't washable *ou* won't wash.

(b) se ~ de *accusation* to clear o.s. of; *affront* to avenge o.s. of; (*fig*) **je m'en lave les mains** I wash my hands of the matter.

3: **lave-glace** *nm, pl* **lave-glaces** windscreen (*Brit*) *ou* windshield (*US*) washer; **lave-mains** *nm inv* wash-stand; **lave-vaisselle** *nm inv* dishwasher.

laverie [lavʀi] *nf* **(a) ~ (automatique)** launderette. **(b)** (*Ind*) washing *ou* preparation plant.

lavette [lavɛt] *nf* (*chiffon*) dish cloth; (*brosse*) dish mop; (*fig, péj: homme*) weak-kneed individual, drip*.

laveur [lavœʀ] *nm* washer. **~ de carreaux** window cleaner; *V* **raton.**

laveuse [lavøz] *nf* washerwoman.

lavis [lavi] *nm* (*procédé*) washing. **(dessin au) ~** wash drawing; **colorier au ~** to wash-paint.

lavoir [lavwaʀ] *nm* (*dehors*) washing-place; (*édifice*) wash house; (*bac*) washtub; (*Tech*) (*machine*) washer; (*atelier*) washing plant.

lavure [lavyʀ] *nf* **(a)** (*lit, fig*) **~ (de vaisselle)** dishwater. **(b)** (*Min*) *[minerai]* washing. **~s** washings.

laxatif, -ive [laksatif, iv] *adj, nm* laxative.

laxisme [laksism(ə)] *nm* laxity. **le gouvernement est accusé de ~ à l'égard des syndicats** the government is accused of being too soft with *ou* too easy on the trade unions.

laxiste [laksist(ə)] 1 *adj* lax. 2 *nmf* laxist.

layette [lɛjɛt] *nf* baby clothes (*pl*), layette. **rayon ~ d'un grand magasin** babywear department in a large store.

layon [lɛjɔ̃] *nm* (forest) track *ou* trail.

lazaret [lazaʀɛ] *nm* lazaret.

lazulite [lazylit] *nf* lazulite.

lazzi [la(d)zi] *nm* gibe. **être l'objet des ~(s) des spectateurs** to be gibed at by the onlookers.

le [l(ə)], **la** [la], **les**¹ [le] *art déf* (*contraction avec à, de* **au, aux, du, des**) **(a)** (*détermination*) the; (*devant nom propre: sg*) *non traduit*; (*pl*) the. **~ propriétaire de l'auto bleue** the owner of the blue car; **la femme de l'épicier** the grocer's wife; **les commerçants de la ville sont en grève** the town's tradesmen are on strike; **je suis inquiète, les enfants sont en retard** I'm worried because the children are late; **~ thé/~ café que je viens d'acheter** the tea/coffee I have just bought; **allons à la gare/à l'église ensemble** let's go to the station/to the church together; **il n'a pas ~ droit/l'intention de le faire** he has no right to do it/no intention of doing it; **il n'a pas eu la patience/l'intelligence d'attendre** he didn't have the patience/the sense to wait; **il a choisi ~ tableau ~ plus original de l'exposition** he chose the most original picture in the exhibition; **~ plus petit des deux frères est ~ plus solide** the smaller of the two brothers is the more robust *ou* the stronger; **l'Italie de Mussolini** Mussolini's Italy; **l'Angleterre que j'ai connue** the England (that) I knew.

(b) (*détermination: temps*) the (*souvent omis*). **~ dimanche de Pâques** Easter Sunday; **venez ~ dimanche de Pâques** come on Easter Sunday; **ne venez pas ~ jour de la lessive** don't come on wash(ing) day; **l'hiver dernier/prochain** last/next winter; **l'hiver 1973** the winter of 1973; **~ premier/dernier lundi du mois** the first/last Monday of *ou* in the month; **il ne travaille pas ~ samedi** he doesn't work on Saturdays *ou* on a Saturday; **il ne sort jamais ~ matin** he never goes out in the morning; **elle travaille ~ matin** she works mornings *ou* in the morning; **vers les 5 heures** at about 5 o'clock; **il est parti ~ 5 mai** he left on the 5th of May *ou* on May the 5th (*style parlé*); he left on May 5th (*style écrit*); **il n'a pas dormi de la nuit** he didn't sleep (a wink) all night.

(c) (*distribution*) a, an. **5 F ~ mètre/~ kg/~ litre/la pièce** 5 francs a metre/a kg/a litre/each *ou* a piece; **60 km à l'heure** 60 km an *ou* per hour; **deux fois la semaine/l'an** twice a week/year.

(d) (*fraction*) a, an. **~ tiers/quart** a third/quarter; **j'en ai fait à peine la moitié/~ dixième** I have barely done (a) half/a tenth of it.

(e) (*généralisation, abstraction*) *gén non traduit.* **~ hibou vole surtout la nuit** owls fly *ou* the owl flies mainly at night; **l'homme est un roseau pensant** man is a thinking reed; **les femmes détestent la violence** women hate violence; **les enfants sont méchants avec les animaux** children are cruel to animals; **l'enfant** *ou* **les enfants n'aime(nt) pas l'obscurité** children don't like the dark; **la tuberculose** tuberculosis; **la grippe** flu; **la jeunesse est toujours pressée** youth is *ou* the young are always in a hurry; **les prix montent en flèche** prices are rocketing; **~ thé et ~ café sont chers** tea and coffee are dear; **il apprend l'histoire et l'anglais** he is learning history and English; **j'aime la musique/la poésie/la danse** I like music/poetry/dancing; **~ beau/grotesque** the beautiful/grotesque; **les riches** the rich; **il aime la bagarre*** he loves a fight; **aller au concert/au restaurant** to go to a concert/out for a meal.

(f) (*possession*) *gén adj poss, parfois art indéf.* **elle ouvrit les yeux/la bouche** she opened her eyes/mouth; **elle est sortie ~ manteau sur ~ bras** she went out, with her coat over her arm; **la tête baissée, elle pleurait** she hung her head and wept; **assis, (les) jambes pendantes** sitting with one's legs dangling; **j'ai mal à la main droite/au pied** I've a pain in my right hand/in my foot, my right hand/my foot hurts; **il a la jambe cassée** he has got a broken leg; **avoir mal à la tête/à la gorge** to have a headache/a sore throat; **croisez les bras** cross your arms; **levez tous la main** all put your hands up, hands up everyone; **il a ~ visage fatigué/~ regard malin** he has a tired look/a mischievous look; **il a les cheveux noirs/~ cœur brisé** he has black hair/a broken heart; **il n'a pas la conscience tranquille** he has a guilty conscience; **il a l'air hypocrite** he looks a hypocrite.

(g) (*valeur démonstrative*) **il ne faut pas agir de la sorte** you must not do that kind of thing *ou* things like that; **que pensez-vous de la pièce/de l'incident?** what do you think of the play/incident?; **faites attention, les enfants!** be careful children!; **oh ~ beau chien!** what a lovely dog!, (just) look at that lovely dog!

le [l(ə)], **la** [la], **les**² [le] *pron m,f,pl* **(a)** (*homme*) him; (*femme, nation, bateau*) her; (*animal, bébé*) it, him, her; (*chose*) it. **les** them; **je ne ~/la/les connais pas** I don't know him/her/them; **regarde-~/-la/-les** look at him *ou* it/her *ou* it/them; **ce sac/cette écharpe est à vous, je l'ai trouvé(e) par terre** this bag/scarf is yours, I found it on the floor; **voulez-vous ces fraises? je les ai apportées pour vous** would you like these strawberries? I brought them for you; **le Canada demande aux USA de ~ soutenir** Canada is asking the USA to give her *ou* their support.

(b) (*emphatique*) **il faut ~ féliciter ce garçon!** you must congratulate this boy!; **cette femme-là, je la déteste** I can't bear that woman; **cela vous ~ savez aussi bien que moi** you know that as well as I; **vous l'êtes, beau** you really DO look smart; *V* **copier, voici, voilà.**

(c) (*neutre: souvent non traduit*) **vous savez qu'il est malade? — je l'ai entendu dire** did you know he's ill? — I have heard it said *ou* I had heard; **elle n'est pas heureuse, mais elle ne l'a jamais été et elle ne ~ sera jamais** she is not happy but she never has been and never will be; **pourquoi il n'est pas venu? — demande-~-lui/je me ~ demande** why hasn't he come? — ask him/I wonder; **il était ministre, il ne l'est plus** he was a minister but he isn't (one) any longer.

lé [le] *nm [étoffe]* width; *[papier peint]* length, strip.

leader [lidœʀ] *nm* (*Pol, Presse, Sport*) leader.

leasing [liziŋ] *nm* leasing.

léchage [leʃaʒ] *nm* (*gén*) licking. **~ (de bottes)*** bootlicking*, toadying; **le ~ d'un tableau*** putting the finishing touches to a picture.

lèche* [lɛʃ] *nf* bootlicking*, toadying. **faire de la ~** to be a bootlicker*; **faire de la ~ à qn** to suck up to sb*, lick sb's boots*.

lèche- [lɛʃ] *préf V* **lécher.**

lèchefrite [lɛʃfʀit] *nf* dripping-pan.

lécher [leʃe] (6) 1 *vt* **(a)** (*gén*) to lick; *assiette* to lick clean; *lait* to lick *ou* lap up. **se ~ les doigts** to lick one's fingers; **~ la confiture d'une tartine** to lick the jam off a slice of bread; *V* **ours.**

(b) *[flammes]* to lick; *[vagues]* to wash against, lap against.

(c) (*: *fignoler*) to polish up. **trop léché** overdone, overpolished.

(d) (*loc*) **~ les bottes de qn*** to suck up to sb*, lick sb's boots*; **~ le cul à** *ou* **de qn**∵ to lick (*Brit*) *ou* kiss (*US*) sb's arse∵; **~ les vitrines*** to go window-shopping; **s'en ~ les doigts/babines** to lick one's lips/chops over it.

2: **lèche-bottes*** *nmf inv* bootlicker*, toady; **lèche-cul**** *nm inv* arse-licker**; **lèche-vitrines*** *nm*: **faire du lèche-vitrines** to go window-shopping.

lécheur, -euse* [leʃœʀ, øz] *nm,f* bootlicker*, toady. **il est du genre ~** he's the bootlicking type*, he's always sucking up to someone*.

leçon [l(ə)sɔ̃] *nf* **(a)** (*Scol*) (*cours*) lesson, class; (*à apprendre*) lesson, homework. **~ de danse/de français/de piano** dancing/French/piano lesson; **~s particulières** private lessons *ou* tuition (*U*); **~s de choses** general science; **faire la ~** to teach; **réciter sa ~** (*lit*) to recite one's lesson; (*fig*) to repeat something parrot fashion, rattle something off; (*fig*) **il peut vous donner des ~s** he could teach you a thing or two.
(b) (*conseil*) advice, teaching. **suivre les ~s de qn** to heed sb's advice, take a lesson from sb; **faire la ~ à qn** (*endoctriner*) to tell sb what he must do, give sb instructions; (*réprimander*) to give sb a lecture; **faire des ~s de morale à qn** to sit in judgment on sb.
(c) (*enseignement*) *[fable, parabole]* lesson. **les ~s de l'expérience** the lessons of experience *ou* that experience teaches; **que cela te serve de ~** let that be a lesson to you, that will teach you a lesson; **cela m'a servi de ~** that taught me a lesson; **nous avons tiré la ~ de notre échec** we learnt a lesson from our failure; **maintenant que notre plan a échoué, il faut en tirer la ~** now that our plan has failed we should draw a lesson from it.
(d) *[manuscrit, texte]* reading.

lecteur, -trice [lɛktœʀ, tʀis] **1** *nm,f* **(a)** (*gén*) reader. **c'est un grand ~ de poésie** he's a great poetry-reader; **'avis au ~'** foreword, 'to the reader'; **le nombre de ~s de ce journal a doublé** the readership of this paper has doubled.
(b) (*Univ*) (foreign language) assistant.
2: (*Aut*) **lecteur de cartes** map-light; **lecteur de cassettes** cassette player; **lecteur de son** (reading) head.

lecture [lɛktyʀ] *nf* **(a)** *[carte, texte]* reading. **la ~ de Proust est difficile** reading Proust is difficult, Proust is difficult to read; **aimer la ~** to like reading; **d'une ~ facile** easy to read, very readable; **livre d'une ~ agréable** book that makes pleasant reading; **~ à haute voix** reading aloud; **faire la ~ à qn** to read to sb; (*frm*) **donner** *ou* **faire ~ de qch** to read sth out (*à qn* to sb); (*Mus*) **~ à vue** sight-reading; *V* **cabinet, livre**[1].
(b) (*livre*) reading (*U*), book. **c'est une ~ à recommander** it is recommended reading *ou* it's a book to be recommended (*à* for); **apportez-moi de la ~** bring me something to read *ou* some reading matter; **~s pour la jeunesse** books for children; **quelles sont vos ~s favorites?** what do you like reading best?; **enrichi par ses ~s** enriched by his reading *ou* by what he has read.
(c) *[projet de loi]* reading. **examiner un projet en première ~** to give a bill its first reading; **le projet a été accepté en seconde ~** the bill passed its second reading.
(d) (*Tech*) *[disque]* reading; *V* **tête.**

Léda [leda] *nf* (*Myth*) Leda.

ledit [lədi], **ladite** [ladit], *m(f)pl* **lesdit(e)s** [ledi(t)] *adj* (*frm*) the aforementioned (*frm*), the aforesaid (*frm*), the said (*frm*).

légal, e, *mpl* **-aux** [legal, o] *adj âge, dispositions, formalité* legal; *armes, moyens* legal, lawful; *adresse* registered, official. **cours ~ d'une monnaie** official rate of exchange of a currency; **monnaie ~e** legal tender, official currency; **recourir aux moyens ~aux contre qn** to take legal action against sb; *V* **fête, heure, médecine.**

légalement [legalmɑ̃] *adv* legally, lawfully.

légalisation [legalizɑsjɔ̃] *nf* (*V* **légaliser**) legalization; authentication.

légaliser [legalize] (1) *vt* (*rendre légal*) to legalize; (*certifier*) to authenticate.

légalisme [legalism(ə)] *nm* legalism.

légaliste [legalist(ə)] **1** *adj* legalist(ic). **2** *nmf* legalist.

légalité [legalite] *nf [régime, acte]* legality, lawfulness. (*loi*) **la ~** the law; **rester dans/sortir de la ~** to keep within/step outside the law.

légat [lega] *nm*: **~ (du Pape)** (papal) legate.

légataire [legatɛʀ] *nmf* legatee. **~ universel** sole legatee.

légation [legɑsjɔ̃] *nf* (*Diplomatie*) legation.

légendaire [leʒɑ̃dɛʀ] *adj* (*gén*) legendary.

légende [leʒɑ̃d] *nf* **(a)** (*histoire, mythe*) legend. **entrer dans la ~** to go down in legend, become legendary; **entrer vivant dans la ~** to become a legend in one's own lifetime.
(b) (*inscription*) *[médaille]* legend; *[dessin]* caption; *[liste, carte]* key.
(c) (*péj: mensonge*) fairy tale.

léger, -ère [leʒe, ɛʀ] *adj* **(a)** (*lit*) *objet, poids, repas, gaz* light; (*délicat*) *parfum, mousseline, style* light. **arme/industrie ~ère** light weapon/industry; **construction ~ère** light *ou* flimsy (*péj*) building; **~ comme une plume** as light as a feather; **se sentir plus ~** (*fig: être soulagé*) to feel a great weight off one's mind; (*hum*) **je me sens plus ~ de 100 F** I feel 100 francs lighter; (*fig*) **faire qch d'un cœur ~** to do sth with a light heart; *V* **poids, sommeil.**
(b) (*agile, souple*) *personne, geste, allure* light, nimble; *taille* light, slender. **se sentir ~ (comme un oiseau)** to feel as light as a bird; **il partit d'un pas ~** he walked away with a light *ou* springy step; **avec une grâce ~ère** with an airy gracefulness; *V* **main.**
(c) (*faible*) (*gén*) slight; *bruit* slight, faint; *couche* thin, light; *thé* weak; *vin* light; *alcool* not very strong; *tabac* mild; *coup* light; *maladie, châtiment* mild, slight. **une ~ère pointe de sel/d'ironie** a (light) touch of salt/irony; **un blessé ~** a slightly injured person; (*Mus*) **soprano/tenor ~** light soprano/tenor.
(d) (*superficiel*) *personne* light-minded, thoughtless; *preuve, argument* lightweight, flimsy; *jugement, propos* thoughtless, careless. **se montrer ~ dans ses actions** to act without proper thought; **pour une thèse, c'est un peu ~** it's rather lightweight *ou* a bit on the flimsy side for a thesis; **parler/agir à la ~ère** to speak/act rashly *ou* thoughtlessly *ou* without giving the matter proper consideration; **il prend toujours tout à la ~ère** he never takes anything seriously.
(e) (*frivole*) *personne, caractère, humeur* fickle; *propos, plaisanterie* ribald, broad. **femme ~ère** *ou* **de mœurs ~ères** woman of easy virtue; **avoir la cuisse ~ère** to be free with one's favours; *V* **musique.**

légèrement [leʒɛʀmɑ̃] *adv* **(a)** *habillé, armé, poser* lightly. **il a mangé ~** he ate a light meal, he didn't eat much.
(b) *courir* lightly, nimbly.
(c) *blesser, bouger, surprendre* slightly. **~ plus grand** slightly bigger.
(d) *agir* thoughtlessly, rashly, without thinking (properly). **parler ~ de la mort de qn** to speak flippantly of sb's death, speak of sb's death in an offhand *ou* a flippant way.

légèreté [leʒɛʀte] *nf* **(a)** *[objet, tissu, style, repas]* lightness.
(b) *[démarche]* lightness, nimbleness. **~ de main** lighthandedness; **avec une ~ d'oiseau** with the lightness of a bird; **marcher/danser avec ~** to walk/dance lightly *ou* with a light step.
(c) *[vin, punition, coup]* lightness; *[tabac]* mildness; *[thé]* weakness.
(d) (*superficialité*) *[conduite, personne, propos]* thoughtlessness; *[preuves, argument]* flimsiness. **faire preuve de ~** to speak (*ou* behave) rashly *ou* irresponsibly *ou* without due thought.
(e) (*frivolité*) *[personne]* fickleness, flightiness; *[propos, plaisanterie]* ribaldry. **sa ~ est bien connue** she is well-known for her free-and-easy morals.

légiférer [leʒifeʀe] (6) *vi* (*lit*) to legislate, make legislation; (*fig*) to lay down the law.

légion [leʒjɔ̃] *nf* (*Hist, fig*) legion. **~ de gendarmerie** corps of gendarmes; **la L~ (étrangère)** the Foreign Legion; **L~ d'honneur** Legion of Honour; **ils sont ~** they are legion, there are any number of them.

légionnaire [leʒjɔnɛʀ] *nm* (*Hist*) legionary; *[Légion étrangère]* legionnaire; *[Légion d'honneur]* holder of the Legion of Honour.

législateur, -trice [leʒislatœʀ, tʀis] *nm,f* legislator, lawmaker.

législatif, -ive [leʒislatif, iv] **1** *adj* legislative. **élections ~ives** elections to the legislature, ≃ general election. **2** *nm* legislature.

législation [leʒislɑsjɔ̃] *nf* legislation.

législature [leʒislatyʀ] *nf* (*Parl*) (*durée*) term (of office); (*corps*) legislature.

légiste [leʒist(ə)] *nm* legist, jurist; *V* **médecin.**

légitimation [leʒitimɑsjɔ̃] *nf [enfant]* legitimatization; *[pouvoir]* recognition; (*littér*) *[action, conduite]* legitimatization, justification.

légitime [leʒitim] **1** *adj* **(a)** (*légal*) *droits* legitimate, lawful; *union, femme* lawful; *enfant* legitimate. **j'étais en état de ~ défense** I was acting in self-defence.
(b) (*juste*) *excuse* legitimate; *colère* justifiable, justified; *revendication* legitimate, rightful; *récompense* just, legitimate. **rien de plus ~ que ...** nothing could be more justified than ... .
2 *nf* (†*) missus*. **ma ~** the missus*, the wife*.

légitimement [leʒitimmɑ̃] *adv* (*gén*) rightfully; (*Jur*) legitimately.

légitimer [leʒitime] (1) *vt enfant* to legitimate, legitimatize; *conduite, action* to legitimate, justify; *titre, pouvoir* to recognize.

légitimisme [leʒitimism(ə)] *nm* (*Hist*) legitimism.

légitimiste [leʒitimist(ə)] (*Hist*) *nmf, adj* legitimist.

légitimité [leʒitimite] *nf* (*gén*) legitimacy.

legs [lɛg] *nm* (*Jur*) legacy, bequest; (*fig: héritage*) legacy, heritage. **faire un ~ à qn** to leave sb a legacy.

léguer [lege] (6) *vt* (*Jur*) to bequeath; *tradition, vertu, tare* to hand down *ou* on, pass on. **~ qch à qn par testament** to bequeath sth to sb (in one's will); (*fig*) **la mauvaise gestion qu'on nous a léguée** the bad management which we inherited.

légume [legym] **1** *nm* vegetable. **~s secs/verts** dry/green vegetables; *V* **bouillon. 2** *nf*: **une grosse ~*** a bigwig*.

légumier, -ière [legymje, jɛʀ] **1** *adj* vegetable (*épith*). **2** *nm* vegetable dish.

légumineuse [legyminøz] *nf* leguminous plant.

leibnizien, ienne [lajbnitsjɛ̃, jɛn] *adj, nm,f* Leibnitzian.

leitmotiv [lajtmɔtif] *nm* (*lit, fig*) leitmotiv, leitmotif.

Léman [lemɑ̃] *nm V* **lac.**

lemme [lɛm] *nm* lemma.

lendemain [lɑ̃dmɛ̃] *nm* **(a)** (*jour suivant*) **le ~** the next *ou* following day, the day after; **le ~ de son arrivée/du mariage** the day after he arrived/after the marriage, the day following his arrival/the marriage; **le ~ matin/soir** the next *ou* following morning/evening; (*Prov*) **il ne faut jamais remettre au ~ ce qu'on peut faire le jour même** never put off till tomorrow what you can do today (*Prov*); **~ de fête** day after a holiday; **au ~ d'un si beau jour** on the morrow of such a glorious day (*littér*); **au ~ de la défaite/de son mariage** soon after *ou* in the days following the defeat/his marriage; *V* **jour.**
(b) (*avenir*) **le ~** tomorrow, the future; **penser au ~** to think of tomorrow *ou* the future, take thought for the morrow (*littér*); **bonheur/succès sans ~** short-lived happiness/success.
(c) **~s** (*conséquences*) consequences, repercussions; (*perspectives*) prospects, future. **cette affaire a eu de fâcheux ~s** this business had unfortunate consequences *ou* repercussions; **des ~s qui chantent** a brighter *ou* better future; **ça nous promet de beaux ~s** the future looks very promising for us.

lénifiant, e [lenifjɑ̃, ɑ̃t] *adj médicament, propos* soothing.
lénifier [lenifje] (7) *vt* to soothe.
Lénine [lenin] *nm* Lenin.
léninisme [leninism(ə)] *nm* Leninism.
léniniste [leninist(ə)] *adj, nmf* Leninist.
lénitif, -ive [lenitif, iv] *adj, nm* lenitive.
lent, e[1] [lɑ̃, lɑ̃t] *adj* (*gén*) slow; *poison* slow, slow-acting; *mort* slow, lingering. **à l'esprit** ~ slow-witted, dim-witted; **il est** ~ **à comprendre** he is slow to understand *ou* slow on the uptake*; **marcher d'un pas** ~ to walk at a slow pace *ou* slowly.
lente[2] [lɑ̃t] *nf* (*Zool*) nit.
lentement [lɑ̃tmɑ̃] *adv* slowly. **progresser** ~ to make slow progress. ~ **mais sûrement** slowly but surely.
lenteur [lɑ̃tœʀ] *nf* slowness. **avec** ~ slowly; ~ **d'esprit** slow-wittedness; **la** ~ **de la construction** the slow progress of the building; **les** ~**s du procès** the slowness of the trial.
lentille [lɑ̃tij] *nf* (*Bot, Culin*) lentil; (*Opt*) lens. **gros comme une** ~ as big as a small pea; ~**s (cornéennes)** contact lenses; ~**s d'eau** duckweed.
Léon [leɔ̃] *nm* Leo.
Léonard [leɔnaʀ] *nm* Leonard.
Léonie [leɔni] *nf* Leonie.
léonin, e [leɔnɛ̃, in] *adj mœurs, aspect, rime* leonine; (*fig*) *contrat, partage* one-sided.
Léonore [leɔnɔʀ] *nf* Leonora.
léopard [leɔpaʀ] *nm* leopard. **manteau de** ~ leopard-skin coat.
Léopold [leɔpɔl(d)] *nm* Leopold.
lépidoptère [lepidɔptɛʀ] **1** *adj* lepidopterous. **2** *nm* lepidopteran, lepidopterous insect. **les** ~**s** the Lepidoptera.
lèpre [lɛpʀ(ə)] *nf* (*Méd*) leprosy; (*fig: mal*) plague. **mur rongé de** ~ flaking *ou* scaling *ou* peeling wall.
lépreux, -euse [lepʀø, øz] **1** *adj* (*lit*) leprous, suffering from leprosy; *mur* flaking, scaling, peeling. **2** *nm,f* (*lit, fig*) leper.
léproserie [lepʀozʀi] *nf* leper-house.
lequel [ləkɛl], **laquelle** [lakɛl], *m(f)pl* **lesquel(le)s** [lekɛl] (*contraction avec à, de* **auquel, auxquels, auxquelles, duquel, desquels, desquelles**) **1** *pron* **(a)** (*relatif*) (*personne: sujet*) who; (*personne: objet*) whom; (*chose*) which. **j'ai écrit au directeur de la banque,** ~ **n'a jamais répondu** I wrote to the bank manager, who has never answered; **la patience avec laquelle il écoute** the patience with which he listens; **le règlement d'après** ~ **...** the ruling whereby ...; **la découverte sur laquelle on a tant parlé** the discovery which has been so much talked about *ou* about which there has been so much talk; **la femme à laquelle j'ai acheté mon chien** the woman from whom I bought my dog; **c'est un problème auquel je n'avais pas pensé** that's a problem I hadn't thought of *ou* which hadn't occurred to me; **le pont sur** ~ **vous êtes passé** the bridge you came over *ou* over which you came; **le docteur/le traitement sans** ~ **elle serait morte** the doctor without whom/the treatment without which she would have died; **cette société sur le compte de laquelle on dit tant de mal** this society about which so much ill is spoken; **la plupart desquels** (*personnes*) most of whom; (*choses*) most of which; **les gens chez lesquels j'ai logé** the people at whose house I stayed; *V* **importer**[2].
(b) (*interrogatif*) which. ~ **des 2 acteurs préférez-vous?** which of the 2 actors do you prefer?; **dans** ~ **de ces hôtels avez-vous logé?** in which of these hotels did you stay?; **laquelle des sonates de Mozart avez-vous entendue?** which of Mozart's sonatas *ou* which Mozart sonata did you hear?; **laquelle des chambres est la sienne?** which is his room?, which of the rooms is his?; **je ne sais à laquelle des vendeuses m'adresser** I don't know which (shop) assistant I should speak to *ou* which (shop) assistant to speak to; **devinez lesquels de ces tableaux elle aimerait avoir** guess which of these pictures she would like to have; **donnez-moi 1 melon/2 melons —** ~**?/lesquels?** give me 1 melon/2 melons — which one?/which ones? *ou* which (2)?; **va voir ma sœur — laquelle?** go and see my sister — which one?
2 *adj:* **son état pourrait empirer, auquel cas je reviendrais** his condition could worsen, in which case I would come back; (*littér, iro*) **il écrivit au ministre,** ~ **ministre ne répondit jamais** he wrote to the minister but the said (*littér, iro*) minister never replied.
lerch(e)* [lɛʀʃ(ə)] *adv:* **pas** ~ not much; **il n'y en a pas** ~ there's not much of it; **c'est pas** ~ that's not much.
les [le] *V* **le**[1], **le**[2].
lesbienne [lɛsbjɛn] *nf* lesbian.
lèse-majesté [lɛzmaʒɛste] *nf* lese-majesty; *V* **crime.**
léser [leze] (6) *vt* **(a)** (*Jur: frustrer*) *personne* to wrong; *intérêts* to damage. **la partie lésée** the injured party; ~ **les droits de qn** to infringe on sb's rights. **(b)** (*Méd: blesser*) *organe* to injure.
lésiner [lezine] (1) *vi* to skimp (*sur qch* on sth).
lésinerie [lezinʀi] *nf* (*avarice*) stinginess; (*action avare*) stingy act.
lésion [lezjɔ̃] *nf* (*Jur, Méd*) lesion.
lésionnel, -elle [lezjɔnɛl] *adj trouble* caused by a lesion; *syndrome* of a lesion.
lessivage [lesivaʒ] *nm* (*gén*) washing; (*Chim*) leaching.
lessive [lesiv] *nf* **(a)** (*produit*) (*gén*) washing powder; (*Tech: soude*) lye.
(b) (*lavage*) washing, wash. **mon jour de** ~ my wash *ou* washing day; **faire la** ~ to do the washing; **faire 4** ~**s par semaine** to do 4 washes a week.
(c) (*linge*) washing (*U*). **porter sa** ~ **à la blanchisserie** to take one's washing to the laundry.
lessivé, e* [lesive] (*ptp de* **lessiver**) *adj* (*fatigué*) **être** ~ to be washed out* *ou* dead beat* *ou* all in*.
lessiver [lesive] (1) *vt* **(a)** (*lit*) *mur, plancher, linge* to wash. **(b)** (*Chim*) to leach. **(c)** (*: *battre*) (*au jeu*) to clean out*; *adversaire* to lick*.
lessiveuse [lesivøz] *nf* boiler (*for washing laundry*).
lest [lɛst] *nm* ballast. (*Naut*) **sur son** ~ in ballast; **garnir un bateau de** ~ to ballast a ship; *V* **jeter.**
lestage [lɛstaʒ] *nm* ballasting.
leste [lɛst(ə)] *adj* **(a)** *animal* nimble, agile; *personne* sprightly, agile; *démarche* sprightly, light, nimble; *V* **main. (b)** (*grivois*) *plaisanterie* risqué; (*cavalier*) *ton, réponse* offhand.
lestement [lɛstəmɑ̃] *adv* (*V* **leste**) nimbly, agilely; in a sprightly manner; lightly; offhandedly. **plaisanter** ~ to make (rather) risqué jokes; **mener** ~ **une affaire** to conduct a piece of business briskly.
lester [lɛste] (1) *vt* **(a)** (*garnir de lest*) to ballast.
(b) (*: *remplir*) *portefeuille, poches* to fill, cram. ~ **son estomac, se** ~ **(l'estomac)** to stuff o.s.*; **lesté d'un repas copieux** weighed down with a heavy meal.
letchi [lɛtʃi] *nm* = **litchi.**
léthargie [letaʀʒi] *nf* (*apathie, Méd*) lethargy. **tomber en** ~ to fall into a state of lethargy.
léthargique [letaʀʒik] *adj* lethargic. **état** ~ lethargic state, state of lethargy.
letton, -onne [lɛtɔ̃, ɔn] **1** *adj* Latvian, Lett, Lettish. **2** *nm* (*Ling*) Latvian, Lett, Lettish. **3** *nm,f:* **L**~**(ne)** Latvian, Lett.
lettre [lɛtʀ(ə)] **1** *nf* **(a)** (*caractère*) letter. ~ **majuscule/minuscule** capital/small letter; **c'est en toutes** ~**s dans les journaux** it's there in black and white *ou* it's there for all to read in the newspapers; **c'est en grosses** ~**s dans les journaux** it's splashed across the newspapers, it has made headlines in the papers; **écrivez la somme en (toutes)** ~**s** write out the sum in words; **un mot de 6** ~**s** a 6-letter word, a word of 6 letters; **c'est écrit en toutes** ~**s sur sa figure** it's written all over his face; **c'est à écrire en** ~**s d'or** it is a momentous event, it is something to celebrate; **inscrit** *ou* **gravé en** ~**s de feu** written in letters of fire; **cette lutte est écrite en** ~**s de sang** this gory struggle will remain engraved on people's minds; *V* **cinq.**
(b) (*missive*) letter. ~**s** (*courrier*) letters, mail; **jeter** *ou* **mettre une** ~ **à la boîte** *ou* **à la poste** to post a letter; **est-ce qu'il y avait des** ~**s aujourd'hui?** were there any letters today?, was there any mail today?; **écris-lui donc une petite** ~ write him a note, drop him a line*; **il a reçu une** ~ **d'injures** he got a rude *ou* an abusive letter; ~ **de condoléances/de félicitations/de réclamation** letter of condolence/of congratulations/of complaint; ~ **d'amour/d'affaires** love/business letter.
(c) (*sens strict*) **à la** ~, **au pied de la** ~ literally; **suivre la** ~ **de la loi** to follow the letter of the law; **exécuter des ordres à la** ~ to carry out orders to the letter.
(d) les ~**s, les belles** ~**s** (*culture littéraire*) literature; **femme/homme/gens de** ~**s** woman/man/men of letters; **le monde des** ~**s** the literary world; **avoir des** ~**s** to be well-read.
(e) (*Scol, Univ*) arts (subjects). **il est très fort en** ~**s** he's very good at arts subjects; **il fait des** ~**s** he's doing an arts degree; **professeur de** ~**s** teacher of French, French teacher (*in France*); ~**s classiques** classics (*sg*); *V* **faculté, licence.**
(f) (*loc*) **rester** ~ **morte** *[remarque, avis, protestation]* to go unheeded; **devenir** ~ **morte** *[loi, traité]* to become a dead letter; **c'est passé comme une** ~ **à la poste*** it went off smoothly *ou* without a hitch; *V* **avant.**
2: (*Hist*) **lettre de cachet** lettre de cachet; (*Comm*) **lettre de change** bill of exchange; (*Admin*) **lettre circulaire** circular; **lettres de créance** credentials; (*Fin*) **lettre de crédit** letter of credit; **lettre exprès** express letter; **lettre de faire-part (de mariage)** ≃ wedding invitation, letter announcing a wedding; (*Admin*) **lettre missive** letter(s) missive; (*Univ*) **section de lettres modernes** French department, department of French (language and literature); **lettres de noblesse** letters patent of nobility; (*Presse*) **lettre ouverte** open letter; **lettres patentes** letters (of) patent; **lettre de recommandation** letter of recommendation, reference; **lettre recommandée** (*attestant sa remise*) recorded delivery letter; (*assurant sa valeur*) registered letter; **lettre de service** notification of command; (*Scol*) **lettres supérieures** *preparatory class (after the baccalauréat) leading to the École Normale Supérieure.*
lettré, e [letʀe] *adj* well-read.
lettrine [letʀin] *nf* **(a)** *[dictionnaire]* headline. **(b)** *[chapitre]* dropped initial.
leu [lø] *nm V* **queue.**
leucémie [løsemi] *nf* leukaemia.
leucémique [løsemik] **1** *adj* leukaemic. **2** *nmf* person suffering from leukaemia.
leucocyte [løkɔsit] *nm* leucocyte. ~ **mononucléaire** monocyte; ~ **polynucléaire** polymorphonuclear leucocyte.
leucorrhée [løkɔʀe] *nf* leucorrhoea.
leur [lœʀ] **1** *pron pers mf* them. **je le** ~ **ai dit** I told them; **il** ~ **est facile de le faire** it is easy for them to do it; **elle** ~ **serra la main** she shook their hand, she shook them by the hand; **je** ~ **en ai donné** I gave them some, I gave some to them.
2 *adj poss* **(a)** their. ~ **jardin à eux est une vraie forêt vierge** their own garden is a real jungle; **à** ~ **vue** at the sight of them, on seeing them; ~ **maladroite de sœur** that clumsy sister of theirs; **ils ont passé tout** ~ **dimanche à travailler** they spent the whole of *ou* all Sunday working; **ils ont** ~**s petites manies** they have their little fads.
(b) (*littér*) theirs, their own. **un** ~ **cousin** a cousin of theirs; **ils ont fait** ~**s ces idées** they made theirs these ideas, they made these ideas their own; **ces terres qui étaient** ~**s** these estates of theirs *ou* which were theirs.
3 *pron poss:* **le** ~, **la** ~, **les** ~**s** theirs, their own; **ces sacs sont les** ~**s** these bags are theirs, these are THEIR bags; **ils sont partis dans une voiture qui n'était pas la** ~ they left in a car which wasn't theirs *ou* their own; **à la (bonne)** ~**!** their good health!, here's to them!; *pour autres exemples V* **sien.**

4 *nm* **(a)** (*U*) **ils ont mis du ~** they pulled their weight, they did their bit*; *V aussi* **sien.**

(b) les ~s (*famille*) their family, their (own) folks*; (*partisans*) their own people; **ils ont encore fait des ~s*** they've (gone and) done it again*, they've been at it again*; **nous étions des ~s** we were with them.

leurre [lœʀ] *nm* (*illusion*) delusion, illusion; (*duperie*) deception; (*piège*) trap, snare; (*Fauconnerie, Pêche: appât*) lure; (*Chasse*) decoy, lure.

leurrer [lœʀe] (1) *vt* to deceive, delude. **ils nous ont leurrés par des promesses fallacieuses** they deluded us with false promises; **ils se sont laissé ~** they let themselves be taken in *ou* deceived; **ne vous leurrez pas** don't delude yourself.

levage [ləvaʒ] *nm* (*Tech*) lifting; (*Culin*) rising, raising; *V* **appareil.**

levain [ləvɛ̃] *nm* [*pain*] leaven. **sans ~** unleavened; (*fig*) **~ de haine/de vengeance** seed of hate/of vengeance.

levant [ləvɑ̃] **1** *adj*: **soleil ~** rising sun; **au soleil ~** at sunrise. **2** *nm*: **du ~ au couchant** from the rising to the setting sun; **le L~** the Levant.

levantin, -ine [ləvɑ̃tɛ̃, in] **1** *adj* Levantine. **2** *nm,f*: **L~(e)** Levantine.

levé[1] [l(ə)ve] *nm* (*plan*) survey. **un ~ de terrain** a land survey; **faire un ~ de terrain** to survey a piece of land.

lève- [lɛv] *préf V* **lever.**

levé[2], e[1] [l(ə)ve] (*ptp de* **lever**) **1** *adj*: **être ~** to be up; **sitôt ~** as soon as he is (*ou* was *etc*) up; **il n'est pas encore ~** he is not up yet; **toujours le premier ~** always the first up; *V* **pierre. 2** *nm* (*Mus*) up-beat.

levée[2] [l(ə)ve] **1** *nf* **(a)** [*blocus, siège*] raising; [*séance*] closing; [*interdiction, punition*] lifting.

(b) (*Poste*) collection. **la ~ du matin est faite** the morning collection has been made, the morning post has gone.

(c) (*Cartes*) trick. **faire une ~** to take a trick.

(d) [*impôts*] levying; [*armée*] raising, levying.

(e) (*remblai*) levee.

2: (*fig*) **levée de boucliers** general outcry, hue and cry; **la levée du corps aura lieu à 10 heures** the funeral will start from the house at 10 o'clock; (*Jur*) **levée d'écrou** release (from prison); (*Jur*) **levée de jugement** transcript (of a verdict); (*Mil*) **levée en masse** levy en masse; (*Jur*) **levée des scellés** removal of the seals; **levée de terre** levee.

lever [l(ə)ve] (5) **1** *vt* **(a)** (*soulever, hausser*) *poids, objet* to lift; *vitre* to put up, raise; *tête* to raise, lift up; *main, bras* (*pour prendre qch, saluer, voter, prêter serment*) to raise; (*en classe*) to put up. **lève ton coude, je veux prendre le papier** lift *ou* raise your elbow, I want to take the paper away; **~ les yeux** to lift up *ou* raise one's eyes, look up (*de* from); **~ les yeux sur qn** (*lit: regarder*) to look at sb; (*fig: vouloir épouser*) to set one's heart on marrying sb; **~ le visage vers qn** to look up at sb; **~ un regard suppliant/éploré vers qn** to look up imploringly/tearfully at sb.

(b) (*faire cesser, supprimer*) *blocus* to raise; *séance, audience* to close; *difficulté* to remove; *interdiction, punition* to lift; (*Comm, Jur*) *option* to exercise, take up. **~ les scellés** to remove the seals; **cela a levé tous ses scrupules** that has removed all his scruples; **on lève la séance?*** shall we break up?, shall we call it a day?*

(c) (*ramasser*) *impôts* to levy; *armée* to raise, levy; (*Cartes*) *pli* to take; [*facteur*] *lettres* to collect.

(d) (*Chasse*) *lièvre* to start; *perdrix* to flush; (*:fig*) *femme* to pick up*. (*fig*) **~ un lièvre** to start a hare (*fig*).

(e) (*établir*) *plan* to draw (up); *carte* to draw.

(f) (†: *prélever*) to cut off.

(g) (*sortir du lit*) *enfant, malade* to get up. **le matin, pour le faire ~, il faut se fâcher** in the morning, you have to get angry before he'll get up *ou* to get him out of bed.

(h) (*loc*) **~ l'ancre** (*Naut*) to weigh anchor; (*fig*) to make tracks*; **~ les bras au ciel** to throw one's arms up in the air; **~ les yeux au ciel** to raise one's eyes heavenwards; **~ le camp** (*lit*) to strike *ou* break camp; (*fig*) to break up a meeting; **~ le siège** (*lit*) to lift *ou* raise the siege; (*fig*) to break up a meeting; **il lève bien le coude*** he enjoys a drink, he drinks a fair bit*; **il n'a pas levé le petit doigt pour m'aider** he didn't lift a finger to help me; **~ l'étendard de la révolte** to raise the standard of revolt; **il ne lève jamais le nez de ses livres** he never takes his nose out of his books; **il ne lève jamais le nez de son travail/son pupitre** he never lifts his nose from his work/his desk; [*chien*] **~ la patte** (*pour pisser*) to cock *ou* lift its leg; (*pour dire bonjour*) to give a paw; **~ le pied** (*disparaître*) to vanish; (*Aut: ralentir*) to slow down; **~ le poing** to raise one's fist; **~ la main sur qn** to raise one's hand to sb; (*Théât*) **~ le rideau** to raise the curtain; **~ le voile** to reveal the truth (*sur* about); **~ le masque** to unmask o.s.; **~ son verre à la santé de qn** to raise one's glass to sb, drink to sb's health.

2 *vi* **(a)** [*plante, blé*] to come up.

(b) (*Culin*) to rise. **faire ~ la pâte** to make the dough rise.

3 se lever *vpr* **(a)** [*rideau, main*] to go up. **toutes les mains se levèrent** every hand went up.

(b) (*se mettre debout*) to get up. **se ~ de table/de sa chaise** to get up from the table/from one's chair; **le maître les fit se lever** the teacher made them stand up *ou* get up *ou* get to their feet.

(c) (*sortir du lit*) to get up. **se ~ tôt** to get up early, rise early; **le convalescent commence à se ~** the convalescent is starting to get up (and about); **c'est l'heure de se ~** it's time to get up; **ce matin, il s'est levé du pied gauche** this morning he got out of bed on the wrong side; **se ~ sur son séant** to sit up.

(d) [*soleil, lune*] to rise; [*jour*] to break. **le soleil n'était pas encore levé** the sun had not yet risen *ou* was not yet up.

(e) (*Mét*) [*vent, orage*] to get up, rise; [*brume*] to lift, clear. **le temps se lève, cela se lève** the weather *ou* it is clearing.

4 *nm* **(a) ~ de soleil** sunrise, sunup*; **~ du jour** daybreak, dawn.

(b) (*au réveil*) **prenez 3 comprimés au ~** take 3 tablets when you get up *ou* on rising; **au ~, à son ~** (*présent*) when he gets up; (*passé*) when he got up; **le ~ du roi** the levee of the king.

(c) (*Théât*) **le ~ du rideau** (*commencement d'une pièce*) the curtain; (*action de lever le rideau*) the raising of the curtain; (*pièce*) **un ~ de rideau** a curtain raiser.

(d) = levé[1].

5: lève-tôt *nm inv* early riser; **lève-tard** *nm inv* late riser.

levier [ləvje] *nm* lever. **~ de commande/de changement de vitesse** control/gear lever; **faire ~ sur qch** to lever sth up (*ou* off *etc*); (*fig*) **être aux ~s de commande** to be in control *ou* command; (*fig*) **l'argent est un puissant ~** money is a powerful lever.

lévitation [levitɑsjɔ̃] *nf* levitation.

lévite [levit] *nm* Levite.

levraut [ləvʀo] *nm* leveret.

lèvre [lɛvʀ(ə)] *nf* (*gén*) lip; (*Géog*) [*faille*] side. (*Géog*) **~ soulevée/abaissée** upthrow/downthrow side; **le sourire aux ~s** with a smile on one's lips; **la cigarette aux ~s** with a cigarette between one's lips; **son nom est sur toutes les ~s** his name is on everyone's lips; (*fig*) **j'ai les ~s scellées** my lips are sealed; *V* **bout, pincer, rouge.**

levrette [ləvʀɛt] *nf* (*femelle*) greyhound bitch; (*variété de lévrier*) Italian greyhound.

lévrier [levʀije] *nm* greyhound. **courses de ~s** greyhound racing; **courir comme un ~** to run like the wind.

levure [l(ə)vyʀ] *nf* (*ferment*) yeast. **~ de bière** brewers' yeast.

lexème [lɛksɛm] *nm* lexeme.

lexical, e, *mpl* -aux [lɛksikal, o] *adj* lexical.

lexicalisation [lɛksikalizɑsjɔ̃] *nf* lexicalization.

lexicaliser [lɛksikalize] (1) *vt* to lexicalize.

lexicographe [lɛksikɔgʀaf] *nmf* lexicographer.

lexicographie [lɛksikɔgʀafi] *nf* lexicography.

lexicographique [lɛksikɔgʀafik] *adj* lexicographical.

lexicologie [lɛksikɔlɔʒi] *nf* lexicology.

lexicologique [lɛksikɔlɔʒik] *adj* lexicological.

lexicologue [lɛksikɔlɔg] *nmf* lexicologist.

lexie [lɛksi] *nf* lexical item.

lexique [lɛksik] *nm* vocabulary; (*glossaire*) lexicon.

lézard [lezaʀ] *nm* (*animal*) lizard; (*peau*) lizardskin. **~ vert** green lizard; **sac/gants en ~** lizardskin bag/gloves; **faire le ~ (au soleil)*** to bask in the sun.

lézarde [lezaʀd(ə)] *nf* (*fissure*) crack.

lézarder[1] [lezaʀde] (1) *vi* to bask in the sun.

lézarder[2] *vt*, **se lézarder** *vpr* [lezaʀde] (1) to crack.

liaison [ljɛzɔ̃] *nf* **(a)** (*fréquentation*) **~ (amoureuse)** (love) affair; **~ (d'affaires)** business relationship *ou* connection; **~ d'amitié††** friendship; **avoir/rompre une ~** to have/break off an affair *ou* a love affair; **avoir une *ou* être en ~ d'affaires avec qn** to have business relations with sb.

(b) (*contact*) **entrer/être en ~ étroite avec qn** to get/be in close contact with sb; **travailler en ~ étroite avec qn** to work closely with *ou* in close collaboration with sb; **en ~ (étroite) avec nos partenaires, nous avons décidé de...** in (close) collaboration with *ou* after close consultation with our partners, we have decided to...; **établir une ~ radio avec un pilote** to establish radio contact with a pilot; (*péj*) **avoir des ~s avec** to have links *ou* dealings with; (*Mil*) **se tenir en ~ avec l'état-major** to keep in contact with headquarters, liaise with headquarters; (*Mil*) **officier *ou* agent de ~** liaison officer.

(c) (*rapport, enchaînement*) connection. **manque de ~ entre 2 idées** lack of connection between 2 ideas; **il n'y a aucune ~ entre les 2 idées/événements** there is no connection *ou* link between the 2 ideas/events; **la ~ des idées n'est pas évidente** the connection of ideas isn't obvious.

(d) (*Phonétique*) liaison. (*Gram*) **mot *ou* terme de ~** link-word; (*Phonétique*) **il ne faut pas faire la ~ devant un h aspiré** one mustn't make a liaison before an aspirate h.

(e) (*Transport*) link. **~ aérienne/routière/ferroviaire/maritime** air/road/rail/sea link.

(f) (*Culin*) liaison.

liane [ljan] *nf* creeper, liana.

liant, e [ljɑ̃, ɑ̃t] **1** *adj* sociable.

2 *nm* **(a)** (*littér: affabilité*) sociable disposition. **il a du ~** he has a sociable disposition *ou* nature, he is sociable.

(b) (*Métal: souplesse*) flexibility.

(c) (*substance*) binder.

liard† [ljaʀ] *nm* farthing. (*fig*) **je n'ai pas un ~** I haven't (got) a farthing.

liasse [ljas] *nf* [*billets, papiers*] bundle, wad.

Liban [libɑ̃] *nm* Lebanon.

libanais, e [libanɛ, ɛz] **1** *adj* Lebanese. **2** *nm,f*: **L~(e)** Lebanese.

libations [libɑsjɔ̃] *nfpl* (*Antiq*) libations. (*fig*) **faire de copieuses ~** to indulge in great libations (*hum*).

libelle [libɛl] *nm* (*satire*) lampoon. **faire des ~s contre qn** to lampoon sb.

libellé [libele] *nm* wording.

libeller [libele] (1) *vt* *acte* to draw up; *chèque* to make out (*au nom de* to); *lettre, demande, réclamation* to word. **sa lettre était ainsi libellée** so went his letter, his letter was worded thus.

libelliste [libelist(ə)] *nm* (*littér*) lampoonist.

libellule [libelyl] *nf* dragonfly.

libérable [libeʀabl(ə)] *adj* *militaire* dischargeable. **permission ~** leave in hand (*allowing early discharge*).

libéral, e, *mpl* -aux [libeʀal, o] *adj, nm,f* (*gén*) liberal; (*Can Pol*) Liberal; *V* **profession.**

libéralement [libeʀalmɑ̃] *adv* liberally.

libéralisation [libeʀalizasjɔ̃] *nf [lois, régime]* liberalization. **la ~ du commerce** the easing of restrictions on trade.
libéraliser [libeʀalize] (1) *vt (V* **libéralisation**) to liberalize.
libéralisme [libeʀalism(ə)] *nm (tous sens)* liberalism.
libéralité [libeʀalite] *nf (littér) (générosité)* liberality; *(gén pl: don)* generous *ou* liberal gift. **vivre des ~s d'un ami** to live off a friend's generosity.
libérateur, -trice [libeʀatœʀ, tʀis] **1** *adj (Pol)* **guerre/croisade ~trice** war/crusade of liberation; *(Psych)* **rire ~** liberating laugh; **expérience ~trice** liberating experience. **2** *nm,f* liberator.
libération [libeʀasjɔ̃] *nf (V* **libérer**) discharge; release; freeing; liberation. **~ conditionnelle** release on parole; *V* **vitesse.**
libératoire [libeʀatwaʀ] *adj (Fin)* **paiement ~** payment in full discharge; **prélèvement ~** levy at source *(on share dividends)*.
libérer [libeʀe] (6) **1** *vt* **(a)** *(relâcher) prisonnier* to discharge, release *(de* from); *soldat* to discharge *(de* from). *(Jur)* **être libéré sous caution/sur parole** to be released on bail/on parole.
(b) *(délivrer) pays, peuple* to free, liberate; *(fig) esprit, personne (de soucis etc)* to free *(de* from); *(d'inhibitions etc)* to liberate *(de* from); **~ qn de** *liens* to release *ou* free sb from; *promesse* to release sb from; *dette* to free sb from.
(c) *(Tech) levier, cran d'arrêt* to release; *(Écon) échanges commerciaux* to ease restrictions on; *(Méd) intestin* to unblock. *(fig)* **~ le passage** to free *ou* unblock the way.
(d) *(soulager)* **~ son cœur/sa conscience** to unburden one's heart/conscience; **~ ses instincts** to give free rein to one's instincts.
(e) *(Phys) énergie, électrons* to release; *(Chim) gaz* to release, give off.
2 se libérer *vpr (de ses liens)* to free o.s. *(de* from); *(d'une promesse)* to release o.s. *(de* from); *(d'une dette)* to clear o.s. *(de* of). **se ~ d'un rendez-vous** to get out of a meeting; **désolé, jeudi je ne peux pas me ~** I'm sorry I can't be free *ou* I'm not free on Thursday; **se ~ du joug de l'oppresseur** to free o.s. from the yoke of one's oppressor.
Libéria [libeʀja] *nm* Liberia.
libérien, -ienne [libeʀjɛ̃, jɛn] **1** *adj* Liberian. **2** *nm,f:* **L~(ne)** Liberian.
libertaire [libɛʀtɛʀ] *adj, nmf* libertarian.
liberté [libɛʀte] **1** *nf* **(a)** *(gén, Jur)* freedom. **mettre en ~** to free, release; **mise en ~** *[prisonnier]* discharge, release; **être en ~** *[animal]* to be free; **animaux en ~** animals in freedom, animals in the wild *ou* natural state; **le voleur est encore en ~** the thief is still at large; **rendre la ~ à un prisonnier** to free *ou* release a prisoner, set a prisoner free; **remettre un animal en ~** to set an animal free (again); **elle a quitté son mari et repris sa ~** she has left her husband and regained her independence; **agir en toute** *ou* **pleine ~** to act with complete freedom, act quite freely; **sans la ~ de critiquer/de choisir aucune opinion n'a de valeur** without the freedom to criticize/to choose any opinion is valueless; **avoir toute ~ pour agir** to have full freedom to act; **donner à qn toute ~ d'action** to give sb complete freedom of action, give sb a free hand to act *ou* carte blanche.
(b) *(gén, Pol: indépendance)* freedom. **~ de la presse/d'opinion/de conscience** *etc* freedom of the press/of thought/of conscience *etc*; **~ du culte/d'expression** freedom of worship/of expression; **~ individuelle/religieuse** personal/religious freedom; **vive la ~!** long live freedom; **~, égalité, fraternité** liberty, equality, fraternity.
(c) *(loisir)* **heures/moments de ~** free hours/moments; **ils ont droit à 2 jours de ~ par semaine** they are allowed 2 free days a week *ou* 2 days off each week; **son travail ne lui laisse pas beaucoup de ~** his work doesn't leave him much free time.
(d) *(absence de retenue, de contrainte)* liberty. **~ d'esprit/de jugement** independence of mind/judgment; **~ de langage/de mœurs** freedom of language/morals; **s'exprimer avec (grande) ~** to express o.s. very freely; *(formule)* **prendre la ~ de faire** to take the liberty of doing; **prendre** *ou* **se permettre des ~s avec** *personne, texte* to take liberties with.
(e) *(droit)* **la ~ du travail** the right *ou* freedom to work; **~ d'association/de réunion** right of association/to meet *ou* hold meetings; **les ~s syndicales** the rights of the unions; *(Hist)* **~s des villes** borough franchises.
2: *(Jur)* **liberté sous caution** release on bail; **mise en liberté sous caution** release on bail; *(Jur)* **liberté conditionnelle** parole; **mettre en liberté conditionnelle** to release on parole; **être mis en liberté conditionnelle** to be granted parole; **mise en liberté conditionnelle** release on parole; *(Jur)* **liberté provisoire** bail; **être mis en liberté provisoire** to be granted bail; *(Jur)* **liberté surveillée** release on probation; **être mis en liberté surveillée** to be put on probation.
libertin, e [libɛʀtɛ̃, in] **1** *adj (littér) (dissolu) personne* libertine, dissolute; *(grivois) roman* licentious; *(Hist: irréligieux) philosophe* libertine.
2 *nm,f (littér: dévergondé)* libertine.
3 *nm (Hist: libre-penseur)* libertine, freethinker.
libertinage [libɛʀtinaʒ] *nm (littér) (débauche) [personne]* debauchery, dissoluteness; *(grivoiserie) [roman]* licentiousness; *(Hist: impiété) [philosophe]* libertine outlook *ou* philosophy.
libidineux, -euse [libidinø, øz] *adj (littér, hum)* libidinous, lustful.
libido [libido] *nf* libido.
libraire [libʀɛʀ] *nmf* bookseller. **~-éditeur** publisher and bookseller.
librairie [libʀeʀi] *nf* **(a)** *(magasin)* bookshop. **~ d'art** art bookshop; **~-papeterie** bookseller's and stationer's; **ça ne se vend plus en ~** it's no longer in the bookshops, the bookshops no longer sell it; **ce livre va bientôt paraître en ~** this book will soon be on sale (in the shops) *ou* will soon be published *ou* out*.
(b) la ~ *(activité)* bookselling *(U)*; *(corporation)* the book trade.
libre [libʀ(ə)] **1** *adj* **(a)** *(gén, Pol: sans contrainte) personne, peuple, presse, commerce* free; *(Comm) prix, concurrence* free; *vente* unrestricted. **médicament en vente ~** medicine on open sale *ou* on sale without prescription; **il est difficile de garder l'esprit** *ou* **la tête ~ quand on a des ennuis** it's difficult to keep one's mind free of worries *ou* to keep a clear mind when one is in trouble; **être ~ comme l'air** to be as free as a bird; **rester ~** *(non marié)* to remain unattached; **il n'est plus ~ (de lui-même)** he is no longer a free agent; **être ~ de ses mouvements** to be free to do what one pleases; *(Jur)* **avoir la ~ disposition de ses biens** to have free disposal of one's goods.
(b) ~ de free from; **~ de tout engagement/préjugé** free from any commitment/all prejudice; **~ de faire** free to do; **~ à vous de poser vos conditions** you are free to *ou* it's (entirely) up to you to state your conditions; **vous êtes parfaitement ~ de refuser l'invitation** you're quite free *ou* at liberty to refuse the invitation.
(c) *(non occupé) passage, voie* clear; *taxi* empty; *personne, place* free; *salle* free, available. **appartement ~ à la vente** flat for sale with vacant possession *ou* immediate entry; *(Téléc)* **la ligne n'est pas ~** the line is engaged; *(Téléc)* **ça ne sonne pas ~** the engaged tone *(Brit) ou* busy signal *(US)* is ringing, it's giving the engaged tone *(Brit) ou* busy signal *(US)*; **est-ce que cette place est ~?** is this seat free? *ou* empty? *ou* vacant?; **avoir du temps ~** to have some spare *ou* free time; **avoir des journées ~s** to have some free days; **êtes-vous ~ ce soir?** are you free this evening?; **vous ne pouvez pas voir M X, il n'est pas ~ aujourd'hui** you can't see Mr X, he is not free *ou* available today; **le jeudi est son jour ~** Thursday is his free day *ou* his day off; **je vais essayer de me rendre ~ pour demain** I'm going to try to make myself free tomorrow *ou* to keep tomorrow free; *V* **air**[1], **champ.**
(d) *(Scol: non étatisé) enseignement* private and Roman Catholic. **école ~** private *ou* independent Roman Catholic school.
(e) *(autorisé, non payant) entrée, accès* free. **'entrée ~'** *(exposition etc)* 'entrance free'; *(galerie d'artisanat, magasin d'exposition-vente etc)* 'please walk round'.
(f) *(lit, fig: non entravé) mouvement, respiration* free; *traduction, improvisation, adaptation* free; *(Tech) pignon, engrenage* disengaged. **robe qui laisse le cou ~** dress which leaves the neck bare *ou* which shows the neck; **robe qui laisse la taille ~** dress which is not tight-fitting round the waist *ou* which fits loosely at the waist; **avoir les cheveux ~s** to have one's hair loose; **de nos jours on laisse les jambes ~s aux bébés** nowadays we leave babies' legs free; **le sujet de la dissertation est ~** the subject of this essay is left open; *V* **main, roue, vers**[2].
(g) *(sans retenue) personne* free *ou* open in one's behaviour; *plaisanteries* broad. **tenir des propos assez ~s sur la politique du gouvernement** to be fairly plain-spoken *ou* make fairly candid remarks about the policies of the government; **être très ~ avec qn** to be very free with sb; **donner ~ cours à sa colère/son indignation** to give free rein *ou* vent to one's anger/indignation.
2: libre arbitre free will; **libre-échange** *nm* free trade; **libre-échangiste** *nm, pl* **libre-échangistes** free trader; **libre entreprise** free enterprise; **libre pensée** freethinking; **libre penseur, -euse** freethinker; **libre-service** *nm, pl* **libres-services** *(restaurant)* self-service restaurant; *(magasin)* self-service store.
librement [libʀəmɑ̃] *adv* freely.
librettiste [libʀetist(ə)] *nmf* librettist.
libretto† [libʀeto], *pl* **~s** *ou* **libretti** [libʀeti] *nm* libretto.
Libye [libi] *nf* Libya.
libyen, -enne [libjɛ̃, ɛn] **1** *adj* Libyan. **2** *nm,f:* **L~(ne)** Libyan.
lice [lis] *nf (Hist)* lists *(pl)*. *(fig)* **entrer en ~** to enter the lists.
licence [lisɑ̃s] *nf* **(a)** *(Univ)* degree. **~ ès lettres** Arts degree, ≃ B.A.; **~ ès sciences** Science degree, ≃ B.Sc.
(b) *(autorisation)* permit; *(Comm, Jur)* licence; *(Sport)* permit *(showing membership of a federation and giving the right of entry into competitions)*.
(c) *(littér: liberté)* **~ (des mœurs)** licentiousness *(U)*; **prendre des ~s avec qn** to take liberties with sb; *(Littérat)* **~ poétique** poetic licence; **'quexé', ça c'est une ~ orthographique!** 'quexé' is an example of the liberties one can take with spelling.
licencié, e [lisɑ̃sje] **1** *adj:* **professeur ~** graduate teacher; **elle est ~e** she is a graduate.
2 *nm,f* **(a)** *(Scol)* **~ ès lettres/ès sciences/en droit** Bachelor of Arts/of Science/of Law, arts/science/law graduate.
(b) *(Sport)* permit-holder.
licenciement [lisɑ̃simɑ̃] *nm (V* **licencier**) making redundant, redundancy; dismissal. **il y a eu des centaines de ~s** there were hundreds of redundancies; **~ collectif** mass redundancy *ou* redundancies.
licencier [lisɑ̃sje] (7) *vt (débaucher)* to make redundant; *(renvoyer)* to dismiss.
licencieusement [lisɑ̃sjøzmɑ̃] *adv* licentiously.
licencieux, -euse [lisɑ̃sjø, øz] *adj (littér)* licentious.
lichen [likɛn] *nm (Bot, Méd)* lichen.
lichette* [liʃɛt] *nf:* **~ de pain/de fromage** nibble of bread/cheese; **tu en veux une ~?** do you want a nibble?; **il n'en restait qu'une ~** there was only a (tiny) taste left.
licite [lisit] *adj* lawful, licit.
licitement [lisitmɑ̃] *adv* lawfully, licitly.
licol [likɔl] *nm* halter.

licorne [likɔʀn(ə)] *nf* unicorn. ~ de mer narwhal, sea unicorn.
licou [liku] *nm* = **licol.**
licteur [liktœʀ] *nm* lictor.
lie [li] **1** *nf [vin]* dregs, sediment. (*fig*) **la ~ (de la société)** the dregs of society. **2: lie de vin** *adj* wine(-coloured); *V* **boire.**
lié, e [lje] (*ptp de* **lier**) *adj*: **être très ~ avec qn** to be very friendly with sb; **ils sont très ~s** they're very close *ou* friendly, they're very close friends.
Liechtenstein [liʃtɛnʃtajn] *nm* Liechtenstein.
liège [ljɛʒ] *nm* cork. **semelle** *etc* **de ~** cork sole *etc*; *V* **bout.**
liégeois, e [ljeʒwa, waz] **1** *adj* of *ou* from Liège. **café/chocolat ~** coffee/chocolate ice cream with crème Chantilly. **2** *nm,f*: **L~(e)** inhabitant *ou* native of Liège.
lien [ljɛ̃] *nm* **(a)** (*lit, fig: attache*) bond. **le prisonnier se libéra de ses ~s** the prisoner freed himself from his bonds; **de solides ~s de cuir** strong leather straps; (*fig*) **les ~s du serment** the bonds of an oath.
(b) (*corrélation*) link, connection. **il y a un ~ entre les 2 événements** there's a link *ou* connection between the 2 events; **servir de ~ entre 2 personnes** to act as a link between 2 people.
(c) (*relation*) tie. **~s affectifs** emotional ties; **~s de parenté/de sang** family/blood ties; **~s d'amitié** bonds of friendship; **~ qui unit 2 personnes** bond which unites 2 people; **~s du mariage** marriage bonds *ou* ties.
lier [lje] (7) **1** *vt* **(a)** (*attacher*) *mains, pieds* to bind, tie up; *fleurs, bottes de paille* to tie up. **~ la paille en bottes** to bind *ou* tie the straw into bales; **~ qn à un arbre/une chaise** to tie sb to a tree/chair; **~ avec une ficelle** to tie with a piece of string; (*fig*) **~ qn par un serment/une promesse** to bind sb with an oath/a promise; *V* **fou, partie**², **pied.**
(b) (*relier*) *mots, phrases* to link up, join up. **~ la cause à l'effet** to link cause to effect; **tous ces événements sont étroitement liés** all these events are closely linked *ou* connected; **la maison est liée à tout son passé** the house is linked to the whole of his past; **tout est lié** everything links up *ou* ties up; (*Mus*) **~ les notes** to slur the notes.
(c) (*unir*) *personnes* to bind, unite. **l'amitié qui nous lie à lui** the friendship which binds us to him; **l'amitié qui les lie** the friendship which unites them; **un goût/un mépris commun pour le théâtre les liait** they were united by a common liking/scorn for the theatre.
(d) (*Culin*) *sauce* to thicken. (*Constr*) **~ des pierres avec du mortier** to bind stones with mortar.
(e) (*loc*) **~ amitié/conversation** to strike up a friendship/conversation; **~ la langue à qn** to make sb tongue-tied.
2 se lier *vpr* to make friends (*avec qn* with sb). **se ~ d'amitié avec qn** to strike up a friendship with sb; **il ne se lie pas facilement** he doesn't make friends easily; **se ~ par un serment** to bind o.s. by an oath.
lierre [ljɛʀ] *nm* ivy.
liesse [ljɛs] *nf* (*joie*) jubilation. **en ~** jubilant.
lieu, *pl* **~x** [ljø] **1** *nm* **(a)** (*gén: endroit*) place; *[événement]* scene. (*Gram*) **adverbe de ~** adverb of place; **~ de pèlerinage/résidence/retraite/travail** place of pilgrimage/residence/retreat/work; **en quelque ~ qu'il soit** wherever he (may) be, wherever he is; **sur les ~x du crime** at the scene of the crime; **en tous ~x** everywhere; **en aucun ~ (du monde)** nowhere (in the world); **cela varie avec le ~** it varies from place to place; **en ~ sûr** in a safe place; *V* **haut, nom.**
(b) sur les ~x: se rendre sur les ~x du crime to go to the scene of the crime; **être sur les ~x de l'accident** to be at *ou* on the scene of the accident; **notre envoyé est sur les ~x** our special correspondent is on the spot.
(c) (*locaux*) **les ~x** the premises; **quitter** *ou* **vider les ~x** (*Admin*) to vacate the premises; (*) to get out; *V* **état.**
(d) (*avec notion temporelle*) **en premier/second ~** in the first/second place, firstly/secondly; **en dernier ~** lastly; **ce n'est pas le ~ d'en parler** this isn't the place to speak about it; **en son ~** in due course; *V* **temps**¹.
(e) au ~ de qch l instead of sth, in place of sth; tu devrais téléphoner au ~ d'écrire you should telephone instead of writing; **il devrait se réjouir, au ~ de cela, il se plaint** he should be glad, instead of which he complains *ou* (but) instead he complains; **signer en ~ et place de qn** to sign for and on behalf of sb; **au ~ que** instead of + *gerund*.
(f) (*loc*) **avoir ~** (*se produire*) to take place; **avoir ~ d'être inquiet/de se plaindre** to have (good) grounds for being worried/for complaining, have (good) reason to be worried/to complain; **il y a ~ d'être inquiet** there is cause *ou* good reason for anxiety; **vous appellerez le docteur, s'il y a ~** you must send for the doctor if necessary; **donner ~ à des critiques** to give rise to criticism; **ça donne ~ de craindre le pire** that tends to make one fear *ou* leads one to fear the worst; **tenir ~ de** to take the place of; **elle lui a tenu ~ de mère** she took the place of his mother; **ce vieux manteau tient ~ de couverture** this old overcoat serves as a blanket *ou* does instead of a blanket.
2: lieux d'aisances† lavatory; **lieu commun** commonplace; († *ou hum*) **lieu de débauche** den of iniquity; **lieu-dit, lieudit,** *pl* **lieux-dits, lieuxdits** locality; (*Math*) **lieu géométrique** locus; **lieu de naissance** (*gén*) birthplace; (*Admin*) place of birth; **lieu de passage** passing through place; **lieu de promenade** place *ou* spot for walking; **lieu public** public place; **les Lieux saints** the Holy Places; **lieu de vacances** (*gén*) place *ou* spot for (one's) holidays (*Brit*) *ou* vacation (*US*); (*ville*) holiday (*Brit*) *ou* vacation (*US*) resort.
lieue [ljø] *nf* league. **j'étais à mille ~s de penser à vous** I was far from thinking of you, you were far from my mind; **j'étais à mille ~s de penser qu'il viendrait** it never occurred to me *ou* I never dreamt for a moment that he'd come; **j'étais à cent ~s de supposer cela** that never occurred to me; **il sent son lexicographe d'une ~** the fact that he's a lexicographer sticks out a mile; **à 20 ~s à la ronde** for 20 leagues round about.
lieuse [ljøz] *nf* (*Agr*) binder; *V* **moissonneur.**
lieutenant [ljøtnɑ̃] **1** *nm* (*armée de terre*) lieutenant; (*armée de l'air*) flying officer; (*marine marchande*) mate; (*gén: second*) lieutenant, second in command.
2: lieutenant-colonel *nm, pl* **lieutenants-colonels** (*armée de terre*) lieutenant colonel; (*armée de l'air*) wing commander; **lieutenant de vaisseau** (*marine nationale*) lieutenant.
lièvre [ljɛvʀ(ə)] *nm* (*Zool*) hare; (*Sport*) pacemaker; *V* **lever.**
liftier [liftje] *nm* lift boy (*Brit*), elevator boy (*US*).
ligament [ligamɑ̃] *nm* ligament.
ligamenteux, -euse [ligamɑ̃tø, øz] *adj* ligamentous, ligamentary.
ligature [ligatyʀ] *nf* **(a)** (*Méd: opération, lien*) ligature. **(b)** (*Agr*) (*opération*) tying up; (*lien*) tie. **(c)** (*Typ*) ligature. **(d)** (*Mus*) ligature, tie.
ligaturer [ligatyʀe] (1) *vt* (*Méd*) to ligature, tie up; (*Agr*) to tie up.
lige [liʒ] *adj* liege. **homme ~** (*Hist*) liegeman; (*fig*) **être l'homme ~ de qn** to be sb's faithful henchman.
lignage [liɲaʒ] *nm* **(a)** lineage. **de haut ~** of noble lineage. **(b)** (*Typ*) number of printed lines.
ligne¹ [liɲ] **1** *nf* **(a)** (*trait, limite*) line; (*Mil*) line. **~ droite/brisée** straight/broken *ou* dotted line; **~ de départ/d'arrivée/de partage** starting/finishing/dividing line; **~ de fortifications** line of fortifications; **~ de tranchées** trench line; **les ~s de la main** the lines of the hand; **~ de vie/de cœur** life/love line; **la ~ des collines dans le lointain** the line of hills in the distance; (*Math*) **la ~ des x/des y** the X/Y axis; (*Math*) **la ~ des abscisses** the abscissa; (*Math*) **la ~ des ordonnées** the ordinate axis; **passer la ~ (de l'équateur)** to cross the line; **courir en ~ droite** to run in a straight line; **en ~ droite, la ville est à 10 km** the town is 10 km from here as the crow flies; (*Aut*) **~ droite** stretch of straight road; **les ~s droites** the straight (*U*).
(b) (*contour*) *[meuble, voiture]* line(s); (*silhouette*) *[femme]* figure. **avoir la ~** to have a good figure; **garder/perdre la ~** to keep/lose one's figure; **la ~ lancée par la dernière mode** the look launched by the most recent collections; **voiture aux ~s aérodynamiques** streamlined car, car built on aerodynamic lines.
(c) (*règle*) line. **~ de conduite/d'action** line of conduct/of action; **une bonne ~ de politique** a good line of action; **la ~ du devoir** the path of duty; **la ~ du parti** the party line; **ne pas dévier de la ~ droite** to keep to the straight and narrow; **les grandes ~s d'un programme** the broad lines *ou* outline of a programme.
(d) (*suite de personnes, de choses*) line; (*rangée*) row. (*Sport*) **la ~ d'avants** *ou* **des avants/d'arrières** *ou* **des arrières** (*Rugby*) the front/back row; (*Ftbl*) the forwards/backs; **enfants placés en ~** children in a line *ou* lined up; **coureurs en ~ pour le départ** runners lined up for the start; **une ~ d'arbres le long de l'horizon** a line *ou* row of trees on the horizon; **mettre des personnes en ~** to line people up, get people lined up; **se mettre en ~** to line up, get lined up, get into line.
(e) (*Rail*) line. (*Aut*) **~ d'autobus** (*service*) bus service; (*parcours*) bus route; (*Aviat, Naut*) **~ d'aviation** *ou* **aérienne/de navigation** (*compagnie*) air/shipping line; (*service*) (air/shipping) service; (*trajet*) (air/shipping) route; **~ de chemin de fer/de métro** railway/underground line; **la ~ d'autobus passe dans notre rue** the bus (route) goes along our street; **~ secondaire** branch line; **~ de banlieue** suburban line; *V* **avion, grand, pilote.**
(f) (*Élec, Téléc*) (*gén*) line; (*câbles*) wires; (*TV: définition*) line. **la ~ est occupée** the line is engaged (*Brit*) *ou* busy (*US*); **être en ~** to be connected; **vous êtes en ~** you're connected *ou* through now; **M X est en ~** Mr X's line is engaged (*Brit*) *ou* busy (*US*); **la ~ passe dans notre jardin** the wires go through our garden.
(g) *[texte écrit]* line. (*dictée*) **'à la ~'** 'new paragraph', 'new line'; **aller à la ~** to start on the next line, begin a new paragraph; **écrire quelques ~s** to write a few lines; **donner 100 ~s à faire à un élève** to give a pupil 100 lines to do; (*Presse*) **tirer à la ~** to pad out an article.
(h) (*Pêche*) fishing line; *V* **pêche**².
(i) (*série de générations*) **~ directe/collatérale** direct/collateral line.
(j) (*loc*) **mettre sur la même ~** to put on the same level; **entrer en ~ de compte** to be taken into account; **mettre** *ou* **faire entrer en ~ de compte** to take into account *ou* consideration; **votre vie privée n'entre pas en ~ de compte** your private life doesn't come *ou* enter into it; **sur toute la ~** all along the line.
2: (*Sport*) **ligne de but** goal line; **ligne de crête = ligne de faîte; ligne de démarcation** (*gén*) boundary; (*Mil*) line of demarcation, demarcation line; **ligne directrice** directrix; (*Géol*) **ligne de faille** fault line; (*Géog*) **ligne de faîte** watershed; **ligne de feu** line of fire; **ligne de flottaison** water line; **ligne de flottaison en charge** load line; (*Pêche*) **ligne de fond** ledger line; **lignes de force** (*Phys*) lines of force; (*fig*) *[discours, politique]* main themes; **ligne à haute tension** high tension line; **ligne d'horizon** skyline; (*Sport*) **ligne médiane** halfway line; **ligne de mire** line of sight; **ligne de partage des eaux** watershed; **ligne de tir = ligne de feu;** (*Sport*) **ligne de touche** touchline; **ligne de visée** line of sight.
ligne² [liɲ] *nf* (*Can*) line (*3,175 mm*).
lignée [liɲe] *nf* (*postérité*) descendants (*pl*); (*race, famille*) line, lineage. **laisser une nombreuse ~** to leave a lot of descendants; **le dernier d'une longue ~** the last (one) of a long line; **de bonne ~ irlandaise** of good Irish stock *ou* lineage; (*fig*) **la ~ des grands romanciers** the tradition of the great novelists.

ligneux, -euse [liɲø, øz] *adj* woody, ligneous.
lignite [liɲit] *nm* lignite, brown coal.
ligoter [ligɔte] (1) *vt personne* to bind hand and foot. ~ **à un arbre** to tie to a tree.
ligue [lig] *nf* league.
liguer [lige] (1) **1** *vt* to unite (*contre* against). **être ligué avec** to be in league with.
2 se liguer *vpr* to league, form a league (*contre* against). **tout se ligue contre moi** everything is in league *ou* is conspiring against me.
ligueur, -euse [ligœʀ, øz] *nm,f* member of a league.
lilas [lilɑ] *nm, adj inv* lilac.
lilliputien, -ienne [lilipysjɛ̃, jɛn] **1** *adj* Lilliputian. **2** *nm,f*: **L~(ne)** Lilliputian.
lillois, e [lilwa, waz] **1** *adj* of *ou* from Lille. **2** *nm,f*: **L~(e)** inhabitant *ou* native of Lille.
limace [limas] *nf* (*Zool*) slug; (*: *chemise*) shirt. (*fig*) **quelle ~!** (*personne*) what a sluggard! *ou* slowcoach! (*Brit*); (*train etc*) this train is just crawling along!, what a dreadfully slow train!
limaçon [limasɔ̃] *nm* (††) snail; (*Anat*) cochlea.
limage [limaʒ] *nm* (*V* **limer**) filing down; filing off.
limaille [limɑj] *nf* filings (*pl*). ~ **de fer** iron filings.
limande [limɑ̃d] *nf* (*poisson*) dab. ~**-sole** lemon sole; *V* **plat**¹.
limbe [lɛ̃b] *nm* **(a)** (*Astron, Bot, Math*) limb. **(b)** (*Rel*) **les ~s** limbo; **dans les ~s** (*Rel*) in limbo; (*fig*) *[projet, science]* **c'est encore dans les ~s** it is still in the air.
lime [lim] *nf* **(a)** (*Tech*) file. ~ **douce** smooth file; ~ **à ongles** nail file. **(b)** (*Zool*) lima. **(c)** (*Bot*) (*fruit*) lime; (*arbre*) lime (tree).
limer [lime] (1) *vt ongles* to file; *métal* to file (down); *aspérité* to file off. **le prisonnier avait limé un barreau pour s'échapper** the prisoner had filed through a bar to escape.
limier [limje] *nm* (*Zool*) bloodhound; (*fig*) sleuth. **c'est un fin ~** he's a really good sleuth.
liminaire [liminɛʀ] *adj discours, note* introductory.
limitable [limitabl(ə)] *adj* capable of being limited (*attrib*).
limitatif, -ive [limitatif, iv] *adj* limiting, restricting.
limitation [limitɑsjɔ̃] *nf* limitation, restriction. ~ **des prix/des naissances** price/birth control; **un accord sur la ~ des armements** an agreement on arms limitation; **sans ~ de temps** without a *ou* with no time limit; (*Aut*) **une ~ de vitesse (à 60 km/h)** a (60 km/h) speed limit; **l'introduction de ~s de vitesse** the introduction of speed restrictions *ou* limits.
limite [limit] **1** *nf* **(a)** *[pays, jardin]* boundary; *[pouvoir, période]* limit. ~ **d'âge/de poids** age/weight limit; **sans ~** boundless, limitless; **homme qui connaît ses ~s** man who knows his limits; **ma patience a des ~s!** there's a limit to my patience!; **la bêtise a des ~s!** foolishness has its limits!; **sa joie ne connaissait pas de ~s** his joy knew no bounds; **sa colère ne connaît pas de ~s** his anger knows no limits; **ce crime atteint les ~s de l'horreur** this crime is too horrible to imagine; **il franchit** *ou* **dépasse les ~s!** he's going a bit too far!
(b) (*Math*) limit.
(c) (*loc*) **à la ~: à la ~ on croirait qu'il le fait exprès** you'd almost think he is doing it on purpose; **à la ~, j'accepterais ces conditions, mais pas plus** if pushed, I'd accept those conditions, but no more; **à la ~ tout roman est réaliste** at a pinch any novel could be said to be realistic; **dans une certaine ~** up to a point, to a certain extent *ou* degree; **dans les ~s du possible/du sujet** within the limits of what is possible/of the subject; **dans les ~s de mes moyens** (*aptitude*) within (the limits of) my capabilities; (*argent*) within my means; **jusqu'à la dernière ~** *rester, résister* till the end; *se battre* to the death; **jusqu'à la ~ de ses forces** to the point of exhaustion, until his strength is (*ou* was *etc*) exhausted; (*Boxe*) **avant la ~** inside *ou* within the distance; (*Boxe*) **aller** *ou* **tenir jusqu'à la ~** to go the distance.
2 *adj*: **cas ~** borderline case; **prix ~** upper price limit; **valeur ~** limiting value; **vitesse/âge ~** maximum speed/age; **date ~** (*pour s'inscrire*) deadline, closing date; (*pour finir*) deadline; **hauteur/longueur/charge ~** maximum height/length/load.
3: **limite d'élasticité** elastic limit; **limite de rupture** breaking point.
limité, e [limite] (*ptp de* **limiter**) *adj durée, choix, portée* limited; *nombre* limited, restricted. **je n'ai qu'une confiance ~e en ce remède** I've got limited confidence in this cure; *V* **société, tirage.**
limiter [limite] (1) **1** *vt* **(a)** (*restreindre*) *dépenses, pouvoirs, temps* to limit, restrict. ~ **les dégâts*: ils en étaient à s'arracher les cheveux quand je suis intervenu pour ~ les dégâts** they were practically tearing each other's hair out when I intervened before things got even worse *ou* to stop things getting any worse; **ils ont dû liquider leur affaire pour ~ les dégâts** they had to sell up the business to cut *ou* minimize their losses; **l'équipe du Brésil menait par 5 à 0 — heureusement on a réussi à ~ les dégâts en marquant 3 buts à la fin du match** the Brazilian team was leading by 5 to nil but fortunately we managed to avert disaster by scoring 3 goals at the end of the match; **nous limiterons notre étude à quelques cas généraux** we'll limit *ou* restrict our study to a few general cases.
(b) (*délimiter*) *[frontière, montagnes]* to border. **les collines qui limitent l'horizon** the hills which bound the horizon.
2 se limiter *vpr [personne]* **se ~ (à qch/à faire)** to limit *ou* confine o.s. (to sth/to doing); *[chose]* **se ~ à** to be limited to.
limitrophe [limitʀɔf] *adj département, population* border (*épith*). **provinces ~s de la France** (*françaises*) border provinces of France; (*étrangères*) provinces bordering on France.
limogeage [limɔʒaʒ] *nm* dismissal.
limoger [limɔʒe] (3) *vt* (*destituer*) to dismiss, fire*.
limon [limɔ̃] *nm* **(a)** (*Géog*) alluvium; (*gén*) silt. **(b)** *[attelage]* shaft; (*Constr*) string-board.
limonade [limɔnad] *nf* **(a)** (*gazeuse*) (fizzy) lemonade. **(b)** (†: *citronnade*) (home-made) lemonade *ou* lemon drink.
limonadier, -ière [limɔnadje, jɛʀ] *nm,f* **(a)** soft drinks manufacturer. **(b)** café owner.
limoneux, -euse [limɔnø, øz] *adj* silt-laden, muddy.
limousin, e¹ [limuzɛ̃, in] **1** *adj* of *ou* from Limousin. **2** *nm* **(a)** (*Ling*) Limousin dialect. **(b)** (*région*) Limousin. **3** *nm,f*: **L~(e)** inhabitant *ou* native of Limousin.
limousine² [limuzin] *nf* (*pèlerine*) cloak; (†: *voiture*) limousine.
limpide [lɛ̃pid] *adj eau, air, ciel, regard* limpid; *explication* lucid; *style* lucid, limpid.
limpidité [lɛ̃pidite] *nf [eau, air, ciel]* clearness; *[regard]* limpidity; *[explication]* clarity, lucidity; *[style]* lucidity, limpidity.
lin [lɛ̃] *nm* flax; *V* **huile, toile.**
linceul [lɛ̃sœl] *nm* (*lit, fig*) shroud.
linéaire [lineɛʀ] *adj* linear.
linéament [lineamɑ̃] *nm* (*littér, gén pl*) **(a)** (*ligne*) *[visage]* lineament, feature; *[forme]* line, outline. **(b)** (*ébauche*) outline.
linge [lɛ̃ʒ] **1** *nm* **(a) le ~, du ~** (*draps, serviettes*) linen; (*sous-vêtements*) underwear; **le gros ~** the household linen, the main items of linen; **le petit ~** the small *ou* light items for washing, the small items of linen.
(b) (*lessive*) **le ~** the washing; **laver/tendre le** *ou* **son ~** to wash/hang out the *ou* one's washing.
(c) (*morceau de tissu*) cloth. **essuyer avec un ~** to wipe with a cloth; **blanc** *ou* **pâle comme un ~** as white as a sheet.
2: (*Rel*) **linges d'autel** altar cloths; **linge de corps** body linen; **linge de maison** household linen; **linge de table** table linen; **linge de toilette** towel.
lingère [lɛ̃ʒɛʀ] *nf* (*personne*) linen maid; (*meuble*) linen cupboard.
lingerie [lɛ̃ʒʀi] *nf* **(a)** (*local*) linen room. **(b)** (*sous-vêtements féminins*) lingerie, underwear. **rayon ~** lingerie department.
lingot [lɛ̃go] *nm* ingot. ~ **d'or** gold ingot.
lingual, e, *pl* **-aux** [lɛ̃gwal, o] *adj* lingual.
linguiste [lɛ̃gɥist(ə)] *nmf* linguist, specialist in linguistics.
linguistique [lɛ̃gɥistik] **1** *nf* linguistics (*sg*). **2** *adj* linguistic.
linguistiquement [lɛ̃gɥistikmɑ̃] *adv* linguistically.
liniment [linimɑ̃] *nm* liniment.
lino [lino] *nm* (*abrév de* **linoléum**) lino.
linoléum [linɔleɔm] *nm* linoleum.
linon [linɔ̃] *nm* lawn (*fabric*).
linotte [linɔt] *nf* linnet; *V* **tête.**
Linotype [linɔtip] *nf* Linotype ®.
linteau, *pl* **~x** [lɛ̃to] *nm* lintel.
lion [ljɔ̃] *nm* (*Zool, fig*) lion. (*Astron*) **le L~** Leo, the Lion; **être (du) L~** to be Leo; ~ **de mer** sea lion; *V* **fosse, part.**
lionceau, *pl* **~x** [ljɔ̃so] *nm* lion cub.
lionne [ljɔn] *nf* lioness.
lipide [lipid] *nm* lipid.
lippe [lip] *nf* (*littér*) (fleshy) lower lip. **faire la ~** (*bouder*) to sulk; (*faire la moue*) to pout; (*faire la grimace*) to make *ou* pull a face.
lippu, e [lipy] *adj* thick-lipped.
liquéfaction [likefaksjɔ̃] *nf* liquefaction.
liquéfiable [likefjabl(ə)] *adj* liquefiable.
liquéfiant, e [likefjɑ̃, ɑ̃t] *adj* liquefying.
liquéfier [likefje] (7) **1** *vt* to liquefy. **2 se liquéfier** *vpr* (*lit*) to liquefy; (*fig*) (*avoir peur*) to turn to a jelly; (*se dégonfler*) to wilt.
liquette* [likɛt] *nf* shirt.
liqueur [likœʀ] *nf* (*boisson*) liqueur; (††: *liquide*) liquid. (*Méd*) ~ **titrée/de Fehling** standard/Fehling's solution.
liquidateur, -trice [likidatœʀ, tʀis] *nm,f* (*Jur*) liquidator. ~ **judiciaire** ≃ official liquidator.
liquidation [likidɑsjɔ̃] *nf* **(a)** (*règlement légal*) *[dettes, compte]* settlement, payment; *[société]* liquidation; *[biens, stock]* selling off, liquidation; *[succession]* settlement; (*fig*) *[problème]* elimination; (*fig*) *[compte]* settling. ~ **judiciaire** compulsory liquidation; **mettre une compagnie en ~** to put a company into liquidation, liquidate a company; **la ~ de vos impôts doit se faire avant la fin de l'année** your taxes must be paid before the end of the year; **afin de procéder à la ~ de la retraite de votre défunt mari** in order to complete the payment of your late husband's pension; *V* **bilan.**
(b) (*vente*) selling (off), sale.
(c) (*: *meurtre*) liquidation, elimination.
(d) (*Bourse*) ~ **de fin de mois** (monthly) settlement.
liquide [likid] **1** *adj corps, son* liquid. **sauce trop ~** sauce which is too runny *ou* too thin; **argent ~** liquid money.
2 *nm* **(a)** (*substance*) liquid.
(b) (*argent*) **du ~** liquid funds *ou* assets; **je n'ai pas beaucoup de ~** I haven't much ready money *ou* ready cash.
3 *nf* (*Ling*) liquid.
liquider [likide] (1) *vt* **(a)** (*Jur: régler légalement*) *succession, dettes, compte* to settle, pay; *société* to liquidate; *biens, stock* to liquidate, sell off; (*fig*) *problème* to eliminate; (*fig*) *compte* to settle.
(b) (*vendre*) to sell (off).
(c) (*) (*tuer*) to liquidate, eliminate; (*se débarrasser de*) to get rid of; (*finir*) to finish off. **c'est liquidé maintenant** it is all finished *ou* over now.
liquidité [likidite] *nf* (*Chim, Jur*) liquidity. **~s** liquid assets.
liquoreux, -euse [likɔʀø, øz] *adj vin* syrupy, sweet and cloying.
lire¹ [liʀ] (43) *vt* **(a)** *roman, journal, partition, carte géographique* to read. **à 5 ans, il ne lit pas encore** *ou* **il ne sait pas encore ~** he's 5 and he still can't read; **~ ses notes avant un cours** to read over *ou* read through *ou* go over one's notes before a lecture; **~ un discours/un rapport devant une assemblée** to read (out) a speech/a report at a meeting; **il l'a lu**

dans le journal he read (about) it in the paper; **chaque soir, elle lit des histoires à ses enfants** every night she reads stories to her children; **à le ~, on croirait que ...** from what he writes *ou* from reading what he writes one would think that ...; **ce roman se lit bien** *ou* **se laisse ~** this novel is very readable; **ce roman se lit très vite** this novel makes quick reading; **ce roman mérite d'être lu** *ou* **est à ~** this novel is worth reading; **elle a continué à ~ malgré le bruit** she continued to read *ou* she went on reading despite the noise; (*fig*) **~ entre les lignes** to read between the lines; **lu et approuvé** read and approved.

(b) (*fig: deviner*) to read. **~ dans le cœur de qn** to see into sb's heart; **la peur se lisait** *ou* **on lisait la peur sur son visage/dans ses yeux** you could see *ou* read fear in her face/eyes, fear showed on her face/in her eyes; **~ l'avenir dans les lignes de la main de qn** to read the future in sb's hand; **~ l'avenir dans le marc de café** ≃ to read (the future in) tea leaves; **elle m'a lu les lignes de la main** she read my hand; **~ dans le jeu de qn** to see sb's (little) game, see what sb is up to*.

(c) (*formule de lettre*) **nous espérons vous ~ bientôt** we hope to hear from you soon; **à bientôt de vous ~** hoping to hear from you soon.

lire[2] [liR] *nf* lira.

lis [lis] *nm* lily; *V* **fleur.**

Lisbonne [lisbɔn] *n* Lisbon.

liseré [lizRe] *nm*, **liséré** [lizeRe] *nm* (*ruban*) border, edging; (*bande, fig*) strip.

lisérer [lizeRe] (6) *vt* to edge with ribbon.

liseron [lizRɔ̃] *nm* bindweed, convolvulus.

liseur, -euse [lizœR, øz] **1** *nm,f* reader. **2: liseuse** *nf* (*couvre-livre*) binder, folder, book-cover; (*vêtement*) bed jacket; (*signet*) paper knife(-cum-bookmark).

lisibilité [lizibilite] *nf* legibility.

lisible [lizibl(ə)] *adj écriture* legible; *livre* (*facile*) which reads easily, readable; (*intéressant*) worth reading.

lisiblement [lizibləmɑ̃] *adv* legibly.

lisière [lizjɛR] *nf* (*Tex*) selvage; *[bois, village]* edge.

lisse[1] [lis] *adj peau, surface* smooth; *cheveux* sleek, smooth.

lisse[2] [lis] *nf* (*Naut*) (*rambarde*) handrail; (*de la coque*) ribband.

lisser [lise] (1) *vt cheveux* to smooth (down); *moustache* to smooth, stroke; *papier, drap froissé* to smooth out; *vêtement* to smooth (out). **l'oiseau lisse ses plumes** *ou* **se lisse les plumes** the bird is preening itself *ou* its feathers.

liste [list(ə)] **1** *nf* list. **en tête/en fin de ~** at the top *ou* head/at the bottom *ou* foot of the list; **faire la ~ de** to make out a list of, list; **s'il fallait faire la ~ de tous ses défauts!** if one had to list *ou* make out a list of all his faults!; **faites-moi la ~ des absents** make me out a list of those absent; *V* **scrutin.**

2: liste civile civil list; **liste électorale** electoral roll; **liste noire** blacklist.

listel, *pl* **~s** *ou* **~eaux** [listɛl, o] *nm* (*Archit*) listel, fillet; *[monnaie]* rim.

lit [li] **1** *nm* **(a)** *[personne, rivière]* bed. **~ d'une/de deux personne(s)** single/double bed; **~ de fer/de bois** iron/wooden bedstead; **les ~s d'hôpital/d'hôtel sont souvent durs** hospital/hotel beds are often hard; **aller** *ou* **se mettre au ~** to go to bed; **prendre le ~** to take to one's bed; **être/lire au ~** to be/read in bed; **faire le ~** to make the bed; **faire ~ à part** to sleep in separate beds; **le ~ n'avait pas été défait** the bed had not been slept in; **au ~ les enfants!** bedtime *ou* off to bed children!; **arracher** *ou* **sortir** *ou* **tirer qn du ~** to drag *ou* haul sb out of bed; (*littér*, †) **sur son ~ de misère** in childbed††; **les pluies ont fait sortir le fleuve de son ~** the river has burst *ou* overflowed its banks because of the rains; *V* **jumeau, saut** *etc.*

(b) (*couche, épaisseur*) bed, layer. **~ d'argile** bed *ou* layer of clay; **~ de cendres** *ou* **de braises** bed of hot ashes.

(c) (*Jur: mariage*) **enfants du premier/deuxième ~** children of the first/second marriage; **enfants d'un autre ~** children of a previous marriage.

2: lit à baldaquin canopied fourposter bed; **lit-cage** *nm,pl* **lits-cages** (folding metal) cot; **lit de camp** campbed; **lit-clos** *nm, pl* **lits-clos** box bed; **lit de coin** bed (standing) against the wall; **lit à colonnes** fourposter bed; **lit de douleur** bed of pain; **lit d'enfant** cot; **lit gigogne** pullout *ou* stowaway bed; **lit de milieu** bed (standing) away from the wall *ou* in the middle of a room; **lit de mort** deathbed; **lit de noces** wedding-bed; **lit-pliant** *nm, pl* **lits-pliants** folding bed; **lit en portefeuille** apple pie bed; **lit de repos** couch; **lit de sangle** trestle bed; (*Naut*) **le lit du vent** the set of the wind.

litanie [litani] *nf* (*Rel, fig péj*) litany.

litchi [litʃi] *nm* litchi.

litée [lite] *nf* (*jeunes animaux*) litter.

literie [litRi] *nf* bedding.

lithiné, e [litine] **1** *adj*: **eau ~e** lithia water. **2** *nmpl*: **~s** lithium salts.

lithographe [litɔgRaf] *nmf* lithographer.

lithographie [litɔgRafi] *nf* (*technique*) lithography; (*image*) lithograph.

lithographier [litɔgRafje] (7) *vt* to lithograph.

lithographique [litɔgRafik] *adj* lithographic.

lithosphère [litɔsfɛR] *nf* lithosphere.

litière [litjɛR] *nf* (*couche de paille*) litter (*U*); (*Hist: palanquin*) litter. **il s'était fait une ~ avec de la paille** he had made himself a bed of sorts in some straw.

litige [litiʒ] *nm* (*gén*) dispute; (*Jur*) lawsuit. **être en ~** (*gén*) to be in dispute; (*Jur*) to be at law *ou* in litigation; **point/objet de ~** point/object of contention.

litigieux, -ieuse [litiʒjø, jøz] *adj* litigious, contentious.

litote [litɔt] *nf* (*Littérat*) litotes. (*hum*) **quand je dis pas très belle, c'est une ~** when I say it's not very beautiful, I'm not exaggerating *ou* that's putting it mildly.

litre [litR(ə)] *nm* (*mesure*) litre; (*récipient*) litre bottle.

litron* [litRɔ̃] *nm*: **~ (de vin)** litre of wine.

littéraire [liteRɛR] **1** *adj* (*gén*) literary; *personne, esprit* with a literary bent; *souffrance, passion* affected.

2 *nmf* (*par don, goût*) literary *ou* arts person; (*étudiant*) arts student; (*enseignant*) arts teacher, teacher of arts subjects.

littérairement [liteRɛRmɑ̃] *adv* in literary terms.

littéral, e, *mpl* **-aux** [liteRal, o] *adj* (*littér, Math*) literal.

littéralement [liteRalmɑ̃] *adv* (*lit, fig*) literally.

littérateur [liteRatœR] *nm* (*péj: écrivain*) literary hack.

littérature [liteRatyR] *nf* **(a) la ~** (*art*) literature; (*profession*) writing; **faire de la ~** to go in for writing, write; (*péj*) **tout cela, c'est de la ~** it's of trifling importance; **écrire de la ~ alimentaire** to write potboilers; **~ de colportage** chapbooks.

(b) (*rare: manuel*) history of literature; (*ensemble d'ouvrages*) literature; (*bibliographie*) literature. **il existe une abondante ~ sur ce sujet** there's a wealth of literature *ou* material on this subject.

littoral, e, *mpl* **-aux** [litɔRal, o] **1** *adj* coastal, littoral (*T*); *V* **cordon. 2** *nm* coast, littoral (*T*).

Lituanie [litɥani] *nf* Lithuania.

lituanien, -ienne [litɥanjɛ̃, jɛn] **1** *adj* Lithuanian. **2** *nm* (*Ling*) Lithuanian. **3** *nm,f*: **L~(ne)** Lithuanian.

liturgie [lityRʒi] *nf* liturgy.

liturgique [lityRʒik] *adj* liturgical.

livide [livid] *adj* (*pâle*) pallid; (*littér: bleuâtre*) livid.

lividité [lividite] *nf* lividness.

living [liviŋ] *nm*, **living-room**, *pl* **living-rooms** [liviŋRum] *nm* living room.

livrable [livRabl(ə)] *adj* which can be delivered. **cet article est ~ dans les 10 jours/à domicile** this article will be delivered within 10 days/can be delivered to your home.

livraison [livRɛzɔ̃] *nf* **(a)** *[marchandise]* delivery. (*avis*) **'~ à domicile'** 'we deliver', 'deliveries carried out'; **payable à la ~** payable on delivery; **la ~ à domicile est comprise dans le prix** the price includes (the cost of) delivery.

(b) *[revue]* part, number, issue, fascicule.

livre[1] [livR(ə)] **1** *nm* **(a)** (*ouvrage*) book. (*commerce*) **le ~** the book trade (*Brit*), the book industry; **~ de géographie** geography book; **il a toujours le nez dans les ~s, il vit dans les ~s** he's always got his nose in a book; **écrire/faire un ~ sur** to write/do a book on; **traduire l'anglais à ~ ouvert** to translate English off the cuff *ou* at sight; *V* **grand.**

(b) (*partie: volume*) book. **le ~ 2** *ou* **le second ~ de la Genèse** book 2 of Genesis, the second book of Genesis.

2: livre blanc white paper; (*Naut*) **livre de bord** logbook; (*Comm*) **livre de caisse** cashbook; **livre de chevet** bedside book; **livre de classe** schoolbook; (*Comm*) **les livres de commerce** the books; **livre de comptes** account(s) book; **livre de cuisine** cookery book (*Brit*), cookbook; **livre d'enfant** children's book; **livre d'heures** book of hours; **livre d'images** picture book; (*Comm*) **livre journal** daybook; **livre de lecture** reader, reading book; **livre de messe** mass book; **livre d'or** visitors' book; **livre de poche** paperback; **livre de prières** prayer book; **livre scolaire** schoolbook; **livre à succès** bestseller.

livre[2] [livR(ə)] *nf* **(a)** (*poids*) ≃ pound, half a kilo; (*Can*) pound (*0,453 kg*).

(b) (*monnaie*) pound; (*Hist française*) livre. **~ sterling** pound sterling; **~ australienne/égyptienne** Australian/Egyptian pound; **ce chapeau coûte 6 ~s** this hat costs £6.

livrée [livRe] *nf* (*uniforme*) livery.

livrer [livRe] (1) **1** *vt* **(a)** (*Comm*) *commande, marchandises* to deliver. **~ un paquet à domicile** to deliver a packet to the home.

(b) (*abandonner*) (*à la police, à l'ennemi*) to hand over (*à* to). **~ qn à la mort** to send sb to his death; **~ qn au bourreau** to deliver sb up *ou* hand sb over to the executioner; **ce pays a été livré au pillage/à l'anarchie** this country was given over to pillage/to anarchy; **~ son âme au diable** to give one's soul to the devil; **se ~ à la police** to give o.s. up to the police; **elle s'est livrée à son amant** she gave herself to her lover; **être livré à soi-même** to be left to o.s. *ou* to one's own devices.

(c) (*confier*) **~ les secrets de son cœur** to give away the secrets of one's heart; **il m'a livré un peu de lui-même** he revealed a bit of himself to me; **se ~ à un ami** to bare one's heart to a friend; **il ne se livre pas facilement** he doesn't unburden himself easily *ou* open up easily.

(d) (*loc*) **~ bataille** to give battle (*à* to); **~ passage à qn** to let sb pass.

2 se livrer *vpr* **(a)** (*se laisser aller à*) **se ~ à** *destin* to abandon o.s. to; *plaisir, excès, douleur* to give o.s. over to; **se ~ à des pratiques répréhensibles** to indulge in undesirable practices.

(b) (*se consacrer à*) **se ~ à** *sport* to practise; *occupation* to be engaged in; *recherches* to do, engage in; *enquête* to hold, set up; **se ~ à l'étude** to study, devote o.s. to study.

livresque [livRɛsk(ə)] *adj* (*gén péj*) bookish.

livret [livRɛ] **1** *nm* **(a)** (*Mus*) libretto. **(b)** (†: *petit livre*) booklet; (*catalogue*) catalogue. **~ de caisse d'épargne** (savings) bank-book; **~ de famille** (official) family record book (*containing registration of births and deaths in a family*); **~ militaire** military record; **~ scolaire** (school) report book. **2:** (*Mil*) **livret matricule** army file.

livreur [livRœR] *nm* delivery man.

livreuse [livRøz] *nf* delivery girl.

lob [lɔb] *nm* (*Tennis*) lob.

lobe [lɔb] *nm* **(a)** (*Anat, Bot*) lobe. **~ de l'oreille** ear lobe. **(b)** (*Archit*) foil.

lobé, e [lɔbe] **1** *ptp de* **lober. 2** *adj* (*Bot*) lobed; (*Archit*) foiled.

lober [lɔbe] (1) **1** *vi* (*Tennis*) to lob. **2** *vt* (*Ftbl, Tennis*) to lob (over).

lobotomie [lɔbɔtɔmi] *nf* lobotomy.

local, e, *mpl* **-aux** [lɔkal, o] **1** *adj* local. **éclaircies ~es** bright spells in places; **averses ~es** scattered *ou* local showers, rain in places; *V* **couleur.**

2 *nm* **(a)** (*salle*) premises. **~ à usage commercial** shop *ou* commercial premises; **~ d'habitation** domestic premises, dwelling house; **le club cherche un ~** the club is looking for premises *ou* a place in which to meet; **il a un ~ au fond de la cour qui lui sert d'atelier** he has got a place *ou* room at the far end of the yard which he uses as a workshop.

(b) (*bureaux*) **~aux** offices, premises; **dans les ~aux de la police** in the police offices *ou* station; **les ~aux de la compagnie sont au 2e étage** the company's offices *ou* premises are on the 2nd floor.

localement [lɔkalmɑ̃] *adv* (*ici*) locally; (*par endroits*) in places.

localisable [lɔkalizabl(ə)] *adj* localizable.

localisation [lɔkalizɑsjɔ̃] *nf* localization. **~s graisseuses** fatty patches *ou* areas.

localiser [lɔkalize] (1) *vt* (*gén*) to localize; *épidémie, incendie* to confine. **l'épidémie s'est localisée dans cette région** the epidemic was confined to this district.

localité [lɔkalite] *nf* locality.

locataire [lɔkatɛʀ] *nmf [appartement]* tenant; *[chambre]* lodger. **les ~s de mon terrain** the people who rent land from me, the tenants of my land; **avoir/prendre des ~s** to have/take in lodgers.

locatif, -ive [lɔkatif, iv] **1** *adj* **(a) local à usage ~** premises for letting; **risques ~s** tenant's risks; **réparations ~ives** repairs incumbent upon the tenant; **valeur ~ive** rental value.

(b) (*Gram*) **préposition ~ive** preposition of place.

2 *nm* (*Gram*) locative (case).

location [lɔkɑsjɔ̃] **1** *nf* **(a)** (*par le locataire*) *[maison, terrain]* renting; *[voiture]* hiring. **prendre en ~** *maison* to rent; *bateau* to hire; **c'est pour un achat ou pour une ~?** is it to buy or to rent?

(b) (*par le propriétaire*) *[maison, terrain]* renting (out), letting; *[voiture]* hiring (out). **donner en ~** *maison* to rent out, let; *véhicule* to hire out; **~ de voitures** (*écriteau*) 'cars for hire'; (*métier*) car rental, car hiring; **c'est pour une vente ou pour une ~?** is it to sell or to let?

(c) (*bail*) lease. **contrat de ~** lease.

(d) (*maison*) **il a 3 ~s dans la région** he has got 3 properties (for letting) in the nearby region; **il a pris une ~ pour un mois au bord de la mer** he has taken *ou* rented a house by the sea for a month.

(e) (*réservation*) **bureau de ~** (advance) booking office; (*Théât*) booking office.

2: location-vente *nf* hire purchase; **acheter un appartement en location-vente** to buy a flat on instalments.

loch [lɔk] *nm* (*Naut*) log.

loche [lɔʃ] *nf* (*poisson*) loach; (*limace*) grey slug.

lock-out [lɔkawt] *nm inv* lockout.

lock-outer [lɔkawte] (1) *vt* to lock out.

locomoteur, -trice[1] [lɔkɔmɔtœʀ, tʀis] *adj* locomotive. **ataxie ~trice** locomotor ataxia.

locomotion [lɔkɔmosjɔ̃] *nf* locomotion; *V* **moyen.**

locomotive [lɔkɔmɔtiv] *nf* (*Rail*) locomotive, engine; (*fig*) (*personnalité mondaine*) pace-setter; (*leader, groupe ou région de pointe*) dynamo, pacemaker, powerhouse.

locomotrice[2] [lɔkɔmɔtʀis] *nf* motive *ou* motor unit.

locuste [lɔkyst(ə)] *nf* (*rare*) locust.

locuteur, -trice [lɔkytœʀ, tʀis] *nm,f* (*Ling*) speaker.

locution [lɔkysjɔ̃] *nf* phrase, locution. **~ figée** set phrase; **~ verbale/adverbiale** verbal/adverbial phrase.

lœss [løs] *nm* loess.

lof [lɔf] *nm* (*Naut*) windward side. **aller** *ou* **venir au ~** to luff; **virer ~ pour ~** to wear (ship).

lofer [lɔfe] (1) *vi* (*Naut*) to luff.

logarithme [lɔgaʀitm(ə)] *nm* logarithm.

logarithmique [lɔgaʀitmik] *adj* logarithmic.

loge [lɔʒ] *nf* **(a)** *[concierge, francs-maçons]* lodge; (†) *[bûcheron]* hut.

(b) (*Théât*) *[artiste]* dressing room; (*spectateur*) box. **secondes ~s** boxes in the upper circle (*Brit*); **premières ~s** boxes in the grand circle (*Brit*); (*fig*) **être aux premières ~s** to have a ringside seat (*fig*).

(c) (*Scol: salle de préparation*) (individual) exam room (*for Prix de Rome*).

(d) (*Archit*) loggia.

logé, e [lɔʒe] (*ptp de* **loger**) *adj*: **être ~ rue X** to live in X street; **être ~, nourri, blanchi** to have board and lodging and one's laundry done; **être bien/mal ~** (*appartement etc*) to have good *ou* comfortable/poor lodgings *ou* accommodation; (*maison*) to be well *ou* comfortably/badly housed; (*fig*) **être ~ à la même enseigne** to be in the same boat (*fig*).

logeable [lɔʒabl(ə)] *adj* (*habitable, confortable*) habitable, fit to live in (*attrib*); (*spacieux, bien conçu*) roomy.

logement [lɔʒmɑ̃] *nm* **(a)** (*hébergement*) housing. **le ~ était un gros problème en 1950** housing was a great problem in 1950; **trouver un ~ provisoire chez des amis** to find temporary accommodation *ou* lodging with friends.

(b) (*appartement*) accommodation (*U*), lodgings (*pl*). **construire des ~s ouvriers** to build flats (*Brit*) *ou* apartments (*US*) *ou* accommodation for workers; **il a réussi à trouver un ~** he managed to find lodgings.

(c) (*Mil*) *[troupes]* (*à la caserne*) quartering; (*chez l'habitant*) billeting. **~s** (*à la caserne*) quarters; (*chez l'habitant*) billet.

(d) (*Tech*) housing.

loger [lɔʒe] (3) **1** *vi* to live (*dans* in, *chez* with, at). **~ à l'hôtel/rue X** to live in a hotel/in X street; **~ à la belle étoile** to live rough; (*Mil*) **~ chez l'habitant** to be billeted on the local inhabitants.

2 *vt* **(a)** *amis* to put up; *clients, élèves* to accommodate; *objet* to put; *soldats* (*chez l'habitant*) to billet. **~ les malles dans le grenier** to put the trunks in the loft.

(b) (*contenir*) to accommodate. **hôtel qui peut ~ 500 personnes** hotel which can accommodate *ou* take (in) 500 people; **salle qui loge beaucoup de monde** room which can hold *ou* accommodate a lot of people.

(c) (*envoyer*) **~ une balle/une bille dans** to lodge a bullet/a marble in; **il s'est logé une balle dans la tête** he lodged a bullet in his head.

3 se loger *vpr* **(a)** (*habiter*) *[jeunes mariés]* to find a house (*ou* flat *etc*), find somewhere to live; *[touristes]* to find accommodation; *[étudiant, saisonnier]* to find lodgings *ou* accommodation. **il n'a pas trouvé à se ~** he hasn't found anywhere to live *ou* any accommodation; **il a trouvé à se ~ chez un ami** he found accommodation with a friend, he was put up by a friend; **il a trouvé à se ~ dans un vieil immeuble** he found lodgings *ou* accommodation in an old block of flats.

(b) (*tenir*) **crois-tu qu'on va tous pouvoir se ~ dans la voiture?** do you think that we'll all be able to fit into the car?

(c) (*se ficher ou coincer dans*) *[balle, ballon]* **se ~ dans/entre** to lodge itself in/between; **le ballon alla se ~ entre les barreaux de la fenêtre** the ball went and lodged itself *ou* went and got stuck between the bars of the window; **le chat est allé se ~ sur l'armoire** the cat went and got itself stuck on the cupboard; (*objet tombé*) **où est-il allé se ~?** where has it gone and hidden itself?

logeur [lɔʒœʀ] *nm* landlord (*who lets furnished rooms*).

logeuse [lɔʒøz] *nf* landlady.

loggia [lɔdʒja] *nf* loggia.

logicien, -ienne [lɔʒisjɛ̃, jɛn] *nm,f* logician.

logique [lɔʒik] **1** *nf* **(a)** logic. **cela manque un peu de ~** that's not very logical; **cela est dans la ~ des choses** it's in the nature of things.

(b) (*façon de raisonner*) logic. **~ déductive** deductive reasoning.

(c) (*science*) **la ~** logic.

2 *adj* logical. **ce n'est pas ~** it's not logical; *V* **analyse.**

3: logique formelle *ou* **pure** formal logic; (*Math*) **logique moderne** modern logic.

logiquement [lɔʒikmɑ̃] *adv* logically.

logis [lɔʒi] *nm* (*littér*) dwelling, abode (*littér*). **rentrer au ~** to return to one's abode (*littér*); **quitter le ~ paternel** to leave the paternal home; **la fée du ~** the perfect housewife *ou* homemaker; *V* **corps, maréchal.**

logistique [lɔʒistik] **1** *adj* logistic. **2** *nf* logistics (*sg*).

logomachie [lɔgɔmaʃi] *nf* (*verbiage*) overweening verbosity, logomachia (*rare*).

logomachique [lɔgɔmaʃik] *adj* verbose.

loi [lwa] **1** *nf* **(a)** (*Jur, Rel, Sci*) law. **la ~ du plus fort** the law of the strongest; **c'est la ~ de la jungle** it's the law of the jungle; (*frm*) **subir la ~ de qn** to be ruled by sb; (*frm*) **se faire une ~ de faire** to make a point *ou* rule of doing, make it a rule to do; **avoir la ~ pour soi** to have the law on one's side; **il n'a pas la ~ chez lui!*** he's not the boss in his own house!*; **tu ne feras pas la ~ ici!*** you're not going to lay down the law here!; **ce qu'il dit fait ~** his word is law, what he says goes*; (*fig*) **c'est la ~ et les prophètes** it's taken as gospel; *V* **coup, force, nom** *etc.*

(b) (*fig: code humain*) **les ~s de la mode** the dictates of fashion; **les ~s de l'honneur** the code of honour; **la ~ du milieu** the law of the underworld; **la ~ du silence** the law of silence; **les ~s de la politesse** the rules of etiquette.

2: loi-cadre *nf, pl* **lois-cadres** outline *ou* blueprint law; **loi de finances** finance law; **loi martiale** martial law; **loi-programme** *nf, pl* **lois-programmes** *act providing framework for government programme (financial, social etc)*; **loi salique** salic law; **la loi du talion** (*Hist*) lex talionis; (*fig*) an eye for an eye; **appliquer la loi du talion** to demand an eye for an eye.

loin [lwɛ̃] *adv* **(a)** (*distance*) far. **plus ~** further, farther; **moins ~** not so far; **la gare n'est pas ~ du tout** the station is no distance at all *ou* isn't far at all; **vous nous gênez, mettez-vous plus ~** you're in our way, go further away *ou* move away; **il est ~ derrière/devant** he's a long way behind/in front, he's far behind/ahead; **il faudrait aller** *ou* **chercher (très) ~ pour trouver un si bon secrétaire** you'd have to look far and wide *ou* far afield to find such a good secretary; **une histoire** *ou* **une affaire qui pourrait aller** *ou* **mener (très) ~** a matter that could lead us (*ou* them *etc*) a long way *ou* which could have untold repercussions; **aussi ~ que vous alliez, vous ne trouverez pas d'aussi beaux jardins** however far you go *ou* wherever you go, you won't find such lovely gardens; *V* **aller, pousser.**

(b) (*temps*) **le temps est ~ où cette banlieue était un village** it's a long time since this suburb was a village; **c'est ~ tout cela!, comme c'est ~!** (*passé*) that was a long time ago!, what a long time ago that was!; (*futur*) that's a long way in the future!, that's (still) a long way off!; **l'été n'est plus ~ maintenant** summer's not far off now, summer's just around the corner; **Noël est encore ~** Christmas is still a long way off; **en remontant plus ~ encore dans le passé** (by) looking even further back into the past; **~ dans le passé** in the remote past, in far-off times; **voir** *ou* **prévoir ~** to see a long way *ou* far ahead, see far *ou* a long way into the future.

(c) ~ de far from, a long way from, far away from; **~ de là** (*lieu*) far from there; (*fig*) far from it; **non ~ de là** not far from there; **il n'est pas ~ de minuit** it isn't far off *ou* far from midnight; **leur maison est ~ de toute civilisation** their house is far *ou* remote from all civilization; **être très ~ du sujet** to be way off the subject; **~ de moi/de lui la pensée de vous blâmer!** far be it from me/him to blame you!; (*littér, hum*) **~ de moi/de nous!**

begone from me/us! (*littér, hum*); **elle est ~ d'être certaine de réussir** she is far from being certain of success; **ils ne sont pas ~ de le croire coupable** they almost believe him to be guilty; **ceci est ~ de lui plaire** he's far from pleased with this; **c'est très ~ de ce que nous attendions de lui** this is a far cry from what we expected of him.

(d) (*loc*) **au ~** in the distance, far off; **partir au ~** to leave for distant parts *ou* places; **de ~** from a distance; **de très ~** from a great distance, from afar (*littér*); (*fig: de beaucoup*) by far; **il voit mal de ~** he can't see distant objects very easily; **il est de très ~ le meilleur** he is by far the best, he is far and away the best; **le directeur voit ces problèmes pratiques de (très) ~** the manager sees these practical problems from a (great) distance *ou* from afar; **d'aussi ~** *ou* **de plus ~ qu'elle le vit, elle courut vers lui** seeing him from afar *ou* seeing him a long way off *ou* seeing him a long way in the distance she ran towards him; **de ~ en ~** (*lieu*) at distant intervals, here and there; (*temps*) every now and then, every now and again; **de ~ en ~ brillaient quelques lumières** a few lights shone at distant intervals *ou* here and there; **d'ici à l'accuser de vol, il n'y a pas ~** we (*ou* they *etc*) are close to *ou* are not far from accusing him of theft; **nous n'avons pas ~ à aller** we don't have far to go, we have no distance to go; **il n'y a pas ~ de 5 ans qu'ils sont partis** it's not far off 5 years since they left; **il ne doit pas y avoir ~ de 5 km d'ici à la gare** there can't be much less than 5 km *ou* it can't be far off 5 km from here to the station; **il leur doit pas ~ de 100 F** he owes them little short of *ou* not far off 100 francs; (*Prov*) **~ des yeux, ~ du cœur** out of sight, out of mind (*Prov*); (*Prov*) **il y a ~ de la coupe aux lèvres** there's many a slip 'twixt (the) cup and (the) lip (*Prov*).

lointain, e [lwɛ̃tɛ̃, ɛn] **1** *adj* **(a)** (*espace*) *région* faraway, distant, remote; *musique* faraway, distant; *horizons, exil* distant.
(b) (*temps*) *passé* distant, remote; *avenir* distant. **les jours ~s** far-off days.
(c) (*vague*) *parent* remote, distant; *regard* faraway; *cause* indirect, distant; *rapport* distant, remote; *ressemblance* remote.
2 *nm* **(a) au ~, dans le ~** in the distance.
(b) (*Peinture*) background.

loir [lwaʀ] *nm* dormouse; *V* **dormir.**

Loire [lwaʀ] *nf*: **la ~** (*fleuve, département*) the Loire.

loisible [lwazibl(ə)] *adj* (*frm*) **il m'est/il vous est ~ de faire** I am/you are at liberty *ou* quite free to do.

loisir [lwaziʀ] *nm* **(a)** (*gén pl: temps libre*) leisure (*U*), spare time (*U*). **pendant mes heures de ~** in my spare time, in my leisure hours *ou* time; **que faites-vous pendant vos ~s?** what do you do in your spare time?
(b) (*activités*) **~s** leisure *ou* spare-time activities; **quels sont vos ~s préférés?** what are your favourite leisure(-time) activities?, what do you like doing best in your spare time?; **~s dirigés** (organized) leisure activities.
(c) (*loc frm*) **avoir (tout) le ~ de faire** to have leisure (*frm*) *ou* time to do; **je n'ai pas eu le ~ de vous écrire** I have not had the leisure *ou* time to write to you; **(tout) à ~** (*en prenant son temps*) at leisure; (*autant qu'on veut*) at will, at one's pleasure (*frm*), as much as one likes; **donner** *ou* **laisser à qn le ~ de faire** to allow sb (the opportunity) to do.

lolo [lolo] *nm* (*langage enfantin*) milk.

lombago [lɔ̃bago] *nm* = **lumbago.**

lombaire [lɔ̃bɛʀ] **1** *adj* lumbar; *V* **ponction. 2** *nf* lumbar vertebra.

lombard, e [lɔ̃baʀ, aʀd(ə)] **1** *adj* Lombard. **2** *nm* (*Ling*) Lombard dialect. **3** *nm,f*: **L~(e)** Lombard.

Lombardie [lɔ̃baʀdi] *nf* Lombardy.

lombes [lɔ̃b] *nmpl* loins.

lombric [lɔ̃bʀik] *nm* earthworm.

londonien, -ienne [lɔ̃dɔnjɛ̃, jɛn] **1** *adj* London (*épith*), of London. **2** *nm,f*: **L~(ne)** Londoner.

Londres [lɔ̃dʀ(ə)] *n* London.

long, longue [lɔ̃, lɔ̃g] **1** *adj* **(a)** (*dans l'espace*) *cheveux, liste, robe* long. **un pont ~ de 30 mètres** a 30-metre bridge, a bridge 30 metres long; **2 cm plus ~/trop ~, plus ~/trop ~ de 2 cm** 2 cm longer/too long, longer/too long by 2 cm; **elle avait de longues jambes maigres** she had long thin legs; **la mode est aux jupes longues** long skirts are the fashion *ou* in fashion; *V* **chaise, culotte.**
(b) (*dans le temps*) *voyage etc* long, lengthy; *amitié, habitude* long-standing. **il écouta (pendant) un ~ moment le bruit** he listened to the noise for a long while; **l'attente fut longue** there was a long *ou* lengthy wait, I (*ou* they *etc*) waited a long time; **la conférence lui parut longue** he found the lecture long; **les heures lui paraissaient longues** the hours seemed long to him *ou* seemed to drag by; **faire de longues phrases** to produce long-winded sentences; **avoir une longue habitude de qch/de faire** to be long accustomed to sth/to doing; **ce travail est ~ à faire** this work takes a long time; **il fut ~ à se mettre en route/à s'habiller** he took a long time *ou* it took him a long time to get started/to get dressed; **il/la réponse était ~/longue à venir** he/the reply was a long time coming; **5 heures, c'est ~** 5 hours is a long time; **ne sois pas trop ~** don't be too long; **nous pouvons vous avoir ce livre, mais ce sera ~** we can get you the book, but it will take some time.
(c) (*Culin*) *sauce* thin.
(d) (*loc*) **au ~ cours** *voyage* ocean (*épith*); *navigation* deep-sea (*épith*), ocean (*épith*); *capitaine* seagoing (*épith*), ocean-going (*épith*); **ils se connaissent de longue date** they have known each other for a very long time; **un ami de longue date** a long-standing friend; **à longue échéance, à ~ terme** *prévoir* in the long term *ou* run; *projet, emprunt* long-term; **à plus ou moins longue échéance, à plus ou moins ~ terme** sooner or later; **faire ~ feu** *[projet]* to fall through; **ce pot de confiture n'a pas fait ~ feu** that jar of jam didn't last long; **de longue haleine** *travail* long-drawn-out; **préparé de longue main** prepared well beforehand *ou* in advance; **à longue portée** *canon* long-range; **boire qch à ~s traits** to drink sth in long draughts; **respirer l'air à ~s traits** to breathe the air in deeply; **il est ~ comme un jour sans pain** he's like a beanpole.
2 *adv*: **s'habiller ~** to wear long clothes; **s'habiller trop ~** to wear one's clothes too long; **en savoir ~/trop ~/plus ~** to know a lot/too much/more (*sur* about); **en dire ~** *[attitude etc]* to speak volumes; **regard qui en dit ~** meaningful *ou* eloquent look; **cela en dit ~ sur ses intentions** that tells you a good deal *ou* speaks volumes about his intentions.
3 *nm* **(a) un bateau de 7 mètres de ~** a boat 7 metres long; **en ~** lengthways, lengthwise; **ils sont venus par le plus ~** they came the longest *ou* long way.
(b) (*vêtements*) long clothes.
(c) (*loc*) **tomber de tout son ~** to measure one's length, go full length; **étendu de tout son ~** spread out at full length; **(tout) le ~ du fleuve/de la route** (all) along the river/the road; **tout le ~ du jour/de la nuit** all *ou* the whole day/night long; **tout au ~ de sa carrière/son récit** throughout his career/his story; **l'eau coule le ~ de la gouttière** the water flows down *ou* along the gutter; **grimper le ~ d'un mât** to climb up a mast; **tout au** *ou* **du ~** from beginning to end; **de ~ en large** back and forth, to and fro, up and down; **en ~ et en large** in great detail, at great length.
4 longue *nf* (*Ling: voyelle*) long vowel; (*Poésie: syllabe*) long syllable; (*Mus: note*) long note. (*Cartes*) **avoir une longue à carreaux** to have a long suit of diamonds; **à la longue: à la longue il s'est calmé** at long last *ou* in the end he calmed down; **à la longue, ça a fini par coûter cher** in the long run *ou* in the end it turned out very expensive; **à la longue ça s'arrangera/ça s'usera** it will sort itself out/wear out in time *ou* eventually.
5: long-courrier, *pl* **long-courriers** (*adj*) (*Naut*) ocean-going (*épith*); (*Aviat*) long-haul (*épith*), long-distance (*épith*); (*nm*) (*Naut*) ocean liner, ocean-going ship; (*Aviat*) long-haul *ou* long-distance aircraft; **long métrage** full-length film; **longue-vue** *nf*, *pl* **longues-vues** telescope.

longanimité [lɔ̃ganimite] *nf* (*littér*) long suffering, forbearance.

longe [lɔ̃ʒ] *nf* **(a)** (*pour attacher*) tether; (*pour mener*) lead. **(b)** (*Boucherie*) loin.

longer [lɔ̃ʒe] (3) *vt [mur, bois]* to border; *[sentier, voie ferrée]* to border, run along(side); *[personne]* to go along, walk along *ou* alongside; *[voiture, train]* to go *ou* pass along *ou* alongside. **le bois longe la voie ferrée** the wood borders the railway line; **la voie ferrée longe la nationale** the railway line runs along(side) the main road; **naviguer en longeant la côte** to sail along *ou* hug the coast; **~ les murs pour ne pas se faire voir** to keep close to the wall to stay out of sight.

longeron [lɔ̃ʒʀɔ̃] *nm* **(a)** *[pont]* (central) girder. **(b)** *[châssis]* side frame; *[fuselage]* longeron; *[aile]* spar.

longévité [lɔ̃ʒevite] *nf* longevity. **il attribue sa ~ à la pratique de la bicyclette** he attributes his long life *ou* longevity to cycling; **étudier la ~ de certaines espèces/races** to study the longevity of certain species/the life expectancy of certain races; **tables de ~** life-expectancy tables.

longitude [lɔ̃ʒityd] *nf* longitude. **à** *ou* **par 50° de ~ ouest/est** at 50° longitude west/east.

longitudinal, e, *mpl* **-aux** [lɔ̃ʒitydinal, o] *adj section, coupe* longitudinal; *vallée, poutre, rainure* running lengthways.

longitudinalement [lɔ̃ʒitydinalmɑ̃] *adv* (*V* **longitudinal**) longitudinally; lengthways.

longtemps [lɔ̃tɑ̃] *adv* **(a)** *parler, attendre etc* (for) a long time; (*dans phrase nég ou interrog*) (for) long. **pendant ~** (for) a long time; (for) long; **absent pendant ~** absent (for) a long time; **pendant ~ ils ne sont pas sortis** for a long time *ou* while they never went out; **avant ~** (*sous peu*) before long; (*dans phrase nég*) **pas avant ~** not for a long time; **~ avant/après** long before/after; **on ne le verra pas de ~** we won't see him for a long time; **il ne reviendra pas d'ici ~** he won't be back for a long time yet; **il vivra encore ~** he'll live (for) a long time yet; **il n'en a plus pour ~** (*pour finir*) he hasn't much longer to go *ou* he won't take much longer now; (*avant de mourir*) he can't hold out *ou* last much longer now; **y a-t-il ~ à attendre?** is there long to wait?, is there a long wait?, will it be long?; **je n'en ai pas pour ~** I shan't be long, it won't take me long; **il a mis** *ou* **été ~, ça lui a pris ~** it took him a long time, he was a long time over it *ou* doing it; **il arrivera dans ~?** will it be long before he gets here?; **rester assez ~ quelque part** (*trop*) to stay somewhere (for) quite *ou* rather a long time *ou* (for) quite a while; (*suffisamment*) to stay somewhere long enough; **tu es resté si ~!** you've stayed so long *ou* (for) such a long time!
(b) (*avec depuis, il y a etc*) (*indiquant une durée*) (for) a long time; (for) long; (*indiquant une action terminée*) a long time ago, long ago. **il habite ici depuis ~, il y a** *ou* **cela fait** *ou* **voilà ~ qu'il habite ici** he has been living here (for) a long time; **il n'était pas là depuis ~ quand je suis arrivé** he hadn't been here (for) long when I arrived; **c'était il y a ~/il n'y a pas ~** that was a long time ago/not long ago; **j'ai fini depuis ~** I finished a long time ago; **il y a** *ou* **cela fait** *ou* **voilà ~ que j'ai fini** I have been finished for a long time *ou* for ages* now; **ça fait ~ qu'il n'est plus venu** it's (been) a long time now since he came, he hasn't been coming for a long time *ou* for ages* now; **je n'y mangeais plus depuis ~** I had given up eating there long before then *ou* ages ago*.

longue [lɔ̃g] *V* **long.**

longuement [lɔ̃gmɑ̃] *adv* (*longtemps*) *regarder, parler* for a long time; (*en détail*) *expliquer, étudier, raconter* at length. **plus ~** for longer; (*en plus grand détail*) at greater length; **plan**

~ **médité** long-considered plan, plan pondered over at length.

longuet, -ette* [lɔ̃gɛ, ɛt] *adj* a bit long (*attrib*), a bit on the long side* (*attrib*).

longueur [lɔ̃gœʀ] *nf* **(a)** (*espace*) length. **mesures/unités de** ~ measures/units of length, linear measures/units; **la pièce fait 3 mètres de** *ou* **en** ~ the room is 3 metres in length *ou* 3 metres long; **la plage s'étend sur une** ~ **de 7 km** the beach stretches for 7 km; **dans le sens de la** ~ lengthways, lengthwise; **s'étirer en** ~ to stretch out lengthways; **pièce tout en** ~ very long room; (*lit, fig*) ~ **d'onde** wavelength.

(b) (*durée*) length. **à** ~ **de journée/de semaine/d'année** all day/week/year long; **à** ~ **de temps** all the time; **traîner** *ou* **tirer en** ~ to drag on; **tirer les choses en** ~ to drag things out; **attente qui tire** *ou* **traîne en** ~ long-drawn-out wait; **les** ~**s de la justice** the slowness of the judicial process.

(c) (*Sport*) length. **saut en** ~ long jump; **l'emporter de plusieurs** ~**s** to win by several lengths; **prendre 2** ~**s d'avance** to go into a 2-length lead.

(d) (*remplissage*) ~**s** monotonous moments *ou* passages, overlong passages; **ce film/livre a des** ~**s** there are some monotonous episodes *ou* some episodes which drag in this film/book.

looping [lupiŋ] *nm* (*Aviat*) looping the loop. **faire des** ~**s** to loop the loop.

lopin [lɔpɛ̃] *nm*: ~ **(de terre)** patch of land, plot (of land).

loquace [lɔkas] *adj* talkative, loquacious (*frm*).

loquacité [lɔkasite] *nf* talkativeness, loquacity (*frm*).

loque [lɔk] *nf* **(a)** (*vêtements*) ~**s** rags, rags and tatters; **être en** ~**s** to be in rags; **vêtu de** ~**s** dressed in rags; **tomber en** ~**s** to be in tatters *ou* all tattered*. **(b)** (*fig péj*) **une** ~ **(humaine)** a (human) wreck; **je suis une vraie** ~ **ce matin** I feel a wreck *ou* like a wet rag this morning.

loquet [lɔkɛ] *nm* latch.

loqueteau, *pl* ~**x** [lɔkto] *nm* (small) latch, catch.

loqueteux, -euse [lɔktø, øz] *adj personne* ragged, (dressed) in rags *ou* in tatters (*attrib*); *vêtement, livre* tattered, ragged.

lorgner* [lɔʀɲe] (1) *vt objet* to peer at, eye; *femme* to ogle, eye up*; *poste, décoration, héritage* to have one's eye on. ~ **qch du coin de l'œil** to look *ou* peer at sth out of the corner of one's eye, cast sidelong glances at sth.

lorgnette [lɔʀɲɛt] *nf* spyglass. (*fig*) **regarder par le petit bout de la** ~ to get things out of proportion.

lorgnon [lɔʀɲɔ̃] *nm* (*face-à-main*) lorgnette; (*pince-nez*) pince-nez.

loriot [lɔʀjo] *nm* (golden) oriole.

lorrain, e [lɔʀɛ̃, ɛn] **1** *adj* of *ou* from Lorraine; *V* **quiche**. **2** *nm* (*Ling*) Lorraine dialect. **3** *nm,f*: **L**~**(e)** inhabitant *ou* native of Lorraine. **4 Lorraine** *nf* (*région*) Lorraine.

lors [lɔʀ] *adv* (*littér*) ~ **de** at the time of; ~ **de sa mort** at the time of his death; ~ **même que** even though *ou* if; ~ **même que la terre croulerait** even though *ou* if the earth should crumble; *V* **dès**.

lorsque [lɔʀsk(ə)] *conj* when. **lorsqu'il entra/entrera** when *ou* as he came/comes in.

losange [lɔzɑ̃ʒ] *nm* diamond, lozenge (*frm*). **en forme de** ~ diamond-shaped; **dallage en** ~**s** diamond tiling.

losangé, e [lɔzɑ̃ʒe] *adj morceau* diamond-shaped; *dessin, tissu* with a diamond pattern.

lot [lo] *nm* **(a)** (*Loterie*) prize. **le gros** ~ the first prize, the jackpot; ~ **de consolation** consolation prize.

(b) (*portion*) share. ~ **(de terre)** plot (of land).

(c) (*assortiment*) *[livres, chiffons]* batch; *[draps, vaisselle]* set; (*aux enchères*) lot. ~ **de 10 chemises** set of 10 shirts; **dans le** ~**, il n'y avait que 2 candidats valables** in the whole batch there were only 2 worthwhile applicants.

(d) (*fig littér: destin*) lot (*littér*), fate.

loterie [lɔtʀi] *nf* (*lit, fig*) lottery; (*dans une kermesse*) raffle. **mettre qch en** ~ to put sth up to be raffled; ~ **foraine** fun fair (*Brit*) *ou* carnival raffle; ~ **nationale** national lottery *ou* sweepstake; **jouer à la** ~ to buy tickets for the raffle *ou* lottery; **gagner à la** ~ to win on the raffle *ou* lottery; (*fig*) **c'est une vraie** ~ it's (all) the luck of the draw.

loti, e [lɔti] (*ptp de* **lotir**) *adj*: **être bien/mal** ~ to be well-/badly off.

lotion [losjɔ̃] *nf* lotion. ~ **capillaire** hair lotion; ~ **après rasage** after-shave lotion; ~ **avant rasage** preshave lotion.

lotionner [losjɔne] (1) *vt* to apply (a) lotion to.

lotir [lɔtiʀ] (2) *vt terrain* (*diviser*) to divided into plots; (*vendre*) to sell by lots; (*Jur*) *succession* to divide up, share out. ~ **qn de qch** to allot sth to sb, provide sb with sth.

lotissement [lɔtismɑ̃] *nm* **(a)** (*terrains à bâtir*) housing estate *ou* site; (*terrains bâtis*) (housing) development *ou* estate; (*parcelle*) plot, lot.

(b) (*action: V* **lotir**) division; sale (by lots); sharing out.

loto [lɔto] *nm* (*jeu traditionnel*) lotto; (*matériel pour ce jeu*) lotto set; (*loterie à numéros*) *numerical lottery in France.*

lotte [lɔt] *nf* (*de rivière*) burbot; (*de mer*) angler, devilfish.

lotus [lɔtys] *nm* lotus.

louable [lwabl(ə)] *adj* **(a)** praiseworthy, commendable, laudable. **(b)** *maison* rentable. **appartement difficilement** ~ **à cause de sa situation** flat that is hard to let because of its situation.

louablement [lwabləmɑ̃] *adv* commendably.

louage [lwaʒ] *nm*: **(contrat de)** ~ rental contract; ~ **de services** work contract.

louange [lwɑ̃ʒ] *nf* praise. **il méprise les** ~**s** he despises praise; **chanter les** ~**s de qn** to sing sb's praises; **faire un discours à la** ~ **de qn** to make a speech in praise of sb; **je dois dire, à sa** ~**, que ...** I must say, to his credit, that ... .

louangeur, -euse [lwɑ̃ʒœʀ, øz] *adj* (*littér*) laudatory (*frm*), laudative (*frm*).

loubar(d) [lubaʀ] *nm* (housing-estate) yobbo‡ *ou* hoodlum.

louche[1] [luʃ] *adj* **(a)** *affaire, manœuvre, milieu, passé* shady; *individu* shifty, shady, dubious; *histoire* dubious, fishy*; *conduite, acte, établissement* dubious, suspicious, shady; *réaction, attitude* dubious, suspicious. **j'ai entendu du bruit, c'est** ~ I heard a noise, that's funny *ou* odd; **il y a du** ~ **dans cette affaire** this business is a bit shady *ou* fishy* *ou* isn't quite above board.

(b) *liquide* cloudy; *couleur, éclairage* murky.

(c) *œil, personne* squinting (*épith*).

louche[2] [luʃ] *nf* ladle.

loucher [luʃe] (1) *vi* (*lit*) to squint, have a squint. (*fig*) ~ **sur*** *objet* to eye; *personne* to ogle, eye up*; *poste, héritage* to have one's eye on.

louer[1] [lwe] (1) **1** *vt* to praise. ~ **qn de qch** to praise sb for sth; **on ne peut que le** ~ **d'avoir agi ainsi** he deserves only praise *ou* one can only praise him for acting in that way; (*Rel*) **louons le Seigneur!** (let us) praise the Lord!; (*fig*) **Dieu soit loué!** thank God!

2 se louer *vpr*: **se** ~ **de** *employé, appareil* to be very happy *ou* pleased with; *action, mesure* to congratulate o.s. on; **se** ~ **d'avoir fait qch** to congratulate o.s. on *ou* for having done sth; **n'avoir qu'à se** ~ **de** *employé, appareil* to have every cause for satisfaction with, be completely satisfied with, have nothing but praise for; **nous n'avons qu'à nous** ~ **de ses services** we have nothing but praise for the service he gives, we have every cause for satisfaction with his services.

louer[2] [lwe] (1) *vt* **(a)** *[propriétaire] maison, chambre* to let, rent; *voiture, tente, téléviseur* to hire out, rent (out). ~ **ses services** *ou* **se** ~ **à un fermier** to hire o.s. (out) to a farmer.

(b) *[locataire] maison, chambre* to rent; *voiture, tente* to hire, rent; *place* to book. **ils ont loué une maison au bord de la mer** they took *ou* rented a house by the sea; **à** ~ *chambre etc* to let; *voiture etc* for hire; **cet appartement doit se** ~ **cher** that flat must be expensive to rent.

loueur, -euse [lwœʀ, øz] *nm,f* (*propriétaire*) hirer.

loufiat‡ [lufja] *nm* waiter.

loufoque* [lufɔk] **1** *adj* wild, crazy, barmy*. **2** *nmf* crackpot*, nut‡.

loufoquerie [lufɔkʀi] *nf* **(a)** (*U*) craziness, barminess*. **(b)** (*acte*) bit of daftness*, crazy goings-on (*U*).

louis [lwi] *nm*: ~ **(d'or)** (gold) louis.

Louis [lwi] *nm* Louis.

louise-bonne, *pl* **louises-bonnes** [lwizbɔn] *nf* louise-bonne pear.

Louisiane [lwizjan] *nf* Louisiana.

louis-philippard, e [lwifilipaʀ, aʀd(ə)] *adj* (*péj*) of *ou* relating to the reign of Louis Philippe.

loukoum [lukum] *nm* Turkish delight (*U*).

loulou[1] [lulu] *nm* spitz. (*chien*) ~ **de Poméranie** Pomeranian dog, Pom.

loulou[2]* [lulu] *nm*, **louloutte*** [lulut] *nf* **(a)** darling; (*péj*) fishy customer, oddball*, nasty bit of work (*Brit*). **(b) = loubar(d).**

loup [lu] **1** *nm* (*carnassier*) wolf; (*poisson*) bass; (*masque*) (eye) mask. **mon (gros** *ou* **petit)** ~* (my) pet* *ou* love; (*Prov*) **les** ~**s ne se mangent pas** *ou* **ne se dévorent pas entre eux** dog does not eat dog, there is honour among thieves (*Prov*); **l'homme est un** ~ **pour l'homme** brother will turn on brother; **enfermer** *ou* **mettre le** ~ **dans la bergerie** to set the fox to mind the geese; *V* **gueule, hurler** *etc.*

2: loup-cervier *nm, pl* **loups-cerviers** lynx; (*Hist*) **loup-garou** *nm, pl* **loups-garous** werewolf; **le loup-garou va te manger!** Mr Bogeyman will get you!; **loup de mer** (*: *marin*) old salt*, old seadog*; (*vêtement*) (short-sleeved) jersey.

loupe [lup] *nf* (*Opt*) magnifying glass; (*Méd*) wen. (*fig*) **regarder qch à la** ~ to put sth under a microscope.

louper* [lupe] (1) *vt* (*rater*) *occasion, train, personne* to miss; *travail, gâteau* to mess up*, make a mess of; *examen* to flunk*. **ma sauce est loupée** my sauce hasn't come off; **ma soirée est loupée** my party is spoilt *ou* is a flop*; **ça n'a pas loupé** sure enough, that was what happened; **loupé!** missed!; (*iro*) **il n'en loupe pas une!** he's forever putting his big foot in it!*; **la prochaine fois je ne te louperai pas** don't think I'll let you get away with it next time; ~ **son entrée** to fluff* *ou* bungle one's entrance; **il a loupé son coup/suicide** he bungled *ou* botched* it/his suicide bid; **ça va tout faire** ~ that'll put everything up the spout* (*Brit*), that'll muck everything up*.

loupiot, -iotte* [lupjo, jɔt] *nm,f* kid*.

loupiote* [lupjɔt] *nf* (*lampe*) (small) light.

lourd, e[1] [luʀ, luʀd(ə)] *adj* **(a)** (*lit, fig: pesant*) *objet, poids, vêtement* heavy; *silence, sommeil* heavy, deep; *chagrin* deep; *ciel, nuage* heavy; *temps, chaleur* sultry, close; *parfum, odeur* heavy, strong; *aliment, vin* heavy; *repas* heavy, big; *paupières* heavy; (*Bourse*) *marché* slack, sluggish; *artillerie, industrie* heavy. **terrain** ~ heavy ground; **marcher d'un pas** ~ to tread heavily, walk with a heavy step; **yeux** ~**s de sommeil/de fatigue** eyes heavy with sleep/tiredness; **c'est** ~ **(à digérer)** it's heavy (on the stomach *ou* the digestion); **se sentir** ~**, avoir l'estomac** ~ to feel bloated; **j'ai** *ou* **je me sens les jambes** ~**es** my legs feel heavy; **j'ai** *ou* **je me sens la tête** ~**e** my head feels fuzzy, I feel a bit headachy; **3 enfants à élever, c'est** ~**/trop** ~ **(pour elle)** bringing up 3 children is a lot/too much (for her) *ou* is a big responsibility/is too heavy a responsibility (for her); *V* **eau, franc**[2]**, hérédité** *etc.*

(b) (*important*) *dettes, impôts, tâche* heavy; *pertes* heavy, severe, serious; *faute* serious, grave; *responsabilité, charge* heavy, weighty. **de** ~**es présomptions pèsent sur lui** suspicion falls heavily on him.

(c) (*massif, gauche*) *construction* heavy(-looking), massive; *silhouette* heavy; *démarche* heavy, cumbersome; *mouvement,* *style* heavy, ponderous; *plaisanterie, compliment* heavy-handed, clumsy. **oiseau au vol ~** bird with a heavy *ou* clumsy flight; **avoir l'esprit ~** to be slow-witted *ou* dull-witted.

(d) (*loc*) **le silence était ~ de menaces** the silence was heavy with threat, there was a threatening *ou* an ominous silence; **le silence était ~ de sous-entendus** the silence was heavy with insinuations; **décision ~e de conséquences** decision charged *ou* fraught (*frm*) with consequence; **en avoir ~ sur la conscience** to have a heavy conscience (about sth); **il n'y a pas ~ de pain*** there isn't much bread; **du bon sens, il n'en a pas ~!*** he hasn't got much *ou* he isn't overendowed with common sense; **il n'en sait/ne fait pas ~** he doesn't know/do much; (*Mét*) **il fait ~** the weather is close, it's sultry; *V* **main, peser.**

lourdaud, e [luʀdo, od] **1** *adj* oafish, clumsy. **2** *nm,f* oaf.

lourde²‡ [luʀd(ə)] *nf* (*porte*) door.

lourdement [luʀdəmɑ̃] *adv* (*gén*) heavily. **marcher ~** to walk with a heavy tread; **se tromper ~** to be sadly mistaken, commit a gross error (*frm*), make a big mistake; **insister ~ sur qch/pour faire** to insist strenuously on sth/on doing; **il cligna ~ de l'œil** he gave a laboured wink.

lourdeur [luʀdœʀ] *nf* **(a)** (*pesanteur*) *[objet, fardeau]* heaviness, weight; (*Bourse*) *[marché]* slackness, sluggishness.

(b) *[édifice]* heaviness, massiveness; *[démarche]* heaviness; *[style, forme]* heaviness, ponderousness. **~ d'esprit** dull-wittedness, slow-wittedness; **s'exprimer avec ~** to express o.s. clumsily *ou* ponderously; **avoir des ~s de tête** to have a fuzzy head, feel headachy.

(c) *[temps]* sultriness, closeness.

loustic* [lustik] *nm* (*enfant*) kid*; (*taquin*) villain* (*hum*); (*type*) (funny) chap* (*Brit*) *ou* fellow* *ou* guy*, oddbod* (*Brit*). **faire le ~** to act the goat*, play the fool; **un drôle de ~** (*type*) an oddball*, an oddbod* (*Brit*); (*enfant*) a little villain* (*hum*) *ou* rascal.

loutre [lutʀ(ə)] *nf* (*animal*) otter; (*fourrure*) otter-skin. **~ de mer** sea-otter.

louve [luv] *nf* she-wolf.

louveteau, *pl* **~x** [luvto] *nm* (*Zool*) (wolf) cub; (*scout*) cub scout, cub, wolf cub† (*Brit*).

louvoiement [luvwamɑ̃] *nm* (*Naut*) tacking (*U*); (*fig*) hedging (*U*), evasion. **assez de ~s** stop hedging.

louvoyer [luvwaje] (8) *vi* (*Naut*) to tack; (*fig*) to hedge, evade the issue, beat about the bush.

lover [lɔve] (1) **1** *vt* to coil. **2 se lover** *vpr [serpent]* to coil up.

loyal, e, *mpl* **-aux** [lwajal, o] *adj* **(a)** (*fidèle*) *sujet, ami* loyal, faithful, trusty. **après 50 ans de bons et ~aux services** after 50 years of good and faithful service.

(b) (*honnête*) *personne, procédé* fair, honest; *conduite* upright, fair; *jeu* fair, straight*. **se battre à la ~e*** to fight cleanly.

loyalement [lwajalmɑ̃] *adv agir* fairly, honestly; *servir* loyally, faithfully; *se battre* cleanly. **accepter ~ une défaite** to take a defeat sportingly *ou* in good part *ou* like a gentleman.

loyalisme [lwajalism(ə)] *nm* loyalty.

loyaliste [lwajalist(ə)] **1** *adj* loyal. **2** *nmf* loyal supporter.

loyauté [lwajote] **(a)** (*fidélité*) loyalty, faithfulness. **(b)** (*honnêteté*) honesty, fairness; *[conduite]* fairness, uprightness. **avec ~** fairly.

loyer [lwaje] *nm* rent. (*Fin*) **~ de l'argent** rate of interest, interest rate.

lubie [lybi] *nf* whim, craze, fad. **avoir des ~s** to have *ou* get whims *ou* crazes *ou* fads; **il lui a pris la ~ de ne plus manger de pain** he has taken it into his head not to eat bread any more, he has got the mad idea of not eating bread any more.

lubricité [lybʀisite] *nf [personne]* lustfulness, lechery; *[propos, conduite]* lewdness.

lubrifiant [lybʀifjɑ̃] **1** *adj* lubricating. **2** *nm* lubricant.

lubrification [lybʀifikɑsjɔ̃] *nf* lubrication.

lubrifier [lybʀifje] (7) *vt* to lubricate.

lubrique [lybʀik] *adj personne* lustful, lecherous; *propos* lewd, libidinous; *danse* lewd; *amour* lustful, carnal. **regarder qch d'un œil ~** to gaze at sth with a lustful eye.

lubriquement [lybʀikmɑ̃] *adv* (*V* **lubrique**) lustfully; lecherously; lewdly; libidinously.

Luc [lyk] *nm* Luke.

lucarne [lykaʀn(ə)] *nf [toit]* skylight; (*en saillie*) dormer window; (*Mus*) opening. (*Ftbl*) **envoyer la balle dans la ~** to send the ball into the top corner of the net.

lucide [lysid] *adj* **(a)** (*conscient*) *malade, vieillard* lucid; *accidenté* conscious. **(b)** (*perspicace*) *personne* lucid, clear-minded, clear-headed; *esprit, analyse, raisonnement* lucid, clear. **le témoin le plus ~ de son temps** the most clear-sighted *ou* perceptive observer of the times he lived in.

lucidement [lysidmɑ̃] *adv* lucidly, clearly.

lucidité [lysidite] *nf* (*V* **lucide**) lucidity; consciousness; clear-mindedness, clear-headedness; clearness. **un vieillard qui a gardé sa ~** an old man who has retained (the use of) his faculties *ou* has remained quite clear-thinking.

Lucie [lysi] *nf* Lucy.

Lucien [lysjɛ̃] *nm* Lucian.

Lucifer [lysifɛʀ] *nm* Lucifer.

luciole [lysjɔl] *nf* firefly.

lucratif, -ive [lykʀatif, iv] *adj entreprise* lucrative, profitable; *emploi* lucrative, well-paid. **association créée dans un but ~/non ~** profit-making/non-profit-making organization.

lucrativement [lykʀativmɑ̃] *adv* lucratively.

lucre [lykʀ(ə)] *nm* (*péj*) lucre (*péj*).

Lucrèce [lykʀɛs] *nm* Lucretius.

ludion [lydjɔ̃] *nm* cartesian diver.

ludique [lydik] *adj* (*Psych*) play (*épith*). **activité ~** play activity.

luette [lɥɛt] *nf* uvula.

lueur [lɥœʀ] *nf* **(a)** *[flamme]* glimmer (*U*); *[étoile, lune, lampe]* (faint) light; *[braises]* glow (*U*). **à la ~ d'une bougie** by candle-light *ou* candle-glow; **les ~s de la ville** the city lights, the glow of the city; **les premières ~s de l'aube/du jour** the first light of dawn/of day; **les ~s du couchant** the glow of sunset, the sunset glow.

(b) (*fig*) *[désir, colère]* gleam; *[raison, intelligence]* glimmer. **une ~ malicieuse dans le regard** a malicious gleam in one's eyes; **pas la moindre ~ d'espoir** not the faintest glimmer of hope.

luge [lyʒ] *nf* sledge (*Brit*), sled (*US*), toboggan. **faire de la ~** to sledge (*Brit*), sled (*US*), toboggan.

luger [lyʒe] (3) *vi* to sledge (*Brit*), sled (*US*), toboggan.

lugeur, -euse [lyʒœʀ, øz] *nm,f* tobogganist.

lugubre [lygybʀ(ə)] *adj personne, pensée, ambiance, récit* lugubrious, gloomy, dismal; *prison, paysage* gloomy, dismal.

lugubrement [lygybʀəmɑ̃] *adv* lugubriously, gloomily, dismally.

lui [lɥi] **1** *pron pers mf* (*objet indirect*) (*homme*) him; (*femme, nation*) her; (*animal, bébé*) it, him, her; (*bateau*) her, it; (*insecte, chose*) it. **je le ~ ai dit** (*à un homme*) I told him; (*à une femme*) I told her; **tu ~ as donné de l'eau?** (*à un animal*) have you given it *ou* him *ou* her some water?; (*à une plante*) have you watered it?; **je ne le ~ ai jamais caché** I have never kept it from him *ou* her; **il ~ est facile de le faire** it's easy for him *ou* her to do it; **elle ~ serra la main** she shook his *ou* her hand, she shook him *ou* her by the hand; **je ne ~ connais pas de défauts** I know of no faults in him *ou* her; **je ~ ai entendu dire que** I heard him *ou* her say that; **la tête ~ a tourné et elle est tombée** her head spun and she fell; **le mur/le bateau est plus propre depuis qu'on ~ a donné un coup de peinture** the wall/the boat is cleaner now they've given it/her *ou* it a coat of paint.

2 *pron m* **(a)** (*fonction objet*) (*personne*) him; (*animal*) him, it; (*chose*) it; (*pays*) her; (*bateau*) her, it. **elle n'admire que ~** she only admires him; **à ~ elle n'a pas dit un mot** she never said a word to him; **~ le revoir?, jamais!** see him again?, never!; **c'est ~, je le reconnais** it's him, I recognize him; **je l'ai bien vu ~!** I saw him all right!, I definitely saw HIM!; **si j'étais ~ j'accepterais** if I were him *ou* he (*frm*) I would accept; *V aussi* **même, non, seul.**

(b) (*sujet, gén emphatique*) (*personne*) he; (*chose*) it; (*animal*) it, he; (*nation*) she. **elle est vendeuse, ~ est maçon** she's a saleswoman and he's a mason; **~, furieux, a refusé** furious, he refused; **l'enfant, ~, avait bien vu les bonbons** the child had seen the sweets all right; **qu'est-ce qu'ils ont dit? — ~ rien** what did they say? — he said nothing; **elle est venue mais pas ~** she came but not him *ou* but he didn't; **mon frère et ~ sont partis ensemble** my brother and he went off together; **~ parti, j'ai pu travailler** with him gone *ou* after he had gone I was able to work; **~ (il) n'aurait jamais fait ça, il n'aurait jamais fait ça ~** HE would never have done that; **est-ce qu'il le sait ~?, est-ce que ~ (il) le sait?** does HE know about it?; **~ se marier?, pas si bête!** HIM get married?, not likely!; **c'est ~ que nous avions invité** it's *ou* it was him we had invited; **c'est à ~ que je veux parler** it's HIM I want to speak to, I want to speak to HIM; **il y a un hibou dans le bois, c'est ~ que j'ai entendu** there is an owl in the wood — that's what I heard.

(c) (*emphatique avec qui, que*) **c'est ~ qui me l'a dit** he told me himself, it's he who told me; (*iro*) **c'est ~ qui le dit!** that's HIS story!, that's what he says!; (*frm*) **ce fut ~ qui le premier découvrit ...** it was he *ou* he it was (*frm*) who first discovered ...; **chasse le chien, c'est ~ qui m'a mordu** chase that dog away — it's the one that bit me; **de tous les arbres c'est ~ qui a le bois le plus dur** of all the trees it's this one that has the hardest wood; **ils ont 3 chats et ~ qui ne voulait pas d'animaux!** they have 3 cats and to think that he didn't want any animals!

(d) (*avec prép*) (*personne*) him; (*animal*) him, it; (*chose*) it. **ce livre est à ~** this book belongs to him *ou* is his; **il a un appartement à ~** he has a flat of his own; **c'est gentil à ~ d'avoir écrit** it was kind of him to write; **un ami à ~** a friend of his, one of HIS friends; **il ne pense qu'à ~** he only thinks of himself; **qu'est-ce qu'elle ferait sans ~!** what would she do without him!; **ce poème n'est pas de ~** this poem is not one of his *ou* not one he wrote; **elle veut une photo de ~** she wants a photo of him; **vous pouvez avoir toute confiance en ~** (*homme*) he is thoroughly reliable, you can have complete confidence in him; (*machine etc*) it is thoroughly reliable.

(e) (*dans comparaisons*) (*sujet*) he, him*; (*objet*) him. **elle est plus mince que ~** she is slimmer than he is *ou* than him*; **j'ai mangé plus/moins que ~** I ate more/less than he did *ou* than him*; **ne fais pas comme ~** don't do as he does *ou* did, don't do like him* *ou* the same as he did; **je ne la connais pas aussi bien que ~** (*que je le connais*) I don't know her as well as (I know) him; (*qu'il la connaît*) I don't know her as well as he does *ou* as him*.

luire [lɥiʀ] (38) *vi [surface mouillée ou polie, étoiles, lune]* to gleam, shine; *[reflets métalliques ou argentés, yeux]* to gleam; *[reflets chauds, cuivrés]* to glow, shine. **l'herbe couverte de rosée/l'étang luisait au soleil du matin** the dew-covered grass/the pond glistened in the morning sunlight; **yeux qui luisent de colère/d'envie** eyes which gleam with anger/desire; **le lac luisait sous la lune** the lake shimmered *ou* glimmered in the moonlight; **l'espoir luit encore** there is still a gleam *ou* glimmer of hope.

luisant, e [lɥizɑ̃, ɑ̃t] **1** *adj* (*V* **luire**) gleaming; shining; glowing. **front ~ de sueur** forehead gleaming *ou* glistening with sweat; **vêtements ~s d'usure** clothes shiny with wear; **yeux ~s de fièvre** eyes bright with fever; *V* **ver.**

2 *nm [étoffe]* sheen; *[poil d'animal]* gloss.

lumbago [lɔ̃bago] *nm* lumbago.

lumière [lymjɛʀ] **1** *nf* **(a)** (*Phys, gén*) light. **la ~ du jour** daylight; **la ~ du soleil l'éblouit** he was dazzled by the sunlight; **à la ~ des étoiles** by the light of the stars, by starlight; **à la ~ artificielle** by artificial light; **la ~ entrait à flots dans la pièce** daylight streamed into the room; **il n'y a pas beaucoup/ça ne donne guère de ~** there isn't/it doesn't give much light; **donnenous de la ~** switch *ou* put the light on, will you?; **il y a de la ~ dans sa chambre** there's a light on in his room; **les ~s de la ville** the lights of the town; *V* **effet.**

(b) (*fig*) light. (*littér*) **avoir/acquérir quelque ~ sur qch** to have/gain some knowledge of sth; **avoir des ~s sur une question** to have some ideas *ou* some knowledge on a question, know something about a question; **aidez-nous de vos ~s** give us the benefit of your wisdom; **mettre qch en ~** to bring sth to light, bring sth out; **jeter une nouvelle ~ sur qch** to throw *ou* shed new light on sth; **à la ~ des récents événements** in the light of recent events; **faire (toute) la ~ sur qch** to make sth (wholly) clear; **la ~ de la foi/de la raison** the light of faith/reason; *V* **siècle**[1].

(c) (*personne*) light. **il fut une des ~s de son siècle** he was one of the (shining) lights of his age; **le pauvre garçon, ce n'est pas une ~** the poor boy doesn't really shine.

(d) (*Tech*) *[machine à vapeur]* port; *[canon]* sight. (*Aut*) **~ d'admission/d'échappement** inlet/exhaust port *ou* valve.

2: (*Phys*) **lumière blanche** white light; (*Astron*) **lumière cendrée** earth-light, earthshine; (*Phys*) **lumière noire** *ou* **de Wood** black light.

lumignon [lymiɲɔ̃] *nm* (*lampe*) (small) light; (*bougie*) candle-end.

luminaire [lyminɛʀ] *nm* (*gén*) light, lamp; (*cierge*) candle.

luminescence [lyminesɑ̃s] *nf* luminescence.

luminescent, e [lyminesɑ̃, ɑ̃t] *adj* luminescent.

lumineusement [lyminøzmɑ̃] *adv expliquer* lucidly, clearly.

lumineux, -euse [lyminø, øz] *adj* **(a)** *corps, intensité* luminous; *fontaine, enseigne* illuminated; *rayon, faisceau, source* of light; *cadran, aiguille* luminous. **onde/source ~euse** light wave/source; **intensité ~euse** luminous intensity; *V* **flèche**[1].

(b) *teint, regard* radiant; *ciel, couleur* luminous.

(c) (*littér: pur, transparent*) luminous (*littér*), lucid; (*hum iro*) *exposé* limpid, brilliant. **j'ai compris, c'est ~** I understand, it's as clear as daylight; *V* **idée.**

luminosité [lyminozite] *nf* **(a)** *[teint, regard]* radiance; *[ciel, couleur]* luminosity. **il y a beaucoup de ~** it is very bright. **(b)** (*Phot, Sci*) luminosity.

lunaire[1] [lynɛʀ] *adj* (*Astron*) *paysage* lunar; (*fig*) *visage* moonlike.

lunaire[2] [lynɛʀ] *nf* (*Bot*) honesty.

lunaison [lynɛzɔ̃] *nf* lunation (*T*), lunar month.

lunatique [lynatik] *adj* quirky, whimsical, temperamental.

lunch [lœntʃ] *nm* buffet lunch.

lundi [lœ̃di] *nm* Monday. **le ~ de Pâques/de Pentecôte** Easter/Whit (*Brit*) Monday; *pour autres loc V* **samedi.**

lune [lyn] *nf* **(a)** (*lit*) moon. **pleine/nouvelle ~** full/new moon; **nuit sans ~** moonless night; **~ rousse** April moon; **croissant/quartier de ~** crescent/quarter moon; *V* **clair**[1].

(b) (*: *derrière*) bottom*, backside*.

(c) (*loc*) **~ de miel** honeymoon; **être dans la ~** to be in the clouds *ou* in a dream; **demander** *ou* **vouloir la ~** to ask for the moon; **promettre la ~** to promise the moon *ou* the earth; **il y a (bien) des ~s†** many moons ago; **vieilles ~s** outdated notions; *V* **face.**

luné, e* [lyne] *adj*: **être bien/mal ~** to be in a good/bad mood.

lunetier, -ière [lyntje, jɛʀ] **1** *adj* spectacle manufacturing. **2** *nm,f* optician, spectacle manufacturer.

lunette [lynɛt] **1** *nf* **(a) ~s** (*correctives*) glasses, specs*, spectacles†; (*de protection*) goggles; (*fig*) **mets tes ~s!** put your specs* on!

(b) (*Astron: télescope*) telescope; *[fusil]* sight(s). **fusil à ~** rifle equipped with sights.

(c) (*Archit*) lunette.

2: lunette d'approche telescope; (*Aut*) **lunette arrière** rear window; **lunette astronomique** astronomical telescope; **lunette des cabinets** (*cuvette*) toilet bowl; (*siège*) toilet rim; **lunettes d'écaille** horn-rimmed spectacles; **lunette méridienne** meridian circle; **lunettes noires** dark glasses; **lunettes de plongée** diving goggles; **lunettes de soleil** sunglasses.

lunetterie [lynɛtʀi] *nf* spectacle trade.

lunule [lynyl] *nf [ongle]* half-moon, lunula (*T*); (*Math*) lune.

lupanar [lypanaʀ] *nm* (*littér*) brothel.

lupin [lypɛ̃] *nm* lupin.

lupus [lypys] *nm* lupus.

lurette [lyʀɛt] *nf V* **beau.**

luron* [lyʀɔ̃] *nm*: **(joyeux** *ou* **gai) ~** gay dog; **un (sacré) ~** a great one for the girls, quite a lad*.

luronne* [lyʀɔn] *nf*: **(gaie) ~** (lively) lass; **une (sacrée) ~** a great one for the men.

lusitanien, -ienne [lyzitanjɛ̃, jɛn] **1** *adj* Lusitanian. **2** *nm,f*: **L~(ne)** Lusitanian.

lustrage [lystʀaʒ] *nm* (*Tech*) *[étoffe, peaux, fourrures]* lustring; *[glace]* shining.

lustral, e, *mpl* **-aux** [lystʀal, o] *adj* (*littér*) lustral (*littér*).

lustre [lystʀ(ə)] *nm* **(a)** *[objet, peaux, vernis]* lustre, shine; (*fig*) *[personne, cérémonie]* lustre. **redonner du ~ à une institution** to give new lustre to an institution. **(b)** (*luminaire*) chandelier. **(c)** (*littér: 5 ans*) lustrum (*littér*). (*fig*) **depuis des ~s** for ages, for aeons.

lustré, e [lystʀe] (*ptp de* **lustrer**) *adj cheveux, fourrure, poil* glossy; *manche usée* shiny.

lustrer [lystʀe] (1) *vt* (*Tech*) *étoffe, peaux, fourrures* to lustre; *glace* to shine; (*gén: faire briller*) to shine, put a shine on; (*par l'usure*) to make shiny. **le chat lustre son poil** the cat is licking its fur; **la pluie lustrait le feuillage** the rain put a sheen on the leaves; **tissue qui se lustre facilement** fabric that soon becomes shiny.

lustrerie [lystʀəʀi] *nf* chandelier trade.

lustrine [lystʀin] *nf* (*Tex*) lustre.

Lutèce [lytɛs] *nf* Lutetia.

lutécien, -ienne [lytesjɛ̃, jɛn] **1** *adj* Lutetian. **2** *nm,f*: **L~(ne)** Lutetian.

luth [lyt] *nm* lute.

luthéranisme [lyteʀanism(ə)] *nm* Lutheranism.

luthérien, -ienne [lyteʀjɛ̃, jɛn] **1** *adj* Lutheran. **2** *nm,f*: **L~(ne)** Lutheran.

luthier [lytje] *nm* (stringed-)instrument maker.

luthiste [lytist(ə)] *nm* lutanist.

lutin, e [lytɛ̃, in] **1** *adj* impish, mischievous. **2** *nm* (*esprit*) imp, sprite, goblin. (*fig*) **(petit) ~** (little) imp.

lutiner [lytine] (1) *vt femme* to fondle, tickle. **il aimait ~ les servantes** he enjoyed a bit of slap and tickle (*Brit*) *ou* fooling around with the serving girls.

lutrin [lytʀɛ̃] *nm* lectern.

lutte [lyt] **1** *nf* **(a)** (*gén: combat*) struggle, fight; (*entre des forces contraires*) conflict, struggle. **les ~s politiques qui ont déchiré le pays** the political struggles which have torn the country apart; **~ contre l'alcoolisme** struggle *ou* fight against alcoholism; **~ pour la vie** (*Bio, fig*) struggle for existence, struggle *ou* fight for survival; **aimer la ~** to enjoy a struggle; **entrer/être en ~ (contre qn)** to enter into/be in conflict (with sb); **en ~ ouverte contre sa famille** in open conflict with his family; **engager/abandonner la ~** to take up/give up the struggle *ou* fight; **nous soutenons une ~ inégale** we're fighting an uneven battle, it's an unequal struggle; **après plusieurs années de ~** after several years of struggling; (*Mil*) **le pays en ~** the country at war; (*Pol*) **les partis en ~** the opposing parties; **gagner** *ou* **conquérir qch de haute ~** to win sth by a hard-fought struggle *ou* after a brave fight *ou* struggle; **~ entre le bien et le mal** conflict *ou* struggle between good and evil; **~ de l'honneur et de l'intérêt** conflict between honour and self-interest.

(b) (*Sport*) wrestling. **~ libre/gréco-romaine** all-in/Graeco-Roman wrestling.

2: lutte armée armed struggle; **en lutte armée** in armed conflict; **lutte des classes** class struggle *ou* war; **lutte d'intérêts** conflict *ou* clash of interests.

lutter [lyte] (1) *vi* (*se battre*) to struggle, fight. **~ contre un adversaire** to struggle *ou* fight against an opponent; **~ contre le vent** to fight against *ou* battle with the wind; **~ contre l'ignorance/un incendie** to fight ignorance/a fire; **~ contre l'adversité/le sommeil** to fight off adversity/sleep; **~ contre la mort** to fight *ou* struggle for (one's) life; **~ avec sa conscience** to struggle *ou* wrestle with one's conscience; **les deux navires luttaient de vitesse** the two ships were racing each other.

lutteur, -euse [lytœʀ, øz] *nm,f* (*Sport*) wrestler; (*fig*) fighter.

lux [lyks] *nm* lux.

luxation [lyksɑsjɔ̃] *nf* dislocation, luxation (*T*).

luxe [lyks(ə)] *nm* **(a)** (*richesse*) wealth, luxury; *[maison, objet]* luxuriousness, sumptuousness. **vivre dans le ~** to live in (the lap of) luxury; **de ~** *voiture, appartement* luxury (*épith*); (*Comm*) *produits* de luxe; **boutique de ~** shop selling luxury goods; **2 salles de bain dans un appartement, c'est du ~!** 2 bathrooms in a flat, it's the height of luxury! *ou* what luxury!; **je me suis acheté un nouveau manteau, ce n'était pas du ~** I bought myself a new coat — I had to have one *ou* I really needed one.

(b) (*plaisir coûteux*) luxury. **il s'est offert** *ou* **payé le ~ d'aller au casino** he allowed himself the indulgence *ou* luxury of a trip to the casino; **je ne peux pas me payer le ~ d'être malade/d'aller au restaurant** I can't afford the luxury of being ill/eating out.

(c) (*fig: profusion*) wealth, host. **un ~ de détails/précautions** a host *ou* wealth of details/precautions.

luxembourgeois, e [lyksɑ̃buʀʒwa, waz] **1** *adj* of *ou* from Luxembourg. **2** *nm,f*: **L~(e)** inhabitant *ou* native of Luxembourg.

luxer [lykse] (1) *vt* to dislocate, luxate (*T*). **se ~ un membre** to dislocate a limb; **avoir l'épaule luxée** to have a dislocated shoulder.

luxueusement [lyksɥøzmɑ̃] *adv* luxuriously.

luxueux, -euse [lyksɥø, øz] *adj* luxurious.

luxure [lyksyʀ] *nf* lust.

luxuriance [lyksyʀjɑ̃s] *nf* luxuriance.

luxuriant, e [lyksyʀjɑ̃, ɑ̃t] *adj végétation* luxuriant, lush; (*fig*) *imagination* fertile, luxuriant (*littér*).

luxurieux, -euse [lyksyʀjø, øz] *adj* lustful, lascivious, sensual.

luzerne [lyzɛʀn(ə)] *nf* lucerne, alfalfa.

lycée [lise] *nm* lycée, ≃ secondary school (*Brit*), high school (*US*). **~ technique** technical school.

lycéen [liseɛ̃] *nm* secondary school (*Brit*) *ou* high-school (*US*) boy *ou* pupil. **lorsque j'étais ~** when I was at secondary school; **quelques ~s étaient attablés à la terrasse** some boys from the secondary school were sitting at a table outside the café; **les ~s sont en grève** pupils at secondary schools are on strike.

lycéenne [liseɛn] *nf* secondary school (*Brit*) *ou* high-school (*US*) girl *ou* pupil.

lymphatique [lɛ̃fatik] *adj* (*Bio*) lymphatic; (*fig*) lethargic, sluggish, lymphatic (*frm*).

lymphe [lɛ̃f] *nf* lymph.

lymphocyte [lɛ̃fɔsit] *nm* lymphocyte.

lymphoïde [lɛ̃fɔid] *adj* lymphoid.

lynchage [lɛ̃ʃaʒ] *nm* lynching.
lyncher [lɛ̃ʃe] (1) *vt* to lynch.
lynx [lɛ̃ks] *nm* lynx.
Lyon [ljɔ̃] *n* Lyons.
lyonnais, e [ljɔnɛ, ɛz] **1** *adj* of *ou* from Lyons; (*Culin*) Lyonnaise. **2** *nm,f*: **L~(e)** inhabitant *ou* native of Lyons.
lyre [liʀ] *nf* (*Mus*) lyre; *V* **oiseau.**
lyrique [liʀik] *adj* **(a)** (*Poésie*) lyric. **(b)** (*Mus, Théât*) **artiste/théâtre ~** opera singer/house; **ténor/soprano ~** lyric tenor/soprano; **drame ~** lyric drama, opera; **comédie ~** comic opera. **(c)** (*enthousiaste*) lyrical.
lyrisme [liʀism(ə)] *nm* lyricism. **s'exprimer avec ~ sur** to wax lyrical about, enthuse over.
lys [lis] *nm* = **lis.**

M

M, m [ɛm] *nm ou nf* (*lettre*) M, m.
m' [m(ə)] *V* **me.**
ma [ma] *adj poss V* **mon.**
maboul, e*† [mabul] *adj, nm,f* (*fou*) loony*.
macabre [makɑbʀ(ə)] *adj histoire, découverte* macabre, gruesome; *humour* macabre, ghoulish.
macache‡† [makaʃ] *adv*: **~! tu ne l'auras pas** not flipping likely!‡ (*Brit*) *ou* nothing doing!* you're not getting it; **~! il n'a pas voulu** nothing doing!* *ou* not a chance!* he wouldn't have it.
macadam [makadam] *nm* **(a)** (*substance*) *[pierres]* macadam; *[goudron]* Tarmac(adam) ®. **~ goudronné** Tarmac(adam) ®. **(b)** (*fig: rue, route*) road.
macadamisage [makadamizaʒ] *nm*, **macadamisation** [makadamizɑsjɔ̃] *nf* (*V* **macadamiser**) macadamization, macadamizing; tarmacking.
macadamiser [makadamize] (1) *vt* (*empierrer*) to macadamize; (*goudronner*) to tarmac. **chaussée** *ou* **route macadamisée** macadamized road; tarmac road.
macaque [makak] *nm* (*Zool*) macaque. **~ rhésus** rhesus (monkey); (*fig*) **qui est ce (vieux) ~?*** who's that ugly (old) ape?‡
macareux [makaʀø] *nm* puffin.
macaron [makaʀɔ̃] *nm* (*Culin*) macaroon; (*insigne*) (round) badge; (*autocollant*) (round) sticker; (*: *décoration*) medal, gong*. **~ publicitaire** publicity badge; (*sur voiture*) advertising sticker; (*Coiffure*) **~s** coils, earphones*.
macaroni [makaʀɔni] *nm* **(a)** (*Culin*) piece of macaroni. **manger des ~s** to eat macaroni; **~(s) au gratin** macaroni cheese. **(b)** (*Italien*) **(mangeur de) ~‡** Eyeti(e)‡, wop‡ (*péj*).
macaronique [makaʀɔnik] *adj vers etc* macaronic.
macchabée‡ [makabe] *nm* stiff‡ (*corpse*).
macédoine [masedwan] *nf* **(a)** (*Culin*) **~ de légumes** mixed vegetables, macedoine (of vegetables); **~ de fruits** fruit salad. **(b)** (**fig: mélange*) jumble, hotchpotch. **(c) M~** Macedonia.
macédonien, -ienne [masedɔnjɛ̃, jɛn] **1** *adj* Macedonian. **2** *nm,f*: **M~(ne)** Macedonian.
macération [maseʀɑsjɔ̃] *nf* (*V* **macérer**) **(a)** (*procédé*) maceration; pickling; steeping, soaking. **pendant leur ~ dans le vinaigre** while they are soaking *ou* pickling in vinegar.
(b) (*Rel: mortification*) maceration, mortification, scourging (of the flesh). **s'infliger des ~s** to scourge one's body *ou* flesh.
macérer [maseʀe] (6) **1** *vt* **(a)** (*dans de l'alcool*) to macerate; (*dans du vinaigre, de la saumure*) to pickle; (*dans de l'eau*) to steep, soak. **faire** *ou* **laisser ~** to macerate; to pickle; to steep, soak.
(b) (*Rel: mortifier*) **~ sa chair** to mortify one's flesh.
2 *vi* **(a)** (*dans de l'alcool*) to macerate; (*dans du vinaigre, de la saumure*) to pickle; (*dans de l'eau*) to steep, soak.
(b) (*fig péj*) **~ dans son ignorance** to wallow in one's ignorance.
macfarlane [makfaʀlan] *nm* (*manteau*) Inverness cape.
Mach [mak] *nm* mach. **voler à ~ 2** to fly at mach 2; **nombre de ~** mach (number).
mâche [mɑʃ] *nf* corn salad, lambs' lettuce.
mâchefer [mɑʃfɛʀ] *nm* clinker (*U*), cinders (*pl*).
mâcher [mɑʃe] (1) *vt [personne]* to chew; (*avec bruit*) to munch; *[animal]* to chomp; (*Tech*) to chew up. **il faut lui ~ tout le travail** you have to do half his work for him *ou* to spoon-feed him*; **il ne mâche pas ses mots** he doesn't mince his words; *V* **papier.**
machette [maʃɛt] *nf* machete.
Machiavel [makjavɛl] *nm* Machiavelli.
machiavélique [makjavelik] *adj* Machiavellian.
machiavélisme [makjavelism(ə)] *nm* Machiavell(ian)ism.
mâchicoulis [mɑʃikuli] *nm* machicolation. **à ~** machicolated.
machin, e[1]* [maʃɛ̃, in] **1** *nm,f* (*chose, truc*) (*dont le nom échappe*) thingummyjig*, whatsit*, what-d'you-call-it*; (*qu'on n'a jamais vu avant*) thing, contraption; (*tableau, statue etc*) thing. **passe-moi ton ~** give me your whatsit*; **les antibiotiques! il faut te méfier de ces ~s-là** antibiotics! you should beware of those things; **espèce de vieux ~!** you doddering old fool!*
2 *nm* (*personne*) **M~ (chouette)** what's-his-name*, what-d'you-call-him*, thingumabob‡; **hé! M~!** hey (you), what's-your-name!*; **le père/la mère M~** Mr/Mrs what's-his-/her-name*.
3 Machine *nf* (*personne*) what's-her-name*, what-d'you-call-her*; **hé! M~e!** hey! (you) what's-your-name!*
machinal, e, *mpl* **-aux** [maʃinal, o] *adj* (*automatique*) mechanical, automatic; (*involontaire*) automatic, unconscious.
machinalement [maʃinalmɑ̃] *adv* (*V* **machinal**) mechanically; automatically; unconsciously. **j'ai fait ça ~** I did it automatically *ou* without thinking.
machination [maʃinɑsjɔ̃] *nf* (*frm: complot*) plot, machination; (*coup monté*) put-up job*, frame-up. **être l'objet d'odieuses ~s** to be the victim of foul machinations *ou* schemings.
machine[2] [maʃin] *nf V* **machin.**
machine[3] [maʃin] **1** *nf* **(a)** (*Tech*) machine; (*Rail: locomotive*) engine, locomotive; (*Aviat: avion*) plane, machine; (*: *bicyclette, moto*) bike*, machine. (*fig*) **il n'est qu'une ~ à penser** he's nothing more than a sort of thinking machine; **le siècle de la ~** the century of the machine.
(b) (*fig: organisation*) machine; (*rouages*) machinery. **la ~ politique/parlementaire** the political/parliamentary machine; **la ~ de l'État** the machinery of state; **la ~ humaine** the human body; **la ~ administrative** the bureaucratic machine *ou* machinery.
(c) à la ~ by machine, with a machine; **faire qch à la ~** to machine sth, do sth on a machine; **fait/cousu/tricoté à la ~** machine-made/-sewn/-knitted; *V* **taper.**
(d) (*Naut*) engine. **faire ~ arrière** (*lit*) to go astern; (*fig*) to back-pedal, draw back; *V* **salle.**
2: machine à affranchir/à calculer franking/calculating machine; **machine composée** complex machine; **machine à composer** composing *ou* typesetting machine; **machine comptable** adding machine, calculating machine; **machine à coudre** sewing machine; **machine à écrire** typewriter; **machine de guerre** (*gén*) machine of war, instrument of warfare; **machine infernale†** time bomb, (explosive) device; **machine à laver** washing machine; **machine à laver la vaisselle** dishwasher; **machine-outil** *nf, pl* **machines-outils** machine tool; **machine simple** simple machine; **machine à sous** (*pour parier de l'argent*) one-armed bandit, fruit machine; (*distributeur automatique*) slot machine; **machine à timbrer = machine à affranchir**; **machine à tisser** power loom; **machine à traduire** translating machine; **machine à tricoter** knitting machine; **machine à vapeur** steam engine; **machine à vapeur à simple effet** simple steam engine; **machine à vapeur à double effet** double-acting engine.
machiner [maʃine] (1) *vt trahison* to plot; *complot* to hatch. **tout était machiné d'avance** the whole thing was fixed beforehand *ou* was prearranged, it was all a put-up job*; **c'est lui qui a tout machiné** the whole thing was contrived *ou* fixed by him; **qu'est-ce qu'il est en train de ~?** what is he hatching?*
machinerie [maʃinʀi] *nf* **(a)** (*équipement*) machinery, plant (*U*). **(b)** (*salle*) (*Naut*) engine room; (*atelier*) machine room.
machinisme [maʃinism(ə)] *nm* mechanization.
machiniste [maʃinist(ə)] *nm* (*Théât*) scene shifter, stagehand; (*Ciné*) (special) effects man; (*Transport*) driver (*of bus, underground train etc*). **'faire signe au ~'** = 'request stop'.
mâchoire [mɑʃwaʀ] *nf* (*Anat, Tech, Zool*) jaw. (*Aut*) **~s de frein** brake shoes; *V* **bâiller.**
mâchonnement [mɑʃɔnmɑ̃] *nm* chewing; (*Méd*) bruxism.
mâchonner [mɑʃɔne] (1) *vt* **(a)** (*) *[personne]* to chew (at); *[cheval]* to munch. **~ son crayon** to chew *ou* bite one's pencil. **(b)** (*fig: marmonner*) to mumble, mutter.
mâchouiller* [mɑʃuje] (1) *vt* to chew at *ou* on.
mâchure [mɑʃyʀ] *nf [drap, velours]* flaw.
mâchurer [mɑʃyʀe] (1) *vt* **(a)** (*salir*) *papier, habit* to stain (black); *visage* to blacken; (*Typ*) to mackle, blur. **(b)** (*Tech: écraser*) to dent. **(c)** (*déchiqueter*) *crayon* to chew, bite; *mouchoir* to chew.
macle[1] [makl(ə)] *nf* water chestnut.
macle[2] [makl(ə)] *nf* (*cristal*) twin; (*Hér*) mascle.
maclé, e [makle] *adj cristal* twinned, hemitrope.
mâcon [mɑkɔ̃] *nm* Mâcon (wine).

maçon [masɔ̃] *nm* **(a)** (*gén*) builder; (*qui travaille la pierre*) (stone)mason; (*qui pose les briques*) bricklayer. **ouvrier** *ou* **compagnon** ~ bricklayer's mate. **(b)** = **franc-maçon**; *V* **franc**[1].
maçonnage [masɔnaʒ] *nm* (*travail*) building; (*en briques*) bricklaying; (*ouvrage*) masonry, stonework; brickwork; (*revêtement*) facing.
maçonne [masɔn] *adj f V* **abeille, fourmi.**
maçonner [masɔne] (1) *vt* (*construire*) to build; (*consolider*) to build up; (*revêtir*) to face; (*boucher*) (*avec briques*) to brick up; (*avec pierres*) to block up (with stone).
maçonnerie [masɔnʀi] *nf* **(a)** *[pierres]* masonry, stonework; *[briques]* brickwork. ~ **de béton** concrete; ~ **en blocage** *ou* **de mœllons** rubble work.
(b) (*travail*) building; bricklaying. **entrepreneur/entreprise de** ~ building contractor/firm; **grosse** ~ erection of the superstructure; **petite** ~ finishing and interior building.
(c) = **franc-maçonnerie**; *V* **franc**[1].
maçonnique [masɔnik] *adj* masonic, Masonic.
macramé [makʀame] *nm* macramé.
macre [makʀ(ə)] *nf* = **macle**[1].
macreuse [makʀøz] *nf* (*Culin*) shoulder of beef; (*Orn*) scoter.
macro ... [makʀɔ] *préf* macro ... .~**céphale** *adj* macrocephalic; ~**cosme** *nm* macrocosm; ~**molécule** *nf* macromolecule; ~**phage** *nm* macrophage; *adj* macrophagic; ~**photographie** *nf* macrophotography; ~**scopique** *adj* macroscopic.
maculage [makylaʒ] *nm*, **maculation** [makylɑsjɔ̃] *nf* **(a)** (*gén*) maculation. **(b)** (*Typ*) (*action*) offsetting; (*tache*) offset, set-off.
maculature [makylatyʀ] *nf* (*Typ*) spoil (sheets), waste (sheets); (*feuille intercalaire*) interleaf.
macule [makyl] *nf [encre]* mackle, smudge; (*Astron, Méd*) macula; (*Typ*) smudge, set-off, blot, mackle.
maculer [makyle] (1) *vt* to stain (*de* with); (*Typ*) to mackle, blur.
Madagascar [madagaskaʀ] *nf* Madagascar.
Madame [madam], *pl* **Mesdames** [medam] *nf* **(a)** (*s'adressant à qn*) **bonjour** ~ (*courant*) good morning; (*nom connu*) good morning, Mrs X; (*frm*) good morning, Madam; **bonjour Mesdames** good morning (ladies); ~, **vous avez oublié quelque chose** excuse me *ou* Madam (*frm*) you've forgotten something; (*devant un auditoire*) **Mesdames** ladies; **Mesdames, Mesdemoiselles, Messieurs** ladies and gentlemen; ~ **votre mère**† your dear mother; ~ **la Présidente** *[société, assemblée]* Madam Chairman; *[gouvernement]* Madam President; **oui** ~ **la Générale/la Marquise** yes Mrs X/Madam; (*Scol*) ~! please Mrs X!, please Miss!; (*au restaurant*) **et pour (vous)** ~? and for (you) madam?; (*frm*) ~ **est servie** dinner is served (Madam); (*iro*) ~ **n'est pas contente!** her ladyship *ou* Madam isn't pleased! (*iro*).
(b) (*parlant de qn*) ~ **X est malade** Mrs X is ill; ~ **votre mère**† your dear *ou* good† mother; (*frm*) ~ **est sortie** Madam *ou* the mistress is not at home; **je vais le dire à** ~ (*parlant à un visiteur*) I will inform Madam (*frm*) *ou* Mrs X; (*parlant à un autre domestique*) I'll tell Mrs X *ou* the missus*†; ~ **dit que c'est à elle** the lady says it belongs to her; ~ **la Présidente** the chairman; **veuillez vous occuper de** ~ please attend to this lady('s requirements).
(c) (*sur une enveloppe*) ~ **X** Mrs X; (*Admin*) ~ **veuve X** Mrs X, widow of the late John *etc* X; **Mesdames X** the Mrs X; **Mesdames X et Y** Mrs X and Mrs Y; **Monsieur X et** ~ Mr and Mrs X; ~ **la Maréchale X** Mrs X; ~ **la Marquise de X** the Marchioness of X; **Mesdames les employées du service de comptabilité** (the ladies on) the staff of the accounts department.
(d) (*en-tête de lettre*) Dear Madam. **Chère** ~ Dear Mrs X; (*Admin*) ~, **Mademoiselle, Monsieur** Dear Sir or Madam; ~ **la Maréchale/Présidente/Duchesse** Dear Madam.
(e) (*Hist: parente du roi*) Madame.
(f) (*sans majuscule, pl* **madames**) (**péj*) lady. **jouer à la m**~ to play the fine lady, put on airs and graces; **toutes ces (belles) madames** all these fine ladies; **c'est une petite m**~ **maintenant** she's quite a (grown-up) young lady now.
madeleine [madlɛn] *nf* **(a)** (*Culin*) madeleine.
(b) M~ Magdalen(e), Madel(e)ine; **pleurer comme une M**~* to cry one's eyes out, weep buckets*.
Madelinot, e [mɑdlino, ɔt] *nm,f* inhabitant *ou* native of the Magdalen Islands.
Madelon [madlɔ̃] *nf dim de* **Madeleine.**
Mademoiselle [madmwazɛl], *pl* **Mesdemoiselles** [medmwazɛl] *nf* **(a)** (*s'adressant à qn*) **bonjour** ~ (*courant*) good morning; (*nom connu: frm*) good morning, Miss X; **bonjour Mesdemoiselles** good morning ladies; (*jeunes filles*) good morning young ladies; ~, **vous avez oublié quelque chose** excuse me miss, you've forgotten something; (*au restaurant*) **et pour vous** ~? and for the young lady?, and for you, miss?; (*devant un auditoire*) **Mesdemoiselles** ladies; (*iro*) ~ **n'est pas contente!** her ladyship isn't pleased!
(b) (*parlant de qn*) ~ **X est malade** Miss X is ill; ~ **votre sœur**† your dear sister; (*frm*) ~ **est sortie** the young lady (of the house) is out; **je vais le dire à** ~ I shall tell Miss X; ~ **dit que c'est à elle** the young lady says it's hers.
(c) (*sur une enveloppe*) ~ **X** Miss X; **Mesdemoiselles X** the Misses X; **Mesdemoiselles X et Y** Miss X and Miss Y.
(d) (*en-tête de lettre*) Dear Madam. **Chère** ~ Dear Miss X.
(e) (*Hist: parente du roi*) Mademoiselle.
Madère [madɛʀ] *nf* Madeira.
madère [madɛʀ] *nm* Madeira (wine); *V* **sauce.**
madériser (se) [maderize] (1) *vpr [eau-de-vie, vin]* to oxidise.
Madone [madɔn] *nf* **(a)** (*Art, Rel*) Madonna. **(b)** (*fig*) **m**~ beautiful woman, madonna-like woman; **elle a un visage de m**~ she has the face of a madonna.

madras [madʀɑs] *nm* (*étoffe*) madras (cotton); (*foulard*) (madras) scarf.
madré, e [madʀe] *adj paysan* crafty, wily, sly. (*hum*) **c'est une petite** ~**e!** she is a crafty *ou* fly* one! (*hum*).
madrépore [madʀepɔʀ] *nm* madrepore. ~**s** Madreporaria.
Madrid [madʀid] *n* Madrid.
madrier [madʀije] *nm* beam.
madrigal, *pl* **-aux** [madʀigal, o] *nm* (*Littérat, Mus*) madrigal; (††: *propos galant*) compliment.
madrilène [madʀilɛn] **1** *adj* of *ou* from Madrid. **2** *nmf*: **M**~ inhabitant *ou* native of Madrid.
maelstrom [malstʀɔm] *nm* (*lit, fig*) maelstrom.
maestria [maɛstʀija] *nf* (masterly) skill, mastery (*à faire qch* in doing sth). **avec** ~ brilliantly, in a masterly fashion, with consummate skill.
maf(f)ia [mafja] *nf* **(a) la M**~ the Maf(f)ia. **(b)** (*fig*) *[bandits, trafiquants]* gang, ring. ~ **d'anciens élèves** old boys' network; **c'est une vraie** ~! what a bunch* *ou* shower‡ of crooks!
mafflu, e [mafly] *adj* (*littér*) *visage, joues* round, full.
magasin [magazɛ̃] **1** *nm* **(a)** (*boutique*) shop, store; (*entrepôt*) warehouse. **faire** *ou* **courir les** ~**s** to go shopping, go (a)round *ou* do the shops; **nous ne l'avons pas en** ~ we haven't got it in stock; *V* **chaîne, grand.**
(b) (*Tech*) *[fusil, appareil-photo]* magazine.
2: (*Théât*) **magasin des accessoires** prop room; **magasin d'alimentation** grocery store; (*Mil*) **magasin d'armes** armoury; **magasin de confection** (ready-to-wear) dress shop *ou* tailor's; (*Théât*) **magasin des décors** scene dock; (*Comm, Jur*) **magasins généraux** bonded warehouse; **magasin à grande surface** hypermarket; (*Mil*) **magasin d'habillement** *ou* **de vivres** quartermaster's stores; **magasin (à) libre service** self-service store; **magasin à prix unique** one-price store, dime store (*US*), ten-cent store (*US*); **magasin à succursales (multiples)** chain *ou* multiple store.
magasinage [magazinaʒ] *nm* **(a)** (*Comm*) warehousing. **frais de** ~ storage costs. **(b)** (*Can*) shopping. **faire son** ~ to do one's shopping.
magasiner [magazine] (1) *vi* (*Can*) to go shopping.
magasinier [magazinje] *nm [usine]* storekeeper, storeman; *[entrepôt]* warehouseman.
magazine [magazin] *nm* (*Presse*) magazine, mag*. (*Rad, TV*) ~ **féminin/pour les jeunes** woman's/children's hour; ~ **hebdomadaire/mensuel** weekly/monthly (magazine); ~ **de luxe** glossy* (magazine).
mage [maʒ] *nm* (*Antiq, fig*) magus. (*Rel*) **les (trois) Rois** ~**s** the Magi, the (Three) Wise Men.
Maghreb [magʀɛb] *nm*: **le** ~ the Maghreb, NW Africa.
maghrébin, e [magʀebɛ̃, in] *adj* of *ou* from the Maghreb.
magicien, -ienne [maʒisjɛ̃, jɛn] *nm,f* (*sorcier, illusionniste*) magician; (*fig*) wizard, magician.
magie [maʒi] *nf* magic. ~ **noire** black magic; **la** ~ **du verbe** the magic of words; **comme par** ~ like magic, (as if) by magic; **c'est de la** ~ it's (like) magic.
magique [maʒik] *adj mot, baguette* magic; (*enchanteur*) *spectacle* magical; *V* **lanterne.**
magiquement [maʒikmɑ̃] *adv* magically.
magister† [maʒistɛʀ] *nm* (village) schoolmaster; (*péj*) pedant.
magistral, e, *mpl* **-aux** [maʒistʀal, o] *adj* **(a)** (*éminent*) *œuvre* masterly, brilliant; *réussite* brilliant, magnificent; *adresse* masterly.
(b) (*hum: gigantesque*) *claque, râclée* thorough, colossal, sound.
(c) (*doctoral*) *ton* authoritative, masterful; (*Univ*) **cours** ~ lecture; **enseignement** ~ lecturing.
(d) (*Pharm*) magistral.
(e) (*Tech*) **ligne** ~**e** magistral line.
magistralement [maʒistʀalmɑ̃] *adv* (*V* **magistral**) in a masterly manner; brilliantly; magnificently.
magistrat [maʒistʀa] *nm* magistrate.
magistrature [maʒistʀatyʀ] *nf* **(a)** (*Jur*) magistracy, magistrature. **la** ~ **assise** *ou* **du siège** the judges, the bench; **la** ~ **debout** the state prosecutors. **(b)** (*Admin, Pol*) public office. **la** ~ **suprême** the supreme *ou* highest office.
magma [magma] *nm* (*Chim, Géol*) magma; (*fig: mélange*) jumble, muddle.
magnanime [maɲanim] *adj* magnanimous. **se montrer** ~ to show magnanimity.
magnanimement [maɲanimmɑ̃] *adv* magnanimously.
magnanimité [maɲanimite] *nf* magnanimity.
magnat [magna] *nm* tycoon, magnate. ~ **de la presse** press baron *ou* lord.
magner (se)‡ [maɲe] (1) *vpr* to get a move on*, hurry up. **magne-toi (le train** *ou* **le popotin)!** get a move on!*, get moving!*, hurry up!
magnésie [maɲezi] *nf* magnesia.
magnésium [maɲezjɔm] *nm* magnesium; *V* **éclair.**
magnétique [maɲetik] *adj* (*Phys, fig*) magnetic. **champ/pôle** ~ magnetic field/pole; *V* **bande**[1].
magnétisable [maɲetizabl(ə)] *adj* hypnotizable.
magnétisation [maɲetizɑsjɔ̃] *nf* (*V* **magnétiser**) magnetization; mesmerization, hypnotization.
magnétiser [maɲetize] (1) *vt* **(a)** (*Phys, fig*) to magnetize. **(b)** (*hypnotiser*) to mesmerize, hypnotize.
magnétiseur, -euse [maɲetizœʀ, øz] *nm,f* hypnotizer.
magnétisme [maɲetism(ə)] *nm* (*Phys, charme*) magnetism; (*hypnotisme*) hypnotism, mesmerism. ~ **terrestre** terrestrial magnetism; **le** ~ **d'un grand homme** the magnetism *ou* charisma of a great man.
magnétite [maɲetit] *nf* magnetite.
magnéto[1] [maɲeto] *nm abrév de* **magnétophone.**

magnéto[2] [maɲeto] *nf* (*Élec*) magneto.
magnéto-cassette, *pl* **magnéto-cassettes** [maɲetɔkasɛt] *nm* cassette deck.
magnéto-électrique [maɲetɔelɛktʀik] *adj* magnetoelectric.
magnétophone [maɲetɔfɔn] *nm* tape recorder. ~ **à cassette(s)** cassette recorder; **enregistré au** ~ (tape-)recorded, taped.
magnétoscope [maɲetɔskɔp] *nm* (*appareil*) video-tape recorder; (*bande*) video-tape.
magnificat [magnifikat] *nm inv* magnificat.
magnificence [maɲifisɑ̃s] *nf* (*littér*) **(a)** (*faste*) magnificence, splendour. **(b)** (*prodigalité*) munificence (*littér*), lavishness.
magnifier [magnifje] (7) *vt* (*littér: louer*) to magnify (*littér*), glorify; (*rare: idéaliser*) to idealize.
magnifique [maɲifik] *adj* **(a)** (*somptueux*) *appartement, repas* magnificent, sumptuous; *cortège* splendid, magnificent; *cadeau, réception* magnificent, lavish.
(b) (*splendide*) *femme, fleur* gorgeous, superb; *paysage, temps* magnificent, glorious, gorgeous; *projet, situation* magnificent, marvellous. ~**!*** fantastic!*, great!*; **il a été ~ hier soir!** he was magnificent *ou* fantastic* *ou* great* last night!
(c) Soliman le M~ Soliman the Magnificent.
magnifiquement [maɲifikmɑ̃] *adv* (*V* **magnifique**) magnificently; sumptuously; lavishly; gorgeously; superbly; marvellously.
magnitude [magnityd] *nf* (*Astron*) magnitude.
magnolia [maɲɔlja] *nm,* **magnolier** [maɲɔlje] *nm* magnolia.
magnum [magnɔm] *nm* magnum.
magot [mago] *nm* **(a)** (*Zool*) Barbary ape, magot.
(b) (*Sculp*) magot.
(c) (*) (*somme d'argent*) pile (of money)*, packet*; (*économies*) savings, nest egg. **ils ont amassé un joli** ~ they've made a nice little pile* *ou* packet*, they've got a tidy sum put by *ou* a nice little nest egg.
magouillage* [maguja3] *nm,* **magouille*** [maguj] *nf* graft* (*péj*), chicanery (*U*).
magouiller* [maguje] (1) *vi* (*péj*) to graft* (*péj*).
magyar, e [magjaʀ] **1** *adj* Magyar. **2** *nm,f*: **M~(e)** Magyar.
mahara(d)jah [maaʀa(d)ʒa] *nm* Maharajah.
maharani [maaʀani] *nf* Maharanee.
mah-jong [maʒɔ̃g] *nm* mah-jong(g).
Mahomet [maɔmɛt] *nm* Mahomet, Mohammed.
mahométan, -ane [maɔmetɑ̃, an] *adj* Mahometan, Mohammedan.
mahométisme [maɔmetism(ə)] *nm* Mohammedanism.
mai [mɛ] *nm* May; *pour loc V* **septembre** *et* **premier.**
maïeutique [majøtik] *nf* maieutics (*sg*).
maigre [mɛgʀ(ə)] **1** *adj* **(a)** *personne* thin, skinny (*péj*); *animal* thin, scraggy; *visage, joue* thin, lean; *membres* thin, scrawny (*péj*), skinny. ~ **comme un clou** *ou* **un chat de gouttière*** as thin as a rake *ou* a lath.
(b) (*Culin: après n*) *bouillon* clear; *viande* lean; *fromage* low-fat.
(c) (*Rel*) **jour** ~ day of abstinence, fish day; day of lean diet; **repas** ~ meal without meat; **faire** ~ **(le vendredi)** not to eat meat (on Fridays).
(d) (*peu important*) *profit, revenu* small, slim, scanty; *ration, salaire* meagre, poor; *résultat* poor; *exposé, conclusion* sketchy, skimpy, slight; *espoir, chance* slim, slight. **comme dîner, c'est un peu** ~ it's a bit of a skimpy dinner, it's not much of a dinner.
(e) (*peu épais*) *végétation* thin, sparse; *récolte, terre* poor. **un ~ filet d'eau** a thin trickle of water; ~ **eau** shallow water; (*hum*) **avoir le cheveu** ~ to be a bit thin on top.
(f) (*Typ*) **caractère** ~ light-faced letter.
2 *nmf*: **grand/petit** ~ tall/small thin person; **les gros et les ~s** fat people and thin people; **c'est une fausse** ~ she looks deceptively thin.
3 *nm* **(a)** (*U: Culin*) (*viande*) lean (meat); (*jus*) thin gravy.
(b) (*Géog*) *[fleuve]* **~s** shallows.
(c) (*Typ*) light face.
maigrelet, -ette [mɛgʀəlɛ, ɛt] *adj* thin, scrawny, skinny. **un gamin** ~ a skinny little kid*; **un petit** ~ a skinny little chap *ou* fellow *ou* man.
maigrement [mɛgʀəmɑ̃] *adv* poorly, meagrely. **être** ~ **payé** to be badly *ou* poorly paid.
maigreur [mɛgʀœʀ] *nf [personne]* thinness, leanness; *[animal]* thinness, scragginess; *[membre]* thinness, scrawniness, skinniness; *[végétation]* thinness, sparseness; *[sol]* poorness; *[profit]* smallness, scantiness; *[salaire]* meagreness, poorness; *[réponse, exposé]* sketchiness, poorness; *[preuve, sujet, auditoire]* thinness; *[style]* thinness, baldness. **il est d'une ~!** he's so thin! *ou* skinny!
maigrichon, -onne [mɛgʀiʃɔ̃, ɔn] *adj,* **maigriot, -otte** [mɛgʀio, ɔt] *adj* = **maigrelet.**
maigrir [megʀiʀ] (2) **1** *vi* to grow *ou* get thinner, lose weight. **je l'ai trouvé maigri** I thought he had got thinner *ou* he was thinner *ou* he had lost weight; **il a maigri de visage** his face has got thinner; **il a maigri de 5 kg** he has lost 5 kg; **régime/pastilles pour** ~ slimming diet/tablets; **se faire** ~ to slim, diet (to lose weight).
2 *vt*: ~ **qn** *[vêtement]* to make sb look slim(mer); **(faire)** ~ **qn** *[maladie, régime]* to make sb lose weight; **faire ~ qn** *[médecin]* to make sb take off *ou* lose weight.
mail [maj] *nm* **(a)** (*promenade*) mall†, tree-lined walk. **(b)** (††) (*jeu, terrain*) (pall-)mall; (*maillet*) mall.
maille [maj] *nf* **(a)** (*Couture*) stitch. *[tissu, tricot]* ~ **qui a filé** stitch which has run; *[bas]* ~ **filée** ladder, run; **une ~ à l'endroit, une ~ à l'envers** knit one, purl one; **tissu à fines ~s** fine-knit material.
(b) *[filet]* mesh. (*lit, fig*) **passer à travers les ~s (du filet)** to slip through the net; **à larges/fines ~s** wide/fine mesh (*épith*).
(c) *[armure, grillage]* link; *V* **cotte.**
(d) avoir ~ à partir avec qn to get into trouble with sb, have a brush with sb.
maillechort [majʃɔʀ] *nm* nickel silver.
maillet [majɛ] *nm* mallet.
mailloche [majɔʃ] *nf* (*Tech*) beetle, maul; (*Mus*) bass drumstick.
maillon [mɑjɔ̃] *nm* **(a)** (*anneau*) link. (*fig*) **il n'est qu'un ~ de la chaîne** he's just one link in the chain. **(b)** (*rare: petite maille*) small stitch.
maillot [majo] **1** *nm* **(a)** (*gén*) vest; (*Danse*) leotard; *[footballeur]* (football) jersey; *[coureur]* vest, singlet. (*Sport*) **porter le ~ jaune, être ~ jaune** to wear the yellow jersey, be leader of the Tour (de France *etc*).
(b) *[bébé]* swaddling clothes††, baby's wrap. **enfant** *ou* **bébé au** ~ babe in arms.
2: maillot de bain *[homme]* swimming *ou* bathing trunks, bathing suit†; *[femme]* swimming *ou* bathing costume, swimsuit; **maillot de corps** vest (*Brit*), undershirt (*US*).
main [mɛ̃] **1** *nf* **(a)** hand. **donner** *ou* **serrer la ~ à qn** to shake hands with sb; **se donner** *ou* **se serrer la** ~ to shake hands; **donner** *ou* **tendre la ~ à qn** to hold out one's hand to sb; **donner** *ou* **tenir la ~ à** *ou* **de qn** to hold sb's hand; **donne-moi la ~ pour traverser** give me your hand *ou* let me hold your hand to cross the street; **ils se tenaient (par) la** ~ they were holding hands; **il me salua de la** ~ he waved to me; **il me fit adieu de la** ~ he waved goodbye to me; **il entra le chapeau à la** ~ he came in with his hat in his hand; **être adroit/maladroit de ses ~s** to be clever/clumsy with one's hands; **d'une ~ experte** with an expert hand; **à ~s nues** *boxer* without gloves, with bare fists *ou* hands; **les ~s nues** (*sans gants*) with bare hands; **prendre des deux ~s/de la ~ gauche** to take with both hands/with one's left hand; (*Ftbl*) **il y a ~!** hands!, hand ball!; **de ~ en ~** from hand to hand; **la ~ dans la ~** *[promeneurs]* hand in hand; *[escrocs]* hand in glove; **regarde, sans les ~s!** look, no hands!; **les ~s en l'air** hands up!, stick 'em up!
(b) (*symbole d'autorité, de possession, d'aide*) hand. **la ~ de Dieu/de la fatalité** the hand of God/of destiny; **trouver une ~ secourable** to find a helping hand; **il lui faut une ~ ferme** he needs a firm hand; **une ~ de fer dans un gant de velours** an iron hand in a velvet glove; **dans des ~s indignes** in unworthy hands; **tomber aux** *ou* **dans les ~s de l'ennemi** to fall into the hands of the enemy; **obtenir la ~ d'une jeune fille (en mariage)** to win a girl's hand (in marriage); **accorder la ~ de sa fille à qn** to give sb one's daughter's hand in marriage.
(c) (*manière, habileté*) **de la ~ de Cézanne** by Cézanne; **reconnaître la ~ de l'artiste/de l'auteur** to recognize the artist's/writer's stamp; **de ~ de maître** with a master's hand; **perdre la** ~ to lose one's touch; **s'entretenir la** ~ to keep one's hand in; **se faire la** ~ to get one's hand in.
(d) (*Cartes*) **avoir/perdre la** ~ to have/lose the lead.
(e) (*écriture*) hand(writing).
(f) (*Comm*) *[papier]* ≃ quire (*25 sheets*).
(g) (*loc*) **à ~ droite/gauche** on the right-/left-hand side; **ce livre est en** ~ this book is in use *ou* is out; **l'affaire est en** ~ the matter is being dealt with *ou* attended to; **en ~s sûres** in(to) safe hands; **avoir une voiture bien en** ~ to have the feel of a car; **de la ~ à la** ~ directly (*without receipt*); **préparé de longue** ~ prepared long beforehand; **de première/seconde** ~ *information, ouvrage* firsthand/secondhand; (*Comm*) **de première** ~ secondhand (*only one previous owner*); **à la** ~ by hand; **fait (à la) ~** handmade; **cousu (à la) ~** hand-sewn; **vol/attaque à ~ armée** armed robbery/attack; **(pris) la ~ dans le sac** caught red-handed, caught in the act; **(en) sous** ~ *négocier, agir* secretly; **les ~s vides** empty-handed; **sous la** ~ to *ou* at hand; **avoir tout sous la** ~ to have everything to *ou* at hand *ou* handy; **on prend ce qui tombe sous la** ~ we take whatever comes to hand; **ce papier m'est tombé sous la** ~ I came across this paper; **à ~ levée** *vote* on *ou* by a show of hands; *dessin* freehand.
(h) (*loc verbales*) **avoir la ~ heureuse: il a eu la ~ heureuse: il a choisi le numéro gagnant** it was a lucky shot his picking the winning number; **en engageant cet assistant on a vraiment eu la ~ heureuse** when we took on that assistant we really picked a winner; **avoir la ~ malheureuse** to be heavy-handed *ou* clumsy; **avoir la ~ lourde** *[commerçant]* to be heavy-handed *ou* overgenerous; *[juge]* to mete out justice with a heavy hand; **ce boucher a toujours la ~ lourde** this butcher always gives *ou* cuts you more than you ask for; **le juge a eu la ~ lourde** the judge gave him a stiff sentence; **avoir la ~ légère** to rule with a light hand; **avoir la ~ leste** to be free *ou* quick with one's hands; (*fig*) **avoir les ~s liées** to have one's hands tied; **être à sa ~: il faudrait être à sa ~ pour réparer ce robinet** you'd have to be able to get at this tap properly to mend it; **je ne suis pas à ma** ~ I can't get a proper hold *ou* grip, I'm not in the right position; **faire ~ basse sur qch** to run off with sth, help o.s. to sth; **laisser les ~s libres à qn** to give sb a free hand *ou* rein; **mettre la ~ au collet de qn** to arrest sb, collar* sb; **en venir aux ~s** to come to blows; **mettre la ~ sur** to lay hands on; *coupable* to arrest, lay hands on, collar*; **je ne peux pas mettre la ~ sur mon passeport** I can't lay hands on my passport; **mettre la ~ à la pâte** to lend a hand, set one's hand to the plough (*fig, littér*); **mettre la dernière ~ à** to put the finishing *ou* crowning touches to; **passer la** ~ to stand down, make way for someone else; **passer la ~ dans le dos à qn** to rub sb up the right way; **se passer la ~ dans le dos** to pat one another on the back; **avoir la situation (bien) en** ~ to have the situation well in hand *ou* well under control; **prendre qch/qn en** ~ to take sth/sb in hand; **remettre qch en ~s propres** to hand sth back to its rightful owner; **reprendre qn/qch en** ~ to take sb/sth in hand again; **il n'y va pas de ~ morte** (*exagérer*) he

doesn't do things by halves; (*frapper*) he doesn't pull his punches; **j'en mettrais ma ~ au feu** *ou* **à couper** I'd stake my life on it; **tu es aussi maladroit que moi, on peut se donner la ~** you're as clumsy as me, we're two of a kind.

2: (*Jeux*) **la main chaude** hot cockles; **main courante** (*câble*) handrail; (*Comm*) rough book, daybook; **main de Fatma** hand of Fatima; **main-forte: prêter** *ou* **donner main-forte à qn** to come to sb's assistance, come to help sb; **main-d'œuvre** *nf* labour, manpower; (*Aut*) **main de ressort** dumb iron.

mainate [mɛnat] *nm* myna(h) bird.

mainlevée [mɛ̃lve] *nf* (*Jur*) withdrawal. (*Fin*) **~ d'hypothèque** release of mortgage.

mainmise [mɛ̃miz] *nf* (*Jur, Pol*) seizure (*de, sur* of).

maint, e [mɛ̃, ɛ̃t] *adj* (*littér*) (a great *ou* good) many (+ *npl*), many a (+ *n sg*). **~ étranger** many a foreigner; **~s étrangers** many foreigners; **à ~es reprises, (~es et) ~es fois** time and (time) again, many a time.

maintenance [mɛ̃tnɑ̃s] *nf* maintenance unit.

maintenant [mɛ̃tnɑ̃] *adv* **(a)** (*en ce moment*) now. **que fait-il ~?** what's he doing now?; **il doit être arrivé ~** he must have arrived by now; *V* **dès, jusque, partir**[1].

(b) (*à ce moment*) now, by now. **ils devaient ~ chercher à se nourrir** they had now to try and find something to eat; **ils étaient ~ très fatigués** by now they were very tired; **ils marchaient ~ depuis 2 heures** they had (by) now been walking for 2 hours.

(c) (*actuellement*) today, nowadays. **les jeunes de ~** young people nowadays *ou* today.

(d) (*ceci dit*) now (then). **~ ce que j'en dis c'est pour ton bien** now (then) what I say is for your own good; **il y a un cadavre, certes: ~, y a-t-il un crime?** we're agreed there's a corpse, now (then), is there a crime?

maintenir [mɛ̃tniʀ] (22) **1** *vt* **(a)** (*soutenir, contenir*) *édifice* to hold *ou* keep up, support; *cheville, os* to give support to, support; *cheval* to hold in. **~ qch fixe/en équilibre** to keep *ou* hold sth in position/balanced; **les oreillers le maintiennent assis** the pillows keep him in a sitting position *ou* keep him sitting up; **~ la tête hors de l'eau** to keep one's head above water; **~ la foule** to keep *ou* hold the crowd back *ou* in check; **~ les prix** to keep prices steady *ou* in check.

(b) (*garder*) (*gén*) to keep; *statu quo, tradition* to maintain, preserve, uphold; *régime* to uphold, support; *décision* to maintain, stand by, uphold; *candidature* to maintain. **~ des troupes en Europe** to keep troops in Europe; **~ l'ordre/la paix** to keep *ou* maintain law and order/the peace; **~ qn en poste** to keep sb on, keep sb at *ou* in his job.

(c) (*affirmer*) to maintain. **je l'ai dit et je le maintiens!** I've said it and I'm sticking to it! *ou* I'm standing by it!; **~ que** to maintain *ou* hold that.

2 se maintenir *vpr [temps]* to stay fair; *[amélioration]* to persist; *[préjugé]* to live on, persist, remain; *[malade]* to hold one's own. **se ~ en bonne santé** to keep in good health, manage to keep well; **les prix se maintiennent** prices are keeping *ou* holding steady; **cet élève devrait se ~ dans la moyenne** this pupil should be able to keep up with the middle of the class; **comment ça va? — ça se maintient*** how are you getting on? — bearing up* *ou* so-so* *ou* not too badly.

maintien [mɛ̃tjɛ̃] *nm* **(a)** (*sauvegarde*) *[tradition]* preservation, upholding, maintenance; *[régime]* upholding. **assurer le ~ de** *tradition* to maintain, preserve, uphold; *régime* to uphold, support; **le ~ des prix/de troupes/de l'ordre** the maintenance of prices/of troops/of law and order; **qu'est-ce qui a pu justifier le ~ de sa décision/candidature?** what(ever) were his reasons for standing by his decision/for maintaining his candidature?

(b) (*posture*) bearing, deportment. **leçon de ~** lesson in deportment; **professeur de ~** teacher of deportment.

maire [mɛʀ] *nm* mayor. (*hum*) **passer devant (monsieur) le ~** to get hitched‡, get married; *V* **adjoint, écharpe.**

mairesse† [mɛʀɛs] *nf* mayoress.

mairie [meʀi] *nf* (*bâtiment*) town hall, city hall; (*administration*) town council, municipal corporation; (*charge*) mayoralty, office of mayor; *V* **secrétaire.**

mais[1] [mɛ] **1** *conj* **(a)** (*objection, restriction, opposition*) but. **ce n'est pas bleu ~ (bien) mauve** it isn't blue, it's (definitely) mauve; **non seulement il boit ~ (encore** *ou* **en outre) il bat sa femme** not only does he drink but on top of that *ou* even worse he beats his wife; **il est peut-être le patron ~ tu as quand même des droits** he may be the boss but you've still got your rights; **il est parti? ~ tu m'avais promis qu'il m'attendrait!** he has left? but you promised he'd wait for me!

(b) (*renforcement*) **je n'ai rien mangé hier, ~ vraiment rien** I ate nothing at all yesterday, absolutely nothing; **tu me crois? — ~ oui** *ou* **~ bien sûr** *ou* **~ certainement** do you believe me? — (but) of course *ou* of course I do; **~ je te jure que c'est vrai!** but I swear it's true!; **~ ne te fais pas de soucis!** don't you worry!

(c) (*transition, surprise*) **~ qu'arriva-t-il?** but what happened (then)?; **~ alors qu'est-ce qui est arrivé?** well then *ou* for goodness' sake what happened?; **~ dites-moi, c'est intéressant tout ça!** well, well *ou* well now that's all very interesting!; **~ j'y pense, vous n'avez pas déjeuné** by the way I've just thought, you haven't had any lunch; **~, vous pleurez** good Lord *ou* gracious, you're crying; **~ enfin, tant pis!** well, too bad!

(d) (*protestation, indignation*) **ah ~! il verra de quel bois je me chauffe** I can tell you he'll soon see what I have to say about it; **non ~ (des fois)!** *ou* **(alors)!*** hey look here!*, for God's sake!‡; **non ~ (des fois)‡ tu me prends pour un imbécile?** I ask you* *ou* come off it‡, do you think I'm a complete idiot?; **~ enfin tu vas te taire?‡** look here, are you going to *ou* will you shut up?*

2 *nm* (*sg*) objection, snag; (*pl*) buts. **je ne veux pas de ~** I don't want any buts; **il n'y a pas de ~ qui tienne** there's no but about it; **il y a un ~** there's one snag *ou* objection; **il va y avoir des si et des ~** there are sure to be some ifs and buts.

mais[2] [mɛ] *adv* (*littér*,†) **il n'en pouvait ~** (*impuissant*) he could do nothing about it; (*épuisé*) he was exhausted *ou* worn out.

maïs [mais] *nm* maize (*Brit*), Indian corn (*Brit*), corn (*US*); *V* **farine.**

maison [mɛzɔ̃] **1** *nf* **(a)** (*bâtiment*) house; (*immeuble*) building; (*locatif*) block of flats. **~ (d'habitation)** dwelling house, private house; **une ~ de 2 étages/de 5 pièces** a 3-storey *ou* -storeyed/5-roomed house; **~ individuelle** detached house; **ils ont une petite ~ à la campagne** they have a cottage in the country; *V* **pâté.**

(b) (*logement, foyer*) home. **être/rester à la ~** to be/stay at home *ou* in; **rentrer à la ~** to go (back); **quitter la ~** to leave home; **tenir la ~ de qn** to keep house for sb; **les dépenses de la ~** household expenses; **fait à la ~** home-made; **c'est la ~ du bon Dieu, c'est une ~ accueillante** they keep open house, their door is always open; *V* **linge, maître, train.**

(c) (*famille, maisonnée*) family. **quelqu'un de la ~ m'a dit** someone in the family told me; **un ami de la ~** a friend of the family; **il n'est pas heureux à la ~** he doesn't have a happy home *ou* family life; **nous sommes 7 à la ~** there are 7 of us at home.

(d) (*entreprise commerciale*) firm, company; (*magasin de vente*) (*grand*) store, (*petit*) shop. **il est dans la ~ depuis 3 ans** he's been *ou* worked with the firm for 3 years; **la ~ n'est pas responsable de ...** the company *ou* management accepts no responsibility for ... ; **la ~ ne fait pas crédit** no credit (given); **la M~ du Disque/du Café** the Record/Coffee Shop; *V* **confiance.**

(e) (*famille royale*) House. **la ~ des Hanovre/des Bourbon** the House of Hanover/of Bourbon.

(f) (*place de domestiques, domesticité*) household. **la ~ du Roi/du Président de la République** the Royal/Presidential Household; **~ civile/militaire** civil/military household; **gens**† *ou* **employés de ~** servants, domestic staff.

(g) (*Astrol*) house, mansion; (*Rel*) house.

2 *adj inv* **(a)** (*fait à la maison*) *gâteau* home-made; (*: *formé sur place*) *ingénieur* trained by the firm. (*Comm: spécialité*) **pâté ~** pâté maison, chef's own pâté.

(b) (*: *très réussi*) first-rate. **il y a eu une bagarre ~** *ou* **une bagarre quelque chose de ~** there was an almighty* *ou* a stand-up row.

3: maison d'arrêt prison (*for prisoners on remand*); **la Maison Blanche** the White House; **maison de campagne** (*grande*) house in the country, (*petite*) (country) cottage; **maison centrale** prison; **maison close** brothel; **maison de commerce** (commercial) firm; (*Jur*†) **maison correction** reformatory†; **maison de couture** couture house; **maison de la culture** ≃ arts centre; **maison d'éducation surveillée** ≃ approved school, ≃ Borstal; **maison d'étudiants** students' hall of residence *ou* hostel; **maison de fous** madhouse, lunatic asylum; **maison de jeu** gambling *ou* gaming club *ou* den; **maison de la jeunesse** *ou* **des jeunes** ≃ youth club; **maison de maître** family mansion; **maison mère** (*Comm*) parent house *ou* company; (*Rel*) mother house; **maison de passe** *hotel used by prostitutes and their customers*; **maison de poupée** doll's house; **maison de rapport** apartment block; **maison de redressement**† reformatory†; **maison religieuse** convent; **maison de rendez-vous** *house used by lovers as a discreet meeting-place;* **maison de repos** convalescent home; **maison de retraite** old people's home; **maison de santé** (*clinique*) nursing home; (*asile*) mental home; **maison de tolérance = maison close.**

maisonnée [mɛzɔne] *nf* household, family.

maisonnette [mezɔnɛt] *nf* small house, maisonette; (*rustique*) cottage.

maistrance [mɛstʀɑ̃s] *nf* petty officers.

maître, maîtresse [mɛtʀ(ə), mɛtʀɛs] **1** *adj* **(a)** (*principal*) *branche* main; *pièce, œuvre* main, major; *qualité* chief, main, major; (*Cartes*) *atout, carte* master (*épith*). **c'est une œuvre maîtresse** it's a major work; **c'est la pièce maîtresse de la collection** it's the major *ou* main *ou* principal piece in the collection; **poutre maîtresse** main beam; **position maîtresse** major *ou* key position; **idée maîtresse** principal *ou* governing idea.

(b) (*avant n: intensif*) **un ~ filou** *ou* **fripon** an arrant *ou* out-and-out rascal; **une maîtresse femme** a managing woman.

2 *nm* **(a)** (*gén*) master; (*Art*) master; (*Pol: dirigeant*) ruler. **parler/agir en ~** to speak/act authoritatively; **ils se sont installés en ~s dans ce pays** they have set themselves up as the ruling power in the country, they have taken command of the country; **d'un ton de ~** in an authoritative *ou* a masterful tone; **je vais t'apprendre qui est le ~ ici!** I'll teach you who is the boss* round here *ou* who's in charge round here!; **la main/l'œil du ~** the hand/eye of a master; (*fig*) **le grand ~ des études celtiques** the greatest authority on Celtic studies; **le ~ de céans** the master of the house; (*Naut*) **seul ~ à bord après Dieu** sole master on board under God; *V* **chauffeur, coup, toile** *etc.*

(b) (*Scol*) **~ (d'école)** teacher, (school)master; **~ de piano/d'anglais** piano/English teacher.

(c) (*artisan*) **~ charpentier/maçon** master carpenter/mason *ou* builder.

(d) (*titre*) **M~** *term of address given to lawyers, artists, professors etc*; **mon cher M~** Dear Mr *ou* Professor *etc* X; (*Art*) maestro; (*Jur*) **M~ X** Mr X.

(e) (*loc*) (*Cartes*) **être ~ à cœur** to have *ou* hold the master *ou* best heart; **le roi de cœur est ~** the king of hearts is master, the king is the master *ou* best heart; **être ~ chez soi** to be master in one's own home; **être son (propre) ~** to be one's own master; **être ~ de refuser/de faire** to be free to refuse/do; **rester ~ de soi** to retain *ou* keep one's self-control; **être ~ de soi** to be in control *ou* have control of o.s.; **être/rester ~ de la situation** to be/remain in control of the situation, have/keep the situation under control; **être/rester ~ de sa voiture** to be/remain in control of one's car; **être/rester ~ du pays** to be/remain in control *ou* command of the country; **être ~ d'un secret** to be in possession of a secret; **se rendre ~ de** *ville, pays* to gain control *ou* possession of; *personne, animal* to bring under control; *incendie, situation* to bring under control; **il est passé ~ dans l'art de mentir** he's a past master in the art of lying.

3 maîtresse *nf* **(a)** (*gén*) mistress; (*amante, petite amie*) mistress.

(b) (*Scol*) **maîtresse (d'école)** teacher, (school)mistress; **maîtresse!** Miss!

(c) (*loc*) **être/rester/se rendre/passer maîtresse (de)** *V* **maître** *nm*.

4: (*Sport*) **maître d'armes** fencing master; (*Univ*) **maître assistant** junior lecturer; (*Rel*) **maître-autel** *nm, pl* **maîtres-autels** high altar; (*Scol*) **maître auxiliaire** auxiliary teacher; (*Danse*) **maître/maîtresse de ballet** ballet master/mistress; **maître de cérémonie** master of ceremonies; **maître chanteur** blackmailer; (*Mus*) Meistersinger, mastersinger; (*Mus*) **maître de chapelle** choirmaster; (*Univ*) **maître de conférences** *mf* (senior) lecturer; **maître d'équipage** boatswain; (*Scol*) **maître/maîtresse d'études** master/mistress in charge of preparation; **maître de forges**† ironmaster; **maître d'hôtel** *[maison]* butler; *[hôtel, restaurant]* head waiter; (*Naut*) chief steward; (*Culin*) **pommes de terre maître d'hôtel** maître d'hôtel potatoes; **maître/maîtresse d'internat** house master/mistress; **maître Jacques** jack-of-all-trades; **maître de maison** host; **maîtresse de maison** housewife; (*hôtesse*) hostess; **maître nageur** swimming teacher *ou* instructor; (*Constr*) **maître d'œuvre** foreman; **maître à penser** intellectual guide *ou* leader; (*Culin*) **maître queux** chef; (*Admin*) **maître des requêtes** *mf counsel of the Conseil d'État.*

maîtrisable [metʀizabl(ə)] *adj* (*gén nég*) controllable. **difficilement** *ou* **guère ~** almost uncontrollable, scarcely controllable.

maîtrise [metʀiz] *nf* **(a)** (*sang-froid*) **~ (de soi)** self-control, self-command, self-possession.

(b) (*contrôle*) mastery, command, control. (*Mil*) **avoir la ~ de la mer** to have control *ou* mastery of the sea, control the sea; (*Comm*) **avoir la ~ d'un marché** to control *ou* have control of a market; **sa ~ du français** his mastery *ou* command of the French language; **avoir la ~ de l'atome** to have mastered the atom.

(c) (*habileté*) skill, mastery, expertise. **faire** *ou* **exécuter qch avec ~** to do sth with skill *ou* skilfully.

(d) (*Ind*) supervisory staff; *V* **agent.**

(e) (*Rel*) (*école*) choir school; (*groupe*) choir.

(f) (*Univ*) *research degree* ≃ master's degree. **~ de conférence** ≃ senior lectureship.

maîtriser [metʀize] (1) **1** *vt* **(a)** (*soumettre*) *cheval, feu, foule, forcené* to control, bring under control; *adversaire* to overcome, overpower; *émeute, révolte* to suppress, bring under control; *problème, difficulté* to master, overcome; *inflation* to curb; *langue* to master.

(b) (*contenir*) *émotion, geste, passion* to control, master, restrain; *larmes, rire* to force back, restrain, control. **il ne peut plus ~ ses nerfs** he can no longer control *ou* contain his temper.

2 se maîtriser *vpr* to control o.s. **elle ne sait pas se ~** she has no self-control.

maïzena [maizena] *nf* ® cornflour (*Brit*), cornstarch (*US*).

majesté [maʒɛste] *nf* **(a)** (*dignité*) majesty; (*splendeur*) majesty, grandeur. **la ~ divine** divine majesty; (*Art*) **de** *ou* **en ~** in majesty, enthroned.

(b) Sa/Votre M~ His *ou* Her/Your Majesty; *V* **lèse-majesté, pluriel.**

majestueusement [maʒɛstɥøzmɑ̃] *adv* majestically, in a stately way.

majestueux, -euse [maʒɛstɥø, øz] *adj* (*solennel*) *personne, démarche* majestic, stately; (*imposant*) *taille* imposing, impressive; (*beau*) *fleuve, paysage* majestic, magnificent.

majeur, e [maʒœʀ] **1** *adj* **(a)** *ennui, empêchement* (*très important*) major; (*le plus important*) main, major, greatest. **ils ont rencontré une difficulté ~e** they came up against a major *ou* serious difficulty; **sa préoccupation ~e** his major *ou* main *ou* greatest concern; **pour des raisons ~es** for reasons of the greatest importance; **en ~e partie** for the most part; **la ~e partie de** the greater *ou* major part of, the bulk of; **la ~e partie des gens sont restés** most of *ou* the majority of the people have stayed on; *V* **cas.**

(b) (*Jur*) of age (*attrib*). **il sera ~ en 1978** he will come of age in 1978; (*hum*) **il est ~ et vacciné** he's old enough to look after himself; (*fig*) **peuple ~** responsible *ou* adult nation; (*fig*) **électorat ~** adult electorate.

(c) (*Mus*) *intervalle, mode* major. **en sol ~** in G major.

(d) (*Logique*) *terme, prémisse* major.

(e) (*Rel*) **ordres ~s** major orders; **causes ~es** causae majores.

(f) (*Cartes*) **tierce/quarte ~e** tierce/quart major.

2 *nm,f* person who has come of *ou* who is of age, person who has attained his *ou* her majority.

3 *nm* middle finger.

major [maʒɔʀ] **1** *nm* **(a)** (*Admin*) adjutant; (*Mil*) **(médecin) ~** medical officer, M.O.; **~ général** (*Mil*) ≃ deputy chief of staff; (*Naut*) ≃ rear admiral.

(b) (*Univ etc*) **être ~ de promotion** ≃ to be first of one's year.

2 *adj inv V* **état-major, infirmière, sergent[1], tambour.**

majoration [maʒɔʀɑsjɔ̃] *nf* (*hausse*) rise, increase (*de* in); (*supplément*) surcharge; (*surestimation*) overvaluation, overestimation. **~ sur une facture** surcharge on a bill.

majordome [maʒɔʀdɔm] *nm* majordomo.

majorer [maʒɔʀe] (1) *vt impôt, prix* to increase, raise, put up (*de* by); *facture* to increase, put a surcharge on.

majorette [maʒɔʀɛt] *nf* (drum) majorette.

majoritaire [maʒɔʀitɛʀ] **1** *adj* majority (*épith*). **2** *nmf* (*Pol*) member of the majority party. **nous sommes ~s** (*gén*) we are in the majority; (*Pol*) we are the majority (party).

majorité [maʒɔʀite] *nf* **(a)** (*électorale*) majority. **~ absolue/relative** absolute/relative majority; **élu à une ~ de** elected by a majority of; **avoir la ~** to have the majority.

(b) (*parti majoritaire*) government, party in power. **député de la ~** ≃ government backbencher; **la ~ et l'opposition** the government and the opposition.

(c) (*majeure partie*) majority. **la ~ silencieuse** the silent majority; **être en ~** to be in (the) majority; **la ~ est d'accord** the majority agree; **les hommes dans leur grande ~** the great majority of mankind; **dans la ~ des cas** in the majority of cases; **groupe composé en ~ de** group mainly composed of.

(d) (*Jur*) **atteindre sa ~** to come of age, attain one's majority; **jusqu'à sa ~** until he comes of age *ou* reaches his majority.

Majorque [maʒɔʀk] *nf* Majorca.

majorquin, e [maʒɔʀkɛ̃, in] **1** *adj* Majorcan. **2** *nm,f*: **M~(e)** Majorcan.

majuscule [maʒyskyl] **1** *adj* capital; (*Typ*) upper case. **A ~** capital A. **2** *nf*: **(lettre) ~** capital letter; (*Typ*) upper case letter.

mal [mal] **1** *adv* **(a)** (*de façon défectueuse*) *jouer, dormir* badly; *fonctionner* not properly, badly. **cette porte ferme ~** this door shuts badly *ou* doesn't shut properly; **il parle ~ l'anglais** he speaks bad English, he speaks English badly; **elle est ~ coiffée aujourd'hui** her hair is not well *ou* nicely done today; **ce travail est ~ fait** this work is badly done; **c'est du travail ~ fait** this is poor *ou* shoddy work; **nous sommes ~ nourris/logés à l'hôtel** the food/accommodation is poor *ou* bad at the hotel; **ils vivent très ~ avec une seule paye** they live very meagrely on *ou* off just one wage; **redresse-toi, tu te tiens ~** stand up straight, you're not holding yourself properly; **il a ~ pris ce que je lui ai dit** he took exception *ou* did not take kindly to what I said to him; **il s'y est ~ pris (pour le faire)** he set about (doing) it the wrong way; **tu le connais ~** you don't know him; **de ~ en pis** from bad to worse.

(b) ~ choisi/informé/inspiré *etc* ill-chosen/-informed/-advised *etc*; **~ acquis** ill-gotten; **~ à l'aise** (*gêné*) ill-at-ease; (*malade*) unwell; **~ avisé** ill-advised; **~ embouché** coarse, ill-spoken; **~ famé** of ill fame, disreputable; **~ pensant** heretical, unorthodox; **~ en point** in a bad state, in a poor condition; **~ à propos** at the wrong moment; **avoir l'esprit ~ tourné** to have a low *ou* dirty mind *ou* that sort of mind; **il est ~ venu de se plaindre** he is scarcely in a position to complain, he should be the last (one) to complain; *V* **ours, vu[2].**

(c) ~ comprendre to misunderstand; **~ interpréter** to misinterpret; **~ renseigner** to misinform; **il comprend ~ ce qu'on lui dit** he doesn't understand properly what he is told; **il a ~ compris ce qu'ils lui ont dit** he didn't understand properly *ou* he misunderstood what they told him; **j'ai été ~ renseigné** I was misinformed *ou* given (the) wrong information; *V* **juger** *etc.*

(d) (*avec difficulté*) with difficulty. **il respire ~** he has difficulty in breathing, he can't breathe properly; **on s'explique** *ou* **comprend ~ pourquoi** it is not easy *ou* it is difficult to understand why; **nous voyons très ~ comment** we fail to see how.

(e) (*de façon répréhensible*) *se conduire* badly, wrongly. **il ne pensait pas ~ faire** he didn't think he was doing the wrong thing *ou* doing wrong; **il ne pense qu'à ~ faire** he's always looking for trouble, he's always thinking up some nasty trick; **se tenir ~ à table** to have bad table manners, behave badly at table; **trouves-tu ~ qu'il y soit allé?** do you think it was wrong of him to go?; **ça lui va ~ d'accuser les autres** who is HE to accuse others?, it ill becomes him to accuse others (*littér*).

(f) (*malade*) **se sentir ~** to feel ill *ou* unwell *ou* sick, not to feel very well; **aller** *ou* **se porter ~, être ~ portant** to be in poor health; **se trouver ~** to be taken ill, feel unwell.

(g) pas ~ (*assez bien*) not badly, rather well; **c'est pas ~*** it's quite good, it's not bad*; **il n'a pas ~ travaillé ce trimestre** he's worked quite well this term; **vous (ne) vous en êtes pas ~ tirés** you haven't done *ou* come off badly, you've done rather well; **vous (ne) feriez pas ~ de le surveiller** it wouldn't be a bad thing if you kept an eye on him; **ça va? — pas ~** how are you? — not (too) bad* *ou* pretty good* *ou* pretty well*.

(h) pas ~ (de)* (*beaucoup*) quite a lot (of); **il y a pas ~ de temps qu'il est parti** it's quite a time since he left, he's been away for quite a time; **on a pas ~ travaillé aujourd'hui** we've done quite a lot of work today, we've worked pretty hard today*; **il est pas ~ fatigué** he is rather *ou* pretty* tired; **je m'en fiche pas ~!** I couldn't care less!, I don't give a damn!‡

2 *adj inv* **(a)** (*contraire à la morale*) wrong, bad. **il est** *ou* **c'est ~ de mentir/de voler** it is bad *ou* wrong to lie/to steal; (*iro*) **(pour elle) il ne peut rien faire de ~** (in her eyes) he can do no wrong; **c'est ~ à lui de dire cela** it's bad *ou* wrong of him to say this.

(b) (*malade*) ill. **il va** *ou* **est (très) ~ ce soir** he is (very) ill tonight; **il est au plus ~** he is very low *ou* poorly.

(c) (*mal à l'aise*) uncomfortable. **vous devez être ~ sur ce banc** you must be uncomfortable on that seat, that seat can't be comfortable (for you); **je marche beaucoup, je ne m'en suis jamais trouvé ~** I walk a lot and I'm none the worse for it *ou* and it's never done me any harm; **il est ~ dans sa peau** he's at odds with himself; **on est pas ~ (assis) dans ces fauteuils** these armchairs are quite comfortable.

(d) être ~ avec qn to be on bad terms with sb, be in sb's bad books*; **se mettre ~ avec qn** to get on the wrong side of sb, get into sb's bad books*; **ils sont au plus ~** they are at daggers drawn.

(e) pas ~ (*bien*) not bad, quite *ou* rather good; (*assez beau*) quite attractive; (*compétent*) quite competent; **vous n'êtes pas ~ sur cette photo** this photo is not bad of you *ou* is rather good of you; *V* **bon**[1].

3 *nm, pl* **maux** [mo] **(a)** (*ce qui est contraire à la morale*) **le ~** evil; **le bien et le ~** good and evil, right and wrong; **faire le ~ pour le ~** to do *ou* commit evil for its own sake *ou* for evil's sake.

(b) (*souffrance morale*) sorrow, pain. **le ~ du siècle** world-weariness; **~ du pays** homesickness; **des paroles qui font du ~** words that hurt, hurtful words; (*fig*) **journaliste en ~ de copie** journalist short of copy.

(c) (*travail pénible, difficulté*) difficulty, trouble. **ce travail/cet enfant m'a donné du ~** this work/child gave me some trouble; **se donner du ~ à faire qch** to take trouble *ou* pains over sth, go to great pains to do sth; **se donner un ~ de chien à faire qch*** to bend over backwards to do sth; **avoir du ~ à faire qch** to have trouble *ou* difficulty doing sth; **on n'a rien sans ~** you get nothing without (some) effort; **faire qch sans trop de ~/non sans ~** to do sth without undue difficulty/not without difficulty; **prendre son ~ en patience** to bear one's difficulties with patience *ou* fortitude (*littér*).

(d) (*ce qui cause un dommage, de la peine*) harm. **mettre qn à ~** to harm sb; **faire du ~ à** to harm, hurt; **il ne ferait pas de ~ à une mouche** he wouldn't hurt *ou* harm a fly; **il n'y a pas de ~ à cela** there's no harm in that; **~ lui en a pris!** he'll rue the day!, he's had *ou* he'll have cause to rue it!; **~ m'en a pris de sortir** going out was a grave mistake (on my part).

(e) (*ce qui est mauvais*) evil, ill. **les maux dont souffre notre société** the ills *ou* evils afflicting our society; **c'est un ~ nécessaire** it's a necessary evil; **de deux maux, il faut choisir le moindre** one must choose the lesser of two evils; **penser/dire du ~ de qn/qch** to think/speak ill of sb/sth; *V* **penser, peur.**

(f) (*douleur physique*) pain, ache; (*maladie*) illness, disease, sickness. **prendre ~** to be taken ill, feel unwell; **avoir ~ partout** to be aching all over; **où avez-vous ~?** where does it hurt?, where is the pain?; **le ~ s'aggrave** (*lit*) the disease is getting worse, he *ou* she is getting worse; (*fig*) the situation is deteriorating; **j'ai ~ dans le dos/à l'estomac** I've got a pain in my back/in my stomach, my back/stomach hurts *ou* aches; **avoir un ~ de tête/de gorge, avoir ~ à la tête/à la gorge** to have a headache/a sore throat; **avoir ~ aux dents/aux oreilles** to have toothache/earache; **avoir ~ au pied** to have a sore foot; **des maux d'estomac** stomach pains, an upset stomach; **un ~ blanc** a whitlow; **il s'est fait (du) ~ en tombant** he hurt himself in falling *ou* when he fell; **se faire ~ au genou** to hurt one's knee; **ces chaussures me font ~ (au pied)** these shoes hurt *ou* pinch (my feet); **avoir le ~ de mer/de l'air/de la route** to be seasick/airsick/carsick; **contre le ~ de mer/de l'air/de la route** against seasickness/airsickness/carsickness; **~ des montagnes** mountain sickness; *V* **cœur, ventre.**

Malabar [malabaʀ] *nm*: **le ~, la côte de ~** the Malabar (Coast).

malabar* [malabaʀ] *nm* muscle man*, hefty fellow*.

malade [malad] **1** *adj* **(a)** (*atteint*) *homme* ill, sick, unwell (*attrib*); *organe* diseased; *plante* diseased; *dent, poitrine* bad; *jambe, bras* bad, game* (*épith*), gammy* (*Brit*) (*épith*). **être bien/gravement/sérieusement ~** to be really/gravely/seriously ill; **être ~ du cœur** to have heart trouble *ou* a bad heart; **être ~ des reins** to have kidney trouble; **tomber ~** to fall ill *ou* sick; **se faire porter ~** to report *ou* go sick; **je me sens (un peu) ~** I feel (a bit) peculiar* *ou* sick, I don't feel very well; **être ~ comme un chien *ou* une bête** (*gén*) to be dreadfully ill; (*euph: vomir*) to be as sick as a dog; **être ~ à crever‡** to be dreadfully ill, feel ghastly* *ou* like death (warmed up)*; **j'ai été ~ après avoir mangé des huîtres** I was ill after eating oysters.

(b) (*fou*) mad. **tu es pas (un peu) ~?‡** are you quite right in the head?*, are you out of your mind?; **être ~ d'inquiétude** to be sick *ou* ill with worry; **être ~ de jalousie** to be mad *ou* sick with jealousy; **rien que d'y penser j'en suis ~, ça me rend ~ rien que d'y penser*** the very thought of it makes me sick *ou* ill, I'm sick at the very thought of it.

(c) (*périclitant*) *objet* in a sorry state. **l'entreprise étant ~ ils durent licencier** the business was failing *ou* was in a dicky* *ou* shaky state and they had to pay people off; **le gouvernement est trop ~ pour durer jusqu'aux élections** the government is too shaky to last till the elections.

2 *nmf* invalid, sick person. **grand ~** seriously *ou* chronically ill person; **~ imaginaire** hypochondriac; **~ mental** mentally sick *ou* ill person; **les ~s** the sick; **les grands ~s** the seriously ill; **le médecin et ses ~s** the doctor and his patients.

maladie [maladi] **1** *nf* **(a)** (*Méd*) illness, disease; *[plante, vin]* disease. **~ bénigne** minor *ou* slight illness, minor complaint; **~ grave** serious illness; **~ de cœur/foie** heart/liver complaint *ou* disease; **ces enfants ont eu une ~ après l'autre** these children have had one sickness *ou* illness after another; **le cancer est la ~ du siècle** cancer is the disease of the times; **il a fait une petite ~*** he's been slightly ill, he's had a minor illness; (**fig*) **il en a fait une ~** he was in a terrible state about it; (**fig*) **tu ne vas pas en faire une ~!** don't you get in (such) a state over it!, don't let it get you down!*.

(b) (*U*) **la ~** sickness, illness, ill health, disease; *V* **assurance.**

(c) (*Vét*) **la ~** distemper.

(d) (*: *obsession*) mania. **avoir la ~ de la vitesse** to be a speed maniac; **quelle ~ as-tu de toujours intervenir!** what a mania you have for interfering!; **c'est une ~ chez lui** it's a mania with him.

2: la maladie bleue the blue disease; **maladie contagieuse** contagious illness *ou* disease; **maladie infantile *ou* d'enfant** childhood *ou* infantile disease *ou* complaint; **maladie infectieuse** infectious disease; **maladie mentale** mental illness; **maladie mortelle** fatal illness *ou* disease; **maladie de peau** skin disease *ou* complaint; **la maladie du sommeil** sleeping sickness; **maladies du travail** occupational diseases; **maladie tropicale** tropical disease; **maladie vénérienne *ou* honteuse†** venereal disease, V.D.

maladif, -ive [maladif, iv] *adj personne* sickly, weak; *air, pâleur* sickly, unhealthy; *obsession, peur* pathological (*fig*). **il faut qu'il mente, c'est ~ chez lui** he has to lie, it's compulsive with him.

maladivement [maladivmɑ̃] *adv* unhealthily.

maladresse [maladʀɛs] *nf* **(a)** (*U: V* **maladroit**) clumsiness; awkwardness; tactlessness. **(b)** (*gaffe*) blunder, gaffe. **~s de style** awkward *ou* clumsy turns of phrase.

maladroit, e [maladʀwa, wat] *adj* **(a)** (*inhabile*) *personne* clumsy; (*embarrassé*) awkward; *ouvrage, style* clumsy. **il est vraiment ~ de ses mains** he's really useless with his hands.

(b) (*indélicat*) *personne, remarque* clumsy, tactless. **ce serait ~ de lui en parler** it would be tactless *ou* ill-considered to mention it to him.

maladroitement [maladʀwatmɑ̃] *adv marcher, dessiner* clumsily, awkwardly; **agir** clumsily, tactlessly.

malaga [malaga] *nm* (*vin*) Malaga (wine); (*raisin*) Malaga grape.

malais, e[1] [malɛ, ɛz] **1** *adj* Malay(an). **2** *nm* (*Ling*) Malay. **3** *nm,f*: **M~(e)** Malay(an).

malaise[2] [malɛz] *nm* **(a)** (*Méd*) feeling of sickness *ou* faintness; (*gén*) feeling of general discomfort *ou* ill-being. **être pris d'un ~, avoir un ~** to feel faint *ou* dizzy, come over faint *ou* dizzy. **(b)** (*fig: trouble*) uneasiness, disquiet. **éprouver un ~** to feel uneasy; **le ~ étudiant/politique** student/political discontent *ou* unrest.

malaisé, e [maleze] *adj* difficult.

malaisément [malezemɑ̃] *adv* with difficulty.

Malaisie [malɛzi] *nf* Malaya.

malandrin [malɑ̃dʀɛ̃] *nm* (†: *littér*) brigand (*littér*), bandit.

malappris, e [malapʀi, iz] *adj* ill-mannered, boorish. **espèce de ~!*** ill-mannered lout!*

malard [malaʀ] *nm* drake; (*sauvage*) mallard.

malaria [malaʀja] *nf* malaria (*U*).

malavisé, e [malavize] *adj personne, remarque* ill-advised, injudicious, unwise.

malaxage [malaksaʒ] *nm* (*V* **malaxer**) kneading; massaging; creaming; blending; mixing.

malaxer [malakse] (1) *vt* **(a)** (*triturer*) *argile, pâte* to knead; *muscle* to massage. **~ du beurre** to cream butter.

(b) (*mélanger*) *plusieurs substances* to blend, mix; *ciment, plâtre* to mix.

malaxeur, -euse [malaksœʀ, øz] **1** *adj* mixing. **2** *nm* mixer.

malchance [malʃɑ̃s] *nf* (*déveine*) bad *ou* ill luck, misfortune; (*mésaventure*) misfortune, mishap. **il a eu beaucoup de ~** he's had a lot of bad luck; **j'ai eu la ~ de** I had the misfortune to, I was unlucky enough to; **par ~** unfortunately, as ill luck would have it; *V* **jouer.**

malchanceux, -euse [malʃɑ̃sø, øz] *adj* unlucky.

malcommode [malkɔmɔd] *adj objet, vêtement* impractical, unsuitable; *horaire* awkward, inconvenient; *outil, meuble* inconvenient; (†) *personne* awkward. **ça m'est vraiment très ~** it's really most inconvenient for me, it really doesn't suit me at all.

maldonne [maldɔn] *nf* (*Cartes*) misdeal. **faire (une) ~** to misdeal, deal the cards wrongly; **il y a ~** (*lit*) there's been a misdeal, the cards have been dealt wrongly; (*fig*) there's been a misunderstanding *ou* a mistake somewhere.

mâle [mɑl] **1** *adj* **(a)** (*Bio, Tech*) male.

(b) (*viril*) *voix, courage* manly; *style, peinture* virile.

2 *nm* male. **c'est un ~ ou une femelle?** is it a he or a she?*, is it a male or a female?; **c'est un beau ~*** he's a real he-man* (*hum*); **(éléphant) ~** bull (elephant); **(lapin) ~** buck (rabbit); **(moineau) ~** cock (sparrow); **(ours) ~** he-bear.

malédiction [malediksjɔ̃] **1** *nf* (*Rel: imprécation, adversité*) curse, malediction (*rare*). **la ~ divine** the curse of God; **n'écoute pas les ~s de cette vieille folle** don't listen to the curses of that old fool; **la ~ pèse sur nous** a curse hangs over us; **donner sa ~ à qn, appeler la ~ sur qn** to call down curses upon sb.

2 *excl* (††, *hum*) curse it!*, damn!* **~! j'ai perdu la clef** curse it!* I've lost the key.

maléfice [malefis] *nm* evil spell.

maléfique [malefik] *adj étoile* malefic, unlucky; *pouvoir* evil, baleful.

malemort [malmɔʀ] *nf* (††, *littér*) cruel death. **mourir de ~** to die a cruel *ou* violent death.

malencontreusement [malɑ̃kɔ̃tʀøzmɑ̃] *adv arriver* at the wrong moment, inopportunely, inconveniently. **faire ~ remarquer que** to make the unfortunate *ou* untoward remark that.

malencontreux, -euse [malɑ̃kɔ̃tʀø, øz] *adj* unfortunate, awkward, untoward.

malentendu [malɑ̃tɑ̃dy] *nm* misunderstanding. **il y a un ~ entre nous** we are at cross purposes.

malfaçon [malfasɔ̃] *nf* fault, defect (*due to bad workmanship*).

malfaisant, e [malfəzɑ̃, ɑ̃t] *adj personne* evil, wicked, harmful; *influence* evil, harmful, baleful; *animal, théories* harmful.

malfaiteur, -trice [malfɛtœʀ, tʀis] *nm,f* (*gén*) lawbreaker; (*voleur*) burglar, thief. **dangereux ~** dangerous criminal.

malformation [malfɔʀmasjɔ̃] *nf* malformation.

malfrat [malfʀa] *nm* crook (*member of the underworld*).

malgache [malgaʃ] **1** *adj* Malagasy, Madagascan.

2 *nm* (*Ling*) Malagasy. **3** *nmf*: **M~** Malagasy, Madagascan.

malgracieux, -euse [malgʀasjø, øz] *adj* (*littér*) *silhouette* ungainly; (†) *caractère* churlish, boorish.

malgré [malgʀe] **1** *prép* **(a)** (*en dépit de*) in spite of, despite. ~ **son père/l'opposition de son père, il devint avocat** despite his *ou* in spite of his father/his father's objections he became a barrister; ~ **son intelligence, il n'a pas réussi** in spite of *ou* for all *ou* notwithstanding (*frm*) his undoubted intelligence he hasn't succeeded in life; **j'ai signé ce contrat** ~ **moi** I signed the contract reluctantly *ou* against my better judgment *ou* against my will; **j'ai fait cela presque** ~ **moi** I did it almost in spite of myself.

(b) (*loc*) ~ **tout** (*en dépit de tout*) in spite of everything, despite everything; (*concession: quand même*) all the same, after all; ~ **tout, c'est dangereux** all the same *ou* after all it's dangerous; **il a continué** ~ **tout** he went on in spite of *ou* despite everything; **je le ferai** ~ **tout** I'll do it all the same *ou* come what may.

2 *conj*: ~ **que*** in spite of the fact that, despite the fact that, although; (*littér*) ~ **qu'il en ait** whether he likes it or not.

malhabile [malabil] *adj* clumsy, awkward. ~ **à** unskilful *ou* bad at.

malhabilement [malabilmɑ̃] *adv* clumsily, awkwardly, unskilfully.

malheur [malœʀ] *nm* **(a)** (*événement pénible*) misfortune; (*très grave*) calamity; (*épreuve*) ordeal, hardship; (*accident*) accident, mishap. **il a supporté ses** ~**s sans se plaindre** he suffered his misfortunes *ou* his hardships without complaint; **cette famille a eu beaucoup de** ~**s** this family has had a lot of misfortune *ou* hardship; **un** ~ **est si vite arrivé** accidents *ou* mishaps happen so easily; (*Prov*) **un** ~ **ne vient jamais seul** it never rains but it pours (*Prov*); **cela a été le grand** ~ **de sa vie** it was the great tragedy of his life; **ce n'est pas un gros** ~**!, c'est un petit** ~**!** it's not such a calamity! *ou* tragedy!

(b) le ~ (*adversité*) adversity; (*malchance*) ill luck, misfortune; **ils ont eu le** ~ **de perdre leur mère** they had the misfortune to lose their mother; **une famille qui est dans le** ~ a family in misfortune *ou* faced with adversity; **le** ~ **des uns fait le bonheur des autres** one man's joy is another man's sorrow; **c'est dans le** ~ **qu'on connaît ses amis** a friend in need is a friend indeed (*Prov*); **le** ~ **a voulu qu'un agent le voie** as ill luck would have it a policeman saw him; *V* **arriver.**

(c) de ~***** (*maudit*) wretched; **cette pluie de** ~ **a tout gâché** this wretched rain has spoilt everything; *V* **oiseau.**

(d) (*loc*) ~**!** oh, lord!*, hell!:; ~ **à (celui) qui**† woe betide him who; **par** ~ unfortunately, as ill luck would have it; **le** ~ *ou* **il n'y a qu'un** ~**, c'est que ...** the trouble *ou* snag is that ...; **son** ~ **c'est qu'il boit** his trouble is that he drinks; **faire le** ~ **de ses parents** to bring sorrow to one's parents, cause one's parents nothing but unhappiness; **faire un** ~ (*: *avoir un gros succès*) [*spectacle*] to be a big hit; [*artiste, joueur*] to make a great hit, be a sensation; **s'il continue à m'ennuyer je fais un** ~***** if he carries on annoying me I'll do something violent *ou* I shall go wild; **quel** ~ **qu'il ne soit pas venu** what a shame he didn't come; **il a eu le** ~ **de dire que cela ne lui plaisait pas** he was unlucky enough to say he didn't like it; **pour son** ~ for his sins; *V* **comble, jouer.**

malheureusement [malœʀøzmɑ̃] *adv* unfortunately.

malheureux, -euse [malœʀø, øz] **1** *adj* **(a)** (*infortuné*) unfortunate. **les** ~**euses victimes des bombardements** the unfortunate *ou* unhappy victims of the bombings.

(b) (*regrettable, fâcheux*) *résultat, jour, geste* unfortunate. **pour un mot** ~ because of an unfortunate remark; **c'est bien** ~ **qu'il ne puisse pas venir** it's very unfortunate *ou* it's a great pity that he can't come; **si c'est pas** ~ **d'entendre ça!*** it makes you sick to hear that!*; **ah te voilà enfin, c'est pas** ~**!*** oh there you are at last and about time too!*

(c) (*triste, qui souffre*) *enfant, vie* unhappy, miserable. **on a été très** ~ **pendant la guerre** we had a miserable life during the war; **il était très** ~ **de ne pouvoir nous aider** he was most distressed *ou* upset at not being able to help us; **prendre un air** ~ to look unhappy *ou* distressed; **rendre qn** ~ to make sb unhappy; **être** ~ **comme les pierres** to be wretchedly unhappy *ou* utterly wretched.

(d) (*après n*) (*malchanceux*) *candidat* unsuccessful, unlucky; *tentative* unsuccessful. **il prit une initiative** ~**euse** he took an unfortunate step; **X a été félicité par ses adversaires** ~ X was congratulated by his defeated opponents; **amour** ~ unhappy love affair; *V* **heureux, main.**

(e) (*: *avant n: insignifiant*) wretched, miserable. **toute une histoire pour un** ~ **billet de 100 F/pour une** ~**euse erreur** such a carry-on for a wretched *ou* mouldy* *ou* measly* 100-franc note/for a miserable mistake; **il y avait 2 ou 3** ~ **spectateurs** there was a miserable handful of spectators.

2 *nm,f* (*infortuné*) poor wretch *ou* soul *ou* devil*; (*indigent*) needy person. **il a tout perdu? le** ~**!** did he lose everything? the poor man!; **un** ~ **de plus** another poor devil*; **ne fais pas cela, (petit)** ~**!** don't do that, you little devil!* *ou* horror!; **aider les** ~ (*indigents*) to help the needy *ou* badly off.

malhonnête [malɔnɛt] *adj* **(a)** (*déloyal, voleur*) *personne, procédé* dishonest, crooked. **(b)** (*impoli*) rude.

malhonnêtement [malɔnɛtmɑ̃] *adv* (*V* **malhonnête**) dishonestly, crookedly; rudely.

malhonnêteté [malɔnɛtte] *nf* **(a)** (*improbité*) dishonesty, crookedness. **faire des** ~**s** to carry on dishonest *ou* crooked dealings.

(b) (*manque de politesse*) rudeness. **dire des** ~**s** to make rude remarks, say rude things.

malice [malis] *nf* **(a)** (*espièglerie*) mischief, mischievousness; roguishness (*littér*). **dit-il non sans** ~ he said somewhat mischievously; **petites** ~**s**† mischievous little ways; **boîte** *ou* **sac à** ~ box *ou* bag of tricks.

(b) (*méchanceté*) malice, spite. **par** ~ out of malice *ou* spite; **il est sans** ~ he is quite guileless; **il n'y voit** *ou* **entend pas** ~ he means no harm by it.

malicieusement [malisjøzmɑ̃] *adv* mischievously, roguishly (*littér*).

malicieux, -euse [malisjø, øz] *adj personne, remarque* mischievous, roguish; *sourire* mischievous, impish, roguish. **notre oncle est très** ~ our uncle is a great tease; **petit** ~**!** little imp! *ou* monkey!

malien, -enne [maljɛ̃, ɛn] **1** *adj* of *ou* from Mali. **2** *nm,f*: **M**~**(ne)** inhabitant *ou* native of Mali.

maligne [maliɲ] *V* **malin.**

malignement [maliɲmɑ̃] *adv* (*rare*) maliciously, spitefully.

malignité [maliɲite] *nf* **(a)** (*malveillance*) malice, spite. **(b)** (*Méd*) malignancy.

malin, -igne [malɛ̃, iɲ] *ou* **-ine*** [in] **1** *adj* **(a)** (*intelligent*) *personne, air* smart, shrewd, cunning. **sourire** ~ cunning *ou* knowing *ou* crafty smile; **il est** ~ **comme un singe** he is as artful as a cartload of monkeys; [*enfant*] he is an artful little monkey; **bien** ~ **qui le dira** it'll take a clever man to say that; **il n'est pas bien** ~ he isn't very bright; (*iro*) **c'est** ~**!** that's clever *ou* bright, isn't it? (*iro*); **si tu te crois** ~ **de faire ça!** do you think it's *ou* you're clever to do that?; *V* **jouer.**

(b) (*: *difficile*) **ce n'est pourtant pas bien** ~ but it isn't so difficult *ou* tricky; **ce n'est pas plus** ~ **que ça** it's as easy *ou* simple as that, it's as easy as pie*, that's all there is to it.

(c) (*mauvais*) *influence* malignant, baneful, malicious. **prendre un** ~ **plaisir à** to take a malicious pleasure in; **l'esprit** ~ the devil.

(d) (*Méd*) malignant.

2 *nm,f*: **c'est un (petit)** ~ he's a crafty one, he knows a thing or two, there are no flies on HIM* (*Brit*); **gros** ~**!** you're a bright one! (*iro*); **ne fais pas ton** *ou* **le** ~***** don't try to show off; **à** ~**,** ~ **et demi** there's always someone cleverer than you; **le M**~ the Devil.

malingre [malɛ̃gʀ(ə)] *adj personne* sickly, puny; *corps* puny.

malintentionné, e [malɛ̃tɑ̃sjɔne] *adj* ill-intentioned, malicious, spiteful (*envers* towards).

malle [mal] **1** *nf* **(a)** (*valise*) trunk. **faire sa** *ou* **ses** ~**(s)** to pack one's trunk; **ils se sont fait la** ~**, ils ont fait la** ~**:** they've scarpered: (*Brit*) *ou* done a bunk: (*Brit*); **on a intérêt à (se) faire la** ~**:** we'd better scarper: (*Brit*) *ou* make ourselves scarce*.

(b) (*Aut*) boot (*Brit*), trunk (*US*).

2: (*Hist*) (*diligence*) **malle-poste** *nf, pl* **malles-poste** mail coach; (*bateau*) packet.

malléabilité [maleabilite] *nf* [*métal*] malleability; [*caractère*] malleability, pliability, flexibility.

malléable [maleabl(ə)] *adj métal* malleable; *caractère* malleable, pliable, flexible.

mallette [malɛt] *nf* (small) suitcase. ~ **de voyage** overnight case.

malmener [malməne] (5) *vt* (*brutaliser*) *personne* to manhandle, handle roughly; (*Mil, Sport*) *adversaire* to give a rough time *ou* handling to. (*fig*) **être malmené par la critique** to be given a rough handling by the critics.

malnutrition [malnytʀisjɔ̃] *nf* malnutrition.

malodorant, e [malɔdɔʀɑ̃, ɑ̃t] *adj personne, pièce* foul- *ou* ill-smelling, malodorous (*frm*), smelly*; *haleine* foul.

malotru, e [malɔtʀy] *nm,f* lout, boor, yob: (*Brit*).

malouin, e [malwɛ̃, in] **1** *adj* of *ou* from Saint Malo. **2** *nm,f*: **M**~**(e)** inhabitant *ou* native of Saint Malo.

malpoli, e [malpɔli] *adj* impolite, discourteous.

malpropre [malpʀɔpʀ(ə)] **1** *adj* **(a)** (*sale*) *personne, objet* dirty, grubby, grimy; *travail* shoddy, slovenly.

(b) (*indécent*) *allusion, histoire* smutty, dirty.

(c) (*indélicat*) *conduite, personne, action* unsavoury, dishonest.

2 *nmf* (*hum*) swine (*pl inv*). **se faire chasser comme un** ~***** to be thrown *ou* kicked* out, be sent packing.

malproprement [malpʀɔpʀəmɑ̃] *adv* in a dirty way. **manger** ~ to be a messy eater.

malpropreté [malpʀɔpʀəte] *nf* **(a)** (*U*) dirtiness, grubbiness, griminess. **(b)** (*acte*) low *ou* shady trick; (*parole*) low *ou* unsavoury remark. **raconter** *ou* **dire des** ~**s** to talk smut, tell dirty stories.

malsain, e [malsɛ̃, ɛn] *adj* unhealthy; *influence, littérature, curiosité* unhealthy, unwholesome. (**fig*) **sauvons-nous, ça devient** ~ let's get out of here, things are turning nasty *ou* things aren't looking too healthy*.

malséant, e [malseɑ̃, ɑ̃t] *adj* (*littér*) unseemly, unbecoming, improper.

malsonnant, e [malsɔnɑ̃, ɑ̃t] *adj* (*littér*) *propos* offensive.

malt [malt] *nm* malt. **pur** ~ malt (whisky).

maltage [maltaʒ] *nm* malting.

maltais, e [maltɛ, ɛz] **1** *adj* Maltese. **2** *nm* (*Ling*) Maltese. **3** *nm,f*: **M**~**(e)** Maltese.

Malte [malt] *nf* Malta.

malter [malte] (1) *vt* to malt.

malthusianisme [maltyzjanism(ə)] *nm* (*Sociol*) Malthusianism. ~ **économique** Malthusian economics (*sg*).

malthusien, -ienne [maltyzjɛ̃, jɛn] **1** *adj* (*Écon, Sociol*) Malthusian. **2** *nm,f* Malthusian.

maltose [maltoz] *nm* maltose, malt sugar.

maltraiter [maltʀete] (1) *vt* **(a)** (*brutaliser*) to manhandle, handle roughly, ill-treat.

(b) (*mal user de*) *langue, grammaire* to misuse.

(c) (*critiquer*) *œuvre, auteur* to slate*, run down*.

malveillance [malvɛjɑ̃s] *nf* **(a)** (*méchanceté*) malevolence; (*désobligeance*) ill will (*pour, envers* towards). **propos dûs à la** ~ **publique** spiteful *ou* malicious public rumour; **regarder qn avec** ~ to look at sb malevolently.

(b) (*visée criminelle*) malicious intent.
malveillant, e [malvɛjɑ̃, ɑ̃t] *adj personne, regard, remarque* malevolent, malicious, spiteful.
malvenu, e [malvəny] *adj* (*déplacé*) out of place (*attrib*), out-of-place (*épith*); (*mal développé*) malformed; *V aussi* **mal.**
malversation [malvɛʀsɑsjɔ̃] *nf* (*gén pl*) embezzlement, misappropriation of funds.
malvision [malvizjɔ̃] *nf* defective eyesight.
malvoisie [malvwazi] *nm* malmsey (wine).
maman [mamɑ̃] *nf* mummy, mother, mum* (*Brit*), mom* (*US*). '~', 'M~' 'mummy', mum* (*Brit*), mom* (*US*); **les ~s attendaient devant l'école** the mothers *ou* mums* (*Brit*) were waiting outside the school; *V* **futur.**
mamelle [mamɛl] *nf* **(a)** (*Zool*) teat; (*pis*) udder, dug. **(b)** (†) *[femme]* breast; (*péj*) tit‡; *[homme]* breast. **à la ~** at the breast; (*fig*) **dès la ~** from infancy; (*fig*) **les deux ~s de** the lifeblood of.
mamelon [mamlɔ̃] *nm* **(a)** (*Anat*) nipple. **(b)** (*Géog*) knoll, hillock.
mamelonné, e [mamlɔne] *adj* hillocky.
mamel(o)uk [mamluk] *nm* Mameluke.
mamie[1] [mami] *nf* (*grand-mère*) granny*, gran*.
mamie[2], **m'amie** [mami] *nf* (††) = **ma mie**; *V* **mie**[2].
mammaire [mamɛʀ] *adj* mammary.
mammifère [mamifɛʀ] **1** *nm* mammal. **les ~s** mammals. **2** *adj* mammalian.
Mammon [mamɔ̃] *nm* Mammon.
mammouth [mamut] *nm* mammoth.
mamours* [mamuʀ] *nmpl* (*hum*) **faire des ~s à qn** to caress *ou* fondle sb; **se faire des ~** to bill and coo.
mam'selle*, mam'zelle* [mamzɛl] *nf abrév de* **mademoiselle.**
manade [manad] *nf* (*Provence*) *[taureaux]* herd of bulls; *[chevaux]* herd of horses.
management [manaʒmɛnt] *nm* management.
manager [manadʒɛʀ] *nm* (*Écon, Sport*) manager; (*Théât*) agent.
manant [manɑ̃] *nm* **(a)** (†, *littér*) churl††. **(b)** (*Hist: villageois*) yokel; (*vilain*) villein.
manceau, -elle, *mpl* **~x** [mɑ̃so, ɛl] **1** *adj* of *ou* from Le Mans. **2** *nm,f*: **M~(-elle)** inhabitant *ou* native of Le Mans.
manche[1] [mɑ̃ʃ] **1** *nf* **(a)** (*Habillement*) sleeve. **à ~s courtes/longues** short-/long-sleeved; **sans ~s** sleeveless; (*fig*) **avoir qn dans sa ~** to be well in with sb*, have sb in one's pocket; **faire la ~‡** to pass the hat round; *V* **autre, chemise, effet.**
(b) (*partie*) (*gén, Pol, Sport*) round (*fig*); (*Bridge*) game. (*fig*) **pour obtenir ce contrat on a gagné la première ~** we've won the first round in the battle for this contract.
(c) (*Aviat*) *[ballon]* neck.
(d) (*Géog*) **la M~** the English Channel.
2: manche à air (*Aviat*) wind sock; (*Naut*) ventilator; **manche ballon** *inv* puff sleeve; **manche à crevés** slashed sleeve; **manche gigot** *inv* leg-of-mutton sleeve; **manche kimono** *inv* kimono *ou* loose sleeve; **manche montée** set-in sleeve; **manche raglan** *inv* raglan sleeve; **manche trois-quarts** three-quarter sleeve; **manche à vent** ventilator.
manche[2] [mɑ̃ʃ] **1** *nm* **(a)** (*gén*) handle; (*long*) shaft; (*Mus*) neck. (*fig*) **tenir le couteau par le ~** *ou* **du côté du ~** to have the whip hand; *V* **branler, jeter.**
(b) (*: *incapable*) clumsy fool *ou* oaf, clot (*Brit*). **conduire comme un ~** to be a hopeless *ou* rotten* driver; **s'y prendre comme un ~ pour faire qch** to set about (doing) sth in a ham-fisted* *ou* ham-handed* way.
2: manche à balai (*gén*) broomstick, broomshaft; (*Aviat*) joystick; **manche à gigot** leg of mutton holder; **manche de gigot** knuckle (of a leg-of-mutton).
manchette [mɑ̃ʃɛt] *nf* **(a)** *[chemise]* cuff; (*protectrice*) oversleeve. **(b)** (*Presse*) (*titre*) headline. **mettre en ~** to headline, put in headlines. **(c)** (*rare: note*) marginal note. **en ~** in the margin. **(d)** forearm blow.
manchon [mɑ̃ʃɔ̃] *nm* **(a)** muff; *V* **chien. (b) ~ à incandescence** incandescent (gas) mantle.
manchot, -ote [mɑ̃ʃo, ɔt] **1** *adj* (*d'un bras*) one-armed; (*des deux bras*) armless; (*d'une main*) one-handed; (*des deux mains*) with no hands, handless. (*fig*) **il n'est pas ~!*** (*adroit*) he's clever *ou* he's no fool with his hands!
2 *nm,f* (*d'un bras*) one-armed person; (*des deux bras*) person with no arms.
3 *nm* (*Orn*) penguin.
mandant, e [mɑ̃dɑ̃, ɑ̃t] *nm,f* (*Jur*) principal. (*Pol frm*) **je parle au nom de mes ~s** I speak on behalf of those who have given me a mandate *ou* of my electors *ou* of my constituents.
mandarin [mɑ̃daʀɛ̃] *nm* (*Hist, péj*) mandarin; (*Orn*) mandarin duck.
mandarinat [mɑ̃daʀina] *nm* **(a)** (*Hist*) mandarinate. **(b)** (*péj*) academic Establishment (*péj*).
mandarine [mɑ̃daʀin] **1** *nf* mandarin (orange), tangerine. **2** *adj inv* tangerine.
mandarinier [mɑ̃daʀinje] *nm* mandarin (orange) tree.
mandat [mɑ̃da] **1** *nm* **(a)** (*gén, Pol*) mandate. **donner à qn ~ de faire** to mandate sb to do; **obtenir le renouvellement de son ~** to be re-elected, have one's mandate renewed; **territoires sous ~** mandated territories, territories under mandate.
(b) (*Comm: aussi* **~-poste**) postal order (*Brit*), money order.
(c) (*Jur: procuration*) power of attorney, proxy; (*Police etc*) warrant.
2: (*Jur*) **mandat d'amener** ≃ summons; **mandat d'arrêt** ≃ warrant for arrest; (*Comm*) **mandat-carte** *nm, pl* **mandats-cartes** money order (*in postcard form*); (*Jur*) **mandat de comparution** ≃ summons (to appear), subpoena; (*Jur*) **mandat de dépôt** ≃ committal order; **placer qn sous mandat de dépôt** ≃ to play sb under a committal order; (*Comm*) **mandat-lettre** *nm, pl* **mandats-lettres** money order (*with space for correspondence*); (*Jur*) **mandat de perquisition** search warrant.
mandataire [mɑ̃datɛʀ] *nmf* (*Jur*) proxy, attorney; (*représentant*) representative. **je ne suis que son ~** I'm only acting as a proxy for him; **~ aux Halles** (sales) agent (at the Halles).
mandater [mɑ̃date] (1) *vt* **(a)** (*donner pouvoir à*) *personne* to appoint, commission; (*Pol*) *député* to give a mandate to, elect. **(b)** (*Fin*) **~ une somme** (*écrire*) to write out a money order for a sum; (*payer*) to pay a sum by money order.
mandchou, e [mɑ̃dʃu] **1** *adj* Manchu(rian). **2** *nm* (*Ling*) Manchu. **3** *nm,f*: **M~(e)** Manchu.
Mandchourie [mɑ̃tʃuʀi] *nf* Manchuria.
mandement [mɑ̃dmɑ̃] *nm* **(a)** (*Rel*) pastoral. **(b)** (††) (*ordre*) mandate, command; (*Jur: convocation*) subpoena.
mander [mɑ̃de] (1) *vt* **(a)** (††) (*ordonner*) to command; (*convoquer*) to summon. **(b)** (*littér: dire par lettre*) **~ qch à qn** to send *ou* convey the news of sth to sb, inform sb of sth.
mandibule [mɑ̃dibyl] *nf* mandible. (*fig*) **jouer des ~s*** to nosh*.
mandoline [mɑ̃dɔlin] *nf* mandolin(e).
mandragore [mɑ̃dʀagɔʀ] *nf* mandrake.
mandrin [mɑ̃dʀɛ̃] *nm* (*pour serrer*) chuck; (*pour percer, emboutir*) punch; (*pour élargir, égaliser des trous*) drift.
...mane [man] *suff V* **mélomane, morphinomane, mythomane etc.**
manécanterie [manekɑ̃tʀi] *nf* (parish) choir school.
manège [manɛʒ] *nm* **(a) ~ (de chevaux de bois)** roundabout, merry-go-round; *V* **tour**[2].
(b) (*Équitation*) (*centre, école*) riding school; (*piste, salle*) ring, school.
(c) (*fig: agissements*) game, ploy. **j'ai deviné son petit ~** I guessed what he was up to, I saw through his little game.
mânes [mɑn] *nmpl* (*Antiq Rel*) manes. (*littér, fig*) **les ~ de ses ancêtres** the shades of one's ancestors (*littér*), the spirits of the dead.
manette [manɛt] *nf* lever, tap. (*Aut*) **~ des gaz** throttle lever.
manganate [mɑ̃ganat] *nm* manganate.
manganèse [mɑ̃ganɛz] *nm* manganese.
mangeable [mɑ̃ʒabl(ə)] *adj* (*lit, fig*) edible, eatable.
mangeaille [mɑ̃ʒaj] *nf* (*péj*) (*nourriture mauvaise*) pigswill, disgusting food; (*grande quantité de nourriture*) mounds of food. **il nous venait des odeurs de ~** we were met by an unappetising smell of food (cooking).
mangeoire [mɑ̃ʒwaʀ] *nf* trough, manger.
manger [mɑ̃ʒe] (3) **1** *vt* **(a)** to eat; *soupe* to drink, eat. **~ dans une assiette/dans un bol** to eat off *ou* from a plate/out of a bowl; **il mange peu** he doesn't eat much; **il ne mange pas** *ou* **rien en ce moment** he's off his food at present, he is not eating at all at present; **ils ont mangé tout ce qu'elle avait (à la maison)** they ate her out of house and home; **vous mangerez bien un morceau avec nous?*** won't you have a bite (to eat) with us?; **il a mangé tout ce qui restait** he has eaten (up) all that was left; **cela se mange?** can you eat it?, is it edible?; **ce plat se mange très chaud** this dish should be eaten very hot; **ils leur ont fait** *ou* **donné à ~ un excellent poisson** they served *ou* gave them some excellent fish (to eat); **faire ~ qn** to feed sb; **faire ~ qch à qn** to give sb sth to eat, make sb eat sth; **donner à ~ à un bébé/un animal** to feed a baby/an animal; **~ goulûment** to wolf down one's food, eat greedily; **~ salement** to be a messy eater; **~ comme un cochon*** to eat like a pig*; **finis de ~!, mange!** eat up!; **on mange bien/mal à cet hôtel** the food is good/bad at this hotel; **les enfants ne mangent pas à leur faim à l'école** the children don't get *ou* are not given enough to eat at school.
(b) (*emploi absolu: faire un repas*) **~ dehors** *ou* **au restaurant** to eat out, have a meal out; **c'est l'heure de ~** (*midi*) it's lunchtime; (*soir*) it's dinnertime; **inviter qn à ~** to invite sb for a meal; **boire en mangeant** to drink with a meal; **~ sur le pouce** to have a (quick) snack, snatch a bite (to eat); *V* **carte.**
(c) (*fig: dévorer*) **~ qn des yeux** to gaze hungrily at sb, devour sb with one's eyes; **~ qn de baisers** to smother sb with kisses; **allez le voir, il ne vous mangera pas** go and see him, he won't eat you; **il va te ~ tout cru** he'll make mincemeat of you, he'll swallow you whole; (*iro*) **~ du curé** to be a priest hater.
(d) (*ronger*) to eat (away). **mangé par les mites** *ou* **aux mites** moth-eaten; **la grille (de fer) a été mangée par la rouille** the (iron) railing is eaten away with rust; **le soleil a mangé la couleur** the sun has taken out *ou* faded the colour.
(e) (*faire disparaître, consommer*) **ce poêle mange beaucoup de charbon** this stove gets through *ou* uses a lot of coal *ou* is heavy on coal; **toutes ces activités lui mangent son temps** all these activities take up his time; (*avaler*) **~ ses mots** to swallow one's words; **de nos jours les grosses entreprises mangent les petites** nowadays the big firms swallow up the smaller ones; **une barbe touffue lui mangeait le visage** his face was half hidden under a bushy beard; **des yeux énormes lui mangeaient le visage** his face seemed to be just two great eyes.
(f) (*dilapider*) *fortune, capital, économies* to go through, squander. **l'entreprise mange de l'argent** the business is eating money; **dans cette affaire il mange de l'argent** he's simply spending money like water in this business.
(g) (*loc*) **~ la consigne** *ou* **la commission** to forget one's errand; **~ comme quatre/comme un oiseau** to eat like a horse/like a bird; **~ du bout des dents** to pick at one's food; (*fig*) **~ le morceau‡** to spill the beans‡, talk, come clean*; **~ son pain blanc le premier** to have it easy at the start; **je ne mange pas de ce pain-là!** I'm having nothing to do with that!, I'm not stooping to anything like that!; **~ de la vache enragée** to have a very lean time of it; **~ son blé en herbe** to spend one's money in advance *ou* before one gets it; **~ à tous les rateliers** to cash in* on all sides; *V* **sang.**

2 *nm* food. **préparer le ~ des enfants*** to get the children's food *ou* meal ready; **'ici on peut apporter son ~'*** 'customers may consume their own food on the premises'; **à prendre après ~** to be taken after meals; *V* **perdre**.

mange-disques [mɑ̃ʒdisk] *nm inv slot-in record player.*

mange-tout [mɑ̃ʒtu] *nm inv*: **pois ~** mange-tout peas; **haricots ~** runner bean, French bean.

mangeur, -euse [mɑ̃ʒœʀ, øz] *nm,f* eater. **être gros *ou* grand/petit ~** to be a big/small eater; **c'est un gros ~ de pain** he eats a lot of bread, he's a big bread-eater*; **~ d'hommes** man-eater.

mangouste [mɑ̃gust(ə)] *nf (Zool)* mongoose.

mangue [mɑ̃g] *nf* mango *(fruit)*.

manguier [mɑ̃gje] *nm* mango *(tree)*.

maniabilité [manjabilite] *nf [objet]* handiness, manageability. **appareil d'une grande ~** implement which is very easy to handle, very handy implement; **c'est un véhicule d'une étonnante ~** this vehicle is incredibly easy to handle.

maniable [manjabl(ə)] *adj* **(a)** *objet, taille* handy, manageable, easy to handle *(attrib)*; *véhicule* easy to handle *(attrib)*. **(b)** *(influençable) électeur* easily swayed *ou* influenced *(attrib)*. **(c)** *(accommodant) homme, caractère* accommodating, amenable.

maniaque [manjak] **1** *adj personne* finicky, fussy, pernickety. **faire qch avec un soin ~** to do sth with almost fanatical care; **c'est un ~ de l'exactitude** he is fanatical about punctuality, he's a stickler for punctuality; **c'est un ~ de la voile** he's sailing mad *ou* a sailing fanatic.

2 *nmf* (†: *Admin, Presse: fou*) maniac, lunatic. **~ sexuel** sex maniac.

maniaquerie [manjakʀi] *nf* fussiness, pernicketiness.

manichéen, -enne [manikeɛ̃, ɛn] *adj, nm,f* Manich(a)ean.

manichéisme [manikeism(ə)] *nm (Philos)* Maniche(an)ism; *(péj)* over-simplification. *(fig)* **il fait du ~** he sees things in black and white, everything is either good or bad to him.

manie [mani] *nf* **(a)** *(habitude)* odd *ou* queer habit. **elle est pleine de (petites) ~s** she's got all sorts of funny little ways *ou* habits; **mais quelle ~ tu as de te manger les ongles!** you've got a terrible habit of biting your nails! **(b)** *(obsession)* mania. *(Méd)* **~ de la persécution** persecution mania.

maniement [manimɑ̃] *nm* **(a)** handling. **d'un ~ difficile** difficult to handle; **le ~ de cet objet est pénible** this object is difficult to handle; **il possède à fond le ~ de la langue** he has a thorough understanding of how to use *ou* handle the language.

(b) *(Mil)* **~ d'armes** arms drill *(Brit)*, manual of arms *(US)*.

manier [manje] (7) **1** *vt objet, langue, foule* to handle; *personne* to handle; *(péj)* to manipulate. **~ l'aviron** to pull *ou* ply *(littér)* the oars; **~ de grosses sommes d'argent** to handle large sums of money; **cheval/voiture facile à ~** horse/car which is easy to handle; **il sait ~ le pinceau, il manie le pinceau avec adresse** he knows how to handle a brush, he's a painter of some skill; **savoir ~ la plume** to be a good writer; **savoir ~ l'ironie** to handle irony skilfully.

2 se manier *vpr* = **se magner**.

manière [manjɛʀ] *nf* **(a)** *(façon)* way. **sa ~ d'agir/de parler** the way he behaves/speaks; **il le fera à sa ~** he'll do it (in) his own way; **~ de vivre** way of life; **~ de voir (les choses)** outlook (on things); **c'est sa ~ d'être habituelle** that's just the way he is, that's just how he usually is; **ce n'est pas la bonne ~ de s'y prendre** this is not the right *ou* best way to go about it; **d'une ~ efficace** in an efficient way; **de quelle ~ as-tu fait cela?** how did you do that?; **à la ~ d'un singe** like a monkey, as a monkey would do.

(b) *(Art: style)* **c'est un Matisse dernière ~** it's a late Matisse *ou* an example of Matisse's later work; **dans la ~ classique** in the classical style; **à la ~ de Racine** in the style of Racine.

(c) *(loc)* **employer la ~ forte** to use strong measures, take a tough line*; **il l'a giflé de belle ~!** he gave him a sound *ou* good slap; **en ~ d'excuse** by way of (an) excuse; **d'une certaine ~, il a raison** in a way *ou* in some ways he is right; **d'une ~ générale** generally speaking, as a general rule; **de toute(s) ~(s)** in any case, at any rate, anyway; **de cette ~** (in) this way; **d'une ~ ou d'une autre** somehow or other; **en aucune ~** in no way; **je n'accepterai en aucune ~** I shall not agree on any account; **de ~ à faire** so as to do; **de ~ (à ce) que nous arrivions à l'heure** so that we get there on time.

(d) ~s: avoir de bonnes/mauvaises ~s to have good/bad manners; **apprendre les belles ~s** to learn good manners; **il n'a pas de ~s, il est sans ~s** he has no manners; **ce ne sont pas des ~s!** that's no way to behave!; **en voilà des ~s!** what a way to behave!; **je n'aime pas ces ~s!** I don't like this kind of behaviour!; **faire des ~s** *(minauderies)* to be affected, put on airs; *(chichis)* to make a fuss.

(e) (†: *genre*) **une ~ de pastiche** a kind of pastiche; **quelle ~ d'homme est-ce?** what kind *ou* sort of a man is he?, what manner of man is he?†

maniéré, e [manjeʀe] *adj* **(a)** *(péj: affecté) personne, style, voix* affected. **(b)** *(Art) genre* mannered. **les tableaux très ~s de ce peintre** the mannered style of this painter.

maniérisme [manjeʀism(ə)] *nm (Art)* mannerism.

manieur, -euse [manjœʀ, øz] *nm,f*: **~ d'argent *ou* de fonds** big businessman.

manif* [manif] *nf (abrév de* **manifestation***)* demo*.

manifestant, e [manifɛstɑ̃, ɑ̃t] *nm,f* demonstrator.

manifestation [manifɛstɑsjɔ̃] *nf* **(a)** *(Pol)* demonstration.

(b) *(expression) [opinion, sentiment]* expression; *[maladie] (apparition)* appearance; *(symptômes)* outward sign *ou* symptom. **~ de mauvaise humeur** show of bad temper; **~ de joie** demonstration *ou* expression of joy; **accueillir qn avec de grandes ~s d'amitié** to greet sb with great demonstrations of friendship.

(c) *[Dieu, vérité]* revelation.

(d) *(réunion, fête)* event. **~ artistique/culturelle/sportive** artistic/cultural/sporting event; **le maire assistait à cette sympathique ~** the mayor was present at this happy gathering *ou* on this happy occasion.

manifeste [manifɛst(ə)] **1** *adj vérité* manifest, obvious, evident; *sentiment, différence* obvious, evident. **erreur ~** glaring error; **il est ~ que vous n'y avez pas réfléchi** obviously you haven't *ou* it is quite obvious *ou* evident that you haven't given it much thought.

2 *nm (Littérat, Pol)* manifesto; *(Aviat, Naut)* manifest.

manifestement [manifɛstəmɑ̃] *adv (V* **manifeste***)* manifestly; obviously, evidently.

manifester [manifɛste] (1) **1** *vt opinion, intention, sentiment* to show, indicate; *courage* to show, demonstrate. **il m'a manifesté son désir de** he indicated to me his wish to, he signified his wish to; *(frm)* **par ce geste la France tient à nous ~ son amitié** France intends this gesture as a demonstration *ou* an indication of her friendship towards us.

2 *vi (Pol)* to demonstrate.

3 se manifester *vpr* **(a)** *(se révéler) [émotion]* to show itself, express itself; *[difficultés]* to emerge, arise. **en fin de journée une certaine détente se manifesta** at the end of the day there was evidence of *ou* there were indications of a certain thaw in the atmosphere, at the end of the day a more relaxed atmosphere could be felt; *(Rel)* **Dieu s'est manifesté aux hommes** God revealed himself to mankind.

(b) *(se présenter) [personne]* to appear, turn up; *[candidat, témoin]* to come forward. **depuis son échec il n'ose pas se ~ ici** since his setback he dare not show his face here.

(c) *(se faire remarquer) [personne]* to make o.s. known, come to the fore. **cette situation difficile lui a permis de se ~** this difficult situation gave him the chance to make himself known *ou* to come to the fore; **il n'a pas eu l'occasion de se ~ dans le débat** he didn't get a chance to assert himself *ou* to make himself heard in the discussion; **il s'est manifesté par une déclaration fracassante** he came to public notice *ou* attracted attention with a shattering pronouncement.

manigance [manigɑ̃s] *nf (gén pl)* scheme, trick. **encore une de ses ~s** another of his little schemes *ou* tricks.

manigancer [manigɑ̃se] (3) *vt* to plot, devise. **qu'est-ce qu'il manigance maintenant?** what's he up to now?, what's his latest little scheme?; **c'est lui qui a tout manigancé** he set the whole thing up*, he engineered it all.

manille[1] [manij] **1** *nm* Manila cigar. **2** *n* **M~** Manila.

manille[2] [manij] *nf* **(a)** *(Cartes) (jeu)* manille; *(dix)* ten. **(b)** *(Tech)* shackle.

manillon [manijɔ̃] *nm* ace *(in game of manille)*.

manioc [manjɔk] *nm* manioc, cassava.

manipulateur, -trice [manipylatœʀ, tʀis] **1** *nm,f* **(a)** *(technicien)* technician. **~ de laboratoire** lab(oratory) technician. **(b)** *(péj)* manipulator. **(c)** *(prestidigitateur)* conjurer. **2** *nm (Téléc)* key.

manipulation [manipylɑsjɔ̃] *nf* **(a)** *(maniement)* handling. **ces produits chimiques sont d'une ~ délicate** these chemicals should be handled with great care, great care should be taken in handling these chemicals.

(b) *(Scol: Chim, Phys)* **~s** experiments.

(c) *(Pol: fig, péj)* manipulation *(U)*. **il y a eu des ~s électorales** there was rigging of the elections, some elections were rigged.

(d) *(prestidigitation)* sleight of hand.

(e) *(Méd: gén pl)* manipulation *(U)*.

manipule [manipyl] *nm (Antiq, Rel)* maniple.

manipuler [manipyle] (1) *vt* **(a)** *objet, produit* to handle.

(b) *(fig, péj) électeurs* to manipulate. **~ une élection** to rig an election; **~ les écritures** to rig *ou* fiddle* the accounts, cook the books* *(Brit)*.

manitobain, e [manitɔbɛ̃, ɛn] **1** *adj* Manitoban. **2** *nm,f*: **M~(e)** Manitoban.

manitou [manitu] *nm* **(a) grand ~*** big shot*, big noise* *(Brit)*. **(b)** *(Rel)* manitou.

manivelle [manivɛl] *nf* crank; *(pour démarrer)* crank, starting handle; *V* **retour**.

manne [man] *nf* **(a)** *(Rel)* **la ~** manna; **recevoir la ~ (céleste)** *(la bonne parole)* to receive the word from on high.

(b) *(fig) (aubaine)* godsend, manna. **ça a été pour nous une ~ (providentielle *ou* céleste)** that was a godsend for us, it was heaven-sent.

(c) *(Bot)* manna.

(d) *(panier)* large wicker basket.

mannequin [mankɛ̃] *nm* **(a)** *(personne)* model, mannequin†; *V* **défilé, taille**[1].

(b) *(objet) [couturière]* dummy; *[vitrine]* model, dummy; *[peintre]* model; *(fig: pantin)* stuffed dummy.

(c) *(panier)* small (gardener's) basket.

manœuvrabilité [manœvʀabilite] *nf* manœuvrability.

manœuvrable [manœvʀabl(ə)] *adj* manœuvrable, easy to handle.

manœuvre [manœvʀ(ə)] **1** *nf* **(a)** *(opération)* manœuvre, operation; *(Rail)* shunting. **diriger/surveiller la ~** to control/supervise the manœuvre *ou* operation; **la ~ d'un bateau n'est pas chose facile** manœuvring a boat is no easy thing to do, it's not easy to manœuvre a boat; *(Aut, Naut)* **il a manqué sa ~** he mishandled *ou* muffed* the manœuvre; **il a réussi sa ~** he carried off the manœuvre successfully; *(Rail)* **faire la ~** to shunt.

(b) *(Mil)* manœuvre. **champ/terrain de ~s** drill *ou* parade ground; **~ d'encerclement** encircling movement; **les grandes ~s de printemps** spring army manœuvres *ou* exercises.

(c) (*agissement, combinaison*) manœuvre; (*machination, intrigue*) manœuvring, ploy. **il a toute liberté de ~** he has complete freedom to manœuvre; **~s électorales** vote-catching manœuvres *ou* ploys; **~s frauduleuses** fraudulent schemes *ou* devices; **~ d'obstruction** obstructive move; **il a été victime d'une ~ de l'adversaire** he was caught out by a clever move *ou* trick on the part of his opponents.
(d) (*Naut*) **~s dormantes/courantes** standing/running rigging.
2 *nm* labourer. **c'est un travail de ~** it's unskilled labour *ou* work; **~ agricole** farm labourer *ou* hand.

manœuvrer [manœvʀe] (1) **1** *vt véhicule* to manœuvre; *machine* to operate, work. **2** *vi* (*gén*) to manœuvre.

manœuvrier, -ère [manœvʀije, ɛʀ] **1** *adj* manœuvring. **2** *nm,f* (*Mil*) tactician; (*Pol*) manœuvrer.

manoir [manwaʀ] *nm* manor *ou* country house.

manomètre [manɔmɛtʀ(ə)] *nm* gauge, manometer.

manométrique [manɔmetʀik] *adj* manometric.

manouvrier† [manuvʀije] *nm* (casual) labourer.

manquant, e [mɑ̃kɑ̃, ɑ̃t] *adj* missing.

manque [mɑ̃k] *nm* **(a)** **~ de** (*pénurie*) lack of, shortage of, want of; (*faiblesse*) lack of, want of; **~ de nourriture/d'argent** lack *ou* shortage *ou* want of food/money; **~ d'intelligence/de goût** lack *ou* want of intelligence/taste; **son ~ de sérieux** his lack of seriousness, his flippancy; **par ~ de** through lack *ou* shortage of, for want of; **quel ~ de chance!** *ou* **de pot!**‡ what bad *ou* hard luck!; **~ à gagner** loss of profit *ou* earnings; **cela représente un sérieux ~ à gagner pour les cultivateurs** that means a serious loss of money *ou* a serious drop in earnings for the farmers.
(b) **~s** (*défauts*) *[roman]* faults; *[personne]* failings, shortcomings; *[mémoire, connaissances]* gaps.
(c) (*vide*) gap, emptiness; (*Drogue*) withdrawal. **je ressens comme un grand ~** it's as if there were a great emptiness inside me; **un ~ que rien ne saurait combler** a gap which nothing could fill; **symptômes de ~** withdrawal symptoms.
(d) (*Tex*) flaw.
(e) (*Roulette*) manque.
(f)(‡) **à la ~: un chanteur à la ~** a crummy‡ *ou* second-rate singer; **lui et ses idées à la ~** him and his half-baked* *ou* crummy‡ ideas.

manqué, e [mɑ̃ke] (*ptp de* **manquer**) *adj essai* failed, abortive; *rendez-vous* missed; *photo* spoilt; *vie* wasted; (*Tech*) *pièce* faulty. **occasion ~e** lost *ou* wasted opportunity; **un roman ~** a novel which doesn't quite succeed *ou* come off*; **c'est un écrivain ~** (*mauvais écrivain*) he is a failure as a writer; (*il aurait dû être écrivain*) he should have been a writer; (*Culin*) **(gâteau) ~** ≃ sponge cake; *V* **garçon.**

manquement [mɑ̃kmɑ̃] *nm* (*frm*) **~ à** *discipline, règle* breach of; **~ au devoir** dereliction of duty; **au moindre ~** at the slightest lapse.

manquer [mɑ̃ke] (1) **1** *vt* **(a)** (*ne pas atteindre ou saisir*) *but, occasion, train* to miss; (*ne pas tuer; ne pas atteindre ou rencontrer*) *personne* to miss. **~ une marche** to miss a step; **~ qn de peu** (*en lui tirant dessus*) to miss sb by a fraction, just to miss sb; (*à un rendez-vous*) just to miss sb; **je l'ai manqué de 5 minutes** I missed him by 5 minutes; **c'est un film/une pièce à ne pas ~** this film/play is a must*, it's a film/play that shouldn't be missed; (*iro*) **il n'en manque jamais une*!** he blunders *ou* boobs‡ every time!, he puts his foot in it every time!*; **vous n'avez rien manqué (en ne venant pas)** you didn't miss anything (by not coming); **je ne le manquerai pas** (*je vais lui donner une leçon*) I won't let him get away with it; (*fig*) **~ le coche** to miss the bus*.
(b) (*ne pas réussir*) *photo, gâteau* to spoil, make a mess of*, botch*; (*rare*) *examen* to fail. **il a manqué sa vie** he has wasted his life; **ils ont (complètement) manqué leur coup** their attempt failed completely, they completely botched* the attempt *ou* the job*.
(c) (*être absent de*) to be absent from, miss. **~ l'école** to be absent from *ou* miss school; **il a manqué deux réunions** he missed two meetings.
2 *vi* **(a)** (*faire défaut*) to be lacking. **l'argent/la nourriture vint à ~** money/food ran out *ou* ran short; **rien ne manque** nothing is lacking; **les occasions ne manquent pas (de faire)** there is no lack of *ou* there are endless opportunities (to do).
(b) (*être absent*) to be absent; (*avoir disparu*) to be missing. **il ne manque jamais** he's never absent, he never misses; **rien ne manque** nothing is missing.
(c) (*échouer*) *[expérience etc]* to fail.
(d) **~ à** (*faire défaut à*): **les mots me manquent pour exprimer** I can't find the words to express, I am at a loss for words to express; **le temps me manque pour m'étendre sur ce sujet** there's no time for me to enlarge on this theme; **le pied lui manqua** his foot slipped, he missed his footing; **la voix lui manqua** words failed him, he stood speechless; **un carreau manquait à la fenêtre** there was a pane missing in *ou* from the window; (*hum*) **qu'est-ce qui manque à ton bonheur?** is there something not to your liking?, what are you unhappy about?
3 manquer à *vt indir* **(a)** (*ne pas respecter*) **~ à son honneur/son devoir** to fail in one's honour/duty; **~ à tous les usages** to flout every convention; **il manque à tous ses devoirs** he neglects all his duties; **sa femme lui a manqué, il l'a battue**† his wife wronged him so he beat her; **~ à qn**† (*être impoli envers qn*) to be disrespectful to sb.
(b) (*être absent de*) *réunion* to be absent from, miss. **~ à l'appel** (*lit*) to be absent from roll call; (*fig*) to be missing.
(c) (*être regretté*) **~ à qn: il nous manque, sa présence nous manque** we miss him; **la campagne nous manque** we miss the country.
4 manquer de *vt indir* **(a)** (*être dépourvu de*) *intelligence, générosité* to lack; *argent, main d'œuvre* to be short of, lack. **ils ne manquent de rien** they want for nothing, they lack nothing; **le pays ne manque pas d'un certain charme** the country is not without a certain charm; **on manque d'air ici** there's no air in here; **nous manquons de personnel** we're short-staffed, we're short of staff, we lack staff; **il ne manque pas d'audace!** he's got a nerve*!
(b) (*faillir*) **elle a manqué (de) se faire écraser** she nearly got run over; **il a manqué mourir** he nearly *ou* almost died.
(c) (*formules nég*) **ne pas ~ de: ne manquez pas de le remercier pour moi** don't forget to thank him for me, be sure to thank him for me; **je ne manquerai pas de le lui dire** I'll be sure to tell him; **il n'a pas manqué de le lui dire** he made sure he told him; **remerciez-la — je n'y manquerai pas** thank her — I won't forget; **on ne peut ~ d'être frappé par** one cannot fail to marvel at, one cannot help but be struck by; **ça ne va pas ~ (d'arriver)*** it's bound to happen; **ça n'a pas manqué (d'arriver)*!** sure enough it was bound to happen!
5 *vt impers*: **il manque un pied à la chaise** there's a leg missing from the chair; **il (nous) manque 10 personnes/2 chaises** (*elles ont disparu*) there are 10 people/2 chairs missing ; (*on en a besoin*) we are 10 people/2 chairs short, we are short of 10 people/2 chairs; **il ne manquera pas de gens pour dire** there'll be no shortage *ou* lack of people to say; **il ne lui manque que d'être intelligent** the only thing he's lacking in is intelligence; **il ne manquait plus que ça** that's all we needed, that beats all*, that's the last straw*; **il ne manquerait plus qu'il parte sans elle!** it would be the last straw if he went off without her!*
6 se manquer *vpr* (*rater son suicide*) to fail (in one's attempt to commit suicide).

mansarde [mɑ̃saʀd(ə)] *nf* (*pièce*) attic, garret.

mansardé, e [mɑ̃saʀde] *adj chambre, étage* attic (*épith*). **la chambre est ~e** the room has a sloping ceiling, it is an attic room.

mansuétude [mɑ̃sɥetyd] *nf* leniency, indulgence.

mante [mɑ̃t] *nf* **(a)** (*Zool*) mantis. **~ religieuse** (*lit*) praying mantis; (*fig*) man-eater (*fig hum*). **(b)** (†: *manteau*) (woman's) mantle, cloak.

manteau, *pl* **~x** [mɑ̃to] **1** *nm* **(a)** (*Habillement*) coat. **~ de pluie** raincoat; (*loc*) **sous le ~** clandestinely, on the sly.
(b) (*fig littér*) *[neige]* mantle, blanket; *[ombre, hypocrisie]* cloak. **sous le ~ de la nuit** under cover of night, under the cloak of darkness.
(c) (*Zool*) *[mollusque]* mantle.
(d) (*Hér*) mantle, mantling.
2: **manteau d'Arlequin** proscenium arch; **manteau de cheminée** mantelpiece.

mantelet [mɑ̃tlɛ] *nm* (*Habillement*) short cape, mantelet; (*Naut*) deadlight.

mantille [mɑ̃tij] *nf* mantilla.

Mantoue [mɑ̃tu] *n* Mantua.

manualiser [manɥalize] (1) *vt* to manualize.

manucure [manykyʀ] *nmf* manicurist.

manuel, -elle [manɥɛl] **1** *adj* manual. **2** *nm,f* (*travailleur manuel*) manual worker; (*qui a du sens pratique*) practical man (*ou* woman). **3** *nm* (*livre*) manual, handbook. **~ de lecture** reader.

manuellement [manɥɛlmɑ̃] *adv fabriquer* by hand, manually. **être bon ~** to be good with one's hands.

manufacturable [manyfaktyʀabl(ə)] *adj* manufacturable.

manufacture [manyfaktyʀ] *nf* **(a)** (*usine*) factory. **~ d'armes/de porcelaine/de tabac** munitions/porcelain/tobacco factory; **~ de tapisserie** tapestry workshop. **(b)** (*fabrication*) manufacture.

manufacturer [manyfaktyʀe] (1) *vt* to manufacture; *V* **produit.**

manufacturier, -ière [manyfaktyʀje, jɛʀ] *adj* manufacturing (*épith*).

manu militari [manymilitaʀi] *adv* by (main) force.

manuscrit, e [manyskʀi, it] **1** *adj* (*écrit à la main*) handwritten. **pages ~es** manuscript pages. **2** *nm* manuscript; (*dactylographié*) manuscript, typescript.

manutention [manytɑ̃sjɔ̃] *nf* (*opération*) handling; (*local*) storehouse.

manutentionnaire [manytɑ̃sjɔnɛʀ] **1** *nm* warehouseman, packer. **2** *nf* warehousewoman, packer.

manutentionner [manytɑ̃sjɔne] (1) *vt* to handle.

maoïsme [maɔism(ə)] *nm* Maoism.

maoïste [maɔist(ə)] *adj, nmf* Maoist.

maousse‡ [maus] *adj personne* hefty; *animal* whacking great‡ (*épith*), colossal.

mappemonde [mapmɔ̃d] *nf* (*carte*) map of the world (in two hemispheres); (*sphère*) globe.

maquereau[1], *pl* **~x** [makʀo] *nm* mackerel; *V* **groseille.**

maquereau[2]‡, *pl* **~x** [makʀo] *nm* pimp, ponce‡.

maquerelle‡ [makʀɛl] *nf* madam*.

maquette [makɛt] *nf* **(a)** (*à échelle réduite*) (*Archit, Ind*) (scale) model; (*Art, Théât*) model.
(b) (*grandeur nature*) (*Ind*) mock-up, model; (*livre*) dummy.
(c) (*Peinture: carton*) sketch.
(d) (*Typ*) (*mise en pages*) paste-up; (*couverture*) artwork.

maquettiste [maketist(ə)] *nmf* model maker.

maquignon [makiɲɔ̃] *nm* (*lit*) horse dealer; (*péj*) shady *ou* crooked dealer.

maquignonnage [makiɲɔnaʒ] *nm* (*lit*) horse dealing; (*fig, péj*) sharp practice, underhand dealings.

maquignonner [makiɲɔne] (1) *vt* (*péj*) *animal* to sell by shady methods; *affaire* to rig, fiddle.

maquillage [makijaʒ] *nm* **(a)** (*résultat*) make-up. **passer du temps à son ~** to spend a long time putting on one's make-up *ou* making up.

(b) (*péj*) *[voiture]* disguising, doing over*; *[document, vérité, faits]* faking, doctoring.

maquiller [makije] (1) **1** *vt* **(a)** *visage, personne* to make up. **très maquillé** heavily made-up.

(b) (*fig*) *document, vérité, faits* to fake, doctor; *résultats, chiffres* to juggle (with), fiddle*; *voiture* to do over*, disguise. **meurtre maquillé en accident** murder faked up to look like an accident.

2 se maquiller *vpr* to make up, put on one's make-up. **elle est trop jeune pour se ~** she is too young to use make-up.

maquilleur [makijœʀ] *nm* make-up artist, make-up man.

maquilleuse [makijøz] *nf* make-up girl.

maquis [maki] *nm* **(a)** (*Géog*) scrub, bush. **le ~ corse** the Corsican scrub; **prendre le ~** to take to the bush.

(b) (*fig: labyrinthe*) tangle, maze.

(c) (*Hist: 2e guerre mondiale*) maquis. **prendre le ~** to take to the maquis, go underground.

maquisard, e [makizaʀ, aʀd(ə)] *nm,f* maquis, member of the Resistance.

marabout [maʀabu] *nm* (*Orn*) marabou(t); (*Rel*) marabout.

maraîcher, -ère [maʀeʃe, maʀɛʃɛʀ] **1** *nm,f* market gardener, truck farmer (*US*). **2** *adj*: **culture ~ère** market gardening (*U*), truck farming (*U*) (*US*); **produit ~** market garden produce (*U*), truck (*U*) (*US*); **jardin ~** market garden, truck farm (*US*).

marais [maʀɛ] *nm* **(a)** marsh, swamp. **~ salant** salt pan, saltern; *V* **gaz**. **(b) le M~** the Marais (*district of Paris*).

marasme [maʀasm(ə)] *nm* **(a)** (*Écon, Pol*) stagnation, paralysis. **les affaires sont en plein ~** business is completely stagnant, there is a complete slump in business.

(b) (*accablement*) dejection, depression.

(c) (*Méd*) marasmus.

marasquin [maʀaskɛ̃] *nm* maraschino.

marathon [maʀatɔ̃] *nm* (*Sport, fig*) marathon.

marâtre [maʀɑtʀ(ə)] *nf* (*mauvaise mère*) cruel *ou* unnatural mother; (††: *belle-mère*) stepmother.

maraud, e[1]†† [maʀo, od] *nm,f* rascal, rogue, scoundrel.

maraudage [maʀodaʒ] *nm* pilfering, thieving (*of poultry, crops etc*).

maraude[2] [maʀod] *nf* **(a)** (*vol*) thieving, pilfering (*of poultry, crops etc*); pillaging (*from farms, orchards*).

(b) taxi en ~ *ou* **qui fait la ~** cruising *ou* prowling taxi, taxi cruising *ou* prowling for fares; **vagabond en ~** tramp on the prowl.

marauder [maʀode] (1) *vi [personne]* to thieve, pilfer; *[taxi]* to cruise *ou* prowl for fares.

maraudeur, -euse [maʀodœʀ, øz] *nm,f* (*voleur*) prowler; (*soldat*) marauder. **oiseau ~** thieving bird; **taxi ~** cruising *ou* prowling taxi.

marbre [maʀbʀ(ə)] *nm* **(a)** (*Géol*) marble. **~ de Carrare** Carrara marble; (*fig*) **rester de ~, garder un visage de ~** to remain stonily indifferent; *V* **froid**.

(b) (*surface*) marble top; (*statue*) marble (statue).

(c) (*Typ*) stone, bed. **être sur le ~** *[journal]* to be put to bed, be on the stone; *[livre]* to be on the press; **rester sur le ~** to be excess copy.

marbrer [maʀbʀe] (1) *vt* **(a)** (*Tech*) *papier, cuir* to marble.

(b) *peau [froid]* to blotch, mottle; *[coup]* to mark, leave marks on; *[coup violent]* to mottle. **peau naturellement marbrée** naturally mottled skin; **visage marbré par le froid** face blotchy *ou* mottled with cold.

(c) (*gén: veiner*) *bois, surface* to vein, mottle.

marbrerie [maʀbʀəʀi] *nf* (*atelier*) marble mason's workshop *ou* yard; (*industrie*) marble industry. **travailler dans la ~** to be a marble mason; (*funéraire*) to be a monumental mason.

marbrier, -ière [maʀbʀije, jɛʀ] **1** *adj industrie* marble (*épith*).

2 *nm* (*funéraire*) monumental mason. **3 marbrière** *nf* marble quarry.

marbrure [maʀbʀyʀ] *nf* (*gén pl*) (*V* **marbrer**) marbling; blotch; mottling; mark; vein.

marc[1] [maʀ] *nm* (*poids, monnaie*) mark. (*Jur*) **au ~ le franc** pro rata, proportionally.

marc[2] [maʀ] *nm [raisin, pomme]* marc. **~ (de café)** (coffee) grounds *ou* dregs; **(eau de vie de) ~** marc brandy.

marcassin [maʀkasɛ̃] *nm* young wild boar.

marchand, e [maʀʃɑ̃, ɑ̃d] **1** *adj valeur* market (*épith*); *prix* trade (*épith*). **navire ~** merchant ship; *V* **galerie, marine**[2].

2 *nm,f* (*boutiquier*) shopkeeper, tradesman (*ou* tradeswoman); (*sur un marché*) stallholder; *[vins, fruits, charbon, grains]* merchant; *[meubles, bestiaux, cycles]* dealer. **~ au détail** retailer; **~ en gros** wholesaler; **la ~e de chaussures me l'a dit** the woman in the shoeshop *ou* the shoeshop owner told me; **rapporte-le chez le ~/chez le ~ de légumes** take it back to the shop *ou* shopkeeper/to the greengrocer's (*Brit*); (*hum, péj*) **c'est un ~ de vacances** he is in the holiday racket (*péj*).

3: marchand ambulant hawker, pedlar (*Brit*), peddler (*US*), door-to-door salesman; (*hum*) **marchande d'amour** lady of pleasure (*hum*); **marchand de biens** estate agent; (*péj*) **marchand de canons** arms dealer *ou* magnate; **marchand de couleurs** ironmonger (*Brit*), hardware dealer; **marchand de fromages** cheesemonger, cheese merchant; **marchand de fruits** fruiterer, fruit merchant; **marchand d'illusions** illusion-monger; **marchand de journaux** newsagent; **marchand de légumes** greengrocer; **marchand de marée** fish merchant; **marchand de marrons** chestnut seller; **marchand de poissons** fishmonger, fish merchant; **marchande de quatre saisons** costermonger (*Brit*); **marchand de rêves** dream-merchant; (*fig*) **marchand de sable** sandman; (*péj*) **marchand de sommeil** *landlord housing immigrant workers in overcrowded conditions*; (*péj*) **marchand de soupe** (*restaurateur*) low-grade restaurateur, profiteering café owner; (*Scol*) money-grubbing *ou* profit-minded headmaster (of a private school); **marchand de tableaux** art dealer; **marchand de tapis** carpet dealer; **marchand de voyages** tour operator.

marchandage [maʀʃɑ̃daʒ] *nm* **(a)** (*au marché*) bargaining, haggling; (*péj: aux élections*) bargaining. **(b)** (*Jur*) **le ~** ≃ the lump (*illegal subcontracting of labour*).

marchander [maʀʃɑ̃de] (1) *vt* **(a)** *objet* to haggle over, bargain over. **il a l'habitude de ~** he is used to haggling *ou* bargaining.

(b) (*fig*) **il ne marchande pas sa peine** he spares no pains, he grudges no effort; **il ne m'a pas marchandé ses compliments** he wasn't sparing with his compliments. **(c)** (*Jur*) to subcontract.

marchandeur, -euse [maʀʃɑ̃dœʀ, øz] *nm,f* **(a)** haggler. **(b)** (*Jur*) subcontractor (of labour).

marchandise [maʀʃɑ̃diz] *nf* **(a)** (*article, unité*) commodity. **~s** goods, merchandise (*U*), wares†; **train/gare de ~s** goods train/station; **~s en gros/au détail** wholesale/retail goods; **il a de la bonne ~** he has *ou* sells good stuff.

(b) (*cargaison, stock*) **la ~** the goods, the merchandise; **la ~ est dans l'entrepôt** the goods are *ou* the merchandise is in the warehouse; **faire valoir** *ou* **vanter la ~*** to show o.s. off *ou* to show off one's wares to advantage, make the most of o.s. *ou* one's wares; **tromper** *ou* **rouler qn sur la ~*** to sell sb a pup*; **elle étale la ~‡** she displays her charms (*hum*), she shows you all she's got*.

marchante [maʀʃɑ̃t] *adj f V* **aile**.

marche[1] [maʀʃ(ə)] **1** *nf* **(a)** (*action, Sport*) walking. **il fait de la ~** he goes in for walking, he does quite a bit of walking; **poursuivre sa ~** to walk on; **chaussures de ~** walking shoes.

(b) (*allure, démarche*) walk, step, gait; (*allure, rythme*) pace, step. **une ~ pesante** a heavy step *ou* gait; **régler sa ~ sur celle de qn** to adjust one's pace *ou* step to sb else's.

(c) (*trajet*) walk. **faire une longue ~** to go for a long walk; **le village est à 2 heures/à 10 km de ~ d'ici** the village is a 2-hour walk/a 10-km walk from here; **une ~ de 10 km** a 10-km walk.

(d) (*mouvement d'un groupe, Mil, Pol*) march. **air/chanson de ~** marching tune/song; **fermer la ~** to bring up the rear; **ouvrir la ~** to lead the way; **faire ~ sur** to march upon; **~ victorieuse sur la ville** victorious march on the town; **en avant, ~!** quick march!, forward march!; *V* **ordre**[1].

(e) (*mouvement, déplacement d'un objet*) (*Aut, Rail*) *[véhicule]* running; (*Tech*) *[machine]* running, working; (*Naut*) *[navire]* sailing; (*Astron*) *[étoile]* course; *[horloge]* working; (*Admin*) *[usine, établissement]* running, working, functioning. **dans le sens de la ~** facing the engine; **ne montez pas dans un véhicule en ~** do not board a moving vehicle; **en (bon) état de ~** in (good) working order; **régler la ~ d'une horloge** to adjust the workings *ou* movement of a clock; **assurer la bonne ~ d'un service** to ensure the smooth running of a service; (*Tech*) **~ — arrêt** on — off.

(f) (*développement*) *[maladie]* progress; *[affaire, événements, opérations]* course; *[histoire, temps, progrès]* march. **la ~ de l'intrigue** the unfolding *ou* development of the plot.

(g) (*loc*) **être en ~** *[personnes, armées]* to be on the move; *[moteur etc]* to be running; **se mettre en ~** *[personne]* to make a move, get moving; *[machine]* to start; **mettre en ~** *moteur, voiture* to start (up); *machine* to put on, turn on, set going; *pendule* to start going; *V* **train**.

(h) (*Mus*) march. **~ funèbre/militaire/nuptiale** funeral/military/wedding march.

2: (*Aut*) **marche arrière** reverse; **entrer/sortir en marche arrière** to reverse in/out; **faire marche arrière** (*Aut*) to reverse; (*fig*) to back-pedal, to backtrack; (*Mil*) **marche forcée** forced march; **se rendre vers un lieu à marche(s) forcée(s)** to get to a place by forced marches; **marche à suivre** (correct) procedure.

marche[2] [maʀʃ(ə)] *nf [escalier, véhicule]* step. **manquer une ~** to miss a step; **attention à la ~** mind the step; **sur les ~s** (*de l'escalier*) on the stairs; (*de l'escalier extérieur, de l'escabeau*) on the steps.

marche[3] [maʀʃ(ə)] *nf* (*gén pl*) (*Géog, Hist*) march. **les ~s** the Marches.

marché [maʀʃe] **1** *nm* **(a)** (*lieu*) market; (*ville*) trading centre. **~ aux bestiaux/aux fleurs/aux poissons** cattle/flower/fish market; **~ couvert/en plein air** covered/open-air market; **aller au ~, aller faire le ~** to go to (the) market; **aller faire son ~** to go to the market; (*plus gén*) to go shopping; *[marchand, acheteur]* **faire les ~s** to go round *ou* do the markets; **vendre/acheter au ~** *ou* **sur les ~s** to buy/sell at the market; **Lyon, le grand ~ des soieries** Lyons, the great trading centre for silk goods.

(b) (*Comm, Écon: débouchés, opérations*) market. **~ financier** money market; **acquérir** *ou* **trouver de nouveaux ~s (pour)** to find new markets (for); **lancer/offrir qch sur le ~** to launch/put sth on the market; **analyse/étude de ~** market analysis/research; **le ~ du travail** the labour market; **étudier un produit en fonction d'un ~** to do research on a product with a view to the possible market; **il n'y a pas de ~ pour ces produits** there is no market for these goods.

(c) (*transaction, contrat*) bargain, transaction, deal. **faire un ~ avantageux** to make *ou* strike a good bargain; **un ~ de dupes** a fool's bargain *ou* deal; **conclure** *ou* **passer un ~ avec qn** to make a deal with sb; **~ conclu!** it's a deal!; **~ ferme** firm deal; (*fig*) **mettre le ~ en main à qn** to force sb to accept or refuse; *V* **bon**[1].

(d) (*Bourse*) market. **le ~ des valeurs** the stockmarket; **le ~ des changes** the exchange market; **~ à prime** option (bargain); **~ au comptant/à terme** spot *ou* cash/forward transaction.

2: Marché commun Common Market; **marché-gare** *nm, pl* **marchés-gares** wholesale food market; **marché noir** black market; **faire du marché noir** to buy and sell on the black market; **marché aux puces** flea market.

marchepied [maʀʃəpje] *nm* (*Rail*) step; (*Aut*) running board; (*fig*) stepping stone.

marcher [maʀʃe] (1) *vi* **(a)** to walk; *[soldats]* to march. ~ **à grandes enjambées** *ou* **à grands pas** to stride (along); **il marche en boitant** he walks with a limp; **venez, on va ~ un peu** come on, let's have a walk *ou* let's go for a walk; **il marchait lentement par les rues** he strolled *ou* wandered along the streets; **il marchait sans but** he walked (along) aimlessly; (*fig*) ~ **sur des œufs** to walk (along) gingerly *ou* cautiously; **faire ~ un bébé** to get a baby to walk, help a baby walk; *V* **pas**[1].

(b) (*mettre le pied sur, dans*) ~ **dans une flaque d'eau** to step in a puddle; **défense de ~ sur les pelouses** keep off the grass; (*lit*) ~ **sur les pieds de qn/sur sa robe** to stand *ou* tread on sb's toes/on one's dress; (*fig*) **ne te laisse pas ~ sur les pieds** don't let anyone tread on your toes (*fig*) *ou* take advantage of you; (*fig*) ~ **sur les plates-bandes** *ou* **les brisées de qn*** to poach *ou* intrude on sb's preserves; ~ **sur les pas de qn** to follow in sb's footsteps.

(c) (*fig: progresser*) ~ **à la conquête de la gloire/vers le succès** to be on the road to fame/success, step out *ou* stride towards fame/success; ~ **au supplice** to walk to one's death *ou* to the stake; ~ **au combat** to march into battle; (*Mil*) ~ **sur une ville/sur un adversaire** to advance on *ou* march against a town/an enemy.

(d) (*fig: obéir*) to toe the line; (*: *consentir*) to agree, play*. (*: *croire naïvement*) **il marche à tous les coups** he is taken in *ou* falls for it* every time; **on lui raconte n'importe quoi et il marche** you can tell him anything and he'll swallow it*; **il n'a pas voulu ~ dans la combine** he did not want to touch the job* *ou* get mixed up in it; **faire ~ qn** (*taquiner*) to pull sb's leg; (*tromper*) to take sb for a ride‡, lead sb up the garden path*; **il sait faire ~ sa grand-mère** he knows how to get round his grandmother; **son père saura le faire ~ (droit)** his father will soon have him toeing the line.

(e) (*avec véhicule*) **le train a/nous avons bien marché jusqu'à Lyon** the train/we made good time as far as Lyons; **nous marchions à 100 à l'heure** we were doing a hundred.

(f) (*fonctionner*) *[appareil]* to work; *[ruse]* to work, come off; *[usine]* to work (well); *[affaires, études]* to go (well). **faire ~** *appareil* to work, operate; *entreprise* to run; **ça fait ~ les affaires** it's good for business; **ça marche à l'électricité** it works by *ou* on electricity; **est-ce que le métro marche aujourd'hui?** is the underground running today?; **ces deux opérations marchent ensemble** these two procedures go *ou* work together; **les affaires marchent mal** things are going badly, business is bad; **les études, ça marche?*** how's the work going? ; **rien ne marche** nothing's going right, nothing's working; *V* **roulette.**

marcheur, -euse [maʀʃœʀ, øz] *nm,f* (*gén*) walker; (*Pol, etc*) marcher.

marcottage [maʀkɔtaʒ] *nm* (*Bot*) layering.

marcotte [maʀkɔt] *nf* (*Bot*) layer, runner.

marcotter [maʀkɔte] (1) *vt* (*Bot*) to layer.

mardi [maʀdi] *nm* Tuesday. **M~ gras** Shrove *ou* Pancake Tuesday; (*hum*) **elle se croit à ~ gras!** she's dressed up like a dog's dinner!; *pour autres loc V* **samedi.**

mare [maʀ] *nf* **(a)** (*étang*) pond. ~ **aux canards** duck pond. **(b)** (*flaque*) pool. ~ **de sang/d'huile** pool of blood/oil.

marécage [maʀekaʒ] *nm* marsh, swamp, bog.

marécageux, -euse [maʀekaʒø, øz] *adj terrain* marshy, swampy, boggy; *plante* marsh (*épith*).

maréchal, *pl* **-aux** [maʀeʃal, o] *nm* (*armée française*) marshal (of France); (*armée britannique*) field marshal. (*Hist*) ~ **de camp** brigadier; **~-ferrant** blacksmith, farrier; **M~ de France** Marshal of France; ~ **des logis** sergeant (*artillery, cavalry etc*); ~ **des logis-chef** battery *ou* squadron sergeant-major; *V* **bâton.**

maréchalat [maʀeʃala] *nm* rank of marshal, marshalcy.

maréchale [maʀeʃal] *nf* marshal's wife; *V* **Madame.**

maréchalerie [maʀeʃalʀi] *nf* (*rare*) (*atelier*) smithy, blacksmith's (shop); (*métier*) blacksmith's trade.

maréchaussée [maʀeʃose] *nf* (*hum*) constabulary (*hum*), police (force); (*Hist*) mounted constabulary.

marée [maʀe] *nf* **(a)** tide. ~ **montante/descendante** flood *ou* rising/ebb tide; **à la ~ montante/descendante** when the tide goes in/out, when the tide is rising/ebbing *ou* falling; **(à) ~ haute** (at) high tide *ou* water; **(à) ~ basse** (at) low tide *ou* water; **grande ~** spring tide; **faible** *ou* **petite ~** neap tide; ~ **noire** oil slick.

(b) (*fig*) *[bonheur, colère]* surge, wave; *[nouveaux immeubles, supermarchés]* flood. ~ **humaine** great flood *ou* surge *ou* influx of people.

(c) (*Comm: poissons de mer*) **la ~** fresh catch, fresh (sea) fish; *V* **marchand.**

marelle [maʀɛl] *nf* (*jeu*) hopscotch; (*dessin*) (drawing of a) hopscotch game.

marémoteur, -trice [maʀemɔtœʀ, tʀis] *adj* (*Élec*) *énergie* tidal. **usine ~trice** tidal power station.

marengo [maʀɛ̃go] **1** *adj inv* (*Culin*) **poulet/veau (à la) ~** chicken/veal marengo. **2** *nm black flecked cloth.*

marennes [maʀɛn] *nf* Marennes oyster.

mareyeur, -euse [maʀɛjœʀ, øz] *nm,f* wholesale fish merchant.

margarine [maʀgaʀin] *nf* margarine, marge*. ~ **de régime** soft margarine.

marge [maʀʒ(ə)] **1** *nf* (*tous sens*) margin. **faire des annotations en ~** to make notes in the margin; **donner de la ~ à qn** (*temps*) to give sb a reasonable margin of time; (*latitude*) to give sb some leeway *ou* latitude *ou* scope; **je ne suis pas pressé, j'ai encore de la ~** I'm not in a hurry, I still have time to spare; **en ~ (de la société)** on the fringe (of society); **il a décidé de vivre en ~ de la société** he has opted out (of society); **vivre en ~ du monde/des affaires** to live cut off from the world/from business; **activités en ~ du festival** fringe activities; **en ~ de cette affaire, on peut aussi signaler** with the *ou* this subject, one might also point out that.

2: marge (bénéficiaire) (profit) margin; **marge d'erreur** margin of error; (*Fin*) **marge de garantie** margin; **marge de manœuvre** room to manœuvre; **marge de sécurité** safety margin; **marge de tolérance** tolerance.

margelle [maʀʒɛl] *nf*: ~ **(de puits)** coping (of a well).

marger [maʀʒe] (3) *vt machine à écrire, feuille* to set the margins on; (*Typ*) to feed (in).

margeur [maʀʒœʀ] *nm [machine à écrire]* margin stop.

marginal, e, *mpl* **-aux** [maʀʒinal, o] *adj* (*gén, Écon*) marginal. **récifs ~aux** fringing reefs; **notes ~es** marginal notes, marginalia (*pl*); (*fig*) **les ~aux** (*contestataires*) the fringe, (the) dropouts; (*déshérités*) second-class citizens.

marginaliser [maʀʒinalize] (1) *vt* to marginalize, edge out*, freeze out*.

margis [maʀʒi] *nm* (*arg Mil abrév de* **maréchal des logis**) sarge (*arg*).

Margot [maʀgo] *nf* (*dim de* **Marguerite**) Maggie.

margoulette‡ [maʀgulɛt] *nf* (*mâchoires, visage*) face, mug‡.

margoulin [maʀgulɛ̃] *nm* (*péj*) swindler, shark (*fig*).

margrave [maʀgʀav] *nm* (*Hist*) margrave.

marguerite [maʀgəʀit] *nf* **(a)** (*Bot*) marguerite, (oxeye) daisy; *V* **effeuiller, reine. (b) M~** Margaret.

marguillier [maʀgije] *nm* (*Hist*) churchwarden.

mari [maʀi] *nm* husband.

mariable [maʀjabl(ə)] *adj* marriageable.

mariage [maʀjaʒ] *nm* **1 (a)** (*institution, union*) marriage. **50 ans de ~** 50 years of married life *ou* of marriage; **au début de leur ~** when they were first married, at the beginning of their marriage; **on parle de ~ entre eux** there is talk of their getting married; **il avait un enfant d'un premier ~** he had a child from his first marriage; **né hors du ~** born out of wedlock; **promettre/donner qn en ~ à** to promise/give sb in marriage to; **elle lui a apporté beaucoup d'argent en ~** she brought him a lot of money when she married him; **faire un riche ~** to marry into money; **faire un ~ d'amour** to marry for love, make a love match; **faire un ~ d'argent** *ou* **d'intérêt** to marry for money; *V* **acte, demande** *etc.*

(b) (*cérémonie*) wedding. **grand ~** society wedding; **cadeau/faire-part/messe de ~** wedding present/invitation/service; *V* **corbeille.**

(c) (*fig: mélange*) *[couleurs, parfums]* marriage, blend.

(d) (*Cartes*) **avoir le ~ à cœur** to have *ou* hold (the) king and queen *ou* king-queen of hearts; **faire des ~s** to collect kings and queens.

2: mariage d'amour love match; **mariage d'argent** marriage for money, money match; **mariage blanc** unconsummated marriage; **mariage en blanc** white wedding; **mariage civil** civil wedding; **mariage de convenance** marriage of convenience; **mariage d'intérêt** money *ou* social match; **mariage mixte** mixed marriage; **mariage de raison** marriage of convenience; **mariage religieux** church wedding.

marial, e, *mpl* **~s** [maʀjal] *adj* (*Rel*) *culte* Marian.

Marianne [maʀjan] *nf* (*prénom*) Marion; Marianne (*symbol of the French Republic*).

marie [maʀi] **1** *nf*: **M~** Mary. **2: marie-couche-toi-là‡†** *nf inv* (*prostituée*) harlot†, strumpet†; **marie-salope** *nf, pl* **maries-salopes** (*bateau*) mud dredger; (‡) slut.

marié, e [maʀje] (*ptp de* **marier**) **1** *adj* married. **non ~** unmarried, single.

2 *nm* (bride)groom. **les ~s** (*jour du mariage*) the bride and (bride)groom; (*après le mariage*) the newly-weds; *V* **jeune, nouveau.**

3 mariée *nf* bride. **trouver** *ou* **se plaindre que la ~e est trop belle** to object that everything's too good to be true; **couronne/robe/voile** *etc* **de ~e** wedding headdress/dress/veil *etc*; *V* **jeune.**

marier [maʀje] (7) **1** *vt* **(a)** *[maire, prêtre]* to marry. **il a marié sa fille à un homme d'affaires** he married his daughter to a businessman; **il a fini par ~ sa fille** he finally got his daughter married, he finally married off his daughter; (*hum*) **demain, je marie mon frère** tomorrow I see my brother (get) married; **nous sommes mariés depuis 15 ans** we have been married for 15 years; **il a encore 2 filles à ~** he still has 2 unmarried daughters, he still has 2 daughters to marry off; **fille à ~** daughter of marriageable age, marriageable daughter.

(b) *couleurs, goûts, parfums, styles* to blend, harmonize.

2 se marier *vpr* **(a)** *[personne]* to get married. **se ~ à** *ou* **avec qn** to marry sb, get married to sb; **se ~ de la main gauche** to live as man and wife.

(b) *[couleurs, goûts, parfums, styles]* to blend, harmonize.

marieur, -euse [maʀjœʀ, øz] *nm,f* matchmaker.

marigot [maʀigo] *nm* backwater, creek.

marihuana [maʀiɥana] *nf*, **marijuana** [maʀiʒɥana] *nf* marijuana, pot (*arg*).

marin, e[1] [maʀɛ̃, in] **1** *adj air* sea (*épith*); *faune, flore* marine (*épith*), sea (*épith*). **bateau (très) ~** seaworthy ship; **costume ~** sailor suit; *V* **mille**[2], **pied** *etc.*

2 *nm* sailor. (*grade*) **(simple) ~** ordinary seaman; **~ d'eau douce** landlubber; **un peuple de ~s** a seafaring nation, a nation of seafarers; **béret/tricot de ~** sailor's hat/jersey; *V* **fusilier.**

marina [maʀina] *nf* marina.

marinade [maʀinad] *nf* **(a)** marinade. **~ de viande** meat in (a) marinade, marinaded meat. **(b)** (*Can*) **~s** pickles.

marine[2] [maʀin] **1** *nf* **(a)** (*flotte, administration*) navy. **terme de ~** nautical term; **au temps de la ~ à voiles** in the days of sailing ships; **~ (de guerre)** navy; **~ marchande** merchant navy; *V* **lieutenant, officier**[1].

(b) (*tableau*) seascape.
2 *nm* (*soldat*) (US) marine.
3 *adj inv* (*couleur*) navy (blue); *V* **bleu.**

mariner [maʀine] (1) **1** *vt* (*Culin: aussi* **faire ~**) to marinade, marinate. **2** *vi* **(a)** (*Culin*) to marinade, marinate; **harengs marinés** soused herrings. **(b)** (*: *attendre*) to hang about*. **~ en prison** to stew* in prison; **faire** *ou* **laisser ~ qn** to keep sb hanging about* *ou* kicking his heels (*Brit*), let sb stew* for a bit.

maringouin [maʀɛ̃gwɛ̃] *nm* (*Can*) mosquito.

marinier [maʀinje] *nm* bargee (*Brit*), bargeman (*US*).

marinière [maʀinjɛʀ] *nf* (*Habillement*) overblouse, smock; (*Nage*) sidestroke; *V* **moule**[2].

mariol(le)* [maʀjɔl] *nm*: **c'est un ~** (*malin*) he is a crafty *ou* sly one; (*peu sérieux*) he's a bit of a joker; **(ne) fais pas le ~** stop trying to be clever *ou* smart*, stop showing off.

marionnette [maʀjɔnɛt] *nf* (*lit, fig: pantin*) puppet. (*spectacle*) **~s** puppet show; **~ à fils** marionette; **~ à gaine** glove puppet; *V* **montreur, théâtre.**

marionnettiste [maʀjɔnetist(ə)] *nmf* puppeteer, puppet-master (*ou* -mistress).

mariste [maʀist(ə)] *nmf* Marist. **frère/sœur ~** Marist brother/sister.

marital, e, *mpl* **-aux** [maʀital, o] *adj* (*Jur*) (*du mari*) marital. **autorisation ~e** husband's permission *ou* authorization.

maritalement [maʀitalmɑ̃] *adv*: **vivre ~** to live as husband and wife, cohabit.

maritime [maʀitim] *adj* **(a)** *localisation* maritime; *ville* seaboard, coastal, seaside; *province* seaboard, coastal, maritime; *V* **gare**[1], **pin, port**[1]. **(b)** *navigation* maritime; *commerce, agence* shipping; *droit* shipping, maritime. **affecté à la navigation ~** sea-going; *V* **arsenal.**

maritorne† [maʀitɔʀn(ə)] *nf* (*souillon*) slut, slattern.

marivaudage [maʀivodaʒ] *nm* (*littér: badinage*) light-hearted gallantries; (*Littérat*) sophisticated banter in the style of Marivaux.

marivauder [maʀivode] (1) *vi* (*littér*) to engage in lively sophisticated banter; (*Littérat*) to write in the style of Marivaux.

marjolaine [maʀʒɔlɛn] *nf* marjoram.

mark [maʀk] *nm* mark (*Fin*).

marketing [maʀkətiŋ] *nm* marketing.

marlou‡ [maʀlu] *nm* pimp.

marmaille* [maʀmɑj] *nf* gang(s) *ou* horde(s) of kids* *ou* brats* (*péj*). **toute la ~ était là** the whole brood was there.

marmelade [maʀməlad] *nf* **(a)** (*Culin*) stewed fruit, compote. **~ de pommes/poires** stewed apples/pears, compote of apples/pears; **~ d'oranges** (orange) marmalade.
(b) (*) **en ~** *légumes, fruits* (*cuits*) cooked to a mush; (*crus*) reduced to a pulp; **avoir le nez en ~** to have one's nose reduced to a pulp; **réduire qn en ~** to smash sb to pulp, reduce sb to a pulp.
(c) (*fig*) **quelle ~!*** what a mess! *ou* shambles!; **être dans la ~*** to be in the soup* (*fig*).

marmite [maʀmit] **1** *nf* (*Culin*) (cooking-)pot; (*arg Mil*) heavy shell. **une ~ de soupe** a pot of soup; *V* **bouillir, nez.**
2: (*Géog*) **marmite (de géants)** pothole; **marmite norvégienne** ≃ haybox.

marmitée [maʀmite] *nf* (††, *hum*) pot(ful).

marmiton [maʀmitɔ̃] *nm* kitchen boy.

marmonnement [maʀmɔnmɑ̃] *nm* mumbling, muttering.

marmonner [maʀmɔne] (1) *vt* to mumble, mutter.

marmoréen, -éenne [maʀmɔʀeɛ̃, eɛn] *adj* (*littér*) marble (*épith*), marmoreal (*littér*).

marmot* [maʀmo] *nm* kid*, brat* (*péj*).

marmotte [maʀmɔt] *nf* (*Zool*) marmot; (*fig*) sleepyhead, dormouse (*fig*); *V* **dormir.**

marmottement [maʀmɔtmɑ̃] *nm* mumbling, muttering.

marmotter [maʀmɔte] (1) *vt* to mumble, mutter. **qu'est-ce que tu as à ~?*** what are you mumbling (on) about? *ou* muttering about?

marmouset [maʀmuzɛ] *nm* (*Sculp*) quaint *ou* grotesque figure; (*†: *enfant*) pixie, pipsqueak†.

marnage[1] [maʀnaʒ] *nm* marling.

marnage[2] [maʀnaʒ] *nm* tidal range.

marne [maʀn(ə)] *nf* (*Géol*) marl.

marner [maʀne] (1) **1** *vt* (*Agr*) to marl. **2** *vi* (*: *travailler dur*) to slog*. **faire ~ qn** to make sb slog*.

marneux, -euse [maʀnø, øz] *adj* marly.

marnière [maʀnjɛʀ] *nf* marlpit.

Maroc [maʀɔk] *nm* Morocco.

marocain, e [maʀɔkɛ̃, ɛn] **1** *adj* Moroccan. **2** *nm,f*: **M~(e)** Moroccan.

maronner* [maʀɔne] (1) *vi* to grouse*, moan*.

maroquin [maʀɔkɛ̃] *nm* **(a)** (*cuir*) morocco (leather). **relié en ~** morocco-bound. **(b)** (*fig: portefeuille*) (minister's) portfolio. **obtenir un ~** to be made a minister.

maroquinerie [maʀɔkinʀi] *nf* (*boutique*) shop selling fancy *ou* fine leather goods; (*atelier*) tannery; (*Ind*) fine leather craft; (*préparation*) tanning. **(articles de) ~** fancy *ou* fine leather goods; **il travaille dans la ~** (*artisan*) he does fine leatherwork; (*commerçant*) he is in the (fine) leather trade.

maroquinier [maʀɔkinje] *nm* (*marchand*) dealer in fine leather goods; (*fabricant*) leather worker *ou* craftsman.

marotte [maʀɔt] *nf* **(a)** (*dada*) fad, hobby. **c'est sa ~!** it's his pet fad! *ou* craze!; **il a la ~ des jeux de patience** he has a craze for jigsaw puzzles; **le voilà lancé sur sa ~!** there he goes on his pet hobby-horse!
(b) (*Hist: poupée*) fool's bauble; (*Coiffure, Habillement: tête*) (milliner's, hairdresser's) dummy head, (milliner's, hairdresser's) model.

marquage [maʀkaʒ] *nm [linge, marchandises]* marking; *[animal]* branding; *[arbre]* blazing; (*Sport*) *[joueur]* marking.

marquant, e [maʀkɑ̃, ɑ̃t] *adj personnage, événement* outstanding; *souvenir* vivid. **je n'ai rien vu de très ~** I saw nothing very striking *ou* nothing worth talking about.

marque [maʀk(ə)] *nf* **(a)** (*repère, trace*) mark; (*signe*) (*lit, fig*) mark, sign; (*fig*) token; *[livre]* bookmark; *[linge]* name tab. **~s de doigts** fingermarks; **~s de pas** footmarks, footprints; **~s d'une blessure/de coups/de fatigue** marks of a wound/of blows/of fatigue; **il porte encore les ~s de son accident** he still bears the scars from his accident; **faites une ~ au crayon devant chaque nom** put a pencil mark beside each name; (*Sport*) **à vos ~s! prêts! partez!** on your marks!, get set!, go!; (*fig*) **~ de confiance/de respect** sign *ou* token *ou* mark of confidence/respect.
(b) (*estampille*) *[or, argent]* hallmark; *[meubles, œuvre d'art]* mark; *[viande, œufs]* stamp. (*fig*) **la ~ du génie** the hallmark *ou* stamp of genius.
(c) (*Comm*) *[nourriture, produits chimiques]* brand; *[automobiles, produits manufacturés]* make. **~ de fabrique** *ou* **de fabrication** *ou* **du fabricant** trademark; **~ d'origine** maker's mark; **~ déposée** registered trademark; **une grande ~ de vin/de voiture** a well-known brand of wine/make of car; **produits de ~** high-class products; (*fig*) **un personnage de ~** a V.I.P.; **visiteur de ~** important *ou* distinguished visitor; *V* **image.**
(d) (*insigne*) *[fonction, grade]* badge. (*frm*) **les ~s de sa fonction** the insignia *ou* regalia of his office.
(e) (*Sport, Cartes: décompte*) **la ~** the score; **tenir la ~** to keep (the) score.

marqué, e [maʀke] (*ptp de* **marquer**) *adj* **(a)** (*accentué*) pronounced; (*Ling*) marked.
(b) (*signalé*) **le prix ~** the price on the label; **au prix ~** at the labelled price, at the price shown on the label; (*fig*) **c'est un homme ~** he's a marked man.

marquer [maʀke] (1) **1** *vt* **(a)** (*par un signe distinctif*) *objet personnel* to mark (*au nom de qn* with sb's name); *animal, criminel* to brand; *arbre* to blaze; *marchandise* to label, stamp.
(b) (*indiquer*) *limite, position* to mark; (*sur une carte*) *village, accident de terrain* to mark, show, indicate; *[horloge]* to show; *[thermomètre]* to show, register; *[balance]* to register. **marquez la longueur voulue d'un trait de crayon** mark off the length required with a pencil; **j'ai marqué nos places avec nos valises** I've reserved our seats with our cases; **j'ai marqué ce jour-là d'une pierre blanche** I'll remember it as a red-letter day; **marquez d'une croix l'emplacement du véhicule** mark the position of the vehicle with a cross; **la pendule marque 6 heures** the clock points to *ou* shows *ou* says 6 o'clock; (*Couture*) **des pinces marquent/une ceinture marque la taille** darts emphasize/a belt emphasizes the waist(line); **une robe qui marque la taille** a dress which shows off the waistline; **cela marque (bien) que le pays veut la paix** that definitely indicates *ou* shows that the country wants peace.
(c) *événement* to mark. **un bombardement a marqué la reprise des hostilités** a bomb attack marked the renewal *ou* resumption of hostilities; **des réjouissances populaires ont marqué la prise de pouvoir par la junte** the junta's takeover was marked by public celebrations; **pour ~ cette journée on a distribué ...** to mark *ou* commemorate this day they distributed ... .
(d) (*écrire*) *nom, rendez-vous, renseignement* to write down, note down, make a note of. **~ les points** *ou* **les résultats** to keep *ou* note the score; **on l'a marqué absent** he was marked absent; **j'ai marqué 3 heures sur mon agenda** I've got 3 o'clock (noted) down in my diary; **il a marqué qu'il fallait prévenir les élèves** he noted down that the pupils should be told, he made a note to tell the pupils; **qu'y a-t-il de marqué?** what does it say?, what's written (on it)?
(e) (*endommager*) *glace, bois* to mark; (*fig: affecter*) *personne* to mark. **la souffrance l'a marqué** suffering has left its mark on him; **visage marqué par la maladie** face marked by illness; **visage marqué par la petite vérole** face pitted with smallpox; **la déception se marquait sur son visage** disappointment showed in his face *ou* was written all over his face.
(f) (*manifester, montrer*) *désapprobation, fidélité, intérêt* to show.
(g) (*Sport*) *joueur* to mark; *but, essai* to score.
(h) (*loc*) **~ le coup*** (*fêter un événement etc*) to mark the occasion; (*accuser le coup*) to react; **j'ai risqué une allusion, mais il n'a pas marqué le coup*** I made an allusion to it, but he didn't react *ou* but he showed no reaction; **~ un** *ou* **des point(s) (sur qn)** to be one up *ou* a few points up (on sb); **~ la mesure** to keep the beat; **~ le pas** (*lit*) to beat *ou* mark time; (*fig*) to mark time; **~ un temps d'arrêt** to mark a pause.
2 *vi* **(a)** *[événement, personnalité]* to stand out, be outstanding; *[coup]* to reach home, tell. **cet incident a marqué dans sa vie** that particular incident stood out in *ou* had a great impact on his life.
(b) *[crayon]* to write; *[tampon]* to stamp. **ne pose pas le verre sur ce meuble, ça marque** don't put the glass down on that piece of furniture, it will leave a mark.
3 se marquer *vpr* to mark.

marqueté, e [maʀkəte] *adj bois* inlaid.

marqueterie [maʀkətʀi] *nf* (*Art*) marquetry, inlaid work; (*fig*) mosaic. **table en ~** inlaid table.

marqueur [maʀkœʀ] *nm [bétail]* brander; (*Sport, Jeux*) *[points]* score-keeper, scorer; (*buteur*) scorer; (*stylo*) felt-tip (marker pen).

marqueuse [maʀkøz] *nf* (*Comm: appareil*) stamp (*for printing brand name on merchandise*), (price) labeller.

marquis [maʀki] *nm* marquis, marquess.
marquisat [maʀkiza] *nm* marquisate.
marquise [maʀkiz] *nf* **(a)** (*noble*) marchioness; *V* **Madame. (b)** (*auvent*) glass canopy *ou* awning. **(c) les (îles) M~s** the Marquesas Islands.
marraine [maʀɛn] *nf [enfant]* godmother; *[navire]* christener *ou* namer. **~ de guerre** (*woman*) *penfriend to soldier etc on active service.*
marrant, e* [maʀɑ̃, ɑ̃t] *adj* **(a)** (*amusant*) funny, killing*. **c'est un ~, il est ~** he's a scream* *ou* a great laugh*; **ce n'est pas ~** it's not funny, it's no joke; **il n'est pas ~** (*ennuyeux, triste*) he's pretty dreary*, he's not much fun; (*sévère*) he's pretty grim*; (*empoisonnant*) he's a pain in the neck*.
(b) (*étrange*) funny, odd.
marre‡ [maʀ] *adv*: **en avoir ~** to be fed up* *ou* cheesed off‡ (*de* with), be sick* (*de* of); **j'en ai ~ de toi** I've just about had enough of you*, I am fed up with you*; **c'est ~!** enough's enough! I'm packing in!*
marrer (se)‡ [maʀe] (1) *vpr* to laugh, have a good laugh*. **il se marrait comme un fou** he was in fits* *ou* kinks‡ (*Brit*); **tu me fais ~ avec ta démocratie!** you kill* me with all your talk about democracy!
marri, e [maʀi] *adj* (*littér*, †) (*triste*) sad, doleful; (*désolé*) sorry, grieved†.
marron¹ [maʀɔ̃] **1** *nm* **(a)** (*Bot, Culin*) chestnut. **~ d'Inde** horse chestnut; **~ glacé** marron glacé; **tirer les ~s du feu** to be sb's cat's paw; *V* **purée.**
(b) (*couleur*) brown.
(c) (‡) thump*, clout‡. **tu veux un ~?** do you want a thick ear*?
2 *adj inv* **(a)** (*couleur*) brown.
(b) (‡) **être ~** (*être trompé, roulé*) to be the sucker‡, be had‡.
marron², -onne [maʀɔ̃, ɔn] *adj*: **médecin ~** (*sans titres*) quack, unqualified doctor; **notaire/avocat ~** (*sans scrupules*) crooked notary/lawyer; (*Hist*) **esclave ~** runaway *ou* fugitive slave.
marronnier [maʀɔnje] *nm* chestnut tree. **~ (d'Inde)** horse chestnut tree.
Mars [maʀs] *nm* (*Astron, Myth*) Mars; *V* **champ.**
mars [maʀs] *nm* (*mois*) March; *pour loc V* **septembre** *et* **arriver.**
marseillais, e [maʀsɛjɛ, ɛz] **1** *adj* of *ou* from Marseilles. **histoire ~e** tall story. **2** *nm,f*: **M~(e)** inhabitant *ou* native of Marseilles. **3** *nf*: **la M~e** the Marseillaise (*French national anthem*).
Marseille [maʀsɛj] *n* Marseilles.
marsouin [maʀswɛ̃] *nm* (*Zool*) porpoise; (*Mil*†) marine.
marsupial, e, *mpl* **-aux** [maʀsypjal, o] *adj, nm* marsupial. **poche ~e** marsupium.
marte [maʀt(ə)] *nf* = **martre.**
marteau, *pl* **~x** [maʀto] **1** *nm* (*Anat, Menuiserie, Mus, Sport*) hammer; *[enchères, médecin]* hammer; *[président]* gavel; *[horloge]* striker; *[porte]* knocker; *[forgeron]* (sledge) hammer. (*fig*) **entre le ~ et l'enclume** between the devil and the deep blue sea; (**fig*) **être ~** to be nuts* *ou* bats* (*Brit*) *ou* cracked*; *V* **coup, faucille, requin.**
2: marteau-perforateur *nm, pl* **marteaux-perforateurs** hammer drill; **marteau-pilon** *nm, pl* **marteaux-pilons** power hammer; **marteau-piqueur** *nm, pl* **marteaux-piqueurs, marteau pneumatique** pneumatic drill.
martel [maʀtɛl] *nm*: **se mettre ~ en tête** to worry o.s. sick, get worked up*.
martelage [maʀtəlaʒ] *nm* (*Métal*) hammering, planishing.
martèlement [maʀtɛlmɑ̃] *nm [bruit, obus]* hammering, pounding; *[pas]* pounding, clanking; *[mots]* hammering out, rapping out.
marteler [maʀtəle] (5) *vt [marteau, obus, coups de poings]* to hammer, pound; *objet d'art* to planish. **~ ses mots** to hammer out *ou* rap out one's words; **ce bruit qui me martèle la tête** that noise hammering *ou* pounding through my head; **ses pas martelaient le sol gelé** his footsteps were pounding on the frozen ground.
martellement [maʀtɛlmɑ̃] *nm* = **martèlement.**
Marthe [maʀt] *nf* Martha.
martial, e, *mpl* **-aux** [maʀsjal, o] *adj* (*hum, littér*) *peuple, discours* martial, warlike, soldier-like; *allure* soldierly, martial; *V* **cour, loi.**
martialement [maʀsjalmɑ̃] *adv* (*hum, littér*) martially, in a soldierly manner.
martien, -ienne [maʀsjɛ̃, jɛn] *adj, nm,f* Martian.
Martin [maʀtɛ̃] *nm* Martin; (*âne*) Neddy.
martinet [maʀtinɛ] *nm* **(a)** small whip (*used on children*), strap. **(b)** (*Orn*) swift. **(c)** (*Tech*) tilt hammer.
martingale [maʀtɛ̃gal] *nf* (*Habillement*) half belt; (*Équitation*) martingale; (*Roulette*) (*combinaison*) winning formula; (*mise double*) doubling-up.
martiniquais, e [maʀtinikɛ, ɛz] **1** *adj* of *ou* from Martinique. **2** *nm,f*: **M~(e)** inhabitant *ou* native of Martinique.
Martinique [maʀtinik] *nf* Martinique.
martin-pêcheur, *pl* **martins-pêcheurs** maʀtɛ̃pɛʃœʀ] *nm* kingfisher.
martre [maʀtʀ(ə)] *nf* marten. **~ zibeline** sable.
martyr, e¹ [maʀtiʀ] **1** *adj soldats, peuple* martyred. **mère ~e** stricken mother; **enfant ~** battered child. **2** *nm,f* martyr (*d'une cause* in *ou* to a cause). **ne prends pas ces airs de ~!** stop acting the martyr, it's no use putting on your martyred look; **c'est le ~ de la classe** he's always being bullied *ou* baited by the class.
martyre² [maʀtiʀ] *nm* (*Rel*) martyrdom; (*fig: souffrance*) martyrdom, agony. **le ~ de ce peuple** the martyrdom *ou* suffering of this people; **sa vie fut un long ~** his life was one long agony; **cette longue attente est un ~** it's agony waiting so long; **mettre au ~** to martyrize, torture; **souffrir le ~** to suffer agonies, go through torture.
martyriser [maʀtiʀize] (1) *vt* **(a)** (*faire souffrir*) *personne, animal* to torture, martyrize; *élève* to bully, bait; *enfant, bébé* to batter. **(b)** (*Rel*) to martyr.
marxien, -ienne [maʀksjɛ̃, jɛn] *adj* Marxian.
marxisme [maʀksism(ə)] *nm* Marxism. **~-léninisme** *nm* Marxism-Leninism.
marxiste [maʀksist(ə)] *adj, nmf* Marxist.
maryland [maʀilɑ̃d] *nm type of Virginia tobacco* = virginia.
mas [mɑ] *nm* mas (*house or farm in South of France*).
mascabina [maskabina] *nm* (*Can*) service tree.
mascarade [maskaʀad] *nf* **(a)** (*péj: tromperie*) farce, masquerade. **(b)** (*réjouissance, déguisement*) masquerade.
mascaret [maskaʀɛ] *nm* (tidal) bore.
mascotte [maskɔt] *nf* mascot.
masculin, e [maskylɛ̃, in] **1** *adj mode, hormone, population, sexe* male; *force, courage* manly; (*péj: hommasse*) *femme, silhouette* mannish, masculine; (*Gram*) masculine. **voix ~e** *[homme]* male voice; *[femme]* masculine *ou* gruff voice; (*virile*) manly voice; *V* **rime.**
2 *nm* (*Gram*) masculine. **'fer' est (du) ~** 'fer' is masculine.
masculiniser [maskylinize] (1) *vt* **(a) ~ qn** to make sb look mannish *ou* masculine. **(b)** (*Bio*) to make masculine.
masculinité [maskylinite] *nf* masculinity; (*virilité*) manliness.
maskinongé [maskinɔ̃ʒe] *nm* (*Can: brochet*) muskellunge, muskie (*Can**), maskinonge.
masochisme [mazɔʃism(ə)] *nm* masochism.
masochiste [mazɔʃist(ə)] **1** *adj* masochistic. **2** *nmf* masochist.
masque [mask(ə)] **1** *nm* **(a)** (*objet, Méd*) mask.
(b) (*faciès*) mask-like features, mask; (*expression*) mask-like expression.
(c) (*fig: apparence*) mask, façade, front. **ce n'est qu'un ~** it's just a mask *ou* front *ou* façade; **présenter un ~ d'indifférence** to put on an air *ou* appearance of indifference; **sous le ~ de la respectabilité** beneath the façade of respectability; **lever** *ou* **jeter le ~** to unmask o.s., reveal o.s. in one's true colours; **arracher son ~ à qn** to unmask sb.
(d) (*Hist: personne déguisée*) mask, masker.
2: masque antirides, masque de beauté face pack; **masque de carnaval** mask; **masque funéraire** funeral mask; **masque à gaz** gas mask; **masque mortuaire** death mask; **masque à oxygène** oxygen mask; **masque de plongée** diving mask.
masqué, e [maske] (*ptp de* **masquer**) *adj bandit* masked; *enfant* wearing *ou* in a mask. (*Aut*) **sortie ~e** concealed exit; (*Aut*) **virage ~** blind corner *ou* bend; (*Naut*) **tous feux ~s** with all lights obscured.
masquer [maske] (1) **1** *vt* (*lit, fig: cacher*) to hide, conceal (*à qn* from sb). **~ un goût** (*exprès*) to hide *ou* disguise *ou* mask a taste; (*involontairement*) to obscure a flavour; **~ la lumière** to screen *ou* shade the light; **~ la vue** to block (out) the view; (*Mil*) **~ des troupes** to screen *ou* mask troops; **ces questions secondaires ont masqué l'essentiel** these questions of secondary importance obscured the essential point; *V* **bal.**
2 se masquer *vpr* (*lit, fig*) to hide, conceal (*derrière* behind).
massacrante [masakʀɑ̃t] *adj f V* **humeur.**
massacre [masakʀ(ə)] *nm* **(a)** (*tuerie*) *[personnes]* slaughter (*U*), massacre; *[animaux]* slaughter (*U*). **c'est un véritable ~** *[prisonniers]* it is an absolute massacre *ou* slaughter; *[gibier]* **c'est du ~** it is sheer butchery; **échapper au ~** to escape being slaughtered; (*Bible*) **le ~ des innocents** the massacre of the innocents; *V* **jeu.**
(b) (*V* **massacrer**) **quel ~!, c'est un vrai ~!*** it's a complete botch-up!*; it's a real mess!; (*Sport*) what a massacre!*
(c) (*Chasse*) stag's head, stag's antlers.
(d) (*Hér*) attire.
massacrer [masakʀe] (1) *vt* **(a)** (*tuer*) *personnes* to slaughter, massacre; *animaux* to slaughter, butcher.
(b) (*: *saboter*) *opéra, pièce* to murder, botch up; *travail* to make a mess *ou* hash* of; (*mal découper, scier*) *viande, planche* to hack to bits, make a mess of; *candidat* to make mincemeat* of; *adversaire* to massacre, slaughter, make mincemeat* of.
massacreur, -euse [masakʀœʀ, øz] *nm,f* (*: *saboteur*) bungler, botcher; (*tueur*) slaughterer, butcher.
massage [masaʒ] *nm* massage.
masse [mas] *nf* **(a)** (*volume, Phys*) mass; (*forme*) massive shape *ou* bulk. **~ d'eau** *[lac]* body *ou* expanse of water; *[chute]* mass of water; **~ de nuages** bank of clouds; **la ~ de l'édifice** the massive structure of the building; **pris** *ou* **taillé dans la ~** carved from the block; **la ~ instrumentale/vocale** massed instruments/voices; **s'écrouler** *ou* **tomber comme une ~** to slump down *ou* fall in a heap.
(b) (*foule*) **les ~s (laborieuses)** the (working) masses; **les ~s paysannes** the agricultural work-force; (†) the peasantry; **la (grande) ~ des lecteurs** the (great) majority of readers; (*péj*) **c'est ce qui plaît à la ~** *ou* **aux ~s** that's the kind of thing that appeals to the masses; **culture/manifestation** *etc* **de ~** mass culture/demonstration *etc.*
(c) une ~ de*, des ~s* de masses of, loads of*; **des ~s de touristes*** crowds *ou* masses of tourists; **des gens comme lui, je n'en connais pas des ~s*** I don't know many people like him, you don't meet his sort every day; **tu as aimé ce film? — pas des ~s!‡** did you like that film? — not desperately!* *ou* not all that much!
(d) (*Élec*) earth. **mettre à la ~** to earth (*Brit*), ground (*US*); **faire ~** to act as an earth.
(e) (*Fin*) (*caisse commune*) kitty; (*Mil*) fund; (*Prison*) prisoner's earnings. (*Fin*) **~ monétaire** (total amount of) money in circulation; (*Comm*) **~ salariale** aggregate remuneration (of employees); (*Jur*) **~ active** assets; **~ passive** liabilities.
(f) (*maillet*) sledgehammer, beetle; *[huissier]* mace. (*Hist*) **~ d'armes** mace.

(g) en ~: exécutions/production *etc* **en ~** mass executions/ production *etc*; **fabriquer** *ou* **produire en ~** to mass-produce; **acheter/vendre en ~** to buy/sell in bulk; **venir en ~** to come in a body *ou* en masse; **il en a en ~, il en a des masses*** he has masses *ou* lots *ou* loads* (of them).

massepain [maspɛ̃] *nm* marzipan.

masser[1] [mase] (1) **1** *vt* **(a)** *gens* to assemble, bring *ou* gather together; *choses* to put *ou* gather together; *troupes* to mass. **(b)** (*Art*) to group. **2 se masser** *vpr [foule]* to gather, assemble.

masser[2] [mase] (1) *vt* **(a)** *personne* to massage. **se faire ~** to have a massage, be massaged; **masse-moi le dos!** massage *ou* rub my back!

(b) (*Billard*) to play a massé shot.

massette [masɛt] *nf* **(a)** (*Tech*) sledgehammer. **(b)** (*Bot*) bulrush, reed mace.

masseur, -euse [masœʀ, øz] **1** *nm,f* masseur, masseuse. **~ kinésithérapeute** physiotherapist. **2** *nm* (*machine: aussi* **vibromasseur**) massager.

massicot [masiko] *nm* (*Typ*) guillotine; (*Chim*) massicot.

massicoter [masikɔte] (1) *vt papier* to guillotine.

massif, -ive [masif, iv] **1** *adj* **(a)** (*d'aspect*) *meuble, bâtiment, porte* massive, solid, heavy; *personne, carrure* sturdily built; *visage* large, heavy. **front ~** massive forehead.

(b) (*pur*) **or/argent/chêne ~** solid gold/silver/oak.

(c) (*intensif*) *bombardements, dose* massive, heavy. **manifestation ~ive** mass demonstration; **départs ~s** mass exodus (*sg*).

2 *nm* (*Géog*) massif; (*Bot*) *[fleurs]* clump, bank; *[arbres]* clump.

massification [masifikɑsjɔ̃] *nf* spreading to the masses.

massique [masik] *adj*: **puissance ~** power-weight ratio; **volume ~** mass volume.

massivement [masivmɑ̃] *adv démissionner, partir, répondre* en masse; *injecter, administrer* in massive doses.

mass(-)media [masmedja] *nmpl* mass media.

massue [masy] *nf* club, bludgeon. **~ de gymnastique** (Indian) club; *V* **argument, coup.**

mastic [mastik] **1** *nm* **(a)** *[vitrier]* putty; *[menuisier]* filler, mastic. **(b)** (*Bot*) mastic. **(c)** (*Typ*) *[caractères, pages]* (faulty) transposition. **2** *adj* putty-coloured. **imperméable (couleur) ~** light-coloured *ou* off-white raincoat.

masticage [mastikaʒ] *nm [vitre]* puttying; *[fissure]* filling.

masticateur, -trice [mastikatœʀ, tʀis] *adj* masticatory.

mastication [mastikɑsjɔ̃] *nf* mastication.

masticatoire [mastikatwaʀ] *adj, nm* masticatory.

mastiquer[1] [mastike] (1) *vt* to chew, masticate.

mastiquer[2] [mastike] (1) *vt* (*Tech*) *vitre* to putty, apply putty to; *fissure* to fill, apply filler to.

mastoc* [mastɔk] *adj inv personne* hefty*, strapping (*épith*); *chose* large and cumbersome. **c'est un (type) ~** he's a big hefty bloke: (*Brit*), he's a great strapping fellow*; **une statue ~** a great hulking statue.

mastodonte [mastɔdɔ̃t] *nm* (*Zool*) mastodon; (*fig hum*) (*personne, animal*) colossus, mountain of a man *ou* an animal; (*véhicule*) great bus (*hum*) *ou* tank (*hum*); (*camion*) juggernaut (*Brit*).

mastroquet*† [mastʀɔkɛ] *nm* (*bar*) pub, bar; (*tenancier*) publican.

masturbation [mastyʀbɑsjɔ̃] *nf* masturbation.

masturber *vt*, **se masturber** *vpr* [mastyʀbe] (1) to masturbate.

m'as-tu-vu* [matyvy] *nmf inv* show-off*, swank*. **il est du genre ~** he's a real show-off*.

masure [mazyʀ] *nf* tumbledown *ou* dilapidated cottage *ou* house.

mat[1] [mat] **1** *adj inv* checkmated. **être ~** to be checkmate; **faire ~** to checkmate; **(tu es) ~!** (you're) checkmate!; **tu m'as fait ~ en 10 coups** you've checkmated me in 10 moves.

2 *nm* checkmate; *V* **échec**[2].

mat[2], **e** [mat] *adj* (*sans éclat*) *métal* mat(t), unpolished, dull; *couleur* mat(t), dull, flat; *peinture, papier* mat(t). **bruit ~** dull noise, thud; **teint ~** mat complexion.

mât [mɑ] **1** *nm* (*Naut*) mast; (*pylône, poteau*) pole, post; (*hampe*) flagpole; (*Sport*) climbing pole; *V* **grand, trois. 2: mât d'artimon** mizzenmast; **mât de charge** derrick; **mât de cocagne** greasy pole; **mât de misaine** foremast.

matage [mataʒ] *nm [dorure, verre]* matting; *[soudure]* caulking.

matamore [matamɔʀ] *nm* (*fanfaron*) braggart, blusterer. **faire le ~** to brag, bluster.

match [matʃ] *nm* (*Sport*) match (*surtout Brit*), game (*US*). **~ aller** first leg; **~ retour** return match, second leg; **~ nul** draw; **~ sur terrain adverse** away match; **~ sur son propre terrain** home match; **ils ont fait ~ nul** they drew; *V* **disputer.**

maté [mate] *nm* maté.

matelas [matla] *nm* mattress. **~ de laine/à ressorts** wool/(interior-)spring mattress; **~ d'air** air space *ou* cavity; **~ (de billets)*** wad of notes; **il a un joli petit ~*** he's got a cosy sum put by*; **dormir sur un ~ de feuilles mortes** to sleep on a carpet of dead leaves; **~ pneumatique** air mattress *ou* bed, Lilo ®; *V* **toile.**

matelasser [matlase] (1) *vt meuble, porte* to pad, upholster; *tissu* to quilt; *vêtement* (*rembourrer*) to pad; (*doubler*) to line; (*avec tissu matelassé*) to quilt.

matelassier, -ière [matlasje, jɛʀ] *nm,f* mattress maker.

matelot [matlo] *nm* **(a)** (*gén: marin*) sailor, seaman. **~ de première/deuxième/troisième classe** leading/able/ordinary seaman. **(b)** (*navire*) **~ d'avant/d'arrière** (next) ship ahead/ astern.

matelote [matlɔt] *nf* (*plat*) matelote; (*sauce*) matelote sauce (*made with wine*). **~ d'anguille** stewed eels.

mater[1] [mate] (1) *vt* **(a)** *rebelles* to bring to heel, subdue; *enfant* to take in hand, curb; *révolution* to put down, quell; *incendie* to bring under control, check. **(b)** (*Échecs*) to checkmate, mate.

mater[2] [mate] (1) *vt* **(a)** (*marteler*) to caulk (*riveted joint*). **(b)** = **matir.**

mater[3]: [matɛʀ] *nf* mum* (*Brit*), mom* (*US*). **ma ~** my old woman *ou* mum: (*Brit*) *ou* mom* (*US*).

mâter [mɑte] (1) *vt* (*Naut*) to mast.

matérialisation [mateʀjalizɑsjɔ̃] *nf [projet, promesse, doute]* materialization; (*Phys*) mass energy conversion; (*Spiritisme*) materialization.

matérialiser [mateʀjalize] (1) **1** *vt* (*concrétiser*) *projet, promesse, doute* to make materialize; (*symboliser*) *vertu, vice* to be a material representation of; (*Philos*) to materialize. **2 se matérialiser** *vpr* to materialize.

matérialisme [mateʀjalism(ə)] *nm* materialism. **~ dialectique** dialectic materialism.

matérialiste [mateʀjalist(ə)] **1** *adj* materialistic. **2** *nmf* materialist.

matérialité [mateʀjalite] *nf* materiality.

matériau [mateʀjo] *nm inv* (*Constr*) material. **un ~ moderne** a modern (building) material.

matériaux [mateʀjo] *nmpl* **(a)** (*Constr*) material(s). **~ de construction** building material; *V* **résistance.**

(b) (*documents*) material (*U*).

matériel, -elle [mateʀjɛl] **1** *adj* **(a)** (*gén, Philos: effectif*) *monde, preuve* material. **être ~** material *ou* physical being; **erreur ~le** material error; **dégâts ~s** material damage; **je suis dans l'impossibilité ~le de le faire** it's materially impossible for me to do it; **je n'ai pas le temps ~ de le faire** I simply have not the time to do it.

(b) *bien-être, confort* material; (*du monde*) *plaisirs, biens, préoccupations* material; (*terre à terre*) *esprit* material, down-to-earth. **sa vie ~le est assurée** she is provided for materially, her material needs are provided for.

(c) (*financier*) *gêne, problèmes* financial; (*pratique*) *organisation, obstacles* practical. **aide ~le** material aid; **de nombreux avantages ~s** a number of material advantages.

2 *nm* (*Agr, Mil*) equipment (*U*), materials; (*Tech*) equipment (*U*), plant (*U*); (*attirail*) gear (*U*), kit (*U*); (*fig: corpus, donnée*) material (*U*). **~ de bureau/d'imprimerie** *etc* office/printing *etc* equipment *ou* materials; **tout son ~ d'artiste** all his artist's materials *ou* gear*.

3: matériel d'exploitation plant (*U*); **matériel humain** human material, labour force; **matériel de pêche** fishing tackle; (*Rail*) **matériel roulant** rolling stock; **matériel scolaire** (*livres, cahiers*) school (reading *ou* writing) materials; (*pupitres, projecteurs*) school equipment.

matériellement [mateʀjɛlmɑ̃] *adv* (*V* **matériel**) materially; financially; practically. **c'est ~ impossible** it's materially impossible.

maternel, -elle [matɛʀnɛl] *adj* **(a)** (*d'une mère*) *instinct, amour* maternal, motherly; (*comme d'une mère*) *geste, soin* motherly.

(b) (*de la mère*) of the mother, maternal. (*Généalogie*) **du côté ~** on the maternal side; **grand-père ~** maternal grandfather; **il avait gardé les habitudes ~les** he had retained his mother's habits; **écoute les conseils ~s!** listen to your mother's advice!; (*Admin*) **la protection ~le et infantile** ≈ mother and infant welfare; *V* **allaitement, lait, langue.**

(c) (école) ~le (state) nursery school.

maternellement [matɛʀnɛlmɑ̃] *adv* maternally, like a mother.

maternité [matɛʀnite] *nf* **(a)** (*bâtiment*) maternity hospital.

(b) (*Bio*) pregnancy. **fatiguée par plusieurs ~s** tired after several pregnancies *ou* after having had several babies.

(c) (*état de mère*) motherhood, maternity. **la ~ l'a mûrie** motherhood *ou* being a mother has made her more mature; *V* **allocation.**

(d) (*Art*) *painting of mother and child or children.*

math(s)* [mat] *nfpl* (*abrév de* **mathématiques**) maths* (*Brit*), math* (*US*).

mathématicien, -ienne [matematisjɛ̃, jɛn] *nm,f* mathematician.

mathématique [matematik] **1** *adj problème, méthode,* (*fig*) *précision, rigueur* mathematical. **c'est ~!*** it's logical!, it's a dead cert!: (*Brit*).

2 *nfpl*: **les ~s** mathematics; **~s élémentaires, math(s) élém*** ≈ sixth form higher maths (class) (*Brit*); **~s supérieures, math(s) sup*** *first year advanced maths class preparing for the Grandes Écoles*; **~s spéciales, math(s) spé*** *second year advanced maths class preparing for the Grandes Écoles.*

mathématiquement [matematikmɑ̃] *adv* (*Math, fig*) mathematically. **~, il n'a aucune chance** logically he hasn't a hope.

matheux, -euse [matø, øz] *nm,f* (*) mathematican, maths specialist; (*arg Scol*) maths student. **leur fille, c'est la ~euse de la famille** their daughter is the mathematician *ou* maths expert in the family.

Mathieu [matjø] *nm* Matthew; *V* **fesse.**

Mathilde [matild] *nf* Matilda.

matière [matjɛʀ] **1** *nf* **(a)** (*Philos, Phys*) **la ~** matter; **la ~ vivante** living matter.

(b) (*substance(s)*) matter (*U*), material. **~ combustible/inflammable** combustible/inflammable material; **~ organique** organic matter; **~s colorantes** *[aliments]* colouring (matter); *[tissus]* dyestuff; **~ précieuse** precious substance; (*Méd*) **~s (fécales)** faeces.

(c) (*fond, sujet*) material, matter, subject matter; (*Scol*) subject. **cela lui a fourni la ~ de son dernier livre** that gave him the material *ou* the subject matter for his latest book; (*Scol*) **il est**

bon dans toutes les ~s he is good at all subjects; **il est très ignorant en la ~** he is completely ignorant on the subject, it's a matter *ou* subject he knows nothing about; *V* **entrée, table.**

(d) (*loc*) **en ~ poétique/commerciale** where *ou* as far as poetry/commerce is concerned, in the matter of poetry/commerce (*frm*); **en ~ d'art/de jardinage** as regards art/gardening; **donner ~ à plaisanter/à la critique** to give cause for laughter/criticism; **il y a là ~ à réflexion** this is a matter for serious thought; **il n'y a pas là ~ à rire** this is no laughing matter; **il n'y a pas là ~ à se réjouir** *ou* **à la réjouissance** this is no matter for rejoicing.

2: matière(s) grasse(s) fat content, fat; (*lit, fig*) **matière grise** grey matter; **matière plastique** plastic; **matière première** raw material.

matin [matɛ̃] **1** *nm* **(a)** morning. **par un ~ de juin** on a June morning, one June morning; **le 10 au ~, le ~ du 10** on the morning of the 10th; **2h du ~** 2 a.m., 2 in the morning; **du ~ au soir** from morning till night, morning noon and night; **je ne travaille que le ~** I only work mornings* *ou* in the morning; (*Méd*) **à prendre ~ midi et soir** to be taken three times a day; **jusqu'au ~** until morning; **de bon** *ou* **de grand ~** early in the morning; **être du ~** to be an early riser, be *ou* get up early; *V* **quatre.**

(b) (*littér*) **au ~ de sa vie** in the morning of one's life.

2 *adv*: **partir/se lever ~** to leave/get up very early *ou* at daybreak.

mâtin, e [mɑtɛ̃, in] **1** *nm,f* (†: *coquin*) cunning devil:, sly dog*. (*hum*) **~e** hussy, minx. **2** *nm* (*chien*) (*de garde*) big watchdog; (*de chasse*) hound. **3** *excl*† by Jove!, my word!

matinal, e, *mpl* **-aux** [matinal, o] *adj tâches, toilette* morning (*épith*). **gelée ~e** early morning frost; **heure ~e** early hour; **être ~** to be an early riser, get up early; **il est bien ~ aujourd'hui** he's up early today.

matinalement [matinalmɑ̃] *adv* (*littér*) early (in the morning), betimes (*littér*).

mâtiné, e [mɑtine] (*ptp de* **mâtiner**) *adj animal* crossbred. **chien ~** mongrel (dog); **~ de** (*Zool*) crossed with; (*fig*) mixed with; **il parle un français ~ d'espagnol** he speaks a mixture of French and Spanish.

matinée [matine] *nf* **(a)** (*matin*) morning. **je le verrai demain dans la ~** I'll see him sometime (in the course of) tomorrow morning; **en début/en fin de ~** at the beginning/at the end of the morning; **après une ~ de chasse** after a morning's hunting; *V* **gras.**

(b) (*Ciné, Théât*) matinée, afternoon performance. **j'irai en ~** I'll go to the matinée; **une ~ dansante** an afternoon dance.

mâtiner [mɑtine] (1) *vt chien* to cross.

matines [matin] *nfpl* matins.

matir [matiʀ] (2) *vt verre, argent* to mat(t), dull.

matois, e [matwa, waz] *adj* (*littér: rusé*) wily, sly, crafty. **c'est un(e) ~(e)** he's (she's) a sly character *ou* a crafty one *ou* a sly one.

matou [matu] *nm* tomcat, tom.

matraquage [matʀakaʒ] *nm* **(a)** (*par la police*) beating (up) (with a truncheon). **(b)** (*Presse, Rad*) plugging. **mettre fin au ~ du public par la chanson** to stop bombarding the public with songs.

matraque [matʀak] *nf [police]* truncheon (*Brit*), billy (*US*); *[malfaiteur]* cosh (*Brit*). **coup de ~** blow from *ou* with a truncheon *ou* cosh.

matraquer [matʀake] (1) *vt* **(a)** *[police]* to beat up (with a truncheon); *[malfaiteur]* to cosh (*Brit*). (**fig*) **~ le client** to soak: *ou* overcharge customers.

(b) (*Presse, Rad*) *chanson, publicité* to plug; *public* to bombard (*de* with).

matraqueur [matʀakœʀ] *nm* (*arg Sport*) dirty player, hatchetman*; (*policier, malfaiteur*) dirty worker:.

matriarcal, e, *mpl* **-aux** [matʀijaʀkal, o] *adj* matriarchal.

matriarcat [matʀijaʀka] *nm* matriarchy.

matrice [matʀis] *nf* **(a)** (*utérus*) womb.

(b) (*Tech*) mould, die; (*Typ*) matrix.

(c) (*Ling, Math*) matrix. **~ réelle/complexe** matrix of real/complex numbers.

(d) (*Admin*) register. **~ cadastrale** cadastre; **~ du rôle des contributions** ≃ original of register of taxes.

matricide [matʀisid] **1** *adj* matricidal. **2** *nmf* matricide. **3** *nm* (*crime*) matricide.

matriciel, -ielle [matʀisjɛl] *adj* (*Math*) matrix (*épith*), done with a matrix; (*Admin*) pertaining to assessment of taxes. **loyer ~** rent assessment (*to serve as basis for calculation of rates*).

matricule [matʀikyl] **1** *nm* (*Mil*) regimental number; (*Admin*) administrative *ou* official *ou* reference number. **dépêche-toi sinon ça va barder pour ton ~!:** hurry up or your number'll be up!* *ou* you'll really get yourself bawled out!: **2** *nf* roll, register. **3** *adj*: **numéro ~ = matricule** *nm*; **registre ~ = matricule** *nf*; *V* **livret.**

matrimonial, e, *mpl* **-aux** [matʀimɔnjal, o] *adj* matrimonial, marriage (*épith*); *V* **agence, régime**[1].

matrone [matʀɔn] *nf* **(a)** matron, matronly woman. **(b)** (*péj: grosse femme laide*) fat old trout: *ou* bag:.

maturation [matyʀɑsjɔ̃] *nf* (*Bot, Méd*) maturation; (*Tech*) *[fromage]* maturing, ripening.

mâture [mɑtyʀ] *nf* masts. **dans la ~** aloft.

maturité [matyʀite] *nf* (*Bio, Bot, fig*) maturity. **venir à ~** *[fruit, idée]* to come to maturity; **manquer de ~** to be immature; **un homme en pleine ~** a man in his prime *ou* at the height of his powers; **~ d'esprit** maturity of mind.

maudire [modiʀ] (2) *vt* to curse.

maudit, e [modi, it] (*ptp de* **maudire**) **1** *adj* **(a)** (*) (*avant n*) blasted:, beastly* (*Brit*), confounded*.

(b) (*littér: réprouvé*) (*après n*) (ac)cursed (*by God, society*). (*Littérat*) **poète/écrivain ~** accursed poet/writer.

(c) (*littér*) **~e soit la guerre!, la guerre soit ~e!** cursed be the war!; **~ soit le jour où ...** cursed be the day on which ..., a curse on the day on which ... .

2 *nm,f* damned soul. **les ~s** the damned.

3 *nm*: **le M~** the Devil.

maugréer [mogʀee] (1) *vi* to grouse, grumble (*contre* about, at).

maure, mauresque [mɔʀ, mɔʀɛsk(ə)] **1** *adj* Moorish. **2** *nm*: **M~** Moor. **3 Mauresque** *nf* Moorish woman.

Maurice [mɔʀis] *nm* Maurice, Morris; *V* **île.**

mauricien, -ienne [mɔʀisjɛ̃, jɛn] **1** *adj* Mauritian. **2** *nm,f*: **M~(ne)** Mauritian.

Mauritanie [mɔʀitani] *nf* Mauritania.

mauritanien, -ienne [mɔʀitanjɛ̃, jɛn] **1** *adj* Mauritanian. **2** *nm,f*: **M~(ne)** Mauritanian.

mausolée [mozɔle] *nm* mausoleum.

maussade [mosad] *adj personne* sullen, glum, morose; *ciel, temps, paysage* gloomy, sullen.

maussadement [mosadmɑ̃] *adv* sullenly, glumly, morosely.

maussaderie [mosadʀi] *nf* sullenness, glumness, moroseness.

mauvais, e [movɛ, ɛz] **1** *adj* **(a)** (*défectueux*) *appareil, instrument* bad, faulty; *marchandise* inferior, shoddy, bad; *route* bad, in bad repair; *santé, vue, digestion, mémoire* poor, bad; *roman, film* poor, bad, feeble. **elle a de ~ yeux** her eyes are *ou* her eyesight is bad, she has bad eyes; **~e excuse** poor *ou* bad *ou* lame excuse; (*Élec*) **un ~ contact** a faulty contact; (*Tennis*) **la balle est ~e** the ball is out; **son français est bien ~** his French is very bad *ou* poor; **son français est plus ~ qu'à son arrivée** his French is worse *ou* poorer than when he arrived.

(b) (*inefficace, incapable*) *père, élève, acteur, ouvrier* poor, bad. **il est ~ en géographie** he's bad *ou* weak at geography; (*Prov*) **les ~ ouvriers ont toujours de ~ outils** a bad workman always blames his tools (*Prov*).

(c) (*inapproprié, erroné*) *méthode, moyens, direction* wrong; *jour, heure* (*qui ne convient pas*) awkward, bad, inconvenient; (*erroné*) wrong. **le ~ numéro/cheval** the wrong number/horse; **il roulait sur le ~ côté de la route** he was driving on the wrong side of the road; **il a choisi un ~ moment** he picked an awkward *ou* a bad time; **il a choisi le ~ moment** he picked the wrong time; **c'est un ~ calcul de sa part** he's badly misjudged it *ou* things; **il ne serait pas ~ de se renseigner** *ou* **que nous nous renseignions** it wouldn't be a bad idea *ou* it would be no bad thing if we found out more about this.

(d) (*dangereux, nuisible*) *maladie, blessure* nasty, bad. **il a fait une ~e grippe/rougeole** he's had a bad *ou* nasty *ou* severe attack *ou* bout of flu/measles; **la mer est ~e** the sea is rough; **c'est ~ pour la santé** it's bad for one's *ou* the health; **il est ~ de se baigner en eau froide** it's bad *ou* it's a bad idea to bathe in cold water; **vous jugez ~ qu'il sorte le soir?** do you think it's a bad thing his going out at night?; **être en ~e posture** to be in a dangerous *ou* tricky *ou* nasty position.

(e) (*défavorable*) *rapport, critique* unfavourable, bad; (*Scol*) *bulletin, note* bad.

(f) (*désagréable*) *temps* bad, unpleasant, nasty; *nourriture, repas* bad, poor; *odeur* bad, unpleasant, offensive; (*pénible*) *nouvelle, rêve* bad. **la soupe a un ~ goût** the soup has an unpleasant *ou* a nasty taste, the soup tastes nasty; **ce n'est qu'un ~ moment à passer** it's just a bad spell *ou* patch you've got to get through; **il a passé un ~ quart d'heure** he had a nasty *ou* an uncomfortable time of it; **ils lui ont fait passer un ~ quart d'heure** they (fairly) put him through it*, they gave him a rough time of it*; *V* **caractère, gré, volonté** *etc.*

(g) (*immoral, nuisible*) *instincts, action, fréquentations, livre, film* bad. **il n'a pas un ~ fond** he's not bad at heart; *V* **génie.**

(h) (*méchant*) *sourire, regard etc* nasty, malicious, spiteful; *personne, joie* malicious, spiteful. **être ~ comme la gale*** to be perfectly poisonous (*fig*); **ce n'est pas un ~ garçon** he's not a bad boy.

(i) (*loc*) **ce n'est pas ~!** it's not bad!, it's quite good!; **quand on l'a renvoyé, il l'a trouvée ~e*** when he was dismissed he didn't appreciate it one little bit* *ou* he was very put out about it; **aujourd'hui il fait ~** today the weather is bad; **il fait ~ le contredire** it is not advisable to contradict him; **prendre qch en ~e part** to take sth in bad part, take sth amiss; **faire contre ~e fortune bon cœur** to put a brave face on things; **se faire du ~ sang** to worry, get in a state.

2 *nm* **(a)** (*U*) **enlève le ~ et mange le reste** cut out the bad part and eat the rest; **la presse ne montre que le ~** the press only shows the bad side (of things).

(b) (*personnes*) **les ~** the wicked; *V* **bon**[1].

3: mauvais coucheur awkward customer; **mauvais coup: recevoir un mauvais coup** to get a nasty blow; **faire un mauvais coup** to commit a crime; **mauvais esprit** troublemaker; **mauvais garçon** tough; **c'est de la mauvaise graine** he's (*ou* she's *ou* they're) a bad lot; **mauvaise herbe** weed; **enlever** *ou* **arracher les mauvaises herbes du jardin** to weed the garden; (*Prov*) **mauvaise herbe croît toujours** ill weeds grow fast; **mauvaise langue** gossip, scandalmonger; **mauvais lieu** place of ill repute; **(avoir) le mauvais œil** (to have) the evil eye; **mauvais pas** tight spot; **mauvaise passe** difficult situation, awkward spot*; **mauvais plaisant** hoaxer; **mauvaise plaisanterie** rotten trick; **mauvais rêve** bad dream, nightmare; **mauvaise saison** rainy season; **mauvais sort** misfortune, ill fate; **mauvais sujet** bad lot; **mauvaise tête: c'est une mauvaise tête** he's headstrong; **faire la mauvaise tête** to sulk; **mauvais traitement** ill treatment; **subir de mauvais traitements** to be ill-treated; **faire subir de mauvais traitements à** to ill-treat.

mauve [mov] **1** *adj, nm* (*couleur*) mauve. **2** *nf* (*Bot*) mallow.

mauviette [movjɛt] *nf (péj)* weakling.

maxi [maksi] **1** *préf*: **maxi ... maxi ...** . **~-jupe** *nf* maxi; **~-bouteille/paquet** giant-size bottle/packet.
2 *adj inv*: **la mode ~** the maxi-length fashion.
3 *nf (robe)* maxi.
4 *nm (mode)* maxi. **elle s'habille en ~** she wears maxis; **la mode est au ~** maxis are in (fashion).

maxillaire [maksilɛʀ] **1** *adj* maxillary. **os ~** jawbone. **2** *nm* maxilla *(T)*. **~ supérieur/inférieur** upper/lower maxilla *(T) ou* jawbone.

maxima [maksima] *V* **appel, maximum.**

maximal, e, *mpl* **-aux** [maksimal, o] *adj* maximal.

Maxime [maksim] *nm* Maximus.

maxime [maksim] *nf* maxim.

maximum [maksimɔm], *f* **~** *ou* **maxima** [maksima], *pl* **maximum(s)** *ou* **maxima 1** *adj* maximum. **la température ~** the maximum *ou* highest temperature; **j'attends de vous une aide ~** I expect a maximum of help *ou* maximum help from you.
2 *nm* **(a)** *(gén, Math)* maximum; *(Jur)* maximum sentence. **avec le ~ de profit** with the maximum (of) profit, with the highest profit, with the greatest possible profit; **il faut travailler au ~** one must work to the utmost of one's ability; **atteindre son ~*** *[production]* to reach its maximum, reach an all-time high*; *[valeur]* to reach its highest *ou* maximum point; *V* **thermomètre.**
(b) *(loc)* **au (grand) ~** at the (very) maximum, at the (very) most; **il faut rester au** *ou* **le ~ à l'ombre** one must stay as much as possible in the shade.

Mayence [majɑ̃s] *n* Mainz.

mayonnaise [majɔnɛz] *nf* mayonnaise. **poisson/œufs (à la) ~** fish/eggs (with *ou* in) mayonnaise.

mazagran [mazagʀɑ̃] *nm* pottery goblet *(for coffee)*.

mazette† [mazɛt] **1** *excl (admiration, étonnement)* my!, my goodness! **2** *nf (incapable)* weakling.

mazout [mazut] *nm* (fuel) oil. **chaudière/poêle à ~** oil-fired boiler/stove; **chauffage central au ~** oil-fired central heating.

me, m' [m(ə)] *pron pers (objet direct ou indirect)* me; *(réfléchi)* myself. **~ voyez-vous?** can you see me?; **elle m'attend** she is waiting for me; **il ~ l'a dit** he told me (it), he told me about it; **il m'en a parlé** he spoke to me about it; **il ~ l'a donné** he gave it to me, he gave it me; **je ne ~ vois pas dans ce rôle-là** I can't see myself in that part.

mea-culpa* [meakylpa] *excl* my fault!, my mistake! **faire son ~** *(lit)* to say one's mea culpa; *(fig)* to blame oneself.

méandre [meɑ̃dʀ(ə)] *nm (Art, Géog)* meander; *(fig) [politique]* twists and turns. **les ~s de sa pensée** the twists and turns *ou* ins and outs *ou* complexities of his thought.

méat [mea] *nm (Anat)* meatus; *(Bot)* lacuna.

mec‡ [mɛk] *nm* guy‡, bloke‡ *(Brit)*.

mécanicien, -ienne [mekanisjɛ̃, jɛn] **1** *adj civilisation* mechanistic.
2 *nm,f* **(a)** *(Aut)* (garage *ou* motor) mechanic. **ouvrier ~** garage hand; **c'est un bon ~** he is a good mechanic, he is good with cars *ou* with machines.
(b) *(Naut)* engineer. *(Aviat)* **~ navigant, ~ de bord** flight engineer.
(c) *(Rail)* train *ou* engine driver *(Brit)*, engineer *(US)*.
(d) *(Méd)* **~-dentiste** dental technician *ou* mechanic.

mécanique [mekanik] **1** *adj* **(a)** *(Tech, gén)* mechanical; *dentelle* machine-made; *jouet* clockwork *(épith)*. **les industries ~s** mechanical engineering industries; *(Aut, Aviat)* **avoir des ennuis ~s** to have engine trouble; *V* **escalier, piano, rasoir.**
(b) *(machinal) geste, réflexe* mechanical.
(c) *(Philos, Sci)* mechanical. **énergie ~** mechanical energy; **lois ~s** laws of mechanics.
2 *nf* **(a)** *(Sci)* (mechanical) engineering; *(Aut, Tech)* mechanics *(sg)*. **la ~, ça le connaît*** he knows what he's doing in mechanics; **~ céleste/ondulatoire** celestial/wave mechanics; **~ hydraulique** hydraulics *(sg)*.
(b) *(mécanisme)* **la ~ d'une horloge** the mechanism of a clock; **cette voiture, c'est de la belle ~** this car is a fine piece of engineering.

mécaniquement [mekanikmɑ̃] *adv* mechanically. **objet fait ~** machine-made object.

mécanisation [mekanizɑsjɔ̃] *nf* mechanization.

mécaniser [mekanize] (1) *vt* to mechanize.

mécanisme [mekanism(ə)] *nm (Bio, Philos, Psych, Tech)* mechanism. **les ~s psychologiques/biologiques** psychological/biological workings *ou* mechanisms; **le ~ administratif** the mechanics of administration; **~(s) politique(s)** political machinery, mechanism of politics; **le ~ d'une action** the mechanics of an action.

mécaniste [mekanist(ə)] *adj* mechanistic.

mécano* [mekano] *nm (abrév de* **mécanicien***)* mechanic.

mécanographe [mekanɔgʀaf] *nmf* comptometer operator, punch card operator.

mécanographie [mekanɔgʀafi] *nf (procédé)* (mechanical) data processing; *(service)* comptometer department.

mécanographique [mekanɔgʀafik] *adj classement* mechanized, automatic. **service ~** comptometer department, (mechanical) data processing department; **machine ~** calculator.

meccano [mɛkano] *nm* ® meccano ®.

mécénat [mesena] *nm (Art)* patronage.

mécène [mesɛn] *nm (Art)* patron. *(Antiq)* **M~** Maecenas.

méchamment [meʃamɑ̃] *adv* **(a)** *(cruellement) rire, agir* spitefully, nastily, maliciously.
(b) (*: *très*) fantastically*, terrifically*. **c'est ~ bon** it's fantastically* *ou* bloody‡ *(Brit)* good.

méchanceté [meʃɑ̃ste] *nf* **(a)** *(U: caractère) [personne, action]* nastiness, spitefulness, maliciousness. **faire qch par ~** to do sth out of spite *ou* malice.
(b) *(action, parole)* mean *ou* spiteful *ou* nasty *ou* malicious action *ou* remark. **~ gratuite** unwarranted piece of unkindness *ou* spitefulness; **dire des ~s à qn** to say spiteful things to sb.

méchant, e [meʃɑ̃, ɑ̃t] **1** *adj* **(a)** *(malveillant)* spiteful, nasty, malicious. **devenir ~** to turn *ou* get nasty; **la mer est ~e** there is a nasty sea; **arrête, tu es ~** stop it, you're wicked *ou* you're (being) horrid *ou* nasty; **ce n'est pas un ~ homme** he's not such a bad fellow; *V* **chien.**
(b) *(dangereux, désagréable)* **ce n'est pas bien ~*** *[blessure, difficulté, dispute]* it's not too serious; *[examen]* it's not too difficult *ou* stiff*; **s'attirer une ~e affaire** *(dangereuse)* to get mixed up in a nasty business; *(désagréable)* to get mixed up in an unpleasant *ou* unsavoury (bit of) business.
(c) (†: *médiocre, insignifiant*) *(avant n)* miserable, pathetic*, mediocre, sorry-looking. **~ vers/poète** poor *ou* second-rate verse/poet; **un ~ morceau de fromage** one miserable *ou* sorry-looking bit of cheese; **que de bruit pour une ~e clef perdue** what a fuss over one wretched lost key.
(d) (*: *sensationnel*) *(avant n)* **il avait (une) ~e allure** he looked terrific*; **il a une ~e moto** he's got a fantastic* *ou* bloody marvellous‡ *(Brit)* bike; **une ~e cicatrice** a hell of a scar‡; **un ~ cigare** a bloody great (big) cigar‡.
2 *nm,f*: **tais-toi, ~!** be quiet you naughty boy!; **les ~s** the wicked; *(dans un western)* the baddies*, the bad guys* *(US)*; **faire le ~*** to be difficult, be nasty.

mèche [mɛʃ] *nf* **(a)** *(inflammable) [bougie, briquet, lampe]* wick; *[bombe, mine]* fuse. **~ fusante** safety fuse; *V* **vendre.**
(b) *[cheveux]* tuft of hair, lock; *(sur le front)* forelock, lock of hair. **~ postiche, fausse ~** hairpiece; **~s folles** straggling locks *ou* wisps of hair; **~ rebelle** cowlick; **se faire faire des ~s** to have highlights put in, have one's hair streaked (blond).
(c) *(Tech)* bit; *(Méd)* pack, dressing; *[fouet]* lash.
(d) *(loc)* **être de ~ avec qn*** to be hand in glove with sb*, be in collusion *ou* league with sb; **y a pas ~**‡ nothing doing*, it's no go*.

mécher [meʃe] (6) *vt (Tech)* to sulphurize; *(Méd)* to pack with gauze.

méchoui [meʃwi] *nm (repas)* barbecue *(whole roast sheep)*.

mécompte [mekɔ̃t] *nm (frm)* **(a)** *(désillusion) (gén pl)* disappointment. **(b)** *(rare: erreur de calcul)* miscalculation, miscount.

méconnaissable [mekɔnɛsabl(ə)] *adj (impossible à reconnaître)* unrecognizable; *(difficile à reconnaître)* hardly recognizable.

méconnaissance [mekɔnɛsɑ̃s] *nf (ignorance)* lack of knowledge *(de* about), ignorance *(de* of); *(mauvais jugement: littér)* lack of comprehension, misappreciation *(de* of); *(refus de reconnaître)* refusal to take into consideration.

méconnaître [mekɔnɛtʀ(ə)] (57) *vt (frm)* **(a)** *(ignorer) faits* to be unaware of, not to know. **je ne méconnais pas que** I am fully *ou* quite aware that, I am alive to the fact that.
(b) *(mésestimer) situation, problème* to misjudge; *mérites, personne* to underrate, underestimate.
(c) *(ne pas tenir compte de) lois, devoirs* to ignore.

méconnu, e [mekɔny] *(ptp de* **méconnaître***)* *adj talent, génie* unrecognized; *musicien, inventeur* unrecognized, misunderstood. **il se prend pour un ~** he sees himself as a misunderstood man.

mécontent, e [mekɔ̃tɑ̃, ɑ̃t] **1** *adj (insatisfait)* discontented, displeased, dissatisfied *(de* with); *(contrarié)* annoyed *(de* with, at). **il a l'air très ~** he looks very annoyed *ou* displeased; **il n'est pas ~ de** he is not altogether dissatisfied *ou* displeased with.
2 *nm,f* grumbler*; *(Pol)* malcontent.

mécontentement [mekɔ̃tɑ̃tmɑ̃] *nm (Pol)* discontent; *(déplaisir)* dissatisfaction, displeasure; *(irritation)* annoyance.

mécontenter [mekɔ̃tɑ̃te] (1) *vt* to dissatisfy; *(contrarier)* to displease; *(irriter)* to annoy.

Mecque [mɛk] *nf*: **la ~** *(lit)* Mecca; *(fig)* the Mecca.

mécréant, e [mekʀeɑ̃, ɑ̃t] *adj, nm,f* **(a)** (†, *hum: non-croyant*) infidel, non-believer. **(b)** (†*péj: bandit*) scoundrel, miscreant†.

médaille [medaj] *nf* **(a)** *(pièce, décoration)* medal. **~ militaire** military decoration; **~ pieuse** medal *(of a saint etc)*; **~ du travail** long-service medal *(in industry etc)*; *V* **revers.**
(b) *(insigne d'identité) [employé]* badge; *[chien]* identification disc, name tag; *[volaille]* guarantee tag.

médaillé, e [medaje] *(ptp de* **médailler***)* **1** *adj (Admin, Mil)* decorated *(with a medal)*; *(Sport)* holding a medal. **2** *nm,f* medal-holder.

médailler [medaje] (1) *vt (rare) (Admin, Sport etc)* to award a medal to; *(Mil)* to decorate, award a medal to.

médaillon [medajɔ̃] *nm (Art)* medallion; *(bijou)* locket; *(Culin)* medaillon *(thin, round slice of meat etc)*.

médecin [mɛdsɛ̃] *nm* doctor, physician *(frm)*. *(fig)* **~ de l'âme** confessor; *(Naut)* **~ du bord** ship's doctor; **~-chef** head doctor; **~ d'hôpital** *ou* **des hôpitaux** ≈ consultant, doctor *ou* physician with a hospital appointment; **~ légiste** forensic surgeon, expert in forensic medicine; **~ généraliste** *ou* **de médecine générale** general practitioner, G.P.; **~ militaire** army medical officer; **~ traitant** attending physician; **votre ~ traitant** your (usual *ou* family) doctor.

médecine [mɛdsin] *nf* **(a)** *(Sci)* medicine. **~ curative** remedial medicine; **~ générale** general medicine; **~ infantile** paediatrics *(sg)*; **~ légale** forensic medicine; **~ opératoire** surgery; **~ du travail** occupational *ou* industrial medicine; **faire des études de ~, faire sa ~** to study *ou* do medicine; **pratiquer une ~ révolutionnaire** to practise a revolutionary type of medicine; **il exerçait la ~ dans un petit village** he had a (medical) practice *ou* he practised in a small village; *V* **docteur, étudiant, faculté.**

(b) (†: *médicament*) medicine.
Médée [mede] *nf* Medea.
media [medja] *nmpl* = **mass media.**
médian, e [medjɑ̃, an] **1** *adj* (*Math, Statistique*) median; (*Ling*) medial. **2 médiane** *nf* (*Math, Statistique*) median; (*Ling*) medial sound, mid vowel; *V* **ligne**[1].
médiat, e [medja, at] *adj* mediate.
médiateur, -trice [medjatœʀ, tʀis] **1** *adj* (*gén, Pol*) mediatory, mediating; (*Ind*) arbitrating. **2** *nm,f* (*gén*) mediator; (*Ind*) arbitrator; (*Brit Pol*) Parliamentary Commissioner, Ombudsman. (*Méd*) ~ **chimique** transmitter substance. **3 médiatrice** *nf* (*Géom*) median.
médiation [medjɑsjɔ̃] *nf* **(a)** (*gén, Philos, Pol*) mediation; (*Ind*) arbitration. **(b)** (*Logique*) mediate inference.
médiatisation [medjatizɑsjɔ̃] *nf* (*Philos*) mediatization.
médiatiser [medjatize] (1) *vt* (*Hist, Philos*) to mediatize.
médiator [medjatɔʀ] *nm* plectrum.
médiatrice [medjatʀis] *V* **médiateur.**
médical, e, *mpl* **-aux** [medikal, o] *adj* medical; *V* **examen, visite.**
médicalement [medikalmɑ̃] *adv* medically.
médicament [medikamɑ̃] *nm* medicine, drug.
médicamenteux, -euse [medikamɑ̃tø, øz] *adj plante, substance* medicinal.
médicastre [medikastʀ(ə)] *nm* (†, *hum*) medical charlatan, quack.
médication [medikɑsjɔ̃] *nf* (medical) treatment, medication.
médicinal, e, *mpl* **-aux** [medisinal, o] *adj plante, substance* medicinal.
medicine-ball, *pl* **medicine-balls** [medisinbol] *nm* medicine ball.
Médicis [medisis] *nmf* Medici.
médico- [medikɔ] *préf*: ~**légal** medico-legal, forensic; ~**social** medico-social; *V* **institut.**
médiéval, e, *mpl* **-aux** [medjeval, o] *adj* medieval.
médiéviste [medjevist(ə)] *nmf* medievalist.
médiocre [medjɔkʀ(ə)] *adj travail, roman, élève* mediocre, indifferent, second-rate; *intelligence, qualité* poor, mediocre, inferior; *revenu, salaire* meagre, poor; *vie, existence* mediocre, narrow. **il occupe une situation** ~ he holds some second-rate position; **gagner un salaire** ~ to earn a mere pittance *ou* a meagre wage; **il a montré un intérêt** ~ **pour ce projet** he showed little or no interest in the project; **c'est un (homme)** ~ he's an uninspiring *ou* a pretty ordinary* sort of person; **génie incompris par les esprits** ~**s** genius misunderstood by the petty-minded *ou* those with small minds.
médiocrement [medjɔkʀəmɑ̃] *adv*: **gagner** ~ **sa vie** to earn a poor living; **être** ~ **intéressé par** not to be particularly interested in; ~ **intelligent** not very *ou* not particularly intelligent; ~ **satisfait** barely satisfied, not very well satisfied; **il joue** ~ **du piano** he plays the piano indifferently, he's not very good at (playing) the piano.
médiocrité [medjɔkʀite] *nf [travail]* poor quality, mediocrity; *[élève, homme politique]* mediocrity; *[revenu, salaire]* meagreness, poorness; *[intelligence]* mediocrity, inferiority; *[vie]* narrowness, mediocrity. **les politiciens de maintenant, quelle** ~! what mediocrity *ou* poor quality in present-day politicians!; **étant donné la** ~ **de ses revenus** given the slimness of his resources, seeing how slight *ou* slim his resources are *ou* were; **cet homme, c'est une (vraie)** ~ this man is a complete mediocrity *ou* second-rater.
médire [mediʀ] (37) *vi*: ~ **de qn** to speak ill of sb; (*à tort*) to malign sb. **elle est toujours en train de** ~ she's always running people down.
médisance [medizɑ̃s] *nf* **(a)** (*diffamation*) scandalmongering. **être en butte à la** ~ to be made a target for scandalmongering *ou* for malicious gossip.
(b) (*propos*) piece of scandal. ~**s** scandal (*U*), gossip (*U*); **ce sont des** ~**s!** that's just scandal! *ou* malicious gossip!; **arrête de dire des** ~**s** stop spreading scandal *ou* gossip.
médisant, e [medizɑ̃, ɑ̃t] **1** *adj paroles* slanderous. **les gens sont** ~**s** people say nasty things.
2 *nm,f* scandalmonger, slanderer.
méditatif, -ive [meditatif, iv] *adj caractère* meditative, thoughtful; *air* musing, thoughtful.
méditation [meditɑsjɔ̃] *nf* (*pensée*) meditation; (*recueillement*) meditation (*U*). **après de longues** ~**s sur le sujet** after giving the subject much *ou* deep thought, after lengthy meditation on the subject; **il était plongé dans la** ~ *ou* **une profonde** ~ he was sunk in deep thought.
méditer [medite] (1) **1** *vt pensée* to meditate on, ponder (over); *livre, projet, vengeance* to meditate. ~ **de faire qch** to contemplate doing sth, plan to do sth.
2 *vi* to meditate. ~ **sur qch** to ponder *ou* muse over sth.
Méditerranée [mediteʀane] *nf*: **la mer** ~, **la** ~ the Mediterranean (Sea).
méditerranéen, -enne [mediteʀaneɛ̃, ɛn] **1** *adj* Mediterranean. **2** *nm,f*: **M**~**(ne)** (French) Southerner; inhabitant *ou* native of a Mediterranean country.
médium [medjɔm] *nm* (*Spiritisme*) medium; (*Mus*) middle register; (*Logique*) middle term.
médius [medjys] *nm* middle finger.
médoc [medɔk] *nm* Médoc (wine).
médullaire [medylɛʀ] *adj* medullary.
méduse [medyz] *nf* jellyfish. (*Myth*) **M**~ Medusa.
méduser [medyze] (1) *vt* (*gén pass*) to dumbfound, paralyze. **je suis resté médusé par ce spectacle** I was rooted to the spot *ou* dumbfounded by this sight.
meeting [mitiŋ] *nm* (*Pol, Sport*) meeting. ~ **d'aviation** air show *ou* display.
méfait [mefɛ] *nm* **(a)** (*ravage*) (*gén pl*) *[temps, drogue]* damage (*U*), ravages; *[passion, épidémie]* ravages, damaging effect. **l'un des nombreux** ~**s de l'alcoolisme** one of the numerous damaging *ou* ill effects of alcoholism.
(b) (*acte*) misdemeanour, wrongdoing; (*hum*) misdeed.
méfiance [mefjɑ̃s] *nf* distrust, mistrust, suspicion. **avoir de la** ~ **envers qn** to mistrust *ou* distrust sb; **apaiser/éveiller la** ~ **de qn** to allay/arouse sb's suspicion(s); **être sans** ~ (*avoir toute confiance*) to be completely trusting; (*ne rien soupçonner*) to be quite unsuspecting.
méfiant, e [mefjɑ̃, ɑ̃t] *adj personne* distrustful, mistrustful, suspicious. **air** *ou* **regard** ~ distrustful *ou* mistrustful *ou* suspicious look, look of distrust *ou* mistrust *ou* suspicion.
méfier (se) [mefje] (7) *vpr* **(a) se** ~ **de qn/des conseils de qn** to mistrust *ou* distrust sb/sb's advice; **je me méfie de lui** I do not trust him, I'm suspicious of him; **méfiez-vous de lui, il faut vous** ~ **de lui** do not trust him, beware of him, be on your guard against him; **je ne me méfie pas assez de mes réactions** I should be more wary of my reactions.
(b) (*faire attention*) **se** ~ **de qch** to be careful about sth; **il faut vous** ~ you must be careful, you've got to be on your guard; **méfie-toi de cette marche** mind *ou* watch the step, look out for that step*; **méfie-toi, tu vas tomber** look out* *ou* be careful or you'll fall.
méforme [mefɔʀm(ə)] *nf* (*Sport*) lack of fitness, unfitness. **traverser une période de** ~ to be (temporarily) off form.
méga [mega] **1** *préf*: **méga ...** mega ... . ~**cycle** *nm* megacycle; ~**tonne** *nf* megaton. **2** *adj inv* (*arg Scol*) ~ **-dissertation** hell of a long essay‡; **un** ~**-cigare à la bouche** a whopping great cigar in his mouth‡; **recevoir une** ~ **dérouillée** to get a hell of a thrashing‡ *ou* a thrashing and a half*.
mégalithe [megalit] *nm* megalith.
mégalithique [megalitik] *adj* megalithic.
mégalomane [megalɔman] *adj, nmf* megalomaniac.
mégalomanie [megalɔmani] *nf* megalomania.
mégaphone† [megafɔn] *nm* (*porte-voix*) megaphone.
mégarde [megaʀd(ə)] *nf*: **par** ~ (*accidentellement*) accidentally, by accident; (*par erreur*) by mistake, inadvertently; (*par négligence*) accidentally; **un livre que j'avais emporté par** ~ a book which I had accidentally *ou* inadvertently taken away with me.
mégère [meʒɛʀ] *nf* (*péj: femme*) shrew.
mégot* [mego] *nm [cigarette]* cigarette butt *ou* end, fag end‡; *[cigare]* stub, butt.
méhari [meaʀi] *nm* fast dromedary, mehari.
méhariste [meaʀist(ə)] *nm* meharist (*rider of mehari or soldier of French Camel corps*).
meilleur, e [mɛjœʀ] **1** *adj* (*comp, superl de bon*) better. **le** ~ **des deux** the better of the two; **le** ~ **de tous, la** ~**e de toutes** the best of the lot; **c'est le** ~ **des hommes, c'est le** ~ **homme du monde** he is the best of men, he's the best man in the world; **il a choisi le** ~ he took the best (one); (*plus charitable*) **il est** ~ **que moi** he's a better person than I am; (*plus doué*) **il est** ~ **que moi (en)** he's better than I am (at); *[aliment]* **avoir** ~ **goût** to taste better; **ce gâteau est (bien)** ~ **avec du rhum** this cake tastes *ou* is (much) better with rum; **il est** ~ **chanteur que compositeur** he makes a better singer than (a) composer, he is better at singing than (at) composing; **de** ~**e qualité** of better *ou* higher quality; **tissu de la** ~**e qualité** best quality material; **les** ~**s spécialistes** the best *ou* top specialists; **son** ~ **ami** his best *ou* closest friend; **servir les** ~**s mets/vins** to serve the best *ou* finest dishes/wines; **information tirée des** ~**es sources** information from the most reliable sources; ~ **marché** cheaper; **le** ~ **marché** the cheapest; **être en** ~**e santé** to be better, be in better health; (*Sport*) **faire un** ~ **temps au deuxième tour** to put up *ou* do a better time on the second lap; **partir de** ~**e heure** to leave earlier; **prendre (une)** ~**e tournure** to take a turn for the better; ~**s vœux** best wishes; **ce sera pour des jours/des temps** ~**s** that will be for better days/happier times; **il n'y a rien de** ~ there is nothing better, there's nothing to beat it.
2 *adv*: **il fait** ~ **qu'hier** it's better *ou* nicer (weather) than yesterday; **sentir** ~ to smell better *ou* nicer.
3 *nm,f* (*celui qui est meilleur*) the best one. **ce ne sont pas toujours les** ~**s qui sont récompensés** it is not always the best (people) who win *ou* who reap the rewards; **que le** ~ **gagne** may the best man win; **j'en passe et des** ~**es** and that's not all — I could go on, and that's the least of them; *V* **raison.**
4 *nm* (*ce qui est meilleur*) the best. **pour le** ~ **et pour le pire** for better or for worse; **donner le** ~ **de soi-même** to give of one's best; **passer le** ~ **de sa vie à faire** to spend the best days *ou* years of one's life doing; **le** ~ **de notre pays fut tué pendant la guerre** the finest *ou* best men of our country were killed during the war; (*Sport*) **prendre le** ~ **sur qn** to get the better of sb; **garder** *ou* **réserver le** ~ **pour la fin** to keep the best till *ou* for the end.
meistre [mɛstʀ(ə)] *nm* = **mestre.**
méjuger [meʒyʒe] (3) (*littér*) **1** *vt* to misjudge. **2** *vi*: ~ **de** to underrate, underestimate. **3 se méjuger** *vpr* to underestimate o.s.
mélancolie [melɑ̃kɔli] *nf* melancholy, gloom; (*Méd*) melancholia; *V* **engendrer.**
mélancolique [melɑ̃kɔlik] *adj personne, paysage, musique* melancholy; *tempérament, personne* melancholic.
mélancoliquement [melɑ̃kɔlikmɑ̃] *adv* with a melancholy air, melancholically.
mélange [melɑ̃ʒ] *nm* **(a)** (*opération*) *[produits]* mixing; *[vins, tabacs]* blending. **faire un** ~ **de** *substances* to make a mixture of; *idées* to mix up; **quand on boit il ne faut pas faire de** ~**s** you shouldn't mix your drinks.

(b) (*résultat*) (*gén, Chim, fig*) mixture; (*vins, tabacs, cafés*) blend. ~ **détonant** explosive mixture; ~ **réfrigérant** freezing mixture; (*Aut etc*) ~ **pauvre/riche** weak/rich mixture; **joie sans** ~ unalloyed *ou* unadulterated joy; (*littér*) **sans** ~ **de** free from, unadulterated by; (*Littérat*) ~**s** miscellanies, miscellany.

mélanger [melɑ̃ʒe] (3) **1** *vt* (*gén, Chim, Culin*) to mix; *couleurs, vins, parfums, tabacs* to blend; *dates, idées* to mix (up), muddle up, confuse; *documents* to mix up, muddle up. ~ **du beurre et de la farine** to rub butter in with flour, mix butter and flour together; **tu mélanges tout!** you're getting it all mixed up! *ou* muddled up!; **un public très mélangé** a very varied *ou* mixed public; (*fig*) **il ne faut pas** ~ **les torchons et les serviettes** we (*ou* you *etc*) must divide *ou* separate the sheep from the goats.

2 se mélanger *vpr [produits]* to mix; *[vins]* to mix, blend. **les dates se mélangent dans ma tête** I'm confused about the dates, I've got the dates mixed up *ou* in a muddle.

mélangeur, -euse [melɑ̃ʒœʀ, øz] **1** *nm,f* mixer.

2 nm (*Plomberie*) mixer tap (*Brit*), mixing faucet (*US*); (*Ciné, Rad*) mixer.

mélasse [melas] *nf* (*Culin*) treacle (*Brit*), molasses (*US*); (*péj: boue*) muck; (*brouillard*) murk. (*fig*) **quelle** ~! what a mess!; **être dans la** ~* (*avoir des ennuis*) to be in the soup*, be in a sticky situation*; (*être dans la misère*) to be on one's beam ends*.

Melba [mɛlba] *adj inv* Melba. **pêche/ananas** ~ peach/pineapple Melba.

mêlé, e [mele] (*ptp de* **mêler**) **1** *adj* **(a)** *sentiments* mixed, mingled; *couleurs, tons* mingled, blending; *monde, société* mixed; *V* **sang.**

(b) ~ **de** mingled with; **joie** ~**e de remords** pleasure mixed with *ou* tinged with remorse; **vin** ~ **d'eau** wine mixed with water.

2 mêlée *nf* **(a)** (*bataille*) mêlée; (*fig hum*) kerfuffle*. ~**e générale** free-for-all; **la** ~**e devint générale** it developed into a free-for-all, scuffles broke out all round *ou* on all sides; (*lit, fig*) **se jeter dans la** ~**e** to plunge into the fray; (*fig*) **rester au-dessus de** *ou* **à l'écart de la** ~**e** to stay on the sidelines, stay *ou* keep aloof.

(b) (*Rugby*) scrum, scrummage.

mêlé-casse† [melekas] *nm* blackcurrant and brandy cocktail.

mêlée [mele] *V* **mêlé.**

mêler [mele] (1) **1** *vt* **(a)** (*unir, mettre ensemble*) *substances* to mingle, mix together; *races* to mix; (*Vét*) to cross; (*Culin: amalgamer, mélanger*) to mix, blend; (*joindre, allier*) *traits de caractère* to combine, mingle. **les deux fleuves mêlent leurs eaux** the two rivers mingle their waters; **elles mêlèrent leurs larmes/leurs soupirs** their tears/their sighs mingled.

(b) (*mettre en désordre, embrouiller*) *papiers, dossiers* to muddle (up), mix up; (*battre*) *cartes* to shuffle. ~ **la réalité et le rêve** to confuse reality and dream.

(c) ~ **à** *ou* **avec** (*ajouter*) to mix *ou* mingle with; ~ **la douceur à la fermeté** to combine gentleness with firmness; ~ **du feuillage à un bouquet** to put some greenery in with a bouquet; **un récit mêlé de détails comiques** a story interspersed with comic(al) details.

(d) (*impliquer*) ~ **à** to involve in; (*fig*) ~ **qn à une affaire** to involve sb in some business, get sb mixed up *ou* involved in an affair; **j'y ai été mêlé contre mon gré** I was dragged into it against my wishes, I got mixed up *ou* involved in it against my will; ~ **qn à la conversation** to bring *ou* draw sb into the conversation.

2 se mêler *vpr* **(a)** to mix, mingle, combine. **ces deux races ne se mêlent jamais** these two races never mix.

(b) se ~ **à** (*se joindre à*) to join; (*s'associer à*) to mix with; *[cris, sentiments]* to mingle with; **il se mêla à la foule** he joined the crowd, he mingled with the crowd; **il ne se mêle jamais aux autres enfants** he never mixes with other children; **se** ~ **à une querelle** to get mixed up *ou* involved in a quarrel; **il se mêlait à toutes les manifestations** he got involved *ou* took part in all the demonstrations; **des rires se mêlaient aux applaudissements** there was laughter mingled with the applause; **se** ~ **à la conversation** to join in *ou* come in on* the conversation.

(c) se ~ **à** *ou* **de** (*s'occuper de*) to meddle with, get mixed up in; **se** ~ **des affaires des autres** to meddle *ou* interfere in other people's business *ou* affairs; **ne vous mêlez pas d'intervenir!** don't you take it into your head to interfere!, just you keep out of it!; **mêle-toi de ce qui te regarde!** *ou* **de tes affaires!** *ou* **de tes oignons!*** mind your own business!; (*iro*) **de quoi je me mêle!*** what business is it of yours?, what's it got to do with you?; **se** ~ **de faire qch** to take it upon o.s. to do sth, make it one's business to do sth; **voilà qu'il se mêle de nous donner des conseils!** who is he to give us advice!, look at him butting in with his advice!

mélèze [melɛz] *nm* larch.

méli-mélo* [melimelo] *nm [situation]* muddle; *[objets]* jumble. **cette affaire est un véritable** ~! what a terrible muddle this business is!

mélisse [melis] *nf* (*Bot*) balm.

mélo* [melo] **1** *adj abrév de* **mélodramatique. 2** *nm abrév de* **mélodrame.**

mélodie [melɔdi] *nf* **(a)** (*motif, chanson*) melody, tune. **les** ~**s de Debussy** Debussy's melodies *ou* songs; **une petite** ~ **entendue à la radio** a little tune heard on the radio. **(b)** (*qualité*) melodiousness.

mélodieusement [melɔdjøzmɑ̃] *adv* melodiously, tunefully.

mélodieux, -euse [melɔdjø, øz] *adj* melodious, tuneful.

mélodique [melɔdik] *adj* melodic.

mélodramatique [melɔdʀamatik] *adj* (*Littérat, péj*) melodramatic.

mélodrame [melɔdʀam] *nm* (*Littérat, péj*) melodrama.

mélomane [melɔman] **1** *adj* music-loving (*épith*), keen on music (*attrib*). **2** *nmf* music lover.

melon [m(ə)lɔ̃] *nm* (*Bot*) (musk) melon, honeydew melon. ~ **(cantaloup)** cantaloupe melon; ~ **d'eau** watermelon; (*Habillement*) **(chapeau)** ~ bowler (hat).

mélopée [melɔpe] *nf* **(a)** (*gén: chant monotone*) monotonous chant, threnody (*littér*). **(b)** (*Hist Mus*) recitative.

membrane [mɑ̃bʀan] *nf* membrane.

membraneux, -euse [mɑ̃bʀanø, øz] *adj* membran(e)ous.

membre [mɑ̃bʀ(ə)] *nm* **(a)** (*Anat, Zool*) limb. ~ **inférieur/supérieur/antérieur/postérieur** lower/upper/fore/rear limb; ~ **(viril)** male member *ou* organ.

(b) *[groupe, société savante]* member; *[académie]* fellow. ~ **fondateur** founder member; ~ **perpétuel** life member; ~ **actif/associé** active/associate member; **un** ~ **de la société/du public** a member of society/of the public; **être** ~ **de** to be a member of; **devenir** ~ **d'un club** to become a member of a club, join a club; **ce club a 300** ~**s** this club has a membership of 300; **pays/états** ~**s (de la Communauté)** member countries/states (of the Community).

(c) (*Math*) member. **premier/second** ~ left-hand/right-hand member.

(d) (*Ling*) ~ **de phrase** (sentence) member.

(e) (*Archit*) member.

(f) (*Naut*) timber, rib.

membré, e [mɑ̃bʀe] *adj* limbed. **bien/mal** ~ strong-/weak-limbed.

membru, e [mɑ̃bʀy] *adj* (*littér*) strong-limbed.

membrure [mɑ̃bʀyʀ] *nf* (*Anat*) limbs, build; (*Naut*) rib; (*collectif*) frame. **homme à** ~ **puissante** strong-limbed *ou* powerfully built man.

même [mɛm] **1** *adj* **(a)** (*identique, semblable: avant n*) same, identical. **des bijoux de** ~ **valeur** jewels of equal *ou* of the same value; **ils ont la** ~ **taille/la** ~ **couleur, ils sont de** ~ **taille/de** ~ **couleur** they are the same size/the same colour; **j'ai exactement la** ~ **robe qu'hier** I am wearing the very same dress I wore yesterday *ou* exactly the same dress as yesterday; **nous sommes du** ~ **avis** we are of the same mind *ou* opinion, we agree; **ils ont la** ~ **voiture que nous** they have the same car as we have *ou* as us*; **que vous veniez ou non c'est la** ~ **chose** whether you come or not it's all one; **c'est toujours la** ~ **chose!** it's always the same (old story)!; **arriver en** ~ **temps (que)** to arrive at the same time (as); **en** ~ **temps qu'il le faisait l'autre s'approchait** as *ou* while he was doing it the other drew nearer.

(b) (*après n ou pron*) very, actual. **ce sont ses paroles** ~**s** those are his very *ou* actual words; **il est la générosité** ~ he is generosity itself, he is the soul of generosity; **la grande maison, celle-là** ~ **que vous avez visitée** the big house, the very one you visited *ou* precisely the one you visited.

(c) moi-~ myself; **toi-**~ yourself; **lui-**~ himself; **elle-**~ herself; **nous-**~**s** ourselves; **vous-**~ yourself; **vous-**~**s** yourselves; **eux-** *ou* **elles-**~**s** themselves; **on est soi-**~ **conscient de ses propres erreurs** one is aware (oneself) of one's own mistakes; **nous devons y aller nous-**~**s** we must go ourselves; **s'apitoyer sur soi-**~ to feel sorry for oneself; **tu n'as aucune confiance en toi-**~ you have no confidence in yourself; **c'est lui-**~ **qui l'a dit, il l'a dit lui-**~ he said it himself, he himself said it; **au plus profond d'eux-**~**s/de nous-**~**s** in their/our heart of hearts; **elle fait ses robes elle-**~ she makes her own clothes, she makes her clothes herself; **c'est ce que je me dis en** *ou* **à moi-**~ that's what I tell myself (inwardly), that's what I think to myself; **elle se disait en elle-**~ **que ...** she thought to herself that ..., she thought privately that ...; **faire qch de soi-**~ to do sth on one's own initiative *ou* off one's own bat* (*Brit*); **faire qch (par) soi-**~ to do sth (by) oneself.

2 *pron indéf* (*avec le, la, les*) **ce n'est pas le** ~ it's not the same (one); **la réaction n'a pas été la** ~ **qu'à Paris** the reaction was not the same as in Paris; **elle est bien toujours la** ~! she's just the same as ever!; (*fig*) **ce sont toujours les** ~**s qui se font tuer** it's always the same ones who catch it*; *V* **pareil, revenir.**

3 *adv* **(a)** even. **ils sont tous sortis,** ~ **les enfants** they are all out, even the children; **il n'a** ~ **pas de quoi écrire** *ou* **pas** ~ **de quoi écrire** he hasn't even got anything to write with; **il est intéressant et** ~ **amusant** he is interesting and amusing too *ou* besides; **elle ne me parle** ~ **plus** she no longer even speaks to me, she doesn't even speak to me anymore; ~ **lui ne sait pas** even he doesn't know; **personne ne sait,** ~ **pas lui** nobody knows, not even him; ~ **si** even if, even though; **c'est vrai,** ~ **que je peux le prouver!*** it's true, and what's more I can prove it!

(b) (*précisément*) **aujourd'hui** ~ this very day; **ici** ~ in this very place, on this very spot; **c'est celui-là** ~ **qui** he's the very one who; **c'est cela** ~ that's just *ou* exactly it.

(c) (*loc*) **boire à** ~ **la bouteille** to drink (straight) from the bottle; **coucher à** ~ **le sol** to lie on the bare ground; **à** ~ **la peau** next to the skin; **mettre qn à** ~ **de faire** to enable sb to do; **être à** ~ **de faire** to be able *ou* to be in a position to do; **je ne suis pas à** ~ **de juger** I am in no position to judge; **il fera de** ~ he'll do the same, he'll do likewise, he'll follow suit; **vous le détestez? moi de** ~ you hate him? so do I *ou* I do too *ou* me too* *ou* same here*; **de** ~ **qu'il nous a dit que ...** just as he told us that ...; **il en est** *ou* **il en va de** ~ **pour moi** it's the same for me, same here*; **quand** ~, **tout de** ~ all the same, for all that, even so; **tout de** ~ *ou* **quand** ~, **il aurait pu nous prévenir** all the same *ou* even so he might have warned us; **il exagère tout de** ~! well really he's going too far!; **il a tout de** ~ **réussi à s'échapper** he managed to escape nevertheless *ou* all the same.

mémé* [meme] *nf* (*langage enfantin: grand-mère*) granny*, grandma; (*péj: vieille dame*) old girl* *ou* dear*.

mêmement [mɛmmɑ̃] *adv* (*frm*) likewise.

mémento [memɛ̃to] *nm* (*agenda*) engagement diary; (*Scol: aide-mémoire*) summary. (*Rel*) ~ **des vivants/des morts** prayers for the living/the dead.

mémère* [memɛʀ] *nf* (*langage enfantin*) granny*, grandma; (*péj: vieille dame*) old girl* *ou* dear*. (*hum*) **le petit chien à sa ~** mummy's little doggy (*hum*).

mémoire[1] [memwaʀ] *nf* **(a)** (*Psych*) memory; *[ordinateur]* memory, store. **de ~** from memory; **de ~ d'homme** in living memory; **de ~ de Parisien, on n'avait jamais vu ça!** no one could remember such a thing happening in Paris before; **pour ~** (*gén*) as a matter of interest; (*Comm*) for the record; *V* **effort, rafraîchir, trou.**

(b) (*loc*) **avoir la ~ des noms** to have a good memory for names; **je n'ai pas la ~ des dates** I have no memory for dates, I can never remember dates; **si j'ai bonne ~** if I remember rightly, if my memory serves me right; **avoir la ~ courte** to have a short memory; **avoir une ~ d'éléphant** to have a memory like an elephant('s); **j'ai gardé la ~ de cette conversation** I remember *ou* recall this conversation, this conversation remains in my memory; **perdre la ~** to lose one's memory; **chercher un nom dans sa ~** to try to recall a name, rack one's brains to remember a name; **ça me revient en ~** it comes back to me; **il me l'a remis en ~** he reminded me of it, he brought it back to me; **son nom restera (gravé) dans notre ~** his name will remain (engraved) in our memories.

(c) (*réputation*) memory, good name; (*renommée*) memory, fame, renown. **soldat de glorieuse ~** soldier of glorious memory *ou* renown; **de sinistre ~** of evil memory, remembered with fear *ou* horror; (*hum*) fearful, ghastly; **à la ~ de** in memory of, to the memory of.

mémoire[2] [memwaʀ] *nm* (*requête*) memorandum; (*rapport*) report; (*exposé*) dissertation, paper; (*facture*) bill; (*Jur*) statement of case. (*souvenirs*) ~**s** memoirs; (*hum*) **tu écris tes ~s?** are you writing your life story? (*hum*).

mémorable [memɔʀabl(ə)] *adj* memorable, unforgettable.

mémorablement [memɔʀabləmɑ̃] *adv* memorably.

mémorandum [memɔʀɑ̃dɔm] *nm* (*Pol*) memorandum; (*Comm*) order sheet, memorandum; (*rare: carnet*) notebook, memo book.

mémorial, *pl* -aux [memɔʀjal, o] *nm* (*Archit*) memorial. (*Littérat*) **M~** Chronicles.

mémorialiste [memɔʀjalist(ə)] *nmf* memorialist, writer of memoirs.

mémorisation [memɔʀizɑsjɔ̃] *nf* memorization, memorizing.

mémoriser [memɔʀize] (1) *vt* to memorize, commit to memory.

menaçant, e [mənasɑ̃, ɑ̃t] *adj geste, paroles, foule, orage* threatening, menacing; *regard, ciel* lowering (*épith*), threatening, menacing.

menace [mənas] *nf* **(a)** (*intimidation*) threat. **il eut un geste de ~** he made a threatening gesture; **il eut des paroles de ~** he said some threatening words; **par/sous la ~** by/under threat; **~ en l'air** idle threat.

(b) (*danger*) imminent *ou* impending danger *ou* threat. **~ d'épidémie** impending epidemic, threat of an epidemic.

(c) (*Jur*) ~s intimidation, threats.

menacer [mənase] (3) *vt* **(a)** to threaten, menace (*gén pass*). **~ qn de mort/d'un revolver** to threaten sb with death/with a gun; **~ de faire qch** to threaten to do sth; **ses jours sont menacés** his life is threatened *ou* in danger; **la guerre menaçait le pays** the country was threatened *ou* menaced by *ou* with war.

(b) (*fig*) **orage qui menace d'éclater** storm which is about to burst *ou* which is threatening to break; **la pluie menace** it looks like rain, it is threatening rain; **le temps menace** the weather looks threatening; **chaise qui menace de se casser** chair which is showing signs of *ou* looks like breaking; **pluie/discours qui menace de durer** rain/speech which threatens to last some time; **la maison menace ruine** the house is in danger of falling down.

ménage [menaʒ] *nm* **(a)** (*entretien d'une maison*) housekeeping. **les soins du ~** the housework, the household duties; **s'occuper de son ~, tenir son ~** to look after one's house, keep house; **faire le ~** to do the housework; **faire le ~ à fond** to clean the house from top to bottom, do the housework thoroughly; **faire des ~s** to go out charring (*surtout Brit*); (*Can*) **le grand ~** the spring-cleaning; *V* **femme, monter**[2].

(b) (*couple, communauté familiale*) married couple, household. **~ sans enfant** childless couple; **~ à trois** eternal triangle, ménage à trois; **jeune/vieux ~** young/old couple; **ils font un gentil petit ~** they make a nice (young) couple; **cela ne va pas dans le ~** (*lit*) they don't get on* in that household, their marriage is a bit shaky *ou* isn't really working; (*fig hum*) they're having a spot of bother (*hum*); **être heureux/malheureux en ~** to have a happy/an unhappy married life; **se mettre en ~ avec qn** to set up house with sb, move in with sb*; **querelles/scènes de ~** domestic quarrels/rows; **il lui a fait une scène de ~** he had a row *ou* showdown* with her; (*fig*) **faire bon/mauvais ~ avec qn** to get on well/badly with sb, hit it off/not hit it off with sb*; **notre chat et la perruche font très bon ~** our cat and the budgie get on famously *ou* like a house on fire*.

ménagement [menaʒmɑ̃] *nm* **(a)** (*douceur*) care; (*attention*) attention. **traiter qn avec ~** to treat sb considerately *ou* tactfully; **il les a congédiés sans ~** he dismissed them without further ado *ou* with scant ceremony; **il lui annonça la nouvelle avec ~** he broke the news to her gently *ou* cautiously; **elle a besoin de ~ car elle est encore très faible** being still very weak she needs care and attention.

(b) (*égards*) ~s (respectful) consideration (*U*) *ou* attention.

ménager[1], **-ère** [menaʒe, ɛʀ] **1** *adj* **(a)** *ustensiles, appareils* household (*épith*), domestic (*épith*). **travaux ~s** housework, domestic chores; **école/collège d'enseignement ~** school/college of domestic science; *V* **art, eau, ordure.**

(b) (†: *économe*) **~ de** sparing of; **être ~ de son argent** to be thrifty with one's money.

2 ménagère *nf* **(a)** (*femme d'intérieur*) housewife.

(b) (*couverts*) canteen of cutlery.

ménager[2] [menaʒe] (3) *vt* **(a)** (*traiter avec prudence*) *personne puissante, adversaire* to handle carefully, treat tactfully *ou* considerately; *sentiments, susceptibilité* to spare, show consideration for. **elle est très sensible, il faut la ~** she is very sensitive, you must treat her gently; **~ les deux partis** to humour both parties; (*fig*) **~ la chèvre et le chou** to keep both parties sweet*; (*hypocritement*) to run with the hare and hunt with the hounds.

(b) (*utiliser avec économie ou modération*) to use carefully *ou* sparingly; *vêtement* to use carefully, treat with care; *argent, temps* to be sparing in the use of, use carefully, economize; (*modérer*) *expressions* to moderate, tone down. **c'est un homme qui ménage ses paroles** he is a man of few words; **~ ses forces** to conserve one's strength; **~ sa santé** to take great care of one's health, look after o.s.; **il faut *ou* vous devriez vous ~ un peu** you should take things easy, you should try not to overtax yourself; **il n'a pas ménagé ses efforts** he spared no effort; **nous n'avons rien ménagé pour vous plaire** we have spared no pains to please you; **il ne lui a pas ménagé les reproches** he didn't spare him his complaints.

(c) (*préparer*) *entretien, rencontre* to arrange, organize, bring about; (*amener*) *transition* to contrive, bring about. **~ l'avenir** to prepare for the future; **il nous ménage une surprise** he has a surprise in store for us; **se ~ une revanche** to plan one's revenge.

(d) (*disposer, pratiquer*) *porte, fenêtre* to put in; *chemin* to cut. **~ un espace entre** to make a space between; **~ une place pour** to make room for; (*fig*) **se ~ une porte de sortie** to leave o.s. a way out *ou* a loophole.

ménagère [menaʒɛʀ] *V* **ménager**[1].

ménagerie [menaʒʀi] *nf* (*lit*) menagerie; (**fig*) zoo.

mendiant, e [mɑ̃djɑ̃, ɑ̃t] *nm,f* beggar, mendicant (†, *littér*). (*Culin*) **les (quatre) ~s** mixed dried fruit(s) and nuts (*raisins, hazelnuts, figs, almonds*); *V* **frère, ordre**[1].

mendicité [mɑ̃disite] *nf* begging. **arrêter qn pour ~** to arrest sb for begging; **être réduit à la ~** to be reduced to beggary; **la ~ est interdite** it is forbidden to beg, no begging allowed.

mendier [mɑ̃dje] (7) **1** *vt argent, nourriture, caresse* to beg (for); (*Pol*) *voix* to solicit, canvass. **~ qch à qn** to beg sb for sth, beg sth from sb; **~ des compliments** to fish for compliments.

2 *vi* to beg (for alms).

mendigot, e* [mɑ̃digo, ɔt] *nm,f* (*péj*) beggar.

meneau, *pl* ~x [məno] *nm* (*horizontal*) transom; (*vertical*) mullion; *V* **fenêtre.**

menées [məne] *nfpl* (*machinations*) intrigues, manœuvres, machinations. **déjouer les ~ de qn** to foil sb's manœuvres *ou* little game*; **~ subversives** subversive activities.

mener [məne] (5) *vt* **(a)** (*conduire*) *personne* to take, lead; (*en voiture*) to drive, take (*à* to, *dans* into). **~ un enfant à l'école/chez le docteur** to take a child to school/to the doctor; **~ la voiture au garage** to take the car to the garage; **mène ton ami à sa chambre** show *ou* take *ou* see your friend to his room; **~ promener le chien** to take the dog for a walk.

(b) *[véhicule] personne* to take; *[route etc]* to lead, go, take; *[profession, action etc]* to lead, get* (*à* to, *dans* into). **c'est le chemin qui mène à la mer** this is the path (leading) to the sea; **le car vous mène à Chartres en 2 heures** the bus will take *ou* get you to Chartres in 2 hours; **cette route vous mène à Chartres** this road will take you to Chartres, you'll get to Chartres on this road; **où tout cela va-t-il nous ~?** where's all this going to get us?, where does all this lead us?; **cela ne (nous) mène à rien** this won't get us anywhere, this will get us nowhere; **ces études les mènent à de beaux postes** this training will get them good jobs; **le journalisme mène à tout** all roads are open to you in journalism; **de telles infractions pourraient le ~ loin** offences such as these could get him into trouble *ou* into deep water; **~ qn à faire ...** to lead sb to do ...; *V* **tout.**

(c) (*diriger, commander*) *personne, cortège* to lead; *pays, entreprise* to run; *navire* to command. **il sait ~ les hommes** he knows how to lead men, he is a good leader; **~ qn par le bout du nez** to lead sb by the nose; **il est mené par le bout du nez par sa femme** his wife has got him on a string; **~ qn à la baguette *ou* au doigt et à l'œil** to have sb under one's thumb, rule sb with an iron hand; **elle se laisse ~ par son frère** she lets herself be led *ou* (*péj*) bossed about* by her brother; (*fig*) **~ qn en bateau*** to take sb for a ride*, lead sb up the garden path*; **l'argent mène le monde** money rules the world; **~ le jeu *ou* la danse** to call the tune, say what goes*; **~ les débats** to chair the discussion.

(d) (*Sport, gén: être en tête*) to lead; (*emploi absolu*) to lead, be in the lead. **il mène par 3 jeux à 1** he is leading by 3 games to 1; **la France mène (l'Écosse par 2 buts à 1)** France is in the lead (by 2 goals to 1 against Scotland), France is leading (Scotland by 2 goals to 1).

(e) (*faire aller, diriger*) *vie* to lead, live; *négociations, lutte, conversation* to carry on; *enquête* to carry out, conduct. **~ les choses rondement** to manage things efficiently, make short work of things; **~ qch à bien *ou* à bonne fin *ou* à terme** to see sth through, carry sth through to a successful conclusion; (*fig*) **il mène bien sa barque** he manages his affairs efficiently; **il mène 2 affaires de front** he runs *ou* manages 2 businesses at once; **~ la vie dure à qn** to make life a misery *ou* hell* for sb, make sb's life a misery; **il n'en menait pas large** his heart was in his boots; **~ grand bruit *ou* tapage autour d'une affaire** to give an affair a lot of publicity, make a great hue and cry about an affair.

(f) (*Math*) ~ **une parallèle à une droite** to draw a line parallel to a straight line.

ménestrel [menɛstʀɛl] *nm* minstrel.

ménétrier† [menetʀije] *nm* (strolling) fiddler.

meneur, -euse [mənœʀ, øz] *nm,f* (*chef*) (ring)leader; (*agitateur*) agitator. ~ **d'hommes** born leader, popular leader; ~ **de jeu** *[spectacles, variétés]* compère; *[jeux-concours]* quizmaster.

menhir [meniʀ] *nm* menhir, standing stone.

méninge [menɛ̃ʒ] *nf* **(a)** (*) ~**s** brain; **se creuser les** ~**s** to rack one's brains; **tu ne t'es pas fatigué les** ~**s!** you didn't strain yourself!*, you didn't overtax your brain!

(b) (*Méd*) meninx. ~**s** meninges.

méningé, e [menɛ̃ʒe] *adj* meningeal.

méningite [menɛ̃ʒit] *nf* meningitis. **ce n'est pas lui qui attrapera une** ~*! he's not one to strain himself!* (*iro*), there's no fear of his getting brain fever!

ménisque [menisk(ə)] *nm* (*Anat, Opt, Phys*) meniscus; (*Bijouterie*) *crescent-shaped jewel.*

ménopause [menɔpoz] *nf* menopause.

menotte [mənɔt] *nf* **(a)** ~**s** handcuffs; **mettre** *ou* **passer les** ~**s à qn** to handcuff sb.

(b) (*langage enfantin*) little *ou* tiny hand, handy (*langage enfantin*).

mensonge [mɑ̃sɔ̃ʒ] *nm* **(a)** (*contre-vérité*) lie, fib*, falsehood (*frm*), untruth. **faire** *ou* **dire un** ~ to tell a lie; **pieux** ~ white lie; (*hum*) **c'est vrai, ce** ~? sure you're telling the truth?, now pull the other one!:; **tout ça, c'est des** ~**s*** it's all a pack of lies*.

(b) (*acte*) **le** ~ lying, untruthfulness; **je hais le** ~ I hate untruthfulness *ou* lies; **il vit dans le** ~ his whole life is a lie.

(c) (*littér: illusion*) illusion.

mensonger, -ère [mɑ̃sɔ̃ʒe, ɛʀ] *adj* (*faux*) *rapport, nouvelle* untrue, false; *promesse* deceitful, false; (*littér: trompeur*) *bonheur* illusory, delusive, deceptive.

mensongèrement [mɑ̃sɔ̃ʒɛʀmɑ̃] *adv* untruthfully, falsely, deceitfully.

menstruation [mɑ̃stʀyasjɔ̃] *nf* menstruation.

menstruel, -elle [mɑ̃stʀyɛl] *adj* menstrual.

menstrues [mɑ̃stʀy] *nfpl* menses.

mensualisation [mɑ̃sɥalizasjɔ̃] *nf* (changeover to a) monthly salary system. **effectuer la** ~ **des salaires** to put weekly-paid workers on monthly salaries.

mensualiser [mɑ̃sɥalize] (1) *vt salaires, employés* to pay on a monthly basis. **être mensualisé** *[salaire, employé]* to be paid monthly *ou* on a monthly basis; *[employé]* to be on a monthly salary; *[contribuable]* to pay income tax monthly, ≈ be on P.A.Y.E. (*Brit*).

mensualité [mɑ̃sɥalite] *nf* (*traite*) monthly payment *ou* instalment; (*salaire*) monthly salary.

mensuel, -elle [mɑ̃sɥɛl] **1** *adj* monthly. **2** *nm,f* employee paid by the month. **3** *nm* (*Presse*) monthly (magazine).

mensuellement [mɑ̃sɥɛlmɑ̃] *adv payer* monthly, every month. **être payé** ~ to be paid monthly *ou* every month.

mensuration [mɑ̃syʀasjɔ̃] *nf* (*rare: mesure, calcul*) mensuration. (*mesures*) ~**s** measurements.

mental, e, *mpl* **-aux** [mɑ̃tal, o] *adj maladie, âge, processus* mental; *V* **calcul, malade.**

mentalement [mɑ̃talmɑ̃] *adv* mentally.

mentalité [mɑ̃talite] *nf* mentality. (*iro*) **quelle** ~**!, jolie** ~**!** what an attitude of mind!, nice mind you've (*ou* he's *etc*) got!* (*iro*).

menterie [mɑ̃tʀi] *nf* (†: *mensonge*) untruth, lie.

menteur, -euse [mɑ̃tœʀ, øz] **1** *adj proverbe* fallacious, false; *rêve, espoir* delusive, illusory, false; *enfant* untruthful, lying. **il est très** ~ he is a great liar.

2 *nm,f* liar, fibber*.

menthe [mɑ̃t] *nf* **(a)** (*Bot*) mint. ~ **poivrée** peppermint; ~ **verte** spearmint, garden mint; **de** ~**, à la** ~ mint (*épith*); *V* **alcool, pastille, thé.**

(b) (*boisson*) peppermint cordial. **une** ~ **à l'eau** a glass of peppermint cordial; *V* **diabolo.**

menthol [mɛ̃tɔl] *nm* menthol.

mentholé [mɛ̃tɔle] *adj* mentholated, menthol (*épith*).

mention [mɑ̃sjɔ̃] *nf* **(a)** (*note brève*) mention. **faire** ~ **de** to mention, make mention of; **faire l'objet d'une** ~ to be mentioned.

(b) (*annotation*) note, comment. **le paquet est revenu avec la** ~ **'adresse inconnue'** the parcel was returned marked 'address unknown'; (*Admin*) **'rayer la** ~ **inutile'** 'delete as appropriate'.

(c) (*Scol: examen*) ~ **passable/assez bien/bien/très bien** ≈ grade D/C/B/A pass; (*Univ: maîtrise*) IIIrd class/lower IInd class/upper IInd class/Ist class Honours; (*doctorat*) ~ **très honorable** (with) distinction; (*Scol*) **être reçu avec** ~ to pass with flying colours *ou* with distinction.

mentionner [mɑ̃sjɔne] (1) *vt* to mention. **la personne mentionnée ci-dessus** the above-mentioned person.

mentir [mɑ̃tiʀ] (16) **1** *vi* **(a)** to lie (*à qn* to sb, *sur* about). **tu mens!** you're a liar!, you're lying!; ~ **effrontément** to lie boldly, be a barefaced liar; **je t'ai menti** I lied to you *ou* told you a lie; **sans** ~ quite honestly, honestly; **il ment comme il respire** *ou* **comme un arracheur de dents** he's a compulsive liar, he lies in *ou* through his teeth*; (*Prov*) **a beau** ~ **qui vient de loin** long ways long lies (*Prov*).

(b) faire ~**: ne me fais pas** ~**!** don't prove me wrong!; **faire** ~ **le proverbe** to give the lie to the proverb, disprove the proverb; *V* **bon**[1].

(c) (*littér*) ~ **à** (*manquer à*) to betray; (*démentir*) to belie; **il ment à sa réputation** he belies *ou* does not live up to his reputation; (†, *hum*) **vous en avez menti** you told an untruth.

2 se mentir *vpr*: **se** ~ **à soi-même** to fool o.s.; **il se ment à lui-même** he's not being honest with himself, he's fooling himself.

menton [mɑ̃tɔ̃] *nm* chin. ~ **en galoche** protruding *ou* jutting chin; ~ **fuyant** receding chin, weak chin; **double/triple** ~ double/treble chin.

mentonnière [mɑ̃tɔnjɛʀ] *nf [coiffure]* (chin) strap; (*Hist*) *[casque]* chin piece; (*Mus*) chin rest; (*Méd*) chin bandage.

mentor [mɛ̃tɔʀ] *nm* (*littér*) mentor.

menu[1] [məny] *nm* (*repas*) meal; (*carte*) menu; (*régime*) diet. **faites votre** ~ **à l'avance** plan your meal in advance; **quel est le** *ou* **qu'y a-t-il au** ~? what's on the menu?; **vous prenez le** ~ **(à prix fixe) ou la carte?** are you having the set menu or the (menu) à la carte?; ~ **du jour** today's menu; ~ **touristique** economy(-price) menu; ~ **gastronomique** gourmet's menu.

menu[2]**, e** [məny] **1** *adj* **(a)** (*fin*) *doigt, tige* slender; *taille, personne* slim, slight; *herbe* fine; *écriture, pas* small, tiny; *voix* thin. **en** ~**s morceaux** in tiny pieces.

(b) (*peu important*) *difficultés, incidents, préoccupations* minor, petty, trifling. **dire/raconter dans les** ~**s détails** to tell/relate in minute detail; ~**s frais** incidental *ou* minor expenses; (*lit, fig*) ~ **fretin** small fry; ~ **gibier** small game; ~**e monnaie** small *ou* loose change; ~ **peuple** humble folk; (*Hist*) **M**~**s Plaisirs** (royal) entertainment (*U*); **se réserver de l'argent pour ses** ~**s plaisirs** to keep some money by for (one's) amusements; ~**s propos** small talk (*U*).

(c) (*loc*) **par le** ~ in detail; **raconter qch par le** ~ to relate sth in great detail; **on fit par le** ~ **la liste des fournitures** they made a detailed list of the supplies.

2 *adv couper, hacher, piler* fine. **écrire** ~ to write small.

menuet [mənɥɛ] *nm* minuet.

menuiserie [mənɥizʀi] *nf* **(a)** (*métier*) joinery; (*Constr*) joinery, carpentry; (*d'amateur*) woodwork, carpentry. ~ **d'art** cabinet work.

(b) (*atelier*) joiner's workshop.

(c) (*ouvrage*) (piece of) woodwork (*U*) *ou* joinery (*U*) *ou* carpentry (*U*).

menuisier [mənɥizje] *nm [meubles]* joiner; *[bâtiment]* carpenter. ~ **d'art** cabinetmaker.

Méphistophélès [mefistɔfelɛs] *nm* Mephistopheles.

méphistophélique [mefistɔfelik] *adj* Mephistophelean.

méphitique [mefitik] *adj* noxious, noisome†, mephitic (*rare*).

méphitisme [mefitism(ə)] *nm* sulphurous (air) pollution.

méplat [mepla] *nm* (*Anat, Archit*) plane.

méprendre (se) [mepʀɑ̃dʀ(ə)] (58) *vpr* (*littér*) to make a mistake, be mistaken (*sur* about). **se** ~ **sur qn** to misjudge sb, be mistaken about sb; **se** ~ **sur qch** to make a mistake about *ou* misunderstand sth; **ils se ressemblent tellement que c'est à s'y** ~ *ou* **qu'on pourrait s'y** ~ they are so alike that you can't tell them apart *ou* that it's difficult to tell which is which.

mépris [mepʀi] *nm* **(a)** (*mésestime*) contempt, scorn. **avoir** *ou* **éprouver du** ~ **pour qn** to despise sb, feel contempt for sb; **sourire/regard de** ~ scornful *ou* contemptuous smile/look; **avec** ~ contemptuously, scornfully, with contempt, with scorn.

(b) (*indifférence*) ~ **de** contempt for, disregard for; **avoir le** ~ **des convenances/traditions** to have no regard for conventions/traditions; **au** ~ **du danger/des lois** regardless *ou* in defiance of danger/the law.

méprisable [mepʀizabl(ə)] *adj* contemptible, despicable.

méprisant, e [mepʀizɑ̃, ɑ̃t] *adj* contemptuous, scornful; (*hautain*) disdainful.

méprise [mepʀiz] *nf* (*erreur de sens*) mistake, error; (*malentendu*) misunderstanding. **par** ~ by mistake.

mépriser [mepʀize] (1) *vt personne* to scorn, despise, look down on; *danger, conseil, offre* to scorn, spurn; *vice, faiblesse* to scorn, despise. ~ **la morale** to scorn *ou* spurn convention.

mer [mɛʀ] **1** *nf* **(a)** (*océan, aussi fig*) sea. ~ **fermée** inland *ou* landlocked sea; ~ **de sable** sea of sand; **naviguer sur une** ~ **d'huile** to sail on a glassy sea *ou* on a sea as calm as a millpond; **vent/port** *etc* **de** ~ sea breeze/harbour *etc*; **gens de** ~ sailors, seafarers, seafaring men; *V* **bras, coup, mal** *etc.*

(b) (*marée*) tide. **la** ~ **est haute** *ou* **pleine/basse** the tide is high *ou* in/low *ou* out; **c'est la haute** *ou* **pleine/basse** ~ it is high/low tide.

(c) (*loc*) **en** ~ at sea; **les pêcheurs sont en** ~ **aujourd'hui** the fishermen are out today *ou* at sea today; **en haute** *ou* **pleine** ~ out at sea, on the open sea; **prendre la** ~ to put out to sea; **mettre (une embarcation) à la** ~ to bring *ou* get out a boat; **bateau qui tient bien la** ~ good seagoing boat; **aller/voyager par** ~ to go/travel by sea; (*fig*) **ce n'est pas la** ~ **à boire!** it's not asking the impossible!, there's nothing to it!

2: la mer Adriatique the Adriatic Sea; **la mer Baltique** the Baltic Sea; **la mer Caspienne** the Caspian Sea; **la mer Égée** the Aegean Sea; **la mer Morte** the Dead Sea; **la mer Noire** the Black Sea; **la mer du Nord** the North Sea; **la mer Rouge** the Red Sea; **la mer des Sargasses** the Sargasso Sea; **les mers du Sud** the South Seas; **la mer Tyrrhénienne** the Tyrrhenian Sea.

mercanti [mɛʀkɑ̃ti] *nm* (*péj*) profiteer, swindler, shark*; (*marchand oriental ou africain*) bazaar merchant.

mercantile [mɛʀkɑ̃til] *adj* mercenary, venal.

mercantilisme [mɛʀkɑ̃tilism(ə)] *nm* (*péj*) mercenary *ou* venal attitude; (*Écon, Hist*) mercantile system, mercantilism.

mercenaire [mɛʀsənɛʀ] **1** *adj* (*péj*) *attitude* mercenary; *soldat* hired. **2** *nm* (*Mil*) mercenary; (*fig péj: salarié*) hireling.

mercerie [mɛʀsəʀi] *nf* (*boutique*) haberdasher's shop (*Brit*), notions store (*US*); (*articles*) haberdashery (*Brit*), notions (*US*); (*profession*) haberdashery (trade) (*Brit*).

merceriser [mɛʀsəʀize] (1) *vt* to mercerize.

merci [mɛʀsi] **1** *excl* **(a)** (*pour remercier*) thank you. ~ **bien** thank you, many thanks; ~ **beaucoup** thank you very much, thanks a lot*; ~ **mille fois** thank you (ever) so much; ~ **de** *ou* **pour votre carte** thank you for your card; ~ **d'avoir répondu** thank you for replying; **sans même me dire** ~ without even thanking me, without even saying thank you; (*iro*) ~ **du compliment!** thanks for the compliment!; *V* **dieu.**

(b) (*pour refuser*) **Cognac? — (non,)** ~ Cognac? — no thank you; **y retourner? ~ (bien), pour me faire traiter comme un chien!** go back there? what, and be treated like a dog?, no thank you!

2 *nm* thank-you. **je n'ai pas eu un** ~ I didn't get *ou* hear a word of thanks; **nous vous devons/nous devons vous dire un grand ~ pour** we owe you/we must say a big thank-you for; **et encore un grand ~ pour votre cadeau** and once again thank you so much *ou* many thanks for your present; **mille ~s** (very) many thanks.

3 *nf* **(a)** (*pitié*) mercy. **crier/implorer** ~ to cry/beg for mercy; **sans** ~ *combat etc* merciless, ruthless.

(b) (*risque, éventualité, pouvoir*) **à la ~ de qn** at the mercy of sb, in sb's hands; **à la ~ d'une erreur** at the mercy of a mistake; **chaque fois que nous prenons la route nous sommes à la ~ d'un accident** every time we go on the road we expose ourselves *ou* lay ourselves open to accidents *ou* we run the risk of an accident; **exploitable à** ~ liable to be ruthlessly exploited, open to ruthless exploitation; *V* **taillable.**

mercier, -ière [mɛʀsje, jɛʀ] *nm,f* haberdasher (*Brit*).

mercredi [mɛʀkʀədi] *nm* Wednesday. **~ des Cendres** Ash Wednesday; *pour autres loc V* **samedi.**

mercure [mɛʀkyʀ] **1** *nm* **(a)** (*Chim*) mercury. **(b)** (*Myth*) **M~** Mercury.

2 *nf* (*Astron*) **M~** Mercury.

mercuriale[1] [mɛʀkyʀjal] *nf* (*littér*) reprimand, rebuke.

mercuriale[2] [mɛʀkyʀjal] *nf* (*Bot*) mercury.

mercuriale[3] [mɛʀkyʀjal] *nf* (*Comm*) market price list.

mercurochrome [mɛʀkyʀɔkʀom] *nm* mercurochrome.

merde [mɛʀd(ə)] **1** *nf* (∵) (*excrément*) shit∵; (*étron*) turd∵. **il y a une ~ (de chien) devant la porte** there's some dog('s) shit∵ *ou* a dog turd∵ in front of the door; (*fig*) **il ne se prend pas pour de la** *ou* **une** ~ he thinks the sun shines out of his arse!∵, he thinks he's one hell of a big nob:; (*fig*) **on est dans la** ~ we're in a bloody mess∵.

2 *excl* (:) (*impatience, contrariété*) hell!:, shit!∵; (*indignation, surprise*) bloody hell!∵. **~ alors!** hell's bells*!; **~ pour X!** to hell with X!:

merdeux, -euse∵ [mɛʀdø, øz] **1** *adj* shitty∵, filthy. **2** *nm,f* squirt:, twerp*.

merdier∵ [mɛʀdje] *nm* pigsty (*fig*). **être dans un beau** ~ to be in a fine bloody mess∵.

merdoyer∵ [mɛʀdwaje] (8) *vi* to be *ou* get in a hell of a mess:, be *ou* get all tied up.

mère [mɛʀ] **1** *nf* **(a)** (*génitrice*) mother. **elle est ~ de 4 enfants** she is a *ou* the mother of 4 (children); (*fig hum*) **tu es une ~ pour moi** you are like a mother to me; (*littér*) **la France, ~ des arts** France, mother of the arts; **frères par la** ~ half-brothers (on the mother's side); **devenir** ~ to become a mother; **rendre qn** ~ to get sb with child (†, *littér*); *V* **fille, madame, reine** *etc.*

(b) (*fig: femme*) (*péj*) **la ~ X*** old mother X, old Ma X (*péj*); **allons la petite ~, dépêchez-vous*!** come on missis, hurry up!*; (*affectueux: à une enfant, un animal*) **ma petite** ~ my little pet *ou* love; (*dial*) **bonjour, ~ Martin** good day to you, Mrs Martin.

(c) (*Rel*) mother. **(la) M~ Catherine** Mother Catherine; **oui, ma** ~ yes, Mother.

(d) (*Tech: moule*) mould.

(e) (*apposition: après n*) *cellule, compagnie* parent. (*Comm*) **maison** ~ parent company, head office; (*Ling*) **langue** ~ mother tongue *ou* language.

2: (*Rel*) **Mère abbesse** mother abbess; (*Admin*) **mère célibataire** unmarried mother; **mère de famille** mother, housewife; **mère-grand†** *nf* grandmama†; **mère patrie** motherland; **mère poule*** motherly mum* (*Brit*) *ou* mom* (*US*); **c'est une vraie mère poule*, elle est très mère poule*** she's a real mother hen, she's a very motherly type; (*Rel*) **Mère Supérieure** Mother Superior; (*Chim*) **mère de vinaigre** mother of vinegar.

méridien, -enne [meʀidjɛ̃, ɛn] **1** *adj* (*Sci*) meridian; (*littér*) meridian (*littér*), midday (*épith*).

2 *nm* (*Astron, Géog*) meridian. **~ d'origine** prime meridian.

3 méridienne *nf* (*Astron*) meridian line; (*Géodésie*) *line of triangulation points.*

méridional, e, *mpl* **-aux** [meʀidjɔnal, o] **1** *adj* (*du Sud*) southern; (*du Sud de la France*) Southern (French).

2 *nm,f*: **M~(e)** (*du Sud*) Southerner; (*du Sud de la France*) Southern Frenchman *ou* Frenchwoman, Southerner.

meringue [məʀɛ̃g] *nf* meringue. **un dessert avec de la ~/des petites ~s** a sweet with meringue/little meringues.

meringuer [məʀɛ̃ge] (1) *vt* (*gén ptp*) to coat *ou* cover with meringue.

mérinos [meʀinos] *nm* merino; *V* **pisser.**

merise [məʀiz] *nf* wild cherry.

merisier [məʀizje] *nm* (*arbre*) wild cherry (tree); (*bois*) cherry.

méritant, e [meʀitɑ̃, ɑ̃t] *adj* deserving.

mérite [meʀit] *nm* **(a)** (*vertu intrinsèque*) merit; (*respect accordé*) credit. **le ~ de cet homme est grand** that man has great merit, he is a man of great merit; **il n'en a que plus de** ~ he deserves all the more credit, it's all the more to his credit; **il n'y a aucun ~ à cela** there's no merit in that, one deserves no credit for that; **tout le ~ lui revient** all the credit is due to him, he deserves all the credit; **il a le grand ~ d'avoir réussi** it's greatly to his credit that *ou* his great merit is that he succeeded; **il a au moins le ~ d'être franc** there's one thing to his credit *ou* in his favour that at least he's frank.

(b) (*valeur*) merit, worth; (*qualité*) quality. **de grand** ~ of great worth *ou* merit; **ce n'est pas sans** ~ it's not without merit; **si nombreux que soient ses ~s** however many qualities he may have; **son intervention n'a eu d'autre ~ que de faire suspendre la séance** the only good point about his intervention was that the sitting was adjourned.

(c) (*décoration*) **l'ordre national du M~** the national order of merit (*French decoration*).

(d) (*Rel*) **~(s) du Christ** merits of Christ.

mériter [meʀite] (1) *vt* **(a)** *louange, châtiment* to deserve, merit. **tu mériterais qu'on t'en fasse autant** you deserve (to get) the same treatment; **cette action mérite des louanges/une punition** this action deserves *ou* merits *ou* warrants praise/punishment; **~ l'estime de qn** to be worthy of *ou* deserve *ou* merit sb's esteem; **tu n'as que ce que tu mérites** you've got (just) what you deserved, it serves you right*; **il mérite la prison/la corde** he deserves to go to gaol/to be hanged; **repos/blâme bien mérité** well-deserved rest/reprimand.

(b) (*valoir*) to deserve, be worth; (*exiger*) to call for, require. **le fait mérite d'être noté** the fact is worth noting, the fact is worthy of note; **ceci mérite réflexion** *ou* **qu'on y réfléchisse** (*exiger*) this calls for *ou* requires careful thought; (*valoir*) this deserves careful thought; **ça lui a mérité le respect de tous** this earned him everyone's respect.

(c) il a bien mérité de la patrie (*frm*) he deserves well of his country;(*hum*) he deserves a (putty) medal for that.

méritocratie [meʀitɔkʀasi] *nf* meritocracy.

méritoire [meʀitwaʀ] *adj* meritorious, praiseworthy, commendable.

merlan [mɛʀlɑ̃] *nm* **(a)** (*Zool*) whiting. **(b)** (†*) barber, hairdresser.

merle [mɛʀl(ə)] *nm* **(a)** (*Orn*) blackbird. (*fig*) **chercher le ~ blanc** to seek (for) the impossible; **elle cherche toujours le ~ blanc** she's still looking for her wonder man *ou* dream man.

(b) (*péj*) **vilain** *ou* (*iro*) **beau** ~ nasty customer.

(c) (*Can Orn*) (American) robin.

merlin [mɛʀlɛ̃] *nm* **(a)** *[bûcheron]* axe; (*Boucherie*) cleaver. **(b)** (*Naut*) marline.

merlu [mɛʀly] *nm* hake.

merluche [mɛʀlyʃ] *nf* **(a)** (*Culin*) dried cod, stockfish. **(b)** = **merlu.**

mérou [meʀu] *nm* grouper.

mérovingien, -ienne [meʀɔvɛ̃ʒjɛ̃, jɛn] **1** *adj* Merovingian. **2** *nm,f*: **M~(ne)** Merovingian.

merveille [mɛʀvɛj] *nf* **(a)** marvel, wonder. **les ~s de la technique moderne** the wonders *ou* marvels of modern technology; **cette montre est une ~ de précision** this watch is a marvel of precision; **les ~s de la nature** the wonders of nature; **cette machine est une (petite)** ~ this machine is a (little) marvel.

(b) (*loc*) **à** ~ perfectly, wonderfully, marvellously; **cela te va à** ~ it suits you perfectly *ou* to perfection; **se porter à** ~ to be in excellent health, be in the best of health; **ça s'est passé à** ~ it went off like a dream* *ou* without a single hitch; **ça tombe à** ~ this comes at an ideal moment *ou* just at the right time; **faire** ~ *ou* **des ~s** to work wonders; **c'est ~ que vous soyez vivant** it's a wonder *ou* a marvel that you are alive; **on en dit ~** *ou* **des ~s** it's praised to the skies *ou* said to be marvellous; *V* **huitième, sept.**

merveilleusement [mɛʀvɛjøzmɑ̃] *adv* marvellously, wonderfully.

merveilleux, -euse [mɛʀvɛjø, øz] **1** *adj* (*magnifique*) marvellous, wonderful; (*après n: surnaturel*) magic.

2 *nm* **(a) le** ~ the supernatural; (*Art, Littérat*) the fantastic element.

(b) (*Hist*) coxcomb††, fop†.

3 merveilleuse *nf* (*Hist*) fine lady, belle.

mes [me] *adj poss V* **mon.**

mésalliance [mezaljɑ̃s] *nf* misalliance, marriage beneath one's station†. **faire une** ~ to marry beneath o.s. *ou* one's station†.

mésallier (se) [mezalje] (7) *vpr* to marry beneath o.s. *ou* one's station†.

mésange [mezɑ̃ʒ] *nf* tit(mouse). **~ bleue** blue tit; **~ charbonnière** coal-tit.

mésaventure [mezavɑ̃tyʀ] *nf* misadventure, misfortune.

mescaline [mɛskalin] *nf* mescaline.

mesdames [medam] *nfpl V* **madame.**

mesdemoiselles [medmwazɛl] *nfpl V* **mademoiselle.**

mésentente [mezɑ̃tɑ̃t] *nf* dissension, disagreement. **la ~ règne dans leur famille** there is constant disagreement in their family, they are always at loggerheads (with each other) in that family.

mésestimation [mezɛstimasjɔ̃] *nf* (*littér*) *[chose]* underestimation.

mésestime [mezɛstim] *nf* (*littér*) *[personne]* low regard, low esteem. **tenir qn en** ~ to have little regard for sb.

mésestimer [mezɛstime] (1) *vt* (*littér: sous-estimer*) *difficulté, adversaire* to underestimate, underrate; *opinion* to set little store by, have little regard for; *personne* to have little regard for.

mésintelligence [mezɛ̃teliʒɑ̃s] *nf* disagreement (*entre* between), dissension, discord.

mesmérisme [mɛsmeʀism(ə)] *nm* mesmerism.

Mésopotamie [mezɔpɔtami] *nf* Mesopotamia.

mésopotamien, -ienne [mezɔpɔtamjɛ̃, jɛn] **1** *adj* Mesopotamian. **2** *nm,f*: **M~(ne)** Mesopotamian.

mesquin, e [mɛskɛ̃, in] *adj personne* mean, stingy; *procédé* mean, petty. **c'est un esprit** ~ he is a mean-minded *ou* small-minded *ou* petty person; **le repas faisait un peu** ~ the meal was a bit stingy.

mesquinement [mɛskinmɑ̃] *adv agir* meanly, pettily; *distribuer* stingily.

mesquinerie [mɛskinʀi] *nf [personne, procédé]* (*étroitesse*) meanness, pettiness; (*avarice*) stinginess, meanness; (*procédé*) mean *ou* petty trick.

mess [mɛs] *nm* mess (*Mil*).
message [mesaʒ] *nm* (*gén, Jur, Littérat, Tech*) message. ~ **chiffré** coded message, message in code *ou* cipher; ~ **publicitaire** advertisement; ~ **téléphoné** telegram (*dictated by telephone*).
messager, -ère [mesaʒe, ɛʀ] *nm,f* messenger. (*littér*) ~ **de bonheur/du printemps** harbinger of glad tidings/of spring (*littér*, †); ~ **de malheur** bearer of bad tidings.
messageries [mesaʒʀi] *nfpl* parcels service; (*Hist*) mail-coach service. ~ **aériennes/maritimes** air freight/shipping company; ~ **de presse** press distributing service.
messe [mɛs] **1** *nf* (*Mus, Rel*) mass. **aller à la** ~ to go to mass; **célébrer la** ~ to celebrate mass; *V* **entendre, livre**[1] *etc.*
2: (*Rel*) **messe basse** low mass; (*fig péj*) **messes basses** muttering, muttered conversation *ou* talk; **finissez vos messes basses** stop muttering *ou* whispering together; **messe de minuit** midnight mass; **messe des morts** mass for the dead; (*Spiritisme*) **messe noire** black mass.
messeigneurs [mesɛɲœʀ] *nmpl V* **monseigneur.**
messeoir [meswaʀ] (26) *vi* (††, *littér*) (*moralement*) to be unseemly (*à* for) (*littér*), ill befit; (*pour l'allure*) to ill become (*littér*), be unbecoming (*à* to) (*littér*). **avec un air qui ne lui messied pas** with a look that does not ill become him *ou* that is not unbecoming to him; **il vous messiérait de le faire** it would be unseemly for you to do it.
messianique [mesjanik] *adj* messianic.
messianisme [mesjanism(ə)] *nm* (*Rel*) messianism. (*fig*) **la tendance au** ~ **de certains révolutionnaires** the messianic tendencies of certain revolutionaries.
messidor [mesidɔʀ] *nm* Messidor (*tenth month in the French Republican Calendar*).
messie [mesi] *nm* messiah. **le M**~ the Messiah.
messieurs [mesjø] *nmpl V* **monsieur.**
messin, e [mesɛ̃, in] **1** *adj* of *ou* from Metz. **2** *nm,f*: **M~(e)** inhabitant *ou* native of Metz.
messire†† [mesiʀ] *nm* (*noblesse*) my lord; (*bourgeoisie*) Master. **oui** ~ yes my lord, yes sir; ~ **Jean** my lord *ou* master John.
mestrance [mɛstʀɑ̃s] *nf* = **maistrance.**
mestre [mɛstʀ(ə)] *nm* (*Naut*) mainmast.
mesurable [məzyʀabl(ə)] *adj grandeur* measurable, mensurable (*rare*); *quantité* measurable. **c'est difficilement** ~ it is hard to measure.
mesurage [məzyʀaʒ] *nm* measuring, measurement.
mesure [m(ə)zyʀ] *nf* **(a)** (*évaluation*) measurement (*U*); (*étalon*) measure; (*dimension*) measurement. ~ **de capacité** liquid measure, dry measure; ~ **de superficie/volume** square/cubic measure; ~ **de longueur** measure of length; **appareil de** ~ gauge; **système de** ~ system of measurement; **prendre les ~s de qch** to take the measurements of sth; *V* **poids.**
(b) (*fig: valeur, dimension de l'homme*) **la** ~ **de ses forces/sentiments** the measure of his strength/feelings; **monde/ville à la** ~ **de l'homme** world/town on a human scale; **il est à ma** ~ *[travail]* it is worthy of me; *[adversaire]* he's a match for me; **prendre la (juste)** ~ **de qn** to size sb up (exactly), get the measure of sb; **donner (toute) sa** ~ to show one's worth, show what one is capable of *ou* made of.
(c) (*récipient, quantité*) measure. ~ **à grains/à lait** corn/milk measure; ~ **graduée** measuring jug; ~ **d'un demi-litre** half-litre measure; **donne-lui 2 ~s d'avoine** give him 2 measures of oats; **faire bonne** ~ to give good measure; (*fig*) **pour faire bonne** ~ for good measure.
(d) (*quantité souhaitable*) **la juste** *ou* **bonne** ~ the happy medium; **la** ~ **est comble** that's the limit; **dépasser** *ou* **excéder** *ou* **passer la** ~ to overstep the mark, go too far; **boire outre** ~ to drink immoderately *ou* to excess.
(e) (*modération*) moderation. **le sens de la** ~ a sense of moderation; **il n'a pas le sens de la** ~ he has no sense of moderation, he knows no measure; **avec** ~ with *ou* in moderation; **il a beaucoup de** ~ he's very moderate; **orgueil sans** ~ immoderate *ou* measureless pride, pride beyond measure; **se dépenser sans** ~ (*se dévouer*) to give one's all; (*se fatiguer*) to overtax one's strength *ou* o.s.
(f) (*disposition, moyen*) measure, step. **prendre des ~s d'urgence** to take emergency action *ou* measures; **des ~s d'ordre social** social measures; **des ~s de rétorsion** reprisals; **j'ai pris mes ~s pour qu'il vienne** I have made arrangements for him to come, I have taken steps to ensure that he comes; **par** ~ **de restriction** as a restrictive measure; *V* **contre, demi**[2].
(g) (*Mus*) (*cadence*) time, tempo; (*division*) bar; (*Poésie*) metre. **en** ~ in time *ou* tempo; ~ **composée/simple/à deux temps** compound/simple/duple time; **être/ne pas être en** ~ to be in/out of time; **jouer quelques ~s** to play a few bars; **2 ~s pour rien** 2 bars for nothing; *V* **battre.**
(h) (*Habillement*) measure, measurement. **prendre les ~s de qn** to take sb's measurements; **est-ce que ce costume est bien à ma ~?** *ou* **à mes ~s?** is this suit my size?, will this suit fit me?; **acheter** *ou* **s'habiller sur** ~ to have one's clothes made to measure; **costume fait à la** ~ *ou* **sur** ~ made-to-measure suit; **tailleur à la** ~ bespoke tail r; (*fig*) **j'ai un emploi du temps/un patron sur** ~ my schedule/boss suits me down to the ground.
(i) (*loc*) **dans la** ~ **de ses forces** *ou* **capacités** as far as *ou* insofar as one is able, to the best of one's ability; **dans la** ~ **de ses moyens** as far as one's circumstances permit, as far as one is able; **dans la** ~ **du possible** as far as possible; **dans la** ~ **où** inasmuch as, insofar as; **dans une certaine** ~ to some *ou* a certain extent; **dans une large** ~ to a large *ou* great extent; **être en** ~ **de faire qch** to be in a position to do sth; **(au fur et) à** ~ **que** as; **il les pliait et me les passait (au fur et) à** ~ he folded them and handed them to me one by one *ou* as he went along; *V* **commun.**
mesuré, e [məzyʀe] (*ptp de* **mesurer**) *adj ton* steady; *pas* measured; *personne* moderate. **il est** ~ **dans ses paroles/ses actions** he is moderate *ou* temperate in his language/actions.
mesurément [məzyʀemɑ̃] *adv* with *ou* in moderation.
mesurer [məzyʀe] (1) **1** *vt* **(a)** *chose* to measure; *personne* to take the measurements of, measure (up); (*par le calcul*) *distance, pression, volume* to calculate; *longueur à couper* to measure off *ou* out. **il mesura 3 cl d'acide** he measured out 3 cl of acid; **il me mesura 3 mètres de tissu** he measured me off *ou* out 3 metres of fabric.
(b) (*évaluer, juger*) *risque, efficacité* to assess, weigh up; *valeur d'une personne* to assess, rate. **vous n'avez pas mesuré la portée de vos actes!** you did not weigh up *ou* consider the consequences of your acts!; **on n'a pas encore mesuré l'étendue des dégâts** the extent of the damage has not yet been assessed; ~ **les efforts aux** *ou* **d'après les résultats (obtenus)** to gauge the effort expended by *ou* according to the results (obtained); ~ **ses forces avec qn** to pit oneself against sb, measure one's strength with sb; ~ **qn du regard** to look sb up and down; **se** ~ **des yeux** to weigh *ou* size each other up.
(c) (*avoir pour mesure*) to measure. **cette pièce mesure 3 mètres sur 10** this room measures 3 metres by 10; **il mesure 1 mètre 80** *[personne]* he's 1 metre 80 tall; *[objet]* it's 1 metre 80 long *ou* high, it measures 1 metre 80.
(d) (*avec parcimonie*) to limit. **elle leur mesure la nourriture** she rations them on food, she limits their food; **le temps nous est mesuré** our time is limited, we have only a limited amount of time.
(e) (*avec modération*) ~ **ses paroles** (*modérer*) to moderate one's language; (*ménager*) to weigh one's words.
(f) (*proportionner*) to match (*à, sur* to), gear (*à, sur* to). ~ **le travail aux forces de qn** to match *ou* gear the work to sb's strength; ~ **le châtiment à l'offense** to make the punishment fit the crime; *V* **brebis.**
2 se mesurer *vpr*: **se** ~ **avec** *personne* to have a confrontation with, pit o.s. against; *difficulté* to confront, tackle.
mesureur [məzyʀœʀ] *nm* (*personne*) measurer; (*appareil*) gauge, measure.
mésuser [mezyze] (1) **mésuser de** *vt indir* (*littér*) to misuse; ~ **de son pouvoir** to abuse one's power.
métabolique [metabɔlik] *adj* metabolic.
métabolisme [metabɔlism(ə)] *nm* metabolism.
métacarpe [metakaʀp(ə)] *nm* metacarpus.
métacarpien, -ienne [metakaʀpjɛ̃, jɛn] **1** *adj* metacarpal. **2** *nmpl*: ~s metacarpals, metacarpal bones.
métairie [meteʀi] *nf* smallholding, farm (*held on a métayage agreement*); *V* **métayage.**
métal, *pl* -aux [metal, o] *nm* **(a)** (*gén, Chim, Fin, Min*) metal. **(b)** (*littér*) metal (*littér*), stuff.
métalangue [metalɑ̃g] *nf*, **métalangage** [metalɑ̃gaʒ] *nm* metalanguage.
métallifère [metalifɛʀ] *adj* metalliferous, metal-bearing.
métallique [metalik] *adj* **(a)** (*gén, Chim*) metallic; *voix, couleur* metallic; *objet* (*en métal*) metal (*épith*); (*qui ressemble au métal*) metallic. **bruit** *ou* **son** ~ *[clefs]* jangle, clank; *[épée]* clash. **(b)** (*Fin*) *V* **encaisse, monnaie.**
métallisation [metalizasjɔ̃] *nf [métal]* plating; *[miroir]* silvering.
métallisé, e [metalize] (*ptp de* **métalliser**) *adj bleu, gris* metallic; *peinture, couleur* metallic, with a metallic finish; *miroir* silvered.
métalliser [metalize] (1) *vt métal* to plate; *miroir* to silver.
métallo* [metalo] *nm* (*abrév de* **métallurgiste**) steel- *ou* metal-worker.
métallographie [metalɔgʀafi] *nf* metallography.
métallographique [metalɔgʀafik] *adj* metallographic.
métalloïde [metalɔid] *nm* metalloid.
métalloplastique [metaloplastik] *adj* copper asbestos (*épith*).
métallurgie [metalyʀʒi] *nf* (*industrie*) metallurgical industry; (*technique, travail*) metallurgy.
métallurgique [metalyʀʒik] *adj* metallurgic.
métallurgiste [metalyʀʒist(ə)] *nm* **(a) (ouvrier)** ~ steel *ou* metal-worker. **(b) (industriel)** ~ metallurgist.
métamorphique [metamɔʀfik] *adj* metamorphic, metamorphous.
métamorphiser [metamɔʀfize] (1) *vt* (*Géol*) to metamorphose.
métamorphisme [metamɔʀfism(ə)] *nm* metamorphism.
métamorphosable [metamɔʀfozabl(ə)] *adj* that can be transformed (*en* into).
métamorphose [metamɔʀfoz] *nf* (*Bio, Myth*) metamorphosis; (*fig*) transformation, metamorphosis.
métamorphoser [metamɔʀfoze] (1) **1** *vt* (*Myth, fig*) to transform, metamorphose (*gén pass*) (*en* into). **son succès l'a métamorphosé** his success has transformed him *ou* made a new man of him.
2 se métamorphoser *vpr* (*Bio*) to be metamorphosed; (*Myth, fig*) to be transformed (*en* into).
métaphore [metafɔʀ] *nf* metaphor.
métaphorique [metafɔʀik] *adj expression, emploi, valeur* metaphoric(al), figurative; *style* metaphoric(al).
métaphoriquement [metafɔʀikmɑ̃] *adv* metaphorically, figuratively.
métaphysicien, -ienne [metafizisjɛ̃, jɛn] **1** *adj* metaphysical. **2** *nm,f* metaphysician, metaphysicist.
métaphysique [metafizik] **1** *adj* (*Philos*) metaphysical; *amour* spiritual; (*péj*) *argument* abstruse, obscure. **2** *nf* (*Philos*) metaphysics (*sg*).
métaphysiquement [metafizikmɑ̃] *adv* metaphysically.
métapsychique [metapsiʃik] *adj* psychic.

métastase [metastɑz] *nf* metastasis.
métatarse [metataʀs(ə)] *nm* metatarsus.
métatarsien, -ienne [metataʀsjɛ̃, jɛn] **1** *adj* metatarsal. **2** *nmpl*: ~s metatarsals, metatarsal bones.
métathèse [metatɛz] *nf* (*Ling*) metathesis.
métayage [metɛjaʒ] *nm* métayage system (*farmer pays rent in kind*), sharecropping (*US*).
métayer [meteje] *nm* (tenant) farmer (*paying rent in kind*), sharecropper (tenant) (*US*).
métayère [metɛjɛʀ] *nf* (*épouse*) farmer's *ou* sharecropper's (*US*) wife; (*paysanne*) (woman) sharecropper.
métazoaire [metazɔɛʀ] *nm* metazoan. ~s Metazoa.
méteil [metɛj] *nm mixed crop of wheat and rye.*
métempsycose [metɑ̃psikoz] *nf* metempsychosis.
météo [meteo] **1** *adj abrév de* **météorologique**. **2** *nf* **(a)** (*Sci, services*) = **météorologie**. **(b)** (*bulletin*) (weather) forecast.
météore [meteɔʀ] *nm* (*lit*) meteor. **passer** *ou* **briller comme un** ~ to have a brief but brilliant career.
météorique [meteɔʀik] *adj* (*Astron, fig*) meteoric.
météorite [meteɔʀit] *nm ou f* meteorite.
météorologie [meteɔʀɔlɔʒi] *nf* (*Sci*) meteorology; (*services*) Meteorological Office, Met Office*.
météorologique [meteɔʀɔlɔʒik] *adj phénomène, observation* meteorological; *carte, prévisions, station* weather (*épith*); *V* **bulletin**.
météorologiste [meteɔʀɔlɔʒist(ə)] *nmf*, **météorologue** [meteɔʀɔlɔg] *nmf* meteorologist.
métèque [metɛk] *nmf* **(a)** (*péj*) wog: (*Brit péj*), wop: (*péj*). **(b)** (*Hist*) metic.
méthane [metan] *nm* methane.
méthanier [metanje] *nm* liquefied gas carrier *ou* tanker.
méthode [metɔd] *nf* **(a)** method. **de nouvelles ~s d'enseignement du français** new methods of *ou* for teaching French, new teaching methods for French; **avoir une bonne ~ de travail** to have a good way *ou* method of working; **avoir sa ~ pour faire qch** to have one's own way of *ou* method for *ou* of doing sth.
(b) (*U*) **il a beaucoup de ~** he's very methodical, he's a man of method; **il n'a aucune ~** he's not in the least methodical, he has no (idea of) method; **faire qch avec/sans ~** to do sth methodically *ou* in a methodical way/unmethodically.
(c) (*livre*) manual, tutor. **~ de piano** piano manual *ou* tutor; **~ de latin** latin primer.
méthodique [metɔdik] *adj* methodical.
méthodiquement [metɔdikmɑ̃] *adv* methodically.
méthodisme [metɔdism(ə)] *nm* Methodism.
méthodiste [metɔdist(ə)] *adj, nmf* Methodist.
méthodologie [metɔdɔlɔʒi] *nf* methodology.
méthyle [metil] *nm* methyl.
méthylène [metilɛn] *nm* (*Comm*) methyl alcohol; (*Chim*) methylene; *V* **bleu**.
méthylique [metilik] *adj* methyl.
méticuleusement [metikyløzmɑ̃] *adv* meticulously.
méticuleux, -euse [metikylø, øz] *adj soin, propreté* meticulous, scrupulous; *personne* meticulous.
méticulosité [metikylozite] *nf* (*rare*) meticulousness.
métier [metje] *nm* **(a)** (*gén: travail*) job; (*Admin*) occupation; (*manuel*) trade; (*artisanal*) craft; (*intellectuel*) profession. **les ~s manuels** (the) manual occupations; **donner un ~ à son fils** to have one's son learn a trade *ou* craft *ou* profession; **enseigner son ~ à son fils** to teach one's son one's trade; **il a fait tous les ~s** he has tried his hand at everything, he has been everything; **après tout ils font leur ~** they are (only) doing their job after all; (*fig*) **le ~ de femme est ardu** a woman's lot is an exacting one; **prendre le ~ des armes** to become a soldier, join the army; **apprendre son ~ de roi** to learn one's job as king; *V* **corps, gâcher** *etc.*
(b) (*technique, expérience*) (acquired) skill, (acquired) technique, experience. **avoir du ~** to have practical experience; **manquer de ~** to be lacking in expertise *ou* in practical technique; **avoir 2 ans de ~** to have been 2 years in the trade *ou* profession.
(c) (*loc*) **homme de ~** expert, professional, specialist; **il est plombier de son ~** he is a plumber by *ou* to trade; **il est du ~** he is in the trade *ou* profession *ou* business; **il connaît son ~** he knows his job (all right)*; **je connais mon ~!, tu ne vas pas m'apprendre mon ~!** I know what I'm doing!, you're not going to teach me my job!; **ce n'est pas mon ~*** it's not my job *ou* line; **quel ~!*** what a job!; (*hum*) **c'est rien, c'est le ~ qui rentre*** it's just learning the hard way.
(d) (*Tech: machine*) loom. **~ à tisser** (weaving) loom; **~ à filer** spinning frame; **~ (à broder)** embroidery frame; (*fig, littér*) **remettre qch sur le ~** to set about recasting sth.
métis, -isse [metis] **1** *adj personne* half-caste, half-breed; (*rare*) *animal* crossbreed, mongrel; (*rare*) *plante* hybrid; *tissu, toile* made of cotton and linen.
2 *nm,f* (*personne*) half-caste, half-breed; (*rare: animal, plante*) mongrel.
3 *nm* (*Tex*) **(toile/drap de) ~** fabric/sheet made of cotton and linen mixture.
métissage [metisaʒ] *nm [gens]* interbreeding; *[animaux]* crossbreeding, crossing; *[plantes]* crossing.
métisser [metise] (1) *vt* to crossbreed, cross.
métonymie [metɔnimi] *nf* metonymy.
métonymique [metɔnimik] *adj* metonymical.
métrage [metʀaʒ] *nm* **(a)** (*Couture*) length, yardage. **grand ~** long length; **petit ~** short length; **quel ~ vous faut-il, Madame?** what yardage do you need, madam?
(b) (*Mesure*) measurement, measuring (in metres). **procéder au ~ de qch** to measure sth out.
(c) (*Ciné*) footage, length; *V* **court[1], long, moyen.**
mètre [mɛtʀ(ə)] *nm* **(a)** (*Math*) metre. **~ carré/cube** square/cubic metre.
(b) (*instrument*) (metre) rule. **~ étalon** standard metre; **~ pliant** folding rule; **~ à ruban** tape measure, measuring tape.
(c) (*Sport*) **un 100 ~s** a 100-metre race; **le 100/400 ~s** the 100/400 metres, the 100-/400-metre race.
(d) (*Littérat*) metre.
métré [metʀe] *nm* (*mesure*) measurement (in metres); (*devis*) estimate of cost (*per metre*).
métrer [metʀe] (6) *vt* (*Tech*) to measure (in metres); *[vérificateur]* to survey.
métreur, -euse [metʀœʀ, øz] *nm,f*: **~ (vérificateur)** quantity surveyor.
métrique [metʀik] **1** *adj* (*Littérat*) metrical, metric; (*Math*) *système, tonne* metric. **géométrie ~** metrical geometry. **2** *nf* (*Littérat*) metrics; (*Math*) metric theory.
métro [metʀo] *nm* underground, subway (*surtout US*). **~ aérien** elevated railway; **le ~ de Paris** the Paris metro *ou* underground; **le ~ de Londres** the London underground *ou* tube.
métrologie [metʀɔlɔʒi] *nf* (*Sci*) metrology; (*traité*) metrological treatise, treatise on metrology.
métrologique [metʀɔlɔʒik] *adj* metrological.
métrologiste [metʀɔlɔʒist(ə)] *nmf* metrologist.
métronome [metʀɔnɔm] *nm* metronome.
métropole [metʀɔpɔl] *nf* **(a)** (*ville*) metropolis; (*état*) home country. **quand est prévu votre retour en ~?** when do you go back home? *ou* back to the home country? **(b)** (*Rel*) metropolis.
métropolitain, e [metʀɔpɔlitɛ̃, ɛn] **1** *adj* (*Admin, Rel*) metropolitan. **la France ~e** metropolitan France; **troupes ~es** home troops. **2** *nm* **(a)** (*Rel*) metropolitan. **(b)** (†: *métro*) underground, subway (*surtout US*).
mets [mɛ] *nm* dish (*Culin*).
mettable [mɛtabl(ə)] *adj* (*gén nég*) wearable, decent. **ça n'est pas ~** this is not fit to wear *ou* to be worn; **je n'ai rien de ~** I've got nothing (decent) to wear *ou* nothing that's wearable; **ce costume est encore ~** you can still wear that suit, that suit is still decent *ou* wearable.
metteur [mɛtœʀ] *nm* (*Bijouterie*) **~ en œuvre** mounter; (*Rad*) **~ en ondes** producer; (*Typ*) **~ en pages** compositor (responsible for upmaking); (*Tech*) **~ au point** adjuster; **~ en scène** (*Théât*) producer; (*Ciné*) director.
mettre [mɛtʀ(ə)] (56) **1** *vt* **(a)** (*placer*) to put (*dans* in, into, *sur* on); (*fig: classer*) to rank,rate. **~ une assiette/une carte sur une autre** to put one *ou* a plate/card on top of another; **ce vase se met sur la cheminée** this vase goes on the mantelpiece; **elle lui mit la main sur l'épaule** she put *ou* laid her hand on his shoulder; **elle met son travail avant sa famille** she puts her work before her family; **je mets Molière parmi les plus grands écrivains** I rank *ou* rate Molière among the greatest writers; **~ qch debout** to stand sth up; **~ qn sur son séant/sur ses pieds** to sit/stand sb up; **~ qch à *ou* par terre** to put sth down (on the ground); **~ qch à l'ombre/au frais** to put sth in the shade/in a cool place; **~ qch à plat** to lay sth down (flat); **~ qch droit** to put *ou* set sth straight *ou* to rights, straighten sth (out *ou* up); **~ qn au *ou* dans le train** to put sb on the train; **mettez-moi à la gare*, s'il vous plaît** take me to *ou* drop me at the station please; **elle a mis la tête à la fenêtre** she put *ou* stuck* her head out of the window; **mettez les mains en l'air** put your hands up, put your hands in the air; **mets le chat dehors *ou* à la porte** put the cat out.
(b) (*ajouter*) **~ du sucre dans son thé** to put sugar in one's tea; **~ une pièce à un drap** to put a patch in *ou* on a sheet, patch a sheet; **~ une idée dans la tête de qn** to put an idea into sb's head; **se ~ une idée dans la tête** to get an idea into one's head; **ne mets pas d'encre sur la nappe** don't get ink on the tablecloth; **il s'est mis de l'encre sur les doigts** he's got ink on his fingers; **il s'en est mis partout*** he's covered in it, he's got it all over him.
(c) (*placer dans une situation*) **~ un enfant à l'école** to send a child to school; **~ qn au régime** to put sb on a diet; **se ~ au régime** to go on a diet; **~ qn dans la nécessité *ou* l'obligation de faire** to oblige *ou* compel sb to do; **~ au désespoir** to throw into despair; **cela m'a mis dans une situation difficile** that has put me in *ou* got me into a difficult position; **on l'a mis* à la manutention/aux réclamations** he was put in the handling/in the complaints department; **~ qn au pas** to bring sb into line, make sb toe the line; *V* **aise, contact, présence** *etc.*
(d) (*revêtir*) *vêtements, lunettes* to put on. **(se) ~ une robe/du maquillage** to put on a dress/some make-up; **depuis qu'il fait chaud je ne mets plus mon cardigan** since it has got warmer I've stopped wearing *ou* I've left off my cardigan; **elle n'a plus rien à se ~** she's got nothing (left) to wear; **mets-lui son chapeau et on sort** put his hat on (for him) and we'll go.
(e) (*consacrer*) **j'ai mis 2 heures à le faire** I took 2 hours to do it *ou* 2 hours over it, I spent 2 hours on *ou* over it *ou* 2 hours doing it; **le train met 3 heures** it takes 3 hours by train, the train takes 3 hours; **~ toute son énergie à faire** to put all one's effort into doing; **~ tous ses espoirs dans** to pin all one's hopes on; **~ beaucoup de soin à faire** to take great care in doing, take great pains to do; **~ de l'ardeur à faire qch** to do sth eagerly *ou* with great eagerness; **il y a mis le temps!** he's taken his time (about it)!, he's taken an age *ou* long enough!; *V* **cœur.**
(f) (*faire fonctionner*) **~ la radio/le chauffage** to put *ou* switch *ou* turn the radio/heating on; **~ les nouvelles** to put *ou* turn the news on; **~ le réveil (à 7 heures)** to set the alarm (for 7 o'clock); **~ le verrou** to bolt up, bolt the door; **mets France Inter/la 2e chaîne** put on France Inter/the 2nd channel; **~ une machine en route** to start up a machine.
(g) (*installer*) **~ l'eau/l'électricité/des placards** to put in *ou* install water/electricity/cupboards.
(h) (*avec à + infin*) **~ qch à cuire/à chauffer** to put sth on to cook/heat; **~ du linge à sécher** (*à l'intérieur*) to put *ou* hang

washing up to dry; (*à l'extérieur*) to put *ou* hang washing out to dry.

(i) (*écrire*) ~ **en anglais/au pluriel** to put into English/the plural; ~ **des vers en musique** to set verse to music; ~ **sa signature (à)** to put *ou* append one's signature (to); ~ **un mot/une carte à qn*** to drop a line/card to sb*; **mets 100 F, ils ne vérifieront pas** put (down) 100 francs, they'll never check up*; **mettez bien clairement que** put (down) quite clearly that; **il met qu'il est bien arrivé** he says in his letter *ou* writes that he arrived safely.

(j) (*dépenser*) ~ **de l'argent sur un cheval** to lay money (down) *ou* put money on a horse; ~ **de l'argent dans une affaire** to put money into a business; **combien avez-vous mis pour cette table?** how much did you give for that table?; ~ **de l'argent sur son compte** to put money into one's account; **je suis prêt à ~ 500 F** I'm willing to give *ou* I don't mind giving 500 francs; **si on veut du beau il faut y ~ le prix** if you want something nice you have to pay the price *ou* pay for it; *V* **caisse.**

(k) (*lancer*) ~ **la balle dans le filet** to put the ball into the net; ~ **une balle dans la peau de qn‡** to put a bullet through sb *ou* in sb's hide*; ~ **son poing dans la figure de qn** to punch sb in the face, give sb a punch in the face.

(l) (*supposer*) **mettons que je me suis** *ou* **sois trompé** let's say *ou* (just) suppose *ou* assume I've got it wrong; **nous arriverons vers 10 heures, mettons, et après?** say we arrive about 10 o'clock then what?, we'll arrive about 10 o'clock, say, then what?

(m) (‡*loc*) ~ **les bouts, les** ~ to clear off‡, beat it‡; (*en vitesse*) to scarper‡ (*Brit*); **qu'est-ce qu'ils nous ont mis!** what a licking* *ou* hiding* they gave us!; **qu'est-ce qu'ils se sont mis!** they didn't half lay into each other!‡ *ou* have a go at each other!*

2 se mettre *vpr* **(a)** (*se placer*) *[personne]* to put o.s.; *[objet]* to go. **mets-toi là** (*debout*) (go and) stand there; (*assis*) (go and) sit there; **se ~ au piano/dans un fauteuil** to sit down at the piano/in an armchair; **se ~ au chaud/à l'ombre** to come *ou* go into the warm/into the shade; (*fig*) **elle ne savait plus où se ~** she didn't know where to hide herself *ou* what to do with herself; **il s'est mis dans une situation délicate** he's put himself in *ou* got himself into an awkward situation; **se ~ autour (de)** to gather round; **ces verres se mettent dans le placard** these glasses go in the cupboard; **l'infection s'y est mise** it has become infected; **les vers s'y sont mis** the maggots have got at it; **il y a un bout de métal qui s'est mis dans l'engrenage** a piece of metal has got caught in the works; **se ~ au vert** to go for a rest in the country; *V* **poil, rang, table** *etc.*

(b) *[temps]* **se ~ au froid/au chaud/à la pluie** to turn cold/warm/wet; **on dirait que ça se met à la pluie** it looks like rain, it looks as though it's turning to rain.

(c) (*s'habiller*) **se ~ en robe/en short** to put on a dress/a pair of shorts; **se ~ en bras de chemise** to take off one's jacket; **se ~ nu** to strip (off *ou* naked), take (all) one's clothes off; **elle s'était mise très simplement** she was dressed very simply.

(d) se ~ à: se ~ à rire/à manger to start laughing/eating, start *ou* begin to laugh/eat; **se ~ au travail** to set to work, get down to work, set about one's work; **se ~ à une traduction** to start *ou* set about (doing) a translation; **se ~ à traduire** to start to translate, start translating, set about translating; **il est temps de s'y ~** it's (high) time we got down to it *ou* got on with it; **se ~ à boire** to take to drink *ou* the bottle*; **se ~ à la peinture** *ou* **à peindre** to take up painting, take to painting; **se ~ au latin** to take up Latin; **il s'est bien mis à l'anglais** he's really taken to English; **voilà qu'il se met à pleuvoir!** and now it's coming on to *ou* beginning to rain!

(e) (*se grouper*) **ils se sont mis à plusieurs/2 pour pousser la voiture** several of them/the 2 of them joined forces to push the car; **se ~ avec qn** (*faire équipe*) to team up with sb; (*prendre parti*) to side with sb; (*: *en ménage*) to shack up‡ with sb; **se ~ d'un parti/d'une société** to join a party/a society; *V* **partie**[2].

(f) (*loc*) **on s'en est mis jusque-là** *ou* **plein la lampe*** we had a real blow-out‡; *V* **dent.**

meublant, e [mœblɑ̃, ɑ̃t] *adj papier, étoffe* decorative, effective. **ce papier est très ~** this paper finishes off the room nicely, this paper really makes* the room; *V* **meuble.**

meuble [mœbl(ə)] **1** *nm* **(a)** (*objet*) piece of furniture. **(les) ~s** (the) furniture; **se cogner à** *ou* **dans un ~** to bump into a *ou* some piece of furniture; **~ de rangement** cupboard, storage unit; **faire la liste des ~s** to make a list *ou* an inventory of the furniture, list each item of furniture; **nous sommes dans nos ~s** the furniture is our own, we own the furniture.

(b) (*U: ameublement*) **le ~** furniture; **le ~ de jardin** garden furniture.

(c) (*Jur*) movable. **~s meublants** furniture, movables.

(d) (*Hér*) charge.

2 *adj* **(a)** *terre, sol* loose, friable; *roche* soft, crumbly.

(b) (*Jur*) **biens ~s** movables, personal estate, personalty.

meublé, e [mœble] (*ptp de* **meubler**) **1** *adj* furnished. **non-~** unfurnished.

2 *nm* (*pièce*) furnished room; (*appartement*) furnished flat. **être** *ou* **habiter en ~** to be *ou* live in furnished accommodation *ou* rooms.

meubler [mœble] (1) **1** *vt pièce, appartement* to furnish (*de* with); *pensée, mémoire, loisirs* to fill (*de* with); *dissertation* to fill out, pad out (*de* with). **~ la conversation** to keep the conversation going; **une table et une chaise meublaient la pièce** the room was furnished with a table and chair; **étoffe/papier qui meuble bien** decorative *ou* effective material/paper.

2 se meubler *vpr* to buy *ou* get (some) furniture, furnish one's home. **ils se sont meublés dans ce magasin/pour pas cher** they got *ou* bought their furniture from this shop/for a pretty reasonable price.

meuglement [møgləmɑ̃] *nm* mooing (*U*), lowing (*U*).

meugler [møgle] (1) *vi* to moo, low.

meule[1] [møl] *nf* (*à moudre*) millstone; (*à polir*) buff wheel. **~ (à aiguiser)** grindstone; **~ courante** *ou* **traînante** upper (mill)-stone; (*Culin*) **~ (de gruyère)** round of gruyère.

meule[2] [møl] *nf* (*Agr*) stack, rick. **~ de foin** haystack, hayrick; **~ de paille** stack of straw; **mettre en ~s** to stack, rick.

meuler [møle] (1) *vt* (*Tech*) to grind down.

meulière [møljɛʀ] *nf*: **(pierre) ~** millstone, buhrstone.

meunerie [mønʀi] *nf* (*industrie*) flour trade; (*métier*) milling. **opérations de ~** milling operations.

meunier, -ière [mønje, jɛʀ] **1** *adj* milling. **2** *nm* miller. **3 meunière** *nf* miller's wife. **sole/truite ~ière** sole/trout meunière.

meurt-de-faim [mœʀdəfɛ̃] *nmf inv* pauper.

meurtre [mœʀtʀ(ə)] *nm* murder. **au ~!** murder!; *V* **incitation.**

meurtrier, -ière [mœʀtʀije, ijɛʀ] **1** *adj intention, fureur* murderous; *arme* deadly, lethal, murderous; *combat* bloody, deadly; *épidémie* fatal; (†) *personne* murderous. **cette route est ~ière** this road is lethal *ou* a deathtrap.

2 *nm* murderer.

3 meurtrière *nf* **(a)** murderess. **(b)** (*Archit*) loophole.

meurtrir [mœʀtʀiʀ] (2) *vt* **(a)** (*lit*) *chair, fruit* to bruise. **être tout meurtri** to be covered in bruises, be black and blue all over. **(b)** (*fig littér*) *personne, âme* to wound, bruise (*littér*).

meurtrissure [mœʀtʀisyʀ] *nf* **(a)** (*lit*) *[chair, fruit]* bruise. **(b)** (*fig littér*) *[âme]* scar, bruise (*littér*). **les ~s laissées par la vie/le chagrin** the scars *ou* bruises (*littér*) left by life/sorrow.

Meuse [møz] *nf*: **la ~** the Meuse, the Maas.

meute [møt] *nf* (*Chasse, fig*) pack.

mévente [mevɑ̃t] *nf* **(a)** slump. **une période de ~** a period of poor sales; **à cause de la ~** because of the slump in sales. **(b)** sale *ou* selling at a loss.

mexicain, e [mɛksikɛ̃, ɛn] **1** *adj* Mexican. **2** *nm,f*: **M~(e)** Mexican.

Mexico [mɛksiko] *n* Mexico City.

Mexique [mɛksik] *nm* Mexico.

mezzanine [mɛdzanin] *nf* (*Archit*) (*étage*) mezzanine (floor); (*fenêtre*) mezzanine window; (*Théât*) mezzanine.

mezzo [mɛdzo] **1** *nm* mezzo (voice). **2** *nf* mezzo.

mezzo-soprano, *pl* mezzo-sopranos [mɛdzosɔpʀano] **1** *nm* mezzo-soprano (voice). **2** *nf* mezzo-soprano.

mezzo-tinto [medzotinto] *nm inv* mezzotint.

mi [mi] *nm* (*Mus*) E; (*en chantant la gamme*) mi.

mi- [mi] **1** *préf* half, mid-. **la mi-janvier** *etc* the middle of January *etc*, mid-January *etc*; **pièce mi-salle à manger mi-salon** room which is half dining-room half lounge, lounge-diner*; **mi-riant mi-pleurant** half-laughing half-crying, halfway between laughing and crying.

2: mi-bas *nm inv* knee *ou* long socks; **la mi-carême** *the third Thursday in Lent*; **à mi-chemin** halfway, midway; **mi-clos, e** *adj* half-closed; **à mi-combat** halfway through the match; **à mi-corps** up to *ou* down to the waist; **portrait à mi-corps** half-length portrait; **à mi-côte** halfway up *ou* down the hill; **à mi-course** halfway through the race, at the halfway mark; **à mi-cuisses: des bottes qui lui venaient à mi-cuisses** boots that came up to his thighs *ou* over his knees; **ils avaient de l'eau (jusqu')à mi-cuisses** they were thigh-deep in water, they were up to their thighs in water; **à mi-distance** halfway (along), midway; **mi-figue mi-raisin** *adj inv sourire* wry; *remarque* half-humorous, wry; **on leur fit un accueil mi-figue mi-raisin** they received a mixed reception; **mi-fil, mi-coton** 50% linen 50% cotton, half-linen half-cotton; **mi-fin** *adj* medium; **à mi-hauteur** halfway up *ou* down; **à mi-jambes** (up *ou* down) to the knees; **mi-long** *bas* knee-length; *manteau* calf-length; *manche* elbow-length; (*Boxe*) **mi-lourd** *adj* light heavyweight; (*Boxe*) **mi-moyen** *adj* welterweight; **à mi-pente = à mi-côte; mi-souriant** with a half-smile, half-smiling; **mi-temps** *V* **mi-temps; à mi-vitesse** at half speed; **à mi-voix** in a low *ou* hushed voice, in an undertone.

miaou [mjau] *nm* miaow. **faire ~** to miaow.

miasmatique [mjasmatik] *adj* (*littér*) miasmic, miasmatic.

miasme [mjasm(ə)] *nm* (*gén pl*) miasma. **~s** putrid fumes, miasmas.

miaulement [mjolmɑ̃] *nm* (*V* **miauler**) mewing; caterwauling.

miauler [mjole] (1) *vi* to mew; (*fortement*) to caterwaul.

mica [mika] *nm* (*roche*) mica; (*vitre*) Muscovy glass.

micaschiste [mikaʃist(ə)] *nm* mica schist.

miche [miʃ] *nf* round loaf, cob loaf. (‡) **~s** (*fesses*) bum‡ (*Brit*), butt‡ (*US*); (*seins*) boobs‡.

Michel [miʃɛl] *nm* Michael.

Michel-Ange [mikɛlɑ̃ʒ] *nm* Michelangelo.

Michèle [miʃɛl] *nf* Michel(l)e.

micheline [miʃlin] *nf* railcar.

Michelle [miʃɛl] *nf* = **Michèle.**

micmac* [mikmak] *nm* (*péj*) (*intrigue*) (little) game* (*péj*), funny business* (*péj*); (*complications*) fuss*, carry-on‡ (*péj*). **je devine leur petit ~** I can guess their little game* *ou* what they're playing at*; **tu parles d'un ~!** what a carry-on!‡ (*Brit*) *ou* fuss!* *ou* mix-up!

micro [mikʀo] *nm* microphone, mike*. (*Rad, TV*) **dites-le au ~** *ou* **devant le ~** say it in front of the mike*.

micro... [mikʀo] *préf* micro .... **~balance** *nf* microbalance; **~climat** *nm* microclimate; **~film** *nm* microfilm; **~photographie** *nf* (*procédé*) photomicrography; (*pellicule*) photomicrograph.

microbe [mikʀɔb] *nm* **(a)** germ, microbe (*T*). **(b)** (*: *enfant*) tich‡; (*péj: nabot*) little runt‡ (*péj*).

microbicide [mikʀɔbisid] **1** *adj* germ-killing. **2** *nm* germ-killer, microbicide (*T*).

microbien, -ienne [mikʀɔbjɛ̃, jɛn] *adj culture* microbial, microbic. **maladie ~ne** bacterial disease.
microcéphale [mikʀɔsefal] *adj, nmf* microcephalic.
microcoque [mikʀɔkɔk] *nm* micrococcus.
microcosme [mikʀɔkɔsm(ə)] *nm* microcosm.
micrographie [mikʀɔgʀafi] *nf* micrography.
micrographique [mikʀɔgʀafik] *adj* micrographic.
micron [mikʀɔ̃] *nm* micron.
microphone [mikʀɔfɔn] *nm* microphone.
microscope [mikʀɔskɔp] *nm* microscope. **examiner au ~** (*lit*) to study under *ou* through a microscope; (*fig*) to study in microscopic detail, subject to a microscopic examination; **~ électronique** electron microscope.
microscopique [mikʀɔskɔpik] *adj* microscopic.
microsillon [mikʀɔsijɔ̃] *nm* (*sillon*) microgroove. **(disque) ~** long-playing record, L.P.
miction [miksjɔ̃] *nf* micturition.
midi [midi] *nm* **(a)** (*heure*) midday, 12 (o'clock), noon. **~ dix** 10 past 12; **de ~ à 2 heures** from 12 *ou* (12) noon to 2; **entre ~ et 2 heures** between 12 *ou* (12) noon and 2; **hier à ~** yesterday at 12 o'clock *ou* at noon *ou* at midday; **pour le ravoir, c'est ~ (sonné)*** there isn't a hope in hell‡ of getting it back, as for getting it back not a hope* *ou* you've had it*; *V* **chercher, coup.**

(b) (*période du déjeuner*) lunchtime, lunch hour; (*période de la plus grande chaleur*) midday, middle of the day. **à/pendant ~** at/during lunchtime, at/during the lunch hour; **demain ~** tomorrow lunchtime; **tous les ~s** every lunchtime *ou* lunch hour; **que faire ce ~?** what shall we do at lunchtime? *ou* midday?, what shall we do this lunch hour?; **le repas de ~** the midday meal, lunch; **qu'est-ce que tu as eu à ~?** what did you have for lunch?; **à ~ on va au café Duval** we're going to the Café Duval for lunch (today); **ça s'est passé en plein ~** it happened right in the middle of the day; **en plein ~ on étouffe de chaleur** at midday *ou* in the middle of the day it's stiflingly hot; *V* **démon.**

(c) (*Géog: sud*) south. **exposé au** *ou* **en plein ~** facing south; **le M~** (*de la France*) the South of France, the Midi; *V* **accent.**
midinette [midinɛt] *nf* (*gén*) office girl, shopgirl; (†: *vendeuse*) shopgirl (*esp in the dress industry*); (†: *ouvrière*) dressmaker's apprentice. (*péj*) **elle a des goûts de ~** she has the tastes of a sixteen-year-old office girl.
mie[1] [mi] *nf* soft part of the bread, crumb (of the loaf); (*Culin*) bread with crusts removed; *V* **pain.**
mie[2] [mi] *nf* (††, *littér: bien-aimée*) lady-love†, beloved (*littér*).
mie[3]†† [mi] *adv* not. **ne le croyez ~** believe it not††.
miel [mjɛl] **1** *nm* honey. **bonbon/boisson au ~** honey sweet/drink; *[personne]* **être tout ~** to be syrupy; **~ rosat** rose honey; *V* **gâteau, lune.**

2 *excl* (*euph**) sugar!*
miellé, e [mjele] *adj* (*littér*) honeyed.
mielleusement [mjɛløzmɑ̃] *adv* (*péj*) unctuously.
mielleux, -euse [mjɛlø, øz] *adj* **(a)** (*péj*) *personne* unctuous, smooth-faced, smooth-tongued; *paroles* honeyed, smooth; *ton* honeyed, sugary; *sourire* sugary, sickly sweet. **(b)** *saveur* sickly sweet.
mien, mienne [mjɛ̃, mjɛn] **1** *pron poss*: **le ~, la mienne, les ~s, les miennes** mine, my own; **ce sac n'est pas le ~** this bag is not mine, this is not MY bag; **vos fils/filles sont sages comparé(e)s aux ~s/miennes** your sons/daughters are well-behaved compared to mine *ou* my own.

2 *nm* **(a)** (*U*) **il n'y a pas à distinguer le ~ du tien** what's mine is yours; *pour autres exemples V* **sien.**

(b) les ~s my family, my (own) folks*.

3 *adj poss* (*littér*) **un ~ cousin** a cousin of mine; **je fais miennes vos observations** I agree wholeheartedly (with you); *V* **sien.**
miette [mjɛt] *nf [pain, gâteau]* crumb. **en ~s** *verre* in bits *ou* pieces; *gâteau* in crumbs *ou* pieces; (*fig*) *bonheur* in pieces *ou* shreds; (*fig*) **les ~s de sa fortune** the (tattered) remnants of his fortune; **je n'en prendrai qu'une ~** I'll just have a tiny bit *ou* a sliver; **il n'en a pas laissé une ~** (*repas*) he didn't leave a scrap; (*fortune*) he didn't leave a ha'penny; **mettre** *ou* **réduire en ~s** to break *ou* smash* to bits *ou* to smithereens; **il ne s'en fait pas une ~** † he doesn't care a jot; **il ne perdait pas une ~ de la conversation/du spectacle** he didn't miss a scrap of the conversation/the show.
mieux [mjø] (*comp, superl de* **bien**) **1** *adv* **(a)** better. **aller** *ou* **se porter ~** to be better; **il ne s'est jamais ~ porté** he's never been in such fine form, he's never been *ou* felt better in his life; **plus il s'entraîne ~ il joue** the more he practises the better he plays; **elle joue ~ que lui** she plays better than he does; **c'est (un peu/beaucoup) ~ expliqué** it's (slightly/much) better explained; **il n'écrit pas ~ qu'il ne parle** he writes no better than he speaks; **s'attendre à ~** to expect better; **espérer ~** to hope for better (things); **il peut faire ~** he can do *ou* is capable of better; *V* **reculer, tant, valoir** *etc.*

(b) le ~, la ~, les ~ (the) best; (*de deux*) (the) better; **c'est à Paris que les rues sont le ~ éclairées** it is Paris that has the best street lighting, it is in Paris that the streets are (the) best lit; **en rentrant je choisis les rues les ~ éclairées** when I come home I choose the better *ou* best lit streets; **c'est ici qu'il dort le ~** he sleeps best here, this is where he sleeps best; **tout va le ~ du monde** everything's going beautifully; **un lycée des ~ conçus/aménagés** one of the best planned/best equipped schools; **un dîner des ~ réussis** a most *ou* highly successful dinner; **j'ai fait le ~** *ou* **du ~ que j'ai pu** I did my best *ou* the best I could; **des deux, elle est la ~ habillée** of the two, she is the better dressed.

(c) (*loc*) **~ que jamais** better than ever; (*Prov*) **~ vaut tard que jamais** better late than never (*Prov*); (*Prov*) **~ vaut prévenir que guérir** prevention is better than cure (*Prov*); **il va de ~ en ~** he's getting better and better, he goes from strength to strength; (*iro*) **de ~ en ~! maintenant il s'est mis à boire** that's great *ou* terrific (*iro*), now he has even taken to the bottle*; **il nous a écrit, ~ il est venu nous voir** he wrote to us, and better still he came to see us; **à qui ~ ~: ils criaient à qui ~ ~** they vied with each other in shouting, each tried to outdo the other in shouting; **c'est on ne peut ~** it's (just) perfect.

2 *adj inv* **(a)** (*plus satisfaisant*) better. **le ~, la ~, les ~** (*de plusieurs*) (the) best; (*de deux*) (the) better; **c'est la ~ de nos secrétaires*** (*de toutes*) she is the best of our secretaries, she's our best secretary; (*de deux*) she's the better of our secretaries; **il est ~ qu'à son arrivée** he's improved since he (first) came, he's better than when he (first) came *ou* arrived; **c'est beaucoup ~ ainsi** it's (much) better this way; **le ~ serait de** the best (thing *ou* plan) would be to; **c'est ce qu'il pourrait faire de ~** it's the best thing he could do.

(b) (*en meilleure santé*) better; (*plus à l'aise*) better, more comfortable. **le ~, la ~, les ~** (the) best, (the) most comfortable; **être ~/le ~ du monde** to be better/in perfect health *ou* excellent form; **je le trouve ~ aujourd'hui** I think he is looking better *ou* he seems better today; **ils seraient ~ à la campagne qu'à la ville** they would be better (off) in the country than in (the) town; **c'est à l'ombre qu'elle sera le ~** she'll be best *ou* most comfortable in the shade; *V* **sentir.**

(c) (*plus beau*) better-looking, more attractive. **le ~, la ~, les ~** (*de plusieurs*) (the) best looking, (the) most attractive; (*de deux*) (the) better looking, (the) more attractive; **elle est ~ les cheveux longs** she looks better with her hair long *ou* with long hair, long hair suits her better; **c'est avec les cheveux courts qu'elle est le ~** she looks best with her hair short *ou* with short hair, short hair suits her best; **il est ~ que son frère** he's better looking than his brother.

(d) (*loc*) **au ~** (*gén*) at best; (*pour le mieux*) for the best; **en mettant les choses au ~** at (the very) best; **faites pour le ~** *ou* **au ~** do what you think best *ou* whatever is best; (*Fin*) **acheter/vendre au ~** to buy/sell at the best price; **être le ~ du monde** *ou* **au ~ avec qn** to be on the best of terms with sb; **c'est ce qui se fait de ~** it's the best there is *ou* one can get; **tu n'as rien de ~ à faire que (de) traîner dans les rues?** haven't you got anything better to do than hang around the streets?; **partez tout de suite, c'est le ~** it's best (that) you leave immediately, the best thing would be for you to leave immediately; **c'est son frère, en ~** he's (just) like his brother only better looking; **ce n'est pas mal, mais il y a ~** it's not bad, but I've seen better; **qui ~ est** even better, better still; **au ~ de sa forme** in peak condition; **au ~ de nos intérêts** in our best interests.

3 *nm* **(a)** best. (*Prov*) **le ~ est l'ennemi du bien** (it's better to) let well alone; (*loc*) **faire de son ~** to do one's best *ou* the best one can; **aider qn de son ~** to do one's best to help sb, help sb the best one can *ou* to the best of one's ability; *V* **changer, faute.**

(b) (*amélioration, progrès*) improvement. **il y a un ~** *ou* **du ~** there's (been) some improvement.

4: mieux-être *nm* greater welfare; (*matériel*) improved standard of living; **mieux-vivre** *nm* improved standard of living.
mièvre [mjɛvʀ(ə)] *adj roman, genre* precious, sickly sentimental; *tableau* pretty-pretty; *sourire* mawkish; *charme* vapid. **elle est un peu ~** she's rather precious *ou* affected.
mièvrerie [mjɛvʀəʀi] *nf* **(a)** (*U: V* **mièvre**) preciousness, sickly sentimentality; pretty-prettiness; mawkishness; vapidity; affectedness.

(b) (*œuvre d'art*) insipid creation; (*comportement*) childish *ou* silly behaviour (*U*); (*propos*) insipid *ou* sentimental talk (*U*).
mignard, e [miɲaʀ, aʀd(ə)] *adj style* mannered, precious; *décor* pretty-pretty, over-ornate; *musique* pretty-pretty, over-delicate; *manières* dainty, simpering (*péj*).
mignardise [miɲaʀdiz] *nf [tableau, poème, style]* preciousness; *[décor]* ornateness; *[manières]* daintiness (*U*), affectation (*péj*).
mignon, -onne [miɲɔ̃, ɔn] **1** *adj* (*joli*) *enfant, objet* sweet, cute*; *bras, pied, geste* dainty; *femme* sweet, pretty; (*gentil, aimable*) nice, sweet. **donne-le-moi, tu seras ~ne*** give it to me there's a dear* *ou* love* (*Brit*), be a dear* and give it to me; **c'est ~ chez vous** you've got a nice little place; *V* **péché.**

2 *nm,f* (little) darling, cutie*. **mon ~, ma ~ne** sweetheart, pet*, lovie* (*Brit*).

3 *nm* (††: *favori*) minion; *V* **filet.**
mignonnement† [miɲɔnmɑ̃] *adv* prettily.
migraine [migʀɛn] *nf* (*gén*) headache; (*Méd*) migraine, sick headache. **j'ai la ~** I've got a bad headache, my head aches.
migrant, -ante [migʀɑ̃, ɑ̃t] *adj, nm,f* migrant.
migrateur, -trice [migʀatœʀ, tʀis] **1** *adj* migratory.

2 *nm* migrant, migratory bird.
migration [migʀɑsjɔ̃] *nf* (*gén*) migration; (*Rel*) transmigration. **oiseau en ~** migrating bird.
migratoire [migʀatwaʀ] *adj* migratory.
mijaurée [miʒɔʀe] *nf* pretentious *ou* affected woman *ou* girl. **faire la ~** to give oneself airs (and graces); **regarde-moi cette ~!** just look at her with her airs and graces!; **petite ~!** little madam!
mijoter [miʒɔte] (1) **1** *vt* **(a)** (*Culin: mitonner*) *plat, soupe* to simmer; (*préparer avec soin*) to cook *ou* prepare lovingly. **un plat mijoté** a dish which has been slow-cooked *ou* simmered; **(faire) ~ un plat** to simmer a dish, allow a dish to simmer; **elle lui mijote de bons petits plats** she lovingly *ou* fondly cooks *ou* prepares him tempting meals.

(b) (**fig: tramer*) to plot, scheme, cook up*. **~ un complot** to hatch a plot; **il mijote un mauvais coup** he's cooking up* *ou* plotting some mischief; **qu'est-ce qu'il peut bien ~?** what's he up to?*, what's he cooking up?*; **il se mijote quelque chose** something's brewing *ou* cooking*.

(c) laisser qn ~ dans son jus* to leave sb stewing* *ou* to stew*.

2 *vi [plat, soupe]* to simmer; *[complot]* to be brewing.

mil¹ [mil] *nm V* **mille¹**.

mil² [mij] *nm* = **millet.**

milady [miledi] *nf (rare: dame anglaise de qualité)* **une ~** a (titled English) lady; **oui ~** yes my lady.

Milan [milɑ̃] *n* Milan.

milan [milɑ̃] *nm (Orn)* kite.

milanais, e [milanɛ, ɛz] **1** *adj* Milanese. (*Culin*) **escalope** *etc* **(à la) ~e** escalope *etc* milanaise. **2** *nm,f*: **M~(e)** Milanese.

mildiou [mildju] *nm* mildew.

mile [majl] *nm* mile.

milice [milis] *nf* militia.

milicien, -ienne [milisjɛ̃, jɛn] **1** *nm* militiaman. **2 milicienne** *nf* woman serving in the Militia.

milieu, *pl* **~x** [miljø] *nm* **(a)** (*centre*) middle. **casser/couper/scier qch en son ~** *ou* **par le ~** to break/cut/saw sth down *ou* through the middle; **le bouton/la porte du ~** the middle *ou* centre knob/door; **je prends celui du ~** I'll take the one in the middle *ou* the middle one; **tenir le ~ de la chaussée** to keep to the middle of the road; **il est venu vers le ~ de l'après-midi/la matinée** he came towards the middle of the afternoon/morning, he came about mid-afternoon/mid-morning; **vers/depuis le ~ du 15e siècle** towards/since the mid-15th century, towards/since the mid-1400s.

(b) au ~ de (*au centre de*) in the middle of; (*parmi*) amid, among, in the midst of, amidst (*littér*). **il est là au ~ de ce groupe** he's over there in the middle of that group; **au beau ~ (de), en plein ~ (de)** right *ou* slap bang* in the middle (of), in the very middle (of); **au ~ de toutes ces difficultés/aventures** in the middle *ou* midst of *ou* amidst all these difficulties/adventures; **au ~ de son affolement** in the middle *ou* midst of his panic; **elle n'est heureuse qu'au ~ de sa famille/de ses enfants** she's only happy when she's among *ou* surrounded by her family/children *ou* with her family/children around her; **au ~ de la journée** in the middle of the day; **au ~ de la nuit** in the middle of the night, at dead of night; **comment travailler au ~ de ce vacarme?** how can anyone work in *ou* surrounded by this din?; **au ~ de la descente** halfway down (the hill); **au ~ de la page** in the middle of the page, halfway down the page; **au ~/en plein ~ de l'hiver** in mid-winter/the depth of winter; **au ~ de l'été** in mid-summer, at the height of summer; **il est parti au beau ~ de la réception** he left when the party was in full swing, he left right in the middle of the party.

(c) (*état intermédiaire*) middle course *ou* way. **il n'y a pas de ~ (entre)** there is no middle course *ou* way (between); **c'est tout noir ou tout blanc, il ne connaît pas de ~** he sees everything as either black or white, he knows no mean (*frm*) *ou* there's no happy medium (for him); **le juste ~** the happy medium, the golden mean; **un juste ~** a happy medium; **il est innocent ou coupable, il n'y a pas de ~** he is either innocent or guilty, he can't be both; **tenir le ~** to steer a middle course.

(d) (*Bio, Géog*) environment. (*Phys*) **~ réfringent** refractive medium; **~ physique/géographique/humain** physical/geographical/human environment; **les animaux dans leur(s) ~(x) naturel(s)** animals in their natural surroundings *ou* environment.

(e) (*entourage social, moral*) milieu, environment; (*groupe restreint*) set, circle; (*provenance*) background. **le ~ familial** the family circle; (*Sociol*) the home *ou* family background, the home environment; **s'adapter à un nouveau ~** to adapt to a different milieu *ou* environment; **il ne se sent pas dans son ~** he feels out of place, he doesn't feel at home; **elle se sent** *ou* **est dans son ~ chez nous** she feels (quite) at home with us; **de quel ~ sort-il?** what is his (social) background?; **les ~x littéraires/financiers** literary/financial circles; **de ~x autorisés/bien informés** from official/well-informed circles; **c'est un ~ très fermé** it is a very closed circle *ou* exclusive set.

(f) le ~ the underworld; **les gens du ~** (people of) the underworld.

militaire [militɛʀ] **1** *adj* military, army (*épith*). **la vie ~** military *ou* army life; **camion ~** army lorry; *V* **attaché, service** *etc.*

2 *nm* serviceman. **il est ~** he is in the forces *ou* services; **~ de carrière** (*terre*) regular (soldier); (*air*) (serving) airman.

militairement [militɛʀmɑ̃] *adv mener une affaire, saluer* in military fashion *ou* style. **la ville a été occupée ~** the town was occupied by the army; **occuper ~ une ville** to (send in the army to) occupy a town.

militant, e [militɑ̃, ɑ̃t] *adj, nm,f* militant. **~ de base** rank and file militant.

militantisme [militɑ̃tism(ə)] *nm* militancy.

militarisation [militaʀizasjɔ̃] *nf* militarization.

militariser [militaʀize] (1) *vt* to militarize.

militarisme [militaʀism(ə)] *nm* militarism.

militariste [militaʀist(ə)] **1** *adj* militaristic. **2** *nmf* militarist.

militer [milite] (1) *vi* **(a)** *[personne]* to be a militant. **il milite au parti communiste** he is a communist party militant, he is a militant in the communist party.

(b) *[arguments, raisons]* **~ en faveur de** *ou* **pour/contre** to militate in favour of/against, argue for/against.

millage [milaʒ] *nm (Can)* mileage.

mille¹ [mil] **1** *adj inv* **(a)** a *ou* one thousand. **~ un** a *ou* one thousand and one; **trois ~** three thousand; **deux ~ neuf cents** two thousand nine hundred; **page ~** page a *ou* one thousand; (*dans les dates: aussi* **mil**) **l'an ~** the year one thousand; **un billet de ~*** a thousand-franc note; *V* **donner.**

(b) (*nombreux*) **~ regrets** I'm *ou* we're terribly *ou* extremely sorry; **~ baisers** fondest love; **je lui ai dit ~ fois** I've told him a thousand times; **c'est ~ fois trop grand** it's far too big.

(c) (*loc*) **~ et un problèmes/exemples** a thousand and one problems/examples; **les ~ et une nuits** the Thousand and One Nights, the Arabian Nights.

2 *nm inv* **(a)** (*Comm, Math*) a *ou* one thousand. **5 pour ~ d'alcool** 5 parts of alcohol to a thousand; **5 pour ~ des enfants, 5 enfants sur ~** 5 children out of *ou* in every thousand; **vendre qch au ~** to sell sth by the thousand; (*Comm*) **2 ~ de boulons** 2 thousand bolts; **ouvrage qui en est à son centième ~** book which has sold 100,000 copies; *V* **gagner.**

(b) (*Sport*) *[cible]* bull, bull's-eye. **mettre** *ou* **taper dans le ~** (*lit*) to hit the bull *ou* bull's-eye; (*fig*) to score a bull's-eye, be bang on target*.

3: (*Culin*) **mille-feuille** *nm, pl* **mille-feuilles** mille feuilles, cream *ou* vanilla slice; **mille-pattes** *nm inv* centipede.

mille² [mil] *nm* **(a) ~ (marin)** nautical mile. **(b)** (*Can*) mile (*1,069 km*).

millénaire [milenɛʀ] **1** *nm* (*période*) millennium, a thousand years; (*anniversaire*) thousandth anniversary, millennium. **c'est le deuxième ~** *ou* **le bi-~ de** it is the two-thousandth anniversary of.

2 *adj* (*lit*) thousand-year-old (*épith*); (*fig: très vieux*) ancient, very old. **des rites plusieurs fois ~s** rites several thousand years old, age-old rites; **ce monument ~** this thousand-year-old monument.

millénium [milenjɔm] *nm* millennium.

mille-pertuis [milpɛʀtɥi] *nm* St.-John's-wort.

millésime [milezim] *nm* (*Admin, Fin: date*) year, date; *[vin]* year, vintage. **vin d'un bon ~** vintage wine; **quel est le ~ de ce vin?** what is the vintage *ou* year of this wine?

millésimé, e [milezime] *adj* vintage. **on a bu un bordeaux ~** we had a vintage Bordeaux.

millet [mijɛ] *nm* (*Agr*) millet. **donner des grains de ~ aux oiseaux** to give the birds some millet *ou* (bird)seed.

milli ... [mili] *préf* milli ... . **~bar** *nm* millibar; **~gramme** *nm* milligram(me).

milliaire [miljɛʀ] *adj* (*Antiq*) milliary. **borne ~** milliary column.

milliard [miljaʀ] *nm* thousand million, milliard (*Brit*), billion (*US*). **un ~ de gens** a thousand million *ou* a billion (*US*) people; **10 ~s de francs** 10 thousand million francs, 10 billion francs (*US*); **des ~s de** thousands of millions of, billions of.

milliardaire [miljaʀdɛʀ] *nmf* multimillionaire (*Brit*), billionaire (*US*). **il est ~** he's a multimillionaire (*Brit*), he's worth millions*; **une compagnie plusieurs fois ~ en dollars** a company worth (many) millions of dollars.

milliardième [miljaʀdjɛm] *adj, nm* thousand millionth (*Brit*), billionth (*US*).

millième [miljɛm] *adj, nm* thousandth.

millier [milje] *nm* thousand. **un ~ de têtes** a thousand (or so) heads, (about) a thousand heads; **par ~s** in (their) thousands, by the thousand; **il y en a des ~s** there are thousands (of them).

millimètre [milimɛtʀ(ə)] *nm* millimetre.

millimétré, e [milimetʀe] *adj* graduated (*in millimetres*); *V* **papier.**

millimétrique [milimetʀik] *adj* millimetric.

million [miljɔ̃] *nm* million. **2 ~s de francs** 2 million francs; **être riche à ~s** to be a millionaire, have millions, be worth millions.

millionième [miljɔnjɛm] *adj, nmf* millionth.

millionnaire [miljɔnɛʀ] *nmf* millionaire. **la société est ~** the company is worth millions *ou* worth a fortune; **il est plusieurs fois ~** he's a millionaire several times over; **~ en dollars** dollar millionaire.

milord†* [milɔʀ] *nm* (*noble anglais*) lord, nobleman; (*riche étranger*) immensely rich foreigner. **oui ~!** yes my lord!

mime [mim] *nm* **(a)** (*personne*) (*Théât: professionnel*) mimer, mime; (*gén: imitateur*) mimic.

(b) (*Théât: art*) (*action*) mime, miming; (*pièce*) mime. **le ~ est un art difficile** miming is a difficult art; **il fait du ~** he is a mime; **aller voir un spectacle de ~** to go to watch *ou* see a mime.

mimer [mime] (1) *vt* (*Théât*) to mime; (*singer*) to mimic, take off*.

mimétique [mimetik] *adj* mimetic.

mimétisme [mimetism(ə)] *nm* (*Bio*) (protective) mimicry; (*fig*) unconscious mimicry, mimetism (*rare*). **par un ~ étrange, il en était venu à ressembler à son chien** through some strange (mimetic) process he had grown to look just like his dog; **le ~ qui finit par faire se ressembler l'élève et le maître** the unconscious imitation through which the pupil grows like his master.

mimique [mimik] *nf* **(a)** (*grimace comique*) comical expression, funny face. **ce singe a de drôles de ~s!** this monkey makes such funny faces!

(b) (*signes, gestes*) gesticulations (*pl*), sign language (*U*). **il eut une ~ expressive pour dire qu'il avait faim** he indicated in expressive sign language that he was hungry.

mimodrame [mimɔdʀam] *nm* (*Théât*) mimodrama.

mimosa [mimoza] *nm* mimosa.

minable [minabl(ə)] *adj* (*décrépit*) *lieu, aspect, personne* shabby(-looking), seedy(-looking); (*médiocre*) *devoir, film, personne* hopeless*, useless*, pathetic*; *salaire, vie* miserable, wretched. **l'histoire ~ de cette veuve avec 15 enfants à nourrir** the sorry *ou* dismal tale of that widow with 15 children to feed; **habillé de façon ~** seedily dressed; **c'est un ~** he's a washout*, he's (just) hopeless* *ou* pathetic*; **une bande de ~s** a pathetic *ou* useless bunch*.

minaret [minaʀɛ] *nm* minaret.

minauder [minode] (1) *vi* to mince, simper. **elle minaudait auprès** *ou* **autour de ses invités** she was fluttering round *ou* she minced round among her guests; **je n'aime pas sa façon de ~** I don't like her (silly) mincing ways.

minauderie [minodʀi] *nf* mincing *ou* simpering ways *ou* manner. **~s** mincing ways, (silly) fluttering(s); **faire des ~s** to flutter about, mince around.

minaudier, -ière [minodje, jɛʀ] *adj* affected, simpering.

mince [mɛ̃s] **1** *adj* **(a)** (*peu épais*) thin; (*svelte, élancé*) slim, slender. **tranche ~** *[pain]* thin slice; *[saucisson, jambon]* sliver, thin slice; **~ comme une feuille de papier à cigarette** *ou* **comme une pelure d'oignon** paper-thin, wafer-thin; **avoir la taille ~** to be slim *ou* slender.

(b) (*fig: faible, insignifiant*) *profit* slender; *salaire* meagre, small; *prétexte* lame, weak; *preuve, chances* slim, slender; *connaissances, rôle, mérite* slight, small. **l'intérêt du film est bien ~** the film is decidedly lacking in interest *ou* is of very little interest; **le prétexte est bien ~** it's a very weak *ou* lame pretext; **ce n'est pas une ~ affaire que de faire** it's quite a job *ou* business doing, it's no easy task to do; **c'est un peu ~ comme réponse** that's a rather lame *ou* feeble reply, that's not much of an answer.

2 *adv couper* thinly, in thin slices.

3 *excl* (*) **~ (alors)!** drat (it)!*, darn (it)!*, blow (it)!*

minceur [mɛ̃sœʀ] *nf* (*V* **mince**) thinness; slimness, slenderness. **la ~ des preuves** the slimness *ou* the insufficiency of the evidence.

mincir [mɛ̃siʀ] (2) *vi* to get slimmer, get thinner.

mine[1] [min] *nf* **(a)** (*physionomie*) expression, look. **dit-il, la ~ réjouie** he said with a cheerful *ou* delighted expression; **ne fais pas cette ~-là** stop making *ou* pulling that face; **elle avait la ~ longue** she was pulling a long face; *V* **gris.**

(b) **~s** *[femme]* simpering airs; *[bébé]* expressions; **faire des ~s** to put on simpering airs, simper; *[bébé]* **il fait ses petites ~s** he makes (funny) little faces, he gives you these funny looks.

(c) (*allure*) exterior, appearance. **ne vous fiez pas à sa ~ affairée/tranquille** don't be taken in by his busy/calm exterior *ou* appearance; **tu as la ~ de quelqu'un qui n'a rien compris** you look as if you haven't understood a single thing; **il cachait sous sa ~ modeste un orgueil sans pareil** his appearance of modesty *ou* his modest exterior concealed an overweening pride; **votre poulet/rôti a bonne ~** your chicken/roast looks good *ou* lovely *ou* inviting; (*iro*) **tu as bonne ~ maintenant!** now you look an utter *ou* a right* idiot! *ou* a fine fool!; *V* **juger, payer.**

(d) (*teint*) **avoir bonne ~** to look well; **il a mauvaise ~** he doesn't look well, he looks unwell *ou* poorly; **avoir une sale ~** to look awful* *ou* dreadful; **avoir une ~ de papier mâché/de déterré** to look washed out/like death warmed up*; **il a meilleure ~ qu'hier** he looks better than (he did) yesterday; **il en a une ~!** he doesn't look at all well; **avoir** *ou* **faire triste ~, avoir** *ou* **faire piètre ~** to cut a sorry figure, look a sorry sight; **faire triste ~ à** to give a cool reception to, greet unenthusiastically.

(e) (*loc*) **faire ~ de faire** to make a show *ou* pretence of doing, go through the motions of doing; **j'ai fait ~ de le croire** I acted as if I believed it, I made a show *ou* pretence of believing it; **j'ai fait ~ de lui donner une gifle** I made as if to slap him; **il n'a même pas fait ~ de résister** he didn't even put up a token resistance, he didn't offer even a show of resistance; **~ de rien*: il est venu nous demander comment ça marchait, ~ de rien*** he came and asked us with a casual air *ou* all casually* how things were going; **~ de rien, tu sais qu'il n'est pas bête*** though you wouldn't think it to look at him, he's not daft* you know.

mine[2] [min] *nf* **(a)** (*gisement*) deposit, mine; (*exploité*) mine. (*lit, fig*) **~ d'or** gold mine; **région de ~s** mining area *ou* district; **~ à ciel ouvert** opencast mine; **la nationalisation des ~s** (*gén*) the nationalization of the mining industry; (*charbon*) the nationalization of coal *ou* of the coalmining industry; **~ de charbon** (*gén*) coalmine; (*puits*) pit, mine; (*entreprise*) colliery; **descendre dans la ~** to go down the mine *ou* pit; *V* **carreau, galerie, puits.**

(b) (*Admin*) **les M~s** ≈ (National) Mining and Geological service; **École des M~s** ≈ (National) School of Mining Engineering; **ingénieur des M~s** (state qualified) mining engineer.

(c) (*fig: source*) mine, source, fund (*de* of). **~ de renseignements** mine of information; **une ~ inépuisable de documents** an inexhaustible source of documents.

(d) **~ (de crayon)** lead (of pencil); **crayon à ~ dure/douce** hard/soft pencil, pencil with a hard/soft lead; **~ de plomb** black lead, graphite; *V* **porter.**

(e) (*Mil*) (*galerie*) gallery, sap, mine; (*explosif*) mine. **~ dormante** unexploded mine; **~ terrestre** landmine; *V* **champ, détecteur** *etc.*

miner [mine] (1) *vt* **(a)** (*garnir d'explosifs*) to mine. **ce pont est miné** this bridge has been mined.

(b) (*ronger*) *falaise, fondations* to undermine, erode, eat away; (*fig*) *société, autorité, santé* to undermine, erode; *force, énergie* to sap, drain, undermine. **la maladie l'a miné** his illness has left him drained (of energy) *ou* has sapped his strength; **être miné par le chagrin/l'inquiétude** to be worn down by grief/anxiety; **miné par la jalousie/le chagrin** wasting away *ou* consumed with jealousy/sorrow; **ses cours sont vraiment minants*** his classes are a real bore *ou* are really deadly*.

minerai [minʀɛ] *nm* ore. **~ de fer/cuivre** iron/copper ore.

minéral, e, *mpl* **-aux** [mineʀal, o] **1** *adj huile, sel* mineral; (*Chim*) inorganic; *V* **chimie, eau.**

2 *nm* mineral.

minéralier [mineʀalje] *nm* ore tanker.

minéralisation [mineʀalizɑsjɔ̃] *nf* mineralization.

minéraliser [mineʀalize] (1) *vt* to mineralize.

minéralogie [mineʀalɔʒi] *nf* mineralogy.

minéralogique [mineʀalɔʒik] *adj* (*Géol*) mineralogical. (*Aut*) **numéro ~** registration (*Brit*) *ou* license (*US*) number; (*Aut*) **plaque ~** number plate.

minéralogiste [mineʀalɔʒist(ə)] *nmf* mineralogist.

minerve [minɛʀv(ə)] *nf* (*Méd*) (surgical) collar; (*Typ*) platen machine. (*Myth*) **M~** Minerva.

minet, -ette [minɛ, ɛt] **1** *nm,f* (*langage enfantin: chat*) puss*, pussy(-cat) (*langage enfantin*). (*terme affectif*) **mon ~, ma ~te** (my) pet*, sweetie(-pie)*.

2 *nm* (*péj: jeune élégant*) young trendy*.

3 minette *nf* (*: *jeune fille*) dollybird*.

mineur[1], **e** [minœʀ] **1** *adj* **(a)** (*Jur*) minor. **enfant ~** minor.

(b) (*peu important*) *soucis, œuvre, artiste* minor; *V* **Asie.**

(c) (*Mus*) *gamme, intervalle* minor. **en do ~** in C minor.

(d) (*Logique*) minor. **terme ~** minor term; **proposition ~e** minor premise.

2 *nm,f* (*Jur*) minor. **un ~ de moins de 18 ans** a minor, a young person under 18 (years of age); *V* **détournement.**

3 *nm* (*Mus*) minor. **en ~** in a minor key.

4 mineure *nf* (*Logique*) minor premise.

mineur[2] [minœʀ] *nm* **(a)** (*Ind*) miner; *[houille]* (coal)miner. **~ de fond** pitface *ou* underground worker, miner at the pitface; **village de ~s** mining village. **(b)** (*Mil*) sapper (*who lays mines*).

mini... [mini] **1** *préf*: **mini...** mini... . **~bus** *nm* minibus; **~-budget** *nm* mini-budget; **~-cassette** *nf* cassette (recorder); **~-jupe** *nf* miniskirt; **~-pull** *nm* shortie pullover; **on va faire un ~-repas** we'll have a snack lunch.

2 *adj inv*: **la mode ~** the mini-length fashion; **c'est ~ chez eux*** they've got a minute *ou* tiny (little) place.

3 *nf* minidress, miniskirt.

4 *nm*: **elle s'habille (en) ~** she wears minis; **la mode est au ~** minis are in (fashion).

miniature [minjatyʀ] **1** *nf* **(a)** (*gén*) miniature. **en ~** in miniature; **cette province, c'est la France en ~** this province is a miniature France *ou* France in miniature.

(b) (*Art*) miniature; (*lettre*) miniature.

(c) (*: *nabot*) (little) shrimp* *ou* tich*. **tu as vu cette ~?** did you see that little shrimp?*

2 *adj* miniature. **train/lampes ~(s)** miniature train/lights.

miniaturisation [minjatyʀizɑsjɔ̃] *nf* miniaturization.

miniaturiser [minjatyʀize] (1) *vt* to miniaturize. **transistor miniaturisé** miniaturized transistor.

miniaturiste [minjatyʀist(ə)] *nmf* miniaturist.

minier, -ière [minje, jɛʀ] *adj* mining.

minima [minima] *V* **appel, minimum.**

minimal, e, *mpl* **-aux** [minimal, o] *adj température, pension* minimum.

minime [minim] **1** *adj dégât, rôle* minor, minimal; *fait* trifling, trivial; *salaire, somme* paltry; *différence* minor, minimal. **2** *nmf* **(a)** (*Sport*) junior (*13-15 years*). **(b)** (*Rel*) Minim.

minimiser [minimize] (1) *vt* to minimize.

minimum [minimɔm], *f* **~** *ou* **minima** [minima], *pl* **~(s)** *ou* **minima 1** *adj* minimum. **vitesse/âge ~** minimum speed/age; **un bikini ~** a scanty bikini; *V* **salaire.**

2 *nm* (*gén, Math*) minimum; (*Jur*) minimum sentence. **dans le ~ de temps** in the shortest time possible; **il faut un ~ de temps/d'intelligence pour le faire** you need a minimum amount of time/a modicum of intelligence to be able to do it; **il faut quand même travailler un ~** you still have to do a minimum of work; **avec un ~ d'efforts il aurait réussi** with a minimum of effort he would have succeeded; **il n'a pris que le ~ de précautions** he took only minimum *ou* minimal precautions; **la production/la valeur des marchandises a atteint son ~** the production/value of the goods has sunk to its lowest level (yet) *ou* an all-time low; **dépenses réduites au/à un ~** expenditure cut (down) to the/a minimum; **avoir tout juste le ~ vital** (*salaire*) to earn barely a living wage; (*subsistence*) to be *ou* live at subsistence level, be on the bread line (*fig*); **au (grand) ~** at the very least; **il faut rester le ~ (de temps) au soleil** you must stay in the sun as little as possible.

ministère [ministɛʀ] *nm* **(a)** (*département*) ministry (*Brit*), department (*US*). **~ des Affaires étrangères** Ministry of Foreign Affairs; **~ de l'Éducation nationale/de la Défense** Ministry of Education/Defence; **~ de l'Économie et des Finances** Ministry of Finance, ≈ the Treasury (*Brit*); **~ de l'Information** Ministry of Information; **~ de l'Intérieur** Ministry of the Interior, ≈ Home Office (*Brit*), Department of the Interior (*US*); **~ de la Justice** Ministry of Justice; **employé de ~** ≈ civil servant.

(b) (*cabinet*) government. **sous le ~ (de) Pompidou** under the premiership of Pompidou, under Pompidou's government; **former un ~** to form one's *ou* a government; **~ de coalition** coalition government.

(c) (*Jur*) **le ~ public** (*partie*) the Prosecution, the State Prosecutor; (*service*) the State Prosecutor's Office; **par ~ d'huissier** served by a bailiff.

(d) (*Rel*) ministry. **exercer son ~ à la campagne** to have a country parish.

(e) (*littér: entremise*) agency. **proposer son ~** to offer to act for sb.

ministériel, -elle [ministeʀjɛl] *adj fonction, circulaire* ministerial; *crise, remaniement* cabinet (*épith*). **solidarité ~le** ministerial solidarity; **département ~** ministry, department; **journal ~** pro-government newspaper, newspaper which backs *ou* supports the government; *V* **arrêté, officier**[1].

ministrable [ministʀabl(ə)] *adj* likely to be appointed minister. **il est ~, c'est un ~** he's a potential minister *ou* likely to be appointed minister.

ministre [ministʀ(ə)] *nm* **(a)** *[gouvernement]* minister, secretary (*surtout US*). ~ **des Affaires étrangères** Minister of Foreign Affairs, Foreign Secretary; ~ **de l'Éducation nationale/de la Défense** Minister of Education/Defence, Education/Defence Minister *ou* Secretary; ~ **de l'Économie et des Finances** Minister of Finance, Finance Minister *ou* Secretary, ≃ Chancellor of the Exchequer (*Brit*), Secretary of the Treasury (*US*); ~ **de l'Information** Minister of Information; ~ **de l'Intérieur** Minister of the Interior, ≃ Home Secretary (*Brit*), Secretary of the Interior (*US*); ~ **de la Justice** Minister of Justice, ≃ Lord Chancellor (*Brit*); ~ **d'État** senior minister (*of Interior or Justice*); ~ **sans portefeuille** minister without portfolio; *V* **bureau, conseil, premier.**

(b) *[ambassade]* envoy. ~ **plénipotentiaire** (minister) plenipotentiary.

(c) (*Rel*) (*protestant*) minister, clergyman; (*catholique*) minister. ~ **(du culte)** minister (of religion); ~ **de Dieu** minister of God; ~ **de l'Évangile** minister of the Gospels.

(d) (*littér: représentant*) agent.

minium [minjɔm] *nm* (*Chim*) red lead, minium; (*Peinture*) red lead paint.

minois [minwa] *nm* (*visage*) little face. **son joli** ~ her pretty little face.

minoration [minɔʀasjɔ̃] *nf* cut, reduction (*de* in).

minorer [minɔʀe] (1) *vt taux, impôts* to cut, reduce.

minoritaire [minɔʀitɛʀ] **1** *adj* minority (*épith*). **groupe** ~ minority group; **ils sont** ~**s** they are a minority *ou* in the minority. **2** *nmf* member of the minority. **les** ~**s** the minority (party).

minorité [minɔʀite] *nf* **(a)** (*âge*) (*gén*) minority; (*Jur*) minority, (legal) infancy, nonage. **pendant sa** ~ while he is *ou* was under age, during his minority *ou* infancy (*Jur*); (*Jur*) ~ **pénale** ≃ legal infancy.

(b) (*groupe*) minority, minority group. ~ **ethnique/nationale** racial *ou* ethnic/national minority; ~ **opprimée/agissante** oppressed/active minority.

(c) ~ **de** minority of; **dans la** ~ **des cas** in the minority of cases; **je m'adresse à une** ~ **d'auditeurs** I'm addressing a minority of listeners.

(d) être en ~ to be in the *ou* a minority; **le gouvernement a été mis en** ~ **sur la question du budget** the government was defeated on the budget.

Minorque [minɔʀk] *nf* Minorca.

minorquin, e [minɔʀkɛ̃, in] **1** *adj* Minorcan. **2** *nm,f*: **M~(e)** Minorcan.

Minotaure [minɔtɔʀ] *nm* Minotaur.

minoterie [minɔtʀi] *nf* (*industrie*) flour-milling (industry); (*usine*) (flour-)mill.

minotier [minɔtje] *nm* miller.

minou [minu] *nm* (*langage enfantin*) pussy(-cat) (*langage enfantin*), puss*. (*terme d'affection*) **oui mon** ~ yes sweetie (-pie)* *ou* (my) pet*.

minuit [minɥi] *nm* midnight, twelve (o'clock) (at night), twelve midnight. ~ **vingt** twenty past twelve *ou* midnight; *V* **messe.**

minus [minys] *nmf* dimwit, moron. ~ **habens** moron; **leur fils est un** ~ their son is moronic *ou* completely lacking*.

minuscule [minyskyl] **1** *adj* **(a)** (*très petit*) minute, tiny, minuscule. **(b)** (*Écriture*) small; (*Typ*) lower case. **h** ~ small h. **2** *nf*: **(lettre)** ~ small letter; (*Typ*) lower case letter.

minutage [minytaʒ] *nm* minute by minute timing, (strict *ou* precise) timing.

minute [minyt] *nf* **(a)** (*division de l'heure, d'un degré*) minute; (*moment*) minute, moment. **je n'ai pas une** ~ **à moi/à perdre** I don't have a minute *ou* moment to myself/to lose; **une** ~ **d'inattention a suffi** a moment's inattention was enough; ~ **(papillon)!*** not so fast!, hey, just a minute!*, hold *ou* hang on (a minute)!*; **une** ~ **de silence** a minute's silence, a minute of silence; **la** ~ **de vérité** the moment of truth; **steak** *ou* **entrecôte** ~ minute steak; *V* **cocotte.**

(b) à la ~: **on me l'a apporté à la** ~ it has just this instant *ou* moment been brought to me; **avec toi il faut toujours tout faire à la** ~ you always have to have things done there and then *ou* on the spot; **réparations à la** ~ on the spot repairs, repairs while you wait; **elle arrive toujours à la** ~ **(près)** she's always there on the dot*, she always arrives to the minute *ou* dead on time*.

(c) (*Jur*) minute, draft.

minuter [minyte] (1) *vt* **(a)** (*organiser*) to time (carefully *ou* to the last minute); (*chronométrer, limiter*) to time. **dans son emploi du temps tout est minuté** everything's worked out *ou* timed down to the last second in his timetable; **emploi du temps minuté** strict schedule *ou* timetable. **(b)** (*Jur*) to draw up, draft.

minuterie [minytʀi] *nf [lumière]* time switch; *[horloge]* regulator. **allumer/éteindre la** ~ to switch on/off the (automatic) light (*on stairs, in passage etc*).

minutie [minysi] *nf* **(a)** (*U*) *[personne, travail]* meticulousness; *[ouvrage, inspection]* minute detail. **j'ai été frappé par la** ~ **de son inspection** I was amazed by the detail of his inspection, I was amazed how detailed his inspection was; **l'horlogerie demande beaucoup de** ~ clock-making requires a great deal of precision; **avec** ~ (*avec soin*) meticulously; (*dans le détail*) in minute detail.

(b) (*détails: péj*) ~**s** trifles, trifling details, minutiae.

minutieusement [minysjøzmɑ̃] *adv* (*avec soin*) meticulously; (*dans le détail*) in minute detail.

minutieux, -euse [minysjø, øz] *adj personne, soin* meticulous; *ouvrage, dessin* minutely detailed; *description, inspection* minute. **il s'agit d'un travail** ~ it's a job that demands painstaking attention to detail; **c'est une opération** ~**euse** it's an operation demanding great care, it's an extremely delicate *ou* finicky operation; **il est très** ~ he is very meticulous *ou* careful of detail.

miocène [mjɔsɛn] *adj, nm* Miocene.

mioche [mjɔʃ] *nmf* (*: *gosse*) kid*, nipper*; (*péj*) brat*. **sale** ~! dirty *ou* horrible little brat!*.

mirabelle [miʀabɛl] *nf* (*prune*) (cherry) plum; (*alcool*) plum brandy.

mirabellier [miʀabelje] *nm* cherry-plum tree, mirabelle (tree).

miracle [miʀɑkl(ə)] **1** *nm* **(a)** (*lit*) miracle; (*fig*) miracle, marvel. ~ **économique** economic miracle; **son œuvre est un** ~ **d'équilibre** his work is a miracle *ou* marvel of balance; **cela tient du** ~ it's a miracle; **faire** *ou* **accomplir des** ~**s** (*lit*) to work *ou* do accomplish miracles; (*fig*) to work wonders *ou* miracles; **c'est** ~ **qu'il résiste dans ces conditions** it's a wonder *ou* a miracle he manages to cope in these conditions; **par** ~ miraculously, by a miracle; *V* **crier.**

(b) (*Hist, lit*) miracle (play).

2 *adj inv*: **le remède/la solution** *etc* ~ the miracle cure/solution *etc.*

miraculé, e [miʀakyle] *adj*: **(malade)** ~ (person) who has been miraculously cured *ou* who has been cured by a miracle; **les 3** ~**s de la route** the 3 (people) who miraculously *ou* who by some miracle survived the accident; (*hum*) **voilà le** ~! here comes the miraculous recovery!

miraculeusement [miʀakyløzmɑ̃] *adv* miraculously, (as if) by a miracle.

miraculeux, -euse [miʀakylø, øz] *adj guérison* miraculous; *progrès, réussite* wonderful. **traitement** *ou* **remède** ~ miracle cure; **ça n'a rien de** ~ there's nothing so extraordinary about that.

mirador [miʀadɔʀ] *nm* (*Mil*) watchtower, mirador; (*Archit*) mirador.

mirage [miʀaʒ] *nm* **(a)** (*lit, fig*) mirage. **tu rêves! c'est un** ~* you're dreaming! you're seeing things! **(b)** *[œufs]* candling.

mire [miʀ] *nf* (*TV*) test card; (*Arpentage*) surveyor's rod; *V* **cran, ligne**[1], **point**[1].

mire-œufs [miʀø] *nm inv* light (*for testing eggs*).

mirer [miʀe] (1) **1** *vt* **(a)** *œufs* to candle. **(b)** (*littér*) to mirror. **2 se mirer** *vpr* (*littér*) *[personne]* to gaze at o.s. (*in the mirror, water etc*); *[chose]* to be mirrored *ou* reflected (*in the water etc*).

mirettes* [miʀɛt] *nfpl* eyes, peepers* (*hum*).

mirifique [miʀifik] *adj* (*hum*) wonderful, fantabulous*, fantastic.

mirliflore†† [miʀliflɔʀ] *nm* fop†, coxcomb††. (*péj*) **faire le** ~ to put on foppish airs, play the fine fellow.

mirliton [miʀlitɔ̃] *nm* (*Mus*) reed pipe, mirliton; *[carnaval]* novelty whistle, kazoo.

mirmidon [miʀmidɔ̃] *nm* = **myrmidon.**

mirobolant, e* [miʀɔbɔlɑ̃, ɑ̃t] *adj* (*hum*) fabulous, fantastic.

miroir [miʀwaʀ] *nm* (*lit*) mirror; (*fig*) mirror, reflection. (*littér*) **le** ~ **des eaux** the glassy waters; **ce roman est-il bien le** ~ **de la réalité?** is this novel a true reflection of reality?, does this novel really mirror reality?; ~ **déformant** distorting mirror; ~ **grossissant** magnifying mirror; ~ **aux alouettes** (*lit*) decoy; (*fig*) lure; (*Aut*) ~ **de courtoisie** vanity mirror.

miroitement [miʀwatmɑ̃] *nm* (*V* **miroiter**) sparkling (*U*), gleaming (*U*); shimmering (*U*).

miroiter [miʀwate] (1) *vi* (*étinceler*) to sparkle, gleam; (*chatoyer*) to shimmer. (*fig*) **il lui fit** ~ **les avantages qu'il aurait à accepter ce poste** he painted in glowing colours the advantages he would gain from taking the job.

miroiterie [miʀwatʀi] *nf* **(a)** (*Comm*) mirror trade; (*Ind*) mirror industry. **(b)** (*usine*) mirror factory.

miroitier, -ière [miʀwatje, jɛʀ] *nm,f* (*vendeur*) mirror dealer; (*fabricant*) mirror manufacturer; (*artisan*) mirror cutter, silverer.

miroton [miʀɔtɔ̃] *nm*, **mironton*** [miʀɔ̃tɔ̃] *nm*: **(bœuf)** ~ boiled beef in onion sauce.

mis, e[1] [mi, miz] (*ptp de* **mettre**) *adj* (†: *vêtu*) attired†, clad. **bien** ~ nicely turned out.

misaine [mizɛn] *nf*: **(voile de)** ~ foresail; *V* **mât.**

misanthrope [mizɑ̃tʀɔp] *nmf* misanthropist, misanthrope. **il est devenu très** ~ he's come to dislike everyone *ou* to hate society, he's turned into a real misanthropist; **une attitude (de)** ~ a misanthropic attitude.

misanthropie [mizɑ̃tʀɔpi] *nf* misanthropy.

misanthropique [mizɑ̃tʀɔpik] *adj* (*littér*) misanthropic, misanthropical.

miscible [misibl(ə)] *adj* miscible.

mise[2] [miz] **1** *nf* **(a)** (*action de mettre*) putting, setting. ~ **en service** putting into service; ~ **en circulation** issue; ~ **en bouteilles** bottling; ~ **en sacs** packing; ~ **en gage** pawning; ~ **en marche** starting; ~ **à jour** updating, bringing up to date; **la** ~ **en service des nouveaux autobus est prévue pour le mois prochain** the new buses are due to be put into service next month; **la** ~ **en pratique ne sera pas aisée** putting it into practice won't be easy, it won't be easy to put it into practice *ou* to carry it out in practice; **la** ~ **à jour de leurs registres sera longue** it will be a lengthy business updating their registers, the updating of their registers will take a long time; **lire les instructions avant la** ~ **en marche de l'appareil** read the instructions before starting the machine; *V* **bière**[2].

(b) (*enjeu*) stake, ante; (*Comm*) outlay; *V* **sauver.**

(c) (*habillement*) attire, clothing, garb (*hum*). **avoir une** ~ **débraillée** to be untidily dressed, have an untidy appearance; **juger qn sur** *ou* **à sa** ~ to judge sb by his clothes *ou* by what he wears; **soigner sa** ~ to take pride in one's appearance.

(d) être de ~ (††: *Fin*) to be in circulation, be legal currency; (*fig*) to be acceptable, be in place *ou* season (*fig*); **ces propos ne sont pas de** ~ those remarks are out of place.

2: **mise en accusation** arraignment, impeachment; (*Vét*) **mise-bas** dropping, birth; **mise en demeure** formal demand; **mise en disponibilité** *[fonctionnaire]* leave of absence; *[officier]* transfer to reserve duty; **mise à exécution** implementation, implementing; *[fusée]* **mise à feu** blast-off; (*Fin*) **mise de fonds** capital outlay; **faire une mise de fonds** to lay out capital; (*Typ*) **mise en forme** imposition; **mise en garde** warning; **mise en jeu** involvement, bringing into play; **mise en liberté** release, freeing; (*Mil*) **mise en ligne** alignment; **mise au monde** birth; **mise à mort** kill; (*Rad*) **mise en ondes** production; (*Typ*) **mise en page** make-up, making up; (*Ind*) **mise à pied** laying off; **mise sur pied** setting up; (*Coiffure*) **mise en plis** set; **se faire faire une mise en plis** to have a set, have one's hair set; **mise au point** (*Aut*) tuning; (*Phot*) focusing; (*Tech*) adjustment; (*fig: explication, correction*) clarification, setting the record straight; **publier une mise au point** to issue a statement (setting the record straight *ou* clarifying a point); **mise à prix** (*enchères*) reserve price (*Brit*), upset price (*US*) (*V aussi* **prix**); (*Ciné, Théât*) **mise en scène** production; (*fig*) **son indignation n'est qu'une mise en scène** his indignation is just for show *ou* is just put on; (*fig*) **toute cette mise en scène pour nous faire croire que ...** this great build-up *ou* performance just to make us believe that ... ; **mise en valeur** *[terre]* development; *[maison]* improvement; *[meuble, tableau]* setting-off; **mise en vigueur** enforcement; **mise aux voix** putting to the vote.

miser [mize] (1) *vt* **(a)** *argent* to stake, bet (*sur* on). **~ sur un cheval** to bet on a horse, put money on a horse; **~ à 8 contre 1** to bet at *ou* accept odds of 8 to 1, take 8 to 1; *V* **tableau.**

(b) (**: compter sur*) **~ sur** to bank on, count on.

misérabilisme [mizeʀabilism(ə)] *nm* (*Littérat*) preoccupation with the sordid aspects of life.

misérabiliste [mizeʀabilist(ə)] *adj* (*Littérat*) who *ou* which concentrates on the sordid aspects of life.

misérable [mizeʀabl(ə)] **1** *adj* **(a)** (*pauvre*) *famille, personne* destitute, poverty-stricken; *région* impoverished, poverty-stricken; *logement, vêtements* seedy, mean. **d'aspect ~** of mean appearance, seedy-looking.

(b) (*pitoyable*) *existence, conditions, logement* miserable, wretched, pitiful; *personne, famille* pitiful, wretched.

(c) (*sans valeur, minable*) *somme d'argent* paltry, miserable. **un salaire ~** a pittance, a miserable salary; **ne te mets pas en colère pour un ~ billet de 10 F** don't get angry about a measly* *ou* mouldy* 10-franc note.

(d) (††, *littér: méprisable*) vile†, base†, contemptible.

2 *nmf* (†, *littér: méchant*) wretch, scoundrel; (*pauvre*) poor wretch. **petit ~!** you (little) rascal! *ou* wretch!

misérablement [mizeʀabləmɑ̃] *adv* (*pitoyablement*) miserably, wretchedly; (*pauvrement*) in great *ou* wretched poverty.

misère [mizɛʀ] *nf* **(a)** (*pauvreté*) (extreme) poverty, destitution (*frm*). **la ~ en gants blancs** *ou* **en faux-col** genteel poverty; **être dans la ~** to be destitute *ou* poverty-stricken; **vivre dans la ~** to live in poverty; **tomber dans la ~** to become impoverished *ou* destitute; **crier** *ou* **pleurer ~** to bewail *ou* bemoan one's poverty; **traitement** *ou* **salaire de ~** starvation wage; **~ dorée** splendid poverty; **~ noire** utter destitution; **réduire qn à la ~** to make sb destitute, reduce sb to a state of (dire) poverty.

(b) (*malheur*) **~s** woes, miseries, misfortunes; (**: ennuis*) **petites ~s** little troubles *ou* adversities, mild irritations; **faire des ~s à qn*** to be nasty* to sb; **les ~s de la guerre** the miseries of war; **c'est une ~ de la voir s'anémier** it's pitiful *ou* wretched to see her growing weaker; **quelle ~!** what a wretched shame!; (†, *hum*) **~!, ~ de nous!** woe is me! (†, *hum*), misery me! (†, *hum*); (*Rel*) **la ~ de l'homme** man's wretchedness; *V* **collier, lit.**

(c) (*somme négligeable*) **il l'a eu pour une ~** he got it for a song *ou* for next to nothing.

miserere, miséréré [mizeʀeʀe] *nm* (*psaume, chant*) Miserere.

miséreux, -euse [mizeʀø, øz] *adj* poverty-stricken. **un ~** a down-and-out, a poverty-stricken man; **les ~** the down-and-out(s), the poverty-stricken.

miséricorde [mizeʀikɔʀd(ə)] **1** *nf* **(a)** (*pitié*) mercy, forgiveness. **la ~ divine** divine mercy; *V* **péché. (b)** (*Constr*) misericord. **2** *excl* (†) mercy me!†, mercy on us!†

miséricordieusement [mizeʀikɔʀdjøzmɑ̃] *adv* mercifully.

miséricordieux, -ieuse [mizeʀikɔʀdjø, jøz] *adj* merciful, forgiving.

misogyne [mizɔʒin] **1** *adj* misogynous. **2** *nmf* misogynist, woman-hater.

misogynie [mizɔʒini] *nf* misogyny.

miss [mis] *nf* **(a)** beauty queen. **M~ France** Miss France. **(b)** English *ou* American governess. **2 enfants et leur ~** 2 children and their (English) governess. **(c)** (*vieille demoiselle*) **~ anglaise** old English spinster.

missel [misɛl] *nm* missal.

missile [misil] *nm* (*Aviat*) missile. **~ antimissile** antimissile missile; **~ autoguidé** self-guiding missile; **~ sol-sol/sol-air** *etc* ground-to-ground/ground-to-air *etc* missile.

mission [misjɔ̃] *nf* **(a)** (*charge*) (*Pol*) mission, assignment; (*Rel*) mission; (*groupe: Pol, Rel*) mission; (*Rel: bâtiment*) mission (station). **~ lui fut donnée de** he was commissioned to; **partir/être en ~** (*Admin, Mil*) to go/be on an assignment; *[prêtre]* to go/be on a mission; **toute la ~ fut massacrée** the entire mission was slaughtered; **~ accomplie** mission accomplished; (*Mil*) **~ de reconnaissance** reconnaissance (mission), recce*; *V* **chargé, ordre**[2].

(b) (*but, vocation*) task, mission. **la ~ de la littérature** the task of literature; **il s'est donné pour ~ de faire** he set himself the task of doing, he has made it his mission (in life) to do.

missionnaire [misjɔnɛʀ] *adj, nmf* missionary.

missive [misiv] *adj, nf* missive.

mistoufle* [mistufl(ə)] *nf*: **être dans la ~** to be down-and-out, be on one's uppers*; **faire des ~s à qn** to play (nasty) tricks on sb.

mistral [mistʀal] *nm* mistral.

mitaine [mitɛn] *nf* († *ou Can*) mitten, mitt.

mitan [mitɑ̃] *nm* (†† *ou dial*) middle, centre.

mite [mit] *nf* clothes moth. **mangé aux ~s** moth-eaten; **~ du fromage** cheese-mite; **avoir la ~ à l'œil†*** to have sleep in one's eyes (*fig*).

mité, e [mite] *adj* moth-eaten.

mi-temps [mitɑ̃] *nf inv* **(a)** (*Sport*) (*période*) half; (*repos*) half-time. **à la ~** at half-time; **première/seconde ~** first/second half; **l'arbitre a sifflé la ~** the referee blew (the whistle) for half-time.

(b) à ~ part-time; **travailler à ~** to work part-time, do part-time work; **elle est dactylo à ~** she's a part-time typist.

miter (se) [mite] (1) *vpr* to be *ou* become moth-eaten. **pour éviter que les vêtements se mitent** to stop the moths getting at the clothes.

miteux, -euse [mitø, øz] *adj lieu* seedy, dingy, grotty: (*Brit*); *vêtement* shabby, tatty*, grotty: (*Brit*); *personne* shabby (-looking), seedy(-looking). **un ~*** a seedy(-looking) character.

Mithridate [mitʀidat] *nm* Mithridates.

mithridatiser [mitʀidatize] (1) *vt* to mithridatize.

mitigation [mitigɑsjɔ̃] *nf* (*Jur*) mitigation.

mitigé, e [mitiʒe] (*ptp de* **mitiger**) *adj ardeur* mitigated; *convictions* lukewarm, reserved. **sentiments ~s** mixed feelings; **joie ~e de regrets** joy mixed *ou* mingled with regret.

mitiger† [mitiʒe] (3) *vt* to mitigate.

mitonner [mitɔne] (1) **1** *vt* **(a)** (*Culin*) (*à feu doux*) to simmer, cook slowly; (*avec soin*) to prepare *ou* cook with loving care. **elle (lui) mitonne des petits plats** she cooks (up) *ou* concocts tasty dishes (for him).

(b) (*) *affaire* to cook up quietly*; *personne* to cosset.

2 *vi* to simmer, cook slowly.

mitose [mitoz] *nf* mitosis.

mitoyen, -enne [mitwajɛ̃, ɛn] *adj*: **mur ~** party *ou* common wall; **le mur est ~** it is a party wall; **cloison ~ne** partition wall; **maisons ~nes** (*deux*) semi-detached houses; (*plus de deux*) terraced houses.

mitoyenneté [mitwajɛnte] *nf [mur]* common ownership. **la ~ des maisons** the (existence of a) party wall between the houses.

mitraillade [mitʀajad] *nf* **(a)** (*coups de feu*) (volley of) shots; (*échauffourée*) exchange of shots. **(b)** (*rare*) = **mitraillage.**

mitraillage [mitʀɑjaʒ] *nm* machine-gunning; (*Scol etc*) quick-fire questioning.

mitraille [mitʀɑj] *nf* **(a)** (*Mil*) (†: *projectiles*) grapeshot; (*décharge*) volley of shots†, hail of bullets. **fuir sous la ~** to flee under a hail of bullets.

(b) (†*: *petite monnaie*) loose *ou* small change.

mitrailler [mitʀɑje] (1) *vt* **(a)** (*Mil*) to machine gun. **~ qn avec des élastiques*** to pelt sb with rubber bands.

(b) (*Phot*) *monument* to take shot after shot of. **les touristes mitraillaient la cathédrale** the tourists' cameras were clicking away madly at the cathedral; **être mitraillé par les photographes** to be bombarded by the photographers.

(c) (*fig*) **~ qn de questions** to bombard *ou* pepper sb with questions, fire questions at sb.

mitraillette [mitʀɑjɛt] *nf* submachine gun, tommy gun*.

mitrailleur [mitʀɑjœʀ] *nm* (*Mil*) machine gunner; (*Aviat*) air gunner; *V* **fusil, pistolet.**

mitrailleuse [mitʀɑjøz] *nf* machine gun. **~ légère/lourde** light/heavy machine gun.

mitre [mitʀ(ə)] *nf* **(a)** (*Rel*) mitre. **recevoir la ~** to be appointed bishop, be mitred. **(b)** (*Tech*) *[cheminée]* cowl.

mitré, e [mitʀe] *adj* mitred; *V* **abbé.**

mitron [mitʀɔ̃] *nm* (*boulanger*) baker's boy; (*pâtissier*) pastry-cook's boy.

mixage [miksaʒ] *nm* (*Ciné, Rad*) (sound) mixing.

mixer[1] [mikse] (1) *vt* (*Ciné, Rad*) to mix.

mixer[2], **mixeur** [miksœʀ] *nm* (*Culin*) (electric) (food) mixer.

mixité [miksite] *nf* (*présence des deux sexes*) coeducation, coeducational system;(*programme intégré*) ≃ comprehensive education *ou* schooling *ou* teaching.

mixte [mikst(ə)] *adj* **(a)** (*deux sexes*) *équipe* mixed; *classe, école, enseignement* mixed, coeducational, coed*; *V* **double.**

(b) (*comportant éléments divers*) *mariage, train* mixed (*épith*); *équipe* combined (*épith*); *tribunal, commission* joint; *rôle* dual (*épith*); *appareil électrique* dual voltage; *radio, électrophone* battery-mains (operated); (*Chim, Géog*) *roche, végétation* mixed. (*Scol*) **enseignement ~** ≃ comprehensive education; **lycée ~** secondary school including technical and/or commercial options; **outil à usage ~** dual-purpose tool; **navire** *ou* **cargo ~** cargo-passenger ship *ou* vessel; **cuisinière ~** gas and electric cooker; **l'opéra-bouffe est un genre ~** comic opera is a mixture of genres.

mixtion [mikstjɔ̃] *nf* (*Chim, Pharm*) (*action*) blending, compounding; (*médicament*) mixture.

mixture [mikstyʀ] *nf* (*Chim, Pharm*) mixture; (*Culin*) mixture, concoction; (*péj, fig*) concoction.

mnémonique [mnemɔnik] *adj* mnemonic.

mnémotechnique [mnemɔtɛknik] **1** *adj* mnemonic. **2** *nf* mnemonics (*sg*), mnemotechnics (*sg*).

mobile [mɔbil] **1** *adj* **(a)** *pièce de moteur* moving; *élément de meuble, casier, panneau* movable; *feuillets (de cahier, calendrier)* loose; *V* **fête.**

(b) *main-d'œuvre, population* mobile.

(c) *reflet* changing; *traits* mobile, animated; *regard, yeux* mobile, darting (*épith*); *esprit* nimble, agile.

(d) *troupes* mobile. **boxeur très ~** boxer who is very quick on his feet, boxer who moves well; **avec la voiture on est très ~** you can really get around *ou* about with a car, having a car makes you very mobile; *V* **garde**[1], **garde**[2].

2 *nm* (a) (*impulsion*) motive (*de* for). **quel était le ~ de son action?** what was the motive for *ou* what prompted his action?

(b) (*Art*) mobile.

(c) (*Phys*) moving object *ou* body.

mobilier, -ière [mɔbilje, jɛʀ] 1 *adj* (*Jur*) *propriété, bien* personal; *valeurs* transferable. **saisie/vente ~ière** seizure/sale of chattels *ou* of personal *ou* movable property; **contribution ~ière** occupancy tax; **cote ~ière** assessment on income.

2 *nm* (a) (*ameublement*) furniture. **le ~ du salon** the lounge furniture; **nous avons un ~ Louis XV** our furniture is Louis XV, our house is furnished in Louis XV (style); (*fig hum*) **il fait partie du ~** he's part of the furniture (*hum*).

(b) (*Jur*) personal *ou* movable property. **~ national** State-owned furniture (*used to furnish buildings of the State*).

mobilisable [mɔbilizabl(ə)] *adj soldat* who can be called up; *énergie, ressources* that can be mobilized, that can be summoned up, summonable; *capitaux* mobilizable. (*Mil*) **il n'est pas ~** he cannot be called up.

mobilisateur, -trice [mɔbilizatœʀ, tʀis] *adj*: **un slogan ~** a slogan which will stir people into action *ou* activate people.

mobilisation [mɔbilizɑsjɔ̃] *nf [citoyens]* mobilization, calling up; *[troupes, ressources]* mobilization. **~ générale/partielle** general/partial mobilization.

mobiliser [mɔbilize] (1) *vt citoyens* to call up, mobilize; *troupes, ressources, adhérents* to mobilize. **~ les enthousiasmes** to summon up *ou* mobilize people's enthusiasm; **~ les esprits (en faveur d'une cause)** to rally people's interest (in a cause); **les (soldats) mobilisés** the mobilized troops; (*fig*) **tout le monde était mobilisé pour la servir** everyone had to run round at her beck and call, everyone had to jump to (it) and attend to her needs; **le gouvernement mobilise** the government is mobilizing.

mobilité [mɔbilite] *nf* (*gén*) mobility. **la ~ de son regard** his darting eyes; **la voiture nous permet une plus grande ~** having the car means we can get around *ou* about more easily *ou* makes us more mobile.

mobylette [mɔbilɛt] *nf* ® Mobylette ®, moped.

mocassin [mɔkasɛ̃] *nm* moccasin.

moche* [mɔʃ] *adj* (a) (*laid*) ugly, awful, ghastly*. **elle est ~ comme un pou** she's got a face like the back of a bus* (*Brit*), she's as ugly as sin.

(b) (*mauvais*) rotten*, lousy‡; (*méchant*) rotten*, nasty. **tu es ~ avec elle** you're rotten* to her.

mocheté* [mɔʃte] *nf* (a) (*laideur*) ugliness. (b) (*femme*) fright; (*objet*) eyesore. **c'est une vraie ~!** she's an absolute fright! *ou* as ugly as sin!

modal, e, *mpl* **-aux** [mɔdal, o] *adj* modal.

modalité [mɔdalite] *nf* (a) (*forme*) form, mode. **~ d'application de la loi** mode of enforcement of the law; **~s de paiement** methods *ou* modes of payment.

(b) (*Ling, Mus, Philos*) modality. **adverbe de ~** modal adverb.

(c) (*Jur: condition*) clause.

mode[1] [mɔd] 1 *nf* (a) fashion. **suivre la ~** to keep in fashion, keep up with the fashions; (*péj*) **une de ces nouvelles ~s** one of these new fads *ou* crazes; **à la ~** fashionable, in fashion; **une femme très à la ~** a very fashionable woman; **c'est la ~ des boucles d'oreilles, les boucles d'oreilles sont à la ~** earrings are in fashion *ou* are in* *ou* are all the rage*; **être habillé très à la ~** (*gén*) to be very fashionably dressed; *[jeunes]* to be very trendily* dressed; **habillé à la dernière ~** dressed in the latest fashion *ou* style; **mettre qch à la ~** to make sth fashionable, bring sth into fashion; **revenir à la ~** to come back into fashion *ou* vogue, to come back (in)*; **marchande de ~s**†† milliner.

(b) (*Comm, Ind: Habillement*) fashion industry *ou* business. **travailler dans la ~** to work *ou* be in the fashion world *ou* industry *ou* business; **journal/présentation de ~** fashion magazine/show; *V* **gravure.**

(c) (†: *mœurs*) custom; (*goût, style*) style, fashion. **selon la ~ de l'époque** according to the custom of the day; **(habillé) à l'ancienne ~** (dressed) in the old style; (*hum*) **cousin à la ~ de Bretagne** distant cousin, cousin six times removed (*hum*); (*Jur, hum*) **oncle** *ou* **neveu à la ~ de Bretagne** first cousin once removed; **à la ~ du 18e siècle** in the style of *ou* after the fashion of the 18th century, in 18th century style; *V* **bœuf, tripe.**

2 *adj inv*: **tissu/coloris/tons ~** fashion fabric/colours/shades.

mode[2] [mɔd] *nm* (a) (*méthode*) form, mode (*frm*), method; (*genre*) way. **quel est le ~ d'action de ce médicament?** how does this medicine work?; **~ de gouvernement/de transport** form *ou* mode of government/of transport; **~ de pensée/de vie** way of thinking/of life; **~ de paiement** method *ou* mode of payment; **~ d'emploi** directions for use.

(b) (*Gram*) mood; (*Mus, Philos*) mode.

modelage [mɔdlaʒ] *nm* (*activité*) modelling; (*ouvrage*) (piece of) sculpture; piece of pottery.

modèle [mɔdɛl] 1 *nm* (a) (*chose*) (*gén, Écon*) model; (*Tech*) pattern; (*type*) type; (*Habillement*) design, style; (*exemple*) example, model; (*Scol: corrigé*) fair copy. **nous avons tous nos ~s en vitrine** our full range is *ou* all our models are in the window; **petit/grand ~** small/large version; (*Mode*) **X présente ses ~s d'automne** X presents his autumn models *ou* styles; **fabriquer qch d'après le ~** to make sth from the model *ou* pattern; **faire qch sur le ~ de** to model sth on, make sth on the pattern *ou* model of; (*Gram*) **~ de conjugaison/déclinaison** conjugation/declension pattern; **son courage devrait nous servir de ~** his courage should be a model *ou* an example to us.

(b) (*personne*) (*gén*) model, example; (*Art*) model. **~ de vertu** paragon of virtue; **X est le ~ du bon élève/ouvrier** X is a model pupil/workman; **elle est un ~ de loyauté** she is a model of *ou* the very model of loyalty; **il restera pour nous un ~** he will remain an example to us; **prendre qn pour ~** to model *ou* pattern o.s. upon sb.

2 *adj conduite, ouvrier* model (*épith*). **c'est une ferme/usine ~** it's a show *ou* model farm/factory.

3: **modèle courant** *ou* **de série** standard *ou* production model; **modèle déposé** registered design; **modèle de fabrique** factory model; **modèle réduit** small-scale model; **modèle réduit au 1/100** model on the scale (of) 1 to 100; **modèle réduit d'avion, avion modèle réduit** scale model of an aeroplane.

modelé [mɔdle] *nm [peinture]* relief; *[sculpture, corps]* contours; (*Géog*) relief.

modeler [mɔdle] (5) *vt* (a) (*façonner*) *statue, poterie, glaise* to model, fashion, mould; *intelligence, caractère* to shape, mould. **l'exercice physique peut ~ les corps jeunes** exercise can shape young bodies; (*Géol*) **le relief a été modelé par la glaciation** the ground *ou* the terrain was moulded *ou* shaped by glaciation; **corps/cuisse bien modelé(e)** shapely *ou* well-shaped *ou* nicely shaped body/thigh; *V* **pâte.**

(b) (*conformer*) **~ ses attitudes/réactions sur** to model one's attitudes/reactions on; **se ~ sur qn/qch** to model *ou* pattern o.s. (up)on sb/sth.

modeleur, -euse [mɔdlœʀ, øz] *nm,f* (*Art*) modeller; (*Tech*) pattern maker.

modéliste [mɔdelist(ə)] *nmf* (a) *[mode]* (dress) designer. **ouvrière ~** dress designer's assistant. (b) *[maquette]* model builder.

Modène [mɔdɛn] *n* Modena.

modérantisme [mɔdeʀɑ̃tism(ə)] *nm* (*Hist*) moderantism.

modérantiste [mɔdeʀɑ̃tist(ə)] *nmf* (*Hist*) moderantist.

modérateur, -trice [mɔdeʀatœʀ, tʀis] 1 *adj action, influence* moderating (*épith*), restraining (*épith*). 2 *nm* (*Tech*) regulator. **~ de pile atomique** moderator (of nuclear reactor); *V* **ticket.**

modération [mɔdeʀɑsjɔ̃] *nf* (a) (*retenue*) moderation, restraint. **avec ~** in moderation.

(b) (*gén, Sci: diminution*) reduction, diminution, lessening.

(c) (*Jur: diminution*) *[peine]* mitigation; *[impôt]* reduction.

modéré, e [mɔdeʀe] (*ptp de* **modérer**) *adj personne* (*dans ses opinions, idées*) moderate; (*dans ses sentiments, désirs*) moderate, restrained; (*Pol*) moderate (*dans* in); *prix* reasonable, moderate; *chaleur, vent* moderate. (*Pol*) **les ~s** the moderates; *V* **habitation.**

modérément [mɔdeʀemɑ̃] *adv boire, manger* in moderation, a moderate amount. **être ~ satisfait** to be moderately *ou* fairly satisfied.

modérer [mɔdeʀe] (6) 1 *vt colère, passion* to restrain, curb, moderate; *ambitions* to curb, restrain; *dépenses, enthousiasme* to curb, moderate; *vitesse* to reduce. **modérez vos expressions!** moderate *ou* mind your language!

2 **se modérer** *vpr* (*s'apaiser*) to calm down, control o.s.; (*montrer de la mesure*) to restrain o.s.

moderne [mɔdɛʀn(ə)] 1 *adj* (*gén*) modern; *cuisine, équipement* up-to-date, modern; *méthode, idées* progressive, modern; (*opposé à classique*) *études* modern. **la jeune fille ~ se libère** the young woman of today *ou* today's young woman is becoming more liberated; *V* **confort.**

2 *nm* (*style*) modern style; (*meubles*) modern furniture. **meublé en ~** with modern furniture, furnished in contemporary style; **ce peintre/romancier est un ~** he is a modern painter/novelist; *V* **ancien.**

modernisation [mɔdɛʀnizɑsjɔ̃] *nf* modernization.

moderniser [mɔdɛʀnize] (1) *vt* to modernize, bring up to date.

modernisme [mɔdɛʀnism(ə)] *nm* modernism.

moderniste [mɔdɛʀnist(ə)] 1 *nmf* modernist. 2 *adj* modernistic.

modernité [mɔdɛʀnite] *nf* modernity.

modern style [mɔdɛʀnstil] *nm* ≃ art nouveau.

modeste [mɔdɛst(ə)] *adj* (a) (*simple*) *vie, appartement, salaire, tenue* modest. **c'est un cadeau bien ~!** it's only a very small gift *ou* thing, it's not much of a present; **un train de vie ~** an unpretentious *ou* a modest way of life; **je ne suis qu'un ~ ouvrier** I'm only a simple working man; **être d'un milieu** *ou* **d'origine ~** to have *ou* come from a modest *ou* humble background; **il est ~ dans ses ambitions** his ambitions are modest, he has modest ambitions.

(b) (*sans vanité*) *héros, attitude* modest. **faire le ~** to put on *ou* make a show of modesty; **tu fais le ~** you're just being modest; **avoir le triomphe ~** to be a modest winner, be modest about one's triumphs *ou* successes.

(c) (*réservé, effacé*) *personne, air* modest, unassuming, self-effacing.

(d) († *ou littér: pudique*) modest.

modestement [mɔdɛstəmɑ̃] *adv* (*V* **modeste**) modestly; unassumingly, self-effacingly.

modestie [mɔdɛsti] *nf* (*absence de vanité*) modesty; (*réserve, effacement*) self-effacement; (*littér: pudeur*) modesty; **fausse ~** false modesty.

modicité [mɔdisite] *nf [prix]* lowness; *[salaire]* lowness, smallness.

modifiable [mɔdifjabl(ə)] *adj* modifiable.

modifiant, e [mɔdifjɑ̃, ɑ̃t] *adj* modifying.

modificateur, -trice [mɔdifikatœʀ, tʀis] 1 *adj* modifying, modificatory. 2 *nm* (*rare*) modifier.

modificatif, -ive [mɔdifikatif, iv] *adj* modifying.

modification [mɔdifikɑsjɔ̃] *nf* modification.

modifier [mɔdifje] (7) 1 *vt* (*gén, Gram*) to modify. 2 **se modifier** *vpr* to alter, be modified.

modique [mɔdik] *adj salaire, prix* modest. **pour la ~ somme de**

for the modest sum of; **il ne recevait qu'une pension ~** he received only a modest *ou* meagre pension.

modiquement [mɔdikmɑ̃] *adv* poorly, meagrely.

modiste [mɔdist(ə)] *nf* milliner.

modulaire [mɔdylɛʀ] *adj* modular.

modulateur [mɔdylatœʀ] *nm* (*Rad*) modulator.

modulation [mɔdylɑsjɔ̃] *nf* (*Ling, Mus, Rad*) modulation. **~ d'amplitude** amplitude modulation; **~ de fréquence** frequency modulation; **poste à ~ de fréquence** VHF *ou* FM radio; **écouter une émission sur ~ de fréquence** to listen to a programme on VHF *ou* on FM.

module [mɔdyl] *nm* (*Archit, Espace, étalon*) module; (*Math, Phys*) modulus.

moduler [mɔdyle] (1) **1** *vt voix* to modulate, inflect; *air* to warble; *son* to modulate; (*Mus, Rad*) to modulate. **les cris modulés des marchands** the singsong cries of the tradesmen. **2** *vi* (*Mus*) to modulate.

modus vivendi [mɔdysvivɛ̃di] *nm inv* modus vivendi, working arrangement.

moelle [mwal] *nf* (*Anat*) marrow, medulla (*T*); (*Bot*) pith; (*fig*) pith, core. (*fig*) **être transi jusqu'à la ~ (des os)** to be frozen to the marrow; **frissonner jusqu'à la ~** to tremble to the very depths of one's being; **~ épinière** spinal chord; (*Culin*) **~ (de bœuf)** beef marrow; *V* **os, substantifique.**

moelleusement [mwaløzmɑ̃] *adv s'étendre* luxuriously.

moelleux, -euse [mwalø, øz] *adj forme, tapis, lit, couleur* soft; *aliment* creamy, smooth; *couleur, son, vin* mellow.

moellon [mwalɔ̃] *nm* (*Constr*) rubble stone.

mœurs [mœʀ(s)] *nfpl* **(a)** (*morale*) morals. **avoir des ~ sévères** to have high morals *ou* strict moral standards; **soupçonner les ~ de qn** to have doubts about sb's morals *ou* standards of behaviour; (*euph*) **il a des ~ particulières** he has certain tendencies (*euph*); **contraire aux bonnes ~** contrary to accepted standards of (good) behaviour; **femme de ~ légères** *ou* **faciles** woman of easy virtue; **femme de mauvaises ~** loose woman; (*Jur, Presse*) **affaire** *ou* **histoire de ~** sex case; **la police des ~, les M~*** ≃ the vice squad; *V* **certificat, outrage.**

(b) (*coutumes, habitudes*) [*peuple, époque*] customs, habits; [*abeilles, fourmis*] habits. **c'est (entré) dans les ~** it's (become) normal practice, it's (become) a standard *ou* an everyday feature of life; **il faut vivre avec les ~ de son temps** one must keep up with present-day customs *ou* habits; **les ~ politiques/littéraires de notre siècle** the political/literary practices *ou* usages of our century; **avoir des ~ simples/aristocratiques** to lead a simple/an aristocratic life, have a simple/an aristocratic life-style; *V* **autre.**

(c) (*manières*) manners, ways; (*Littérat*) manners. **ils ont de drôles de ~** they have some peculiar ways *ou* manners; **quelles ~!, drôles de ~!** what a way to behave! *ou* carry on!, what manners!; **peinture/comédie de ~** portrayal/comedy of manners.

mohair [mɔɛʀ] *nm* mohair.

moi [mwa] **1** *pron pers* **(a)** (*objet direct ou indirect*) me. **aide-~** help me, give me a hand; **donne-~ ton livre** give me your book, give your book to me; **donne-le-~** give it to me, give me it*; **si vous étiez ~ que feriez vous?** if you were me *ou* in my shoes what would you do?; **il nous a regardés ma femme et ~** he looked at my wife and me; **écoute-~ ça!*** just listen to that!; **elle me connaît bien, ~** she knows me all right!; **il n'obéit qu'à ~** he only obeys me, I'm the only one he obeys; **~, elle me déteste** she hates me *ou* ME; *V aussi* **même, non, seul.**

(b) (*sujet*) I (*emphatique*), I myself (*emphatique*), me*. **qui a fait cela? — (c'est) ~/(ce n'est) pas ~** who did this? — I did/I didn't *ou* me*/not me*; **~, le saluer?, jamais!** me, greet him?, never!; **mon mari et ~ (nous) refusons** my husband and I refuse; **~ parti/malade que ferez-vous?** when I'm gone/ill what will you do?, what will you do with me away/ill?; **et ~ de rire de plus belle!** and so I (just) laughed all the more!; **je ne l'ai pas vu, ~** I didn't see him myself, I myself didn't see him; **~, je ne suis pas d'accord** for my part I don't agree; **alors ~, je ne compte pas?** hey, what about me? *ou* where do I come in?*

(c) (*emphatique avec qui, que*) **c'est ~ qui vous le dis!** you can take it from me!, I'm telling you!; **merci — c'est ~ (qui vous remercie)** thank you — thank YOU; **et ~ qui n'avais pas le sou!** there was me without a penny!*, and to think I didn't have a penny!; **~ qui vous parle, je l'ai vu** I saw him personally; **c'est ~ qu'elle veut voir** it's me she wants to see; **il me dit cela à ~ qui l'ai tant aidé** he says that to ME after I've helped him so much; **et ~ qui avais espéré gagner!** and to think that I had hoped to win!; **~ que le théâtre passionne, je n'ai jamais vu cette pièce** even I, with all my great love for the theatre, have never seen that play.

(d) (*avec prép*) **à ~ il le dira** he'll tell ME (all right); **avec/sans ~** with/without me; **sans ~ il ne les aurait jamais retrouvés** but for me *ou* had it not been for me, he would never have found them; **venez chez ~** come to my place; **le poème n'est pas de ~** the poem isn't one I wrote *ou* isn't one of mine; **un élève à ~** a pupil of mine; **j'ai un appartement à ~** I have a flat of my own; **ce livre est à ~** this book belongs to me *ou* is mine; **mes livres à ~ sont bien rangés** MY books are arranged tidily; **elle l'a appris par ~** she heard about it from me *ou* through me; **cette lettre ne vient pas de ~** this letter isn't from me *ou* isn't one I wrote; **il veut une photo de ~** he wants a photo of me; **c'est à ~ de décider** it's up to me to decide.

(e) (*dans comparaisons*) I, me. **il est plus grand que ~** he is taller than I (am) *ou* than me; **il mange plus/moins que ~** he eats more/less than I (do) *ou* than me; **fais comme ~** do as I do, do like me*, do the same as me; **il l'aime plus que ~** (*plus qu'il ne m'aime*) he loves her more than (he loves) me; (*plus que je ne l'aime*) he loves her more than I do.

2 *nm*: **le ~** the self, the ego; **le ~ est haïssable** the ego *ou* self is detestable; **notre vrai ~** our true self.

moignon [mwaɲɔ̃] *nm* stump. **il n'avait plus qu'un ~ de bras** he had just the *ou* a stump of an arm left.

moi-même [mwamɛm] *pron V* **autre, même.**

moindre [mwɛ̃dʀ(ə)] *adj* **(a)** (*comp*) (*moins grand*) less, lesser; (*inférieur*) lower, poorer. **les dégâts sont bien** *ou* **beaucoup ~s** the damage is much less; **à un ~ degré, à un degré ~** to a lesser degree *ou* extent; **à ~ prix** at a lower price; **de ~ qualité, de qualité ~** of lower *ou* poorer quality; **enfant de ~ intelligence** child of lower *ou* less intelligence; **une épidémie de ~ étendue** a less widespread epidemic; *V* **mal.**

(b) (*superl*) **le ~, la ~, les ~s** the least, the slightest; (*de deux*) the lesser; **le ~ bruit** the slightest noise; **la ~ chance/idée** the slightest *ou* remotest chance/idea; **jusqu'au ~ détail** down to the smallest detail; **le ~ de deux maux** the lesser of two evils; **sans se faire le ~ souci** without worrying in the slightest; **c'est la ~ de mes difficultés** that's the least of my difficulties; **c'est la ~ des choses!** it's a pleasure!; **remerciez-le de m'avoir aidé — c'était la ~ des choses** thank him for helping me — it was the least he could do; **certains spécialistes et non des ~s disent que** some specialists and important ones at that say that; **la ~ des politesses veut que ...** common politeness demands that ... ; **il n'a pas fait le ~ commentaire** he didn't make a single comment; **la loi du ~ effort** the line of least resistance *ou* effort, the law of least effort.

moindrement [mwɛ̃dʀəmɑ̃] *adv* (*littér*) (*avec nég*) **il n'était pas le ~ surpris** he was not in the least surprised, he was not surprised in the slightest; **sans l'avoir le ~ voulu** without having in any way wanted this.

moine [mwan] *nm* **(a)** (*Rel*) monk, friar. **~ bouddhiste** buddhist monk; *V* **habit.**

(b) (*Zool*) monk seal; (*Orn*) black vulture.

(c) (*Hist: chauffe-lit*) bedwarmer.

moineau, *pl* **~x** [mwano] *nm* (*Orn*) sparrow. (*péj rare*) **sale** *ou* **vilain ~** dirty dog.

moinillon [mwanijɔ̃] *nm* (*hum*) little monk (*hum*).

moins [mwɛ̃] **1** *adv* **(a)** (*avec adj, adv ou vb*) less. (*en comparatifs*) **~ que ...** less ... than, not so ... as; **~ ... plus** the less ... the more ... ; **~ je mange, ~ j'ai d'appétit** the less I eat the less hungry I feel; **beaucoup/un peu ~** much/a little less; **tellement ~** so much less; **encore ~** even less; **3 fois ~** 3 times less; **il est ~ grand/intelligent que son frère/que nous/que je ne pensais** he is not as tall/intelligent as his brother/as us *ou* as we are/as I thought, he is less tall/intelligent than his brother/than us *ou* than we are/than I thought; **il travaille ~/~ vite que vous** he works less/less quickly than you (do), he does not work as hard/as quickly as you do; **il a fait encore ~ beau en août qu'en juillet** the weather was even worse in August than in July; **sortez ~ (souvent)** go out less often, don't go out so often *ou* so much; **j'aime ~ la campagne en hiver (qu'en été)** I don't like the country so much in winter *ou* I like the country less in winter (than in summer); **rien n'est ~ sûr, il n'y a rien de ~ sûr** nothing is less certain; **c'est tellement ~ cher** it's so much cheaper *ou* less expensive; **~ je fume, plus je mange** the less I smoke the more I eat; **il ressemble à son père, en ~ grand** he looks like his father only he's not so tall, he looks like a smaller version of his father; **c'est le même genre de livre, en ~ bien** it's the same kind of book, only (it's) not so good *ou* but not so good.

(b) (*superl*) **le~, la~, les ~** least, the least; **c'est la ~ douée de mes élèves** she is the least gifted of my pupils; **la température la ~ haute de l'été** the lowest temperature of the summer; **c'est celui que j'aime le ~/que je lis le ~ souvent** it's the one I like (the) least/I read (the) least often.

2 *nm* **(a)** (*quantité*) less. **exiger/donner ~** to demand/give less; **je gagne (un peu) ~ que lui** I earn (a little) less than him *ou* than he does; **cela m'a coûté ~ que rien** it cost me next to nothing; **vous ne l'obtiendrez pas à ~** you won't get it for less.

(b) **~ de** (*quantité*) less, not so much; (*nombre*) fewer, not so many; (*heure*) before, not yet; (*durée, âge, distance*) less than, under; **mange ~ de bonbons et de chocolat** eat fewer sweets and less chocolate; **il y a ~ de 2 ans qu'il vit ici** he has been living here (for) less than 2 years; **les enfants de ~ de 4 ans voyagent gratuitement** children under 4 *ou* of less than 4 years of age travel free; **il est ~ de minuit** it is not yet midnight; **vous ne pouvez pas lui donner ~ de 100 F** you can't give him less than 100 francs; **vous ne trouverez rien à ~ de 100 F** you won't find anything under 100 francs *ou* for less than 100 francs; **il a eu ~ de mal que nous à trouver une place** he had less trouble than we had *ou* than us (in) finding a seat; **ils ont ~ de livres que de jouets** they have fewer books than toys; **nous l'avons fait en ~ de 5 minutes** we did it in less than *ou* in under 5 minutes; **en ~ de deux** in a flash *ou* a trice, in the twinkling of an eye; **il y aura ~ de monde demain** there will be fewer people tomorrow, there will not be so many people tomorrow; **il devrait y avoir ~ de 100 personnes** there should be under 100 people *ou* less than a hundred people; **en ~ de rien** in less than no time.

(c) (*superl*) **c'est (bien) le ~ qu'on puisse faire** it's the least one can do; **de nous tous c'est lui qui a bu le ~** he's the one who drank the least of all of us, of all of us he drank the least; **si vous êtes le ~ du monde soucieux** if you are the slightest bit *ou* the least bit *ou* in the least worried.

(d) (*quantité qui se soustrait*) **il gagne 500 F de ~ qu'elle** he earns 500 francs less than she does; **vous avez 5 ans de ~ qu'elle** you are 5 years younger than her *ou* than she is; **il y a 3 verres en ~** (*qui manquent*) there are 3 glasses missing; (*trop peu*) we are 3 glasses short; **c'est le même climat, le brouillard en ~** it's the same climate except for the fog *ou* minus the fog.

(e) (*signe algébrique*) minus (sign).

(f) (*loc*) **à ~ qu'il ne vienne** unless he comes; **à ~ de faire une**

bêtise il devrait gagner unless he does something silly he should win; **à ~ d'un accident ça devrait marcher** barring accidents it should work; **au ~** at (the) least; **elle a payé cette robe au ~ 1.000 F** she paid at least 1,000 francs for this dress; **cela fait au ~ 10 jours qu'il est parti** it is at least 10 days since he left; **vous avez (tout) au ~ appris la nouvelle** you must at least have heard the news; **à tout le ~, pour le ~** to say the least, at the very least; **sa décision est pour le ~ bizarre** his decision is odd to say the least; **de ~ en ~** less and less; **du ~** (*restriction*) at least; **il ne pleuvra pas, du ~ c'est ce qu'annonce la radio** it's not going to rain, at least that's what it says on the radio *ou* at least so the radio says; **si du ~** that is if; **laissez-le sortir, si du ~ il ne fait pas froid** let him go out, that is (only) if it is not cold; *V* **autant, plus.**

3 *prép* **(a)** (*soustraction*) **6 ~ 2 font 4** 6 minus 2 equals 4, 2 from 6 makes 4; **j'ai retrouvé mon sac, ~ le portefeuille** I found my bag, minus the wallet.

(b) (*heure*) to. **il est 4 heures ~ 5 (minutes)** it is 5 (minutes) to 4; **nous avons le temps, il n'est que ~ 10*** we have plenty of time, it's only 10 to*.

(c) (*température*) below. **il fait ~ 5°** it is 5° below freezing *ou* minus 5°.

4: (*Comm*) **moins-value** *nf* depreciation.

moirage [mwaʀaʒ] *nm* (*procédé*) watering; (*reflet*) watered effet.

moire [mwaʀ] *nf* (*tissu*) moiré, watered fabric; (*procédé*) watering. **on voit la ~ du papier** you can see the mottled effect in the paper.

moiré, e [mwaʀe] (*ptp de* **moirer**) **1** *adj* (*Tech*) watered, moiré; (*fig*) shimmering. **2** *nm* (*Tech*) moiré, water; (*littér*) shimmering ripples.

moirer [mwaʀe] (1) *vt* (*Tech*) to water. (*littér*) **la lune moirait l'étang de reflets argentés** the moon cast a shimmering silvery light over the pool.

moirure [mwaʀyʀ] *nf* (*Tech*) moiré; (*littér*) shimmering ripples.

mois [mwa] *nm* **(a)** (*période*) month. (*Rel*) **~ de Marie** month of Mary; (*Culin*) **les ~ en R** when there is an R in the month; **au ~ de janvier** in (the month of) January; **dans un ~** in a month('s time); (*Comm*) **le 10 de ce ~** the 10th inst(ant) *ou* the 10th of this month; **être payé au ~** to be paid monthly; **louer au ~** to rent by the month; **30 F par ~** 30 francs a *ou* per month; (*Comm*) **billet à 3 ~** bill at 3 months; **un bébé de 6 ~** a 6-month(-old) baby; **tous les 4 ~** every 4 months; **devoir 3 ~ de loyer** to owe 3 months' rent; **devoir 3 ~ (de factures)** to owe 3 months' bills; *V* **enceinte[1], tout.**

(b) (*salaire*) monthly pay, monthly salary. **toucher son ~*** to draw one's pay *ou* salary for the month *ou* one's month's pay *ou* salary; **~ double** extra month's pay (*as end-of-year bonus*); *V* **fin[2].**

Moïse [mɔiz] *nm* Moses.

moïse [mɔiz] *nm* (*berceau*) Moses basket.

moisi, e [mwazi] (*ptp de* **moisir**) **1** *adj* mouldy, mildewed. **2** *nm* mould, mildew. **odeur de ~** musty *ou* fusty smell; **goût de ~** musty taste; **ça sent le ~** it smells musty *ou* fusty.

moisir [mwaziʀ] (2) **1** *vt* to make mouldy.

2 *vi* **(a)** to go mouldy, mould.

(b) (*fig*) **~ en province** to stagnate in the country; **~ dans un cachot** to rot in a dungeon; **on ne va pas ~ ici jusqu'à la nuit!*** we're not going to stay here and rot* till night-time!

moisissure [mwazisyʀ] *nf* **(a)** (*V* **moisir**) mould, mouldiness.

(b) (*Bio*) mould (*U*).

(c) (*moisi*) mould (*U*), mildew (*U*). **enlever les ~s sur un fromage** to scrape the mould *ou* mildew off a piece of cheese.

moisson [mwasɔ̃] *nf* (*saison, travail*) harvest; (*récolte*) harvest, crop; (*fig*) wealth. **à l'époque de la ~** at harvest time; **la ~ est en avance/en retard** the harvest is early/late; **rentrer la ~** to bring in the harvest; **faire la ~** to harvest, reap; (*fig*) **faire (une) ample ~ de renseignements/souvenirs** to gather *ou* amass a wealth of information/memories; (*fig*) **faire une ample ~ de lauriers** to carry off a rich booty of prizes.

moissonner [mwasɔne] (1) *vt* (*Agr*) *céréale* to harvest, reap, gather in; *champ* to reap; († *ou littér*) *récompenses* to collect, carry off; *renseignements, souvenirs* to gather, collect. (*littér*) **cette génération moissonnée par la guerre** this generation cut down by the war.

moissonneur, -euse [mwasɔnœʀ, øz] **1** *nm,f* harvester, reaper († *ou littér*).

2 **moissonneuse** *nf* (*machine*) harvester.

3: **moissonneuse-batteuse** *nf, pl* **moissonneuses-batteuses** combine harvester; **moissonneuse-batteuse-lieuse** *nf, pl* **moissonneuses-batteuses-lieuses** combine harvester; **moissonneuse-lieuse** *nf, pl* **moissonneuses-lieuses** self-binder.

moite [mwat] *adj peau, mains* sweaty, sticky; *atmosphère* sticky, muggy; *chaleur* sticky.

moiteur [mwatœʀ] *nf* (*V* **moite**) sweatiness; stickiness; mugginess. **essuyer la ~ de ses paumes** to wipe the stickiness from one's hands.

moitié [mwatje] *nf* **(a)** (*partie*) half. **partager qch en deux ~s** to halve sth, divide sth in half *ou* into (two) halves; **quelle est la ~ de 40?** what is half of 40?; **donne-m'en la ~** give me half (of it); **faire la ~ du chemin avec qn** to go halfway *ou* half of the way with sb; **la ~ des habitants a été sauvée** *ou* **ont été sauvés** half (of) the inhabitants were rescued; **la ~ du temps** half the time; **il en faut ~ plus/moins** you need half as much again/half (of) that; **~ anglais, ~ français** half English, half French.

(b) (*milieu*) halfway mark, half. **parvenu à la ~ du trajet** having completed half the journey, having reached halfway *ou* the halfway mark; **parvenu à la ~ de la vie** when one reaches the middle of one's life, when one has completed half one's life-span; **arrivé à la ~ du travail** having done half the work *ou* got halfway through the work.

(c) (*hum: épouse*) **ma/sa ~** my/his better half* (*hum*); **ma tendre ~** my ever-loving wife (*hum*).

(d) **à ~** half; **il a fait le travail à ~** he has (only) half done the work; **il a mis la table à ~** he has half set the table; **il ne fait jamais rien à ~** he never does things by halves; **à ~ plein/mûr** half-full/-ripe; **à ~ chemin** (at) halfway, at the halfway mark; **à ~ prix** (at) half-price.

(e) (*loc*) **de ~** by half; **réduire de ~** *trajet, production, coût* to cut *ou* reduce by half, halve; **plus grand de ~** half as big again, bigger by half; **être/se mettre de ~ dans une entreprise** to have half shares/go halves in a business; **par ~** in two, in half; **diviser qch par ~** to divide sth in two *ou* in half; **il est pour ~ dans cette faillite** he is half responsible *ou* half to blame for this bankruptcy; **~ ~: on a partagé le pain ~ ~** we halved the bread between us, we shared the bread half-and-half *ou* fifty-fifty*; **ils ont partagé** *ou* **fait ~ ~** they went halves; **ça a marché? — ~ ~*** how did it go? — so-so*.

moka [mɔka] *nm* (*gâteau*) coffee cream cake, mocha cake; (*café*) mocha coffee.

mol [mɔl] *adj m V* **mou[1].**

molaire[1] [mɔlɛʀ] *nf* (*dent*) molar.

molaire[2] [mɔlɛʀ] *adj* (*Chim*) molar.

molasse [mɔlas] *nf* = **mollasse[2].**

moldave [mɔldav] **1** *adj* Moldavian. **2** *nmf*: **M~** Moldavian.

Moldavie [mɔldavi] *nf* Moldavia.

mole [mɔl] *nf* (*Chim*) mole, mol.

môle [mol] *nm* (*digue*) breakwater, mole, jetty; (*quai*) pier, jetty.

moléculaire [mɔlekylɛʀ] *adj* molecular.

molécule [mɔlekyl] *nf* molecule. **~-gramme** gram molecule.

moleskine [mɔlɛskin] *nf* imitation leather. **il avait usé ses pantalons sur la ~ des cafés** he had spent half his life sitting around in cafés.

molester [mɔlɛste] (1) *vt* to manhandle, maul (about). **molesté par la foule** mauled by the crowd.

moleté, e [mɔlte] *adj roue, vis* milled, knurled.

molette [mɔlɛt] *nf* **(a)** (*Tech*) toothed wheel, cutting wheel; *V* **clef. (b)** *[briquet, clef]* knurl; *[éperon]* rowel.

moliéresque [mɔljeʀɛsk(ə)] *adj* Molieresque.

mollard‡ [mɔlaʀ] *nm* (*crachat*) gob of spit‡.

mollasse[1]* [mɔlas] **1** *adj* (*péj*) sluggish, lethargic; (*flasque*) flabby, flaccid. **une grande fille ~** a great lump* of a girl. **2** *nmf* lazy lump*.

mollasse[2] [mɔlas] *nf* (*Géol*) molasse.

mollasserie [mɔlasʀi] *nf* sluggishness, lethargy.

mollasson, -onne* [mɔlasɔ̃, ɔn] (*péj*) **1** *adj* sluggish, lethargic. **2** *nm,f* lazy lump*.

molle [mɔl] *adj f V* **mou[1].**

mollement [mɔlmɑ̃] *adv* (*doucement*) *tomber* softly; *couler* gently, sluggishly; (*paresseusement*) *travailler* half-heartedly, lethargically, unenthusiastically; (*faiblement*) *réagir, protester* feebly, weakly. **les jours s'écoulaient ~** the days slipped gently by.

mollesse [mɔlɛs] *nf* **(a)** (*au toucher*) *[substance, oreiller]* softness; *[poignée de main]* limpness, flabbiness.

(b) (*à la vue*) *[contours, lignes]* softness; *[relief]* softness, gentleness; *[traits du visage]* flabbiness, sagginess; (*Peinture*) *[dessin, traits]* lifelessness, weakness.

(c) (*manque d'énergie*) *[geste]* lifelessness, feebleness; *[protestations, opposition]* weakness, feebleness; (†) *[vie]* indolence, softness; *[style]* woolliness; (*Mus*) *[exécution]* lifelessness, dullness; *[personne]* (*indolence*) sluggishness, lethargy; (*manque d'autorité*) spinelessness; (*grande indulgence*) laxness. **vivre dans la ~** to live the soft life.

mollet[1], -ette [mɔlɛ, ɛt] *adj V* **œuf.**

mollet[2] [mɔlɛ] *nm* (*Anat*) calf. (*fig*) **~s de coq** wiry legs.

molletière [mɔltjɛʀ] *nf V* **bande[1].**

molleton [mɔltɔ̃] *nm* (*tissu*) flannelette, duffel; (*pour table etc*) felting.

molletonner [mɔltɔne] (1) *vt* to line *ou* cover with flannelette. **gants molletonnés** fleece-lined gloves.

mollir [mɔliʀ] (2) *vi* **(a)** (*fléchir*) *[sol]* to give (way), yield; *[ennemi]* to yield, give way, give ground; *[père, créancier]* to come round, relent; *[courage]* to be failing, flag. **nos prières l'ont fait ~** our pleas softened his attitude *ou* made him relent; (*fig*) **sentir ses jambes/genoux ~ sous soi** to feel one's legs/knees give way beneath one.

(b) *[substance]* to soften, go soft.

(c) *[vent]* to abate, die down.

mollo‡ [mɔlo] *adv*: **(vas-y) ~!** take it easy!*, (go) easy*!, easy does it!

mollusque [mɔlysk(ə)] *nm* (*Zool*) mollusc; (** péj*) lazy lump*, spineless lump* (*péj*).

molosse [mɔlɔs] *nm* (*littér*) big (ferocious) dog, huge hound (*hum*).

môme [mom] *nmf* (**: enfant*) kid*; (*péj*) brat*; (*‡: fille*) bird‡. **belle ~‡** nice-looking piece‡.

moment [mɔmɑ̃] *nm* **(a)** (*long instant*) while, moment. **pendant un court ~ elle le crut** for a moment *ou* a few moments she believed him; **je ne l'ai pas vu depuis un (bon) ~** I haven't seen him for a (good) while *ou* for quite a time *ou* while; **cette réparation va prendre un ~** this repair job will take some time *ou* a good while; **elle en a pour un petit ~** (*lit*) she won't be long *ou* a moment, it'll only take her a moment; (*iro*) she'll be some *ou* a little while.

(b) (*court instant*) **il réfléchit un ~** he thought for a moment; **c'est l'affaire d'un ~** it won't take a minute *ou* moment, it will only take a minute, it'll be done in a jiffy*; **ça ne dure qu'un ~** it doesn't last long, it (only) lasts a minute; **un ~ de silence** a moment of silence, a moment's silence; **j'ai eu un ~ de panique** for a moment I panicked; **en un ~** in a matter of minutes; **dans un ~ de colère** in a moment of anger, in a momentary fit of anger; **dans un ~** in a little while, in a moment; **un ~, il arrive!** just a moment *ou* a minute *ou* a mo'*, he's coming!

(c) (*période caractérisée*) time. **à quel ~ est-ce arrivé?** at what point in time *ou* when exactly did this occur?; **connaître/passer de bons ~s** to have/spend (some) happy times; **les ~s que nous avons passés ensemble** the times we spent together; **il a passé un mauvais *ou* sale ~*** he went through *ou* had a difficult time, he had a rough* time *ou* passage; **je n'ai pas un ~ à moi** I haven't a moment to myself; **le ~ présent** the present time; **à ses ~s perdus** in his spare time; **les grands ~s de l'histoire** the great moments of history; **il a ses bons et ses mauvais ~s** he has his good times and his bad (times); **il est dans un de ses mauvais ~s** it's one of *ou* he's having one of his off spells; **la célébrité/le succès du ~** the celebrity/success of the moment *ou* day.

(d) (*instant spécifique*) **il faut profiter du ~** you must take advantage of *ou* seize this opportunity; **ce n'est pas le ~ (de protester)** this is no time *ou* not the time (to protest *ou* for protesting), this is not the (right) moment (to protest); **tu arrives au bon ~** you've come just at the right time; **le ~ psychologique** the psychological moment; *V* **jamais.**

(e) (*Tech*) moment; (*Phys*) momentum.

(f) (*loc*) **en ce ~** at the moment, at present, just now; **au ~ de l'accident** at the time of the accident, when the accident took place; **au ~ de partir** just as I (*ou* he *etc*) was about to leave, just as I (*ou* he *etc*) was on the point of leaving; **au ~ où elle entrait, lui sortait** as she was going in he was coming out; **au ~ où il s'y attendait le moins** (at a time) when he was least expecting it; **à un ~ donné il cesse d'écouter** at a certain point he stops listening; **il se prépare afin de savoir quoi dire le ~ venu** he's getting ready so that he'll know what to say when the time comes; **le ~ venu ils s'élancèrent** when the time came they hurled themselves forward; **des voitures arrivaient à tout ~** *ou* **tous ~s** cars were constantly *ou* continually arriving, cars kept on arriving; **il peut arriver à tout ~** he may arrive (at) any time (now) *ou* any moment (now); **à ce ~-là** (*temps*) at that point *ou* time; (*circonstance*) in that case, if that's the case, if that's so; **à aucun ~ je n'ai dit que** I never at any time said that; **le bruit grandissait de ~ en ~** the noise grew louder every moment *ou* grew ever louder; **on l'attend d'un ~ à l'autre** he is expected any moment now *ou* (at) any time now; **du ~ où *ou* que** since, seeing that; **dès le ~ que *ou* où** as soon as, from the moment *ou* time when; **par ~s** now and then, at times, every now and again; **pour le ~** for the time being *ou* the moment, at present; **sur le ~** at the time.

momentané, e [mɔmɑ̃tane] *adj gêne, crise, arrêt* momentary (*épith*); *espoir, effort* short-lived, brief. **cette crise n'est que ~e** this is only a momentary crisis.

momentanément [mɔmɑ̃tanemɑ̃] *adv* (*en ce moment*) at *ou* for the moment, at present; (*un court instant*) for a short while, momentarily.

momeries [mɔmʀi] *nfpl* (*littér*) mummery, mumbo jumbo.

momie [mɔmi] *nf* mummy. (**fig*) **ne reste pas là comme une ~** don't stand there like a stuffed dummy*.

momification [mɔmifikɑsjɔ̃] *nf* mummification.

momifier [mɔmifje] (7) **1** *vt* to mummify. **2 se momifier** *vpr* (*fig*) *[corps]* to atrophy, shrivel up; *[esprit]* to fossilize.

mon [mɔ̃], **ma** [ma], **mes** [me] *adj poss* **(a)** (*possession, relation*) my, my own (*emphatique*). **~ fils et ma fille** my son and (my) daughter; *pour autres exemples V* **son**[1].

(b) (*valeur affective, ironique, intensive*) **alors voilà ~ type/~ François qui se met à m'injurier*** and then the fellow/our François starts bawling insults at me; **on a changé ~ Paris** they've changed the Paris I knew *ou* what I think of as Paris; **j'ai ~ samedi cette année*** I've got Saturday(s) off this year; *V* **son**[1].

(c) (*dans termes d'adresse*) my. **viens ~ petit/ma chérie** come along lovie*/(my) darling; **~ cher ami** my dear friend; **~ cher monsieur** my dear sir; **~ vieux** my dear fellow; **ma vieille** my dear girl; **eh bien ~ vieux, si j'avais su!*** well I can tell you old chap*, if I'd known!; (*Rel*) **oui ~ Père/ma Sœur/ma Mère** yes Father/Sister/Mother; (*Rel*) **mes (bien chers) frères** my (dear) brethren; (*Rel*) **~ Dieu, ayez pitié de nous** dear Lord *ou* O God, have mercy upon us; (*Mil*) **oui ~ lieutenant/général** yes sir/sir *ou* general; **eh bien ~ salaud *ou* cochon, tu as du toupet‡** you so-and-so *ou* you old devil, you've got some cheek!‡; **~ Dieu, j'ai oublié mon sac** oh dear, *ou* heavens, I've forgotten my bag.

monacal, e, *mpl* **-aux** [mɔnakal, o] *adj* (*lit, fig*) monastic.

Monaco [mɔnako] *nm* Monaco.

monade [mɔnad] *nf* monad.

monarchie [mɔnaʀʃi] *nf* monarchy.

monarchique [mɔnaʀʃik] *adj* monarchistic, monarchial.

monarchisme [mɔnaʀʃism(ə)] *nm* monarchism.

monarchiste [mɔnaʀʃist(ə)] *adj, nmf* monarchist.

monarque [mɔnaʀk(ə)] *nm* monarch.

monastère [mɔnastɛʀ] *nm* monastery.

monastique [mɔnastik] *adj* monastic.

monaural, e, *mpl* **-aux** [mɔnoʀal, o] *adj* monophonic, monaural.

monceau, *pl* **~x** [mɔ̃so] *nm*: **un ~ de** (*amoncellement*) a heap *ou* pile of; (*accumulation*) a heap *ou* load* of; **des ~x de** heaps *ou* piles of; heaps *ou* loads* *ou* stacks* of.

mondain, e [mɔ̃dɛ̃, ɛn] **1** *adj* **(a)** *réunion, vie* society (*épith*); *public* fashionable. **plaisirs ~s** pleasures of society; **mener une vie ~e** to lead a busy social life, be in the social round, move in fashionable circles; **goût pour la vie ~e** taste for society life *ou* living; **carnet/romancier ~** society news/novelist; **chronique ~e** society gossip column; **leurs obligations ~es** their social obligations; **ils sont très ~s** they are great society people *ou* great socialites, they like moving in fashionable society *ou* circles.

(b) *politesse, ton* refined, urbane, sophisticated.

(c) (*Philos*) mundane; (*Rel*) worldly, earthly.

(d) la police *ou* brigade ~, la M~* ≃ the vice squad.

2 *nm,f* society man (*ou* woman), socialite.

mondanité [mɔ̃danite] *nf* **(a) ~s** (*divertissements, soirées*) society life; (*politesses, propos*) society *ou* polite small talk; (*Presse: chronique*) society gossip column; **toutes ces ~s sont fatigantes** we are exhausted by this social whirl *ou* round.

(b) (*goût*) taste for society life, love of society life; (*habitude, connaissance des usages*) savoir-faire.

(c) (*Rel*) worldliness.

monde [mɔ̃d] *nm* **(a)** (*univers, terre*) world. **dans le ~ entier,** (*littér*) **de par le ~** all over the world, the world over, throughout the world; **le ~ entier s'indigna** the whole world was outraged; **le ~ des vivants** the land of the living; **il se moque *ou* se fiche* *ou* se fout‡ du ~** he's got a nerve* *ou* cheek*, he's got a damn‡ *ou* bloody‡ nerve; **venir au ~** to come into the world; **mettre un enfant au ~** to bring a child into the world; **si je suis encore de ce ~** if I'm still here *ou* in the land of the living *ou* of this world; **depuis qu'il est de ce ~** since he was born; **rêver à un ~ meilleur** to dream of a better world; **où va le ~?** whatever is the world coming to?; **dans ce (bas) ~** here below, in this world; **l'Ancien/le Nouveau M~** the Old/New World; *V* **unique.**

(b) (*ensemble, groupement spécifique*) world. **le ~ végétal/animal** the vegetable/animal world; **le ~ des affaires/du théâtre** the world of business/(the) theatre, the business/theatre world; **le ~ chrétien/communiste/capitaliste** the Christian/communist/capitalist world.

(c) (*domaine*) world, realm. **le ~ de l'illusion/du rêve** the realm of illusion/dreams; **le ~ de la folie** the world *ou* realm of madness.

(d) (*intensif*) **du ~, au ~** in the world, on earth; **produit parmi les meilleurs au *ou* du ~** product which is among the best in the world *ou* among the world's best; (*littér*) **au demeurant, le meilleur homme du *ou* au ~** even so, the finest man alive; **tout s'est passé le mieux du ~** everything went (off) perfectly *ou* like a dream*; **il n'était pas le moins du ~ anxieux** he was not the slightest *ou* least bit worried, he wasn't worried in the slightest *ou* least; **je ne m'en séparerais pour rien au ~** I wouldn't part with it for anything (in the world) *ou* for all the world *ou* for all the tea in China; **nul au ~ ne peut ...** nobody in the world can ...; **j'en pense tout le bien du ~** I have the highest opinion of him *ou* her *ou* it.

(e) (*loc*) **c'est le ~ à l'envers *ou* renversé** it's a topsy-turvy *ou* crazy world; **comme le ~ est petit!** it's a small world!; **se faire (tout) un ~ de qch** to make a (great deal of) fuss about *ou* a (great) song and dance about sth; **se faire un ~ de rien** to make a mountain out of a molehill, make a fuss over nothing; **se faire un ~ de tout** to make a fuss over everything, make everything into a great issue; **c'est un ~!*** if that doesn't beat all!*; **il y a un ~ entre ces deux personnes/conceptions** these two people/concepts are worlds apart, there is a world of difference between these two people/concepts.

(f) (*gens*) **j'entends du ~ à côté** I can hear people in the next room; **est-ce qu'il y a du ~?** (*qn est-il présent*) is there anybody there?; (*y a-t-il foule*) are there many there?, are there a lot of people there?; **il y a du ~** (*ce n'est pas vide*) there are some people there; (*il y a foule*) there's quite a crowd; **il y a beaucoup de ~** there's a real crowd, there are a lot of people; **il y avait un ~!** *ou* **un ~ fou!*** there were crowds!, the place was packed!; **ils voient beaucoup de ~** they have a busy social life; **ils reçoivent beaucoup de ~** they entertain a lot, they do a lot of entertaining; **ce week-end nous avons du ~** we have people coming *ou* visitors *ou* company this weekend; (*fig*) **il y a du ~ au balcon!‡** what a frontage‡ she's got!; **elle promène tout son petit ~** she's out with all her brood; **tout ce petit ~ s'est bien amusé?** and have all these children had a nice time?; **il connaît son ~** he knows the people he deals with; **je n'ai pas encore tout mon ~** my set *ou* group *ou* lot* isn't all here yet; *V* **monsieur, tout.**

(g) (*Rel*) **le ~** the world; **les plaisirs du ~** worldly pleasures, the pleasures of the world.

(h) (*milieu social*) set, circle. (*la bonne société*) **le (grand *ou* beau) ~** (high) society; **aller dans le ~** to mix with high society; **appartenir au meilleur ~** to move in the best circles; **il n'est pas de notre ~** he is from a different set, he's not one of our set *ou* crowd*; **nous ne sommes pas du même ~** we don't move in *ou* belong to the same circles (of society); **cela ne se fait pas dans le ~** that isn't done in the best of circles *ou* in polite society; **homme/femme/gens du ~** society man/woman/people; *V* **beau, grand** *etc.*

monder [mɔ̃de] (1) *vt orge* to hull.

mondial, e, *mpl* **-aux** [mɔ̃djal, o] *adj* world (*épith*), world-wide. **guerre/population/production ~e** world war/population/production; **influence/crise ~e** world-wide influence/crisis; **à l'échelle ~e** on a world-wide scale, world-wide; **une célébrité ~e** a world-famous personality *ou* celebrity.

mondialement [mɔ̃djalmɑ̃] *adv* throughout the world. **il est ~ connu** he is known the (whole) world over *ou* throughout the world, he is world-famous.

mondialisation [mɔ̃djalizɑsjɔ̃] *nf [technique]* world-wide application. **redoutant la ~ du conflit** fearing that the conflict will (*ou* would) spread throughout the world, fearing the spread of the conflict world-wide *ou* throughout the world.

mond(i)ovision [mɔ̃d(j)ɔvizjɔ̃] *nf* television broadcast by satellite.
monégasque [mɔnegask(ə)] 1 *adj* Monegasque. 2 *nmf*: **M~** Monegasque.
monème [mɔnɛm] *nm* moneme.
monétaire [mɔnetɛʀ] *adj valeur, unité, système* monetary. **la circulation ~** the circulation of currency; *V* **masse**.
monétiser [mɔnetize] (1) *vt* to monetize.
mongol, e [mɔ̃gɔl] 1 *adj* Mongol, Mongolian. 2 *nm* (*Ling*) Mongolian. 3 *nm,f* (*Géog*) **M~(e)** (*gén*) Mongol, Mongoloid; (*habitant ou originaire de la Mongolie*) Mongolian.
Mongolie [mɔ̃gɔli] *nf* Mongolia. **République populaire de ~** Mongolian People's Republic, People's Republic of Mongolia.
mongolien, -ienne [mɔ̃gɔljɛ̃, jɛn] *adj, nm,f* (*Méd*) mongol.
mongolique [mɔ̃gɔlik] *adj* (*rare: Géog*) Mongol(ic), Mongolian.
mongolisme [mɔ̃gɔlism(ə)] *nm* mongolism.
monisme [mɔnism(ə)] *nm* monism.
moniste [mɔnist(ə)] 1 *adj* monistic.
2 *nmf* monist.
moniteur [mɔnitœʀ] *nm* **(a)** (*Sport*) instructor. **(b)** *[colonie de vacances]* supervisor (*Brit*), (camp) counsellor (*US*).
monitrice [mɔnitʀis] *nf* **(a)** (*Sport*) instructress. **(b)** *[colonie de vacances]* supervisor (*Brit*), (camp) counsellor (*US*).
monnaie [mɔnɛ] 1 *nf* **(a)** (*Écon, Fin: espèces, devises*) currency. **une ~ forte** a strong currency; **~ d'or/d'argent** gold/silver currency; **~ décimale** decimal coinage *ou* currency; *V* **battre, faux²**, **hôtel**.
(b) (*pièce, médaille*) coin. **une ~ d'or** a gold coin; **émettre/retirer une ~** to issue/withdraw a coin.
(c) (*pièces inférieures à l'unité, appoint*) change; (*petites pièces*) (loose) change. **petite** *ou* **menue ~** small change; **vous n'avez pas de ~?** (*pour payer*) haven't you got (the) change? *ou* any change?; **auriez-vous de la ~?, pourriez-vous me faire de la ~?** could you give me some change?; **faire de la ~** to get (some) change; **faire la ~ de 100 F** to get change for *ou* change a 100-franc note *ou* 100 francs; **faire** *ou* **donner à qn la ~ de 10 F** to change 10 francs for sb, give sb the change for 10 francs; **elle m'a rendu la ~ sur 10 F** she gave me the change out of *ou* from 10 francs; **passez la ~!*** let's have the money!, cough up* everyone!
(d) (*loc*) **c'est ~ courante** *[faits, événements]* it's common *ou* widespread, it's a common occurrence; *[actions, pratiques]* it's common practice, it's widespread, it's a common occurrence; (*fig*) **donner** *ou* **rendre à qn la ~ de sa pièce** to pay sb back in the same *ou* in his own coin, repay sb in kind; **à l'école les billes servent de ~ d'échange** at school marbles are used as money *ou* as a currency; **payer qn en ~ de singe** to fob sb off with empty promises.
2: (*Fin*) **monnaie divisionnaire** fractional currency; (*Fin*) **monnaie fiduciaire** fiduciary currency, paper money; (*Fin*) **monnaie légale** legal tender; (*Fin*) **monnaie métallique** coin (*U*); (*Bot*) **monnaie-du-pape** *nf, pl* **monnaies-du-pape** honesty; (*Fin*) **monnaie de papier** paper money; (*Fin*) **monnaie scripturale** *ou* **de banque** representative *ou* bank money.
monnayable [mɔnɛjabl(ə)] *adj* (*V* **monnayer**) convertible into cash. (*fig*) **ses talents/ses diplômes ne sont pas ~s** he can't capitalize on his talents/his diplomas.
monnayer [mɔneje] (8) *vt terres, titres* to convert into cash. (*fig*) **~ son talent/ses capacités** to capitalize on one's talents/abilities.
monnayeur [mɔnɛjœʀ] *nm V* **faux²**.
mono [mɔno] 1 *nm* (*arg Scol*) *abrév de* **moniteur**. 2 *nf* (*abrév de* **monophonie**) **en ~** in mono.
mono... [mɔnɔ] *préf* mono... .
monoacide [mɔnɔasid] *adj* mon(o)acid.
monocaméral *pl*, **-aux** [mɔnɔkameʀal, o] *adj m* unicameral.
monocamérisme [mɔnɔkameʀism(ə)] *nm* unicameralism.
monochrome [mɔnɔkʀom] *adj* monochrome, monochromatic.
monocle [mɔnɔkl(ə)] *nm* monocle, eyeglass.
monocoque [mɔnɔkɔk] *adj* monocoque.
monocorde [mɔnɔkɔʀd(ə)] 1 *adj instrument* with a single chord; *voix, timbre, discours* monotonic. 2 *nm* monochord.
monoculture [mɔnɔkyltyʀ] *nf* single-crop farming, monoculture.
monodie [mɔnɔdi] *nf* monody.
monogame [mɔnɔgam] *adj* monogamous.
monogamie [mɔnɔgami] *nf* monogamy.
monogamique [mɔnɔgamik] *adj* monogamistic.
monogramme [mɔnɔgʀam] *nm* monogram.
monographie [mɔnɔgʀafi] *nf* monograph.
monokini [mɔnɔkini] *nm* topless swimsuit.
monolingue [mɔnɔlɛ̃g] *adj* monolingual.
monolinguisme [mɔnɔlɛ̃gɥism(ə)] *nm* monolingualism.
monolithe [mɔnɔlit] 1 *nm* monolith. 2 *adj* monolithic.
monolithique [mɔnɔlitik] *adj* (*lit, fig*) monolithic.
monolithisme [mɔnɔlitism(ə)] *nm* (*Archit, Constr*) monolithism.
monologue [mɔnɔlɔg] *nm* monologue, soliloquy. (*Littérat*) **~ intérieur** stream of consciousness.
monologuer [mɔnɔlɔge] (1) *vi* to soliloquize. (*péj*) **il monologue pendant des heures** he talks away *ou* holds forth for hours.
monomane [mɔnɔman] *nmf*, **monomaniaque** [mɔnɔmanjak] *nmf* monomaniac.
monomanie [mɔnɔmani] *nf* monomania.
monôme [mɔnom] *nm* (*Math*) monomial; (*arg Scol*) students' rag procession (*in single file through the streets*).
monométallisme [mɔnɔmetalism(ə)] *nm* (*Écon*) monometallism.
monomoteur, -trice [mɔnɔmɔtœʀ, tʀis] 1 *adj* single-engined. 2 *nm* single-engined aircraft.
mononucléaire [mɔnɔnykleɛʀ] 1 *adj* (*Bio*) mononuclear. 2 *nm* mononuclear (cell), mononucleate.
mononucléose [mɔnɔnykleoz] *nf* mononucleosis (*T*), glandular fever.
monophasé, e [mɔnɔfɑze] 1 *adj* single-phase (*épith*).
2 *nm* single-phase current.
monophonie [mɔnɔfɔni] *nf* monaural reproduction.
monophonique [mɔnɔfɔnik] *adj* monaural, monophonic.
monoplace [mɔnɔplas] *nmf* (*Aut, Aviat*) single-seater, one-seater.
monoplan [mɔnɔplɑ̃] *nm* monoplane.
monopole [mɔnɔpɔl] *nm* (*Écon, fig*) monopoly.
monopolisateur, -trice [mɔnɔpɔlizatœʀ, tʀis] *nm,f* monopolizer.
monopolisation [mɔnɔpɔlizɑsjɔ̃] *nf* monopolization.
monopoliser [mɔnɔpɔlize] (1) *vt* (*lit, fig*) to monopolize.
monoprix [mɔnɔpʀi] *nm* ® department store (*for inexpensive goods*).
monorail [mɔnɔʀɑj] *nm* (*voie*) monorail; (*voiture*) monorail coach.
monosyllabe [mɔnɔsilab] *nm* (*lit, fig*) monosyllable.
monosyllabique [mɔnɔsilabik] *adj* (*lit, fig*) monosyllabic.
monosyllabisme [mɔnɔsilabism(ə)] *nm* monosyllabism.
monothéique [mɔnɔteik] *adj* monotheistic.
monothéisme [mɔnɔteism(ə)] *nm* monotheism.
monothéiste [mɔnɔteist(ə)] 1 *adj* monotheistic. 2 *nmf* monotheist.
monotone [mɔnɔtɔn] *adj son, voix* monotonous; *spectacle, style, discours* monotonous, dull, dreary; *existence, vie* monotonous, humdrum, dull, dreary.
monotonie [mɔnɔtɔni] *nf [son, voix]* monotony; *[discours, spectacle, vie]* monotony, dullness, dreariness.
monotype [mɔnɔtip] *nm* monotype.
monovalent, e [mɔnɔvalɑ̃, ɑ̃t] *adj* (*Chim*) monovalent, univalent.
monseigneur [mɔ̃sɛɲœʀ], *pl* **messeigneurs** [mesɛɲœʀ] *nm* **(a)** (*formule d'adresse*) (*à archevêque, duc*) Your Grace; (*à cardinal*) Your Eminence; (*à évêque*) Your Grace, Your Lordship, My Lord (Bishop); (*à prince*) Your (Royal) Highness. **(b)** (*à la troisième personne*) His Grace; His Eminence; His Lordship; His (Royal) Highness. **(c)** *V* **pince**.
Monsieur [məsjø], *pl* **Messieurs** [mesjø] *nm* **(a)** (*s'adressant à qn*) **bonjour ~** (*courant*) good morning; (*nom connu*) good morning Mr X; (*nom inconnu*) good morning, good morning sir (*frm*); **bonjour Messieurs** good morning (gentlemen); (*hum*) **(bonjour) Messieurs Dames*** morning all *ou* everyone*; **~, vous avez oublié quelque chose** excuse me, you've forgotten something; (*au restaurant*) **et pour (vous) ~/Messieurs?** and for you, sir/gentlemen?; (*devant un auditoire*) **Messieurs** gentlemen; **Messieurs et chers collègues** gentlemen; **~ le Président** *[gouvernement]* Mr President; *[compagnie]* Mr Chairman; **oui, ~ le Juge** ≃ yes, Your Honour *ou* My Lord *ou* Your Worship; **~ l'abbé** Father; **~ le curé** Father; **~ le ministre** Minister; **~ le duc** Your Grace; (*frm*) **~ devrait prendre son parapluie** I suggest you take your umbrella, sir (*frm*), Your Lordship should take his umbrella; (*frm*) **~ est servi** dinner is served, sir (*frm*); (*iro*) **~ n'est pas content?** is something not to Your Honour's (*iro*) *ou* Your Lordship's (*iro*) liking?; **mon bon** *ou* **pauvre ~*** my dear sir; *V* **Madame**.
(b) (*parlant de qn*) **~ X est malade** Mr X is ill; († *ou iro*) **~ votre fils** your dear son; (*frm*) **~ est sorti** Mr X *ou* the Master (of the house) is not at home; **~ dit que c'est à lui** the gentleman says it's his; **~ le Président** the President; the Chairman; **~ le juge X** ≃ (His Honour) Judge X; **~ le duc de X** (His Grace) the Duke of X; **~ l'abbé (X)** Father X; **~ le curé** the parish priest; **~ le curé X** Father X; **~ tout le monde** the average man.
(c) (*sur une enveloppe*) **~ X** Mr X, John X Esq.; (*à un enfant*) Master John X; **Messieurs Dupont** Messrs Dupont and Dupont, Messrs J and M Dupont; (*Comm*) **MM Dupont et fils** Messrs Dupont and Son; **Messieurs X et Y** Messrs X and Y; *V* **Madame**.
(d) (*en-tête de lettre*) **~** (*gén*) Dear Sir; (*personne connue*) Dear Mr X; **cher ~** Dear Mr X; **~ et cher collègue** My dear Sir, Dear Mr X; **~ le Président** Dear Mr President; Dear Mr Chairman.
(e) (*Hist: parent du roi*) Monsieur.
(f) (*sans majuscule*) gentleman; (*personnage important*) great man. **ces messieurs désirent?** what would you like, gentlemen?, what is it for you, gentlemen?; **maintenant il se prend pour un m~** he thinks he's quite the gentleman now, he fancies himself as a (proper) gentleman now; **c'est un grand m~** he is a great man, he's quite someone.
monstre [mɔ̃stʀ(ə)] 1 *nm* **(a)** (*Bio, Zool*) (*par la difformité*) freak (of nature), monster; (*par la taille*) monster.
(b) (*Myth*) monster.
(c) (*fig péj*) monster, brute. **c'est un ~ de laideur** he is monstrously *ou* hideously ugly, he is a hideous brute; **c'est un ~ de méchanceté** he is a wicked *ou* an absolute monster.
(d) (*: *affectueux*) **viens ici, petit ~!** come here, you little monster* *ou* horror!*
(e) (*Ciné, Théât*) **~ sacré** superstar, public idol.
2 *adj* (*) monstrous, colossal. **rabais ~s** gigantic *ou* colossal reductions; **elle a un culot ~** she's got fantastic cheek*; **faire une publicité ~ à qch** to launch a massive publicity campaign for sth; **j'ai un travail ~** I've got (absolute) loads* of work to do; **un dîner ~** a whacking* great dinner, a colossal dinner.
monstrueusement [mɔ̃stʀyøzmɑ̃] *adv laid* monstrously, hideously; *intelligent* prodigiously, stupendously.
monstrueux, -euse [mɔ̃stʀyø, øz] *adj* (*difforme*) monstrous, freakish, freak (*épith*); (*abominable*) monstrous, wicked; (*: *gigantesque*) monstrous.

monstruosité [mɔ̃stʀyozite] *nf* **(a)** (*U*) *[crime]* monstrousness, monstrosity.
(b) (*acte*) outrageous *ou* monstrous act, monstrosity; (*propos*) monstrous *ou* horrifying remark. **dire des ~s** to say monstrous *ou* horrifying things, make horrifying remarks.
(c) (*Méd*) deformity.

mont [mɔ̃] **1** *nm* **(a)** (*montagne: littér*) mountain. (*avec un nom propre*) **le ~ X** Mount X; (*littér*) **par ~s et par vaux** up hill and down dale (*littér*); **être toujours par ~s et par vaux*** to be always on the move*; *V* **promettre**.
(b) *[main]* mount (*Palmistry*).
2: les monts d'Auvergne the mountains of Auvergne, the Auvergne mountains; **le mont Blanc** Mont Blanc; (*Culin*) **mont-blanc** *nm, pl* **monts-blancs** chestnut cream dessert (*topped with cream*); **le mont Everest** Mount Everest; **le mont des Oliviers** the Mount of Olives; **mont-de-piété** *nm, pl* **monts-de-piété** (state-owned) pawnshop; **mettre qch au mont-de-piété** to pawn sth; (*Anat*) **mont de Vénus** mons veneris.

montage [mɔ̃taʒ] *nm* **(a)** (*assemblage*) *[appareil, montre]* assembly; *[bijou]* mounting, setting; *[manche]* setting in; *[tente]* pitching, putting up; *V* **chaîne**.
(b) (*Ciné*) (*opération*) editing. **ce film est un bon ~** this film has been well edited *ou* is a good piece of editing; **~ réalisé par** edited by, editing by; **~ de photographies** photomontage.
(c) (*Élec*) wiring (up); (*Rad etc*) assembly. **~ en parallèle/en série** connection in parallel/series.

montagnard, e [mɔ̃taɲaʀ, aʀd(ə)] **1** *adj* mountain (*épith*), highland (*épith*); (*Hist*) Mountain (*épith*). **2** *nm,f* **(a)** mountain dweller. **~s** mountain people *ou* dwellers. **(b)** (*Hist*) **M~(e)** Montagnard.

montagne [mɔ̃taɲ] **1** *nf* **(a)** (*sommet*) mountain. (*région montagneuse*) **la ~** the mountains; **vivre à** *ou* **habiter la ~** to live in the mountains; **haute/moyenne/basse ~** high/medium/low mountains; **plantes des ~s** mountain plants; *V* **chaîne, guide**.
(b) (*fig*) **une ~ de** a mountain of, masses* of; **une ~ de travail l'attendait** a mountain of work was waiting for him, there was masses* of work waiting for him.
(c) (*loc*) **se faire une ~ de rien** to make a mountain out of a molehill; **il se fait une ~ de cet examen** he's making far too much of this exam; (*Prov*) **il n'y a que les ~s qui ne se rencontrent pas** there are none so distant that fate cannot bring them together; **c'est la ~ qui accouche d'une souris** after all that it's (a bit of) an anticlimax, what a great to-do with precious little to show for it.
(d) (*Hist*) **la M~** the Mountain.
2: les montagnes Rocheuses the Rocky Mountains, the Rockies; **montagnes russes** switchback, big dipper; (*hum*) **montagne à vaches*** gentle slope, easy climb; **nous ne faisons que de la montagne à vaches*, mais pas d'escalade** we only go hill walking, not rock climbing.

montagneux, -euse [mɔ̃taɲø, øz] *adj* (*gén, Géog*) mountainous; (*basse montagne: accidenté*) hilly.

montant, e [mɔ̃tɑ̃, ɑ̃t] **1** *adj* *mouvement* upward, rising; *bateau* (travelling) upstream; *col* high; *robe, corsage* high-necked; *chemin* uphill. **chaussures ~es** boots; **train/voie ~(e)** up train/line; *V* **colonne, garde**[1].
2 *nm* **(a)** (*portant*) *[échelle]* upright; *[lit]* post. **les ~s de la fenêtre** the uprights of the window frame.
(b) (*somme*) (sum) total, total amount. **le ~ s'élevait à** the total added up to, the total (amount) came to *ou* was.
(c) (*Équitation*) cheek-strap.

monte [mɔ̃t] *nf* **(a)** (*Équitation*) horsemanship. **(b)** (*Vét*) **station/service de ~** stud farm/service; **mener une jument à la ~** to take a mare to be covered.

monte- [mɔ̃t] *V* **monter**[1].

montée [mɔ̃te] *nf* **(a)** (*escalade*) climb, climbing. **la ~ de la côte** the ascent of the hill, climbing *ou* going up the hill; **la ~ de l'escalier** climbing the stairs; **c'est une ~ difficile** it's a hard *ou* difficult climb; **en escalade, la ~ est plus facile que la descente** when you're climbing, going up is easier than coming down; **la côte était si raide qu'on a fait la ~ à pied** the hill was so steep that we walked up *ou* we went up on foot.
(b) (*ascension*) *[ballon, avion]* ascent. **pendant la ~ de l'ascenseur** while the lift is (*ou* was) going up.
(c) (*mouvement ascendant*) *[eaux]* rise, rising; *[lait]* inflow; *[sève]* rise. **la soudaine ~ des prix/de la température** the sudden rise in prices/(the) temperature.
(d) (*côte, pente*) hill, uphill slope. **la maison était en haut de la ~** the house stood at the top of the hill *ou* rise; **une petite ~ mène à leur maison** there is a little slope leading up to their house.

monter[1] [mɔ̃te] (1) **1** *vi* **(a)** (*gén*) to go up (*à* to, *dans* into); *[oiseau]* to fly up; *[avion]* to climb. **~ à pied/à bicyclette/en voiture** to walk/cycle/drive up; **~ en courant/en titubant** to run/stagger up; **~ en train/par l'ascenseur** to go up by train/in the lift; **~ dans** *ou* **à sa chambre** to go up(stairs) to one's room; **~ sur la colline** to go up *ou* climb up *ou* walk up the hill; **j'ai dû ~ en courant de la cave au grenier** I had to run upstairs from the cellar (up) to the attic; **monte me voir** come up and see me; **monte le prévenir** go up and *ou* to warn him; **~ à Paris** (*lit: en voyage*) to go up *ou* drive up to Paris; (*fig: pour une promotion*) to go to work in Paris.
(b) ~ sur *table, rocher, toit* to climb (up) on *ou* on to; **monté sur une chaise, il accrochait un tableau** he was standing on a chair hanging a picture; **~ sur une échelle** to climb up a ladder; **monté sur un cheval gris** riding *ou* on a grey horse.
(c) (*moyen de transport*) **~ en voiture** to get into a car; **~ dans un train/un avion** to get on *ou* into a train/into *ou* on an aircraft, board a train/an aircraft; **beaucoup de voyageurs sont montés à Lyon** a lot of people got on at Lyons; (*Naut*) **~ à bord (d'un navire)** to go on board *ou* aboard (a ship); **~ à cheval** (*se mettre en selle*) to get on *ou* mount a horse; (*faire du cheval*) to ride, go riding; **~ à bicyclette** to get on a bicycle; to ride a bicycle.
(d) (*progresser*) *[vedette]* to be on the way up; *[réputation]* to rise, go up. **~ en grade** to be promoted; **artiste qui monte** up-and-coming artist; **les générations montantes** the rising generations.
(e) *[eau, vêtements]* **~ à** *ou* **jusqu'à** to come up to; **robe qui monte jusqu'au cou** high-necked dress; **la vase lui montait jusqu'aux genoux** the mud came right up to his knees.
(f) (*s'élever*) *[colline, route]* to go up, rise; *[soleil, flamme, brouillard]* to rise. **~ en pente douce** to slope gently upwards, rise gently; **le chemin monte en lacets** the path winds *ou* twists upwards; **de nouveaux gratte-ciel montent chaque jour** new skyscrapers are going *ou* springing up every day; **un bruit/une odeur montait de la cave** there was a noise/a smell coming from (down) in the cellar, noise was drifting up/a smell was wafting up from the cellar.
(g) (*hausser de niveau*) *[mer, marée]* to come in; *[fleuve]* to rise; *[prix, température, baromètre]* to rise, go up; (*Mus*) *[voix, note]* to go up. **le lait monte** (*sur le feu*) the milk is on the boil; (*dans le sein*) the milk is coming in; **~ dans l'estime de qn** to go up *ou* rise in sb's estimation; **les prix montent en flèche** prices are rocketing (up) *ou* soaring; **ça a fait ~ les prix** it sent *ou* put prices up; **la colère monte** tempers are rising; **le ton monte** (*colère*) the discussion is getting heated, voices are beginning to be raised; (*animation*) voices are rising, the conversation is getting noisier; **le tricot monte vite avec cette laine*** this wool knits up quickly, the knitting grows quickly with this wool; (*Culin*) **(faire) ~ des blancs en neige** to whisk up egg whites.
(h) (*exprimant des émotions*) **le sang** *ou* **le rouge lui monta au visage** the blood rushed to his face; **les larmes lui montent aux yeux** tears are welling up in her eyes, tears come into her eyes; **le succès/le vin lui monte à la tête** success/wine goes to his head; **un cri lui monta à la gorge** a cry rose (up) in his throat; **ça lui a fait ~ le rouge aux joues** it made him blush; **ça lui a fait ~ les larmes aux yeux** it brought tears to his eyes; *V* **moutarde**.
(i) (*Agr*) *[plante]* to bolt, go to seed. **salade qui monte en graine** lettuce which bolts *ou* goes to seed; **la salade est (toute) montée** the lettuce has (all) bolted.
(j) (*loc*) (*Mil*) **~ à l'assaut** *ou* **à l'attaque** to go into the attack; **~ à l'assaut de la forteresse** to launch an attack on the fortress; **~ en chaire** to go up into *ou* ascend the pulpit; **~ à l'échafaud** to climb the scaffold; **~ sur ses ergots** to get one's hackles up; (*Tennis*) **~ au filet** to go up to the net; (*Mil*) **~ au front, ~ en ligne** to go to the front (line); **~ sur ses grands chevaux** to get on one's high horse; (*Théât*) **~ sur les planches** to go on the stage; (*Parl etc*) **~ à la tribune** to come forward to speak, ≃ take the floor; **~ sur le trône** to come to *ou* ascend the throne.
2 *vt* **(a)** to go up. **~ l'escalier** *ou* **les marches précipitamment** to rush upstairs *ou* up the steps; **~ l'escalier** *ou* **les marches quatre à quatre** to go upstairs *ou* up the steps four at a time; **~ la rue** to walk *ou* go *ou* come up the street; (*en courant*) to run up the street; (*Mus*) **~ la gamme** to go up the scale.
(b) (*porter*) *valise, meuble* to take *ou* carry *ou* bring up. **montez-lui son petit déjeuner** take his breakfast up to him; **faire ~ ses valises** to have one's luggage brought *ou* taken *ou* sent up.
(c) ~ un cheval to ride a horse; **ce cheval n'a jamais été monté** this horse has never been ridden.
(d) (*exciter*) **~ qn contre qn** to set sb against sb; **être monté contre qn** to be dead set against sb; **quelqu'un lui a monté la tête** someone has put him up to it* *ou* given him (grand) ideas; **il se monte la tête pour un rien** he gets het up* *ou* worked up over nothing.
(e) (*couvrir*) to cover *ou* serve.
(f) (*Mil*) **~ la garde** to mount guard, go on guard.
3 se monter *vpr* **(a)** *[prix, frais]* **se ~ à** to come to, amount to; **ça va se ~ à 2.000 F** it will come to *ou* amount to *ou* add up to 2,000 francs.
(b) se ~ la tête *ou* **le bourrichon*** to get (all) worked up *ou* het up*.
4: monte-charge *nm inv* goods lift (*Brit*), hoist, service elevator (*US*); (*: *voleur*) **monte-en-l'air** *nm inv* cat burglar; **monte-plats** *nm inv* service lift (*Brit*), dumbwaiter.

monter[2] [mɔ̃te] (1) *vt* **(a)** (*assembler*) *machine* to assemble; *tente* to pitch, put up; *film* to edit, cut; *robe* to assemble, sew together. **~ des mailles** to cast on stitches; (*Élec, Rad*) **~ en parallèle/en série** to connect in parallel/in series.
(b) (*organiser*) *pièce de théâtre* to put on, produce, stage; *affaire* to set up; *farce, canular* to play. **~ un coup** to plan a job; **~ le coup à qn‡** to take sb for a ride‡; **~ un bateau (à qn)** to play a practical joke (on sb); **coup monté** put-up job*, frame-up*; **~ un complot** to hatch a plot; **~ une histoire pour déshonorer qn** to cook up* *ou* fix* a scandal to ruin sb's good name.
(c) (*pourvoir, équiper*) to equip. **~ son ménage** *ou* **sa maison** to set up house; **être bien/mal monté en qch** to be well-/ill-equipped with sth; **tu es bien montée, avec deux garnements pareils*** you're well set up with that pair of rascals!; **se ~ en linge** to equip o.s. with linen; **se ~** to get o.s. (well) set up.
(d) (*fixer*) *diamant, perle* to set, mount; *pneu* to put on. (*fig*) **~ qch en épingle** to blow sth up out of all proportion, make a thing of sth*.

monteur, -euse [mɔ̃tœʀ, øz] *nm,f* **(a)** (*Tech*) fitter. **(b)** (*Ciné*) (film) editor.

montgolfière [mɔ̃gɔlfjɛʀ] *nf* montgolfier, hot air balloon.

monticule [mɔ̃tikyl] *nm* (*colline*) hillock, mound; (*tas*) mound, heap.

montmartrois, e [mɔ̃maʀtʀwa, waz] **1** *adj* of *ou* from Montmartre. **2** *nm,f*: **M~(e)** inhabitant *ou* native of Montmartre.

montmorency [mɔ̃mɔʀɑ̃si] *nf inv* morello cherry.

montrable [mɔ̃tʀabl(ə)] *adj* fit to be seen (*attrib*).

montre[1] [mɔ̃tʀ(ə)] *nf* **(a)** watch. **~-bracelet** wrist watch; **~ de gousset** fob watch; **~ de plongée** diver's watch; **~ de précision** precision watch; **~ à répétition** repeating *ou* repeater watch.

(b) (*loc*) **il est 2 heures à ma ~** it is 2 o'clock by my watch; (*fig*) **j'ai mis 2 heures ~ en main** it took me exactly *ou* precisely 2 hours, it took me 2 hours exactly by the clock; *V* **chaîne, course, sens.**

montre[2] [mɔ̃tʀ(ə)] *nf* **(a) faire ~ de** *courage, ingéniosité* to show, display.

(b) (*littér: ostentation*) **pour la ~** for show, for the sake of appearances.

(c) (*Comm*†: *en vitrine*) display, show. **publication interdite à la ~** publication banned from public display; **un ouvrage qu'il avait en ~** a work that he had on display *ou* show.

Montréal [mɔ̃ʀeal] *n* Montreal.

montréalais, e [mɔ̃ʀealɛ, ɛz] **1** *adj* of *ou* from Montreal. **2** *nm,f*: **M~(e)** Montrealer.

montrer [mɔ̃tʀe] (1) **1** *vt* **(a)** (*gén*) to show (*à* to); (*par un geste*) to point to; (*faire remarquer*) *détail, personne, faute* to point out (*à* to); (*avec ostentation*) to show off, display (*à* to). (*faire visiter*) **je vais vous ~ le jardin** I'll show you (round) the garden; **~ un enfant au docteur** to let the doctor see a child; **l'aiguille montre le nord** the needle points north.

(b) (*laisser voir*) to show. **elle montrait ses jambes en s'asseyant** she showed her legs as she sat down; (*hum*) **elle montre ses charmes** she's showing off *ou* displaying her charms (*hum*).

(c) (*mettre en évidence*) to show, prove. **il a montré que l'histoire était fausse** he has shown *ou* proved the story to be false *ou* that the story was false; **l'avenir montrera qui avait raison** the future will show *ou* prove who was right; **~ la complexité d'un problème** to show how complex a problem is, demonstrate the complexity of a problem; **l'auteur montre un pays en décadence** the author shows *ou* depicts a country in decline.

(d) (*manifester*) *humeur, surprise, courage* to show, display. **son visage montra de l'étonnement** his face registered (his) surprise.

(e) (*apprendre*) **~ à qn à faire qch, ~ à qn la manière de faire qch** to show sb how *ou* the way to do sth.

(f) (*loc*) **c'est l'avocat/le maître d'école qui montre le bout de l'oreille** it's the lawyer/the schoolteacher coming out in him, it's the lawyer/the schoolteacher in him showing through; **je lui montrerai de quel bois je me chauffe** I'll show him (what I'm made of), I'll give him something to think about; (*lit, fig*) **~ les dents** to bare one's teeth; **~ le bon exemple** to set a good example; (*lit, fig*) **~ le chemin** to show the way; **~ le** *ou* **son nez, ~ le bout du nez** to put in an appearance, show one's face; **~ patte blanche** to show one's pass; **~ le poing** to shake one's fist; **~ la porte à qn** to show sb the door.

2 se montrer *vpr* **(a)** *[personne]* to appear, show o.s.; *[chose]* to appear. **se ~ à son avantage** to show o.s. (off) to advantage; (*fig*) **ton père devrait se ~ davantage** your father should assert himself more *ou* show his authority more.

(b) (*s'avérer*) *[personne]* to show o.s. (to be), prove (o.s.) (to be); *[chose]* to prove (to be). **se ~ digne de sa famille** to show o.s. (to be) *ou* prove o.s. worthy of one's family; **il s'est montré très désagréable** he was very unpleasant, he behaved very unpleasantly; **le traitement s'est montré efficace** the treatment proved (to be) effective; **se ~ d'une lâcheté révoltante** to show *ou* display despicable cowardice; **si les circonstances se montrent favorables** if conditions prove (to be) *ou* turn out to be favourable; **il faut se ~ ferme** you must appear firm, you must show firmness.

montreur, -euse [mɔ̃tʀœʀ, øz] *nm,f*: **~ de marionnettes** puppet master, puppeteer; **~ d'ours**†† bear leader††.

montueux, -euse [mɔ̃tɥø, øz] *adj* (*littér*) (very) hilly.

monture [mɔ̃tyʀ] *nf* **(a)** (*cheval*) mount. **(b)** (*Tech*) mounting; *[lunettes]* frame; *[bijou, bague]* setting.

monument [mɔnymɑ̃] *nm* **(a)** (*statue, ouvrage commémoratif*) monument, memorial. **~ élevé à la gloire d'un grand homme** monument *ou* memorial erected in remembrance of a great man; **~ (funéraire)** monument; **~ aux morts (de la guerre)** war memorial.

(b) (*bâtiment, château*) monument. **~ historique** ancient monument, historic building; **~ public** public building.

(c) (*fig*) (*roman, traité scientifique*) monument. **la 'Comédie humaine' est un ~ de la littérature française** the 'Comédie Humaine' is one of the monuments of French literature; **ce buffet est un ~, on ne peut pas le soulever** this sideboard is colossal, we can't shift it*; **c'est un ~ de bêtise!*** what colossal *ou* monumental stupidity!

monumental, e, *mpl* **-aux** [mɔnymɑ̃tal, o] *adj* **(a)** *taille, erreur* monumental, colossal. **être d'une bêtise ~e** to be incredibly *ou* monumentally *ou* unbelievably stupid. **(b)** (*Archit*) monumental.

moquer [mɔke] (1) **1** *vt* († *ou littér*) to mock. **j'ai été moqué** I was laughed at *ou* mocked.

2 se moquer *vpr*: **se ~ de (a)** (*ridiculiser*) to make fun of, laugh at, poke fun at. **tu vas te faire ~ de toi, on va se ~ de toi** people will laugh at you *ou* make fun of you, you'll make yourself a laughing stock; († *ou frm*) **vous vous moquez, j'espère** I trust that you are not in earnest (*frm*).

(b) (*tromper*) **non mais, vous vous moquez du monde!** really you've got an absolute nerve! *ou* a damn‡ cheek! *ou* nerve!

(c) (*mépriser*) **il se moque bien de nous maintenant qu'il est riche** he looks down on us *ou* looks down his nose at us now that he's rich; **je m'en moque (pas mal)*** I couldn't care less*; **je m'en moque comme de l'an quarante** *ou* **comme de ma première chemise*** I don't care twopence (*Brit*), I don't give a tinker's cuss*; **il se moque du tiers comme du quart** he doesn't care about anything or anybody; **je me moque d'y aller*** I'm darned* if I'll go; **elle se moque du qu'en-dira-t-on** she doesn't care what people say (about her).

moquerie [mɔkʀi] *nf* **(a)** (*U*) mockery, mocking. **(b)** (*quolibet, sarcasme*) mockery (*U*). **en butte aux ~s continuelles de sa sœur** the target of constant mockery from his sister *ou* of his sister's constant mockery.

moquette [mɔkɛt] *nf* (*tapis*) fitted carpet, wall-to-wall carpeting (*U*); (*Tex*) moquette.

moqueur, -euse [mɔkœʀ, øz] *adj remarque, réplique* mocking. **il est très ~, c'est un ~** he's always making fun of people.

moqueusement [mɔkøzmɑ̃] *adv* mockingly.

moraine [mɔʀɛn] *nf* moraine.

morainique [mɔʀenik] *adj* morainic, morainal.

moral, e, *mpl* **-aux** [mɔʀal, o] **1** *adj* **(a)** (*éthique*) *valeurs, problème* moral. **j'ai pris l'engagement ~ de le faire** I've morally committed myself to doing it; **avoir l'obligation ~e de faire** to be under a moral obligation *ou* be morally obliged to do; **sens/conscience ~(e)** moral sense/conscience; **conduite ~e** moral *ou* ethical conduct.

(b) (*mental, psychologique*) *courage, support, victoire* moral. **il a fait preuve d'une grande force ~e** he showed great moral fibre; **j'ai la certitude ~e que** I am morally certain that, I feel deep down that; **les douleurs ~es et physiques** mental and physical pain.

2 *nm* **(a) au ~ comme au physique** mentally as well as physically; **au ~ il est irréprochable** morally he is beyond reproach.

(b) (*état d'esprit*) morale. **les troupes ont bon/mauvais ~** the morale of the troops is high/low; **le malade a bon ~** *ou* **le ~*** the patient is in good spirits; **le malade a mauvais ~** the patient is in low *ou* poor spirits; **avoir le ~ à zéro*** to be (feeling) down in the dumps*; **le ~ est atteint** it has shaken *ou* undermined his morale *ou* his confidence; *V* **remonter.**

3 morale *nf* **(a)** (*doctrine*) moral doctrine *ou* code, ethic (*Philos*); (*mœurs*) morals; (*valeurs traditionnelles*) morality, moral standards, ethic (*Philos*). (*Philos*) **la ~e** moral philosophy, ethics; **action conforme à la ~e** act in keeping with morality *ou* moral standards; **faire la ~e à qn** to lecture sb, preach at sb; **avoir une ~e relâchée** to have loose morals.

(b) *[fable]* moral. **la ~e de cette histoire** the moral of this story.

moralement [mɔʀalmɑ̃] *adv agir, se conduire* morally. **une action ~ bonne** a morally *ou* an ethically sound act; **il était ~ vainqueur** he scored a moral victory.

moralisateur, -trice [mɔʀalizatœʀ, tʀis] **1** *adj ton* moralizing, sententious, sanctimonious; *histoire* edifying, elevating. **2** *nm,f* moralizer.

moraliser [mɔʀalize] (1) **1** *vi* to moralize, sermonize (*péj*). **2** *vt* (†: *sermonner*) **~ qn** to preach at sb, lecture sb.

moralisme [mɔʀalism(ə)] *nm* moralism.

moraliste [mɔʀalist(ə)] **1** *adj* moralistic. **2** *nmf* moralist.

moralité [mɔʀalite] *nf* **(a)** (*mœurs*) morals, morality, moral standards. **d'une ~ douteuse** *personne* of doubtful morals; *film* of dubious morality; **d'une haute ~** of high moral standards; **la ~ publique** public morality; *V* **témoin.**

(b) (*valeur*) *[attitude, action]* morality.

(c) (*enseignement*) *[fable]* moral. **~: il ne faut jamais mentir!** the moral is: never tell lies!; **~, j'ai eu une indigestion*** the result was (that) I had indigestion.

(d) (*Littérat*) morality play.

morasse [mɔʀas] *nf* (*Typ*) final *ou* foundry proof.

moratoire[1] [mɔʀatwaʀ] *adj* moratory. **intérêts ~s** interest on arrears.

moratoire[2] [mɔʀatwaʀ] *nm*, **moratorium** [mɔʀatɔʀjɔm] *nm* (*Jur*) moratorium.

morave [mɔʀav] **1** *adj* Moravian. **2** *nmf*: **M~** Moravian.

Moravie [mɔʀavi] *nf* Moravia.

morbide [mɔʀbid] *adj curiosité, goût, imagination* morbid, unhealthy; *littérature, personne* morbid; (*Méd*) morbid.

morbidement [mɔʀbidmɑ̃] *adv* morbidly.

morbidité [mɔʀbidite] *nf* morbidity.

morbleu†† [mɔʀblø] *excl* zounds!††, gadzooks!††

morceau, *pl* **~x** [mɔʀso] *nm* **(a)** (*comestible*) *[pain]* piece, bit; *[sucre]* lump; *[viande]* (*à table*) piece, bit; (*chez le boucher*) piece, cut. **~ de choix** choice cut; **c'était un ~ de roi** it was fit for a king; **manger** *ou* **prendre un ~** to have a bite (to eat) *ou* a snack; (*fig*) **manger** *ou* **lâcher le ~‡** to spill the beans*, come clean*, talk*; (*fig*) **emporter le ~** to carry something off, win the day; *V* **bas**[1]**, sucre.**

(b) (*gén*) piece; *[bois]* piece, lump; *[fer]* block; *[ficelle]* bit, piece; *[terre]* piece, patch, plot; *[tissu]* piece, length. **en ~x** in pieces; **couper en ~x** to cut into pieces; **mettre qch en ~x** to pull sth to bits *ou* pieces; **essayant d'assembler les ~x du vase** trying to piece together the broken vase.

(c) (*Littérat*) passage, extract, excerpt; (*Art, Mus*) piece, item, passage; (*poème*) piece. **(recueil de) ~x choisis** (collection of) selected extracts *ou* passages; **un beau ~ d'éloquence** a fine piece of eloquence; **~ de bravoure** purple passage; **~ de concours** competition piece; **~ de piano/violon** piece for piano/violin.

(d) (**loc*) **beau ~** (*femme*) nice bit of stuff‡ (*surtout Brit*), nice little piece*; **sacré ~** (*personne, objet*) great *ou* solid lump*.

morceler [mɔʀsəle] (4) *vt domaine, terrain* to parcel out, break up, divide up; *troupes, territoire* to divide up, split up.

morcellement [mɔʀsɛlmɑ̃] *nm* (*V* **morceler**) (*action*) parcelling (out); division; dividing (up); splitting (up); (*état*) division.

mordant, e [mɔʀdɑ̃, ɑ̃t] **1** *adj* **(a)** (*caustique*) *ton, réplique* cutting, scathing, mordant, caustic; *pamphlet* scathing, cutting; *polémiste, critique* scathing. **avec une ironie ~e** with caustic *ou* biting *ou* mordant irony.
(b) *froid* biting (*épith*).
2 *nm* **(a)** (*dynamisme, punch*) *[personne]* spirit, drive; *[troupe, équipe]* spirit, keenness; *[style, écrit]* bite, punch. **discours plein de ~** speech full of bite *ou* punch.
(b) *[scie]* bite.
(c) (*Tech*) mordant.
(d) (*Mus*) mordent.
mordicus* [mɔʀdikys] *adv soutenir, affirmer* obstinately, stubbornly.
mordieu†† [mɔʀdjø] *excl* 'sdeath!††
mordillage [mɔʀdijaʒ] *nm*, **mordillement** [mɔʀdijmɑ̃] *nm* nibble, nibbling (*U*).
mordiller [mɔʀdije] (1) *vt* to chew at, nibble at.
mordoré, e [mɔʀdɔʀe] *adj, nm* lustrous bronze.
mordorer [mɔʀdɔʀe] (1) *vt* (*littér*) to bronze.
mordorure [mɔʀdɔʀyʀ] *nf* (*littér*) bronze. **les ~s de l'étoffe** the bronze lustre of the cloth.
mordre [mɔʀdʀ(ə)] (41) **1** *vt* **(a)** *[animal, insecte, personne]* to bite; *[oiseau]* to peck. **~ qn à la main** to bite sb's hand; **un chien l'a mordu à la jambe, il s'est fait ~ à la jambe par un chien** a dog bit him on the leg, he was bitten on the leg by a dog; **~ une pomme (à belles dents)** to bite (greedily) into an apple; **~ un petit bout de qch** to bite off a small piece of sth, take a small bite (out) of sth; **le chien l'a mordu (jusqu')au sang** the dog bit him and drew blood; **approche, il ne mord pas** come closer, he doesn't *ou* won't bite; (*fig*) **~ la poussière** to bite the dust; **faire ~ la poussière à qn** to make sb bite the dust.
(b) *[lime, vis]* to bite into; *[acide]* to bite (into), eat into; *[froid]* to bite, nip. **les crampons mordaient la glace** the crampons gripped *ou* bit (into) the ice; **l'inquiétude/la jalousie lui mordait le cœur** worry/jealousy was eating at *ou* gnawing at his heart.
(c) (*empiéter sur*) **la balle a mordu la ligne** the ball (just) touched the line; **~ (sur) la ligne de départ** to be touching the starting line.
2 mordre sur *vt indir* (*empiéter sur*) to go over into, overlap into; (*corroder*) to bite into. **ça va ~ sur l'autre semaine** that will go over into *ou* overlap into *ou* cut into the following week; **~ sur la marge** to go over into the margin.
3 *vi* **(a) ~ dans: ~ dans une pomme** to bite into an apple; (*Naut*) *[ancre]* **~ dans le sable** to grip *ou* hold the sand.
(b) (*Pêche, fig*) to bite; (*lit, fig*) **~ (à l'hameçon *ou* à l'appât)** to bite, rise (to the bait); (*Pêche*) **ça mord aujourd'hui?** are the fish biting *ou* rising today?; (*fig*) **~ à: il a mordu au latin/aux maths*** he's taken to Latin/maths.
(c) (*Gravure*) to bite; (*Tex*) *[étoffe]* to take the dye; *[teinture]* to take.
(d) (*Tech*) **l'engrenage ne mord plus** the gear won't bite *ou* catch any more.
4 se mordre *vpr*: **se ~ la langue** (*lit*) to bite one's tongue; (*fig*) (*se retenir*) to hold one's tongue; (*se repentir*) to bite one's tongue; (*fig*) **se ~** *ou* **s'en ~ les doigts** to kick o.s. (*fig*); **maintenant il s'en mord les doigts** he could kick himself now.
mordu, e [mɔʀdy] (*ptp de* **mordre**) *adj* **(a)** (*: *amoureux*) madly in love (*de* with). **il en est bien ~** he is mad* *ou* wild* about her, he is crazy* over *ou* about her.
(b) (*: *fanatique*) **~ de football/jazz** crazy* *ou* mad* about *ou* mad keen* on football/jazz; **c'est un ~ du football** he is a great one for football, he is a great football fan *ou* buff (*US*).
more, moresque [mɔʀ, mɔʀɛsk(ə)] = **maure.**
morfondre (se) [mɔʀfɔ̃dʀ(ə)] (42) *vpr* (*après une déception*) to mope, fret; (*dans l'attente de qch*) to fret. **il se morfondait en attendant le résultat des examens** he moped about *ou* fretted as he awaited the exam results.
morfondu, e [mɔʀfɔ̃dy] (*ptp de* **morfondre**) *adj* dejected, crestfallen.
morganatique [mɔʀganatik] *adj* morganatic.
morganatiquement [mɔʀganatikmɑ̃] *adv* morganatically.
morgue¹ [mɔʀg(ə)] *nf* (*littér*) pride, haughtiness. **il me répondit plein de ~ que** he answered me haughtily that.
morgue² [mɔʀg(ə)] *nf* (*Police*) morgue; *[hôpital]* mortuary.
moribond, e [mɔʀibɔ̃, ɔ̃d] *adj* (*lit, fig*) dying, moribund. **un ~** a dying man; **les ~s** the dying.
moricaud, e [mɔʀiko, od] **1** *adj* (*rare*) dark(-skinned). **2** *nm,f* darkie (*hum*); (*péj*) wog: (*péj*).
morigéner [mɔʀiʒene] (6) *vt* (*littér*) to take to task, reprimand. **il faut le ~** he will have to be taken to task (over it) *ou* reprimanded (for it).
morille [mɔʀij] *nf* morel.
mormon, e [mɔʀmɔ̃, ɔn] *adj, nm,f* Mormon. **la secte ~e** the Mormon sect.
mormonisme [mɔʀmɔnism(ə)] *nm* Mormonism.
morne [mɔʀn(ə)] *adj personne, visage* doleful, glum; *ton, temps* gloomy, dismal; *silence* mournful, gloomy, dismal; *conversation, vie, paysage, ville* dismal, dreary. **passer un après-midi ~** to spend a dreary *ou* dismal afternoon.
mornifle: [mɔʀnifl(ə)] *nf* clout*, clip* round the ear.
morose [mɔʀoz] *adj humeur, personne, ton* sullen, morose.
morosité [mɔʀozite] *nf* sullenness, moroseness.
Morphée [mɔʀfe] *nm* Morpheus.
morphème [mɔʀfɛm] *nm* morpheme.
morphine [mɔʀfin] *nf* morphine.
morphinisme [mɔʀfinism(ə)] *nm* morphinism.
morphinomane [mɔʀfinɔman] **1** *adj* addicted to morphine. **2** *nmf* morphine addict.
morphinomanie [mɔʀfinɔmani] *nf* morphine addiction, morphinomania.
morphologie [mɔʀfɔlɔʒi] *nf* morphology.
morphologique [mɔʀfɔlɔʒik] *adj* morphological.
morphologiquement [mɔʀfɔlɔʒikmɑ̃] *adv* morphologically.
morpion [mɔʀpjɔ̃] *nm* (*Jeux*) ≈ noughts and crosses; (*: *pou du pubis*) crab:; (*péj: gamin*) brat*.
mors [mɔʀ] *nm* **(a)** (*Équitation*) bit. **prendre le ~ aux dents** (*lit*) to take the bit between its teeth; (*fig*) (*se lancer*) to swing into action, get going*; (*s'emporter*) to fly off the handle*, get carried away*. **(b)** (*Tech*) jaw; (*Reliure*) joint.
morse¹ [mɔʀs(ə)] *nm* (*Zool*) walrus.
morse² [mɔʀs(ə)] *nm* (*code*) Morse (code).
morsure [mɔʀsyʀ] *nf* bite.
mort¹ [mɔʀ] *nf* **(a)** death. **~ relative, ~ clinique** brain death; **~ absolue, ~ définitive** clinical death; **~ apparente** apparent death; **~ naturelle** natural death; **souhaiter la ~** to long for death *ou* long to die; **souhaiter la ~ de qn** to wish death upon sb (*littér*), wish sb (were) dead; **donner la ~ (à qn)** to kill (sb); **il est en danger *ou* en péril de ~** he is in danger of dying *ou* of his life; **périr *ou* mourir de ~ violente** to die a violent death; **~ volontaire** suicide; **mourir dans son sommeil, c'est une belle ~** dying in one's sleep is a good way to go; **à la ~ de sa mère** on the death of his mother, when his mother died; **il a vu la ~ de près** he has been face to face with death; **il n'y a pas eu ~ d'homme** no one was killed, there was no loss of life; **être à la ~** to be at death's door; *V* **hurler, pâle** *etc*.
(b) de ~: silence de ~ deathly *ou* deathlike hush; **d'une pâleur de ~** deathly *ou* deadly pale; **engin de ~** lethal *ou* deadly weapon; **arrêt/peine de ~** death warrant/penalty; **menaces de ~** threats of death; **proférer des menaces de ~ (contre qn)** to threaten (sb with) death.
(c) à ~: lutte à ~ fight to the death; **détester qn à ~** to hate sb like poison; **blessé à ~** (*dans un combat*) mortally wounded; (*dans un accident*) fatally injured; **condamnation à ~** death sentence; **frapper qn à ~** to strike sb dead; **mettre qn à ~** to put sb to death; (*fig*) **nous sommes fâchés à ~** we're at daggers drawn (with each other); (*fig*) **en vouloir à qn à ~** to be bitterly resentful of sb; **il m'en veut à ~** he hates me *ou* my guts: (for it); (*fig*) **défendre qch à ~** to defend sth to the bitter end; **freiner à ~*** to jam on the brakes *ou* the anchors*; **s'ennuyer à ~** to be bored to death; *V* **mise²**.
(d) (*destruction, fin*) death, end. **c'est la ~ de ses espoirs** that puts paid to his hopes, that puts an end to *ou* is the end of his hopes; **le supermarché sera la ~ du petit commerce** supermarkets will mean the end of *ou* the death of *ou* will put an end to small businesses; **notre secrétaire est la ~ des machines à écrire*** our secretary is lethal to *ou* the ruin of typewriters; **cet enfant sera ma ~*** this child will be the death of me!*
(e) (*douleur*) **souffrir mille ~s** to suffer agonies, be in agony; **la ~ dans l'âme** with an aching *ou* a heavy heart, grieving inwardly; **il avait la ~ dans l'âme** his heart ached.
(f) ~ au tyran!, à ~ le tyran! down with the tyrant!, death to the tyrant!; **~ aux vaches!:** down with the cops!*; *V* **mort²**.
mort², e [mɔʀ, mɔʀt(ə)] (*ptp de* **mourir**) **1** *adj* **(a)** *être animé, arbre, feuille* dead. **il est ~ depuis 2 ans** he's been dead (for) 2 years, he died 2 years ago; **laissé pour ~** left for dead; **il est ~ et bien ~, il est ~ et enterré** he's dead and gone, he's dead and buried; **ramenez-les ~s ou vifs** bring them back dead or alive; (*Mil*) **~ au champ d'honneur** killed in action; **il était comme ~** he looked (as though he were) dead; **tu es un homme ~!*** you're a dead man!*
(b) (*fig*) **je suis ~ (de fatigue)!** I'm dead (tired)! *ou* dead beat!*, I'm all in!*; **il était ~ de peur *ou* plus ~ que vif** he was frightened to death *ou* scared stiff*; *V* **ivre.**
(c) (*inerte, sans vie*) *chair, peau* dead; *pied, doigt etc* dead, numb; (*yeux*) lifeless, dull; (*Fin*) *marché* dead. **la ville est ~e le dimanche** the town is dead on a Sunday; *V* **poids, point¹, temps¹** *etc*.
(d) (*qui n'existe plus*) *civilisation* extinct, dead; *langue* dead. **leur vieille amitié est ~e** their old friendship is dead; **le passé est bien ~** the past is over and done with *ou* is dead and gone.
(e) (*: *usé, fini*) *pile, radio, moteur* dead.
2 *nm* **(a)** dead man. **les ~s** the dead; **les ~s de la guerre** those *ou* the men killed in the war, the war dead; **il y a eu un ~** one man was killed; **il y a eu de nombreux ~s** many (people) were killed, there were many killed; **jour *ou* fête des ~s** All Souls' Day; (*Rel*) **office/messe/prière des ~s** office/mass/prayer for the dead; **cet homme est un ~ vivant/un ~ en sursis** this man is more dead than alive/is living on borrowed time; **faire le ~** (*lit*) to pretend to be dead, sham death; (*fig*) to lie low; *V* **monument, tête.**
(b) (*Cartes*) dummy. **être le ~** to be dummy.
3 morte *nf* dead woman.
4: morte-eau *nf, pl* **mortes-eaux** neap tide; **mort-né, mort-née**, *mpl* **mort-nés** *adj enfant* stillborn; *projet* abortive, stillborn; **mort-aux-rats** *nf* rat poison; **morte-saison** *nf, pl* **mortes-saisons** slack *ou* off season.
mortadelle [mɔʀtadɛl] *nf* mortadella.
mortaise [mɔʀtɛz] *nf* (*Menuiserie*) mortise.
mortalité [mɔʀtalite] *nf* mortality, death rate. **taux de ~** death rate, mortality (rate); **~ infantile** infant mortality; **régression de la ~** fall in the death rate.
mortel, -elle [mɔʀtɛl] **1** *adj* **(a)** (*sujet à la mort*) mortal; *V* **dépouille.**
(b) (*entraînant la mort*) *chute* fatal; *blessure, plaie* fatal, mortal; *poison* deadly, lethal. **être en danger ~** to be in mortal danger; **coup ~** lethal *ou* fatal *ou* mortal blow, death-blow; **cette révélation lui serait ~le** such a discovery would kill him *ou* would be fatal to him.
(c) (*intense*) *frayeur, jalousie* mortal; *pâleur, silence* deadly, deathly; *ennemi, haine* mortal, deadly. **il fait un froid ~** it is

deathly cold, it is as cold as death; **cette attente ~le se prolongeait** this deadly wait dragged on; **allons, ce n'est pas ~!*** come on, it's not all that bad! *ou* it's not the end of everything!*

(d) (*: *ennuyeux*) *livre, soirée* deadly*, deadly boring *ou* dull. **il est ~** he's a deadly* *ou* crashing* bore.

2 *nm,f* (*littér, hum*) mortal. **heureux ~!*** lucky chap!*; *V* **commun.**

mortellement [mɔʀtɛlmɑ̃] *adv blesser* fatally, mortally; (*fig*) *offenser, vexer* mortally, deeply. **~ pâle** deadly *ou* deathly pale; (*fig*) **c'est ~ ennuyeux** it's deadly boring *ou* dull.

mortier [mɔʀtje] *nm* (*Constr, Culin, Mil, Pharm*) mortar; (*toque*) cap (*worn by certain French judges*).

mortification [mɔʀtifikɑsjɔ̃] *nf* mortification.

mortifier [mɔʀtifje] (7) *vt* (*Méd, Rel, aussi vexer*) to mortify.

mortinatalité [mɔʀtinatalite] *nf* rate of stillbirths.

mortuaire [mɔʀtɥɛʀ] *adj chapelle* mortuary (*épith*); *rites* mortuary (*épith*), funeral (*épith*); *cérémonie* funeral (*épith*). **acte/avis ~** death certificate/announcement; **drap ~** pall; (*Can*) **salon ~** funeral home *ou* parlor (*US, Can*); **la chambre ~** the death chamber; **la maison ~** the house of the departed *ou* deceased; *V* **couronne.**

morue [mɔʀy] *nf* **(a)** (*Zool*) cod; *V* **brandade, huile. (b)** (**:**) tart:, whore.

morutier, -ière [mɔʀytje, jɛʀ] **1** *adj* cod-fishing. **2** *nm* (*pêcheur*) cod-fisherman; (*bateau*) cod-fishing boat.

morvandeau, -elle, *mpl* **~x** [mɔʀvɑ̃do, ɛl] **1** *adj* of *ou* from the Morvan region. **2** *nm,f*: **M~(-elle)** inhabitant *ou* native of the Morvan region.

morve [mɔʀv(ə)] *nf* snot:, (nasal) mucus; (*Zool*) glanders (*sg*).

morveux, -euse [mɔʀvø, øz] **1** *adj* **(a)** *enfant* snotty(-nosed):. (*Prov*) **qui se sent ~ qu'il se mouche** if the cap fits wear it. **(b)** (*Zool*) glandered. **2** *nm,f* (:) (little) jerk:.

mosaïque[1] [mozaik] *nf* (*Art, Bot*) mosaic; *[états, champs]* chequered pattern, patchwork; *[idées, peuples]* medley.

mosaïque[2] [mozaik] *adj* (*Bible*) Mosaic(al), of Moses.

Moscou [mɔsku] *n* Moscow.

moscovite [mɔskɔvit] **1** *adj* of *ou* from Moscow, Moscow (*épith*). **2** *nmf*: **M~** Muscovite.

mosquée [mɔske] *nf* mosque.

mot [mo] **1** *nm* **(a)** (*gén*) word. **le ~ (d')orange** the word 'orange'; **les ~s me manquent pour exprimer** words fail me when I try to express, I can't find the words to express; **ce ne sont que des ~s** it's just (so many) empty words; **je n'en crois pas un (traître) ~** I don't believe a (single) word of it; **qu'il soit paresseux, c'est bien le ~!** lazybones is the right word to describe him!; **à/sur ces ~s** at/with these words; **à ~s couverts** in veiled terms; **en d'autres ~s** in other words; **en un ~** in a word; **en un ~ comme en cent** in a nutshell, in brief; **faire du ~ à ~, traduire ~ à ~** to translate word for word; **c'est du ~ à ~** it's a word for word rendering *ou* translation; **rapporter une conversation ~ pour ~** to give a word for word *ou* a verbatim report of a conversation.

(b) (*message*) word; (*courte lettre*) note, line. (*Scol*) **~ d'excuse** excuse note; **en dire** *ou* **en toucher un ~ à qn** to have a word with sb about sth; **glisser un ~ à qn** to have a word in sb's ear; **se donner** *ou* **se passer le ~** to send *ou* pass the word round, pass the word on; **mettez-lui un petit ~** drop* him a line *ou* note, write him a note.

(c) (*expression frappante*) saying. **~s célèbres/historiques** famous/historic sayings.

(d) (*loc*) **avoir** *ou* **échanger des ~s avec qn** to have words with sb; **avoir toujours le ~ pour rire** to be a born joker, always be able to raise a laugh; **avoir** *ou* **tenir le ~ de l'énigme** to have *ou* hold the key to the mystery; **avoir** *ou* **dire le ~ de la fin** to get the last word, come out with the punch line; **vous n'avez qu'un ~ à dire et je le ferai** you have only to say the word and I'll do it; **j'estime avoir mon ~ à dire dans cette affaire** I think I'm entitled to have my say in this matter; **je vais lui dire deux ~s** I'll give him a piece of my mind; **prendre qn au ~** to take sb at his word; **il ne sait pas le premier ~ de sa leçon** he doesn't know a word of his lesson; **il ne sait pas un (traître) ~ d'allemand** he doesn't know a (single) word of German; **je n'ai pas pu lui tirer un ~** I couldn't get a word out of him.

2: mot d'auteur revealing *ou* witty remark from the author; **c'est un mot d'auteur** it's the author having his say; **mot-clé** *nm, pl* **mots-clés** keyword; **mot composé** compound; **mots croisés** crossword (puzzle); **faire les mots croisés** (*en général*) to do crosswords; *[journal particulier]* to do the crossword (puzzle); **mot d'emprunt** loanword; **mot d'enfant** child's (funny) remark *ou* saying; **mot d'esprit, bon mot** witticism, witty remark; **mot d'ordre** watchword, slogan; **mot-outil** *nm, pl* **mots-outils** grammatical word; **mot de passe** password; **mot souche** root-word.

motard [mɔtaʀ] *nm* (*Police*) motorcycle policeman *ou* cop*; (*Mil: dans l'armée*) motorcyclist. **les ~s de l'escorte** the motorcycle escort.

motel [mɔtɛl] *nm* motel.

motet [mɔtɛ] *nm* motet.

moteur[1] [mɔtœʀ] *nm* **(a)** (*Tech*) motor, engine. **~ à combustion interne, ~ à explosion** internal combustion engine; **~ diesel** diesel engine; **~ électrique** electric motor; **~ à injection** fuel injection engine; **~ à réaction** jet engine; **~ à 2/4 temps** 2-/4-stroke engine; **à ~** power-driven, motor (*épith*); *V* **bloc, frein.**

(b) (*fig*) mover, mainspring. (*littér*) **le grand ~ de l'univers** the prime mover of the universe; **être le ~ de qch** to be the mainspring of sth, be the driving force behind sth.

moteur[2], **-trice**[1] [mɔtœʀ, tʀis] *adj* **(a)** (*Anat*) *muscle, nerf* motor (*épith*). **troubles ~s** motory troubles.

(b) (*Tech*), *force* (*lit, fig*) driving. **arbre ~** driving shaft; **voiture à roues ~trices avant/arrière** front-/rear-wheel drive car.

motif [mɔtif] *nm* **(a)** (*raison*) motive (*de* for), grounds (*de* for); (*but*) purpose (*de* of). **quel est le ~ de votre visite?** what is the motive for *ou* the purpose of your visit?; **quel ~ as-tu de te plaindre?** what grounds have you got for complaining?; **il a de bons ~s pour le faire** he has good grounds for doing it; († *ou hum*) **fréquenter une jeune fille pour le bon ~** to court a girl with honourable intentions; **faire qch sans ~** to have no motive for doing sth; **colère sans ~** groundless *ou* irrational anger.

(b) (*ornement*) motif, design, pattern; (*Peinture*) (*sujet*) motif; (*Mus*) motif.

(c) (*Jur*) *[jugement]* grounds (*de* for).

motion [mosjɔ̃] *nf* (*Pol*) motion. **~ de censure** censure motion, motion of censure.

motivation [mɔtivɑsjɔ̃] *nf* motivation. (*Écon*) **études** *ou* **recherche de ~** motivation(al) research.

motivé, e [mɔtive] (*ptp de* **motiver**) *adj* **(a)** *action* (*dont on donne les motifs*) reasoned, justified; (*qui a des motifs*) well-founded, motivated. **non ~** unexplained, unjustified.

(b) *personne* motivated. **non ~** unmotivated.

motiver [mɔtive] (1) *vt* **(a)** (*justifier, expliquer*) *action, attitude, réclamation* to justify, account for. **il a motivé sa conduite en disant que** he justified his behaviour by saying that; **rien ne peut ~ une telle conduite** nothing can justify *ou* warrant such behaviour.

(b) (*fournir un motif à*) *décision, refus, intervention,* (*Jur*) *jugement* to motivate, found; (*Psych*) to motivate.

moto* [mɔto] *nf* (*abrév de* **motocyclette**) (motor)bike*. **~ de trial, ~ verte** trail bike.

moto-cross [mɔtɔkʀɔs] *nm inv* motocross.

motoculteur [mɔtɔkyltœʀ] *nm* (motorized) cultivator.

motocycle [mɔtɔsikl(ə)] *nm* (*Admin*) motor bicycle.

motocyclette [mɔtɔsiklɛt] *nf* motorcycle.

motocyclisme [mɔtɔsiklism(ə)] *nm* motorcycle racing.

motocycliste [mɔtɔsiklist(ə)] *nmf* motorcyclist.

motonautique [mɔtɔnotik] *adj*: **sport ~** speedboat *ou* motorboat racing.

motonautisme [mɔtɔnotism(ə)] *nm* speedboat *ou* motorboat racing.

motoneige [mɔtɔnɛʒ] *nf* snow-bike, skidoo (*Can*).

motopompe [mɔtɔpɔ̃p] *nf* motor-pump, power-driven pump.

motorisation [mɔtɔʀizɑsjɔ̃] *nf* motorization.

motoriser [mɔtɔʀize] (1) *vt* (*Mil, Tech*) to motorize. **être motorisé*** to have transport, have one's *ou* a car, be car-borne*.

motrice[1] [mɔtʀis] *adj V* **moteur**[2].

motrice[2] [mɔtʀis] *nf* motive *ou* motor unit.

motricité [mɔtʀisite] *nf* motor functions.

motte [mɔt] *nf* **(a)** (*Agr*) **~ (de terre)** lump of earth, clod (of earth); **~ de gazon** turf, sod.

(b) (*Culin*) **~ de beurre** lump *ou* block of butter; **acheter du beurre en** *ou* **à la ~** to buy a slab of butter.

motus [mɔtys] *excl*: **~ (et bouche cousue)!** mum's the word!*, keep it under your hat!, not a word!

mou[1], **molle** [mu, mɔl] (**mol** [mɔl] *devant voyelle ou h muet*) **1** *adj* **(a)** (*au toucher*) *substance, oreiller* soft; *tige, tissu* limp; *chair, visage* flabby. **ce melon est tout ~** this melon has gone all soft *ou* mushy; *V* **chapeau.**

(b) (*à la vue*) *contours, lignes, relief, collines* soft, gentle; *traits du visage,* (*Art*) *dessin, trait* weak, slack.

(c) (*à l'oreille*) **bruit ~** muffled noise, soft thud; **voix aux molles inflexions** gently lilting voice.

(d) (*sans énergie*) *geste, poignée de main* limp, lifeless; *protestations, opposition* weak, feeble; (†) *vie* soft, indolent; (*Littérat*) *style* feeble, dull, woolly; (*Mus*) *exécution* dull, lifeless. **personne molle** indolent *ou* lethargic *ou* sluggish person; (*sans autorité*) spineless character; (*trop indulgent*) lax *ou* soft person; **il est ~ comme une chiffe** *ou* **chique, c'est un ~** he is spineless *ou* a spineless character.

(e) *temps* muggy; *tiédeur* languid.

2 *adv* **jouer/dessiner ~** to play/draw without energy *ou* languidly; (:) **vas-y ~** go easy*, take it easy*.

3 *nm* **(a)** (*qualité*) softness.

(b) *[corde]* **avoir du ~** to be slack *ou* loose; **donner du ~** to slacken, loosen.

mou[2] [mu] *nm* **(a)** (*Boucherie*) lights, lungs; *V* **rentrer. (b)** (:*loc*) **bourrer le ~ à qn** to have sb on*, take sb in.

mouchard [muʃaʀ] *nm* **(a)** (*) (*Scol*) sneak*; (*Police*) grass (*arg*). **(b)** (*Tech*) *[avion, train]* black box; *[veilleur de nuit]* control clock; (*Mil*) spy plane.

mouchardage* [muʃaʀdaʒ] *nm* (*V* **moucharder**) sneaking; grassing.

moucharder* [muʃaʀde] (1) *vt* (*Scol*) to split on*, sneak on*; (*arg Police*) to grass on (*arg*). **arrête de ~!** stop sneaking!*

mouche [muʃ] **1** *nf* **(a)** (*Zool*) fly. **quelle ~ t'a piqué?** what has bitten you?*, what has got into you?; **faire la ~ du coche** to fuss *ou* buzz around importantly (doing nothing); **mourir/tomber comme des ~s** to die (off)/fall like flies; **prendre la ~** to take the huff*, get huffy; (*Prov*) **on ne prend pas les ~s avec du vinaigre** you won't get him (*ou* me *etc*) to swallow that bait; *V* **entendre, fin**[1]**, mal.**

(b) (*Sport*) (*Escrime*) button; (*Pêche*) fly. **faire ~** (*Tir*) to score a *ou* hit the bull's-eye; (*fig*) to score, hit home; *V* **poids.**

(c) (*en taffetas*) patch, beauty spot; (*touffe de poils sous la lèvre*) short goatee.

(d) (*Opt*) **~s** specks, spots.

2: mouche bleue = mouche de la viande; (*Naut*) **mouche d'escadre** advice boat; (*Can*) **mouche à feu** firefly; **mouche tsé-tsé** tsetse fly; **mouche à vers** blowfly; **mouche de la viande** bluebottle; **mouche du vinaigre** fruit fly.

moucher [muʃe] (1) **1** *vt* **(a) ~ (le nez de) qn** to blow sb's nose; **mouche ton nez*** blow your nose; **il mouche du sang** there are

traces of blood (in his handkerchief) when he blows his nose.
(b) (**fig: remettre à sa place*) ~ **qn** to snub sb, put sb in his place; **se faire** ~ to get snubbed, get put in one's place.
(c) *chandelle* to snuff (out).
2 se moucher *vpr* to blow one's nose. **mouche-toi** blow your nose; (*loc*) **il ne se mouche pas du coude*** he thinks he's it* *ou* the cat's whiskers*, he thinks himself no small beer; *V* **morveux.**

moucheron [muʃʀɔ̃] *nm* (*Zool*) midge; (*: *enfant*) kid*.

moucheté, e [muʃte] (*ptp de* **moucheter**) *adj œuf* speckled; *laine* flecked; *fleuret* buttoned.

moucheter [muʃte] (4) *vt* (*tacheter*) to speckle, fleck (*de* with); (*Escrime*) to button.

mouchetis [muʃti] *nm* (*Constr*) roughcast.

mouchettes [muʃɛt] *nfpl* (*Hist*) snuffers.

moucheture [muʃtyʀ] *nf* (*sur les habits*) speck, spot, fleck; (*sur un animal*) spot, patch. (*Hér*) ~**s d'hermine** ermine tips.

mouchoir [muʃwaʀ] *nm* (*dans la poche*) handkerchief; (†: *autour du cou*) neckerchief. ~ **en papier** tissue, paper hanky; **grand comme un** ~ **de poche** as big as *ou* the size of *ou* no bigger than a pocket handkerchief; (*fig*) **ils sont arrivés dans un** ~ it was a close finish; *V* **nœud.**

moudre [mudʀ(ə)] (47) *vt blé* to mill, grind; *café, poivre* to grind; (†: *Mus*) *air* to grind out. ~ **qn de coups**† to thrash sb; *V* **moulu.**

moue [mu] *nf* pout. **faire la** ~ (*gén: tiquer*) to pull a face; *[enfant gâté]* to pout.

mouette [mwɛt] *nf* (sea)gull. ~ **rieuse** black-headed gull.

mou(f)fette [mufɛt] *nf* skunk.

moufle [mufl(ə)] **1** *nf* mitt, mitten. **2** *nm ou f* (*Tech*) pulley block.

mouflet, -ette* [muflɛ, ɛt] *nm,f* brat* (*péj*), kid*.

mouflon [muflɔ̃] *nm* mouf(f)lon.

mouillage [mujaʒ] *nm* **(a)** (*Naut: action*) *[navire]* anchoring, mooring; *[ancre]* casting; *[mine]* laying. **(b)** (*Naut: abri, rade*) anchorage, moorage. **(c)** (*Tech*) *[cuir, linge]* moistening, damping; *[vin, lait]* watering(-down).

mouillé, e [muje] (*ptp de* **mouiller**) *adj herbe, vêtement, personne* wet. **tout** ~, ~ **comme une soupe** *ou* **jusqu'aux os** soaked through and through, soaked *ou* drenched to the skin; **tu sens le chien** ~ you smell like a wet dog; **ne marche pas dans le** ~ don't walk in the wet; *V* **poule**[1].

mouiller [muje] (1) **1** *vt* **(a)** (*gén*) to wet. ~ **son doigt pour tourner la page** to moisten one's finger to turn the page.
(b) (*pluie: tremper*) *route* to wet; *personne* to wet; (*complètement*) to drench, soak. **se faire** ~ to get wet *ou* drenched *ou* soaked; **un sale brouillard qui mouille** a horrible wetting fog.
(c) (*Culin*) *vin, lait* to water (down); *viande* to cover with stock *ou* wine *etc*, add stock *ou* wine *etc* to.
(d) (*Naut*) *mine* to lay; *sonde* to heave. ~ **l'ancre** to cast *ou* drop anchor.
(e) (*Ling*) to palatalize.
2 *vi* **(a)** (*Naut*) to lie *ou* be at anchor. **ils mouillèrent 3 jours à Papeete** they anchored *ou* they lay at anchor at Papeete for 3 days.
(b) (∵: *avoir peur*) to be scared shitless∵ *ou* be shit-scared∵.
3 se mouiller *vpr* **(a)** (*au bord de la mer: se tremper*) (*accidentellement*) to get o.s. wet; (*pour un bain rapide*) to have a quick dip. **se** ~ **les pieds** (*sans faire exprès*) to get one's feet wet; (*exprès*) to dabble one's feet in the water.
(b) *[yeux]* to fill *ou* brim (*littér*) with tears.
(c) (‡*fig: prendre des risques*) to get one's feet wet, commit o.s.

mouillette [mujɛt] *nf* finger of bread, sippet†.

mouilleur [mujœʀ] *nm* **(a)** *[timbres]* (stamp) sponge. **(b)** (*Naut*) *[ancre]* tumbler. ~ **de mines** minelayer.

mouillure [mujyʀ] *nf* **(a)** (*trace*) wet mark. **(b)** (*Ling*) palatalization.

mouise‡ [mwiz] *nf*: **être dans la** ~ to be on one's beam-ends*; **c'est la** ~ **chez eux** they've hit hard times.

moujik [muʒik] *nm* mujik, muzhik.

moujingue‡ [muʒɛ̃g] *nmf* brat* (*péj*), kid*.

moukère [mukɛʀ] *nf* Arab woman; (†‡) woman, female.

moulage[1] [mulaʒ] *nm* **(a)** (*V* **mouler**) moulding; casting. **le** ~ **d'un bas-relief** making *ou* taking a cast of a bas-relief.
(b) (*objet*) (*d'un moule plein*) cast. (*d'un moule creux*) **sur la cheminée il y avait le** ~ **en plâtre d'une statue** there was a plaster (of Paris) figure on the mantelpiece; **prendre un** ~ **de** to take a cast of; (*Art*) **ce n'est qu'un** ~ it is only a copy.

moulage[2] [mulaʒ] *nm* (*rare*) *[grain]* milling, grinding.

moule[1] [mul] **1** *nm* (*lit, fig*) mould; (*Typ*) matrix. **il n'a jamais pu sortir du** ~ **étroit de son éducation** he has never been able to free himself from the strait jacket of his education; (*lit, fig*) **fait sur le même** ~ cast in the same mould; (*rare: être beau*) **être fait au** ~ to be shapely.
2: moule à briques brick mould; **moule à beurre** butter print; **moule à gâteaux** cake tin (*for baking*); **moule à gaufre** waffle-iron; **moule à manqué** (deep) sandwich tin; **moule à pisé** clay mould; **moule à tarte** pie plate, flan case.

moule[2] [mul] *nf* **(a)** (*Zool*) mussel. ~**s marinières** mussels (cooked) in white wine.
(b) (*: *idiot*) idiot, twit*.

mouler [mule] (1) *vt* **(a)** (*faire*) *briques* to mould; *caractères d'imprimerie* to cast; *statue, buste* to cast. ~ **un buste en plâtre** to cast a bust in plaster.
(b) (*reproduire*) *bas-relief, buste* to make *ou* take a cast of. ~ **en plâtre** *visage, buste* to make a plaster cast of.
(c) (*écrire avec soin*) *lettre, mot* to shape *ou* form with care.
(d) (*conformer à*) ~ **son style/sa conduite sur** to model one's style/conduct on; (*littér*) ~ **sa pensée dans l'alexandrin** to express o.s. *ou* cast one's thoughts in the mould of the alexandrine.
(e) (*coller à*) *[robe, pantalons] cuisses, hanches* to hug, fit closely round. **une robe qui moule** a close- *ou* tight-fitting dress, a dress which hugs the figure; **des pantalons qui moulent** tight(-fitting) trousers; **une robe qui lui moulait les hanches** a dress which clung to *ou* around her hips, a dress which fitted closely round her hips; **son corps se moulait au sien** her body pressed closely against his.

mouleur [mulœʀ] *nm* caster, moulder.

moulin [mulɛ̃] *nm* **(a)** (*instrument, bâtiment*) mill. ~ **à eau** water mill; ~ **à vent** windmill; ~ **à café/poivre** coffee/pepper mill; ~ **à légumes** vegetable mill; (*fig*) ~ **à paroles** chatterbox; ~ **à prières** prayer wheel; *V* **entrer.**
(b) (‡: *moteur*) engine.

mouliner [muline] (1) *vt* (*Culin*) to put through a vegetable mill; (*Pêche*) to reel in.

moulinet [mulinɛ] *nm* (*Pêche*) reel; (*Tech*) winch; (*Escrime*) flourish. **faire des** ~**s avec une canne** to twirl *ou* whirl a walking stick; **faire des** ~**s avec les bras** to whirl one's arms about *ou* round.

moulinette [mulinɛt] *nf* ® vegetable mill. **passer qch à la** ~ to put sth through the vegetable mill.

moult [mult] *adv* (†† *ou hum*) (*beaucoup*) many; (*très*) very. ~ **(de) gens** many people, many a person; ~ **fois** oft(en)times (*hum*), many a time.

moulu, e [muly] (*ptp de* **moudre**) *adj* (†: *meurtri*) bruised, black and blue. (*battu*) ~ **(de coups)** thrashed; ~ **(de fatigue)*** dead-beat*, worn-out, all-in*.

moulure [mulyʀ] *nf* moulding.

moulurer [mulyʀe] (1) *vt* to decorate with mouldings. **machine à** ~ moulding machine; **panneau mouluré** moulded panel.

moumoute* [mumut] *nf* (*hum*) wig.

mouquère [mukɛʀ] *nf* = **moukère.**

mourant, e [muʀɑ̃, ɑ̃t] *adj* **(a)** *personne* dying; *voix* faint; *regard* languishing; *feu, jour* dying. **un** ~ a dying man; **les** ~**s** the dying.
(b) (*: *lent, ennuyeux*) *rythme, allure* deadly* (dull).

mourir [muʀiʀ] (19) *vi* **(a)** *[être animé, arbre, plante]* to die. ~ **dans son lit** to die in one's bed; ~ **de vieillesse** to die of old age; ~ **de sa belle mort** to die a natural death; ~ **avant l'âge** to die young *ou* before one's time; ~ **d'une maladie/d'une blessure/de chagrin** to die of a disease/from a wound/of grief; ~ **à la peine** *ou* **à la tâche** to die in harness; ~ **assassiné** to be murdered; ~ **empoisonné** to die of poisoning; ~ **en héros** to die a hero's death; **il est mort très jeune** he died very young, he was very young when he died; ~ **de faim** to starve to death, die of hunger; **faire** ~ **qn de faim** to starve sb to death; ~ **de froid** to die of exposure; **faire** ~ **qn** *[maladie, meurtrier]* to kill sb; (*littér*) **se** ~ to be dying; (*hum*) **une simple piqûre, tu n'en mourras pas!*** it's only a little injection, it won't kill you!*; **il attend que quelqu'un meure pour prendre sa place** he is waiting to step into a dead man's shoes.
(b) *[civilisation, empire, feu, coutume]* to die out; *[bruit]* to die away; *[jour]* to fade, die; *[feu, flamme]* to die down. **la vague vint** ~ **à ses pieds** the wave died away at his feet; **le ballon vint** ~ **à ses pieds** the ball came to rest at his feet.
(c) (*fig*) ~ **de chagrin/de tristesse** to be weighed down with grief/sadness; ~ **d'inquiétude** to be worried to death; **il me fera** ~ **d'inquiétude** he'll drive me to my death with worry; (*littér, hum*) **(se)** ~ **d'amour pour qn** to pine for sb; **il meurt d'envie de le faire** he's dying to do it; **s'ennuyer à** ~ to be bored to death *ou* to tears; ~ *ou* **être mort de peur** to be scared to death, be dying of fright; ~ **de faim** to be famished *ou* starving; ~ **de soif** to be parched; **faire** ~ **qn à petit feu** (*lit*) to kill sb slowly *ou* by inches; (*fig*) to torment the life out of sb; **faire** ~ **qn d'impatience** to keep sb on tenterhooks; **ennuyeux à** ~ deadly boring; **c'est à** ~ **de rire** it would make you die laughing*, it's hilarious*; **il me fera** ~ **de peur** he'll frighten the life out of me.

mouroir [muʀwaʀ] *nm* (*péj*) old people's home.

mouron [muʀɔ̃] *nm* pimpernel. ~ **rouge** scarlet pimpernel; ~ **blanc** *ou* **des oiseaux** chickweed; (*fig*) **se faire du** ~* to worry o.s. sick*.

mouscaille* [muskɑj] *nf*: **être dans la** ~ (*misère*) to be on one's beam-ends*; (*ennuis*) to be up the creek‡.

mousquet [muskɛ] *nm* musket.

mousquetaire [muskətɛʀ] *nm* musketeer.

mousqueterie [muskətʀi] *nf* (††: *salve*) musketry.

mousqueton [muskətɔ̃] *nm* (*boucle*) snap hook, clasp; (*Mil*) carbine.

moussaillon* [musajɔ̃] *nm* ship's boy.

moussant, e [musɑ̃, ɑ̃t] *adj savon* foaming; *crème à raser* lathering. **bain** ~ bubble bath.

mousse[1] [mus] **1** *nf* **(a)** (*Bot*) moss; *V* **pierre.**
(b) (*écume*) *[bière, eau]* froth, foam; *[savon]* lather; *[champagne]* bubbles. **la** ~ **sur le verre de bière** the head on the beer.
(c) (*Culin*) mousse. ~ **au chocolat** chocolate mousse.
(d) (*caoutchouc*) **balle (en)** ~ rubber ball; (*nylon*) **collant/bas** ~ stretch tights/stockings; ~ **de caoutchouc** foam rubber.
(e) se faire de la ~* to worry o.s. sick*, get all het up*.
2: mousse carbonique (fire-fighting) foam; **mousse de nylon** (*tissu*) stretch nylon; (*pour rembourrer*) foam; **mousse de platine** platinum sponge; *V* **point**[2].

mousse[2] [mus] *nm* ship's boy.

mousseline [muslin] *nf* (*Tex*) (*coton*) muslin; (*soie, tergal*) chiffon; *V* **pomme, sauce.**

mousser [muse] (1) *vi* **(a)** *[bière, eau]* to froth, foam; *[champagne]* to bubble, sparkle; *[détergent]* to foam, lather; *[savon]* to lather.
(b) faire ~ **qch/qn‡** to crack sth/sb up*, boost sth/sb*; **se faire**

~ (*auprès d'un supérieur, d'un ami*) to give o.s. a boost* (*auprès de* with); (*auprès d'un supérieur*) to sell o.s. hard* (*auprès de* to).
mousseron [musʀɔ̃] *nm* meadow mushroom.
mousseux, -euse [musø, øz] **1** *adj vin* sparkling (*épith*); *bière, eau, chocolat* frothy. **2** *nm* sparkling wine.
mousson [musɔ̃] *nf* monsoon.
moussu, e [musy] *adj sol, arbre* mossy; *banc* moss-covered.
moustache [mustaʃ] *nf [homme]* moustache. *[animal]* ~**s** whiskers; **porter la** ~ *ou* **des** ~**s** to have *ou* wear a moustache; ~ **en brosse** toothbrush moustache; ~ **en croc** *ou* **en guidon de vélo** handlebar moustache; ~ **(à la) gauloise** walrus moustache.
moustachu, e [mustaʃy] *adj* with a moustache.
moustiquaire [mustikɛʀ] *nf* (*rideau*) mosquito net; *[fenêtre, porte]* screen; (*Can*) (window, door) screen.
moustique [mustik] *nm* (*Zool*) mosquito; (*: *enfant*) tich*, (little) kid*.
moût [mu] *nm [raisin etc]* must; *[bière]* wort.
moutard* [mutaʀ] *nm* brat* (*péj*), kid*.
moutarde [mutaʀd(ə)] **1** *nf* mustard. ~ **(extra-)forte** English mustard; ~ **à l'estragon** French mustard; (*fig*) **la** ~ **me monta au nez!** I flared up!, I lost my temper! **2** *adj inv* mustard (-coloured); *V* **gaz.**
moutardier [mutaʀdje] *nm* (*pot*) mustard pot; (*avec salière etc*) cruet; (*fabricant*) mustard maker *ou* manufacturer.
mouton[1] [mutɔ̃] **1** *nm* **(a)** (*Zool*) sheep. **doublé de** ~ lined with sheepskin; **relié en** ~ bound in sheepskin, sheepskin-bound; (*fig*) **compter les** ~**s pour s'endormir** to count sheep to help one get to sleep; *V* **revenir, sauter.**
(b) (*Culin*) mutton.
(c) (*: *personne*) (*grégaire, crédule*) sheep; (*doux, passif*) sheep, lamb. **c'est un** ~ (*grégaire*) he is easily led, he goes with the crowd; (*doux*) he is as mild *ou* gentle as a lamb; **il m'a suivi comme un** ~ he followed me like a lamb; **se conduire en** ~**s de Panurge** to behave like a lot of sheep, follow one another (around) like sheep.
(d) (*arg Police: dans une prison*) stool pigeon*, grass (*arg*).
(e) ~**s** (*sur la mer*) white horses; (*sur le plancher*) (bits of) fluff; (*dans le ciel*) fluffy *ou* fleecy clouds.
(f) (*Constr*) ram, monkey.
2: mouton à cinq pattes rara avis (*littér*), world's wonder; **mouton à laine** sheep reared for wool; **mouton à viande** sheep reared for meat.
mouton[2]**, -onne** [mutɔ̃, ɔn] *adj* sheeplike.
moutonnant, e [mutɔnɑ̃, ɑ̃t] *adj mer* flecked with white horses; (*littér*) *collines* rolling (*épith*).
moutonné, e [mutɔne] (*ptp de* **moutonner**) *adj ciel* flecked with fleecy *ou* fluffy clouds.
moutonnement [mutɔnmɑ̃] *nm [mer]* breaking into *ou* becoming flecked with white horses *ou* foam. (*littér*) **le** ~ **des collines** the rolling hills.
moutonner [mutɔne] (1) **1** *vi [mer]* to be covered in white horses, be flecked with foam; (*littér*) *[collines]* to roll.
2 se moutonner *vpr [ciel]* to be flecked with fleecy *ou* fluffy clouds.
moutonneux, -euse [mutɔnø, øz] *adj mer* flecked with white horses; *ciel* flecked with fleecy *ou* fluffy clouds.
moutonnier, -ière [mutɔnje, jɛʀ] *adj* (*fig*) sheeplike.
mouture [mutyʀ] *nf [blé]* milling, grinding; *[café]* grinding. (*fig péj*) **c'est la 3e** ~ **du même livre** it's the 3rd rehash of the same book.
mouvance [muvɑ̃s] *nf* (*Hist*) tenure; (*Philos*) mobility; (*fig littér*) domain, sphere of influence.
mouvant, e [muvɑ̃, ɑ̃t] *adj situation* unsettled, fluid; *ombre, flamme* moving, changing; *pensée, univers* changing; *terrain* unsteady, shifting. (*fig*) **être en terrain** ~ to be on shaky *ou* uncertain ground; *V* **sable**[1].
mouvement [muvmɑ̃] *nm* **(a)** (*geste*) movement, motion. ~**s de gymnastique** (physical) exercises; **il a des** ~**s très lents** he is very slow in his movements; **il approuva d'un** ~ **de tête** he nodded his approval, he gave a nod of approval; **elle eut un** ~ **de recul** she started back; **un** ~ **de dégoût** *etc* a movement of disgust *etc*; *V* **temps**[1].
(b) (*impulsion, réaction*) impulse, reaction. **avoir un bon** ~ to make a nice *ou* kind gesture; **dans un bon** ~ on a kindly impulse; **dans un** ~ **de colère/d'indignation** in a fit *ou* a burst *ou* an upsurge of anger/indignation; **les** ~**s de l'âme** the impulses of the soul; ~**s dans l'auditoire** a stir in the audience; **discours accueilli avec des** ~**s divers** speech which got a mixed reception; **son premier** ~ **fut de refuser** his first impulse was to refuse; **agir de son propre** ~ to act of one's own accord.
(c) (*activité*) *[ville, entreprise]* activity, bustle. **une rue pleine de** ~ a busy *ou* lively street; **prendre** *ou* **se donner du** ~ to take some exercise; **il aime le** ~ he likes to be on the go*.
(d) (*déplacement*) (*Astron, Aviat, Naut*) movement; (*Mil*) (*déplacement*) movement; (*manœuvre*) move. **être sans cesse en** ~ to be constantly on the move *ou* on the go*; **mettre qch en** ~ to set sth in motion, set sth going; **suivre le** ~ to follow the general movement; **le** ~ **perpétuel** perpetual motion; ~ **de foule** movement *ou* sway in the crowd; (*Sociol*) ~**s de population** shifts in population; (*Mil*) ~ **de repli** withdrawal; ~ **tournant** (out)flanking movement; ~**s de troupes** troop movements; (*Écon*) ~ **de marchandises/de capitaux** *ou* **de fonds** movement of goods/capital; (*Admin*) ~ **de personnel** changes in staff *ou* personnel; *V* **guerre.**
(e) (*Philos, Pol etc: évolution*) **le** ~ **des idées** the evolution of ideas; **le parti du** ~ the party in favour of change, the progressive party; **être dans le** ~ to keep up-to-date; **un** ~ **d'opinion se dessine en faveur de** one can detect a trend of opinion in favour of; (*Fin*) **le** ~ **des prix** the trend of prices; (*Fin*) ~ **de baisse (sur les ventes)** downward movement *ou* trend (in sales).
(f) (*rythme*) *[phrase]* rhythm; *[tragédie]* movement, action; *[mélodie]* tempo.
(g) (*Pol, Sociol: groupe*) movement. ~ **politique/de jeunesse** political/youth movement; **le** ~ **syndical** the trade-union *ou* labor-union (*US*) movement.
(h) (*Mus*) *[symphonie etc]* movement.
(i) (*Tech: mécanisme*) movement. **par un** ~ **d'horlogerie** by clockwork.
(j) (*ligne, courbe*) *[sculpture]* contours; *[draperie, étoffe]* drape; *[collines]* undulations, rise and fall (*U*).
mouvementé, e [muvmɑ̃te] *adj vie, poursuite, récit* eventful; *séance* turbulent, stormy; (*rare*) *terrain* rough.
mouvoir [muvwaʀ] (27) **1** *vt* (*gén ptp*) **(a)** *machine* to drive, power; *bras, levier* to move. **faire** ~ to drive, power; move; **il se leva comme mû par un ressort** he sprung up as if propelled by a spring *ou* like a Jack-in-the-box.
(b) *[motif, sentiment]* to drive, prompt.
2 se mouvoir *vpr* to move.
moyen, -enne [mwajɛ̃, ɛn] **1** *adj* **(a)** (*qui tient le milieu*) *taille* medium (*épith*), average; *prix* moderate, medium (*épith*). **de taille** ~**ne** of medium height; **une maison de dimensions** ~**nes** a medium- *ou* moderate-sized house; (*Comm*) **il ne reste plus de tailles** ~**nes** there are no medium sizes left; **les régions de la** ~**ne Loire** the middle regions of the Loire, the mid-Loire regions; **la solution** ~**ne** the middle-of-the-road solution; **une** ~**ne entreprise** a medium-sized company; *V* **cours, onde, poids.**
(b) (*du type courant*) average. **le Français/le lecteur** ~ the average Frenchman/reader.
(c) (*ni bon ni mauvais*) *résultats, intelligence* average. **nous avons eu un temps** ~ we had mixed weather, the weather was so-so*; **un élève qui est** ~ **en géographie** a pupil who is average at geography; **bien** ~, **très** ~ mediocre, pretty poor*.
(d) (*d'après des calculs*) *température* average, mean (*épith*); *âge, prix etc* average.
2 *nm* **(a)** means, way. **il y a toujours un** ~ there's always a way, there are ways and means; **par quel** ~ **allez-vous le convaincre?** how will you manage to convince him?; **connaissez-vous un bon** ~ **pour ...?** do you know a good way to ... ?; (*péj*) **par tous les** ~**s** by fair means or foul; **j'ai essayé par tous les** ~**s de le convaincre** I've done everything to try and convince him; **tous les** ~**s lui sont bons** he'll stick at nothing; **c'est l'unique** ~ **de s'en sortir** it's the only way out, it's the only way we can get out of it; **employer les grands** ~**s** to have to resort to drastic means *ou* measures; **se débrouiller avec les** ~**s du bord** to get by as best one can, make do with what's available; **au** ~ **de, par le** ~ **de** by means of, with the help of; *V* **fin**[2].
(b) est-ce qu'il y a ~ **de lui parler?** is it possible to speak to him?; **il n'y a pas** ~ **de sortir par ce temps** you can't get out in this weather; (*Téléc*) **pas** ~ **d'obtenir la communication** I can't get through; **le** ~ **de dire autre chose!** what else could I say!; **le** ~ **de lui refuser!** how could I possibly refuse!; **non, il n'y a pas** ~**!** no, nothing doing!*; **il n'y a jamais** ~ **qu'il fasse attention** you will never get him to take care, he'll never take care; *V* **trouver.**
(c) (*capacités intellectuelles, physiques*) ~**s** means; **il a de grands** ~**s** he is well-equipped; **ça lui a enlevé tous ses** ~**s** it completely cramped his style, it left him completely floored; **être en (pleine) possession de tous ses** ~**s** to be really on top of things; **c'est au-dessus de ses** ~**s** it's beyond him; **par ses propres** ~**s** all by himself, on his own; **ils ont dû rentrer par leurs propres** ~**s** they had to go home under their own steam*, they had to make their own way home; *V* **perdre.**
(d) (*ressources financières*)~**s** means; **il n'a pas les** ~**s de s'acheter une voiture** he can't afford to buy a car; **c'est au-dessus de ses** ~**s** he can't afford it, it's beyond his means; **il a les** ~**s** he's got the means, he can afford it; **avoir de gros/petits** ~**s** to have a large/small income, be well/badly off.
3 moyenne *nf* **(a)** (*gén*) average; (*Aut*) average speed. **au-dessus/au-dessous de la** ~**ne** above/below average; **faites-moi la** ~**ne de ces chiffres** work out the average of these figures; **la** ~**ne d'âge/des températures/des gens** the average age/temperature/person; **faire du 100 de** ~**ne** to average 100 km/h, drive at an average speed of 100 km/h, do 100 km/h on average; (*Math*) ~**ne géométrique/arithmétique** geometric/arithmetic mean; **en** ~**ne** on (an) average.
(b) (*Scol*) **avoir la** ~**ne** (*devoir*) to get fifty per cent, get half marks; (*examen*) to get a pass *ou* the passmark; ~**ne générale (de l'année)** average (for the year); **cet élève est dans la** ~**ne/la bonne** ~**ne** this pupil is about/above average.
4: moyen d'action measures, means of action; **moyen âge** Middle Ages (*V* **haut**); **moyenâgeux, -euse** *ville, costumes* medieval, historic, quaint; (*péj*) *attitudes, théories* antiquated, outdated, old-fashioned; **moyen anglais** Middle English; (*Aviat*) **moyen-courrier** *nm, pl* **moyens-courriers** medium-haul (aeroplane); **moyen de défense** means of defence; **moyen d'existence** means of existence; **moyen d'expression** means of expression; **moyen de fortune** makeshift device *ou* means; **moyen de locomotion** means of transport; (*Ciné*) **moyen métrage** medium-length film; **le Moyen-Orient** the Middle East; **moyen de pression** means of applying pressure; **moyen de production** means of production; **moyen terme** (*gén*) middle course; (*Logique*) middle term; **moyen de transport** means of transport; **moyens de trésorerie** *means of raising revenue.*
moyennant [mwajɛnɑ̃] *prép argent* for; *service* in return for; *travail, effort* with. ~ **finance** for a fee *ou* a consideration; ~ **quoi** in return for which, in consideration of which.
moyenne [mwajɛn] *nf V* **moyen.**
moyennement [mwajɛnmɑ̃] *adv* fairly, moderately; *s'entendre, travailler* fairly well, moderately well. **ça va?** — ~*

how are things? — so-so* *ou* not too bad* *ou* average.
moyeu, *pl* **~x** [mwajø] *nm [roue]* hub; *[hélice]* boss.
mozartien, -ienne [mɔzaʀtjɛ̃, jɛn] *adj, nm,f* Mozartian.
mû, mue[1] [my] *ptp de* **mouvoir.**
mucosité [mykozite] *nf (gén pl)* mucus (*U*).
mucus [mykys] *nm* mucus (*U*).
mue[2] [my] *nf* **(a)** (*transformation*) *[oiseau]* moulting; *[serpent]* sloughing; *[mammifère]* shedding, moulting; *[cerf]* casting; *[voix]* breaking. **la ~ (de la voix) intervient vers 12 ans** the voice breaks at round about 12 years of age.
(b) (*époque*) moulting *etc* season. *[voix]* **au moment de la ~** when the voice is breaking.
(c) (*peau, plumes*) *[serpent]* slough; *[oiseau, mammifère]* moulted *ou* shed hair, feathers *etc.*
(d) (*Agr: cage*) coop.
muer [mɥe] (1) **1** *vi [oiseau]* to moult; *[serpent]* to slough; *[mammifère]* to moult, shed hair *ou* skin *etc.* **sa voix mue, il mue** his voice is breaking.
2 *vt* (*littér*) **~ qch en** to transform *ou* change *ou* turn sth into.
3 se muer *vpr* (*littér*) **se ~ en** to transform *ou* change *ou* turn into.
muet, -ette [mɥɛ, ɛt] **1** *adj* **(a)** (*infirme*) dumb; *V* **sourd.**
(b) (*silencieux*) *colère, prière, personne* silent, mute (*littér*); (*littér*) *forêt* silent. **~ de colère/surprise** speechless with anger/surprise; **~ de peur** dumb with fear; **le code est ~ à ce sujet** the law is silent on this matter; **en rester ~ (d'étonnement)** to stand speechless, be struck dumb (with astonishment); **~ comme une tombe** (as) silent as the grave; **il est resté ~ comme une carpe** he never opened his mouth.
(c) (*Ciné*) *film, cinéma* silent; *V* **jeu, rôle.**
(d) (*Ling*) mute, silent.
(e) (*Scol*) (*Géog*) *carte, clavier de machine à écrire* blank. (*Mus*) **clavier ~** dummy keyboard.
2 *nm* **(a)** (*infirme*) mute, dumb man.
(b) (*Ciné*) **le ~** the silent cinema.
3 muette *nf* dumb woman.
mufle [myfl(ə)] *nm* **(a)** (*Zool: museau*) *[bovin]* muffle; *[chien, lion]* muzzle. **(b)** (*‡: goujat*) boor, lout*, yob‡ (*Brit*). **ce qu'il est ~ alors!‡** what a yob‡ (*Brit*) *ou* lout* he is!, what a boorish fellow he is!
muflerie [myflǝʀi] *nf* boorishness.
muflier [myflije] *nm* antirrhinum.
mufti [myfti] *nm* (*Rel*) mufti.
mugir [myʒiʀ] (2) *vi* **(a)** *[vache]* to low, moo; *[bœuf]* to bellow. **(b)** (*littér*) *[vent]* to howl, roar, bellow; *[mer]* to howl, roar, boom; *[sirène]* to howl.
mugissement [myʒismɑ̃] *nm* (*V* **mugir**) lowing, mooing; bellowing; howling; roaring; booming.
muguet [mygɛ] *nm* (*Bot*) lily of the valley; (*Méd*) thrush; (††: *élégant*) fop, coxcomb††, popinjay††.
muid [mɥi] *nm* (††: *tonneau*) hogshead.
mulâtre, -esse [mylɑtʀ(ə), ɛs] *nm,f,* **mulâtre** *adj inv* mulatto.
mule [myl] *nf* **(a)** (*Zool*) (she-)mule; *V* **tête, têtu. (b)** (*pantoufle*) mule.
mulet [mylɛ] *nm* (*Zool*) (he-)mule; (*poisson*) mullet.
muletier, -ière [myltje, jɛʀ] **1** *adj*: **sentier** *ou* **chemin ~** mule track. **2** *nm,f* mule-driver, muleteer.
mulot [mylo] *nm* field mouse.
multicellulaire [myltiselylɛʀ] *adj* multicellular.
multicolore [myltikɔlɔʀ] *adj* multicoloured, many-coloured.
multiculturalisme [myltikyltyʀalism(ə)] *nm* multiculturalism.
multiflore [myltiflɔʀ] *adj* multiflorous.
multiforme [myltifɔʀm(ə)] *adj apparence* multiform; *problème* many-sided.
multilatéral, e, *mpl* **-aux** [myltilateʀal, o] *adj* multilateral.
multilingue [myltilɛ̃g] *adj* multilingual.
multimilliardaire [myltimiljaʀdɛʀ] *adj, nmf,* **multimillionnaire** [myltimiljɔnɛʀ] *adj, nmf* multimillionaire.
multinational, e, *mpl* **-aux** [myltinasjɔnal, o] *adj* multinational.
multipare [myltipaʀ] **1** *adj* multiparous. **2** *nf* (*femme*) multipara; (*animal*) multiparous animal.
multiplace [myltiplas] *adj, nm*: **cet avion est (un) ~** it's a passenger aircraft.
multiple [myltipl(ə)] **1** *adj* **(a)** (*nombreux*) numerous, multiple, many; (*Méd*) *fracture, blessures* multiple. **dans de ~s cas** in numerous instances; **en de ~s occasions** on numerous *ou* multiple occasions; **pour des raisons ~s** *ou* **de ~s raisons** for multiple reasons; **à de ~s reprises** time and again, repeatedly; **à têtes ~s** *missile* multiple-warhead; *outil* with (range of) attachments; **à usages ~s** multi-purpose; *V* **magasin.**
(b) (*variés*) *activités, aspects* many, multifarious, manifold.
(c) (*complexe*) *pensée, problème, homme* many-sided; *monde* complex, mixed.
(d) (*Math*) **100 est ~ de 10** 100 is a multiple of 10.
2 *nm* multiple. **plus petit commun ~** lowest common multiple.
multipliable [myltiplijabl(ə)] *adj* multipli(c)able.
multiplicande [myltiplikɑ̃d] *nm* multiplicand.
multiplicateur, -trice [myltiplikatœʀ, tʀis] **1** *adj* multiplying. **2** *nm* multiplier.
multiplicatif, -ive [myltiplikatif, iv] *adj* (*Math*) multiplying; (*Gram*) multiplicative.
multiplication [myltiplikasjɔ̃] *nf* **(a)** (*prolifération*) increase in the number of. (*Bible*) **la ~ des pains** the miracle of the loaves and fishes. **(b)** (*Bot, Math*) multiplication. **(c)** (*Tech*) gear ratio.
multiplicité [myltiplisite] *nf* multiplicity.
multiplier [myltiplije] (7) **1** *vt* (*Math*) to multiply (*par* by); *attaques, difficultés, avertissements* to multiply, increase. **malgré nos efforts multipliés** in spite of our increased efforts.
2 se multiplier *vpr* **(a)** *[incidents, attaques, difficultés]* to multiply, increase, grow in number; *[progrès]* to expand, increase.
(b) (*se reproduire*) *[animaux]* to multiply.
(c) (*fig: se donner à fond*) *[infirmier, soldat]* to do one's utmost, give of one's best (*pour faire* in order to do).
multipolaire [myltipɔlɛʀ] *adj* multipolar.
multirisque [myltiʀisk(ə)] *adj* multiple-risk (*épith*).
multitude [myltityd] *nf* **(a)** (*grand nombre*) **(toute) une ~ de** *personnes* a multitude of, a vast number of; *objets, idées* a vast number of; **la ~ des gens** the (vast) majority of people.
(b) (*ensemble, masse*) *[lois, idées]* body; *[objets]* mass. **on pouvait voir d'en haut la ~ des champs** from the air you could see the mass of fields.
(c) († *ou littér: foule de gens*) multitude, throng.
munichois, e [mynikwa, waz] **1** *adj* of *ou* from Munich, Munich (*épith*). **bière ~e** Munich beer. **2** *nm,f*: **M~(e)** inhabitant *ou* native of Munich; (*Pol*) **les ~** the men of Munich.
municipal, e, *mpl* **-aux** [mynisipal, o] *adj élection, taxe, théâtre, stade* municipal; *conseil, conseiller* local, town (*épith*), borough (*épith*). **règlement/arrêté ~** local by-law; **piscine/ bibliothèque ~e** public swimming pool/library.
municipalité [mynisipalite] *nf* **(a)** (*ville*) town, municipality.
(b) (*conseil*) town council, corporation.
munificence [mynifisɑ̃s] *nf* (*littér*) munificence.
munir [myniʀ] (2) **1** *vt*: **~ de: ~ un objet de** to provide *ou* fit an object with; **~ une machine de** to equip *ou* fit a machine with; **~ un bâtiment de** to equip *ou* fit up *ou* fit out a building with; **~ qn de** to provide *ou* supply *ou* equip sb with; **muni de ces conseils** armed with this advice; (*Rel*) **muni des sacrements de l'Église** fortified with the rites of the Church.
2 se munir *vpr*: **se ~ de** *papiers, imperméable* to provide *ou* equip o.s. with; *argent, nourriture* to provide *ou* supply o.s. with; **se ~ de patience** to arm o.s. with patience; **se ~ de courage** to pluck up one's courage.
munitions [mynisjɔ̃] *nfpl* ammunition (*U*).
munster [mœ̃stɛʀ] *nm* Munster (cheese).
muphti [myfti] *nm* = **mufti.**
muqueux, -euse [mykø, øz] **1** *adj* mucous. **2 muqueuse** *nf* mucous membrane.
mur [myʀ] **1** *nm* **(a)** (*gén*) wall. **leur jardin est entouré d'un ~** their garden is walled (in) *ou* is surrounded by a wall; **une maison aux ~s de brique** a brick house; **~ d'appui** parapet; **mettre/pendre qch au ~** to put/hang sth on the wall; **sauter** *ou* **faire le ~*** to leap over *ou* jump the wall; (*Sport*) **faire le ~** to make a wall; **ils n'ont laissé que les (quatre) ~s** they left nothing but the bare walls; **l'ennemi est dans nos ~s** the enemy is within our gates; **M X est dans nos ~s aujourd'hui** we have Mr X with us today; (*fig*) **les ~s ont des oreilles** walls have ears; (*Mil, Pol*) **le ~ de Berlin/de l'Atlantique** the Berlin/the Atlantic Wall.
(b) (*obstacle*) *[feu, pluie]* wall; *[silence, hostilité]* barrier. **il y a un ~ entre nous** there is a barrier between us; **se heurter à** *ou* **se trouver devant un ~** to come up against a brick wall; **être** *ou* **avoir le dos au ~** to have one's back to the wall; **on parle à un ~** it's like talking to a brick wall; *V* **pied.**
(c) (*Aviat*) **~ du son/de la chaleur** sound/heat barrier; **passer** *ou* **franchir le ~ du son** to break the sound barrier.
2: mur de clôture enclosing wall; **mur d'enceinte** outer wall(s); **le Mur des Lamentations** the Wailing Wall; **mur mitoyen** party wall; **mur de pierres sèches** dry-stone wall; **mur portant** load-bearing wall; **mur de refend** supporting (partition) wall; **mur de séparation** dividing wall; **mur de soutènement** retaining *ou* breast wall.
mûr, e[1] [myʀ] *adj fruit, projet* ripe; *toile, tissu* worn; *personne, esprit* mature. **pas ~** *fruit* unripe, not ripe; *personne* immature, not mature; **des fruits trop ~s** overripe fruit; **il est ~ pour le mariage** he is ready for marriage; **il est très ~ pour son âge** he is very mature for his age; **une femme assez ~e** a woman advanced in years *ou* who is getting on* (in years); **après ~e réflexion** after mature reflection; (‡: *ivre*) **il est complètement ~** he's pretty far gone‡.
murage [myʀaʒ] *nm [ouverture]* walling up, bricking up, blocking up.
muraille [myʀɑj] *nf* (high) wall. **la Grande M~ de Chine** the Great Wall of China; **~ de glace/roche** wall of ice/rock, ice/rock barrier; **couleur (de) ~** (stone) grey.
mural, e, *mpl* **-aux** [myʀal, o] *adj* wall (*épith*); (*Art*) mural.
mûre[2] [myʀ] *nf [ronce]* blackberry, bramble; *[mûrier]* mulberry.
mûrement [myʀmɑ̃] *adv*: **ayant ~ réfléchi** *ou* **délibéré sur cela** after giving it much thought, after lengthy deliberation.
murène [myʀɛn] *nf* moray, mur(a)ena.
murer [myʀe] (1) **1** *vt* **(a)** *ouverture* to wall up, brick up, block up; *lieu, ville* to wall (in).
(b) *personne* (*lit*) to wall in, wall up; (*fig*) to isolate.
2 se murer *vpr* (*chez soi*) to wall o.s. up. **se ~ dans sa douleur/son silence** to immure o.s. in one's grief/in silence.
muret [myʀɛ] *nm,* **murette** [myʀɛt] *nf* low wall.
murex [myʀɛks] *nm* murex.
mûrier [myʀje] *nm* mulberry tree; (*ronce*) blackberry bush, bramble bush.
mûrir [myʀiʀ] (2) **1** *vi [fruit]* to ripen; *[idée]* to mature, develop; *[personne]* to mature; *[abcès, bouton]* to come to a head.
2 *vt fruit* to ripen; *idée, projet* to nurture; *personne* to (make) mature. **faire ~** *fruit* to ripen.
mûrissant, e [myʀisɑ̃, ɑ̃t] *adj fruit* ripening; *personne* of mature years.

mûrissement [myʀismɑ̃] *nm [fruit]* ripening; *[idée]* maturing, development; *[projet]* nurturing.
murmure [myʀmyʀ] *nm* **(a)** (*chuchotement*) *[personne]* murmur; *[ruisseau]* murmur(ing), babble; *[vent]* murmur(ing); *[oiseaux]* twitter(ing).
(b) (*commentaire*) murmur. **~ d'approbation/de protestation** murmur of approval/of protest; **obéir sans ~** to obey without a murmur; **~s** (*protestations*) murmurings, mutterings, grumblings; (*objections*) objections.
murmurer [myʀmyʀe] (1) **1** *vt* to murmur. **on murmure que ...** it's whispered that ..., rumour has it that ... .
2 *vi* **(a)** (*chuchoter*) *[personne, vent]* to murmur; *[ruisseau]* to murmur, babble; *[oiseaux]* to twitter.
(b) (*protester*) to mutter, complain, grumble (*contre* about). **il a consenti sans ~** he agreed without a murmur (of protest).
musaraigne [myzaʀɛɲ] *nf* (*Zool*) shrew.
musarder [myzaʀde] (1) *vi* (*littér*) (*en se promenant*) to dawdle (along); (*en perdant son temps*) to idle (about).
musc [mysk] *nm* musk.
muscade [myskad] *nf* **(a)** (*Culin*) nutmeg; *V* **noix.**
(b) (conjurer's) ball. **passez ~!** (*lit*) *[jongleur]* hey presto!; (*fig*) quick as a flash!
muscadet [myskadɛ] *nm* muscadet (wine).
muscadier [myskadje] *nm* nutmeg (tree).
muscadin [myskadɛ̃] *nm* (*Hist††: élégant*) fop†, coxcomb††, popinjay††.
muscat [myska] *nm* (*raisin*) muscat grape; (*vin*) muscatel (wine).
muscle [myskl(ə)] *nm* muscle. (*Anat*) **~s lisses/striés** smooth/striated muscles; **il est tout en ~** he's all muscle; **il a des ~s** *ou* **du ~*** he is brawny, he's got plenty of beef*.
musclé, e [myskle] (*ptp de* **muscler**) *adj corps, membre* muscular; *homme* brawny; (*fig*) *style* sinewy; *pièce de théâtre* powerful; *régime, appariteur* strong-arm (*épith*). (*arg Scol*) **un problème ~** a stinker: of a problem.
muscler [myskle] (1) *vt* to develop the muscle of.
musculaire [myskylɛʀ] *adj force* muscular. **fibre ~** muscle fibre.
musculation [myskylɑsjɔ̃] *nf*: **(exercices de) ~** muscle-development exercises.
musculature [myskylatyʀ] *nf* muscle structure, musculature (*T*). **il a une ~ imposante** he has an impressive set of muscles.
musculeux, -euse [myskylø, øz] *adj corps, membre* muscular; *homme* muscular, brawny.
muse [myz] *nf* (*Littérat, Myth*) Muse. **les (neuf) ~s** the Muses; (*hum*) **cultiver** *ou* **taquiner la ~** to court the Muse (*hum*).
museau, *pl* **~x** [myzo] *nm* **(a)** *[chien, bovin]* muzzle; *[porc]* snout.
(b) (*Culin*) brawn.
(c) (*) *[visage]* face, snout*.
musée [myze] *nm* (*art, peinture*) art gallery; (*technique, scientifique*) museum. **Nîmes est une ville-~** Nîmes is a historical town, Nîmes is a town of great historical interest; (*hum*) **~ des horreurs** junkshop (*hum*); **elle ferait bien dans un ~ des horreurs** she should be in a chamber of horrors; (*lit, fig*) **objet** *ou* **pièce de ~** museum piece.
museler [myzle] (4) *vt* (*lit*) *animal* to muzzle; (*fig*) *personne, liberté, presse* to muzzle (*fig*), gag (*fig*), silence.
muselière [myzəljɛʀ] *nf* muzzle. **mettre une ~ à** to muzzle.
musellement [myzɛlmɑ̃] *nm* (*lit*) *[animal]* muzzling; (*fig*) *[personne, liberté, presse]* muzzling (*fig*), gagging (*fig*), silencing.
muséobus [myzeobys] *nm* mobile museum.
muser [myze] (1) *vi* († *ou littér*) (*en se promenant*) to dawdle (along); (*en perdant son temps*) to idle (about).
musette [myzɛt] **1** *nf* **(a)** (*sac*) *[ouvrier]* lunchbag; (††) *[écolier]* satchel; *[soldat]* haversack.
(b) (*Mus: instrument, air*) musette.
(c) (*Zool*) common shrew.
2 *nm* (*bal*) popular dance (*to the accordion*). (*genre*) **le ~** accordion music.
3 *adj inv genre, style, orchestre* accordion (*épith*); *V* **bal.**
muséum [myzeɔm] *nm*: **~ (d'histoire naturelle)** (natural history) museum.
musical, e, *mpl* **-aux** [myzikal, o] *adj* musical. **avoir l'oreille ~e** to have a good ear for music; *V* **comédie.**
musicalement [myzikalmɑ̃] *adv* musically.
musicalité [myzikalite] *nf* musicality, musical quality.
music-hall, *pl* **music-halls** [myzikol] *nm* (*salle*) variety theatre, music hall. **faire du ~** to be in *ou* do variety; **spectacle/numéro de ~** variety show/turn *ou* act *ou* number.
musicien, -ienne [myzisjɛ̃, jɛn] **1** *adj* musical. **2** *nm,f* musician.
musicographe [myzikɔgʀaf] *nm* musicographer.
musicographie [myzikɔgʀafi] *nf* musicography.
musicologie [myzikɔlɔʒi] *nf* musicology.
musicologue [myzikɔlɔg] *nmf* musicologist.
musique [myzik] **1** *nf* **(a)** (*art, harmonie, notations*) music. **~ militaire/sacrée** military/sacred music; **~ pour piano** piano music; (*Rad*) **programme de ~ variée** programme of selected music; **la ~ adoucit les mœurs** music has a civilizing influence; **elle fait de la ~** she plays; **si on faisait de la ~** let's make some music; **mettre un poème en ~** to set a poem to music; **déjeuner en ~** to lunch against a background of music; **travailler en ~** to work to music; **je n'aime pas travailler en ~** I don't like working against *ou* with music; (*fig*) **c'est toujours la même ~*** it's always the same old refrain *ou* song; *V* **boîte, papier.**
(b) (*orchestre, fanfare*) band. (*Mil*) **marcher** *ou* **aller ~ en tête** to march with the band leading; *V* **chef**[1].
2: musique d'ambiance background music; **musique de ballet** ballet music; **musique de chambre** chamber music; **musique classique** classical music; **musique concrète** concrete music, musique concrète; **musique douce** soft music; **musique folklorique** folk music; **musique de fond** background music; **musique légère** light music; **musique pop** pop music; **musique de scène** incidental music.
musiquette [myzikɛt] *nf* rubbishy* music.
musoir [myzwaʀ] *nm* (*Naut*) pierhead.
musqué, e [myske] *adj odeur, goût* musky. **rat ~** muskrat; **bœuf ~** musk ox; **rose ~e** musk rose.
musulman, e [myzylmɑ̃, an] *adj, nm,f* Moslem, Muslim.
mutabilité [mytabilite] *nf* (*Bio, Jur etc*) mutability.
mutation [mytɑsjɔ̃] *nf* **(a)** (*transfert*) *[fonctionnaire]* transfer.
(b) (*changement*) (*gén*) transformation; (*Bio*) mutation. **(c)** (*Jur*) transfer; (*Mus*) mutation. (*Ling*) **~ consonantique/vocalique** consonant/vowel shift.
muter [myte] (1) *vt* (*Admin*) to transfer, move.
mutilateur, -trice [mytilatœʀ, tʀis] (*littér*) **1** *adj* mutilating, mutilative. **2** *nm,f* mutilator.
mutilation [mytilɑsjɔ̃] *nf [corps]* mutilation, maiming; *[texte, statue, arbre]* mutilation.
mutilé, e [mytile] (*ptp de* **mutiler**) *nm,f* (*infirme*) cripple, disabled person. **les (grands) ~s** the (badly *ou* severely) disabled; **~ de la face** disfigured person; **~ de guerre** disabled ex-serviceman; **~ du travail** disabled worker.
mutiler [mytile] (1) *vt personne* to mutilate, maim; *tableau, statue, arbre* to mutilate, deface; *texte* to mutilate. **gravement mutilé** badly disabled; **se ~ (volontairement)** to injure o.s. (on purpose), inflict an injury on o.s.
mutin, e [mytɛ̃, in] **1** *adj* (*espiègle*) mischievous, impish. **2** *nm* (*Mil, Naut*) mutineer; (*gén: révolté*) rebel.
mutiné, e [mytine] (*ptp de* **se mutiner**) **1** *adj marin, soldat* mutinous. **2** *nm* mutineer.
mutiner (se) [mytine] (1) *vpr* (*Mil, Naut*) to mutiny; (*gén*) to rebel, revolt.
mutinerie [mytinʀi] *nf* (*Mil, Naut*) mutiny; (*gén*) rebellion, revolt.
mutisme [mytism(ə)] *nm* **(a)** silence. **la presse observe un ~ total** the press is maintaining a complete silence *ou* blackout on the subject. **(b)** (*rare: Méd*) dumbness, muteness; (*Psych*) mutism.
mutité [mytite] *nf* (*Méd*) muteness.
mutualisme [mytɥalism(ə)] *nm* mutualism.
mutualiste [mytɥalist(ə)] **1** *adj* mutualistic. **2** *nmf* mutualist.
mutualité [mytɥalite] *nf* mutual benefit insurance; (*réciprocité*) mutuality (*rare*).
mutuel, -elle [mytɥɛl] **1** *adj* (*réciproque*) mutual; *V* **pari. 2 mutuelle** *nf* mutual benefit society, mutual benefit insurance company, ≃ Friendly Society (*Brit*).
mutuellement [mytɥɛlmɑ̃] *adv* one another, each other. **~ ressenti** mutually felt; **s'aider ~** to give each other mutual help, help one another.
mycénien, -ienne [misenjɛ̃, jɛn] **1** *adj* Mycenaean. **2** *nm,f*: **M~(ne)** Mycenaean.
mycologie [mikɔlɔʒi] *nf* mycology.
mycologique [mikɔlɔʒik] *adj* mycologic(al).
mycologue [mikɔlɔg] *nmf* mycologist.
mycose [mikoz] *nf* mycosis. **la ~ du pied** athlete's foot.
myéline [mjelin] *nf* myelin.
myélite [mjelit] *nf* myelitis.
myocarde [mjɔkaʀd(ə)] *nm* myocardium.
myope [mjɔp] *adj* short- *ou* near-sighted, myopic (*T*). **~ comme une taupe*** (as) blind as a bat*.
myopie [mjɔpi] *nf* short- *ou* near-sightedness, myopia (*T*).
myosotis [mjozɔtis] *nm* forget-me-not.
myriade [miʀjad] *nf* myriad.
myriapode [miʀjapɔd] *nm* myriapod. **~s** Myriapoda.
myrmidon [miʀmidɔ̃] *nm* († *péj: nabot*) pipsqueak*.
myrrhe [miʀ] *nf* myrrh.
myrte [miʀt(ə)] *nm* myrtle.
myrtille [miʀtij] *nf* bilberry, whortleberry.
mystère [mistɛʀ] *nm* **(a)** (*énigme, dissimulation*) mystery. **pas tant de ~(s)!** don't be so mysterious! *ou* secretive!; **faire (un) ~ de** to make a mystery out of. **(b)** (*Littérat, Rel*) mystery.
mystérieusement [misteʀjøzmɑ̃] *adv* mysteriously.
mystérieux, -euse [misteʀjø, øz] *adj* mysterious; (*cachottier*) secretive.
mysticisme [mistisism(ə)] *nm* mysticism.
mystificateur, -trice [mistifikatœʀ, tʀis] **1** *adj*: **j'ai reçu un coup de fil ~** I had a phone call which was a hoax; **tenir des propos ~s à qn** to say things to trick sb.
2 *nm,f* (*farceur*) hoaxer, practical joker.
mystification [mistifikɑsjɔ̃] *nf* (*farce*) hoax, practical joke; (*péj: mythe*) myth.
mystifier [mistifje] (7) *vt* to fool, take in, bamboozle*.
mystique [mistik] **1** *adj* mystic(al). **2** *nmf* (*personne*) mystic. **3** *nf* (*science, pratiques*) mysticism; (*péj: vénération*) blind belief (*de* in). **avoir la ~ du travail** to have a blind belief in work.
mystiquement [mistikmɑ̃] *adv* mystically.
mythe [mit] *nm* (*gén*) myth.
mythique [mitik] *adj* mythical.
mythologie [mitɔlɔʒi] *nf* mythology.
mythologique [mitɔlɔʒik] *adj* mythological.
mythomane [mitɔman] *adj, nmf* mythomaniac.
mythomanie [mitɔmani] *nf* mythomania.
myxomatose [miksɔmatoz] *nf* myxomatosis.

N

N, n [ɛn] *nm* (*lettre*) N, n; (*Math*) n.
n' [n] *V* **ne.**
na [na] *excl* (*langage enfantin*) so there! **je n'en veux pas, ~!** I don't want any, so there!
nabab [nabab] *nm* (*Hist ou* †) nabob.
nabot, e [nabo, ɔt] **1** *adj* dwarfish, tiny. **2** *nm,f* (*péj*) dwarf, midget.
nabuchodonosor [nabykɔdɔnɔzɔʀ] *nm* (*bouteille*) nebuchadnezzar. **N~** Nebuchadnezzar.
nacelle [nasɛl] *nf* [*ballon*] nacelle; (*littér: bateau*) skiff, barque (*littér*).
nacre [nakʀ(ə)] *nf* mother-of-pearl.
nacré, e [nakʀe] (*ptp de* **nacrer**) *adj* pearly.
nacrer [nakʀe] (1) *vt* (*iriser*) to cast a pearly sheen over; (*Tech*) to give a pearly gloss to.
nadir [nadiʀ] *nm* nadir.
nævus [nevys], *pl* **nævi** [nevi] *nm* naevus.
nage [naʒ] *nf* **(a)** swimming; (*manière*) stroke, style of swimming. **~ sur le dos** backstroke; **~ indienne** sidestroke; **~ libre** freestyle; **~ sous-marine** underwater swimming, skin diving; **~ de vitesse** speed stroke.
(b) à la ~: se sauver à la ~ to swim away *ou* off; **gagner la rive/traverser une rivière à la ~** to swim to the bank/across a river; **faire traverser son chien à la ~** to get one's dog to swim across; *V* **homard.**
(c) il était tout en ~ he was pouring with sweat *ou* bathed in sweat; **cela m'a mis en ~** that made me sweat.
(d) (*Naut*) **~ à couple/en pointe** double-/single-banked rowing; **chef de ~** coxswain, cox.
nageoire [naʒwaʀ] *nf* [*poisson*] fin; [*phoque etc*] flipper. **~ anale/dorsale/ventrale** *etc* anal/dorsal/ventral *etc* fin.
nager [naʒe] (3) **1** *vi* **(a)** [*personne, poisson*] to swim; [*objet*] to float. **~ comme un fer à repasser*/comme un poisson** to swim like a brick/like a fish; **~ entre deux eaux** to swim *ou* float under water; **la viande nage dans la graisse** the meat is swimming in fat; **attention, tes manches nagent dans la soupe** look out, your sleeves are dipping *ou* getting in the soup; **on nageait dans le sang** the place was swimming in *ou* with blood, the place was awash with blood; *V* **apprendre, savoir.**
(b) (*fig*) **il nage dans la joie** he is overjoyed, his joy knows no bounds; **~ dans l'opulence** to be rolling in money*; **il nage dans ses vêtements** he is lost in his clothes; **en allemand, je nage complètement*** I'm completely at sea* *ou* lost in German.
(c) (*Naut*) to row.
2 *vt* to swim. **~ la brasse/le 100 mètres** to swim breaststroke/the 100 metres.
nageur, -euse [naʒœʀ, øz] *nm,f* swimmer; (*rameur*) rower. (*Mil*) **~ de combat** naval frogman.
naguère [nagɛʀ] *adv* (*frm*) (*il y a peu de temps*) not long ago, a short while ago; (*autrefois*) formerly.
naïade [najad] *nf* (*Bot, Myth*) naïad; (*hum, littér*) nymph.
naïf, naïve [naif, naiv] **1** *adj personne* (*ingénu*) innocent, naïve; (*crédule*) naïve; *réponse, foi, gaieté* naïve. (*Art*) **peintre/art ~** naïve painter/art.
2 *nm,f* gullible fool, innocent. **vous me prenez pour un ~** you must think I'm a gullible fool *ou* a complete innocent.
nain, e [nɛ̃, nɛn] **1** *adj* dwarfish, dwarf (*épith*). **chêne/haricot ~** dwarf oak/runner bean; (*Astron*) **étoile ~e** dwarf star. **2** *nm,f* dwarf. (*Cartes*) **le ~ jaune** pope Joan.
naissain [nɛsɛ̃] *nm* seed oyster, spat.
naissance [nɛsɑ̃s] *nf* **(a)** [*personne, animal*] birth. **à la ~** at birth; **de ~: il est aveugle/muet/sourd de ~** he has been blind/dumb/deaf from birth, he was born blind/dumb/deaf; **français de ~** French by birth; **chez lui, c'est de ~*** he was born like that; **~ double** birth of twins; *V* **contrôle, extrait, limitation** *etc.*
(b) (*frm: origine, source*) **de ~ obscure/illustre** of obscure/illustrious birth; **de haute** *ou* **bonne ~** of high birth.
(c) (*point de départ*) [*rivière*] source; [*langue, ongles*] root; [*cou, colonne*] base. **à la ~ des cheveux** at the roots of the hair.
(d) (*littér: commencement*) [*printemps, monde, idée*] birth; [*amour*] dawn, birth. **la ~ du jour** daybreak.
(e) (*loc*) **prendre ~** [*projet, idée*] to originate, take form; [*rivière*] to rise, originate; [*soupçon*] to arise, take form; **donner ~ à** (*lit*) to give birth to; (*fig*) to give rise to.
naissant, e [nɛsɑ̃, ɑ̃t] *adj* (*littér, Chim*) nascent.
naître [nɛtʀ(ə)] (59) **1** *vi* **(a)** [*personne, animal*] to be born. **quand l'enfant doit-il ~?** when is the child to be born?, when is the child due?; **il vient tout juste de ~** he has only just been born, he is just newly born; **X est né** *ou* **X naquit** (*frm*) **le 4 mars** X was born on March 4; **l'homme naît libre** man is born free; **il est né poète** he is a born *ou* natural poet; **l'enfant qui naît aveugle/infirme** the child who is born blind/disabled *ou* a cripple; **l'enfant qui va ~, l'enfant à ~** the unborn child; **l'enfant qui vient de ~** the newborn child; **en naissant** at birth; **prématuré né à 7 mois** baby born prematurely at 7 months premature baby born at 7 months; **enfant né de père inconnu** child of an unknown father; **Mme Durand, née Dupont** Mme Durand, née Dupont; **être né de parents français** to be of French parentage, be born of French parents; **être né d'une mère anglaise** to be born of an English mother; (*Bible*) **un sauveur nous est né** a saviour is born to us; (*fig*) **être né coiffé** *ou* **sous une bonne étoile** to be born lucky *ou* under a lucky star; (*fig*) **il n'est pas né d'hier** *ou* **de la dernière pluie** he wasn't born yesterday, he is not as green as he looks; *V* **terme.**
(b) (*fig*) [*sentiment, craintes*] to arise, be born, spring; [*idée, projet*] to be born; [*ville, industrie*] to spring up; [*jour*] to break; [*difficultés*] to arise; [*fleur, plante*] to burst forth. **la rivière naît au pied de ces collines** the river has its source *ou* rises at the foot of these hills; **je vis ~ un sourire sur son visage** I saw the beginnings of a smile on his face, I saw a smile creep over his face; **faire ~ une industrie/des difficultés** to create an industry/difficulties; **faire ~ des soupçons/le désir** to arouse suspicions/desire.
(c) ~ de (*résulter de*) to spring from, arise from; **la haine née de ces querelles** the hatred caused by *ou* which sprang from these quarrels; **de cette rencontre naquit le mouvement qui ...** from this meeting sprang the movement which ... .
(d) être né pour (*être destiné à*): **il était né pour commander/pour la magistrature** he was born to command/to be a magistrate; **ils sont nés l'un pour l'autre** they were made for each other.
(e) (*littér*) **~ à** (*s'éveiller à*): **~ à l'amour/la poésie** to awaken to love/poetry.
2 *vb impers*: **il naît plus de filles que de garçons** there are more girls born than boys, more girls are born than boys; (*littér*) **il vous est né un fils** a son has been born to you (*littér*).
naïvement [naivmɑ̃] *adv* (*V* **naïf**) innocently; naïvely.
naïveté [naivte] *nf* (*V* **naïf**) innocence; naïvety. **il a eu la ~ de le croire** he was naïve enough to believe him.
naja [naʒa] *nm* cobra.
nana* [nana] *nf* (*femme*) bird: (*Brit*), chick:.
nanan* [nanɑ̃] *nm*: **c'est du ~** (*agréable*) it's a bit of all right* (*Brit*); (*facile*) it's a walkover* *ou* a doddle* (*Brit*); (*succulent*) it's scrumptious*.
nanisme [nanism(ə)] *nm* dwarfism, nanism (*T*).
nantais, e [nɑ̃tɛ, ɛz] **1** *adj* of *ou* from Nantes. **2** *nm,f*: **N~(e)** inhabitant *ou* native of Nantes.
nanti, e [nɑ̃ti] (*ptp de* **nantir**) *adj* rich, affluent, well-to-do. **les ~s** the rich, the affluent, the well-to-do.
nantir [nɑ̃tiʀ] (2) **1** *vt* († *Jur*) *créancier* to secure. (*fig, littér: munir*) **~ qn de** to provide sb with. **2 se nantir** *vpr* († *Jur*) to secure o.s. (*fig, littér*) **se ~ de** to provide o.s. with, equip o.s. with.
nantissement [nɑ̃tismɑ̃] *nm* (*Jur*) security, pledge.
napalm [napalm] *nm* napalm.
naphthaline [naftalin] *nf* (*antimite*) mothballs (*pl*).
naphte [naft(ə)] *nm* naphtha.
Naples [napl(ə)] *n* Naples.
Napoléon [napɔleɔ̃] *nm* Napoleon.
napoléon [napɔleɔ̃] *nm* (*Fin*) napoleon.
napoléonien, -ienne [napɔleɔnjɛ̃, jɛn] *adj* Napoleonic.
napolitain, e [napɔlitɛ̃, ɛn] **1** *adj* Neapolitan. **2** *nm,f*: **N~(e)** Neapolitan.
nappe [nap] **1** *nf* tablecloth. (*fig*) **~ de gaz/de pétrole** layer of gas/oil; **~ d'eau** sheet *ou* expanse of water; **mettre la ~** to put the tablecloth on. **2: nappe d'autel** altar cloth; **nappe de brouillard** blanket *ou* layer of fog; **nappe de charriage** nappe; **nappe de feu** sheet of flame; **nappe de mazout** oil slick.
napper [nape] (1) *vt* (*Culin*) to coat (*de* with).
napperon [napʀɔ̃] *nm* tablemat; (*pour vase, lampe etc*) mat. **~ individuel** place mat.
narcisse [naʀsis] *nm* (*Bot*) narcissus; (*péj: égocentrique*) narcissistic individual. (*Myth*) **N~** Narcissus.
narcissique [naʀsisik] *adj* narcissistic.
narcissisme [naʀsisism(ə)] *nm* narcissism.
narcose [naʀkoz] *nf* narcosis.
narcotique [naʀkɔtik] *adj, nm* narcotic.
narghileh [naʀgilɛ] *nm* nargileh *ou* narghile, hookah.
narguer [naʀge] (1) *vt danger, traditions* to flout, thumb one's nose at; *personne* to deride, scoff at.
narguilé [naʀgile] *nm* = **narghileh.**
narine [naʀin] *nf* nostril.
narquois, e [naʀkwa, waz] *adj* (*railleur*) mocking, derisive, sardonic.
narquoisement [naʀkwazmɑ̃] *adv* mockingly, derisively, sardonically.
narrateur, -trice [naʀatœʀ, tʀis] *nm,f* narrator.
narratif, -ive [naʀatif, iv] *adj* narrative.
narration [naʀɑsjɔ̃] *nf* **(a)** (*U*) narration; *V* **infinitif. (b)** (*récit*) narration, narrative, account; (*Scol: rédaction*) essay, composition; (*Rhétorique*) narration.
narrer [naʀe] (1) *vt* (*frm*) to narrate, relate.
narval [naʀval] *nm* narwhal.
nasal, e, *mpl* -aux [nazal, o] **1** *adj* nasal. **2 nasale** *nf* nasal; *V* fosse.

nasalisation [nazalizɑsjɔ̃] *nf* nasalization.
nasaliser [nazalize] (1) *vt* to nasalize.
nasalité [nazalite] *nf* nasality.
nasarde [nazaʀd(ə)] *nf* (*littér: chiquenaude*) flick on the nose; (*fig: affront*) snub.
naseau, *pl* **~x** [nazo] *nm [cheval, bœuf]* nostril.
nasillard, e [nazijaʀ, aʀd(ə)] *adj voix* nasal; *instrument* nasal; *gramophone* whiny.
nasillement [nazijmɑ̃] *nm [voix]* (nasal) twang; *[microphone, gramophone]* whine; *[instrument]* nasal sound; *[canard]* quack.
nasiller [nazije] (1) **1** *vt* to say (*ou* sing *ou* intone) with a (nasal) twang. **2** *vi [personne]* to have a (nasal) twang, speak with *ou* in a nasal voice; *[instrument]* to give a nasal sound; *[microphone, gramophone]* to whine; (*rare*) *[canard]* to quack.
nasse [nas] *nf* hoop net.
natal, e, *mpl* **~s** [natal] *adj* native. **ma maison ~e** the house where I was born; **ma terre ~e** my native soil.
nataliste [natalist(ə)] *adj politique* which supports a rising birth rate.
natalité [natalite] *nf* birth rate.
natation [natɑsjɔ̃] *nf* swimming.
natatoire [natatwaʀ] *adj* (*rare*) swimming (*épith*); *V* **vessie.**
natif, -ive [natif, iv] *adj, nm,f* (*gén*) native. **~ de Nice** native of Nice.
nation [nɑsjɔ̃] *nf* (*pays, peuple*) nation. **les N~ Unies** the United Nations; *V* **société.**
national, e, *mpl* **-aux** [nasjɔnal, o] **1** *adj* national. **obsèques ~es** state funeral; **éducation ~e** state education; **(route) ~e** ≈ 'A' *ou* trunk road (*Brit*), state highway (*US*); *V* **assem blée, fête.**
2 *nmpl* (*citoyens*) nationals.
3: national-socialisme *nm* national socialism; **national(e)-socialiste,** *mpl* **nationaux-socialistes** *adj, nm,f* national socialist.
nationalement [nasjɔnalmɑ̃] *adv* nationally.
nationalisation [nasjɔnalizɑsjɔ̃] *nf* nationalization.
nationaliser [nasjɔnalize] (1) *vt* to nationalize.
nationalisme [nasjɔnalism(ə)] *nm* nationalism.
nationaliste [nasjɔnalist(ə)] *adj, nmf* nationalist.
nationalité [nasjɔnalite] *nf* nationality.
nativisme [nativism(ə)] *nm* (*Philos*) nativism.
nativiste [nativist(ə)] *adj* (*Philos*) nativistic.
nativité [nativite] *nf* nativity; (*Art*) (painting of the) nativity, nativity scene.
natte [nat] *nf* (*tresse*) pigtail, plait, braid†; (*paillasse*) mat, matting (*U*).
natter [nate] (1) *vt cheveux* to plait, braid; *laine etc* to weave.
naturalisation [natyʀalizɑsjɔ̃] *nf* (*Bot, Ling, Pol*) naturalization; *[animaux morts]* stuffing; *[plantes séchées]* pressing, drying.
naturalisé, e [natyʀalize] (*ptp de* **naturaliser**) **1** *adj:* **Français ~** naturalized Frenchman; **il est ~ (français)** he's a naturalized Frenchman. **2** *nm,f* naturalized person.
naturaliser [natyʀalize] (1) *vt* (*Bot, Ling, Pol*) to naturalize; *animal mort* to stuff; *plante séchée* to press *ou* dry. **se faire ~ français** to become a naturalized Frenchman.
naturalisme [natyʀalism(ə)] *nm* naturalism.
naturaliste [natyʀalist(ə)] **1** *adj* naturalistic. **2** *nmf* (*Littérat, Sci*) naturalist; (*empailleur*) taxidermist; (*pour les plantes*) flower-preserver.
nature [natyʀ] **1** *nf* **(a)** (*caractère*) *[personne, substance, sentiment]* nature. **la ~ humaine** human nature; **c'est une** *ou* **il est de** *ou* **d'une ~ arrogante** he has an *ou* he is of an arrogant nature; **il est arrogant de** *ou* **par ~** he is naturally arrogant *ou* arrogant by nature; **ce n'est pas dans sa ~** it is not (in) his nature (*d'être* to be); **c'est/ce n'est pas de ~ à** it's liable to/not likely to; **il n'est pas de ~ à** he's not the sort of person who would; **avoir une heureuse ~** to have a happy nature, be of a happy disposition; **c'est dans la ~ des choses** it's in the nature of things; *V* **habitude, second.**
(b) (*monde physique, principe fondamental*) **la ~** nature; **vivre (perdu) dans la ~** to live (out) in the country *ou* in the wilds *ou* at the back of beyond (*Brit*) *ou* in the boondocks (*US*); **la ~ a horreur du vide** nature abhors a vacuum; **laisser agir la ~** to leave it to nature, let nature take its course; **disparaître dans la ~*** *[personne]* to vanish into thin air; *[ballon]* to disappear into the undergrowth *ou* bushes; **actions/crimes/vices/goûts contre ~** unnatural acts/crimes/vices/tastes, acts/crimes/vices/tastes which go against nature *ou* which are contrary to nature; *V* **force, retour.**
(c) (*sorte*) nature, kind, sort. **de toute(s) ~(s)** of all kinds, of every kind.
(d) (*Art*) **peindre d'après ~** to paint from life; **plus grand que ~** more than life-size, larger than life; **~ morte** still life; *V* **grandeur.**
(e) (*Fin*) **en ~** *payer, don* in kind.
2 *adj inv* **(a) café ~** black coffee; **eau ~** plain water; **thé ~** tea without milk; **boire le whisky ~** to drink whisky neat; **manger les fraises** *etc* **~** to eat strawberries *etc* without anything on them.
(b) il est ~!* he is so natural!, he is completely uninhibited!
naturel, -elle [natyʀɛl] **1** *adj* **(a)** *caractère, frontière, produit, phénomène* natural; *besoins, fonction* bodily (*épith*); *soie, laine* pure.
(b) (*inné*) natural. **son intelligence ~le** his natural intelligence, his native wit; **elle a un talent ~ pour le piano** playing the piano comes naturally to her, she has a natural talent for the piano.
(c) (*normal, habituel*) natural. **avec sa voix ~le** in his normal voice; **c'est un geste ~ chez lui** it's a natural gesture *ou* quite a normal gesture for him, this gesture comes (quite) naturally to him; **votre indignation est bien ~le** your indignation is quite *ou* very natural *ou* understandable; **ne me remerciez pas, c'est bien** *ou* **tout ~** don't thank me, anybody would have done the same *ou* it was the obvious thing to do; **il est bien ~ qu'on en vienne à cette décision** it's only natural that this decision should have been reached; **il trouve ça tout ~** he finds it the most natural thing in the world *ou* perfectly normal.
(d) (*simple, spontané*) *voix, style, personne* natural, unaffected. **elle sait rester très ~le** she manages to stay very natural; **être ~ sur les photos** to be very natural in photos, take a good photo.
(e) (*Mus*) natural.
2 *nm* **(a)** (*caractère*) nature, disposition. **être d'un** *ou* **avoir un bon ~** to have a good *ou* happy nature *ou* disposition; *V* **chasser.**
(b) (*absence d'affectation*) naturalness. **avec (beaucoup de) ~** (completely) naturally; **manquer de ~** to be affected, have a rather self-conscious manner.
(c) (*indigène*) native.
(d) (*loc*) **au ~** (*Culin: sans assaisonnement*) served plain, au naturel; (*en réalité*) **elle est mieux en photo qu'au ~** she's better in photos than in real life.
naturellement [natyʀɛlmɑ̃] *adv* **(a)** (*sans artifice, normalement*) naturally; (*avec aisance*) naturally, unaffectedly. **(b)** (*bien sûr*) naturally, of course.
naturisme [natyʀism(ə)] *nm* (*nudisme*) naturism; (*Philos*) naturism; (*Méd*) naturopathy.
naturiste [natyʀist(ə)] *adj, nmf* (*nudiste*) naturist; (*Philos*) naturist; (*Méd*) naturopath.
naufrage [nofʀaʒ] *nm* **(a)** *[bateau]* wreck. **le ~ de ce navire** the wreck of this ship; **un ~** a shipwreck; **faire ~** *[bateau]* to be wrecked; *[marin etc]* to be shipwrecked.
(b) (*fig: déchéance*) *[ambitions, réputation]* ruin, ruination; *[projet, pays]* foundering, ruination. **sauver du ~** *personne* to save from disaster; *argent, biens* to salvage (from the wreckage).
naufragé, e [nofʀaʒe] **1** *adj marin* shipwrecked; *bateau* (ship-) wrecked. **2** *nm,f* shipwrecked person; (*sur une île*) castaway.
naufrageur, -euse [nofʀaʒœʀ, øz] *nm,f* (*lit, fig*) wrecker.
nauséabond, e [nozeabɔ̃, ɔ̃d] *adj* (*lit, fig*) nauseating, sickening.
nausée [noze] *nf* (*U*) feeling of nausea *ou* sickness, nausea (*U*); (*haut-le-cœur*) bout of nausea. **avoir la ~** to feel sick; **avoir des ~s** to have bouts of nausea; (*lit, fig*) **ça me donne la ~** it makes me (feel) sick.
nautile [notil] *nm* (*Zool*) nautilus.
nautique [notik] *adj* nautical. **sports ~s** water sports; **fête ~** water festival; *V* **ski.**
nautisme [notism(ə)] *nm* water sport(s).
naval, e, *mpl* **~s** [naval] *adj combat, base* naval; *industrie* shipbuilding. **école ~e** naval college; *V* **chantier, construction, force.**
navarin [navaʀɛ̃] *nm* mutton stew, navarin lamb.
navarrais, e [navaʀɛ, ɛz] **1** *adj* Navarrian. **2** *nm,f:* **N~(e)** Navarrian.
Navarre [navaʀ] *nf* Navarre.
navet [navɛ] *nm* **(a)** turnip; *V* **sang. (b)** (*péj*) (*film*) rubbishy *ou* third-rate film; (*roman*) rubbishy *ou* third-rate novel; (*tableau*) daub. **c'est un ~** it's (a piece of) rubbish, it's tripe.
navette[1] [navɛt] *nf* **(a)** (*Tex*) shuttle.
(b) (*service de transport*) shuttle (service). **faire la ~ entre** *[banlieusard, homme d'affaires]* to commute between; *[véhicule]* to operate a shuttle (service) between; *[bateau]* to ply between; *[projet de loi, circulaire]* to be sent backwards and forwards between; **elle fait la ~ entre la cuisine et la chambre** she comes and goes between the kitchen and the bedroom.
navette[2] [navɛt] *nf* (*Bot*) rape.
navigabilité [navigabilite] *nf [rivière]* navigability; *[bateau]* seaworthiness; *[avion]* airworthiness.
navigable [navigabl(ə)] *adj rivière* navigable.
navigant, e [navigɑ̃, ɑ̃t] *adj, nm:* **le personnel ~, les ~s** (*Aviat*) flying personnel; (*Naut*) seagoing personnel.
navigateur [navigatœʀ] *nm* (*littér, Naut: marin*) navigator, sailor; (*Aut, Aviat: co-pilote*) navigator. **~ solitaire** single-handed sailor.
navigation [navigɑsjɔ̃] *nf* **(a)** (*Naut*) sailing (*U*), navigation (*U*); (*voyage*) voyage, trip; (*trafic*) (sea) traffic (*U*); (*pilotage*) navigation, sailing (*U*). **les récifs rendent la ~ dangereuse/difficile** the reefs make sailing *ou* navigation dangerous/difficult; **canal ouvert/fermé** *ou* **interdit à la ~** canal open/closed to shipping *ou* ships; **~ côtière/intérieure** coastal/inland navigation; **~ de plaisance** pleasure sailing; **~ à voiles** sailing; **compagnie de ~** shipping company; **terme de ~** nautical term.
(b) (*Aviat*) (*trafic*) (air) traffic (*U*); (*pilotage*) navigation, flying (*U*). **~ aérienne** aerial navigation; **compagnie de ~ aérienne** airline company.
naviguer [navige] (1) *vi* **(a)** (*voyager*) *[bateau, passager, marin]* to sail; *[avion, passager, pilote]* to fly. **~ à la voile** to sail; **ce bateau/marin a beaucoup/n'a jamais navigué** this ship/sailor has been to sea a lot *ou* has done a lot of sailing/has never been to sea *ou* has never sailed; **bateau en état de ~** seaworthy ship; **~ à 800 mètres d'altitude** to fly at an altitude of 800 metres.
(b) (*piloter*) *[marin]* to navigate, sail; *[aviateur]* to navigate, fly. **~ au compas** to navigate by (the) compass; **~ à travers Glasgow** (*en voiture*) to find one's way through Glasgow, negotiate Glasgow; (*fig*) **pour réussir ici, il faut savoir ~** to succeed here you need to know how to get around *ou* you need to know the ropes.
(c) (*: *errer*) **c'est un type qui a beaucoup navigué** he's a guy*

who has been around a lot *ou* who has knocked about quite a bit*; **après avoir navigué pendant une heure entre les rayons du supermarché** after having spent an hour finding one's way around the supermarket shelves; **le dossier a navigué de bureau en bureau** the file found its way from office to office.

navire [naviʀ] *nm* (*bateau*) ship; (*Jur*) vessel. ~ **amiral** flagship; ~**-citerne** tanker; ~ **marchand** *ou* **de commerce** merchant ship, merchantman; ~**-école** training ship; ~ **de guerre** warship; ~**-hôpital** hospital ship.

navrant, e [navʀɑ̃, ɑ̃t] *adj* (*V* **navrer**) distressing, upsetting; (most) annoying. **tu es** ~! you're hopeless!

navré, e [navʀe] (*ptp de* **navrer**) *adj* sorry (*de* to). **avoir l'air** ~ (*pour s'excuser, compatir*) to look sorry; (*d'une nouvelle*) to look distressed *ou* upset; **d'un ton** ~ (*pour s'excuser*) in an apologetic tone, apologetically; (*pour compatir*) in a sympathetic tone; (*par l'émotion*) in a distressed *ou* an upset voice.

navrer [navʀe] (1) *vt* (*désoler*) [*spectacle, conduite, nouvelle*] to grieve, distress, upset; [*contretemps, malentendu*] to annoy.

nazaréen, enne [nazaʀeɛ̃, ɛn] **1** *adj* Nazarene. **2** *nm,f*: N~(ne) Nazarene.

Nazareth [nazaʀɛt] *n* Nazareth.

nazi, e [nazi] *adj, nm,f* Nazi.

nazisme [nazism(ə)] *nm* Nazism.

ne [n(ə)] *adv nég*, **n'** *devant voyelles et h muet* **(a)** (*valeur nég: avec nég avant ou après*) **il n'a rien dit** he didn't say anything, he said nothing; **elle** ~ **nous a pas vus** she didn't *ou* did not see us, she hasn't *ou* has not seen us; **personne** *ou* (*frm*) **nul n'a compris** nobody *ou* no one *ou* not a soul understood; **il n'y a aucun mal à ça** there's no harm *ou* there's nothing wrong in that; **il n'est pas du tout** *ou* **nullement idiot** he is by no means stupid; **s'il n'est jamais monté en avion ce n'est pas qu'il n'en ait jamais eu l'occasion** if he has never been up in an aeroplane it's not that he has never had the opportunity *ou* it's not for lack of opportunities; **je n'ai pas** *ou* († *ou hum*) **point d'argent** I have no money, I haven't any money; **il** ~ **sait plus ce qu'il dit** he no longer knows what he's saying; **plus rien** ~ **l'intéresse, rien** ~ **l'intéresse plus** nothing interests him any more, he's not interested in anything any more; ~ **me dérangez pas** don't *ou* do not disturb me; **je** ~ **connais ni son fils ni sa fille** I know neither his son nor his daughter, I don't know his son or his daughter; **je n'ai pas du tout** *ou* **aucunement l'intention de refuser** I have not the slightest intention of refusing; **je n'ai guère le temps** I have scarcely *ou* hardly the time; **il** ~ **sait pas parler** he can't *ou* cannot speak; **pas un seul** ~ **savait sa leçon** not (a single) one (of them) knew his lesson.

(b) (*valeur nég: sans autre nég: gén littér*) **il** ~ **cesse de se plaindre** he does not stop complaining; **je** ~ **sais qui a eu cette idée** I do not know *ou* I know not (*littér* ††) who had that idea; **elle** ~ **peut jouer du violon sans qu'un voisin** (~) **proteste** she cannot play her violin without some neighbour's objecting; **il n'a que faire de vos conseils** he has no use for your advice; **que n'a-t-il songé à me prévenir** if only he had thought to warn me; **n'était la situation internationale, il serait parti** had it not been for *ou* were it not for the international situation he would have left; **il n'est de paysage qui** ~ **soit maintenant gâché** nowadays there is no landscape that is not spoilt *ou* there is no unspoilt countryside; **il n'est de jour qu'elle** ~ **se plaigne** not a day goes by but she complains (about something), not a day goes by without her complaining; **cela fait des années que je n'ai été au cinéma** it's years since I (last) went to the cinema; **il a vieilli depuis que je** ~ **l'ai vu** he has aged since I (last) saw him; **si je** ~ **me trompe** if I'm not mistaken; *V* **cure**[2], **empêcher, importer**[2].

(c) ~ ... **que** only; **elle n'a confiance qu'en nous** she trusts only us, she only has confidence in us; **c'est mauvais de** ~ **manger que des conserves** it is bad to eat only tinned foods *ou* nothing but tinned foods; **il n'a que trop d'assurance** he is only too self-assured; **il n'a d'autre idée en tête que de se lancer dans la politique** his (one and) only thought is to embark upon politics; **il n'y a que lui pour dire des choses pareilles!** only he *ou* nobody but he would say such things!; **il n'y a pas que vous qui le dites!** you're not the only one who says so! *ou* to say this!; **et il n'y a pas que ça!** and that's not all!; *V* **demander**.

(d) (*explétif sans valeur nég, gén omis dans la langue parlée*) **je crains** *ou* **j'ai peur** *ou* **j'appréhende qu'il** ~ **vienne** I am afraid *ou* I fear (that) he is coming *ou* (that) he will come; **je** ~ **doute pas/je** ~ **nie pas qu'il** ~ **soit compétent** I don't doubt/deny that he is competent; **empêche que les enfants** ~ **touchent aux animaux** stop the children touching *ou* prevent the children from touching the animals; **mangez avant que le rôti** ~ **refroidisse** do eat before the roast gets cold; **j'irai la voir avant qu'il/à moins qu'il** ~ **pleuve** I shall go and see her before/unless it rains; **il est parti avant que je** ~ **l'aie remercié** he left before I had thanked him; **il est parti sans que je** ~ **l'aie remercié** he left without my having thanked him; **peu s'en faut qu'il n'ait oublié la réunion** he all but *ou* he very nearly forgot the meeting; **il est plus/moins malin qu'on** ~ **pense** he is more cunning than/not as cunning as you think.

né, e [ne] (*ptp de* **naître**) *adj, nm,f* born; (*fig: causé*) caused (*de* by), due (*de* to). **orateur/acteur** ~ born orator/actor; **bien/mal** ~ of noble *ou* high/humble *ou* low birth; **Paul est son premier/dernier** ~ Paul is her first-/last-born *ou* her first/last child; *V* **naître, mort**[2], **nouveau**.

néanmoins [neɑ̃mwɛ̃] *adv* (*pourtant*) nevertheless, yet. **il était malade, il est** ~ **venu** he was ill, (and) nevertheless *ou* (and) yet he came; **il est agressif et** ~ **patient** he is aggressive yet patient, he is aggressive but nevertheless patient.

néant [neɑ̃] *nm* nothingness (*U*), void. **le** ~ **de la vie/de l'homme** the worthlessness of life/man; **signes particuliers:** ~ special peculiarities: none; *V* **réduire**.

nébuleuse[1] [nebyløz] *nf* (*Astron*) nebula.

nébuleusement [nebyløzmɑ̃] *adv* (*rare*) nebulously, vaguely.

nébuleux, -euse[2] [nebylø, øz] *adj* (*lit*) *ciel* cloudy, overcast; (*fig*) *écrivain, discours* nebulous, obscure; *projet, idée* nebulous, vague.

nébulosité [nebylozite] *nf* [*ciel*] cloud covering, nebulosity (*T*); (*rare*) [*discours*] obscureness.

nécessaire [nesesɛʀ] **1** *adj* **(a)** (*gén, Math, Philos*) necessary. **il est** ~ **de le faire** it needs to be done, it has (got) to be done, it must be done, it's necessary to do it; **il est** ~ **qu'on le fasse** we need to do it, we have (got) to do it, we must do it, it's necessary for us to do it; **est-ce (bien)** ~ **(de le faire)?** have we (really) got to (do it)?, do we (really) need *ou* have to (do it)?, is it (really) necessary (for us to do it)?; **non, ce n'est pas** ~ **(de le faire)** no, there's no need to (do it), no, you don't need *ou* have to (do it), it's not (really) necessary (for you to do it); **l'eau est** ~ **à la vie/aux hommes/pour vivre** water is necessary for life/to man/to live; **un bon repos vous est** ~ you need a good rest; **cette attitude lui est** ~ **pour réussir** he has to have *ou* maintain this attitude to succeed; **cette attitude est** ~ **pour réussir** this is a necessary attitude *ou* this attitude is necessary *ou* needed if one wants to get on; **c'est une condition** ~ it's a necessary condition (*pour faire* for doing, *de qch* for sth); **c'est une conséquence** ~ it's a necessary consequence (*de qch* of sth); **avoir le talent/le temps/l'argent** ~ **(pour qch/pour faire)** to have the (necessary *ou* requisite) talent/time/money (for sth/to do), have the talent/time/money (required) (for sth/to do); **a-t-il les moyens** ~**s?** does he have the necessary *ou* requisite means?, does he have the means required?; **faire les démarches** ~**s** to take the necessary *ou* requisite steps.

(b) *personne* indispensable (*à* to). **se sentir** ~ to feel indispensable.

2 *nm* **(a)** (*l'indispensable*) **as-tu emporté le** ~? have you got all *ou* everything we need?; **je n'ai pas le** ~ **pour le faire** I haven't got what's needed *ou* the necessary stuff to do it; **il peut faire froid, prenez le** ~ it may be cold so take the necessary clothes; **emporter le strict** ~ to take the bare *ou* absolute essentials; **il faut d'abord penser au** ~ one must first consider the essentials; **manquer du** ~ to lack the (basic) necessities of life; **faire le** ~ to do what is necessary *ou* what has to be done; **j'ai fait le** ~ I've settled it *ou* seen to it, I've done what was necessary; **je vais faire le** ~ I'll see to it, I'll make the necessary arrangements, I'll do the necessary*.

(b) (*Philos*) **le** ~ the necessary.

3: **nécessaire à couture** workbag, sewing box; **nécessaire à ongles** manicure set; **nécessaire à ouvrage** = **nécessaire à couture**; **nécessaire de toilette** toilet *ou* sponge bag (*Brit*); **nécessaire de voyage** grip.

nécessairement [nesesɛʀmɑ̃] *adv* necessarily. **dois-je** ~ **m'en aller?** is it (really) necessary for me to go?, must I (really) go?, do I (really) have to go?; **il devra** ~ **s'y faire** he will (just) have to get used to it; **il y a** ~ **une raison** there must (needs) be a reason; **ce n'est pas** ~ **faux** it isn't necessarily wrong; **s'il s'y prend ainsi, il va** ~ **échouer** if he sets about it this way, he's bound to fail *ou* he'll inevitably fail; (*Philos*) **causes et effets sont liés** ~ causes and effects are necessarily linked *ou* are of necessity linked.

nécessité [nesesite] *nf* **(a)** (*obligation*) necessity. **c'est une** ~ **absolue** it's an absolute necessity; **sévère sans** ~ unnecessarily severe; **je ne vois pas la** ~ **de le faire** I don't see the necessity of doing that *ou* the need for (doing) that; **se trouver** *ou* **être dans la** ~ **de faire qch** to have no choice *ou* alternative but to do sth; **mettre qn dans la** ~ **de faire** to make it necessary for sb to do; **la** ~ **où je suis de faire cela** having no choice *ou* alternative but to do that; **la** ~ **d'être le lendemain à Paris nous fit partir de très bonne heure** the need to be *ou* our having to be in Paris the next day made us leave very early.

(b) ~**s**: **les** ~**s de la vie** the necessities *ou* essentials of life; **les** ~**s du service** the demands *ou* requirements of the job; ~**s financières** (financial) liabilities.

(c) (*Philos*) **la** ~ necessity; **la** ~ **de mourir** the inevitability of death.

(d) (††: *pauvreté*) destitution. **être dans la** ~ to be in need, be poverty-stricken.

(e) (*loc*) **faire qch par** ~ to do sth out of necessity; **faire de** ~ **vertu** to make a virtue of necessity; (*Prov*) ~ **fait loi** necessity knows no law (*Prov*).

nécessiter [nesesite] (1) *vt* (*requérir*) to necessitate, require, make necessary.

nécessiteux, -euse [nesesitø, øz] **1** *adj* needy, necessitous. **2** *nm,f* needy person. **les** ~ the needy, the poor.

nec plus ultra [nɛkplysyltʀa] *nm*: **c'est le** ~ it's the last word (*de* in).

nécrologie [nekʀɔlɔʒi] *nf* (*liste*) obituary column; (*notice biographique*) obituary.

nécrologique [nekʀɔlɔʒik] *adj* obituary (*épith*).

nécromancie [nekʀɔmɑ̃si] *nf* necromancy.

nécromancien, -ienne [nekʀɔmɑ̃sjɛ̃, jɛn] *nm,f* necromancer.

nécropole [nekʀɔpɔl] *nf* necropolis.

nectar [nɛktaʀ] *nm* (*Bot, Myth, fig*) nectar.

néerlandais, e [neɛʀlɑ̃dɛ, ɛz] **1** *adj* Dutch, of the Netherlands. **2** *nm* **(a)** N~ Dutchman; **les N~** the Dutch. **(b)** (*Ling*) Dutch. **3** **Néerlandaise** *nf* Dutchwoman.

nef [nɛf] *nf* **(a)** (*Archit*) nave. ~ **latérale** side aisle.

(b) (†† *ou littér: bateau*) vessel, ship.

néfaste [nefast(ə)] *adj* (*nuisible*) harmful (*à* to); (*funeste*) ill-fated, unlucky. **cela lui fut** ~ it had disastrous consequences for him.

nèfle [nɛfl(ə)] *nf* medlar. **des** ~**s!**‡ nothing doing!*, not likely!*.

néflier [neflije] *nm* medlar (tree).

négateur, -trice [negatœʀ, tʀis] (*littér*) **1** *adj* given to denying, contradictory. **2** *nm,f* denier.

négatif, -ive [negatif, iv] **1** *adj* negative; *quantité, nombre* negative, minus (*épith*). **2** *nm* (*Phot*) negative. **3 négative** *nf*: **dans la ~ive** in the negative.

négation [negɑsjɔ̃] *nf* negation.

négativement [negativmɑ̃] *adv* negatively.

négativisme [negativism(ə)] *nm* negativism.

négativité [negativite] *nf* (*Phys*) negativity; [*attitude*] negativeness, negativity.

négligé, e [negliʒe] (*ptp de* **négliger**) **1** *adj épouse, ami* neglected; *personne, tenue* slovenly, sloppy; *travail* slapdash, careless; *style* slipshod; *occasion* missed (*épith*).

2 *nm* (*laisser-aller*) slovenliness; (*vêtement*) négligée. **je suis en ~** I'm in déshabillé, I'm not dressed; **le ~ de sa tenue** the slovenliness of his dress.

négligeable [negliʒabl(ə)] *adj* negligible; *détail* unimportant, trivial, trifling; *adversaire* insignificant. **qui n'est pas ~, non ~** *facteur, élément* not inconsiderable; *adversaire, aide, offre* which is not to be sneezed at; *détail, rôle* not insignificant; *V* **quantité.**

négligemment [negliʒamɑ̃] *adv* (*sans soin*) carelessly, negligently, in a slovenly way; (*nonchalamment*) casually.

négligence [negliʒɑ̃s] *nf* (*manque de soin*) negligence, slovenliness; (*faute, erreur*) omission, piece of negligence. **~ (de style)** stylistic blunder, carelessness (*U*) of style.

négligent, e [negliʒɑ̃, ɑ̃t] *adj* (*sans soin*) negligent, careless; (*nonchalant*) casual.

négliger [negliʒe] (3) **1** *vt* **(a)** (*gén*) to neglect; *style, tenue* to be careless about; *conseil* to neglect, pay no attention *ou* no heed to, disregard; *occasion* to miss, fail to grasp, pass up*. **une plaie négligée peut s'infecter** a wound if neglected *ou* if left unattended can become infected, if you don't attend to a wound it can become infected; **ce n'est pas à ~** (*offre*) it's not to be sneezed at; (*difficulté*) it mustn't be overlooked; **rien n'a été négligé** nothing has been missed, no stone has been left unturned, nothing has been left to chance; **ne rien ~ pour réussir** to leave no stone unturned *ou* leave nothing to chance in an effort to succeed.

(b) ~ de (*ne pas prendre la peine de*) **il a négligé de le faire** he did not bother *ou* he neglected to do it; **ne négligez pas de prendre vos papiers** be sure to *ou* don't neglect to take your papers.

2 se négliger *vpr* (*santé*) to neglect o.s., not to look after o.s.; (*tenue*) to neglect one's appearance, not to look after one's appearance.

négoce [negɔs] *nm* (†: *commerce*) trade, commerce, business. **dans mon ~** in my trade *ou* business; **il fait le ~ de** he trades *ou* deals in; **il tenait un ~ de** he had a business in.

négociabilité [negɔsjabilite] *nf* negotiability.

négociable [negɔsjabl(ə)] *adj* negotiable.

négociant, e [negɔsjɑ̃, ɑ̃t] *nm,f* merchant. **~ en gros** wholesaler; **~ en vin** wine merchant.

négociateur, -trice [negɔsjatœʀ, tʀis] *nm,f* (*Comm, Pol*) negotiator.

négociation [negɔsjɑsjɔ̃] *nf* (*Comm, Pol*) negotiation. **engager des ~s** to enter into negotiations.

négocier [negɔsje] (7) **1** *vi* (*Pol*) to negotiate; (†† *Comm*) to trade. **2** *vt* (*Fin, Pol*) to negotiate. **~ un virage** to negotiate a bend.

nègre [nɛgʀ(ə)] **1** *nm* (†*péj: indigène*) Negro, nigger (*Brit péj*); (*Littérat: péj: écrivain*) ghost (writer). **~ blanc** white Negro.

2 *adj tribu, art* Negro (*épith*); (*rare*) *couleur* nigger brown (*Brit*), dark brown.

négresse [negʀɛs] *nf* Negress. **~ blanche** white Negress.

négrier [negʀije] *nm* (*marchand d'esclaves*) slave trader; (*fig péj: patron*) slave driver*. **(bateau) ~** slave ship; **(capitaine) ~** slave-ship captain.

négrillon [negʀijɔ̃] *nm* piccaninny (*surtout Brit*), Negro boy.

négrillonne [negʀijɔn] *nf* Negro girl.

négritude [negʀityd] *nf* negritude.

négro [negʀo] *nm* (†*péj*) nigger (*Brit péj*), negro.

négroïde [negʀɔid] *adj* negroid.

neige [nɛʒ] **1** *nf* snow; (*arg Drogue: cocaïne*) snow (*arg*). **aller à la ~*** to go to the ski resorts, go on a skiing holiday; **cheveux/teint de ~** snow-white hair/complexion.

2: neige artificielle artificial snow; **neige carbonique** dry ice; **neiges éternelles** eternal *ou* everlasting snow(s); **neige fondue** (*pluie*) sleet; (*par terre*) slush; **neige poudreuse** powder snow; *V* **bonhomme, train** *etc.*

neiger [neʒe] (3) *vb impers* to snow, be snowing.

neigeux, -euse [nɛʒø, øz] *adj sommet* snow-covered, snow-clad; *temps* snowy; *aspect* snowy.

nenni [nani] *adv* (†† *ou dial: non*) nay.

nénuphar [nenyfaʀ] *nm* water lily.

néo- [neɔ] *préf* neo-. (*Can*) **N~Canadien, -ienne** *nm,f* New Canadian; **~classicisme** *nm* neo-classicism; **N~Écossais, e** *nm,f* Nova Scotian; **~gothique** *adj, nm* neo-gothic; (*Can*) **N~Québécois, e** *nm,f* New Quebec(k)er *ou* Québécois; **~zélandais, e** *adj* New Zealand (*épith*); **N~Zélandais, e** *nm,f* New Zealander.

néolithique [neɔlitik] *adj, nm* neolithic.

néologisme [neɔlɔʒism(ə)] *nm* neologism.

néon [neɔ̃] *nm* (*gaz*) neon; (*éclairage*) neon lighting (*U*).

lneophyte.

hyte **Népal** [nepal] *nm* Nepal.

népalais, e [nepalɛ, ɛz] **1** *adj* Nepalese. **2** *nm* (*Ling*) Nepalese. **3** *nm,f*: **N~(e)** Nepalese.

néphrétique [nefʀetik] *adj, nmf* nephritic; *V* **colique.**

néphrite [nefʀit] *nf* **(a)** (*Méd*) nephritis. **(b)** (*jade*) nephrite.

népotisme [nepɔtism(ə)] *nm* nepotism.

Neptune [nɛptyn] *nm* Neptune.

néréide [neʀeid] *nf* (*Myth, Zool*) nereid.

nerf [nɛʀ] **1** *nm* **(a)** (*Anat*) nerve.

(b) ~s: avoir les ~s malades to suffer with one's nerves *ou* from nerves; **avoir les ~s fragiles** to have sensitive nerves; **avoir les ~s à vif** to be very nervy (*Brit*) *ou* edgy, be on edge; **avoir les ~s à fleur de peau** to be nervy (*Brit*) *ou* excitable; **avoir les ~s en boule*** *ou* **en pelote*** to be very tensed up *ou* tense *ou* edgy, be in a nervy (*Brit*) state; **avoir les ~s à toute épreuve** *ou* **des ~s d'acier** to have nerves of steel; **avoir ses ~s** to have an attack *ou* a fit of nerves, have a temperamental outburst; **être sur les ~s** to be all keyed up*; **vivre sur les ~s** to live on one's nerves; **porter** *ou* **taper*** *ou* (*rare*) **donner sur les ~s de qn** to get on sb's nerves; **ça me met les ~s à vif** that gets on my nerves; **ça va te calmer les ~s** that will calm you down, that will calm *ou* settle your nerves; **ses ~s ont été ébranlés** that shook him *ou* his nerve; **ses ~s ont craqué*** *ou* **lâché*** his nerves have gone to pieces, he has cracked up*; *V* **bout, crise, guerre.**

(c) (*vigueur*) **allons du ~!** *ou* **un peu de ~!** come on, buck up!* *ou* show some spirit!; **ça a du ~** it has really got some go* about it; **ça manque de ~** it has got no go* about it; **l'argent est le ~ de la guerre** money is the sinews of war.

(d) (*Typ*) cord.

2: nerf de bœuf bull's pizzle, cosh (*Brit*); **nerf centrifuge** centrifugal nerve; **nerf centripète** centripetal nerve; **nerf gustatif** gustatory nerve; **nerf moteur** motor nerve; **nerf optique** optic nerve; **nerf sensitif** sensory nerve.

Néron [neʀɔ̃] *nm* Nero.

nerveusement [nɛʀvøzmɑ̃] *adv* (*d'une manière excitée*) nervously, tensely; (*de façon irritable*) irritably, touchily, nervily; (*rare: avec vigueur*) energetically, vigorously. **ébranlé ~** shaken, with shaken nerves.

nerveux, -euse [nɛʀvø, øz] *adj* **(a)** (*Méd*) *tension, dépression* nervous; (*Anat*) *cellule, centre, tissu* nerve (*épith*). **système ~** nervous system; **grossesse ~euse** false pregnancy, phantom pregnancy.

(b) (*agité*) *personne, animal, rire* nervous, tense; (*irritable*) irritable, touchy, nervy (*Brit*), nervous. **ça me rend ~** it makes me nervous; **c'est un grand ~** he's very highly strung.

(c) (*vigoureux*) *personne, corps* energetic, vigorous; *animal* spirited, energetic, skittish; *moteur, voiture* responsive; *style* energetic, vigorous. **pas très ~ dans ce qu'il fait** not very energetic in what he does, not doing anything with very much dash *ou* spirit.

(d) (*sec*) *personne* sinewy, wiry; *main* sinewy; *viande* fibrous, stringy.

nervi [nɛʀvi] *nm* (*gén pl*) thug.

nervosité [nɛʀvozite] *nf* **(a)** (*agitation*) (*permanente*) nervousness, excitability; (*passagère*) agitation, tension. **dans un état de grande ~** in a state of great agitation *ou* tension.

(b) (*irritabilité*) (*permanente*) irritability; (*passagère*) irritability, nerviness, touchiness.

nervure [nɛʀvyʀ] *nf* (*Bot, Zool*) nervure, vein; (*Archit, Tech*) rib; (*Typ*) raised band.

nervurer [nɛʀvyʀe] (1) *vt feuille, aile* to vein; (*Archit, Tech*) to rib; (*Typ*) to put raised bands on.

n'est-ce pas [nɛspɑ] *adv* **(a)** (*appelant l'acquiescement*) isn't it?, doesn't he? *etc* (*selon le verbe qui précède*). **il est fort, ~?** he is strong, isn't he?; **c'est bon, ~?** it's nice, isn't it? *ou* don't you think?; **il n'est pas trop tard, ~?** it's not too late, is it?

(b) (*intensif*) **~ que c'est bon/difficile?** it is nice/difficult, isn't it?; (*iro*) **eux, ~, ils peuvent se le permettre** of course THEY can afford to do it.

net, nette [nɛt] **1** *adj* **(a)** (*propre*) (*après n*) *surface, ongles, mains* clean; *intérieur, travail, copie* neat, tidy. **elle est toujours très nette (dans sa tenue)** she is always neatly dressed *ou* very neat and tidy; **avoir la conscience nette** to have a clear conscience; **mettre au ~** to copy out, make a neat *ou* fair copy of; *V* **cœur, place.**

(b) (*Comm, Fin*) (*après n*) *bénéfice, prix, poids* net. **~ de** free of; **emprunt ~ de tout impôt** tax-free loan.

(c) (*clair, précis*) (*après n*) *idée, explication, esprit* clear; (*sans équivoque*) *réponse* straight, clear, plain; *refus* flat (*épith*); *situation, position* clear-cut. **je serai ~ avec vous** I shall be (quite) candid *ou* frank with you; **sa conduite** *ou* **son attitude dans cette affaire n'est pas très nette** his behaviour *ou* attitude in this matter is slightly questionable.

(d) (*marqué, évident*) *différence, amélioration etc* marked, distinct. **il y a une très nette odeur** *ou* **une odeur très nette de brûlé** there's a distinct *ou* a very definite smell of burning; **il est très ~ qu'il n'a aucune intention de venir** it is quite clear *ou* obvious *ou* plain that he does not intend to come *ou* has no intention of coming.

(e) (*distinct*) (*après n*) *dessin, écriture* clear; *ligne, contour,* (*Phot*) *image* sharp; *voix, son* clear, distinct; *cassure, coupure* clean. **j'ai un souvenir très ~ de sa visite** I have a very clear memory of his visit.

2 *adv* **(a)** (*brusquement*) *s'arrêter* dead. **se casser ~** to snap *ou* break clean through; **il a été tué ~** he was killed outright.

(b) (*franchement, carrément*) bluntly; *dire, parler* frankly, bluntly; *refuser* flatly. **il (m')a dit tout ~ que** he made it quite clear (to me) that, he told me frankly *ou* bluntly that; **je vous le dis tout ~** I'm telling you *ou* I'm giving it to you straight*, I'm telling you bluntly *ou* frankly; **à** *ou* **pour vous parler ~** to be blunt *ou* frank with you.

(c) (*Comm*) net. **il reste 200 F ~** there remains 200 francs net; **cela pèse 2 kg ~** it weighs 2 kg net.

nettement [nɛtmɑ̃] *adv* **(a)** (*clairement, sans ambiguïté*) *expliquer, répondre* clearly. **il refusa ~** he flatly refused, he refused point-blank; **je lui ai dit ~ ce que j'en pensais** I told him bluntly *ou* frankly *ou* plainly *ou* straight* what I thought of it; **il a ~ pris position contre nous** he has clearly *ou* quite obviously taken up a stance against us.

(b) (*distinctement*) *apercevoir, entendre* clearly, distinctly; *se détacher, apparaître* clearly, distinctly, sharply; *se souvenir* clearly, distinctly.

(c) (*incontestablement*) *s'améliorer, se différencier* markedly, decidedly, distinctly; *mériter* decidedly, distinctly. **j'aurais ~ préféré ne pas venir** I would have definitely *ou* distinctly preferred not to come; **ça va ~ mieux** things are going decidedly *ou* distinctly better; **~ fautif** distinctly *ou* decidedly faulty; **~ meilleur/plus grand** markedly *ou* decidedly *ou* distinctly better/bigger.

netteté [nɛtte] *nf* **(a)** (*propreté*) *[tenue, travail]* neatness.

(b) (*clarté*) *[explication, expression, esprit, idées]* clearness, clarity.

(c) (*caractère distinct*) *[dessin, écriture]* clearness; *[contour, image]* sharpness, clarity, clearness; *[souvenir, voix, son]* clearness, clarity; *[cassure]* cleanness.

nettoiement [nɛtwamɑ̃] *nm [rues]* cleaning; (*Agr*) *[terre]* clearing. **service du ~** refuse disposal *ou* collection service.

nettoyage [nɛtwajaʒ] *nm* (*gén*) cleaning; (*Mil, Police*) cleaning up, cleaning out. **faire le ~ par le vide*** to throw everything out; **~ de printemps** spring-cleaning; **~ à sec** dry cleaning; **un ~ complet** a thorough cleanup.

nettoyer [nɛtwaje] (8) *vt* **(a)** (*gén*) *objet* to clean; *jardin* to clear; *canal etc* to clean up. **~ au chiffon** *ou* **avec un chiffon** to dust; **~ au balai** to sweep (out); **~ à l'eau/avec du savon** to wash in water/with soap; **~ à la brosse** to brush (out); **~ à l'éponge** to sponge (down); **~ à sec** to dry-clean; **~ une maison à fond** to spring-clean a house from top to bottom; **nettoyez-vous les mains au robinet** run your hands under the tap, give your hands a rinse under the tap; (*hum*) **le chien avait nettoyé le réfrigérateur*** the dog had cleaned out *ou* emptied the fridge.

(b) (*) *personne* (*tuer*) to eliminate; (*ruiner*) to clean out; (*rare: fatiguer*) to wear out. **~ son compte en banque** to clear one's bank account; **se faire ~ au jeu** to be cleaned out at gambling.

(c) (*Mil, Police*) to clean out *ou* up.

nettoyeur, -euse [nɛtwajœʀ, øz] *nm,f* (*rare*) cleaner.

neuf[1] [nœf] *adj inv, nm inv* nine; *pour loc V* **six** *et* **preuve.**

neuf[2], **neuve** [nœf, nœv] **1** *adj* (*gén*) new; *vision, esprit, pensée* fresh, new, original; *pays* young, new. **quelque chose de ~** something new; **regarder qch avec un œil ~** to look at sth with a new *ou* fresh eye; **être ~ dans le métier/en affaires** to be new to the trade/to business; **à l'état ~, comme ~** as good as new, as new; *V* **flambant, peau, tout.**

2 *nm* new. **il y a du ~** something new has turned up, there has been a new development; **faire du ~** (*politique*) to introduce new *ou* fresh ideas; (*artisanat*) to make new things; **de ~: être vêtu/habillé de ~** to be dressed in new clothes, be wearing new clothes, have new clothes on; **à ~: remettre** *ou* **refaire à ~** to do up like new *ou* as good as new; **repeindre un appartement à ~** to redecorate a flat.

neurasthénie [nøʀasteni] *nf* (*gén*) depression; (*Méd*) neurasthenia. **faire de la ~** to be depressed, be suffering from depression.

neurasthénique [nøʀastenik] **1** *adj* depressed, depressive; (*Méd*) neurasthenic (*T*). **2** *nmf* depressed person, depressive; (*Méd*) neurasthenic (*T*).

neuro... [nøʀɔ] *préf* neuro ... .

neurologie [nøʀɔlɔʒi] *nf* neurology.

neurologiste [nøʀɔlɔʒist(ə)] *nmf*, **neurologue** [nøʀɔlɔg] *nmf* neurologist.

neurone [nøʀɔn] *nm* neuron.

neutralisation [nøtʀalizɑsjɔ̃] *nf* neutralization.

neutraliser [nøtʀalize] (1) *vt* (*Mil, Pol, Sci*) to neutralize. **les deux influences/produits se neutralisent** the two influences/products neutralize each other *ou* cancel each other out.

neutralisme [nøtʀalism(ə)] *nm* neutralism.

neutraliste [nøtʀalist(ə)] *adj, nmf* neutralist.

neutralité [nøtʀalite] *nf* neutrality. **rester dans la ~** to remain neutral.

neutre [nøtʀ(ə)] **1** *adj* (*gén, Chim, Élec, Pol*) neutral; (*Ling, Zool*) neuter; *style* neutral, colourless. **rester ~ (dans)** to remain neutral (in), not to take sides (in).

2 *nm* (*Ling*) (*genre*) neuter; (*nom*) neuter noun; (*Élec*) neutral; (*Zool*) neuter (animal); (*Pol*) neutral (country). **les ~s** the neutral nations.

neutron [nøtʀɔ̃] *nm* neutron.

neuvaine [nœvɛn] *nf* novena. **faire une ~** to make a novena.

neuvième [nœvjɛm] *adj, nmf* ninth; *pour loc V* **sixième.**

neuvièmement [nœvjɛmmɑ̃] *adv* ninthly, in the ninth place; *pour loc V* **sixièmement.**

névé [neve] *nm* névé, firn.

neveu, *pl* **~x** [n(ə)vø] *nm* nephew; (††: *descendant*) descendant. **un peu, mon ~!*** you bet!*, of course!, and how!*

névralgie [nevʀalʒi] *nf* (*Méd*) neuralgia; (*mal de tête*) headache.

névralgique [nevʀalʒik] *adj* neuralgic. **centre** *ou* **point ~** (*Méd*) nerve centre; (*fig*) (*point sensible*) sensitive spot; (*point capital*) nerve centre.

névrite [nevʀit] *nf* neuritis.

névritique [nevʀitik] *adj* neuritic.

névropathe [nevʀɔpat] **1** *adj* neuropathic, neurotic. **2** *nmf* neuropath, neurotic.

névropathie [nevʀɔpati] *nf* neuropathy.

névrose [nevʀoz] *nf* neurosis.

névrosé, e [nevʀoze] *adj, nm,f* neurotic.

névrotique [nevʀɔtik] *adj* neurotic.

newtonien, -ienne [njutɔnjɛ̃, jɛn] *adj* Newtonian.

new yorkais, e [njujɔʀkɛ, ɛz] **1** *adj* of *ou* from New York. **2** *nm,f*: **New Yorkais(e)** New Yorker.

nez [ne] *nm* **(a)** (*organe*) nose. **avoir le ~ grec/aquilin** to have a Grecian/an aquiline nose; **~ en pied de marmite** *ou* **en trompette** turned-up nose; **ton ~ remue, tu mens** I can tell by looking at you that you're fibbing*; **parler du ~** to talk through one's nose; **cela se voit comme le ~ au milieu du visage** it's as plain as the nose on your face *ou* as a pikestaff; **cela sent le brûlé à plein ~** there's a strong smell of burning.

(b) (*visage, face*) **le ~ en l'air** with one's nose in the air; **où est mon sac? — tu as le ~ dessus!** where's my bag? — under your nose!; **baisser/lever le ~** to bow/raise one's head; **il ne lève jamais le ~ de son travail** he never looks up from his work; **mettre le ~** *ou* **son ~ à la fenêtre/au bureau** to show one's face at the window/at the office; **je n'ai pas mis le ~ dehors hier** I didn't put my nose outside the door yesterday; **rire/fermer la porte au ~ de qn** to laugh/shut the door in sb's face; **faire qch au ~ et à la barbe de qn** to do sth under sb's very nose; **regarder qn sous le ~** to stare sb in the face, stare sb out; **sous son ~** (right) under his nose, under his (very) nose; **se trouver ~ à ~ avec qn** to find o.s. face to face with sb; **faire un (drôle de) ~** to pull a (funny) face.

(c) (*flair*) flair. **avoir du ~, avoir le ~ fin** to have flair; **j'ai eu le ~ creux de m'en aller*** I was quite right to leave, I did well to leave; *V* **vue**[2].

(d) (*Aviat, Naut*) nose. (*Naut*) **sur le ~** down at the bows; *V* **piquer.**

(e) (*loc*) **avoir qn dans le ~*** to have something against sb; **il m'a dans le ~*** he can't stand me*, he has got something against me; **se manger** *ou* **se bouffer le ~*** to be at each others' throats; **mettre** *ou* **fourrer* le** *ou* **son ~ dans qch** to poke *ou* stick* one's nose into sth, nose *ou* pry into sth; **l'affaire lui est passée sous le ~*** the bargain slipped through his fingers; **le ~ au vent** in a daydream, with one's head in the clouds; *V* **bout, casser, doigt** *etc.*

ni [ni] *conj* (*après la négation*) nor, or. **ni ... ni ...**neither ... nor ...; **il ne boit ~ ne fume** he doesn't drink or smoke, he neither drinks nor smokes; **il ne pouvait (~) parler ~ entendre** he could neither speak nor hear, he couldn't speak or hear; **il ne pouvait pas parler ~ son frère entendre** he couldn't speak nor could his brother hear; **personne ne l'a (jamais) aidé ~ (même) encouragé** nobody (ever) helped or (even) encouraged him; **je ne veux ~ ne peux accepter** I neither wish to nor can accept, I don't wish to accept, nor can I; **elle est secrétaire, ~ plus ~ moins** she's just a secretary, no more no less; **il n'est ~ plus bête ~ plus paresseux qu'un autre** he is neither more stupid nor lazier than anyone else, he's no more stupid and no lazier than anyone else; **il ne veut pas, ~ moi non plus** he doesn't want to and neither do I *ou* and nor do I; **~ lui ~ moi** neither he *ou* him* nor I *ou* me*, neither of us; **~ l'un ~ l'autre** neither one nor the other, neither of them; **~ d'un côté ~ de l'autre** on neither one side nor the other, on neither side; **~ vu ~ connu*** no one'll be any the wiser*; **~ vu ~ connu je t'embrouille:** before you (*ou* he *etc*) know (*ou* knows *etc*) what's up* *ou* see (*ou* sees *etc*) the game*; **cela ne me fait ~ chaud ~ froid** it makes no odds to me, I don't feel strongly (about it) one way or the other; *V* **feu**[1], **foi.**

niable [njabl(ə)] *adj* deniable. **cela n'est pas ~** that cannot be denied, you can't deny that.

Niagara [njagaʀa] *nm* Niagara.

niais, e [njɛ, ɛz] **1** *adj personne* silly, simple; *air, sourire* simple; *rire* silly, inane. **2** *nm,f* simpleton. **pauvre ~** poor innocent *ou* fool.

niaisement [njɛzmɑ̃] *adv rire* inanely.

niaiserie [njɛzʀi] *nf* (*U: V* **niais**) silliness; simpleness; inaneness; (*action*) foolish *ou* inane behaviour (*U*); (*parole*) foolish *ou* inane talk (*U*). **dire des ~s** to talk rubbish *ou* twaddle.

niaule* [njol] *nf* = **gnôle*.**

Nicaragua [nikaʀagwa] *nm* Nicaragua.

nicaraguayen, enne [nikaʀagwajɛ̃, jɛn] **1** *adj* Nicaraguan. **2** *nm,f*: **N~(ne)** Nicaraguan.

niche [niʃ] *nf* **(a)** (*alcôve*) niche, recess; *[chien]* kennel. **à la ~!** (*à un chien*) (into your) kennel!; (**hum: à une personne*) scram!:, make yourself scarce!* **(b)** (*farce*) trick. **faire des ~s à qn** to play tricks on sb.

nichée [niʃe] *nf [oiseaux]* brood. **~ de chiens** litter of puppies; **une ~ de pinsons** a nest *ou* brood of chaffinches; **la mère/l'instituteur et toute sa ~ (d'enfants)*** the mother/teacher and her/his entire brood.

nicher [niʃe] (1) **1** *vi [oiseau]* to nest; (*) *[personne]* to hang out:.

2 se nicher *vpr [oiseau]* to nest; (*littér: se blottir*) *[village etc]* to nestle; (*: *se cacher*) *[personne]* to stick* *ou* put o.s.; *[objet]* to lodge itself. (*hum*) **où la vertu va-t-elle se ~!** of all the places to find such virtue!; **les cerises nichées dans les feuilles** the cherries nestling among the leaves.

nichon: [niʃɔ̃] *nm* tit**, boob** (*Brit*).

nickel [nikɛl] **1** *nm* nickel.

2 *adj* (*: *impeccable*) **chez eux, c'est ~** their flat is really spick and span.

nickelage [niklaʒ] *nm* nickel-plating.

nickeler [nikle] (4) *vt* to nickel-plate. **en acier nickelé** nickel-plated steel.

niçois, e [niswa, waz] **1** *adj* of *ou* from Nice. **2** *nm,f*: **N~(e)** inhabitant *ou* native of Nice.

Nicolas [nikɔla] *nm* Nicholas.

nicotine [nikɔtin] *nf* nicotine.

nid [ni] **1** *nm* **(a)** (*Zool*) nest. **~ d'oiseau/de vipères/de guêpes** bird's/vipers'/wasps' nest.

(b) (*fig: abri*) (*foyer*) cosy little nest; (*repaire*) den. **trouver le ~ vide** to find the bird has *ou* the birds have flown, find the nest empty; **surprendre qn au ~, trouver l'oiseau au ~** to find *ou* catch sb at home *ou* in.

2: nid(s) d'abeilles (*point*) honeycomb stitch; (*tissu*) waffle cloth; **radiateur en nid(s) d'abeilles** cellular radiator; (*Zool, fig*) **nid d'aigle** eyrie; **nid d'amoureux** love nest; **nid de brigands** robbers' den; (*Culin*) **nids d'hirondelles** birds' nest; **potage aux nids d'hirondelles** birds' nest soup; **nid de mitrailleuses** nest of machine guns; (*Naut*) **nid de pie** crow's-nest; **nid de poule** pothole; **nid à poussière** dust trap; (*Méd, Mil*) **nid de résistance** centre of resistance.

nidifier [nidifje] (7) *vi* (*rare*) to nest.

nièce [njɛs] *nf* niece.

nielle [njɛl] **1** *nf* (*Agr*) (*plante*) corn-cockle. (*maladie*) **~ (du blé)** blight. **2** *nm* (*incrustation*) niello.

nieller [njele] (1) *vt* (*Agr*) to blight; (*Tech*) to niello.

niellure [njelyʀ] *nf* (*Agr*) blight; (*Tech*) niello.

nième [ɛnjɛm] *adj* nth. **x à la ~ puissance** x to the power n, x to the nth power; **je te le dis pour la ~ fois** I'm telling you for the nth *ou* umpteenth time.

nier [nje] (7) *vt* (*gén*) to deny; (*Jur*††: *désavouer*) *dette, fait* to repudiate. **il nie l'avoir fait** he denies having done it; **~ l'évidence** to deny the evidence; **je ne le nie pas** I'm not denying it, I don't deny it; **on ne peut ~ que** one cannot deny that; **l'accusé nia** the accused denied the charges.

nietzschéen, -éene [nitʃeɛ̃, eɛn] *adj, nm,f* Nietzschean.

nigaud, e [nigo, od] **1** *adj* silly, simple. **2** *nm,f* simpleton. **grand** *ou* **gros ~!** big silly!, big ninny!*

nigauderie [nigodʀi] *nf* (*U: caractère*) silliness, simpleness; (*action*) silly action.

Niger [niʒɛʀ] *nm* Niger.

Nigéria [niʒeʀja] *nm ou f* Nigeria.

nigérian, e [niʒeʀjɑ̃, an] **1** *adj* Nigerian. **2** *nm,f*: **N~(e)** Nigerian.

nigérien, -ienne [niʒeʀjɛ̃, jɛn] **1** *adj* of *ou* from Niger. **2** *nm,f*: **N~(ne)** inhabitant *ou* native of Niger.

nihilisme [niilism(ə)] *nm* nihilism.

nihiliste [niilist(ə)] **1** *adj* nihilistic. **2** *nmf* nihilist.

Nil [nil] *nm*: **le ~** the Nile.

nilotique [nilɔtik] *adj* of *ou* from the Nile.

nimbe [nɛ̃b] *nm* (*Rel, fig*) nimbus, halo.

nimber [nɛ̃be] (1) *vt* (*auréoler*) to halo. **nimbé de lumière** radiant *ou* suffused with light.

nimbus [nɛ̃bys] *nm* (*Mét*) nimbus.

n'importe [nɛ̃pɔʀt(ə)] *V* **importer**[2].

ninas [ninas] *nm* small cigar.

niôle* [njol] *nf* = **gnôle***.

nipper* [nipe] (1) **1** *vt* (*habiller*) to tog out*, deck out. **bien/mal nippé** well/badly got up*, in a nice/an awful getup* *ou* rig-out*. **2 se nipper** *vpr* to get togged up*, tog o.s. up*.

nippes†* [nip] *nfpl* togs*, gear*. **de vieilles ~** old togs*.

nippon, e *ou* **-onne** [nipɔ̃, ɔn] **1** *adj* Japanese, Nippon(ese). **2** *nm,f*: **N~(e), N~(ne)** Japanese, Nippon(ese). **3** *nm* (*pays*) **N~** Nippon.

nique [nik] *nf* (†: *lit, fig*) **faire la ~ à qn** to thumb one's nose at sb, cock a snook at sb (*surtout Brit*).

niquedouille* [nikduj] = **nigaud.**

nirvāna [niʀvana] *nm* nirvana.

nitouche [nituʃ] *nf V* **saint.**

nitrate [nitʀat] *nm* nitrate. **~ d'argent** silver nitrate.

nitrique [nitʀik] *adj* nitric.

nitroglycérine [nitʀɔgliseʀin] *nf* nitroglycerine.

niveau, pl ~x [nivo] **1** *nm* **(a)** (*hauteur*) *[huile, eau]* level. **le ~ de l'eau** the water level; **au ~ de l'eau/du sol** at water/ground level; **au-dessus du ~ de la mer** above sea level; **l'eau est arrivée au ~ du quai** the water has risen to the level of the embankment; **la neige m'arrivait au ~ des genoux** the snow came up to my knees *ou* was knee-deep; **une tache au ~ du coude** a mark at the elbow; **serré au ~ de la taille** tight at the waist; **il avait une cicatrice sur la joue au ~ de la bouche** he had a scar on his cheek about level with his mouth; **au ~ du village, il s'arrêta** once level with the village, he stopped; **de ~ avec, au même ~ que** level with; **les deux vases sont au même ~** the two vases are level *ou* at the same height; **de ~** level; **mettre qch de** *ou* **à ~** to make sth level; **le plancher n'est pas de ~** the floor isn't level; **les deux pièces ne sont pas de ~** the two rooms are not on a level; *V* **courbe, passage.**

(b) (*degré*) *[connaissances, études]* standard; *[intelligence, qualité]* level. **le ~ des études en France** the standard of French education; **cet élève est d'un bon ~** this pupil keeps up a good level of attainment *ou* a good standard; **son anglais est d'un bon ~** his English is of a good standard; **ils ne sont pas du même ~** they're not (of) the same standard, they're not on a par *ou* on the same level; **le ~ intellectuel de la classe moyenne** the intellectual level of the middle class; **la production littéraire a atteint son ~ le plus bas** literary production has reached its lowest ebb *ou* level; (*Scol*) **au ~** up to standard; **les cours ne sont pas à son ~** the classes aren't up to his standard; **il faut se mettre au ~ des enfants** you have to put yourself on the same level as the children; (*Écon, Pol*) **au ~ de l'usine/des gouvernements** at factory/government level; **au ~ européen** at a European level.

(c) (*objet*) (*Constr*) level; (*Aut: gauge*) gauge.

2: (*Géog*) **niveau de base** base level; (*Tech*) **niveau à bulle (d'air)** spirit level; (*Tech*) **niveau d'eau** water level; (*Phys*) **niveau d'énergie** energy level; (*Ling*) **niveau de langue** register (*Ling*); (*Constr*) **niveau de maçon** plumb level; (*Psych*) **niveau mental** mental age; (*Écon*) **niveau social** social standing *ou* rank; (*Écon*) **niveau de vie** standard of living.

nivelage [nivlaʒ] *nm* (*V* **niveler**) levelling; levelling out, evening out, equalizing.

niveler [nivle] (4) *vt* **(a)** (*égaliser*) *surface* to level; *fortunes, conditions sociales* to level *ou* even out, equalize. **l'érosion nivelle les montagnes** erosion wears down *ou* wears away the mountains; **sommets nivelés** mountain tops worn down *ou* worn away by erosion; **~ par le bas** to level down.

(b) (*mesurer avec un niveau*) to measure with a spirit level, level.

nivellement [nivɛlmɑ̃] *nm* **(a)** (*V* **niveler**) levelling; levelling out, evening out, equalizing. **(b)** (*mesure*) surveying.

nivo-glaciaire [nivɔglasjɛʀ] *adj* snow and ice (*épith*).

nivo-pluvial, e, *mpl* **-aux** [nivɔplyvjal, o] *adj* snow and rain (*épith*).

nivôse [nivoz] *nm* Nivôse (*fourth month of French Republican calendar*).

nobiliaire [nɔbiljɛʀ] **1** *adj* nobiliary. **2** *nm* (*livre*) peerage list.

noble [nɔbl(ə)] **1** *adj* **(a)** (*de haute naissance*) noble.

(b) (*généreux, digne*) *ton, attitude* noble, dignified. **une âme/un cœur ~** a noble spirit/heart; **le ~ art (de la boxe)** the noble art (of boxing).

2 *nm* **(a)** (*personne*) nobleman. **les ~s** the nobility. **(b)** (*monnaie*) noble.

3 *nf* noblewoman.

noblement [nɔbləmɑ̃] *adv* (*généreusement*) nobly; (*dignement*) with dignity.

noblesse [nɔblɛs] *nf* **(a)** (*générosité, dignité*) nobleness, nobility. **~ d'esprit/de cœur** nobleness *ou* nobility of spirit/heart.

(b) (*caste*) nobility (*U*). **la ~ d'épée** the old nobility; **la ~ de robe** the noblesse de robe; **la ~ de cour** the courtiers, the nobility at court; **la haute ~** the nobility; **~ oblige** noblesse oblige; **la petite ~** the gentry.

nobliau, *pl* **~x** [nɔblijo] *nm* (*péj*) one of the lesser nobility, petty noble.

noce [nɔs] *nf* **(a)** (*cérémonie*) wedding; (*cortège, participants*) wedding party. (*frm*) **~s** wedding, nuptials (*frm*); **être de la ~** to be (a member) of the wedding party, be among the wedding guests; **être de ~** to be invited to a wedding; **aller à la ~ de qn** to go to sb's wedding; **repas/robe/nuit** *etc* **de ~(s)** wedding banquet/dress/night *etc*; **~s d'argent/d'or/de diamant** silver/golden/diamond wedding; (*Bible*) **les N~s de Cana** the wedding at Cana; **il l'avait épousée en premières/secondes ~s** she was his first/second wife; (†, *hum*) **épouser en justes ~s** to take as one's lawful wedded wife; *V* **convoler.**

(b) (*loc*) **faire la ~** to live it up*, have a wild time; **je n'étais pas à la ~** I wasn't exactly enjoying myself, I was having a pretty uncomfortable time; **il n'avait jamais été à pareille ~** he'd never been so happy, he was having the time of his life.

noceur, -euse* [nɔsœʀ, øz] *nm,f* fast liver, reveller. **il est assez ~** he likes to live it up*.

nocif, -ive [nɔsif, iv] *adj* noxious, harmful.

nocivité [nɔsivite] *nf* noxiousness, harmfulness.

noctambule [nɔktɑ̃byl] **1** *adj* (*noceur*) night (*épith*); (*rare: qui veille la nuit*) wakeful at night (*attrib*); (††: *somnambule*) noctambulant†.

2 *nmf* (*noceur*) night-bird, late-nighter; (*rare: qui veille la nuit*) night-bird, night-owl; (††: *somnambule*) noctambulist†.

noctambulisme [nɔktɑ̃bylism(ə)] *nm* (*rare: débauche*) night-time revelling, night revels; (*habitudes nocturnes*) nocturnal habits; (††: *somnambulisme*) noctambulism†.

nocturne [nɔktyʀn(ə)] **1** *adj* nocturnal, night (*épith*); *V* **tapage.** **2** *nm* **(a)** (*Zool*) night hunter (*bird*). **(b)** (*Rel*) nocturn. **(c)** (*Mus*) nocturne; (*Peinture*) nocturne, night scene; (*Sport*) evening meeting.

nodal, e, *mpl* **-aux** [nɔdal, o] *adj* (*Phys*) nodal.

nodosité [nɔdozite] *nf* (*corps dur*) node, nodule; (*état*) knottiness, nodosity (*T*).

Noé [nɔe] *nm* Noah.

Noël [nɔɛl] *nm* (*fête*) Christmas; (*chant*) (Christmas) carol; (*cadeau*) Christmas present. **à la (fête de) ~** at Christmas (time); **que faites-vous pour (la) ~?** what are you doing for *ou* at Christmas?; **pendant (l'époque de) ~** during Christmas *ou* the Christmas period; **que veux-tu pour ton (petit) ~?** what would you like for Christmas?; **joyeux ~!** merry Christmas!; *V* **bûche, sapin, veille** *etc.*

nœud [nø] **1** *nm* **(a)** (*gén: pour attacher etc*) knot; (*ornemental: de ruban*) bow. **faire/défaire un ~** to make *ou* tie/untie *ou* undo a knot *ou* bow; **la fillette avait des ~s dans les cheveux** the little girl had bows *ou* ribbons in her hair; **fais un ~ à ton mouchoir!** tie *ou* make a knot in your hanky!; (*fig*) **avoir un ~ dans la gorge** to have a lump in one's throat; (*fig*) **il y a un ~!** there's a hitch *ou* snag!; **les ~s d'un serpent** the coils of a snake; **~ de perles/de diamants** pearl/diamond knot; *V* **corde.**

(b) (*Naut: vitesse*) knot; *V* **filer.**

(c) (*protubérance*) *[planche, canne]* knot; *[branche, tige]* knot, node.

(d) (*fig*) **le ~ de** *problème, débat* the crux of; (*Littérat, Théât*) **le ~ de l'intrigue** the knot of the intrigue.

(e) (*littér: lien*) **le (saint) ~ du mariage** the bonds of (holy) wedlock; **les ~s de l'amitié** the bonds *ou* ties of friendship.

(f) (*Astron, Élec, Géog, Phys, Tech*) node.

2: nœud coulant slipknot, running knot; **nœud de cravate** tie knot; **faire son nœud de cravate** to knot one's tie; **nœud ferroviaire** rail junction; **nœud gordien** Gordian knot; **couper** *ou* **trancher le nœud gordien** to cut the Gordian knot; **nœud papillon** bow tie; **nœud plat** reef knot; **nœud routier** road junction; **nœud de vache** granny knot; **nœud de vipères** nest of vipers; **nœud vital** vital centre.

noir, e [nwaʀ] **1** *adj* **(a)** (*couleur*) black; *peau, personne* (*par le soleil*) tanned; (*par les coups etc*) black and blue (*attrib*); *yeux,* *cheveux* dark; *fumée, mer, ciel, nuage, temps* black, dark. ~ **comme du jais/de l'encre** jet/ink(y) black, black as jet/ink; ~ **comme du cirage** as black as boot-polish; ~ **comme l'ébène** jet-black; **mets-moi ça ~ sur blanc** put it down in black and white for me; **je l'ai vu/c'est écrit ~ sur blanc** I saw it/it is (down) in black and white; **les murs étaient ~s de saleté/suie** the walls were black with dirt/soot; *V* **beurre, blé, lunette** *etc.*

(b) *personne, race* black, coloured. **l'Afrique ~e** black Africa; **le problème ~** the colour problem.

(c) (*obscur*) dark. **il faisait ~ comme dans un four*** it was as black as pitch; **il faisait nuit ~e** it was pitch-dark *ou* pitch-black; **dans/à la nuit ~e** in the/at dead of night; *(fig)* **rue ~e de monde** street teeming *ou* swarming with people; *V* **chambre.**

(d) (*fig*) *désespoir* black, deep; *humeur, pressentiment, colère* black; *idée* gloomy; (*macabre*) *film* macabre. **faire un tableau assez ~ de la situation** to paint a rather black picture of the situation; **plongé dans le plus ~ désespoir** *ou* **le désespoir le plus ~** plunged in the depths of despair; *V* **bête, humour, série** *etc.*

(e) (*hostile, mauvais*) *âme, ingratitude, trahison* black; *regard* black. **regarder qn d'un œil ~** to give sb a black look; **il se trame un ~ complot** some dark plot is being hatched.

(f) (*: *ivre*) drunk, sloshed*, tight.

2 *nm* **(a)** (*couleur*) black, blackness; (*matière colorante*) black. **une photo en ~ et blanc** a black and white *ou* monochrome photo; **le ~ et blanc** black and white *ou* monochrome photography; **le ~ de ses cheveux accentuait sa pâleur** her dark *ou* black hair accentuated her pallor; **la mer était d'un ~ d'encre** the sea was inky black; **elle avait du ~ sur le menton** she had a black mark *ou* smudge on her chin; **se mettre du ~ aux yeux** to put on mascara *ou* eye-liner; **~ de fumée** lampblack.

(b) (*Habillement*) **elle ne porte jamais de ~, elle n'est jamais en ~** she never wears black; **elle est en ~** she is in *ou* is wearing black; (*en deuil*) she is in mourning.

(c) (*obscurité*) dark, darkness. **avoir peur du ~** to be afraid of the dark; **dans le ~** in the dark *ou* darkness.

(d) (*pessimisme*) **peindre les choses en ~** to paint things black; **voir les choses en ~** to look on the black side; *V* **broyer, pousser, voir.**

(e) (*: *café*) black coffee.

(f) (*illégalement*) **au ~: acheter/vendre au ~** to buy/sell on the black market; **travailler au ~** to work on the side, moonlight*.

(g) N~ black; **les N~s d'Amérique** the blacks of America.

3 noire *nf* **(a)** (*personne*) **Noire** black, black woman.

(b) (*Mus*) crotchet.

noirâtre [nwaʀɑtʀ(ə)] *adj* blackish.

noiraud, e [nwaʀo, od] **1** *adj* dark, swarthy. **2** *nm,f* dark *ou* swarthy person.

noirceur [nwaʀsœʀ] *nf* (*littér*) **(a)** (*U*: *V* **noir**) blackness; darkness. **(b)** (*acte perfide*) black *ou* evil deed.

noircir [nwaʀsiʀ] (2) **1** *vt* **(a)** (*salir*) *[fumée]* to blacken; *[encre, charbon]* to dirty. (*fig*) **~ du papier** to cover paper with writing.

(b) (*colorer*) to blacken; (*à la cire, peinture*) to darken. **le soleil l'a noirci/lui a noirci le visage** the sun has tanned him/his face.

(c) (*fig*) *réputation* to blacken. **~ qn** to blacken sb's reputation *ou* name; **~ la situation** to paint a black picture of the situation.

2 *vi [personne, peau]* to tan; *[fruit]* to ripen; *[ciel]* to darken, grow black *ou* dark; *[couleur]* to darken.

3 se noircir *vpr [ciel]* to darken, grow black *ou* dark; *[temps]* to turn stormy; *[couleur, bois]* to darken.

noircissement [nwaʀsismɑ̃] *nm* (*V* **noircir**) blackening; dirtying; darkening.

noircissure [nwaʀsisyʀ] *nf* black smudge.

noise [nwaz] *nf*: **chercher ~ à qn** to try to pick a quarrel with sb.

noisetier [nwaztje] *nm* hazel tree.

noisette [nwazɛt] **1** *adj inv* hazel. **2** *nf* (*fruit*) hazel(nut). (*morceau*) **~ de beurre** knob of butter.

noix [nwa] **1** *nf* (*fruit*) walnut; (‡: *rare: idiot*) nut*; (*Culin*) *[côtelette]* eye. **à la ~*** rubbishy, crummy‡; *V* **brou, coquille, gîte**[1].

2: noix de beurre knob of butter; **noix du Brésil** Brazil nut; **noix de coco** coconut; **noix de galle** oak-gall; **noix (de) muscade** nutmeg; **noix de veau** cushion of veal; **noix vomique** nux vomica.

nom [nɔ̃] **1** *nm* **(a)** (*nom propre*) name. **petit ~** Christian *ou* first name, forename, given name (*US*); **Henri le troisième du ~** Henry III; **un homme du ~ de Dupont** *ou* **qui a ~ Dupont** a man called Dupont, a man with *ou* by the name of Dupont; **il ne connaît pas ses élèves par leur ~** he doesn't know his pupils by (their) name; **je le connais de ~** I know him by name; **il écrit sous le ~ de X** he writes under the name of X; **c'est un ~** *ou* **ce n'est qu'un ~ pour moi!** he *ou* it is just a name to me!; (**péj*) **un ~ à coucher dehors** an unpronounceable *ou* an impossible-sounding name; (*péj*) **~ à charnière** *ou* **à rallonge** *ou* **à tiroirs** double-barrelled name; **sous un ~ d'emprunt** under an assumed name; *V* **faux**[2], **répondre.**

(b) (*désignation*) name. **quel est le ~ de cet arbre?** what is the name of this tree?, what's this tree called?; **c'est une sorte de fascisme qui n'ose pas dire son ~** it's fascism of a kind hiding behind another name; **comme son ~ l'indique** as is indicated by its *ou* his name, as the name indicates; **le ~ ne fait rien à la chose** what's in a name?; **les beaux ~s de justice, de liberté** these fine-sounding words of justice and liberty; **il n'est spécialiste que de ~** he is only nominally a specialist, he is a specialist in name only; **un crime sans ~** an unspeakable crime; **ce qu'il a fait n'a pas de ~** what he did was unspeakable.

(c) (*célébrité*) name; (*noblesse*) name. **se faire un ~** to make a name for o.s.; **laisser un ~** to make one's mark; **c'est un (grand) ~ dans l'histoire** he's one of the great names of history.

(d) (*Gram*) noun; *V* **complément.**

(e) (*loc*) **en mon/votre ~** in my/your name; **il a parlé au ~ de tous les employés** he spoke for all *ou* on behalf of all the employees; **au ~ de la loi, ouvrez** open up in the name of the law; **au ~ de quoi vous permettez-vous ...?** whatever gives you the right to ...?; **au ~ du Père, du Fils ...** in the name of the Father and of the Son ...; **au ~ du ciel!** in heaven's name!; **au ~ de ce que vous avez de plus cher** in the name of everything you hold most dear; **~ de Dieu!‡** bloody hell!‡ (*Brit*), hell fire!‡; **~ de ~** *ou* **d'un chien** *ou* **d'une pipe** *ou* **d'un petit bonhomme*** jings!*, (flipping) heck!* (*Brit*), blimey!* (*Brit*), strewth!* (*Brit*); **donner à qn des ~s d'oiseaux** to call sb names; **traiter qn de tous les ~s** to call sb everything under the sun.

2: nom de baptême Christian name, given name (*US*); **nom de chose** concrete noun; **nom commun** common noun; **nom composé** compound (word *ou* noun); **nom déposé** (registered) trademark; **nom d'emprunt** alias, assumed name; **nom de famille** surname; **nom de femme mariée** married name; **nom de fille/garçon** girl's/boy's name; **nom de guerre** nom de guerre; **nom de jeune fille** maiden name; **nom de lieu** place-name; **nom de marque** trade name; **nom de plume** nom de plume, pen name; **nom propre** proper noun; **nom de rue** street name; **nom de théâtre** stage name.

nomade [nɔmad] **1** *adj* nomadic; (*Zool*) migratory. **2** *nmf* nomad.

nomadisme [nɔmadism(ə)] *nm* nomadism.

nombrable [nɔ̃bʀabl(ə)] *adj* countable, numerable. **difficilement ~** difficult to count.

nombre [nɔ̃bʀ(ə)] **1** *nm* **(a)** (*Ling, Math*) number. (*Bible*) **les N~s** (the Book of) Numbers.

(b) (*quantité*) number. **le ~ des victimes** the number of victims; **un certain/grand ~ de** a certain/great number of; **(un) bon ~ de** a good *ou* fair number of; **je lui ai dit ~ de fois que ...** I've told him several *ou* many *ou* a number of times that ...; **depuis ~ d'années** for several *ou* many years, for a number of years; **les gagnants sont au ~ de 3** there are 3 winners, the winners are 3 in number; **être supérieur en ~** to be superior in numbers; **être en ~ suffisant** to be in sufficient number *ou* sufficient in number; **ils sont en ~ égal** their numbers are equal *ou* even, they are equal in number; **à ~ égal** with equal *ou* even numbers; **des ennemis sans ~** innumerable enemies.

(c) (*masse*) numbers. **être/venir en ~** to be/come in large numbers; **faire ~** to make up the numbers; **être submergé par le ~, succomber sous le ~** to be overcome by sheer weight of *ou* force of numbers; **il y en avait dans le ~ qui riaient** there were some among them who were laughing; **ça ne se verra pas dans le ~** it won't be seen among all the rest *ou* when they're all together; **le (plus) grand ~** the (great) majority (of people).

(d) au ~ de, du ~ de (*parmi*): **je le compte au ~ de mes amis** I count him as *ou* consider him one of my friends, I number him among my friends; **il n'est plus du ~ des vivants** he is no longer of this world; **est-il du ~ des reçus?** is he among those who passed?, is he one of the ones who passed?

2: nombre atomique atomic number; **nombre entier** whole number, integer; **nombre imaginaire** imaginary number; **nombre de Mach** mach number; **nombre d'or** golden section; **nombre parfait** perfect number; **nombre premier** prime number.

nombrer [nɔ̃bʀe] (1) *vt* (†, *littér*) to number†, count.

nombreux, -euse [nɔ̃bʀø, øz] *adj* **(a)** (*en grand nombre*) **être ~** *[exemples, visiteurs]* to be numerous; *[accidents]* to be frequent; **les gens étaient venus ~** a great number of people had come, people had come in great numbers; **certains, et ils sont ~** certain people, and there are quite a few of them; **peu ~** few; **le public était moins/plus ~ hier** there were fewer/more spectators yesterday; **les visiteurs arrivaient sans cesse plus/de plus en plus ~** visitors kept on arriving in greater *ou* increasing/in greater and greater *ou* in ever-increasing numbers.

(b) (*le grand nombre de*) numerous, many. **parmi les ~euses personnalités** amongst the numerous *ou* many personalities.

(c) (*un grand nombre de*) **de ~** many, numerous; **de ~ accidents se sont produits** many *ou* numerous accidents have occurred; **ça se voit à de ~ exemples** many *ou* numerous examples illustrate this.

(d) (*important*) *foule, assistance, collection* large.

(e) (*littér: harmonieux*) *vers, style* harmonious, rounded, rich.

nombril [nɔ̃bʀi] *nm [personne]* navel, belly button*. **il se prend pour le ~ du monde*** he thinks he is the cat's whiskers*.

nomenclature [nɔmɑ̃klatyʀ] *nf* (*gén: liste*) list; (*Ling, Sci*) nomenclature.

nominal, e, *mpl* **-aux** [nɔminal, o] **1** *adj* (*gén*) nominal; (*Ling*) *syntagme, groupe, phrase* noun (*épith*). **liste ~e** list of names; **procéder à l'appel ~** to call the register *ou* the roll, do the roll call. **2** *nm* (*Ling*) pronoun.

nominalement [nɔminalmɑ̃] *adv* (*gén, Ling*) nominally. **appeler qn ~** to call sb by name.

nominalisme [nɔminalism(ə)] *nm* nominalism.

nominaliste [nɔminalist(ə)] *adj, nmf* nominalist.

nominatif, -ive [nɔminatif, iv] **1** *adj* (*Fin*) *titre, action* registered. (*Comm*) **état ~** list of items; **liste ~ive** list of names. **2** *nm* (*Ling*) nominative.

nomination [nɔminɑsjɔ̃] *nf* (*promotion*) appointment, nomination (*à* to); (*titre, acte*) appointment *ou* nomination papers.

obtenir sa ~ to be nominated *ou* appointed (*au poste de* to the post of).

nominativement [nɔminativmɑ̃] *adv* by name.

nommément [nɔmemɑ̃] *adv* **(a)** (*par son nom*) by name. **(b)** (*spécialement*) notably, especially, particularly.

nommer [nɔme] (1) **1** *vt* **(a)** (*promouvoir*) *fonctionnaire* to appoint; *candidat* to nominate. **~ qn à un poste** to appoint *ou* nominate sb to a post; **~ qn son héritier** to name *ou* appoint sb (as) one's heir; **il a été nommé gérant/ministre** he was appointed manager/minister.

(b) (*appeler*) *personne* to call, name; (*dénommer*) *découverte, produit* to name, give a name to. **ils l'ont nommé Richard** they called *ou* named him Richard, they gave him the name of Richard; **un homme nommé Martin** a man named *ou* called Martin; **le nommé Martin** the man named *ou* called Martin; **ce que nous nommons le bonheur** what we name *ou* call happiness; *V* **point**[1].

(c) (*citer, fleuves, batailles, auteurs* to name, give the name(s) of; (*Police*) *complices* to name, give the name(s) of. **M Martin, pour ne pas le ~ ...** without mentioning any names, Mr Martin ...; **quelqu'un que je ne nommerai pas** somebody who shall remain nameless, somebody whose name I shall not mention.

2 se nommer *vpr* **(a)** (*s'appeler*) to be called. **comment se nomme-t-il?** what is he called?, what is his name?; **il se nomme Paul** he's called Paul, his name is Paul.

(b) (*se présenter*) to introduce o.s. **il entra et se nomma** he came in and gave his name *ou* introduced himself.

non [nɔ̃] **1** *adv* **(a)** (*réponse négative*) no. **le connaissez-vous? — ~** do you know him? — no (I don't); **est-elle chez elle? — ~** is she at home? — no (she isn't *ou* she's not); **je vais ouvrir la fenêtre — ~ il y aura des courants d'air** I'll open the window — no (don't), it'll make a draught; **il n'a pas encore dit ~!** he hasn't said no yet!, he hasn't refused (as) yet; **je ne dis pas ~** (*ce n'est pas de refus*) I wouldn't say no; (*je n'en disconviens pas*) I don't disagree; **ah ça ~!** certainly *ou* definitely not!, I should say not!; **~ et ~!** no, no, no!, absolutely not!; **que ~!** I should say not!, definitely not!; **~ merci!** no thank you!; **certes ~!** most certainly *ou* definitely not!, indeed no!, no indeed!; **vous n'y allez pas? — mais ~! *ou* bien sûr que ~!** aren't you going? — of course not! *ou* I (most) certainly shall not! *ou* I should think not!; **répondre (par) ~ à toutes les questions** to answer no *ou* answer in the negative to all the questions; **faire ~ de la tête, faire signe que ~** to shake one's head; **dire/répondre que ~** to say/answer it isn't (*ou* it won't *etc, selon le contexte*).

(b) (*remplaçant une proposition*) not. **est-ce que c'est nécessaire? — je pense *ou* crois que ~** is that necessary? — I don't think so *ou* I don't think it is *ou* I think not; **je crains que ~** I fear not, I am afraid not; **il nous quitte? — j'espère que ~** is he leaving us? — I hope not *ou* I hope he isn't; **je le crois — moi ~** I believe him — I (*emphatique*) don't *ou* not me*; **vous avez aimé le film? — moi ~ mais les autres oui** did you like the film? — (no) I didn't *ou* not me* but the others did; **il l'aime bien, moi ~** he likes him but I don't *ou* not me*; **j'ai demandé si elle était venue, lui dit que ~** I asked if she had been - he says not *ou* he says no *ou* he says she hasn't; **ah ~? really?, no?; partez-vous ou ~?** are you going or not?, are you going or aren't you?; **il se demandait s'il irait ou ~** he wondered whether to go or not; **erreur ou ~/qu'il l'ait voulu ou ~ le mal est fait** mistake or no mistake/whether he meant it or not the damage is done.

(c) (*frm: pas*) not. **c'est par paresse et ~ (pas) par prudence que ...** it is through laziness and not caution that ...; **je veux bien de leur aide mais ~ (pas) de leur argent** I am willing to accept their help but not their money *ou* but I want none of their money; **c'est mon avis ~ (pas) le vôtre** it's my opinion not yours; **~ (pas) que ...** not that ...; **~ (pas) qu'il eût peur mais ...** not that he was frightened but ...; **il n'a pas reculé, ~ plus qu'eux d'ailleurs** he didn't go back any more than they did in fact.

(d) (*exprimant l'impatience, l'indignation*) **tu vas cesser de pleurer ~?** WILL you stop crying?, just stop that crying (will you?); **~ par exemple!** for goodness sake!, good gracious!; **~ mais alors*, ~ mais (des fois)!** for goodness sake!*; **~ mais des fois, tu me prends pour qui?*** look here* *ou* for God's sake! what do you take me for?

(e) (*exprimant le doute*) no? **il me l'a dit lui-même — ~?** he told me so himself — no!; **c'est bon ~?** it's good isn't it?, it's good – no?

(f) ~ plus neither, not either; **il ne l'a pas vu ni moi ~ plus** he didn't see him - (and) neither did I *ou* (and) I didn't either; **nous ne l'avons pas vu — nous ~ plus** we didn't see him — neither did we *ou* we didn't either; **nous ~ plus nous ne l'avons pas vu** we didn't see him either; **il n'a pas compris lui ~ plus** HE didn't understand either; **il parle ~ plus en médecin mais en ami** he is talking now not as a doctor but as a friend.

(g) (*modifiant adv*) not. **~ loin de là il y a ...** not far from there there's ...; **c'est une expérience ~ moins intéressante** it's an experience that is no less interesting; **je l'aime ~ moins que toi** I love him no less than you (do), I do not love him less than you (do); **un homme ~ pas érudit mais instruit** a man (who is) not (at all) erudite but well-informed; **il a continué ~ plus en auto mais en train** he continued on his way not by car (any more) but by train; **il l'a fait ~ sans raison/~ sans peine** he did it not without reason/difficulty; **il y est allé ~ sans protester** he went (but) not without protest *ou* protesting; **~ seulement il est impoli mais ...** not only is he *ou* he is not only impolite but...; **~ seulement il ne travaille pas mais (encore) il empêche les autres de travailler** not only does he not work but he (also) stops the others working too; **~ seulement le directeur mais aussi *ou* encore les employés** not only the manager but the employees too *ou* as well.

(h) (*modifiant adj ou participe*) **les objets ~ réclamés** unclaimed items; **produit ~ polluant** non-polluting product; **une quantité ~ négligeable** an appreciable amount; **toutes les places ~ réservées** all the unreserved seats, all seats not reserved; **les travaux ~ terminés** the unfinished work; **~ coupable** not guilty.

2 *nm inv* no. **répondre par un ~ catégorique** to reply with a categorical no; **il y a eu 30 ~** there were 30 votes against *ou* 30 noes; *V* **oui**.

3 *préf* non-, un-. **~-ferreux/-gazeux** non-ferrous/-gaseous; **~-vérifié** unverified; **~-spécialisé** unspecialized, non-specialized.

4: non-activité *nf* inactivity; **non-agression** *nf* non-aggression; **non-alignement** *nm* non-alignment; (*Jur*) **non-assistance** *nf:* **non-assistance à personne en danger** failure to render assistance to a person in danger; **non-combattant, e** *nm,f, adj, mpl* **non-combattants** non-combatant; (*Jur*) **non-comparution** *nf* non-appearance; **non-conformisme** *nm* nonconformism; **non-conformiste** *adj, nmf, pl* **non-conformistes** nonconformist; **non-conformité** *nf* nonconformity; **non-croyant, e** *nm,f, mpl* **non-croyants** unbeliever, non-believer; (*Jur*) **non-cumul** *nm:* **non-cumul de peines** sentences to run concurrently; **non(-)engagé, e** *adj, nm,f, mpl* **non(-)engagés** non-aligned; (*Philos*) **non-être** *nm* non-being; (*Jur*) **non-exécution** *nf* failure to carry out (*de: non traduit*); **non-existant, e** *adj* non-existent; **non(-)figuratif, -ive** *adj* non-representational; **non-ingérence** *nf* non-interference; **non-inscrit, e** *adj* (*Pol*) independent; **non-intervention** *nf* non-intervention; **non-interventionniste** *nmf, adj, pl* **non-interventionnistes** non-interventionist; (*Jur*) **non-jouissance** *nf* non-enjoyment; (*Jur*)**non-lieu** *nm, pl* **non-lieux** withdrawal of case; (*Philos*) **non-moi** *nm* non-ego; **non-paiement** *nm* non-payment; **non-parution** *nf* failure to appear *ou* be published; **non-recevoir** *nm V* **fin**[2]; **non-retour** *nm* no return (*V* **point**[1]); **non-rétroactivité** *nf* (*Jur*) non-retroactivity; **non-sens** *nm inv* (*absurdité*) (piece of) nonsense; (*erreur de traduction etc*) meaningless word (*ou* phrase etc); **non-stop** *adj inv* non-stop; **non-syndiqué, e,** *mpl* **non-syndiqués** (*nm,f*) non-union member, non-member (of a *ou* the union); (*adj*) non-union; **non-valeur** *nf* (*Jur*) unproductiveness; (*Fin*) bad debt; (*fig*) non-productive asset, wasted asset; **non-violence** *nf* non-violence; **non-violent, e** *adj* non-violent.

nonagénaire [nɔnaʒenɛʀ] *adj, nmf* nonagenarian.

nonante [nɔnɑ̃t] *adj* (*Belgique, Suisse*) ninety.

nonantième [nɔnɑ̃tjɛm] *adj* (*Belgique, Suisse*) ninetieth.

nonce [nɔ̃s] *nm* nuncio. **~ apostolique** apostolic nuncio.

nonchalamment [nɔ̃ʃalamɑ̃] *adv* nonchalantly.

nonchalance [nɔ̃ʃalɑ̃s] *nf* nonchalance.

nonchalant, e [nɔ̃ʃalɑ̃, ɑ̃t] *adj* nonchalant.

nonne [nɔn] *nf* (††, *hum*) nun.

nonobstant [nɔnɔpstɑ̃] **1** *prép* († *ou Jur: malgré*) notwithstanding, despite, in spite of. **2** *adv* (†: *néanmoins*) notwithstanding†, nevertheless.

nonpareil, -eille†† [nɔ̃paʀɛj] *adj* nonpareil, peerless.

noosphère [noosfɛʀ] *nf* noosphere.

nord [nɔʀ] **1** *nm* **(a)** (*point cardinal*) north. **~ géographique/magnétique** true/magnetic north; **le vent du ~** the north wind; **un vent du ~** a north(erly) wind, a northerly (*Naut*); **le vent tourne/est au ~** the wind is veering north (wards) *ou* towards the north/is blowing from the north; **regarder vers le ~ *ou* dans la direction du ~** to look north(wards) *ou* towards the north; **au ~** (*situation*) in the north; (*direction*) to the north, north(wards); **au ~ de** north of, to the north of; **l'appartement est (exposé) au ~/en plein ~** the flat faces (the) north *ou* northwards/due north, the flat looks north (wards)/due north; **l'Europe/l'Italie/la Bourgogne du ~** Northern Europe/Italy/Burgundy; *V* **mer**.

(b) (*partie, régions septentrionales*) north. **pays/peuples du ~** northern countries/peoples, countries/peoples of the north; **le ~ de la France, le N~** the North (of France); *V* **grand**.

2 *adj inv région, partie* northern (*épith*); *entrée, paroi* north (*épith*); *versant, côte* north(ern) (*épith*); *côté* north(ward) (*épith*); *direction* northward (*épith*), northerly (*Mét*); *V* **hémisphère, latitude, pôle**.

3 nord-africain, e *adj* North African; **Nord-Africain, e** *nm,f, mpl* **Nord-Africains** North African; **nord-américain, e** *adj* North American; **Nord-Américain, e** *nm,f, mpl* **Nord-Américains** North American; **nord-coréen, -enne** *adj* North Korean; **Nord-Coréen, -enne** *nm,f, mpl* **Nord-Coréens** North Korean; **nord-est** *adj inv, nm* north-east; **nord-nord-est** *adj inv, nm* north-north-east; **nord-nord-ouest** *adj inv, nm* north-north-west; **nord-ouest** *adj inv, nm* north-west; **nord-vietnamien, -ienne** *adj* North Vietnamese; **Nord-Vietnamien, -ienne** *nm,f, mpl* **Nord-Vietnamiens** North Vietnamese.

nordique [nɔʀdik] **1** *adj pays, race* Nordic; *langues* Scandinavian, Nordic. **2** *nmf:* **N~** Scandinavian.

nordiste [nɔʀdist(ə)] **1** *adj* Northern, Yankee. **2** *nmf:* **N~** Northerner, Yankee.

noria [nɔʀja] *nf* noria.

normal, e, *mpl* **-aux** [nɔʀmal, o] **1** *adj* (*gén, Chim, Math, Méd*) normal; (*courant, habituel*) normal, usual. **de dimension ~e** normal-sized, standard-sized; **c'est une chose très ~e, ça n'a rien que de très ~** that's quite usual *ou* normal, it's quite the usual thing, it's the normal thing; **c'est bien ~** it's quite understandable; **il n'est pas ~** (*mentalement*) he's not normal; (*physiquement*) there's something wrong with him; **c'est ~!** it's (quite) natural!; **ce n'est pas ~** there must be something wrong; *V* **école, état, temps**[1].

2 normale *nf* **(a) s'écarter de la ~e** to diverge from the norm; **revenir à la ~e** to return to normality, get back to normal; **au-dessus de la ~e** above average. **(b)** (*Math*) normal (*à* to).

normalement [nɔʀmalmɑ̃] *adv* (*comme prévu*) normally; (*habituellement*) normally, usually, ordinarily. **~, il devrait être là demain** normally he'd be there tomorrow, in the usual *ou* ordinary course of events he'd be there tomorrow.

normalien, -ienne [nɔʀmaljɛ̃, jɛn] *nm,f* student at teachers' training college; student at the *École Normale Supérieure*.

normalisation [nɔʀmalizɑsjɔ̃] *nf* (*V* **normaliser**) normalization; standardization.

normaliser [nɔʀmalize] (1) *vt situation, relations* to normalize; *produit* to standardize.

normalité [nɔʀmalite] *nf* normality.

normand, e [nɔʀmɑ̃, ɑ̃d] **1** *adj* (*de Normandie*) Norman; (*Hist: scandinave*) Norse; *V* **armoire, trou.**

2 *nm* (*Ling*) Norman (French).

3 *nm,f*: **N~(e)** (*de Normandie*) Norman; (*Hist: Scandinave*) Norseman, Northman. **faire une réponse de N~** to give a non-committal answer.

Normandie [nɔʀmɑ̃di] *nf* Normandy.

normatif, -ive [nɔʀmatif, iv] *adj* normative.

norme [nɔʀm(ə)] *nf* (*gén*) norm; (*Tech*) standard. **~s de fabrication** standards of manufacture, manufacturing standards; **tant que ça reste dans la ~** as long as it is kept within limits; **pourvu que vous restiez dans la ~** provided you do not overdo it *ou* you don't overstep the limits.

normé, e [nɔʀme] *adj* (*Math*) normed.

norois[1]**, e** [nɔʀwa, waz] **1** *adj* Old Norse. **2** *nm* Old Norse.

norois[2]**, noroît** [nɔʀwa] *nm* northwester.

Norvège [nɔʀvɛʒ] *nf* Norway.

norvégien, -ienne [nɔʀveʒjɛ̃, jɛn] **1** *adj* Norwegian; *V* **marmite. 2** *nm* (*Ling*) Norwegian. **3** *nm,f*: **N~(ne)** Norwegian.

nos [no] *adj poss V* **notre.**

nostalgie [nɔstalʒi] *nf* nostalgia. **avoir la ~ de** to feel nostalgia for; **garder la ~ de** to retain a nostalgia for.

nostalgique [nɔstalʒik] *adj* nostalgic.

nota (bene) [nɔta(bene)] *nm inv* nota bene.

notabilité [nɔtabilite] *nf* notability.

notable [nɔtabl(ə)] **1** *adj fait* notable, noteworthy; *changement, progrès* notable. **c'est quelqu'un de ~** he's somebody of note. **2** *nm* notable.

notablement [nɔtabləmɑ̃] *adv* notably.

notaire [nɔtɛʀ] *nm* ≃ solicitor, notary (public).

notamment [nɔtamɑ̃] *adv* (*entre autres*) notably, among others; (*plus particulièrement*) notably, in particular, particularly.

notarial, e, *mpl* **-aux** [nɔtaʀjal, o] *adj* notarial.

notariat [nɔtaʀja] *nm* (*fonction*) profession of (a) notary (public); (*corps des notaires*) body of notaries (public).

notarié, e [nɔtaʀje] *adj* drawn up by a notary (public) *ou* by a solicitor, notarized (*T*).

notation [nɔtɑsjɔ̃] *nf* **(a)** (*symboles, système*) notation.

(b) (*touche, note*) *[couleurs]* touch; *[sons]* variation. (*Littérat*) **une ~ intéressante** an interesting touch *ou* variation.

(c) (*transcription*) *[sentiment, geste, son]* expression.

(d) (*jugement*) *[devoir, employé]* marking.

note [nɔt] **1** *nf* **(a)** (*remarque, communication*) note. **~ diplomatique/officielle** diplomatic/official note; **prendre des ~s** to take notes; **prendre (bonne) ~ de qch** to take (good) note of sth; **prendre qch en ~** to make a note of sth, write sth down; (*hâtivement*) to jot sth down; **remarque en ~** marginal comment, comment in the margin; **c'est écrit en ~** it's written in the margin.

(b) (*appréciation chiffrée*) mark. **mettre une ~ à une dissertation** to mark an essay; **c'est une mauvaise ~ pour lui** it's a black mark against him.

(c) (*compte*) *[gaz, blanchisserie]* bill; *[restaurant, hôtel]* bill, check (*US*). **demander/présenter/régler la ~** to ask for/present/settle the bill; **vous me donnerez la ~, s'il vous plaît** may I have the bill, please?, I'd like my bill please.

(d) (*Mus, fig*) note. **donner la ~** (*Mus*) to give the key; (*fig*) to give an idea; **la ~ juste** the right note; **c'est tout à fait dans la ~** it fits in perfectly with the rest; **ses paroles étaient tout à fait dans la ~/n'étaient pas dans la ~** his words struck exactly the right note/struck the wrong note (altogether); **ce n'est pas dans la ~** it doesn't fit in with the rest at all; **mettre une ~ triste** *ou* **de tristesse dans qch** to lend a touch *ou* note of sadness to sth; **une ~ de fierté perçait sous ses paroles** a note of pride was discernible in his words; *V* **faux**[2]**, forcer.**

2: note en bas de page footnote; **note marginale** marginal note, note in the margin; **note de service** memorandum.

noter [nɔte] (1) *vt* **(a)** (*inscrire*) *adresse, rendez-vous* to write down, note down, make a note of; *idées* to jot down, write down, note down; (*Mus*) *air* to write down, take down. **si vous pouviez le ~ quelque part** could you make a note of it *ou* write it down somewhere; **notez que nous serons absents** note that we'll be away.

(b) (*remarquer*) *faute, progrès* to notice. **notez (bien) que je n'ai rien dit, je n'ai rien dit notez-le** *ou* **notez (bien)** note that I didn't say anything, mark you (*surtout Brit*), I didn't say anything; **il faut ~ qu'il a des excuses** admittedly he has an excuse, he has an excuse mark you; **ceci est à ~** *ou* **mérite d'être noté** this is worth noting, this should be noted.

(c) (*cocher, souligner*) *citation, passage* to mark. **~ d'une croix** to mark with a cross, put a cross against.

(d) (*juger*) *devoir* to mark; *élève, employé* to give a mark to. **~ sur 10/20** to mark out of 10/20; **devoir bien/mal noté** homework with a good/bad mark; **employé bien/mal noté** highly/poorly rated employee, employee with a good/bad record.

notice [nɔtis] *nf* (*préface*) note; (*résumé*) note; (*mode d'emploi*) directions, instructions. **~ biographique/bibliographique** biographical/bibliographical note; **~ explicative** directions for use, explanatory leaflet; **~ nécrologique** obituary.

notification [nɔtifikɑsjɔ̃] *nf* (*Admin*) notification. **~ vous a été envoyée de vous présenter** notification has been sent to you to present yourself; **recevoir ~ de** to be notified of, receive notification of.

notifier [nɔtifje] (7) *vt* to notify. **~ qch à qn** to notify sb of sth, notify sth to sb; **on lui a notifié que...** he was notified that..., he received notice that... .

notion [nosjɔ̃] *nf* **(a)** (*conscience*) notion. **je n'ai pas la moindre ~ de** I haven't the faintest notion of; **perdre la ~ du temps** *ou* **de l'heure** to lose all notion *ou* idea of time.

(b) (*connaissances*) **~s** notion, elementary knowledge; **avoir quelques ~s de grammaire** to have some notion of grammar; (*titre*) **~s d'algèbre/d'histoire** algebra/history primer.

notionnel, -elle [nosjɔnɛl] *adj* notional.

notoire [nɔtwaʀ] *adj criminel, méchanceté* notorious; *fait, vérité* well-known, acknowledged (*épith*). **il est ~ que** it is common *ou* public knowledge that, it's an acknowledged fact that.

notoirement [nɔtwaʀmɑ̃] *adv*: **c'est ~ reconnu** it's generally recognized, it's well known; **il est ~ malhonnête** he's notoriously dishonest.

notoriété [nɔtɔʀjete] *nf [fait]* notoriety; (*renommée*) fame. **c'est de ~ publique** that's common *ou* public knowledge.

notre [nɔtʀ(ə)], *pl* **nos** [no] *adj poss* **(a)** (*possession, relation*) our; (*emphatique*) our own; (*majesté ou modestie de convention = mon, ma, mes*) our; (*emphatique*) our own. **~ fils et ~ fille** our son and daughter; **nous avons tous laissé ~ manteau et ~ chapeau au vestiaire** we have all left our coats and hats in the cloakroom; **~ bonne ville de Tours est en fête** our fine city of Tours is celebrating; **car tel est ~ bon plaisir** for such is our wish, for so it pleases us; **dans cet exposé ~ intention est de ...** in this essay we intend to ...; *pour autres exemples V* **son**[1].

(b) (*valeur affective, ironique, intensive*) **et comment va ~ malade aujourd'hui?** and how's the *ou* our patient today?; **~ héros décide alors ...** and so our hero decides ...; **~ homme a filé sans demander son reste** the chap *ou* fellow has run off without asking for his dues; (*‡: dial*) **~ maître** the master; *V* **son**[1].

(c) (*représentant la généralité des hommes*) **~ planète** our planet; **~ corps/esprit** our body/mind, our bodies/minds; **~ maître à tous** our master, the master of us all; **N~ Seigneur/Père** Our Lord/Father; **N~ Dame** Our Lady; (*église*) Notre Dame; **le N~ Père** the Lord's Prayer, Our Father.

nôtre [notʀ(ə)] **1** *pron poss*: **le ~, la ~, les ~s** ours, our own; **cette voiture n'est pas la ~** this car is not ours, this is not OUR car; **leurs enfants sont sortis avec les ~s** their children are out with ours *ou* our own; **à la (bonne) ~!** our good health!, here's to us!; *pour autres exemples V* **sien.**

2 *nm* **(a)** (*U*) **nous y mettrons du ~** we'll pull our weight, we'll do our bit*; *V aussi* **sien.**

(b) les ~s (*famille*) our family, our (own) folks*; (*partisans*) our own people; **j'espère que vous serez des ~s ce soir** I hope you will join our party *ou* join us tonight.

3 *adj poss* (*littér*) ours, our own. **ces idées ne sont plus exclusivement ~s** these ideas are no longer ours alone *ou* exclusively; **ces principes, nous les avons faits ~s** we have made these principles our own.

nouba: [nuba] *nf*: **faire la ~** to live it up*.

nouer [nwe] (1) **1** *vt* **(a)** (*faire un nœud avec*) *ficelle* to tie, knot; *lacets, ceinture* to tie, fasten; *cravate* to knot, fasten. **~ les bras autour de la taille de qn** to put one's arms round sb's waist; **l'émotion lui nouait la gorge** his throat was tight with emotion; **avoir la gorge nouée (par l'émotion)** to have a lump in one's throat.

(b) (*entourer d'une ficelle*) *bouquet, paquet* to tie up, do up; *cheveux* to tie up *ou* back.

(c) (*former*) *complot* to hatch; *alliance* to make, form; *amitié* to form, build up. **~ conversation avec qn** to start (up) *ou* strike up a conversation with sb.

(d) (*Tech*) **~ la chaîne/la trame** to splice the warp/weft.

(e) (*Littérat*) *action, intrigue* to build up, bring to a head *ou* climax.

2 *vi* (*Bot*) to set.

3 se nouer *vpr* **(a)** (*s'unir*) *[mains]* to join together. **sa gorge se noua** a lump came to his throat.

(b) (*se former*) *[complot]* to be hatched; *[alliance]* to be made, be formed; *[amitié]* to be formed, build up; *[conversation]* to start, be started.

(c) (*Littérat*) *[intrigue]* to build up towards a climax.

noueux, -euse [nwø, øz] *adj branche* knotty, gnarled; *main* gnarled; *vieillard* wizened.

nougat [nuga] *nm* (*Culin*) nougat. (*pieds*) **~s:** feet; **c'est du ~*** it's dead easy*, it's a cinch* *ou* a piece of cake* (*Brit*); **c'est pas du ~*** it's not so easy.

nougatine [nugatin] *nf* nougatine.

nouille [nuj] *nf* **(a)** (*Culin*) **~s** noodles; (*gén*) pasta. **(b)** (*) (*imbécile*) noodle*, idiot; (*mollasson*) big lump*. **ce que c'est ~*** how idiotic (it is).

noumène [numɛn] *nm* noumenon.

nounou* [nunu] *nf* nanny.

nounours [nunuʀs] *nm* teddy (bear).

nourri, e [nuʀi] (*ptp de* **nourrir**) *adj fusillade* heavy; *applaudissements* hearty, prolonged; *conversation* lively; *style* rich.

nourrice [nuʀis] *nf* **(a)** (wet-)nurse. **~ sèche** dry nurse; **mettre**

un enfant en ~ to put a child out to nurse *ou* in the care of a nurse; *V* **épingle. (b)** (*bidon*) jerrycan (*Brit*).

nourricier, -ière [nuʀisje, jɛʀ] *adj* (*Anat*) *canal, artère* nutrient; (*Bot*) *suc, sève* nutritive; (††: *adoptif*) *mère, père* foster (*épith*). (*littér*) **la terre ~ière** the nourishing earth.

nourrir [nuʀiʀ] (2) **1** *vt* **(a)** (*alimenter*) *animal, personne* to feed; *feu* to stoke; *récit, devoir* to fill out. **~ au biberon** to bottle-feed; **~ au sein** to breast-feed; **~ à la cuiller** to spoon-feed; **~ un oiseau au grain** to feed a bird (on) seed; **les régions qui nourrissent la capitale** the areas which provide food for the capital *ou* provide the capital with food; **bien/mal nourri** well-/poorly-fed; *V* **logé.**

(b) (*faire vivre*) *famille, pays* to feed, provide for. **cette entreprise nourrit 10.000 ouvriers** this firm gives work to *ou* provides work for 10,000 workers; **ce métier ne nourrit pas son homme** this job doesn't earn a man his bread *ou* doesn't give a man a living wage.

(c) (*fig: caresser*) *projet* to nurse; *désir, espoir, illusion* to nourish, nurture, cherish; *haine* to nourish, harbour a feeling of; *vengeance* to nourish, harbour thoughts of.

(d) (*littér: former*) **être nourri dans les bons principes** to be nurtured on good principles; **la lecture nourrit l'esprit** reading improves the mind.

2 *vi* to be nourishing.

3 se nourrir *vpr* to eat. **se ~ de** *viande* to feed (o.s.) on, eat; *illusions* to feed on, live on; (*fig*) **il se nourrit de romans** novels are his staple diet.

nourrissant, e [nuʀisɑ̃, ɑ̃t] *adj* nourishing, nutritious.

nourrisson [nuʀisɔ̃] *nm* (unweaned) infant, nursling (*littér*).

nourriture [nuʀityʀ] *nf* **(a)** (*aliments, fig*) food. **assurer la ~ de qn** to provide sb's meals *ou* sb with food. **(b)** (*alimentation*) nourishment, nutrition. **il lui faut une ~ saine** he needs a healthy diet.

nous [nu] **1** *pron pers* **(a)** (*sujet*) we. **~ vous écrirons** we'll write *ou* be writing to you; **~ avons bien ri tous les deux** the two of us had a good laugh, we both had a good laugh; **eux ont accepté, ~ non** *ou* **pas ~** they accepted but we didn't, they accepted but not us*; **c'est enfin ~, ~ voilà enfin** here we are at last; **qui l'a vu? — ~/pas ~** who saw him? — we did/we didn't *ou* us/not us*; **~ accepter?, jamais!** us accept that?, never!, you expect us to accept that?, never!; *V aussi* **même.**

(b) (*objet dir ou indir, complément*) us. **aide-~** help us, give us a hand; **donne-~ ton livre** give us your book, give your book to us; **si vous étiez ~ que feriez-vous?** if you were us *ou* if you were in our shoes what would you do?; **donne-le-~** give it to us, give us it; **écoutez-~** listen to us; **il n'obéit qu'à ~** we are the only ones he obeys, he obeys only us.

(c) (*emphatique: insistance*) (*sujet*) WE, we ourselves; (*objet*) US. **~, nous le connaissons bien — mais ~ aussi** WE know him well *ou* we know him well ourselves — but so do we *ou* we do too; **pourquoi ne le ferait-il pas?, nous l'avons bien fait, ~** why shouldn't he do it?, WE did it (all right); **alors ~, nous restons pour compte?** and what about us, are we to be left out?; **~, elle nous déteste** she hates us *ou* US; **elle nous connaît bien, ~** she knows us *ou* US all right.

(d) (*emphatique avec qui, que*) (*sujet*) we; (*objet*) us. **c'est ~ qui sommes fautifs** we are the culprits, we are the ones to blame; **merci — c'est ~ qui vous remercions** thank you — it's WE who should thank you; **et ~ (tous) qui vous parlons l'avons vu** we (all) saw him personally; **est-ce ~ qui devons vous le dire?** do WE have to tell you?; **et ~ qui n'avions pas le sou!** and there were we without a penny!, and to think we didn't have a penny!; **~ que le théâtre passionne, nous n'avons jamais vu cette pièce** great theatre lovers that we are we have still never seen that play, even we with all our great love for the theatre have never seen that play; **il nous dit cela à ~ qui l'avons tant aidé** and that's what he says to US who have helped him so much; **c'est ~ qu'elle veut voir** it's us she wants to see.

(e) (*avec prép*) us. **à ~ cinq, nous devrions pouvoir soulever ça** between the 5 of us we should be able to lift that; **cette maison est à ~** this house belongs to us *ou* is ours; **nous avons une maison à ~** we have a house of our own, we have our own house; **avec/sans ~** with/without us; **c'est à ~ de décider** it's up to us *ou* to ourselves to decide; **elle l'a appris par ~** she heard about it through *ou* from us; **un élève à ~** one of our pupils; **l'un de ~** *ou* **d'entre ~ doit le savoir** one of us must know (it); **nos enfants à ~** our children; **l'idée vient de ~** the idea comes from us *ou* is ours; **elle veut une photo de ~ tous** she wants a photo of us all *ou* of all of us.

(f) (*dans comparaisons*) we, us. **il est aussi fort que ~** he is as strong as we are *ou* as us*; **il mange plus/moins que ~** he eats more/less than we do *ou* than us*; **faites comme ~** do as we do, do like us*, do the same as us*; **il vous connaît aussi bien que ~** (*aussi bien que nous vous connaissons*) he knows you as well as we do *ou* as us*; (*aussi bien qu'il nous connaît*) he knows you as well as (he knows *ou* does) us.

(g) (*avec vpr*) **nous ~ sommes bien amusés** we had a good time, we thoroughly enjoyed ourselves; **(lui et moi) nous ~ connaissons depuis le lycée** we have known each other since we were at school; **nous ~ détestons** we hate (the sight of) each other; **asseyons-~ donc** let's sit down, shall we sit down?; **nous ~ écrirons** we'll write to each other.

(h) (*pl: de majesté, modestie etc = moi*) we. **~, préfet de X, décidons que** we, (the) prefect of X, decide that; **dans cet exposé, ~ essaierons d'expliquer** in this paper, we shall try to explain.

2 *nm*: **le ~ de majesté** the royal we.

nous-même, *pl* **nous-mêmes** [numɛm] *pron V* **même.**

nouveau, nouvelle [nuvo, nuvɛl] (**nouvel** [nuvɛl] *devant nm commençant par une voyelle ou h muet*) *mpl* **nouveaux** [nuvo] **1** *adj* **(a)** (*gén après n: qui apparaît pour la première fois*) new. **pommes de terre nouvelles** new potatoes; **vin ~** new wine; **carottes nouvelles** spring carrots; **la mode nouvelle** the latest fashion; **la mode nouvelle du printemps** the new spring fashion(s); **un sentiment si ~ pour moi** such a new feeling for me; **montrez-moi le chemin, je suis ~ ici** show me the way, I'm new here; *V* **art, quoi, tout.**

(b) (*après n: original*) *idée* novel, new, original; *style* new, original; (*moderne*) *méthode* new, up-to-date, new-fangled (*péj*). **le dernier de ses romans, et le plus ~** his latest and most original novel; **présenter qch sous un jour ~** to present sth in a new light; **c'est tout ~, ce projet** this project is brand-new; **il n'y a rien de/ce n'est pas ~!** there's/it's nothing new.

(c) (*inexpérimenté*) new (*en, dans* to). **il est ~ en affaires** he's new to business; **ce travail est ~ pour lui** he's new to this job, this work is new to him.

(d) (*avant n: qui succède*) new; (*qui s'ajoute*) new, fresh. **le ~ président** the new president, the newly-elected president; **le nouvel élu** the newly-elected representative; **nous avons un ~ président/une nouvelle voiture** we have a new president/car; **avez-vous lu son ~ livre?** have you read his new *ou* latest book?; **un ~ Napoléon** a second Napoleon; **il y a eu un ~ tremblement de terre** there has been a further *ou* a new *ou* a fresh earthquake; **c'est là une nouvelle preuve que** it's fresh proof *ou* further proof that; **je ferai un nouvel essai** I'll make another *ou* a new *ou* a fresh attempt; (*fig*) **c'est la nouvelle mode maintenant** it's the new fashion now, it's the latest thing *ou* fashion; *V* **jusque.**

2 *nm* **(a)** (*homme, ouvrier etc*) new man; (*Scol*) new boy.

(b) du ~: y a-t-il du ~ à ce sujet? is there anything new on this?; **il y a du ~ dans cette affaire** there has been a fresh *ou* a new development in this business; **le public veut sans cesse du ~** the public always wants something new.

(c) (*loc*) **de ~** again; **faire qch de ~** to do sth again, repeat sth; **à ~** (*d'une manière différente*) anew, afresh, again; (*encore une fois*) again; **nous examinerons la question à ~** we'll examine the question anew *ou* afresh *ou* again.

3 nouvelle *nf* **(a)** (*femme, ouvrière etc*) new woman *ou* girl; (*Scol*) new girl.

(b) (*écho*) news (*U*). **une nouvelle** a piece of news; **bonne/mauvaise nouvelle** good/bad news; **ce n'est pas une nouvelle!** that's not news!, that's nothing new!; **vous connaissez la nouvelle?** have you heard the news?; **la nouvelle de cet événement nous a surpris** we were surprised by the news of this event; **annoncer/apprendre la nouvelle de la mort de qn** to announce/hear the news of sb's death; **aller aux nouvelles** to go and find out what is (*ou* was *etc*) happening; *V* **dernier, faux², premier.**

(c) nouvelles news (*U*); **avez-vous de ses nouvelles?** (*de sa propre main*) have you heard from him?, have you had any news from him?; (*par un tiers*) have you heard anything about *ou* of him?, have you had any news of him?; **j'irai prendre de ses nouvelles** I'll go and see how he's getting on; **il a fait prendre de mes nouvelles (par qn)** he asked for news of me (from sb); **il ne donne plus de ses nouvelles** you never hear from him any more; **je suis sans nouvelles (de lui) depuis huit jours** I haven't heard anything (of him) for a week, I've had no news (of him) for a week; **pas de nouvelles, bonnes nouvelles** no news is good news; **il aura/entendra de mes nouvelles!*** I'll give him what for!*; **(goûtez mon vin) vous m'en direz des nouvelles** (taste my wine,) I'm sure you'll like it.

(d) (*Presse, Rad, TV*) **les nouvelles** the news (*U*); **écouter/entendre les nouvelles** to listen to/hear the news; **voici les nouvelles** here is the news.

(e) (*court récit*) short story.

4: Nouvel An, Nouvelle Année New Year; **Nouvelle-Angleterre** New England; **Nouvelle-Calédonie** *nf* New Caledonia; **Nouvelle-Écosse** *nf* Nova Scotia; **Nouvelle-Galles du Sud** *nf* New South Wales; **Nouvelle-Guinée** *nf* New Guinea; **Nouvelles-Hébrides** *nfpl* New Hebrides; **nouvelle lune** new moon; **nouveaux mariés** newly-weds, newly married couple; **Nouveau Monde** New World; **nouveau-né, e,** *mpl* **nouveau-nés** (*adj*) newborn; (*nm,f*) newborn child; **La Nouvelle-Orléans** New Orleans; **nouveau riche** nouveau riche; **Nouveau Testament** New Testament; **nouvelle vague** (*adj*) (*gén*) with-it*; (*Ciné*) nouvelle vague; (*nf*) (*nouvelle génération*) new generation; (*Ciné*) nouvelle vague; **nouveau venu, nouvelle venue,** *mpl* **nouveaux venus** newcomer; **Nouvelle-Zélande** *nf* New Zealand.

nouveauté [nuvote] *nf* **(a)** (*actualité*) novelty, newness; (*originalité*) novelty; (*chose*) new thing, something new; (*livre*) new publication. **il n'aime pas la ~** he hates anything new *ou* new ideas, he hates change; **il travaille? c'est une ~!** he's working? that's new! *ou* that's a new departure!

(b) (*Habillement*) **~s de printemps** (the) new spring fashions, (the) spring fashions; **le commerce de la ~** the fashion trade; **magasin de ~s** draper's shop (*Brit*), dry goods store (*US*).

nouvel [nuvɛl] *adj m V* **nouveau.**

nouvellement [nuvɛlmɑ̃] *adv* recently, newly.

nouvelliste [nuvelist(ə)] *nmf* short story writer, writer of short stories.

novateur, -trice [nɔvatœʀ, tʀis] **1** *adj* innovatory, innovative. **2** *nm,f* innovator.

novembre [nɔvɑ̃bʀ(ə)] *nm* November; *pour loc V* **septembre** *et* **onze.**

novice [nɔvis] **1** *adj* inexperienced (*dans* in), green* (*dans* at). **2** *nmf* (*débutant*) novice, beginner, greenhorn*; (*Rel*) novice.

noviciat [nɔvisja] *nm* (*bâtiment, période*) noviciate, novitiate.

novocaïne [nɔvɔkain] *nf* novocaine.

noyade [nwajad] nf drowning; (événement) drowning accident, death by drowning. il y a eu de nombreuses ~s à cet endroit there have been many drowning accidents ou many deaths by drowning ou many people drowned at this spot; sauver qn de la ~ to save sb from drowning.

noyau, pl ~x [nwajo] nm (a) (lit) [fruit] stone, pit (US); (Astron, Bio, Ling, Phys) nucleus; (Géol) core; (Art) centre, core; (Élec) core (of induction coil etc); (Constr) newel. enlevez les ~x remove the stones (from the fruit).
(b) (fig) [personnes] (cellule originelle) nucleus; (groupe de fidèles) circle; (groupe de manifestants) small group; (groupe d'opposants) cell, small group. il ne restait maintenant qu'un ~ d'opposants now there only remained a hard core of opponents; ~ de résistance centre of resistance.

noyautage [nwajotaʒ] nm (Pol) infiltration.

noyauter [nwajote] (1) vt (Pol) to infiltrate.

noyé, e [nwaje] (ptp de noyer[2]) 1 adj (a) être ~ (fig: ne pas comprendre) to be out of one's depth, be all at sea (en in).
(b) avoir le regard ~ to have a faraway ou vague look in one's eyes; regard ~ de larmes tearful look, eyes swimming with tears.
2 nm,f drowned person.

noyer[1] [nwaje] nm (arbre) walnut (tree); (bois) walnut.

noyer[2] [nwaje] (8) 1 vt (a) (gén) personne, animal, incendie, flamme to drown; (Aut) moteur to flood. la crue a noyé les champs riverains the high water has flooded ou drowned ou swamped the riverside fields; il avait les yeux noyés de larmes his eyes were brimming ou swimming with tears; la nuit noyait la campagne the countryside lay plunged in darkness; ~ une révolte dans le sang to put down a revolt violently, spill blood in quelling a revolt; (Mil) ~ la poudre to wet the powder; ~ son chagrin dans l'alcool to drown one's sorrows; (fig) ~ le poisson to draw a red herring across the trail.
(b) (gén pass: perdre) ~ qn sous un déluge d'explications to swamp sb with explanations; (Scol) quelques bonnes idées noyées dans des détails inutiles a few good ideas lost ou buried in ou swamped by a mass of irrelevant detail; être noyé dans l'obscurité to be plunged in darkness; être noyé dans la foule to be lost in the crowd; noyé dans la masse, cet écrivain n'arrive pas à percer because he's (just) one amongst (so) many, this writer can't manage to make a name for himself; cette dépense ne se verra pas, noyée dans la masse this expense won't be noticed when it's lumped ou put together with the rest; ses paroles furent noyées par ou dans le vacarme his words were drowned in the din.
(c) (Culin) alcool, vin to water down; sauce to thin too much, make too thin.
(d) (Tech) clou to drive right in; pilier to embed. noyé dans la masse embedded.
(e) (effacer) contours, couleur to blur.
2 se noyer vpr (a) (lit) (accidentellement) to drown; (volontairement) to drown o.s. une personne qui se noie a drowning person; il s'est noyé he drowned ou was drowned.
(b) (fig) se ~ dans un raisonnement to become tangled up ou bogged down in an argument; se ~ dans les détails to get bogged down in details; se ~ dans un verre d'eau to make a mountain out of a molehill, make heavy weather of the simplest thing; se ~ l'estomac to overfill one's stomach (by drinking too much liquid).

nu, e[1] [ny] 1 adj (a) (sans vêtement) personne naked, nude, bare; torse, membres naked, bare; crâne bald. ~-pieds, (les) pieds ~s barefoot, with bare feet; ~-tête, (la) tête ~e bareheaded; ~-jambes, (les) jambes ~es barelegged, with bare legs; (les) bras ~s barearmed, with bare arms; (le) torse ~, ~ jusqu'à la ceinture stripped to the waist, naked from the waist up; à moitié ~, à demi ~ half-naked; il est ~ comme un ver ou comme la main he is as naked as the day he was born, he is stark naked; se mettre ~ to strip (off), take one's clothes off; V épée, main, œil.
(b) (sans ornement) mur, chambre bare; arbre, pays, plaine bare, naked; style plain; vérité plain, naked.
(c) (Jur) en ~e-propriété without usufruct.
(d) (Bot, Zool) naked.
(e) (loc) à ~: mettre à ~ fil électrique to strip; erreurs, vices to expose, lay bare; mettre son cœur à ~ to lay bare one's heart ou soul; monter un cheval à ~ to ride bareback.
2 nm nude.
3 nu-pieds nmpl (sandales) flip-flops; (Jur) nu-propriétaire nmf owner without usufruct.

nuage [nɥaʒ] nm (lit, fig) cloud. ~ de grêle/de pluie hail/rain cloud; ~ de fumée/de tulle/de poussière/de sauterelles cloud of smoke/tulle/dust/locusts; (lit, fig) il y a des ~s noirs à l'horizon there are dark clouds on the horizon; le ciel se couvre de ~s/est couvert de ~s the sky is clouding over/is cloudy ou overcast ou has clouded over; juste un ~ (de lait) just a drop (of milk); (fig) il est (perdu) dans les ~s he has his head ou he is in the clouds; sans ~s ciel cloudless; bonheur unmarred, unclouded; une amitié qui n'est pas sans ~s a friendship which is not entirely untroubled ou is not entirely quarrelfree.

nuageux, -euse [nɥaʒø, øz] adj (a) temps cloudy; ciel cloudy, overcast. système ~ cloud system. (b) (rare: vague) nebulous, hazy.

nuance [nɥɑ̃s] nf (a) [couleur] shade; (Littérat) shade of meaning, nuance; (Mus) nuance.
(b) (différence) slight difference. il y a une ~ entre mentir et se taire there's a slight difference between lying and keeping quiet; je ne lui ai pas dit non, ~! je lui ai dit peut-être I didn't say no to him, understand, I said perhaps; d'une ~ politique différente of a different shade of political opinion; de toutes les ~s politiques of all shades of political opinion.
(c) (subtilité, variation) les ~s du cœur/de l'amour the subtleties of the heart/of love; apporter des ~s à une affirmation to qualify a statement; faire ressortir les ~s to bring out the finer ou subtler points; tout en ~s esprit, discours, personne very subtle, full of nuances; sans ~ discours unsubtle, cut and dried; esprit, personne unsubtle.
(d) (petit élément) touch. avec une ~ de tristesse with a touch ou a slight note of sadness.

nuancé, e [nɥɑ̃se] (ptp de nuancer) adj tableau finely shaded; opinion qualified; (Mus) nuanced.

nuancer [nɥɑ̃se] (3) vt tableau to shade; opinion to qualify; (Mus) to nuance.

nubile [nybil] adj nubile.

nubilité [nybilite] nf nubility.

nucléaire [nykleɛʀ] adj nuclear.

nucléé, e [nyklee] adj nucleate(d).

nucléine [nyklein] nf nuclein.

nucléique [nykleik] adj nucleic.

nucléon [nykleɔ̃] nm nucleon.

nudisme [nydism(ə)] nm nudism.

nudiste [nydist(ə)] adj, nmf nudist.

nudité [nydite] nf [personne] nakedness, nudity; (fig) [mur] bareness; (rare: Art) nude. la laideur des gens s'étale dans toute sa ~ people are exposed in all their ugliness, people's ugliness is laid bare for all to see.

nue[2] [ny] nf (a) (†† ou littér) (nuage) ~, ~s clouds; (ciel) la ~, les ~s the skies.
(b) porter ou mettre qn aux ~s to praise sb to the skies; tomber des ~s to be completely taken aback ou flabbergasted; je suis tombé des ~s you could have knocked me down with a feather, I was completely taken aback.

nuée [nɥe] nf (a) (littér: nuage) thick cloud. ~s d'orage storm clouds; ~ ardente nuée ardente, glowing cloud.
(b) (multitude) [insectes] cloud, horde; [flèches] cloud; [photographes, spectateurs, ennemis] horde, host. (fig) comme une ~ de sauterelles like a plague ou a swarm of locusts.

nuire [nɥiʀ] (38) 1 nuire à vt indir (desservir) personne to harm, injure; santé, réputation to damage, harm, injure; action to prejudice. sa laideur lui nuit beaucoup his ugliness is very much against him ou is a great disadvantage to him; il a voulu le faire mais ça va lui ~ he wanted to do it, but it will bring him into discredit ou it will go against him; chercher à ~ à qn to try to do ou run sb down; cela risque de ~ à nos projets there's a risk that it will damage ou harm our plans.
2 se nuire vpr (à soi-même) to do o.s. a lot of harm; (l'un l'autre) to work against each other's interests.

nuisance [nɥizɑ̃s] nf (gén pl) (environmental) nuisance.

nuisible [nɥizibl(ə)] adj climat, temps harmful, injurious (à to); gaz harmful, noxious (à to). animaux ~s vermin, pests; insectes ~s pests.

nuit [nɥi] 1 nf (a) (obscurité) darkness, night. il fait ~ it is dark; il fait ~ à 5 heures it gets dark at 5 o'clock; il fait ~ noire it's pitch dark ou black; la ~ tombe night is falling; à la ~ tombante at nightfall, at dusk; pris ou surpris par la ~ overtaken by night; rentrer avant la ~ to come home before dark; rentrer à la ~ to come home in the dark; la ~ polaire the polar night ou darkness; (Prov) la ~ tous les chats sont gris every cat in the twilight is grey.
(b) (espace de temps) night. cette ~ (passée) last night; (qui vient) tonight; dans la ~ de jeudi during Thursday night; dans la ~ de jeudi à vendredi during Thursday night, during the night of Thursday to Friday; souhaiter (une) bonne ~ à qn to wish sb goodnight; (Prov) la ~ porte conseil let's (let them etc) sleep on it; une ~ blanche ou sans sommeil a sleepless night; faire sa ~* to go through the night; ~ et jour night and day; au milieu de la ~, en pleine ~ in the middle of the night; elle part cette ~ ou dans la ~ she's leaving tonight; ouvert la ~ open at night; sortir/travailler la ~ to go out/work at night; rouler ou conduire la ~ ou de ~ to drive at night; conduire la ~ ne me gêne pas I don't mind night-driving ou driving at night; de ~ service, travail, garde, infirmière etc night (épith).
(c) (littér) darkness. dans la ~ de ses souvenirs in the darkness of his memories; dans la ~ des temps in the mists of time; la ~ du tombeau/de la mort the darkness of the grave/of death.
2: nuit d'hôtel night spent in a hotel room, overnight stay in a hotel; payer sa nuit (d'hôtel) to pay one's hotel bill; nuit de noces wedding night; nuit de Noël Christmas Eve; (rare) nuit des Rois Twelfth Night.

nuitamment [nɥitamɑ̃] adv by night.

nuitée [nɥite] nf (gén pl) ~s overnight stays, beds occupied (in statistics for tourism).

nul, nulle [nyl] 1 adj indéf (a) (aucun: devant n) il n'avait ~ besoin/nulle envie de sortir he had no need/no desire to go out at all; ~ doute qu'elle ne l'ait vu there is no doubt (whatsoever) that she saw him; ~ autre que lui (n'aurait pu le faire) no one (else) but him (could have done it); il ne l'a trouvé nulle part he couldn't find it anywhere, he could find it nowhere; sans ~ doute/nulle exception without any doubt/any exception.
(b) (après n) (proche de zéro) résultat, différence, risque nil (attrib); (invalidé) testament, élection null and void (attrib); (inexistant) récolte etc non-existent. (Sport) le résultat ou le score est ~ (zéro à zéro) the result is a goalless ou a nil draw; (2 à 2 etc) the result is a draw; (Jur) ~ et non avenu invalid, null and void; (Jur) rendre ~ to annul, nullify; V match.
(c) (qui ne vaut rien) personne useless, hopeless; intelligence nil; travail worthless, useless. être ~ en géographie to be hopeless ou useless at geography; il est ~ pour ou dans tout ce qui est manuel he's hopeless ou useless at anything manual.
2 pron indéf (sujet sg: personne, aucun) no one. ~ n'est prophète en son pays no man (ou woman) is a prophet in his (ou

her) own country; ~ **n'est censé ignorer la loi** ignorance of the law is no excuse; ~ **d'entre vous n'ignore que** ... none of you is ignorant of the fact that ...; *V* **à**.

nullard, e* [nylaʀ, aʀd(ə)] 1 *adj* hopeless, useless (*en* at). 2 *nm,f* dunce, numskull.

nullement [nylmɑ̃] *adv* not at all, not in the least.

nullité [nylite] *nf* **(a)** (*Jur*) nullity; *[personne]* uselessness; incompetence; *[raisonnement, objection]* invalidity. **(b)** (*personne*) nonentity, wash-out*.

nûment [nymɑ̃] *adv* (*littér*) (*sans fard*) plainly, frankly; (*crûment*) bluntly. **dire (tout)** ~ **que** ... to say (quite) frankly that ... .

numéraire [nymeʀɛʀ] 1 *adj* (*rare*) **pierres** ~**s** milestones; **espèces** ~**s** legal tender *ou* currency; **valeur** ~ face value.
2 *nm* specie (*T*), cash. **paiement en** ~ cash payment, payment in specie (*T*).

numéral, e, *mpl* **-aux** [nymeʀal, o] *adj, nm* numeral.

numérateur [nymeʀatœʀ] *nm* numerator.

numération [nymeʀɑsjɔ̃] *nf* numeration. (*Math*) ~ **décimale/binaire** decimal/binary number system; (*Méd*) ~ **globulaire** blood count.

numérique [nymeʀik] *adj* numerical.

numériquement [nymeʀikmɑ̃] *adv* numerically.

numéro [nymeʀo] *nm* **(a)** (*gén, Aut, Phys*) number. **j'habite au** ~ **6** I live at number 6; ~ **d'ordre** queue ticket, number; ~ **minéralogique** *ou* **d'immatriculation** *ou* **de police** registration (*Brit*) *ou* license (*US*) number, car number; ~ **(de téléphone)** (tele)phone number; **quel est votre** ~ **d'appel?** what number do you require?; **faire** *ou* **composer un** ~ to dial a number; **tirer un bon/mauvais** ~ to draw a lucky/an unlucky number; ~ **un** *ennemi, problème* number one (*épith*).
(b) (*Presse*) issue, number. **le** ~ **du jour** the day's issue; **vieux** ~ back number, back issue; *V* **suite**.
(c) (*spectacle*) *[chant, danse]* number; *[cirque, music-hall]* act, turn. (*fig*) **il nous a fait son** ~ **habituel** *ou* **son petit** ~ he gave us *ou* put on his usual (little) act.
(d) (*personne*) **quel** ~**!*, c'est un drôle de** ~**!*** what a character!

numérotage [nymeʀɔtaʒ] *nm,* **numérotation** [nymeʀɔtɑsjɔ̃] *nf* numbering, numeration.

numéroter [nymeʀɔte] (1) *vt* to number. ~ **ses abattis‡** to check that one hasn't lost any limbs (*hum*).

numide [nymid] 1 *adj* Numidian. 2 *nmf:* **N**~ Numidian.

Numidie [nymidi] *nf* Numidia.

numismate [nymismat] *nmf* numismatist.

numismatique [nymismatik] 1 *adj* numismatic. 2 *nf* numismatics (*sg*), numismatology.

nuptial, e, *mpl* **-aux** [nypsjal, o] *adj bénédiction, messe* nuptial (*littér*); *robe, marche, anneau, cérémonie* wedding (*épith*); *lit, chambre* bridal, nuptial (*littér*).

nuptialité [nypsjalite] *nf* marriage rate.

nuque [nyk] *nf* nape (of the neck).

nurse [nœʀs(ə)] *nf* nanny, (children's) nurse.

nutritif, -ive [nytʀitif, iv] *adj* (*nourrissant*) nourishing, nutritious; (*Méd*) *besoins, fonction, appareil* nutritive. (*Bio*) **qualité** *ou* **valeur** ~**ive** food value, nutritional value.

nutrition [nytʀisjɔ̃] *nf* nutrition.

nyctalope [niktalɔp] 1 *adj* day-blind, nyctalopic (*T*), hemeralopic (*T*). 2 *nmf* day-blind *ou* nyctalopic *ou* hemeralopic person. **les chats sont** ~**s** cats see well in the dark *ou* are hemeralopic (*T*).

nyctalopie [niktalɔpi] *nf* day blindness, nyctalopia (*T*), hemeralopia (*T*).

nylon [nilɔ̃] *nm* ® nylon. **bas (de)** ~ (*pl*) nylons, nylon stockings.

nymphe [nɛ̃f] *nf* (*Myth, fig*) nymph; (*Zool*) nymph, nympha, pupa; (*Anat*) nymphae, labia minora.

nymphéa [nɛ̃fea] *nm* white water lily.

nymphomane [nɛ̃fɔman] *adj, nf* nymphomaniac.

nymphomanie [nɛ̃fɔmani] *nf* nymphomania.

O

O, o [o] *nm* (*lettre*) O, o.

ô [o] *excl* oh!, O!

oasis [ɔazis] *nf* (*lit, fig*) oasis.

obédience [ɔbedjɑ̃s] *nf* **(a)** (*appartenance*) **d'**~ **communiste** of Communist allegiance; **de même** ~ **religieuse** of the same religious persuasion. **(b)** (*Rel, littér: obéissance*) obedience.

obéir [ɔbeiʀ] (2) **obéir à** *vt indir* **(a)** *personne* to obey; *ordre* to obey, comply with; *loi, principe* to obey. **il sait se faire** ~ **de ses élèves** he knows how to command *ou* exact obedience from his pupils *ou* how to get his pupils to obey him *ou* how to make his pupils obey him; **on lui obéit** *ou* **il est obéi au doigt et à l'œil** he commands strict obedience; **je lui ai dit de le faire mais il n'a pas obéi** I told him to do it but he took no notice *ou* didn't obey (me); **ici, il faut** ~ you have to toe the line *ou* obey orders here.
(b) (*fig*) ~ **à** *conscience, mode* to follow the dictates of. ~ **à une impulsion** to act on an impulse; **obéissant à un sentiment de pitié** prompted *ou* moved by a feeling of pity; ~ **à ses instincts** to submit to *ou* obey one's instincts.
(c) *[voilier, moteur, monture]* to respond to. **le cheval obéit au mors** the horse responds to the bit; **le moteur/voilier obéit bien** the engine/boat responds well.

obéissance [ɔbeisɑ̃s] *nf* obedience (*à* to). **le refus d'**~ **est puni** any refusal to obey will be punished.

obéissant, e [ɔbeisɑ̃, ɑ̃t] *adj* obedient (*à* to, towards).

obélisque [ɔbelisk(ə)] *nm* obelisk (*monument*).

obérer [ɔbeʀe] (6) *vt* (*frm*) to burden with debt. **obéré (de dettes)** burdened with debt.

obèse [ɔbɛz] *adj* obese.

obésité [ɔbezite] *nf* obesity.

objecter [ɔbʒɛkte] (1) *vt* **(a)** (*à une suggestion ou opinion*) ~ **une raison à un argument** to put forward a reason against an argument; **il m'objecta une très bonne raison, à savoir que** ... against that he argued convincingly that ..., he gave me *ou* he put forward a very sound reason against (doing) that, namely that ...; ~ **que** ... to object that ...; **il m'objecta que** ... he objected to me that ..., the objection he mentioned *ou* raised to me was that ...; **je n'ai rien à** ~ I have no objection (to make); **elle a toujours quelque chose à** ~ she always has some objection or other (to make), she always raises some objection or other.
(b) (*à une demande*) **il objecta le manque de temps/la fatigue pour ne pas y aller** he pleaded lack of time/tiredness to save himself going; **quand je lui demandai de m'emmener, il m'objecta mon manque d'expérience/le manque de place** when I asked him to take me with him, he objected on the grounds of my lack of experience/on the grounds that there was not enough space *ou* he objected that I lacked experience/that there was not enough space.

objecteur [ɔbʒɛktœʀ] *nm:* ~ **(de conscience)** conscientious objector.

objectif, -ive [ɔbʒɛktif, iv] 1 *adj* **(a)** *article, jugement, observateur* objective, unbiased.
(b) (*Ling, Philos*) objective; (*Méd*) *symptôme* objective.
2 *nm* **(a)** (*but*) objective; (*Mil: cible*) objective, target.
(b) *[télescope, lunette]* objective, object glass, lens; *[caméra]* lens, objective. ~ **grand-angulaire** *ou* **(à) grand-angle** wide-angle lens; **braquer son** ~ **sur** to train one's camera on.

objection [ɔbʒɛksjɔ̃] *nf* objection. **faire une** ~ to raise *ou* make an objection, object; **si vous n'y voyez aucune** ~ if you have no objection (to that); ~ **de conscience** conscientious objection.

objectivement [ɔbʒɛktivmɑ̃] *adv* objectively.

objectiver [ɔbʒɛktive] (1) *vt* to objectivize.

objectivisme [ɔbʒɛktivism(ə)] *nm* objectivism.

objectivité [ɔbʒɛktivite] *nf* objectivity.

objet [ɔbʒɛ] 1 *nm* **(a)** (*article*) object, thing. **emporter quelques** ~**s de première nécessité** to take a few basic essentials *ou* a few essential items *ou* things; **femme-/homme-**~ woman/man as an object; *V* **bureau**.
(b) (*sujet*) *[méditation, rêve, désir]* object; *[discussion, recherches, science]* subject. **l'**~ **de la psychologie est le comportement humain** human behaviour forms the subject matter of psychology, psychology is the study of human behaviour.
(c) (*cible*) **un** ~ **de raillerie/de grande admiration** an object of fun/great admiration; **il était l'**~ **de la curiosité/de l'envie des autres** he was an object of curiosity/an object of envy to (the) others.
(d) faire *ou* **être l'**~ **de** *discussion, recherches* to be *ou* form the subject of; *surveillance, enquête* to be subjected to; *soins, dévouement* to be given *ou* shown; **les prisonniers font l'**~ **d'une surveillance constante** the prisoners are subject *ou* subjected to constant surveillance; **le malade fit** *ou* **fut l'**~ **d'un dévouement de tous les instants** the patient was shown *ou* was given every care and attention.
(e) (*but*) *[visite, réunion, démarche]* object, purpose. **cette enquête a rempli son** ~ the investigation has achieved its purpose *ou* object *ou* objective; **votre plainte est dès lors sans** ~ your complaint therefore no longer applies *ou* is no longer applicable.
(f) (*Ling, Philos*) object; *V* **complément**.
(g) (*Jur*) *[procès, litige]* **l'**~ **du litige** the matter at issue, the subject of the case.
2: (†† *ou hum*) **l'objet aimé** the beloved one; **objet d'art** objet

d'art; **objets de toilette** toilet requisites *ou* articles; **objets trouvés** lost property (office).
objurgations [ɔbʒyʀgɑsjɔ̃] *nfpl* (*exhortations*) objurgations (*frm*); (*prières*) pleas, entreaties.
obligation [ɔbligɑsjɔ̃] *nf* **(a)** (*devoir moral ou réglementaire*) obligation. **avoir l'~ de faire** to be under an obligation to do, be obliged to do; **il se fait une ~ de cette visite/lui rendre visite** he feels himself obliged *ou* he feels he is under an obligation to make this visit/to visit him; **être** *ou* **se trouver dans l'~ de faire** to be obliged to do; **sans ~ d'achat** with no *ou* without obligation to buy; **c'est sans ~ de votre part** there's no obligation on your part, you're under no obligation.
(b) (*gén pl: devoirs*) obligation, duty. **~s sociales/professionnelles** social/professional obligations; **~s de citoyen/de chrétien** one's obligations *ou* responsibilities *ou* duties as a citizen/Christian; **~s militaires** military obligations *ou* duties, duties *ou* obligations as a soldier; **~s scolaires** *[professeur]* teaching obligations; *[élève]* obligations *ou* duties as a pupil; **~s familiales** family obligations *ou* responsibilities.
(c) (*littér: devoir de reconnaissance*) ~(s) obligation; **avoir de l'~ à qn** to be under an obligation to sb.
(d) (*Jur*) obligation; (*dette*) obligation. **~ légale** legal obligation; **~ alimentaire** maintenance obligation; **contracter une ~ envers qn** to contract an obligation towards sb.
(e) (*Fin*) bond, debenture.
obligatoire [ɔbligatwaʀ] *adj* **(a)** compulsory, obligatory, mandatory. **le service militaire est ~ pour tous** military service is obligatory *ou* compulsory for all.
(b) (*: *inévitable*) **il est arrivé en retard? — c'était ~!** he arrived late? — he was bound to! *ou* it was inevitable!
obligatoirement [ɔbligatwaʀmɑ̃] *adv* **(a)** (*frm*) **devoir ~ faire** to be under a strict obligation to do, be strictly obliged to do.
(b) (*: *sans doute*) inevitably. **il aura ~** des ennuis **s'il continue comme ça** he's bound to *ou* he'll be bound to *ou* he'll inevitably make trouble for himself if he carries on like that.
obligé, e [ɔbliʒe] (*ptp de* **obliger**) **1** *adj* **(a)** (*forcé de*) **~ de faire** obliged *ou* compelled to do; **j'étais bien ~** I was forced to, I HAD to.
(b) (*frm: redevable*) **être ~ à qn** to be (most) obliged to sb, be indebted to sb (*de qch* for sth, *d'avoir fait* for having done, for doing).
(c) (*: *inévitable*) **c'est ~!** it never fails!, it's inevitable!; **c'était ~** it had to happen!, it was sure *ou* bound to happen!
2 *nm,f* **(a)** (*Jur*) obligee, debtor. (*Jur*) **le principal ~** the principal obligee.
(b) (*frm*) **être l'~ de qn** to be under an obligation to sb.
obligeamment [ɔbliʒamɑ̃] *adv* obligingly.
obligeance [ɔbliʒɑ̃s] *nf*: **ayez l'~ de vous taire pendant que je parle** (kindly) oblige me by keeping quiet while I'm speaking, have the goodness *ou* be good enough to keep quiet while I'm speaking; **il a eu l'~ de me reconduire en voiture** he was obliging *ou* kind enough to take me back in the car *ou* to drive me back.
obligeant, e [ɔbliʒɑ̃, ɑ̃t] *adj personne* obliging; *offre* kind, helpful; *paroles, termes* kind, obliging.
obliger [ɔbliʒe] (3) *vt* **(a)** (*forcer*) **~ qn à faire** *[règlement, autorités]* to require sb to do, make it compulsory for sb to do; *[principes moraux]* to oblige sb to do; *[circonstances, parents, agresseur]* to force *ou* oblige sb to do; **le règlement vous y oblige** you are required to *ou* bound to by the regulation; **mes principes m'y obligent** I'm bound by my principles (to do it); **l'honneur m'y oblige** I'm honour bound to do it; **quand le temps l'y oblige, il travaille dans sa chambre** when forced *ou* obliged to by the weather, he works in his room; **ses parents l'obligent à aller à la messe** her parents make her go *ou* force her to go to mass; **rien ne l'oblige à partir** nothing's forcing him to leave, he's under no obligation to leave; **le manque d'argent l'a obligé à emprunter** lack of money compelled *ou* forced him to borrow; **je suis obligé de vous laisser** I have to *ou* I must leave you, I'm obliged to leave you; **il va accepter? — il (y) est bien obligé** is he going to accept? — he has no choice! *ou* alternative! *ou* he jolly* (*Brit*) *ou* damned: well has to!; *V* **noblesse.**
(b) (*Jur*) to bind.
(c) (*rendre service à*) to oblige. **vous m'obligeriez en acceptant** *ou* **si vous acceptiez** you would greatly oblige me by accepting *ou* if you accepted; (*formule de politesse*) **je vous serais très obligé de bien vouloir** I should be greatly obliged if you would kindly; **entre voisins, il faut bien s'~** we neighbours have to help each other *ou* be of service to each other.
oblique [ɔblik] **1** *adj* (*gén, Ling, Math*) oblique. **regard ~** sidelong *ou* side glance; **en ~** obliquely; **il a traversé la rue en ~** he crossed the street diagonally. **2** *nf* (*Math*) oblique line.
obliquement [ɔblikmɑ̃] *adv planter, fixer* at an angle, slantwise, obliquely; *se diriger, se mouvoir* obliquely. **regarder qn ~** to look sideways *ou* sidelong at sb, give sb a sidelong look *ou* glance.
obliquer [ɔblike] (1) *vi*: **obliquez juste avant l'église** turn off just before the church; **~ à droite** to turn off *ou* bear right; **obliquez en direction de la ferme** (*à travers champs*) cut across towards the farm; (*sur un sentier*) turn off towards the farm.
obliquité [ɔblikɥite] *nf [rayon]* (*Math*) obliqueness, obliquity; (*Astron*) obliquity.
oblitérateur [ɔbliteʀatœʀ] *nm* canceller.
oblitération [ɔbliteʀɑsjɔ̃] *nf* (*V* **oblitérer**) cancelling, cancellation; obliteration; obstruction. (*Poste*) **cachet d'~** postmark.
oblitérer [ɔbliteʀe] (6) *vt* **(a)** *timbre* to cancel. **(b)** (*† ou littér: effacer*) to obliterate. **(c)** (*Méd*) *artère* to obstruct.
oblong, -ongue [ɔblɔ̃, ɔ̃g] *adj* oblong.
obnubiler [ɔbnybile] (1) *vt* to obsess. **se laisser ~ par** to become obsessed by; **elle a l'esprit obnubilé par l'idée que** her mind is obsessed with the idea that, she is possessed with the idea that; **il a l'esprit obnubilé par les préjugés** his mind is clouded by prejudice.
obole [ɔbɔl] *nf* **(a)** (*contribution*) mite, offering. **(b)** (*monnaie française*) obole; (*monnaie grecque*) obol.
obscène [ɔpsɛn] *adj film, propos, geste* obscene, lewd.
obscénité [ɔpsenite] *nf* **(a)** (*U: V* **obscène**) obscenity, lewdness. **(b)** (*propos, écrit*) obscenity.
obscur, e [ɔpskyʀ] *adj* **(a)** (*sombre*) dark; *V* **salle.**
(b) (*fig*) (*incompréhensible*) obscure; (*vague*) *malaise* vague; *pressentiment* vague, dim; (*méconnu*) *œuvre, auteur* obscure; (*humble*) *vie, situation, besogne* obscure, humble, lowly. **des gens ~s** humble folk; **de naissance ~e** of obscure *ou* lowly *ou* humble birth.
obscurantisme [ɔpskyʀɑ̃tism(ə)] *nm* obscurantism.
obscurantiste [ɔpskyʀɑ̃tist(ə)] *adj, nmf* obscurantist.
obscurcir [ɔpskyʀsiʀ] (2) **1** *vt* **(a)** (*rendre obscur*) to darken. **ce tapis obscurcit la pièce** this carpet makes the room (look) dark *ou* darkens the room; **des nuages obscurcissent le ciel** clouds darken the sky.
(b) (*rendre inintelligible*) to obscure. **ce critique aime ~ les choses les plus simples** this critic likes to obscure *ou* cloud the simplest issues; **cela obscurcit encore plus l'énigme** that deepens the mystery even more; **le vin obscurcit les idées** wine muddles one's brain.
2 s'obscurcir *vpr* **(a)** *[ciel]* to darken, grow dark; *[temps, jour]* to grow dark.
(b) *[style]* to become obscure; *[esprit]* to become confused; *[vue]* to grow dim.
obscurcissement [ɔpskyʀsismɑ̃] *nm* (*V* **obscurcir, s'obscurcir**) darkening; obscuring; confusing; dimming.
obscurément [ɔpskyʀemɑ̃] *adv* obscurely. **il sentait ~ que** he felt in an obscure *ou* a vague (sort of) way that, he felt obscurely that.
obscurité [ɔpskyʀite] *nf* **(a)** (*V* **obscur**) darkness; obscurity. (*lit*) **dans l'~** in the dark, in darkness; (*fig*) **vivre/travailler dans l'~** to live/work in obscurity; **il a laissé cet aspect du problème dans l'~** he did not cast *ou* throw any light on that aspect of the problem, he passed over *ou* neglected that aspect of the problem.
(b) (*littér: passage peu clair*) obscurity.
obsédant, e [ɔpsedɑ̃, ɑ̃t] *adj musique, souvenir* haunting, obsessive; *question, idée* obsessive.
obsédé, e [ɔpsede] (*ptp de* **obséder**) *nm,f* obsessive. (*Psych, hum*) **un ~ (sexuel)** a sex maniac; (*hum*) **un ~ du tennis/de l'alpinisme** a tennis/climbing fanatic.
obséder [ɔpsede] (6) *vt* **(a)** (*obnubiler*) to haunt, obsess. **le remords l'obsédait** he was haunted *ou* obsessed by remorse; **être obsédé par** *souvenir, peur* to be haunted *ou* obsessed by; *idée, problème* to be obsessed with *ou* by; (*hum*) **il est obsédé** (*sexuellement*) he's obsessed, he's got a one-track mind (*hum*).
(b) (*littér: importuner*) **~ qn de ses assiduités** to pester *ou* importune sb with one's attentions.
obsèques [ɔpsɛk] *nfpl* funeral. **~ civiles/religieuses/nationales** civil/religious/state funeral.
obséquieusement [ɔpsekjøzmɑ̃] *adv* obsequiously.
obséquieux, -euse [ɔpsekjø, øz] *adj* obsequious.
obséquiosité [ɔpsekjozite] *nf* obsequiousness.
observable [ɔpsɛʀvabl(ə)] *adj* observable.
observance [ɔpsɛʀvɑ̃s] *nf* observance.
observateur, -trice [ɔpsɛʀvatœʀ, tʀis] **1** *adj personne, esprit, regard* observant, perceptive. **2** *nm,f* observer. **avoir des talents d'~** to have a talent for observation.
observation [ɔpsɛʀvɑsjɔ̃] *nf* **(a)** (*obéissance*) *[règle]* observance.
(b) (*examen, surveillance*) observation. (*Méd*) **être/mettre en ~** to be/put under observation; (*Mil*) **~ aérienne** aerial observation; (*Sport*) **round/set d'~** round/set in which one plays a guarded *ou* a wait-and-see game; *V* **poste**[2].
(c) (*chose observée*) *[savant, auteur]* observation. **il consignait ses ~s dans son carnet** he noted down his observations *ou* what he had observed in his notebook.
(d) (*remarque*) observation, remark; (*objection*) remark; (*reproche*) reproof. **il fit quelques ~s judicieuses** he made one or two judicious remarks *ou* observations; **je lui en fis l'~** I pointed it out to him; **ce film appelle quelques ~s** this film calls for some comment; **pas d'~s je vous prie** no remarks please; **faire une ~ à qn** to reprove sb.
observatoire [ɔpsɛʀvatwaʀ] *nm* **(a)** (*Astron*) observatory.
(b) (*Mil, gén: lieu*) observation *ou* look-out post.
observer [ɔpsɛʀve] (1) **1** *vt* **(a)** (*gén: regarder*) to observe, watch; *adversaire, proie* to watch; (*Sci*) *phénomène, réaction* to observe; (*au microscope*) to examine. **les invités s'observaient avec hostilité** the guests examined *ou* observed each other hostilely; **se sentant observée, ella se retourna** she felt she was being watched *ou* observed so she turned round; **il ne dit pas grand-chose mais il observe** he doesn't say much but he observes what goes on around him *ou* he watches keenly what goes on around him.
(b) (*contrôler*) **~ ses manières/ses gestes** to be mindful of *ou* to watch one's manners/one's gestures.
(c) (*remarquer*) to notice, observe. **elle n'observe jamais rien** she never notices anything.
(d) faire ~ que to point out *ou* remark *ou* observe that; **faire ~ un détail à qn** to point out a detail to sb, bring a detail to sb's attention; **je vous ferai ~ que vous n'avez pas le droit de fumer ici** I should like to *ou* I must point out (to you) that you're not allowed to smoke here.
(e) (*respecter*) *règlement* to observe, abide by; *fête, jeûne* to keep, observe; *coutume* to observe.

(f) (*littér*) *attitude, maintien* to keep (up), maintain.

2 s'observer *vpr* (*surveiller sa tenue, son langage*) to keep a check on o.s., be careful of one's behaviour. **il ne s'observe pas assez en public** he's not careful enough of his behaviour in public, he doesn't keep sufficient check on himself in public.

obsession [ɔpsesjɔ̃] *nf* obsession. **il avait l'~ de la mort/l'argent** he had an obsession with death/money.

obsessionnel, -elle [ɔpsesjɔnɛl] *adj* obsessional.

obsidienne [ɔpsidjɛn] *nf* obsidian, volcanic glass.

obstacle [ɔpstakl(ə)] *nm* (*lit*) obstacle; (*lit, fig*) obstacle, hurdle; (*Équitation*) jump, fence. **course d'~s** obstacle race; **faire ~ à la lumière** to block (out) *ou* obstruct the light; (*fig*) **faire ~ à un projet** to hinder a plan, put obstacles *ou* an obstacle in the way of a plan; **tourner l'~** (*Équitation*) to go round *ou* outside the jump; (*fig*) to get round the obstacle *ou* difficulty; (*lit, fig*) **progresser sans rencontrer d'~s** to make progress without meeting any obstacles *ou* hitches.

obstétrical, e, *mpl* **-aux** [ɔpstetʀikal, o] *adj* obstetric(al).

obstétrique [ɔpstetʀik] **1** *adj* obstetric(al). **clinique ~** obstetric clinic. **2** *nf* obstetrics (*sg*).

obstination [ɔpstinɑsjɔ̃] *nf* [*personne, caractère*] obstinacy, stubbornness. **~ à faire** obstinate *ou* stubborn determination to do; **son ~ au refus** his persistency in refusing, his persistent refusal.

obstiné, e [ɔpstine] (*ptp de* **s'obstiner**) *adj personne, caractère* obstinate, stubborn, unyielding, mulish (*péj*); *efforts, résistance* obstinate, dogged, persistent; *travail, demandes* persistent, obstinate; (*fig*) *brouillard, pluie, malchance* persistent, unyielding, relentless.

obstinément [ɔpstinemɑ̃] *adv* (*V* **obstiné**) obstinately; stubbornly; doggedly; persistently; relentlessly.

obstiner (s') [ɔpstine] (1) *vpr* to insist, dig one's heels in (*fig*). **s'~ sur un problème** to keep working *ou* labour away stubbornly at a problem; **s'~ dans une opinion** to cling stubbornly *ou* doggedly to an opinion; **s'~ à faire** to persist obstinately *ou* stubbornly in doing, obstinately *ou* stubbornly insist on doing; **s'~ au silence** to remain obstinately silent, maintain an obstinate *ou* a stubborn silence.

obstruction [ɔpstʀyksjɔ̃] *nf* **(a)** (*U: V* **obstruer**) obstruction, blockage.

(b) (*tactique*) obstruction. **faire de l'~** (*Pol*) to obstruct (the passage of) legislation; (*gén*) to use obstructive tactics, be obstructive; (*Ftbl*) to obstruct.

obstructionnisme [ɔpstʀyksjɔnism(ə)] *nm* obstructionism (*Brit*), filibustering (*US*).

obstructionniste [ɔpstʀyksjɔnist(ə)] **1** *adj* obstructionist (*Brit*), filibustering (*épith*) (*US*). **2** *nmf* obstructionist (*Brit*), filibuster (*US*).

obstruer [ɔpstʀye] (1) **1** *vt passage, circulation, artère* to obstruct, block. **~ la vue/le passage** to block *ou* obstruct the view/the way. **2 s'obstruer** *vpr* [*passage*] to get blocked up; [*artère*] to become blocked.

obtempérer [ɔptɑ̃peʀe] (6) **obtempérer à** *vt indir* to obey, comply with. **il refusa d'~** he refused to comply *ou* obey.

obtenir [ɔptəniʀ] (22) *vt* **(a)** *permission, explication, diplôme* to obtain, get. **~ satisfaction** to obtain satisfaction; **~ la main de qn** to gain *ou* win sb's hand; **je peux vous ~ ce livre rapidement** I can get you this book promptly, I can obtain this book promptly for you; **il m'a fait ~** *ou* **il m'a obtenu de l'avancement** he got promotion for me, he got me promoted; **il obtint de lui parler** he was (finally) allowed to speak to him; **elle a obtenu qu'il paie** she got him to pay up, she managed to make him pay up; **j'ai obtenu de lui qu'il ne dise rien** I managed to induce him *ou* to get him to agree not to say anything.

(b) *résultat, température* to achieve, obtain; *total* to reach, arrive at. **~ un corps à l'état gazeux** to obtain a body in the gaseous state; **~ un succès aux élections** to obtain *ou* achieve success in the elections; **cette couleur s'obtient par un mélange** this colour is obtained through *ou* by mixing; **en additionnant ces quantités, on obtient 2.000** when you add these amounts together you arrive at *ou* get 2,000.

obtention [ɔptɑ̃sjɔ̃] *nf* (*V* **obtenir**) obtaining; achievement. **pour l'~ du visa** to obtain the visa.

obturateur, -trice [ɔptyʀatœʀ, tʀis] **1** *adj* (*Tech*) *plaque* obturating; *membrane, muscle* obturator (*épith*). **2** *nm* **(a)** (*Phot*) shutter. **(b)** (*Tech*) obturator; [*fusil*] gas check.

obturation [ɔptyʀɑsjɔ̃] *nf* **(a)** (*V* **obturer**) closing (up), sealing; filling. **faire une ~ (dentaire)** to fill a tooth, do a filling. **(b)** (*Phot*) **vitesse d'~** shutter speed.

obturer [ɔptyʀe] (1) *vt conduit, ouverture* to close (up), seal; *dent* to fill.

obtus, e [ɔpty, yz] *adj* (*Math*) *angle* obtuse; (*fig: stupide*) dull-witted, obtuse.

obus [ɔby] *nm* shell. **~ explosif** high-explosive shell; **~ incendiaire** incendiary *ou* fire bomb; **~ de mortier** mortar shell; **~ perforant** armour-piercing shell; *V* **éclat, trou.**

obusier [ɔbyzje] *nm* howitzer. **~ de campagne** field howitzer.

obvier [ɔbvje] (7) **obvier à** *vt indir danger, mal* to take precautions against, obviate (*frm*); *inconvénient* to obviate (*frm*).

oc [ɔk] *nm V* **langue.**

ocarina [ɔkaʀina] *nm* ocarina.

occase‡ [ɔkɑz] *nf* (*abrév de* **occasion**) bargain, snip*.

occasion [ɔkɑzjɔ̃] *nf* **(a)** (*circonstance*) occasion; (*conjoncture favorable*) opportunity, chance. **avoir l'~ de faire** to have the *ou* a chance *ou* the *ou* an opportunity of doing *ou* to do; **sauter sur*** *ou* **saisir l'~** to jump at *ou* seize *ou* grab* the opportunity *ou* chance; **laisser échapper** *ou* **passer l'~** to let the opportunity pass one by *ou* slip; (*iro*) **tu as manqué une belle ~ de te taire** you should have held your tongue, why couldn't you have kept quiet *ou* kept your mouth shut; **cela a été l'~ d'une grande discussion** it gave rise to *ou* occasioned a great discussion; **à l'~ de** on the occasion of; **à cette ~** on that occasion; **si l'~ se présente** if the opportunity arises, should the opportunity arise; **dans/pour les grandes ~s** on/for important *ou* special occasions; **la bouteille/la robe des grandes ~s** the bottle put by/the dress kept for special *ou* great occasions.

(b) (*Comm*) secondhand buy, bargain; (*: *acquisition très avantageuse*) bargain, snip*. **(le marché de) l'~** the secondhand market; **faire le neuf et l'~** to deal in new and secondhand goods; **d'~** (*adj, adv*) secondhand.

(c) (*loc*) **à l'~** sometimes, on occasions; **à l'~ venez dîner** come and have dinner some time; **à la première ~** at the earliest *ou* first opportunity; **d'~** *amitié, rencontre* casual; (*frm*) **passer par ~** to chance *ou* pass by, happen to be passing by; (*Prov*) **l'~ fait le larron** opportunity makes the thief.

occasionnel, -elle [ɔkazjɔnɛl] *adj* **(a)** (*non régulier*) *rencontres, disputes* occasional (*épith*); *client, visiteur* casual, occasional (*épith*); (*fortuit*) *incidents, rencontre* chance (*épith*). **(b)** (*Philos*) occasional.

occasionnellement [ɔkazjɔnɛlmɑ̃] *adv* occasionally, from time to time.

occasionner [ɔkazjɔne] (1) *vt frais, accident, dérangement* to cause, bring about. **en espérant ne pas vous ~ trop de dérangement** hoping not to put you to *ou* to cause you a great deal of trouble; **cet accident va m'~ beaucoup de frais** this accident is going to involve me in *ou* to cause me a great deal of expense.

occident [ɔksidɑ̃] *nm* (*littér: ouest*) west. **l'O~** the West, the Occident (*littér*); *V* **empire.**

occidental, e, *mpl* **-aux** [ɔksidɑ̃tal, o] **1** *adj* (*littér: d'ouest*) western; (*Pol*) *pays, peuple* Western, Occidental (*littér*). **les Indes ~es** the West Indies. **2** *nm,f*: **O~(e)** Westerner, Occidental (*littér*).

occidentaliser [ɔksidɑ̃talize] (1) *vt* to westernize.

occipital, e, *mpl* **-aux** [ɔksipital, o] **1** *adj* occipital. **2** *nm* occipital bone.

occiput [ɔksipyt] *nm* back of the head, occiput (*T*).

occire [ɔksiʀ] *vt* (†† *ou hum*) to slay.

occitan, e [ɔksitɑ̃, an] *adj littérature* of the langue d'oc, of Provençal French.

occlure [ɔklyʀ] (35) *vt* (*Chim, Méd*) to occlude.

occlusif, -ive [ɔklyzif, iv] *adj, nf* (*Ling*) **(consonne) ~ive** occlusive.

occlusion [ɔklyzjɔ̃] *nf* (*Ling, Méd, Mét, Tech*) occlusion. (*Méd*) **~ intestinale** obstruction of the bowels *ou* intestines, ileus (*T*).

occultation [ɔkyltɑsjɔ̃] *nf* occultation.

occulte [ɔkylt(ə)] *adj* **(a)** (*surnaturel*) supernatural, occult. **les sciences ~s** the occult, the occult sciences. **(b)** (*littér: secret*) hidden, secret, occult.

occulter [ɔkylte] (1) *vt* (*Astron, Tech*) to occult; (*fig*) to overshadow.

occultisme [ɔkyltism(ə)] *nm* occultism.

occultiste [ɔkyltist(ə)] *adj, nmf* occultist.

occupant, e [ɔkypɑ̃, ɑ̃t] **1** *adj* (*Pol*) *autorité, puissance* occupying. **l'armée ~e** the army of occupation.

2 *nm,f* [*maison*] occupant, occupier; [*place, compartiment, voiture*] occupant. (*gén, Jur*) **le premier ~** the first occupier.

3 *nm*: **l'~** the occupying forces.

occupation [ɔkypɑsjɔ̃] *nf* **(a)** (*Mil, Pol*) occupation. **les forces/l'armée d'~** the forces/army of occupation, the occupying forces/army; **durant l'~** during the Occupation.

(b) (*Jur*) [*logement*] occupancy, occupation.

(c) (*passe-temps*) occupation; (*emploi*) occupation, job. **vaquer à ses ~s** to go about one's business, attend to one's affairs; **une ~ fixe/temporaire** a permanent/temporary job *ou* occupation.

occupé, e [ɔkype] (*ptp de* **occuper**) *adj* **(a)** (*affairé*) busy; (*non disponible*) busy, engaged. **je suis très ~ en ce moment** I'm very busy at present; **il ne peut pas vous recevoir, il est ~** he cannot see you as he is busy *ou* engaged.

(b) *ligne téléphonique* engaged (*Brit*) (*attrib*), busy (*US*) (*attrib*); *toilettes* engaged (*attrib*); *places, sièges* taken (*attrib*). **c'est ~** it's engaged; it's taken.

(c) (*Mil, Pol*) *zone, usine* occupied.

occuper [ɔkype] (1) **1** *vt* **(a)** *endroit, appartement* to occupy; *place, surface* to occupy, take up. **le bureau occupait le coin de la pièce** the desk stood in *ou* occupied the corner of the room; **leurs bureaux occupent tout l'étage** their offices take up *ou* occupy the whole floor; **le piano occupe très peu/trop de place** the piano takes up very little/too much room; **l'appartement qu'ils occupent est trop exigu** the flat they are living in *ou* occupying is too small.

(b) *moment, période* (*prendre*) to occupy, fill, take up; (*faire passer*) to occupy, spend, employ. **cette besogne occupait le reste de la journée** this task took (up) *ou* occupied the rest of the day; **la lecture occupe une trop petite/très grande part de mon temps** reading takes up *ou* fills *ou* occupies far too little/a great deal of my time; **comment ~ ses loisirs?** how should one spend *ou* occupy *ou* employ one's free time?

(c) *poste, fonction* to hold, occupy.

(d) (*absorber*) to occupy; (*employer*) *main d'œuvre* to employ. **mon travail m'occupe beaucoup** my work keeps me very busy; **la ganterie occupait naguère un millier d'ouvriers dans cette région** the glove industry used to employ *ou* give employment to about a thousand workers in this area.

(e) (*Mil, Pol*) (*envahir*) to take over, occupy; (*être maître de*) to occupy. **ils ont occupé tout le pays/l'immeuble** they took over *ou* occupied the whole country/the whole building; **les forces qui occupaient le pays** the forces occupying the country.

2 s'occuper *vpr* **(a) s'~ de qch** (*s'attaquer à*) to deal with sth, take care *ou* charge of sth; (*être chargé de*) to be in charge of sth, be dealing with *ou* taking care of sth; (*s'intéresser à*) to take an interest in sth, interest o.s. in sth; **je vais m'~ de ce problème/cette affaire** I'll deal with *ou* take care of this problem/ this matter; **c'est lui qui s'occupe de cette affaire** he's the one in charge of *ou* who is dealing with this matter; **il s'occupe de vous trouver un emploi** he is undertaking to find you a job, he'll see about finding you a job; **je vais m'~ de rassembler les documents nécessaires** I'll set about *ou* see about gathering (together) the necessary documents; **il s'occupe un peu de politique** he takes a bit of an interest *ou* he dabbles a bit in politics; **je m'occupe de tout** I'll see to everything, I'll take care of everything; **il veut s'~ de trop de choses à la fois** he tries to take on *ou* to do too many things at once; **occupe-toi de tes affaires* *ou* oignons*** mind your own business; **t'occupe (pas)!‡** don't worry yourself*.

(b) s'~ de (*se charger de*) *enfants, malades* to take charge *ou* care of, look after; *client* to attend to; (*être responsable de*) *enfants, malades* to be in charge of, look after; **je vais m'~ des enfants** I'll take charge *ou* care of *ou* I'll look after the children; **qui s'occupe des malades?** who is in charge of *ou* looks after the patients?; **un instant et je m'occupe de vous** one moment and I'll attend to you *ou* and I'll be with you; **est-ce qu'on s'occupe de vous Madame?** is someone serving you?, are you being attended to? *ou* served?

(c) (*s'affairer*) to occupy o.s., keep o.s. busy. **s'~ à faire qch/à qch** to busy o.s. doing sth/with sth; **il a trouvé à s'~** he has found something to do *ou* to occupy his time *ou* to fill his time with; **il y a de quoi s'~** there is plenty to do *ou* to keep one busy *ou* occupied; **je ne sais pas à quoi m'~** I don't know what to do with myself *ou* how to keep myself busy *ou* occupied.

occurrence [ɔkyʀɑ̃s] *nf* **(a)** (*frm*) instance, case. **en cette/toute autre ~** in this/in any other instance; **en l'~** in this case; **en pareille ~** in such circumstances, in such a case; (*frm*) **suivant *ou* selon l'~** according to the circumstances. **(b)** (*Ling*) occurrence.

océan [ɔseɑ̃] *nm* (*lit*) ocean. (*comparé à la Méditerranée*) **l'O~** the Atlantic (Ocean); **un ~ de verdure/de sable** a sea of greenery/sand; **l'~ Arctique** the Arctic Ocean; **l'~ Atlantique** the Atlantic Ocean; **l'~ glacial** the polar sea; **l'~ Indien** the Indian Ocean; **l'~ Pacifique** the Pacific Ocean.

Océanie [ɔseani] *nf* Oceania.

océanique [ɔseanik] *adj* oceanic.

océanographe [ɔseanɔgʀaf] *nmf* oceanographer.

océanographie [ɔseanɔgʀafi] *nf* oceanography.

océanographique [ɔseanɔgʀafik] *adj* oceanographical.

ocelot [ɔslo] *nm* (*Zool*) ocelot; (*fourrure*) ocelot fur.

ocre [ɔkʀ(ə)] *nf, adj inv* ochre.

ocré, e [ɔkʀe] *adj* ochred.

ocreux, -euse [ɔkʀø, øz] *adj* (*littér*) ochreous.

octaèdre [ɔktaɛdʀ(ə)] **1** *adj* octahedral. **2** *nm* octahedron.

octaédrique [ɔktaedʀik] *adj* octahedral.

octane [ɔktan] *nm* octane; *V* **indice.**

octante [ɔktɑ̃t] *adj inv* (*dial*) eighty.

octave [ɔktav] *nf* **(a)** (*Mus*) octave. **jouer à l'~** to play an octave higher *ou* lower. **(b)** (*Escrime, Rel*) octave.

octobre [ɔktɔbʀ(ə)] *nm* October; *pour loc V* **septembre.**

octogénaire [ɔktɔʒenɛʀ] *adj, nmf* octogenarian.

octogonal, e, *mpl* **-aux** [ɔktɔgɔnal, o] *adj* octagonal, eight-sided.

octogone [ɔktɔgɔn] *nm* octagon.

octopode [ɔktɔpɔd] **1** *adj* (*Zool*) octopod. **2** *nm* octopod. **~s** Octopoda.

octosyllabe [ɔktɔsilab] **1** *adj* octosyllabic. **2** *nm* octosyllable.

octosyllabique [ɔktɔsilabik] *adj* octosyllabic.

octroi [ɔktʀwa] *nm* **(a)** (*V* **octroyer**) granting; bestowing. **(b)** (*Hist*) octroi, city toll.

octroyer [ɔktʀwaje] (8) **1** *vt* (*frm*) *charte* to grant (*à* to); *faveur, pardon* to bestow (*à* on, upon), grant (*à* to); *répit, permission* to grant (*à* to). **2 s'octroyer** *vpr répit, vacances* to treat o.s. to, grant o.s.

octuor [ɔktɥɔʀ] *nm* (*Mus*) octet.

oculaire [ɔkylɛʀ] **1** *adj* (*Anat*) ocular; *V* **globe, témoin. 2** *nm* (*Opt*) eyepiece, ocular (*T*).

oculiste [ɔkylist(ə)] *nmf* eye specialist, oculist.

odalisque [ɔdalisk(ə)] *nf* odalisque.

ode [ɔd] *nf* ode.

odeur [ɔdœʀ] *nf* **(a)** (*gén: bonne ou mauvaise*) smell, odour (*frm*); (*agréable: de fleurs etc*) fragrance, scent. **sans ~** odourless, which has no smell; **produit qui combat les (mauvaises) ~s** air freshener; **mauvaise ~** bad *ou* unpleasant smell; **~ suave/délicieuse** sweet/delicious smell *ou* scent; **à l'~ fétide** stinking, evil-smelling; **~ de brûlé/de moisi** smell of burning/of damp; **~ de renfermé** musty *ou* fusty smell; **avoir une bonne/une mauvaise ~** to smell nice/bad; *V* **argent.**

(b) (*loc*) **être en ~ de sainteté auprès de qn** to be in sb's good graces; **ne pas être en ~ de sainteté auprès de qn** not to be well looked upon by sb, be out of favour with sb; (*Rel*) **mourir en ~ de sainteté** to die in the odour of sanctity.

odieusement [ɔdjøzmɑ̃] *adv* (*V* **odieux**) hatefully; obnoxiously; odiously.

odieux, -euse [ɔdjø, øz] *adj* **(a)** (*infâme*) *personne, caractère, tâche* hateful, obnoxious, odious; *conduite* odious, obnoxious; *crime* heinous, odious. **la vie m'est ~euse** life is unbearable to me; **cette personne m'est ~euse** I cannot bear this person, I find this person (quite) unbearable.

(b) (*insupportable*) *gamin, élève* obnoxious, unbearable.

odontologie [ɔdɔ̃tɔlɔʒi] *nf* odontology.

odorant, e [ɔdɔʀɑ̃, ɑ̃t] *adj* sweet-smelling, odorous (*frm*).

odorat [ɔdɔʀa] *nm* (sense of) smell. **avoir l'~ fin** to have a keen sense of smell.

odoriférant, e [ɔdɔʀifeʀɑ̃, ɑ̃t] *adj* sweet-smelling, fragrant, odoriferous (*frm*).

odyssée [ɔdise] *nf* odyssey. (*littér*) **l'O~** the Odyssey.

œcuménique [ekymenik] *adj* oecumenical; *V* **concile.**

œcuménisme [ekymenism(ə)] *nm* oecumenicalism, oecumenism.

œcuméniste [ekymenist(ə)] *adj, nmf* oecumenist.

œdémateux, -euse [edematø, øz] *adj* oedematous, oedematose.

œdème [edɛm] *nm* oedema.

Oedipe [edip] *nm* Oedipus; *V* **complexe.**

œil [œj], *pl* **yeux** [jø] **1** *nm* **(a)** (*Anat*) eye. **avoir les yeux bleus/bridés** to have blue/slit eyes; **il a les yeux bleus** he has blue eyes, his eyes are blue; **aux yeux bleus** blue-eyed, with blue eyes; **aux grands yeux** wide-eyed, with big eyes; **des yeux de biche *ou* de gazelle** doe eyes; **avoir de bons/mauvais yeux** to have good/bad eyes *ou* eyesight; (*fig*) **les yeux lui sortaient de la tête** his eyes were (nearly) popping out of his head, his eyes were out on stalks* (*surtout Brit*); **je l'ai vu de mes (propres) yeux** I saw it with my own eyes; **à l'~ nu** with the naked eye; **avoir un ~ au beurre noir *ou* un ~ poché*** to have a black eye.

(b) (*fig: expression*) look. **il a un ~ malin/spirituel/méchant** there's a mischievous/humorous/malicious look in his eye; **il a l'~ vif** he has a lively look about him *ou* a lively expression; **il le regardait l'~ méchant *ou* d'un ~ méchant** he fixed him with a threatening stare *ou* look, he looked *ou* stared at him threateningly.

(c) (*fig: jugement*) **considérer *ou* voir qch d'un bon/mauvais ~** to look on *ou* view sth favourably/unfavourably, view sth in a favourable/unfavourable light; **considérer qch d'un ~ critique** to consider sth with a critical eye, look at sth critically; **il ne voit pas cela du même ~ qu'elle** he doesn't see *ou* view that in the same light as she does.

(d) (*fig: coup d'œil*) **avoir l'~ du spécialiste/du maître** to have a trained/an expert eye, have the eye of a specialist/an expert; **il a l'~** he has sharp *ou* keen eyes; **avoir l'~ américain** to have a quick eye; **risquer un ~ au dehors/par-dessus la barrière** to take a peep *ou* a quick look outside/over the fence, poke one's nose outside/over the fence; *V* **compas.**

(e) (*fig: regard*) **se consulter de l'~** to exchange glances, glance questioningly at one another; **attirer *ou* tirer l'~ (de qn)** to catch the eye (of sb); **sous l'~ (vigilant/inquiet) de** under the (watchful/anxious) eye *ou* gaze of; **ils jouaient sous l'~ de leur mère** they played under the watchful eye of their mother *ou* with their mother looking on; **faire qch aux yeux de tous** to do sth in full view of everyone; **sous les yeux de** before the very eyes of; **cela s'est passé devant *ou* sous nos yeux** it happened in front of *ou* before our very eyes; **vous avez l'article sous les yeux** you have the article there before you *ou* right in front of you *ou* your eyes; **couver/dévorer qn des yeux** to gaze devotedly/hungrily at sb, fix sb with a devoted/hungry look; **chercher qn des yeux** to glance *ou* look (a)round for sb; **suivre qn des yeux** to watch sb; **n'avoir d'yeux que pour qch/qn** to have eyes only for sth/sb, have eyes for nothing/nobody else but sth/sb.

(f) *[aiguille, marteau]* eye; (*Typ*) *[caractère]* (*pl* **œils**) face; *[fromage, pain]* eye, hole; *[pomme de terre]* eye; (*Mét*) *[cyclone]* eye; (*Bot: bourgeon*) bud; (*Naut: boucle*) eye, loop. **les yeux du bouillon** the globules *ou* droplets of fat in the stock.

(g) (*loc avec* **œil**) **à l'~*** (*gratuitement*) for nothing, for free*; **mon ~!*** (*je n'y crois pas*) my eye!*, my foot!*; (*je ne le donnerai pas*) nothing doing!*, not likely!*; **avoir l'~ à qch** to keep an eye on sth; **garder l'~ ouvert** to keep one's eyes open, stay on the alert; **avoir *ou* tenir qn à l'~** to keep a watch *ou* an eye on sb; **je vous ai à l'~!** I've got my eye on you!; **faire de l'~ à qn** to make eyes at sb, give sb the eye*; (*Prov*) **~ pour ~, dent pour dent** an eye for an eye, a tooth for a tooth; *V* **clin, coin, rincer** *etc.*

(h) (*loc avec* **yeux**) **à ses yeux, cela n'a aucune valeur** in his eyes that has no value; **faire *ou* ouvrir de grands yeux** to look surprised, stare in amazement; **coûter/payer les yeux de la tête** to cost/pay the earth *ou* a (small) fortune; (*fig*) **faire/acheter qch les yeux fermés** to do/buy sth with one's eyes closed *ou* shut; **il a les yeux plus grands que le ventre** *[affamé]* his eyes are bigger than his belly *ou* stomach; *[ambitieux]* he has bitten off more than he can chew; **voir avec *ou* avoir les yeux de la foi** to see with the eyes of a believer; **ne pas avoir les yeux dans sa poche** to be very observant, keep one's eyes skinned* (*Brit*); **il n'a pas les yeux en face des trous** he's half asleep, he's not thinking straight; **faire des yeux de velours à qn, faire les yeux doux à qn** to make sheep's eyes at sb; **faire *ou* ouvrir des yeux comme des soucoupes** to stare with eyes like saucers; **faire *ou* ouvrir des yeux ronds** to stare round-eyed *ou* wide-eyed; **avoir les yeux battus** to have blue rings under one's eyes.

2: œil-de-bœuf *nm, pl* **œils-de-bœuf** bull's-eye (window), œil-de-bœuf; **œil cathodique** cathode eye, magic eye; (*Minér*) **œil-de-chat** *nm, pl* **œils-de-chat** tiger's eye; **œil magique**† = **œil cathodique**; **œil-de-perdrix** *nm, pl* **œils-de-perdrix** (*cor au pied*) soft corn; (*Naut*) **œil-de-pie** *nm, pl* **œils-de-pie** eyelet; **œil de verre** glass eye.

œillade [œjad] *nf* wink. **faire des ~s à qn** to make eyes at sb, give sb the eye*; **jeter *ou* décocher une ~ à qn** to wink at sb, give sb a wink.

œillère [œjɛʀ] *nf* **(a) ~s** *[cheval]* blinkers; (*fig péj*) **avoir des ~s** to wear blinkers, be blinkered. **(b)** (*Méd*) eyebath, eyecup.

œillet [œjɛ] *nm* **(a)** (*fleur*) carnation. **~ d'Inde** French marigold. **(b)** (*petit trou, bordure*) eyelet.

œnologie [enɔlɔʒi] *nf* oenology.

œnologue [enɔlɔg] nmf oenologist.
œsophagien, -ienne [ezɔfaʒjɛ̃, jɛn] adj, œsophagique [ezɔfaʒik] adj oesophageal.
œstrogène [østʀɔʒɛn] nm oestrogen.
œuf [œf], pl ~s [ø] 1 nm (a) (Bio, Culin) egg. ~ du jour/frais new-laid/fresh egg; en (forme d')~ egg-shaped; ~s de marbre/de faïence marble/china eggs; V blanc, jaune.
(b) (imbécile) quel ~ ce type! what a blockhead* this fellow is!
(c) (loc) étouffer ou écraser ou détruire qch dans l'~ to nip sth in the bud; mettre tous ses ~s dans le même panier to put all one's eggs in one basket; c'est comme l'~ de Colomb (fallait y penser)! it's simple when you know how!, it's easy once you think of it!; va te faire cuire un ~!‡ (go and) take a running jump!*, get stuffed!‡; V marcher, omelette.
2: œufs brouillés scrambled eggs; œuf en chocolat chocolate egg; œuf à la coque (soft-)boiled egg; œuf dur hard-boiled egg; œuf mollet soft-boiled egg; œufs à la ou en neige œufs à la neige, floating islands; œuf de Pâques Easter egg; œuf sur le plat ou au plat fried egg; œuf poché poached egg; œuf à repriser darning egg.
œuvre [œvʀ(ə)] 1 nf (a) (livre, tableau etc) work; (production artistique ou littéraire) works. c'est une ~ de jeunesse it's an early work; toute l'~ de Picasso Picasso's entire works; les ~s complètes/choisies de Victor Hugo the complete/selected works of Victor Hugo; l'~ romanesque de Balzac the novels of Balzac, Balzac's works of fiction; V chef[1].
(b) (tâche) undertaking, task; (travail achevé) work. ce sera une ~ de longue haleine it will be a long-term task ou undertaking; admirant leur ~ admiring their work; la satisfaction de l'~ accomplie the satisfaction of seeing the ou a task complete ou well done; ce beau gâchis, c'est l'~ des enfants this fine mess is the children's doing ou work; ces formations sont l'~ du vent et de l'eau these formations are the work of wind and water; V main, maître, pied.
(c) (acte) ~(s) deed, work; être jugé selon ses ~s to be judged by one's works ou deeds; (frm, hum) enceinte de ses ~s with child by him, bearing his child; (bonnes) ~s good ou charitable works; (littér) faire ~ pie to do a pious deed; aide-le, ce sera une bonne ~ help him, that will be a kind act ou an act of kindness; V fils.
(d) (organisation) ~ (de bienfaisance ou de charité) charitable organization, charity; les ~s charity, charities.
(e) (loc) être/se mettre à l'~ to be at/get down to work; voir qn à l'~ (lit) to see sb at work; (iro) to see sb in action; faire ~ utile to do worthwhile ou valuable work; faire ~ de pionnier/médiateur to act as a pioneer/mediator; la mort avait fait son ~ death had (already) claimed its own; le feu avait fait son ~ the fire had wrought its havoc; faire ~ durable to create a work of lasting significance ou importance; mettre en ~ moyens to implement, make use of, bring into play; il avait tout mis en ~ pour éviter la dévaluation/pour les aider he had done everything possible ou had taken all possible steps to avoid devaluation/to help them; la mise en ~ d'importants moyens the implementation ou the bringing into play of considerable resources; (Prov) à l'~ on ou c'est à l'~ qu'on connaît l'ouvrier a man is judged ou known by his works ou by the work he does.
2 nm (littér) l'~ gravé/sculpté de Picasso the etchings/sculptures of Picasso; V grand, gros.
3: (lit, fig) œuvre d'art work of art; (Naut) œuvres mortes deadwork; œuvres vives (Naut) quickwork; (fig littér) vitals.
œuvrer [œvʀe] (1) vi (littér) to work.
off [ɔf] adj inv (Ciné) voix, son off. dire qch en voix ~ to say sth in a voice off.
offensant, e [ɔfɑ̃sɑ̃, ɑ̃t] adj insulting, offensive.
offense [ɔfɑ̃s] nf (a) (frm: affront) insult. faire ~ à to offend, insult; (hum) il n'y a pas d'~* no offence (taken); (frm) soit dit sans ~ let this not be taken amiss.
(b) (Rel: péché) transgression, trespass, offence. pardonnez-nous nos ~s forgive us our trespasses; ~ à ou envers chef d'État libel against; Dieu offence against.
offensé, e [ɔfɑ̃se] (ptp de offenser) 1 adj offended, hurt. 2 nm,f offended ou injured party.
offenser [ɔfɑ̃se] (1) 1 vt (a) personne to offend, hurt (the feelings of), give offence to. je n'ai pas voulu vous ~ I didn't mean to give offence (to you) ou to offend you; ~ Dieu to offend ou trespass against God.
(b) (littér) sentiments, souvenir to offend, insult; personne, bon goût to offend; règles, principes to offend against.
2 s'offenser vpr to take offence (de qch at sth).
offenseur [ɔfɑ̃sœʀ] nm offender.
offensif, -ive [ɔfɑ̃sif, iv] 1 adj (Mil, Pol) offensive.
2 offensive nf offensive. prendre l'~ive to take the offensive; passer à l'~ive to go into the attack ou offensive; (fig) l'~ive de l'hiver/du froid the onslaught of winter/of the cold.
offertoire [ɔfɛʀtwaʀ] nm (Rel) offertory.
office [ɔfis] 1 nm (a) (littér: tâche) duties, office; (Hist) charge, office; (Admin) office. remplir l'~ de directeur/chauffeur to hold the office ou post of manager/chauffeur; ~ ministériel ministerial office; ~ d'avoué office of solicitor.
(b) (usage) faire ~ de to act ou serve as; faire ~ de chauffeur to act as (a) chauffeur; remplir son ~ to fulfil its function, do its job*.
(c) (bureau) bureau, agency. ~ de publicité advertising agency ou organization; ~ du tourisme/des changes tourist/foreign exchange bureau; ~ de commerce trade organization.
(d) (Rel) (messe) (church) service. (prières) l'~ (divin) the divine office; l'~ des morts the service for the dead; aller à/manquer l'~ to go to/miss church ou the church service.
(e) (loc) d'~: être nommé/mis à la retraite d'~ to be appointed/retired automatically ou as a matter of course; faire qch d'~ (Admin) to do sth automatically; (gén) to do sth as a matter of course ou automatically; avocat/expert d'~ (officially) appointed lawyer/expert.
(f) (littér: service) office; (Pol) bons ~s good offices.
2 nm ou nf (cuisine) pantry, staff dining quarters.
officialisation [ɔfisjalizasjɔ̃] nf officializing, officialization.
officialiser [ɔfisjalize] (1) vt to make official, officialize.
officiant, e [ɔfisjɑ̃, ɑ̃t] (Rel) 1 adj m, nm: (prêtre) ~ officiant, officiating priest.
2 adj f, nf (sœur) ~e officiating sister.
officiel, -elle [ɔfisjɛl] 1 adj (gén) official. (c'est) ~!* it's no joke!, it's for sure!* 2 nm, f official.
officiellement [ɔfisjɛlmɑ̃] adv officially.
officier[1] [ɔfisje] nm officer. ~ subalterne/supérieur/général junior/field/general officer; ~ de marine naval officer; ~ de police ≃ police officer; ~ ministériel member of the legal profession; ~ de l'état civil (mayor considered in his capacity as) registrar.
officier[2] [ɔfisje] (7) vi (Rel, hum) to officiate.
officieusement [ɔfisjøzmɑ̃] adv unofficially.
officieux, -euse [ɔfisjø, øz] adj unofficial. à titre ~ unofficially, in an unofficial capacity.
officinal, e, mpl -aux [ɔfisinal, o] adj plante medicinal.
officine [ɔfisin] nf [pharmacie] dispensary; (Admin, Jur: pharmacie) pharmacy; (péj: repaire) headquarters, agency.
offrande [ɔfʀɑ̃d] nf (don) offering. (Rel: cérémonie) l'~ the offertory.
offrant [ɔfʀɑ̃] nm: au plus ~ to the highest bidder; (petites annonces) 'au plus ~' 'highest offer secures sale'.
offre [ɔfʀ(ə)] nf (gén) offer; (aux enchères) bid; (Admin: soumission) tender. (Écon) l'~ et la demande supply and demand; appel d'~s invitation to tender; as-tu regardé les ~s d'emploi? have you checked the situations vacant column? ou the job ads?*; il y avait plusieurs ~s d'emploi pour des ingénieurs there were several jobs advertised for engineers, there were several advertisements ou ads* for engineering jobs; (Fin) ~ publique d'achat takeover bid; (frm) ~(s) de service offer of service; (Pol) ~s de paix peace overtures.
offrir [ɔfʀiʀ] (18) 1 vt (a) cadeau (donner) to give (à to); (acheter) to buy (à for). c'est pour ~? is it for a present? ou a gift?; la joie d'~ the joy of giving; il lui a offert un bracelet he gave her a bracelet, he presented her with a bracelet; il nous a offert à boire (chez lui) he gave us a drink; (au café) he bought ou stood us a drink.
(b) (proposer) aide, marchandise, excuse to offer; sacrifice to offer up; choix, possibilité to offer, give; démission to tender, offer. puis-je vous ~ à boire/une cigarette? can I offer you a drink/a cigarette?; ~ l'hospitalité à qn to offer sb hospitality; ~ le mariage à qn to offer to marry sb; il m'offrit un fauteuil he offered me a chair; ~ son bras à qn to offer sb one's arm; ~ de faire to offer to do; combien m'en offrez-vous? how much will you give me for it? ou will you offer for it?; ~ sa vie à la patrie/à Dieu to offer up one's life to the homeland/to God.
(c) (présenter) spectacle, image to present, offer; vue to offer. ~ son corps aux regards to reveal ou expose one's body to the world at large; ~ sa poitrine aux balles to proffer (frm) ou present one's chest to the bullets; le paysage n'offrait rien de particulier the countryside had no particular features.
(d) (apporter) avantage, inconvénient to offer, present; exemple, explication to provide, afford (frm); analogie to offer, have; échappatoire to offer. cela n'offre rien de condamnable there is nothing blameworthy about that; ~ de la résistance [coffre-fort] to resist, offer resistance; [personne] to put up ou offer resistance (à to).
2 s'offrir vpr (a) [femme] to offer o.s. s'~ à Dieu to offer o.s. (up) to God; s'~ aux regards [personne] to expose ou reveal o.s. to the public gaze; [spectacle] to present itself to the gaze, meet ou greet our (ou your etc) eyes; s'~ aux coups to let the blows rain down on one, submit to the blows.
(b) repas, vacances to treat o.s. to; disque to buy o.s., treat o.s. to.
(c) s'~ à faire qch to offer to do sth.
offset [ɔfsɛt] nm, adj inv (Typ) offset.
offusquer [ɔfyske] (1) 1 vt to offend. ses manières offusquent beaucoup de gens his manners offend many people. 2 s'offusquer vpr to take offence ou umbrage (de at), be offended (de at, by).
ogival, e, mpl -aux [ɔʒival, o] adj voûte rib (épith), ogival (T); arc pointed, ogival (T); architecture, art gothic (medieval).
ogive [ɔʒiv] nf (a) (Archit) diagonal rib. croisée d'~s intersection of the ribs (of a vault); arc d'~s pointed ou equilateral arch; voûte en ~ rib vault; arc en ~ lancet arch.
(b) (Mil) [fusée etc] nose cone. ~ nucléaire nuclear warhead.
ogre [ɔgʀ(ə)] nm ogre. manger comme un ~, être un vrai ~ to eat like a horse.
ogresse [ɔgʀɛs] nf ogress. elle a un appétit d'~ she's got an appetite like a horse.
oh [o] excl oh! pousser des ~ to exclaim.
ohé [oe] excl: ~ du bateau! ahoy (there)!, hey (there)!, hullo (there)!
ohm [om] nm ohm.
ohmmètre [ommɛtʀ(ə)] nm ohmmeter.
oie [wa] nf (Zool) goose; (péj: niaise) silly goose. ~ sauvage wild goose; (péj) ~ blanche innocent young thing; V caca, jeu, patte d'oie.
oignon [ɔɲɔ̃] nm (légume) onion; [tulipe etc] bulb; (Méd) bunion; (montre) turnip watch. petits ~s pickling onions; aux petits ~s (Culin) with (pickling) onions; (fig) first-rate, tophole*; ce n'est pas ou ce ne sont pas mes ~s‡ it's no business of

mine, it's nothing to do with me; **occupe-toi de tes ~s!** mind your own business; *V* **pelure, rang.**

oïl [ɔjl] *nm V* **langue.**

oindre [wɛ̃dʀ(ə)] (49) *vt* to anoint.

oint, e [wɛ̃, wɛ̃t] (*ptp de* **oindre**) *adj* anointed.

oiseau, *pl* **~x** [wazo] **1** *nm* (*Zool*) bird; (*gén péj: personne*) customer*, fellow*. **être comme l'~ sur la branche** to be here today and gone tomorrow, be very unsettled (*in a place*); **trouver l'~ rare** to find the man (*ou* woman) in a million; (*fig*) **l'~ s'est envolé** the bird has flown; **drôle d'~** queer fish* (*Brit*) *ou* bird* *ou* customer*; *V* **appétit, cervelle, petit.**

2: oiseau chanteur songbird; **oiseau des îles** exotic bird; **oiseau-lyre** *nm, pl* **oiseaux-lyres** lyrebird; (*fig*) **oiseau de malheur** *ou* **de mauvais augure** bird of ill omen; **oiseau-mouche** *nm, pl* **oiseaux-mouches** hummingbird; **oiseau de nuit** bird of the night, night-bird; **oiseau de paradis** bird of paradise; **oiseau de proie** bird of prey.

oiseleur [wazlœʀ] *nm* bird-catcher.

oiselier, -ière [wazəlje, jɛʀ] *nm,f* bird-seller.

oisellerie [wazɛlʀi] *nf* (*magasin*) birdshop; (*commerce*) bird-selling.

oiseux, -euse [wazø, øz] *adj dispute, digression, commentaire* pointless; *propos* idle (*épith*), pointless; *question* trivial, trifling.

oisif, -ive [wazif, iv] **1** *adj* idle. **une vie ~ive** a life of leisure, an idle life. **2** *nm,f* man (*ou* woman) of leisure. **les ~s** the idle.

oisillon [wazijɔ̃] *nm* young bird, fledgeling.

oisivement [wazivmɑ̃] *adv* idly. **vivre ~** to live a life of leisure.

oisiveté [wazivte] *nf* idleness. (*Prov*) **l'~ est la mère de tous les vices** idleness is the root of all evil; **~ forcée** forced inactivity.

oison [wazɔ̃] *nm* gosling.

O.K.* [okɛ] *excl* O.K.!*, right-oh!*

okapi [ɔkapi] *nm* okapi.

okoumé [ɔkume] *nm* gaboon (mahogany).

oléacée [ɔlease] *nf* member of the Oleaceae family. **~s** Oleaceae.

oléagineux, -euse [ɔleaʒinø, øz] **1** *adj* oil-producing, oleaginous. **2** *nm* oil-producing *ou* oleaginous plant.

oléiculteur [ɔleikyltœʀ] *nm* olive grower.

oléiculture [ɔleikyltyʀ] *nf* olive growing.

oléifère [ɔleifɛʀ] *adj* oil-producing, oleiferous (*T*).

oléoduc [ɔleɔdyk] *nm* oil pipeline.

olfactif, -ive [ɔlfaktif, iv] *adj* olfactory.

olibrius [ɔlibʀijys] *nm* (*péj*) (queer) customer* *ou* fellow*.

olifant [ɔlifɑ̃] *nm* (ivory) horn.

oligarchie [ɔligaʀʃi] *nf* oligarchy.

oligarchique [ɔligaʀʃik] *adj* oligarchic.

oligo-élément, *pl* **oligo-éléments** [ɔligɔelemɑ̃] *nm* trace element.

oligopole [ɔligɔpɔl] *nm* oligopoly.

olivaie [ɔlivɛ] *nf* = **oliveraie.**

olivâtre [ɔlivɑtʀ(ə)] *adj* (*gén*) olive-greenish; *teint* sallow.

olive [ɔliv] **1** *nf* **(a)** (*fruit*) olive; *V* **huile. (b)** (*ornement*) bead *ou* pearl moulding; (*interrupteur*) switch. **(c)** (*Anat*) olivary body. **2** *adj inv* olive(-green).

oliveraie [ɔlivʀɛ] *nf* olive grove.

olivier [ɔlivje] *nm* (*arbre*) olive tree; (*bois*) olive(-wood); *V* **jardin, mont, rameau.**

Olivier [ɔlivje] *nm* Oliver.

olographe [ɔlɔgʀaf] *adj V* **testament.**

Olympe[1] [ɔlɛ̃p] *nm* Mount Olympus.

Olympe[2] [ɔlɛ̃p] *nf* Olympia.

olympiade [ɔlɛ̃pjad] *nf* Olympiad.

olympien, -ienne [ɔlɛ̃pjɛ̃, jɛn] *adj* (*Myth*) **les dieux ~s** the Olympic gods; (*fig*) **un calme ~** an Olympian calm; (*fig*) **un air ~** an air of Olympian aloofness.

olympique [ɔlɛ̃pik] *adj* Olympic; *V* **jeu.**

ombelle [ɔ̃bɛl] *nf* umbel. **en ~** umbellate (*T*), parasol-shaped.

ombellifère [ɔ̃belifɛʀ] **1** *adj* umbelliferous. **2** *nf* member of the Umbelliferae family. **~s** Umbelliferae.

ombilic [ɔ̃bilik] *nm* **(a)** (*nombril*) umbilicus, navel. **(b)** (*plante*) navelwort. **(c)** (*Bot*) hilum; (*renflement*) *[bouclier etc]* boss; (*Math*) umbilic.

ombilical, e, *mpl* **-aux** [ɔ̃bilikal, o] *adj* (*Anat*) umbilical; (*Sci, Tech*) navel-like; *V* **cordon.**

omble(-chevalier), *pl* **ombles(-chevaliers)** [ɔ̃bl(ə)(ʃ(ə) val je)] *nm* char (*fish*).

ombrage [ɔ̃bʀaʒ] *nm* **(a)** (*ombre*) shade. (*feuillage*) **sous les ~s (du parc)** in the shade of the trees (in the park), in the leafy shade (of the park).

(b) (*loc frm*) **prendre ~ de qch** to take umbrage *ou* offence at sth; **porter ~ à qn,** († *ou littér*) **causer** *ou* **donner de l'~ à qn** to offend sb.

ombragé, e [ɔ̃bʀaʒe] (*ptp de* **ombrager**) *adj* shaded, shady.

ombrager [ɔ̃bʀaʒe] (3) *vt [arbres]* to shade. (*fig littér*) **une frange ombrageait son front** a fringe shaded his brow.

ombrageux, -euse [ɔ̃bʀaʒø, øz] *adj* **(a)** *personne* touchy, quick to take offence (*attrib*), easily offended; *caractère* touchy. **(b)** *âne, cheval* skittish, nervous.

ombre[1] [ɔ̃bʀ(ə)] **1** *nf* **(a)** (*lit*) shade (*U*); (*ombre portée*) shadow; (*littér: obscurité*) darkness. **25° à l'~** 25° in the shade; **dans l'~ de l'arbre/du vestibule** in the shade of the tree/of the hall; **ces arbres font de l'~** these trees give (us) shade; **enlève-toi, tu me fais de l'~** get out of my light, move — you're in my light; **places sans ~/pleines d'~** shadeless/shady squares; **tapi dans l'~** crouching in the darkness; *V* **théâtre.**

(b) (*forme vague*) shadow, shadowy figure *ou* shape.

(c) (*fig*) (*anonymat*) obscurity; (*secret, incertitude*) dark. **laisser une question dans l'~** to leave a question in the dark, deliberately ignore a question; **tramer quelque chose dans l'~** to plot something in the dark; **sortir de l'~** *[auteur]* to emerge from one's obscurity; *[terroriste]* to come out into the open; **rester dans l'~** *[artiste]* to remain in obscurity; *[meneur]* to keep in the background; *[détail]* to be still obscure.

(d) (*soupçon*) **une ~ de moustache** a hint *ou* suspicion of a moustache; **il n'y a pas l'~ d'un doute** there's not the (slightest) shadow of a doubt; (*littér*) **une ~ de tristesse passa sur son visage** a shadow of sadness passed over his face; (*littér*) **il y avait dans sa voix l'~ d'un reproche** there was a hint of reproach in his voice.

(e) (*fantôme*) shade.

(f) (*loc*) **à l'~ de** (*tout près de*) in the shadow of, close beside; (*à l'abri de*) in the shade of; **vivre dans l'~ de qn** to live in the shadow of sb; **être l'~ de qn** to be sb's (little) shadow; **mettre qn à l'~*** to put sb behind bars, lock sb up; **il y a une ~ au tableau** there's a fly in the ointment; **n'être plus que l'~ de soi-même** to be the mere shadow of one's former self; *V* **peur, proie, suivre.**

2: ombres chinoises (*improvisées*) shadowgraph; (*spectacle*) shadow show *ou* pantomime; **ombre méridienne** noonday shadow; **ombre portée** shadow.

ombre[2] [ɔ̃bʀ(ə)] *nm* = **omble(-chevalier).**

ombrelle [ɔ̃bʀɛl] *nf* (*parasol*) parasol, sunshade; (*Zool*) *[méduse]* umbrella.

ombrer [ɔ̃bʀe] (1) *vt dessin* to shade. **~ les paupières** to put eyeshadow on; **un maquillage qui ombre les paupières** a make-up which darkens the eyelids.

ombreux, -euse [ɔ̃bʀø, øz] *adj* (*littér*) *pièce, forêt* shady.

oméga [ɔmega] *nm* omega; *V* **alpha.**

omelette [ɔmlɛt] *nf* omelette. **~ aux fines herbes** omelette with herbs; **~ aux champignons/au fromage** mushroom/cheese omelette; (*Prov*) **on ne fait pas d'~ sans casser des œufs** you can't make an omelette without breaking eggs.

omettre [ɔmɛtʀ(ə)] (56) *vt* to leave out, miss out, omit. **~ de faire qch** to fail *ou* omit *ou* neglect to do sth.

omission [ɔmisjɔ̃] *nf* (*action*) omission; (*chose oubliée*) omission, oversight. **pécher par ~** to commit the sin of omission.

omnibus [ɔmnibys] *nm* (*aussi* **train ~**) slow *ou* stopping train; (*Hist: bus*) omnibus.

omnidirectionnel, -elle [ɔmnidiʀɛksjɔnɛl] *adj* omnidirectional.

omnipotence [ɔmnipɔtɑ̃s] *nf* omnipotence.

omnipotent, e [ɔmnipɔtɑ̃, ɑ̃t] *adj* omnipotent, all-powerful.

omnipraticien, -ienne [ɔmnipʀatisjɛ̃, jɛn] *nm,f* general practitioner.

omniprésence [ɔmnipʀezɑ̃s] *nf* omnipresence.

omniprésent, e [ɔmnipʀezɑ̃, ɑ̃t] *adj* omnipresent.

omniscience [ɔmnisjɑ̃s] *nf* omniscience.

omniscient, e [ɔmnisjɑ̃, ɑ̃t] *adj* omniscient.

omnisports [ɔmnispɔʀ] *adj inv salle* multi-purpose (*épith*); *terrain* general-purpose (*épith*). **association ~** (general) sports club.

omnium [ɔmnjɔm] *nm* **(a)** (*Cyclisme*) prime; (*Courses*) open handicap. **(b)** (*Comm*) corporation.

omnivore [ɔmnivɔʀ] **1** *adj* omnivorous. **2** *nm* omnivorous creature, omnivore (*T*).

omoplate [ɔmɔplat] *nf* shoulder blade, scapula (*T*).

on [ɔ̃] *pron* **(a)** (*indétermination: souvent traduit par pass*) **~ les interrogea sans témoins** they were questioned without (any) witnesses; **~ va encore augmenter l'essence** (the price of) petrol is going up again, they are putting up the price of petrol again; (*annonce*) **~ demande jeune fille** young girl wanted *ou* required; **~ ne nous a pas demandé notre avis** nobody asked our opinion, our opinion wasn't asked; **~ ne devrait pas poser des questions si ambiguës** you *ou* one shouldn't ask such ambiguous questions; **dans cet hôtel ~ ne vous permet pas d'avoir des chiens** you aren't allowed to *ou* they won't let you keep a dog in this hotel; **~ prétend que** they say that, it is said that; **~ se précipita sur les places vides** there was a rush for the empty seats; (*Prov*) **~ n'est jamais si bien servi que par soi-même** a job is never so well done as when you do it yourself; *V* **dire.**

(b) (*quelqu'un*) someone, anyone. **~ a déposé ce paquet pendant que vous étiez sorti** someone left this parcel *ou* this parcel was left while you were out; **qu'est-ce que je dis si (l')~ demande à vous parler?** what shall I say if someone *ou* anyone asks to speak to you?; **~ vous demande au téléphone** you're wanted on the phone, there's someone on the phone for you; **~ frappa à la porte** there was a knock at the door; **est-ce qu'~ est venu réparer la porte?** has anyone *ou* someone been to repair the door?; **~ peut très bien aimer la pluie** some people may well like the rain; **je n'admets pas qu'~** *ou* **que l'~ ne sache pas nager** I can't understand how (some) people can't swim.

(c) (*indéf: celui qui parle*) you, one, we. **~ ne dort pas par cette chaleur** you (*ou* one) can't sleep in this heat; **est-ce qu'~ est censé s'habiller pour le dîner?** is one *ou* are we expected to dress for dinner?; **~ aimerait être sûr que ...** one *ou* we would like to be sure that ... ; **de nos fenêtres, ~ voit les collines** from our windows you (*ou* we) can see the hills; **~ a trop chaud ici** it's too hot here; **quand ~ est inquiet rien ne peut vous** *ou* **nous distraire** when you are (*ou* one is) worried nothing can take your (*ou* one's) mind off it; **~ comprend difficilement pourquoi** it is difficult to understand why; **~ ne pense jamais à tout** one (*ou* you) can't think of everything; **~ ne lui donnerait pas 70 ans** you wouldn't think she was 70; **~ ne dirait pas que** you wouldn't think that.

(d) (*éloignement dans temps, espace*) they, people. **autrefois, ~ se préoccupait peu de l'hygiène** years ago, they (*ou* people) didn't worry about hygiene; **en Chine ~ mange avec des baguettes** in China they eat with chopsticks; **dans aucun pays ~ ne semble pouvoir arrêter l'inflation** it doesn't seem as if inflation can be stopped in any country, no country seems (to be) able to stop inflation.

(e) (*: *nous*) we; (*: *je*) one; (*frm: je*) we. **~ a décidé tous les trois de partir chacun de son côté** the three of us decided to go (each) our separate ways; **chez nous ~ mange beaucoup de pain** we eat a lot of bread in our family; **lui et moi ~ n'est pas d'accord** we don't see eye to eye, him and me*; **nous, ~ a amené notre chien** we've brought along the dog; **nous, ~ a tous réclamé une augmentation** we all (of us) demanded a rise; **~ fait ce qu'~ peut** *ou* **de son mieux** you can only do your best; **il faut bien qu'~ vive** a fellow (*ou* a girl) has got to eat*; **dans ce chapitre ~ essaiera de prouver** in this chapter we (*frm*) shall attempt to prove.

(f) (*gén langue parlée: familiarité, reproche etc*) **~ est bien sage aujourd'hui!** aren't we a good boy (*ou* girl) today!, we ARE a good boy (*ou* girl) today!; **alors ~ ne dit plus bonjour aux amis!** don't we say hullo to our friends any more?; (*iro*) **~ n'a pas un sou mais ~ s'achète une voiture!** he hasn't (*ou* they haven't *etc*) a penny to his (*ou* their *etc*) name but he goes and buys (*ou* they go and buy *etc*) a car!; **~ parle ~ parle et puis ~ finit par dire des sottises** talk, talk, talk and it's all nonsense in the end.

(g) (*intensif*) **c'est ~ ne peut plus beau/ridicule** it couldn't be lovelier/more ridiculous; **je suis ~ ne peut plus heureux de vous voir** I couldn't be more delighted to see you, I'm absolutely delighted to see you.

onagre[1] [ɔnagʀ(ə)] *nm* (*Archéol, Zool*) onager.

onagre[2] [ɔnagʀ(ə)] *nf* (*Bot*) oenothera, evening primrose.

onanisme [ɔnanism(ə)] *nm* onanism.

once[1] [ɔ̃s] *nf* (*mesure, aussi Can*) ounce. **il n'a pas une ~ de bon sens** he hasn't an ounce of common sense.

once[2] [ɔ̃s] *nf* (*Zool*) ounce, snow leopard.

oncial, e, *mpl* **-aux** [ɔ̃sjal, o] **1** *adj* uncial. **2 onciale** *nf* uncial.

oncle [ɔ̃kl(ə)] *nm* uncle. (*fig*) **~ d'Amérique** rich uncle; **l'O~ Sam** Uncle Sam; **l'O~ Tom** Uncle Tom; *V* **héritage.**

oncques†† [ɔ̃k] *adv* never.

onction [ɔ̃ksjɔ̃] *nf* (*Rel, fig*) unction; *V* **extrême.**

onctueusement [ɔ̃ktɥøzmɑ̃] *adv couler* unctuously; *parler* with unction, suavely.

onctueux, -euse [ɔ̃ktɥø, øz] *adj crème* smooth, creamy, unctuous; *manières, voix* unctuous, smooth.

onctuosité [ɔ̃ktɥozite] *nf* (*V* **onctueux**) unctuousness, smoothness; creaminess.

onde [ɔ̃d] *nf* **(a)** (*gén, Phys*) wave. **~s herziennes** *ou* **radioélectriques/sonores** Hertzian *ou* radio/sound waves; (*Rad*) **~s courtes** short waves; **petites ~s, ~s moyennes** medium waves; **grandes ~s** long waves; **transmettre sur ~s courtes/petites ~s/grandes ~s** to broadcast on short/medium/long wave; *V* **longueur.**

(b) (*loc Rad*) **sur les ~s et dans la presse** on the radio and in the press; **nous espérons vous retrouver sur les ~s demain à 6 heures** we hope to join you again on the air tomorrow at 6 o'clock; **il passe sur les ~s demain** he's going on the air tomorrow; **mettre en ~s** *pièce etc* to produce for the radio; **par ordre d'entrée en ~s** in order of appearance.

(c) (*littér: lac, mer*) **l'~** the waters; **l'~ amère** the briny deep (*littér*).

ondé, e[1] [ɔ̃de] *adj* (*littér*) *tissu* watered; *cheveux* wavy.

ondée[2] [ɔ̃de] *nf* shower (*of rain*).

ondin, e [ɔ̃dɛ̃, in] *nm,f* water sprite.

on-dit [ɔ̃di] *nm inv* rumour, hearsay (*U*). **ce ne sont que des ~** it's only hearsay.

ondoiement [ɔ̃dwamɑ̃] *nm* **(a)** (*littér*) *[blés, surface moirée]* undulation. **(b)** (*Rel*) provisional baptism.

ondoyant, e [ɔ̃dwajɑ̃, ɑ̃t] *adj* **(a)** *eaux, blés* undulating; *flamme* wavering; *reflet* shimmering; *démarche* swaying, supple. **(b)** († *ou littér*) *caractère, personne* unstable, changeable.

ondoyer [ɔ̃dwaje] (8) **1** *vi [blé]* to undulate, ripple; *[drapeau]* to wave, ripple. **2** *vt* (*Rel*) to baptize (*in an emergency*).

ondulant, e [ɔ̃dylɑ̃, ɑ̃t] *adj* **(a)** *démarche* swaying, supple; *ligne, profil, surface* undulating. **(b)** (*Méd*) *pouls* uneven.

ondulation [ɔ̃dylɑsjɔ̃] *nf* **(a)** *[vagues, blés, terrain]* undulation. **~s** *[sol]* undulations; *[cheveux]* waves.

(b) (†: *coiffure*) **~ indéfrisable** *ou* **permanente** permanent wave; **se faire faire une ~** to have one's hair waved *ou* permed.

ondulatoire [ɔ̃dylatwaʀ] *adj* (*Phys*) undulatory, wave (*épith*); *V* **mécanique.**

ondulé, e [ɔ̃dyle] (*ptp de* **onduler**) *adj surface* undulating; *chevelure* wavy.

onduler [ɔ̃dyle] (1) **1** *vi* (*gén*) to undulate; *[drapeau]* to ripple, wave; *[route]* to snake up and down, undulate; *[cheveux]* to be wavy, wave. **2** *vt* (†) *cheveux* to wave.

onduleux, -euse [ɔ̃dylø, øz] *adj courbe, ligne* wavy; *plaine* undulating; *silhouette, démarche* sinuous, swaying, supple.

onéreux, -euse [ɔneʀø, øz] *adj* costly; *V* **titre.**

ongle [ɔ̃gl(ə)] *nm [personne]* (finger)nail; *[animal]* claw. **~ des pieds** toenail; **porter** *ou* **avoir les ~s longs** to have long nails; **vernis/ciseaux à ~s** nail varnish/scissors; **avoir les ~s en deuil*** to have dirty (finger)nails; **avoir bec et ~s** *ou* **dents et ~s** to be well equipped to hit back; *V* **bout, payer.**

onglée [ɔ̃gle] *nf*: **avoir l'~** to have fingers numb with cold.

onglet [ɔ̃glɛ] *nm* **(a)** *[tranche de livre]* (*dépassant*) tab; (*en creux*) thumb index. **dictionnaire à ~s** dictionary with a thumb index. **(b)** *[lame de canif]* (thumbnail) groove. **(c)** (*Menuiserie*) mitre, mitred angle. **boîte à ~s** mitre box. **(d)** (*Math*) ungula; (*Bot*) unguis; (*Reliure*) guard.

onglier [ɔ̃glije] **1** *nm* manicure set. **2** *nmpl*: **~s** nail scissors.

onguent [ɔ̃gɑ̃] *nm* **(a)** (*Pharm*) ointment, salve. **(b)** (††: *parfum*) unguent.

ongulé, e [ɔ̃gyle] **1** *adj* hoofed, ungulate (*T*). **2** *nm* hoofed *ou* ungulate (*T*) animal. **~s** Ungulata.

onirique [ɔniʀik] *adj* (*Art, Littérat*) dreamlike, dream (*attrib*).

onirisme [ɔniʀism(ə)] *nm* (*Psych*) hallucinosis; (*Littérat*) fantasizing.

onomatopée [ɔnɔmatɔpe] *nf* onomatopoeia.

onomatopéique [ɔnɔmatɔpeik] *adj* onomatopoeic.

onques†† [ɔ̃k] *adv* = **oncques**††.

ontarien, -ienne [ɔ̃taʀjɛ̃, jɛn] **1** *adj* Ontarian. **2** *nm,f*: **O~(ne)** Ontarian.

ontologie [ɔ̃tɔlɔʒi] *nf* ontology.

ontologique [ɔ̃tɔlɔʒik] *adj* ontological.

onyx [ɔniks] *nm* onyx.

onze [ɔ̃z] **1** *adj inv* eleven. **le ~ novembre** Armistice Day; *pour autres loc V* **six. 2** *nm inv* (*Sport*) **le ~ de France** the French eleven *ou* team; *pour autres loc V* **six.**

onzième [ɔ̃zjɛm] *adj, nmf* eleventh. (*péj*) **les ouvriers de la ~ heure** last-minute helpers; *pour autres loc V* **sixième.**

onzièmement [ɔ̃zjɛmmɑ̃] *adv* in the eleventh place; *pour loc V* **sixièmement.**

oolithe [ɔɔlit] *nm* oolite.

oolithique [ɔɔlitik] *adj* oolitic.

opacifier [ɔpasifje] (7) *vt* to make opaque.

opacité [ɔpasite] *nf* (*V* **opaque**) opaqueness; impenetrableness.

opale [ɔpal] *nf* opal.

opalescence [ɔpalesɑ̃s] *nf* opalescence.

opalescent, e [ɔpalesɑ̃, ɑ̃t] *adj* opalescent.

opalin, e[1] [ɔpalɛ̃, in] *adj* opaline.

opaline[2] [ɔpalin] *nf* opaline.

opaque [ɔpak] *adj verre, corps* opaque (*à* to); *brouillard, nuit* impenetrable.

op' art [ɔpaʀt] *nm* op art.

open [ɔpɛn] *adj inv* open.

opéra [ɔpeʀa] *nm* (*œuvre, genre, spectacle*) opera; (*édifice*) opera house. **~ bouffe** opera bouffe, comic opera; **grand ~** grand opera; **~-ballet** opéra ballet; **~-comique** light opera, opéra comique.

opérable [ɔpeʀabl(ə)] *adj* operable. **le malade est-il ~?** can the patient be operated on?; **ce cancer n'est plus ~** this cancer is too far advanced for an operation *ou* to be operable.

opérateur, -trice [ɔpeʀatœʀ, tʀis] **1** *nm,f* (*sur machine*) operator. **~ (de prise de vue)** cameraman.

2 *nm* **(a)** (*Math*)operator.

(b) *[calculateur]* processing unit.

opération [ɔpeʀɑsjɔ̃] *nf* **(a)** (*Méd*) operation. **~ à cœur ouvert** open heart surgery (*U*); **salle/table d'~** operating theatre/table.

(b) (*Math*) operation. **les ~s fondamentales** the fundamental operations; **ça peut se résoudre en 2 ou 3 ~s** that can be solved in 2 or 3 calculations *ou* operations.

(c) (*Mil, gén*) operation. **~ de police/de sauvetage** police/rescue operation; (*fig Comm*) **'~ baisse des prix'** 'operation price cut'; *V* **théâtre.**

(d) (*Comm*) deal. **~ financière/commerciale** financial/commercial deal; **~s de bourse** stock exchange dealings.

(e) (*Tech, gén*) process, operation. **les diverses ~s de la fabrication du papier** the different operations *ou* processes in the making of paper; **l'~ de la digestion** the operation of the digestive system; **les ~s de la raison** the processes of thought; **par l'~ du Saint-Esprit** (*Rel*) through the workings of the Holy Spirit; (*iro*) by magic.

opératoire [ɔpeʀatwaʀ] *adj* (*Méd*) *méthodes, techniques* operating; *maladie, commotion, dépression* post-operative; *V* **bloc.**

opercule [ɔpɛʀkyl] *nm* (*Bot, Zool*) operculum; (*Tech*) protective cap *ou* cover.

opéré, e [ɔpeʀe] (*ptp de* **opérer**) *nm,f* (*Méd*) patient (*who has undergone an operation*).

opérer [ɔpeʀe] (6) **1** *vt* **(a)** (*Méd*) *malade, organe* to operate on (*de* for); *tumeur* to remove. **on l'a opéré d'une tumeur** he had an operation for a tumour *ou* to remove a tumour; **se faire ~ des amygdales** to have one's tonsils removed *ou* out*; **il faut ~** we'll have to operate.

(b) (*exécuter*) *transformation, réforme* to carry out, implement; *choix* to make. **la Bourse a opéré un redressement spectaculaire** the Stock Exchange made a spectacular recovery; **cette méthode a opéré des miracles** this method has worked wonders; **seule la foi peut ~ le salut des fidèles** faith alone can bring about the salvation of the faithful; **ce traitement a opéré sur lui un changement remarquable** this treatment has brought about an amazing change in him; **un changement considérable s'était opéré** a major change had taken place *ou* occurred.

2 *vi* (*agir*) *[remède]* to act, work, take effect; (*procéder*) *[photographe, technicien etc]* to proceed. **comment faut-il ~ pour nettoyer le moteur?** how does one go about *ou* what's the procedure for cleaning the engine?, how does one proceed to clean the engine?

opérette [ɔpeʀɛt] *nf* operetta, light opera.

Ophélie [ɔfeli] *nf* Ophelia.

ophidien [ɔfidjɛ̃] *nm* ophidian. **~s** Ophidia.

ophtalmie [ɔftalmi] *nf* ophthalmia.

ophtalmique [ɔftalmik] *adj* ophthalmic.

ophtalmologie [ɔftalmɔlɔʒi] *nf* ophthalmology.

ophtalmologique [ɔftalmɔlɔʒik] *adj* opthalmological.

ophtalmologiste [ɔftalmɔlɔʒist(ə)] *nmf,* **ophtalmologue** [ɔftalmɔlɔg] *nmf* ophthalmologist.

ophtalmoscope [ɔftalmɔskɔp] *nm* ophthalmoscope.

opiacé, e [ɔpjase] *adj médicament, substance* opiate, opium-containing. **odeur ~e** smell of *ou* like opium.

opiner [ɔpine] (1) *vi* (*littér*) (*se prononcer*) **~ pour/contre qch** to come out in favour of/come out against sth, pronounce o.s. in favour of/against sth; (*acquiescer*) **~ de la tête** to nod one's agreement, nod assent; (*hum*) ~ **du bonnet** to bow assent; ~ **à qch** to give one's consent to sth.

opiniâtre [ɔpinjɑtʀ(ə)] *adj personne, caractère* stubborn, obstinate; *efforts, haine* unrelenting, persistent; *résistance* stubborn, dogged (*épith*), obstinate, persistent; *fièvre* persistent; *toux* persistent, obstinate, stubborn.

opiniâtrement [ɔpinjɑtʀəmɑ̃] *adv* (*V* **opiniâtre**) stubbornly; obstinately; unrelentingly; persistently; doggedly.

opiniâtrer (s') [ɔpinjɑtʀe] (1) *vpr* (†† *ou littér*) s'~ **dans son erreur/dans un projet** to persist in one's mistaken belief/in pursuing a project.

opiniâtreté [ɔpinjɑtʀəte] *nf* (*V* **opiniâtre**) stubbornness; obstinacy; unrelentingness; persistency; doggedness.

opinion [ɔpinjɔ̃] *nf* **(a)** (*jugement, conviction, idée*) opinion (*sur* on, about). **avoir une ~/des ~s** to have an opinion *ou* a point of view/(definite) opinions *ou* views *ou* points of view; **j'ai la même ~** I hold *ou* I am of the same opinion *ou* view, I agree with your (*ou* their *etc*) views; **avoir l'~ *ou* être de l'~ que** to be of the opinion that; **être de l'~ du dernier qui a parlé** to agree with whoever spoke last; **avoir bonne/mauvaise ~ de qn/de soi** to have a good/bad opinion of sb/o.s.

(b) (*U: manière générale de penser*) **l'~ publique** public opinion; **l'~ ouvrière** working-class opinion; **l'~ française** French public opinion; **informer l'~** to inform the public; **braver l'~** to defy public opinion; **l'~ est unanime/divisée** opinion is unanimous/divided; **il se moque de l'~ des autres** he doesn't care (a hoot) (about) what (other) people think.

opiomane [ɔpjɔman] *nmf* opium addict.

opiomanie [ɔpjɔmani] *nf* opium addiction.

opium [ɔpjɔm] *nm* opium.

opportun, e [ɔpɔʀtœ̃, yn] *adj démarche, visite, remarque* timely, opportune. **il serait ~ de faire** it would be appropriate *ou* advisable to do; **nous le ferons en temps ~** we shall do it at the appropriate *ou* right time.

opportunément [ɔpɔʀtynemɑ̃] *adv* opportunely. **il est arrivé ~** his arrival was timely *ou* opportune, he arrived opportunely *ou* just at the right time.

opportunisme [ɔpɔʀtynism(ə)] *nm* opportunism.

opportuniste [ɔpɔʀtynist(ə)] *adj, nmf* opportunist.

opportunité [ɔpɔʀtynite] *nf* [*mesure, démarche*] (*qui vient au bon moment*) timeliness, opportuneness; (*qui est approprié*) appropriateness.

opposable [ɔpozabl(ə)] *adj* opposable (*à* to).

opposant, e [ɔpozɑ̃, ɑ̃t] **1** *nm,f* opponent (*à* of). **2** *adj* **(a)** *minorité*, (*Jur*) *partie* opposing (*épith*). **(b)** (*Anat*) *muscle* opponent.

opposé, e [ɔpoze] (*ptp de* **opposer**) **1** *adj* **(a)** *rive, direction* opposite; *parti, équipe* opposing (*épith*). **venant en sens ~** coming in the opposite *ou* other direction; **garé en sens ~** parked facing the wrong way, parked on the wrong side of the road; **~ à: la maison ~e à la nôtre** the house opposite *ou* facing ours; **l'équipe ~e à la nôtre** the team playing against ours.

(b) (*contraire*) *intérêts* conflicting, opposing; *opinions* conflicting; *caractères* opposite; *forces, pressions* opposing; *couleurs, styles* contrasting; (*Math*) *nombres, angles* opposite. **~ à** conflicting *ou* contrasting with, opposed to; **opinions totalement ~es** totally conflicting *ou* opposed opinions, opinions totally at variance; **ils sont d'un avis ~** (*au nôtre*) they are of a different *ou* the opposite opinion; (*l'un à l'autre*) they are of conflicting opinions, their opinions are at variance with each other; (*Math*) **angles ~s par le sommet** vertically opposite angles; *V* **diamétralement**.

(c) (*hostile à*) **~ à** opposed to, against; **je suis ~ à la publicité/à ce mariage** I am opposed to *ou* against advertising/this marriage.

2 *nm* **(a)** (*contraire*) **l'~** the opposite, the reverse; **il fait tout l'~ de ce qu'on lui dit** he does the opposite *ou* the reverse of what he is told; **à l'~, il serait faux de dire ...** on the other hand *ou* conversely it would be wrong to say ...; **ils sont vraiment à l'~ l'un de l'autre** they are totally unalike; **à l'~ de Paul, je pense que ...** contrary to *ou* unlike Paul, I think that ... .

(b) (*direction*) **à l'~** (*dans l'autre direction*) the other *ou* opposite way (*de* from); (*de l'autre côté*) on the other *ou* opposite side (*de* from).

opposer [ɔpoze] (1) **1** *vt* **(a)** *équipes, boxeurs* to bring together; *rivaux, pays* to bring into conflict (*à* with); *idées, personnages* to contrast (*à* with); *couleurs* to contrast (*à* with); *objets, meubles* to place opposite each other. **le match opposant l'équipe de Lyon et *ou* à celle de Reims** the match bringing together the team from Lyons and the team from Rheims; **des questions d'intérêts les ont opposés/les opposent** matters of personal interest have brought them into conflict/divide them; **quel orateur peut-on ~ à Cicéron?** what orator could be put *ou* set beside Cicero?; **~ un vase à une statue** to place *ou* set a vase opposite a statue.

(b) (*utiliser comme défense contre*) **~ à qn/qch** *armée, tactique* to set against sb/sth; **~ son refus le plus net** to give an absolute refusal (*à* to); **~ de véhémentes protestations à une accusation** to protest vehemently at an accusation; **opposant son calme à leurs insultes** setting his calmness against their insults; **il nous opposa une résistance farouche** he put up a fierce resistance to us; **~ la force à la force** to match strength with strength.

(c) (*objecter*) **~ des raisons à** to put forward objections to, raise objections to; **~ des prétextes à** to put forward pretexts for; **que va-t-il ~ à notre proposition/nous ~?** what objections will he make *ou* raise to our proposals/to us?; **il nous opposa que cela coûtait cher** he objected that it was expensive.

2 s'opposer *vpr* **(a)** [*équipes, boxeurs*] to confront each other, meet; [*rivaux, partis*] to clash (*à* with); [*opinions, théories*] to conflict; [*couleurs, styles*] to contrast (*à* with); [*immeubles*] to face each other. **haut s'oppose à bas** high is the opposite of low.

(b) (*se dresser contre*) **s'~ à** *parents* to rebel against; *mesure, mariage, progrès* to oppose; **je m'oppose à lui en tout** I am opposed to him in everything; **rien ne s'oppose à leur bonheur** nothing stands in the way of their happiness; **je m'oppose formellement à ce que vous y alliez** I am strongly opposed to *ou* I am strongly against your going there; **ma conscience s'y oppose** it goes against my conscience; **sa religion s'y oppose** it is against his religion; **votre état de santé s'oppose à tout excès** your state of health makes any excess extremely inadvisable.

opposite [ɔpozit] *nm* (*frm*) **à l'~** on the other *ou* opposite side (*de* from).

opposition [ɔpozisjɔ̃] **1** *nf* **(a)** (*résistance*) opposition (*à* to). **faire de l'~ systématique (à tout ce qu'on propose)** to oppose systematically (everything that is put forward); (*Jur, Pol*) **loi passée sans ~** law passed unopposed.

(b) (*conflit, contraste*) (*gén*) opposition; [*idées, intérêts*] conflict; [*couleurs, style, caractères*] contrast. **l'~ des 2 partis en cette circonstance ...** (*divergence de vue*) the opposition between the 2 parties on that occasion ...; (*affrontement*) the clash *ou* confrontation between the 2 parties on that occasion ...; **l'~ du gris et du noir a permis de ...** contrasting grey with *ou* and black has made it possible to ...; **mettre 2 styles/théories en ~** to oppose *ou* contrast 2 styles/theories.

(c) (*Pol*) **l'O~** the opposition.

(d) (*loc*) **entrer en ~ sur un point** to come into conflict over a point; **en ~ avec** (*contraste, divergence*) at variance with; (*résistance, rébellion*) in conflict with; (*situation dans l'espace*) in apposition to; **agir en ~ avec ses principes** to act contrary to one's principles; **ceci est en ~ avec les faits** this conflicts with the facts; **faire *ou* mettre ~ à** *loi, décision* to oppose; *chèque* to stop; **par ~** in contrast; **par ~ à** as opposed to, in contrast with.

2: (*Jur*) **opposition à mariage** objection to a marriage; (*Jur*) **opposition à paiement** *objection by unpaid creditor to payment being made to a debtor.*

oppositionnel, -elle [ɔpozisjɔnɛl] **1** *adj* oppositional. **2** *nm,f* oppositionist.

oppressant, e [ɔpʀesɑ̃, ɑ̃t] *adj temps, souvenirs, ambiance* oppressive.

oppresser [ɔpʀese] (1) *vt* [*chaleur, ambiance, souvenirs*] to oppress; [*poids, vêtement serré*] to suffocate; [*remords, angoisse*] to oppress, weigh heavily on, weigh down. **avoir une respiration oppressée** to have difficulty with one's breathing.

oppresseur [ɔpʀesœʀ] **1** *nm* oppressor. **2** *adj* oppressive.

oppressif, -ive [ɔpʀesif, iv] *adj* oppressive.

oppression [ɔpʀesjɔ̃] *nf* (*asservissement*) oppression; (*gêne, malaise*) feeling of suffocation *ou* oppression.

opprimer [ɔpʀime] (1) *vt* **(a)** *peuple* to oppress; *opinion, liberté* to suppress, stifle. **les opprimés** (*gén*) the oppressed; (*socialement*) the downtrodden, the oppressed classes. **(b)** (*oppresser*) [*chaleur etc*] to suffocate, oppress.

opprobre [ɔpʀɔbʀ(ə)] *nm* (*littér: honte*) opprobrium (*littér*), disgrace. **accabler *ou* couvrir qn d'~** to cover sb with opprobrium; **jeter l'~ sur** to heap opprobrium on; **être l'~ de la famille** to be a source of shame to the family; **vivre dans l'~** to live in infamy.

optatif, -ive [ɔptatif, iv] *adj, nm* optative.

opter [ɔpte] (1) *vi* (*se décider*) **~ pour** *carrière, solution* to opt for, decide upon; (*choisir*) **~ entre** *nationalité* to choose *ou* decide between.

opticien, -ienne [ɔptisjɛ̃, jɛn] *nm,f* optician.

optimal, e, *mpl* **-aux** [ɔptimal, o] *adj* optimal, optimum (*épith*).

optimiser [ɔptimize] (1) *vt* to optimize.

optimisme [ɔptimism(ə)] *nm* optimism.

optimiste [ɔptimist(ə)] **1** *adj* optimistic. **2** *nmf* optimist.

optimum, *pl* **~s *ou* optima** [ɔptimɔm, a] **1** *nm* optimum. **2** *adj* optimum (*épith*), optimal.

option [ɔpsjɔ̃] **1** *nf* (*littér: choix*) option, choice; (*Jur, Scol*) option. (*Scol*) **matière/texte à ~** optional subject/text; (*Scol*) **avec ~ mathématique(s)** with a mathematics option, with optional mathematics; (*Fin*) **prendre une ~ sur** to take (out) an option on.

2: (*Fin*) **option d'achat** option to buy *ou* call; (*Fin*) **option de vente** option to sell *ou* put.

optique [ɔptik] **1** *adj verre* optical; *nerf* optic. **une bonne qualité ~** a good optical quality; *V* **angle, télégraphie**.

2 *nf* **(a)** (*science, technique, commerce*) optics (*sg*). **~ médicale/photographique** medical/photographic optics; **instrument d'~** optical instrument; *V* **illusion**.

(b) (*lentilles etc*) [*caméra, microscope*] optics.

(c) (*manière de voir*) perspective. **il faut situer ses arguments dans une ~ sociologique** we must situate his arguments in a sociological perspective; **voir qch avec *ou* dans une certaine ~** to look at sth from a certain angle *ou* viewpoint.

opulence [ɔpylɑ̃s] *nf* **(a)** (*richesse*) (*V* **opulent**) wealthiness; richness; opulence. **(b) ~ des formes** richness *ou* fullness of form; **l'~ de sa poitrine** the ampleness of her bosom.

opulent, e [ɔpylɑ̃, ɑ̃t] *adj* **(a)** (*riche*) *province, région, pays* wealthy, rich; *prairie* rich; *personne* opulent, wealthy, rich; *luxe, vie* opulent. **(b)** *femme* buxom; *poitrine* ample, generous.

opuscule [ɔpyskyl] *nm* (*pamphlet*) opuscule.

or[1] [ɔʀ] *nm* **(a)** (*métal*) gold; (*dorure*) gilt, gilding, gold. **~ blanc *ou* gris** white gold; **~ jaune/rouge** yellow/red gold; **~ noir** (*fig: pétrole*) black gold; **en lettres d'~** in gilt *ou* gold lettering; **ses cheveux d'~** his golden hair; **les blés d'~** the golden cornfields; **les ~s des coupoles/de l'automne** the golden tints of the cupolas/of autumn; **peinture/étalon/franc ~** gold paint/standard/franc; *V* **cœur, cousu, lingot** *etc*.

(b) (*loc*) en ~ *objet* gold; *occasion* golden (*épith*); *mari, enfant, sujet* marvellous, wonderful; **c'est une affaire en ~** (*achat*) it's a real bargain!; (*commerce, magasin*) it's a gold mine; **c'est de l'~ en barre** (*commerce, investissement*) it's a rock-solid investment, it's as safe as houses (*surtout Brit*); **pour (tout) l'~ du monde** for all the money in the world, for all the tea in China (*hum*); **faire des affaires d'~** to run a gold mine.

or[2] [ɔʀ] *conj* (*gén*) now; (*dans un syllogisme*) *non traduit.* **ceci n'aurait pas manqué de provoquer des jalousies, ~ nous ne désirions nullement nous brouiller avec eux** this would unfailingly have led to jealousy, when in fact *ou* whereas we had not the slightest wish to quarrel with them; († *ou frm*) **~ donc** thus, therefore.

oracle [ɔʀakl(ə)] *nm* (*gén*) oracle. **rendre un ~** to pronounce an oracle; (*hum*) **l'oncle Jean était l'~ de la famille** Uncle John was the oracle of the family; **il parlait en ~ *ou* comme un ~** he talked like an oracle.

orage [ɔʀaʒ] **1** *nm* **(a)** (*tempête*) thunderstorm, (electric) storm. **pluie/temps d'~** thundery (*surtout Brit*) *ou* stormy shower/weather; **vent d'~** stormy wind; **il va y avoir de l'~** *ou* **un ~** there's going to be a (thunder)storm.

(b) (*fig: dispute*) upset. **un ~ familial** a family row *ou* upset; **elle sentait venir l'~** she could sense the storm brewing.

(c) (*fig littér: tumulte*) **les ~s de la vie** the turmoils of life; **les ~s des passions** the tumult *ou* storm of the passions.

(d) (*loc*) **il y a de l'~ dans l'air** (*lit*) there is a (thunder)storm brewing; (*fig*) there is trouble *ou* a storm brewing; **le temps est à l'~** there's thunder in the air, the weather is thundery; **sa voix est à l'~** his tone is ominous.

2: orage de chaleur heat storm; **orage magnétique** magnetic storm.

orageusement [ɔʀaʒøzmɑ̃] *adv* (*fig*) tempestuously.

orageux, -euse [ɔʀaʒø, øz] *adj* **(a)** (*lit*) *ciel* stormy, lowering (*épith*); *région, saison* stormy; *pluie, chaleur, atmosphère* thundery. **temps ~** thundery weather, threatening weather.

(b) (*fig: mouvementé*) *époque, vie, adolescence* turbulent, stormy; *discussion, séance* stormy, turbulent, tempestuous.

oraison [ɔʀɛzɔ̃] *nf* orison, prayer. **l'~ dominicale** the Lord's Prayer; **~ funèbre** funeral oration.

oral, e, *mpl* **-aux** [ɔʀal, o] **1** *adj tradition, littérature, épreuve* oral; *confession, déposition* verbal, oral; (*Ling, Méd, Psych*) oral; *V* **stade, voie. 2** *nm* (*Scol*) oral, viva (voce).

oralement [ɔʀalmɑ̃] *adv transmettre des contes, des rumeurs* orally, by word of mouth; *conclure un accord, confesser* verbally, orally; (*Méd, Scol*) orally.

orange [ɔʀɑ̃ʒ] **1** *nf* (*fruit*) orange. **2** *nm* (*couleur*) orange. **3** *adj inv* orange. **4: orange amère** bitter orange; **orange douce** sweet orange; **orange sanguine** blood orange.

orangé, e [ɔʀɑ̃ʒe] **1** *adj* orangey, orange-coloured. **2** *nm* orangey colour. **l'~ de ces rideaux ...** the orangey shade of these curtains ... .

orangeade [ɔʀɑ̃ʒad] *nf* orangeade.

oranger [ɔʀɑ̃ʒe] *nm* orange tree; *V* **fleur.**

orangeraie [ɔʀɑ̃ʒʀɛ] *nf* orange grove.

orangerie [ɔʀɑ̃ʒʀi] *nf* (*serre*) orangery.

Orangiste [ɔʀɑ̃ʒist(ə)] **1** *nm* (*Hist, Pol*) Orangeman. **2** *nf* Orangewoman.

orang-outan(g), *pl* **orangs-outan(g)s** [ɔʀɑ̃utɑ̃] *nm* orang-outang.

orateur, -trice [ɔʀatœʀ, tʀis] *nm,f* (*homme politique, tribun*) orator, speaker; (*à un banquet etc*) speaker; (*Can*) Speaker (of House of Commons).

oratoire [ɔʀatwaʀ] **1** *adj art, morceau* oratorical, of oratory; *ton, style* oratorical; *V* **joute, précaution. 2** *nm* (*lieu, chapelle*) oratory, small chapel; (*au bord du chemin*) (wayside) shrine.

oratorio [ɔʀatɔʀjo] *nm* oratorio.

orbe[1] [ɔʀb(ə)] *nm* (*littér: globe*) orb; (*Astron*) (*surface*) plane of orbit; (*orbite*) orbit.

orbe[2] [ɔʀb(ə)] *adj*: **mur ~** blind wall.

orbital, e, *mpl* **-aux** [ɔʀbital, o] *adj* orbital.

orbite [ɔʀbit] *nf* **(a)** (*Anat*) (eye-)socket, orbit (*T*). **aux yeux enfoncés dans les ~s** with sunken eyes.

(b) (*Astron, Phys*) orbit. **mettre *ou* placer sur ~, mettre en ~** *satellite* to put into orbit; **la mise en *ou* sur ~ d'un satellite** the putting into orbit of a satellite, putting a satellite into orbit; **être sur *ou* en ~** *[satellite]* to be in orbit.

(c) (*fig: sphère d'influence*) sphere of influence, orbit. **être/entrer dans l'~ de** to be in/enter the sphere of influence of; **vivre dans l'~ de** to live in the sphere of influence of; **attirer qn dans son ~** to draw sb into one's orbit.

(d) (*loc*) **mettre *ou* placer sur ~** *auteur, projet, produit* to launch; **être sur ~** *[auteur, produit, méthode, projet]* to be successfully launched; **se mettre *ou* se placer sur ~** *[auteur, région]* to launch o.s. *ou* itself.

orbiter [ɔʀbite] (1) *vt [satellite]* to orbit.

Orcades [ɔʀkad] *nfpl*: **les ~** the Orkneys.

orchestral, e, *mpl* **-aux** [ɔʀkɛstʀal, o] *adj* orchestral.

orchestration [ɔʀkɛstʀɑsjɔ̃] *nf* (*V* **orchestrer**) orchestration; scoring; organization. (*Mus*) **une bonne ~** good scoring, a good orchestration.

orchestre [ɔʀkɛstʀ(ə)] **1** *nm* **(a)** (*musiciens*) *[grande musique, bal]* orchestra; *[jazz, danse]* band. **grand ~** full orchestra; *V* **chef**[1], **homme.**

(b) (*Ciné, Théât: emplacement*) stalls (*Brit*); (*fauteuil*) seat in the (orchestra) stalls (*Brit*). **l'~ applaudissait** applause came from the stalls (*Brit*); *V* **fauteuil, fosse.**

2: orchestre de chambre chamber orchestra; **orchestre de jazz** jazz band; **orchestre symphonique** symphony orchestra.

orchestrer [ɔʀkɛstʀe] (1) *vt* **(a)** (*Mus*) (*composer*) to orchestrate; (*adapter*) to orchestrate, score. **(b)** (*fig*) *couleurs* to orchestrate; *propagande* to organize.

orchidée [ɔʀkide] *nf* orchid.

ordalie [ɔʀdali] *nf* (*Hist*) ordeal.

ordinaire [ɔʀdinɛʀ] **1** *adj* **(a)** (*habituel*) ordinary, normal; (*Jur*) *session* ordinary. **avec sa maladresse ~** with his customary *ou* usual clumsiness; **personnage/fait peu ~** unusual character/fact; **avec un culot pas *ou* peu ~*** with incredible *ou* extraordinary cheek; **ça alors, ce n'est pas ~!*** that's (really) unusual *ou* out of the ordinary.

(b) (*courant*) *vin* ordinary; *vêtement* ordinary, everyday (*épith*); *service de table* everyday (*épith*); *qualité* standard.

(c) (*péj: commun*) *personne, manière* common; *conversation* ordinary, run-of-the-mill. **un vin très ~** a very indifferent wine; **mener une existence très ~** to lead a humdrum existence.

2 *nm* **(a)** (*la banalité*) **l'~** the ordinary; **qui sort de l'~** which is out of the ordinary.

(b) (*nourriture, menu ordinaire*) **l'~** ordinary *ou* everyday fare.

(c) (*loc*) (*littér*) **à l'~** usually, ordinarily; **comme à l'~** as usual; **d'~** usually, normally, as a rule; **il fait plus chaud que d'~ *ou* qu'à l'~** it's warmer than usual; **(comme) à son/mon ~** in his/my usual way, as was his/my wont (*littér, hum*).

3: l'ordinaire de la messe the ordinary of the Mass.

ordinairement [ɔʀdinɛʀmɑ̃] *adv* usually, normally, as a rule.

ordinal, e, *mpl* **-aux** [ɔʀdinal, o] **1** *adj* ordinal. **2** *nm* ordinal number.

ordinateur [ɔʀdinatœʀ] *nm* computer. **mettre sur ~** to computerize, put onto a computer; **mise sur ~** computerization; **la facturation est faite à l'~** the invoicing is computerized *ou* done by computer.

ordonnance [ɔʀdɔnɑ̃s] **1** *nf* **(a)** (*Méd*) prescription. **préparer une ~** to make up a prescription.

(b) (*Jur: arrêté*) *[gouvernement]* order, edict; *[juge]* order, ruling.

(c) (*disposition*) *[poème, phrase, tableau]* organization, layout; *[bâtiment]* plan, layout; *[cérémonie]* organization.

2 *nm ou nf* (*Mil*) **(a)** (*subalterne*) orderly, batman.

(b) d'~ *revolver, tunique* regulation (*épith*).

3: ordonnance de paiement authorization of payment; **ordonnance de police** police regulation; **ordonnance royale** royal decree *ou* edict.

ordonnancement [ɔʀdɔnɑ̃smɑ̃] *nm* (*Fin*) order to pay.

ordonnancer [ɔʀdɔnɑ̃se] (3) *vt* (*Fin*) *dépense* to authorize.

ordonnateur, -trice [ɔʀdɔnatœʀ, tʀis] *nm,f* **(a)** *[fête, cérémonie]* organizer, arranger. **(b)** (*Fin*) official with power to authorize expenditure. (*Hist Mil*) **commissaire ~** ≃ ordnance officer.

ordonné, e [ɔʀdɔne] (*ptp de* **ordonner**) **1** *adj* **(a)** (*méthodique*) *enfant* tidy; *employé* methodical.

(b) (*bien arrangé*) *maison* orderly, tidy; *vie* (well-)ordered, orderly; *discours* well-ordered; *V* **charité.**

(c) (*Math*) ordered. **couple ~** ordered pair.

2 ordonnée *nf* (*Math*) ordinate, Y-axis.

ordonner [ɔʀdɔne] (1) **1** *vt* **(a)** (*arranger*) *espace, idées, éléments* to arrange, organize; *discours, texte* to organize; (*Math*) *polynôme* to arrange in (*ascending ou descending*) order. **il avait ordonné sa vie de telle façon que ...** he had arranged *ou* organized his life in such a way that ... .

(b) (*commander*) (*Méd*) *traitement, médicament* to prescribe; (*Jur*) *huis-clos etc* to order. **~ à qn de faire qch** to order sb to do sth; **il nous ordonna le silence** he ordered us to be quiet; **ils ordonnèrent la fermeture des cafés *ou* qu'on fermât les cafés** they ordered the closure of the cafés *ou* that the cafés be closed; **le travail qui m'a été ordonné** the work which I've been ordered to do; **je vais ~ que cela soit fait immédiatement** I'm going to order that that be done immediately.

(c) (*Rel*) *prêtre* to ordain.

2 s'ordonner *vpr [idées, faits]* to organize themselves. **les idées s'ordonnaient dans sa tête** the ideas began to organize themselves *ou* sort themselves out in his head.

ordre[1] [ɔʀdʀ(ə)] **1** *nm* **(a)** (*succession régulière*) order. (*Ling*) **l'~ des mots** word order; **par ~ alphabétique** in alphabetical order; **par ~ d'ancienneté** in order of seniority; **alignez-vous par ~ de grandeur** line up in order of height *ou* size; **par ~ d'importance** in order of importance; **dans l'~** in order; **dans le bon ~** in the right order; **par ~ *ou* dans l'~ d'entrée en scène** in order of appearance; (*Mil*) **en ~ de bataille/de marche** in battle/marching order; (*Jur*) **~ des descendants *ou* héritiers** order of descent; *V* **numéro, procéder.**

(b) (*Archit, Bio: catégorie*) order. (*Archit*) **l'~ ionique/dorique** Ionic/Doric order.

(c) (*nature, catégorie*) **dans le même ~ d'idées** similarly; **dans un autre ~ d'idées** in a different *ou* another connection; **pour des motifs d'~ personnel/différent** for reasons of a personal/different nature; **c'est dans l'~ des choses** it's in the nature of things; **une affaire/un chiffre du même ~** a matter/figure of the same nature *ou* order; **un chiffre de l'~ de 2 millions** a figure in the region of *ou* of the order of 2 millions; **avec une somme de cet ~** with a sum of this order; **~ de grandeur: donnez-nous un ~ de grandeur** give us a rough estimate *ou* a rough idea; **dans cet ~ de grandeur** in this region; **de premier/deuxième/troisième ~** first-/second-/third-rate; **de dernier ~** third-rate; **considérations d'~ pratique/général** considerations of a practical/general nature.

(d) (*principe d'organisation*) **l'~** order; **l'~ établi** the established order; **l'~ public** law and order; **le maintien de l'~ (public)** the maintenance of law and order *ou* of public order; **quand tout fut rentré dans l'~** when order had been restored, when all was back to order; **le parti de l'~** the party of the establishment; **un homme d'~** a man of the establishment; *V* **force, rappeler, service** *etc.*

(e) (*méthode, bonne organisation*) *[personne, chambre]* tidiness, orderliness. **sans ~** untidy, disorderly; **avoir de l'~** (*rangements*) to be tidy *ou* orderly; (*travail*) to have method, be systematic *ou* methodical; **manquer d'~** to be untidy *ou* disorderly; to have no method, be unsystematic *ou* unmethodical; **en ~** *tiroir, maison, bureau* tidy, orderly; *comptes* in order; **tenir en ~** *chambre* to keep tidy; *comptes* to keep in order; **mettre en ~, mettre de l'~ dans** *affaires* to set in order, tidy up; *papiers, bureau* to tidy (up), clear up; **mettre bon ~ à qch** to put sth to rights, sort out sth; **défiler en ~** to go past in an orderly manner; **travailler avec ~ et méthode** to work in a methodical *ou* systematic way; **un homme d'~** a man who likes order.

(f) (*condition, état*) **en ~ de marche** in (full) working order.

(g) (*association, congrégation*) order. **les ~s de chevalerie** the orders of knighthood; **les ~s monastiques** the monastic orders; **les ~s mendiants** the mendicant orders; **l'~ de la jarretière/du mérite** the Order of the Garter/of merit; (*Rel*) **les ~s** (holy) orders; (*Rel*) **les ~s majeurs/mineurs** major/minor orders; (*Rel*) **entrer dans les ~s** to take (holy) orders.

2: l'ordre des avocats ≃ the Bar; **ordre du jour** *[conférence etc]* agenda (*V aussi* **ordre**[2]); **passons à l'ordre du jour** let us turn to the business of the day; **inscrit à l'~ du jour** on the agenda; **être à l'ordre du jour** (*lit*) to be on the agenda; (*fig*) *[problème, question]* to be (very) topical; **l'ordre des médecins** ≃ the British Medical Association.

ordre[2] [ɔʀdʀ(ə)] **1** *nm* **(a)** (*commandement, directive*) (*gén*) order; (*Mil*) order, command. **je n'ai pas d'~ à recevoir de vous** I won't take orders from you; **donner (l')~ de** to give an order *ou* the order to, give orders to; **par ~** *ou* **sur les ~s du ministre** by order of the minister; **j'ai reçu des ~s formels** I have formal instructions; **être aux ~s de qn** to be at sb's disposal; (*formule de politesse*) **je suis à vos ~s** I am at your service; **dis donc, je ne suis pas à tes ~s!** I'm not at your beck and call; (*Mil*) **à vos ~s!** yes sir!; **être/combattre sous les ~s de qn** to be/fight under sb's command; *V* **désir, jusque, mot.**

(b) (*Comm, Fin*) order. **à l'~ de** payable to, to the order of; **chèque à mon ~** cheque made out to me; *V* **billet, chèque, citer.**

2: (*Fin*) **ordre d'achat** buying order; (*Mil*) **ordre d'appel** call-up papers; (*Fin*) **ordre de Bourse** Stock Exchange order; **ordre de grève** strike call; (*Mil*) **ordre du jour** order of the day; **citer qn à l'ordre du jour** to mention sb in dispatches; (*Mil*) **ordre de mission** orders (*for a mission*); (*Mil*) **ordre de route** marching orders (*pl*).

ordure [ɔʀdyʀ] *nf* **(a)** (*saleté, immondices*) dirt (*U*), filth (*U*). **les chiens qui font leurs ~s sur le trottoir** dogs which leave their dirt on the pavement.

(b) (*détritus*) **~s** rubbish (*U*), refuse (*U*), garbage (*U*) (*US*); **~s ménagères** household refuse; **l'enlèvement** *ou* **le ramassage des ~s** refuse *ou* rubbish *ou* garbage (*US*) collection; **jeter qch aux ~s** to throw sth into the dustbin *ou* rubbish bin *ou* garbage can (*US*); **c'est juste bon à mettre aux ~s** it's fit for the dustbin (*Brit*) *ou* rubbish bin (*Brit*) *ou* garbage can (*US*); *V* **boîte, vider.**

(c) (*péj: chose, personne abjecte*) **ce film est une ~** this film is pure filth; **ce type est une belle ~** this guy is a real bastard‡; **cette ~ a fait tirer dans la foule** this bastard‡ had them shoot into the crowd.

(d) (*grossièretés*) **~s** obscenities, filth; **dire des ~s** to utter obscenities, talk filth; **écrire des ~s** to write filth.

(e) (*littér: abjection*) mire (*littér*). **il aime à se vautrer dans l'~** he likes to wallow in filth.

ordurier, -ière [ɔʀdyʀje, jɛʀ] *adj* lewd, filthy.

orée [ɔʀe] *nf* (*littér*) *[bois]* edge.

oreillard [ɔʀɛjaʀ] *nm* (*chauve-souris*) long-eared bat.

oreille [ɔʀɛj] *nf* **(a)** (*Anat*) ear. **l'~ moyenne/interne** the middle/inner ear; **l'~ externe** the outer *ou* external ear, the auricle (*T*); **~s décollées** protruding *ou* sticking-out ears; **~s en feuille de chou** big flappy ears; **le béret sur l'~** his beret cocked over one ear *ou* tilted to one side; **avoir des bourdonnements d'~, avoir les ~s qui bourdonnent** to have (a) buzzing *ou* (a) ringing in the ears; (*fig hum*) **les ~s ont dû lui tinter** his ears must have been burning; **animal aux longues ~s** long-eared animal; **aux ~s pointues** with pointed ears; *V* **boucher**[1]**, boucle, dresser** *etc.*

(b) (*ouïe*) hearing, ear. **avoir l'~ fine** to be sharp of hearing, have a sharp ear; **avoir de l'~** to have a good ear (for music); **ne pas avoir d'~** to have no ear for music; *V* **casser, écorcher, écouter.**

(c) (*comme organe de communication*) ear. **avoir l'~ de qn** to have sb's ear; **écouter de toutes ses ~s** to be all ears; **porter qch/venir aux ~s de qn** to let sth be/come to be known to sb, bring sth/come to sb's attention; **dire qch à l'~ de qn, dire qch à qn dans le creux** *ou* **dans le tuyau de l'~** to have a word in sb's ear about sth; **cela entre par une ~ et ressort par l'autre** it goes in (at) one ear and out (at) the other; **n'écouter que d'une ~** to listen with (only) one ear, only half listen; **écouter d'une ~ distraite** to only half listen, listen with (only) one ear; *V* **bouche, prêter, sourd.**

(d) *[écrou, fauteuil]* wing; *[soupière]* handle.

(e) (*loc*) **avoir les ~s rebattues de qch** to have heard enough of sth, be sick of hearing sth; **tirer les ~s à qn** (*lit*) to pull *ou* tweak sb's ears; (*fig*) to give sb a (good) telling off*, tell sb off*; (*fig*) **se faire tirer l'~** to take *ou* need a lot of persuading; **ouvre tes ~s** (will you) listen to what you are told; **l'~ basse** crestfallen, (with) one's tail between one's legs; **ferme tes ~s** don't (you) listen!; *V* **échauffer, montrer, puce** *etc.*

oreiller [ɔʀeje] *nm* pillow. **se raccommoder sur l'~** to make it up in bed; *V* **confidence, taie.**

oreillette [ɔʀɛjɛt] *nf [cœur]* auricle; *[casquette]* ear-flap.

oreillons [ɔʀɛjɔ̃] *nmpl*: **les ~** (the) mumps.

ores [ɔʀ] *adv*: **d'~ et déjà** already.

orfèvre [ɔʀfɛvʀ(ə)] *nm* silversmith, goldsmith. (*fig*) **M X, qui est ~ en la matière, va nous éclairer** Mr X, who's an expert (on the subject) is going to enlighten us.

orfèvrerie [ɔʀfɛvʀəʀi] *nf* (*art, commerce*) silversmith's *ou* goldsmith's trade; (*magasin*) silversmith's *ou* goldsmith's shop; (*ouvrage*) (silver) plate, (gold) plate.

orfraie [ɔʀfʀɛ] *nf* white-tailed eagle.

organdi [ɔʀgɑ̃di] *nm* organdie.

organe [ɔʀgan] **1** *nm* **(a)** (*Anat, Physiol*) organ. **~s des sens/sexuels** sense/sexual organs; *V* **fonction, greffe**[1].

(b) (*fig*) (*véhicule, instrument*) instrument, medium, organ; (*institution, organisme*) organ. **le juge est l'~ de la loi** the judge is the instrument of the law; **la parole est l'~ de la pensée** speech is the medium *ou* vehicle of thought; **un des ~s du gouvernement** one of the organs of government.

(c) (*porte-parole*) (*magistrat, fonctionnaire*) representative, spokesman; (*journal*) mouthpiece, organ.

(d) († *ou littér: voix*) voice.

2: organes de commande *[machine]* controls; **organes de transmission** *[machine]* transmission system.

organigramme [ɔʀganigʀam] *nm* (*tableau hiérarchique, structurel*) organization chart; (*tableau des opérations, de synchronisation*) flow chart, flow diagram.

organique [ɔʀganik] *adj* (*Chim, Jur, Méd*) organic; *V* **chimie.**

organiquement [ɔʀganikmɑ̃] *adv* organically.

organisateur, -trice [ɔʀganizatœʀ, tʀis] **1** *adj faculté, puissance* organizing (*épith*). **2** *nm,f* organizer.

organisation [ɔʀganizɑsjɔ̃] *nf* **(a)** (*action*) (*V* **organiser**) organization; arranging; getting up; setting up; setting out. **il a l'esprit d'~** he has an organizing mind *ou* a mind for organization.

(b) (*arrangement*) *[soirée, manifestation]* organization.

(c) (*structure*) *[service]* organization, setup; *[armée, travail]* organization; *[texte]* organization, layout. **une ~ syndicale encore primitive** a still primitive union setup; **l'~ infiniment complexe du corps humain** the infinitely complex organization of the human body.

(d) (*parti, syndicat*) organization.

organisationnel, -elle [ɔʀganizɑsjɔnɛl] *adj problème, moyens* organizational.

organisé, e [ɔʀganize] (*ptp de* **organiser**) *adj foule, groupe, citoyens* organized; *travail, affaire* organized; *esprit* organized, methodical. **personne bien ~e** well-organized person; **c'est du vol ~!** it's legalized robbery; *V* **voyage.**

organiser [ɔʀganize] (1) **1** *vt* **(a)** (*préparer*) *voyage, fête, réunion* to organize, arrange; *campagne* to organize; *pétition* to organize, get up; *service, coopérative* to set up.

(b) (*structurer*) *travail, opérations, armée, parti* to organize; *emploi du temps* to organize, set out; *journée* to organize.

2 s'organiser *vpr [personne, société]* to organize o.s. (*ou* itself), get (o.s. *ou* itself) organized. **il ne sait pas s'~** he does not know how to organize himself.

organisme [ɔʀganism(ə)] *nm* **(a)** (*organes, corps*) body, organism (*T*). **les besoins/les fonctions de l'~** the needs/functions of the body *ou* organism, bodily needs/functions.

(b) (*Zool: individu*) organism. **un pays est un ~ vivant** a country is a living organism.

(c) (*institution, bureaux*) body, organism. **un ~ nouvellement mis sur pied** a recently established body *ou* organism.

organiste [ɔʀganist(ə)] *nmf* organist.

orgasme [ɔʀgasm(ə)] *nm* orgasm, climax.

orge [ɔʀʒ(ə)] *nf* barley; *V* **sucre.**

orgeat [ɔʀʒa] *nm* orgeat; *V* **sirop.**

orgelet [ɔʀʒəlɛ] *nm* (*Méd*) sty(e).

orgiaque [ɔʀʒjak] *adj* orgiastic.

orgie [ɔʀʒi] *nf* **(a)** (*Hist, repas*) orgy; (*beuverie*) drinking orgy. **faire une ~** to have an orgy; **faire des ~s de gâteaux** to have an orgy of cakes *ou* of cake-eating.

(b) (*fig*) **~ de** profusion of; **~ de fleurs** profusion of flowers; **~ de couleurs** riot of colour.

orgue [ɔʀg(ə)] *nm* (*V aussi* **orgues**) organ. **tenir l'~** to play the organ; **~ de chœur/de cinéma/électrique/portatif** choir/theatre/electric/portable organ; **~ de Barbarie** barrel organ, hurdy-gurdy; *V* **point**[1].

orgueil [ɔʀgœj] *nm* **(a)** (*défaut: fierté exagérée*) pride, arrogance; (*justifiable: amour-propre*) pride. **gonflé d'~** puffed up *ou* bursting with pride; **~ démesuré** overweening pride *ou* arrogance; **il a l'~ de son rang** he has all the arrogance associated with his rank; **avec l'~ légitime du vainqueur** with the victor's legitimate pride; **le péché d'~** the sin of pride.

(b) (*loc*) **~ de: ce tableau, ~ de la collection** this picture, pride of the collection; **l'~ de se voir confier les clefs lui fit oublier sa colère** his pride at being entrusted with the keys made him forget his anger; **avoir l'~ de qch** to take pride in sth, pride o.s. on sth; **tirer ~ de qch** to take pride in sth; **mettre son ~ à faire qch** to take a pride in doing sth.

orgueilleusement [ɔʀgœjøzmɑ̃] *adv* (*V* **orgueilleux**) proudly, arrogantly.

orgueilleux, -euse [ɔʀgœjø, øz] *adj* (*défaut*) proud, arrogant; (*qualité*) proud. **~ comme un paon** as proud as a peacock; **c'est un ~** he's a (very) proud man; **c'est une ~euse** she's a (very) proud woman; (*littér*) **un chêne ~** a proud oak.

orgues [ɔʀg(ə)] *nfpl* **(a)** (*Mus*) organ. **les grandes ~** the great organs. **(b)** (*Géol*) **~ basaltiques** basalt columns.

orient [ɔʀjɑ̃] *nm* **(a)** (*littér: est*) orient (*littér*), east. **l'O~** the

Orient (*littér*), the East; **les pays d'O~** the countries of the Orient (*littér*), the oriental countries; *V* **extrême, moyen, proche.**
(b) *[perle]* orient.
(c) *V* **grand.**
orientable [ɔʀjɑ̃tabl(ə)] *adj bras d'une machine* swivelling, rotating; *lampe, antenne, lamelles de store* adjustable.
oriental, e, *mpl* **-aux** [ɔʀjɑ̃tal, o] **1** *adj côte, frontière, région* eastern; *langue, produits* oriental; *musique, arts* oriental, eastern; *V* **Inde. 2** *nm*: **O~** Oriental. **3** *nf*: **O~e** Oriental woman.
orientalisme [ɔʀjɑ̃talism(ə)] *nm* orientalism.
orientaliste [ɔʀjɑ̃talist(ə)] *nmf, adj* orientalist.
orientation [ɔʀjɑ̃tɑsjɔ̃] *nf* **(a)** (*V* **orienter**) positioning; adjusting, adjustment; directing; orientating, orientation. (*Scol*) **l'~ professionnelle** careers advising; **conseiller d'~** careers adviser.
(b) (*V* **s'orienter**) **~ vers** *[science]* trend towards; *[parti]* move towards; *[élève]* turning towards; *V* **sens, table.**
(c) (*position*) *[maison]* aspect; *[phare, antenne]* direction. **l'~ du jardin au sud** the garden's southern aspect *ou* the fact that the garden faces south.
(d) (*tendance, direction*) *[science]* trends orientation; *[magazine]* leanings, (political) tendencies. **l'~ générale de notre enquête/de ses recherches** the general direction *ou* orientation of our inquiry/of his research.
orienté, e [ɔʀjɑ̃te] (*ptp de* **orienter**) *adj* **(a)** (*disposé*) **~ à l'est/au sud** *maison* facing east/south, with an eastern/a southern aspect; *antenne* directed *ou* turned towards the east/the south; **bien/mal ~** *maison* well/badly positioned; *antenne* properly/badly directed.
(b) (*tendancieux, partial*) *article* slanted.
(c) (*marqué*) *plan, carte* orientated; (*Math*) *droite, vecteur* oriented.
orienter [ɔʀjɑ̃te] (1) **1** *vt* **(a)** (*disposer*) *maison* to position; *lampe, phare* to adjust; *miroir, bras de machine* to position, adjust; *antenne* to direct, adjust, turn. **~ un transistor pour améliorer la réception** to turn a transistor round to get better reception; **~ vers** to turn (on)to; **~ une maison vers le** *ou* **au sud** to build a house facing south; **~ une antenne vers le** *ou* **au nord** to turn *ou* direct an aerial towards the north; **~ la lampe** *ou* **la lumière vers** *ou* **sur son livre** to turn *ou* direct the light onto one's book; **la lampe peut s'~ dans toutes les positions** the lamp can be put into any position, the light can be turned in all directions.
(b) (*guider*) *élèves* to orientate, orient (*vers* towards); *touristes, voyageurs* to direct (*vers* to); *science, recherches* to direct (*vers* towards). **~ la conversation vers un sujet** to turn the conversation onto a subject.
(c) (*marquer*) *carte* to orientate; (*Math*) *droite* to orient.
(d) (*Naut*) *voiles* to trim.
2 s'orienter *vpr* **(a)** (*trouver son chemin*) *[touriste, voyageur]* to find one's bearings.
(b) (*se diriger vers*) **s'~ vers** (*lit*) to turn towards; (*fig*) *[science, goûts]* to turn towards; *[chercheur, parti, société]* to move towards; *[élève]* to turn towards.
orienteur, -euse [ɔʀjɑ̃tœʀ, øz] **1** *nm,f* (*Scol*) careers adviser. **2** *nm* (*Tech*) orientator.
orifice [ɔʀifis] *nm [mur de caverne, digue]* opening, orifice, aperture; *[puits, gouffre, four, tuyau, canalisation]* opening, mouth; *[organe]* orifice. (*Tech*) **~ d'admission/d'échappement (des gaz)** intake/exhaust part.
oriflamme [ɔʀiflam] *nf* (*bannière*) banner, standard; (*Hist*) oriflamme.
origan [ɔʀigɑ̃] *nm* origan(um).
originaire [ɔʀiʒinɛʀ] *adj* **(a) ~ de** (*natif de*) *famille, personne* originating from; (*provenant de*) *plante, coutume, mets* native to; **il est ~ de** he is a native of, he was born in.
(b) (*originel*) *titulaire, propriétaire* original, first; *vice, défaut* innate, inherent.
originairement [ɔʀiʒinɛʀmɑ̃] *adv* originally, at first.
original, e, *mpl* **-aux** [ɔʀiʒinal, o] **1** *adj* (*premier, originel*) original; (*neuf, personnel*) *idée, décor* original, novel; *artiste, talent* original; (*péj: bizarre*) eccentric, odd.
2 *nm,f* (*péj: excentrique*) eccentric; (*fantaisiste*) clown*, joker*. **c'est un ~** he's a (real) character *ou* a bit of an eccentric.
3 *nm* (*exemplaire premier*) (*ouvrage, tableau*) original; (*document*) original (copy); (*texte dactylographié*) top copy. **l'~ de ce personnage** the model for *ou* the original of this character.
originalement [ɔʀiʒinalmɑ̃] *adv* (*de façon personnelle*) originally, in an original way; (*rare: originellement*) originally.
originalité [ɔʀiʒinalite] *nf* **(a)** (*U: V* **original**) originality; novelty; eccentricity, oddness. **(b)** (*élément, caractéristique*) original aspect *ou* feature; (*action*) eccentric behaviour (*U*).
origine [ɔʀiʒin] *nf* **(a)** (*gén*) origin; (*commencement*) origin, beginning. **cette coutume a son ~ dans ...** this custom has its origins in *ou* originated in ...; **tirer son ~ de, avoir son ~ dans** to have one's origins in, originate in; (*titre d'ouvrage*) **'l'Automobile, des O~s à nos Jours'** 'the Motor Car, from its Origin(s) to the Present Day'; **ce coup de chance, ainsi que ses relations, sont à l'~ de sa fortune** this lucky break, as well as his connections, are at the origin *ou* root of his wealth.
(b) d'~ *nationalité, pays* of origin; *appellation, région de production* of origin; *pneus, garniture* original; (*Sci*) *méridien* prime, zero; **d'~ française/noble** of French/noble origin *ou* extraction; **mot d'~ française** word of French origin; **coutume d'~ ancienne** long-standing custom, custom of long standing.
(c) (*loc*) **à l'~** originally, to begin with; **dès l'~** at *ou* from the outset, at *ou* from the very beginning; **à l'~ de** *maladie, évolution* at the origin of; **souvent de telles rencontres sont à l'~ d'une vocation** such encounters are often the origin of a vocation.
originel, -elle [ɔʀiʒinɛl] *adj innocence, pureté, beauté* original, primeval; *état, sens* original; *V* **péché.**
originellement [ɔʀiʒinɛlmɑ̃] *adv* (*primitivement*) originally; (*dès le début*) from the (very) beginning, from the outset.
orignal, *pl* **-aux** [ɔʀiɲal, o] *nm* moose, Canadian elk.
oripeaux [ɔʀipo] *nmpl* (*haillons*) rags; (*guenilles clinquantes*) showy *ou* flashy rags.
orlon [ɔʀlɔ̃] *nm* ® Orlon.
orme [ɔʀm(ə)] *nm* elm.
ormeau, *pl* **~x** [ɔʀmo] *nm* (*Bot*) (young) elm; (*Zool*) ormer, abalone.
orné, e [ɔʀne] (*ptp de* **orner**) *adj style* ornate, florid. **lettres ~es** illuminated letters.
ornement [ɔʀnəmɑ̃] *nm* (*gén*) ornament; (*Archit, Art*) embellishment, adornment; (*Mus*) grace-note(s), ornament. **sans ~(s)** *élégance, toilette, style* plain, unadorned; **d'~** *arbre, jardin* ornamental; **les ~s du style** the ornaments *ou* ornamentation of style; (*Rel*) **~s sacerdotaux** vestments.
ornemental, e, *mpl* **-aux** [ɔʀnəmɑ̃tal, o] *adj style, plante* ornamental; *motif* decorative.
ornementation [ɔʀnəmɑ̃tɑsjɔ̃] *nf* ornamentation.
ornementer [ɔʀnəmɑ̃te] (1) *vt* to ornament.
orner [ɔʀne] (1) *vt* **(a)** (*décorer*) *chambre, vêtement* to decorate (*de* with); (*embellir*) *discours, récit* to embellish (*de* with). **~ une rue de drapeaux** to deck out a street with flags; **sa robe était ornée d'un galon** her dress was trimmed with braid; **discours orné de citations** speech embellished with quotations; (*littér*) **~ la vérité** to adorn *ou* embellish the truth; (*littér*) **~ son esprit** to enrich one's mind.
(b) (*servir d'ornement à*) to adorn, decorate, embellish. **la fleur qui ornait sa boutonnière** the flower which adorned *ou* decorated his buttonhole; **les sculptures qui ornaient la façade** the sculpture which adorned *ou* decorated *ou* embellished the façade.
ornière [ɔʀnjɛʀ] *nf* (*lit*) rut. (*fig*) **il est sorti de l'~ maintenant** he's made the grade now.
ornithologie [ɔʀnitɔlɔʒi] *nf* ornithology.
ornithologique [ɔʀnitɔlɔʒik] *adj* ornithological.
ornithologiste [ɔʀnitɔlɔʒist(ə)] *nmf*, **ornithologue** [ɔʀnitɔlɔg] *nmf* ornithologist.
ornithorynque [ɔʀnitɔʀɛ̃k] *nm* duck-billed platypus, ornithorynchus (*T*).
orogénèse [ɔʀɔʒenɛz] *nf* (*processus*) orogenesis; (*période*) orogeny.
orogénie [ɔʀɔʒeni] *nf* orology.
orogénique [ɔʀɔʒenik] *adj* orogenic, orogenetic.
orographie [ɔʀɔgʀafi] *nf* or(e)ography.
orographique [ɔʀɔgʀafik] *adj* or(e)ographic(al).
oronge [ɔʀɔ̃ʒ] *nf* agaric. **~ vraie** imperial mushroom; **fausse ~** fly agaric.
Orphée [ɔʀfe] *nm* Orpheus.
orphelin, e [ɔʀfəlɛ̃, in] **1** *adj* orphan(ed). **2** *nm,f* orphan. **être ~ de père/de mère** to be fatherless/motherless, have lost one's father/mother; *V* **veuf.**
orphelinat [ɔʀfəlina] *nm* (*lieu*) orphanage; (*orphelins*) children of the orphanage.
orphéon [ɔʀfeɔ̃] *nm* (*fanfare*) (village *ou* town) band.
orphie [ɔʀfi] *nf* garfish.
orteil [ɔʀtɛj] *nm* toe. **gros ~** big toe.
orthocentre [ɔʀtɔsɑ̃tʀ(ə)] *nm* orthocentre.
orthodoxe [ɔʀtɔdɔks(ə)] **1** *adj* **(a)** (*Rel, gén*) orthodox; *V* **église.**
(b) peu ~, pas très ~ rather unorthodox, not very orthodox.
2 *nmf* (*Rel*) orthodox; (*Pol*) one who follows the orthodox (party) line. **les ~s grecs/russes** the Greek/Russian orthodox.
orthodoxie [ɔʀtɔdɔksi] *nf* orthodoxy.
orthogénèse [ɔʀtɔʒenɛz] *nf* orthogenesis.
orthogonal, e, *mpl* **-aux** [ɔʀtɔgɔnal, o] *adj* orthogonal.
orthographe [ɔʀtɔgʀaf] *nf* (*gén*) spelling, orthography (*T*); (*forme écrite correcte*) spelling; (*système*) spelling (system). **réforme de l'~** spelling *ou* orthographical reform, reform of the spelling system; *V* **faute.**
orthographier [ɔʀtɔgʀafje] (7) *vt* to spell (*in writing*). **un mot mal orthographié** a word incorrectly *ou* wrongly spelt.
orthographique [ɔʀtɔgʀafik] *adj* (*Ling*) spelling (*épith*), orthographical. **signe ~** orthographical sign.
orthonormé, e [ɔʀtɔnɔʀme] *adj* orthonormal.
orthopédie [ɔʀtɔpedi] *nf* orthopaedics (*sg*).
orthopédique [ɔʀtɔpedik] *adj* orthopaedic.
orthopédiste [ɔʀtɔpedist(ə)] *nmf* orthopaedic specialist, orthopaedist. **chirurgien ~** orthopaedic surgeon.
orthophonie [ɔʀtɔfɔni] *nf* (*Ling: prononciation correcte*) correct pronunciation; (*Méd: traitement*) speech therapy.
orthophoniste [ɔʀtɔfɔnist(ə)] *nmf* speech therapist.
ortie [ɔʀti] *nf* (stinging) nettle. **~ blanche** white dead-nettle; *V* **jeter, piqûre.**
ortolan [ɔʀtɔlɑ̃] *nm* ortolan.
orvet [ɔʀvɛ] *nm* slow worm.
os [ɔs] **1** *nm* **(a)** (*gén*) bone. **avoir de petits/gros ~** to be small-boned/big-boned; **viande avec ~** meat on the bone; **viande sans ~** boned meat, meat off the bone; **fait en ~** made of bone; **jetons/manche en ~** bone counters/handle; **à manche en ~** bone-handled.
(b) (*loc*) **c'est un paquet** *ou* **sac d'~** he's a bag of bones, he's (mere) skin and bone(s); **mouillée** *ou* **trempé jusqu'aux ~** soaked to the skin, wet through; **donner** *ou* **jeter un ~ à ronger à qn** to give sb something to keep him occupied; **l'avoir dans l'~:**

(*être roulé*) to be done‡ *ou* had‡; (*être bredouille*) to get egg all over one's face‡; **il y a un ~*** there's a snag *ou* hitch; **il va trouver un** *ou* **tomber sur un ~*** he'll come across *ou* hit* a snag; *V* **chair, rompre, vieux.**

2: os à moelle marrowbone; **os de seiche** cuttle-bone.

oscar [ɔskaʀ] *nm* (*Ciné*) Oscar; (*autres domaines*) prize (*de* for).

oscillateur [ɔsilatœʀ] *nm* (*Phys*) oscillator.

oscillation [ɔsilɑsjɔ̃] *nf* (*Élec, Phys*) oscillation; *[pendule]* swinging (*U*), oscillation; *[navire]* rocking (*U*); *[température, grandeur variable, opinion]* fluctuation, variation (*de* in). **les ~s de son esprit** his (mental) fluctuations.

oscillatoire [ɔsilatwaʀ] *adj* (*Sci*) oscillatory; *mouvement* swinging, oscillatory (*T*).

osciller [ɔsile] (1) *vi* (*Sci*) to oscillate; *[pendule]* to swing, oscillate; *[navire]* to rock. **le vent fit ~ la flamme/la statue** the wind made the flame flicker/made the statue rock; **sa tête oscillait de droite à gauche** his head rocked from side to side; **il oscillait sur ses pieds** he rocked on his feet; (*fig*) **~ entre** *[personne]* to waver *ou* oscillate between; *[prix, température]* to fluctuate *ou* vary between.

oscillographe [ɔsilɔgʀaf] *nm* oscillograph.

oscilloscope [ɔsilɔskɔp] *nm* oscilloscope.

osé, e [oze] (*ptp de* **oser**) *adj tentative, démarche, toilette* bold, daring; *sujet, plaisanterie* risqué, daring.

oseille [ozɛj] *nf* **(a)** (*Bot*) sorrel. **(b)** (‡: *argent*) dough‡. **avoir de l'~** to be in the money*, have plenty of dough‡ *ou* bread‡.

oser [oze] (1) *vt* **(a)** to dare. **il faut ~!** one must take risks; **~ faire qch** to dare (to) do sth; (*littér*) **~ qch** to dare sth; **il n'osait (pas) bouger** he did not dare (to) move; **je voudrais bien mais je n'ose pas** I'd like to but I dare not *ou* I daren't; **approche si tu l'oses!** come over here if you dare!; **il a osé m'insulter** he dared *ou* presumed to insult me; *V* **qui.**

(b) (*loc*) **si j'ose dire** if I may say so, if I may make so bold; **si j'ose m'exprimer ainsi** if I can put it that way, if you'll pardon the expression; **j'ose espérer/croire que** I like to hope/think that; **j'ose l'espérer** I like to hope so; **je n'ose y croire** I dare not *ou* daren't believe it; **j'oserais même dire que** I'd even venture to *ou* go as far as to say that.

osier [ozje] *nm* (*Bot*) willow, osier; (*fibres*) wicker (*U*). **corbeille en ~** wicker(work) basket; **fauteuil en ~** wicker(work) chair, basket chair; *V* **brin.**

osmose [ɔsmoz] *nf* (*lit, fig*) osmosis.

ossature [ɔsatyʀ] *nf [corps]* frame, skeletal structure (*T*); *[tête, visage]* bone structure; *[machine, appareil]* framework; *[voûte]* frame(work); (*fig*) *[société, texte, discours]* framework. **à ~ grêle/robuste** slender-/heavy-framed.

osselet [ɔslɛ] *nm* **(a)** (*jeu*) **~s** knucklebones. **(b)** (*Anat*) *[oreille]* ossicle. **(c)** (*Vét*) osselet.

ossements [ɔsmɑ̃] *nmpl* (*squelettes*) bones.

osseux, -euse [ɔsø, øz] *adj* **(a)** (*Anat*) *tissu* bone (*épith*), osseus (*T*); *charpente, carapace* bony; (*Méd*) *greffe* bone (*épith*); *maladie* bone (*épith*), of the bones. **(b)** (*maigre*) *main, visage* bony.

ossification [ɔsifikɑsjɔ̃] *nf* ossification (*Méd*).

ossifier *vt*, **s'ossifier** *vpr* [ɔsifje] (7) (*lit, fig*) to ossify.

ossu, e [ɔsy] *adj* (*littér*) large-boned.

ossuaire [ɔsɥɛʀ] *nm* (*lieu*) ossuary.

Ostende [ɔstɑ̃d] *n* Ostend.

ostensible [ɔstɑ̃sibl(ə)] *adj* (*bien visible*) *mépris, indifférence* conspicuous, patent; *charité, compassion, attitude, geste* conspicuous. **de façon ~** conspicuously.

ostensiblement [ɔstɑ̃sibləmɑ̃] *adv* conspicuously.

ostensoir [ɔstɑ̃swaʀ] *nm* monstrance.

ostentation [ɔstɑ̃tɑsjɔ̃] *nf* ostentation. **il détestait toute ~** he hated all ostentation *ou* show, he hated all manner of ostentation *ou* display; **agir avec ~** to act with ostentation *ou* ostentatiously; **courage/élégance sans ~** unostentatious courage/elegance; **faire qch sans ~** to do sth without ostentation *ou* unostentatiously; (*littér*) **faire ~ de qch** to make a display *ou* show of sth, parade sth.

ostentatoire [ɔstɑ̃tatwaʀ] *adj* (*littér*) ostentatious.

ostraciser [ɔstʀasize] (1) *vt* to ostracize.

ostracisme [ɔstʀasism(ə)] *nm* ostracism. **être frappé d'~** to be ostracized; **leur ~ m'était indifférent** being ostracised by them didn't bother me.

ostréicole [ɔstʀeikɔl] *adj* oyster-farming (*épith*).

ostréiculteur, -trice [ɔstʀeikyltœʀ, tʀis] *nm,f* oyster-farmer, ostreiculturist (*T*).

ostréiculture [ɔstʀeikyltyʀ] *nf* oyster-farming, ostreiculture (*T*).

ostrogot(h), e [ɔstʀɔgo, ɔt] **1** *adj* Ostrogothic. **2** *nm,f*: **O~(e)** Ostrogoth. **3** *nm* († *ou hum*) (*mal élevé*) barbarian; (*original, olibrius*) queer fish* *ou* fellow.

otage [ɔtaʒ] *nm* hostage.

otarie [ɔtaʀi] *nf* sea-lion, otary (*T*), eared seal (*T*).

ôter [ote] (1) **1** *vt* **(a)** (*enlever*) *ornement* to take away, remove (*de* from); *vêtement* to take off, remove; *arêtes* to take out (*de* of), remove (*de* from); *tache* to take out (*de* of), remove (*de* from), lift (*de* from); *hésitation, scrupule* to remove, take away; *remords* to take away. **ôte les assiettes (de la table)** clear the table, clear the dishes off the table; **un produit qui ôte l'acidité (à une** *ou* **d'une substance)** a product which removes the acidity (from a substance); **ôte tes mains de la porte!** take your hands off the door!; **cela lui a ôté un gros poids (de dessus la poitrine)** that took a great weight off his chest *ou* lifted a great weight from his chest; **comment est-ce que ça s'ôte?** how do you remove it? *ou* take it off?; **on lui ôta ses menottes** they took his handcuffs off, they unhandcuffed him.

(b) (*retrancher*) *somme* to take away; *paragraphe* to remove, cut out (*de* from). **~ un nom d'une liste** to remove a name from a list, take a name off a list; **5 ôté de 8 égale 3** 5 (taken away) from 8 equals *ou* leaves 3.

(c) (*prendre*) **~ qch à qn** to take sth (away) from sb; **~ un enfant à sa mère** to take a child (away) from its mother; **s'~ la vie** to take one's (own) life; **~ à qn ses illusions** to rid *ou* deprive sb of his illusions; **~ à qn ses forces/son courage** to deprive sb of his strength/his courage; **ça lui ôtera toute envie de recommencer** that will stop him wanting to do it again, that will rid him of any desire to do it again; **ôte-lui le couteau, ôte-lui le couteau des mains** take the knife (away) from him, take the knife out of *ou* from his hands; **on m'ôte le pain de la bouche** they are taking the bread out of my mouth; **on ne m'ôtera pas de l'idée que ..., je ne peux m'~ de l'idée que ...** I can't get it out of my mind *ou* head that ... ; **il faut absolument lui ~ cette idée de la tête** we must get this idea out of his head.

2 s'ôter *vpr*: **ôtez-vous de là** move yourself!, get out of there!; **ôtez-vous de la lumière,** (*hum*) **ôte-toi de mon soleil** get out of my light; (*hum*) **ôte-toi de là (que je m'y mette)!*** (get) out of the way!, move *ou* shift* out of the way (and give me some room)!

otite [ɔtit] *nf* ear infection, otitis (*T*). **~ moyenne/interne** otitis media/interna.

oto-rhino, *pl* **oto-rhinos** [ɔtɔʀino] *nmf* = **oto-rhino- laryngologiste.**

oto-rhino-laryngologie [ɔtɔʀinɔlaʀɛ̃gɔlɔʒi] *nf* otorhinolaryngology.

oto-rhino-laryngologiste, *pl* **oto-rhino-laryngologistes** [ɔtɔʀinɔlaʀɛ̃gɔlɔʒist(ə)] *nmf* ear, nose and throat specialist.

otoscope [ɔtɔskɔp] *nm* otoscope.

ottoman, e [ɔtɔmɑ̃, an] **1** *adj* Ottoman. **2** *nm* **(a)** (*personne*) **O~** Ottoman. **(b)** (*tissu*) ottoman. **3 ottomane** *nf* **(a)** (*personne*) **O~e** Ottoman woman. **(b)** (*canapé*) ottoman.

ou [u] *conj* **(a)** (*alternative*) or. **est-ce qu'il doit venir aujourd'hui ~ demain?** is he coming today or tomorrow?; **il faut qu'il vienne aujourd'hui ~ demain** he must come (either) today or tomorrow; **vous le préférez avec ~ sans sucre?** do you prefer it with or without sugar?; **que vous alliez chez cet épicier ~ chez l'autre, c'est le même prix** it's the same price whether you go to this grocer or (to) the other one; **un kilo de plus ~ de moins, cela ne se sent pas** one kilo more or less doesn't show up; **que vous le vouliez ~ non** whether you like it or not; **jolie ~ non elle plaît** (whether she's) pretty or not, she's attractive; **est-ce qu'elle veut se lever ~ préfère-t-elle attendre demain?** does she want to get up or does she prefer to wait till tomorrow?; **il nous faut 3 pièces, ~ plutôt/~ même 4** we need 3 rooms, or preferably/or even 4; **apportez-moi une bière, ~ plutôt non un café** bring me a beer, or rather a coffee *ou* or no a coffee instead; **~ pour mieux dire** or rather, or I SHOULD say.

(b) (*approximation*) or. **à 5 ~ 6 km d'ici** 5 or 6 km from here; **ils étaient 10 ~ 12 (à vouloir parler à la fois)** there were (some) 10 or 12 of them (wanting to speak at the same time).

(c) (*alternative avec exclusion*) **~ ... ~** either ... or; **~ il est malade ~ (bien) il est fou** he's either sick or mad, either he's sick or (else) he's mad; **~ (bien) tu m'attends ~ (bien) alors tu pars à pied** either you wait for me or (else) you'll have to walk, you (can) either wait for me or (else) go on foot; **il faut qu'il travaille ~ (bien) il échouera à son examen** he'll have to work or (else) *ou* otherwise he'll fail his exam; *V* **tôt.**

où [u] **1** *pron* **(a)** (*lit: situation, direction*) where. **l'endroit ~ je vais/je suis** the place where I'm going/I am, the place I'm going to/I'm in; **l'endroit idéal ~ s'établir** the ideal place to settle; **je cherche un endroit ~ m'asseoir** I'm looking for a place to sit down *ou* for somewhere to sit; **la ville ~ j'habite** the town I live in *ou* where I live; **la maison ~ j'habite** the house I live in; **le mur ~ il est accoudé** the wall he's leaning against; **le tiroir ~ tu as rangé le livre** the drawer you put the book in *ou* where you put the book; **le tiroir ~ tu a pris le livre** the drawer (where) you took the book from; **le livre ~ il a trouvé ce renseignement** the book where he found this piece of information; **le livre ~ il a copié ceci** the book he copied this from *ou* from which he copied this; **le chemin par ~ il est passé** the road he went along *ou* he took; **le village par ~ il est passé** the village he went through; **l'endroit d'~ je viens** the place I've come from; **la pièce d'~ il sort** the room he's come out of; **la crevasse d'~ on l'a retiré** the crevasse they rescued him from; **une chambre d'~ s'échappent des gémissements** a room from which moans are coming; **l'endroit jusqu'~ ils ont grimpé** the place (where) they have climbed to *ou* to which they've climbed; *V* **là, partout.**

(b) (*antécédent abstrait: institution, groupe, état, condition*) **la famille ~ il est entré** the family he has become part of; **la famille/la firme d'~ il sort** the family/firm he comes *ou* has come from; **la ville d'~ il vient** (*origine*) the town he comes from; **l'école ~ il est inscrit** the school where *ou* in which he is enrolled; **les mathématiques, branche ~ je ne suis guère compétent** mathematics, a branch in which I have little skill; **dans l'état ~ il est** in the state he is in *ou* in which he is; **la colère ~ il est entré** the rage he went into; **dans l'embarras ~ j'étais** in the embarrassed state I was in; **les conditions ~ ils travaillent** the conditions they work in *ou* in which they work; **la rêverie ~ il est plongé/d'~ je l'ai tiré** the daydream he's in/from which I roused him; **les extrêmes ~ il s'égare** the extremes into which he is straying; **le but ~ tout homme tend** the goal towards which all men strive; **la mélancolie ~ il se complaît** the melancholy in which he wallows; **au rythme ~ ça va** at the speed it's going; **au prix ~ c'est** at the price it is; **au tarif ~ ils font payer ça** at the rate they charge for it; **à l'allure ~ ils vont** at the rate they're going; *V* **prix, train** *et pour autres constructions V vbs appropriés.*

(c) (*temporel*) **le siècle ~ se passe cette histoire** the century in which this story takes place; **le jour ~ je l'ai rencontré** the day (on which) I met him; **à l'instant ~ il est arrivé** the moment he arrived; *V* **moment.**

2 *adv rel* **(a)** (*situation et direction*) where. **j'irai ~ il veut** I'll go where *ou* wherever he wants; **s'établir ~ l'on veut** to settle where one likes; **je ne sais pas d'~ il vient** I don't know where he comes from; **on ne peut pas passer par ~ on veut** you can't just go where you like; **d'~ je suis on voit la mer** you can see the sea from where I am; **~ que l'on aille/soit** wherever one goes/is; **d'~ que l'on vienne** wherever one comes from; **par ~ que l'on passe** wherever one goes.

(b) (*abstrait*) **~ cela devient grave, c'est lorsqu'il prétend que ...** where it gets serious is when he claims that ... ; **savoir ~ s'arrêter** to know where *ou* when to stop; **d'~ l'on peut conclure que ...** from which one may conclude that ... ; **d'~ son silence/ma méfiance** hence his silence/my wariness; (*titre de chapitre*) **'~ l'on voit que ...'** 'in which the reader sees *ou* learns that ...'; (*littér*) **les récriminations sont vaines ~ les malheurs viennent de notre propre incurie** recrimination is in vain when misfortune comes of our own negligence; (*Prov*) **~ il y a de la gêne, il n'y a pas de plaisir** comfort comes first, there's no sense in being uncomfortable; (*péj*) talk about making yourself at home!, some people think only of their own comfort.

3 *adv interrog* **(a)** (*situation et direction*) where. **~ vas-tu/es-tu/l'as-tu mis?** where are you going/are you/did you put it?; **d'~ viens-tu?** where have you come from?; **par ~ y aller?** which way should we (*ou* I *etc*) go?; **~ aller?** where should I (*ou* he *etc*) go?

(b) (*abstrait*) **~ en étais-je?** where was I?, where had I got to?; **~ en êtes-vous?** where are you up to?; **~ allons-nous?** where are we going?; **d'~ vient cette attitude?** what's the reason for this attitude?; **d'~ vient qu'il n'a pas répondu?** how come he hasn't replied?*, what's the reason for his not having replied?; **d'~ le tenez-vous?** where did you hear that?; **~ voulez-vous en venir?** what are you leading up to? *ou* getting at?

ouailles [waj] *nfpl* (*Rel, hum*) flock. **l'une de ses ~** one of his flock.

ouais* [wɛ] *excl* (*oui*) yeah*; (*sceptique*) oh yeah?*

ouananiche [wananiʃ] *nm* (*Can*) lake trout *ou* salmon.

ouaouaron* [wawaʀɔ̃] *nm* (*Can*) bull frog.

ouate [wat] **1** *nf* **(a)** (*pour pansement*) cotton wool. (*fig*) **élever un enfant dans de la ~ *ou* dans l'~** to keep a child (wrapped up) in cotton wool (*Brit*).

(b) (*pour rembourrage*) padding, wadding. **doublé d'~** quilted.

2: ouate hydrophile cotton wool (*Brit*), absorbent cotton (*US*); **ouate thermogène** Thermogene ®.

ouaté, e [wate] (*ptp de* **ouater**) *adj* **(a)** (*lit*) *pansement* cotton-wool (*épith*); *vêtement* quilted. **(b)** (*fig*) *pas, bruit* muffled; *ambiance* cocoon-like.

ouater [wate] (1) *vt manteau, couverture* to quilt. **les collines ouatées de neige** the hills covered *ou* blanketed in snow.

ouatine [watin] *nf* wadding, padding.

ouatiner [watine] (1) *vt* to quilt.

oubli [ubli] *nm* **(a)** (*V* **oublier**) forgetting; leaving behind; missing; leaving-out; neglecting. **l'~ de cette date/cet objet a eu des conséquences graves** forgetting this date/forgetting *ou* leaving behind this thing has had serious repercussions; **l'~ de soi(-même)** self-effacement, self-negation; **l'~ de tout problème matériel** disregard for all material problems.

(b) (*trou de mémoire, omission*) lapse of memory. **ses ~s répétés m'inquiètent** his constant lapses of memory worry me, his constant forgetfulness worries me; **réparer un ~** to make up for having forgotten something *ou* for a lapse of memory; **cet ~ lui coûta la vie** this omission *ou* oversight cost him his life.

(c) l'~ oblivion, forgetfulness; **tirer qch de l'~** to bring sth out of oblivion; **l'~ guérit toutes les blessures** oblivion *ou* forgetfulness heals all wounds.

oublier [ublije] (7) *vt* **(a)** (*ne pas se souvenir de*) to forget; (*ne plus penser à*) *soucis, chagrin, client, visiteur* to forget (about). **~ de faire/pourquoi** to forget to do/why; **ça s'oublie facilement** it's easily forgotten; **j'ai oublié qui je dois prévenir** I can't remember who (it is) *ou* I've forgotten who (it is) I should warn; **j'ai oublié si j'ai bien éteint le gaz** I forget *ou* I can't remember if I turned off the gas; **n'oublie pas que nous sortons ce soir** remember *ou* don't forget we're going out tonight; **il oubliera avec le temps** he'll forget in time, time will help him forget; **j'avais complètement oublié sa présence** I had completely forgotten that he was there *ou* forgotten his presence; **il essaie de se faire ~** he's trying to keep out of the limelight.

(b) (*laisser*) *chose* to forget, leave behind; *fautes d'orthographe* to miss; *virgule, phrase* to leave out. **tu as oublié (de laver) une vitre** you forgot *ou* have forgotten (to wash) one of the panes.

(c) (*négliger*) *famille, devoir, travail, promesse* to forget, neglect. **~ les règles de la politesse** to forget *ou* neglect the rules of etiquette; **n'oubliez pas le guide!** don't forget the guide!; **il ne faut pas ~ que c'est un pays pauvre** we must not lose sight of the fact *ou* forget that it's a poor country; **~ qn dans son testament** to leave sb out of one's will, forget (to include) sb in one's will; **~ qn dans ses pensées** to forget (to include) sb in one's thoughts, forget to think about sb; **il ne vous oublie pas** he hasn't forgotten (about) you; **on l'a oublié sur la liste** he's been left off the list; (*iro*) **il ne s'est pas oublié (dans le partage)** he didn't forget himself (in the share-out).

ouest [wɛst] **1** *nm* **(a)** (*point cardinal*) west. **le vent d'~** the west wind; **un vent d'~** a west(erly) wind, a westerly (*T*); **le vent tourne/est à l'~** the wind is veering west(wards) *ou* towards the west/is blowing from the west; **regarder vers l'~ *ou* dans la direction de l'~** to look west(wards) *ou* towards the west; **à l'~** (*situation*) in the west; (*direction*) to the west, west(wards); **le soleil se couche à l'~** the sun sets in the west; **à l'~ de** west of, to the west of; **l'appartement est (exposé) à l'~/exposé plein ~** the flat faces (the) west *ou* westwards/due west, the flat looks west(wards)/due west; **l'Europe/la France/la Bourgogne de l'~** Western Europe/France/Burgundy; *V* **Allemagne.**

(b) (*partie, régions occidentales*) west. (*Pol*) **l'O~** the West; **l'O~ de la France, l'O~** the West of France.

2 *adj inv région, partie* western; *entrée, paroi* west; *versant, côte* west(ern); *côté* west(ward); *direction* westward, westerly; *V* **longitude.**

3: ouest-allemand, e *adj* West German; **Ouest-allemand, e** *nm,f* West German; **ouest-nord-ouest** *adj inv, nm* west-north-west; **ouest-sud-ouest** *adj inv, nm* west-south-west.

ouf [uf] *excl* phew! **ils ont dû repartir sans avoir le temps de dire ~*** they had to leave again before they had time to catch their breath *ou* before they knew where they were.

Ouganda [ugɑ̃da] *nm* Uganda.

ougrien, -ienne [ugʀijɛ̃, ijɛn] *V* **finno-ougrien.**

oui [wi] **1** *adv* **(a)** (*réponse affirmative*) yes, aye (*Naut, régional*), yea (†† *ou littér*). **le connaissez-vous? — ~** do you know him? — yes (I do); **est-elle chez elle? — ~** is she at home? — yes (she is); **vous avez aimé le film? — ~ et non** did you like the film? — yes and no *ou* I did and I didn't; **je vais ouvrir la fenêtre — ~ cela fera un peu d'air** I'll open the window — yes (do), we could do with some fresh air; **il n'a pas encore dit ~!** he hasn't said yes yet, he hasn't agreed *ou* accepted (as) yet; **ah, ça ~!** you can say that again!*, and how!*; **que ~!** rather! (*surtout Brit*), I should say so!; **certes ~!** (yes) most definitely *ou* certainly, yes indeed; **vous en voulez? — mais ~! *ou* bien sûr que ~ *ou* ~, bien sûr** do you want some? — of course (I do) *ou* I most certainly do; **~ mais, il y a un obstacle** yes but there is a difficulty; **eh bien ~, j'avoue** all right (then), I confess; **contraception ~, avortement non** yes to contraception, no to abortion; **répondre (par) ~ à toutes les questions** to answer yes *ou* answer in the affirmative to all the questions; **répondez par ~ ou par non** answer yes or no; **faire ~ de la tête, faire signe que ~** to nod (one's head); **ah ~?** really?, yes?; (†, *hum*) **~-da** yes indeed, absolutely; (*Naut*) **~, capitaine** aye aye captain.

(b) (*remplaçant une proposition*) **est-il chez lui?/est-ce qu'il travaille? — je pense *ou* crois que ~** is he at home?/is he working? — (yes) I think so *ou* believe he is; **il nous quitte? — je crains bien/j'espère que ~** is he leaving us? — I am afraid so *ou* I am afraid he is/I hope so *ou* I hope he is; **est-ce qu'elle sort souvent? — j'ai l'impression que ~** does she often go out? — I have an idea *ou* the impression that she does; **tu as aimé ce film? — moi ~/moi non** did you like the film? — I (*emphatique*) did/I didn't; **j'ai demandé si elle était venue, lui dit que ~** I asked if she had been and he says she has.

(c) (*intensif*) **c'est un escroc, ~, un escroc** he's an absolute rogue, he's a rogue, an absolute rogue; **~ vraiment, il a répondu ça?** (really), did he really answer that?; **tu vas cesser de pleurer, ~?** have you quite finished crying?, WILL you stop crying?; **~ (évidemment), c'est toujours bien facile de critiquer** of course it's always easy enough to criticize; **c'est bon, ~?** isn't that good?; **il va accepter, ~ ou non?** is he or isn't he going to accept?; **tu te presses, ~ ou non?** will you PLEASE hurry up, WILL you hurry up?

2 *nm inv* yes, aye. **il y a eu 30 ~** there were 30 votes for, there were 30 ayes; **j'aimerais un ~ plus ferme** I should prefer a more definite yes; **il ne dit ni ~ ni non** he's not saying either yes or no, he's not committing himself either way; **pleurer/réclamer pour un ~ ou pour un non** to cry/protest at the drop of a hat.

ouï-dire [widiʀ] *nm inv*: **par ~** by hearsay.

ouïe¹ [uj] *excl* = **ouille.**

ouïe² [wi] *nf* hearing (*U*). **avoir l'~ fine** to have sharp hearing, have a keen sense of hearing; *V* **tout.**

ouïes [wi] *nfpl* (*Zool*) gills; (*Mus*) sound-hole.

ouille [uj] *excl* ouch!

ouïr [wiʀ] (10) *vt* (††, *littér, hum*) to hear; (*Jur*) *témoins* to hear. **j'ai ouï dire à mon père que ...** I've heard my father say that ... ; **j'ai ouï dire que** it has come to my ears that, I've heard it said that; († *ou hum*) **oyez!** harken! († *ou hum*), hear ye! († *ou hum*).

ouistiti [wistiti] *nm* (*Zool*) marmoset. (*type*) **un drôle de ~*** a queer bird*.

oukase [ukɑz] *nm* = **ukase.**

ouragan [uʀagɑ̃] *nm* **(a)** (*lit*) hurricane.

(b) (*fig*) storm. **cet homme est un véritable ~** he's like a whirlwind, he's a human tornado; **ce livre va déchaîner un ~** this book is going to create a storm; **arriver en *ou* comme un ~** to arrive like a whirlwind *ou* tornado.

Oural [uʀal] *nm* (*fleuve*) **l'~** the Ural. **l'~, les monts ~** the Urals, the Ural Mountains.

ouralo-altaïque [uʀalɔaltaik] *adj, nm* Ural-Altaic.

ourdir [uʀdiʀ] (2) *vt complot* to hatch; *intrigue* to weave.

ourdou [uʀdu] **1** *adj inv* Urdu. **2** *nm* (*Ling*) Urdu.

ourlé, e [uʀle] (*ptp de* **ourler**) *adj* hemmed. **oreilles délicatement ~es** delicately rimmed ears.

ourler [uʀle] (1) *vt* (*Couture*) to hem. (*fig littér*) **~ de** to fringe with.

ourlet [uʀlɛ] *nm* **(a)** (*Couture*) hem. **faux ~** false hem; **faire un ~ à** to hem. **(b)** (*Tech*) hem. **(c)** (*Anat*) [*oreille*] rim, helix (*T*).

ours [uʀs] **1** *nm* **(a)** (*Zool*) bear. **tourner comme un ~ en cage** to pace up and down like a caged animal; *V* **fosse, montreur, vendre.**

(b) (*jouet*) **~ (en peluche)** teddy bear.

(c) (*péj: misanthrope*) (old) bear. **vivre comme un *ou* en ~** to live at odds with the world; elle est un peu ~ she's a bit of an old bear *ou* a gruff individual.

2: ours blanc polar bear; ours brun brown bear; (*péj*) ours mal léché uncouth fellow; ours marin fur-seal; ours polaire = ours blanc; ours savant trained *ou* performing bear.

ourse [uʀs(ə)] *nf* (a) (*Zool*) she-bear. (b) (*Astron*) la Petite O~ the Little Bear, Ursa Minor; la Grande O~ the Great Bear, Ursa Major.

oursin [uʀsɛ̃] *nm* sea urchin, sea hedgehog.

ourson [uʀsɔ̃] *nm* (bear-)cub.

oust(e)* [ust(ə)] *excl* hop it!* (*surtout Brit*), buzz off!*, off with you!

outarde [utaʀd(ə)] *nf* bustard; (*Can: bernache*) Canada goose.

outil [uti] *nm* (*lit, fig*) tool; (*agricole, de jardin*) implement, tool; *V* machine³, mauvais.

outillage [utijaʒ] *nm* [*mécanicien, bricoleur*] (set of) tools; [*fermier, jardinier*] implements (*pl*), equipment (*U*); [*atelier, usine*] equipment (*U*).

outiller [utije] (1) *vt ouvrier* to supply *ou* provide with tools, equip, kit out; *atelier* to fit out, equip. je suis bien/mal outillé pour ce genre de travail I'm well-/badly-equipped for this kind of work; pour ce travail, il faudra qu'on s'outille to do this job, we'll have to kit ourselves out *ou* equip ourselves properly; les ouvriers s'outillent à leurs frais the workers buy their own tools.

outilleur [utijœʀ] *nm* tool-maker.

outrage [utʀaʒ] 1 *nm* insult. accabler qn d'~s to heap insults on sb; faire ~ à *réputation, mémoire* to dishonour; *pudeur, honneur* to outrage, be an outrage to; (*fig*) ~ au bon sens/à la raison insult to common sense/reason; (*fig littér*) les ~s du temps the ravages of time; *V* dernier.

2: (*Jur*) outrage à agent insulting behaviour (*to police officer*); (*Jur*) outrage aux bonnes mœurs outrage *ou* affront to public decency; (*Jur*) outrage à magistrat contempt of court; (*Jur*) outrage à la pudeur indecent behaviour (*U*).

outragé, e [utʀaʒe] (*ptp de* outrager) *adj air, personne* gravely offended.

outrageant, e [utʀaʒɑ̃, ɑ̃t] *adj* offensive.

outrager [utʀaʒe] (3) *vt* (*littér*) *personne* to offend gravely; *mœurs, morale* to outrage; *bon sens, raison* to insult. outragée dans son honneur with outraged honour.

outrageusement [utʀaʒøzmɑ̃] *adv* (*excessivement*) outrageously, excessively.

outrageux, -euse [utʀaʒø, øz] *adj* (*excessif*) outrageous, excessive. de manière ~euse outrageously, excessively.

outrance [utʀɑ̃s] *nf* (a) (*U*) excessiveness. pousser le raffinement jusqu'à l'~ to take refinement to extremes *ou* to excess.

(b) (*excès*) excess. il y a des ~s dans ce roman there are some extravagant passages in this novel.

(c) à ~: raffiner à ~ to refine excessively *ou* to excess; dévot/méticuleux à ~ excessively pious/meticulous, pious/meticulous in the extreme *ou* to excess; *V* guerre.

outrancier, -ière [utʀɑ̃sje, jɛʀ] *adj personne, propos* extreme. son caractère ~ the extreme nature of his character, the extremeness of his character.

outre¹ [utʀ(ə)] *nf* goatskin, wine *ou* water skin. gonflé *ou* plein comme une ~ full to bursting.

outre² [utʀ(ə)] 1 *prép* (a) (*en plus de*) as well as, besides. ~ sa cargaison, le bateau transportait des passagers besides *ou* as well as its cargo the boat was carrying passengers; ~ son salaire, il a des pourboires on top of *ou* in addition to his salary, he gets tips; ~ le fait que as well as *ou* besides the fact that.

(b) (*loc*) en ~ moreover, besides, further(more); en ~ de over and above, on top of; ~ mesure to excess, overmuch, inordinately; manger/boire ~ mesure to eat/drink to excess *ou* immoderately; cela ne lui plaît pas ~ mesure he doesn't like that overmuch, he's not overkeen on that; cet auteur a été louangé ~ mesure this author has been praised overmuch *ou* unduly; passer ~ to carry on regardless, let it pass; passer ~ à to disregard, carry on regardless of; ~ que: ~ qu'il a le temps, il a les capacités pour le faire not only does he have the time but he also has the ability to do it, apart from having the time *ou* besides having the time he also has the ability to do it; (†) d'~ en ~ through and through.

2: outre-Atlantique across the Atlantic; outre-Manche across the Channel; outre-mer overseas; les territoires d'outre-mer overseas territories; outre-Rhin across the Rhine; les pays d'outre-rideau de fer the iron curtain countries, the countries behind the iron curtain; outre-tombe beyond the grave; d'une voix d'outre-tombe in a lugubrious voice; *V* outrecuidance, outremer, outrepasser *etc*.

outré, e [utʀe] (*ptp de* outrer) *adj* (a) (*littér: exagéré*) *éloges, flatterie* excessive, exaggerated, overdone (*attrib*); *description* exaggerated, extravagant, overdone (*attrib*). (b) (*indigné*) outraged (*de, par* at, by).

outrecuidance [utʀəkɥidɑ̃s] *nf* (a) (*littér: présomption*) presumptuousness. parler avec ~ to speak presumptuously.

(b) (*effronterie*) impertinence. répondre à qn avec ~ to answer sb impertinently; ~s impudence (*U*), impertinences.

outrecuidant, e [utʀəkɥidɑ̃, ɑ̃t] *adj* (a) (*présomptueux*) presumptuous. (b) (*effronté*) *attitude, réponse* impertinent.

outremer [utʀəmɛʀ] 1 *nm* (*pierre*) lapis lazuli; (*couleur*) ultramarine. 2 *adj inv* ultramarine.

outrepasser [utʀəpɑse] (1) *vt droits* to go beyond; *pouvoir, ordres* to exceed; *limites* to go beyond, overstep.

outrer [utʀe] (1) *vt* (a) (*littér*) (*exagérer*) to exaggerate. cet acteur outre son jeu this actor overacts.

(b) (*indigner*) to outrage. votre ingratitude m'a outré your ingratitude has outraged me, I am outraged at *ou* by your ingratitude.

outsider [awtsajdœʀ] *nm* (*Sport, fig*) outsider.

ouvert, e [uvɛʀ, ɛʀt(ə)] (*ptp de* ouvrir) *adj* (a) *porte, magasin, valise, lieu, espace* open; *voiture* open, unlocked; (*Ling*) *voyelle, syllabe* open; *angle* wide; *série, ensemble* open-ended; *robinet* on, running; *col, chemise* open, undone (*attrib*). la bouche ~e open-mouthed, with open mouth; entrez, c'est ~! come in, the door isn't locked!; ~ au public open to the public; (*Comm*) je suis ~ jusqu'à Noël* I'm open till Christmas; ~ à la circulation open to traffic; le col du Simplon est ~ the Simplon pass is open (to traffic); ~ à la navigation open to ships *ou* for sailing; une rose trop ~e a rose which is too (far) open; elle est partie en laissant le robinet/gaz ~ she went away leaving the tap *ou* the water on *ou* running/the gas on; *V* bras, ciel *etc*.

(b) (*commencé*) open. la chasse/pêche est ~e the shooting season/fishing season is open; *V* pari.

(c) (*percé, incisé*) *plaie* open. il a le crâne/le bras ~ he has a gaping wound in his head/arm; *V* cœur, fracture.

(d) *débat*, (*Sport*) *compétition* open. une partie très ~e an open-ended game; pratiquer un jeu ~ to play an open game.

(e) (*déclaré, non dissimulé*) *guerre, haine* open. de façon ~e openly.

(f) (*communicatif, franc*) *personne, caractère* open, frank; *visage, physionomie* open; (*éveillé, accessible*) *esprit, intelligence, milieu* open. à l'esprit ~ open-minded.

ouvertement [uvɛʀtəmɑ̃] *adv dire, avouer* openly; *agir* openly, overtly.

ouverture [uvɛʀtyʀ] *nf* (a) (*action: V* ouvrir) opening; unlocking; opening up; opening out; unfastening; cutting open; starting up; turning on; switching on. (*Comm*) jours d'~ days of opening; (*Comm*) heures d'~ [*magasin*] opening hours, hours of business *ou* of opening; [*musée*] opening hours, hours of opening; à l'heure d'~, à l'~ at opening time; l'~ de la porte est automatique the door opens *ou* is operated automatically; cérémonie d'~ opening ceremony; c'est demain l'~ de la chasse tomorrow sees the opening of *ou* the first day of the shooting season; (*Chasse*) faire l'~ to go on *ou* be at the first shoot.

(b) (*passage, issue, accès*) opening; [*puits*] mouth, opening. toutes les ~s sont gardées all means of access (*ou* exit) are guarded, all the access points (*ou* exit points) are guarded.

(c) (*avances*) ~s overtures; faire des ~s à qn to make overtures to sb; faire des ~s de paix/conciliation to make peace/conciliatory overtures; faire des ~s de négociation to make steps towards instigating negotiations.

(d) (*fig: largeur, compréhension*) open-mindedness. (*Pol*) l'~ the opening up of the political spectrum; il a une grande ~ d'esprit he is extremely broad-minded; (*Pol*) être partisan de l'~ to be in favour of *ou* support the opening up of the political spectrum; le besoin d'(une) ~ sur le monde the need of (an) opening onto the world.

(e) (*Mus*) overture.

(f) (*Math*) [*angle*] magnitude; [*compas*] degree of opening; (*Phot*) aperture.

(g) (*Cartes*) opening. (*Échecs*) avoir l'~ to have the first *ou* opening move.

(h) (*Ftbl, Rugby*) forward kick *ou* pass; *V* demi².

ouvrable [uvʀabl(ə)] *adj*: jour ~ weekday, working day; heures ~s business hours.

ouvrage [uvʀaʒ] 1 *nm* (a) (*travail*) work (*U*). se mettre à l'~ to set to *ou* get (down) to *ou* start work; (*littér*) l'~ du temps/du hasard the work of time/chance; *V* cœur.

(b) (*objet produit*) piece of work; (*Couture*) work (*U*). ~ d'orfèvrerie piece of goldwork; ~ à l'aiguille (piece of) needlework; *V* boîte, corbeille, panier *etc*.

(c) (*livre*) (*œuvre, écrit*) work; (*volume*) book.

(d) (*Constr*) work.

2 *nf* (†, *hum: travail*) de la belle ~ a nice piece of work.

3: (*Génie civil*) ouvrage d'art structure (*bridge or tunnel etc*); (*Mil*) ouvrage avancé outwork; ouvrage de dames fancy work (*U*); (*Mil*) ouvrage défensif defences, defence work(s); ouvrage de maçonnerie masonry work; ouvrage militaire fortification.

ouvragé, e [uvʀaʒe] *adj meuble, bois* (finely) carved; *napperon* (finely) embroidered; *signature* elaborate; *métal, bijou* finely worked.

ouvrant, e [uvʀɑ̃, ɑ̃t] *adj V* toit.

ouvre- [uvʀə] *préf V* ouvrir.

ouvré, e [uvʀe] *adj* (*Tech, littér*) *meuble, bois* (finely) carved; *napperon* (finely) embroidered; *métal, bijou* finely worked.

ouvreur [uvʀœʀ] *nm* (*Cartes*) opener; (*Ski*) forerunner, vorläufer.

ouvreuse [uvʀøz] *nf* usherette.

ouvrier, -ière [uvʀije, ijɛʀ] 1 *adj enfance, éducation, quartier* working-class; *conflit, agitation, législation* industrial (*épith*), labour (*épith*); *questions* labour (*épith*). association ~ière workers' *ou* working men's association; *V* cité, classe, syndicat.

2 *nm* worker, workman. ~ d'usine factory worker *ou* hand; les revendications des ~s the workers' claims; des mains d'~ workman's hands; 150 ~s ont été mis en chômage technique 150 men *ou* workers have been laid off; comme ~, dans un petit atelier, il ... as a workman *ou* worker in a small workshop, he ... ; *V* mauvais, œuvre.

3 ouvrière *nf* (a) (*gén, Admin*) female worker. ~ière (d'usine) female factory worker *ou* factory hand; (*jeune*) factory girl, young factory hand; il allait à l'usine attendre la sortie des ~ières he went to the factory to wait for the women *ou* girls to come out; on voyait à son visage fatigué que c'était une ~ière you could see by her tired look that she was a factory worker *ou* factory hand.

(b) (*Zool*) **(abeille) ~ière** worker (bee).
4: ouvrier agricole agricultural *ou* farm worker, farm labourer, farmhand; **ouvrier de chantier** labourer; **ouvrier à la journée** day labourer; **ouvrier qualifié** skilled workman; **ouvrier spécialisé** unskilled worker.

ouvriérisme [uvʀijeʀism(ə)] *nm* worker control, worker power.

ouvrir [uvʀiʀ] (18) **1** *vt* **(a)** *fenêtre, porte, tiroir, paquet, magasin, chambre* to open; *rideaux* to open, draw back; *porte fermée à clef* to unlock; *huîtres, coquillages* to open (up). **~ par *ou* avec effraction** *porte, coffre* to break open; **~ la porte toute grande/le portail tout grand** to open the door/gate wide; **il a ouvert brusquement la porte** he opened the door abruptly, he threw *ou* flung the door open; (*fig*) **~ sa porte *ou* sa maison à qn** to throw open one's doors *ou* one's house to sb; (*fig*) **ça lui a ouvert toutes les portes** this opened all doors to him; (*fig*) **~ la porte toute grande aux abus/excès** to throw the door wide open to abuses/excesses; **on a frappé: va ~!** there was a knock: go and open *ou* answer the door!; **fais-toi ~ par la concierge** ask *ou* get the caretaker to let you in; **le boulanger ouvre de 7 heures à 19 heures** the baker('s shop) is open *ou* opens from 7 a.m. till 7 p.m.; **ils ouvrent leur maison au public tous les étés** they open up their house to the public every summer, they throw their house open to the public every summer; *V* **parenthèse.**
(b) *bouche, yeux, paupières* to open. **~ le bec, l'~‡** to open one's trap‡; **~ la *ou* sa gueule**** to open one's gob**; (*fig*) **~ l'œil** to keep one's eyes open (*fig*); (*lit*) **~ les yeux** to open one's eyes; (*fig*) **ce voyage en Asie m'a ouvert les yeux** this trip through Asia opened my eyes *ou* was an eye-opener (to me); **ouvre l'œil, et le bon!*** keep your eyes skinned!* (*Brit*) *ou* peeled!*; **~ les oreilles** to pin back one's ears; **elle m'a ouvert son cœur** she opened her heart to me; **ça m'a ouvert l'appétit** that whetted my appetite; (*fig*) **~ l'esprit à qn** to open up sb's mind.
(c) *journal, couteau* to open; *parapluie* to open (out), put up; *éventail, bras, ailes, main* to open (out); *manteau, gilet* to undo, unfasten, open; *lit, drap* to turn down. (*Mil*) **ouvrez les rangs!** dress!; (*fig*) **~ ses rangs à qn** to welcome sb among one's ranks; (*fig*) **~ sa bourse (à qn)** to put one's hand in one's pocket (to help sb).
(d) (*faire un trou dans*) *chaussée, mur* to open up; *membre, ventre* to open up, cut open. **les roches lui ont ouvert la jambe** he has cut his leg open on the rocks; **le médecin pense qu'il faudra ~** the doctor thinks that they will have to operate.
(e) (*faire, construire*) *porte, passage* to open up, make; *autoroute* to build; (*fig*) *horizons, perspectives* to open up. **il a fallu ~ une porte dans ce mur** a doorway had to be opened up *ou* made in this wall; **~ un passage dans le roc à la dynamite** to open up *ou* blast a passage in the rock with dynamite; **cette autoroute a été ouverte pour desservir la nouvelle banlieue** this motorway has been built to serve the new suburb; **ils lui ont ouvert un passage *ou* le passage dans la foule** they made way for him through the crowd; **s'~ un passage à travers la forêt** to open up *ou* cut a path for o.s. through the forest; (*fig*) **~ des horizons à qn** to open up new horizons for sb.
(f) (*débloquer*) *chemin, passage* to open. **le chasse-neige a ouvert la route** the snowplough opened up the road; (*Sport*) **~ le jeu** to open up the game; (*fig*) **~ la voie (à qn)** to lead the way (for sb).
(g) (*autoriser l'accès de*) *route, col, frontière* to open (up).
(h) (*commencer l'exploitation de*) *restaurant, théâtre, magasin* to open (up), start up; *école, succursale* to open (up).
(i) (*constituer*) *souscription, compte bancaire, enquête* to open; (*inaugurer*) *festival, exposition, bal* to open. **~ un compte à un client** to open an account for a customer *ou* in a customer's name; **~ les hostilités** to start up *ou* begin hostilities; **~ le feu** to open fire, open up; (*Ski*) **~ la piste** to be the forerunner; (*Cartes*) **~ le jeu** to open play; (*Cartes*) **il a ouvert à pique** he opened on *ou* with spades; (*Ftbl, Rugby*) **il ouvre toujours sur un joueur faible** he always passes to a weak player.
(j) (*être au début de*) *liste, œuvre* to head; *procession* to lead. **~ la marche** to take the lead, walk in front.
(k) *électricité, gaz, radio* to turn on, switch on, put on; *eau, robinet* to turn on; *vanne* to open.
2 *vi* **(a)** *[fenêtre, porte]* to open. **cette fenêtre ouvre sur la cour** this window opens onto the yard; **la porte de derrière n'ouvre pas** the back door doesn't open.
(b) *[magasin]* to open. **ça ouvre de 2 à 5** they open *ou* are open from 2 to 5.
(c) (*commencer*) to open. **la pièce ouvre par un discours du vainqueur** the play opens with a speech from the victor.
3 s'ouvrir *vpr* **(a)** *[porte, fenêtre, parapluie, livre]* to open; *[fleur, coquillage]* to open (out); *[bouche, yeux]* to open; *[bras, main, ailes]* to open (out); *[esprit]* to open out; *[gouffre]* to open. **robe qui s'ouvre par devant** dress that undoes *ou* unfastens at the front; **sa robe s'est ouverte** her dress came undone *ou* unfastened; **la fenêtre s'ouvre sur une cour** the window opens (out) onto a courtyard; **la foule s'ouvrit pour le laisser passer** the crowd parted to let him through; **la porte s'ouvrit violemment** the door flew open *ou* was flung open *ou* was thrown open; **la porte/boîte a dû s'~** the door/box must have come open.
(b) (*commencer*) *[récit, séance, exposition]* to open (*par* with). **la séance s'ouvrit par un chahut** the meeting opened in (an) uproar *ou* with an uproar.
(c) (*se présenter*) **s' ~ devant** *[paysage, vie]* to open in front of *ou* before; **un chemin poussiéreux s'ouvrit devant eux** a dusty path opened in front of *ou* before them; **la vie qui s'ouvre devant elle est pleine d'embûches** the life which is opening in front of *ou* before her is full of obstacles.
(d) (*béer*) to open (up). **la terre s'ouvrit devant eux** the ground opened up before them; **le gouffre s'ouvrait à leurs pieds** the chasm lay open *ou* gaped at their feet.
(e)(*devenir sensible à*) **s'~ à** *amour, art, problèmes économiques* to open one's mind to, become aware of; **son esprit s'est ouvert aux souffrances d'autrui** his mind opened to *ou* he became aware of others' suffering.
(f) (*se confier*) **s'~ à qn de** to open one's heart to sb about; **il s'en est ouvert à son confesseur** he opened his heart to his confessor about it.
(g) (*se blesser*) to cut open. **elle s'est ouvert les veines** she slashed *ou* cut her wrists; **il s'ouvrit la jambe en tombant sur une faux** he cut open his leg by falling on a scythe.
4: ouvre-boîte(s) *nm inv* tin opener; **ouvre-bouteille(s)** *nm inv* bottle-opener.

ouvroir [uvʀwaʀ] *nm [couvent]* workroom; *[paroisse]* sewing room.

ovaire [ɔvɛʀ] *nm* ovary.

ovale [ɔval] **1** *adj table, surface* oval; *volume* egg-shaped; *V* **ballon. 2** *nm* oval. **l'~ du visage** the oval of the face; **en ~** oval (-shaped).

ovariectomie [ɔvaʀjɛktɔmi] *nf* ovariotomy.

ovarien, -ienne [ɔvaʀjɛ̃, jɛn] *adj* ovarian.

ovariotomie [ɔvaʀjɔtɔmi] *nf* = **ovariectomie.**

ovarite [ɔvaʀit] *nf* ovaritis, oophoritis.

ovation [ɔvɑsjɔ̃] *nf* ovation. **faire une ~ à qn** to give sb an ovation; **ils se levèrent pour lui faire une ~** they gave him a standing ovation.

ovationner [ɔvɑsjɔne] (1) *vt*: **~ qn** to give sb an ovation.

ove [ɔv] *nm* ovum (*Archit*).

Ovide [ɔvid] *nm* Ovid.

ovin, e [ɔvɛ̃, in] **1** *adj* ovine. **2** *nm*: **les ~s** the ovine race.

ovipare [ɔvipaʀ] **1** *adj* oviparous. **2** *nm* oviparous animal. **~s** ovipara.

ovoïde [ɔvɔid] *adj* egg-shaped, ovoid (*T*).

ovulaire [ɔvylɛʀ] *adj* ovular.

ovulation [ɔvylɑsjɔ̃] *nf* ovulation.

ovule [ɔvyl] *nm* (*Physiol*) ovum; (*Bot*) ovule; (*Pharm*) pessary.

oxacide [ɔksasid] *nm* oxyacid, oxygen acid.

oxfordien, -ienne [ɔksfɔʀdjɛ̃, jɛn] **1** *adj* Oxfordian. **2** *nm,f*: **O~(ne)** Oxfordian.

oxhydrique [ɔksidʀik] *adj* oxyhydrogen (*épith*).

oxonien, -ienne [ɔksɔnjɛ̃, jɛn] **1** *adj* Oxonian. **2** *nm,f*: **O~(ne)** Oxonian.

oxyacétylénique [ɔksiasetilenik] *adj* oxyacetylene (*épith*).

oxydable [ɔksidabl(ə)] *adj* liable to rust, oxidizible (*T*).

oxydant, e [ɔksidɑ̃, ɑ̃t] **1** *adj* oxidizing. **2** *nm* oxidizer, oxidizing agent.

oxydation [ɔksidɑsjɔ̃] *nf* oxidization, oxidation.

oxyde [ɔksid] *nm* oxide. **~ de carbone** carbon monoxide; **~ de plomb** lead oxide *ou* monoxide; **~ de cuivre/de fer** copper/iron oxide.

oxyder [ɔkside] (1) **1** *vt* to oxidize. **2 s'oxyder** *vpr* to become oxidized.

oxygénation [ɔksiʒenɑsjɔ̃] *nf* oxygenation.

oxygène [ɔksiʒɛn] *nm* oxygen. **masque/tente à ~** oxygen mask/tent.

oxygéner [ɔksiʒene] (6) *vt* (*Chim*) to oxygenate; *cheveux* to peroxide, bleach. **s'~ (les poumons)*** to get some fresh air (into one's lungs); *V* **blond, eau.**

oyez [ɔje] *V* **ouïr.**

ozone [ozɔn] *nm* ozone.

ozonisation [ozɔnizɑsjɔ̃] *nf* ozonization.

ozoniser [ozɔnize] (1) *vt* to ozonize.

P

P, p [pe] *nm (lettre)* P, p.
pacage [pakaʒ] *nm* pasture (land).
pacha [paʃa] *nm* pasha. **mener une vie de ~, faire le ~** *(vivre richement)* to live like a lord; *(se prélasser)* to live a life of ease.
pachyderme [paʃidɛʀm(ə)] *nm (éléphant)* elephant; *(ongulé)* pachyderm *(T)*. *(fig)* **de ~** elephantine, heavy.
pacificateur, -trice [pasifikatœʀ, tʀis] **1** *adj* pacificatory. **2** *nm,f (personne)* peacemaker; *(chose)* pacifier.
pacification [pasifikɑsjɔ̃] *nf* pacification. **mesures de ~** pacification *ou* pacificatory measures.
pacifier [pasifje] (7) *vt pays* to pacify, bring peace to; *(fig) esprits* to pacify.
pacifique [pasifik] **1** *adj* **(a)** *coexistence* peaceful; *humeur* peaceable; *personne* peace-loving, peaceable; *mesure, intention* pacific. **utilisé à des fins ~s** used for peaceful purposes. **(b)** *(Géog)* Pacific. **2** *nm (Géog)* **le P~** the Pacific.
pacifiquement [pasifikmɑ̃] *adv (V* **pacifique***)* peacefully; peaceably; pacifically.
pacifisme [pasifism(ə)] *nm* pacifism.
pacifiste [pasifist(ə)] **1** *nmf* pacifist. **2** *adj* pacifistic, pacifist.
pacotille [pakɔtij] *nf* **(a)** *(de mauvaise qualité)* poor-quality stuff, cheap and nasty goods; *(clinquant)* showy stuff. *(péj)* **c'est de la ~** it's rubbishy stuff, it's cheap rubbish; **leur maison, c'est de la ~** it's just a jerry-built house, their house is just a shack; **meubles/bijoux de ~** cheap furniture/jewellery.
(b) *(Hist) goods carried free of freightage.*
pacte [pakt(ə)] *nm* pact, treaty. **~ d'alliance** treaty of alliance; **~ de non-agression** pact of non-aggression.
pactiser [paktize] (1) *vt (péj) (se liguer)* to take sides *(avec* with); *(transiger)* to come to terms *(avec* with). **c'est ~ avec le crime** it amounts to being in league with crime.
pactole [paktɔl] *nm (fig)* gold mine. *(Géog)* **le P~** the Pactolus.
paddock [padɔk] *nm* **(a)** *[champ de courses]* paddock. **(b)** *(*✱*: lit)* bed. **aller au ~** to hit the sack* *ou* the hay*, turn in*.
Padoue [padu] *n* Padua.
paf [paf] **1** *excl (chute)* bam!; *(gifle)* slap!, wham! **2** *adj inv (*✱*: ivre)* tight*. **complètement ~** plastered✱.
pagaie [pagɛ] *nf* paddle.
pagaie, pagaille [pagaj] *nf* **(a)** *(objets en désordre)* mess, shambles *(U)*; *(cohue, manque d'organisation)* chaos *(U)*. **quelle ~ dans la pièce!** what a mess this room is in!, what a shambles in this room!; **c'est la ~ sur les routes/dans le gouvernement!** there is (complete) chaos on the roads/in the government!; **il a mis la ~ dans mes affaires/dans la réunion** he has messed up all my things/the meeting. **(b)** *(beaucoup)* **il y en a en ~** there are loads* *ou* masses of them.
paganiser [paganize] (1) *vt* to paganize, heathenize.
paganisme [paganism(ə)] *nm* paganism, heathenism.
pagaye [pagaj] *nf* = **pagaïe.**
pagayer [pageje] (8) *vi* to paddle.
pagayeur, -euse [pagɛjœʀ, øz] *nm,f* paddler.
page[1] [paʒ] **1** *nf* **(a)** *(feuillet)* page; *(fig) (passage)* passage, page; *(événement)* page, chapter, episode. **une ~ d'écriture** a page of writing; **les plus belles ~s de Corneille** the finest passages of Corneille; **une ~ glorieuse de l'histoire de France** a glorious page *ou* chapter in the history of France; **une ~ est tournée** a page has been turned; *(Typ)* **mettre en ~** to make up (into pages); *V* **mise[2], tourner.**
(b) *(loc)* **être à la ~** *(mode)* to be up-to-date *ou* with it*; *(actualité)* to keep in touch *ou* up-to-date, keep up with what's new; **ne plus être à la ~** to be out of touch *ou* behind the times.
2: page blanche blank page; **page de garde** flyleaf; *(Presse)* **page des petites annonces** small-ads page.
page[2] [paʒ] *nm (Hist)* page (boy).
page[3]✱ [paʒ] *nm*, **pageot**✱ [paʒo] *nm* bed. **se mettre au ~** to hit the sack*, turn in*.
pageoter (se)✱ [paʒɔte] (1) *vpr* to turn in*, hit the sack* *ou* the hay*.
pagination [paʒinɑsjɔ̃] *nf* pagination.
paginer [paʒine] (1) *vt* to paginate.
pagne [paɲ] *nm* loincloth.
pagode [pagɔd] *nf* pagoda.
paie [pɛ] *nf [militaire]* pay; *[ouvrier]* pay, wages. **jour de ~** payday; **bulletin** *ou* **feuille de ~** paysheet; **toucher sa ~** to be paid, get one's wages; *(fig)* **il y a** *ou* **ça fait une ~ que nous ne nous sommes pas vus*** it's ages *ou* donkey's years* *(Brit)* since we last saw each other.
paiement [pɛmɑ̃] *nm* payment. **faire un ~** to make a payment; **~ comptant** cash payment; **~ par chèque/d'avance** payment by cheque/in advance; *V* **facilité.**
païen, -ïenne [pajɛ̃, jɛn] *adj, nm,f* pagan, heathen.
paillage [pɑjaʒ] *nm* mulching.
paillard, e* [pajaʀ, aʀd(ə)] *adj personne* bawdy, coarse; *histoire* bawdy, lewd, dirty. **chanson ~e** ≈ rugby song.
paillardise [pajaʀdiz] *nf (débauche)* bawdiness; *(plaisanterie)* dirty *ou* lewd joke *(ou* story *ou* remark *etc)*.
paillasse[1] [pajas] *nf* **(a)** *(matelas)* straw mattress. **(b)** *[évier]* draining board.
paillasse[2] [pajas] *nm (clown)* clown.
paillasson [pɑjasɔ̃] *nm [porte]* doormat; *(péj: personne)* doormat *(fig)*; *(Agr)* matting; *V* **clef.**
paille [pɑj] **1** *nf* **(a)** straw; *(pour boire)* (drinking) straw. **chapeau/panier de ~** straw hat/basket; **botte de ~** bale of hay; **boire avec une ~** to drink through a straw.
(b) *(loc)* **être sur la ~** to be penniless; **mettre sur la ~** to reduce to poverty; **mourir sur la ~** to die penniless *ou* in poverty; **voir la ~ dans l'œil du prochain** to see the mote in one's neighbour's eye *ou* one's brother's eye; **c'est la ~ et la poutre** it's the pot calling the kettle black; **2 millions de francs? une ~!*** 2 million francs? that's peanuts!*; *V* **court[1], homme.**
(c) *(Tech: défaut)* flaw.
2 *adj inv* straw-coloured.
3: paille de fer steel wool; **paille de riz** straw.
pailler [pɑje] (1) *vt chaise* to put a straw bottom in; *arbre, fraisier* to mulch. **chaise paillée** straw-bottomed chair.
pailleté, e [pajte] *(ptp de* **pailleter***) adj robe* sequined.
pailleter [pajte] (4) *vt* to spangle.
paillette [pajɛt] *nf* **(a)** *(Habillement)* sequin, spangle. **(b)** *[or]* speck; *[mica, lessive]* flake. **savon en ~s** soapflakes.
paillis [pɑji] *nm* mulch.
paillote [pɑjɔt] *nf* straw hut.
pain [pɛ̃] **1** *nm* **(a)** *(gén)* bread *(U)*; *(miche)* loaf. **un ~ (de 2 livres)** a (2-lb) loaf; **du gros ~** bread sold by weight; *(Rel)* **le ~ et le vin** the bread and wine; **le ~ quotidien** one's daily bread.
(b) *(en forme de pain) [cire]* bar; *[savon]* bar, cake. *(Culin)* **~ de poisson/de légumes** *etc* fish/vegetable *etc* loaf.
(c) *(loc)* **avoir du ~ sur la planche*** to have a lot on one's plate *(Brit)*; **ôter** *ou* **retirer le ~ de la bouche à qn** to take the bread out of sb's mouth; **faire passer** *ou* **ôter le goût du ~ à qn*** to do sb in*.
2: pain azyme unleavened bread; **pain bis** brown bread; **pain brioché** brioche loaf; **pain à cacheter** sealing wax *(U)*; **pain de campagne** farmhouse bread; **pain au chocolat** *puff pastry with chocolate filling;* **pain complet** wholemeal bread; **pain d'épice(s)** ≃ gingerbread; **pain de Gênes** Genoa cake; **pain grillé** toast; **pain de gruau** wheaten bread; **pain de mie** sandwich loaf; **pain perdu** French toast; **pain aux raisins** currant bun; **pain de seigle** rye bread; **pain de sucre** sugar loaf; **montagne en pain de sucre** sugar loaf mountain; **tête en pain de sucre** egg-shaped head; **pain viennois** wheaten bread.
pair[1] [pɛʀ] *nm* **(a)** *(dignitaire)* peer.
(b) *(égaux)* **~s** peers.
(c) *(Fin)* par. **valeur remboursée au ~** stock repayable at par; **cours au ~** par rate.
(d) au ~: travailler au ~ to work in exchange for board and lodging; **jeune fille au ~** au pair girl.
(e) de ~: ces 2 conditions/qualités vont *ou* **marchent de ~** these 2 conditions/qualities go hand in hand *ou* go together; **ça va de ~ avec** it goes hand in hand with; *V* **hors.**
pair[2], e[1] [pɛʀ] *adj nombre* even. **le côté ~ de la rue** the even-numbers side of the street; **jours ~s** even dates; **jouer ~** to bet on the even numbers.
paire[2] [pɛʀ] *nf* **(a)** *[ciseaux, lunettes, tenailles, chaussures]* pair; *[bœufs]* yoke; *[pistolets, pigeons]* brace. **ils forment une ~ d'amis** the two of them are great friends; **donner une ~ de gifles à qn** to box sb's ears; **avoir une bonne ~ de joues** to be chubby-cheeked.
(b) *(loc)* **les deux font la ~** they're two of a kind; **c'est une autre ~ de manches*** that's another story; **se faire la ~**✱ to clear off✱, beat it✱.
pairesse [pɛʀɛs] *nf* peeress.
pairie [peʀi] *nf* peerage.
paisible [pezibl(ə)] *adj (sans remous)* peaceful, calm, quiet; *(sans agressivité)* peaceful, peaceable, quiet. **dormir d'un sommeil ~** to be sleeping peacefully.
paisiblement [pezibləmɑ̃] *adv (V* **paisible***)* peacefully; calmly; quietly; peaceably.
paître [pɛtʀ(ə)] (57) **1** *vi* to graze. **faire ~** to take to pasture; **le pâturage où ils font ~ leur troupeau pendant l'été** the pasture where they graze their herd in the summer; **envoyer ~ qn**✱ to send sb packing*.
2 *vt:* **~ l'herbe d'un pré** to be grazing in a meadow.
paix [pɛ] *nf* **(a)** *(Mil, Pol)* peace. **~ armée** armed peace; **demander la ~** to sue for peace; **signer la ~** to sign the *ou* a peace treaty; **en temps de ~** in peacetime; **traité/pourparlers de ~** peace treaty/talks; *(Prov)* **si tu veux la ~, prépare la guerre** if you wish to have peace, prepare for war.
(b) *(état d'accord)* peace. **ramener la ~ entre** to make peace between; **il a fait la ~ avec son frère** he has made his peace with his brother, he and his brother have made it up; *V* **baiser, gardien, juge.**
(c) *(tranquillité)* peace, quiet; *(silence)* stillness, peacefulness. **tout le monde est sorti, quelle ~ dans la maison!** how peaceful *ou* quiet it is in the house now everyone has gone out!; **est-ce qu'on pourrait avoir la ~?** could we have a bit of peace and quiet? *ou* a bit of hush?*

(d) (*calme intérieur*) peace. **la ~ de l'âme** inner peace; (*Rel*) **allez** *ou* **partez en ~** go in peace; (*hum*) **~ à sa mémoire** *ou* **à ses cendres** God rest his soul; **avoir la conscience en ~, être en ~ avec sa conscience** to have a clear conscience; **laisser qn en ~, laisser la ~ à qn** to leave sb alone *ou* in peace; **fous-moi:** *ou* **fiche-moi* la ~!** stop pestering me!, clear off!:; **la ~!** shut up!*, quiet!

Pakistan [pakistɑ̃] *nm* Pakistan.

pakistanais, e [pakistanɛ, ɛz] **1** *adj* Pakistani. **2** *nm,f*: **P~(e)** Pakistani.

pal, *pl* **~s** [pal] *nm* (*Hér*) pale; (*pieu*) stake. **le (supplice du) ~** torture by impalement.

palabrer [palabʀe] (1) *vi* (*parlementer*) to argue endlessly; (*bavarder*) to chat, waffle on* (*Brit*).

palabres [palabʀ(ə)] *nmpl ou nfpl* never-ending *ou* interminable discussions.

palace [palas] *nm* luxury hotel.

paladin [paladɛ̃] *nm* paladin.

palais [palɛ] **1** *nm* **(a)** (*édifice*) palace.

(b) (*Jur*) law courts. **en argot du P~, en termes de P~** in legal parlance.

(c) (*Anat*) palate. **~ dur/mou** hard/soft palate; **avoir le ~ desséché** to be parched; (*fig*) **avoir le ~ fin** to have a delicate palate; *V* **flatter, voile**[2].

2: le Palais-Bourbon *the French National Assembly;* **palais des expositions** exhibition hall; **le Palais de Justice** the Law Courts; **palais des sports** sports stadium.

palan [palɑ̃] *nm* hoist.

palanque [palɑ̃k] *nf* stockade.

palanquin [palɑ̃kɛ̃] *nm* palanquin, palankeen.

palatal, e, *mpl* **-aux** [palatal, o] **1** *adj* (*Ling*) *consonne* palatal (*épith*); *voyelle* front (*épith*); (*Anat*) palatal. **2 palatale** *nf* palatal consonant; front vowel.

palatalisation [palatalizɑsjɔ̃] *nf* palatalization.

palataliser [palatalize] (1) *vt* to palatalize.

palatin, e [palatɛ̃, in] **1** *adj* **(a)** (*Hist*) Palatine. **le Comte/l'Électeur ~** the Count/Elector Palatine. **(b)** (*Géog*) **le (mont) P~** the Palatine Hill. **2** *nm* (*Hist*) palatine.

Palatinat [palatina] *nm*: **le ~** the Palatinate.

pale [pal] *nf* [*hélice, rame*] blade; [*roue, écluse*] paddle.

pâle [pɑl] *adj* **(a)** *teint, personne* pale; (*maladif*) pallid, pale. **~ comme un linge** as white as a sheet; **~ comme la mort** deathly pale *ou* white; **~ de peur/de colère** white with fear/with anger; **se faire porter ~:** to report *ou* go sick; *V* **visage.**

(b) *lueur* pale, weak, faint; *couleur, soleil, ciel* pale.

(c) *style* weak; *imitation* pale, poor; *sourire* faint, wan. (*péj*) **un ~ crétin** a downright *ou* an utter fool.

palefrenier [palfʀənje] *nm* [*auberge*] ostler; [*château*] groom.

palefroi [palfʀwa] *nm* (*Hist*) palfrey.

paléographe [paleɔgʀaf] *nmf* paleographer.

paléographie [paleɔgʀafi] *nf* paleography.

paléographique [paleɔgʀafik] *adj* paleographic(al).

paléolithique [paleɔlitik] **1** *adj* paleolithic. **2** *nm* Paleolithic (age).

paléontologie [paleɔ̃tɔlɔʒi] *nf* paleontology.

paléontologique [paleɔ̃tɔlɔʒik] *adj* paleontologic(al).

paléontologiste [paleɔ̃tɔlɔʒist(ə)] *nmf*, **paléontologue** [paleɔ̃tɔlɔg] *nmf* paleontologist.

paleron [palʀɔ̃] *nm* (*Boucherie*) chuck.

Palestine [palɛstin] *nf* Palestine.

palestinien, -ienne [palɛstinjɛ̃, jɛn] **1** *adj* Palestinian. **2** *nm,f*: **P~(ne)** Palestinian.

palet [palɛ] *nm* (*gén*) (metal *ou* stone) disc; [*hockey*] puck.

paletot [palto] *nm* (thick) cardigan. **il m'est tombé sur le ~:** he jumped on me.

palette [palɛt] *nf* **(a)** (*Peinture: lit, fig*) palette. **(b)** (*Boucherie*) shoulder. **(c)** (*aube de roue*) paddle; (*battoir à linge*) beetle.

palétuvier [paletyvje] *nm* mangrove.

pâleur [pɑlœʀ] *nf* [*teint*] paleness; (*maladive*) pallor, paleness; [*couleur, ciel*] paleness.

pâlichon, -onne* [pɑliʃɔ̃, ɔn] *adj personne* (a bit) pale *ou* peaky*; *soleil* sorry-looking *ou* weakish.

palier [palje] *nm* **(a)** [*escalier*] landing. **être voisins de ~, habiter sur le même ~** to live on the same floor. **(b)** (*fig: étape*) stage. **les prix ont atteint un nouveau ~** prices have found a *ou* risen to a new level; **procéder par ~s** to proceed in stages. **(c)** [*route, voie*] level, flat. (*Aviat*) **voler en ~** to fly level. **(d)** (*Tech*) bearing. **~ de butée** thrust bearing.

palière [paljɛʀ] *adj f V* **porte.**

palinodie [palinɔdi] *nf* (*Littérat*) palinode. (*fig*) **~s** recantations.

pâlir [pɑliʀ] (2) **1** *vi* [*personne*] to turn *ou* go pale; [*lumière, étoiles*] to grow dim; [*ciel*] to grow pale; [*couleur, encre*] to fade; (*fig*) [*souvenir*] to fade (away), dim. **~ de colère/de crainte** to go *ou* turn pale *ou* white with anger/fear; **faire ~ qn (d'envie)** to make sb green with envy. **2** *vt* to turn pale.

palissade [palisad] *nf* [*pieux*] fence; [*planches*] boarding; (*Mil*) stockade.

palissandre [palisɑ̃dʀ(ə)] *nm* rosewood.

pâlissant, e [pɑlisɑ̃, ɑ̃t] *adj teinte, lumière* wan, fading.

palladium [paladjɔm] *nm* (*Chim, fig*) palladium.

palliatif, -ive [paljatif, iv] **1** *adj* (*Méd*) palliative. **2** *nm* (*Méd*) palliative; (*mesure*) palliative, stopgap measure; (*réparation sommaire*) makeshift.

pallier [palje] (7) **1** *vt difficulté* to get round; *manque* to offset, compensate for, make up for; (*littér*) *défaut* to cover up, disguise.

2 pallier à *vt indir difficulté, manque* = **pallier.**

palmarès [palmaʀɛs] *nm* (*Scol*) prize list; (*Sport*) (list of) medal winners; [*athlète etc*] record (of achievements).

palme [palm(ə)] *nf* **(a)** (*Bot*) palm leaf; (*symbole*) palm. **vin/huile de ~** palm wine/oil; **~s académiques** *decoration for services to education in France.* **(b)** [*nageur*] flipper.

palmé, e [palme] *adj feuille* palmate (*T*); *patte* webbed; *oiseau* webfooted, palmate (*T*).

palmer [palmɛʀ] *nm* (*Tech*) micrometer.

palmeraie [palməʀɛ] *nf* palm grove.

palmier [palmje] *nm* **(a)** (*Bot*) palm tree. **(b)** (*gâteau*) palmier.

palmipède [palmipɛd] **1** *nm* palmiped (*T*). **2** *adj* webfooted.

palmiste [palmist(ə)] *adj m V* **chou**[1].

palois, e [palwa, waz] **1** *adj* of *ou* from Pau. **2** *nm,f*: **P~(e)** inhabitant *ou* native of Pau.

palombe [palɔ̃b] *nf* woodpigeon, ringdove.

palonnier [palɔnje] *nm* (*Aviat*) rudder bar; (*Aut*) compensator; [*cheval*] swingletree.

pâlot, -otte* [pɑlo, ɔt] *adj personne* (a bit) pale *ou* peaky*.

palourde [paluʀd(ə)] *nf* clam.

palpable [palpabl(ə)] *adj* (*lit, fig*) palpable.

palper [palpe] (1) *vt objet* to feel, finger; (*Méd*) to palpate; (:) *argent* to get, make. **qu'est-ce qu'il a dû ~ (comme argent)!:** he must have made a fortune *ou* a mint out of it!*

palpitant, e [palpitɑ̃, ɑ̃t] **1** *adj livre, moment* thrilling, exciting. **d'un intérêt ~, ~ d'intérêt** terribly exciting, thrilling; **être ~ d'émotion** to be quivering with emotion. **2** *nm* (*: cœur*) ticker*.

palpitation [palpitɑsjɔ̃] *nf* [*cœur*] pounding (*U*), throbbing (*U*); [*lumière, flamme*] quivering (*U*). (*Méd*) **avoir des ~s** to have palpitations; (*fig*) **ça m'a donné des ~s** it gave me quite a turn.

palpiter [palpite] (1) *vi* [*cœur*] (*battre*) to beat; (*battre violemment*) to pound, throb; [*cadavre*] to twitch; [*chair*] to quiver; [*blessure*] to throb; [*narines, lumière, flamme*] to quiver.

palsambleu†† [palsɑ̃blø] *excl* zounds!††

paltoquet [paltɔkɛ] *nm* (*littér péj*) (*rustre*) boor; (*freluquet*) pompous fool.

paluche: [palyʃ] *nf* (*main*) hand, paw*.

paludéen, -éenne [palydeɛ̃, eɛn] *adj* (*gén, Méd*) paludal.

paludisme [palydism(ə)] *nm* paludism (*T*), malaria.

palustre [palystʀ(ə)] *adj* (*gén, Méd*) paludal.

pâmer (se) [pɑme] (1) *vpr* (*littér*) to swoon†. (*fig*) **se ~** *ou* **être pâmé devant qch** to be in raptures *ou* be ecstatic over sth; **se ~ d'admiration/d'amour** to be overcome with admiration/love; **se ~ de rire** to be convulsed with laughter.

pâmoison [pɑmwazɔ̃] *nf* (*littér, hum*) swoon. (*lit*) **tomber en ~** to swoon†; (*fig*) **tomber en ~ devant un tableau** to go into raptures over a painting.

pampa [pɑ̃pa] *nf* pampas (*pl*).

pamphlet [pɑ̃flɛ] *nm* satirical tract, lampoon.

pamphlétaire [pɑ̃fletɛʀ] *nmf* lampoonist.

pampille [pɑ̃pij] *nf* pendant.

pamplemousse [pɑ̃pləmus] *nm* grapefruit.

pampre [pɑ̃pʀ(ə)] *nm* (*littér*) vine branch.

pan[1] [pɑ̃] **1** *nm* (*lit, fig: morceau*) piece; (*basque*) tail; (*face, côté*) side, face.

2: pan de chemise shirt tail; **se promener en pan de chemise** to wander about with just one's shirt on; **pan de ciel** patch of sky; **pan coupé** *cut-off corner (of room)*; **maison en pan coupé** house with a slanting *ou* cut-off corner; **mur en pan coupé** wall with a cut-off corner; **pan de mur** (section of) wall.

pan[2] [pɑ̃] *excl* [*coup de feu*] bang!; [*gifle*] slap!, whack! (*langage enfantin*) **je vais te faire ~ ~** you'll get your bottom smacked.

Pan [pɑ̃] *nm* Pan.

panacée [panase] *nf* panacea.

panachage [panaʃaʒ] *nm* **(a)** (*Pol*) *voting for candidates from different parties instead of for the set list of one party.* **(b)** (*mélange*) [*couleurs*] blend; [*programmes, plats*] selection.

panache [panaʃ] *nm* **(a)** (*plumet*) plume, panache. (*fig*) **~ de fumée** plume of smoke. **(b)** (*héroïsme*) gallantry. **se battre avec ~** to fight gallantly, put up a spirited resistance.

panaché, e [panaʃe] (*ptp de* **panacher**) **1** *adj* **(a)** *fleur* variegated, many-coloured. **(b)** *foule, assortiment* motley; *glace* two- *ou* mixed-flavour (*épith*); *salade* mixed. **bière ~e** shandy. **2** *nm* (*boisson*) shandy.

panacher [panaʃe] (1) *vt* **(a)** (*Pol*) **~ une liste électorale** *to vote for candidates from different parties instead of for the set list of one party.* **(b)** (*mélanger*) *couleurs* to blend; (*varier*) *programmes, exercices* to vary, give variety to. **dois-je prendre l'un des menus ou puis-je ~ (les plats)?** do I have to take a set menu or can I make my own selection (of courses)?

panachure [panaʃyʀ] *nf* (*gén pl*) motley colours.

panade [panad] *nf* bread soup. (*fig*) **être dans la ~:** (*avoir des ennuis*) to be in the soup*, be in a sticky situation; (*avoir des ennuis d'argent*) to be on one's beam-ends*.

panafricain, e [panafʀikɛ̃, ɛn] *adj* Pan-African.

panafricanisme [panafʀikanism(ə)] *nm* Pan-Africanism.

panais [panɛ] *nm* parsnip.

panama [panama] *nm* **(a)** (*Géog*) **P~** Panama. **(b)** (*chapeau*) Panama hat.

panaméen, -enne [panameɛ̃, ɛn] **1** *adj* Panamanian. **2** *nm,f*: **P~(ne)** Panamanian.

panaméricain, e [panameʀikɛ̃, ɛn] *adj* Pan-American.

panaméricanisme [panameʀikanism(ə)] *nm* Pan-Americanism.

panarabisme [panaʀabism(ə)] *nm* Pan-Arabism.

panard: [panaʀ] *nm* foot, hoof:. **~s** plates of meat:, hooves:.

panaris [panaʀi] *nm* whitlow.

pancarte [pɑ̃kaʀt(ə)] *nf* (*gén*) sign, notice; (*Aut*) (road)sign; [*manifestant*] placard.

pancréas [pɑ̃kʀeɑs] *nm* pancreas.

pancréatique [pɑ̃kʀeatik] *adj* pancreatic.

panda [pɑ̃da] *nm* panda.

pandit [pɑ̃di(t)] *nm* pandit, pundit.

panégyrique [paneʒiʀik] *nm* (*frm*) panegyric. **faire le ~ de qn** to extol sb's merits; (*fig péj*) **quel ~ de sa belle-mère il a fait!** what a tribute to pay to his mother-in-law!
panel [panɛl] *nm* (*Can: jury*) panel.
paner [pane] (1) *vt* to coat *ou* dress with breadcrumbs. **escalope panée** escalope (coated) with breadcrumbs.
pangermanisme [pɑ̃ʒɛʀmanism(ə)] *nm* Pan-Germanism.
pangermaniste [pɑ̃ʒɛʀmanist(ə)] **1** *nmf* Pan-German. **2** *adj* Pan-German(ic).
panier [panje] **1** *nm* (*gén, Sport*) basket; (*contenu*) basket(ful). (*Sport*) **réussir un ~** to score a basket; (*fig*) **ils sont tous à mettre dans le même ~** they are all much of a muchness; **mettre** *ou* **jeter au ~** to throw out, throw in the dustbin (*Brit*) *ou* garbage can (*US*) *ou* wastepaper basket; *V* **anse, dessus, œuf.**
2: panier à bouteilles bottle-carrier; (*fig*) **c'est un panier de crabes** they're always fighting among themselves, they're always at each other's throats; **panier à ouvrage** workbasket; (*fig*) **c'est un panier percé** he's a spendthrift; **panier à provisions** shopping basket; **panier-repas** *nm, pl* **paniers-repas** packed lunch; **panier à salade** (*Culin*) salad shaker *ou* basket; (**fig*) police van, Black Maria*, sweat box**:**.
panifiable [panifjabl(ə)] *adj* (suitable for) bread-making.
panification [panifikasjɔ̃] *nf* bread-making.
panifier [panifje] (7) *vt* to make bread from.
panique [panik] **1** *nf* panic. **pris de ~** panic-stricken; **un vent de ~** a wave of panic. **2** *adj* panic. **terreur** *ou* **peur ~** panic fear.
paniquer [panike] (1) *vi* to panic. **commencer à ~** *ou* **se ~*** to get panicky*; **il ne s'est pas paniqué*** he didn't panic, he kept his head; **être paniqué*** to be in a panic.
panne [pan] *nf* **(a)** breakdown. *[machine]* **être** *ou* **tomber en ~** to break down; **je suis tombé en ~ (de moteur)** my car has broken down; **je suis tombé en ~ sèche** *ou* **en ~ d'essence** I have run out of petrol (*Brit*) *ou* gasoline (*US*); **~ de courant** *ou* **d'électricité** power *ou* electrical failure; *[avion, voiture de course]* **~ de moteur** engine failure.
(b) (**fig*) **être en ~** to be *ou* get stuck; **je suis en ~ de cigarettes** I've run out of *ou* I'm out of* cigarettes; **rester en ~ devant une difficulté** to be stumped* (by a problem), stick at a difficulty; **laisser qn en ~** to leave sb in the lurch, let sb down.
(c) (*Naut*) **mettre en ~** to bring to.
panneau, *pl* **~x** [pano] **1** *nm* (*Art, Habillement, gén*) panel; (*écriteau*) sign, notice; (*Constr*) prefabricated section. **les ~x qui ornent la salle** the panelling round the room; **à ~x** panelled; (*fig*) **tomber** *ou* **donner dans le ~*** to fall *ou* walk (right) into the trap, fall for it*.
2: panneau d'affichage (*pour résultats etc*) notice board; (*pour publicité*) hoarding (*Brit*), billboard (*US*); (*Naut*) **panneau d'écoutille** hatch cover; **panneaux électoraux** *notice boards for election posters;* **panneau indicateur** signpost; **panneau publicitaire, panneau-réclame** *nm, pl* **panneaux-réclame** hoarding (*Brit*), billboard (*US*); **panneau de signalisation** roadsign; **panneau vitré** glass panel.
panonceau, *pl* **~x** [panɔ̃so] *nm* (*plaque de médecin*) plaque; (*écriteau publicitaire*) sign.
panoplie [panɔpli] *nf* **(a)** (*jouet*) outfit. **~ d'Indien** Red Indian outfit; **~ d'armes** display of weapons.
(b) (*fig: gamme*) *[armes]* armoury; *[mesures]* package.
panorama [panɔʀama] *nm* (*lit, fig*) panorama.
panoramique [panɔʀamik] **1** *adj vue* panoramic; *carrosserie* with panoramic *ou* wrap-round windows. (*Ciné*) **écran ~** wide *ou* panoramic screen. **2** *nm* (*Ciné, TV*) panoramic shot.
pansage [pɑ̃saʒ] *nm* grooming.
panse [pɑ̃s] *nf [ruminant]* paunch; (*) *[personne]* paunch, belly**:**; (*fig*) *[bouteille]* belly. **s'en mettre plein la ~*** to stuff o.s.* *ou* one's belly**:**; **je me suis bien rempli la ~*** I've eaten my fill.
pansement [pɑ̃smɑ̃] *nm* (*V* **panser**) dressing; bandage; plaster. **faire un ~** to dress a wound; **refaire un ~** to put a clean dressing on a wound; **couvert de ~s** all bandaged up; **~ adhésif** sticking plaster.
panser [pɑ̃se] (1) *vt* **(a)** (*Méd*) *plaie* to dress; *bras, jambe* to put a dressing on; (*avec un bandage*) to bandage; (*avec du sparadrap*) to put a plaster on; *blessé* to dress the wounds of. (*fig*) **le temps panse les blessures (du cœur)** time heals the wounds of the heart; (*fig*) **~ ses blessures** to lick one's wounds.
(b) *cheval* to groom.
panslavisme [pɑ̃slavism(ə)] *nm* Pan-Slavism.
panslaviste [pɑ̃slavist(ə)] **1** *adj* Pan-Slav(onic). **2** *nmf* Pan-Slavist.
pansu, e [pɑ̃sy] *adj personne* potbellied, paunchy; *vase* potbellied.
pantagruélique [pɑ̃tagʀyelik] *adj* pantagruelian.
pantalon [pɑ̃talɔ̃] *nm* **(a)** (*Habillement*) *[homme]* (pair of) trousers, (pair of) pants*; *[femme]* (pair of) trousers *ou* slacks; (††: *sous-vêtement*) knickers. **un ~ neuf** a new pair of trousers, new trousers; **10 ~s** 10 pairs of trousers; **~ court** short trousers *ou* pants*.
(b) (*Théât*) **P~** Pantaloon.
pantalonnade [pɑ̃talɔnad] *nf* (*Théât*) knockabout farce; (*péj*) tomfoolery.
pantelant, e [pɑ̃tlɑ̃, ɑ̃t] *adj personne* gasping for breath (*attrib*), panting (*attrib*); *gorge* heaving; *cadavre, animal* twitching; *chair* throbbing, heaving. **~ de peur** panting with fear.
panthéisme [pɑ̃teism(ə)] *nm* pantheism.
panthéiste [pɑ̃teist(ə)] **1** *nmf* pantheist. **2** *adj* pantheistic.
panthéon [pɑ̃teɔ̃] *nm* pantheon.
panthère [pɑ̃tɛʀ] *nf* panther. **sa femme est une vraie ~** his wife is a real hellcat*.
pantin [pɑ̃tɛ̃] *nm* (*jouet*) jumping jack; (*péj: personne*) puppet.
pantographe [pɑ̃tɔgʀaf] *nm* pantograph.
pantois [pɑ̃twa] *adj m* flabbergasted. **j'en suis resté ~** I was flabbergasted.
pantomime [pɑ̃tɔmim] *nf* (*art*) mime (*U*); (*spectacle*) mime show; (*fig*) scene, fuss (*U*).
pantouflard, e* [pɑ̃tuflaʀ, aʀd(ə)] **1** *adj personne, caractère* stay-at-home (*épith*); *vie* quiet, uneventful, humdrum. **2** *nm* stay-at-home.
pantoufle [pɑ̃tufl(ə)] *nf* slipper. **il était en ~s** he was in his slippers.
paon [pɑ̃] *nm* peacock.
paonne [pan] *nf* peahen.
papa [papa] *nm* (*gén*) dad; (*langage enfantin*) daddy; (*langage de bébé*) dada. **la musique/les voitures de ~*** old-fashioned music/cars; **c'est vraiment l'usine de ~!*** this factory isn't half antiquated!* *ou* behind the times!*; **conduire à la ~*** to potter along, drive at a snail's pace; **c'est un ~ gâteau** he spoils his (grand)children, he's a doting (grand)father; *V* **fils.**
papal, e, *mpl* **-aux** [papal, o] *adj* papal.
papauté [papote] *nf* papacy.
papaye [papaj] *nf* pawpaw, papaya.
papayer [papaje] *nm* pawpaw *ou* papaya (tree).
pape [pap] *nm* pope; (*fig*) *[école littéraire etc]* leading light.
papelard[1]* [paplaʀ] *nm* (*feuille*) (bit of) paper; (*article de journal*) article; (*journal*) paper.
papelard[2], e [paplaʀ, aʀd(ə)] *adj* (*littér*) suave, smarmy.
papelardise [paplaʀdiz] *nf* (*littér*) suavity, suaveness, smarminess.
paperasse [papʀas] *nf* (*péj*) **~(s)** (wretched) papers; (*à remplir*) forms; **je n'ai pas le temps de lire toutes les ~s** *ou* **toute la ~ qu'on m'envoie** I've no time to read all the bumf**:** (*Brit*) *ou* stuff that people send me.
paperasserie [papʀasʀi] *nf* (*péj*) (*à lire*) bumf**:** (*Brit*); (*à remplir*) forms; (*tracasserie, routine*) red tape. **il y a trop de ~ à faire dans ce travail** there's too much paperwork in this job.
paperassier, -ière [papʀasje, jɛʀ] (*péj*) **1** *adj personne* fond of red tape *ou* paperwork; *administration* cluttered with red tape (*attrib*), obsessed with form filling (*attrib*).
2 *nm,f* (*bureaucrate*) penpusher (*péj*). **quel ~!** he's forever poring over his old papers *ou* scribbling away on his papers.
papeterie [papetʀi] *nf* (*magasin*) stationer's (shop); (*fourniture*) stationery; (*fabrique*) paper mill; (*fabrication*) paper-making industry; (*commerce*) stationery trade.
papetier, -ière [paptje, jɛʀ] *nm,f* (*vendeur*) stationer; (*fabricant*) paper-maker.
papier [papje] **1** *nm* **(a)** (*U: matière*) paper. **morceau/bout de ~** piece/bit *ou* slip of paper; **de** *ou* **en ~** paper (*épith*); **mets-moi cela sur ~** (*pour ne pas oublier*) write that down for me; (*pour confirmation écrite*) let me have that in writing; **écrire qch sur ~ libre** to write sth on plain paper; **sur le ~** (*en projet, théoriquement*) on paper; **jeter une idée sur le ~** to jot down an idea; *V* **pâte.**
(b) (*feuille écrite*) paper; (*feuille blanche*) sheet *ou* piece of paper; (*Presse: article*) article. **~ personnels/d'affaires** personal/business papers; **un ~ à signer/à remplir** a form to be signed/filled in.
(c) ~s (d'identité) (identity) papers; **vos ~s, s'il vous plaît!** could I see your identity papers, please?; (*Aut*) may I see your (driving) licence, please?; **ses ~s ne sont pas en règle** his papers are not in order; (*fig*) **rayez cela de vos ~s!** you can forget about that!; *V* **petit.**
2: papier aluminium aluminium foil, tinfoil; **papier d'argent** silver foil *ou* paper, tinfoil; **papier d'Arménie** incense paper; **papier bible** bible paper, India paper; **papier buvard** blotting paper; **papier calque** tracing paper; **papier carbone** carbon paper; **papier à cigarettes** cigarette paper; **papier chiffon** rag paper; **papier collant** gummed paper; (*transparent*) Sellotape ® (*Brit*), Scotch tape (*US*), sticky tape; **papier couché** art paper; **papier cul**✠ bog-paper**:** (*Brit*), bumf**:** (*Brit*); **papier à dessin** drawing paper; **papier d'emballage** wrapping paper; **papier émeri** emery paper; **papier à en-tête** headed notepaper, letterhead (*Comm*); **papier d'étain** tinfoil, silver paper; **papier filtre** filter paper; **papier glacé** glazed paper; **papier hygiénique** toilet paper; **papier journal** newspaper; **papier à lettres** writing paper, notepaper; **papier mâché** papier-mâché; (*fig*) **mine de papier mâché** pasty complexion; **papier machine** typing paper; **papiers militaires** army papers; **papier millimétré** graph paper; **papier ministre** official paper (*approx quarto size*); **écrit sur papier ministre** written on official paper; **papier monnaie** paper money; **papier à musique** manuscript paper; **papier paraffiné** (*gén*) wax paper; (*Culin*) greaseproof paper; **papier peint** wallpaper; **papier pelure** India paper; (*Phot*) **papier sensible** bromide paper; **papier de soie** tissue paper; **papier timbré** stamped paper; **papier de tournesol** litmus paper; **papier de verre** glass-paper, sandpaper.
papille [papij] *nf* papilla. **~s gustatives** taste buds.
papillon [papijɔ̃] *nm* (*insecte*) butterfly; (*fig: personne*) fickle person; (*Tech: écrou*) wing *ou* butterfly nut; (*Police: contravention*) (parking) ticket; (*autocollant*) sticker. **~ de nuit** moth; *V* **brasse, minute, nœud.**
papillonnant, e [papijɔnɑ̃, ɑ̃t] *adj esprit* fickle; *personne* fickle-minded.
papillonnement [papijɔnmɑ̃] *nm* (*V* **papillonner**) flitting about *ou* around; chopping and changing.
papillonner [papijɔne] (1) *vi* (*entre personnes, objets*) to flit about *ou* around; (*entre activités diverses*) to chop and change. **~ d'un sujet/d'une femme à l'autre** to flit from one subject/woman to another; **~ autour d'une femme** to hover round a woman.
papillote [papijɔt] *nf [cheveux]* curlpaper; *[bonbon]* (sweet) paper; *[gigot]* frill; (*papier beurré*) buttered paper.

papillotement [papijɔtmɑ̃] *nm* (*V* **papilloter**) twinkling; sparkling; flickering; blinking.
papilloter [papijɔte] (1) *vi [lumière, étoiles]* to twinkle; *[reflets]* to sparkle; *[paupières]* to flicker; *[yeux]* to blink.
papisme [papism(ə)] *nm* papism, popery.
papiste [papist(ə)] *nmf* papist.
papotage [papɔtaʒ] *nm* (*U: action*) chattering; (*propos*) (idle) chatter.
papoter [papɔte] (1) *vi* to chatter, have a natter* (*surtout Brit*).
papou, e [papu] **1** *adj* Papuan. **2** *nm* (*Ling*) Papuan. **3** *nm,f:* **P~(e)** Papuan.
papouille* [papuj] *nf* tickling (*U*). **faire des ~s à qn** to give sb a bit of a feel:.
paprika [papʀika] *nm* paprika (pepper).
papule [papyl] *nf* papule.
papyrus [papiʀys] *nm* papyrus.
pâque [pɑk] *nf:* **la ~** Passover; *V aussi* **Pâques.**
paquebot [pakbo] *nm* liner, (steam)ship.
pâquerette [pɑkʀɛt] *nf* daisy.
Pâques [pɑk] **1** *nm* Easter. (*fig*) **à ~ ou à la Trinité** never in a month of Sundays; *V* **dimanche, œuf. 2** *nfpl:* **bonnes** *ou* **joyeuses ~** Happy Easter; **faire ses ~** to do one's Easter duties.
paquet [pakɛ] *nm* **(a)** (*pour emballer etc*) *[sucre, café]* bag; *[cigarettes]* packet, pack (*US*); *[cartes]* pack; *[linge]* bundle. **il fume deux ~s par jour** he smokes forty a day; (*fig*) **malmener** *ou* **secouer qn comme un ~ de linge sale** to shake *ou* handle sb roughly; (*fig*) **c'est un vrai ~ de nerfs/d'os** he's a bag of nerves/bones.
(b) (*colis*) parcel. **mettre en ~** to parcel up, bundle up; **faire un ~** to make up a parcel.
(c) (*fig: tas*) **~ de neige** pile *ou* mass of; *boue* lump of; *billets, actions* wad of; **il a touché un bon ~*** he got a fat sum*; **par ~s** in waves.
(d) (*Rugby*) **~ (d'avants)** pack.
(e) (*Naut*) **~ de mer** heavy sea (*U*), big wave.
(f) (**loc*) **faire son ~** *ou* **ses ~s** to pack one's bags; **y mettre le ~** (*argent*) to spare no expense; (*efforts*) to give all one has got; **lâcher son ~ à qn*** to tell sb a few home truths; *V* **risquer.**
paquetage [paktaʒ] *nm* (*Mil*) pack, kit. **faire son ~** to get one's pack *ou* kit ready.
par [paʀ] *prép* **(a)** (*agent, cause*) by. **le carreau a été cassé ~ l'orage/un enfant** the pane was broken by the storm/a child; **accablé ~ le désespoir** overwhelmed with despair; **elle nous a fait porter des fraises ~ son jardinier** she got her gardener to bring us some strawberries, she had her gardener bring us some strawberries; **il a appris la nouvelle ~ le journal/~ un ami** he learned the news from the paper/from *ou* through a friend; **elle veut tout faire ~ elle-même** she wants to do everything (for) herself; **la découverte ~ Fleming de la pénicilline** Fleming's discovery of penicillin, the discovery of penicillin by Fleming.
(b) (*manière, moyen*) by, with, through. **obtenir qch ~ la force/la torture/la persuasion/la ruse** to obtain sth by force/by torture/with persuasion/by *ou* through cunning; **essayer ~ tous les moyens** to try every possible means; **arriver ~ l'intelligence/le travail** to succeed through intelligence/hard work; **la porte ferme ~ un verrou** the gate is locked with *ou* by means of a bolt; **prendre qn ~ le bras/la main/la taille** to take sb by the arm/hand/waist; **payer ~ chèque** to pay by cheque; **prendre qn ~ les sentiments/son faible** to appeal to sb's feelings/weak spot; **~ le train/l'avion** by rail *ou* train/air *ou* plane; **~ la poste** by post *ou* mail, through the post; **ils se ressemblent ~ leur sens de l'humour** they are alike in their sense of humour; **il descend des Bourbon ~ sa mère** he is descended from the Bourbons through his mother *ou* on his mother's side; **ils diffèrent ~ bien des côtés** they are different *ou* they differ in many ways *ou* aspects; **il est honnête ~ nature** he is honest by nature, he is naturally honest; **il ne jure que ~ elle** he swears by her alone; *V* **cœur, excellence, mégarde** *etc.*
(c) (*gén sans art: cause, motif etc*) through, out of, from, by. **étonnant ~ son érudition** amazing for his learning; **~ manque de temps** owing to lack of time, because time is (*ou* was) short *ou* lacking; **~ habitude** by *ou* out of *ou* from (sheer) habit; **faire qch ~ plaisir/pitié** to do sth for pleasure/out of pity; **~ souci d'exactitude** for the sake of accuracy, out of a concern for accuracy; **~ hasard/erreur** by chance/mistake; **~ pure bêtise/négligence** through *ou* out of sheer stupidity/negligence; *V* **principe.**
(d) (*lit, fig: lieu, direction*) by (way of), through, across, along. **il est sorti ~ la fenêtre** he went out by (way of) *ou* through the window; **il est venu ~ le chemin le plus court** he came (by) the shortest way; **je dois passer ~ le bureau avant de rentrer** I must drop in at the office on my way home; **nous sommes venus ~ la côte/~ Lyon/~ l'Espagne** we came along (by) the coast/via *ou* by way of Lyons/via *ou* through Spain; **~ terre ou ~ mer** by land or (by) sea; **se promener ~ les rues/les champs** to walk through the streets/through *ou* across the fields; **~ tout le pays** throughout *ou* all over the (entire) country; **il habite ~ ici** he lives round *ou* around here *ou* here somewhere; **sortez ~ ici/là** go out this/that way; **~ où est-il venu?** which way did he come (by)?; **passer ~ de dures épreuves** to go through some very trying times; **la rumeur s'était répandue ~ la ville** the rumour had spread (a)round the town; **elle est passée ~ toutes les couleurs de l'arc-en-ciel** she went through all the colours of the rainbow; **~ 5 mètres de fond** at a depth of 5 metres; **~ 10° de latitude sud** at a latitude of 10° south; **arriver ~ le nord/la gauche/le haut** *ou* **en haut** to arrive from the north/the left/the top; *V* **ailleurs, mont** *etc et aussi* **par-devant** *etc.*
(e) (*distribution, mesure*) a, per, by. **marcher 2 ~ 2/3 ~ 3** to walk 2 by 2/3 by 3 *ou* in 2's/3's; **faites-les entrer un ~ un** let them in one at a time *ou* one by one; **nous avons payé 50 F ~ personne** we paid 50 francs per person *ou* a head; **3 fois ~ jour/semaine/mois** 3 times daily *ou* a day/weekly *ou* a week/monthly *ou* a month; **6 étudiants ~ appartement** 6 students to a flat *ou* per flat; **gagner tant ~ semaine/mois** to earn so much a *ou* per week/month; **~ an** a *ou* per year, per annum; **ils déduisent 5F ~ enfant** they take off 5 francs for each child *ou* per child; **~ moments** *ou* **instants, je crois rêver** at times I think I'm dreaming; **ils s'abattirent sur les plantes ~ milliers** they swooped down onto the plants in their thousands; **~ poignées/charretées** in handfuls/cartloads, by the handful/cartload; **~ 3 fois, on lui a demandé** 3 times he has been asked.
(f) (*atmosphère*) in; (*atmosphère, moment*) on. **~ une belle nuit d'été** on a beautiful summer('s) night; **il partit ~ une pluvieuse journée de mars** he left on a rainy *ou* wet March day; **ne restez pas dehors ~ ce froid/cette chaleur** don't stay out in this cold/heat; **évitez cette route ~ temps de pluie/de brouillard** avoid that road in wet weather/in fog *ou* when it's wet/foggy; **sortir ~ moins 10°** to go out when it's minus 10°; **~ les temps qui courent** these days.
(g) (*avec finir, commencer etc*) **commencer ~ qch/~ faire** to begin with sth/by doing; **il a fini ~ ennuyer tout le monde** he ended up *ou* finished up boring everyone; **~ où allons-nous commencer?** where shall we begin?; **on a clôturé la séance ~ des élections** elections brought the meeting to a close, the meeting closed with elections; **il finit ~ m'agacer avec ses plaisanteries!** I've really had enough of his jokes!
(h) (*dans exclamations, serments*) by. **~ tous les dieux du ciel** by *ou* in the name of heaven; **~ tout ce que j'ai de plus cher, je vous promets** I promise you by all that I hold most dear; *V* **jurer, pitié** *etc.*
(i) (*loc frm*) **~ trop** far too, excessively; **de ~ ...** in the name of ..., by order of ... .
para* [paʀa] *nm* (*abrév de* **parachutiste**) para*.
parabole [paʀabɔl] *nf* (*Math*) parabola; (*Rel*) parable.
parabolique [paʀabɔlik] **1** *adj* parabolic. **2** *nm* (*radiateur*) electric fire.
parachèvement [paʀaʃɛvmɑ̃] *nm* perfection, perfecting.
parachever [paʀaʃve] (5) *vt* to perfect, put the finishing touches to.
parachutage [paʀaʃytaʒ] *nm* parachuting, dropping *ou* landing by parachute.
parachute [paʀaʃyt] *nm* parachute. **~ ventral/dorsal** lap-pack/back-type parachute.
parachuter [paʀaʃyte] (1) *vt* to parachute, drop *ou* land by parachute. (**fig*) **ils m'ont parachuté à ce poste** I was pitch-forked into this job; **ils nous ont parachuté un nouveau directeur de Paris** a new manager from Paris has suddenly been landed on us.
parachutisme [paʀaʃytism(ə)] *nm* parachuting. **faire du ~** to go parachuting.
parachutiste [paʀaʃytist(ə)] **1** *nmf* parachutist; (*Mil*) paratrooper. **nos unités de ~s** our paratroops. **2** *adj unité* paratrooper (*épith*).
parade [paʀad] *nf* **(a)** (*ostentation*) show, ostentation. **faire ~ de** *érudition* to parade, display, show off; *relations* to boast about, brag about; **de ~** *uniforme, épée* ceremonial; (*péj*) **afficher une générosité de ~** to make an outward *ou* a superficial show *ou* display of generosity.
(b) (*spectacle*) parade. **~ militaire/foraine** military/circus parade; **les troupes s'avancèrent comme à la ~** the troops moved forward as if they were (still) on the parade ground *ou* on parade.
(c) (*Équitation*) pulling up.
(d) (*Escrime*) parry, parade; (*Boxe*) parry; (*fig*) answer, reply; (*orale*) riposte, rejoinder. **trouver la bonne ~ (à une attaque/un argument)** to find the right answer *ou* reply (to an attack/an argument).
parader [paʀade] (1) *vi* to strut about, show off.
paradigmatique [paʀadigmatik] **1** *adj* paradigmatic. **2** *nf* study of paradigmatic relationships.
paradigme [paʀadigm(ə)] *nm* paradigm.
paradis [paʀadi] *nm* **(a)** (*lit, fig*) paradise, heaven. **le P~ terrestre** (*Bible*) the Garden of Eden; (*fig*) heaven on earth. **(b)** (*Théât**) **le ~** the gods* (*pl*).
paradisiaque [paʀadizjak] *adj* heavenly, paradisiacal.
paradisier [paʀadizje] *nm* bird of paradise.
paradoxal, e, *mpl* **-aux** [paʀadɔksal, o] *adj* paradoxical.
paradoxalement [paʀadɔksalmɑ̃] *adv* paradoxically.
paradoxe [paʀadɔks(ə)] *nm* paradox.
parafe [paʀaf] *nm* = **paraphe.**
parafer [paʀafe] (1) *vt* = **parapher.**
paraffinage [paʀafinaʒ] *nm* paraffining.
paraffine [paʀafin] *nf* (*gén: solide*) paraffin wax; (*Chim*) paraffin (*Chim*).
paraffiner [paʀafine] (1) *vt* to paraffin(e); *V* **papier.**
parages [paʀaʒ] *nmpl* **(a) dans les ~** (*dans la région*) in the area, in the vicinity; (**: pas très loin*) round about; **dans ces ~** in these parts; **dans les ~ de** near, round about, in the vicinity of. **(b)** (*Naut*) waters, region(s).
paragraphe [paʀagʀaf] *nm* paragraph; (*Typ*) section (mark).
paraguayen, -enne [paʀagwajɛ̃, ɛn] **1** *adj* Paraguayan. **2** *nm,f:* **P~(ne)** Paraguayan.
paraître [paʀɛtʀ(ə)] (57) **1** *vi* **(a)** (*se montrer*) (*gén*) to appear; *[personne]* to appear, make one's appearance. **~ en scène/à** *ou* **sur l'écran/au balcon** to appear on stage/on the screen/on the balcony; (*Jur*) **~ à la barre** to appear before the court; **il n'a pas paru de la journée** I (*ou* we *etc*) haven't seen him all day, he

hasn't shown up* *ou* appeared all day; **il n'a pas paru à la réunion** he didn't appear *ou* turn up *ou* show up* at the meeting; ~ **en public** to appear in public, make a public appearance; **un sourire parut sur ses lèvres** a smile appeared on his lips.

(b) (*Presse*) to appear, be published, come out. **faire ~ qch** *[éditeur]* to bring out *ou* publish sth; *[auteur]* to have sth published; **'vient de ~'** 'just out', 'just published'.

(c) (*briller*) to be noticed. **chercher à ~** to show off; **le désir de ~** the desire to be noticed *ou* to show off.

(d) (*être visible*) to show (through). **il en paraît toujours quelque chose** one can always see some sign of it *ou* traces of it; **il n'y paraîtra bientôt plus** (*tache, cicatrice*) there will soon be no trace left of it *ou* nothing left to show (of it); (*maladie*) soon no one will ever know you've had it; **laisser ~ ses sentiments/son irritation** to let one's feelings/one's annoyance show; **sans qu'il y paraisse rien** without anything being obvious, without letting anything show.

(e) (*sembler*) to look, seem, appear. **elle paraît heureuse** she seems (to be) happy; **cela me paraît une erreur** it looks *ou* seems like a mistake to me; **elle paraissait l'aimer** she seemed *ou* appeared to love him; **il paraît 20 ans** (*il est plus jeune*) he looks (at least) 20; (*il est plus âgé*) he only looks 20; **le voyage a paru long** the journey seemed long; **cette robe la fait ~ plus grande** that dress makes her look taller; **essayer de ~ ce qu'on n'est pas** to try to appear to be what *ou* something one isn't.

2 *vb impers* **(a)** (*il semble*) **il me paraît difficile qu'elle puisse venir** it seems to me that it will be difficult for her to come; **il ne lui paraît pas essentiel qu'elle sache** he doesn't think it essential for her to know; **il lui paraissait impossible de refuser** he didn't see how he could refuse; **il paraîtrait ridicule de s'offenser** it would seem stupid to take offence.

(b) (*le bruit court*) **il va se marier, paraît-il** *ou* **à ce qu'il paraît** he's apparently getting married; **il paraît** *ou* **il paraîtrait qu'on va construire une autoroute** apparently *ou* it seems they're going to build a motorway, they're going to build a motorway, so they say; **il paraît que oui** so it seems *ou* appears, apparently so.

3 *nm* **le ~** appearance(s).

paralittérature [paʀaliteʀatyʀ] *nf* marginal literature.

parallactique [paʀalaktik] *adj* parallactic.

parallaxe [paʀalaks(ə)] *nf* parallax.

parallèle [paʀalɛl] **1** *adj* **(a)** (*Math*) parallel (*à* to); *V* **barre**. **(b)** (*fig*) (*comparable*) parallel, similar; (*indépendent*) separate; (*non officiel*) *marché, cours, police* unofficial. **mener une action ~** to take similar action, act on *ou* along the same lines.

2 *nf* (*Math*) parallel (line). (*Élec*) **monté en ~** wired (up) in parallel.

3 *nm* (*Géog, fig*) parallel. **~ de latitude** parallel of latitude; **établir un ~ entre 2 textes** to draw a parallel between 2 texts; **mettre en ~** *choses opposées* to compare; *choses semblables* to parallel; **mettre en ~ deux problèmes semblables** to parallel one problem with another.

parallèlement [paʀalɛlmɑ̃] *adv* (*lit*) parallel (*à* to); (*fig*) (*ensemble*) at the same time; (*similairement*) in the same way.

parallélépipède [paʀalelepipɛd] *nm* parallelepiped.

parallélisme [paʀalelism(ə)] *nm* (*lit, fig*) parallelism; (*Aut*) wheel alignment.

parallélogramme [paʀalelɔgʀam] *nm* parallelogram.

paralysé, e [paʀalize] (*ptp de* **paralyser**) **1** *adj* paralysed. **rester ~** to be left paralysed; **il est ~ des jambes** his legs are paralysed. **2** *nm,f* paralytic.

paralyser [paʀalize] (1) *vt* (*Méd, fig*) to paralyse.

paralysie [paʀalizi] *nf* (*Méd, fig*) paralysis; palsy (*Bible*). **~ infantile** infantile paralysis.

paralytique [paʀalitik] *adj, nmf* paralytic.

paramètre [paʀamɛtʀ(ə)] *nm* parameter.

paramilitaire [paʀamilitɛʀ] *adj* paramilitary.

parangon [paʀɑ̃gɔ̃] *nm* paragon.

paranoïa [paʀanɔja] *nf* paranoia.

paranoïaque [paʀanɔjak] *adj, nmf* paranoiac.

paranoïde [paʀanɔid] *adj* paranoid.

parapet [paʀapɛ] *nm* parapet.

paraphe [paʀaf] *nm* (*trait*) paraph, flourish; (*initiales*) initial; (*littér: signature*) signature.

parapher [paʀafe] (1) *vt* (*Admin*) to initial; (*littér: signer*) to sign.

paraphrase [paʀafʀɑz] *nf* paraphrase.

paraphraser [paʀafʀɑze] (1) *vt* to paraphrase.

paraphrastique [paʀafʀastik] *adj* paraphrastic.

paraplégie [paʀapleʒi] *nf* paraplegia.

paraplégique [paʀapleʒik] *adj, nmf* paraplegic.

parapluie [paʀaplɥi] *nm* umbrella.

parasitaire [paʀazitɛʀ] *adj* parasitic(al).

parasite [paʀazit] **1** *nm* (*Bot, Vét*) parasite; (*fig: personne*) parasite, sponger*. (*Rad, TV*) **~s** interference, atmospherics. **2** *adj* parasitic(al). (*Rad, TV*) **bruits ~s** interference, atmospherics.

parasiter [paʀazite] (1) *vt* (*Bot, Vét*) to live as a parasite on; (*Rad, TV*) to cause interference on.

parasitique [paʀazitik] *adj* parasitic(al).

parasitisme [paʀazitism(ə)] *nm* parasitism.

parasol [paʀasɔl] *nm* *[plage]* beach umbrella, parasol; *[café, terrasse]* sunshade, parasol; (†: *ombrelle*) parasol, sunshade; *V* **pin**.

paratonnerre [paʀatɔnɛʀ] *nm* lightning conductor.

paratyphique [paʀatifik] *adj* paratyphoid.

paratyphoïde [paʀatifɔid] *nf* paratyphoid fever.

paravent [paʀavɑ̃] *nm* folding screen *ou* partition; (*fig*) screen.

parbleu†† [paʀblø] *excl* of course!

parc [paʀk] **1** *nm* (*jardin public*) park; (*jardin de château*) grounds; (*Mil: entrepôt*) depot; (*fig, Écon: ensemble*) stock.

2: parc d'attractions amusement park; **parc automobile** *[pays]* number of vehicles on the road; *[entreprise]* car (*ou* bus *etc*) fleet; **parc à bébé** playpen; **parc à bestiaux** cattle pen *ou* enclosure; **parc ferroviaire** rolling stock; **parc à huîtres** oyster bed; **parc à moules** mussel bed; **parc à moutons** sheep pen, sheepfold; **parc national** national park; **parc naturel** nature reserve; **parc de stationnement** car park (*Brit*), parking lot (*US*); **parc zoologique** zoological gardens.

parcage [paʀkaʒ] *nm* *[moutons]* penning; *[voitures]* parking.

parcellaire [paʀsɛlɛʀ] *adj* (*fig: fragmentaire*) *plan, travail* bitty*.

parcelle [paʀsɛl] *nf* fragment, particle, bit; (*sur un cadastre*) parcel (*of land*). **~ de terre** plot of land; **~ de vérité** grain *ou* scrap of truth; **une ~ de bonheur/gloire** a bit of happiness/fame.

parcellisation [paʀselizɑsjɔ̃] *nf* breakdown into individual operations.

parce que [paʀsk(ə)] *conj* because. **Robert, de mauvaise humeur ~ fatigué, répondit que ...** Robert, being tired, was in a bad temper and replied that ..., Robert was in a bad temper because he was tired and replied that ...; **pourquoi n'y vas-tu pas?** — **~!** why aren't you going? — (just) because (I'm not!).

parchemin [paʀʃəmɛ̃] *nm* parchment (*U*), piece of parchment; (*Univ fig*) diploma, degree.

parcheminé [paʀʃəmine] (*ptp de* **parcheminer**) *adj* *peau* wrinkled; *visage* wizened.

parcheminer [paʀʃəmine] (1) **1** *vt* to give a parchment finish to. **2 se parcheminer** *vpr* to wrinkle up.

parcimonie [paʀsimɔni] *nf* parsimony, parsimoniousness. **avec ~** (*par économie*) sparingly; (*à contrecœur*) grudgingly.

parcimonieusement [paʀsimɔnjøzmɑ̃] *adv* (*V* **parcimonie**) parsimoniously; sparingly; grudgingly.

parcimonieux, -euse [paʀsimɔnjø, øz] *adj* *personne* parsimonious; *distribution* niggardly, stingy.

par-ci par-là [paʀsipaʀla] *adv* (*espace*) here and there; (*temps*) now and then, from time to time. **il m'agace avec ses bien sûr par-ci, bien sûr par-là** he gets on my nerves saying of course, right, left and centre.

parcmètre [paʀkmɛtʀ(ə)] *nm*, **parcomètre** [paʀkɔmɛtʀ(ə)] *nm* (parking) meter.

parcourir [paʀkuʀiʀ] (11) *vt* **(a)** *trajet, distance* to cover, travel; (*en tous sens*) *lieu* to go all over; *pays* to travel up and down. **ils ont parcouru toute la région en un mois** they've been over *ou* through *ou* they've covered the whole region in a month; **~ la ville à la recherche de qch** to search for sth all over (the) town, scour the town for sth; **les navires parcourent les mers** ships sail all over the seas; **un frisson parcourut tout son corps** a shiver ran through his body; **le ruisseau parcourt toute la vallée** the stream runs along *ou* through the whole valley *ou* right along the valley; **l'obus parcourut le ciel** the shell flew through *ou* across the sky.

(b) (*regarder rapidement*) *lettre, livre* to glance *ou* skim through. **il parcourut la foule des yeux** he ran his eye over the crowd.

parcours [paʀkuʀ] *nm* (*distance*) distance; (*trajet*) journey; (*itinéraire*) route; *[fleuve]* course; *[golf]* round. (*Sport*) **sur un ~ difficile** over a difficult course; **le prix du ~** the fare; *V* **accident**.

par-delà [paʀdəla] *prép*: **~ les montagnes/les mers** beyond the mountains/the seas; **~ les querelles, la solidarité demeure** there is a feeling of solidarity which goes beyond the quarrels.

par-derrière [paʀdɛʀjɛʀ] **1** *prép* (round) behind, round the back of. **2** *adv passer* round the back; *attaquer, emboutir* from behind; *être endommagé* at the back *ou* rear; *se boutonner* at the back. **dire du mal de qn ~** to speak ill of sb behind his back.

par-dessous [paʀd(ə)su] *prép, adv* under(neath); *V* **jambe**.

pardessus [paʀdəsy] *nm* overcoat.

par-dessus [paʀd(ə)sy] **1** *prép* over (the top of). **il a mis un pullover ~ sa chemise** he has put a pullover over *ou* on top of his shirt; **~ tout** above all; **j'en ai ~ la tête de toutes ces histoires** I'm sick and tired of all this business; **~ le marché** into the bargain, on top of all that; **~ bord** overboard; *V* **jambe**.

2 *adv* over (the top).

par-devant [paʀd(ə)vɑ̃] **1** *prép* (*Jur*) **~ notaire** in the presence of *ou* before a lawyer. **2** *adv passer* round the front; *attaquer, emboutir* from the front; *être abîmé, se boutonner* at the front.

par-devers [paʀdəvɛʀ] *prép* (*Jur*) before. (*frm*) **~ soi** (*en sa possession*) in one's possession; (*fig: dans son for intérieur*) to *ou* within onself.

pardi† [paʀdi] *excl* of course!

pardieu†† [paʀdjø] *excl* of course!

pardon [paʀdɔ̃] *nm* **(a)** (*grâce*) forgiveness, pardon (*frm, Jur*).

(b) (*en Bretagne*) pardon (*religious festival*).

(c) (*loc*) **demander ~ à qn d'avoir fait qch** to apologize to sb for doing sth; **demande ~!** say you're sorry!; **(je vous demande) ~** (I'm) sorry, I beg your pardon, excuse me; **~ Monsieur, avez-vous l'heure?** excuse me, have you got the time?; **tu n'y es pas allé — (je te demande bien) ~, j'y suis allée ce matin** you didn't go — oh yes I did *ou* excuse ME, I went this morning *ou* I certainly did go this morning; **et puis ~!* il travaille dur** he works hard, I'm telling you *ou* I can tell you *ou* you can take it from me*; **je suis peut-être un imbécile mais alors lui, ~!*** maybe I'm stupid but he's even worse! *ou* HE takes the biscuit!* (*Brit*) *ou* cake!* (*US*).

pardonnable [paʀdɔnabl(ə)] *adj* pardonable, forgivable, excusable. **il l'a oublié mais c'est ~** he can be forgiven *ou* excused for forgetting it, he has forgotten it but you have to forgive *ou* excuse him.

pardonner [paʀdɔne] (1) **1** *vt* *péché* to forgive, pardon;

indiscrétion to forgive, excuse. ~ **(à) qn** to forgive sb, let sb off*; ~ **qch à qn/à qn d'avoir fait qch** to forgive sb for sth/for doing sth; **pour se faire ~ son erreur** to try to win forgiveness for his mistake, so as to be forgiven for his mistake; **pardonnez-moi de vous avoir dérangé** excuse me for disturbing you, excuse my disturbing you; **vous êtes tout pardonné** I'll let you off*, you're forgiven (*hum*); **je ne me le pardonnerai jamais** I'll never forgive myself; **ce genre d'erreur ne se pardonne pas** this is an unforgivable mistake.

2 *vi* to forgive. (*fig*) **c'est une maladie/une erreur qui ne pardonne pas** it's a fatal illness/mistake.

pare- [paʀ] *préf V* **parer²**.

paré, e [paʀe] (*ptp de* **parer²**) *adj* (*prêt*) ready, all set; (*préparé*) prepared. **être ~ contre le froid** to be prepared for the cold weather.

parégorique [paʀegɔʀik] *adj, nm* paregoric; *V* **élixir.**

pareil, -eille [paʀɛj] **1** *adj* **(a)** (*identique*) the same, similar, alike (*attrib*). **il n'y en a pas deux ~s** there aren't two the same *ou* alike; **~ que, ~ à** the same as, similar to, just like; **comment va-t-elle? — c'est toujours ~** how is she? — (she's) just the same (as ever); **c'est toujours ~, il ne peut pas être à l'heure** it's always the same, he never manages to be on time; **il est ~ à lui-même** he doesn't change, he's the same as ever; **tu as vu son sac? j'en ai un ~/presque ~** have you seen her bag? I've got the same one *ou* one just like it/one very similar; (*littér*) **à nul autre ~** peerless (*littér, épith*), unrivalled, unmatched; **l'an dernier à ~le époque** this time last year.

(b) (*tel*) such (a), of the sort. **je n'ai jamais entendu ~ discours** *ou* **un discours ~** I've never heard such a speech *ou* a speech like it *ou* a speech of the sort (*péj*); **en ~ cas** in such a case; **en ~le occasion** on such an occasion; **à ~le heure, il devrait être debout** he ought to be up at this hour; **se coucher à une heure ~le!** what a time to be going to bed (at)!

2 *nm,f*: **nos ~s** (*semblables*) our fellow men; (*égaux*) our equals *ou* peers; **je ne retrouverai jamais son ~** (*chose*) I'll never find another one like it; (*employé*) I'll never find another one like him *ou* to match him; **ne pas avoir son ~ (ou sa ~le)** to be second to none; **vous et vos ~s** you and your kind, people like you; **sans ~** unparalleled, unequalled; **c'est du ~ au même*** it doesn't make the slightest difference, it comes to the same thing; *V* **rendre.**

3 *adv* (*) *s'habiller* the same, in the same way, alike. **faire ~** to do the same thing (*que* as).

pareillement [paʀɛjmɑ̃] *adv* (*de la même manière*) *s'habiller* in the same way (*à* as); (*également*) likewise, also, equally. **cela m'a ~ surpris** it surprised me also *ou* too; **~ heureux** equally happy; **mon père va bien et ma mère ~** my father is well and so is my mother *ou* and my mother too; **à vous ~!** the same to you!

parement [paʀmɑ̃] *nm* (*Constr, Habillement*) facing.

parenchyme [paʀɑ̃ʃim] *nm* parenchyma.

parent, e [paʀɑ̃, ɑ̃t] **1** *adj* related (*de* to).

2 *nm,f* **(a)** relative, relation. **être ~ de qn** to be related to *ou* a relative of sb; **nous sommes ~s par alliance/par ma mère** we are related by marriage/on my mother's side; **~s en ligne directe** blood relations; **~s proches** close relations *ou* relatives; **~s et amis** friends and relations *ou* relatives; **nous ne sommes pas ~s** we aren't related; (*fig*) **traiter qn en ~ pauvre** to treat sb like a poor relation.

(b) (*Bio*) parent.

3 *nmpl*: **~s** (*père et mère*) parents; (*littér: ancêtres*) ancestors, forefathers; **accompagné de l'un de ses ~s** accompanied by one parent *ou* one of his parents; **nos premiers ~s** our first parents, Adam and Eve.

parental, e, *mpl* **-aux** [paʀɑ̃tal, o] *adj* parental.

parenté [paʀɑ̃te] *nf* (*rapport*) relationship, kinship; (*ensemble des parents*) relations (*pl*), relatives (*pl*), kith and kin (*pl*).

parenthèse [paʀɑ̃tɛz] *nf* (*digression*) parenthesis, digression; (*signe*) bracket, parenthesis. **ouvrir/fermer la ~** to open/close the brackets; **mettre qch entre ~s** to put sth in *ou* between brackets; **entre ~s** (*lit*) in brackets; (*fig*) incidentally, in parenthesis; **il vaut mieux mettre cet aspect entre ~s** it would be better to leave that aspect aside; (*fig*) **ouvrir une ~** to digress, make a digression; **je me permets d'ouvrir une ~ pour dire ...** may I interrupt *ou* digress for a moment to say ... .

parer¹ [paʀe] (1) **1** *vt* **(a)** (*orner*) *chose* to adorn, bedeck; *personne* to adorn, deck out (*de* with). **robe richement parée** richly trimmed *ou* ornamented dress; (*fig*) **~ qn de toutes les vertus** to attribute every virtue to sb.

(b) (*préparer*) *viande* to dress, trim; *cuir* to dress.

2 se parer *vpr* (*littér: se faire beau*) to put on all one's finery. **se ~ de** *bijoux* to adorn o.s. with; (*péj*) *faux titre* to assume, invest o.s. with; (*fig*) **se ~ des plumes du paon** to take all the credit (for o.s.).

parer² [paʀe] (1) **1** *vt* (*se protéger de*) *coup* to ward off, stave off, fend off; (*Boxe, Escrime*) to parry; (*fig*) *attaque* to stave off, parry. **2 parer à** *vt indir* **(a)** (*remédier*) *inconvénient* to deal with, remedy, overcome; *danger* to ward off. **(b)** (*pourvoir à*) *éventualité* to prepare for, be prepared for. **~ au plus pressé** to attend to the most urgent things first; **il faut ~ au plus pressé** first things first. **3: pare-balles** (*nm inv*) bullet sheild; (*adj inv*) bulletproof; **pare-brise** *nm inv* windscreen (*Brit*), windshield (*US*); **pare-chocs** *nm inv* (*Aut*) bumper (*Brit*), fender (*US*); **pare-étincelles** *nm inv* fireguard; **pare-feu** *nm inv [forêt]* firebreak; *[foyer]* fireguard; **pare-soleil** *nm inv* sun visor.

paresse [paʀɛs] *nf* (*V* **paresseux**) laziness; idleness; slowness; sluggishness; (*défaut*) laziness; (*péché*) sloth. **~ d'esprit** laziness *ou* sluggishness of mind.

paresser [paʀese] (1) *vi* to laze about *ou* around. **~ au lit** to laze in bed.

paresseusement [paʀɛsøzmɑ̃] *adv* (*V* **paresseux**) lazily; idly; sluggishly.

paresseux, -euse [paʀɛsø, øz] **1** *adj personne* lazy, idle; *esprit* slow; *allure, pose* lazy; *attitude mentale* casual; *estomac* sluggish. **solution ~euse** easy way out, line of least resistance; **~ comme une couleuvre** bone-idle*; **il est ~ pour se lever** he's not very good at getting up.

2 *nm,f* **(a)** lazy *ou* idle person, lazybones*.

(b) (*Zool*) sloth.

parfaire [paʀfɛʀ] (60) *vt travail* to perfect, bring to perfection; *connaissances* to perfect, round off; *décor, impression* to complete, put the finishing touches to; *somme* to make up.

parfait, e [paʀfɛ, ɛt] (*ptp de* **parfaire**) **1** *adj* **(a)** (*impeccable*) (*gén*) *travail, condition, exemple* perfect; *exécution, raisonnement* perfect, flawless; *manières* perfect, faultless; *V* **filer.**

(b) (*absolu*) *bonne foi, tranquillité* complete, total, perfect; *ressemblance* perfect. **il a été d'une discrétion ~e** *ou* (*frm*) **~ de discrétion** he has shown absolute discretion, he has been the soul of discretion; **dans la plus ~e ignorance** in total *ou* utter *ou* complete ignorance; **en ~ accord avec** in perfect *ou* total agreement with.

(c) (*accompli, achevé*) *élève, employé* perfect; (*péj*) *crétin, crapule* utter, downright, perfect. **le type même du ~ mari** the epitome of the perfect husband; **~ homme du monde** perfect gentleman.

(d) (*à son plein développement*) *fleur, insecte* perfect; *V* **accord, gaz, nombre.**

(e) (*très bon*) **(c'est) ~!** (that's) fine! *ou* excellent! *ou* great!*; (*iro*) (that's) marvellous *ou* great*; **vous refusez? (voilà qui est) ~, vous l'aurez voulu!** you won't? (that's) fine — it's your own affair!

2 *nm* **(a)** (*Culin*) parfait. **~ au café** coffee parfait.

(b) (*Ling*) perfect.

parfaitement [paʀfɛtmɑ̃] *adv* **(a)** (*très bien*) *connaître* perfectly. **je comprends ~** I quite understand, I understand perfectly.

(b) (*tout à fait*) *heureux, clair, exact* perfectly, quite; *hermétique, étanche* completely; *idiot* utterly, absolutely, perfectly. **cela m'est ~ égal** that makes absolutely no difference to me, it's all the same to me; **vous avez ~ le droit de le garder** you have a perfect right *ou* you're perfectly entitled to keep it.

(c) (*certainement*) (most) certainly, oh yes. **tu as fait ce tableau tout seul? — ~!** you did this picture all on your own? — I (most) certainly did!; **tu ne vas pas partir sans moi! — ~!** you're not going to leave without me! — oh yes *ou* indeed I am!; **je refuse d'obéir, ~, et j'en suis fier** I'm refusing to obey, most certainly *ou* definitely, and I'm proud of it.

parfois [paʀfwa] *adv* (*dans certains cas*) sometimes; (*de temps en temps*) sometimes, occasionally, at times. **~ je lis, ~ je sors** sometimes I (may) read, other times I (may) go out; **il y a ~ du brouillard en hiver** there's occasional fog *ou* occasionally there's fog in winter.

parfum [paʀfœ̃] *nm* **(a)** (*substance*) perfume, scent, fragrance. **(b)** (*odeur*) *[fleur, herbe]* scent, fragrance; *[tabac, vin, café]* aroma; *[glace]* flavour; *[savon]* scent; (*fig littér*) *[louanges, vertu]* odour. (*fig*) **ceci a un ~ de scandale/d'hérésie** that has a whiff of scandal/heresy about it. **(c)** (‡) **être au ~** to be in the know*; **mettre qn au ~** to put sb in the picture*, gen sb up‡.

parfumé, e [paʀfyme] (*ptp de* **parfumer**) *adj papier à lettres, savon* scented; *air, fleur, vin* fragrant; *effluves* aromatic. **femme trop ~e** woman wearing too much scent; **~ au café** coffee-flavour(ed).

parfumer [paʀfyme] (1) **1** *vt pièce, air [fleurs]* to perfume, scent; *[café, tabac]* to fill with its aroma; *mouchoir* to put scent *ou* perfume on; (*Culin*) to flavour (*à* with).

2 se parfumer *vpr* to use *ou* wear perfume *ou* scent. **elle se parfuma rapidement** she quickly put *ou* dabbed some scent *ou* perfume on.

parfumerie [paʀfymʀi] *nf* (*usine, industrie*) perfumery; (*boutique*) perfume shop; (*rayon*) perfumery (department); (*produits*) perfumery, perfumes, fragrances.

parfumeur, -euse [paʀfymœʀ, øz] *nm,f* perfumer.

pari [paʀi] *nm* bet, wager; (*Sport*) bet; (*activité*) betting. **faire/tenir un ~** to make *ou* lay/take up a bet; **~ mutuel (urbain)** ≃ tote, parimutuel (*US*); (*fig*) **les ~s sont ouverts** there's no knowing, it's anyone's bet*.

paria [paʀja] *nm* outcast, pariah; *[Indes]* Pariah.

parier [paʀje] (7) *vt* **(a)** (*gager*) to bet, wager. **je (te) parie que c'est lui/tout ce que tu veux** I bet you it's him/anything you like; **il y a gros à ~ que ...** the odds are that ...; **je l'aurais parié** I might have known.

(b) (*Courses*) *argent* to bet, lay, stake. **~ 100 F sur le favori** to bet *ou* lay 100 francs on the favourite; **~ gros sur un cheval** to bet heavily on *ou* lay a big bet on a horse; (*emploi absolu*) **~ sur un cheval** to bet on a horse, back a horse; **~ aux courses** to bet on the races.

pariétal, e, *mpl* **-aux** [paʀjetal, o] **1** *adj* (*Anat*) parietal; (*Art*) wall (*épith*). **2** *nm* parietal bone.

parieur, -euse [paʀjœʀ, øz] *nm,f* punter.

parigot, e* [paʀigo, ɔt] **1** *adj* Parisian. **2** *nm,f*: **P~(e)** Parisian.

Paris [paʀi] *n* Paris.

parisianisme [paʀizjanism(ə)] *nm* (*habitude*) Parisian habit; (*façon de parler*) Parisian way of speaking.

parisien, -ienne [paʀizjɛ̃, jɛn] **1** *adj* (*gén*) Paris (*épith*), of Paris; *société, goûts, ambiance* Parisian. **le bassin/la région ~(ne)** the Paris basin/region *ou* area; **la vie ~ne** Paris life, life in Paris. **2** *nm,f*: **P~(ne)** Parisian.

paritaire [paʀitɛʀ] *adj commission* joint (*épith*), with equal representation of both sides; *représentation* equal.

parité [paʀite] *nf* parity.

parjure [parʒyʀ] **1** *adj personne* faithless, disloyal; *serment* false. **2** *nm* (*violation de serment*) betrayal; (*faux serment*) false witness. **3** *nmf* traitor; false witness.
parjurer (se) [parʒyʀe] (1) *vpr* (*V* **parjure**) to be faithless *ou* a traitor to one's oath *ou* promise; to give *ou* bear false witness.
parking [parkiŋ] *nm* (*lieu*) car park (*Brit*), parking lot (*US*); (*action*) parking.
parlant, e [parlɑ̃, ɑ̃t] **1** *adj* **(a)** (*doué de parole*) speaking (*épith*), talking (*épith*). **il n'est pas très ~** he's not very talkative. **(b)** (*fig*) *portrait* lifelike; *comparaison, description* graphic, vivid; *geste, regard* eloquent, meaningful. **les chiffres sont ~s** the figures speak for themselves. **2** *adv*: **scientifiquement/économiquement** *etc* **~** scientifically/economically *etc* speaking.
parlé, e [parle] (*ptp de* **parler**) **1** *adj langue* spoken; *V* **chaîne, journal. 2** *nm* (*Théât*) spoken part.
parlement [parləmɑ̃] *nm* parliament. **le P~ (britannique)** Parliament; le **~ américain** the American parliament, the US Congress.
parlementaire [parləmɑ̃tɛʀ] **1** *adj* (*Pol*) parliamentary. **2** *nmf* **(a)** (*Pol*) member of Parliament; (*Brit Hist: partisan*) Parliamentarian. **(b)** (*négociateur*) negociator, mediator.
parlementairement [parləmɑ̃tɛʀmɑ̃] *adv* parliamentarily.
parlementarisme [parləmɑ̃taʀism(ə)] *nm* parliamentary government.
parlementer [parləmɑ̃te] (1) *vi* (*négocier*) to parley; (**: discuter*) to argue things over. **~ avec qn** to parley *ou* talk with sb.
parler [parle] (1) **1** *vi* **(a)** (*faculté physique*) to talk. **il a commencé à ~ à 2 ans** he started talking when he was 2; **votre perroquet parle?** can your parrot talk?; **~ du nez** to talk through one's nose; **~ distinctement** to speak distinctly; **il parle entre ses dents** he talks between his teeth, he mumbles; **je n'aime pas sa façon de ~** I don't like the way he talks *ou* speaks; **parlez plus fort!** talk *ou* speak louder!, speak up!; *V* **façon.**
(b) (*exprimer sa pensée*) to speak; (*bavarder*) to talk. **~ franc/crûment** to speak frankly/bluntly; **~ bien/mal** to be a good/not to be a (very) good speaker; **~ d'or** to speak words of wisdom; (*péj*) **~ comme un livre** to talk like a book; **il aime s'écouter ~** he likes the sound of his own voice; **~ pour qn** to speak for sb; (*iro*) **parle pour toi!** speak for yourself!; (*Cartes*) **c'est à vous de ~** it's your bid; **au lieu de ~ en l'air, renseigne-toi/agis** instead of coming out with a lot of vague talk, find out/do something; **plutôt que de ~ en l'air, allons lui demander** instead of talking (wildly) let's go and ask him; **~ à tort et à travers** to blether, talk drivel, talk through one's hat; **~ pour ne rien dire** to talk for the sake of talking, say nothing at great length; **voilà qui est (bien) ~!** hear hear!, well said!
(c) (*converser*) **~ à qn** to talk *ou* speak to sb; **il faut que je lui parle** I must talk to him *ou* have a word with him; **nous ne nous parlons pas** we're not on speaking terms; **moi qui vous parle** I myself; (*fig*) **trouver à qui ~** to meet one's match; (*fig*) **c'est ~ à un mur** it's like talking to a (brick) wall.
(d) (*s'entretenir*) **~ de qch/qn** to talk about sth/sb; (*fig*) **~ de la pluie et du beau temps** to talk about the weather; **faire ~ de soi** to get o.s. talked about; **~ mal de qn** to speak ill of sb; **on parle beaucoup de lui comme ministre** he is being talked about *ou* spoken of as a possible *ou* future minister, he's tipped as a likely minister; **on ne parle que de ça** it's the only topic of conversation, it's the only thing people are talking about; **tout le monde en parle** everybody's talking about it, it's common gossip; **toute la ville en parle** it's the talk of the town; **il n'en parle jamais** he never mentions it *ou* refers to it *ou* talks about it; **quand on parle du loup (on en voit la queue)** talk (*Brit*) *ou* speak of the devil (and he will appear).
(e) (*entretenir*) **~ de qch à qn** to tell sb about sth; **parlez-nous de vos vacances/projets** tell us about your holidays/plans; **on m'avait parlé d'une vieille maison** I had been told about an old house; **je lui parlerai de cette affaire** I'll speak to him *ou* I'll have a word with him about this business; **il a parlé de moi au patron** he put in a word for me with the boss; **on m'a beaucoup parlé de vous** I've heard a lot about you.
(f) (*annoncer l'intention*) **~ de faire qch** to talk of doing sth; **elle a parlé d'aller voir un docteur** she has talked of going to see a doctor; **on parle de construire une route** they're talking of builing a road, there is talk of a road being built *ou* of building a road.
(g) (*fig*) **~ par gestes** to use sign language; **~ aux yeux/à l'imagination** to appeal to the eye/the imagination; **~ au cœur** to speak to the heart; **les faits parlent (d'eux-mêmes)** the facts speak for themselves; **faire ~ la poudre** to resort to war; **de quoi ça parle, ton livre? — ça parle de bateaux*** what is your book about? — it's about ships; **le jardin lui parlait de son enfance** the garden brought back memories of his childhood (to him); **le devoir a parlé** I (*ou* he *etc*) heard the call of duty; **son cœur a parlé** he heeded the call of his heart.
(h) (*révéler les faits*) to talk. **faire ~** *suspect* to make talk, loosen the tongue of; *introverti, timide* to draw out.
(i) (*loc*) **tu parles!*, vous parlez!*** (*bien sûr*) you're telling me!*, you bet!*; (*iro*) no chance!*, you must be joking!*; **tu as été dédommagé, non? — parlons-en!** (*ça ne change rien*) you've been compensated, haven't you? — some good *ou* a lot of use that is (to me)!*; (*pas du tout*) you've been compensated, haven't you? — not likely!* *ou* you must be joking!*; **tu parles *ou* vous parlez d'une brute!** talk about a brute!; **leur proposition, tu parles si on s'en fiche!*** a fat lot we think of their idea!*; (*iro*) **tu parles si ça nous aide/c'est pratique*** that helps us/it's very helpful and I don't think!*; **ne m'en parlez pas!** you're telling me!*, I don't need telling!*; **n'en parlons plus!** let's forget (about) it, let's not mention it again; **sans ~ de ...** not to mention ..., to say nothing of ...; **tu peux ~!*** YOU can talk!*; **vous n'avez qu'à ~** just say the word, you've only to say the word.
2 *vt* **(a)** *langue* to speak. **~ (l')anglais** to speak English.
(b) ~ politique/affaires to talk politics/business; **~ boutique*** to talk shop; (*hum*) **si nous parlions finances?** how about talking cash?*
3 *nm* **(a)** (*manière de parler*) speech. **le ~ de tous les jours** everyday speech, common parlance; **il a un ~ vulgaire** he has a coarse way of speaking.
(b) (*langue régionale*) dialect.
parleur, -euse [parlœʀ, øz] *nm,f* talker. **beau ~** fine talker.
parloir [parlwaʀ] *nm [école, prison]* visiting room; *[couvent]* parlour.
parlot(t)e* [parlɔt] *nf* chitchat* (*U*). **toutes ces ~s ne mènent à rien** all this chitchat* is a waste of time; **faire la ~ avec qn** to have a natter* (*surtout Brit*) *ou* rap* (*US*) with sb.
Parme [parm(ə)] *n* Parma.
Parmentier [parmɑ̃tje] *adj inv V* **hachis.**
parmesan [parməzɑ̃] *nm* (*Culin*) Parmesan (cheese).
parmi [parmi] *prép* among(st). **~ la foule** among *ou* in the crowd; **venez ici ~ nous** come over here with us; **c'est un cas ~ d'autres** it's one case among many, it's one of many cases; **allant ~ les ruelles désertes** going through the deserted alleys.
Parnasse [parnas] *nm* Parnassus.
parnassien, -ienne [parnasjɛ̃, jɛn] *adj, nm* Parnassian.
parodie [parɔdi] *nf* parody. (*fig*) **une ~ de procès** a mockery of a trial.
parodier [parɔdje] (7) *vt* to parody.
parodique [parɔdik] *adj style* parodic(al).
parodiste [parɔdist(ə)] *nmf* parodist.
paroi [parwa] *nf* (*gén, Anat, Bot*) wall; *[récipient]* (inside) surface, (inner) wall; *[véhicule]* side; (*cloison*) partition. **~ (rocheuse)** rock face.
paroisse [parwas] *nf* parish.
paroissial, e, *mpl* -aux [parwasjal, o] *adj* parish (*épith*). **salle ~e** church hall; **à l'échelon ~** at the parochial *ou* parish level.
paroissien, -ienne [parwasjɛ̃, jɛn] **1** *nm,f* parishioner. (*fig*) **un drôle de ~*** a funny customer*. **2** *nm* (*missel*) prayer book, missal.
parole [parɔl] *nf* **(a)** (*mot*) word. **comprenez-vous le sens de ses ~s?** can you understand (the meaning of) what he says?; (*Prov*) **les ~s s'envolent, les écrits restent** verba volant, scripta manent; (*hum*) **voilà une bonne ~!** sound thinking!, that's what I like to hear!; **la ~ de Dieu** the word of God; **c'est ~ d'évangile** it's the gospel truth, it's gospel*; (*iro*) **de belles ~s** fair *ou* fine words! (*iro*); **~ célèbre** famous words *ou* saying; **prononcer une ~ historique** to make a historic remark; **il est surtout courageux en ~s** he's brave enough when it's just a matter of words *ou* talking about it; **tout cela est bien joli en ~s mais ...** this sounds all very well but ...; *V* **boire, payer.**
(b) (*texte*) **~s** *[chanson]* words, lyrics; *[dessin]* words; **histoire sans ~s** wordless cartoon.
(c) (*promesse*) word. **tenir ~** to keep one's word; **il a tenu ~** he kept his word, he was as good as his word; **c'est un homme de ~, il est de ~, il n'a qu'une ~** he's a man of his word, his word is his bond; **il n'a aucune ~** you (just) can't trust a word he says; **je l'ai cru sur ~** I took his word for it; **(je vous donne *ou* vous avez ma) ~ d'honneur!** I give you *ou* you have my word (of honour), cross my heart!*; (*fig*) **ma ~!*** (upon) my word!, well I never!; **prisonnier sur ~** prisoner on parole.
(d) (*faculté d'expression*) speech. **l'homme est doué de ~** man is endowed with speech. **avoir la ~ facile** to be a fluent speaker, have the gift of the gab*; **avoir le don de la ~** to be a gifted speaker; (*Prov*) **la ~ est d'argent, le silence est d'or** speech is silver, silence is golden; *[animal]* **il ne lui manque que la ~** it *ou* he does everything but talk; **perdre/retrouver la ~** to lose/recover one's speech, lose/find one's tongue*.
(e) (*Ling*) speech, parole (*T*). **acte de ~** speech act.
(f) (*Cartes*) **~!** (I) pass!
(g) (*dans un débat*) **droit de ~** right to speak; **temps de ~** speaking time; **vous avez la ~** you have the floor, over to you*; **passer la ~ à qn** to hand over to sb; **prendre la ~** to speak.
parolier, ière [parɔlje, jɛʀ] *nm,f [chanson]* lyric writer; *[opéra]* librettist.
paronyme [parɔnim] *nm* paronym.
paronymie [parɔnimi] *nf* paronymy.
paroxysme [parɔksism(ə)] *nm [maladie]* crisis (point); *[sensation, sentiment]* height. **être au ~ de la joie/colère** to be beside o.s. with joy/anger; **le bruit était au ~** the noise was at its height; **l'incendie/la douleur avait atteint son ~** the fire/pain was at its height *ou* at its fiercest; **le combat avait atteint son ~** the fight had reached fever pitch *ou* its height *ou* a climax.
parpaillot, e [parpajo, ɔt] *nm,f* (*Hist, péj*) Protestant.
parpaing [parpɛ̃] *nm* (*pierre pleine*) parpen; (*aggloméré*) breeze-block.
Parque [park(ə)] *nf* (*Myth*) Fate. **les ~s** the Parcae, the Fates.
parquer [parke] (1) **1** *vt voiture, artillerie* to park; *moutons, bétail* to pen (in *ou* up); (*fig*) *personnes* to pen *ou* pack in; (*à l'intérieur*) to pack in, shut up. **2 se parquer** *vpr* (*Aut*) to park.
parquet [parkɛ] *nm* **(a)** (*plancher*) (wooden *ou* parquet) floor. **(b)** (*Jur*) Public Prosecutor's department. **(c)** (*Bourse*) **le ~** (*enceinte*) the (dealing) floor; (*agents*) the Stock Exchange.
parqueter [parkəte] (4) *vt* to lay a wooden *ou* parquet floor in. **pièce parquetée** room with a (polished) wooden *ou* parquet floor.
parrain [parɛ̃] *nm* **(a)** (*Rel*) godfather. **accepter d'être le ~ d'un enfant** to agree to be a child's godfather *ou* to stand godfather to a child. **(b)** (*dans un cercle, une société*) sponsor, proposer; *[navire]* christener, namer; *[entreprise, initiative]* promoter; *[œuvre, fondation]* patron.

parrainage [paʀɛnaʒ] *nm* (*V* **parrain**) sponsorship, proposing (for membership); christening, naming; promoting; patronage.

parrainer [paʀene] (1) *vt* (*V* **parrain**) to sponsor, propose (for membership); to christen, name; to promote; to patronize.

parricide [paʀisid] **1** *adj* parricidal. **2** *nmf* parricide. **3** *nm* (*crime*) parricide.

parsec [paʀsɛk] *nm* parsec.

parsemer [paʀsəme] (5) *vt* **(a)** (*répandre*) **~ de** to sprinkle with, strew with; **~ le sol de mines** to scatter mines over the ground, strew the ground with mines; **~ un tissu de paillettes d'or** to sprinkle material with gold sequins, strew gold sequins over material; (*fig*) **~ un texte de citations** to scatter quotations through a text, strew a text with quotations.

(b) (*être répandu sur*) to be scattered *ou* sprinkled over. **les feuilles qui parsèment le gazon** the leaves which are scattered *ou* which lie scattered over the lawn; **ciel parsemé d'étoiles** sky sprinkled *ou* strewn *ou* studded with stars; **champ parsemé de fleurs** field dotted with flowers; (*fig*) **parsemé de difficultés/de fautes** riddled with difficulties/mistakes.

parsi, e [paʀsi] **1** *adj* Parsee. **2** *nm* (*Ling*) Parsee. **3** *nm,f*: **P~(e)** Parsee.

part [paʀ] *nf* **(a)** (*portion*) (*gén*) share; [*légumes, gâteau*] portion. **~ d'héritage/de soucis** share of the inheritance/of worries; (*fig*) **avoir/vouloir sa ~ du gâteau** to have/want one's slice *ou* share of the cake; **la ~ du lion** the lion's share; **~ à deux!** share and share alike!; **chacun paie sa ~** everyone pays his share, everyone chips in*.

(b) (*participation*) part. **cela prend une grande ~ dans sa vie** it plays a great part in his life; **il a pris une ~ importante dans l'élaboration du projet** he played an important part in the development of the project; **prendre ~ à un débat** to participate in *ou* take part in a debate; **je prends ~ à vos soucis** I share in your worries; **avoir ~ à** to have a share in; **faire la ~ de la fatigue/du hasard** to take tiredness/chance into account *ou* consideration, allow for *ou* make allowance for tiredness/chance; **faire la ~ des choses** to take things into account *ou* consideration, make allowances; (*fig*) **faire la ~ du feu** to cut one's losses, make a deliberate sacrifice.

(c) (*partie*) part, portion. **c'est une toute petite ~ de sa fortune** it's only a tiny fraction *ou* part of his fortune; **pour une bonne** *ou* **large ~** largely, to a great extent; **pour une ~** partly, to some extent; **pour une petite ~** in a small way.

(d) (*Fin*) ≃ share (*giving right to participate in profits but not running of firm*).

(e) à ~ (*de côté*) aside, on one side; (*séparément*) separately, on its (*ou* their) own; (*excepté*) except for, apart from; (*exceptionnel*) special, extraordinary; **nous mettrons ces livres à ~ pour vous** we'll put these books aside *ou* on one side for you; **prendre qn à ~** to take sb aside; **étudier chaque problème à ~** to study each problem separately *ou* on its own; **à ~ vous, je ne connais personne ici** apart from *ou* except for you I don't know anyone here; **à ~ cela** apart from that, otherwise; **plaisanterie à ~** joking apart; **c'est un homme à ~** he's an extraordinary *ou* exceptional man, he's in a class of his own; **un cas/une place à ~** a special case/place; **il est vraiment à ~*** there aren't many like him around*; (*littér*) **garder qch à ~ soi** to keep sth to o.s.; (*littér*) **je pensais à ~ moi** I thought within *ou* to myself; *V* **bande[2], chambre.**

(f) (*loc*) **faire ~ de qch à qn** to announce sth to sb, inform sb of sth, let sb know *ou* tell sb about sth; **de la ~ de** (*provenance*) from; (*au nom de*) on behalf of; **il vient de la ~ de X** he has been sent by X; **cette machine demande un peu de bon sens de la ~ de l'utilisateur** this machine requires a little common sense on the part of the user *ou* from the user; **cela m'étonne de sa ~** I'm surprised at that (coming) from him; **pour ma ~** as for me, for my part (*frm*), as far as I'm concerned; **dites-lui bonjour de ma ~** give him my regards; **c'est gentil de sa ~** that's nice of him; (*Téléc*) **c'est de la ~ de qui?** who's calling? *ou* speaking?; **prendre qch en bonne ~** to take sth in good part; **prendre qch en mauvaise ~** to take sth amiss, take offence at sth; **de toute(s) ~(s)** from all sides *ou* quarters; **d'autre ~** (*de plus*) moreover; **d'une ~ ... d'autre ~** on the one hand ... on the other hand; **de ~ et d'autre** on both sides, on either side; **de ~ en ~** right through; **membre/citoyen à ~ entière** full member/citizen; *V* **nul, quelque.**

partage [paʀtaʒ] *nm* **(a)** (*fractionnement, division*) [*terrain, surface*] dividing up, division; [*gâteau*] cutting; (*Math*) [*nombre*] factorizing. **faire le ~ de qch** to divide sth up; **le ~ du pays en 2 camps** the division of the country into 2 camps; *V* **ligne[1].**

(b) (*distribution*) [*butin, héritage*] sharing out. **procéder au ~ de qch** to share sth out; **le ~ n'est pas juste** the way it's shared out isn't fair, it isn't fairly shared out; **j'ai été oublié, dans le ~** I've been forgotten in the share-out; **quel a été le ~ des voix entre les candidats?** how were the votes divided among the candidates?; (*Pol*) **en cas de ~ des voix** in the event of a tie in the voting.

(c) (*participation*) sharing. **l'enquête a conclu au ~ des responsabilités** the inquiry came to the conclusion that the responsibility was shared; **le ~ du pouvoir avec nos adversaires** the sharing of power with our adversaries; (*fig*) **fidélité sans ~** undivided loyalty.

(d) (*part*) share; (*fig: sort*) portion, lot. **donner/recevoir qch en ~** to give/receive sth in a will; **la maison lui échut en ~** the house came to him in the will; (*fig*) **le bon sens qu'il a reçu en ~** the common sense with which he has been endowed.

partagé, e [paʀtaʒe] (*ptp de* **partager**) *adj* **(a)** (*divisé*) *avis, opinions* divided. **les experts sont ~s** the experts are divided. **(b)** (*littér: doté*) endowed. **il est bien/mal ~ par le sort** fate has been/has not been kind to him.

partageable [paʀtaʒabl(ə)] *adj* divisible, which can be shared out *ou* divided up. **frais ~s entre tous** costs that are shared by all.

partager [paʀtaʒe] (3) **1** *vt* **(a)** (*fractionner*) *terrain, feuille, gâteau* to divide up. **~ en 2/en 2 bouts/par moitié** to divide in 2/into 2 bits/in half.

(b) (*distribuer, répartir*) *butin, gâteau* to share (out) (*entre 2/plusieurs personnes* between 2/among several people). **il partage son temps entre son travail et sa famille** he divides his time between his work and his family; **il partage son affection entre plusieurs personnes** several people have to share his affections.

(c) (*avoir une part de*) *héritage, responsabilités, sort* to share (*avec* with). **voulez-vous ~ notre repas?** will you share our meal?; **~ le lit de qn** to share sb's bed; **il n'aime pas ~** he doesn't like sharing; **les torts sont partagés** all *ou* both parties are at fault.

(d) (*s'associer à*) *sentiments, bonheur, goûts* to share (in); *opinion, idée* to share, agree with. **je partage votre douleur/bonheur/surprise** I share your sorrow/happiness/surprise; **amour partagé** mutual love.

(e) (*fig: diviser*) [*problème, conflit*] to divide. **partagé entre l'amour et la haine** torn between love and hatred.

(f) (*frm: douer*) to endow. **la nature l'a bien partagé** Nature has been generous to him.

2 se partager *vpr* **(a)** (*se fractionner*) to be divided. **ça peut facilement se ~ en 3/en 3 morceaux** it can easily be divided (up) *ou* cut in 3/into 3 bits; **se ~ entre diverses tendances** to have differing viewpoints; **le monde se partage en deux: les bons et les méchants** the world falls *ou* can be divided into two groups, the good and the wicked; **à l'endroit où les branches se partagent** where the branches fork *ou* divide; **le reste des voix s'est partagé entre les autres candidats** the remaining votes are distributed *ou* shared among the other candidates; **le pouvoir ne se partage pas** power is not something which can be shared; **il se partage entre son travail et son jardin** he divides his time between his work and his garden.

(b) (*se distribuer*) **se ~ qch** to share *ou* divide sth between *ou* among themselves; **ils se sont partagé le butin** they shared the booty between them; **nous nous sommes partagé le travail** we shared the work between us; **les 3 meilleurs candidats se sont partagé les suffrages** the votes were divided among the 3 best candidates; **se ~ les faveurs du public** to vie for the public's favour.

partageur, -euse [paʀtaʒœʀ, øz] *adj* ready *ou* willing to share. **il n'est pas ~** he doesn't like sharing (his things), he's not a good sharer.

partageux, -euse† [paʀtaʒø, øz] *nm,f* distributionist.

partance [paʀtɑ̃s] *nf*: **en ~** *train* due to leave; *avion* outbound; *bateau* sailing (*attrib*); **en ~ pour Londres** *train, avion* for London, London (*épith*); *bateau* bound *ou* sailing for London.

partant[1] [paʀtɑ̃] *nm* **(a)** (*coureur*) starter; (*cheval*) runner. **tous ~s** all horses running; **non ~** non-runner. **(b)** (*personne*) person leaving, departing traveller *ou* visitor *etc*. **les ~s et les arrivants** the departures and arrivals.

partant[2] [paʀtɑ̃] *conj* (*littér*) hence, therefore, consequently.

partenaire [paʀtənɛʀ] *nmf* partner.

parterre [paʀtɛʀ] *nm* **(a)** (*plate-bande*) border, (flower)bed; (*: *plancher*) floor. **(b)** (*Théât*) (*emplacement*) stalls (*Brit*), orchestra (*US*); (*public*) (audience in the) stalls (*Brit*) *ou* orchestra (*US*).

Parthe [paʀt] *nm* Parthian; *V* **flèche[1].**

parthénogénèse [paʀtenɔʒenɛz] *nf* parthenogenesis.

parthénogénétique [paʀtenɔʒenetik] *adj* parthenogenetic.

parthénogénétiquement [paʀtenɔʒenetikmɑ̃] *adv* parthenogenetically.

Parthénon [paʀtenɔ̃] *nm*: **le ~** the Parthenon.

parti[1] [paʀti] **1** *nm* **(a)** (*groupe*) (*gén, Pol*) party. **le ~ des mécontents** the malcontents; **le ~ de la défaite** the defeatists; **se mettre** *ou* **se ranger du ~ de qn** to take sides with sb, side with sb; **prendre le ~ de qn** to stand up for sb; **prendre ~ pour qn** to take sb's side; **il ne veut pas prendre ~ (dans cette affaire)** he does not want to take a stand (on this matter); **le ~ (communiste)** the Communist party.

(b) (*solution*) option, course of action. **hésiter entre 2 ~s** to wonder which of 2 courses *ou* which course to follow; **prendre un ~** to come to *ou* make a decision, make up one's mind; **prendre le ~ de faire** to make up one's mind to do, decide *ou* resolve to do; **mon ~ est pris** my mind is made up; **crois-tu que c'est le meilleur ~ (à prendre)?** do you think that's the best course (to take)? *ou* the best idea?; **prendre son ~ de qch** to come to terms with sth, reconcile o.s. to sth; **il faut bien en prendre son ~** you just have to come to terms with it *ou* put up with it*.

(c) (*personne à marier*) match. **beau** *ou* **bon** *ou* **riche ~** good match.

(d) (*loc*) **tirer ~ de** *situation, occasion* to take advantage of, turn to (good) account; *outil, ressources* to put to (good) use; **tirer le meilleur ~ possible d'une situation** to turn a situation to best account, get the most one can out of a situation; **faire un mauvais ~ à qn** to deal roughly with sb, give sb rough treatment.

2: parti pris prejudice, bias; **je crois, sans parti pris ...** I think, without bias (on my part) ... *ou* being quite objective about it ...; **juger sans parti pris** to take an unbiased *ou* objective view; **être de/éviter le parti pris** to be/avoid being prejudiced *ou* biased.

parti[2], e[1]* [paʀti] (*ptp de* **partir**) *adj* (*ivre*) tipsy, tight*. **il est bien ~** he's well away*.

partial, e, *mpl* **-aux** [paʀsjal, o] *adj* biased, partial.

partialement [paʀsjalmɑ̃] *adv* in a biased way. **juger qch ~** to take a biased view of sth.

partialité [paʀsjalite] *nf*: ~ **(en faveur de qn)** partiality (for sb); ~ **(contre qn)** bias (against sb); **faire preuve de ~ envers** *ou* **contre qn** to be unfair to sb, be biased against sb, show bias against sb.

participant, e [paʀtisipɑ̃, ɑ̃t] **1** *adj* participant, participating. **2** *nm,f* (*à un concours, une course*) entrant (*à* in); (*à un débat, un projet*) participant, person taking part (*à* in); (*à une association*) member (*à* of); (*à une cérémonie, un complot*) person taking part (*à* in). **~s aux bénéfices** those sharing in the profits; **les ~s à la manifestation/au concours** those taking part in the demonstration/competition.

participation [paʀtisipɑsjɔ̃] *nf* **(a)** (*U: V* **participer**) **~ à** taking part in; participation in; appearance in; involvement in; contributing to; sharing in; **la réunion aura lieu sans leur ~** the meeting will take place without their taking part *ou* without them; **peu importe l'habileté: c'est la ~ qui compte** skill doesn't really matter: what counts is taking part; **nous nous sommes assurés la ~ de 2 équilibristes** we have arranged for 2 tightrope walkers to appear; **c'est la ~ de X qui va attirer les spectateurs** it's X (performing) who'll *ou* it's the fact that X is appearing *ou* performing that will draw the crowds; **ce soir grand gala avec la ~ de plusieurs vedettes** tonight, grand gala with appearances by several stars; '**~ aux frais: 50 F**' 'cost: 50 francs'.

(b) (*Écon*) (*détention d'actions*) interest. **prendre une ~ majoritaire dans une firme** to acquire a majority interest in a firm; **la ~ (ouvrière)** worker participation; **~ aux bénéfices** profit-sharing.

participe [paʀtisip] *nm* participle.

participer [paʀtisipe] (1) **1 participer à** *vt indir* **(a)** (*prendre part à*) *concours, colloque, cérémonie* to take part in. **je compte ~ au concours/à l'épreuve de fond** I intend to enter *ou* take part in the competition/the long-distance event.

(b) (*prendre une part active à*) *entreprise, discussion, jeu* to participate in, take part in; *spectacle [artiste]* to appear in; *aventure, complot, escroquerie* to take part in, be involved in. **en sport, l'important n'est pas de gagner mais de ~** in sport the important thing is not winning but taking part; **~ à la joie/au chagrin de qn** to share sb's joy/sorrow; **ils ont participé à l'allégresse générale** they joined in the general mood of joyfulness.

(c) (*payer sa part de*) *frais, dépenses* to contribute to. **~ (financièrement) à** *entreprise, projet* to cooperate in.

(d) (*avoir part à*) *profits, pertes, succès* to share in.

2 participer de *vt indir* (*littér: tenir de*) to partake of (*frm*), have something of the nature of.

participial, e, *mpl* **-iaux** [paʀtisipjal, jo] **1** *adj* participial. **2 participiale** *nf* participial phrase *ou* clause.

particularisation [paʀtikylaʀizɑsjɔ̃] *nf* particularization.

particulariser [paʀtikylaʀize] (1) **1** *vt* to particularize. **2 se particulariser** *vpr* to be distinguished *ou* characterized (*par* by).

particularisme [paʀtikylaʀism(ə)] *nm* **(a)** (*Pol: attitude*) sense of identity. (*particularité*) **~(s)** specific (local) character (*U*), specific characteristic(s). **(b)** (*Rel*) particularism.

particularité [paʀtikylaʀite] *nf* **(a)** (*U: littér*) particularity. **(b)** (*caractéristique*) *[individu, caractère, religion]* particularity, (distinctive) characteristic; *[texte, paysage]* (distinctive) characteristic *ou* feature; *[appareil, modèle]* (distinctive) feature. **ces modèles ont en commun la ~ d'être ...** these models all have the distinctive feature of being ..., these models are all distinguished by being ...; **cet animal présente la ~ d'être herbivore** a distinctive feature *ou* characteristic of this animal is that it is herbivorous.

(c) (†, *littér: détail*) particular.

particule [paʀtikyl] *nf* (*Ling, Phys*) particle. **~ (nobiliaire)** nobiliary particle; **nom à ~** name with a handle; **il a un nom à ~** he has a handle to his name.

particulier, -ière [paʀtikylje, jɛʀ] **1** *adj* **(a)** (*spécifique*) *aspect, point, exemple* particular, specific; *trait, style, manière de parler* characteristic, distinctive. **dans ce cas ~** in this particular case; **il n'avait pas d'aptitudes ~ières** he had no particular *ou* special aptitudes; **cette habitude lui est ~ière** this habit is peculiar to him; **signes ~s** (*gén*) distinctive signs; (*sur un passeport*) special peculiarities.

(b) (*spécial*) exceptional, special, particular. **la situation est un peu ~ière** the situation is rather exceptional; **ce que j'ai à dire est un peu ~** what I have to say is slightly unusual; **cela constitue un cas ~** this is a special *ou* an unusual *u* an exceptional case; **rien de ~ à signaler** nothing in particular *ou* unusual to report; **je l'ai préparé avec un soin tout ~** I prepared it with very special care *ou* with particular care.

(c) (*étrange*) *mœurs* peculiar, odd. **il a toujours été un peu ~** he has always been a bit peculiar *ou* odd.

(d) (*privé*) *voiture, secrétaire, conversation, intérêt* private. **leçons ~ières** private lessons *ou* tuition; **l'entreprise a son service ~ de livraison** the company has its own delivery service; **intervenir à titre ~** to intervene in a private capacity; *V* **hôtel**.

(e) en ~ (*en privé*) *parler* in private; (*séparément*) *examiner* separately; (*surtout*) in particular, particularly, especially; (*entre autres choses*) in particular.

2 *nm* **(a)** (*personne*) person; (*Admin, Comm*) private individual. **comme un simple ~** like any ordinary person; (*petites annonces*) **vente/location de ~ à ~** private sale/let.

(b) (*: *individu*) individual, character. **un drôle de ~** an odd character *ou* individual.

(c) (*chose*) **le ~** the particular; **du général au ~** from the general to the particular.

particulièrement [paʀtikyljɛʀmɑ̃] *adv* particularly, especially. **~ bon/évolué** particularly good/developed; **je ne le connais pas ~** I don't know him very *ou* particularly well; **il aime tous les arts et tout ~ la peinture** he is keen on all the arts, especially painting; **je voudrais plus ~ vous faire remarquer ce détail** I'd particularly like to draw your attention to this detail; **voulez-vous du café? — je n'y tiens pas ~** would you like a coffee? — not particularly.

partie[2] [paʀti] **1** *nf* **(a)** (*portion, fraction*) part; (*quantité*) part, amount. **diviser en trois ~s** to divide into three parts; **il y a des ~s amusantes dans le film** the film is funny in parts, the film has its funny moments; **il ne possède qu'une ~ du terrain** he only owns (one) part of the land; **une petite ~ de l'argent** a small part *ou* amount of the money; **une grande *ou* bonne ~ du travail** a large *ou* good part of *ou* a good deal of the work; **la majeure *ou* plus grande ~ du temps/du pays** most of *ou* the greater *ou* the best part of the time/the country; **la plus grande ~ de ce qu'on vous a dit** the greater part *ou* most of what you were told; **tout ou ~ de** all or part of; **en ~** partly, in part; **en grande *ou* majeure ~** largely, in large part, mainly, for the most part; **faire ~ de** *ensemble, obligations, risques* to be part of; *club, association* to belong to, be a member of; *catégorie, famille* to belong to; *élus, gagnants* to be among, be one of; **la rivière fait ~ du domaine** the river is part of the estate; **elle fait ~ de notre groupe** she belongs to our group, she's one of our group; **faire ~ intégrante de** to be an integral part of, be part and parcel of.

(b) (*spécialité*) field, subject. **moi qui suis de la ~** knowing the field *ou* subject as I do; **il n'est pas dans *ou* de la ~** it's not his line *ou* field; **quand on lui parle électricité, il est dans sa ~** when it's a matter of electricity, he knows what he's talking about; **demande à ton frère, c'est sa ~ *ou* il est de la ~** ask your brother — it's his field *ou* his line.

(c) (*Cartes, Sport*) game; (*fig: lutte*) struggle, fight. **faisons une ~ de ...** let's have a game of ...; **on a fait une bonne ~** we had a good game; (*fig*) **abandonner la ~** to give up the fight; **la ~ est délicate** it's a tricky situation *ou* business; **la ~ n'est pas égale** it's an unequal *ou* uneven match.

(d) (*Jur*) *[contrat]* party; *[procès]* litigant; (*Mil: adversaire*) opponent. **la ~ adverse** the opposing party; **les ~s en présence** the parties; **les ~s belligérantes** the warring factions; **avoir affaire à forte ~** to have no mean opponent *ou* a tough opponent to contend with; **être ~ prenante dans une négociation** to be a party to a negotiation; *V* **juge**.

(e) (*Mus*) part.

(f) (*Anat euph*) **~s sexuelles *ou* génitales, ~s honteuses**† private parts; **~s viriles** male organs; **les ~s*** the privates*.

(g) (*loc*) **avoir la ~ belle** to be sitting pretty*; **se mettre de la ~** to join in; **je veux être de la ~** I don't want to miss this, I want to be in on this*; (*littér*) **avoir ~ liée (avec qn)** to be hand in glove (with sb); **ce n'est que ~ remise** it will be for another time; **prendre qn à ~** (*apostropher*) to take sb to task; (*malmener*) to set on sb; (*Comm*) **comptabilité en ~ simple/double** single-/double-entry book-keeping.

2: partie de campagne day *ou* outing in the country; **partie carrée** wife-swapping party; **partie de chasse** shooting party *ou* expedition; (*Jur*) **partie civile** *private party associating in action with public prosecutor;* **se porter *ou* se constituer partie civile** *to associate in an action with the public prosecutor*; (*Ling*) **les parties du discours** the parts of speech; **partie fine** pleasure party; **partie de pêche** fishing party *ou* trip; **partie de plaisir** (†: *sortie*) outing; (*fig*) **ce n'est pas une partie de plaisir!** it's no holiday! (*Brit*) *ou* vacation! (*US*), it's not my idea of fun!

partiel, -elle [paʀsjɛl] **1** *adj* (*gén*) partial. **paiement ~** part payment; *V* **élection**. **2** *nm* (*Univ*) class exam.

partiellement [paʀsjɛlmɑ̃] *adv* partially, partly.

partir[1] [paʀtiʀ] (16) *vi* **(a)** (*quitter un lieu*) to go, leave; (*se mettre en route*) to leave, set off, set out; (*s'éloigner*) to go away *ou* off; (*disparaître*) to go. **pars, tu vas être en retard** go *ou* off you go, you're going to be late; **pars, tu m'embêtes** go away, you're annoying me; **es-tu prêt à ~?** are you ready to go?; **allez, je pars** I'm off now; **nos voisins sont partis il y a 6 mois** our neighbours left *ou* moved *ou* went (away) 6 months ago; **depuis que mon pauvre mari est parti** since my poor husband passed on, since the departure of my poor husband; **ma lettre ne partira pas ce soir** my letter won't go this evening; **quand partez-vous (pour Paris)?** when are you going off (to Paris)? *ou* leaving (for Paris)?, when are you off (to Paris)?*; **~ pour le bureau** to leave *ou* set off for the office; **elle est partie de Nice à 9 heures** she left Nice *ou* set off from Nice at 9 o'clock; **sa femme est partie de la maison** his wife has left home; **sa femme est partie avec un autre** his wife has gone off with another man; (*fig*) **~ en fumée** to go up in smoke; **le mauvais temps a fait ~ les touristes** the bad weather has driven the tourists away; **j'espère que je ne vous fais pas ~** I hope I'm not chasing you away; **ceux-là, quand ils viennent bavarder, c'est dur de les faire ~** when that lot come round to talk it's a hard job to get rid of them*; **fais ~ le chat de ma chaise** get the cat off my chair.

(b) (*aller*) to go. **il est parti dans sa chambre/acheter du pain** he has gone to his room/to buy some bread; **~ faire des courses/se promener** to go (out) shopping/for a walk; **pars devant acheter les billets** go on ahead and buy the tickets; **~ à la chasse/à la pêche** to go shooting/fishing; **~ en vacances/en voyage** to go (off) on holiday/on a journey; **tu pars en avion ou en voiture?** are you flying or driving?, are you going by plane or by car?; **~ à la guerre/au front** to go (off) to the war/to the front; **~ en guerre contre les abus** to mount a campaign against abuses; **~ à la recherche de** to go in search of; **~ à la conquête d'un pays/de la gloire** to set off to conquer a country/to win glory.

(c) (*démarrer*) *[moteur]* to start; *[avion]* to take off; *[train]* to leave; *[coureur]* to be off; *[plante]* to take. **la voiture partit sous son nez** the car started up *ou* drove off and left him standing; **il partit en courant** he dashed *ou* ran off; **il partit en trombe** *ou* comme une flèche he was off *ou* set off like a shot; attention, le train va ~ look out, the train's leaving; l'avion va ~ dans quelques minutes the plane is taking off in a few minutes; ce cheval est bien/mal parti that horse got off to a good/bad start; les voilà partis! they're off!; attention, prêts? partez! ready, steady, go!; (*fig*) il faut ~ du bon pied one must set off on the right foot; c'est parti mon kiki!‡ here we go!*; faire ~ une voiture/un moteur to start (up) a car/an engine.

(d) (*être lancé*) [*fusée*] to go off *ou* up; [*fusil, coup de feu*] to go off; [*bouchon*] to pop *ou* shoot out. le coup est parti tout seul the gun went off on its own; le coup ne partit pas the shot didn't go off, the shot misfired; le bouchon est parti au plafond the cork shot up to the ceiling; ces cris partaient de la foule these cries came from the crowd; l'obus qui part du canon the shell fired from the gun; le pétard n'a pas voulu ~ the banger wouldn't go off; le mot partit malgré lui the word came out before he could stop it; le ballon partit comme un boulet de canon the ball shot off like a bullet; faire ~ *fusée* to launch; *pétard* to set off, light.

(e) (*être engagé*) ~ sur une idée fausse/une mauvaise piste to start off with the wrong idea/on the wrong track; ~ bien/mal to be *ou* get off to a good/bad start, start (off) well/badly; le pays est mal parti the country is in a bad way *ou* in a mess*; nous sommes mal partis pour arriver à l'heure we've made a bad start as far as arriving on time is concerned; son affaire est bien partie his business has got off to a good start; il est bien parti pour gagner he's all set to win; ~ dans des digressions sans fin to wander off *ou* launch into endless digressions; quand ils sont partis à discuter, il y en a pour des heures* once they're off* *ou* launched on one of their discussions they'll be at it for hours*; ~ à rire* *ou* d'un éclat de rire to burst out laughing; il est (bien) parti pour parler deux heures the way he's going, he'll be talking for *ou* he looks all set to talk for two hours; la pluie est partie pour (durer) toute la journée the rain has set in for the day; on est parti pour ne pas déjeuner at this rate *ou* the way things are going, we won't get any lunch.

(f) (*commencer*) ~ de [*contrat, vacances*] to begin on, run from; [*course, excursion*] to start *ou* leave from; l'autoroute part de Lille the motorway starts at Lille; un chemin qui part de l'église a path going from *ou* leaving the church; les branches qui partent du tronc the branches going out from the trunk; cet industriel est parti de rien *ou* de zéro this industrialist started from scratch *ou* from nothing; cette rumeur est partie de rien this rumour grew up out of nothing; notre analyse part de cette constatation our analysis is based on this observation *ou* takes this observation as its starting point; si tu pars du principe que tu as toujours raison/qu'ils ne peuvent pas gagner if you start from the notion that *ou* if you start off by assuming that you're always right/that they can't win; en partant de ce principe, rien n'est digne d'intérêt on that basis, nothing's worthy of interest; en partant de là, on peut faire n'importe quoi looking at things that way, one can do anything.

(g) (*provenir*) ~ de to come from; mot qui part du cœur word which comes from the heart; cela part d'un bon sentiment/d'un bon naturel that comes from his (*ou* her *etc*) kindness/good nature.

(h) (*disparaître*) [*tache*] to go, come out; [*bouton, crochet*] to go, come off; [*douleur*] to go; [*rougeurs, boutons*] to go, clear up; [*odeur*] to go, clear. la tache est partie au lavage the stain has come out in the wash *ou* has washed out; toute la couleur est partie all the colour has gone *ou* faded; faire ~ *tache* to remove; *odeur* to clear, get rid of; lessive qui fait ~ la couleur washing powder which fades *ou* destroys the colours.

(i) (*loc*) à ~ de from; à ~ d'aujourd'hui (as) from today, from today onwards; à ~ de maintenant from now on; à ~ de 4 heures from 4 o'clock on(wards); à ~ d'ici le pays est plat from here on(wards) the land is flat; à ~ de *ou* en partant de la gauche, c'est le troisième it is (the) third along from the left; pantalons à ~ de 50 F trousers from 50 francs (upwards); lire à ~ de la page 5 to start reading at page 5; allez jusqu'à la poste et à ~ de là, c'est tout droit go as far as the post office and after that it's straight on; à ~ de ces 3 couleurs vous pouvez obtenir toutes les nuances with *ou* from these 3 colours you can get any shade; c'est fait à ~ de produits chimiques it's made from chemicals; à ~ de ce moment-là, ça ne sert à rien de discuter plus longtemps once you've reached that stage, it's no use discussing things any further.

partir[2] [paʀtiʀ] *vt V* maille.

partisan, e [paʀtizɑ̃, an] 1 *adj* (a) partisan. (b) être ~ de qch/de faire qch to be in favour of sth/of doing sth. 2 *nm,f* [*personne, thèse, régime*] supporter; [*action*] supporter, advocate; [*doctrine, réforme*] partisan, supporter, advocate; (*Mil*) partisan. c'est un ~ de la fermeté he's an advocate of firm measures, he supports *ou* advocates firm measures.

partitif, -ive [paʀtitif, iv] 1 *adj* partitive. 2 *nm* partitive (article).

partition [paʀtisjɔ̃] *nf* (a) (*Mus*) score. as-tu ta ~? have you got your score? *ou* music?* (b) (*frm, gén Pol: division*) partition.

partouse‡ [paʀtuz] *nf* orgy.

partout [paʀtu] *adv* everywhere. ~ où everywhere (that), wherever; avoir mal ~ to ache all over; tu as mis des papiers ~ you've put papers all over the place; (*Sport*) 2/15 ~ 2/15 all; (*Tennis*) 40 ~ deuce.

partouze‡ [paʀtuz] *nf* = partouse‡.

parturition [paʀtyʀisjɔ̃] *nf* parturition.

parure [paʀyʀ] *nf* (a) (*toilette*) costume, finery (*U*); (*bijoux*) jewels; (*sous-vêtements*) set of lingerie; (*fig littér*) finery, livery (*littér*). ~ de table/de lit set of table/bed linen; ~ de salle de bain bathroom set; ~ de diamants set of diamonds, diamond ornament; les arbres ont revêtu leur ~ de feuilles the trees have put on their leafy finery (*littér*). (b) (*déchet*) trimming.

parution [paʀysjɔ̃] *nf* appearance, publication.

parvenir [paʀvəniʀ] (22) 1 parvenir à *vt indir* (a) (*arriver*) *sommet* to get to, reach; *honneurs* to achieve; *état, âge* to reach. ~ aux oreilles de qn to reach sb's ears; ~ à maturité to become ripe; ma lettre lui est parvenue my letter reached him, he got my letter; faire ~ qch à qn to send sth to sb; ~ à ses fins to achieve one's ends; sa renommée est parvenue jusqu'à notre époque *ou* nous his fame has come down to our own day *ou* to us.

(b) (*réussir*) ~ à faire qch to manage to do sth, succeed in doing sth; il y est parvenu he managed it; il n'y parvient pas tout seul he can't manage on his own.

2 *vi* (*parfois péj: faire fortune*) to succeed *ou* get on in life, arrive*.

parvenu, e [paʀvəny] (*ptp de* parvenir) *adj, nm,f* (*péj*) parvenu, upstart.

parvis [paʀvi] *nm* square (*in front of church*).

pas[1] [pɑ] 1 *nm* (a) (*gén*) step; (*bruit*) footstep; (*trace*) footprint. faire un ~ en arrière/en avant, reculer/avancer d'un ~ to step *ou* take a step *ou* a pace back/forward; faire de grands/petits ~ to take long strides/short steps; marcher à grands ~ to stride along; il reconnut son ~ dans le couloir he recognized his footsteps *ou* his step in the corridor; je vais là où me conduisent mes ~ I am going where my steps take me; à ~ mesurés *ou* comptés with measured steps; (*lit, fig*) ~ à ~ step by step; à chaque ~ at every step; il ne peut pas faire un ~ sans elle/sans la rencontrer he can't go anywhere without her/without meeting her; ne le quittez pas d'un ~ follow him wherever he goes; arriver sur les ~ de qn to arrive just after sb, follow close on sb's heels.

(b) (*distance*) pace. à 20 ~ at 20 paces; c'est à deux ~ d'ici it's only a minute away, it's just a stone's throw from here.

(c) (*vitesse*) pace; (*Mil*) step; [*cheval*] walk. aller bon ~, aller *ou* marcher d'un bon ~ to walk at a good *ou* brisk pace; marcher d'un ~ lent to walk slowly; changer de ~ to change step; allonger *ou* hâter *ou* presser le ~ to hurry on, quicken one's step *ou* pace; ralentir le ~ to slow down; au ~: marcher au ~ to march; se mettre au ~ to get in step; mettre son cheval au ~ to walk one's horse; (*Aut*) rouler *ou* aller au ~ to crawl along, go dead slow*; au ~ cadencé in quick time; au ~ de charge at the charge; au ~ de course at a run; au ~ de gymnastique at a jog trot; au ~ redoublé in double time, double-quick.

(d) (*démarche*) tread. d'un ~ lourd *ou* pesant with a heavy tread; ~ d'éléphant elephantine tread.

(e) (*Danse*) step. ~ de danse/valse dance/waltz step; esquisser un ~ de danse to do a little dance, dance a few steps.

(f) (*Géog: passage*) [*montagne*] pass; [*mer*] strait.

(g) (*Tech*) [*vis, écrou*] thread.

(h) (*loc*) faire un grand ~ en avant to take a big step *ou* a great leap forward; la science avance à grands ~/à ~ de géant science is taking great/gigantic steps forward, science is striding forward/advancing by leaps and bounds; à ~ de loup, à ~ feutrés stealthily, with (a) stealthy tread; d'un ~ léger (*agilement*) with an airy tread; (*avec insouciance*) airily, blithely; (*joyeusement*) with a spring in one's step; j'y vais de ce ~ I'll go straightaway *ou* at once; mettre qn au ~ to bring sb to heel, make sb toe the line; avoir le ~ sur qn to rank before sb; prendre le ~ sur *considérations, préoccupations* to override; *théorie, méthode* to supplant; *personne* to steal a lead over; franchir *ou* sauter le ~ to take the plunge; *V* céder, faux[2], premier *etc*.

2: (*Danse*) pas battu pas battu; le pas de Calais (*détroit*) the Straits of Dover; le Pas de Calais (*département*) the Pas de Calais; (*littér*) pas de clerc blunder; (*Danse*) pas de deux pas de deux; (*Mil*) pas de l'oie goose-step; (*Mil*) faire le pas de l'oie to goose-step; (*Jur*) pas de porte ≈ key money (*for shop etc*); pas de la porte doorstep; sur le pas de la porte on the doorstep, in the doorway; pas de vis thread.

pas[2] [pɑ] 1 *adv nég* (a) (*avec ne: formant nég verbale*) not, n't (*dans la langue courante*). je ne vais ~ à l'école (*aujourd'hui*) I'm not *ou* I am not going to school; (*habituellement*) I don't *ou* I do not go to school; ce n'est ~ vrai, c'est ~ vrai* it isn't *ou* it's not *ou* it is not true; je ne suis ~/il n'est ~ allé à l'école I/he didn't *ou* did not go to school; je ne trouve ~ mon sac I can't *ou* cannot find my bag; je ne vois ~ I can't *ou* cannot *ou* don't see; c'est ~ vrai!‡ no kidding!‡, you don't say!‡; je ne prends ~ de pain I won't have any bread; ils n'ont ~ de voiture/d'enfants they don't have *ou* haven't got a car/any children, they have no car/children; il m'a dit de (ne) ~ le faire he told me not to do it; je pense qu'il ne viendra ~ I don't think he'll come; ce n'est ~ sans peine que je l'ai convaincu it was not without (some) difficulty that I convinced him; non ~ *ou* ce n'est ~ qu'il soit bête (it's) not that he's a fool; je n'en sais ~ plus que vous I know no more *ou* I don't know any more about it than you (do); il n'y avait ~ plus de 20 personnes there weren't *ou* were not more than 20 people; il n'est ~ plus/moins intelligent que vous he is no more/no less intelligent than you.

(b) (*indiquant ou renforçant opposition*) elle travaille, (mais) lui ~ she works, but he doesn't; il aime ça, ~ toi? he likes it, don't you?; ils sont 4 et non (~) 3 there are 4 of them, not 3; vient-il ou (ne vient-il) ~? is he coming or (is he) not?, is he coming or isn't he?; leur maison est chauffée, la nôtre ~ their house is heated but ours isn't *ou* is not.

(c) (*dans réponses négatives*) not. ~ de sucre, merci! no sugar, thanks!; ~ du tout not at all, not a bit; il t'a remercié, au moins? — ~ du tout *ou* absolument ~ he did at least thank you? — he certainly didn't *ou* did not; ~ encore not yet; ~ plus que ça so-so*; ~ tellement*, ~ tant que ça not (all) that much*, not so very much; ~ des masses‡ not a lot*, not an awful lot*; qui l'a prévenu? — ~ moi/elle *etc* who told him? — not me/she *etc* *ou* I didn't/she didn't *etc*.

(d) (*devant adj, n, dans excl, souvent* *) **ce sont des gens ~ fiers** they're not proud people; **elle est ~ mal* cette secrétaire!** she's not bad at all*, that secretary!; **il est dans une situation ~ banale** *ou* **ordinaire** he's in an unusual situation; **~ un n'est venu** not one *ou* none (of them) came; **~ possible!*** no!, you don't say!*; **~ de chance!*** hard *ou* bad luck!*, too bad!*; **~ vrai?*** isn't that so?, (isn't that) right?; **tu es content, ~ vrai?*** you're pleased, aren't you? *ou* admit it; **t'es ~ un peu fou?*** you must be *ou* you are off (*Brit*) *ou* out of (*US*) your head!*; **~ d'histoires** *ou* **de blagues, il faut absolument que j'arrive à l'heure** (now) no nonsense, I absolutely MUST be on time; **(c'est) ~ bête, cette idée!** that's not a bad idea (at all)!; **si c'est ~ malheureux!*** *ou* **honteux!*** isn't that *ou* it a shame!; **tu viendras, ~?*** you're coming, aren't you?, you'll come, won't you?; **~ de ça!** none of that!; *V* **falloir, fou, mal.**

(e) (*loc*) **~ de sitôt: je ne reviendrai ~ de sitôt, ce n'est ~ de sitôt que je reviendrai** I (certainly) shan't be coming back *ou* I'm (certainly) not coming back for a long time *ou* for quite some time; **il ne recommencera ~ de sitôt** he won't do that again in a hurry*, he won't be in a hurry to do that again; **ce n'est ~ trop tôt!** it's not before time!, about time too!*; **~ plus tard qu'hier/que l'an dernier** only *ou* just yesterday/last year; **~ mal (de)*** (*quantité*) quite a lot (of), quite a bit (of)*; (*nombre*) quite a few, a fair number (of), quite a lot (of); **il gagne ~ mal*** he earns quite a bit* *ou* quite a lot, he doesn't get a bad wage; **il a ~ mal vieilli ces derniers temps** he's aged quite a lot *ou* a good bit* lately; **ils ont ~ mal d'argent/d'enfants** they have quite a lot of money/children, they have a fair bit* of money/a fair number of *ou* quite a few children.

2: (*péj*) **pas grand-chose** *nmf inv* good-for-nothing.

pascal, e, *mpl* **-aux** [paskal, o] *adj agneau* paschal; *messe* Easter.

pascalien, -ienne [paskaljɛ̃, jɛn] *adj* of Pascal.

passable [pɑsabl(ə)] *adj* passable, tolerable. (*Univ*) **mention ~** pass(mark); **à peine ~** barely passable, not so good (*attrib*).

passablement [pɑsabləmɑ̃] *adv* (*moyennement*) *jouer, travailler* tolerably *ou* passably well; (*assez*) *irritant, long* rather, fairly, pretty*; (*beaucoup*) quite a lot *ou* a bit*. **il faut ~ de courage pour ...** it requires a fair amount of courage to ... .

passade [pɑsad] *nf* passing fancy, whim, fad; (*amoureuse*) passing fancy.

passage [pɑsaʒ] **1** *nm* **(a)** (*venue*) **guetter le ~ du facteur** to watch for the postman to come by, be on the look-out for the postman; **attendre le ~ de l'autobus** to wait for the bus to come; **agrandir une voie pour permettre le ~ de gros camions** to widen a road to allow large lorries to use it; **observer le ~ des oiseaux dans le ciel** to watch the birds fly by; **pour empêcher le ~ de l'air sous la porte** to stop draughts (coming in) under the door; **lors de votre ~ à la douane** when you go through Customs; **lors d'un récent ~ à Paris** when I (*ou* he *etc*) was in *ou* visiting Paris recently; **la navette d'autobus fait 4 ~s par jour** the shuttle bus goes past 4 times a day; **prochain ~ de notre représentant le 8 mai** our representative will call next on May 8th; **'~ de troupeaux'** 'cattle crossing'; **livrer ~** to make way; **il y a beaucoup de ~ l'été** there are a lot of people passing *ou* coming through here in the summer; **commerçant qui travaille avec le ~** *ou* **les clients de ~** shopkeeper catering for customers passing through *ou* the casual trade; **Dijon est un lieu de ~** Dijon is a stopping-off place; **il est de ~ à Paris** he is in *ou* visiting Paris at the moment; **amours/amant de ~** casual *ou* passing affairs/lover; **je l'ai saisi au ~** (*je passais devant*) I grabbed him as I went by *ou* past; (*il passait devant*) I grabbed him as he went by *ou* past.

(b) (*transfert*) **le ~ de l'état solide à l'état gazeux** the change from the solid to the gaseous state; **le ~ de l'enfance à l'adolescence** the transition from childhood to adolescence; **le ~ du jour à la nuit** the change from day to night; **le ~ du grade de capitaine à celui de commandant** promotion from captain to major; **le ~ de l'alcool dans le sang** the entry of alcohol into the bloodstream; **son ~ en classe supérieure est problématique** there are problems about his moving up to the next class.

(c) (*lieu*) passage; (*chemin*) way, passage; (*itinéraire*) route; (*rue*) passage(way), alley(way). **un ~ dangereux sur la falaise** a dangerous passage on the cliff; **il faut trouver un ~ dans ces broussailles** we must find a way through (all) this undergrowth; **on a mis des barrières sur le ~ de la procession** barriers have been put up along the route of *ou* taken by the procession; **on se retourne sur son ~** people turn round and look when he goes past; **l'ennemi dévasta tout sur son ~** the enemy left total devastation in their wake; **barrer le ~ à qn** to block sb's way; **laisser le ~ à qn** to let sb pass *ou* past; **va plus loin, tu gênes le ~** move along, you're in the way; **ne laissez pas vos valises dans le ~** don't leave your cases in the passage; *V* **frayer.**

(d) (*Naut*) **payer son ~** to pay for one's passage, pay one's fare.

(e) (*fragment*) *[livre, symphonie]* passage.

(f) (*traversée*) *[rivière, limite]* crossing. (*Naut*) **le ~ de la ligne** crossing the Line.

2: passage clouté pedestrian crossing; **passage inperdit** no entry, no thoroughfare; **passage à niveau** level crossing; **passage pour piétons** pedestrian subway (*Brit*), underpass (*US*); (*Aut*) **passage protégé** priority over secondary roads; **passage souterrain** subway (*Brit*), underground passage (*US*); **passage à tabac** beating up; **passage à vide** loss of stamina *ou* power.

passager, -ère [pɑsaʒe, ɛʀ] **1** *adj* **(a)** (*de passage*) *hôte* making a short stay (*attrib*), staying (only) a short while (*attrib*); *oiseau* migrating (*épith*), migratory.

(b) (*de courte durée*) *malaise* passing (*épith*), brief; *inconvénient* temporary; *bonheur, beauté* passing (*épith*), transient, ephemeral. **j'avais cru à un malaise ~** I thought this uneasiness would quickly pass over; **pluies ~ères** intermittent *ou* occasional showers *ou* rain.

(c) *rue* busy.

2 *nm,f* passenger. **~ clandestin** stowaway.

passagèrement [pɑsaʒɛʀmɑ̃] *adv* for a short while, temporarily.

passant, e [pɑsɑ̃, ɑ̃t] **1** *adj rue* busy. **2** *nm,f* passer-by. **3** *nm* *[ceinture]* loop.

passation [pɑsasjɔ̃] *nf [contrat]* signing; (*Comm*) *[écriture]* entry. **~ de pouvoirs** handing over of office *ou* power, transfer of power.

passavant [pɑsavɑ̃] *nm* **(a)** (*Comm, Jur*) transire. **(b)** (*Naut*) catwalk.

passe[1] [pɑs] **1** *nf* **(a)** (*Escrime, Ftbl, Tauromachie*) pass. **faire une ~ en avant** to make a forward pass.

(b) *[magnétiseur]* pass.

(c) (*Roulette*) passe.

(d) (*Naut: chenal*) pass, channel.

(e) (*loc*) **être en ~ de faire** to be on one's *ou* the way to doing; **il est en ~ de réussir** he is poised to succeed; **cette espèce est en ~ de disparaître** this species is on the way to dying out *ou* looks likely to die out; **être dans une bonne ~** to be in a healthy situation; **être dans une mauvaise ~** to be in a bad way; **traverser une mauvaise ~** (*gén*) to be going through a bad patch; (*santé*) to be in a poor state; **est-ce qu'il va sortir de cette mauvaise ~?** will he manage to pull through (this time)?; *V* **hôtel, maison, mot.**

2: (*fig*) **passe d'armes** heated exchange; (*Comm*) **passe de caisse** *sum allowed for cashier's errors*; **passes magnétiques** hypnotic passes.

passe[2]* [pɑs] *nm abrév de* **passe-partout;** *V* **passer.**

passe- [pɑs] *préf V* **passer.**

passé, e [pɑse] (*ptp de* **passer**) **1** *adj* **(a)** (*dernier*) last. **c'est arrivé le mois/l'année ~(e)** it happened last month/year; **au cours des semaines/années ~es** over these last *ou* the past (few) weeks/years.

(b) (*révolu*) *action, conduite* past. **~ de mode** out of fashion, out of date; **songeant à sa gloire/ses angoisses ~e(s)** thinking of his past *ou* former glory/distress; **regrettant sa jeunesse/sa beauté ~e** yearning for her departed youth/beauty; **si l'on se penche sur les événements ~s** if one looks back over past events; **cette époque est ~e maintenant** that era is now over; **ce qui est ~ est ~** what is past is dead and gone; **où sont mes années ~es?** where has my life gone?; **il se rappelait le temps ~** he was thinking back to days *ou* time gone by.

(c) (*fané*) *couleur, fleur* faded. **tissu ~ de ton** material that has lost its colour, faded material.

(d) (*plus de*) **il est 8 heures ~es** it's past *ou* gone 8 o'clock; **il est rentré à 9 heures ~es** it was past *ou* gone 9 o'clock when he got back; **ça fait une heure ~e que je t'attends** I've been waiting for you for more than *ou* over an hour.

2 *nm* **(a) le ~** the past; **il faut oublier le ~** the past should be forgotten; **c'est du ~, n'en parlons plus** it's (all) in the past now, let's not say any more about it; **il est revenu nous voir comme par le ~** he came back to see us as he used to in the past; **il a eu plusieurs condamnations dans le ~** he had several previous convictions.

(b) (*vie écoulée*) past. **pays fier de son ~** country proud of its past; **bandit au ~ chargé** gangster with an eventful past; **son ~ m'est inconnu** I know nothing of his past.

(c) (*Gram*) past tense. **les temps du ~** the past tenses; **mettez cette phrase au ~** put this sentence into the past (tense); **~ antérieur** past anterior; **~ composé** perfect; **~ simple** past historic, preterite.

3 *prép* after. **~ 6 heures on ne sert plus les clients** after 6 o'clock we stop serving (customers); **~ cette maison, on quitte le village** after this house, you are out of the village.

passéisme [pɑseism(ə)] *nm* (*péj*) attachment to the past.

passéiste [pɑseist(ə)] **1** *adj* (*péj*) backward-looking. **2** *nmf* (*péj*) devotee of the past.

passement [pɑsmɑ̃] *nm* braid (*U*).

passementer [pɑsmɑ̃te] (1) *vt* to braid.

passementerie [pɑsmɑ̃tʀi] *nf* (*objets*) braid (*U*), trimmings; (*commerce*) haberdashery trade (*Brit*), notions trade (*US*). **rayon de ~** haberdashery (*Brit*) *ou* notions (*US*) department.

passementier, -ière [pɑsmɑ̃tje, jɛʀ] **1** *adj* haberdashery (*Brit*) (*épith*), notions (*US*) (*épith*). **2** *nm,f* haberdasher (*Brit*).

passepoil [pɑspwal] *nm* piping.

passeport [pɑspɔʀ] *nm* passport.

passer [pɑse] (1) **1** *vi* **(a)** to pass, go *ou* come past. **~ devant la maison/sous les fenêtres de qn** to pass *ou* go past sb's house/sb's window; **~ en courant** to run past; **~ à pas lents** to go slowly past; **les camions ne passent pas dans notre rue** lorries don't come along *ou* down our street; **il passait dans la rue avec son chien/en voiture** he was walking down the street with his dog/ driving down the street; **le train va bientôt ~** the train will soon come past; **l'air passe sous la porte** a draught is coming in under the door; **où passe la route?** where does the road go?; **la Seine passe à Paris** the Seine flows through Paris; **la voie ferrée passe le long du fleuve** the railway line runs alongside the river; **faire ~ les piétons** to let the pedestrians cross; **faire ~ les femmes et les enfants d'abord** to let the women and children go first; **une lueur cruelle passa dans son regard** a cruel gleam came into his eyes; *V* **bouche, coup, main.**

(b) (*faire une halte rapide*) **~ au bureau/chez un ami** to call (in) *ou* drop in* at the office/at a friend's; **je ne fais que ~** I'm not stopping*; **~ à la radio/à la visite médicale** to go for an X-ray/one's medical (examination); **~ à la douane** to go through *ou* clear Customs; **~ chercher** *ou* **prendre qn** to call for sb, (go *ou* come and) pick sb up; ~ **voir qn** *ou* **rendre visite à qn** to call (in) on sb, call to see sb; **le facteur est passé** the postman has been; **à quelle heure passe le laitier?** what time does the milkman come?; **le releveur du gaz passera demain** the gasman will call tomorrow; **j'irai le voir en passant** I'll call to see him *ou* I'll call in and see him on my way.

(c) (*changer de lieu, d'attitude, d'état*) to go. ~ **d'une pièce dans une autre** to go from one room to another; **si nous passions au salon?** shall we go into the sitting room?; ~ **à table** to sit down to eat; ~ **en Belgique** to go over to Belgium; ~ **à l'ennemi/l'opposition** to go over *ou* defect to the enemy/the opposition; **la photo passa de main en main** the photo was passed *ou* handed round; ~ **d'un extrême à l'autre** to go from one extreme to the other; ~ **de l'état solide à l'état liquide** to pass *ou* change from the solid to the liquid state; ~ **à un ton plus sévère** to take a harsher tone; ~ **aux actes** to go into action, act; ~ **aux ordres** to collect one's orders; ~ **aux aveux** to make a confession; ~ **dans les mœurs/les habitudes** to become the custom/the habit; ~ **dans la langue** to pass *ou* come into the language; ~ **en proverbe** to become proverbial; **son argent de poche passe en bonbons** his pocket money (all) goes on sweets; **l'alcool passe dans le sang** alcohol enters the bloodstream; **le restant des légumes est passé dans le potage** the left-over vegetables went into the soup.

(d) (*franchir un obstacle*) *[véhicule]* to get through; *[cheval, sauteur]* to get over.

(e) *[temps]* to go by, pass. **comme le temps passe!** how time flies!; **cela fait** ~ **le temps** it passes the time.

(f) *[liquide]* to go *ou* come through, seep through; *[café]* to go through; *[courant électrique]* to get through.

(g) (*être digéré, avalé*) to go down. **le déjeuner ne passe pas** that lunch won't go down; **prendre un cachet pour faire** ~ **le déjeuner** to take a tablet to help one's lunch down; **ce vin passe bien** this wine goes down nicely.

(h) (*être accepté*) *[demande, proposition]* to pass; (*réussir un examen*) to pass, get through. **je ne pense pas que ce projet de loi passera** I don't think this bill will be passed *ou* will go through; **cette plaisanterie ne passe pas dans certains milieux** that joke doesn't go down well *ou* isn't appreciated in some circles; **il y a des plaisanteries/des erreurs qui passent dans certaines circonstances mais pas dans d'autres** there are some jokes/mistakes which are all right in some circumstances but not in others; **il est passé de justesse à l'examen** he only just scraped through *ou* passed the exam; **il est passé dans la classe supérieure** he's moved up to the next class.

(i) (*devenir*) to become. ~ **directeur/président** to become *ou* be appointed director/president.

(j) (*Ciné*) *[film]* to be showing, be on; (*TV*) *[émission]* to be on; *[personne]* to be on, appear. ~ **à la radio/à la télé*** to be on the radio/on TV*; ~ **sur l'antenne** to go on the air.

(k) (*dépasser*) **le panier est trop petit, la queue du chat passe** the basket is too small — the cat's tail is sticking out; **son manteau est trop court, la robe passe** her coat is too short — her dress is showing; **ne laisse pas** ~ **ton bras par la portière** don't put your arm out of the window.

(l) (*disparaître*) *[couleur]* to fade; *[mode]* to die out; *[douleur]* to pass (off), wear off; *[colère]* to die down; (*lit, fig*) *[orage]* to blow over, die down; *[beauté]* to fade; *[jeunesse]* to pass; (*mourir*) *[personne]* to pass on *ou* away. **faire** ~ **à qn le goût** *ou* **l'envie de faire** to cure sb of doing, make sb give up doing; **il voulait être pompier mais ça lui a passé** he wanted to be a fireman but he got over it; **cela fera** ~ **votre rhume** that will get you over your cold *ou* get rid of your cold for you; **le plus dur est passé** the worst is over now; (*fig*) **ça lui passera!*** he'll grow out of it!

(m) (*Cartes*) to pass.

(n) (*Jur, Parl: être présenté*) to come up. **le projet de loi va** ~ **devant la Chambre** the bill will come *ou* be put before Parliament; **il est passé devant le conseil de discipline de l'école** he came up *ou* was brought up before the school disciplinary committee; ~ **en justice** to come up before the courts.

(o) (*Aut*) ~ **en première/marche arrière** to go into first/reverse; ~ **en seconde/quatrième** to change into second/fourth *ou* top; **les vitesses passent mal** the gears are stiff.

(p) ~ **par** *lieu* to go *ou* come through; *intermédiaire* to go through; *expérience* to go through, undergo; **par où êtes-vous passé?** which way did you go? *ou* come?; **le chien est trop gros pour** ~ **par le trou** the dog is too big to get through the hole; ~ **par l'université/par un collège technique** to go through university/technical school; **pour lui parler, j'ai dû** ~ **par sa secrétaire** I had to go through his secretary *ou* I had to see his secretary before I could speak to him; **pour téléphoner, il faut** ~ **par le standard** you have to go through the switchboard to make a call; ~ **par des difficultés** to have difficulties *ou* a difficult time; **il est passé par des moments difficiles** he had some hard times; **nous sommes tous passés par là** we've all been through it, it's happened to all of us; **il faudra bien en** ~ **par là** there's no way round it; **il faudra bien en** ~ **par ce qu'il demande** we'll have to give him what he wants, we'll have to comply with *ou* give in to his request.

(q) ~ **pour: je ne voudrais pas** ~ **pour un imbécile** I wouldn't like to be taken for a fool; **il pourrait** ~ **pour un Allemand** you could take him for a German, he could pass as a German; **auprès de ses amis, il passait pour un séducteur/un excentrique** he was regarded by his friends as (being) a seducer/an eccentric; **il passe pour intelligent** he is thought of *ou* supposed to be intelligent; **il passe pour beau auprès de certaines femmes** some women think *ou* find him attractive; **cela passe pour vrai** it's thought to be true; **se faire** ~ **pour** to pass o.s. off as; **faire** ~ **qn pour** to make sb out to be.

(r) ~ **sous/sur/devant/derrière** *etc* to go under/over/in front of/behind *etc*; **passez donc devant** you go first; **l'autobus lui est passé dessus, il est passé sous l'autobus** he was run over by the bus; **le travail passe avant tout/avant les loisirs** work comes first/before leisure; **les poissons sont passés au travers du filet** the fish slipped through the net; (*fig*) **passer sur** *faute* to pass over, overlook; *détail inutile ou scabreux* to pass over; **je veux bien** ~ **sur cette erreur** I'm willing to pass over *ou* overlook this mistake; **je passe sur les détails** I shall pass over *ou* leave out *ou* skip* the details; *V* **corps, côté, ventre.**

(s) y ~*: **on a eu la grippe, tout le monde y a** *ou* **est passé** we've had the flu and everybody got it *ou* nobody escaped it; **si tu conduis comme ça on va tous y** ~ if you go on driving like that, we've all had it*; **toute sa fortune y a passé** *ou* **y est passée** he spent all his fortune on it, his whole fortune went on it.

(t) laisser ~ *air, lumière* to let in; *personne, procession* to let through (*ou* past, in, out *etc*); *erreur* to overlook, miss; *occasion* to let slip, miss; **s'écarter pour laisser** ~ **qn** to move back to let sb (get) through *ou* past; **nous ne pouvons pas laisser** ~ **cette affaire sans protester** we cannot let this pass without a protest, we can't let this matter rest there — we must make a protest.

(u) (*loc*) **en passant** (*accessoirement*) in passing, by the way; **soit dit en passant** let me say in passing; **qu'il soit menteur, passe (encore), mais voleur c'est plus grave** he may be a liar, that's one thing but a thief, that's more serious; **passe pour cette erreur, mais une malhonnêteté, c'est impardonnable** a mistake is one thing, but being dishonest is unforgivable; **passons** let's say no more (about it).

2 *vt* **(a)** *rivière, frontière, seuil* to cross; *porte* to go through; *haie* to jump *ou* get over. ~ **une rivière à la nage/en bac** to swim across/take the ferry across a river.

(b) *examen* to sit, take; *douane* to go through, clear. ~ **son permis (de conduire)** to take one's driving test; ~ **une visite médicale** to have a medical (examination); ~ **un examen avec succès** to pass an exam.

(c) *temps, vacances* to spend. ~ **le temps/sa vie à faire** to spend the time/one's life doing; ~ **son temps à ne rien faire** to idle one's time away; **(faire qch) pour** ~ **le temps** (to do sth) to while away *ou* pass the time; ~ **la soirée chez qn** to spend the evening at sb's (house).

(d) (*assouvir*) ~ **sa colère/sa mauvaise humeur sur qn** to work off *ou* vent one's anger/one's bad temper on sb.

(e) (*omettre*) *mot, ligne* to miss out, leave out. ~ **son tour** to miss one's turn; **et j'en passe!** and that's not all!

(f) (*permettre*) ~ **une faute à qn** to overlook sb's mistake; ~ **un caprice à qn** to humour *ou* indulge sb's whim; **on lui passe tout** *bêtises* he gets away with anything; *désirs* he gets everything he wants; **il faut bien se** ~ **quelques fantaisies** you've got to allow yourself a few *ou* indulge in a few extravagances; **passez-moi l'expression** (if you'll) pardon the expression.

(g) (*transmettre*) *consigne, message, maladie* to pass on; (*Sport*) *ballon* to pass. ~ **qch à qn** to give *ou* hand sth to sb; **tu (le) fais** ~ pass *ou* hand it round; ~ **une affaire/un travail à qn** to hand a matter/a job over to sb; **passe-moi une cigarette** pass *ou* give me a cigarette; **passer-moi du feu** give me a light; **il m'a passé un livre** he's lent me a book; **je suis fatigué, je vous passe le volant** I am tired, you take the wheel *ou* you drive; (*au téléphone*) **je vous passe M X** *(standard)* I'm putting you through to Mr X; (*je lui passe l'appareil*) here's Mr X; **passe-lui un coup de fil** give him a ring (*Brit*) *ou* call, phone *ou* ring (*Brit*) *ou* call him (up); **passez-moi tous vos paquets** let me have all your parcels.

(h) (*Douane*) ~ **des marchandises en transit** to carry goods in transit; ~ **qch en fraude** to smuggle sth (in, out, through *etc*); ~ **des faux billets** to pass forged notes.

(i) (*enfiler*) *pull* to slip on; *robe* to slip into. ~ **une bague au doigt de qn** to slip a ring on sb's finger; ~ **un lacet dans qch** to thread a lace through sth.

(j) ~ **la tête à la porte** to poke one's head round the door; ~ **la main/la tête à travers les barreaux** to stick one's hand/head through the bars.

(k) (*dépasser*) *gare, maison* to pass, go past. ~ **le poteau** to pass the post, cross the finishing line; ~ **les limites** *ou* **les bornes** to go too far (*fig*); **tu as passé l'âge (de ces jeux)** you are too old (for these games); **il ne passera pas la nuit/la semaine** he won't last the night/the week *ou* see the night/week out.

(l) (*Culin*) *soupe, thé* to strain; *café* to pour the water on.

(m) (*Aut*) ~ **la seconde/la troisième** to go *ou* change (up *ou* down) into second/third (gear).

(n) *film, diapositives* to show; *disque* to put on, play. **que passent-ils au cinéma?** what's on *ou* showing at the cinema?

(o) (*Comm*) *écriture* to enter; *commande* to place; *marché, accord* to reach, come to; *contrat* to sign.

(p) (*faire subir une action*) ~ **le balai/l'aspirateur/le chiffon** to sweep up/hoover/dust; **passe le chiffon dans le salon** go and dust the sitting room, give the sitting room a dust; ~ **une pièce à l'aspirateur** to hoover (*Brit*) *ou* vacuum a room, go over a room with the vacuum cleaner; ~ **la serpillière dans la cuisine,** ~ **la cuisine à la serpillière** to wash (down) the kitchen floor; ~ **une couche de peinture sur qch** to give sth a coat of paint; ~ **un mur à la chaux** to whitewash a wall; ~ **qch sous le robinet** to rinse *ou* run sth under the tap; **elle lui passa la main dans les cheveux** she ran her hand through his hair; **se** ~ **les mains à l'eau** to rinse one's hands; **passe-toi de l'eau sur le visage** give your face a (quick) wash; *V* **arme, menotte, tabac.**

3 se passer *vpr* **(a)** (*avoir lieu*) to take place; (*arriver*) to happen. **la scène se passe à Paris** the scene takes place in Paris; **qu'est-ce qui s'est passé?** what (has) happened?; **que se passe-t-il?, qu'est-ce qu'il se passe?** what's going on?; **tout s'est bien passé** everything went off smoothly; **je ne sais pas ce qui se passe en lui** I don't know what's the matter with him *ou* what's got into him; cela ne se passera pas ainsi! I shan't stand for that!, I shan't let it rest at that!; il ne se passe pas un seul jour sans qu'il ne pleuve not a day goes by *ou* passes without it *ou* its raining.

(b) (*finir*) to pass off, be over. il faut attendre que ça se passe you'll have to wait till it passes off *ou* is over.

(c) se ~ de qch to do without sth; on peut se ~ d'aller au théâtre we can do without going to the theatre; se ~ de qn to manage without sb; (*iro*) je peux me ~ de ta présence I can manage without you around; je me passerais bien d'y aller! I could do without having to go; s'il n'y en a plus, je m'en passerai if there isn't any more, I'll do without; nous nous voyons dans l'obligation de nous ~ de vos services we find ourselves obliged to dispense with your services; il se passerait de manger plutôt que de faire la cuisine he'd go without eating *ou* food rather than cook; (*iro*) tu pourrais te ~ de fumer do you have to smoke?; la citation se passe de commentaires the quotation needs no comment *ou* speaks for itself.

4: passe-crassane *nf, pl* passe-crassanes *type of winter pear*; passe-droit *nm, pl* passe-droits (undeserved) privilege, favour; il a eu un passe-droit he got preferential treatment; passe-lacet *nm, pl* passe-lacets bodkin (*V* raide); passe-montagne *nm, pl* passe-montagnes balaclava; passe-partout (*nm inv: clef*) master *ou* skeleton key; (*adj inv*) *tenue, formule* for all occasions, all-purpose (*épith*); passe-plat *nm, pl* passe-plats serving hatch; passe-temps *nm inv* pastime; passe-thé *nm inv* tea strainer.

passereau, *pl* ~x [pɑsʀo] *nm* (*Orn*) passerine; (†: *moineau*) sparrow.

passerelle [pɑsʀɛl] *nf* (*pont*) footbridge; (*Naut: pont supérieur*) bridge; (*Aviat, Naut: voie d'accès*) gangway; (*fig: passage*) (inter)link.

passeur [pɑsœʀ] *nm* [*rivière*] ferryman, boatman; [*frontière*] smuggler (*of drugs, refugees etc*).

passible [pasibl(ə)] *adj*: ~ d'une amende/peine *personne* liable to a fine/penalty; *délit* punishable by a fine/penalty; ~ d'un impôt liable for (a) tax.

passif, -ive [pasif, iv] 1 *adj* (*gén*) passive. rester ~ devant une situation to remain passive in the face of a situation; *V* défense[1].

2 *nm* (*Ling*) passive; (*Fin*) liabilities. le ~ d'une succession the liabilities on an estate.

passion [pasjɔ̃] *nf* (a) passion. avoir la ~ du jeu/des voitures to have a passion for gambling/cars; le sport est sa ~ he is mad* *ou* crazy* about sport, his one passion is sport.

(b) (*amour*) passion. déclarer sa ~ to declare one's love; aimer avec *ou* à la ~ to love passionately.

(c) (*émotion, colère*) passion. emporté par la ~ carried away by passion; discuter avec/sans ~ to argue passionately/dispassionately; œuvre pleine de ~ work full of passion.

(d) (*Rel*) P~ Passion; le dimanche de la P~ Passion Sunday; le jour de la P~ the day of the Passion; la semaine de la P~ Passion week; la P~ selon saint Matthieu (*Rel*) the Passion according to St Matthew; (*Mus*) the St Matthew Passion.

passionnant, e [pasjɔnɑ̃, ɑ̃t] *adj personne* fascinating; *livre, film* fascinating, gripping, enthralling; *match* fascinating, exciting, gripping.

passionné, e [pasjɔne] (*ptp de* passionner) 1 *adj personne, tempérament, haine* passionate; *description, orateur, jugement* impassioned. être ~ de *ou* pour to have a passion for.

2 *nm,f* (a) (*artiste, jeune homme*) passionate person.

(b) ~ de: c'est un ~ de voitures de course he's a racing car fanatic.

passionnel, -elle [pasjɔnɛl] *adj sentiment* inspired by passion; *crime* of passion.

passionnément [pasjɔnemɑ̃] *adv* passionately, with passion. ~ amoureux de madly *ou* passionately in love with.

passionner [pasjɔne] (1) 1 *vt personne* [*mystère, match*] to fascinate, grip; [*livre, sujet*] to fascinate; [*sport, science*] to be a passion with; *débat* to inflame. ce film/ce roman m'a passionné I found that film/novel fascinating; la musique le passionne music is his passion, he has a passion for music.

2 se passionner *vpr*: se ~ pour *livre, mystère* to be fascinated by; *sport, science* to have a passion for, be mad keen on*.

passivement [pasivmɑ̃] *adv* passively.

passivité [pasivite] *nf* passivity, passiveness.

passoire [pɑswaʀ] *nf* (*gén*) sieve; [*thé*] strainer; [*légumes*] colander. (*fig*) être une (vraie) ~ to be like a sieve; troué comme une ~ with as many holes as a sieve.

pastel [pastɛl] 1 *nm* (*Bot*) woad, pastel; (*teinture bleue*) pastel; (*bâtonnet de couleur*) pastel (crayon); (*œuvre*) pastel. au ~ in pastels. 2 *adj inv tons* pastel. un bleu/vert ~ a pastel blue/green.

pastelliste [pastelist(ə)] *nmf* pastellist.

pastèque [pastɛk] *nf* watermelon.

pasteur [pastœʀ] *nm* (a) (*Rel: prêtre*) minister, pastor. (b) (*littér, Rel: berger*) shepherd. le bon P~ the Good Shepherd.

pasteurisation [pastœʀizasjɔ̃] *nf* pasteurization.

pasteuriser [pastœʀize] (1) *vt* to pasteurize.

pastiche [pastiʃ] *nm* (*imitation*) pastiche.

pasticher [pastiʃe] (1) *vt* to write a pastiche of.

pasticheur, -euse [pastiʃœʀ, øz] *nm,f* author of pastiches.

pastille [pastij] *nf* [*médicament, sucre*] pastille, lozenge; [*encens, couleur*] block; [*papier, tissu*] round spot, disc. ~s de menthe mints; ~s pour la toux cough pastilles *ou* drops *ou* lozenges; ~s pour la gorge throat pastilles.

pastis [pastis] *nm* (*boisson*) pastis; (*: *dial: ennui*) fix*. être dans le ~ to be in a fix* *ou* a jam*.

pastoral, e, *mpl* **-aux** [pastɔʀal, o] 1 *adj* (*gén*) pastoral. 2 pastorale *nf* (*Littérat, Peinture, Rel*) pastoral; (*Mus*) pastorale.

pastorat [pastɔʀa] *nm* pastorate.

pastoureau, *pl* ~x [pastuʀo] *nm* (*littér*) shepherd boy.

pastourelle [pastuʀɛl] *nf* (*littér*) shepherd girl; (*Mus*) pastourelle.

pat [pat] 1 *adj inv* stalemate(d). 2 *nm*: le ~ stalemate; faire ~ (*vi*) to end in (a) stalemate; (*vt*) to stalemate.

patachon [pataʃɔ̃] *nm V* vie.

patagon, -onne [patagɔ̃, ɔn] 1 *adj* Patagonian. 2 *nm,f*: P~(ne) Patagonian.

Patagonie [patagɔni] *nf* Patagonia.

pataphysique [patafizik] *nf* pataphysics (*sg*).

patapouf [patapuf] 1 *excl* (*langage enfantin*) whoops! faire ~ to tumble (down). 2 *nmf* (*) fatty*.

pataquès [patakɛs] *nm* pronunciation mistake (*faulty liaison*).

patata* [patata] *excl V* patati*.

patate [patat] *nf* (*Bot*) sweet potato; (*: *pomme de terre*) spud*; (*: *imbécile*) fathead*, chump*, clot* (*Bot*). ~ (douce) sweet potato; *V* gros.

patati* [patati] *excl*: et ~ et patata and so on and so forth.

patatras [patatʀa] *excl* crash!

pataud, e [pato, od] 1 *adj* lumpish, clumsy. 2 *nm,f* lump. 3 *nm* (*chien*) pup(py) (*with large paws*).

patauger [patoʒe] (3) *vi* (*avec effort*) to wade about; (*avec plaisir*) to splash about; (*fig: être perdu*) to flounder. on a dû ~ dans la boue pour y aller we had to wade through *ou* squelch through the mud to get there.

patchouli [patʃuli] *nm* patchouli.

pâte [pɑt] 1 *nf* (a) (*Culin*) (*à tarte*) pastry; (*à gâteaux*) mixture; (*à pain*) dough; (*à frire*) batter. (*fig*) il est de la ~ dont sont faits les héros* he's (of) the stuff heroes are made of; *V* bon[1], coq[1], main.

(b) [*fromage*] cheese. fromage à ~ dure/molle hard/soft cheese.

(c) ~s (alimentaires) pasta; (*dans la soupe*) noodles.

(d) (*gén: substance*) paste; (*crème*) cream.

(e) (*Art*) paste.

2: pâte d'amandes almond paste; pâte brisée shortcrust pastry (*Brit*); pâte à choux choux pastry; pâte à crêpes pancake batter; pâte dentifrice toothpaste; pâte feuilletée puff *ou* flaky (*Brit*) pastry; pâte à frire batter; pâte de fruits fruit jelly, crystallized fruit (*U*); une framboise en pâte de fruit a raspberry jelly, a crystallized raspberry; pâte à modeler modelling clay, Plasticine ®; (*péj*) pâte molle milksop, spineless individual; pâte à pain (bread) dough; pâte à papier paper pulp; pâtes pectorales cough drops *ou* pastilles; pâte sablée sablé pastry; pâte de verre molten glass.

pâté [pɑte] *nm* (a) (*Culin*) pâté. ~ en croûte ≈ pork pie; petit ~ meat patty, small pork pie. (b) (*tache d'encre*) (ink) blot. (c) ~ de maisons block (of houses). (d) ~ (de sable) sandpie, sandcastle.

pâtée [pɑte] *nf* (a) [*chien, volaille*] mash (*U*), feed (*U*); [*porcs*] swill (*U*). (b) (*) hiding*. recevoir la *ou* une ~ to get a hiding*; donner la *ou* une ~ à qn to give sb a hiding*.

patelin[1]* [patlɛ̃] *nm* village.

patelin[2], **e** [patlɛ̃, in] *adj* (*littér péj*) bland, smooth, ingratiating.

patelinerie [patlinʀi] *nf* (*littér péj*) blandness (*U*), smoothness (*U*).

patelle [patɛl] *nf* (*Zool*) limpet.

patène [patɛn] *nf* paten.

patenôtre [patnotʀ(ə)] *nf* (†, *péj*) (*prière*) paternoster, oraison (†, *littér*); (*marmonnement*) gibberish (*U*).

patent, e[1] [patɑ̃, ɑ̃t] *adj* obvious, manifest, patent (*frm*). il est ~ que it is patently obvious that; *V* lettre.

patentable [patɑ̃tabl(ə)] *adj* (*Comm*) liable to trading dues, subject to a (trading) licence.

patente[2] [patɑ̃t] *nf* (*Comm*) trading dues *ou* licence; (*Naut*) bill of health.

patenté, e [patɑ̃te] *adj* (*Comm*) licensed; (*fig hum: attitré*) established, officially recognized. c'est un menteur ~ he's a thoroughgoing liar.

pater [patɛʀ] *nm inv* (a) (*: *père*) old man*, governor† (*Brit hum*). (b) (*Rel*) P~ pater, paternoster. (c) (*Antiq, fig*) ~ familias paterfamilias.

patère [patɛʀ] *nf* (hat- *ou* coat-)peg.

paternalisme [patɛʀnalism(ə)] *nm* paternalism.

paternaliste [patɛʀnalist(ə)] *adj* paternalistic.

paterne [patɛʀn(ə)] *adj* (*littér*) fatherly, avuncular.

paternel, -elle [patɛʀnɛl] 1 *adj autorité, descendance* paternal; (*bienveillant*) *personne, regard, conseil* fatherly. quitter le domicile ~ to leave one's father's house; du côté ~ on one's father's side, on the paternal side; ma tante ~le my aunt on my father's side, my paternal aunt.

2 *nm* (*) old man*, governor† (*Brit hum*).

paternellement [patɛʀnɛlmɑ̃] *adv* (*V* paternel) paternally; in a fatherly way.

paternité [patɛʀnite] *nf* (*lit*) paternity, fatherhood; (*fig*) paternity, authorship.

pâteux, -euse [pɑtø, øz] *adj* (*gén*) pasty; *pain* doughy; *langue* coated, furred; *voix* thick, husky; *style* woolly. avoir la bouche ~euse to have a furred *ou* coated tongue.

pathétique [patetik] 1 *adj* moving, pathetic; (*Anat*) pathetic. 2 *nm* pathos.

pathétiquement [patetikmɑ̃] *adv* movingly, pathetically.

pathétisme [patetism(ə)] *nm* (*littér*) pathos.

pathogène [patɔʒɛn] *adj* pathogenic.

pathologie [patɔlɔʒi] *nf* pathology.

pathologique [patɔlɔʒik] *adj* pathological.

pathologiquement [patɔlɔʒikmɑ̃] *adv* pathologically.

pathologiste [patɔlɔʒist(ə)] *nmf* pathologist.

pathos [patos] *nm* (overdone) pathos, emotionalism. **rédigé avec un ~ irritant** written with irritating pathos *ou* emotionalism.
patibulaire [patibylɛʀ] *adj* sinister. **avoir une mine ~** to be sinister-looking.
patiemment [pasjamɑ̃] *adv* patiently.
patience[1] [pasjɑ̃s] *nf* **(a)** (*gén*) patience; (*résignation*) long-suffering. **souffrir avec ~** to bear one's sufferings with patience *ou* patiently; **perdre ~** to lose (one's) patience; **prendre** *ou* **s'armer de ~** to be patient, have patience; **il faut avoir une ~ d'ange pour le supporter** it takes the patience of a saint *ou* of Job to put up with him; **je suis à bout de ~** my patience is exhausted, I'm at the end of my patience; *V* **mal.**
(b) (*Cartes*) patience. **faire des ~s** to play patience.
(c) (*loc*) **~, j'arrive** wait a minute! *ou* hang on!*, I'm coming; **~, j'aurai ma revanche** I'll get even in the end.
patience[2] [pasjɑ̃s] *nf* (*Bot*) (patience) dock.
patient, e [pasjɑ̃, ɑ̃t] **1** *adj* patient; *travail* patient, laborious. **2** *nm,f* (*Méd*) patient.
patienter [pasjɑ̃te] (1) *vi* to wait. **faites-le ~** ask him to wait, have him wait; **si vous voulez ~ un instant** could you wait *ou* hang on* *ou* hold on* a moment?; **lisez ce journal, ça vous fera ~** read this paper to fill in *ou* pass the time; **pour ~ il regardait les tableaux** to fill in *ou* pass the time he looked at the paintings.
patin [patɛ̃] *nm* **(a)** *[patineur]* skate; *[luge]* runner; *[rail]* base; (*pour le parquet*) cloth pad (*used as slippers on polished wood floors*). **~ (de frein)** brake block; **~s à glace** iceskates; **~s à roulettes** roller skates; **faire du ~ à glace/à roulettes** to go ice-skating/roller-skating.
(b) (‡: *baiser*) French kiss.
patinage[1] [patinaʒ] *nm* (*Sport*) skating; (*Aut*) *[roue]* spinning; *[embrayage]* slipping. **~ artistique** figure skating; **~ à roulettes** roller-skating; **~ de vitesse** speed skating.
patinage[2] [patinaʒ] *nm* (*Tech*) patination.
patine [patin] *nf* patina, sheen.
patiner[1] [patine] (1) *vi* (*Sport*) to skate; (*Aut*) *[roue]* to spin; *[embrayage]* to slip. **la voiture patina sur la chaussée verglacée** the wheels of the car spun on the icy road; **faire ~ l'embrayage** to slip the clutch.
patiner[2] [patine] (1) *vt* (*naturellement*) *bois, bronze, pierre* to give a sheen to; (*artificiellement*) to patinate, give a patina to.
patinette [patinɛt] *nf* scooter.
patineur, -euse [patinœʀ, øz] *nm,f* skater.
patinoire [patinwaʀ] *nf* skating rink, ice rink. (*fig*) **cette route est une vraie ~** this road is like an ice rink *ou* a skidpan (*Brit*).
patio [patjo] *nm* patio.
pâtir [pɑtiʀ] (2) *vi* (*littér*) to suffer (*de* because of, on account of).
pâtisserie [pɑtisʀi] *nf* **(a)** (*magasin*) cake shop, confectioner's; (*gâteau*) cake, pastry; (*art ménager*) cake- *ou* pastry-making, baking; (*métier, commerce*) confectionery. **apprendre la ~** (*comme métier*) to learn to be a pastrycook, learn confectionery; **faire de la ~** (*en amateur*) to do some baking, make cakes and pastries; **moule/ustensiles à ~** pastry dish/utensils; *V* **rouleau.**
(b) (*stuc*) fancy (plaster) moulding.
pâtissier, -ière [pɑtisje, jɛʀ] *nm,f* confectioner, pastrycook. **~-glacier** confectioner and ice-cream maker; *V* **crème.**
patois, e [patwa, waz] **1** *adj* patois (*épith*), dialectal, dialect (*épith*). **2** *nm* patois, (provincial) dialect. **parler (en) ~** to speak (in) patois.
patoisant, e [patwazɑ̃, ɑ̃t] **1** *adj* patois- *ou* dialect-speaking. **2** *nm,f* patois *ou* dialect speaker.
patoiser [patwaze] (1) *vi* to speak (in) dialect *ou* patois.
patraque* [patʀak] **1** *adj* peaky* (*Brit*), off-colour (*Brit*) (*attrib*), out of sorts (*attrib*). **2** *nf* (†: *montre*) timepiece, ticker*.
pâtre [pɑtʀ(ə)] *nm* (*littér*) shepherd.
patriarcal, e, *mpl* **-aux** [patʀijaʀkal, o] *adj* patriarchal.
patriarcat [patʀijaʀka] *nm* (*Rel*) patriarchate; (*Sociol*) patriarchy, patriarchate.
patriarche [patʀijaʀʃ(ə)] *nm* patriarch.
patricien, -ienne [patʀisjɛ̃, jɛn] *adj, nm,f* patrician.
patrie [patʀi] *nf* homeland; (*berceau*) homeland, home. **mourir pour la ~** to die for one's homeland *ou* country; **la Grèce, ~ de l'art** Greece, the homeland of art; **Limoges, ~ de la porcelaine** Limoges, the home of porcelain.
patrimoine [patʀimwan] *nm* (*gén*) inheritance, patrimony (*frm*); (*Jur*) patrimony; (*bien commun*) (*fig*) heritage, patrimony (*frm*). (*Bio*) **~ héréditaire** genetic inheritance, genotype.
patriotard, e [patʀijɔtaʀ, aʀd(ə)] (*péj*) **1** *adj* jingoistic. **2** *nm,f* jingoist.
patriote [patʀijɔt] **1** *adj* patriotic. **2** *nmf* patriot.
patriotique [patʀijɔtik] *adj* patriotic.
patriotiquement [patʀijɔtikmɑ̃] *adv* patriotically.
patriotisme [patʀijɔtism(ə)] *nm* patriotism.
patron[1] [patʀɔ̃] **1** *nm* **(a)** (*propriétaire*) owner, boss*; (*gérant*) manager, boss*; (*employeur*) employer. **le ~ est là?** is the boss* *ou* governor†‡ (*Brit*) in?; **le ~ de l'usine** the factory owner; the factory manager; **le ~ du restaurant** the proprietor of the restaurant, the restaurant owner; **il est ~ d'hôtel** he's a hotel proprietor; **la bonne garde la maison quand ses ~s sont absents** the maid looks after the house when her employers are away; **~ boulanger/boucher** master baker/butcher.
(b) (*Hist, Rel: protecteur*) patron. **saint ~** patron saint.
(c) (*: *mari*) (old) man‡. **il est là, le ~?** is your (old) man in?‡
(d) (*Hôpital*) ≃ senior consultant (*of teaching hospital*).
2: (*Naut*) **patron (pêcheur)** skipper; (*Univ*) **patron de thèse** supervisor *ou* director of postgraduate doctorate.

patron[2] [patʀɔ̃] *nm* (*Couture*) pattern; (*pochoir*) stencil. **~ de robe** dress pattern; **(taille) demi-~/~/grand ~** small/medium/large (size).
patronage [patʀɔnaʒ] *nm* **(a)** (*protection*) patronage. **sous le (haut) ~ de** under the patronage of. **(b)** (*organisation*) youth club; (*Rel*) youth fellowship.
patronal, e, *mpl* **-aux** [patʀɔnal, o] *adj* (*Ind*) *responsabilité, cotisation* employer's, employers'; (*Rel*) *fête* patronal.
patronat [patʀɔna] *nm* (*Ind*) **le ~** the employers.
patronne [patʀɔn] *nf* **(a)** (*V* **patron**) (lady) owner, boss*; (lady) manager; (lady) employer; proprietress. **(b)** (*: *épouse*) missus‡, old lady‡. **(c)** (*sainte*) patron saint.
patronner [patʀɔne] (1) *vt personne* to patronize, sponsor; *entreprise* to patronize, support; *candidature* to support.
patronnesse [patʀɔnɛs] *nf V* **dame.**
patronyme [patʀɔnim] *nm* patronymic.
patronymique [patʀɔnimik] *adj* patronymic.
patrouille [patʀuj] *nf* patrol. **partir** *ou* **aller en/être de ~** to go/be on patrol.
patrouiller [patʀuje] (1) *vi* to patrol, be on patrol. **~ dans les rues** to patrol the streets.
patrouilleur [patʀujœʀ] *nm* (*soldat*) soldier on patrol (duty), patroller; (*Naut*) patrol boat; (*Aviat*) patrol *ou* scout plane.
patte [pat] **1** *nf* **(a)** (*jambe d'animal*) leg; (*pied*) *[chat, chien]* paw; *[oiseau]* foot. **~s de devant** forelegs; forefeet; **~s de derrière** hindlegs; hind feet; **le chat retomba sur ses ~s** the cat fell on its feet; **le chien tendit la ~** the dog put its paw out *ou* gave a paw; **faire ~ de velours** *[chat]* to draw in *ou* sheathe its claws; (*fig*) to hide one's true intentions behind a show of goodwill; *V* **bas**[1]**, mille**[1]**, mouton**[1]**.**
(b) (‡: *jambe*) leg. **nous avons 50 km dans les ~s** we've walked 50 km; **à ~s** on foot; **nous y sommes allés à ~s** we walked *ou* hoofed‡ it, we went on Shanks' pony* (*Brit*) *ou* mare* (*US*); **bas** *ou* **court sur ~s** *personne* short-legged; *table, véhicule* low; **il est toujours dans mes ~s** he's always under my feet.
(c) (‡: *main*) hand, paw*. **ce peintre a de la ~** *ou* **un bon coup de ~** this painter has real talent; **s'il me tombe sous la ~, gare à lui!** if I get my hands *ou* paws* on him he'd better look out!; **tomber dans les/se tirer des ~s de qn** to fall into/get out of sb's clutches.
(d) *[ancre]* palm, fluke; (*languette*) *[poche]* flap; *[vêtement]* strap; (*sur l'épaule*) epaulette; *[porte-feuilles]* tongue; *[chaussure]* tongue.
(e) (*favoris*) **~s (de lapin)** sideburns; *V* **fil, graisser, quatre** *etc.*
2: pantalon (à) pattes d'éléphant bell-bottom *ou* flared trousers, bell-bottoms, flares; **patte folle** gammy (*Brit*) *ou* game leg; **patte à glace** mirror clamp; **patte(s) de mouche** spidery scrawl; **faire des pattes de mouche** to write (in) a spidery scrawl; **patte-d'oie** *nf, pl* **pattes-d'oie** (*à l'œil*) crow's-foot; (*carrefour*) branching crossroads *ou* junction.
pattemouille [patmuj] *nf* damp cloth (*for ironing*).
pâturage [pɑtyʀaʒ] *nm* (*lieu*) pasture; (*action*) grazing, pasturage; (*droits*) grazing rights.
pâture [pɑtyʀ] *nf* **(a)** (*nourriture*) food. (*fig*) **il fait sa ~ de romans noirs** he is an avid reader of detective stories, detective stories form his usual reading matter; (*lit, fig*) **donner qn en ~ aux fauves** to throw sb to the lions.
(b) (*pâturage*) pasture.
pâturer [pɑtyʀe] (1) **1** *vi* to graze. **2** *vt*: **~ l'herbe** to be grazing.
paturon [patyʀɔ̃] *nm* pastern.
Paul [pɔl] *nm* Paul.
Paule [pɔl] *nf* Paula.
paume [pom] *nf [main]* palm. (*Sport*) **jouer à la ~** to play real tennis.
paumé, e‡ [pome] (*ptp de* **paumer**) *adj* (*péj*) (*dans un lieu*) lost; (*dans une explication*) lost, at sea*; (*dans un milieu inconnu*) bewildered. **un pauvre ~** a poor bum**; **habiter un bled** *ou* **trou ~** (*isolé*) to live in a godforsaken place *ou* hole‡; (*sans attrait*) to live in a real dump *ou* a godforsaken hole‡; (*fig: socialement inadapté*) **la jeunesse ~e d'aujourd'hui** the young wasters* *ou* drop-outs* of today.
paumelle [pomɛl] *nf* split hinge.
paumer‡ [pome] (1) **1** *vt* (*perdre*) to lose. **2 se paumer** *vpr* to get lost.
paupérisation [popeʀizasjɔ̃] *nf* pauperization.
paupérisme [popeʀism(ə)] *nm* pauperism.
paupière [popjɛʀ] *nf* eyelid.
paupiette [popjɛt] *nf* (*Culin*) **~ de veau** veal olive.
pause [poz] *nf* (*arrêt*) break; (*en parlant*) pause; (*Mus*) pause; (*Sport*) half-time. **faire une ~** to have a break, break off; **~-café** coffee break.
pauser*† [poze] *vi* **faire ~ qn** to keep sb waiting.
pauvre [povʀ(ə)] **1** *adj* **(a)** *personne, pays, sol* poor; *végétation* sparse; *minerai, gisement* poor; *style,* (*Aut*) *mélange* weak; *mobilier, vêtements* shabby; *nourriture, salaire* meagre, poor. **minerai ~ en cuivre** ore with a low copper content, ore poor in copper; **air ~ en oxygène** air low in oxygen; **pays ~ en ressources/en hommes** country short of *ou* lacking resources/men; **nourriture ~ en calcium** (*par manque*) diet lacking in calcium; (*par ordonnance*) low-calcium diet; **~ comme Job** as poor as a church mouse; **les couches ~s de la population** the poorer *ou* deprived sections of the population; *V* **rime.**
(b) (*avant n: piètre*) *excuse, argument* weak, pathetic; *devoir* poor; *orateur* weak, bad. **de ~s chances de succès** only a slim *ou* slender chance of success; **il esquissa un ~ sourire** he smiled weakly *ou* gave a weak smile.
(c) (*avant n: malheureux*) poor. **laisse-le tranquille, c'est un ~ type!** leave the poor chap* (*Brit*) *ou* guy* alone!; **~ con!**** you poor sod!**; **c'est un ~ type, tu sais!‡** he's just a poor bum**;

(*littér, hum*) ~ hère down-and-out; ~ d'esprit (*simple d'esprit*) half-wit; (*Rel*) les ~s d'esprit the poor in spirit; comme disait mon ~ mari as my poor (dear) husband used to say; (*hum*) ~ de moi! poor (little) me!; mon ~ ami my dear friend; elle me faisait pitié, avec son ~ petit air I felt sorry for her, she looked so wretched *ou* miserable.

2 *nmf* (a) (*personne pauvre*) poor man *ou* woman, pauper††. les ~s the poor; ce pays compte encore beaucoup de ~s there's still a lot of poverty *ou* there are still many poor people in this country.

(b) (*: *marquant dédain ou commisération*) mon (*ou* ma) ~, si tu voyais comment ça se passe ... but my dear fellow (*ou* girl *etc*) *ou* friend, if you saw what goes on...; le ~, il a dû en voir! the poor chap* (*Brit*) *ou* guy*, he must have had a hard time of it!

pauvrement [povʀəmɑ̃] *adv meublé, éclairé, vivre* poorly; *vêtu* poorly, shabbily.

pauvresse† [povʀɛs] *nf* poor woman *ou* wretch.

pauvret, -ette [povʀɛ, ɛt] 1 *adj visage, air* pathetic. 2 *nm,f* poor (little) thing.

pauvreté [povʀəte] *nf* [*personne*] poverty; [*vêtement, mobilier*] shabbiness; [*langage*] weakness, poorness; [*sol*] poorness. (*Prov*) ~ n'est pas vice there is no shame in being poor.

pavage [pavaʒ] *nm* (*V* paver) (*action*) paving; cobbling; (*revêtement*) paving; cobbles.

pavane [pavan] *nf* pavane.

pavaner (se) [pavane] (1) *vpr* to strut about. se ~ comme un dindon to strut about like a turkey-cock.

pavé [pave] *nm* [*chaussée*] cobblestone; [*cour*] paving stone; (*fig péj: livre*) hefty tome*. déraper sur le ~ *ou* les ~s to skid on the cobbles; ~ de viande thick piece of steak; être sur le ~ (*sans domicile*) to be on the streets *ou* homeless; (*sans emploi*) to be out of a job; mettre *ou* jeter qn sur le ~ (*domicile*) to turn *ou* throw sb out (onto the streets); (*emploi*) to give sb the sack*, throw sb out; j'ai l'impression d'avoir un ~ sur l'estomac* I feel as if I've got a great *ou* lead weight in my stomach; (*fig*) jeter un ~ dans la mare to set the cat among the pigeons; *V* battre, brûler, haut.

pavement [pavmɑ̃] *nm* ornamental tiling.

paver [pave] (1) *vt cour* to pave; *chaussée* to cobble. cour pavée paved yard; *V* enfer.

paveur [pavœʀ] *nm* paver.

pavillon [pavijɔ̃] 1 *nm* (a) (*villa*) house; (*loge de gardien*) lodge; (*section d'hôpital*) ward, pavilion; (*corps de bâtiment*) wing, pavilion.

(b) (*Naut*) flag. sous ~ panaméen *etc* under the Panamanian *etc* flag; *V* baisser, battre.

(c) (*Mus*) [*instrument*] bell; [*phonographe*] horn.

(d) [*oreille*] pavilion, pinna.

2: pavillon de banlieue house in the suburbs; pavillon de chasse hunting lodge; pavillon de guerre war flag; pavillon noir Jolly Roger; pavillon de quarantaine yellow flag; pavillon de verdure leafy arbour *ou* bower.

pavlovien, -ienne [pavlɔvjɛ̃, jɛn] *adj* Pavlovian.

pavois [pavwa] *nm* (*Naut: bordage*) bulwark; (*Hist: bouclier*) shield. (*lit*) hisser qn sur le ~ to carry sb shoulder-high.

pavoiser [pavwaze] (1) 1 *vt navire* to dress; *monument* to deck with flags.

2 *vi* to put out flags; (*fig: Sport*) [*supporters*] to wave the banners, exult. toute la ville a pavoisé there were flags out all over the town; (*fig*) il pavoise maintenant qu'on lui a donné raison publiquement he's rejoicing openly now that he has been publicly acknowledged to be in the right.

pavot [pavo] *nm* poppy.

payable [pɛjabl(ə)] *adj* payable. ~ en 3 fois *somme* payable in *ou* that must *ou* may be paid in 3 instalments; *objet* that must *ou* can be paid for in 3 instalments; l'impôt est ~ par tous taxes must be paid by everyone; (*Fin*) billet ~ à vue bill payable at sight.

payant, e [pɛjɑ̃, ɑ̃t] *adj spectateur* who pays (for his seat); *billet, place* which one must pay for, not free (*attrib*); *spectacle* where one must pay to go in, where there is a charge for admission; (*rentable*) *affaire* profitable; *politique, conduite* which pays off.

paye [pɛj] *nf* = **paie.**

payement [pɛjmɑ̃] *nm* = **paiement.**

payer [peje] (8) 1 *vt* (a) [*somme, cotisation, intérêt*] to pay; *facture, dette* to pay, settle. ~ comptant to pay cash; ~ rubis sur l'ongle† to pay cash on the nail; c'est lui qui paie he's paying.

(b) *employé* to pay; *entrepreneur* to pay, settle up with. être payé par chèque/en espèces/en nature/à l'heure to be paid by cheque/in cash/in kind/by the hour; être payé à la pièce to be on piecework; ~ qn de *ou* en paroles/promesses to fob sb off with (empty) words/promises; je ne suis pas payé pour ça* that's not what I'm paid for; (*fig iro*) il est payé pour le savoir he has learnt the hard way, he has learnt that to his cost.

(c) *travail, service, maison, marchandise* to pay for. je l'ai payé de ma poche I paid for it with my own money, the money for it came out of my own pocket; les réparations ne sont pas encore payées the repairs haven't been paid for yet; il m'a fait ~ 10F he charged me 10 francs (*pour* for); ~ le déplacement de qn to pay sb's travelling expenses; ~ la casse *ou* les pots cassés (*lit*) to pay for the damage; (*fig*) to pick up the pieces, carry the can* (*Brit*); travail bien/mal payé well-/badly-paid work; *V* congé.

(d) (*: *offrir*) ~ qch à qn to buy sth for sb; c'est moi qui paie (à boire) the drinks are on me*, have this one on me*; ~ des vacances/un voyage à qn to pay for sb to go on holiday/on a trip.

(e) (*récompenser*) to reward. le succès le paie de tous ses efforts his success makes all his efforts worthwhile *ou* rewards him for all his efforts; il l'aimait et elle le payait de retour he loved her and she returned his love.

(f) (*expier*) *faute, crime* to pay for. ~ qch de 5 ans de prison to get 5 years in jail for sth; il l'a payé de sa vie/santé it cost him his life/health; il a payé cher son imprudence he paid dearly for his rashness, his rashness cost him dearly; (*en menace*) il me le paiera! he'll pay for this!, I'll make him pay for this!

2 *vi* (a) [*effort, tactique*] to pay off; [*métier*] to be well-paid. le crime ne paie pas crime doesn't pay; ~ pour qn (*lit*) to pay for sb; (*fig*) to carry the can (*Brit*) for sb*.

(b) ~ de: pour y parvenir il a dû ~ de sa personne he had to sacrifice himself in order to succeed; ce poisson ne paie pas de mine, mais il est très bon this fish isn't much to look at but it's very tasty; ~ d'audace to act with great daring.

3 se payer *vpr* (a) payez-vous et rendez-moi la monnaie take what I owe you and give me the change; tout se paie (*lit*) everything must be paid for; (*fig*) everything has its price.

(b) (*: *s'offrir*) *objet* to buy o.s., treat o.s. to. on va se ~ un bon dîner/le restaurant we're going to treat ourselves to a slap-up* meal/to a meal out; se ~ une pinte de bon sang to have a good laugh*; se ~ la tête de qn (*ridiculiser*) to take the mickey* out of sb; (*tromper*) to take sb for a ride‡; se ~ une bonne grippe to get a bad dose of flu; se ~ une bonne cuite‡ to get stoned‡; il s'est payé un arbre/le trottoir/un piéton he has wrapped his car round a tree/run into the pavement/mown a pedestrian down.

(c) se ~ d'illusions to delude o.s.; se ~ de culot to use one's nerve; il se paie de mots he's talking a lot of hot air*.

payeur, -euse [pɛjœʀ, øz] 1 *adj*: organisme/service ~ payments department/office. 2 *nm,f* payer; (*Mil, Naut*) paymaster. mauvais ~ bad debtor.

pays[1] [pei] 1 *nm* (a) (*contrée, habitants*) country. des ~ lointains far-off countries *ou* lands; les ~ membres du marché commun the countries which are members of *ou* the member countries of the Common Market; la France est le ~ du vin France is the land of wine; *V* mal.

(b) (*région*) region. il est du ~ he's from these parts *ou* this area; les gens du ~ the local people, the locals; un ~ de légumes, d'élevage et de lait a vegetable-growing, cattle-breeding and dairy region; c'est le ~ de la tomate it's famous tomato-growing country; nous sommes en plein ~ du vin we're in the heart of the wine country; vin de *ou* du ~ local wine; melons/pêches de *ou* du ~ local-grown melons/peaches.

(c) (*village*) village.

(d) (*loc*) (*fig*) le ~ des rêves the land of dreams, dreamland; voir du ~ to travel around (a lot); se comporter comme en ~ conquis to lord it over everyone, act all high and mighty; être en ~ de connaissance (*dans une réunion*) to be among friends *ou* familiar faces; (*sur un sujet, dans un lieu*) to be on home ground.

2: pays de Cocagne land of plenty; pays de Galles Wales.

pays[2], **e** [pei, peiz] *nm,f* (*dial: compatriote*) nous sommes ~ we come from the same village *ou* region *ou* part of the country; elle est ma ~e she comes from the same village *ou* region *ou* part of the country as me.

paysage [peizaʒ] *nm* (*point de vue*) landscape; (*décor*) scenery (*U*); (*Peinture*) landscape. on découvrait un ~ magnifique/un ~ de montagne a magnificent/mountainous landscape lay before us; nous avons traversé des ~s magnifiques we drove through some magnificent scenery.

paysagiste [peizaʒist(ə)] *nmf* (*Peinture*) landscape painter. (*Agr*) (jardinier) ~ landscape gardener.

paysan, -anne [peizɑ̃, an] 1 *adj* (*agricole*) *monde, problème* farming (*épith*); *agitation, revendications* farmers', of the farmers; (*rural*) *vie, coutumes* country (*épith*); (*péj*) *air, manières* peasant (*épith*).

2 *nm* countryman, farmer; (*péj*) peasant.

3 paysanne *nf* peasant woman, countrywoman; (*péj*) peasant.

paysannerie [peizanʀi] *nf* peasantry, farmers.

Pays-Bas [peiba] *nmpl*: les ~ the Netherlands.

péage [peaʒ] *nm* (*droit*) toll; (*barrière*) tollgate. autoroute/pont à ~ toll motorway/bridge.

peau, *pl* ~x [po] 1 *nf* (a) [*personne*] skin. avoir une ~ de pêche to have a peach-like complexion; soins de la/maladie de ~ skin care/disease; n'avoir que la ~ et les os to be all skin and bones; attraper qn par la ~ du cou *ou* du dos *ou* des fesses‡ (*empoigner rudement*) to grab sb by the scruff of his *ou* her neck; (*s'en saisir à temps*) to grab hold of sb in the nick of time; faire ~ neuve [*parti politique, administration*] to adopt *ou* find a new image; [*personne*] (*en changeant d'habit*) to change (one's clothes); (*en changeant de conduite*) to turn over a new leaf; *V* fleur.

(b) (*: *corps, vie*) jouer *ou* risquer sa ~ to risk one's neck* *ou* hide*; sauver sa ~ to save one's skin *ou* bacon* (*Brit*); tenir à sa ~ to value one's life; se faire crever *ou* trouer la ~‡ to get killed, get a bullet in one's hide*; on lui fera la ~‡ we'll bump him off‡; je veux/j'aurai sa ~! I'm out to get him!*, I'll have his hide for this!*; être bien/mal dans sa ~ (*physiquement*) to feel great*/awful; (*mentalement*) to be always quite at ease/always ill-at-ease; avoir qn dans la ~* to be crazy about sb*; avoir le jeu *etc* dans la ~ to have gambling *etc* in one's blood; se mettre dans la ~ de qn to put o.s. in sb's place *ou* shoes; entrer dans la ~ du personnage to get (right) into the part; je ne voudrais pas être dans sa ~ I wouldn't like to be in his shoes *ou* place.

(c) [*animal*] (*gén*) skin; (*cuir*) hide; (*fourrure*) pelt; [*éléphant, buffle*] hide. gants/vêtements de ~ leather gloves/clothes; *V* vendre.

(d) [*fruit, lait, peinture*] skin; [*fromage*] rind; (*épluchure*) peel. glisser sur une ~ de banane to slip on a banana skin; enlever la ~ de *fruit* to peel; *fromage* to take the rind off.

(e) ~ de balle!‡ nothing doing!*, not a chance!*, no way!‡.

2: **peau d'âne**† (*diplôme*) diploma, sheepskin (*US*); (*lit*) **peau de chagrin** shagreen; (*fig*) **diminuer comme une peau de chagrin** to shrink away; **peau de chamois** chamois leather, shammy; **peau de mouton** sheepskin; **en peau de mouton** sheepskin (*épith*); **peau de porc** pigskin; **Peau-Rouge** *nmf, pl* **Peaux-Rouges** Red Indian, redskin; **peau de serpent** snakeskin; **peau de vache: c'est une peau de vache*** (*homme*) he's a bastard‡; (*femme*) she's a bitch‡; **peau de zénana: c'est en peau de zénana** it's made of some sort of cheap stuff.

peaucier [posje] *adj m, nm:* **(muscle)** ~ platysma.

peausserie [posʀi] *nf* (*articles*) leatherwear (*U*); (*commerce*) skin trade; (*boutique*) suede and leatherware shop.

peaussier [posje] **1** *adj m* leather (*épith*). **2** *nm* (*ouvrier*) leatherworker; (*commerçant*) leather dealer.

pébroque* [pebʀɔk] *nm* brolly*.

pécari [pekaʀi] *nm* peccary.

peccadille [pekadij] *nf* (*vétille*) trifle; (*délit*) peccadillo.

pechblende [pɛʃblɛ̃d] *nf* pitchblende.

pêche[1] [pɛʃ] *nf* (*fruit*) peach; (‡: *coup*) slap, clout*. **~-abricot, ~ jaune** *ou* **abricotée** yellow peach; **~ blanche** white peach; **~ de vigne** bush peach; **donner une ~ à qn‡** to slap *ou* clout* sb across the face; *V* **melba, peau.**

pêche[2] [pɛʃ] *nf* **(a)** (*U: activité*) fishing; (*saison*) fishing season. **la ~ à la ligne** (*mer*) line fishing; (*rivière*) angling; **la ~ à la baleine** whaling; **la ~ à la truite** trout fishing; **la ~ aux moules** the gathering of mussels; **aller à la ~** to go fishing, go angling; **filet/barque de ~** fishing net/boat; *V* **canne.**

(b) (*poissons*) catch. **faire une belle ~** to have *ou* make a good catch. (*Rel*) **~ miraculeuse** the miraculous draught of fishes.

péché [peʃe] **1** *nm* sin. **pour mes ~s** for my sins; **à tout ~ miséricorde** every sin can be forgiven *ou* pardoned; **vivre dans le ~** (*gén*) to lead a sinful life; (*sans être marié*) to live in sin; **mourir en état de ~** to die a sinner.

2: péché capital: les sept péchés capitaux the seven deadly sins; **péché de chair**† sin of the flesh; **péché de jeunesse** youthful indiscretion; **péché mignon: c'est son péché mignon** he is partial to it, he has a weakness for it; **péché mortel** mortal sin; **le péché d'orgueil** the sin of pride; **le péché originel** original sin; **péché véniel** venial sin.

pécher [peʃe] (6) *vi* **(a)** (*Rel*) to sin. **~ par orgueil** to commit the sin of pride.

(b) ~ contre la politesse/l'hospitalité to break the rules of courtesy/hospitality; **~ par négligence/imprudence** to be too careless/reckless; **~ par ignorance** to err through ignorance; **~ par excès de prudence/d'optimisme** to be over-careful/over-optimistic, err on the side of caution/optimism; **ça pèche par bien des points** *ou* **sur bien des côtés** it has a lot of weaknesses *ou* shortcomings.

pêcher[1] [peʃe] (1) **1** *vt* (*être pêcheur de*) to fish for; (*attraper*) to catch, land. **~ des coquillages** to gather shellfish; **~ la baleine/la crevette** to go whaling/shrimping; **~ la truite/la morue** to fish for trout/cod, go trout-/cod-fishing; **~ qch à la ligne/à l'asticot** to fish for *ou* catch sth with rod and line/with maggots; **~ qch au chalut** to trawl for sth; (*fig*) **où as-tu été ~ cette idée/cette boîte?*** where did you dig that idea/box up from?*

2 *vi* to go fishing; (*avec un chalut*) to trawl, go trawling. **~ à la ligne** to go angling; **~ à l'asticot** to fish with maggots; **~ à la mouche** to fly-fish; (*fig*) **~ en eau trouble** to fish in troubled waters.

pêcher[2] [peʃe] *nm* (*arbre*) peach tree.

pécheresse [peʃʀɛs] *nf V* **pécheur.**

pêcherie [pɛʃʀi] *nf* fishery, fishing ground.

pécheur, pécheresse [peʃœʀ, peʃʀɛs] **1** *adj* sinful. **2** *nm,f* sinner.

pêcheur [pɛʃœʀ] **1** *nm* fisherman; (*à la ligne*) angler. **~ de crevettes** shrimper; **~ de baleines** whaler; **~ de perles** pearl diver; **c'est un ~ de coquillages** he gathers shellfish. **2** *adj* **bateau** fishing.

pêcheuse [pɛʃøz] *nf* fisherwoman; (*à la ligne*) (woman) angler.

pécore [pekɔʀ] **1** *nf* (*péj: imbécile*) silly goose*. **2** *nmf* (*péj: paysan*) country bumpkin.

pectine [pɛktin] *nf* pectin.

pectique [pɛktik] *adj* pectic.

pectoral, e, *mpl* **-aux** [pɛktɔʀal, o] **1** *adj* **(a)** (*Anat, Zool*) pectoral. **(b)** (*Méd*) *sirop* throat (*épith*), cough (*épith*). **2** *nm* **(a)** (*Anat*) pectoral muscle. **(b)** (*Méd*) throat *ou* cough mixture.

pécule [pekyl] *nm* (*économies*) savings, nest egg; *[détenu, soldat]* earnings, wages (*paid on release or discharge*).

pécuniaire [pekynjɛʀ] *adj embarras* financial, pecuniary (*frm*); *aide, avantage, situation* financial.

pécuniairement [pekynjɛʀmɑ̃] *adv* financially.

pédagogie [pedagɔʒi] *nf* (*V* **pédagogique**) pedagogy; educational methods.

pédagogique [pedagɔʒik] *adj intérêt, contenu, théorie* pedagogical (*T*), educational; *moyens, méthodes* educational. **stage (de formation) ~** teacher-training course; **il a fait un exposé très ~** he gave a very clear lecture.

pédagogiquement [pedagɔʒikmɑ̃] *adv* (*V* **pédagogique**) pedagogically (*T*); from an educational standpoint; clearly.

pédagogue [pedagɔg] *nmf* (*professeur*) teacher; (*spécialiste*) teaching specialist. **c'est un bon ~, il est bon ~** he's a good teacher.

pédale [pedal] *nf* **(a)** *[bicyclette, piano, voiture]* pedal; *[machine à coudre, tour]* treadle; *V* **perdre. (b)** (‡*péj*) queer‡.

pédaler [pedale] (1) *vi* to pedal; (**fig: se dépêcher*) to hurry.

pédaleur, -euse [pedalœʀ, øz] *nm,f* cyclist.

pédalier [pedalje] *nm [bicyclette]* pedal and gear mechanism; *[orgue]* pedal-board, pedals.

pédalo [pedalo] *nm* pedalo, pedal-boat.

pédant, e [pedɑ̃, ɑ̃t] **1** *adj* pedantic. **2** *nm,f* pedant.

pédanterie [pedɑ̃tʀi] *nf* (*littér*) pedantry.

pédantesque [pedɑ̃tɛsk(ə)] *adj* pedantic.

pédantisme [pedɑ̃tism(ə)] *nm* pedantry.

pédé‡ [pede] *nm* (*abrév de* **pédéraste**) queer‡, gay*.

pédéraste [pedeʀast(ə)] *nm* homosexual, pederast.

pédérastie [pedeʀasti] *nf* homosexuality, pederasty.

pédestre [pedɛstʀ(ə)] *adj* (*littér, hum*) **promenade** *ou* **circuit ~** walk.

pédestrement [pedɛstʀəmɑ̃] *adv* (*littér, hum*) on foot.

pédiatre [pedjatʀ(ə)] *nmf* paediatrician.

pédiatrie [pedjatʀi] *nf* paediatrics (*sg*).

pédibus (cum jambis) [pedibys(kumʒɑ̃bis)] *adv* on foot, on Shanks' pony* (*Brit*) *ou* mare* (*US*).

pédicule [pedikyl] *nm* (*Anat*) pedicle; (*Bot, Zool*) peduncle.

pédicure [pedikyʀ] *nmf* chiropodist.

pedigree [pedigʀi] *nm* pedigree.

pédologie [pedɔlɔʒi] *nf* (*Géol*) pedology.

pédologue [pedɔlɔg] *nmf* (*Géol*) pedologist.

pédoncule [pedɔ̃kyl] *nm* (*Anat, Bot, Zool*) peduncle.

pedzouille‡ [pɛdzuj] *nm* (*péj*) peasant, country bumpkin.

peeling [piliŋ] *nm* peeling.

Pégase [pegaz] *nm* Pegasus.

pègre [pɛgʀ(ə)] *nf:* **la ~** the underworld.

peignage [pɛɲaʒ] *nm [laine]* carding; *[lin, chanvre]* carding, hackling.

peigne [pɛɲ] *nm [cheveux]* comb; (*Tex*) *[laine]* card; *[lin, chanvre]* card, hackle; *[métier]* reed. (*fig*) **passer qch au ~ fin** to go through sth with a fine-tooth comb; **se donner un coup de ~** to run a comb through one's hair.

peigne-cul‡, *pl* **peigne-culs** [pɛɲky] *nm* (*péj*) (*mesquin*) creep‡; (*inculte*) yob‡ (*Brit*).

peignée* [peɲe] *nf* (*raclée*) thrashing, hiding*. **donner/recevoir une** *ou* **la ~** to give/get a thrashing *ou* hiding*.

peigner [peɲe] (1) **1** *vt cheveux* to comb; *enfant* to comb the hair of; (*Tex*) *laine* to card; *lin, chanvre* to card, hackle. **mal peigné** dishevelled, tousled; **laine peignée** *[pantalon, veston]* worsted wool; *[pull]* combed wool; (*hum*) **~ la girafe** to fill in time on a pointless task. **2 se peigner** *vpr* to comb one's hair, give one's hair a comb.

peignoir [pɛɲwaʀ] *nm* (*robe de chambre*) dressing gown; *[boxeur]* (boxer's) dressing gown. **~ (de bain)** bathrobe.

peinard, e* [penaʀ, aʀd(ə)] *adj travail, vie* cushy‡. **on est ~ dans l'armée** it's a cushy‡ *ou* soft life in the army; **rester** *ou* **se tenir ~** to keep out of trouble, keep one's nose clean‡; **tout le monde est couché, on va être ~** everybody's asleep so now we'll have a bit of peace *ou* now we can take it easy.

peinardement* [penaʀdəmɑ̃] *adv* quietly.

peindre [pɛ̃dʀ(ə)] (52) **1** *vt* (*gén*) to paint; (*fig*) *mœurs* to paint, depict. **~ qch en jaune** to paint sth yellow; **~ à la chaux** to whitewash; **tableau peint à l'huile** picture painted in oils; **se faire ~ par X** to have one's portrait painted by X; (*fig*) **romancier qui sait bien ~ ses personnages** novelist who portrays his characters well; **il l'avait peint sous les traits d'un vieillard dans son livre** he had depicted *ou* portrayed him as an old man in his book.

2 se peindre *vpr* (*se décrire*) to portray o.s. **Montaigne s'est peint dans 'Les Essais'** 'Les Essais' are a self-portrayal of Montaigne; **le désespoir se peignait sur leur visage** despair was written on their faces; **la cruauté était peinte sur ses traits** cruelty was reflected in his features.

peine [pɛn] *nf* **(a)** (*chagrin*) sorrow, sadness (*U*). **avoir de la ~** to be sad *ou* (*moins fort*) upset; **être dans la ~** to be grief-stricken; **faire de la ~ à qn** to upset sb, make sb sad, distress sb; **elle m'a fait de la ~ et je lui ai donné de l'argent** I felt sorry for her and gave her some money; **je ne voudrais pas te faire de (la) ~* mais ...** I don't want to disappoint you but ...; **~s de cœur** emotional troubles; **il faisait ~ à voir** he looked a sorry *ou* pitiful sight; *V* **âme.**

(b) (*gén: U: effort*) effort, trouble (*U*). **il faut se donner de la ~, cela demande de la ~** that requires an effort, you have to make an effort; **se donner de la ~ pour faire** to go to a lot of trouble to do; **si tu te mettais seulement en ~ d'essayer, si tu te donnais seulement la ~ d'essayer** if you would only bother to try *ou* take the trouble to try; **il ne se donne aucune ~** he just doesn't try *ou* bother; (*formule de politesse*) **donnez-vous** *ou* **prenez donc la ~ d'entrer/de vous asseoir** please *ou* do come in/sit down; **est-ce que c'est la ~ d'y aller?** is it worth going?; **ce n'est pas la ~ de me le répéter** there's no point in repeating that, you've no need to repeat that; **ce n'est pas la ~** don't bother; (*iro*) **c'était bien la ~ de sortir!** *ou* **qu'il sorte!** it was a waste of time (his) going out, he wasted his time going out; **c'est ~ perdue** it's a waste of time (and effort); **on lui a donné 100 F pour sa ~** he was given 100 francs for his trouble; **tu as été sage, pour la ~, tu auras un bonbon** here's a sweet for being good; **ne vous mettez pas en ~ pour moi** don't go to *ou* put yourself to any trouble for me; *V* **mourir, valoir.**

(c) (*difficulté*) difficulty. **il a eu de la ~ à finir son repas/la course** he had difficulty finishing his meal/the race; **il a eu de la ~ mais il y est arrivé** it wasn't easy (for him) but he managed it; **avoir de la ~ à faire** to have difficulty in doing, find it difficult *ou* hard to do; **j'avais (de la) ~ à croire** I found it hard to believe, I could hardly believe it; **avec ~** with difficulty; **à grand-~** with great difficulty; **sans ~** without (any) difficulty, easily; **il n'est pas en ~ pour trouver des secrétaires** he has no difficulty *ou* trouble finding secretaries; **j'ai eu toutes les ~s du monde à le convaincre/à démarrer** I had no end of a job* *ou* a hell of a job‡ convincing him/getting the car started; **je serais bien en ~ de vous le dire/d'en trouver** I'd be hard pushed* to tell you/to find any.

(d) (*punition*) punishment, penalty; (*Jur*) sentence. ~ **capitale** *ou* **de mort** capital punishment, death sentence; **sous ~ de mort** on pain of death; **défense d'afficher sous ~ d'amende** billposters will be fined; **défense d'entrer sous ~ de poursuites** trespassers will be prosecuted; **on ne peut rien lui dire, sous ~ d'être renvoyé** you daren't *ou* can't say anything to him for fear of dismissal *ou* the sack*; **pour la** *ou* **ta ~ tu mettras la table** for that you can lay the table.

(e) à ~ hardly, only just, scarcely, barely; **il est à ~ 2 heures** it's only just 2 o'clock, it's only just turned 2; **il leur reste à ~ de quoi manger** they've scarcely *ou* hardly any food left; **il parle à ~** *[personne silencieuse]* he hardly says anything; *[enfant]* he can hardly *ou* barely talk; **il était à ~ rentré qu'il a dû ressortir** he had only just got in *ou* he had scarcely got in when he had to go out again; **à ~ dans la voiture, il s'est endormi** no sooner had he got in the car than he fell asleep; **c'est à ~ si on l'entend** you can hardly hear him; **il était à ~ aimable** he was barely *ou* scarcely civil.

peiner [pene] (1) **1** *vi [personne]* to work hard; *[moteur]* to labour. ~ **sur un problème** to struggle with a problem; **le coureur peinait dans les derniers mètres** the runner had a hard time *ou* was struggling over the last few metres.

2 *vt* to grieve, sadden, distress. **j'ai été peiné de l'apprendre** I was upset *ou* distressed to hear it; **dit-il d'un ton peiné** he said in an aggrieved tone; **il avait un air peiné** he looked upset.

peintre [pɛ̃tʀ(ə)] *nmf (lit)* painter; *(fig: écrivain)* portrayer. ~ **en bâtiment** house painter, painter and decorator; ~**-décorateur** painter and decorator.

peinture [pɛ̃tyʀ] **1** *nf* **(a)** (*action, art*) painting. **faire de la ~ (à l'huile/à l'eau)** to paint (in oils/in watercolours).

(b) (*ouvrage*) painting, picture. **vendre sa ~** to sell one's paintings.

(c) (*surface peinte*) paintwork. **la ~ est craquelée** the paintwork is cracked.

(d) (*matière*) paint. **attention à la ~!** wet paint!

(e) (*fig*) portrayal. **c'est une ~ des mœurs de l'époque** it portrays *ou* depicts the social customs of the period.

2: peinture abstraite (*U*) abstract art; (*tableau*) abstract (painting); **peinture en bâtiment** house painting, painting and decorating; **peinture brillante** gloss paint; **peinture à l'eau** (*tableau, matière*) watercolour; (*pour le bâtiment*) water paint; **peinture à l'huile** (*tableau*) oil painting; (*matière*) oil paint; (*pour le bâtiment*) oil-based paint; **peinture laquée** gloss paint; **peinture mate** matt emulsion (paint); **peinture murale** mural; **peinture au pistolet** spray painting; **peinture au rouleau** roller painting.

peinturlurer [pɛ̃tyʀlyʀe] (1) *vt* to daub (with paint). ~ **qch de bleu** to daub sth with blue paint; **visage peinturluré** painted face.

péjoratif, -ive [peʒɔʀatif, iv] **1** *adj* derogatory, pejorative. **2** *nm (Ling)* pejorative word.

péjorativement [peʒɔʀativmɑ̃] *adv* in a derogatory fashion, pejoratively.

pékin [pekɛ̃] *nm (arg Mil)* civvy (*arg*). **s'habiller en ~** to dress in civvies.

Pékin [pekɛ̃] *n* Peking.

pékinois, e [pekinwa, waz] **1** *adj* Pekinese. **2** *nm* **(a)** (*chien*) pekinese, peke*. **(b)** (*Ling*) Mandarin (Chinese), Pekinese. **3** *nm,f*: **P~(e)** Pekinese.

pelade [pəlad] *nf* alopecia.

pelage [pəlaʒ] *nm* coat, fur.

pelé, e [pəle] (*ptp de* **peler**) **1** *adj personne* bald(-headed); *animal* hairless; *vêtement* threadbare; *terrain* bare.

2 *nm* (*) bald-headed man, baldie*. (*fig*) **il n'y avait que quatre ~s et un tondu** there was hardly anyone there, there was only a handful of people there.

pêle-mêle [pɛlmɛl] **1** *adv* any old how, higgledy-piggledy*. **ils s'entassaient ~ dans l'autobus** they piled into the bus one on top of the other. **2** *nm inv* jumble.

peler [pəle] (5) *vti* (*gén*) to peel. **ce fruit se pèle bien** this fruit peels easily *ou* is easy to peel.

pèlerin [pɛlʀɛ̃] *nm* pilgrim. **(faucon) ~** peregrine falcon; **(requin) ~** basking shark.

pèlerinage [pɛlʀinaʒ] *nm* (*voyage*) pilgrimage; (*lieu*) place of pilgrimage, shrine. **aller en** *ou* **faire un ~ à** to go on a pilgrimage to.

pèlerine [pɛlʀin] *nf* cape.

pélican [pelikɑ̃] *nm* pelican.

pelisse [pəlis] *nf* pelisse.

pelle [pɛl] **1** *nf* (*gén*) shovel; *[enfant, terrassier]* spade. (*fig*) **on en ramasse** *ou* **il y en a à la ~** there are loads of them *; (*fig*) **avoir de l'argent** *ou* **remuer l'argent à la ~** to have pots* *ou* loads* of money, be rolling (in money)*; **ramasser** *ou* **prendre une ~‡** to fall flat on one's back *ou* face.

2: pelle à charbon coal shovel; **pelle mécanique** mechanical shovel *ou* digger; **pelle à ordures** dustpan; **pelle à tarte** cake *ou* pie server.

pelletée [pɛlte] *nf* (*V* **pelle**) shovelful; spadeful.

pelleter [pɛlte] (4) *vt* to shovel (up).

pelleterie [pɛltʀi] *nf* (*commerce*) fur trade, furriery; (*préparation*) fur dressing; (*peau*) pelt.

pelleteuse [pɛltøz] *nf* mechanical shovel *ou* digger.

pelletier, -ière [pɛltje, jɛʀ] *nm,f* furrier.

pellicule [pelikyl] *nf* (*couche fine*) film, thin layer; (*Phot*) film. (*Méd*) **~s** dandruff (*U*); **lotion contre les ~s** dandruff lotion.

Péloponnèse [pelɔpɔnɛz] *nm*: **le ~** the Peloponnese.

pelotage* [p(ə)lɔtaʒ] *nm* petting* (*U*).

pelote [p(ə)lɔt] *nf* **(a)** *[laine]* ball; *[épingles]* pin cushion. (*fig*) **faire sa ~** to feather one's nest, make one's pile*; *V* **nerf. (b)** (*Sport*) **~ (basque)** pelota.

peloter [p(ə)lɔte] (1) *vt* **(a)** (*: *caresser*) to pet*, paw*; (*fig: flatter*) to fawn on, suck up to*. **arrêtez de me ~!** stop pawing me!*, keep your hands to yourself!; **ils se pelotaient** they were petting* *ou* necking*.

(b) (†) *laine* to wind into a ball.

peloteur, -euse [p(ə)lɔtœʀ, øz] **1** *adj* **(a)** (*vicieux*) **il a des gestes ~s** *ou* **des manières ~euses** he can't keep his hands to himself.

(b) (*flatteur*) fawning.

2 *nm* (*) **(a)** (*vicieux*) dirty old man*. **c'est un ~** he can't keep his hands to himself.

(b) (*flatteur*) fawner.

peloton [p(ə)lɔtɔ̃] **1** *nm* **(a)** *[laine]* small ball.

(b) (*groupe*) cluster, group; *[pompiers]* squad; (*Mil*) platoon; (*Sport*) pack, main body of runners *ou* riders *etc.*

2: peloton d'exécution firing squad; (*Sport*) **peloton de tête** leaders, leading runners *ou* riders *etc*; **être dans le peloton de tête** (*Sport*) to be up with the leaders; (*en classe*) to be among the top few.

pelotonner [p(ə)lɔtɔne] (1) **1** *vt laine* to wind into a ball. **2 se pelotonner** *vpr* to curl (o.s.) up. **se ~ contre qn** to snuggle up to sb, nestle close to sb.

pelouse [p(ə)luz] *nf* lawn; (*Courses*) *area for spectators inside racetrack*; (*Ftbl, Rugby*) field, ground.

peluche [p(ə)lyʃ] *nf* (*Tex*) plush; (*poil*) fluff (*U*), bit of fluff. **jouets en ~** soft toys; **chien/lapin en ~** fluffy dog/rabbit; *V* **ours.**

pelucher [p(ə)lyʃe] (1) *vi* (*par l'aspect*) to become *ou* go fluffy; (*perdre des poils*) to leave fluff.

pelucheux, -euse [p(ə)lyʃø, øz] *adj* fluffy.

pelure [p(ə)lyʀ] *nf* (*épluchure*) peel (*U*), peeling, piece of peel; (‡: *manteau*) (over)coat. (*Bot*) **~ d'oignon** onion skin; *V* **papier.**

pelvien, -enne [pɛlvjɛ̃, ɛn] *adj* pelvic.

pelvis [pɛlvis] *nm* pelvis.

pénal, e, *mpl* **-aux** [penal, o] *adj* penal; *V* **clause.**

pénalisation [penalizasjɔ̃] *nf* (*Sport*) penalty. **points de ~** penalty points.

pénaliser [penalize] (1) *vt contrevenant, faute, joueur* to penalize.

pénalité [penalite] *nf* (*Fin, Sport: sanction*) penalty.

penalty [penalti], *pl* **penalties** [penaltiz] *nm* (*Ftbl*) penalty (kick). **siffler le** *ou* **un ~** to award a penalty.

pénard, e [penaʀ, aʀd(ə)] *adj* = **peinard.**

pénardement [penaʀdəmɑ̃] *adv* = **peinardement.**

pénates [penat] *nmpl* (*Myth*) Penates; (*fig hum*) home. **regagner ses ~** to go back home.

penaud, e [pəno, od] *adj* sheepish, contrite. **d'un air ~** sheepishly, contritely.

penchant [pɑ̃ʃɑ̃] *nm* (*tendance*) tendency, propensity (*à faire* to do); (*faible*) liking, fondness (*pour qch* for sth). **avoir un ~ à faire qch** to be inclined *ou* have a tendency to do sth; **avoir un ~ pour qch** to be fond of *ou* have a liking *ou* fondness for sth; **avoir un ~ pour la boisson** to be partial to drink; (*littér*) **avoir du ~ pour qn** to be in love with sb; **mauvais ~s** baser instincts.

penché, e [pɑ̃ʃe] (*ptp de* **pencher**) *adj tableau* slanting, tilted, lop-sided; *mur, poteau* slanting, leaning over (*attrib*); *objet déséquilibré* tilting, tipping; *écriture* sloping, slanting. *[personne]* **être ~ sur ses livres** to be bent over one's books.

pencher [pɑ̃ʃe] (1) **1** *vt meuble, bouteille* to tip up, tilt. **~ son assiette** to tip one's plate up; **~ la tête** (*en avant*) to bend one's head forward; (*sur le côté*) to lean *ou* tilt one's head to one side.

2 *vi* **(a)** (*être incliné*) *[mur]* to lean over, tilt, be slanting; *[arbre]* to tilt, lean over; *[navire]* to list; *[objet en déséquilibre]* to tilt, tip (to one side). **le tableau penche un peu de ce côté** the picture is slanting *ou* tilting a bit this way; (*fig*) **faire ~ la balance** to tip the scales.

(b) (*être porté à*) **je penche pour la première hypothèse** I'm inclined to favour the first hypothesis; **je penche à croire qu'il est sincère** I'm inclined to believe he is sincere.

3 se pencher *vpr* **(a)** (*s'incliner*) to lean over; (*se baisser*) to bend down. **se ~ en avant** to lean forward; **se ~ par-dessus bord** to lean overboard; **se ~ sur un livre** to bend *ou* be bent over a book; **défense de se ~ (au dehors** *ou* **par la fenêtre)** do not lean out, do not lean out of the window.

(b) (*examiner*) **se ~ sur un problème/cas** to study *ou* look into a problem/case; **se ~ sur les malheurs de qn** to turn one's attention to sb's misfortunes.

pendable [pɑ̃dabl(ə)] *adj V* **cas, tour**[2].

pendaison [pɑ̃dɛzɔ̃] *nf* hanging. **~ de crémaillère** house warming, house-warming party.

pendant[1]**, e** [pɑ̃dɑ̃, ɑ̃t] *adj* **(a)** (*qui pend*) *bras, jambes* hanging, dangling; *langue* hanging out (*attrib*); *oreilles* drooping; (*Jur*) *fruits* on the tree (*attrib*). **ne reste pas là les bras ~s** don't just stand there (with your arms at your sides); **assis sur le mur les jambes ~es** sitting on the wall with his legs hanging down; **le chien haletait la langue ~e** the dog was panting with its tongue hanging out; **chien aux oreilles ~es** dog with drooping ears; **les branches ~es du saule** the hanging *ou* drooping branches of the willow.

(b) (*Admin: en instance*) *question* outstanding, in abeyance (*attrib*); *affaire* pending (*attrib*); (*Jur*) *procès* pending (*attrib*).

pendant[2] [pɑ̃dɑ̃] *nm* **(a)** (*objet*) **~ (d'oreille)** drop earring, pendant earring; **~ d'épée** frog.

(b) (*contrepartie*) **le ~ de** *œuvre d'art, meuble* the matching piece to; *personne, institution* the counterpart of; **faire ~ à** to match, be matched by; to be the counterpart of, parallel; **se faire ~** to match; to be counterparts, parallel each other; **j'ai un chandelier et je cherche le ~** I've got a candlestick and I'm looking for one to match it *ou* and I'm trying to make up a pair.

pendant[3] [pɑ̃dɑ̃] **1** *prép* (*au cours de*) during; (*indique la durée*) for. ~ **la journée/son séjour** during the day/his stay; ~ **ce temps Paul attendait** during this time *ou* meanwhile Paul was waiting; **qu'est-ce qu'il faisait ~ ce temps-là?** what was he doing during that time? *ou* meanwhile? *ou* in the meantime?; **on a marché ~ des kilomètres** we walked for miles; **il a vécu en France ~ plusieurs années** he lived in France for several years; ~ **quelques mois, il n'a pas pu travailler** for several months he was unable to work; **on est resté sans nouvelles de lui ~ longtemps** we had no news from him for a long time; ~ **un moment on a cru qu'il ne reviendrait pas** for a while we thought he would not return; **avant la guerre et ~, il ...** before and during the war, he ... , before the war and while it was on*, he ... ; **il n'a pas fait ses devoirs après les cours, mais ~!** he didn't do his homework after school but in class!

2: ~ **que** *conj* while, whilst (*frm*); ~ **qu'elle se reposait, il écoutait la radio** while she was resting he would listen to the radio; ~ **que vous serez à Paris, pourriez-vous aller le voir?** while you're in Paris could you go and see him?; ~ **que j'y pense, n'oubliez pas de fermer la porte à clef** while I think of it, don't forget to lock the door; **arrosez le jardin et ~ que vous y êtes, arrachez les mauvaises herbes** water the garden and do some weeding while you're at it; (*iro*) **finissez le plat ~ que vous y êtes** why don't you eat it all (up) while you're at it (*iro*); **dire que des gens doivent suivre un régime pour maigrir ~ que des enfants meurent de faim** to think that some people have to go on diets to lose weight while there are children dying of hunger.

pendard, e [pɑ̃daʀ, aʀd(ə)] *nm,f* (††, *hum*) scoundrel.

pendeloque [pɑ̃dlɔk] *nf* [*boucle d'oreille*] pendant; [*lustre*] lustre, pendant.

pendentif [pɑ̃dɑ̃tif] *nm* (*bijou*) pendant; (*Archit*) pendentive.

penderie [pɑ̃dʀi] *nf* (*meuble*) wardrobe (*only for hanging things up*); (*débarras*) walk-in cupboard (*Brit*) *ou* closet (*US*); **le placard du couloir nous sert de ~** we hang our things in the hall cupboard (*Brit*) *ou* closet (*US*).

pendiller [pɑ̃dije] (1) *vi* to flap about.

pendouiller* [pɑ̃duje] (1) *vi* to dangle (about *ou* down), hang down.

pendre [pɑ̃dʀ(ə)] (41) **1** *vt* **(a)** *rideau* to hang, put up (*à* at); *tableau, manteau* to hang (up) (*à* on); *lustre* to hang (up) (*à* from). ~ **le linge pour le faire sécher** (*dans la maison*) to hang up the washing to dry; (*dehors*) to hang out the washing to dry; ~ **la crémaillère** to have a house-warming party *ou* a house warming.

(b) *criminel* to hang. (*Hist*) ~ **qn haut et court** to hang sb; ~ **qn en effigie** to hang sb in effigy; **qu'il aille se faire ~ ailleurs!*** let him go hang!*, he can take a running jump!*; **je veux être pendu si ...** I'll be hanged if ... ; **dussé-je être pendu** over my dead body; *V* **pis**[2].

2 *vi* **(a)** (*être suspendu*) to hang (down). **des fruits pendaient aux branches** there was fruit hanging from the branches; **cela lui pend au nez*** he's got it coming to him*, that's what he's in for*.

(b) (*fig*) [*bras, jambes*] to dangle; [*joue*] to sag; [*robe, cheveux*] to hang down. **un lambeau de papier pendait** a strip of wallpaper was hanging off; **laisser ~ ses jambes** to dangle one's legs.

3 se pendre *vpr* **(a)** (*se tuer*) to hang o.s.

(b) (*se suspendre*) **se ~ à une branche** to hang from a branch; **se ~ au cou de qn** to throw one's arms round sb *ou* sb's neck.

pendu, e [pɑ̃dy] (*ptp de* **pendre**) **1** *adj* **(a)** *chose* hung up, hanging up. ~ **à** hanging from; *V* **langue.**

(b) *personne* hanged. **être toujours ~ aux basques de qn** to keep pestering sb; **il est toujours ~ aux jupes de sa mère** he's always clinging to his mother's skirts; ~ **au bras de qn** holding on to sb's arm; **être ~ au téléphone*** to spend all one's time on the telephone; **être ~ aux lèvres de qn** to drink in sb's words, hang on sb's every word.

2 *nm,f* hanged man (*ou* woman).

pendulaire [pɑ̃dylɛʀ] *adj* pendular.

pendule [pɑ̃dyl] **1** *nf* clock. ~ **à coucou** cuckoo clock. **2** *nm* pendulum.

pendulette [pɑ̃dylɛt] *nf* small clock. ~ **de voyage** travelling clock.

pêne [pɛn] *nm* bolt (*of lock*).

Pénélope [penelɔp] *nf* Penelope.

pénéplaine [peneplɛn] *nf* peneplain.

pénétrabilité [penetʀabilite] *nf* penetrability.

pénétrable [penetʀabl(ə)] *adj matière* penetrable (*à* by); (*fig*) *mystère, mobile* penetrable, understandable (*à* by). **peu** *ou* **difficilement ~** difficult to penetrate; (*fig*) impenetrable, enigmatic.

pénétrant, e [penetʀɑ̃, ɑ̃t] *adj* **(a)** (*lit*) *pluie* drenching, that soaks right through you; *froid* piercing, biting, bitter; *odeur* penetrating, pervasive.

(b) (*fig*) *regard* penetrating, searching, piercing; *esprit* penetrating, keen, shrewd; *analyse, remarque* penetrating, shrewd; *personne* shrewd.

pénétration [penetʀasjɔ̃] *nf* **(a)** (*action*) penetration. (*Mil*) **force de ~** force of penetration; **la ~ des mobiles/pensées d'autrui** the divination of others' motives/thoughts. **(b)** (*sagacité*) penetration, perception.

pénétré, e [penetʀe] (*ptp de* **pénétrer**) *adj* **(a)** (*convaincu*) **être ~ de: être ~ de son importance** *ou* **de soi-même** to be full of one's own importance; **être ~ de ses obligations/de la nécessité de faire** to be (fully) alive to *ou* highly conscious of one's obligations/of the need to do.

(b) (*sérieux*) *air, ton* earnest, of deep conviction.

pénétrer [penetʀe] (6) **1** *vi* **(a)** [*personne, véhicule*] ~ **dans** *pièce, bâtiment, pays* to enter; (*fig*) *groupe, milieu* to penetrate; **personne ne doit ~ ici** nobody must be allowed to enter; ~ **chez qn par la force** to force an entry *ou* one's way into sb's home; **les envahisseurs/les troupes ont pénétré dans le pays** the invaders/the troops have entered the country; **il est difficile de ~ dans les milieux de la finance** it is hard to penetrate financial circles; **faire ~ qn dans le salon** to show *ou* let sb into the lounge; **des voleurs ont pénétré dans la maison en son absence** thieves broke into his house while he was away; **l'habitude n'a pas encore pénétré dans les mœurs** the habit hasn't established itself yet *ou* made its way into general behaviour yet; **faire ~ une idée dans la tête de qn** to instil an idea in sb.

(b) [*soleil*] to shine *ou* come in; [*vent*] to blow *ou* come in; [*air, liquide, insecte*] to come *ou* get in. ~ **dans** to shine into; to come into; to blow into; to get into; **la lumière pénétrait dans la cellule (par une lucarne)** light came into *ou* entered the cell (through a skylight); **le liquide pénètre à travers une membrane** the liquid comes through a membrane; **la fumée/l'odeur pénètre par tous les interstices** the smoke/the smell comes *ou* gets in through all the gaps; **faire ~ de l'air (dans)** to let fresh air in(to).

(c) (*en s'enfonçant*) ~ **dans** [*balle, verre*] to penetrate; [*idée, habitude*] to make its way into; [*huile, encre*] to soak into; **ce vernis pénètre dans le bois** this varnish soaks (down) into the wood; **faire ~ une crème (dans la peau)** to rub a cream in(to the skin).

2 *vt* **(a)** (*percer*) [*froid, air*] to penetrate; [*odeur*] to spread through, fill; [*liquide*] to penetrate, soak through; [*regard*] to penetrate, go through. **le froid les pénétrait jusqu'aux os** the cold cut *ou* went right through them.

(b) (*découvrir*) *secret* to penetrate; *intentions, idées, plans* to penetrate, fathom, perceive. **il est difficile à ~** it is difficult to fathom him.

(c) (*fig*) **son sang-froid me pénètre d'admiration** his composure fills me with admiration; **il se sentait pénétré de pitié/d'effroi** he was filled with pity/fright; **le remords pénétra sa conscience** he was filled with remorse, he was conscience-stricken.

3 se pénétrer *vpr* **(a) se ~ d'une idée** to get an idea firmly set in one's mind; **s'étant pénétré de l'importance de qch** firmly convinced of *ou* with a clear realization of the importance of sth; **il faut bien vous ~ du fait que ...** you must be utterly clear in your mind that *ou* have it firmly in your mind that ... ; **j'ai du mal à me ~ de l'utilité de cette mesure** I find it difficult to convince myself of the usefulness of this measure.

(b) (*s'imbiber*) **se ~ d'eau/de gaz** to become permeated with water/gas.

pénible [penibl(ə)] *adj* **(a)** (*fatigant, difficile*) *travail, voyage, ascension* hard, tiresome, tedious; *personne* tiresome. ~ **à lire/supporter** hard *ou* difficult to read/bear; **les derniers kilomètres ont été ~s (à parcourir)** the last few kilometres were heavy going *ou* hard going; **l'hiver a été ~** the winter has been unpleasant; **tout effort lui est ~** any effort is difficult for him, he finds it hard to make the slightest effort; **il est vraiment ~*** [*enfant*] he's a real nuisance; [*personne*] he's a real pain in the neck*.

(b) (*douloureux*) *sujet, séparation, moment, maladie* painful (*à* to); *nouvelle, spectacle* sad, painful; *respiration* laboured. **la lumière violente lui est ~** bright light hurts his eyes, he finds bright light painful (to his eyes); **il m'est ~ de constater/d'avoir à vous dire que** I am sorry to find/to have to tell you that.

péniblement [penibləmɑ̃] *adv* (*difficilement*) with difficulty; (*tristement*) painfully; (*tout juste*) just about, only just.

péniche [peniʃ] *nf* barge. (*Mil*) ~ **de débarquement** landing craft.

pénicilline [penisilin] *nf* penicillin.

péninsulaire [penɛ̃sylɛʀ] *adj* peninsular.

péninsule [penɛ̃syl] *nf* peninsula. **la ~ Ibérique** the Iberian peninsula.

pénis [penis] *nm* penis.

pénitence [penitɑ̃s] *nf* **(a)** (*Rel*) (*repentir*) penitence; (*peine, sacrement*) penance. **faire ~** to repent (*de* of); **pour votre ~** as a penance.

(b) (*gén, Scol: châtiment*) punishment. **infliger une ~ à qn** to punish sb; **mettre qn en ~** to make sb stand in the corner; **pour ta ~** as a punishment (to you).

(c) [*jeux*] forfeit.

pénitencier [penitɑ̃sje] *nm* (*Jur, Rel*) penitentiary.

pénitent, e [penitɑ̃, ɑ̃t] *adj, nm,f* penitent.

pénitentiaire [penitɑ̃sjɛʀ] *adj* penitentiary, prison (*épith*).

Pennsylvanie [pɛnsilvani] *nf* Pennsylvania.

pénombre [penɔ̃bʀ(ə)] *nf* (*faible clarté*) half-light, shadowy light; (*obscurité*) darkness; (*Astron*) penumbra. (*fig*) **demeurer dans la ~** to stay in the background.

pensant, e [pɑ̃sɑ̃, ɑ̃t] *adj* thinking; *V* **bien, mal.**

pense-bête, *pl* **pense-bêtes** [pɑ̃sbɛt] *nm* aide-mémoire, crib*.

pensée[1] [pɑ̃se] *nf* **(a)** (*ce que l'on pense*) thought. **sans déguiser sa ~** without hiding one's thoughts *ou* feelings; **je l'ai fait dans la seule ~ de vous être utile** I only did it thinking it would help you, my only thought in doing it was to help you; **recevez mes plus affectueuses ~s** with fondest love; **saisir/deviner les ~s de qn** to grasp/guess sb's thoughts *ou* what sb is thinking (about); **si vous voulez connaître le fond de ma ~** if you want to know what I really think (about it) *ou* how I really feel about it; **à la ~ de faire qch** at the thought of doing sth; **à la ~ que ...** to think that ..., when one thinks that ... .

(b) (*faculté, fait de penser*) thought. **la dignité de l'homme est dans la ~** human dignity lies in man's capacity for thought; (*littér*) **arrêter sa ~ sur qch** to pause to think about sth.

(c) (*manière de penser*) thinking. ~ **claire/obscure** clear/muddled thinking.
(d) (*esprit*) thought, mind. **venir à la ~ de qn** to occur to sb; **se représenter qch par la ~ ou en ~** to imagine sth in one's mind, conjure up a mental picture of sth; **les soucis qui hantent sa ~** the worries that haunt his thoughts *ou* his mind.
(e) (*doctrine*) thought, thinking. **la ~ marxiste** Marxist thinking; **la ~ de Gandhi** the thought of Gandhi; **la ~ de cet auteur est difficile à comprendre** it is difficult to understand what this author is trying to say.
(f) (*maxime*) thought. **les ~s de Pascal** the thoughts of Pascal.
pensée[2] [pɑ̃se] *nf* (*Bot*) pansy.
penser [pɑ̃se] (1) **1** *vi* **(a)** (*réfléchir*) to think. **façon de ~** way of thinking; **une nouvelle qui donne** *ou* **laisse à ~** a piece of news which makes you (stop and) think *ou* which gives (you) food for thought.
(b) ~ **à** (*songer à*) *ami* to think of *ou* about; (*réfléchir à*) *problème, offre* to think about *ou* over, turn over in one's mind; **pensez donc à ce que vous dites** just think about what you're saying; ~ **aux autres/aux malheureux** to think of others/of those who are unhappy; **faire ~ à** to make one think of, remind one of; **cette mélodie fait ~ à Debussy** this tune reminds you of Debussy; **il ne pense qu'à jouer** playing is all he ever thinks about; **pensez-y avant d'accepter** think it over *ou* give it some thought before you accept; (*fig*) **il ne pense qu'à ça*** he's got a one-track mind*; **fais m'y ~** don't let me forget, remind me about that; **faire/dire qch sans y ~** to do/say sth without thinking about it.
(c) ~ **à** (*prévoir*) to think of; (*se souvenir de*) to remember; **il pense à tout** he thinks of everything; ~ **à l'avenir/aux conséquences** to think of the future/of the consequences; **a-t-il pensé à rapporter du pain?** did he think of bringing *ou* did he remember to bring some bread?; **pense à l'anniversaire de ta mère** remember *ou* don't forget your mother's birthday; **il suffisait d'y ~** it was just a matter of thinking of it; **sans ~ à mal** without meaning any harm; **voyons, pense un peu au danger!** just think of *ou* consider the danger!
(d) (*loc excl*) **il vient? — penses-tu! ou pensez-vous!** is he coming? — is he heck!: *ou* you must be joking!*; **tu penses! ou vous pensez! je le connais trop bien pour le croire** not likely!* I know him too well to believe him; **il va accepter? — je pense bien!** will he accept? — of course he will! *ou* I should hope so!
2 *vt* **(a)** (*avoir une opinion*) to think (*de* of, about). ~ **du bien/du mal de qch/qn** to have a high/poor opinion of sth/sb, think highly/not think much of sth/sb; **que pense-t-il du film?** what does he think of the film?; **que pensez-vous de ce projet?** what do you think *ou* how do you feel about this plan?; **il est difficile de savoir ce qu'il pense** it's difficult to know what he's thinking *ou* what's in his mind; **que penseriez-vous d'un voyage à Rome?** what would you say to *ou* how would you fancy *ou* how about a trip to Rome?
(b) (*supposer*) to think, suppose, believe; (*imaginer*) to think, expect, imagine. **il n'aurait jamais pensé qu'elle ferait cela** he would never have thought *ou* imagined *ou* dreamt she would do that, he would never have expected her to do that; **quand on lui dit musique, il pense ennui** when you mention the word music to him it just spells boredom to him *ou* his only thought is that it's boring; **je pense que non** I don't think so; **je pense que oui** I think so; **ce n'est pas si bête qu'on le pense** it's not such a silly idea as you might think *ou* suppose; **pensez-vous qu'il vienne? ou viendra?** do you think he'll come?, are you expecting him to come?; **je vous laisse à ~ s'il était content** you can imagine how pleased he was; **ils pensent avoir trouvé une maison** they think *ou* believe they've found a house; **c'est bien ce que je pensais!** I thought as much!, just as *ou* what I thought!; **vous pensez bien qu'elle a refusé** you can well imagine (that) she refused, as you may well expect, she refused; **j'ai pensé mourir/m'évanouir** I thought I was going to die/faint.
(c) ~ **faire** (*avoir l'intention de*) to be thinking of doing, consider doing; (*espérer*) to hope *ou* expect to do; **il pense partir jeudi** he's thinking of going *ou* he intends to leave on Thursday; **il pense arriver demain** he's hoping *ou* expecting to arrive tomorrow.
(d) (*concevoir*) *problème, projet, machine* to think out. **c'est bien/fortement pensé** it's well/very well thought out.
3 *nm* (*littér*) thought.
penseur [pɑ̃sœʀ] *nm* thinker; *V* **libre**.
pensif, -ive [pɑ̃sif, iv] *adj* pensive, thoughtful.
pension [pɑ̃sjɔ̃] **1** *nf* **(a)** (*allocation*) pension. ~ **de guerre/de retraite** war/retirement *ou* old age pension; ~ **d'invalidité** disablement pension; **toucher sa ~** to draw one's pension.
(b) (*hôtel*) boarding house.
(c) (*Scol*) (boarding) school. **mettre qn en ~** to send sb to boarding school.
(d) (*hébergement*) board and lodgings, bed and board. **la ~ coûte 80 F par jour** board and lodging is 80 francs a day; **être en ~ chez qn** to board with sb *ou* at sb's, be in digs* at sb's; **prendre ~ chez qn** to take board and lodgings at sb's; **prendre qn en ~** to take sb (in) as a lodger, board sb; **chambre sans ~** room (*with no meals provided*); **chambre avec demi-~** room with breakfast and dinner provided; **chambre avec ~ complète** full board; (*Scol*) **être en demi-~** to be a day boarder, be a day boy *ou* girl.
2: **pension alimentaire** *[étudiant]* living allowance; *[divorcée]* maintenance allowance, alimony; **pension de famille** ≈ boarding house, guesthouse.
pensionnaire [pɑ̃sjɔnɛʀ] *nmf* (*Scol*) boarder; *[famille]* lodger; *[hôtel]* resident; *[sanatorium]* patient; *V* **demi-**.
pensionnat [pɑ̃sjɔna] *nm* (boarding) school.
pensionné, e [pɑ̃sjɔne] (*ptp de* **pensionner**) **1** *adj* who gets *ou* draws a pension. **2** *nm,f* pensioner.
pensionner [pɑ̃sjɔne] (1) *vt* to give a pension to.
pensivement [pɑ̃sivmɑ̃] *adv* pensively, thoughtfully.
pensum [pɑ̃sɔm] *nm* (*Scol*†) imposition; (*fig*) chore.
pentaèdre [pɛ̃taɛdʀ(ə)] **1** *nm* pentahedron. **2** *adj* pentahedral.
pentagonal, e, *mpl* **-aux** [pɛ̃tagɔnal, o] *adj* pentagonal.
pentagone [pɛ̃tagɔn] **1** *nm* pentagon. **2** *adj* pentagonal.
pentamètre [pɛ̃tamɛtʀ(ə)] *adj, nm* pentameter.
Pentateuque [pɛ̃tatøk] *nm* Pentateuch.
pentathlon [pɛ̃tatlɔ̃] *nm* pentathlon.
pente [pɑ̃t] *nf* (*gén*) slope. **être en ~ douce/raide** to slope (down) gently/steeply; **en ~** *toit* sloping; *allée, pelouse* on a slope (*attrib*); **de petites rues en ~** steep little streets; **garé dans une rue en ~** parked on a slope; (*fig*) **être sur une mauvaise ~** to be going downhill, be on a downward path; (*fig*) **remonter la ~** to get on one's feet again, fight one's way back again; (*fig*) **être sur une ~ glissante** to be on a slippery slope (*fig*); *V* **dalle, rupture**.
Pentecôte [pɑ̃tkot] *nf* **(a)** (*Rel: dimanche*) Whit Sunday, Pentecost; (*gén: période*) Whit(suntide), Whitsun. **lundi de ~** Whit Monday. **(b)** (*fête juive*) Pentecost.
pénultième [penyltjɛm] **1** *adj* penultimate. **2** *nf* penultimate (syllable).
pénurie [penyʀi] *nf* shortage. ~ **de** shortage *ou* lack of; ~ **de main-d'œuvre/sucre** labour/sugar shortage; **on ne peut guère qu'organiser la ~** we must just make the best of a bad job* *ou* the best of what we've got.
pépé* [pepe] *nm* grandad*, grandpa*.
pépée: [pepe] *nf* (*fille*) bird: (*Brit*), chick:.
pépère* [pepɛʀ] **1** *nm* **(a)** (*pépé*) grandad*, grandpa*.
(b) **un gros ~** (*enfant*) a bonny (*surtout Brit*) child; (*homme*) an old fatty*; **un petit ~ à vélo** a little (old) man on a bike.
2 *adj* **(a)** (*tranquille*) quiet, cosy. **un petit coin ~** a nice quiet spot.
(b) (*peinard*) *vie* quiet, uneventful; (*Aut*) *conduite* pottering, dawdling; *travail* cushy*.
pépettes: [pepɛt] *nfpl* dough:, lolly:.
pépie [pepi] *nf* (*Orn*) pip. (*fig*) **avoir la ~** to have a terrible thirst, be parched.
pépiement [pepimɑ̃] *nm* chirping (*U*), chirruping (*U*), tweeting (*U*).
pépier [pepje] (7) *vi* to chirp, chirrup, tweet.
pépin [pepɛ̃] *nm* **(a)** (*Bot*) pip. **sans ~s** seedless. **(b)** (** fig: ennui*) snag, hitch. **avoir un ~** to hit a snag*, have a spot of bother. **(c)** (*: *parapluie*) brolly*.
pépinière [pepinjɛʀ] *nf* (*lit*) tree nursery; (*fig*) nest, breeding-ground.
pépiniériste [pepinjeʀist(ə)] *nm* nurseryman.
pépite [pepit] *nf* nugget.
péplum [peplɔm] *nm* peplos.
pepsine [pɛpsin] *nf* pepsin.
peptique [pɛptik] *adj* peptic.
péquenaud, e: [pɛkno, od] **1** *adj* peasant (*épith*). **2** *nm,f* country bumpkin.
pequenot [pɛkno] *adj, nm* = **péquenaud**.
péquiste [pekist(ə)] (*Québec*) **1** *adj* of the Parti Québécois. **2** *nmf* member of the Parti Québécois.
perçage [pɛʀsaʒ] *nm [trou]* boring, drilling; *[matériau]* boring through.
percale [pɛʀkal] *nf* percale, percaline.
perçant, e [pɛʀsɑ̃, ɑ̃t] *adj cri, voix* piercing, shrill; *froid* piercing, biting, bitter; *vue* sharp, keen; (*fig*) *regard* piercing; *esprit* penetrating.
perce [pɛʀs(ə)] *nf*: **mettre en ~** *tonneau, vin* to broach, tap.
perce- [pɛʀs(ə)] *préf V* **percer**.
percée [pɛʀse] *nf* (*dans une forêt*) opening, clearing; (*dans un mur*) breach, gap; (*Mil, Sci*) breakthrough; (*Rugby*) break.
percement [pɛʀsəmɑ̃] *nm [trou]* piercing; drilling, boring; *[rue, tunnel]* building, driving; *[fenêtre]* making.
percepteur, -trice [pɛʀsɛptœʀ, tʀis] **1** *adj* perceptive, of perception. **2** *nm* tax collector, tax man*.
perceptibilité [pɛʀsɛptibilite] *nf* perceptibility.
perceptible [pɛʀsɛptibl(ə)] *adj* **(a)** *son, ironie* perceptible (*à* to). **(b)** *impôt* collectable, payable.
perceptiblement [pɛʀsɛptibləmɑ̃] *adv* perceptibly.
perceptif, -ive [pɛʀsɛptif, iv] *adj* perceptive.
perception [pɛʀsɛpsjɔ̃] *nf* **(a)** (*sensation*) perception. **(b)** *[impôt, amende, péage]* collection; (*bureau*) tax (collector's) office.
percer [pɛʀse] (3) **1** *vt* **(a)** (*gén: perforer*) to pierce, make a hole in; (*avec perceuse*) to drill *ou* bore (a hole) through *ou* in; *lobe d'oreille* to pierce; *chaussette, chaussure* to wear a hole in; *coffre-fort* to break open, crack*; *tonneau* to broach, tap; (*Méd*) *abcès* to lance, burst; *tympan* to burst. **avoir une poche/une chaussure percée** to have a hole in one's pocket/shoe; **percé de trous** full of holes, riddled with holes; **il a eu le bras percé par une balle** his arm was pierced by a bullet; **la rouille avait percé le métal** rust had eaten into the metal; **on a retrouvé son corps percé de coups de couteau** his body was found full of stab wounds; *V* **chaise, panier**.
(b) *fenêtre, ouverture* to make; *canal* to build; *tunnel* to build, bore, drive (*dans* through). ~ **un trou dans** to pierce *ou* make a hole in; (*avec perceuse*) to drill *ou* bore a hole through *ou* in; **ils ont percé une nouvelle route à travers la forêt** they have driven *ou* built a new road through the forest; ~ **une porte dans un mur** to make *ou* open a doorway in a wall; **mur percé de petites fenêtres** wall with (a number of) small windows set in it.
(c) (*fig: traverser*) ~ **l'air/le silence** to pierce the air/the silence; ~ **les nuages/le front ennemi** to break through the clouds/the enemy lines; ~ **la foule** to force *ou* elbow one's way

through the crowd; **bruit qui perce les oreilles** ear-piercing *ou* ear-splitting noise; **~ qn du regard** to give sb a piercing look; **ses yeux essayaient de ~ l'obscurité** he tried to peer through the darkness; **cela m'a percé le cœur** it cut me to the heart.

(d) (*découvrir*) *mystère* to penetrate; *complot* to uncover. **~ qch à jour** to see (right) through sth.

(e) ~ des *ou* ses dents to be teething, cut one's teeth; **il a percé 2 dents** he has cut 2 teeth, he has got 2 teeth through.

2 *vi* **(a)** *[abcès]* to burst; *[plante]* to come up; *[soleil]* to come out, break through; (*Mil*) to break through; (*Sport*) to make a break. **il a une dent qui perce** he's cutting a tooth.

(b) *[sentiment, émotion]* to show; *[nouvelle]* to filter through *ou* out. **rien n'a percé des négociations** no news of the negotiations has filtered through; **il ne laisse jamais ~ ses sentiments** he never lets his feelings show.

(c) (*réussir, acquérir la notoriété*) to make a name for o.s., become famous.

3: perce-neige *nm inv* snowdrop; **perce-oreille** *nm, pl* **perce-oreilles** earwig.

perceur [pɛʀsœʀ] *nm* driller. **~ de muraille*** burglar; **~ de coffre-fort*** safe-breaker.

perceuse [pɛʀsøz] *nf* drill.

percevable [pɛʀsəvabl(ə)] *adj impôt* collectable, payable.

percevoir [pɛʀsəvwaʀ] (28) *vt* **(a)** (*ressentir*) to perceive, detect, sense, make out. **(b)** (*faire payer*) *taxe, loyer* to collect; (*recevoir*) *indemnité* to receive, be paid, get.

perche¹ [pɛʀʃ(ə)] *nf* (*poisson*) perch.

perche² [pɛʀʃ(ə)] *nf* **(a)** (*gén*) pole; *[tuteur]* stick; (*Ciné, Rad, TV*) boom; *V* **saut, tendre¹**. **(b)** (**: personne*) **(grande) ~** beanpole*.

percher [pɛʀʃe] (1) **1** *vi [oiseau]* to perch; *[volailles]* to roost; (‡) *[personne]* to live, hang out‡; (*pour la nuit*) to stay, kip*; *V* **chat**.

2 *vt* to stick*. **~ qch sur une armoire** to stick* sth up on top of a cupboard; **village perché sur la montagne** village set high up in the mountains.

3 se percher *vpr [oiseau]* to perch; (**: se jucher*) to perch.

percheron, -onne [pɛʀʃəʀɔ̃, ɔn] **1** *adj* of *ou* from the Perche. **2** *nm,f*: **P~(ne)** inhabitant *ou* native of the Perche.

perchiste [pɛʀʃist(ə)] *nmf* (*Sport*) pole vaulter; (*Ciné, Rad, TV*) boom operator.

perchoir [pɛʀʃwaʀ] *nm* (*lit, fig*) perch; *[volailles]* roost.

perclus, e [pɛʀkly, yz] *adj* (*paralysé*) crippled, paralyzed (*de* with); (*ankylosé*) stiff; (*fig*) paralyzed.

percolateur [pɛʀkɔlatœʀ] *nm* percolator (*in café*).

perçu, e [pɛʀsy] *ptp de* **percevoir**; *V* **trop-perçu**.

percussion [pɛʀkysjɔ̃] *nf* (*Méd, Mus, Phys*) percussion. **instrument à *ou* de ~** percussion instrument.

percussionniste [pɛʀkysjɔnist(ə)] *nmf* percussionist.

percutant, e [pɛʀkytɑ̃, ɑ̃t] *adj* **(a)** (*Mil*) percussion (*épith*); (*Phys*) percussive. **(b)** (*fig*) *argument, discours* forceful, explosive.

percuter [pɛʀkyte] (1) **1** *vt* (*Mil, Phys*) to strike; (*Méd*) to percuss. **~ un arbre** *[voiture]* to smash into *ou* strike a tree. **2** *vi*: **~ contre** *[avion, voiture]* to crash into; *[obus]* to strike, thud into.

percuteur [pɛʀkytœʀ] *nm* firing pin.

perdant, e [pɛʀdɑ̃, ɑ̃t] **1** *adj numéro, cheval* losing (*épith*). **je suis ~** I'm out of pocket, I lose out*. **2** *nm,f* loser. **partir ~** to have lost before one starts.

perdition [pɛʀdisjɔ̃] *nf* **(a)** (*Rel*) perdition. **lieu de ~** den of vice *ou* iniquity. **(b)** (*Naut*) **en ~** in distress.

perdre [pɛʀdʀ(ə)] (41) **1** *vt* **(a)** *match, guerre, procès* to lose; *situation, avantage* to lose; *habitude* to lose, get out of; (*volontairement*) to break, get out of. **vous n'avez rien à ~** you've (got) nothing to lose; **il a perdu son père à la guerre** he lost his father in the war; **ce quartier est en train de ~ son cachet** this district is losing its distinctive charm; **~ qn/qch de vue** to lose sight of sb/sth; **~/ne pas ~ un ami de vue** to lose touch/keep in touch with a friend; **j'ai perdu le goût de rire/de manger** I've lost all interest in jokes and laughter/food, I don't feel like laughing/eating any longer.

(b) *objet* (*ne plus trouver*) to lose; (*égarer*) to mislay; (*oublier*) *nom, date* to forget. **~ sa page *ou* place** (*en lisant*) to lose one's place; **j'ai perdu le nom de cet auteur** I've forgotten *ou* I can't recall the name of this author.

(c) *bras, cheveux, dent* to lose. **~ du poids** to lose weight; **~ l'appétit/la mémoire/la vie** to lose one's appetite/one's memory/one's life; **il perd la vue** his sight is failing; **il a perdu le souffle** he's out of breath; **courir à ~ haleine** to run until one pants for breath *ou* is quite out of breath; **~ la parole** to lose the power of speech; **~ espoir/patience** to lose hope/(one's) patience; **~ l'esprit *ou* la raison** to go out of one's mind, take leave of one's senses; **~ connaissance** to lose consciousness, pass out; **~ courage** to lose heart, be downhearted; (*Méd*) **elle a perdu les eaux** her waters have broken; (*hum*) **as-tu perdu ta langue?** have you lost your tongue?

(d) *feuille, pétale, [animal] corne* to lose, shed. **il perd son pantalon** his trousers are falling down; **il perd sa chemise** his shirt is sticking out (of his trousers); **ce réservoir perd beaucoup d'eau** this tank leaks badly *ou* loses a lot of water.

(e) (*gaspiller*) *temps, peine, souffle, argent* to waste (*à qch* on sth); (*abîmer*) *aliments, vêtements* to spoil. **il a perdu une heure à la chercher** he wasted an hour looking for her; **vous n'avez pas une minute à ~** you haven't (got) a minute to lose; **sans ~ une minute** without wasting a minute.

(f) (*manquer*) *occasion* to lose, miss. **tu ne l'as jamais vu? tu n'y perds rien!** you've never seen him? you haven't missed anything!; **il n'a pas perdu un mot/une miette de la conversation** he didn't miss a single word/syllable of the conversation; **il ne perd rien pour attendre!** I can wait!, he won't get off lightly when I get hold of him!

(g) (*causer préjudice à*) to ruin, be the ruin of. **~ qn dans l'esprit de qn** to send sb down in sb's esteem; **son ambition l'a perdu** ambition was his downfall *ou* the ruin of him, ambition proved his undoing.

(h) (*loc fig*) **~ la boule*** to go round the bend* (*Brit*), go crazy*; **~ le fil*** to lose the thread (*of an explanation*), forget where one is up to; **~ le nord*** to panic, go to pieces; **~ les pédales** (*dans une explication*) to get all mixed-up; (*s'affoler*) to lose one's head *ou* one's grip; **j'y perds mon latin** I can't make head nor tail of it; **~ ses moyens** to crack up*; **~ pied** (*lit: en nageant, aussi fig*) to be *ou* get out of one's depth; (*en montagne*) to lose one's footing; **~ la tête** (*s'affoler*) to lose one's head; (*devenir fou*) to be off one's rocker‡, be crackers* *ou* crazy*; *V* **équilibre, face, terrain**.

2 *vi* **(a)** (*gén*) to lose. (*Comm*) **~ sur un article** to lose on an article, sell an article at a loss; **vous y perdez** you lose on *ou* by it, you lose out on it; **tu as perdu en ne venant pas** you missed something by not coming; **tu ne perds pas au change** you get the better of the deal.

(b) *[citerne, réservoir]* to leak.

3 se perdre *vpr* **(a)** (*s'égarer*) to get lost, lose one's way.

(b) (*fig*) **se ~ dans les détails/dans ses explications** to get bogged down *ou* get lost in the details/in one's explanations; **se ~ en conjectures** to become lost in conjecture; **se ~ dans ses pensées** to be lost in thought; **il y a trop de chiffres, je m'y perds** there are too many figures, I'm all confused *ou* all at sea*.

(c) (*disparaître*) to disappear, vanish; *[coutume]* to be dying out; (*Naut*) to sink, be wrecked. **se ~ dans la foule** to disappear *ou* vanish into the crowd; **son cri se perdit dans le vacarme** his shout was lost in the din *ou* was drowned by the din; **leurs silhouettes se perdirent dans la nuit** their figures vanished into the night *ou* were swallowed up by the darkness; **ce sens s'est perdu** this meaning has died out *ou* has been lost.

(d) (*devenir inutilisable*) to be wasted, go to waste; *[denrées]* to go bad. (*fig*) **il y a des gifles/des coups de pied qui se perdent** he (*ou* she *etc*) deserves to be slapped *ou* a good slap/deserves a kick in the pants*.

perdreau, *pl* **~x** [pɛʀdʀo] *nm* (young) partridge.

perdrix [pɛʀdʀi] *nf* partridge.

perdu, e [pɛʀdy] (*ptp de* **perdre**) **1** *adj* **(a)** *bataille, cause, réputation, aventurier* lost; *malade* done for (*attrib*). **je suis ~!** I'm done for!, it's all up with me!*; **quand il se vit ~** when he saw he was lost *ou* done for; **tout est ~** all is lost; **rien n'est ~** nothing's lost, there's no harm done; *V* **corps**.

(b) (*égaré*) *personne, chien, objet* lost; *balle* stray. **ce n'est pas ~ pour tout le monde** it came in handy for somebody; **une de ~e, dix de retrouvées** there are lots of good fish in the sea, there are plenty more as good as her *ou* like her; *V* **salle**.

(c) (*gaspillé*) *occasion* lost, wasted, missed; *temps* wasted. **c'était une soirée de ~e** it was a waste of an evening; **c'est de l'argent ~** it's money down the drain; **il y a trop de place ~e** there's too much space wasted; **pendant ses moments ~s, à temps ~** in his spare time; *V* **pain, peine**.

(d) (*abîmé*) *aliment* spoilt, wasted; *vêtement* ruined, spoilt. **ma récolte est ~e** my harvest is ruined.

(e) (*écarté*) *pays, endroit* out-of-the-way, isolated, miles from anywhere (*attrib*).

(f) (*non consigné*) *emballage, verre* non-returnable, no-deposit (*épith*).

(g) *personne* (*embrouillé*) lost, all at sea* (*attrib*); (*absorbé*) lost, plunged (*dans* in).

2 *nm* (††) madman. **crier/rire comme un ~** to shout/laugh like a mad thing.

père [pɛʀ] **1** *nm* **(a)** father. **marié et ~ de 3 enfants** married with 3 children *ou* and father of 3 children; **il est ~ depuis hier** he became a father yesterday; **Martin (le) ~** Martin senior; **de ~ en fils** from father to son, from one generation to the next; **ils sont bouchers de ~ en fils** they've been butchers for generations.

(b) (*pl: ancêtres*) **~s** forefathers, ancestors.

(c) (*fondateur*) father.

(d) (*Zool*) *[animal]* sire.

(e) (*Rel*) father. **le P~ X** Father X; **mon P~** Father; *V* **dieu**.

(f) (**: monsieur*) **le ~ Benoit** old (man) Benoit*; **le ~ Hugo** old Hugo*; **un gras ~** a big fat fellow* *ou* lump of a fellow*; **dis-donc, petit ~** tell me old man (*surtout Brit*) *ou* buddy*.

(g) (**: enfant*) **un brave petit ~** a fine little fellow*; **un bon gros ~** a fine chubby fellow*.

2: (*Rel*) **père abbé** abbot; (*Rel*) **le Père éternel** our Heavenly Father; (*Jur*) **père de famille** father; **tu es père de famille, ne prends pas de risques** you have a wife and family to think about *ou* you're a family man, don't take risks; **en bon père de famille, il s'occupait de l'éducation de ses enfants** as a good father should, he looked after his children's education; (*hum*) **maintenant, c'est le vrai père de famille** now he's the sober head of the family *ou* the serious family man; **le père Fouettard** Mr Bogeyman; **le père Noël** Father Christmas, Santa Claus; **père peinard, père tranquille: sous ses allures de père tranquille *ou* de père peinard, c'était en fait un redoutable malfaiteur** he seemed on the surface a genial *ou* benign sort of fellow but was in fact a fearsome criminal; *V* **placement**.

pérégrination [peʀegʀinɑsjɔ̃] *nf* peregrination.

péremption [peʀɑ̃psjɔ̃] *nf* lapsing.

péremptoire [peʀɑ̃ptwaʀ] *adj argument, ton* peremptory.

péremptoirement [peʀɑ̃ptwaʀmɑ̃] *adv* peremptorily.

pérenniser [peʀenize] (1) *vt* to perpetuate.

pérennité [peʀenite] *nf* durability.

péréquation [peʀekwɑsjɔ̃] *nf* *[prix, impôts]* balancing out, evening out; *[notes]* coordination, adjustment; *[salaires]* adjustment, realignment.

perfectibilité [pɛʀfɛktibilite] *nf* perfectibility.
perfectible [pɛʀfɛktibl(ə)] *adj* perfectible.
perfectif, -ive [pɛʀfɛktif, iv] *adj* perfective.
perfection [pɛʀfɛksjɔ̃] *nf* perfection. **à la ~** to perfection; **c'est une ~!** it's (just) perfect!
perfectionné, e [pɛʀfɛksjɔne] (*ptp de* **perfectionner**) *adj dispositif, machine* advanced, sophisticated.
perfectionnement [pɛʀfɛksjɔnmɑ̃] *nm* perfection (*U*) (*de* of); improvement (*de* in). **cours de ~** proficiency course.
perfectionner [pɛʀfɛksjɔne] (1) **1** *vt* (*améliorer*) to improve, perfect. **2 se perfectionner** *vpr [chose]* to improve; *[personne]* to improve o.s., increase one's knowledge. **se ~ en anglais** to improve one's English.
perfectionnisme [pɛʀfɛksjɔnism(ə)] *nm* perfectionism.
perfectionniste [pɛʀfɛksjɔnist(ə)] *nmf* perfectionist.
perfide [pɛʀfid] **1** *adj* (*littér*) *personne, manœuvre* perfidious, treacherous; *promesse* deceitful, false; *chose* treacherous. **2** *nmf* (*littér*) traitor; (*en amour*) perfidious *ou* false-hearted person.
perfidement [pɛʀfidmɑ̃] *adv* (*littér*) perfidiously, treacherously.
perfidie [pɛʀfidi] *nf* (*U*) perfidy; (*acte*) act of perfidy.
perforage [pɛʀfɔʀaʒ] *nm* (*V* **perforer**) punching; perforation.
perforant, e [pɛʀfɔʀɑ̃, ɑ̃t] *adj instrument* perforating; *balle, obus* armour-piercing.
perforateur, -trice [pɛʀfɔʀatœʀ, tʀis] **1** *adj* perforating. **2** *nm,f* (*ouvrier*) punch-card operator. **3 perforatrice** *nf* (*perceuse*) drilling *ou* boring machine; (*Ordinateurs*) card punch. **4** *nm* (*Méd*) perforator.
perforation [pɛʀfɔʀasjɔ̃] *nf* (*Méd*) perforation; (*Ordinateurs*) punch.
perforer [pɛʀfɔʀe] (1) *vt* (*trouer*) to pierce; (*poinçonner*) to punch; (*Méd*) to perforate. (*Ordinateurs*) **carte perforée** punch card; **bande perforée** punched tape.
perforeuse [pɛʀfɔʀøz] *nf* card punch.
performance [pɛʀfɔʀmɑ̃s] *nf* performance.
perfusion [pɛʀfyzjɔ̃] *nf* (*Méd*) perfusion.
pergola [pɛʀgɔla] *nf* pergola.
péri [peʀi] *adj, m, nm*: (*marin*) **~ en mer** sailor lost at sea; **au profit des ~s en mer** in aid of those lost at sea.
péricarde [peʀikaʀd(ə)] *nm* pericardium.
péricliter [peʀiklite] (1) *vi [affaire]* to be in a state of collapse, collapse.
péridot [peʀido] *nm* peridot.
périgée [peʀiʒe] *nm* perigee.
périglaciaire [peʀiglasjɛʀ] *adj* periglacial.
périgourdin, e [peʀiguʀdɛ̃, in] **1** *adj* of *ou* from the Perigord. **2** *nm,f*: **P~(e)** inhabitant *ou* native of the Perigord.
péril [peʀil] *nm* (*littér*) peril, danger. **mettre en ~** to imperil, endanger, jeopardize; **au ~ de sa vie** at the risk of one's life; (*fig*) **il n'y a pas ~ en la demeure** there's no great need to hurry; **il y a ~ à faire** it is perilous to do; **le ~ rouge/jaune** the red/yellow peril; *V* **risque.**
périlleusement [peʀijøzmɑ̃] *adv* (*littér*) perilously.
périlleux, -euse [peʀijø, øz] *adj* perilous; *V* **saut.**
périmé, e [peʀime] (*ptp de* **périmer**) *adj billet, bon* out-of-date (*épith*), expired, no longer valid (*attrib*); *idée* dated, outdated. **ce billet/bon est ~** this ticket/voucher is out of date *ou* has expired.
périmer [peʀime] (1) **1** *vi*: **laisser ~ un passeport/un billet** to let a passport/ticket expire. **2 se périmer** *vpr* (*Jur*) to lapse; *[passeport, billet]* to expire; *[idée]* to date, become outdated.
périmètre [peʀimɛtʀ(ə)] *nm* (*Math*) perimeter; (*zone*) area.
périnée [peʀine] *nm* perineum.
période [peʀjɔd] *nf* (*gén*) period; (*Math*) *[fraction]* repetend; (*Méd: intervalle*) intermission. **pendant la ~ des vacances** during the holiday period; **une ~ de chaleur** a hot period *ou* spell; **pendant la ~ électorale** at election time; (*Mil*) **~ (d'instruction)** training (*U*).
périodicité [peʀjɔdisite] *nf* periodicity.
périodique [peʀjɔdik] **1** *adj* (*gén, Chim, Phys*) periodic; (*Presse*) periodical; (*Méd*) *fièvre* recurring. (*Math*) **fraction ~** recurring decimal; (*Math*) **fonction ~** periodic function; *V* **garniture. 2** *nm* (*Presse*) periodical.
périodiquement [peʀjɔdikmɑ̃] *adv* periodically.
périoste [peʀjɔst(ə)] *nm* periosteum.
péripatéticien, -ienne [peʀipatetisjɛ̃, jɛn] **1** *adj, nm,f* (*Philos*) peripatetic. **2 péripatéticienne** *nf* (*hum: prostituée*) streetwalker.
péripétie [peʀipesi] *nf* **(a)** (*épisode*) event, episode. **les ~s d'une révolution/d'une exploration** the turns taken by a revolution/an exploration; **après bien des ~s** after many ups and downs. **(b)** (*Littérat*) peripeteia.
périphérie [peʀifeʀi] *nf* (*limite*) periphery; (*banlieue*) outskirts.
périphérique [peʀifeʀik] **1** *adj* (*Anat, Math*) peripheral; *quartier* outlying (*épith*). **2** *nm*: **(boulevard) ~** ring road (*Brit*), circular route (*US*).
périphrase [peʀifʀaz] *nf* circumlocution, periphrasis (*T*), periphrase (*T*).
périphrastique [peʀifʀastik] *adj* circumlocutory, periphrastic.
périple [peʀipl(ə)] *nm* (*par mer*) voyage; (*par terre*) journey.
périr [peʀiʀ] (2) *vi* (*littér*) to perish (*littér*), die; *[navire]* to go down, sink; *[empire]* to perish, fall. **~ noyé** to drown, be drowned; **faire ~** *personne, plante* to kill; **son souvenir ne périra jamais** his memory will never die *ou* perish (*littér*); (*fig*) **~ d'ennui** to die of boredom.
périscope [peʀiskɔp] *nm* periscope.
périscopique [peʀiskɔpik] *adj* periscopic.
périssable [peʀisabl(ə)] *adj* perishable. **denrées ~s** perishable goods, perishables.
périssoire [peʀiswaʀ] *nf* canoe.
péristyle [peʀistil] *nm* peristyle.
péritoine [peʀitwan] *nm* peritoneum.
péritonite [peʀitɔnit] *nf* peritonitis.
perle [pɛʀl(ə)] **1** *nf* **(a)** (*bijou*) pearl; (*boule*) bead. **jeter** *ou* **donner des ~s aux pourceaux** to cast pearls before swine; *V* **enfiler.**
(b) (*littér: goutte*) *[eau, sang]* drop(let); *[sueur]* bead.
(c) (*fig: personne, chose de valeur*) gem. **la cuisinière est une ~** the cook is an absolute gem *ou* a perfect treasure; **c'est la ~ des maris** you couldn't hope for a better husband; **vous êtes une ~** you're a (real) gem; **la ~ d'une collection** the gem of a collection.
(d) (*erreur*) gem, howler.
2: perle de culture cultured pearl; **perle fine, perle naturelle** natural pearl; **perle de rosée** dewdrop.
perlé, e [pɛʀle] (*ptp de* **perler**) *adj orge* pearl (*épith*); *riz* polished; *tissu* beaded; *travail* perfect, exquisite; *rire* rippling; *V* **grève.**
perler [pɛʀle] (1) **1** *vi [sueur]* to form. **la sueur perlait sur son front** beads of sweat stood out *ou* formed on his forehead. **2** *vt travail* to take great pains over.
perlier, -ière [pɛʀlje, jɛʀ] *adj* pearl (*épith*).
perlimpinpin [pɛʀlɛ̃pɛ̃pɛ̃] *nm V* **poudre.**
permanence [pɛʀmanɑ̃s] *nf* **(a)** (*durée*) permanence, permanency. **en ~** *siéger* permanently; *crier* continuously; **dans ce pays ce sont des émeutes/c'est la guerre en ~** in that country there are constant *ou* continuous riots/there is a permanent state of war.
(b) (*service*) **être de ~** to be on duty *ou* on call; **une ~ est assurée le dimanche** there is someone on duty on Sundays, the office is manned on Sundays.
(c) (*bureau*) (duty) office; (*Pol*) committee room; (*Scol*) study room.
permanent, e [pɛʀmanɑ̃, ɑ̃t] **1** *adj* (*gén*) permanent; *armée, comité* standing (*épith*); *spectacle* continuous; (*Presse*) *envoyé, correspondant* permanent; (*Phys*) *aimantation, gaz* permanent. (*Ciné*) **~ de 2 heures à minuit** continuous showings from 2 o'clock to midnight; **un cinéma ~** a cinema showing a continuous programme.
2 *nm* (*Pol*) official (*of union, political party*).
3 permanente *nf* (*Coiffure*) perm, permanent wave.
permanganate [pɛʀmɑ̃ganat] *nm* permanganate.
perme [pɛʀm(ə)] *nf* (*arg Mil*) leave.
perméabilité [pɛʀmeabilite] *nf* (*lit*) (*Phys*) permeability; (*à l'eau*) perviousness, permeability; (*fig*) *[personne]* receptiveness, openness; *[frontière etc]* openness.
perméable [pɛʀmeabl(ə)] *adj* (*V* **perméabilité**) permeable; pervious; receptive, open (*à* to).
permettre [pɛʀmɛtʀ(ə)] (56) **1** *vt* **(a)** (*tolérer*) to allow, permit, let. **~ à qn de faire, ~ que qn fasse** to allow *ou* permit sb to do, let sb do; **la loi le permet** it is allowed *ou* permitted by law, the law allows *ou* permits it; **le docteur me permet l'alcool** the doctor allows *ou* permits me to drink *ou* lets me drink; **il se croit tout permis** he thinks he can do what he likes *ou* as he pleases; **est-il permis d'être aussi bête!** how can anyone be so stupid!; **il est permis à tout le monde de se tromper!** anyone can make a mistake!; **le professeur lui a permis de ne pas aller à l'école aujourd'hui** the teacher has given him permission to stay off school *ou* not to go to school today.
(b) (*rendre possible*) to allow, permit. **ce diplôme va lui ~ de trouver du travail** this qualification will allow *ou* enable *ou* permit him to find a job; **mes moyens ne me le permettent pas** I cannot afford it; **mes occupations ne me le permettent pas** I'm too busy to be able to do it; **sa santé ne le lui permet pas** his health doesn't allow *ou* permit him to do it; **son attitude permet tous les soupçons** his attitude gives cause for suspicion *ou* reinforces one's suspicions; **si le temps le permet** weather permitting; **autant qu'il est permis d'en juger** as far as one can tell.
(c) (*idée de sollicitation*) **vous permettez?** may I?; **permettez-moi de vous présenter ma sœur/de vous interrompre** may I introduce my sister/interrupt (you)?; **s'il m'est permis de faire une objection** if I may *ou* might (be allowed to) raise an objection; **vous permettez que je fume?** do you mind if I smoke?; **vous permettez que je passe!*** if you don't mind I'd like to come past!, do you mind if I come past!; **permettez! je ne suis pas d'accord** if you don't mind! *ou* pardon me! I disagree; **permets-moi de te le dire** let me tell you.
2 se permettre *vpr* **(a)** (*s'offrir*) *fantaisie, excès* to allow o.s., indulge o.s. in. **je ne peux pas me ~ d'acheter ce manteau** I can't afford to buy this coat.
(b) (*risquer*) *grossièreté, plaisanterie* to allow o.s. to make, dare to make. **ce sont des plaisanteries qu'on ne peut se ~ qu'entre amis** these jokes are only acceptable among friends; **je me suis permis de sourire** *ou* **un sourire** I had *ou* gave *ou* ventured a smile, I ventured to *ou* allowed myself to smile; **il s'est permis de partir sans permission** he took the liberty of going without permission; **il se permet bien des choses** he takes a lot of liberties; **je me permettrai de vous faire remarquer que ...** I'd like to point out (to you) that ...; **puis-je me ~ de vous offrir un whisky?** will you have a whisky?; (*formule épistolaire*) **je me permets de vous écrire au sujet de ...** I am writing to you in connection with ... .
permis, e [pɛʀmi, iz] (*ptp de* **permettre**) **1** *adj limites* permitted. (*frm*) **il est ~ de s'interroger sur la nécessité de ...** one might *ou* may well question the necessity of ... .
2 *nm* permit, licence. **~ de chasse** hunting permit; **~ de conduire** (*carte*) driving licence; (*épreuve*) driving test; **~ de con-**

struire planning permission; ~ **d'inhumer** burial certificate; ~ **de pêche** fishing permit; ~ **de séjour** residence permit; ~ **de travail** work permit.

permission [pɛʀmisjɔ̃] *nf* **(a)** permission. **avec votre** ~ with your permission; **accorder à qn la** ~ **de faire** to give sb permission to do; **demander la** ~ to ask permission (*de* to); **demander à qn la** ~ to ask sb his permission (*de* to); **est-ce qu'il t'a donné la** ~ **(de le faire)?** did he give you permission (to do it)?

(b) (*Mil*) (*congé*) leave; (*certificat*) pass. **en** ~ on leave; ~ **de minuit** late pass.

permissionnaire [pɛʀmisjɔnɛʀ] *nm* soldier on leave.

permutabilité [pɛʀmytabilite] *nf* permutability.

permutable [pɛʀmytabl(ə)] *adj* which can be changed *ou* swapped *ou* switched round; (*Math*) permutable.

permutation [pɛʀmytɑsjɔ̃] *nf* permutation.

permuter [pɛʀmyte] (1) **1** *vt* (*gén*) to change *ou* swap *ou* switch round, permutate; (*Math*) to permutate, permute. **2** *vi* to change, swap, switch (seats *ou* positions *ou* jobs *etc*).

pernicieusement [pɛʀnisjøzmɑ̃] *adv* (*littér*) perniciously.

pernicieux, -euse [pɛʀnisjø, øz] *adj* (*gén, Méd*) pernicious. ~ **pour** injurious *ou* harmful to.

péroné [peʀɔne] *nm* fibula.

péroniste [peʀɔnist(ə)] **1** *adj* Peronist. **2** *nmf*: **P**~ Peronist.

péronnelle [peʀɔnɛl] *nf* (*péj*) silly goose* (*péj*).

péroraison [peʀɔʀɛzɔ̃] *nf* (*Littérat: conclusion*) peroration, summing up; (*péj: discours*) windy discourse (*péj*).

pérorer [peʀɔʀe] (1) *vi* to hold forth (*péj*), declaim (*péj*).

Pérou [peʀu] *nm* Peru. (*fig*) **ce qu'il gagne, ce n'est pas le** ~ it's no great fortune what he earns.

peroxyde [pɛʀɔksid] *nm* peroxide.

perpendiculaire [pɛʀpɑ̃dikylɛʀ] *adj, nf* perpendicular (*à* to).

perpendiculairement [pɛʀpɑ̃dikylɛʀmɑ̃] *adv* perpendicularly. ~ **à** at right angles to, perpendicular to.

perpète [pɛʀpɛt] *nf* (*arg Prison: perpétuité*) **il a eu la** ~ he got life (*arg*); (*loin*) **à** ~* miles away*; (*longtemps*) **jusqu'à** ~* till doomsday*, till the cows come home*.

perpétration [pɛʀpetʀɑsjɔ̃] *nf* perpetration.

perpétrer [pɛʀpetʀe] (6) *vt* to perpetrate.

perpette [pɛʀpɛt] *nf* = **perpète.**

perpétuation [pɛʀpetɥɑsjɔ̃] *nf* (*littér*) perpetuation.

perpétuel, -elle [pɛʀpetɥɛl] *adj* (*pour toujours*) perpetual, everlasting; (*incessant*) perpetual, constant; *fonction, secrétaire* permanent; *rente* life (*épith*), for life (*attrib*); *V* **calendrier, mouvement.**

perpétuellement [pɛʀpetɥɛlmɑ̃] *adv* perpetually, constantly.

perpétuer [pɛʀpetɥe] (1) **1** *vt* (*immortaliser*) to perpetuate; (*maintenir*) to perpetuate, carry on.

2 se perpétuer *vpr* [*usage, abus*] to be perpetuated, be carried on; [*espèce*] to survive. **se** ~ **dans son œuvre/dans ses enfants** to live on in one's works/children.

perpétuité [pɛʀpetɥite] *nf* perpetuity, perpetuation. **à** ~ *condamnation* for life; *concession* in perpetuity.

perplexe [pɛʀplɛks(ə)] *adj* perplexed, confused, puzzled. **rendre** *ou* **laisser** ~ to perplex, confuse, puzzle.

perplexité [pɛʀplɛksite] *nf* perplexity, confusion. **je suis dans une grande** ~ I just don't know what to think, I'm greatly perplexed *ou* highly confused; **être dans la plus complète** ~ to be completely baffled *ou* utterly perplexed *ou* confused, be at an absolute loss (to know what to think).

perquisition [pɛʀkizisjɔ̃] *nf* (*Police*) search. **ils ont fait une** ~ they've carried out *ou* made a search, they've searched the premises; *V* **mandat.**

perquisitionner [pɛʀkizisjɔne] (1) **1** *vi* to carry out a search, make a search. ~ **au domicile de qn** to search sb's house, carry out *ou* make a search of sb's house. **2** *vt* (*) to search.

perron [pɛʀɔ̃] *nm* steps (*leading to entrance*), perron (*T*).

perroquet [pɛʀɔkɛ] *nm* **(a)** (*Orn, fig*) parrot. **répéter qch comme un** ~ to repeat sth parrot fashion. **(b)** (*Naut*) topgallant.

perruche [peʀyʃ] *nf* **(a)** (*Orn*) budgerigar, budgie*; (*femelle du perroquet*) female parrot; (*fig: femme bavarde*) chatterbox*, gas bag‡ (*péj*), windbag‡ (*péj*). **(b)** (*Naut*) mizzen topgallant (sail).

perruque [peʀyk] *nf* (*gén*) wig; (*Hist*) wig, periwig, peruke; (*Pêche*: enchevêtrement*) bird's nest.

perruquier, -ière [peʀykje, jɛʀ] *nm,f* wigmaker.

pers [pɛʀ] *adj yeux* greenish-blue, blue-green.

persan, e [pɛʀsɑ̃, an] **1** *adj* Persian; *V* **tapis. 2** *nm* (*Ling*) Persian. **3** *nm,f*: **P**~**(e)** Persian.

perse [pɛʀs(ə)] **1** *adj* Persian. **2** *nm* (*Ling*) Persian. **3** *nmf*: **P**~ Persian. **4** *nf* (*Géog*) **P**~ Persia.

persécuter [pɛʀsekyte] (1) *vt* (*opprimer*) to persecute; (*harceler*) to harass, plague.

persécuteur, -trice [pɛʀsekytœʀ, tʀis] **1** *adj* persecuting. **2** *nm,f* persecutor.

persécution [pɛʀsekysjɔ̃] *nf* persecution. **délire** *ou* **folie de la** ~ persecution mania.

Persée [pɛʀse] *nm* Perseus.

Perséphone [pɛʀsefɔn] *nf* Persephone.

persévérance [pɛʀseveʀɑ̃s] *nf* perseverance.

persévérant, e [pɛʀseveʀɑ̃, ɑ̃t] *adj* persevering. **être** ~ to persevere, be persevering.

persévérer [pɛʀseveʀe] (6) *vi* to persevere. ~ **dans** *effort, entreprise, recherches* to persevere with *ou* in; *erreur, voie* to persevere in.

persienne [pɛʀsjɛn] *nf* (metal) shutter.

persiflage [pɛʀsiflaʒ] *nm* mockery (*U*).

persifler [pɛʀsifle] (1) *vt* to mock, make mock of (*littér*), make fun of.

persifleur, -euse [pɛʀsiflœʀ, øz] **1** *adj* mocking. **2** *nm,f* mocker.

persil [pɛʀsi] *nm* parsley.

persillé, e [pɛʀsije] *adj plat* sprinkled with chopped parsley; *viande* marbled; *fromage* veined.

persique [pɛʀsik] *adj* Persian; *V* **golfe.**

persistance [pɛʀsistɑ̃s] *nf* [*pluie, fièvre, douleur, odeur*] persistence; [*personne*] persistence, persistency (*à faire* in doing). **sa** ~ **dans l'erreur** his persistently mistaken attitude; **cette** ~ **dans le mensonge** this persistence in lying, this persistent lying; **avec** ~ (*tout le temps*) persistently; (*avec obstination*) persistently, doggedly, stubbornly.

persistant, e [pɛʀsistɑ̃, ɑ̃t] *adj* (*gén*) persistent; *feuilles* evergreen, persistent (*T*). **arbre à feuillage** ~ evergreen (tree).

persister [pɛʀsiste] (1) *vi* [*pluie*] to persist, keep up; [*fièvre, douleur, odeur*] to persist; [*personne*] to persist. ~ **dans qch/à faire** to persist in sth/in doing; **la pluie/la douleur n'a pas persisté** the rain/the pain didn't last *ou* persist; **il persiste dans son refus** he won't go back on *ou* he persists in his refusal; ~ **dans son opinion/ses projets** to stick to one's opinion/one's plans; **il persiste dans son silence** he persists in keeping quiet; **il persiste à faire cela** he persists in doing *ou* keeps (on) doing that, he does that persistently; **je persiste à croire que ...** I still believe that ...; **il persistait une odeur de moisi** a musty smell persisted.

persona [pɛʀsɔna] *nf*: ~ **grata/non grata** persona grata/non grata.

personnage [pɛʀsɔnaʒ] *nm* **(a)** (*individu*) character, individual.

(b) (*célébrité*) (very) important person, personage (*frm, hum*). ~ **influent/haut placé** influential/highly placed person; ~ **connu** celebrity, well-known person *ou* personage (*frm, hum*); ~ **officiel** V.I.P.; **un grand** ~ a great figure; **grands** ~**s de l'État** State dignitaries; ~**s de l'Antiquité/historiques** great names of Antiquity/of history; **il est devenu un** ~ he's become a very important person *ou* a big name*; **il se prend pour un grand** ~ he really thinks he is someone important, he really thinks he's somebody*.

(c) (*Littérat*) character. **liste des** ~**s** dramatis personae, list of characters; (*lit, fig*) **jouer un** ~ to play a part, act a part *ou* role; *V* **peau.**

(d) (*Art*) [*tableau*] figure.

personnalisation [pɛʀsɔnalizɑsjɔ̃] *nf* personalization.

personnaliser [pɛʀsɔnalize] (1) *vt* (*gén*) to personalize; *voiture, appartement* to give a personal touch to, personalize.

personnalité [pɛʀsɔnalite] *nf* (*gén*) personality.

personne [pɛʀsɔn] **1** *nf* **(a)** (*être humain*) person. **deux** ~**s** two people; (*Jur*) **les droits de la** ~ the rights of the individual; **les** ~**s qui ...** those who ..., the people who ...; **c'est une** ~ **sympathique** he *ou* she is a very pleasant person; **une** ~ **de connaissance m'a dit** someone *ou* a person I know told me; **il n'y a pas** ~ **de plus discrète que lui** there is no one more discreet than he; **c'est une drôle de petite/une jolie** ~† she's a funny little/a pretty little thing; **par** ~: **3 gâteaux par** ~ 3 cakes per person, 3 cakes each; **100 F par** ~ 100 francs each *ou* per head *ou* a head *ou* per person; **par** ~ **interposée** through an intermediary, through a third party *ou* person; *V* **grand, tierce**[2].

(b) (*personnalité*) **toute sa** ~ **inspire confiance** his whole being inspires confidence; **j'admire son œuvre mais je le méprise en tant que** ~ I admire his works but I despise him as a person; **la** ~ **et l'œuvre de Balzac** Balzac, the man and his work.

(c) (*corps*) **être bien (fait) de sa** ~ to be good-looking; **exposer** *ou* **risquer sa** ~ to risk one's life *ou* one's neck; **sur ma** ~ on my person; **il semble toujours très content de sa petite** ~ he always seems very pleased with his little self *ou* with himself; **il prend soin de sa petite** ~ he looks after himself; **en** ~: **je l'ai vu en** ~ I saw him in person; **je m'en occupe en** ~ I'll see to it personally; **c'est la paresse/la bonté en** ~ he's *ou* she's laziness/kindness itself *ou* personified; *V* **payer.**

(d) (*Gram*) person. **à la première/troisième** ~ in the first/third person.

2 *pron* **(a)** (*quelqu'un*) anyone, anybody. **elle le sait mieux que** ~ **(au monde)** she knows that better than anyone *ou* anybody (else); **il est entré sans que** ~ **le voie** he came in without anyone *ou* anybody seeing him; ~ **de blessé?** is anyone *ou* anybody injured?

(b) (*avec ne: aucun*) no one, nobody. **presque** ~ hardly anyone *ou* anybody, practically no one *ou* nobody; ~ **(d'autre) ne l'a vu** no one *ou* nobody (else) saw him; **il n'a vu** ~ **(d'autre)** he didn't see anyone *ou* anybody (else), he saw no one *ou* nobody (else); ~ **d'autre que lui** no one *ou* nobody but he; **il n'y a** ~ there's no one *ou* nobody in, there isn't anyone *ou* anybody in; **il n'y a eu** ~ **de blessé** no one *ou* nobody was injured, there wasn't anyone *ou* anybody injured; **à qui as-tu demandé? — à** ~ who did you ask? — no one *ou* nobody *ou* I didn't ask anyone *ou* anybody; **ce n'est la faute de** ~ it's no one's *ou* nobody's fault; **il n'y avait** ~ **d'intéressant à qui parler** there was no one *ou* nobody interesting to talk to; **il n'y est pour** ~ he doesn't want to see anyone *ou* anybody; (*iro*) **pour le travail, il n'y a plus** ~* as soon as there's a bit of work to be done, everyone disappears *ou* clears off* *ou* there's suddenly no one *ou* nobody around*; **n'y a-t-il** ~ **qui sache où il est?** doesn't anyone *ou* anybody know where he is?

3: personne âgée elderly person; **mesure en faveur des personnes âgées** measure benefiting the elderly; **personne à charge** dependent; (*Jur*) **personne civile** artificial person; (*Pol*) **personnes déplacées** displaced persons; **la personne humaine** human dignity; (*Jur*) **personne morale** = **personne civile**; (*Jur*) **personne physique** individual.

personnel, -elle [pɛʀsɔnɛl] **1** *adj* **(a)** (*particulier, privé*) personal. **fortune** ~**le** personal *ou* private fortune; **strictement** ~ *lettre* highly confidential, private and personal; *billet* not

transferable (*attrib*); **il a des idées/des opinions très ~les sur la question** he has ideas/opinions of his own *ou* he has his own ideas/opinions on the subject.
(b) (*égoïste*) selfish, self-centred.
(c) (*Gram*) *pronom, nom, verbe* personal; *mode* finite.
2 *nm [école]* staff; *[château, hôtel]* staff, employees; *[usine]* workforce, employees, personnel; *[service public]* personnel, employees. **manquer de ~** to be shortstaffed *ou* understaffed; **faire partie du ~** to be on the staff; (*Aviat, Mil*) **~ à terre/navigant** ground/flight personnel *ou* staff; **bureau/chef du ~** personnel office/officer.
personnellement [pɛʀsɔnɛlmɑ̃] *adv* personally.
personnification [pɛʀsɔnifikɑsjɔ̃] *nf* personification. **c'est la ~ de la cruauté** he's the embodiment of cruelty.
personnifier [pɛʀsɔnifje] (7) *vt* to personify. **cet homme personnifie le mal** this man is the embodiment of evil *ou* is evil itself *ou* is evil personified; **être la bêtise personnifiée** to be stupidity itself *ou* personified; **il personnifie son époque** he typifies his age, he's the embodiment of his age.
perspectif, -ive [pɛʀspɛktif, iv] **1** *adj* perspective.
2 **perspective** *nf* **(a)** (*Art*) perspective.
(b) (*point de vue*) (*lit*) view; (*fig*) angle, viewpoint. **dans une ~ive historique** from a historical angle *ou* viewpoint, in a historical perspective; **examiner une question sous des ~ives différentes** to examine a question from different angles *ou* viewpoints.
(c) (*événement en puissance*) prospect; (*idée*) prospect, thought. **en ~ive** in prospect; **des ~ives d'avenir** future prospects; **quelle ~ive!** what a thought! *ou* prospect!; **à la ~ive de** at the prospect *ou* thought *ou* idea of.
perspicace [pɛʀspikas] *adj* clear-sighted, penetrating, perspicacious.
perspicacité [pɛʀspikasite] *nf* clear-sightedness, insight, perspicacity.
persuader [pɛʀsɥade] (1) **1** *vt* (*convaincre*) to persuade, convince (*qn de qch* sb of sth). **~ qn (de faire qch)** to persuade sb (to do sth); **il les a persuadés que tout irait bien** he persuaded *ou* convinced them that all would be well; **on l'a persuadé de partir** he was persuaded to leave; **j'en suis persuadé** I'm quite sure *ou* convinced (of it); **il sait ~** he's very persuasive, he knows how to convince people.
2 *vi*: **~ à qn (de faire)** to persuade sb (to do); **on lui a persuadé de rester** he was persuaded to stay.
3 se persuader *vpr* to be persuaded, be convinced. **il s'est persuadé qu'on le déteste** he is persuaded *ou* convinced that *ou* he has convinced himself that everyone hates him; **elle s'est persuadée de l'inutilité de ses efforts** she has convinced herself of the uselessness of her efforts.
persuasif, -ive [pɛʀsɥazif, iv] *adj ton, éloquence* persuasive; *argument, orateur* persuasive, convincing.
persuasion [pɛʀsɥɑzjɔ̃] *nf* (*action, art*) persuasion; (*croyance*) conviction, belief.
perte [pɛʀt(ə)] **1** *nf* **(a)** (*gén*) loss, losing (*U*); (*Comm*) loss. **vendre à ~** to sell at a loss; **la ~ d'une bataille/d'un procès** the loss of a battle/case, losing a battle/case; **essuyer une ~ importante** to suffer heavy losses; (*Mil*) **de lourdes ~s (en hommes)** heavy losses (in men); *V* **profit.**
(b) (*ruine*) ruin. **il a juré sa ~** he has sworn to ruin him; **il court à sa ~** he is on the road to ruin.
(c) (*déperdition*) loss; (*gaspillage*) waste. **~ de chaleur/d'énergie** loss of heat/energy, heat/energy loss; **~ de lumière** loss of light; **c'est une ~ de temps** it's a waste of time; **il devrait s'économiser: c'est une ~ d'énergie** he ought to save his efforts: he's wasting energy *ou* it's a waste of energy.
(d) (*loc*) **à ~ de vue** (*lit*) as far as the eye can see; (*fig*) interminably; **mis à la porte avec ~ et fracas** thrown out.
2: (*Méd*) **pertes blanches** vaginal discharge, leucorrhoea (*T*); **perte de charge** pressure drop, drop in *ou* loss of pressure; (*Méd*) **pertes de sang** flooding (*during menstruation*); (*Fin*) **perte sèche** dead loss (*Fin*); (*Élec*) **perte à la terre** earth leakage; **perte de vitesse: être en perte de vitesse** (*Aviat*) to stall, lose lift; (*fig*) to be losing momentum.
pertinemment [pɛʀtinamɑ̃] *adv parler* pertinently, to the point. **il a répondu ~** his reply was to the point; **savoir ~ que** to know full well that, know for a fact that.
pertinence [pɛʀtinɑ̃s] *nf* (*V* **pertinent**) aptness; pertinence; appositeness; judiciousness; relevance; significance, distinctive nature.
pertinent, e [pɛʀtinɑ̃, ɑ̃t] *adj remarque* apt, pertinent, apposite; *analyse, jugement, esprit* judicious, discerning; *idée* relevant, apt, pertinent; (*Ling*) significant, distinctive.
pertuis [pɛʀtɥi] *nm* (*détroit*) strait(s), channel; *[fleuve]* narrows.
pertuisane [pɛʀtɥizan] *nf* partisan (*weapon*).
perturbateur, -trice [pɛʀtyʀbatœʀ, tʀis] **1** *adj* disruptive.
2 *nm,f* troublemaker, rowdy.
perturbation [pɛʀtyʀbɑsjɔ̃] *nf* **(a)** (*V* **perturber**) disruption; disturbance; perturbation. **jeter la ~ dans** to disrupt; to disturb; **facteur de ~** disruptive factor; **~s dans l'acheminement du courrier** disruption(s) of the mail.
(b) (*Mét*) **~ (atmosphérique)** (atmospheric) disturbance.
perturber [pɛʀtyʀbe] (1) *vt services publics, travaux* to disrupt; *cérémonie, réunion* to disrupt, disturb; (*Rad, TV*) *transmission* to disrupt; *personne* to perturb, disturb; (*Astron*) to perturb; (*Mét*) to disturb.
péruvien, -ienne [peʀyvjɛ̃, jɛn] **1** *adj* Peruvian. **2** *nm* (*Ling*) Peruvian. **3** *nm,f*: **P~(ne)** Peruvian.
pervenche [pɛʀvɑ̃ʃ] **1** *nf* periwinkle (*plant*).
2 *adj inv* periwinkle blue.
pervers, e [pɛʀvɛʀ, ɛʀs(ə)] **1** *adj* (*littér: diabolique*) perverse; (*vicieux*) perverted, depraved. **2** *nm,f* pervert.
perversion [pɛʀvɛʀsjɔ̃] *nf* perversion, corruption; (*Méd, Psych*) perversion.
perversité [pɛʀvɛʀsite] *nf* perversity, depravity.
perverti, e [pɛʀvɛʀti] (*ptp de* **pervertir**) *nm,f*: **~(e) (sexuel(le))** (sexual) pervert.
pervertir [pɛʀvɛʀtiʀ] (2) **1** *vt* (*dépraver*) to corrupt, pervert, deprave; (*altérer*) to pervert. **2 se pervertir** *vpr* to become corrupt(ed) *ou* perverted *ou* depraved.
pesage [pəzaʒ] *nm* weighing; *[jockey]* weigh-in; (*salle*) weighing room; (*enceinte*) enclosure.
pesamment [pəzamɑ̃] *adv chargé, tomber* heavily; *marcher* with a heavy step *ou* tread, heavily.
pesant, e [pəzɑ̃, ɑ̃t] **1** *adj paquet* heavy, weighty; (*lit, fig*) *fardeau, joug, charge* heavy; *sommeil* deep; *démarche, pas* heavy; *esprit* slow, sluggish; *architecture* massive; *style, ton* heavy, weighty, ponderous; *présence* burdensome.
2 *nm*: **valoir son ~ d'or** to be worth one's weight in gold.
pesanteur [pəzɑ̃tœʀ] *nf* **(a)** (*Phys*) gravity.
(b) (*lourdeur: V* **pesant**) heaviness; weightiness; depth; slowness, sluggishness; massiveness; ponderousness; burdensomeness. **avoir des ~s d'estomac** to have something lying (heavy) on one's stomach.
pèse- [pɛz] *préf V* **peser.**
pesée [pəze] *nf* (*action*) *[objet]* weighing; (*fig*) *[motifs, termes]* weighing up; (*pression, poussée*) push, thrust. **effectuer une ~** to carry out a weighing operation.
peser [pəze] (5) **1** *vt* **(a)** *objet, personne* to weigh. **~ qch dans sa main** to feel the weight of sth (in one's hand); **se ~** to weigh o.s.
(b) (*évaluer*) to weigh (up). **~ le pour et le contre** to weigh (up) the pros and cons; **~ ses mots** to weigh one's words; **tout bien pesé** having weighed everything up, everything considered; **ce qu'il dit est toujours pesé** what he says is always carefully weighed up.
2 *vi* **(a)** to weigh. **cela pèse beaucoup** it weighs a lot; **cela pèse peu** it doesn't weigh much; **~ 60 kg** to weigh 60 kg; **~ lourd** to be heavy; (*fig*) **ce ministre ne pèse pas lourd** this minister doesn't carry much weight *ou* doesn't count for much; (*fig*) **il n'a pas pesé lourd (devant son adversaire)** he was no match (for his opponent).
(b) (*appuyer*) to press, push; (*fig*) to weigh heavy. **~ sur/contre qch (de tout son poids)** to press *ou* push down on/against sth (with all one's weight); (*fig*) *[aliment, repas]* **~ sur l'estomac** to lie (heavy) on the stomach; (*fig*) **cela lui pèse sur le cœur** that makes him heavy-hearted; **les remords lui pèsent sur la conscience** remorse lies heavy on his conscience, his conscience is weighed down by remorse; **cela pèsera sur la décision** that will influence the decision; **le soupçon/l'accusation qui pèse sur lui** the suspicion/the accusation which hangs over him; **la menace/sentence qui pèse sur sa tête** the threat/sentence which hangs over his head; **toute la responsabilité pèse sur lui *ou* sur ses épaules** all the responsibility is on him *ou* on his shoulders, he has to shoulder all the responsibility.
(c) (*accabler*) **~ à qn** to weigh sb down, weigh heavy on sb; **le silence/la solitude lui pèse** the silence/solitude is getting him down* *ou* weighs heavy on him; **le temps lui pèse** time hangs heavy on his hands; **ses responsabilités de maire lui pèsent** he feels the weight of *ou* weighed down by his responsibilities as mayor, his responsibilities as mayor weigh heavy on him.
(d) (*avoir de l'importance*) to carry weight. **cela va ~ (dans la balance)** that will carry some weight; **sa timidité a pesé dans leur décision** his shyness influenced their decision.
3: pèse-acide *nm, pl* **pèse-acides** acidimeter; **pèse-alcool** *nm, pl* **pèse-alcools** alcoholometer; **pèse-bébé** *nm, pl* **pèse-bébés** (baby) scales; **pèse-lait** *nm, pl* **pèse-laits** lactometer; **pèse-lettre** *nm, pl* **pèse-lettres** letter scales; **pèse-personne** *nm, pl* **pèse-personnes** scales; *[salle de bains]* (bathroom) scales.
pessimisme [pesimism(ə)] *nm* pessimism.
pessimiste [pesimist(ə)] **1** *adj* pessimistic (*sur* about). **2** *nmf* pessimist.
peste [pɛst(ə)] **1** *nf* (*Méd*) plague; (*fig: personne*) pest, nuisance. (*fig*) **fuir qch/qn comme la ~** to avoid sth/sb like the plague. **2** *excl* (*littér*) good gracious! **~ soit de ...** a plague on ... .
pester [pɛste] (1) *vi* to curse. **~ contre qn/qch** to curse sb/sth.
pestiféré, e [pɛstifeʀe] **1** *adj* plague-stricken.
2 *nm,f* plague victim. (*fig*) **fuir qn comme un ~** to avoid sb like the plague.
pestilence [pɛstilɑ̃s] *nf* stench.
pestilentiel, -elle [pɛstilɑ̃sjɛl] *adj* stinking, foul(-smelling).
pet [pɛ] **1** *nm* **(a)** (∵) fart∵. **ça ne vaut pas un ~ (de lapin)‡** it's worth damn all‡; **faire un ~** to fart∵.
(b) faire le ~* to be on (the) watch *ou* on (the) look-out; **~! les voilà!*** look out! here they come!
2: pet-de-nonne *nm, pl* **pets-de-nonne** fritter (*made with choux pastry*).
pétainiste [petenist(ə)] **1** *adj* Pétain (*épith*). **2** *nmf*: **P~** Pétain supporter.
pétale [petal] *nm* petal.
pétanque [petɑ̃k] *nf* petanque (*type of bowls played in the Midi*).
pétant, e* [petɑ̃, ɑ̃t] *adj*: **à deux heures ~es** at two on the dot*, on the dot of two*.
pétarade [petaʀad] *nf [moteur, véhicule]* backfire (*U*); *[feu d'artifice, fusillade]* crackling.
pétarader [petaʀade] (1) *vi [moteur, véhicule]* to backfire. **il les entendait ~ dans la cour** he could hear them revving up their engines in the backyard.
pétard [petaʀ] *nm* **(a)** (*feu d'artifice*) banger, firecracker; (*accessoire de cotillon*) cracker; (*Rail*) detonator (*Brit*), torpedo (*US*); (*Mil*) petard, explosive charge. **tirer *ou* faire partir**

un ~ to let off a banger (Brit) ou firecracker; to pull a cracker.
(b) (‡: tapage) din*, racket*, row*. il va y avoir du ~ sparks will fly, there's going to be a hell of a row‡; faire du ~ [nouvelle] to cause a stir, raise a stink‡; [personne] to kick up a row* ou fuss* ou stink‡; être en ~ to be raging mad*, be in a flaming temper.
(c) (‡: revolver) gun, gat‡.
(d) (‡: derrière) bum‡ (Brit), ass‡ (US), bottom*, rump*.

pétaudière [petodjɛʀ] nf bedlam, bear garden.

péter [pete] (6) 1 vi (a) (∵) to fart∵. (fig) il veut ~ plus haut que son cul he aims too bloody (Brit) ou damned high∵; (fig) il m'a envoyé ~ he told me to go to hell‡ ou to bugger off∵ (Brit) ou fuck off∵.
(b) (*) [détonation] to go off; [tuyau] to burst, bust; [ballon] to pop, burst; [ficelle] to bust*, snap. l'affaire lui a pété dans la main the deal fell through.
2 vt (*) (a) ficelle to bust*, snap; transistor, vase to bust*.
(b) (fig) ~ du feu ou des flammes to be full of go* ou beans*; ~ la santé to be bursting with health; ça va ~ des flammes there's going to be a heck of a row*.

pète-sec [pɛtsɛk] nm inv, adj inv disciplinarian.

péteux, -euse‡ [petø, øz] 1 adj cowardly, yellow(-bellied)‡. 2 nm,f coward, yellowbelly‡.

pétillant, e [petijɑ̃, ɑ̃t] adj eau bubbly, (slightly) fizzy; vin bubbly, sparkling; yeux sparkling, twinkling. discours ~ d'esprit speech sparkling with wit.

pétillement [petijmɑ̃] nm (U: V pétiller) crackling; bubbling; sparkling; twinkling. entendre des ~s to hear crackling ou crackles ou a crackle; ce ~ de malice qui animait son regard this malicious sparkle in his eye; un ~ de lumière envahit la pièce the room was filled with (a) sparkling light.

pétiller [petije] (1) vi [feu] to crackle; [champagne, vin, eau] to bubble; [joie] to sparkle (dans in); [yeux] (de malice) to sparkle, glisten; (de joie) to sparkle, twinkle (de with). ses yeux pétillaient de malice his eyes were sparkling ou glistening evilly; il pétillait de bonne humeur he was bubbling (over) with good humour; ~ d'esprit to sparkle with wit.

pétiole [pesjɔl] nm leafstalk, petiole (T).

petiot, e* [pətjo, ɔt] 1 adj weeny (little)*, teenyweeny*, tiny (little). 2 nm little laddie*. 3 petiote nf little lassie*.

petit, e [p(ə)ti, it] 1 adj (a) (gén) main, personne, objet, colline small, little (épith); pointure small. ~ et mince short and thin; ~ et carré squat; ~ et rond dumpy; il est tout ~ he's very small ou a very small man; (nuance affective) he's a little ou a tiny (little) man; (fig) se faire tout ~ to retreat into one's shell; être de ~e taille to be short ou small; un ~ vieux a little old man; ces chaussures sont un peu/trop ~es pour moi these shoes are a bit small ou rather a small fit/too small for me.
(b) (mince) personne, taille slim, slender; membre thin, slender. avoir de ~s os to be small-boned; avoir une ~e figure/de ~s bras to have a thin face/slender ou thin arms; une ~e pluie (fine) tombait a (fine) drizzle was falling.
(c) (jeune) small, young; (avec nuance affective) little. quand il était ~ when he was small ou little; son ~ frère his younger ou little brother, (très petit) his baby ou little brother; ~ chat/chien (little) kitten/puppy; un ~ Anglais an English boy; les ~s Anglais English children; ~ lion/tigre/ours little lion/tiger/bear, lion/tiger/bear cub; dans sa ~e enfance when he was very small; le ~ Jésus Infant Jesus, baby Jesus; comment va la ~e famille? how are the young ones?; tout ce ~ monde s'amusait all these youngsters were enjoying themselves; (péj) je vous préviens mon ~ ami ou monsieur I warn you my good man ou dear fellow.
(d) (court) promenade, voyage short, little. par ~es étapes in short ou easy stages; sur une ~e distance over a short distance; il est resté deux (pauvres) ~es heures he only stayed for two short hours; il en a pour une ~e heure it will take him an hour at the most, it won't take him more than an hour; attendez une ~e minute can you wait just a ou half a minute?; j'en ai pour un ~ moment (longtemps) it'll take me quite a while; (peu de temps) it won't take me long, I shan't be long over it; elle est sortie pour un bon ~ moment she won't be back for a (good) while ou for quite a while yet; écrivez-lui un ~ mot write him a (short) note ou a line; c'est à un ~ kilomètre d'ici it's no more than ou just under a kilometre from here.
(e) (faible) bruit faint, slight; cri little, faint; coup, tape light, gentle; pente gentle, slight; somme d'argent small. on entendit 2 ~s coups à la porte we heard 2 light ou gentle knocks on the door; il a un ~ appétit he hasn't much of an appetite; avoir une ~e santé to be in delicate health, be frail; c'est une ~e nature he's (ou she's) a humdrum sort of person; une toute ~e voix a tiny voice.
(f) (minime) opération, détail small, minor; inconvénient slight, minor; espoir, chance faint, slight; cadeau, bibelot little; odeur, rhume slight. avec un ~ effort with a bit of an ou with a little effort; ce n'est pas une ~e affaire que de le faire obéir getting him to obey is no easy matter ou no mean task; ce n'est qu'une ~e robe d'été it's just a light summer dress.
(g) (peu important) commerçant, pays, firme small; fonctionnaire, employé, romancier minor; soirée, réception little. la ~e industrie light industry; le ~ commerce small businesses; les ~es gens ordinary people; le ~ épicier du coin the small street-corner grocer('s); la ~e noblesse minor nobility; la ~e histoire the footnotes of history.
(h) (peu nombreux) groupe small. cela n'affecte qu'un ~ nombre it only affects a small number of people ou a few people.
(i) (péj: mesquin) attitude, action mean, petty, low; personne petty. c'est ~ ce qu'il a fait là that was a mean thing to do, that was mean of him.
(j) (avec nuance affective ou euph) little. vous prendrez bien un ~ dessert/verre you'll have a little dessert/drink won't you?; comment va la ~e santé? how are you keeping?*; ma ~e maman my mummy; mon ~ papa my daddy; mon ~ chou ou rat etc (my little) pet*, darling; un ~ coin tranquille a nice quiet spot; on va se faire un bon ~ souper we'll make ourselves a nice little (bit of) supper; (euph) le ~ coin ou endroit the bathroom (euph); (euph) faire son ~ besoin ou sa ~e commission to spend a penny (Brit); un ~ chapeau ravissant a lovely little hat; avoir ses ~es habitudes/manies to have one's little habits/ways; espèce de ~ impertinent you cheeky little so-and-so*; cela coûte une ~e fortune it costs a small fortune.
(k) (loc) (fig hum) le ~ oiseau va sortir watch the birdie!; être/ne pas être dans les ~s papiers de qn to be in sb's good/bad books; c'est de la ~e bière it's small stuff; ce n'est pas de la ~e bière its not without importance; se réunir en ~ comité to have a small get-together; à ~s pas (lit) with short steps; (fig) slowly but surely; un ~ peu a little (bit); un Balzac/un Versailles au ~ pied a poor man's Balzac/Versailles; mettre les ~s plats dans les grands to put on a first rate meal, go to town on the meal*; à la ~e semaine (adj) small-time; être aux ~s soins pour qn to give sb every attention, wait on sb hand and foot; être dans ses ~s souliers to be shaking in one's shoes; (hum) en ~e tenue V tenu; (Prov) les ~s ruisseaux font les grandes rivières little streams make big rivers.
2 adv: ~ à ~ little by little, gradually.
3 nm (a) (enfant) (little) boy; (Scol) junior (boy). les ~s children; viens ici, ~ come here, son; pauvre ~ poor little thing; le ~ Durand young Durand, the Durand boy; les ~s Durand the Durand children; les tout ~s the very young, the tiny tots; (Scol) the infants; jeu pour ~s et grands game for old and young (alike).
(b) (jeune animal) (gén) young. la chatte et ses ~s the cat and her kittens; la lionne et ses ~s the lioness and her young ou cubs; faire des ~s to have little kittens (ou puppies ou lambs etc); (fig) son argent a fait des ~s his money has bred more money.
(c) (personne de petite taille) small man; (personne inférieure) little man. les ~s small people; c'est toujours le ~ qui a tort it's always the little man who's in the wrong.
(d) une cour d'école, c'est le monde en ~ a school playground is the world in miniature.
4 petite nf (enfant) (little) girl; (femme) small woman. la ~e Durand (la fillette des Durand) the Durand's daughter; (péj: Mlle Durand) the Durand girl; pauvre ~e poor little thing; viens ici, ~e come here, little one.
5: petit ami boyfriend; petite amie girlfriend; petit banc low bench; petit-beurre nm, pl petits-beurre petit beurre biscuit; les petits blancs poor white settlers; petit bleu wire (telegram); petit bois kindling (U); petit-bourgeois, petite-bourgeoise, mpl petits-bourgeois (adj) petit-bourgeois, middle-class; (nm) petit-bourgeois, middle-class man; (nf) petit-bourgeois ou middle-class woman; petits chevaux: jouer aux petits chevaux to play ludo (Brit); petite classe junior form; les petites classes the junior ou lower school; petit cousin, petite cousine (enfant) little ou young cousin; (parent éloigné) distant cousin; petit déjeuner breakfast; le petit doigt the little finger; mon petit doigt me l'a dit a little bird told me; le petit écran television, TV; petit-enfant nm, pl petits-enfants grandchild; petite-fille nf, pl petites-filles granddaughter; petit-fils nm, pl petits-fils grandson; petit four petit four; petit garçon: il fait très petit garçon there's something of the little boy about him; (fig) à côté de lui, c'est un petit garçon next to him, he's a babe in arms; petit gâteau (sec) biscuit; petit-gris nm, pl petits-gris (escargot) garden snail; (écureuil) Siberian squirrel; (fourrure) squirrel fur; petit-lait nm whey; petit-maître†† nm, pl petits-maîtres dandy, toff†, fop†; (péj) petit-nègre nm pidgin French; (péj: galimatias) gibberish, gobbledygook*; petit-neveu nm, pl petits-neveux great- ou grand-nephew; petite-nièce nf, pl petites-nièces great- ou grand-niece; petit nom* Christian name (Brit), first name; (Couture) petit point petit point; petit-pois nm, pl petits-pois (garden) pea; le Petit Poucet Tom Thumb; (fig) la petite reine the bicycle; (Culin) petit salé ≈ streaky bacon; petit-suisse nm, pl petits-suisses petit-suisse; la petite vérole smallpox; petite voiture (d'infirme) invalid carriage.

petitement [pətitmɑ̃] adv (chichement) poorly; (mesquinement) meanly, pettily. nous sommes ~ logés our accommodation is cramped.

petitesse [p(ə)titɛs] nf [taille, endroit] smallness, small size; [somme] smallness, modesty; (fig) [esprit, acte] meanness (U), pettiness (U).

pétition [petisjɔ̃] nf (a) petition. faire une ~ auprès de qn to petition sb; faire signer une ~ to set up a petition. (b) (Philos) ~ de principe petitio principii (T), begging the question (U).

pétitionnaire [petisjɔnɛʀ] nmf petitioner.

pétoche‡ [petɔʃ] nf blue funk‡. avoir la ~ to be in a blue funk‡, have the wind up‡; flanquer la ~ à qn to scare the living daylights out of sb*, put the wind up sb‡.

pétoire [petwaʀ] nf (sarbacane) peashooter; (péj: fusil) peashooter (péj), popgun (péj).

peton* [pətɔ̃] nm (pied) foot, tootsy*.

pétoncle [petɔ̃kl(ə)] nm scallop.

Pétrarque [petʀaʀk] nm Petrarch.

pétrarquisme [petʀaʀkism(ə)] nm Petrarchism.

pétrel [petʀɛl] nm petrel.

pétri, e [petʀi] (ptp de pétrir) adj: ~ d'orgueil filled with pride; ~ d'ignorance steeped in ignorance.

pétrifiant, e [petʀifjɑ̃, ɑ̃t] adj petrifactive.

pétrification [petʀifikɑsjɔ̃] nf (a) (Géol) petrifaction, petrification. **(b)** (*fig*) *[cœur]* hardening; *[idées]* fossilization.

pétrifier [petʀifje] (7) **1** *vt* **(a)** (*Géol*) to petrify. **(b)** (*fig*) *personne* to paralyze, transfix; *cœur* to freeze; *idées* to fossilize, ossify. **être pétrifié de terreur** to be petrified (with terror), be paralyzed *ou* transfixed with terror.

2 se pétrifier *vpr* **(a)** (*Géol*) to petrify, become petrified. **(b)** (*fig*) *[sourire]* to freeze; *[personne]* to be paralyzed *ou* transfixed; *[cœur]* to freeze; *[idées]* to become fossilized *ou* ossified.

pétrin [petʀɛ̃] *nm* **(a)** (*: *ennui*) mess*, jam*, fix*. **tirer qn du ~** to get sb out of a mess* *ou* fix* *ou* tight spot*; **laisser qn dans le ~** to leave sb in a mess* *ou* jam* *ou* fix*; **se mettre dans un beau ~** to get (o.s.) into a fine mess*; **être dans le ~** to be in a mess* *ou* jam* *ou* fix*.

(b) (*Boulangerie*) kneading-trough; (*mécanique*) kneading-machine.

pétrir [petʀiʀ] (2) *vt pâte, argile* to knead; *muscle, main* to knead; *personne, esprit* to mould, shape.

pétrochimie [petʀɔʃimi] *nf* petrochemistry.

pétrochimique [petʀɔʃimik] *adj* petrochemical.

pétrochimiste [petʀɔʃimist(ə)] *nmf* petrochemist.

pétrographie [petʀɔgʀafi] *nf* petrography.

pétrographique [petʀɔgʀafik] *adj* petrographic(al).

pétrole [petʀɔl] *nm* (*brut*) oil, petroleum. **~ (lampant)** paraffin (oil); **~ brut** crude (oil), petroleum; **puits de ~** oil well; **gisement de ~** oilfield; **lampe/réchaud à ~** paraffin *ou* oil lamp/heater.

pétrolette [petʀɔlɛt] *nf* moped.

pétroleuse [petʀɔløz] *nf* (*Hist*) pétroleuse (*female fire-raiser during the Commune*).

pétrolier, -ière [petʀɔlje, jɛʀ] **1** *adj industrie, produits* petroleum (*épith*), oil (*épith*); *société* oil (*épith*); *pays* oil-producing (*épith*).

2 *nm* (*navire*) (oil) tanker; (*personne*) (*financier*) oil magnate, oilman; (*technicien*) petroleum engineer.

pétrolifère [petʀɔlifɛʀ] *adj roches, couches* oil-bearing. **gisement ~** oilfield.

pétulance [petylɑ̃s] *nf* exuberance, vivacity.

pétulant, e [petylɑ̃, ɑ̃t] *adj* exuberant, vivacious.

pétunia [petynja] *nm* petunia.

peu [pø] **1** *adv* **(a)** (*petite quantité*) little, not much. **il gagne/mange/lit (assez) ~** he doesn't earn/eat/read (very) much; **il gagne/mange/lit très ~** he earns/eats/reads very little *ou* precious little*; **il s'intéresse ~ à la peinture** he isn't very *ou* greatly interested in painting, he takes little interest in painting; **il se contente de ~** he is satisfied with little, it doesn't take much to satisfy him; **il a donné 10 F, c'est ~** he gave 10 francs, which isn't (very) much; **il y a (bien) ~ à faire/à voir ici** there's very little *ou* precious little* to do/see here, there's not much (at all) to do/see here; **il mange trop ~** he doesn't eat (nearly) enough; **je le connais trop ~ pour le juger** I don't know him (nearly) well enough to judge him.

(b) (*modifiant adj etc*) (a) little, not very. **il est (très) ~ sociable** he is not very sociable (at all), he is (very) unsociable; **fort ~ intéressant** decidedly uninteresting, of very little interest; **il conduit ~ prudemment** he drives carelessly *ou* with little care, he doesn't drive very carefully; **ils sont (bien) trop ~ nombreux** there are (far) too few of them; **un auteur assez ~ connu** a relatively little-known *ou* relatively unknown author; **c'est un ~ grand/petit** it's a little *ou* a bit (too) big/small; **elle n'est pas ~ soulagée d'être reçue** she's more than a little relieved *ou* not a little relieved at passing her exam; **~ avant** shortly before.

(c) ~ de (*quantité*) little, not much; (*nombre*) few, not (very) many; **nous avons eu (très) ~ de soleil/d'orages** we had (very) little sunshine/(very) few storms, we didn't have (very) much sunshine/(very) many storms (at all); **je peux vous céder du pain, bien qu'il m'en reste ~** I can let you have some bread though I haven't (very) much left; **on attendait des touristes mais il en est venu (très) ~** we expected tourists but not (very) many came *ou* but (very) few came; **~ de monde** *ou* **de gens** few people, not many people; **il est ici depuis ~ de temps** he hasn't been here long, he has been here (only) for a short while *ou* time; **il est ici pour ~ de temps** he isn't here for long, he is here for (only) a short time *ou* while; **en ~ de mots** briefly, in a few words; **cela a ~ d'importance** that's not (very) important, that doesn't matter (very) much, that's of little importance.

(d) (*employé seul: personnes*) **ils sont ~ à croire que** few believe that, there are few *ou* there aren't many who believe that; **bien ~/trop ~ le savent** very few/too few (people) know; **~ d'entre eux sont restés** few (of them) stayed, not many (of them) stayed.

(e) de ~: il est le plus âgé de ~ he is slightly *ou* a little older, he is just older; **il l'a battu de ~** he just beat him; **il a manqué le train de ~** he just missed the train; *V* **falloir**.

(f) (*loc*) **à ~ près** (just) about, near enough*; **à ~ près terminé/cuit** almost finished/cooked, more or less finished/cooked; **à ~ près 10 minutes/kilos** roughly *ou* approximately 10 minutes/kilos; **rester dans l'à ~ près** to remain vague; **à ~ de chose près: c'est terminé à ~ de chose près** it's more or less *ou* pretty well* finished, it's finished as near as damn it‡; **(c'est) ~ de chose** it's nothing; **c'est pas ~ dire!*** and THAT'S saying something!; (*littér*) **c'est ~ dire que** it is an understatement to say that; **~ à ~** gradually, little by little, bit by bit; (*littér*) **~ ou prou** to a greater or lesser degree, more or less; *V* **avant, depuis, si**[1] *etc.*

2 *nm* **(a)** little. **j'ai oublié le ~ (de français) que j'avais appris** I have forgotten the little (French) I had learnt; **elle se contente du ~ (d'argent) qu'elle a** she is satisfied with what little (money) *ou* the little (money) she has; **son ~ de compréhension/patience lui a nui** his lack of understanding/patience has done him harm; **elle s'est aliéné le ~ d'amis qu'elle avait** she has alienated the few friends *ou* the one or two friends she had.

(b) un ~ (*avec vb, modifiant adv mieux, moins, plus, trop etc*) a little, slightly, a bit; **un (tout) petit ~** a little bit, a trifle; **essaie de manger un ~** try to eat a little *ou* bit; **il boite un ~** he limps slightly *ou* a little *ou* a bit, he is slightly *ou* a bit lame; **elle va un tout petit ~ mieux** she is a trifle better *ou* ever so* slightly better; **il est un ~ artiste** he's a bit of* an artist, he's something of an artist; **il travaille un ~ trop/un ~ trop lentement** he works a little *ou* a bit too much/too slowly; **restez encore un ~** stay a little longer; **il y a un ~ moins de bruit** it is slightly *ou* a little less noisy, there's slightly *ou* a little less noise; **nous avons un ~ moins/plus de clients aujourd'hui** we have slightly fewer/more customers today; (*en effeuillant la marguerite*) **un ~, passionnément, pas du tout** he loves me, he loves me not; **un ~ plus: un ~ plus il écrasait le chien/oubliait son rendez-vous** he all but *ou* he very nearly ran over the dog/forgot his appointment; **pour un ~: pour un ~ il m'aurait accusé d'avoir volé** he all but *ou* just about* accused me of stealing; **pour un ~ je l'aurais giflé** for two pins (*Brit*) *ou* cents (*US*) I'd have slapped his face.

(c) un ~ de a little, a bit of; **un ~ d'eau** a little water, a drop of water; **un ~ de patience** a little patience, a bit of patience; **un ~ de silence/de calme, s'il vous plaît!** let's have some quiet *ou* a bit of quiet/some peace *ou* a bit of peace please!; **il a un ~ de sinusite/bronchite** he has a touch of sinusitis/bronchitis.

(d) (*: *intensif*) **un ~!** and how!* ; **tu as vraiment vu l'accident? — un ~! ou un ~ mon neveu!‡†** did you really see the accident? — you bet!* *ou* and how!* *ou* I sure did!* (*US*); **je me demande un ~ où sont les enfants** I just wonder where the children are *ou* can be; **montre-moi donc un ~ comment tu fais** just (you) show me then how you do it; **va-t-en voir un ~ si c'est vrai!** just you go and see if it's true!; **être un ~ là!: comme menteur il est un ~ là!** he's a darned good liar!*; **un ~ qu'il nous a menti!** he didn't half lie to us!*, I'll say he lied to us!*; **on en trouve un ~ partout** you find them just about everywhere; **c'est un ~ beaucoup*** that's a bit much* (*surtout Brit*).

peuchère [pøʃɛʀ] *excl* (*dial Midi*) strewth!*

peuh [pø] *excl* pooh!, bah!

peuplade [pœplad] *nf* (small) tribe, people.

peuple [pœpl(ə)] *nm* **(a)** (*Pol, Rel: communauté*) people, nation. **les ~s d'Europe** the peoples *ou* nations of Europe; (*Rel*) **le ~ élu** the chosen people.

(b) (*prolétariat*) **le ~** the people; **les gens du ~** the common people, ordinary people; (††, *péj*) **le bas** *ou* **petit ~** the lower classes (*péj*); (*fig*) **il se moque du ~** who does he think he is?, he's trying it on*; (*péj*) **faire ~** (*ne pas être distingué*) to be common (*péj*); (*vouloir paraître simple*) to try to appear working-class.

(c) (*foule*) crowd (of people). (*littér*) **un ~ de badauds/d'admirateurs** a crowd of gawkers/of admirers; **il y a du ~!*** there's a big crowd!

peuplé, e [pœple] (*ptp de* **peupler**) *adj ville, région* populated, inhabited. **très/peu/sous-~** densely-/sparsely-/under-populated.

peuplement [pœpləmɑ̃] *nm* **(a)** (*action*) *[colonie]* peopling, populating; *[étang]* stocking; *[forêt]* planting (with trees). **(b)** (*population*) population.

peupler [pœple] (1) **1** *vt* **(a)** (*pourvoir d'une population*) *colonie* to people, populate; *étang* to stock; *forêt* to plant out, plant with trees; (*fig littér*) to fill (*de* with). **les rêves/les souvenirs qui peuplent mon esprit** the dreams/memories that dwell in my mind (*littér*) *ou* that fill my mind.

(b) (*habiter*) *terre* to inhabit, populate; *maison* to live in, inhabit. **maison peuplée de souvenirs** house filled with *ou* full of memories.

2 se peupler *vpr [ville, région]* to become populated *ou* peopled; (*fig: s'animer*) to fill (up), be filled (*de* with). **la rue se peuplait de cris/de boutiques** the street filled with shouts/shops.

peupleraie [pøplәʀɛ] *nf* poplar grove.

peuplier [pøplije] *nm* poplar (tree).

peur [pœʀ] *nf* **(a) la ~** fear; **inspirer de la ~** to cause *ou* inspire fear; **ressentir de la ~** to feel afraid, feel fear; **la ~ lui donnait des ailes** fear lent him wings; **être vert** *ou* **mort de ~** to be frightened *ou* scared out of one's wits, be petrified (with fear); **la ~ de la punition/de mourir/du qu'en-dira-t-on** (the) fear of punishment/of dying/of what people might say; **prendre ~** to take fright; **la ~ du gendarme*** the fear of being caught; **cacher sa ~** to hide one's fear; **sans ~** (*adj*) fearless (*de* of); (*adv*) fearlessly.

(b) une ~: une ~ irraisonnée de se blesser s'empara de lui he was seized by *ou* with an irrational fear of injuring himself; **je n'ai qu'une ~, c'est qu'il ne revienne pas** I have only one fear, that he doesn't *ou* won't come back; **il a eu une ~ bleue** he had a bad fright *ou* scare; **des ~s irraisonnées/enfantines** irrational/childish fears; **il a une ~ bleue de sa femme** he's scared stiff* of his wife, he goes *ou* lives in fear and trembling of his wife; **il m'a fait une de ces ~s!** he gave me a dreadful fright *ou* scare, he didn't half* give me a fright! *ou* scare!

(c) avoir ~ to be frightened *ou* afraid *ou* scared (*de* of); **avoir ~ pour qn** to be afraid for sb *ou* on sb's behalf, fear for sb; **n'ayez pas ~** (*craindre*) don't be afraid *ou* frightened *ou* scared; (*s'inquiéter*) have no fear; **il veut faire ce voyage en 2 jours, il n'a pas ~, lui, au moins!*** he wants to do the trip in 2 days — you can't say he hasn't got nerve!; **il prétend qu'il a téléphoné, il n'a pas ~, lui, au moins!*** he says he phoned — he has some nerve! *ou* you can't say he hasn't got nerve!; **n'ayez pas ~ de dire la vérité** don't be afraid *ou* frightened *ou* scared of telling the truth; **il n'a ~ de rien** he's afraid of nothing, nothing frightens him; **avoir ~ d'un rien** to frighten easily; **avoir ~ de son ombre** to be frightened *ou* scared of one's own shadow; **j'ai bien ~/très ~ qu'il ne pleuve** I'm afraid/very much afraid it's going to rain *ou* it might rain; **il va échouer? — j'en ai (bien) ~** is he going to fail? — I'm (very much) afraid so *ou* I'm afraid he is; **j'ai ~ qu'il ne vous ait menti/que cela ne vous gêne** I'm afraid *ou* worried *ou* I fear that he might have lied to you/that it might inconvenience you; **je n'ai pas ~ qu'il dise la vérité** I'm not afraid *ou* frightened of his telling the truth; **il a eu plus de ~ que de mal** he was more frightened than hurt, he wasn't hurt so much as frightened; **il y a eu *ou* ça a fait plus de ~ que de mal** it caused more fright than real harm, it was more frightening than anything else.

(d) faire ~ à qn (*intimider*) to frighten *ou* scare sb; (*causer une frayeur à*) to give sb a fright, frighten *ou* scare sb; **pour faire ~ aux oiseaux** to frighten *ou* scare the birds away *ou* off; **l'idée de l'examen lui fait ~** the idea of sitting the exam frightens *ou* scares him, he's frightened *ou* scared at the idea of sitting the exam; **cette pensée fait ~** the thought is frightening, it's a frightening thought; **tout lui fait ~** he's afraid *ou* frightened *ou* scared of everything; **laid *ou* hideux à faire ~** frighteningly ugly; (*iro*) **ça fait ~!*: il fait chaud, ça fait ~!** it's not exactly roasting!* (*iro*).

(e) de *ou* par ~ de: de ~ de faire for fear of doing, for fear that one might *ou* should do, lest one (should) do (*littér*); **il a couru de ~ de manquer le train** he ran for fear of missing the train, he ran for fear that he might *ou* should miss the train, he ran because he was afraid he might miss the train; **il a accepté de ~ de les vexer** he accepted for fear of annoying them *ou* lest he (should) annoy them (*littér*); **ferme la porte, de ~ qu'il ne prenne froid** close the door so that he doesn't catch cold; **il renonça, de ~ du ridicule** he gave up for fear of ridicule.

peureusement [pœʀøzmɑ̃] *adv* fearfully, timorously.
peureux, -euse [pœʀø, øz] **1** *adj* fearful, timorous. **2** *nm,f* fearful *ou* timorous person.
peut-être [pøtɛtʀ(ə)] *adv* perhaps, maybe. **il est ~ intelligent, ~ est-il intelligent** he's perhaps clever, perhaps he's clever, he may *ou* might (well) be clever, maybe he's clever; **il n'est ~ pas beau mais il est intelligent** he may *ou* might not be handsome but he is clever, perhaps *ou* maybe he's not handsome but he's clever; **~ bien** perhaps (so), it could well be; **~ pas** perhaps *ou* maybe not; **~ bien mais ...** that's as may be *ou* perhaps so but ...; **~ que ...** perhaps ...; **~ bien qu'il pleuvra** it may well rain; **~ que oui** perhaps so, perhaps he will (*ou* they are *etc*); **je ne sais pas conduire ~?** who's (doing the) driving? (*iro*), I do know how to drive, you know!; **tu le sais mieux que moi ~?** so (you think) you know more about it than I do, do you?, I DO know more about it than you, you know!
pèze‡ [pɛz] *nm* (*argent*) dough‡, bread‡.
pff(t) [pf(t)] *excl*, **pfut** [pfyt] *excl* pooh!, bah!
phacochère [fakɔʃɛʀ] *nm* wart hog.
phaéton [faetɔ̃] *nm* (*calèche*) phaeton. (*Myth*) **P~** Phaëton.
phagocyte [fagɔsit] *nm* phagocyte.
phagocyter [fagɔsite] (1) *vt* (*Bio*) to phagocytose; (*fig*) to absorb, engulf.
phagocytose [fagɔsitoz] *nf* phagocytosis.
phalange [falɑ̃ʒ] *nf* (*Anat*) phalanx; (*Antiq, littér: armée*) phalanx. (*Pol espagnole*) **la ~** the Falange.
phalangien, -ienne [falɑ̃ʒjɛ̃, jɛn] *adj* (*Anat*) phalangeal.
phalangiste [falɑ̃ʒist(ə)] *adj, nmf* Falangist.
phalanstère [falɑ̃stɛʀ] *nm* phalanstery.
phalène [falɛn] *nf* emerald, geometrid (*T*).
phallique [falik] *adj* phallic.
phallocrate [falɔkʀat] *nm* (*hum*) male chauvinist pig* (*hum*).
phallocratie [falɔkʀasi] *nf* (*hum*) male chauvinism.
phalloïde [falɔid] *adj* phalloid; *V* **amanite.**
phallus [falys] *nm* phallus.
phantasme [fɑ̃tasm(ə)] *nm* = **fantasme.**
pharamineux, -euse [faʀaminø, øz] *adj* = **faramineux.**
pharaon [faʀaɔ̃] *nm* (*Antiq*) Pharaoh.
pharaonien, -ienne [faʀaɔnjɛ̃, jɛn] *adj*, **pharaonique** [faʀaɔnik] *adj* Pharaonic.
phare [faʀ] *nm* **(a)** (*tour*) lighthouse; (*Aviat, fig*) beacon. (*Naut*) **~ à feu fixe/tournant** fixed/revolving light *ou* beacon.
(b) (*Aut*) headlight, headlamp. **rouler pleins ~s *ou* en ~s** to drive on full beam (*Brit*) *ou* high beams (*US*) *ou* on full headlights *ou* with headlights full on; **mettre ses ~s en veilleuse/en code** to dim/dip one's headlights; **~s code** dipped headlights *ou* beam; **~ antibrouillard** fog lamp; **~ de recul** reversing light; **~ à iodes** quartz halogen lamp; *V* **appel.**
pharisaïque [faʀizaik] *adj* (*Hist*) Pharisaic; (*fig*) pharisaic(al).
pharisaïsme [faʀizaism(ə)] *nm* (*Hist*) Pharisaism, Phariseeism; (*fig*) pharisaism, phariseeism.
pharisien, -ienne [faʀizjɛ̃, jɛn] *nm,f* (*Hist*) Pharisee; (*fig*) pharisee.
pharmaceutique [faʀmasøtik] *adj* pharmaceutical, pharmaceutic.
pharmacie [faʀmasi] *nf* **(a)** (*magasin*) chemist's (shop), pharmacy, drugstore (*Can, US*); (*officine*) dispensary; [*hôpital*] dispensary, pharmacy.
(b) (*science*) pharmacology; (*profession*) pharmacy. **laboratoire de ~** pharmaceutical laboratory; **préparateur en ~** pharmacist.
(c) (*produits*) pharmaceuticals, medicines. **(armoire à) ~** medicine chest *ou* cabinet *ou* cupboard, first-aid cabinet *ou* cupboard; **~ portative** first-aid kit.
pharmacien, -ienne [faʀmasjɛ̃, jɛn] *nm,f* (*qui tient une pharmacie*) (dispensing) chemist, pharmacist, druggist (*US*); (*préparateur*) pharmacist, chemist.
pharmacologie [faʀmakɔlɔʒi] *nf* pharmacology.
pharmacologique [faʀmakɔlɔʒik] *adj* pharmacological.
pharmacopée [faʀmakɔpe] *nf* pharmacopoeia.
pharyngé, e [faʀɛ̃ʒe] *adj*, **pharyngien, -ienne** [faʀɛ̃ʒjɛ̃, jɛn] *adj* pharyngeal, pharyngal.
pharyngite [faʀɛ̃ʒit] *nf* pharyngitis.
pharynx [faʀɛ̃ks] *nm* pharynx.
phase [fɑz] *nf* (*gén, Méd*) phase, stage; (*Astron, Chim, Phys*) phase.
Phébus [febys] *nm* Phoebus.
Phèdre [fɛdʀ(ə)] *nf* Phaedra.
Phénicie [fenisi] *nf* Phoenicia.
phénicien, -ienne [fenisjɛ̃, jɛn] **1** *adj* Phoenician. **2** *nm* (*Ling*) Phoenician. **3** *nm,f*: **P~(ne)** Phoenician.
phénix [feniks] *nm* (*Myth*) phoenix; (*fig†, littér*) paragon.
phénol [fenɔl] *nm* phenol.
phénoménal, e, *mpl* -aux [fenɔmenal, o] *adj* (*gén*) phenomenal.
phénoménalement [fenɔmenalmɑ̃] *adv* phenomenally.
phénomène [fenɔmɛn] *nm* (*gén, Philos*) phenomenon; (*monstre de foire*) freak (of nature); (*: *personne*) (*génial*) phenomenon; (*excentrique*) character*; (*anormal*) freak*.
phénoménologie [fenɔmenɔlɔʒi] *nf* phenomenology.
phénoménologique [fenɔmenɔlɔʒik] *adj* phenomenological.
philanthrope [filɑ̃tʀɔp] *nmf* philanthropist.
philanthropie [filɑ̃tʀɔpi] *nf* philanthropy.
philanthropique [filɑ̃tʀɔpik] *adj* philanthropic(al).
philatélie [filateli] *nf* philately, stamp collecting.
philatélique [filatelik] *adj* philatelic.
philatéliste [filatelist(ə)] *nmf* philatelist, stamp collector.
philarmonie [filaʀmɔni] *nf* (local) philharmonic society.
philharmonique [filaʀmɔnik] *adj* philharmonic.
philhellénisme [filelenism(ə)] *nm* philhellenism.
Philippe [filip] *nm* Philip.
philippin, e [filipɛ̃, in] **1** *adj* Philippine. **2** *nm,f*: **P~(e)** Filipino.
Philippines [filipin] *nfpl*: **les ~** the Philippines.
philistin [filistɛ̃] *adj m, nm* (*Hist*) Philistine; (*fig*) philistine.
philistinisme [filistinism(ə)] *nm* philistinism.
philo [filo] *nf* (*arg Scol*) *abrév de* **philosophie.**
philodendron [filɔdɛ̃dʀɔ̃] *nm* philodendron.
philologie [filɔlɔʒi] *nf* philology.
philologique [filɔlɔʒik] *adj* philological.
philologiquement [filɔlɔʒikmɑ̃] *adv* philologically.
philologue [filɔlɔg] *nmf* philologist.
philosophale [filozɔfal] *adj f V* **pierre.**
philosophe [filozɔf] **1** *nmf* philosopher. **2** *adj* philosophical.
philosopher [filozɔfe] (1) *vi* to philosophize.
philosophie [filozɔfi] *nf* philosophy; (*Scol*) (*enseignement*) philosophical studies, ≃ arts subjects; (*classe*) philosophy class, ≃ arts sixth (form (*Brit*) *ou* grade (*US*)).
philosophique [filozɔfik] *adj* philosophical.
philosophiquement [filozɔfikmɑ̃] *adv* philosophically.
philtre [filtʀ(ə)] *nm* philtre, love potion.
phlébite [flebit] *nf* phlebitis.
phlegmon [flɛgmɔ̃] *nm* phlegmon.
phlox [flɔks] *nm inv* phlox.
phobie [fɔbi] *nf* phobia. **avoir la ~ de** to have a phobia about.
phobique [fɔbik] *adj* phobic.
phocéen, -enne [fɔseɛ̃, ɛn] **1** *adj* Phocaean. **2** *nm,f*: **P~(ne)** Phocaean.
phonateur, -trice [fɔnatœʀ, tʀis] *adj* phonatory.
phonation [fɔnɑsjɔ̃] *nf* phonation.
phonatoire [fɔnatwaʀ] *adj* = **phonateur.**
phone [fɔn] *nm* phone.
phonématique [fɔnematik] *nf* phonology, phonemics (*sg*).
phonème [fɔnɛm] *nm* phoneme.
phonémique [fɔnemik] **1** *adj* phonemic. **2** *nf* = **phonématique.**
phonéticien, -ienne [fɔnetisjɛ̃, jɛn] *nm,f* phonetician.
phonétique [fɔnetik] **1** *nf* phonetics (*sg*). **2** *adj* phonetic.
phonétiquement [fɔnetikmɑ̃] *adv* phonetically.
phoniatre [fɔnjatʀ(ə)] *nmf* speech therapist.
phoniatrie [fɔnjatʀi] *nf* speech therapy.
phonie [fɔni] *nf* wireless telegraphy (*Brit*), radiotelegraphy.
phonique [fɔnik] *adj* phonic.
phono [fono] *nm* (*abrév de* **phonographe**) (*phonographe*) (wind-up) gramophone (*Brit*), phonograph (*US*); (*électrophone*) record player.
phonographe [fɔnɔgʀaf] *nm* (wind-up) gramophone (*Brit*), phonograph (*US*).
phonologie [fɔnɔlɔʒi] *nf* phonology.
phonologique [fɔnɔlɔʒik] *adj* phonological.
phonologue [fɔnɔlɔg] *nmf* phonologist.
phonothèque [fɔnɔtɛk] *nf* sound archives.
phoque [fɔk] *nm* (*animal*) seal; (*fourrure*) sealskin; *V* **souffler.**
phosphate [fɔsfat] *nm* phosphate.
phosphaté, e [fɔsfate] (*ptp de* **phosphater**) *adj* phosphatic, phosphated.
phosphater [fɔsfate] (1) *vt* to phosphate, treat with phosphate.
phosphène [fɔsfɛn] *nm* phosphene.
phosphine [fɔsfin] *nf* phosphine.
phosphore [fɔsfɔʀ] *nm* phosphorus.
phosphoré, e [fɔsfɔʀe] *adj* phosphorous.
phosphorescence [fɔsfɔʀesɑ̃s] *nf* luminosity, phosphorescence (*T*).
phosphorescent, e [fɔsfɔʀesɑ̃, ɑ̃t] *adj* luminous, phosphorescent (*T*).
phosphoreux, -euse [fɔsfɔʀø, øz] *adj acide* phosphorous; *bronze* phosphor (*épith*).
phosphorique [fɔsfɔʀik] *adj* phosphoric.
phosphure [fɔsfyʀ] *nm* phosphide.

photo [fɔto] 1 *nf* (*abrév de* **photographie**) (*image*) photo, snap(shot), shot. **en ~: prendre qn en ~** to take a photo *ou* snap(shot) *ou* shot of sb; **en ~ ça rend bien** it looks good in *ou* on a photo; *V* **appareil.**
2: photo-électricité *nf* photo-electricity; **photo-électrique** *adj* photo-electric; **photo-finish** *nf* (*film*) film (of the end of a race); (*appareil*) camera (at the finishing line); **photo-robot** *nf, pl* **photos-robot** identikit (picture).
photochimie [fɔtɔʃimi] *nf* photochemistry.
photochimique [fɔtɔʃimik] *adj* photochemical.
photocopie [fɔtɔkɔpi] *nf* (*action*) photocopying, photostatting; (*copie*) photocopy, photostat (copy).
photocopier [fɔtɔkɔpje] (7) *vt* to photocopy, photostat.
photocopieur [fɔtɔkɔpjœʀ] *nm* photocopier, photostat.
photogénique [fɔtɔʒenik] *adj* photogenic.
photographe [fɔtɔgʀaf] *nmf* (*artiste*) photographer; (*commerçant*) camera dealer. **vous trouverez cet article chez un ~** you will find this item at a camera shop (*Brit*) *ou* store (*US*).
photographie [fɔtɔgʀafi] *nf* **(a)** (*art*) photography. **faire de la ~** (*comme passe-temps*) to be an amateur photographer, take photographs; (*en vacances*) to take photographs.
(b) (*image*) photograph. **~ d'identité/en couleur/aérienne** passport/colour/aerial photograph; **prendre une ~** to take a photograph *ou* a picture; **prendre qn en ~** to take a photograph *ou* a picture of sb, photograph sb.
photographier [fɔtɔgʀafje] (7) *vt* to photograph, take a photo(graph) of, take a picture of. **se faire ~** to have one's photo(graph) *ou* picture taken; (*fig: mémoriser*) **il avait photographié l'endroit** he had got the place firmly fixed in his mind.
photographique [fɔtɔgʀafik] *adj* photographic; *V* **appareil.**
photographiquement [fɔtɔgʀafikmɑ̃] *adv* photographically.
photograveur [fɔtɔgʀavœʀ] *nm* photoengraver.
photogravure [fɔtɔgʀavyʀ] *nf* photoengraving.
photolithographie [fɔtɔlitɔgʀafi] *nf* photolithography.
photométrie [fɔtɔmetʀi] *nf* photometry.
photométrique [fɔtɔmetʀik] *adj* photometric(al).
photomontage [fɔtɔmɔ̃taʒ] *nm* photomontage.
photon [fɔtɔ̃] *nm* photon.
photophobie [fɔtɔfɔbi] *nf* photophobia.
photosensible [fɔtɔsɑ̃sibl(ə)] *adj* photosensitive.
photostat [fɔtɔsta] *nm* photostat.
photosynthèse [fɔtɔsɛ̃tɛz] *nf* photosynthesis.
photothèque [fɔtɔtɛk] *nf* photographic library, picture library.
phrase [fʀɑz] *nf* (*Ling*) sentence; (*propos*) phrase; (*Mus*) phrase. **faire des ~s** to talk in flowery language; **~ tout faite** stock phrase; **citer une ~ célèbre** to quote a famous phrase *ou* saying; **sans ~s** without mincing matters; *V* **membre.**
phrasé [fʀɑze] *nm* (*Mus*) phrasing.
phraséologie [fʀazeɔlɔʒi] *nf* (*vocabulaire spécifique*) phraseology; (*péj*) fine words (*péj*), high-flown language (*péj*).
phraséologique [fʀazeɔlɔʒik] *adj* *dictionnaire* of phrases; (*péj*) *style* high-flown (*péj*), pretentious.
phraser [fʀɑze] (1) 1 *vt* (*Mus*) to phrase. 2 *vi* (*péj*) to use fine words (*péj*) *ou* high-flown language (*péj*).
phraseur, -euse [fʀɑzœʀ, øz] *nm,f* man (*ou* woman) of fine words (*péj*).
Phrygie [fʀiʒi] *nf* Phrygia.
phrygien, -ienne [fʀiʒjɛ̃, jɛn] 1 *adj* Phrygian; *V* **bonnet.** 2 *nm,f*: **P~(ne)** Phrygian.
phtaléine [ftalein] *nf* phthalein.
phtisie [ftizi] *nf* consumption, phthisis (*T*). **~ galopante** galloping consumption.
phtisiologie [ftizjɔlɔʒi] *nf* phthisiology.
phtisiologue [ftizjɔlɔg] *nmf* phthisiologist.
phtisique [ftizik] *adj* consumptive, phthisical (*T*).
phylloxéra [filɔkseʀa] *nm* phylloxera.
physicien, -ienne [fizisjɛ̃, jɛn] *nm,f* physicist. **~ de l'atome** atomic *ou* nuclear physicist.
physico-chimie [fizikɔʃimi] *nf* physical chemistry.
physico-chimique [fizikɔʃimik] *adj* physio-chemical.
physiocrate [fizjɔkʀat] 1 *nmf* physiocrat. 2 *adj* physiocratic.
physiocratie [fizjɔkʀasi] *nf* physiocracy.
physiologie [fizjɔlɔʒi] *nf* physiology.
physiologique [fizjɔlɔʒik] *adj* physiological.
physiologiquement [fizjɔlɔʒikmɑ̃] *adv* physiologically.
physiologiste [fizjɔlɔʒist(ə)] 1 *nmf* physiologist. 2 *adj* physiological.
physionomie [fizjɔnɔmi] *nf* (*traits du visage*) facial appearance (*U*), physiognomy (*frm*); (*expression*) countenance (*frm*), face; (*fig: aspect*) face, physiognomy (*frm*).
physionomiste [fizjɔnɔmist(ə)] *adj, nmf*: **c'est un ~, il est ~** (*bon jugement*) he's a good judge of faces; (*bonne mémoire*) he has a good memory for faces.
physique [fizik] 1 *adj* (*gén*) physical; *V* **amour, culture, personne.** 2 *nm* (*aspect*) physique; (*visage*) face. **au ~** physically; **avoir un ~ agréable** to be quite good-looking; **avoir le ~ de l'emploi** to look the part. 3 *nf* physics (*sg*).
physiquement [fizikmɑ̃] *adv* physically.
piaf* [pjaf] *nm* sparrow.
piaffement [pjafmɑ̃] *nm* [*cheval*] stamping, pawing.
piaffer [pjafe] (1) *vi* [*cheval*] to stamp, paw the ground; [*personne*] to stamp one's feet. **~ d'impatience** to fidget with impatience *ou* impatiently.
piaillard, e* [pjɑjaʀ, aʀd(ə)] (*V* **piailler**) 1 *adj* squawking (*épith*); screeching (*épith*); squealing (*épith*). 2 *nm,f* squawker, squealer.
piaillement* [pjɑjmɑ̃] *nm* (*V* **piailler**) squawking (*U*); screeching (*U*); squealing (*U*).
piailler* [pjɑje] (1) *vi* [*oiseau*] to squawk, screech; [*personne*] to squawk, squeal.
piaillerie* [pjɑjʀi] *nf* = **piaillement*.**
piailleur, -euse* [pjɑjœʀ, øz] = **piaillard*.**
piane-piane* [pjanpjan] *adv* gently. **allez-y ~** go gently *ou* easy*, easy *ou* gently does it*.
pianiste [pjanist(ə)] *nmf* pianist, piano player.
pianistique [pjanistik] *adj* pianistic.
piano [pjano] 1 *nm* piano. **~ droit/à queue/de concert/demi-queue** upright/grand/concert grand/baby grand (piano); **~ mécanique** player piano.
2 *adv* (*Mus*) piano; (**fig*) gently. **allez-y ~** easy *ou* gently does it*, go easy* *ou* gently.
pianotage [pjanɔtaʒ] *nm* (*V* **pianoter**) tinkling (at the piano *ou* typewriter *etc*); drumming.
pianoter [pjanɔte] (1) 1 *vi* (*sur un clavier*) to tinkle away (at the piano *ou* typewriter *etc*); (*fig*) to drum one's fingers. 2 *vt*: **~ un air** to strum (out) *ou* tinkle out a tune on the piano.
piastre [pjastʀ(ə)] *nf* piastre; (*Can**) dollar.
piaule* [pjol] *nf* pad*.
piaulement [pjolmɑ̃] *nm* (*V* **piauler**) cheeping (*U*); whimpering (*U*); singing (*U*).
piauler [pjole] (1) *vi* [*oiseau*] to cheep; [*enfant*] to whimper; (*fig*) [*balle de fusil*] to sing.
pic [pik] *nm* **(a)** (*montagne, cime*) peak.
(b) (*pioche*) pick(axe). **~ à glace** ice pick.
(c) (*oiseau*) **~ (vert)** (green) woodpecker.
(d) (*loc*) **à ~** (*adv*) vertically, sheer, straight down; (*adj*) sheer; **couler à ~** to go straight down; (*fig*) **arriver** *ou* **tomber à ~*** to come just at the right time *ou* moment; **vous arrivez à ~*** you couldn't have come at a better time *ou* moment, you've come just at the right time ou moment.
picaillons* [pikajɔ̃] *nmpl* cash* (*U*).
picard, e [pikaʀ, aʀd(ə)] 1 *adj* Picardy. 2 *nm* (*Ling*) Picardy dialect. 3 *nm,f*: **P~(e)** inhabitant *ou* native of Picardy.
Picardie [pikaʀdi] *nf* Picardy.
picaresque [pikaʀɛsk(ə)] *adj* picaresque.
piccolo [pikɔlo] *nm* piccolo.
pichenette* [piʃnɛt] *nf* flick. **faire tomber d'une ~** to flick off *ou* away.
pichet [piʃɛ] *nm* pitcher, jug.
pickpocket [pikpɔkɛt] *nm* pickpocket.
pick-up [pikœp] *nm* (*bras*) pickup; (*électrophone*) record player.
picoler* [pikɔle] (1) *vi* to booze*, knock it back*, tipple*. **qu'est-ce qu'il peut ~!** he can't half knock it back!*
picorer [pikɔʀe] (1) 1 *vi* to peck (about). 2 *vt* to peck, peck (away) at.
picotement [pikɔtmɑ̃] *nm* [*gorge*] tickle (*U*), tickling (*U*); [*peau, membres*] smarting (*U*), prickling (*U*); [*yeux*] smarting (*U*), stinging (*U*).
picoter [pikɔte] (1) 1 *vt* **(a)** (*piquer*) *gorge* to tickle; *peau* to make smart *ou* prickle; *yeux* to make smart, sting; (*avec une épingle*) to prick. **la fumée lui picote les yeux** the smoke is making his eyes smart *ou* is stinging his eyes; **j'ai les yeux qui me picotent** my eyes are smarting *ou* stinging.
(b) (*picorer*) to peck, peck (away) at.
2 *vi* [*gorge*] to tickle; [*peau*] to smart, prickle; [*yeux*] to smart, sting.
picotin [pikɔtɛ̃] *nm* (*ration d'avoine*) oats (*pl*), ration of oats; (*mesure*) peck.
picrate* [pikʀat] *nm* (*péj*) plonk* (*Brit*), cheap wine.
Pictes [pikt(ə)] *nmpl* Picts.
pictographie [piktɔgʀafi] *nf* pictography.
pictographique [piktɔgʀafik] *adj* pictographic.
pictural, e, *mpl* **-aux** [piktyʀal, o] *adj* pictorial.
pie[1] [pi] 1 *nf* (*oiseau*) magpie; (**fig: bavarde*) chatterbox*, gasbag* (*péj*), windbag*. 2 *adj inv* *cheval* piebald; *vache* black and white; *V* **voiture.**
pie[2] [pi] *adj f V* **œuvre.**
Pie [pi] *nm* Pius.
pièce [pjɛs] 1 *nf* **(a)** (*fragment*) piece. **en ~s** in pieces; **mettre en ~s** (*lit*) (*casser*) to smash to pieces; (*déchirer*) to pull *ou* tear to pieces; (*fig*) to tear *ou* pull to pieces; **c'est inventé** *ou* **forgé de toutes ~s** it's made up from start to finish, it's a complete fabrication; *V* **tailler, tout.**
(b) (*gén: unité, objet*) piece; [*jeu d'échecs, de dames*] piece; [*tissu, drap*] length, piece; (*Mil*) gun; (*Chasse, Pêche: prise*) specimen. (*Comm*) **se vendre à la ~** to be sold separately *ou* individually; **2 F (la) ~** 2 francs each *ou* apiece; **travail à la ~** *ou* **aux ~s** piecework; **payé à la ~** *ou* **aux ~s** on piece rate, on piecework; (*fig*) **on n'est pas aux ~s!** there's no rush!; (*Habillement*) **un deux ~s** (*costume, tailleur*) a two-piece (suit); (*maillot de bain*) a two-piece (swimsuit); *V* **chef**[1].
(c) [*machine, voiture*] part, component. **~s (de rechange)** spares, (spare) parts.
(d) (*document*) paper, document. **avez-vous toutes les ~s nécessaires?** have you got all the necessary papers? *ou* documents?; **juger/décider sur ~s** to judge/decide on actual evidence; **avec ~s à l'appui** with supporting documents.
(e) (*Couture*) patch. **mettre une ~ à qch** to put a patch on sth.
(f) [*maison*] room. **appartement de 5 ~s** 5-room(ed) flat; **un deux-~s cuisine** a 2-room(ed) flat (*Brit*) *ou* apartment (*US*) with kitchen.
(g) (*Théât*) play; (*Littérat, Mus*) piece. **jouer** *ou* **monter une ~ de Racine** to put on a Racine play; **une ~ pour hautbois** a piece for oboe.
(h) **(de monnaie)** coin; **~ d'argent/d'or** silver/gold coin; **une ~ de 5 francs/de 50 centimes** a 5-franc/50-centime piece *ou*

coin; **donner la ~ à qn*** to give *ou* slip* sb a tip, tip sb; *V* **rendre.**

2: pièce d'artifice firework; **pièce d'artillerie** piece of ordnance; **pièce de bétail** head of cattle; **50 pièces de bétail** 50 head of cattle; **pièce de blé** wheat field, cornfield; **pièce de bois** piece of wood *ou* timber *(for joinery etc)*; **pièce de charpente** member; **pièce de collection** collector's item *ou* piece; **pièce comptable** accounting record; *(Jur)* **pièce à conviction** exhibit; **pièce détachée** spare, (spare) part; **livré en pièces détachées** (delivered) in kit form; **pièce d'eau** ornamental lake *ou* pond; **pièce d'identité** identity paper; **avez-vous une pièce d'identité?** have you (got) any identification? *ou* some means of identification?; *(Admin)* **pièces jointes** enclosures; **pièces justificatives** supporting documents; *(Culin)* **pièce montée** (ornamental) tiered cake; *(à une noce)* wedding cake; **pièce de musée** museum piece; **pièce rapportée** *(Couture)* patch; *[marqueterie, mosaïque]* insert, piece; **pièce de rechange** spare, (spare) part; **pièce de résistance** main dish, pièce de résistance; **pièce de terre** piece *ou* patch of land; **pièce de théâtre** play; **pièce de vers** piece of poetry, short poem; **pièce de viande** side of meat; **pièce de vin** cask of wine.

piécette [pjesɛt] *nf* small coin.

pied [pje] **1** *nm* **(a)** *(gén) [personne, animal]* foot; *(sabot) [cheval, bœuf]* hoof; *(Zool) [mollusque]* foot. **aller ~s nus** *ou* **nu-pieds** to go barefoot(ed); **avoir les ~s plats** to have flat feet, be flatfooted; **avoir les ~s en dedans/dehors** to have turned-in/turned-out feet, be pigeon-toed/splay-footed; **marcher les ~s en dedans/dehors** to walk with one's feet turned in/turned out, walk pigeon-toed/splay-footed; **à ~s joints** with one's feet together; **le ~ lui a manqué** he lost his footing, his foot slipped; **aller à ~** to go on foot, walk; **nous avons fait tout le chemin à ~** we walked all the way, we came all the way on foot; **il est incapable de mettre un ~ devant l'autre** he can't walk straight, he can't put one foot in front of the other; **il ne tient pas sur ses ~s** *(alcool)* he can hardly stand up; *(maladie)* he's dead on his feet; **sauter d'un ~ sur l'autre** to hop from one foot to the other; *(lit, fig)* **~s et poings liés** tied *ou* bound hand and foot.

(b) *[table]* leg; *[arbre, colline, échelle, lit, mur]* foot, bottom; *[appareil-photo]* stand, tripod; *[lampe]* base; *[lampadaire]* stand; *[verre]* stem; *[colonne]* base, foot; *[chaussette]* foot; *(Math) [perpendiculaire]* foot.

(c) *(Agr) [salade, tomate]* plant. **~ de laitue** lettuce (plant); **~ de céleri** head of celery; **~ de vigne** vine; **blé sur ~** uncut corn.

(d) *(Culin) [porc, mouton, veau]* trotter.

(e) *(mesure, aussi Can)* foot. **un poteau de 6 ~s** a 6-foot pole.

(f) *(Poésie)* foot.

(g) *(niveau)* **vivre sur un grand ~** to live in (great *ou* grand) style; **sur un ~ d'amitié** on a friendly footing; **sur un ~ d'égalité** on an equal footing, as equals.

(h) (‡: *idiot*) twit* *(Brit)*, idiot. **quel ~!** what a useless twit!* *(Brit)*, what an idiot!; **jouer comme un ~** to be a useless* *ou* lousy‡ player; **il s'y prend comme un ~** he hasn't a clue how to go about it*; **il conduit/chante comme un ~** he hasn't a clue about driving/singing*.

(i) *(loc: avec prép)* **~ à ~** *se défendre, lutter* every inch of the way; **au ~ de la lettre** literally; **au ~ levé** at a moment's notice; **à ~ d'œuvre** ready to get down to the job; **à ~ sec** without getting one's feet wet; **de ~ ferme** resolutely; **en ~** *portrait* full-length; *statue* full-scale, full-size; **se jeter aux ~s de qn** to throw o.s. at sb's feet; **des ~s à la tête** from head to foot; **de ~ en cap** from head to foot, from top to toe; **sur le ~ de guerre** (all) ready to go, ready for action; *V* **petit.**

(j) *(loc: avec verbes)* **avoir ~** to be able to touch the bottom *(in swimming)*; **je n'ai plus ~** I'm out of my depth *(lit)*; **perdre ~** *(lit: en nageant, aussi fig)* to be *ou* get out of one's depth; *(en montagne)* to lose one's footing; **avoir bon ~ bon œil** to be as fit as a fiddle, be fighting fit; **avoir le ~ léger** to be light of step; **avoir le ~ marin** to be a good sailor; **avoir les (deux) ~s sur terre** to have one's feet firmly (planted) on the ground; **avoir le ~ à l'étrier** to be well on the way; *(fig)* **mettre le ~ à l'étrier à qn** to give sb a leg up; **avoir un ~ dans la tombe** to have one foot in the grave; **être sur ~** *[projet]* to be under way; *[malade]* to be up and about; **faire du ~ à qn** *(prévenir)* to give sb a kick *(to warn him)*; *(galamment)* to play footsy with sb*; **faire le ~ de grue** to stand about (waiting), kick one's heels; **faire des ~s et des mains pour faire qch*** to move heaven and earth to do sth, pull out all the stops to do sth*; **faire un ~ de nez à qn** to thumb one's nose at sb, cock a snook at sb *(Brit)*; **cela lui fera les ~s*** that'll teach him (a thing or two)*; **mettre qn à ~** to dismiss sb; **mettre ~ à terre** to dismount; **mettre les ~s chez qn** to set foot in sb's house; **je n'y remettrai jamais le(s) ~(s)** I'll never set foot (in) there again; **je n'ai pas mis les ~s dehors aujourd'hui** I haven't stepped *ou* been outside all day; **mettre qn au ~ du mur** to get sb with his back to the wall *(fig)*; **mettre les ~s dans le plat** to put one's foot in it; **mettre qch sur ~** to set sth up; **remettre qn sur ~** to set sb back on his feet again; **prendre ~ dans/sur** to get a foothold in/on; *(Comm)* **"les pieds dans l'eau"** "your own access to the waterfront"; **prendre son ~‡** to get a real kick (out of something)*; **c'est le ~!‡** it's a real turn-on!‡, it's great!*; *V* **casser, lâcher, retomber** *etc.*

2: pied-de-biche *nm, pl* **pieds-de-biche** *[machine à coudre]* presser foot; *[meuble]* cabriole leg; *(levier)* claw; **pied-bot** *nm, pl* **pieds-bots** person with a club-foot; **pied à coulisse** calliper rule; **pied de fer** (cobbler's) last; **pied de lit** footboard; **pied-noir** *nm, pl* **pieds-noirs** pied-noir *(Algerian-born Frenchman)*; **pied-de-poule** *(adj inv)* hound's-tooth; *(nm, pl* **pieds-de-poule***)* hound's-tooth cloth *(U) ou* material *(U)*; *(Can)* **pied-de-roi** *nm, pl* **pieds-de-roi** folding foot-rule; **pied-à-terre** *nm inv* pied-à-terre.

piédestal, *pl* **-aux** [pjedɛstal, o] *nm (lit, fig)* pedestal.

piège [pjɛʒ] *nm (lit, fig)* trap; *(fosse)* pit; *(collet)* snare. **les ~s d'une version/dictée** the pitfalls of a translation/dictation; **~ à rats/à moineaux** rat-/sparrow-trap; **prendre au ~** to (catch in a) trap; **être pris à son propre ~** to be caught in *ou* fall into one's own trap; **tendre un ~ (à qn)** to set a trap (for sb); **traduction pleine de ~s** translation full of traps; **donner** *ou* **tomber dans le ~** to fall into the trap, be trapped; **~ à loups** mantrap.

piégé, e [pjeʒe] *(ptp de* **piéger***) adj*: **engin ~** booby trap; **voiture/lettre ~e** car-/letter-bomb; **colis ~** parcel-bomb.

piégeage [pjeʒaʒ] *nm (rare: V* **piéger***)* trapping; setting of traps *(de* in); setting of booby traps *(de* in).

piéger [pjeʒe] (3) *vt* **(a)** *animal, (fig) personne* to trap. **se faire ~** to be trapped, find o.s. in a trap. **(b)** *bois, arbre* to set a trap *ou* traps in; *(avec des explosifs) engin, porte* to booby-trap.

pie-grièche, *pl* **pies-grièches** [pigʀijɛʃ] *nf* shrike.

pie-mère, *pl* **pies-mères** [pimɛʀ] *nf* pia mater.

Piémont [pjemɔ̃] *nm* Piedmont.

piémontais, e [pjemɔ̃tɛ, ɛz] **1** *adj* Piedmontese. **2** *nm (Ling)* Piedmontese. **3** *nm,f*: **P~(e)** Piedmontese.

piéride [pjeʀid] *nf* pierid, pieridine butterfly.

pierraille [pjɛʀɑj] *nf [route, sentier]* loose stones *(pl)*, chippings *(pl)*; *[pente, montagne]* scree *(U)*, loose stones *(pl)*, chippings *(pl)*.

pierre [pjɛʀ] **1** *nf* **(a)** *(gén, Méd)* stone. *[fruits]* **~s†** grit *(U)*; **maison de** *ou* **en ~** stone(-built) house, house built of stone; **attaquer qn à coups de ~s** to throw stones at sb, stone sb; *(fig)* **il resta** *ou* **son visage resta de ~** he remained stony-faced; *(fig)* **cœur de ~** heart of stone, stony heart; *V* **âge, casseur,** *etc.*

(b) *(loc)* **faire d'une ~ deux coups** to kill two birds with one stone; *(Prov)* **~ qui roule n'amasse pas mousse** a rolling stone gathers no moss *(Prov)*; **c'est une ~ dans son jardin** it's directed at him, it's a dig at him; **jour à marquer d'une ~ blanche/noire** red-letter/black day; **bâtir qch ~ à ~** to build sth up piece by piece *ou* stone by stone; **ils n'ont pas laissé ~ sur ~** they didn't leave a stone standing; **apporter sa ~ à qch** to add one's contribution to sth.

2: pierre d'achoppement stumbling block; **pierre à aiguiser** whetstone; *(lit, fig)* **pierre angulaire** cornerstone; **pierre à bâtir** building stone; **pierre à briquet** flint; **pierre à chaux** limestone; **pierre à feu** flint; **pierre fine** semiprecious stone; **pierre funéraire** tombstone, gravestone; **pierre à fusil** gunflint; **pierre levée** standing stone; **pierre ollaire** soapstone, steatite *(T)*; **pierre philosophale** philosopher's stone; **pierre ponce** pumice stone, pumice *(U)*; **pierre (précieuse)** (precious) stone, gem; **pierre sèche: mur en pierres sèches** drystone wall *ou* dyke; **pierre de taille** freestone; **pierre tombale** tombstone; *(lit, fig)* **pierre de touche** touchstone.

Pierre [pjɛʀ] *nm* Peter.

pierreries [pjɛʀʀi] *nfpl* gems, precious stones.

pierreux, -euse [pjɛʀø, øz] *adj terrain* stony; *fruit* gritty; *(Méd)* calculous.

pierrot [pjɛʀo] *nm* **(a)** *(Théât)* pierrot. **(b)** *(Orn)* sparrow.

Pierrot [pjɛʀo] *nm* **(a)** *(prénom)* Pete. **(b)** *(Théât)* Pierrot.

piétaille [pjetɑj] *nf (Mil péj)* rank and file; *(fig: subalternes)* rank and file, menials; *(fig: piétons)* pedestrians.

piété [pjete] *nf (Rel)* piety; *(attachement)* devotion, reverence. **~ filiale** filial devotion *ou* respect; **articles de ~** devotional articles; **images de ~** pious images; *V* **mont.**

piétinement [pjetinmɑ̃] *nm* **(a)** *(stagnation)* **le ~ de la discussion** the fact that the discussion is not *(ou* was not) making (any) progress; **vu le ~ de l'enquête** given that the investigation is *(ou* was) at a virtual standstill.

(b) *(marche sur place)* standing about. **le ~ auquel nous contraignait la foule** being forced to stand about because of the crowd.

(c) *(bruit)* stamping.

piétiner [pjetine] (1) **1** *vi* **(a)** *(trépigner)* to stamp (one's foot *ou* feet). **~ de colère/d'impatience** to stamp (one's feet) angrily/impatiently.

(b) *(ne pas avancer) [personne]* to stand about; *[cortège]* to mark time; *[discussion]* to make no progress; *[affaire, enquête]* to be at a virtual standstill, hang fire; *[économie, science]* to stagnate, be at a standstill. **~ dans la boue** to trudge through the mud.

2 *vt sol* to trample on; *victime, (fig) adversaire* to trample underfoot; *parterres* to trample on, trample underfoot, tread on; *fleurs* to trample down *ou* underfoot *ou* on, tread on. **plusieurs personnes furent piétinées** several people were trampled on *ou* trampled underfoot; *(fig)* **~ les principes de qn** to trample sb's principles underfoot, ride roughshod over sb's principles; *V* **plat**[1].

piétisme [pjetism(ə)] *nm* pietism.

piétiste [pjetist(ə)] **1** *adj* pietistic. **2** *nmf* pietist.

piéton[1] [pjetɔ̃] *nm* pedestrian.

piéton[2]**, -onne** [pjetɔ̃, ɔn] *adj*, **piétonnier, -ière** [pjetɔnje, jɛʀ] *adj* pedestrian *(épith)*. **rue ~ne** *ou* **~ière** pedestrian precinct.

piètre [pjɛtʀ(ə)] *adj (frm) adversaire, écrivain, roman* very poor, very mediocre; *excuse* paltry, lame. **c'est une ~ consolation** it's small *ou* little comfort; **faire ~ figure** to cut a sorry figure; **avoir ~ allure** to be a sorry *ou* wretched sight.

piètrement [pjɛtʀəmɑ̃] *adv* very poorly, very mediocrely.

pieu, *pl* **~x** [pjø] *nm* **(a)** *(poteau)* post; *(pointu)* stake, pale; *(Constr)* pile. **(b)** (‡: *lit*) bed. **se mettre au ~** to hit the hay* *ou* sack*, turn in*.

pieusement [pjøzmɑ̃] *adv (Rel)* piously; *(respectueusement)* reverently. *(hum)* **un vieux tricot qu'il avait ~ conservé** an old sweater which he had religiously kept.

pieuter (se)‡ [pjøte] (1) *vpr* to hit the hay* *ou* sack*, turn in*.

pieuvre [pjœvʀ(ə)] *nf* octopus.

pieux, -euse [pjø, øz] *adj personne (religieux)* pious, devout; *(dévoué)* devoted, dutiful; *pensée, souvenir, lecture, image* pious; *silence* reverent, respectful. ~ **mensonge** white lie (*told out of pity etc*).

pif[1]‡ [pif] *nm* (*nez*) conk‡, hooter‡, beak‡. **au** ~ at a rough guess.

pif[2] [pif] *excl*: ~! *ou* ~ **paf!** (*explosion*) bang! bang!; (*gifle*) smack! smack!, slap! slap!

pif(f)er‡ [pife] *vt*: **je ne peux pas le** ~ I can't stand‡ *ou* stick‡ him.

pifomètre‡ [pifɔmɛtʀ(ə)] *nm* intuition, instinct. **au** ~ at a rough guess; **faire qch au** ~ to do sth by guesswork; **aller (quelque part) au** ~ to follow one's nose*.

pige [piʒ] *nf* **(a)** (‡) **avoir 40/50** ~**s** to be 40/50, have 40/50 years behind one; **à 60** ~**s** at 60, when one is 60.
(b) (*Presse, Typ*) **être payé à la** ~ *[typographe]* to be paid at piecework rates; *[journaliste]* to be paid by the line.
(c) faire la ~ **à qn‡** to leave sb standing*.

pigeon [piʒɔ̃] **1** *nm* (*oiseau*) pigeon; (*: *dupe*) mug‡. **2: pigeon d'argile** clay pigeon; **pigeon ramier** woodpigeon, ring dove; (*jeu*) **pigeon vole** *game of forfeits* = Simon says; **pigeon voyageur** carrier *ou* homing pigeon.

pigeonnant, e [piʒɔnɑ̃, ɑ̃t] *adj soutien-gorge* uplift (*épith*). **poitrine** ~**e** high rounded bust.

pigeonne [piʒɔn] *nf* hen-pigeon.

pigeonneau, *pl* ~**x** [piʒɔno] *nm* young pigeon, squab (*T*).

pigeonner‡ [piʒɔne] (1) *vt*: ~ **qn** to do sb‡, take sb for a ride‡; **se laisser** *ou* **se faire** ~ to be done‡, be taken for a ride‡, be had*.

pigeonnier [piʒɔnje] *nm* pigeon house *ou* loft, dovecot(e); (*: *logement*) garret, attic room.

piger‡ [piʒe] (3) *vi* **(a)** (*comprendre*) to twig‡. **il a pigé** he has twigged‡, the penny has dropped*, he has cottoned on* *ou* caught on*; **tu piges?** (d'you) get it?*, dig?‡; **je ne pige pas** I don't get it*, I don't twig‡; **je ne pige rien à la chimie** chemistry's all Greek* *ou* double Dutch* to me, chemistry just doesn't register with me*; **je n'y pige rien** I just don't get it (at all)*, I can't make head nor tail of it; **tu y piges quelque chose, toi?** do you get it?*, can you make anything of it?
(b) (*regarder*) **pige-moi un peu ça!** just have *ou* take a dekko‡ *ou* a butchers‡ at this!

pigiste [piʒist(ə)] *nmf* (*typographe*) (piecework) typesetter; (*journaliste*) freelance journalist.

pigment [pigmɑ̃] *nm* pigment.

pigmentaire [pigmɑ̃tɛʀ] *adj* pigmentary, pigmental.

pigmentation [pigmɑ̃tɑsjɔ̃] *nf* pigmentation.

pigmenter [pigmɑ̃te] (1) *vt* to pigment.

pignocher [piɲɔʃe] (1) *vi* to pick *ou* nibble at one's food.

pignon [piɲɔ̃] *nm* **(a)** (*Archit*) gable. **à** ~ gabled; (*fig*) **avoir** ~ **sur rue** to have *ou* run a prosperous business. **(b)** (*Tech*) cog(wheel), gearwheel; (*petite roue*) pinion. **(c)** (*Bot*) pine kernel.

pignouf‡ [piɲuf] *nm* peasant*, boor.

pilage [pilaʒ] *nm* crushing, pounding.

pilastre [pilastʀ(ə)] *nm* pilaster.

Pilate [pilat] *nm* Pilate.

pile [pil] **1** *nf* **(a)** (*tas*) pile, stack.
(b) *[pont]* support, pile, pier.
(c) (*Élec*) battery. **à** ~**(s)** battery (*épith*), battery-operated; ~ **sèche** dry cell *ou* battery; ~ **atomique** nuclear reactor, (atomic) pile.
(d) (‡) (*volée*) belting‡, hammering‡; (*défaite*) hammering‡, thrashing*, licking*. **donner une** ~ **à qn** (*rosser*) to give sb a belting‡ *ou* hammering‡, lay into sb‡; (*vaincre*) to lick sb*, beat sb hollow*; **prendre** *ou* **recevoir une** ~ (*volée*) to get a belting‡ *ou* hammering‡; (*défaite*) to be licked*, be beaten hollow*.
(e) *[pièce]* (*côté*) ~: **c'est tombé sur (le côté)** ~ it came down tails; ~ **ou face?** heads or tails?; ~ **c'est moi, face c'est toi** tails it's me, heads it's you; **sur le côté** ~ **il y a ...** on the reverse side there's ... ; **on va jouer** *ou* **tirer ça à** ~ **ou face** we'll toss (up) for it, we'll toss up to decide that; **tirer à** ~ **ou face pour savoir si ...** to toss up to find out if ... .
2 *adv* (*) (*net*) dead*; (*juste*) just, right. **s'arrêter** ~ to stop dead*; **ça l'a arrêté** ~ it stopped him dead* *ou* in his tracks, it brought him up dead*; **tomber** ~: *[personne]* **vous êtes tombé** ~ **en m'offrant ce cadeau** you've chosen exactly the right present for me; **j'ai ouvert le bottin et je suis tombé** ~ **sur le numéro** I opened the directory and came straight *ou* right upon the number *ou* came up with* the number straight away *ou* right away; *[chose]* **il lâcha sa gomme qui tomba** ~ **dans l'encrier** he let go of his rubber which fell straight *ou* right into the inkwell; **ça tombe** ~! that's just *ou* exactly what I (*ou* we *etc*) need(ed)!; (*survenir*) **tomber** *ou* **arriver** ~ *[personne]* to turn up* just at the right moment *ou* time; *[chose]* to come just at the right moment *ou* time; **à 2 heures** ~ (at) dead on 2*, at 2 on the dot*, on the dot of 2*.

piler [pile] (1) *vt* **(a)** (*lit*) to crush, pound. **(b)** (**fig*) ~ **qn** (*rosser*) to lay into sb‡, give sb a hammering‡ *ou* belting‡; (*vaincre*) to beat sb hollow*, lick sb*.

pileux, -euse [pilø, øz] *adj follicule* hair (*épith*); *V* **système.**

pilier [pilje] *nm* (*Anat, Constr, fig*) pillar; (*Rugby*) prop (forward). **c'est un** ~ **de cabaret** *ou* **de bistro** he spends his life propping up a bar, he spends his life in the pub.

pillage [pijaʒ] *nm* (*V* **piller**) pillaging; plundering; looting; fleecing; wholesale borrowing (*de* from); plagiarizing; pirating. **mettre au** ~ to pillage; to plunder; to loot; to borrow wholesale from; to plagiarize; to pirate.

pillard, e [pijaʀ, aʀd(ə)] (*V* **piller**) **1** *adj nomades, troupes* pillaging (*épith*); looting (*épith*); *oiseau* thieving (*épith*). **2** *nm,f* pillager; plunderer; looter.

piller [pije] (1) *vt ville* to pillage, plunder; *magasin, maison* to loot; (*voler*) *objet* to plunder, take as booty; *personne* to fleece; (*fig: plagier*) *ouvrage, auteur* to borrow wholesale from, plagiarize, pirate.

pilleur, -euse [pijœʀ, øz] (*V* **piller**) **1** *adj* pillaging; plundering; looting. **2** *nm,f* pillager; plunderer; looter; (†) literary pirate, plagiarist. ~ **d'épaves** wrecker (*of ships*).

pilon [pilɔ̃] *nm* (*instrument*) pestle; (*jambe*) wooden leg, pegleg*; *[poulet]* drumstick. (*Typ*) **mettre un livre au** ~ to pulp a book.

pilonnage [pilɔnaʒ] *nm* (*V* **pilonner**) pestling; pounding; crushing; shelling, bombardment.

pilonner [pilɔne] (1) *vt* (*Culin, Pharm*) to pestle, pound, crush; (*Mil*) to pound, shell, bombard.

pilori [pilɔʀi] *nm* pillory. (*lit, fig*) **mettre** *ou* **clouer au** ~ to pillory.

pilosité [pilozite] *nf* pilosity.

pilotage [pilɔtaʒ] *nm* (*Aviat*) piloting, flying; (*Naut*) piloting. **école de** ~ flying school; ~ **automatique** automatic piloting; *V* **poste**[2].

pilote [pilɔt] **1** *adj* (*expérimental*) *école, ferme, réalisation* experimental; (*Comm*) *magasin* cut-price (*épith*); *boisson* low-priced; *V* **bateau.**
2 *nm* (*Aviat, Naut*) pilot; (*Aut*) driver; (*poisson*) pilotfish; (*fig: guide*) guide. **servir de** ~ **à qn** to show *ou* guide sb round, serve as a guide for sb.
3: pilote automatique automatic pilot; **pilote automobile** racing driver; **pilote de chasse** fighter pilot; **pilote de course** = **pilote automobile**; **pilote d'essai** test pilot; **pilote de guerre** fighter pilot; **pilote de ligne** airline pilot.

piloter [pilɔte] (1) *vt avion* to pilot, fly; *navire* to pilot; *voiture* to drive. (*fig*) ~ **qn** to show *ou* guide sb round.

pilotis [pilɔti] *nm* pile, pilotis (*T*). **sur** ~ on piles.

pilou [pilu] *nm* flannelette.

pilule [pilyl] *nf* pill. **prendre la** ~ (*contraceptive*) to be on *ou* take the pill; (‡*fig*) **prendre une** *ou* **la** ~ to take a hammering‡, be thrashed*; *V* **avaler, dorer.**

pimbêche [pɛ̃bɛʃ] **1** *adj f* stuck-up*, full of herself (*attrib*). **2** *nf* stuck-up thing*. **cette jeune fille est une horrible** ~ that girl is full of herself *ou* is horribly stuck-up*.

pimbina [pɛ̃bina] *nm* (*Can*) pembina (*Can*) (*type of cranberry*).

piment [pimɑ̃] *nm* **(a)** (*plante*) pepper, capsicum. (*Culin*) ~ **rouge** chilli, hot red pepper; ~ **doux** pepper, capsicum.
(b) (*fig*) spice, piquancy. **avoir du** ~ to be spicy *ou* piquant; **donner du** ~ **à une situation** to add *ou* give spice to a situation; **trouver du** ~ **à qch** to find sth spicy *ou* piquant.

pimenté, e [pimɑ̃te] (*ptp de* **pimenter**) *adj plat* hot; (*fig*) *récit* spicy.

pimenter [pimɑ̃te] (1) *vt* (*Culin*) to put chillis in; (*fig*) to add *ou* give spice to.

pimpant, e [pɛ̃pɑ̃, ɑ̃t] *adj robe, femme* trim and fresh-looking.

pimprenelle [pɛ̃pʀənɛl] *nf* (*à fleurs verdâtres*) (salad) burnet; (*à fleurs rouges*) great burnet.

pin [pɛ̃] *nm* (*arbre*) pine (tree); (*bois*) pine(wood). ~ **maritime/parasol** maritime/umbrella pine; ~ **sylvestre** Scotch fir, Scots pine; *V* **aiguille, pomme.**

pinacle [pinakl(ə)] *nm* (*Archit*) pinnacle. (*fig*) **être au** ~ to be at the top; (*fig*) **porter qn au** ~ to praise sb to the skies.

pinacothèque [pinakɔtɛk] *nf* art gallery.

pinailler* [pinɑje] (1) *vi* to quibble, split hairs. ~ **sur** to pick holes in*.

pinailleur, -euse* [pinɑjœʀ, øz] **1** *adj* pernickety, fussy, nit-picking* (*épith*). **2** *nm,f* nitpicker*, quibbler, fusspot*.

pinard‡ [pinaʀ] *nm* plonk* (*Brit*), (cheap) wine.

pinasse [pinas] *nf* (fishing) smack.

pince [pɛ̃s] **1** *nf* **(a)** (*outil*) ~**(s)** (*gén*) pair of pliers, pliers (*pl*); (*à charbon*), *[forgeron]* pair of tongs, tongs (*pl*).
(b) (*levier*) crowbar.
(c) (*Zool*) *[crabe]* pincer, claw.
(d) (*Couture*) dart. **faire des** ~**s à** to put darts in, dart.
(e) (‡: *main*) mitt‡, paw‡.
(f) (‡: *jambe*) leg. **aller à** ~**s** to foot* *ou* hoof‡ it; **j'ai fait 15 km à** ~**s** I footed it for 15 km*.
2: pince de chirurgien forceps (*pl*); **pince de cycliste** bicycle clip; **pince à épiler** (eyebrow) tweezers (*pl*); **pince à linge** clothes peg; **pince-monseigneur** *nf, pl* **pinces-monseigneur** jemmy; **pince à ongles** nail clippers (*pl*); **pince à sucre** sugar tongs (*pl*); **pince universelle** (universal) pliers (*pl*).

pince- [pɛ̃s] *préf V* **pincer.**

pincé, e[1] [pɛ̃se] (*ptp de* **pincer**) *adj personne, air* stiff, starchy; *sourire* stiff, tight-lipped; *ton* stiff. **d'un air** ~ stiffly; **les lèvres** ~**es** with pursed lips, tight-lipped; (*minces*) thin-lipped.

pinceau, *pl* ~**x** [pɛ̃so] *nm* (*gén*) brush; (*Peinture*) (paint)brush; (*fig: manière de peindre*) brushwork; (‡: *pied*) foot, hoof‡. ~ **lumineux** pencil of light; *V* **coup.**

pincée[2] [pɛ̃se] *nf [sel, poivre]* pinch.

pincement [pɛ̃smɑ̃] *nm* (*Mus*) plucking; (*Agr*) pinching out. ~ **au cœur** lump in one's throat.

pincer [pɛ̃se] (3) **1** *vt* **(a)** (*accidentellement, pour faire mal*) to pinch, nip; *[froid, chien]* to nip. **je me suis pincé dans la porte/avec l'ouvre-boîte** I caught myself in the door/with the tin opener; **se** ~ **le doigt** to catch one's finger; **se** ~ **le doigt dans la porte** to trap *ou* catch one's finger in the door; ~ **son manteau dans la porte** to catch one's coat in the door; **il s'est fait** ~ **par un crabe/un chien** he was nipped by a crab/a dog.
(b) (*tenir, serrer*) to grip. ~ **les lèvres** to purse (up) one's lips; ~ **la bouche** to screw up one's mouth; **se** ~ **le nez** to hold one's nose; **une robe qui pince la taille** a dress which is tight at the waist.
(c) (*Mus*) to pluck.
(d) (*Couture*) *veste* to put darts in, dart.
(e) (**fig: arrêter, prendre*) to catch, cop‡; *[police]* to nick‡ (*Brit*), cop‡, catch.
(f) (*Agr*) to pinch out.
(g) en ~ **pour qn‡** to be stuck on sb‡, be mad about sb*.

2 *vi* (:) **ça pince (dur)** it's freezing (cold), it's biting *ou* hellish: (*surtout Brit*) cold.

3: **pince-fesse(s)**: *nm inv* dance, hop*; **pince-nez** *nm inv* pince-nez; **pince-sans-rire** (*nm inv*): **c'est un pince-sans-rire** he's the deadpan type; (*adj inv*) deadpan.

pincette [pɛ̃sɛt] *nf* (*gén pl*) (*pour le feu*) pair of (fire) tongs, (fire) tongs; *[horloger]* pair of tweezers, tweezers. **il n'est pas à toucher avec des** ~**s** (*sale*) he's filthy dirty; (*mécontent*) he's like a bear with a sore head.

pinçon [pɛ̃sɔ̃] *nm* pinch-mark.

Pindare [pɛ̃daʀ] *nm* Pindar.

pindarique [pɛ̃daʀik] *adj* Pindaric.

pinède [pinɛd] *nf*, **pineraie** [pinʀɛ] *nf* pinewood, pine forest.

pingouin [pɛ̃gwɛ̃] *nm* penguin; (*alcidé*) auk.

ping-pong [piŋpɔ̃g] *nm* table tennis, ping-pong.

pingre [pɛ̃gʀ(ə)] (*péj*) **1** *adj* stingy, niggardly. **2** *nmf* skinflint, niggard.

pingrerie [pɛ̃gʀəʀi] *nf* (*péj*) stinginess, niggardliness.

pin-pon [pɛ̃pɔ̃] *excl sound made by two-tone siren.*

pinson [pɛ̃sɔ̃] *nm* chaffinch; *V* **gai.**

pintade [pɛ̃tad] *nf* guinea-fowl.

pintadeau, *pl* ~**x** [pɛ̃tado] *nm* young guinea-fowl, guinea-poult (*T*).

pinte [pɛ̃t] *nf* (*ancienne mesure*) ≈ quart (*0.93 litre*); (*mesure anglo-saxonne*) pint; (*Can*) quart (*1,136 litre*). (*fig*) **se payer une** ~ **de bon sang** (*s'amuser*) to have a good time; (*rire*) to have a good laugh.

pinté, e: [pɛ̃te] (*ptp de* **pinter**) *adj* sloshed:, smashed:, stoned:.

pinter: [pɛ̃te] (1) **1** *vi*, **se pinter**: *vpr* to booze:. **2** *vt* to knock back:.

pin up [pinœp] *nf inv* pinup.

pioche [pjɔʃ] *nf* (*à deux pointes*) pick, pickaxe; (*à pointe et à houe*) mattock, pickaxe; *V* **tête.**

piocher [pjɔʃe] (1) **1** *vt terre* to dig up *ou* over (with a pick), use a pick on; (*) *sujet* to swot at* (*Brit*) cram for, slave *ou* slog away at*; *examen* to swot (*Brit*) *ou* cram for*; (*Jeu*) *carte, domino* to take (from the pile).

2 *vi* (*creuser*) to dig (with a pick); (*: *bûcher*) to swot*, slave* *ou* slog* away; (*Jeu*) to take a card (*ou* domino) (from the pile). ~ **dans le tas** to dig into the pile.

piocheur, -euse* [pjɔʃœʀ, øz] **1** *adj* hard-working. **2** *nm,f* swot* (*Brit*), crammer, slogger*.

piolet [pjɔlɛ] *nm* ice axe.

pion [pjɔ̃] *nm* **(a)** (*Échecs*) pawn; (*Jeu*) piece, draught. (*fig*) **n'être qu'un** ~ **(sur l'échiquier)** to be nothing but a pawn; *V* **damer.**

(b) (*Scol: surveillant*) ≈ prefect (*student paid to supervise schoolchildren*).

pioncer: [pjɔ̃se] (3) *vi* to have a kip:. **je n'ai pas pioncé de la nuit** I got no kip at all last night:; **laisse-le** ~ leave him to his kip:, let him have his kip:; **je vais** ~ I'm going for a kip: *ou* to have a kip:.

pionne [pjɔn] *nf* (*Scol: V* **pion**) ≈ (girl) prefect.

pionnier [pjɔnje] *nm* (*lit, fig*) pioneer.

pioupiou*† [pjupju] *nm* young soldier, tommy*†.

pipe [pip] *nf* pipe. **fumer la** ~ to smoke a pipe, be a pipe-smoker; ~ **de bruyère/de terre** briar/clay pipe; *V* **casser, fendre, tête.**

pipeau, *pl* ~**x** [pipo] *nm* (*Mus*) (reed-)pipe; *[oiseleur]* bird call. (*gluaux*) ~**x** limed twigs.

pipelet, -ette* [piplɛ, ɛt] *nm,f* (*péj*) concierge.

pipe-line, *pl* **pipe-lines** [pajplajn] *nm* pipeline.

piper [pipe] (1) *vt cartes* to mark; *dés* to load. (*fig*) **les dés sont pipés** the dice are loaded; **ne pas** ~ **(mot)*** not to breathe a word, keep mum*.

pipette [pipɛt] *nf* pipette.

pipi* [pipi] *nm* wee(wee) (* *ou langage enfantin*). **faire** ~: **va faire** ~ go and (have a) wee(wee)*; **j'irais bien faire** ~ I want to go to the loo* (*Brit*) *ou* john* (*US*); **faire** ~ **au lit** to wet the bed; **le chien a fait** ~ **sur le tapis** the dog has weed on *ou* has done a wee on the carpet*; (*fig*) **c'est du** ~ **de chat** (*boisson*) it's just coloured water, it's absolute dishwater*; (*livre, film, théorie*) it's pathetic*, it's a waste of time.

pipit [pipit] *nm* pipit.

piquage [pikaʒ] *nm* (*Couture*) sewing up, stitching, machining.

piquant, e [pikɑ̃, ɑ̃t] **1** *adj* **(a)** *barbe* prickly; (*Bot*) *tige* thorny, prickly.

(b) *sauce, moutarde* hot, pungent; *goût, odeur, fromage* pungent; *vin* sour, tart; *radis* hot. **eau** ~**e*** fizzy water (*hum*); soda water; (*Culin*) **sauce** ~**e** sauce piquante, piquant sauce.

(c) *air, froid* biting.

(d) *détail* titillating; *description, style* racy, piquant, titillating; *conversation, charme, beauté* piquant, titillating.

(e) (*mordant*) *mot, réplique* biting, cutting.

2 *nm* **(a)** *[hérisson]* quill, spine; *[oursin]* spine, prickle; *[rosier]* thorn, prickle; *[chardon]* prickle; *[barbelé]* barb.

(b) (*fig*) *[style, description]* raciness; *[conversation]* piquancy; *[aventure]* spice. **le** ~ **de l'histoire, c'est que ...** the most entertaining thing (about it) is that ... ; **et, détail qui ne manque pas de** ~, ... and here's a diverting detail ... .

pique [pik] **1** *nf* (*arme*) pike; *[picador]* lance; (*fig: parole blessante*) cutting remark. **lancer des** ~**s à qn** to make cutting remarks to sb. **2** *nm* (*carte*) spade; (*couleur*) spades (*pl*).

pique- [pik] *préf V* **piquer.**

piqué, e [pike] (*ptp de* **piquer**) **1** *adj* **(a)** (*Couture*) (*cousu*) (machine-)stitched; *couvre-lit* quilted.

(b) (*marqué*) *glace, livre, linge* mildewed, mildewy; *meuble* worm-eaten; (*aigre*) *vin* sour. **visage** ~ **de taches de rousseur** freckled face, face dotted with freckles; ~ **par la rouille** *métal* pitted with rust; *linge* covered in rust spots; ~ **par l'acide** pitted with acid marks; (*fig*) **ce problème/cet orage n'était pas** ~ **des hannetons!*** *ou* **des vers!*** it was one heck of a problem/storm*.

(c) (*: *fou*) nuts*, barmy* (*Brit*). **il est** ~, **c'est un** ~ he's a nutter* (*Brit*), he's nuts* *ou* barmy* (*Brit*).

(d) (*Mus*) *note* staccato.

2 *nm* **(a)** (*Aviat*) dive. **attaque** *ou* **bombardement en** ~ dive bombing; **faire un** ~ to (go into a) dive.

(b) (*tissu*) piqué.

piquer [pike] (1) **1** *vt* **(a)** *[guêpe]* to sting; *[moustique, serpent]* to bite; (*avec une épingle, une pointe*) to prick; (*Méd*) to give an injection to, give a jab* (*Brit*) *ou* shot* to. **se faire** ~ **contre la variole** to have a smallpox injection *ou* jab* (*Brit*) *ou* shot*; **faire** ~ **qn contre qch** to have sb vaccinated *ou* inoculated against sth; (*euph*) **faire** ~ **un chat/un chien** to have a cat/dog put down (*Brit*) (*euph*) *ou* put to sleep (*euph*); **se** ~ **le doigt** to prick one's finger; **les ronces, ça pique** brambles prickle *ou* scratch; *V* **mouche.**

(b) *aiguille, fourche, fléchette* to stick, stab, jab (*dans* into). **rôti piqué d'ail** joint stuck with cloves of garlic; **piqué de lardons** larded; ~ **la viande avec une fourchette** to prick the meat with a fork; ~ **des petits pois avec une fourchette** to stab peas with a fork; ~ **qch au mur** to put *ou* stick sth up on the wall; ~ **une fleur sur un corsage** to pin a flower on(to) a blouse; ~ **une fleur dans ses cheveux** to stick a flower in one's hair; ~ **(une frite/un haricot) dans le plat*** to help o.s. (to a chip/a bean or two); ~ **au hasard*** *ou* **dans le tas*** to choose *ou* pick at random.

(c) (*Couture*) ~ **qch (à la machine)** to machine sth, (machine) stitch sth, sew sth up; **ta mère sait-elle** ~? can your mother use a sewing machine?

(d) *[barbe]* to prick, prickle; *[ortie]* to sting. **tissu qui pique (la peau)** prickly cloth, cloth that prickles the skin *ou* is prickly on the skin; **moutarde/liqueur qui pique la gorge** mustard/liqueur which burns the throat; **la fumée me pique les yeux** the smoke is stinging my eyes *ou* making my eyes smart; **le froid/le vent nous piquait le** *ou* **au visage** the cold/the wind was biting *ou* stinging our faces; *[démangeaison]* **ça (me) pique** it's itching *ou* itchy, it's making me itch; **les yeux me piquent, j'ai les yeux qui piquent** my eyes are smarting *ou* stinging; **ma gorge me pique** my throat's burning; **tu piques avec ta barbe** you're all prickly with that beard of yours, your beard prickles *ou* is prickly; **attention, ça pique** *[alcool sur une plaie]* careful, it's going to sting; *[liquide dans la bouche]* careful, it burns your throat; *V* **qui.**

(e) (*exciter*) *curiosité* to arouse, excite; *intérêt* to arouse, stir up; (†: *vexer*) *personne* to pique, nettle; *amour-propre* to pique, hurt. ~ **qn au vif** to cut sb to the quick.

(f) (*: *faire brusquement*) ~ **un cent mètres** *ou* **un sprint** to (put on a) sprint, put on a burst of speed; ~ **un roupillon** *ou* **un somme** to have forty winks* *ou* a nap; ~ **un galop** to break into a gallop; ~ **une** *ou* **sa crise** to throw a fit; ~ **une crise de larmes** to have a fit of tears; ~ **une colère** to fly into a rage, have a fit*; ~ **un soleil** *ou* **un fard** to go (bright) red; ~ **une suée** to break out in a sweat; ~ **un plongeon** to dive; ~ **une tête dans la piscine** to dive (headfirst) into the pool.

(g) (*: *attraper*) *accent* to pick up; *manie, maladie* to pick up, catch, get.

(h) (*: *voler*) *portefeuille* to pinch*, nick: (*Brit*), whip:; *idée* to pinch* (*à qn* from sb).

(i) (:: *arrêter*) *voleur* to cop:, nab:, nick: (*Brit*).

(j) (*Mus*) to play staccato.

2 *vi* **(a)** *[avion]* to go into a dive; *[oiseau]* to swoop down. **le cavalier piqua droit sur nous** the horseman came straight towards us; **il faudrait** ~ **vers le village** we'll have to head towards the village; ~ **du nez** *[avion]* to go into a nose-dive; *[bateau]* to dip her head; *[fleurs]* to droop; *[personne]* to fall headfirst; ~ **du nez dans son assiette*** (*s'endormir*) to nod off* *ou* doze off* (during a meal); (*avoir honte*) to hang one's head in shame; ~ **des deux** to go full tilt.

(b) *[moutarde, radis]* to be hot; *[vin]* to be sour, have a sour taste; *[fromage]* to be pungent. **eau qui pique*** fizzy water (*hum*); soda water.

3 se piquer *vpr* **(a)** (*se blesser*) (*avec une aiguille*) to prick o.s.; (*dans les orties*) to get stung, sting o.s.

(b) *[morphinomane]* to give o.s. a shot of *ou* inject o.s. with heroin (*ou* morphine *etc*); *[diabétique]* to give o.s. an injection, inject o.s.

(c) *[livres, miroir, bois, linge]* to go mildewed *ou* mildewy; *[métal]* to be pitted; *[vin, cidre]* to go *ou* turn sour.

(d) (*avoir la prétention*) **se** ~ **de littérature/psychologie** to like to think one knows a lot about literature/psychology, pride o.s. on one's knowledge of literature/psychology; **se** ~ **de faire qch** to pride o.s. on one's ability to do sth.

(e) (*se vexer*) to take offence.

(f) (*loc*) **il s'est piqué au jeu** it grew on him; **se** ~ **le nez**: **c'est quelqu'un qui se pique le nez**: he's a right boozer:, he's on the bottle*; **il se pique le nez toute la journée**: he knocks it back: *ou* boozes: all day long.

4: pique-assiette* *nmf inv* scrounger*, sponger* (*for a free meal*); **pique-fleurs** *nm inv* flower-holder; **pique-fruit(s)** *nm inv* cocktail stick; **pique-nique** *nm, pl* **pique-niques** picnic; **faire un pique-nique** to have a picnic, picnic; **demain nous allons faire un pique-nique** tomorrow we're going for *ou* on a picnic; **pique-niquer** to have a picnic, picnic; **pique-niqueur, -euse** *nm,f, mpl* **pique-niqueurs** picknicker.

piquet [pikɛ] *nm* **(a)** (*pieu*) post, stake, picket; *[tente]* peg; *V* **raide. (b)** (*personne*) (*Ind*) ~ **(de grève)** (strike-) picket; (*Mil*) ~ **d'incendie** fire-fighting squad. **(c)** (*Scol*) **mettre qn au** ~ to make sb stand *ou* put sb in the corner. **(d)** (*Cartes*) piquet.

piquetage [piktaʒ] *nm* staking (out).

piqueter [pikte] (4) *vt* **(a)** *allée* to stake out, put stakes along. **(b)** (*moucheter*) to dot (*de* with). **ciel piqueté d'étoiles** star-studded *ou* star-spangled sky, sky studded with stars.

piquette [pikɛt] *nf* **(a)** (*cru local*) local wine; (*mauvais vin*) (cheap) wine, plonk* (*Brit*). **(b)** (‡: *défaite*) hammering‡, licking*, thrashing*. **prendre une ~** to be hammered‡ *ou* thrashed* *ou* licked*.

piqueur, -euse [pikœʀ, øz] **1** *adj insecte* stinging (*épith*). **2** *nm* **(a)** *[écurie]* groom; (*Chasse*) whip. **(b)** (*mineur*) hewer. **(c)** (*surveillant*) foreman. **3** *nm,f* (*Couture*) machinist.

piquier [pikje] *nm* pikeman.

piqûre [pikyʀ] *nf* **(a)** *[épingle]* prick; *[guêpe, ortie]* sting; *[moustique]* bite. **~ d'épingle** pinprick; (*plaie*) **la ~ faite par l'aiguille** the hole made by the needle; (*fig*) **~ d'amour-propre** injury to one's pride.

(b) (*Méd*) injection, jab* (*Brit*), shot*. **faire une ~ à qn** to give sb an injection *ou* a jab* (*Brit*); **se faire faire une ~** to have an injection *ou* a jab* (*Brit*), get jabbed* (*Brit*) *ou* injected.

(c) *[miroir, papier]* spot of mildew, mildew (*U*); *[métal]* hole, pitting (*U*); *[bois]* hole. **~ de ver** wormhole.

(d) (*Couture*) (*point*) (straight) stitch; (*rang*) (straight) stitching (*U*). **rang de ~s** row *ou* line of straight stitching.

piranha [piʀana] *nm* piranha.

pirate [piʀat] **1** *adj bateau, émission* pirate (*épith*). **2** *nm* pirate; (*fig: escroc*) swindler, shark*. **~ de l'air** hijacker, skyjacker*.

pirater [piʀate] (1) *vi* to pirate.

piraterie [piʀatʀi] *nf* (*U*) piracy; (*acte*) act of piracy; (*fig*) swindle, swindling (*U*). **acte de ~** act of piracy; **~ aérienne** hijacking, skyjacking*; **c'est de la ~!** it's daylight robbery!

piraya [piʀaja] *nm* = **piranha.**

pire [piʀ] **1** *adj* **(a)** (*comp*) worse. **c'est bien ~** it's even worse; **quelque chose de ~** something worse; **il y a quelque chose de ~** there is worse; **c'est ~ que jamais** it's worse than ever; (*Prov*) **il n'est ~ eau que l'eau qui dort** still waters run deep (*Prov*); (*Prov*) **il n'est ~ sourd que celui qui ne veut pas entendre** there is none so deaf as he who will not hear (*Prov*).

(b) (*superl*) **le ~, la ~** the worst.

2 *nm*: **le ~** the worst; **le ~ de tout c'est de ...** the worst thing of all is to ...; **le ~ c'est que ...** the worst of it (all) is that ... ; **pour le meilleur et pour le ~** for better or for worse; **(en mettant les choses) au ~** at (the very) worst; *V* **politique.**

Pirée [piʀe] *nm* Piraeus.

piriforme [piʀifɔʀm(ə)] *adj* pear-shaped.

pirogue [piʀɔg] *nf* dugout (canoe), pirogue.

piroguier [piʀɔgje] *nm* boatman (*in a pirogue*).

pirouette [piʀwɛt] *nf* (*lit*) pirouette; (*fig: volte-face*) about-turn (*fig*); (*fig: faux-fuyant*) evasive reply. (*fig*) **répondre par une ~** to side-step *ou* evade the question, refuse to give a straight answer.

pirouetter [piʀwete] (1) *vi* to pirouette.

pis[1] [pi] *nm [vache]* udder.

pis[2] [pi] (*littér*) **1** *adj* worse. **qui ~ est** what is worse.

2 *adv* worse. **aller de ~ en ~** to get worse and worse; **dire ~ que pendre de qn** to sling mud at sb (*fig*); *V* **mal, tant.**

3 *nm*: **le ~** the worst (thing); **au ~ aller** if the worst comes to the worst.

4: pis-aller *nm inv* (*personne, solution*) last resort, stopgap; (*chose*) makeshift, stopgap; (*mesure*) stopgap measure.

piscicole [pisikɔl] *adj* piscicultural, fish-breeding (*épith*).

pisciculteur [pisikyltœʀ] *nm* pisciculturist (*T*), fish breeder.

pisciculture [pisikyltyʀ] *nf* pisciculture (*T*), fish breeding.

pisciforme [pisifɔʀm(ə)] *adj* pisciform.

piscine [pisin] *nf* swimming pool; (*publique*) (swimming) baths (*pl*), swimming pool.

piscivore [pisivɔʀ] **1** *adj* fish-eating (*épith*), piscivorous (*T*). **2** *nm* fish eater.

Pise [piz] *n* Pisa.

pisé [pize] *nm* clay, cob, pisé (*T*).

pisse‡ [pis] *nf* pee‡, piss**. (*fig*) **de la ~ d'âne** duck's *ou* cat's piss** (*fig*), a disgusting brew.

pisse-froid‡ [pisfʀwa] *nm inv* wet blanket*.

pissement [pismɑ̃] *nm* (‡) peeing‡, pissing**. (*Méd*) **~ de sang** passing of blood (with the urine).

pissenlit [pisɑ̃li] *nm* dandelion. **manger *ou* sucer les ~s par la racine** to be pushing up the daisies.

pisser‡ [pise] (1) **1** *vi* (*uriner*) *[personne]* to (have a) pee‡ *ou* piss**; *[animal]* to pee‡, piss**; (*couler*) to gush; (*fuir*) to gush out, piss out**. **je vais ~ un coup** I'm going out for a pee‡ *ou* a slash** (*Brit*) *ou* a piss**; **il a pissé dans sa culotte** he wet his trousers, he peed in his pants‡; **~ au lit** to wet the *ou* one's bed, pee in the bed‡; **ça pisse** (*il pleut*) it's chucking it down*, it's pissing down** (*surtout Brit*); **c'est comme si on pissait dans un violon** it's like banging your head against a brick wall; **laisse ~ (le mérinos)** forget it!*, let him (*ou* them *etc*) get on with it!

2 *vt* (*Méd*) **~ du sang** to pass blood (with the urine); **son nez pisse le sang** his nose is gushing *ou* pissing** (*Brit*) blood, blood's gushing from his nose; **réservoir qui pisse l'eau** tank which is gushing *ou* pissing** out water.

pissette* [pisɛt] *nf* (*filet de liquide*) trickle.

pisseur, -euse[1] [pisœʀ, øz] **1** *nm,f* (‡) person who is always going for a pee‡ *ou* a piss**. **2 pisseuse‡** *nf* brat*. **3: pisseur de copie*** writer who churns out rubbish.

pisseux, -euse[2]‡ [pisø, øz] *adj couleur* wishy-washy*, insipid; *aspect* tatty*, scruffy*. **odeur ~euse** smell of pee‡ *ou* piss**.

pissoir [piswaʀ] *nm* (*dial*) urinal.

pissotière‡ [pisɔtjɛʀ] *nf* urinal (*in the street*), ≃ (public) loo* (*Brit*) *ou* john* (*US*) *ou* bog‡ (*Brit*).

pistache [pistaʃ] **1** *nf* pistachio (nut). **2** *adj inv* pistachio (green).

pistachier [pistaʃje] *nm* pistachio (tree).

pistage [pistaʒ] *nm* (*V* **pister**) tracking; trailing; tailing, tagging.

pistard [pistaʀ] *nm* track cyclist.

piste [pist(ə)] *nf* **(a)** (*traces*) *[animal, suspect]* track, tracks, trail. **suivre/perdre la ~** to follow/lose the trail; **être/mettre qn sur la (bonne) ~** to be/put sb on the right track; **être sur/perdre la ~ du meurtrier** to be on/lose the murderer's trail; **se lancer sur la ~ de qn** to follow sb's trail, set out to track sb down; *V* **brouiller, faux**[2].

(b) (*Police: indice*) lead. **nous avons plusieurs ~s** we have several leads.

(c) *[hippodrome]* course; *[vélodrome, autodrome, stade]* track; *[patinage]* rink; *[danse]* (dance) floor; *[skieurs]* (ski) run; *[cirque]* ring. **~ cavalière** bridle path; **~ cyclable** cycle track; (*Athlétisme*) **~ 3** lane 3; **en ~!** (*lit*) into the ring!; (*fig*) set to it!; (*fig*) **se mettre en ~** to get down to it.

(d) (*Aviat*) runway; *[petit aéroport]* airstrip. **~ d'atterrissage/d'envol** landing/takeoff runway.

(e) (*sentier*) track; *[désert]* trail.

(f) *[magnétophone]* track. **à 2/4 ~s** 2/4 track; (*Ciné*) **~ sonore** sound track.

pister [piste] (1) *vt gibier* to track; trail; *[police] personne* to tail, tag.

pistil [pistil] *nm* pistil.

pistole [pistɔl] *nf* pistole.

pistolet [pistɔlɛ] **1** *nm* (*arme*) pistol, gun; (*jouet*) (toy) pistol, (toy) gun; *[peintre]* spray gun; (*: *urinal*) bed-bottle. **peindre au ~** to spray-paint; (**fig*) **un drôle de ~** a queer fish* (*Brit*) *ou* duck* (*US*) *ou* customer*.

2: pistolet à air comprimé airgun; **pistolet d'arçon** horse pistol; **pistolet à bouchon** popgun; **pistolet à capsules** cap gun; **pistolet à eau** water pistol; **pistolet mitrailleur** submachine gun, sten gun (*Brit*), tommy gun.

piston [pistɔ̃] *nm* **(a)** (*Tech*) piston; (*Mus*) valve.

(b) (*) string-pulling*. **avoir du ~** to have friends in the right places* *ou* who can pull strings*; **il a eu le poste par ~** someone pulled strings to get him the job*, he got the job through a bit of string-pulling*.

pistonner* [pistɔne] (1) *vt* to pull strings for* (*auprès de* with). **se faire ~** to get sb to pull (some) strings (for one)*.

pitance [pitɑ̃s] *nf* (*péj*, †) (means of) sustenance (†, *frm*).

pitchpin [pitʃpɛ̃] *nm* pitch pine.

piteusement [pitøzmɑ̃] *adv* pathetically; *échouer* miserably.

piteux, -euse [pitø, øz] *adj* (*minable*) *apparence* sorry (*épith*), pitiful, pathetic; *résultats* pitiful, pathetic; (*honteux*) *personne, air* ashamed, shamefaced. **en ~ état** in a sorry *ou* pitiful state; **faire ~euse figure** to cut a sorry figure, be a sorry *ou* pitiful sight; **avoir ~euse mine** to be shabby-looking; **avoir la mine ~euse** to be shamefaced.

pithécanthrope [pitekɑ̃tʀɔp] *nm* pithecanthrope.

pitié [pitje] *nf* **(a)** (*compassion*) pity. **avoir ~ de qn** to pity sb, feel pity for sb; **prendre qn/le sort de qn en ~** to pity sb/sb's fate; **faire ~ à qn** to inspire pity in sb; **il me fait ~** I feel sorry for him, I pity him; **cela nous faisait ~ de les voir si mal vêtus** we felt great pity to see them so badly dressed; **son sort me fit ~** I pitied his fate; **c'est (une vraie) ~ *ou* quelle ~ de voir ça** it's pitiful to see (that); **cela fait plus peur que ~** it inspires more fear than pity *ou* fear more than pity; **il était si maigre que c'en était ~ *ou* que c'était à faire ~** he was so thin it was pitiful (to see him), he was pitifully *ou* pathetically thin; **chanter à faire ~** to sing pitifully *ou* pathetically.

(b) (*miséricorde*) pity, mercy. **avoir ~ d'un ennemi** to take pity on an enemy, have pity *ou* mercy on an enemy; **~!** (*lit: grâce*) (have) mercy!; (*: *assez*) for goodness' *ou* pity's *ou* Pete's sake!*; **par ~!** for pity's sake!; **sans ~** *agir* pitilessly, mercilessly, ruthlessly; *regarder* pitilessly; **il est sans ~** he's pitiless *ou* merciless *ou* ruthless.

piton [pitɔ̃] *nm* **(a)** (*à anneau*) eye; (*à crochet*) hook; *[alpiniste]* piton, peg. **(b)** (*Géog*) peak.

pitoyable [pitwajabl(ə)] *adj* (*gén*) pitiful, pitiable.

pitoyablement [pitwajabləmɑ̃] *adv* pitifully.

pitre [pitʀ(ə)] *nm* (*lit, fig*) clown. **faire le ~** to clown *ou* fool about *ou* around, act the fool.

pitrerie [pitʀəʀi] *nf* tomfoolery. **il n'arrête pas de faire des ~s** he's always *ou* he never stops clowning around *ou* acting the fool.

pittoresque [pitɔʀɛsk(ə)] **1** *adj site* picturesque; *personnage, tenu* picturesque, colourful; *récit, style, détail* colourful, picturesque, vivid. **2** *nm* colour. **le ~ de qch** the picturesque quality of sth; the colourfulness *ou* vividness of sth.

pivert [pivɛʀ] *nm* green woodpecker.

pivoine [pivwan] *nf* peony; *V* **rouge.**

pivot [pivo] *nm* (*gén, Mil*) pivot; (*fig*) mainspring, pivot; *[dent]* post; (*Bot*) taproot.

pivotant, e [pivɔtɑ̃, ɑ̃t] *adj bras, panneau* pivoting (*épith*), revolving (*épith*); *fauteuil* swivel (*épith*); *V* **racine.**

pivoter [pivɔte] (1) *vi [porte]* to revolve, pivot; (*Mil*) to wheel round. *[personne]* **~ (sur ses talons)** to turn *ou* swivel round, turn on one's heels; **faire ~ qch** to swing *ou* swivel sth round.

placage [plakaʒ] *nm* **(a)** (*en bois*) veneering (*U*), veneer; (*en marbre, pierre*) facing. **~ en acajou** mahogany veneer. **(b)** (*Rugby*) = **plaquage.**

placard [plakaʀ] *nm* **(a)** (*armoire*) cupboard. **~ à balai/de cuisine** broom/kitchen cupboard. **(b)** (*affiche*) poster, notice. *[journal]* **~ publicitaire** display advertisement. **(c)** (*Typ*) galley (proof). **(d)** (*: *couche*) thick layer, thick coating (*U*).

placarder [plakaʀde] (1) *vt* to stick up, put up; *mur* to stick posters on, placard. **mur placardé d'affiches** wall covered with *ou* placarded with posters.

place [plas] *nf* **(a)** (*esplanade*) square. (*fig*) **étaler ses divergences sur la ~ publique** to wash one's dirty linen in public; (*fig*) **clamer qch sur la ~ publique** to proclaim sth from the roof-tops.

(b) *[objet]* place. **remettre qch à sa ~** *ou* **en ~** to put sth back where it belongs *ou* in its proper place; **la ~ des mots dans la phrase** word order in sentences; **changer la ~ de qch** to move *ou* shift sth, put sth in a different place, change the place of sth.

(c) *[personne]* (*lit, fig*) place; (*assise*) seat. **~ d'honneur** place *ou* seat of honour; **à vos ~s!, en ~!** to your places! *ou* seats!; **tout le monde est en ~** everyone is in (his) place *ou* is seated; **prenez ~** take your place *ou* seat; **prendre la ~ de qn** to take sb's place; (*remplacer*) to take over from sb, take sb's place; **il ne tient pas en ~** he can't keep still, he's always fidgeting; (*fig*) **remettre qn à sa ~** to put sb in his place; **laisser la ~ à qn** (*lit*) to give (up) one's seat to sb; (*fig*) to hand over to sb; **savoir rester à sa ~** to know one's place; **tenir sa ~** (*faire bonne figure*) to put up a good show; **il n'est pas à sa ~ dans ce milieu** he feels out of place in this sphere; **se faire une ~ dans le monde/dans la littérature** to carve out a place for o.s. in society/in literature; **avoir sa ~ dans la littérature** to have found a place in literature; **se faire une ~ au soleil** to find o.s. a place in the sun (*fig*); **avoir sa ~ dans le cœur de qn** to have a place in sb's heart; **trouver** *ou* **prendre ~ parmi/dans** to find a place (for o.s.) among/in; **il ne donnerait pas sa ~ pour un empire** *ou* **pour un boulet de canon*** he wouldn't change places with anyone for all the tea in China* *ou* for the world; **être en bonne ~ pour gagner** to be well-placed *ou* in a good position to win; **se mettre à la ~ de qn** to put o.s. in sb's place *ou* in sb's shoes; **à votre/sa ~** if I were you/him *ou* he (*frm*), in your/his place.

(d) (*espace libre*) room, space. **tenir** *ou* **prendre de la ~** to take up a lot of room *ou* space; **faire de la ~** to make room *ou* space; **j'ai trouvé une ~** *ou* **de la ~ pour me garer** I've found room *ou* (a) space to park; **pouvez-vous me faire une petite ~?** can you make a bit of room for me?; **on n'a pas de ~ pour se retourner** there's no room to move *ou* not enough room to swing a cat* (*surtout Brit*).

(e) (*siège, billet*) seat; (*prix, trajet*) fare; (*emplacement réservé*) space. **louer** *ou* **réserver sa ~** to book one's seat; **il n'a pas payé sa ~** he hasn't paid for his seat; he hasn't paid his fare; **payer ~ entière** (*au cinéma etc*) to pay full price; (*dans le tram etc*) to pay full fare; **~ de parking** parking space; **parking de 500 ~s** parking (space) for 500 cars; **cinéma de 400 ~s** cinema seating 400 (people) *ou* with a seating capacity of 400; **~ assise** seat; **~s assises 20, ~s debout 40** seating capacity 20, standing passengers 40; **il n'y a que des ~s debout** it's standing room only; **une (voiture de) 4 ~s** a 4-seater (car); **tente à 4 ~s** tent that sleeps 4, 4-man tent; **j'ai 3 ~s dans ma voiture** I've room for 3 in my car.

(f) (*rang*) (*Scol*) place; (*Sport*) place, placing. **il a eu une bonne ~** he got a good place, he got a good placing; **être reçu dans les premières ~s** to get one of the top places, be amongst the top; **il a eu une 2e ~** *ou* **une ~ de 2e en histoire** he came *ou* was 2nd in history.

(g) (*emploi*) job; *[domestique]* position, situation. **une ~ d'employé/de dactylo** a job as a clerk/a typist; *[domestique]* **être en ~** to be in service (*chez* with); (*Pol*) **les gens en ~** influential people, people with influence.

(h) (*Mil*) **~ (forte** *ou* **de guerre)** fortified town; **le commandant de la ~** the fortress commander; **s'introduire/avoir des contacts dans la ~** to get/have contacts on the inside; (*fig*) **maintenant il est dans la ~** now he's on the inside; **~ d'armes** parade ground.

(i) (*Comm, Fin*) market. **vous n'en trouverez pas de moins cher sur la ~ de Paris** you won't find cheaper on the Paris market; **dans toutes les ~s financières du monde** in all the money markets of the world.

(j) (*loc*) **par ~s, de ~ en ~** here and there, in places; **rester sur/se rendre sur ~** to stay on/go to the spot, stay/go there; **on peut faire la réparation sur ~** we can repair it right here *ou* on the spot; **être cloué sur ~** to be *ou* stand rooted to the spot; **faire du sur ~*** *[cycliste]* to balance; (*fig*) *[enquête, automobilistes]* to move at a snail's pace; **à la ~ (de)** (*en échange*) instead (of), in place (of); **faire une démarche à la ~ de qn** to take steps on sb's behalf; **répondre à la ~ de qn** to reply in sb's place *ou* on sb's behalf; **être en ~** *[plan]* to be ready; *[forces de l'ordre]* to be in place *ou* stationed; **mettre qch en ~** to set sth up, get sth ready; **la mise en ~ du projet** the setting up of the plan; **faire ~ à qch** to give way to sth; **faire ~ à qn** (*lit*) to let sb pass; (*fig*) to give way to sb; **faire ~ nette** to make a clean sweep; **~ aux jeunes!** make way for the young!

placé, e [plase] (*ptp de* **placer**) *adj* **(a)** (*gén*) **la fenêtre/leur maison est ~e à gauche** the window/their house is (situated) on the left; **je suis** *ou* **je me trouve ~ dans une position délicate** I am (placed) in *ou* I find myself (placed) in a tricky position; **être bien/mal ~** *[terrain]* to be well/badly situated, be favourably/unfavourably situated; *[objet]* to be well/badly placed; *[spectateur]* to have a good/a poor seat; *[concurrent]* to be in a good/bad position, be well/badly placed; **leur confiance a été bien/mal ~e** their trust was not/was misplaced; **sa fierté est mal ~e** his pride is misplaced *ou* out of place; **il est bien ~ pour gagner** he is in a good position *ou* well placed to win; **il est bien ~ pour le savoir** he is in a position to know; **je suis bien/mal ~ pour vous répondre** I'm in a/in no position to answer; **tu es mal ~ pour te plaindre!*** you've got nothing to complain about!; *V* **haut.**

(b) (*Courses*) **arriver ~** to be placed; **jouer (un cheval) ~** to back a horse each way (*Brit*) *ou* to win, put an each-way (*Brit*) bet on (a horse).

placement [plasmɑ̃] *nm* **(a)** (*Fin*) investment. **faire un ~ d'argent** to invest (some) money; **~ de père de famille** gilt-edged investment, safe investment. **(b)** *[employés]* placing; *V* **bureau.**

placenta [plasɛ̃ta] *nm* placenta; (*arrière-faix*) afterbirth, placenta.

placentaire [plasɛ̃tɛʀ] *adj* placental.

placer [plase] (3) **1** *vt* **(a)** (*assigner une place à*) *objet, personne* to place, put; *invité* to seat, put; *spectateur* to seat, give a seat to, put; *sentinelle* to post, station; (*Ftbl*) *balle* to place; (*Boxe*) *coup* to land, place; (*Tech: installer*) to put in, fit in. **vous me placez dans une situation délicate** you're placing *ou* putting me in a tricky position; **~ sa voix** to pitch one's voice; **~ ses affaires bien en ordre** to put one's things tidy *ou* straight.

(b) (*situer*) to place, set, put. **il a placé l'action de son roman en Provence** he has set *ou* situated the action of his novel in Provence; **où placez-vous Lyon?** whereabouts do you think Lyons is?, where would you put Lyons?; **~ l'honnêteté avant l'intelligence** to set *ou* put *ou* place honesty above intelligence; **~ le bonheur dans la vie familiale** to consider that happiness is found in family life; **~ un nom sur un visage** to put a name to a face; **je ne peux pas ~ de nom sur son visage** I can't place him *ou* his face, I can't put a name to his face *ou* to him; **~ ses espérances en qn/qch** to set *ou* pin one's hopes on sb/sth.

(c) (*introduire*) *remarque, anecdote, plaisanterie* to come out with, put in, get in. **il n'a pas pu ~ un mot** he couldn't get a word in (edgeways).

(d) *ouvrier, malade, écolier* to place (*dans* in). **~ qn comme vendeur/chez X** to get *ou* find sb a job as a salesman/with X; **~ qn comme apprenti (chez X)** to apprentice sb (to X); **~ qn à la comptabilité** to give sb a job *ou* place sb in the accounts department; (*hum*) **ils n'ont pas encore pu ~ leur fille** they've still not been able to marry off their daughter (*hum*) *ou* to get their daughter off their hands (*hum*); **l'orchestre est placé sous la direction de ...** the orchestra is under the direction of ... *ou* conducted by ...; **~ qn/qch sous l'autorité/les ordres de** to place *ou* put sb/sth under the authority/orders of.

(e) (*Comm: vendre*) *marchandise* to place, sell. (*fig hum*) **elle a réussi à ~ sa vieille machine à laver** she managed to find a home (*hum*) *ou* a buyer for her old washing machine.

(f) *argent* (*à la Bourse*) to invest; (*à la Caisse d'Épargne, sur un compte*) to deposit. **~ une somme sur son compte** to put *ou* pay a sum into one's account.

2 se placer *vpr* **(a)** *[personne]* to take up a position; (*debout*) to stand; (*assis*) to sit (down); *[événement, action]* to take place. **se ~ de face/contre le mur/en cercle** to stand face on/against the wall/in a circle; **se ~ sur le chemin de qn** to stand in sb's path; **cette démarche se place dans le cadre de nos revendications** these steps should be seen in the context of our claims; **ça se place bien avant sa mort** this took place *ou* occurred *ou* happened long before he died; (*fig*) **si nous nous plaçons à ce point de vue** *ou* **dans cette perspective** if we look at things from this point of view, if we view the situation in this way; **plaçons-nous dans le cas où cela arriverait** let us suppose that this happens, let us put ourselves in the situation where this actually happens.

(b) (*Scol, Sport*) **se ~ 2e** to be *ou* come 2nd, be in 2nd place; **il s'est bien placé dans la course** he was well placed in the race.

(c) (*prendre une place*) **se ~ comme vendeuse** to get *ou* find a job as a salesgirl; **retraité qui voudrait bien se ~ (dans une institution)** pensioner who would like to find a place in a home; (*hum*) **ce célibataire n'a pas encore réussi à se ~** this bachelor still hasn't been able to find anyone to marry him.

placet [plasɛ] *nm* (*Hist, Jur*) petition.

placeur [plasœʀ] *nm* *[spectateurs, invités]* usher; *[domestiques]* (domestic) employment agent.

placeuse [plasøz] *nf* (*au cinéma*) usherette.

placide [plasid] *adj* placid, calm.

placidement [plasidmɑ̃] *adv* placidly, calmly.

placidité [plasidite] *nf* placidity, placidness, calmness.

placier [plasje] *nm* travelling salesman, traveller.

plafond [plafɔ̃] *nm* **(a)** (*lit*) *[salle]* ceiling; *[voiture, caverne]* roof. **~ à caissons** coffered ceiling; *V* **araignée.**

(b) (*fig: limite*) *[prix, loyer]* ceiling; (*Mét: nuages*) ceiling, cloud cover; (*Aviat*) ceiling, maximum height; (*Aut*) top *ou* maximum speed. **haut/bas de ~** high-/low-ceilinged; **prix ~** ceiling, ceiling *ou* maximum price.

plafonnement [plafɔnmɑ̃] *nm* reaching a ceiling (*fig*).

plafonner [plafɔne] (1) **1** *vi* *[prix, écolier, salaire]* to reach a ceiling *ou* maximum; (*Aviat*) to reach one's ceiling; (*Aut*) to reach one's top speed *ou* maximum speed.

2 *vt* (*Constr*) to put a ceiling in. **grenier plafonné** loft which has had a ceiling put in.

plafonnier [plafɔnje] *nm* *[voiture]* courtesy *ou* interior light; *[chambre]* ceiling light *ou* lamp.

plage [plaʒ] **1** *nf* **(a)** *[mer, rivière, lac]* beach. **~ de sable/de galets** sandy/pebble beach; **sac/serviette/robe de ~** beach bag/towel/robe.

(b) (*ville*) (seaside) resort.

(c) (*zone*) (*dans un barème, une progression*) range, bracket; (*dans un horaire etc*) (time) segment. **~ d'ombre** band of shadow (*fig*), shadowy area (*fig*); **temps d'écoute divisé en ~s (horaires)** listening time divided into segments; **~ de prix** price range *ou* bracket.

(d) *[disque]* track, band.

2: plage arrière (*Naut*) quarter-deck; (*Aut*) parcel *ou* back shelf; (*Naut*) **plage avant** forecastle (head *ou* deck), fo'c'sle; **plage lumineuse** illuminated area.

plagiaire [plaʒjɛʀ] *nmf* plagiarist, plagiarizer.

plagiat [plaʒja] *nm* plagiarism, plagiary. **c'est un véritable ~** it's absolute plagiarism.

plagier [plaʒje] (7) *vt* to plagiarize.

plagiste [plaʒist(ə)] *nm* beach manager.

plaidant, e [plɛdɑ̃, ɑ̃t] *adj partie* litigant; *avocat* pleading.

plaider [plede] (1) **1** *vt* to plead. ~ coupable/non-coupable/la légitime défense to plead guilty/not guilty/self-defence; ~ la cause de qn (*fig*) to plead sb's cause, argue *ou* speak in favour of sb; (*Jur*) to plead for sb, plead sb's case, defend sb; ~ sa propre cause to speak in one's own defence; (*fig*) ~ le faux pour savoir le vrai to tell a lie (in order) to get at the truth; l'affaire s'est plaidée à Paris/à huis clos the case was heard in Paris/in closed court *ou* in camera.

2 *vi* **(a)** *[avocat]* to plead (*pour* for, on behalf of, *contre* against).

(b) (*intenter un procès*) to go to court, litigate. ~ contre qn to take sb to court, take (out) proceedings against sb; ils ont plaidé pendant des années their case has been dragging on for years.

(c) (*fig*) ~ pour *ou* en faveur de qn *[personne]* to speak for sb, defend sb; *[mérites, qualités]* to be a point in sb's favour.

plaideur, -euse [plɛdœʀ, øz] *nm,f* litigant.

plaidoirie [plɛdwaʀi] *nf* speech for the defence, defence speech.

plaidoyer [plɛdwaje] *nm* (*Jur*) speech for the defence; (*fig*) defence, plea. (*fig*) ~ en faveur de/contre qch plea for/against sth.

plaie [plɛ] *nf* (*physique, morale*) wound; (*coupure*) cut; (*fig: fléau*) scourge. (*fig*) rouvrir une ~ to reopen an old sore; quelle ~!* (*personne*) what a bind* (*Brit*) *ou* nuisance he is!, what a pest* (he is)!; (*chose*) what a bind!* (*Brit*) *ou* pest!* *ou* nuisance!; remuer *ou* tourner le couteau *ou* le fer dans la ~ to twist *ou* turn the knife in the wound; (*Prov*) ~ d'argent n'est pas mortelle money isn't everything; (*Bible*) les ~s d'Égypte the plagues of Egypt; *V* rêver.

plaignant, e [plɛɲɑ̃, ɑ̃t] **1** *adj partie* litigant. **2** *nm,f* plaintiff.

plain-chant, *pl* plains-chants [plɛ̃ʃɑ̃] *nm* plainchant, plainsong (*U*).

plaindre [plɛ̃dʀ(ə)] (52) **1** *vt* **(a)** *personne* to pity, feel sorry for. aimer se faire ~ to like to be pitied; il est bien à ~ he is to be pitied; elle n'est pas à ~ (*c'est bien fait*) she doesn't deserve (any) sympathy, she doesn't deserve to be pitied; (*elle a de la chance*) she's got nothing to complain about; je vous plains de vivre avec elle I pity you *ou* I sympathize with you (for) having to live with her.

(b) (*: *donner chichement*) to begrudge, grudge. donne-moi plus de papier, on dirait que tu le plains give me some more paper — anybody would think you begrudged it (me); il ne plaint pas son temps/sa peine he doesn't grudge his time/his efforts.

2 se plaindre *vpr* (*gémir*) to moan; (*rouspéter*) to complain, grumble, moan* (*de* about); (*frm, Jur: réclamer*) to make a complaint (*de* about, *auprès de* to). (*souffrir*) se ~ de *maux de tête etc* to complain of; se ~ de qn/qch à qn to complain to sb about sb/sth; de quoi te plains-tu? (*lit*) what are you complaining *ou* grumbling *ou* moaning* about?; (*iro*) what have you got to complain *ou* grumble *ou* moan* about?; il se plaint que les prix montent he's complaining about rising prices *ou* that prices are going up; ne viens pas te ~ si tu es puni don't come and complain *ou* moan* (to me) if you're punished; se ~ à qui de droit to make a complaint *ou* to complain to the appropriate person.

plaine [plɛn] *nf* plain.

plain-pied [plɛ̃pje] *adv:* de ~ (*pièce*) on the same level (*avec* as); (*maison*) (built) at street-level; (*fig*) entrer de ~ dans le sujet to come straight to the point.

plainte [plɛ̃t] *nf* **(a)** (*gémissement*) moan, groan; (*littér*) *[vent]* moaning. **(b)** (*doléance*) complaint, moaning (*U: péj*). **(c)** (*Jur*) complaint. porter ~ *ou* déposer une ~ contre qn to lodge a complaint against *ou* about sb.

plaintif, -ive [plɛ̃tif, iv] *adj* plaintive, sorrowful, doleful.

plaintivement [plɛ̃tivmɑ̃] *adv* plaintively, sorrowfully, dolefully.

plaire [plɛʀ] (54) **1** *vi* **(a)** (*être apprécié*) ce garçon me plaît I like that boy; ce garçon ne me plaît pas I don't like that boy, I don't care for that boy; ce spectacle/dîner/livre m'a plu I liked *ou* enjoyed that show/dinner/book; ce genre de musique ne me plaît pas beaucoup I'm not (very *ou* terribly) keen on *ou* I don't (really) care for *ou* go for* that kind of music, that kind of music doesn't appeal to me very much; ton nouveau travail te plaît? (how) do you like your new job?, how are you enjoying your new job?; les brunes me plaisent I like *ou* go for* dark-haired girls, dark-haired girls appeal to me; c'est une chose qui me plairait beaucoup à faire it's something I'd very much like to do *ou* I'd love to do; on ne peut pas ~ à tout le monde one cannot be liked by everyone; il cherche à ~ à tout le monde he tries to please everyone; il cherchait à ~ à toutes les femmes he was trying to impress all the women *ou* appeal to all the women; c'est le genre d'homme qui plaît aux femmes he's the sort of man that women like; le désir de ~ the desire to please; c'est le genre de personne qui plaît en société he's the type of person who gets on well with people *ou* that people like.

(b) (*convenir à*) ce plan me plaît this plan suits me; ça te plairait d'aller au cinéma? would you like to go to the pictures?, do you fancy* *ou* do you feel like going to the pictures?; ce qui vous plaira le mieux whichever *ou* whatever suits you best; j'irai si ça me plaît I'll go if I feel like it *ou* if it suits me; je travaille quand ça me plaît I work when I feel like it *ou* when it suits me *ou* when the fancy takes me*; je fais ce qui me plaît I do what I like *ou* as I please.

(c) (*réussir*) fais un gâteau, cela plaît toujours make a cake, it always goes down well; achète des fleurs, cela pla ît toujours buy some flowers, they're always appreciated *ou* welcome; la pièce a plu the play was a success *ou* hit* *ou* went down well; cette réponse a plu this reply went down well *ou* was appreciated.

2 *vb impers* **(a)** ici, je fais ce qu'il me plaît here, I do as I please *ou* like; et s'il me plaît d'y aller? and what if I want to go?; (*littér*) il lui plaît de croire que ... he likes to think that ...; comme il vous plaira just as you like *ou* please *ou* choose.

(b) (*loc*) s'il te plaît, s'il vous plaît please; et elle a un manteau de vison, s'il vous plaît!* and she's got a mink coat if you please!* *ou* no less!; (*littér*) plaise *ou* plût à Dieu *ou* au ciel, qu'il réussisse! please God that *ou* would to God that *ou* heaven grant that he succeeds! (*littér*); (*frm*) plaît-il? I beg your pardon? (*frm*); *V* dieu.

3 se plaire *vpr* **(a)** (*se sentir bien, à l'aise*) il se plaît à Londres he likes *ou* enjoys being in London, he likes it in London; j'espère qu'il s'y plaira I hope he'll like it there; te plais-tu avec tes nouveaux amis? do you like being with your new friends?; les fougères se plaisent dans les sous-bois ferns do well *ou* thrive in the undergrowth.

(b) (*s'apprécier*) je me plais en robe longue I like myself in *ou* I like wearing a long dress; tu te plais avec ton chapeau? do you like *ou* fancy* yourself in your hat?; ces deux-là se plaisent those two get on well together, those two (have) hit it off (together)*.

(c) (*littér: prendre plaisir à*) se ~ à lire to take pleasure in reading, like *ou* be fond of reading; se ~ à tout critiquer to delight in criticizing everything.

plaisamment [plɛzamɑ̃] *adv* (*V* plaisant) pleasantly; agreeably; amusingly; laughably, ridiculously.

plaisance [plɛzɑ̃s] *nf:* la (navigation de) ~ boating; (*à voile*) sailing, yachting; bateau de ~ pleasure boat; maison de ~ country house.

plaisancier [plɛzɑ̃sje] *nm* (amateur) sailor.

plaisant, e [plɛzɑ̃, ɑ̃t] *adj* **(a)** (*agréable*) *personne, séjour* pleasant, agreeable; *maison* pleasant; *souvenir* pleasant, agreeable. ~ à l'œil pleasing to *ou* on the eye, nice to look at; ce n'est guère ~ it's not exactly pleasant, it's not very nice; *V* mauvais.

(b) (*amusant*) *histoire, aventure* amusing, funny. le ~ de la chose the funny side *ou* part of it, the funny thing about it.

(c) (*ridicule*) laughable, ridiculous.

(d) (†: *bizarre*) bizarre, singular. voilà qui est ~! it's quite bizarre!; je vous trouve bien ~ de parler de la sorte I consider it most bizarre *ou* singular of you to speak in that way.

plaisanter [plɛzɑ̃te] (1) **1** *vi* to joke, have a joke (*sur* about). je ne suis pas d'humeur à ~ I'm in no mood for jokes *ou* joking, I'm in no joking mood; et je ne plaisante pas! and I mean it!, and I'm not joking!, and I'm serious!; c'est quelqu'un qui ne plaisante pas he's not the sort you can have a joke with; vous plaisantez you must be joking *ou* kidding*, you're joking *ou* kidding*; pour ~ for fun *ou* a joke *ou* a laugh*; on ne plaisante pas avec cela it's no joking *ou* laughing matter, this is a serious matter; il ne plaisante pas sur la discipline/cette question there's no joking with him over matters of discipline/this subject; on ne plaisante pas avec la police there's no joking where the police are concerned, the police are not to be trifled with.

2 *vt* to make fun of, tease. ~ qn sur qch to tease sb about sth.

plaisanterie [plɛzɑ̃tʀi] *nf* **(a)** (*blague*) joke (*sur* about). aimer la ~ to be fond of a joke; ~ de corps de garde barrack-room joke; par ~ for fun *ou* a joke *ou* a laugh*; faire une ~ to tell *ou* crack a joke; tourner qch en ~ to make a joke of sth, laugh sth off.

(b) (*raillerie*) joke. il est en butte aux ~s de ses amis his friends are always making fun of him *ou* poking fun at him, his friends treat him as a figure of fun; faire des ~s sur to joke *ou* make jokes about *ou* at the expense of; il comprend *ou* prend bien la ~ he knows how to *ou* he can take a joke; il ne faudrait pas pousser la ~ trop loin we mustn't take the joke too far.

(c) (*farce*) (practical) joke, prank. mauvaise ~ (nasty) practical joke.

(d) (*loc fig*) c'est une ~ pour lui de résoudre ce problème/gagner la course he could solve this problem/win the race with his eyes shut *ou* standing on his head*; lui, se lever tôt? c'est une ~! him, get up early? what a joke! *ou* you must be kidding!*

plaisantin [plɛzɑ̃tɛ̃] *nm* **(a)** (*blagueur*) joker. c'est un petit ~ he's quite a joker. **(b)** (*fumiste*) jester.

plaisir [pleziʀ] *nm* **(a)** (*joie*) pleasure. avoir du ~ *ou* prendre ~ à faire qch to find *ou* take pleasure in doing sth, delight in doing sth; prendre (un malin) ~ à faire qch to take (a mischievous) delight in doing sth; j'ai le ~ de vous annoncer que ... it is with great pleasure that I am able to announce that ...; c'est un ~ de le voir it's a pleasure to see him; par ~, pour le ~ (*gén*) for pleasure; *bricoler, peindre* as a hobby; ranger pour le ~ de ranger to tidy up just for the sake of it; (*iro*) je vous souhaite bien du ~! good luck to you! (*iro*), I wish you (the best of) luck! (*iro*); (*iro*) ça nous promet du ~ (en perspective) I can hardly wait! (*iro*); avec (le plus grand) ~ with (the greatest of) pleasure; au ~ de vous revoir, au ~* (I'll) see you again sometime, (I'll) be seeing you*; le ~ solitaire self-abuse; les ~s de la chair the pleasures of the flesh; *V* durer, gêne.

(b) (*distraction*) pleasure. les ~s de la vie life's (little) pleasures; courir après les ~s to be a pleasure-seeker; le tennis est un ~ coûteux tennis is an expensive hobby *ou* pleasure; lieu de ~ house of pleasure.

(c) (*littér: volonté*) pleasure (*littér*), wish. si c'est votre (bon) ~ if such is your will (*littér*) *ou* wish (*littér*), if you so desire (*littér*); à ~: les faits ont été grossis à ~ the facts have been wildly exaggerated; il s'inquiète à ~ he seems to take a perverse delight in worrying himself; il ment à ~ he lies for the sake of lying *ou* for the sake of it.

(d) (*loc*) faire ~ à qn to please sb; ce cadeau m'a fait ~ I was very pleased with this gift, this gift gave me great pleasure; **cela me fait ~ de vous entendre dire cela** I'm pleased *ou* delighted to hear you say that, it gives me great pleasure to hear you say that; **mine/appétit qui fait ~ à voir** healthy face/appetite that is a pleasure to see *ou* to behold; **pour me faire ~** (just) to please me; **fais-moi ~: mange ta soupe/arrête la radio** eat your soup/turn off the radio for me, there's a dear — eat your soup/turn off the radio; (*frm*) **voulez-vous me faire le ~ de venir dîner?** I should be most pleased if you would come to dinner, would you do me the pleasure of dining with me (*ou* us)? (*frm*); **fais-moi le ~ de te taire!** would you mind just being quiet!, do me a favour and shut up!*; **il se fera un ~ de vous reconduire** he'll be (only too) pleased *ou* glad to drive you back, it will be a pleasure for him to drive you back; **bon, c'est bien pour vous faire ~ *ou* si cela peut vous faire ~** all right, if it will make you happy *ou* give you pleasure; **j'irai, mais c'est bien pour vous faire ~** I'll go (just) to keep you happy.

plan[1] [plɑ̃] **1** *nm* **(a)** *[maison]* plan, blueprint; *[machine]* plan, scale drawing; *[ville, métro]* map, plan; *[région]* map. **acheter un appartement sur ~** to buy a flat after seeing the plans; **tirer des ~s** to draw up plans; (*fig*) **tirer des ~s sur la comète*** to count one's chickens before they are hatched.

(b) (*Math, Phys: surface*) plane.

(c) (*Ciné*) shot. (*Peinture, Phot*) **premier ~** foreground; **dernier ~** background; (*Peinture*) **au deuxième ~** in the middle distance; *V* **gros**.

(d) (*fig: niveau*) plane, level. **mettre qch au deuxième ~** to consider sth of secondary importance; **ce problème est au premier ~ de nos préoccupations** this problem is uppermost in our minds *ou* is one of our foremost preoccupations; **parmi toutes ces questions, l'inflation vient au premier ~ *ou* nous mettons l'inflation au premier ~** of all these questions, inflation comes uppermost in our minds *ou* we consider inflation to be the most important; **personnalité de premier ~** key figure; **personnalité de second ~** background figure; **un savant de tout premier ~** a scientist of the first rank, one of our foremost scientists; **au premier ~ de l'actualité** very much in the news; **mettre sur le même ~** to put on the same plane *ou* level; **sur le ~ de la communauté** as far as the community is concerned; **sur le ~ moral/intellectuel** morally/intellectually speaking, on the moral/intellectual plane; *V* **arrière**.

(e) (*projet*) plan; (*Écon*) plan, programme. **avoir/exécuter un ~** to have/carry out a plan; **~ de cinq ans** five-year plan.

(f) *[livre]* plan; *[dissertation, devoir]* plan, framework. **faire un ~ de qch** to make a plan for sth, plan sth out.

(g) (**loc*) **rester en ~** *[personne]* to be left stranded, be left high and dry; *[voiture]* to be abandoned *ou* ditched*; *[projets]* to be abandoned in midstream, be left (hanging) in mid air; **laisser en ~** *personne* to leave in the lurch *ou* high and dry *ou* stranded; *voiture* to leave (behind), abandon, ditch*; *affaires* to abandon; *projet, travail* to drop, abandon; **il a tout laissé en ~ pour venir me voir** he dropped everything to come and see me.

2: plan d'action plan of action *ou* campaign; **plan directeur** (*Mil*) *map of the combat area*; (*Écon*) blueprint, master plan; **plan d'eau** stretch of water; **plan d'équipement** industrial development programme; **plan d'études** study plan *ou* programme; (*Géol*) **plan de faille** fault plane; (*Ciné*) **plan fixe** static shot; **plan incliné** inclined plane; **en plan incliné** sloping; **plan de modernisation** modernization plan *ou* project; (*Ciné*) **plan rapproché** close-up (shot); (*Ciné*) **plan séquence** sequence shot; **plan de travail** (*dans une cuisine*) work-top, work(ing) surface; (*planning*) work plan *ou* programme *ou* schedule; *V* **plan-concave, plan-convexe**.

plan[2], **plane** [plɑ̃, plan] *adj miroir* flat; *surface* flat, level, plane; (*Math*) *angle, géométrie* plane.

planche [plɑ̃ʃ] **1** *nf* **(a)** (*en bois*) plank; (*plus large*) board; (*rayon*) shelf; (*Naut: passerelle*) gangplank; (*plongeoir*) diving board; (**: ski*) ski. **cabine/sol en ~s** wooden hut/floor; **dormir sur une ~** to sleep on a wooden board; *V* **pain**.

(b) (*Typ, illustration*) plate.

(c) (*Horticulture*) bed.

(d) (*Théât*) **les ~s** the boards, the stage (*U*); **monter sur les ~s** (*entrer en scène*) to go on stage; (*faire du théâtre*) to go on the stage; *V* **brûler**.

(e) (*Natation*) floating (on one's back). **faire la ~** to float on one's back.

2: planche à billets banknote plate; **faire marcher la planche à billets*** to print money; **planche à découper** *[cuisinière]* chopping board; *[boucher]* chopping block; **planche à dessin *ou* à dessiner** drawing board; **planche à laver** washboard; **planche à pain** (*lit*) breadboard; (*péj*) flat-chested woman, woman who is as flat as a board (*péj*); **planche à pâtisserie** pastry board; **planche à repasser** ironing board; **planche de salut** (*appui*) mainstay; (*dernier espoir*) last hope, sheet anchor.

planchéié, e [plɑ̃ʃeje] *adj* floored (*lit*).

plancher[1] [plɑ̃ʃe] *nm* **(a)** (*Constr*) floor; (*fig: Écon*) minimum holdings (*of Government stocks*). (*Aut*) **mettre le pied au ~** to put one's foot down to the floor, step on it* *ou* on the gas*; (*fig*) **le ~ des vaches*** dry land; **prix ~** minimum *ou* floor *ou* bottom price. **(b)** (*Anat*) floor.

plancher[2] [plɑ̃ʃe] (1) *vi* (*arg Scol*) to spout* (*Brit*). **sur quoi as-tu planché?** what did they get you to spout (*Brit*) on?*

planchette [plɑ̃ʃɛt] *nf* (*gén*) (small) board; (*rayon*) (small) shelf.

plan-concave [plɑ̃kɔ̃kav] *adj* plano-concave.

plan-convexe [plɑ̃kɔ̃vɛks(ə)] *adj* plano-convex.

plancton [plɑ̃ktɔ̃] *nm* plankton.

planéité [planeite] *nf* (*V* **plan**[2]) flatness; levelness; planeness.

planer [plane] (1) *vi* **(a)** *[oiseau]* to glide, soar; (*en tournoyant*) to hover; *[avion]* to glide, volplane; *[fumée]* to float, hover.

(b) *[danger, soupçons]* **~ sur** to hang over; **laisser ~ le mystère (sur)** to let mystery hang (over).

(c) (*se détacher*) *[savant]* to take a detached view, be detached; *[rêveur]* to have one's head in the clouds. **~ au-dessus de** *querelles, détails* to be above; **il plane dans un univers de rêve** he is lost in a dream world.

(d) (*littér*) *[regard]* **~ sur** to look down on *ou* over; **le regard planait au loin sur la mer** one had a commanding view over the sea.

planétaire [planetɛʀ] *adj* (*Astron, Tech*) planetary.

planétarium [planetaʀjɔm] *nm* planetarium.

planète [planɛt] *nf* planet.

planeur [planœʀ] *nm* (*Aviat*) glider.

planificateur, -trice [planifikatœʀ, tʀis] (*Écon*) **1** *adj* economic. **2** *nm,f* planner.

planification [planifikɑsjɔ̃] *nf* (economic) planning.

planifier [planifje] (7) *vt* to plan. **économie planifiée** planned economy.

planisphère [planisfɛʀ] *nm* planisphere.

planning [planiŋ] *nm* (*Écon, Ind*) programme, schedule. **~ familial** family planning.

planque‡ [plɑ̃k] *nf* (*cachette*) hideaway, hideout, hidey-hole*; (*travail tranquille*) cushy job*, cushy *ou* soft (*Brit*) *ou* real easy number‡. **c'est la ~!** it's dead cushy!‡, it's a real cushy number!‡

planqué [plɑ̃ke] *nm* (*arg Mil*) funker* (*Brit*).

planquer‡ [plɑ̃ke] (1) **1** *vt* to hide (away), stash away*. **2 se planquer** *vpr* to take cover.

plant [plɑ̃] *nm* (*plante*) *[légume]* seedling, young plant; *[fleur]* bedding plant; (*plantation*) *[légumes]* bed, (vegetable) patch; *[fleurs]* (flower) bed; *[arbres]* plantation. **un ~ de salade** a lettuce seedling, a young lettuce (plant); **un ~ de vigne/de bégonia** a young vine/begonia.

plantain [plɑ̃tɛ̃] *nm* plantain.

plantaire [plɑ̃tɛʀ] *adj* plantar. **verrue ~** verruca on the sole of the foot; *V* **voûte**.

plantation [plɑ̃tɑsjɔ̃] *nf* **(a)** (*Horticulture*) (*action*) planting; (*culture*) plant; (*terrain*) *[légumes]* bed, (vegetable) patch; *[fleurs]* (flower) bed; *[arbres, café, coton]* plantation. **faire des ~s de fleurs** to plant flowers (out).

(b) (*Théât*) *[décor]* setting up.

plante[1] [plɑ̃t] *nf* (*Bot*) plant. **~ d'appartement** house *ou* pot plant; **~ à fleurs** flowering plant; **~ fourragère** fodder plant; **~ grasse** succulent (plant); **~ grimpante** creeper; (*lit, fig*) **~ de serre** hothouse plant; **~ textile** fibre plant; **~ verte** green (foliage) plant.

plante[2] [plɑ̃t] *nf* (*Anat*) **~ (des pieds)** sole (of the foot).

planté, e [plɑ̃te] (*ptp de* **planter**) *adj*: **bien ~** *enfant* sturdy; *dents* well-formed; **mal ~** *dents* badly-formed; **ses cheveux sont ~s très bas** he has a very low hairline; **être bien ~ (sur ses jambes)** to be sturdily built; **il est resté ~ au milieu de la rue** he stood stock-still in the middle of the road; **ne restez pas ~ (debout *ou* comme un piquet) à ne rien faire!** don't just stand there doing nothing!; **rester ~ devant une vitrine** to stand looking in a shop window.

planter [plɑ̃te] (1) *vt* **(a)** *plante, graine* to plant, put in; *jardin* to put plants in; (*repiquer*) to plant out. **~ une région en vignes** to plant a region with vines; **~ un terrain en gazon** to plant out a piece of ground with grass, grass a piece of ground; **avenue plantée d'arbres** tree-lined avenue; (*fig*) **aller ~ ses choux** to retire to the country.

(b) (*enfoncer*) *clou* to hammer in, knock in; *pieu* to drive in. **~ un poignard dans le dos de qn** to stick a knife into sb's back, knife *ou* stab sb in the back; **l'ours planta ses griffes dans le bras de l'enfant** the bear stuck its claws into the child's arm; **se ~ une épine dans le doigt** to get a thorn stuck in one's finger; **la flèche se planta dans la cible** the arrow sank into the target.

(c) (*mettre*) to stick*, put. **~ son chapeau sur sa tête** to stick one's hat on one's head*; **il a planté sa voiture au milieu de la rue et il est parti** he stuck* *ou* dumped* his car in the middle of the road and went off; **il nous a plantés sur le trottoir pour aller chercher un journal** he left us hanging about* *ou* standing on the pavement while he went to get a paper; **~ un baiser sur la joue de qn** to plant a kiss on sb's cheek; **~ son regard *ou* ses yeux sur qn** to fix one's eyes on sb; **il se planta devant moi** he planted *ou* plonked* himself in front of me; **~ là** (*laisser sur place*) *personne* to dump*, leave behind; *voiture* to dump*, ditch*; *travail, outils* to dump*, drop; (*délaisser*) *épouse* to walk out on*, ditch*; *travail* to pack in*.

(d) (*installer*) *échelle, drapeau* to put up; *tente* to put up, pitch; (*Théât*) *décors* to put *ou* set up. **~ une échelle contre un mur** to put a ladder (up) *ou* stand a ladder (up) against a wall; (*fig*) **cet auteur sait ~ ses personnages** this author is good at characterization, this author knows how to build up *ou* give substance to his characters.

planteur [plɑ̃tœʀ] *nm* (*colon*) planter.

planteuse [plɑ̃tøz] *nf* (*Agr*) (potato) planter.

plantigrade [plɑ̃tigʀad] *adj, nm* plantigrade.

plantoir [plɑ̃twaʀ] *nm* dibble.

planton [plɑ̃tɔ̃] *nm* (*Mil*) orderly. **être de ~** to be on orderly duty; (*fig*) ou4faire **le ~*** to hang about*, stand around *ou* about (waiting).

plantureusement [plɑ̃tyʀøzmɑ̃] *adv* copiously.

plantureux, -euse [plɑ̃tyʀø, øz] *adj* **(a)** *repas* copious, lavish; *femme* buxom; *poitrine* ample. **(b)** *région, terre* fertile. **récolte/année ~euse** bumper crop/year.

plaquage [plakaʒ] *nm* **(a)** (*Rugby*) tackling (*U*), tackle.

(b) (‡: *abandon: V* **plaquer**) jilting*; ditching*; chucking (in *ou* up)*; packing in*.

plaque [plak] **1** *nf* **(a)** *[métal, verre]* sheet, plate; *[marbre]* slab; *[chocolat]* block, slab; (*revêtement*) plate, cover(ing).

(b) *[verglas]* sheet, patch; *[boue]* patch.
(c) (*tache sur la peau*) patch, blotch, plaque (*T*); *[eczéma]* patch; *V* **sclérose.**
(d) (*portant une inscription*) plaque; (*insigne*) badge; (*au casino*) chip.
(e) (*Élec, Phot*) plate.
2: plaque de blindage armour-plate (*U*), armour-plating (*U*); (*Culin*) **plaque chauffante** hotplate; **plaque de cheminée** fireback; **plaque commémorative** commemorative plaque *ou* plate; **plaque d'égout** manhole cover; **plaque d'identité** *[soldat]* identity disc; *[chien]* name tag, identity disc; *[bracelet]* nameplate; (*Aut*) **plaque d'immatriculation** *ou* **minéralogique** *ou* **de police** number plate (*Brit*), license plate (*US*), registration plate (*Brit*); **plaque de propreté** fingerplate; **plaque tournante** (*Rail*) turntable; (*fig*) centre.

plaqué, e [plake] (*ptp de* **plaquer**) **1** *adj bracelet* plated; *poches* patch (*épith*); *accord* non-arpeggiated. **~ or/argent** gold-/silver-plated. **2** *nm* plate. **en ~** plated; **c'est du ~** it's plated.

plaquer [plake] (1) *vt* **(a)** *bois* to veneer; *bijoux* to plate. **~ du métal sur du bois** to plate wood with metal; **~ des bijoux d'or/d'argent** to plate jewellery with gold/silver, gold-plate/silver-plate jewellery; (*fig*) **ce passage semble plaqué sur le reste du texte** this passage seems to be stuck on *ou* tacked on to the rest of the text.
(b) (‡: *abandonner*) *fiancé* to jilt*, ditch*, chuck*; *épouse* to ditch*, chuck*, walk out on; *emploi* to chuck (in *ou* up)*, pack in*. **elle a tout plaqué pour le suivre** she chucked up* *ou* packed in* everything to follow him.
(c) (*aplatir*) *cheveux* to plaster down. **la sueur plaquait sa chemise contre son corps** the sweat made his shirt cling *ou* stick to his body; **~ une personne contre un mur/au sol** to pin a person to a wall/to the ground; **se ~ les cheveux** to plaster one's hair down (*sur* on, over); **se ~ au sol/contre un mur** to flatten o.s. on the ground/against a wall; **le vent plaquait la neige contre le mur** the wind was blowing the snow up against the wall.
(d) (*Rugby*) to tackle, bring down.
(e) (*Mus*) *accord* to play (*non-arpeggio*).

plaquette [plakɛt] *nf* **(a)** (*petite plaque*) *[métal]* plaque; *[marbre]* tablet; *[chocolat]* block, bar; (*Physiol*) platelet. **(b)** (*livre*) small volume.

plasma [plasma] *nm* (*Anat, Phys*) plasma. **~ sanguin** blood plasma.

plastic [plastik] *nm* plastic explosive.

plasticage [plastikaʒ] *nm* planting of a plastic bomb.

plasticité [plastisite] *nf* (*lit*) plasticity; (*fig*) malleability, plasticity.

plastifier [plastifje] (7) *vt* to coat with plastic. **plastifié** plastic-coated.

plastiquage [plastikaʒ] *nm* = **plasticage.**

plastique [plastik] **1** *adj* **(a)** (*Art*) plastic. **(b)** (*malléable*) malleable, plastic. **en matière ~** plastic. **2** *nm* plastic. **en ~** plastic. **3** *nf* *[sculpteur]* art of modelling, plastic art; *[statue]* modelling; (*arts*) plastic arts (*pl*).

plastiquement [plastikmɑ̃] *adv* from the point of view of form, plastically (*rare*).

plastiquer [plastike] (1) *vt* to plant a plastic bomb in (*ou* on, under *etc*).

plastiqueur [plastikœʀ] *nm* bomber (*planting a plastic bomb*).

plastron [plastʀɔ̃] *nm* (*Habillement*) *[corsage]* front; *[chemise]* shirt front; (*amovible*) false shirt front, dicky*; *[escrimeur]* plastron; *[armure]* plastron, breastplate.

plastronner [plastʀɔne] (1) **1** *vi* to swagger. **2** *vt* to put a plastron on.

plat[1], plate [pla, plat] **1** *adj* **(a)** *surface, pays, casquette, couture, pli* flat; *mer* smooth, still; (*Géom*) *angle* straight; *ventre, poitrine* flat; *cheveux* straight. **bateau à fond ~** flat-bottomed boat; **chaussure plate** *ou* **à talon ~** flat(-heeled) *ou* low(-heeled) shoe; **elle est plate de poitrine, elle a la poitrine plate** she is flat-chested; **elle est plate comme une galette*** *ou* **une limande*** *ou* **une planche à pain*** she's as flat as a board*; *V* **assiette, battre** *etc.*
(b) (*fade*) *style* flat, dull, unimaginative; *dissertation, livre* dull, unremarkable, unimaginative; *adaptation* unimaginative, unremarkable; *voix* flat, dull; *vin* weak-tasting, flat; *personne, vie* dull, uninteresting. **ce qu'il écrit est très ~** what he writes is very dull *ou* flat.
(c) (*obséquieux*) *personne* obsequious, ingratiating (*épith*). **il nous a fait ses plus plates excuses** he made the humblest of apologies to us.
(d) à ~: mettre *ou* **poser qch à ~** to lay sth (down) flat; **poser la main à ~ sur qch** to lay one's hand flat on sth; **être à ~** *[pneu, batterie]* to be flat; *[personne]* to be washed out* *ou* run down; **la grippe l'a mis à ~*** his flu laid him low *ou* completely knocked him out*; (*Aut*) **être/rouler à ~** to have a/drive on a flat (tyre); (*fig*) **tomber à ~** *[remarque, plaisanterie, pièce]* to fall flat; **tomber à ~ ventre** to fall flat on one's face, fall full-length; **se mettre à ~ ventre** to lie face down; (*fig*) **se mettre à ~ ventre devant qn** to crawl *ou* toady to sb.
2 *nm* (*partie plate*) flat (part); *[main]* flat. **une course de ~** a flat race; (*Natation*) **faire un ~** to (do a) belly flop; (*fig*) **faire du ~ à*** *supérieur* to crawl to; *femme* to chat up* (*Brit*), sweet-talk*.
3 plate *nf* (*bateau*) punt, flat-bottomed boat.
4: plate-bande *nf, pl* **plates-bandes** (*Horticulture*) flower bed; (*fig*) **marcher sur** *ou* **piétiner les plates-bandes de qn*** to trespass on sb's preserves, tread on sb else's patch; **plat-bord** *nm, pl* **plats-bords** gunwale; **plat de côtes, plates côtes** middle *ou* best rib; **plate-forme** *nf, pl* **plates-formes** (*gén: terrasse, estrade*) platform; *[autobus]* platform; (*Rail: wagon*) flat wagon (*Brit*) *ou* car (*US*); (*Pol, fig*) platform; **toit en plate-forme** flat roof; (*Géog*) **plate-forme continentale** continental shelf; (*Pol*) **plate-forme électorale** election platform.

plat[2] [pla] **1** *nm* (*récipient, mets*) dish; (*partie du repas*) course; (*contenu*) dish, plate(ful). **~ à légumes/à poisson** vegetable/fish dish; **on en était au ~ de viande** we had reached the meat course; **2 ~s de viande au choix** a choice of 2 meat dishes *ou* courses; (*fig*) **il en a fait tout un ~*** he made a song and dance* *ou* a great fuss* about it; **il voudrait qu'on lui apporte tout sur un ~ (d'argent)** he wants everything handed to him on a silver platter, he expects to be waited on hand and foot; **mettre les petits ~s dans les grands** to put on a first-rate meal, go to town on the meal*; **elle lui prépare de bons petits ~s** she makes the most succulent of dishes for him; *V* **œuf, pied.**
2: plat à barbe shaving mug; **plat garni** main course (served with vegetables); **plat du jour** today's special, ≈ (today's) set menu, plat du jour; **plat de résistance** main course; (*fig*) pièce de résistance.

platane [platan] *nm* plane tree. (*Aut*) **rentrer dans un ~** to crash into a tree.

plateau, *pl* ~x [plato] **1** *nm* **(a)** tray. **~ de fromages** cheese-board, choice of cheeses (*on a menu*); **~ d'huîtres/de fruits de mer** plate of oysters/seafood; (*fig*) **il faut tout lui apporter sur un ~ (d'argent)** he expects everything to be handed to him on a silver platter, he wants waiting on hand and foot.
(b) *[balance]* pan; *[électrophone]* turntable, deck; *[table]* top; *[graphique]* plateau, tableland (*U*). **la courbe fait un ~ avant de redescendre** the curve levels off *ou* reaches a plateau before falling again.
(c) (*Géog*) plateau. **haut ~** high plateau.
(d) (*Théât*) stage; (*Ciné, TV*) set.
(e) (*Rail: wagon*) flat wagon (*Brit*) *ou* truck (*US*); (*plate-forme roulante*) trailer.
2: plateau continental continental shelf; (*Aut*) **plateau d'embrayage** pressure plate; **plateau à fromages** cheese-board; **plateau sous-marin** submarine plateau.

platée [plate] *nf* (*Culin*) dish(ful), plate(ful).

platement [platmɑ̃] *adv écrire, s'exprimer* dully, unimaginatively; *s'excuser* obsequiously.

platine[1] [platin] **1** *nm* platinum. **~ iridié** platinum-iridium alloy. **2** *adj inv* (*couleur*) platinum (*épith*). **blond ~** platinum blond.

platine[2] [platin] *nf* *[électrophone]* deck, turntable; *[microscope]* stage; *[presse]* platen; *[montre, serrure]* plate; *[machine à coudre]* throat plate.

platiné, e [platine] *adj cheveux* platinum (*épith*). **une blonde ~e** a platinum blonde; *V* **vis[1].**

platitude [platityd] *nf* **(a)** (*U*) *[style]* flatness, dullness; *[livre, film, discours, remarque]* dullness, lack of imagination (*de* in, of); *[vie, personnage]* dullness.
(b) (*propos*) platitude. **dire des ~s** to make trite remarks, utter platitudes.
(c) (†: *servilité*) (*U*) *[personne]* obsequiousness; *[excuse]* humility; (*acte*) obsequiousness (*U*).

Platon [platɔ̃] *nm* Plato.

platonicien, -ienne [platɔnisjɛ̃, jɛn] **1** *adj* Platonic. **2** *nm,f* Platonist.

platonique [platɔnik] *adj amour* platonic; *protestation* futile, vain (*épith*).

platoniquement [platɔnikmɑ̃] *adv* (*V* **platonique**) platonically; vainly.

platonisme [platɔnism(ə)] *nm* Platonism.

plâtrage [plɑtʀaʒ] *nm* (*V* **plâtrer**) plastering; liming; setting *ou* putting in plaster; lining.

plâtras [plɑtʀa] *nm* (*débris*) rubble; (*morceau de plâtre*) chunk *ou* lump of plaster.

plâtre [plɑtʀ(ə)] *nm* **(a)** (*matière*) (*Chirurgie, Constr, Sculp*) plaster; (*Agr*) lime. (*Méd*) **mettre dans le ~** to put *ou* set in plaster; (*fig: fromage*) **c'est du ~!** it's like chalk!; *V* **battre.**
(b) (*Chirurgie, Sculp: objet*) plaster cast. (*Constr*) **les ~s** the plasterwork (*U*); (*Chirurgie*) **~ de marche** walking plaster; *V* **essuyer.**
(c) (††*péj: maquillage*) war paint (*hum péj*).

plâtrer [plɑtʀe] (1) *vt mur* to plaster; *prairie* to lime; *jambe* to set *ou* put in plaster; *estomac* to line. **jambe plâtrée** leg in plaster; (*péj*) **~ son visage††** to plaster one's face with war paint (*hum péj*).

plâtrerie [plɑtʀəʀi] *nf* (*usine*) plaster works.

plâtreux, -euse [plɑtʀø, øz] *adj sol* limey, chalky; *surface* plastered, coated with plaster; (*fig*) *fromage* chalky(-textured).

plâtrier [plɑtʀije] *nm* plasterer.

plâtrière [plɑtʀijɛʀ] *nf* (*carrière*) gypsum *ou* lime quarry; (*four*) gypsum kiln.

plausibilité [plozibilite] *nf* plausibility, plausibleness.

plausible [plozibl(ə)] *adj* plausible.

plausiblement [plozibləmɑ̃] *adv* plausibly.

Plaute [plot] *nm* Plautus.

plèbe [plɛb] *nf* (*péj*) plebs, proles. (*Hist*) **la ~** the plebeians (*pl*).

plébéien, -ienne [plebejɛ̃, jɛn] **1** *adj* (*Hist*) plebeian; *goûts* plebeian, common. **2** *nm,f* plebeian.

plébiscitaire [plebisitɛʀ] *adj* of a plebiscite.

plébiscite [plebisit] *nm* plebiscite.

plébisciter [plebisite] (1) *vt* (*Pol*) to elect by plebiscite; (*fig: approuver*) to elect by an overwhelming majority. **se faire ~** to be elected by an overwhelming majority, have a landslide victory.

plectre [plɛktʀ(ə)] *nm* plectrum.

pléiade [plejad] *nf* **(a)** (*groupe*) group, pleiad. (*Littérat*) **la P~** the Pléiade. **(b)** (*Astron*) **P~** Pleiad; **la P~** the Pleiades.

plein, pleine [plɛ̃, plɛn] **1** *adj* **(a)** (*rempli*) *boîte* full; *bus, salle* full (up); *joue, visage* full, plump; *crustacé, coquillage* full; *vie, journée* full, busy. **~ à déborder** full to overflowing; **~ à craquer** *valise* full to bursting, crammed full; *salle* packed (out), crammed full, full to bursting; **un ~ verre de vin** a full glass of wine; **un ~ panier de pommes** a whole basketful of apples, a full basket of apples; **j'ai les mains pleines** my hands are full, I've got my hands full; **parler la bouche pleine** to speak with one's mouth full; **avoir l'estomac** *ou* **le ventre ~*** to be full, have eaten one's fill, be replete (*frm*); **~ comme un œuf*** *tiroir* chock-a-block*, chock-full*; *estomac* full to bursting; *nez* stuffed up; **être ~ aux as‡** to be rolling in money* *ou* in it*, be filthy rich‡; (*péj*) **un gros ~ de soupe*** a big fatty* (*péj*).

(b) ~ de *bonne volonté, admiration, idées, attentions, fautes, vie* full of; *taches, graisse* covered in *ou* with; **salle pleine de monde** room full of people, crowded room; **journée pleine d'événements** day packed with incidents; **entreprise pleine de risques** undertaking fraught with risk(s); **voilà une remarque pleine de finesse** that's a very shrewd remark; **il est ~ de santé/d'idées** he's bursting with health/ideas; **il est ~ de son sujet/de sa nouvelle voiture** he's full of his subject/his new car; **être ~ de soi** to be full of o.s. *ou* of one's own importance.

(c) (*complet*) *succès* complete; *confiance* complete, total; *satisfaction* full, complete, total. **vous avez mon accord ~ et entier** you have my wholehearted consent *ou* approval; **absent un jour ~** absent for a whole day; **à ~ temps, à temps ~** *travailler, emploi* full-time; **il a ~ pouvoir pour agir** he has full power *ou* authority to act; **avoir les ~s pouvoirs** to have full powers; *V* **arc**.

(d) *lune* full. **la mer est pleine, c'est la pleine mer** the tide is in, it is high tide.

(e) (*non creux*) *paroi, porte, pneu* solid; *roue* solid; *trait* unbroken, continuous; *son* solid; *voix* rich, sonorous. (*fig*) **mot employé dans son sens ~** word used in its full sense *ou* meaning.

(f) (‡: *ivre*) stoned‡, plastered‡. **~ comme une barrique** to be as drunk as a lord*.

(g) (*Vét*) pregnant, in calf (*ou* foal, lamb *etc*).

(h) (*indiquant l'intensité*) **la pleine lumière le fatiguait** he found the bright light tiring; **avoir pleine conscience de qch** to be fully aware of sth; **en pleine possession de ses moyens** in full possession of one's faculties; **être en pleine forme*** to be in *ou* on top form; **de son ~ gré** of one's own free will; **réclamer qch de ~ droit** to claim sth as one's right; **heurter qch de ~ fouet** to crash headlong into sth; **entreprise qui marche à ~ rendement** business that is working at full capacity; **à ~ régime** (*Aut*) at maximum revs; (*fig: à toute vitesse*) at full speed; (*fig*) **la production/l'économie marche à ~ régime** production/the economy is going full steam ahead*; **rouler (à) ~s gaz*** *ou* **tubes‡** to drive flat out*; **rouler ~s phares** to drive on full beam *ou* full headlights; **rincer le sol à ~s seaux** to rinse the floor with bucketfuls of water; **embrasser qn à pleine bouche** to kiss sb full on the mouth; **ça sent l'ammoniaque à ~ nez** there's a terrible smell of ammonia; **rire à pleine gorge** to laugh heartily, laugh one's head off*; **crier à ~s poumons** to shout at the top of one's voice, shout one's head off*; **respirer l'air frais à ~s poumons** to take deep breaths of fresh air; **ramasser qch à ~s bras/à pleines mains** to pick up armfuls/handfuls of sth; **prendre qch à pleines mains** to lay a firm hold on sth, grasp sth firmly.

(i) (*au milieu de, au plus fort de*) **en ~ milieu** right *ou* bang* in the middle; **en pleine poitrine** full *ou* right in the chest; **en pleine tête** right in the head; **arriver en ~ (milieu du) cours/en pleine répétition** to arrive (right) in the middle of the class/rehearsal; **oiseau en ~ vol** bird in full flight; **tué en pleine jeunesse** killed in the bloom *ou* fullness (*littér*) of youth; **c'est arrivé en ~ Paris/en pleine rue** it happened in the middle of Paris/in the middle of the street; **en ~ midi** (*à l'heure du déjeuner*) in the middle of the lunch hour; (*en plein zénith*) at the height of noon *ou* at high noon; (*exposé plein sud*) facing south, south-facing; **en ~ jour** in broad daylight; **en pleine nuit** in the middle of the night, at dead of night; **en ~ hiver** in the depths *ou* middle of winter; **rester en ~ soleil** to stay (out) in the heat of the sun; **le jardin est en ~ soleil** the sun is shining right on(to) the garden; **son visage était en pleine lumière** the light was shining straight into his face *ou* at him; **affaire en ~ essor** *ou* **en pleine croissance** rapidly expanding *ou* growing business; **en ~ vent** right in the wind; **arbre planté en pleine terre** tree planted in open ground *ou* out in the open; **en pleine saison** at the height of the season; (*touristique*) when the season is (*ou* was) in full swing, at the middle of the (tourist) season; **je suis en ~ travail** I'm in the middle of (my) work, I'm hard at work; **en pleine obscurité** in complete *ou* utter darkness.

2 *adv* **(a) avoir des bonbons ~ les poches** to have one's pockets full of *ou* stuffed with sweets; **avoir de l'encre ~ les mains** to have ink all over one's hands *ou* one's hands covered in ink; **avoir de l'argent ~ les poches** to have plenty of money, be rolling in money*, be a moneybags*; **il a des jouets ~ un placard** he's got a cupboardful *ou* a cupboard full of toys; **se diriger/donner ~ ouest** to head/face due west; **en avoir ~ la bouche de qn/qch** to be full of sb/sth, be always talking about sb/sth; **en avoir ~ le dos*** *ou* **le cul**** **de qch** to be fed up with sth*, be sick and tired of sth*, be pissed off** with sth; **en avoir ~ les jambes*** *ou* **les bottes*** to be all-in*, have walked one's legs off*; **il a voulu nous en mettre ~ la vue*** he wanted to dazzle us (with his brilliance *ou* intelligence *etc*); **on s'en est mis ~ la lampe*** we had a slap-up meal*; *V* **tout**.

(b) (*: *beaucoup de*) **~ de** lots of; **il y a ~ de bouteilles dans la cave/de gens dans la rue** the cellar/street is full of bottles/people, there are lots *ou* loads* of bottles in the cellar/people in the street; **un gâteau avec ~ de crème** a cake filled with lots of *ou* plenty of cream; **il a mis ~ de chocolat sur sa veste** he has got chocolate all over his jacket.

(c) en ~: la lumière frappait son visage en ~ the light was shining straight *ou* right into his face; **en ~ devant toi** right *ou* straight *ou* bang* in front of you; **en ~ dans l'eau/l'œil** right *ou* straight in the water/eye; **mettre en ~ dans le mille** (*lit*) to strike right *ou* (slap-)bang* in (the middle of) the bull's-eye; (*fig*) to hit the nail on the head.

(d) (*au maximum*) **à ~** at full capacity; **entreprise qui tourne à ~** business that is working at full capacity; **les légumes donnent à ~** it is the height of the vegetable season; **utiliser à ~ son potentiel/une machine/ses connaissances** to use one's potential/a machine/one's knowledge to the full, make full use of one's potential/a machine/one's knowledge; **cet argument a porté à ~** this argument struck home *ou* made its point.

3 *nm* **(a) faire le ~** (*d'essence*) (*Aut*) to fill up; **(faites) le ~, s'il vous plaît** fill it *ou* her* up please; **faire le ~ d'eau/d'huile** to top up the water/oil; (*fig*) **théâtre qui fait le ~ (de monde) tous les soirs** theatre which has a full house every night.

(b) (*plénitude*) [*animation, fête*] height. **donner son ~** to do one's utmost, give one's all, give of one's best; *V* **battre**.

(c) (*Archit*) solid; (*Calligraphie*) downstroke.

4: plein air open air; (*Scol*) **les enfants ont plein air le mercredi** the children have games *ou* sport on Wednesdays; **jeux de plein air** outdoor games; **en plein air** *spectacle, cirque* open-air (*épith*); *s'asseoir* (out) in the open (air); **plein-emploi** *nm* full employment; **pleine mer** (*le large*) open sea; (*la marée haute*) high tide; **en pleine mer** out at sea, on the open sea.

pleinement [plɛnmɑ̃] *adv vivre, jouir* to the full; *approuver* wholeheartedly, fully. **utiliser qch ~** to make full use of sth, use sth to the full *ou* fully; **~ responsable/satisfait de** wholly *ou* entirely *ou* fully responsible for/satisfied with.

pléistocène [pleistɔsɛn] *adj, nm* Pleistocene.

plénier, -ière [plenje, jɛʀ] *adj* plenary.

plénipotentiaire [plenipɔtɑ̃sjɛʀ] *adj, nm* plenipotentiary. **ministre ~** minister plenipotentiary.

plénitude [plenityd] *nf* [*forme*] plenitude (*frm, littér*), fullness; [*son*] fullness, richness; [*droit*] completeness. **réaliser ses désirs dans leur ~** to realize one's desires in their entirety; **vivre la vie avec ~** to live one's life to the full; **dans la ~ de sa jeunesse/de sa beauté** in the fullness of his youth/beauty (*littér*).

pléonasme [pleɔnasm(ə)] *nm* pleonasm.

pléonastique [pleɔnastik] *adj* pleonastic.

pléthore [pletɔʀ] *nf* overabundance, plethora.

pléthorique [pletɔʀik] *adj nombre* excessive; *effectifs, documentation* overabundant; *classe* overcrowded.

pleur [plœʀ] *nm* **(a)** (*littér*) (*larme*) tear; (*sanglot*) sob. (*hum*) **verser un ~** to shed a tear.

(b) (*loc*) **en ~s** in tears; **il y aura des ~s et des grincements de dents quand ...** there'll be much wailing and gnashing of teeth when ... .

pleural, e, *mpl* -aux [plœʀal, o] *adj* pleural.

pleurard, e [plœʀaʀ, aʀd(ə)] (*péj*) **1** *adj enfant* whining (*épith*), who never stops crying; *ton* whimpering (*épith*), whining (*épith*), grizzling* (*épith*). **2** *nm,f* crybaby*, whiner, grizzler*.

pleurer [plœʀe] (1) *vi* **(a)** (*larmoyer*) [*personne*] to cry, weep; [*yeux*] to water, run. **~ bruyamment** to cry noisily, howl*, bawl*; **~ de rire** to shed tears of laughter, laugh until one cries; **~ de rage** to weep *ou* cry with rage, shed tears of rage; **~ de joie** to cry for joy, shed tears of joy; **~ d'avoir fait qch** to cry *ou* weep at *ou* over having done sth; **j'ai perdu mon sac, j'en aurais pleuré** I lost my bag — I could have cried *ou* wept; **il vaut mieux en rire que d'en ~** it's better to laugh (about it) than cry about *ou* over it; **faire ~ qn** to make sb cry, bring tears to sb's eyes; **les oignons me font ~** onions make my eyes water *ou* make me cry *ou* bring tears to my eyes; **~ comme un veau** (*péj*) *ou* **une madeleine** *ou* **à chaudes larmes** to cry one's eyes *ou* one's heart out; **être sur le point de ~** to be almost in tears, be on the point *ou* verge of tears; **aller ~ dans le gilet de qn*** to run crying to sb, go and cry *ou* weep on sb's shoulder; **triste à (faire) ~** dreadfully *ou* terribly sad; **bête à (faire) ~** pitifully stupid; **c'est bête à (faire) ~** it's enough to make you weep.

(b) ~ sur to lament (over); **~ sur son propre sort** to bemoan one's lot.

(c) (*péj: réclamer*) **elle est tout le temps à ~** she's always shouting for something; **~ après qch** to shout for sth; **il a été ~ à la direction pour obtenir une augmentation** he has been to the management shouting for a rise.

(d) (*littér*) [*sirène, violon*] to wail.

2 *vt* **(a)** *personne* to mourn (for); *chose* to bemoan; *faute* to bewail, bemoan, lament. **mourir sans être pleuré** to die unwept *ou* unmourned; **~ des larmes de joie** to weep tears of joy, weep for joy, shed tears of joy; **~ des larmes de sang** to shed tears of blood; **~ tout son soûl** to have a good cry; **~ toutes les larmes de son corps** to cry one's eyes out; **~ misère** to bewail *ou* bemoan one's destitution *ou* impoverished state; **~ sa jeunesse** to mourn *ou* lament the loss of one's youth, mourn for one's lost youth.

(b) (*péj*) (*quémander*) *augmentation, objet* to shout for; (*lésiner sur*) *nourriture, fournitures* to begrudge, stint. **il ne pleure pas sa peine*** he spares no effort, he doesn't stint his efforts; **il ne pleure pas son argent*** he doesn't stint his money.

pleurésie [plœʀezi] *nf* pleurisy.

pleurétique [plœʀetik] *adj* pleuritic.

pleureur, -euse [plœʀœʀ, øz] **1** *adj enfant* whining (*épith*), always crying (*attrib*); *ton* tearful, whimpering (*épith*). **c'est un ~/une ~euse** (*pleurard*) he/she is always crying; (*péj: quémandeur*) he/she is always shouting for something; *V* **saule**.

2 pleureuse *nf* (hired) mourner.

pleurnichard, e [plœʀniʃaʀ, aʀd(ə)] = **pleurnicheur.**

pleurnichement [plœʀniʃmɑ̃] *nm* = **pleurnicherie.**

pleurnicher [plœʀniʃe] (1) *vi* to snivel*, grizzle*, whine.

pleurnicherie [plœʀniʃʀi] *nf* snivelling* (*U*), grizzling* (*U*), whining (*U*).

pleurnicheur, -euse [plœʀniʃœʀ, øz] **1** *adj enfant* snivelling* (*épith*), grizzling* (*épith*), whining (*épith*); *ton* whining (*épith*), grizzling* (*épith*). **2** *nm,f* crybaby*, grizzler*, whiner.

pleuropneumonie [plœʀɔpnømɔni] *nf* pleuropneumonia.

pleutre [pløtʀ(ə)] (*littér*) **1** *adj* cowardly. **2** *nm* coward.

pleutrerie [pløtʀəʀi] *nf* (*littér*) (*caractère*) cowardice; (*acte*) act of cowardice.

pleuvasser [pløvase] (1) *vi*, **pleuviner** [pløvine] (1) *vi* (*crachiner*) to drizzle, spit (with rain); (*par averses*) to be showery.

pleuvoir [pløvwaʀ] (23) **1** *vb impers* to rain. **il pleut** it's raining; **les jours où il pleut** on rainy days; **on dirait qu'il va ~** it looks like rain; **il pleut à grosses gouttes** heavy drops of rain are falling; **il pleut à flots** *ou* **à torrents** *ou* **à seaux** *ou* **à verse, il pleut des cordes** *ou* **des hallebardes** it's pouring (down) *ou* it's teeming down (with rain), it's raining cats and dogs*; **qu'il pleuve** *ou* **qu'il vente** rain or shine, come wind or foul weather; **il ramasse de l'argent comme s'il en pleuvait*** he's raking it in*, he's raking in the money*.

2 *vi [coups, projectiles]* to rain down; *[critiques, invitations]* to shower down. **faire ~ des coups sur qn** to rain blows (up)on sb; **faire ~ des injures sur qn** to shower insults (up)on sb, subject sb to a torrent of abuse; **les invitations pleuvaient sur lui** he was showered with invitations, invitations were showered (up)on him.

pleuvoter [pløvɔte] (1) *vi* = **pleuvasser.**

plèvre [plɛvʀ(ə)] *nf* pleura.

plexiglas [plɛksiglɑs] *nm* ® plexiglass ®.

plexus [plɛksys] *nm* plexus. **~ solaire** solar plexus.

pli [pli] **1** *nm* **(a)** *[tissu, rideau, ourlet, accordéon]* fold; (*Couture*) pleat. **(faux) ~** crease; **jupe/robe à ~s** pleated skirt/dress; **son manteau est plein de ~s** his coat is all creased; **ton manteau fait un ~ dans le dos** your coat has a crease at the back, your coat creases (up) at the back; **son corsage est trop étroit, il fait des ~s** her blouse is too tight — it's all puckered (up); **les ~s et les replis de sa cape** the many folds of her cloak; (*fig*) **il va refuser, cela ne fait pas un ~*** he'll refuse, no doubt about it*.

(b) (*jointure*) *[genou, bras]* bend; (*bourrelet*) *[menton, ventre]* (skin-)fold; (*ligne*) *[bouche, yeux]* crease; (*ride*) *[front]* crease, furrow, line. **sa peau faisait des ~s au coin des yeux/sur son ventre** his skin was creased round his eyes/made folds on his stomach; **le ~ de l'aîne** the (fold of the) groin; **les ~s et les replis de son menton** the many folds under his chin, his quadruple chin (*hum*).

(c) (*forme*) *[vêtement]* shape. **suspends ton manteau pour qu'il garde un beau ~** hang up your coat so that it will keep its shape; **garder un bon ~** to keep its shape; **prendre un mauvais ~** *[vêtement]* to go out of shape, lose its shape; *[cheveux]* to get messed up, go funny*; *V* **mise**[2].

(d) (*fig: habitude*) habit. **prendre le ~ de faire** to get into the habit of doing; **il a pris un mauvais ~** he has got into a bad habit; **c'est un ~ à prendre!** you get used to it!

(e) (*enveloppe*) envelope; (*Admin: lettre*) letter. **sous ce ~** enclosed, herewith; **sous ~ cacheté** in a sealed envelope.

(f) (*Cartes*) trick. **faire un ~** to win a trick, take a trick.

(g) (*Géol*) fold.

2: (*Couture*) **pli d'aisance** inverted pleat; (*Couture*) **pli creux** box pleat; **pli de pantalon** trouser crease; (*Couture*) **pli plat** flat pleat; **pli de terrain** undulation.

pliable [plijabl(ə)] *adj* pliable, flexible.

pliage [plijaʒ] *nm* folding.

pliant, e [plijɑ̃, ɑ̃t] **1** *adj lit, table, vélo* collapsible, folding (*épith*); *mètre* folding (*épith*); *canot* collapsible. **2** *nm* folding *ou* collapsible (canvas) stool, campstool.

plie [pli] *nf* plaice.

plier [plije] (7) **1** *vt* **(a)** *papier, tissu* (*gén*) to fold; (*ranger*) to fold up. **~ le coin d'une page** to fold over *ou* fold down *ou* turn down the corner of a page.

(b) (*rabattre*) *lit, table, tente* to fold up; *éventail* to fold; *livre, cahier* to close (up); *volets* to fold back. (*fig*) **~ bagage** to pack up (and go); **on leur fit rapidement ~ bagage** we quickly sent them packing *ou* made them clear out*.

(c) (*ployer*) *branche* to bend; *genou, bras* to bend, flex. (*fig*) **~ le genou devant qn** to bow before sb, bend the knee before sb; **être plié par l'âge** to be bent (double) with age; **être plié (en deux) de rire/par la douleur** to be doubled up with laughter/pain.

(d) ~ qn à une discipline to force a discipline upon sb; **~ qn à sa volonté** to bend sb to one's will; **~ qn à sa loi** to lay down the law to sb; **~ ses désirs à la situation** to adjust *ou* adapt one's desires to suit the situation.

2 *vi* **(a)** *[arbre, branche]* to bend (over); *[plancher, paroi]* to sag, bend over. **faire ~ le plancher sous son poids** to make the floor sag beneath one's weight; **~ sous le poids des soucis/des ans** to be weighed down by worry/years.

(b) (*céder*) *[personne]* to yield, give in; *[armée]* to give way, lose ground; *[résistance]* to give way. **~ devant l'autorité** to give in *ou* yield to authority; **faire ~ qn** to make sb give in *ou* knuckle under.

3 se plier *vpr* **(a)** *[lit, chaise]* to fold (up).

(b) se **~ à** *règle* to submit to, abide by; *discipline* to submit o.s. to; *circonstances* to bow to, submit to, yield to; *désirs, caprices de qn* to give in to, submit to.

Pline [plin] *nm* Pliny.

plinthe [plɛ̃t] *nf* skirting (board); (*Archit*) plinth.

pliocène [plijɔsɛn] *adj, nm* Pliocene.

plissage [plisaʒ] *nm* pleating.

plissé, e [plise] (*ptp de* **plisser**) **1** *adj jupe* pleated; *terrain* folded; *peau* creased, wrinkled. **2** *nm* pleats (*pl*). **~ soleil** sunray pleats.

plissement [plismɑ̃] *nm* (*V* **plisser**) puckering (up); screwing up; creasing; folding. (*Géol*) **~ de terrain** fold; **le ~ alpin** the folding of the Alps.

plisser [plise] (1) **1** *vt* **(a)** (*froncer*) *jupe* to pleat, put pleats in; *papier* to fold (over).

(b) (*rider*) *lèvres* to pucker (up); *yeux* to screw up; *front* to crease. **un sourire plissa son visage** his face creased (up) into a smile; **il plissa le front** he knit *ou* creased his brow; **une ride lui plissa le front** a wrinkle furrowed his brow.

(c) (*chiffonner*) to crease.

(d) (*Géol*) to fold.

2 *vi* to become creased.

3 se plisser *vpr [front]* to crease (up), furrow; *[lèvres]* to pucker (up).

plissure [plisyʀ] *nf* pleats (*pl*).

pliure [plijyʀ] *nf* fold; *[bras, genou]* bend; (*Typ*) folding.

ploc [plɔk] *excl* plop! **~ ~** plip plop, plop plop.

ploiement [plwamɑ̃] *nm* bending.

plomb [plɔ̃] *nm* **(a)** (*métal*) lead. **de ~** *tuyau* lead; *soldat* tin; *ciel* leaden; *soleil* blazing; *sommeil* deep, heavy; **j'ai des jambes de ~** my legs are *ou* feel like lead; **il n'a pas de ~ dans la tête** he's featherbrained; **cela lui mettra du ~ dans la tête** that will knock some sense into him; **avoir du ~ dans** *ou* **sur l'estomac** to have something lying heavy on one's stomach, have a lump in one's stomach.

(b) (*Chasse*) (lead) shot (*U*). **j'ai trouvé 2 ~s dans le lièvre en le mangeant** I found 2 pieces of (lead) shot in the hare when I was eating it; **du gros ~** buckshot; **du petit ~** small shot; (*fig*) **avoir du ~ dans l'aile** to be in a bad way.

(c) (*Pêche*) sinker; (*Typ*) type; *[vitrail]* lead; (*sceau*) (lead) seal; (*Élec: fusible*) fuse; (*Couture*) lead weight. (*Naut*) **~ (de sonde)** sounding lead.

(d) (*loc*) **mettre un mur à ~** to plumb a wall; **le soleil tombe à ~** the sun is blazing straight down.

plombage [plɔ̃baʒ] *nm* **(a)** (*U: V* **plomber**) weighting (with lead); filling, stopping; sealing (with lead).

(b) (*sur une dent*) filling.

plombé, e [plɔ̃be] (*ptp de* **plomber**) **1** *adj teint, couleur* leaden. **canne ~e** *ou* **à bout ~** stick with a lead(en) tip. **2 plombée** *nf* (*arme*) bludgeon; (*Pêche*) sinkers (*pl*), weights (*pl*).

plomber [plɔ̃be] (1) **1** *vt canne, ligne* to weight (with lead); *dent* to fill, stop, put a filling in; *colis* to seal (with lead), put a lead seal on; *mur* to plumb; (*Agr*) to roll; (*colorer*) to turn leaden. (*Pêche*) **ligne pas assez plombée** insufficiently weighted line, line that hasn't enough weights on it.

2 se plomber *vpr* to turn leaden.

plomberie [plɔ̃bʀi] *nf* (*métier, installations*) plumbing; (*atelier*) plumber's (work)shop; (*industrie*) lead industry.

plombier [plɔ̃bje] *nm* plumber. **c'est le ~!** plumber!

plombières [plɔ̃bjɛʀ] *nf inv* tutti-frutti (ice cream).

plonge [plɔ̃ʒ] *nf* washing-up (*in restaurant*). **faire la ~** to be a washer-up (*Brit*) *ou* dish-washer.

plongé, e[1] [plɔ̃ʒe] (*ptp de* **plonger**) *adj*: **~ dans** *obscurité, désespoir, misère* plunged in; *vice* steeped in; *méditation, pensées* immersed in, deep in; **~ dans la lecture d'un livre** engrossed in reading a book, buried *ou* immersed in a book; **~ dans le sommeil** sound asleep, in a deep sleep.

plongeant, e [plɔ̃ʒɑ̃, ɑ̃t] *adj décolleté, tir* plunging. **vue ~e** view from above.

plongée[2] [plɔ̃ʒe] *nf* **(a)** (*action*) *[nageur]* diving; *[sous-marin]* submersion. **effectuer plusieurs ~s** to make several dives; to carry out several submersions; **sous-marin en ~** submerged submarine; **~ sous-marine** (*gén*) diving; (*sans scaphandre*) skin diving. **(b)** (*Ciné: prise de vue*) high angle shot.

plongeoir [plɔ̃ʒwaʀ] *nm* diving board.

plongeon [plɔ̃ʒɔ̃] *nm* (*Ftbl, Natation*) dive. **faire un ~** *[nageur]* to dive; *[gardien de but]* to make a dive, dive; (*fig*) **faire le ~** to make heavy losses.

plonger [plɔ̃ʒe] (3) **1** *vi* **(a)** (*gén*) *[personne, sous-marin, avion]* to dive (*dans* into, *sur* on, onto). **avion qui plonge sur son objectif** plane that dives (down) onto its target; **oiseau qui plonge sur sa proie** bird that dives *ou* plunges onto its prey; **il plongea dans sa poche pour prendre son mouchoir** he plunged his hand *ou* he dived into his pocket to get his handkerchief out.

(b) (*fig*) *[route, terrain]* to plunge (down), dip (sharply *ou* steeply); *[racines]* to go down. **l'origine de cette coutume plonge dans la nuit des temps** the origin of this custom is buried in the mists of time; **~ dans le sommeil** to fall (straight) into a deep sleep; **mon regard plongeait sur la vallée** I cast my eyes down upon the valley.

2 *vt*: **~ qch dans** *sac* to plunge *ou* thrust sth into; *eau* to plunge sth into; **~ qn dans** *obscurité, misère* to plunge sb into; *désespoir* to throw *ou* plunge sb into; *sommeil, méditation, vice* to plunge sb into; **~ qn dans la surprise** to surprise sb greatly; **vous me plongez dans l'embarras** you have thrown me into a difficult position; **il lui plongea un poignard dans le cœur** he plunged *ou* thrust a dagger into his heart; **plante qui plonge ses racines dans le sol** plant that plunges its roots into the ground; **~ son regard sur/vers** to cast one's eyes at/towards.

3 se plonger *vpr*: se **~ dans** *études, lecture* to bury *ou* immerse o.s. in, throw o.s. into, plunge into; *eau, bain* to plunge into, immerse o.s. in; se **~ dans le vice** to throw *ou* hurl o.s. into a life of vice.

plongeur, -euse [plɔ̃ʒœʀ, øz] 1 *adj* diving. 2 *nm,f* (a) (*Sport*) diver. ~ **sous-marin** (*gén*) diver; (*sans scaphandre*) skin diver; *V* **cloche.** (b) *[restaurant]* washer-up (*Brit*), dishwasher. 3 *nm* (*Orn*) diver.
plosive [ploziv] *nf* plosive.
plot [plo] *nm* (*Élec*) contact; (*butée*) pin.
plouc* [pluk] *nm* (*péj: rustre*) country bumpkin.
plouf [pluf] *excl* splash! **il est tombé dans l'eau avec un gros ~** he slipped and fell into the water with a splash; **la pierre a fait ~ en tombant dans l'eau** the stone made a splash as it fell into the water.
ploutocrate [plutɔkʀat] *nm* plutocrat.
ploutocratie [plutɔkʀasi] *nf* plutocracy.
ploutocratique [plutɔkʀatik] *adj* plutocratic.
ployer [plwaje] (8) (*littér*) 1 *vi [branche, dos]* to bend; *[poutre, plancher]* to sag; *[genoux, jambes]* to give way, bend; *[armée]* to yield, give in; *[résistance]* to give way. **faire ~ le plancher sous son poids** to make the floor sag beneath one's weight; **~ sous l'impôt** to be weighed down by taxes; (*fig*) **~ sous le joug** to bend beneath the yoke.
2 *vt* to bend. **~ un pays sous son autorité** to make a country bow down *ou* submit to one's authority.
plucher [plyʃe] (1) *vi* = **pelucher.**
pluches [plyʃ] *nfpl* (*arg Mil*) spud-bashing (*arg*). **être de (corvée de) ~** to be spud-bashing.
plucheux, -euse [plyʃø, øz] *adj* = **pelucheux.**
pluie [plɥi] *nf* (a) rain; (*averse*) shower (of rain). **les ~s** the rains; **la saison des ~s** the rainy season; **le temps est à la ~** we're in for rain, it looks like rain; **jour/temps de ~** wet *ou* rainy day/weather; **~ battante** driving *ou* lashing rain; **~ diluvienne** pouring rain (*U*), downpour; **~ fine** drizzle; **une ~ fine tombait** it was drizzling.
(b) (*fig*) *[cadeaux, cendres]* shower; *[balles, pierres, coups]* hail, shower. **en ~** in a shower; **tomber en ~** to shower down; (*Culin*) **jeter le riz en ~** to sprinkle in *ou* on the rice.
(c) (*loc*) (*Prov*) **après la ~ le beau temps** every cloud has a silver lining (*Prov*); (*fig*) **faire la ~ et le beau temps** to carry a lot of weight, be very influential; **il n'est pas né *ou* tombé de la dernière ~** he wasn't born yesterday; *V* **ennuyeux, parler.**
plum(-pudding) [plum(pudiŋ)] *nm* (rich) fruit cake.
plumage [plymaʒ] *nm* plumage (*U*), feathers (*pl*).
plumard‡ [plymaʀ] *nm* bed. **aller au ~** to turn in*, hit the hay* *ou* the sack*.
plume [plym] 1 *nf* (a) *[oiseau]* feather. **chapeau à ~s** feathered hat, hat with feathers; **oreiller/lit de ~s** feather pillow/bed; **ne pas peser plus lourd qu'une ~** to be as light as a feather; **soulever qch comme une ~** to lift sth up as if it were a featherweight; **il y a laissé des ~s*** he came off badly, he got his fingers burnt; **il perd ses ~s*** his hair is falling out, he's going bald; *V* **gibier, poids.**
(b) (*pour écrire*) (*d'oiseau*) quill (pen); (*en acier*) (pen) nib. **~ d'oie** goose quill; **dessin à la ~** pen and ink drawing; **écrire au courant de la ~** to write just as the ideas come to one *ou* come into one's head; **il a la ~ facile** writing comes easy to him; **vivre de sa ~** to live by one's pen; **prendre la ~** to take up one's pen; (*dans une lettre*) **je lui passe la ~** I'll hand over to him, I'll let him carry on; (*fig*) **tremper sa ~ dans le poison** to steep one's pen in venom; *V* **homme.**
2 *nm* = **plumard.**
3: plume à vaccin vaccine point.
plumeau, *pl* **~x** [plymo] *nm* feather duster.
plumer [plyme] (1) *vt volaille* to pluck; (‡*fig*) *personne* to fleece*.
plumet [plymɛ] *nm* plume.
plumetis [plymti] *nm* (*tissu*) Swiss muslin; (*broderie*) raised satin stitch.
plumeux, -euse [plymø, øz] *adj* feathery.
plumier [plymje] *nm* pencil box.
plumitif [plymitif] *nm* (*péj*) (*employé*) penpusher (*péj*); (*écrivain*) scribbler (*péj*).
plupart [plypaʀ] *nf*: **la ~: la ~ des gens** most people, the majority of people; **la ~ des gens qui se trouvaient là** most of the people there; **la ~ (d'entre eux) pensent que ...** most (of them) *ou* the majority (of them) think that ...; **dans la ~ des cas** in most cases, in the majority of cases; **pour la ~** mostly, for the most part; **ces gens qui, pour la ~, avaient tout perdu** these people who, for the most part, had lost everything, these people, most of whom had *ou* who had mostly lost everything; **la ~ du temps** most of the time; **la ~ de mon temps** most of my time, the greater part of my time.
plural, e, *mpl* **-aux** [plyʀal, o] *adj vote* plural.
pluralisme [plyʀalism(ə)] *nm* pluralism.
pluraliste [plyʀalist(ə)] 1 *adj* pluralistic. 2 *nmf* pluralist.
pluralité [plyʀalite] *nf* multiplicity, plurality.
pluridisciplinaire [plyʀidisiplinɛʀ] *adj* (*Scol*) interdisciplinary, pluridisciplinary.
pluridisciplinarité [plyʀidisiplinaʀite] *nf* interdisciplinarity, pluridisciplinarity.
pluriel, -elle [plyʀjɛl] 1 *adj* plural.
2 *nm* plural. **au ~** in the plural; **la première personne du ~** the first person plural; **le ~ de majesté** the royal plural, the royal 'we'; **le ~ de 'cheval' est 'chevaux'** the plural of 'cheval' is 'chevaux'.
plurifonctionnalité [plyʀifɔ̃ksjɔnalite] *nf* commercial flexibility.
plus 1 *adv nég* [ply] (a) (*temps*) **ne ... ~** not any longer *ou* any more, no longer; **il ne la voit ~** he no longer sees her, he doesn't see her any more; **je ne reviendrai ~/~ jamais** I shan't/I'll never come back again *ou* any more; **il n'a ~ besoin de son parapluie** he doesn't need his umbrella any longer *ou* any more; **il n'a ~ à s'inquiéter/travailler maintenant** he does not need to worry/work any more now; **il n'a ~ dit un mot** he didn't say another word (after that); **il n'est ~ là** he's gone (away); (*euph*) **son père n'est ~** his father has passed away (*euph*); **elle n'est ~ très jeune** she's not as young as she was, she's getting on in years; **~ de doute** no doubt now, no longer any doubt about it; **~ besoin de rester*** no need to stay now; (*hum*) **il n'y a ~ d'enfants/de jeunesse!** children/young people aren't what they used to be.
(b) (*quantité*) **ne ... ~** no more, not any more; **elle n'a ~ de pain/d'argent** she's got no more *ou* she hasn't got any more bread/money, she's got no (more) bread/money left; **elle ne veut ~ de pain** she doesn't want any more bread; **des fruits? il n'y en a ~** fruit? there is none left *ou* there isn't any more left; **~ de vin, merci** no more wine, thank you; **(il n'y a) ~ personne à la maison** there's no one left in the house, they've all left the house, they've all gone (away); **il n'y a ~ rien** there's nothing left; **il n'y a ~ rien d'autre à faire** there's nothing else to do; **il n'y a ~ guère *ou* beaucoup de pain** there's hardly any bread left; **on n'y voit presque ~ rien** you can hardly see anything now; *V* **non.**
(c) (*avec que: seulement*) **il n'y a ~ que des miettes** there are only crumbs left, there's nothing left but crumbs; **cela ne tient ~ qu'à elle** it's up to her now; **il n'y a (guère) ~ que huit jours avant les vacances** there's only (about) a week to go before the holidays; **~ que 5 km à faire** only another 5 km to go.
2 *adv emploi comparatif:* [ply] *devant consonne,* [plyz] *devant voyelle,* [plys] *à la finale* (a) (*avec adj*) **il est ~ intelligent (que vous/moi)** he is more intelligent (than you (are)/than me *ou* than I am *ou* than I (*frm*)); **elle n'est pas ~ grande (que sa sœur)** she isn't any taller *ou* she is no taller (than her sister); **il est ~ bête que méchant** he's stupid rather than malicious; **il est ~ vieux qu'elle de 10 ans** he's 10 years older than her *ou* than she is *ou* than she (*frm*); **il est deux fois ~ âgé qu'elle** he's twice as old as her, he's twice her age; **deux ou trois fois ~ cher que ...** two or three times more expensive than ... *ou* as expensive as ...; **il est ~ qu'intelligent** he's clever to say the least, he isn't just intelligent; **un résultat ~ qu'honorable** an honourable result to say the least.
(b) (*avec adv*) **il court ~ vite (qu'elle)** he runs faster (than her); **beaucoup ~ facilement** much more *ou* a lot more easily; **ne venez pas ~ tard que 6 heures** don't come any later than 6 o'clock; **deux fois ~ souvent que ...** twice as often as ...; **j'en ai ~ qu'assez!** I've had more than enough!
(c) [ply(s)] (*avec vb*) **vous travaillez ~ (que nous)** you work more *ou* harder (than us); **il ne gagne pas ~ (que vous)** he doesn't earn any more (than you); **j'aime la poésie ~ que tout au monde** I like poetry more than anything (else) in the world; **j'aime dix fois ~ le théâtre que le cinéma** I like the theatre ten times better than the cinema.
(d) [ply(s)] (*davantage de*) **~ de: (un peu) ~ de pain** (a little *ou* a bit) more bread; **j'ai ~ de pain que vous** I've got more bread than you (have); **il y aura (beaucoup) ~ de monde demain** there will be (a lot *ou* many) more people tomorrow; **il n'y aura pas ~ de monde demain** there won't be any more people tomorrow.
(e) [ply] (*au-delà de*) **~ de: il y aura ~ de 100 personnes** there will be more than *ou* over 100 people; **à ~ de 100 mètres d'ici** more than *ou* over 100 metres from here; **les enfants de ~ de 4 ans** children over 4; **il n'y avait pas ~ de 10 personnes** there were no more than 10 people; **il est ~ de 9 heures** it's after *ou* past 9 o'clock; **100.000 F et ~** [ply(s)] 100,000 francs and more *ou* and over; **~ d'un** more than one.
(f) [ply], *devant voyelle* [plyz] **~ ... ~: ~ on est de fous, ~ on rit *ou* s'amuse** the more the merrier; **~ il en a, ~ il en veut** the more he has, the more he wants; **~ on boit, ~ on a soif** the more you drink, the thirstier you get; **~ il gagne, moins il est content** the more he earns, the less happy he is.
(g) [ply(s)] **de ~, en ~: elle a 10 ans de ~ (que lui)** she's 10 years older (than him); **il y a 10 personnes de ~ qu'hier** there are 10 more people than yesterday; **une fois de ~** once more; **les frais de poste en ~** postal charges extra *ou* on top of that *ou* not included; **on nous a donné deux verres de ~ *ou* en ~** we were given two more *ou* extra glasses; (*de trop*) we were given two glasses too many; **en ~ de son travail, il prend des cours du soir** on top of *ou* besides his work, he's taking evening classes; **en ~ de cela** on top of (all) that, in addition to that, into the bargain.
(h) (*loc*) **de ~ en ~** more and more; **il fait de ~ en ~ beau chaque jour** the weather gets better and better every day; **aller de ~ en ~ vite** to go faster and faster; **~ ou moins** more or less; **il a réussi ~ ou moins bien** he didn't manage too badly, he just about managed; **~ que jamais** more than ever; **qui ~ est** what is more, moreover, into the bargain; (*Prov*) **~ fait douceur que violence** kindness succeeds where force will fail; *V* **autant, raison, tant.**
3 (*prononciation V 2*) *adv emploi superlatif* (a) (*avec adj*) **le ~ beau de tous mes livres** the most beautiful of all my books; **l'enfant le ~ intelligent que je connaisse/de la classe** the cleverest child I've (ever) met/in the class; **il était dans une situation des ~ embarrassantes** he was in a most embarrassing situation *ou* the most embarrassing of situations; **la ~ grande partie de son temps** most of his time, the best part of his time; **c'est ce que j'ai de ~ précieux** it's the most precious thing I possess; **la ~ belle fille du monde ne peut donner que ce qu'elle a** one can only give as much as one has got.
(b) (*avec adv*) **c'est le livre que je lis le ~ souvent** it's the book I read most often; **il a couru le ~ vite** he ran the fastest; **il a couru le ~ vite possible** he ran as fast as possible *ou* as fast as

he could; **prends-en le ~ possible** [ply(s)] take as much (*ou* as many) as possible *ou* as you can.

(c) [ply(s)] (*avec vb*) **c'est le livre que j'aime le ~** it's the book I most like *ou* I like (the) most *ou* (the) best; **ce qui nous frappe le ~** what strikes us most.

(d) [ply(s)] **le ~ de: c'est nous qui avons cueilli le ~ de fleurs** we've picked the most flowers; **c'est le samedi qu'il y a le ~ de monde** it's on Saturdays that there are (the) most people; **prends le ~ possible de livres/de beurre** take as many books/as much butter as possible.

(e) [ply(s)] **au ~** at the most, at the outside; **tout au ~** at the very most.

4 *conj* [plys] **(a)** (*addition*) plus, and. **deux ~ deux font quatre** two and two are four, two plus two make four; **tous les voisins, ~ leurs enfants** all the neighbours, plus their children *ou* and their children (as well); **il paie sa chambre, ~ le gaz et l'électricité** he pays for his room, plus gas and electricity.

(b) (*avec un chiffre*) plus. **il fait ~ deux aujourd'hui** it's plus two (degrees) today, it's two above freezing today; (*Math*) **~ cinq** plus five.

5 *nm* [plys] (*Math*) **(signe) ~** plus (sign).

6: plus-que-parfait [plyskəparfɛ] *nm* (*Gram*) pluperfect (tense), past perfect; **plus-value** [plyvaly] *nf, pl* **plus-values** *[investissement, terrain]* appreciation (*U*), increase in value; (*excédent*) *[budget]* surplus; (*bénéfice*) profit, surplus; (*V* **impôt**).

plusieurs [plyzjœr] **1** *adj indéf pl* several. **on ne peut pas être en ~ endroits à la fois** you can't be in more than one place at once; **ils sont ~** there are several (of them), there are a number of them; **un ou ~** one or more. **2** *pron indéf pl* several (people). **~ (d'entre eux)** several (of them); **se mettre à ~: ils se sont mis à ~ pour ...** several people banded *ou* got together to ...; **nous nous sommes mis à ~ pour ...** several of us got together to ... .

Plutarque [plytark] *nm* Plutarch.

Pluton [plytɔ̃] *nm* (*Astron, Myth*) Pluto.

plutonium [plytɔnjɔm] *nm* plutonium.

plutôt [plyto] *adv* **(a)** (*de préférence*) rather; (*à la place*) instead. **ne lis pas ce livre, prends ~ celui-ci** don't read that book but rather take this one *ou* take this one instead; **prends ce livre ~ que celui-là** take this book rather than *ou* instead of that one; **cette maladie affecte ~ les enfants** this illness affects children for the most part; **je préfère ~ celui-ci** (*je voudrais de préférence*) I'd rather *ou* sooner have this one; (*j'aime mieux*) I prefer this one, I like this one better; **~ souffrir que mourir** it is better to suffer (rather) than to die; **~ que de me regarder, viens m'aider** rather than *ou* instead of (just) watching me, come and help; **n'importe quoi ~ que cela!** anything but that!, anything rather than that!

(b) (*plus exactement*) rather. **il n'est pas paresseux mais ~ apathique** he's apathetic rather than *ou* more than lazy, he's not so much lazy as apathetic; **il est ignorant ~ que sot** he's ignorant rather *ou* more than stupid, he's more ignorant than stupid, he's not so much stupid as ignorant; **ou ~, c'est ce qu'il pense** or rather that's what he thinks; **c'est un journaliste ~ qu'un romancier** he's more of a journalist than a novelist, he's a journalist more *ou* rather than a novelist; **il s'y habitue ~ qu'il n'oublie** he's getting used to it rather than *ou* more than forgetting about it.

(c) (*assez*) *chaud, bon* rather, quite. **il remange, c'est ~ bon signe** he's eating again — that's quite *ou* rather a good sign; **nos vacances sont ~ compromises avec cet événement** our holidays are rather *ou* somewhat jeopardized by this incident; **un homme brun, ~ petit** a dark man, rather *ou* somewhat on the short side *ou* rather short; **il est ~ pénible, celui-là!** he's a bit of a pain in the neck, that one!*; **il faisait beau? — non, il faisait ~ frais** was the weather good? — no, it was cool if anything; **qu'est-ce qu'il est pénible, celui-là — ah oui, ~!*** what a pain in the neck he is!* — you said it!* *ou* you're telling me!*

pluvial, e, *mpl* **-aux** [plyvjal, o] *adj régime, écoulement* pluvial. **eau ~e** rainwater.

pluvier [plyvje] *nm* plover.

pluvieux, -euse [plyvjø, øz] *adj* rainy, wet.

pluviner [plyvine] (1) *vi* = **pleuvasser.**

pluviomètre [plyvjɔmɛtr(ə)] *nm* pluviometer (*T*), rain gauge.

pluviométrie [plyvjɔmetri] *nf* pluviometry.

pluviométrique [plyvjɔmetrik] *adj* pluviometric(al).

pluviôse [plyvjoz] *nm* Pluviôse (*fifth month in the French Republican calendar*).

pluviosité [plyvjozite] *nf [temps, saison]* raininess, wetness; (*pluie tombée*) (average) rainfall.

pneu [pnø] *nm* (*abrév de* **pneumatique**) **(a)** *[véhicule]* tyre (*Brit*), tire (*US*). **(b)** (*message*) letter sent by pneumatic despatch *ou* tube. **par ~** by pneumatic dispatch *ou* tube.

pneumatique [pnømatik] **1** *adj* (*Sci*) pneumatic; (*gonflable*) inflatable; *V* **canot, marteau, matelas. 2** *nf* pneumatics (*sg*). **3** *nm* = **pneu.**

pneumocoque [pnømɔkɔk] *nm* pneumococcus.

pneumologie [pnømɔlɔʒi] *nf* pneumology.

pneumologue [pnømɔlɔg] *nmf* lung specialist.

pneumonie [pnømɔni] *nf* pneumonia (*U*).

pneumonique [pnømɔnik] **1** *adj* pneumonic. **2** *nmf* pneumonia patient.

pneumothorax [pnømɔtɔraks] *nm* pneumothorax; (*Chirurgie*) artificial pneumothorax.

Pô [po] *nm*: **le ~** the Po.

pochade [pɔʃad] *nf* (*dessin*) quick sketch (in colour); (*histoire*) humorous piece.

pochard, e: [pɔʃar, ard(ə)] *nm,f* drunk, soak*.

pochardise† [pɔʃardiz] *nf* drunkenness.

poche¹ [pɔʃ] *nf* **(a)** *[vêtement, cartable, portefeuille]* pocket. **~ revolver/intérieure** hip/inside pocket; **~ de pantalon** trouser pocket; **de ~** *sous-marin, couteau, mouchoir* pocket (*épith*); *collection, livre* paperback (*épith*); **format de ~** pocket-size; **j'avais 10 F/je n'avais pas un sou en ~** I had 10 francs/I hadn't a penny on me; **en être de sa ~*** to be out of pocket, lose out* (financially); **il a payé de sa ~** it came *ou* he paid for it out of his (own) pocket; (*fig*) **mettre qn dans sa ~** to (be able to) twist sb round one's little finger; **il a sa nomination en ~** his appointment is in the bag*; **c'est dans la ~!*** it's in the bag!*; **faire les ~s à qn*** to go through *ou* rifle sb's pockets; **connaître un endroit comme sa ~** to know a place like the back of one's hand *ou* inside out; *V* **argent, langue** *etc.*

(b) (*déformation*) **faire des ~s** *[veste]* to bag, go out of shape; *[pantalon]* to bag, go baggy; **avoir des ~s sous les yeux** to have bags *ou* pouches under one's eyes.

(c) (*Comm: sac*) (paper *ou* plastic) bag.

(d) *[kangourou]* pouch.

(e) (*cavité*) pocket. **~ d'air** air pocket; **~ d'eau** pocket of water; **~ de pus** pus sac; **~ de sang** haematoma.

poche² [pɔʃ] *nm* (*livre*) paperback.

pocher [pɔʃe] (1) *vt* (*Culin*) to poach. **~ un œil à qn** to give sb a black eye.

pochetée: [pɔʃte] *nf* oaf, twit* (*Brit*).

pochette [pɔʃɛt] *nf* (*mouchoir*) (breast) pocket handkerchief; (*petite poche*) breast pocket; *[timbres, photos]* wallet, envelope; *[serviette, aiguilles]* case. **~ surprise** lucky bag; **~ d'allumettes** book of matches.

pocheuse [pɔʃøz] *nf* (egg) poacher.

pochoir [pɔʃwar] *nm* (*cache*) stencil; (*tampon*) transfer.

podagre [pɔdagr(ə)] **1** *nf* (††) gout. **2** *adj* (†) suffering from gout.

podium [pɔdjɔm] *nm* podium.

podomètre [pɔdɔmɛtr(ə)] *nm* pedometer.

poêle¹ [pwal] *nf*: **~ (à frire)** frying pan; **passer à la ~** to fry.

poêle², poële [pwal] *nm* stove. **~ à mazout/à pétrole** oil/paraffin stove.

poêle³ [pwal] *nm [cercueil]* pall.

poêlée [pwale] *nf*: **une ~ de** a frying pan full of.

poêler [pwale] (1) *vt* to fry.

poêlon [pwalɔ̃] *nm* casserole.

poème [pɔɛm] *nm* poem. **~ en prose/symphonique** prose/symphonic poem; **c'est tout un ~*** (*c'est compliqué*) it's a real palaver*, what a carry-on*; (*c'est indescriptible*) it defies description.

poésie [pɔezi] *nf* (*U*) poetry; (*poème*) poem, piece of poetry. **faire de la ~** to write poetry.

poète [pɔɛt] **1** *nm* poet; (*fig: rêveur*) dreamer.

2 *adj tempérament* poetic. **être ~** to be a poet; **femme ~** poetess.

poétesse [pɔetɛs] *nf* poetess.

poétique [pɔetik] **1** *adj* poetic(al). **2** *nf* poetics (*sg*).

poétiquement [pɔetikmɑ̃] *adv* poetically.

poétisation [pɔetizasjɔ̃] *nf* (*action*) poetizing; (*résultat*) poetic depiction.

poétiser [pɔetize] (1) *vt* to poetize.

pogne: [pɔɲ] *nf* mitt:, paw:.

pognon: [pɔɲɔ̃] *nm* dough:, lolly: (*Brit*), bread:.

pogrom(e) [pɔgrɔm] *nm* pogrom.

poids [pwa] **1** *nm* **(a)** (*U*) weight. **prendre/perdre du ~** to gain/lose weight; **Georges a encore pris du ~** George has been putting on *ou* gaining weight again; **vendu au ~** sold by weight; **quel ~ pèse-t-il?** what weight is he?, what does he weigh?, what's his weight?; **quel ~ cela pèse!** what a weight this is!; **ces bijoux d'argent seront vendus au ~ du métal** this silver jewellery will be sold by the weight of the metal; **la branche pliait sous le ~ des fruits** the branch was weighed down with (the) fruit *ou* was bending beneath the weight of the fruit; **elle s'appuyait contre lui de tout son ~** she leaned against him with all her weight; **elle a ajouté une pomme pour faire le ~** she put in an extra apple to make up the weight; (*fig*) **il ne fait vraiment pas le ~** *[acteur, homme politique]* he really doesn't measure up; **il ne fait pas le ~ face à son adversaire** he's no match for his opponent; *V* **bon¹**.

(b) (*objet*) *[balance, horloge etc]* weight; (*Sport*) shot. (*Sport*) **lancer le ~** to put(t) the shot; *V* **deux.**

(c) (*fig: charge*) weight. **tout le ~ de l'entreprise repose sur lui** he carries the weight of the whole business on his shoulders; **plier sous le ~ des soucis/des impôts** to be weighed down by worries/taxes, be bent beneath the weight of one's worries/of taxes; **être courbé sous le ~ des ans** to be weighed down by (the weight of) years; (*hum*) **c'est le ~ des ans** old age never comes alone (*hum*); **enlever un ~ (de la conscience) à qn** to take a weight *ou* a load off sb's mind; **c'est un ~ sur sa conscience** it lies *ou* weighs heavy on his conscience; (*fig*) **avoir** *ou* **se sentir un ~ sur l'estomac** to have something lying heavy on one's stomach; **j'ai un ~ sur la poitrine** I feel *ou* I am tight-chested, my chest feels tight.

(d) (*force, influence*) weight. **argument de ~** weighty argument, argument of great weight; **homme de ~** man who carries weight (*fig*); **cela donne du ~ à son hypothèse** that gives *ou* lends weight to his hypothesis.

2: poids coq *nm* bantam-weight; (*Sport*) **poids et haltères** *nmpl* weight lifting; **faire des poids et haltères** (*spécialité*) to be a weight lifter; (*pour s'entraîner*) to do weight-training *ou*-lifting; **poids léger** *nm* lightweight; **poids lourd** *nm* (*Sport, *fig: personne grosse*) heavyweight; (*camion*) lorry (*Brit*), truck (*US*), heavy goods vehicle (*Brit Admin*); **poids et mesures** *nmpl* weights and measures; **poids mi-lourd** *nm* light heavyweight; **poids mi-moyen** *nm* welterweight; **poids moléculaire** molecular weight; (*Tech*) **poids mort** dead load;

(*fig péj*) **cet employé est un poids mort** this employee is being carried *ou* is not pulling his weight; **poids mouche** flyweight; **poids moyen** middleweight; **poids plume** (*Sport*, **fig: personne menue*) featherweight; **poids spécifique** specific gravity; **poids total en charge** gross weight; **poids utile** net weight; **poids welter** welterweight.

poignant, e [pwaɲɑ̃, ɑ̃t] *adj adieux, chagrin* poignant, heartrending, agonizing; *souvenir, récit* poignant, harrowing, agonizing; *regard* heartrending; *situation* deeply distressing, harrowing, agonizing.

poignard [pwaɲaʀ] *nm* dagger. **coup de ~** stab; **frappé d'un coup de ~ en plein cœur** stabbed in *ou* through the heart.

poignarder [pwaɲaʀde] (1) *vt* to stab, knife. (*lit, fig*) **~ qn dans le dos** to stab sb in the back; **la jalousie/la douleur le poignardait** he felt stabs of jealousy/pain, jealousy/pain cut through him like a knife.

poigne [pwaɲ] *nf* (*étreinte*) grip; (*main*) hand; (*fig: autorité*) firm-handedness. **avoir de la ~** (*lit*) to have a strong grip; (*fig*) to rule with a firm hand; **à ~** *homme, gouvernement* firm-handed.

poignée [pwaɲe] *nf* **(a)** (*lit: quantité*) handful, fistful; (*fig: petit nombre*) handful. **à** *ou* **par ~s** in handfuls; **ajoutez une ~ de sel** add a handful of salt.

(b) *[porte, tiroir, valise]* handle; *[épée]* handle, hilt.

(c) ~ de main handshake; **donner une ~ de main à qn** to shake hands with sb, shake sb's hand *ou* sb by the hand.

poignet [pwaɲɛ] *nm* (*Anat*) wrist; (*Habillement*) cuff; *V* **force.**

poil [pwal] **1** *nm* **(a)** (*Anat*) hair. **avoir du ~** *ou* **des ~s sur la poitrine** to have hairs on one's chest, have a hairy chest; **les ~s de sa barbe** (*entretenue*) the bristles *ou* hairs of his beard; (*mal rasée*) the stubble on his face; **sans ~s** *poitrine, bras* hairless; **il n'a pas un ~ sur le caillou*** he's as bald as a coot*; **il n'a pas un ~ de sec*** he's sweating in streams* *ou* like a pig‡.

(b) *[animal]* hair; (*pelage*) coat. **monter un cheval à ~**†† to ride a horse bareback; **en ~ de chèvre** goatskin (*épith*); **en ~ de lapin** rabbit-skin (*épith*); **en ~ de chameau** camel hair (*épith*); *V* **gibier.**

(c) *[brosse à dents, pinceau]* bristle; *[tapis, étoffe]* strand; (*Bot*) *[plante]* down (*U*); *[artichaut]* choke (*U*). **les ~s d'un tapis** the pile of a carpet; **les ~s d'un tissu** the pile *ou* nap of a fabric.

(d) (*: *un petit peu*) **s'il avait un ~ de bon sens** if he had an iota *ou* an ounce of good sense; **à un ~ près: à un ~ près, l'armoire ne passait pas sous la porte** but for a hair's breadth the cupboard wouldn't go through the doorway; **ça mesure environ un mètre, à un ~ près** it measures one metre as near as makes no difference; **il n'y a pas un ~ de différence entre les deux** there isn't the slightest difference between the two (of them); **pousser qch d'un ~** to shift sth a fraction; **il s'en est fallu d'un ~** it was a near *ou* close thing *ou* a close shave*; *V* **quart.**

(e) (*loc*) **à ~‡** starkers‡, in the altogether*, in one's birthday suit*; **se mettre à ~‡** to strip off; **au ~*** (*magnifique*) great*, fantastic*; (*précisément*) perfectly; **tu arrives au ~, j'allais partir** you've come just at the right moment — I was just about to leave; **ça me va au ~*** it suits me fine* *ou* to a T*; **de tout ~** of all kinds, in all shapes and sizes; **avoir un ~ dans la main*** to be bone-idle*; (*péj*) **un jeune blanc-bec qui n'a même pas de ~ au menton*** a lad who's still wet behind the ears* (*péj*), a babe in arms (*péj*); **tu parleras quand tu auras du ~ au menton** you can have your say when you're out of short pants*; **être de bon/de mauvais ~*** to be in a good/bad mood; **tomber sur le ~ à qn** to go for* *ou* lay into* sb; **reprendre du ~ de la bête** *[maladie, plante]* to pick up (again), regain strength; *[rebelles]* to regain strength, be on the way up again.

2: poil de carotte *personne* red-haired, red-headed; *cheveux* red, carroty; **poils follets** down (*U*); **poil à gratter** itching powder.

poilant, e‡ [pwalɑ̃, ɑ̃t] *adj* killing‡, killingly funny*.

poiler (se)‡ [pwale] (1) *vpr* to kill o.s. (laughing)‡.

poilu, e [pwaly] **1** *adj* hairy. **2** *nm* poilu (*French soldier in First World War*).

poinçon [pwɛ̃sɔ̃] *nm* **(a)** (*outil*) *[cordonnier]* awl; *[menuisier]* awl, bradawl; *[brodeuse]* bodkin; *[graveur]* style; *[bijou, or]* die, stamp. **(b)** (*estampille*) hallmark. **(c)** (*matrice*) pattern.

poinçonnage [pwɛ̃sɔnaʒ] *nm*, **poinçonnement** [pwɛ̃sɔnmɑ̃] *nm* (*V* **poinçonner**) stamping; hallmarking; punching, clipping.

poinçonner [pwɛ̃sɔne] (1) *vt marchandise* to stamp; *pièce d'orfèvrerie* to hallmark; *billet* to punch (a hole in), clip.

poinçonneur, -euse [pwɛ̃sɔnœʀ, øz] **1** *nm,f* (*Hist: personne*) ticket-puncher. **2 poinçonneuse** *nf* (*machine*) punching machine, punch press.

poindre [pwɛ̃dʀ(ə)] (49) **1** *vi* (*littér*) *[jour]* to break, dawn; *[aube]* to break; *[plante]* to come up, peep through. **2** *vt* (††) *[tristesse]* to afflict; *[douleur, amour]* to sting (*littér*).

poing [pwɛ̃] *nm* fist. **taper du ~** *ou* **donner des coups de ~ sur la table** to thump the table (with one's fist), bang *ou* thump one's fist on the table; **les ~s sur les hanches** with (one's) hands on (one's) hips, with (one's) arms akimbo; **revolver au ~** revolver in hand; **je vais t'envoyer** *ou* **te coller* mon ~ dans la figure** you'll get my fist in your face*, I'm going to thump* *ou* punch you; **montrer les ~s** to shake one's fist; **menacer qn du ~** to shake one's fist at sb; *V* **dormir, pied.**

point[1] [pwɛ̃] **1** *nm* **(a)** (*endroit*) point, place, spot; (*Astron, Géom*) point; (*fig: situation*) point, stage. **pour aller d'un ~ à un autre** to go from one point *ou* place *ou* spot to another; **fixer un ~ précis dans l'espace** to stare at a fixed point in space; **déborder en plusieurs ~s** to overflow at several points *ou* in several places; **ils étaient venus de tous les ~s de l'horizon** they had come from all corners of the earth *ou* from all the points of the compass; **je reprends mon discours au ~ où je l'ai laissé** I take up my speech where *ou* at the point at which I left off; **avoir atteint le ~ où ..., en être arrivé au ~ où ...** to have reached the point *ou* stage where ...; **nous en sommes toujours au même ~** we haven't got any further, we're no further forward; **c'est bête d'en être (arrivé) à ce ~-là et de ne pas finir** it's silly to have got so far *ou* to have reached this point *ou* stage and not to finish; **au ~ où on en est, cela ne changera pas grand-chose** considering the situation we're in, it won't make much difference.

(b) (*degré*) (*Sci*) point; (*fig: niveau*) point, stage. **~ d'ébullition/de congélation** boiling/freezing point; **jusqu'à un certain ~** to some extent *ou* degree, up to a point, to a certain extent; **au plus haut ~** *détester, aimer, admirer* intensely; **se méfier au plus haut ~ de qch** to be extremely mistrustful of *ou* highly sceptical about sth; **être au plus haut ~ de la gloire** to be at the peak *ou* summit of glory; **est-il possible d'être bête à ce ~(-là)!** how can anyone be so (incredibly) stupid?, how stupid can you get?*; **vous voyez à quel ~ il est généreux** you see how (very) generous he is *ou* the extent of his generosity; **il ne pleut pas au ~ de mettre des bottes** it isn't raining enough for you to put boots on, it isn't raining so much that you need boots; **tirer sur une corde au ~ de la casser** to pull on a rope so much that it breaks, pull a rope to the point where it breaks; **sa colère avait atteint un ~ tel** *ou* **un tel ~ que ...** he was so (very) angry that ..., his anger was such that ...; **il en était arrivé à ce ~** *ou* **à un tel ~ d'avarice que ...** he had become so miserly that ..., his avarice had reached such proportions that ...; **il a mangé au ~ de se rendre malade** he ate so much that he was sick; **c'était à ce ~ absurde que** it was so (very) absurd that.

(c) (*aspect, détail, subdivision*) point. **exposé en 3/4 ~s** 3/4-point exposé; **~ de théologie/de philosophie/de droit** point of theology/philosophy/law; **passons au ~ suivant de l'ordre du jour** let us move on to the next item on the agenda; **~ d'accord/de désaccord** point of agreement/disagreement; **~ mineur** *ou* **de détail** minor point, point of detail; **voilà déjà un ~ acquis** *ou* **de réglé** that's one thing *ou* point settled; **ils sont d'accord sur ce ~/sur tous les ~s** they are agreed on this point *ou* score/on all points *ou* scores *ou* counts; **se ressembler en tout ~** to resemble each other in every respect; **nous avons repris la question ~ par ~** we went over the question point by point; **de ~ en ~** point by point, in every detail, down to the last detail.

(d) (*position*) (*Aviat, Naut*) position. **recevoir le ~ par radio** to be given one's position by radio; (*Naut*) **faire le ~** to take a bearing, plot one's position; **faire le ~ de la situation** to take stock of the situation; (*faire un compte-rendu*) to sum up the situation.

(e) (*marque*) (*gén, Mus, en morse, sur i*) dot; (*ponctuation*) full stop (*Brit*), period; (*tache*) spot, speck; *[dé]* pip. **le bateau n'était plus qu'un ~ à l'horizon** the ship was now nothing but a dot *ou* speck *ou* spot on the horizon; (*fig*) **mettre les ~s sur les i** to spell it out; **~, à la ligne** (*lit*) new paragraph; (*fig*) full stop (*Brit*), period; **tu n'iras pas, un ~ c'est tout** you're not going, and that's all there is to it *ou* and that's that, you're not going — period *ou* full stop; *V* **deux.**

(f) *[score]* (*Cartes, Sport*) point; (*Scol, Univ*) mark, point; *[retraite]* unit; *[salaire]* point. (*Boxe*) **aux ~s** on points; **il a échoué d'un ~** he failed by one mark *ou* point; **la partie se joue en 15 ~s** the winner is the first person to get to *ou* to score 15 (points); (*fig*) **donner** *ou* **rendre des ~s à qn** to give sb points, give sb a (head) start; **bon/mauvais ~** (*Scol*) good/bad mark (*for conduct etc*); (*fig*) plus/minus (mark).

(g) (*Méd*) *[pleurésie, congestion]* site. **avoir un ~ dans le dos** to have a twinge (of pain) in one's back.

(h) (*loc*) (*Culin*) **à ~** *viande* medium; *fruit* just ripe (*attrib*), nicely ripe; *fromage* just right for eating (*attrib*); **arriver à ~ (nommé)** to arrive just at the right moment *ou* just when needed; **cela tombe à ~** that's just *ou* exactly what I (*ou* we *etc*) need; **au ~** *image, photo* in focus; *affaire* completely finalized *ou* settled; *procédé, technique, machine* perfected; *discours, ouvrage* up to scratch (*attrib*), in its final form; **mettre au ~** to (bring into) focus; to finalize; to settle; to perfect; **mettre une affaire au ~ avec qn** to finalize *ou* settle all the details of a matter with sb; **ce n'est pas encore au ~** *[machine, spectacle]* it isn't quite up to scratch yet; **être sur le ~ de faire qch** to be (just) about to do sth, be just going to do sth, be on the point of doing sth; **j'étais sur le ~ de faire du café** I was just going to *ou* (just) about to make some coffee; *V* **mal, mise**[2].

2: point d'appui (*Mil*) base of operations; *[levier]* fulcrum; *[personne]* something to lean on; **chercher un point d'appui** to look for something to lean on; **chercher un point d'appui pour placer une échelle** to look for somewhere to lean a ladder *ou* something to lean a ladder on *ou* against; **l'échelle a glissé de son point d'appui** the ladder slipped from where it was leaning; **point d'attache** *[bateau]* mooring (post); (*fig*) base; **points cardinaux** points of the compass, cardinal points; **point chaud** (*Mil*) trouble spot, hot spot; (*fig: endroit*) trouble spot; (*fait*) **c'est un des points chauds de l'actualité** it's one of today's major issues; **point de chute** (*lit*) landing place; (*fig*) stopping-off place; **point de contrôle** checkpoint; **point de côté** stitch (*pain in the side*); (*Phys, fig*) **point critique** critical point; **point culminant** *[gloire, réussite, panique, épidémie]* height; *[affaire, scandale]* climax, culmination; *[montagne]* peak, summit; *[carrière]* height, zenith; **point de départ** *[train, autobus]* point of departure; *[science, réussite, aventure]* starting point; *[enquête]* point of departure, starting point; (*Sport*) start; **revenir à son point de départ** to come back to where it (*ou* one) started; (*fig*) **nous voilà revenus au point de départ** (so) we're back to square one*, we're back where we started; **point de droit** point of law; **point d'eau** (*source*) watering place; *[camping]* water (supply) point; **point d'exclamation** exclamation mark (*Brit*) *ou* point (*US*); **point faible** weak point; **point de**

fait point of fact; **point final** (*lit*) full stop (*Brit*), period; (*fig*) **mettre un point final à qch** to put an end to sth, bring sth to an end; **point fort** strong point; **point d'honneur** point of honour; **mettre un point d'honneur à** *ou* **se faire un point d'honneur de faire qch** to make it a point of honour to do sth; **point d'impact** point of impact; **point d'information** point of information; **point d'interrogation** question mark; **qui sera élu, c'est là le point d'interrogation** who will be elected — that's the big question (mark) *ou* that's the 64,000-dollar question*; **point d'intersection** point of intersection; **point du jour** daybreak, break of day; **point lumineux** dot *ou* spot of light; **point de mire** (*lit*) target; (*fig*) focal point; **point mort** (*Tech*) dead centre; (*Aut*) neutral; **au point mort** (*Aut*) in neutral; (*fig*) at a standstill; **point névralgique** (*Méd*) nerve centre; (*fig*) sensitive spot; **point noir** *[visage]* blackhead; (*fig: problème*) problem, difficulty; (*Aut*) blackspot; **point de non-retour** point of no return; **point d'ordre** point of order; (*Mus*) **point d'orgue** pause; **point de ralliement** rallying point; **point de ravitaillement** refreshment point; **point de rencontre** meeting point; **point de repère** (*dans l'espace*) landmark; (*dans le temps*) point of reference; (*Mus*) **points de reprise** repeat marks; **point de rouille** spot *ou* speck of rust; **point de rupture** breaking point; (*Sci, fig*) **point de saturation** saturation point; **point sensible** (*sur la peau*) tender spot; (*Mil*) trouble spot; (*fig*) sensitive area, sore point; **point de soudure** spot *ou* blob of solder; **point stratégique** key point; **points de suspension** suspension points; (*Comm*) **point de vente** sales outlet; **'points de vente dans toute la France'** 'on sale throughout France'; **point virgule** semicolon; (*Ling*) **point voyelle** vowel point; **point de vue** (*lit*) view(point); (*fig*) point of view, standpoint; **du** *ou* **au point de vue argent** from the financial point of view *ou* standpoint *ou* viewpoint, as regards money, moneywise*; **nous aimerions connaître votre point de vue sur ce sujet** we should like to know your standpoint *ou* where you stand in this matter.

point[2] [pwɛ̃] **1** *nm* (*Couture, Tricot*) stitch. **bâtir à grands ~s** to tack; **coudre à grands ~s** to sew *ou* stitch using a long stitch; **faire un (petit) ~ à qch** to put a stitch in sth.

2: point d'Alençon Alençon lace; **point d'arrêt** finishing-off stitch; **point arrière** backstitch; **point de chaînette** chain stitch; **point de chausson** (*Couture*) blind hem stitch; (*Broderie*) closed herringbone stitch; **point de couture** stitch; **point de croix** cross-stitch; **point devant** running stitch; **point d'épine** feather stitch; **point de feston** blanket stitch; **point de jersey** stocking stitch; **point mousse** moss stitch; **point d'ourlet** hemstitch; (*Med*) **point de suture** stitch; **faire des points de suture à** to put stitches in, stitch up; **point de tapisserie** canvas stitch; **point de tige** stem stitch; **point de tricot** knitting stitch; **point de Venise** rose point.

point[3] [pwɛ̃] *adv* (*littér, hum*) = **pas**[2].

pointage [pwɛ̃taʒ] *nm* **(a)** (*action: V* **pointer**[1]) ticking *ou* checking *ou* marking off; checking in; checking out; pointing, aiming, levelling; training; directing; dotting; starting off; clocking in; clocking out. **(b)** (*contrôle*) check.

pointe [pwɛ̃t] **1** *nf* **(a)** (*extrémité*) *[aiguille, épée]* point; *[flèche, lance]* head, point; *[couteau, crayon, clocher, clou]* point, tip; *[canne]* (pointed) end, tip, point; *[montagne]* peak, top; *[menton, nez, langue]* tip; *[moustache, seins, col]* point; *[chaussure]* toe. **à la ~ de l'île** at the tip of the island; (*fig*) **chasser l'ennemi à la ~ de l'épée** *ou* **de la baïonnette** to chase away the enemy with swords drawn.

(b) (*partie saillante*) *[grillage]* spike; *[côte]* headland. **la côte forme une ~** *ou* **s'avance en ~ à cet endroit** the coast juts out (into the sea) *ou* forms a headland at that point; **objet qui forme une ~** object that tapers (in)to a point; (*Danse*) **faire des ~s** to dance on points; **en ~** *barbe* in a point, pointed; *col* pointed; **décolleté en ~** plunging V-neckline; **tailler en ~** *arbre, barbe* to cut *ou* trim into a point; *crayon* to sharpen (in)to a point; **clocher/canne qui se termine en ~** bell-tower/stick with a pointed tip *ou* that ends in a point.

(c) (*clou*) tack; (*Sport*) *[chaussure]* spike; (*outil pointu*) point. **tu cours avec des tennis ou avec des ~s?** do you run in plimsolls or spikes?

(d) (*foulard*) triangular (neck)scarf; (*couche de bébé*) (triangular-)shaped nappy.

(e) (*allusion ironique*) pointed remark; (*trait d'esprit*) witticism.

(f) (*petite quantité*) **~ de** *ail* touch *ou* dash *ou* hint of; *ironie, jalousie* touch *ou* tinge *ou* hint of; **il a une ~ d'accent** he has a hint of an accent.

(g) (*maximum*) peak. (*Aut*) **faire des ~s (de vitesse) de 140** to have the occasional burst of 140 km/h; **à la ~ du combat** in the forefront of (the) battle; **à la ~ de l'actualité** in the forefront of current affairs *ou* of the news; **à la ~ du progrès** in the forefront *ou* the front line of progress; **de ~** *industrie* leading; *technique* latest, ultramodern; *vitesse* top, maximum; **heure** *ou* **période de ~** *[gaz, électricité]* peak period; *[circulation]* rush *ou* peak hour; **faire** *ou* **pousser une ~ jusqu'à Paris** to push *ou* press on as far as Paris; **faire** *ou* **pousser une ~ de vitesse** *[athlète, cycliste, automobiliste]* to put on a burst of speed, put on a spurt, step on it*; (*Aut*) **faire du 200 km/h en ~** to have a top *ou* maximum speed of 200 km/h.

(h) (*Naut*) *[compas]* point.

2: pointe d'asperge asparagus tip; **pointe Bic** ® biro ® (*Brit*), ball-point (pen), ball pen; (*Méd*) **pointes de feu** ignipuncture (*Brit*); **faire des pointes de feu à qn** to perform ignipuncture (*Brit*) on sb; (*littér*) **pointe du jour** daybreak; **la pointe des pieds** the toes; **(se mettre) sur la pointe des pieds** (to stand) on tiptoe *ou* on one's toes; **marcher/entrer sur la pointe des pieds** to walk/come in on tiptoe *ou* on one's toes; (*Art*) **pointe sèche** dry-point; **(gravure à la) pointe sèche** dry-point (engraving); **pointe de terre** spit *ou* tongue of land, headland.

pointeau, *pl* **~x** [pwɛ̃to] *nm* **(a)** *[carburateur, graveur]* needle. **(b)** (*Ind: surveillant*) timekeeper.

pointer[1] [pwɛ̃te] (1) **1** *vt* **(a)** (*cocher*) to tick off, check off, mark off. (*Naut*) **~ (sa position sur) la carte** to prick off *ou* plot one's position; *V* **zéro**.

(b) (*Ind*) *employé* (*à l'arrivée*) to check in; (*au départ*) to check out.

(c) (*braquer*) *fusil* to point, aim, level (*vers, sur* at); *jumelles* to train (*vers, sur* on); *lampe* to direct (*vers, sur* towards); *boule* (*de pétanque*) to roll (*as opposed to throw*). **il pointa vers elle un index accusateur** he pointed *ou* directed an accusing finger at her.

(d) (*Mus*) *note* to dot.

(e) (*Tech*) *trou de vis* to start off.

2 *vi [employé]* (*arrivée*) to clock in, check in; (*départ*) to clock out, check out.

3 se pointer* *vpr* (*arriver*) to turn up*, show up*.

pointer[2] [pwɛ̃te] (1) **1** *vt* **(a)** (*piquer*) to stick. **il lui pointa sa lance dans le dos** he stuck his lance into his back.

(b) (*dresser*) **église qui pointe ses tours vers le ciel** church whose towers soar (up) into the sky; **chien qui pointe les oreilles** dog which pricks up its ears.

2 *vi* (*littér*) **(a)** (*s'élever*) *[tour]* to soar up.

(b) (*apparaître*) *[plante]* to peep out; (*fig*) *[ironie]* to pierce through. **ses seins pointaient sous la robe** the points of her breasts showed beneath her dress; **le jour pointait** day was breaking *ou* dawning; **le bateau pointait à l'horizon** the boat appeared as a dot on the horizon.

pointer[3] [pwɛ̃tœʀ] *nm* (*chien*) pointer.

pointeur [pwɛ̃tœʀ] *nm* (*Ind, Sport*) timekeeper; *[boules] player who rolls the bowl (as opposed to throwing it)*; *[canon]* gun-layer.

pointillage [pwɛ̃tijaʒ] *nm* stipple, stippling.

pointillé, e [pwɛ̃tije] (*ptp de* **pointiller**) **1** *adj* dotted.

2 *nm* **(a)** (*Art*) (*procédé*) stipple, stippling; (*gravure*) stipple.

(b) (*trait*) dotted line; (*perforations*) perforation(s). **en ~** dotted; **'détacher suivant le ~'** 'tear along the dotted line'.

pointillement [pwɛ̃tijmɑ̃] *nm* = **pointillage**.

pointiller [pwɛ̃tije] (1) (*Art*) **1** *vi* to draw (*ou* engrave) in stipple. **2** *vt* to stipple.

pointilleux, -euse [pwɛ̃tijø, øz] *adj* particular, pernickety (*péj*).

pointillisme [pwɛ̃tijism(ə)] *nm* pointillism.

pointilliste [pwɛ̃tijist(ə)] *adj, nmf* pointillist.

pointu, e [pwɛ̃ty] **1** *adj* **(a)** (*lit*) (*en forme de pointe*) pointed; (*aiguisé*) sharp.

(b) (*péj*) *air* touchy, peevish, peeved; *caractère* touchy, peevish, crabbed; *voix, ton* shrill. **accent ~** northern accent (*expression used by people from South of France*).

2 *adv*: **parler ~** to speak with *ou* have a northern accent.

pointure [pwɛ̃tyʀ] *nf [gant, chaussure]* size. **quelle est votre ~?, quelle ~ faites-vous?** what size do you take *ou* are you?

poire [pwaʀ] **1** *adj*: **être ~*** to be a mug* (*Brit*) *ou* a sucker*.

2 *nf* **(a)** (*fruit*) pear. **il m'a dit cela entre la ~ et le fromage** ≈ he told me that (casually) over coffee (*at the end of a meal*); *V* **couper, garder**.

(b) (*: tête*) mug‡, face. **il a une bonne ~** he's got a nice enough face; **se ficher de** *ou* **se payer la ~ de qn** (*ridiculiser*) to have a good laugh at sb's expense; (*tromper*) to take sb for a ride*; **en pleine ~** right in the face.

(c) (*: dupe*) mug* (*Brit*), sucker*. **c'est une bonne ~** he's a real mug* (*Brit*) *ou* sucker*.

3: poire électrique switch (*pear-shaped*); **poire à injections** syringe; **poire à lavement** enema; **poire à poudre** powder horn.

poiré [pwaʀe] *nm* perry.

poireau, *pl* **~x** [pwaʀo] *nm* leek. (*fig*) **faire le ~*** to be left kicking *ou* cooling one's heels*; **elle m'a fait faire le ~ pendant 2 heures*** she left me to kick *ou* cool my heels *ou* she left me kicking *ou* cooling my heels for 2 hours*.

poireauter* [pwaʀote] (1) *vi* to be left kicking *ou* cooling one's heels*. **faire ~ qn** to leave sb to kick *ou* cool his (*ou* her) heels*, leave sb kicking *ou* cooling his (*ou* her) heels*.

poirier [pwaʀje] *nm* pear tree. (*fig*) **faire le ~** to do a headstand.

pois [pwa] **1** *nm* **(a)** (*légume*) pea. **petits ~** (garden) peas. **(b)** (*Habillement*) (polka) dot, spot. **robe à ~** dotted *ou* spotted *ou* polka dot dress. **2: pois cassés** split peas; **pois chiche** chickpea; **pois de senteur** sweet pea.

poison [pwazɔ̃] **1** *nm* (*lit, fig*) poison. **on a mis du ~ dans sa soupe** his soup was poisoned. **2** *nmf* (**fig: personne*) misery*, misery-guts*; (*chose*) drag*, bind* (*Brit*).

poissard, e [pwasaʀ, aʀd(ə)] **1** *adj accent, langage* vulgar, coarse. **2 poissarde** *nf*: **parler comme une ~e** to talk like a fish-wife.

poisse‡ [pwas] *nf* rotten luck*, bad luck. **avoir la ~** to have rotten* *ou* bad luck; **quelle ~!, c'est la ~!** just my (*ou* our) (rotten) luck!*; **ne le fais pas, ça porte la ~** don't do that — it's bad luck *ou* it's unlucky; **ça leur a porté la ~** that brought them bad luck.

poisser [pwase] (1) *vt* **(a)** (*‡: attraper*) to nab‡, cop‡. **(b)** (*salir*) to make sticky; (*engluer*) *cordage* to pitch.

poisseux, -euse [pwasø, øz] *adj mains, surface* sticky.

poisson [pwasɔ̃] **1** *nm* **(a)** fish. **pêcher du ~** to fish; **2/3 ~s** 2/3 fish *ou* fishes; **fourchette/couteau à ~** fish fork/knife; **être (heureux) comme un ~ dans l'eau** to be in one's element, be as happy as a sandboy; **insulter** *ou* **engueuler qn comme du ~ pourri** to call sb all the names under the sun, bawl at sb; *V* **queue**.

(b) (*Astron*) **les P~s** Pisces, the Fishes; **être (des) P~s** to be Pisces *ou* a Piscean.

2: poisson d'avril (*excl*) April fool!; (*nm: blague*) April fool's trick; **poisson(-)chat** *nm, pl* **poissons(-)chats** catfish; **poisson d'eau douce** freshwater fish; **poisson épée** swordfish; **poisson lune** moon-fish, sunfish; **poisson de mer** saltwater fish; **poisson perroquet** parrotfish; **poisson pilote** pilotfish; **poisson plat** flatfish; **poisson rouge** goldfish; **poisson scie** sawfish; **poisson volant** flying fish.

poissonnerie [pwasɔnʀi] *nf* (*boutique*) fishmonger's (shop), fish-shop; (*métier*) fish trade.

poissonneux, -euse [pwasɔnø, øz] *adj* full of fish (*attrib*), abounding in fish (*attrib*).

poissonnier [pwasɔnje] *nm* fishmonger.

poissonnière [pwasɔnjɛʀ] *nf* **(a)** (*personne*) (woman) fishmonger, fishwife. **(b)** (*ustensile*) fish kettle.

poitevin, e [pwatvɛ̃, in] **1** *adj* Poitou (*épith*), of Poitou; Poitiers (*épith*), of Poitiers. **2** *nm,f*: **P~(e)** inhabitant *ou* native of Poitou *ou* Poitiers.

poitrail [pwatʀaj] *nm* (*Zool*) breast; (*hum: poitrine*) chest.

poitrinaire [pwatʀinɛʀ] **1** *adj*: être ~ to have TB, be tuberculous (*T*). **2** *nmf* tuberculosis sufferer.

poitrine [pwatʀin] *nf* (*gén*) chest, breast (*littér*); (*seins*) bust, bosom; (*Culin*) *[veau, mouton]* breast; *[porc]* belly. ~ **de bœuf** brisket (of beef); **maladie de** ~† chest complaint; **elle a beaucoup de** ~ she has a big bust *ou* bosom, she's big-busted; **elle n'a pas de** ~ she's flat-chested; *V* **fluxion, tour²,** voix.

poivrade [pwavʀad] *nf* (*Culin*) vinaigrette (sauce) with pepper. (**à la**) ~ with salt and pepper.

poivre [pwavʀ(ə)] **1** *nm* pepper; *V* **moulin, steak. 2: poivre blanc** white pepper; **poivre de Cayenne** Cayenne pepper; **poivre en grains** whole pepper, peppercorns (*pl*); **poivre gris** black pepper; **poivre moulu** ground pepper; **poivre noir** black pepper; **poivre en poudre** = **poivre moulu**; **poivre rouge** red pepper; **poivre et sel** *adj inv cheveux* pepper-and-salt.

poivré, e [pwavʀe] (*ptp de* **poivrer**) *adj plat, goût, odeur* peppery; (*fig*) *histoire* spicy, juicy*, saucy*; (**:** *soûl*) pickled**:**, plastered**:**.

poivrer [pwavʀe] (1) **1** *vt* to pepper, put pepper in *ou* on. **2 se poivrer:** *vpr* (*se soûler*) to get pickled**:** *ou* plastered**:**.

poivrier [pwavʀije] *nm* **(a)** (*Bot*) pepper plant. **(b)** (*Culin*) pepperpot.

poivrière [pwavʀijɛʀ] *nf* **(a)** (*Culin*) pepperpot. **(b)** (*plantation*) pepper plantation. **(c)** (*Archit*) pepper-box.

poivron [pwavʀɔ̃] *nm*: ~ **(vert)** green pepper, capsicum; ~ **rouge** red pepper, capsicum.

poivrot, e* [pwavʀo, ɔt] *nm,f* drunkard.

poix [pwa] *nf* pitch (*tar*).

poker [pɔkɛʀ] *nm* (*Cartes*) (*jeu*) poker; (*partie*) game of poker. **faire un** ~ to have a game of poker; ~ **d'as/de dames** four aces/queens; ~ **d'as** (*jeu*) poker dice; (*fig*) **coup de** ~ gamble.

polaire [pɔlɛʀ] **1** *adj* (*Chim, Géog, Math*) polar. **froid** ~ arctic cold; *V* **cercle, étoile. 2** *nf* (*Math*) polar.

polaque [pɔlak] *nm* (*péj*) Polack (*péj*).

polarisant, e [pɔlaʀizɑ̃, ɑ̃t] *adj* (*Élec, Phys*) polarizing.

polarisation [pɔlaʀizɑsjɔ̃] *nf* (*Élec, Phys*) polarization; (*fig*) focusing.

polariser [pɔlaʀize] (1) **1** *vt* **(a)** (*Élec, Phys*) to polarize.

(b) (*fig: faire converger sur soi*) *attention, regards* to attract. **problème qui polarise toute l'activité/tout le mécontentement** problem around *ou* upon which all the activity/discontent centres *ou* is centred.

(c) (*fig: concentrer*) ~ **son attention sur qch** to focus *ou* centre one's attention on sth; ~ **son énergie sur qch** to bring all one's energies to bear on sth.

2 se polariser *vpr* (*Phys*) to polarize. **se** ~ **sur qch** *[mécontentement, critiques]* to be centred (a)round *ou* upon sth, be focused upon sth; *[personne]* to focus *ou* centre one's attention on sth.

polariseur [pɔlaʀizœʀ] *adj, nm*: **(prisme)** ~ polarizer.

polarité [pɔlaʀite] *nf* (*Bio, Math, Phys*) polarity.

polaroïd [pɔlaʀɔid] *nm* ® polaroid ®.

polder [pɔldɛʀ] *nm* polder.

pôle [pol] *nm* (*Sci, fig*) pole. **P~ Nord/Sud** North/South Pole; ~ **magnétique** magnetic pole; (*fig*) ~ **d'attraction** centre of attraction, focus of attention.

polémique [pɔlemik] **1** *adj* controversial, polemic(al) (*frm*).

2 *nf* controversy, argument, polemic (*frm*). **engager une** ~ **avec qn** to enter into an argument with sb; **chercher à faire de la** ~ to try to be controversial.

polémiquer [pɔlemike] (1) *vi* to be involved in controversy.

polémiste [pɔlemist(ə)] *nmf* polemist, polemicist.

polémologie [pɔlemɔlɔʒi] *nf* study of war.

poli, e¹ [pɔli] *adj* polite. **être** ~ **avec qn** to be polite to sb; **être trop** ~ **pour être honnête** to be hiding something beneath a courteous exterior; **soyez** ~! don't be so rude!

poli, e² [pɔli] (*ptp de* **polir**) **1** *adj bois, ivoire* polished; *métal* burnished, polished; *caillou* smooth. **2** *nm* shine. **donner du** ~ **à** to put a shine on, polish (up).

police¹ [pɔlis] **1** *nf* **(a)** (*corps*) police (*U*), police force. **inspecteur/voiture de** ~ police inspector/car; **être dans** *ou* **de la** ~ to be in the police (force), be a policeman; **la** ~ **est à ses trousses** the police are after him *ou* are on his tail; *V* **plaque, salle.**

(b) (*maintien de l'ordre*) enforcement of (law and) order. **les pouvoirs de** ~ **dans la société** powers to maintain law and order in society; **exercer** *ou* **faire la** ~ to keep (law and) order; **faire la** ~ **dans une classe** to police a class, keep order in a class, keep a class in order; **faire sa propre** ~ to do one's own policing, keep (law and) order for o.s.

(c) (*règlements*) regulations (*pl*). ~ **intérieure d'un lycée** internal regulations of a school.

(d) (*tribunal*) **passer en simple** ~ to be tried in a police *ou* magistrates' court; *V* **tribunal.**

2: police de la circulation traffic police; **police judiciaire** ≃ Criminal Investigation Department, CID; **police des mœurs** *ou* **mondaine** ≃ vice squad; (*Can*) **police montée** mounted police, mounties*; **police parallèle** *unofficial governmental police agency*; **police privée** (private) detective agency; **police secours** police (*special service for emergencies*), ≃ emergency services (*pl*); **appeler police secours** ≃ to dial 999 (*Brit*); **police secrète** secret police.

police² [pɔlis] *nf* (insurance) policy. ~ **d'assurance vie** life insurance *ou* assurance policy; ~ **d'assurance contre l'incendie** fire insurance policy.

policer [pɔlise] (3) *vt* (*littér*, ††) to civilize.

polichinelle [pɔliʃinɛl] *nm* **(a)** (*Théât*) **P~** Punchinello; *V* **secret. (b)** (*marionnette*) Punch. **(c)** (*fig péj: personne*) buffoon. **faire le** ~ to act the buffoon. **(d) : avoir un** ~ **dans le tiroir** to have a bun in the oven.

policier, -ière [pɔlisje, jɛʀ] **1** *adj chien, enquête, régime* police (*épith*); *film, roman* detective (*épith*). **2** *nm* **(a)** (*agent*) policeman. **(b)** (*roman*) detective novel.

poliment [pɔlimɑ̃] *adv* politely.

polio [pɔljo] *nf* (*abrév de* **poliomyélite**) polio.

poliomyélite [pɔljɔmjelit] *nf* poliomyelitis (*T*).

poliomyélitique [pɔljɔmjelitik] *adj* suffering from polio.

polir [pɔliʀ] (2) *vt* **(a)** *meuble, objet, souliers* to polish (up), put a shine on; *pierre, verre* to polish; *métal* to polish, burnish, buff; *ongles* to polish, buff. **(b)** (*fig*) *discours* to polish (up); *style* to polish; *caractère* to refine.

polissage [pɔlisaʒ] *nm* (*V* **polir**) polishing; burnishing.

polisseur, -euse [pɔlisœʀ, øz] *nm,f* polisher.

polissoir [pɔliswaʀ] *nm* polisher, polishing machine. ~ **à ongles** nail buffer.

polisson, -onne [pɔlisɔ̃, ɔn] **1** *adj* **(a)** (*espiègle*) *enfant* naughty, bad; *air* naughty.

(b) (*grivois*) *chanson* naughty, saucy; *regard* saucy, randy*.

2 *nm,f* (*enfant*) (little) rascal, (little) devil*; (*personne égrillarde*) saucy *ou* randy devil*; (††: *petit vagabond*) street urchin.

polissonner [pɔlisɔne] (1) *vi* to be naughty.

polissonnerie [pɔlisɔnʀi] *nf* **(a)** (*espièglerie*) naughty trick. **(b)** (*grivoiserie*) (*parole*) naughty remark; (*action*) naughty thing.

politesse [pɔlitɛs] *nf* **(a)** (*U: savoir-vivre*) politeness, courtesy. **par** ~ out of politeness, to be polite; *V* **brûler, formule, visite.**

(b) (*parole*) polite remark; (*action*) polite gesture. **rendre une** ~ to return a favour; **se faire des** ~**s** (*paroles*) to exchange polite remarks; (*actions*) to make polite gestures to one another.

politicard [pɔlitikaʀ] *nm* (*péj*) politician, political schemer.

politicien, -ienne [pɔlitisjɛ̃, jɛn] (*péj*) **1** *adj* politicking (*péj*). **2** *nm,f* politician, political schemer.

politico- [pɔlitiko] *préf* politico-.

politique [pɔlitik] **1** *adj* **(a)** *institutions, économie, parti, prisonnier* political; *carrière* political, in politics. **homme** ~ politician.

(b) (*littér: habile*) *personne* diplomatic; *acte, invitation* diplomatic, politic.

2 *nf* **(a)** (*science, carrière*) politics (*sg*). **faire de la** ~ (*militantisme*) to be a political activist; (*métier*) to be in politics.

(b) (*Pol, fig: ligne de conduite*) policy; (*manière de gouverner*) policies. **la** ~ **extérieure du gouvernement** the government's foreign policy; **l'opposition se plaint de la** ~ **du gouvernement** the opposition is complaining about the government's policies; **avoir une** ~ **de gauche/droite** to follow left-/right-wing policies; (*fig*) **il est de bonne** ~ **de faire** it is good policy to do; **la** ~ **du moindre effort** the principle of least effort; **la** ~ **du pire** the policy of painting things as black as possible (*in order to further one's own ends*); **pratiquer la** ~ **de l'autruche** to bury one's head in the sand; **c'est faire la** ~ **de l'autruche** it's like burying one's head in the sand.

3 *nm* (*politicien*) politician; (*aspects politiques*) politics, the political side of things.

politiquement [pɔlitikmɑ̃] *adv* (*lit*) politically; (*fig littér*) diplomatically.

politiquer*† [pɔlitike] (1) *vi* to talk (about) politics, politicize.

politisation [pɔlitizɑsjɔ̃] *nf* politicization.

politiser [pɔlitize] (1) *vt débat* to politicize, bring politics into; *événement* to make a political issue of.

polka [pɔlka] *nf* polka.

pollen [pɔlɛn] *nm* pollen.

polluant, e [pɔlɥɑ̃, ɑ̃t] *adj* polluting. **produit** ~ pollutant, polluting agent.

polluer [pɔlɥe] (1) *vt* to pollute.

pollution [pɔlysjɔ̃] *nf* pollution. (*Méd*) ~**s nocturnes** wet dreams.

polo [pɔlo] *nm* **(a)** (*Sport*) polo. **(b)** (*chemise*) sweat shirt.

polochon* [pɔlɔʃɔ̃] *nm* bolster.

Pologne [pɔlɔɲ] *nf* Poland.

polonais, e [pɔlɔnɛ, ɛz] **1** *adj* Polish. **2** *nm* **(a) P~** Pole; *V* **soûl. (b)** (*Ling*) Polish. **3 polonaise** *nf* **(a) P~e** Pole. **(b)** (*Mus*) polonaise. **(c)** (*gâteau*) polonaise (*meringue-covered sponge cake containing preserved fruit*).

poltron, -onne [pɔltʀɔ̃, ɔn] **1** *adj* cowardly, craven (*littér*). **2** *nm,f* coward.

poltronnerie [pɔltʀɔnʀi] *nf* cowardice.

poly... [pɔli] *préf* poly... .

polyacide [pɔliasid] *adj, nm* polyacid.

polyamide [pɔliamid] *nm* polyamide.

polyandre [pɔljɑ̃dʀ(ə)] *adj femme, plante* polyandrous.
polyandrie [pɔliɑ̃dʀi] *nf* polyandry.
polychrome [pɔlikʀom] *adj* polychrome, polychromatic.
polyclinique [pɔliklinik] *nf* polyclinic.
polycopie [pɔlikɔpi] *nf* duplication, stencilling. **tiré à la ~** duplicated, stencilled.
polycopié [pɔlikɔpje] *nm* (*Univ*) (*payant*) duplicated lecture notes (*sold to students*); (*gratuit*) handout.
polycopier [pɔlikɔpje] (7) *vt* to duplicate, stencil. **cours polycopiés** duplicated lecture notes (*sold to students*); **machine à ~** duplicator.
polyculture [pɔlikyltyʀ] *nf* mixed farming.
polyèdre [pɔljɛdʀ(ə)] **1** *adj angle, solide* polyhedral. **2** *nm* polyhedron.
polyédrique [pɔliedʀik] *adj* polyhedral.
polyester [pɔliɛstɛʀ] *nm* polyester.
polygame [pɔligam] **1** *adj* polygamous. **2** *nm* polygamist.
polygamie [pɔligami] *nf* polygamy.
polyglotte [pɔliglɔt] *adj, nmf* polyglot.
polygonal, e, *mpl* **-aux** [pɔligɔnal, o] *adj* polygonal, many-sided.
polygone [pɔligɔn] *nm* (*Math*) polygon; (*fig: zone*) area, zone. (*Mil*) **~ de tir** rifle range.
polygraphe [pɔligʀaf] *nmf* polygraph.
polymère [pɔlimɛʀ] **1** *adj* polymeric. **2** *nm* polymer.
polymérisation [pɔlimeʀizɑsjɔ̃] *nf* polymerization.
polymériser *vt*, **se polymériser** *vpr* [pɔlimeʀize] (1) to polymerize.
polymorphe [pɔlimɔʀf(ə)] *adj* polymorphous, polymorphic.
polymorphie [pɔlimɔʀfi] *nf*, **polymorphisme** [pɔlimɔʀfism(ə)] *nm* polymorphism.
Polynésie [pɔlinezi] *nf* Polynesia.
polynésien, -ienne [pɔlinezjɛ̃, jɛn] **1** *adj* Polynesian. **2** *nm* (*Ling*) Polynesian. **3** *nm,f*: **P~(ne)** Polynesian.
Polynice [pɔlinis] *nm* Polynices.
polynôme [pɔlinom] *nm* polynomial (*Math*).
polynucléaire [pɔlinykleɛʀ] **1** *adj* polynuclear, multinuclear. **2** *nm* polymorphonuclear leucocyte.
polype [pɔlip] *nm* (*Zool*) polyp; (*Méd*) polyp, polypus.
polyphasé, e [pɔlifɑze] *adj* polyphase.
Polyphème [pɔlifɛm] *nm* Polyphemus.
polyphonie [pɔlifɔni] *nf* polyphony (*Mus*).
polyphonique [pɔlifɔnik] *adj* polyphonic (*Mus*).
polysémie [pɔlisemi] *nf* polysemy.
polysémique [pɔlisemik] *adj* polysemous.
polysyllabe [pɔlisilab] **1** *adj* polysyllabic. **2** *nm* polysyllable.
polysyllabique [pɔlisilabik] *adj* polysyllabic.
polytechnicien, -ienne [pɔlitɛknisjɛ̃, jɛn] *nm,f* polytechnician (*student or ex-student at the Paris polytechnic*).
polytechnique [pɔlitɛknik] *adj* (†) polytechnic. **(l'École) ~** École Polytechnique.
polythéisme [pɔliteism(ə)] *nm* polytheism.
polythéiste [pɔliteist(ə)] **1** *adj* polytheistic. **2** *nmf* polytheist.
polyvalent, e [pɔlivalɑ̃, ɑ̃t] **1** *adj* (*Chim*) *corps* polyvalent; (*Méd*) *sérum, vaccin* polyvalent; (*fig*) *rôle, traitement, enseignement* varied; *attributions, usages* various, many; *personne* versatile. **2** *nm* tax inspector (*sent to examine company's books*).
Poméranie [pɔmeʀani] *nf* Pomerania; *V* **loulou**[1].
pommade [pɔmad] *nf* [*peau*] ointment; [*cheveux*] cream, pomade. (*fig*) **passer de la ~ à qn*** to lay it on thick*, butter sb up*, soft-soap sb*.
pommader [pɔmade] (1) *vt* (*péj*) *cheveux* to pomade; *joues* to paint.
pomme [pɔm] **1** *nf* **(a)** (*fruit*) apple; (*pomme de terre*) potato. (*fig*) **grand *ou* haut comme trois ~s*** knee-high to a grasshopper*; (*fig*) **tomber dans les ~s*** to faint, pass out*.
(b) [*chou, laitue*] heart; [*canne, lit*] knob; [*arrosoir, douche*] rose; [*mât*] truck.
(c) (*) (*tête*) head, nut*; (*visage*) face, mug‡. **c'est pour ma ~** it's for my own sweet self*.
2: pomme d'Adam Adam's apple; **pomme d'api** *type of small apple*; **pomme cannelle** sweetsop, custard apple; **(pommes) chips** (potato) crisps (*Brit*) *ou* chips (*US*); **pomme à cidre** cider apple; **pomme à couteau** eating apple; **pomme à cuire** cooking apple, cooker*; (*fig*) **pomme de discorde** bone of contention, apple of discord (*Myth*); **pommes frites** (*gén*) chips (*Brit*), French fries (*US*); (*au restaurant*) French fried potatoes; **bifteck (aux) pommes frites** steak and chips (*Brit*) *ou* French fries (*US*); **pommes mousseline** mashed potatoes; **pomme de pin** pine *ou* fir cone; **pomme de reinette** Cox's orange pippin (*Brit*); **pomme de terre** potato; **pommes vapeur** boiled potatoes.
pommé, e [pɔme] (*ptp de* **pommer**) *adj chou* firm and round; *laitue* with a good heart.
pommeau, *pl* **~x** [pɔmo] *nm* [*épée, selle*] pommel; [*canne*] knob.
pommelé, e [pɔmle] (*ptp de* **pommeler**) *adj cheval* dappled; *ciel* full of fluffy *ou* fleecy clouds, mackerel (*épith*). **gris ~** dapple-grey.
pommeler (se) [pɔmle] (4) *vpr* [*ciel*] to become full of fluffy *ou* fleecy clouds; [*chou, laitue*] to form a head *ou* heart.
pommelle [pɔmɛl] *nf* filter (*over a pipe*).
pommer [pɔme] (1) *vi* (*Bot*) to form a head *ou* heart.
pommette [pɔmɛt] *nf* cheekbone. **le rouge lui monta aux ~s** a flush came to his cheeks.
pommier [pɔmje] *nm* apple tree.
Pomone [pɔmɔn] *nf* Pomona.
pompage [pɔ̃paʒ] *nm* pumping.
pompe[1] [pɔ̃p] **1** *nf* **(a)** (*machine*) pump. **~ à air/à vide/de bicyclette** air/vacuum/bicycle pump; *V* **bateau, château, coup.**
(b) (**fig: chaussure*) shoe.
(c) (**loc*) **à toute ~** at top speed, flat out*; (*Mil*) **(soldat de) deuxième ~** private.
2: pompe aspirante suction *ou* lift pump; **pompe aspirante et foulante** suction and force pump; **pompe à essence** (*distributeur*) petrol (*Brit*) *ou* gasoline (*US*) pump; (*station*) petrol station (*Brit*), gas station (*US*); **pompe foulante** force pump; **pompe à incendie** fire engine (*apparatus*).
pompe[2] [pɔ̃p] *nf* **(a)** (*littér: solennité*) pomp. **en grande ~** with great pomp and ceremony. **(b)** (*Rel: vanités*) **~s** pomps and vanities; **renoncer au monde et à ses ~s** to renounce the world and all its pomps and vanities. **(c) ~s funèbres** funeral director's, undertaker's; **entreprise de ~s funèbres** funeral parlour.
pompé, e‡ [pɔ̃pe] (*ptp de* **pomper**) *adj* (*fatigué*) whacked‡ (*Brit*), pooped‡ (*US*), dead-beat‡, all-in*.
Pompée [pɔ̃pe] *nm* Pompey.
Pompéi [pɔ̃pei] *n* Pompeii.
pompéien, -enne [pɔ̃pejɛ̃, ɛn] **1** *adj* Pompeian. **2** *nm,f*: **P~(ne)** Pompeian.
pomper [pɔ̃pe] (1) *vt* **(a)** *air, liquide* to pump; [*moustique*] to suck (up); (*évacuer*) to pump out; (*faire monter*) to pump up. **~ de l'eau** to get water from the pump, pump water out; **tu nous pompes l'air‡** you're getting us down*, we're getting fed up with you‡.
(b) [*éponge, buvard*] to soak up.
(c) (*arg Scol: copier*) to crib* (*sur* from).
(d) (‡: *boire*) to swill down‡, knock back‡. **qu'est-ce qu'il pompe!** he can't half knock it back!‡
(e) (‡: *épuiser*) to wear out, tire out. **tout ce travail m'a pompé** I'm worn out* *ou* whacked‡ (*Brit*) *ou* pooped‡ (*US*) after (doing) all that work.
pompette* [pɔ̃pɛt] *adj* tipsy*.
pompeusement [pɔ̃pøzmɑ̃] *adv* pompously, pretentiously.
pompeux, -euse [pɔ̃pø, øz] *adj* (*ampoulé*) pompous; (*imposant*) solemn.
pompier, -ière [pɔ̃pje, jɛʀ] **1** *adj* (*) *style, écrivain* pompous, pretentious; *morceau de musique* slushy*. **2** *nm* fireman. **appeler les ~s** to call the fire brigade.
pompiste [pɔ̃pist(ə)] *nmf* petrol (*Brit*) *ou* gasoline (*US*) pump attendant.
pompon [pɔ̃pɔ̃] *nm* [*chapeau, coussin*] pompom; [*frange, instrument*] bobble. **avoir son ~†*** to be tipsy*; (*fig iro*) **avoir *ou* tenir le ~** to take the biscuit* (*Brit*) *ou* cake*, be the limit*; **c'est le ~!** it's the last straw!, that beats everything!*, that's the limit!*; *V* **rose.**
pomponner [pɔ̃pɔne] (1) **1** *vt* to titivate, doll up*; *bébé* to dress up. **bien pomponné** all dolled up* *ou* dressed up. **2 se pomponner** *vpr* to titivate (o.s.), doll o.s. up*, get dolled up* *ou* dressed up.
ponant [pɔnɑ̃] *nm* (*littér*) west.
ponçage [pɔ̃saʒ] *nm* (*V* **poncer**) sanding (down); rubbing down; sandpapering; pumicing.
ponce [pɔ̃s] *nf* **(a) (pierre) ~** pumice (stone). **(b)** (*Art*) pounce box.
Ponce Pilate [pɔ̃spilat] *nm* Pontius Pilate.
poncer [pɔ̃se] (3) *vt* **(a)** (*décaper*) (*avec du papier de verre*) to sand (down), rub down, sandpaper; (*avec une ponceuse*) to sand (down), rub down; (*avec une pierre ponce*) to pumice. **il faut ~ d'abord** it needs sanding down first.
(b) (*Art*) *dessin* to pounce.
ponceuse [pɔ̃søz] *nf* sander.
poncho [pɔ̃tʃo] *nm* poncho.
poncif [pɔ̃sif] *nm* (*cliché*) commonplace, cliché; (*Art*) stencil (*for pouncing*).
ponction [pɔ̃ksjɔ̃] *nf* (*Méd*) (*lombaire*) puncture; (*pulmonaire*) tapping; (*fig*) [*argent*] withdrawal. **par de fréquentes ~s il a épuisé son capital** he has dipped into *ou* drawn on his capital so often he has used it all up; **faire une sérieuse ~ dans ses économies** [*impôt*] to make a large hole in *ou* make serious inroads into one's savings; (*pour vacances etc*) to draw heavily on one's savings; (*hum*) **faire une ~ dans les bonbons** to raid the sweets; (*hum*) **faire une ~ dans une bouteille** to help o.s. to plenty out of a bottle.
ponctionner [pɔ̃ksjɔne] (1) *vt région lombaire* to puncture; *poumon* to tap.
ponctualité [pɔ̃ktɥalite] *nf* (*exactitude*) punctuality; (*assiduité*) punctiliousness (*frm*), meticulousness.
ponctuation [pɔ̃ktɥɑsjɔ̃] *nf* punctuation.
ponctuel, -elle [pɔ̃ktɥɛl] *adj* **(a)** (*à l'heure*) punctual; (*scrupuleux*) punctilious (*frm*), meticulous. **(b)** (*Phys*) punctual; (*fig: isolé*) limited; (*aspect d'un verbe*) punctual.
ponctuellement [pɔ̃ktɥɛlmɑ̃] *adv* (*à l'heure*) punctually; (*scrupuleusement*) punctiliously (*frm*), meticulously.
ponctuer [pɔ̃ktɥe] (1) *vt* (*lit, fig*) to punctuate (*de* with); (*Mus*) to phrase.
pondérateur, -trice [pɔ̃deʀatœʀ, tʀis] *adj influence* stabilizing, steadying.
pondération [pɔ̃deʀɑsjɔ̃] *nf* **(a)** [*personne*] level-headedness. **(b)** (*équilibrage*) balancing; (*Écon*) weighting. **~ des pouvoirs** balance of powers.
pondéré, e [pɔ̃deʀe] (*ptp de* **pondérer**) *adj* **(a)** *personne, attitude* level-headed. **(b)** (*Écon*) *indice* **~** weighted index.
pondérer [pɔ̃deʀe] (6) *vt* (*équilibrer*) to balance; (*compenser*) to counterbalance (*par* by); (*Écon*) *indice* to weight.
pondéreux, -euse [pɔ̃deʀø, øz] **1** *adj marchandises, produits* heavy. **2** *nmpl*: **les ~** heavy goods.
pondeur [pɔ̃dœʀ] *nm* (*péj*) **~ de romans** writer who churns out books.
pondeuse [pɔ̃døz] *nf*: **(poule) ~** good layer; **~ (d'enfants)*** prolific child-bearer (*hum*).

pondre [pɔ̃dʀ(ə)] (41) **1** *vt œuf* to lay; (*) *enfant* to produce; *devoir, texte* to produce, turn out*. **œuf frais pondu** new-laid egg. **2** *vi [poule]* to lay; *[poisson, insecte]* to lay its eggs.

poney [pɔnɛ] *nm* pony.

pongiste [pɔ̃ʒist(ə)] *nmf* table tennis player.

pont [pɔ̃] **1** *nm* **(a)** (*Constr*) bridge; (*fig: lien*) bridge, link. **passer un ~** to go over *ou* cross a bridge; **vivre** *ou* **coucher sous les ~s** to be a tramp; **se porter comme le P~-Neuf*** to be hale and hearty; **faire un ~ d'or à qn (pour l'employer)** to offer sb a fortune to take on a job; *V* **couper, eau, jeter.**

(b) (*Naut*) deck. **~ avant/arrière/supérieur** fore/rear/upper *ou* top deck; **navire à 2/3 ~s** 2/3 decker.

(c) (*Aut*) axle. **~ avant/arrière** front/rear axle.

(d) (*vacances*) extra day(s) off (*taken between two public holidays or a public holiday and a weekend*). **on a un ~ de 3 jours pour Noël** we have 3 extra days (off) for *ou* at Christmas; **faire le ~** to take the extra day (off), make a long weekend of it.

(e) (*Antiq*) **(royaume du) P~** Pontus.

2: pont aérien airlift; **pont aux ânes** pons asinorum; **pont basculant** bascule bridge; **pont de bateaux** floating bridge, pontoon bridge; **les Ponts et chaussées** (*service*) the highways department, department of civil engineering; (*école*) school of civil engineering; **ingénieur des Ponts et chaussées** civil engineer; (*Naut*) **pont d'envol** flight deck; (*Antiq*) **le Pont-Euxin** the Euxine Sea; (*Can*) **pont de glace** ice bridge *ou* road; (*Aut*) **pont de graissage** ramp (*in a garage*); **pont-levis** *nm, pl* **ponts-levis** drawbridge; **pont mobile** movable bridge; **pont à péage** tollbridge; (*Naut*) **pont promenade** promenade deck; (*Rail*) **pont roulant** travelling crane; **pont suspendu** suspension bridge; **pont tournant** swing bridge; **pont transbordeur** transporter bridge.

pontage [pɔ̃taʒ] *nm* decking (*Naut*).

ponte[1] [pɔ̃t] *nf* (*action*) laying (of eggs); (*œufs*) eggs, clutch; (*saison*) (egg-)laying season.

ponte[2] [pɔ̃t] *nm* **(a)** (*: *pontife*) big shot*, big boy*, big noise*. **(b)** (*Jeu*) punter.

ponter[1] [pɔ̃te] (1) *vt* (*Naut*) to deck, lay the deck of.

ponter[2] [pɔ̃te] (1) (*Jeu*) **1** *vi* to punt. **2** *vt* to bet.

pontife [pɔ̃tif] *nm* **(a)** (*Rel*) pontiff; *V* **souverain. (b)** (**fig*) big shot*, pundit*.

pontifiant, e [pɔ̃tifjɑ̃, ɑ̃t] *adj personne, ton* pontificating.

pontifical, e, *mpl* **-aux** [pɔ̃tifikal, o] *adj* (*Antiq*) pontifical; (*Rel*) *messe* pontifical; *siège, gardes, états* papal.

pontificat [pɔ̃tifika] *nm* pontificate.

pontifier* [pɔ̃tifje] (7) *vi* to pontificate.

ponton [pɔ̃tɔ̃] *nm* (*plate-forme*) pontoon, (floating) landing stage; (*chaland*) lighter; (*navire*) hulk.

pontonnier [pɔ̃tɔnje] *nm* (*Mil*) pontoneer, pontonier.

pool [pul] *nm* pool (*Comm*).

pop [pɔp] **1** *adj inv musique, art* pop. **ambiance ~** trendy atmosphere.

2 *nm* (*musique*) pop (music); (*art*) pop art.

pope [pɔp] *nm* (Orthodox) priest.

popeline [pɔplin] *nf* poplin.

popote [pɔpɔt] **1** *nf* **(a)** (*: *cuisine*) cooking. **(b)** (*Mil*) mess, canteen. **2** *adj inv* (*) stay-at-home. **il est très ~** he's a real stay-at-home, he never goes out of the house.

popotin* [pɔpɔtɛ̃] *nm* bottom*; *V* **magner.**

populace [pɔpylas] *nf* (*péj*) rabble.

populaire [pɔpylɛʀ] *adj* **(a)** (*du peuple*) *gouvernement, front, croyance, tradition* popular; *démocratie* popular, people's; *république* people's; *mouvement, manifestation* mass, of the people.

(b) (*pour la masse*) *roman, art, chanson* popular; *édition* cheap. **mesures fiscales qui ne sont guère ~s** financial measures which are hardly of help to ordinary people; *V* **bal, soupe.**

(c) (*plébéien*) *goût* common; (*ouvrier*) *milieu, quartier, origines* working-class. **les classes ~s** the working classes.

(d) (*qui plaît*) popular, well-liked. **très ~ auprès des jeunes** very popular with young people, greatly liked by young people.

(e) (*Ling*) *mot, expression* vernacular; *étymologie* popular; *latin* popular.

populairement [pɔpylɛʀmɑ̃] *adv* (*gén*) popularly; *parler* in the vernacular.

populariser [pɔpylaʀize] (1) *vt* to popularize.

popularité [pɔpylaʀite] *nf* popularity.

population [pɔpylasjɔ̃] *nf* (*gén, Bot, Zool*) population. **région à ~ dense/faible** densely/sparsely populated region *ou* area; **~ active/agricole** working/farming population; **la ~ du globe** the world's population, world population; **la ~ scolaire** the school population.

populeux, -euse [pɔpylø, øz] *adj pays, ville* densely populated, populous; *rue* crowded.

populisme [pɔpylism(ə)] *nm* (*Littérat*) populisme (*a literary movement of the 1920s and 1930s which sets out to describe the lives of ordinary people*).

populiste [pɔpylist(ə)] *adj, nmf* (*V* **populisme**) populiste.

populo‡ [pɔpylo] *nm* (*péj: peuple*) ordinary people *ou* folks*; (*foule*) crowd (of people).

porc [pɔʀ] *nm* (*animal*) pig, hog (*US*); (*viande*) pork; (*péj: personne*) pig; (*peau*) pigskin.

porcelaine [pɔʀsəlɛn] *nf* **(a)** (*matière*) porcelain, china; (*objet*) a piece of porcelain. **~ vitreuse** vitreous china; **~ de Saxe/de Sèvres** Dresden/Sèvres china; **~ de Limoges** Limoges porcelain *ou* china(ware). **(b)** (*Zool*) cowrie.

porcelainier, -ière [pɔʀsəlenje, jɛʀ] **1** *adj* china (*épith*), porcelain (*épith*). **2** *nm* (*fabricant*) porcelain *ou* china manufacturer.

porcelet [pɔʀsəlɛ] *nm* piglet.

porc-épic, *pl* **porcs-épics** [pɔʀkepik] *nm* porcupine; (*fig: personne irritable*) prickly customer* *ou* person. (*homme mal rasé*) **tu es un vrai ~** you're all bristly.

porche [pɔʀʃ(ə)] *nm* porch. **sous le ~ de l'immeuble** in the porch *ou* porchway of the flats.

porcher, -ère [pɔʀʃe, ɛʀ] *nm,f* pig-keeper, swineherd†.

porcherie [pɔʀʃəʀi] *nf* (*lit, fig*) pigsty.

porcin, e [pɔʀsɛ̃, in] **1** *adj* (*lit*) porcine; (*fig*) piglike. **2** *nm* pig. **les ~s** swine, pigs.

pore [pɔʀ] *nm* pore. **il sue l'arrogance par tous les ~s** he exudes arrogance from every pore.

poreux, -euse [pɔʀø, øz] *adj* porous.

porno* [pɔʀno] (*abrév de* **pornographique**) **1** *adj* pornographic. **2** *nm* pornography, porn*.

pornographe [pɔʀnɔgʀaf] **1** *nmf* pornographer. **2** *adj* of pornography, pornographic.

pornographie [pɔʀnɔgʀafi] *nf* pornography.

pornographique [pɔʀnɔgʀafik] *adj* pornographic.

porosité [pɔʀozite] *nf* porosity.

porphyre [pɔʀfiʀ] *nm* porphyry.

porphyrique [pɔʀfiʀik] *adj* porphyritic.

port[1] [pɔʀ] **1** *nm* **(a)** (*bassin*) harbour, port; (*Comm*) port; (*ville*) port; (*fig, littér: abri*) port, haven. **sortir du ~** to leave port *ou* harbour; **arriver au ~** (*Naut*) to dock; (*fig*) to reach the finishing straight; **arriver à bon ~** to arrive intact, arrive safe and sound; **~ de commerce/de pêche** commercial/fishing port; (*fig*) **un ~ dans la tempête** a port in a storm.

(b) *[Pyrénées]* pass.

2: port artificiel artificial harbour; **port d'attache** (*Naut*) port of registry; (*fig*) home base; **port fluvial** river port; **port franc** free port; **port maritime** seaport.

port[2] [pɔʀ] *nm* **(a)** (*fait de porter*) *[objet]* carrying; *[habit, barbe, décoration]* wearing. **le ~ du casque est obligatoire** safety helmets *ou* crash helmets (*Aut*) must be worn; **~ d'armes prohibées** illegal carrying of firearms; (*Mil*) **se mettre au ~ d'armes** to shoulder arms.

(b) (*prix*) (*poste*) postage; (*transport*) carriage. **franco** *ou* **franc de ~** carriage paid; **(en) ~ dû/payé** postage due/paid.

(c) (*comportement*) bearing, carriage. **elle a un ~ majestueux** *ou* **de reine** she has a noble *ou* majestic *ou* queenly bearing; **elle a un joli ~ de tête** she holds her head very nicely.

(d) (*Mus*) **~ de voix** portamento.

portable [pɔʀtabl(ə)] *adj vêtement* wearable; (*portatif*) portable.

portage [pɔʀtaʒ] *nm [marchandise]* porterage; (*Naut, aussi Can*) portage.

portager [pɔʀtaʒe] (3) *vi* (*Can*) to portage.

portail [pɔʀtaj] *nm* portal.

portant, e [pɔʀtɑ̃, ɑ̃t] **1** *adj* **(a)** *mur* structural, supporting; *roue* running. (*Aviat*) **surface ~e** aerofoil (*Brit*), airfoil (*US*).

(b) être bien/mal ~ to be healthy *ou* in good health/in poor health; *V* **bout.**

2 *nm* (*anse*) handle; (*Théât*) upright.

portatif, -ive [pɔʀtatif, iv] *adj* portable.

porte [pɔʀt(ə)] **1** *nf* **(a)** *[maison, voiture, meuble]* door; *[forteresse, jardin]* gate; (*seuil*) doorstep; (*embrasure*) doorway. **franchir** *ou* **passer la ~** to go through *ou* come through the door(way); **sonner à la ~** to ring the (door)bell; **c'est à ma ~** it's close by, it's on the doorstep; **le bus me descend à ma ~** the bus stops at my (front) door *ou* takes me to my door; **le bus me met à ma ~** the bus stops at my (front) door *ou* takes me to my door; **j'ai trouvé ce colis à ma ~** I found this parcel on my doorstep; **ils se réfugièrent sous la ~** they took shelter in the doorway; **nous habitons ~ à ~** we live next door to each other, they are our next-door neighbours; **il y a 100 km/j'ai mis 2 heures de ~ à ~** it's 100 km/it took me 2 hours from door to door; **de ~ en ~** from house to house; **faire du ~ à ~** (*vendre*) to sell from door to door, be a door-to-door salesman; (*chercher du travail*) to go from firm to firm, go round all the firms; **l'ennemi est à nos ~s** the enemy is at our gate(s); **Dijon, ~ de la Bourgogne** Dijon, the gateway to Burgundy; *V* **aimable, casser, clef** *etc.*

(b) *[écluse]* (lock) gate; (*Ski*) gate.

(c) (*loc*) **à la ~!** (get) out!; **être à la ~** to be locked out; **mettre** *ou* **flanquer* qn à la ~** (*licencier*) to sack sb*, give sb the sack*; (*Scol*) to expel sb; (*Univ*) to send sb down; (*éjecter*) to throw *ou* boot* sb out; **claquer/fermer la ~ au nez de qn** to slam/shut the door in sb's face; (*fig*) **entrer** *ou* **passer par la petite ~/la grande ~** to start at the bottom/at the top; **fermer** *ou* **refuser sa ~ à qn** to close the door to sb, bar sb from one's house; **frapper à la bonne ~** to strike lucky, hit on* *ou* get hold of the right person; **frapper à la mauvaise ~** to be out of luck, get hold of the wrong person; **c'est la ~ ouverte** *ou* **c'est ouvrir la ~ à tous les abus** it means leaving the door wide open *ou* the way open to all sorts of abuses, if that happens, it'll mean anything goes*; **toutes les ~s lui sont ouvertes** every door is open to him; **laisser la ~ ouverte à un compromis** to leave the door open for a compromise; **aux ~s de la mort** at death's door; **parler à qn entre deux ~s** to have a quick word with sb, speak to sb very briefly *ou* in passing; **recevoir qn entre deux ~s** to meet sb very briefly *ou* in passing; **prendre la ~** to go away, leave; **aimable** *ou* **souriant comme une ~ de prison** like a bear with a sore head.

2: portes du Ciel gates of Heaven; **porte cochère** carriage entrance, porte-cochère; **porte à deux battants** double door *ou* gate; (*Aviat*) **porte d'embarquement** departure gate; **portes de l'Enfer** gates of Hell; **porte d'entrée** front door; **porte-fenêtre** *nf, pl* **portes-fenêtres** French window; (*Géog*) **les Portes de Fer** the Iron Gate(s); **porte palière** landing door, door opening onto the landing; **porte de secours** emergency exit *ou* door; **porte de service** tradesman's (*surtout Brit*) *ou* rear entrance; **porte de sortie** (*lit*) exit, way out; (*fig*) way out, let-out*; (*Hist*) **la Porte Sublime** the Sublime Porte.

porte- [pɔʀt(ə)] *préf V* **porter.**
porté, e[1] [pɔʀte] (*ptp de* **porter**) *adj*: **être ~ à faire** to be apt *ou* inclined to do, tend to do; **nous sommes ~s à croire que ...** we are inclined to believe that ... ; **être ~ à la colère/à l'exagération** to be prone to anger/exaggeration; **être ~ sur qch** to be keen on *ou* fond of sth, be partial to sth; **être ~ sur la chose*** to be always at it* *ou* on the job*, to be a randy one.
portée[2] [pɔʀte] *nf* **(a)** (*distance*) range, reach; *[fusil]* range; *[cri, voix]* carrying-distance, reach. **canon à faible/longue ~** short-/long-range cannon; **à ~ de la main** within (arm's) reach, at *ou* on hand; **restez à ~ de voix** stay within earshot; **restez à ~ de vue** don't go out of sight; (*fig*) **cet hôtel est/n'est pas à la ~ de toutes les bourses** this hotel is/is not within everyone's means *ou* reach, this hotel suits/does not suit everyone's purse; **ne laissez pas les médicaments à ~ de main** *ou* **à la ~ des enfants** keep medicines out of reach of children; **hors de ~** out of reach *ou* range; **hors de ~ de fusil/de voix** out of rifle range/earshot.
(b) (*capacité*) *[intelligence]* reach, scope, capacity; (*niveau*) level. **ce concept dépasse la ~ de l'intelligence ordinaire** this concept is beyond the reach *ou* scope *ou* capacity of the average mind; **être à la ~ de qn** to be understandable to sb, be at sb's level, be within sb's capability; **il faut savoir se mettre à la ~ des enfants** you have to be able to come down to a child's level.
(c) (*effet*) *[parole, écrit]* impact, import; *[acte]* significance, consequences. **il ne mesure pas la ~ de ses paroles/ses actes** he doesn't think about the import of what he's saying/the consequences of his actions; **la ~ de cet événement est incalculable** this event will have far-reaching consequences *ou* repercussions; **sans ~ pratique** of no practical consequence *ou* importance *ou* significance.
(d) (*Archit*) (*poussée*) loading; (*distance*) span.
(e) (*Mus*) stave, staff.
(f) (*Vét*) litter.
portefaix†† [pɔʀtəfɛ] *nm inv* porter.
portefeuille [pɔʀtəfœj] *nm [argent]* wallet, billfold (*US*); (*Bourse, Pol*) portfolio. **avoir un ~ bien garni** to be well-off; *V* **lit, ministre.**
portemanteau, *pl* **~x** [pɔʀtmɑ̃to] *nm* **(a)** (*cintre*) coat hanger; (*accroché au mur*) coat rack; (*sur pied*) hat stand. **accrocher une veste au ~** to hang up a jacket. **(b)** (††: *malle*) portmanteau.
porter [pɔʀte] (1) **1** *vt* **(a)** *parapluie, paquet, valise* to carry; (*fig*) *responsabilité* to bear, carry. **~ un enfant dans ses bras/sur son dos** to carry a child in one's arms/on one's back; **pouvez-vous me ~ ma valise?** can you carry my case for me?; **laisse-toi ~ par la vague pour bien nager** to swim well let yourself be carried by the waves; **ses jambes ne le portent plus** his legs can no longer carry him; **ce pont n'est pas fait pour ~ des camions** this bridge isn't meant to carry lorries *ou* for lorries *ou* can't take the weight of a lorry; (*Mil*) **portez ... armes!** present ... arms!; **la tige qui porte la fleur** the stem which bears the flower; **cette poutre porte tout le poids du plafond** this beam bears *ou* carries *ou* takes the whole weight of the ceiling; (*fig*) **~ sa croix** to carry one's cross; (*fig*) **~ le poids de ses fautes** to bear the weight of one's mistakes.
(b) (*amener*) to take. **~ qch à qn** to take sth to sb; **porte-lui ce livre** take this book to him, take him this book; **~ des lettres/un colis à qn** to deliver letters/a parcel to sb; **je vais ~ la lettre à la boîte** I'm going to take the letter to the postbox, I'm going to put this letter in the postbox; **~ les plats sur la table** to put the dishes on the table; **~ qn sur le lit** to put *ou* lay sb on the bed; **~ la main à son front** to put one's hand to one's brow; **~ la main à son chapeau** to lift one's hand to one's hat; **~ qch à sa bouche** to lift *ou* put sth to one's lips; **~ de l'argent à la banque** to take some money to the bank; **se faire ~ à manger** to have food brought (to one); **~ l'affaire sur la place publique/devant les tribunaux** to take *ou* carry the matter into the public arena/before the courts; **~ la nouvelle à qn** to take *ou* carry the news to sb, let sb know *ou* have the news; (*Ciné, Théât*) **~ une œuvre à l'écran/à la scène** to transfer a work to the screen/to the stage; **cela porte chance/malheur** it brings (good) luck/misfortune, it's lucky/unlucky; **cela porte bonheur** it brings good fortune, it's lucky; **~ chance/malheur à qn** to be lucky/unlucky for sb, bring sb (good) luck/misfortune; **~ bonheur à qn** to be lucky for sb, bring sb good fortune; (*Prov*) **~ de l'eau à la rivière** to carry coals to Newcastle; (*littér*) **portant partout la terreur et la mort** carrying fear and death everywhere.
(c) *vêtement, bague, laine* to wear; *armes héraldiques* to bear; *barbe* to have, wear; *nom* to have, bear. **~ les cheveux longs** to wear one's hair long, have long hair; **~ le nom d'une fleur** to be called after a flower, bear the name of a flower (*frm*); **~ le nom de Jérôme** to be called Jerome; **il porte bien son nom** his name suits him; **elle porte bien le pantalon** trousers suit her; **le chameau porte deux bosses** the camel has two humps; **les jupes se portent très courtes** very short skirts are in fashion *ou* are the fashion, skirts are being worn very short; **cela ne se porte plus** that's out of fashion, nobody wears that any more.
(d) (*tenir*) to hold, keep. **~ la tête haute** (*lit*) to hold *ou* keep one's head up; (*fig*) to hold one's head high; **~ le corps en avant** to lean *ou* stoop forward.
(e) (*montrer*) *signe, trace* to show, bear; *blessure, cicatrice* to bear; *inscription, date* to bear. **il porte la bonté sur son visage** he has a very kind(-looking) face, his face is a picture of kindness; **ce livre porte un beau titre** this book has a fine title; **la lettre porte la date du 12 mai** the letter bears the date of *ou* is dated May 12th.
(f) (*inscrire*) *nom* to write down, put down (*sur* on, in); (*Comm*) *somme* to enter (*sur* in). **~ de l'argent au crédit d'un compte** to credit an account with some money; **nous portons cette somme à votre débit** we are debiting this sum to your account; **se faire ~ absent** to go absent; **se faire ~ malade** to report sick; **porté disparu/au nombre des morts** reported missing/dead; **porté manquant** unaccounted for.
(g) (*diriger*) *regard* to direct, turn (*sur, vers* towards); *choix* to direct (*sur* towards); *attention* to turn, give (*sur* to), focus (*sur* on); *effort* to direct (*sur* towards); *pas* to turn (*vers* towards); *coup* to deal (*à* to); *accusation* to make (*contre* against); *attaque* to make (*contre* on). **il fit ~ son attention sur ce détail** he turned *ou* focused his attention on this detail; **il fit ~ son choix sur ce livre** his choice fell on this book.
(h) (*ressentir*) *amour, haine* to have, feel, bear (*à* for); *reconnaissance* to feel (*à* to, towards). **~ de l'amitié à qn** to feel friendship towards sb.
(i) (*faire arriver*) to bring. **~ qn au pouvoir** to bring *ou* carry sb to power; **~ qch à sa perfection/à son paroxysme/à l'apogée** to bring sth to perfection/to a peak/to a climax; **~ la température à 800°/le salaire à 2.000 F/la vitesse à 30 nœuds** to bring the temperature up to 800°/the salary up to 2,000 francs/the speed up to 30 knots; **cela porte le nombre de blessés à 20** that brings the number of casualties (up) to 20.
(j) (*inciter*) **~ qn à faire qch** to prompt *ou* induce *ou* lead sb to do sth; **cela le portera à l'indulgence** that will prompt him to be indulgent *ou* make him indulgent; **tout (nous) porte à croire que...** everything leads us to believe that ... ; *V* **porté.**
(k) (*Méd*) *enfant* to carry; (*Vét*) *petits* to carry; (*Fin*) *intérêts* to yield; (*Bot*) *graines, fruit* to bear; *récolte, moisson* to yield. **cette ardeur/haine qu'il portait en lui** this ardour/hatred which he carried with him; **je ne le porte pas dans mon cœur** I am not exactly fond of him; **idée qui porte en soi les germes de sa propre destruction** idea which carries (within itself) *ou* bears the seeds of its own destruction; (*fig*) **~ ses fruits** to bear fruit.
(l) (*conduire*) to carry; (*entraîner*) *[foi]* to carry along; *[vent]* to carry away. **se laisser ~ par la foule** to (let o.s.) be carried away by the crowd.
2 *vi* **(a)** *[bruit, voix, canon]* to carry. **le son/le coup a porté à 500 mètres** the sound/the shot carried 500 metres.
(b) *[reproche, coup]* **~ (juste)** to hit *ou* strike home; **tous les coups portaient** every blow told; **un coup qui porte** a telling blow; **ses conseils ont porté** his advice had some effect *ou* was of some use.
(c) (*Méd*) *[femme]* to carry her child *ou* baby; (*Vét*) *[animal]* to carry its young.
(d) **~ sur** *[édifice, pilier]* to be supported by *ou* on; (*fig*) *[débat, cours]* to turn on, revolve around, be about; *[revendications, objection]* to concern; *[étude, effort, action]* to be concerned with, focus on; *[accent]* to fall on. **tout le poids du plafond porte sur cette poutre** the whole weight of the ceiling falls on *ou* is supported by this beam; **la question portait sur des auteurs au programme** the question turned on *ou* revolved around some of the authors on the syllabus; **il a fait ~ son exposé sur la situation économique** in his talk he concentrated *ou* focused on the economic situation.
(e) (*frapper*) **sa tête a porté sur le bord du trottoir** his head struck the edge of the pavement; **c'est la tête qui a porté** his head took the blow.
(f) **~ à faux** *[mur]* to be out of plumb *ou* true; *[rocher]* to be precariously balanced; (*fig*) *[remarque]* to come *ou* go amiss.
3 se porter *vpr* **(a)** *[personne]* **se ~ bien/mal** to be well/unwell; **comment vous portez-vous? — je me porte bien** how are you? — I'm fine *ou* I'm very well; **se ~ comme un charme** to be fighting fit, be as fit as a fiddle*; **buvez moins, vous ne vous en porterez que mieux** drink less and you'll feel better for it; **et je ne m'en suis pas plus mal porté** and I didn't come off any worse for it, and I was no worse off for it; *V* **pont.**
(b) (*se présenter comme*) **se ~ candidat** to put o.s. up *ou* stand as a candidate; **se ~ acquéreur (de)** to put in a bid (for).
(c) (*se diriger*) *[soupçon, choix]* **se ~ sur** to fall on; **son regard se porta sur moi** his eyes fell on me, his gaze focused on me; **son attention se porta sur ce point** he focused *ou* concentrated his attention on this point.
(d) (*aller*) to go. **se ~ à la rencontre** *ou* **au-devant de qn** to go to meet sb.
(e) (*se laisser aller*) **se ~ à** *voies de fait, violences* to commit; **se ~ à des extrémités** to go to extremes.
4: porte-aiguille *nm, pl* **porte-aiguille(s)** needle case; **porte-avions** *nm inv* aircraft carrier; **porte-bagages** *nm inv* (luggage) rack; **porte-bonheur** *nm inv* lucky charm; **acheter du muguet porte-bonheur** to buy lily of the valley for good luck; **porte-bouteilles** *nm inv* (*à anse*) bottle-carrier; (*à casiers*) wine rack; (*hérisson*) bottle-drainer; **porte-carte(s)** *nm inv [cartes d'identité]* card holder; *[cartes géographiques]* map wallet; **porte-cigares** *nm inv* cigar case; **porte-cigarettes** *nm inv* cigarette case; **porte-clefs** *nm inv* (*anneau*) key ring; (*étui*) key case; (††: *geôlier*) turnkey††; **porte-couteau** *nm, pl* **porte-couteau(x)** knife rest; **porte-crayon** *nm, pl* **porte-crayon(s)** pencil holder; **porte-documents** *nm inv* attaché case, document case; (*lit, fig*) **porte-drapeau** *nm, pl* **porte-drapeau(x)** standard bearer; **porte-étendard**†† *nm inv* standard bearer; **porte-à-faux** *nm inv [mur]* slant; *[rocher]* precarious balance, overhang; (*Archit*) cantilever; **en porte-à-faux** slanting, out of plumb; precariously balanced, overhanging; cantilevered; (*fig*) *personne* in an awkward position (*fig*); **porte-greffe** *nm, pl* **porte-greffe(s)** stock (*for graft*); **porte-hélicoptères** *nm inv* helicopter carrier; **porte-jarretelles** *nm inv* suspender belt (*Brit*), garter belt (*US*); **porte-jupe** *nm, pl* **porte-jupe(s)** skirt hanger; **porte-menu** *nm inv* menu holder; **porte-mine** *nm, pl* **porte-mine(s)** propelling pencil; **porte-monnaie** *nm inv* purse; **faire appel au porte-monnaie de qn** to ask sb to dip into his pocket; **avoir le porte-monnaie bien garni** to be well-off; **porte-musique** *nm inv*

music case; porte-outil *nm, pl* porte-outil(s) chuck (*Tech*); porte-parapluies *nm inv* umbrella stand; porte-parole *nm inv* (*homme*) spokesman; (*femme*) spokeswoman; se faire le porte-parole de qn to act as spokesman for sb, speak on sb's behalf; journal qui est le porte-parole d'un parti newspaper which is the mouthpiece *ou* organ of a party; porte-plume *nm inv* penholder; porte-revues *nm inv* magazine rack; porte-savon *nm, pl* porte-savon(s) soapdish; porte-serviettes *nm inv* towel rail; porte-valise *nm, pl* porte-valise(s) luggage stand; porte-voix *nm inv* megaphone; (*électrique*) loudhailer; mettre ses mains en porte-voix to cup one's hands round one's mouth.

porteur, -euse [pɔʀtœʀ, øz] 1 *adj fusée* booster; *courant* carrier. onde ~euse carrier (wave).

2 *nm,f [valise, colis]* porter; *[message]* messenger; *[chèque]* bearer; *[titre, actions]* holder. ~ d'eau water carrier; ~ de journaux newsboy, paper boy; le ~ du message the bearer of the message; il arriva ~ d'une lettre/d'une nouvelle alarmante he came bearing a letter/an alarming piece of news; il était ~ de faux papiers he was carrying forged papers; (*Méd*) être ~ de germes to be a germ carrier; (*Sport*) le ~ du ballon the holder of the football, the person who is holding the football; (*Fin*) payable au ~ payable to bearer; (*Fin*) les petits/gros ~s small/big shareholders.

portier [pɔʀtje] *nm* commissionaire, porter. (*Rel*) (frère) ~ porter.

portière [pɔʀtjɛʀ] *nf* (a) (*Aut, Rail*) door. (b) (*rideau*) portiere. (c) (*Rel*) (sœur) ~ portress.

portillon [pɔʀtijɔ̃] *nm* gate; *[métro]* gate, barrier; *V* bousculer.

portion [pɔʀsjɔ̃] *nf [héritage]* portion, share; (*Culin*) portion, helping; (*partie*) portion, section, part. (*fig*) être réduit à la ~ congrue to get the smallest *ou* meanest share; bonne/mauvaise ~ de route good/bad stretch of road.

portique [pɔʀtik] *nm* (*Archit*) portico; (*Sport*) crossbar.

porto [pɔʀto] *nm* port (wine).

Porto [pɔʀto] *n* Oporto.

portoricain, e [pɔʀtɔʀikɛ̃, ɛn] 1 *adj* Puerto Rican. 2 *nm,f*: P~(e) Puerto Rican.

Porto Rico [pɔʀtɔʀiko] *nf* Puerto Rico.

portrait [pɔʀtʀɛ] *nm* (a) (*peinture*) portrait; (*photo*) photograph; (*: *visage*) face, mug*. ~ fidèle good likeness; (*Police*) ~-robot Identikit picture ®, photo-fit picture; (*fig*) identikit picture, profile; c'est tout le ~ de son père he's the spitting image *ou* the very spit* (*Brit*) of his father; faire le ~ de qn to paint sb's portrait; se faire tirer le ~* to have one's photograph taken; se faire abîmer le ~* to have one's face *ou* head bashed in* *ou* smashed*.

(b) (*description*) portrait, description. faire *ou* tracer le ~ de qn to draw a portrait of *ou* describe sb; ~-charge caricature; jouer aux ~s to play twenty questions.

(c) (*genre*) le ~ portraiture.

portraitiste [pɔʀtʀetist(ə)] *nmf* portrait painter, portraitist.

portraiturer [pɔʀtʀetyʀe] (1) *vt* (*lit, fig*) to portray.

portuaire [pɔʀtɥɛʀ] *adj* port (*épith*), harbour (*épith*).

portugais, e [pɔʀtygɛ, ɛz] 1 *adj* Portuguese.

2 *nm* (a) P~ Portuguese.

(b) (*Ling*) Portuguese.

3 portugaise *nf* (a) P~e Portuguese.

(b) (*huître*) Portuguese oyster. (*: *oreille*) il a les ~es ensablées he's a real cloth-ears* (*Brit*).

Portugal [pɔʀtygal] *nm* Portugal.

pose [poz] *nf* (a) (*installation*) *[tableau, rideaux]* hanging, putting up; *[tapis]* laying, putting down; *[moquette]* fitting, laying; *[vitre]* putting in, fixing (in); *[serrure]* fixing (on), fitting; *[chauffage]* installation, putting in; *[gaz, électricité]* laying on, installation; *[canalisations]* laying, putting in; *[fondations, mines, voie ferrée]* laying.

(b) (*attitude*) pose, posture; (*Art*) pose. garder la ~ to hold the pose; prendre une ~ to strike a pose.

(c) (*Phot*) (*vue*) exposure. un film (de) 36 ~s a 36-exposure film; déterminer le temps de ~ to decide on the exposure (time); mettre le bouton sur ~ to set the button to time exposure; prendre une photo en ~ *ou* à la ~ to take a photo in time exposure.

(d) (*fig: affectation*) posing, pretention. parler avec/sans ~ to speak pretentiously/quite unpretentiously *ou* naturally.

posé, e [poze] (*ptp de* poser) *adj* (a) (*pondéré*) *personne, caractère, air* serious, sedate, staid; *attitude, allure* steady, sober. c'est un garçon ~ he has his head firmly on his shoulders, he's level-headed; d'un ton ~ mais ferme calmly but firmly.

(b) (*Mus*) bien/mal ~ *voix* steady/unsteady.

posément [pozemɑ̃] *adv parler* calmly, deliberately, steadily; *agir* calmly, unhurriedly.

posemètre [pozmɛtʀ(ə)] *nm* exposure meter.

poser [poze] (1) 1 *vt* (a) (*placer*) *objet* to put (down), lay (down), set down; (*debout*) to stand (up), put (up); (*Math*) *opération, chiffres* to write, set down. (*ôter*) ~ son manteau/chapeau to take off one's coat/hat; ~ qch sur une table/par terre to put sth (down) on the table/on the floor; ~ sa main/tête sur l'épaule de qn to put *ou* lay one's hand/head on sb's shoulder; ~ sa tête sur l'oreiller to lay one's head on the pillow; ~ une échelle contre un mur to lean *ou* stand *ou* put (up) a ladder against a wall; où ai-je posé mes lunettes? where have I put my glasses?; (*fig*) il a posé son regard *ou* les yeux sur la fille he looked at the girl, his gaze came to rest on the girl; le pilote posa son avion en douceur the pilot brought his plane down *ou* landed his plane gently; (*Mus*) ~ la voix de qn to train sb's voice; (*Math*) je pose 4 et je retiens 3 (I) put down 4 and carry 3, 4 and 3 to carry; ~ un lapin à qn* to stand sb up*.

(b) (*installer*) *tableau, rideaux* to hang, put up; *tapis, carrelage* to lay, put down; *moquette* to fit, lay; *vitre* to put in, fix in; *serrure* to fix on, fit; *chauffage* to put in, install; *gaz, électricité* to lay on, install; *canalisations* to lay, put in; *fondations, mines, voie ferrée* to lay. ~ la première pierre (*lit, fig*) to lay the foundation stone; ~ des étagères au mur to fix *ou* put some shelves *ou* shelving on the wall, fix *ou* put up some wall-shelves; ~ des jalons (*lit*) to put stakes up; (*fig*) to prepare the ground, pave the way.

(c) (*fig: énoncer*) *principe, condition* to lay *ou* set down, set out, state; *question* to ask; (*à un examen*) to set; *problème* to pose, formulate; *devinette* to set. ~ une question à qn to ask sb a question, put a question to sb; l'ambiguïté de son attitude pose la question de son honnêteté his ambivalent attitude makes you wonder how honest he is; son cas nous pose un sérieux problème his case poses a difficult problem for us, his case presents us with a difficult problem; la question me semble mal posée I think the question is badly put; (*Pol*) ~ la question de confiance to ask for a vote of confidence; ~ sa candidature à un poste to apply for a post, submit an application for a post; (*Pol*) ~ sa candidature to put o.s. up *ou* run (*US*) for election; dire cela, c'est ~ que ... in saying that, one is supposing that *ou* taking it for granted that ... ; ceci posé supposing that this is (*ou* was *etc*) the case, assuming this to be the case; posons que ... let us suppose *ou* take it that ... .

(d) (*donner de l'importance*) to give standing to; (*professionnellement*) to establish the reputation of. voilà ce qui pose un homme that's what sets a man up; avoir un frère ministre, ça vous pose!* having a brother who's a cabinet minister really makes people look up to you! *ou* gives you real status!; une maison comme ça, ça (vous) pose* with a house like that people really think you are somebody.

2 *vi* (a) (*Art, Phot*) to pose, sit (*pour* for); (*fig*) to swank, show off, put on airs. (*hum*) ~ pour la postérité to pose for posterity; (*fig*) ~ pour la galerie to play to the gallery.

(b) (*jouer à*) ~ au grand patron/à l'artiste to play *ou* act the big businessman/the artist, pretend to be a big businessman/an artist.

(c) (*Constr*) *[poutre]* ~ sur to bear *ou* rest on, be supported by.

3 se poser *vpr* (a) *[insecte, oiseau]* to come down, land, settle, alight (*sur* on); *[avion]* to land, touch down; *[regard]* to (come to) rest, settle, fix (*sur* on). (*Aviat*) se ~ en catastrophe/sur le ventre to make an emergency landing/a belly-landing; son regard se posa sur la pendule he turned his eyes to the clock; une main se posa soudain sur son épaule a hand was suddenly laid on his shoulder; pose-toi là* sit down here.

(b) *[personne]* se ~ comme *ou* en tant que victime to pretend *ou* claim to be a victim; se ~ en chef/en expert to pass o.s. off as *ou* pose as a leader/an expert.

(c) *[question, problème]* to come up, crop up, arise. la question qui se pose the question which must be asked *ou* considered; le problème qui se pose the problem we are faced with *ou* we must face; le problème ne se pose pas dans ces termes the problem shouldn't be stated in these terms; il se pose la question des passeports the question of passports arises, there's the question of passports; il se pose la question de savoir s'il viendra there's the question of (knowing) whether he'll come; je me pose la question that's the question, that's what I'm wondering; il commence à se ~ des questions he's beginning to wonder *ou* to have his doubts; il y a une question que je me pose there's one thing I'd like to know, there's one question I ask myself.

(d) (**loc*) se ~ là: comme menteur, vous vous posez (un peu) là! you're a terrible *ou* an awful liar!; comme erreur, ça se posait (un peu) là! that was (quite) some mistake!*; tu as vu leur chien? il se pose là! have you seen their dog? it's enormous! *ou* a whopper!*

poseur, -euse [pozœʀ, øz] 1 *adj* affected. 2 *nm,f* (a) (*péj*) show-off, poseur. (b) (*ouvrier*) ~ de carrelage/de tuyaux tile/pipe layer; ~ d'affiches billsticker.

positif, -ive [pozitif, iv] 1 *adj* (*gén, Ling, Sci*) positive; *fait, preuve* positive, definite; *personne, esprit* pragmatic, down-to-earth; *action, idée* positive, constructive; *avantage* positive, real. (*sang*) Rhésus ~ Rhesus positive.

2 *nm* (a) (*réel*) positive, concrete. je veux du ~! I want something positive!

(b) (*Mus*) (*clavier d'un orgue*) choir organ (*division of organ*); (*instrument*) positive organ.

(c) (*Phot*) positive.

(d) (*Ling*) positive (degree). au ~ in the positive (form).

position [pozisjɔ̃] *nf* (a) (*gén, Ling, Mil: emplacement*) position. ~ de défense/fortifiée defensive/fortified position; (*lit, fig*) rester sur ses ~s to stand one's ground; abandonner ses ~s to retreat, abandon one's position, withdraw; se replier *ou* se retirer sur des ~s préparées à l'avance to fall back on positions prepared in advance; avoir une ~ de repli (*Mil*) to have a position to fall back on; (*fig*) to have secondary proposals to make, have other proposals to fall back on *ou* other proposals in reserve; la ville jouit d'une ~ idéale the town is ideally situated; les joueurs ont changé de ~ the players have changed position(s); être en première/seconde/dernière ~ (*dans une course*) to be in the lead/in second place/last; (*sur une liste*) to be at the top of the list/second on the list/at the bottom *ou* end of the list; arriver en première/deuxième/dernière ~ to come first/second/last; (*Ling*) syllabe en ~ forte/faible stressed/unstressed syllable, syllable in (a) stressed/(an) unstressed position; (*Ling*) voyelle en ~ forte/faible stressed *ou* strong/unstressed *ou* weak vowel; *V* feu[1], guerre.

(b) (*posture*) position. dormir dans une mauvaise ~ to sleep in the wrong position; (*Mil, gén*) se mettre en ~ to take up (one's) position(s), get into position; **en ~!** (get to your) positions!; **en ~ de combat** in a fighting position; **en ~ allongée/assise/verticale** in a reclining/sitting/vertical *ou* upright position.

(c) (*fig: situation*) position, situation; (*dans la société*) position. **être dans une ~ délicate/fausse** to be in a difficult *ou* an awkward position/in a false position; **être en ~ de faire** to be in a position to do; **dans sa ~ il ne peut se permettre une incartade** a man in his position dare not commit an indiscretion; **il occupe une ~ importante** he holds an important position; (†, *hum*) **femme dans une ~ intéressante** woman in a certain condition (*hum, euph*).

(d) (*attitude*) position, stance. **le gouvernement doit définir sa ~ sur cette question** the government must make its position *ou* stance on this question clear; **prendre ~** to take a stand, declare o.s.; *V* **pris**.

(e) (*Fin*) *[compte bancaire]* position. **demander sa ~** to ask how one's account stands.

positivement [pozitivmɑ̃] *adv* (*gén, Sci*) positively. **je ne le sais pas ~** I'm not positive about it.

positivisme [pozitivism(ə)] *nm* positivism.

positiviste [pozitivist(ə)] *adj, nmf* positivist.

positivité [pozitivite] *nf* positivity.

posologie [pozɔlɔʒi] *nf* (*étude*) posology; (*indications*) directions for use, dosage.

possédant, e [pɔsedɑ̃, ɑ̃t] **1** *adj* propertied, wealthy. **2** *nmpl*: **les ~s** the wealthy, the moneyed.

possédé, e [pɔsede] (*ptp de* **posséder**) **1** *adj* possessed (*de* by). **~ du démon** possessed by the devil. **2** *nm,f* person possessed. **crier comme un ~** to cry like one possessed.

posséder [pɔsede] (6) **1** *vt* **(a)** *bien, maison* to possess, own, have; *fortune* to have, possess. **c'est tout ce que je possède** it's all I possess *ou* all I've got; (*fig*) **~ une femme** to possess a woman; **~ le cœur d'une femme** to have captured a woman's heart.

(b) *caractéristique, qualité, territoire* to have, possess; *expérience* to have (had); *diplôme* to have, hold. **cette maison possède une vue magnifique/2 entrées** this house has a magnificent view/2 entrances; **il croit ~ la vérité** he believes that he is in possession of truth *ou* that he possesses the truth.

(c) (*connaître*) *métier, langue* to have a thorough knowledge of, know inside out, know backwards*. **~ la clef de l'énigme** to possess *ou* have the key to the mystery; **~ bien son rôle** to be really on top of *ou* into* one's role *ou* part.

(d) (*égarer*) *[démon]* to possess. **la fureur/jalousie le possède** he is beside himself with *ou* he is overcome with rage/jealousy; **quel démon *ou* quelle rage te possède?** what's got into you?, what's come over you?; *V* **possédé**.

(e) (*: *duper*) **~ qn** to take sb in*; **se faire ~** to be taken in*, be had*.

2 se posséder *vpr*: **elle ne se possédait plus de joie** she was beside herself *ou* was overcome with joy; **lorsqu'il est en colère, il ne se possède pas** when he's angry he loses all self-control.

possesseur [pɔsesœʀ] *nm [bien]* possessor, owner; *[diplôme]* holder; *[titre]* holder, possessor; *[secret]* possessor; *[billet de loterie]* holder. **être ~ de** *objet* to have; *diplôme* to hold; *secret* to possess, have.

possessif, -ive [pɔsesif, iv] **1** *adj* (*gén, Ling*) possessive. **2** *nm* (*Ling*) possessive.

possession [pɔsesjɔ̃] *nf* **(a)** (*fait de posséder*) *[bien]* possession, ownership; *[diplôme]* holding; *[titre]* holding, possession; *[secret]* possession; *[billet de loterie]* holding. **la ~ d'une arme/de cet avantage le rendait confiant** having a weapon/this advantage made him feel confident; **avoir qch en sa ~** to have sth in one's possession; **être en ~ de qch** to be in possession of sth; **tomber en la ~ de qn** to come into sb's possession; **prendre ~ de, entrer en ~ de** *fonction* to take up; *bien, héritage* to take possession of, enter into possession of; *appartement* to take possession of; *voiture* to take delivery of; **être en ~ de toutes ses facultés** to be in possession of all one's faculties; **être en pleine ~ de ses moyens** to be in full possession of one's health.

(b) (*chose possédée*) possession. **nos ~s à l'étranger** our overseas possessions.

(c) (*maîtrise*) **~ de soi** self-control; **reprendre ~ de soi-même** to regain one's self-control *ou* one's composure.

(d) (*connaissance*) *[langue]* command, mastery.

(e) (*Rel: envoûtement*) possession.

possibilité [pɔsibilite] *nf* (*gén*) possibility; *[entreprise, projet]* feasibility. **il y a plusieurs ~s** there are several possibilities; **je ne vois pas d'autre ~ (que de faire)** I don't see any other possibility (than to do); **ai-je la ~ de faire du feu/de parler librement?** is it possible for me to light a fire/speak freely?, is there the possibility of (my) lighting a fire/speaking freely?; **~s** (*moyens*) means; (*potentiel*) possibilities, potential; **quelles sont vos ~s de logement?** what means do you have of putting people up?; **les ~s d'une découverte/d'un pays neuf** the possibilities *ou* potential of a discovery/of a new country.

possible [pɔsibl(ə)] **1** *adj* **(a)** (*faisable*) *solution* possible; *projet, entreprise* feasible. **il est ~/il n'est pas ~ de faire** it is possible/impossible to do; **nous avons fait tout ce qu'il était humainement ~ de faire** we've done everything that was humanly possible; **lui serait-il ~ d'arriver plus tôt?** could he possibly *ou* would it be possible for him to come earlier?; **arrivez tôt si (c'est) ~** arrive early if possible *ou* if you can; **c'est parfaitement ~** it's perfectly possible *ou* feasible; **ce n'est pas ~ autrement** there's no other way, otherwise it's impossible; **il n'est pas ~ qu'il soit aussi bête qu'il en a l'air** he can't possibly be as stupid as he looks; **c'est dans les choses ~s** it's a possibility; **la paix a rendu ~ leur rencontre** peace has made a meeting between them possible *ou* has made it possible for them to meet.

(b) (*éventuel*) (*gén*) possible; *danger* possible, potential. **une erreur est toujours ~** a mistake is always possible; **il est ~ qu'il vienne/qu'il ne vienne pas** he may *ou* might (possibly) come/not come, it's possible (that) he'll come/he won't come; **il est bien ~ qu'il se soit perdu en route** he may very well have *ou* it could well be *ou* it's quite possible that he has lost his way; **c'est (bien) ~/très ~** possibly/very possibly.

(c) (*indiquant une limite*) possible. **dans le meilleur des mondes ~s** in the best of all possible worlds; **il a essayé tous les moyens ~s** he tried every possible means *ou* every means possible; **il a eu toutes les difficultés ~s et imaginables à obtenir un visa** he had all kinds of problems getting a visa, he had every possible difficulty getting a visa; **venez aussi vite/aussitôt que ~** come as quickly as possible *ou* as you (possibly) can/as soon as possible *ou* as you (possibly) can; **venez le plus longtemps ~** come for as long as you (possibly) can; **venez le plus vite/tôt ~** come as quickly/as soon as you (possibly) can; **il sort le plus (souvent)/le moins (souvent) ~** he goes out as often/as little as possible *ou* as he can; **il a acheté la valise la plus légère ~** he bought the lightest possible suitcase *ou* the lightest suitcase possible; **le plus grand nombre ~ de personnes** as many people as possible, the greatest possible number of people; *V* **autant**.

(d) (*: *nég: acceptable*) **cette situation n'est plus ~** this situation has become impossible *ou* intolerable *ou* unbearable; **il n'est pas ~ de travailler dans ce bruit** it just isn't possible *ou* it's (quite) impossible to work in this noise.

(e) (*loc*) **est-ce ~!** I don't believe it!; **c'est pas ~!*** (*faux*) that can't be true *ou* right!; (*étonnant*) well I never!*; (*irréalisable*) it's out of the question!, it's impossible!; **ce n'est pas ~ d'être aussi bête!** how can anyone be so stupid!, how stupid can you get!*; **c'est (bien) ~** (quite) possibly; **elle voudrait vous parler — c'est (bien) ~, mais il faut que je parte** she'd like a word with you — that's as may be *ou* quite possibly, but I've got to go; **il devrait se reposer! — c'est (bien) ~, mais il n'a pas le temps** he ought to take a rest! — maybe (he should), but he's too busy.

2 *nm* what is possible. **il fera le ~ et l'impossible pour avoir la paix** he will move heaven and earth *ou* he'll do anything possible to get some peace; **c'est dans le ~ *ou* dans les limites du ~** it is within the realms of possibility; **faire (tout) son ~** to do one's utmost *ou* one's best, do all one can (*pour* to, *pour que* to make sure that); **il a été grossier/aimable au ~** he couldn't have been ruder/nicer (if he'd tried), he was as rude/nice as it's possible to be; **c'est énervant au ~** it's extremely annoying; *V* **mesure**.

post- [pɔst] *préf* post-. **~électoral/surréaliste** *etc* post-election/-surrealist *etc*; *V* **postdater** *etc*.

postal, e, *mpl* **-aux** [pɔstal, o] *adj service, taxe, voiture* postal; *colis* sent by post *ou* mail. **sac ~** postbag, mailbag; *V* **carte, chèque, franchise**.

postdater [pɔstdate] (1) *vt* to postdate.

poste[1] [pɔst(ə)] **1** *nf* **(a)** (*administration, bureau*) post office. **employé/ingénieur des ~s** post office worker/engineer; **les P~s et Télécommunications** Post(s) and Telecommunications, ≃ the G.P.O. (*Brit*), the Post Office Corporation (*Brit*); **la grande ~, la ~ principale, le bureau de ~ principal** the main *ou* head post office.

(b) (*service postal*) post, postal *ou* mail service. **envoyer qch par la ~** to send sth by post *ou* mail; **mettre une lettre à la ~** to post *ou* mail a letter; *V* **cachet**.

(c) (*Hist*) post. **maître de ~** postmaster; **cheval de ~** post horse; **courir la ~** to go posthaste; *V* **chaise, voiture**.

2: **poste aérienne** airmail; **poste auxiliaire** sub post office; **poste restante** poste restante.

poste[2] [pɔst(ə)] **1** *nm* **(a)** (*emplacement*) post. **~ de douane** customs post; **être/rester à son ~** to be/stay at one's post; **mourir à son ~** to die at one's post; **à vos ~s!** to your stations! *ou* posts!; **à vos ~s de combat!** action stations!; (*fig*) **être solide au ~** to be hale and hearty; (*fig*) **toujours fidèle au ~?*** still on the job?*, still manning the fort?*

(b) (*Police*) **~ (de police)** (police) station; **conduire *ou* emmener qn au ~** to take sb to the police station *ou* into custody; **il a passé la nuit au ~** he spent the night in the cells.

(c) (*emploi*) (*gén*) job; *[fonctionnaire]* post, appointment (*frm*); (*dans une hiérarchie*) position; (*nomination*) appointment. **être en ~ à Paris/à l'étranger** to hold an appointment *ou* a post in Paris/abroad; **il a trouvé un ~ de bibliothécaire** he has found a job as a librarian; **il a un ~ de professeur/en fac** he's a teacher/a university lecturer; **la liste des ~s vacants** the list of positions available *ou* of unfilled appointments.

(d) (*Rad, TV*) set. **~ émetteur/récepteur** transmitting/receiving set, transmitter/receiver; **~ de radio/de télévision** radio/television (set); **~ portatif** (*radio*) portable radio; (*télévision*) portable television; **éteindre le ~** to turn the radio *ou* television off.

(e) (*Téléc*) **~ 23** extension 23.

(f) (*Fin*) (*opération*) item, entry; *[budget]* item, element.

(g) (*Ind*) shift. **~ de 8 heures** 8-hour shift.

2: (*Rail*) **poste d'aiguillage** signal box; (*Mil*) **poste avancé** advanced post; **poste budgétaire** post (*budgeted for*); **poste de commandement** headquarters; **poste de contrôle** checkpoint; (*Naut*) **poste d'équipage** crew's quarters; **poste d'essence** petrol *ou* filling station, gas station (*US*); **poste frontière** border *ou* frontier post; (*Mil*) **poste de garde** guardroom; **poste d'incendie** fire point; (*Aut*) **poste de lavage** car wash; **poste d'observation** observation post; (*Aviat*) **poste de pilotage** cockpit; **poste de police** (*Police*) police station; (*Mil*) guardroom, guardhouse; **poste de secours** first-aid post.

poster[1] [pɔste] (1) **1** *vt* **(a)** *lettre* to post, mail. **(b)** *sentinelle* to

post, station. **2 se poster** *vpr* to take up (a) position, position o.s., station o.s.
poster[2] [pɔstɛʀ] *nm* poster.
postérieur, e [pɔsteʀjœʀ] **1** *adj* (*dans le temps*) *date, document* later; *événements* subsequent, later; (*dans l'espace*) *partie* back, posterior (*frm*); *membres* hind, back. **ce document est légèrement/très ~ à cette date** this document dates from slightly later/much later; **l'événement est ~ à 1850** the event took place later than *ou* after 1850; **~ à 1800** after 1800.
2 *nm* (*) behind*, posterior (*hum*).
postérieurement [pɔsteʀjœʀmɑ̃] *adv* later, subsequently. **~ à** after.
posteriori [pɔsteʀjɔʀi] *loc adv*: **à ~** a posteriori.
postériorité [pɔsteʀjɔʀite] *nf* posteriority.
postérité [pɔsteʀite] *nf* (*descendants*) descendants, posterity; (*avenir*) posterity. (*frm*) **mourir sans ~** to die without issue; **entrer dans la ~** to come down to posterity.
postface [pɔstfas] *nf* postscript, postface.
posthume [pɔstym] *adj* posthumous.
postiche [pɔstiʃ] **1** *adj cheveux, moustache* false; (*fig*) *ornement, fioriture* postiche, superadded; *sentiment* pretended. **2** *nm* hairpiece, postiche.
postier, -ière [pɔstje, jɛʀ] *nm,f* post office worker. **grève des ~s** postal *ou* mail strike.
postillon [pɔstijɔ̃] *nm* (*Hist: cocher*) postilion; (*: *salive*) sputter. **envoyer des ~s** to sputter, splutter.
postillonner* [pɔstijɔne] (1) *vi* to sputter, splutter.
postnatal, e, *mpl* **~s** [pɔstnatal] *adj* postnatal.
postopératoire [pɔstɔpeʀatwaʀ] *adj* post-operative.
postposer [pɔstpoze] (1) *vt* to place after. **sujet postposé** postpositive subject, subject placed after the verb.
postposition [pɔstpozisjɔ̃] *nf* postposition. **verbe à ~** phrasal verb.
postscolaire [pɔstskɔlɛʀ] *adj enseignement* further (*épith*).
post-scriptum [pɔstskʀiptɔm] *nm inv* postscript.
postsynchronisation [pɔstsɛ̃kʀɔnizasjɔ̃] *nf* dubbing (*of a film*).
postsynchroniser [pɔstsɛ̃kʀɔnize] (1) *vt* to dub (*a film*).
postulant, e [pɔstylɑ̃, ɑ̃t] *nm,f* applicant; (*Rel*) postulant.
postulat [pɔstyla] *nm* postulate.
postuler [pɔstyle] (1) **1** *vt* **(a)** *emploi* to apply for, put in for. **(b)** *principe* to postulate. **2** *vi* (*Jur*) **~ pour** to represent.
posture [pɔstyʀ] *nf* posture, position. **être en bonne/mauvaise ~** to be in a good/bad position; (†, *littér*) **en ~ de faire** in a position to do.
pot [po] **1** *nm* **(a)** (*récipient*) (*en verre*) jar; (*en terre*) pot; (*en métal*) tin (*Brit*), can (*US*); (*en carton*) carton. **petit ~ pour bébé** jar of baby food; **~ à confiture** jamjar, jampot (*Brit*); **~ de confiture** jar *ou* pot (*Brit*) of jam; **mettre en ~** *fleurs* to pot; *confiture* to put in jars, pot (*Brit*); **plantes en ~** pot plants; **mettre un enfant sur le ~** to put a child on the potty, pot a child; **un particulier qui se bat contre l'administration c'est le ~ de terre contre le ~ de fer** one individual struggling against the authorities can't hope to win; **tu viens prendre** *ou* **boire un ~?*** are you coming for a drink? *ou* for a jar?* (*Brit*); *V* **cuiller, découvrir, fortune** *etc.*
(b) (*: *chance*) luck. **avoir du ~** to be lucky *ou* in luck; **manquer de ~** to be unlucky *ou* out of luck; **pas de** *ou* **manque de ~!** just his (*ou* your *etc*) luck!; **tu as du ~!** some people have all the luck!, you're a lucky begger!* *ou* blighter!* (*Brit*); **c'est un vrai coup de ~!** what a stroke of luck!
(c) (*Cartes*) (*enjeu*) kitty; (*restant*) pile.
2: pot à bière (*en verre*) beer mug; (*en terre ou en métal*) tankard; **pot de chambre** chamberpot; **pot de colle** (*lit*) pot of glue; (*péj: crampon*) leech; **il est du genre pot de colle!** you just can't shake him off!, he sticks like a leech!; **pot à eau** (*pour se laver*) water jug, pitcher; (*pour boire*) water jug; (*Aut*) **pot d'échappement** exhaust pipe; (*silencieux*) silencer; **pot-au-feu** (*nm inv*) (*plat*) (beef) stew; (*viande*) stewing beef; (*adj inv*) (*) stay-at-home; **pot de fleurs** (*récipient*) plant pot, flowerpot; (*fleurs*) pot plant, pot of flowers; **pot à lait** (*pour transporter*) milk can; (*sur la table*) milk jug; **pot-pourri** *nm, pl* **pots-pourris** (*Mus*) potpourri, medley; **pot à tabac** (*lit*) tobacco jar; (*fig*) dumpy little person; **pot de terre** earthenware pot; **pot-de-vin** *nm, pl* **pots-de-vin** bribe, backhander* (*Brit*); **donner un pot-de-vin à qn** to bribe sb, give sb a backhander* (*Brit*), grease sb's palm.
potable [pɔtabl(ə)] *adj* (*lit*) drinkable; (**fig*) reasonable, passable, decent. **eau ~** drinking water; **il ne peut pas faire un travail ~** he can't do a decent piece of work; **le film est ~** the film isn't bad; **ce travail est tout juste ~** this piece of work is barely passable *ou* acceptable.
potache* [pɔtaʃ] *nm* schoolboy, schoolkid*.
potage [pɔtaʒ] *nm* soup.
potager, -ère [pɔtaʒe, ɛʀ] **1** *adj plante* vegetable (*épith*), edible; *jardin* kitchen (*épith*), vegetable (*épith*). **2** *nm* kitchen *ou* vegetable garden.
potasse [pɔtas] *nf* (*hydroxide*) potassium hydroxide, caustic potash; (*carbonate*) potash (*impure potassium carbonate*).
potasser* [pɔtase] (1) **1** *vt livre, discours* to swot up (*Brit*) *ou* cram for; *examen* to swot (*Brit*) *ou* cram for. **2** *vi* to swot (*Brit*), cram.
potassique [pɔtasik] *adj* potassic.
potassium [pɔtasjɔm] *nm* potassium.
pote* [pɔt] *nm* pal*, mate*, chum*, buddy* (*US*).
poteau, *pl* **~x** [pɔto] **1** *nm* **(a)** post. (*Courses*) **rester au ~** to be left at the (starting) post; **elle a les jambes comme des ~x*** she's got legs like tree trunks*.
(b) ~ (d'exécution) execution post, stake (*for execution by shooting*); **envoyer au ~** to sentence to execution by firing squad; **au ~!** lynch him!; **le directeur au ~!** down with the boss!
(c) (*†: *ami*) pal*, buddy* (*US*).
2: poteau d'arrivée winning *ou* finishing post; **poteau de but** goal-post; **poteau de départ** starting post; **poteau indicateur** signpost; **poteau télégraphique** telegraph post *ou* pole.
potée [pɔte] *nf* (*Culin*) ≈ hotpot (*of pork and cabbage*).
potelé, e [pɔtle] *adj enfant* plump, chubby; *bras* plump.
potence [pɔtɑ̃s] *nf* **(a)** (*gibet*) gallows (*sg*); *V* **gibier. (b)** (*support*) bracket. **en ~** (*en équerre*) L-shaped; (*en T*) T-shaped.
potentat [pɔtɑ̃ta] *nm* (*lit*) potentate; (*fig péj*) despot.
potentialité [pɔtɑ̃sjalite] *nf* potentiality.
potentiel, -elle [pɔtɑ̃sjɛl] *adj, nm* (*gén*) potential.
potentiellement [pɔtɑ̃sjɛlmɑ̃] *adv* potentially.
potentiomètre [pɔtɑ̃sjɔmɛtʀ(ə)] *nm* potentiometer.
poterie [pɔtʀi] *nf* (*atelier, art*) pottery; (*objet*) earthenware bowl (*ou* dish *ou* jug *etc*), piece of pottery.
poterne [pɔtɛʀn(ə)] *nf* postern.
potiche [pɔtiʃ] *nf* (large) oriental vase; (*fig*) figurehead.
potier [pɔtje] *nm* potter.
potin* [pɔtɛ̃] *nm* **(a)** (*vacarme*) din*, racket*. **faire du ~** (*lit*) to make a noise; (*fig*) to kick up a fuss*; **ça va faire du ~** (*lit*) there'll be a lot of noise, it'll be noisy; (*fig*) this is going to stir things up*, there'll be quite a rumpus (over this).
(b) (*commérage*) **~s** gossip, tittle-tattle.
potiner [pɔtine] (1) *vi* to gossip.
potion [posjɔ̃] *nf* (*lit*) potion; (*fig*) concoction.
potiron [pɔtiʀɔ̃] *nm* pumpkin.
potron-minet* [pɔtʀɔ̃minɛ] *nm*: **dès ~** at the crack of dawn.
pou, *pl* **~x** [pu] *nm* louse. **couvert de ~x** covered in lice, lice-ridden; *V* **chercher, laid.**
pouah [pwa] *excl* ugh!
poubelle [pubɛl] *nf* [*ordures*] (dust)bin (*Brit*), trash *ou* garbage can (*US*). **c'est bon à mettre à la ~** it's only fit for the dustbin (*Brit*) *ou* trash can (*US*).
pouce [pus] *nm* **(a)** (*Anat*) [*main*] thumb; [*pied*] big toe. **se tourner** *ou* **se rouler les ~s** to twiddle one's thumbs; **se tenir les ~s pour qn*** to cross one's fingers for sb; **mettre les ~s*** to give in *ou* up; (*au jeu*) **~!** pax!, truce!; **on a déjeuné** *ou* **on a pris un morceau sur le ~*** we had a quick snack *ou* a bite to eat*; (*Can**) **faire du ~, voyager sur le ~** to thumb* (a lift), hitch-hike; *V* **coup.**
(b) (*mesure, aussi Can*) inch. (*fig*) **il n'a pas avancé/reculé d'un ~** he refused to budge, he wouldn't budge an inch; **son travail n'a pas avancé d'un ~** his work hasn't progressed at all; **un ~ de terrain** a tiny plot of land; **et le ~!*** and a bit more besides!
Poucet [pusɛ] *nm*: **le Petit ~** Tom Thumb.
Pouchkine [puʃkin] *nm* Pushkin.
pouding [pudiŋ] *nm* = **pudding.**
poudre [pudʀ(ə)] **1** *nf* (*gén*) powder; (*poussière*) dust; (*fard*) (face) powder; (*explosif*) (gun)powder; (*Méd*) powder. **~ d'or/de diamant** gold/diamond dust; **réduire qch en ~** to reduce *ou* grind sth to powder, powder sth; **en ~** *lait, œufs* dried, powdered; *chocolat* drinking (*épith*); **se mettre de la ~** to powder one's face *ou* nose; **se mettre de la ~ sur** to powder; **prendre la ~ d'escampette*** to take to one's heels, skedaddle*; **de la ~ de perlimpinpin** the universal remedy (*iro*), a magic cure-all; *V* **feu**[1]**, inventer, jeter** *etc.*
2: poudre à canon gunpowder; **poudre dentifrice** tooth powder; **poudre à éternuer** sneezing powder; **poudre à laver** washing powder (*Brit*), soap powder; **poudre à récurer** scouring powder; **poudre de riz** face powder.
poudrer [pudʀe] (1) **1** *vt* to powder. **2** *vi* (*Can*) [*neige*] to drift. **3 se poudrer** *vpr* to powder one's face *ou* nose.
poudrerie [pudʀəʀi] *nf* gunpowder factory; (*Can*) blizzard, drifting snow.
poudreux, -euse [pudʀø, øz] **1** *adj* (*poussiéreux*) dusty. **neige ~euse** powder snow; (*Can*) drifting snow. **2 poudreuse** *nf* powder snow.
poudrier [pudʀije] *nm* (powder) compact.
poudrière [pudʀijɛʀ] *nf* powder magazine; (*fig*) powder keg (*fig*).
poudroiement [pudʀwamɑ̃] *nm* dust haze.
poudroyer [pudʀwaje] (8) *vi* [*poussière*] to rise in clouds; [*neige*] to rise in a flurry. **la route poudroie** clouds of dust rise up from the road.
pouf [puf] **1** *nm* pouffe. **2** *excl* thud! **faire ~** to tumble (over).
pouffer [pufe] (1) *vi*: **~ (de rire)** to snigger.
pouffiasse‡ [pufjas] *nf* (*péj*) (*grosse femme*) fat bag‡; (*prostituée*) whore (*péj*), tart‡, broad‡ (*US*).
pouh [pu] *excl* pooh!
pouillerie [pujʀi] *nf* squalor.
pouilleux, -euse [pujø, øz] **1** *adj* **(a)** (*lit*) lousy, flea-ridden, verminous.
(b) (*fig: sordide*) *quartier, endroit* squalid, seedy, shabby; *personne* dirty, filthy.
2 *nm,f* (*pauvre*) down-and-out; (*couvert de poux*) flea-ridden *ou* verminous person.
poulailler [pulaje] *nm* henhouse. (*Théât*) **le ~*** the gods* (*Brit*).
poulain [pulɛ̃] *nm* foal; (*fig*) promising young athlete (*ou* writer *ou* singer *etc*); (*protégé*) protégé.
poulaine [pulɛn] *nf* (*Hist: soulier*) poulaine, long pointed shoe.
poularde [pulaʀd(ə)] *nf* fatted chicken. (*Culin*) **~ demi-deuil** poularde demi-deuil.
poulbot [pulbo] *nm* street urchin (*in Montmartre*).
poule[1] [pul] **1** *nf* **(a)** (*Zool*) hen; (*Culin*) (boiling) fowl. (*fig*) **se lever avec les ~s** to get up with the lark (*Brit*) *ou* birds (*US*), be an early riser; **se coucher avec les ~s** to go to bed early; **quand les ~s auront des dents** when pigs can fly *ou* have wings; **être**

comme une ~ qui a trouvé un couteau to be flustered, be all hot and bothered; *V* **chair, cul, lait.**

(b) (*) (*maîtresse*) mistress; (*fille*) girl, lass*, bird* (*Brit*), chick*; (*prostituée*) whore, broad: (*US*). **ma ~** (my) pet.

2: poule d'eau moorhen; **poule faisane** hen pheasant; **poule mouillée** softy*, coward; **la poule aux œufs d'or** the goose that lays the golden eggs; **poule pondeuse** laying hen, layer; **poule au pot** boiled chicken; **poule au riz** chicken and rice.

poule[2] [pul] *nf* **(a)** (*enjeu*) pool, kitty. **(b)** (*tournoi*) (*gén*) tournament; (*Escrime*) pool; (*Rugby*) group.

poulet [pulɛ] *nm* (*Culin, Zool*) chicken; (*: *flic*) cop*; (††: *billet doux*) love letter. **~ de grain/fermier** corn-fed/free-range (*Brit*) chicken; (*fig*) **mon (petit) ~!*** (my) pet! *ou* love!

poulette [pulɛt] *nf* (*Zool*) pullet; (*: *fille*) girl, lass*, bird* (*Brit*), chick* (*US*). (*fig*) **ma ~!*** (my) pet! *ou* love!; (*Culin*) **sauce ~** sauce poulette.

pouliche [puliʃ] *nf* filly.

poulie [puli] *nf* pulley; (*avec sa caisse*) block. **~ simple/double/fixe** single/double/fixed block; **~ folle** loose pulley.

pouliner [puline] (1) *vi* to foal.

poulinière [pulinjɛʀ] *adj f, nf*: **(jument) ~** brood mare.

poulot, -otte†* [pulo, ɔt] *nm,f*: **mon ~!, ma ~te!** (my) pet! *ou* love! (*said to a child*).

poulpe [pulp(ə)] *nm* octopus.

pouls [pu] *nm* pulse. **prendre** *ou* **tâter le ~ de qn** (*lit*) to feel sb's pulse; (*fig*) to sound sb (out); (*fig*) **prendre** *ou* **tâter le ~ de** *opinion publique* to test, sound out; *économie* to feel the pulse of.

poumon [pumɔ̃] *nm* lung. **respirer à pleins ~s** to breathe in deeply, take deep breaths; **chanter/crier à pleins ~s** to sing/shout at the top of one's voice; **avoir des ~s** *[chanteur, coureur]* to have a good pair of lungs; **~ d'acier** iron lung.

poupard [pupaʀ] **1** *adj* (†) chubby(-cheeked). **2** *nm* bonny (*Brit*) baby, bouncing baby.

poupe [pup] *nf* (*Naut*) stern; *V* **vent.**

poupée [pupe] *nf* **(a)** (*jouet*) doll, dolly*. **~ gigogne** nest of dolls; **elle joue à la ~** she's playing with her doll(s); *V* **maison.**

(b) (**fig*) (*femme jolie ou pomponnée*) doll*; (*fille, maîtresse*) bird*. **bonjour, ~** hullo, sweetie*.

(c) (*pansement*) finger bandage. **faire une ~ à qn** to bandage sb's finger.

poupin, e [pupɛ̃, in] *adj* chubby.

poupon [pupɔ̃] *nm* little baby, babe-in-arms.

pouponner [pupɔne] (1) *vi* to play mother. **tu vas bientôt (pouvoir) ~** soon you'll be the fond mother (*ou* father *etc*).

pouponnière [pupɔnjɛʀ] *nf* day nursery, crèche.

pour [puʀ] **1** *prép* **(a)** (*direction*) for, to. **partir ~ l'Espagne** to leave for Spain; **il part ~ l'Espagne demain** he leaves for Spain *ou* he is off to Spain tomorrow; **partir ~ l'étranger** to go abroad; **le train ~ Londres** the London train, the train for London.

(b) (*temps*) for. **demander/promettre qch ~ le mois prochain/~ dans huit jours/~ après les vacances** to ask for/promise sth for next month/for next week/for after the holidays; **il lui faut sa voiture ~ demain** he must have his car for *ou* by tomorrow; **ne m'attendez pas, j'en ai encore ~ une heure** don't wait for me, I'll be another hour (yet); **~ le moment** *ou* **l'instant** for the moment; **~ toujours** for ever; (*iro*) **c'est ~ aujourd'hui ou ~ demain?** are we getting it *ou* is it coming today? (*iro*) *ou* this side of Christmas? (*iro*); **ce sera ~ des jours meilleurs** we'll have to wait for better days; **garder le meilleur ~ la fin** to keep the best till last *ou* till the end.

(c) (*intention, destination*) for. **faire qch ~ qn** to do sth for sb; **il ferait tout ~ elle/sa mère** he would do anything for her/his mother *ou* for her sake/his mother's sake; **faire qch ~ la gloire/le plaisir** to do sth for the glory/for the pleasure of it *ou* for pleasure; **son amour ~ les bêtes** his love of animals; **quêter ~ les hôpitaux** to collect for *ou* in aid of hospitals; **il travaille ~ un cabinet d'architectes** he works for a firm of architects; **ce n'est pas un livre ~ (les) enfants** it's not a book for children, it's not a children's book; **c'est mauvais/bon ~ vous/~ la santé** it's bad/good for you/for the health; **il a été très gentil ~ ma mère** he was very kind to my mother; **sirop ~ la toux** cough mixture; **pastilles ~ la gorge** throat tablets; **il n'est pas fait ~ le travail de bureau** he's not made for office work; **le plombier est venu/a téléphoné ~ la chaudière** the plumber came/phoned about the boiler; **~ le meilleur et ~ le pire** for better or for worse; **l'art ~ l'art** art for art's sake; *V* **amour, craindre** *etc.*

(d) (*approbation*) for, in favour of. **être ~ la peine de mort** to be for *ou* in favour of the death penalty; **il est ~ protester** he's in favour of protesting *ou* he's (all) for protesting*; **je suis ~!*** I'm all for it*, I'm all in favour (of it); *V* **voter.**

(e) (*point de vue*) **~ moi, le projet n'est pas réalisable** as I see it *ou* in my opinion *ou* in my view the plan cannot be carried out; **~ moi, je suis d'accord** personally *ou* for my part I agree; **ce n'est un secret ~ personne** it's no secret from anyone; **sa fille est tout ~ lui** his daughter is everything to him; **c'est trop compliqué ~ elle** it's too complicated for her.

(f) (*cause*) **être condamné ~ vol** to be convicted for theft; **il a été félicité ~ son audace** he was congratulated on his boldness; **fermé ~ cause de maladie** closed owing to *ou* because of *ou* on account of illness; **fermé ~ réparations** closed for repairs; **quelle histoire ~ si peu** what a fuss *ou* to-do* over *ou* about such a little thing; **il n'en est pas plus heureux ~ cela!** he is none the happier for all that!; **il est furieux et ~ cause!** he's furious and with good reason!; **pourquoi se faire du souci ~ cela?** why worry about that?; **il est ~ quelque chose/~ beaucoup dans le succès de la pièce** he is partly/largely responsible for the success of the play, he had something/a lot to do with the play's success; *V* **beau, oui.**

(g) (*à la place de; en échange de*) **payer ~ qn** to pay for sb; **signez ~ moi** sign in my place *ou* for me; (*Comm etc*) **~ le directeur** p.p. Manager; **il a parlé ~ nous tous** he spoke on behalf of all of us *ou* on our behalf, he spoke for all of us; **en avoir ~ son argent** to have *ou* get one's money's worth; **donnez-moi ~ 30 F d'essence** give me 30 francs' worth of petrol; **il l'a eu ~ 5 F/une bouchée de pain** he got it for 5 francs/for a song; *V* **chacun.**

(h) (*rapport, comparaison*) for. **~ cent/mille** per cent/thousand; **il est petit ~ son âge** he is small for his age; **il fait chaud ~ la saison** it's warm for the time of year; **~ un Anglais, il parle bien le français** he speaks French well for an Englishman; **~ un qui s'intéresse, il y en a 6 qui bâillent** for every one that takes an interest there are 6 (who are) yawning; **c'est mot ~ mot ce qu'il a déjà dit** it's word for word what he has already said; **jour/heure ~ jour/heure** to the (very) day/hour; **mourir ~ mourir, je préfère que ce soit ici** if I have to die I should prefer it to be here; *V* **coup, œil.**

(i) (*rapport d'équivalence: comme*) for, as. **prendre qn ~ femme** to take sb as one's wife; **prendre qn ~ un imbécile** to take sb for an idiot; **il a ~ adjoint son cousin** he has his cousin as his deputy; **il passe ~ filou** he's said to be a crook; **il s'est fait passer ~ fou/~ son patron** he passed himself off as a madman/as his boss; **il a ~ principe/méthode de faire ...** it is his principle/method to do ..., his principle/method is to do ...; **cela a eu ~ effet de** that had the effect of; **~ de bon*** *ou* **de vrai*** truly, really, for real*; *V* **compter, laisser.**

(j) (*emphatique*) **~ (ce qui est de) notre voyage, il faut y renoncer** as for our journey *ou* as far as our journey goes, we'll have to forget it, we'll have to give up all idea of going on that journey; **~ une malchance c'est une malchance!** of all the unfortunate things (to happen)!, that WAS unfortunate and no mistake!; **~ être furieux, je le suis!** talk about furious, I really am!*; **~ sûr*†** for sure *ou* certain.

(k) (+ *infin: but, succession*) to. **trouvez un argument ~ le convaincre** find an argument to convince him *ou* that will convince him; **il est d'accord ~ nous aider** he agrees *ou* he has agreed to help us; **nous avons assez d'argent ~ l'aider** we have enough money to help him; **~ mûrir, les tomates ont besoin de soleil** tomatoes need sunshine to ripen; **je n'ai rien dit ~ ne pas le blesser** I didn't say anything so as not to hurt him; **je n'ai rien dit ~ le blesser** I said nothing to hurt him; **creuser ~ trouver de l'eau/du pétrole** to dig for water/oil; **elle se pencha ~ ramasser son gant** she bent down to pick up her glove; **il étendit le bras ~ prendre la boîte** he reached for the box; **il finissait le soir tard ~ reprendre le travail tôt le lendemain** he finished late at night (only) to start work again early the next morning; **il y a des gens assez innocents ~ le croire** SOME people are unsuspecting enough to believe him; **le travail n'est pas ~ l'effrayer** *ou* **~ lui faire peur** he's not afraid of hard work *ou* of working hard; **il a dit ça ~ rire** *ou* **~ plaisanter** he said it in fun *ou* as a joke; **il est parti ~ ne plus revenir** he left never to return, he left and never came back again; **j'étais ~ partir*** I was just going, I was just about to go; *V* **assez, trop.**

(l) (+ *infin: cause, concession*) **elle a été punie ~ avoir menti** she was punished for lying *ou* having lied; **~ avoir réussi, il n'en est pas plus riche** he's no richer *ou* none the richer for having succeeded *ou* for his success.

(m) ~ que + *subj* so that, in order that (*frm*); **écris vite ta lettre ~ qu'elle parte ce soir** write your letter quickly so (that) it will go *ou* it goes this evening; **il a mis une barrière ~ que les enfants ne sortent pas** he has put up a fence so that the children won't get out; **il est trop tard ~ qu'on le prévienne** it's too late to warn him *ou* for him to be warned; (*iro*) **c'est ça, laisse ton sac là ~ qu'on te le vole!** that's right, leave your bag there for someone to steal it! *ou* so that someone steals it!; **elle est assez grande ~ qu'on puisse la laisser seule** she is old enough (for her) to be left on her own.

(n) (*restriction, concession*) **~ riche qu'il soit, il n'est pas généreux** (as) rich as he is *ou* rich though he is, he's not generous; **~ peu que lui aussi soit sorti sans sa clef ...** if on top of it all he should have come out without his key too ...; **~ autant que je sache** as far as I know, to the best of my knowledge.

2 *nm*: **le ~ et le contre** the arguments for and against, the pros and the cons; **il y a du ~ et du contre** there are arguments on both sides *ou* arguments for and against.

pourboire [puʀbwaʀ] *nm* tip. **~ interdit** tipping not allowed, our staff do not accept gratuities.

pourceau, *pl* **~x** [puʀso] *nm* (*littér, péj*) pig, swine (*inv, littér*); *V* **perle.**

pourcentage [puʀsɑ̃taʒ] *nm* percentage; (*Comm*) percentage, cut*. **travailler au ~** to work on commission.

pourchasser [puʀʃase] (1) *vt [police, chasseur, ennemi]* to pursue, hunt down; *[créancier]* to hound, harry; *[importun]* to hound. **~ la misère/le crime** to hunt out *ou* seek out poverty/crime; **~ les fautes d'orthographe** to hunt out the spelling mistakes.

pourfendeur [puʀfɑ̃dœʀ] *nm* (*hum*) destroyer.

pourfendre [puʀfɑ̃dʀ(ə)] (41) *vt* (*littér*) *adversaire* to set about, assail; (*fig*) *abus* to fight against, combat.

pourlécher (se) [puʀleʃe] (6) *vpr* to lick one's lips.

pourparlers [puʀpaʀle] *nmpl* talks, negotiations, discussions. **entrer en ~ avec** to start negotiations *ou* discussions with, enter into talks with; **être en ~ avec** to negotiate with, have talks *ou* discussions with.

pourpier [puʀpje] *nm* portulaca; (*comestible*) purslane.

pourpoint [puʀpwɛ̃] *nm* doublet, pourpoint.

pourpre [puʀpʀ(ə)] **1** *adj* crimson. **il devint ~** he turned crimson *ou* scarlet.

2 *nm* (*couleur*) crimson. **le ~ de la honte** the crimson (colour) of shame; **~ rétinien** visual purple.

3 *nf* (*matière colorante, étoffe, symbole*) purple; (*couleur*) scarlet. ~ **royale** royal purple; **accéder à la** ~ **cardinalice** to be given the red hat; **né dans la** ~ born in the purple.
pourpré, e [puʀpʀe] *adj* (*littér*) crimson.
pourquoi [puʀkwa] 1 *conj* why. ~ **est-il venu?** why did he come?, what did he come for?; ~ **les avoir oubliés?** why did he (*ou* they *etc*) forget them?; **c'est** *ou* **voilà** ~ **il n'est pas venu** that's (the reason) why he didn't come.
2 *adv* why. **tu me le prêtes? — ~ (donc)?** can you lend me it? — why? *ou* what for?; **tu viens? — ~ pas?** are you coming? — why(ever) not? *ou* why shouldn't I?; **il a réussi, ~ pas vous?** (*dans le futur*) he succeeded so why shouldn't you?; (*dans le passé*) he succeeded so why didn't you?; **je vais vous dire ~** I'll tell you why; **il faut que ça marche, ou que ça dise ~*** it had better work or else ...*, it had better work, or I'll want to know why (not); **allez savoir** *ou* **comprendre ~*, je vous demande bien ~** I don't know why, I just can't imagine why!, don't ask me!, search me!*
3 *nm inv* (*raison*) reason (*de* for); (*question*) question. **le ~ de son attitude** the reason for his attitude; **il veut toujours savoir le ~ et le comment** he always wants to know the whys and wherefores; **il est difficile de répondre à tous les ~ des enfants** it isn't easy to find an answer for everything children ask you.
pourri, e [puʀi] (*ptp de* **pourrir**) 1 *adj* (a) *fruit* rotten, bad, spoilt; *bois* rotten; *feuille* decayed, rotting; *viande* bad *œuf* rotten, addled, bad; *cadavre* decomposed, putrefied. **être ~** *[pomme]* to have gone rotten *ou* bad; *[œuf]* to have gone bad; *V* **poisson.**
(b) *roche* rotten; *neige* melting, half-melted.
(c) (*mauvais*) *temps, été* wet, rainy; *personne, société* rotten. **~ de fric**: stinking: *ou* filthy: rich, lousy with money:; **~ de défauts** full of *ou* riddled with faults.
2 *nm* (a) **enlever le ~** (*d'un fruit etc*) to take out the rotten *ou* bad part; **sentir le ~** to smell rotten *ou* bad.
(b) (:: *crapule*) swine:, sod∵ (*Brit*). **bande de ~s!** (you) bastards!:, (you) lousy sods!∵ (*Brit*).
pourrir [puʀiʀ] (2) 1 *vi [fruit]* to go rotten *ou* bad, spoil; *[bois]* to rot (away); *[œuf]* to go bad; *[cadavre]* to rot away; *[corps, membre]* to be eaten away. **récolte qui pourrit sur pied** harvest which is rotting on the stalk; (*fig*) **~ dans la misère** to languish in poverty; **~ en prison** to rot (away) in prison; **laisser ~ la situation** to let the situation deteriorate *ou* get worse.
2 *vt* (a) *fruit* to make rotten, rot, spoil; *bois* to make rotten, rot; (*infecter*) *corps* to eat away (at).
(b) (*fig*) (*gâter*) *enfant* to spoil through and through; (*corrompre*) *personne* to corrupt, spoil. **les ennuis qui pourrissent notre vie** the worries which spoil our lives.
3 **se pourrir** *vpr [fruit]* to go rotten *ou* bad, spoil; *[bois]* to rot (away); *[situation]* to deteriorate, get worse.
pourrissement [puʀismɑ̃] *nm [situation]* deterioration, worsening (*de* in, of).
pourriture [puʀityʀ] *nf* (a) (*lit, Agr*) rot; *[société]* rottenness. **odeur de ~** putrid smell. (b) (*péj: personne*) louse*, swine:.
pour-soi [puʀswa] *nm* (*Philos*) pour-soi.
poursuite [puʀsɥit] *nf* (a) *[voleur, animal]* chase (*de* after), pursuit (*de* of); (*fig*) *[bonheur, gloire]* pursuit (*de* of). **se mettre** *ou* **se lancer à la ~ de qn** to chase *ou* run after sb, go in pursuit of sb.
(b) (*Jur*) **~s (judiciaires)** legal proceedings; **engager des ~s contre** to start legal proceedings against, take legal action against; **s'exposer à des ~s** to lay o.s. open to *ou* run the risk of prosecution.
(c) (*continuation*) continuation.
(d) (*Sport*) (**course**) ~ track race.
poursuiteur [puʀsɥitœʀ] *nm* track rider, track cyclist.
poursuivant, e [puʀsɥivɑ̃, ɑ̃t] 1 *adj* (*Jur*) **partie ~e** plaintiff. 2 *nm,f* pursuer; (*Jur*) plaintiff.
poursuivre [puʀsɥivʀ(ə)] (40) 1 *vt* (a) (*courir après*) *fugitif, ennemi* to pursue; *animal* to chase (after), hunt down, pursue; *malfaiteur* to chase (after), pursue. **un enfant poursuivi par un chien** a child (being) chased *ou* pursued by a dog; **les motards poursuivaient la voiture** the police motorcylists were chasing the car *ou* were in pursuit of the car.
(b) (*harceler*) *[importun, souvenir]* to hound. **être poursuivi par ses créanciers** to be hounded *ou* harried by one's creditors; **~ qn de sa colère/de sa haine** to hound sb through anger/hatred; **~ une femme de ses assiduités** to force one's attentions on a woman; **cette idée le poursuit** he can't get this idea out of his mind, he's haunted by this idea; **les photographes ont poursuivi l'actrice jusque chez elle** the photographers followed the actress all the way home.
(c) (*chercher à atteindre*) *fortune, gloire* to seek (after); *vérité* to pursue, seek (after); *rêve* to pursue; *but, idéal* to strive towards, pursue.
(d) (*continuer*) (*gén*) to continue, go *ou* carry on with; *avantage* to follow up, pursue. **~ sa marche** to keep going, walk on, carry on walking *ou* on one's way.
(e) (*Jur*) **~ qn (en justice)** (*au criminel*) to prosecute sb, bring proceedings against sb; (*au civil*) to sue sb, bring proceedings against sb; **être poursuivi pour vol** to be prosecuted for theft.
2 *vi* (a) (*continuer*) to carry on, go on, continue. **poursuivez, cela m'intéresse** go on *ou* tell me more, it interests me; **puis il poursuivit: 'voici pourquoi ...'** then he went on, 'that's why ...'.
(b) (*persévérer*) to keep at it, keep it up.
3 **se poursuivre** *vpr [négociations, débats]* to go on, continue; *[enquête, recherches, travail]* to be going on, be carried out. **les débats se sont poursuivis jusqu'au matin** discussions went on *ou* continued until morning.
pourtant [puʀtɑ̃] *adv* (*néanmoins, en dépit de cela*) yet, nevertheless, all the same, even so; (*cependant*) (and) yet. **et ~** and yet, but nevertheless; **frêle mais ~ résistant** frail but nevertheless *ou* but even so *ou* but all the same *ou* (and *ou* but) yet resilient; **il faut ~ le faire** it's got to be done all the same *ou* even so *ou* nevertheless, (and) yet it's got to be done; **il n'est ~ pas très intelligent** (and) yet he's not very clever, he's not very clever though; (*intensif*) **c'est ~ facile!** but it's easy!, but it's not difficult!; **on lui a ~ dit de faire attention** (and) yet we told him *ou* did tell him to be careful.
pourtour [puʀtuʀ] *nm [cercle]* circumference; *[rectangle]* perimeter; (*bord*) surround. **sur le ~** de around, on the sides of.
pourvoi [puʀvwa] *nm* (*Jur*) appeal. **~ en grâce** appeal for clemency.
pourvoir [puʀvwaʀ] (25) 1 *vt*: **~ qn de qch** to provide *ou* equip *ou* supply sb with sth, provide sth for sb; **~ un enfant de vêtements chauds** to provide a child with warm clothes, provide warm clothes for a child; **la nature l'a pourvu d'une grande intelligence** he is gifted with great natural intelligence; **la nature l'a pourvue d'une grande beauté** she is graced with great natural beauty; **~ sa maison de tout le confort moderne** to equip one's house with all mod cons*; **~ sa cave de vin** to stock one's cellar with wine; *V* **pourvu**[1].
2 **pourvoir à** *vt indir éventualité* to provide for, cater for; *emploi* to fill. **~ aux besoins de qn** to provide for *ou* cater for *ou* supply sb's needs; **~ à l'entretien du ménage** to provide for the upkeep of the household; **j'y pourvoirai** I'll see to it *ou* deal with it.
3 **se pourvoir** *vpr* (a) **se ~ de** *argent, vêtements* to provide o.s. with; *provisions, munitions* to provide o.s. with, equip o.s. with.
(b) (*Jur*) to appeal, lodge an appeal. **se ~ en cassation** to take one's case to the Court of Appeal.
pourvoyeur, -euse [puʀvwajœʀ, øz] 1 *nm,f* supplier; *[drogue]* supplier, pusher*. 2 *nm* (*Mil: servant de pièce*) artilleryman.
pourvu[1], **e** [puʀvy] (*ptp de* **pourvoir**) *adj* (a) *[personne]* **être ~ de** *intelligence, imagination* to be gifted with, be endowed with; *beauté* to be endowed with, be graced with; **avec ces provisions nous voilà ~s pour l'hiver** with these provisions we're stocked up *ou* well provided for for the winter; **nous sommes très bien/très mal ~s en commerçants** we're very well-off/very badly off for shops, we're very well/very badly provided with shops; **après l'héritage qu'il a fait c'est quelqu'un de bien ~** with the inheritance he's received, he's very well-off *ou* very well provided for.
(b) *[chose]* **être ~ de** to be equipped *ou* fitted with; **feuille de papier ~e d'une marge** sheet of paper with a margin; **animal (qui est) ~ d'écailles** animal which has scales *ou* which is equipped with scales.
pourvu[2] [puʀvy] *conj*: **~ que** (*souhait*) let's hope; (*condition*) provided (that), so long as.
poussa(h) [pusa] *nm* (*jouet*) tumbler; (*péj: homme*) potbellied man.
pousse [pus] *nf* (a) (*bourgeon*) shoot. **~s de bambou** bamboo shoots. (b) (*action*) *[feuilles]* sprouting; *[dent, cheveux]* growth.
poussé, e[1] [puse] (*ptp de* **pousser**) *adj études* advanced; *enquête* extensive, exhaustive. **très ~** *organisation, technique, dessin* elaborate; *technicité, précision* high-level (*épith*), advanced; **une plaisanterie un peu ~e** a joke which goes a bit too far.
pousse-café* [puskafe] *nm inv* (after-dinner) liqueur.
poussée[2] [puse] *nf* (a) (*pression*) *[foule]* pressure, pushing, shoving; (*Archit, Géol, Phys*) thrust (*U*). **sous la ~** under the pressure.
(b) (*coup*) push, shove; *[ennemi]* thrust. **écarter qn d'une ~** to thrust *ou* push *ou* shove sb aside; **enfoncer une porte d'une ~ violente** to break a door down with a violent heave *ou* shove.
(c) (*éruption*) *[acné]* attack, eruption; *[prix]* rise, upsurge, increase. **~ de fièvre** (sudden) high temperature; **la ~ de la gauche/droite aux élections** the upsurge of the left/right in the elections; **la ~ révolutionnaire de 1789** the revolutionary upsurge of 1789.
pousse-pousse [puspus] *nm inv* rickshaw.
pousser [puse] (1) 1 *vt* (a) (*gén*) *charrette, meuble, personne* to push; *brouette, landau* to push, wheel; *verrou* (*ouvrir*) to slide, push back; (*fermer*) to slide, push to *ou* home; *objet gênant* to move, shift*, push aside. **~ une chaise contre le mur/près de la fenêtre/dehors** to push a chair (up) against the wall/(over) near the window/outside; **~ les gens vers la porte** to push the people towards *ou* to the door; **il me pousse du genou/du coude** he nudged me with his knee/(with his elbow); **~ un animal devant soi** to drive an animal (in front of one); **~ la porte/la fenêtre** (*fermer*) to push the door/window to *ou* shut; (*ouvrir*) to push the door/window open; **~ un caillou du pied** to kick a stone (along); **le vent nous poussait vers la côte** the wind was blowing us towards the shore; **le courant poussait le bateau vers les rochers** the current was carrying the boat towards the rocks; (*balançoire*) **peux-tu me ~?** can you give me a push?; **peux-tu ~ ta voiture?** can you move *ou* shift* your car (out of the way)?; **pousse tes fesses!:** shift your backside!:, shove over!:; **(ne) poussez pas, il y a des enfants!** don't push *ou* stop pushing, there are children here!; **il m'a poussé** he jostled me; (*fig*) **faut pas ~ grand-mère (dans les orties)!:** that *ou* this is going a bit far!, that *ou* this is overdoing things a bit!; *V* **pointe.**
(b) (*stimuler*) *élève, ouvrier* to urge on, egg on, push; *cheval* to ride hard, push; *moteur* to flog* (*surtout Brit*), drive hard; *voiture* to drive hard *ou* fast; *machine* to work hard; *feu* to stoke up; *chauffage* to turn up; (*mettre en valeur*) *candidat, protégé* to push. **c'est le même modèle, avec un moteur poussé** it's the same model with a souped-up* *ou* tuned-up engine; **c'est**

l'ambition qui le pousse he is driven by ambition, it's ambition which drives him on; **dans ce lycée on pousse trop les élèves** the pupils are worked *ou* driven *ou* pushed too hard in this school; **ce prof l'a beaucoup poussé en maths** this teacher has really made him get on in maths.

(c) ~ **qn à faire qch** *[faim, curiosité]* to drive sb to do sth; *[personne]* (*inciter*) to urge *ou* press sb to do sth; (*persuader*) to persuade *ou* induce sb to do sth, talk sb into doing sth; **ses parents le poussent à entrer à l'université/vers une carrière médicale** his parents are urging *ou* encouraging him to go to university/to take up a career in medicine; **c'est elle qui l'a poussé à acheter cette maison** she talked him into *ou* pushed him into* buying this house, she induced him to buy this house; **son échec nous pousse à croire que ...** his failure leads us to think that ..., because of his failure we're tempted to think that ...; ~ **qn au crime/au désespoir** to drive sb to crime/to despair; ~ **qn à la consommation** to encourage sb to buy (*ou* eat, drink *etc*) more than he wants; ~ **qn à la dépense** to encourage sb to spend (more) money, drive sb into spending (more) money; **le sentiment qui le poussait vers sa bien-aimée** the feeling which drove him to his beloved; ~ **qn sur un sujet** to get sb onto a subject.

(d) (*poursuivre*) *études, discussion* to continue, carry on (with), go *ou* press on with; *avantage* to press (home), follow up; *affaire* to follow up, pursue; *marche, progression* to continue, carry on with. ~ **l'enquête/les recherches plus loin** to carry on *ou* press on with the inquiry/research; ~ **la curiosité/la plaisanterie un peu (trop) loin** to carry *ou* take curiosity/the joke a bit (too) far; ~ **les choses au noir** always to look on the black side, always take a black view of things; ~ **qch à la perfection** to carry *ou* bring sth to perfection; **il a poussé le dévouement/la gentillesse/la malhonnêteté jusqu'à faire** he was devoted/kind/dishonest enough to do, his devotion/kindness/dishonesty was such that he did; ~ **l'indulgence jusqu'à la faiblesse** to carry indulgence to the point of weakness; ~ **qn dans ses derniers retranchements** to get sb up against a wall *ou* with his back to the wall; ~ **qn à bout** to push sb to breaking point, drive sb to his wits' end.

(e) *cri, hurlement* to let out, utter, give; *soupir* to heave. ~ **des cris** to shout, scream; ~ **des rugissements** to roar; **les enfants poussaient des cris perçants** the children were shrieking; **le chien poussait de petits jappements plaintifs** the dog was yelping pitifully; ~ **une gueulante‡** (*douleur*) to be screaming with pain; (*colère*) to be shouting and bawling (with anger); (*hum*) ~ **sa chanson** *ou* **la romance, en** ~ **une*** to sing a song.

2 *vi* **(a)** (*grandir*) *[barbe, enfant, plante]* to grow; *[dent]* to come through; *[ville]* to grow, expand. *[enfant]* ~ **bien** *ou* **comme un champignon** to be growing well, be shooting up; **alors, les enfants, ça pousse?** and how are the kids doing?*; **mes choux poussent bien** my cabbages are coming on *ou* doing nicely *ou* well; **tout pousse bien dans cette région** everything grows well in this region; **ils font** ~ **des tomates par ici** they grow tomatoes in these parts, this is a tomato-growing area; **la pluie fait** ~ **les mauvaises herbes** the rain makes the weeds grow; **ça pousse comme du chiendent** they grow like weeds; **il se fait** *ou* **se laisse** ~ **la barbe** he's growing a beard; **il se fait** *ou* **se laisse** ~ **les cheveux** he's letting his hair grow; **il a une dent qui pousse** he's cutting a tooth, he's got a tooth coming through; **de nouvelles villes poussaient partout comme des champignons** new towns were springing up all over the place.

(b) (*faire un effort*) (*pour accoucher, aller à la selle*) to push. (*fig*) ~ **à la roue** to do a bit of pushing, push a bit; ~ **(à la roue) pour que qn fasse qch** to keep nudging *ou* pushing sb to get him to do sth; (*Fin*) ~ **à la hausse/à la baisse** to press for *ou* push for* reflation/deflation of the economy.

(c) (*aller*) **nous allons** ~ **un peu plus avant** we're going to go on *ou* push on a bit further; ~ **jusqu'à Lyon** to go on *ou* push on as far as *ou* carry on to Lyons; **l'ennemi poussait droit sur nous** the enemy was coming straight for *ou* towards us.

(d) (*‡: exagérer*) to go too far, overdo it. **tu pousses!** that's going a bit far!; **faut pas** ~! that *ou* this is going a bit far!, that *ou* this is overdoing it a bit!

3 se pousser *vpr* (*se déplacer*) to move, shift*; (*faire de la place*) to move *ou* shift* over (*ou* up *ou* along *ou* down); (*en voiture*) to move. (*fig*) **se** ~ **(dans la société)** to make one's way up, push o.s. up in society *ou* in the world.

poussette [pusɛt] *nf* push chair.

poussier [pusje] *nm* coaldust, screenings (*T*).

poussière [pusjɛʀ] *nf* dust. ~ **de charbon** coaldust; ~ **d'étoiles** stardust; ~ **d'or** gold dust; **faire** *ou* **soulever de la** ~ to raise a dust; **couvert de** ~ dusty, covered in dust; **avoir une** ~ **dans l'œil** to have a speck of dust in one's eye; (*frm*) **leur** ~ **repose dans ces tombes** their ashes *ou* mortal remains lie in these tombs; (*fig*) **3 F et des** ~**s*** just over 3 francs, 3 and a bit francs*; (*fig*) **une** ~ **de** a myriad of; ~ **radioactive** radioactive particles *ou* dust (*U*); ~ **volcanique** volcanic ash (*U*) *ou* dust (*U*); **réduire/tomber en** ~ to reduce to/crumble into dust.

poussiéreux, -euse [pusjeʀø, øz] *adj* (*lit*) dusty; (*fig*) fusty.

poussif, -ive [pusif, iv] *adj personne* wheezy, short-winded; *cheval* broken-winded; *moteur* puffing, wheezing; *style* flabby, tame.

poussin [pusɛ̃] *nm* chick. **mon** ~**!*** pet!

poussivement [pusivmɑ̃] *adv*: **il monta** ~ **la côte/l'escalier** he wheezed up *ou* puffed up the hill/the stairs.

poussoir [puswaʀ] *nm [sonnette]* button.

poutre [putʀ(ə)] *nf* (*en bois*) beam; (*en métal*) girder. ~**s apparentes** exposed beams; *V* **paille**.

poutrelle [putʀɛl] *nf* girder.

pouvoir[1] [puvwaʀ] (33) **1** *vb aux* **(a)** (*permission*) can, may (*frm*), to be allowed to. **il ne peut pas venir** he can't *ou* cannot *ou* may not (*frm*) come, he isn't allowed to come; **peut-il/ne peut-il pas venir?** can he/can't he come?, may he/may he not come? (*frm*); **il peut ne pas venir** he doesn't have to come, he's not bound to come; **il pourra venir** he will be able *ou* allowed to come; **il pourrait venir s'il nous prévenait** he could come *ou* he would be able *ou* allowed to come if he notified us; **il pouvait venir, il a pu venir** he could come, he was allowed *ou* able to come; **il aurait pu venir** he could have come, he would have been allowed *ou* able to come; **s'il avait pu venir** if he could have come, if he had been allowed *ou* able to come; **les élèves peuvent se promener le dimanche** the pupils may *ou* can go *ou* are allowed to go for walks on Sundays; **maintenant, tu peux aller jouer** now you can *ou* may go and play; **est-ce qu'on peut fermer la fenêtre?** may *ou* can we *ou* do you mind if we shut the window?; **on ne peut pas laisser ces enfants seuls** we can't leave these children on their own; **dans le famille victorienne, on ne pouvait pas jouer du piano le dimanche** in Victorian families, you weren't allowed to *ou* could not play the piano on Sundays.

(b) (*possibilité*) can, to be able to; (*: *réussir*) to manage to. **il ne peut pas venir** he can't come, he isn't able to *ou* is unable to come; **peut-il venir?** can he *ou* is he able to come?; **ne peut-il pas venir?** can't he *ou* isn't he able to *ou* is he unable to come?; **il ne peut pas ne pas venir** he can't not come, he HAS to *ou* he MUST come; (*littér*) **je puis venir** I can come; **il aurait pu venir** he could have come, he would have been able to come; **s'il avait pu venir** if he could have come, if had been able to come; **il n'a (pas) pu** *ou* (*littér*) **ne put venir** he couldn't *ou* wasn't able to *ou* was unable to come; **il ne peut pas s'empêcher de tousser** he can't help coughing; **peut-il marcher sans canne?** can he (manage to) walk *ou* is he able to walk without a stick?; **il peut bien faire cela** that's the least he can do; **venez si vous pouvez/dès que vous pourrez** come if/as soon as you can (manage) *ou* are able; **puis-je vous être utile?** can I be of any help (to you)?, can *ou* may I be of assistance?; **la salle peut contenir 100 personnes** the room can seat *ou* hold 100 people *ou* has a seating capacity of 100; **comme il pouvait comprendre la fiche technique, il a pu réparer le poste** since he could understand the technical information he was able to *ou* he managed to repair the set; **il ne pourra jamais plus marcher** he will never be able to walk again; **il pourrait venir demain si vous aviez besoin de lui** he could come tomorrow if you needed him; **pourriez-vous nous apporter du thé?** could you bring us some tea?

(c) (*éventualité*) **il peut être français** he may *ou* might *ou* could be French; **il ne peut pas être français** he can't be French; **peut-il être français?** could *ou* might he be French?; **ne peut-il pas être français?** couldn't *ou* mightn't he *ou* may he not (*frm*) be French?; **il peut ne pas être français** he may *ou* might not be French; **il ne peut pas ne pas être français** he MUST be French; **il pourrait être français** he might *ou* could be French; **il aurait pu être français** he might *ou* could have been French; **quel âge peut-il (bien) avoir?** (just) how old might he be?; **l'émeute peut éclater d'un moment à l'autre** rioting may *ou* might *ou* could break out any minute; **qu'est-ce que cela peut bien lui faire?*** what's that (got) to do with him?; **il peut être très méchant, parfois** he can be very nasty at times; **où ai-je bien pu mettre mon stylo?** where on earth can I have put my pen?; **vous pourrez en avoir besoin** you may *ou* might need it; **les cambrioleurs ont pu entrer par la fenêtre** the burglars could *ou* may *ou* might have got in through the window; **il a très bien pu entrer sans qu'on le voie** he may very well *ou* he could easily have come in unseen; **songez un peu à ce qui pourrait arriver** just imagine what might *ou* could happen; **cela pourrait se faire** that might *ou* could be arranged.

(d) (*suggestion*) might, could. **elle pourrait arriver à l'heure!** she might *ou* could (at least) be punctual!; **il aurait pu me dire cela plus tôt!** he might *ou* could have told me sooner!; **vous pouvez bien lui prêter votre livre** you can lend him your book, can't you?, surely you can lend him your book!

(e) (*littér: souhait*) **puisse Dieu/le Ciel les aider!** may God/Heaven help them!; **puisse-t-il guérir rapidement!** would to God (*littér*) *ou* let us hope he recovers soon!, may he soon recover (*littér*); **puissiez-vous dire vrai!** let us pray *ou* hope you're right!

2 *vb impers* may, might, could, to be possible. **il peut** *ou* **pourrait pleuvoir** it may *ou* might *ou* could rain, it is possible that it will rain; **il pourrait y avoir du monde** there may *ou* might *ou* could be a lot of people there; **il aurait pu y avoir un accident!** there could *ou* might have been an accident!; **il pourrait se faire qu'elle ne soit pas chez elle** she may *ou* might well not be at home, it may *ou* might well be that she isn't at home.

3 *vt* **(a)** can, to be able to. **est-ce qu'on peut quelque chose pour lui?** is there anything we can do for him?; **il partira dès qu'il le pourra** he will leave as soon as he can *ou* is able (to); **il fait ce qu'il peut** he does what he can, he does the best he can; **il a fait tout ce qu'il a pu** he did all he could *ou* all that was in his power; **il peut beaucoup** he's very capable; (*frm*) **que puis-je pour vous?** what can I do for you?, can I do anything to assist you?; **personne ne peut rien sur lui** he won't listen to anyone, no one has any hold on him.

(b) (+ *adj ou adv comp*) **on ne peut plus/mieux: il a été on ne peut plus aimable/compréhensif/impoli** he couldn't have been kinder/more understanding/ruder, he was as kind/understanding/rude as it's possible to be; **elle le connaît on ne peut mieux** she knows him as well as it's possible to know anyone, no one knows him better than she does; **ils sont on ne peut plus mal avec leurs voisins** they couldn't (possibly) be on worse terms with their neighbours, they're on the worst possible terms with their neighbours.

(c) (*loc*) il n'en peut plus (*fatigué*) he's all-in *ou* tired out; (*à bout de nerfs*) he can't go on, he's had enough, he can't take any more; je n'en peux plus de fatigue I'm all-in* *ou* tired out *ou* worn out; (*littér*) il n'en pouvait mais there was nothing he could do about it, he could do nothing about it; qu'y pouvons-nous? — on n'y peut rien what can we do about it? — there's nothing we can do (about it); je m'excuse, mais je n'y peux rien I'm sorry, but it can't be helped *ou* there's nothing I can do *ou* there's nothing to be done.

4 se pouvoir *vpr:* il se peut/se pourrait qu'elle vienne she may *ou* could/might *ou* could (well) come; se peut-il que ...? is it possible that ...?, could *ou* might it be that ...?; il se peut, éventuellement, que ... it may possibly be that ...; cela se pourrait bien that's quite possible, that may *ou* could well be, that's a clear possibility; ça se peut* possibly, perhaps, maybe, could be*; ça ne se peut pas* that's impossible, that's not possible; *V* autant.

pouvoir[2] [puvwaʀ] 1 *nm* (a) (*faculté*) (*gén*) power; (*capacité*) ability, capacity; (*Phys, gén: propriété*) power. avoir le ~ de faire to have the power *ou* ability to do; il a le ~ de se faire des amis partout he has the ability *ou* he is able to make friends everywhere; il a un extraordinaire ~ d'éloquence/de conviction he has remarkable *ou* exceptional powers of oratory/persuasion; ce n'est pas en mon ~ it is not within *ou* in my power, it is beyond my power; il n'est pas en son ~ de vous aider it is beyond *ou* it does not lie within his power to help you; il fera tout ce qui est en son ~ he will do everything (that is) in his power *ou* all that he possibly can; ~ couvrant/éclairant covering/lighting power; ~ absorbant absorption power, absorption factor (*T*).

(b) (*autorité*) power; (*influence*) influence. avoir beaucoup de ~ to have a lot of power *ou* influence, be very powerful *ou* influential; avoir du ~ sur qn to have influence *ou* power over sb, exert an influence over sb; le père a ~ sur ses enfants a father has power over his children; tenir qn en son ~ to hold sb in one's power; le pays entier est en son ~ the whole country is in his power, he has the whole country in his power; avoir du ~ sur soi-même to have will power.

(c) (*droit, attribution*) power. dépasser ses ~s to exceed one's powers; en vertu des ~s qui me sont conférés by virtue of the power which has been vested in me; séparation des ~s division of powers; avoir ~ de faire (*autorisation*) to have authority to do; (*droit*) to have the right to do; je n'ai pas ~ pour vous répondre I have no authority to reply to you; *V* plein.

(d) (*Pol*) le ~ (*direction des pays*) power; (*dirigeants*) the government; le parti (politique) au ~ the (political) party in power *ou* in office, the ruling party; avoir le ~ to have *ou* hold power; exercer le ~ to exercise power, rule, govern; prendre le ~ (*légalement*) to come to power *ou* into office; (*illégalement*) to seize power; des milieux proches du ~ sources close to the government; le ~ actuel, dans ce pays the present régime, in this country; l'opinion et le ~ public opinion and the authorities, us and them*.

(e) (*Jur: procuration*) proxy. ~ par-devant notaire power of attorney; donner ~ à qn de faire to give sb proxy to do (*Jur*), empower sb to do, give sb authority to do; des ~s credentials.

2: pouvoir d'achat purchasing power; pouvoir de concentration powers of concentration; pouvoirs constitués powers that be; pouvoir de décision decision-making power(s); pouvoir disciplinaire disciplinary power(s); pouvoirs exceptionnels emergency powers; pouvoir exécutif executive power; pouvoir judiciaire judiciary, judicial power; pouvoir législatif legislative power; pouvoirs publics authorities; pouvoir spirituel spiritual power; pouvoir temporel temporal power.

pragmatique [pʀagmatik] *adj, nf* pragmatic.

pragmatisme [pʀagmatism(ə)] *nm* pragmatism.

pragmatiste [pʀagmatist(ə)] 1 *adj* pragmatic, pragmatist. 2 *nmf* pragmatist.

praire [pʀɛʀ] *nf* clam.

prairial [pʀɛʀjal] *nm* Prairial (*9th month of French Republican calendar*).

prairie [pʀɛʀi] *nf* meadow. (*aux USA*) la ~ the prairie; des hectares de ~ acres of grassland.

praline [pʀalin] *nf* praline, sugared almond.

praliné, e [pʀaline] 1 *adj amande* sugared; *glace, crème* praline-flavoured, almond-flavoured. 2 *nm* praline- *ou* almond-flavoured ice cream.

prame [pʀam] *nf* (*Naut*) pram, praam.

praticable [pʀatikabl(ə)] 1 *adj* (a) *projet, moyen, opération* practicable, feasible; *chemin* passable, negotiable, practicable. (b) (*Théât*) *porte, décor* practicable. 2 *nm* (*Théât: décor*) practicable scenery; (*plate-forme*) gantry.

praticien, -ienne [pʀatisjɛ̃, jɛn] *nm,f* (*Méd*) practitioner; (*gén*) practician.

pratiquant, e [pʀatikɑ̃, ɑ̃t] 1 *adj* practising (*épith*). il est très/peu ~ he goes to *ou* attends church regularly/infrequently, he's a regular/an infrequent attender at church *ou* churchgoer.

2 *nm,f* (regular) churchgoer, practising Christian (*ou* Catholic *etc*); (*adepte*) follower. cette religion compte 30 millions de ~s this faith has 30 million followers *ou* 30 million faithful.

pratique [pʀatik] 1 *adj* (a) (*non théorique*) *jugement, philosophe, connaissance* practical; (*Scol*) *exercice, cours* practical. considération d'ordre ~ practical consideration; *V* travail[1].

(b) (*réaliste*) *personne* practical(-minded). il faut être ~ dans la vie you have to be practical in life; avoir le sens ~ to be practical-minded; avoir l'esprit ~ to have a practical turn of mind.

(c) (*commode*) *livre, moyen, vêtement, solution* practical; *instrument* practical, handy; *emploi du temps* convenient. c'est très ~, j'habite à côté du bureau it's very convenient *ou* handy*, I live next door to the office.

2 *nf* (a) (*application*) practice. dans la ~ in (actual) practice; en ~ in practice; mettre qch en ~ to put sth into practice.

(b) (*expérience*) practical experience. il a une longue ~ des élèves he has a long practical experience of teaching, he is well-practised at teaching; il a perdu la ~ he is out of practice, he's lost the knack*; avoir la ~ du monde†† to be well-versed in *ou* have a knowledge of *ou* be familiar with the ways of society.

(c) (*coutume, procédé*) practice. c'est une ~ générale it is a widespread practice; des ~s malhonnêtes dishonest practices, sharp practice; ~s religieuses religious practices.

(d) (*exercice, observance*) *[règle]* observance; *[médecine]* practising, exercise; *[sport]* practising; *[vertu]* exercise, practice. la ~ de l'escrime/du cheval/du golf développe les réflexes fencing/horse-riding/golfing *ou* (playing) golf develops the reflexes; ~ (religieuse) church attendance; condamné pour ~ illégale de la médecine convicted of the illegal practising of medicine.

(e) (††: *clientèle*) *[commerçant]* custom (*U*), clientèle (*U*); *[avocat]* practice, clientèle (*U*). donner sa ~ à un commerçant to give a tradesman one's custom.

(f) (††: *client*) *[commerçant]* customer; *[avocat]* client.

(g) (††: *fréquentation*) *[personne, société]* frequenting, frequentation; *[auteur]* close study.

pratiquement [pʀatikmɑ̃] *adv* (*en pratique*) in practice; (*en réalité*) in (actual) practice; (*presque*) practically, virtually.

pratiquer [pʀatike] (1) 1 *vt* (a) (*mettre en pratique*) *philosophie, politique* to practise (*Brit*), practice (*US*), put into practice; *règle* to observe; *vertu, charité* to practise, exercise; *religion* to practise.

(b) (*exercer*) *profession, art* to practise; *football, golf* to play. ~ l'escrime/le cheval/la pêche to go (in for) fencing/horse-riding/fishing; ~ la photo to go in for photography; ils pratiquent l'exploitation systématique du touriste they systematically exploit *ou* make a practice of systematically exploiting the tourist.

(c) (*faire*) *ouverture* to make; *trou* to pierce, bore, open up; *route* to make, build, open up; (*Méd*) *intervention* to carry out (*sur* on).

(d) (*utiliser*) *méthode* to practise, use; *système* to use. ~ le chantage/le bluff to use blackmail/bluff.

(e) (††: *fréquenter*) *auteur* to study closely; *personne, haute société* to frequent.

2 *vi* (a) (*Rel*) to go to church, be a churchgoer, be a practising Christian *etc*.

(b) (*Méd*) to be in practice, have a practice.

3 se pratiquer *vpr* to be the practice. cela se pratique encore dans les villages it is still the practice in the villages; comme cela se pratique en général as is the usual practice; les prix qui se pratiquent à Paris prices which prevail *ou* are current in Paris; le vaudou se pratique encore dans cette région voodoo is still practised in this region.

praxis [pʀaksis] *nf* praxis.

Praxitèle [pʀaksitɛl] *nm* Praxiteles.

pré [pʀe] 1 *nm* meadow. aller sur le ~ to fight a duel. 2: pré-salé *nm, pl* prés-salés (*mouton*) salt meadow sheep; (*viande*) (salt meadow) lamb.

pré ... [pʀe] *préf* pre ....

préalable [pʀealabl(ə)] 1 *adj* preliminary. ~ à preceding; lors des entretiens ~s aux négociations during (the) discussions (which took place) prior to the negotiations; vous ne pouvez pas partir sans l'accord ~ du directeur you cannot leave without first obtaining *ou* having obtained the agreement of the director *ou* without the prior *ou* previous agreement of the director; ceci n'allait pas sans une certaine inquiétude ~ a certain initial anxiety was experienced; sans avis ~ without prior *ou* previous notice.

2 *nm* (*condition*) precondition, prerequisite; (†: *préparation*) preliminary. au ~ first, beforehand.

préalablement [pʀealabləmɑ̃] *adv* first, beforehand. ~ à prior to; ~ à toute négociation before any negotiation can take place, prior to any negotiation.

Préalpes [pʀealp(ə)] *nfpl:* les ~ the Pre-Alps.

préalpin, e [pʀealpɛ̃, in] *adj* of the Pre-Alps.

préambule [pʀeɑ̃byl] *nm [discours, loi]* preamble (*de* to); (*fig: prélude*) prelude (*à* to). sans ~ without any preliminaries, straight off*.

préau, *pl* ~x [pʀeo] *nm [école]* covered playground; *[prison, couvent]* inner courtyard.

préavis [pʀeavi] *nm* (advance) notice. un ~ d'un mois a month's notice; ~ de grève strike notice; sans ~ *faire grève, partir* without (previous) notice, without advance warning; *retirer de l'argent* on demand, without advance *ou* previous notice.

prébende [pʀebɑ̃d] *nf* (*Rel*) prebend; (*péj*) emoluments, payment (*U*).

prébendé, e [pʀebɑ̃de] *adj* prebendal.

prébendier [pʀebɑ̃dje] *nm* prebendary.

précaire [pʀekɛʀ] *adj position, situation, bonheur* precarious; *santé* shaky, precarious. (*Jur*) possesseur/possession (à titre) ~ precarious holder/tenure.

précairement [pʀekɛʀmɑ̃] *adv* precariously.

précambrien, -ienne [pʀekɑ̃bʀijɛ̃, ijɛn] *adj, nm* Precambrian.

précarité [pʀekaʀite] *nf* (*gén, Jur*) precariousness.

précaution [pʀekosjɔ̃] *nf* (a) (*disposition*) precaution. prendre des *ou* ses ~s to take precautions; s'entourer de ~s to take a lot of precautions; ~s oratoires carefully phrased remarks.

(b) (*prudence*) caution, care. par ~ as a precaution (*contre* against); par mesure de ~ as a precautionary measure; pour

plus de ~ to be on the safe side; **avec ~** cautiously.

précautionner (se) [pʀekosjɔne] (1) *vpr* to take precautions (*contre* against).

précautionneusement [pʀekosjɔnøzmɑ̃] *adv* (*par précaution*) cautiously; (*avec soin*) carefully.

précautionneux, -euse [pʀekosjɔnø, øz] *adj* (*prudent*) cautious; (*soigneux*) careful.

précédemment [pʀesedamɑ̃] *adv* before, previously.

précédent, e [pʀesedɑ̃, ɑ̃t] **1** *adj* previous. **un discours/article ~** a previous *ou* an earlier speech/article; **le discours/film ~** the preceding *ou* previous speech/film; **le jour/mois ~** the previous day/month, the day/month before.

2 *nm* (*fait, décision*) precedent. **sans ~** unprecedented, without precedent.

précéder [pʀesede] (6) **1** *vt* **(a)** (*venir avant*) (*dans le temps, une hiérarchie*) to precede, come before; (*dans l'espace*) to precede, be in front of, come before; (*dans une file de véhicules*) to be in front *ou* ahead of, precede. **les jours qui ont précédé le coup d'État** the days preceding *ou* which led up to the coup d'état; **être précédé de** (*gén*) to be preceded by; *[discours]* to be preceded by *ou* prefaced with; **faire ~ son discours d'un préambule** to precede one's speech by *ou* preface one's speech with an introduction, give a short introduction at the start of one's speech.

(b) (*devancer*) (*dans le temps, l'espace*) to precede, go in front *ou* ahead of; (*dans une carrière etc*) to precede, get ahead of. **quand j'y suis arrivé, j'ai vu que quelqu'un m'avait précédé** when I got there I saw that someone had got there before me *ou* ahead of me *ou* had preceded me; **il le précéda dans la chambre** he went into the room in front of him, he entered the room ahead of *ou* in front of him; **il m'a précédé de 5 minutes** he got there 5 minutes before me *ou* ahead of me.

2 *vi* to precede, go before. **les jours qui ont précédé** the preceding days; **dans tout ce qui a précédé** in all that has been said (*ou* written *etc*) before *ou* so far; **dans le chapitre/la semaine qui précède** in the preceding chapter/week.

précepte [pʀesɛpt(ə)] *nm* precept.

précepteur [pʀesɛptœʀ] *nm* private tutor.

préceptorat [pʀesɛptɔʀa] *nm* tutorship, tutorage (*frm*).

préceptrice [pʀesɛptʀis] *nf* governess.

prêche [pʀɛʃ] *nm* (*lit, fig*) sermon.

prêcher [pʀeʃe] (1) **1** *vt* (*Rel, fig*) to preach; *personne* to preach to. **~ un converti** to preach to the converted; (*hum*) **~ la bonne parole** to spread the good word.

2 *vi* (*Rel*) to preach; (*fig*) to preach, preachify, sermonize. (*fig*) **~ dans le désert** to talk to a brick wall; **~ d'exemple** to practise what one preaches, preach by example; **~ pour son saint** *ou* **sa paroisse** to look after one's own interests, look after *ou* take care of number one*.

prêcheur, -euse [pʀɛʃœʀ, øz] **1** *adj personne, ton* moralizing. **frères ~s** preaching friars. **2** *nm,f* (*Rel*) preacher; (*fig*) moralizer.

prêchi-prêcha [pʀeʃipʀeʃa] *nm inv* (*péj*) preachifying (*U*), continuous moralizing (*U*) *ou* sermonizing (*U*).

précieusement [pʀesjøzmɑ̃] *adv* (*V* **précieux**) preciously; in an affected way.

précieux, -euse [pʀesjø, øz] **1** *adj* **(a)** *pierre, métal, temps, qualité, objet* precious; *collaborateur, aide, conseil* invaluable; *ami* valued, precious.

(b) (*Littérat*) *écrivain, salon* précieux, precious; (*fig: affecté*) precious, mannered, affected.

2 précieuse *nf* précieuse.

préciosité [pʀesjozite] *nf* **(a)** (*U*) (*Littérat*) preciosity; (*affectation*) preciosity, affectation.

(b) (*expression*) affectation.

précipice [pʀesipis] *nm* **(a)** (*gouffre*) chasm. **un ~ de plusieurs centaines de mètres** a drop of several hundred metres; **la voiture s'immobilisa au bord du ~/tomba dans le ~** the car stopped at the very edge of the precipice/went over the precipice; **d'affreux ~s s'ouvraient de tous côtés** frightful chasms opened up on all sides; **ne t'aventure pas près du ~** you mustn't go too near the edge (of the precipice).

(b) (*fig*) abyss. **être au bord du ~** to be at the edge of the abyss.

précipitamment [pʀesipitamɑ̃] *adv* hurriedly, hastily, precipitately. **sortir ~** to rush *ou* dash out.

précipitation [pʀesipitasjɔ̃] *nf* **(a)** (*hâte*) haste; (*hâte excessive*) great haste, violent hurry. **(b)** (*Chim*) precipitation. **(c)** (*Mét*) **~s** precipitation.

précipité, e [pʀesipite] (*ptp de* **précipiter**) **1** *adj départ* hurried, precipitate; *décision, personne* hasty, precipitate; *fuite* headlong; *pas* hurried; *pouls, respiration* fast; *rythme* rapid, swift. **tout cela est trop ~** it's all happening too fast, it's all far too hasty.

2 *nm* (*Chim*) precipitate.

précipiter [pʀesipite] (1) **1** *vt* **(a)** (*jeter*) *personne* to throw (down), hurl (down), push headlong; *objet* to throw, hurl (*contre* against, at, *vers* towards, at). **~ qn du haut d'une falaise** to hurl *ou* throw sb (down) from the top of a cliff, push sb headlong off a cliff; (*fig*) **~ qn dans le malheur** to plunge sb into misfortune.

(b) (*hâter*) *pas* to quicken, speed up; *événement* to hasten, precipitate. **il ne faut rien ~** we mustn't be hasty, we mustn't rush (into) things.

(c) (*Chim*) to precipitate.

2 *vi* (*Chim*) to precipitate.

3 se précipiter *vpr* **(a)** (*se jeter*) *[personne]* **se ~ dans le vide** to hurl o.s. *ou* plunge (headlong) into space; **se ~ du haut d'une falaise** to throw o.s. off the edge of *ou* over a cliff.

(b) (*se ruer*) to rush over *ou* forward. **se ~ vers** to rush *ou* race towards; **se ~ sur** to rush at; **se ~ contre** *[personne]* to throw o.s. against; *[voiture]* to tear into, smash into; **se ~ au devant de qn/aux pieds de qn** to throw o.s. in front of sb/at sb's feet; **se ~ sur l'ennemi** to rush at *ou* hurl o.s. on *ou* at the enemy; **elle se précipita dans ses bras** she rushed into *ou* threw herself into *ou* flew into his arms; **il se précipita à la porte pour ouvrir** he rushed to open the door; **il se précipita sur le balcon** he raced *ou* dashed *ou* rushed out onto the balcony.

(c) (*s'accélérer*) *[rythme]* to speed up; *[pouls]* to quicken, speed up. **les choses** *ou* **événements se précipitaient** things began to happen all at once *ou* in a great rush, events started to move fast *ou* faster.

(d) (*se dépêcher*) to hurry, rush.

précis, e [pʀesi, iz] **1** *adj* **(a)** (*juste*) *style, témoignage, vocabulaire* precise; *sens* precise, exact; *description, indication* precise, exact, clear, accurate; *instrument, tir* precise, accurate.

(b) (*défini*) *idée, donnée, règle* precise, definite; *heure* precise; *ordre, demande* precise; *fait, raison* precise, particular, specific. **sans raison ~e** for no particular *ou* precise reason; **je ne pense à rien de ~** I'm not thinking of anything in particular; **à cet instant ~** at that precise *ou* very moment; **à 4 heures ~es** at 4 o'clock sharp *ou* on the dot*, at 4 o'clock precisely; **sans que l'on puisse dire de façon ~e ...** although we can't say precisely *ou* with any precision ...; **se référer à un texte de façon ~e** to make precise reference to a text.

(c) (*net*) *point* precise, exact; *contours* precise, distinct; *geste, esprit* precise; *trait* distinct.

2 *nm* (*résumé*) précis, summary; (*manuel*) handbook.

précisément [pʀesizemɑ̃] *adv* **(a)** (*avec précision: V* **précis**) precisely; exactly; clearly, accurately; distinctly. **... ou plus ~ ...** or more precisely *ou* exactly, ... or to be more precise.

(b) (*justement*) **je venais ~ de sortir** I had in fact just gone out, as it happened I'd just gone out; **c'est lui ~ qui m'avait conseillé de le faire** as a matter of fact it was he *ou* it so happens that it was he who advised me to do it; **c'est ~ la raison pour laquelle** *ou* **c'est ~ pour cela que je viens vous voir** that's precisely *ou* just why I've come to see you, it's for that very *ou* precise reason that I've come to see you; **il fallait ~ ne rien lui dire** in actual fact he shouldn't have been told anything; **mais je ne l'ai pas vu! — ~!** but I didn't see him! — precisely! *ou* exactly! *ou* that's just it! *ou* that's just the point!

(c) (*exactement*) exactly, precisely. **c'est ~ ce que je cherchais** that's exactly *ou* precisely *ou* just what I was looking for; **il est arrivé ~ à ce moment-là** he arrived right *ou* just at that moment *ou* at that exact *ou* precise *ou* very moment; **ce n'est pas ~ ce que j'appelle un chef-d'œuvre** it's not exactly what I'd call a masterpiece.

préciser [pʀesize] (1) **1** *vt idée, intention* to specify, make clear, clarify; *faits, points* to be more specific about, clarify. **je vous préciserai la date de la réunion plus tard** I'll let you know the exact date of the meeting later; **il a précisé que ...** he explained that ..., he made it clear that ...; **je dois ~ que ...** I must point out *ou* add that ...; **pourriez-vous ~ quand cela est arrivé?** could you be more exact *ou* specific about when it happened?; **pourriez-vous ~?** could you be more precise? *ou* explicit?

2 se préciser *vpr [idée]* to take shape; *[danger, intentions]* to become clear *ou* clearer. **la situation commence à se ~** we are beginning to see the situation more clearly.

précision [pʀesizjɔ̃] *nf* **(a)** (*U*) (*gén*) precision, preciseness; *[description, instrument]* precision, preciseness, accuracy; *[contours]* precision, preciseness, distinctness; *[trait]* distinctness. **avec ~** precisely, with precision; **de ~** precision (*épith*).

(b) (*détail*) point, piece of information. **j'aimerais vous demander une ~/des ~s** I'd like to ask you to explain one thing/for further explanation *ou* information; **il a apporté des ~s intéressantes** he revealed some interesting points *ou* facts *ou* information; **encore une ~** one more point *ou* thing.

précité, e [pʀesite] *adj* aforesaid, aforementioned; (*par écrit*) aforesaid, above(-mentioned).

précoce [pʀekɔs] *adj fruit, saison, gelée* early; *plante* early-flowering *ou* -fruiting, precocious (*T*); *calvitie, sénilité* premature; *mariage* young (*épith*), early (*épith*); *enfant* (*intellectuellement*) precocious, advanced for his *ou* her age (*attrib*); (*sexuellement*) sexually precocious *ou* forward.

précocement [pʀekɔsmɑ̃] *adv* precociously.

précocité [pʀekɔsite] *nf [fruit, saison]* earliness; *[enfant]* (*intellectuelle*) precocity, precociousness; (*sexuelle*) sexual precocity, sexual precociousness.

précolombien, -ienne [pʀekɔlɔ̃bjɛ̃, jɛn] *adj* pre-Colombian.

précombustion [pʀekɔ̃bystjɔ̃] *nf* precombustion.

précompte [pʀekɔ̃t] *nm* deduction (from sb's pay).

précompter [pʀekɔ̃te] (1) *vt* to deduct (*sur* from).

préconception [pʀekɔ̃sɛpsjɔ̃] *nf* preconception.

préconçu, e [pʀekɔ̃sy] *adj* preconceived. **idée ~e** preconceived idea.

préconiser [pʀekɔnize] (1) *vt remède* to recommend; *méthode, mode de vie* to advocate.

précontraint, e [pʀekɔ̃tʀɛ̃, ɛ̃t] *adj, nm:* **(béton) ~** prestressed concrete.

précurseur [pʀekyʀsœʀ] **1** *adj m* precursory. **~ de** preceding; *V* signe. **2** *nm* forerunner, precursor.

prédateur, -trice [pʀedatœʀ, tʀis] **1** *adj* predatory. **2** *nm* predator.

prédécesseur [pʀedesesœʀ] *nm* predecessor.

prédestination [pʀedɛstinɑsjɔ̃] *nf* predestination.

prédestiné, e [pʀedestine] (*ptp de* **prédestiner**) *adj* predestined (*à qch* for sth, *à faire* to do), fated (*à faire* to do).

prédestiner [pʀedɛstine] (1) *vt* to predestine (*à qch* for sth, *à faire* to do).

prédétermination [pʀedetɛʀminɑsjɔ̃] *nf* predetermination.

prédéterminer [pʀedetɛʀmine] (1) *vt* to predetermine.

prédicant [pʀedikɑ̃] *nm* preacher.

prédicat [pʀedika] *nm* predicate.

prédicateur [pʀedikatœʀ] *nm* preacher.

prédicatif, -ive [pʀedikatif, iv] *adj* predicative.

prédication [pʀedikɑsjɔ̃] *nf* (*U*) preaching; (*sermon*) sermon.

prédiction [pʀediksjɔ̃] *nf* prediction.

prédigéré, e [pʀediʒeʀe] *adj* predigested.

prédilection [pʀedilɛksjɔ̃] *nf* (*pour qn, qch*) predilection, partiality (*pour* for). **avoir une ~ pour la cuisine française** to have a partiality for *ou* be partial to French cooking; **de ~** favourite, preferred (*frm*).

prédire [pʀediʀ] (37) *vt [prophète]* to foretell; (*gén*) to predict. **~ l'avenir** to tell *ou* predict the future; **~ qch à qn** to predict sth for sb; **il m'a prédit que je ...** he predicted (that) I ..., he told me (that) I ... .

prédisposer [pʀedispoze] (1) *vt* to predispose (*à qch* to sth, *à faire* to do). **être prédisposé à une maladie** to be predisposed *ou* prone to an illness; **être prédisposé en faveur de qn** to be predisposed in sb's favour.

prédisposition [pʀedispozisjɔ̃] *nf* predisposition (*à qch* to sth, *à faire* to do).

prédominance [pʀedɔminɑ̃s] *ne* (*gén*) predominance, predominancy; *[couleur]* predominance, prominence.

prédominant, e [pʀedɔminɑ̃, ɑ̃t] *adj* (*gén*) predominant, most dominant; *avis, impression* prevailing; *couleur* predominant, most prominent.

prédominer [pʀedɔmine] (1) *vi* (*gén*) to predominate, be most dominant; *[avis, impression]* to prevail; *[couleur]* to predominate, be most prominent. **le souci qui prédomine dans mon esprit** the worry which is uppermost in my mind.

prééminence [pʀeeminɑ̃s] *nf* pre-eminence.

prééminent, e [pʀeeminɑ̃, ɑ̃t] *adj* pre-eminent.

préemption [pʀeɑ̃psjɔ̃] *nf* pre-emption. **droit de ~** pre-emptive right.

préétablir [pʀeetabliʀ] (2) *vt* to pre-establish.

préexistant, e [pʀeɛgzistɑ̃, ɑ̃t] *adj* pre-existent, pre-existing.

préexistence [pʀeɛgzistɑ̃s] *nf* pre-existence.

préexister [pʀeɛgziste] (1) *vi* to pre-exist. **~ à** to exist before.

préfabrication [pʀefabʀikɑsjɔ̃] *nf* prefabrication.

préfabriqué, e [pʀefabʀike] **1** *adj* prefabricated. **2** *nm* (*maison*) prefabricated house, prefab*; (*matériau*) prefabricated material.

préface [pʀefas] *nf* preface; (*fig: prélude*) preface, prelude (*à* to).

préfacer [pʀefase] (3) *vt livre* to write a preface for, preface.

préfacier [pʀefasje] *nm* preface writer.

préfectoral, e, *mpl* **-aux** [pʀefɛktɔʀal, o] *adj* (*Admin française, Antiq*) prefectorial, prefectural.

préfecture [pʀefɛktyʀ] *nf* (*Admin française, Antiq*) prefecture. **~ de police** Paris police headquarters.

préférable [pʀefeʀabl(ə)] *adj* preferable (*à qch* to sth), better (*à qch* than sth). **il est ~ que je parte** it is preferable *ou* better that I should leave *ou* for me to leave; **il serait ~ d'y aller** *ou* **que vous y alliez** it would be better if you went *ou* for you to go; **il est ~ de faire** it is preferable *ou* better to do.

préférablement [pʀefeʀabləmɑ̃] *adv* preferably. **~ à** in preference to.

préféré, e [pʀefeʀe] (*ptp de* **préférer**) **1** *adj* favourite, pet* (*épith*), preferred (*frm*). **2** *nm,f* favourite, pet*. **le ~ du professeur** the teacher's pet*.

préférence [pʀefeʀɑ̃s] *nf* preference. **de ~** preferably; **de ~ à** in preference to, rather than; **donner la ~ à** to give preference to; **avoir une ~ marquée pour ...** to have a marked preference for ... ; **avoir la ~ sur** to have preference over; **je n'ai pas de ~** I have no preference, I don't mind.

préférentiel, -ielle [pʀefeʀɑ̃sjɛl] *adj* preferential.

préférer [pʀefeʀe] (6) *vt* to prefer (*à* to). **je préfère ce manteau à l'autre** I prefer this coat to that, I like this coat better than that one *ou* the other; **je te préfère avec les cheveux courts** I like you better *ou* prefer you with short hair; **je préfère aller au cinéma** I prefer to go *ou* I would rather go to the cinema; **il préfère que ce soit vous qui le fassiez** he prefers that you should do it, he would rather you did it; **nous avons préféré attendre avant de vous le dire** we preferred to wait *ou* we thought it better to wait before telling you; **nous avons préféré attendre que d'y aller tout de suite** we preferred to wait *ou* thought it better to wait rather than go straight away; **que préférez-vous: du thé ou du café?** what would you rather have *ou* would you prefer — tea or coffee?; **si tu préfères** if you prefer, if you like.

préfet [pʀefɛ] *nm* (*Admin française, Antiq*) prefect. **~ de police** prefect of police.

préfète [pʀefɛt] *nf* prefect's wife.

préfiguration [pʀefigyʀɑsjɔ̃] *nf* prefiguration, foreshadowing.

préfigurer [pʀefigyʀe] (1) *vt* to prefigure, foreshadow.

préfixal, e, *mpl* **-aux** [pʀefiksal, o] *adj* prefixal.

préfixation [pʀefiksɑsjɔ̃] *nf* prefixation.

préfixe [pʀefiks] *nm* prefix.

préfixer [pʀefikse] (1) *vt* to prefix.

préglaciaire [pʀeglasjɛʀ] *adj* preglacial.

préhenseur [pʀeɑ̃sœʀ] *adj m* prehensile.

préhensile [pʀeɑ̃sil] *adj* prehensile.

préhension [pʀeɑ̃sjɔ̃] *nf* prehension.

préhistoire [pʀeistwaʀ] *nf* prehistory.

préhistorique [pʀeistɔʀik] *adj* prehistoric; (*fig: suranné*) antediluvian, ancient.

préjudice [pʀeʒydis] *nm* (*matériel, financier*) loss; (*moral*) harm (*U*), damage (*U*), wrong. **subir un ~** (*matériel*) to suffer a loss; (*moral*) to be wronged; **porter ~ à qn** to do sb harm, harm sb, do sb a disservice; **ce supermarché a porté ~ aux petits commerçants** this supermarket was detrimental to (the interests of) small tradesmen; **je ne voudrais pas vous porter ~ en leur racontant cela** I wouldn't like to harm you *ou* your case *ou* make difficulties for you by telling them about this; **au ~ de sa santé/de la vérité** to the prejudice (*frm*) *ou* at the expense *ou* at the cost of his health/the truth; **au ~ de M X** to the prejudice (*frm*) *ou* at the expense of Mr X; **~ moral** moral wrong; **sans ~ de** without prejudice to.

préjudiciable [pʀeʒydisjabl(ə)] *adj* prejudicial, detrimental, harmful (*à* to).

préjugé [pʀeʒyʒe] *nm* prejudice. **avoir un ~ contre** to be prejudiced *ou* biased against; **sans ~** unprejudiced, unbiased; **bénéficier d'un ~ favorable** to be favourably considered.

préjuger [pʀeʒyʒe] (3) *vt,* **préjuger (de)** *vt indir* to prejudge. **~ d'une réaction** to foresee a reaction, judge what a reaction might be; **autant qu'on peut le ~, à ce qu'on en peut ~** as far as it is possible to judge in advance.

prélasser (se) [pʀelɑse] (1) *vpr* (*dans un fauteuil*) to sprawl, lounge; (*au soleil*) to bask.

prélat [pʀela] *nm* prelate.

prélature [pʀelatyʀ] *nf* prelacy.

pré-lavage [pʀelavaʒ] *nm* pre-wash.

pré-laver [pʀelave] (1) *vt* to pre-wash.

prélèvement [pʀelɛvmɑ̃] *nm* (*V* **prélever**) taking (*U*); levying (*U*), imposition; deduction; withdrawal, drawing out (*U*); removal. **faire un ~ de sang** to take a blood sample; **~ bancaire** standing *ou* banker's order.

prélever [pʀelve] (5) *vt échantillon* to take (*sur* from); *impôt* to levy, impose (*sur* on); *retenue, montant* to deduct (*sur* from); *argent* (*sur un compte*) to withdraw, draw out (*sur* from); (*Méd*) *sang* to take (a sample of); *organe* to remove. **ses factures d'électricité sont automatiquement prélevées sur son compte** his electricity bills are automatically deducted from his account.

préliminaire [pʀelimineʀ] **1** *adj* preliminary. **2** *nmpl*: **~s** preliminaries; *[négociations]* preliminary talks.

prélude [pʀelyd] *nm* (*Mus*) (*morceau*) prelude; (*pour se préparer*) warm-up; (*fig*) prelude (*à* to).

préluder [pʀelyde] (1) **1** *vi* (*Mus*) to warm up. **~ par** to begin with. **2 préluder à** *vt indir* to be a prelude to, lead up to, prelude.

prématuré, e [pʀematyʀe] **1** *adj bébé, nouvelle* premature; *mort* untimely, premature. **il est ~ de** it is premature to, it's too early to. **2** *nm,f* premature baby.

prématurément [pʀematyʀemɑ̃] *adv* prematurely. **une cruelle maladie l'a enlevé ~ à notre affection** a grievous illness took him too soon from his loving family *ou* brought his untimely departure from our midst.

préméditation [pʀemeditɑsjɔ̃] *nf* premeditation. **avec ~** (*adj*) premeditated; (*adv*) with intent, with malice aforethought†.

préméditer [pʀemedite] (1) *vt* to premeditate. **~ de faire** to plan to do.

prémices [pʀemis] *nfpl* (*littér*) beginnings; *[récolte]* first fruits; *[animaux]* first-born (animals).

premier, -ière [pʀəmje, jɛʀ] **1** *adj* **(a)** (*dans le temps, l'espace*) (*gén*) first; *impression* first, initial; *enfance, jeunesse* early; *rang* front; *ébauche, projet* first, rough; *branche* lower, bottom; *barreau d'échelle* bottom. **arriver/être ~** to arrive/be first; **arriver bon ~** to get there well ahead of the others; (*dans une course*) to come an easy first; **dans le ~ café venu** in the first café they came to; **la ~ière fille venue** the first girl to come along; (*Sport*) **être en/venir en ~ière position** to be in/come into the lead; (*Équitation*) **en ~ière position: Brutus** (and it's) Brutus leading *ou* in the lead; (*Presse*) **en ~ière page** on the front page; **les 100 ~ières pages** the first 100 pages; **la ~ière marche de l'escalier** the bottom step; **le ~ mouchoir de la pile** the first handkerchief in the pile, the top handkerchief in the pile; **les ~ières heures du jour** the early hours, the (wee) small hours*; **dès les ~s jours** from the very first days; **ses ~s poèmes** his first *ou* early poems; **les ~s habitants de la terre** the earliest *ou* first inhabitants of the earth; **les ~ières années de sa vie** the first few *ou* the early years of his life; **lire qch de la ~ière à la dernière ligne** to read sth from beginning to end *ou* from cover to cover; **c'est la ~ière et la dernière fois que je suis tes conseils** it's the first and last time I follow your advice; **acheter une voiture de ~ière main** to buy a car which has only had one owner; **poser la ~ière pierre** (*lit, fig*) to lay the foundation stone *ou* first stone; **au ~ signe de résistance** at the first *ou* slightest sign of resistance; **à mon ~ signal** at the first signal from me, as soon as you see my signal; *V* **lit, sixième, tête.**

(b) (*dans un ordre*) first; (*à un examen*) first, top; (*en importance*) leading, foremost, top*. **~ secrétaire/lieutenant** first secretary/lieutenant; **~ commis/clerc** chief shop assistant/clerk; **~ danseur** leading dancer; **article de ~ière qualité** top-quality article, article of the first quality; **de ~ ordre** first-rate; (*Rail*) **~ière classe** first-class; (*Boucherie*) **morceau de ~ choix** prime cut; **affaire à traiter en ~ière urgence** question to be dealt with as a matter of the utmost urgency *ou* as (a) top priority; (*Gram*) **à la ~ière personne (du singulier)** in the first person (singular); **être reçu ~** to come first *ou* top; **il est toujours ~ en classe** he's always top of the class *ou* first in the class; **avoir le ~ prix** to get *ou* win first prize; (*Mus*) **c'est un ~ prix du conservatoire de Paris** he won first prize at the Paris Conservatoire; **un événement/document de ~ière importance** an event/a document of paramount *ou* prime *ou* the highest *ou* the first importance; **de ~ière nécessité** absolutely essential; **objets de ~ière nécessité** basic essentials; **cela m'intéresse au ~ chef** it's of the greatest *ou* utmost interest to me; **c'est lui le ~ intéressé dans cette histoire** he's the one who has most at stake in this business; **le ~ constructeur automobile du monde** the world's leading car manufacturer; **c'est le ~ écrivain français vivant** he's the leading *ou* greatest *ou* foremost *ou* top* French writer alive today.

(c) (*du début*) *échelon, grade, prix* bottom. **c'était le ~ prix** it was the cheapest; **apprendre les ~s rudiments d'une science** to learn the first *ou* basic rudiments of a science.

(d) (*après n: originel, fondamental*) *cause, donnée* basic; *principe* first, basic; *objectif* basic, primary, prime; *état* initial, original. **la qualité ~ière d'un chef d'État est ...** the prime *ou* essential quality of a head of state is ... ; **retrouver sa vivacité ~ière/son éclat ~** to regain one's former *ou* initial liveliness/sparkle; *V* **matière, nombre, vérité.**

(e) (*loc*) **au ~ abord** at first sight, to begin with; **au** *ou* **du ~ coup** at the first attempt *ou* go *ou* try; **demain, à la ~ière heure** tomorrow at first light; **il n'est plus de la ~ière jeunesse** he's not as young as he was *ou* as he used to be; **en ~ lieu** in the first place; **il veut acheter une maison mais il n'en a pas le ~ sou** he wants to buy a house but he hasn't got two pennies (*Brit*) *ou* cents (*US*) to rub together *ou* a penny (*Brit*) *ou* a cent (*US*) (to his name); **il n'en connaît** *ou* **n'en sait pas le ~ mot** he doesn't know the first thing about it; **il s'en moque** *ou* **fiche comme de sa ~ière chemise*** he doesn't give a damn about it*, he doesn't care a fig* *ou* a rap* about it; **~ière nouvelle!** that's the first I've heard about it!, it's news to me!; **à la ~ière occasion** at the first opportunity, as soon as one can; **il a fait ses ~ières armes dans le métier en 1960/comme manœuvre** he started out on the job in 1960/as an unskilled worker; **faire ses ~s pas** to start walking; **faire les ~s pas** to take the initiative, make the first move; **il n'y a que le ~ pas qui coûte** the first step is the hardest; **dans un ~ temps** to start *ou* begin with, at first; **dans les ~s temps** in the earliest times; **à ~ière vue** at first sight.

2 *nm,f* first (one). **parler/passer/sortir le ~** to speak/go/go out first; **arriver les ~s** to arrive (the) first; **les ~s arrivés seront les ~s servis** first come, first served; **il a été le ~ à reconnaître ses torts** he was the first to admit that he was in the wrong; **elle sera servie la ~ière** she will be served first; **au ~ de ces messieurs** next gentleman please; (*Scol, Univ*) **il a été reçu dans** *ou* **parmi les ~s** he was in the top *ou* first few; **il est le ~ de sa classe** he is top of his class; **les ~s seront les derniers** the last shall be first, and the first last; **les ~s venus** (*lit*) the first to come *ou* to arrive; (*fig*) anybody, anybody who happens by; **il n'est pas le ~ venu** he isn't just anyone; **elle n'épousera pas le ~ venu** she won't marry the first man that comes along; **le ~ semble mieux** (*entre deux*) the first one seems better; (*dans une série*) the first one seems best; *V* **jeune, né.**

3 *nm* (*gén*) first; (*étage*) first floor (*Brit*), second floor (*US*). (*enfant*) **c'est leur ~** it's their first child; **le ~ de l'an** New Year's Day; (*charade*) **mon ~ est ...** my first is in ... ; **il était arrivé en ~** he had arrived first; **en ~ je dirai que ...**firstly *ou* first *ou* in the first place *ou* to start with I'd like to say that ... .

4 première *nf* **(a)** (*gén*) first; (*Aut*) first (gear); (*Hippisme*) first (race). (*Aut*) **être en/passer la ~ière** to be in/go into first (gear).

(b) (*Théât*) first night; (*Ciné*) première; (*gén: exploit*) first; (*Alpinisme*) first ascent. **le public des grandes ~ières** first-nighters; **~ière mondiale** (*Ciné*) world première; (*gén*) world first.

(c) (*Aviat, Rail etc*) first class. **voyager en ~ière** to travel first-class; **billet de ~ière** first-class ticket.

(d) (*Scol*) ≃ lower sixth.

(e) (*Couture*) head seamstress.

(f) (*semelle*) insole.

(g) (**loc*) **c'est de ~ière!** it's first-class!; **il est de ~ière pour trouver les bons restaurants/pour les gaffes!** he's got a great knack* for *ou* he's great* at finding good restaurants/making blunders!

5: le premier âge the first 3 months; **le premier avril** the first of April, April Fool's Day; (*Théât*) **premiers balcons** lower circle; (*Mil*) **première classe** *nm* ≃ private (*Brit*), private first class (*US*); **premier communiant/première communiante** young boy/girl making his/her first communion; **première communion** first communion; **faire sa première communion** to make one's first communion; (*Alpinisme*) **premier de cordée** leader; (*Typ*) **première épreuve** first proof; **premier jet** first *ou* rough draft; **premier jour** *[exposition]* first *ou* opening day; (*Théât*) **premières loges** first-tier boxes; (*fig*) **être aux premières loges** to have a front seat (*fig*); **le Premier Mai** the first of May, May Day; (*Naut*) **premier-maître** *nm, pl* **premier-maîtres** chief petty officer; **Premier ministre** Prime Minister, Premier; **premier plan** (*Phot*) foreground; (*fig*) forefront; **personnage/rôle de (tout) premier plan** principal character/role; (*Théât*) **premier rôle** leading role *ou* part; (*fig*) **avoir le premier rôle dans une affaire** to play the leading part in an affair; **les premiers secours** first aid; **premier violon** leader.

premièrement [pʀəmjɛʀmɑ̃] *adv* (*d'abord*) first(ly); (*en premier lieu*) in the first place; (*introduisant une objection*) firstly, for a start. **~ il ne m'a rien dit** to begin with *ou* first of all *ou* at first he didn't say anything to me.

prémisse [pʀemis] *nf* premise, premiss.

prémolaire [pʀemɔlɛʀ] *nf* premolar (tooth).

prémonition [pʀemɔnisjɔ̃] *nf* premonition.

prémonitoire [pʀemɔnitwaʀ] *adj* premonitory.

prémunir [pʀemyniʀ] (2) **1** *vt* (*littér*) (*mettre en garde*) to warn; (*protéger*) to protect (*contre* against).

2 se prémunir *vpr* to protect o.s. (*contre* from), guard (*contre* against).

prenable [pʀənabl(ə)] *adj ville* pregnable.

prénaissance [pʀenesɑ̃s] *nf* pregnancy. **robe de ~** maternity dress.

prenant, e [pʀənɑ̃, ɑ̃t] *adj* **(a)** (*captivant*) *film, livre* absorbing, engrossing, compelling; *voix* fascinating, captivating.

(b) (*absorbant*) *activité* absorbing, engrossing. **ce travail est trop ~** this job is too absorbing *ou* is over-absorbing.

(c) (*Zool*) *queue* prehensile.

prénatal, e, *mpl* **~s** [pʀenatal] *adj* antenatal; *allocation* maternity (*épith*).

prendre [pʀɑ̃dʀ(ə)] (58) **1** *vt* **(a)** (*saisir*) *objet* to take. **prends-le dans le placard/sur l'étagère** take it out of the cupboard/off *ou* (down) from the shelf; **il l'a pris dans le tiroir** he took *ou* got it out of the drawer; **il prit un journal/son crayon sur la table** he picked up *ou* took a newspaper/his pencil from the table; **prends tes lunettes pour lire** put your glasses on to read; **il la prit par le cou/par la taille** he put his arms round her neck/round her waist; **ils se prirent par le cou/par la taille** they put their arms round one another('s necks/waists); **il y a plusieurs livres, lequel prends-tu?** there are several books — which one are you going to take? *ou* which one do you want?; **il a pris le bleu** he took the blue one; **~ qch des mains de qn** (*débarrasser*) to take sth out of sb's hands; (*enlever*) to take sth off sb *ou* away from sb.

(b) (*aller chercher*) *chose* to pick up, get, fetch; *personne* to pick up; (*emmener*) to take. **passer ~ qn à son bureau** to pick sb up *ou* call for sb at his office; **je passerai les ~ chez toi** I'll come and collect *ou* get them *ou* I'll call in for them at your place; **pouvez-vous me ~ (dans votre voiture)?** can you give me a lift?; **si tu sors, prends ton parapluie** if you go out, take your umbrella (with you); **as-tu pris les valises?** have you brought the suitcases?; **je ne veux plus de ce manteau, tu peux le ~** I don't want this coat any more so you can take *ou* have it; **prends ta chaise et viens t'asseoir ici** bring your chair and come and sit over here; **prends du beurre dans le frigo** go and get *ou* go and fetch some butter from the fridge, get some butter out of the fridge.

(c) (*s'emparer de*) *poisson, voleur* to catch; *argent, place, otage* to take; (*Mil*) *ville* to take, capture; (*Cartes, Échecs*) to take. **un voleur lui a pris son portefeuille** a thief has taken *ou* stolen his wallet *ou* has robbed him of his wallet; **il m'a pris mon idée** he has used *ou* pinched* my idea; **il prend tout ce qui lui tombe sous la main** he takes *ou* grabs everything he can lay his hands on; **le voleur s'est fait ~** the robber was caught; **~ une femme** to take a woman.

(d) (*surprendre*) to catch. **~ qn à faire qch** to catch sb doing sth; **je vous y prends!** caught you!; (*menace*) **si je t'y prends (encore), que je t'y prenne** just *ou* don't let me catch you doing that (again) *ou* at it (again); **le brouillard nous a pris dans la descente** we were caught in the fog on the way down the hill; **on ne m'y prendra plus** I won't be taken in again, I won't be had a second time*; **se laisser ~ à des paroles aimables** to let o.s. be taken in by soft talk.

(e) *boisson, repas* to have; *médicament* to take; *bain, douche* to take, have. **est-ce que vous prenez du sucre?** do you take sugar?; **est-ce que vous prendrez du café?** will you have *ou* would you like (some) coffee?; **fais-lui ~ son médicament** give him his medicine; **à ~ avant les repas** to be taken before meals; **ce médicament se prend dans de l'eau** this medicine must be taken in water; **as-tu pris de ce bon gâteau?** have you had some of this nice cake?; **il n'a rien pris depuis hier** he hasn't eaten anything since yesterday; **le docteur m'interdit de ~ de l'alcool** the doctor won't allow me (to take *ou* drink) alcohol.

(f) (*voyager par*) *métro, taxi* to take, travel *ou* go *ou* come by; *voiture* to take; (*s'engager dans*) *direction, rue* to take. **il prit le train puis l'avion de Paris à Londres** he took the train *ou* went by train then flew from Paris to London; **je prends l'avion/le train de 4 heures** I'm catching the 4 o'clock plane/train; (*d'habitude*) I catch the 4 o'clock plane/train; **je préfère ~ ma voiture** I'd rather take the car *ou* go in the car; **~ la mauvaise direction** to take the wrong direction, go the wrong way; **ils prirent un chemin défoncé** they went down a bumpy lane.

(g) (*se procurer*) *billet, essence* to get; (*acheter*) *voiture* to buy; (*réserver*) *couchette, place* to book. **il prend toujours son pain à côté** he always gets *ou* buys his bread from the shop next door; **peux-tu me ~ du pain?** can you get me some bread?; **nous avons pris une maison** (*loué*) we have taken *ou* rented a house; (*acheté*) we have bought a house.

(h) (*accepter*) *client* to take; *passager* to pick up; *locataire* to take (in); *personnel* to take on; *domestique* to engage, take on. **l'école ne prend plus de pensionnaires** the school no longer takes boarders; **ce train ne prend pas de voyageurs** this train does not pick up passengers; **il l'a prise comme interprète** he took her on as an interpreter.

(i) *photo, film* to take. **~ qn en photo/en film** to take a photo/a film of sb, photograph *ou* snap*/film sb.

(j) (*noter*) *renseignement, adresse, nom, rendez-vous* to write down, take down, jot down, make a note of; *mesures, température, empreintes* to take; (*sous la dictée*) *lettre* to take (down). **~ des notes** to take notes.

(k) (*adopter, choisir*) *air, ton* to put on, assume; *décision* to take, make, come to; *risque, mesure* to take; *attitude* to strike, take up. **il prit un ton menaçant** a threatening note crept into his voice, his voice took on a threatening tone.

(l) (*acquérir*) *assurance* to gain. **~ du ventre** to get fat; **~ du poids** *[adulte]* to put on weight; *[bébé]* to gain weight; **~ de l'autorité** to gain authority; **cela prend un sens** it's beginning to make sense; **les feuilles prenaient une couleur dorée** the leaves were turning golden-brown *ou* taking on a golden-brown colour.

(m) (*Méd*) *maladie* to catch. ~ **froid** to catch cold; ~ **un rhume** to catch a cold.

(n) (*s'accorder*) *congé* to take; *vacances* to take, have, go on; *repos* to have, take. **il a pris son temps!** he took his time (over *ou* about it)!; ~ **le temps de faire** to find time to do.

(o) (*coûter*) *temps, place, argent* to take. **cela me prend tout mon temps** it takes up all my time; **la réparation a pris des heures** the repair took hours *ou* ages.

(p) (*faire payer*) to charge. **ils prennent un pourcentage sur la vente** they charge a commission on the sale; **ils (m')ont pris 100 F pour une petite réparation** they charged (me) 100 francs for a minor repair; **ce spécialiste prend très cher** this specialist charges very high fees, this specialist's charges *ou* fees are very high; **ce plombier prend cher de l'heure** this plumber's hourly rate is high.

(q) (*prélever*) *pourcentage* to take. **il prend sa commission sur la vente** he takes his commission on the sale; ~ **de l'argent à la banque/sur son compte** to draw (out) *ou* withdraw money from the bank/from one's account; **la cotisation à la retraite est prise sur le salaire** the pension contribution is taken off one's salary *ou* deducted from one's salary; **il a dû** ~ **sur ses économies pour payer les dégâts** he had to dip into *ou* go into his savings to pay for the damage; **il a pris sur son temps pour venir m'aider** he gave up some of his time to help me.

(r) (*: *recevoir, subir*) *coup, choc* to get, receive. **il a pris la porte en pleine figure** the door hit *ou* got* him right in the face; **nous avons pris l'averse sur le dos** we got caught in the shower; **on a pris toute l'averse** we got drenched; **qu'est-ce qu'on a pris!** (*reproches*) we didn't half* catch *ou* cop‡ (*Brit*) it!; (*défaite*) we got hammered!‡; (*averse*) we got drenched!; (*emploi absolu*) **il a pris pour les autres** he took the rap; **le seau d'eau s'est renversé et c'est moi qui ai tout pris** the bucket of water tipped over and I caught the lot.

(s) (*manier*) *personne* to handle; *problème* to handle, tackle, deal with, cope with. ~ **qn par la douceur** to use gentle persuasion on sb; **elle sait le** ~ she knows how to handle *ou* approach *ou* get round him; **on ne sait jamais par quel bout le** ~ you never know how to handle him *ou* how he's going to react; **il y a plusieurs façons de** ~ **le problème** there are several ways of going about *ou* tackling the problem.

(t) (*réagir à*) *nouvelle* to take. **il a bien/mal pris la chose, il l'a bien/mal pris** he took it well/badly; **si vous le prenez ainsi ...** if that's how you want it ... ; ~ **qch avec bonne humeur** to take sth good-humouredly *ou* in good part; ~ **les choses comme elles sont/la vie comme elle vient** to take things as they come/life as it comes.

(u) ~ **qn/qch pour** (*considérer*) to take sb/sth for; (*se servir de*) to take sb/sth as; **pour qui me prenez-vous?** what do you take me for?, what do you think I am?; ~ **qn pour un autre** to take sb for *ou* think sb is somebody else, mistake sb for somebody else; **je n'aime pas qu'on me prenne pour un imbécile** I don't like being taken for a fool; ~ **qch pour prétexte/pour cible** to take sth as a pretext/target.

(v) (*assaillir*) *[colère]* to come over; *[fièvre]* to strike; *[doute]* to seize, sweep over; *[douleur]* to strike, get*. **la colère le prit soudain** he was suddenly overcome with anger, anger suddenly came over him; **être pris de vertige** to come over (*surtout Brit*) *ou* go dizzy; **être pris de remords** to be stricken by remorse; **être pris de panique** to be panic-stricken; **l'envie me prend** *ou* **il me prend l'envie de faire** I feel like doing, I've got an urge to do; **la douleur m'a pris au genou** the pain got me in the knee; **les douleurs la prirent** her labour pains started; **qu'est-ce qui te prend?*** what's the matter *ou* what's up* with you?, what's come over you?*; **ça te prend souvent?‡** are you often like that? (*iro*), do you often get these fits?* (*iro*); **quand le froid vous prend** when the cold hits you; **ça vous prend aux tripes‡** it gets you right there, it hits you right in the guts‡.

(w) (*accrocher, coincer*) to catch, trap. **le chat s'est pris la patte dans un piège** the cat got its paw trapped, the cat caught its paw in a trap; **le rideau se prend dans la fenêtre** the curtain gets caught (up) *ou* stuck in the window; **j'ai pris mon manteau dans la porte, mon manteau s'est pris dans la porte** I caught *ou* trapped my coat in the door, my coat got stuck *ou* trapped *ou* caught in the door.

(x) (*loc*) **à tout** ~ on the whole, all in all; **c'est à** ~ **ou à laisser** (you can) take it or leave it; **avec lui j'en prends et j'en laisse** I take everything he says with a pinch of salt; **c'est toujours ça** *ou* **autant de pris** that's something at least; ~ **qch sur soi** to take sth upon o.s.; ~ **sur soi de faire qch** to take it upon o.s. to do sth.

2 *vi* **(a)** (*durcir*) *[ciment, pâte, crème]* to set.

(b) (*réussir*) *[plante]* to take (root); *[vaccin]* to take; *[mouvement, mode]* to catch on; *[livre, spectacle]* to be a success. **la plaisanterie a pris** the joke was a great success; **avec moi, ça ne prend pas*** it won't wash with me* (*Brit*), it doesn't work with me.

(c) *[feu]* (*foyer*) to go; *[incendie]* to start; *[allumette]* to light; *[bois]* to catch fire. **le feu ne veut pas** ~ the fire won't go; **le feu a pris au toit** the fire took hold in the roof.

(d) (*se diriger*) to go. ~ **à gauche** to go *ou* turn *ou* bear left; ~ **par les petites rues** to take to *ou* go along *ou* keep to the side streets.

3 se prendre *vpr* **(a)** (*se considérer*) **se** ~ **au sérieux** to take o.s. seriously; **il se prend pour un intellectuel** he thinks *ou* likes to think he's an intellectual; **pour qui se prend-il?** (just) who does he think he is?

(b) (*littér: commencer*) **se** ~ **à faire qch** to begin to do *ou* begin doing sth, start doing sth.

(c) s'y ~ to set about (doing) it; **il fallait s'y** ~ **à temps** you should have set about it *ou* started before it was too late; **s'y** ~ **bien/mal pour faire qch** to set about doing sth the right/wrong way; **il s'y est pris drôlement pour le faire** he chose the oddest way of doing it, he went about it in the strangest way; **s'y** ~ **à deux fois/plusieurs fois pour faire qch** to try twice/several times to do sth, take two/several attempts to do sth; **il faut s'y** ~ **à deux** it needs two of us (to do it); **il ne sait pas s'y** ~ he doesn't know how to do it *ou* set about it; **je ne sais pas comment tu t'y prends** I don't know how you manage it; **il ne s'y serait pas pris autrement s'il avait voulu tout faire échouer** he couldn't have done better if he had actually set out to ruin the whole thing; **s'y** ~ **bien** *ou* **savoir s'y** ~ **avec qn** to handle sb the right way.

(d) s'en ~ **à** *personne* (*agresser*) to lay into, set about; (*passer sa colère sur*) to take it out on; (*blâmer*) to lay *ou* put the blame on, attack; *traditions, préjugés* (*remettre en question*) to challenge; *autorité, organisation* (*critiquer*) to attack, take on; **s'en** ~ **à qch** to take it out on sth; **tu ne peux t'en** ~ **qu'à toi** you've only got yourself to blame; **s'en** ~ **aux traditions** to let fly at tradition.

(e) (*se solidifier*) to set hard. **l'eau s'est prise en glace** the water has frozen over.

preneur, -euse [pʀənœʀ, øz] *nm,f* (*acheteur*) buyer; (*locataire*) lessee (*Jur*), taker, tenant. **trouver** ~ to find a buyer; (*fig*) **ces restes de gâteau vont vite trouver** ~ someone will soon eat (up) what's left of this cake, there'll be no problem finding a taker for the rest of this cake; **je suis** ~ **à 100 F** I'll buy *ou* take it for 100 francs.

prénom [pʀenɔ̃] *nm* (*gén*) Christian name, first name; (*Admin*) forename, given name (*US*). ~ **usuel** name by which one is known, name one is usually called.

prénommé, e [pʀenɔme] (*ptp de* **prénommer**) **1** *adj*: **le** ~ **Paul** the said Paul. **2** *nm,f* (*Jur*) above-named.

prénommer [pʀenɔme] (1) **1** *vt* to call, name, give a (Christian) name to. **on l'a prénommé comme son oncle** he was called *ou* named after his uncle, he was given the same name as his uncle.

2 se prénommer *vpr* to be called *ou* named.

prénuptial, e, *mpl* **-aux** [pʀenypsjal, o] *adj* premarital.

préoccupant, e [pʀeɔkypɑ̃, ɑ̃t] *adj* worrying.

préoccupation [pʀeɔkypɑsjɔ̃] *nf* **(a)** (*souci*) worry, anxiety. **sa mauvaise santé était une** ~ **supplémentaire pour ses parents** his ill health was a further worry to *ou* cause for concern to his parents.

(b) (*priorité*) preoccupation, concern. **sa seule** ~ **était de** his one concern *ou* preoccupation was to.

préoccupé, e [pʀeɔkype] (*ptp de* **préoccuper**) *adj* (*absorbé*) preoccupied (*de qch* with sth, *de faire* with doing); (*soucieux*) concerned (*de qch* about sth, *de faire* to do), worried (*de qch* about sth, *de faire* over doing). **tu as l'air** ~ you look worried.

préoccuper [pʀeɔkype] (1) **1** *vt* **(a)** (*inquiéter*) to worry. **il y a quelque chose qui le préoccupe** something is worrying *ou* bothering* him, he has something on his mind; **l'avenir de son fils le préoccupe** he is concerned *ou* anxious about his son's future.

(b) (*absorber*) to preoccupy. **cette idée lui préoccupe l'esprit** *ou* **le préoccupe** he is preoccupied with that idea; **il est uniquement préoccupé de sa petite personne** he only thinks about himself.

2 se préoccuper *vpr* to concern o.s. (*de* with), be concerned (*de* with); to worry (*de* about). **se** ~ **de la santé de qn** to show (great) concern about sb's health; **il ne se préoccupe pas beaucoup de notre sort** he isn't greatly concerned *ou* very worried *ou* he doesn't care very much about what happens to us; **il ne s'en préoccupe guère** he hardly gives it a thought.

préopératoire [pʀeɔpeʀatwaʀ] *adj* preoperative.

prépa [pʀepa] *nf* (*arg Scol: abrév de* **classe préparatoire**) *class preparing for entrance to the grandes écoles.*

préparateur, -trice [pʀepaʀatœʀ, tʀis] *nm,f* assistant.

préparatifs [pʀepaʀatif] *nmpl* preparations (*de* for). **nous en sommes aux** ~ **de départ** we're getting ready *ou* we're preparing to leave.

préparation [pʀepaʀɑsjɔ̃] *nf* **(a)** (*confection*) (*gén*) preparation; *[repas]* preparation, making; *[médicament]* preparation, making up; *[complot]* laying, hatching; *[plan]* preparation, working out, drawing up. **plat dont la** ~ **demande des soins minutieux** dish which requires very careful preparation.

(b) (*apprêt*) (*gén*) preparation; *[table]* laying, getting ready; *[peaux, poisson, volaille]* dressing; *[attaque, départ, voyage]* preparation (*de* for). **la** ~ **de l'avenir** preparing *ou* preparation for the future; **attaque après** ~ **d'artillerie** attack following initial assault by the artillery; (*fig*) ~ **du terrain** preparing the ground; **auteur qui a plusieurs livres en** ~ author who has several books in hand *ou* in preparation.

(c) (*étude*) *[examen]* preparation, getting ready (*de* for).

(d) (*entraînement*) *[personne]* (*à un examen*) preparation (*à* for); (*à une épreuve sportive*) preparation, training (*à* for). **annoncer quelque chose sans** ~ to announce something abruptly *ou* without preparation, spring something on someone.

(e) (*Chim, Pharm*) preparation.

(f) (*Scol*) (*classe préparatoire*) **faire une** ~ **à Polytechnique** to prepare for entrance to the École Polytechnique (*in one of the classes préparatoires*); (*devoir*) **une** ~ **française** a French exercise, a piece of French homework.

préparatoire [pʀepaʀatwaʀ] *adj travail, démarche, conversations* preparatory, preliminary; *V* **cours.**

préparer [pʀepaʀe] (1) **1** *vt* **(a)** (*confectionner*) (*gén*) to prepare; *repas* to prepare, make; *médicament* to prepare, make up; *piège, complot* to lay, hatch; *plan* to draw up, work out, prepare; *cours, discours* to prepare; *thèse* to be doing, be working on, prepare. **elle nous prépare une tasse de thé** she's making a cup of tea for us, she's getting us a cup of tea; **elle lui prépare de bons petits plats** she makes *ou* cooks *ou* prepares tasty dishes for him; **acheter un plat tout préparé** to buy a ready-cooked *ou* pre-cooked dish.

(b) (*apprêter*) (*gén*) to prepare; *table* to lay, get ready; *affaires, bagages, chambre* to prepare, get ready; *peaux, poisson, volaille* to dress; (*Agr*) *terre* to prepare; *attaque, rentrée, voyage* to prepare (for), get ready for; *transition* to prepare for. ~ **le départ** to get ready *ou* prepare to leave; ~ **l'avenir** to prepare for the future; ~ **ses effets** to time one's effects carefully, prepare one's effects; **il a préparé la rencontre des 2 ministres** he made the preparations for *ou* he organized the meeting of the 2 ministers; **l'attaque avait été soigneusement préparée** the attack had been carefully prepared *ou* organized; **le coup avait été préparé de longue main** they (*ou* he *etc*) had been preparing for it for a long time; (*Mil, fig*) ~ **le terrain** to prepare the ground.

(c) (*Scol*) *examen* to prepare for, study for.

(d) (*habituer, entraîner*) ~ **qn à qch/à faire qch** to prepare sb for sth/to do sth; ~ **les esprits** to prepare people's minds (*à qch* for sth); ~ **qn à un examen** to prepare *ou* coach sb for an exam; **il a essayé de la ~ à la triste nouvelle** he tried to prepare her for the sad news; **je n'y étais pas préparé** I wasn't prepared for it, I wasn't expecting it.

(e) (*réserver*) ~ **qch à qn** to have sth in store for sb; **on ne sait pas ce que l'avenir nous prépare** we don't know what the future holds (in store) *ou* has in store for us; **il nous prépare une surprise** he has a surprise in store for us; (*iro*) **ce temps nous prépare de joyeuses vacances!** if this weather continues, the holidays will be just great!*; **il nous prépare un bon rhume** he's in for a cold.

2 se préparer *vpr* **(a)** (*s'apprêter*) to prepare (o.s.), get ready (*à qch* for sth, *à faire* to do). **attendez, elle se prépare** wait a minute, she's getting ready; **se ~ à une mauvaise nouvelle** to prepare o.s. *ou* be prepared for some bad news; **se ~ au combat** *ou* **à combattre** to prepare to fight *ou* to do battle; **se ~ pour les Jeux olympiques** to prepare *ou* train for the Olympics; **préparez-vous au pire** prepare yourself for the worst; **je ne m'y étais pas préparé** I hadn't prepared myself for it, I wasn't expecting it; **se ~ pour le bal/pour sortir dîner en ville** to get ready *ou* dressed for the dance/to go out to dinner; **préparez-vous à être appelé d'urgence** be prepared to be called out urgently.

(b) (*approcher*) *[orage]* to be brewing. **il se prépare une bagarre** there's going to be a fight, there's a fight brewing; **il se prépare quelque chose de louche** there's something fishy in the air.

prépondérance [prepɔ̃deʀɑ̃s] *nf [nation, groupe]* ascendancy, preponderance, supremacy; *[idée, croyance, théorie]* supremacy; *[trait de caractère]* domination.

prépondérant, e [pʀepɔ̃deʀɑ̃, ɑ̃t] *adj rôle* dominating. **voix ~e** casting vote.

préposé [prepoze] *nm* (*gén*) employee; (*facteur*) postman; *[douane]* official, officer; *[vestiaire]* attendant.

préposée [pʀepoze] *nf* (*gén*) employee; (*factrice*) postwoman; *[vestiaire]* attendant.

préposer [pʀepoze] (1) *vt* to appoint (*à* to). **être préposé à** to be in charge of.

prépositif, -ive [prepozitif, iv] *adj* prepositional.

préposition [pʀepozisjɔ̃] *nf* preposition.

prépositivement [prepozitivmɑ̃] *adv* prepositionally, as a preposition.

prépuce [prepys] *nm* foreskin, prepuce (*T*).

préraphaélisme [pʀeʀafaelism(ə)] *nm* Pre-Raphaelitism.

préraphaélite [pʀeʀafaelit] *adj, nm* Pre-Raphaelite.

préretraite [pʀeʀ(ə)tʀɛt] *nf* early retirement.

prérogative [pʀeʀɔgativ] *nf* prerogative.

préromantique [pʀeʀɔmɑ̃tik] *adj* preromantic. **les ~s** the preromantics, the preromantic poets.

préromantisme [pʀeʀɔmɑ̃tism(ə)] *nm* preromanticism.

près [pʀɛ] **1** *adv* **(a)** (*dans l'espace*) near(by), close (by), near *ou* close at hand; (*dans le temps*) near, close. **la gare est tout ~** we're very close to the station, the station is very near by *ou* close at hand; **il habite assez/tout ~** he lives quite/very near *ou* close (by) *ou* near at hand *ou* close at hand; **ne te mets pas trop ~** don't get (*ou* sit *ou* stand *etc*) too close *ou* near; **c'est plus/moins ~ que je ne croyais** (*espace*) it's nearer *ou* closer than/further than I thought *ou* not as near *ou* close as I thought; (*temps*) it's nearer *ou* sooner *ou* closer than/not as near *ou* soon as I thought *ou* further off than I thought; **Noël est très ~ maintenant** Christmas is (getting) very near *ou* close now, it'll very soon be Christmas now.

(b) ~ de (*dans le temps*) close to; (*dans l'espace*) close to, near (to); (*approximativement*) nearly, almost; **leur maison est ~ de l'église** their house is close to *ou* near the church; **le plus/moins ~ possible de la porte/de Noël** as close *ou* near to/as far away as possible from the door/Christmas; **une robe ~ du corps** a slim-fitting dress; **ils étaient très ~ l'un de l'autre** (*lit*) they were very close to each other; (*fig*) *[candidats]* they were very close (to each other); *[enfants]* they were very close (to each other) in age; **il est ~ de minuit** it is close to *ou* on midnight, it's nearly midnight; **elle est ~ de sa mère** she's with her mother; **être très ~ du but** to be very close *ou* near to one's goal; **être très ~ d'avoir trouvé la solution** to have almost *ou* nearly found the solution; **il est ~ de la retraite** he is close to *ou* nearing retirement; **arriver ~ de la fin d'un voyage/des vacances** to be nearing the end *ou* coming near *ou* close to the end of a journey/the holidays; **il est ~ de la cinquantaine** he's nearly *ou* almost fifty, he's coming up to fifty*; **il a dépensé ~ de la moitié de son mois** he has spent nearly *ou* almost half his month's salary; **il y a ~ de 5 ans qu'ils sont partis** they left nearly *ou* close on 5 years ago; **il a été très ~ de refuser** he was on the point of *ou* on the verge of refusing *ou* about to refuse; **je suis très ~ de croire que ...** I'm (almost) beginning to think that ... ; (*iro*) **je ne suis pas ~ de partir/réussir** at this rate, I'm not likely to be going (yet)/to succeed; (*iro*) **je ne suis pas ~ d'y retourner/de recommencer** I shan't go back there/do that again in a hurry!; (*fig*) **être ~ de son argent** *ou* **de ses sous*** to be close- *ou* tight-fisted.

(c) de (très) ~ (very) closely; **le coup a été tiré de ~** the shot was fired at close range; **il voit mal/bien de ~** he can't see very well/he can see all right close to; **surveiller qn de ~** to keep a close watch on sb, watch carefully over sb; **il faudra examiner cette affaire de plus ~** we must have *ou* take a closer look at *ou* look more closely into this business; **il a vu la mort de ~** he has stared *ou* looked death in the face; **on a frôlé de très ~ la catastrophe** we came within an inch of disaster, we had a close shave *ou* a narrow escape; *V* **connaître, rasé, regarder** *etc.*

(d) (*loc*) **à peu de chose ~** more or less (*V aussi* **peu**); **ce n'est pas aussi bon, à beaucoup ~** it's nothing like *ou* nowhere near as good, it's not as good by a long way *ou* chalk* (*Brit*); **ils sont identiques, à la couleur ~** they are identical apart from *ou* except for the colour, colour apart, they are identical; **à cela ~ que ...** if it weren't for *ou* apart from the fact that ... ; **je vais vous donner le chiffre à un franc/à un centimètre ~** I'll give you the figure to within about a franc/a centimetre; **cela fait 100 F à quelque chose** *ou* **à peu de chose(s) ~** that comes to 100 francs, as near as makes no difference *ou* as near as damn it*; **il n'en est pas à 100 F ~** he's not going to quibble over an odd *ou* a mere 100 francs, he can spare (another) 100 francs, (another) 100 francs isn't going to ruin him; **il a raté le bus à une minute ~** he missed the bus by a minute or so; **il n'est pas à 10 minutes/à un kilo de sucre ~** he can spare 10 minutes/a kilo of sugar; **il n'est pas à un crime ~** he won't let a crime stop him; **il n'est plus à 10 minutes ~** he can wait another 10 minutes.

2 *prép* (*littér, Admin*) *lieu* near. **ambassadeur ~ le roi de** ambassador to the king of.

présage [pʀezaʒ] *nm* omen, sign, presage (*littér*), portent (*littér*). **mauvais ~** ill omen; **~ de malheur** sign of misfortune.

présager [pʀezaʒe] (3) *vt* (*annoncer*) to be a sign *ou* an omen of, presage (*littér*), portend (*littér*); (*prévoir*) to predict, foresee. **cela ne présage rien de bon** nothing good will come of it, that's an ominous sign; **cela nous laisse ~ que** it leads us to predict *ou* expect that; **rien ne laissait ~ que** there was nothing to make me (*ou* him *etc*) expect that.

presbyte [pʀɛsbit] *adj* long-sighted, presbyopic (*T*).

presbytère [pʀɛsbitɛʀ] *nm* presbytery.

presbytérianisme [pʀɛsbiteʀjanism(ə)] *nm* Presbyterianism.

presbytérien, -ienne [pʀɛsbiteʀjɛ̃, jɛn] *adj, nm,f* Presbyterian.

presbytie [pʀɛsbisi] *nf* long-sightedness, presbyopia (*T*).

prescience [pʀesjɑ̃s] *nf* prescience, foresight.

prescient, e [pʀesjɑ̃, ɑ̃t] *adj* prescient, far-sighted.

préscolaire [pʀeskɔlɛʀ] *adj* preschool (*épith*).

prescriptible [pʀɛskʀiptibl(ə)] *adj* prescriptible.

prescription [pʀɛskʀipsjɔ̃] *nf* (*Méd*) prescription, directions; (*Jur*) prescription; (*ordre*) (*gén*) order, instruction; *[morale, règlement]* dictate.

prescrire [pʀɛskʀiʀ] (39) *vt* (*Méd*) to prescribe; (*Jur*) *droit* to prescribe; *[morale, honneur, loi]* to stipulate, lay down; (*ordonner*) to order, command. **à la date prescrite** on the date stipulated; (*Méd*) **ne pas dépasser la dose prescrite** do not exceed the prescribed dose; **être prescrit, se ~** *[peine, dette]* to lapse.

préséance [pʀeseɑ̃s] *nf* precedence (*U*).

présélection [pʀeselɛksjɔ̃] *nf* (*gén*) preselection; *[candidats]* short-listing (*Brit*). (*Aut*) **boîte de vitesses à ~** preselector (gearbox); (*Rad*) **bouton de ~** preset switch.

présélectionner [pʀeselɛksjɔne] (1) *vt chaîne de radio* to preset; *candidats* to short-list (*Brit*).

présence [pʀezɑ̃s] **1** *nf* **(a)** *[personne, chose, pays]* presence; (*au bureau, à l'école*) attendance; (*Rel*) presence. **fuir la ~ de qn** to avoid sb, keep well away from sb; (*frm*) **Monsieur le maire a honoré la cérémonie de sa ~** the Mayor honoured them with his presence at the ceremony; **j'ai juste à faire de la ~** I just have to be there; **~ assidue au bureau** regular attendance at the office; *V* **acte, feuille, jeton.**

(b) (*personnalité*) presence. **avoir de la ~** to have (a) great presence.

(c) (*être*) **sentir une ~** to be aware of sb's presence *ou* of a presence.

(d) (*loc*) **en ~** *armées* opposing (each other); *personnes* face to face (with each other); **mettre deux personnes en ~** to bring two people together *ou* face to face; (*Jur*) **les parties en ~** the litigants, the opposing parties; **en ~ de** in (the) presence of; **cela s'est produit en ma/hors de ma ~** it happened while I was there *ou* in my presence/while I was not there *ou* in my absence; **en ~ de tels incidents** faced with *ou* in the face of such incidents; **mettre qn en ~ de qn/qch** to bring sb face to face with sb/sth.

2: présence d'esprit presence of mind.

présent[1], **e** [pʀezɑ̃, ɑ̃t] **1** *adj* **(a)** *personne* present; (*Rel*) present. (*frm*) **les personnes ici ~es** the persons here present (*frm*), the people here present; **les personnes (qui étaient) ~es au moment de l'incident** the people who were present *ou* there when the incident occurred; **être ~ à une cérémonie** to be present at *ou* attend a ceremony; **être ~ à l'appel** to be present at roll call; **~!** present!; (*hum*) **pour un bon repas, il est toujours ~!** you can always count on him to be there for a good meal, he's always around* *ou* there when there's a good meal on the go!; **je suis ~ en pensée** my thoughts are with you (*ou* him *etc*), I'm thinking of you (*ou* him *etc*).

(b) *chose* present. **métal ~ dans un minerai** metal present *ou* found in an ore; **son pessimisme est partout ~ dans son dernier roman** his pessimism runs right through his latest novel; **sa gentillesse est ~e dans chacun de ses actes** his kindness is evident in *ou* is to be found in everything he does; **avoir qch ~ à l'esprit** to have sth fresh in one's mind, not to forget about sth; **je n'ai pas les chiffres ~s à l'esprit** I can't have the figures to mind, I can't remember the figures offhand; **j'aurai toujours ce souvenir ~ à l'esprit** this memory will be ever-present in my mind *ou* will always be fresh in my mind; **gardez ceci ~ à l'esprit** keep this in the forefront of your mind.

(c) (*actuel*) *circonstances, état, heure, époque* present. **le 15 du mois ~** on the 15th instant (*Admin*) *ou* of this month.

(d) (*Gram*) *temps, participe* present.

(e) (*dont il est question*) present. **le ~ récit** the present *ou* this account; (*Admin*) **par la ~e lettre** hereby.

2 *nm* **(a)** (*époque*) **le ~** the present.

(b) (*Gram*) present (tense). **~ de l'indicatif** present indicative; **~ historique** historic(al) present.

(c) (*personne*) **les ~s et les absents** those present and those absent; **il n'y avait que 5 ~s** there were only 5 people present *ou* there.

(d) (*loc*) **à ~** (*en ce moment*) at present, presently (*US*); (*maintenant*) now; (*de nos jours*) now, nowadays; **à ~ que nous savons** now that we know; **d'à ~** present-day (*épith*), of today; **la jeunesse/les gens d'à ~** youngsters/people of today, youngsters/people nowadays; *V* **dès, jusque.**

3 présente *nf* (*Admin: lettre*) **veuillez recevoir par la ~e** please accept by the present letter *ou* by this letter.

présent[2] [prezɑ̃] *nm* (*littér*) gift, present. **faire ~ de qch à qn** to present sb with sth.

présentable [prezɑ̃tabl(ə)] *adj plat, personne* presentable.

présentateur, -trice [prezɑ̃tatœr, tris] *nm,f* (*Rad, TV*) introducer, presenter.

présentation [prezɑ̃tɑsjɔ̃] *nf* **(a)** (*gén*) presentation. **sur ~ d'une pièce d'identité** on presentation of proof of identity.

(b) *[nouveau venu, conférencier]* introduction; (*frm: à la cour*) presentation. **faire les ~s** to make the introductions, introduce people to one another.

(c) (*au public*) *[tableaux, pièce]* presentation; *[marchandises]* presentation, display; *[film]* presentation, showing; (*Rad, TV*) *[émission]* presentation, introduction. **~ de mode** fashion show.

(d) (*manière de présenter*) *[idées, produit, travail]* presentation. (*fig*) *[personne]* **avoir une bonne/mauvaise ~** to have a good *ou* pleasant/an unattractive *ou* off-putting (*surtout Brit*) appearance.

(e) (*Rel*) **la P~** the Presentation.

(f) (*Méd*) *[fœtus]* presentation. **~ par la tête/le siège** head/breech presentation.

présentement [prezɑ̃tmɑ̃] *adv* (*en ce moment*) at present, presently (*US*); (*maintenant*) now.

présenter [prezɑ̃te] (1) **1** *vt* **(a)** (*introduire*) *connaissance, conférencier* to introduce (*à* to, *dans* into); (*au roi, à la cour*) to present (*à* to). **je vous présente ma femme** this is my wife, have you met my wife?, may I introduce my wife (to you)?

(b) (*proposer au public*) *marchandises* to present, display (*à* to), set out (*à* before); (*Théât*) *acteur, pièce* to present; (*Rad, TV*) *émission* to introduce, compere; *modes, tableaux* to present.

(c) (*exposer*) *problème* to set out, explain; *idées* to present, set *ou* lay out; *théorie* to expound, set out. **c'est un travail bien/mal présenté** it's a well-/badly presented *ou* well/badly laid-out piece of work; **~ qch sous un jour favorable** to present sth in a favourable light; **présentez-lui cela avec tact** explain it to him *ou* put it to him tactfully; **il nous a présenté son ami comme un héros** he spoke of his friend as a hero.

(d) (*montrer*) *billet, passeport* to present, show. **il présentait un tel air de consternation** he presented such a picture of consternation; **il présenta sa joue au baiser de sa mère** he presented *ou* offered his cheek for his mother to kiss.

(e) (*tourner*) to turn. **~ le flanc à l'ennemi** to turn one's flank towards the enemy; **bateau qui présente le travers au vent** ship which turns *ou* sails broadside on to the wind.

(f) (*exprimer*) *excuses* to present, offer, make; *condoléances, félicitations* to present, offer; *respects* to present, pay; *objection* to raise.

(g) (*laisser paraître*) *avantage, intérêt* to present, afford; *différences* to reveal, present; *danger, difficulté, obstacle* to present. **cette route présente beaucoup de détours** there are a lot of bends on this road; **ce malade présente des symptômes de tuberculose** this patient presents *ou* shows symptoms of tuberculosis.

(h) (*offrir*) *plat* to present, hold out; *rafraîchissements* to offer, hand round; *bouquet* to present. **~ son bras à qn** to offer one's arm to sb.

(i) (*soumettre*) *addition, facture, devis* to present, submit; *thèse* to submit; *motion* to move; *projet de loi* to present, introduce; *rapport, requête* to present, put in, submit. **~ sa candidature à un poste** to apply for *ou* put in for a job; **~ un candidat à un concours** to put a candidate in for a competition; (*Scol*) **~ un texte de Camus à un examen** to choose *ou* do a text by Camus for an exam.

(j) (*Mil*) *armes* to present; *troupes* to present (*for inspection*). **présentez armes!** present arms!

(k) (*Tech: placer*) to position, line up.

2 *vi* *[personne]* **~ bien/mal** to have a good *ou* pleasant/an unattractive *ou* off-putting (*surtout Brit*) appearance, be of good/poor appearance.

3 se présenter *vpr* **(a)** (*se rendre*) to go, come, appear. **se ~ chez qn** to go to sb's house; **il ose encore se ~ chez toi!** does he still dare to show himself ou6ou to appear at your house!; **il ne s'est présenté personne** no one came *ou* appeared; **je ne peux pas me ~ dans cette tenue** I can't appear dressed like this; (*Comm*) **ne pas écrire, se ~** (interested) applicants should apply in person; (*Jur*) **se ~ à l'audience** to appear in court, make a court appearance.

(b) (*être candidat*) to come forward. **se ~ pour un emploi** to put in for a job; **se ~ à** *élection* to stand at; *examen* to sit, take; *concours* to go in for, enter (for); **se ~ comme candidat** (*à un poste*) to apply, be an applicant (*à* for); (*aux élections*) to be a candidate, stand (*Brit*) *ou* run (*US*) as a candidate (*à* at).

(c) (*se faire connaître*) (*gén*) to introduce o.s.; (*à un patron*) to introduce o.s., report (*à* to).

(d) (*surgir*) *[occasion]* to arise, present itself; *[difficulté]* to crop *ou* come up, arise, present itself; *[solution]* to come to mind, present itself. **un problème se présente à nous** we are faced *ou* confronted with a problem; **il lit tout ce qui se présente** he reads everything he can get his hands on; **il faut attendre que quelque chose se présente** we must wait until something turns up; **deux noms se présentent à l'esprit** two names come *ou* spring to mind; **un spectacle magnifique se présenta à ses yeux** a magnificent sight met his eyes.

(e) (*apparaître*) **cela se présente sous forme de cachets** it's presented *ou* it comes in the form of pills; **l'affaire se présente bien/mal** things are looking good/aren't looking too good; **le problème se présente sous un nouveau jour** the problem takes on (quite) a different aspect *ou* appears in a new light; **comment le problème se présente-t-il?** what exactly is the problem?, what is the nature of the problem?; (*Méd*) **comment l'enfant se présente-t-il?** how is the baby presenting?; **comment cela se présente-t-il?** (*lit*) what does it look like?; (**fig*) how's it going?*

présentoir [prezɑ̃twar] *nm* (*étagère*) display shelf.

préservateur, -trice [prezervatœr, tris] *adj* preventive, protective.

préservatif, -ive [prezervatif, iv] **1** *adj* preventive, protective. **2** *nm* condom, sheath.

préservation [prezervɑsjɔ̃] *nf* preservation, protection.

préserver [prezerve] (1) *vt* (*protéger*) to protect (*de* from, against); (*sauver*) to save (*de* from); (*sauvegarder*) to protect, safeguard. **se ~ du soleil** to protect o.s. from the sun; **le ciel** *ou* **Dieu m'en préserve!** Heaven forbid!

présidence [prezidɑ̃s] *nf* **(a)** *[état, tribunal]* presidency; *[comité, réunion]* chairmanship; *[firme]* chairmanship, directorship; *[université]* vice-chancellorship (*Brit*), presidency (*US*). (*Pol*) **candidat à la ~** presidential candidate.

(b) (*résidence*) presidential residence *ou* palace.

président [prezidɑ̃] **1** *nm* **(a)** (*Pol*) president. **Monsieur le ~** Mr President.

(b) *[comité, réunion]* chairman; *[club, société savante]* president; *[firme]* chairman, president; *[jury d'examen]* chairman, chief examiner; *[université]* vice-chancellor (*Brit*), president (*US*).

(c) (*Jur*) *[tribunal]* presiding judge *ou* magistrate; *[jury]* foreman.

2: (*Hist*) **président du conseil** prime minister; **président directeur général** chairman and managing director (*Brit*).

présidente [prezidɑ̃t] *nf* **(a)** (*en titre: V* **président**) (lady *ou* woman) president; chairwoman; presiding judge *ou* magistrate. **(b)** (*épouse: V* **président**) president's wife, first lady; president's *ou* chairman's wife.

présidentialisme [prezidɑ̃sjalism(ə)] *nm* presidentialism.

présidentiel, -elle [prezidɑ̃sjel] **1** *adj* presidential. **2 présidentielles** *nfpl* presidential election(s).

présider [prezide] (1) **1** *vt tribunal, conseil, assemblée* to preside over; *comité, débat, séance* to chair. **~ un dîner** to be the guest of honour at a dinner; **c'est X qui préside** (*séance*) X is in *ou* taking the chair, X is chairing; (*club*) X is the president, X is presiding. **2 présider à** *vt indir préparatifs, décisions, exécution* to direct, be in charge *ou* command of; *destinées* to rule over. **règles qui président à qch** rules which govern sth; **la volonté de conciliation a présidé aux discussions** a conciliatory spirit prevailed throughout the talks.

présidium [prezidjɔm] *nm* presidium.

présomptif, -ive [prezɔ̃ptif, iv] *adj:* **héritier ~** heir apparent.

présomption [prezɔ̃psjɔ̃] *nf* **(a)** (*supposition*) presumption, assumption; (*Jur*) presumption. **(b)** (*U: prétention*) presumptuousness, presumption.

présomptueusement [prezɔ̃ptɥøzmɑ̃] *adv* presumptuously.

présomptueux, -euse [prezɔ̃ptɥø, øz] *adj* presumptuous, self-assured. **ton/air ~** presumptuous *ou* brash tone/air.

presque [presk(ə)] *adv* **(a)** almost, nearly. **j'ai ~ terminé** I've almost *ou* nearly *ou* as good as finished; **~ à chaque pas** at almost every step; **une espèce d'inquiétude, ~ d'angoisse** a kind of anxiety — almost anguish; **c'est ~ de la folie** it's little short of madness; **c'est ~ impossible** it's almost *ou* next to *ou* well-nigh impossible; **c'est sûr ou ~** it's almost *ou* practically certain.

(b) (*contexte négatif*) hardly, scarcely, almost. **personne/rien ou ~, ~ personne/rien** hardly *ou* scarcely anyone/anything, almost nobody/nothing, next to nobody/nothing; **as-tu trouvé des fautes? — ~ pas** did you find any mistakes? — only a few *ou* — no, hardly *ou* scarcely any *ou* — no, practically none; **a-t-il dormi? — ~ pas** has he had a sleep? — no, not really, did he sleep? — no, hardly at all *ou* no, not really; **je ne l'ai ~ pas entendu** I hardly *ou* scarcely heard him; **il n'y a ~ plus de vin** there's almost no *ou* hardly any wine left, the wine has nearly all gone; **ça n'arrive ~ jamais** it hardly *ou* scarcely ever happens, it almost never happens.

(c) (*avant n*) **dans la ~ obscurité** in the near darkness; **la ~ totalité des lecteurs** almost *ou* nearly all the readers; **j'en ai la ~ certitude** I'm almost certain.

presqu'île [pʀɛskil] *nf* peninsula.

pressage [pʀɛsaʒ] *nm [disque, raisin]* pressing.

pressant, e [pʀɛsɑ̃, ɑ̃t] *adj besoin, danger, invitation* urgent, pressing (*épith*); *situation, travail, désir* urgent; *demande, personne* insistent, urgent. **demander qch de façon ~e** to ask for sth urgently; **le créancier a été/s'est fait ~** the creditor was insistent/started to insist *ou* started to press him (*ou* me *etc*); (*euph*) **avoir un besoin ~** to need to spend a penny (*euph*) (*Brit*) *ou* go to the restroom (*US*).

presse [pʀɛs] *nf* **(a)** (*institution*) press; (*journaux*) (news)papers. **la grande ~, la ~ à grand tirage** the popular press; **c'est dans toute la ~** it's in all the papers; **~ régionale/mensuelle** regional/monthly press *ou* papers; **~ féminine/automobile** women's/car magazines; **avoir bonne/mauvaise ~** (*lit*) to get *ou* have a good/bad press; (*fig*) to be well/badly thought of; **agence/attaché/conférence de ~** press agency/attaché/conference; *V* **délit, liberté**.

(b) (*appareil*) (*gén*) press; (*Typ*) (printing) press. **~ à cylindres/à bras** cylinder/hand press; **mettre sous ~** *livre* to send to press; *journal* to put to bed; **le livre a été mis sous ~** the book has gone to press; **le journal a été mis sous ~** the (news)paper has gone to bed; **livre sous ~** book in press.

(c) (*littér: foule*) throng (*littér*), press (*littér*).

(d) (*urgence*) **pendant les moments de ~** when things get busy; **il n'y a pas de ~*** there's no rush *ou* hurry.

presse- [pʀɛs] *préf V* **presser**.

pressé, e [pʀese] (*ptp de* **presser**) *adj* **(a)** *pas* hurried. **avoir un air ~** to look as though one is in a hurry; **marcher d'un pas ~** to hurry along; **je suis (très) ~/ne suis pas ~** I'm in a (great) hurry *ou* (very) pressed for time/in no hurry; **être ~ de partir** to be in a hurry to leave.

(b) (*urgent*) *travail, lettre* urgent. **c'est ~?** is it urgent?, are you in a hurry for it?; **il n'a eu rien de plus ~ que de faire ...** he wasted no time doing ..., he just couldn't wait to do ...; **si tu n'as rien de plus ~ à faire que de ...** if you have nothing more urgent to do than ...; **il faut parer au plus ~** we must do the most urgent thing(s) first, first things first.

(c) **citron** *etc* **~** (fresh) lemon *etc* juice.

pressentiment [pʀesɑ̃timɑ̃] *nm* (*intuition*) foreboding, presentiment, premonition; (*idée*) feeling. **j'ai comme un ~ qu'il ne viendra pas** I've got a feeling *ou* a premonition he won't come.

pressentir [pʀesɑ̃tiʀ] (16) *vt* **(a)** *danger* to sense, have a foreboding of. **~ que ...** to have a feeling *ou* a premonition that ...; **j'avais pressenti quelque chose** I had sensed something; **il n'a rien laissé ~ de ses projets** he gave no hint of his plans; **rien ne laissait ~ une mort si soudaine** there was nothing to forewarn of *ou* to hint at such a sudden death.

(b) *personne* to sound out, approach. **il a été pressenti pour le poste** he has been sounded out *ou* approached about taking the job, he's in line for the job; **ministre pressenti** prospective minister.

presser [pʀese] (1) **1** *vt* **(a)** *éponge* to squeeze; *fruit* to squeeze (the juice out of); *raisin* to press.

(b) (*serrer*) *objet* to squeeze. **les gens étaient pressés les uns contre les autres** people were squashed up *ou* crushed up against one another; **~ qn dans ses bras** to squeeze sb in one's arms, hug sb; **~ qn contre sa poitrine** to clasp sb to one's chest; **~ la main de** *ou* **à qn** to squeeze sb's hand, give sb's hand a squeeze.

(c) (*appuyer sur*) *bouton, sonnette* to press, push. **~ une matrice dans la cire** to press a mould into the wax; **il faut ~ ici** you must press here.

(d) (*façonner*) *disque, pli de pantalon* to press.

(e) (*inciter à*) **~ qn de faire** to urge *ou* press sb to do.

(f) (*hâter*) *affaire* to speed up; *départ* to hasten, speed up. **(faire) ~ qn** to hurry sb (up); **(faire) ~ les choses** to speed things up; **~ le pas** *ou* **l'allure** to speed up, hurry on; **il fit ~ l'allure** he quickened *ou* speeded up the pace; **qu'est-ce qui vous presse?** what's the hurry?; **rien ne vous presse** there's no hurry, we're in no rush.

(g) (*harceler*) *débiteur* to press; (*littér: Mil*) *ennemi* to press. **être pressé par le besoin** to be driven *ou* pressed by need; (*littér*) **le désir qui le presse** the desire which drives him; (*fig*) **~ qn de questions** to bombard *ou* ply sb with questions.

2 *vi* (*être urgent*) to be urgent. **l'affaire presse** it's urgent; **le temps presse** time is short, time presses; **cela ne presse pas, rien ne presse** there's no hurry, there's no need to rush.

3 se presser *vpr* **(a)** (*se serrer*) **se ~ contre qn** to squeeze up against sb; **les gens se pressaient pour entrer** people were pushing to get in, there was a crush to get in; **les gens se pressaient autour de la vedette** people were pressing *ou* crowding round the star.

(b) (*se hâter*) to hurry (up). **ils allaient/travaillaient sans se ~** they went/were working without hurrying *ou* at a leisurely pace; **pressez-vous, il est tard** hurry up *ou* get a move on*, it's getting late; **il faut se ~** we must hurry up *ou* get cracking* *ou* get a move on*; **presse-toi de partir** hurry up and go; **allons, pressons(-nous)!** come on, come on!, come on, we must hurry!

4: presse-bouton *adj inv* push-button; **presse-citron** *nm inv* lemon squeezer; **presse-livres** *nm inv* book-ends; **presse-papiers** *nm inv* paperweight; **presse-purée** *nm inv* potato-masher; **presse-raquette** *nm inv* racket press.

pressing [pʀesiŋ] *nm* **(a)** (*repassage*) steam-pressing; (*établissement*) dry-cleaner's. **(b)** (*Sport*) pressure.

pression [pʀɛsjɔ̃] *nf* **(a)** (*action*) pressure. **je sentais la ~ de sa main sur la mienne** I could feel the pressure of his hand on mine *ou* his hand pressing on mine; **une simple ~ du doigt suffit** one push with the finger is all that is needed; **faire ~ sur le couvercle d'une boite** (*pour fermer*) to press (down) on the lid of a box; (*pour ouvrir*) to push up *ou* twist open the lid of a box; **il inséra le levier sous la pierre et fit ~ pour la lever** he inserted the lever under the stone and pressed on it to lift the stone.

(b) (*Méd, Phys*) pressure. **~ artérielle/atmosphérique** blood/atmospheric pressure; **à haute/basse ~** high/low pressure (*épith*); **être sous ~** *[machine]* to be under pressure, be at full pressure; *[cabine]* to be pressurized; (*fig*) to be keyed up, be tense; **mettre sous ~** to pressurize.

(c) (*fig: contrainte*) pressure. **sous la ~ des événements** under the pressure of events; **faire ~** *ou* **exercer une ~ sur qn** to put pressure on sb, bring pressure to bear on sb, pressurize sb; **être soumis à des ~s** to be subject to pressures, be under pressure; *V* **groupe**.

(d) **bière à la ~** draught beer, beer on draught; **deux ~(s)* s'il vous plaît** two (draught) beers, please.

(e) (*bouton*) press stud (*surtout Brit*), snap fastener (*US*), popper*.

pressoir [pʀɛswaʀ] *nm* **(a)** (*appareil*) *[vin]* wine press; *[cidre]* cider press; *[huile]* oil press. **(b)** (*local*) press-house.

pressurage [pʀesyʀaʒ] *nm [fruit]* pressing.

pressurer [pʀesyʀe] (1) *vt fruit* to press; (*fig*) *personne* to squeeze.

pressurisation [pʀesyʀizɑsjɔ̃] *nf* pressurization.

pressuriser [pʀesyʀize] (1) *vt* to pressurize.

prestance [pʀɛstɑ̃s] *nf* imposing bearing, presence.

prestataire [pʀɛstatɛʀ] *nm* person receiving benefits *ou* allowances.

prestation [pʀɛstɑsjɔ̃] **1** *nf* **(a)** (*allocation*) *[assurance]* benefit.

(b) (*gén pl: services*) *[hôtel, restaurant]* service.

(c) (*performance*) *[artiste, sportif]* performance. **faire une bonne ~** to put up a good performance, perform well.

2: prestations familiales State benefits paid to the family (*maternity benefit, family income supplement, rent rebate etc*); **prestation d'invalidité** disablement benefit *ou* allowance; **prestation de serment** taking the oath; **la prestation de serment du président a eu lieu hier** the president was sworn in yesterday; **prestations sociales** social security benefits; **prestation de vieillesse** old age pension.

preste [pʀɛst(ə)] *adj* (*littér*) nimble.

prestement [pʀɛstəmɑ̃] *adv* (*littér*) nimbly.

prestesse [pʀɛstɛs] *nf* (*littér*) nimbleness.

prestidigitateur, -trice [pʀɛstidiʒitatœʀ, tʀis] *nm,f* conjurer.

prestidigitation [pʀɛstidiʒitɑsjɔ̃] *nf* conjuring. (*fig*) **c'est de la ~!** it's like a conjuring trick!

prestige [pʀɛstiʒ] *nm* prestige. **le ~ de l'uniforme** the glamour of the uniform; **de ~** *politique, opération, voiture* prestige (*épith*).

prestigieux, -euse [pʀɛstiʒjø, øz] *adj* prestigious; (*Comm*) renowned, prestigious. **X est une marque ~euse de voiture** X is a famous *ou* prestigious make of car *ou* name in cars.

presto [pʀɛsto] *adv* (*Mus*) presto; (**fig*) double-quick*.

présumable [pʀezymabl(ə)] *adj* presumable.

présumer [pʀezyme] (1) **1** *vt* to presume, assume. **présumé innocent** presumed innocent; **l'auteur présumé du livre** the presumed author of the book.

2 présumer de *vt indir*: **trop ~ de qch/qn** to overestimate *ou* overrate sth/sb; **trop ~ de ses forces** to overestimate one's strength.

présupposé [pʀesypoze] *nm* presupposition.

présupposer [pʀesypoze] (1) *vt* to presuppose.

présupposition [pʀesypozisjɔ̃] *nf* presupposition.

présure [pʀezyʀ] *nf* rennet.

prêt¹, e [pʀɛ, ɛt] *adj* **(a)** (*préparé*) *personne, repas* ready. **~ à** *ou* **pour qch/à** *ou* **pour faire qch** ready for sth/to do sth; **~ à fonctionner** ready for use; **poulet ~ à cuire** *ou* **rôtir** oven-ready chicken; **~ au départ** *ou* **à partir** ready to go *ou* leave, ready for off*; **être fin ~ (au départ)** to be all set *ou* be raring* to go; **tout est (fin) ~** everything is (quite) ready *ou* is at the ready, everything is in readiness; **se tenir ~ à qch/à faire qch** to hold o.s. *ou* be ready for sth/to do sth; **tiens ta monnaie ~e pour payer** have your money ready to pay; **il est ~ à tout** he will do anything, he will stop at nothing; **on m'a averti: je suis ~ à tout** they've warned me and I'm ready for anything; *V* **marque**.

(b) (*disposé*) **~ à** ready *ou* prepared *ou* willing to; **être tout ~ à faire qch** to be quite ready *ou* prepared *ou* willing to do sth.

prêt² [pʀɛ] **1** *nm* **(a)** (*action*) loaning, lending; (*somme*) loan. **le service de ~ d'une bibliothèque** the lending department of a library; **~ sur gages** (*U*) pawnbroking; (*somme*) loan against security; *V* **bibliothèque**.

(b) (*Mil*) pay.

(c) (*avance*) advance.

2: prêt à la construction building loan; **prêt d'honneur** *repayable student grant*.

prêt-à-porter [pʀɛtapɔʀte] *nm* ready-to-wear (clothes). **acheter qch en ~** to buy sth off the peg (*surtout Brit*); **je n'achète que du ~** I only buy off-the-peg (*surtout Brit*) clothes *ou* ready-to-wear clothes.

prêté [pʀete] *nm*: **c'est un ~ (pour un) rendu** it's tit for tat.

prétendant, e [pʀetɑ̃dɑ̃, ɑ̃t] **1** *nm* (*prince*) pretender; (*littér: galant*) suitor. **2** *nm,f* (*candidat*) candidate (*à* for).

prétendre [pʀetɑ̃dʀ(ə)] (41) **1** *vt* **(a)** (*affirmer*) to claim, maintain, assert, say. **il prétend être** *ou* **qu'il est le premier à avoir trouvé la réponse** he claims to be the first to have found the answer, he claims *ou* maintains *ou* asserts (that) he's the first to have found the answer; **il se prétend insulté/médecin** he makes out *ou* claims he's insulted/a doctor; **je ne prétends pas qu'il**

l'ait fait I don't say *ou* I'm not saying he did it; **on le prétend très riche** he is said *ou* alleged to be very rich; **en prétendant qu'il venait chercher un livre** on the pretence of coming to get a book, claiming that he had come to get a book; **à ce qu'il prétend** according to him *ou* to what he says, if what he says is true; **à ce qu'on prétend** allegedly, according to what people say.

(b) (*avoir la prétention de*) to claim. **il prétend savoir jouer du piano** he claims he can play the piano; **tu ne prétends pas le faire tout seul?** you don't pretend *ou* expect to do it on your own?; **je ne prétends pas me défendre** I don't pretend *ou* I'm not trying to justify myself.

(c) (*littér*) (*vouloir*) to want; (*avoir l'intention de*) to mean, intend. **que prétendez-vous de moi?** what do you want of me? (*littér*); **que prétend-il faire?** what does he mean *ou* intend to do?; **je prétends être obéi ou qu'on m'obéisse** I mean to be obeyed.

2 prétendre à *vt indir honneurs, emploi* to lay claim to, aspire to; *femme* to aspire to. **~ à faire** to aspire to do.

prétendu, e [pretɑ̃dy] (*ptp de* **prétendre**) **1** *adj chose* so-called, alleged; *personne* so-called, would-be; *preuves* alleged. **2** *nm,f* (*fiancé*) intended (†, *littér*).

prétendument [pretɑ̃dymɑ̃] *adv* supposedly, allegedly.

prête-nom, *pl* **prête-noms** [prɛtnɔ̃] *nm* figurehead.

prétentaine† [pretɑ̃tɛn] *nf*: **courir la ~** to go gallivanting.

prétentieusement [pretɑ̃sjøzmɑ̃] *adv* pretentiously.

prétentieux, -euse [pretɑ̃sjø, øz] *adj personne, manières, ton* pretentious, conceited; *appellation* pretentious, fancy; *maison* pretentious, showy. **c'est un petit ~!** he's a conceited little blighter!* (*Brit*) *ou* jerk*.

prétention [pretɑ̃sjɔ̃] *nf* **(a)** (*exigence*) claim. (*salaire*) **~s** expected salary; **avoir des ~s à ou sur** to lay claim to; **quelles sont vos ~s?** what sort of salary do you expect? *ou* are you looking for?*

(b) (*ambition*) pretension, claim (*à* to). **avoir la ~ de faire** to claim to be able to do, (like to) think one can do; **je n'ai pas la ~ de rivaliser avec lui** I don't claim *ou* expect (to be able) to compete with him; **il n'a pas la ~ de tout savoir** he makes no pretence of knowing everything, he doesn't pretend *ou* claim to know everything; **sa ~ à l'élégance** her claims *ou* pretensions to elegance; **sans ~** *maison, repas* unpretentious; *robe* simple.

(c) (*vanité*) pretentiousness, pretension, conceitedness. **avec ~** pretentiously, conceitedly.

prêter [prete] (1) **1** *vt* **(a)** *objet, argent* to lend. **~ qch à qn** to lend sth to sb, lend sb sth; **peux-tu me ~ ton stylo?** can you lend me *ou* can I borrow your pen?; **ils prêtent à 10%** they lend (money) at 10%, they give loans at 10%; **ils m'ont prêté 100 F** they lent me 100 francs; (*Prov*) **on ne prête qu'aux riches** it's easiest to do favours to those who don't need them.

(b) (*attribuer*) *sentiment, facultés* to attribute, ascribe. **on lui prête l'intention de démissionner** he is alleged *ou* claimed to be intending *ou* going to resign, he is supposed to be going to resign; **on me prête des paroles que je n'ai pas dites** people attribute to me words that I never said, people put words in my mouth that I never said, people say I said things that I didn't; **nous prêtons une grande importance à ces problèmes** we consider these problems of great importance, we accord a great deal of importance to these problems.

(c) (*apporter, offrir*) *aide, appui* to give, lend. **~ assistance/secours à qn** to go to sb's assistance/aid; **~ main forte à qn** to lend sb a hand, go to sb's help; **~ son concours à** to give one's assistance to; **~ sa voix à une cause** to speak on behalf of *ou* in support of a cause; **~ sa voix pour un gala** to sing at a gala performance; **dans cette émission il prêtait sa voix à Napoléon** in this broadcast he played *ou* spoke the part of Napoleon; **~ son nom à** to lend one's name to; **~ la main à une entreprise/un complot** to be *ou* get involved in *ou* take part in an undertaking/a plot; **~ attention à** to pay attention to, take notice of; **il faut ~ la plus grande attention à mes paroles** you must listen very closely *ou* you must pay very close attention to what I have to say; **~ le flanc à la critique** to lay o.s. open to criticism, invite criticism; **~ l'oreille** to listen, lend an ear† (*à* to); **~ serment** to take an *ou* the oath; (*hum*) **si Dieu me prête vie** if God grants me life.

2 prêter à *vt indir*: **son attitude prête à équivoque/à la critique/aux commentaires** his attitude is ambiguous/is open to *ou* gives rise to *ou* invites criticism/makes people talk; **décision qui prête à (la) discussion** decision which is open to debate, debatable decision; **sa conduite prête à rire** his behaviour makes you (want to) laugh *ou* is ridiculous *ou* laughable.

3 *vi* [*tissu, cuir*] to give, stretch.

4 se prêter *vpr* **(a)** (*consentir*) **se ~ à** *expérience, arrangement* to lend o.s. to; *projet, jeu* to fall in with, go along with; **il n'a pas voulu se ~ à leurs manœuvres** he didn't want any part in *ou* wouldn't lend himself to *ou* refused to have anything to do with their schemes.

(b) (*s'adapter*) [*chaussures, cuir*] to give, stretch. **se ~ (bien) à qch** to lend itself (well) to sth; **la salle se prête mal à une réunion intime** the room doesn't lend itself to an informal meeting.

prétérit [preterit] *nm* preterite.

prétérition [preterisjɔ̃] *nf* paralipsis, paraleipsis.

préteur [pretœr] *nm* (*Antiq*) praetor.

prêteur, -euse [prɛtœr, øz] **1** *adj* unselfish. **il n'est pas ~** [*enfant*] he's possessive about his toys *ou* belongings, he doesn't like lending his things; [*adulte*] he isn't willing to lend things, he doesn't believe in lending (things).

2 *nm,f* (money)lender. **~ sur gages** pawnbroker.

prétexte [pretɛkst(ə)] *nm* pretext, pretence, excuse. **mauvais ~** poor *ou* lame excuse; **sous ~ d'aider son frère** on the pretext *ou* pretence *ou* under (the) pretext of helping his brother; **sous (le) ~ que** ... on *ou* under the pretext that ..., on the pretence that ...; **sous aucun ~** on no account; **il a pris ~ du froid ou il a donné le froid comme ~ pour rester chez lui** he used *ou* took the cold weather as a pretext *ou* an excuse for staying at home; **servir de ~ à qch/à faire qch** to be a pretext *ou* an excuse for sth/to do sth; **ça lui a servi de ~ ou ça lui a donné un ~ pour refuser** it provided him with an excuse to refuse *ou* with a pretext for refusing; **il saisit le premier ~ venu pour partir** he made the first excuse he could think of for leaving.

prétexter [pretɛkste] (1) *vt* to give as a pretext *ou* an excuse. **il a prétexté/en prétextant qu'il était trop fatigué** he said *ou* he gave as a pretext *ou* as his excuse/on the pretext *ou* excuse that he was too tired; **~ une angine pour refuser une invitation** to plead a bad throat to excuse oneself from an invitation.

prétoire [pretwar] *nm* (*Antiq*) praetorium; (*Jur: frm*) court.

prétorien, -ienne [pretɔrjɛ̃, jɛn] *adj, nm* (*Antiq*) praetorian.

prêtraille [prɛtrɑj] *nf* (*péj*) **la ~** priests, the clergy.

prêtre [prɛtr(ə)] *nm* priest.

prêtre-ouvrier, *pl* **prêtres-ouvriers** [prɛtruvrije] *nm* worker priest.

prêtresse [prɛtrɛs] *nf* priestess.

prêtrise [prɛtriz] *nf* priesthood.

preuve [prœv] **1** *nf* **(a)** (*U*) proof, evidence. **faire la ~ de qch/que** to prove sth/that; **avoir la ~ de/que** to have proof *ou* evidence of/that; **sur la ~ de son identité** on proof of one's identity; **pouvez-vous apporter la ~ de ce que vous dites?** can you prove *ou* can you produce proof *ou* evidence of what you're saying?; **c'est la ~ que** that proves that; **j'avais prévu cela, la ~, j'ai déjà mon billet*** I'd thought of that, witness the fact that *ou* and to prove it I've already got my ticket; **jusqu'à ~ (du) contraire** until we find proof *ou* evidence to the contrary, until there's proof *ou* evidence that it's not the case; **n'importe qui peut conduire, à ~ ma femme*** anyone can drive, just look at *ou* take my wife (for instance); **il a réussi, à ~ qu'il ne faut jamais désespérer*** he succeeded, which just goes to show *ou* prove you should never give up hope.

(b) (*indice*) proof, piece of evidence, evidence (*U*). **je n'ai pas de ~s** I have no proof(s) *ou* evidence; **c'est une ~ supplémentaire de sa culpabilité** it's (a) further proof *ou* it's further evidence of his guilt; **il y a 3 ~s irréfutables qu'il ment** there are 3 definite pieces of evidence to show that he's lying *ou* which prove quite clearly that he's lying; **affirmer qch ~s en mains** to back up a statement with concrete proof *ou* evidence.

(c) (*marque*) proof. **c'est une ~ de bonne volonté/d'amour** it's (a) proof of his good intentions/of his love.

(d) (*Math*) [*opération*] proof. **faire la ~ par neuf** to cast out the nines.

(e) (*loc*) **faire ~ de** to show; **faire ses ~s** [*personne*] to prove o.s., show one's ability; [*technique*] to be well-tried, be tried and tested; [*voiture*] to prove itself; **cette nouvelle technique n'a pas encore fait ses ~s** this new technique hasn't yet been thoroughly tested *ou* fully tried and tested; **professeur qui a fait ses ~s** experienced teacher.

2: preuve par l'absurde reductio ad absurdum; **preuve concluante** conclusive *ou* positive proof; **preuve à contrario** a contrario proof; **preuve matérielle** material evidence (*U*).

preux†† [prø] **1** *adj* valiant†, gallant†. **2** *nm* valiant knight†.

prévaloir [prevalwar] (29) **1** *vi* (*littér*) to prevail (*sur* over, *contre* against). **faire ~ ses droits** to insist upon one's rights; **faire ~ son opinion** to win agreement *ou* acceptance for one's opinion; **son opinion a prévalu sur celle de ses collègues** his opinion overrode that of his colleagues; **rien ne peut ~ contre ses préjugés** nothing can overcome his prejudices.

2 se prévaloir *vpr* **(a)** (*se flatter*) **se ~ de** to pride o.s. on.

(b) (*profiter*) **se ~ de** to take advantage of.

prévaricateur, -trice [prevarikatœr, tris] **1** *adj* corrupt. **2** *nm,f* corrupt official.

prévarication [prevarikɑsjɔ̃] *nf* corrupt practices.

prévariquer [prevarike] (1) *vi* to be guilty of corrupt practices.

prévenance [prevnɑ̃s] *nf* thoughtfulness (*U*), consideration (*U*), kindness (*U*). **toutes les ~s que vous avez eues pour moi** all the consideration *ou* kindness you've shown me; **entourer qn de ~s** to be very considerate to *ou* towards sb; **il n'a aucune ~ pour les autres** he has no consideration for others, he is quite thoughtless of others.

prévenant, e [prɛvnɑ̃, ɑ̃t] *adj personne* considerate, kind (*envers* to), thoughtful; *manières* kind, attentive.

prévenir [prevnir] (22) *vt* **(a)** (*avertir*) to warn (*de qch* about *ou* against sth); (*aviser*) to inform, tell, let know (*de qch* about sth). **qui faut-il ~ en cas d'accident?** who should be informed *ou* told if there's an accident?; **~ le médecin/la police** to call the doctor/the police; **tu es prévenu!** you've been warned!; **partir sans ~** to leave without warning, leave without telling anyone; **il aurait pu ~** he could have let us know.

(b) (*empêcher*) *accident* to prevent, avert, avoid; *maladie* to prevent, guard against; *danger, catastrophe* to avert; *malheur* to ward off, avoid, provide against. (*Prov*) **mieux vaut ~ que guérir** prevention is better than cure (*Prov*).

(c) (*devancer*) *besoin, désir* to anticipate; *question, objection* to forestall. (*littér*) **il voulait arriver le premier mais son frère l'avait prévenu** he wanted to be the first to arrive but his brother had anticipated him *ou* had got there before him.

(d) (*frm: influencer*) **~ qn contre qn** to prejudice *ou* bias sb against sb; **~ qn en faveur de qn** to prejudice *ou* predispose sb in sb's favour.

préventif, -ive [prevɑ̃tif, iv] *adj mesure, médecine* preventive. **à titre ~** as a precaution *ou* preventive; (*Jur*) **il a fait 6 mois de prison ~ive** he was remanded in custody for 6 months (while awaiting trial).

prévention [pʀevɑ̃sjɔ̃] *nf* **(a)** *[accident, crime]* prevention. **~ routière** road safety. **(b)** (*Jur*) custody, detention. **mettre en ~** to detain, remand in *ou* take into custody. **(c)** (*préjugé*) prejudice (*contre* against). **considérer qch sans ~** to take an unprejudiced *ou* unbiased view of sth.

préventivement [pʀevɑ̃tivmɑ̃] *adv agir* preventively, as a precaution *ou* preventive. (*Jur*) **être incarcéré ~** to be remanded *ou* held in custody *ou* detention (awaiting trial).

préventorium [pʀevɑ̃tɔʀjɔm] *nm* tuberculosis sanatorium.

prévenu, e [pʀevny] (*ptp de* **prévenir**) **1** *adj* (*Jur*) charged. **être ~ d'un délit** to be charged with *ou* accused of a crime. **2** *nm,f* (*Jur*) defendant, accused (person).

préverbe [pʀevɛʀb(ə)] *nm* verbal prefix.

prévisible [pʀevizibl(ə)] *adj* foreseeable. **difficilement ~** difficult to foresee.

prévision [pʀevizjɔ̃] *nf* **(a)** (*gén pl: prédiction*) prediction; expectation; (*Fin*) forecast, estimate, prediction. **~s budgétaires** budget estimates; **~s météorologiques** weather forecast.

(b) (*U: action*) **la ~ du temps** weather forecasting, forecasting of the weather; **la ~ de ses réactions est impossible** predicting his reactions is quite impossible, it's impossible to predict his reactions *ou* to foresee what his reactions will be; **en ~ de son arrivée/d'une augmentation du trafic** in anticipation *ou* expectation of his arrival/of an increase in the traffic.

prévisionnel, -elle [pʀevizjɔnɛl] *adj mesure, budget, plan* forward-looking, orientated towards future requirements.

prévoir [pʀevwaʀ] (24) *vt* **(a)** (*anticiper*) *événement, conséquence* to foresee, anticipate; *temps* to forecast; *réaction, contretemps* to expect, reckon on, anticipate. **il faut ~ les erreurs éventuelles** we must allow for *ou* make provision for possible errors; **nous n'avions pas prévu qu'il refuserait** we hadn't reckoned on his refusing, we hadn't anticipated *ou* foreseen (that) he'd refuse; **cela fait *ou* laisse ~ un malheur** it bodes ill; **rien ne laisse ~ une amélioration rapide** there's no prospect of a quick improvement; **tout laisse ~ une issue rapide/qu'il refusera** everything points *ou* all the signs point to a rapid outcome/to his refusing; **rien ne faisait *ou* ne laissait ~ que ...** there was nothing to suggest *ou* to make us think that ...; **on ne peut pas tout ~** you can't think of everything; **plus tôt que prévu** earlier than expected *ou* anticipated; **ce n'était pas prévu au programme*** we weren't expecting that (to happen) *ou* reckoning on that (happening).

(b) (*projeter*) *voyage, construction* to plan. **~ de faire qch** to plan to do *ou* on doing sth; **pour quand prévoyez-vous votre arrivée?** when do you plan to arrive?; **au moment prévu** at the appointed *ou* scheduled time; **comme prévu** as planned, according to plan; *[autoroute]* **ouverture prévue pour la fin de l'année** scheduled to open at the end of the year.

(c) (*préparer, envisager*) to allow. **il faudra ~ des trous pour l'écoulement des eaux** you must leave *ou* provide some holes for the water to drain away; **prévoyez de l'argent en plus pour les faux frais** allow some extra money *ou* put some money on one side for incidental expenses; **il vaut mieux ~ quelques couvertures en plus** you'd better allow a few extra blankets *ou* bring (along) a few extra blankets; **tout est prévu pour l'arrivée de nos hôtes** everything is in hand *ou* organized for the arrival of our guests; **cette voiture est prévue pour 4 personnes** this car is designed *ou* supposed to take 4 people; **vous avez prévu grand** you've allowed a lot of (extra) space, you've planned things on a grand scale; **déposez vos lettres dans la boîte prévue à cet effet** put your letters in the box provided; **on a prévu un coin pour les enfants/des douches** they have laid on *ou* provided a children's corner/showers.

(d) (*Jur*) *[loi]* to provide for, make provision for. **c'est prévu à l'article 8** article 8 makes provision for that, it's provided for in article 8.

prévôt [pʀevo] *nm* (*Hist, Rel*) provost; (*Mil*) provost marshal.

prévôtal, e, *mpl* **-aux** [pʀevotal, o] *adj* of a provost.

prévôté [pʀevote] *nf* (*Hist*) provostship; (*Mil*) military police.

prévoyance [pʀevwajɑ̃s] *nf* foresight, forethought. **caisse de ~** contingency fund; **société de ~** provident society.

prévoyant, e [pʀevwajɑ̃, ɑ̃t] *adj* provident.

prie-Dieu [pʀidjø] *nm inv* prie-dieu.

prier [pʀije] (7) **1** *vt* **(a)** *Dieu, saint* to pray to. **~ Dieu de faire un miracle** to pray for a miracle; **je prie Dieu que cela soit vrai** pray God that it is true.

(b) (*implorer*) to beg, beseech (*littér*). **elle le pria de rester** she begged *ou* urged *ou* pressed him to stay; **je vous prie de me pardonner** I beg you to forgive me, please forgive me; **dites oui, je vous en prie** please say yes, say yes, I beg *ou* beseech (*littér*) you; **Pierre, je t'en prie, calme-toi** Peter, for heaven's sake, calm down; **je t'en prie, ça suffit!** please, that's quite enough!

(c) (*inviter*) to invite, ask; (*frm*) to request (*frm*). **il m'a prié à déjeuner *ou* de venir déjeuner** he has invited *ou* asked me to lunch; **vous êtes prié de vous présenter à 9 heures** you are requested to present yourself at 9 o'clock; **on l'a prié d'assister à la cérémonie** he was invited to be present *ou* his presence was requested at the ceremony.

(d) (*ordonner*) **je vous prie de sortir** will you please leave the room; **vous êtes prié de répondre quand on vous parle/de rester assis** please reply when spoken to/remain seated; **taisez-vous, je vous prie** please shut up*, be quiet, will you.

(e) (*formules de politesse*) **je vous en prie** (*faites donc*) please do, of course; (*après vous*) after you; **excusez-moi — je vous en prie** I'm sorry — don't mention it *ou* not at all; **voulez-vous ouvrir la fenêtre je vous prie?** would you mind opening the window please?, would you be so kind as to open the window please?; (*formule épistolaire*) **je vous prie d'agréer mes sentiments les meilleurs** yours sincerely.

(f) (*loc*) **se faire ~:** **il s'est fait ~** he needed coaxing *ou* persuading; **il ne s'est pas fait ~** he didn't need persuading, he didn't wait to be asked twice, he was only too willing (to do it); **il a accepté l'offre sans se faire ~** he accepted the offer without hesitation.

2 *vi* to pray (*pour* for). **prions, mes frères** brothers, let us pray.

prière [pʀijɛʀ] *nf* **(a)** (*Rel: oraison, office*) prayer. **être en ~** to be praying *ou* at prayer; **dire *ou* faire ses ~s** to say one's prayers; (*fig*) **ne m'oubliez pas dans vos ~s*** remember me in your prayers, pray for me; *V* **livre**[1], **moulin.**

(b) (*demande*) plea, entreaty. **céder aux ~s de qn** to give in to sb's requests; **à la ~ de qn** at sb's request *ou* behest (*littér*); **j'ai une ~ à vous adresser** I have a request to make to you; **il est resté sourd à mes ~s** he turned a deaf ear to my pleas *ou* entreaties.

(c) (*loc*) **~ de: ~ de répondre par retour du courrier** please reply by return of post; **~ de vous présenter à 9 heures** you are requested to present yourself *ou* please present yourself at 9 o'clock; **~ de ne pas fumer** no smoking (please).

prieur [pʀijœʀ] *nm*: (**père**) **~** prior.

prieure [pʀijœʀ] *nf*: (**mère**) **~** prioress.

prieuré [pʀijœʀe] *nm* (*couvent*) priory; (*église*) priory (church).

primaire [pʀimɛʀ] **1** *adj* **(a)** (*Écon, Élec, Méd, Pol, Scol*) primary; (*Géol*) *ère* primary, palaeozoic; (*Jur*) *délinquant* first; (*Psych*) *personne, caractère, fonction* primary (*T*).

(b) (*péj: simpliste*) *personne* simple-minded, of limited outlook, limited*; *raisonnement* simplistic.

2 *nm* (*Scol*) primary school *ou* education; (*Élec*) primary; (*Géol*) Primary, Palaeozoic. (*Scol*) **être en ~** to be in primary school.

3 *nf* (*Pol*) primary (election).

primarité [pʀimaʀite] *nf* primarity.

primat [pʀima] *nm* **(a)** (*Rel*) primate. **(b)** (*littér: primauté*) primacy.

primate [pʀimat] *nm* (*Zool*) primate.

primauté [pʀimote] *nf* (*Rel*) primacy; (*fig*) primacy, pre-eminence.

prime[1] [pʀim] *nf* **(a)** (*cadeau*) free gift. **objet donné en ~ avec qch** object given away *ou* given as a free gift with sth.

(b) (*bonus*) bonus; (*subvention*) premium, subsidy; (*indemnité*) allowance. **~ de fin d'année/de rendement** Christmas/productivity bonus; **~ à l'exportation** export premium *ou* subsidy; **~ de transport** transport allowance; **~ d'allaitement** nursing mother's allowance; (*fig*) **c'est donner une ~ à la paresse!** it's like actively encouraging laziness!

(c) (*Assurance, Bourse*) premium. **~ d'émission/de remboursement** issuing/redemption premium; *V* **marché.**

(d) **faire ~** to be at a premium.

prime[2] [pʀim] *adj* **(a)** **de ~ abord** at first glance, at the outset; **dès sa ~ jeunesse** from his earliest youth; **il n'est plus de ~ jeunesse** he's no longer in the prime of youth. **(b)** (*Math*) prime. **n ~** n prime.

prime[3] [pʀim] *nf* (*Escrime, Rel*) prime.

primer [pʀime] (1) **1** *vt* **(a)** (*surpasser*) to outdo, prevail over, take precedence over *ou* of. **chez elle, l'intelligence prime la sagesse** in her case, intelligence takes precedence over *ou* is more in evidence than wisdom.

(b) (*récompenser*) to award a prize to; (*subventionner*) to subsidize. **invention primée dans un concours** prize-winning invention in a competition; **bête primée** prize(-winning) animal.

2 *vi* (*dominer*) to be the prime *ou* dominant feature, dominate; (*compter, valoir*) to be of prime importance, take first place. **c'est le bleu qui prime dans ce tableau** blue is the prime *ou* dominant colour in this picture; **pour moi ce sont les qualités de cœur qui priment** the qualities of the heart are what take first place for me *ou* are of prime importance to me.

primesautier, -ière [pʀimsotje, jɛʀ] *adj* impulsive.

primeur [pʀimœʀ] **1** *nfpl* (*Comm*) **~s** early fruit and vegetables; **marchand de ~s** greengrocer (*Brit*) (specializing in early produce).

2 *nf*: **avoir la ~ d'une nouvelle** to be the first to hear a piece of news; **je vous réserve la ~ de mon manuscrit** I'll let you be the first to read my manuscript.

primevère [pʀimvɛʀ] *nf* primrose, primula.

primigeste [pʀimiʒɛst(ə)] *nf* primagravida.

primipare [pʀimipaʀ] **1** *adj* primiparous. **2** *nf* primipara.

primitif, -ive [pʀimitif, iv] **1** *adj* **(a)** (*originel*) *forme, état* original, primitive; *projet, question, préoccupation* original, first; *église* primitive, early; (*Logique*) *proposition, concept* basic; (*Art*) *couleurs* primary; (*Géol*) *terrain* primitive, primeval. **ville construite sur le site ~ d'une cité romaine** town built on the original site of a Roman city; **je préfère revenir à mon projet ~/à mon idée ~ive** I'd rather revert to my original *ou* first plan/idea.

(b) (*Sociol*) *peuple, art, mœurs* primitive.

(c) (*sommaire*) *installation* primitive, crude.

(d) (*Ling*) *temps, langue* basic; *mot* primitive; *sens* original.

(e) (*Math*) **fonction ~ive** primitive.

2 *nm, f* (*Art, Sociol*) primitive.

3 primitive *nf* (*Math*) primitive.

primitivement [pʀimitivmɑ̃] *adv* originally.

primo [pʀimo] *adv* first (of all), firstly.

primogéniture [pʀimɔʒenityʀ] *nf* primogeniture.

primo-infection, *pl* **primo-infections** [pʀimɔɛ̃fɛksjɔ̃] *nf* primary infection.

primordial, e, *mpl* **-aux** [pʀimɔʀdjal, o] *adj* **(a)** (*vital*) essential, primordial. **d'une importance ~e** of the utmost *ou* of paramount *ou* primordial importance. **(b)** (*littér: originel*) primordial.

primordialement [pʀimɔʀdjalmɑ̃] *adv* essentially.

prince [pʀɛ̃s] **1** *nm* **(a)** (*lit*) prince. (*fig*) le ~ **des chanteurs** *etc* the prince *ou* king of singers *etc*; *V* **fait**[2].

(b) (*loc*) **être bon** ~ to be magnanimous *ou* generous, behave generously; **être habillé comme un** ~ to be dressed like a prince.

2: prince des apôtres Prince of the apostles; **prince charmant** Prince Charming; **prince consort** Prince Consort; **prince des démons** prince of darkness; **prince de l'Église** prince of the Church; **prince de Galles** Prince of Wales; (*tissu*) check cloth; **prince héritier** crown prince; **prince du sang** prince of royal blood.

princeps [pʀɛ̃sɛps] *adj édition* first.

princesse [pʀɛ̃sɛs] *nf* princess; *V* **frais**[2].

princier, -ière [pʀɛ̃sje, jɛʀ] *adj* (*lit, fig*) princely.

princièrement [pʀɛ̃sjɛʀmɑ̃] *adv* in (a) princely fashion.

principal, e, *mpl* **-aux** [pʀɛ̃sipal, o] **1** *adj* **(a)** *entrée, bâtiment, résidence* main; *clerc, employé* chief, head; *question* main, principal; *raison, but* principal, main; *personnage, rôle* leading, main, principal. **il a eu l'un des rôles** ~**aux dans l'affaire** he played a major role *ou* he was one of the leading *ou* main figures in the business.

(b) (*Gram*) *proposition* main.

2 *nm* **(a)** (*Fin*) principal.

(b) (*Scol*) principal, head(master); (*Admin*) chief clerk.

(c) (*chose importante*) most important thing, main point. **c'est le** ~ that's the main thing.

3 principale *nf* (*Gram*) main clause.

principalement [pʀɛ̃sipalmɑ̃] *adv* principally, mainly, chiefly.

principat [pʀɛ̃sipa] *nm* princedom.

principauté [pʀɛ̃sipote] *nf* principality.

principe [pʀɛ̃sip] *nm* **(a)** (*règle*) [*science, géométrie*] principle. **il nous a expliqué le** ~ **de la machine** he explained to us the principle on which the machine worked; **le** ~ **d'Archimède** Archimedes' principle; *V* **pétition.**

(b) (*hypothèse*) principle, assumption. **partir du** ~ **que ..., poser comme** ~ **que ...** to work on the principle *ou* assumption that ...; *V* **accord.**

(c) (*règle morale*) principle. **il a des** ~**s** he's a man of principle, he's got principles; **il n'a pas de** ~**s** he is unprincipled, he has no principles; **avoir pour** ~ **de faire** to make it a principle to do, make a point of doing; **il n'est pas dans mes** ~**s de ...** I make it a principle not to ... .

(d) (*origine*) principle. **remonter jusqu'au** ~ **des choses** to go back to first principles.

(e) (*élément*) principle, element, constituent. ~ **nécessaire à la nutrition** necessary principle of nutrition.

(f) (*rudiment*) ~**s** rudiments, principles.

(g) (*loc*) **par** ~ on principle; **en** ~ (*d'habitude, en général*) as a rule; (*théoriquement*) in principle, theoretically; **de** ~ mechanical, automatic; **faire qch pour le** ~ to do sth on principle *ou* for the sake of (doing) it.

printanier, -ière [pʀɛ̃tanje, jɛʀ] *adj soleil* spring; *temps* spring(-like); *vêtement, atmosphère* spring-like.

printemps [pʀɛ̃tɑ̃] *nm* spring. **au** ~ in (the) spring(time); (*littér*) **au** ~ **de la vie** in the springtime of (one's) life; (*hum*) **mes 40** ~**s** my 40 summers (*hum*).

priorat [pʀijɔʀa] *nm* priorate.

priori [pʀijɔʀi] *V* **a priori.**

prioritaire [pʀijɔʀitɛʀ] **1** *adj* **(a)** *projet* having priority, priority (*épith*); *personne* having priority.

(b) (*Aut*) *véhicule* having priority *ou* right of way. **il était sur une route** ~ he had right of way, he was on the main road.

2 *nmf* (*Aut*) person who has right of way *ou* priority.

priorité [pʀijɔʀite] *nf* **(a)** (*gén*) priority. **discuter qch en** ~ to discuss sth as a (matter of) priority; **l'une des choses à faire en grande** ~, **l'une des** ~**s essentielles** one of the first *ou* top* priorities; **il nous faudrait en** ~ **des vivres** first and foremost we need supplies, we need supplies as a matter of urgency.

(b) (*Aut*) priority, right of way. **avoir la** ~ to have right of way; **avoir** ~ **sur un autre véhicule** to have right of way over another vehicle; ~ **à droite** (*principe*) *system of giving priority ou right of way to traffic coming from the right;* (*panneau*) give way to the vehicles on your right.

pris, prise [pʀi, pʀiz] (*ptp de* **prendre**) **1** *adj* **(a)** *place* taken. **avoir les mains prises** to have one's hands full; **tous les billets sont** ~ the tickets are sold out, all the tickets have been sold; **toutes les places sont prises** all the seats are taken *ou* have gone.

(b) *personne* busy, engaged (*frm*). **le directeur est très** ~ **cette semaine** the manager is very busy this week; **si vous n'êtes pas** ~ **ce soir ...** if you're free *ou* if you've got nothing on this evening ...; **désolé, je suis** ~ I'm sorry, but I've got something on.

(c) (*Méd*) *nez* stuffy, stuffed-up; *gorge* hoarse. **j'ai le nez** ~ my nose is stuffed up; **j'ai la gorge prise** my throat is hoarse; **la paralysie gagne, le bras droit est** ~ the paralysis is spreading, and has reached *ou* taken hold of the right arm; **les poumons sont** ~ the lungs are (now) affected.

(d) avoir la taille bien prise† to have a neat waist; **la taille prise dans un manteau de bonne coupe** wearing a well-cut coat to show off a neat waist.

(e) (*fig*) (*Culin*) *crème, mayonnaise* set; (*gelé*) *eau* frozen.

(f) ~ **de peur/remords** stricken with *ou* by fear/remorse; ~ **d'une inquiétude soudaine/d'une envie** seized by a sudden anxiety/a fancy; ~ **de boisson** under the influence*, the worse for drink.

2 prise *nf* **(a)** (*moyen d'empoigner, de prendre*) hold (*U*), grip (*U*); (*pour soulever, faire levier*) purchase (*U*); (*Catch, Judo*) hold; (*Alpinisme*) hold. **on n'a pas de prise pour soulever la caisse** there's no purchase to lift the chest, you can't get a hold on this chest to lift it; **cette construction offre trop de prise au vent** this building is too open to the wind; *V* **lâcher.**

(b) (*Chasse, Pêche: butin*) catch; (*Mil: capture*) capture, seizure; (*Dames, Échecs*) capture.

(c) (*Aut*) **être/mettre en prise** to be in/put the car into gear; **en prise (directe)** in direct drive; (*fig*) **en prise directe avec, en prise (directe) sur** in direct contact with.

(d) (*Élec*) **prise (de courant)** (*mâle*) plug; (*femelle*) socket, point, power point (*T*); (*boîtier*) socket. **prise multiple** adaptor.

(e) [*tabac*] pinch of snuff.

(f) (*Méd*) dose.

(g) (*loc*) **avoir prise sur** to have a hold over; **personne n'a aucune prise sur lui** no one has any hold *ou* influence over him; **les passions n'ont que trop de prise sur elle** her passions have all too great a hold over her; **donner prise à** to give rise to, lay one open to; **son attitude donne prise aux soupçons** his attitude gives rise to *ou* lays him open to suspicion; **être** *ou* **se trouver aux prises avec des difficultés** to be battling *ou* grappling with difficulties; **être** *ou* **se trouver aux prises avec un créancier** to be battling against *ou* doing battle with a creditor; **on les a mis/laissés aux prises** we set them by the ears/left them to fight it out.

3: prise d'air air inlet *ou* intake; **prise d'armes** military review *ou* parade; **prise de bec*** row*, set-to*; **avoir une prise de bec avec qn** to have a row* *ou* a set-to* with *ou* fall out with sb; **prise en charge** (*par taxi*) [*passager*] picking up; (*taxe*) pick-up charge; (*par Sécurité sociale etc*) *undertaking to reimburse medical expenses*; **prise de conscience** awareness, realization; **il faut qu'il y ait une prise de conscience du problème** people must be made aware of *ou* must be alive to the problem, a new awareness *ou* full realization of the problem is needed; **prise en considération: la prise en considération de qch** taking sth into consideration *ou* account; **prise de contact** initial contact *ou* meeting; (*Jur*) **prise de corps** arrest; **prise de courant** *V* **2d**; **prise d'eau** water (supply) point; (*robinet*) tap; **prise de guerre** spoils of war (*pl*); (*Rel*) **prise d'habit** taking the cloth (*U*); **prise d'otages** taking *ou* seizure of hostages, hostage-taking (*U*); (*Jur*) **prise à partie** *action against a judge*; **prise de position** taking a stand (*U*), stand; **prise de possession** taking possession, taking over; (*Méd*) **prise de sang** blood test, taking a blood sample (*U*); (*Ciné, Rad, TV*) **prise de son** sound recording; **prise de son J Dupont** sound (engineer) J Dupont; (*Élec, Rad*) **prise de terre** earth (*Brit*), ground (*US*); (*Rel*) **prise de voile** taking the veil; **prise de vue(s)** (*opération: Ciné, TV*) filming, shooting; **prise de vue(s) J Dupont** camera(work) J Dupont; **prise de vue** (*photo*) shot.

priser[1] [pʀize] (1) *vt* (*littér*) to prize, value. **je prise fort peu ce genre de plaisanterie** I don't appreciate this sort of joke at all.

priser[2] [pʀize] (1) **1** *vt tabac, héroïne* to take; *V* **tabac. 2** *vi* to take snuff.

priseur, -euse [pʀizœʀ, øz] *nm,f* snuff taker; *V* **commissaire.**

prismatique [pʀismatik] *adj* prismatic.

prisme [pʀism(ə)] *nm* prism.

prison [pʀizɔ̃] *nf* **(a)** (*lieu*) prison, jail; (*fig: demeure sombre*) prison. (*Hist*) ~ **pour dettes** debtors' prison; **mettre en** ~ to send to prison *ou* jail, imprison; *V* **porte.**

(b) (*emprisonnement*) imprisonment, prison, jail. **peine de** ~ prison sentence; **faire de la** ~ to go to *ou* be in prison; **faire 6 mois de** ~ to spend 6 months in jail *ou* prison; **condamné à 3 mois de** ~ **ferme/à la** ~ **à vie** sentenced to 3 months' imprisonment/to life imprisonment; **faire de la** ~ **préventive** to be remanded in custody.

prisonnier, -ière [pʀizɔnje, jɛʀ] **1** *adj soldat* captive. **être** ~ (*enfermé*) to be trapped, be a prisoner; (*en prison*) to be imprisoned, be a prisoner; **être** ~ **de ses vêtements** to be imprisoned in *ou* hampered by one's clothes; **être** ~ **de ses préjugés/de l'ennemi** to be a prisoner of one's prejudices/of the enemy.

2 *nm,f* prisoner. **faire/retenir qn** ~ to take/hold sb prisoner; ~ **de guerre** prisoner of war; *V* **camp, constituer.**

privatif, -ive [pʀivatif, iv] **1** *adj* **(a)** (*Gram*) privative. **(b)** (*Jur: qui prive*) which deprives of rights (*ou* liberties *etc*). **(c)** (*Jur: privé*) private. **2** *nm* (*Gram*) privative (prefix *ou* element).

privation [pʀivɑsjɔ̃] *nf* **(a)** (*suppression*) deprivation, deprival. (*Jur*) **la** ~ **des droits civiques** the forfeiture *ou* deprival *ou* deprivation of civil rights; **la** ~ **de la vue/d'un membre** losing one's sight/a limb.

(b) (*gén pl: sacrifice*) privation, hardship. **les** ~**s que je me suis imposées** the things I went *ou* did *ou* managed without, the hardships I bore.

privatisation [pʀivatizɑsjɔ̃] *nf* putting into private hands, taking over by a private concern.

privatiser [pʀivatize] (1) *vt entreprise* to put into private hands, hand over to a private concern.

privautés [pʀivote] *nfpl* liberties. **prendre des** ~ **avec** to take liberties with; ~ **de langage** familiar *ou* coarse language.

privé, e [pʀive] **1** *adj* (*gén*) private; (*Presse*) *source* unofficial; (*Jur*) *droit* civil. **2** *nm* (*vie*) private life; (*Comm: secteur*) private sector. **en** ~ in private.

privément [pʀivemɑ̃] *adv* (*littér*) privately.

priver [pʀive] (1) **1** *vt* **(a)** (*délibérément, pour punir*) ~ **qn de** to deprive sb of; **il a été privé de dessert** he was deprived of sweet, he had to go without his sweet; **il a été privé de récréation** he was kept in at playtime; **on l'a privé de sa liberté/de ses droits** he was deprived of his freedom/his rights.

(b) (*faire perdre*) ~ **qn de ses moyens** to deprive sb of *ou* strip sb of his means; **cette perte m'a privé de ma seule joie** this loss has deprived me of my only joy *ou* has taken my only joy from me; **l'accident l'a privé d'un bras** he lost an arm in the accident; **privé de connaissance** unconscious; **privé de voix** speechless, unable to speak; **un discours privé de l'essentiel** a speech from which the main content had been removed *ou* which was stripped of its essential content.

(c) (*supprimer*) **nous avons été privés d'électricité pendant 3 jours** we were without *ou* we had no *ou* we were deprived of electricity for 3 days; **il a été privé de sommeil** he didn't get any sleep; **on m'interdit le sel, ça me prive beaucoup** I'm not allowed salt and I must say I miss it *ou* and I don't like having to go *ou* do without it; **cela ne me prive pas du tout** (*de vous le donner*) I can spare it (quite easily); (*de ne plus en manger*) I don't miss it at all; (*de ne pas y aller*) I don't mind at all.

2 se priver *vpr* **(a)** (*par économie*) to go without, do without. **se ~ de qch** to go without sth, do without sth, manage without sth; **ils ont dû se ~ pour leurs enfants** they had to go *ou* do without because of their children; **je n'ai pas l'intention de me ~** I've no intention of going *ou* doing without, I don't intend to go short.

(b) (*se passer de*) **se ~ de** to manage without, do without; **il se prive de dessert par crainte de grossir** he does without sweet *ou* he misses out on the sweet* for fear of putting on weight; **ils ont dû se ~ d'une partie de leur personnel** they had to manage without *ou* do without some of their staff; **tu te prives d'un beau spectacle en refusant d'y aller** you'll miss out on* *ou* you'll deprive yourself of a fine show by not going.

(c) (*gén nég: se retenir*) **il ne s'est pas privé de le dire/le critiquer** he made no bones about *ou* he had no hesitation in saying it/criticizing him; **j'aime bien manger et quand j'en ai l'occasion je ne m'en prive pas** I love eating and whenever I get the chance I don't hold back; **si tu veux y aller, ne t'en prive pas pour moi** if you want to go don't hold back for me *ou* don't deny yourself *ou* stop yourself because of me.

privilège [pʀivilɛʒ] *nm* (*gén*) privilege. **j'ai eu le ~ d'assister à la cérémonie** I had the privilege of attending *ou* I was privileged to attend the ceremony; **avoir le triste ~ de faire** to have the unhappy privilege of doing.

privilégié, e [pʀivileʒje] (*ptp de* **privilégier**) **1** *adj personne* privileged, favoured; *site, climat* privileged; (*Fin*) *action* preference (*épith*); *créancier* preferential. **~ par le sort** fortunate, lucky; **il a été ~ par la nature** he has been favoured by nature; **~ pour le temps** lucky with the weather.

2 *nm,f* privileged person. **c'est un ~** he is fortunate *ou* lucky; **quelques ~s** a privileged few.

privilégier [pʀivileʒje] (7) *vt* to favour, give greater place *ou* importance to.

prix [pʀi] **1** *nm* **(a)** (*coût*) *[objet]* price; *[location, transport]* cost. **le ~ d'un billet Paris-Lyon** the fare between Paris and Lyons; **à quel ~ vend-il/sont ses tapis?** what price is he asking for/are his carpets?, how much is he charging for/are his carpets?; **au ~ que ça coûte** for what it costs, for the price it is; **au ~ où sont les choses *ou* où est le beurre!*** with prices what they are; **votre ~ sera le mien** name *ou* state your price; **acheter qch à ~ d'or** to pay a (small) fortune for sth; **au ~ fort** at the highest possible price, for a tremendous price; **ça n'a pas de ~** it is priceless; **je vous fais un ~ (d'ami)** I'll let you have it cheap *ou* at a reduced price, I'll knock a bit off for you*; **j'y ai mis le ~ (qu'il fallait)** I had to pay a lot *ou* quite a price for it, it cost me a lot; **il faut y mettre le ~** you have to be prepared to pay for it; **il n'a pas voulu y mettre le ~** he didn't want to pay that much; **c'est dans mes ~** that's affordable *ou* within my price-range; (*enchères*) **mettre qch à ~** to set a reserve price (*Brit*) *ou* an upset price (*US*) on sth; **mettre à ~ la tête de qn** to put a price on sb's head, offer a reward for sb's capture; **objet de ~** expensive *ou* pricey object; *V* **bas**[1], **hors, premier.**

(b) (*fig*) price. **le ~ du succès/de la gloire** the price of success/glory; **j'apprécie votre geste à son juste ~** I appreciate your gesture for what it's worth; **donner du ~ à** *exploit, aide* to make (even) more worthwhile; **leur pauvreté donne encore plus de ~ à leur cadeau** their poverty makes their present even more valuable *ou* increases the value *ou* worth of their gift even more; **à tout ~** at all costs, at any price; **à aucun ~** on no account, not at any price; **au ~ de grands efforts/sacrifices** at the expense of great efforts/sacrifices.

(c) (*Scol, gén: récompense*) prize. (*Scol*) **(livre de) ~** prize (-book); **le ~ Nobel de la paix** the Nobel Peace Prize.

(d) (*vainqueur*) (*personne*) prizewinner; (*livre*) prize winning book. **premier ~ du Conservatoire** first prizewinner at the Conservatoire; **as-tu lu le dernier ~ Goncourt?** have you read the book that won the last Prix Goncourt?

(e) (*Courses*) race. (*Aut*) **Grand ~ (automobile)** Grand Prix.

2: prix de consolation consolation prize; **prix coûtant** cost price; **prix de détail** retail price; **prix d'encouragement** special *ou* consolation prize (*for promising entrant*); (*Scol*) **prix d'excellence** prize for excellence; **prix de fabrique** factory price; **prix fixe** (*gén*) set price; (*menu*) set (price) menu; **(repas à) prix fixe** set (price) meal; **prix de gros** wholesale price; (*Comm*) **prix imposé** regulation price; (*Ciné, Théât*) **prix d'interprétation** *prize for the interpretation of a role;* **prix de revient** cost price; **prix de vertu** paragon of virtue.

pro [pʀo] *nm* (*abrév de* **professionnel**) pro.

pro- [pʀo] *préf* pro-. **~américain/chinois** pro-American/-Chinese.

probabiliste [pʀɔbabilist(ə)] *adj* (*Statistique*) probability (*épith*).

probabilité [pʀɔbabilite] *nf* (*V* **probable**) (*U*) probability; likelihood; (*chance*) probability. **selon toute ~, il est perdu** in all probability *ou* likelihood it has been lost, the chances are it has been lost*.

probable [pʀɔbabl(ə)] *adj événement, hypothèse* probable, likely; (*Math, Statistique*) probable. **il est ~ qu'il gagnera** it is likely *ou* probable that he will win, he is likely to win, the chances are (that) he'll win*; **il est peu ~ qu'il vienne** he is unlikely to come, there is little chance of his coming, the chances are (that) he won't come*; **c'est (très) ~** it's (very *ou* highly) probable, (very) probably, it's (highly) likely.

probablement [pʀɔbabləmɑ̃] *adv* probably. **il viendra ~** he's likely to come, he'll probably come; **~ pas** probably not.

probant, e [pʀɔbɑ̃, ɑ̃t] *adj argument, expérience* convincing; (*Jur*) probative.

probation [pʀɔbasjɔ̃] *nf* (*Rel*) probation.

probatoire [pʀɔbatwaʀ] *adj examen, test* grading, preliminary. **stage ~** trial *ou* probationary period.

probe [pʀɔb] *adj* (*littér*) upright, honest.

probité [pʀɔbite] *nf* probity, integrity.

problématique [pʀɔblematik] *adj* problematic(al).

problème [pʀɔblɛm] *nm* (*difficulté*) problem; (*question débattue*) problem, issue; (*Math*) problem. (*Scol*) **~s de robinets** sums about the volume of water in containers; **c'est tout un ~** it's a real problem; **le ~ du logement** the housing problem, the problem of housing; **enfant/cheveux à ~s** problem child/hair; *V* **faux**[2].

procédé [pʀɔsede] *nm* **(a)** (*méthode*) process.

(b) (*conduite*) behaviour (*U*), conduct (*U*). **avoir recours à un ~ malhonnête** to do sth in a dishonest way, resort to dishonest behaviour; **ce sont là des ~s peu recommandables** that's pretty disreputable behaviour; *V* **échange.**

(c) (*Billard*) tip.

procéder [pʀɔsede] (6) **1** *vi* (*agir*) to proceed; (*moralement*) to behave. **~ par ordre** to take things one by one, do one thing at a time; **~ avec prudence/par élimination** to proceed with caution/by elimination; **je n'aime pas sa façon de ~ (envers les gens)** I don't like the way he behaves (towards people).

2 procéder à *vt indir* (*opérer*) *enquête, expérience* to conduct, carry out; *dépouillement* to start. **~ à l'ouverture du coffre** to proceed to open the chest, set about *ou* start opening the chest; **nous avons fait ~ à une étude sur** we have initiated *ou* set up a study on.

3 procéder de *vt indir* (*frm: provenir de*) to come from, proceed from, originate in; (*Rel*) to proceed from. **cette philosophie procède de celle de Platon** this philosophy originates in *ou* is a development from that of Plato; **cela procède d'une mauvaise organisation** it comes from *ou* is due to a lack of organization.

procédure [pʀɔsedyʀ] *nf* **(a)** (*marche à suivre*) procedure.

(b) (*Jur: règles*) procedure; (*procès*) proceedings. **quelle ~ doit-on suivre pour obtenir ...?** what procedure must one follow to obtain ...?, what's the (usual) procedure for obtaining ...?; **~ de conciliation** conciliation procedure; **~ civile** civil (law) procedure; **~ pénale** criminal (law) procedure.

procédurier, -ière [pʀɔsedyʀje, jɛʀ] *adj* (*péj*) *tempérament, attitude* quibbling (*épith*), pettifogging (*épith*), nit-picking* (*épith*).

procès [pʀɔsɛ] **1** *nm* **(a)** (*Jur*) (*poursuite*) (legal) proceedings, (court) action, lawsuit; *[cour d'assises]* trial. **faire/intenter un ~ à qn** to take/start *ou* institute (*frm*) (legal) proceedings against sb; **engager un ~ contre qn** to take (court) action against sb, bring an action against sb, take sb to court, sue sb; **intenter un ~ en divorce** to institute divorce proceedings; **être en ~ avec qn** to be involved in a lawsuit with sb; **gagner/perdre son ~** to win/lose one's case; **réviser un ~** to review a case *ou* judgment.

(b) (*fig*) **faire le ~ de la société capitaliste** to put capitalism on trial *ou* in the dock; **faire le ~ de qn** to put sb in the dock; **faire le ~ de qch** to pick holes in* *ou* criticize sth; **faire un ~ d'intention à qn** to accuse sb on the basis of his supposed intentions, make a case against sb based on assumptions not facts; **vous me faites un mauvais ~** you're making unfounded *ou* groundless accusations against me; *V* **forme.**

(c) (*Anat*) process.

(d) (*Ling*) process.

2: procès civil civil proceedings *ou* action; **procès criminel** criminal proceedings *ou* trial; **procès-verbal** *nm, pl* **procès-verbaux** (*compte-rendu*) minutes; (*Jur: constat*) report, statement; (*de contravention*) statement; **dresser un procès-verbal contre un automobiliste** to book a motorist.

procession [pʀɔsesjɔ̃] *nf* (*gén*) procession. **marcher en ~** to walk in procession.

processionnaire [pʀɔsesjɔnɛʀ] **1** *adj* processionary.

2 *nf* processionary caterpillar.

processionnel, -elle [pʀɔsesjɔnɛl] *adj* processional.

processionnellement [pʀɔsesjɔnɛlmɑ̃] *adv* in procession.

processus [pʀɔsesys] *nm* **(a)** process; *[maladie]* progress. **(b)** (*Anat*) process.

prochain, e [pʀɔʃɛ̃, ɛn] **1** *adj* **(a)** (*suivant*) *réunion, numéro, semaine* next. **lundi/le mois ~** next Monday/month; **la ~e rencontre aura lieu à Paris** the next meeting will take place in Paris; **la ~e fois que tu viendras** (the) next time you come; **la ~e fois *ou* la fois ~e, je le saurai** I'll know next time; **à la ~e occasion** at the next *ou* first opportunity; **à la ~e!*** be seeing you!*; **au revoir, à une ~e fois!** bye, see you again!*; **je ne peux pas rester dîner aujourd'hui, ce sera pour une ~e fois** I can't stay for dinner today — it'll have to be *ou* I'll have to come some other time; **je descends à la ~e*** I'm getting off at the next stop (*ou* station *etc*); **au ~ (client)** next (one) please!

(b) (*proche*) *arrivée, départ* impending, imminent; *mort* imminent; *avenir* near, immediate. **un jour ~** soon, in the near future; **un de ces ~s jours** one of these days, before long.

(c) *village* (*suivant*) next; (*voisin*) neighbouring, nearby; (*plus près*) nearest.

(d) (*littér*) *cause* immediate.

2 *nm* fellow man; (*Rel*) neighbour.

prochainement [pʀɔʃɛnmɑ̃] *adv* soon, shortly. (*Ciné*) ~ **(sur vos écrans) ...** coming soon ....

proche [pʀɔʃ] **1** *adj* **(a)** (*dans l'espace*) *village* neighbouring (*épith*), nearby (*épith*); *rue* nearby (*épith*). **être (tout)** ~ to be (very) near *ou* close, be (quite) close by; ~ **de la ville** near the town, close to the town; **le magasin le plus** ~ the nearest shop; **les maisons sont très** ~**s les unes des autres** the houses are very close together; **de** ~ **en** ~ step by step, gradually; **la nouvelle se répandit de** ~ **en** ~ the news spread from one person to the next.

(b) (*imminent*) *mort* close (*attrib*), at hand (*attrib*); *départ* imminent, at hand (*attrib*). **dans un** ~ **avenir** in the near *ou* immediate future; **être** ~ *[fin]* to be drawing near; *[but, dénouement]* to be near at hand; **être** ~ **de** *fin, victoire* to be nearing, be close to; *dénouement* to be reaching, be drawing close to; **être** ~ **de la mort** to be near death *ou* close to death; **la nuit est** ~ it's nearly nightfall; **l'heure est** ~ **où ...** the time is at hand when ...; *V* **futur.**

(c) (*récent*) *événement* close (*attrib*), recent.

(d) *parent* close, near. **mes plus** ~**s parents** my nearest *ou* closest relatives, my next of kin (*Admin*).

(e) ~ **de** (*avoisinant*) close to; (*parent de*) closely related to; **l'italien est** ~ **du latin** Italian is closely related to Latin; **une désinvolture** ~ **de l'insolence** an offhandedness verging on insolence.

2 *nmpl*: ~**s** close relations, nearest and dearest*, next of kin (*Admin*).

3: le Proche-Orient the Near East; **du Proche-Orient** Near Eastern, in *ou* from the Near East.

proclamateur, -trice [pʀɔklamatœʀ, tʀis] *nm,f* proclaimer.

proclamation [pʀɔklamɑsjɔ̃] *nf* (*V* **proclamer**) proclamation; declaration; announcement; (*écrite*) proclamation.

proclamer [pʀɔklame] (1) *vt* **(a)** (*affirmer*) *conviction, vérité* to proclaim. ~ **son innocence** to proclaim *ou* declare one's innocence; ~ **que** to proclaim *ou* declare *ou* assert that; **il se proclamait le sauveur du pays** he proclaimed *ou* declared himself (to be) the saviour of the country; (*littér*) **chez eux, tout proclamait la pauvreté** everything in their house evinced poverty (*littér*).

(b) *république, état d'urgence* to proclaim, declare; *décret* to publish; *verdict, résultats d'élection* to declare, announce; *résultats d'examen* to announce. ~ **qn roi** to proclaim sb king.

proclitique [pʀɔklitik] *adj, nm* proclitic.

proconsul [pʀɔkɔ̃syl] *nm* proconsul.

procréateur, -trice [pʀɔkʀeatœʀ, tʀis] (*littér*) **1** *adj* procreative. **2** *nm,f* procreator.

procréation [pʀɔkʀeɑsjɔ̃] *nf* (*littér*) procreation.

procréer [pʀɔkʀee] (1) *vt* (*littér*) to procreate.

procuration [pʀɔkyʀɑsjɔ̃] *nf* (*Jur*) (*pour voter, représenter qn*) proxy; (*pour toucher de l'argent*) power of attorney. **par** ~ by proxy; **avoir une** ~ to have power of attorney *ou* an authorization; **donner une** ~ **à qn** to give sb power of attorney, authorize sb.

procurer [pʀɔkyʀe] (1) **1** *vt* **(a)** (*faire obtenir*) ~ **qch à qn** to get *ou* obtain sth for sb, find sth for sb, provide sb with sth.

(b) (*apporter*) *joie, ennuis* to bring; *avantage* to bring, give. **le plaisir que procure le jardinage** the pleasure that gardening brings *ou* that one gets from gardening.

2 se procurer *vpr* (*obtenir*) to get, procure, obtain (for o.s.); (*trouver*) to find, come by; (*acheter*) to get, buy (o.s.).

procureur [pʀɔkyʀœʀ] *nm* (*Jur*) ~ **(de la République)** public *ou* state prosecutor; ~ **général** public prosecutor (*in appeal courts*); (*Can*) ~ **général, juge en chef** Attorney General, Chief Justice; (*Can*) ~ **de la Couronne** Crown attorney (*Can*).

prodigalité [pʀɔdigalite] *nf* **(a)** (*U: caractère*) prodigality, extravagance. **(b)** (*dépenses*) ~**s** extravagance, extravagant expenditure (*U*). **(c)** (*littér: profusion*) *[détails]* abundance, profusion, wealth.

prodige [pʀɔdiʒ] **1** *nm* (*événement*) marvel, wonder; (*personne*) prodigy. **un** ~ **de la nature/science** a wonder of nature/science; **tenir du** ~ to be astounding *ou* extraordinary; **faire des** ~**s** to do *ou* work wonders; **grâce à des** ~**s de courage/patience** thanks to his (*ou* her *etc*) prodigious *ou* extraordinary courage/patience.

2 *adj*: **enfant** ~ child prodigy.

prodigieusement [pʀɔdiʒjøzmɑ̃] *adv* fantastically, incredibly, phenomenally, tremendously.

prodigieux, -euse [pʀɔdiʒjø, øz] *adj foule, force, bêtise* fantastic, incredible, phenomenal; *personne, génie* prodigious, phenomenal; *effort* tremendous, fantastic.

prodigue [pʀɔdig] **1** *adj* (*dépensier*) extravagant, wasteful, prodigal; (*généreux*) generous. **être** ~ **de ses compliments** to be lavish with one's praise; **être** ~ **de conseils** to be full of advice *ou* free with one's advice; **lui en général si peu** ~ **de compliments/conseils** he who is usually so sparing of compliments/advice; **être** ~ **de son temps** to be unsparing *ou* unstinting of one's time; **être** ~ **de son bien** to be lavish with one's money; (*Rel*) **l'enfant** *ou* **le fils** ~ the prodigal son.

2 *nmf* spendthrift.

prodiguer [pʀɔdige] (1) *vt énergie, talent* to be unsparing *ou* unstinting of; *compliments, conseils* to be full of, pour out; *argent* to be lavish with. ~ **des compliments/conseils à qn** to lavish compliments/advice on sb, pour out compliments/advice to sb; **elle me prodigua ses soins** she lavished care on me; **malgré les soins que le médecin lui a prodigués** in spite of the care *ou* treatment the doctor gave him; **se** ~ **sans compter** to spare no efforts, give unsparingly *ou* unstintingly of o.s.

producteur, -trice [pʀɔdyktœʀ, tʀis] **1** *adj* producing (*épith*), growing (*épith*). **pays** ~ **de pétrole** oil-producing country, oil producer; **pays** ~ **de blé** wheat-growing country, wheat producer; (*Ciné*) **société** ~**trice** film company.

2 *nm,f* **(a)** (*Comm*) producer; (*Agr*) *[œufs]* producer; *[blé, tomates]* grower, producer.

(b) (*Ciné*) producer.

productible [pʀɔdyktibl(ə)] *adj* producible.

productif, -ive [pʀɔdyktif, iv] *adj* productive. (*Fin*) ~ **d'intérêts** that bears interest, interest-bearing.

production [pʀɔdyksjɔ̃] *nf* **(a)** (*U: V* **produire**) production; generation; growing; writing; painting.

(b) (*rendement, fabrication, récolte*) (*Ind*) production, output; (*Agr*) production, yield. **notre** ~ **est inférieure à nos besoins** our output does not meet our needs *ou* is lower than our needs; **restreindre la** ~ to restrict output *ou* production; **la** ~ **dramatique du 20e siècle** 20th-century plays; *V* **moyen.**

(c) (*produit*) product. ~**s** (*Agr*) produce; (*Comm, Ind*) goods; **les** ~**s de l'esprit** creations of the mind.

(d) (*Ciné*) production.

productivité [pʀɔdyktivite] *nf* productivity, productiveness; (*Écon, Ind: rendement*) productivity.

produire [pʀɔdɥiʀ] (38) **1** *vt* **(a)** (*fabriquer*) *acier, voiture* to produce, make, turn out*; *électricité* to produce, generate; *maïs, tomates* to produce, grow; *charbon, pétrole* to produce; *rouille, humidité, son* to produce, make; *roman* to produce, write, turn out*; *tableau* to produce, paint, turn out*; (*Fin*) *intérêt* to yield, return. **arbre/terre qui produit de bons fruits** tree/soil which yields *ou* produces good fruit; **certains sols produisent plus que d'autres** some soils are more productive than others; **un poète qui ne produit pas beaucoup** a poet who doesn't write much *ou* turn out* very much; **cette école a produit plusieurs savants** this school has produced several scientists.

(b) (*causer*) *effet* to produce, have; *changement* to produce, bring about; *résultat* to produce, give; *sensation* to cause, create. ~ **une bonne/mauvaise impression sur qn** to produce *ou* make a good/bad impression on sb; **il a produit une forte impression sur les examinateurs** he made a great impression on the examiners, the examiners were highly impressed by him.

(c) (*présenter*) *document, témoin* to produce.

(d) (*Ciné*) *film* to produce.

2 se produire *vpr* **(a)** (*survenir*) to happen, occur, take place. **il s'est produit un revirement dans l'opinion** there has been a complete change in public opinion; **le changement qui s'est produit en lui** the change that has come over him *ou* taken place in him.

(b) *[personne]* (*paraître en public*) to perform, give a performance, appear. **se** ~ **sur scène** to appear on the stage; **se** ~ **en public** to appear in public, give a public performance.

produit [pʀɔdɥi] **1** *nm* **(a)** (*denrée, article*) product. ~**s** (*Agr*) produce; (*Comm, Ind*) goods, products; ~**s finis/semi-finis,** ~**s ouvrés/semi-ouvrés** finished/semi-finished goods *ou* products; **il faudrait acheter un** ~ **pour nettoyer les carreaux** we'll have to buy something to clean the windows (with); (*fig*) **un** ~ **typique de notre université** a typical product of our university.

(b) (*U*) (*rapport*) product, yield; (*bénéfice*) profit; (*revenu*) income. **le** ~ **de la collecte sera donné à une bonne œuvre** the proceeds *ou* takings from the collection will be given to charity; **vivre du** ~ **de sa terre** to live on the produce of *ou* the income from one's land.

(c) (*Math*) product.

(d) (*Chim*) product, chemical.

(e) (*Zool: petit*) offspring (*inv*).

2: produits agricoles agricultural *ou* farm produce; **produits alimentaires** foodstuffs; **produits de beauté** cosmetics, beauty products; **produit brut** (*bénéfice*) gross profit; (*objet*) unfinished product; **produit chimique** chemical; **produit d'entretien** clean(s)ing product; **produits de grande consommation** consumer goods; **produit de l'impôt** tax yield; **produits industriels** industrial goods *ou* products; **produits manufacturés** manufactured goods; **produit national brut** gross national product; **produit net** net profit; **produit pharmaceutique** pharmaceutical (product); **produit pour la vaisselle** washing-up (*Brit*) *ou* dish-washing (*US*) liquid; **produit des ventes** income *ou* proceeds from sales.

proéminence [pʀɔeminɑ̃s] *nf* prominence, protuberance.

proéminent, e [pʀɔeminɑ̃, ɑ̃t] *adj* prominent, protuberant.

prof* [pʀɔf] *nmf* (*abrév de* **professeur**) (*Scol*) teacher; (*Univ*) ≃ lecturer; (*avec chaire*) prof*.

profanateur, -trice [pʀɔfanatœʀ, tʀis] **1** *adj* profaning (*épith*), profane. **2** *nm,f* profaner.

profanation [pʀɔfanɑsjɔ̃] *nf* (*V* **profaner**) desecration; profanation; violation; defilement; debasement; prostitution.

profane [pʀɔfan] **1** *adj* **(a)** (*non-spécialiste*) **je suis** ~ **en la matière** I'm a layman in the field, I don't know anything about the subject.

(b) *fête* secular; *auteur, littérature, musique* secular, profane (*littér*).

2 *nmf* **(a)** (*gén*) layman, lay person. **aux yeux du** ~ to the layman *ou* the uninitiated; **un** ~ **en art** a person who is uninitiated in the field of art, a person who knows nothing about art.

(b) (*Rel*) non-believer.

3 *nm* (*Rel*) **le** ~ the secular, the profane (*littér*).

profaner [pʀɔfane] (1) *vt église* to desecrate, profane; *tombe* to desecrate, violate, profane; *sentiments, souvenir, nom* to defile, profane (*littér*); *institution* to debase; *talent* to prostitute, debase.

proférer [pʀɔfeʀe] (6) *vt parole* to utter; *injures* to utter, pour out.

professer [pʀɔfese] (1) *vt* **(a)** *opinion* to profess, declare, state; *théorie* to profess; *sentiment* to profess, declare. ~ **que ...** to profess *ou* declare *ou* claim that .... **(b)** (*Scol*) to teach.

professeur [pʀɔfesœʀ] *nm* (*gén*) teacher; (*Scol*) (school)-teacher, schoolmaster (*ou* schoolmistress); (*Univ*) ≃ lecturer; (*avec chaire*) professor. **elle est** ~ she's a (school)teacher *ou* schoolmistress; (*Univ*) **(Monsieur) le** ~ **X** Professor X; ~ **de piano/de chant** piano/singing teacher *ou* master (*ou* mistress); ~ **de droit** lecturer in law; professor of law; (*Can*) ~ **adjoint** assistant professor; (*Can*) ~ **agrégé** associate professor; (*Can*) ~ **titulaire** full professor.

profession [pʀɔfesjɔ̃] **1** *nf* **(a)** (*gén*) occupation; (*manuelle*) trade; (*libérale*) profession. **exercer la** ~ **de médecin** to be a doctor by profession, practise as a doctor; **menuisier de** ~ carpenter by *ou* to trade; (*fig*) **menteur de** ~ professional liar; (*Admin*) **'sans** ~**'** (*gén*) 'unemployed'; (*femme mariée*) 'housewife'.

(b) faire ~ **de non-conformisme** to profess nonconformism; **faire** ~ **d'être non-conformiste** to profess *ou* declare o.s. a nonconformist.

2: (*Rel*) **profession de foi** profession of faith; (*fig*) declaration of principles; **profession libérale** (liberal) profession; **les membres des professions libérales** professional people, the members of the (liberal) professions.

professionnalisme [pʀɔfesjɔnalism(ə)] *nm* professionalism.

professionnel, -elle [pʀɔfesjɔnel] **1** *adj* **(a)** *activité, maladie* occupational (*épith*); *école* vocationally-orientated. **faute** ~**le** (professional) negligence (*U*); (*Méd*) malpractice; **formation/orientation** ~**le** vocational training/guidance; **(être tenu par) le secret** ~ (to be bound by) professional secrecy; *V* **certificat, conscience, déformation.**

(b) *écrivain, sportif,* (*fig*) *menteur* professional.

2 *nm,f* **(a)** (*gén, Sport*) professional. **c'est un travail de** ~ it's a job for a professional; (*bien fait*) it's a professional job; **passer** ~ to turn professional.

(b) (*Ind*) skilled worker.

professionnellement [pʀɔfesjɔnelmɑ̃] *adv* professionally.

professoral, e, *mpl* **-aux** [pʀɔfesɔʀal, o] *adj ton, attitude* professorial. **le corps** ~ (*gén*) (the) teachers (*pl*), the teaching profession; (*d'une école*) the teaching staff.

professorat [pʀɔfesɔʀa] *nm*: **le** ~ the teaching profession; **le** ~ **de français** French teaching, the teaching of French.

profil [pʀɔfil] *nm* **(a)** (*silhouette*) [*personne*] profile; [*édifice*] outline, profile, contour; [*voiture*] line, contour. **de** ~ *dessiner* in profile; *regarder* sideways on, in profile; (*fig*) **un** ~ **de médaille** a finely chiselled profile.

(b) (*coupe*) [*bâtiment, route*] profile; (*Géol*) [*sol*] section.

(c) (*Psych*) profile.

profilé, e [pʀɔfile] (*ptp de* **profiler**) *adj* (*gén*) shaped; (*aérodynamique*) streamlined.

profiler [pʀɔfile] (1) **1** *vt* **(a)** (*Tech*) (*dessiner*) to profile, represent in profile; (*fabriquer*) to shape; (*rendre aérodynamique*) to streamline.

(b) (*faire ressortir*) **la cathédrale profile ses tours contre le ciel** the cathedral towers stand out *ou* stand outlined *ou* are silhouetted against the sky.

2 se profiler *vpr* [*objet*] to stand out (in profile), be outlined (*sur, contre* against); (*fig*) [*ennuis, solution*] to emerge. **les obstacles qui se profilent à l'horizon** the obstacles which are looming *ou* emerging *ou* which stand out on the horizon.

profit [pʀɔfi] *nm* **(a)** (*Comm, Fin: gain*) profit. **c'est une source illimitée de** ~ it's an endless source of profit; **compte de** ~**s et pertes** profit and loss account; (*fig*) **faire passer qch dans les** ~**s et pertes** to write sth off (as a loss).

(b) (*avantage*) benefit, advantage, profit. **être d'un grand** ~ **à qn** to be of great benefit *ou* most useful to sb; **faire du** ~ (*gén*) to be economical, be good value (for money); (*) [*vêtement*] to wear well; [*rôti*] to go a long way; **ce rôti n'a pas fait de** ~ that joint didn't go very far; **ses vacances lui ont fait beaucoup de** ~ *ou* **lui ont été d'un grand** ~ his holiday greatly benefited him *ou* did him a lot of good, he greatly benefited from his holiday; **vous avez** ~ **à faire cela** it's in your interest *ou* to your advantage to do that; **s'il le fait, c'est qu'il y trouve son** ~ if he does it, it's because it's to his advantage *ou* in his interest *ou* because he's getting something out of it; **il a suivi les cours sans (en tirer) aucun** ~**/avec** ~ he attended the classes without deriving any benefit *ou* advantage *ou* profit from them/and got a lot out of them *ou* and gained a lot from them; **tirer** ~ **de** *leçon, affaire* to profit *ou* benefit from; **tirer** ~ **du malheur des autres** to profit from *ou* take advantage of other people's misfortune; **collecte au** ~ **des aveugles** collection in aid of the blind; **il fait (son)** ~ **de tout** he turns everything to (his) advantage; **mettre à** ~ *idée, invention* to turn to (good) account; *jeunesse, temps libre, sa beauté* to make the most of, take advantage of; **tourner qch à** ~ to turn sth to good account; **il a mis à** ~ **le mauvais temps pour ranger le grenier** he made the most of *ou* took advantage of the bad weather to tidy the attic, he turned the bad weather to (good) account by tidying (up) the attic.

profitable [pʀɔfitabl(ə)] *adj* (*utile*) beneficial, of benefit (*attrib*); (*lucratif*) profitable (*à* to).

profitablement [pʀɔfitabləmɑ̃] *adv* profitably.

profiter [pʀɔfite] (1) **1 profiter de** *vt indir* (*tirer avantage*) *situation, privilège, occasion, crédulité* to take advantage of; *jeunesse, vacances* to make the most of, take advantage of. **ils ont profité de ce que le professeur était sorti pour se battre** they took advantage of the teacher's being absent *ou* of the fact that the teacher had gone out to have a fight.

2 profiter à *vt indir* (*rapporter*) ~ **à qn** [*affaire, circonstances*] to be profitable *ou* of benefit to sb, be to sb's advantage; [*repos*] to benefit sb, be beneficial to sb; [*conseil*] to benefit *ou* profit sb, be of benefit to sb; **à qui cela profite-t-il?** who stands to gain by it?, who will that help?; *V* **bien.**

3 *vi* (*) (*se développer*) [*enfant*] to thrive, grow; (*être économique*) [*plat*] to go a long way, be economical; [*vêtement*] to wear well.

profiterole [pʀɔfitʀɔl] *nf* profiterole.

profiteur, -euse [pʀɔfitœʀ, øz] *nm,f* profiteer. ~ **de guerre** war profiteer.

profond, e [pʀɔfɔ̃, ɔ̃d] **1** *adj* **(a)** (*lit*) deep. **peu** ~ shallow; ~ **de 3 mètres** 3 metres deep.

(b) (*grand, extrême*) *soupir* deep, heavy; *sommeil* deep, sound; *silence, mystère* deep, profound; (*littér*) *nuit* deep (*littér*), dark; *joie, foi, différence, influence, erreur* profound; *ignorance* profound, extreme; *intérêt, sentiment* profound, keen; *ennui* profound, acute; *forage* penetrating; *révérence* low, deep.

(c) (*caché, secret*) *cause, signification* underlying, deeper; *tendance* deep-seated, underlying.

(d) (*pénétrant*) *penseur, réflexion* profound, deep; *esprit, remarque* profound.

(e) *voix, couleur, regard* deep.

2 *nm*: **au plus** ~ **de** *forêt, désespoir* in the depths of; **au plus** ~ **de la mer** at the (very) bottom of the sea, in the depths of the sea; **au plus** ~ **de la nuit** at dead of night; **au plus** ~ **de mon être** in the depths of my being, in my deepest being.

3 *adv creuser* deep; *planter* deep (down).

profondément [pʀɔfɔ̃demɑ̃] *adv ému, choqué* deeply, profoundly; *convaincu* deeply, utterly; *différent* profoundly, vastly; *influencer, se tromper* profoundly; *réfléchir* deeply, profoundly; *aimer, ressentir* deeply; *respirer* deep(ly); *creuser, pénétrer* deep; *s'incliner* low. **il dort** ~ (*en général*) he sleeps soundly, he is a sound sleeper; (*en ce moment*) he is sound *ou* fast asleep; **s'ennuyer** ~ to be utterly *ou* acutely *ou* profoundly bored; **idée** ~ **ancrée dans les esprits** idea deeply rooted in people's minds; **ça m'est** ~ **égal** I really couldn't care less.

profondeur [pʀɔfɔ̃dœʀ] *nf* **(a)** (*lit*) [*trou, boîte, mer*] depth; [*plaie*] deepness, depth. **à cause du peu de** ~ because of the shallowness; **cela manque de** ~ it's not deep enough; **creuser en** ~ to dig deep; **creuser jusqu'à 3 mètres de** ~ to dig down to a depth of 3 metres; **avoir 10 mètres de** ~ to be 10 metres deep *ou* in depth; **à 10 mètres de** ~ 10 metres down, at a depth of 10 metres; **cette pommade agit en** ~ this cream works deep into the skin; (*Phot*) ~ **de champ** depth of field.

(b) (*fond*) [*mine, métro, poche*] ~**s** depths; (*fig*) **les** ~**s de l'être** the depths of the human psyche.

(c) (*fig*) [*personne*] profoundness, profundity, depth; [*esprit, remarque*] profoundness, profundity; [*sentiment*] depth, keenness; [*sommeil*] soundness, depth; [*regard*] depth. **en** ~ *agir, exprimer* in depth; **c'est une réforme en** ~ **qu'il faut** what is needed is a radical *ou* thorough(going) reform.

profus, e [pʀɔfy, yz] *adj* (*littér*) profuse.

profusément [pʀɔfyzemɑ̃] *adv* (*littér*) profusely, abundantly.

profusion [pʀɔfyzjɔ̃] *nf* [*fleurs, lumière*] profusion; [*idées, conseils*] wealth, abundance, profusion. **à** ~**: il y a des fruits à** ~ **sur le marché** there is fruit galore* *ou* in plenty *ou* there is plenty of fruit on the market; **nous en avons à** ~ we've got plenty *ou* masses*.

progéniture [pʀɔʒenityʀ] *nf* [*homme, animal*] offspring, progeny (*littér*); (*hum: famille*) offspring (*hum*).

programmateur, -trice [pʀɔgʀamatœʀ, tʀis] *nm,f* (*Rad, TV*) programme planner.

programmation [pʀɔgʀamɑsjɔ̃] *nf* (*Rad, TV*) programming, programme planning; [*ordinateur*] programming.

programme [pʀɔgʀam] *nm* **(a)** [*concert, spectacle, télévision, radio*] programme (*Brit*), program (*US*). **au** ~ in the programme; **numéro hors** ~ item not (billed *ou* announced) in the programme; **cette excursion n'est pas prévue au** ~ this trip is not on the programme; **changement de** ~ change in (the) *ou* of programme.

(b) (*calendrier*) programme (*Brit*), program (*US*). **quel est le** ~ **de la journée?** *ou* **des réjouissances?*** what's the programme for the day?, what's on the agenda?*; **j'ai un** ~ **très chargé** I have a very busy timetable.

(c) (*Scol*) (*d'une matière*) syllabus; (*d'une classe, d'une école*) curriculum. **le** ~ **de maths** the maths syllabus; **quel est le** ~ **en sixième?** what's (on) the curriculum in the first year?; **les œuvres du** ~ the set books *ou* works, the books on the syllabus.

(d) (*projet*) programme. ~ **d'action/de travail** programme of action/work; **il y a un changement de** ~ there's a change of plan *ou* programme; **c'est tout un** ~**!** that'll take some doing!

(e) [*ordinateur*] (computer) program; [*machine à laver*] programme.

programmé, e [pʀɔgʀame] (*ptp de* **programmer**) *adj opération, (Typ) composition* computerized; *V* **enseignement.**

programmer [pʀɔgʀame] (1) *vt émission* to bill; *ordinateur* to program; (*: *prévoir*) *vacances* to plan.

programmeur, -euse [pʀɔgʀamœʀ, øz] *nm,f* (computer) programmer.

progrès [pʀɔgʀe] *nm* **(a)** (*amélioration*) progress (*U*). **faire des** ~**/de petits** ~ to make progress/some little progress; **élève en** ~ pupil who is making progress *ou* who is progressing *ou* getting on (well); **il y a du** ~ there is some progress *ou* improvement; **c'est un grand** ~ it's a great advance, much progress has been made; **il a fait de grands** ~ he has made great progress *ou* shown (a) great improvement.

(b) (*évolution*) progress (*U*). **croire au** ~ to believe in progress; **suivre les** ~ **de** to follow the progress of.

(c) (*progression*) [*incendie, inondation*] spread, progress;

[maladie] progression, progress; *[armée]* progress, advance.
progresser [pʀɔgʀese] (1) *vi* **(a)** (*s'améliorer*) *[malade, élève]* to progress, make progress, get *ou* come on (well).
(b) (*avancer*) *[explorateurs, sauveteurs, ennemi]* to advance, make headway *ou* progress; *[maladie]* to progress; *[science, recherches]* to advance, progress; *[idée, théorie]* to gain ground, make headway. **afin que notre monde/la science progresse** so that our world/science goes forward *ou* progresses *ou* makes progress.
progressif, -ive [pʀɔgʀesif, iv] *adj* (*gén, Ling*) progressive.
progression [pʀɔgʀesjɔ̃] *nf* **(a)** *[élève, explorateurs]* progress; *[ennemi]* advance; *[maladie]* progression; *[science]* progress, advance. **la ~ très rapide de ces idées** the fact that these ideas have gained ground so rapidly.
(b) (*Math, Mus*) progression. **~ arithmétique/géométrique** arithmetic/geometric progression; **~ économique** economic advance.
progressiste [pʀɔgʀesist(ə)] *adj, nmf* progressive.
progressivement [pʀɔgʀesivmɑ̃] *adv* progressively.
progressivité [pʀɔgʀesivite] *nf* progressiveness.
prohibé, e [pʀɔibe] (*ptp de* **prohiber**) *adj marchandise, action* prohibited, forbidden; *arme* illegal.
prohiber [pʀɔibe] (1) *vt* to prohibit, ban, forbid.
prohibitif, -ive [pʀɔibitif, iv] *adj prix* prohibitive; *mesure* prohibitory, prohibitive.
prohibition [pʀɔibisjɔ̃] *nf* prohibition.
prohibitionniste [pʀɔibisjɔnist(ə)] *adj, nmf* prohibitionist.
proie [pʀwa] *nf* **(a)** (*lit*) prey (*U*); *V* **oiseau**.
(b) (*fig*) prey. *[personne]* **être la ~ de** to fall (a) prey to, be the prey of; **le pays fut la ~ des envahisseurs** the country fell (a) prey to invaders; **la maison était la ~ des flammes** the house fell (a) prey to *ou* was claimed by the flames; **c'est une ~ facile pour des escrocs** he's (*ou* she's) easy prey *ou* game* *ou* meat* for swindlers.
(c) (*loc*) **être en ~ à** *maladie* to be a victim of; *douleur* to be racked *ou* tortured by; *doute, émotion* to be (a) prey to; **il était en ~ au remords** he was (a) prey to remorse, remorse preyed on him; **en ~ au désespoir** racked by despair, a prey to despair; **lâcher** *ou* **laisser la ~ pour l'ombre** to give up what one has (already) for some uncertain *ou* fanciful alternative.
projecteur [pʀɔʒɛktœʀ] *nm* **(a)** *[diapositive, film]* projector. **~ sonore** sound projector. **(b)** (*lumière*) *[théâtre]* spotlight; *[prison, bateau]* searchlight; *[monument public, stade]* floodlight.
projectif, -ive [pʀɔʒɛktif, iv] *adj* projective.
projectile [pʀɔʒɛktil] *nm* (*gén*) missile; (*Mil, Tech*) projectile.
projection [pʀɔʒɛksjɔ̃] *nf* **(a)** *[ombre]* casting, projection, throwing; *[film]* (*action*) projection; (*séance*) showing. **appareil de ~** projector, projection equipment (*U*); **salle de ~** film theatre; **cabine de ~** projection room.
(b) (*lancement*) *[liquide, vapeur]* discharge, ejection; *[pierre]* throwing (*U*). (*Géol*) **~s volcaniques** volcanic ejections *ou* ejecta.
(c) (*Math, Psych*) projection (*sur* onto).
projet [pʀɔʒɛ] *nm* **(a)** (*dessein*) plan. **~s criminels/de vacances** criminal/holiday plans; **faire des ~s d'avenir** to make plans for the future, make future plans; **faire** *ou* **former le ~ de faire** to make plans to do; **ce ~ de livre/d'agrandissement** this plan for a book/for an extension; **quels sont vos ~s pour le mois prochain?** what are your plans *ou* what plans have you for next month?; **ce n'est encore qu'un ~, c'est encore à l'état de ~** *ou* **encore en ~** it's still only at the planning stage.
(b) (*ébauche*) *[roman]* (preliminary) draft; *[maison, ville]* plan. **~ de loi** bill; **établir un ~ d'accord/de contrat** to draft an agreement/a contract, produce a draft agreement/contract.
projeter [pʀɔʒte] (4) **1** *vt* **(a)** (*envisager*) to plan (*de faire* to do). **as-tu projeté quelque chose pour les vacances?** have you made any plans *ou* have you planned anything for your holidays?
(b) (*jeter*) *gravillons* to throw up; *étincelles* to throw off; *fumée* to send out, discharge; *lave* to eject, throw out. **attention! la poêle projette de la graisse** careful! the frying pan is spitting (out) fat; **être projeté hors de** to be thrown *ou* hurled *ou* flung out of; **on lui a projeté de l'eau dans les yeux** water was thrown *ou* flung into his eyes.
(c) (*envoyer*) *ombre, reflet* to cast, project, throw; *film, diapositive* to project; (*montrer*) to show. **on peut ~ ce film sur un petit écran** this film may be projected onto a small screen; **on nous a projeté des diapositives** we were shown some slides.
(d) (*Math, Psych*) to project (*sur* onto).
2 se projeter *vpr [ombre]* to be cast, fall (*sur* on).
prolégomènes [pʀɔlegɔmɛn] *nmpl* prolegomena.
prolepse [pʀɔlɛps(ə)] *nf* (*Littérat*) prolepsis.
prolétaire [pʀɔletɛʀ] *nm* proletarian.
prolétariat [pʀɔletaʀja] *nm* proletariat.
prolétarien, -ienne [pʀɔletaʀjɛ̃, jɛn] *adj* proletarian.
prolétarisation [pʀɔletaʀizɑsjɔ̃] *nf* proletarianization.
prolétariser [pʀɔletaʀize] (1) *vt* to proletarianize.
prolifération [pʀɔlifeʀɑsjɔ̃] *nf* proliferation.
proliférer [pʀɔlifeʀe] (6) *vi* to proliferate.
prolifique [pʀɔlifik] *adj* prolific.
prolixe [pʀɔliks(ə)] *adj orateur* verbose, prolix (*frm*); *discours* wordy, verbose, prolix (*frm*).
prolixement [pʀɔliksəmɑ̃] *adv* (*V* **prolixe**) verbosely, prolixly (*frm*); wordily.
prolixité [pʀɔliksite] *nf* (*V* **prolixe**) verbosity, prolixity (*frm*); wordiness.
prolo* [pʀɔlo] *nm* (*abrév de* **prolétaire**) pleb* (*péj*), prole* (*péj*).
prologue [pʀɔlɔg] *nm* prologue (*à* to).
prolongation [pʀɔlɔ̃gɑsjɔ̃] *nf* (*V* **prolonger**) prolongation; extension. (*Ftbl*) **~s** extra time (*U*); (*Ftbl*) **ils ont joué les ~s** they played extra time, the game *ou* they went into extra time.
prolonge [pʀɔlɔ̃ʒ] *nf*: **~ d'artillerie** gun carriage.
prolongé, e [pʀɔlɔ̃ʒe] (*ptp de* **prolonger**) *adj débat, séjour* prolonged, lengthy; *rire, cri* prolonged; *effort* prolonged, sustained. **exposition ~e au soleil** prolonged exposure to the sun; (*hum*) **jeune fille ~e** old maid, girl left on the shelf; **rue de la Paix ~e** continuation of Rue de la Paix; **en cas d'arrêt ~** in case of prolonged stoppage.
prolongement [pʀɔlɔ̃ʒmɑ̃] *nm* **(a)** *[route]* continuation; *[bâtiment]* extension; (*fig*) *[affaire, politique]* extension. **décider le ~ d'une route** to decide to extend *ou* continue a road; **cette rue se trouve dans le ~ de l'autre** this street runs on from the other *ou* is the continuation of the other.
(b) (*suites*) **~s** repercussions, effects.
prolonger [pʀɔlɔ̃ʒe] (3) **1** *vt* **(a)** (*dans le temps*) *séjour, trêve, séance* to prolong, extend; *billet* to extend; *vie, maladie* to prolong; (*Mus*) *note* to prolong. **nous ne pouvons ~ notre séjour** we cannot stay any longer, we cannot prolong our stay any longer (*frm*).
(b) (*dans l'espace*) *rue* to extend, continue; (*Math*) *ligne* to prolong, produce. **on a prolongé le mur jusqu'au garage** we extended *ou* continued the wall as far as *ou* up to the garage; **ce bâtiment prolonge l'aile principale** this building is the *ou* an extension *ou* a continuation of the main wing.
2 se prolonger *vpr* **(a)** (*persister*) *[attente]* to go on; *[situation]* to go on, last, persist; *[effet]* to last, persist; *[débat]* to last, go on, carry on; *[maladie]* to continue, persist. **il voudrait se ~ dans ses enfants** he would like to live on in his children.
(b) (*s'étendre*) *[rue, chemin]* to go on, carry on, continue.
promenade [pʀɔmnad] *nf* **(a)** (*à pied*) walk, stroll; (*en voiture*) drive, ride; (*en bateau*) sail; (*en vélo, à cheval*) ride. **partir en ~, faire une ~** to go for a walk *ou* stroll (*ou* drive *etc*); **être en ~** to be out walking *ou* out for a walk; **faire faire une ~ à qn** to take sb (out) for a walk; (*Sport*) **cette course a été une vraie ~ pour lui** this race was a real walkover for him.
(b) (*avenue*) walk, esplanade.
promener [pʀɔmne] (5) **1** *vt* **(a)** (**emmener**) **~ qn** to take sb (out) for a walk *ou* stroll; **~ le chien** to take the dog out (walking *ou* for a walk); **~ des amis à travers une ville** to show *ou* take friends round a town; **cela te promènera** that will get you out for a while; **il promène son nounours partout*** he trails his teddy bear (around) everywhere with him; **est-ce qu'il va nous ~ encore longtemps à travers ces bureaux?*** is he going to trail us round these offices much longer?; *V* **envoyer**.
(b) (*fig*) **~ ses regards sur qch** to run *ou* cast one's eyes over sth; **~ ses doigts sur qch** to run *ou* pass one's fingers over sth; **~ sa tristesse** to carry one's sadness around with one.
2 se promener *vpr* **(a)** (*V* **promenade**) to go for a walk *ou* stroll (*ou* drive *etc*). **aller se ~** to go (out) for a walk *ou* stroll (*ou* drive *etc*); **viens te ~ avec maman** come (out) (for a walk *ou* stroll *ou* drive *etc*) with mummy; **se ~ dans sa chambre** to walk *ou* pace up and down in one's room; **allez vous ~!*** go and take a running jump!*, (go and) get lost!*; **je ne vais pas laisser tes chiens se ~ dans mon jardin** I'm not going to let your dogs wander round my garden; (*Sport*) **il s'est vraiment promené dans cette course** this race was a real walkover for him.
(b) (*fig*) *[pensées, regards, doigts]* to wander. **son crayon se promenait sur le papier** he let his pencil wander over the paper, his pencil wandered over the paper; **ses affaires se promènent toujours partout*** his things are always lying around all over the place *ou* are always scattered about the place.
promeneur, -euse [pʀɔmnœʀ, øz] *nm,f* walker, stroller. **les ~s du dimanche** Sunday strollers, people out for a Sunday walk *ou* stroll.
promenoir [pʀɔm(ə)nwaʀ] *nm* (*Théât*) promenade gallery, standing gallery; *[école, prison]* (covered) walk.
promesse [pʀɔmɛs] *nf* (*assurance*) promise; (*parole*) promise, word; (*Comm*) commitment, undertaking. **~ de mariage** promise of marriage; **~ en l'air** *ou* **d'ivrogne** *ou* **de Gascon** empty *ou* vain promise; **~ d'achat/de vente** commitment to buy/to sell; **faire une ~** to make a promise, give one's word; **il m'en a fait la ~** he gave me his word for it; **tenir/manquer à sa ~** to keep/break one's promise *ou* word; **j'ai sa ~** I have his word for it, he has promised me; (*fig*) **auteur plein de ~s** writer showing much promise *ou* full of promise, very promising writer; **sourire plein de ~s** smile that promised (*ou* promises) much.
Prométhée [pʀɔmete] *nm* Prometheus.
prometteur, -euse [pʀɔmɛtœʀ, øz] *adj début, signe* promising.
promettre [pʀɔmɛtʀ(ə)] (56) **1** *vt* **(a)** *chose, aide* to promise. **je lui ai promis un cadeau** I promised him a present; **je te le promets** I promise (you); **il n'a rien osé ~** he couldn't promise anything, he didn't dare commit himself; **il a promis de venir** he promised to come; **il m'a promis de venir** *ou* **qu'il viendrait** he promised me that he would come; **~ la lune, ~ monts et merveilles** to promise the moon *ou* the earth; **tu as promis, il faut y aller** you've promised *ou* you've given your word so you have to go; **il ne faut pas ~ quand on ne peut pas tenir** one mustn't make promises that one cannot keep; **~ le secret** to promise to keep a secret; **~ son cœur/sa main/son amour** to pledge one's heart/hand/love.
(b) (*prédire*) to promise. **je vous promets qu'il ne recommencera pas** I (can) promise you he won't do that again; **il sera furieux, je te le promets** he will be furious, I (can) promise you *ou* I can tell you; **on nous promet du beau temps/un été pluvieux** we are promised *ou* we are in for* some fine weather/a rainy summer; **ces nuages nous promettent de la pluie** these clouds promise rain; **cela ne nous promet rien de bon** this promises to be pretty bad for us, this doesn't look at all hopeful for us.

(c) (*faire espérer*) to promise. **le spectacle/dîner promet d'être réussi** the show/dinner promises to be a success; **cet enfant promet** this child shows promise *ou* is promising, he's (*ou* she's) a promising child; (*iro*) **ça promet!** that's a good start! (*iro*), that's promising! (*iro*); (*iro*) **ça promet pour l'avenir/pour l'hiver!** that bodes well for the future/(the) winter! (*iro*).

2 se promettre *vpr*: **se ~ de faire** to mean *ou* resolve to do sth; **se ~ du bon temps** *ou* **du plaisir** to promise o.s. a good time; **je me suis promis un petit voyage** I've promised myself a little trip.

promis, e [pRɔmi, iz] (*ptp de* **promettre**) **1** *adj*: **être ~ à qch** to be destined *ou* set for sth; *V* **chose, terre. 2** *nm,f* (††, *dial*) betrothed††.

promiscuité [pRɔmiskɥite] *nf [lieu public]* crowding (*U*) (*de* in); *[chambre]* (degrading) lack of privacy (*U*) (*de* in).

promontoire [pRɔmɔ̃twaR] *nm* (*Géog*) headland, promontory.

promoteur, -trice [pRɔmɔtœR, tRis] *nm,f* (*Constr*) property developer; (*instigateur*) instigator, promoter; (*Chim*) promoter.

promotion [pRɔmosjɔ̃] *nf* **(a)** (*avancement*) promotion (*à un poste* to a job). **~ sociale** social advancement.

(b) (*Scol*) year. **être le premier de sa ~** to be first in one's year.

(c) (*Comm: réclame*) **notre ~ de la semaine** this week's special offer; **article en ~** item on special offer; (*Comm*) **~ des ventes** sales promotion.

promotionnel, -elle [pRɔmosjɔnɛl] *adj article* on (special) offer; *vente* promotional.

promouvoir [pRɔmuvwaR] (27) *vt personne* to promote (*à* to); *politique, recherche* to promote, further; (*Comm*) *produit* to promote. **il a été promu directeur** he was promoted to (the rank of) manager.

prompt, prompte [pRɔ̃, pRɔ̃t] *adj* (*gén*) swift, rapid, speedy, quick; *repartie* ready (*épith*), quick; *esprit* ready (*épith*), quick, sharp; *réaction* prompt, swift; *départ, changement* sudden. **~ rétablissement!** get well soon!, I (*ou* we) wish you a speedy recovery; **~ à l'injure/aux excuses/à se décider** quick to insult/to apologize/to make up one's mind; **avoir le geste ~** to be quick to act; **~ comme l'éclair** *ou* **la foudre** as quick as lightning.

promptement [pRɔ̃tmɑ̃] *adv* (*V* **prompt**) swiftly; rapidly; speedily; quickly; promptly; suddenly.

promptitude [pRɔ̃tityd] *nf* (*V* **prompt**) swiftness; rapidity; speed; quickness; promptness, promptitude (*frm*); suddenness.

promulgation [pRɔmylgɑsjɔ̃] *nf* promulgation.

promulguer [pRɔmylge] (1) *vt* to promulgate.

prône [pRon] *nm* sermon.

prôner [pRone] (1) *vt* (*vanter*) to laud, extol; (*préconiser*) to advocate, commend.

pronom [pRɔnɔ̃] *nm* pronoun.

pronominal, e, *mpl* **-aux** [pRɔnɔminal, o] *adj* pronominal. **(verbe) ~** reflexive (verb).

pronominalement [pRɔnɔminalmɑ̃] *adv* (*V* **pronominal**) pronominally; reflexively.

prononçable [pRɔnɔ̃sabl(ə)] *adj* pronounceable.

prononcé, e [pRɔnɔ̃se] (*ptp de* **prononcer**) **1** *adj accent, goût, trait* marked, pronounced. **2** *nm* (*Jur*) pronouncement.

prononcer [pRɔnɔ̃se] (3) **1** *vt* **(a)** (*articuler*) *mot, son* to pronounce. **son nom est impossible à ~** his name is impossible to pronounce *ou* is unpronounceable; **comment est-ce que ça se prononce?** how is it pronounced?, how do you pronounce it?; **cette lettre ne se prononce pas** that letter is silent *ou* is not pronounced; **tu prononces mal** your pronunciation is bad; **mal ~ un mot** to mispronounce a word, pronounce a word badly; **~ distinctement** to speak clearly, pronounce one's words clearly.

(b) (*dire*) *parole, nom* to utter; *souhait* to utter, make; *discours* to make, deliver. **~ qch entre ses dents** to mutter *ou* mumble sth; **sortir sans ~ un mot** to go out without uttering a word; **ne prononcez plus jamais ce nom!** don't you ever mention *ou* utter that name again!; (*Rel*) **~ ses vœux** to take one's vows.

(c) *sentence* to pronounce, pass; *dissolution, excommunication* to pronounce. **~ le huis clos** to order that a case (should) be heard in camera.

2 *vi* (*Jur*) to deliver *ou* give a verdict. (*littér*) **~ en faveur de/contre** to come down *ou* pronounce in favour of/against.

3 se prononcer *vpr* to reach *ou* come to a decision (*sur* on, about), reach *ou* give a verdict (*sur* on). **le médecin ne s'est toujours pas prononcé** the doctor still hasn't given a verdict *ou* a firm opinion *ou* still hasn't come to a decision; **se ~ en faveur de qn/pour qch** to come down in favour of sb/in favour of sth.

prononciation [pRɔnɔ̃sjɑsjɔ̃] *nf* **(a)** (*Ling*) pronunciation. **il a une bonne/mauvaise ~** he speaks/doesn't speak clearly, he pronounces/does not pronounce his words clearly; (*dans une langue étrangère*) he has a good/bad pronunciation; **faute** *ou* **erreur de ~** error of pronunciation; **faire une faute de ~** to mispronounce a word (*ou* a sound *etc*); **défaut** *ou* **vice de ~** speech impediment *ou* defect.

(b) (*Jur*) pronouncement.

pronostic [pRɔnɔstik] *nm* forecast, prognostication (*frm*); (*Méd*) prognosis; (*Sport*) forecast. **quels sont vos ~s?** what is your forecast?; **au ~ infaillible** unerring in his (*ou* her *etc*) forecasts.

pronostiquer [pRɔnɔstike] (1) *vt* (*prédire*) to forecast, prognosticate (*frm*); (*être le signe de*) to foretell, be a sign of.

pronostiqueur, -euse [pRɔnɔstikœR, øz] *nm,f* (*gén*) forecaster, prognosticator (*frm*); (*Courses*) tipster.

pronunciamiento [pRɔnunsjamjɛnto] *nm* pronunciamento.

propagande [pRɔpagɑ̃d] *nf* propaganda. **film/discours de ~** propaganda film/speech; **faire de la ~ pour qch/qn** to push *ou* plug* sth/sb; **je ne ferai pas de ~ pour ce commerçant/ce produit** I certainly shan't be doing any advertising for this trader/product.

propagandiste [pRɔpagɑ̃dist(ə)] *nmf* propagandist.

propagateur, -trice [pRɔpagatœR, tRis] *nm,f [méthode, religion, théorie]* propagator, disseminator; *[nouvelle]* spreader, disseminator.

propagation [pRɔpagɑsjɔ̃] *nf* **(a)** (*V* **propager**) propagation; dissemination; diffusion; spreading (abroad); putting about. **la ~ de l'espèce** the propagation of the species. **(b)** (*V* **se propager**) spread, spreading; propagation.

propager [pRɔpaʒe] (3) **1** *vt* **(a)** *foi, idée* to propagate, disseminate, diffuse; *nouvelle* to spread (abroad), disseminate; *maladie* to spread; *fausse nouvelle* to spread (abroad), put about; (*Phys*) *son* to propagate.

(b) (*Bio*) *espèce* to propagate.

2 se propager *vpr [incendie, idée, nouvelle, maladie]* to spread; (*Phys*) *[onde]* to be propagated; (*Bio*) *[espèce]* to propagate.

propane [pRɔpan] *nm* propane.

propédeutique† [pRɔpedøtik] *nf* (*Univ*) *foundation course for first-year university students.*

propension [pRɔpɑ̃sjɔ̃] *nf* proclivity (*à qch* to *ou* towards sth, *à faire* to do), propensity (*à qch* for sth, *à faire* to do). (*Écon*) **~ à consommer/économiser** propensity to spend/save.

prophète [pRɔfɛt] *nm* (*gén*) prophet, seer; (*Rel*) prophet. **~ de malheur** prophet of doom, Jeremiah; *V* **nul.**

prophétesse [pRɔfetɛs] *nf* (*gén*) prophetess, seer; (*Rel*) prophetess.

prophétie [pRɔfesi] *nf* (*Rel, gén*) prophecy.

prophétique [pRɔfetik] *adj* prophetic.

prophétiquement [pRɔfetikmɑ̃] *adv* prophetically.

prophétiser [pRɔfetize] (1) *vt* to prophesy.

prophylactique [pRɔfilaktik] *adj* prophylactic.

prophylaxie [pRɔfilaksi] *nf* disease prevention, prophylaxis (*T*).

propice [pRɔpis] *adj circonstance* favourable, auspicious, propitious (*frm*); *milieu, terrain* favourable; *occasion* good (*épith*), favourable. **attendre le moment ~** to wait for the right *ou* an opportune moment; **attendre un moment ~** to wait for a suitable *ou* an opportune moment; **être ~ à qch** to favour sth, be favourable to sth; (*littér, hum*) **que les dieux vous soient ~s!** may the gods look kindly *ou* smile upon you! (*littér, hum*).

propitiation [pRɔpisjɑsjɔ̃] *nf* propitiation. **victime de ~** propitiatory victim.

propitiatoire [pRɔpisjatwaR] *adj* propitiatory.

proportion [pRɔpɔRsjɔ̃] *nf* **(a)** (*gén, Art, Math*) proportion. **selon** *ou* **dans une ~ de 100 contre** *ou* **pour 1** in a proportion of 100 to 1; **quelle est la ~ entre la hauteur et la largeur?** *ou* **de la hauteur et de la largeur?** what is the proportion *ou* relation of height to width?, what's the ratio between height and width?; **~ égale de réussites et d'échecs** equal proportion of successes and failures, equal ratio of successes to failures; **il n'y a aucune ~ entre la faute et la peine** the punishment is out of all proportion to the offence *ou* bears no relation to the offence.

(b) **~s** (*taille, importance*) proportions; **de vastes ~s** of vast proportions *ou* dimensions; **édifice de belles ~s** well-proportioned building; **cela a pris des ~s considérables** it took on considerable proportions.

(c) (*loc*) **à ~ de** in proportion to, proportionally to; **en ~ de** (*adj*) in proportion *ou* relation to, proportional to; (*adv*) in proportion *ou* relation to, proportionally to; **en ~** in proportion; **on lui a donné un poste élevé et un salaire en ~** he was given a high position and a salary in proportion; **quand on veut avoir des domestiques, il faut avoir des revenus en ~** when you want to have servants, you must have a commensurate income *ou* an income to match; **hors de (toute) ~** out of (all) proportion (*avec* to); **toute(s) ~(s) gardée(s)** relatively speaking, making due allowance(s).

proportionnalité [pRɔpɔRsjɔnalite] *nf* proportionality; (*Pol*) proportional representation. **~ de l'impôt** proportional taxation (system).

proportionné, e [pRɔpɔRsjɔne] (*ptp de* **proportionner**) *adj*: **~ à** proportional *ou* proportionate to; **bien ~** well-proportioned; **admirablement ~** admirably well-proportioned.

proportionnel, -elle [pRɔpɔRsjɔnɛl] **1** *adj* (*gén, Math, Pol*) proportional; *impôt, retraite* proportional. **~ à** proportional *ou* proportionate to, in proportion to *ou* with; **directement/inversement ~ à** directly/inversely proportional to, in direct/inverse proportion to.

2 proportionnelle *nf* (*Math*) proportional. (*Pol*) **la ~le** proportional representation.

proportionnellement [pRɔpɔRsjɔnɛlmɑ̃] *adv* proportionally *ou* proportionately. **~ plus grand** proportionally *ou* proportionately bigger; **~ à** in proportion to, proportionally to.

proportionner [pRɔpɔRsjɔne] (1) *vt* to proportion, make proportional, adjust (*à* to).

propos [pRɔpo] *nm* **(a)** (*gén pl*) talk (*U*), remarks (*pl*), words (*pl*). **ce sont des ~ en l'air** it's just empty *ou* idle talk *ou* hot air*; **tenir des ~ blessants** to say hurtful things, make hurtful remarks; (*péj*) **des ~ de femme soûle** drunken ramblings; *V* **avant.**

(b) (*littér: intention*) intention, aim. **mon ~ est de vous expliquer ...** my intention *ou* aim is to explain to you ...; **avoir le ferme ~ de faire** to have the firm intention of doing; **faire qch de ~ délibéré** to do sth deliberately *ou* on purpose.

(c) (*sujet*) **à quel ~ voulait-il me voir?** what did he want to see me about?; **à quel ~ est-il venu?** what was his reason for coming?, what brought him?*; **c'est à quel ~?** what is it about?, what is it in connection with?; **à ~ de ta voiture** about your car, on the subject of your car; **je vous écris à ~ de l'annonce** I am writing regarding *ou* concerning the advertisement *ou* in connection with the advertisement; **il se met en colère à ~ de tout et de rien** *ou* **à tout ~** he loses his temper at the drop of a hat* *ou* at the slightest (little) thing *ou* for no reason at all; **à ce ~** in this connection, (while) on this subject; *V* **hors.**

(d) à ~ *décision* well-timed, opportune, timely; *remarque* apt, pertinent, apposite; *arriver* at the right moment *ou* time; **tomber** *ou* **arriver mal à ~** to happen (just) at the wrong moment *ou* time; **voilà qui tombe à ~/mal à ~!** it couldn't have come at a better/worse time! *ou* moment!; **il a jugé à ~ de nous prévenir** he thought it right to let us know, he thought *ou* saw fit to let us know; **à ~, dis-moi ...** incidentally *ou* by the way, tell me ... .

proposable [pʀɔpozabl(ə)] *adj* which may be proposed.

proposer [pʀɔpoze] (1) **1** *vt* **(a)** (*suggérer*) *arrangement, interprétation, projet, appellation* to suggest, propose; *solution, interprétation* to suggest, put forward, propose; *candidat* to nominate, put forward; (*Scol, Univ*) *sujet, texte* to set. **on a proposé mon nom pour ce poste** my name has been put forward for this post; **~ qch à qn** to suggest sth to sb; **~ de faire qch** to suggest *ou* propose doing sth; (*TV*) **le film que nous vous proposons (de voir) ce soir** the film which you will be able to watch this evening; **l'homme propose et Dieu dispose** man proposes, God disposes (*Prov*); **je vous propose de passer me voir** I would suggest that you come round and see me; **~ qu'une motion soit mise aux voix** to move that a motion be put to the vote; **~ qu'un comité soit établi** to propose the setting-up of a committee, move *ou* propose that a committee be set up.

(b) (*offrir*) *aide, prix, situation* to offer. **~ qch à qn** to offer sth to sb, offer sb sth; **~ de faire qch** to offer to do sth; **on me propose une nouvelle voiture** I have been offered *ou* I have had the offer of a new car; **je lui ai proposé de la raccompagner** I offered to see her home.

2 se proposer *vpr* **(a)** (*offrir ses services*) to offer one's services. **elle s'est proposée pour garder les enfants** she offered to look after the children.

(b) (*envisager*) *but, tâche* to set o.s. **se ~ de faire qch** to intend *ou* mean *ou* propose to do sth; **il se proposait de prouver que ...** he set out to prove that ... .

proposition [pʀɔpozisjɔ̃] *nf* **(a)** (*suggestion*) suggestion, proposal, proposition; (*Pol: recommandation*) proposal; (*offre*) offer, proposal. **~s de paix** peace proposals; (*Pol*) **~ de loi** private bill; **sur (la) ~ de** at the suggestion of; **sur sa ~, il a été décidé d'attendre** at his suggestion, it was decided to wait; **la ~ de qn à un grade supérieur** putting forward sb for *ou* the nomination of sb to a higher grade; **faire des ~s à une femme** to proposition a woman; *V* **contre.**

(b) (*Math, Philos: postulat*) proposition; (*déclaration*) statement, assertion.

(c) (*Gram*) clause. **~ principale/subordonnée/ indépendante** main/subordinate/independent clause; **~ consécutive** *ou* **de conséquence** consecutive *ou* result clause.

propre[1] [pʀɔpʀ(ə)] **1** *adj* **(a)** (*pas sali*) *linge, mains, maison* clean; (*net*) *personne, vêtement* neat, tidy; *travail, exécution d'un morceau de musique* neat, neatly done; (*Scol*) *cahier, copie* neat. **~ comme un sou neuf** as neat *ou* clean as a new pin; **leurs enfants sont toujours (tenus) très ~s** their children are always very neat and tidy *ou* very neatly turned out; **a-t-il les mains ~s?** are his hands clean?; **ce n'est pas ~ de manger avec les doigts** it's dirty to eat with your fingers; **nous voilà ~s!*** now we're in a fine *ou* proper mess!*

(b) (*qui ne salit pas*) *chien, chat* house-trained; *enfant* toilet-trained, potty-trained*, clean. **il n'est pas encore ~** he still isn't clean *ou* toilet-trained *ou* potty-trained*.

(c) (*honnête*) *personne* honest, decent; *affaire, argent* honest; *mœurs* decent. **il n'a jamais rien fait de ~** he's never done a decent *ou* an honest thing in his life; **une affaire pas très ~** a shady piece of business; **ce garçon-là, ce n'est pas grand-chose de ~** that lad hasn't got much to recommend him *ou* isn't up to much*.

2 *nm*: **sentir le ~** to smell clean; **avoir une apparence de ~** to have a neat *ou* tidy appearance; (*Scol*) **mettre** *ou* **recopier qch au ~** to make a fair copy of sth, copy sth out neatly; **c'est du ~!*** (*gâchis*) what a mess!, what a shambles!*; (*comportement*) it's an absolute disgrace!

propre[2] [pʀɔpʀ(ə)] **1** *adj* **(a)** (*intensif possessif*) own. **il a sa ~ voiture** he's got *ou* he has his own car *ou* a car of his own; **par ses ~s moyens** *réussir* on one's own, by oneself; *rentrer* under one's own steam; **ce sont ses ~s mots** those are his own *ou* his very *ou* his actual words; **de mes ~s yeux** with my own (two) eyes; **de sa ~ initiative** on his own initiative; (*frm*) **de son ~ chef** on his own initiative, on his own authority; **ils ont leurs caractères/qualités ~s** they have their own (specific) characters/qualities; **au lieu de critiquer nos enfants, il devrait surveiller les siens ~s** instead of criticizing our children, he ought to keep his own in order; *V* **amour, main.**

(b) (*particulier, spécifique*) **~ à: c'est un trait qui lui est ~** it's a distinctive *ou* specific characteristic of his; **les coutumes ~s à certaines régions** the customs peculiar to *ou* characteristic of *ou* proper to (*frm*) certain regions; *V* **nom, sens.**

(c) (*qui convient*) suitable, appropriate (*à* for). **le mot ~** the right *ou* proper word; **ce n'est pas un lieu ~ à la conversation** it isn't a suitable *ou* an appropriate place for talking; **sol ~ à la culture du blé** soil suitable for *ou* suited to wheat-growing; **on l'a jugé ~ à s'occuper de l'affaire** he was considered the right man for *ou* suitable for the job.

(d) (*de nature à*) **~ à: un poste ~ à lui apporter des satisfactions** a job likely to bring him satisfaction; **exercice ~ à développer les muscles des épaules** exercise that will develop the shoulder muscles; **c'est bien ~ à vous dégoûter de la politique** it's (exactly) the sort of thing that turns you *ou* to turn you right off politics.

2 *nm* **(a)** (*qualité distinctive*) peculiarity, (exclusive *ou* distinctive) feature. **la raison est le ~ de l'homme** reason is a peculiarity *ou* (distinctive) feature of man, reason is peculiar to man; **le rire/la parole est le ~ de l'homme** laughter/speech is man's special gift *ou* attribute; **c'est le ~ de ce système d'éducation de fabriquer des paresseux** it's a peculiarity *ou* feature of this educational system that it turns out idlers; **c'est le ~ des ambitieux de vouloir réussir à tout prix** it's a peculiarity *ou* (specific) feature of ambitious people to want to succeed at any price; **en ~: avoir un domaine en ~** to be the sole owner of an estate, have exclusive possession of an estate; **cette caractéristique que la France possède en ~** this feature which is peculiar *ou* exclusive to France.

(b) (*Ling*) **au ~** in the literal sense *ou* meaning, literally.

propre-à-rien, *pl* **propres-à-rien** [pʀɔpʀaʀjɛ̃] *nmf* good-for-nothing, ne'er-do-well.

proprement [pʀɔpʀəmɑ̃] *adv* **(a)** (*avec propreté*) cleanly; (*avec netteté*) neatly, tidily; (*comme il faut*) properly; (*fig: décemment*) decently. **tenir une maison très ~** to keep a house very clean; **mange ~!** don't make such a mess (when you're eating)!, eat properly!

(b) (*exactement*) exactly, literally; (*exclusivement*) specifically, strictly; (*vraiment*) absolutely. **à ~ parler** strictly speaking; **~ dit: le village ~ dit** the actual village, the village itself; **la linguistique ~ dite** linguistics proper; **c'est un problème ~ français** it's a specifically French problem; **c'est ~ scandaleux** it's absolutely disgraceful; **il m'a ~ fermé la porte au nez** he jolly well shut the door in my face*.

propret, -ette [pʀɔpʀɛ, ɛt] *adj personne* neat (and tidy), spruce; *chose* neat (and tidy), spick-and-span (*attrib*).

propreté [pʀɔpʀəte] *nf* (*V* **propre**[1]) cleanliness, cleanness; neatness; tidiness. **ils n'ont aucune notion de ~** they have no notion of hygiene; **l'éducation de la ~ chez l'enfant** toilet-training in the child.

propriétaire [pʀɔpʀijetɛʀ] **1** *nm* **(a)** (*gén*) *[voiture, chien, maison]* owner; *[hôtel, entreprise]* proprietor, owner. **il est ~ (de sa maison)** he owns his (own) house; **quand on est ~, il faut ...** when one is a house-owner *ou* householder one has to ...; **faire le tour du ~** to look *ou* go round *ou* over one's property; **je vais te faire faire le tour du ~** I'll show you over *ou* round the place.

(b) *[location]* landlord, owner. **mis à la porte par son ~** thrown out by one's landlord.

(c) *[terres, immeubles etc]* landowner, owner. **~-éleveur** breeder; **~ récoltant** grower; **achat direct au ~** direct purchase from the grower; **~ terrien** landowner; **~ foncier** property owner; **les petits ~s** (the) smallholders.

2 *nf* (*gén*) owner; *[hôtel, entreprise]* proprietress, owner; *[location]* landlady, owner.

propriété [pʀɔpʀijete] **1** *nf* **(a)** (*droit*) ownership, property (*frm, Jur*); (*possession*) property. **~ de l'État/collective/publique** state/collective/public ownership; **posséder en toute ~** to be the sole owner of, have sole ownership of; **accession à la ~** possibility of home-ownership; *V* **titre.**

(b) (*immeuble, maison*) property; (*terres*) property (*gén U*), land (*gén U*), estate. **revenu d'une ~** revenue from a property *ou* a piece of land.

(c) (*gén, Chim, Phys: qualité*) property.

(d) (*correction*) *[mot]* appropriateness, suitability, correctness.

2: propriété artistique artistic copyright; **propriété bâtie** developed property; **propriété commerciale** security of tenure (*of industrial or commercial tenant*); **propriété foncière** property ownership; **propriétés immobilières** real estate (*U*), realty (*U*) (*Jur*); **propriété industrielle** patent rights; **propriété littéraire** author's copyright; **propriété non-bâtie** undeveloped *ou* unbuilt-on property; **propriété privée** private property; **propriété publique** public property.

proprio* [pʀɔpʀio] *nm* (*abrév de* **propriétaire**) (*homme*) landlord; (*femme*) landlady.

propulser [pʀɔpylse] (1) **1** *vt* **(a)** *[moteur]* to propel, drive (along *ou* forward).

(b) (*projeter*) to hurl, fling. (*fig*) **on l'a propulsé chef de service** he was propelled speedily up the ladder to departmental head.

2 se propulser* *vpr* (*aller*) to trot*; (*se hâter*) to shoot*.

propulseur [pʀɔpylsœʀ] **1** *adj* propulsive, driving (*épith*). **2** *nm* propeller.

propulsif, ive [pʀɔpylsif, iv] *adj* propelling, propellent.

propulsion [pʀɔpylsjɔ̃] *nf* propulsion. **à ~ atomique** atomic-powered.

prorata [pʀɔʀata] *nm inv* proportional share, proportion. **au ~ de** in proportion to, on the basis of.

prorogatif, -ive [pʀɔʀɔgatif, iv] *adj* (*V* **proroger**) extending; deferring.

prorogation [pʀɔʀɔgɑsjɔ̃] *nf* (*V* **proroger**) extension; putting back, deferment; adjournment; prorogation.

proroger [pʀɔʀɔʒe] (3) *vt* **(a)** *délai, durée* to extend; *échéance* to put back, defer. **(b)** *séance* to adjourn; (*Parl*) to prorogue.

prosaïque [pʀozaik] *adj esprit, personne, vie* mundane, prosaic; *style* pedestrian, mundane, prosaic; *goûts* mundane, commonplace.

prosaïquement [pʀozaikmɑ̃] *adv* mundanely, prosaically. **vivre ~** to lead a mundane life *ou* a prosaic existence.

prosaïsme [pʀozaism(ə)] *nm* (*V* **prosaïque**) mundaneness; prosaicness; pedestrianism.

prosateur [pʀozatœʀ] *nm* prose-writer, writer of prose.

proscription [pʀɔskʀipsjɔ̃] *nf* (*V* **proscrire**) banning; prohibition; proscription (*frm*); outlawing (*U*); banishment, exiling (*U*).

proscrire [pʀɔskʀiʀ] (39) *vt idéologie, activité* to ban, prohibit, proscribe (*frm*); *drogue, mot* to ban, prohibit the use of, proscribe (*frm*); *personne* (*mettre hors la loi*) to outlaw, proscribe (*littér, frm*); (*exiler*) to banish, exile. ~ **une expression de son style** to banish an expression from one's style.

proscrit, e [pʀɔskʀi, it] (*ptp de* **proscrire**) *nm,f* (*hors-la-loi*) outlaw; (*exilé*) exile.

prose [pʀoz] *nf* (*gén*) prose; (*style*) prose (style). **poème/tragédie en** ~ prose poem/tragedy; **écrire en** ~ to write in prose; **faire de la** ~ to write prose; (*péj*) **la** ~ **administrative** officialese; (*péj*) **je viens de lire sa** ~ (*lettre*) I've just read his epistle (*hum*); (*devoir, roman*) I've just read his great work (*iro, hum*).

prosélyte [pʀozelit] *nmf* proselyte, convert.

prosélytisme [pʀozelitism(ə)] *nm* proselytism.

prosodie [pʀɔzɔdi] *nf* prosody.

prosodique [pʀɔzɔdik] *adj* prosodic.

prosopopée [pʀɔzɔpɔpe] *nf* prosopopoeia, prosopopeia.

prospecter [pʀɔspɛkte] (1) *vt* (*Min*) to prospect; (*Comm*) to canvass.

prospecteur, -trice [pʀɔspɛktœʀ, tʀis] *nm,f* prospector.

prospectif, -ive [pʀɔspɛktif, iv] **1** *adj* prospective. **2 prospective** *nf* futurology.

prospection [pʀɔspɛksjɔ̃] *nf* (*V* **prospecter**) prospecting; canvassing. (*Comm*) **faire de la** ~ to canvass for business.

prospectus [pʀɔspɛktys] *nm* (*feuille*) handbill, leaflet, handout; (*dépliant*) brochure, leaflet.

prospère [pʀɔspɛʀ] *adj* **(a)** *commerce* thriving, flourishing; *finances* thriving; *pays, collectivité* prosperous, affluent; *période* prosperous.
 (b) *santé, mine* flourishing; *personne* in flourishing health (*attrib*), blooming with health (*attrib*).

prospérer [pʀɔspeʀe] (6) *vi [commerce, activité, plante]* to thrive, flourish; *[personne]* to prosper, do well; *[animal]* to thrive.

prospérité [pʀɔspeʀite] *nf* **(a)** (*matérielle*) prosperity; (*économique*) prosperity, affluence. **étant donné la** ~ **de mes finances ...** in view of the thriving state of my finances .... **(b)** (*santé*) (flourishing) health.

prostate [pʀɔstat] *nf* prostate (gland).

prostatique [pʀɔstatik] **1** *adj* prostatic. **2** *nm* prostate sufferer.

prosternation [pʀɔstɛʀnɑsjɔ̃] *nf* prostration.

prosterné, e [pʀɔstɛʀne] (*ptp de* **prosterner**) *adj* prostrate.

prosternement [pʀɔstɛʀnəmɑ̃] *nm* (*action*) prostration; (*attitude*) prostrate attitude; (*fig*) grovelling.

prosterner [pʀɔstɛʀne] (1) **1** *vt* (*littér*) to bow low. **il prosterna le corps** he prostrated himself.
 2 se prosterner *vpr* (*s'incliner*) to bow low, bow down, prostrate o.s. (*devant* before); (*fig: s'humilier*) to grovel (*devant* before), kowtow (*devant* to).

prostituée [pʀɔstitɥe] *nf* prostitute.

prostituer [pʀɔstitɥe] (1) **1** *vt* (*lit*) ~ **qn** to make a prostitute of sb; ~ **qn (à qn)** to prostitute sb (to sb); (*fig*) to prostitute. **2 se prostituer** *vpr* (*lit, fig*) to prostitute o.s.

prostitution [pʀɔstitysjɔ̃] *nf* (*lit, fig*) prostitution.

prostration [pʀɔstʀɑsjɔ̃] *nf* (*Méd, Rel*) prostration.

prostré, e [pʀɔstʀe] *adj* (*fig*) prostrate, prostrated; (*Méd*) prostrate.

protagoniste [pʀɔtagɔnist(ə)] *nm* protagonist.

protecteur, -trice [pʀɔtɛktœʀ, tʀis] **1** *adj* **(a)** (*gén, Chim, Écon*) protective (*de* of); *V* **société.**
 (b) *ton, air* patronizing.
 2 *nm,f* (*défenseur*) protector, guardian; *[arts]* patron.
 3 *nm [femme]* (*souteneur*) pimp (*péj*); (†: *galant*) fancy man†. (*Québec*) ~ **du citoyen** ombudsman.

protection [pʀɔtɛksjɔ̃] **1** *nf* **(a)** (*défense*) protection (*contre* against, from). **mesures/rideau de** ~ protective measures/curtain; **sous la** ~ **de** under the protection of; **prendre qn sous sa** ~ to give sb one's protection, take sb under one's wing; **assurer la** ~ **de** to protect.
 (b) (*patronage*) patronage. **prendre qn sous sa** ~ to give sb one's patronage, take sb under one's wing; **obtenir une place par** ~ to get a post through string-pulling; **air/sourire de** ~ protective air/smile.
 (c) (*blindage*) *[navire]* armour(-plating).
 2: protection civile ≈ civil defence; **protection de l'enfance** child welfare; **protection de la nature** preservation *ou* protection of the countryside; **protection des sites** preservation *ou* protection of beauty spots.

protectionnisme [pʀɔtɛksjɔnism(ə)] *nm* protectionism.

protectionniste [pʀɔtɛksjɔnist(ə)] *adj, nmf* protectionist.

protectorat [pʀɔtɛktɔʀa] *nm* protectorate.

protège- [pʀɔtɛʒ] *préf V* **protéger.**

protégé, e [pʀɔteʒe] (*ptp de* **protéger**) **1** *adj V* **passage. 2** *nm* protégé; (*: *chouchou*) favourite, pet*. **3 protégée** *nf* protégée; (*: *favorite*) favourite, pet*.

protéger [pʀɔteʒe] (6 *et* 3) **1** *vt* **(a)** *personne* (*veiller à la sécurité de*) to protect, guard; (*abriter*) to protect, shield; (*moralement*) to protect, guard, shield; *plantes, lieu* (*des éléments*) to protect, shelter; *équipement, matériel, membres* (*des chocs etc*) to protect; *institution, tradition* to protect (*de, contre* from). **se** ~ **du froid/contre les piqûres d'insectes** to protect o.s. from the cold/against insect bites.
 (b) (*patronner*) *personne* to be a patron of; *carrière* to further; *arts, sports, artisanat* to patronize.
 (c) (*Comm*) *produits locaux* to protect.
 2: protège-cahier *nm, pl* **protège-cahiers** exercise-book cover; **protège-dents** *nm inv* gum-shield; **protège-tibia** *nm, pl* **protège-tibias** shin guard.

protéiforme [pʀɔteifɔʀm(ə)] *adj* protean.

protéine [pʀɔtein] *nf* protein.

protéique [pʀɔteik] *adj* protein (*épith*), proteinic.

protestable [pʀɔtɛstabl(ə)] *adj* protestable, which may be protested.

protestant, e [pʀɔtɛstɑ̃, ɑ̃t] *adj, nm,f* Protestant.

protestantisme [pʀɔtɛstɑ̃tism(ə)] *nm* Protestantism.

protestataire [pʀɔtɛstatɛʀ] **1** *adj personne* protesting (*épith*); *marche, mesure* protest (*épith*). **2** *nmf* protestor, protester.

protestation [pʀɔtɛstɑsjɔ̃] *nf* (*plainte*) protest; (*déclaration*) protestation, profession; (*Jur*) protesting, protestation. **en signe de** ~ as a (sign of) protest; **faire des** ~**s d'amitié à qn** to profess one's friendship to sb.

protester [pʀɔtɛste] (1) **1** *vi* to protest (*contre* against, about). ~ **de son innocence/de sa loyauté** to protest one's innocence/loyalty; **'mais non', protesta-t-il** 'no' he protested.
 2 *vt* (*Jur*) to protest; (*frm: déclarer*) to declare, affirm, profess. (*frm*) **il protesta la plus vive admiration pour elle** he declared that he had the keenest admiration for her.

protêt [pʀɔtɛ] *nm* (*Comm, Jur*) protest.

prothèse [pʀɔtɛz] *nf* (*appareil*) prosthesis; (*science, technique*) prosthetics (*gén sg*), prosthesis. ~ **(dentaire)** denture, dentures (*pl*), false teeth (*pl*); **(appareil de)** ~ artificial limb (*ou* hand *ou* arm *etc*), prosthesis (*T*).

protide [pʀɔtid] *nm* protein.

protocolaire [pʀɔtɔkɔlɛʀ] *adj invitation, cérémonie* formal. **question** ~ question of protocol; **ce n'est pas très** ~! it's not showing much regard for etiquette!

protocole [pʀɔtɔkɔl] *nm* **(a)** (*étiquette*) etiquette; (*Pol*) protocol. **(b)** (*procès-verbal*) protocol. **établir un** ~ **d'accord** to draw up a draft treaty.

proton [pʀɔtɔ̃] *nm* proton.

protoplasma [pʀɔtɔplasma] *nm*, **protoplasme** [pʀɔtɔplasm(ə)] *nm* protoplasm.

protoplasmique [pʀɔtɔplasmik] *adj* protoplasmic.

prototype [pʀɔtɔtip] *nm* prototype.

protozoaire [pʀɔtɔzɔɛʀ] *nm* protozoon. ~**s** protozoa.

protubérance [pʀɔtybeʀɑ̃s] *nf* bulge, protuberance.

protubérant, e [pʀɔtybeʀɑ̃, ɑ̃t] *adj ventre, yeux* bulging, protuberant, protruding; *nez, menton* protuberant, protruding.

prou [pʀu] *adv V* **peu.**

proue [pʀu] *nf* bow, bows (*pl*), prow; *V* **figure.**

prouesse [pʀuɛs] *nf* (*littér*) feat. (*fig*) **il a fallu faire des** ~**s pour le convaincre** we had to work minor miracles *ou* stand on our heads to convince him.

proustien, -ienne [pʀustjɛ̃, jɛn] *adj* Proustian, Proust (*épith*).

prouvable [pʀuvabl(ə)] *adj* provable. **allégations difficilement** ~**s** allegations which are difficult to prove.

prouver [pʀuve] (1) *vt* (*gén*) to prove. ~ **qch par l'absurde** to prove sth by reducing it to the absurd; **les faits ont prouvé qu'il avait raison/qu'il était innocent** the facts proved him (to be) right/innocent *ou* proved that he was right/innocent; **il est prouvé que ...** it has been proved that ...; **cela prouve que ...** it proves *ou* shows that ...; **il n'est pas prouvé qu'il soit coupable** there is no proof that he is guilty *ou* of his guilt; **cela n'est pas prouvé** there's no proof of it, that hasn't been proved, that remains to be proved; **cette réponse prouve de l'esprit** that answer gives proof of his (*ou her etc*) wit *ou* shows wit; **comment vous** ~ **ma reconnaissance?** how can I show *ou* demonstrate my gratitude to you?; **il a voulu se** ~ **(à lui-même) qu'il en était capable** he wanted to prove to himself that he was capable of it.

provenance [pʀɔvnɑ̃s] *nf [produit, objet, famille]* origin, provenance (*frm*); *[mot, coutume]* source, provenance (*frm*). **j'ignore la** ~ **de cette lettre** I don't know where this letter comes *ou* came *ou* was sent from; **pays de** ~ country of origin; **des objets de toutes** ~**s** articles of every possible origin; **de** ~ **étrangère** of foreign origin; **en** ~ **de l'Angleterre** from England.

provençal, e, *mpl* **-aux** [pʀɔvɑ̃sal, o] **1** *adj* Provençal. (*Culin*) **(à la)** ~**e** (à la) Provençale. **2** *nm* (*Ling*) Provençal. **3** *nmf*: **P**~**(e)** Provençal.

Provence [pʀɔvɑ̃s] *nf* Provence.

provenir [pʀɔvniʀ] (22) **provenir de** *vt indir* (*venir de*) *pays* to come from, be from; (*résulter de*) *cause* to be due to, be the result of. **son genre de vie provient de son éducation** his life style stems *ou* proceeds from *ou* is the product of his upbringing; **mot qui provient d'une racine grecque** word which comes *ou* derives from a Greek root *ou* source; **fortune qui provient d'une lointaine cousine** fortune whose source is a distant cousin *ou* that comes from a distant cousin; **vase provenant de Chine** vase (that comes) from China.

proverbe [pʀɔvɛʀb(ə)] *nm* proverb. **comme dit le** ~ as the saying goes.

proverbial, e, *mpl* **-aux** [pʀɔvɛʀbjal, o] *adj* proverbial.

proverbialement [pʀɔvɛʀbjalmɑ̃] *adv* proverbially.

providence [pʀɔvidɑ̃s] *nf* (*Rel*) providence; (*fig: sauveur*) guardian angel. (*fig*) **cette bouteille d'eau a été notre** ~ that bottle of water was our salvation *ou* was a lifesaver.

providentiel, -elle [pʀɔvidɑ̃sjɛl] *adj* providential.

providentiellement [pʀɔvidɑ̃sjɛlmɑ̃] *adv* providentially.

province [pʀɔvɛ̃s] *nf* **(a)** (*région*) province. **Paris et la** ~ Paris and the provinces; **vivre en** ~ to live in the provinces; **ville de** ~ provincial town; (*péj*) **il arrive de sa** ~ where has he been?; (*péj*) **elle fait très** ~ she is very provincial.
 (b) (*Can Pol*) province (*main political division*) (*Can*). **les P**~**s maritimes** the Maritime Provinces, the Maritimes (*Can*);

habitant des P~s maritimes Maritimer; **les P~s des prairies** the Prairie Provinces (*Can*).

provincial, e, *mpl* **-aux** [pʀɔvɛ̃sjal, o] **1** *adj* **(a)** (*gén, Rel*) provincial, small-townish (*péj*). **(b)** (*Can Pol*) **gouvernement ~** Provincial government (*Can*). **2** *nm,f* provincial. **les ~aux** people who live in the provinces, provincials. **3** *nm* **(a)** (*Rel*) Provincial. **(b)** (*Can*) **le ~** the Provincial Government.

provincialisme [pʀɔvɛ̃sjalism(ə)] *nm* provincialism.

proviseur [pʀɔvizœʀ] *nm* head(master) (*of a lycée*).

provision [pʀɔvizjɔ̃] *nf* **(a)** (*réserve*) *[vivres, cartouches]* stock, supply; *[eau]* supply. **faire (une) ~ de** *nourriture, papier* to stock up with, lay *ou* get in a stock of; *énergie, courage* to build up a stock of; **j'ai acheté toute une ~ de bonbons** I've bought in a whole supply *ou* stock of sweets; **j'ai une bonne ~ de conserves** I have a good stock of tinned food, I've plenty of tinned food in; **avoir une bonne ~ de courage** to have a good stock of courage. **(b)** (*vivres*) **~s** provisions, food (*U*); **faire ses ~s, aller aux ~s*** to go shopping (for groceries *ou* food); **elle posa ses ~s sur la table** she put her groceries on the table; **faire des ~s pour l'hiver** to buy in food *ou* provisions for the winter, stock up (with food *ou* provisions) for the winter; **~s de guerre** war supplies; **~s de bouche** provisions; **filet/panier à ~s** shopping bag/basket; **placard à ~s** food cupboard; **armoire à ~s** food *ou* store cupboard. **(c)** (*arrhes*) (*chez un avocat*) retainer, retaining fee; (*pour un achat*) deposit. (*Banque*) **y a-t-il ~ au compte?** are there sufficient funds in the account?; *V* **chèque.**

provisionnel, -elle [pʀɔvizjɔnɛl] *adj* (*Jur*) provisional; *V* **tiers.**

provisoire [pʀɔvizwaʀ] **1** *adj arrêt, jugement* provisional; *mesure, solution* provisional, temporary; *bonheur, liaison* temporary; *installation* temporary; *adjoint* temporary, acting (*épith*); *gouvernement* provisional, interim (*épith*). **à titre ~** temporarily, provisionally; *V* **liberté.** **2** *nm*: **c'est du ~** it's a temporary arrangement.

provisoirement [pʀɔvizwaʀmɑ̃] *adv* (*pour l'instant*) for the time being.

provocant, e [pʀɔvɔkɑ̃, ɑ̃t] *adj* provocative.

provocateur, -trice [pʀɔvɔkatœʀ, tʀis] **1** *adj* provocative; *V* **agent. 2** *nm* agitator.

provocation [pʀɔvɔkɑsjɔ̃] *nf* provocation. **~ à (faire) qch** incitement to (do) sth; **~ en duel** challenge to a duel.

provoquer [pʀɔvɔke] (1) *vt* **(a)** (*inciter, pousser à*) **~ qn à** to incite sb to. **(b)** (*défier*) to provoke. **~ qn en duel** to challenge sb to a duel; **elle aime ~ les hommes** she likes to provoke men; **les 2 adversaires s'étaient provoqués** the 2 opponents had provoked each other. **(c)** (*causer*) *accident, incendie, explosion* to cause; *réaction, changement d'attitude* to provoke, prompt, produce; *courant d'air* to create, cause; *révolte* to cause, bring about, instigate; *commentaires* to give rise to, provoke, prompt; *colère* to arouse, spark off; *curiosité* to arouse, excite, prompt; *gaieté* to cause, give rise to, provoke; *aveux, explications* to prompt. **blessures qui ont provoqué la mort** injuries which led to *ou* brought about death; **médicament qui provoque le sommeil** medicine which brings on *ou* induces sleep; **le malade est sous sommeil/évanouissement provoqué** the patient is in an induced sleep/a state of induced unconsciousness; (*Chim*) **l'élévation de température a provoqué cette réaction** the rise in temperature brought about *ou* triggered off *ou* started up this reaction.

proxénète [pʀɔksenɛt] *nm* procurer.

proxénétisme [pʀɔksenetism(ə)] *nm* procuring.

proximité [pʀɔksimite] *nf* (*dans l'espace*) nearness, closeness, proximity; (*dans le temps*) imminence, closeness. **à ~** near *ou* close by, near *ou* close at hand; **à ~ de** near (to), close to, in the vicinity of.

pruche [pʀyʃ] *nf* (*Can*) hemlock spruce.

prude [pʀyd] **1** *adj* prudish. **2** *nf* prude.

prudemment [pʀydamɑ̃] *adv* (*V* **prudent**) carefully; cautiously; prudently; wisely, sensibly; cagily. **garder ~ le silence** to keep a cautious silence.

prudence [pʀydɑ̃s] *nf* (*V* **prudent**) care; caution, cautiousness; prudence (*frm*); wisdom; caginess. **manquer de ~** not to be careful *ou* cautious enough; **par (mesure de) ~** as a precaution; **il a eu la ~ de partir** he had the good sense *ou* he was wise *ou* sensible enough to leave; (*Prov*) **~ est mère de sûreté** safety is born of caution.

prudent, e [pʀydɑ̃, ɑ̃t] *adj* (*circonspect*) careful, cautious, prudent; (*sage*) wise, sensible; (*réservé*) cautious, cagey. **il est ~ de faire** it is wise *ou* advisable *ou* a good idea to do; **il serait ~ de vous munir d'un parapluie** it would be wise *ou* sensible *ou* a good idea to *ou* you would be well-advised to take an umbrella; **ce n'est pas ~** it's not advisable *ou* a good idea; **ce n'est pas ~ de boire avant de conduire** it's not sensible *ou* wise *ou* advisable to drink before driving; **c'est plus ~** it's wiser *ou* safer *ou* more sensible; **soyez ~!** be careful!, take care!; **il s'est montré très ~ au sujet du résultat** he was very cautious *ou* cagey about the result; **il jugea plus ~ de se taire** he thought it wiser *ou* more sensible to keep quiet; **c'est un ~** he's a careful *ou* cautious *ou* prudent type.

pruderie [pʀydʀi] *nf* (*littér*) prudishness (*U*), prudery.

prud'homie [pʀydɔmi] *nf* (*V* **prud'homme**) jurisdiction of an industrial tribunal.

prud'homme [pʀydɔm] *nm*: **conseil de ~s** ≈ industrial tribunal (*with wider administrative and advisory powers*).

prudhommerie [pʀydɔmʀi] *nf* sententiousness, pomposity.

prudhommesque [pʀydɔmɛsk(ə)] *adj* sententious, pompous.

prune [pʀyn] **1** *nf* (*fruit*) plum; (*alcool*) plum liqueur. (*fig*) **pour des ~s:** for nothing; **des ~s!:** not likely!*, not on your life!* **2** *adj inv* plum-coloured.

pruneau, *pl* **~x** [pʀyno] *nm* prune; (*: *balle*) slug*.

prunelle [pʀynɛl] *nf* **(a)** (*Bot*) sloe; (*eau-de-vie*) sloe gin. **(b)** (*Anat: pupille*) pupil; (*œil*) eye. **il y tient comme à la ~ de ses yeux** (*objet*) he treasures *ou* cherishes it; (*personne*) she (*ou* he) is very precious to him; **jouer de la ~*** to give the eye*.

prunellier [pʀynelje] *nm* sloe, blackthorn.

prunier [pʀynje] *nm* plum tree; *V* **secouer.**

prunus [pʀynys] *nm* (ornamental) plum tree.

prurigineux, -euse [pʀyʀiʒinø, øz] *adj* pruriginous.

prurigo [pʀyʀigo] *nm* prurigo.

prurit [pʀyʀit] *nm* pruritus.

Prusse [pʀys] *nf* Prussia; *V* **bleu.**

prussien, -ienne [pʀysjɛ̃, jɛn] **1** *adj* Prussian. **2** *nm,f*: **P~(ne)** Prussian.

prussique [pʀysik] *adj m*: **acide ~** prussic acid.

prytanée [pʀitane] *nm* (*Mil*) school, academy.

psallette [psalɛt] *nf* choir.

psalmiste [psalmist(ə)] *nm* psalmist.

psalmodie [psalmɔdi] *nf* (*Rel*) psalmody; (*fig littér*) drone.

psalmodier [psalmɔdje] (7) **1** *vt* (*Rel*) to chant; (*fig littér*) to drone out. **2** *vi* to chant; to drone (on *ou* away).

psaume [psom] *nm* psalm.

psautier [psotje] *nm* psalter.

pseudo- [psødɔ] *préf* (*gén*) pseudo-; *employé, officier* bogus.

pseudonyme [psødɔnim] *nm* (*gén*) assumed name, fictitious name; *[écrivain]* pen name, pseudonym, nom de plume; *[comédien]* stage name.

psi [psi] *nm* psi.

psitt [psit] *excl* ps(s)t!

psittacisme [psitasism(ə)] *nm* (*répétition mécanique*) parrotry; (*Psych*) psittacism.

psittacose [psitakoz] *nf* psittacosis.

psychanalyse [psikanaliz] *nf [personne]* psychoanalysis; *[texte]* psychoanalytical study.

psychanalyser [psikanalize] (1) *vt personne* to psychoanalyze; *texte* to study from a psychoanalytical viewpoint. **se faire ~** to have o.s. psychoanalyzed.

psychanalyste [psikanalist(ə)] *nmf* psychoanalyst.

psychanalytique [psikanalitik] *adj* psychoanalytic(al).

psyché [psiʃe] *nf* **(a)** (*Psych*) psyche. **(b)** (*miroir*) cheval glass, swing mirror. **(c)** (*Myth*) **P~** Psyche.

psychédélique [psikedelik] *adj* psychedelic.

psychédélisme [psikedelism(ə)] *nm* psychedelic state.

psychiatre [psikjatʀ(ə)] *nmf* psychiatrist.

psychiatrie [psikjatʀi] *nf* psychiatry.

psychiatrique [psikjatʀik] *adj troubles* psychiatric; *hôpital* psychiatric, mental (*épith*).

psychique [psiʃik] *adj* psychological, psychic(al).

psychisme [psiʃism(ə)] *nm* psyche, mind.

psychodrame [psikɔdʀam] *nm* psychodrama.

psycholinguistique [psikɔlɛ̃gɥistik] **1** *adj* psycholinguistic. **2** *nf* psycholinguistics (*sg*).

psychologie [psikɔlɔʒi] *nf* psychology. **~ de l'enfant** child psychology; **la ~ des foules** crowd psychology.

psychologique [psikɔlɔʒik] *adj* psychological. **tu sais, mon vieux, c'est ~!** it's psychological *ou* it's all in the mind, old boy!; *V* **moment.**

psychologiquement [psikɔlɔʒikmɑ̃] *adv* psychologically.

psychologue [psikɔlɔg] **1** *adj*: **il est ~** (*de profession*) he is a psychologist; (*il a de l'intuition*) he is a good psychologist; **il n'est pas (très) ~** he's not much of a psychologist. **2** *nmf* psychologist. **~ d'entreprise** industrial psychologist.

psychomoteur, -trice [psikɔmɔtœʀ, tʀis] *adj* psychomotor.

psychopathe [psikɔpat] *nmf* person who is mentally ill; (*agressif, criminel*) psychopath.

psychopathie [psikɔpati] *nf* mental illness; psychopathy.

psychopathologie [psikɔpatɔlɔʒi] *nf* psychopathology.

psychopédagogie [psikɔpedagɔʒi] *nf* (application of) experimental psychology in education.

psychopédagogique [psikɔpedagɔʒik] *adj*: **études ~s** studies in education involving experimental psychology.

psychophysiologie [psikɔfizjɔlɔʒi] *nf* psychophysiology.

psychophysiologique [psikɔfizjɔlɔʒik] *adj* psychophysiological.

psychose [psikoz] *nf* (*Psych*) psychosis; (*fig: obsession*) obsessive fear (*de* of).

psychosensoriel, -elle [psikɔsɑ̃sɔʀjɛl] *adj* psychosensory.

psychosomatique [psikɔsɔmatik] **1** *adj* psychosomatic. **2** *nf* psychosomatics (*sg*).

psychotechnicien, -ienne [psikɔtɛknisjɛ̃, jɛn] *nm,f* psychotechnician, psychotechnologist.

psychotechnique [psikɔtɛknik] **1** *adj* psychotechnical, psychotechnological. **2** *nf* psychotechnics (*sg*), psychotechnology.

psychothérapie [psikɔteʀapi] *nf* psychotherapy.

psychothérapique [psikɔteʀapik] *adj* psychotherapeutic.

psychotique [psikɔtik] *adj, nmf* psychotic.

ptérodactyle [pteʀɔdaktil] *nm* pterodactyl.

Ptolémée [ptɔleme] *nm* Ptolemy.

puant, e [pɥɑ̃, ɑ̃t] *adj* (*lit*) stinking, foul-smelling; (*fig*) *personne, attitude* bumptious, overweening. **il est ~, c'est un type ~** he's full of himself, he's a bumptious *ou* an overweening character; **~ d'orgueil** bloated with pride.

puanteur [pɥɑ̃tœʀ] *nf* stink, stench.

pubère [pybɛʀ] *adj* pubescent.

puberté [pybɛʀte] *nf* puberty.

pubien, -ienne [pybjɛ̃, jɛn] *adj* pubic. **région ~ne** pubic region, pubes.
pubis [pybis] *nm* (*os*) pubis; (*bas-ventre*) pubes. **os ~** pubic bone.
publiable [pyblijabl(ə)] *adj* publishable. **ce n'est pas ~** it's not fit for publication.
public, -ique [pyblik] **1** *adj* **(a)** (*non privé*) *intérêt, lieu, opinion, vie* public; *vente, réunion* public, open to the public (*attrib*). **danger/ennemi/homme ~** public danger/enemy/figure; **la nouvelle est maintenant ~ique** the news is now common knowledge *ou* public knowledge; *V* **domaine, droit**[3], **notoriété.**
(b) (*de l'État*) *services, secteur, finances* public; *école, instruction* State (*épith*); *V* **charge, chose, dette** *etc.*
2 *nm* **(a)** (*population*) (general) public. **interdit au ~** no admittance to the public.
(b) (*audience, assistance*) audience. **œuvre conçue pour un jeune ~** work written for a young audience; **en matière d'opéra, le ~ parisien est très exigeant** the opera-going public of Paris is very demanding, where opera is concerned Paris audiences are very demanding; **des huées s'élevèrent du ~** boos rose from the audience *ou* public; **cet écrivain s'adresse à un vaste ~** this author writes for a large readership; **cet ouvrage plaira à tous les ~s** this work will be appreciated by all types of readership *ou* reading public; **un ~ clairsemé assistait au match** the match was attended by very few spectators; **le ~ est informé que ...** the public is advised that ...; **en ~** in public; **le grand ~** the general public; **roman destiné au grand ~** novel written for the general reader *ou* public; (*fig*) **il lui faut toujours un ~** he always needs an audience; **ses romans ont conquis un vaste ~** his novels have won a vast readership; **être bon/mauvais ~** to be a good/poor audience.
publicain [pyblikɛ̃] *nm* (*Hist romaine*) publican, tax-gatherer.
publication [pyblikɑsjɔ̃] *nf* (*action*) publication, publishing; (*écrit publié*) publication.
publiciste [pyblisist(ə)] *nmf* (*publicitaire*) adman*. **il est ~** he's in advertising, he's an adman*.
publicitaire [pyblisitɛʀ] **1** *adj budget, affiche, agence, campagne* advertising (*épith*); *film* publicity (*épith*); *voiture* publicity (*épith*). **annonce ~** advertisement; **grande vente ~** big promotional sale; **rédacteur ~** copywriter.
2 *nmf* adman*, advertising executive.
publicité [pyblisite] *nf* **(a)** (*Comm: méthode, profession*) advertising. **agence de ~** advertising agency; (*Comm, fig*) **faire de la ~ pour qch** to advertise sth; **cette marque fait beaucoup de ~** this make does a lot of advertising.
(b) (*annonce*) advertisement, ad(vert)*. **page de ~** page of advertisements.
(c) (*révélations*) publicity. **on a fait trop de ~ autour de cette affaire** this affair has had *ou* has been given too much publicity.
(d) (*Jur*) **la ~ des débats** the public nature of the proceedings.
publier [pyblije] (7) *vt* **(a)** *livre [auteur]* to publish; *[éditeur]* to publish, bring out.
(b) *bans, décret* to publish; (*littér*) *nouvelle* to publish (abroad) (*littér*), make public. **ça vient d'être publié** it's just out*, it has just come out *ou* been published.
publiquement [pyblikmɑ̃] *adv* publicly.
puce [pys] **1** *nf* **(a)** flea. **~ de mer** *ou* **de sable** sand flea; (*fig*) **cela m'a mis la ~ à l'oreille** that started me thinking; **les ~s, le marché aux ~s** the flea market; **oui, ma ~*** yes, pet* *ou* lovie*; (*fig*) **c'est une vraie ~** he's (*ou* she's) a real midget; *V* **secouer.**
(b) jeu de ~s tiddly-winks; **jouer aux ~s** to play tiddly-winks.
2 *adj inv* puce.
puceau‡, *pl* **~x** [pyso] **1** *adj m*: **être ~** to be a virgin. **2** *nm* virgin.
pucelage‡ [pyslaʒ] *nm* virginity.
pucelle [pysɛl] (††, *hum*,*) **1** *adj f*: **être ~** to be a virgin; **elle n'est plus ~** she has lost her virginity, she's not a virgin. **2** *nf* virgin, maid(en) (*littér*). (*Hist*) **la ~ d'Orléans** the Maid of Orleans.
puceron [pysʀɔ̃] *nm* aphid, greenfly, plant louse.
pucier‡ [pysje] *nm* bed.
pudding [pudiŋ] *nm* plum pudding, plum duff.
puddlage [pydlaʒ] *nm* puddling.
pudeur [pydœʀ] *nf* **(a)** (*sexuelle*) (sense of) modesty, sense of decency. **elle a beaucoup de ~** she has a keen sense of modesty *ou* decency; **sans ~** (*adj*) immodest; (*adv*) immodestly, unblushingly; *V* **attentat, outrage. (b)** (*délicatesse*) sense of propriety. **agir sans ~** to act with no regard to propriety.
pudibond, e [pydibɔ̃, ɔ̃d] *adj* (excessively) prudish, prim and proper.
pudibonderie [pydibɔ̃dʀi] *nf* (excessive) prudishness, (excessive) primness.
pudicité [pydisite] *nf* (*littér: V* **pudique**) modesty; discretion.
pudique [pydik] *adj* (*chaste*) modest; (*discret*) discreet.
pudiquement [pydikmɑ̃] *adv* (*V* **pudique**) modestly; discreetly. **ils détournaient les yeux ~** they looked away discreetly *ou* out of a sense of decency.
puer [pɥe] (1) **1** *vi* to stink, reek, smell foul. (*fig*) **il pue de vanité** he is bloated with vanity. **2** *vt* to stink *ou* reek of.
puéricultrice [pɥeʀikyltʀis] *nf* paediatric nurse.
puériculture [pɥeʀikyltyʀ] *nf* paediatric nursing. **donner des cours de ~ aux mamans** to give courses on infant care to mothers.
puéril, e [pɥeʀil] *adj* puerile, childish.
puérilement [pɥeʀilmɑ̃] *adv* childishly, puerilely.
puérilité [pɥeʀilite] *nf* (*caractère*) puerility, childishness; (*acte*) puerility.
pugilat [pyʒila] *nm* (fist)fight.
pugiliste [pyʒilist(ə)] *nm* (*littér*) pugilist (*littér, frm*).
pugilistique [pyʒilistik] *adj* (*littér*) pugilistic (*littér, frm*).
pugnacité [pygnasite] *nf* (*littér*) pugnacity.
puîné, e† [pɥine] **1** *adj* (*de deux*) younger; (*de plusieurs*) youngest. **2** *nm,f* younger; youngest.
puis [pɥi] *adv* (*ensuite*) then; (*dans une énumération*) then, next. (*en outre*) **et ~** and besides; **et ~ ensuite** and then, and after that; **et ~ c'est tout** and that's all *ou* that's it; **et ~ après tout** and after all; **et ~ après?** *ou* **ensuite?** (*ensuite*) and what next?, and then (what)?; (*et alors?*) so what?, what of it?; **et ~ quoi?** (*quoi d'autre*) well, what?, and then what?; (*et alors?*) so what?, what of it?
puisage [pɥizaʒ] *nm* drawing (of water).
puisard [pɥizaʀ] *nm* (*gén*) cesspool, sink; (*Naut*) well; (*Min*) sump.
puisatier [pɥizatje] *nm* well-digger.
puiser [pɥize] (1) *vt* (*lit*) *eau* to draw (*dans* from); (*fig*) *exemple, renseignement* to draw, take (*dans* from). **~ des exemples dans un auteur** to draw examples from an author, draw on an author for one's examples; **~ dans son sac** to dip into one's bag.
puisque [pɥisk(ə)] *conj* **(a)** (*du moment que*) since, seeing that. **ces animaux sont donc des mammifères, puisqu'ils allaitent leurs petits** these animals are therefore mammals, seeing that *ou* since they suckle their young; **ça doit être vrai, puisqu'il le dit** it must be true since he says so.
(b) (*comme*) as, since, seeing that. **~ vous êtes là, venez m'aider** as *ou* since *ou* seeing that you're here come and help me; **ces escrocs, puisqu'il faut les appeler ainsi, ...** these crooks — as *ou* since one must call them that ... .
(c) (*valeur intensive*) **~ je te le dis!** I'm telling you (so)!; **~ je te dis que c'est vrai!** I'm telling you it's true!
puissamment [pɥisamɑ̃] *adv* (*fortement*) powerfully; (*beaucoup*) greatly. (*iro*) **~ raisonné!** what brilliant reasoning! (*iro*).
puissance [pɥisɑ̃s] **1** *nf* **(a)** (*force*) *[armée, muscle, impulsion]* power, strength; *[moteur, haut-parleur]* power; *[éclairage]* brightness, power; *[vent]* strength, force. **avoir une grande ~ de travail** to have a great capacity for work; **avoir une grande ~ d'imagination** to have a very powerful imagination *ou* great powers of imagination; **la ~ de son regard** the power of his gaze; **grâce à la ~ de sa volonté** thanks to his will power *ou* his strength of will.
(b) (*pouvoir*) *[classe sociale, pays, argent]* power; (*efficacité*) *[exemple]* power. **une grande ~ de séduction/suggestion** great seductive/suggestive power(s), great powers of seduction/suggestion; **user de sa ~ pour faire qch** to use one's power to do sth; **l'or/le pétrole est une ~** gold/oil confers power; **les ~s qui agissent sur le monde** the powers that influence the world.
(c) (*Pol: état*) power. **les grandes ~s** the great powers.
(d) (*Élec, Phys*) power; (*Opt*) *[microscope]* (magnifying) power. (*Math*) **élever un nombre à la ~ 10** to raise a number to the power of 10; **10 ~ 4** 10 to the power of 4, 10 to the 4th.
(e) (*Jur, hum*) **être en ~ de mari** to be under a husband's authority.
(f) (*loc*) **en ~** *adj* potential; **exister en ~** to have a potential existence; **c'est là en ~** it is potentially present; **l'homme est en ~ dans l'enfant** the man is latent in the child.
2: les puissances d'argent the forces of money; (*Mil*) **puissance de feu** fire power; (*Aut*) **puissance fiscale** engine rating; (*Aut*) **puissance au frein** brake horsepower; (*Jur*) **puissance maritale** marital rights; **les puissances occultes** unseen *ou* hidden powers; (*Jur*) **puissance paternelle** parental authority; **les puissances des ténèbres** the powers of darkness.
puissant, e [pɥisɑ̃, ɑ̃t] **1** *adj* (*gén*) powerful; *drogue, remède* potent, powerful. **2** *nm*: **les ~s** the mighty *ou* powerful.
puits [pɥi] **1** *nm [eau, pétrole]* well; (*Min*) shaft; (*Constr*) well, shaft.
2: puits d'aérage *ou* **d'aération** ventilation shaft; **puits artésien** artesian well; (*Min*) **puits à ciel ouvert** opencast mine; **puits d'extraction** winding shaft; **puits de mine** mine shaft; **puits perdu** cesspool, sink; **puits de pétrole** oil well; (*fig*) **puits de science** well of erudition *ou* learning.
pull* [pyl] *nm* sweater, jumper (*Brit*), pullover.
pullman [pulman] *nm* Pullman (car).
pull-over, *pl* **pull-overs** [pulɔvœʀ] *nm* sweater, jumper (*Brit*), pullover.
pullulation [pylylɑsjɔ̃] *nf*, **pullulement** [pylylmɑ̃] *nm* (*action*) proliferation; (*profusion*) *[fourmis, moustiques]* swarm, multitude; *[erreurs]* abundance, multitude.
pulluler [pylyle] (1) *vi* (*se reproduire*) to proliferate, multiply, pullulate (*frm*); (*grouiller*) to swarm, pullulate (*frm*); (*fig*) *[erreurs, contrefaçons]* to abound, pullulate (*frm*). **la ville pullule de touristes** the town is swarming with tourists; **la rivière pullule de truites** the river is teeming with trout.
pulmonaire [pylmɔnɛʀ] *adj maladie* pulmonary, lung (*épith*); *artère* pulmonary. **congestion ~** congestion of the lungs.
pulpe [pylp(ə)] *nf* pulp.
pulpeux, -euse [pylpø, øz] *adj* pulpy.
pulsation [pylsɑsjɔ̃] *nf* (*Méd*) *[cœur, pouls]* beating (*U*), beat, pulsation (*T*); (*Phys*) pulsation; (*Élec*) pulsatance. **~s** (**du cœur**) (*rythme cardiaque*) heartbeat; (*battements*) heartbeats.
pulsion [pylsjɔ̃] *nf* (*Psych*) drive, urge. **la ~ sexuelle** the sex drive.
pulvérisateur [pylveʀizatœʀ] *nm* (*à parfum*) spray, atomizer; (*à peinture*) spray; (*pour médicament*) spray, vaporizer.
pulvérisation [pylveʀizɑsjɔ̃] *nf* (*V* **pulvériser**) pulverizing, pulverization; spraying; demolition, demolishing; shattering*, smashing*. (*Méd*) **'trois ~s dans chaque narine'** 'spray three

times into each nostril'; (*Méd*) **le médecin a ordonné des ~s** the doctor prescribed a nasal spray.
pulvériser [pylveʀize] (1) *vt* **(a)** *solide* to pulverize, reduce to powder; *liquide* to spray.
(b) (*fig: anéantir*) *adversaire* to pulverize, demolish; *record* to shatter*, smash*; *argument* to demolish, pull to pieces.
pulvériseur [pylveʀizœʀ] *nm* disc harrow.
pulvérulence [pylveʀylɑ̃s] *nf* pulverulence.
pulvérulent, e [pylveʀylɑ̃, ɑ̃t] *adj* pulverulent.
puma [pyma] *nm* puma, cougar, mountain lion.
punaise [pynɛz] *nf* **(a)** (*Zool*) bug. (*péj*) **c'est une vraie ~** he's a real mischief-maker; (*excl*) **~!*** blimey!* (*Brit*), well!; (*péj*) **~ de sacristie*** church hen. **(b)** (*clou*) drawing pin (*Brit*), thumbtack (*US*).
punch[1] [pɔ̃ʃ] *nm* (*boisson*) punch.
punch[2] [pœnʃ] *nm* (*Boxe*) punching ability; (*fig*) punch. **avoir du ~** (*Boxe*) to pack *ou* have a good punch; (*fig*) to have punch.
puncheur [pœnʃœʀ] *nm* good puncher, hard hitter.
punching-ball, *pl* **punching-balls** [pœnʃiŋbol] *nm* punchball.
punique [pynik] *adj* Punic.
punir [pyniʀ] (2) *vt* **(a)** *criminel, enfant* to punish (*pour* for). **être puni de prison/de mort** to be sentenced to prison/death.
(b) (*faire souffrir*) to punish. **il a été puni de son imprudence** he was punished for his recklessness, he suffered for his recklessness; **tu as été malade, ça te punira de ta gourmandise** you've been ill – that will teach you not to be greedy *ou* it's no more than you deserve for being greedy; **il est orgueilleux, et l'en voilà bien puni** he is paying the penalty for *ou* being made to suffer for his pride; **il est puni par où il a péché** he has got his (just) deserts, he is paying for his sins.
(c) (*sanctionner*) *faute, infraction, crime* to punish. **tout abus sera puni (de prison)** all abuses are punishable *ou* will be punished (by prison); **ce crime est puni par la loi/puni de mort** this crime is punishable by law/by death.
punissable [pynisabl(ə)] *adj* punishable (*de* by).
punitif, -ive [pynitif, iv] *adj* *expédition* punitive.
punition [pynisjɔ̃] *nf* punishment (*de qch* for sth). (*Scol*) **avoir une ~** to be given a punishment; **~ corporelle** corporal punishment (*U*); **en ~ de ses fautes** in punishment for his mistakes; **pour ta ~** for your punishment.
pupille[1] [pypij] *nf* (*Anat*) pupil.
pupille[2] [pypij] *nmf* (*enfant*) ward. **~ de l'État** child in (local authority) care; **~ de la Nation** war orphan.
pupitre [pypitʀ(ə)] *nm* (*Scol*) desk; (*Rel*) lectern; (*Mus*) *[musicien]* music stand; *[piano]* music rest; *[chef d'orchestre]* rostrum. (*Mus*) **au ~, Henri Dupont** at the rostrum – Henri Dupont, conducting – Henri Dupont; (*Mus*) **chef de ~** head of section.
pur, e [pyʀ] **1** *adj* **(a)** (*sans mélange*) *alcool, eau, race, métal, voix, style* pure; *vin* undiluted; *whisky, gin* neat, straight; *ciel* clear, pure. **~e laine** pure wool; **boire son vin ~** to drink one's wine without water *ou* undiluted; (*Chim*) **à l'état ~** in the pure state; **~ sang** thoroughbred, purebred; *V* **pur-sang**.
(b) (*innocent*) *âme, cœur, fille* pure; *homme* pure-hearted; *intentions* pure, honourable, honest; *regard* frank. **~ de tout soupçon** free of *ou* above all suspicion; **~ de toute tache** free of all blemish, unblemished, unsullied.
(c) (*valeur intensive*) **c'est de la folie ~e** it's pure *ou* sheer *ou* utter madness; **c'est de la poésie/de l'imagination toute ~e** it's pure *ou* sheer poetry/imagination; **~ et simple: c'est de l'insubordination ~e et simple** it's insubordination pure and simple; **il donna sa démission ~e et simple** he purely and simply gave in his notice; **œuvre de ~e imagination** work of pure imagination; **c'est une question de ~e forme** it's merely *ou* purely a formal question; **c'est par ~ hasard que je l'ai vu** I saw it by sheer chance *ou* purely by chance; **c'est la ~e vérité** it's the plain *ou* simple (unadulterated) truth; **en ~e perte** for absolutely nothing, fruitlessly; **il a travaillé en ~e perte** he worked for absolutely nothing, his work was fruitless.
2 *nm,f* (*Pol*) hard-liner.
purée [pyʀe] *nf*: **~ (de pommes de terre)** mashed potato(es); **~ de marrons/de tomates** chestnut/tomato purée; (*fig*) **de la ~ de pois** peasoup, a peasouper; (*fig*) **être dans la ~‡** to be in a right mess‡; **~, je l'ai oublié!*** darn (it)*, I forgot!
purement [pyʀmɑ̃] *adv* purely. **~ et simplement** purely and simply.
pureté [pyʀte] *nf* **(a)** (*perfection*) *[race, style, métal]* purity; *[air, eau, son]* purity, pureness. **(b)** (*innocence: V* **pur**) purity; honourableness, honesty; frankness.
purgatif, -ive [pyʀgatif, iv] **1** *adj* purgative. **2** *nm* purgative, purge.
purgation [pyʀgɑsjɔ̃] *nf* (*Méd*) (*action*) purgation; (*remède*) purgative, purge.
purgatoire [pyʀgatwaʀ] *nm* (*Rel, fig*) purgatory.
purge [pyʀʒ(ə)] *nf* (*Méd*) purge, purgative; (*Pol*) purge; (*Tech*) *[conduite]* flushing out, draining; *[freins]* bleeding.
purger [pyʀʒe] (3) **1** *vt* **(a)** (*vidanger*) *conduite, radiateur* to flush (out), drain; *circuit hydraulique, freins* to bleed.
(b) (*Méd*) to purge, give a purgative to.
(c) (*Jur*) *peine* to serve.
(d) (*débarrasser*) to purge, cleanse, rid (*de* of).
2 se purger *vpr* to take a purgative *ou* purge.
purgeur [pyʀʒœʀ] *nm* *[tuyauterie]* drain-cock *ou* tap; *[radiateur]* bleed-tap.
purifiant, e [pyʀifjɑ̃, ɑ̃t] *adj* purifying, cleansing.
purificateur, -trice [pyʀifikatœʀ, tʀis] **1** *adj* purifying, cleansing, purificatory. **2** *nm* (*appareil*) (air) purifier.
purification [pyʀifikɑsjɔ̃] *nf* (*V* **purifier**) purification, purifying; cleansing; refinement; purging.
purificatoire [pyʀifikatwaʀ] *adj* (*littér*) purificatory, purifying, cleansing.
purifier [pyʀifje] (7) **1** *vt* (*gén*) to purify, cleanse; *air, langue, liquide* to purify; *métal* to refine; *âme* to cleanse, purge. **2 se purifier** *vpr* to cleanse o.s.
purin [pyʀɛ̃] *nm* liquid manure.
purisme [pyʀism(ə)] *nm* purism.
puriste [pyʀist(ə)] **1** *adj* purist(ic). **2** *nmf* purist.
puritain, e [pyʀitɛ̃, ɛn] **1** *adj* puritan(ical); (*Hist*) Puritan. **2** *nm,f* puritan; (*Hist*) Puritan.
puritanisme [pyʀitanism(ə)] *nm* puritanism; (*Hist*) Puritanism.
purpurin, e [pyʀpyʀɛ̃, in] *adj* (*littér*) crimson.
pur-sang [pyʀsɑ̃] *nm inv* thoroughbred, purebred.
purulence [pyʀylɑ̃s] *nf* purulence, purulency.
purulent, e [pyʀylɑ̃, ɑ̃t] *adj* purulent.
pus [py] *nm* pus.
pusillanime [pyzilanim] *adj* (*littér*) pusillanimous (*littér*), fainthearted.
pusillanimité [pyzilanimite] *nf* (*littér*) pusillanimity (*littér*), faintheartedness.
pustule [pystyl] *nf* pustule.
pustuleux, -euse [pystylø, øz] *adj* pustular.
putain‡ [pytɛ̃] *nf* pro‡, whore; (*fille facile*) whore, tart‡, tramp‡. (*lit*) **faire la ~** to be a prostitute; (*fig*) to sell one's soul; **ce ~ de réveil!** that goddamn‡ alarm clock!; **~!** bloody hell!** (*Brit*), bugger me!** (*Brit*), goddam it!‡
putatif, -ive [pytatif, iv] *adj* putative, presumed. **père ~** putative father.
pute** [pyt] *nf* pro‡, whore.
putois [pytwa] *nm* (*animal*) polecat; (*fourrure*) polecat (fur); *V* **crier**.
putréfaction [pytʀefaksjɔ̃] *nf* putrefaction. **cadavre en ~** body in a state of putrefaction, putrifying *ou* rotting body.
putréfier [pytʀefje] (7) **1** *vt* to putrefy, rot. **2 se putréfier** *vpr* to putrefy, rot, go rotten.
putrescence [pytʀesɑ̃s] *nf* putrescence.
putrescent, e [pytʀesɑ̃, ɑ̃t] *adj* putrescent.
putrescible [pytʀesibl(ə)] *adj* putrescible.
putride [pytʀid] *adj* putrid.
putridité [pytʀidite] *nf* putridity, putridness.
putsch [putʃ] *nm* putsch.
puzzle [pœzl(ə)] *nm* (*lit*) jigsaw (puzzle); (*fig*) jigsaw.
pygmée [pigme] *nm* pygmy, pigmy. (*fig, péj*) **c'est un vrai ~** he's just a little squirt* (*péj*), he's a little runt* (*péj*).
pyjama [piʒama] *nm* pyjamas (*pl*), pajamas (*pl*) (*US*). **il était en ~(s)** he was in his pyjamas; **acheter un ~** to buy a pair of pyjamas, buy some pyjamas; **2 ~s** 2 pairs of pyjamas; *V* **veste**.
pylône [pilon] *nm* pylon.
pylore [pilɔʀ] *nm* pylorus.
pylorique [pilɔʀik] *adj* pyloric.
pyorrhée [pjɔʀe] *nf* pyorrhoea, pyorrhea.
pyramidal, e, mpl -aux [piʀamidal, o] *adj* pyramid-shaped, pyramid-like, pyramidal (*T*).
pyramide [piʀamid] *nf* (*Anat, Archit, Géom, fig*) pyramid. **~ humaine** human pyramid; **~ des âges** *pyramid-shaped diagram representing population by age-groups.*
pyrénéen, -enne [piʀeneɛ̃, ɛn] **1** *adj* Pyrenean. **2** *nm,f*: **P~(ne)** inhabitant *ou* native of the Pyrenees, Pyrenean.
Pyrénées [piʀene] *nfpl*: **les ~** the Pyrenees.
pyrex [piʀɛks] *nm* ® Pyrex ®. **assiette en ~** Pyrex plate.
pyrite [piʀit] *nf* pyrites.
pyrograveur, -euse [piʀɔgʀavœʀ, øz] *nm,f* pyrographer.
pyrogravure [piʀɔgʀavyʀ] *nf* (*Art*) pyrography, poker-work; (*objet*) pyrograph.
pyrolyse [piʀɔliz] *nf* pyrolysis.
pyromane [piʀɔman] *nmf* (*Méd*) pyromaniac; (*gén, Jur*) arsonist.
pyromètre [piʀɔmɛtʀ(ə)] *nm* pyrometer.
pyrométrie [piʀɔmetʀi] *nf* pyrometry.
pyrométrique [piʀɔmetʀik] *adj* pyrometric.
pyrotechnie [piʀɔtɛkni] *nf* pyrotechnics (*sg*), pyrotechny.
pyrotechnique [piʀɔtɛknik] *adj* pyrotechnic.
Pyrrhon [piʀɔ̃] *nm* Pyrrho.
pyrrhonien, -ienne [piʀɔnjɛ̃, jɛn] **1** *adj* Pyrrhonic, Pyrrhonian. **2** *nm,f* Pyrrhonist, Pyrrhonian.
pyrrhonisme [piʀɔnism(ə)] *nm* Pyrrhonism.
Pyrrhus [piʀys] *nm* Pyrrhus; *V* **victoire**.
Pythagore [pitagɔʀ] *nm* Pythagoras.
pythagoricien, -ienne [pitagɔʀisjɛ̃, jɛn] *adj, nm,f* Pythagorean.
pythagorique [pitagɔʀik] *adj* Pythagorean.
pythagorisme [pitagɔʀism(ə)] *nm* Pythagoreanism, Pythagorism.
Pythie [piti] *nf* Pythia. (*fig: devineresse*) **p~** prophetess.
python [pitɔ̃] *nm* python.
pythonisse [pitɔnis] *nf* prophetess.

Q

Q, q [ky] *nm* (*lettre*) Q, q.
qu' [k(ə)] *V* **que.**
quadragénaire [kwadʀaʒenɛʀ] *adj* (*de quarante ans*) forty-year-old (*épith*); (*de quarante à cinquante ans*) in his (*ou* her) forties. (*hum*) **maintenant que tu es ~** now that you're forty (years old), now that you've reached forty.
Quadragésime [kwadʀaʒezim] *nf* Quadragesima.
quadrangulaire [kwadʀɑ̃gylɛʀ] *adj* quadrangular.
quadrant [kadʀɑ̃] *nm* quadrant.
quadrature [kwadʀatyʀ] *nf* (*gén*) quadrature. (*Math*) **~ du cercle** quadrature of the circle; (*fig*) **c'est la ~ du cercle** it's like trying to square the circle, it's attempting the impossible.
quadriceps [kwadʀisɛps] *nm* quadriceps.
quadriennal, e, *mpl* **-aux** [kwadʀijenal, o] *adj* four-year (*épith*), quadrennial. (*Agr*) **assolement ~** four-year rotation.
quadrijumeaux [kwadʀiʒymo] *adj mpl*: **tubercules ~** corpora quadrigemina, quadrigeminal *ou* quadrigeminate bodies.
quadrilatère [kadʀilatɛʀ] *nm* (*Géom, Mil*) quadrilateral.
quadrillage [kadʀijaʒ] *nm* **(a)** (*action*) (*Mil, Police*) covering, control(ling); (*Admin, Écon*) covering. **la police a établi un ~ serré du quartier** the police have set up a tight control over the area. **(b)** (*dessin*) *[papier]* square pattern; *[tissu]* check pattern; *[rues]* criss-cross *ou* grid pattern *ou* layout.
quadrille [kadʀij] *nm* (*danse, danseurs*) quadrille. **~ des lanciers** lancers.
quadrillé, e [kadʀije] (*ptp de* **quadriller**) *adj papier, feuille* squared.
quadriller [kadʀije] (1) *vt* (*Mil, Police*) to cover, control; (*Admin, Écon*) to cover; *papier* to mark out in squares. **la ville est étroitement quadrillée par la police** the town is well covered by the police, the town is under close *ou* tight police control, the police are positioned throughout the whole town; **la ville est quadrillée par un réseau de rues** the town is criss-crossed by a network of streets, the town has a criss-cross network *ou* a grid pattern of streets.
quadrimoteur [kadʀimɔtœʀ] **1** *adj m* four-engined. **2** *nm* four-engined plane.
quadriparti, e [kwadʀipaʀti] *adj,* **quadripartite** [kwadʀipaʀtit] *adj* (*Bot*) quadripartite. (*Pol*) **conférence quadripartite** *[pays]* four-power conference; *[parti]* four-party conference.
quadriphonie [kadʀifɔni] *nf* quadrophony.
quadriréacteur [kadʀiʀeaktœʀ] *nm* four-engined jet.
quadrisyllabe [kwadʀisilab] *nm* quadrisyllable.
quadrisyllabique [kwadʀisilabik] *adj* quadrisyllabic.
quadrumane [kadʀyman] **1** *adj* quadrumanous. **2** *nm* quadrumane.
quadrupède [kadʀypɛd] **1** *adj* fourfooted, quadruped. **2** *nm* quadruped.
quadruple [kadʀypl(ə)] **1** *adj quantité, rangée, nombre* quadruple. **une quantité ~ de l'autre** a quantity four times (as great as) the other; **en ~ exemplaire/partie** in four copies/parts; *V* **croche.**
2 *nm* (*Math, gén*) quadruple (*de* of). **je l'ai payé le ~/le ~ de l'autre** I paid four times as much for it/four times as much as the other for it; **je vous le rendrai au ~** I'll repay you four times over; **augmenter au ~** to increase fourfold.
quadrupler [kadʀyple] (1) *vti* to quadruple, increase fourfold.
quadruplés, -ées [kadʀyple] (*ptp de* **quadrupler**) *nm,f pl* quadruplets, quads*.
quai [ke] **1** *nm [port]* (*gén*) quay; (*pour marchandises*) wharf, quay; *[gare]* platform; *[rivière]* embankment. **être à ~** *[bateau]* to be alongside (the quay); *[train]* to be in (the station); **sur les ~s de la Seine** on the banks *ou* embankments of the Seine; *V* **accès, billet.**
2: le Quai des Orfèvres police headquarters (in Paris), ≃ (New) Scotland Yard (*Brit*); **le Quai (d'Orsay)** the French Foreign Office.
quaker, -keresse [kwɛkœʀ, kʀɛs] *nm,f* Quaker.
quakerisme [kwɛkœʀism(ə)] *nm* Quakerism.
qualifiable [kalifjabl(ə)] *adj*: **une telle conduite n'est pas ~** such behaviour is beyond description *ou* defies description.
qualificatif, -ive [kalifikatif, iv] **1** *adj adjectif* qualifying. **2** *nm* (*Gram*) qualifier; (*fig: terme, mot*) term.
qualification [kalifikɑsjɔ̃] *nf* **(a)** (*désignation*) label, description.
(b) (*Sport*) **obtenir sa ~** to qualify; **épreuves de ~** qualifying heats *ou* rounds; **la ~ de notre équipe demeure incertaine** it's still not certain whether our team will qualify.
(c) (*aptitude*) qualification. **~ professionnelle** professional qualification.
(d) (*Gram*) qualification.
qualifié, e [kalifje] (*ptp de* **qualifier**) *adj* **(a)** (*compétent*) (*gén*) qualified; (*Ind*) *main d'œuvre, ouvrier* skilled (*épith*). **non ~** unskilled (*épith*).
(b) (*Jur*) *vol, délit* aggravated. (*fig*) **c'est de l'hypocrisie ~e** it's blatant hypocrisy; (*fig*) **c'est du vol ~** it's daylight *ou* sheer robbery.
qualifier [kalifje] (7) **1** *vt* **(a)** *conduite, projets* to describe (*de* as). **~ qn de menteur** to call *ou* label sb a liar, describe sb as a liar; **sa maison qu'il qualifiait pompeusement (de) manoir** his house which he described pompously as a manor, his house which he pompously labelled *ou* termed manor.
(b) (*Sport, gén: rendre apte*) to qualify (*pour* for).
(c) (*Gram*) to qualify.
2 se qualifier *vpr* (*Sport*) to qualify (*pour* for). (*hum*) **il se qualifie d'artiste** he labels *ou* qualifies himself as an artist, he calls himself an artist.
qualitatif, -ive [kalitatif, iv] *adj* qualitative.
qualitativement [kalitativmɑ̃] *adv* qualitatively.
qualité [kalite] *nf* **(a)** *[marchandise]* quality. **de bonne/mauvaise ~** of good *ou* high/bad *ou* poor quality; **produits de ~** high-quality products; **fruits de ~ supérieure** fruit of superior quality, superior-quality fruit; **la ~ de la vie** the quality of life.
(b) *[personne]* (*vertu*) quality; (*don*) skill. **ses ~s de cœur l'ont fait aimer de tous** his noble-heartedness made everyone like him; **il a les ~s requises pour faire ce travail** he has the necessary skills for this job; **cette œuvre a de grandes ~s littéraires** this work has great literary qualities.
(c) (*fonction*) position; (††: *noblesse*) quality. **sa ~ de directeur** his position as manager; **en sa ~ de maire** in his capacity as mayor; (*Admin*) **vos nom, prénom et ~** surname, Christian name and occupation; (*Jur*) **avoir ~ pour** to have authority to; (*frm*) **ès ~s** in an official capacity; **homme de ~††** man of quality.
quand [kɑ̃] **1** *conj* **(a)** (*lorsque*) when. **~ ce sera fini, nous irons prendre un café** when it's finished we'll go and have a coffee; **prête-le-moi pour ~ j'en aurai besoin** lend it to me for when I'll next need it; **sais-tu de ~ était sa dernière lettre?** do you know when his last letter was written? *ou* what was the date of his last letter?; **~ je te le disais!** didn't I tell you so!, I told you so!; **~ je pense que ...!** when I think that...; (*hum*) **~ les poules auront des dents** when pigs learn to fly, when pigs have wings; (*Prov*) **~ le vin est tiré, il faut le boire** once the wine is drawn it must be drunk, once the first step is taken there's no going back; (*Prov*) **~ le chat est loin, les sourls dansent** when the cat's away the mice will play.
(b) (*alors que*) when. **pourquoi ne pas acheter une voiture ~ nous pouvons nous le permettre?** why not buy a car when we can afford it?; **pourquoi vivre ici ~ tu pourrais avoir une belle maison?** why live here when you could have a beautiful house?
(c) ~ bien même even though *ou* if; **~ bien même tu aurais raison, je n'irais pas** even though *ou* even if you were right, I wouldn't go.
(d) ~ même: malgré tous ses défauts elle est ~ même gentille in spite of all her faults she's nevertheless pleasant *ou* she's pleasant nonetheless; **tu aurais ~ même pu me le dire!** even so, you might have told me; **~ même, il exagère!** really, he overdoes it!; **quel crétin ~ même!** what a downright idiot!, really, what an idiot!; (*lit, hum*) **merci ~ même** thanks all the same *ou* just the same; **tu aurais pu venir ~ même** even so you could have come, you could have come all the same *ou* just the same.
2 *adv* when. **~ pars-tu?, ~ est-ce que tu pars?, tu pars ~?*** when are you leaving?; **dis-moi ~ tu pars** tell me when you're leaving *ou* when you'll be leaving; **à ~ le voyage?** when is the journey?; **c'est pour ~?** *[devoir]* when is it due? *ou* for?; *[rendez-vous]* when is it?; *[naissance]* when is it to be?; **ça date de ~?** *[événement]* when did it take place?; *[lettre]* what's the date of it?, when was it written?; *V* **depuis, importer², jusque.**
quant [kɑ̃] **1** *adv*: **~ à** (*pour ce qui est de*) as for, as to; (*au sujet de*) as regards, regarding; **~ à moi** as for me; **~ à affirmer cela** ... as for stating that ... ; **je n'ai rien su ~ à ce qui s'est passé** I knew nothing about *ou* of *ou* as to what happened; **~ à cela, tu peux en être sûr** you can be quite sure about THAT; **~ à cela, je n'en sais rien** as to that *ou* as regards that, I know nothing about it. **2: quant-à-moi** *nm inv*, **quant-à-soi** *nm inv* reserve; **il est resté sur son quant-à-soi** he remained aloof, he held himself *ou* kept himself aloof.
quanta [kwɑ̃ta] *nmpl de* **quantum.**
quantième [kɑ̃tjɛm] *nm* (*Admin*) day (*of the month*).
quantifiable [kɑ̃tifjabl(ə)] *adj* quantifiable. **facteurs non ~s** factors which cannot be quantified, unquantifiable factors.
quantification [kɑ̃tifikɑsjɔ̃] *nf* (*V* **quantifier**) quantification; quantization.
quantifier [kɑ̃tifje] (7) *vt* (*gén, Philos*) to quantify; (*Phys*) to quantize.
quantique [kɑ̃tik] *adj* quantum (*épith*).
quantitatif, -ive [kɑ̃titatif, iv] *adj* quantitative.
quantitativement [kɑ̃titativmɑ̃] *adv* quantitatively.
quantité [kɑ̃tite] *nf* **(a)** (*somme, nombre*) quantity, amount. **la ~ d'eau nécessaire à l'organisme** the amount *ou* quantity of water necessary for the body; **il s'indignait de la ~ de gens qui ne paient pas leurs impôts** he was outraged by the number of people who don't pay their taxes; **en ~s industrielles** in massive *ou* huge amounts.

(b) (*grand nombre*) **(une) ~ de** a great deal of, a lot of; (*nombre*) a great many, a lot of; **des ~s** *ou* **(une) ~ de gens croient que** a great many people *ou* a lot of people believe that; **~ d'indices révèlent que** many signs *ou* a (great) number of signs indicate that; **il y a des fruits en (grande) ~** there is fruit in plenty, fruit is in good supply; **il y a eu des accidents en ~** there have been a great number of *ou* a lot of *ou* a great many accidents; **du travail en ~** a great deal of work.

(c) (*Ling, Sci*) quantity. (*Sci*) **~ négligeable** negligible quantity *ou* amount; (*fig*) **considérer qn comme ~ négligeable** to consider sb as totally insignificant, consider sb of minimal importance, disregard sb.

quantum [kwɑ̃tɔm], *pl* **quanta** *nm* (*Jur, Phys*) quantum.

quarantaine [kaʀɑ̃tɛn] *nf* **(a)** (*âge, nombre*) about forty; *V* **soixantaine. (b)** (*Méd, Naut*) quarantine. **mettre en ~** (*lit*) *malade, animal, navire* to quarantine, put in quarantine; (*fig: ostraciser*) to send to Coventry; *V* **pavillon.**

quarante [kaʀɑ̃t] *adj, nm inv* forty; *pour loc V* **soixante** *et* **an.**

quarantenaire [kaʀɑ̃tnɛʀ] **1** *adj période* forty-year (*épith*); (*Méd, Naut*) quarantine (*épith*). **2** *nm* (*anniversaire*) fortieth anniversary.

quarantième [kaʀɑ̃tjɛm] *adj, nmf* fortieth.

quarantièmement [kaʀɑ̃tjɛmmɑ̃] *adv* in the fortieth place.

quart [kaʀ] **1** *nm* **(a)** (*fraction*) quarter. **un ~ de poulet/de fromage** a quarter chicken/cheese; **un ~ de beurre** a quarter (kilo) of butter; **un ~ de vin** a quarter-litre bottle of wine; **un kilo/une livre un ~** *ou* **et ~** a kilo/a pound and a quarter; **on n'a pas fait le ~ du travail** we haven't done a quarter of the work; **au ~ de poil*** perfectly; **un ~ de siècle** a quarter century; *V* **quatre, tiers, trois.**

(b) (*Mil: gobelet*) beaker (*of 1/4 litre capacity*).

(c) ~ d'heure quarter of an hour; **3 heures moins le ~** (a) quarter to 3; **3 heures et ~, 3 heures un ~** (a) quarter past 3; **il est le ~/moins le ~** it's (a) quarter past/(a) quarter to; **de ~ d'heure en ~ d'heure** every quarter of an hour; **passer un mauvais** *ou* **sale ~ d'heure** to have a bad *ou* nasty time of it; **il lui a fait passer un mauvais ~ d'heure** he gave her a bad time.

(d) (*Naut*) watch. **être de ~** to keep the watch; **prendre le ~** to take the watch; **de ~** *homme, matelot* on watch; **officier de ~** officer of the watch; **petit ~** dogwatch; **grand ~** six-hour watch.

2: (*Sport*) **quarts de finale** quarter finals; **quart-de-rond** *nm, pl* **quarts-de-rond** ovolo, quarter round; (*Mus*) **quart de soupir** semiquaver rest (*Brit*), sixteenth rest (*US*); (*Mus*) **quart de ton** quarter tone; **quart de tour: donner un quart de tour à un bouton** to turn a knob round a quarter (of the way), give a knob a quarter turn; (*Aut*) **partir** *ou* **démarrer au quart de tour** to start (up) first time; **comprendre au quart de tour*** to understand first time off *ou* straight off*, be quick on the uptake.

quarte [kaʀt(ə)] **1** *nf* (*Escrime*) quarte; (*Cartes*) quart; (*Mus*) fourth; (*Hist: deux pintes*) quart. **2** *adj f V* **fièvre.**

quarteron, -onne [kaʀtəʀɔ̃, ɔn] **1** *nm,f* (*métis*) quadroon. **2** *nm* (*péj: groupe*) small *ou* insignificant band, minor group.

quartette [kwaʀtɛt] *nm* (*Mus*) jazz quartet(te).

quartier [kaʀtje] **1** *nm* **(a)** [*ville*] (*Admin: division*) district, area; (*gén: partie*) neighbourhood, district, area, quarter. **~ commerçant/résidentiel** shopping/residential area *ou* quarter; **les vieux ~s de la ville** the old quarter *ou* part of the town; **les gens du ~** the local people, the people of the area *ou* district *ou* neighbourhood; **vous êtes du ~?** do you come from the area? *ou* district? *ou* neighbourhood?, are you (a) local?*; **de ~** *cinéma, épicier* local (*épith*); **le ~ est/ouest de la ville** the east/west end of (the) town; **le ~ des affaires** the business district *ou* quarter; **le ~ latin** the Latin Quarter; *V* **bas**[1], **beau.**

(b) (*Mil*) **~(s)** quarters; **rentrer au(x) ~(s)** to return to quarters; **avoir ~(s) libre(s)** (*Mil*) to have leave from barracks; (*Scol*) to be free *ou* off (for a few hours); (*lit, fig*) **prendre ses ~s d'hiver** to go into winter quarters; (*fig*) **c'est là que nous tenons nos ~s** here's where we have our headquarters (*fig*) *ou* where we hang out*.

(c) (*portion*) [*bœuf*] quarter; [*viande*] large piece, chunk; [*fruit*] piece, segment. (*lit, fig*) **mettre en ~s** to tear to pieces.

(d) (*Astron, Hér*) quarter.

(e) (†: *grâce, pitié*) quarter†. **demander/faire ~** to ask for/give quarter; **ne pas faire de ~** to give no quarter; **pas de ~!** (give) no quarter!

2: (*Mil, fig*) **quartier général** headquarters; (*Mil*) **grand quartier général** general headquarters; (*Naut*) **quartier-maître** *nm, pl* **quartiers-maîtres** ≃ leading seaman; **quartier de noblesse** (*lit*) degree of noble lineage (*representing one generation*); (*fig*) **avoir ses quartiers de noblesse** to be well established and respected; **quartier réservé** red-light district.

quarto [kwaʀto] *adv* fourthly.

quartz [kwaʀts] *nm* quartz.

quartzite [kwaʀtsit] *nm* quartzite.

quasi[1] [kazi] *nm* (*Culin*) *cut of meat from upper part of leg of veal.*

quasi[2] [kazi] **1** *adv* almost, nearly.

2 *préf* near. **~-certitude/-obscurité** near certainty/darkness; **la ~-totalité des dépenses** the near total of the expenditure *ou* expenses, almost the whole of the expenditure.

quasiment [kazimɑ̃] *adv* almost, nearly. **c'est ~ fait** it's almost *ou* nearly done, it's as good as done, it's just about done.

Quasimodo [kazimɔdo] *nf*: **la ~,** *ou* **le dimanche de ~** Low Sunday.

quaternaire [kwatɛʀnɛʀ] **1** *adj* (*gén, Chim*) quaternary; (*Géol*) Quaternary. **2** *nm* (*Géol*) Quaternary.

quatorze [katɔʀz(ə)] *adj, nm inv* fourteen. **avant/après (la guerre de) ~** before/after the First World War; **le ~ juillet** the Fourteenth of July, Bastille Day (*French national holiday*); *pour autres loc V* **six** *et* **chercher.**

quatorzième [katɔʀzjɛm] *adj, nmf* fourteenth; *pour loc V* **sixième.**

quatorzièmement [katɔʀzjɛmmɑ̃] *adv* in the fourteenth place, fourteenthly.

quatrain [katʀɛ̃] *nm* quatrain.

quatre [katʀ(ə)] **1** *adj, nm inv* four. **une robe de ~ sous** a cheap dress; **il avait ~ sous d'économies** he had a modest amount of savings; **s'il avait ~ sous de bon sens** if he had a scrap *ou* modicum of common sense; (*lit, fig*) **aux ~ coins de** in the four corners of; (*Mus*) **à ~ mains** (*adj*) *morceau* for four hands, four-handed; (*adv*) *jouer* four-handed; **à ~ pattes** on all fours; **se disperser aux ~ vents** to scatter to the four winds; **être tiré à ~ épingles** to be dressed up to the nines; **un de ces ~ (matins)*** one of these (fine) days; **faire les ~ cents coups** to get into a lot of trouble, be a real troublemaker; **tomber les ~ fers en l'air** to fall flat on one's back; **faire ses ~ volontés** to do exactly as one pleases; **faire les ~ volontés de qn** to satisfy sb's every whim; **dire à qn ses ~ vérités** to tell sb a few plain *ou* home truths; (*Pol*) **les ~ grands** the Big Four; **monter/descendre (l'escalier) ~ à ~** to rush up/down the stairs four at a time; **manger comme ~** to eat like a wolf *ou* enough for four (people); **se mettre en ~ pour qn** to go out of one's way for sb, put o.s. out for sb; **elle se tenait à ~ pour ne pas rire/pour ne pas le gifler** it was all she could do *ou* she was doing all she could to keep from laughing/smacking him; **ne pas y aller par ~ chemins** not to beat about the bush, make no bones about it; **entre ~ murs** within *ou* between four walls; *V* **couper, entre, trèfle** *etc*; *pour autres loc V* **six.**

2: (*Naut*) **quatre barré** *nm* coxed four; (*Dés*) **quatre(-cent)-vingt-et-un** *nm dice game in casinos*; **quatre heures** *nm inv* afternoon tea *ou* snack; (*Mus*) **(mesure à) quatre-huit** *nm inv* common time; **quatre-mâts** *nm inv* four-master; (*Culin*) **quatre-quarts** *nm inv* pound cake; (*Naut*) **quatre sans barreur** coxless four; **quatre-vingt-dix** *adj, nm inv* ninety; **quatre-vingt-dixième** *adj, nmf* ninetieth; **quatre-vingtième** *adj, nmf* eightieth; **quatre-vingt-onze** *adj, nm inv* ninety-one; **quatre-vingts** *adj, nm inv* eighty; **quatre-vingt-un** *adj, nm inv* eighty-one.

quatrième [katʀijɛm] **1** *adj* fourth. (*fig*) **faire qch en ~ vitesse** to do sth at great speed. **2** *nmf* (*joueur de cartes*) fourth player. **3** *nf* (*Aut: vitesse*) fourth gear; (*Cartes: quarte*) quart; *pour autres loc V* **sixième.**

quatrièmement [katʀijɛmmɑ̃] *adv* fourthly, in the fourth place.

quatrillion [katʀiljɔ̃] *nm* quadrillion (*Brit*), septillion (*US*).

quatuor [kwatɥɔʀ] *nm* (*œuvre, musiciens, fig*) quartet(te). **~ à cordes** string quartet.

que [k(ə)] **1** *conj* **(a)** (*introduisant subordonnée complétive*) that (*souvent omis; avec vb de volonté on emploie la proposition infinitive*). **elle sait ~ tu es prêt** she knows (that) you're ready; **il est agréable qu'il fasse beau** it's nice that the weather's fine; **il est possible qu'elle vienne** it's possible (that) she'll come; **c'est dommage qu'il pleuve** it's a pity (that) it's raining; **l'idée qu'il pourrait échouer** the idea of him *ou* his failing, the idea that he might fail; **je veux/j'aimerais qu'il vienne** I want him/would like him to come **je veux qu'il ne vienne pas** I want him not to come; **j'aimerais qu'il ne vienne pas** I'd rather he didn't come; *V* **craindre, douter, peur** *etc.*

(b) (*remplaçant si, quand, comme etc: non traduit*) **si vous êtes sage et qu'il fasse beau, nous sortirons** if you are good and the weather is fine, we'll go out; **si vous le voyez ou ~ vous lui téléphoniez ...** if you see him or phone him ... ; **il vous recevra quand il rentrera et qu'il aura déjeuné** he'll see you when he comes home and he's had a meal; **comme la maison était petite et qu'il n'y avait pas de jardin** as the house was small and there was no garden; **bien qu'il soit en retard et ~ nous soyons pressés** although he's late and we're in a hurry.

(c) (*hypothèse*) **il ira qu'il le veuille ou qu'il ne le veuille pas** he'll go whether he wants to or not *ou* whether he likes it or not; (*conséquence*) **il cria si fort qu'on le fit sortir** he shouted so loudly that he was sent out; **la classe n'est pas si avancée qu'il ne puisse suivre** the class is not too advanced for him to keep up *ou* is not so advanced that he can't keep up; (*but*) **tenez-le qu'il ne tombe pas** hold him in case he falls *ou* so that he won't fall; **venez ~ nous causions** come along and we'll have *ou* so that we can have a chat; (*temps*) **elle venait à peine de sortir qu'il se mit à pleuvoir** she had no sooner gone out than *ou* she had hardly *ou* just gone out when it started raining; **ils se connaissaient depuis 10 minutes qu'ils étaient déjà amis** they had known each other for only 10 minutes and already they were friends; **ça fait 2 ans qu'il est là** he has been here (for) 2 years; **ça fait 2 ans qu'il est parti** it is 2 years since he left, he left 2 years ago; *V* **attendre, ne.**

(d) (*3e personne: ordre, souhait, résignation etc*) **qu'il se taise!** I wish he would be quiet!; **~ la lumière soit** let there be light; **~ la guerre finisse!** if only the war would end!; **eh bien, qu'il vienne!** all right, he can come *ou* let him come; **~ m'importe!** what do I care?, I don't care!; **~ le Seigneur ait pitié de lui!** (may) the Lord have mercy upon him.

(e) (*comparaison*) (*avec plus, moins*) than; (*avec aussi, autant, tel*) as. **la campagne est plus reposante ~ la mer** the country is more restful than the sea; **il est plus petit qu'elle** he's smaller than her *ou* than she is; **elle est tout aussi capable ~ vous** she's just as capable as you (are); **j'ai laissé la maison telle ~ je l'avais trouvée** I left the house (just) as I found it; *V* **bien, condition, moins** *etc.*

2 *adv* **(a)** (*excl*) (*devant adj, adv*) how; (*devant n sg*) what a; (*devant npl*) what a lot of. **~ tu es lent!** aren't you slow!; **ce ~ tu**

es lent!* you're so slow!; **qu'est-ce ~ tu es lent!** how slow you are!; **~ de monde, ce qu'il y a du monde*, qu'est-ce qu'il y a comme monde** what a crowd (there is)!, what a lot of people!; **~ de mal vous vous donnez!** what a lot of trouble you're taking!; **qu'il joue bien!, ce qu'il joue bien!*, qu'est-ce qu'il joue bien!** doesn't he play well!, what a good player he is!

(b) (*avec ne: excl ou interrog*) why. **~ n'es-tu venu me voir?** why didn't you come to see me?

3 *pron* **(a)** (*relatif: objet direct*) (*personne*) that, whom (*frm*); (*chose, animal*) which, that (*gén omis*); (*temps*) when. **Paul, ~ je ne voyais même pas, m'a appelé** Paul, who *ou* whom I couldn't even see, called me; **les enfants ~ tu vois jouer dans la rue** the children that *ou* whom you see playing in the street; **c'est le concert le plus beau ~ j'aie jamais entendu** it's the finest concert (that) I have ever heard; **l'étiquette, ~ j'avais pourtant bien collée, est tombée** the label, which I stuck on properly, fell off all the same; **la raison qu'il a donnée** the reason (that *ou* which) he gave; **tu te souviens de l'hiver qu'il a fait si froid?*** do you remember the winter (when) it was so cold?; **un jour/un été ~** one day/one summer when.

(b) (*attrib*) **quel homme charmant ~ votre voisin!** what a charming man your neighbour is; **distrait qu'il est, il n'a rien vu** dreamy as he is, he didn't notice anything; **pour ignorante qu'elle soit** ignorant though she may be, however ignorant she is *ou* may be; **c'est un inconvénient ~ de ne pas avoir de voiture** it's inconvenient not having a car; **plein d'attentions qu'il était ce jeune homme*** he was so considerate that young man was*; **de brune qu'elle était, elle est devenue blonde** once brunette *ou* brunette at one time, she has now turned blonde; **en bon fils qu'il est** being the good son (that) he is.

(c) (*interrog: dir, indir*) what; (*discriminatif*) which. **~ fais-tu?, qu'est-ce ~ tu fais?** what are you doing?; **qu'est-ce qui vous prend?** what has come over you?; **qu'en sais-tu?** what do you know?; **qu'est-ce qu'il y a?, qu'est-ce?** what is it?, what's the matter?; **qu'est-ce ~ c'est ~ cette histoire?** what's all this about?, what's it all about?; **il ne dit pas ce qu'il fait** he doesn't say what he's doing; **je pense ~ oui/non** I think/don't think so; **mais il n'a pas de voiture! — il dit ~ si** but he has no car! — he says he has; **qu'est-ce ~ tu préfères, le rouge ou le noir?** which (one) do you prefer, the red or the black?; *V* **ce, depuis, voici** *etc.*

(d) (*loc*) **je ne l'y ai pas autorisé, ~ je sache** I didn't give him permission to do so, as far as I know, I don't know that *ou* I'm not aware that I gave him permission to do so; **(il n'est pas venu) ~ je sache** (he didn't come) as far as I know *ou* am aware; **qu'il dit!*** that's what he says!, that's his story!, so he says!; **~ tu crois!*** that's what you think!; **~ oui!** yes indeed!, quite so!; **~ non!** certainly not!, not at all!; **mais il n'en veut pas! — ~ si/non** but he doesn't want any! — yes, he does/no, he doesn't.

Québec [kebɛk] *n* Quebec.

québécois, -e [kebekwa, waz] **1** *adj* Quebec. **le Parti ~** the Parti Québécois. **2** *nm* (*Ling*) Quebec French. **3** *nm,f*: **Q~(e)** Quebecker, Quebecer, Québécois (*Can*).

quel, quelle [kɛl] **1** *adj* **(a)** (*interrog: dir, indir*) (*être animé: attrib*) who; (*être animé: épith*) what; (*chose*) what. **~ est cet auteur?** who is that author?; **sur ~ auteur va-t-il parler?** what author is he going to talk about?; **quelles ont été les raisons de son départ?** what were the reasons for his leaving? *ou* departure?; **dans ~s pays êtes-vous allé?** what countries have you been to?; **lui avez-vous dit à quelle adresse (il faut) envoyer la lettre?** have you told him the *ou* what address to send the letter to?; **j'ignore ~ est l'auteur de ces poèmes** I don't know who wrote these poems *ou* who the author of these poems is.

(b) (*interrog discriminatif*) which. **~ acteur préférez-vous?** which actor do you prefer?; **~ est le vin le moins cher des trois?** which wine is the cheapest of the three?

(c) (*excl*) what. **quelle surprise/coïncidence!** what a surprise/coincidence!; **~ courage/temps!** what courage/weather!; **~s charmants enfants!** what charming children!; **~ dommage qu'il soit parti!** what a pity he's gone!; **~ imbécile je suis!** what a fool I am!; **quelle chance!** what (a stroke of) luck!; **~ toupet!*** what (a) cheek!; **~ sale temps!** what filthy weather!; **il a vu ~s amis fidèles il avait** he saw what faithful friends he had; **j'ai remarqué avec quelle attention ils écoutaient** I noticed how attentively they were listening.

(d) (*relatif*) (*être animé*) whoever; (*chose*) whatever; (*discriminatif*) whichever, whatever. **quelle que soit votre décision, écrivez-nous** write to us whatever your decision (may be) *ou* whatever you decide; **~ que soit le train que vous preniez, vous arriverez trop tard** whichever *ou* whatever train you take, you will be too late; **quelles que soient les conséquences** whatever the consequences; **quelle que soit la personne qui vous répondra** whoever answers you, whichever person answers you; **~ qu'il soit, le prix sera toujours trop élevé** whatever the price (is), it will still be too high; **les hommes, ~s qu'ils soient** men, whoever they may be.

2 *pron interrog* which. **de tous ces enfants, ~ est le plus intelligent?** of all these children which (one) is the most intelligent?; **des deux solutions quelle est celle que vous préférez?** of the two solutions, which (one) do you prefer?

quelconque [kɛlkɔ̃k] *adj* **(a)** (*n'importe quel*) some (or other), any. **une lettre envoyée par un ami ~ ou par un ~ de ses amis** a letter sent by some friend of his *ou* by some friend or other (of his); **choisis un stylo ~ parmi ceux-là** choose any pen from among those; **sous un prétexte ~** on some pretext or other; **pour une raison ~** for some reason (or other); **à partir d'un point ~ du cercle** from any point on the circle; *V* **triangle.**

(b) (*moindre*) **un ou une ~** any, the least *ou* slightest; **il n'a pas manifesté un désir ~ d'y aller** he didn't show the slightest *ou* least desire *ou* any desire to go.

(c) (*médiocre*) *repas* poor, indifferent; *élève, devoir* poor; *acteur* poor, second-rate. **c'est un repas/devoir ~** this meal/piece of homework isn't up to much*, this is a poor meal/piece of homework; **c'est quelqu'un de très ~** (*laid*) he's a very plain-looking *ou* ordinary-looking sort of person; (*ordinaire*) he's a very ordinary *ou* nondescript sort of person.

quelque [kɛlk(ə)] **1** *adj indéf* **(a)** (*sans pl*) some. **il habite à ~ distance d'ici** he lives some distance *ou* way from here; **cela fait ~ temps que je ne l'ai vu** I haven't seen him for some time *ou* for a while, it's some time *ou* a while since I've seen him; **il faut trouver ~ autre solution** we'll have to find some other solution; **j'ai ~ peine à croire cela** I find it rather *ou* somewhat *ou* a little difficult to believe; **avec ~ impatience/inquiétude** with some impatience/anxiety; **désirez-vous ~ autre chose?** would you like something *ou* anything else?

(b) (*pl*) a few, some. **M Dupont va vous dire ~s mots** Mr Dupont is going to say a few words (to you); **~s milliers (de)** a few *ou* several thousand; **il ne peut rester que ~s instants** he can only stay (for) a few moments; **~s autres** some *ou* a few others; **avez-vous ~s feuilles de papier à me passer?** have you any *ou* some *ou* a few sheets of paper you could let me have?

(c) (*pl avec art: petit nombre*) few. **les ~s enfants qui étaient venus** the few children who had come; **ces ~s poèmes** these few poems; **les ~s centaines/milliers de personnes qui ...** the several *ou* few hundred/thousand people who ... .

(d) ~ ... que whatever; (*discriminatif*) whichever, whatever; **de ~ façon que l'on envisage le problème** whatever *ou* whichever way you look at the problem; **par ~ temps qu'il fasse** whatever the weather (may be *ou* is like).

(e) ~ part somewhere; **posez votre paquet ~ part dans un coin** put your parcel down in a corner somewhere; (*euph: W.-C.*) **je vais ~ part** I'm going to wash my hands (*euph*); (**euph: derrière*) **tu veux mon pied ~ part?** do you want a kick somewhere where it hurts?* (*euph*).

(f) en ~ sorte (*pour ainsi dire*) as it were, so to speak; (*bref*) in a word; **le liquide s'était en ~ sorte solidifié** the liquid had solidified as it were *ou* so to speak; **en ~ sorte, tu refuses** in a word, you refuse.

2 *adv* **(a)** (*environ, à peu près*) some, about. **il y a ~ 20 ans qu'il enseigne ici** he has been teaching here for some *ou* about 20 years *ou* for 20 years or so; **ça a augmenté de ~ 50 F** it's gone up by about 50 francs *ou* by 50 francs or so *ou* by some 50 francs.

(b) et ~(s)*: 20 kg et ~(s) a bit over 20 kg*; **il doit être 3 heures et ~s** it must be a bit after 3*.

(c) ~ peu rather, somewhat; **~ peu déçu** rather *ou* somewhat disappointed; **il est ~ peu menteur** he is something of *ou* a bit of a liar.

(d) (*littér*) **~ ... que** however; **~ lourde que soit la tâche** however heavy the task may be.

quelque chose [kɛlkəʃoz] *pron indéf* **(a)** something. **~ d'extraordinaire** something extraordinary; **~ d'autre** something else; **puis-je faire ~ pour vous?** is there anything *ou* something I can do for you?; **il a ~ (qui ne va pas)** (*maladie*) there's something wrong *ou* the matter with him; (*ennuis*) there's something the matter (with him); **vous prendrez bien ~ (à boire)** you'll have something to drink; **il est ~ aux PTT*** he's got something to do with the Post Office; **il/ça y est pour ~** he/it has got something to do with it; **il y a ~ comme une semaine** something like a week ago, a week or so ago.

(b) (*: *intensif*) **il a plu ~!** it rained something dreadful!*, it didn't half rain!*; **je tiens ~ (de bien) comme rhume!** I've got a really dreadful cold, I don't half have a (dreadful) cold*; **il se prend pour ~** he thinks he's quite something.

(c) (*loc*) (*lit, fig*) **faire ~ à qn** to have an effect on sb; **ça alors, c'est ~!** that's (a bit) too much!, that's a bit stiff!*; **je t'ai apporté un petit ~** I've brought you a little something; *V* **déjà, dire.**

quelquefois [kɛlkəfwa] *adv* sometimes, occasionally, at times.

quelques-uns, -unes [kɛlkəzœ̃, yn] *pron indéf pl* some, a few. **~ de nos lecteurs/ses amis** some *ou* a few of our readers/his friends; **privilège réservé à ~** privilege reserved for a very few.

quelqu'un [kɛlkœ̃] *pron indéf* somebody, someone; (*avec nég*) anybody, anyone. **~ d'autre** somebody *ou* someone else; **c'est ~ de sûr/d'important** he's a reliable/an important person, he's someone reliable/important; **il faudrait ~ de plus** one more person *ou* somebody *ou* someone else would be needed; **ce savant, c'est ~** this scientist is (a) somebody; **ça alors, c'est ~!*†** that's (a bit) too much!, that's a bit stiff!*

quémander [kemɑ̃de] (1) *vt argent, faveur* to beg for; *louanges* to beg *ou* fish *ou* angle for.

quémandeur, -euse [kemɑ̃dœʀ, øz] *nm,f* (*littér*) beggar.

qu'en-dira-t-on [kɑ̃diʀatɔ̃] *nm inv* (*commérage*) gossip. **il se moque du ~** he doesn't care what people say *ou* about gossip.

quenelle [kənɛl] *nf* (*Culin*) quenelle.

quenotte [kənɔt] *nf* (*langage enfantin*) tooth, toothy-peg (*langage enfantin*).

quenouille [kənuj] *nf* distaff; *V* **tomber.**

querelle [kəʀɛl] *nf* **(a)** (*dispute*) quarrel. **~ d'amoureux** lovers' tiff; **~ d'Allemand, mauvaise ~** quarrel over nothing, unreasonable quarrel; **chercher une ~ d'Allemand ou une mauvaise ~ à qn** to pick a quarrel with sb for nothing *ou* for no reason at all; **~ de famille ou familiale** family quarrel *ou* squabble; *V* **chercher, vider.**

(b) (††, *littér: cause, parti*) cause, quarrel†. **épouser ou embrasser la ~ de qn** to take up *ou* fight sb's cause, fight sb's quarrels.

quereller [kəʀele] (1) **1** *vt* (†: *gronder*) to scold. **2 se quereller** *vpr* to quarrel (with one another).

querelleur, -euse [kɔʀɛlœʀ, øz] *adj* quarrelsome.
quérir [keʀiʀ] *vt* (*littér: chercher*) **envoyer** *ou* **faire ~ qn** to summon sb, bid sb (to) come†; **aller ~ qn** to go seek sb†, go in quest of sb†.
questeur [kɥɛstœʀ] *nm* (*Antiq*) quaestor; (*Pol française*) questeur (*administrative and financial officer elected to the French Parliament*).
question [kɛstjɔ̃] *nf* **(a)** (*demande*) (*gén*) question; (*pour lever un doute*) query, question. **sans (poser de) ~s** without asking any questions; without raising any queries; **évidemment! cette ~!** *ou* **quelle ~!** obviously! what a question!; **~ piège** (*d'apparence facile*) trick question; (*pour nuire à qn*) loaded question; **~ subsidiaire** decisive *ou* deciding question (*in a competition*); (*Pol*) **poser la ~ de confiance** to ask for a vote of confidence.
(b) (*problème*) question, matter, issue. **la ~ est délicate** it's a delicate question *ou* matter; **la ~ est de savoir si** the question is whether; **~s économiques/sociales** economic/social questions *ou* matters *ou* issues; (*Presse*) **~ d'actualité** topical question; **la ~ sociale** the social question *ou* issue; **sortir de la ~** to stray *ou* wander from the point; **la ~ n'est pas là** that's not the point; **c'est toute la ~, c'est la grosse ~*** that's the big question, that's the crux of the matter, that's the whole point; **il n'y a pas de ~, c'est lui le meilleur** without question he's the best, there's no question about it — he's the best; **c'est une ~ de temps** it's a question *ou* matter of time; **c'est une ~ d'heures/de vie ou de mort/d'habitude** it's a matter *ou* question of hours/of life or death/of habit; *V* **autre.**
(c) (*: *en ce qui concerne*) **~ argent** as far as money goes, money-wise*; **l'aider oui, mais ~ de tout faire, sûrement pas** help him I will but as for doing everything for him, I certainly won't.
(d) il est ~: de quoi est-il ~? what is it about?; **il fut d'abord ~ du budget** first they spoke about *ou* discussed the budget; **il est ~ de lui comme ministre** *ou* **qu'il soit ministre** there's some question of him *ou* his being *ou* becoming a minister; **il n'est plus ~ de ce fait dans la suite** no further mention of this fact is made subsequently; **il n'est pas ~ que nous y renoncions/d'y renoncer** there's no question of our *ou* us giving it up/of giving it up; **il n'en est pas ~!** there's no question of it!; **moi y aller? pas ~!*** me go? nothing doing!* *ou* no way!‡
(e) en ~ in question; **hors de ~** out of the question; **la personne en ~** the person in question; **mettre** *ou* **remettre en ~** *autorité* to question, challenge; *science* to question, call *ou* bring in(to) question; **c'est notre vie même qui est en ~ ici** it's our very lives that are at stake here; **tout est remis en ~ à cause du mauvais temps** the bad weather throws the whole thing back into question; **la remise en ~ de nos accords** the renewed doubt surrounding our agreements, the fact that our agreements are once again in doubt *ou* question.
(f) (*Hist: torture*) question. **soumettre qn à la ~, infliger la ~ à qn** to put sb to the question.
questionnaire [kɛstjɔnɛʀ] *nm* questionnaire.
questionner [kɛstjɔne] (1) *vt* (*interroger*) to question (*sur* about). **arrête de ~ toujours comme ça** stop pestering me with questions all the time, stop questioning me all the time.
questionneur, -euse [kɛstjɔnœʀ, øz] *nm,f* questioner.
quête [kɛt] *nf* **(a)** (*collecte*) collection. **faire la ~** *[prêtre]* to take (the) collection; *[jongleur]* to go round with the hat; *[quêteur]* to collect for charity.
(b) (*littér: recherche*) *[Graal]* quest; *[absolu]* pursuit. **âme en ~ d'absolu** soul in pursuit *ou* quest *ou* search of the absolute.
(c) se mettre en ~ de *pain* to set out to look for *ou* to find, go in search of; *appartement* to (go on the) hunt for; **être en ~ de travail** to be looking for work.
quêter [kete] (1) **1** *vi* (*à l'église*) to take the collection; (*dans la rue*) to collect money. **~ pour les aveugles** to collect for the blind.
2 *vt louanges* to seek (after), fish *ou* angle for; *suffrages, sourire, regard* to seek.
quêteur, -euse [kɛtœʀ, øz] *nm,f* (*dans la rue, à l'église*) collector.
quetsche [kwɛtʃ(ə)] *nf* (*variety of*) damson.
queue [kø] **1** *nf* **(a)** *[animal, lettre, note, avion, comète]* tail; *[orage]* tail end; *[classement]* bottom; *[casserole, poêle]* handle; *[fruit, feuille]* stalk; *[fleur]* stem, stalk; *[train, colonne]* rear. **en ~ de phrase** at the end of the sentence; **en ~ de liste/classe** at the bottom of the list/class; **en ~ (de train)** at the rear of the train; **compartiments de ~** rear compartments; **commencer par la ~** to begin at the end.
(b) (*file de personnes*) queue (*Brit*), line (*US*). **faire la ~** to queue (up) (*Brit*), stand in line (*US*); **il y a 2 heures de ~** there's 2 hours' queuing (*Brit*) *ou* standing in line (*US*); **mettez-vous à la ~** join the queue (*Brit*) *ou* line (*US*); **à la ~** in the queue (*Brit*), in line (*US*).
(c) (*loc*) **la ~ basse*** *ou* **entre les jambes*** with one's tail between one's legs; **à la ~ leu leu** *marcher, arriver* in single *ou* Indian file; *venir se plaindre* one after the other; **il n'y en avait pas la ~ d'un*** there wasn't the sniff of one*; (*Aut*) **faire une ~ de poisson à qn** to cut in front of sb; **finir en ~ de poisson** to finish up in the air, come to an abrupt end; **histoire sans ~ ni tête*** cock-and-bull story.
2: queue d'aronde dovetail; **assemblage en queue d'aronde** dovetail joint; **queue de billard** billiard cue; **queue de cheval** ponytail; **queue-de-morue** *nf, pl* **queues-de-morue** (*pinceau*) (medium) paintbrush; (*habit*) tails (*pl*), tail coat; **queue-de-pie** *nf, pl* **queues-de-pie** (*basques*) tails (*pl*); (*habit*) tails (*pl*), tail coat; **queue-de-rat** *nf, pl* **queues-de-rat** round file; **queue de vache** *adj inv couleur, cheveux* reddish-brown.
queux [kø] *nm V* **maître.**
qui [ki] **1** *pron* **(a)** (*interrog sujet*) who. **~** *ou* **~ est-ce ~ l'a vu?** who saw him?; **~ est-il/elle?** who is he/she?; **on m'a raconté ... — ~ ça?** somebody told me ... — who was that?; **~ d'entre eux/parmi vous saurait?** which of them/ of you would know?; **~ va là?** (*Mil*) who goes there?; (*gén*) who's there?; *V* **que.**
(b) (*interrog objet*) who, whom. **elle a vu ~?*, ~ est-ce qu'elle a vu?*** who did she see?; **~ a-t-elle vu?** who *ou* whom (*frm*) did she see?; (*surprise*) **elle a vu ~?** she saw WHO?, WHO did she see?; **à** *ou* **avec ~ voulez-vous parler?** who would you like to *ou* do you wish to speak to?, who is it you want to speak to?, to whom (*frm*) do you wish to speak?; **à ~ est ce sac?** whose bag is this?, who does this bag belong to?, whose is this bag?; **à ~ donc parlais-tu?** who was it you were talking to?, who were you talking to?; **de ~ est la pièce?** who is the play by?; **chez ~ allez-vous?** whose house are you going to?
(c) (*interrog indir*) (*sujet*) who; (*objet*) who, whom (*frm*). **je me demande ~ est là/~ il a invité** I wonder who's there/who *ou* whom (*frm*) he has invited; **elle ne sait à ~ se plaindre/pour ~ voter** she doesn't know who to complain to/who to vote for, she doesn't know to whom to complain/for whom to vote (*frm*); **vous devinez ~ me l'a dit! c'est ~ vous savez!** you can guess who told me! it was you-know-who!*
(d) (*relatif sujet*) (*être animé*) who, that*; (*chose*) which, that. **Paul, ~ traversait le pont, trébucha** Paul, who was crossing the bridge, tripped; **les amis ~ viennent ce soir sont américains** the friends who *ou* that* are coming tonight are American; **il a un perroquet ~ parle** he's got a talking parrot, he's got a parrot which *ou* that talks; **c'est le plus grand peintre ~ ait jamais vécu** he is the greatest painter that ever lived; **prenez les assiettes ~ sont sur la table** take the plates (which *ou* that are) on the table; **la table, ~ était en acajou, était très lourde** the table, which was mahogany, was very heavy; **je la vis ~ nageait vers le rivage** I saw her (as she was) swimming towards the bank; **j'en connais ~ seraient heureux ...** I know some who would be happy ... ; *V* **ce, moi, voici** *etc.*
(e) (*relatif avec prép*) **l'ami de ~ je vous ai parlé** the friend (that *ou* who* *ou* whom (*frm*) I spoke to you about; **l'auteur sur l'œuvre de ~ elle a écrit une thèse** the author whose work she wrote a thesis on *ou* on whose work she wrote a thesis, the author on the work of whom she wrote a thesis (*frm*); **le patron pour ~ il travaille** the employer (that *ou* who* *ou* whom (*frm*)) he works for, the employer for whom he works (*frm*); **les docteurs sans ~ il n'aurait pu être sauvé** the doctors without whom he couldn't have been saved.
(f) (*relatif sans antécédent: être animé*) whoever, anyone who. **amenez ~ vous voulez** bring along whoever *ou* anyone *ou* who you like *ou* please; **cela m'a été dit par ~ vous savez** I was told that by you-know-who*; **ira ~ voudra** let whoever wants *ou* anyone who wants to go go; **c'est à ~ des deux mentira le plus** each tries to outdo the other in lying *ou* in lies; **il a dit à ~ voulait l'écouter que ...** he told anyone who *ou* whoever would listen *ou* cared to listen that ... ; **je le dirai à ~ de droit** I will tell whoever is concerned *ou* is the proper authority; **j'interdis à ~ que ce soit d'entrer ici** I'm not letting anybody (come) in here, I forbid anyone to come in here; **(~ que ce soit) ~ a fait cette faute ne va pas aller le dire!** whoever (the person is who) made this mistake is not going to say so!; **~ les verrait ensemble ne devinerait jamais qu'ils se détestent** anyone seeing them together would never guess (that) they can't stand one another; **à ~ mieux mieux** (*gén*) each one more so than the other; *crier* each one louder than the other; *frapper* each one harder than the other; **ils ont sauvé des flammes tout ce qu'ils ont pu: ~ une chaise, ~ une table, ~ une radio** they saved whatever they could from the fire: some took a chair, some a table, others a radio.
(g) (*Prov*) **~ m'aime me suive** come all ye faithful (*hum*), come along you folks; **~ va lentement va sûrement** more haste less speed (*Prov*); **~ vivra verra** what will be will be (*Prov*); **~ a bu boira** a leopard never changes its spots, once a thief always a thief (*Prov*); **~ aime bien châtie bien** spare the rod and spoil the child (*Prov*); **~ donne aux pauvres prête à Dieu** charity will be rewarded in heaven; **~ dort dîne** he who sleeps forgets his hunger; **~ ne dit mot consent** silence gives consent; **~ ne risque rien** *ou* **n'ose rien n'a rien** nothing venture(d) nothing gain(ed); **~ paie ses dettes s'enrichit** the rich man is the one who pays his debts; **~ peut le plus peut le moins** he who can do more can do less; **~ casse les verres les paye** you pay for your mistakes; **~ sème le vent récolte la tempête** he who sows the wind shall reap the whirlwind; **~ se ressemble s'assemble** birds of a feather flock together (*Prov*); **~ se sent morveux, qu'il se mouche** if the cap *ou* shoe (*US*) fits, wear it (*Prov*); **~ s'y frotte s'y pique** beware the man who crosses swords with us; **~ trop embrasse mal étreint** he who grasps at too much loses everything; **~ va à la chasse perd sa place** he who leaves his place loses it; **~ veut voyager loin ménage sa monture** he who takes it slow and easy goes a long way; **~ veut la fin veut les moyens** he who wills the end wills the means; **~ veut noyer son chien l'accuse de la rage** give a dog a bad name and hang him; **~ n'entend qu'une cloche n'entend qu'un son** one should hear both sides of a question; **~ vole un œuf vole un bœuf** he that will steal a pin will steal a pound (*surtout Brit*).
2: qui-vive? *excl* who goes there?; **être sur le qui-vive** to be on the alert.
quia [kɥija] *adv* **à ~†: mettre à ~** to confound sb†, nonplus sb; **être à ~** to be at a loss for an answer.
quiche [kiʃ] *nf*: **~ (lorraine)** quiche (Lorraine).
quiconque [kikɔ̃k] (*frm*) **1** *pron rel* (*celui qui*) whoever, anyone who, whosoever†. **~ a tué sera jugé** whoever has killed will be judged; **la loi punit ~ est coupable** the law punishes anyone who is guilty.
2 *pron indéf* (*n'importe qui, personne*) anyone, anybody. **je le sais mieux que ~** I know better than anyone (else); **il ne veut**

recevoir d'ordres de ~ he won't take orders from anyone *ou* anybody.
quidam [kɥidam] *nm* (†, *hum: individu*) chap, cove (†, *hum*).
quiet, quiète [kjɛ, kjɛt] *adj* (*littér*,††) calm, tranquil.
quiétisme [kɥijetism(ə)] *nm* quietism.
quiétiste [kɥijetist(ə)] *adj, nmf* quietist.
quiétude [kjetyd] *nf* (*littér*) *[lieu]* quiet, tranquility; *[personne]* peace (of mind). **en toute** ~ (*sans soucis*) with complete peace of mind; (*sans obstacle*) in (complete) peace.
quignon [kiɲɔ̃] *nm*: ~ **(de pain)** (*croûton*) crust (of bread); (*morceau*) hunk *ou* chunk of bread.
quille [kij] *nf* **(a)** skittle. **(jeu de)** ~**s** ninepins, skittles; *V* **chien. (b)** (*: *jambe*) pin*. (*arg Mil*) **la** ~ demob (*arg Brit*). **(c)** (*Naut*) keel. **la** ~ **en l'air** bottom up(wards), keel up.
quincaillerie [kɛ̃kɑjʀi] *nf* (*ustensiles, métier*) hardware, ironmongery (*Brit*); (*magasin*) hardware shop *ou* store, ironmonger's (shop) (*Brit*); (*fig péj: bijoux*) jewellery. **elle a sorti toute sa** ~ she has decked herself out *ou* loaded herself down with every available piece of jewellery.
quincaillier, -ière [kɛ̃kɑje, jɛʀ] *nm,f* hardware dealer, ironmonger (*Brit*).
quinconce [kɛ̃kɔ̃s] *nm*: **en** ~ in staggered rows.
quinine [kinin] *nf* quinine.
quinquagénaire [kɛ̃kaʒenɛʀ] *adj* (*de cinquante ans*) fifty-year-old (*épith*); (*de cinquante à soixante ans*) in his (*ou* her) fifties. (*hum*) **maintenant que tu es** ~ now that you're fifty (years old), now that you've reached fifty.
Quinquagésime [kɥɛ̃kwaʒezim] *nf* Quinquagesima.
quinquennal, e, *mpl* **-aux** [kɥɛ̃kɥenal, o] *adj* five-year (*épith*), quinquennial. (*Agr*) **assolement** ~ five-year rotation.
quinquet [kɛ̃kɛ] *nm* (*Hist*) oil lamp. (*yeux*) ~**s*** peepers* (*hum*).
quinquina [kɛ̃kina] *nm* (*Bot, Pharm*) cinchona. **(apéritif au)** ~ *quinine tonic wine.*
quint, e[1] [kɛ̃, kɛ̃t] *adj V* **Charles.**
quintal, *pl* **-aux** [kɛ̃tal, o] *nm* quintal (*100 kg*); (*Can*) hundredweight.
quinte[2] [kɛ̃t] *nf* **(a)** (*Méd*) ~ **(de toux)** coughing fit. **(b)** (*Mus*) fifth; (*Escrime*) quinte; (*Cartes*) quint.
quintessence [kɛ̃tesɑ̃s] *nf* (*Chim, Philos, fig*) quintessence. (*hum*) **abstracteur de** ~ hair-splitter.
quintette [kɛ̃tɛt] *nm* (*morceau, musiciens*) quintet(te).
quinteux, -euse [kɛ̃tø, øz] *adj* (††, *littér*) *vieillard* crotchety, crabbed†.
quintillion [kɛ̃tiljɔ̃] *nm* quintillion (*Brit*), nonillion (*US*).
quintuple [kɛ̃typl(ə)] **1** *adj quantité, rangée, nombre* quintuple. **une quantité** ~ **de l'autre** a quantity five times (as great as) the other; **en** ~ **exemplaire/partie** in five copies/parts.
2 *nm* (*Math, gén*) quintuple (*de* of). **je l'ai payé le** ~**/le** ~ **de l'autre** I paid five times as much for it/five times as much as the other for it; **je vous le rendrai au** ~ I'll repay you five times over; **augmenter au** ~ to increase fivefold.
quintupler [kɛ̃typle] (1) *vti* to quintuple, increase fivefold.
quintuplés, -ées [kɛ̃typle] (*ptp de* **quintupler**) *nm,f pl* quintuplets, quins*.
quinzaine [kɛ̃zɛn] *nf* (*nombre*) about fifteen, fifteen or so; (*salaire*) fortnightly (*Brit*) *ou* fortnight's (*Brit*) *ou* two weeks' pay. (*deux semaines*) ~ **(de jours)** fortnight (*Brit*), two weeks; ~ **publicitaire** *ou* **commerciale** (two-week) sale; **la** ~ **du blanc** (two-week) white sale; **'**~ **des soldes'** 'sales fortnight' (*Brit*); *pour autres loc V* **soixantaine.**
quinze [kɛ̃z] **1** *nm inv* fifteen. (*Rugby*) **le** ~ **de France** the French fifteen; *pour autres loc V* **six.**
2 *adj inv* fifteen. **le** ~ **août** Assumption; **demain en** ~ a fortnight tomorrow (*Brit*), two weeks tomorrow; **lundi en** ~ a fortnight (*Brit*) *ou* two weeks on Monday; **dans** ~ **jours** in a fortnight (*Brit*), in a fortnight's time (*Brit*), in two weeks, in two weeks' time.
quinzième [kɛ̃zjɛm] *adj, nmf* fifteenth; *pour loc V* **sixième.**
quinzièmement [kɛ̃zjɛmmɑ̃] *adv* in the fifteenth place, fifteenthly.
quiproquo [kipʀɔko] *nm* **(a)** (*méprise sur une personne*) mistake; (*malentendu sur un sujet*) misunderstanding. **le** ~ **durait depuis un quart d'heure, sans qu'ils s'en rendent compte** they had been talking at cross-purposes for a quarter of an hour without realizing it.
(b) (*Théât*) (case of) mistaken identity.
quittance [kitɑ̃s] *nf* (*reçu*) receipt; (*facture*) bill. (*frm*) **donner** ~ **à qn de qch** to acquit sb of sth (*frm*).
quitte [kit] *adj* **(a) être** ~ **envers qn** to be quits *ou* all square with sb, be no longer in sb's debt (*frm*); **être** ~ **envers sa patrie** to have served one's country; **être** ~ **envers la société** to have paid one's debt to society; **nous sommes** ~**s** (*dette*) we're quits *ou* all square; (*méchanceté*) we're even *ou* quits *ou* all square; **tu es** ~ **pour cette fois** I'll let you off this time, I'll let you get off *ou* away with it this time, you'll get off *ou* away with it this time; **je ne vous tiens pas** ~ I don't consider your debt paid.
(b) être/tenir qn ~ **d'une dette/obligation** to be/consider sb rid *ou* clear of a debt/an obligation; **je suis** ~ **de mes dettes envers vous** I'm clear as far as my debts to you are concerned, all my debts to you are clear *ou* are paid off; **tu en es** ~ **à bon compte** you got off lightly; **nous en sommes** ~**s pour la peur/un bain glacé** we got off with a fright/an icy dip.
(c) ~ à even if it means *ou* does mean, although it may mean; ~ **à s'ennuyer, ils préfèrent rester chez eux** they prefer to stay (at) home even if it means *ou* does mean getting bored *ou* although it may mean getting bored.
(d) ~ **ou double** (*jeu*) ≃ double your money; (*fig*) **c'est du** ~ **ou double, c'est jouer à** ~ **ou double** it's a big gamble, it's risking a lot.
quitter [kite] (1) *vt* **(a)** *personne, pays, école* to leave; *métier* to leave, quit (*US*), give up. **il n'a pas quitté la maison depuis 3 jours** he hasn't been outside *ou* set foot outside the house for 3 days, he hasn't left the house for 3 days; **ne pas** ~ **la chambre** to be confined to one's room; **les clients sont priés de** ~ **la chambre avant midi** guests are requested to vacate their rooms before midday; **le camion a quitté la route** the lorry left *ou* ran off the road; **se** ~ *[couple, interlocuteurs]* to part; **nous nous sommes quittés bons amis** we parted good friends; (†, *hum*) **il a quitté ce monde** he has departed this world; (*fig*) ~ **la place** to withdraw, retire; **ne pas** ~ **qn d'un pas** *ou* **d'une semelle** not to leave sb for a second; *V* **lieu.**
(b) (*fig*) (*renoncer à*) *espoir, illusion* to give up, forsake; (*abandonner*) *[crainte, énergie]* to leave, desert. **tout son courage l'a quitté** all his courage left *ou* deserted him.
(c) (*enlever*) *vêtement* to take off. ~ **le deuil** to come out of mourning; (*fig*) ~ **l'habit** *ou* **la robe** to leave the priesthood.
(d) (*loc*) **si je le quitte des yeux une seconde** if I take my eyes off him for a second, if I let him out of my sight for a second; (*Téléc*) **ne quittez pas** hold the line, hold on a moment.
quitus [kitys] *nm* (*Comm*) full discharge, quietus.
quoi [kwa] *pron* **(a)** (*interrog*) what. **de** ~ **parles-tu?, tu parles de** ~**?*** what are you talking about?, what are you on about?*; **on joue** ~ **au cinéma?*** what's on at the cinema?; **en** ~ **puis-je vous aider?** how can I help you?; **en** ~ **est cette statue?** what is this statue made of?; **vers** ~ **allons-nous?** what are we heading for?; **à** ~ **reconnaissez-vous le cristal?** how can you tell (that) it is crystal?; ~ **faire/lui dire?** what are we (going) to do/to say to him?; ~ **encore?** what else?; (*exaspération*) what is it now?; ~ **de plus beau que ...?** what can be more beautiful than ...?; ~ **de neuf?** *ou* **de nouveau?** any news?, what's the news?; **à** ~ **bon?** what's the use? (*faire* of doing).
(b) (*interrog indir*) what. **dites-nous à** ~ **cela sert** tell us what that's for; **il voudrait savoir de** ~ **il est question/en** ~ **cela le concerne** he would like to know what it's about/what that's got to do with him; **je ne vois pas avec** ~**/sur** ~ **vous allez écrire** I don't see what you are going to write with/on; **devinez** ~ **j'ai mangé*** guess what I've eaten; **je ne sais** ~ **lui donner** I don't know what to give him.
(c) (*relatif*) **je sais la chose à** ~ **tu fais allusion** I know what (it is) you're referring to; **c'est en** ~ **tu te trompes** that's where you're wrong; **as-tu de** ~ **écrire?** have you got anything to write with?; **ils n'ont même pas de** ~ **vivre** they haven't even got enough to live on; **il n'y a pas de** ~ **rire** it's no laughing matter, there's nothing to laugh about; **il n'y a pas de** ~ **pleurer** it's not worth crying over *ou* about, there's nothing to cry about; **il n'y a pas de** ~ **s'étonner** there's nothing surprising about *ou* in that; **il n'y a pas de** ~ **fouetter un chat** it's not worth making a fuss about; **ils ont de** ~ **occuper leurs vacances** they've got enough *ou* plenty to occupy their holiday; **avoir/emporter de** ~ **écrire/manger** to have/take something to write with/to eat; *V* **ce, comme, sans** *etc.*
(d) ~ **qu'il arrive** whatever happens; ~ **qu'il en soit** be that as it may, however that may be; ~ **qu'on en dise/qu'elle fasse** whatever *ou* no matter what people say/she does; **si vous avez besoin de** ~ **que ce soit** if there's anything (at all) you need.
(e) (*loc*) (*excl*) ~**! tu oses l'accuser?** what! you dare to accuse him!; (*pour faire répéter*) ~**? qu'est-ce qu'il a dit?** what was it *ou* what was that he said?; (*iro*) **et puis** ~ **encore!** what next! (*iro*); **puisque je te le dis,** ~**!*** damn it all! I'm telling you!‡; **de** ~ **(de** ~**)!‡** what's all this nonsense!; **merci beaucoup! — il n'y a pas de** ~ many thanks! — don't mention it *ou* (it's) a pleasure *ou* not at all; **ils n'ont pas de** ~ **s'acheter une voiture** they can't afford to buy a car, they haven't the means *ou* the wherewithal to buy a car; **avoir de** ~ to have means; **des gens qui ont de** ~ people of means.
quoique [kwak(ə)] *conj* (*bien que*) although, though. **quoiqu'il soit malade et qu'il n'ait pas d'argent** although *ou* though he is ill and has no money.
quolibet† [kɔlibɛ] *nm* (*raillerie*) gibe, jeer. **couvrir qn de** ~**s** to gibe *ou* jeer at sb.
quorum [kɔʀɔm] *nm* quorum. **le** ~ **a/n'a pas été atteint** there was/was not a quorum, we (*ou* they *etc*) had/did not have a quorum.
quota [kɔta] *nm* (*Admin*) quota.
quote-part, *pl* **quotes-parts** [kɔtpaʀ] *nf* (*lit, fig*) share.
quotidien, -ienne [kɔtidjɛ̃, jɛn] **1** *adj* (*journalier*) *travail, trajet, nourriture* daily (*épith*); (*banal*) *incident* everyday (*épith*), daily (*épith*); *existence* everyday (*épith*), humdrum. **dans la vie** ~**ne** in everyday *ou* daily life; *V* **pain.**
2 *nm* daily (paper), news(paper). **les grands** ~**s** the big national dailies (*Brit*).
quotidiennement [kɔtidjɛnmɑ̃] *adv* daily, every day.
quotient [kɔsjɑ̃] *nm* (*Math*) quotient. ~ **intellectuel** intelligence quotient, IQ.
quotité [kɔtite] *nf* (*Fin*) quota. (*Jur*) ~ **disponible** *portion of estate of which testator may dispose at his discretion.*

R

R, r [ɛʀ] *nm (lettre)* R, r; *V* **mois.**
rab‡ [ʀab] *nm abrév de* **rabiot‡.**
rabâchage [ʀabɑʃaʒ] *nm* constant harping on (*U*).
rabâcher [ʀabɑʃe] (1) **1** *vt* (*ressasser*) *histoire* to harp on, keep (on) repeating; (*réviser*) *leçon* to go over and over, keep going back over. **il rabâche toujours la même chose** he's always harping on the same theme, he keeps on harping on about the same (old) thing.
2 *vi* (*radoter*) to keep on, keep harping on, keep repeating o.s.
rabâcheur, -euse [ʀabɑʃœʀ, øz] *nm,f* repetitive *ou* repetitious bore. **il est du genre ~** he's one of these *ou* he's the type who never stops repeating himself *ou* harping on.
rabais [ʀabɛ] *nm* reduction, discount. **10 centimes de ~, ~ de 10 centimes** reduction *ou* discount of 10 centimes, 10 centimes off*; **faire un ~ de 2 F sur qch** to give a reduction *ou* discount of 2 francs on sth, knock 2 francs off (the price of) sth*; **au ~** *acheter, vendre* at a reduced price, (on the) cheap; (*péj*) *acteur, enseignement* third-rate, paltry; (*péj*) **je ne veux pas travailler au ~** I won't work for a pittance *ou* do underpaid work.
rabaisser [ʀabese] (1) **1** *vt* **(a)** (*dénigrer*) *personne* to humble, belittle, disparage; *efforts, talent, travail* to belittle, disparage.
(b) (*réduire*) *pouvoirs* to reduce, decrease; *orgueil* to humble; *exigences* to moderate, reduce. **ces défauts rabaissent la qualité de l'ensemble** these defects impair the quality of the whole; *V* **caquet.**
(c) (*diminuer*) *prix* to reduce, knock down*, bring down.
(d) (*baisser*) *robe, store* to pull (back) down.
2 se rabaisser *vpr* to belittle o.s. **elle se rabaisse toujours** she never gives herself enough credit, she always belittles herself; **se ~ devant qn** to humble o.s. *ou* bow before sb.
rabat [ʀaba] *nm* **(a)** *[table]* flap, leaf; *[poche, enveloppe]* flap; *[drap]* fold (*over the covers*); *[avocat, prêtre]* bands. **poche à ~** flapped pocket. **(b) = rabattage.**
rabat- [ʀaba] *préf V* **rabattre.**
rabattage [ʀabataʒ] *nm* (*Chasse*) beating.
rabatteur, -euse [ʀabatœʀ, øz] **1** *nm,f* (*Chasse*) beater; (*fig péj*) tout; *[prostituée]* procurer, pimp. **le ~ de l'hôtel** the hotel tout. **2** *nm [moissonneuse]* reel.
rabattre [ʀabatʀ(ə)] (41) **1** *vt* **(a)** *capot, clapet* to close *ou* shut down; *couvercle* to put on, close; *drap* to fold over *ou* back; *col* to turn down; *bord de chapeau* to turn *ou* pull down; *strapontin* (*ouvrir*) to pull down; (*fermer*) to put up; *jupe* to pull down. **le vent rabat la fumée** the wind blows the smoke back down; **il rabattit ses cheveux sur son front** he brushed his hair down over his forehead; **le chapeau rabattu/les cheveux rabattus sur les yeux** his hat pulled down/hair brushed down over his eyes; **~ les couvertures** (*se couvrir*) to pull the blankets up; (*se découvrir*) to push *ou* throw back the blankets.
(b) (*diminuer*) to reduce; (*déduire*) to deduct, take off. **il n'a pas voulu ~ un centime (du prix)** he wouldn't take *ou* knock* a centime off (the price), he wouldn't come down (by) one centime (on the price); **~ l'orgueil de qn** to humble sb's pride; **en ~** (*de ses prétentions*) to climb down, come down off one's high horse; (*de ses illusions*) to lose one's illusions; *V* **caquet.**
(c) (*Chasse*) *gibier* to drive; *terrain* to beat. **~ des clients*** to tout for customers.
(d) (*Tricot*) **~ des mailles** to decrease; (*Couture*) **~ une couture** to stitch down a seam.
2 se rabattre *vpr* **(a)** *[voiture]* to cut in; *[coureur]* to cut in, cut across. **se ~ devant qn** *[voiture]* to cut *ou* pull in front of sb; *[coureur]* to cut *ou* swing in front of *ou* across sb; **le coureur s'est rabattu à la corde** the runner cut *ou* swung across to the inside lane.
(b) (*prendre faute de mieux*) **se ~ sur** *marchandise, personne* to fall back on, make do with.
(c) (*se refermer*) *[porte]* to fall *ou* slam shut; *[couvercle]* to close. **la porte se rabattit sur lui** the door closed *ou* shut on *ou* behind him.
3: rabat-joie *nm inv* killjoy, spoilsport*; **faire le rabat-joie** to spoil the fun, act like *ou* be a spoilsport*; **il est drôlement rabat-joie** he's an awful killjoy *ou* spoilsport*.
rabattu, e [ʀabaty] (*ptp de* **rabattre**) *adj col, bords* turned down; *poche* flapped; *V* **couture.**
rabbin [ʀabɛ̃] *nm* rabbi. **grand ~** chief rabbi.
rabbinat [ʀabina] *nm* rabbinate.
rabbinique [ʀabinik] *adj* rabbinic(al).
rabbinisme [ʀabinism(ə)] *nm* rabbinism.
rabelaisien, -ienne [ʀablezjɛ̃, jɛn] *adj* Rabelaisian.
rabibochage* [ʀabibɔʃaʒ] *nm* (*réconciliation*) reconciliation.
rabibocher* [ʀabibɔʃe] (1) **1** *vt* (*réconcilier*) *amis, époux* to bring together (again), reconcile, patch things up between*. **2 se rabibocher** *vpr* to make it up*, patch things up* (*avec* with).
rabiot‡ [ʀabjo] *nm* (*supplément*) **(a)** *[nourriture]* extra. **est-ce qu'il y a du ~?** is there any extra (left)?, is there any extra food (left)?; **qui veut du ~?** anyone for extras? *ou* seconds?*; **va me chercher du ~ de frites** go and get me some extra chips *ou* seconds* of chips; **il reste un ~ de frites, il reste des frites en ~** there are still (some) extra chips left (over); **que font-ils du ~?** what'll they do with the extra (food)?
(b) *[temps]* (*Mil*) extra time. **un ~ de 5 minutes *ou* 5 minutes de ~ pour finir le devoir** 5 minutes' extra time *ou* 5 minutes extra to finish off the exercise; **faire du ~** (*travail*) to do *ou* work extra time; (*Mil*) to do *ou* serve extra time.
rabioter‡ [ʀabjɔte] (1) *vt* **(a)** (*s'approprier*) to scrounge* (*qch à qn* sth from sb). **il a rabioté tout le vin** he scrounged* all the extra wine; **~ 5 minutes de sommeil** to snatch 5 minutes' extra sleep.
(b) (*voler*) *temps, argent* to fiddle*. **l'ouvrier m'a rabioté 10 F/un quart d'heure** the workman swindled *ou* did* me out of 10 francs/a quarter of an hour; **commerçant qui rabiote** shopkeeper who fiddles* a bit extra *ou* makes a bit extra on the side; **~ sur la quantité** to give short measure.
rabioteur, -euse‡ [ʀabjɔtœʀ, øz] *nm,f* (*V* **rabioter**) scrounger*; fiddler*.
rabique [ʀabik] *adj* rabies (*épith*).
râble [ʀɑbl(ə)] *nm [lapin, lièvre]* back; (‡: *dos*) small of the back. (*Culin*) **~ de lièvre** saddle of hare; *V* **tomber.**
râblé, e [ʀɑble] *adj homme* well-set, stocky; *cheval* broad-backed.
rabot [ʀabo] *nm* plane. **passer qch au ~** to plane sth (down).
rabotage [ʀabɔtaʒ] *nm* planing (down).
raboter [ʀabɔte] (1) *vt* **(a)** (*Menuiserie*) to plane (down).
(b) (*: *racler*) *chaussure, objet* to scrape, rub; *main* to graze, scrape. **ne rabote pas le mur avec ton manteau** don't brush *ou* rub your coat along the wall; **baisse-toi si tu ne veux pas te ~ la tête contre le plafond** bend down if you don't want to graze your head on the ceiling.
raboteur [ʀabɔtœʀ] *nm* (*ouvrier*) planer.
raboteuse[1] [ʀabɔtøz] *nf* (*machine*) planing machine.
raboteux, -euse[2] [ʀabɔtø, øz] *adj* (*rugueux*) *surface, arête* uneven, rough; *chemin* rugged, uneven, bumpy; (*littér*) *style* rough, rugged; *voix* rough.
rabougri, e [ʀabugʀi] (*ptp de* **rabougrir**) *adj* (*chétif*) *plante* stunted, scraggy; *personne* stunted, puny; (*desséché*) *plante* shrivelled; *vieillard* wizened, shrivelled.
rabougrir [ʀabugʀiʀ] (2) **1** *vt personne* to (cause to) shrivel up; *plante* (*dessécher*) to shrivel (up); (*étioler*) to stunt. **2 se rabougrir** *vpr [personne]* to become shrivelled (with age), become wizened; *[plante]* to shrivel (up), become stunted.
rabougrissement [ʀabugʀismɑ̃] *nm* (*action*) stunting, shrivelling (up); (*résultat*) scragginess, stunted appearance, shrivelled appearance.
rabouter [ʀabute] (1) *vt tubes, planches* to join (together) (end to end); *étoffes* to seam *ou* sew together.
rabrouer [ʀabʀue] (1) *vt* to snub, rebuff, give the brush-off to*. **elle me rabroue tout le temps** she's always snapping at me.
racaille [ʀakɑj] *nf* rabble, riffraff, scum.
raccommodable [ʀakɔmɔdabl(ə)] *adj vêtement* repairable, mendable.
raccommodage [ʀakɔmɔdaʒ] *nm* **(a)** (*action*) *[vêtement, accroc, filet]* mending, repairing; *[chaussettes]* darning, mending. **faire du ~ *ou* des ~s** (*pour soi*) to do some mending; (*comme métier*) to take in mending.
(b) (*endroit réparé*) mend; repair; darn.
raccommodement [ʀakɔmɔdmɑ̃] *nm* (*réconciliation*) reconciliation.
raccommoder [ʀakɔmɔde] (1) **1** *vt* **(a)** *vêtements, accroc* to mend, repair; *chaussette* to darn, mend. **(b)** (*) *ennemis* to bring together again, reconcile. **2 se raccommoder*** *vpr* to make it up*, be reconciled.
raccommodeur, -euse [ʀakɔmɔdœʀ, øz] *nm,f [linge, filets]* mender. **~ de porcelaines**†† china mender *ou* restorer.
raccompagner [ʀakɔ̃paɲe] (1) *vt* to take *ou* see back (*à* to). **~ qn (chez lui)** to take *ou* see *ou* accompany sb home; **~ qn au bureau en voiture/à pied** to drive sb back/walk back with sb to the office; **~ qn à la gare** to see sb off at *ou* take sb (back) to the station; **~ qn (jusqu')à la porte** to see sb to the door.
raccord [ʀakɔʀ] *nm* **(a)** *[papier peint]* join. **~ (de maçonnerie)** pointing (*U*); **~ (de peinture)** (*liaison*) join (*in the paintwork*); (*retouche*) touch up; **on ne voit pas les ~s (de peinture)** you can't see where the paint has been touched up; **elle procéda à un rapide ~ (de maquillage)** she quickly touched up her make-up; **papier peint sans ~s** random match wallpaper.
(b) *[texte, discours]* link, join; (*Ciné*) (*séquence*) continuity; (*scène*) link scene. (*Ciné*) **à cause des coupures, nous avons dû faire des ~s** because of the cuts, we had to do some linking up.
(c) (*pièce, joint*) link.
raccordement [ʀakɔʀdəmɑ̃] *nm* **(a)** (*V* **raccorder**) linking; joining; connecting. (*Téléc*) **~ (au réseau)** connection (of one's phone); **ils sont venus faire le ~** they've come to connect the (*ou* our *etc*) phone; *V* **bretelle, ligne**[1]**, voie.**
(b) (*soudure, épissure*) join; (*tunnel, passage*) connecting passage; (*carrefour*) junction.
raccorder [ʀakɔʀde] (1) **1** *vt routes, bâtiments* to link up, join (up), connect (*à* with, to); *fils électriques* to join; *tuyaux* to join,

link (à to); (*Ciné*) *plans* to link up. (*fig*) ~ **à** *faits* to link (up) with, tie up with; (*Téléc*) ~ **qn au réseau** to connect sb's phone; **quand les 2 tuyaux seront raccordés** when the 2 pipes are joined *ou* linked (up) *ou* connected together.

2 se raccorder *vpr [routes]* to link *ou* join up (*à* with). *[faits]* se ~ à to tie up *ou* in with.

raccourci [RakuRsi] *nm* **(a)** (*chemin*) short cut.

(b) (*fig: formule frappante*) compressed turn of phrase; (*résumé*) summary. **en** ~ (*en miniature*) in miniature; (*dans les grandes lignes*) in (broad) outline; (*en bref*) in a nutshell, in brief.

(c) (*Art*) foreshortening. **figure en** ~ foreshortened figure; *V* **bras.**

raccourcir [RakuRsiR] (2) **1** *vt distance, temps* to shorten; *vêtement* to shorten, take up; *vacances, textes* to shorten, curtail, cut short. **passons par là, ça (nous) raccourcit** let's go this way, it's shorter *ou* quicker *ou* it cuts a bit off*; ~ **qn**: to chop sb's head off.

2 *vi [jours]* to grow shorter, draw in; *[vêtement]* (*au lavage*) to shrink. (*Mode*) **les jupes ont raccourci cette année** skirts are shorter *ou* have got shorter this year.

raccourcissement [RakuRsismɑ̃] *nm* **(a)** (*V* **raccourcir**) shortening; curtailing, curtailment. **(b)** *[jour]* shortening, drawing in; *[vêtement]* (*au lavage*) shrinkage.

raccoutumer [Rakutyme] (1) *vt* = **réaccoutumer.**

raccroc [RakRo] *nm* (*frm*) **par** ~ (*par hasard*) by chance; (*par un heureux hasard*) by a stroke of good fortune.

raccrocher [RakRɔʃe] (1) **1** *vi* (*Téléc*) to hang up, ring off. **ne raccroche pas** hold on, don't hang up *ou* ring off.

2 *vt* **(a)** *vêtement, tableau* to hang back up, put back on the hook; *écouteur* to put down. (*arg Boxe*) ~ **les gants** to hang up one's gloves (*arg*).

(b) (*racoler*) *[vendeur, portier]* to tout for; *[prostituée]* to accost.

(c) (*attraper*) *personne, bonne affaire* to grab *ou* get hold of. **il m'a raccroché dans la rue** he stopped *ou* waylaid me in the street.

(d) (*relier*) *wagons, faits* to link, connect (*à* to, with).

(e) (*: *rattraper*) *affaire, contrat* to save, rescue.

3 se raccrocher *vpr*: se ~ à *branche* to catch *ou* grab (hold of); *espoir, personne* to cling to, hang on to; **cette idée se raccroche à la précédente** this idea links with *ou* ties in with the previous one.

race [Ras] *nf* **(a)** (*ethnique*) race. **être de** ~ **indienne** to be of Indian stock *ou* blood.

(b) (*Zool*) breed. **de** ~ (*gén*) pedigree (*épith*), purebred (*épith*); *cheval* thoroughbred; **avoir de la** ~ to be of good stock; *V* **bon**[1], **chien.**

(c) (*ancêtres*) stock, race. **être de** ~ **noble** to be of noble stock *ou* blood *ou* race; **avoir de la** ~ to have a certain (natural) distinction.

(d) (*catégorie*) breed. **lui et les gens de sa** ~ him and people of the same breed, him and the likes of him*.

racé, e [Rase] *adj animal* purebred (*épith*), pedigree (*épith*); *cheval* thoroughbred; *personne* thoroughbred, of natural distinction; (*fig*) *voiture, ligne* thoroughbred.

rachat [Raʃa] *nm* (*V* **racheter**) buying back; repurchase (*frm*); purchase; buying up; redemption; ransom; ransoming; atonement, expiation.

rachetable [Raʃtabl(ə)] *adj dette, rente* redeemable; *péché* expiable; *pécheur* redeemable. **cette faute n'est pas** ~ you can't make up for this mistake.

racheter [Raʃte] (5) **1** *vt* **(a)** *objet qu'on possédait avant* to buy back, repurchase (*frm*); *nouvel objet* to buy *ou* purchase another; *pain, lait* to buy some more; *objet d'occasion* to buy, purchase (*frm*); *usine en faillite* to buy up. **je lui ai racheté son vieux transistor** I've bought his old transistor from him; **il a racheté toutes les parts de son associé** he bought his partner out, he bought up all his partner's shares.

(b) (*se libérer de*) *dette, rente* to redeem.

(c) *esclave, otage* to ransom, pay a ransom for; (*Rel*) *pécheur* to redeem.

(d) (*réparer*) *péché, crime* to atone for, expiate; *mauvaise conduite, faute* to make amends for, make up for; *imperfection* to make up *ou* compensate for (*par* by).

(e) (*Archit*) to modify.

2 se racheter *vpr [pécheur]* to redeem o.s.; *[criminel]* to make amends. **essaie de te** ~ **en t'excusant** try and make up for it *ou* try to make amends by apologizing.

rachidien, -ienne [Raʃidjɛ̃, jɛn] *adj* of the spinal column, rachidian (*T*).

rachitique [Raʃitik] *adj* (*Méd*) *personne* suffering from rickets, rachitic (*T*), rickety; *arbre, poulet* scraggy, scrawny. **c'est un** ~, il est ~ he suffers from rickets.

rachitisme [Raʃitism(ə)] *nm* rickets, rachitis (*T*). **faire du** ~ to have rickets.

racial, e, *mpl* **-aux** [Rasjal, o] *adj* racial.

racine [Rasin] **1** *nf* **(a)** (*gén*) root. (*Bot*) **la carotte est une** ~ the carrot is a root *ou* root vegetable, carrots are a root crop; (*fig: attaches*) ~s roots; (*fig*) **il est sans** ~s he's rootless, he belongs nowhere; **prendre** ~ (*lit*) to take *ou* strike root, put out roots; (*fig*) (*s'attacher*) to take root; (*s'établir*) to put down (one's) roots (*fig*); *V* **rougir.**

(b) (*Math*) *[équation]* root. *[nombre]* ~ **carrée/cubique/dixième** square/cube/tenth root; **prendre** *ou* **extraire la** ~ **de** to take the root of.

(c) (*Ling*) *[mot]* root.

2: racine adventive adventitious root; **racine aérienne** aerial root; **racine pivotante** taproot.

racinien, -ienne [Rasinjɛ̃, jɛn] *adj* Racinian.

racisme [Rasism(ə)] *nm* racialism, racism. ~ **antijeunes** anti-youth prejudice.

raciste [Rasist(ə)] *adj, nmf* racialist, racist.

racket [Rakɛt] *nm* (*action*) racketeering (*U*); (*vol*) racket (*extortion through blackmail etc*).

racketter, racketteur [Rakɛtœr] *nm* racketeer.

raclage [Rɑklaʒ] *nm* (*Tech*) scraping.

raclée* [Rɑkle] *nf* (*coups*) hiding*, thrashing*; (*défaite*) thrashing*, licking:. **il a pris une** ~ **à l'élection** he got thrashed* *ou* licked: *ou* he got a licking: in the election.

raclement [Rɑkləmɑ̃] *nm* (*bruit*) scraping (noise). **il émit un** ~ **de gorge** he cleared his throat noisily *ou* raucously.

racler [Rɑkle] (1) **1** *vt* **(a)** (*gén, Méd, Tech*) to scrape; *fond de casserole* to scrape out; *parquet* to scrape (down). (*fig*) ~ **les fonds de tiroir** to scrape some money together, raid the piggy bank*; **ce vin racle le gosier** this wine is harsh *ou* rough on the throat.

(b) (*ratisser*) *allée, gravier, sable* to rake.

(c) (*enlever*) *tache, croûte* to scrape away; *peinture, écailles* to scrape off. ~ **la boue de ses semelles** to scrape the mud off one's shoes, scrape off the mud from one's shoes.

(d) (*péj*) *violon* to scrape *ou* saw (a tune) on; *guitare* to scrape (a tune) on.

2 se racler *vpr*: se ~ **la gorge** to clear one's throat.

raclette [Rɑklɛt] *nf* **(a)** (*outil*) scraper. **(b)** (*Culin*) raclette (*Swiss cheese dish*).

racloir [Rɑklwar] *nm* scraper.

raclure [Rɑklyr] *nf* (*gén pl: déchet*) scraping.

racolage [Rakɔlaʒ] *nm* (*V* **racoler**) soliciting; touting. **faire du** ~ to solicit; to tout.

racoler [Rakɔle] (1) *vt [prostituée]* to solicit, accost; (*fig péj*) *[agent électoral, portier, vendeur]* to solicit, tout for. **elle racolait** she was soliciting, she was touting for customers.

racoleur, -euse [Rakɔlœr, øz] **1** *nm* tout. **2 racoleuse** *nf* (*prostituée*) streetwalker, whore.

racontable [Rakɔ̃tabl(ə)] *adj* tellable, relatable.

racontar [Rakɔ̃tar] *nm* story, lie.

raconter [Rakɔ̃te] (1) **1** *vt* **(a)** (*relater*) *histoire, légende* to tell, relate, recount; *vacances, malheurs* to tell about, relate, recount. ~ **qch à qn** to tell sb sth, relate *ou* recount sth to sb; ~ **que** to tell that; **on raconte que** people say that, it is said that, the story goes that; ~ **ce qui s'est passé** to say *ou* relate *ou* recount what happened; ~ **à qn ce qui s'est passé** to tell sb *ou* relate *ou* recount to sb what happened.

(b) (*dire de mauvaise foi*) to tell, say. **qu'est-ce que tu racontes?** what on earth do you think you're talking about? *ou* saying?; **il raconte n'importe quoi** he's talking rubbish *ou* nonsense *ou* through his hat* (*fig*); ~ **des histoires, en** ~ to tell stories, spin yarns.

2 se raconter *vpr [écrivain]* to talk about o.s.

raconteur, -euse [Rakɔ̃tœr, øz] *nm,f* storyteller. ~ **de** narrator of.

racornir [RakɔRniR] (2) **1** *vt* (*durcir*) to toughen, harden; (*dessécher*) to shrivel (up). **vieillard racorni** shrivelled(-up) *ou* wizened old man; **dans son cœur racorni** in his hard heart.

2 se racornir *vpr* to become tough *ou* hard; to shrivel (up), become shrivelled (up).

racornissement [RakɔRnismɑ̃] *nm* (*V* **racornir**) toughening, hardening; shrivelling (up).

radar [Radar] *nm* radar.

radariste [Radarist(ə)] *nmf* radar operator.

rade [Rad] *nf* **(a)** (*port*) (natural) harbour, roads (*T*), roadstead (*T*). **en** ~ in harbour, in the roads (*T*); **en** ~ **de Brest** in Brest harbour.

(b) (*loc) **laisser en** ~ *personne* to leave in the lurch, leave stranded *ou* behind; *projet* to forget about, drop, shelve; *voiture* to leave behind; **elle/sa voiture est restée en** ~ she/her car was left stranded *ou* behind.

radeau, *pl* ~**x** [Rado] *nm* raft; (*train de bois*) timber float *ou* raft. ~ **de sauvetage/pneumatique** rescue/inflatable raft.

radial, e, *mpl* **-aux** [Radjal, o] *adj* (*gén*) radial.

radian [Radjɑ̃] *nm* radian.

radiant, e [Radjɑ̃, ɑ̃t] *adj énergie* radiant. (*Astron*) **(point)** ~ radiant.

radiateur [RadjatœR] *nm* (*à eau, à huile*) radiator; (*à gaz, à barres chauffantes*) heater; *[voiture]* radiator. ~ **soufflant** fan heater; ~ **parabolique** electric fire.

radiation [Radjɑsjɔ̃] *nf* **(a)** (*Phys*) radiation. **(b)** *[nom, mention]* crossing *ou* striking off. **sa** ~ **du club** his being struck off the club register.

radical, e, *mpl* **-aux** [Radikal, o] **1** *adj* (*gén, Bot, Math*) radical; (*Hist, Pol*) Radical. **essayez ce remède, c'est** ~ try this cure — it has a radical effect; (*Ling*) **voyelle** ~**e** stem *ou* radical vowel.

2 *nm [mot]* stem, radical; (*Pol*) radical; (*Chim*) radical; (*Math*) radical sign.

3: radical-socialisme *nm* radical-socialism; **radical-socialiste** *adj, nmf, mpl* **radicaux-socialistes** radical-socialist.

radicalement [Radikalmɑ̃] *adv* **(a)** *modifier* radically; *guérir* completely. **(b)** ~ **faux** completely wrong; ~ **opposé à** radically opposed to.

radicalisation [Radikalizɑsjɔ̃] *nf* (*V* **radicaliser**) toughening; intensification; radicalization.

radicaliser *vt*, **se radicaliser** *vpr* [Radikalize] (1) *position* to toughen, harden; *conflit* to intensify; *régime* to radicalize.

radicalisme [Radikalism(ə)] *nm* (*Pol*) radicalism.

radicelle [Radisɛl] *nf* rootlet, radicle (*T*).

radiculaire [RadikylɛR] *adj* radicular.

radicule [Radikyl] *nf* radicule.

radié, e [Radje] **1** *ptp de* **radier. 2** *adj* (*rayonné*) rayed, radiate.

radier [ʀadje] (7) *vt mention, nom* to cross off, strike off. **ce médecin a été radié** this doctor has been struck off (the list).
radiesthésie [ʀadjɛstezi] *nf* (power of) divination (*based on the detection of radiation emitted by various bodies*).
radiesthésiste [ʀadjɛstezist(ə)] *nmf* diviner (*who uses radiation detector*).
radieusement [ʀadjøzmɑ̃] *adv* radiantly. **~ beau** *personne* radiantly *ou* dazzlingly beautiful; *temps* brilliantly *ou* gloriously fine.
radieux, -euse [ʀadjø, øz] *adj personne* glowing *ou* radiant with happiness, beaming *ou* radiant with joy; *air, sourire* radiant, beaming (*épith*); *soleil, beauté* radiant, dazzling; *journée, temps* brilliant, glorious.
radin, e* [ʀadɛ̃, in] **1** *adj* stingy*, tight-fisted. **2** *nm,f* skinflint.
radinerꜝ *vi*, **se radiner**ꜝ *vpr* [ʀadine] (1) (*arriver*) to turn up, show up*, roll upꜝ; (*accourir*) to rush over, dash over. **allez, radine(-toi)!** come on, step on it!* *ou* get your skates on!*
radinerie* [ʀadinʀi] *nf* stinginess* (*U*), tight-fistedness (*U*).
radio [ʀadjo] **1** *nf* **(a)** (*poste*) radio (set), wireless (set)† (*surtout Brit*). **mets la ~** turn *ou* put on the radio; *V* **poste**².
(b) (*radiodiffusion*) **la ~** (the) radio; **avoir la ~** to have a radio; **parler à la ~** to speak on the radio, broadcast; **passer à la ~** to be on the radio *ou* on the air.
(c) (*radiographie*) X-ray (photograph). **passer une ~** to have an X-ray (taken), be X-rayed.
2 *nm* (*opérateur*) radio operator; (*message*) radiogram, radiotelegram.
3: radio-actif = radioactif; radio-isotope *nm, pl* **radio-isotopes** radioisotope.
radioactif, -ive [ʀadjɔaktif, iv] *adj* radioactive.
radioactivité [ʀadjɔaktivite] *nf* radioactivity.
radioalignement [ʀadjɔaliɲmɑ̃] *nm* radio navigation system.
radioastronomie [ʀadjɔastʀɔnɔmi] *nf* radio astronomy.
radiobalisage [ʀadjɔbalizaʒ] *nm* radio beacon signalling.
radiocarbone [ʀadjɔkaʀbɔn] *nm* radiocarbon, radioactive carbon.
radiocobalt [ʀadjɔkɔbalt] *nm* radio cobalt, radioactive cobalt.
radiocommunication [ʀadjɔkɔmynikɑsjɔ̃] *nf* radio communication.
radiocompas [ʀadjɔkɔ̃pa] *nm* radio compass.
radioconducteur [ʀadjɔkɔ̃dyktœʀ] *nm* detector.
radiodiffuser [ʀadjɔdifyze] (1) *vt* to broadcast (*by radio*). **interview radiodiffusé** broadcast *ou* radio interview.
radiodiffusion [ʀadjɔdifyzjɔ̃] *nf* broadcasting (*by radio*).
radioélectricien, -ienne [ʀadjɔelɛktʀisjɛ̃, jɛn] *nm,f* radio-engineer.
radioélectricité [ʀadjɔelɛktʀisite] *nf* radio-engineering.
radioélectrique [ʀadjɔelɛktʀik] *adj* radio (*épith*).
radioélément [ʀadjɔelemɑ̃] *nm* radio-element.
radiogoniomètre [ʀadjɔgɔnjɔmɛtʀ(ə)] *nm* direction finder, radiogoniometer.
radiogoniométrie [ʀadjɔgɔnjɔmetʀi] *nf* radio direction finding, radiogoniometry.
radiogramme [ʀadjɔgʀam] *nm* radiogram, radiotelegram.
radiographie [ʀadjɔgʀafi] *nf* **(a)** (*technique*) radiography, X-ray photography. **passer une ~** to have an X-ray (taken). **(b)** (*photographie*) X-ray (photograph), radiograph.
radiographier [ʀadjɔgʀafje] (7) *vt* to X-ray.
radiographique [ʀadjɔgʀafik] *adj* X-ray (*épith*).
radioguidage [ʀadjɔgidaʒ] *nm* (*Aviat*) radio control, radiodirection. (*Rad*) **le ~ des automobilistes** broadcasting traffic reports to motorists.
radioguidé, e [ʀadjɔgide] *adj* radio-controlled.
radiologie [ʀadjɔlɔʒi] *nf* radiology.
radiologiste [ʀadjɔlɔʒist(ə)] *nmf*, **radiologue** [ʀadjɔlɔg] *nmf* radiologist.
radionavigant [ʀadjɔnavigɑ̃] *nm* radio officer.
radionavigation [ʀadjɔnavigɑsjɔ̃] *nf* radio navigation.
radiophare [ʀadjɔfaʀ] *nm* radio beacon.
radiophonie [ʀadjɔfɔni] *nf* radiotelephony.
radiophonique [ʀadjɔfɔnik] *adj* radio (*épith*).
radioreportage [ʀadjɔʀ(ə)pɔʀtaʒ] *nm* radio report; *V* **car**¹.
radioreporter [ʀadjɔʀəpɔʀtɛʀ] *nm* radio reporter.
radioscopie [ʀadjɔskɔpi] *nf* radioscopy.
radiosondage [ʀadjɔsɔ̃daʒ] *nm* (*Mét*) radiosonde exploration; (*Géol*) seismic prospecting.
radiosonde [ʀadjɔsɔ̃d] *nf* radiosonde.
radiotechnique [ʀadjɔtɛknik] **1** *nf* radio technology. **2** *adj* radiotechnological.
radiotélégraphie [ʀadjɔtelegʀafi] *nf* radiotelegraphy, wireless telegraphy.
radiotélégraphique [ʀadjɔtelegʀafik] *adj* radiotelegraphic.
radiotélégraphiste [ʀadjɔtelegʀafist(ə)] *nmf* radiotelegrapher.
radiotéléphonie [ʀadjɔtelefɔni] *nf* radiotelephony, wireless telephony.
radiotélescope [ʀadjɔtelɛskɔp] *nm* radio telescope.
radiotélévisé, e [ʀadjɔtelevize] *adj* broadcast on both radio and television, broadcast and televised.
radiothérapie [ʀadjɔteʀapi] *nf* radiotherapy.
radis [ʀadi] *nm* **(a)** radish. **~ noir** horseradish.
(b) (ꜝ: *sou*) penny (*Brit*), cent (*US*). **je n'ai pas un ~** I haven't got a penny (to my name)* *ou* a cent (*US*) *ou* a bean*; **ça ne vaut pas un ~** it's not worth a penny *ou* a bean*.
radium [ʀadjɔm] *nm* radium.
radius [ʀadjys] *nm* (*Aviat*) radius.
radjah [ʀadʒa] *nm* = **rajah.**
radotage [ʀadɔtaʒ] *nm* (*péj*) drivel (*U*), rambling.
radoter [ʀadɔte] (1) *vi* (*péj*) to ramble on *ou* drivel (on) (in a senile way). **tu radotes**ꜝ you're talking a load of drivelꜝ.
radoteur, -euse [ʀadɔtœʀ, øz] *nm,f* (*péj*) drivelling (old) fool, (old) driveller.
radoub [ʀadu] *nm* (*Naut*) refitting. **navire au ~** ship under repair; *V* **bassin.**
radouber [ʀadube] (1) *vt navire* to repair, refit; *filet de pêche* to repair, mend.
radoucir [ʀadusiʀ] (2) **1** *vt personne, voix, ton, attitude* to soften; *temps* to make milder. **2 se radoucir** *vpr* [*personne*] to calm down, be mollified; [*voix*] to soften, become milder; [*temps*] to become milder.
radoucissement [ʀadusismɑ̃] *nm* **(a)** (*Mét*) **à cause du ~ (du temps)** because of the milder weather; **~ (de la température)** rise in (the) temperature; **on prévoit pour demain un léger ~** slightly milder weather *ou* a slightly milder spell (of weather) is forecast *ou* slightly higher temperatures are forecast for tomorrow.
(b) [*ton, attitude*] softening; [*personne*] calming down.
rafale [ʀafal] *nf* [*vent*] gust, blast; [*pluie, mitrailleuse*] gust, burst. **une soudaine ~ (de vent)** a sudden gust *ou* blast of wind, a sudden squall; **en *ou* par ~s** in gusts; in bursts; **une ~ *ou* des ~s de balles** a hail of bullets.
raffermir [ʀafɛʀmiʀ] (2) **1** *vt muscle* to strengthen, harden, tone up; *chair, sol* to make firm(er); *voix* to steady; *gouvernement, popularité* to strengthen, reinforce; *courage, résolution* to fortify, strengthen.
2 se raffermir *vpr* [*muscle*] to grow stronger, harden; [*chair, sol*] to become firm(er); [*autorité*] to become strengthened *ou* reinforced; [*voix*] to become steady *ou* steadier. **ma résolution se raffermit** my resolution grew stronger; **son visage se raffermit** his face became *ou* he looked more composed.
raffermissement [ʀafɛʀmismɑ̃] *nm* (*V* **raffermir**) strengthening; firming; steadying; reinforcement; fortifying.
raffinage [ʀafinaʒ] *nm* (*gén*) refining.
raffiné, e [ʀafine] (*ptp de* **raffiner**) *adj* **(a)** *pétrole, sucre* refined. **(b)** *personne, mœurs, style* refined, polished, sophisticated; *esprit, goûts, gourmet* discriminating, refined; *élégance, cuisine* refined.
raffinement [ʀafinmɑ̃] *nm* **(a)** (*U: V* **raffiné**) refinement, sophistication.
(b) (*gén pl: détail*) [*langage etc*] nicety, subtlety, refinement.
(c) (*exagération*) **c'est du ~** that's being oversubtle.
(d) (*surenchère*) **~ de** refinement of; **avec un ~ de luxe/de cruauté** with refinements of luxury/cruelty.
raffiner [ʀafine] (1) **1** *vt* **(a)** *pétrole, sucre, papier* to refine. **(b)** *langage, manières* to refine, polish. **2** *vi* (*dans le raisonnement*) to be oversubtle; (*sur les détails*) to be (over)meticulous.
raffinerie [ʀafinʀi] *nf* refinery.
raffineur, -euse [ʀafinœʀ, øz] *nm,f* refiner.
raffoler [ʀafɔle] (1) **raffoler de** *vt indir* to be very keen on *ou* fond of, be wild about*.
raffut* [ʀafy] *nm* (*vacarme*) row*, racket*, din. **faire du ~** (*être bruyant*) to kick up* *ou* make a row* *ou* racket* *ou* din; (*protester*) to kick up a row* *ou* fuss *ou* stinkꜝ; **sa démission va faire du ~** his resignation will cause a row* *ou* stinkꜝ.
rafiot [ʀafjo] *nm* (*péj: bateau*) (old) tub (*péj*).
rafistolage* [ʀafistɔlaʒ] *nm* (*action*) patching *ou* botching up. **ce n'est qu'un ~** it's only a patched-up *ou* makeshift repair.
rafistoler* [ʀafistɔle] (1) *vt* (*réparer*) to patch up, botch up.
rafle [ʀɑfl(ə)] *nf* (police) roundup *ou* raid. **la police a fait une ~** the police made a roundup (of suspects); (*fig*) **les voleurs ont fait une ~ chez le bijoutier/sur les montres** the thieves cleaned out the jewellery shop/cleaned out *ou* made a clean sweep of all the watches.
rafler* [ʀɑfle] (1) *vt récompenses, bijoux* to run off with*, swipe*; *place* to bag*, grab*, swipe*. **les ménagères avaient tout raflé** the housewives had swept up *ou* snaffled* everything.
rafraîchir [ʀafʀɛʃiʀ] (2) **1** *vt* **(a)** (*refroidir*) *air* to cool (down), freshen; *vin* to chill; *boisson* to cool, make cooler.
(b) (*revivifier*) *visage, corps* to freshen (up); [*boisson*] to refresh.
(c) (*rénover*) *vêtement* to smarten up, brighten up; *tableau, couleur* to brighten up, freshen up; *appartement* to do up, brighten up; *connaissances* to brush up. **se faire ~ les cheveux** to have a trim, have one's hair trimmed; (*fig*) **~ la mémoire *ou* les idées de qn** to jog *ou* refresh sb's memory.
2 *vi* [*vin etc*] to cool (down). **mettre à ~** *vin, dessert* to chill.
3 se rafraîchir *vpr* **(a)** (*Mét*) **le temps/ça* se rafraîchit** the weather/it's getting cooler *ou* colder.
(b) (*en se lavant*) to freshen (o.s.) up; (*en buvant*) to refresh o.s. **on se rafraîchirait volontiers** a cool drink would be most acceptable.
rafraîchissant, e [ʀafʀɛʃisɑ̃, ɑ̃t] *adj vent* refreshing, cooling; *boisson* refreshing; (*fig*) *idée, œuvre* refreshing.
rafraîchissement [ʀafʀɛʃismɑ̃] *nm* **(a)** [*température*] cooling. **dû au ~ de la température** due to the cooler weather *ou* the cooling of the weather; **on s'attend à un ~ rapide de la température** we expect the weather to get rapidly cooler.
(b) (*boisson*) cool *ou* cold drink. (*glaces, fruits*) **~s** refreshments.
ragaillardir [ʀagajaʀdiʀ] (2) *vt* to perk up*, buck up*. **tout ragaillardi par cette nouvelle** bucked up by this news*.
rage [ʀaʒ] *nf* **(a)** (*colère*) rage, fury. **la ~ au cœur** seething with rage *ou* anger, seething inwardly; **mettre qn en ~** to infuriate *ou* enrage sb, make sb's blood boil; **être dans une ~ folle, être ivre *ou* fou (*f* folle) de ~** to be mad with rage, be in a furious rage *ou* a raging temper; **suffoquer *ou* étouffer de ~** to choke with anger *ou* rage; **dans sa ~ de ne pouvoir l'obtenir, il ...** in his rage *ou* fury at not being able to obtain it, he ...; *V* **amour.**

(b) (*manie*) **avoir la ~ de faire/qch** (*besoin irraisonné*) to have a mania for doing/sth; (*habitude irritante*) **cette ~ qu'il a de tout le temps ricaner** this infuriating *ou* maddening habit he has of sniggering all the time.

(c) faire ~ *[incendie, tempête]* to rage.

(d) (*Méd*) rabies.

(e) ~ de dents raging toothache.

rageant, e* [ʀaʒɑ̃, ɑ̃t] *adj* infuriating, maddening.

rager [ʀaʒe] (3) *vi* to fume. **ça (me) fait ~!** it makes me fume! *ou* furious! *ou* mad!; **rageant de voir que les autres n'étaient pas punis** furious *ou* fuming that the others weren't punished.

rageur, -euse [ʀaʒœʀ, øz] *adj enfant* hot- *ou* quick-tempered; *ton, voix* bad-tempered, angry. **il était ~** he was furious *ou* livid.

rageusement [ʀaʒøzmɑ̃] *adv* angrily.

raglan [ʀaglɑ̃] *nm, adj inv* raglan.

ragondin [ʀagɔ̃dɛ̃] *nm* (*animal*) coypu; (*fourrure*) nutria.

ragot* [ʀago] *nm* piece of (malicious) gossip *ou* tittle-tattle. **~s** gossip, tittle-tattle.

ragougnasse [ʀaguɲas] *nf* (*péj*) pigswill (*fig: U*).

ragoût [ʀagu] *nm* stew. **viande en ~** meat stew.

ragoûtant, e [ʀagutɑ̃, ɑ̃t] *adj*: **peu ~** *mets* unsavoury, unpalatable; *individu* unsavoury; *travail* unwholesome, unpalatable, unappetising; **ce n'est guère ~** that's not very inviting *ou* tempting.

ragrafer [ʀagʀafe] (1) *vt* to do up. **elle se ragrafa** she did herself up (again).

rahat-lo(u)koum [ʀaatlukum] *nm* = **loukoum.**

rai [ʀɛ] *nm* (*littér: rayon*) ray ; (*Tech*) spoke (*of wooden wheel*).

raid [ʀɛd] *nm* (*Mil*) raid, hit-and-run attack. (*Sport: parcours*) **~ automobile/aérien/à skis** long-distance car trek/flight/ski trek.

raide [ʀɛd] **1** *adj* **(a)** (*rigide*) *corps, membre, geste, étoffe* stiff; *cheveux* straight; *câble* taut, tight. **être *ou* se tenir ~ comme un échalas *ou* un piquet *ou* la justice** to be (as) stiff as a poker; **assis ~ sur sa chaise** sitting bolt upright on his chair; *V* **corde.**

(b) (*abrupt*) steep, abrupt.

(c) (*inflexible*) *attitude, morale, personne* rigid, inflexible; (*guindé*) *manières* stiff, starchy; *démarche* stiff.

(d) (*fort, âpre*) *alcool* rough.

(e) (*: *difficile à croire*) **l'histoire est un peu ~** that's a bit hard to swallow* (*fig*) *ou* a bit far-fetched; **elle est ~ celle-là** (*je n'y crois pas*) that's a bit hard to swallow* (*fig*), that's a bit far-fetched; (*ils vont trop loin*) that's a bit steep* *ou* stiff*; **il en a vu de ~s** he's seen a thing or two*; **il (t')en raconte de ~s** he's always spinning (you) a yarn.

(f) (*osé*) **assez *ou* un peu ~** *propos, passage, scène* daring, bold; **il s'en passe de ~s, chez eux** all sorts of things go on at their place; **il en raconte de ~s** he's always telling pretty daring stories.

(g) (*: *sans argent*) broke*. **être ~ comme un passe-lacet** to be stony *ou* flat broke*.

2 *adv* **(a)** (*en pente*) **ça montait/descendait ~** *[ascension]* it was a steep climb/climb down; *[pente]* it climbed/fell steeply.

(b) (*net*) **tomber ~** to drop to the ground *ou* floor; **tomber ~ mort** to drop *ou* fall down stone dead; **tuer qn ~** to kill sb outright *ou* stone dead; **il l'a étendu ~ (mort)*** he laid him out cold.

raideur [ʀɛdœʀ] *nf* (*V* **raide**) stiffness; straightness; tautness, tightness; steepness, abruptness; rigidity, inflexibility; starchiness; roughness. **avec ~** *répondre* stiffly, abruptly; *marcher* stiffly.

raidillon [ʀedijɔ̃] *nm* (steep) rise *ou* incline (*in a narrow path or road*).

raidir [ʀedíʀ] (2) **1** *vt drap, tissu* to stiffen; *corde, fil de fer* to pull taut *ou* tight, tighten. **~ ses muscles** to tense *ou* stiffen one's muscles; **le corps raidi par la mort** his body stiffened by death; (*fig*) **~ sa position** to harden *ou* toughen one's position, take a hard *ou* tough line.

2 se raidir *vpr* **(a)** *[toile, tissu]* to stiffen, become stiff(er); *[corde]* to grow taut; (*fig*) *[position]* to harden.

(b) *[personne]* (*perdre sa souplesse*) to become stiff(er); (*bander ses muscles*) to tense *ou* stiffen o.s.; (*se préparer moralement*) to brace *ou* steel o.s.; (*s'entêter*) to take a hard *ou* tough line.

raidissement [ʀedismɑ̃] *nm* (*perte de souplesse*) stiffening. (*fig: intransigeance*) **ce ~ soudain du parti adverse** this sudden tough line taken by the opposing party.

raidisseur [ʀedisœʀ] *nm* (*tendeur*) tightener.

raie[1] [ʀɛ] *nf* **(a)** (*trait*) line; (*Agr: sillon*) furrow; (*éraflure*) mark, scratch. **faire une ~** to draw a line; **attention, tu vas faire des ~s** careful, you'll make marks *ou* scratches.

(b) (*bande*) stripe. **chemise avec des ~s** striped *ou* stripy shirt; **les ~s de son pelage** the stripes on its fur; (*Phys*) **~ d'absorption/d'émission** absorption/emission line.

(c) (*Coiffure*) parting. **avoir la ~ au milieu/sur le côté** to have a centre/side parting, have one's hair parted in the middle/to the side.

raie[2] [ʀɛ] *nf* (*Zool*) skate, ray; *V* **gueule.**

raifort [ʀɛfɔʀ] *nm* horseradish.

rail [ʀɑj] *nm* rail. (*voie*) **les ~s** the rails, the track; **~ conducteur** live rail; **le ~ est plus pratique que la route** the railway (*Brit*) *ou* railroad (*US*) is more practical than the road, rail is more practical than road; (*lit, fig*) **remettre sur les ~s** to put back on the rails; **quitter les ~s, sortir des ~s** to jump the rails, go off the rails.

railler [ʀɑje] (1) **1** *vt* (*frm: se moquer de*) *personne* to scoff at, jeer at, mock at; *chose* to scoff at. **2** *vi* (††: *plaisanter*) to jest. **... dit-il en raillant ...** he said in jest. **3 se railler** *vpr*: **se ~ de**†† to scoff at, jeer at, mock at.

raillerie [ʀɑjʀi] *nf* (*frm*) (*U: ironie*) mockery, scoffing; (*sarcasme*) mocking remark, scoff.

railleur, -euse [ʀɑjœʀ, øz] **1** *adj* mocking, derisive, scoffing. **2** *nmpl*: **les ~s** the scoffers, the mockers.

railleusement [ʀɑjøzmɑ̃] *adv répondre, suggérer* mockingly, derisively, scoffingly.

rainer [ʀene] (1) *vt* to groove.

rainette [ʀenɛt] *nf* **(a)** (*grenouille*) tree frog. **(b)** = **reinette.**

rainure [ʀenyʀ] *nf* (*gén: longue, formant glissière*) groove; (*courte, pour emboîtage*) slot.

rainurer [ʀenyʀe] (1) *vt* to groove.

rais [ʀɛ] *nm* = **rai.**

raisin [ʀɛzɛ̃] **1** *nm* **(a)** (*gén*) **~(s)** grapes; **~ noir/blanc** black/white grape; **c'est un ~ qui donne du bon vin** it's a grape that yields a good wine; *V* **grain, grappe, jus.**

(b) (*papier*) ≃ royal.

2: raisins de Corinthe currants; **raisins secs** raisins; **raisins de Smyrne** sultanas; **raisins de table** dessert *ou* eating grapes.

raisiné [ʀɛzine] *nm* (*jus*) grape jelly; (*confiture*) *pear or quince jam made with grape jelly*; (*: *sang*) claret‡, blood.

raison [ʀɛzɔ̃] **1** *nf* **(a)** (*gén, Philos: faculté de discernement*) reason. **seul l'homme est doué de ~** man alone is endowed with reason; **conforme à la ~** within the bounds of reason; **contraire à la ~** contrary to reason; **il n'a plus sa ~, il a perdu la ~** he has lost his reason, he has taken leave of his senses, he is not in his right mind; **si tu avais toute ta ~ tu verrais que ...** if you were in your right mind *ou* right senses, you would see that ...; **manger/boire plus que de ~** to eat/drink more than is sensible *ou* more than one should *ou* more than is good for one; *V* **âge, mariage, rime.**

(b) (*motif*) reason. **la ~ pour laquelle je suis venu** the reason (why *ou* that *ou* for which) I came; **pour quelles ~s l'avez-vous renvoyé?** on what grounds did you sack him?, what were your reasons for sacking him?; **la ~ de cette réaction** the reason for this reaction; **il n'y a pas de ~ de s'arrêter** there's no reason to stop; **j'ai mes ~s** I have my reasons; **pour des ~s politiques/de famille** for political/family reasons; **pour ~s de santé** for reasons of health, on grounds of (ill) health, for health reasons; **~s cachées** hidden motives *ou* reasons.

(c) (*argument, explication, excuse*) reason. **sans ~** without reason; **sans ~ valable** for no valid reason; (*iro*) **il a toujours de bonnes ~s!** he's always got a good excuse! *ou* reason!; (*Prov*) **la ~ du plus fort est toujours la meilleure** might is right; **ce n'est pas une ~!** that's no excuse! *ou* reason!; *V* **comparaison, rendre.**

(d) (*Math*) ratio. **~ directe/inverse** direct/inverse ratio *ou* proportion.

(e) (*loc*) **avec (juste) ~** rightly, justifiably, with good reason; **~ de plus** all the more reason (*pour faire* for doing); **à plus forte ~, je n'irai pas** all the more reason for me not to go; **comme de ~** as one might expect; **pour une ~ ou pour une autre** for one *ou* some reason or other *ou* another; **non sans ~** not without reason; **avoir ~** to be right (*de faire* in doing, to do); **avoir ~ de qn/qch** to get the better of sb/sth; **donner ~ à qn** *[événement]* to prove sb right; **tu donnes toujours ~ à ta fille** you're always siding with your daughter; **se faire une ~** to accept it, put up with it; **mettre qn à la ~** to bring sb to his senses, make sb see reason, talk (some) sense into sb*; (†, *littér*) **demander ~ à qn de** *offense* to demand satisfaction from sb for (†, *littér*); **en ~ du froid** because of *ou* owing to the cold weather; **en ~ de son jeune âge** because of *ou* on the grounds of his youth; **on est payé en ~ du travail fourni** we are paid according to *ou* in proportion to the work produced; **à ~ de 5 F par caisse** at the rate of 5 francs per crate.

2: raison d'État reason of State; **raison d'être: cet enfant est toute sa raison d'être** this child is her whole life *ou* her entire reason for living *ou* her entire raison d'être; **cette association n'a aucune raison d'être** this association has no reason for being *ou* no grounds for existence *ou* no raison d'être; (*Comm*) **raison sociale** corporate name.

raisonnable [ʀɛzɔnabl(ə)] *adj* **(a)** (*sensé*) *personne* sensible, reasonable; *conseil* sensible, sound, sane; *opinion, propos, conduite* sensible, sane. **soyez ~** be reasonable; **elle devrait être plus ~, à son âge** she should know better *ou* she should have more sense at her age; **réaction bien peu ~** very unreasonable reaction; **ce n'est vraiment pas ~** it's not really sensible *ou* reasonable at all.

(b) (*décent*) *prix, demande, salaire, quantité* reasonable, fair. **ils vous accordent une liberté ~** they grant you reasonable freedom, they grant you a reasonable *ou* fair *ou* tolerable amount of freedom.

(c) (*littér: doué de raison*) rational, reasoning.

raisonnablement [ʀɛzɔnabləmɑ̃] *adv conseiller* sensibly, soundly; *agir* sensibly, reasonably; *dépenser* moderately; *travailler, rétribuer* reasonably *ou* fairly. **tout ce qu'on peut ~ espérer est que ...** all that one can reasonably hope for is that ... .

raisonné, e [ʀɛzɔne] (*ptp de* **raisonner**) *adj* **(a)** (*mûri, réfléchi*) *attitude, projet* well-thought-out, reasoned. **(b)** (*systématique*) **grammaire/méthode ~e de français** reasoned grammar/primer of French.

raisonnement [ʀɛzɔnmɑ̃] *nm* **(a)** (*U*) (*façon de réfléchir*) reasoning (*U*); (*faculté de penser*) power *ou* faculty of reasoning; (*cheminement de la pensée*) thought process. **~ analogique/par déduction** analogical/deductive reasoning; **prouver qch par le ~** to prove sth by one's reasoning *ou* by the use of reason; **ses ~s m'étonnent** his reasoning surprises me.

(b) (*argumentation*) argument. **un ~ logique** a logical argument, a logical line *ou* chain of reasoning.

(c) (*péj: ergotages*) **~s** arguing, argument, quibbling; **tous les ~s ne feront rien pour changer ma décision** no amount of arguing *ou* argument will alter my decision.

raisonner [ʀɛzɔne] (1) **1** *vi* **(a)** (*penser, réfléchir*) to reason (*sur* about). ~ **par induction/déduction** to reason by induction/deduction; **il raisonne mal** he doesn't reason very well, his reasoning *ou* way of reasoning isn't very sound; **il raisonne juste** his reasoning is sound; **il raisonne comme un panier percé* *ou* une pantoufle*** he can't follow his own argument; **c'est bien raisonné** it's well *ou* soundly reasoned.

(b) (*discourir, argumenter*) to argue (*sur* about). **on ne peut pas** ~ **avec lui** you (just) can't argue *ou* reason with him.

(c) (*péj: ergoter*) to argue, quibble (*avec* with).

(d) ~ **de**† *question, problème* to argue about.

2 *vt* **(a)** (*sermonner*) to reason with. **inutile d'essayer de le** ~ it's useless to try and reason with him, it's useless to try and make him listen to *ou* see reason.

(b) (*justifier par la raison*) *croyance, conduite, démarche* to reason out. **explication bien raisonnée** well-reasoned explanation.

3 se raisonner *vpr* to reason with o.s., make o.s. see reason. **raisonne-toi** try to be reasonable *ou* to make yourself see reason; **l'amour ne se raisonne pas** love cannot be reasoned *ou* knows no reason.

raisonneur, -euse [ʀɛzɔnœʀ, øz] **1** *adj* (*péj*) quibbling (*épith*), argumentative; (*réfléchi*) reasoning (*épith*).

2 *nm,f* **(a)** (*péj: ergoteur*) arguer, quibbler. **c'est un** ~ he's always arguing *ou* quibbling, he's an arguer *ou* a quibbler; **ne fais pas le** ~ stop arguing *ou* quibbling.

(b) (*rare: penseur*) reasoner.

rajah [ʀadʒa] *nm* rajah.

rajeunir [ʀaʒœniʀ] (2) **1** *vt* **(a)** ~ **qn** *[cure]* to rejuvenate sb; *[repos, expérience]* to make sb feel younger; *[soins de beauté, vêtement]* to make sb look younger; **l'amour/ce chapeau la rajeunit de 10 ans** love/this hat takes 10 years off her* *ou* makes her look 10 years younger; **tu le rajeunis (de 5 ans), il est né en 1950** you're making him (5 years) younger than he is — he was born in 1950; (*hum*) **ça ne nous rajeunit pas!** we're not getting any younger!

(b) *manuel* to update, bring up to date; *institution* to modernize; *installation, mobilier* to modernize, give a new look to; *vieux habits* to give a new look to, brighten up; *personnel* to infuse *ou* bring new *ou* young blood into, recruit younger people into; *thème, théorie* to inject new life into. **firme qui a besoin d'être rajeunie** firm that needs new *ou* young blood (brought *ou* infused into it) *ou* that needs an influx of new people.

2 *vi [personne]* (*se sentir plus jeune*) to feel younger; (*paraître plus jeune*) to look younger; *[institution, quartier]* (*modernisation*) to be modernized; (*membres plus jeunes*) to take on a younger air. **avec les enfants, la vieille demeure rajeunissait** with the children around, the old house seemed to take on a younger air *ou* had a younger atmosphere about it.

3 se rajeunir *vpr* (*se prétendre moins âgé*) to make o.s. younger; (*se faire paraître moins âgé*) to make o.s. look younger.

rajeunissant, e [ʀaʒœnisɑ̃, ɑ̃t] *adj traitement, crème* rejuvenating.

rajeunissement [ʀaʒœnismɑ̃] *nm [personne]* rejuvenation; *[manuel]* updating; *[installation, mobilier]* modernization; *[vieux habits]* brightening up. ~ **du personnel** infusion of new *ou* young blood into the staff.

rajout [ʀaʒu] *nm* addition.

rajouter [ʀaʒute] (1) *vt sel, sucre* to put on *ou* put in *ou* add (some) more; *commentaire* to add another. **il rajouta que ...** he added that ...; (*fig*) **en** ~* to lay it on (thick)*; **ayant déjà donné 50 F, il rajouta 10 F** having already given 50 francs he added another 10.

rajustement [ʀaʒystəmɑ̃] *nm [salaires, prix]* adjustment.

rajuster [ʀaʒyste] (1) **1** *vt* **(a)** (*remettre en place*) *mécanisme* to readjust; *vêtement* to straighten (out), tidy; *cravate, lunettes* to straighten, adjust; *coiffure* to rearrange, tidy. **elle rajusta sa toilette** she arranged herself *ou* her dress.

(b) (*recentrer*) *tir* to (re)adjust; (*fig*) *prix, salaire* to adjust.

2 se rajuster *vpr [personne]* to tidy *ou* straighten o.s. up, rearrange o.s.

râlant, e* [ʀɑlɑ̃, ɑ̃t] *adj* infuriating.

râle[1] [ʀɑl] *nm* **(a)** *[blessé]* groan; *[mourant]* (death) rattle. ~ **d'agonie *ou* de la mort** death rattle. **(b)** (*Méd*) rale.

râle[2] [ʀɑl] *nm* (*Orn*) rail.

ralenti, e [ʀalɑ̃ti] (*ptp de* **ralentir**) **1** *adj vie* slow-moving, easy-paced, slow; *mouvement* slow.

2 *nm* **(a)** (*Ciné*) slow motion. **en *ou* au** ~ *filmer, projeter* in slow motion.

(b) (*Aut*) **régler le** ~ to adjust the tick-over (*Brit*); **le moteur est un peu faible au** ~ the engine doesn't tick over (*Brit*) *ou* doesn't idle too well; **tourner au** ~ to tick over (*Brit*), idle.

(c) (*fig*) **vivre au** ~ to live at a slower pace; **cette existence paisible, au** ~ that peaceful slow *ou* easy-paced existence; **usine qui tourne au** ~ factory which is just ticking over *ou* idling.

ralentir [ʀalɑ̃tiʀ] (2) **1** *vt processus, véhicule* to slow down; *mouvement, expansion* to slow down *ou* up; (*Mil*) *avance* to check, hold up; *effort, zèle* to slacken. ~ **l'allure** to slow down *ou* up, reduce speed; ~ **sa marche *ou* le pas** to slacken one's *ou* the pace, slow down.

2 *vi [marcheur]* to slow down, slacken one's pace; *[véhicule, automobiliste]* to slow down, reduce speed. (*Aut*) '~' 'slow', 'reduce speed now'.

3 se ralentir *vpr [production]* to slow down *ou* up, slacken (off), fall off; (*Mil*) *[offensive]* to let up, ease off; *[ardeur, zèle]* to flag; (*Physiol*) *[fonctions]* to slow up.

ralentissement [ʀalɑ̃tismɑ̃] *nm* **(a)** (*V* **ralentir**) slowing down; slowing up; checking, holding up; slackening.

(b) *[marcheur, véhicule, automobiliste]* slowing down.

(c) (*V* **se ralentir**) slowing down; slowing up; slackening (off), falling off; letting up, easing off; flagging.

râler [ʀɑle] (1) *vi* **(a)** *[blessé]* to groan, moan; *[mourant]* to give the death rattle.

(b) (*: *rouspéter*) to grouse*, moan (and groan)*. **il est allé** ~ **chez le prof** he went to grouse* *ou* moan* to the teacher; **faire** ~ **qn** to infuriate sb; **ça (vous) fait** ~ it makes you fume, it makes you want to blow your top*; **qu'as tu à** ~**?** what have you got to grouse* *ou* moan* about?

râleur, -euse [ʀɑlœʀ, øz] **1** *adj* grousing* (*épith*). **il est (trop)** ~ he's (too much of) a grouser* *ou* moaner*. **2** *nm,f* grouser*, moaner*.

ralliement [ʀalimɑ̃] *nm* **(a)** (*V* **rallier**) rallying; winning over; uniting. **le** ~ **des troupes** the rallying *ou* rally of troops.

(b) (*V* **se rallier**) ~ **à** joining; going over to, siding with; coming over *ou* round to; being won over to; rallying to; rallying around; **je suis étonné de son** ~ **(à notre cause)** I am surprised by the fact that he joined (our cause).

(c) (*Mil*) rallying, rally. **signe/cri de** ~ rallying sign/cry.

rallier [ʀalje] (7) **1** *vt* **(a)** (*Chasse, Mil, Naut: regrouper*) to rally.

(b) (*gagner*) *personne, groupe* to win over, rally (*à* to); *suffrages* to bring in, win. ~ **qn à son avis** to bring sb round *ou* win sb over to one's opinion.

(c) (*unir*) *groupe, parti* to rally, unite. **groupe rallié autour d'un idéal** group united by an ideal.

(d) (*rejoindre: Mil, Naut*) to rejoin. (*Pol*) ~ **la majorité** to rejoin the majority; (*Naut*) ~ **le bord** to rejoin ship.

2 se rallier *vpr* **(a)** (*suivre*) **se** ~ **à** *parti* to join; *ennemi* to go over to, side with; *chef* to rally round *ou* to; *avis* to come over *ou* round to; *doctrine* to be won over to; *cause* to join, rally to, be won over to.

(b) (*Mil, Naut: se regrouper*) to rally.

rallonge [ʀalɔ̃ʒ] *nf* **(a)** *[table]* (extra) leaf; *[fil électrique]* extension cord *ou* flex; *[vêtement]* piece (*used to lengthen an item of clothing*); *[compas]* extension arm; *[perche]* extension piece. **table à** ~**(s)** extendable table.

(b) (*: *supplément*) **une** ~ **d'argent/de vacances** a bit of extra *ou* some extra money/holiday; **une** ~ **de deux jours** an extra two days, a two-day extension.

(c) (*péj*) **histoire à** ~ never-ending story; **nom à** ~ double-barrelled name.

rallongement [ʀalɔ̃ʒmɑ̃] *nm* (*V* **rallonger**) lengthening; letting down; extension.

rallonger [ʀalɔ̃ʒe] (3) **1** *vt vêtement* (*en ajoutant*) to lengthen, make longer; (*en défaisant l'ourlet*) to let down; *texte, service militaire, piste* to lengthen, extend, make longer; *vacances, fil, table, bâtiment* to extend.

2 *vi* (*) **les jours rallongent** the days are getting longer.

rallumer [ʀalyme] (1) **1** *vt* **(a)** (*lit*) *feu* to light (up) again, relight, rekindle (*littér*); *cigarette* to relight, light up again; *lampe* to switch *ou* turn *ou* put on again, relight. ~ **(l'électricité *ou* la lumière)** to switch *ou* turn *ou* put the light(s) on again; ~ **(dans) le bureau** to switch *ou* turn *ou* put the light(s) on again in the office.

(b) (*fig*) *courage, haine, querelle* to revive, rekindle; *conflit, guerre* to stir up again, revive, rekindle.

2 se rallumer *vpr* **(a)** *[incendie]* to flare up again; *[lampe]* to come on again. **le bureau se ralluma** the light(s) in the office came on again.

(b) *[guerre, querelle]* to flare up again; *[haine, courage]* to revive, be revived.

rallye [ʀali] *nm*: ~ **(automobile)** (car) rally.

ramadan [ʀamadɑ̃] *nm*: **(R)**~ Ramadan.

ramage [ʀamaʒ] *nm* **(a)** (*littér: chant*) song, warbling (*U*). **(b)** (*branchages, dessin*) ~**(s)** foliage; **tissu à** ~**s** fabric *ou* material with a leafy design *ou* pattern.

ramassage [ʀamɑsaʒ] *nm* **(a)** (*gén*) collection. ~ **des pommes de terre** lifting *ou* digging up of potatoes; ~ **scolaire** (*service*) school bus service; (*action*) picking up of pupils; **point de** ~ pick-up point.

(b) (*cueillette*) *[bois mort, coquillages, foin]* gathering; *[épis, fruits tombés]* gathering (up); *[champignons]* picking, gathering; *[pommes de terres]* digging up, lifting; *[balles de tennis]* picking up.

ramasse- [ʀamɑs] *préf V* **ramasser.**

ramassé, e [ʀamɑse] (*ptp de* **ramasser**) *adj* (*pour se protéger*) huddled (up); (*pour bondir*) crouched; (*trapu*) squat, stocky; (*concis*) compact, condensed. **le petit village** ~ **dans le fond de la vallée** the little village nestling in the heart of the valley.

ramasser [ʀamɑse] (1) **1** *vt* **(a)** (*lit, fig: prendre*) *objet, personne* to pick up. **il l'a ramassée dans le ruisseau** he picked her up out of the gutter; **se faire** ~ **dans une manif** to get picked up at a demo; **on l'a ramassé à la petite cuiller*** they had to scrape him off the ground; ~ **une bûche* *ou* une pelle*** to come a cropper*.

(b) (*collecter*) *objets épars* to pick up, gather up; *élèves* to pick up, collect; *copies, cahiers* to collect, take in, gather up; *cotisations, ordures* to collect; (*) *idée* to pick up; (*) *argent* to pick up, pocket*.

(c) (*récolter*) *bois, feuilles, coquillages* to gather, collect; *fruits tombés* to gather (up); *foin* to gather; *pommes de terre* to lift, dig up; *champignons* to pick, gather. ~ **à la pelle** (*lit*) to shovel up; (*fig: en abondance*) to gather (up) by the shovelful.

(d) (*resserrer*) *jupons, draps* to gather (up); (*fig*) *style* to condense.

(e) (*: *attraper*) *rhume, maladie* to pick up, catch, get;

réprimande, coups to collect, get; *amende* to pick up, collect, get. **il va se faire ~ par sa mère** he'll get told off *ou* ticked off (*surtout Brit*) by his mother*; **il a ramassé 100 F (d'amende)** he picked up *ou* collected a 100-franc fine, he was done for 100 francs*.

2 se ramasser *vpr* (*se pelotonner*) to curl up; (*pour bondir*) to crouch; (*: *se relever*) to pick o.s. up; (‡: *tomber*) to come a cropper*, fall over *ou* down. se faire ~ *[candidat]* to come a cropper*.

3: ramasse-miettes *nm inv* table tidy; **ramasse-monnaie** *nm inv* (change-)tray.

ramasseur, -euse [ʀamɑsœʀ, øz] **1** *nm,f* (*personne*) collector. **~ de lait** milk collector; **~ de balles (de tennis)** ballboy; **~ de mégots** collector of fag ends; **~ de pommes de terre** potato-picker.

2 *nm* (*outil*) *[machine]* pickup.

3 ramasseuse *nf* (*machine*) **~euse-presse** baler.

ramassis [ʀamɑsi] *nm* (*péj*) **~ de** *voyous* pack *ou* bunch *ou* horde of; *doctrines, objets* jumble of.

rambarde [ʀɑ̃baʀd(ə)] *nf* guardrail.

ramdam‡ [ʀamdam] *nm* (*tapage*) hullabaloo‡, row*, racket*. **faire du ~** (*bruit*) to kick up *ou* make a racket* *ou* row*; (*protestation*) to kick up a row*.

rame [ʀam] *nf* **(a)** (*aviron*) oar. **aller à la ~** to row; (*littér*) **faire force de ~s** to ply the oars (*littér*), row hard; **il n'en fiche pas une ~‡** he doesn't do a damned‡ *ou* ruddy‡ (*Brit*) thing.

(b) (*Rail*) train. **~ (de métro)** (underground (*Brit*) *ou* subway) train.

(c) (*Typ*) ream; (*Tex*) tenter; (*Agr*) stake, stick; *V* **haricot.**

rameau, *pl* **~x** [ʀamo] *nm* (*lit*) (small) branch; (*fig*) branch; (*Anat*) ramification. (*lit, fig*) **~ d'olivier** olive branch; (*Rel*) **(dimanche des) R~x** Palm Sunday.

ramée [ʀame] *nf* (*littér: feuillage*) leafy boughs (*littér*); (*coupé*) leafy *ou* green branches. **il n'en fiche pas une ~‡** he doesn't do a damned‡ *ou* ruddy‡ (*Brit*) thing.

ramener [ʀamne] (5) **1** *vt* **(a)** *personne, objet* to bring back, take back; *paix, ordre* to bring back, restore. **je vais te ~ en voiture** I'll drive you back (home), I'll take you back (home) in the car; **ramène du pain/les enfants** bring *ou* fetch some bread/the children back (*de* from); **ça l'a ramené en prison** it brought *ou* sent him back to prison; **l'été a ramené les accidents/la mode des chapeaux** summer has brought the return of accidents/has brought back *ou* brought the return of the fashion for hats.

(b) (*tirer*) *voile* to draw; *couverture* to pull, draw. **~ ses cheveux sur son front** to brush down one's hair onto *ou* over one's forehead; **~ ses cheveux en arrière** to brush one's hair back; **~ ses jambes/épaules en arrière** to draw back one's legs/shoulders.

(c) (*faire revenir à*) **~ à** to bring back to; **~ à la vie** *personne, région* to revive, bring back to life; **~ qn à la raison** to bring sb to reason *ou* to his senses; **~ le compteur à zéro** to put the meter back to zero, reset the meter at zero; **~ les prix à un juste niveau** to bring prices back (down) *ou* restore prices to a reasonable level; **~ la conversation sur un sujet** to bring *ou* lead the conversation back (on)to a subject; **~ son cheval au pas** to rein in one's horse to a walk; **il ramène toujours tout à lui** he always relates eveything to himself.

(d) (*réduire à*) **~ à** to reduce to; **ils ont ramené ces bagarres au rang de simple incident** they played down the fighting, passing it off as a mere incident.

(e) (*loc*) **~ sa fraise‡, la ~‡** (*protester*) to kick up a row* *ou* fuss*; (*intervenir*) to put *ou* shove one's oar in*.

2 se ramener *vpr* **(a)** (*se réduire à*) **se ~ à** *[problèmes]* to come down to, boil down to; (*Math*) *[fraction]* to reduce to, be reduced to.

(b) (‡: *arriver*) to roll up‡, turn up*.

ramequin [ʀamkɛ̃] *nm* ramekin, ramequin.

ramer[1] [ʀame] (1) *vi* to row. **~ en couple** to scull.

ramer[2] [ʀame] (1) *vt* (*Agr*) to stake.

rameur [ʀamœʀ] *nm* (*sportif*) oarsman, rower; (*galérien*) rower.

rameuse [ʀamøz] *nf* (*sportive*) oarswoman, rower.

rameuter [ʀamøte] (1) *vt* *foule, partisans* to gather together, round up; *chiens* to round up, form into a pack again. **les gens s'étaient rameutés** people had gathered (themselves) together (again).

rami [ʀami] *nm* rummy.

ramier [ʀamje] *nm*: **(pigeon) ~** woodpigeon, ringdove.

ramification [ʀamifikɑsjɔ̃] *nf* (*gén*) ramification.

ramifier (se) [ʀamifje] (7) *vpr* *[veines]* to ramify; *[routes, branches, famille]* to branch out (*en* into). **cette science s'est ramifiée en plusieurs autres** this science has branched out into several others.

ramolli, e [ʀamɔli] (*ptp de* **ramollir**) **1** *adj* *biscuit, beurre* soft; *personne* (*avachi*) soft; (*stupide*) soft (in the head), soft-headed. (*péj*) **il a le cerveau ~** he is *ou* has gone soft in the head.

2 *nm,f* (*péj*) soft-headed fool.

ramollir [ʀamɔliʀ] (2) **1** *vt* *matière* to soften; (*fig*) *courage, résolution* to weaken. **~ qn** *[plaisir]* to soften sb, make sb soft; *[climat]* to enervate sb.

2 se ramollir *vpr* (*lit, fig*) to get *ou* go soft. **son cerveau se ramollit** (*hum*) he's going soft in the head; (*Méd*) his brain is softening.

ramollissement [ʀamɔlismɑ̃] *nm* softening. **~ cérébral** softening of the brain.

ramollo* [ʀamɔlo] *adj* (*avachi*) droopy*; (*gâteux*) soft (in the head), soft-headed.

ramonage [ʀamɔnaʒ] *nm* chimney-sweeping.

ramoner [ʀamɔne] (1) *vt* *cheminée* to sweep.

ramoneur [ʀamɔnœʀ] *nm* (chimney)sweep.

rampant, e [ʀɑ̃pɑ̃, ɑ̃t] **1** *adj* **(a)** *animal* crawling, creeping; *plante* creeping; *caractère, employé* grovelling, cringing. (*arg Aviat*) **personnel ~** ground crew *ou* staff; *V* **arc.**

(b) (*Hér*) rampant.

2 *nm* **(a)** (*arg Aviat*) member of the ground crew *ou* staff. **les ~s** the ground crew *ou* staff.

(b) (*Archit*) pitch.

rampe [ʀɑ̃p] **1** *nf* **(a)** (*voie d'accès*) ramp, slope; (*côte*) slope, incline, gradient.

(b) *[escalier]* banister(s); *[chemin, escarpe etc]* handrail.

(c) (*projecteurs*) (*Théât*) **la ~** the footlights, the floats.

(d) (*loc*) (*fig*) **tenez bon la ~*** hold on to your hat*; **elle tient bon la ~*** she's still going strong; (*fig*) **lâcher la ~*** to kick the bucket*; **passer la ~** to get across to the audience.

2: rampe d'accès approach ramp; **rampe de balisage** runway lights (*pl*); **rampe de débarquement** disembarcation ramp; **rampe de graissage** oil gallery; **rampe de lancement** launching pad.

ramper [ʀɑ̃pe] (1) *vi* **(a)** *[serpent]* to crawl, creep, slither (along); *[quadrupède, homme]* to crawl; *[plante, ombre, feu]* to creep; *[sentiment, brouillard]* to lurk. **entrer/sortir en rampant** to crawl in/out; **le lierre rampe contre le mur** the ivy creeps up the wall.

(b) (*fig péj: s'abaisser*) to grovel (*devant* before), crawl *ou* cringe (*devant* to).

ramponneau‡, *pl* **~x** [ʀɑ̃pɔno] *nm* poke, bump, knock. **donner un ~ à qn** to poke *ou* bump *ou* knock sb.

ramure [ʀamyʀ] *nf* *[cerf]* antlers; *[arbre]* boughs, foliage.

rancard‡ [ʀɑ̃kaʀ] *nm* **(a)** (*tuyau*) tip; (*explication*) gen* (*Brit*) (*U*), info* (*U*). **il m'avait donné le ~** he had tipped me off *ou* given me the tip-off.

(b) (*rendez-vous*) (*gén*) meeting, date; (*amoureux*) date. **donner (un) ~ à qn** to arrange to meet sb, make a date with sb; **avoir (un) ~ avec qn** to have a meeting with sb, have a date with sb.

rancarder‡ [ʀɑ̃kaʀde] (1) *vt* (*V* **rancard**) to tip off; to give the gen* (*Brit*) *ou* info* to; to arrange to meet; to make a date with*. **se ~ sur qch** to get the info* *ou* gen* (*Brit*) about sth.

rancart[1]**‡** [ʀɑ̃kaʀ] *nm* = **rancard‡.**

rancart[2]**‡** [ʀɑ̃kaʀ] *nm*: **mettre au ~** *objet, idée, projet* to chuck out‡, sling out‡, get shot of‡ (*Brit*), scrap; **bon à mettre au ~** ready for the scrap heap.

rance [ʀɑ̃s] *adj* *beurre* rancid; *odeur* rank, rancid; (*fig*) stale. **sentir le ~** to smell rancid *ou* rank *ou* off* (*Brit*); **odeur de ~** rank *ou* rancid smell.

ranch [ʀɑ̃tʃ] *nm* ranch.

rancir [ʀɑ̃siʀ] (2) *vi* *[lard, beurre]* to go rancid *ou* off* (*Brit*); (*fig*) to grow stale.

rancœur [ʀɑ̃kœʀ] *nf* (*frm*) rancour (*U*), resentment (*U*). **avoir de la ~ contre qn** to be full of rancour against sb, feel resentment against sb.

rançon [ʀɑ̃sɔ̃] *nf* (*lit*) ransom. (*fig*) **c'est la ~ de la gloire** that's the price you have to pay for being famous, that's the price of fame; (*littér*) **mettre à ~** to hold to ransom.

rançonnement [ʀɑ̃sɔnmɑ̃] *nm* (*V* **rançonner**) demanding a ransom; fleecing; holding to ransom.

rançonner [ʀɑ̃sɔne] (1) *vt* **(a)** (*voler*) *convoi, voyageurs* to demand *ou* exact a ransom from; (*fig*) *contribuables, locataires* to fleece. **(b)** (†: *exiger une rançon*) *prisonnier* to hold to ransom.

rançonneur, -euse [ʀɑ̃sɔnœʀ, øz] *nm,f* (*lit*) person demanding a ransom; (*fig*) extortioner, extortionist.

rancune [ʀɑ̃kyn] *nf* grudge, rancour (*U: littér*). **avoir** *ou* **nourrir de la ~ à l'égard de** *ou* **contre qn** to harbour a grudge *ou* harbour feelings of rancour against sb; **garder ~ à qn (de qch)** to hold a grudge against sb (for sth), bear sb a grudge (for sth); **sans ~!** no hard *ou* ill feelings!

rancunier, -ière [ʀɑ̃kynje, jɛʀ] *adj* vindictive, rancorous (*littér*), spiteful.

randonnée [ʀɑ̃dɔne] *nf*: **~ (en voiture)** drive, ride; **~ (à bicyclette)** ride; **~ (à pied)** (*courte, à la campagne*) walk, ramble; (*longue, en montagne etc*) hike; **faire une ~ (en voiture)** to go for a drive *ou* ride; **cette ~ nocturne se termina mal** this night escapade ended badly.

rang [ʀɑ̃] *nm* **(a)** (*rangée*) *[maisons]* row, line; *[personnes, objets, tricot]* row. **collier à 3 ~s (de perles)** necklace with 3 rows of pearls; **porter un ~ de perles** to wear a string *ou* rope *ou* row of pearls; **en ~ d'oignons** in a row *ou* line.

(b) (*Scol*) row; (*Mil*) rank. **en ~s serrés** in close order, in serried ranks; **en ~ par 2/4** 2/4 abreast; **sur 2/4 ~s** 2/4 deep; **se mettre sur un ~** to get into *ou* form a line; (*fig*) **grossir les ~s de** to swell the ranks of; **se mettre en ~s par 4** (*Scol*) to get into *ou* form rows of 4; (*Mil*) to form fours; (*Mil*) **servir dans les ~s de** to serve in the ranks of; (*Mil*) **à vos ~s, marche!** fall in!; (*Mil, fig*) **sortir du ~** to come up *ou* rise *ou* be promoted from the ranks; *V* **rentrer, rompre, serrer.**

(c) (*Can*) country road (*bordered by farms at right angles*), concession road (*Québec*). **les ~s** the country.

(d) (*condition*) station. **du plus haut ~** of the highest standing *ou* station. **tenir** *ou* **garder son ~** to maintain one's rank.

(e) (*hiérarchique, grade, place*) rank. **avoir ~ de** to hold the rank of; **par ~ d'âge/de taille** in order of age/size *ou* height; **13e, c'est un bon ~** that's not bad — 13th place, 13th — that's a good position; **être placé au deuxième ~** to be ranked second; **mettre qn au ~ de** to count sb among; **c'est au premier/dernier ~ de mes préoccupations** that's the first/last thing on my mind; **il est au premier ~ des artistes contemporains** he is one of the highest ranking of *ou* he ranks among the best of the contemporary artists.

(f) (*loc*) **être/se mettre sur le ~** to be in/get into the running; **prendre ou avoir ~ parmi** to rank among.
rangé, e[1] [Rɑ̃ʒe] (*ptp de* **ranger**) *adj* (*ordonné*) orderly; (*sans excès*) settled, steady. **il est ~ ou il est ~ des voitures‡ maintenant** he has settled *ou* steadied down now; **petite vie bien ~e** well-ordered existence; *V* **bataille.**
rangée[2] [Rɑ̃ʒe] *nf [maisons, arbres]* row, line; *[objets, spectateurs]* row.
rangement [Rɑ̃ʒmɑ̃] *nm* **(a)** (*action*) *[objets, linge]* putting away; *[pièce, meuble]* tidying (up). **faire du ~ ou des ~s** to do some tidying (up).
(b) (*espace*) *[appartement]* cupboard space; *[remise]* storage space. **capacité de ~ d'une bibliothèque** shelf space of a bookcase; *V* **meuble.**
(c) (*arrangement*) arrangement.
ranger [Rɑ̃ʒe] (3) **1** *vt* **(a)** (*mettre en ordre*) *tiroir, maison* to tidy (up); *dossiers, papiers* to tidy (up), arrange; *mots, chiffres* to arrange, order. **tout est toujours bien rangé chez elle** it's always (nice and) tidy at her place; **rangé par ordre alphabétique** listed *ou* arranged alphabetically *ou* in alphabetical order.
(b) (*mettre à sa place*) *papiers, vêtements* to put away; *bateau* to moor, berth; *voiture, vélo* (*au garage*) to put away, park; (*dans la rue*) to park. **où se rangent les tasses?** where do the cups go? *ou* belong?; **je le range parmi les meilleurs** I rank *ou* put it among the best; **ce roman est à ~ parmi les meilleurs** this novel ranks *ou* is to be ranked among the best.
(c) (*disposer*) *écoliers* to line up, put *ou* form into rows; *soldats* to draw up; *invités* to place. (*fig*) **~ qn sous son autorité** to bring sb under one's authority.
2 se ranger *vpr* **(a)** *[automobiliste]* (*stationner*) to park; (*venir s'arrêter*) to pull in. **la voiture se rangea contre le trottoir** the car pulled in at the kerb; **le navire se rangea contre le quai** the ship moored *ou* berthed *ou* came alongside the quay.
(b) (*s'écarter*) *[piéton]* to step *ou* stand aside, make way; *[véhicule]* to pull over. **il se rangea pour la laisser passer** he stepped *ou* stood aside to let her go by *ou* past, he made way for her (to get by *ou* past).
(c) (*se mettre en rang*) to line up, get into line *ou* rows. **se ~ par deux/par quatre** to line up in twos/fours, get into rows of two/four.
(d) (*se rallier à*) **se ~ à** *décision* to go along with, abide by; *avis* to come round *ou* over to, fall in with; **se ~ du côté de qn** to side with *ou* take sides with sb.
(e) (*: *se caser*) to settle down; *V* **rangé.**
ranimation [Ranimɑsjɔ̃] *nf* = **réanimation.**
ranimer [Ranime] (1) **1** *vt blessé* to revive, restore to consciousness, bring round*, bring to*; *feu, braises* to rekindle; *région, souvenir, époque, conversation* to revive, bring back to life; *rancune, querelle* to rake up, revive; *forces, ardeur* to renew, restore; *amour, haine* to rekindle, renew; *douleur* to revive, renew; *espoir* to reawaken, rekindle, renew; *couleurs* to brighten up, revive.
2 se ranimer *vpr* (*V* **ranimer**) to revive, be revived; to come round*, come to*; to rekindle, be rekindled; to come back to life; to be raked up; to be renewed; to be restored; to reawaken, be reawakened.
raout† [Raut] *nm* (*réception*) rout††.
rapace [Rapas] **1** *nm* (*Orn*) bird of prey, raptor (*T*). **2** *adj* predatory, raptorial (*T*); (*fig*) rapacious, grasping, money-grabbing*.
rapacité [Rapasite] *nf* (*lit, fig*) rapaciousness, rapacity.
râpage [Rɑpaʒ] *nm* (*V* **râper**) grating; rasping; grinding.
rapatrié, e [RapatRije] (*ptp de* **rapatrier**) **1** *adj* repatriated. **2** *nm,f* repatriate.
rapatriement [RapatRimɑ̃] *nm* repatriation.
rapatrier [RapatRije] (7) *vt personne* to repatriate; *capital, objet* to bring back (home).
râpe [Rɑp] *nf* (*V* **râper**) grater; rasp; grinder.
râpé, e [Rɑpe] (*ptp de* **râper**) **1** *adj* (*usé*) *veste, coude* threadbare, worn to threads (*attrib*); (*Culin*) grated. **2** *nm* (*fromage*) grated cheese.
râper [Rɑpe] (1) *vt* (*Culin*) to grate; *bois* to rasp; *tabac* to grind. (*fig*) **vin qui râpe la gorge** wine that's rough on the throat.
rapetassage* [Raptasaʒ] *nm* patching up, botching up*.
rapetasser* [Raptase] (1) *vt* to patch up, botch up*.
rapetissement [Raptismɑ̃] *nm* (*V* **rapetisser**) taking up, shortening; taking in; shrinking; belittling; dwarfing. **le ~ des objets dû à la distance** the reduction in the size of objects when seen from a distance.
rapetisser [Raptise] (1) **1** *vt* **(a)** (*raccourcir*) *manteau* to take up, shorten; *taille, encolure* to take in; *objet* to shorten. (*fig*) **l'âge l'avait rapetissé** he had shrunk with age (*fig*).
(b) (*dénigrer*) to belittle.
(c) (*faire paraître plus petit*) to make seem *ou* look small(er). **le château rapetissait toutes les maisons qui l'entouraient** the castle dwarfed all the surrounding houses, the castle made all the surrounding houses look *ou* seem small in *ou* by comparison.
2 *vi*, **se rapetisser** *vpr* **(a)** *[vieillard]* to shrink, grow shorter *ou* smaller; (*) *[jours]* to get shorter. **les objets rapetissent à distance** objects look smaller at a distance.
(b) se ~ aux yeux de qn to belittle o.s. in sb's eyes.
râpeux, -euse [Rɑpø, øz] *adj* (*gén*) rough.
raphaélique [Rafaelik] *adj* Raphaelesque.
raphia [Rafja] *nm* raffia.
rapiat, e [Rapja, at] *nm,f* (*péj*) niggard, skinflint. **elle est ~(e)** she's niggardly *ou* stingy* *ou* tight-fisted, she's a niggard *ou* a skinflint.
rapide [Rapid] **1** *adj* **(a)** (*en déplacement*) *coureur, marche, pas* fast, quick, rapid, swift, speedy; *véhicule, route* fast; *animal* fast(-moving), swift; *fleuve* fast(-flowing), swift-flowing, rapid. **~ comme l'éclair** (as) quick as a flash; **il est ~ à la course** he's a good *ou* fast runner.
(b) (*dans le temps*) *travail, guérison, progrès, remède, réponse* speedy, quick, rapid, swift, fast; *accord* speedy, swift, rapid; *fortune, recette* quick. **examen (trop) ~ de qch** cursory examination of sth; **décision trop ~** hasty decision.
(c) (*vif*) *mouvement* quick, brisk, rapid, swift; *coup d'œil* rapid, quick, swift; *intelligence* quick, lively, nimble; *travailleur* quick, rapid, fast, swift, speedy. **d'une main ~** (*vite*) quickly, rapidly, swiftly; (*adroitement*) deftly; **tu n'es pas très ~ ce matin** you're not very lively *ou* bright *ou* you're not on the ball* this morning.
(d) (*en fréquence*) *pouls, rythme, respiration* fast, rapid.
(e) (*concis*) *style, récit* brisk, lively, fast-flowing.
(f) (*raide*) *pente* steep, abrupt, rapid (*littér*).
2 *nm* **(a)** (*train*) express (train), fast train. **le ~ Paris-Nice** the Paris-Nice express.
(b) *[rivière]* rapid.
rapidement [Rapidmɑ̃] *adv* (*V* **rapide**) fast; quickly; rapidly; swiftly; speedily; cursorily; hastily; deftly; steeply; abruptly.
rapidité [Rapidite] *nf* (*gén*) speed; *[allure, pas, coup d'œil]* speed, rapidity, quickness; *[opération, remède, réponse]* speed, speediness, swiftness, quickness; *[geste, travailleur]* speed, quickness; *[pouls, rythme]* speed, rapidity; *[style]* briskness, liveliness.
rapiéçage [Rapjesaʒ] *nm*, **rapiècement** [Rapjɛsmɑ̃] *nm* **(a)** (*V* **rapiécer**) patching (up); mending, cobbling. **(b)** (*pièce*) patch.
rapiécer [Rapjese] (3 *et* 6) *vt vêtement, pneu* to patch (up), put a patch in; *chaussure* to mend, cobble.
rapière [RapjɛR] *nf* rapier.
rapin [Rapɛ̃] *nm* († *ou péj: artiste peintre*) painter, dauber†.
rapine [Rapin] *nf* (*littér*) (*U*) plundering, plunder. **vivre de ~(s)** to live by plunder.
rapiner [Rapine] (1) *vti* (*littér*) to plunder.
raplapla‡ [Raplapla] *adj inv* (*fatigué*) washed out*, tuckered out‡; (*plat*) flat.
raplatir* [RaplatiR] (2) *vt* (*aplatir*) to flatten out. (*fig*) **être tout raplati** to be (completely) washed out*.
rappareiller [RapaReje] (1) *vt* to match up.
rapparier [RapaRje] (7) *vt* to pair up, match up.
rappel [Rapɛl] *nm* **(a)** *[ambassadeur]* recall, recalling; (*Mil*) *[réservistes]* recall. (*Théât*) **il y a eu 3 ~s** there were 3 curtain calls; *V* **battre.**
(b) *[événement]* reminder; (*Comm*) *[référence]* quote; (*Admin: deuxième avis*) reminder; (*Admin: somme due*) back pay (*U*); (*Méd: vaccination*) booster. **rougissant au ~ de cette bévue** blushing at being reminded of that blunder; **toucher un ~ (de salaire)** to get some back pay; (*Aut*) **~ de limitation de vitesse** speed limit sign; **~ à l'ordre** call to order; **~ de couleur** repeat of colour.
(c) (*Tech*) *[pièce, levier]* return. (*Alpinisme*) **~ (de corde)** (*technique*) abseiling, roping down; (*opération*) abseil; **faire un ~** to abseil, rope down; (*Naut*) **faire du ~** to sit out; (*Tech*) **ressort de ~** return spring; *V* **descente.**
rappelé [Raple] *nm* recalled soldier.
rappeler [Raple] (4) **1** *vt* **(a)** (*faire revenir*) *personne* to call back; (*Mil*) *réservistes, classe* to recall, call up again; *diplomate* to recall; *acteur* to bring back, call back; *chien* to call back. **~ qn au chevet d'un malade ou auprès d'un malade** to call *ou* summon sb back to a sick man's bedside; (*frm*) **Dieu l'a rappelé à lui** he departed this world (*frm*) *ou* life (*frm*); (*Mil*) **~ des réservistes au front** to recall reservists to the front.
(b) ~ qch à qn (*évoquer*) to recall sth to sb, remind sb of sth; (*remettre en mémoire*) to remind sb of sth; **il rappela les qualités du défunt** he evoked *ou* mentioned the qualities of the deceased, he reminded the audience of the qualities of the deceased; **faut-il ~ que ...** must I remind you that ..., must it be repeated that ... ; **ces dessins rappellent l'art arabe** those drawings are reminiscent of *ou* remind one of Arabian art; **le motif des poches rappelle celui du bas de la robe** the design on the pockets is repeated round the hem of the dress; **cela ne te rappelle rien?** doesn't that remind you of anything?, doesn't that bring anything to mind?; **tu me rappelles ma tante** you remind me of my aunt; **rappelle-moi mon rendez-vous** remind me about my appointment; **attends, ça me rappelle quelque chose** wait, it rings a bell; (*frm*) **rappelez-moi à son bon souvenir** kindly remember me to him (*frm*).
(c) ~ qn à la vie ou à lui to bring sb back to life, bring sb to *ou* round, revive sb; **~ qn à l'ordre** to call sb to order; **~ qn à son devoir** to remind sb of his duty; **~ qn aux bienséances** to recall sb to a sense of propriety; **~ qn à de meilleurs sentiments** to bring sb round to a better frame of mind.
(d) (*retéléphoner à*) to call *ou* ring *ou* phone back. **il vient de ~** he's just called *ou* rung *ou* phoned back.
(e) (*Comm*) *référence* to quote.
(f) (*tirer*) (*Tech*) *pièce, levier* to return; (*Alpinisme*) *corde* to pull to.
2 se rappeler *vpr* (*gén*) to remember, recollect, recall. **se ~ que** to remember *ou* recall *ou* recollect that; (*frm*) **je me permets de me ~ à votre bon souvenir** I am sending you my kindest regards (*frm*); **rappelle-toi que ton honneur est en jeu** remember (that) your honour is at stake; **il ne se rappelle plus (rien)** he doesn't *ou* can't remember *ou* recall anything *ou* a thing.
rappliquer‡ [Raplike] (1) *vi* (*revenir*) to come back; (*arriver*) to turn up*, show up*.
rapport [RapɔR] *nm* **(a)** (*lien, corrélation*) connection, relationship, link. **~ de parenté** relationship, tie of kinship (*frm*); **il y a**

un ~ de parenté entre nous we're related, there's a relationship *ou* tie of kinship (*frm*) between us; **~ de** *ou* **des forces** (*dans un conflit*) balance of power; **établir un ~/des ~s entre deux incidents** to establish a link *ou* connection *ou* relation/links *ou* connections between two incidents; **avoir un certain ~/beaucoup de ~ avec qch** to have something/a lot to do with sth, have some/a definite connection with sth; **n'avoir aucun ~ avec** *ou* **être sans ~ avec qch** to bear no relation to sth, have nothing to do with sth; **avoir ~ à qch** to bear some relation to sth, have something to do with sth; **les deux incidents n'ont aucun ~** the two incidents have nothing to do with each other *ou* have no connection (with each other), the two incidents are unconnected *ou* unrelated; **être en ~ avec qch** to be in keeping with sth; **une situation en ~ avec ses goûts** a job in keeping *ou* in harmony *ou* in line with his tastes; **son train de vie n'est pas en ~ avec son salaire** his salary isn't in keeping with his life style.

(b) ~s (*relations*) relations; **ses ~s avec les autres sont difficiles** she has lots of problems with relationships *ou* in dealing with *ou* getting on with people; **entretenir de bons/mauvais ~s avec qn** to be on good/bad terms *ou* have good/bad relations with sb; **avoir des ~s (sexuels)** to have (sexual) intercourse *ou* sexual relations *ou* sex*; **les ~s d'amitié entre les deux peuples** the friendly relations *ou* ties of friendship between the two nations; **~s de force** power struggle; **les ~s entre les professeurs et les étudiants** relations between teachers and students, student-teacher *ou* student-staff relations.

(c) (*exposé, compte rendu*) report; (*Mil: réunion*) (post-exercise) conference. **~ de police** police report.

(d) (*revenu, profit*) yield, return, revenue. **vivre du ~ d'une terre** to live from the yield *ou* revenue of *ou* on *ou* from the return on a piece of land; **être d'un bon ~** to give a good profit, have a good yield, give a good return; **ces champs sont en plein ~** these fields are bringing in a full yield; **immeuble de ~** block of flats (used *ou* for use as a letting concern), apartment block; **maison de ~** residential property (used *ou* for use as a letting concern).

(e) (*Math, Tech*) ratio. **dans le ~ de 1 à 100/de 100 contre 1** in a *ou* the ratio of 1 to 100/of 100 to 1.

(f) (*loc*) **être en ~ avec qn** to have connections *ou* dealings with sb; **nous n'avons jamais été en ~ avec cette compagnie** we have never had any dealings *ou* anything to do with that company; **se mettre en ~ avec qn** to get in touch *ou* contact with sb; **mettre qn en ~ avec qn d'autre** to put sb in touch *ou* contact with sb else; **par ~ à** (*comparé à*) in comparison with, in relation to; (*en fonction de*) in relation to; (*envers*) with respect *ou* regard to, towards; **~ à**‡ about, in connection with, concerning; **je viens vous voir ~ à votre annonce**‡ I've come (to see you) about your advertisement; **il n'y a aucune inquiétude à avoir sous le ~ de l'honnêteté** from the point of view of honesty *ou* as far as honesty is concerned there's nothing to worry about; **sous tous les ~s** in every respect.

rapportage [RapɔRtaʒ] *nm* (*arg Scol: mouchardage*) tale-telling (*U*).

rapporter [RapɔRte] (1) **1** *vt* **(a)** (*apporter*) *objet, souvenir, réponse* to bring back; *[chien] gibier* to retrieve. **~ qch à qn** to bring *ou* take sth back to sb; **n'oublie pas de lui ~ son parapluie** don't forget to bring *ou* take him back *ou* return him his umbrella; **il rapportera le pain en rentrant** he'll bring home the bread when he comes in; **~ une bonne impression de qch** to come back *ou* come away with a good impression of sth; **quand doit il ~ la réponse?** when does he have to come *ou* be back with the answer?

(b) (*Fin, fig: produire un gain*) *[actions, terre]* to yield (a return of), bring in (a yield *ou* revenue of); *[métier]* to bring in; *[vente]* to bring in (a profit *ou* revenue of). **placement qui rapporte 5%** investment that yields (a return of) 5% *ou* that brings in (a yield *ou* revenue of) 5%; **ça rapporte beaucoup d'argent** it's extremely profitable, it brings in a lot of money; **cette mauvaise action ne lui rapportera rien** that bad deed won't do him any good; **ça leur a rapporté 100 F net** they netted 100 francs, it brought them in 100 francs net.

(c) (*faire un compte rendu de*) *fait* to report; (*mentionner*) to mention; (*citer*) *mot célèbre* to quote; (*répéter pour dénoncer*) to report. **on nous a rapporté que son projet n'avait pas été bien accueilli** we were told that *ou* we heard that *ou* it was reported to us that his project hadn't been well received; **~ à qn les actions de qn** to report sb's actions to sb; **il a rapporté à la maîtresse ce qu'avaient dit ses camarades** he told the teacher what his classmates had said, he reported what his classmates had said to the teacher.

(d) (*ajouter*) (*gén*) to add; *bande de tissu, poche* to sew on. **~ une aile à une maison** to annex a wing to a house; **~ un peu de terre pour surélever** to bank up with earth *ou* pile up some earth to raise the level of the ground; **c'est un élément rapporté** this element has been added on; **poches rapportées** sewn-on pockets.

(e) (*rattacher à*) **~ à** to relate to; **il faut tout ~ à la même échelle de valeurs** everything has to be related *ou* referred to the same scale of values; **on lui rapporte des découvertes dues à d'autres savants** discoveries are attributed *ou* ascribed to him which have been made by other learned men; **il rapporte tout à lui** he sees everything in relation to himself, he views everything in terms of himself.

(f) (*annuler*) *décret, décision, mesure* to revoke.

(g) (*Math*) **~ un angle** to plot an angle.

2 *vi* **(a)** (*Chasse*) *[chien]* to retrieve.

(b) (*Fin*) *[investissement]* to give a good return *ou* yield. **ça rapporte bien** *ou* **gros** it brings in a lot of money, it pays very well, it's very profitable.

(c) (*arg Scol: moucharder*) **~ (sur ses camarades)** to tell tales *ou* sneak* (on one's friends), tell on* *ou* sneak on* one's friends.

3 se rapporter *vpr* **(a) se ~ à qch** to relate to sth; **se ~ à** (*Gram*) *antécédent* to relate *ou* refer to; **ce paragraphe ne se rapporte pas du tout au sujet** this paragraph bears no relation *ou* connection at all to the subject, this paragraph is totally irrelevant to *ou* unconnected with the subject; **ça se rapporte à ce que je disais tout à l'heure** that ties *ou* links up with *ou* relates to what I was saying just now.

(b) s'en ~ à qn to rely on sb; **s'en ~ au jugement/au témoignage de qn** to rely on sb's judgment/account.

rapporteur, -euse [RapɔRtœR, øz] **1** *nm,f* (*mouchard*) telltale, sneak*, talebearer. **elle est ~euse** she's a telltale *ou* sneak* *ou* talebearer.

2 *nm* **(a)** (*Jur*) *[tribunal]* (court) reporter; *[commission]* reporter (*member acting as spokesman*).

(b) (*Géom*) protractor.

rapprendre [RapRɑ̃dR(ə)] (58) *vt* = **réapprendre.**

rapproché, e [RapRoʃe] (*ptp de* **rapprocher**) *adj* **(a)** *échéance* which is near *ou* close at hand; (*proche*) *objet, date* which is close *ou* near; *bruit* which is close. **l'objet le plus ~ de toi** the object closest *ou* nearest to you; **à une date ~e, dans un avenir ~** in the near *ou* not too distant future; **il faut faire un film aussi ~ de la réalité que possible** we have to make a film as close *ou* faithful to reality as possible; *V* **combat.**

(b) (*répété*) *crises, bruits* (increasingly) frequent. **des crises de plus en plus ~es** increasingly frequent crises, crises which have become more and more frequent; **à intervalles ~s** at (increasingly) frequent intervals, at short *ou* close intervals; **grossesses ~es** (a series of) pregnancies at short *ou* close intervals; **échecs ~s** (a series of) failures in close succession.

rapprochement [RapRoʃmɑ̃] *nm* **(a)** (*U: V* **rapprocher**) *[objet, meuble etc]* bringing closer *ou* nearer; *[objets, meubles]* bringing closer *ou* nearer to each other; (*fig*) *[personnes brouillées, ennemis]* bringing together, reconciliation; *[partis, factions]* bringing together; *[points de vue, textes]* comparison, bringing together, comparing. (*Méd*) **le ~ des lèvres d'une plaie** joining the edges of a wound, closing (the lips of) a wound.

(b) (*U: V* **se rapprocher**) *[bruit]* coming closer; *[ennemis, famille]* coming together, reconciliation; *[partis, factions]* coming together, rapprochement (*Pol*). (*Pol*) **ce ~ avec la droite nous inquiète** their moving closer to the right worries us; **le ~ des bruits de pas** the noise of footsteps drawing *ou* coming closer.

(c) (*lien, rapport*) parallel. **je n'avais pas fait le ~ (entre ces deux affaires)** I hadn't made *ou* established the connection *ou* link *ou* parallel (between these two matters); **il y a de nombreux ~s intéressants/troublants** there are numerous interesting/disquieting parallels *ou* comparisons.

rapprocher [RapRoʃe] (1) **1** *vt* **(a)** (*approcher*) to bring closer *ou* nearer (*de* to). **~ sa chaise (de la table)** to pull *ou* draw one's chair up (to the table); **~ deux objets l'un de l'autre** to move two objects (closer) together; **~ les lèvres d'une plaie** to join the edges of a wound, close (the lips of) a wound; **il a changé de métier: ça le rapproche de chez lui** he has changed jobs — that brings him closer *ou* nearer to home.

(b) (*réconcilier, réunir*) *ennemis* to bring together. **nous nous sentions rapprochés par un malheur commun** we felt drawn together by a common misfortune, we felt that a common misfortune had brought *ou* drawn us together; **leur amour de la chasse les rapproche** their love of hunting brings them together *ou* draws them to *ou* towards each other.

(c) (*mettre en parallèle, confronter*) *indices, textes* to put together *ou* side by side, compare, bring together; (*établir un lien entre, assimiler*) *indices, textes* to establish a *ou* the connection *ou* link *ou* parallel between. **essayons de ~ ces indices de ceux-là** let's try and put *ou* bring these two sets of clues together, let's try and compare these two sets of clues; **on peut ~ cela du poème de Villon** we can relate *ou* connect that to Villon's poem, we can establish a *ou* the connection *ou* link *ou* parallel between that and Villon's poem; **c'est à ~ de ce qu'on disait tout à l'heure** that ties up *ou* connects with *ou* relates to what was being said earlier.

2 se rapprocher *vpr* **(a)** (*approcher*) *[échéance, personne, véhicule, orage]* to get closer *ou* nearer, approach. **rapproche-toi (de moi)** come *ou* move *ou* draw closer *ou* nearer (to me); **il se rapprocha d'elle sur la banquette** he edged his way towards her *ou* drew closer to her on the bench; **pour se ~ de chez lui, il a changé de métier** to get closer *ou* nearer to home he changed jobs; **plus on se rapprochait de l'examen** the closer *ou* nearer we came *ou* got to the exam, the nearer *ou* closer the exam got *ou* came; **se ~ de la vérité** to come close *ou* get near *ou* close to the truth; **les bruits se rapprochèrent** (*cadence*) the noises became more frequent; (*proximité*) the noises got closer *ou* nearer.

(b) (*se réconcilier*) *[ennemis]* to come together, be reconciled; (*trouver un terrain d'entente*) *[points de vue]* to draw closer together. **il s'est rapproché de ses parents** he became *ou* drew closer to his parents; (*Pol*) **il a essayé de se ~ de la droite** he tried to move *ou* draw closer to the right; **leur position s'est rapprochée de la nôtre** their position has drawn closer to ours.

(c) (*s'apparenter à*) to be close to. **ça se rapproche de ce qu'on disait tout à l'heure** that's close to *ou* ties up *ou* connects with what was being said earlier; **ses opinions se rapprochent beaucoup des miennes** his opinions are very close *ou* similar to mine.

rapprovisionnement [RapRovizjɔnmɑ̃] *nm* = **réapprovisionnement.**

rapprovisionner [RapRovizjɔne] (1) = **réapprovisionner.**

rapsode [Rapsɔd] *nm* = **rhapsode.**

rapsodie [Rapsɔdi] *nf* = **rhapsodie.**

rapt [ʀapt] *nm* (*enlèvement*) abduction.
raquer: [ʀake] (1) *vi* (*payer*) to cough up:, pay up.
raquette [ʀakɛt] *nf* **(a)** (*Tennis*) racket; (*Ping-Pong*) bat. **c'est une bonne** ~ he's a good tennis player. **(b)** (*à neige*) snowshoe. **(c)** (*Bot*) nopal, prickly pear.
raquetteur, -euse [ʀakɛtœʀ, øz] *nm,f* (*Can*) snowshoer (*Can*).
rare [ʀaʀ] *adj* **(a)** (*peu commun*) *objet, mot, édition* rare. **ça n'a rien de** ~ there's nothing uncommon *ou* unusual about it, it's not a rare occurrence; **il était** ~ **qu'il ne sache pas** he rarely *ou* seldom did not know; **il n'était pas** ~ **de le rencontrer** it was not unusual *ou* uncommon to meet him; **c'est** ~ **de le voir fatigué** it's rare *ou* unusual to see him tired, one rarely *ou* seldom sees him tired; **c'est bien** ~ **s'il ne vient pas*** I'd be surprised *ou* it would be unusual if he doesn't *ou* didn't come; *V* **oiseau.**
(b) (*peu nombreux*) *cas, exemples* rare, few; *visites* rare; *passants, voitures* few. **les** ~**s voitures qui passaient** the few *ou* odd cars that went by; **les** ~**s amis qui lui restent** the few friends still left to him; **à de** ~**s intervalles** at rare intervals; **il est l'un des** ~**s qui** he's one of the few (people) who; **à cette heure les clients sont** ~s at this time of day customers are scarce *ou* are few and far between; **à de** ~**s exceptions près** with one or two odd exceptions.
(c) (*peu abondant*) *nourriture, main d'œuvre* scarce; *barbe, cheveux* thin, sparse; *végétation* sparse; *gaz* rare. **se faire** ~ *[argent]* to become scarce, be tight; *[légumes]* to become scarce, be in short supply; (*hum*) **vous vous faites** ~ we haven't seen a lot of you recently, we rarely see you these days.
(d) (*exceptionnel*) *talent, qualité, sentiment, beauté* rare; *homme, énergie* exceptional; *saveur, moment* exquisite; (*hum*) *imbécile, imprudence* singular. **avec un** ~ **courage** with rare *ou* singular courage.
raréfaction [ʀaʀefaksjɔ̃] *nf [oxygène]* rarefaction; *[nourriture]* (*action*) increased scarcity; (*résultat*) scarcity, short supply.
raréfiable [ʀaʀefjabl(ə)] *adj* rarefiable.
raréfier [ʀaʀefje] (7) **1** *vt air* to rarefy. **2 se raréfier** *vpr [oxygène]* to rarefy; *[argent, nourriture]* to grow *ou* become scarce, become in short supply.
rarement [ʀaʀmɑ̃] *adv* rarely, seldom.
rareté [ʀaʀte] *nf* **(a)** (*U*) *[édition, objet]* rarity; *[mot, cas]* rareness, rarity; *[vivres, argent]* scarcity. **la** ~ **des touristes/visiteurs** the small *ou* scattered numbers of tourists/visitors; **se plaindre de la** ~ **des lettres/visites de qn** to complain of the infrequency of sb's letters/visits.
(b) (*objet précieux etc*) rarity, rare object. **une telle erreur de sa part, c'est une** ~ it's a rare *ou* an unusual occurrence for him to make a mistake like that.
rarissime [ʀaʀisim] *adj* extremely rare.
ras[1] [ʀɑs] *nm* (*titre éthiopien*) ras.
ras[2], **e** [ʀɑ, ʀɑz] *adj* **(a)** *poil, herbe* short; *cheveux* close-cropped; *étoffe* with a short pile; *mesure* full. **il avait la tête** ~**e** he had close-cropped hair; **à poil** ~ *chien* short-haired; *étoffe* with a short pile.
(b) ongles/cheveux coupés ~ *ou* **à** ~ nails/hair cut short; **à** ~ **de terre, au** ~ **de la terre** level with the ground; **au** ~ **de l'eau** level with the water; **arbre coupé à** ~ **de terre** tree cut down to the ground; **voler au** ~ **de la terre/au** ~ **de l'eau** to fly close to *ou* just above the ground/water, skim the ground/water; **le projectile lui est passé au** ~ **de la tête/du visage** the projectile skimmed his head/face.
(c) à ~ **bords** to the brim; **remplir un verre à** ~ **bords** to fill a glass to the brim *ou* top; **plein à** ~ **bords** *verre* full to the brim, brimful; *baignoire* full to overflowing *ou* to the brim; **en** ~**e campagne** in open country; **pull** ~ **du cou** crew-neck jumper, round-neck jumper; **(j'en ai)** ~ **le bol (de tout ça)*** I've had my fill (of all that)*, I'm fed up to the teeth (with all that):; *V* **table.**
rasade [ʀazad] *nf* glassful.
rasage [ʀɑzaʒ] *nm* **(a)** *[barbe]* shaving; *V* **lotion. (b)** (*Tex*) shearing.
rasant, e [ʀɑzɑ̃, ɑ̃t] *adj* **(a)** (*: *ennuyeux*) boring. **qu'il est** ~! he's a (real) bore! *ou* drag!* **(b)** *lumière* low-angled; (*Mil*) *fortification* low-built. (*Mil*) **tir** ~ grazing fire.
rascasse [ʀaskas] *nf* scorpionfish.
rase- [ʀɑz] *préf V* **raser.**
rasé, e [ʀɑze] (*ptp de* **raser**) *adj menton* (clean-)shaven; *tête* shaven. **être bien/mal** ~ to be shaven/unshaven; ~ **de près** close-shaven; **avoir les cheveux** ~**s** to have one's hair shaved off *ou* a shaven head.
raser [ʀɑze] (1) **1** *vt* **(a)** (*tondre*) *barbe, cheveux* to shave off; *menton, tête* to shave; *malade* etc to shave. ~ **un prêtre/condamné** to shave a priest's/convict's head; **se faire** ~ **la tête** to have one's head shaved; *V* **crème.**
(b) (*effleurer*) *[projectile, véhicule]* to graze, scrape; *[oiseau, balle de tennis]* to skim (over). ~ **les murs** to hug the walls.
(c) (*abattre*) *maison* to raze (to the ground).
(d) (*: *ennuyer*) to bore. **ça me rase!** it bores me stiff*, it bores me to tears*.
(e) (*Tech*) *mesure à grains* to strike; *velours* to shear.
2 se raser *vpr* **(a)** (*toilette*) to shave, have a shave. **se** ~ **la tête/les jambes** to shave one's head/legs.
(b) (*: *s'ennuyer*) to be bored stiff* *ou* to tears*.
3: rase-mottes *nm inv* hedgehopping; **faire du rase-mottes, voler en rase-mottes** to hedgehop; **vol en rase-mottes** hedgehopping flight.
raseur, -euse* [ʀɑzœʀ, øz] *adj, nm,f* (*importun*) bore. **qu'il est** ~! he's a (real) bore *ou* drag*.
rasibus: [ʀazibys] *adv couper* very close *ou* fine. **passer** ~ *[projectile]* to whizz past very close; **avoir un examen** ~ to pass an exam by the skin of one's teeth*.
rasoir [ʀɑzwaʀ] *nm* **(a)** razor. ~ **électrique** (electric) shaver, electric razor; ~ **mécanique** *ou* **de sûreté** safety razor; *V* **feu**[1], **fil** etc. **(b)** (*: *importun*) bore. **quel** ~, **qu'il est** ~! what a bore *ou* drag* he is!
rassasier [ʀasazje] (7) (*frm*) **1** *vt* **(a)** (*assouvir*) *faim, curiosité, désirs* to satisfy.
(b) (*nourrir*) ~ **qn** *[aliment]* to satisfy sb *ou* sb's appetite *ou* sb's hunger; *[hôte, aubergiste]* to satisfy sb's appetite *ou* hunger, nourish sb (*frm*); ~ **qn de qch** (*lui en donner suffisamment*) to satisfy sb with sth *ou* sb's appetite *ou* hunger with sth; (*lui en donner trop*) to overfeed sb with sth, surfeit sb with sth; **être rassasié** (*n'avoir plus faim*) to be satisfied, have eaten one's fill; (*en être dégoûté*) to be satiated *ou* sated, have had more than enough; **je suis rassasié de toutes ces histoires!** I've had quite enough of *ou* I've had more than my fill of all these stories!; **on ne peut pas le** ~ **de petits chocolats** you can't give him too many chocolates; (*fig*) ~ **ses yeux d'un spectacle** to tire one's eyes of a sight.
2 se rassasier *vpr* (*se nourrir*) to satisfy one's hunger, eat one's fill. **se** ~ **d'un spectacle** to tire of a sight; **je ne me rassasierai jamais de ...** I'll never tire *ou* have enough of ... .
rassemblement [ʀasɑ̃bləmɑ̃] *nm* **(a)** (*U*) (*V* **rassembler**) rallying; rounding up; gathering, collecting, assembling; (*V* **se rassembler**) gathering. (*Mil*) **le** ~ **a lieu à 8 heures** parade is at 8 o'clock; (*Mil*) ~! fall in!; ~ **à 9 heures sur le quai** we'll meet at 9 o'clock on the platform.
(b) (*groupe*) gathering; (*parti, organisation*) union.
rassembler [ʀasɑ̃ble] (1) **1** *vt* **(a)** (*regrouper*) *troupes* to rally; *troupeau* to round up; *objets épars* to gather together, collect, assemble. **il rassembla les élèves dans la cour** he gathered *ou* assembled the pupils in the playground.
(b) (*accumuler*) *documents, manuscrits, notes* to gather together, collect, assemble.
(c) (*fig: faire appel à, reprendre*) *idées, esprits* to collect; *courage, forces* to summon up, muster (up).
(d) (*après démontage*) *pièces, mécanisme* to put back together, reassemble.
(e) (*Équitation*) *cheval* to collect.
2 se rassembler *vpr [foule, badauds]* to gather; *[soldats, participants]* to assemble, gather. **rassemblés autour du feu** gathered round the fire.
rasseoir [ʀaswaʀ] (26) **1** *vt bébé* to sit back up (straight); *objet* to put back up straight. **2 se rasseoir** *vpr* to sit down again. **faire (se)** ~ **qn** to make sb sit down again.
rasséréné, e [ʀaseʀene] (*ptp de* **rasséréner**) *adj ciel, personne, visage* serene.
rasséréner [ʀaseʀene] (6) **1** *vt* (*rare*) to make serene again. **2 se rasséréner** *vpr [personne, visage, ciel]* to become serene again, recover one's *ou* its serenity.
rassir *vi*, **se rassir** *vpr* [ʀasiʀ] (2) to go stale.
rassis, e [ʀasi, iz] (*ptp de* **rassir, rasseoir**) *adj* **(a)** *pain* stale. **(b)** *personne* (*pondéré*) composed, sober, calm; (*péj*) stale.
rassortiment [ʀasɔʀtimɑ̃] *nm* = **réassortiment.**
rassortir [ʀasɔʀtiʀ] (2) = **réassortir.**
rassurant, e [ʀasyʀɑ̃, ɑ̃t] *adj nouvelle* reassuring, comforting, cheering; *voix* reassuring, comforting; *visage* reassuring; *indice* encouraging. (*iro*) **c'est** ~! that's very reassuring! (*iro*), that's a fat lot of comfort!*
rassurer [ʀasyʀe] (1) **1** *vt*: ~ **qn** to put sb's mind at ease *ou* rest, reassure sb; **je ne me sentais pas rassuré dans sa voiture** I didn't feel easy *ou* at ease in his car; **te voilà rassuré maintenant** you've got nothing to worry about now, your mind's at ease *ou* at rest now, you're reassured now.
2 se rassurer *vpr*: **à cette nouvelle il se rassura** his mind was put at ease *ou* rest *ou* he felt reassured on hearing the news; **il essayait de se** ~ **en se disant que c'était impossible** he tried to put his mind at ease *ou* rest *ou* to reassure himself by saying it was impossible; **rassure-toi** put your mind at ease *ou* rest, don't worry.
rastaquouère [ʀastakwɛʀ] *nm* (*péj*) flashy wog: (*Brit péj*), flashy foreigner (*péj*).
rat [ʀa] **1** *nm* (*Zool*) rat; (*péj: avare*) miser. **c'est un vrai** ~, **ce type** he's really stingy* *ou* he's a real skinflint, that fellow; **il est fait comme un** ~ he's cornered, he has no escape; (*fig*) **quand il y a du danger, les** ~**s quittent le navire** in times of danger the rats leave the sinking ship (*fig*); (*terme d'affection*) **mon (petit)** ~ pet, darling; *V* **à, mort**[2].
2: rat d'Amérique musquash (*fur*); **rat de bibliothèque** bookworm (*who spends all his time in libraries*); **rat de cave** wax taper (*used for lighting one's way in a cellar or on a staircase*); **rat des champs** fieldmouse; **rat d'eau** water vole; **rat d'égout** sewer rat; **rat d'hôtel** hotel thief; **rat musqué** muskrat, musquash; **(petit) rat de l'Opéra** pupil of the Opéra de Paris ballet class (working as an extra).
rata [ʀata] *nm* (*arg Mil*) (*nourriture*) grub*; (*ragoût*) stew.
ratafia [ʀatafja] *nm* (*liqueur*) ratafia.
ratage* [ʀataʒ] *nm* (*U: V* **rater**) missing; messing up, spoiling; failing, flunking*. **ces** ~**s successifs** these successive failures.
ratatiner [ʀatatine] (1) **1** *vt* **(a)** *pomme* to dry up, shrivel; *visage, personne* to wrinkle, make wrinkled *ou* wizened *ou* shrivelled.
(b) (:: *détruire*) *maison* to knock to bits *ou* pieces, wreck; *machine, voiture* to smash to bits *ou* pieces. **se faire** ~ (*battre*) to get thrashed *ou* a thrashing; (*tuer*) to get done in:; **sa voiture a été complètement ratatinée** his car was completely smashed up *ou* written off, his car was a complete write-off.
2 se ratatiner *vpr [pomme]* to shrivel *ou* dry up; *[visage]* to become wrinkled *ou* shrivelled *ou* wizened; *[personne]* (*par l'âge*) to become wrinkled *ou* shrivelled *ou* wizened; (*pour tenir moins de place*) to curl up.
ratatouille [ʀatatuj] *nf* (*Culin*) ~ **(niçoise)** ratatouille (*aubergines, courgettes, peppers, tomatoes etc cooked in olive oil*);

(*péj*) (*ragoût*) bad stew; (*cuisine*) lousy* food.

rate[1] [ʀat] *nf* spleen; *V* **dilater, fouler.**

rate[2] [ʀat] *nf* she-rat.

raté, e [ʀate] (*ptp de* **rater**) **1** *nm,f* (*personne*) failure. **2** *nm* **(a)** (*Aut: gén pl*) misfiring (*U*). **avoir des ~s** to misfire. **(b)** *[arme à feu]* misfire.

râteau, *pl* **~x** [ʀɑto] *nm* (*Agr, Roulette*) rake; *[métier à tisser]* comb.

râtelier [ʀɑtəlje] *nm [bétail]* rack; *[armes, outils]* rack; (*: *dentier*) set of dentures. **~ à pipes** pipe rack; *V* **manger.**

rater [ʀate] (1) **1** *vi [arme, coup]* to misfire, fail to go off; *[projet, affaire]* to go wrong, backfire. **ce contretemps/cette erreur risque de tout faire ~** this hitch/mistake could well ruin everything; **je t'avais dit qu'elle y allait: ça n'a pas raté*** I told you she'd go and (so) she did *ou* and I was dead right*.

2 *vt* (*) **(a)** (*ne pas attraper ou saisir*) *balle, cible, occasion, train* to miss. **raté!** missed!; (*iro*) **il n'en rate pas une** he's always putting his foot in it*; **tu crois être le plus fort mais je ne te raterai pas!** you think you're the toughest but don't you worry, I'll get you!* *ou* I'll show you!; **il voulait faire le malin mais je ne l'ai pas raté** he tried to be smart but I soon sorted him out* *ou* I didn't let him get away with it.

(b) (*ne pas réussir*) *mayonnaise, travail, affaire* to mess up*, spoil, botch*; *examen* to fail, flunk*. **~ son effet** to spoil one's effect; **~ sa vie** to mess up* *ou* make a mess of one's life; **il a raté son coup** he didn't bring *ou* carry *ou* pull it off; **il a raté son suicide, il s'est raté** he failed in his suicide attempt *ou* bid.

ratiboiser‡ [ʀatibwaze] (1) *vt* **(a)** (*rafler*) **~ qch à qn** (*au jeu*) to clean sb out of sth*; (*en le volant*) to nick‡ (*Brit*) *ou* pinch* sth from sb; **on lui a ratiboisé son portefeuille, il s'est fait ~ son portefeuille** he got his wallet nicked‡ (*Brit*) *ou* pinched*.

(b) (*dépouiller*) **~ qn** to skin sb (alive)‡, pluck sb‡, clean sb out*.

(c) (*abattre*) *maison* to knock to bits *ou* pieces, wreck. *[personne]* **il a été ratiboisé en moins de deux** he was done for in no time.

ratier [ʀatje] *nm*: **(chien) ~** ratter.

ratière [ʀatjɛʀ] *nf* rattrap.

ratification [ʀatifikɑsjɔ̃] *nf* (*Admin, Jur*) ratification. **~ de vente** sales confirmation.

ratifier [ʀatifje] (7) *vt* (*Admin, Jur*) to ratify; (*littér: confirmer*) to confirm, ratify.

ratine [ʀatin] *nf* (*Tex*) ratine.

ratiocination [ʀasjɔsinɑsjɔ̃] *nf* (*littér péj*) (*action*) hair-splitting, quibbling; (*raisonnement*) hair-splitting argument, quibbling (*U*).

ratiociner [ʀasjɔsine] (1) *vi* (*littér péj*) to split hairs, quibble (*sur* over).

ration [ʀɑsjɔ̃] *nf* **(a)** *[soldat]* rations (*pl*); *[animal]* (feed) intake; *[organisme]* ration, (food) intake. **~ alimentaire** *ou* **d'entretien** food intake; (*Mil etc*) **toucher une ~ réduite** to be on *ou* get short rations.

(b) (*portion*) ration. **~ de viande/fourrage** meat/fodder ration; (*fig*) **il a eu sa ~ d'épreuves/de soucis** he had his share of trials/quota *ou* share of worries.

rationalisation [ʀasjɔnalizɑsjɔ̃] *nf* rationalization.

rationaliser [ʀasjɔnalize] (1) *vt* to rationalize.

rationalisme [ʀasjɔnalism(ə)] *nm* rationalism.

rationaliste [ʀasjɔnalist(ə)] *adj, nmf* rationalist.

rationalité [ʀasjɔnalite] *nf* rationality.

rationnel, -elle [ʀasjɔnɛl] *adj* rational.

rationnellement [ʀasjɔnɛlmɑ̃] *adv* rationally.

rationnement [ʀasjɔnmɑ̃] *nm* rationing; *V* **carte.**

rationner [ʀasjɔne] (1) **1** *vt pain, charbon* to ration; *personne* (*lit*) to put on rations; (*fig hum: ne pas donner assez*) to give short rations to. **2 se rationner** *vpr* to ration o.s.

ratissage [ʀatisaʒ] *nm* (*Agr*) raking; (*Mil, Police*) combing.

ratisser [ʀatise] (1) *vt gravier* to rake; *feuilles* to rake up; (*Mil, Police*) to comb; (*Rugby*) *ballon* to heel; (*: *dépouiller au jeu*) to clean out*, fleece*.

raton [ʀatɔ̃] *nm* **(a)** (*Zool*) young rat. **~ laveur** racoon. **(b)** (*péj*) *term applied to North African in France.* **(c)** (*terme d'affection*) **mon ~!** (my) pet!

rattachement [ʀataʃmɑ̃] *nm* (*Admin, Pol*) uniting (*à* with), joining (*à* to).

rattacher [ʀataʃe] (1) *vt* **(a)** (*attacher de nouveau*) *animal, prisonnier, colis* to tie up again; *ceinture, lacets, jupe* to do up *ou* fasten again.

(b) (*annexer, incorporer*) *territoire, commune, service* to join (*à* to), unite (*à* with).

(c) (*comparer, rapprocher*) *problème, question* to link, connect, tie up (*à* with); *fait* to relate (*à* to). **cela peut se ~ au premier problème** that can be related to *ou* tied up with the first problem; **on peut ~ cette langue au groupe slave** this language can be related to *ou* linked with the Slavonic group.

(d) (*relier*) *personne* to bind, tie (*à* to). **rien ne le rattache plus à sa famille** he has no more ties with his family, nothing binds *ou* ties him to his family any more.

rattrapage [ʀatʀapaʒ] *nm [maille]* picking up; *[erreur]* making good; *[candidat d'examen]* passing. **le ~ d'une bêtise/d'un oubli** making up for something silly/an omission; **le ~ du retard** *[élève]* catching up, making up (for) lost time; *[conducteur]* making up (for) lost time; **~ scolaire** remedial teaching *ou* classes; **suivre des cours de ~** to go to remedial classes.

rattraper [ʀatʀape] (1) **1** *vt* **(a)** (*reprendre*) *animal échappé, prisonnier* to recapture. (*fig*) **on m'a eu une fois mais on ne m'y rattrapera plus** I was caught once but I won't be caught (at it) again.

(b) (*retenir*) *objet, enfant qui tombe* to catch (hold of).

(c) (*réparer*) *maille* to pick up; *mayonnaise* to salvage; *erreur* to make good, make up for; *bêtise, parole malheureuse, oubli* to make up for.

(d) (*regagner*) *argent perdu* to recover, get back, recoup; *sommeil* to catch up on; *temps perdu* to make up for. **le conducteur a rattrapé son retard** the driver made up (for) lost time; **cet élève ne pourra jamais ~ son retard** this pupil will never be able to make up (for) lost time *ou* catch up; **ce qu'il perd d'un côté, il le rattrape de l'autre** what he loses on the swings he gains on the roundabout (*surtout Brit*).

(e) (*rejoindre*) (*lit, fig*) **~ qn** to catch sb up, catch up with sb; **le coût de la vie a rattrapé l'augmentation de salaire** the cost of living has caught up with the increase in salaries.

(f) (*Scol: repêcher*) **~ qn** to allow sb to pass, pass sb, let sb get through.

2 se rattraper *vpr* **(a)** (*reprendre son équilibre*) to stop o.s. falling, catch o.s. (just) in time. **se ~ à une branche/à qn** to stop o.s. falling by catching hold of a branch/sb.

(b) (*prendre une compensation*) to make up for it. **j'ai dû passer trois nuits sans dormir, mais hier je me suis rattrapé** I had to spend three sleepless nights, but I made up for it last night.

(c) (*se ressaisir*) to make good, make up for it. **il avait perdu gros, mais il s'est rattrapé en un soir à la roulette** he had lost heavily but he made good (his losses) *ou* recovered his losses *ou* made up for it in one evening at roulette; **le joueur français avait perdu les deux premiers sets, mais il s'est rattrapé au troisième** the French player had lost the first two sets but he made good *ou* made up for it *ou* caught up in the third.

rature [ʀatyʀ] *nf* deletion, erasure, crossing out. **faire une ~** to make a deletion *ou* an erasure; (*Admin*) **sans ~s ni surcharges** without deletions or alterations.

raturer [ʀatyʀe] (1) *vt* (*corriger*) *mot, phrase, texte* to make an alteration *ou* alterations to; (*rare: barrer*) *lettre, mot* to cross out, erase, delete.

raugmenter* [ʀɔgmɑ̃te] (1) *vi* (*augmenter*) to go up again. **le beurre a raugmenté** butter is up again*, butter has gone up again.

rauque [ʀok] *adj voix* (*gén*) hoarse; *[chanteuse de blues etc]* husky; *cri* raucous.

ravage [ʀavaʒ] *nm* **(a)** (*littér: action*) *[pays, ville]* laying waste, ravaging, devastation.

(b) (*gén pl: dévastation*) *[guerre, maladie]* ravages (*pl*), devastation (*U*); *[vieillesse]* ravages (*pl*). **la grêle a fait du ~ dans les vignes** the hailstorm has wrought havoc in the vineyards *ou* played havoc with the vines; **l'épidémie a fait de terribles ~s parmi les jeunes** the epidemic has caused terrible loss among *ou* has destroyed huge numbers of young people; (*fig hum*) **faire des ~s** *[séducteur]* to break hearts (*fig*); *[doctrine]* to gain (too much) ground.

ravagé, e [ʀavaʒe] (*ptp de* **ravager**) *adj* **(a)** (*tourmenté*) *visage* harrowed. **avoir les traits ~s** to have harrowed *ou* ravaged features; **visage ~ par la maladie** face ravaged by illness.

(b) (‡: *fou*) **il est complètement ~** he's completely nuts* *ou* bonkers‡ (*Brit*).

ravager [ʀavaʒe] (3) *vt pays* to lay waste, ravage, devastate; *maison, ville* to ravage, devastate; *visage [maladie]* to ravage; *[chagrin, soucis]* to harrow; *personne, vie* to wreak havoc upon.

ravageur, -euse [ʀavaʒœʀ, øz] **1** *adj passion* devastating. **animaux/insectes ~s** animals/insects which cause damage to *ou* which devastate the crops. **2** *nm,f* (*pillard*) ravager, devastator.

ravalement [ʀavalmɑ̃] *nm* **(a)** (*V* **ravaler**) cleaning; restoration; face lift*. **faire le ~ de** to clean; to restore; to give a face lift to*. **(b)** (*littér: avilissement*) lowering.

ravaler [ʀavale] (1) *vt* **(a)** (*Constr*) (*nettoyer*) to clean; (*remettre en état*) *façade, mur* to restore; *immeuble* to give a face lift to*.

(b) (*avaler*) *salive* to swallow; *sanglots* to swallow, choke back; *colère* to stifle; *larmes* to hold *ou* choke back. (*fig*) **faire ~ ses paroles à qn** to make sb swallow his words.

(c) (*littér: rabaisser*) *dignité, personne, mérite* to lower. **~ qn au niveau de la brute** to reduce *ou* lower sb to the level of a brute.

ravaudage [ʀavodaʒ] *nm [vêtement]* mending, repairing; *[chaussette]* darning. **faire du ~** to mend; to darn.

ravauder [ʀavode] (1) *vt* (*littér: repriser*) *vêtement* to repair, mend; *chaussette* to darn.

rave [ʀav] *nf* (*Bot*) rape; *V* **céleri, chou**[1].

ravi, e [ʀavi] (*ptp de* **ravir**) *adj* (*enchanté*) delighted.

ravier [ʀavje] *nm* hors d'oeuvres dish.

ravigote [ʀavigɔt] *nf* (*vinaigrette*) (oil and vinegar) dressing (*with shallot and herbs*).

ravigoter* [ʀavigɔte] (1) *vt [alcool]* to buck up*, pick up; *[repas, douche, nouvelle, chaleur]* to buck up*, put new life into. **(tout) ravigoté par une bonne nuit** feeling refreshed after a good night's sleep; **ce vin est ravigotant** this wine bucks you up* *ou* puts new life into you.

ravin [ʀavɛ̃] *nm* (*gén*) gully; (*assez encaissé*) ravine.

ravine [ʀavin] *nf* (small) ravine, gully.

ravinement [ʀavinmɑ̃] *nm* (*action*) gullying (*Géog*). (*rigoles, ravins*) **~s** gullies; (*aspect*) **le ~ de ces pentes** the (numerous) gullies furrowing these slopes; **le ~ affecte particulièrement ces sols** gully erosion *ou* gullying affects these kinds of soil in particular.

raviner [ʀavine] (1) *vt versant* to gully (*Géog*); *visage* to furrow. **les bords ravinés de la rivière** the gullied (*Géog*) *ou* furrowed banks of the river.

ravir [ʀaviʀ] (2) *vt* (*littér*) **(a)** (*charmer*) to delight. **à ~: cela lui va à ~** that suits her beautifully, she looks delightful in it.

(b) *(enlever)* ~ **à qn** *trésor, être aimé, honneur* to rob sb of, take (away) from sb.

(c) (†: *kidnapper*) to ravish†.

raviser (se) [ʀavize] (1) *vpr* to change one's mind, decide otherwise. **après avoir dit oui, il s'est ravisé** after saying yes he changed his mind *ou* decided otherwise *ou* decided against it; **il s'est ravisé** he decided against it, he thought better of it.

ravissant, e [ʀavisɑ̃, ɑ̃t] *adj beauté* ravishing; *femme, robe* ravishing, beautiful; *maison, tableau* delightful, beautiful.

ravissement [ʀavismɑ̃] *nm* **(a)** *(gén, Rel)* rapture. **plonger qn dans le** ~ to send sb into raptures; **plongé dans le** ~ in raptures; **regarder qn avec** ~ to look at sb rapturously. **(b)** († *ou littér: enlèvement*) ravishing†.

ravisseur, -euse [ʀavisœʀ, øz] *nm,f* kidnapper, abductor.

ravitaillement [ʀavitajmɑ̃] *nm* **(a)** *(U: V* **ravitailler)** resupplying; refuelling. ~ **en vol** in-flight refuelling; **le** ~ **des troupes (en vivres/munitions)** resupplying the troops (with food/ammunition), the provision *ou* providing of the troops with fresh supplies (of food/ammunition); **aller au** ~ *(Mil)* to go for fresh supplies; *(fig) [campeur, ménagère]* to go and stock up, go for fresh supplies.

(b) *(réserves)* supplies.

ravitailler [ʀavitaje] (1) **1** *vt (en vivres, munitions) armée, ville, navire* to provide with fresh supplies, resupply; *coureurs, skieurs* to give fresh supplies to; *(en carburant) véhicule, avion, embarcation* to refuel. ~ **une ville en combustible** to provide a town with fresh supplies of fuel, resupply a town with fuel.

2 se ravitailler *vpr [ville, armée]* to get fresh supplies, be resupplied; *[coureurs, skieurs]* to take on fresh supplies; *(fig hum) [campeur, ménagère]* to stock up (*à* at); *[véhicule, avion]* to refuel. *(Sport)* **se** ~ **à l'étape** to take on fresh supplies at the next leg.

ravitailleur [ʀavitajœʀ] **1** *nm (Mil) (navire)* supply ship; *(avion)* supply plane; *(véhicule)* supply vehicle.

2 *adj navire, avion, véhicule* supply *(épith)*.

raviver [ʀavive] (1) *vt feu, sentiment, douleur* to revive, rekindle; *couleur* to brighten up; *souvenir* to revive, bring back to life; *(Méd) plaie* to reopen. **sa douleur/sa jalousie s'est ravivée** his grief/jealousy was revived *ou* rekindled.

ravoir [ʀavwaʀ] *vt* **(a)** *(recouvrer)* to have *ou* get back. **(b)** (*: *nettoyer: gén nég) tissu, métal* to get clean.

rayé, e [ʀeje] *(ptp de* **rayer)** *adj* **(a)** *tissu, pelage* striped; *papier à lettres etc* ruled, lined. **(b)** *disque, surface* scratched. **(c)** *(Tech) canon* rifled.

rayer [ʀeje] (8) *vt* **(a)** *(marquer de raies) papier à lettres etc* to rule, line. **des cicatrices lui rayaient le visage** scars lined *ou* scored his face; *(fig)* **le fouet lui raya le visage** the whip lashed his face.

(b) *(érafler)* to scratch.

(c) *(Tech) canon* to rifle.

(d) *(biffer)* to cross *ou* score out.

(e) *(exclure)* ~ **qn de** to cross sb *ou* sb's name off; **il a été rayé de la liste** he *ou* his name has been crossed *ou* struck off the list; ~ **qch de sa mémoire** to blot out *ou* erase sth from one's memory.

rayon [ʀɛjɔ̃] **1** *nm* **(a)** *(gén: trait, faisceau) (Opt, Phys)* ray; *[astre]* ray; *[lumière, jour]* ray, beam; *[phare]* beam.

(b) *(radiations)* ~**s** radiation; ~**s infrarouges** infrared rays; ~**s X** X-rays; **traitement par les** ~**s** radiation treatment; **passer aux** ~**s X** to be X-rayed.

(c) *(fig: lueur)* ray. ~ **d'espoir** ray *ou* gleam of hope.

(d) *(Math)* radius.

(e) *[roue]* spoke.

(f) *(planche)* shelf; *[bibliothèque]* (book)shelf.

(g) *(Comm) (section)* department; *(petit: comptoir)* counter. **le** ~ **(de l')alimentation/(de la) parfumerie** the food/perfume counter; the food/perfume department; *(fig: spécialité)* **c'est (de) son** ~**/ce n'est pas son** ~ that's/that isn't his line; *(fig: responsabilité)* **c'est son** ~ that's his concern *ou* responsibility *ou* department* *(fig)*; **ce n'est pas son** ~ that's not his concern *ou* responsibility *ou* department* *(fig)*, that's nothing to do with him.

(h) *[ruche]* (honey)comb.

(i) *(périmètre)* radius. **dans un** ~ **de 10 km** within a radius of 10 km *ou* a 10-km radius; **il continuait ses excursions, dans le** ~ **restreint auquel le limitait son grand âge** he continued his walks within the limited range imposed on him by his great age.

(j) *(Agr)* drill.

2: **rayon d'action** *(lit)* range; *(fig)* field of action, scope, range; **engin à grand rayon d'action** long-range missile; *(Aut)* **rayon de braquage** turning circle; *(Élec)* **rayon cathodique** cathode ray; **rayons cosmiques** cosmic rays; **rayons gamma** gamma rays; *(Phys)* **rayon laser** laser beam; **rayon de lune** moonbeam; **le rayon de la mort** the death ray; **rayon de soleil** *(lit)* ray of sunlight *ou* sunshine, sunbeam; *(fig)* ray of sunshine; *(Opt)* **rayon visuel** line of vision *ou* sight.

rayonnage [ʀɛjɔnaʒ] *nm* set of shelves, shelving *(U)*. ~**s** (sets of) shelves, shelving.

rayonnant, e [ʀɛjɔnɑ̃, ɑ̃t] *adj* **(a)** *(radieux) beauté, air, personne* radiant; *sourire* radiant, beaming *(épith)*; *visage* wreathed in smiles, beaming. **visage** ~ **de joie/santé** face radiant with joy/glowing *ou* radiant with health.

(b) *(en étoile) motif, fleur* radiating. **le style (gothique)** ~ High Gothic; **chapelles** ~**es** radiating chapels.

(c) *(rare: Phys) énergie, chaleur* radiant.

rayonne [ʀɛjɔn] *nf* rayon.

rayonnement [ʀɛjɔnmɑ̃] *nm* **(a)** *(influence bénéfique) [culture, civilisation]* influence; *[influence]* extension; *(magnétisme) [personnalité]* radiance. **le** ~ **de la culture hellénique s'étendit au monde entier** the influence of Greek culture extended over *ou* made itself felt over the whole world.

(b) *(éclat) [jeunesse, beauté]* radiance. **dans tout le** ~ **de sa jeunesse** in the full radiance of his youth; **le** ~ **de son bonheur** his radiant happiness.

(c) *(lumière) [astre, soleil]* radiance.

(d) *(radiations) [chaleur, lumière, astre]* radiation.

rayonner [ʀɛjɔne] (1) *vi* **(a)** *(étinceler) [influence, culture, personnalité]* to shine forth. *(se répandre)* ~ **sur/dans** *[influence, prestige]* to extend over/in, make itself felt over/in; *[culture]* to extend over/in, be influential over/in, exert its influence over/in; *[personnalité]* to be influential over/in.

(b) *(être éclatant) [joie, bonheur]* to shine *ou* beam forth; *[beauté]* to shine forth, be radiant; *[visage, personne] (de joie, de beauté)* to be radiant. **le bonheur faisait** ~ **son visage** his face glowed with happiness; **l'amour rayonne dans ses yeux** love shines *ou* sparkles in his eyes; ~ **de bonheur** to be radiant *ou* glowing *ou* beaming with happiness; ~ **de beauté** to be radiant *ou* dazzling with beauty.

(c) *(littér: briller) [lumière, astre]* to shine (forth), be radiant.

(d) *(Phys: émettre un rayonnement) [chaleur, énergie, lumière]* to radiate.

(e) *(faire un circuit)* ~ **autour d'une ville** *[touristes]* to use a town as a base for touring (around a region); *[cars]* to service the area around a town; ~ **dans une région** *[touristes]* to tour around a region (from a base); *[cars]* to service a region.

(f) *(aller en rayons) [avenues, lignes]* to radiate *(autour de* from, out from).

rayure [ʀejyʀ] *nf (dessin)* stripe; *(éraflure)* scratch; *[fusil]* groove. **papier/tissu à** ~**s** striped paper/material; **à** ~**s noires** with black stripes, black-striped.

raz-de-marée [ʀɑdmaʀe] *nm inv (Géog, fig)* tidal wave. ~ **électoral** big swing *(to a party in an election)*; **le** ~ **communiste** *ou* **le** ~ **électoral en faveur des communistes qui s'est produit aux dernières élections** the big swing to the Communists in the last elections, the massive Communist vote *ou* the Communist landslide vote in the last elections.

razzia [ʀazja] *nf* raid, foray, razzia. *(fig)* **faire une** ~ **dans une maison/le frigo*** to raid *ou* plunder a house/the fridge.

razzier [ʀazje] (7) *vt (lit, fig: piller)* to raid, plunder.

ré [ʀe] *nm (Mus)* D; *(en chantant la gamme)* re. **en** ~ **mineur** in D minor.

réabonnement [ʀeabɔnmɑ̃] *nm* renewal of subscription. **le** ~ **doit se faire dans les huit jours** renewal of subscription must be made within a week, subscriptions must be renewed within a week.

réabonner [ʀeabɔne] (1) **1** *vt:* ~ **qn** to renew sb's subscription (*à* to). **2 se réabonner** *vpr* to renew one's subscription, take out a new subscription (*à* to).

réabsorber [ʀeapsɔʀbe] (1) *vt* to reabsorb.

réabsorption [ʀeapsɔʀpsjɔ̃] *nf* reabsorption.

réac* [ʀeak] *abrév de* **réactionnaire.**

réaccoutumer [ʀeakutyme] (1) **1** *vt* to reaccustom. **2 se réaccoutumer** *vpr* to reaccustom o.s., become reaccustomed (*à* to).

réacteur [ʀeaktœʀ] *nm (Aviat)* jet engine; *(Chim, Phys nucléaire)* reactor.

réactif, -ive [ʀeaktif, iv] **1** *adj* reactive. **papier** ~ reagent *ou* test paper. **2** *nm (Chim, fig)* reagent.

réaction [ʀeaksjɔ̃] *nf* **(a)** *(gén)* reaction. **être** *ou* **rester sans** ~ to show no reaction; **être en** ~ **contre** to be in reaction against; ~ **de défense/en chaîne** defence/chain reaction; *(Méd)* **faire à qn des** ~**s de floculation** to test sb for a flocculation reaction; *V* **cuti-réaction.**

(b) *(Pol)* **la** ~ reaction; **les forces de la** ~ the forces of reaction.

(c) *(Aviat)* **moteur à/propulsion par** ~ jet engine/propulsion *(V* **avion)**; **cette voiture a de bonnes** ~**s** this car responds well.

réactionnaire [ʀeaksjɔnɛʀ] *adj, nmf* reactionary.

réactivation [ʀeaktivasjɔ̃] *nf* reactivation.

réactiver [ʀeaktive] (1) *vt* to reactivate.

réadaptation [ʀeadaptasjɔ̃] *nf (V* **réadapter)** readjustment; rehabilitation; re-education.

réadapter [ʀeadapte] (1) **1** *vt personne* to readjust (*à* to); *(Méd)* to rehabilitate; *muscle* to re-educate. **2 se réadapter** *vpr* to readjust, become readjusted (*à* to).

réadmettre [ʀeadmɛtʀ(ə)] (56) *vt* to readmit.

réadmission [ʀeadmisjɔ̃] *nf* readmission, readmittance.

réaffirmer [ʀeafiʀme] (1) *vt* to reaffirm, reassert.

réagir [ʀeaʒiʀ] (2) *vi* to react (*à* to, *contre* against, *sur* upon).

réajustement [ʀeaʒystəmɑ̃] *nm* = **rajustement.**

réajuster [ʀeaʒyste] (1) *vt* = **rajuster.**

réalisable [ʀealizabl(ə)] *adj (fig) rêve* attainable; *(Fin) capital* realizable; *projet* workable, feasible.

réalisateur, -trice [ʀealizatœʀ, tʀis] *nm,f (Ciné)* (film) director, film-maker; *(Rad, TV)* director; *[plan]* realizer.

réalisation [ʀealizasjɔ̃] *nf* **(a)** *(action) (V* **réaliser)** *[projet]* realization; carrying out; *[rêve]* fulfilment, realization; *[exploit]* achievement; *[valeurs, fortune]* realization; *(Comm) [vente, contrat]* conclusion; *(V* **se réaliser)** *[projet, rêve]* fulfilment, realization.

(b) *(ouvrage)* achievement, creation.

(c) *(Ciné)* production.

réaliser [ʀealize] (1) **1** *vt* **(a)** *(concrétiser) ambition, rêve* to realize, fulfil; *effort* to make, exercise; *exploit* to achieve, carry off; *projet* to carry out, carry through, realize. **il réalise (en soi) le meilleur exemple de** he is the best (material) example of.

(b) (*: *se rendre compte de)* to realize. ~ **l'importance de qch** to realize the importance of sth.

(c) *(Ciné)* to produce.

(d) (*Comm*) to realize; *achat, vente, bénéfice* to make; *contrat* to conclude.
(e) (*Fin*) *capital* to realize.
(f) (*Mus*) to realize.
2 se réaliser *vpr* **(a)** (*se concrétiser*) *[rêve]* to come true, be realized; *[projet]* to be carried out, be achieved, be realized.
(b) (*s'épanouir*) *[caractère, personnalité]* to fulfil o.s.

réalisme [Realism(ə)] *nm* realism.

réaliste [Realist(ə)] **1** *adj description, négociateur* realistic; (*Art, Littérat*) realist. **2** *nmf* realist.

réalité [Realite] *nf* **(a)** (*existence effective*) reality (*U*). **différentes ~s** different types of reality; **en ~** in (actual) fact, in reality; **parfois la ~ dépasse la fiction** (sometimes) truth can be stranger than fiction.
(b) (*chose réelle*) reality. **ce que je dis est une ~, pas une chose fictive** what I say is reality *ou* fact, not fiction; **oublieux des ~s de la vie en communauté** neglecting the realities *ou* facts of communal life; **détaché des ~s de ce monde** divorced from the realities of this world; **son rêve est devenu (une) ~** his dream became (a) reality *ou* came true; *V* **désir, sens.**

réanimation [Reanimɑsjɔ̃] *nf* resuscitation.

réanimer [Reanime] (1) *vt* to resuscitate, revive.

réapparaître [ReapaRetR(ə)] (57) *vi* to reappear.

réapparition [ReapaRisjɔ̃] *nf* reappearance.

réapprendre [ReapRɑ̃dR(ə)] (58) *vt* (*gén*) to relearn, learn again; (*littér*) *solitude, liberté* to get to know again, relearn (*littér*), learn again (*littér*). **~ qch à qn** to teach sth to sb again, teach sb sth again; **~ à faire qch** to learn to do sth again.

réapprentissage [ReapRɑ̃tisaʒ] *nm* (*V* **réapprendre**) **le ~ de qch** relearning sth, learning sth again; getting to know sth again; **cela va demander un long ~** that will take a long time to relearn *ou* to learn again.

réapprovisionnement [ReapRɔvizjɔnmɑ̃] *nm* (*V* **réapprovisionner**) restocking; stocking up again.

réapprovisionner [ReapRɔvizjɔne] (1) **1** *vt* to restock (*en* with). **2 se réapprovisionner** *vpr* to stock up again (*en* with).

réargenter [ReaRʒɑ̃te] (1) **1** *vt* to resilver. **2 se réargenter*** *vpr* (*se renflouer*) to replenish the coffers*, get back on a sound financial footing.

réarmement [ReaRməmɑ̃] *nm* (*V* **réarmer**) reloading; refitting; rearmament.

réarmer [ReaRme] (1) **1** *vt fusil, appareil-photo* to reload; *bateau* to refit. **2** *vi*, **se réarmer** *vpr [pays]* to rearm.

réarrangement [ReaRɑ̃ʒmɑ̃] *nm* rearrangement. (*Phys*) **~ moléculaire** molecular rearrangement.

réarranger [ReaRɑ̃ʒe] (3) *vt coiffure, fleurs, chambre* to rearrange; *cravate, jupe* to straighten (up) again; *entrevue* to rearrange.

réassignation [Reasiɲɑsjɔ̃] *nf* (*Jur*) resummons (*sg*); (*Fin*) reallocation.

réassigner [Reasiɲe] (1) *vt* (*gén*) to reassign; (*Jur*) to resummon; (*Fin*) to reallocate (*pay from other monies*).

réassortiment [ReasɔRtimɑ̃] *nm [stock]* replenishment; *[verres]* replacement, matching (up); *[service de table, tissu]* matching (up); *[marchandises]* new *ou* fresh stock.

réassortir [ReasɔRtiR] (2) **1** *vt magasin* to restock (*en* with); *stock* to replenish; *service de table, tissu* to match (up); *verres* to replace, match (up).
2 se réassortir *vpr* (*Comm*) to stock up again (*de* with), replenish one's stock(s) (*de* of).

réassurance [ReasyRɑ̃s] *nf* reinsurance.

réassurer *vt*, **se réassurer** *vpr* [ReasyRe] (1) to reinsure.

réassureur [ReasyRœR] *nm* reinsurer.

rebaisser [R(ə)bese] (1) **1** *vi [prix]* to go down again; *[température, niveau d'eau]* to fall again.
2 *vt prix* to bring back down *ou* down again, lower again; *radio, son, chauffage* to turn down again; *store, levier* to pull down again, lower again.

rebaptiser [R(ə)batize] (1) *vt enfant* to rebaptize; *rue* to rename; *navire* to rechristen.

rébarbatif, -ive [RebaRbatif, iv] *adj* (*rebutant*) *mine* forbidding, unprepossessing; *sujet, tâche* daunting, forbidding; *style* crabbed, off-putting (*surtout Brit*).

rebâtir [R(ə)bɑtiR] (2) *vt* to rebuild.

rebattre [R(ə)batR(ə)] (41) *vt* **(a)** (*Cartes*) to reshuffle.
(b) il m'a rebattu les oreilles de son succès he kept harping on about his success; **il en parlait toute la journée, j'en avais les oreilles rebattues** he talked of it all day long until I was sick and tired of hearing about it*.

rebattu, e [R(ə)baty] (*ptp de* **rebattre**) *adj sujet, citation* hackneyed.

rebec [Rəbɛk] *nm* rebec(k).

rebelle [Rəbɛl] **1** *adj* **(a)** *troupes, soldat* rebel (*épith*); *enfant, cheval* rebellious, refractory; *esprit* intractable, rebellious; (*fig*) *fièvre, maladie* stubborn; (*fig*) *mèche, cheveux* unruly; (*fig hum*) *cœur* rebellious; (*fig*) *matière* unworkable, refractory, stubborn. (*fig hum*) **découragé par un steak ~, il passa aux légumes** disheartened by a steak which refused to allow itself to be cut *ou* which resisted all attempts at being eaten, he turned his attention to the vegetables.
(b) ~ à *patrie, souverain* unwilling to serve; *discipline* unamenable to; *maths, latin* unwilling to understand; **il est ~ à la poésie** poetry is a closed book to him; **virus ~ à certains remèdes** virus resistant to certain medicines; **cheveux ~s à la brosse** hair which won't be brushed smooth *ou* which a brush cannot tame.
2 *nmf* rebel.

rebeller (se) [R(ə)bele] (1) *vpr* to rebel (*contre* against).

rébellion [Rebeljɔ̃] *nf* (*révolte*) rebellion. (*rebelles*) **la ~** the rebels.

rebiffer (se)* [R(ə)bife] (1) *vpr* (*résister*) *[personne]* to hit *ou* strike back (*contre* at); (*fig*) *[corps, conscience]* to rebel (*contre* against).

rebiquer* [R(ə)bike] (1) *vi* (*se redresser*) *[mèche de cheveux]* to stick up; *[chaussures, col]* to curl up at the ends.

reboisement [R(ə)bwazmɑ̃] *nm* reafforestation.

reboiser [R(ə)bwaze] (1) *vt* to reafforest.

rebond [R(ə)bɔ̃] *nm* (*V* **rebondir**) bounce; rebound.

rebondi, e [R(ə)bɔ̃di] (*ptp de* **rebondir**) *adj objet, bouteille, forme* potbellied; *croupe* rounded; *poitrine* well-developed; *ventre* fat; *joues, visage* chubby, plump, fat; *femme* curvaceous, amply proportioned; *homme* portly, corpulent; *porte-monnaie* well-lined. **elle avait des formes ~es** she was amply proportioned; **il a un ventre ~** he has a paunch *ou* a corporation *ou* a fat stomach.

rebondir [R(ə)bɔ̃diR] (2) *vi* **(a)** *[balle]* (*sur le sol*) to bounce; (*contre un mur etc*) to rebound.
(b) (*être relancé*) *[conversation]* to get going *ou* moving again, spring to life again; *[scandale, affaire, procès]* to be revived; (*Théât*) *[action, intrigue]* to get moving again, spring to life again. **faire ~** *conversation* to give new impetus to, set *ou* get going again; *action d'une tragédie* to get *ou* set moving again; *scandale, procès* to revive.

rebondissement [R(ə)bɔ̃dismɑ̃] *nm [affaire]* (sudden new) development (*de* in), sudden revival (*U*) (*de* of).

rebord [R(ə)bɔR] *nm* **(a)** *[assiette, tuyau, plat, pot]* rim; *[puits, falaise]* edge; *[corniche, table, buffet]* (projecting) edge. **le ~ de la cheminée** the mantelpiece *ou* mantelshelf; **le ~ de la fenêtre** the windowsill, the window ledge. **(b)** hem.

rebours [R(ə)buR] *nm*: **à ~ (a)** (*à rebrousse-poil*) **caresser un chat à ~** to stroke a cat the wrong way; **lisser un tissu à ~** to smooth out a fabric against the nap *ou* pile; (*fig*) **prendre qn à ~** to rub sb up the wrong way.
(b) (*à l'envers*) **faire un trajet à ~** to make a journey *ou* trip the other way round; **prendre une rue en sens unique à ~** to go the wrong way up a one-way street; **feuilleter un magazine à ~** to flip through a magazine from back to front; **compter à ~** to count backwards; (*Mil*) **prendre l'ennemi à ~** to surprise the enemy from behind; *V* **compte.**
(c) (*de travers*) **comprendre à ~** to misunderstand, get the wrong idea, get the wrong end of the stick* (*surtout Brit*); **faire tout à ~** to do everything the wrong way round *ou* upside down.
(d) (*à l'opposé de*) **à ~ de** against; **aller à ~ de la tendance générale** to go against *ou* run counter to the general trend; **c'est à ~ du bon sens!** it goes against *ou* flies in the face of common sense!

rebouteur, -euse [R(ə)butœR, øz] *nm,f*, **rebouteux, -euse** [R(ə)butø, øz] *nm,f* bonesetter.

reboutonner [R(ə)butɔne] (1) **1** *vt* to button up again, rebutton. **2 se reboutonner** *vpr* to do o.s. up again, do up one's buttons again.

rebrousse- [R(ə)bRus] *préf V* **rebrousser.**

rebrousser [R(ə)bRuse] (1) **1** *vt* **(a) ~ chemin** to turn back, turn round and go back, retrace one's steps.
(b) *poil* to brush up; *cheveux* to brush back. **tu as les cheveux tout rebroussés par le vent** your hair is all ruffled up *ou* tousled by the wind.
2: à rebrousse-poil *caresser* the wrong way; **lisser un tissu à rebrousse-poil** to smooth out a fabric against the pile *ou* nap; (*fig*) **prendre qn à rebrousse-poil** to rub sb up the wrong way.

rebuffade [R(ə)byfad] *nf* rebuff.

rébus [Rebys] *nm* rebus. (*fig*) **sa lettre est un vrai ~** reading his letter is a real puzzle.

rebut [Rəby] *nm* **(a)** (*déchets*) scrap. **c'est du ~** (*objets*) it's scrap; (*vêtements*) they're just cast-offs; **c'est le ~ de la cave** it's what's to be thrown out of the cellar, it's all the unwanted stuff in the cellar; **mettre** *ou* **jeter au ~** to put on the scrap heap *ou* rubbish heap; *objets* to scrap, throw out, discard; *vêtements* to discard, throw out; **ces vieux journaux vont aller au ~** these old papers are going to be thrown out *ou* discarded *ou* are going to be put on the rubbish heap; **marchandises de ~** trash goods; **bois de ~** old wood.
(b) (*péj: racaille*) **le ~ de la société** the scum *ou* dregs of society.
(c) (*Poste*) **~s** dead letters.

rebutant, e [R(ə)bytɑ̃, ɑ̃t] *adj* (*dégoûtant*) repellent; (*décourageant*) off-putting (*surtout Brit*), disheartening.

rebuter [R(ə)byte] (1) *vt* (*décourager*) to put off (*surtout Brit*), dishearten, discourage; (*répugner*) to repel; (*repousser durement*) to repulse. **il ne faut pas te ~ tout de suite** don't be deterred straight away.

recacheter [R(ə)kaʃte] (4) *vt* to reseal.

recalage [R(ə)kalaʒ] *nm* (*Scol*) *[candidat]* failure.

récalcitrant, e [RekalsitRɑ̃, ɑ̃t] **1** *adj* (*indocile*) *animal* refractory, stubborn; *personne* recalcitrant, refractory; (*fig*) *appareil, pièce* unmanageable. **2** *nm,f* recalcitrant.

recaler [R(ə)kale] (1) *vt* (*Scol: ajourner*) to fail. **se faire ~ (en histoire)** to fail *ou* flunk* (history); **j'ai été recalé en histoire** I failed (in) *ou* flunked* history; **les recalés** the failed candidates, the failures.

récapitulatif, -ive [Rekapitylatif, iv] *adj chapitre* recapitulative, recapitulatory; *état, tableau* summary (*épith*). **dresser un état ~ (d'un compte etc)** to draw up a summary statement (of an account *etc*).

récapitulation [Rekapitylɑsjɔ̃] *nf* recapitulation, summing up, recap*. **faire la ~ de** to recapitulate, sum up, recap*.

récapituler [Rekapityle] (1) *vt* to recapitulate, sum up, recap*.

recarreler [R(ə)kaRle] (4) *vt* to retile.

recaser* [R(ə)kɑze] (1) *vt* **(a)** *travailleur* to find a new job for; *résident* to rehouse. **il a été recasé** *[chômeur]* he has been found

a new job; **il a pu se** ~ he managed to find a new job.
(b) (*refiler*) ~ **qch à qn** to palm sth off on sb*.
recauser* [ʀ(ə)koze] (1) *vi*: ~ **de qch** to talk about sth again; **je vous en recauserai** we'll talk about it again.
recéder [ʀ(ə)sede] (6) *vt* (*rétrocéder*) to give *ou* sell back; (*vendre*) to resell.
recel [ʀəsɛl] *nm*: ~ **(d'objets volés)** (*action*) receiving stolen goods, receiving (*T*); (*résultat*) possession of *ou* possessing stolen goods; ~ **de malfaiteur** harbouring a wrongdoer; **condamné pour** ~ sentenced for possession of *ou* for receiving stolen goods *ou* for receiving (*T*).
receler [ʀəs(ə)le] (5) *vt* **(a)** (*Jur*) *objet volé* to receive; *voleur* to harbour. **(b)** (*contenir*) *secret, erreur, trésor* to conceal.
receleur, -euse [ʀəs(ə)lœʀ, øz] *nm,f* (*Jur*) receiver.
récemment [resamɑ̃] *adv* **(a)** (*depuis peu*) recently. **la pluie** ~ **tombée rendait la route glissante** the rain which had fallen recently *ou* had just fallen made the road slippery; **ce livre,** ~ **publié** *ou* **publié** ~ this book which has been published recently *ou* which has just been published.
(b) (*dernièrement*) recently, lately (*gén dans phrases nég ou interrog*). **l'as-tu vu** ~? have you seen him lately? *ou* recently?; **encore** ~ **il était très en forme** just recently *ou* even quite recently he was still in tiptop form.
recensement [ʀ(ə)sɑ̃smɑ̃] *nm [population]* census; *[objets]* inventory. (*Mil*) ~ **du contingent** *registration of young men eligible for French military service, carried out by a mayor*; **faire le** ~ to take a *ou* the census of the population, make *ou* take a population census.
recenser [ʀ(ə)sɑ̃se] (1) *vt population* to take a *ou* the census of, make a census of; *objets* to make *ou* take an inventory of; (*Mil*) to compile a register of.
recenseur [ʀ(ə)sɑ̃sœʀ] *adj m, nm*: **(agent)** ~ census taker.
récent, e [ʀesɑ̃, ɑ̃t] *adj* (*survenu récemment*) *événement, traces* recent; (*nouveau, de fraîche date*) *propriétaire, bourgeois* new.
récépissé [ʀesepise] *nm* (*reçu*) (acknowledgment of) receipt.
réceptacle [ʀesɛptakl(ə)] *nm* (*Bot*) *[fleur]* receptacle; (*déversoir*) (*gén*) receptacle; (*Géog*) catchment basin; (*fig*) gathering place; (*péj*) dumping place.
récepteur, -trice [ʀesɛptœʀ, tʀis]. **1** *adj* receiving. **poste** ~ receiving set, receiver.
2 *nm* (*gén, Téléc*) receiver; (*Rad, TV*) (receiving) set, receiver. ~ **(de télévision)** television receiver *ou* (receiving) set.
réceptif, -ive [ʀesɛptif, iv] *adj* receptive (*à* to).
réception [ʀesɛpsjɔ̃] *nf* **(a)** (*réunion, gala*) reception; *V* **jour.**
(b) (*accueil*) reception, welcome. **faire bonne/mauvaise** ~ **à qn** to give a good/bad reception to sb; **un discours de** ~ **(à un nouveau sociétaire)** a welcoming speech *ou* an address of welcome (given to a new member of a society).
(c) (*entrée, salon*) *[appartement, villa]* reception room; *[hôtel]* entrance hall; (*bureau*) *[hôtel]* reception desk, reception. **salle de** ~ function room, stateroom; **salons de** ~ reception rooms.
(d) (*action de recevoir*) *[paquet, lettre]* receipt; (*Bio, Rad, TV*) reception. **à la** ~ **de sa lettre** on receipt of *ou* on receiving his letter; **c'est lui qui s'occupe de la** ~ **des marchandises** he is the one who takes delivery of the goods; *V* **accusé, accuser.**
(e) (*Sport*) (*prise, blocage*) *[ballon]* trapping, catching; (*atterrissage*) *[sauteur, parachutiste]* landing. **le footballeur manqua sa** ~ **et le ballon roula en touche** the footballer failed to trap *ou* catch the ball and it rolled into touch; **après une bonne** ~ **du ballon** after trapping *ou* catching the ball well; **le sauteur manqua sa** ~ the jumper made a bad landing *ou* landed badly.
réceptionnaire [ʀesɛpsjɔnɛʀ] *nmf [hôtel]* head of reception; (*Comm*) *[marchandises]* receiving clerk; (*Jur*) receiving agent.
réceptionner [ʀesɛpsjɔne] (1) *vt marchandises* to receive, take delivery of, check and sign for.
réceptionniste [ʀesɛpsjɔnist(ə)] *nmf* receptionist. ~**-standardiste** receptionist-telephonist.
réceptivité [ʀesɛptivite] *nf* (*gén*) receptivity, receptiveness; (*Méd*) sensitivity, liability (*à* to).
récessif, -ive [ʀesesif, iv] *adj* (*Bio*) recessive.
récession [ʀesesjɔ̃] *nf* recession.
récessivité [ʀesesivite] *nf* recessiveness.
recette [ʀ(ə)sɛt] *nf* **(a)** (*Culin*) recipe; (*Chim*) *[teinture, produit]* formula; (*fig: truc, secret*) formula, recipe (*de* for).
(b) (*encaisse*) takings (*pl*). **aujourd'hui, j'ai fait une bonne** ~ I've made a good day's takings, today the takings were good; (*fig: avoir du succès*) **faire** ~ to be a big success, be a winner.
(c) (*rentrées d'argent*) ~**s** receipts; **l'excédent des** ~**s sur les dépenses** the excess of receipts *ou* revenue over expenses.
(d) (*Impôts*) (*fonction*) position of tax *ou* revenue collector; (*bureau*) tax (collector's) office, revenue office. ~**-perception** tax office.
(e) (*recouvrement*) collection. **faire la** ~ **des sommes dues** to collect the money due; *V* **garçon.**
recevabilité [ʀəsvabilite] *nf* (*Jur*) *[pourvoi, témoignage]* admissibility.
recevable [ʀəsvabl(ə)] (*Jur*) *adj demande, appel, pourvoi* admissible, allowable; *personne* competent. **témoignage non** ~ inadmissible evidence.
receveur [ʀəsvœʀ] *nm* **(a)** (*Méd*) recipient. ~ **universel** universal recipient. **(b)** ~ **(d'autobus)** conductor; ~ **(des contributions)** tax collector *ou* officer; ~ **(des postes)** postmaster.
receveuse [ʀəsvøz] *nf* **(a)** (*Méd*) recipient. ~ **universelle** universal recipient. **(b)** ~ **(d'autobus)** conductress; ~ **(des contributions)** tax collector *ou* officer; ~ **(des postes)** postmistress.
recevoir [ʀəsvwaʀ] (28) **1** *vt* **(a)** (*gén*) *lettre, ordre, argent, blessure, ovation etc* to receive, get; *approbation, refus* to meet with, receive, get; *modifications* to undergo, receive; (*Rel*) *confession* to hear; (*Rel*) *vœux, sacrement* to receive. (*Rel*) ~ **les ordres** to take holy orders; **nous avons bien reçu votre lettre du 15 courant** we acknowledge receipt of your letter of the 15th instant; **je n'ai d'ordre à** ~ **de personne** I don't take orders from anyone; **procédé qui a reçu le nom de son inventeur** process which has taken *ou* got its name from the inventor; **l'affaire recevra toute notre attention** the matter will receive our full attention; **nous avons reçu la pluie** we got *ou* had rain; **j'ai reçu le caillou sur la tête** the stone hit me on the head, I got hit on the head by the stone; **il a reçu un coup de pied/un coup de poing dans la figure** he got kicked/punched in the face, he got a kick/punch in the face; **c'est lui qui a tout reçu** (*blâme, coups*) he got the worst of it, he bore *ou* got the brunt of it; (*sauce, éclaboussures*) he got the worst of it; (*formule épistolaire*) **recevez, cher Monsieur** (*ou* **chère Madame**) **l'expression de mes sentiments distingués/mes salutations sincères/l'assurance de mon dévouement** yours faithfully/sincerely/truly.
(b) *invité* (*accueillir*) to receive, welcome, greet; (*traiter*) to entertain; (*loger*) to take in, receive; (*Admin*) *employé, demandeur* to see; *demande, déposition* to receive, admit. ~ **qn à dîner** to entertain *ou* invite sb to dinner; **ils ont reçu le roi** they entertained the *ou* were host to the king; **être bien/mal reçu** *[proposition, nouvelles]* to be well/badly received; *[personne]* to receive a good/bad welcome; *[invités]* to be entertained well/badly; **il est reçu partout dans la haute société** all doors are open to him in society; **les Dupont reçoivent beaucoup** the Duponts entertain a lot; **la baronne reçoit le jeudi** the baroness is at home (to visitors) on Thursdays; **le directeur reçoit le jeudi** the principal receives visitors on Thursdays; **le docteur reçoit de 10h à 12h** the doctor's surgery (*Brit*) *ou* office (*US*) is from 10 a.m. till noon; ~ **la visite de qn/d'un cambrioleur** to receive *ou* have a visit from sb/from a burglar; **elles se connaissent mais ne se reçoivent pas** they know each other but they are not on visiting terms; *V* **chien.**
(c) (*Scol, Univ etc*) *candidat* to pass. **être reçu à un examen** to pass an exam, be successful in an exam; **il a été reçu dans les premiers/dans les derniers** he was near the top/bottom in the exam; **il a été reçu premier/deuxième/dernier** he came first/second/last *ou* bottom in the exam; *V* **reçu.**
(d) (*contenir*) *[hôtel, lycée]* to take, hold, accommodate; (*récolter*) *[gouttière]* to collect. **par manque de locaux on n'a pas pu** ~ **plus d'élèves cette année** lack of space prevented us from taking *ou* admitting more pupils this year; (*Géog*) ~ **un affluent** to be joined by a tributary; **leur chambre ne reçoit jamais le soleil** their room never gets any sun.
(e) (*Tech*) *pièce mobile* to receive (*T*). **cette encoche reçoit le crochet qui assure la fermeture de la porte** this notch receives (*T*) *ou* takes the hook which keeps the door shut.
2 se recevoir *vpr* (*tomber*) to land. **se** ~ **sur une jambe/sur les mains** to land on one leg/on one's hands; **il s'est mal reçu** he landed badly.
rechange [ʀ(ə)ʃɑ̃ʒ] *nm* **(a)** ~ **(de vêtements)** change of clothes; **as-tu ton** ~? have you got a change of clothes?
(b) de ~ (*de remplacement*) *solution, politique* alternative; (*de secours*) *outil* spare; **avoir du linge de** ~ to have a change of underwear; **j'ai apporté des chaussures de** ~ I brought a spare *ou* an extra pair of shoes; *V* **pièce.**
rechanger [ʀ(ə)ʃɑ̃ʒe] (3) *vt* to change again.
rechanter [ʀ(ə)ʃɑ̃te] (1) *vt* to sing again.
rechapage [ʀ(ə)ʃapaʒ] *nm* retreading, remoulding. **le** ~ **n'a pas duré** the retread *ou* remould didn't last long.
rechaper [ʀ(ə)ʃape] (1) *vt pneu* to retread, remould. **pneus rechapés** remoulds, retreads.
réchapper [ʀeʃape] (1) *vi*: ~ **de** *ou* **à** *accident, maladie* to come through; **tu as eu de la chance d'en** ~ you were lucky to escape with your life; **si jamais j'en réchappe** if ever I come through this.
recharge [ʀ(ə)ʃaʀʒ(ə)] *nf* **(a)** (*action*) (*Élec*) recharging; (*Mil*) reloading. **(b)** (*cartouche*) *[arme]* reload; *[stylo]* refill.
rechargement [ʀ(ə)ʃaʀʒəmɑ̃] *nm* (*V* **recharger**) reloading; refilling; recharging; refuelling; remetalling; relaying.
recharger [ʀ(ə)ʃaʀʒe] (3) *vt véhicule, arme, appareil-photo* to reload; *briquet, stylo* to refill; *accumulateur* to recharge; *poêle* to refuel; (*Tech*) *route* to remetal; (*Tech*) *voie, rails* to relay.
réchaud [ʀeʃo] *nm* **(a)** (portable) stove. **(b)** (*chauffe-plat*) plate-warmer. **(c)** (*cassolette*) burner (*for incense etc*).
réchauffage [ʀeʃofaʒ] *nm [aliment]* reheating.
réchauffé, e [ʀeʃofe] (*ptp de* **réchauffer**) *adj nourriture* reheated, warmed-up, rehashed (*péj*); (*péj*) *plaisanterie* stale, old hat (*attrib*); *théories* rehashed, old hat (*attrib*). **c'est du** ~ it's reheated *ou* warmed-up *ou* rehashed (*péj*); it's stale *ou* old hat; it's rehashed *ou* old hat.
réchauffement [ʀeʃofmɑ̃] *nm [eau, membres, personne]* warming (up). **on constate un** ~ **de la température** we notice a rise *ou* an increase in the temperature (of the weather); **on espère un** ~ **de la température pour la moisson** we're hoping for warmer weather for the harvest.
réchauffer [ʀeʃofe] (1) **1** *vt* **(a)** (*Culin*) *aliment* to reheat, heat *ou* warm up again. **réchauffe** *ou* **fais** ~ **la soupe, mets la soupe à** ~ reheat the soup, heat *ou* warm the soup up again.
(b) *personne* to warm up. **une bonne soupe, ça réchauffe** a good soup warms you up; (*littér, hum*) ~ **un serpent dans son sein** to nurse a viper in one's bosom.
(c) (*réconforter*) *cœur* to warm; (*ranimer*) *courage* to stir up, rekindle.

(d) *[soleil]* to heat up, warm up. **le soleil réchauffe la terre** the sun heats up the land; **ce rayon de soleil va ~ l'atmosphère** this ray of sunshine will warm up the air.

2 se réchauffer *vpr* **(a)** *[temps, température]* to get warmer, warm up. **on dirait que ça se réchauffe** it feels as if it's getting warmer *ou* warming up.

(b) *[personne]* to warm o.s. (up). **alors tu te réchauffes un peu?** are you warming up now? *ou* feeling a bit warmer now?; **se ~ les doigts, ~ ses doigts** to warm one's fingers (up).

réchauffeur [reʃofœr] *nm* (re)heater.

rechausser [r(ə)ʃose] (1) **1** *vt*: **~ un enfant** (*chaussures enlevées*) to put a child's shoes back on; (*chaussures neuves*) to buy a child new shoes. **2 se rechausser** *vpr* to put one's shoes back on; to buy (o.s.) new shoes.

rêche [rɛʃ] *adj* (*au toucher*) *tissu, peau* rough, harsh; (*au goût*) *vin* rough; *fruit vert* harsh.

recherche [r(ə)ʃɛrʃ(ə)] *nf* **(a)** (*action de rechercher*) search (*de* for). **la ~ de ce papier m'a pris plusieurs heures** the search for this paper took me several hours; **la ~ de l'albumine dans le sang est faite en laboratoire** tests to detect albumin in the blood are performed in the laboratory; **à la ~ de** in search of; **être/se mettre à la ~ de qch/qn** to be/go in search of sth/sb, search for sth/sb; **je suis à la ~ de mes lunettes** I'm searching *ou* hunting *ou* looking for my glasses; **ils sont à la ~ d'un appartement/d'une maison** they are flat-hunting/house-hunting, they're looking for *ou* on the look-out for a flat/house; **il a dû se mettre à la ~ d'une nouvelle situation** he had to start looking *ou* hunting for a new job; **il est toujours à la ~ d'une bonne excuse** he's always on the look-out for a good excuse, he's always trying to come up with *ou* find a good excuse.

(b) (*enquête*) **~s** investigations; **faire des ~s** to make *ou* pursue investigations; **malgré toutes leurs ~s, ils n'ont pas trouvé le document nécessaire** in spite of all their searching *ou* hunting they haven't found the necessary document; **toutes nos ~s pour retrouver l'enfant sont demeurées sans résultat** all our attempts to find the child remained fruitless; **jusqu'ici il a échappé aux ~s de la police** until now he has escaped the police hunt *ou* search.

(c) (*fig: poursuite*) pursuit (*de* of), search (*de* for). **la ~ des plaisirs** the pursuit of pleasure, pleasure-seeking; **la ~ de la gloire** the pursuit of glory; **la ~ de la perfection** the search *ou* quest for perfection.

(d) (*Scol, Univ*) (*métier, spécialité*) **la ~** research; (*études, enquêtes*) **~s** research; **faire des ~s sur un sujet** to do *ou* carry out research into a subject; **que fait-il comme ~s?** what (kind of) research does he do?, what is he doing research on? *ou* in?; **être dans la ~, faire de la ~** to be (engaged) in research, do research (work); **il fait de la ~ en maths** he's doing research in maths; **bourse/étudiant de ~** research grant/student; **c'est un travail de ~** it's a piece of research (work).

(e) (*raffinement*) *[tenue, ameublement]* meticulousness, studied elegance; (*péj: affectation*) affectation. **être habillé avec ~** to be dressed with studied elegance; **être habillé sans ~** to be dressed carelessly.

recherché, e [r(ə)ʃɛrʃe] (*ptp de* **rechercher**) *adj* **(a)** *édition, tableau, livre* much sought-after; (*très demandé*) *produits, acteur, conférencier* in great demand (*attrib*), much sought-after; (*apprécié des connaisseurs*) *morceau délicat, plaisir* choice (*épith*), exquisite. **c'est quelqu'un de très ~** he's in great demand, he's much sought-after.

(b) (*étudié, soigné*) *style* mannered; *expression* studied; *tenue* meticulous; (*péj*) affected, studied.

rechercher [r(ə)ʃɛrʃe] (1) *vt* **(a)** (*chercher à trouver*) *objet égaré ou désiré, enfant perdu* to search for, hunt for; *coupable, témoin* to try to trace *ou* find, look for, seek; *cause d'accident* to try to determine *ou* find out *ou* ascertain, inquire into. **~ l'albumine dans le sang** to look for (evidence of *ou* the presence of) albumin in the blood; **~ comment/pourquoi** to try to find out how/why; **~ qch dans sa mémoire** to search one's memory for sth; **il faudra ~ ce document dans tous les vieux dossiers** we'll have to search through all the old files to find this document; (*dans une annonce*) **'on recherche femme de ménage'** 'cleaning lady required'; **recherché pour meurtre** wanted for murder; **les policiers le recherchent depuis 2 ans** the police have been looking for him *ou* have been after him for 2 years.

(b) (*viser à*) *honneurs, compliment* to seek; *danger* to court, seek; *succès, plaisir* to pursue. **~ la perfection** to strive for *ou* seek perfection; **~ l'amitié/la compagnie de qn** to seek sb's friendship/company; **un écrivain qui recherche l'insolite** a writer who strives to capture the unusual.

(c) (*chercher à nouveau*) to search for *ou* look for again. **il faudra que je recherche dans mon sac** I must have another look (for it) in my bag, I must look in *ou* search my bag again; **recherche donc cette lettre** search *ou* look for that letter again, have another look *ou* search for that letter.

rechigner [r(ə)ʃiɲe] (1) *vi* (*renâcler*) to balk, jib. **quand je lui ai dit de m'aider, il a rechigné** when I told him to help me he balked *ou* jibbed *ou* made a sour face; **faire qch en rechignant** to do sth with bad grace *ou* with a sour face; **il m'a obéi sans trop ~** he obeyed me without making too much fuss; **~ à faire qch** to balk *ou* jib at doing sth; **~ à *ou* devant qch** to balk *ou* jib at sth.

rechute [r(ə)ʃyt] *nf* (*Méd*) relapse; (*fig: dans l'erreur, le vice*) lapse (*dans* into). (*Méd*) **faire *ou* avoir une ~** to have a relapse.

rechuter [r(ə)ʃyte] (1) *vi* (*Méd*) to relapse, have a relapse.

récidive [residiv] *nf* **(a)** (*Jur*) second *ou* subsequent offence *ou* crime. **en cas de ~** in the event of a second *ou* subsequent offence, in the event of a repetition of the offence; **escroquerie avec ~** second offence of fraud; **être en ~** to be a recidivist; **les cas de ~ se multiplient chez les jeunes délinquants** recidivism is on the increase among juvenile delinquents; **à la première ~, je le fiche à la porte** at the first (sign of) repetition *ou* if he repeats that once again, I shall throw him out.

(b) (*Méd*) recurrence; (*fig: nouvelle incartade*) repetition (*of one's bad ways*).

récidiver [residive] (1) *vi* (*Jur*) to commit a second *ou* subsequent offence *ou* crime; (*fig*) *[enfant, élève]* to do it again; (*Méd*) to recur.

récidiviste [residivist(ə)] *nmf* second offender, recidivist (*T*); (*plusieurs répétitions*) habitual offender, recidivist (*T*). **un condamné ~** a recidivist.

récif [resif] *nm* reef.

récipiendaire [resipjɑ̃dɛr] *nm* (*Univ*) recipient (*of a diploma*); *[société]* newly elected member, member elect.

récipient [resipjɑ̃] *nm* container, receptacle.

réciprocité [resiprɔsite] *nf* reciprocity.

réciproque [resiprɔk] **1** *adj sentiments, confiance, tolérance, concessions* reciprocal, mutual; (*Math*) *figure, transformation* reciprocal; (*Gram*) *verbe* reciprocal. (*Logique*) **propositions ~s** converse propositions.

2 *nf*: **la ~** (*l'inverse*) (*Logique*) the converse; (*gén*) the opposite, the reverse; (*la pareille*) the same (treatment); **il me déteste mais la ~ n'est pas vraie** he hates me but the opposite *ou* reverse isn't true, he hates me but conversely I don't hate him; **il m'a joué un sale tour, mais je lui rendrai la ~** he played a dirty trick on me, but I'll be quits with him yet *ou* I'll pay him back (in kind *ou* in his own coin); **encore merci, j'espère qu'un jour j'aurai l'occasion de vous rendre la ~** thanks again, I hope that one day I'll have the opportunity to do the same for you *ou* to pay you back; **s'attendre à la ~** to expect the same (treatment) *ou* to be paid back.

réciproquement [resiprɔkmɑ̃] *adv* **(a)** (*l'un l'autre*) each other, one another, mutually. **ils se félicitaient ~** they congratulated each other *ou* one another.

(b) (*vice versa*) vice versa. **il me déteste et ~** he hates me and vice versa *ou* and I hate him; **un employé doit avoir de l'estime pour son chef et ~** an employee must have regard for his boss and the other way round *ou* and vice versa.

récit [resi] *nm* **(a)** (*action de raconter*) account, story; (*histoire*) story; (*genre*) narrative. **~ d'aventures** adventure story; **faire le ~ de** to give an account of, tell the story of; **au ~ de ces exploits** on hearing an *ou* the account of *ou* the story of these exploits.

(b) (*Théât: monologue*) (narrative) monologue.

(c) (*Mus*) solo.

récital, *pl* ~s [resital] *nm* recital.

récitant, e [resitɑ̃, ɑ̃t] **1** *adj* (*Mus*) solo. **2** *nm,f* (*Mus, Rad, Théât, TV*) narrator.

récitatif [resitatif] *nm* recitative.

récitation [resitasjɔ̃] *nf* **(a)** (*matière, classe*) recitation. **composition de ~** recitation test; **leçon de ~** lesson to be recited by heart.

(b) (*texte, poème*) recitation, piece (to be recited).

(c) (*action*) recital, reciting.

réciter [resite] (1) *vt* **(a)** *leçon, chapelet, prière* to recite. **(b)** (*péj*) *profession de foi, témoignage* to trot out, recite.

réclamation [reklamasjɔ̃] *nf* **(a)** (*plainte*) complaint; (*Sport*) objection. **faire une ~** to make *ou* lodge a complaint; **adressez vos ~s à, pour toute ~ s'adresser à** all complaints should be referred to; **'(bureau des) ~s'** 'complaints department *ou* office'; (*Téléc*) **téléphonez aux ~s** ring the engineers.

(b) (*récrimination*) protest, complaint.

réclame [reklam] *nf* (*annonce publicitaire*) advertisement, advert. (*publicité*) **la ~** advertising; **faire de la ~ pour un produit** to advertise a product; **ça ne leur fait pas de ~** that's no advert for them; (*fig*) **je ne vais pas lui faire de la ~** I'm not going to boost his business for him *ou* spread his name around (for him); **en ~** on offer; **article ~** special offer.

réclamer [reklame] (1) **1** *vt* **(a)** (*solliciter*) *silence, paix, aide* to ask *ou* call for; *argent* to ask for; *pain* to ask *ou* beg for. **~ l'indulgence de qn** to beg *ou* crave sb's indulgence; **je réclame la parole!** I ask *ou* beg to speak!; **il m'a réclamé à boire/un jouet** he asked me for a drink/a toy; **je n'aime pas les enfants qui réclament** I don't like children who are always asking for things; **l'enfant malade réclame sa mère** the sick child is calling *ou* asking for his mother, the sick child wants his mother.

(b) (*revendiquer*) *augmentation, droit, dû* to claim, demand; *part* to claim, lay claim to. **je lui ai réclamé le stylo que je lui avais prêté** I asked him for the pen back which I had lent him.

(c) (*nécessiter*) *patience, soin* to call for, demand, require.

2 *vi* (*protester*) to complain. **si vous n'êtes pas content, allez ~ ailleurs** if you're not happy, go and complain *ou* make your complaints elsewhere; **~ contre** to cry out against.

3 se réclamer *vpr*: **se ~ de**: **se ~ de ses ancêtres** to call on the spirit of one's ancestors; **doctrine politique qui se réclame de la révolution française** political doctrine that claims to go back to the spirit of the French Revolution; **il se réclame de l'école romantique** he claims to draw *ou* take his inspiration from the romantic school; **il s'est réclamé du ministre pour obtenir ce poste** he used the minister's name (as a reference) to obtain this position; **je me réclame de Descartes quand je dis cela** I use Descartes as my authority when I say that.

reclassement [r(ə)klasmɑ̃] *nm* (*V* **reclasser**) placement; rehabilitation; regrading; reclassifying.

reclasser [r(ə)klase] (1) *vt chômeur* to place, find a new placement for; *ex-prisonnier* to rehabilitate; *fonctionnaire* to regrade; *objet* to reclassify.

reclus, e [rəkly, yz] **1** *adj* cloistered. **elle vit ~e, elle a *ou* mène une vie ~e** she leads the life of a recluse, she leads a cloistered life. **2** *nm,f* recluse.

réclusion [ʀeklyzjɔ̃] *nf* (*littér*) reclusion (*littér*). (*Jur*) ~ **(criminelle)** imprisonment.

réclusionnaire [ʀeklyzjɔnɛʀ] *nmf* (*Jur*) convict.

recoiffer [ʀ(ə)kwafe] (1) **1** *vt*: ~ **ses cheveux** to do one's hair; ~ **qn** to do sb's hair. **2 se recoiffer** *vpr* (*se peigner*) to do one's hair; (*remettre son chapeau*) to put one's hat back on.

recoin [ʀəkwɛ̃] *nm* (*lit*) nook; (*fig*) hidden *ou* innermost recess. **les ~s du grenier** the nooks and crannies of the attic.

recollage [ʀ(ə)kɔlaʒ] *nm*, **recollement** [ʀ(ə)kɔlmɑ̃] *nm* (*V* **recoller**) resticking; sticking back together again.

recoller [ʀ(ə)kɔle] (1) **(1)** *vt* **(a)** (*lit*) *étiquette* to stick back on *ou* down, restick; *morceau, vase* to stick back together; *enveloppe* to stick back down, restick. (*fig*) **le coureur recolla au peloton** the runner closed the gap with the rest of the bunch.

(b) (*remettre*) ~ **son oreille à la porte** to stick one's ear against *ou* to the door again; ~ **qn en prison*** to stick sb back in prison*; **ne recolle pas tes affaires dans ce coin!*** don't stick your things back down in that corner!*

(c) (*: *redonner*) ~ **une amende** *etc* **à qn** to give another fine *etc* to sb; **je ne veux pas qu'on nous recolle le grand-père!** I don't want them to dump *ou* palm off grandfather on us again!*

2 se recoller *vpr* **(a)** *[os]* to mend, knit (together).

(b) (*: *subir*) **il a fallu se ~ la lessive** we had to take on the washing-up again.

(c) (*: *se remettre*) **on va se ~ au boulot** let's knuckle down to the job again*, let's get back down to the job.

(d) (*: *se remettre en ménage*) to go back (to live) together. **après leur brouille ils se sont recollés (ensemble)** after their quarrel they went back (to live) together.

récoltant, e [ʀekɔltɑ̃, ɑ̃t] *adj, nm,f*: **(propriétaire-)~** owner (*who harvests his own crop*), grower.

récolte [ʀekɔlt(ə)] *nf* **(a)** (*action*) (*V* **récolter**) harvesting; gathering (in); collecting. **faire la ~ des pommes de terre** to harvest *ou* gather (in) the potatoes *ou* the potato crop; **la saison des ~s** the harvest *ou* harvesting season.

(b) (*produit*) *[blé]* harvest, crop; *[pommes de terre, miel]* crop. **cette année, on a fait une excellente ~ (de fruits)** this year we had an excellent *ou* a bumper crop (of fruit); ~ **sur pied** standing crop.

(c) (*fig*) *[documents, souvenirs]* collection, crop (*fig*); (*argent récolté*) takings (*pl*); (*observations récoltées*) findings (*pl*).

récolter [ʀekɔlte] (1) *vt* **(a)** *blé, pommes de terre* to harvest, gather (in); *miel* to collect, gather. (*Prov*) ~ **ce qu'on a semé** to reap what one has sown; *V* **qui.**

(b) (*recueillir*) *souvenirs, documents, signatures* to collect, gather; *argent* to collect; (*) *contravention, coups* to get, collect*. **je n'ai récolté que des ennuis** all I got was a lot of trouble.

recommandable [ʀ(ə)kɔmɑ̃dabl(ə)] *adj* (*estimable*) commendable. **peu ~** not very commendable.

recommandation [ʀ(ə)kɔmɑ̃dɑsjɔ̃] *nf* **(a)** (*conseil: gén, Pol*) recommendation. **faire des ~s à qn** to make recommendations to sb. **(b)** (*louange*) *[hôtel, livre]* recommendation. **(c)** (*appui*) recommendation. **sur la ~ de qn** on sb's recommendation; **donner une ~ à qn pour un patron** to give sb a recommendation for an employer; *V* **lettre. (d)** (*Poste: V* **recommander**) recording; registration.

recommandé, e [ʀ(ə)kɔmɑ̃de] (*ptp de* **recommander**) *adj* **(a)** (*Poste: V* **recommander**) recorded; registered. **'envoi ~'** 'recorded delivery' (*Brit*); 'registered post' (*Brit*), 'registered mail'; **envoyer qch en ~** to send sth recorded delivery (*Brit*); to send sth by registered post (*Brit*) *ou* mail; *V* **lettre.**

(b) (*conseillé*) *produit* recommended; *hôtel* approved, recommended; *mesure, initiative* advisable, recommended. **est-ce bien ~?** is it advisable? *ou* recommended? (*de faire* to do).

recommander [ʀ(ə)kɔmɑ̃de] (1) **1** *vt* **(a)** (*appuyer*) *candidat* to recommend (*à* to). **est-il recommandé?** has he been recommended?; **un savant que sa probité intellectuelle recommande autant que ses découvertes** a scholar whose intellectual honesty commends him as much as (do) his discoveries.

(b) (*conseiller*) *hôtel, livre, produit* to recommend (*à* to). **~ à qn de faire** to recommend *ou* advise sb to do; **le médecin lui recommande le repos** the doctor advises *ou* recommends (him to) rest; **je te recommande la modération/la discrétion** I advise you to be moderate/discreet, I recommend that you be moderate/discreet; **je te recommande (de lire) ce livre** I recommend you (to read) this book, I recommend that you read this book; (*ton de menace*) **je te recommande de partir** I strongly advise you to leave; **est-ce bien à ~?** is it to be recommended?, is it advisable?

(c) (*Rel*) **~ son âme à Dieu** to commend one's soul to God.

(d) (*tournure impersonnelle*) **il est recommandé de** it's advisable *ou* recommended to.

(e) (*Poste*) *lettre* (*pour attester sa remise*) to record; (*pour assurer sa valeur*) *lettre, paquet* to register.

2 se recommander *vpr*: **se ~ de qn** to give sb's name as a reference; **se ~ à qn/Dieu** to commend o.s. to sb/God; **il se recommande par son talent/son ambition** his talent/ambition commends him.

recommencement [ʀ(ə)kɔmɑ̃smɑ̃] *nm*: **le ~ des hostilités/combats** the renewal of hostilities/(the) fighting; **l'histoire est un perpétuel ~** history is a process of constant renewal *ou* a series of new beginnings; **les ~s sont toujours difficiles** beginning again *ou* making a fresh start is always difficult.

recommencer [ʀ(ə)kɔmɑ̃se] (3) **1** *vt* **(a)** (*continuer*) *récit, lecture* to begin *ou* start again, resume; *lutte, combat* to start up again, start afresh, renew. **soyez attentifs, ça fait la 3e fois que je recommence** pay attention, that's the 3rd time I've had to start *ou* begin again.

(b) (*refaire*) *travail, expérience* to start (over) again, start afresh. **~ sa vie** to make a fresh start (in life), start *ou* begin one's life (over) again; **si c'était à ~** if I could start *ou* have it over again.

(c) (*répéter*) *erreur* to make *ou* commit again.

2 *vi [pluie, orage]* to begin *ou* start again; *[combat]* to start up again, start afresh, resume. **la pluie recommence** it's beginning *ou* starting to rain again, the rain is beginning *ou* starting again; **en septembre, l'école recommence** in September school begins *ou* starts again *ou* resumes; **année après année, les saisons recommencent** year after year the seasons begin afresh *ou* anew; **je leur ai dit de se taire, et voilà que ça recommence!** I told them to be quiet and yet there they go again!; **~ à** *ou* **de faire** to begin *ou* start to do again, begin *ou* start doing again; **tu ne vas pas ~ de sitôt!** you won't do that again in a hurry!*; **on lui dit de ne pas le faire, mais deux minutes plus tard, il recommence (à le faire)** he is told not to do it but two minutes later he does it again *ou* he's at it again.

recomparaître [ʀ(ə)kɔ̃paʀɛtʀ(ə)] (57) *vi* (*Jur*) to appear (in court) again.

récompense [ʀekɔ̃pɑ̃s] *nf* (*action, chose*) reward; (*prix*) award. **en ~ de** in return for, as a reward for; **je me sacrifie et voilà ma ~** I make sacrifices and that's all the reward I get.

récompenser [ʀekɔ̃pɑ̃se] (1) *vt* to reward. **être récompensé d'avoir fait qch** to be rewarded *ou* recompensed (*frm*) for having done sth.

recomposer [ʀ(ə)kɔ̃poze] (1) *vt puzzle* to put together again, reconstruct; (*Chim*) to recompose; (*Téléc*) *numéro* to dial again, redial; (*Typ*) *ligne* to reset. **il parvint à ~ la scène** (*par la mémoire*) he succeeded in reconstructing the scene; **l'œil/la télévision recompose l'image** the eye/television reconstitutes the image.

recomposition [ʀ(ə)kɔ̃pozisjɔ̃] *nf* (*V* **recomposer**) reconstruction; recomposition; redialling; resetting; reconstitution.

recompter [ʀ(ə)kɔ̃te] (1) *vt* to count again, recount.

réconciliateur, -trice [ʀekɔ̃siljatœʀ, tʀis] *nm,f* reconciler.

réconciliation [ʀekɔ̃siljɑsjɔ̃] *nf* reconciliation.

réconcilier [ʀekɔ̃silje] (7) **1** *vt personnes, théories* to reconcile (*avec, et* with, and). **~ qn avec une idée** to reconcile sb to an idea. **2 se réconcilier** *vpr* to be *ou* become reconciled (*avec* with).

reconductible [ʀ(ə)kɔ̃dyktibl(ə)] *adj* renewable.

reconduction [ʀ(ə)kɔ̃dyksjɔ̃] *nf* renewal.

reconduire [ʀ(ə)kɔ̃dɥiʀ] (38) *vt* **(a)** (*continuer*) *politique, budget, bail* to renew. **commande tacitement reconduite** order renewed by tacit agreement.

(b) (*raccompagner*) **~ qn chez lui/à la gare** to see *ou* take *ou* escort sb (back) home/to the station; **il a été reconduit à la frontière par les policiers** he was escorted (back) to the frontier by the police; **~ qn à pied/en voiture chez lui** to walk/drive sb (back) home; **il m'a reconduit à la porte** he showed me to the door.

réconfort [ʀekɔ̃fɔʀ] *nm* comfort.

réconfortant, e [ʀekɔ̃fɔʀtɑ̃, ɑ̃t] *adj* (*rassurant*) *parole, idée* comforting; (*stimulant*) *remède* tonic (*épith*), fortifying; *aliment* fortifying.

réconforter [ʀekɔ̃fɔʀte] (1) **1** *vt [paroles, présence]* to comfort; *[alcool, aliment, remède]* to fortify. **2 se réconforter** *vpr* (*boire, manger*) to have *ou* take some refreshment.

reconnaissable [ʀ(ə)kɔnɛsabl(ə)] *adj* recognizable (*à* by, from). **il n'était pas ~** he was unrecognizable, you wouldn't have recognized him.

reconnaissance [ʀ(ə)kɔnɛsɑ̃s] **1** *nf* **(a)** (*gratitude*) gratitude, gratefulness (*à qn* to *ou* towards sb). **avoir/éprouver de la ~ pour qn** to be/feel grateful to sb; **en ~ de ses services/de son aide** in recognition of *ou* acknowledgement of *ou* gratitude for his services/his help; **être pénétré de ~ pour la générosité de qn** to be filled with gratitude to sb for his generosity; (*hum*) **il a la ~ du ventre** he's grateful now that his belly* is full.

(b) (*Pol: d'un état*) recognition; (*Jur: d'un droit*) recognition, acknowledgement.

(c) (*exploration*) reconnaissance, survey; (*Mil*) reconnaissance, recce*. (*lit, fig*) **envoyer en ~** to send (out) on reconnaissance *ou* on a recce*; (*lit, fig*) **partir en ~** to go and reconnoitre (the ground); (*Mil*) **faire** *ou* **pousser une ~** to make a reconnaissance, go on reconnaissance; **mission/patrouille de ~** reconnaissance mission/patrol.

(d) (*action de reconnaître*) recognition. **il lui fit un petit signe de ~** he gave her a little sign of recognition.

(e) (*littér: aveu*) acknowledgement, admission.

2: reconnaissance de dette acknowledgement of a debt, IOU; **reconnaissance d'enfant** legal recognition of a child; **reconnaissance du mont-de-piété** pawn ticket.

reconnaissant, e [ʀ(ə)kɔnɛsɑ̃, ɑ̃t] *adj* grateful (*à qn de qch* to sb for sth). **je vous serais ~ de me répondre rapidement** I would be grateful if you would reply quickly *ou* for a speedy reply.

reconnaître [ʀ(ə)kɔnɛtʀ(ə)] (57) **1** *vt* **(a)** (*gén: identifier*) to recognize. **je l'ai reconnu à sa voix** I recognized him *ou* I knew it was him *ou* I could tell it was him from *ou* by (the sound of) his voice; **je le reconnaîtrais entre mille** I'd recognize him *ou* pick him out anywhere; **elle reconnut l'enfant à son foulard rouge** she recognized the child by his red scarf; **~ la voix/le pas de qn** to recognize sb's voice/walk; **ces jumeaux sont impossibles à ~** these twins are impossible to tell apart, it's impossible to tell which of these twins is which; **on reconnaît un fumeur à ses doigts jaunis** you can tell *ou* recognize *ou* spot a smoker by his stained fingers; **on reconnaît bien là sa paresse** that's just typical of him and his lazy ways, that's just typical of his laziness; **je le reconnais bien là** that's just like him, that's him all over!;

méfiez-vous, il sait ~ un mensonge be careful — he knows *ou* recognizes *ou* he can spot a lie when he hears one; **on ne le reconnaît plus** you wouldn't know *ou* recognize him now.

(b) (*convenir de*) *innocence, supériorité, valeur* to recognize, acknowledge; (*avouer*) *torts* to recognize, acknowledge, admit. **il reconnut peu à peu la difficulté de la tâche** he gradually came to realize *ou* recognize the difficulty of the task; **il faut ~ les faits** we must face *ou* recognize the facts; **on lui reconnaît une qualité, il est honnête** he is recognized as having one quality – he is honest; **il faut ~ qu'il faisait très froid** admittedly, it was very cold, you must admit it was very cold; **il a reconnu s'être trompé/qu'il s'était trompé** he admitted to making a mistake/that he had made a mistake; **je reconnais que j'avais tout à fait oublié ce rendez-vous** I must confess *ou* admit (that) I had completely forgotten this appointment.

(c) (*admettre*) *maître, chef* to recognize; (*Pol*) *état, gouvernement* to recognize; (*Jur*) *enfant* to recognize legally, acknowledge; *dette* to acknowledge. **~ qn pour *ou* comme chef** to acknowledge *ou* recognize sb as (one's) leader; (*Jur*) **~ la compétence d'un tribunal** to acknowledge *ou* recognize the competence of a court; (*Jur*) **~ qn coupable** to find sb guilty; **~ sa signature** to acknowledge one's signature; **il ne reconnaît à personne le droit d'intervenir** he doesn't recognize in anyone *ou* acknowledge that anyone has the right to intervene.

(d) (*Mil*) *terrain, île, côte* to reconnoitre. **on va aller ~ les lieux *ou* le terrain** we're going to see how the land lies, we're going to reconnoitre (the ground); **les gangsters étaient certainement venus ~ les lieux auparavant** the gangsters had certainly been to look over the place *ou* spy out the land beforehand.

(e) (*littér: montrer de la gratitude*) to recognize, acknowledge.

2 se reconnaître *vpr* **(a)** (*dans la glace*) to recognize o.s.; (*entre personnes*) to recognize each other. **elle ne se reconnaît pas du tout dans ses filles** she just can't see any likeness between herself and her daughters.

(b) (*lit, fig: se retrouver*) to find one's way about *ou* around. **je ne m'y reconnais plus** I'm completely lost; **je commence à me ~** I'm beginning to find my bearings.

(c) (*être reconnaissable*) to be recognizable (*à* by). **le pêcher se reconnaît à ses fleurs roses** the peach tree is recognizable by its pink flowers, you can tell a peach tree by its pink flowers.

(d) (*s'avouer*) **se ~ vaincu** to admit *ou* acknowledge defeat; **se ~ coupable** to admit *ou* acknowledge one's guilt.

reconnu, e [R(ə)kɔny] (*ptp de* **reconnaître**) *adj fait* recognized, accepted; *auteur, chef* recognized. **c'est un fait ~ que ...** it's a recognized *ou* an accepted fact that ... ; **il est ~ que ...** it is recognized *ou* acknowledged that ... .

reconquérir [R(ə)kɔ̃keRiR] (21) *vt* (*Mil*) to reconquer, recapture, capture back; *femme* to win back; *dignité, liberté* to recover, win back.

reconquête [R(ə)kɔ̃kɛt] *nf* (*Mil*) reconquest, recapture; *[droit, liberté]* recovery.

reconsidérer [R(ə)kɔ̃sideRe] (6) *vt* to reconsider.

reconstituant, e [R(ə)kɔ̃stitɥɑ̃, ɑ̃t] **1** *adj aliment, régime* which builds up *ou* boosts (up) one's strength. **2** *nm* tonic, pick-me-up*.

reconstituer [R(ə)kɔ̃stitɥe] (1) *vt* **(a)** *parti, armée* to re-form, reconstitute; *fortune* to build up again, rebuild; *crime* to reconstruct; *faits, puzzle* to piece together; *texte* to restore, reconstitute; *édifice, vieux quartier* to restore, reconstruct; *objet brisé* to put together again. **le parti s'est reconstitué** the party was re-formed *ou* reconstituted.

(b) (*Bio*) *organisme* to regenerate.

reconstitution [R(ə)kɔ̃stitysjɔ̃] *nf* (*V* **reconstituer**) re-formation; reconstitution; rebuilding; reconstruction; piecing together; restoration; regeneration. **~ historique** reconstruction *ou* recreation of history.

reconstruction [R(ə)kɔ̃stRyksjɔ̃] *nf* (*V* **reconstruire**) rebuilding; reconstruction.

reconstruire [R(ə)kɔ̃stRɥiR] (38) *vt maison* to rebuild, reconstruct; *fortune* to build up again, rebuild.

reconversion [R(ə)kɔ̃vɛRsjɔ̃] *nf* (*V* **reconvertir, se reconvertir**) reconversion; redeployment.

reconvertir [R(ə)kɔ̃vɛRtiR] (2) **1** *vt usine* to reconvert (*en* to); *personnel* to redeploy.

2 se reconvertir *vpr [usine]* to be reconverted, be turned over to a new type of production; *[personne]* to move into *ou* turn to a new type of employment. **il s'est reconverti dans le secrétariat** he has given up his old job and gone into secretarial work; **nous nous sommes reconvertis dans le textile** we have moved over *ou* gone over into textiles.

recopier [R(ə)kɔpje] (7) *vt* (*transcrire*) to copy out, write out; (*recommencer*) to copy out *ou* write out again. **~ ses notes au propre** to write up one's notes, make a fair copy of one's notes.

record [R(ə)kɔR] **1** *nm* (*Sport*) record. **~ masculin/féminin** men's/women's record. **2** *adj inv chiffre, production* record (*épith*). **en un temps ~** in record time.

recordman [R(ə)kɔRdman], *pl* **recordmen** [R(ə)kɔRdmɛn] *nm* (men's) record holder.

recordwoman [R(ə)kɔRdwɔman], *pl* **recordwomen** [R(ə)kɔRdwɔmɛn] *nf* (women's) record holder.

recorriger [R(ə)kɔRiʒe] (3) *vt* to recorrect, correct again; (*Scol*) to mark again, re-mark.

recors [R(ə)kɔR] *nm* (*Hist*) bailiff's assistant.

recoucher [R(ə)kuʃe] (1) **1** *vt enfant* to put back to bed; *objet* to lay *ou* put down again. **2 se recoucher** *vpr* to go back to bed.

recoudre [R(ə)kudR(ə)] (48) *vt* (*Couture*) *ourlet* to sew up again; *bouton* to sew back on, sew on again; (*Méd*) *plaie* to stitch up (again), put stitches (back) in; *opéré* to stitch (back) up.

recoupement [R(ə)kupmɑ̃] *nm* cross-check, cross-checking (*U*). **par ~** by cross-checking; **faire un ~** to cross-check.

recouper [R(ə)kupe] (1) **1** *vt* **(a)** (*gén*) to cut again; *vêtement* to recut; *vin* to blend; *route* to intersect. **~ du pain** to cut (some) more bread; **elle m'a recoupé une tranche de viande** she cut me another slice of meat.

(b) *[témoignage]* to tie up *ou* match up with, confirm, support.

2 *vi* (*Cartes*) to cut again.

3 se recouper *vpr [faits]* to tie up *ou* match up, confirm *ou* support one another; *[droites, cercles]* to intersect.

recourbé, e [R(ə)kuRbe] (*ptp de* **recourber**) *adj* (*gén*) curved; (*accidentellement*) bent; *bec* curved, hooked. **nez ~** hooknose.

recourbement [R(ə)kuRbəmɑ̃] *nm* bending.

recourber [R(ə)kuRbe] (1) **1** *vt bois* to bend (over); *métal* to bend, curve. **2 se recourber** *vpr* to curve (up), bend (up).

recourir [R(ə)kuRiR] (11) **1** *vt* (*Sport*) to run again.

2 recourir à *vt indir chose* to resort to, have recourse to; *personne* to turn to, appeal to. **j'ai recouru à son aide** I turned *ou* appealed to him for help.

3 *vi* **(a)** (*Sport*) to race again, run again. **j'ai recouru le chercher*** I ran back *ou* raced back *ou* nipped back* to fetch it.

(b) (*Jur*) **~ contre qn** to (lodge an) appeal against sb.

recours [R(ə)kuR] **1** *nm* resort, recourse; (*Jur*) appeal. **le ~ à la violence ne sert à rien** resorting to violence doesn't do any good; **en dernier ~** as a last resort, in the last resort; **nous n'avons plus qu'un ~** we've only got one resort *ou* recourse left, there's only one course left open to us; **il n'y a aucun ~ contre cette décision** there is no way of changing this decision, there is no appeal possible *ou* no recourse against this decision; **il n'y a aucun ~ contre cette maladie** there is no cure *ou* remedy for this disease; **la situation est sans ~** there's nothing we can do about the situation, there's no way out of the situation; **avoir ~ à** *chose* to resort to, have recourse to; *personne* to turn to, appeal to.

2: recours en cassation appeal to the Supreme Court; **recours contentieux** *submission for an out-of-court settlement*; **recours en grâce** (*remise de peine*) plea for pardon; (*commutation de peine*) plea for clemency; **recours gracieux** *submission for a legal decision.*

recouvrable [R(ə)kuvRabl(ə)] *adj* **(a)** *impôt* collectable, which can be collected; *créance* recoverable, reclaimable, retrievable. **(b)** *peinture* **~ après 24 heures** allow to dry 24 hours *ou* leave 24 hours before applying a second coat.

recouvrement [R(ə)kuvRəmɑ̃] *nm* **(a)** (*couverture: action*) covering (up); (*résultat*) cover. (*Constr*) **assemblage à ~** lap joint.

(b) (*Fin*) *[cotisations]* collection, payment; *[impôt]* collection, levying; (*littér*) *[créance]* recovery.

(c) (*littér*) *[forces, santé]* recovery.

recouvrer [R(ə)kuvRe] (1) *vt* **(a)** *santé, vue* to recover, regain; *amitié* to win back. **~ la raison** to recover one's senses, come back to one's senses.

(b) (*Fin*) *cotisation* to collect; *impôt* to collect, levy; (*littér*) *créance* to recover.

recouvrir [R(ə)kuvRiR] (18) **1** *vt* **(a)** (*entièrement*) to cover. **la neige recouvre le sol** snow covers the ground; **recouvert d'écailles/d'eau** covered in *ou* with scales/water; **~ un mur de papier peint/de carreaux** to paper/tile a wall; **le sol était recouvert d'un tapis** the floor was carpeted, there was a carpet on the floor; **les ouvriers recouvrirent la maison** the workmen put the roof on the house *ou* roofed over the house; **recouvre la casserole/les haricots** put the lid on the saucepan/on *ou* over the beans.

(b) (*à nouveau*) *fauteuil, livre* to re-cover, put a new cover on; *casserole* to put the lid back on. **~ un enfant qui dort** to cover (up) a sleeping child again.

(c) (*cacher*) *intentions* to conceal, hide, mask; (*englober*) *aspects, questions* to cover.

2 se recouvrir *vpr*: **se ~ d'eau/de terre** to become covered in *ou* with water/earth; **le ciel se recouvre** the sky is getting cloudy *ou* becoming overcast again; **les 2 feuilles se recouvrent partiellement** the 2 sheets overlap slightly.

recracher [R(ə)kRaʃe] (1) **1** *vt* to spit out (again). **2** *vi* to spit again.

récré [RekRe] *nf* (*arg Scol*) *abrév de* **récréation.**

récréatif, -ive [RekReatif, iv] *adj lecture* light (*épith*). **soirée ~ive** evening's recreation *ou* entertainment.

récréation [RekReɑsjɔ̃] *nf* **(a)** (*Scol*) (*au lycée*) break; (*à l'école primaire*) playtime, break. **aller en ~** to go out for (the) break; **les enfants sont en ~** the children are having their playtime *ou* break; *V* **cour. (b)** recreation, relaxation.

recréer [R(ə)kRee] (1) *vt* to re-create.

récréer [RekRee] (1) (*littér*) **1** *vt* to entertain, amuse. **2 se récréer** *vpr* to amuse o.s.

recrépir [R(ə)kRepiR] (2) *vt* to resurface (with roughcast *ou* pebble dash). **faire ~ sa maison** to have the roughcast *ou* pebble dash redone on one's house.

recreuser [R(ə)kRøze] (1) *vt* (*lit*) (*de nouveau*) to dig again; (*davantage*) to dig deeper; (*fig*) to go further *ou* deeper into, dig deeper into.

récrier (se) [RekRije] (7) *vpr* to exclaim, cry out in admiration (*ou* indignation, surprise *etc*).

récriminateur, -trice [RekRiminatœR, tRis] *adj* remonstrative, complaining.

récrimination [RekRiminɑsjɔ̃] *nf* remonstration, complaint.

récriminatoire [RekRiminatwaR] *adj discours, propos* remonstrative.

récriminer [RekRimine] (1) *vi* to remonstrate (*contre* against), complain bitterly (*contre* about).

récrire [RekRiR] (39) *vt roman, inscription* to rewrite; *lettre* to write again. **il m'a récrit** he has written to me again, he has written me another letter.

recroqueviller (se) [ʀ(ə)kʀɔkvije] (1) *vpr [papier, fleur]* to shrivel up, curl up; *[personne]* to huddle *ou* curl o.s. up. **il était tout recroquevillé dans un coin** he was all hunched up *ou* huddled up in a corner.

recru, e[1] [ʀ(ə)kʀy] *adj (littér)* ~ **(de fatigue)** exhausted, tired out.

recrudescence [ʀ(ə)kʀydesɑ̃s] *nf [criminalité, combats]* upsurge, new and more serious wave *ou* outburst; *[épidémie]* upsurge, further and more serious outbreak *ou* outburst. **il y a eu une ~ de froid** the cold weather suddenly set in even worse again, there was another spell of even colder weather.

recrudescent, e [ʀ(ə)kʀydesɑ̃, ɑ̃t] *adj (littér)* recrudescent. **épidémie ~e** epidemic which is on the increase *ou* upsurge again.

recrue[2] [ʀ(ə)kʀy] *nf (Mil)* recruit; *(fig)* recruit, new member. *(fig)* **faire une (nouvelle) ~** to gain a (new) recruit, recruit a new member.

recrutement [ʀ(ə)kʀytmɑ̃] *nm (action)* recruiting, recruitment; *(recrues)* recruits.

recruter [ʀ(ə)kʀyte] (1) *vt (Mil, fig)* to recruit. **se ~ dans** *ou* **parmi** to be recruited from.

recruteur [ʀ(ə)kʀytœʀ] **1** *nm* recruiting officer. **2** *adj m* recruiting. **agent ~** recruiting agent.

recta‡ [ʀɛkta] *adv payer* promptly, on the nail*; *arriver* on the dot*. **quand j'ai les pieds mouillés, c'est ~ j'attrape un rhume** whenever I get my feet wet that's it*, I catch a cold *ou* I catch a cold straight off*.

rectal, e, *mpl* **-aux** [ʀɛktal, o] *adj* rectal.

rectangle [ʀɛktɑ̃gl(ə)] **1** *nm (gén)* rectangle, oblong; *(Math)* rectangle. **2** *adj* right-angled.

rectangulaire [ʀɛktɑ̃gylɛʀ] *adj* rectangular, oblong.

recteur [ʀɛktœʀ] *nm* **(a)** *(Univ)* ≃ director of education (for a region). **(b)** *(Rel) (prêtre)* priest; *(directeur)* rector.

rectifiable [ʀɛktifjabl(ə)] *adj erreur* rectifiable, which can be put right *ou* corrected; *alcool* rectifiable.

rectificateur [ʀɛktifikatœʀ] *nm (Chim)* rectifier.

rectificatif, -ive [ʀɛktifikatif, iv] **1** *adj compte* rectified, corrected. **acte ~, note ~ive** correction. **2** *nm* correction.

rectification [ʀɛktifikɑsjɔ̃] *nf (V* **rectifier***)* rectification; correction; straightening.

rectifier [ʀɛktifje] (7) *vt calcul* to rectify, correct; *erreur* to rectify, correct, put right; *paroles* to correct; *route, tracé* to straighten; *virage* to straighten (out); *mauvaise position* to correct; *(Tech) pièce* to true (up), adjust; *(Chim, Math)* to rectify. **il rectifia la position du rétroviseur/son chapeau** he adjusted *ou* straightened his driving mirror/his hat; **non, ils étaient 2, rectifia-t-il** no, there were 2 of them, he added, correcting himself; *(Mil)* **~ la position/l'alignement** to correct one's stance/the alignment; **~ le tir** *(lit)* to adjust the fire; *(fig)* to get one's aim right.

rectiligne [ʀɛktiliɲ] **1** *adj (gén)* straight; *mouvement* rectilinear; *(Géom)* rectilinear. **2** *nm (Géom)* rectilinear angle.

rectitude [ʀɛktityd] *nf [caractère]* rectitude, uprightness; *[jugement]* soundness, rectitude; *(littér) [ligne]* straightness.

recto [ʀɛkto] *nm* front (of a page), first side, recto *(frm)*. **~ verso** on both sides (of the page); **voir au ~** see on first *ou* other side.

rectoral, e, *pl* **-aux** [ʀɛktɔʀal, o] *adj (Univ)* rectorial.

rectorat [ʀɛktɔʀa] *nm (Univ) (fonction)* rectorship; *(durée)* rector's term of office; *(bureaux)* Education Offices.

rectum [ʀɛktɔm] *nm* rectum.

reçu, e [ʀ(ə)sy] *(ptp de* **recevoir***)* **1** *adj* **(a)** *usages, coutumes* accepted; *V* **idée**. **(b)** *candidat* successful. **les ~s** the successful candidates; **il y a eu 50 ~s** there were 50 passes *ou* successful candidates. **2** *nm (quittance)* receipt.

recueil [ʀ(ə)kœj] *nm (gén)* book, collection; *[documents]* compendium. **~ de poèmes** anthology *ou* collection of poems; **~ de morceaux choisis** anthology; *(fig)* **~ de faits** collection of facts.

recueillement [ʀ(ə)kœjmɑ̃] *nm (Rel, gén)* meditation, contemplation. **écouter avec un grand ~** to listen reverently; **écouter avec un ~ quasi religieux** to listen with an almost religious respect *ou* reverence.

recueilli, e [ʀ(ə)kœji] *(ptp de* **recueillir***)* *adj* meditative, contemplative.

recueillir [ʀ(ə)kœjiʀ] (12) **1** *vt* **(a)** *(récolter) graines* to gather, collect; *argent, documents, liquide* to collect; *suffrages* to win; *héritage* to inherit. **~ le fruit de ses efforts** to reap the rewards of one's efforts; **il a recueilli 100 voix** he got *ou* polled 100 votes.

(b) *(accueillir) réfugié* to take in.

(c) *(enregistrer) déposition, chansons anciennes* to take down, take note of; *opinion* to record.

2 se recueillir *vpr (Rel, gén)* to collect *ou* gather one's thoughts, commune with o.s. **aller se ~ sur la tombe de qn** to go and meditate at sb's grave.

recuire [ʀ(ə)kɥiʀ] (38) **1** *vt viande* to recook, cook again; *pain, gâteaux* to rebake, bake again; *poterie* to bake *ou* fire again; *(Tech) métal* to anneal. **2** *vi [viande]* to cook for a further length of time. **faire ~** to recook; to rebake.

recul [ʀ(ə)kyl] *nm* **(a)** *(retraite) [armée]* retreat; *(revirement) [patron, négociateur]* retreat. **j'ai été étonné de son ~ devant la menace de grève** I was amazed at how he retreated *ou* climbed down at the threat of strike action; **cela constitue un ~ important par rapport aux premières propositions** that represents quite a considerable retreat from the initial proposals; **avoir un mouvement de ~** to recoil, start back, shrink back *(par rapport à* from).

(b) *(déclin) [épidémie, maladie]* recession; *[civilisation, langue]* decline; *[valeur boursière]* decline. **être en ~** *[épidémie]* to be on the decline, be subsiding; *[chômage]* to be on the decline, be going down *ou* subsiding; *[monnaie]* to be falling; *[parti]* to be losing ground; *(Pol)* **~ de la majorité aux élections** setback for the government in the election; **~ du franc sur les marchés internationaux** setback for the franc *ou* drop in the franc on the international markets; **le ~ de l'influence française en Afrique** the decline in French influence in Africa.

(c) *(éloignement dans le temps, l'espace)* distance. **avec le ~ (du temps), on juge mieux les événements** with the passing of time one can stand back and judge events better; **le village paraissait plus petit avec le ~** from a distance *ou* from further away the village looked smaller; **prendre du ~** *(lit)* to step back, stand back; *(fig)* to stand back *(par rapport à* from); **cette salle n'a pas assez de ~** there isn't enough room to move back in this room, you can't move back *ou* get back far enough in this room.

(d) *[arme à feu]* recoil, kick.

(e) *(report) [échéance]* postponement.

(f) *(déplacement) [véhicule]* backward movement; *V* **phare**.

reculade [ʀ(ə)kylad] *nf (Mil)* retreat, withdrawal; *(fig péj)* retreat, climb-down*. **c'est la ~ générale** they're all backing down.

reculé, e [ʀ(ə)kyle] *(ptp de* **reculer***)* *adj époque* remote, distant; *ville, maison* remote, out-of-the-way.

reculer [ʀ(ə)kyle] (1) **1** *vi* **(a)** *[personne]* to move *ou* step back; *(par peur)* to draw back, back away; *[automobiliste, automobile]* to reverse, back (up), move back; *[cheval]* to back; *(Mil)* to retreat. **~ de 2 pas** to go back *ou* move back 2 paces, take 2 paces back; **~ devant l'ennemi** to retreat from *ou* draw back from the enemy; **~ d'horreur** to draw back *ou* shrink back in horror; *(fig)* **c'est ~ pour mieux sauter** it's just putting off the evil day *ou* delaying the day of reckoning; **faire ~** *foule* to move back, force back; *cheval* to move back; *ennemi* to push *ou* force back; **ce spectacle le fit ~** this sight made him draw back *ou* made him back away.

(b) *(hésiter)* to shrink back; *(changer d'avis)* to back down, back out. **tu ne peux plus ~ maintenant** you can't back out *ou* back down now; **~ devant la dépense/difficulté** to shrink from the expense/difficulty; **je ne reculerai devant rien, rien ne me fera ~** I'll stop *ou* stick at nothing, nothing will stop me; **il ne faut pas ~ devant ses obligations** you mustn't shrink from your obligations; **il ne recule pas devant la dénonciation** he doesn't flinch at informing on people, he doesn't shrink from informing on people; **cette condition ferait ~ de plus braves** this condition would make braver men (than I *ou* you *etc*) hesitate *ou* draw back.

(c) *(diminuer) (gén)* to be on the decline; *[patois]* to be on the decline, lose ground; *[chômage]* to decline, subside, go down; *[eaux]* to subside, recede, go down; *[incendie]* to subside, lose ground; *[élève, science, civilisation]* to be on the downgrade, decline. **faire ~ l'épidémie/le chômage** to bring about a reduction in the epidemic/the number of unemployed.

(d) *[arme à feu]* to recoil.

2 *vt chaise, meuble* to move back, push back; *véhicule* to reverse, back (up); *frontières* to extend, push *ou* move back; *livraison, date* to put back, postpone; *décision* to put off, postpone; *échéance* to defer, postpone.

3 se reculer *vpr* to stand *ou* step *ou* move back, take a step back. **se ~ d'horreur** to draw back *ou* shrink back in horror, back away in horror.

reculons [ʀ(ə)kylɔ̃] *loc adv*: **à ~**: **aller à ~** *(lit)* to go backwards; *(fig)* to move *ou* go backwards; **sortir à ~ d'une pièce/d'un garage** to back out of a room/a garage.

récupérable [ʀekypeʀabl(ə)] *adj créance* recoverable; *heures* which can be made up; *ferraille* which can be salvaged; *vieux habits* retrievable, which are worth rescuing. **délinquant qui n'est plus ~** irredeemable delinquent, delinquent who is beyond redemption.

récupérateur [ʀekypeʀatœʀ] **1** *nm [chaleur]* recuperator, regenerator; *[arme]* recuperator. **2** *adj m (péj) procédé, discours* designed to win over dissenting opinion *ou* groups *etc*.

récupération [ʀekypeʀɑsjɔ̃] *nf* **(a)** *[argent, biens, forces]* recovery. **la capacité de ~ de l'organisme** the body's powers of recuperation *ou* recovery.

(b) *[ferraille]* salvage, reprocessing; *[chiffons]* reprocessing; *[chaleur]* recovery; *[délinquant]* rehabilitation.

(c) *[journées de travail]* making up.

(d) *(Pol: péj)* **assister à la ~ du mouvement anarchique par le gouvernement** to watch the takeover *ou* the harnessing of the anarchist movement by the government.

récupérer [ʀekypeʀe] (6) *vt* **(a)** *argent, biens* to get back, recover; *forces* to recover, get back, regain. **coureur qui récupère vite** runner who recovers *ou* recuperates quickly.

(b) *ferraille* to salvage, reprocess; *chiffons* to reprocess; *chaleur* to recover; *délinquant* to rehabilitate; *(*fig) bonbon, gifle* to get. **toutes les pêches étaient pourries, je n'ai rien pu ~** all the peaches were rotten and I wasn't able to save *ou* rescue a single one; **regarde si tu peux ~ quelque chose dans ces vieux habits** have a look and see if there's anything you can rescue *ou* retrieve from among these old clothes; **où es-tu allé ~ ce chat?*** wherever did you pick up *ou* get that cat (from) ? *ou* find that cat?

(c) *journées de travail* to make up. **on récupérera samedi** we'll make it up *ou* the time up on Saturday.

(d) *(Pol: péj) personne, mouvement* to take over, harness, bring into line. **se faire ~ par la gauche/droite** to find o.s. taken over *ou* won over by the left/the right.

récurage [rekyraʒ] *nm* scouring.
récurer [rekyre] (1) *vt* to scour; *V* **poudre.**
récurrence [rekyrɑ̃s] *nf* (*littér: répétition*) recurrence.
récurrent, e [rekyrɑ̃, ɑ̃t] *adj* (*Anat, Méd*) recurrent. (*Math*) série ~e recursion series.
récusable [rekyzabl(ə)] *adj témoin* challengeable; *témoignage* impugnable.
récusation [rekyzɑsjɔ̃] *nf* (*V* **récusable**) challenging (*U*), challenge; impugnment.
récuser [rekyze] (1) **1** *vt témoin* to challenge; *témoignage* to impugn, challenge. **2 se récuser** *vpr* to decline to give an opinion *ou* accept responsibility *etc.*
recyclage [r(ə)siklaʒ] *nm* (*V* **recycler**) reorientation; retraining; recyling.
recycler [r(ə)sikle] (1) **1** *vt* **(a)** *élève* to reorientate; *professeur, ingénieur* (*perfectionner*) to send on a refresher course, retrain; (*reconvertir*) to retrain.
(b) (*Tech*) to recycle.
2 se recycler *vpr* to retrain; to go on a refresher course. **je ne peux pas me ~ à mon âge** I can't keep up with the latest developments *ou* techniques at my age; **se ~ en permanence** to be constantly updating one's skills.
rédacteur, -trice [redaktœr, tris] **1** *nm,f* (*Presse*) sub-editor; *[article]* writer; *[loi]* drafter; *[encyclopédie]* compiler. **~ politique/économique** political/economics editor. **2: rédacteur en chef** chief editor; **rédacteur publicitaire** copywriter.
rédaction [redaksjɔ̃] *nf* **(a)** *[contrat, projet]* drafting, drawing up; *[thèse, article]* writing; *[encyclopédie, dictionnaire]* compiling, compilation. **ce n'est que la première ~** it's only the first draft. **(b)** (*Presse*) (*personnel*) editorial staff; (*bureaux*) editorial offices; *V* **salle, secrétaire. (c)** (*Scol*) essay, composition.
rédactionnel, -elle [redaksjɔnɛl] *adj* editorial.
reddition [redisjɔ̃] *nf* (*Mil*) surrender; (*Admin*) rendering.
redécouverte [r(ə)dekuvɛrt(ə)] *nf* rediscovery.
redécouvrir [r(ə)dekuvrir] (18) *vt* to rediscover.
redéfaire [r(ə)defɛr] (60) *vt paquet, lacet* to undo again; *manteau* to take off again; *couture* to unpick again. **le nœud s'est redéfait** the knot has come undone *ou* come untied again.
redemander [rədmɑ̃de] (1) *vt adresse* to ask again for; *aliment* to ask for more. **redemande-le-lui** (*une nouvelle fois*) ask him for it again; (*récupère-le*) ask him to give it you back, ask him for it back; **~ du poulet** to ask for more chicken *ou* another helping of chicken.
rédempteur, -trice [redɑ̃ptœr, tris] **1** *adj* redemptive, redeeming. **2** *nm,f* redeemer.
rédemption [redɑ̃psjɔ̃] *nf* **(a)** (*Rel*) redemption. **(b)** (*Jur*) *[rente]* redemption; *[droit]* recovery.
redescendre [r(ə)desɑ̃dr(ə)] (41) **1** *vt* **(a)** *escalier* to go *ou* come (back) down again. **la balle a redescendu la pente** the ball rolled down the slope again *ou* rolled back down the slope.
(b) *objet* (*à la cave*) to take downstairs again; (*du grenier*) to bring downstairs again; (*d'un rayon*) to get *ou* lift (back) down again; (*d'un crochet*) to take (back) down again. **~ qch d'un cran** to put sth one notch lower down.
2 *vi* **(a)** (*dans l'escalier*) to go *ou* come (back) downstairs again; (*d'une colline*) to go *ou* come (back) down again. **l'alpiniste redescend** (*à pied*) the mountaineer climbs down again; (*avec une corde*) the mountaineer ropes down again; **~ de voiture** to get *ou* climb out of the car again.
(b) *[ascenseur, avion]* to go down again; *[marée]* to go out again, go back out; *[chemin]* to go *ou* slope down again; *[baromètre, fièvre]* to fall again.
redevable [rədvabl(ə)] *adj* **(a)** (*Fin*) être **~ de 10 F à qn** to owe sb 10 francs; **~ de l'impôt** liable for tax. **(b) ~ à qn de** *aide, service* indebted to sb for; **je vous suis ~ de la vie** I owe you my life.
redevance [rədvɑ̃s] *nf* (*gén: impôt*) tax; (*Rad, TV*) licence fee (*Brit*); (*Téléc*) rental charge; (*bail, rente*) dues, fees.
redevenir [rədvənir] (22) *vi* to become again. **le temps est redevenu glacial** the weather has become *ou* gone very cold again; **il est redevenu lui-même** he is his old self again.
redevoir [rədvwar] (28) *vt*: **il me redoit 10.000 F** he still owes me 10,000 francs.
rédhibitoire [redibitwar] *adj défaut* crippling, damning. **sa mauvaise foi est vraiment ~** his insincerity puts him quite beyond the pale; **il est un peu menteur, mais ce n'est pas ~** he's a bit of a liar but that doesn't rule him out altogether; (*Jur*) vice ~ redhibitory defect.
rédiger [rediʒe] (3) *vt article, lettre* to write, compose (*frm*); (*à partir de notes*) to write up; *encyclopédie, dictionnaire* to compile, write; *contrat* to draw up, draft. **bien rédigé** well-written.
redingote [r(ə)dɛ̃gɔt] *nf* (*Hist*) frock coat. *[femme]* **manteau ~** fitted coat.
rédintégration [redɛ̃tegrɑsjɔ̃] *nf* redintegration.
redire [r(ə)dir] (37) *vt* **(a)** *affirmation* to say again, repeat; *histoire* to tell again, repeat; *médisance* to (go and) tell, repeat. **~ qch à qn** to say sth to sb again, tell sb sth again, repeat sth to sb; **il redit toujours la même chose** he's always saying *ou* he keeps saying the same thing; **je te l'ai dit et redit** I've told you that over and over again *ou* time and time again; **je lui ai redit cent fois que ...** I've told him countless times that ... ; **redis-le après moi** repeat after me; **ne le lui redites pas** don't go and tell him *ou* don't go and repeat (to him) what I've said; **elle ne se le fait pas ~ deux fois** she doesn't need telling *ou* to be told twice.
(b) (*loc*) **avoir** *ou* **trouver à ~ à qch** to find fault with sth; **je ne vois rien à ~ (à cela)** I've no complaint with that, I can't see anything wrong with that.
rediscuter [r(ə)diskyte] (1) *vt* to discuss again, have further discussion on.
redistribuer [r(ə)distribɥe] (1) *vt biens* to redistribute; *cartes* to deal again.
redistribution [r(ə)distribysjɔ̃] *nf* redistribution.
redite [r(ə)dit] *nf* (needless) repetition.
redondance [r(ə)dɔ̃dɑ̃s] *nf* **(a)** *[style]* redundancy (*U*), diffuseness (*U*); (*Ling*) redundancy (*U*). **(b)** (*expression*) unnecessary *ou* superfluous expression.
redondant, e [r(ə)dɔ̃dɑ̃, ɑ̃t] *adj mot* superfluous, redundant; *style* redundant, diffuse; (*Ling*) redundant.
redonner [r(ə)dɔne] (1) **1** *vt* **(a)** (*rendre*) *objet, bien* to give back, return; *forme, idéal* to give back, give again; *espoir, énergie* to restore, give back. **l'air frais te redonnera des couleurs** the fresh air will put some colour back in your cheeks *ou* bring some colour back to your cheeks; **~ de la confiance/du courage à qn** to give sb new *ou* fresh confidence/courage, restore sb's confidence/courage; **ça a redonné le même résultat** that gave the same result again; **cela te redonnera des forces** that will build your strength back up *ou* put new strength into you *ou* restore your strength.
(b) (*resservir*) *boisson, pain* to give more; *légumes, viande* to give more, give a further *ou* another helping of. **~ une couche de peinture** to give another coat of paint; **redonne-lui un coup de peigne** give his hair another quick comb, run a comb through his hair again quickly.
(c) (*Théât*) to put on again.
2 *vi* (*frm*) **~ dans** to fall *ou* lapse back into.
redorer [r(ə)dɔre] (1) *vt* to regild. **~ son blason** to boost the family fortunes by marrying into money.
redormir [r(ə)dɔrmir] (16) *vi* to sleep again, sleep for a further length of time.
redoublant, e [r(ə)dublɑ̃, ɑ̃t] *nm,f* (*Scol*) pupil who is repeating (*ou* has repeated) a year at school, repeater (*US*).
redoublement [r(ə)dubləmɑ̃] *nm* (*Ling*) reduplication; (*accroissement*) increase (*de* in), intensification (*de* of). **je vous demande un ~ d'attention** I need you to pay even closer attention, I need your increased attention; **avec un ~ de larmes** with a fresh flood of tears; (*Scol*) **le ~ permet aux élèves faibles de rattraper** repeating a year *ou* a grade (*US*) helps the weaker pupils to catch up.
redoubler [r(ə)duble] (1) **1** *vt* **(a)** (*accroître*) *joie, douleur, craintes* to increase, intensify; *efforts* to step up, redouble. **frapper à coups redoublés** to bang twice as hard, bang even harder; **hurler à cris redoublés** to yell twice as loud.
(b) (*Ling*) *syllabe* to reduplicate; (*Couture*) *vêtement* to reline. (*Scol*) **~ (une classe)** to repeat a year *ou* a grade (*US*).
2 redoubler de *vt indir*: **~ d'efforts** to step up *ou* redouble one's efforts, try extra hard; **~ de prudence/de patience** to be extra careful/patient, be doubly careful/patient; **~ de larmes** to cry even harder; **le vent redouble de violence** the wind is getting even stronger *ou* is blowing even more strongly.
3 *vi* (*gén*) to increase, intensify; *[froid, douleur]* to become twice as bad, get even worse; *[vent]* to become twice as strong; *[joie]* to become twice as great; *[larmes]* to flow *ou* fall even faster; *[cris]* to get even louder *ou* twice as loud.
redoutable [r(ə)dutabl(ə)] *adj maladie, arme, adversaire* fearsome, formidable; *concurrence* fearsome, fearful.
redoute [r(ə)dut] *nf* (*Mil*) redoubt.
redouter [r(ə)dute] (1) *vt ennemi, avenir, conséquence* to dread, fear. **je redoute de l'apprendre** I dread finding out about it; **je redoute qu'il ne l'apprenne** I dread him finding out about it.
redoux [r(ə)du] *nm* spell of milder weather.
redressement [r(ə)drɛsmɑ̃] *nm* **(a)** *[poteau]* setting upright, righting; *[tige]* straightening (up); *[tôle]* straightening out, knocking out; (*Élec*) *[courant]* rectification; *[buste, corps]* straightening up.
(b) *[bateau]* righting; *[roue, voiture, avion]* straightening up.
(c) *[économie, situation]* (*action*) putting right; (*résultat*) recovery.
(d) *[erreur]* righting, putting right; *[abus, torts]* righting, redress; *[jugement]* correcting. (*Fin*) **~ fiscal** payment of back taxes; *V* **maison.**
redresser [r(ə)drese] (1) **1** *vt* **(a)** (*relever*) *arbre, statue, poteau* to right, set upright; *tige, poutre* to straighten (up); *tôle cabossée* to straighten out, knock out; (*Élec*) *courant* to rectify; (*Opt*) *image* to straighten. **~ un malade sur son oreiller** to sit *ou* prop a patient up against his pillow; **~ les épaules** to throw one's shoulders back; **~ le corps (en arrière)** to stand up straight, straighten up; **~ la tête** (*lit*) to hold up *ou* lift (up) one's head; (*fig: être fier*) to hold one's head up high; (*fig: se révolter*) to show signs of rebellion.
(b) (*rediriger*) *barre, bateau* to right; *avion* to lift the nose of, straighten up; *roue, voiture* to straighten up. **redresse!** straighten up!
(c) (*rétablir*) *économie* to redress, put *ou* set right; *situation* to put right, straighten out. **~ le pays** to get *ou* put the country on its feet again.
(d) (*littér: corriger*) *erreur* to rectify, put right, redress; *torts, abus* to right, redress. **~ le jugement de qn** to correct sb's opinion.
2 se redresser *vpr* **(a)** (*se mettre assis*) to sit up; (*se mettre debout*) to stand up; (*se mettre droit*) to stand up straight; (*fig: être fier*) to hold one's head up high.
(b) *[bateau]* to right itself; *[avion]* to flatten out, straighten up; *[voiture]* to straighten up; *[pays, économie]* to recover; *[situation]* to correct itself, put itself to rights.
(c) *[coin replié, cheveux]* to stick up. **les blés, couchés par le vent, se redressèrent** the corn which had been blown flat by the wind straightened up again *ou* stood up straight again.
redresseur [r(ə)drɛsœr] **1** *nm* **(a)** (*Hist iro*) **~ de torts** righter

of wrongs. **(b)** *(Élec)* rectifier. **2** *adj m muscle* erector; *prisme* erecting.
réducteur, -trice [ʀedyktœʀ, tʀis] **1** *adj (Chim)* reducing; *(Tech) engrenage* reduction. **2** *nm (Chim)* reducing agent; *(Phot)* reducer. *(Tech)* **~ (de vitesse)** speed reducer; **~ de tête** head shrinker *(lit)*.
réductibilité [ʀedyktibilite] *nf* reducibility.
réductible [ʀedyktibl(ə)] *adj (Chim, Math)* reducible *(en, à* to); *(Méd)* which can be set; *quantité* which can be reduced. **leur philosophie n'est pas ~ à la nôtre** their philosophy can't be simplified to ours.
réduction [ʀedyksjɔ̃] *nf* **(a)** *(diminution) [dépenses, impôts, production]* reduction, cut *(de* in). **~ de salaire/d'impôts** wage/tax cut; **obtenir une ~ de peine** to get a reduction in one's sentence, get one's sentence cut; **il faut s'attendre à une ~ du personnel** we must expect a reduction in staff *ou* expect staff cuts; **ils voudraient obtenir une ~ des heures de travail** they would like a reduction *ou* a cut in working hours.
(b) *(rabais)* discount, reduction. **faire/obtenir une ~** to give/get a discount *ou* a reduction.
(c) *(reproduction) [plan, photo]* reduction. *(fig)* **un adulte en ~** a miniature adult, an adult in miniature.
(d) *(Méd) [fracture]* reduction *(T)*, setting; *(Bio, Chim, Math)* reduction.
(e) *(Culin)* reduction (by boiling).
(f) *(Mil) [ville]* capture; *[rebelles]* quelling.
réduire [ʀedɥiʀ] (38) **1** *vt* **(a)** *(diminuer) peine, impôt, consommation* to reduce, cut; *hauteur, vitesse* to reduce; *prix* to reduce, cut, bring down; *pression* to reduce, lessen; *texte* to shorten, cut; *production* to reduce, cut (back), lower; *dépenses* to reduce, cut, cut down *ou* back (on); *tête coupée* to shrink. **il va falloir ~ notre train de vie** we'll have to cut down *ou* curb our spending.
(b) *(reproduire) dessin, plan* to reduce, scale down; *photographie* to reduce, make smaller; *figure géométrique* to scale down.
(c) *(contraindre)* **~ à** *soumission, désespoir* to reduce to; **~ qn au silence/à l'obéissance/en esclavage** to reduce sb to silence/to obedience/to slavery; **après son accident, il a été réduit à l'inaction** since his accident he has been reduced to doing nothing; **il en est réduit à mendier** he has been reduced to begging.
(d) **~ à** *(ramener à)* to reduce to, bring down to; *(limiter à)* to limit to, confine to; **~ des fractions à un dénominateur commun** to reduce *ou* bring down fractions to a common denominator; **~ des éléments différents à un type commun** to reduce different elements to one general type; **je réduirai mon étude à quelques aspects** I shall limit *ou* confine my study to a few aspects; **~ à sa plus simple expression** *(Math) polynôme* to reduce to its simplest expression; *(fig) mobilier, repas* to reduce to the absolute *ou* bare minimum; **~ qch à néant** *ou* **à rien** *ou* **à zéro** to reduce sth to nothing.
(e) *(transformer)* **~ en** to reduce to; **réduisez les grammes en milligrammes** convert the grammes to milligrammes; **~ qch en miettes/morceaux** to smash sth to tiny pieces/to pieces; **~ qch en bouillie** to crush *ou* reduce sth to pulp; **~ des grains en poudre** to grind *ou* reduce seeds to powder; **sa maison était réduite en cendres** his house was reduced to ashes *ou* burnt to the ground; **les cadavres étaient réduits en charpie** the bodies were torn to shreds.
(f) *(Méd) fracture* to set, reduce *(T)*; *(Chim) minerai, oxyde* to reduce; *(Culin) sauce* to reduce (by boiling).
(g) *(Mil) place forte* to capture; *rebelles* to quell. **~ l'opposition** to silence the opposition.
2 *vi (Culin) [sauce]* to reduce. **faire** *ou* **laisser ~ la sauce** to cook *ou* simmer the sauce to reduce it; **les épinards réduisent à la cuisson** spinach shrinks when you cook it.
3 se réduire *vpr* **(a) se ~ à** *[affaire, incident]* to boil down to, amount to; *[somme, quantité]* to amount to; **mon profit se réduit à bien peu de chose** my profit amounts to very little; **notre action ne se réduit pas à quelques discours** the action we are taking involves more than *ou* isn't just a matter of a few speeches; **je me réduirai à quelques exemples** I'll limit *ou* confine myself to a few examples, I'll just select *ou* quote a few examples.
(b) se ~ en to be reduced to; **se ~ en cendres** to be burnt *ou* reduced to ashes; **se ~ en poussière** to be reduced *ou* crumble away *ou* turn to dust; **se ~ en bouillie** to be crushed to pulp.
(c) *(dépenser moins)* to cut down on one's spending *ou* expenditure.
réduit, e [ʀedɥi, it] *(ptp de* **réduire***)* **1** *adj* **(a)** *mécanisme, objet (à petite échelle)* small-scale, scaled-down; *(en miniature)* miniature; *(miniaturisé)* miniaturized. **reproduction à échelle ~e** small-scale reproduction; tête ~e shrunken head; *V* **modèle.**
(b) *tarif, prix* reduced; *moyens, débouchés* limited. **livres à prix ~s** cut-price books, books at a reduced price *ou* at reduced prices; **avancer à vitesse ~e** to move forward at low speed *ou* at a reduced speed *ou* at a crawl.
2 *nm (pièce)* tiny room; *(péj)* cubbyhole, poky little hole; *(recoin)* recess; *(Mil) [maquisards]* hideout.
réécrire [ʀeekʀiʀ] (39) *vt* = **récrire.**
réédification [ʀeedifikasjɔ̃] *nf* rebuilding, reconstruction.
réédifier [ʀeedifje] (7) *vt* to rebuild, reconstruct; *(fig)* to rebuild.
rééditer [ʀeedite] (1) *vt (Typ)* to republish; *(* fig)* to repeat.
réédition [ʀeedisjɔ̃] *nf (Typ)* new edition; *(* fig)* repetition, repeat.
rééducation [ʀeedykasjɔ̃] *nf* **(a)** *(Méd) [malade]* rehabilitation; *[membre]* re-education; *(spécialité médicale)* physiotherapy. **faire de la ~** to undergo *ou* have physiotherapy; **exercice/centre de ~** physiotherapy exercise/clinic; **~ de la parole** speech therapy.
(b) *(gén, lit)* re-education; *[délinquant]* rehabilitation.
rééduquer [ʀeedyke] (1) *vt* **(a)** *(Méd) malade* to rehabilitate; *membre* to re-educate. **(b)** *(gén, Pol, lit)* to re-educate; *délinquant* to rehabilitate.
réel, -elle [ʀeɛl] **1** *adj* **(a)** *fait, chef, existence, avantage* real; *besoin, cause* real, true; *danger, plaisir, amélioration, douleur* real, genuine. **dans la vie ~le** in real life; **faire de ~les économies** to make significant *ou* real savings; **son héros est très ~** his hero is very lifelike *ou* realistic.
(b) *(Math, Opt, Philos, Phys)* real; *(Fin) valeur, salaire* real, actual.
2 *nm*: **le ~** reality.
réélection [ʀeelɛksjɔ̃] *nf* re-election.
rééligibilité [ʀeeliʒibilite] *nf* re-eligibility.
rééligible [ʀeeliʒibl(ə)] *adj* re-eligible.
réélire [ʀeeliʀ] (43) *vt* to re-elect.
réellement [ʀeɛlmɑ̃] *adv* really, truly. **je suis ~ désolé** I'm really *ou* truly sorry; **ça m'a ~ consterné/aidé** that really worried/helped me, that was a genuine worry/help to me; **~, tu exagères!** really *ou* honestly, you go too far!
réembarquer [ʀeɑ̃baʀke] (1) = **rembarquer.**
réembobiner [ʀeɑ̃bɔbine] (1) *vt* = **rembobiner.**
réemploi [ʀeɑ̃plwa] *nm (V* **réemployer***)* re-use; reinvestment; re-employment.
réemployer [ʀeɑ̃plwaje] (8) *vt méthode, produit* to re-use; *argent* to reinvest; *ouvrier* to re-employ, take back on.
réengagement [ʀeɑ̃gaʒmɑ̃] *nm* = **rengagement.**
réengager [ʀeɑ̃gaʒe] (3) *vt* = **rengager.**
réentendre [ʀeɑ̃tɑ̃dʀ(ə)] (41) *vt* to hear again.
réescompte [ʀeɛskɔ̃t] *nm* rediscount.
réescompter [ʀeɛskɔ̃te] (1) *vt* to rediscount.
réessayage [ʀeɛsɛjaʒ] *nm* second fitting.
réessayer [ʀeɛseje] (8) *vt robe* to try on again, have a second fitting of.
réévaluation [ʀeevalɥasjɔ̃] *nf* revaluation.
réévaluer [ʀeevalɥe] (1) *vt* to revalue.
réexamen [ʀeɛgzamɛ̃] *nm (V* **réexaminer***)* re-examination; reconsideration.
réexaminer [ʀeɛgzamine] (1) *vt étudiant, candidature, malade* to re-examine; *problème, situation* to examine again, reconsider.
réexpédier [ʀeɛkspedje] (7) *vt (à l'envoyeur)* to return, send back; *(au destinataire)* to send on, forward.
réexpédition [ʀeɛkspedisjɔ̃] *nf (V* **réexpédier***)* return; forwarding.
réexportation [ʀeɛkspɔʀtasjɔ̃] *nf* re-export.
refaçonner [ʀ(ə)fasɔne] (1) *vt* to refashion, remodel, reshape.
refaire [ʀ(ə)fɛʀ] (60) **1** *vt* **(a)** *(recommencer) (gén) travail, dessin, maquillage* to redo, do again; *voyage* to make *ou* do again; *pansement* to put on *ou* do up again, renew; *article, devoir* to rewrite; *nœud, paquet* to do up again, tie again. **elle a refait sa vie avec lui** she started a new life *ou* she made a fresh start (in life) with him; **il m'a refait une visite** he paid me another call, he called on me again *ou* on another occasion; **il refait du soleil** the sun is shining *ou* is out again; **tu refais toujours la même faute** you always make *ou* you keep on making *ou* repeating the same mistake; **il a refait de la fièvre/de l'asthme** he has had another bout of fever/another dose *ou* bout of asthma; **il refait du vélo** he goes cycling again; **il va falloir tout ~ depuis le début** it will have to be done all over again, we'll have to start again from scratch; **si vous refaites du bruit** if you start making a noise again, if there's any further noise from you; **il va falloir ~ de la soupe** we'll have to make some more soup; **son éducation est à ~** he'll have to be re-educated; **si c'était à ~!** if I had to do it again! *ou* begin again!; *(Cartes)* **à ~** re-deal.
(b) *(retaper) toit* to redo, renew; *meuble* to do up, renovate, restore; *chambre (gén)* to do up, renovate, redecorate; *(en peinture)* to repaint; *(en papier)* to repaper. **on refera les peintures/les papiers au printemps** we'll repaint/repaper in the spring, we'll redo the paintwork/the wallpaper in the spring; **~ qch à neuf** to do sth up like new; *(fig)* **~ ses forces/sa santé** to recover one's strength/health.
(c) (*: *duper*) to take in. **il a été refait, il s'est fait ~** he has been taken in *ou* had*; **il m'a refait** *ou* **je me suis fait ~ de 5 F** he did me out of 5 francs*, he diddled me out of 5 francs*.
2 se refaire *vpr (retrouver la santé)* to recuperate, recover; *(regagner son argent)* to make up one's losses. **se ~ (la santé) dans le Midi** to (go and) recuperate in the south of France, recover *ou* regain one's health in the south of France; **que voulez-vous, on ne se refait pas!** what can you expect — you can't change how you're made!* *ou* your own character!
réfection [ʀefɛksjɔ̃] *nf [route]* repairing, remaking; *[mur, maison]* rebuilding, repairing. **la ~ de la route va durer 3 semaines** the road repairs *ou* the repairs to the road will last 3 weeks.
réfectoire [ʀefɛktwaʀ] *nm (Scol)* dining hall, canteen; *(Rel)* refectory; *[usine]* canteen.
référé [ʀefeʀe] *nm (Jur)* **procédure/arrêt en ~** *emergency interim proceedings/ruling.*
référence [ʀefeʀɑ̃s] *nf* **(a)** *(renvoi)* reference; *(en bas de page)* reference, footnote. **par ~ à** in reference to; **ouvrage/numéro de ~** reference book/number; **prendre qch comme point/année de ~** to use sth as a point/year of reference; **faire ~ à** to refer to, make (a) reference to.
(b) *(recommandation) (gén)* reference. **cet employé a-t-il des ~s?** *(d'un employeur)* has this employee got a reference?

ou a testimonial?; (de plusieurs employeurs) has this employee got references? ou testimonials?; **il a un doctorat, c'est quand même une ~** he has a doctorate which is not a bad recommendation; (iro) **ce n'est pas une ~** that's no recommendation.
référendum [refeʀɛ̃dɔm] nm referendum.
référentiel [refeʀɑ̃sjɛl] nm system of reference.
référer [refeʀe] (6) **1 en référer à** vt indir: **en ~ à qn** to refer ou submit a matter ou question to sb.
2 se référer vpr: **se ~ à** (consulter) to consult; (faire référence à) to refer to; (s'en remettre à) to refer to; **s'en ~ à qn** to refer ou submit a question ou matter to sb.
refermer [ʀ(ə)fɛʀme] (1) **1** vt to close ou shut again. **peux-tu ~ la porte?** can you shut the door (again)?
2 se refermer vpr [plaie] to close up, heal up; [fleur] to close up (again); [porte, fenêtre] to close ou shut (again). **le piège se referma sur lui** the trap closed ou shut on him.
refiler‡ [ʀ(ə)file] (1) vt to palm off*, fob off* (à qn on sb). **refile-moi ton livre** let me have your book, give me your book; **il m'a refilé la rougeole** I've caught measles off him, he has passed his measles on to me; **il s'est fait ~ une fausse pièce** someone has palmed ou fobbed a forged coin off on him*.
réfléchi, e [refleʃi] (ptp de **réfléchir**) **1** adj **(a)** (pondéré) action well-thought-out, well-considered; personne reflective, thoughtful; air thoughtful. **tout bien ~** after careful consideration ou thought; **c'est tout ~** my decision is made.
(b) (Gram) reflexive.
(c) (Opt) reflected.
2 nm (Gram) reflexive.
réfléchir [refleʃiʀ] (2) **1** vi to think. **prends le temps de ~** take time to think about it ou to consider it; **cela donne à ~** that gives you food for thought, that makes you think; **je demande à ~** I must have time to consider it ou to think things over; **la prochaine fois, tâche de ~** next time just try and think a bit ou try and use your brains a bit.
2 réfléchir à ou **sur** vt indir: **~ à** ou **sur qch** to think about sth, turn sth over in one's mind; **réfléchissez-y** think about it, think it over; **réfléchis à ce que tu vas faire** think about what you're going to do.
3 vt **(a) ~ que** to realize that; **il n'avait pas réfléchi qu'il ne pourrait pas venir** he hadn't thought ou realized that ou it hadn't occurred to him that he wouldn't be able to come.
(b) lumière, son to reflect. **les arbres se réfléchissent dans le lac** the trees are reflected in the lake, you can see the reflection of the trees in the lake.
réfléchissant, e [refleʃisɑ̃, ɑ̃t] adj reflective.
réflecteur, -trice [reflɛktœʀ, tʀis] **1** adj reflecting. **2** nm (gén) reflector.
reflet [ʀ(ə)flɛ] nm **(a)** (éclat) (gén) reflection; [cheveux] (naturel) glint, light; (artificiel) highlight. **~s moirés de la soie** shimmering play of light on silk; **~s du soleil sur la mer** reflection ou glint ou flash of the sun on the sea; **la lame projetait des ~s sur le mur** the reflection of the blade shone on the wall, the blade threw a reflection onto the wall.
(b) (lit: image) reflection. **le ~ de son visage dans le lac** the reflection of his face in the lake.
(c) (fig: représentation) reflection. **les habits sont le ~ d'une époque/d'une personnalité** clothes reflect ou are the reflection of an era/one's personality; **c'est le pâle ~ de son prédécesseur** he's a pale reflection of his predecessor; **c'est le ~ de son père** he's the image of his father.
refléter [ʀ(ə)flete] (6) **1** vt (lit) to reflect, mirror; (fig) to reflect. **son visage reflète la bonté** goodness shines in his face.
2 se refléter vpr to be reflected; to be mirrored.
refleurir [ʀ(ə)flœʀiʀ] (2) **1** vi (Bot) to flower ou blossom again; (renaître) to flourish ou blossom again. **2** vt tombe to put fresh flowers on.
reflex [reflɛks] **1** adj reflex. **2** nm reflex camera.
réflexe [reflɛks(ə)] **1** adj reflex.
2 nm reflex. **~ conditionné** conditioned reflex; **avoir de bons/mauvais ~s** to have quick ou good/slow ou poor reflexes; **il eut le ~ de couper l'électricité** his immediate ou instant reaction was to switch off the electricity, he instinctively switched off the electricity.
réflexibilité [reflɛksibilite] nf reflexibility.
réflexible [reflɛksibl(ə)] adj reflexible.
réflexif, -ive [reflɛksif, iv] adj (Math) reflexive; (Psych) introspective.
réflexion [reflɛksjɔ̃] nf **(a)** (méditation) thought, reflection (U). **plongé ou absorbé dans ses ~s** deep ou lost in thought ou reflection, absorbed in thought ou in one's thoughts; **ceci donne matière à ~** this gives (you) food for thought, this gives you something to think about; **ceci mérite ~** [offre] this is worth thinking about ou considering; [problème] this needs thinking about ou over; **il a agi sans ~** he acted without thinking ou thoughtlessly; **avec ~** thoughtfully; **laissez-moi un moment de ~** let me think about it for a moment, let me have a moment's reflection; **~ faite ou à la ~, je reste** on reflection ou on second thoughts, I'll stay; **à la ~, on s'aperçoit que c'est faux** when you think about it you can see that it's wrong.
(b) (remarque) remark, reflection; (idée) thought, reflection. **consigner ses ~s dans un cahier** to write down one's thoughts ou reflections in a notebook; **garde tes ~s pour toi** keep your remarks ou reflections ou comments to yourself; **les clients commencent à faire des ~s** the customers are beginning to pass ou make remarks; **on m'a fait des ~s sur son travail** people have complained to me ou made complaints to me about his work.
(c) (Phys) reflection.
réflexivité [reflɛksivite] nf reflexiveness; (Math) reflexivity.
refluer [ʀ(ə)flye] (1) vi [liquide] to flow back; [marée] to go back, ebb; (fig) [foule] to pour ou surge back; [sang] to rush back. **faire ~ la foule** to push ou force the crowd back.
reflux [ʀəfly] nm [foule] backward surge; [marée] ebb; V **flux**.
refondre [ʀ(ə)fɔ̃dʀ(ə)] (41) **1** vt métal to remelt, melt down again; cloche to recast; texte to recast. **2** vi to melt again.
refonte [ʀ(ə)fɔ̃t] nf (V **refondre**) remelting; recasting.
réformable [refɔʀmabl(ə)] adj (gén) reformable; jugement which may be reversed; loi which may be amended ou reformed.
réformateur, -trice [refɔʀmatœʀ, tʀis] **1** adj reforming. **2** nm,f reformer.
réformation [refɔʀmɑsjɔ̃] nf reformation, reform.
réforme [refɔʀm(ə)] nf **(a)** (changement) reform. **~ agraire/de l'orthographe** land/spelling reform.
(b) (Mil) [appelé] declaration of unfitness for service; [soldat] discharge. **mettre à la ~** (Mil, fig) objets to scrap; cheval to put out to grass; **mise à la ~** [soldat] discharge; [objets] scrapping.
(c) (Rel) reformation.
réformé, e [refɔʀme] (ptp de **réformer**) **1** adj (Rel) reformed; (Mil) appelé declared unfit for service; soldat discharged, invalided out. **2** nm,f (Rel) Protestant.
reformer [ʀ(ə)fɔʀme] (1) **1** vt to re-form. (Mil) **~ les rangs** to fall in again, fall into line again. **2 se reformer** vpr [armée, nuage] to re-form; [parti] to re-form, be re-formed; [groupe, rangs] to form up again.
réformer [refɔʀme] (1) **1** vt **(a)** (améliorer) loi, mœurs, religion to reform; abus to correct, (put) right, reform; méthode to improve, reform; administration to reform, overhaul.
(b) (Jur) jugement to reverse.
(c) (Mil) appelé to declare unfit for service; soldat to discharge, invalid out; matériel to scrap. **il s'est fait ~** he got himself declared unfit for service; he got himself discharged on health grounds ou invalided out.
2 se réformer vpr to change one's ways, turn over a new leaf.
réformisme [refɔʀmism(ə)] nm reformism.
réformiste [refɔʀmist(ə)] adj, nmf reformist.
refoulé, e [ʀ(ə)fule] (ptp de **refouler**) adj personne frustrated, inhibited.
refoulement [ʀ(ə)fulmɑ̃] nm **(a)** (V **refouler**) driving back; repulsing; turning back; forcing back; holding back; repression; suppression; backing, reversing, reversal ou inversion of the flow of; stemming.
(b) (Psych: complexe) repression.
refouler [ʀ(ə)fule] (1) vt **(a)** envahisseur, attaque to drive back, repulse; immigrant, étranger to turn back.
(b) larmes to force ou hold back, repress; personnalité, désir, souvenir to repress, suppress; colère to repress, hold in check; sanglots to choke back, force back.
(c) (Rail) to back, reverse.
(d) liquide to force back, reverse ou invert the flow of.
(e) (Naut) to stem.
réfractaire [refʀaktɛʀ] **1** adj **(a) ~ à** autorité, virus resistant to; influence resistant to; musique impervious to; (lit, hum) **être ~ à la discipline** to resist discipline; **prêtre ~** non-juring priest. **(b)** métal refractory; brique, argile fire (épith); plat ovenproof, heat-resistant. **2** nm (Hist Mil) draft dodger, draft evader.
réfracter [refʀakte] (1) **1** vt to refract. **2 se réfracter** vpr to be refracted.
réfracteur, -trice [refʀaktœʀ, tʀis] adj refractive, refracting (épith).
réfraction [refʀaksjɔ̃] nf refraction.
refrain [ʀ(ə)fʀɛ̃] nm (Mus: en fin de couplet) refrain, chorus; (chanson monotone) strains (pl), refrain. **c'est toujours le même ~*** it's always the same old story.
refréner [ʀ(ə)fʀene] (6) vt désir, impatience, envie to curb, hold in check, check.
réfrigérant, e [refʀiʒeʀɑ̃, ɑ̃t] **1** adj fluide refrigerant, refrigerating; accueil, personne icy, frosty; V **mélange**. **2** nm (Tech) cooler.
réfrigérateur [refʀiʒeʀatœʀ] nm refrigerator, fridge* (surtout Brit). (fig) **mettre un projet au ~** to put a plan in cold storage ou on ice.
réfrigération [refʀiʒeʀɑsjɔ̃] nf refrigeration; (Tech) cooling.
réfrigérer [refʀiʒeʀe] (6) vt **(a)** (gén) to refrigerate; (Tech) to cool; local to cool. **je suis réfrigéré*** I'm frozen stiff*.
(b) (fig) enthousiasme to put a damper on, cool; personne to have a cooling ou dampening effect on.
réfringence [refʀɛ̃ʒɑ̃s] nf refringence.
réfringent, e [refʀɛ̃ʒɑ̃, ɑ̃t] adj refringent.
refroidir [ʀ(ə)fʀwadiʀ] (2) **1** vt **(a)** nourriture to cool (down).
(b) (fig) personne to put off, have a cooling effect on; zèle to cool, put a damper on, dampen.
(c) (‡: tuer) to do in‡, bump off‡.
2 vi (cesser d'être trop chaud) to cool (down); (devenir trop froid) to get cold. **laisser ou faire ~** mets trop chaud to let cool (down); (involontairement) to let get cold; moteur to let cool; (péj) projet to let slide ou slip; **mettre qch à ~** to put sth to cool (down).
3 se refroidir vpr [ardeur] to cool (off); [mets] to get cold; [temps] to get cooler ou colder; [personne] (avoir froid) to get ou catch cold; (attraper un rhume) to catch a chill.
refroidissement [ʀ(ə)fʀwadismɑ̃] nm **(a)** [air, liquide] cooling. **~ par air/eau** air-/water-cooling; **~ de la température** drop in the temperature; **on observe un ~ du temps** the weather appears to be getting cooler ou colder.

(b) (*Méd*) chill. **prendre un ~** to catch a chill.
(c) *[passion]* cooling (off).

refroidisseur, -euse [ʀ(ə)fʀwadisœʀ, øz] **1** *adj* cooling. **2** *nm* cooler.

refuge [ʀ(ə)fyʒ] *nm* (*gén*) refuge; (*pour piétons*) refuge, (traffic) island; (*en montagne*) refuge, (mountain) hut. **lieu de ~** place of refuge *ou* safety; (*Bourse*) **valeur ~** tried and tested share.

réfugié, e [ʀefyʒje] (*ptp de* **se réfugier**) *adj, nm,f* refugee.

réfugier (se) [ʀefyʒje] (7) *vpr* (*lit, fig*) to take refuge.

refus [ʀ(ə)fy] *nm* refusal. (*Jur*) **~ de comparaître** refusal to appear (in court); **~ d'obéissance** refusal to obey; (*Mil*) insubordination; **ce n'est pas de ~*** I won't say no (to that).

refusable [ʀ(ə)fyzabl(ə)] *adj* which can be refused.

refuser [ʀ(ə)fyze] (1) **1** *vt* **(a)** (*ne pas accepter*) *cadeau* to refuse; *offre, invitation* to refuse, decline, turn down, reject; *marchandise, racisme, inégalité* to reject, refuse to accept; *manuscrit, politique, méthodes* to refuse, reject. **il l'a demandée en mariage mais il a été refusé** he asked her to marry him but she turned him down *ou* refused him; **~ la lutte** *ou* **le combat** to refuse battle; **le cheval a refusé (l'obstacle)** the horse refused (the fence); **~ le risque** to refuse to take risks; **il a toujours refusé la vie routinière** he has always refused to accept a routine life.

(b) (*ne pas accorder*) *permission, entrée, consentement* to refuse; *demande* to refuse, turn down; *compétence, qualité* to deny. **on lui a refusé la permission d'y aller** he was refused permission to go, they refused him permission to go; **~ l'entrée à qn** to refuse admittance *ou* entry to sb; **~ sa porte à qn** to bar one's door to sb; **je me suis vu ~ un verre d'eau** I was refused a glass of water; **on lui a refusé l'accès aux archives** he was refused *ou* denied access to the records; **je lui refuse toute générosité** I refuse to accept *ou* admit that he has any generosity.

(c) *client* to turn away; *candidat* (*à un examen*) to fail; (*à un poste*) to turn down. **il s'est fait ~ au permis de conduire** he failed his driving test.

(d) ~ de faire qch to refuse to do sth; **il a refusé net (de le faire)** he refused point-blank (to do it).

2 se refuser *vpr* **(a)** (*se priver de*) to refuse o.s., deny o.s. (*iro*) **tu ne te refuses rien!** I can see you deny yourself nothing!, I can see you don't have to stint yourself!

(b) (*être décliné*) **ça ne se refuse pas** *[offre]* it is not to be refused; *[apéritif]* I wouldn't say no (to it).

(c) se ~ à *méthode, solution* to refuse (to accept), reject; **se ~ à l'évidence** to refuse to accept *ou* admit the obvious; **se ~ à tout commentaire** to refuse to make any comment; **elle s'est refusée à lui** she refused to give herself to him; **se ~ à faire qch** to refuse to do sth.

réfutable [ʀefytabl(ə)] *adj* refutable, which can be disproved *ou* refuted. **facilement ~** easily refuted *ou* disproved.

réfutation [ʀefytɑsjɔ̃] *nf* refutation. **fait qui apporte la ~ d'une allégation** fact which refutes *ou* disproves an allegation.

réfuter [ʀefyte] (1) *vt* to refute, disprove.

regagner [ʀ(ə)gɑɲe] (1) *vt* **(a)** (*récupérer*) *amitié, faveur* to regain, win *ou* gain back; *argent* to win back, get back. **~ le temps perdu** to make up (for) lost time; (*Mil, fig*) **~ du terrain** to regain ground, win *ou* gain ground again; **~ le terrain perdu** to win back lost ground.

(b) (*arriver à*) *lieu* to get *ou* go back to; *pays* to arrive back in, get back to. **il regagna enfin sa maison** he finally arrived back home *ou* got back home *ou* reached home again.

regain [ʀ(ə)gɛ̃] *nm* **(a) ~ de** *jeunesse* renewal of; *santé, popularité* revival of; *activité, influence* renewal *ou* revival of; **~ de vie** new lease of life. **(b)** (*Agr*) aftermath, second crop of hay.

régal, *pl* **~s** [ʀegal] *nm* delight, treat. **ce gâteau est un ~** this cake is absolutely delicious; **c'est un ~ pour les yeux** it is a delight *ou* treat to look at; **quel ~ de manger des cerises** what a treat to have cherries (to eat).

régalade [ʀegalad] *nf*: **boire à la ~** to drink without letting one's lips touch the bottle (*ou* glass *etc*).

régaler [ʀegale] (1) **1** *vt personne* to treat to a slap-up* (*Brit*) *ou* delicious meal. **c'est moi qui régale** I'm treating everyone, it's my treat; **c'est le patron qui régale** it's on the house.

2 se régaler *vpr* (*bien manger*) to have a delicious *ou* a slap-up* (*Brit*) meal. **se ~ de gâteaux** to treat o.s. to some delicious cakes; **on s'est bien régalé** it was delicious; (*fig péj*) **il y en a qui se sont régalés dans cette vente** some people made a packet* (*Brit*) *ou* did really well out of that sale; (*hum, péj*) **les cafetiers se régalent avec cette vague de chaleur** the café owners are coining it in* (*surtout Brit*) *ou* making a mint* *ou* doing really well in this heatwave; **se ~ de romans** (*habituellement*) to be very keen on *ou* be a keen reader of novels; (*en vacances etc*) to gorge o.s. on novels, have a feast of novel-reading.

regard [ʀ(ə)gaʀ] *nm* **(a)** (*vue*) glance, eye. **parcourir qch du ~, promener son ~ sur qch** to cast a glance *ou* an eye over sth; **son ~ se posa sur moi** his glance *ou* eye *ou* gaze came to rest on me; **soustraire qch aux ~s** to hide sth from sight *ou* from view, put sth out of sight; **cela attire tous les ~s** it catches everyone's eye *ou* attention; **nos ~s sont fixés sur vous** our eyes are turned on you.

(b) (*expression*) look *ou* expression (in one's eye). **son ~ était dur/tendre** the look *ou* expression in his eye was hard/tender, he had a hard/tender look *ou* expression in his eye; **~ fixe/perçant** fixed/penetrating stare.

(c) (*coup d'œil*) look, glance. **échanger des ~s avec qn** to exchange looks *ou* glances with sb; **lancer un ~ de colère à qn** to glare at sb, cast an angry look *ou* glare *ou* glance at sb; **au premier ~** at first glance *ou* sight.

(d) *[égout]* manhole; *[four]* peephole, window.

(e) (*loc*) **au ~ de la loi** in the eyes *ou* the sight of the law, from the legal viewpoint; **texte avec photos en ~** text with photos on the opposite page *ou* facing; **en ~ de ce qu'il gagne** compared with *ou* in comparison with what he earns; *V* **droit**[2].

regardant, e [ʀ(ə)gaʀdɑ̃, ɑ̃t] *adj* careful with money. **il n'est pas ~** he's quite free with his money; **ils sont/ne sont pas ~s sur l'argent de poche** they are quite/they are not very generous with pocket money.

regarder [ʀ(ə)gaʀde] (1) **1** *vt* **(a)** *paysage, scène* to look at; *action en déroulement, film, match* to watch. **elle regardait les voitures sur le parking** she was looking at the cars in the car park; **elle regardait les voitures défiler** *ou* **qui défilaient** she was watching the cars driving past *ou* the cars as they drove past; **~ tomber la pluie** *ou* **la pluie tomber** to watch the rain falling; **il regarda sa montre** he looked at *ou* had a look at his watch; **regarde, il pleut** look, it's raining; **regarde bien, il va sauter** watch, he's going to jump; **~ la télévision/une émission à la télévision** to watch television/a programme on television; **~ le journal** to look at *ou* have a look at the paper; **~ sur le livre de qn** (*partager*) to share sb's book; (*tricher*) to look *ou* peep at sb's book; **~ par la fenêtre** (*du dedans*) to look out of the window; (*du dehors*) to look in through the window; **regarde les oiseaux par la fenêtre** look through *ou* out of the window at the birds, watch the birds through *ou* out of the window; **regarde devant toi/derrière toi** look in front of you/behind you; **regarde où tu marches*** watch *ou* look where you're going *ou* putting your feet; **regarde voir dans l'armoire** take *ou* have a look in the wardrobe; **regarde voir s'il arrive** look *ou* have a look and see if he's coming; **attends, je vais ~** hang on, I'll go and look *ou* I'll take a look; **regardez-moi ça/son écriture*** just (take a) look at that/at his writing; **vous ne m'avez pas regardé!‡** what do you take me for!*, who do you think I am!*; **j'ai regardé partout, je n'ai rien trouvé** I looked everywhere but I couldn't find anything; **regarde à la pendule quelle heure il est** look at the clock to see what time it is, look and see what time it is by the clock; **regardez-le faire** (*gén*) watch him *ou* look at him do it; (*pour apprendre*) watch *ou* look how he does it; **elles sont allées ~ les vitrines/les magasins** they've gone to do some window-shopping/to have a look around the shops; **sans ~** *traverser* without looking; *payer* regardless of cost *ou* the expense; *acheter* without stopping to look carefully.

(b) (*rapidement*) to glance at, have a glance *ou* a (quick) look at; (*longuement*) to gaze at; (*fixement*) to stare at. **~ un texte rapidement** to glance at *ou* through a text, have a quick look *ou* glance at *ou* through a text; **~ (qch) par le trou de la serrure** to peep *ou* look (at sth) through the keyhole; **~ de près/de plus près** to have a close/closer look at, look closely/more closely at; **~ sans voir** to look with unseeing eyes; **~ bouche bée** to gape at; **~ à la dérobée** *ou* **par en-dessous** to steal a glance at, glance sidelong at; **~ qn avec colère** to glare angrily at sb; **~ qn avec méfiance** to look at *ou* eye sb suspiciously; **~ qn du coin de l'œil** to look at *ou* watch sb from the corner of one's eye; **~ qn sous le nez** to look at sb defiantly; **~ qn de travers** to scowl at sb; **~ qn/qch d'un bon/mauvais œil** to look favourably/unfavourably upon sb/sth, view sb/sth favourably/unfavourably; **~ qn de haut** to give sb a scornful look, look scornfully at sb; (*lit, fig*) **~ qn droit dans les yeux/bien en face** to look sb straight in the eye/straight in the face; **~ qn dans le blanc des yeux** to look sb straight in the face *ou* eye; **~ la vie/le danger en face** to look life/danger in the face, face up to life/danger.

(c) (*vérifier*) *appareil, malade* to look at, check; *huile, essence* to look at, check. **regarde la lampe, elle ne marche pas** have a look at the lamp — it doesn't work; **~ dans l'annuaire** to look in the phone book; **~ un mot dans le dictionnaire** to look up *ou* check a word in the dictionary.

(d) (*envisager*) *situation, problème* to view. **~ l'avenir avec appréhension** to view the future with trepidation; **il ne regarde que son propre intérêt** he is only concerned with *ou* he only thinks about his own interests; **nous le regardons comme un ami** we look upon him *ou* we regard him *ou* we consider him as a friend.

(e) (*concerner*) to concern. **cette affaire me regarde quand même un peu** this business does concern me a bit *ou* is a little bit my concern; **en quoi cela te regarde-t-il?** (*se mêler de*) what business is it of yours?, what has it to do with you?; (*être touché par*) how does it affect *ou* concern you?; **fais ce que je te dis, la suite me regarde** do what I tell you and I'll take care of what happens next *ou* and what happens next is my concern *ou* business; **que vas-tu faire? — cela me regarde** what will you do? — that's my business *ou* my concern; **non mais, ça vous regarde?*** really, is it any of your business? *ou* what business is it of yours?; **cela ne le regarde pas, cela ne le regarde en rien** that's none of his business, that's no concern *ou* business of his; **mêlez-vous de ce qui vous regarde** mind your own business.

(f) *[maison]* **~ (vers)** to face.

2 regarder à *vt indir* to think of *ou* about. **y ~ à deux fois avant de faire qch** to think twice before doing sth; **il n'y regarde pas de si près** he's not that fussy *ou* particular; **à y bien ~** on thinking it over; **c'est quelqu'un qui va ~ à 2 F** he's the sort of person who will niggle over 2 francs *ou* worry about 2 francs; **il regarde à s'acheter un costume neuf** he can't make up his mind to buy a new suit, he hums and haws* about buying a new suit; **quand il fait un cadeau, il ne regarde pas à la dépense** when he gives (somebody) a present he doesn't worry how much he spends *ou* he spares no expense; **acheter qch sans ~ à la dépense** to buy sth without thought for expense *ou* without bothering about the expense.

3 se regarder *vpr* **(a) se ~ dans une glace** to look at o.s. in a mirror; (*iro*) **il ne s'est pas regardé!** he should take a look at himself!

(b) *[personnes]* to look at each other *ou* one another; *[maisons]* to face each other *ou* one another. **les deux enfants restaient là à se ~ en chiens de faïence** the two children sat (*ou* stood) glaring at each other *ou* one another.

regarnir [ʀ(ə)gaʀniʀ] (2) *vt magasin, rayon* to stock up again, restock; *trousse* to refill, replenish; *plat* to fill (up) again.

régate [ʀegat] *nf*: **~(s)** regatta.

regeler [ʀəʒle] (5) *vt, vb impers* to freeze again.

régence [ʀeʒɑ̃s] **1** *nf* (*Pol*) regency. (*Hist*) **la R~** the Regency. **2** *adj inv meuble* (*en France*) (French) Regency; (*en Grande-Bretagne*) Regency; (*fig*) *personne, mœurs* overrefined.

régénérateur, -trice [ʀeʒeneʀatœʀ, tʀis] **1** *adj* regenerative. **2** *nm,f* regenerator.

régénération [ʀeʒeneʀɑsjɔ̃] *nf* regeneration.

régénérer [ʀeʒeneʀe] (6) *vt* (*Bio, Rel*) to regenerate; *personne, forces* to revive, restore.

régent, e [ʀeʒɑ̃, ɑ̃t] **1** *adj* regent. **prince ~** prince regent. **2** *nm,f* (*Pol*) regent; (††: *professeur*) master; (*Admin: directeur*) manager.

régenter [ʀeʒɑ̃te] (1) *vt* (*gén*) to rule over; *personne* to dictate to. **il veut tout ~** he wants to run the whole show.

régicide [ʀeʒisid] **1** *adj* regicidal. **2** *nmf* (*personne*) regicide. **3** *nm* (*crime*) regicide.

régie [ʀeʒi] *nf* **(a)** (*gestion*) *[État]* state control; *[commune]* local government control (*de* over). **en ~** under state (*ou* local government) control.

(b) (*compagnie*) **~ (d'État)** state-owned company.

(c) (*Ciné, Théât, TV*) production department.

regimber [ʀ(ə)ʒɛ̃be] (1) *vi [personne]* to rebel (*contre* against); *[cheval]* to jib. **fais-le sans ~** do it without grumbling; **quand je lui ai demandé de le faire, il a regimbé** when I asked him to do it he jibbed at the idea.

régime[1] [ʀeʒim] *nm* **(a)** (*Pol*) (*mode*) system (of government); (*péj*) régime; (*gouvernement*) government; (*péj*) régime. **~ monarchique/républicain** monarchical/republican system (of government); **les opposants au ~** the opponents to the régime; *V* **ancien.**

(b) (*Admin*) (*système*) system; (*règlements*) regulations. **~ douanier/des hôpitaux** customs/hospital system; customs/hospital regulations.

(c) (*Jur*) **~ (matrimonial)** marriage settlement; **se marier sous le ~ de la communauté/de la séparation de biens** to opt for a marriage settlement based on joint ownership of property/on separate ownership of property.

(d) (*Méd*) diet. **être/mettre qn au ~** to be/put sb on a diet; **suivre un ~** (*gén*) to be on a diet; (*scrupuleusement*) to follow *a ou* keep to a diet; **~ sans sel/sec/lacté** salt-free/alcohol-free/milk diet.

(e) *[moteur]* (engine *ou* running) speed. **ce moteur est bruyant à haut ~** this engine is noisy when it is revving hard; (*Tech, fig*) **marcher** *ou* **aller à plein ~** to go (at) full speed, go flat out; (*fig*) **à ce ~, nous n'aurons bientôt plus d'argent** (if we go on) at this rate *ou* at the rate we're going we'll soon have no money left.

(f) (*Géog, Mét*) régime.

(g) (*Gram*) object. **~ direct/indirect** direct/indirect object; **cas ~** objective case.

(h) (*Phys*) *[écoulement]* rate of flow.

régime[2] [ʀeʒim] *nm [dattes]* cluster, bunch; *[bananes]* bunch, hand.

régiment [ʀeʒimɑ̃] *nm* **(a)** (*Mil*) (*corps*) regiment; (*: *service militaire*) military *ou* national service. **être au ~*** to be doing (one's) national *ou* military service; **aller au ~*** to go into the army, be called up.

(b) (*: *masse*) *[personnes]* regiment, army; *[choses]* mass(es), loads. **il y en a pour tout un ~** there's enough for a whole army.

régimentaire [ʀeʒimɑ̃tɛʀ] *adj* regimental.

région [ʀeʒjɔ̃] *nf* (*Admin, Géog*) (*étendue*) region; (*limitée*) area; (*Anat*) region, area; (*fig: domaine*) region. **~s polaires/équatoriales** polar/equatorial regions; **la ~ parisienne/londonienne** the Paris/London area *ou* region; **ça se trouve dans la ~ de Lyon** it's in the Lyons area *ou* around Lyons *ou* in the region of Lyons; **si vous passez dans la ~, allez les voir** if you are in the area *ou* in thosparts *ou* if you go that way, go and see them; **dans nos ~s** in these regions, in the regions we live in.

régional, e, *mpl* **-aux** [ʀeʒjɔnal, o] *adj* regional.

régionalisation [ʀeʒjɔnalizɑsjɔ̃] *nf* regionalization.

régionaliser [ʀeʒjɔnalize] (1) *vt* to regionalize.

régionalisme [ʀeʒjɔnalism(ə)] *nm* regionalism.

régionaliste [ʀeʒjɔnalist(ə)] **1** *adj* regionalist(ic). **2** *nmf* regionalist.

régir [ʀeʒiʀ] (2) *vt* (*gén*) to govern.

régisseur [ʀeʒisœʀ] *nm* **(a)** (*Théât*) stage manager; (*Ciné, TV*) assistant director. **(b)** *[propriété]* steward.

registre [ʀəʒistʀ(ə)] **1** *nm* **(a)** (*livre*) register. **~ maritime/d'hôtel/du commerce** shipping/hotel/trade register.

(b) (*Mus*) *[orgue]* stop; *[voix]* (*étage*) register; (*étendue*) register, range.

(c) (*Ling*) (*niveau*) register, level (of language); (*style*) register, style.

(d) (*Tech*) *[fourneau]* damper, register; (*Ordinateurs, Typ*) register.

2: registre de comptabilité ledger; **registre de l'état civil** register of births, marriages and deaths; **registre mortuaire** register of deaths; **registre de vapeur** throttle valve.

réglable [ʀeglabl(ə)] *adj* adjustable. **siège à dossier ~** reclining seat.

réglage [ʀeglaʒ] *nm* **(a)** *[mécanisme, débit]* regulation, adjustment; *[moteur]* tuning; *[allumage, thermostat]* setting, adjustment; *[dossier, tir]* adjustment. **(b)** *[papier]* ruling.

règle [ʀɛgl(ə)] *nf* **(a)** (*loi, principe*) rule. **~ de conduite** rule of conduct; **~ de 3** rule of 3; **les ~s de la bienséance/de l'honneur** the rules of propriety/honour; **sa parole nous sert de ~** his word is our rule; **ils ont pour ~ de se réunir chaque jour** they make it a rule to meet every day; (*lit, fig*) **c'est la ~ du jeu** it's one of the rules of the game, those are the rules of the game; (*lit, fig*) **se plier aux ~s du jeu** to play the game according to the rules; **c'est la ~ (de la maison)!** that's the rule (of the house)!; **cela n'échappe pas à la ~** that's no exception to the rule.

(b) (*instrument*) ruler. **trait tiré à la ~** line drawn with a ruler; **~ à calcul** *ou* **à calculer** slide rule.

(c) (*Rel: U*) rule.

(d) (*menstruation*) **~s** period(s); **avoir ses ~s** to have one's period(s).

(e) (*loc*) **il est de ~ qu'on fasse un cadeau** it's usual *ou* it's standard practice *ou* the done thing to give a present; **en ~** *comptabilité, papiers* in order; *avertissement* given according to the rules; *réclamation* made according to the rules; **bataille en ~** proper *ou* right old* fight; **il lui fait une cour en ~** he's courting her according to the rule book *ou* by the book; **être/se mettre en ~ avec les autorités** to be/put o.s. straight with the authorities; **je ne suis pas en ~** I'm not straight with the authorities, my papers *etc* are not in order; **en ~ générale** as a (general) rule; **il faut faire la demande dans** *ou* **selon les ~s** you must make the request through the proper channels *ou* according to the rules; (*hum*) **dans les ~s de l'art** according to the rule book.

réglé, e [ʀegle] (*ptp de* **régler**) *adj* **(a)** (*régulier*) *vie* (well-)ordered, regular; *personne* steady, stable. **c'est ~ comme du papier à musique*, il arrive tous les jours à 8 heures** he arrives at 8 o'clock every day, as regular as clockwork.

(b) *fille* pubescent, who has reached puberty. **femme (bien) ~e** woman whose periods are regular.

(c) *papier* ruled, lined.

règlement [ʀɛgləmɑ̃] *nm* **(a)** (*Admin, Police, Univ*) (*règle*) regulation; (*réglementation*) rules, regulations. **~ de service** administrative rule *ou* regulation.

(b) *[affaire, conflit]* settlement, settling; *[facture, dette]* settlement, payment. **faire un ~ par chèque** to pay *ou* make a payment by cheque; (*Jur*) **~ judiciaire** (compulsory) liquidation; (*fig*) **~ de compte(s)** settling of scores; (*de gangsters*) gangland killing.

réglementaire [ʀɛgləmɑ̃tɛʀ] *adj uniforme, taille* regulation (*épith*); *procédure* statutory, laid down in the regulations. **ça n'est pas très ~** that isn't really allowed, that's really against the rules; **dans le temps ~** in the prescribed time; **ce certificat n'est pas ~** this certificate doesn't conform to the regulations; **dispositions ~s** regulations; **pouvoir ~** power to make regulations.

réglementairement [ʀɛgləmɑ̃tɛʀmɑ̃] *adv* in accordance with *ou* according to the regulations, statutorily.

réglementation [ʀɛgləmɑ̃tɑsjɔ̃] *nf* (*règles*) regulations; (*contrôle*) *[prix, loyers]* control, regulation.

réglementer [ʀɛgləmɑ̃te] (1) *vt* to regulate, control.

régler [ʀegle] (6) *vt* **(a)** (*conclure*) *affaire, conflit* to settle; *problème* to settle, sort out. **~ qch à l'amiable** (*gén*) to settle sth amicably; (*Jur*) to settle sth out of court; **alors, c'est une affaire réglée** *ou* **c'est réglé, vous acceptez?** that's it settled then — do you accept?; **on va ~ ça tout de suite** we'll get that settled *ou* sorted out straightaway.

(b) (*payer*) *note, dette* to settle (up), pay (up); *compte* to settle; *commerçant, créancier* to settle up with, pay; *travaux* to settle up for, pay for. **est-ce que je peux ~?** can I settle up (with you)? *ou* settle *ou* pay the bill?; **je viens ~ mes dettes** I've come to settle my debts *ou* to square up with you*; **est-ce que je peux (vous) ~ par chèque?** can I make you a cheque out?, can I pay you by cheque?; **j'ai un compte à ~ avec lui** I've got a score to settle with him; **on lui a réglé son compte!*** they've settled his hash* *ou* settled him.

(c) *mécanisme, débit, machine* to regulate, adjust; *dossier, tir* to adjust; *moteur* to tune; *allumage, ralenti* to set, adjust. **~ le thermostat à 18°** to set the thermostat to *ou* at 18°; **~ une montre** (*mettre à l'heure*) to put a watch right (*sur* by); (*réparer*) to regulate a watch; **le carburateur est mal réglé** the carburettor is badly tuned.

(d) (*fixer*) *modalités, date, programme* to settle (on), fix (up), decide on; *conduite, réactions* to determine. **~ l'ordre d'une cérémonie** to settle *ou* fix (up) the order of (a) ceremony; **il ne sait pas ~ l'emploi de ses journées** he is incapable of planning out *ou* organizing his daily routine; **~ le sort de qn** to decide *ou* determine sb's fate.

(e) ~ qch sur to model sth on, adjust sth to; **~ sa vie sur (celle de) son père** to model one's life on that of one's father; **~ sa conduite sur les circonstances** to adjust one's conduct *ou* behaviour to the circumstances; **se ~ sur qn d'autre** to model o.s. on sb else; **il essaya de ~ son pas sur celui de son père** he tried to walk in step with his father; **~ sa vitesse sur celle de l'autre voiture** to adjust *ou* match one's speed to that of the other car.

(f) *papier* to rule (lines on).

réglette [ʀeglɛt] *nf* (*Typ*) setting stick.

régleur, -euse [ʀeglœʀ, øz] **1** *nm,f* (*ouvrier*) setter, adjuster. **2** **régleuse** *nf* ruling machine.

réglisse [ʀeglis] *nf ou nm* liquorice.

régnant, e [ʀeɲɑ̃, ɑ̃t] *adj famille, prince* reigning; *théorie, idée* reigning, prevailing.

règne [ʀɛɲ] *nm* **(a)** *[roi, tyran]* (*période*) reign; (*domination*) rule, reign. **sous le ~ de Louis XIV** (*période*) in the reign of Louis XIV; (*domination*) under the reign *ou* rule of Louis XIV.

(b) *[mode, banquiers]* reign; *[justice, liberté]* reign, rule. **(c)** (*Bot, Zool etc*) kingdom. **~ animal/végétal/minéral** animal/vegetable/mineral kingdom.

régner [ʀeɲe] (6) *vi* **(a)** (*être sur le trône*) to reign; (*exercer sa domination*) to rule (*sur* over). **les 20 ans qu'il a régné** during the 20 years of his reign; (*fig*) **il règne (en maître) sur le village** he reigns *ou* rules (supreme) over the village; **elle règne dans la cuisine** she reigns over *ou* rules in the kitchen; (*littér*) **~ sur nos passions** to rule over *ou* govern our passions.

(b) (*prédominer*) *[paix, silence]* to reign, prevail (*sur* over); *[accord, confiance, opinion]* to prevail; *[peur]* to reign, hold sway (*sur* over). **la confusion la plus totale régnait dans la chambre** utter confusion prevailed in the room, the room was in utter confusion; **maison où l'ordre règne** house where order reigns; **faire ~ l'ordre** to maintain law and order; **faire ~ la terreur/le silence** to make terror/silence reign; (*iro*) **la confiance règne!** that's *ou* there's confidence *ou* trust for you! (*iro*).

regonflage [ʀ(ə)gɔ̃flaʒ] *nm* (*V* **regonfler**) blowing up (again); reinflation; pumping up (again).

regonfler [ʀ(ə)gɔ̃fle] (1) **1** *vt* **(a)** (*gonfler à nouveau*) *pneu de voiture* to blow up again, reinflate; *pneu de vélo, matelas, ballon* to blow up again; (*avec pompe à main*) to pump up again.

(b) (*gonfler davantage*) to blow up harder, put some more air in, pump up further.

(c) (*) *personne* to cheer up, bolster up. **il est regonflé** he's his usual cheerful self *ou* he's his old self again; **~ le moral de qn** to bolster up sb's spirits, bolster sb up.

2 *vi [rivière]* to swell *ou* rise again; (*Méd*) to swell (up) again.

regorgement [ʀ(ə)gɔʀʒəmɑ̃] *nm* overflow.

regorger [ʀ(ə)gɔʀʒe] (3) *vi* **(a) ~ de** *[région, pays]* to abound in, be abundant in, overflow with; *[maison, magasin]* to be packed *ou* crammed with, overflow with; *[rue]* to be swarming *ou* milling *ou* bursting with; **la région regorge d'ananas** the region abounds in *ou* is abundant in pineapples, there is an abundance of pineapples in the region; **cette année le marché regorge de fruits** this year there is a glut of fruit *ou* there is an abundance of fruit on the market; **le pays regorge d'argent** there is an abundance of wealth in the country; **sa maison regorgait de livres/d'invités** his house was packed with *ou* crammed with *ou* cram-full of books/guests; **il regorge d'argent** he is rolling in money*, he has got plenty of money.

(b) *[liquide]* to overflow.

régresser [ʀegʀese] (1) *vi [science, enfant]* to regress; *[douleur, épidémie]* to recede, diminish, decrease.

régressif, -ive [ʀegʀesif, iv] *adj évolution, raisonnement* regressive; *marche* backward (*épith*). (*Géol*) **érosion ~ive** headward erosion; **forme ~ive** regressive *ou* recessive form.

régression [ʀegʀesjɔ̃] *nf* (*gén*) regression, decline; (*Bio, Psych*) regression. **être en (voie de) ~** to be on the decline *ou* decrease, be declining *ou* decreasing; (*Géol*) **~ marine** marine regression.

regret [ʀ(ə)gʀɛ] *nm* **(a)** *[décision, faute]* regret (*de* for); *[passé]* regret (*de* about). **le ~ d'une occasion manquée la faisait pleurer** she wept with regret at the lost opportunity, she wept in regret at losing the opportunity; **les ~s causés par une occasion manquée** the regrets felt at *ou* for a missed opportunity; **le ~ du pays natal** homesickness; **le ~ d'avoir échoué** the regret that he had failed *ou* at having failed; **vivre dans le ~ d'une faute** to spend one's life regretting a mistake; **le ~ de sa jeunesse/de son ami mort le rendait triste** his heart was heavy with the sorrow *ou* grief he felt for his lost youth/his departed friend, he grieved for the sad loss of his youth/his friend; **c'est avec ~ que je vous le dis** I'm sorry *ou* I regret to have to tell you this; **sans ~** with no regrets; (*sur une tombe*) **~s éternels** sorely missed.

(b) (*loc*) **à ~** *partir* with regret, regretfully; *accepter, donner* with regret, reluctantly; **je suis au ~ de ne pouvoir ...** I'm sorry *ou* I regret that I am unable to ... ; **j'ai le ~ de vous informer ...** I regret to have to point out that ... , I must regretfully inform you that ... (*frm*); **à mon grand ~** to my great regret.

regrettable [ʀ(ə)gʀɛtabl(ə)] *adj incident, conséquence* regrettable, unfortunate. **il est ~ que** it's unfortunate *ou* regrettable that.

regrettablement [ʀ(ə)gʀɛtabləmɑ̃] *adv* (*littér*) regrettably.

regretter [ʀ(ə)gʀete] (1) *vt* **(a)** *personne, pays natal* to miss; *jeunesse* to miss, regret; *occasion manquée, temps perdu* to regret. **nous avons beaucoup regretté votre absence** we were very sorry *ou* we greatly regretted that you weren't able to join us; **il regrette son argent** he regrets the expense, he wishes he had his money back; **c'était cher, mais je ne regrette pas mon argent** it was expensive but I don't regret buying it *ou* spending the money; **notre regretté président** our late lamented president; **on le regrette beaucoup dans le village** he is greatly *ou* sadly missed in the village.

(b) (*se repentir de*) *décision, imprudence, péché* to regret. **tu le regretteras** you'll regret it, you'll be sorry for it; **tu ne le regretteras pas** you won't regret it; **je ne regrette rien** I have no regrets; **je regrette mon geste** I'm sorry I did that, I regret doing that.

(c) (*désapprouver*) *mesure, décision hostile* to regret, deplore. **nous regrettons votre attitude** we regret *ou* deplore your attitude.

(d) (*être désolé*) to be sorry, regret. **je regrette, mais il est trop tard** I'm sorry, but it's too late, I'm afraid it's too late; **ah non! je regrette, il était avec moi** no! I'm sorry *ou* I'm sorry to contradict you but he was with me; **nous regrettons qu'il soit malade** we regret *ou* are sorry that he is ill; **je regrette de ne pas lui avoir écrit** I'm sorry *ou* I regret that I didn't write to him, I regret not writing *ou* not having written to him; **je regrette de vous avoir fait attendre** I'm sorry to have kept you waiting; **je ne regrette pas d'être venu** I'm not sorry *ou* I'm glad I came.

regrimper [ʀ(ə)gʀɛ̃pe] (1) **1** *vt pente, escalier* to climb (up) again.

2 *vi [route]* to climb (up) again; *[fièvre]* to go up *ou* rise again; *[prix]* to go up again, climb again. **~ dans le train** to climb back into the train; **ça va faire ~ la fièvre/les prix** it'll send his temperature/prices (back) up again.

regrossir [ʀ(ə)gʀosiʀ] (2) *vi* to put on weight again, put weight back on.

regroupement [ʀ(ə)gʀupmɑ̃] *nm* (*V* **regrouper**) grouping together; bringing *ou* gathering together; reassembly; roundup.

regrouper [ʀ(ə)gʀupe] (1) **1** *vt* **(a)** (*réunir*) *objets* to put *ou* group together; *pièces de collection* to bring *ou* gather together; *industries, partis* to unite, group together; *parcelles* to group together.

(b) (*réunir de nouveau*) *armée, personnes* to reassemble; *parti* to regroup; *bétail* to round up, herd together.

2 se regrouper *vpr* to gather (together), assemble (*autour de* (a)round, *derrière* behind).

régularisation [ʀegylaʀizɑsjɔ̃] *nf* (*V* **régulariser**) regularization; straightening out; putting in order; regulation.

régulariser [ʀegylaʀize] (1) *vt* **(a)** *position* to regularize, straighten out, sort out; *passeport* to put in order. **~ sa situation** (*gén*) to regularize *ou* straighten out one's position; (*se marier*) to regularize *ou* legalize one's situation; **faire ~ ses papiers** to have one's papers put in order.

(b) (*régler*) *mécanisme, débit* to regulate.

régularité [ʀegylaʀite] *nf* (*V* **régulier**) regularity; steadiness; evenness; consistency; neatness; equability. **contester la ~ d'une élection/d'un jugement/d'une opération** to question the lawfulness *ou* legality of an election/a sentence/an operation.

régulateur, -trice [ʀegylatœʀ, tʀis] **1** *adj* regulating. **2** *nm* (*Tech, fig*) regulator.

régulation [ʀegylɑsjɔ̃] *nf [économie, trafic]* regulation; *[mécanisme]* regulation, adjustment; *[circulation, naissances]* control. (*Physiol*) **~ thermique** regulation of body temperature, thermotaxis (*T*).

régulier, -ière [ʀegylje, jɛʀ] **1** *adj* **(a)** (*fixe, constant*) *pouls, travail, effort, élève* regular, steady; *qualité, résultats* steady, even, consistent; *habitudes, vie* regular; *vitesse, vent* steady; *paiement, visites, service de car* regular; *train, avion* regular, scheduled. **rivière ~ière** river which has a regular *ou* steady flow; **frapper qch à coups ~s** to strike sth with regular *ou* steady blows; **à intervalles ~s** at regular intervals; **il est ~ dans son travail** he's steady in his work, he's a regular *ou* steady worker; **exercer une pression ~ière sur qch** to press steadily *ou* exert a steady pressure on sth; **la compagnie a 13 lignes ~ières avec le Moyen-Orient** the airline has 13 scheduled services to the Middle East; **être en correspondance ~ière avec qn** to be in regular correspondence with sb.

(b) (*égal*) *répartition, couche, ligne* even; *façade* regular; *traits, paysage* regular, even; *écriture* regular, neat; (*Math*) *polygone* regular; (*fig*) *humeur* steady, even, equable. **avoir un visage ~** to have regular features; **il faut que la pression soit bien ~ière partout** the pressure must be evenly distributed over the whole area.

(c) (*légal*) *gouvernement* legitimate; *élection, procédure* in order (*attrib*); *jugement* regular, in order (*attrib*); *tribunal* legal, official. **être en situation ~ière** to be in line with the law.

(d) (*honnête*) *opération, coup* aboveboard (*attrib*), on the level (*attrib*); *homme d'affaires* on the level (*attrib*), straightforward, straight (*attrib*). **vous me faites faire quelque chose qui n'est pas très ~** you're getting me into something that is not quite on the level *ou* aboveboard; **être ~ en affaires** to be straight *ou* honest in business; **coup ~** (*Boxe*) fair blow; (*Échecs*) correct move.

(e) (*Mil*) *troupes* regular; *armée* regular, standing; (*Rel*) *clergé, ordre* regular.

(f) *vers, verbe* regular.

2 *nm* (*Mil, Rel*) regular.

3 régulière‡ *nf* (*femme*) missus‡, old woman‡; (*maîtresse*) lady-love.

régulièrement [ʀegyljɛʀmɑ̃] *adv* **(a)** (*V* **régulier**) regularly; steadily; evenly; consistently; neatly; equably; lawfully. **élu ~** properly elected, elected in accordance with the rules; **opération effectuée ~** operation carried out in the correct *ou* proper fashion; **coup porté ~** fairly dealt blow. **(b)** (*en principe*) normally, in principle; (*d'habitude*) normally, usually.

régurgitation [ʀegyʀʒitɑsjɔ̃] *nf* regurgitation.

régurgiter [ʀegyʀʒite] (1) *vt* to regurgitate.

réhabilitation [ʀeabilitɑsjɔ̃] *nf* (*V* **réhabiliter**) clearing (the name of), rehabilitation; discharge; restoring to favour; reinstatement. **obtenir la ~ de qn** to get sb's name cleared, get sb rehabilitated; to obtain a discharge for sb.

réhabiliter [ʀeabilite] (1) **1** *vt condamné* to clear (the name of), rehabilitate; *failli* to discharge; *profession, art* to bring back into favour, restore to favour. **~ la mémoire de qn** to restore sb's good name; **~ qn dans ses fonctions** to reinstate sb (in his job); **~ qn dans ses droits** to restore sb's rights (to him).

2 se réhabiliter *vpr [condamné, criminel]* to rehabilitate o.s.; (*fig*) *[candidat etc]* to redeem o.s.

réhabituer [ʀeabitɥe] (1) **1** *vt*: **~ qn à (faire) qch** to get sb used to (doing) sth again, reaccustom sb to (doing) sth.

2 se réhabituer *vpr*: **se ~ à (faire) qch** to get used to (doing) sth again, reaccustom o.s. to (doing) sth; **ça va être dûr de se ~** it will be difficult to get used to it again.

rehaussement [ʀəosmɑ̃] *nm* (*V* **rehausser**) heightening; raising.

rehausser [ʀəose] (1) *vt* **(a)** (*relever*) *mur, clôture* to heighten, make *ou* build higher; *plafond, chaise* to raise, heighten.
(b) (*fig: souligner*) *beauté, couleur* to set off, enhance; *goût* to bring out; *mérite, prestige* to enhance, increase; *courage* to increase; *détail* to bring out, emphasize, accentuate; *tableau, robe* to brighten up, liven up. **rehaussé de** embellished with.
réifier [ʀeifje] (7) *vt* to reify.
réimperméabilisation [ʀeɛ̃pɛʀmeabilizɑsjɔ̃] *nf* reproofing.
réimperméabiliser [ʀeɛ̃pɛʀmeabilize] (1) *vt* to reproof.
réimportation [ʀeɛ̃pɔʀtɑsjɔ̃] *nf* reimportation.
réimporter [ʀeɛ̃pɔʀte] (1) *vt* to reimport.
réimposer [ʀeɛ̃poze] (1) *vt* **(a)** (*Fin*) to impose a new *ou* further tax on. **(b)** (*Typ*) to reimpose.
réimposition [ʀeɛ̃pozisjɔ̃] *nf* (*V* **réimposer**) further taxation; reimposition.
réimpression [ʀeɛ̃pʀesjɔ̃] *nf* (*action*) reprinting, reimpression; (*livre*) reprint.
réimprimer [ʀeɛ̃pʀime] (1) *vt* to reprint.
Reims [ʀɛ̃s] *n* Rheims.
rein [ʀɛ̃] *nm* **(a)** (*organe*) kidney. **~ artificiel** kidney machine.
(b) (*région*) **~s** (small of the) back, loins (*littér*); **avoir mal aux ~s** to have backache (*low down in one's back*), have an ache in the small of one's back; **avoir les ~s solides** (*lit*) to have a strong *ou* sturdy back; (*fig*) to be on a sound (financial) footing, have a solid financial backing; (*fig*) **casser** *ou* **briser les ~s à qn** to ruin *ou* break sb; *V* **coup, creux** *etc*.
réincarcération [ʀeɛ̃kaʀseʀɑsjɔ̃] *nf* reimprisonment, reincarceration.
réincarcérer [ʀeɛ̃kaʀseʀe] (6) *vt* to reimprison, reincarcerate.
réincarnation [ʀeɛ̃kaʀnɑsjɔ̃] *nf* reincarnation.
réincarner (se) [ʀeɛ̃kaʀne] (1) *vpr* to be reincarnated.
réincorporer [ʀeɛ̃kɔʀpɔʀe] (1) *vt* to re-enlist.
reine [ʀɛn] **1** *nf* (*Échecs, Pol, Zool, fig*) queen. **la ~ d'Angleterre** the Queen of England; **la ~ Élisabeth** Queen Elizabeth; **la ~ mère** (*lit*) the Queen mother; (**fig*) her ladyship*; **la ~ du bal** the queen *ou* the belle of the ball; **~ de beauté** beauty queen; (*fig*) **l'infanterie est la ~ des batailles** the infantry reigns supreme in battle; **la ~ des abeilles/des fourmis** the queen bee/ant; *V* **bouchée, petit, port²**.
2: reine-claude *nf, pl* **reine(s)-claudes** greengage; **reine-marguerite** *nf, pl* **reines-marguerites** (China) aster; **reine des prés** meadowsweet; **reine des reinettes** rennet.
reinette [ʀɛnɛt] *nf* rennet, pippin. **~ grise** russet.
réinfecter [ʀeɛ̃fɛkte] (1) *vt* to reinfect. **la plaie s'est réinfectée** the wound has become infected again.
réinfection [ʀeɛ̃fɛksjɔ̃] *nf* reinfection.
réinscription [ʀeɛ̃skʀipsjɔ̃] *nf* reregistration, re-enrolment.
réinscrire [ʀeɛ̃skʀiʀ] (39) **1** *vt épitaphe* to reinscribe; *date, nom* to put down again; *élève* to re-enrol, reregister. **je n'ai pas réinscrit** *ou* **fait ~ mon fils à la cantine cette année** I haven't reregistered my son for school meals this year.
2 se réinscrire *vpr* to re-enrol, reregister.
réinsérer [ʀeɛ̃seʀe] (6) *vt publicité, feuillet* to reinsert; *délinquant, handicapé* to reintegrate, rehabilitate. **se ~ dans la société** to rehabilitate o.s. in society.
réinsertion [ʀeɛ̃sɛʀsjɔ̃] *nf* (*V* **réinsérer**) reinsertion; reintegration, rehabilitation.
réinstallation [ʀeɛ̃stalɑsjɔ̃] *nf* (*V* **réinstaller**) putting back; reinstallation; putting up again; connecting up again. **notre ~ à Paris/dans l'appartement va poser des problèmes** (our) settling back in Paris/into the flat is going to create problems.
réinstaller [ʀeɛ̃stale] (1) **1** *vt cuisinière* to put back, reinstall; *étagère* to put back up, put up again, reinstall; *téléphone* to connect up again, put back in, reinstall. **~ qn chez lui** to reinstall sb in *ou* move sb back into his (own) home; **~ qn dans ses fonctions** to reinstate sb (in his job), give sb his job back.
2 se réinstaller *vpr* (*dans un fauteuil*) to settle down again (*dans* in); (*dans une maison*) to settle back (*dans* into). **il s'est réinstallé à Paris** (*gén*) he has gone back to live in Paris; *[commerçant]* he has set up in business again in Paris.
réintégration [ʀeɛ̃tegʀɑsjɔ̃] *nf* (*V* **réintégrer**) reinstatement (*dans* in); return (*de* to).
réintégrer [ʀeɛ̃tegʀe] (6) *vt* **(a) ~ qn (dans ses fonctions)** to reinstate sb (in his job), restore sb to his (former) position. **(b)** *lieu* to return to, go back to. **~ le domicile conjugal** to return to the marital home.
réintroduction [ʀeɛ̃tʀɔdyksjɔ̃] *nf* (*V* **réintroduire**) reintroduction; putting back.
réintroduire [ʀeɛ̃tʀɔdɥiʀ] (38) *vt personne, mode* to reintroduce, introduce again. **~ qch dans une lettre** to put sth back in a letter; **~ des erreurs dans un texte** to reintroduce errors *ou* put errors back into a text.
réinventer [ʀeɛ̃vɑ̃te] (1) *vt* to reinvent.
réinviter [ʀeɛ̃vite] (1) *vt* to invite back, ask back again, reinvite.
réitératif, -ive [ʀeiteʀatif, iv] *adj* reiterative.
réitération [ʀeiteʀɑsjɔ̃] *nf* reiteration, repetition.
réitérer [ʀeiteʀe] (6) *vt promesse, ordre, question* to reiterate, repeat; *demande, exploit* to repeat. **attaques réitérées** repeated attacks; **le criminel a réitéré** the criminal has repeated his crime *ou* has done it again.
reître [ʀɛtʀ(ə)] *nm* (*littér*) ruffianly *ou* roughneck soldier.
rejaillir [ʀ(ə)ʒajiʀ] (2) *vi [liquide]* to splash back *ou* up (*sur* onto, at); (*avec force*) to spurt back *ou* up (*sur* onto, at); *[boue]* to splash up (*sur* onto, at). **~ sur qn** *[scandale, honte]* to rebound on sb; *[gloire]* to be reflected on sb; **l'huile bouillante m'a rejailli à la figure** the boiling oil splashed up in my face; **les bienfaits de cette invention rejailliront sur tous** the benefits of this invention will fall upon everyone, everyone will have a share in the benefits of this invention.
rejaillissement [ʀ(ə)ʒajismɑ̃] *nm* (*V* **rejaillir**) splashing up; spurting up; rebounding; reflection.
rejet [ʀ(ə)ʒɛ] *nm* **(a)** (*action: V* **rejeter**) bringing *ou* throwing up, vomiting; spewing out; throwing out; casting up, washing up; discharge; pushing back, driving back, repulsion; casting out, expulsion; rejection; dismissal; throwing back, tossing back. **en anglais, le ~ de la préposition à la fin de la phrase est courant** putting the preposition at the end of the sentence is quite usual *ou* is common practice in English.
(b) (*Bot*) shoot; (*Littérat*) enjambment, rejet; (*Méd*) *[greffe]* rejection.
rejetable [ʀəʒtabl(ə)] *adj* (*littér*) which must be rejected. **difficilement ~** difficult to reject.
rejeter [ʀəʒte] (4) **1** *vt* **(a)** (*relancer*) *objet* to throw back (*à* to).
(b) (*vomir, recracher*) *nourriture, dîner, sang* to bring *ou* throw up, vomit. **son estomac rejette toute nourriture** his stomach rejects everything; **le volcan rejette de la lave** the volcano is spewing *ou* throwing out lava; **le cadavre a été rejeté par la mer** the corpse was cast up *ou* washed up by the sea; **les déchets que rejettent les usines polluent les rivières** the waste thrown out *ou* discharged by factories pollutes the rivers.
(c) (*repousser*) *envahisseur* to push back, drive back, repulse; *indésirable* to cast out, expel; *domination* to reject; *projet de loi* to reject, throw out; *offre, demande, conseil* to reject, turn down; *recours en grâce, hypothèse* to reject, dismiss. **la machine rejette les mauvaises pièces de monnaie** the machine rejects *ou* refuses invalid coins; **le village l'a rejeté après ce dernier scandale** the village has rejected him *ou* cast him out after this latest scandal; **~ d'un parti les éléments suspects** to cast out *ou* eject *ou* expel the suspicious elements from a party.
(d) ~ une faute sur qn/qch to shift *ou* transfer the blame *ou* responsibility for a mistake onto sb/sth; **il rejette la responsabilité sur moi** he lays the responsibility at my door.
(e) (*placer*) **la préposition est rejetée à la fin** the preposition is put at the end; **~ la tête en arrière** to throw *ou* toss one's head back; **~ ses cheveux en arrière** (*avec la main*) to push one's hair back; (*en se coiffant*) to comb *ou* brush one's hair back; **~ les épaules en arrière pour se tenir droit** to pull one's shoulders back to stand up straight; **le chapeau rejeté en arrière** with his hat tilted back; **~ la terre en dehors d'une tranchée** to throw the earth out of a trench.
2 se rejeter *vpr* **(a) se ~ sur qch** to fall back on sth; **faute de viande, on se rejette sur le fromage*** as there is no meat we'll have to fall back on cheese.
(b) se ~ en arrière to jump *ou* leap back(wards); **il s'est rejeté dans l'eau** he jumped back *ou* threw himself back into the water; **ils se rejettent (l'un l'autre) la responsabilité de la rupture** they lay the responsibility for the break-up at each other's door, each wants the other to take responsibility for the break-up.
rejeton [ʀəʒtɔ̃] *nm* **(a)** (*: *enfant*) kid*. **il veut que son ~ soit dentiste** he wants his son and heir (*hum*) *ou* his kid* to be a dentist; **la mère et ses ~s** the mother and her kids* *ou* her offspring (*hum*).
(b) (*Bot*) shoot; (*fig*) offshoot.
rejoindre [ʀ(ə)ʒwɛ̃dʀ(ə)] (49) **1** *vt* **(a)** (*regagner, retrouver*) *lieu* to get (back) to; *route* to get (back) (on)to; *personne* to (re)join, meet (again); *poste, régiment* to rejoin, return to. **la route rejoint la voie ferrée à X** the road meets (up with) *ou* joins the railway line at X.
(b) (*rattraper*) to catch up (with). **je n'arrive pas à le ~** I can't manage to catch up with him *ou* to catch him up.
(c) (*se rallier à*) *parti* to join; *point de vue* to agree with. **je vous rejoins sur ce point** I agree with you *ou* I'm at one with you on that point; **mon idée rejoint la vôtre** my idea is closely akin to yours *ou* is very much like yours; **c'est ici que la prudence rejoint la lâcheté** this is where prudence comes close to *ou* is closely akin to cowardice.
(d) (*réunir*) *personnes* to reunite, bring back together; *choses* to bring together (again); *lèvres d'une plaie* to close.
2 se rejoindre *vpr [routes]* to join, meet; *[idées]* to concur, be closely akin to each other; *[personnes] (pour rendez-vous)* to meet (up) (again); (*sur point de vue*) to agree, be at one.
rejointoyer [ʀ(ə)ʒwɛ̃twaje] (8) *vt* to repoint, regrout.
rejouer [ʀ(ə)ʒwe] (1) **1** *vt* (*gén*) to play again; *match* to replay. (*Cartes*) **~ cœur** to lead hearts again; **on rejoue une partie?** shall we have *ou* play another game?; **~ une pièce** *[acteurs]* to perform a play again, give another performance of a play; *[théâtre]* to put on a play again; **nous rejouons demain à Marseille** *[acteurs]* we're performing again tomorrow at Marseilles; *[joueurs]* we're playing again tomorrow at Marseilles.
2 *vi [enfants, joueurs]* to play again; *[musicien]* to play *ou* perform again. **acteur qui ne pourra plus jamais ~** actor who will never be able to act *ou* perform again.
réjoui, e [ʀeʒwi] (*ptp de* **réjouir**) *adj air, mine* joyful, joyous.
réjouir [ʀeʒwiʀ] (2) **1** *vt personne, regard, estomac* to delight; *cœur* to gladden. **cette perspective le réjouit** this prospect delights *ou* thrills him, he is delighted *ou* thrilled at this prospect; **cette idée ne me réjouit pas beaucoup** I don't find the thought of it particularly appealing.
2 se réjouir *vpr* to be delighted *ou* thrilled (*de faire* to do). **se ~ de** *nouvelle, événement* to be delighted *ou* thrilled about *ou* at; *malheur* to take delight in, rejoice over; **vous avez gagné et je m'en réjouis pour vous** you've won and I'm delighted for you; **se ~ (à la pensée) que** to be delighted *ou* thrilled (at the thought) that; **je me réjouis à l'avance de les voir** I am greatly looking forward to seeing them; **réjouissez-vous!** rejoice!
réjouissance [ʀeʒwisɑ̃s] *nf* rejoicing. **~s** festivities, merrymaking (*U*); (*fig hum*) **quel est le programme des ~s pour la**

journée? what delights are in store (for us) today? (*hum*), what's on the agenda for today?*

réjouissant, e [ʀeʒwisɑ̃, ɑ̃t] *adj histoire* amusing, entertaining; *nouvelle* cheering, cheerful, joyful. (*iro*) **quelle perspective ~e!** what a delightful *ou* heartening prospect! (*iro*); **ce n'est pas ~!** it's no joke!; (*iro*) **c'est ~!** that's great!* (*iro*).

rejuvénation [ʀəʒyvenɑsjɔ̃] *nf* rejuvenation.

relâche [ʀ(ə)lɑʃ] **1** *nm ou nf* **(a)** (*littér: répit*) respite (*littér*), rest. **prendre un peu de ~** to take a short rest *ou* break; **se donner ~** to give o.s. a rest; **sans ~** without (a) respite (*littér*).

(b) (*Théât*) closure. **faire ~** to be closed, close; '**~**' 'no performance(s) (today *ou* this week *etc*)'; **le lundi est le jour de ~ du cinéma local** the local cinema is closed on Monday(s).

2 *nf* (*Naut*) port of call. **faire ~ dans un port** to put in at *ou* call at a port.

relâché, e [ʀ(ə)lɑʃe] (*ptp de* **relâcher**) *adj style* loose, limp; *conduite, mœurs* loose, lax; *discipline, autorité* lax, slack.

relâchement [ʀ(ə)lɑʃmɑ̃] *nm* (*V* **relâcher**) relaxation; loosening; slackening; release; laxity; flagging. **il y a du ~ dans la discipline** discipline is getting lax *ou* slack, there is some slackening *ou* relaxation of discipline.

relâcher [ʀ(ə)lɑʃe] (1) **1** *vt* **(a)** (*desserrer*) *étreinte* to relax, loosen; *lien* to loosen, slacken (off); *muscle* to relax; *ressort* to release. **~ les intestins** to loosen the bowels.

(b) (*affaiblir*) *attention, discipline, effort* to relax, slacken; *surveillance* to relax.

(c) (*libérer*) *prisonnier, otage, gibier* to release, let go, set free.

(d) (*refaire tomber*) *objet* to drop again, let go of again; *corde* to let go of again. **ne relâche pas la corde** don't let go of the rope again.

2 *vi* (*Naut*) **~ (dans un port)** to put into port.

3 se relâcher *vpr* **(a)** *[courroie]* to loosen, go *ou* get loose *ou* slack; *[muscle]* to relax.

(b) *[surveillance, discipline]* to become *ou* get lax *ou* slack; *[mœurs]* to become *ou* get lax *ou* loose; *[style]* to become loose *ou* limp; *[courage, attention]* to flag; *[effort, zèle]* to slacken, flag, fall off. **il se relâche** he's growing slack; **ne te relâche pas maintenant!** don't let up *ou* slack(en) off now!; **il se relâche dans son travail** he's growing slack in his work, his work is getting slack.

relais [ʀ(ə)lɛ] *nm* **(a)** (*Sport*) relay (race). **400 mètres ~, ~ 4 fois 100 mètres** 400 metres relay.

(b) (*Ind*) **travailler par ~** to work shifts, do shift work; **ouvriers/équipe de ~** shift workers/team; **prendre le ~ (de qn)** to take over (from sb); (*fig*) **la pluie ayant cessé, c'est la neige qui a pris le ~** once the rain had stopped the snow took over *ou* set in.

(c) (*chevaux, chiens*) relay. (*Hist: auberge*) **~ (de poste)** post house, coaching inn; **~ routier** transport café; *V* **cheval**.

(d) (*Élec, Rad, Téléc*) (*action*) relaying; (*dispositif*) relay. **~ de télévision** television relay station; **avion/satellite de ~** relay plane/satellite.

relance [ʀ(ə)lɑ̃s] *nf* **(a)** (*action: reprise*) *[économie, industrie]* boosting, stimulation; *[idée, projet]* revival, relaunching. (*résultat*) **la ~ de l'économie n'a pas duré** the boost (given) to the economy did not last; **la ~ du terrorisme est due à ...** the fresh outburst of terrorism is due to ... ; **provoquer la ~ de** *économie* to give a boost to, boost, stimulate; *projet* to revive, relaunch.

(b) (*Poker*) **faire une ~** to raise the stakes, make a higher bid; **limiter la ~** to limit the stakes.

relancer [ʀ(ə)lɑ̃se] (3) *vt* **(a)** (*renvoyer*) *objet, ballon* to throw back (again).

(b) (*faire repartir*) *gibier* to start (again); *moteur* to restart; *idée, projet* to revive, relaunch; *économie, industrie* to boost, give a boost to, stimulate.

(c) (*harceler*) *débiteur* to pester, badger; *femme* to pester, chase after.

(d) (*Cartes*) *enjeu* to raise.

relaps, e [ʀ(ə)laps, aps(ə)] **1** *adj* relapsed. **2** *nm,f* relapsed heretic.

rélargir [ʀelaʀʒiʀ] (2) *vt* **(a)** (*agrandir*) *rue* to widen further; *vêtement* to let out further *ou* more. **(b)** (*à nouveau*) to widen again; to let out again.

rélargissement [ʀelaʀʒismɑ̃] *nm [route]* widening.

relater [ʀ(ə)late] (1) *vt* (*littér*) *événement, aventure* to relate, recount; (*Jur*) *pièce, fait* to record. **le journaliste relate que** the journalist says that *ou* tells us that; **pourriez-vous ~ les faits tels que vous les avez observés** could you state *ou* recount the facts exactly as you observed them.

relatif, -ive [ʀ(ə)latif, iv] **1** *adj* (*gén, Gram, Mus*) relative; *silence, luxe* relative, comparative. **tout est ~** everything is relative; **discussions ~ives à un sujet** discussions relative to *ou* relating to *ou* connected with a subject.

2 *nm* **(a)** (*Gram*) relative pronoun.

(b) avoir le sens du ~ to have a sense of proportion.

3 relative *nf* (*Gram*) relative clause.

relation [ʀ(ə)lɑsjɔ̃] *nf* **(a)** (*gén, Math, Philos*) relation(ship). **~ de cause à effet** relation(ship) of cause and effect; **la ~ entre l'homme et l'environnement** the relation(ship) between man and the environment; **il y a une ~ évidente entre** there is an obvious connection *ou* relation(ship) between; **c'est sans ~** *ou* **cela n'a aucune ~ avec** it has no connection with, it bears no relation to; **~ causale** causal relation(ship).

(b) (*rapports*) **~s** (*gén*) relations; (*sur le plan personnel*) relationship, relations; **~s diplomatiques/culturelles/publiques** diplomatic/cultural/public relations; **les ~s sont tendues/cordiales entre nous** relations between us are strained/cordial, the relationship between us *ou* our relationship is strained/cordial; **avoir des ~s avec une femme** to have sexual relations *ou* intercourse with a woman; **avoir des ~s amoureuses avec qn** to have an affair *ou* a love affair with sb; **avoir de bonnes ~s/des ~s amicales avec qn** to be on good/friendly terms with sb, have a good/friendly relationship with sb; **avoir des ~s de bon voisinage avec qn** to be on neighbourly terms with sb; **être en ~s d'affaires avec qn** to have business relations *ou* business dealings *ou* a business relationship with sb; **être/rester en ~(s) avec qn** to be/keep in touch *ou* contact with sb; **entrer** *ou* **se mettre en ~(s) avec qn** to get in touch *ou* make contact with sb; **être en ~s épistolaires avec qn** to be in correspondence with sb; **nous sommes en ~s suivies** we have frequent contact with each other, we are in constant contact *ou* touch (with each other).

(c) (*connaissance*) acquaintance. **une de mes ~s** an acquaintance of mine, someone I know; **trouver un poste par ~s** to find a job through one's connections, find a job by knowing somebody *ou* by knowing the right people; **avoir des ~s** to have (influential) connections, know (all) the right people.

(d) (*récit*) account, report. **~ orale/écrite** oral/written account *ou* report; **d'après la ~ d'un témoin** according to a witness's account; **faire la ~ des événements/de son voyage** to give an account of *ou* relate the events/one's journey.

relativement [ʀ(ə)lativmɑ̃] *adv* **(a)** *facile, honnête, rare* relatively, comparatively. **(b) ~ à** (*par comparaison*) in relation to, compared to; (*concernant*) with regard to, concerning.

relativisme [ʀ(ə)lativism(ə)] *nm* relativism.

relativiste [ʀ(ə)lativist(ə)] **1** *adj* relativistic. **2** *nmf* relativist.

relativité [ʀ(ə)lativite] *nf* relativity.

relaver [ʀ(ə)lave] (1) *vt* to wash again, rewash.

relax* [ʀ(ə)laks] *adj* = **relaxe**[2]*****.

relaxation [ʀ(ə)laksɑsjɔ̃] *nf* relaxation. **j'ai besoin de ~** I need to relax, I need a bit of relaxation.

relaxe[1] [ʀ(ə)laks(ə)] *nf* (*V* **relaxer**) acquittal, discharge; release.

relaxe[2]***** [ʀ(ə)laks(ə)] *adj ambiance* relaxed, informal; *tenue* informal, casual; *personne* relaxed, easy-going. **siège** *ou* **fauteuil ~** reclining chair.

relaxer [ʀ(ə)lakse] (1) **1** *vt* **(a)** (*acquitter*) *prisonnier* to acquit, discharge; (*relâcher*) to release. **(b)** *muscles* to relax. **2 se relaxer** *vpr* to relax.

relayer [ʀ(ə)leje] (8) **1** *vt* **(a)** to relieve, take over from. **se faire ~** to get somebody to take over (from one), hand over to somebody else.

(b) (*Rad, TV*) to relay.

2 se relayer *vpr* to take turns (*pour faire* to do, at doing), take it in turns (*pour faire* to do); (*dans un relais*) to take over from one another.

relayeur, -euse [ʀ(ə)lɛjœʀ, øz] *nm,f* relay runner.

relecture [ʀ(ə)lɛktyʀ] *nf* rereading.

relégation [ʀ(ə)legɑsjɔ̃] *nf* (*V* **reléguer**) relegation; banishment.

reléguer [ʀ(ə)lege] (6) *vt* **(a)** (*confiner*) *personne, problème* to relegate (*à* to); *objet* to consign, relegate (*à, dans* to); (*Sport*) to relegate (*en* to). **~ qch/qn au second plan** to relegate sth/sb to a position of secondary importance.

(b) (*Jur: exiler*) to relegate, banish.

relent [ʀ(ə)lɑ̃] *nm* foul smell, stench (*U*). **un ~** *ou* **des ~s de poisson pourri** the *ou* a stench *ou* foul smell of rotten fish, the reek of rotten fish; (*fig*) **ça a des ~s de vengeance** it reeks of vengeance.

relevable [ʀəlvabl(ə)] *adj siège* tip-up (*épith*).

relevage [ʀəlvaʒ] *nm [objet]* standing up again, raising.

relève [ʀ(ə)lɛv] *nf* **(a)** (*personne*) relief; (*travailleurs*) relief (team); (*troupe*) relief (troops); (*sentinelles*) relief (guard).

(b) (*action*) relief. **la ~ de la garde** the changing of the guards; **assurer** *ou* **prendre la ~ de qn** (*lit*) to relieve sb, take over from sb; (*fig*) to take over (from sb).

relevé, e [ʀəlve] (*ptp de* **relever**) **1** *adj* **(a)** *col* turned-up; *virage* banked; *manches* rolled-up; *tête* (*lit*) held up; (*fig*) held high. **chapeau à bords ~s** hat with a turned-up brim; **porter les cheveux ~s** to wear one's hair up.

(b) (*noble*) *style, langue, sentiments* elevated, lofty. **cette expression n'est pas très ~e** it's not a very choice *ou* refined expression.

(c) (*Culin*) *sauce, mets* highly-seasoned, spicy.

2 *nm [dépenses]* summary, statement; (*repérage, résumé*) *[cote]* plotting; (*liste*) *[citations, adresses]* list; (*facture*) bill. **faire un ~ de** *citations, erreurs* to list, note down; *notes* to take down; *compteur* to read; **prochain ~ du compteur le mois prochain** next meter reading *ou* reading of the meter next month; **~ de gaz/de téléphone** gas/telephone bill; **~ bancaire** *ou* **de compte** bank statement; **~ de condamnations** police record; **~ d'identité bancaire** (bank) account number; **~ de notes** ≃ (school) report.

3 relevée†† *nf*: **à 2/3 heures de ~e** at 2/3 o'clock in the afternoon.

relèvement [ʀ(ə)lɛvmɑ̃] *nm* (*V* **relever**) standing up again; picking up; righting; setting upright; banking; turning up; raising; tipping up; lifting up; rebuilding; putting back on its feet; rise (*de* in); increase (*de* in); putting up; plotting. **le ~ du salaire minimum** (*action*) the raising of the minimum wage; (*résultat*) the rise in the minimum wage; **on assiste à un ~ spectaculaire du pays/de l'économie** we are witnessing a spectacular recovery of the country/economy; (*Naut*) **faire un ~ de sa position** to plot one's position.

relever [ʀəlve] (5) **1** *vt* **(a)** (*redresser*) *statue, meuble* to stand up again; *chaise* to stand up (again), pick up; *véhicule* to right, set upright again; *bateau* to right; *personne* to help (back) up, help (back) to his feet; *blessé* to pick up; (*Aut*) *virage* to bank. ~ **une vieille dame tombée dans la rue** to help up an old lady who has fallen in the street; ~ **la tête** (*lit*) to lift *ou* hold up one's head; (*fig: se rebeller*) to show signs of rebelling; (*fig: être fier*) to hold one's head up *ou* high again.

(b) (*remonter*) *col* to turn up; *chaussettes* to pull up; *jupe* to raise, lift; *manche, pantalon* to roll up; *cheveux* to put up; *mur, étagère, plafond* to raise, heighten; *vitre* (*en poussant*) to push up; (*avec manivelle*) to wind up; *store* to roll up, raise; *niveau* to raise, bring up; *siège* to tip up; *couvercle* to lift (up). **elle releva son voile** she lifted *ou* raised her veil; **lorsqu'il releva les yeux** when he lifted (up) *ou* raised his eyes, when he looked up.

(c) (*remettre en état*) *mur en ruines* to rebuild; *pays, entreprise, économie* to put back on its feet. (*fig*) ~ **le courage de qn** to restore sb's courage; (*fig*) ~ **le moral de qn** to boost *ou* raise sb's spirits, cheer sb up.

(d) (*augmenter*) *salaire, impôts* to raise, increase, put up; *niveau de vie* to raise; *chiffre d'affaires* to increase. **les devoirs étaient si mauvais que j'ai dû ~ toutes les notes de 2 points** the exercises were so badly done that I had to put up *ou* raise *ou* increase all the marks by 2 points; **cela ne l'a pas relevé dans mon estime** that didn't improve my opinion of him, that did nothing to heighten my opinion of him.

(e) *sauce, plat* to season, add seasoning *ou* spice to. ~ **le goût d'un mets avec des épices** to pep up the flavour of a dish with spice *ou* by adding spice; **ce plat aurait pu être un peu plus relevé** this dish could have done with a bit more seasoning; (*fig*) **mettre des touches de couleurs claires pour ~ un tableau un peu terne** to add dabs of light colour to brighten *ou* liven up a rather dull picture; (*fig*) **bijoux qui relèvent la beauté d'une femme** jewellery that sets off *ou* enhances a woman's beauty.

(f) (*relayer*) *sentinelle* to relieve, take over from. **à quelle heure viendra-t-on me ~?** when will I be relieved?, when is someone coming to take over from me?; ~ **la garde** to change the guard.

(g) (*remarquer*) *faute* to pick out, find; *empreintes, faits* to find, discover. (*Jur*) **les charges relevées contre l'accusé** the charges laid against the accused.

(h) (*inscrire*) *adresse, renseignement* to take down, note (down); *notes* to take down; *plan* to copy out, sketch; (*Naut*) *point* to plot; *compteur, électricité* to read. **j'ai fait ~ le nom des témoins** I had the name of the witnesses noted (down) *ou* taken down; ~ **une cote** to plot an altitude.

(i) *injure, calomnie* to react to, reply to; *défi* to accept, take up, answer. **je n'ai pas relevé cette insinuation** I ignored this insinuation, I did not react *ou* reply to this insinuation; **il a dit un gros mot mais je n'ai pas relevé** he said a rude word but I didn't react *ou* I ignored it; ~ **le gant** to take up the gauntlet.

(j) (*ramasser*) *copies, cahiers* to collect (in), take in; (††) *mouchoir, gerbe* to pick up.

(k) ~ **qn de qch** to release sb from sth; **je te relève de ta promesse** I release you from your promise; ~ **un fonctionnaire de ses fonctions** to relieve an official of his position.

2 relever de *vt indir* **(a)** (*se rétablir*) ~ **de maladie** to recover from *ou* get over an illness, get back on one's feet (after an illness)*; ~ **de couches** to recover from *ou* get over one's confinement.

(b) (*être du ressort de*) to be a matter for, be the concern of; (*être sous la tutelle de*) to come under. **cela relève de la Sécurité sociale** that is a matter for *ou* the concern of the Social Security; **cela relève de la théologie** that is a matter for the theologians, that comes *ou* falls within the province of theology; **ce service relève du ministère de l'Intérieur** this service comes under the Home Office; **ça relève de l'imagination la plus fantaisiste** that is a product of the wildest imagination.

3 *vi* (*remonter*) *[vêtement]* to pull up, go up. **jupe qui relève par devant** skirt that rides up at the front.

4 se relever *vpr* **(a)** (*se remettre debout*) to stand *ou* get up (again), get back (on)to one's feet (again). **le boxeur se releva** the boxer got up again *ou* got back to his feet *ou* picked himself up; **l'arbitre a fait (se) ~ les joueurs** the referee made the players get up.

(b) (*sortir du lit*) to get up; (*ressortir du lit*) to get up again. (*lit, euph*) **se ~ la nuit** to get up in the night; **il m'a fait (me) ~ pour que je lui apporte à boire** he made me get up to fetch him a drink.

(c) (*remonter*) *[col]* to turn up, be turned up; *[strapontin]* to tip up; *[couvercle, tête de lit]* to lift up. **ses lèvres se relevaient dans un sourire** his mouth turned up in a smile; **est-ce que cette fenêtre se relève?** does this window go up?; **à l'heure où tous les stores de magasins se relèvent** when all the shop-blinds are going up.

(d) (*se remettre de*) **se ~ de** *deuil, chagrin, honte* to recover from, get over; **se ~ de ses ruines/cendres** to rise from its ruins/ashes.

releveur [ʀəlvœʀ] **1** *adj m*: **muscle ~** levator (muscle). **2** *nm* **(a)** (*Anat*) levator. **(b)** *[compteur]* meter reader, meter man*. ~ **du gaz** gasman*.

relief [ʀəljɛf] *nm* **(a)** (*Géog*) relief. **avoir un ~ accidenté** to be hilly; **région de peu de ~** fairly flat region; **le ~ sous-marin** the relief of the sea bed.

(b) (*saillies*) *[visage]* contours (*pl*); *[médaille]* relief, embossed *ou* raised design; (*Art*) relief. **la pierre ne présentait aucun ~** the stone was quite smooth.

(c) (*profondeur, contraste*) *[dessin]* relief, depth; *[style]* relief. **portrait/photographie qui a beaucoup de ~** portrait/photograph which has plenty of relief *ou* depth; ~ **acoustique** *ou* **sonore** depth of sound; **personnage qui manque de ~** rather flat *ou* uninteresting character; **votre dissertation manque de ~** your essay is lacking in relief *ou* is rather flat.

(d) en ~ *motif* in relief, raised; *caractères* raised, embossed; *photographie, cinéma* three-dimensional, 3-D*, stereoscopic; **l'impression est en ~** the printing stands out in relief; **carte en ~** relief map; **mettre en ~** *intelligence* to bring out; *beauté, qualités* to set off, enhance, accentuate; *idée* to bring out, accentuate; **l'éclairage mettait en ~ les imperfections de son visage** the lighting brought out *ou* accentuated the imperfections of her face; **je tiens à mettre ce point en ~** I wish to underline *ou* stress *ou* emphasize this point; **il essayait de se mettre en ~ en monopolisant la conversation** he was trying to get himself noticed by monopolizing the conversation.

(e) ~s (†: *d'un repas*) remains, left-overs; (*littér*) **les ~s de sa gloire** the remnants of his glory.

relier [ʀəlje] (7) *vt* **(a)** *points, mots* to join *ou* link up *ou* together; (*Élec*) to connect (up); *villes* to link (up); *idées* to link (up *ou* together); *faits* to connect (together), link (up *ou* together). ~ **deux choses entre elles** to link *ou* join up two things, link *ou* join two things together; **des vols fréquents relient Paris à New York** frequent flights link Paris and New York; **nous sommes reliés au studio par voiture-radio** we have a radio-car link to the studio; (*Téléc*) **nous sommes reliés à Paris par l'automatique** we are linked to Paris by the automatic dialling system; **ce verbe est relié à son complément par une préposition** this verb is linked to its complement by a preposition; ~ **le passé au présent** to link the past to the present, link the past and the present (together).

(b) *livre* to bind; *tonneau* to hoop. **livre relié** bound volume, hard-back (book); **livre relié (en) cuir** leather-bound book, book bound in leather.

relieur, -euse [ʀəljœʀ, øz] *nm,f* (book)binder.

religieusement [ʀ(ə)liʒjøzmɑ̃] *adv* (*Rel, fig*) religiously; *écouter* religiously, reverently; *tenir sa parole* scrupulously, religiously. **vivre ~** to lead a religious life.

religieux, -euse [ʀ(ə)liʒjø, øz] **1** *adj* **(a)** (*Rel*) *édifice, secte, cérémonie, opinion* religious; *art* sacred; *école, mariage, musique* church (*épith*); *vie, ordres, personne* religious. **l'habit ~** the monk's (*ou* nun's) habit.

(b) (*fig*) *respect, soin* religious; *silence* religious, reverent; *V* **mante**.

2 *nm* (*moine*) monk.

3 religieuse *nf* **(a)** (*nonne*) nun.

(b) (*Culin*) cream bun (*made with choux pastry*).

religion [ʀ(ə)liʒjɔ̃] *nf* **(a)** (*U*) **la ~** religion.

(b) (*culte*) (*Rel*) religion, (religious) faith; (*fig*) religion. **la ~ musulmane** the Islamic religion *ou* faith; **la ~ réformée** Calvinism; **se faire une ~ de qch** to make a religion of sth; **elle a la ~ de la propreté** cleanliness is a religion with her.

(c) (*foi*) (religious) faith. **sa ~ est profonde** he is a man of great (religious) faith; (*frm*) **avoir de la ~** to be religious.

(d) (*vie monastique*) monastic life. **elle est entrée en ~** she has taken her vows, she has become a nun.

religiosité [ʀ(ə)liʒjozite] *nf* religiosity.

reliquaire [ʀ(ə)likɛʀ] *nm* reliquary.

reliquat [ʀ(ə)lika] *nm [dette]* remainder, outstanding amount *ou* balance; *[compte]* balance; *[somme]* remainder. **il subsiste un ~ très important/un petit ~** there's a very large/a small amount left (over) *ou* remaining; **arrangez-vous pour qu'il n'y ait pas de ~** work it so that there is nothing left over.

relique [ʀ(ə)lik] *nf* (*Rel, fig*) relic. **garder** *ou* **conserver qch comme une ~** to treasure sth.

relire [ʀ(ə)liʀ] (43) **1** *vt roman* to read again, reread; *manuscrit* to read through again, read over (again), reread. **2 se relire** *vpr* to read (through *ou* over) what one has written.

reliure [ʀəljyʀ] *nf* (*couverture*) binding; (*art, action*) (book)binding. ~ **pleine** full binding; **donner un livre à la ~** to send a book for binding *ou* to the binder('s).

relogement [ʀ(ə)lɔʒmɑ̃] *nm* rehousing.

reloger [ʀ(ə)lɔʒe] (3) *vt* to rehouse.

relouer [ʀəlwe] (1) *vt [locataire]* to rent again; *[propriétaire]* to relet, rent out again. **cette année je reloue dans le Midi** this year I'm renting a place in the South of France again.

reluire [ʀəlɥiʀ] (38) *vi [meuble, chaussures]* to shine, gleam; *[métal, carrosserie]* (*au soleil*) to gleam, shine; (*sous la pluie*) to glisten. **faire ~ qch** to polish *ou* shine sth up, make sth shine; *V* **brosse**.

reluisant, e [ʀəlɥizɑ̃, ɑ̃t] *adj* **(a)** *meubles, parquet, cuivres* shining, shiny, gleaming. ~ **de graisse** shiny with grease; ~ **de pluie** glistening in the rain.

(b) (*fig iro*) **peu ~** *avenir, résultat, situation* far from brilliant (*attrib*); *personne* despicable.

reluquer‡ [ʀ(ə)lyke] (1) *vt femme* to eye (up)*; *passant* to eye, squint at*; *objet* to have one's eye on.

remâcher [ʀ(ə)mɑʃe] (1) *vt [ruminant]* to ruminate; *[personne] passé, soucis, échec* to ruminate over *ou* on, chew over, brood on *ou* over; *colère* to nurse.

remaillage [ʀ(ə)mɑjaʒ] *nm* = **remmaillage**.

remailler [ʀ(ə)mɑje] (1) *vt* = **remmailler**.

remake [ʀimɛk] *nm* (*Ciné*) remake.

rémanence [ʀemanɑ̃s] *nf* (*Phys*) remanence. ~ **des images visuelles** after-imagery.

rémanent, e [ʀemanɑ̃, ɑ̃t] *adj magnétisme* residual. **image ~e** after-image.

remanger [ʀ(ə)mɑ̃ʒe] (3) **1** *vt* (*manger de nouveau*) to have again; (*reprendre*) to have *ou* eat some more. **on a remangé du poulet aujourd'hui** we had chicken again today; **j'en remangerais bien** I'd like to have that again, I could eat that again.

2 *vi* to eat again, have something to eat again.

remaniement [ʀ(ə)manimɑ̃] *nm* (*V* **remanier**) revision; reshaping, recasting; modification, reorganization; amendment; reshuffle. (*Pol*) **~ ministériel** cabinet reshuffle; **apporter un ~ à** to revise; to reshape, recast; to modify, reorganize; to amend; to reshuffle.

remanier [ʀ(ə)manje] (7) *vt roman, discours* to revise, reshape, recast; *encyclopédie* to revise; *programme* to modify, reorganize; *plan, constitution* to revise, amend; *cabinet, ministère* to reshuffle.

remaquiller [ʀ(ə)makije] (1) **1** *vt*: **~ qn** to make sb up again. **2 se remaquiller** *vpr* (*complètement*) to make o.s. up again, redo one's face; (*rapidement*) to touch up one's make-up.

remariage [ʀ(ə)maʀjaʒ] *nm* second marriage, remarriage.

remarier [ʀ(ə)maʀje] (7) **1** *vt*: **~ sa fille** to remarry one's daughter; **il cherche à ~ sa fille** he is trying to find another husband for his daughter. **2 se remarier** *vpr* to remarry, marry again.

remarquable [ʀ(ə)maʀkabl(ə)] *adj personne, exploit, réussite* remarkable, outstanding; *événement, fait* striking, noteworthy, remarkable. **il est ~ par sa taille** he is notable for *ou* he stands out because of his height.

remarquablement [ʀ(ə)maʀkabləmɑ̃] *adv beau, doué* remarkably, outstandingly; *réussir, jouer* remarkably *ou* outstandingly well.

remarque [ʀ(ə)maʀk(ə)] *nf* **(a)** (*observation*) remark, comment; (*critique*) critical remark; (*annotation*) note. **il m'en a fait la ~** he remarked *ou* commented on it to me, he made *ou* passed a remark *ou* made a comment about it to me; **je m'en suis moi-même fait la ~** that occurred to me as well, I thought that myself; **faire une ~ à qn** to make a critical remark to sb, criticize sb; **il m'a fait des ~s sur ma tenue** he passed comment *ou* he remarked on the way I was dressed.

(b) (†, *littér*) **digne de ~** worthy of note, noteworthy.

remarquer [ʀ(ə)maʀke] (1) *vt* **(a)** (*apercevoir*) to notice. **je l'ai remarqué dans la foule** I caught sight of *ou* noticed him in the crowd; **avec ce chapeau, comment ne pas la ~!** with that hat on, how can you fail to notice her?; **l'impresario avait remarqué la jeune actrice lors d'une audition** the impresario had noticed the young actress at an audition, the young actress had come to the notice of the impresario at an audition; **il entra sans être remarqué** *ou* **sans se faire ~** he came in unnoticed *ou* without being noticed; **cette tache se remarque beaucoup/à peine** this stain is quite/hardly noticeable, this stain shows badly/hardly shows; **c'est une femme qui aime se faire ~** she's a woman who likes to be noticed *ou* to draw attention to herself; **je remarque que vous avez une cravate** I see *ou* note that you are wearing a tie; **je remarque que vous ne vous êtes pas excusé** I note that you did not apologize; **ça finirait par se ~** people would start to notice *ou* start noticing.

(b) (*faire une remarque*) to remark, observe. **tu es sot, remarqua son frère** you're stupid, his brother remarked *ou* observed; **il remarqua qu'il faisait froid** he remarked *ou* commented *ou* observed that it was cold; **remarquez (bien) que je n'en sais rien** mark you *ou* mind you I don't know; **ça m'est tout à fait égal, remarque!** I couldn't care less, mark you! *ou* mind you!* *ou* I can tell you!

(c) faire ~ *détail, erreur* to point out, draw attention to; **il me fit ~ qu'il faisait nuit/qu'il était tard** he pointed out to me that *ou* he drew my attention to the fact that it was dark/late; **il me fit ~ qu'il était d'accord avec moi** he pointed out (to me) that he agreed with me; **je te ferai seulement ~ que tu n'as pas de preuves** I should just like to point out (to you) that you have no proof.

(d) (*marquer de nouveau*) to remark, mark again.

remballage [ʀɑ̃balaʒ] *nm* (*V* **remballer**) packing (up) again; rewrapping.

remballer [ʀɑ̃bale] (1) *vt* to pack (up) again; (*dans du papier*) to rewrap. **remballe ta marchandise!**‡ you can clear off (*Brit*) and take that stuff with you!‡; **tu n'as qu'à ~ tes commentaires!**‡ you can stuff your remarks!‡ (*Brit*).

rembarquement [ʀɑ̃baʀkəmɑ̃] *nm* (*V* **rembarquer**) re-embarkation; reloading.

rembarquer [ʀɑ̃baʀke] (1) **1** *vt passagers* to re-embark; *marchandises* to reload. **2** *vi* to re-embark, go back on board (ship). **faire ~ les passagers** to re-embark the passengers. **3 se rembarquer** *vpr* to re-embark, go back on board (ship).

rembarrer [ʀɑ̃baʀe] (1) *vt*: **~ qn** (*recevoir avec froideur*) to brush sb aside, rebuff sb; (*remettre à sa place*) to put sb in his place.

remblai [ʀɑ̃blɛ] *nm* (*Rail, pour route*) embankment; (*Constr*) cut. **(terre de) ~** (*Rail*) ballast, remblai; (*pour route*) hard core; (*Constr*) backfill; **travaux de ~** (*Rail, pour route*) embankment work; (*Constr*) cutting work; (*Aut*) **~s récents** soft verges.

remblaver [ʀɑ̃blave] (1) *vt* (*Agr*) to resow.

remblayage [ʀɑ̃blɛjaʒ] *nm* (*V* **remblayer**) banking up; filling in *ou* up.

remblayer [ʀɑ̃bleje] (8) *vt route, voie ferrée* to bank up; *fossé* to fill in *ou* up.

rembobiner [ʀɑ̃bɔbine] (1) *vt film, bande magnétique* to rewind, wind back; *fil* to rewind, wind up again.

remboîtage [ʀɑ̃bwataʒ] *nm*, **remboîtement** [ʀɑ̃bwatmɑ̃] *nm* (*V* **remboîter**) putting back; reassembly; recasing.

remboîter [ʀɑ̃bwate] (1) *vt tuyaux* to fit together again, reassemble; *os* to put back into place; *livre* to recase.

rembourrage [ʀɑ̃buʀaʒ] *nm* (*V* **rembourrer**) stuffing; padding.

rembourrer [ʀɑ̃buʀe] (1) *vt fauteuil, matelas* to stuff; *vêtement* to pad. (*lit, hum*) **bien rembourré** well-padded; (*hum*) **mal rembourré, rembourré avec des noyaux de pêches** as hard as rock *ou* iron.

remboursable [ʀɑ̃buʀsabl(ə)] *adj billet* refundable; *emprunt* repayable.

remboursement [ʀɑ̃buʀsəmɑ̃] *nm* (*V* **rembourser**) repayment; settlement; reimbursement. **obtenir le ~ de son repas** to get one's money back for one's meal, get a refund on one's meal; **envoi contre ~** cash with order.

rembourser [ʀɑ̃buʀse] (1) *vt dette* to pay back *ou* off, repay, settle (up); *emprunt* to pay back *ou* off, repay; *somme* to reimburse, repay, pay back; *créancier* to pay back *ou* off, repay, reimburse. **~ qn de qch** to reimburse sth to sb, reimburse sb sth, repay sb sth; **~ qn de ses dépenses** to refund *ou* reimburse sb's expenses; **je te rembourserai demain** I'll pay you back *ou* repay you *ou* square up with you* tomorrow; **je me suis fait ~ mon repas/mon voyage** I got my money back for my meal/journey, I got back the cost of my meal/journey, I got the cost of my meal/journey refunded; **est-ce remboursé par la Sécurité sociale?** is it reimbursed by the Social Security?, can we get it back from Social Security?; **~ un billet de loterie** to refund the price of a lottery ticket; (*Théât*) **remboursez!** we want our money back! *ou* a refund!; **puisqu'il n'avait pas l'argent qu'il me devait, je me suis remboursé en prenant son manteau!** since he didn't have the money he owed me, I helped myself to his coat by way of repayment!

rembrunir (se) [ʀɑ̃bʀyniʀ] (2) *vpr [visage, traits]* to darken, cloud over; *[ciel]* to become overcast, darken, cloud over. **le temps se rembrunit** it's clouding over, it's going cloudy.

rembrunissement [ʀɑ̃bʀynismɑ̃] *nm* (*littér*) *[visage, front]* darkening.

remède [ʀ(ə)mɛd] *nm* **(a)** (*Méd*) (*traitement*) remedy, cure; (*médicament*) medicine. **prescrire/prendre un ~ pour un lumbago** to give/take something *ou* some medicine for lumbago; **~ de bonne femme** old wives' *ou* folk cure *ou* remedy; **~ souverain/de cheval** sovereign/drastic remedy; **~ universel** cure-all, universal cure.

(b) (*fig*) remedy, cure. **porter ~ à qch** to cure sth, find a cure for sth, remedy sth; **la situation est sans ~** there is no remedy for the situation, the situation cannot be remedied *ou* is beyond remedy; **le ~ est pire que le mal** the cure is worse than the disease, the solution is even worse than the evil it is designed to remedy; **c'est un ~ à** *ou* **contre l'amour!*** she's (*ou* he's) enough to put you off the opposite sex altogether!*; *V* **à**.

remédiable [ʀ(ə)medjabl(ə)] *adj mal* that can be remedied.

remédier [ʀ(ə)medje] (7) **remédier à** *vt indir* (*lit*) *maladie* to cure; (*fig*) *mal, situation* to remedy, put right; *abus* to remedy, right; *perte* to remedy, make good; *besoin* to remedy; *inconvénient* to remedy, find a remedy for; *difficulté* to find a solution for, solve.

remembrement [ʀ(ə)mɑ̃bʀəmɑ̃] *nm* regrouping of lands.

remembrer [ʀ(ə)mɑ̃bʀe] (1) *vt terres* to regroup; *exploitation* to regroup the lands of.

remémoration [ʀ(ə)memɔʀasjɔ̃] *nf* recall, recollection.

remémorer (se) [ʀ(ə)memɔʀe] (1) *vpr* to recall, recollect.

remerciement [ʀ(ə)mɛʀsimɑ̃] *nm* **(a)** **~s** thanks; (*dans un livre*) acknowledgements; **avec tous mes ~s** with many thanks, with my grateful thanks; **faire ses ~s à qn** to thank sb, express one's thanks to sb.

(b) (*action*) thanks (*pl*), thanking. **le ~ est souvent hypocrite** thanking is often hypocritical; **il lui fit un ~ embarrassé** he thanked him in an embarrassed way; **lettre de ~** thank-you letter, letter of thanks; **lire un ~ à qn** to read a message of thanks to sb.

remercier [ʀ(ə)mɛʀsje] (7) *vt* **(a)** (*dire merci*) to thank (*qn de ou pour qch* sb for sth, *qn d'avoir fait qch* sb for doing sth). **~ le ciel** *ou* **Dieu** to thank God; **~ qn par un cadeau/d'un pourboire** to thank sb with a present/with a tip, give sb a present/a tip by way of thanks; **je ne sais comment vous ~** I can't thank you enough, I don't know how to thank you; **il me remercia d'un sourire** he thanked me with a smile, he smiled his thanks; **je vous remercie** (I) thank you; **tu peux me ~!** you've got me to thank for that!; (*iro*) **je te remercie de tes conseils** thanks for the advice (*iro*), I can do without your advice (thank you) (*iro*).

(b) (*refuser poliment*) **vous voulez boire? — je vous remercie** would you like a drink? — no thank you.

(c) (*euph: renvoyer*) *employé* to dismiss (*from his job*).

remettre [ʀ(ə)mɛtʀ(ə)] (56) **1** *vt* **(a)** (*replacer*) *objet* to put back, replace (*dans* in(to), *sur* on); *os luxé* to put back in place. **~ un enfant au lit** to put a child back (in)to bed; **~ un enfant à l'école** to send a child back to school; **~ qch à cuire** to put sth on to cook again; **~ debout** *enfant* to stand back on his feet; *objet* to stand up again; **~ qch droit** to put *ou* set sth straight again; **~ un bouton à une veste** to sew *ou* put a button back on a jacket; **il a remis l'étagère/la porte qu'il avait enlevée** he put the shelf back up/rehung the door that he had taken down; **~ qn sur la bonne voie** to put sb back on the right track; **~ un enfant insolent à sa place** to put an insolent child in his place.

(b) (*porter de nouveau*) *vêtement, chapeau* to put back on, put on again. **j'ai remis mon manteau d'hiver** I'm wearing my winter coat again.

(c) (*replacer dans une situation*) **~ un appareil en marche** to restart a machine, start a machine (up) again; **~ une coutume en usage** to revive a custom; **~ en question** *institution, autorité* to (call into) question, challenge; *projet, accord* to cast doubt over, throw back into question; **tout est remis en question à cause du mauvais temps** the bad weather throws the whole thing back into question; **~ une pendule à l'heure** to put *ou* set a clock right; **~ qch à neuf** to make sth as good as new again; **~ qch en état** to repair *ou* mend sth; **le repos l'a remise (sur pied)** the rest has set her back on her feet; **~ de l'ordre dans qch** (*ranger*) to tidy sth up, sort sth out; (*classer*) to sort sth out.

(d) (*donner*) *lettre, paquet* to hand over, deliver; *clefs* to hand in *ou* over, give in, return; *récompense* to present; *devoir* to hand in, give in; *rançon* to hand over; *démission* to hand in, give in, tender (*à* to). **il s'est fait ~ les clefs par la concierge** he got *ou* had the keys given to him by the concierge; **~ un enfant à ses parents** to return a child to his parents; **~ un criminel à la justice** to hand a criminal over to the law; **~ à qn un porte-monnaie volé** to hand *ou* give back *ou* return a stolen purse to sb.

(e) (*ajourner*) *réunion* to put off, postpone (*à* until), put back (*à* to); (*Jur*) to adjourn (*à* until); *décision* to put off (*à* until); *date* to put back (*à* to). **une visite qui ne peut se ~ (à plus tard)** a visit that can't be postponed *ou* put off; **~ un rendez-vous à jeudi/au 8** to put off *ou* postpone an appointment till Thursday/the 8th; **il ne faut jamais ~ à demain** *ou* **au lendemain ce qu'on peut faire le jour même** procrastination is the thief of time, never put off till tomorrow what you can do today.

(f) (*se rappeler*) to remember. **je vous remets très bien**† I remember you very well; **je ne me le remets pas**† I can't place him, I don't remember him; (*rappeler*) **~ qch en esprit** *ou* **en mémoire à qn** to remind sb of sth, recall sth to sb; **ce livre m'a remis ces événements en mémoire** this book reminded me of these events *ou* brought these events to mind.

(g) (*rajouter*) *vinaigre, sel* to add more, put in (some) more; *verre, coussin* to add; *maquillage* to put on (some) more. **j'ai froid, je vais ~ un tricot** I'm cold — I'll go and put another jersey on; **~ de l'huile dans le moteur** to top up the engine with oil; **en remettant un peu d'argent, vous pourriez avoir le grand modèle** if you put a little more (money) to it you could have the large size; **il faut ~ de l'argent sur le compte, nous sommes débiteurs** we'll have to put some money into the account as we're overdrawn; **en ~*** to overdo it.

(h) *radio, chauffage* to put *ou* turn *ou* switch on again. **il y a eu une coupure mais le courant a été remis à midi** there was a power cut but the electricity came back on again *ou* was put back on again at midday; **~ le contact** to turn the ignition on again.

(i) (*faire grâce de*) *dette, peine* to remit; *péché* to forgive, pardon, remit. **~ une dette à qn** to remit sb's debt, let sb off a debt; **~ une peine à un condamné** to remit a prisoner's sentence.

(j) (*confier*) **~ son sort/sa vie entre les mains de qn** to put one's fate/life into sb's hands; **~ son âme à Dieu** to commit one's soul to God *ou* into God's keeping.

(k) ~ ça*: (*démarches*) **dire qu'il va falloir ~ ça!** to think that we'll have to go through all that again! *ou* through a repeat performance!*; **quand est-ce qu'on remet ça?** when will the next time be?; **on remet ça?** (*partie de cartes*) shall we have another game?; (*au café*) shall we have another drink? *ou* round?; (*travail*) let's get back to it*, let's get down to it again, let's get going again*; **garçon remettez-nous ça!** (the) same again please!*; (*bruit*) **les voilà qui remettent ça!** here *ou* there they go again!*, they're at it again!*; **tu ne vas pas ~ ça avec tes critiques** no more of your criticism(s); **le gouvernement va ~ ça avec les économies d'énergie** the government is going to get going on energy saving again*.

2 se remettre *vpr* **(a)** (*recouvrer la santé*) to recover, get better, pick up*. **se ~ d'une maladie/d'un accident** to recover from *ou* get over an illness/an accident; **le temps se remet** the weather's getting better; **remettez-vous!** pull yourself together!

(b) (*recommencer*) **se ~ à (faire) qch** to start (doing) sth again; **se ~ à fumer** to take up *ou* start smoking again; **il s'est remis au tennis/au latin** he has taken up tennis/Latin again; **après son départ il se remit à travailler** *ou* **au travail** after she had gone he started working again *ou* went back *ou* got back to work; **il se remet à faire froid** the weather *ou* it is getting *ou* turning cold again; **le temps s'est remis au beau** the weather has turned fine again; **se ~ en selle** to remount, get back on one's horse; **se ~ debout** to get back to one's feet, get (back) up again, stand up again.

(c) (*se confier*) **se ~ entre les mains de qn** to put o.s. in sb's hands; **je m'en remets à vous** I'll leave it (up) to you, I'll leave the matter in your hands; **s'en ~ à la décision de qn** to leave it to sb to decide; **s'en ~ à la discrétion de qn** to leave it to sb's discretion.

(d) (*se réconcilier*) **se ~ avec qn** to make it up with sb, make *ou* patch up one's differences with sb; **ils se sont remis ensemble** they've come back *ou* they are back together again.

remeubler [ʀ(ə)mœble] (1) **1** *vt* to refurnish. **2 se remeubler** *vpr* to refurnish one's house, get new furniture.

rémige [ʀemiʒ] *nf* remix.

remilitarisation [ʀ(ə)militaʀizɑsjɔ̃] *nf* remilitarization.

remilitariser [ʀ(ə)militaʀize] (1) *vt* to remilitarize.

réminiscence [ʀeminisɑ̃s] *nf* (*U: Philos, Psych*) reminiscence; (*souvenir*) reminiscence, vague recollection. **sa conversation était truffée de ~s littéraires** literary influences were constantly in evidence in his conversation; **mon latin est bien rouillé, mais j'ai encore quelques ~s** my Latin is very rusty but I've retained *ou* I still recollect a little; **on trouve des ~s de Rabelais dans l'œuvre de cet auteur** there are echoes of Rabelais in this author's work, parts of this author's work are reminiscent of Rabelais.

remisage [ʀ(ə)mizaʒ] *nm* [*outil, voiture*] putting away.

remise [ʀ(ə)miz] **1** *nf* **(a)** (*livraison*) [*lettre, paquet*] delivery; [*clefs*] handing over; [*récompense*] presentation; [*devoir*] handing in; [*rançon*] handing over, hand-over. (*Jur*) **~ de parts** transfer *ou* conveyance of legacy.

(b) (*grâce*) [*péchés*] remission, forgiveness, pardon; [*dette*] remission; [*peine*] reduction (*de* of, in). **le condamné a bénéficié d'une importante ~ de peine** the prisoner was granted a large reduction in his sentence.

(c) (*Comm: rabais*) discount, reduction. **ils font une ~ de 5% sur les livres scolaires** they're giving *ou* allowing (a) 5% discount *ou* reduction on school books.

(d) (*local: pour outils, véhicules*) shed.

(e) (*ajournement*) [*réunion*] postponement, putting off *ou* back; [*décision*] putting off. **~ à quinzaine d'un débat** postponement of a debate for a fortnight.

2: remise en cause calling into question; **remis en état** [*machine*] repair(ing); [*tableau, meuble ancien*] restoration; (*Sport*) **remise en jeu** throw-in; **remise à jour** updating, bringing up to date; **remise en marche** restarting, starting (up) again; **remise à neuf** restoration; **remise en ordre** reordering, sorting out; **remise en place** [*os, étagère*] putting back in place; **remise en question** calling into question.

remiser [ʀ(ə)mize] (1) **1** *vt* **(a)** *voiture, outil, valise* to put away. **(b)** (*: *rembarrer*) *personne* to send sb packing*. **2** *vi* (*Jeu*) to make another bet, bet again. **3 se remiser** *vpr* [*gibier*] to take cover.

rémissible [ʀemisibl(ə)] *adj* remissible.

rémission [ʀemisjɔ̃] *nf* **(a)** [*péchés*] remission, forgiveness; (*Jur*) remission.

(b) (*Méd*) [*maladie*] remission; [*douleur*] subsidence, abatement; [*fièvre*] subsidence, lowering, abatement; (*fig littér: dans la tempête, le travail*) lull.

(c) sans ~ *travailler, torturer, poursuivre* unremittingly, relentlessly; *payer* without fail; *mal, maladie* irremediable; **si tu recommences tu seras puni sans ~** if you do it again you'll be punished without fail.

remmaillage [ʀɑ̃majaʒ] *nm* (*V* **remmailler**) darning; mending.

remmailler [ʀɑ̃maje] (1) *vt tricot, bas* to darn; *filet* to mend.

remmailleuse [ʀɑ̃majøz] *nf* darner.

remmailloter [ʀɑ̃majɔte] (1) *vt bébé* to change.

remmancher [ʀɑ̃mɑ̃ʃe] (1) *vt couteau, balai* (*remettre le manche*) to put the handle back on; (*remplacer le manche*) to put a new handle on, rehandle.

remmener [ʀɑ̃mne] (5) *vt* to take back, bring back. **~ qn chez lui** to take sb back home; **~ qn à pied/en voiture** to walk/drive sb back.

remodelage [ʀ(ə)mɔdlaʒ] *nm* (*V* **remodeler**) remodelling; replanning; reorganization, restructuring.

remodeler [ʀ(ə)mɔdle] (5) *vt visage* to remodel; *ville* to remodel, replan; *profession, organisation* to reorganize, restructure.

rémois, e [ʀemwa, waz] **1** *adj* of *ou* from Rheims. **2** *nm,f*: **R~(e)** inhabitant *ou* native of Rheims.

remontage [ʀ(ə)mɔ̃taʒ] *nm* [*montre*] rewinding, winding up; [*machine, meuble*] reassembly, putting back together; [*tuyau*] putting back.

remontant, e [ʀ(ə)mɔ̃tɑ̃, ɑ̃t] **1** *adj* **(a)** *boisson* invigorating, fortifying. **(b)** (*Horticulture*) *rosier* remontant; *fraisier, framboisier* double-cropping *ou* -fruiting. **2** *nm* tonic, pick-me-up*.

remonte [ʀ(ə)mɔ̃t] *nf* **(a)** [*bateau*] sailing upstream, ascent; [*poissons*] run. **(b)** (*Équitation*) (*fourniture de chevaux*) remount; (*service*) remount department.

remontée [ʀ(ə)mɔ̃te] *nf* [*côte*] ascent, climbing; [*rivière*] ascent; [*eaux*] rising. **la ~ des mineurs par l'ascenseur** bringing miners up by lift; **il ne faut pas que la ~ du plongeur soit trop rapide** the diver must not go back up *ou* rise too quickly; **la ~ de l'or à la Bourse** the rise in the price *ou* value of gold on the Stock Exchange; **faire une (belle) ~** to catch up the lost ground (well), make a (good) recovery; **faire une ~ spectaculaire (de la 30e à la 2e place)** to make a spectacular recovery (from 30th to 2nd place); (*Sport*) **~ mécanique** skilift.

remonte-pente, *pl* remonte-pentes [ʀ(ə)mɔ̃tpɑ̃t] *nm* skilift.

remonter [ʀ(ə)mɔ̃te] (1) **1** *vi* **(a)** (*monter à nouveau*) to go *ou* come back up. **il remonta à pied** he walked back up; **remonte me voir** come back up and see me; **je remonte demain à Paris (en voiture)** I'm driving back up to Paris tomorrow; **il remonta sur la table** he climbed back (up) onto the table; **~ sur le trône** to come back *ou* return to the throne; (*Théât*) **~ sur les planches** to go back on the stage *ou* the boards.

(b) (*dans un moyen de transport*) **~ en voiture** to get back into one's car, get into one's car again; **~ à cheval** (*se remettre en selle*) to remount (one's horse), get back on(to) one's horse; (*se remettre à faire du cheval*) to take up riding again; (*Naut*) **~ à bord** to go back on board (a ship).

(c) (*s'élever de nouveau*) [*marée*] to come in again; [*prix, température, baromètre*] to rise again, go up again; [*colline, route*] to go up again, rise again. **la mer remonte** the tide is coming in again; **la fièvre remonte** his temperature is rising *ou* going up again, the fever is getting worse again; **les prix ont remonté en flèche** prices shot up *ou* rocketed again; (*fig*) **ses actions remontent** things are looking up for him (again), his fortunes are picking up (again); **il remonte dans mon estime** my opinion of him is growing again, he is redeeming himself in my eyes; **il est remonté de la 7e à la 3e place** he has come up *ou* recovered from 7th to 3rd place.

(d) [*vêtement*] to go up, pull up. **sa robe remonte sur le côté** her dress goes *ou* pulls up at the side *ou* is higher on one side; **sa jupe remonte quand elle s'assoit** her skirt rides up *ou* pulls up *ou* goes up when she sits down.

(e) (*réapparaître*) to come back. **les souvenirs qui remontent à ma mémoire** memories which come back to me *ou* to my mind; **~ à la surface** to come back up to the surface, resurface; **une mauvaise odeur remontait de l'égout** a bad smell was coming *ou* wafting up out of the drain.

(f) (*retourner*) to return, go back. **~ à la source/cause** to go back *ou* return to the source/cause; **~ de l'effet à la cause** to go back from the effect to the cause; (*Naut*) **~ au vent** *ou* **dans le vent** to tack close to the wind; **il faut ~ plus haut** *ou* **plus loin pour comprendre l'affaire** you must go *ou* look further back to understand this business; **aussi loin que remontent ses souvenirs** as far back as he can remember; **cette histoire remonte à une époque reculée/à plusieurs années** this story dates back *ou* goes back a very long time/several years; (*hum*) **tout cela remonte au déluge!** (*c'est vieux comme le monde*) all that's as old as the hills!; (*c'est passé depuis longtemps*) all that was donkey's years ago!* (*Brit hum*); **la famille remonte aux croisades** the family goes *ou* dates back to the time of the Crusades.

2 *vt* **(a)** *étage, côte, marche* to go *ou* climb back up; *rue* to go *ou* come back up. ~ **l'escalier en courant** to rush *ou* run back upstairs; ~ **la rue à pas lents** to walk slowly (back) up the street; ~ **le courant/une rivière** (*à la nage*) to swim (back) upstream/up a river; (*en barque*) to sail *ou* row (back) upstream/up a river; (*fig*) ~ **le courant** *ou* **la pente** to begin to get back on one's feet again *ou* pick up again.

(b) (*rattraper*) *adversaire* to catch up with. ~ **la procession** to move up towards *ou* work one's way towards the front of the procession; **se faire ~ par un adversaire** to let o.s. be caught up by an opponent; **il a 15 points/places à ~ pour être 2e** he has 15 marks/places to catch up in order to be 2nd.

(c) (*relever*) *mur* to raise, heighten; *tableau, étagère* to raise, put higher up; *vitre* (*en poussant*) to push up; (*avec manivelle*) to wind up; *store* to roll up, raise; *pantalon, manche* to pull up, roll up; *chaussettes* to pull up; *col* to turn up; *jupe* to pick up, raise; (*fig*) *mauvaise note* to put up, raise.

(d) (*reporter*) to take *ou* bring back up. ~ **une malle au grenier** to take *ou* carry a trunk back up to the attic.

(e) *montre, mécanisme* to wind up. **il est remonté, il n'arrête pas de parler!*** he's full of beans and won't stop talking!*

(f) (*réinstaller*) *machine, moteur, meuble* to put together again, put back together (again), reassemble; *robinet, tuyau* to put back. **ils ont remonté une usine à Lyon** they have set up *ou* built a factory in Lyons again; **il a eu du mal à ~ les roues de sa bicyclette** he had a job putting *ou* getting the wheels back on his bicycle.

(g) (*réassortir*) *garde-robe* to renew, replenish; *magasin* to restock. **mon père nous a remontés en vaisselle** my father has given us a whole new stock of crockery; **~ son ménage** (*meubles*) to buy all new furniture, refurnish one's house; (*linge*) to buy all new linen.

(h) (*remettre en état*) *personne* (*physiquement*) to set *ou* buck* up (again); (*moralement*) to cheer *ou* buck* up (again); *entreprise* to put *ou* set back on its feet; *mur en ruines* to rebuild. ~ **le moral de qn** to raise sb's spirits, cheer *ou* buck* sb up; **le nouveau directeur a bien remonté cette firme** the new manager has really got this firm back on its feet; **ce contrat remonterait bien mes affaires** this contract would really give a boost to business for me.

(i) (*Théât*) *pièce* to restage, put on again.

3 se remonter *vpr* **(a) se ~ en boîtes de conserves** to get in (further) stocks of tinned food, replenish one's stocks of tinned food; **se ~ en linge** to build up one's stock of linen again; **se ~ en chaussures** to get some new shoes; **tu as besoin de te ~ en chemises** you need a few new shirts.

(b) (*physiquement*) to buck* *ou* set o.s. up (again). (*moralement*) **se ~ (le moral)** to raise (one's spirits), cheer *ou* buck* o.s. up.

remontoir [R(ə)mɔ̃twaR] *nm* [*montre*] winder; [*jouet, horloge*] winding mechanism.

remontrance [R(ə)mɔ̃tRɑ̃s] *nf* **(a)** reproof, reprimand, admonition (*frm*). **faire des ~s à qn** to reprove *ou* reprimand *ou* admonish (*frm*) sb. **(b)** (*Hist*) remonstrance.

remontrer [R(ə)mɔ̃tRe] (1) *vt* **(a)** (*montrer de nouveau*) to show again. **remontrez-moi la bleue** show me the blue one again, let me have another look at the blue one; **ne te remontre plus ici** don't show your face *ou* yourself here again.

(b) en ~ à qn: dans ce domaine, il pourrait t'en ~ he could teach you a thing or two in this field; **il a voulu m'en ~, mais je l'ai remis à sa place** he wanted to prove his superiority to me *ou* to show he knew better than I but I soon put him in his place; **ce n'est pas la peine de m'en ~, je connais cela mieux que toi** don't bother trying to teach me anything — I know all that better than you, it's no use your trying to prove you know better than I — you can't teach me anything about that.

(c) (†, *littér*) *faute* to point out (*à* to).

remordre [R(ə)mɔRdR(ə)] (41) *vt* (*lit*) to bite again. (*fig*) ~ **à** *peinture, sport* to take to again; *travail* to tackle again; (*fig*) **~ à l'hameçon** to rise to the bait again.

remords [R(ə)mɔR] *nm* remorse (*U*). **j'éprouve quelques ~ à l'avoir laissé seul** I am somewhat conscience-stricken *ou* I feel some remorse at having left him alone; **j'ai eu un ~ de conscience, je suis allé vérifier** I had second thoughts *ou* I thought better of it and went to check; **~ cuisants** agonies of remorse; **avoir des ~** to feel remorse, be smitten with remorse, be conscience-stricken; **n'avoir aucun ~** to have no (feeling of) remorse, feel no remorse; **je le tuerais sans (le moindre) ~** I should kill him without (the slightest) compunction *ou* remorse.

remorquage [R(ə)mɔRkaʒ] *nm* (*V* **remorquer**) towing; pulling, hauling; tugging.

remorque [R(ə)mɔRk(ə)] *nf* **(a)** (*véhicule*) trailer; (*câble*) towrope, towline; *V* **camion, semi-**.

(b) (*loc*) **prendre une voiture en ~** to tow a car; **'en ~'** 'on tow'; (*péj*) **être à la ~ de** (*lit, fig*) to tag behind; **quand ils vont se promener ils ont toujours la belle-mère en ~** whenever they go for a walk they always have the mother-in-law in tow *ou* tagging along *ou* they always drag along the mother-in-law; **pays à la ~ d'une grande puissance** country that is being carried by a great power (*péj*).

remorquer [R(ə)mɔRke] (1) *vt* *voiture, caravane* to tow; *train* to pull, haul; *bateau, navire* to tow, tug. **je suis tombé en panne et j'ai dû me faire ~ jusqu'au village** I had a breakdown and had to get a tow *ou* get myself towed as far as the village; (*fig*) **~ toute la famille derrière soi** to have the whole family in tow, trail *ou* drag the whole family along (with one).

remorqueur [R(ə)mɔRkœR] *nm* tug(boat).

remoudre [R(ə)mudR(ə)] (47) *vt* *café, poivre* to regrind, grind again.

remouiller [R(ə)muje] (1) *vt* **(a)** to wet again. **~ du linge à repasser** to (re)dampen washing ready for ironing; **se faire ~ (par la pluie)** to get wet (in the rain) again; **je viens de m'essuyer les mains, je ne veux pas me les ~** I've just dried my hands and I don't want to get them wet *ou* to wet them again.

(b) (*Naut*) **~ (l'ancre)** to drop anchor again.

rémoulade [Remulad] *nf* remoulade, rémoulade (*dressing containing mustard and herbs*); *V* **céleri**.

remoulage [R(ə)mulaʒ] *nm* **(a)** (*Art*) recasting. **(b)** (*Tech*) [*café*] regrinding; [*farine*] remilling.

remouler [R(ə)mule] (1) *vt* *statue* to recast.

rémouleur [RemulœR] *nm* (knife- *ou* scissor-)grinder.

remous [R(ə)mu] *nm* **(a)** [*bateau*] (back)wash (*U*); [*eau*] swirl, eddy; [*air*] eddy; (*fig*) [*foule*] bustle (*U*), bustling. **emporté par les ~ de la foule** swept along by the bustling *ou* milling crowd *ou* by the bustle of the crowd.

(b) (*agitation*) upheaval, stir (*U*). **~ d'idées** whirl *ou* swirl of ideas; **les ~ provoqués par ce divorce** the stir caused by this divorce.

rempaillage [Rɑ̃pɑjaʒ] *nm* reseating, rebottoming (*with straw*).

rempailler [Rɑ̃pɑje] (1) *vt* *chaise* to reseat, rebottom (*with straw*).

rempailleur, -euse [Rɑ̃pɑjœR, øz] *nm,f* [*chaise*] upholsterer, chair-bottomer; [*animal*] taxidermist.

rempaqueter [Rɑ̃pakte] (4) *vt* to wrap up again, rewrap.

rempart [Rɑ̃paR] *nm* **(a)** (*Mil*) rampart. **~s** [*ville*] city walls, ramparts; [*château fort*] battlements, ramparts. **(b)** (*fig*) defence, rampart (*littér*). **faire à qn un ~ de son corps** to shield sb with one's (own) body.

rempiler [Rɑ̃pile] (1) **1** *vt* to pile *ou* stack up again. **2** *vi* (*arg Mil*) to join up again, re-enlist.

remplaçable [Rɑ̃plasabl(ə)] *adj* replaceable.

remplaçant, e [Rɑ̃plasɑ̃, ɑ̃t] *nm,f* replacement, substitute; (*Méd*) locum (*Brit*); (*Sport*) reserve; (*pendant un match*) substitute; (*Théât*) understudy; (*Scol*) supply teacher. **être le ~ de qn** to stand in for sb; **trouver un ~ à un professeur malade** to get sb to stand in *ou* substitute for a sick teacher; **il faut lui trouver un ~** we must find a replacement *ou* a substitute for him.

remplacement [Rɑ̃plasmɑ̃] *nm* **(a)** (*intérim: V* **remplacer**) standing in (*de* for); substitution (*de* for), deputizing (*de* for). **assurer le ~ d'un collègue pendant sa maladie** to stand in for *ou* deputize for a colleague during his illness; **secrétaire intérimaire qui fait des ~s** secretary who does temporary replacement work; **j'ai fait 3 ~s cette semaine** I've had 3 temporary replacement jobs this week.

(b) (*substitution, changement: V* **remplacer**) replacement (*de* of); taking over (*de* from); acting as a substitute (*de* for). **effectuer le ~ d'une pièce défectueuse** to replace a faulty part; **film présenté en ~ d'une émission annulée** film shown as a replacement *ou* substitute for a cancelled programme; **je n'ai plus de stylos à billes, en ~ je vous donne un marqueur** I have no more ball-point pens so I'll give you a felt tip instead; **le ~ du nom par le pronom** the replacement of the noun by the pronoun; **il va falloir trouver une solution de ~** we'll have to find an alternative solution; **produit de ~** substitute (product).

remplacer [Rɑ̃plase] (3) *vt* **(a)** (*assurer l'intérim de*) *acteur malade* to stand in for; *joueur, professeur malade* to stand in for, substitute for, deputize for; *médecin en vacances* to stand in for, do a locum for (*Brit*). **je me suis fait ~** I found myself a deputy *ou* a stand-in, I got someone to stand in for me.

(b) (*substitution: succéder à*) to replace, take over from, take the place of. **le train a maintenant remplacé la diligence** the train has now replaced *ou* taken the place of the stagecoach; **son fils l'a remplacé comme directeur** his son has taken over from him *ou* has taken his place *ou* has replaced him as director; **~ une sentinelle** to take over from *ou* relieve a sentry.

(c) (*substitution: tenir lieu de*) to take the place of, act as a substitute for, replace. **le miel peut ~ le sucre** honey can be used in place of *ou* as a substitute for sugar *ou* can take the place of sugar; **le pronom remplace le nom dans la phrase** the pronoun stands for *ou* takes the place of *ou* replaces the noun in the sentence; **quand on n'a pas d'alcool, on peut le ~ par de l'eau de Cologne** when you have no alcohol you can use eau de Cologne in its place *ou* you can substitute eau de Cologne.

(d) (*changer*) *employé démissionnaire* to replace; *objet usagé* to replace, change. **~ le vieux lit par un neuf** to replace the old bed with a new one, change the old bed for a new one; **les pièces défectueuses seront remplacées gratuitement** faulty parts will be replaced free; **~ les pointillés par des pronoms** to replace the dotted lines by *ou* with pronouns, put pronouns in place of the dotted lines.

rempli, e [Rɑ̃pli] (*ptp de* **remplir**) **1** *adj* *théâtre, récipient* full (*de* of), filled (*de* with); *joue, visage* full, plump; *journée, vie* full, busy. **il est ~ de son importance** he's full of his own importance; **avoir l'estomac bien ~** to have a full stomach, have eaten one's fill; **texte ~ de fautes** text riddled *ou* packed with mistakes; **être ~ de colère** to be filled with anger; **sa tête était ~e de souvenirs** his mind was filled with *ou* full of memories.

2 *nm* (*Couture*) tuck.

remplir [ʀɑ̃pliʀ] (2) **1** *vt* **(a)** (*gén*) to fill (*de* with); *récipient* to fill (up); (*à nouveau*) to refill; *questionnaire* to fill in *ou* out. ~ **qch à moitié** to half fill sth, fill sth half full; **il en a rempli 15 pages** he filled 15 pages with it, he wrote 15 pages on it; **ce chanteur ne remplira pas la salle** this singer won't fill the hall *ou* won't get a full house; **ces tâches routinières ont rempli sa vie** these routine tasks have filled his life, his life has been filled with these routine tasks; **ça remplit la première page des journaux** it fills *ou* covers the front page of the newspapers; **ce résultat me remplit d'admiration** this result fills me with admiration, I am filled with admiration at this result; ~ **son temps** to fill one's time; **il remplit bien ses journées** he gets a lot done in (the course of) a day, he packs a lot into his days.

(b) (*s'acquitter de*) *promesse* to fulfil; *devoir* to fulfil, carry out, do; *travail* to carry out, do; *rôle* to fill, play; *besoin* to answer, meet, satisfy. **objet qui remplit une fonction précise** object that fulfils a precise purpose; **vous ne remplissez pas les conditions** you do not fulfil *ou* satisfy *ou* meet the conditions; ~ **ses fonctions** to do *ou* carry out one's job, carry out *ou* perform one's functions.

2 se remplir *vpr* [*récipient, salle*] to fill (up) (*de* with). **se ~ les poches*** to line one's pockets; **on s'est bien rempli la panse*** we had a good stuff-out‡ (*Brit*).

remplissage [ʀɑ̃plisaʒ] *nm* [*tonneau, bassin*] filling (up); (*péj: dans un livre*) padding. **faire du ~** to pad out one's work (*ou* speech *etc*).

remploi [ʀɑ̃plwa] *nm* = **réemploi.**

remployer [ʀɑ̃plwaje] (8) *vt* = **réemployer.**

remplumer* (se) [ʀɑ̃plyme] (1) *vpr* (*physiquement*) to fill out again, get a bit of flesh on one's bones again; (*financièrement*) to get back on one's feet.

rempocher [ʀɑ̃pɔʃe] (1) *vt* to put back into one's pocket.

rempoissonnement [ʀɑ̃pwasɔnmɑ̃] *nm* restocking (with fish).

rempoissonner [ʀɑ̃pwasɔne] (1) *vt* to restock (with fish).

remporter [ʀɑ̃pɔʀte] (1) *vt* **(a)** (*reprendre*) to take away (again), take back. **remportez ce plat!** take this dish away!

(b) *victoire, championnat* to win; *prix* to carry off, win. ~ **un (vif) succès** to achieve (a great) success.

rempotage [ʀɑ̃pɔtaʒ] *nm* repotting.

rempoter [ʀɑ̃pɔte] (1) *vt* to repot.

remprunter [ʀɑ̃pʀœ̃te] (1) *vt* (*une nouvelle fois*) to borrow again; (*davantage*) to borrow more.

remuant, e [ʀəmɥɑ̃, ɑ̃t] *adj enfant* restless, always on the go (*attrib*). **politicien ~** politician who likes stirring things up.

remue-ménage [ʀ(ə)mymenaʒ] *nm inv* (*bruit*) commotion (*U*); (*activité*) hurly-burly (*U*), commotion (*U*). **il y a du ~ chez les voisins** the neighbours are making a great commotion; **faire du ~** to make a commotion; **le ~ électoral** the electoral hurly-burly.

remuement [ʀ(ə)mymɑ̃] *nm* moving, movement.

remuer [ʀ(ə)mɥe] (1) **1** *vt* **(a)** (*bouger*) *tête, bras* to move; *oreille* to twitch. ~ **la queue** [*vache, écureuil*] to flick its tail; [*chien*] to wag its tail; ~ **les bras** *ou* **les mains en parlant** to wave one's arms about *ou* gesticulate as one speaks; ~ **les épaules/les hanches en marchant** to swing *ou* sway one's shoulders/hips as one walks; (*fig*) **il n'a pas remué le petit doigt** he didn't lift a finger (to help).

(b) *objet* (*déplacer*) to move, shift; (*secouer*) to shake. **il essaya de ~ la pierre** he tried to move *ou* shift the stone; **sa valise est si lourde que je ne peux même pas la ~** his case is so heavy that I can't even shift *ou* move *ou* budge it; **arrête-toi de ~ ta chaise** stop moving your chair about; **ne remue pas** *ou* **ne fais pas ~ la table, je suis en train d'écrire** don't shake *ou* move *ou* wobble the table — I'm trying to write.

(c) (*brasser*) *café, sauce* to stir; *braises* to poke, stir; *sable* to stir up; *salade* to toss; *terre* to dig *ou* turn over. **il a tout remué dans le tiroir** he turned the whole drawer *ou* everything in the drawer upside down; (*fig*) ~ **de l'argent (à la pelle)** to handle a great deal of money; (*fig*) ~ **la boue** *ou* **l'ordure** to rake *ou* stir up dirt *ou* muck; (*fig*) ~ **ciel et terre pour** to move heaven and earth (in order) to; (*fig*) ~ **des souvenirs** [*personne nostalgique*] to turn *ou* go over old memories in one's mind; [*évocation*] to stir up *ou* arouse old memories.

(d) (*émouvoir*) *personne* to move. **ça vous remue les tripes*** it really tugs at your heartstrings.

2 *vi* **(a)** (*bouger*) [*personne*] to move; [*dent, tuile*] to be loose. **cesse de ~!** keep still!; **le vent faisait ~ les branchages** the wind was stirring the branches, the branches were stirring *ou* swaying in the wind; *V* **nez.**

(b) (*fig: se rebeller*) to show signs of unrest.

3 se remuer *vpr* **(a)** (*bouger*) to move; (*se déplacer*) to move about.

(b) (*) (*se mettre en route*) to get going; (*s'activer*) to shift *ou* stir o.s.*, get a move on*. **il s'est beaucoup remué pour leur trouver un appartement** he's gone to a lot of trouble to find them a flat; **il ne s'est pas beaucoup remué** he didn't stir himself much*.

rémunérateur, -trice [ʀemyneʀatœʀ, tʀis] *adj emploi* remunerative, lucrative.

rémunération [ʀemyneʀasjɔ̃] *nf* remuneration, payment (*de* for).

rémunérer [ʀemyneʀe] (6) *vt personne* to remunerate, pay. ~ **le travail de qn** to remunerate *ou* pay sb for his work; **travail mal rémunéré** badly-paid job.

renâcler [ʀ(ə)nakle] (1) *vi* [*animal*] to snort; (*fig*) [*personne*] to grumble, show (one's) reluctance. ~ **à un travail** to balk at a job, show reluctance to do a job; ~ **à faire qch** to grumble at having to do sth, do sth reluctantly *ou* grudgingly; **sans ~** uncomplainingly, without grumbling.

renaissance [ʀ(ə)nɛsɑ̃s] **1** *nf* (*Rel, fig*) rebirth. (*Hist*) **la R~** the Renaissance. **2** *adj inv mobilier, style* Renaissance.

renaissant, e [ʀ(ə)nɛsɑ̃, ɑ̃t] *adj* **(a)** *forces* returning; *économie* reviving, recovering. **toujours** *ou* **sans cesse ~** *difficultés* constantly recurring, that keep cropping up; *obstacles* that keep cropping up; *intérêt, hésitations, doutes* constantly renewed.

(b) (*Hist*) Renaissance (*épith*).

renaître [ʀ(ə)nɛtʀ(ə)] (59) *vi* **(a)** [*joie*] to spring up again, be revived (*dans* in); [*espoir, doute*] to be revived (*dans* in); to be reborn (*littér*); [*conflit*] to spring up again, break out again; [*difficulté*] to recur, crop up again; [*économie*] to revive, recover; [*sourire*] to return (*sur* to), reappear (*sur* on); [*plante*] to come *ou* spring up again; [*jour*] to dawn, break. **le printemps renaît** spring is reawakening; **la nature renaît au printemps** nature comes back to life in spring; **faire ~** *sentiment, passé* to bring back, revive; *problème, sourire* to bring back; *espoir, conflit* to revive.

(b) (*revivre*) (*gén*) to come to life again; (*Rel*) to be born again. (*Myth, fig*) ~ **de ses cendres** to rise from one's ashes; **je me sens ~** I feel as if I've been given a new lease of life.

(c) (*littér*) ~ **au bonheur** to find happiness again; ~ **à l'espérance** to find fresh hope; ~ **à la vie** to take on a new lease of life.

rénal, e, *mpl* **-aux** [ʀenal, o] *adj* renal (*T*), kidney (*épith*).

renard [ʀ(ə)naʀ] *nm* (*Zool*) fox; (*fourrure*) fox(-fur). (*fig*) **c'est un fin ~** he's a crafty *ou* sly fox *ou* dog; ~ **argenté/bleu** silver/blue fox.

renarde [ʀ(ə)naʀd(ə)] *nf* vixen.

renardeau, *pl* **~x** [ʀ(ə)naʀdo] *nm* fox cub.

renardière [ʀ(ə)naʀdjɛʀ] *nf* (*Can*) fox farm.

rencaisser [ʀɑ̃kese] (1) *vt* **(a)** (*Comm*) *argent* to put back in the till. **(b)** (*Horticulture*) to rebox.

rencard‡, rencart‡ [ʀɑ̃kaʀ] *nm* = **rancard‡.**

renchérir [ʀɑ̃ʃeʀiʀ] (2) *vi* **(a)** (*en paroles*) to go further, add something, go one better (*péj*); (*en actes*) to go further, go one better (*péj*). ~ **sur ce que qn dit** to add something to what sb says, go further *ou* one better (*péj*) than sb; ~ **sur ce que qn fait** to go further than sb; **'et je n'en ai nul besoin' renchérit-il** 'and I don't need it in the least' he added (further); **il faut toujours qu'il renchérisse (sur ce qu'on dit)** he always has to add something (to what anyone says), he always has to go one better (than anyone else) (*péj*).

(b) [*prix*] to get dearer *ou* more expensive. **la vie renchérit** the cost of living is going up *ou* rising.

renchérissement [ʀɑ̃ʃeʀismɑ̃] *nm* [*marchandises*] rise *ou* increase in (the) price (*de* of); [*loyers*] rise, increase (*de* in). **le ~ de la vie** the rise *ou* increase in the cost of living.

rencogner* [ʀɑ̃kɔɲe] (1) **1** *vt* to corner. **2 se rencogner** *vpr* to huddle up, curl up (in a corner).

rencontre [ʀɑ̃kɔ̃tʀ(ə)] *nf* **(a)** [*amis, diplomates, étrangers*] meeting; (*imprévue*) encounter, meeting. **faire la ~ de qn** to meet sb; (*imprévue*) to run into sb, encounter sb (*frm*); **j'ai peur que dans ces milieux il ne fasse de mauvaises ~s** I am afraid that in these circles he might meet (up with) *ou* fall in with the wrong sort of people; **faire une ~ inattendue/une mauvaise ~** to have an unexpected/unpleasant encounter; **le hasard d'une ~ a changé ma vie** a chance encounter *ou* meeting has changed my life.

(b) (*gén*) [*éléments*] conjunction; [*rivières*] confluence; [*routes*] junction; [*voitures*] collision; [*voyelles*] juxtaposition. **la ~ des deux lignes/routes/rivières se fait ici** the two lines/roads/rivers meet *ou* join here; *V* **point**[1].

(c) (*Sport*) meeting. **la ~ (des 2 équipes) aura lieu le 15** the 2 teams will meet on the 15th; ~ **de boxe** boxing match.

(d) (*Mil*) skirmish, encounter, engagement; (*duel*) encounter, meeting.

(e) (*loc*) **aller à la ~ de qn** to go and meet sb, go to meet sb; **(partir) à la ~ des Incas** (to go) in search of the Incas; **amours de ~** (brief) casual love affairs; **compagnons/voyageurs de ~** chance/travelling companions.

rencontrer [ʀɑ̃kɔ̃tʀe] (1) **1** *vt* **(a)** (*gén*) to meet; (*par hasard*) to meet, run *ou* bump into*, encounter (*frm*). **j'ai rencontré Paul en ville** I met *ou* ran into* *ou* bumped into* Paul in town; **le Premier ministre a rencontré son homologue allemand** the Prime Minister has had a meeting with *ou* has met his German counterpart; **mon regard rencontra le sien** our eyes met, my eyes met his.

(b) (*trouver*) *expression* to find, come across; *occasion* to meet with. **des gens/sites comme on n'en rencontre plus** the sort of people/places you don't find any more; **arrête-toi au premier garage que nous rencontrerons** stop at the first garage you come across *ou* find; **avec lui, j'ai rencontré le bonheur** with him I have found happiness.

(c) (*heurter*) to strike; (*toucher*) to meet (with). **la lame rencontra un os** the blade struck a bone; **sa main ne rencontra que le vide** his hand met with nothing but empty space.

(d) *obstacle, difficulté, opposition* to meet with, encounter, come up against; *résistance* to meet with, come up against.

(e) (*Sport*) *équipe* to meet, play (against); *boxeur* to meet, fight (against).

2 se rencontrer *vpr* **(a)** [*personnes, regards*] to meet; [*rivières, routes*] to meet, join; [*équipes*] to meet, play (each other); [*boxeurs*] to meet, fight (each other); [*véhicules*] to collide (with each other). **faire se ~ 2 personnes** to arrange for 2 people to meet, arrange a meeting between 2 people; (*frm*) **je me suis déjà rencontré avec lui** I have already met him.

(b) (*avoir les mêmes idées*) to be at one, be of the same opinion *ou* mind. **se ~ avec qn** to be at one with sb, be of the same opinion *ou* mind as sb; *V* **grand.**

(c) (*exister*) [*coïncidence, curiosité*] to be found. **cela ne se rencontre plus de nos jours** that isn't found *ou* one doesn't come across that any more nowadays; **il se rencontre des gens qui ...**

you do find people who ..., people are to be found who ...

rendement [Rɑ̃dmɑ̃] *nm [champ]* yield; *[machine]* output; *[entreprise]* (*productivité*) productivity; (*production*) output; *[personne]* output; *[investissement]* return (*de* on), yield (*de* of); (*Phys*) efficiency. **il travaille beaucoup, mais il n'a pas de ~*** he works hard but he hasn't *ou* there isn't much to show for it*; **champ/placement qui est d'un mauvais ~** low-yield field/investment.

rendez-vous [Rɑ̃devu] *nm inv* **(a)** (*rencontre*) appointment; (*d'amoureux*) date. **donner** *ou* **fixer un ~ à qn, prendre ~ avec qn** to make an appointment with sb, arrange to see *ou* meet sb; **j'ai (un) ~ à 10 heures** I have an appointment *ou* I have to meet someone at 10 o'clock; **ma parole, vous vous êtes donné ~** my goodness, you must have seen each other coming!; (*littér*) **avoir ~ avec la mort** to have a date with death; **~ d'affaires** business appointment; **~ galant** amorous meeting; **~ spatial** docking (in space).

(b) (*lieu*) meeting place. **~ de chasse** meet; *V* **maison.**

rendormir [Rɑ̃dɔRmiR] (16) **1** *vt* to put to sleep again, put back to sleep. **2 se rendormir** *vpr* to go back to sleep, fall asleep again.

rendosser [Rɑ̃dose] (1) *vt* to put on again.

rendre [Rɑ̃dR(ə)] (41) **1** *vt* **(a)** (*restituer*) (*gén*) to give back, return, take *ou* bring back; *marchandises défectueuses, bouteille vide* to return, take back; *argent* to pay *ou* give back, return; *objet volé* to give back, return, restore; *otage* to return; *cadeau, bague* to return, give *ou* send back. **quand pourriez-vous me ~ votre réponse?** when will you be able to give me *ou* let me have your reply?; **~ son devoir en retard** to hand *ou* give in one's homework late; **~ à qn sa parole** to release sb from a promise, let sb off (his promise); **~ la liberté à qn** to set sb free, give sb his freedom; **~ la santé à qn** to restore sb to health; **~ la vue à qn** to restore sb's sight, give sb back his sight; **cela lui a rendu toutes ses forces/son courage** that gave him back *ou* restored all his strength/courage; **~ la vie à qn** to save sb's life (*fig*); **rendu à la vie civile** restored to *ou* back in civilian life; (*fig*) **~ son tablier** to give (in) one's notice.

(b) (*Jur*) *justice* to administer, dispense; *jugement, arrêt* to pronounce, render; *verdict* to return. (*fig*) **~ justice à qn** to do justice to sb; **il faut lui ~ cette justice qu'il a essayé** he did try – (we must) grant *ou* give him that.

(c) (*donner en retour*) *hospitalité, invitation* to return, repay; *salut, coup, baiser* to return. **~ à qn son dîner** to invite sb back to dinner *ou* to dinner in return, return sb's invitation to dinner; **je lui ai rendu sa visite** I returned *ou* repaid his visit; **~ coup pour coup** to return blow for blow; **il m'a joué un sale tour, mais je le lui rendrai** he played a dirty trick on me, but I'll get even with him; **je lui ai rendu injure pour injure** I answered insult by insult, I gave him as good as I got; **il la déteste, et elle le lui rend bien** he hates her and she returns his feelings; **~ la monnaie à qn** to give sb his change; **il m'a donné 10 F et je lui en ai rendu 5** he gave me 10 francs and I gave him 5 francs back *ou* 5 francs change; (*fig*) **~ à qn la monnaie de sa pièce** to pay sb back in his own coin.

(d) (+ *adj*) to make. **~ qn heureux** to make sb happy; **~ qch public** to make sth public; **~ qn responsable de** to make sb responsible for; **son discours l'a rendu célèbre** his speech has made him famous; **c'est à vous ~ fou!** it's enough to drive you mad!; **se ~ utile/indispensable** to make o.s. useful/indispensable; **il se rend ridicule** he's making himself ridiculous, he's making a fool of himself, he's making himself look foolish; **~ qn/qch meilleur** to make sb/sth better.

(e) *expression, traduction* to render. **cela ne rend pas bien sa pensée** that doesn't render *ou* convey his thoughts very well; **le portrait ne rend pas son expression** this portrait has not caught his expression.

(f) (*produire*) *liquide* to give out; *son* to produce, make. **le concombre rend beaucoup d'eau** cucumbers give out a lot of water; (*fig*) **l'enquête n'a rien rendu** the inquiry drew a blank *ou* didn't come to anything *ou* produced nothing.

(g) (*vomir*) *bile* to vomit, bring up; *déjeuner* to vomit, bring back *ou* up. **~ tripes et boyaux*** to be as sick as a dog*; **~ du sang (par la bouche)** to cough up *ou* vomit blood; **~ du sang par le nez** to bleed from the nose.

(h) (*Sport*) *[cheval]* **~ du poids** to have a weight handicap; **~ 3 kg** to give *ou* carry 3 kg; *[coureur]* **~ de la distance** to have a handicap; **~ 100 mètres** to have a 100-metre handicap; (*fig*) **~ des points à qn** to give sb points *ou* a head start.

(i) (*Mil*) *place forte* to surrender. **~ les armes** to lay down one's arms.

(j) (*loc*) **~ l'âme** *ou* **le dernier soupir** to breathe one's last, give up the ghost; **~ des comptes à qn** to be accountable to sb; **je n'ai de comptes à ~ à personne** I am accountable to no one, I don't have to account to anyone for my actions; **~ compte de qch à qn** to give sb an account of sth; **~ un culte à** to worship; **~ gloire à** *Dieu* to glorify; *hommes* to pay homage to; **~ gorge** to restitute ill-gotten gains; **~ grâces à** to render (*frm*) *ou* give thanks to; **~ hommage/honneur à** to pay hommage/tribute to; **le régiment rendait les honneurs** the regiment was paying honour; **rendre les derniers honneurs à qn** to pay the last tributes to sb; **~ la pareille à qn** to do the same for sb, pay sb back the same way; **~ raison de qch à qn** to give sb an explanation for sth; **~ (des) service(s) à qn** to be of service *ou* help to sb, help sb; **cela m'a bien rendu service** that was a great help to me; **ce petit couteau rend bien des services** this little knife comes in *ou* is very handy (for a variety of purposes); **~ visite à qn** to visit sb, call on sb, pay sb a visit *ou* a call.

2 *vi* **(a)** *[arbres, terre]* to yield, be productive. **les pommiers ont bien rendu** the apple trees have given a good yield *ou* crop; **la pêche a bien rendu** we have got a good catch (of fish); (*fig*) **ma petite expérience n'a pas rendu** my little experiment didn't pay off *ou* didn't come to anything.

(b) (*vomir*) to be sick, vomit. **avoir envie de ~** to feel sick.

3 se rendre *vpr* **(a)** (*céder*) *[soldat, criminel]* to give o.s. up, surrender; *[troupe]* to surrender. **se ~ aux ordres de qn** to comply with *ou* obey sb's orders; **se ~ à l'avis de qn** to bow to sb's opinion; **se ~ à l'évidence** (*regarder les choses en face*) to face facts; (*admettre son tort*) to bow before the evidence; **se ~ aux prières de qn** to give way *ou* give in *ou* yield to sb's pleas.

(b) (*aller*) **se ~ à** to go to; **il se rend à son travail à pied/en voiture** he walks/drives to work, he goes to work on foot/by car; **alors qu'il se rendait à ...** as he was on his way to ... *ou* going to ...; **la police s'est rendue sur les lieux** the police arrived on the scene; **se ~ à l'appel de qn** to respond to sb's appeal.

(c) se ~ compte de qch to realize sth, be aware of sth; **se ~ compte que** to realize that, be aware that; **je me rends très bien compte de la situation** I am very well aware of the situation; **est-ce que tu te rends vraiment compte de ce que tu dis/fais?** do you really realize *ou* are you really aware of what you are saying/doing?; **tu ne te rends pas compte du travail que ça représente** you have no idea of the amount of work *ou* you just don't realize how much work that represents; **rendez-vous compte!** just imagine! *ou* think!; **il a osé me dire ça, à moi, tu te rends compte!** he dared say that to ME – can you imagine!

rendu, e [Rɑ̃dy] (*ptp de* **rendre**) **1** *adj* **(a)** (*arrivé*) **être ~** to have arrived; **nous voilà ~s!** here we are then!; **on est plus vite ~ par le métro** you get there quicker by tube.

(b) (*remis*) **~ à domicile** delivered to the house.

(c) (*fatigué*) exhausted, tired out, worn out.

2 *nm* (*Comm*) return; *V* **prêté.**

rêne [REn] *nf* rein. (*fig*) **prendre les ~s d'une affaire** to take over a business, assume control *ou* take control of a business; **lâcher les ~s** (*lit*) to loose *ou* slacken the reins; (*fig*) to let go; (*fig*) **c'est lui qui tient les ~s du gouvernement** it's he who holds the reins of government *ou* who is in the saddle.

renégat, e [Rənega, at] *nm,f* (*Rel*) renegade; (*Pol, gén*) renegade, turncoat.

reneiger [R(ə)neʒe] (3) *vb impers* to snow again.

renfermé, e [Rɑ̃fERme] (*ptp de* **renfermer**) **1** *adj* withdrawn, closed in upon oneself (*attrib*). **2** *nm*: **odeur de ~** fusty *ou* stale smell; **ça sent le ~** it smells stuffy *ou* fusty (in here), it's stuffy in here.

renfermer [Rɑ̃fERme] (1) **1** *vt* **(a)** (*contenir*) *trésors* to contain, hold; *vérités, erreurs* to contain. **phrase qui renferme plusieurs idées** sentence that encompasses *ou* contains several ideas.

(b) (†: *à clef*) to lock again, lock back up.

2 se renfermer *vpr*: **se ~ (en soi-même)** to withdraw into o.s.; **se ~ dans sa coquille** to withdraw into one's shell.

renfiler [Rɑ̃file] (1) *vt perles* to restring; *aiguille* to thread again, rethread; *bas, manteau* to slip back into.

renflammer [Rɑ̃flame] (1) *vt* to rekindle.

renflé, e [Rɑ̃fle] (*ptp de* **renfler**) *adj* bulging (*épith*), bulbous.

renfler [Rɑ̃fle] (1) **1** *vt* to make a bulge in; *joues* to blow out. **2 se renfler** *vpr* to bulge (out).

renflouement [Rɑ̃flumɑ̃] *nm* (*V* **renflouer**) refloating; bailing out.

renflouer [Rɑ̃flue] (1) *vt bateau* to refloat; (*fig*) *entreprise, personne* to bail out, set back on its (*ou* his *etc*) feet.

renfoncement [Rɑ̃fɔ̃smɑ̃] *nm* recess. **caché dans le ~ d'une porte** hidden in a doorway.

renfoncer [Rɑ̃fɔ̃se] (3) *vt* **(a)** *clou* to knock further in; *bouchon* to push further in. **il renfonça son chapeau (sur sa tête)** he pulled his hat down (further). **(b)** (*Typ*) to indent.

renforcement [Rɑ̃fɔRsəmɑ̃] *nm* (*V* **renforcer**) reinforcement; trussing; strengthening; intensification.

renforcer [Rɑ̃fɔRse] (3) **1** *vt* **(a)** *vêtement, mur* to reinforce; *poutre* to reinforce, truss. **bas à talon renforcé** stocking with reinforced heel.

(b) *équipe, armée* to reinforce. **ils sont venus ~ nos effectifs** they came to strengthen *ou* swell our numbers.

(c) *crainte, argument, amitié* to reinforce, strengthen; *paix* to consolidate; *pression, effort* to add to, intensify; *position* to strengthen; *couleur, ton, expression* to intensify. **~ qn dans une opinion** to confirm sb's opinion, confirm sb in an opinion; **ça renforce ce que je dis** that backs up *ou* reinforces what I'm saying.

2 se renforcer *vpr [craintes, amitié]* to strengthen; *[pression]* to intensify. **notre équipe s'est renforcée de 2 nouveaux joueurs** our team has been strengthened by 2 new players.

renfort [Rɑ̃fɔR] *nm* **(a)** (*Mil*) **~s** (*hommes*) reinforcements; (*matériel*) (further) supplies.

(b) (*Tech*) reinforcement, strengthening piece.

(c) (*loc*) **de ~** *barre, toile* strengthening; *armée* back-up, supporting; *personnel* extra, additional; **envoyer qn en ~** to send sb as an extra *ou* sb to augment the numbers; **recevoir un ~ de troupes/d'artillerie, recevoir des troupes/de l'artillerie de** *ou* **en ~** to receive more troops/guns, receive reinforcements/a further supply of guns; **embaucher du personnel de** *ou* **en ~** to employ extra *ou* additional staff; **à grand ~ de gestes/d'explications** accompanied by a great many gestures/explanations.

renfrogné, e [Rɑ̃fRɔɲe] (*ptp de* **se renfrogner**) *adj visage* sullen, scowling (*épith*), sulky; *air* sullen, sulky; *personne* sullen *ou* sulky (looking).

renfrognement [Rɑ̃fRɔɲmɑ̃] *nm* scowling, sullenness.

renfrogner (se) [Rɑ̃fRɔɲe] (1) *vpr [personne]* to scowl, pull a sour face.

rengagé [Rɑ̃gaʒe] **1** *adj m soldat* re-enlisted. **2** *nm* re-enlisted soldier.

rengagement [ʀɑ̃gaʒmɑ̃] *nm* (*V* **rengager**) starting up again; reinvestment; re-engagement; repawning; re-enlistment.

rengager [ʀɑ̃gaʒe] (3) **1** *vt discussion* to start up again; *fonds* to reinvest; *combat* to re-engage; *bijoux* to repawn; *soldat* to re-enlist; *ouvrier* to take on *ou* engage again, re-engage. ~ **la clef dans la serrure** to insert the key back *ou* reinsert the key into the lock; ~ **sa voiture dans une rue** to drive (back) into a street again.
2 *vi* (*Mil*) to join up again, re-enlist.
3 se rengager *vpr* (*Mil*) to join up again, re-enlist; *[discussion]* to start up again. **se ~ dans une rue** to enter a street again.

rengaine [ʀɑ̃gɛn] *nf* (*formule*) hackneyed expression; (*chanson*) old (repetitive) song *ou* melody. (*fig*) **c'est toujours la même ~*** it's always the same old chorus (*Brit*) *ou* refrain* (*Brit*) *ou* song* (*US*).

rengainer [ʀɑ̃gene] (1) *vt* **(a)** (*) *compliment* to save, withhold; *sentiments* to contain, hold back. **rengaine tes beaux discours!** (you can) save *ou* keep your fine speeches!*
(b) *épée* to sheathe, put up; *revolver* to put back in its holster.

rengorgement [ʀɑ̃gɔʀʒəmɑ̃] *nm* puffed-up pride.

rengorger (se) [ʀɑ̃gɔʀʒe] (3) *vpr [oiseau]* to puff out its throat; *[personne]* to puff o.s. up. **se ~ d'avoir fait qch** to be pleased with o.s. for having done sth.

rengraisser [ʀɑ̃gʀese] (1) *vi* to put on weight again, put (some) weight back on.

reniement [ʀ(ə)nimɑ̃] *nm* (*V* **renier**) renunciation; disowning, repudiation; breaking; denial.

renier [ʀənje] (7) **1** *vt foi, opinion* to renounce; *frère, patrie, signature, son passé* to disown, repudiate; *promesse* to go back on, break. (*Rel*) **il renia Jésus Christ** he denied Christ; ~ **Dieu** to renounce God.
2 se renier *vpr* to go back on what one has said *ou* done.

reniflement [ʀ(ə)nifləmɑ̃] *nm* (*V* **renifler**) (*action*) sniffing (*U*); snorting (*U*); sniffling (*U*), snuffling (*U*); (*bruit*) sniff; snort; sniffle, snuffle.

renifler [ʀ(ə)nifle] (1) **1** *vt tabac* to sniff up, take a sniff of; *fleur, objet* to sniff (at); (**fig*) *bonne affaire* to sniff out*. (*fig*) ~ **quelque chose de louche** to smell a rat*.
2 *vi [personne]* to sniff; *[cheval]* to snort. **arrête de ~, mouche-toi!** stop sniffling *ou* snuffling and blow your nose!

renifleur, -euse [ʀ(ə)niflœʀ, øz] **1** *adj* sniffling, snuffling. **2** *nm,f* (*) sniffler, snuffler.

rennais, e [ʀɛnɛ, ɛz] **1** *adj* of *ou* from Rennes. **2** *nm,f*: **R~(e)** inhabitant *ou* native of Rennes.

renne [ʀɛn] *nm* reindeer.

renom [ʀ(ə)nɔ̃] *nm* **(a)** (*notoriété*) renown, fame. **vin de grand ~** celebrated *ou* renowned *ou* famous wine, wine of high renown; **restaurant en ~** celebrated *ou* renowned *ou* famous restaurant; **acquérir du ~** to win renown, become famous; **avoir du ~** to be famous.
(b) (*frm: réputation*) reputation. **son ~ de sévérité** his reputation for severity; **bon/mauvais ~** good/bad reputation *ou* name.

renommé, e [ʀ(ə)nɔme] (*ptp de* **renommer**) **1** *adj* celebrated, famous. ~ **pour** renowned *ou* famed for. **2 renommée** *nf* **(a)** (*célébrité*) fame, renown. **marque/savant de ~ mondiale** world-famous make/scholar. **(b)** (*littér: opinion publique*) public report. **(c)** (*littér: réputation*) reputation. **bonne/mauvaise ~** good/bad reputation *ou* name; *V* **bon**[1].

renommer [ʀ(ə)nɔme] (1) *vt* to reappoint.

renonce [ʀ(ə)nɔ̃s] *nf* (*Cartes*) **faire une ~** to fail to follow suit, renounce.

renoncement [ʀ(ə)nɔ̃smɑ̃] *nm* (*action*) renouncement (*à* of). (*sacrifice*) **le ~** renunciation, abnegation; ~ **à soi-même** self-abnegation, self-renunciation; **mener une vie de ~** to live a life of renunciation *ou* abnegation.

renoncer [ʀ(ə)nɔ̃se] (3) **1 renoncer à** *vt indir* (*gén*) to give up, renounce; *héritage, titre, pouvoir* to renounce, relinquish; *habitude* to give up; *métier* to abandon, give up. ~ **à un voyage/au mariage** to give up the idea of *ou* abandon all thought of a journey/of marriage; ~ **à qn** to give sb up; ~ **au tabac** to give up smoking; ~ **à lutter/à comprendre** to give up struggling/trying to understand; ~ **à se marier** to give up *ou* abandon the idea of getting married; ~ **aux plaisirs/au monde** to renounce pleasures/the world; **je** *ou* **j'y renonce** I give up; (*Cartes*) ~ **à cœur** to fail to follow (in) hearts.
2 *vt* (*littér*) *ami* to give up, withdraw one's friendship from.

renonciation [ʀ(ə)nɔ̃sjɑsjɔ̃] *nf* (*V* **renoncer**) giving up; renunciation; relinquishment; abandonment.

renoncule [ʀ(ə)nɔ̃kyl] *nf* (*sauvage*) buttercup; (*cultivée*) ranunculus.

renouer [ʀənwe] (1) **1** *vt lacet, nœud* to tie (up) again, re-tie; *cravate* to reknot, knot again; *conversation, liaison* to renew, resume, take up again.
2 *vi*: ~ **avec qn** to take up with sb again, become friends with sb again; ~ **avec une habitude** to take up a habit again; ~ **avec une tradition** to revive a tradition.

renouveau, *pl* ~**x** [ʀ(ə)nuvo] *nm* **(a)** (*transformation*) revival. **le ~ des sciences et des arts à la Renaissance** the revival of the sciences and the arts *ou* the renewed interest in *ou* the renewal of interest in the sciences and arts during the Renaissance.
(b) (*regain*) ~ **de succès/faveur** renewed success/favour; **connaître un ~ de faveur** to enjoy renewed favour, come back into favour.
(c) (*littér: printemps*) **le ~** springtide (*littér*).

renouvelable [ʀ(ə)nuvlabl(ə)] *adj passeport, bail* renewable; *expérience* which can be tried again *ou* repeated; *congé* which can be re-granted; *assemblée* that must be re-elected. **le mandat présidentiel est ~ tous les 7 ans** the president must stand for re-election every 7 years.

renouveler [ʀ(ə)nuvle] (4) **1** *vt* **(a)** (*remplacer*) *outillage, personnel* to renew, replace; *stock* to renew, replenish; *pansement* to renew, change; *conseil d'administration* to re-elect. ~ **l'air d'une salle** to air a room; ~ **l'eau d'une piscine** to renew *ou* replenish the water in a swimming pool; ~ **sa garde-robe** to renew one's wardrobe, buy some new clothes; (*Pol*) **la chambre doit être renouvelée tous les 5 ans** the house must be re-elected every 5 years.
(b) (*transformer*) *mode, théorie* to renew, revive. **les poètes de la Pléiade renouvelèrent la langue française** the poets of the Pléiade gave new *ou* renewed life to the French language; **je préfère la pièce dans sa version renouvelée** I prefer the new version of the play.
(c) (*reconduire*) *passeport, contrat, abonnement* to renew; *congé* to re-grant. (*Méd*) **à ~** to be renewed; **la chambre a renouvelé sa confiance au gouvernement** the house reaffirmed its confidence *ou* expressed its renewed confidence in the government.
(d) (*recommencer*) *candidature* to renew; *demande, offre, promesse, erreur* to renew, repeat; *expérience, exploit* to repeat, do again; (*littér*) *douleur* to renew, revive. **l'énergie sans cesse renouvelée que requiert ce métier** the constantly renewed energy which this job requires; (*dans une lettre*) **avec mes remerciements renouvelés** with renewed thanks, thanking you once more *ou* once again; (*littér*) **épisode renouvelé de l'Antiquité** episode taken *ou* borrowed from Antiquity.
(e) (*Rel*) to renew.
2 se renouveler *vpr* **(a)** (*se répéter*) to recur, be repeated. **cette petite scène se renouvelle tous les jours** this little scene recurs *ou* is repeated every day; **et que ça ne se renouvelle plus!** and (just) don't let that happen again!
(b) (*être remplacé*) to be renewed *ou* replaced. **les cellules de notre corps se renouvellent constamment** the cells of our body are constantly being renewed *ou* replaced; **les hommes au pouvoir ne se renouvellent pas assez** men in power aren't replaced often enough.
(c) (*innover*) *[auteur, peintre]* to change one's style, try something new. *[comique]* **il ne se renouvelle pas** he never has any new jokes *ou* stories, he always tells the same old jokes *ou* stories.

renouvellement [ʀ(ə)nuvɛlmɑ̃] *nm* (*V* **renouveler**) renewal; replacement; replenishment; changing; revival; repetition; recurrence. (*Pol*) **solliciter le ~ de son mandat** to stand for re-election; (*Rel*) **faire son ~** to renew one's first communion promises.

rénovateur, -trice [ʀenɔvatœʀ, tʀis] **1** *adj doctrine* which seeks a renewal, reformist; *influence* renewing (*épith*), reforming (*épith*).
2 *nm,f* (*de la morale*) reformer. **il est considéré comme le ~ de cette science/de cet art** he's considered as having been the one to inject new life into this science/this art.

rénovation [ʀenɔvɑsjɔ̃] *nf* (*V* **rénover**) renovation, modernisation; restoration; reform; remodelling; renewal; bringing up to date.

rénover [ʀenɔve] (1) *vt* **(a)** *maison* to renovate, modernize; *meuble* to restore. **(b)** *enseignement, institutions* to reform, remodel; *science* to renew, bring up to date; *méthodes* to reform.

renseignement [ʀɑ̃sɛɲmɑ̃] *nm* **(a)** information (*U*), piece of information. **un ~ intéressant** an interesting piece of information, some interesting information; **demander un ~** *ou* **des ~s à qn** to ask sb for (some) information, inquire about sth; **il est allé aux ~s** he has gone to make inquiries *ou* to see what he can find out (about it); **prendre ses ~s** *ou* **demander des ~s sur qn** to make inquiries *ou* ask for information *ou* for particulars about sb, try to find out about sb; **~s pris** upon inquiry; **avoir de bons ~s sur le compte de qn** to have good *ou* favourable reports about *ou* on sb; **pourriez-vous me donner un ~?** I'd like some information, could you give me some information?; **je peux te demander un ~?** can you give me some information?, can I ask you something?, could you tell me something?; **merci pour le ~** thanks for the information, thanks for telling me *ou* letting me know; **bureau des ~s** inquiry office; (*panneau*) '**~s**' 'inquiries', 'information'; (*Téléc*) **(service des) ~s** directory inquiries.
(b) (*Mil*) intelligence (*U*), piece of intelligence. **agent/service de ~s** intelligence agent/service; **les ~s généraux** the secret police.

renseigner [ʀɑ̃seɲe] (1) **1** *vt*: ~ **un client/un touriste** to give some information to a customer/a tourist; ~ **la police/l'ennemi** to give information to the police/the enemy (*sur* about); ~ **un passant/un automobiliste** to give directions to a passer-by/a driver, tell a passer-by/a driver the way; **qui pourrait me ~ sur le prix de la voiture/sur lui?** who could tell me the price of the car/something about him?, who could give me some information *ou* particulars about the price of the car/about him?; **il pourra peut-être te ~** perhaps he'll be able to give you some information (about it) *ou* to tell you *ou* to help you; **document qui renseigne utilement** document which gives useful information; **ça ne nous renseigne pas beaucoup!** that doesn't get us very far!, that doesn't tell us very much! *ou* give us much to go on!; **il a l'air bien renseigné** he seems to be well informed *ou* to know a lot about it; **il est mal renseigné** he doesn't know much about it, he isn't very well informed about it; **on vous a mal renseigné** you have been misinformed.
2 se renseigner *vpr* (*demander des renseignements*) to make inquiries, ask for information (*sur* about); (*obtenir des renseignements*) to find out (*sur* about). **je vais me ~ auprès de lui** I'll ask him for information *ou* for particulars, I'll ask him about it; **j'essaierai de me ~** I'll try to find out, I'll try and get some information; **je vais me ~ sur son compte** I'll make

inquiries about him, I'll find out about him; **je voudrais me ~ sur les chaînes hi-fi** I'd like some information *ou* particulars about hi-fi equipment.

rentabiliser [ʀɑ̃tabilize] (1) *vt* to make profitable, make pay.

rentabilité [ʀɑ̃tabilite] *nf* profitability.

rentable [ʀɑ̃tabl(ə)] *adj* profitable. **c'est un exercice très ~** this is a really profitable operation, this operation really pays; **au prix où est l'essence, les transports privés ne sont pas ~s** with petrol the price it is, private transport isn't a paying *ou* viable proposition *ou* doesn't pay.

rentamer [ʀɑ̃tame] (1) *vt discours* to begin *ou* start again.

rente [ʀɑ̃t] *nf* **(a)** (*pension*) annuity, pension; (*fournie par la famille*) allowance. **~ viagère** life annuity.

(b) (*emprunt d'État*) government stock *ou* loan *ou* bond. **~s perpétuelles** perpetual loans, irredeemable securities.

(c) (*loc*) **avoir des ~s** to have a private *ou* an unearned income, have private *ou* independent means; **vivre de ses ~s** to live on *ou* off one's private income; (*fig*) **cette voiture est une ~, il faut tout le temps la réparer** this car costs a fortune (to run) because it needs constant repairs.

rentier, -ière [ʀɑ̃tje, jɛʀ] *nm,f* person of independent *ou* private means. **c'est un petit ~** he has a small private income; **mener une vie de ~** to live a life of ease *ou* leisure.

rentrant, e [ʀɑ̃tʀɑ̃, ɑ̃t] *adj train d'atterrissage* retractable; (*Math*) *angle* reflex.

rentré, e[1] [ʀɑ̃tʀe] (*ptp de* **rentrer**) *adj colère* suppressed; *yeux* sunken; *joues* sunken, hollow.

rentrée[2] [ʀɑ̃tʀe] *nf* **(a)** (*Scol*) start of the new school year; (*Univ*) start of the new academic year; (*du trimestre*) start of the new term. **acheter des cahiers pour la ~ (des classes)** to buy exercise books for the new school year; **la ~ aura lieu lundi** the new term begins on Monday, school starts again on Monday, pupils go back *ou* return to school again *ou* start school again on Monday; **à la ~ de Noël/Pâques** at the start of (the) term after the Christmas/Easter holidays, at the start of the second/third term.

(b) *[tribunaux]* reopening; *[parlement]* reopening, reassembly; *[députés]* return, reassembly. **la ~ parlementaire aura lieu cette semaine** parliament reassembles *ou* reopens this week, the new session of parliament starts this week; **c'est la ~ des théâtres parisiens** it's the start of the theatrical season in Paris; **les députés font leur ~ aujourd'hui** the deputies are returning *ou* reassembling today (for the start of the new session); **on verra ça à la ~** we'll see about that after the holidays *ou* when we come back from holiday.

(c) *[acteur]* (stage) comeback; *[sportif]* comeback. **faire sa ~ politique** to make a *ou* one's political come-back.

(d) (*retour*) **pour faciliter la ~ dans la capitale** to make getting back into *ou* the return into the capital easier; **la ~ des ouvriers à l'usine le lundi matin** the workers' return to work on a Monday morning; **à l'heure des ~s dans Paris** when everyone is coming back into Paris *ou* returning to Paris, when the roads into Paris are full of returning motorists *ou* motorists on their way back home; **le concierge n'aime pas les ~s tardives** the concierge doesn't like people coming in late; (*Espace*) **~ dans l'atmosphère** re-entry into the atmosphere; **effectuer sa ~ dans l'atmosphère** to re-enter the atmosphere; (*Sport*) **~ en touche** throw-in.

(e) *[récolte]* bringing in. **faire la ~ du blé** to bring in the wheat.

(f) (*Cartes*) cards picked up.

(g) (*Comm*) **~s** income; **~ d'argent** sum of money (coming in); **je compte sur une ~ d'argent très prochaine** I'm expecting a sum of money *ou* some money very soon; (*Fin*) **les ~s de l'impôt** the revenue from tax.

rentrer [ʀɑ̃tʀe] (1) **1** *vi* **(a)** (*entrer à nouveau*) (*aller*) to go back in; (*venir*) to come back in. **il pleut trop, rentrez un instant** it's raining too hard so come back in for a while; **il était sorti sans ses clefs, il a dû ~ par la fenêtre** he'd gone out without his keys and he had to get back in through the window; **il est rentré dans la maison/la pièce** he went back (*ou* came back) into the house/the room.

(b) (*revenir chez soi*) to come back, come (back) home, return (home); (*s'en aller chez soi*) to go (back) home, return home; (*arriver chez soi*) to get (back) home, return home. **est-ce qu'il est rentré?** is he back?, is he (back) home?, has he got *ou* come back home?; **~ de l'école/du bureau** to come back from school/from the office, come (*ou* go) home from school/from the office; **il a dû ~ de voyage d'urgence** he had to come back *ou* come home from his trip urgently, he had to return home urgently; **~ à Paris/de Paris** to go back *ou* come back *ou* return to Paris/from Paris; (*Aviat*) **~ à sa base** to return *ou* go back to base; **je rentre en voiture** I'm driving back, I'm going back by car; **dépêche-toi de ~, ta mère a besoin de toi** hurry home *ou* back because your mother needs you; **elle est rentrée très tard hier soir** she came *ou* got in *ou* back very late last night.

(c) (*reprendre ses activités*) *[élèves]* to go back to school, start school again; *[université]* to start again; *[tribunaux]* to reopen; *[parlement]* to reassemble; *[députés]* to return, reassemble. **les enfants rentrent en classe *ou* au lycée lundi** the children go back to school *ou* start school again on Monday, school resumes *ou* starts again *ou* goes back on Monday; **le trimestre prochain, on rentrera un lundi** next term starts *ou* next term we start on a Monday.

(d) (*entrer*) *[personne]* to go in; to come in; *[chose]* to go in. **les voleurs sont rentrés par la fenêtre** the thieves got in by the window; **il pleuvait, nous sommes rentrés dans un café** it was raining so we went into a cafe; **il faut trouver une clef qui rentre dans cette serrure** we must find a key that goes *ou* fits into this lock; **cette clef ne rentre pas (dans la serrure)** this key doesn't fit (into the lock), I can't get this key in (the lock) *ou* into the lock; (*fig*) **il a le cou qui lui rentre dans les épaules** he is very short-necked, he has a very short neck; **il était exténué, les jambes lui rentraient dans le corps** he was so exhausted his legs were giving way under him; **tout cela ne rentrera pas dans la valise** that won't all go *ou* fit into the suitcase, you (*ou* we *etc*) won't get all that into the suitcase; **pour les enfants, il y a des cubes qui rentrent les uns dans les autres** there are cubes that fit into one another *ou* one inside the other for children.

(e) (*travailler dans*) **~ dans** *police, firme, fonction publique* to join, go into; *industrie, banque* to go into; **c'est son père qui l'a fait ~ dans l'usine** his father helped him (to) get a job in the factory *ou* (to) get into the factory.

(f) (*se jeter dans*) **~ dans** to crash into, collide with; **sa voiture a dérapé, il est rentré dans un arbre** his car skidded and he crashed into a tree; **furieux, il voulait lui ~ dedans*;** *ou* **lui ~ dans le chou*;** he was furious and he felt like pitching into him *ou* smashing his head in*; **il lui est rentré dans le lard*;** *ou* **le mou*;** he bashed him up*; **les deux voitures se sont rentrées dedans à grande vitesse** the two cars crashed into each other *ou* collided (with each other) at high speed.

(g) (*être compris dans*) **~ dans** to be included in, be part of; **cela ne rentre pas dans ses attributions** that is not included in *ou* part of his duties; **les frais de déplacement ne devraient pas ~ dans la note** travelling expenses should not be included in the bill *ou* should not be put on the bill; **~ dans une catégorie** to fall into *ou* come into *ou* go under a category.

(h) *[argent]* to come in. **l'argent ne rentre pas en ce moment** the money isn't coming in at the moment; **l'argent rentre difficilement/bien en ce moment** there isn't much money/there's plenty of money coming in at the moment; **faire ~ les impôts/les fonds** to collect the taxes/the funds; **faire ~ l'argent** to get the money in.

(i) (*) *[connaissances]* **la grammaire/les maths, ça ne rentre pas** he can't take grammar/maths in, he can't get the hang of grammar/maths*; **faire ~ qch dans la tête de qn** to drum *ou* get sth into sb *ou* sb's head; **vous aurez du mal à lui faire ~ cela dans la tête** you'll have a job drumming that into him *ou* making him take that in *ou* getting that into his head*.

(j) (*loc*) **~ dans sa coquille** to go back into one's shell; **~ dans ses droits** to recover one's rights; **~ dans son argent/dans ses frais** to recover *ou* get back one's money/expenses; **tout est rentré dans l'ordre** (*dans son état normal*) everything is back to normal again, everything is straight again *ou* in order again; (*dans le calme*) order has returned, order has been restored; (*tout a été clarifié*) everything is sorted out now; **~ dans le rang** to come *ou* fall back into line; **~ en grâce *ou* faveur auprès de qn** to get back into sb's good graces.

2 *vt* **(a)** *foins, moisson* to bring in, get in; *marchandises, animaux* (*en venant*) to bring in; (*en allant*) to take in. **~ sa voiture (au garage)** to put the car away (in the garage), put the car in the garage; **ne laisse pas ta bicyclette à la pluie, rentre-la** don't leave your bicycle out in the rain, put it away *ou* bring it in; **~ les bêtes à l'étable** to bring the cattle into the cowshed, bring in the cattle, put the cattle in the cowshed.

(b) *train d'atterrissage* to raise; (*lit, fig*) *griffes* to draw in. **~ sa chemise (dans son pantalon)** to tuck one's shirt in (one's trousers); **~ le cou dans les épaules** to hunch up one's shoulders; **ne me rentre pas ton coude dans le ventre** don't jab *ou* stick your elbow in(to) my stomach; **~ le ventre** to pull one's stomach in; **~ ses larmes** to hold back *ou* choke back (one's) tears, fight back tears; **~ sa rage** to hold back *ou* suppress one's anger.

renvelopper [ʀɑ̃vlɔpe] (1) *vt* to rewrap, wrap up again.

renversable [ʀɑ̃vɛʀsabl(ə)] *adj obstacle* (*lit*) which can be knocked down; (*fig*) which can be overcome; *ordre établi* which can be overthrown; *termes* which can be reversed; *fraction* which can be inverted. **facilement ~** *objet* easily overturned, easily knocked over; *canot* easily overturned *ou* capsized.

renversant, e* [ʀɑ̃vɛʀsɑ̃, ɑ̃t] *adj nouvelle* staggering, astounding; *personne* amazing, incredible.

renverse [ʀɑ̃vɛʀs(ə)] *nf*: **à la ~** on one's back; **tomber à la ~** to fall backwards; (*fig*) **il y a de quoi tomber à la ~!** it's astounding! *ou* staggering!, it (quite) bowls you over!

renversé, e [ʀɑ̃vɛʀse] (*ptp de* **renverser**) *adj* **(a)** (*à l'envers*) upside down (*attrib*); *fraction* inverted; *image* inverted, reversed. **c'est le monde ~** it's a topsy-turvy world, what's the world coming to?; *V* **crème**.

(b) (*stupéfait*) être **~** to be bowled over, be staggered.

(c) (*penché*) *écriture* backhand (*épith*).

renversement [ʀɑ̃vɛʀsəmɑ̃] *nm* **(a)** *[image, fraction]* inversion; *[ordre des mots]* inversion, reversal; *[vapeur]* reversing; *[situation]* reversal; (*Mus*) *[intervalles, accord]* inversion.

(b) *[alliances, valeurs]* reversal; *[ministre]* removal from office; *[gouvernement]* (*par un coup d'État*) overthrow; (*par un vote*) defeat, voting *ou* turning out of office.

(c) *[buste, tête]* tilting *ou* tipping back.

(d) *[courant]* changing of direction; *[marée]* turning, changing of direction.

renverser [ʀɑ̃vɛʀse] (1) **1** *vt* **(a)** (*faire tomber*) *personne* to knock over *ou* down; *chaise* to knock down, overturn; *vase, bouteille* to knock over, upset, overturn; (*Aut*) *piéton* to knock over *ou* down, run over. **il l'a renversé d'un coup de poing** he gave it a blow that knocked it over; **le cheval a renversé son cavalier** the horse threw *ou* unseated its rider.

(b) (*répandre*) *liquide* to spill, upset. **~ du vin sur la nappe** to spill *ou* upset some wine on the tablecloth.

(c) (*mettre à l'envers*) to turn upside down. **~ un seau (pour monter dessus)** to turn a bucket upside down (so as to stand on it).

(d) (*abattre*) *obstacles* (*lit*) to knock down; (*fig*) to overcome; *ordre établi, tradition, royauté* to overthrow; *ministre* to put *ou* throw out of office, remove from office. **~ le gouvernement** (*par un coup d'État*) to overthrow *ou* overturn the government; (*par un vote*) to defeat the government, vote *ou* throw the government out of office.

(e) (*pencher*) **~ la tête en arrière** to tip *ou* tilt one's head back; **~ le corps en arrière** to lean back; **elle lui renversa la tête en arrière** she tipped *ou* put his head back.

(f) (*inverser*) *ordre des mots, courant* to reverse; *fraction* to invert; (*Opt*) *image* to invert, reverse. **~ la situation** to reverse the situation; **~ la vapeur** (*lit*) to reverse steam; (*fig*) to change course.

(g) (*: *étonner*) to bowl over, stagger. **la nouvelle l'a renversé** the news bowled him over *ou* staggered him, he couldn't get over the news.

2 se renverser *vpr* **(a)** **se ~ en arrière** to lean back; **se ~ sur le dos** to lie down (on one's back); **se ~ sur sa chaise** to tilt *ou* tip *ou* lean back on one's chair, tilt *ou* tip one's chair back.

(b) *[voiture, camion]* to overturn; *[bateau]* to overturn, capsize; *[verre, vase]* to fall over, be overturned.

renvoi [rɑ̃vwa] *nm* **(a)** (*V* **renvoyer**) dismissal; expulsion; suspension; discharge; sending back; return; kicking back; throwing back; referral; postponement. **menacer de ~** *employé* to threaten with dismissal; (*Scol*) to threaten to expel; **le ~ d'un projet de loi en commission** sending a bill to a committee *ou* for further discussion; (*Sport*) **à la suite d'un mauvais ~ du gardien, la balle fut interceptée par l'équipe adverse** as a result of a poor return *ou* throw by the goalkeeper, the ball was intercepted by the opposing team.

(b) (*référence*) cross-reference; (*en bas de page*) footnote. **faire un ~ aux notes de l'appendice** to cross-refer to the notes in the appendix.

(c) (*rot*) belch. **avoir un ~** to belch; **avoir des ~s** to have wind; **ça me donne des ~s** it gives me wind, it repeats on me, it makes me belch.

(d) (*Tech*) **levier de ~** reversing lever; **poulie de ~** return pulley.

renvoyer [rɑ̃vwaje] (8) *vt* **(a)** (*congédier*) *employé* to dismiss; *élève* (*définitivement*) to expel; (*temporairement*) to suspend; *étudiant* to expel, send down. **il s'est fait ~ de son travail** he was dismissed from his job.

(b) (*faire retourner*) to send back; (*faire repartir*) to send away; (*libérer*) *accusé, troupes* to discharge. **je l'ai renvoyé chez lui** I sent him back home; **~ les soldats dans leurs foyers** to discharge soldiers, send soldiers back home; **~ le projet de loi en commission** to send the bill for further discussion, send the bill to a committee; **ils se renvoient les clients de service en service** they send the customers *ou* hand on the customers from one office to the next.

(c) (*réexpédier*) *lettre, colis* to send back, return; *bague de fiançailles* to return, give back.

(d) (*relancer*) *balle* (*gén*) to send back; (*au pied*) to kick back; (*à la main*) to throw back; (*Tennis*) to return (*à* to). **il m'a renvoyé la balle** (*argument*) he threw the *ou* my argument back at me, he came back at me with the same argument; (*responsabilité*) he handed the responsibility over to me, he left it up to me, he passed the buck to me*; **ils se renvoient la balle** (*argument*) they throw the same argument at each other, they come back at each other with the same argument; (*responsabilité*) they each refuse to take the responsibility, they each want to off-load the responsibility, they're each trying to pass the buck*.

(e) (*référer*) *lecteur* to refer (*à* to). **~ aux notes de l'appendice** to (cross-)refer to notes in the appendix; **~ un procès en Haute cour** to refer a case to the high court; **~ le prévenu en cour d'assises** to send the accused for trial by the assize court.

(f) (*différer*) *rendez-vous* to postpone, put off. (*Jur*) **l'affaire a été renvoyée à huitaine** the case was postponed *ou* put off for a week; **~ qch aux calendes grecques** to postpone sth *ou* put sth off indefinitely.

(g) (*réfléchir*) *son* to echo; *lumière, chaleur, image* to reflect.

(h) (*Cartes*) **~ carreau/pique** to play diamonds/spades again, lead diamonds/spades again.

réoccupation [reɔkypasjɔ̃] *nf* reoccupation.

réoccuper [reɔkype] (1) *vt territoire* to reoccupy; *fonction* to take up again; *local* to take over again.

réorchestration [reɔrkɛstrasjɔ̃] *nf* reorchestration.

réorchestrer [reɔrkɛstre] (1) *vt* to reorchestrate.

réorganisateur, -trice [reɔrganizatœr, tris] *nm,f* reorganizer.

réorganisation [reɔrganizasjɔ̃] *nf* reorganization.

réorganiser [reɔrganize] (1) **1** *vt* to reorganize. **2 se réorganiser** *vpr [pays, parti]* to be reorganized. **il faudrait qu'on se réorganise** we must get reorganized, we must reorganize ourselves.

réorientation [reɔrjɑ̃tasjɔ̃] *nf [politique]* redirecting, reorientation. **~ scolaire** restreaming (*Brit*).

réorienter [reɔrjɑ̃te] (1) *vt politique* to redirect, reorient(ate); (*Scol*) *élève* to restream (*Brit*).

réouverture [reuvɛrtyr] *nf [magasin, théâtre]* reopening; *[débat]* resumption, reopening.

repaire [r(ə)pɛr] *nm* (*Zool*) den, lair; (*fig*) den, hideout. **cette taverne est un ~ de brigands** this inn is a thieves' den *ou* a haunt of robbers.

repaître [rəpɛtr(ə)] (57) **1** *vt* (*littér*) **~ ses yeux de qch** to feast one's eyes on sth; **~ son esprit de lectures** to feed one's mind on books.

2 se repaître *vpr* **(a)** (*fig*) **se ~ de** *crimes* to wallow in; *lectures, films* to revel in; *illusions* to revel in, feed on.

(b) (*manger*) to eat its fill. **se ~ de viande crue** to feed on *ou* eat raw meat.

répandre [repɑ̃dr(ə)] (41) **1** *vt* **(a)** (*renverser*) *soupe, vin* to spill; *grains* to scatter; (*volontairement*) *sciure, produit* to spread. **le camion a répandu son chargement sur la chaussée** the lorry shed *ou* spilled its load in the road; **~ du sable sur le sol** to spread *ou* sprinkle sand on the ground; **~ sa petite monnaie (sur la table) pour la compter** to spread one's change out (on the table) to count it; **la rivière répand ses eaux dans la vallée** the waters of the river spread over *ou* out across the valley.

(b) (*littér*) *larmes* to shed. **~ son sang** to shed one's blood; **~ le sang** to spill *ou* shed blood; **beaucoup de sang a été répandu** a lot of blood was shed *ou* spilled, there was a lot of bloodshed.

(c) (*être source de*) *lumière* to shed, give out; *odeur* to give off; *chaleur* to give out *ou* off. **~ de la fumée** *[cheminée]* to give out smoke; *[feu]* to give off *ou* out smoke.

(d) (*fig: propager*) *nouvelle, mode, joie, terreur* to spread; *dons* to lavish, pour out.

2 se répandre *vpr* **(a)** (*couler*) *[liquide]* to spill, be spilled; *[grains]* to scatter, be scattered (*sur* over). **le verre a débordé, et le vin s'est répandu par terre** the glass overflowed and the wine spilled onto the floor; **le sang se répand dans les tissus** blood spreads through the tissues; **la foule se répand dans les rues** the crowd spills out *ou* pours out into the streets.

(b) (*se dégager*) *[chaleur, odeur, lumière]* to spread; *[son]* to carry (*dans* through). **il se répandit une forte odeur de caoutchouc brûlé** a strong smell of burning rubber was given off.

(c) (*se propager*) *[doctrine, mode, nouvelle]* to spread (*dans, à travers* through); *[opinion, méthode]* to become widespread (*dans, parmi* among). **la peur se répandit sur son visage** fear spread over his face; **l'horreur/la nouvelle se répandit à travers la ville comme une traînée de poudre** horror/the news spread round *ou* through the town like wildfire.

(d) **se ~ en calomnies/condoléances/menaces** to pour out *ou* pour forth slanderous remarks/condolences/threats; **se ~ en invectives** to let out a torrent of abuse, pour out a stream of abuse.

répandu, e [repɑ̃dy] (*ptp de* **répandre**) *adj opinion, préjugé* widespread; *méthode* widespread, widely used. **c'est une idée très ~e** it's a widely *ou* commonly held idea.

réparable [reparabl(ə)] *adj objet* repairable, which can be repaired *ou* mended; *erreur* which can be put right *ou* corrected; *perte, faute* which can be made up for. **ce n'est pas ~** *[objet]* it is beyond repair; *[faute]* there's no way of making up for it; *[erreur]* it can't be put right.

reparaître [r(ə)parɛtr(ə)] (57) *vi [personne, trait héréditaire]* to reappear; *[lune]* to reappear, come out again.

réparateur, -trice [reparatœr, tris] **1** *adj sommeil* refreshing.

2 *nm,f* repairer. **~ d'objets d'art** restorer of works of art; **~ de porcelaine** porcelain restorer; **~ de télévision** television *ou* TV repairman *ou* engineer.

réparation [reparasjɔ̃] *nf* **(a)** (*remise en état*) (*action: V* **réparer**) mending; repairing; fixing*; restoring, restoration; (*résultat*) repair. **la voiture est en ~** the car is under repair *ou* is being repaired; **on va faire des ~s dans la maison** we're going to have some repair work *ou* some repairs done in the house; **pendant les ~s** during the repairs, while the repairs are being carried out; **l'atelier de ~** the repair shop.

(b) (*correction*) *[erreur]* correction; *[oubli, négligence]* putting right, rectification.

(c) (*compensation*) *[faute, offense]* atonement (*de* for); *[tort]* redress (*de* for); *[perte]* compensation (*de* for). **en ~ du dommage causé** to make up for *ou* to compensate for *ou* to make amends for the harm that has been done; **obtenir ~ (d'un affront)** to obtain redress (for an insult); **demander ~ par les armes** to demand a duel.

(d) (*Ftbl*) **coup de pied/surface de ~** penalty kick/area.

(e) (*régénérescence*) *[forces]* restoring, restoration, recovery. **la ~ des tissus sera longue** the tissues will take a long time to heal.

(f) (*dommages-intérêts*) damages, compensation. (*Hist*) **~s** reparations.

réparer [repare] (1) *vt* **(a)** (*remettre en état*) (*gén*) to mend; *chaussure, machine* to mend, repair, fix*; *déchirure, fuite* to mend; *maison* to repair, have repairs done to; *objet d'art* to restore, repair. **donner qch à ~** to take sth to be mended *ou* repaired; **faire ~ qch** to get *ou* have sth mended *ou* repaired; **~ qch sommairement** to patch sth up, do a temporary repair job on sth.

(b) (*corriger*) *erreur* to correct, put right; *oubli, négligence* to put right, rectify.

(c) (*compenser*) *faute* to make up for, make amends for; *tort* to put right, redress; *offense* to atone for, make up for; *perte* to make good, make up for, compensate for. **tu ne pourras jamais ~ le mal que tu m'as fait** you can never put right *ou* never undo the harm you've done me; **comment pourrais-je ~ ma bêtise?** how could I make amends for *ou* make up for my stupidity?; **cela ne pourra jamais ~ le dommage que j'ai subi** that'll never make up for *ou* compensate for the harm I've suffered; **vous devez ~ en l'épousant** you'll have to make amends by marrying her; **comment pourrais-je ~?** what could I do to make up for it? *ou* to make amends (for it)?

(d) (*régénérer*) *forces, santé* to restore.

(e) (*loc*) **il va falloir ~ les dégâts** (*lit*) we'll have to repair the damage; (**fig*) we'll have to repair the damage *ou* pick up the pieces; (*littér*) **~ le désordre de sa toilette** to straighten *ou* tidy one's dress.

reparler [ʀ(ə)paʀle] (1) **1** *vi*: ~ **de qch** to talk about sth again; ~ **à qn** to speak to sb again; **nous en reparlerons** we'll talk about it again *ou* discuss it again later.

2 se reparler *vpr* to speak to each other again, be on speaking terms again, be back on speaking terms.

repartie [ʀəpaʀti] *nf* retort. **avoir de la** ~, **avoir la** ~ **facile** to be good *ou* quick at repartee.

repartir[1] [ʀəpaʀtiʀ] (16) *vt* (*littér: répliquer*) to retort, reply.

repartir[2] [ʀ(ə)paʀtiʀ] (16) *vi [voyageur]* to set *ou* start off again; *[machine]* to start (up) again, restart; *[affaire]* to get going again, pick up again. ~ **chez soi** to go back *ou* return home; **il est reparti hier** he left again yesterday; ~ **à zéro** to start from scratch again, go back to square one; **heureusement, c'est bien reparti** fortunately, things are going smoothly *ou* have got off to a good start this time; *[discussion]* **c'est reparti!*** they're off again!*, they're at it again!*, there they go again!

répartir [ʀepaʀtiʀ] (2) **1** *vt* **(a)** (*diviser*) *ressources, travail* to share out, divide up (*en* into, *entre* among), allocate, distribute (*entre* among); *impôts, charges* to share out (*en* into, *entre* among), apportion, allot, allocate (*entre* among); (*distribuer*) *butin, récompenses, rôles* to share out, divide up, distribute (*entre* among). **on avait réparti les joueurs en 2 groupes** the players had been divided *ou* split (up) into 2 groups.

(b) (*égaliser*) *poids, masses, chaleur* to distribute; (*étaler*) *paiement, cours, horaire* to spread (*sur* over). **on a mal réparti les bagages dans le coffre** the luggage has been badly *ou* unevenly distributed *ou* hasn't been evenly distributed in the boot; **les troupes sont réparties le long de la frontière nord** troops are spread out *ou* distributed *ou* scattered along the northern frontier; **le programme est réparti sur 2 ans** the programme is spread (out) over 2 years.

2 se répartir *vpr*: **les charges se répartissent comme suit** the expenses are divided up as follows *ou* in the following way; **ils se répartissent en 2 ensembles** they can be divided into 2 sets; **ils se sont répartis en 2 groupes** they divided themselves *ou* they split into 2 groups; **ils se sont réparti le travail** they shared the work out *ou* divided the work up among themselves.

répartiteur [ʀepaʀtitœʀ] *nm* (*gén: littér*) distributor, apportioner; *[impôt]* assessor.

répartition [ʀepaʀtisjɔ̃] *nf* **(a)** (*action: V* **répartir**) sharing out (*U*), share-out; dividing up (*U*); allocation (*U*); distribution (*U*); apportionment (*U*), allotment (*U*); spreading (*U*). **cette** ~ **est injuste et favorise certains** this is a very unfair way to share things out because it gives some more than others; **il a fallu procéder à une deuxième** ~ **des tâches** the tasks had to be divided up *ou* shared out again.

(b) (*résultat*) *[population, flore, richesses]* distribution; *[pièces, salles]* layout, distribution.

repas [ʀ(ə)pɑ] *nm* meal. ~ **léger** light meal, snack; ~ **de midi** midday meal, lunch; ~ **de noces** wedding meal *ou* breakfast; ~ **de Noël** Christmas dinner; **faire son** ~ **d'un œuf et d'un fruit** to eat an egg and a piece of fruit for one's meal, dine off an egg and a piece of fruit (*frm, hum*); **il prend tous ses** ~ **au restaurant** he has all his meals at the restaurant, he always eats (out) at the restaurant, he always eats out; **assister au** ~ **des fauves** to watch the big cats being fed; **à l'heure du** ~ at mealtimes, at our mealtime; **aux heures des** ~ at mealtimes; **panier** ~ lunch *ou* dinner *ou* picnic basket; **plateau** ~ meal tray.

repassage [ʀ(ə)pɑsaʒ] *nm [linge]* ironing; *[couteau]* sharpening. **faire le** ~ to do the ironing.

repasser [ʀ(ə)pɑse] (1) **1** *vt* **(a)** *rivière, montagne, frontière* to cross again, go *ou* come back across.

(b) *examen* to resit, take again; *permis de conduire* to take again; *visite médicale* to undergo again.

(c) *plat* to hand round again; *film* to show again; *émission* to repeat. ~ **un plat au four** to put a dish in the oven again *ou* back in the oven.

(d) (*au fer à repasser*) to iron; (*à la pattemouille*) to press. **le nylon ne se repasse pas** nylon doesn't need ironing *ou* must not be ironed; **planche/table à** ~ ironing board/table; *V* **fer**.

(e) *couteau, lame* to sharpen (up).

(f) *souvenir, leçon, rôle* to go (back) over, go over again. ~ **qch dans son esprit** to go over sth again *ou* go back over sth in one's mind.

(g) (*: *transmettre*) *affaire, travail* to hand over *ou* on; *maladie* to pass on (*à qn* to sb). **il m'a repassé le tuyau** he passed *ou* handed me on the tip; **je te repasse ta mère** (*au téléphone*) I'm handing you back to your mother; **je vous repasse le standard** I'll put you back through to the operator.

2 *vi* **(a)** (*retourner*) to come back, go back. **je repasserai** I'll come *ou* call back, I'll call (in) again; **si vous repassez par Paris** (*au retour*) if you come back through Paris; (*une autre fois*) if you're passing through Paris again; **ils sont repassés en Belgique** they crossed back *ou* went back over into Belgium; **il va falloir que je repasse sur le billard* pour une autre opération** I've got to go through another operation, they want to open me up again*; **tu peux toujours** ~**!‡** you've got a hope!* (*Brit*), not on your nelly!‡ (*Brit*).

(b) (*devant un même lieu*) to go *ou* come past again; (*sur un même trait*) to go over again, go back over. **je passai et repassai devant la vitrine** I kept walking backwards and forwards in front of the shop window; **souvenirs qui repassent dans la mémoire** memories that are running through one's mind; (*fig*) **quand elle fait un travail, il faut toujours** ~ **derrière elle** when she does some work it always has to be done again *ou* gone over again afterwards.

repasseur [ʀ(ə)pɑsœʀ] *nm* knife-grinder *ou* -sharpener.

repasseuse [ʀ(ə)pɑsøz] *nf* (*femme*) ironer; (*machine*) ironer, ironing machine.

repavage [ʀ(ə)pavaʒ] *nm*, **repavement** [ʀ(ə)pavmɑ̃] *nm* repaving.

repaver [ʀ(ə)pave] (1) *vt* to repave.

repayer [ʀ(ə)peje] (8) *vt* to pay again.

repêchage [ʀ(ə)peʃaʒ] *nm* (*V* **repêcher**) recovery; fishing out; recovery of the body of; letting through; passing. **épreuve/question de** ~ exam/question to give candidates a second chance.

repêcher [ʀ(ə)peʃe] (1) *vt* **(a)** *corps* to recover, fish out; *noyé* to recover the body of, fish out.

(b) (*Scol*) *candidat* to let through, pass (*with less than the official pass mark*); *athlète* to give a second chance to. **élève repêché à l'oral** student who scrapes through *ou* just gets a pass thanks to the oral exam.

repeindre [ʀ(ə)pɛ̃dʀ(ə)] (52) *vt* to repaint.

repenser [ʀ(ə)pɑ̃se] (1) **1 repenser à** *vt indir*: ~ **à qch** to think about sth again; **plus j'y repense** the more I think of it; **je n'y ai plus repensé** I haven't thought about it again (since), I haven't given it any further thought (since); **j'y repenserai** I'll think about it again, I'll have another think about it.

2 *vt concept* to rethink. **il faut** ~ **tout l'enseignement** the whole issue of education will have to be rethought; ~ **la question** to think the question out again, have a second think about the question.

repentant, e [ʀ(ə)pɑ̃tɑ̃, ɑ̃t] *adj* repentant, penitent.

repenti, e [ʀ(ə)pɑ̃ti] (*ptp de* **se repentir**) *adj* repentant, penitent.

repentir[1] **(se)** [ʀ(ə)pɑ̃tiʀ] (16) *vpr* **(a)** (*Rel*) to repent. **se** ~ **d'une faute/d'avoir commis une faute** to repent (of) a fault/(of) having committed a fault.

(b) (*regretter*) **se** ~ **de qch/d'avoir fait qch** to regret sth/having done sth, be sorry for sth/for having done sth; **tu t'en repentiras!** you'll be sorry (for that), you'll regret that.

repentir[2] [ʀ(ə)pɑ̃tiʀ] *nm* (*Rel*) repentance (*U*); (*regret*) regret.

repérable [ʀ(ə)peʀabl(ə)] *adj* which can be spotted. **un chapeau rouge** ~ **de loin** a red hat easily spotted from a distance; **difficilement** ~ difficult to spot; (*Mil*) difficult to locate.

repérage [ʀ(ə)peʀaʒ] *nm* (*Aviat, Mil*) location. **le** ~ **d'un point sur la carte** locating *ou* spotting a point on the map, pinpointing a spot on the map.

répercussion [ʀepɛʀkysjɔ̃] *nf* (*gén*) repercussion (*sur, dans* on).

répercuter [ʀepɛʀkyte] (1) **1** *vt* **(a)** *son* to echo; *écho* to send back, throw back; *lumière* to reflect.

(b) (*transmettre*) ~ **des charges/une augmentation sur le client** to pass the cost of sth/an increase in cost on to the customer.

2 se répercuter *vpr* **(a)** *[son]* to reverberate, echo; *[lumière]* to be reflected, reflect.

(b) se ~ **sur** to have repercussions on, affect.

reperdre [ʀ(ə)pɛʀdʀ(ə)] (41) *vt* to lose again.

repère [ʀ(ə)pɛʀ] *nm* (*gén: marque, trait*) line, mark; (*jalon, balise*) marker, indicator; (*monument, accident de terrain etc*) landmark; (*fig*) landmark. **j'ai laissé des branches comme** ~**s pour retrouver notre chemin** I've left branches as markers *ou* to mark our way so that we can find the way back again; ~ **de niveau** bench mark; *V* **point**[1].

repérer [ʀ(ə)peʀe] (6) **1** *vt* **(a)** (*: *localiser*) *personne, erreur* to spot, pick out; *endroit, chemin* to discover, locate, find. **se faire** ~ to be spotted, be picked out; **il avait repéré un petit restaurant où l'on mange bien** he had discovered *ou* located *ou* tracked down a little restaurant where the food was good; **tu vas nous faire** ~ we'll be noticed *ou* spotted because of you, you'll get us caught; **il s'est fait** ~ **par le concierge** he was spotted by the concierge.

(b) (*Mil*) to locate, pinpoint.

(c) (*Tech*) *niveau, alignement* to mark out *ou* off, stake out.

2 se repérer *vpr* (*gén: se diriger*) to find one's way about *ou* around; (*établir sa position*) to find *ou* get one's bearings. (*fig*) **j'ai du mal à me** ~ **dans cette intrigue** I have difficulty getting my bearings in this plot.

répertoire [ʀepɛʀtwaʀ] **1** *nm* **(a)** (*carnet*) index notebook, notebook with thumb index; (*liste*) (alphabetical) list; (*catalogue*) catalogue. **noter un mot dans un** ~ to write a word down in an alphabetical index, index a word.

(b) (*Théât*) repertoire, repertory; *[chanteur, musicien]* repertoire. **jouer une pièce du** ~ to put on a stock play; (*fig*) **elle a tout un** ~ **de jurons/d'histoires drôles** she has quite a repertoire of swearwords/jokes; **c'est un** ~ **vivant** he's a real storehouse *ou* a mine of information (*de* about, on).

2: répertoire d'adresses address book; **répertoire alphabétique** alphabetical index *ou* list; (*sur un plan*) **répertoire des rues** street index.

répertorier [ʀepɛʀtɔʀje] (7) *vt* to itemize, make a list of, list.

repeser [ʀ(ə)pəze] (5) *vt* to reweigh, weigh again.

répéter [ʀepete] (6) **1** *vt* **(a)** (*redire*) *explication, question* to repeat; *mot* to repeat, say again; *histoire* to repeat, retell. ~ **à qn que** to tell sb again that, repeat that; **pourriez-vous me** ~ **cette phrase?** could you repeat that sentence?, could you say that sentence (to me) again?; **je l'ai répété/je te l'ai répété dix fois** I've said that/I've told you that a dozen times; **il répète toujours la même chose** he keeps saying *ou* repeating the same thing; (*ton de menace*) **répète!** just you dare repeat that! *ou* say that again!; **il ne se l'est pas fait** ~ he didn't have to be told *ou* asked twice, he didn't need asking *ou* telling twice.

(b) (*rapporter*) *calomnie* to repeat, spread about; *histoire* to repeat. **elle est allée tout** ~ **à son père** she went and related *ou* repeated everything to her father, she went and told her father everything; **je vais vous** ~ **exactement ce qu'il m'a dit** I'll repeat exactly what he said; **c'est un secret, ne le répétez pas!**

it's a secret, don't repeat it! *ou* don't tell anyone!; **il m'a répété tous les détails de l'événement** he went over all the details of the event for me, he related all the details of the event to me.

(c) (*refaire*) *expérience, exploit* to repeat, do again; *proposition* to repeat, renew; *essai* to repeat. **nous répéterons une nouvelle fois la tentative** we'll repeat the attempt one more time, we'll have another try (at it), we'll try (it) again one more time; **tentatives répétées de suicide** repeated attempts at suicide; **tentatives répétées d'évasion** repeated escape attempts, repeated attempts to escape.

(d) *pièce, symphonie, émission* to rehearse; *rôle, leçon* to learn, go over; *morceau de piano* to practise. **nous répétons à 4 heures** we rehearse at 4 o'clock, the rehearsal is at 4 o'clock; **ma mère m'a fait ~ ma leçon/mon rôle** I had to go over my homework/my part with my mother.

(e) (*reproduire*) *motif* to repeat; (*Mus*) *thème* to repeat, restate.

2 se répéter *vpr* **(a)** (*redire, radoter*) to repeat o.s. **se ~ qch à soi-même** to repeat sth to o.s.; **la nouvelle que toute la ville se répète** the news that everyone in town is passing round, the news which is being repeated all round the town; **je ne voudrais pas me ~, mais ...** I don't want to repeat myself *ou* say the same thing twice, but ... .

(b) (*se reproduire*) to be repeated, reoccur, recur. **ces incidents se répétèrent fréquemment** these incidents were frequently repeated, these incidents kept recurring *ou* occurred repeatedly; **que cela ne se répète pas!** (just) don't let that happen again!

répétiteur, -trice [ʀepetitœʀ, tʀis] *nm,f* (*Scol*) tutor, coach.

répétition [ʀepetisjɔ̃] *nf* **(a)** (*redite*) repetition. **il y a beaucoup de ~s** there is a lot of repetition, there are numerous repetitions.

(b) (*Théât: représentation*) rehearsal. **~ générale** (final) dress rehearsal.

(c) (*action*) (*gén*) repetition; *[pièce, symphonie]* rehearsal; *[rôle]* learning; *[morceau de piano]* practising. **pour éviter la ~ d'une telle mésaventure** to prevent the repetition *ou* the recurrence of such a mishap, to prevent such a mishap recurring; **la ~ d'un tel exploit est difficile** repeating a feat like that *ou* doing a feat like that again is difficult.

(d) (*Hist Scol*) private lesson, private coaching (*U*).

(e) (*Tech*) **fusil/montre à ~** repeater rifle/watch.

repeuplement [ʀəpœpləmɑ̃] *nm* (*V* **repeupler**) repopulation; restocking; replanting.

repeupler [ʀəpœple] (1) **1** *vt région* to repopulate; *bassin, chasse* to restock (*de* with); *forêt* to replant (*de* with). **2 se repeupler** *vpr* to be *ou* become repopulated.

repincer [ʀ(ə)pɛ̃se] (3) *vt* (*lit*) to pinch *ou* nip again; (**fig*) to catch again, nab* again. **se faire ~** to get nabbed* again.

repiquage [ʀ(ə)pikaʒ] *nm* (*V* **repiquer**) planting *ou* pricking *ou* bedding out; subculturing; touching up, retouching; rerecording; recording, taping.

repiquer [ʀ(ə)pike] (1) **1** *vt* **(a)** (*Bot*) to plant out, prick out, bed (out); (*Bio*) to subculture. **plantes à ~** bedding plants.

(b) (*Phot*) to touch up, retouch; *enregistrement* to rerecord; *disque* to record, tape.

(c) (*: *attraper*) to nab* again.

(d) *[moustique]* to bite again; *[épine]* to prick again. (*Couture*) **~ un vêtement à la machine** to restitch a garment.

2 repiquer à: *vt indir*: **~ au plat** to take a second helping; **~ au truc** to go back to one's old ways, be at it again*.

répit [ʀepi] *nm* (*rémission*) respite; (*repos*) respite, rest. **la douleur ne lui laisse pas de ~** he never has any respite from the pain, the pain never gives him any respite; **s'accorder un peu de ~** to take a bit of a rest *ou* a breather*; **accordez-nous 5 minutes de ~** give us 5 minutes' rest *ou* respite; **travailler sans ~** to work continuously *ou* without respite; **harceler qn sans ~** to harass sb relentlessly; **donnez-moi un petit ~ pour vous payer** give me some breathing space to pay you.

replacement [ʀ(ə)plasmɑ̃] *nm* (*V* **replacer**) replacing, putting back; re-employment.

replacer [ʀ(ə)plase] (3) **1** *vt objet* to replace, put back (in its place); *employé* to find a new job for, re-employ. **il faut ~ les choses dans leur contexte** we must put things back in their context.

2 se replacer *vpr [employé]* to find a new job. **se ~ dans les mêmes conditions** to put o.s. in the same situation.

replanter [ʀ(ə)plɑ̃te] (1) *vt plante* to replant, plant out; *forêt, arbre* to replant. **~ un bois en conifères** to replant a wood with conifers.

replat [ʀəpla] *nm* projecting ledge, shelf.

replâtrage [ʀ(ə)plɑtʀaʒ] *nm* (*V* **replâtrer**) replastering; patching up. (*Pol*) **~ ministériel*** minor cabinet reshuffle, patching together *ou* patch-up of the cabinet.

replâtrer [ʀ(ə)plɑtʀe] (1) *vt* **(a)** *mur* to replaster. **(b)** (*) *amitié* to patch up; *gouvernement* to patch up.

replet, -ète [ʀəplɛ, ɛt] *adj* podgy, fat; *personne, visage* chubby.

réplétion [ʀeplesjɔ̃] *nf* (*frm*) repletion (*frm*).

repleuvoir [ʀ(ə)plœvwaʀ] (23) *vb impers* to rain again, start raining again. **il repleut** it is raining again, it has started raining again.

repli [ʀ(ə)pli] *nm* **(a)** *[terrain, papier]* fold; *[intestin, serpent]* coil, fold; *[rivière]* bend, twist, winding (*U*); *[peau]* (*de l'âge*) wrinkle; (*de l'embonpoint*) fold (*de* in).

(b) (*Couture*) *[ourlet, étoffe]* fold, turn (*de* in).

(c) (*Mil*) withdrawal, falling back.

(d) (*réserve*) withdrawal. **~ sur soi-même** withdrawal into oneself *ou* into one's shell, turning in on oneself.

(e) (*recoin*) *[cœur, conscience]* hidden *ou* innermost recess, innermost reaches.

repliable [ʀ(ə)plijabl(ə)] *adj* folding.

repliement [ʀ(ə)plimɑ̃] *nm*: **~ (sur soi-même)** withdrawal (into oneself), turning in on oneself.

replier [ʀ(ə)plije] (7) **1** *vt* **(a)** *carte, journal, robe* to fold up (again), fold back up; *manche, bas de pantalon* to roll up, fold up; *coin de feuille* to fold over; *ailes* to fold (back); *jambes* to tuck up. **les jambes repliées sous lui** sitting back with his legs tucked under him; **~ le drap sur la couverture** to fold the sheet back over *ou* down over the blanket.

(b) (*Mil*) *troupes* to withdraw; *civils* to move back *ou* away.

2 se replier *vpr [serpent]* to curl up, coil up; *[chat]* to curl up; *[lame de couteau]* to fold back; (*Mil*) to fall back, withdraw (*sur* to). **se ~ (sur soi-même)** to withdraw into oneself, turn in on oneself; **la province est repliée sur elle-même** the provinces are very inward-looking.

réplique [ʀeplik] *nf* **(a)** (*réponse*) reply, retort. **il a la ~ facile** he's always ready with a quick answer, he's never at a loss for an answer *ou* a reply; **et pas de ~!** and don't answer back!, and let's not have any backchat!* (*Brit*); **argument sans ~** unanswerable *ou* irrefutable argument; **il n'y a pas de ~ à cela** there's no answer to that.

(b) (*contre-attaque*) counter-attack. **la ~ ne se fit pas attendre: ils attaquèrent** they weren't slow to retaliate and attacked at once.

(c) (*Théât*) line. **dialogue aux ~s spirituelles** dialogue with some witty lines; **oublier sa ~** to forget one's lines *ou* words; **l'acteur a manqué sa ~** the actor missed his cue; **c'est X qui vous donnera la ~** (*pour répéter*) X will give you your cue; (*dans une scène*) X will play opposite you, X will play the supporting role; (*fig*) **je saurai lui donner la ~** I can match him (in an argument), I can give as good as I get*; **les 2 orateurs se donnent la ~** the 2 speakers indulge in a bit of verbal sparring.

(d) (*Art*) replica. (*fig*) **il est la ~ de son jumeau** he is the (spitting) image of his twin brother.

répliquer [ʀeplike] (1) **1** *vt* to reply. **il (lui) répliqua que** he replied *ou* retorted that; **il n'y a rien à ~ à cela** what can we say to that?, there's no answer to that; **il trouve toujours quelque chose à ~** he always has a ready answer, he's always got an answer for everything.

2 *vi* **(a)** (*répondre*) to reply. **~ à la critique** to reply to criticism; **et ne réplique pas!** (*insolence*) and don't answer back!; (*protestation*) and no protests! *ou* objections!

(b) (*contre-attaquer*) to retaliate. **il répliqua par des coups de poing/des injures** he retaliated with his fists/with foul language.

replonger [ʀ(ə)plɔ̃ʒe] (3) **1** *vt rame, cuiller* to dip back (*dans* into). **replongé dans la pauvreté/la guerre/l'obscurité** plunged into poverty/war/obscurity again, plunged back into poverty/war/obscurity; **replongeant sa main dans l'eau** plunging *ou* putting *ou* sticking his hand into the water again *ou* back in(to) the water.

2 *vi* (*dans une piscine*) to dive back, dive again (*dans* into).

3 se replonger *vpr* to dive back *ou* dive again (*dans* into). **il se replongea dans sa lecture** he immersed himself in his book *ou* his reading again, he went back to his reading.

repolir [ʀ(ə)pɔliʀ] (2) *vt objet* to repolish; (*fig*) *discours* to polish up again, touch up again.

répondant, e [ʀepɔ̃dɑ̃, ɑ̃t] **1** *nm,f* guarantor, surety. **servir de ~ à qn** (*Fin*) to stand surety for sb, be sb's guarantor; (*fig*) to vouch for sb.

2 *nm* **(a)** (*Fin*) **il a du ~** (*compte approvisionné*) he has money behind him; (*: *beaucoup d'argent*) he has something *ou* plenty to fall back on*.

(b) (*Rel*) server.

répondeur, -euse [ʀepɔ̃dœʀ, øz] **1** *adj* (*) impertinent, cheeky*. **je n'aime pas les enfants ~s** I don't like children who answer back. **2** *nm* (telephone) answering machine. **~ (téléphonique)** Ansafone ®.

répondre [ʀepɔ̃dʀ(ə)] (41) **1** *vt* **(a)** to answer, reply. **il a répondu une grossièreté** he replied with a rude remark, he made a rude remark in reply; **il m'a répondu une lettre** he sent me a letter in reply; **il a répondu qu'il le savait** he answered *ou* replied that he knew, he said in reply that he knew; **il m'a répondu qu'il viendrait** he told me (in reply) that he would come; **je lui ai répondu de se taire** *ou* **qu'il se taise** I told him to be quiet; **vous me demandez si j'accepte, je (vous) réponds que non** you're asking me if I accept and I'm telling you I don't *ou* won't *ou* and my answer is no *ou* that I won't; **je me suis vu ~ que, il me fut répondu que** I was told that; **~ présent à l'appel** (*lit*) to answer present at roll call; (*fig*) to come forward, make oneself known, volunteer; **réponds quelque chose, même si c'est faux** give an answer (of some sort), even if it's wrong; **(c'est) bien répondu!** well said!; **qu'avez-vous à ~?** what have you got to say in reply?; **il n'y a rien à ~** there's no reply *ou* answer to that; **qu'est-ce que vous voulez ~ à cela?** what can you reply *ou* say to that?; **il n'a répondu que des sottises** he only replied with stupid remarks.

(b) (*Rel*) **~ la messe** to serve (at) mass.

2 *vi* **(a)** to answer, reply. **réponds donc!** well answer (then)!; **~ en claquant la porte** to slam the door by way of reply *ou* by way of an answer; **~ à qn/à une question/à une convocation** to reply to *ou* answer sb/a question/a summons; **seul l'écho lui répondit** only the echo answered him; **je ne lui ai pas encore répondu** I haven't yet replied to his letter *ou* answered his letter *ou* written back to him; **je lui répondrai par écrit** I'll reply *ou* answer in writing, I'll let him have a written reply *ou* answer; **avez-vous répondu à son invitation?** did you reply to *ou* acknowledge his invitation?; **il répond au nom de Dick** he answers to the name of Dick; **~ par oui ou par non** to reply *ou* answer *ou* say yes or no; **~ par monosyllabes** to reply in monosyllables, give monosyllabic answers; **instruments de musique qui se répondent** musical instruments that answer each other; ~ **par un sourire/en hochant la tête** to smile/nod in reply; **elle répondit à son salut par un sourire** she replied to *ou* answered his greeting with a smile, she acknowledged his greeting with a smile; **il a répondu par des injures** he replied with a string of insults, he replied by insulting us (*ou* them *etc*); (*Jur*) **prévenu qui doit** ~ **à plusieurs chefs d'accusation** defendant who must answer several charges *ou* who has several charges to answer.

(b) ~ **(à la porte** *ou* **sonnette)** to answer the bell; ~ **(au téléphone)** to answer the telephone; **personne ne répond, ça ne répond pas** there's no answer *ou* reply, no one's answering; **on a sonné, va** ~ the doorbell rang — go and see who's there, that was the bell — go and answer the door; **personne n'a répondu à mon coup de sonnette** no one answered the door *ou* the bell when I rang, I got no answer when I rang the bell.

(c) (*être impertinent*) to answer back. **il a répondu à la maîtresse** he answered the teacher back, he was cheeky to the teacher*.

(d) (*réagir*) *voiture, commandes, membres* to respond (*à* to). **son cerveau ne répond plus aux excitations** his brain no longer responds to stimuli; **les freins ne répondaient plus** the brakes were no longer working *ou* had given up *ou* had failed.

3 répondre à *vt indir* **(a)** (*correspondre à*) *besoin* to answer; *signalement* to answer, fit. **ça répond tout à fait à l'idée que je m'en faisais** that corresponds exactly to *ou* fits exactly the idea I had of it; **cela répond/ne répond pas à ce que nous cherchons** this meets/doesn't meet *ou* falls short of our requirements; **ça répond/ne répond pas à mon attente** *ou* **à mes espérances** it comes up to/falls short of my expectations.

(b) (*payer de retour*) *attaque, avances* to respond to; *amour, affection, salut* to return; *politesse, gentillesse, invitation* to repay, pay back. **peu de gens ont répondu à cet appel** few people responded to this appeal *ou* heeded this appeal, there was little response to this appeal; ~ **à la force par la force** to answer force with force; **s'ils lancent une attaque, nous saurons y** ~ if they launch an attack we'll fight back *ou* retaliate.

(c) (*être identique à*) *dessin, façade* to match. **les 2 ailes du bâtiment se répondent** the 2 wings of the building match (each other).

4 répondre de *vt indir* (*garantir*) *personne* to answer for. ~ **de l'innocence/l'honnêteté de qn** to answer *ou* vouch for sb's innocence/honesty; ~ **des dettes de qn** to answer for sb's debts, be answerable for sb's debts; **il viendra, je vous en réponds!** mark my words, he'll come!, he'll come all right, you can take it from me!* *ou* you can take my word for it!; **si vous agissez ainsi, je ne réponds plus de rien** if you behave like that, I'll accept no further responsibility; **je te réponds bien que cela ne se passera pas comme ça!** you can take it from me* *ou* you can be sure that it won't happen like that!; (*Jur*) ~ **de ses crimes devant la cour d'assises** to answer for one's crimes in the Crown Court.

répons [ʀepɔ̃] *nm* (*Rel*) response.

réponse [ʀepɔ̃s] *nf* **(a)** (*à une lettre, demande, objection*) reply, response; (*à une question, une prière, un coup de sonnette*) answer, reply; *[problème, énigme, examen]* answer (*à, de* to); (*Mus*) answer. **en** ~ **à votre question** in answer *ou* reply *ou* response to your question; **ma lettre est restée sans** ~ my letter remained unanswered; **sa demande est restée sans** ~ there has been no reply *ou* response to his request; (*Mil*) **on a tiré sur l'ennemi et la** ~ **ne se fit pas attendre** we fired at the enemy and they were quick to fire back *ou* to return the fire; **télégramme avec** ~ **payée** reply-paid telegram; **bulletin-/coupon-**~ reply slip/coupon.

(b) (*Physiol, Tech: réaction*) response; (*écho: à un appel, un sentiment*) response.

(c) (*loc*) **avoir** ~ **à tout** to have an answer for everything; (*en se justifiant*) never to be at a loss for an answer; **c'est la** ~ **du berger à la bergère** it's tit for tat; **il me fit une** ~ **de Normand** he gave me an evasive answer, he wouldn't say yes or no, he wouldn't give me a straight answer.

repopulation [ʀəpɔpylɑsjɔ̃] *nf [ville]* repopulation; *[étang]* restocking.

report [ʀ(ə)pɔʀ] *nm* (*V* **reporter**) postponement, putting off; deferment; putting back; transfer; writing out, copying out; posting; carrying forward *ou* over; rebetting. **les** ~**s de voix entre les 2 partis se sont bien effectués au deuxième tour** the votes were satisfactorily transferred to *ou* shared (out) among the 2 parties left in the second round of the election; **faire le** ~ **de** *somme* to carry forward *ou* over; *écriture* to post; (*sur livre de compte*) '~' (*en bas de page*) 'carried forward'; (*en haut de page*) 'brought forward'.

reportage [ʀ(ə)pɔʀtaʒ] *nm* **(a)** (*Presse*) report, article; (*Rad, TV*) report (*sur* on); (*sur le vif*) *[match, événement]* (live) commentary. ~ **photographique/télévisé** illustrated/television report; ~ **en direct** live commentary; **faire un** ~ **sur** (*Presse*) to write a report *ou* an article on; (*Rad, TV*) to report on; **faire** *ou* **assurer le** ~ **d'une cérémonie** to cover a ceremony, do the coverage of a ceremony; **être en** ~ (*Presse*) to be out on a story, be covering a story; (*Rad, TV*) to be (out) reporting; **c'était un** ~ **de X** that was X reporting.

(b) (*métier*) (news) reporting. **il fait du** ~ he's a (news) reporter.

reporter¹ [ʀ(ə)pɔʀte] (1) **1** *vt* **(a)** (*ramener*) *objet* to take back; (*par la pensée*) to take back (*à* to). **cette chanson nous reporte aux années trente** this song takes us back to the thirties.

(b) (*différer*) *match* to postpone, put offt *décision* to put off, defer; *date* to put back, defer. **la réunion est reportée à demain** the meeting has been postponed until tomorrow; (*Jur*) **le jugement est reporté à huitaine** (the) sentence has been deferred for a week.

(c) (*recopier*) *chiffres, indications* to transfer (*sur* to), write out, copy out (*sur* on); (*Comm*) *écritures* to post; (*Phot*) to transfer (*sur* to). ~ **une somme sur la page suivante** to carry an amount forward *ou* over to the next page.

(d) (*transférer*) ~ **son affection/son vote sur** to transfer one's affection/one's vote to; ~ **son gain sur un autre cheval/numéro** to put *ou* place one's winnings on *ou* transfer one's bet to another horse/number.

2 se reporter *vpr* **(a)** (*se référer à*) **se** ~ **à** to refer to; **reportez-vous à la page 5** turn to *ou* refer to *ou* see page 5.

(b) (*par la pensée*) **se** ~ **à** to think back to; **reportez-vous par l'esprit au début du siècle** cast your mind back to the turn of the century; **si l'on se reporte à l'Angleterre de cette époque** if one thinks back to the England of that period.

reporter² [ʀ(ə)pɔʀtɛʀ] *nm* reporter. **grand** ~ international reporter; ~ **photographe** reporter and photographer; *V* **radioreporter.**

repos [ʀ(ə)po] *nm* **(a)** (*détente*) rest. **prendre du** ~**/un peu de** ~ to take *ou* have a rest/a bit of a rest; **il ne peut pas rester** *ou* **demeurer en** ~ **5 minutes** he can't rest *ou* relax for (even) 5 minutes; **le médecin lui a ordonné le** ~ the doctor has ordered him to rest *ou* ordered him complete rest; **après une matinée/journée de** ~ **il allait mieux** after a morning's/day's rest he felt better; **respecter le** ~ **dominical** to respect Sunday as a day of rest; *V* **cure¹, jour, maison.**

(b) (*congé*) **avoir droit à un jour de** ~ **hebdomadaire** to have the right to one day off a week; **le médecin lui a donné du** ~**/huit jours de** ~ the doctor has given him some time off/a week off.

(c) (*tranquillité*) peace and quiet; (*quiétude morale*) peace of mind; (*littér: sommeil, mort*) rest, sleep. **il n'y aura pas de** ~ **pour lui tant que ...** he'll have no peace of mind until ..., he won't get any rest until ...; **le** ~ **de la tombe** the sleep of the dead; **le** ~ **éternel** eternal rest; **avoir la conscience en** ~ to have an easy *ou* a clear conscience; **pour avoir l'esprit en** ~ to put my (*ou* your *etc*) mind at rest, so that I (*ou* you *etc*) can feel easy in my (*ou* your *etc*) mind; **laisse ton frère en** ~ leave your brother in peace; *V* **lit.**

(d) (*pause*) *[discours]* pause; *[vers]* rest; (*Mus*) cadence.

(e) (*loc*) (*Mil*) ~! (stand) at ease!; **au** ~ *soldat* standing at ease; *masse, machine, animal* at rest; **muscle au** ~ *ou* **à l'état de** ~ relaxed muscle; **sans** ~ *travailler* without stopping, without taking a rest, relentlessly; *marcher* without a break *ou* a rest, without stopping; *quête* uninterrupted, relentless; **de tout** ~ *situation, entreprise* secure, safe; *placement* gilt-edged, safe; **ce n'est pas de tout** ~! it's not exactly restful!, it's no picnic!*; (*Agr*) **laisser la terre en** ~ to let the land lie fallow; **en hiver la nature est en** ~ nature rests in winter.

reposant, e [ʀ(ə)pozɑ̃, ɑ̃t] *adj sommeil* refreshing; *lieu, couleur* restful; *vacances* restful, relaxing. **c'est** ~ **pour la vue** it's (very) restful on *ou* to the eyes.

repose [ʀ(ə)poz] *nf [appareil]* refitting, reinstallation; *[tapis]* relaying, putting (back) down again.

repose- [ʀ(ə)poz] *préf V* **reposer.**

reposé, e [ʀ(ə)poze] (*ptp de* **reposer**) *adj visage, air, teint* fresh, rested (*attrib*); *cheval* fresh (*attrib*), rested (*attrib*). **j'ai l'esprit** ~ my mind is fresh *ou* rested; **maintenant que vous êtes bien** ~ ... now (that) you have had a good rest ... ; *V* **tête.**

reposer [ʀ(ə)poze] (1) **1** *vt* **(a)** (*poser à nouveau*) *verre etc* to put back down, put down again; *tapis* to relay, put back down; *objet démonté* to refit, put back. ~ **ses yeux sur qch** to look at sth again; **va** ~ **ce livre où tu l'as trouvé** go and put that book back where you found it; (*Mil*) **reposez armes!** order arms!

(b) (*soulager, délasser*) *yeux, corps, membres* to rest; *esprit* to rest, relax. **se** ~ **l'esprit** to rest one's mind, give one's mind *ou* brain a rest; **les lunettes de soleil reposent les yeux** *ou* **la vue** sunglasses rest the eyes, sunglasses are restful to the eyes; ~ **sa tête/sa jambe sur un coussin** to rest one's head/leg on a cushion; **cela repose de ne voir personne (pendant une journée)** it's restful not to see anyone (for a whole day).

(c) (*répéter*) *question* to repeat, ask again; *problème* to bring up again, raise again. **cela va** ~ **le problème** that will raise the (whole) problem again *ou* bring the (whole) problem up again; **cet incident va (nous)** ~ **un problème** this incident is going to pose us a new problem *ou* bring up a new problem for us.

2 reposer sur *vt indir [bâtiment]* to be built on; *[route]* to rest on, be supported by; *[supposition]* to rest on, be based on; *[résultat]* to depend on. **sa théorie ne repose sur rien de précis** his theory doesn't rest on *ou* isn't based on anything specific; **tout repose sur son témoignage** everything hinges on *ou* rests on his evidence.

3 *vi* **(a)** (*littér*) (*être étendu*) to rest, lie (down); (*dormir*) to sleep, rest; (*être enterré*) to rest. **tout reposait dans la campagne** everything was sleeping *ou* resting in the country(side); **ici repose ...** here lies ... ; **qu'il repose en paix** may he rest in peace; (*Naut*) **l'épave repose par 20 mètres de fond** the wreck is lying 20 metres down.

(b) laisser ~ *liquide* to leave to settle, let settle *ou* stand; *pâte à pain* to leave to rise, let rise; *pâte feuilletée* to (allow to) rest; *pâte à crêpes* to leave (to stand); **laisser** ~ **la terre** to let the earth lie fallow; **faire** ~ **son cheval** to rest one's horse.

4 se reposer *vpr* **(a)** (*se délasser*) to rest. **se** ~ **sur ses lauriers** to rest on one's laurels.

(b) se ~ **sur qn** to rely on sb; **je me repose sur vous pour régler cette affaire** I'll leave it to you *ou* I'm relying on you to sort this business out; **elle se repose de tout sur lui** she relies on him for everything.

(c) (*se reposer à nouveau*) *[oiseau, poussière]* to settle again; *[problème]* to crop up again.

5: repose-pieds *nm inv* footrest; **repose-tête** *nm, pl* **repose-têtes** headrest.

reposoir [ʀ(ə)pozwaʀ] *nm [église, procession]* altar of repose; (*rare*) *[maison privée]* temporary altar.

repoussage [ʀ(ə)pusaʒ] *nm [cuir, métal]* repoussé work, embossing.

repoussant, e [ʀ(ə)pusɑ̃, ɑ̃t] *adj odeur, saleté, visage* repulsive, repugnant; *laideur* repulsive.

repousse [ʀ(ə)pus] *nf [cheveux, gazon]* regrowth. **pour accélérer la ~ des cheveux** to help the hair grow again.

repousser [ʀ(ə)puse] (1) **1** *vt* **(a)** (*écarter, refouler*) *objet encombrant* to push out of the way, push away; *ennemi, attaque* to repel, repulse, drive back; *coups* to ward off; *soupirant, quémandeur, malheureux* to turn away, repulse. **~ qch du pied** to kick sth out of the way, kick sth away; **il me repoussa avec brusquerie** he pushed me away *ou* out of the way roughly; **elle parvint à ~ son agresseur** she managed to repel *ou* drive off *ou* beat off her attacker; **les électrons se repoussent** electrons repel each other.

(b) (*fig: décliner*) *demande, conseil, aide* to turn down, reject; *hypothèse* to reject, dismiss, rule out; *tentation* to reject, resist, repel; *projet de loi* to reject. **la police ne repousse pas l'hypothèse du suicide** the police do not rule out the possibility of suicide.

(c) (*remettre en place*) *meuble* to push back; *tiroir* to push back in; *porte* to push to. **~ la table contre le mur** to push the table back *ou* up against the wall.

(d) (*différer*) *date* to put back; *réunion* to put off, postpone. **la date de l'examen a été repoussée (à huitaine/à lundi)** the date of the exam has been put back (a week/till Monday), the exam has been put off *ou* postponed (for a week/till Monday).

(e) (*dégoûter*) to repel, repulse. **tout en lui me repousse** everything about him repels *ou* repulses me.

(f) (*Tech*) *cuir, métal* to emboss (by hand), work in repoussé. **en cuir/métal repoussé** in repoussé leather/metal.

2 *vi [feuilles, cheveux]* to grow again.

repoussoir [ʀ(ə)puswaʀ] *nm* **(a)** (*à cuir, métal*) snarling iron; (*à ongles*) cuticle remover. **(b)** (*Art*) repoussoir, high-toned foreground; (*fig: faire-valoir*) foil. **servir de ~ à qn** to act as a foil to sb.

répréhensible [ʀepʀeɑ̃sibl(ə)] *adj acte, personne* reprehensible. **je ne vois pas ce qu'il y a de ~ à ça!** I don't see what's wrong with (doing) that!

reprendre [ʀ(ə)pʀɑ̃dʀ(ə)] (58) **1** *vt* **(a)** (*récupérer*) *ville* to recapture; *prisonnier* to recapture, catch again; *employé* to take back; *objet prêté* to take back, get back. **~ sa place** to go back to one's seat, resume one's seat; **le directeur malade n'a pas pu ~ sa place parmi ses collègues** the director who was ill was unable to take his place with his colleagues again; **la photo avait repris sa place sur la cheminée** the photo was back in its (usual) place on the mantelpiece; **passer ~ qn** to go back *ou* come back for sb, go *ou* come and fetch sb; **il a repris sa parole** he went back on his word; **j'irai ~ mon manteau chez le teinturier** I'll go and get *ou* fetch my coat (back) from the cleaner's; **~ son nom de jeune fille** to take one's maiden name again, go back to *ou* revert to one's maiden name.

(b) *pain, viande* to have *ou* take (some) more. **voulez-vous ~ des légumes?** would you like a second helping of vegetables?, would you like some more vegetables?

(c) (*retrouver*) *espoir, droits, forces* to regain, recover. **~ des couleurs** to get some colour back in one's cheeks; **~ confiance/courage** to regain *ou* recover one's confidence/courage; **~ ses habitudes** to get back into one's old habits, take up one's old habits again; **~ contact avec qn** to get in touch with sb again; **~ ses esprits** *ou* **ses sens** to come to, come round, regain consciousness; *V* **connaissance, conscience** *etc.*

(d) (*Comm*) *marchandises* to take back; (*contre un nouvel achat*) to take in part exchange; *fonds de commerce, usine* to take over. **les articles en solde ne sont pas repris** sale goods cannot be returned *ou* exchanged; **ils m'ont repris ma vieille télé** they bought my old TV set off me (in part exchange); **j'ai acheté une voiture neuve et ils ont repris la vieille** I bought a new car and traded in the old one *ou* and they took the old one in part exchange.

(e) (*recommencer, poursuivre*) *travaux* to resume; *études* to take up again, resume; *livre* to pick up again, go back to; *lecture* to go back to, resume; *conversation, récit* to resume, carry on (with); *promenade* to resume, continue; *hostilités* to reopen, start again; *lutte* to take up again, resume; *pièce de théâtre* to put on again. **après déjeuner ils reprirent la route** after lunch they resumed *ou* continued their journey *ou* they set off again; **~ la plume** to take up the pen again; **reprenez votre histoire au début** start your story from the beginning again, go back to the beginning of your story again; **reprenons les faits un par un** let's go over the facts one by one again; **il reprendra la parole après vous** he will speak again after you; **~ le travail** (*après maladie, grève*) to go back to work, start work again; (*après le repas*) to get back to work, start work again; **~ la route** *ou* **son chemin** to go on *ou* set off on one's way again; **~ la mer/la route** *[marin, routier etc]* to go back to sea/back on the road again.

(f) (*saisir à nouveau*) **son mal de gorge l'a repris** he's suffering from *ou* has got a sore throat again, his sore throat is troubling *ou* bothering him again; **ses douleurs l'ont repris** he is in pain again; (*iro*) **voilà que ça le reprend!** there he goes again!, he's off again!*; **ses doutes le reprirent** he started feeling doubtful again, he was seized with doubts once more.

(g) (*attraper à nouveau*) to catch again. (*fig*) **on ne m'y reprendra plus** I won't let myself be caught (out) *ou* had* again *ou* a second time; (*menace*) **que je ne t'y reprenne pas!** don't let me catch you at it *ou* catch you doing that again!

(h) (*Sport: rattraper*) *balle* to catch. (*Tennis*) **revers bien repris par X** backhand well returned by X.

(i) (*retoucher, corriger*) *tableau* to touch up; *article, chapitre* to go over again; *manteau* (*gén*) to alter; (*trop grand*) to take in; (*trop petit*) to let out; (*trop long*) to take up; (*trop court*) to let down. **il n'y a rien à ~** there's not a single correction *ou* alteration to be made; **il y a beaucoup de choses à ~ dans ce travail** there are lots of improvements to be made to this work, there are a lot of things that need tidying up *ou* improving in this work; (*Couture*) **il faut ~ un centimètre à droite** we'll have to take it in half an inch on the right.

(j) (*réprimander*) *personne* to reprimand, tell off*, tick off*; (*pour faute de langue*) to pull up. **~ un élève qui se trompe** to correct a pupil.

(k) (*répéter*) *refrain* to take up; *argument, critique* to repeat. **il reprend toujours les mêmes arguments** he always repeats the same arguments, he always comes out with *ou* trots out the same old arguments*; (*Mus*) **reprenez les 5 dernières mesures** let's have *ou* take the last 5 bars again; **ils reprirent la chanson en chœur** they all joined in *ou* took up the song.

(l) (*se resservir de*) *idée, suggestion* to take up (again), use (again). **l'incident a été repris par les journaux** the incident was taken up by the newspapers.

2 *vi* **(a)** (*retrouver la vigueur*) *[plante]* to take again; *[affaires]* to pick up. **la vie reprenait peu à peu** life gradually resumed as usual *ou* as normal; **il a bien repris depuis son opération** he's picked up well *ou* made a good recovery since his operation.

(b) (*recommencer*) *[bruit, pluie]* to start again; (*Scol, Univ*) to start again, go back. **le froid a repris depuis hier** it has turned cold again since yesterday.

(c) (*dire*) **'ce n'est pas moi' reprit-il** 'it's not me' he went on.

3 se reprendre *vpr* **(a)** (*se corriger*) to correct o.s.; (*s'interrompre*) to stop o.s. **il allait plaisanter, il s'est repris à temps** he was going to joke but he stopped himself *ou* pulled himself up in time.

(b) (*recommencer*) **se ~ à plusieurs fois pour faire qch** to make several attempts to do sth *ou* at doing sth; **il a dû s'y ~ à 2 fois pour ouvrir la porte** he had to make 2 attempts before he could open the door; **il se reprit à penser à elle** he started thinking *ou* he went back to thinking about her, his thoughts went back to her; **il se reprit à craindre que** once more he began to be afraid *ou* to fear that; **chacun se reprit à espérer** everyone began to hope again, everyone's hopes began to revive again.

(c) (*réagir*) to take a grip on o.s., pull o.s. together (again), take o.s. in hand. **après une période de découragement, il s'est repris** after a period of discouragement he's taken himself in hand *ou* got a grip on himself *ou* pulled himself together (again); **le coureur s'est bien repris sur la fin** the runner made a good recovery *ou* caught up well towards the end.

représailles [ʀ(ə)pʀezɑj] *nfpl* (*Pol, fig*) reprisals, retaliation (*U*). **user de ~, exercer des ~** to take reprisals (*envers, contre, sur* against); **par ~** in retaliation, as a reprisal; **en ~ de** by way of reprisal for, as a reprisal for, in retaliation for; **attends-toi à des ~!** you can expect reprisals!

représentable [ʀ(ə)pʀezɑ̃tabl(ə)] *adj phénomène* representable, that can be represented. **c'est difficilement ~** it is difficult to represent it.

représentant, e [ʀ(ə)pʀezɑ̃tɑ̃, ɑ̃t] *nm,f* (*gén*) representative. **~ de commerce** sales representative, travelling salesman, commercial traveller, rep* (*Brit*); **~ en justice** legal representative; **il est ~ en parapluies** he's a representative *ou* a rep* (*Brit*) for an umbrella firm, he travels in umbrellas*.

représentatif, -ive [ʀ(ə)pʀezɑ̃tatif, iv] *adj* (*gén*) representative. **~ de** (*typique de*) representative of; **signes ~s d'une fonction** signs representing *ou* which represent a function.

représentation [ʀ(ə)pʀezɑ̃tɑsjɔ̃] *nf* **(a)** (*notation, transcription*) *[objet, phénomène, son]* representation; *[paysage, société]* portrayal; *[faits]* representation, description. **~ graphique** graphic(al) representation; **c'est une ~ erronée de la réalité** it's a misrepresentation of reality.

(b) (*évocation, perception*) representation. **~s visuelles/auditives** visual/auditory representations.

(c) (*Théât: action, séance*) performance.

(d) *[pays, citoyens, mandant]* representation; (*mandataires, délégation*) representatives. **il assure la ~ de son gouvernement auprès de notre pays** he represents his government *ou* he is his government's representative in our country; **~ diplomatique/proportionnelle/en justice** diplomatic/proportional/legal representation.

(e) (*Comm*) (*métier*) commercial travelling; (*publicité, frais*) sales representation. **faire de la ~** to be a (sales) representative *ou* a commercial traveller; **la ~ entre pour beaucoup dans les frais** sales representation is a major factor in costs.

(f) (*réception*) entertainment. **frais de ~** entertainment allowance.

(g) (*frm: reproches*) **faire des ~s à** to make representations to.

(h) (*loc*) **être en ~** to be on show (*fig*).

représentativité [ʀ(ə)pʀezɑ̃tativite] *nf* representativeness.

représenter [ʀ(ə)pʀezɑ̃te] (1) **1** *vt* **(a)** (*décrire*) *[peintre, romancier]* to depict, portray, show; *[photographie]* to represent, show. (*Théât*) **la scène représente une rue** the scene represents a street; **~ fidèlement les faits** to describe *ou* set out the facts faithfully; **on le représente comme un escroc** he's represented as a crook, he's made out to be a crook; **il a voulu ~ un paysage sous la neige/la société du 19e siècle** he wanted to show *ou* depict a snowy landscape/to depict *ou* portray 19th-century society.

(b) (*symboliser, correspondre à*) to represent; (*signifier*) to represent, mean. **les parents représentent l'autorité** parents represent *ou* embody authority; **ce trait représente un arbre** this stroke represents a tree; **ça va ~ beaucoup de travail** that will mean *ou* represent *ou* involve a lot of work.

(c) (*Théât*) (*jouer*) to perform, play; (*mettre à l'affiche*) to perform, put on; *superproduction, adaptation* to stage. **on va ~ 4 pièces cette année** we (*ou* they *etc*) will perform *ou* put on 4 plays this year; **Hamlet fut représenté pour la première fois en 1603** Hamlet was first performed *ou* acted in 1603.

(d) (*agir au nom de*) *ministre, pays* to represent. **il s'est fait ~ par son notaire** he was represented by his solicitor, he sent his solicitor to represent him, he had his solicitor represent him; **les personnes qui ne peuvent pas assister à la réunion doivent se faire ~ (par un tiers)** those who are unable to attend the meeting should send someone to replace them *ou* should send a stand-in *ou* a deputy.

(e) ~ une maison de commerce to represent a firm, be a representative *ou* a traveller for a firm.

(f) (*littér*) **~ qch à qn** to point sth out to sb, (try to) impress sth on sb; **il lui représenta les inconvénients de l'affaire** he pointed out to him the drawbacks of the matter.

2 *vi* (*en imposer*) **il représente bien** he cuts a fine figure; **le directeur est un petit bonhomme qui ne représente pas** the manager is a little fellow with no presence at all *ou* who cuts a poor *ou* sorry figure.

3 se représenter *vpr* **(a)** (*s'imaginer*) to imagine. **je ne pouvais plus me ~ son visage** I could no longer bring his face to mind *ou* recall *ou* visualize his face; **on se le représente bien en Hamlet** you can well imagine him as Hamlet; **représentez-vous cet enfant maintenant seul au monde** just think of that child now alone in the world; **tu te représentes la scène quand il a annoncé sa démission!** you can just imagine the scene when he announced his resignation!

(b) (*survenir à nouveau*) **l'idée se représenta à lui** the idea came back to his mind *ou* occurred to him again *ou* crossed his mind again; **si l'occasion se représente** if the occasion presents itself again, if the opportunity arises again; **le même problème va se ~** the same problem will crop up again, we'll be faced *ou* confronted with the same problem again.

(c) (*se présenter à nouveau*) (*Scol*) to resit; (*Pol*) to stand again (*Brit*), run again (*US*). **se ~ à un examen** to resit an exam; **se ~ à une élection** to stand for election again.

répressible [ʀepʀesibl(ə)] *adj* repressible.

répressif, -ive [ʀepʀesif, iv] *adj* repressive.

répression [ʀepʀesjɔ̃] *nf* repression.

réprimandable [ʀepʀimɑ̃dabl(ə)] *adj* reprovable.

réprimande [ʀepʀimɑ̃d] *nf* reprimand, rebuke. **adresser une sévère ~ à un enfant** to give a child a severe reprimand, reprimand *ou* scold *ou* rebuke a child severely; **son attitude mérite une ~** he deserves a reprimand *ou* he deserves reprimanding for his attitude; **faire des ~s à qn** to sermonize sb.

réprimander [ʀepʀimɑ̃de] (1) *vt* to reprimand, rebuke.

réprimer [ʀepʀime] (1) *vt* *insurrection* to quell, repress, suppress, put down; *crimes* to curb, suppress; *abus* to curb, repress; *sentiment* to repress, suppress; *rire, bâillement* to suppress, stifle; *larmes, colère* to hold back, swallow, suppress.

reprisage [ʀ(ə)pʀizaʒ] *nm* (*V* **repriser**) darning; mending.

repris de justice [ʀ(ə)pʀidʒystis] *nm inv* ex-prisoner, ex-convict. **il s'agit d'un ~** the man has previous convictions, the man is an ex-prisoner *ou* an ex-convict; **un dangereux ~** a dangerous known criminal.

reprise [ʀ(ə)pʀiz] *nf* **(a)** (*recommencement*) *[activité, cours, travaux]* resumption; *[hostilités]* resumption, re-opening, renewal; *[froid]* return; (*Théât*) revival; (*Ciné*) rerun, reshowing (*U*); (*Mus: passage répété*) repeat; (*Rad, TV: rediffusion*) repeat. (*Mus*) **la ~ des violons** the re-entry of the violins; **la ~ des combats est imminente** fighting will begin again *ou* will be resumed again very soon; **avec la ~ du mauvais temps** with the return of the bad weather, with the bad weather setting in again, with the new spell of bad weather; **les ouvriers ont décidé la ~ du travail** the men have decided to go back to work; **on espère une ~ des affaires** we're hoping for a recovery in business *ou* hoping that business will pick up again; **la ~ (économique) est assez forte dans certains secteurs** the (economic) revival *ou* recovery is quite marked in certain sectors.

(b) (*Aut*) **avoir de bonnes ~s** to have good acceleration, accelerate well; **sa voiture n'a pas de ~s** his car has no acceleration.

(c) (*Boxe*) round; (*Escrime*) reprise. (*Ftbl*) **à la ~** at the start of the second half, when play resumed (*ou* resumes) after half-time.

(d) (*Comm*) *[marchandise]* taking back; (*pour nouvel achat*) part exchange. **valeur de ~ d'une voiture** part-exchange value *ou* trade-in value of a car; **nous vous offrons une ~ de 500 F pour votre vieux téléviseur, à l'achat d'un modèle en couleur** we'll give you 500 francs for your old television when you buy a colour set *ou* when you part-exchange it for a colour set; **~ des bouteilles vides** return of empties; **la maison ne fait pas de ~** goods cannot be returned *ou* exchanged; **payer une ~ de 500 F à l'ancien locataire** to pay the outgoing tenant 500 francs for improvements made to the property.

(e) (*réutilisation*) *[idée, suggestion]* re-using, taking up again.

(f) *[chaussette]* darn; *[drap, chemise]* mend. **faire une ~ perdue** to darn (*ou* mend) invisibly; **faire une ~ *ou* des ~s à un drap** to mend a sheet, stitch up the tear(s) in a sheet.

(g) (*loc*) **à 2 ou 3 ~s** on 2 or 3 occasions, 2 or 3 times; **à maintes/plusieurs ~s** on many/several occasions, many/several times.

repriser [ʀ(ə)pʀize] (1) *vt* *chaussette, lainage* to darn; *collant* to mend; *drap* to mend, stitch up (a tear in); *accroc* to mend, stitch up; *V* **aiguille, coton.**

réprobateur, -trice [ʀepʀɔbatœʀ, tʀis] *adj* reproving.

réprobation [ʀepʀɔbɑsjɔ̃] *nf* **(a)** (*blâme*) reprobation. **air/ton de ~** reproving look/tone. **(b)** (*Rel*) reprobation.

reproche [ʀ(ə)pʀɔʃ] *nm* reproach. **faire *ou* adresser des ~s à qn** to direct *ou* level reproaches at sb, reproach sb; **conduite qui mérite des ~s** blameworthy *ou* reprehensible behaviour; (*frm*) **faire ~ à qn d'avoir menti** to reproach *ou* upbraid sb for having lied; **je me fais de grands ~s** I blame *ou* reproach myself bitterly; **avec ~** reproachfully; **ton/regard de ~** reproachful tone/look; **homme sans ~** man beyond *ou* above reproach; **sans ~, permettez-moi *ou* je ne vous fais pas de ~ mais permettez-moi de vous dire que ...** I'm not blaming *ou* criticizing *ou* reproaching you but let me say that ... .

reprocher [ʀ(ə)pʀɔʃe] (1) *vt* **(a) ~ qch à qn** to reproach sb for sth; **~ à qn de faire qch** to reproach sb for *ou* with doing sth; **on lui a reproché sa maladresse** they reproached *ou* criticized him for his clumsiness; **on lui reproche de nombreuses malhonnêtetés** they are reproaching him with *ou* accusing him of several instances of dishonesty; **il me reproche mon succès/ma fortune** he reproaches me with *ou* resents my success/my good fortune, he holds my success/my good fortune against me; **je ne te reproche rien** I'm not blaming you for anything; **je n'ai rien à me ~** I've nothing to reproach myself with; **il est trop minutieux mais il n'y a rien à ~ à cela** he's a bit on the meticulous side but there's nothing wrong with that *ou* but that's no bad thing.

(b) (*critiquer*) **qu'as-tu à ~ à mon plan/à ce tableau?** what have you got (to say) against my plan/this picture?, what don't you like about my plan/this picture?; **je reproche à ce tissu d'être trop salissant** the thing I have against this material *ou* the fault I find with this material is that it gets dirty too easily; **je ne vois rien à ~ à ce devoir/à son travail** I can't find any faults *ou* I can't find anything to criticize in this piece of homework/in his work.

reproducteur, -trice [ʀ(ə)pʀɔdyktœʀ, tʀis] **1** *adj* (*Bio*) reproductive. **cheval ~** studhorse, stallion. **2** *nm* breeder. **~s** breeding stock (*U*).

reproductible [ʀ(ə)pʀɔdyktibl(ə)] *adj* which can be reproduced.

reproductif, -ive [ʀ(ə)pʀɔdyktif, iv] *adj* reproductive.

reproduction [ʀ(ə)pʀɔdyksjɔ̃] *nf* (*V* **reproduire**) reproduction; copy; repeat; duplication; reprinting; breeding. **livre contenant de nombreuses ~s** book containing many reproductions; **organes de ~** reproductive organs; **garder quelques mâles pour la ~ et vendre les autres pour la viande** to keep a few males for reproduction *ou* breeding and sell the rest for meat; (*sur un livre, album*) **'~ interdite'** 'all rights (of reproduction) reserved'.

reproduire [ʀ(ə)pʀɔdɥiʀ] (38) **1** *vt* *son* to reproduce; *modèle, tableau* to reproduce, copy; *erreur* to repeat; (*par reprographie*) to reproduce, duplicate. **essayant de ~ les gestes de son professeur** trying to copy *ou* imitate his teacher's gestures; **la photo est reproduite en page 3** the picture is shown *ou* reproduced on page 3; **le texte de la conférence sera reproduit dans notre magazine** the text of the lecture will be reprinted in our magazine.

2 se reproduire *vpr* (*Bio, Bot*) to reproduce, breed; *[phénomène]* to recur, re-occur; *[erreur]* to reappear, recur. **et que ça ne se reproduise plus!** and don't let that happen again!

reprographie [ʀəpʀɔgʀafi] *nf* reprography (*T*).

reprographier [ʀəpʀɔgʀafje] (7) *vt* to reproduce.

reprographieur [ʀəpʀɔgʀafjœʀ] *nm* copying machine.

reprographique [ʀəpʀɔgʀafik] *adj* reprographic (*T*).

réprouvé, e [ʀepʀuve] (*ptp de* **réprouver**) *nm,f* (*Rel*) reprobate; (*fig*) outcast, reprobate.

réprouver [ʀepʀuve] (1) *vt* **(a)** *personne* to reprove; *attitude, comportement* to reprove, condemn; *projet* to condemn, disapprove of. **des actes que la morale réprouve** acts which the moral code condemns, immoral acts.

(b) (*Rel*) to damn, reprobate.

reps [ʀɛps] *nm* rep(p).

reptation [ʀɛptɑsjɔ̃] *nf* crawling.

reptile [ʀɛptil] *nm* (*Zool*) reptile; (*serpent*) snake; (*péj: personne*) creep* (*péj*).

reptilien, -ienne [ʀɛptiljɛ̃, jɛn] *adj* reptilian.

repu, e [ʀəpy] (*ptp de* **repaître**) *adj* *animal* sated, satisfied, which has gorged itself; (**péj*) *personne* full up* (*attrib*). **je suis ~** I'm full, I've eaten my fill; (*fig*) **il est ~ de cinéma** he has had his fill of the cinema.

républicain, e [ʀepyblikɛ̃, ɛn] *adj nm,f* republican; (*US Pol*) Republican; *V* **garde**[2].

republier [ʀəpyblije] (7) *vt* to republish.

république [ʀepyblik] *nf* republic. **on est en ~!*** this is *ou* it's a free country!; (*fig*) **~ des lettres** republic of letters; **la R~ Arabe Unie** the United Arab Republic; **la R~ d'Irlande** the Irish Republic.

répudiation [ʀepydjɑsjɔ̃] *nf* (*V* **répudier**) repudiation; renouncement; relinquishment.

répudier [ʀepydje] (7) *vt* *conjoint* to repudiate; *opinion, foi* to renounce; *engagement* to renounce, go back on; (*Jur*) *nationalité, succession* to renounce, relinquish.

répugnance [ʀepyɲɑ̃s] *nf* **(a)** (*répulsion*) (*pour personnes*) repugnance (*pour* for), disgust (*pour* for), loathing (*pour* of); (*pour nourriture, mensonge*) disgust (*pour* for), loathing (*pour* of). **avoir de la ~ pour les épinards/le travail scolaire** to loathe *ou* have a loathing of spinach/schoolwork; **j'éprouve de la ~ à la vue de ce spectacle** this sight fills me with disgust, I find this sight quite repugnant *ou* disgusting.

(b) (*hésitation*) reluctance (*à faire qch* to do sth). **il éprouvait une certaine ~ à nous le dire** he was rather loath *ou* reluctant to tell us; **faire qch avec ~** to do sth reluctantly, to do sth unwillingly.

répugnant, e [ʀepyɲɑ̃, ɑ̃t] *adj individu* repugnant; *laideur* revolting; *action* disgusting, loathsome; *travail, odeur* disgusting, revolting, repugnant; *nourriture* disgusting, revolting.

répugner [ʀepyɲe] (1) **1 répugner à** *vt indir* **(a)** (*dégoûter*) to repel, disgust, be repugnant to. **cet individu me répugne profondément** I am utterly repelled by that fellow, I am filled with repugnance *ou* disgust for that fellow; **manger du poisson/vivre dans la crasse lui répugnait** it was (quite) repugnant to him to eat fish/to live in squalor, he was repelled at the notion of eating fish/a life of squalor; **cette odeur lui répugnait** the smell was repugnant to him, he was repelled by the smell; **cette idée ne lui répugnait pas du tout** he wasn't in the least repelled by *ou* disgusted at this idea, he didn't find this idea off-putting (*surtout Brit*) *ou* repellent in the least.

(b) ~ à faire qch to be loath *ou* reluctant to do sth; **il répugnait à parler en public/à accepter cette aide** he was loath *ou* reluctant to speak in public/to accept this help; **il ne répugnait pas à mentir quand cela lui semblait nécessaire** he didn't hesitate to lie *ou* he had no qualms about lying if he thought he needed to.

2 *vb impers* (*frm*) **il me répugne de devoir vous le dire** it's very distasteful to me to have to tell you this.

3 *vt* (†,*) = **1a.**

répulsif, -ive [ʀepylsif, iv] *adj* (*gén, Phys*) repulsive.

répulsion [ʀepylsjɔ̃] *nf* (*gén*) repulsion, repugnance, disgust; (*Phys*) repulsion. **éprouver** *ou* **avoir de la ~ pour** to feel repulsion for, be absolutely repelled by.

réputation [ʀepytɑsjɔ̃] *nf* **(a)** (*honneur*) reputation, good name. **préserver sa ~** to keep up *ou* protect one's reputation *ou* good name.

(b) (*renommée*) reputation. **se faire une ~** to make a name *ou* a reputation for o.s.; **avoir bonne/mauvaise ~** to have a good/bad reputation; **produit de ~ mondiale** product which has a world-wide reputation; **connaître qn/qch de ~ (seulement)** to know sb/sth (only) by repute; **sa ~ de gynécologue** his reputation as a gynaecologist; **il a une ~ d'avarice** he has a reputation for miserliness; **il a la ~ d'être avare** he has a reputation for being miserly, he is reputed to be miserly.

réputé, e [ʀepyte] *adj* **(a)** (*célèbre*) *vin, artiste* reputable, renowned, of repute. **l'un des médecins les plus ~s de la ville** one of the town's most reputable doctors, one of the best-known doctors in the town; **c'est un fromage/vin hautement ~** it's a cheese/wine of great repute *ou* renown; **orateur ~ pour ses bons mots** speaker who is renowned for his witticisms; **ville ~e pour sa cuisine/ses monuments** town which is renowned for *ou* which has a great reputation for its cooking/its monuments; **il n'est pas ~ pour son honnêteté!** he's not exactly renowned *ou* famous for his honesty!

(b) (*prétendu*) **remède ~ infaillible** cure which is reputed *ou* supposed *ou* said to be infallible; **professeur ~ pour être très sévère** teacher who has the reputation of being *ou* who is reputed to be *ou* said to be very strict.

requérant, e [ʀəkeʀɑ̃, ɑ̃t] *nm,f* (*Jur*) applicant.

requérir [ʀəkeʀiʀ] (21) *vt* **(a)** (*nécessiter*) *soins, prudence* to call for, require. **ceci requiert toute notre attention** this calls for *ou* requires *ou* demands our full attention; **l'honneur requiert que vous acceptiez** honour requires *ou* demands that you accept.

(b) (*solliciter*) *aide, service* to request; (*exiger*) *justification* to require, necessitate, call for; (*réquisitionner*) *personne* to call upon. **~ l'intervention de la police** to require *ou* necessitate police intervention; (*frm*) **je vous requiers de me suivre** I call on you *ou* I summon you to follow me.

(c) (*Jur*) *peine* to call for, demand. **le procureur était en train de ~** the prosecutor was summing up *ou* making his closing speech.

requête [ʀəkɛt] *nf* **(a)** (*Jur*) petition. **adresser une ~ à un juge** to petition a judge; **~ en cassation** appeal; **~ civile** *appeal to a court against its judgment.*

(b) (*supplique*) request, petition. **à** *ou* **sur la ~ de qn** at sb's request, at the request of sb.

requiem [ʀekɥijɛm] *nm inv* requiem.

requin [ʀ(ə)kɛ̃] *nm* (*Zool, fig*) shark. **~ marteau** hammerhead (shark).

requinquer* [ʀ(ə)kɛ̃ke] (1) **1** *vt* to pep up*, buck up*. **un bon grog vous requinquera** a good grog will pep you up* *ou* buck you up*; **avec un peu de repos, dans 3 jours vous serez requinqué** with a bit of a rest in 3 days you'll be your old (perky) self again* *ou* you'll be back on form again.

2 se requinquer *vpr* to perk up*.

requis, e [ʀəki, iz] (*ptp de* **requérir**) *adj* **(a)** (*nécessaire*) (*gén*) required; *âge, diplôme, conditions* requisite, required. **(b)** (*réquisitionné*) **les ~** labour conscripts (*civilians*).

réquisition [ʀekizisjɔ̃] *nf* **(a)** *[biens]* requisition, requisitioning, commandeering; *[hommes]* requisition, requisitioning, conscription. **~ de la force armée** requisitioning of *ou* calling out of the army.

(b) (*Jur: aussi* **~s**) closing speech for the prosecution.

réquisitionner [ʀekizisjɔne] (1) *vt biens* to requisition, commandeer; *hommes* to requisition, conscript. **j'ai été réquisitionné pour faire la vaisselle*** I have been requisitioned to do the washing-up (*hum*).

réquisitoire [ʀekizitwaʀ] *nm* **(a)** (*Jur*) (*plaidoirie*) closing speech for the prosecution (*specifying appropriate sentence*); (*acte écrit*) instruction, brief (*to examining magistrate*).

(b) (*fig*) indictment (*contre* of). **son discours fut un ~ contre le capitalisme** his speech was an indictment of capitalism.

resaler [ʀ(ə)sale] (1) *vt* to add more salt to, put more salt in.

resalir [ʀ(ə)saliʀ] (2) *vt tapis, mur, sol, vêtement* to get dirty again. **ne va pas te ~** don't go and get yourself dirty *ou* in a mess again; **se ~ les mains** to get one's hands dirty *ou* dirty one's hands again.

rescapé, e [ʀɛskape] **1** *adj personne* surviving. **2** *nm,f* survivor (*de* of).

rescousse [ʀɛskus] *nf*: **venir** *ou* **aller à la ~ de qn** to go to sb's rescue *ou* aid; **appeler qn à la ~** to call on *ou* to sb for help; **ils arrivèrent à la ~** they came to the rescue, they rallied round.

rescrit [ʀɛskʀi] *nm* rescript.

réseau, *pl* **~x** [ʀezo] *nm* **(a)** (*gén, fig*) network. **~ ferroviaire/commercial/de résistance/téléphonique** rail/sales/resistance/telephone network; **~ fluvial** river system, network of rivers; **~ d'espionnage** spy network *ou* ring; **~ d'intrigues** network *ou* web of intrigue(s); **~ d'habitudes** pattern of habits; **les abonnés du ~ sont avisés que** telephone subscribers are advised that; **sur l'ensemble du ~** over the whole network.

(b) (*Zool*) reticulum.

(c) (*Phys*) **~ de diffraction** diffraction pattern; **~ cristallin** crystal lattice.

réséda [ʀezeda] *nm* reseda, mignonette.

réservation [ʀezɛʀvɑsjɔ̃] *nf* (*à l'hôtel*) reservation; (*des places*) reservation, booking; (*Jur*) reservation.

réserve [ʀezɛʀv(ə)] *nf* **(a)** (*provision*) reserve; *[marchandises]* reserve, stock. **les enfants ont une ~ énorme d'énergie** children have an enormous reserve *ou* enormous reserves of energy; **faire des ~s de sucre** to get in *ou* lay in a stock of *ou* reserves of sugar; **heureusement ils avaient une petite ~ (d'argent)** fortunately they had a little money put by *ou* a little money in reserve; **les ~s mondiales de pétrole** the world's oil reserves; **~s (nutritives) de l'organisme** the organism's food reserves; **il peut jeûner, il a des ~s!** he can afford to do without food — he's got plenty of reserves!; **avoir des provisions en ~** *ou* **en ~** to have provisions in reserve *ou* put by; **mettre qch en ~** to put sth by, put sth in reserve; **avoir/tenir qch en ~** (*gén*) to have/keep sth in reserve; (*Comm*) to have/keep sth in stock.

(b) (*restriction*) reservation, reserve. **faire** *ou* **émettre des ~s sur l'opportunité de qch** to have reservations *ou* reserves about the timeliness of sth; **sous toutes ~s** *publier* with all reserve, with all proper reserves; *dire* with reservations; **je vous le dis sous toutes ~s** I can't vouch for *ou* guarantee the truth of what I'm telling you; **tarif/horaire publié sous toute ~** no guarantee as to the accuracy of the price/timetable shown; **sous ~ de** subject to; **sans ~** *admiration, consentement* unreserved, unqualified; *approuver, accepter* unreservedly, without reservation, unhesitatingly; *dévoué* unreservedly.

(c) (*prudence, discrétion*) reserve. **être/demeurer** *ou* **se tenir sur la ~** to be/stay on the reserve, be/remain very reserved about sth; **il m'a parlé sans ~** he talked to me quite unreservedly *ou* openly; **elle est d'une grande ~** she's very reserved, she keeps herself to herself.

(d) (*Mil*) **la ~** the reserve; **les ~s** the reserves; **officiers/armée de ~** reserve officers/army.

(e) (*territoire*) *[nature, animaux]* reserve; *[Indiens]* reservation. **~ de pêche/chasse** fishing/hunting preserve.

(f) *[bibliothèque]* reserve collection. **le livre est à la ~** the book is in reserve.

(g) (*entrepôt*) storehouse, storeroom.

réservé, e [ʀezɛʀve] (*ptp de* **réserver**) *adj place, salle* reserved (*à qn/qch* for sb/sth); *personne, caractère* reserved. **chasse/pêche ~e** private hunting/fishing; **j'ai une table ~e** I've got a table reserved *ou* booked; **les médecins sont très ~s à son sujet** the doctors are very guarded *ou* cautious in their opinions about him; **tous droits ~s** all rights reserved; *V* **quartier.**

réserver [ʀezɛʀve] (1) **1** *vt* **(a)** (*mettre à part*) to keep, save, reserve (*à, pour* for); *marchandises* to keep, put aside *ou* on one side (*à* for). **il nous a réservé 2 places à côté de lui** he's kept *ou* saved us 2 seats beside him; **on vous a réservé ce bureau** we've reserved you this office, we've set this office aside for you; **~ le meilleur pour la fin** to keep *ou* save the best till last; **ils réservent ces fauteuils pour les cérémonies** they reserve *ou* keep these armchairs for (special) ceremonies; **pouvez-vous me ~ 5 mètres de ce tissu?** could you put 5 metres of that material aside *ou* on one side for me?, could you keep me 5 metres of that material?; **ces emplacements sont strictement réservés aux voitures du personnel** these parking places are strictly reserved for staff cars; **nous réservons toujours un peu d'argent pour les dépenses imprévues** we always keep *ou* put a bit of money on one side *ou* earmark a bit of money for unexpected expenses.

(b) (*louer*) *place, chambre, table [voyageur]* to book, reserve; *[agence]* to reserve.

(c) (*fig: destiner*) *dangers, désagréments, joies* to have in store (*à* for); *accueil, châtiment* to have in store, reserve (*à* for). **cette expédition devait leur ~ bien des surprises** that expedition was to have many surprises in store for them, there were to be many surprises in store for them on that expedition; **nous ne savons pas ce que l'avenir nous réserve** we don't know what the future has in store for us *ou* holds for us; **le sort qui lui est réservé est peu enviable** he has an unenviable fate in store for him *ou* reserved for him; **il lui était réservé de mourir jeune** he was destined to die young; **c'est à lui qu'il était réservé de marcher le premier sur la lune** he was to be the first to walk on the moon; **c'est à lui que fut réservé l'honneur de porter le drapeau** the honour of carrying the flag fell to him.

(d) (*remettre à plus tard*) *réponse, opinion* to reserve. **le médecin préfère ~ son diagnostic** the doctor would rather reserve his diagnosis.

2 se réserver *vpr* **(a)** (*prélever*) to keep *ou* reserve for o.s. **il s'est réservé le meilleur morceau** he kept *ou* saved the best bit for himself.

(b) (*se ménager*) **se ~ pour une autre occasion** to wait for another opportunity, wait until another opportunity comes along; **il ne mange pas maintenant, il se réserve pour le banquet/pour plus tard** he isn't eating now — he's saving *ou* reserving himself for the banquet/for later; (*Sport*) **il faut savoir se ~** one must learn to hold back *ou* to conserve *ou* save one's strength.

(c) se ~ de faire: il se réserve d'intervenir plus tard he's waiting to see whether he'll need to intervene later, he's reserving the possibility of intervening later; **se ~ le droit de faire qch** to reserve the right to do sth.

réserviste [ʀezɛʀvist(ə)] *nm* reservist.

réservoir [ʀezɛʀvwaʀ] *nm* (*cuve*) tank; (*plan d'eau*) reservoir; *[poissons]* fishpond; *[usine à gaz]* gasometer, gasholder. (*fig*) **ce pays est un ~ de talents/de main-d'œuvre** this country has a wealth of talents/a huge pool of labour to draw on; **~ d'eau** (*gén, Aut*) water tank; (*pour une maison*) water cistern; (*pour eau de pluie*) (*en bois*) water butt; (*en ciment*) water tank.

résidant, e [ʀezidɑ̃, ɑ̃t] *adj* resident.

résidence [ʀezidɑ̃s] **1** *nf* (*gén*) residence; (*immeuble*) (block of) residential flats. **établir sa ~ à** to take up residence in; **changer de ~** to move (house); (*Admin*) **en ~ à** in residence at; **en ~ surveillée** *ou* **forcée** under house arrest; (*Diplomatie*) **la ~** the residency; *V* **certificat**.

2: résidence principale main home; **résidence secondaire** second home, weekend cottage; **résidence universitaire** (university) hall of residence.

résident, e [ʀezidɑ̃, ɑ̃t] *nm,f* (*étranger*) foreign national *ou* resident; (*diplomate*) resident.

résidentiel, -ielle [ʀezidɑ̃sjɛl] *adj* residential.

résider [ʀezide] (1) *vi* (*lit, fig*) to reside (*en, dans* in). **il réside à cet hôtel/à Dijon** he resides (*frm*) at this hotel/in Dijon; **après avoir résidé quelques temps en France** after living *ou* residing (*frm*) in France for some time, after having been resident in France for some time; **le problème réside en ceci que ...** the problem lies in the fact that ... .

résidu [ʀezidy] *nm* **(a)** (*reste*) (*Chim, fig*) residue (*U*); (*Math*) remainder. **(b)** (*déchets*) **~s** remnants, residue (*U*); **~s industriels** industrial waste.

résiduel, -elle [ʀezidɥɛl] *adj* residual.

résignation [ʀeziɲɑsjɔ̃] *nf* resignation (*à* to). **avec ~** with resignation, resignedly.

résigné, e [ʀeziɲe] (*ptp de* **résigner**) *adj air, geste, ton* resigned. **~ à son sort** resigned to his fate; **il est ~** he's resigned to it; **dire qch d'un air ~** to say sth resignedly.

résigner [ʀeziɲe] (1) **1 se résigner** *vpr* to resign o.s. (*à* to). **il faudra s'y ~** we'll have to resign ourselves to it *ou* put up with it. **2** *vt* (*littér*) *charge, fonction* to relinquish, resign.

résiliable [ʀeziljabl(ə)] *adj* (*V* **résilier**) which can be terminated, terminable; which can be cancelled, cancellable.

résiliation [ʀeziljɑsjɔ̃] *nf* (*V* **résilier**) termination; cancellation.

résilience [ʀeziljɑ̃s] *nf* (*Tech*) ductility.

résilient, e [ʀeziljɑ̃, ɑ̃t] *adj* (*Tech*) ductile.

résilier [ʀezilje] (7) *vt contrat* (*à terme*) to terminate; (*en cours*) to cancel.

résille [ʀezij] *nf* (*gén: filet*) net, netting (*U*); (*pour les cheveux*) hairnet; *[vitrail]* cames, lead(s), leading (*U*).

résine [ʀezin] *nf* resin.

résiné, e [ʀezine] *adj, nm*: **(vin) ~** retsina.

résineux, -euse [ʀezinø, øz] **1** *adj* resinous. **2** *nm* coniferous tree. **forêt de ~** coniferous forest.

résistance [ʀezistɑ̃s] *nf* **(a)** (*opposition*) resistance (*U*) (*à* to). (*Hist*) **la R~** the (French) Resistance; **l'armée dut se rendre après une ~ héroïque** the army was forced to surrender after putting up a heroic resistance *ou* a heroic fight; **opposer une ~ farouche à un projet** to put up a fierce resistance to a project, make a very determined stand against a project; **cela ne se fera pas sans ~** that won't be done without some opposition *ou* resistance; **~ passive/armée** passive/armed resistance; *V* **noyau**.

(b) (*endurance*) resistance, stamina. **~ à la fatigue** resistance to fatigue; **il a une grande ~** *ou* **beaucoup de ~** he has great *ou* a lot of resistance *ou* stamina; **coureur qui a de la ~/qui n'a pas de ~** runner who has lots of/who has no staying power; **ces plantes-là n'ont pas de ~** those plants have no resistance; **ce matériau offre une grande ~ au feu/aux chocs** this material is very heat-/shock-resistant; *V* **pièce, plat**[2].

(c) (*Élec*) (*U*) resistance; *[réchaud, radiateur]* element. **unité de ~** unit of (electrical) resistance.

(d) (*Phys: force*) resistance. **~ d'un corps/de l'air** resistance of a body/of the air; **~ mécanique** mechanical resistance; **~ des matériaux** strength of materials; **quand il voulut ouvrir la porte, il sentit une ~** when he tried to open the door he felt some resistance.

résistant, e [ʀezistɑ̃, ɑ̃t] **1** *adj personne* robust, tough; *plante* hardy; *vêtements, tissu* strong, hard-wearing; *couleur* fast; *acier* resistant; *métal* resistant, strong; *bois* resistant, hard. **il est très ~** (*gén*) he is very robust, he has a lot of resistance *ou* stamina; *[athlète]* he has lots of staying power; **~ à la chaleur** heatproof, heat-resistant.

2 *nm,f* (*Hist*) (French) Resistance worker *ou* fighter.

résister [ʀeziste] (1) **résister à** *vt indir* **(a)** (*s'opposer à*) *ennemi, agresseur, police* to resist; *passion, tentation, argument* to resist; *attaque* to hold out against, withstand, resist. **inutile de ~** it's useless to resist, it's *ou* there's no use resisting; **~ au courant d'une rivière** to fight against *ou* hold one's own against the current of a river; **~ à la volonté de qn** to hold out against *ou* resist sb's will; **il n'ose pas ~ à sa fille** he doesn't dare (to) stand up to his daughter; **je n'aime pas que mes enfants me résistent** I don't like my children opposing me; **je n'ai pas résisté à cette petite robe** I couldn't resist (buying) this dress.

(b) (*surmonter*) *fatigue, émotion, privations* to stand up to, withstand; *chagrin, adversité* to withstand; *douleur* to stand, withstand. **leur amour ne résista pas à cette infidélité** their love could not stand up to *ou* could not withstand this infidelity.

(c) (*supporter*) *sécheresse, gelée, vent* to withstand, stand up to, resist. **ça a bien résisté à l'épreuve du temps** it has really stood the test of time, it has stood up to the passing centuries; **le plancher ne pourra pas ~ au poids** the floor won't support *ou* withstand *ou* take the weight; **la porte a résisté** the door didn't give, the door stood firm *ou* resisted; **ça n'a pas résisté longtemps** it didn't resist *ou* hold out for long; **couleur qui résiste au lavage** colour which is fast in the wash, fast colour; **tissu qui résiste au lavage en machine** material which can be machine-washed *ou* which will stand up to machine washing; **cette vaisselle résiste au feu** this crockery is heat-resistant *ou* heatproof; **ce raisonnement ne résiste pas à l'analyse** this reasoning does not stand up to analysis.

résolu, e [ʀezɔly] (*ptp de* **résoudre**) *adj personne, ton, air* resolute. **il est bien ~ à partir** he is firmly resolved *ou* he is determined to leave, he is set on leaving.

résoluble [ʀezɔlybl(ə)] *adj problème* soluble; (*Chim*) resolvable; (*Jur*) *contrat* annullable, cancellable.

résolument [ʀezɔlymɑ̃] *adv* (*totalement*) resolutely; (*courageusement*) resolutely, steadfastly. **je suis ~ contre** I'm firmly against it, I'm resolutely opposed to it.

résolutif, -ive [ʀezɔlytif, iv] *adj, nm* resolvent.

résolution [ʀezɔlysjɔ̃] *nf* **(a)** (*gén, Pol: décision*) resolution. **prendre la ~ de faire** to make a resolution to do, resolve to do, make up one's mind to do; **ma ~ est prise** I've made my resolution; **bonnes ~s** good resolutions.

(b) (*énergie*) resolve, resolution, determination. **avec un visage plein de ~** his face full of resolve *ou* resolution, with a determined expression on his face.

(c) (*solution*) solution. **il attendait de moi la ~ de son problème** he expected me to give him a solution to his problem *ou* to solve his problem for him.

(d) (*Jur*) *[contrat, vente]* cancellation, annulment.

(e) (*Méd, Mus, Phys*) resolution. **~ de l'eau en vapeur** resolution of water into steam.

résolutoire [ʀezɔlytwaʀ] *adj* (*Jur*) resolutive.

résonance [ʀezɔnɑ̃s] *nf* (*gén, Élec, Phys*) resonance (*U*); (*fig*) echo. **être/entrer en ~** to be/start resonating; (*littér*) **ce poème éveille en moi des ~s** this poem awakens echoes in me; *V* **caisse**.

résonateur [ʀezɔnatœʀ] *nm* resonator. **~ nucléaire** nuclear resonator.

résonnant, e [ʀezɔnɑ̃, ɑ̃t] *adj voix* resonant. **cour ~e de bruits** yard resounding *ou* resonant *ou* ringing with noise.

résonner [ʀezɔne] (1) *vi* *[son]* to resonate, reverberate, resound; *[salle]* to be resonant. **cloche qui résonne bien/faiblement** bell which resounds well/rings feebly; **ne parle pas trop fort, ça résonne** don't speak too loudly because it *ou* the noise resonates *ou* reverberates *ou* echoes; **~ de** to resound *ou* ring *ou* resonate with.

résorber [ʀezɔʀbe] (1) **1** *vt* (*Méd*) to resorb; *chômage* to bring down, reduce gradually; *déficit, surplus* to absorb; *inflation* to bring down, reduce gradually, curb. **trouver un moyen pour ~ la crise économique** to find some way of solving the economic crisis from within.

2 se résorber *vpr* (*Méd*) to be resorbed; (*fig*) *[chômage]* to be brought down *ou* reduced; *[déficit]* to be absorbed. **l'embouteillage se résorbe peu à peu** the traffic jam is gradually breaking up *ou* sorting itself out *ou* resolving itself.

résorption [ʀezɔʀpsjɔ̃] *nf* (*V* **résorber**) resorption; bringing down, gradual reduction (*de* in); absorption; curbing.

résoudre [ʀezudʀ(ə)] (51) **1** *vt* **(a)** *mystère, équation* to solve; *problème, dilemme* to solve, resolve; *difficultés* to solve, resolve, settle, sort out; *conflit* to settle, resolve; *crise* to solve. **j'ignore comment ce problème va se ~** *ou* **va être résolu** I can't see how this problem will be solved *ou* resolved.

(b) (*décider*) *exécution, mort* to decide on, determine on. **~ de faire qch** to decide *ou* resolve to do sth, make up one's mind to do sth; **~ qn à faire qch** to prevail upon sb *ou* induce sb to do sth.

(c) (*Méd*) *tumeur* to resolve.

(d) (*Jur*) *contrat, vente* to cancel, annul.

(e) (*Mus*) *dissonance* to resolve.

(f) (*transformer*) **~ qch en cendres** to reduce sth to cinders; **les nuages se résolvent en pluie/grêle** the clouds break up *ou* resolve into rain/hail.

2 se résoudre *vpr*: **se ~ à faire qch** (*se décider*) to resolve *ou* decide to do sth, make up one's mind to do sth; (*se résigner*) to bring o.s. to do sth.

respect [ʀɛspɛ] *nm* **(a)** respect (*de, pour* for). **avoir du ~ pour qn** to have respect fr sb, hold sb in respect; **il n'a aucun ~ pour le bien d'autrui** he has no respect *ou* consideration *ou* regard for other people's property; **par ~ pour sa mémoire** out of respect *ou* consideration for his memory; **malgré le ~ que je vous dois, sauf votre ~** with (all) respect, with all due respect; **le ~ humain** respect for the individual; **~ de soi** self-respect.

(b) (*formule de politesse*) **présenter ses ~s à qn** to present one's respects to sb; **présentez mes ~s à votre femme** give my regards *ou* pay my respects† to your wife; **mes ~s, mon colonel** good day to you, sir.

(c) (*loc*) **tenir qn en ~** (*avec une arme*) to keep sb at a respectful distance *ou* at bay; **au ~ de**†† compared with, in comparison to *ou* with.

respectabilité [ʀɛspɛktabilite] *nf* respectability.

respectable [ʀɛspɛktabl(ə)] *adj* (*honorable*) respectable; (*important*) respectable, sizeable. **il avait un ventre ~*** he had quite a pot-belly*, he had a fair-sized corporation*.

respecter [ʀɛspɛkte] (1) **1** *vt* **(a)** *personne* to respect, have respect for. **~ une femme** to respect a woman's honour; **se faire ~** to be respected, make o.s. respected (*par* by), command respect (*par* from).

(b) *formes, loi* to respect; *traditions* to respect, have respect for, honour. **~ les opinions/sentiments de qn** to show consideration *ou* respect for people's opinions/feelings; **~ le sommeil de qn** to respect sb's right to get some sleep; **respectez le matériel!** treat the equipment with respect!, show some respect for the equipment!; **la jeunesse ne respecte rien** young people show no respect for anything *ou* do not respect anything; **classer des livres en respectant l'ordre alphabétique** to classify books, keeping them in alphabetical order; **faire ~ la loi** to enforce the law; **~ les termes d'un contrat** to abide by the terms of a contract.

2 se respecter *vpr* to respect o.s. (*hum*) **le professeur/juge/plombier qui se respecte** any self-respecting teacher/judge/plumber; **il se respecte trop pour faire cela** he is above doing that sort of thing, he has too much self-respect to do that sort of thing.

respectif, -ive [ʀɛspɛktif, iv] *adj* respective.

respectivement [ʀɛspɛktivmɑ̃] *adv* respectively.

respectueusement [ʀɛspɛktɥøzmɑ̃] *adv* respectfully, with respect.

respectueux, -euse [ʀɛspɛktɥø, øz] **1** *adj silence, langage, personne* respectful (*envers, pour* to). **se montrer ~ du bien d'autrui** to show respect *ou* consideration for other people's property; **~ des traditions** respectful of traditions; **~ de la loi** respectful of the law, law-abiding; **veuillez agréer mes salutations ~euses** yours respectfully; **je vous envoie mes hommages ~** yours (most) sincerely, your humble servant†; *V* **distance.**

2 respectueuse* *nf* (*prostituée*) tart*, whore, prostitute.

respirable [ʀɛspiʀabl(ə)] *adj* breathable. **l'air n'y est pas ~** the air there is unbreathable; (*fig*) **l'atmosphère n'est pas ~ dans cette famille** the atmosphere in this family is suffocating.

respiration [ʀɛspiʀɑsjɔ̃] *nf* (*fonction, action naturelle*) breathing, respiration (*T*); (*souffle*) breath. **~ pulmonaire/cutanée/artificielle** pulmonary/cutaneous/artificial respiration; **~ difficile** difficulty in breathing; **~ entrecoupée** irregular breathing; **~ courte** shortness of breath; **avoir la ~ difficile** to have difficulty (in) *ou* trouble breathing; **avoir la ~ bruyante** to breathe heavily *ou* noisily; **retenir sa ~** to hold one's breath; **faites 3 ~s complètes** breathe in and out 3 times; *V* **couper.**

respiratoire [ʀɛspiʀatwaʀ] *adj système, voies* respiratory; *troubles* breathing (*épith*), respiratory.

respirer [ʀɛspiʀe] (1) **1** *vi* **(a)** (*lit, Bio*) to breathe, respire (*T*). (*chez le médecin*) **'respirez'** 'breathe in!', 'take a deep breath!'; **~ par la bouche/le nez** to breathe through one's mouth/nose; **est-ce qu'il respire (encore)?** is he (still) breathing?; **~ avec difficulté** to have difficulty (in) *ou* trouble breathing, breathe with difficulty; **~ profondément** to breathe deeply, take a deep breath.

(b) (*fig*) (*se détendre*) to get one's breath (*fig*), have a break; (*se rassurer*) to breathe again *ou* easy (*fig*). **ouf, on respire** phew, we can breathe again.

2 *vt* **(a)** (*inhaler*) to breathe (in), inhale. **~ un air vicié/le grand air** to breathe in foul air/the fresh air; **faire ~ des vapeurs à qn** to make sb inhale vapours.

(b) (*exprimer*) *calme, bonheur* to radiate; *honnêteté, franchise, orgueil* to exude, emanate. **son attitude respirait la méfiance** his whole attitude was mistrustful, his attitude was clearly one of mistrust.

resplendir [ʀɛsplɑ̃diʀ] (2) *vi [soleil]* to shine, beam; *[lune]* to beam; *[surface métallique]* to gleam, shine. **le lac/la neige resplendissait sous le soleil** the lake/snow glistened *ou* glittered in the sun; **le ciel resplendit au coucher du soleil** the sky blazes with light *ou* is radiant at sunset; **toute la cuisine resplendissait** the whole kitchen gleamed; (*fig*) **il resplendissait de joie/de bonheur** he was aglow *ou* radiant with joy/happiness.

resplendissant, e [ʀɛsplɑ̃disɑ̃, ɑ̃t] *adj* **(a)** (*lit: brillant*) *soleil* radiant, beaming, dazzling; *lune* beaming, glowing; *surface métallique* gleaming, shining; *lac, neige* glistening, glittering; *ciel* radiant.

(b) (*fig: éclatant*) *beauté, santé, mine* radiant; *yeux, visage* shining. **être ~ de santé/de joie** to be aglow *ou* radiant with health/joy.

responsabilité [ʀɛspɔ̃sabilite] **1** *nf* **(a)** (*légale*) liability (*de* for); (*morale*) responsibility (*de* for); (*ministérielle*) responsibility. **emmener ces enfants en montagne, c'est une ~** it's a responsibility taking these children to the mountains; **la ~ pénale des parents** the legal responsibility of parents; *V* **assurance, société.**

(b) (*charge*) responsibility. **de lourdes ~s** heavy responsibilities; **assumer la ~ d'une affaire** to take on the responsibility for a matter; **avoir la ~ de la gestion/de la sécurité** to be responsible for the management/for security; **il fuit les ~s** he shuns (any) responsibility; **ce poste comporte d'importantes ~s** this post involves *ou* carries considerable responsibilities; **accéder à une haute ~** to reach a position of great responsibility.

2: (*Jur*) **responsabilité atténuée** diminished responsibility; **responsabilité civile** civil liability; **responsabilité collective** collective responsibility; **responsabilité contractuelle** contractual liability; **responsabilité pénale** criminal responsibility; (*Jur*) **responsabilité pleine et entière** full and entire responsibility.

responsable [ʀɛspɔ̃sabl(ə)] **1** *adj* **(a)** (*comptable*) (*légalement*) (*de dégâts*) liable, responsible (*de* for); (*de délits*) responsible (*de* for); (*moralement*) responsible, accountable (*de* for, *devant qn* to sb). **reconnu ~ de ses actes** recognized as responsible *ou* accountable for his actions; **il n'est pas ~ des délits/dégâts commis par ses enfants** he is not responsible for the misdemeanours of/liable *ou* responsible for damage caused by his children; **un père est ~ de la santé morale de ses enfants** a father is responsible for the moral well-being of his children; **civilement/pénalement ~** liable in civil/criminal law; **le ministre est ~ de ses décisions (devant le parlement)** the minister is responsible *ou* accountable (to Parliament) for his decisions.

(b) (*chargé de*) **~ de** responsible for, in charge of.

(c) (*coupable*) responsible, to blame. **X, ~ de l'échec, a été renvoyé** X, who was responsible *ou* to blame for the failure, has been dismissed; **ils considèrent l'état défectueux des freins comme ~ (de l'accident)** they consider that defective brakes were to blame *ou* were responsible for the accident.

(d) (*sérieux*) *attitude, employé, étudiant* responsible.

2 *nmf* **(a)** (*coupable*) **il s'agit de trouver et de punir le ~/les ~s (de cette action)** we must find and punish the person responsible/those responsible *ou* the person who is to blame/those who are to blame (for this act); **le seul ~ est l'alcool** alcohol alone is to blame *ou* is the culprit.

(b) (*personne compétente*) person in charge. **adressez-vous au ~** see the person in charge.

(c) (*dirigeant*) **les ~s d'un parti** the officials of a party; **une table ronde réunissant des ~s de l'industrie** a round table discussion bringing together representatives *ou* leaders of industry; **~ syndical** trade union official.

responsabiliser [ʀɛspɔ̃sabilize] (1) *vt*: **~ qn** to make sb aware of his responsibilities.

resquillage [ʀɛskijaʒ] *nm*, **resquille** [ʀɛskij] *nf* (*dans l'autobus*) grabbing a free ride; (*au match, cinéma*) sneaking in, getting in on the sly.

resquiller [ʀɛskije] (1) *vi* (*ne pas payer*) (*dans l'autobus etc*) to fiddle* a free seat *ou* ride; (*au match, cinéma*) to get in on the sly; (*ne pas faire la queue*) to jump the queue (*Brit*).

resquilleur, -euse [ʀɛskijœʀ, øz] *nm,f* (*qui n'attend pas son tour*) queue-jumper (*Brit*); (*qui ne paie pas*) (*dans l'autobus etc*) fare-dodger; (*au stade etc*) **expulser les ~s** to throw out the people who have wangled their way in without paying.

ressac [ʀəsak] *nm*: **le ~** (*mouvement*) the backwash, the undertow; (*vague*) the surf.

ressaisir [ʀ(ə)seziʀ] (2) **1** *vt* **(a)** *branche, bouée* to catch hold of again; *fuyard* to recapture, seize again; (*fig*) *pouvoir, occasion, prétexte* to seize again; (*Jur*) *biens* to recover possession of.

(b) *[peur]* to grip (once) again; *[délire, désir]* to take hold of again.

(c) (*Jur*) **~ un tribunal d'une affaire** to lay a matter before a court again.

2 se ressaisir *vpr* **(a)** (*reprendre son sang-froid*) to regain one's self control; (*Sport: après avoir flanché*) to rally. **ressaisissez-vous!** pull yourself together!, take a grip on yourself!; **le coureur s'est bien ressaisi sur la fin** the runner rallied well towards the end.

(b) **se ~ de** *objet, fugitifs* to recover; *pouvoir* to seize again.

ressassé, e [ʀ(ə)sɑse] (*ptp de* **ressasser**) *adj plaisanterie, thème* worn out, hackneyed.

ressasser [ʀ(ə)sɑse] (1) *vt pensées, regrets* to keep turning over; *plaisanteries, conseil* to keep trotting out.

ressaut [ʀ(ə)so] *nm* (*Géog*) (*plan vertical*) rise; (*plan horizontal*) shelf; (*Archit*) projection.

ressauter [ʀ(ə)sote] (1) **1** *vi* to jump again. **2** *vt obstacle* to jump (over) again.

ressayage [ʀesejaʒ] *nm* = **réessayage.**

ressayer [ʀeseje] (8) *vt, vi* (*gén*) to try again; (*Couture*) = **réessayer.**

ressemblance [ʀ(ə)sɑ̃blɑ̃s] *nf* **(a)** (*U*) (*similitude visuelle*) resemblance, likeness; (*analogie de composition*) similarity. **~ presque parfaite entre 2 substances** near perfect similarity of 2 substances; **avoir *ou* offrir une ~ avec qch** to bear a resemblance *ou* likeness to sth; **la ~ entre père et fils/ces montagnes est frappante** the resemblance between father and son/these mountains is striking; **ce peintre s'inquiète peu de la ~** this painter cares very little about likenesses; **toute ~ avec des personnes ayant existé ne peut être que fortuite** any resemblance to any person living or dead is purely accidental.

(b) (*trait*) resemblance; (*analogie*) similarity.

ressemblant, e [ʀ(ə)sɑ̃blɑ̃, ɑ̃t] *adj photo, portrait* likelife, true to life. **vous êtes très ~ sur cette photo** this photo is very like you; **il a fait d'elle un portrait très ~** he painted a very good likeness of her.

ressembler [ʀ(ə)sɑ̃ble] (1) **1 ressembler à** *vt indir* **(a)** (*être semblable à*) *[personne]* (*physiquement*) to resemble, be *ou* look like; (*moralement, psychologiquement*) to resemble, be like; *[choses]* (*visuellement*) to resemble, look like; (*par la composition*) to resemble, be like; *[faits, événements]* to resemble, be like. **il me ressemble beaucoup**

physiquement/moralement he is very like me *ou* he resembles me closely in looks/in character; **juste quelques accrochages, rien qui ressemble à une offensive** just a few skirmishes — nothing that would pass as *ou* that you could call a proper offensive; **il ne ressemble en rien à l'image que je me faisais de lui** he's nothing like how I imagined him; **à quoi ressemble-t-il?*** what does he look like?, what's he like?*; **ton fils s'est roulé dans la boue, regarde à quoi il ressemble!*** your son has been rolling in the mud — just look at the state of him!*; **ça ne ressemble à rien!*** (*attitude*) that has no rhyme or reason to it, it makes no sense at all; (*peinture, objet*) it's like nothing on earth!*; **à quoi ça ressemble de crier comme ça!*** what's the idea of* *ou* what do you mean by shouting like that!

(b) (*être digne de*) **cela lui ressemble bien, de dire ça** it's just like him *ou* it's typical of him to say that; **cela te ressemble peu** that's (most) unlike you *ou* not like you.

2 se ressembler *vpr* (*physiquement, visuellement*) to look *ou* be alike, resemble each other; (*moralement, par ses éléments*) to be alike, resemble each other. **ils se ressemblent comme deux gouttes d'eau** they're as like as two peas (in a pod); **tu ne te ressembles plus depuis ton accident** you're not yourself since your accident; **aucune ville ne se ressemble** *ou* **ne ressemble à une autre** no town is like another, no two towns are alike; **toutes les grandes villes se ressemblent** all big towns are *ou* look alike; *V* **jour, qui.**

ressemelage [ʀ(ə)səmlaʒ] *nm* soling, resoling.

ressemeler [ʀ(ə)səmle] (4) *vt* to sole, resole.

ressemer [ʀəsme] (5) **1** *vt* to resow, sow again.

2 se ressemer *vpr* to (re)seed itself. **cette plante se ressème toute seule** this plant reseeds itself.

ressentiment [ʀ(ə)sɑ̃timɑ̃] *nm* resentment (*contre* against, *de* at). **éprouver du ~** to feel resentful; **éprouver un ~ légitime à l'égard de qn** to feel justifiably resentful towards sb; **il en a gardé du ~** it has remained a sore point with him, he has harboured resentment over it; **avec ~** resentfully, with resentment.

ressentir [ʀ(ə)sɑ̃tiʀ] (16) **1** *vt douleur, sentiment, coup* to feel; *sensation* to feel, experience; *perte, insulte, privation* to feel, be affected by. **il ressentit les effets de cette nuit de beuverie** he felt the effects of that night's drinking; **il ressent toute chose profondément** he feels everything deeply, he is deeply affected by anything *ou* everything.

2 se ressentir *vpr* **(a)** *[travail, qualité]* **se ~ de** to show the effects of; **la qualité/son travail s'en ressent** the quality/his work is showing the effect, it is telling on the quality/his work.

(b) *[personne, communauté]* **se ~ de** to feel the effects of; **il se ressentait du manque de préparation** he felt the effects of his lack of preparation, his lack of preparation told on his performance.

(c) (*) **s'en ~ pour** to feel up to*; **il ne s'en ressent pas pour faire ça** he doesn't feel up to doing that*.

resserre [ʀ(ə)sɛʀ] *nf* (*cabane*) shed; (*réduit*) store, storeroom.

resserré, e [ʀ(ə)seʀe] (*ptp de* **resserrer**) *adj chemin, vallée* narrow. **une petite maison ~e entre des immeubles** a little house squeezed between high buildings.

resserrement [ʀ(ə)sɛʀmɑ̃] *nm* **(a)** (*U: action*) *[nœud, étreinte]* tightening; *[pores]* closing; *[liens, amitié]* strengthening; *[vallée]* narrowing; *[crédit]* tightening. **(b)** (*goulet*) *[route, vallée]* narrow part.

resserrer [ʀ(ə)seʀe] (1) **1** *vt boulon, souliers, nœud* to tighten up; *étreinte* to tighten; (*fig*) *cercle, filets* to draw tighter, tighten; (*fig*) *liens, amitié* to strengthen; (*fig*) *récit* to tighten up, compress; (*fig*) *crédits* to tighten, squeeze*. **la peur resserra le cercle des fugitifs autour du feu** fear drew the group of fugitives in *ou* closer around the fire; **produit qui resserre les pores de la peau** product which helps (to) close the pores of the skin.

2 se resserrer *vpr [nœud, étau, étreinte]* to tighten; *[liens affectifs]* to grow stronger; *[cercle, groupe]* to draw in; *[pores, mâchoire]* to close; (*fig*) *[chemin, vallée]* to narrow. **le filet/l'enquête se resserrait autour de lui** the net/inquiry was closing in on him.

resservir [ʀ(ə)sɛʀviʀ] (14) **1** *vt* **(a)** (*servir à nouveau*) *plat* to serve (up) again (*à* to), dish up again* (*péj*) (*à* for); *dîneur* to give a second helping to (*de, en* of). **ils (nous) ont resservi la soupe de midi** they served (us) up the lunchtime soup again; **ils nous ont resservi (de viande)** they gave us a second helping *ou* second helpings (of meat).

(b) (*servir davantage de*) **~ de la soupe/viande** to give another *ou* a second helping of soup/meat; **ils (nous) ont resservi de la viande** they gave (us) a second helping of meat.

(c) (*fig*) *thème, histoire* to trot out again* (*péj*). **les thèmes qu'ils nous resservent depuis des années** the themes that they have been feeding us with *ou* trotting out* to us for years.

2 *vi* **(a)** *[vêtement usagé, outil]* to serve again, do again. **ça peut toujours ~** it may come in handy* *ou* be useful again; **cet emballage peut ~** this packaging can be used again; **ce manteau pourra te ~** you may find this coat useful again (some time).

(b) (*Tennis*) to serve again.

3 se resservir *vpr* **(a)** *[dîneur]* to help o.s. again, take another helping. **se ~ de fromage/viande** to help o.s. to some more cheese/meat, take another helping of cheese/meat.

(b) (*réutiliser*) **se ~ de** *outil* to use again; *vêtement* to wear again.

ressort[1] [ʀ(ə)sɔʀ] **1** *nm* **(a)** (*pièce de métal*) spring. **faire ~** to spring back; **à ~** *mécanisme, pièce* spring-loaded; *V* **matelas, mouvoir.**

(b) (*énergie*) spirit. **avoir du/manquer de ~** to have/lack spirit; **un être sans ~** a spiritless individual.

(c) (*littér: motivation*) **les ~s qui le font agir** the forces which motivate him, the motivating forces behind his actions; **les ~s de l'âme** the moving forces of the soul.

(d) (†: *élasticité*) resilience.

(e) (†: *moyen*) means.

2: ressort à boudin spiral spring; **ressort à lames** leafspring; **ressort de montre** hairspring; **ressort de suspension** suspension spring; **ressort de traction** drawspring.

ressort[2] [ʀ(ə)sɔʀ] *nm* **(a)** (*Admin, Jur: de la compétence de*) **être du ~ de** to be *ou* fall within the competence of; **c'est du ~ de la justice/du chef de service** that is for the law/head of department to deal with, that is the law's/the head of department's responsibility; (*fig*) **ce n'est pas de mon ~** this is not my responsibility, this doesn't come within my province, this falls outside my scope.

(b) (*Jur: circonscription*) jurisdiction. **dans le ~ du tribunal de Paris** in the jurisdiction of the courts of Paris; *V* **dernier.**

ressortir[1] [ʀ(ə)sɔʀtiʀ] (2) **1** *vi* **(a)** (*à nouveau: V aussi* **sortir**) *[personne]* (*aller*) to go out again, leave again; (*venir*) to come out again, leave again; (*en voiture*) to drive out again; *[objet, pièce]* to come out again. **je suis ressorti faire des courses** I went out shopping again; **ils sont ressortis du pays une troisième fois** they left the country again for the third time; **le rouge/7 est ressorti** the red/7 came out *ou* up again.

(b) (*sortir*) *[personne]* to go (*ou* come) out (again), leave; *[objet, pièce]* to come out (again). **il a jeté un coup d'œil aux journaux et il est ressorti** he glanced at the newspapers and went (back) out again; (*fig*) **des désirs refoulés/souvenirs qui ressortent** repressed desires/memories which come back up to the surface.

(c) (*contraster*) *[détail, couleur, qualité]* to stand out. **faire ~ qch** to make sth stand out, bring out sth.

2 ressortir de *vt indir* (*résulter*) to emerge from, be the result of.

3 *vt* (*à nouveau: V aussi* **sortir**) *vêtements d'hiver, outil etc* to take out again; (*Comm*) *modèle* to bring out again. **le soleil revenant, ils ont ressorti les chaises sur la terrasse** when the sun came out again, they took the chairs back onto the terrace; **j'ai encore besoin du registre, ressors-le** I still need the register so take *ou* get it (back) out again.

ressortir[2] [ʀ(ə)sɔʀtiʀ] (2) **ressortir à** *vt indir* (*Jur*) *cour, tribunal* to come under the jurisdiction of; (*frm*) *domaine* to be the concern *ou* province of, pertain to. (*Jur*) **ceci ressort à une autre juridiction** this comes under *ou* belongs to a separate jurisdiction.

ressortissant, e [ʀ(ə)sɔʀtisɑ̃, ɑ̃t] *nm,f* national.

ressouder [ʀ(ə)sude] (1) **1** *vt objet brisé* to solder together again; *amitié* to mend, strengthen the bonds of; (*souder à nouveau*) to resolder, reweld. **2 se ressouder** *vpr [os, fracture]* to knit, mend; *[amitié]* to mend.

ressource [ʀ(ə)suʀs(ə)] *nf* **(a)** (*moyens matériels, financiers*) **~s** *[pays]* resources; *[personne, famille]* resources, means; **~s personnelles** personal finances, private resources; **avoir de maigres ~s** to have very limited resources, be of slender means; **une famille sans ~s** a family with no means of support *ou* no resources; **les ~s en hommes d'un pays** the manpower resources of a country.

(b) (*possibilités*) **~s** *[artiste, sportif, aventurier]* resources; *[art, technique, système]* possibilities; **les ~s de son talent/imagination** the resources of one's talent/imagination; **cet appareil/cette technique/ce système a des ~s variées** this camera/technique/system has a wide range of possible applications; **les ~s de la langue française** the resources of the French language; **les ~s de la photographie** the various possibilities of photography; **être à bout de ~s** to have exhausted all the possibilities, be at the end of one's resources; **homme/femme de ~(s)** man/woman of resource, resourceful man/woman.

(c) (*recours*) **n'ayant pas la ~ de lui parler** having no means *ou* possibility of speaking to him; **je n'ai d'autre ~ que de lui téléphoner** the only course open to me is to phone him; **sa seule/dernière ~ était de** the only way *ou* course open to him/the only way *ou* course left *ou* remaining open to him was to; **vous êtes ma dernière ~** you are my last resort.

(d) avoir de la ~ *[sportif, cheval]* to have strength in reserve.

ressouvenir (se) [ʀ(ə)suvniʀ] (22) *vpr* (*littér*) **se ~ de** to remember, recall; **faire se ~ qn de qch,** (*littér*) **faire ~ qn de qch** to remind sb of sth; **ce bruit le fit se ~** *ou* (*littér*) **lui fit ~ de son accident** hearing that noise he was reminded of his accident.

ressurgir [ʀ(ə)syʀʒiʀ] (2) *vi* = **resurgir.**

ressusciter [ʀesysite] (1) **1** *vi* **(a)** (*Rel*) to rise (from the dead). **le Christ ressuscité** the risen Christ; **ressuscité d'entre les morts** risen from the dead.

(b) (*fig: renaître*) *[malade]* to come back to life, revive; *[sentiment, souvenir]* to revive, reawaken; *[pays]* to come back to life.

2 *vt* **(a)** (*lit*) *mourant* to resuscitate, restore *ou* bring back to life; (*Rel*) to raise (from the dead). **buvez ça, ça ressusciterait un mort*** drink that — it'll put new life into you; **bruit à ~ les morts** noise that would wake *ou* awaken the dead.

(b) (*fig: régénérer*) *malade, projet, entreprise* to bring back to life, inject new life into, revive.

(c) (*fig: faire revivre*) *sentiment* to revive, reawaken; *héros, mode* to bring back, resurrect (*péj*); *passé, coutume, loi* to revive, resurrect (*péj*).

restant, e [ʀɛstɑ̃, ɑ̃t] **1** *adj* remaining. **le seul cousin ~** the sole *ou* one remaining cousin, the only *ou* one cousin left *ou* remaining; *V* **poste**[1].

2 *nm* **(a)** (*l'autre partie*) **le ~** the rest, the remainder; **tout le ~ des provisions était perdu** all the rest *ou* remainder of the supplies were lost; **employant le ~ de ses journées à lire** spending the rest *ou* remainder of his days reading.

(b) (*ce qui est en trop*) **accommoder un ~ de poulet** to make a dish with some left-over chicken; **faire une écharpe dans un ~ de tissu** to make a scarf out of some left-over material; **un ~ de lumière** a last glimmer of light.

restaurant [ʀɛstɔʀɑ̃] **1** *nm* restaurant. **on mange à la maison ou on va au ~?** shall we eat at home or shall we eat out? *ou* have a meal out?; *V* **café, hôtel** *etc.*

2: restaurant d'entreprise staff canteen, staff dining room; **restaurant gastronomique** gourmet restaurant; **restaurant libre-service** *ou* **self-service** self-service restaurant; **restaurant universitaire** university refectory *ou* canteen.

restaurateur, -trice [ʀɛstɔʀatœʀ, tʀis] *nm,f* **(a)** *[tableau, dynastie]* restorer. **(b)** (*aubergiste*) restaurant owner, restaurateur.

restauration [ʀɛstɔʀasjɔ̃] *nf* **(a)** *[tableau, dynastie]* restoration. **(b)** (*hôtellerie*) catering. **il travaille dans la ~** he works in catering.

restaurer [ʀɛstɔʀe] (1) **1** *vt* to restore. **2 se restaurer** *vpr* to take some refreshment, have something to eat.

restauroute [ʀɛstɔʀut] *nm* = **restoroute.**

reste [ʀɛst(ə)] *nm* **(a)** (*l'autre partie*) **le ~** the rest, what is left; **le ~ de sa vie/du temps/des hommes** the rest of his life/of the time/of humanity; **j'ai lu 3 chapitres, je lirai le ~ (du livre) demain** I've read 3 chapters and I'll read the rest (of the book) tomorrow; **le ~ du lait** the rest of the milk, what is left of the milk; **préparez les bagages, je m'occupe du ~** get the luggage ready and I'll see to the rest *ou* everything else.

(b) (*ce qui est en trop*) **il y a un ~ de fromage/de tissu** there's some *ou* a piece of cheese/material left over; **s'il y a un ~, je fais une omelette/une écharpe** if there's some *ou* any left *ou* left over I'll make an omelette/a scarf; **ce ~ de poulet ne suffira pas** this (piece of) left-over chicken won't be enough; **s'il y a un ~ (de laine), j'aimerais faire une écharpe** if there's some spare (wool) *ou* some (wool) to spare, I'd like to make a scarf; **un ~ de tendresse/de pitié le poussa à rester** a last trace *ou* a remnant of tenderness/pity moved him to stay.

(c) les ~s (*nourriture*) the left-overs; (*frm: dépouille mortelle*) the (mortal) remains; **les ~s de** *repas* the remains of, the left-overs from; *fortune, ville incendiée etc* the remains of, what is (*ou* was) left of; **donner les ~s au chien** to give the scraps *ou* left-overs to the dog; (*hum*) **elle a de beaux ~s** she is a fine woman yet.

(d) (*Math: différence*) remainder.

(e) (*loc*) **avoir de l'argent/du temps de ~** to have money/time left over *ou* in hand *ou* to spare; **être/demeurer en ~** to be outdone; **il ne voulait pas être en ~ avec eux** he didn't want to be outdone by them *ou* one down on them* *ou* indebted to them; (*littér*) **au ~, du ~** besides, moreover; **nous la connaissons, du ~, très peu** besides *ou* moreover, we hardly know her at all; **il est parti sans attendre** *ou* **demander son ~** he left without asking (any) questions *ou* without waiting to hear more; **il est menteur, paresseux et (tout) le ~** he's untruthful, lazy and everything else as well; **pour le ~** *ou* **quant au ~ (nous verrons bien)** (as) for the rest (we'll have to see); **avec la grève, la neige et (tout) le ~, ils ne peuvent pas venir** with the strike, the snow and everything else *ou* all the rest, they can't come.

rester [ʀɛste] (1) **1** *vi* **(a)** (*dans un lieu*) to stay, remain; (*: *habiter*) to live. **~ au lit** *[paresseux]* to stay *ou* lie in bed; *[malade]* to stay in bed; **~ à la maison/chez soi** to stay *ou* remain in the house *ou* indoors/at home *ou* in; **~ au** *ou* **dans le jardin/à la campagne/à l'étranger** to stay *ou* remain in the garden/in the country/abroad; **~ (à) dîner/déjeuner** to stay for *ou* to dinner/lunch; **je ne peux ~ que 10 minutes** I can only stay *ou* stop* 10 minutes; **la voiture est restée dehors/au garage** the car stayed *ou* remained outside/in the garage; **la lettre va certainement ~ dans sa poche** the letter is sure to stay in his pocket; **un os lui est resté dans la gorge** a bone was caught *ou* got stuck* in his throat; **restez où vous êtes** stay *ou* remain where you are; **~ à regarder la télévision** to stay watching television; **nous sommes restés 2 heures à l'attendre** we stayed there waiting for him for 2 hours; **naturellement ça reste entre nous** of course we shall keep this to ourselves *ou* this is strictly between ourselves.

(b) (*dans un état*) to stay, remain. **~ éveillé/immobile** to keep *ou* stay awake/still; **~ sans bouger/sans rien dire** to stay *ou* remain motionless/silent *ou* without saying anything; **~ dans l'ignorance** to remain in ignorance; **~ en fonction** to remain in office; **~ debout** (*lit*) to stand, remain standing; (*ne pas se coucher*) to stay up; **je suis resté assis/debout toute la journée** I spent the (whole) day sitting/standing, I've been sitting/standing (up) all day; **ne reste pas là les bras croisés** don't just stand there with your arms folded; **il est resté très timide** he has remained *ou* he is still very shy; **il est et restera toujours maladroit** he is clumsy and he always will be; **cette coutume est restée en honneur dans certains pays** this custom is still honoured in certain countries; **~ en carafe*** to be left stranded, be left high and dry, be left in mid air; *V* **panne, plan**[1].

(c) (*subsister*) to be left, remain. **rien ne reste de l'ancien château** nothing is left *ou* remains of the old castle; **c'est le seul parent qui leur reste** he's their only remaining relative, he's the only relative they have left; **c'est tout l'argent qui leur reste** that's all the money they have left; **10 km restaient à faire** there were still 10 km to go.

(d) (*durer*) to last, live on. **c'est une œuvre qui restera** it's a work which will live on *ou* which will last; **le désir passe, la tendresse reste** desire passes, tenderness lives on; **le surnom lui est resté** the nickname stayed with him, the nickname stuck*.

(e) ~ sur: ~ sur une impression to retain an impression; (*lit, fig*) **~ sur sa faim** *ou* **son appétit** to be left unsatisfied; **sa remarque m'est restée sur le cœur** his remark (still) rankles (in my mind); **ça m'est resté sur l'estomac*** it still riles me*, I still feel sore about it*, it still rankles with me.

(f) en ~ à (*ne pas dépasser*) to go no further than; **ils en sont restés à quelques baisers bien innocents/des discussions préliminaires** they got no further than a few quite innocent kisses/preliminary discussions; **les gens du village en sont restés à la lampe à pétrole** the villagers never moved on from the paraffin lamp, the villagers are still at the stage of paraffin lamps; **ils en sont restés là des pourparlers** they only got that far *ou* that is as far as they got in their discussions; **où en étions-nous restés dans notre lecture?** where did we leave off in our reading?; **restons-en là** let's leave off there, let's leave it at that.

(g) (*: *mourir*) **y ~** to meet one's end; **il a bien failli y ~** he nearly met his end, that was nearly the end of him.

2 *vb impers:* **il reste encore un peu de jour/de pain** there's still a little daylight/bread left; **il leur reste juste de quoi vivre** they've just enough left to live on; **il me reste à faire ceci** I still have this to do, there's still this for me to do; **il reste beaucoup à faire** much remains to be done, there's a lot left to do *ou* to be done, there's still a lot to do *ou* to be done; **il nous reste son souvenir** we still have our memories of him; **il ne me reste que toi** you're all I have left; **il n'est rien resté de leur maison/des provisions** nothing remained *ou* was left of their house/the supplies; **le peu de temps qu'il lui restait à vivre** the short time that he had left to live; **il ne me reste qu'à vous remercier** it only remains for me to thank you; **il restait à faire 50 km** there were 50 km still *ou* left to go; **est-ce qu'il vous reste assez de force pour terminer ce travail?** have you enough strength left to finish this job?; **quand on a été en prison il en reste toujours quelque chose** when you've been in prison something of it always stays with you; **(il) reste à savoir si/à prouver que** it remains to be seen if/to be proved that; **il reste que, il n'en reste pas moins que** the fact remains (nonetheless) that, it is nevertheless a fact that; **il reste entendu que** it remains *ou* is still quite understood that.

restituer [ʀɛstitɥe] (1) *vt* **(a)** (*rendre*) *objet volé* to return, restore (*à qn* to sb); *somme d'argent* to return, refund (*à qn* to sb).

(b) (*reconstituer*) *fresque, texte, inscription* to reconstruct, restore. **un texte enfin restitué dans son intégralité** a text finally restored in its entirety; **appareil qui restitue fidèlement les sons** apparatus which gives faithful sound reproduction; **l'énergie emmagasinée est entièrement restituée sous forme de chaleur** the energy stored up is entirely released in the form of heat.

restitution [ʀɛstitysjɔ̃] *nf* (*V* **restituer**) return; restoration; restitution; reconstruction; reproduction; release.

restoroute [ʀɛstɔʀut] *nm [route]* roadside restaurant; *[autoroute]* motorway (*Brit*) *ou* turnpike (*US*) restaurant.

restreindre [ʀɛstʀɛ̃dʀ(ə)] (52) **1** *vt quantité, production, dépenses* to restrict, limit, cut down; *ambition* to restrict, limit, curb. **nous restreindrons notre étude à quelques exemples** we will restrict our study to a few examples.

2 se restreindre *vpr* **(a)** (*dans ses dépenses, sur la nourriture*) to cut down.

(b) (*diminuer*) *[production, tirage]* to decrease, go down; *[espace]* to decrease, diminish; *[ambition, champ d'action]* to narrow; *[sens d'un mot]* to become more restricted. **le champ de leur enquête se restreint** the scope of their inquiry is narrowing.

restreint, e [ʀɛstʀɛ̃, ɛ̃t] (*ptp de* **restreindre**) *adj production, autorité, emploi, vocabulaire* limited, restricted; *personnel, espace, moyens, nombre* limited; *sens* restricted. **~ à** confined *ou* restricted *ou* limited to; *V* **suffrage.**

restrictif, -ive [ʀɛstʀiktif, iv] *adj* restrictive.

restriction [ʀɛstʀiksjɔ̃] *nf* **(a)** (*action*) restriction, limiting, limitation.

(b) (*de personnel, de consommation*) **~s** restrictions; **~s d'électricité** electricity restrictions, restrictions on the use of electricity.

(c) (*condition*) qualification. (*réticence*) **~ (mentale)** mental reservation; **faire des ~s** to make qualifications, express some reservations; **avec ~** *ou* **des ~s** with some qualification(s) *ou* reservation(s).

restructuration [ʀəstʀyktyʀasjɔ̃] *nf* restructuring.

restructurer [ʀəstʀyktyʀe] (1) *vt* to restructure.

resucée* [ʀ(ə)syse] *nf* (*plagiat*) rehash*.

résultante [ʀezyltɑ̃t] *nf* (*Sci*) resultant; (*fig: conséquence*) outcome, result, consequence.

résultat [ʀezylta] *nm* **(a)** (*conséquence*) result, outcome (*U*). **cette tentative a eu des ~s désastreux** this attempt had disastrous results *ou* a disastrous outcome; **cette démarche eut pour ~ une amélioration de la situation** *ou* **d'améliorer la situation** this measure resulted in *ou* led to an improvement in the situation *ou* resulted in the situation's improving; **on l'a laissé seul: ~, il a fait des bêtises** we left him alone — so what happens *ou* what's the result — he goes and does something silly.

(b) (*chose obtenue, réalisation*) result. **c'est un ~ remarquable** it's a remarkable result *ou* achievement; **il a promis d'obtenir des ~s** he promised to get results; (*iro*) **beau ~!** well done! (*iro*); **il essaya, sans ~, de le convaincre** he tried to convince him, but to no effect.

(c) (*solution*) *[problème, addition]* result.

(d) (*classement*) *[examen, élection]* results. **et maintenant les ~s sportifs** and now for the sports results; **le ~ des courses** the racing results; **voici quelques ~s partiels de l'élection** here are some of the election results so far.

résulter [ʀezylte] (1) **1** *vi:* ~ **de** to result from, be the result of; **rien de bon ne peut en** ~ no good can come of it *ou* result from it; **les avantages économiques qui en résultent** the resulting economic benefits; **ce qui a résulté de la discussion est que ...** the result *ou* outcome of the discussion was that... .

2 *vb impers:* **il résulte de tout ceci que** the result of all this is that; **il en résulte que c'est impossible** as a result it's impossible, the result is that it's impossible; **qu'en résultera-t-il?** what will be the result? *ou* outcome?

résumé [ʀezyme] *nm* (*texte, ouvrage*) summary, résumé. '~ **des chapitres précédents'** 'the story (in brief) so far'; **en** ~ (*en bref*) in short, in brief; (*pour conclure*) to sum up; (*en miniature*) in miniature.

résumer [ʀezyme] (1) **1** *vt* (*abréger*) to summarize; (*récapituler, aussi Jur*) to sum up; (*reproduire en petit*) to epitomize, typify.

2 se résumer *vpr* **(a)** *[personne]* to sum up (one's ideas).

(b) (*être contenu*) **toutes les facettes du bien et du mal se résumaient en lui** every aspect of good and evil was typified in him.

(c) (*se réduire à*) **se** ~ **à** to amount to, come down to, boil down to*; **l'affaire se résume à peu de chose** the affair amounts to *ou* comes down to nothing really, that's all the affair boils down to*.

résurgence [ʀezyʀʒɑ̃s] *nf* (*Géol*) reappearance (*of river*), resurgence.

résurgent, e [ʀezyʀʒɑ̃, ɑ̃t] *adj* (*Géol*) *eaux* re-emergent.

resurgir [ʀ(ə)syʀʒiʀ] (2) *vi* to reappear, re-emerge.

résurrection [ʀezyʀɛksjɔ̃] *nf [mort]* resurrection; (*fig: renouveau*) revival. (*Rel*) **la R**~ the Resurrection; **c'est une véritable** ~! he has really come back to life!

retable [ʀətabl(ə)] *nm* retable, reredos.

rétablir [ʀetabliʀ] (2) **1** *vt* **(a)** (*remettre*) *courant, communications* to restore.

(b) (*restaurer*) *monarchie* to restore, re-establish; *droit, ordre, équilibre* to restore; *forces, santé* to restore; *fait, vérité* to re-establish.

(c) (*réintégrer*) to reinstate. ~ **qn dans son emploi** to reinstate sb in *ou* restore sb to his post; ~ **qn dans ses droits** to restore sb's rights.

(d) (*guérir*) ~ **qn** to restore sb to health, bring about sb's recovery.

2 se rétablir *vpr* **(a)** (*guérir*) to recover. **après sa maladie, il s'est vite rétabli** he soon recovered after his illness.

(b) (*revenir*) to return, be restored. **le silence/le calme s'est rétabli** silence/calm returned *ou* was restored.

(c) (*faire un rétablissement*) to pull o.s. up (*onto a ledge etc*).

rétablissement [ʀetablismɑ̃] *nm* **(a)** (*U: V* **rétablir**) restoring; re-establishment.

(b) (*guérison*) recovery. **en vous souhaitant un prompt** ~ with my good wishes for your swift recovery, hoping you will get better soon*.

(c) (*Sport*) **faire** *ou* **opérer un** ~ to do a pull-up (*into a standing position, onto a ledge etc*).

retailler [ʀ(ə)tɑje] (1) *vt vêtement* to re-cut; *crayon* to sharpen; *arbre* to (re-)prune.

rétamage [ʀetamaʒ] *nm* re-coating, re-tinning (*of pans*).

rétamé, e: [ʀetame] (*ptp de* **rétamer**) *adj* (*fatigué*) knackered: (*Brit*), worn out*; (*ivre*) stoned:, loaded:; (*détruit, démoli*) wiped out; (*sans argent*) broke*.

rétamer [ʀetame] (1) **1** *vt* **(a)** *casseroles* to re-coat, re-tin.

(b) (:) (*fatiguer*) to knacker: (*Brit*), wear out*; (*rendre ivre*) to knock out:; (*démolir*) to wipe out; (*dépouiller au jeu*) to clean out*. **se faire** ~ **au poker** to go broke* *ou* be cleaned out* at poker.

2 se rétamer: *vpr* (*tomber*) **se** ~ **(par terre)** to take a dive*, crash to the ground; **la voiture s'est rétamée contre un arbre** the car crashed into a tree.

rétameur [ʀetamœʀ] *nm* tinker.

retapage [ʀ(ə)tapaʒ] *nm [maison, vêtement]* doing up; *[voiture]* fixing up; *[lit]* straightening.

retape: [ʀ(ə)tap] *nf:* **faire (de) la** ~ *[prostituée]* to be on the game: (*Brit*), walk the streets*; *[agent publicitaire]* to tout (around); **faire de la** ~ **pour une compagnie de bateaux-mouches** to tout for a pleasure boat company.

retaper [ʀ(ə)tape] (1) **1** *vt* **(a)** (*: *remettre en état*) *maison, vêtement* to do up; *voiture* to fix up; *lit* to straighten; (* *fig*) *malade, personne fatiguée* to set up (again), buck up*. **ça m'a retapé, ce whisky** that whisky has set me up again.

(b) (*dactylographier*) to retype, type again.

2 se retaper* *vpr* (*guérir*) to get back on one's feet. **il va se** ~ **en quelques semaines** he'll get back on his feet in a few weeks.

retapisser [ʀ(ə)tapise] (1) *vt* to re-paper.

retard [ʀ(ə)taʀ] **1** *nm* **(a)** *[personne attendue]* lateness (*U*). **ces** ~**s continuels seront punis** this constant lateness will be punished; **plusieurs** ~**s dans la même semaine, c'est inadmissible** it won't do being late several times in one week; **son** ~ **m'inquiète** I'm worried by his lateness; **vous avez du** ~, **vous êtes en** ~ you're late; **vous avez 2 heures de** ~ *ou* **un** ~ **de 2 heures, vous êtes en** ~ **de 2 heures** you're 2 hours late; **ça/il m'a mis en** ~ it/he made me late; **je me suis mis en** ~ I made myself late; *V* **billet.**

(b) *[train etc]* delay. **le train est en** ~ **sur l'horaire** the train is running behind schedule; **un** ~ **de 3 heures est annoncé sur la ligne Paris-Brest** there will be a delay of 3 hours *ou* trains will run 3 hours late on the Paris-Brest line; **le conducteur essayait de combler son** ~ the driver was trying to make up for the delay; (*Sport*) **être en** ~ **(de 2 heures/2 km) sur le peloton** to be (2 hours/2 km) behind the pack; (*Sport*) **avoir 2 secondes de** ~ **sur le champion/record** to be 2 seconds slower than *ou* behind the champion/outside the record.

(c) *[montre]* **cette montre a du** ~ this watch is slow; **la pendule prend un** ~ **de 3 minutes par jour** the clock loses 3 minutes a day.

(d) (*non-observation des délais*) delay. **si l'on apporte du** ~ **dans l'exécution d'une commande** if one is late in carrying out an order; **paiement en** ~ (*effectué*) late payment; (*non effectué*) overdue payment, payment overdue; **vous êtes en** ~ **pour les inscriptions** *ou* **pour vous inscrire** you are late (in) registering; **il est toujours en** ~ **sur les autres pour payer ses cotisations** he is always behind the others *ou* later than the others in paying his subscriptions; **payer/livrer qch avec** ~ *ou* **en** ~ to pay/deliver sth late, be late (in) paying/delivering sth; **sans** ~ without delay.

(e) (*sur un programme*) delay. **nous sommes/les recherches sont en** ~ **sur le programme** we are/the research is behind schedule; **j'ai du travail/courrier en** ~ I'm behind *ou* behindhand with my work/mail, I have a backlog of work/mail; **il avait un** ~ **scolaire considérable** he had fallen *ou* was considerably behind at school; **pour combler son** ~ **en anglais** to make up for the ground he has (*ou* had *etc*) lost in English; **j'ai pris du** *ou* **je me suis mis en** ~ **dans mes révisions** I have fallen behind in *ou* I am behindhand in my revision.

(f) (*infériorité*) *[peuple, pays]* backwardness. **il est en** ~ **pour son âge** he's backward for his age; ~ **de croissance** slow development; **pays qui a 100 ans de** ~ **économique** *ou* **est en** ~ **de 100 ans du point de vue économique** country whose economy is 100 years behind *ou* which is economically 100 years behind; **être en** ~ **sur son temps** *ou* **siècle** to be behind the times; **il vit avec un siècle de** ~ he's 100 years behind the times, he's living in the last century; **tu es en** ~ **d'un métro*** you must have been asleep!

(g) (*Mus*) retardation.

2 *adj inv* (*Pharm*) **insuline** ~ delayed insulin.

3: (*Aut*) **retard à l'allumage** retarded spark.

retardataire [ʀ(ə)taʀdatɛʀ] **1** *adj arrivant* late; *théorie, méthode* obsolete, outmoded. **2** *nmf* latecomer.

retardateur, -trice [ʀ(ə)taʀdatœʀ, tʀis] *adj* (*Sci, Tech*) retarding.

retardé, e [ʀ(ə)taʀde] (*ptp de* **retarder**) *adj* (*scolairement*) backward, slow; (*intellectuellement*) retarded, backward. **classe pour** ~**s** class for backward children.

retardement [ʀ(ə)taʀdəmɑ̃] *nm* **(a) à** ~ *engin, torpille* with a timing device; *dispositif* delayed action (*épith*); (*Phot*) *mécanisme* self-timing; (*) *souhaits* belated; *V* **bombe.**

(b) à ~ *comprendre, rire, se fâcher* after the event, in retrospect; (*péj*) **il comprend tout à** ~ he's slow on the uptake*; (*péj*) **il rit toujours à** ~ he's always slow in seeing the joke.

retarder [ʀ(ə)taʀde] (1) **1** *vt* **(a)** (*mettre en retard sur un horaire*) *arrivant, arrivée* to delay, make late; *personne ou véhicule en chemin* to delay, hold up. **une visite inattendue m'a retardé** I was delayed by an unexpected visit; **je ne veux pas vous** ~ I don't want to delay you *ou* make you late; **ne te retarde pas (pour ça)** don't make yourself late for that; **il a été retardé par les grèves** he has been delayed *ou* held up by the strikes.

(b) (*mettre en retard sur un programme*) to hinder, set back; *opération, vendange, chercheur* to delay, hold up. **ça l'a retardé dans sa mission/ses études** this has set him back in *ou* hindered him in his mission/studies.

(c) (*remettre*) *départ, opération* to delay, put back; *date* to put back. ~ **son départ d'une heure** to put back one's departure by an hour, delay one's departure for an hour.

(d) *montre, réveil* to put back. ~ **l'horloge d'une heure** to put the clock back an hour.

2 *vi* **(a)** *[montre]* to be slow; (*d'habitude*) to lose. **je retarde (de 10 minutes)** my watch is (10 minutes) slow, I'm (10 minutes) slow.

(b) (*être à un stade antérieur*) ~ **sur son époque** *ou* **temps** *ou* **siècle** to be behind the times.

(c) (*: *n'être pas au courant*) **ma voiture? tu retardes, je l'ai vendue il y a 2 ans** my car? you're a bit behind the times* *ou* you're a bit out of touch — I sold it 2 years ago.

retâter [ʀ(ə)tɑte] (1) **1** *vt pouls, objet etc* to feel again. **2** *vi:* ~ **de** to taste again. **3 se retâter** *vpr* (*après une chute*) to feel o.s. over.

reteindre [ʀ(ə)tɛ̃dʀ(ə)] (52) *vt* to dye again, redye.

retéléphoner [ʀ(ə)telefɔne] (1) *vi* to phone again, call back. **je lui retéléphonerai demain** I'll phone him again *ou* call him back tomorrow, I'll give him another call tomorrow.

retendre [ʀ(ə)tɑ̃dʀ(ə)] (41) *vt* **(a)** *câble* to stretch again, pull taut again; (*Mus*) *cordes* to retighten.

(b) *piège, filets* to reset, set again.

(c) ~ **la main à qn** to stretch out one's hand again to sb.

retenir [ʀətniʀ] (22) **1** *vt* **(a)** (*lit, fig: maintenir*) *personne, objet qui glisse* to hold back; *cheval, chien* to hold back, check. ~ **qn par le bras** to hold sb back by the arm; **il allait tomber, une branche l'a retenu** he was about to fall but a branch held him back; **le barrage retient l'eau** the barrage holds back the water; ~ **la foule qui se rue vers ...** to hold back the crowd rushing towards ... ; **il se serait jeté par la fenêtre si on ne l'avait pas retenu** he would have thrown himself out of the window if he hadn't been held back *ou* stopped; **retenez-moi ou je fais un malheur** hold me back *ou* stop me or I'll do something I'll regret; (*fig*) **une certaine timidité le retenait** a certain shyness held him back; ~ **qn de faire qch** to keep sb from *ou* stop sb doing sth; **je ne sais pas ce qui me retient de lui dire ce que je pense** I don't know what keeps me from *ou* stops me telling him what I think.

(b) (*garder*) *personne* to keep. ~ **qn à dîner** to have sb stay for dinner, keep sb for dinner; **j'ai été retenu** I was kept back *ou* detained *ou* held up; **il m'a retenu une heure** he kept me for an hour; **si tu veux partir, je ne te retiens pas** if you want to leave, I shan't hold you back *ou* keep you; **c'est la maladie de sa femme qui l'a retenu à Brest** it was his wife's illness that kept *ou* detained him in Brest; **son travail le retenait ailleurs** his work kept *ou* detained him elsewhere; **la grippe l'a retenu au lit/à la maison** flu kept him in bed/kept him in *ou* indoors *ou* at home; ~ **qn prisonnier** to hold sb prisoner.

(c) *eau d'infiltration, odeur* to retain; *chaleur* to retain, keep in; *lumière* to reflect. **cette terre retient l'eau** this soil retains water; **le noir retient la chaleur** black retains the heat *ou* keeps in the heat; **une texture qui retient la lumière** a texture which reflects the light.

(d) (*fixer*) *[clou, nœud etc]* to hold. **c'est un simple clou qui retient le tableau au mur** there's just a nail holding the picture on the wall; **un ruban retenait ses cheveux** a ribbon kept *ou* held her hair in place.

(e) ~ **l'attention de qn** to hold sb's attention; **ce détail retient l'attention** this detail holds one's attention; (*frm*) **sa demande a retenu notre attention** his request has been accorded our attention.

(f) (*réserver, louer*) *chambre, place, table* to book, reserve; *domestique* to engage.

(g) (*se souvenir de*) *leçon, nom, donnée* to remember; *impression* to retain. **je n'ai pas retenu son nom/la date** I can't remember his name/the date; **je retiens de cette aventure qu'il est plus prudent de bien s'équiper** I've learnt from this adventure that it's wiser to be properly equipped; **j'en retiens qu'il est pingre et borné, c'est tout** the only thing that stands out *ou* that sticks in my mind is that he's stingy and narrow-minded; **un nom qu'on retient** a name that stays in your mind, a name you remember; **retenez bien ce qu'on vous a dit** don't forget *ou* make sure you remember what you were told; (*fig*) **celui-là, je le retiens!*** I'll remember him all right!, I shan't forget him in a hurry!*

(h) (*contenir, réprimer*) *larmes, cri* to hold back *ou* in; *colère* to hold back, restrain. ~ **son souffle** *ou* **sa respiration** to hold one's breath; **il ne put** ~ **un sourire/un rire** he could not hold back a smile/a laugh, he could not help smiling/laughing; **il retint les mots qui lui venaient à la bouche** he bit back (*surtout Brit*) the words that came to him.

(i) (*Math*) to carry. **je pose 4 et je retiens 2** 4 down and 2 to carry, put down 4 and carry 2.

(j) (*garder*) *salaire* to stop, withhold; *possessions, bagages d'un client* to retain.

(k) (*retrancher, prélever*) to deduct, keep back. **il nous retiennent 100 F (sur notre salaire) pour les assurances** they deduct 100 francs (from our wages) for insurance; ~ **une certaine somme pour la retraite** to keep back a certain sum for retirement; ~ **les impôts à la base** to deduct taxes at source.

(l) (*accepter*) *proposition, plan* to accept. (*Jur*) **le jury a retenu la préméditation** the jury accepted the charge of premeditation; **c'est notre projet qui a été retenu** it's our project that has been accepted.

2 se retenir *vpr* **(a)** (*s'accrocher*) to hold o.s. back. **se** ~ **pour ne pas glisser** to stop o.s. sliding; **se** ~ **à** to hold on to.

(b) (*se contenir*) to restrain o.s.; (*s'abstenir*) to stop o.s. (*de faire* doing); (*besoins naturels*) to hold on. **se** ~ **pour ne pas pleurer** *ou* **de pleurer** to stop o.s. crying; **malgré sa colère, il essaya de se** ~ despite his anger, he tried to restrain *ou* contain himself; **il se retint de lui faire remarquer que ...** he refrained from pointing out to him that ...

retenter [ʀ(ə)tɑ̃te] (1) *vt* to try again, make another attempt at, have another go at*; *saut, épreuve* to try again; *opération, action* to reattempt. ~ **sa chance** to try one's luck again; ~ **de faire qch** to try to do sth again.

rétenteur, -trice [ʀetɑ̃tœʀ, tʀis] *adj muscle* retaining.

rétention [ʀetɑ̃sjɔ̃] *nf* (*Jur, Méd*) retention. (*Méd*) ~ **d'eau/d'urine** retention of water/urine.

retentir [ʀ(ə)tɑ̃tiʀ] (2) *vi* **(a)** *[sonnerie]* to ring; *[cris, bruit métallique]* to ring out. **ces mots retentissent encore à mes oreilles** those words are still ringing *ou* echoing in my ears.

(b) ~ **de** (*résonner de*) to ring *ou* resound with, be full of the sound of.

(c) (*affecter*) ~ **sur** to have an effect upon, affect.

retentissant, e [ʀ(ə)tɑ̃tisɑ̃, ɑ̃t] *adj* **(a)** (*fort, sonore*) *voix, son* ringing (*épith*); *choc, claque, bruit* resounding (*épith*). **(b)** (*frappant, éclatant*) *succès* resounding (*épith*); *scandale* tremendous; *déclarations, discours* remarkable, outstanding.

retentissement [ʀ(ə)tɑ̃tismɑ̃] *nm* **(a)** (*répercussion*) repercussion, (after-)effect. **les ~s de l'affaire** the repercussions of the affair.

(b) (*éclat*) stir, effect. **cette nouvelle eut un grand** ~ **dans l'opinion** this piece of news created a considerable stir in public opinion; **son œuvre fut sans grand** ~ his work went virtually unnoticed *ou* caused little stir.

(c) (*littér*) *[son]* ringing.

retenu, e[1] [ʀətny] (*ptp de* **retenir**) *adj* (*littér: discret*) *grâce, charme* reserved, restrained.

retenue[2] [ʀətny] *nf* **(a)** (*prélèvement*) deduction, stoppage*. **opérer une** ~ **(de 10%) sur un salaire** to deduct (10%) from a salary; ~ **pour la retraite/la Sécurité sociale** deductions *ou* stoppages* for a pension scheme/ ≈ National Insurance; **système de** ~ **à la source** pay-as-you-earn system (*Brit*).

(b) (*modération*) self-control, (self-)restraint; (*réserve*) reserve, reticence. **avoir de la** ~ to be reserved; **(rire) sans** ~ (to laugh) without restraint *ou* unrestrainedly; **il n'a aucune** ~ **dans ses propos** he shows no restraint in his speech.

(c) (*Math*) **n'oublie pas la** ~ don't forget what to carry (over).

(d) (*Scol*) detention. **être en** ~ to be in detention, be kept in; **il a eu 2 heures de** ~ he got 2 hours' detention, he was kept in for 2 hours (after school).

(e) (*Tech*) *[barrage]* **barrage à faible** ~ low-volume dam; **bassin de** ~ balancing *ou* compensating reservoir.

réticence [ʀetisɑ̃s] *nf* **(a)** (*hésitation*) hesitation, reluctance (*U*), reservation. **avec** ~ reluctantly, with some reservation *ou* hesitation; **sans** ~ without (any) hesitation *ou* reservation(s).

(b) (*littér: omission*) omission, reticence (*U*).

réticent, e [ʀetisɑ̃, ɑ̃t] *adj* **(a)** (*hésitant*) hesitant, reluctant. **(b)** (*réservé*) reticent, reserved. **le gouvernement se montre** ~ the government is retaining its reserve *ou* is not letting anything through.

réticule [ʀetikyl] *nm* (*Opt*) reticle; (*sac*) reticule.

réticulé, e [ʀetikyle] *adj* (*Anat, Géol*) reticulate; (*Archit*) reticulated.

rétif, -ive [ʀetif, iv] *adj animal, personne* restive.

rétine [ʀetin] *nf* retina.

rétinien, -ienne [ʀetinjɛ̃, jɛn] *adj* retinal.

retiré, e [ʀ(ə)tiʀe] (*ptp de* **retirer**) *adj* **(a)** (*solitaire*) *lieu* remote, out-of-the-way; *vie* secluded. **ils habitent un endroit** ~ they live in a remote *ou* an out-of-the-way place; **vivre** ~, **mener une vie** ~**e** to live in isolation *ou* seclusion, lead a secluded *ou* sequestered (*littér*) life; **il vivait** ~ **du reste du monde** he lived withdrawn *ou* cut off from the rest of the world.

(b) (*en retraite*) retired. ~ **des affaires** retired from business.

retirer [ʀ(ə)tiʀe] (1) **1** *vt* **(a)** (*lit, fig: enlever*) *gants, manteau, lunettes* to take off, remove. ~ **son collier au chien** to take the dog's collar off, remove the dog's collar; **retire-lui ses chaussures** take his shoes off (for him); **retire-lui ce couteau des mains (il va se blesser)** take that knife (away) from him (he's going to hurt himself); ~ **à qn son emploi** to take sb's job away (from him), deprive sb of his job; ~ **son permis (de conduire) à qn** to take away sb's (driving) licence, disqualify sb from driving; ~ **une pièce de l'affiche** to take off a play; **on lui a retiré la garde des enfants** he had the care of the children taken away from him, he was deprived of the care of the children; ~ **à qn sa confiance** to withdraw one's confidence in sb; **il m'a retiré son amitié** he has deprived me of his friendship; **vous allez lui** ~ **l'envie de recommencer** you're going to stop him wanting to start up again; ~ **à qn ses privilèges** to withdraw sb's privileges; ~ **la parole à qn** to make sb stand down (*Brit*).

(b) (*faire sortir*) to take out, remove (*de* from). ~ **un bouchon** to pull out *ou* take out *ou* remove a cork; ~ **un noyé de l'eau/qn de dessous les décombres** to pull a drowning man out of the water/sb out of *ou* out from under the rubble; ~ **un plat du four/les bagages du coffre** to take a dish out of the oven/the luggage out of the boot; **ils ont retiré leur fils du lycée** they have taken their son away from *ou* removed their son from the school; **je ne peux pas** ~ **la clef de la serrure** I can't get the key out of the lock; ~ **un flan d'un moule** to turn a flan out of a mould; **retire les mains de tes poches** take your hands out of your pockets; (*fig*) **on lui retirera difficilement de l'idée** *ou* **de la tête qu'il est menacé*** we'll have difficulty *ou* a job* convincing him that he's not being threatened.

(c) (*reprendre possession de*) *bagages, billets réservés* to collect, pick up; *argent en dépôt* to withdraw, take out; *gage* to redeem. **où peut-on** ~ **ses bagages?** where can we collect *ou* pick up our luggage?; **vous pouvez** ~ **vos billets dès demain** you can collect *ou* pick up your tickets as from tomorrow; ~ **de l'argent (de la banque)** to withdraw money (from the bank), take money out (of the bank).

(d) (*ramener en arrière*) to take away, remove, withdraw. ~ **sa tête/sa main (pour éviter un coup)** to take one's head/hand away *ou* remove *ou* withdraw one's head/hand (to avoid being hit); **il retira prestement sa main** he whisked his hand away.

(e) (*annuler*) *candidature* to withdraw; *plainte, accusation* to withdraw, take back. **je retire ce que j'ai dit** I take back what I said; (*Pol*) ~ **sa candidature** to stand down, withdraw one's candidature.

(f) (*obtenir*) ~ **des avantages de qch** to get *ou* gain *ou* derive advantages from sth; **les avantages/bénéfices qu'on en retire** the benefits/profits to be had *ou* gained from it; **il en a retiré un grand profit** he profited *ou* gained greatly by it; **il n'en a retiré que des ennuis** he only got worry out of it; **tout ce qu'il en a retiré, c'est ...** the only thing he has got out of it is ... , all he has gained is ... .

(g) (*extraire*) *minerai, extrait, huile* to obtain. **une substance dont on retire une huile précieuse** a substance from which a valuable oil is obtained.

2 se retirer *vpr* **(a)** (*partir*) to retire, withdraw; (*aller se coucher*) to retire (to bed); (*prendre sa retraite*) to retire; (*retirer sa candidature*) to withdraw, stand down (*en faveur de* in favour of). **se** ~ **discrètement** to withdraw discreetly; **ils se sont retirés dans un coin pour discuter affaires** they withdrew *ou* retired to a corner to talk (about) business; **se** ~ **dans sa chambre** to withdraw *ou* retire *ou* go to one's room; (*fig*) **se** ~ **dans sa tour d'ivoire** to take refuge *ou* lock o.s. up in one's ivory tower (*fig*); **ils ont décidé de se** ~ **à la campagne** they've decided to retire to the country; **elle s'est retirée dans un couvent** she retired *ou* withdrew to a convent.

(b) (*reculer*) (*pour laisser passer qn, éviter un coup etc*) to move out of the way; (*Mil*) *[troupes]* to withdraw; *[mer, marée]* to recede, go back, ebb; *[eaux d'inondation]* to recede, go down; *[glacier]* to recede. **retire-toi d'ici** *ou* **de là, tu me gênes** mind *ou* get out of the way — you're bothering me, stand *ou* move back a bit — you're in my way.

(c) (*quitter*) **se** ~ **de** to withdraw from; **se** ~ **des affaires** to retire from business; **se** ~ **d'une compétition** to withdraw from a competition; **se ~ du monde** to withdraw from society; **se ~ de la partie** to drop out.

retombée [ʀ(ə)tɔ̃be] *nf* **(a)** **~s (radioactives *ou* atomiques)** (radioactive) fallout (*U*). **(b)** (*fig: gén pl*) (*répercussions*) fallout (*U*); *[invention etc]* spin-off. **(c)** (*Archit*) spring, springing.

retomber [ʀ(ə)tɔ̃be] (1) *vi* **(a)** (*faire une nouvelle chute*) to fall again. **le lendemain, il est retombé dans la piscine** the next day he fell into the swimming pool again; (*fig*) **~ dans la misère** to fall on hard times again; **~ sous le joug de qn** to come under sb's yoke again; **~ dans le découragement** to lose heart again; **~ dans l'erreur/le péché** to fall back *ou* lapse into error/sin; **son roman est retombé dans l'oubli** his novel has sunk back *ou* lapsed into oblivion; **le pays retomba dans la guerre civile** the country lapsed into civil war again; **je vais retomber dans l'ennui** I shall start being bored again, boredom is going to set in again; **la conversation retomba sur le même sujet** the conversation turned once again *ou* came round again to the same subject.

(b) (*redevenir*) **~ amoureux/malade** to fall in love/fall ill again; **ils sont retombés d'accord** they reached agreement again.

(c) *[pluie, neige]* to fall again, come down again. **la neige retombait de plus belle** the snow came down again *ou* was falling again still more heavily.

(d) (*tomber après s'être élevé*) *[personne]* to land; *[chose lancée, liquide]* to come down; *[abattant, capot, herse]* to fall back down; *[fusée, missile]* to land, come back to earth; (*fig*) *[conversation]* to fall away, die; (*fig*) *[intérêt]* to fall away, fall off. **il est retombé lourdement (sur le dos)** he landed heavily (on his back); **elle saute bien mais elle ne sait pas ~** she can jump well but she doesn't know how to land; **le chat retombe toujours sur ses pattes** cats always land on their feet; (*fig*) **il retombera toujours sur ses pattes *ou* pieds** he'll always land *ou* fall on his feet; **les nuages retombent en pluie** the clouds come down *ou* fall again as rain; **l'eau retombait en cascades** the water fell back in cascades; (*fig*) **après quelques leçons, l'intérêt retombait** after a few lessons interest was falling away *ou* falling off; (*fig*) **ça lui est retombé sur le nez** that's rebounded on him; **le brouillard est retombé en fin de matinée** the fog fell again *ou* came down again *ou* closed in again towards lunchtime; **laisser ~ le couvercle d'un bureau avec bruit** to let a desk lid fall back noisily; **se laisser ~ sur son oreiller** to fall back *ou* sink back onto one's pillow; (*Sport*) **laissez ~ les bras** let your arms drop *ou* fall (by your sides).

(e) (*pendre*) *[cheveux, rideaux]* to fall, hang (down). **de petites boucles blondes retombaient sur son front** little blond curls tumbled *ou* fell onto her forehead.

(f) (*fig: échoir à*) **~ sur: le péché du père retombera sur la tête des enfants** the sin of the father will fall on the heads of the children, the sins of the fathers will be visited on the sons; **la responsabilité retombera sur toi** the responsibility will fall *ou* land* on you; **les frais retombèrent sur nous** we were landed* *ou* saddled* with the expense; **faire ~ sur qn la responsabilité de qch/les frais de qch** to pass the responsibility for sth/the cost of sth on to sb, land* sb with the responsibility for sth/the cost of sth.

(g) (*loc*) **Noël retombe un samedi** Christmas falls on a Saturday again; **retomber en enfance** to lapse into second childhood; **je suis retombé sur lui le lendemain, au même endroit** I came across him again the next day in the same place; **ils nous sont retombés dessus le lendemain** they landed* on us again the next day.

retordre [ʀ(ə)tɔʀdʀ(ə)] (41) *vt* **(a)** (*Tech*) *câbles, fils* to twist again; *V* **fil**. **(b)** *linge* to wring (out) again; *fil de fer* to rewind.

rétorquer [ʀetɔʀke] (1) *vt* to retort.

retors, e [ʀətɔʀ, ɔʀs(ə)] *adj* (*rusé*) sly, wily, underhand.

rétorsion [ʀetɔʀsjɔ̃] *nf* (*frm, Jur, Pol*) retortion, retaliation. **user de ~ envers un état** to retaliate *ou* use retortion against a state; *V* **mesure**.

retouchable [ʀ(ə)tuʃabl(ə)] *adj photo* which can be touched up; *vêtement* which can be altered.

retouche [ʀ(ə)tuʃ] *nf [photo, peinture]* touching up (*U*); *[texte, vêtement]* alteration. **faire une ~ à une photo** to touch up a photograph; **faire une ~** (*à une photo*) to do some touching up; (*à un vêtement*) to make an alteration.

retoucher [ʀ(ə)tuʃe] (1) **1** *vt* **(a)** (*améliorer*) *photo, peinture* to touch up, retouch; *vêtement, texte* to alter, make alterations to. **il faudra ~ cette veste au col** this jacket will have to be altered at the neck; **on voit tout de suite que cette photo est retouchée** you can see straight away that this photo has been touched up.

(b) (*toucher de nouveau*) to touch again; (*blesser de nouveau*) to hit again.

2 *vi*: **~ à qch** to lay hands on sth again, touch sth again; **s'il retouche à ma sœur, gare à lui!** if he lays hands on *ou* touches my sister again he'd better look out!

retoucheur, -euse [ʀ(ə)tuʃœʀ, øz] *nm,f*: **~ (en confection)** dressmaker in charge of alterations; **~ photographe** retoucher.

retour [ʀ(ə)tuʀ] **1** *nm* **(a)** (*fait d'être revenu*) (*gén*) return; (*à la maison*) homecoming, return home; (*chemin, trajet*) return (journey), way back, journey back; (*billet*) return (ticket). **il fallait déjà penser au ~** it was already time to think about going back *ou* about the return journey; **être sur le (chemin du) ~** to be on one's way back; **pendant le ~** on the way back, during the return journey, on the journey back; **elle n'a pas assez pour payer son ~** she hasn't enough to pay for her return journey; **(être) de ~ (de)** (to be) back (from); **à votre ~, écrivez-nous** write to us when you are *ou* get back; **à leur ~, ils trouvèrent la maison vide** when they got back *ou* on their return, they found the house empty; **de ~ à la maison** back home; **au ~ de notre voyage** when we got back from our journey, arriving back from our journey; **(à son) ~ d'Afrique/du service militaire** on his return *ou* on returning from Africa/military service; *V* **cheval**.

(b) (*à un état antérieur*) **~ à** return to; **le ~ à une vie normale** the return *ou* reversion to (a) normal life; **~ à la nature/à la terre** return to nature/the land; **~ aux sources** return to basics, return to the basic *ou* simple life; **~ au calme/à l'Antiquité** return to a state of calm/to Antiquity; **son ~ à la politique** his return to politics.

(c) (*réapparition*) return; (*répétition régulière*) *[thème, motif, cadence]* recurrence. **le ~ du printemps/de la paix** the return of spring/peace; **on prévoit un ~ du froid** a return of the cold weather is forecast; **un ~ offensif de la grippe** a renewed outbreak of flu.

(d) (*Comm, Poste*) *[emballage, récipient]* return; *[objets invendus]* return. **~ à l'envoyeur *ou* à l'expéditeur** return to sender; **avec faculté de ~** on approval, on sale or return; (*Fin*) **clause de ~** no protest clause.

(e) (*Jur*) reversion. **(droit de) ~** reversion.

(f) (*littér*) (*changement d'avis*) change of heart. (*revirements*) **~s** reversals; **les ~s de la fortune** the turns of fortune; **un ~ soudain dans l'opinion publique** a sudden turnabout in public opinion.

(g) (*Tech*) *[pièce mobile, chariot de machine]* return. **le ~ du chariot est automatique** the carriage return is automatic.

(h) (*Élec*) **~ à la terre *ou* à la masse** earth return.

(i) (*loc*) **en ~** in return; **choc *ou* effet en ~** backlash; (*péj*) **être sur le ~*** to be over the hill*, be a bit past it*; **faire ~ à** to revert to; **par un juste ~ des choses, il a été cette fois récompensé** events went his way *ou* fate was fair to him this time and he got his just reward; **par ~ (du courrier)** by return (of post); **sans ~** irredeemably, irrevocably, for ever; **~ sur soi-même** soul-searching (*U*); **faire un ~ sur soi-même** to take stock of o.s., do some soul-searching; *V* **payer**.

2: **retour d'âge** change of life; **retour en arrière** (*Littérat*) flashback; (*souvenir*) look back; (*mesure rétrograde*) retreat; **faire un ~ en arrière** to take a look back, look back; (*Ciné*) to flash back; **retour de bâton** kickback; (*Philos*) **retour éternel** eternal recurrence; (*Tech*) **retour de flamme** backfire; **retour en force** return in strength; **retour de manivelle** (*lit*) backfire, kick; (*fig*) **il y aura un retour de manivelle** it'll backfire (on them); **retour offensif** renewed attack.

retourner [ʀ(ə)tuʀne] (1) **1** *vt* **(a)** (*mettre dans l'autre sens*) *seau, caisse* to turn upside down; *matelas* to turn (over); *carte* to turn up; (*Culin*) *viande, poisson, omelette* to turn over; *crêpe* (*avec une spatule*) to turn over; (*en lançant*) to toss. **~ un tableau/une carte contre le mur** to turn a picture/a map against the wall; (*fig*) **elle l'a retourné (comme une crêpe *ou* un gant)*** she soon changed his mind for him; **~ la situation** to reverse the situation.

(b) (*en remuant, secouant*) *sol, terre* to turn over; *salade* to toss. **~ le foin** to toss (the) hay, turn (over) the hay.

(c) (*mettre l'intérieur à l'extérieur*) *sac, vêtement, parapluie* to turn inside out; (*Couture*) *vêtement, col* to turn. (*fig*) **~ sa veste** to turn one's coat; **~ ses poches pour trouver qch** to turn one's pockets inside out *ou* turn out one's pockets to find sth; **son col/revers est retourné** (*par mégarde*) his collar/lapel is turned up.

(d) (*orienter dans le sens opposé*) *mot, phrase* to turn round. **~ un argument contre qn** to turn an argument back on sb *ou* against sb; **~ contre l'ennemi ses propres armes** to turn the enemy's own weapons on him; **il retourna le pistolet contre lui-même** he turned the gun on himself; **on pourrait vous ~ votre compliment/votre critique** one might return the compliment/your criticism.

(e) (*renvoyer*) *marchandise, lettre* to return, send back.

(f) (*fig*: bouleverser*) *pièce, maison* to turn upside down; *personne* to shake. **il a tout retourné dans la maison pour retrouver ce livre** he turned the whole house upside down to find that book; **la nouvelle l'a complètement retourné** the news has severely shaken him; (*fig*) **ce spectacle m'a retourné*** the sight of this shook me *ou* gave me quite a turn*.

(g) (*tourner plusieurs fois*) **~ une pensée/une idée dans sa tête** to turn a thought/an idea over (and over) in one's mind; **~ le couteau *ou* le poignard dans la plaie** to twist the knife in the wound; *V* **tourner**.

2 *vi* **(a)** (*aller à nouveau*) to return, go back. **~ en Italie/à la mer** to return *ou* go back to Italy/the seaside; **je devrai ~ chez le médecin** I'll have to go back to the doctor's; **~ en arrière *ou* sur ses pas** to turn back, retrace one's steps; **il retourne demain à son travail/à l'école** he's going back to work/school tomorrow; (*rentrer*) **elle est retournée chez elle chercher son parapluie** she went back home to get her umbrella.

(b) (*à un état antérieur*) **~ à** to return to, go back to; **~ à la vie sauvage** to revert *ou* go back to the wild state; **~ à Dieu** to return to God; **il est retourné à son ancien métier/à la physique** he has gone back to his old job/to physics.

3 *vb impers*: **nous voudrions bien savoir de quoi il retourne** we should really like to know what is going on.

4 se retourner *vpr* **(a)** *[personne couchée]* to turn over; *[véhicule, automobiliste]* to turn over, overturn. **se ~ sur le dos/le ventre** to turn (over) onto one's back/stomach; **se ~ dans son lit toute la nuit** to toss and turn all night in bed; (*hum*) **il doit se ~ dans sa tombe** he must be turning in his grave! (*hum*); **la voiture s'est retournée *ou* ils se sont retournés (dans un fossé)** the car *ou* they overturned (into a ditch); (*fig*) **laissez-lui le temps de se ~** give him time to sort himself out *ou* to find his feet; (*fig*) **il sait se ~** he knows how to cope.

(b) (*tourner la tête*) to turn round. **partir sans se ~** to leave without looking back *ou* without a backward glance; **tout le monde se retournait sur son passage** everyone turned round as he went by.

(c) (*fig*) se ~ **contre qn** *[personne]* to turn against sb; *[acte, situation]* to backfire on sb, rebound on sb; **il ne savait vers qui se** ~ he didn't know who to turn to.

(d) (*tordre*) *pouce* to wrench, twist.

(e) (*littér*) **s'en** ~ (*cheminer*) to journey back; (*partir*) to depart, leave; (*fig*) **il s'en retourna comme il était venu** he left as he had come; **s'en** ~ **dans son pays (natal)** to return to one's native country.

retracer [R(ə)tRase] (3) *vt* **(a)** (*raconter*) *vie, histoire* to relate, recount. **(b)** (*tracer à nouveau*) *trait effacé* to redraw, draw again.

rétractable [RetRaktabl(ə)] *adj* (*Jur*) revocable.

rétractation [RetRaktɑsjɔ̃] *nf* (*désaveu*) retraction, retractation; (*Jur*) revocation.

rétracter [RetRakte] (1) **1** *vt* **(a)** (*contracter, rentrer*) *corne, griffe* to draw in, retract.

(b) (*littér: revenir sur*) *parole, opinion* to retract, withdraw.

2 se rétracter *vpr* **(a)** (*se retirer*) *[griffe, antenne]* to retract. (*fig littér*) **au moindre reproche, elle se rétractait** she would shrink at the slightest reproach.

(b) (*se dédire*) to retract, back down, climb down.

rétractile [RetRaktil] *adj* retractile.

rétraction [RetRaksjɔ̃] *nf* retraction.

retraduction [R(ə)tRadyksjɔ̃] *nf* (*V* **retraduire**) retranslation; back translation.

retraduire [R(ə)tRadɥiR] (38) *vt* (*traduire de nouveau*) to translate again; (*traduire dans la langue de départ*) to translate back.

retrait [R(ə)tRɛ] *nm* **(a)** (*départ*) *[mer]* ebb; *[eaux, glacier]* recession; *[troupes, candidat]* withdrawal.

(b) (*fait de retirer*) *[somme d'argent]* withdrawal; *[bagages]* collection; *[objet en gage]* redemption. **le** ~ **des bagages peut se faire à toute heure** luggage may be collected at all times.

(c) (*fait d'ôter*) *[candidature]* withdrawal. ~ **du permis (de conduire)** disqualification from driving, driving ban; (*Admin*) ~ **d'emploi** deprivation of office.

(d) (*rétrécissement*) *[ciment]* shrinkage, contraction; *[tissu]* shrinkage. **il y a du** ~ there's some shrinkage.

(e) en ~: **situé en** ~ set back; **se tenant en** ~ standing back; **en** ~ **de** set back from; **une petite maison, un peu en** ~ **de la route** a little house, set back a bit from the road; (*fig*) **rester en** ~ to stand aside.

retraite [R(ə)tRɛt] **1** *nf* **(a)** (*Mil: déroute, fuite*) retreat. **battre/sonner la** ~ to beat/sound the retreat; *V* **battre.**

(b) (*cessation de travail*) retirement. **être en** *ou* **à la** ~ to be retired *ou* in retirement; **en** ~ retired; **travailleur en** ~ retired worker, pensioner; **mettre qn à la** ~ to pension sb off, superannuate sb; **mise à la** ~ retirement; **prendre sa** ~ to retire, go into retirement; **prendre une** ~ **anticipée** to retire early; **pour lui, c'est la** ~ **forcée** he has had retirement forced on him, he has had to retire early.

(c) (*pension*) pension. **toucher** *ou* **percevoir une petite** ~ to receive *ou* draw a small pension; *V* **caisse, maison.**

(d) (*littér: refuge*) *[poète, amants]* retreat, refuge; *[ours, loup]* lair; *[voleurs]* hideout, hiding place.

(e) (*Rel: récollection*) retreat. **faire** *ou* **suivre une** ~ to be in retreat, go into retreat.

2: retraite des cadres management pension; **retraite complémentaire** supplementary pension; (*Mil*) **retraite aux flambeaux** torchlight tattoo; **retraite des vieux** (old age) pension; **retraite des vieux travailleurs** retirement pension.

retraité, e [R(ə)tRete] **1** *adj* retired. **2** *nm,f* (old age) pensioner.

retranchement [R(ə)tRɑ̃ʃmɑ̃] *nm* (*Mil*) entrenchment, retrenchment. (*fig*) **poursuivre** *ou* **pourchasser qn jusque dans ses derniers** ~**s** to drive *ou* hound sb into a corner.

retrancher [R(ə)tRɑ̃ʃe] (1) **1** *vt* **(a)** (*enlever*) *quantité, somme* to take away, subtract (*de* from); *somme d'argent* to deduct, dock, take off; *passage, mot* to take out, remove, omit (*de* from). ~ **10 de 15** to take 10 (away) from 15, subtract 10 from 15; ~ **une somme d'un salaire** to deduct *ou* dock a sum from a salary, take a sum out of a salary; **si l'on retranche ceux qui n'ont pas de licence** if you leave out *ou* omit the non-graduates; (*hum*) **ils étaient décidés à me** ~ **du monde des vivants** they were set on removing me from the land of the living.

(b) (*littér: couper*) *chair gangrenée* to remove, cut off; *organe malade* to remove, cut out.

(c) (*littér: séparer*) to cut off. **son argent le retranchait des autres** his money cut him off from other people.

(d) (†: *Mil: fortifier*) to entrench.

2 se retrancher *vpr* **(a)** (*Mil: se fortifier*) **se** ~ **derrière/dans** to entrench o.s. behind/in; **se** ~ **sur une position** to entrench o.s. in a position.

(b) (*fig*) **se** ~ **dans son mutisme/sa douleur** to take refuge in one's dumbness/pain; **se** ~ **derrière la loi/le secret professionnel** to take refuge behind *ou* hide behind the law/professional secrecy.

retranscription [R(ə)tRɑ̃skRipsjɔ̃] *nf* retranscription.

retranscrire [R(ə)tRɑ̃skRiR] (39) *vt* to retranscribe.

retransmetteur [R(ə)tRɑ̃smɛtœR] *nm* relay station.

retransmettre [R(ə)tRɑ̃smɛtR(ə)] (56) *vt match, émission, concert* (*Rad*) to broadcast, relay; (*TV*) to show. ~ **en différé** to broadcast a recording of; to show a recording of; ~ **en direct** to relay *ou* broadcast live; to show live.

retransmission [R(ə)tRɑ̃smisjɔ̃] *nf* (*V* **retransmettre**) broadcast; showing. ~ **en direct/différé** live/recorded broadcast; live/recorded showing; **la** ~ **du match aura lieu à 23 heures** the match will be shown at 11 p.m.

retravailler [R(ə)tRavaje] (1) **1** *vi* **(a)** (*recommencer le travail*) to start work again. **il retravaille depuis le mois dernier** he has been back at work since last month.

(b) (*se remettre à*) ~ **à qch** to start work on sth again, work at sth again.

2 *vt question* to give (some) more thought to; *discours, ouvrage* to work on again; *argile* to work again; *minerai* to reprocess.

retraverser [R(ə)tRavɛRse] (1) *vt* (*de nouveau*) to recross; (*dans l'autre sens*) to cross back.

rétréci, e [RetResi] (*ptp de* **rétrécir**) *adj tricot, vêtement* shrunken; *pupille* contracted; (*péj*) *esprit* narrow. (*Aut*) **'chaussée** ~**e'** 'road narrows'; (*Comm, Tex*) ~ **(à la coupe)** preshrunk.

rétrécir [RetResiR] (2) **1** *vt* **(a)** *vêtement* to take in; *tissu* to shrink; *pupille* to contract; *rue, conduit, orifice* to narrow, make narrower; *bague* to tighten, make smaller; (*fig*) *esprit* to narrow.

(b) faire ~ *tissu* to shrink.

2 *vi,* **se rétrécir** *vpr [laine, tissu]* to shrink; *[pupilles]* to contract; *[rue, vallée]* to narrow, become *ou* get narrower; *[esprit]* to grow narrow; *[cercle d'amis]* to grow smaller, dwindle.

rétrécissement [RetResismɑ̃] *nm* **(a)** (*le fait de se rétrécir*) *[tricot, laine]* shrinkage; *[pupille]* contraction; *[rue, vallée]* narrowing.

(b) (*rare: le fait de rétrécir*) *[tissu]* shrinking; *[vêtement]* taking in; *[conduit]* narrowing.

(c) (*Méd*) *[rectum, aorte]* stricture.

retremper [R(ə)tRɑ̃pe] (1) **1** *vt* **(a)** (*Tech*) *acier* to requench. (*fig*) ~ **son courage aux dangers du front** to try *ou* test one's courage again at the dangers of the front.

(b) (*réimprégner*) to resoak.

2 se retremper *vpr [baigneur]* to go back into the water. (*fig*) **se** ~ **dans l'ambiance familiale** to reimmerse o.s. in the family atmosphere.

rétribuer [RetRibɥe] (1) *vt ouvrier* to paye. ~ **le travail/les services de qn** to pay sb for his work/his services.

rétribution [RetRibysjɔ̃] *nf* (*paiement*) payment, remuneration (*U*); (*littér: récompense*) reward, recompense (*de* for).

rétro[1] [RetRo] *nm abrév de* **rétroviseur.**

rétro[2] [RetRo] *adj inv*: **la mode/le style** ~ the Twenties fashion/style.

rétroactif, -ive [RetRɔaktif, iv] *adj effet, action, mesure* retrospective; (*Jur*) retroactive. (*Admin*) **mesure/augmentation avec effet** ~ backdated measure/pay rise.

rétroaction [RetRɔaksjɔ̃] *nf* retrospective effect.

rétroactivement [RetRɔaktivmɑ̃] *adv* (*gén*) retrospectively, in retrospect; (*Jur*) retroactively.

rétroactivité [RetRɔaktivite] *nf* retroactivity; *V* **non.**

rétrocéder [RetRɔsede] (6) *vt* (*Jur*) to retrocede, cede back.

rétrocession [RetRɔsesjɔ̃] *nf* (*Jur*) retrocession, retrocedence.

rétrofusée [RetRɔfyze] *nf* retrorocket.

rétrogradation [RetRɔgRadɑsjɔ̃] *nf* (*littér: régression*) regression, retrogression; (*Admin*) *[officier]* demotion; *[fonctionnaire]* demotion, downgrading; (*Astron*) retrogradation.

rétrograde [RetRɔgRad] *adj* **(a)** (*péj: arriéré*) *esprit* reactionary; *mesures, idées, politique* retrograde, reactionary.

(b) (*de recul*) *mouvement, sens* backward, retrograde; (*Littérat*) *vers, rimes* palindromic; (*Astron*) retrograde.

rétrograder [RetRɔgRade] (1) **1** *vi* **(a)** (*Aut*) to change down. ~ **de troisième en seconde** to change down from third to second.

(b) (*régresser*) (*dans une hiérarchie*) to regress, move down; (*contre le progrès*) to go backward, regress; (*perdre son avance*) to fall back; (*reculer*) to move back.

(c) (*Astron*) to retrograde.

2 *vt officier* to demote, reduce in rank; *fonctionnaire* to demote, downgrade.

rétropédalage [RetRɔpedalaʒ] *nm* (*rare*) back-pedalling (*lit*).

rétrospectif, -ive [RetRɔspɛktif, iv] **1** *adj étude* retrospective.

2 rétrospective *nf* (*Art: exposition*) retrospective. (*Ciné: projections*) ~**ive Buster Keaton** Buster Keaton season.

rétrospectivement [RetRɔspɛktivmɑ̃] *adv apparaître* in retrospect, retrospectively; *avoir peur, être jaloux* in retrospect, looking back. **ces faits me sont apparus** ~ **sous un jour inquiétant** looking back on it *ou* in retrospect I saw the worrying side of these facts.

retroussé, e [R(ə)tRuse] (*ptp de* **retrousser**) *adj jupe* hitched up; *manche, pantalon* rolled *ou* turned up; *nez* turned-up, retroussé; *moustaches, lèvres* curled up.

retroussement [R(ə)tRusmɑ̃] *nm* (*action: V* **retrousser**) hitching up; rolling up; curling; flaring.

retrousser [R(ə)tRuse] (1) **1** *vt jupe* to hitch up, tuck up; *manche, pantalon* to roll up; *lèvres* to curl up; *narines* to dilate.

2 se retrousser *vpr [femme]* to hitch up one's skirt(s); *[bords]* to turn outwards.

retroussis [R(ə)tRusi] *nm* (*littér: partie retroussée*) lip; *[lèvres]* curl.

retrouvailles [R(ə)tRuvɑj] *nfpl* reunion.

retrouver [R(ə)tRuve] (1) **1** *vt* **(a)** (*récupérer*) *objet personnel, enfant* to find (again); *fugitif, objet égaré par un tiers* to find. ~ **son chemin** to find one's way again; **on retrouva son cadavre sur une plage** his body was found on a beach; **on les a retrouvés vivants** they were found alive; **une chienne n'y retrouverait pas ses petits, une poule n'y retrouverait pas ses poussins** it's in absolute chaos, it's an unholy mess*.

(b) (*se remémorer*) to think of, remember. **je ne retrouve plus son nom** I can't think of *ou* remember his name.

(c) (*revoir*) *personne* to meet (up with) again; *endroit* to be back in, see again. **je l'ai retrouvé par hasard en Italie** I met up with him again by chance in Italy, I happened to come across him again in Italy; **je l'ai retrouvé grandi/vieilli** I found him taller/aged *ou* looking older; **et que je ne te retrouve pas ici!** and don't let me catch *ou* find you here again!; **je serai ravi de vous ~** I'll be delighted to see *ou* meet you again.

(d) (*rejoindre*) to join, meet (again), see (again). **je vous retrouve à 5 heures au Café de la Poste** I'll join *ou* meet *ou* see you at 5 o'clock at the Café de la Poste.

(e) (*recouvrer*) *forces, santé, calme* to regain; *joie, foi* to find again. **~ le sommeil** to go back to sleep (again); **elle mit longtemps à ~ la santé/le calme** she took a long time to regain her health/composure, it was a long time before her health/composure returned *ou* before she regained her health/composure; **très vite elle retrouva son sourire** she very soon found her smile again.

(f) (*redécouvrir*) *secret* to rediscover; *recette* to rediscover, uncover; *article en vente* to find again; *situation, poste* to find again. **je voudrais ~ des rideaux de la même couleur** I'd like to find curtains in the same colour again; **~ du travail** to find work again; **il a bien cherché, mais une situation pareille ne se retrouve pas facilement** he looked around but it's not easy to come by *ou* find another job like that; **une telle occasion ne se retrouvera jamais** an opportunity like this will never occur again *ou* crop up again.

(g) (*reconnaître*) to recognize. **on retrouve chez Jacques le sourire de son père** you can see *ou* recognize his father's smile in Jacques, you can see Jacques has the same smile as his father *ou* has his father's smile; **je retrouve bien là mon fils!** that's my son all right!

(h) (*trouver, rencontrer*) to find, encounter. **on retrouve sans cesse les mêmes tournures dans ses romans** you find the same expressions all the time in his novels, you are constantly coming across *ou* meeting the same expressions in his novels; **ces caractéristiques se retrouvent aussi chez les cervidés** these characteristics are also found *ou* encountered in the deer family.

2 se retrouver *vpr* **(a)** (*se réunir*) to meet, meet up; (*se revoir après une absence*) to meet again. **après le travail, ils se sont tous retrouvés au café** after work they all met in the café; **ils se sont retrouvés par hasard à Paris** they met again by chance in Paris; **un club où l'on se retrouve entre sportifs** a club where one meets with other sportsmen *ou* where sportsmen get together; **on se retrouvera!** I'll get even with you!, I'll get my own back!; **comme on se retrouve!** fancy meeting *ou* seeing you here!

(b) (*être de nouveau*) to find o.s. back. **il se retrouva place de la Concorde** he found himself back at the Place de la Concorde; **se ~ dans la même situation** to find o.s. back in the same situation; **se ~ seul** (*sans amis etc*) to be left on one's own *ou* with no one; (*loin des autres, de la foule*) to be alone *ou* on one's own.

(c) (*: *finir*) **il s'est retrouvé en prison/dans le fossé** he ended up in prison/in the ditch, he landed up* *ou* wound up* in prison/in the ditch.

(d) (*voir clair, mettre de l'ordre*) **se ~, s'y ~ (dans): il ne se** *ou* **s'y retrouve pas dans ses calculs/la numération binaire** he can't make sense of his calculations/binary notation; **on a de la peine à s'y ~, dans ces digressions/ces raisonnements** it's hard to find one's way through *ou* to make sense of these digressions/arguments; **allez donc vous (y) ~ dans un désordre pareil!** let's see you try and straighten out this awful mess!; **je ne m'y retrouve plus** I'm completely lost.

(e) (*: *rentrer dans ses frais*) **s'y ~** to break even; **les frais furent énormes mais il s'y est largement retrouvé** his outgoings were enormous but he made handsomely on the deal; **tout ce que j'espère c'est qu'on s'y retrouve** all I hope is that we break even; **s'il te prête cet argent c'est qu'il s'y retrouve** if he lends you this money, it's because there's something in it for him.

(f) (*trouver son chemin*) **se ~, s'y ~** to find one's way; **la ville où je suis né a changé et je ne m'y retrouve plus** the town where I was born has changed, and I can't find my way any more.

(g) (*littér: faire un retour sur soi-même*) to find o.s. again.

rétroviseur [ʀetʀɔvizœʀ] *nm* rear-view mirror, (driving) mirror. **~ (d'aile)** wing mirror.

rets [ʀɛ] *nmpl* (*littér: piège*) snare. **prendre** *ou* **attraper qn dans les ~** to ensnare sb; **se laisser prendre** *ou* **tomber dans les ~ de qn** to be ensnared by sb.

réuni, e [ʀeyni] (*ptp de* **réunir**) *adj* **(a)** (*pris ensemble*) **~s** (put) together; **aussi fort que les Français et les Anglais ~s** as strong as the French and the English put together.

(b) (*Comm: associés*) associated. **les Transporteurs R~s** Associated Carriers.

réunification [ʀeynifikasjɔ̃] *nf* reunification.

réunifier [ʀeynifje] (7) *vt* to reunify.

réunion [ʀeynjɔ̃] **1** *nf* **(a)** *[objets, faits]* collection, gathering; *[fonds]* raising; *[membres d'une famille, d'un club]* bringing together, reunion, reuniting; *[éléments, parties]* combination. **~ d'une province à un état** the union of a province with a state.

(b) *[amis]* reuniting, reunion; *[compagnies]* merging; *[états]* union; *[fleuves]* confluence, merging; *[rues]* junction, joining; *[idées]* meeting.

(c) (*séance*) meeting. **notre prochaine ~ sera le 10** our next meeting will be on the 10th.

(d) (*journée sportive*) **~ cycliste** cycle rally; **~ hippique** gymkhana, horse show.

2: réunion électorale adoption meeting; **réunion de famille** family gathering; **réunion sportive** sports meeting.

Réunion [ʀeynjɔ̃] *nf* (*Géog*) **la ~, l'île de la ~** Reunion Island.

réunir [ʀeyniʀ] (2) **1** *vt* **(a)** (*rassembler*) *objets* to gather *ou* collect (together); *faits, preuves* to put together. **~ tout son linge en un paquet** to collect all one's washing into a bundle; **~ des papiers par une épingle** to pin papers together, fix papers together with a pin.

(b) (*recueillir*) *fonds* to raise, get together*; *preuves* to collect, gather (together); *pièces de collection, timbres* to collect.

(c) (*cumuler*) to combine. **ce livre réunit diverses tendances stylistiques** this book combines various styles, this book is a combination of different styles.

(d) (*assembler*) *participants* to gather, collect; (*convoquer*) *membres d'un parti* to call together, call a meeting of; (*inviter*) *amis, famille* to entertain, have round*; (*rapprocher*) *ennemis, antagonistes* to bring together, reunite; *anciens amis* to bring together again, reunite. **on avait réuni les participants dans la cour** they had gathered those taking part in the yard; **ce congrès a réuni des écrivains de toutes tendances** this congress gathered *ou* brought together writers of all types; **nous réunissons nos amis tous les mercredis** we have our friends round* every Wednesday; **après une brouille de plusieurs années, ce deuil les a réunis** after a quarrel which lasted several years, this bereavement brought them together again *ou* reunited them.

(e) (*raccorder*) *parties, éléments* to join. **le couloir réunit les deux ailes du bâtiment** the corridor joins *ou* links the two wings of the building.

(f) (*rare: relier*) to join (up *ou* together). **~ deux fils** to tie two threads together; **~ les bords d'une plaie/d'un accroc** to bring together the edges of a wound/tear.

(g) (*rattacher à*) **~ à** *province etc* to unite to.

2 se réunir *vpr* **(a)** (*se rencontrer*) to meet, get together*, have a get-together*. **se ~ entre amis** to get together with (some) friends*, have a friendly get-together*; **le petit groupe se réunissait dans un bar** the little group would meet *ou* get together* in a bar.

(b) (*s'associer*) *[compagnies]* to combine; *[états]* to unite.

(c) (*se joindre*) *[états]* to unite; *[fleuves]* to flow into each other, merge; *[rues]* to join, converge; *[idées]* to unite, be united.

réussi, e [ʀeysi] (*ptp de* **réussir**) *adj* **(a)** (*couronné de succès*) *dîner, soirée, mariage* successful, a success (*attrib*); (*bien exécuté*) *mouvement* good, well executed (*frm*); *repas, photo, roman* successful; *mélange, tournure* effective. **c'était vraiment très ~** it really was a great success *ou* very successful; (*iro*) **eh bien, c'est ~!** well that's just great!* (*iro*), very clever! (*iro*).

(b) (*exécuté*) **une photo/une tourte/une soirée bien/mal ~** a successful/an unsuccessful photo/pie/evening; **un mouvement assez bien ~** a good *ou* well-executed movement.

réussir [ʀeysiʀ] (2) **1** *vi* **(a)** *[affaire, projet, entreprise]* to succeed, be a success, be successful; *[culture, plantation]* to thrive, do well. **pourquoi l'entreprise n'a-t-elle pas réussi?** why wasn't the undertaking a success?; **le culot réussit parfois où la prudence échoue** sometimes nerve succeeds *ou* works where caution fails; **la vigne ne réussit pas partout** vines don't thrive everywhere *ou* do not do well everywhere; **~ à qn: tout lui/rien ne lui réussit** everything/nothing goes *ou* comes right for him, everything/nothing works for him; **cela lui a mal réussi, cela ne lui a pas réussi** that didn't do him any good.

(b) *[personne]* (*dans une entreprise, la vie*) to succeed, be successful, be a success; (*à un examen*) to pass. **~ dans la vie** to succeed *ou* get on in life; **~ dans les affaires/dans ses études** to succeed *ou* do well in business/one's studies; **et leur expédition au Pôle, ont-ils réussi? — ils n'ont pas réussi** what about their expedition to the Pole – did they succeed? *ou* did they pull it off?* — they didn't *ou* they failed; **il a réussi dans tout ce qu'il a entrepris** he has made a success of *ou* been successful *ou* succeeded in all his undertakings; **il a réussi à son examen** he passed his exam; **tous leurs enfants ont bien réussi** all their children have done well; **il réussit bien en maths/à l'école** he's a success at maths/school.

(c) ~ à faire to succeed in doing, manage to do; **il a réussi à les convaincre** he succeeded in convincing them, he managed to convince them; (*iro*) **cette maladroite a réussi à se brûler*** this clumsy girl has managed to burn herself *ou* has gone and burnt herself*.

(d) (*être bénéfique à*) **~ à** to agree with; **l'air de la mer/la vie active lui réussit** sea air/an active life agrees with him; **le curry ne me réussit pas** curry doesn't agree with me.

2 *vt* **(a)** (*bien exécuter*) *film, entreprise, plat* to make a success of. **elle a bien réussi sa sauce** her sauce was a great success; **vont-ils ~ leur coup?** will they manage to carry *ou* pull it off?*; **il a réussi son coup: 10.000 F de raflés en 10 minutes!** he pulled the job off – 10,000 francs pinched in 10 minutes flat*; (*hum*) **je l'ai bien réussi, mon fils** I did a good job on my son (*hum*).

(b) (*exécuter*) *but, essai* to bring off, pull off*; *tâche* to bring off, manage successfully. **il a réussi 2 très jolies photos** he managed 2 very nice photographs.

réussite [ʀeysit] *nf* **(a)** *[entreprise]* success, successful outcome; *[culture, soirée]* success. **ce fut une ~ complète** it was a complete *ou* an unqualified success. **(b)** *[personne]* success. **une réussite bien méritée** a well-deserved success. **(c)** (*Cartes*) patience. **faire une ~** to play patience.

revaccination [ʀ(ə)vaksinasjɔ̃] *nf* revaccination.

revacciner [ʀ(ə)vaksine] (1) *vt* to revaccinate.

revaloir [ʀ(ə)valwaʀ] (29) *vt* to pay back. **je te revaudrai ça, je te le revaudrai** (*hostile*) I'll pay you back for this, I'll get even with you for this; (*reconnaissant*) I'll repay you some day.

revalorisation [ʀ(ə)valɔʀizasjɔ̃] *nf* (*V* **revaloriser**) revaluation; raising; fresh promotion. **une ~ du mariage** a reassertion of the value of marriage.

revaloriser [ʀ(ə)valɔʀize] (1) *vt monnaie* to revalue; *salaire* to raise; *méthode* to promote again; *valeur morale, institution* to reassert the value of.

revanchard, e [ʀ(ə)vɑ̃ʃaʀ, aʀd(ə)] *(péj)* **1** *adj politique* of revenge *(esp against enemy country)*; *politicien* who is an advocate of *ou* who advocates revenge; *pays* bent on revenge *(attrib)*. **2** *nm,f* advocate of revenge, revanchist *(frm)*.

revanche [ʀ(ə)vɑ̃ʃ] *nf (après défaite, humiliation)* revenge; *(Jeux, Sport)* revenge match; *(Boxe)* return fight *ou* bout. **prendre sa ~ (sur qn)** take one's revenge (on sb), get one's own back (on sb)*; **prendre une ~ éclatante (sur qn)** to take a spectacular revenge (on sb); *(Jeux, Sport)* **donner sa ~ à qn** to let sb have *ou* give sb his revenge; **le mépris est la ~ des faibles** contempt is the revenge of the weak; **en ~** on the other hand; *V* **charge**.

rêvasser [ʀevase] (1) *vi* to daydream, let one's mind wander, muse *(littér)*.

rêvasserie [ʀɛvasʀi] *nf (U: rêve)* daydreaming; *(chimère)* (idle) dream, (idle) fancy, daydreaming *(U)*.

rêve [ʀɛv] *nm* **(a)** *(pendant le sommeil, chimère)* dream; *(éveillé)* dream, daydream. *(Psych)* **le ~, les ~s** dreaming, dreams; *(Psych)* **le ~ éveillé** daydreaming; **j'ai fait un ~ affreux** I had a horrible dream; **faire des ~s** to dream, have dreams; **faites de beaux ~s!** sweet dreams!; **il est dans un ~** he's (day)dreaming; **sortir d'un ~** to come out of a dream; *V* **mauvais**.

(b) *(loc)* **c'était un beau ~!** it was a lovely dream!; **une voiture/maison de ~** a dream car/house; **son ~ de jeunesse** his youthful dream; **une créature/un silence de ~** a dream creature/silence; **la voiture/la femme de ses ~s** the car/woman of his dreams, his dream car/woman; **disparaître comme dans un ~** to be gone *ou* disappear in a trice; **voir/entendre qch en ~** to see/hear sth in a dream; **créer qch en ~** to dream sth up; **ça, c'est le ~*** that would be ideal *ou* (just) perfect; **une maison comme ça, ce n'est pas le ~*** it's not the sort of house you dream about.

revêche [ʀəvɛʃ] *adj* surly, sour-tempered.

réveil [ʀevɛj] *nm* **(a)** *[dormeur]* waking (up) *(U)*, wakening *(littér)*; *(fig: retour à la réalité)* awakening. **au ~, je le trouvai déjà parti** when I woke up *ou* on waking I found he was already gone; **il a le ~ difficile** he finds it hard to wake up, he finds waking up difficult; **il eut un ~ brutal** he was rudely woken up *ou* awakened; **dès le ~, il chante** as soon as he's awake *ou* he wakes up he starts singing, he's singing from the moment he's awake; **ils assistaient au ~ du roi** they were present at the awakening of the king; **il a passé une nuit entrecoupée de ~s en sursaut** he spent a broken night coming awake *ou* waking with a start every so often; *(fig)* **après tous ces châteaux en Espagne, le ~ fut pénible** after building all these castles in the air, he had a rude awakening.

(b) *(fig: renaissance) [nature, sentiment, souvenir]* reawakening; *[volcan]* fresh stirrings *(pl)*; *[douleur]* return.

(c) *(Mil)* reveille. **sonner le ~** to sound the reveille; **battre le ~** *to wake soldiers up to the sound of drums*; **~ en fanfare** reveille on the bugle; *(fig)* **mes enfants m'ont gratifié d'un ~ en fanfare ce matin!** my children treated me to a rowdy awakening this morning!

(d) *(réveille-matin)* alarm (clock). **mets le ~ à 8 heures** set the alarm for 8 (o'clock).

réveillé, e [reveje] *(ptp de* **réveiller***) adj (à l'état de veille)* awake; (*: *dégourdi*) bright, all there* *(attrib)*. **à moitié ~** half asleep; **il était mal ~** he was still half asleep, he hadn't woken up properly.

réveille-matin [ʀevɛjmatɛ̃] *nm inv* alarm clock.

réveiller [reveje] (1) **1** *vt* **(a)** *dormeur* to wake (up), waken, awaken *(littér)*; *(ranimer) personne évanouie* to bring round, revive; *(ramener à la réalité) rêveur* to wake up, waken. **réveillez-moi à 5 heures** wake me (up) at 5 (o'clock); **être réveillé en sursaut** to be woken (up) with a start; **faire un vacarme à ~ les morts** to make a row that would waken the dead; *(Prov)* **ne réveillez pas le chat qui dort** let sleeping dogs lie *(Prov)*.

(b) *(raviver) appétit, courage* to rouse, awaken; *douleur (physique)* to start up again; *(mentale)* to revive, reawaken; *rancune, jalousie* to reawaken, rouse.

(c) *(ranimer) souvenir* to awaken, revive, bring back; *membre ankylosé* to bring some sensation *ou* feeling back into. **~ les consciences** to awaken *ou* stir people's consciences.

2 se réveiller *vpr* **(a)** *[dormeur]* to wake (up), awake, awaken *(littér)*; *[personne évanouie]* to come round, regain consciousness; *(fig) [rêveur, paresseux]* to wake up *(de* from). **réveille-toi!** wake up!; *(fig)* **se réveillant de sa torpeur** rousing himself from his lethargy.

(b) *(se raviver) [appétit, courage]* to be roused; *[douleur]* to return; *[rancune, jalousie]* to be rearoused; *[souvenir]* to return, come back, to reawaken *(littér)*.

(c) *(se ranimer) [nature]* to reawaken; *[volcan]* to stir again; *[membre ankylosé]* to regain some sensation *ou* feeling in.

réveillon [ʀevɛjɔ̃] *nm (Noël/Nouvel An) (repas)* Christmas Eve/New Year's Eve dinner; *(fête)* Christmas Eve/New Year's party; *(date)* Christmas Eve; New Year's Eve.

réveillonner [ʀevɛjɔne] (1) *vi* to celebrate Christmas *ou* New Year's Eve *(with a dinner and a party)*.

réveillonneur [ʀevɛjɔnœʀ] *nm* party-goer, reveller *(on Christmas or New Year's Eve)*. **un des ~s proposa un jeu** one of the people at the party suggested a game.

révélateur, -trice [ʀevelatœʀ, tʀis] **1** *adj indice, symptôme* revealing. **~ de** revealing; **film ~ d'une mode/d'une tendance** film revealing a fashion/a tendency; **c'est ~ d'un malaise profond** it reveals a deep malaise.

2 *nm (Phot)* developer; *(littér: qui dévoile) (personne)* enlightener; *(événement, expérience)* revelation. **ces manies sont un ~ de la personnalité** these quirks are revealing of personality.

révélation [ʀevelɑsjɔ̃] *nf* **(a)** *(U: V* **révéler***) [fait, projet, secret]* revelation; disclosure; *[artiste]* revelation; *(Phot) [image]* developing. **ce jeune auteur a été la ~ de l'année** this young author was the discovery of the year.

(b) *(U) [sensations, talent, tendances]* revelation.

(c) *(chose avouée)* disclosure, revelation. **faire des ~s importantes** to make important disclosures *ou* revelations.

(d) *(illuminations, surprise, Rel)* revelation. **ce fut une ~!** it was (quite) a revelation!

révélé, e [ʀevele] *(ptp de* **révéler***) adj (Rel) dogme, religion* revealed.

révéler [ʀevele] (6) **1** *vt* **(a)** *(divulguer) fait, projet* to reveal, make known, disclose; *secret* to disclose, reveal; *opinion* to make known. **ça l'avait révélée à elle-même** this had opened her eyes to herself, this had given her a new awareness of herself; **je ne peux encore rien ~** I can't disclose *ou* reveal anything yet, I can't give anything away yet*; **~ que** to reveal that.

(b) *(témoigner de) aptitude, caractère* to reveal, display, show; *sentiments* to show. **œuvre qui révèle une grande sensibilité** work which reveals *ou* displays great sensibility; **sa physionomie révèle la bonté/une grande ambition** his features show *ou* evince *(frm)* goodness/great ambition.

(c) *(faire connaître) artiste [impresario]* to discover; *[œuvre]* to bring to fame; *(Rel)* to reveal.

(d) *(Phot)* to develop.

2 se révéler *vpr* **(a)** *(apparaître) [vérité, talent, tendance]* to be revealed, reveal itself; *(Rel)* to reveal o.s. *[artiste]* **il ne s'est révélé que vers la quarantaine** he didn't show his *ou* display his talent until he was nearly forty; **des sensations nouvelles se révélaient à lui** he was becoming aware of new feelings.

(b) *(s'avérer)* **se ~ cruel/ambitieux** to show o.s. *ou* prove to be cruel/ambitious; **se ~ difficile/aisé** to prove difficult/easy; **son hypothèse se révéla fausse** his hypothesis proved *ou* was shown to be false.

revenant, e [ʀəvnɑ̃, ɑ̃t] *nm,f* ghost. **tiens, un ~!*** hello stranger!*; *V* **histoire**.

revendeur, -euse [ʀ(ə)vɑ̃dœʀ, øz] *nm,f (détaillant)* retailer; *(d'occasion)* secondhand dealer. **chez votre ~ habituel** at your local stockist.

revendicateur, -trice [ʀ(ə)vɑ̃dikatœʀ, tʀis] *adj*: **dans notre lettre ~trice** in the letter stating our claims; **déclaration ~trice** declaration of claims.

revendicatif, -ive [ʀ(ə)vɑ̃dikatif, iv] *adj mouvement, journée* of protest. **organiser une journée ~ive** to organize a day of action *ou* protest (in support of one's claims).

revendication [ʀ(ə)vɑ̃dikɑsjɔ̃] *nf* **(a)** *(U)* claiming.

(b) *(Pol, Syndicats: demande)* claim, demand. **des ~s légitimes** rightful claims *ou* demands; **le parti de la ~** the claim-makers; **journée de ~** day of action *ou* protest (in support of one's claim); **lettre de ~** letter putting forward one's claims.

revendiquer [ʀ(ə)vɑ̃dike] (1) *vt* **(a)** *(demander, réclamer) chose due, droits* to claim, demand. **les ouvriers ont décidé de ~** the workers have decided to put in a claim; **ils passent leur temps à ~** they spend their time putting forward claims.

(b) *(assumer) responsabilité, paternité* to claim.

revendre [ʀ(ə)vɑ̃dʀ(ə)] (41) *vt* **(a)** *(vendre d'occasion)* to resell. **ça se revend facilement** that's easily resold, that's easily sold again.

(b) *(vendre au détail)* to sell.

(c) *(vendre davantage)* **j'en ai vendu 2 en janvier et j'en ai revendu 4 en février** I sold 2 in January and I sold another 4 in February; **j'en ai vendu la semaine dernière mais je n'en ai pas revendu depuis** I sold some last week but I've sold no more since then.

(d) *(loc)* **à ~: avoir de l'énergie/de l'intelligence à ~** to have energy/brains to spare, have energy/brains enough and to spare; **si tu veux un tableau, on en a à ~** if you want a picture, we've got them by the score.

revenez-y [ʀəvnezi] *nm inv V* **goût**.

revenir [ʀəvniʀ] (22) **1** *vi* **(a)** *(repasser, venir de nouveau)* to come back, come again. **il doit ~ nous voir demain** he's coming back to see us tomorrow, he's coming to see us again tomorrow; **pouvez-vous ~ plus tard?** can you come back later?

(b) *(réapparaître) [saison, mode]* to come back, return; *[soleil, oiseaux]* to return, reappear; *[fête, date]* to come (round) again; *[calme, ordre]* to return. **cette expression revient souvent dans sa conversation** that expression often crops up in his conversation; **Noël revient chaque année à la même date** Christmas comes (round) on the same date every year; **sa lettre est revenue parce qu'il avait changé d'adresse** his letter was returned *ou* came back because he had left that address *ou* had changed his address.

(c) *(rentrer)* to come back, return. **~ quelque part/de quelque part** to come back *ou* return (to) somewhere/from somewhere; **~ chez soi** to come back *ou* return home; **~ dans son pays** to come back *ou* return to one's country; **~ en bateau/avion** to sail/fly back, come back by boat/air; **~ à la hâte** to hurry back; **~ de voyage** to return from a journey; **en revenant de l'école** coming back *ou* coming home from school, on the way back from school; **sa femme lui est revenue** his wife has come back to him; **je reviens dans un instant** I'll be back in a minute, I'll be right back*.

(d) *(recommencer, reprendre)* **~ à** *études, sujet* to go back to, return to; *méthode, procédé* to go back to, return to, revert to; **~ à la religion** to come back to religion; **~ à ses premières**

amours to go back *ou* return to one's first love; ~ **à de meilleurs sentiments** to return to a better frame of mind; **on y reviendra, à cette mode** this fashion will come back; **nous y reviendrons dans un instant** we'll come back to that in a moment; **n'y revenez plus!** don't (you) do that again!, don't start that again!; **j'en reviens toujours là, il faut ...** I still come back to this, we must ...; **il n'y a pas à y** ~ there's no going back on it.

(e) (*réexaminer*) ~ **sur** *affaire, problème* to go back over; **ne revenons pas là-dessus** let's not go back over that; ~ **sur le passé** to go back over the past, hark back to the past.

(f) (*revenir à la mémoire*) ~ **à qn** to come back to sb; **son nom me revient maintenant** his name has come back to me now; **ça me revient!** I've got it now!, it's coming back to me now!

(g) (*être redonné à*) ~ **à qn** *[courage, appétit, parole]* to come back to sb, return (to sb); **à la vue de sa résistance farouche, le courage me revint** seeing his fierce resistance, my courage came back to me *ou* returned; **à la vue de cette ratatouille, l'appétit m'est revenu** my appetite returned at the sight of *ou* when I saw that ratatouille.

(h) (*se remettre de*) ~ **de** *maladie* to recover from, get over; *syncope* to come round from; *égarement, surprise* to get over; *illusions* to lose, shake off; *erreurs, théories* to leave behind, throw over, cast aside; **ils sont déjà revenus de ces théories** they have already thrown over these theories; **elle est revenue de tout** she's seen it all before.

(i) (*se dédire de*) ~ **sur** *promesse* to go back on; *décision* to go back on, reconsider.

(j) (*parvenir à la connaissance de*) ~ **à qn,** ~ **aux oreilles de qn** to reach the ears of sb, get back to sb*; (*frm, hum*) **il m'est revenu que** word has come back to me *ou* reached me that.

(k) ~ **à qn** (*être la prérogative de*) to fall to sb; (*échoir à*) to come *ou* pass to sb; (*être la part de*) to come *ou* go to sb; (*incomber à*) **il lui revient de décider** it is for him *ou* up to him to decide; **ce titre lui revient de droit** this title is his by right; **les biens de son père sont revenus à l'État** his father's property passed to the state; **là-dessus, 100 F me reviennent** 100 francs of that comes to me.

(l) (*équivaloir à*) ~ **à** to come down to, amount to, boil down to*; **cette hypothèse revient à une proposition très simple** this hypothesis comes down *ou* amounts to a very simple proposition; **ça revient à une question d'argent** it all boils down* to a question of money; **cela revient à dire que** that amounts to saying that; **cela revient au même** it amounts *ou* comes to the same thing.

(m) (*coûter*) ~ **à** to amount to *ou* come to, cost; **ça revient à 10 F** it comes to *ou* amounts to 10 francs; **ça revient cher** it's expensive, it's an expensive business; **à combien est-ce que cela va vous** ~? how much will that cost you?, how much will that set you back?*

(n) (*Culin*) **faire** ~ to brown; **'faire** ~ **les oignons dans le beurre'** 'brown *ou* fry the onions gently in the butter'.

(o) (*loc*) (*en réchapper*) **en** ~ to pull through; **crois-tu qu'il en reviendra?** do you think he'll pull through?; ~ **à soi** to come round; ~ **à la vie** to come back to life; **il revient de loin** it's a miracle he's still with us; **je n'en reviens pas!** I can't get over it!; **il a une tête qui ne me revient pas** I don't like the look of him; ~ **à la charge** to return to the attack; **revenons à nos moutons** let's get back to the subject; *V* **tapis.**

2 s'en revenir *vpr*: **comme il s'en revenait (du village), il aperçut un aigle** as he was coming back from the village, he noticed an eagle; **il s'en revenait la queue basse** he was coming away with his tail between his legs; **il s'en revint le cœur plein d'allégresse** he came away with a joyful heart.

revente [ʀ(ə)vɑ̃t] *nf* resale.

revenu [ʀəvny] **1** *nm* **(a)** *[particulier]* income (*U*) (*de* from); *[état]* revenue (*de* from); *[domaine, terre]* income (*de* from); *[investissement, capital]* yield (*de* from, on). ~ **annuel/brut** annual/gross income; (*Fin*) **à** ~ **fixe** *valeurs* fixed yield; **avoir de gros** ~**s** to have a large income, have substantial means; **être sans** ~**s** to have no income *ou* means.

(b) (*Tech*) tempering.

2: (*Écon*) **revenus de l'État** public revenue; **revenu national** gross national product; **revenus publics** = **revenus de l'État; revenu du travail** earned income.

rêver [ʀeve] (1) **1** *vi* **(a)** *[dormeur]* to dream (*de, à* of, about). ~ **que** to dream that; **j'ai rêvé de toi** I dreamt about *ou* of you; **il en rêve la nuit*** he dreams about it at night; ~ **tout éveillé** to be lost in a daydream; **je ne rêve pas, c'est bien vrai?** I'm not imagining it *ou* dreaming, am I — it's really true!; **tu m'as appelé? — moi? tu rêves!** did you call me? — me? you must have been dreaming! *ou* you're imagining things!; **une révolution, maintenant? vous rêvez!** a revolution now? your imagination's running away with you!; **on croit** ~**!*** I can hardly believe it!, the mind boggles!*

(b) (*rêvasser*) to dream, muse (*littér*), daydream. **travaille au lieu de** ~! get on with your work instead of (day)dreaming!; ~ **à des jours meilleurs** to dream of better days.

(c) (*désirer*) ~ **de qch/de faire** to dream of sth/of doing; **elle rêve d'une chaumière en pleine forêt** she dreams of a cottage in the heart of a forest; ~ **de réussir** to long to succeed, long for success; ~ **de rencontrer l'épouse idéale** to dream of meeting *ou* long to meet the ideal wife.

2 *vt* **(a)** (*en dormant*) to dream. **j'ai rêvé la même chose qu'hier** I dreamt the same (thing) as last night.

(b) (*littér: imaginer*) to dream. **il rêve sa vie au lieu de la vivre** he's dreaming his life away instead of living it; (*péj*) **où as-tu été** ~ **ça?** where did you dream that up?; (*péj*) **je n'ai jamais dit ça, c'est toi qui l'as rêvé!** I never said that — you must have dreamt it!

(c) (*désirer*) to dream of. (*littér*) ~ **mariage/succès** to dream of marriage/success; (*littér*) **il se rêve conquérant** he dreams of being a conqueror; **il ne rêve que plaies et bosses** his mind is full of warlike *ou* heroic dreams, he lives in a dream world of bold and bloody deeds.

réverbération [ʀevɛʀbeʀɑsjɔ̃] *nf* reverberation.

réverbère [ʀevɛʀbɛʀ] *nm* (*d'éclairage*) street lamp *ou* light; (*Tech*) reflector; *V* **allumeur.**

réverbérer [ʀevɛʀbeʀe] (6) *vt son* to send back, reverberate; *chaleur, lumière* to reflect.

reverdir [ʀ(ə)vɛʀdiʀ] (2) **1** *vi [plantes]* to grow green again. **2** *vt* (*Tech*) to soak.

révérence [ʀeveʀɑ̃s] *nf* **(a)** (*salut*) *[homme]* bow; *[femme]* curtsey. **faire une** ~ to bow; to curtsey (*à qn* to sb); **tirer sa** ~ **(à qn)** (*lit*) to bow out (from sb's presence), make one's bow (and leave); (*fig*) to take one's leave (of sb).

(b) (*littér: respect*) reverence (*envers, pour* for). ~ **parler**† with all due respect.

révérencieux, -euse [ʀeveʀɑ̃sjø, øz] *adj* (*littér*) reverent. **être peu** ~ **envers** to show scant respect for.

révérend, e [ʀeveʀɑ̃, ɑ̃d] *adj, nm* reverend.

révérer [ʀeveʀe] (6) *vt* (*littér*) (*gén*) to revere; (*Rel*) to revere, reverence.

rêverie [ʀɛvʀi] *nf* **(a)** (*U*) daydreaming, reverie (*littér*), musing (*littér*). **(b)** (*moment de rêverie*) daydream, reverie (*littér*). **(c)** (*péj: chimère*) ~s daydreams, delusions, illusions.

revernir [ʀ(ə)vɛʀniʀ] (2) *vt* to revarnish.

revers [ʀ(ə)vɛʀ] *nm* **(a)** *[papier, feuille]* back; *[étoffe]* wrong side. (*fig littér*) **le** ~ **de la charité/vérité** the reverse of charity/truth; **prendre l'ennemi de** *ou* **à** ~ to take the enemy from *ou* in the rear.

(b) *[pièce d'argent, médaille]* reverse, reverse side, back. **pièce frappée au** ~ **d'une effigie** coin struck with a portrait on the reverse; (*fig*) **c'est le** ~ **de la médaille** that's the other side of the coin; **toute médaille a son** ~ every rose has its thorn.

(c) *[main]* back. **d'un** ~ **de main** with the back of one's hand.

(d) (*Tennis*) backhand. **faire un** ~ to play a backhand shot; **volée de** ~ backhand volley.

(e) (*Habillement*) *[veste, manteau]* lapel; *[pantalon]* turn-up (*Brit*), cuff (*US*); *[bottes]* top; *[manche]* (turned-back) cuff. **bottes à** ~ turned-down boots; **pantalons à** ~ trousers with turn-ups (*Brit*) *ou* cuffs (*US*).

(f) (*coup du sort*) ~ **(de fortune)** reverse (of fortune); ~ **économiques/militaires** economic/military setbacks *ou* reverses.

reverser [ʀ(ə)vɛʀse] (1) *vt* **(a)** *liquide* (*verser davantage*) to pour out some more. **reverse-moi du vin/un verre de vin** pour me (out) some more wine/another glass of wine; (*remettre*) **reversez le vin dans la bouteille** pour the wine back into the bottle.

(b) (*Fin*) *excédent, somme* to put back, pay back (*dans, sur* into).

réversible [ʀevɛʀsibl(ə)] *adj mouvement, vêtement* reversible; (*Jur*) revertible (*sur* to).

réversion [ʀevɛʀsjɔ̃] *nf* (*Bio, Jur*) reversion.

revêtement [ʀ(ə)vɛtmɑ̃] *nm* (*enduit*) coating; (*surface*) *[route]* surface; (*placage, garniture*) *[mur extérieur]* facing; *[mur intérieur]* covering. ~ **(du sol)** flooring (*U*), floor-covering (*U*).

revêtir [ʀ(ə)vetiʀ] (20) **1** *vt* **(a)** (*frm, hum: mettre*) *uniforme, habit* to don (*frm*), put on, array o.s. in (*frm*).

(b) (*prendre, avoir*) *caractère, importance* to take on, assume; *apparence, forme* to assume, appear in, take on. **une rencontre qui revêt une importance particulière** a meeting which takes on particular importance; **le langage humain revêt les formes les plus variées** human language appears in *ou* takes on the most varied forms.

(c) (*frm, hum: habiller*) *[vêtement]* to adorn. *[personne]* ~ **qn de** to dress *ou* array (*frm*) sb in; ~ **un prélat des vêtements sacerdotaux** to array (*frm*) *ou* clothe a prelate in his priestly robes.

(d) (*couvrir, déguiser*) ~ **qch de** to cloak sth in, cover sth with; ~ **la pauvreté d'un vernis respectable** to conceal poverty behind *ou* beneath a gloss of respectability.

(e) (*frm: investir de*) ~ **qn de** *dignité* to endow *ou* invest sb with; ~ **qn de l'autorité suprême** to endow *ou* invest sb with supreme authority; **l'autorité dont il était revêtu** the authority with which he was endowed *ou* invested.

(f) (*Admin, Jur*) ~ **un document de sa signature/d'un sceau** to append one's signature/a seal to a document.

(g) (*Tech*) (*enduire*) to coat (*de* with); (*couvrir*) *route* to surface (*de* with); *mur, sol* to cover (*de* with). ~ **un mur de boiseries** to (wood-)panel a wall; ~ **un mur de carreaux** to tile a wall, cover a wall with tiles; ~ **de plâtre** to plaster; ~ **de crépi** to face with roughcast, roughcast; ~ **d'un enduit imperméable** to cover with a waterproof coating, give a waterproof coating to; **rue revêtue d'un pavage** street which has been paved over; **les falaises que la tempête avait revêtues de neige** the cliffs (which) the storm had covered in snow.

2 se revêtir *vpr* (*mettre*) **se** ~ **de** (*frm*) to array o.s. in (*frm*), don (*frm*), dress o.s. in; (*littér*) **vers l'automne les sommets se revêtent de neige** as autumn draws near, the mountain tops don their snowy mantle (*littér*) *ou* are bedecked (*frm*) with snow.

revêtu, e [ʀ(ə)vety] (*ptp de* **revêtir**) *adj* **(a)** (*habillé de*) ~ **de** dressed in, wearing. **(b)** (*Tech*) *route* surfaced. **chemin non** ~ unsurfaced road. **(c)** (*Tech*) ~ **de** (*enduit de*) coated with.

rêveur, -euse [ʀɛvœʀ, øz] **1** *adj air, personne* dreamy. **il a l'esprit** ~ he's inclined to be a dreamer; **ça vous laisse** ~* the mind boggles*, it makes you wonder. **2** *nm,f* (*lit, péj*) dreamer.

rêveusement [ʀɛvøzmɑ̃] *adv* (*distraitement*) dreamily, as (if) in a dream; (*avec perplexité*) distractedly.

revient [ʀ(ə)vjɛ̃] *V* **prix.**

revigorer [R(ə)vigɔRe] (1) *vt [vent, air frais]* to invigorate; *[repas, boisson]* to revive, buck up*; *[discours, promesse]* to cheer, invigorate, buck up*. **un petit vent frais qui revigore** a bracing *ou* an invigorating cool breeze.

revirement [R(ə)viRmɑ̃] *nm* (*changement d'avis, volte-face*) change of mind, reversal (of opinion); (*changement brusque*) *[tendances]* reversal (*de* of); *[goûts]* (abrupt) change (*de* in); *[opinions]* change, turnaround (*de* in), revulsion (*frm*) (*de* of). ~ **d'opinion** change *ou* turnaround in public opinion, revulsion (*frm*) of public opinion; **un ~ soudain de la situation** a sudden reversal of the situation.

réviser [revize] (1) *vt*, **reviser** [Rəvize] (1) *vt* **(a)** *procès, règlement, constitution* to review; (*fig*) *croyance, opinion* to review, reappraise.
(b) *comptes* to audit; *liste* to revise; *texte, manuscrit* to revise, look over again; (*Typ*) *épreuves* to revise. **nouvelle édition complètement révisée** new and completely revised edition.
(c) (*Scol*) *sujet* to revise. ~ **son histoire** to revise history, do one's history revision; **commencer à** ~ to start revising *ou* (one's) revision.
(d) *moteur, installation* to overhaul, service; *montre* to service.

réviseur [revizœR] *nm*, **reviseur** [RəvizœR] *nm* reviser.

révision [revizjɔ̃] *nf*, **revision** [Rəvizjɔ̃] *nf* (*action, séance: V* **réviser**) review; reappraisal; auditing (*U*); revision (*U*); overhauling (*U*); servicing (*U*). ~ **des listes électorales** revision *ou* revising of the electoral register; (*Scol*) **faire ses ~s** to do one's revision, revise; (*Aut*) **prochaine ~ après 10.000 km** next major service after 10,000 km.

révisionnisme [revizjɔnism(ə)] *nm*, **revisionnisme** [Rəvizjɔnism(ə)] *nm* revisionism.

révisionniste [revizjɔnist(ə)] *nmf*, **revisionniste** [Rəvizjɔnist(ə)] *nmf* revisionist.

revisser [R(ə)vise] (1) *vt* to screw back again.

revitaliser [R(ə)vitalize] (1) *vt* to revitalize.

revivifier [R(ə)vivifje] (7) *vt* (*littér*) *personne* to re-enliven, revitalize; *souvenir* to revive, bring alive again.

revivre [RəvivR(ə)] (46) **1** *vi* **(a)** (*être ressuscité*) to live again. **on peut vraiment dire qu'il revit dans son fils** it's really true to say that he is living (over) again in his son.
(b) (*être revigoré*) to come alive again. **je me sentais ~** I felt alive again, I felt a new man (*ou* woman); **ouf, je revis!** whew! what a relief!, whew! I can breathe again!*
(c) (*se renouveler*) *[institution, coutumes, mode]* to be revived.
(d) faire ~ (*ressusciter*) to bring back to life, restore to life; (*revigorer*) to revive, put new life in *ou* into; (*remettre en honneur*) *mode, époque, usage* to revive; (*remettre en mémoire*) to bring back; **faire ~ un personnage/une époque dans un roman** to bring a character/an era back to life in a novel; **le grand air m'a fait ~** the fresh air put new life in me; **ce spectacle faisait ~ tout un monde que j'avais cru oublié** this sight brought back a whole world I thought I had forgotten.
2 *vt passé, période* (*lit*) to relive, live (through) again; (*en imagination*) to relive, live (over) again (*fig*).

révocabilité [revɔkabilite] *nf [contrat]* revocability; *[fonctionnaire]* removability.

révocable [revɔkabl(ə)] *adj legs, contrat* revocable; *fonctionnaire* removable, dismissible.

révocation [revɔkɑsjɔ̃] *nf* (*V* **révoquer**) removal (from office), dismissal; revocation.

revoici* [R(ə)vwasi] *prép*, **revoilà*** [R(ə)vwala] *prép*: ~ **Paul!** Paul's back (again)!, here's Paul again!; **me ~!** it's me again!, here I am again!; **nous ~ à la maison/en France** here we are, back home/in France (again); ~ **la mer** here's the sea again; **le ~ qui se plaint!** there he goes complaining again!

revoir [R(ə)vwaR] (30) *vt* **(a)** (*retrouver*) *personne* to see *ou* meet again; *village, patrie* to see again. **je l'ai revu deux ou trois fois depuis** I've seen him two or three times since, we've met two or three times since; **quand le revois-tu?** when are you seeing *ou* meeting him again?, when are you meeting again?; **au ~!** goodbye!; **au ~ Monsieur/Madame** goodbye Mr X/Mrs X; **dire au ~ à qn** to say goodbye to sb; **faire au ~ de la main** to wave goodbye; **ce n'était heureusement qu'un au ~** fortunately it was only a temporary farewell *ou* goodbye; *V* **plaisir.**
(b) (*apercevoir de nouveau*) to see again.
(c) (*regarder de nouveau*) *photos* to see again, have another look at; *film, exposition* to see again. **je suis allé ~ ce film** I went to (see) that film again.
(d) (*être à nouveau témoin de*) *atrocités, scène* to witness *ou* see again; *conditions* to see again. **craignant de ~ s'installer le chômage** afraid of seeing unemployment settle in again.
(e) (*imaginer de nouveau*) to see again. **je la revois encore, dans sa cuisine** I can still see her there in her kitchen; **je me revoyais écolier, dans mon village natal** I saw myself as a schoolboy again, back in the village where I was born.
(f) (*réviser*) *texte, édition* to revise; (*Scol*) *leçons* to revise, go over again. **édition revue et corrigée** revised and corrected edition.

revoler[1] [R(ə)vɔle] (1) *vi [pilote, oiseau]* to fly again.

revoler[2] [R(ə)vɔle] (1) *vt*: ~ **qch** to steal sth again.

révoltant, e [revɔltɑ̃, ɑ̃t] *adj* revolting, appalling.

révolte [revɔlt(ə)] *nf* **(a)** (*rébellion*) revolt, rebellion. **les paysans sont en ~ contre** the peasants are in revolt against *ou* up in arms against. **(b)** (*indignation, opposition*) rebellion, revolt.

révolté, e [revɔlte] (*ptp de* **révolter**) **1** *adj* **(a)** rebellious, in revolt (*attrib*). **(b)** (*outré*) outraged, incensed. **2** *nm,f* rebel.

révolter [revɔlte] (1) **1** *vt* (*indigner*) to revolt, outrage, appal. **ceci nous révolte** we are revolted *ou* outraged by this.
2 se révolter *vpr* **(a)** *[personne]* (*s'insurger*) to revolt, rebel, rise up (*contre* against); (*se cabrer*) to rebel (*contre* against).
(b) (*s'indigner*) to be revolted *ou* repelled (*contre* by); to rebel (*contre* against). **à cette vue tout mon être se révolte** my whole being revolts *ou* rebels at this sight; **l'esprit se révolte contre une telle propagande** the mind revolts at *ou* against *ou* is repelled *ou* revolted by such propaganda.

révolu, e [revɔly] *adj* **(a)** (*littér: de jadis*) *jours, époque* past, bygone (*épith*), gone by. **des jours ~s** past *ou* bygone days, days gone by; **rêvant à l'époque ~e des diligences** dreaming of the bygone days of stagecoaches.
(b) (*fini*) *époque, jours* past, in the past (*attrib*). **cette époque est ~e — nous devons penser à l'avenir** that era is in the past — we have to think of the future.
(c) (*Admin: complété*) **âgé de 20 ans ~s** over 20 years of age; **avoir 20 ans ~s** to be over 20 years of age; **après 2 ans ~s** when two full years had (*ou* have) passed.

révolution [revɔlysjɔ̃] *nf* **(a)** (*rotation*) revolution.
(b) (*changement, révolte*) revolution. ~ **violente/pacifique** violent/peaceful revolution; **la R~ (française)** the French Revolution; **la ~ industrielle** the industrial revolution.
(c) la ~ (*parti, forces de la révolution*) the forces of revolution.
(d) (*loc*) **être en ~** to be in (an) uproar; *[invention, procédé, idée]* **faire ~ dans** to revolutionize.

révolutionnaire [revɔlysjɔnɛR] **1** *adj* (*gén*) revolutionary; (*Hist*) Revolutionary, of the French Revolution. **2** *nmf* (*gén*) revolutionary; (*Hist*) Revolutionary (*in the French Revolution*).

révolutionner [revɔlysjɔne] (1) *vt* **(a)** (*transformer radicalement*) to revolutionize.
(b) (*: *bouleverser*) *personne* to stir up. **son arrivée a révolutionné le quartier** his arrival stirred up the whole neighbourhood *ou* caused a great stir in the neighbourhood.

revolver [revɔlvɛR] *nm* (*pistolet*) (*gén*) gun; (*à barillet*) revolver; **microscope à ~** microscope with a revolving nose-piece; **tour ~** capstan lathe, turret lathe; *V* **coup, poche**[1].

révoquer [revɔke] (1) *vt* **(a)** (*destituer*) *magistrat, fonctionnaire* to remove from office, dismiss. **(b)** (*annuler*) *legs, contrat, édit* to revoke, repeal, rescind. **(c)** (*littér*) ~ **qch en doute** to call sth into question, question sth, cast doubt on sth.

revouloir* [R(ə)vulwaR] (31) *vt* **(a)** (*désirer à nouveau*) *jouer etc* to want again. **(b) en ~: il en reveut** he wants some more.

revoyure‡ [R(ə)vwajyR] *excl*: **à la ~!** see you!‡, (I'll) be seeing you!‡

revue [R(ə)vy] **1** *nf* **(a)** (*examen*) ~ **de** review of; **faire la ~ de** to review, go through; **une ~ de la presse hebdomadaire** a review of the weekly press.
(b) (*Mil: inspection des troupes*) inspection, review; (*parade*) march-past, review.
(c) (*magazine*) (*à fort tirage, illustré*) magazine; (*spécialisée*) journal; (*érudite*) review.
(d) (*spectacle*) (*satirique*) revue; (*de variétés*) variety show *ou* performance. ~ **à grand spectacle** revue spectacular.
(e) (*loc*) **passer en ~** (*Mil*) to pass in review, review, inspect; (*fig: énumérer mentalement*) to pass in review, go through.
2: (*Mil*) **revue d'armement** arms inspection; (*Mil*) **revue de détail** kit inspection; **revue de presse** review of the press *ou* papers.

révulsé, e [revylse] (*ptp de* **se révulser**) *adj yeux* rolled upwards (*attrib*); *visage* contorted.

révulser (se) [revylse] (1) *vpr [visage]* to contort; *[yeux]* to roll upwards.

révulsif, -ive [revylsif, iv] (*Méd*) **1** *adj* revulsant. **2** *nm* revulsant, revulsive.

rez-de-chaussée [redʃose] *nm inv* ground floor (*Brit*), first floor (*US*). **au ~** on the ground floor; **habiter un ~** to live in a ground-floor flat.

rhabillage [Rabijaʒ] *nm*: **pendant le ~ des mannequins** while the models were (*ou* are) dressing (themselves) (again) *ou* were (*ou* are) putting their clothes back on.

rhabiller [Rabije] (1) **1** *vt* **(a)** ~ **qn** (*lit*) to dress sb again, put sb's clothes back on; (*lui racheter des habits*) to fit sb out again, reclothe sb.
(b) (*rare*) *édifice* to renovate. **un immeuble rhabillé façon moderne** a renovated and modernized building.
2 se rhabiller *vpr* to put one's clothes back on, dress (o.s.) again. **va te ~!‡, tu peux aller te ~!‡** (you can go and) get lost!‡.

rhabituer [Rabitɥe] (1) = **réhabituer.**

rhapsode [Rapsɔd] *nm* rhapsode.

rhapsodie [Rapsɔdi] *nf* rhapsody.

rhénan, e [Renɑ̃, an] *adj* (*Géog*) Rhine (*épith*), of the Rhine; (*Art*) Rhenish.

Rhénanie [Renani] *nf* Rhineland.

rhéostat [Reɔsta] *nm* rheostat.

rhésus [Rezys] *nm* **(a)** (*Méd*) Rhesus. **(b)** (*Zool*) rhesus monkey. ~ **positif/négatif** Rhesus *ou* Rh positive/negative; *V* **facteur.**

rhéteur [RetœR] *nm* (*Hist*) rhetor.

rhétoricien, -ienne [RetɔRisjɛ̃, jɛn] *nm,f* (*lit, péj*) rhetorician.

rhétorique [RetɔRik] **1** *nf* rhetoric; *V* **figure, fleur. 2** *adj* rhetorical.

rhéto-roman, e [RetɔRɔmɑ̃, an] **1** *adj* Rhaeto-Romanic. **2** *nm* (*Ling*) Rhaeto-Romanic.

Rhin [Rɛ̃] *nm*: **le ~** the Rhine.

rhinite [Rinit] *nf* rhinitis (*T*).

rhinocéros [RinɔseRɔs] *nm* rhinoceros.

rhinolaryngite [RinɔlaRɛ̃ʒit] *nf* sore throat, throat infection, rhinolaryngitis (*T*).

rhinologie [ʀinɔlɔʒi] *nf* rhinology.

rhinopharyngien, -ienne [ʀinɔfaʀɛ̃ʒjɛ̃, jɛn] *adj* rhinopharyngeal.

rhinopharyngite [ʀinɔfaʀɛ̃ʒit] *nf* sore throat, throat infection, rhinopharyngitis (*T*).

rhizome [ʀizom] *nm* rhizome.

rhodanien, -ienne [ʀɔdanjɛ̃, jɛn] *adj* Rhone (*épith*), of the Rhone.

Rhodes [ʀɔd] *n* Rhodes. **l'île de ~** the island of Rhodes; *V* colosse.

Rhodésie [ʀɔdezi] *nf* Rhodesia.

rhodésien, -ienne [ʀɔdezjɛ̃, jɛn] **1** *adj* Rhodesian. **2** *nm,f*: **R~(ne)** Rhodesian.

rhododendron [ʀɔdɔdɛ̃dʀɔ̃] *nm* rhododendron.

Rhône [ʀon] *nm*: **le ~** the (river) Rhone.

rhovyl [ʀɔvil] *nm* vinyl.

rhubarbe [ʀybaʀb(ə)] *nf* rhubarb.

rhum [ʀɔm] *nm* rum.

rhumatisant, e [ʀymatizɑ̃, ɑ̃t] *adj, nm,f* rheumatic.

rhumatismal, e, *mpl* **-aux** [ʀymatismal, o] *adj* rheumatic.

rhumatisme [ʀymatism(ə)] *nm* rheumatism (*U*). **avoir un ~** *ou* **des ~s dans le bras** to have rheumatism in one's arm; **~ articulaire** rheumatoid arthritis (*U*); **~ déformant** polyarthritis.

rhumatologie [ʀymatɔlɔʒi] *nf* rheumatology.

rhumatologue [ʀymatɔlɔg] *nmf* rheumatologist.

rhume [ʀym] *nm* cold. **attraper un (gros) ~** to catch a (bad *ou* heavy) cold; **~ de cerveau** head cold; **~ des foins** hay fever.

rhumerie [ʀɔmʀi] *nf* (*distillerie*) rum distillery.

ria [ʀija] *nf* ria.

riant, e [ʀjɑ̃, ɑ̃t] *adj paysage* smiling; *atmosphère, perspective* cheerful, pleasant, happy; *visage* cheerful, smiling, happy.

ribambelle [ʀibɑ̃bɛl] *nf*: **~ de** *enfants* swarm *ou* herd *ou* flock of; *animaux* herd of; *noms* string of.

ribaud [ʀibo] *nm* (†† *ou hum*) bawdy *ou* ribald fellow.

ribaude†† [ʀibod] *nf* trollop†‡, bawdy wench††.

ribonucleïque [ʀibonykleik] *adj*: **acide ~** ribonucleic acid.

ribote [ʀibɔt] *nf* († *ou* *) merrymaking (*U*), revel, carousing† (*U*). **être en ~, faire ~** to make merry, carouse†.

ribouldingue*† [ʀibuldɛ̃g] *nf* spree, binge*. **deux jours de ~** two days on the spree *ou* the binge*; **faire la ~** to go on the spree *ou* the binge*.

ricain, e‡ [ʀikɛ̃, ɛn] (*péj*) **1** *adj* Yank(ee)* (*péj*). **2** *nm,f*: **R~(e)** Yank(ee)*.

ricanement [ʀikanmɑ̃] *nm* (*V* **ricaner**) snigger, sniggering (*U*); giggle, giggling (*U*); nervous *ou* self-conscious *ou* an embarrassed laugh *ou* laughter (*U*).

ricaner [ʀikane] (1) *vi* (*méchamment*) to snigger; (*bêtement*) to giggle (away); (*avec gêne*) to laugh nervously *ou* self-consciously, give a nervous *ou* an embarrassed laugh.

ricaneur, -euse [ʀikanœʀ, øz] (*V* **ricaner**) **1** *adj* sniggering; giggling. **2** *nm,f* sniggerer; giggler.

Richard [ʀiʃaʀ] *nm* Richard.

richard, e* [ʀiʃaʀ, aʀd(ə)] *nm,f* (*péj*) moneybags* (*inv*).

riche [ʀiʃ] **1** *adj* **(a)** (*nanti*) *personne* rich, wealthy, well-off (*attrib*); *pays* rich. **il est ~ à millions** he is enormously wealthy; **~ comme Crésus** as rich as Croesus, fabulously rich *ou* wealthy; **c'est un ~ parti** he (*ou* she) is an excellent match; **faire un ~ mariage** to marry into a wealthy family, marry (into) money; **vous savez, nous ne sommes pas ~s** we're by no means rich *ou* we're not very well-off, you know.

(b) (*luxueux*) *étoffes, bijoux* rich, costly; *coloris* rich; *mobilier* sumptuous, costly. **je vous donne ce stylo, mais ce n'est pas un ~ cadeau** I'll give you this pen but it's not much of a gift; **ça fait ~*** it looks plush(y)* *ou* expensive *ou* posh*.

(c) (*fertile, consistant*) *terre, aliment, mélange, sujet* rich. **le français est une langue ~** French is a rich language; **c'est une ~ idée** that's a great* *ou* grand idea; **c'est une ~ nature** he (*ou* she) is a person of immense resources *ou* qualities.

(d) (*abondant*) *moisson* rich; *végétation* rich, lush; *collection* large, rich; *vocabulaire* rich, wide. **il y a une documentation très ~ sur ce sujet** there is a wealth of *ou* a vast amount of information on this subject.

(e) ~ en *calories, gibier, monuments* rich in; **~ de** *possibilités, espérances* full of; **~ en protéines** with a high protein content, rich in protein; **je ne suis pas ~ en sucre** I'm not very well-off for sugar; **c'est une aventure ~ d'enseignements** you learn a great deal from this venture, this venture is a tremendous learning experience; **il est revenu, ~ de souvenirs** he returned with a wealth of memories.

2 *nmf* rich *ou* wealthy person. **les ~s** the rich, the wealthy.

richement [ʀiʃmɑ̃] *adv récompenser, vêtir* richly; *décoré, meublé* richly, sumptuously. **marier ~ sa fille** to marry one's daughter into a wealthy family, find a rich *ou* wealthy match *ou* husband for one's daughter; **~ illustré** richly *ou* lavishly illustrated, with lavish *ou* copious illustrations.

richesse [ʀiʃɛs] *nf* **(a)** *[personne, pays]* wealth. **la ~ ne l'a pas changé** wealth *ou* being rich hasn't altered him; **vivre dans la ~** to be wealthy *ou* very comfortably off; **ce n'est pas la ~, mais c'est mieux que rien*** it's not exactly the lap of luxury but it's better than nothing.

(b) *[ameublement, décor]* sumptuousness, costliness, richness; *[étoffe, coloris]* richness.

(c) *[sol, texte, aliment, collection]* richness; *[végétation]* richness, lushness. **la ~ de son vocabulaire** the richness of his vocabulary, his wide *ou* rich vocabulary; **la ~ de cette documentation** the abundance *ou* fullness of the information; **la ~ en calcium de cet aliment** the high calcium content of this food; **la ~ en matières premières/en gibier de cette région** the abundance of raw materials/of game in this region; **la ~ en pétrole/en minéraux du pays** the country's abundant *ou* vast oil/mineral resources.

(d) (*fig: bien*) blessing. **la santé est une ~** good health is a great blessing *ou* is a boon, it's a blessing to be healthy.

(e) ~s (*argent*) riches, wealth; (*ressources*) wealth; (*fig: trésors*) treasures; **entasser des ~s** to pile up riches; **la répartition des ~s d'un pays** the distribution of a country's wealth; **l'exploitation des ~s naturelles** the exploitation of natural resources; **découvrir les ~s d'un art/d'un musée** to discover the treasures of an art/a museum; **montrez-nous toutes vos ~s** show us all your precious possessions *ou* all your treasures.

richissime [ʀiʃisim] *adj* fabulously rich *ou* wealthy.

ricin [ʀisɛ̃] *nm* castor oil plant; *V* **huile**.

ricocher [ʀikɔʃe] (1) *vi [balle de fusil]* to rebound, ricochet; *[pierre etc]* to rebound; (*sur l'eau*) to bounce. **~ sur** to rebound *ou* ricochet off, rebound *ou* glance off, bounce on *ou* off; **faire ~ un caillou sur l'eau** to skim a pebble across the water, make a pebble bounce on the water.

ricochet [ʀikɔʃɛ] *nm* (*gén*) rebound; *[balle de fusil]* ricochet; *[caillou sur l'eau]* bounce. **faire ~** (*lit*) to rebound (*sur* off), bounce (*sur* on, off); (*fig*) to rebound; **il a été blessé par ~** he was wounded on the rebound *ou* as the bullet rebounded; (*fig*) **par ~, il a perdu son emploi** as an indirect result he lost his job; **(s'amuser à) faire des ~s** to skim pebbles, play ducks and drakes; **il a fait 4 ~s** he made the pebble bounce 4 times.

ric-rac‡ [ʀikʀak] *adv* (*de justesse*) by the skin of one's teeth; *payer* on the nail*. **quand on lui confie un travail, il le fait toujours ~** when you give him a job to do he's always spot on with it*.

rictus [ʀiktys] *nm* (*sourire grimaçant*) grin; *[animal, dément]* (snarling) grimace. **~ moqueur/cruel** mocking *ou* sardonic/cruel grin.

ride [ʀid] *nf [peau, pomme]* wrinkle (*de* in); *[eau, sable]* ripple (*de* on, in), ridge (*de* in). **les ~s de son front** the wrinkles *ou* lines on his forehead; **visage creusé de ~s** deeply lined face, wrinkled face.

rideau, *pl* **~x** [ʀido] **1** *nm* **(a)** (*draperie*) curtain. **tirer les ~x** (*fermer*) to draw *ou* close the curtains (*Brit*) *ou* drapes (*US*), draw the curtains to; (*ouvrir*) to draw the curtains, pull *ou* draw the curtains back; (*fig*) **tirer le ~ sur** *passé, défaut* to draw a veil over.

(b) (*Théât*) curtain. **~ à 8 heures** the curtain rises at 8 o'clock, (the) curtain's at 8 (o'clock); **~!** (*cri des spectateurs*) curtain!; (**fig: assez*) that's enough!, I've had enough!

(c) *[boutique]* shutter; *[cheminée]* register, blower; *[secrétaire, classeur]* roll shutter; *[appareil-photo]* shutter.

(d) (*fig: écran*) **~ de** *arbres, verdure* curtain *ou* screen of; *policiers, troupes* curtain of; *pluie* curtain *ou* sheet of.

2: rideaux bonne femme looped curtains (*Brit*) *ou* drapes (*US*); **rideau de fer** *[boutique]* metal shutter(s); *[théâtre]* (metal) safety curtain; (*Pol*) **le rideau de fer** the Iron Curtain; **les pays au-delà du rideau de fer** the Iron Curtain countries; **rideau de fumée** smoke screen; **rideaux de lit** bed hangings *ou* curtains.

ridelle [ʀidɛl] *nf [camion, charrette]* slatted side, raves (*pl*).

rider [ʀide] (1) **1** *vt peau, fruit* to wrinkle; *front [colère, soucis]* to wrinkle; *[âge]* to line with wrinkles; *eau* to ripple, ruffle the surface of; *sable, neige* to ruffle *ou* wrinkle the surface of.

2 se rider *vpr* to become wrinkled, become lined with wrinkles; to ripple, become rippled. **à ces mots, son front se rida** his forehead wrinkled *ou* he wrinkled his forehead at these words.

ridicule [ʀidikyl] **1** *adj* **(a)** (*grotesque*) *personne, conduite, vêtement* ridiculous, ludicrous, absurd; *prétentions* ridiculous, laughable; *superstition* ridiculous, silly. **se rendre ~ aux yeux de tous** to make o.s. (look) ridiculous *ou* make a fool of o.s. *ou* make o.s. look a fool in everyone's eyes; **ça le rend ~** it makes him look ridiculous *ou* a fool; **ne sois pas ~** don't be ridiculous *ou* silly *ou* absurd.

(b) (*infime*) *prix* ridiculous, ridiculously low; *quantité* ridiculous, ridiculously small.

2 *nm* **(a)** (*U: absurdité*) ridiculousness, absurdity. **le ~ de la conversation ne lui échappait pas** he was well aware of the absurdity of the conversation; **je ne sais pas si vous saisissez tout le ~ de la situation** I don't know if you realize just how absurd *ou* ridiculous the situation is *ou* if you realize the full absurdity of the situation; **il y a quelque ~ à faire ...** it is rather ridiculous to do ... ; **c'est d'un ~ achevé** it's perfectly *ou* utterly ridiculous; **se donner le ~ de ...** to be ridiculous enough to ... ; *V* **tourner**.

(b) le ~ ridicule; **tomber dans le ~** *[personne]* to make o.s. ridiculous, become ridiculous; *[film]* to become ridiculous; **s'exposer au ~** to expose o.s. *ou* lay o.s. open to ridicule; **avoir le sens du ~** to have a sense of the ridiculous; **la peur du ~** (the) fear of ridicule *ou* of appearing ridiculous; **le ~ ne tue pas** ridicule has never been the unmaking of anyone, ridicule never killed anyone; **couvrir qn de ~** to heap ridicule on sb, make sb look ridiculous.

(c) (*travers*) **~s** silliness (*U*), ridiculous *ou* silly ways, absurdities; **les ~s humains** the absurdities of human nature; **les ~s d'une classe sociale** the ridiculous ways *ou* the (little) absurdities of a social class.

ridiculement [ʀidikylmɑ̃] *adv vêtu, bas* ridiculously; *marcher, chanter* in a ridiculous way.

ridiculiser [ʀidikylize] (1) **1** *vt personne, défaut, doctrine* to ridicule, hold up to ridicule. **2 se ridiculiser** *vpr* to make o.s. (look) ridiculous, make a fool of o.s.

rien [ʀjɛ̃] **1** *pron indéf* **(a)** (*avec ne*) nothing. **je n'ai ~ entendu** I didn't hear anything, I didn't hear a thing, I heard nothing; **~ ne le fera reculer** nothing will make him go back; **il n'y a ~ qui**

puisse m'empêcher de there's nothing that could prevent me from; **il n'y a ~ que je ne fasse pour elle** there's nothing I wouldn't do for her; **on ne pouvait plus ~ pour elle** there was nothing more *ou* else to be done for her, nothing more could be done for her; **il n'y a plus ~** there's nothing left; *V* **comprendre, risquer, valoir.**

(b) ~ de + *adj, ptp* nothing; **~ d'autre** nothing else; **~ de plus** nothing more *ou* else *ou* further; **~ de moins** nothing less; **~ de neuf** nothing new; **il n'y a ~ eu de volé** nothing was stolen, there was nothing stolen; **nous n'avons ~ d'autre** *ou* **de plus à ajouter** we have nothing else *ou* more *ou* further to add; **il n'est ~ de tel qu'une bonne pêche** there's nothing like *ou* nothing to beat a good peach, you can't beat a good peach*; **cela n'a ~ d'impossible** there's nothing impossible about it; **~ de plus facile** nothing easier; **elle a fait ce qu'il fallait, ~ de plus, ~ de moins** she did all she had to, nothing more nor less *ou* nothing more, nothing less.

(c) ~ que: ~ que la chambre coûte déjà très cher the room alone already costs a great deal; **la vérité, ~ que la vérité** the truth and nothing but the truth; **~ qu'à le voir, j'ai deviné** just looking at him I guessed, just looking at him was enough to let me guess; **je voudrais vous voir, ~ qu'une minute** could I see you just for a minute; **il le fait ~ que pour l'embêter*** he does it just to annoy him.

(d) (= *quelque chose*) anything. **avez-vous jamais ~ fait pour l'aider?** have you ever done anything to help him?; **as-tu jamais lu ~ de plus drôle?** have you ever read anything funnier?; **sans ~ qui le prouve** without anything to prove it; **sans que/avant que tu en saches ~** without your knowing/before you know anything about it; **avez-vous jamais ~ vu de pareil?** have you ever seen such a thing? *ou* anything like it? *ou* the like?

(e) (*intensif*) **~ au monde** nothing on earth *ou* in the world; **~ du tout** nothing at all; **~ de ~*** nothing, absolutely nothing; **il ne fait ~, mais ~ de ~*** he does nothing, and I mean nothing *ou* but nothing (at all); **je ne connais ~ au monde de plus bête** I know of nothing on earth more stupid; **deux** *ou* **trois fois ~** next to nothing.

(f) (*Sport*) nil, nothing; (*Tennis*) love. **~ à ~, ~ partout** nothing all; love all; (*Tennis*) **15 à ~** 15 love.

(g) (*avec avoir, être, faire*) **n'avoir ~ contre qn** to have nothing against sb; **il n'a ~ d'un politicien/d'un dictateur** *etc* he's got nothing of the politician/dictator *etc* in *ou* about him; **il n'a ~ de son père** he's nothing *ou* not a bit like his father; **n'être ~** *[personne]* to be a nobody; *[chose]* to be nothing; **n'être ~ en comparaison de ...** to be nothing compared to ... ; **il n'est ~ dans la maison** he's a nobody *ou* he's nothing in the firm; **n'être ~ à qn** to be nothing to do with sb; **il ne nous est ~** he's not connected with us, he's nothing to do with us; **n'être pour ~ dans une affaire** to have no hand in *ou* have nothing to do with an affair; **on le croyait blessé, mais il n'en est ~** we thought he was injured but he's not at all *ou* he's nothing of the sort; **élever 4 enfants, ça n'est pas ~** bringing up 4 children is not exactly a picnic* *ou* is no mean feat; **ne ~ faire: il ne fait (plus) ~** he doesn't work (any more); **huit jours sans ~ faire** a week doing nothing; **il ne nous a ~ fait** he hasn't done anything to us; **cela ne lui fait ~** he doesn't mind *ou* care, it doesn't make any odds* (*surtout Brit*) *ou* it doesn't matter to him; **ça ne fait ~*** it doesn't matter, never mind; **~ à faire!** it's no good!, nothing doing!*, it's not on!* (*surtout Brit*).

(h) (*loc*) **je vous remercie — de ~*** thank you — you're welcome *ou* don't mention it *ou* not at all; **c'est cela ou ~** take it or leave it; **(c'est) mieux que ~** it's better than nothing; **(c'est) moins que ~** it's nothing at all; **ce que tu fais ou ~!** your efforts are useless, you may as well not bother; **c'est à moi, ~ qu'à moi** it's mine and mine alone; (*iro*) **il voulait 500 F, ~ que ça!** he wanted a mere 500 francs (*iro*), he just *ou* only wanted 500 francs (*iro*); **~ (du tout): une petite blessure de ~ (du tout)** a trifling *ou* trivial little injury; (*péj*) **une fille de ~** a worthless girl; **cela ne nous gêne en ~ (du tout)** it doesn't bother us in any way *ou* at all; **pour ~** (*peu cher*) for a song, for next to nothing; (*inutilement*) for nothing; **on n'a ~ pour ~** you get nothing for nothing, you get what you pay for; **ce n'est pas pour ~ que ...** it is not without cause *ou* good reason *ou* it's not for nothing that ... ; **~ moins que sûr** anything but sure, not at all sure; **il ne s'agit de ~ moins qu'un crime** it's nothing less than a crime; **il ne s'agit de ~ (de) moins que d'abattre 2 forêts** it will mean nothing less than chopping down 2 forests; (*Prov*) **~ ne sert de courir, il faut partir à point** *ou* **temps** slow and steady wins the race; *V* **comme, compter, dire** *etc.*

2 *nm* **(a)** (*néant*) nothingness.

(b) un ~ a mere nothing; **des ~s** trivia; **il a peur d'un ~, un ~ l'effraie** every little thing *ou* anything frightens him; **un ~ le fait rire** he laughs at every little thing *ou* anything at all; **un ~ l'habille** she looks good in the simplest thing; **il pleure pour un ~** he cries at the drop of a hat *ou* at the slightest little thing; **comme un ~*** no bother*, no trouble (at all); **on fait Paris-Tokyo comme un ~ de nos jours*** these days you can go from Paris to Tokyo no bother* (at all) *ou* (with) no trouble (at all).

(c) un ~ de a touch *ou* hint of; **mettez-y un ~ de muscade** add a touch *ou* a tiny pinch of nutmeg; **un ~ de vin** a taste of wine; **un ~ de fantaisie** a touch of fantasy; **avec un ~ d'ironie** with a hint *ou* touch of irony; **en un ~ de temps** in no time (at all), in next to no time.

(d) un ~ (*adv: gén **) a tiny bit, a shade; **c'est un ~ bruyant ici** it's a bit *ou* a shade noisy in here.

(e) c'est un/une ~ du tout (*social*) he/she is a nobody; (*moral*) he/she is no good.

3 *adv* (**:**) (*très*) not half**:**. **c'est ~ impressionnant cette cérémonie** this ceremony isn't half impressive**:**; **il fait ~ froid ici** it isn't half cold *ou* it's damned cold here**:**; **ils sont ~ snobs** they aren't half snobs**:**.

rieur, rieuse [RjœR, Rjøz] **1** *adj personne* cheerful, merry; *yeux, expression* cheerful, laughing.

2 *nm,f*: **les ~s se turent** people stopped laughing; **avoir les ~s de son côté** to have the laughs on one's side, have people laughing with one rather than at one.

rififi [Rififi] *nm* (*arg Crime*) trouble.

riflard*† [RiflaR] *nm* (*parapluie*) brolly*.

rigaudon [Rigodɔ̃] *nm* rigadoon.

rigide [Riʒid] *adj* **(a)** *armature, tige* rigid, stiff; *muscle* stiff; *carton* stiff. **livre à couverture ~** hardback (book), book with a stiff cover.

(b) *caractère* rigid, inflexible; *règle* strict, rigid, hard and fast; *classification, éducation* strict; *morale, politique* strict, rigid.

rigidement [Riʒidmɑ̃] *adv élever un enfant* strictly; *appliquer un règlement* strictly, rigidly.

rigidité [Riʒidite] *nf* (*V* **rigide**) rigidity, rigidness; stiffness; inflexibility; strictness. **~ cadavérique** rigor mortis.

rigodon [Rigodɔ̃] *nm* = **rigaudon.**

rigolade* [Rigɔlad] *nf* **(a)** (*amusement*) **il aime la ~** he likes a bit of fun *ou* a laugh*; **on a eu une bonne partie** *ou* **séance de ~** it was *ou* we had a good laugh* *ou* a lot of fun; **quelle ~, quand il est entré!** what a laugh* *ou* a kill**:** (*Brit*) when he came in!; **il n'y a pas que la ~ dans la vie** having fun isn't the only thing in life; **il prend tout à la ~** he thinks everything's a big joke *ou* laugh*, he makes a joke of everything.

(b) (*loc*) **démonter ça, c'est une** *ou* **de la ~** taking that to pieces is child's play *ou* is a cinch*; **ce qu'il dit là, c'est de la ~** what he says is a lot of *ou* a load of hooey**:**; **ce procès est une (vaste) ~** this trial is a (big) joke* *ou* farce; **cette crème amaigrissante c'est de la ~** this slimming cream is a complete con**:**.

rigolard, e* [RigɔlaR, aRd(ə)] *adj personne, air* grinning. **c'est un ~** he's always ready for a laugh*, he likes a good laugh*.

rigole [Rigɔl] *nf* (*canal*) channel; (*filet d'eau*) rivulet; (*Agr: sillon*) furrow. **la pluie avait creusé des ~s dans le sol** the rain had cut channels in the earth; **~ d'irrigation** irrigation channel; **~ d'écoulement** drain.

rigoler* [Rigɔle] (1) *vi* **(a)** (*rire*) to laugh. **quand il l'a su, il a bien rigolé** when he found out, he had a good laugh about it*; **il nous a bien fait ~** he had us all laughing *ou* in stitches*; (*iro*) **tu me fais ~** you make me laugh; (*iro*) **ne me fais pas ~** don't make me laugh; **il n'y a pas de quoi ~** that's nothing to laugh about, what's so funny?*

(b) (*s'amuser*) to have (a bit of) fun, have a (bit of a) laugh*. **il aime ~** he likes a bit of fun *ou* a good laugh*; **on a bien rigolé, en vacances** we had great fun *ou* a good laugh* on holiday; **chez eux on ne doit pas ~ tous les jours!** it can't be much fun at home for them!

(c) (*plaisanter*) to joke. **tu rigoles!** you're kidding!**:** *ou* joking!; **je ne rigole pas** I'm not joking *ou* kidding**:**; **il ne faut pas ~ avec ces médicaments** you shouldn't mess about* with medicines like these; **il ne faut pas ~ avec ce genre de maladie** an illness like this has to be taken seriously *ou* can't be taken lightly; **j'ai dit ça pour ~** it was only a joke, I only said it in fun *ou* for a laugh*.

rigolo, -ote* [Rigɔlo, ɔt] **1** *adj film, histoire* funny, killing*; *personne* funny, comical. **il est ~** (*plaisantin*) he's a laugh* *ou* a kill**:**, he's funny; (*original*) he's comical *ou* funny, he's a comic; **ce qui lui est arrivé n'est pas ~** what's happened to him is no joke *ou* is not funny; (*iro*) **vous êtes ~, vous, mettez-vous à ma place!** funny aren't you?* *ou* you make me laugh — put yourself in my shoes!; **c'est ~, je n'avais jamais remarqué cela** that's funny *ou* odd, I had never noticed that.

2 *nm,f* (*amusant*) comic, wag; (*péj: fumiste*) fraud, phoney, chancer**:** (*Brit*). **c'est un sacré ~** he likes a good laugh*, he's a real scream*; (*péj*) **c'est un (petit) ~** he's a (little) chancer**:** (*Brit*) *ou* fraud.

3 *nm* (*arg Crime: revolver*) rod (*US*), gat (*arg*).

rigorisme [Rigɔrism(ə)] *nm* rigorism, austerity, rigid moral standards.

rigoriste [Rigɔrist(ə)] **1** *adj* rigoristic, austere, rigid. **2** *nmf* rigorist, rigid moralist.

rigoureusement [RiguRøzmɑ̃] *adv* **(a)** *punir, traiter* harshly; *raisonner, démontrer* rigorously; *appliquer, classifier* rigorously, strictly. **(b)** (*absolument*) *authentique, vrai* absolutely, utterly, entirely; *exact* rigorously; *interdit* strictly. **ce n'est pas ~ vrai** it's not entirely *ou* strictly true.

rigoureux, -euse [RiguRø, øz] *adj* **(a)** (*sévère*) *punition, discipline* rigorous, harsh, severe; *mesures* rigorous, stringent, harsh; (*fig*) *climat* rigorous, harsh; *maître, moraliste* rigorous, strict, rigid. **hiver ~** hard *ou* harsh winter.

(b) (*exact*) *raisonnement, style, méthode* rigorous; *définition, classification* rigorous, strict.

(c) (*absolu*) *interdiction, sens d'un mot* strict. **observation ~euse du règlement** strict observation of the rule; **ce n'est pas une règle ~euse** it's not a hard-and-fast *ou* an absolute and unbreakable rule.

rigueur [RigœR] *nf* **(a)** (*sévérité*) *[condamnation, discipline]* harshness, severity, rigour; *[mesures]* harshness, stringency, rigour; *[climat, hiver]* rigour, harshness. **punir qn avec toute la ~ de la loi** to punish sb with the utmost rigour of the law; **faire preuve de ~ à l'égard de qn** to be strict *ou* harsh with sb, be hard on sb; **traiter qn avec la plus grande ~** to treat sb with the utmost rigour *ou* harshness *ou* severity; (*littér*) **les ~s du sort/de l'hiver** the rigours of fate/winter; *jv* **arrêt, délai.**

(b) (*austérité*) *[morale]* rigour, rigidness, strictness; *[personne]* sternness, strictness.

(c) (*précision*) *[raisonnement, style, pensée]* rigour; *[calcul]* precision, exactness; *[définition, classification]* strictness, rigour, rigorousness. **manquer de ~** to lack rigour.

(d) tenir ~ à qn de n'être pas venu to hold it against sb that he didn't come *ou* for not coming, refuse to forgive sb for not coming; **je ne vous en tiens pas ~** I don't hold it against you; **à la ~** at a pinch, if need be, in extreme circumstances (*frm*); **on peut à l'extrême ~ remplacer le curry par du poivre** at a pinch *ou* if the worst comes to the worst *ou* if need be you can use pepper instead of curry powder; **un délit, à la ~, mais un crime non: le mot est trop fort** a minor offence possibly *ou* perhaps, but not a crime — that's too strong a word; **il pourrait à la ~ avoir gagné la côte, mais j'en doute** there is a faint possibility that he made it *ou* he may just possibly have made it back to the shore but I doubt it; **il est de ~ d'envoyer un petit mot de remerciement** it is the done thing to send a note of thanks; **la tenue de ~ est ...** the dress to be worn is ... , the accepted dress *ou* attire (*frm*) is ... ; **'tenue de soirée de ~'** 'evening dress', 'dress: formal'.

rikiki* [ʀikiki] *adj V* **riquiqui.**

rillettes [ʀijɛt] *nfpl* potted meat (*made from pork or goose*), rillettes.

rimailler [ʀimɑje] (1) *vi* (*péj*) to write bits of verse, write poetry of a sort.

rimailleur, -euse [ʀimɑjœʀ, øz] *nm,f* (*péj*) would-be poet, poet of a sort, rhymester.

rimaye [ʀimɑj] *nf* bergschrund.

rimbaldien, -ienne [ʀɛ̃baldjɛ̃, jɛn] *adj* of Rimbaud.

rime [ʀim] *nf* rhyme. **~ masculine/féminine** masculine/feminine rhyme; **~ pauvre/riche** poor/rich rhyme; **~s croisées** *ou* **alternées** alternate rhymes; **~s plates** *ou* **suivies** rhyming couplets; **~s embrassées** abba rhyme scheme; **~s tiercées** terza rima; **~ pour l'œil/l'oreille** rhyme for the eye/ear; **faire qch sans ~ ni raison** to do sth without either rhyme or reason; **cela n'a ni ~ ni raison** there's neither rhyme nor reason to it; *V* **dictionnaire.**

rimer [ʀime] (1) **1** *vi* **(a)** *[mot]* to rhyme (*avec* with). (*fig*) **cela ne rime à rien** it does not make sense, there's no sense *ou* point in it; **à quoi cela rime-t-il?** what's the point of it? *ou* sense in it?

(b) *[poète]* to write verse *ou* poetry.

2 *vt* to put into verse. **poésie rimée** rhyming poetry *ou* verse.

rimeur, -euse [ʀimœʀ, øz] *nm,f* (*péj*) rhymester, would-be poet.

rimmel [ʀimɛl] *nm* ® mascara.

rinçage [ʀɛ̃saʒ] *nm* (*V* **rincer**) (*action*) rinsing out *ou* through; rinsing; (*opération*) rinse. **cette machine à laver fait 3 ~s** this washing machine does 3 rinses.

rinceau, *pl* **~x** [ʀɛ̃so] *nm* (*Archit*) foliage (*U*), foliation (*U*).

rince- [ʀɛ̃s] *préf V* **rincer.**

rincée [ʀɛ̃se] *nf* (*: *averse*) downpour; (‡: *défaite, volée*) thrashing*, licking*.

rincer [ʀɛ̃se] (3) **1** *vt* (*laver*) to rinse out *ou* through; (*ôter le savon*) to rinse. **rince le verre** give the glass a rinse, rinse the glass out; (*fig*) **se faire ~*** (*par la pluie*) to get drenched *ou* soaked; (*au jeu*) to get cleaned out*.

2 se rincer *vpr*: **se ~ la bouche** to rinse out one's mouth; **se ~ les mains** to rinse one's hands; **se ~ l'œil‡** to get an eyeful*; **se ~ la dalle‡** to wet one's whistle*.

3: rince-bouteilles *nm inv* (*machine*) bottle-washing machine; (*brosse*) bottle-brush; **rince-doigts** *nm inv* finger-bowl.

rincette* [ʀɛ̃sɛt] *nf* nip of brandy *etc*, little drop of wine (*ou* brandy *etc*).

rinçure [ʀɛ̃syʀ] *nf* (*eau de lavage*) rinsing water; (*péj: mauvais vin*) dishwater (*péj*), foul-tasting *ou* lousy* wine (*ou* beer).

ring [ʀiŋ] *nm* (boxing) ring. **les champions du ~** boxing champions; **monter sur le ~** (*pour un match*) to go into the ring; (*faire carrière*) to take up boxing.

ringard [ʀɛ̃gaʀ] *nm* poker.

ripaille*† [ʀipɑj] *nf* (*festin*) feast. **faire ~** to (have a) feast, have a good blow-out*.

ripailler*† [ʀipɑje] (1) *vi* (*festoyer*) to feast, have a good blow-out*.

ripaton‡ [ʀipatɔ̃] *nm* (*pied*) foot, tootsy*.

riper [ʀipe] (1) **1** *vi* (*déraper*) to slip. **2** *vt* (*aussi* **faire ~**: *déplacer*) *meuble, pierre, véhicule* to slide along.

ripolin [ʀipɔlɛ̃] *nm* ® enamel paint. **passer qch au ~** to give sth a coat of enamel paint.

ripoliné, e [ʀipɔline] *adj* enamel-painted.

riposte [ʀipɔst(ə)] *nf* (*réponse*) retort, riposte; (*contre-attaque*) counter-attack, reprisal; (*Escrime*) riposte. **il est prompt à la ~** he always has a ready answer *ou* a quick retort.

riposter [ʀipɔste] (1) **1** *vi* **(a)** (*répondre*) to answer back, riposte, retaliate. **~ à une insulte** to reply to an insult; **il riposta (à cela) par une insulte** he answered back *ou* retorted *ou* retaliated *ou* riposted with an insult, he flung back an insult; **~ à une accusation par une insulte** to counter an accusation by an insult; **savoir ~ à propos** to be ready with the right retort.

(b) (*contre-attaquer*) to counter-attack, retaliate. **~ à coups de grenades** to retaliate by throwing grenades; **~ à une attaque** to counter an attack (*par* by).

(c) (*Escrime*) to riposte.

2 *vt*: **~ que** to retort *ou* riposte *ou* answer back that.

riquiqui* [ʀikiki] *adj inv portion* tiny, mean, stingy*. **elle portait un chapeau ~** she was wearing a shabby little hat; **ça fait un peu ~** (*portion*) it looks a bit stingy*; (*manteau*) it looks pretty shabby*.

rire [ʀiʀ] (36) **1** *vi* **(a)** to laugh. **~ aux éclats** *ou* **à gorge déployée** to roar with laughter, shake with laughter, laugh one's head off; **~ aux larmes** to laugh until one cries; **~ franchement** *ou* **de bon cœur** to laugh heartily; **~ bruyamment** to guffaw, roar with laughter; (*péj*) **~ comme un bossu** *ou* **comme une baleine** to laugh o.s. silly, be doubled up with laughter, split one's sides (laughing); **c'est à mourir** *ou* **crever* de ~** it's hilarious, it's awfully funny, you'd die laughing*; **la plaisanterie fit ~** the joke raised a laugh *ou* made everyone laugh; **ça ne me fait pas ~** I don't find it funny, I'm not amused, it doesn't make me laugh; **nous avons bien ri (de notre mésaventure)** we had a good laugh* (over our mishap); **ça m'a bien fait ~** that really made me laugh, that had me in fits*; **on va ~: il va essayer de sauter** we're in for a laugh* because he's going to try and jump; **il vaut mieux en ~ qu'en pleurer** it's better to look *ou* we (*ou* you *etc*) may as well look on the bright side of things; **il a pris les choses en riant** (*avec bonne humeur*) he saw the funny side of it; (*à la légère*) he laughed it off; **il n'y a pas de quoi ~** there's nothing to laugh about, it's no laughing matter; (*Prov*) **rira bien qui rira le dernier** he who laughs last laughs longest (*Prov*).

(b) (*littér*) *[yeux]* to sparkle *ou* shine with happiness *ou* laughter; *[visage]* to shine with happiness.

(c) (*s'amuser*) to have fun, have a laugh*. **il ne pense qu'à ~** he only thinks of having fun; **il passe son temps à ~ avec ses camarades** he spends his time playing about *ou* larking about with his friends; **~ aux dépens de qn** to laugh *ou* have a laugh at sb's expense; **c'est un homme qui aime bien ~** he is a man who likes a bit of fun *ou* a good laugh*; **c'est maintenant qu'on va ~!** this is where the fun starts!; *V* **histoire.**

(d) (*plaisanter*) **vous voulez ~!** you're joking!, you must be joking!; **et je ne ris pas** and I'm not joking!; **sans ~, c'est vrai?** joking apart, is it true?, seriously, is it true?; **il a dit cela pour ~** he was only joking, he said it in fun, he didn't mean it; **il a fait cela pour ~** he did it for a joke *ou* laugh*; **c'était une bagarre pour ~** it was only a pretend fight, it wasn't a real fight.

(e) (*loc*) **~ dans sa barbe** *ou* **tout bas** to laugh to o.s., chuckle (away) to o.s.; **~ dans sa barbe** *ou* **sous cape** to laugh up one's sleeve, have a quiet laugh; **~ aux anges** *[personne]* to have a great beam *ou* a vacant grin on one's face, beam (away); *[bébé]* to smile happily in one's sleep; **~ au nez** *ou* **à la barbe de qn** to laugh in sb's face; **~ du bout des dents** *ou* **des lèvres** to force o.s. to laugh, laugh politely; **~ jaune: il faisait semblant de trouver ça drôle, mais en fait il riait jaune** he pretended he found it funny but in fact he had to force himself to laugh; **quand il apprendra la nouvelle il rira jaune** when he hears the news he'll laugh on the other side of his face; (*iro*) **vous me faites ~!, laissez-moi ~!** don't make me laugh!, you make me laugh (*iro*).

2 rire de *vt indir* (*se moquer de*) *personne, défaut, crainte* to laugh *ou* scoff at; **il fait ~ de lui** people laugh at him *ou* make fun of him, he makes himself a laughing stock.

3 se rire *vpr*: **se ~ de** (*se jouer de*) *difficultés, épreuve* to make light of, take in one's stride; (*se moquer de*) *menaces, recommandations* to laugh off *ou* at; *personne* to laugh at, scoff at.

4 *nm* (*façon de rire*) laugh; (*éclat de rire*) laughter (*U*), laugh. **~s** laughter; **le ~** laughter; **un gros ~** a loud laugh, a guffaw; **un petit ~ bête** a stupid giggle *ou* titter; **il y eut des ~s dans la salle quand ...** there was laughter in the room when ... ; **elle a un ~ bête** she has a stupid laugh; **elle eut un petit ~ méchant** she gave a wicked little laugh, she laughed wickedly; **il eut un petit ~ de satisfaction** he gave a little chuckle of satisfaction, he chuckled with satisfaction; **les ~s l'obligèrent à se taire** he was laughed down; *V* **éclater, fou, mourir** *etc.*

ris[1] [ʀi] *nm* **(a)** (*Culin*) **~ de veau** calf sweetbread. **(b)** (*Naut*) reef.

ris[2] [ʀi] *nm* (*littér: rire*) laugh, laughter (*U*).

risée [ʀize] *nf* **(a) s'exposer à la ~ générale** to lay o.s. open to ridicule; **être un objet de ~** to be a laughing stock, be an object of ridicule; **être la ~ de toute l'Europe** to be *ou* make o.s. the laughing stock of Europe.

(b) (*Naut*) **~(s)** light breeze.

risette [ʀizɛt] *nf*: **faire (une) ~ à qn** to give sb a nice *ou* little smile; **fais ~ (au monsieur)** smile nicely (at the gentleman); (*fig*) **être obligé de faire des ~s au patron** to have to smile politely to the boss.

risible [ʀizibl(ə)] *adj* (*ridicule*) *attitude* ridiculous, silly; (*comique*) *aventure* laughable, funny.

risiblement [ʀizibləmɑ̃] *adv* ridiculously.

risque [ʀisk(ə)] *nm* **(a)** (*gén, Jur: danger*) risk. **~ calculé** calculated risk; **c'est un ~ à courir** it's a risk one has to take *ou* run, one has to take *ou* run the risk; **il y a du ~ à faire cela** it's taking a risk doing that, it's risky doing *ou* to do that; **le goût du ~** a taste for danger; **ce qui paie, c'est le ~** it pays off to take risks, taking risks pays off; **on n'a rien sans ~** you don't get anywhere without taking risks, nothing ventured, nothing gained (*Prov*); **prendre tous les ~s** to take any number of risks; **il y a (un) ~ d'émeute/d'épidémie** there's a risk of an uprising/an epidemic; **à cause du ~ d'incendie** because of the fire risk *ou* the risk of fire; **cela constitue un ~ pour la santé** that is a health hazard *ou* health risk; *V* **assurance.**

(b) (*loc*) (*hum*) **ce sont les ~s du métier** that's an occupational hazard (*hum*); **il n'y a pas de ~ qu'il refuse** there's no risk *ou* chance of his refusing, he isn't likely to refuse; **au ~ de le mécontenter/de se tuer/de sa vie** at the risk of displeasing him/of killing o.s./of his life; **c'est à tes ~s et périls** it's at your own risk, on your own head be it!

risqué, e [ʀiske] (*ptp de* **risquer**) *adj* (*hasardeux*) risky; (*licencieux*) risqué, daring, coarse, off-color (*US*).

risquer [ʀiske] (1) **1** *vt* **(a)** (*mettre en danger*) *réputation, fortune, vie* to risk.

(b) (*s'exposer à*) *prison, renvoi, ennuis* to risk. **il risque la mort** he's risking death; **tu risques gros** you're taking a big risk, you're sticking your neck out*; **tu risques qu'on te le vole** you risk having it stolen; **qu'est-ce qu'on risque?** (*quels sont les risques?*) what do we risk?, what are the risks? *ou* dangers?; (*c'est sans danger*) what have we got to lose?, where's *ou* what's the risk?; **bien emballé, ce vase ne risque rien** packed like this the vase is *ou* will be quite safe; **ce vieux pantalon ne risque rien** these old trousers don't matter at all.

(c) (*tenter*) to risk. ~ **le tout pour le tout,** ~ **le paquet*** to risk *ou* chance the lot; **risquons le coup** let's chance it, let's take the chance; (*Prov*) **qui ne risque rien n'a rien** nothing ventured, nothing gained (*Prov*).

(d) (*hasarder*) *allusion, regard* to venture, hazard. **je ne risquerais pas un gros mot devant mon père** I wouldn't risk swearing *ou* take the risk of swearing in front of my father; ~ **un œil derrière un mur** to venture a peep behind a wall; (*hum*) ~ **un orteil dans l'eau** to venture a toe in the water.

(e) ~ **de: tu risques de le perdre** (*éventualité*) you might (well) *ou* could well lose it; (*forte possibilité*) you could easily lose it; (*probabilité*) you're likely to lose it; **il risque de pleuvoir** it could *ou* may (well) rain, there's a chance of rain; **le feu risque de s'éteindre** the fire may (well) go out, there's a risk the fire may go out; **pourquoi ~ de tout perdre?** why should we risk losing *ou* take the risk of losing everything?; **ça ne risque pas (d'arriver)!** not a chance, there's no chance *ou* danger of that (happening)!, that's not likely to happen; **il ne risque pas de gagner** he hasn't got much chance of winning, there isn't much chance of him winning, he isn't likely to win.

2 se risquer *vpr*: **se ~ dans une grotte/sur une corniche** to venture inside a cave/onto a ledge; **se ~ dans une entreprise** to venture (up)on *ou* launch o.s. into an enterprise; **se ~ dans une aventure dangereuse** to risk one's neck *ou* chance one's luck in a dangerous adventure; **se ~ à faire qch** to venture *ou* dare to do sth; **je vais me ~ à faire un soufflé** I'll have a try *ou* a go* *ou* a shot* at making a soufflé.

risque-tout [riskətu] *nmf inv* daredevil. **elle est ~, c'est une ~** she's a daredevil.

rissole [risɔl] *nf* rissole.

rissoler [risɔle] (1) **1** *vt* (*Culin: aussi* **faire** ~) to brown. **pommes rissolées** fried potatoes. **2** *vi* **(a)** (*Culin*) to brown. **(b)** (*hum: bronzer*) **se faire** *ou* **se laisser ~ sur la plage** to (lie and) roast (o.s.) on the beach.

ristourne [risturn(ə)] *nf* (*sur achat*) rebate, discount; (*sur cotisation*) rebate, refund. **faire une ~ à qn** to give sb a rebate *ou* a refund.

ristourner [risturne] (1) *vt* to refund, give a rebate *ou* a refund of. **il m'a ristourné 2 F** he refunded me 2 francs, he gave me a 2 francs rebate, he gave me 2 francs back.

rital‡ [rital] *nm* (*péj: Italien*) wop‡ (*péj*).

rite [rit] *nm* (*gén, Rel*) rite; (*fig: habitude*) ritual.

ritournelle [riturnɛl] *nf* (*Mus*) ritornello. (*fig*) **c'est toujours la même ~** it's always the same (old) story *ou* tune, he (*ou* she *etc*) is always harping on about that.

ritualisme [ritɥalism(ə)] *nm* ritualism.

ritualiste [ritɥalist(ə)] **1** *adj* ritualistic. **2** *nmf* ritualist.

rituel, -elle [ritɥɛl] *adj, nm* (*gén*) ritual.

rituellement [ritɥɛlmɑ̃] *adv* (*religieusement*) religiously, ritually; (*hum: invariablement*) invariably, unfailingly.

rivage [rivaʒ] *nm* shore.

rival, e, *mpl* **-aux** [rival, o] *adj, nm,f* rival. **sans ~** unrivalled.

rivaliser [rivalize] (1) *vi*: ~ **avec** *[personne]* to rival, compete with, vie with, emulate; *[chose]* to hold its own against, compare with; ~ **de générosité/de bons mots avec qn** to vie with sb *ou* try to outdo sb in generosity/wit, rival sb in generosity/wit; **ils rivalisaient de générosité** they vied with each other *ou* they tried to outdo each other in generosity; **il essaie de ~ avec moi** he's trying to emulate me *ou* to vie with me; **ses œuvres rivalisent avec les plus grands chefs d'œuvre** his works rival the greatest masterpieces *ou* can hold their own against *ou* compare with the greatest masterpieces.

rivalité [rivalite] *nf* rivalry.

rive [riv] *nf* **(a)** *[mer, lac]* shore; *[rivière]* bank. **la R~ gauche** the Left Bank (*in Paris: a district noted for its student and intellectual life*). **(b)** (*Tech*) *[four]* lip.

rivé, e [rive] (*ptp de* **river**) *adj*: ~ **à** *bureau, travail* tethered *ou* tied to; *chaise* glued *ou* riveted to; **les yeux ~s sur moi/la tache de sang** (with) his eyes riveted on me/the bloodstain; **rester ~ sur place** to be *ou* stand riveted *ou* rooted to the spot.

river [rive] (1) *vt* **(a)** (*Tech*) *clou* to clinch; *plaques* to rivet together. (*fig*) ~ **son clou à qn*** to shut sb up*.

(b) (*littér: fixer*) ~ **qch au mur/au sol** to nail sth to the wall/floor; **la poigne qui le rivait au sol** the tight grip which held him down on *ou* pinned him to the ground; **la haine/le sentiment qui les rivait ensemble** *ou* **l'un à l'autre** the hate/the sentiment which bound them to each other.

riverain, e [rivrɛ̃, ɛn] **1** *adj* (*d'un lac*) lakeside, waterside, riparian (*T*); (*d'une rivière*) riverside, waterside, riparian (*T*). (*d'une route*) **les propriétés ~es** the houses along the road; **les propriétés ~es de la Seine** the houses bordering on the Seine *ou* along the banks of the Seine.

2 *nm,f* lakeside resident; riverside resident; riparian (*T*). **les ~s se plaignent du bruit des voitures** the residents of *ou* in the street complain about the noise of cars; **'interdit sauf aux ~s'** (*d'une rue*) 'no entry except for access'; (*de la rive*) 'residents only'.

rivet [rivɛ] *nm* rivet.

rivetage [rivtaʒ] *nm* riveting.

riveter [rivte] (4) *vt* to rivet (together).

riveteuse [rivtøz] *nf*, **riveuse** [rivøz] *nf* riveting machine.

rivière [rivjɛr] *nf* (*lit, fig*) river; (*Équitation*) water jump. ~ **de diamants** diamond rivière; *V* **petit.**

rixe [riks(ə)] *nf* brawl, fight, scuffle.

riz [ri] *nm* rice. ~ **Caroline** *ou* **à grains longs** long-grain rice; ~ **au lait** rice pudding; (*Culin*) ~ **créole creole rice;** *V* **curry, gâteau, paille** *etc.*

rizerie [rizri] *nf* rice-processing factory.

riziculture [rizikyltyr] *nf* rice-growing.

rizière [rizjɛr] *nf* paddy-field, ricefield.

robe [rɔb] **1** *nf* **(a)** *[femme, fillette]* dress, frock. ~ **courte/décolletée/d'été** short/low-necked/summer dress.

(b) *[magistrat, prélat]* robe; *[professeur]* gown. (*Hist Jur*) **la ~** the legal profession; *V* **gens**[1]**, homme, noblesse.**

(c) (*pelage*) *[cheval, fauve]* coat.

(d) (*peau*) *[oignon]* skin; *[fève]* husk.

(e) *[cigare]* wrapper, outer leaf.

(f) (*couleur*) *[vin]* colour.

2: robe bain de soleil sundress; **robe de bal** ball gown *ou* dress, evening dress *ou* gown; **robe de baptême** christening robe; **robe de chambre** dressing gown; (*Culin*) **pommes de terre en robe de chambre** *ou* **des champs** jacket potatoes *ou* potatoes in their jackets; **robe chemisier** shirtwaister (dress); **robe de communion** *ou* **de communiante** first communion dress; **robe de grossesse** maternity dress; **robe d'intérieur** housecoat; **robe-manteau** *nf, pl* **robes-manteaux** coat-dress; **robe de mariée** wedding dress *ou* gown; **robe-sac** *nf, pl* **robes-sacs** sack dress; **robe du soir** evening dress *ou* gown; **robe-tablier** *nf, pl* **robes-tabliers** overall; **robe tunique** smock.

Robert [rɔbɛr] *nm* Robert.

roberts‡ [rɔbɛr] *nmpl* (*seins*) tits‡, boobs‡.

robin†† [rɔbɛ̃] *nm* (*péj*) lawyer.

robinet [rɔbinɛ] *nm [évier, baignoire, tonneau]* tap (*Brit*), faucet (*US*). ~ **d'eau chaude/froide** hot/cold (water) tap (*Brit*) *ou* faucet (*US*); ~ **mélangeur** mixer tap; ~ **du gaz** gas tap; ~ **d'arrêt** stopcock; *V* **problème.**

robinetterie [rɔbinɛtri] *nf* (*installations*) taps, plumbing (*U*); (*usine*) tap factory; (*commerce*) tap trade.

roboratif, -ive [rɔbɔratif, iv] *adj* (*littér*) *climat* bracing; *activité* invigorating; *vin, liqueur* tonic, stimulating.

robot [rɔbo] *nm* (*lit, fig*) robot. ~ **ménager** multi-purpose kitchen aid *ou* gadget; **avion ~** remote-controlled aircraft; *V* **photo, portrait.**

robre [rɔbr(ə)] *nm* (*Bridge*) rubber.

robuste [rɔbyst(ə)] *adj personne* robust, sturdy; *santé* robust, sound; *plante* robust, hardy; *voiture* robust, sturdy; *moteur, machine* robust; *foi* firm, strong.

robustement [rɔbystəmɑ̃] *adv* robustly, sturdily.

robustesse [rɔbystɛs] *nf* (*V* **robuste**) robustness; sturdiness; soundness; hardiness; firmness, strength.

roc [rɔk] *nm* (*lit, fig*) rock; *V* **bâtir, dur.**

rocade [rɔkad] *nf* (*route*) by-road; bypass; (*Mil*) communications line.

rocaille [rɔkaj] **1** *adj objet, style* rocaille.

2 *nf* **(a)** (*cailloux*) loose stones; (*terrain*) rocky *ou* stony ground.

(b) (*jardin*) rockery, rock garden. **plantes de ~** rock plants.

(c) (*Constr*) **grotte/fontaine en ~** grotto/fountain in rockwork.

rocailleux, -euse [rɔkajø, øz] *adj terrain* rocky, stony; *style* rugged, harsh; *son, voix* harsh, grating.

rocambolesque [rɔkɑ̃bɔlɛsk(ə)] *adj aventures, péripéties* fantastic, incredible.

rochassier, -ière [rɔʃasje, jɛr] *nm,f* rock climber.

roche [rɔʃ] *nf* (*gén*) rock. ~**s sédimentaires/volcaniques** sedimentary/volcanic rock(s); (*Naut*) **fond de ~** rock-bottom; *V* **aiguille, coq**[1]**, cristal** *etc.*

rocher [rɔʃe] *nm* **(a)** (*bloc*) rock; (*gros, lisse*) boulder; (*substance*) rock. **le ~ de Sisyphe** the rock of Sisyphus; (*Alpinisme*) **faire du ~** to go rock climbing. **(b)** (*Anat*) petrosal bone.

rochet [rɔʃɛ] *nm* **(a)** (*Rel*) ratchet. **(b)** (*Tech*) **roue à ~** ratchet wheel.

rocheux, -euse [rɔʃø, øz] *adj récit, terrain, lit* rocky. **paroi ~euse** rock face; *V* **montagne.**

rock (and roll) [rɔk(ɛnrɔl)] *nm* (*musique*) rock-'n'-roll; (*danse*) jive.

rocking-chair, *pl* **rocking-chairs** [rɔkiŋʃɛr] *nm* rocking chair.

rococo [rɔkɔko] **1** *nm* (*Art*) rococo. **2** *adj inv* (*Art*) rococo; (*péj*) old-fashioned, outdated.

rodage [rɔdaʒ] *nm* (*V* **roder**) running in (*surtout Brit*), breaking in (*US*); grinding. **'en ~'** 'running in' (*surtout Brit*), 'breaking in' (*US*); **pendant le ~** during the running-in (*surtout Brit*) *ou* breaking-in (*US*) period; **ce spectacle a demandé un certain ~** the show took a little while to get over its teething troubles *ou* get into its stride.

rodéo [rɔdeo] *nm* rodeo; (*fig*) free-for-all.

roder [rɔde] (1) *vt véhicule, moteur* to run in (*Brit*), break in (*US*); *soupape* to grind. (*fig*) **il faut ~ ce spectacle/ce nouveau service** we have to let this show/this new service get into its stride, we have to give this show/this new service time to get over its teething troubles; **il n'est pas encore rodé** *[personne]* he hasn't yet got the hang of things* *ou* got into the way of things, he is not yet broken in; *[organisme]* it hasn't yet got into its stride, it is not yet run in properly; **ce spectacle est maintenant bien rodé** the show is really running well *ou* smoothly now, all the initial problems in the show have been ironed out.

rôder [rode] (1) *vi* (*au hasard*) to roam *ou* wander about; (*de façon suspecte*) to loiter *ou* lurk (about *ou* around); (*être en maraude*) to prowl about, be on the prowl. ~ **autour d'un magasin** to hang *ou* lurk around a shop; ~ **autour d'une femme** to hang around a woman.

rôdeur, -euse [rodœr, øz] *nm,f* prowler.

Rodolphe [rɔdɔlf] *nm* Rudolph, Rudolf.

rodomontade [Rɔdɔmɔ̃tad] *nf (littér) (vantarde)* bragging (*U*), boasting (*U*); (*menaçante*) sabre rattling (*U*); bluster (*U*).

Rogations [Rɔgɑsjɔ̃] *nfpl (Rel)* Rogations.

rogatoire [Rɔgatwar] *adj (Jur)* rogatory; *V* **commission.**

rogatons [Rɔgatɔ̃] *nmpl (péj)* scraps (of food), left-overs.

Roger [Rɔʒe] *nm* Roger.

rogne* [Rɔɲ] *nf* anger. **être en ~** to be (hopping) mad* *ou* really ratty* (*Brit*); **se mettre en ~** to get (hopping) mad* *ou* really ratty* (*Brit*), blow one's top* (*contre* at); **mettre qn en ~** to make *ou* get sb (hopping) mad* *ou* really ratty* (*Brit*), get sb's temper up; **il était dans une telle ~ que ...** he was in such a (foul) temper that ... , he was so mad* *ou* ratty* (*Brit*) that ... ; **ses ~s duraient des jours** his tempers lasted for days.

rogner [Rɔɲe] (1) *vt* **(a)** (*couper*) *ongle, page, plaque* to trim; *griffe* to clip, trim; *aile, pièce d'or* to clip. **~ les ailes à qn** to clip sb's wings.

(b) (*réduire*) *prix* to whittle down, cut down; *salaire* to cut back *ou* down, whittle down. **~ sur** *dépense, prix* to cut down on, cut back on.

rognon [Rɔɲɔ̃] *nm (Culin)* kidney.

rognures [Rɔɲyr] *nfpl [métal]* clippings, trimmings; *[papier, cuir]* clippings; *[ongles]* clippings, parings; *[viande]* scraps.

rogomme [Rɔgɔm] *nm*: **voix de ~** husky *ou* rasping (*péj*) voice.

rogue [Rɔg] *adj* offensive, haughty, arrogant.

roi [Rwa] **1** *nm* **(a)** (*souverain, Cartes, Échecs*) king. (*Rel*) **les R~s** the Three Wise Men; **le jour des R~s** (*gén*) Twelfth Night; (*Rel*) Epiphany; **tirer les ~s** to eat Twelfth Night cake; **le ~ n'est pas son cousin!** he's very full of himself *ou* very conceited (*péj*), he's as pleased *ou* as proud as Punch; **travailler pour le ~ de Prusse** to receive no reward for one's pains; *V* **bleu, camelot** *etc.*

(b) (*fig*) **le ~ des animaux/de la forêt** the king of beasts/of the forest; **~ du pétrole** oil king; **les ~s de la finance** the kings of finance; **un des ~s de la presse/du textile** one of the press/textile barons *ou* kings *ou* magnates *ou* tycoons; **X, le ~ des fromages X,** the leading *ou* first name in cheese(s), X, the cheese king (*hum*); **c'est le ~ de la resquille!*** he's a master *ou* an ace at getting something for nothing; **tu es vraiment le ~ (des imbéciles)!*** you really are a prize idiot!*, you really take the cake (for sheer stupidity)!*; **c'est le ~ des cons**⁑ he's the world's biggest blockhead*, for sheer bloody stupidity he's got everybody beat⁑; **c'est le ~ des salauds**⁑ he's the world's biggest bastard⁑.

2: (*Hist*) **les rois fainéants** *the last Merovingian kings;* (*Bible*) **les Rois mages** the Magi, the Three Wise Men; **le Roi des Rois** the Kings of Kings; **le Roi-Soleil** the Sun-King.

roide [Rwad], **roideur** [Rwadœr], **roidir** [Rwadir] = **raide, raideur, raidir.**

roitelet [Rwatlɛ] *nm (péj)* kinglet, petty king; (*Orn*) wren.

Roland [Rɔlɑ̃] *nm* Roland.

rôle [Rol] *nm* **(a)** (*Théât, fig*) role, part. **premier ~** lead, leading *ou* major role *ou* part; **second/petit ~** supporting/minor role *ou* part; **~ muet** non-speaking part; **~ de composition** character part *ou* role; **savoir son ~** to know one's part *ou* lines; **distribuer les ~s** to cast the parts; **je lui ai donné le ~ de Lear** I gave him the role *ou* part of Lear, I cast him as Lear; **jouer un ~** to play a part, act a role; (*fig*) **il joue toujours les seconds ~s** he always plays second fiddle; **il joue bien son ~ de jeune cadre** he acts his role of young executive *ou* plays the part of a young executive well; **renverser les ~s** to reverse the roles; *V* **beau.**

(b) (*fonction, statut*) *[personne]* role, part; *[institution, système]* role, function; (*contribution*) part; (*travail, devoir*) job. **il a un ~ important dans l'organisation** he plays an important part *ou* he has an important part to play *ou* he has an important role in the organization; **quel a été son ~ dans cette affaire?** what part did he play in this business?; **ce n'est pas mon ~ de vous sermonner mais ...** it isn't my job *ou* place to lecture you but ...; **le ~ de la métaphore chez Lawrence** the role of metaphor *ou* the part played by metaphor in Lawrence; **la télévision a pour ~ de ...** the role *ou* function of television is to ... .

(c) (*registre*) (*Admin*) roll; (*Jur*) cause-list. **~ d'équipage** muster (roll); **~ d'impôt** tax list *ou* roll; *V* **tour**[2].

rollmops [Rɔlmɔps] *nm* rollmop.

romain, e [Rɔmɛ̃, ɛn] **1** *adj* (*gén*) Roman. **2** *nm,f*: **R~(e)** Roman; *V* **travail**[1]. **3 romaine** *nf*: (*laitue*) **~e** cos (lettuce); (*balance*) **~e** steelyard.

romaïque [Rɔmaik] *adj, nm* Romaic, demotic Greek.

roman[1] [Rɔmɑ̃] **1** *nm* **(a)** (*livre*) novel; (*fig: récit*) story. (*genre*) **le ~** the novel; **ils ne publient que des ~s** they only publish novels *ou* fiction; **ça n'arrive que dans les ~s** it only happens in novels *ou* fiction *ou* stories; **sa vie est un vrai ~** his life is a real storybook *ou* is like something out of a storybook; **c'est tout un ~*** it's a long story, it's a real saga; *V* **eau, nouveau.**

(b) (*Littérat: œuvre médiévale*) romance. **~ courtois** courtly romance; **le R~ de la Rose/de Renart** the Roman de la Rose/de Renart, the Romance of the Rose/of Renart.

2: roman d'amour (*lit*) love story; (*fig*) love story, (storybook) romance; **roman d'analyse** psychological novel; **roman d'anticipation** futuristic novel, science-fiction novel; **roman d'aventures** adventure story; **roman de cape et d'épée** cloak and dagger story; **roman de chevalerie** tale of chivalry; **roman à clefs** roman à clef; **roman d'épouvante** horror story; **roman d'espionnage** spy story; **roman-feuilleton** *nm, pl* **romans-feuilletons** serialized novel, serial; **roman fleuve** roman fleuve, saga; **roman historique** historical novel; **roman de mœurs** social novel; **roman noir** Gothic novel, horror story; **roman photo** romantic picture story (*using photographs*); **roman policier** detective novel *ou* story; **roman de science-fiction** science fiction novel; **roman (de) série noire** thriller.

roman[2], **e** [Rɔmɑ̃, an] **1** *adj* (*Ling*) Romance (*épith*), Romanic; (*Archit*) Romanesque. **2** *nm* (*Ling*) **le ~ (commun)** late vulgar Latin; (*Archit*) **le ~** the Romanesque.

romance [Rɔmɑ̃s] *nf* **(a)** (*chanson*) sentimental ballad, lovesong. **les ~s napolitaines** the Neapolitan lovesongs; *V* **pousser. (b)** (*Littérat, Mus*) ballad, romance.

romancer [Rɔmɑ̃se] (3) *vt* (*présenter sous forme de roman*) to make into a novel; (*agrémenter*) to romanticize; *V* **biographie, histoire.**

romanche [Rɔmɑ̃ʃ] *adj, nm* Ro(u)mansh.

romancier [Rɔmɑ̃sje] *nm* novelist.

romancière [Rɔmɑ̃sjɛr] *nf* (woman) novelist.

romand, e [Rɔmɑ̃, ɑ̃d] *adj* of French-speaking Switzerland. **les R~s** the French-speaking Swiss; *V* **suisse.**

romanesque [Rɔmanɛsk(ə)] **1** *adj* **(a)** *histoire* fabulous, fantastic; *amours* storybook (*épith*); *aventures* storybook (*épith*), fabulous; *personne, tempérament, imagination* romantic.

(b) (*Littérat*) *récit, traitement* novelistic. **la technique ~** the technique(s) of the novel; **œuvre ~** novels, fiction (*U*).

2 *nm [imagination, personne]* romantic side. **elle se réfugiait dans le ~** she took refuge in fancy.

romanichel, -elle [Rɔmaniʃɛl] *nm,f* gipsy.

romanisant, e [Rɔmanizɑ̃, ɑ̃t] **1** *adj* (*Rel*) romanist; (*Ling*) specializing in Romance languages. **2** *nm,f* (*linguiste*) romanist, specialist in Romance languages.

romaniser [Rɔmanize] (1) *vt* (*gén*) to romanize.

romaniste [Rɔmanist(ə)] *nmf* (*Jur, Rel*) romanist; (*Ling*) romanist, specialist in Romance languages.

romano [Rɔmano] *nm* (*péj*) gippo* (*péj*).

romantique [Rɔmɑ̃tik] **1** *adj* romantic. **2** *nmf* romantic(ist).

romantisme [Rɔmɑ̃tism(ə)] *nm* romanticism.

romarin [Rɔmarɛ̃] *nm* rosemary.

rombière⁑ [Rɔ̃bjɛr] *nf* (*péj*) old biddy⁑ (*péj*).

Rome [Rɔm] *n* Rome; *V* **tout.**

rompre [Rɔ̃pr(ə)] (41) **1** *vt* **(a)** (*faire cesser*) *relations diplomatiques, fiançailles, pourparlers* to break off; *silence, monotonie, enchantement* to break; (*ne pas respecter*) *traité, marché* to break. **~ l'équilibre** to upset the balance; **~ le Carême** to break Lent *ou* the Lenten fast; (*littér*) **~ le charme** to break the spell.

(b) (*casser*) *branche* to break; *pain* to break (up). **il faut ~ le pain, non le couper** bread should be broken not cut; **il rompit le pain et distribua les morceaux** he broke (up) the bread and handed the pieces around; (*fig littér*) **tu nous romps la tête avec ta musique** you're deafening us with your music; (*fig littér*) **je vais lui ~ les côtes** I'm going to tan his hide; (*lit, fig*) **~ ses chaînes** to break one's chains; (*Naut*) **~ ses amarres** to break (loose from) its moorings; (*Mil*) **~ le front de l'ennemi** to break through the enemy front; **la mer a rompu les digues** the sea has broken (through) *ou* burst the dikes; *V* **applaudir, glace**[1].

(c) (*littér*) **~ qn à un exercice** to break sb in to an exercise.

(d) (*loc*) **~ une lance** *ou* **des lances pour qn** to take up the cudgels for sb; **~ une lance** *ou* **des lances contre qn** to cross swords with sb; (*Mil*) **~ les rangs** to fall out, dismiss; (*Mil*) **rompez (les rangs)!** dismiss!, fall out!

2 *vi* **(a)** (*se séparer de*) **~ avec qn** to break with sb, break off one's relations with sb; **ils ont rompu (leurs fiançailles)** they've broken it off, they've broken off their engagement; **~ avec de vieilles habitudes/la tradition** to break with old habits/tradition; **il n'a pas le courage de ~** he hasn't got the courage to break it off.

(b) *[corde]* to break, snap; *[digue]* to burst, break.

(c) (*Boxe, Escrime*) to break. (*fig*) **~ en visière avec** to quarrel openly with; (*Mil*) **~ le combat** to withdraw from the engagement.

3 se rompre *vpr* (*se briser*) *[câble, corde, branche, chaîne]* to break, snap; *[digue]* to burst, break; *[veine]* to burst, rupture. **se ~ une veine** to burst *ou* rupture a blood vessel; **il va se ~ les os** *ou* **le cou** he's going to break his neck.

rompu, e [Rɔ̃py] (*ptp de* **rompre**) *adj* **(a)** (*fourbu*) **~ (de fatigue)** exhausted, worn-out, tired out; **~ de travail** exhausted by overwork.

(b) (*expérimenté*) **~ aux affaires** with wide business experience; **~ aux privations/à la discipline** accustomed *ou* inured to deprivation/discipline; **il est ~ à toutes les ficelles du métier/au maniement des armes** he is experienced in all the tricks of the trade/in the handling of firearms; *V* **bâton.**

romsteck [Rɔmstɛk] *nm* (*viande*) rumpsteak (*U*); (*tranche*) piece of rumpsteak.

ronce [Rɔ̃s] *nf* **(a)** (*branche*) bramble branch. (*buissons*) **~s** brambles, thorns; (*Bot*) **~ (des haies)** blackberry bush, bramble (bush); **il a déchiré son pantalon dans les ~s** he tore his trousers on *ou* in the brambles.

(b) (*Menuiserie*) **~ de noyer** burr walnut; **~ d'acajou** figured mahogany.

ronceraie [Rɔ̃srɛ] *nf* bramble patch, briar patch.

ronchon [Rɔ̃ʃɔ̃] **1** *adj* grumpy, grouchy*. **2** *nm* grumbler, grouch(er)*, grouser*.

ronchonnement [Rɔ̃ʃɔnmɑ̃] *nm* grumbling, grousing*, grouching*.

ronchonner [Rɔ̃ʃɔne] (1) *vi* to grumble, grouse*, grouch* (*après* at). **..., ronchonna-t-il** ..., he grumbled.

ronchonneur, -euse [Rɔ̃ʃɔnœr, øz] **1** *adj* grumpy, grouchy*. **2** *nm,f* grumbler, grouser*, grouch(er)*.

rond, e [Rɔ̃, Rɔ̃d] **1** *adj* **(a)** (*gén*) *objet, forme, visage* round; *pièce, lit* circular, round; *V* **dos, table, tourner** *etc.*

(b) (*gras*) *visage* round, chubby, plump; *joue, fesse* chubby, plump, well-rounded; *mollet* (well-)rounded, well-turned; *poitrine* full, (well-)rounded; *ventre* plump, tubby. **une petite femme toute ~e** a plump little woman.

(c) (*net*) round. **chiffre ~** round number *ou* figure; **ça fait 50**

F tout ~ it comes to exactly 50 francs, it comes to a round 50 francs; **ça coûte 29 F/31 F, disons 30 F pour faire un compte** ~ it costs 29 francs/31 francs, let's round it up/down to 30 francs *ou* let's say 30 francs to make a round figure; **être** ~ **en affaires** to be straightforward *ou* straight* *ou* on the level* in business matters, do a straight deal*.

(d) (*: *soûl*) drunk, tight*. **être** ~ **comme une bille** to be blind *ou* rolling drunk*.

2 *nm* **(a)** (*cercle dessiné*) circle, ring. **faire des** ~**s de fumée** to blow smoke rings; **faire des** ~**s dans l'eau** to make (circular) ripples in the water; **le verre a fait des** ~**s sur la table** the glass has made rings on the table.

(b) (*tranche*) *[carotte, saucisson]* slice, round (*Brit*); (*objet*) *[cuisinière]* ring. ~ **de serviette** serviette *ou* napkin ring; *V* **baver, flan.**

(c) (*: *sou*) ~**s** lolly‡ (*U*), cash* (*U*); **avoir des** ~**s** to be loaded*, be rolling in it*, have plenty of cash*; **il n'a pas le** *ou* **un** ~ he hasn't got a penny (to his name) *ou* a cent *ou* a brass farthing (*Brit*); **il n'a plus le** *ou* **un** ~ he hasn't got a penny left, he's (stony (*Brit*) *ou* stone (*US*) *ou* flat) broke*; **ça doit valoir des** ~**s!** that must cost a heck of a lot (of cash)!*; **pièce de 10/20** ~**s** 10-centime/20-centime piece.

(d) (*loc*) **en** ~ in a circle *ou* ring; **s'asseoir/danser en** ~ to sit/dance in a circle *ou* ring; *V* **empêcheur, tourner.**

3 ronde *nf* **(a)** (*tour de surveillance*) *[gardien, soldats]* rounds (*pl*); *[policier]* beat, patrol, rounds (*pl*); (*patrouille*) patrol. **faire sa** ~**e** to be on one's rounds *ou* on the beat *ou* on patrol; **sa** ~**e dura plus longtemps** he took longer doing his rounds; **il a fait 3** ~**es aujourd'hui** he has been on his rounds 3 times today, he has covered his beat 3 times today; ~**e de nuit** (*tour*) night rounds (*pl*), night beat *ou* patrol; (*patrouille*) night patrol; **ils virent passer la** ~**e** they saw the soldiers pass on their rounds; *V* **chemin.**

(b) (*danse*) round (dance), dance in a ring; (*danseurs*) circle, ring. ~**e villageoise/enfantine** villagers'/children's dance (*in a ring*); **faites la** ~**e** dance round in a circle *ou* ring.

(c) (*Mus: note*) semibreve (*Brit*), whole note (*US*).

(d) (*Écriture*) roundhand.

(e) (*loc*) **à 10 km à la** ~**e** for 10 km round, within a 10-km radius; **à des kilomètres à la** ~**e** for miles around; **passer qch à la** ~**e** to pass sth round; **boire à la** ~**e** to pass *ou* hand the bottle (*ou* cup *etc*) round.

4: ronde(-)bosse *nf, pl* **rondes(-)bosses** (sculpture in the) round; (*péj*) **rond-de-cuir** *nm, pl* **ronds-de-cuir** penpusher (*péj*), clerk; (*Danse*) **rond de jambes** rond de jambe; (*fig*) **faire des ronds de jambes** to bow and scrape (*péj*); **rond-point** *nm, pl* **ronds-points** (*carrefour*) roundabout (*Brit*), traffic circle (*US*); (*dans nom de lieu: place*) circus (*Brit*).

rondeau, *pl* ~**x** [ʀɔ̃do] *nm* (*Littérat*) rondeau; (*Mus*) rondo.

rondelet, -ette [ʀɔ̃dlɛ, ɛt] *adj femme* plumpish, nicely rounded; *enfant* chubby, plumpish; *bourse* well-lined; *salaire, somme* tidy (*épith*).

rondelle [ʀɔ̃dɛl] *nf* **(a)** (*Culin*) *[carotte, saucisson]* slice, round (*Brit*). **couper en** ~**s** to slice, cut into rounds (*Brit*) *ou* slices.

(b) (*disque de carton, plastique etc*) disc; *[boulon]* washer; *[canette de bière]* ring; *[bâton de ski]* basket.

rondement [ʀɔ̃dmɑ̃] *adv* **(a)** (*efficacement*) briskly. **mener** ~ **une affaire** to deal briskly with a piece of business.

(b) (*franchement*) frankly, outspokenly. **je vais parler** ~ I shan't beat about the bush, I'm going to be frank *ou* to speak frankly.

rondeur [ʀɔ̃dœʀ] *nf* **(a)** *[bras, personne, joue]* plumpness, chubbiness; *[visage]* roundness, plumpness, chubbiness; *[poitrine]* fullness; *[mollet]* roundness. (*hum*) **les** ~**s d'une femme** (*formes*) a woman's curves *ou* curviness; (*embonpoint*) a woman's plumpness *ou* chubbiness.

(b) *[terre]* roundness.

(c) (*bonhomie*) friendly straightforwardness, easy-going directness. **avec** ~ with (an) easy-going directness.

rondin [ʀɔ̃dɛ̃] *nm* log; *V* **cabane.**

rondo [ʀɔ̃do] *nm* rondo.

rondouillard, e* [ʀɔ̃dujaʀ, aʀd(ə)] *adj* (*péj*) tubby, podgy. **c'est un petit** ~ he's a dumpy *ou* tubby *ou* podgy little chap (*Brit*) *ou* guy.

ronéoter [ʀɔneɔte] (1) *vt,* **ronéotyper** [ʀɔneɔtipe] (1) *vt* to duplicate, roneo.

ronflant, e [ʀɔ̃flɑ̃, ɑ̃t] *adj* (*péj*) *promesse* high-flown, grand(-sounding).

ronflement [ʀɔ̃fləmɑ̃] *nm* (*V* **ronfler**) snore, snoring (*U*); humming (*U*); roar, roaring (*U*); purr(ing) (*U*); throbbing (*U*).

ronfler [ʀɔ̃fle] (1) *vi* **(a)** *[dormeur]* to snore; *[toupie]* to hum; *[poêle, feu]* (*sourdement*) to hum; (*en rugissant*) to roar; *[moteur]* (*sourdement*) to purr, throb; (*en rugissant*) to roar. **faire** ~ **son moteur** to rev up one's engine; **il actionna le démarreur et le moteur ronfla** he pressed the starter and the engine throbbed *ou* roared into action.

(b) (*: *dormir*) to snore away, be out for the count* (*surtout Brit*).

ronfleur, -euse [ʀɔ̃flœʀ, øz] **1** *nm,f* snorer. **2** *nm [téléphone]* buzzer.

ronger [ʀɔ̃ʒe] (3) **1** *vt* **(a)** *[souris]* to gnaw *ou* eat away at, gnaw *ou* eat into; *[rouille, acide, vers, pourriture]* to eat into; *[mer]* to wear away, eat into; *[eczéma]* to pit. ~ **un os** *[chien]* to gnaw (at) a bone; *[personne]* to pick a bone, gnaw (at) a bone; **les chenilles rongent les feuilles** caterpillars are eating away *ou* are nibbling (at) the leaves; **rongé par les vers** worm-eaten; **rongé par la rouille** eaten into by rust, pitted with rust; ~ **son frein** *[cheval]*, (*fig*) to champ (at) the bit; *V* **os.**

(b) (*fig*) *[maladie]* to sap (the strength of); *[chagrin, pensée]* to gnaw *ou* eat away at. **le mal qui le ronge** the evil which is gnawing *ou* eating away at him; **rongé par la maladie** sapped by illness.

2 se ronger *vpr*: **se** ~ **les ongles** to bite one's nails; **se** ~ **de soucis, se** ~ **les sangs** to worry o.s., fret; **elle se ronge (de chagrin)** she is eating her heart out, she is tormented with grief.

rongeur, -euse [ʀɔ̃ʒœʀ, øz] *adj, nm* rodent.

ronron [ʀɔ̃ʀɔ̃] *nm [chat]* purr(ing) (*U*); *[moteur]* purr(ing) (*U*), hum(ming) (*U*); (*péj*) *[discours]* drone (*U*), droning (on) (*U*).

ronronnement [ʀɔ̃ʀɔnmɑ̃] *nm* (*V* **ronronner**) purr (*U*), purring (*U*); hum (*U*), humming (*U*).

ronronner [ʀɔ̃ʀɔne] (1) *vi [chat]* to purr; *[moteur]* to purr, hum. (*fig*) **il ronronnait de satisfaction** he was purring with satisfaction.

roque [ʀɔk] *nm* (*Échecs*) castling. **grand/petit** ~ castling queen's/king's site.

roquefort [ʀɔkfɔʀ] *nm* Roquefort (cheese).

roquer [ʀɔke] (1) *vi* (*Échecs*) to castle; (*Croquet*) to roquet.

roquet [ʀɔkɛ] *nm* (*péj*) (*chien*) (nasty little) lap-dog; (*personne*) ill-tempered little runt*.

roquette [ʀɔkɛt] *nf* (*Mil*) rocket; *V* **lancer.**

rosace [ʀozas] *nf [cathédrale]* rose window, rosace; *[plafond]* (ceiling) rose; (*Broderie*) Tenerife motif; (*figure géométrique*) rosette.

rosacé, e [ʀozase] **1** *adj* (*Bot*) rosaceous. **2 rosacée** *nf* **(a)** (*Méd*) rosacea. **(b)** (*Bot*) rosaceous plant. ~**es** Rosaceae, rosaceous plants.

rosaire [ʀozɛʀ] *nm* rosary. **réciter son** ~ to say *ou* recite the rosary, tell one's beads†.

Rosalie [ʀozali] *nf* Rosalyn, Rosalind, Rosalie.

rosat [ʀoza] *adj inv pommade, miel* rose (*épith*). **huile** ~ oil of roses.

rosâtre [ʀozɑtʀ(ə)] *adj* pinkish.

rosbif [ʀɔsbif] *nm* **(a)** (*rôti*) roast beef (*U*); (*à rôtir*) roasting beef (*U*). **un** ~ a joint of (roast) beef; a joint of (roasting) beef.

(b) (‡*péj: Anglais*) ≃ limey* (*péj*).

rose [ʀoz] **1** *nf* (*fleur*) rose; (*vitrail*) rose window; (*diamant*) rose diamond. (*Prov*) **pas de** ~**s sans épines** no rose without a thorn (*Prov*); *V* **bois, bouton** *etc.*

2 *nm* (*couleur*) pink; *V* **vieux.**

3 *adj* **(a)** (*gén*) pink; *joues, teint* pink; (*plein de santé*) rosy. ~ **bonbon** candy-pink; ~ **saumoné** *ou* **saumon** salmon pink; *V* **crevette, flamant, tendre**[2].

(b) (*loc*) **tout n'est pas** ~**, ce n'est pas tout** ~ it's not all roses, it's not all rosy; **voir la vie** *ou* **tout en** ~ to see everything through rose-coloured glasses; **sa vie n'était pas bien** ~ his life was not a bed of roses.

4: Rose-croix (*nf inv*) (*confrérie*) Rosicrucians; (*nm inv*) (*membre*) Rosicrucian; (*grade de franc-maçonnerie*) Rose-croix; **rose de Noël** Christmas rose; **rose pompon** button rose; **rose des sables** gypsum flower; **rose-thé** *nf, pl* **roses-thé** tea rose; **rose trémière** hollyhock; **rose des vents** compass card.

rosé, e[1] [ʀoze] **1** *adj couleur* pinkish; *vin* rosé. **2** *nm* rosé (wine).

roseau, *pl* ~**x** [ʀozo] *nm* reed.

rosée[2] [ʀoze] *nf* dew. **couvert** *ou* **humide de** ~ *prés, herbe* dewy, covered in *ou* with dew; *sac de couchage, objet laissé dehors* wet with dew; *V* **goutte.**

roseraie [ʀozʀɛ] *nf* (*jardin*) rose garden; (*plantation*) rose-nursery.

rosette [ʀozɛt] *nf* (*nœud*) bow; (*insigne*) rosette; (*Archit, Art, Bot*) rosette. **avoir la** ~ to be an officer of the Légion d'Honneur; (*Culin*) ~ **de Lyon** (*type of*) slicing sausage.

rosier [ʀozje] *nm* rosebush, rose tree. ~ **nain/grimpant** dwarf/climbing rose.

rosière [ʀozjɛʀ] *nf* (*Hist*) *village maiden publicly rewarded for her chastity*; (*hum*) innocent maiden.

rosiériste [ʀozjeʀist(ə)] *nmf* rose grower.

rosir [ʀoziʀ] (2) **1** *vi [ciel, neige]* to grow *ou* turn pink; *[visage, personne]* to go pink, blush slightly. **2** *vt ciel, neige* to give a pink(ish) hue *ou* tinge to.

rosse [ʀɔs] **1** *nf* **(a)** († *péj: cheval*) nag.

(b) (**péj: méchant*) (*homme*) beast*, swine‡; (*femme*) beast*, bitch‡. **ah les** ~**s!** the (rotten) swine!‡, the (rotten) beasts!*

2 *adj* (*péj*) *critique, chansonnier* beastly* (*Brit*), nasty, vicious; *caricature* nasty, vicious; *coup, action* lousy*, rotten*, beastly* (*Brit*); *maître, époux* beastly* (*Brit*), horrid; *femme, patronne* bitchy‡, beastly* (*Brit*), horrid. **tu as vraiment été** ~ **(envers lui)** you were really beastly* (*Brit*) *ou* horrid (to him).

rossée [ʀɔse] *nf* (*, †) thrashing, (good) hiding, hammering*.

rosser [ʀɔse] (1) *vt* **(a)** (*frapper*) to thrash, give a (good) hiding to. **se faire** ~ to get a (good) hiding *ou* a thrashing *ou* a hammering*. **(b)** (*: *vaincre*) to thrash, lick*, hammer*.

rosserie [ʀɔsʀi] *nf* (*V* **rosse**) **(a)** (*U*) beastliness* (*Brit*); nastiness, viciousness; lousiness*, rottenness*; horridness; bitchiness‡.

(b) (*propos*) beastly* (*Brit*) *ou* nasty *ou* bitchy‡ remark; (*acte*) lousy* *ou* rotten* *ou* beastly* (*Brit*) trick.

rossignol [ʀɔsiɲɔl] *nm* **(a)** (*Orn*) nightingale. **(b)** (*: *invendu*) unsaleable article, piece of junk*. **(c)** (*clef*) picklock.

rossinante [ʀɔsinɑ̃t] *nf* (†, *hum*) (old) jade, old nag.

rot [ʀo] *nm* belch, burp*; *[bébé]* burp. **faire** *ou* **lâcher un** ~ to belch, burp*, let out a belch *ou* burp*; **le bébé a fait son** ~ the baby has done his (little) burp *ou* has got his wind up.

rôt†† [ʀo] *nm* roast.

rotatif, -ive [ʀɔtatif, iv] **1** *adj* rotary. **2 rotative** *nf* rotary press.

rotation [ʀɔtasjɔ̃] *nf* **(a)** (*mouvement*) rotation. **mouvement de** ~ rotating movement, rotary movement *ou* motion; **corps en** ~ rotating body, body in rotation; **vitesse de** ~ speed of rotation.

(b) (*alternance*) *[matériel, stock]* turnover; *[avions, bateaux]* frequency (of service). **la** ~ **du personnel** (*à des tâches successives*) the rotation *ou* swap-around of staff; (*départs et* *embauche*) the turnover of staff; **médecin qui est de garde par ~ tous les mois** doctor who is on duty each month on a rota basis *ou* system; **~ des cultures** rotation of crops.

rotatoire [ʀɔtatwaʀ] *adj* rotatory, rotary.

roter* [ʀɔte] (1) *vi* to burp*, belch. **en ~‡** to have a rough *ou* tough time of it, go through the mill* *ou* through it*; **il nous en a fait ~‡** he gave us a rough time, he put us through the mill* *ou* through it*.

rôti [ʀoti] *nm* (*Culin*) (*au magasin*) joint, roasting meat (*U*); (*au four, sur la table*) joint, roast, roast meat (*U*). **~ de bœuf/porc** joint of beef/pork, roasting beef/pork (*U*); joint of beef/pork, roast beef/pork (*U*).

rôtie [ʀoti] *nf* (†, *dial*) piece *ou* slice of toast.

rotin [ʀɔtɛ̃] *nm* **(a)** (*fibre*) rattan (cane). **fauteuil de ~** cane (arm)chair. **(b)** (†, *: *sou*) penny, cent. **il n'a pas un ~** he hasn't got a penny *ou* cent to his name.

rôtir [ʀotiʀ] (2) **1** *vt* (*Culin: aussi* **faire ~**) to roast. **poulet/agneau rôti** roast chicken/lamb.

2 *vi* (*Culin*) to roast; *[estivants, baigneur]* to roast, be roasting hot. **on rôtit ici!** it's roasting *ou* scorching (hot) *ou* sweltering here!, we're roasting (hot) *ou* sweltering here!

3 se rôtir *vpr*: **se ~ au soleil** to bask in the sun.

rôtisserie [ʀotisʀi] *nf* (*dans noms de restaurant*) steakhouse, grill and griddle; (*boutique*) shop selling roast meat.

rôtisseur, -euse [ʀotisœʀ, øz] *nm,f* (*traiteur*) seller of roast meat; (*restaurateur*) steakhouse proprietor.

rôtissoire [ʀotiswaʀ] *nf* (roasting) spit.

rotogravure [ʀɔtɔgʀavyʀ] *nf* rotogravure.

rotonde [ʀɔtɔ̃d] *nf* (*Archit*) rotunda; (*Rail*) engine shed (*Brit*), roundhouse (*US*). **édifice en ~** circular building.

rotondité [ʀɔtɔ̃dite] *nf* **(a)** (*sphéricité*) roundness, rotundity (*frm*). **(b)** (*hum: embonpoint*) plumpness, rotundity (*hum*). **~s** *[femme]* plump curves.

rotor [ʀɔtɔʀ] *nm* rotor.

rotule [ʀɔtyl] *nf* **(a)** (*Anat*) kneecap, patella (*T*). **être sur les ~s*** to be dead beat* *ou* all in*. **(b)** (*Tech*) ball-and-socket joint.

rotulien, -ienne [ʀɔtyljɛ̃, jɛn] *adj* patellar.

roture [ʀɔtyʀ] *nf* (*absence de noblesse*) common rank. **la ~** (*roturiers*) the commoners, the common people; *[fief]* roture.

roturier, -ière [ʀɔtyʀje, jɛʀ] **1** *adj* (*Hist*) common, of common birth; (*fig: vulgaire*) common, plebeian. **2** *nm,f* commoner.

rouage [ʀwaʒ] *nm* *[engrenage]* cog(wheel), gearwheel; *[montre]* part. **les ~s d'une montre** the works *ou* parts of a watch; (*fig*) **il n'est qu'un ~ dans cette organisation** he's merely a cog in this organization; (*fig*) **les ~s de l'État/de l'organisation** the wheels of State/of the organization; (*fig*) **organisation aux ~s compliqués** organization with complex structures.

roublard, e* [ʀublaʀ, aʀd(ə)] **1** *adj* crafty, wily, artful. **2** *nm,f* crafty *ou* artful devil*. **ce ~ de Paul** crafty old Paul*.

roublardise [ʀublaʀdiz] *nf* (*caractère*) craftiness, wiliness, artfulness; (*acte, tour*) crafty *ou* artful trick.

rouble [ʀubl(ə)] *nm* rouble.

roucoulade [ʀukulad] *nf* (*V* **roucouler**) (*gén pl*) coo(ing) (*U*); (billing and) cooing (*U*); warble, warbling (*U*).

roucoulement [ʀukulmɑ̃] *nm* (*V* **roucouler**) coo(ing) (*U*); (billing and) cooing (*U*); warble, warbling (*U*).

roucouler [ʀukule] (1) **1** *vi [oiseau]* to coo; (*péj*) *[amoureux]* to bill and coo; (*péj*) *[chanteur]* to warble. **venir ~ sous la fenêtre de sa bien-aimée** to come cooing under the window of one's beloved.

2 *vt* (*péj*) *chanson* to warble; *mots d'amour* to coo.

roue [ʀu] **1** *nf [véhicule, loterie, montre]* wheel; *[engrenage]* cog(wheel), (gear)wheel. **véhicule à deux/quatre ~s** two-/four-wheeled vehicle; **~ avant/arrière** front/back wheel; **(supplice de) la ~** (torture of) the wheel; (*fig*) **la ~ de la Fortune** the wheel of Fortune; **faire la ~** *[paon]* to spread *ou* fan its tail; *[personne]* (*se pavaner*) to strut about, swagger (about); (*Gymnastique*) to do a cartwheel; *V* **bâton, chapeau, cinquième** *etc.*

2: roue à aubes *[bateau]* paddle wheel; **roue dentée** cog-wheel; **roue à godets** bucket wheel; (*Naut*) **roue de gouvernail** (steering) wheel, helm; **roue hydraulique** waterwheel; (*Aut*) **roue libre** freewheel; **descendre une côte en roue libre** to freewheel *ou* coast down a hill; **pédaler en roue libre** to freewheel, coast (along); (*Aut*) **roue motrice** driving wheel; **vehicule à 4 roues motrices** 4-wheel drive vehicle; (*Aut*) **roue de secours** spare wheel; **roue de transmission** driving wheel.

roué, e [ʀwe] (*ptp de* **rouer**) **1** *adj* (*rusé*) cunning, wily, sly.

2 *nm,f* cunning *ou* sly individual. **c'est une petite ~e** she's a cunning *ou* wily *ou* sly little minx.

3 *nm* (*Hist: débauché*) rake, roué.

4 rouée *nf* (*Hist: débauchée*) hussy.

rouennais, e [ʀwanɛ, ɛz] **1** *adj* of *ou* from Rouen. **2** *nm,f*: **R~(e)** inhabitant *ou* native of Rouen.

rouer [ʀwe] (1) *vt* **(a) ~ qn de coups** to give sb a beating *ou* thrashing, beat sb black and blue. **(b)** (*Hist*) *condamné* to put on the wheel.

rouerie [ʀuʀi] *nf* (*U: caractère*) cunning, wiliness, slyness; (*tour*) cunning *ou* wily *ou* sly trick.

rouet [ʀwɛ] *nm* (*à filer*) spinning wheel.

rouflaquettes* [ʀuflakɛt] *nfpl* (*favoris*) sideboards (*Brit*), sideburns.

rouge [ʀuʒ] **1** *adj* **(a)** (*gén, Pol*) red; *V* **armée**[2], **chaperon** *etc.*

(b) (*porté à l'incandescence*) *fer* red-hot; *tison* glowing red (*attrib*), red-hot.

(c) *visage, yeux* red. **~ de colère/de confusion/de honte** red *ou* flushed with anger/embarrassment/shame; **~ d'émotion** flushed with emotion; **devenir ~ comme une cerise** to blush, go quite pink; **il est ~ comme un coq** *ou* **un coquelicot** *ou* **une pivoine** *ou* **une écrevisse** *ou* **une tomate** he's as red as a beetroot *ou* a lobster; **il était ~ d'avoir couru** he was red in the face *ou* his face was flushed from running; *V* **fâcher.**

(d) *cheveux, pelage* red.

2 *nm* **(a)** (*couleur*) red. (*Pol*) **voter ~** to vote Communist; (*Aut*) **le feu est au ~** the lights are red; **passer au ~** to jump the lights, go through red lights; *V* **bordeaux.**

(b) (*signe d'émotion*) **le ~ lui monta aux joues** his cheeks flushed, he went red (in the face); **le ~ (de la confusion/de la honte) lui monta au front** his face went red *ou* flushed *ou* he blushed (with embarrassment/shame).

(c) (*vin*) red wine; (*: *verre de vin*) glass of red wine; *V* **coup, gros.**

(d) (*fard*) rouge; (*à lèvres*) lipstick; *V* **bâton, tube.**

(e) (*incandescence*) **fer porté au ~** red-hot iron.

3 *nmf* (*péj: communiste*) Red* (*péj*), Commie* (*péj*).

4: rouge-cerise *adj inv* cherry-red; **rouge-gorge** *nm, pl* **rouges-gorges** robin (redbreast); **rouge à lèvres** lipstick; **rouge-queue** *nm, pl* **rouges-queues** redstart; **rouge-sang** *adj inv* blood red.

rougeâtre [ʀuʒɑtʀ(ə)] *adj* reddish.

rougeaud, e [ʀuʒo, od] *adj* red-faced. **ce gros ~ la dégoûtait** she found this fat red-faced man repellent.

rougeoiement [ʀuʒwamɑ̃] *nm [incendie, couchant]* red *ou* reddish glow; *[ciel]* reddening.

rougeole [ʀuʒɔl] *nf*: **la ~** (the) measles (*sg*); **il a eu une très forte ~** he had a very bad bout of measles.

rougeoyant, e [ʀuʒwajɑ̃, ɑ̃t] *adj ciel* reddening; *cendres* glowing red (*attrib*), glowing. **des reflets ~s** a glimmering red glow.

rougeoyer [ʀuʒwaje] (8) *vi [feu, incendie, couchant]* to glow red; *[ciel]* to turn red, take on a reddish hue.

rouget [ʀuʒɛ] *nm* mullet. **~ barbet** red mullet; **~ grondin** gurnard.

rougeur [ʀuʒœʀ] *nf* **(a)** (*teinte*) redness.

(b) *[personne] (due à la course, un échauffement, une émotion)* red face, flushing (*U*); (*due à la honte, gêne*) red face, blushing (*U*), blushes (*pl*); *[visages, joues]* redness, flushing (*U*). **sa ~ a trahi son émotion/sa gêne** her red face *ou* her blushes betrayed her emotion/embarrassment; **la ~ de ses joues** his red face *ou* cheeks, his flushing, his blushing; **avoir des ~s de jeune fille** to blush like a young girl; **elle était sujette à des ~s subites** she was given to sudden flushes *ou* blushing.

(c) (*Méd: tache*) red blotch *ou* patch.

rougir [ʀuʒiʀ] (2) **1** *vi* **(a)** (*de honte, gêne*) to blush, go red, redden, colour (up) (*de* with); (*de plaisir, d'émotion*) to flush, go red, redden (*de* with). **il rougit de colère** he *ou* his face flushed *ou* reddened with anger; **à ces mots, elle rougit** she blushed *ou* coloured (up) *ou* went red *ou* reddened at the words; **~ jusqu'au blanc des yeux** *ou* **jusqu'aux yeux, ~ jusqu'aux oreilles, ~ jusqu'à la racine des cheveux** to go bright red, blush to the roots of one's hair; (*lit, fig*) **faire ~ qn** to make sb blush; **dire qch sans ~** to say sth without blushing *ou* unblushingly.

(b) (*fig: avoir honte*) **~ de** to be ashamed of; **je n'ai pas à ~ de cela** that is nothing for me to be ashamed of; **il ne rougit de rien** he's quite shameless, he has no shame.

(c) (*après un coup de soleil*) to go red.

(d) *[ciel, neige, feuille]* to go *ou* turn red, redden; *[métal]* to become *ou* get red-hot; (*Culin*) *[crustacés]* to go *ou* turn red, redden; (*Agr*) *[tomates, fraises]* to redden, turn red.

2 *vt ciel* to turn red, give a red glow to, redden; *feuilles, arbres* to turn red, redden; *métal* to heat to red heat, make red-hot. **~ son eau** to put a dash *ou* drop of red wine in one's water; **~ la terre de son sang** (*lit*) to stain the ground with one's blood; (*fig*) to shed one's blood.

rougissant, e [ʀuʒisɑ̃, ɑ̃t] *adj visage, jeune fille* blushing; *feuille, ciel* reddening.

rougissement [ʀuʒismɑ̃] *nm* (*de honte etc*) blush, blushing (*U*); (*d'émotion*) flush, flushing (*U*).

rouille [ʀuj] **1** *nf* **(a)** (*Bot, Chim*) rust. **(b)** (*Culin*) *spicy Provençal sauce accompanying fish.* **2** *adj inv* rust(-coloured), rusty.

rouillé, e [ʀuje] (*ptp de* **rouiller**) *adj* **(a)** *métal* rusty, rusted; (*littér*) *roche, écorce* rust-coloured. **tout ~** rusted over.

(b) (*fig*) *mémoire* rusty; *muscles* stiff; *athlète* rusty, out of practice (*attrib*). **j'étais ~ en latin*** my Latin was rusty.

(c) (*Bot*) *blé* rusty.

rouiller [ʀuje] (1) **1** *vi* to rust, go *ou* get rusty. **laisser ~ qch** to let sth go *ou* get rusty.

2 *vt métal, esprit* to make rusty. **l'inaction rouillait les hommes** the lack of action was making the men rusty.

3 se rouiller *vpr [métal]* to go *ou* get rusty, rust; *[esprit, mémoire]* to become *ou* go rusty; *[corps, muscles]* to grow *ou* get stiff; *[athlète]* to get rusty, get out of practice.

rouir [ʀwiʀ] (2) *vt* (*aussi* **faire ~**) to ret.

rouissage [ʀwisaʒ] *nm* retting.

roulade [ʀulad] *nf* **(a)** (*Mus*) roulade, run; *[oiseau]* trill. **(b)** (*Culin*) rolled meat (*U*). **~ de veau** rolled veal (*U*). **(c)** (*Sport*) roll. **~ avant/arrière** forward/backward roll.

roulage [ʀulaʒ] *nm* (*Min*, †: *transport, camionnage*) haulage; (*Agr*) rolling.

roulant, e [ʀulɑ̃, ɑ̃t] **1** *adj* **(a)** (*mobile*) *meuble* on wheels; *V* **cuisine, fauteuil, table.**

(b) (*Rail*) **matériel ~** rolling stock; **personnel ~** train crews (*pl*).

(c) *trottoir, surface transporteuse* moving; *V* **escalier, feu**[1], **pont.**

(d) *route* fast; *voiture* smooth-running.

(e) (*: *drôle*) *chose, événement* killing*, killingly funny*. **elle est ~e!** she's a scream!*, she's killingly funny!*

2 *nmpl* (*arg Rail*) **les ~s** train crews.

3 roulante *nf* (*arg Mil*) field kitchen.

roulé, e [Rule] (*ptp de* **rouler**) **1** *adj* **(a)** **être bien ~*** to be shapely, have a good shape *ou* figure.
(b) *bord de chapeau* curved; *bord de foulard, morceau de boucherie* rolled; 'r' rolled, trilled; *V* **col.**
2 *nm* (*gâteau*) Swiss roll; (*pâte*) = turnover; (*viande*) rolled meat (*U*). **~ de veau** rolled veal (*U*).
3: (*Sport*) **roulé-boulé** *nm, pl* **roulés-boulés** roll.

rouleau, *pl* **~x** [Rulo] **1** *nm* **(a)** (*bande enroulée*) roll. **~ de papier/tissu/pellicule** roll of paper/material/film; **un ~ de cheveux blonds** a ringlet of blond hair; *V* **bout.**
(b) (*cylindre*) *[tabac, pièces]* roll. **~ de réglisse** liquorice roll.
(c) (*ustensile, outil*) roller; *[machine à écrire]* platen, roller. **passer une pelouse au ~** to roll a lawn; **avoir des ~x dans les cheveux** to have one's hair in curlers *ou* rollers, have curlers *ou* rollers in one's hair; **peindre au ~** to paint with a roller.
(d) (*vague*) roller.
(e) (*Sport: saut*) roll.
2: rouleau compresseur steamroller, roadroller; (*Sport*) **rouleau dorsal** Fosbury flop; **rouleau encreur** = **rouleau imprimeur; rouleau essuie-mains** roller towel; **rouleau imprimeur** ink roller; **rouleau de papier hygiénique** toilet roll, roll of toilet paper *ou* tissue; **rouleau de parchemin** scroll *ou* roll of parchment; **rouleau à pâtisserie** rolling pin; (*Sport*) **rouleau ventral** western roll.

roulement [Rulmɑ̃] **1** *nm* **(a)** (*rotation*) *[équipe, ouvriers]* rotation. **travailler par ~** to work on a rota basis *ou* system, work in rotation.
(b) (*geste*) **avoir un ~** *ou* **des ~s d'épaules/de hanches** to sway one's shoulders/wiggle one's hips; **un ~ d'yeux** a roll of the eyes; **faire des ~s d'yeux** to roll one's eyes.
(c) (*circulation*) *[voiture, train]* movement. **route usée/pneu usé par le ~** road/tyre worn through use; *V* **bande**[1].
(d) (*bruit*) *[train, camion]* rumble, rumbling (*U*); *[charrette]* rattle, rattling (*U*). **entendre le ~ du tonnerre** to hear the rumble *ou* peal *ou* roll of thunder, hear thunder rumbling; **il y eut un ~ de tonnerre** there was a rumble *ou* peal *ou* roll of thunder; **~ de tambour** drum roll.
(e) *[capitaux]* circulation; *V* **fonds.**
2: roulement (à billes) ball bearings (*pl*); **monté sur roulement à billes** mounted on ball bearings.

rouler [Rule] (1) **1** *vt* **(a)** (*pousser*) *meuble* to wheel (along), roll (along); *chariot, brouette* to wheel (along), trundle along; *boule, tonneau* to roll (along). **~ un bébé dans sa poussette** to wheel *ou* push a baby (along) in his push chair.
(b) (*enrouler*) *tapis, tissu, carte* to roll up; *cigarette* to roll; *ficelle, fil de fer* to wind up, roll up; *viande, parapluie, mèche de cheveux* to roll (up). **~ qn dans une couverture** to wrap *ou* roll sb (up) in a blanket; **~ un pansement autour d'un bras** to wrap *ou* wind a bandage round an arm; **~ ses manches jusqu'au coude** to roll up one's sleeves to one's elbows.
(c) (*tourner et retourner*) to roll. **~ des boulettes dans de la farine** to roll meatballs in flour; **la mer roulait les galets sur la plage** the sea rolled the pebbles along the beach; (*fig*) **il roulait mille projets dans sa tête** he was turning thousands of plans over (and over) in his mind; (*littér*) **le fleuve roulait des flots boueux** the river flowed muddily along.
(d) (*passer au rouleau*) *court de tennis, pelouse* to roll; (*Culin*) *pâte* to roll out.
(e) (*: *duper*) to con‡; (*sur le prix, le poids*) to diddle* (*sur* over). **je l'ai bien roulé** I really conned him‡, I really took him for a ride*; **se faire ~** to be conned‡ *ou* had* *ou* done* *ou* diddled*.
(f) ~ les *ou* **des épaules** *ou* **des mécaniques‡ (en marchant)** to sway one's shoulders (when walking); **~ les** *ou* **des hanches** to wiggle one's hips; **~ les yeux** to roll one's eyes; (*fig*) **il a roulé sa bosse** he has knocked about the world*, he has certainly been places*.
(g) (*Ling*) **~ les 'r'** to roll one's r's.
2 *vi* **(a)** *[voiture, train]* to go, run. **le train roulait/roulait à vive allure à travers la campagne** the train was going along/was racing (along) through the countryside; **cette voiture est comme neuve, elle a très peu roulé** this car is like new, it has a very low mileage; **cette voiture a 10 ans et elle roule encore** this car is 10 years old but it's still going *ou* running; **la voiture roule bien depuis la révision** the car is running *ou* going well since its service; **les voitures ne roulent pas bien sur le sable** cars don't run well on sand; **le véhicule roulait à gauche** the vehicle was driving (along) on the left; **~ au pas** (*prudence*) to go dead slow; (*dans un embouteillage*) to crawl along; **le train roulait à 150 à l'heure au moment de l'accident** the train was doing 150 *ou* going at 150 at the time of the accident.
(b) *[passager, conducteur]* to drive. **~ à 80 km à l'heure** to do 80 km *ou* 50 miles per hour, drive at 80 km *ou* 50 miles per hour; **on a bien roulé*** we kept up a good speed, we made good time; **ça roule/ça ne roule pas bien** the traffic is/is not flowing well; **nous roulions sur la N7 quand soudain ...** we were driving along the N7 when suddenly ...; **dans son métier, il roule beaucoup** in his job, he does a lot of driving; **il roule en 2CV** he drives a 2CV; **il roule en Rolls** he drives (around) in a Rolls; (†, *hum*) **~ carrosse** to live in high style.
(c) *[boule, bille, dé]* to roll; *[presse]* to roll, run. **allez, roulez!** let's roll it!*, off we go!; **une larme roula sur sa joue** a tear rolled down his cheek; **une secousse le fit ~ à bas de sa couchette** a jerk sent him rolling down from his couchette, a jerk made him roll off his couchette; **il a roulé en bas de l'escalier** he rolled right down the stairs; **un coup de poing l'envoya ~ dans la poussière** a punch sent him rolling in the dust; **faire ~** *boule* to roll; *cerceau* to roll along; *V* **pierre.**
(d) *[bateau]* to roll. **ça roulait*** the boat was rolling quite a bit.
(e) (*: *bourlinguer*) to knock about*, drift around. **il a pas mal roulé** he has knocked about* *ou* drifted around quite a bit.
(f) *[argent, capitaux]* to be put to (good) use. **il faut que l'argent roule** money must be made to work *ou* be put to (good) use.
(g) (*faire un bruit sourd*) *[tambour]* to roll; *[tonnerre]* to roll, rumble, peal.
(h) *[conversation]* **~ sur** to turn on, be centred on.
(i) ~ sur l'or to be rolling in money*, have pots of money*; **ils ne roulent pas sur l'or depuis qu'ils sont à la retraite** they're not exactly living in the lap of luxury *ou* they're not terribly well-off now they've retired.
3 se rouler *vpr* **(a)** to roll (about). **se ~ de douleur** to roll about in *ou* with pain; **se ~ par terre/dans l'herbe** to roll on the ground/in the grass; (*fig*) **se ~ par terre de rire** to fall about* (laughing); **c'est à se ~ (par terre)*** it's a scream*, it's killing*; *V* **pouce.**
(b) (*s'enrouler*) **se ~ dans une couverture** to roll *ou* wrap o.s. up in a blanket; **se ~ en boule** to roll o.s. (up) into a ball.

roulette [Rulɛt] *nf* **(a)** *[meuble]* castor. **fauteuil à ~s** armchair on castors; **ça a marché** *ou* **été comme sur des ~s*** *[plan]* it went like clockwork *ou* very smoothly; *[soirée, interview]* it went off very smoothly; *V* **patin.**
(b) (*outil*) *[pâtissière]* pastry (cutting) wheel; *[relieur]* fillet; *[couturière]* tracing wheel. **~ de dentiste** dentist's drill.
(c) (*jeu*) roulette; (*instrument*) roulette wheel. **~ russe** Russian roulette.

rouleur [RulœR] *nm* (*Cyclisme*) flat racer.
roulier [Rulje] *nm* (*Hist*) cart driver, wagoner.
roulis [Ruli] *nm* (*Naut*) roll(ing) (*U*). **il y a beaucoup de ~** the ship is rolling a lot; *V* **coup.**
roulotte [Rulɔt] *nf* caravan (*Brit*), trailer (*US*).
roulotter [Rulɔte] (1) *vt* (*Couture*) *ourlet* to roll; *foulard* to roll the edges of, roll a hem on.
roulure‡ [RulyR] *nf* (*péj*) slut (*péj*), trollop† (*péj*).
roumain, e [Rumɛ̃, ɛn] **1** *adj* Rumanian, Romanian. **2** *nm* (*Ling*) Rumanian, Romanian. **3** *nm,f*: **R~(e)** Rumanian, Romanian.
Roumanie [Rumani] *nf* Rumania, Romania.
roupie [Rupi] *nf* **(a)** (*Fin*) rupee. **(b)** (†*) **c'est de la ~ de sansonnet** it's a load of (old) rubbish *ou* junk*, it's absolute trash*; **ce n'est pas de la ~ de sansonnet** it's none of your cheap rubbish *ou* junk*.
roupiller* [Rupije] (1) *vi* (*dormir*) to sleep; (*faire un petit somme*) to have a snooze* *ou* a kip‡ *ou* a nap. **j'ai besoin de ~** I must get some shut-eye‡ *ou* kip‡; **je n'arrive pas à ~** I can't get any shut-eye‡ *ou* kip‡; **je vais ~** I'll be turning in*, I'm off to hit the hay*; **viens ~ chez nous** come and kip down at our place‡; **secouez-vous, vous roupillez!** pull yourself together — you're half asleep! *ou* you're dozing!
roupillon* [Rupijɔ̃] *nm* snooze*, kip‡, nap. **piquer** *ou* **faire un ~** to have a snooze* *ou* a kip‡ *ou* a nap.
rouquin, e* [Rukɛ̃, in] **1** *adj personne* red-haired; *cheveux* red. **2** *nm,f* redhead. **3** *nm* (‡: *vin rouge*) red plonk* (*Brit*), (cheap) red wine.
rouscailler‡ [Ruskɑje] (1) *vi* to moan*, bellyache‡.
rouspétance* [Ruspetɑ̃s] *nf* (*V* **rouspéter**) moaning* (*U*); grousing* (*U*), grouching* (*U*); grumbling (*U*).
rouspéter* [Ruspete] (6) *vi* (*ronchonner*) to moan*, grouse*, grouch*; (*protester*) to moan*, grumble (*après* at).
rouspéteur, -euse* [RuspetœR, øz] **1** *adj* grumpy. **c'est un ~** he's a proper moaner* *ou* grumbler, he's a grumpy individual. **2** *nm,f* (*ronchonneur*) moaner*, grouser*, grouch*; (*qui proteste*) grumbler, moaner*.
roussâtre [RusɑtR(ə)] *adj* reddish, russet.
rousse[1] [Rus] *adj f V* **roux.**
rousse[2] [Rus] *nf* (*arg Crime*) **la ~** the fuzz (*arg*).
rousseauiste [Rusoist(ə)] *adj* Rousseauistic.
roussette [Rusɛt] *nf* (*poisson*) dogfish; (*chauve-souris*) flying fox; (*grenouille*) common frog.
rousseur [RusœR] *nf* **(a)** (*U: V* **roux**) redness; gingery colour; russet colour; *V* **tache. (b)** (*sur la peau, le papier*) **~s** brownish marks *ou* stains.
roussi [Rusi] *nm*: **odeur de ~** smell of (something) burning *ou* scorching *ou* singeing; **ça sent le ~!** (*lit*) there's a smell of (something) burning *ou* scorching *ou* singeing; (*fig*) I can smell trouble.
roussin†† [Rusɛ̃] *nm* horse.
roussir [RusiR] (2) **1** *vt* *[fer à repasser]* to scorch, singe; *[flamme]* to singe. **~ l'herbe** *[gelée]* to turn the grass brown *ou* yellow; *[chaleur]* to scorch the grass.
2 *vi* **(a)** *[feuilles, forêt]* to turn *ou* go brown *ou* russet.
(b) (*Culin*) **faire ~** to brown.

route [Rut] *nf* **(a)** road. **~ nationale/départementale** = trunk (*Brit*) *ou* main/secondary road; **~ de montagne** mountain road; **prenez la ~ de Lyon** take the road to Lyons *ou* the Lyons road; *V* **course, grand.**
(b) (*moyen de transport*) **la ~** road; **la ~ est plus économique que le rail** road is cheaper than rail; **la ~ est meurtrière** the road is a killer, driving is treacherous; **arriver par la ~** to arrive by road; **faire de la ~** to do a lot of mileage; **accidents/blessés de la ~** road accidents/casualties; *V* **code.**
(c) (*chemin à suivre*) way; (*Naut: direction, cap*) course. **je ne l'emmène pas, ce n'est pas ma ~** I'm not taking him because it's not on my way; **perdre/retrouver sa ~** to lose/find one's way.
(d) (*ligne de communication*) route. **~ aérienne/maritime** air/sea route; **la ~ du sel/de l'opium/des épices** the salt/opium/spice route *ou* trail; **la ~ des Indes** the route *ou* road to India; **indiquer/montrer la ~ à qn** to point out/show the way to sb; **ils ont fait toute la ~ à pied/à bicyclette** they did the whole journey on foot/by bicycle, they walked/cycled the whole way; **la ~ sera longue** (*gén*) it'll be a long journey; (*en voiture*) it'll be

a long drive *ou* ride; **il y a 3 heures de ~** (*en voiture*) it's a 3-hour drive *ou* ride *ou* journey; (*à bicyclette*) it's a 3-hour (cycle-)ride *ou* journey; *V* **barrer, compagnon** *etc.*

(e) (*fig: ligne de conduite, voie*) path, road, way. **la ~ à suivre** the path *ou* road to follow; **la ~ du bonheur** the road *ou* path *ou* way to happinesss; **votre ~ est toute tracée** your path is set out for you; **la ~ s'ouvre devant lui** the road *ou* way opens (up) before him; **être sur la bonne ~** (*dans la vie*) to be on the right road *ou* path; (*dans un problème*) to be on the right track; **remettre qn sur la bonne ~** to put sb back on the right road *ou* path, put sb back on the right track; **c'est lui qui a ouvert la ~** he's the one who opened (up) the road *ou* way.

(f) (*loc*) **faire ~ vers** (*gén*) to head towards *ou* for; *[bateau]* to steer a course for, head for; **en ~ pour, faisant ~ vers** bound for, heading for, on its way to; **faire ~ avec qn** to travel with sb; **prendre la ~, se mettre en ~** to start out, set off *ou* out, get under way; **en ~** on the way *ou* journey, en route; **en ~!** let's go!, let's be off; **reprendre la ~, se remettre en ~** to resume one's journey, start out again, set off *ou* out again; **bonne ~!** have a good journey! *ou* trip!; **mettre en ~** *machine, moteur* to start (up); *affaire* to set in motion, get under way; **mise en ~** starting up, setting in motion; **carnet** *ou* **journal de ~** travel diary *ou* journal; **tenir bien la ~** to hold the road well; *V* **tenu.**

routier, -ière [rutje, jɛr] **1** *adj circulation, carte, réseau, transport* road (*épith*); *V* **gare**[1].

2 *nm* (*camionneur*) long-distance lorry (*Brit*) *ou* truck (*US*) driver; (*restaurant*) ≈ transport café (*Brit*); (*cycliste*) road racer; (*Naut: carte*) route chart; (*scout*) rover; *V* **vieux.**

3 routière *nf* (*Aut*) tourer (*Brit*), touring car.

routine [rutin] *nf* routine. **par ~** as a matter of routine; **opération/visite de ~** routine operation/visit.

routinier, -ière [rutinje, jɛr] *adj procédé, travail, vie* humdrum, routine; *personne* routine-minded, addicted to routine (*attrib*). **il a l'esprit ~** he's completely tied to (his) routine; **c'est un travail un peu ~** the work is a bit routine *ou* humdrum; **c'est un ~** he's a creature of habit.

rouvrir *vti*, **se rouvrir** *vpr* [ruvrir] (18) to reopen, open again. **la porte se rouvrit** the door opened again; **~ le débat** to reopen the debate.

roux, rousse[1] [ru, rus] **1** *adj cheveux* red, auburn; (*orangé*) ginger; *barbe* red; (*orangé*) ginger; *pelage, robe, feuilles* russet, reddish-brown. **il aime les rousses** he likes redheads; *V* **beurre, blond, brun** *etc.*

2 *nm* **(a)** (*couleur*) (*V adj*) red; auburn; ginger; russet, reddish-brown.

(b) (*Culin*) roux.

royal, e, *mpl* **-aux** [rwajal, o] *adj* **(a)** *couronne, palais, appartement* royal; *pouvoir, autorité* royal, regal; *prérogative, décret, charte* royal. **la famille ~e** the Royal Family *ou* royal family.

(b) *maintien, magnificence* kingly, regal; *repas, demeure, cadeau* fit for a king (*attrib*); *salaire* princely; *V* **aigle, tigre.**

(c) (*intensif*) *indifférence, mépris* majestic, lofty, regal; *paix* blissful.

(d) (*Culin*) **lièvre à la ~e** hare royale.

royalement [rwajalmɑ̃] *adv vivre* in (a) royal fashion; *recevoir, traiter* royally, in (a) regal *ou* royal fashion. **il se moque ~ de sa situation*** he couldn't care less* *ou* he doesn't care two hoots* about his position; (*iro*) **il m'a ~ offert 3 F d'augmentation*** he offered me a princely 3-franc rise (*iro*).

royalisme [rwajalism(ə)] *nm* royalism.

royaliste [rwajalist(ə)] **1** *adj* royalist. **être plus ~ que le roi** to out-Herod Herod (*in the defence of sb or in following a doctrine etc*). **2** *nmf* royalist.

royalties [rwajalti] *nfpl* royalties (*on patent, on the use of oil-fields or pipeline*).

royaume [rwajom] **1** *nm* (*lit*) kingdom, realm; (*fig: domaine*) realm, (private) world. **le vieux grenier était son ~** the old attic was his (private) world *ou* his realm; *V* **à.**

2: le royaume céleste *ou* **de Dieu** the kingdom of heaven *ou* God; **le Royaume-Uni** the United Kingdom.

royauté [rwajote] *nf* (*régime*) monarchy; (*fonction, dignité*) kingship.

ru†† [ry] *nm* brook, rivulet (*littér*).

ruade [ryad] *nf* kick (*of a horse's hind legs*). **tué par une ~** killed by a kick from a horse; **le cheval lui a cassé la jambe d'une ~** the horse kicked *ou* lashed out at him and broke his leg; **décocher** *ou* **lancer une ~** to lash *ou* kick out.

ruban [rybɑ̃] **1** *nm* (*gén, fig*) ribbon; *[machine à écrire]* ribbon; *[téléscripteur, magnétophone]* tape; *[ourlet, couture]* binding, tape. **le ~ (de la Légion d'honneur)** the ribbon of the Légion d'Honneur; (*fig*) **le ~ argenté du Rhône** the silver ribbon of the Rhone; **le double ~ de l'autoroute** the two *ou* twin lines of the motorway; *V* **mètre, scie.**

2: ruban d'acier steel band *ou* strip; **ruban adhésif** adhesive tape, sticky tape; (*Naut*) **le ruban bleu** the Blue Riband *ou* Ribbon (*of the Atlantic*); **ruban de chapeau** hat band; **ruban encreur** typewriter ribbon.

rubéole [rybeɔl] *nf* German measles (*sg*), rubella (*T*).

Rubicon [rybikɔ̃] *nm* *V* **franchir.**

rubicond, e [rybikɔ̃, ɔ̃d] *adj* rubicund, ruddy.

rubis [rybi] **1** *nm* (*pierre*) ruby; (*couleur*) ruby (colour); *[horloge, montre]* jewel; *V* **payer. 2** *adj inv* ruby(-coloured).

rubrique [rybrik] *nf* **(a)** (*article, chronique*) column. **~ sportive/littéraire des spectacles** sports/literary/entertainments column.

(b) (*titre, catégorie*) heading, rubric. **sous cette même ~** under the same heading *ou* rubric.

(c) (*Rel*) rubric.

ruche [ryʃ] *nf* **(a)** (*en bois*) (bee)hive; (*essaim*) hive; (*en paille*) (bee)hive, skep (*T*). (*fig*) **l'école se transforme en ~ dès 8 heures** the school turns into a (regular) hive of activity at 8 o'clock.

(b) (*Couture*) ruche.

ruché [ryʃe] *nm* (*Couture*) ruching (*U*), ruche.

rucher [ryʃe] *nm* apiary.

rude [ryd] *adj* **(a)** (*au toucher*) *surface, barbe, peau* rough; (*à l'ouïe*) *voix, sons* harsh.

(b) (*pénible*) *métier, vie, combat* hard, tough; *adversaire* tough; *montée* stiff, tough, hard; *climat, hiver* harsh, hard, severe. **être mis à ~ épreuve** *[personne]* to be put through a severe trial; *[tissu, métal]* to receive *ou* have rough treatment; **mes nerfs ont été mis à ~ épreuve** it was a great strain on my nerves; **il a été à ~ école dans sa jeunesse** he learned life the hard way when he was young; **en faire voir de ~s à qn** to give sb a hard *ou* tough time; **en voir de ~s** to have a hard *ou* tough time (of it).

(c) (*fruste*) *manières* unpolished, crude, unrefined; *traits* rugged; *montagnards* rugged, tough.

(d) (*sévère, bourru*) *personne, caractère* harsh, hard, severe; *manières* rough.

(e) (*intensif: fameux*) **un ~ gaillard** a hearty fellow; **avoir un ~ appétit/estomac** to have a hearty appetite/an iron stomach; **il a une ~ veine** he's a lucky beggar*; **ça m'a fait une ~ peur** it gave me a dreadful *ou* real fright; **recevoir un ~ coup de poing** to get a real *ou* proper* thump.

rudement [rydmɑ̃] *adv* **(a)** *heurter, tomber, frapper* hard; *répondre* harshly; *traiter* roughly, harshly.

(b) (*: *très, beaucoup*) *content, bon* terribly*, awfully*, jolly* (*Brit*); *fatigant, mauvais, cher* dreadfully*, terribly*, awfully*. **travailler ~** to work terribly *ou* awfully *ou* jolly (*Brit*) hard*; **se dépêcher ~** to really hurry, rush like mad*; **elle danse ~ bien** she dances terribly *ou* awfully *ou* jolly (*Brit*) well*, she's quite a dancer; **ça me change ~ de faire ça** it's a real change *ou* quite a change for me to do that; **elle avait ~ changé** she had really changed, she hadn't half changed*; **il est ~ plus généreux que toi** he's a great deal *ou* darned sight* more generous than you; **j'ai eu ~ peur** I had quite a scare, I had a dreadful *ou* an awful fright.

rudesse [rydɛs] *nf* (*V* **rude**) roughness; harshness; hardness; toughness; severity; crudeness; ruggedness. **traiter qn avec ~** to treat sb roughly *ou* harshly.

rudiment [rydimɑ̃] *nm* **(a)** **~s** *[discipline]* rudiments; *[théorie, système]* principles; **~s d'algèbre** principles *ou* rudiments of algebra; **avoir quelques ~s de chimie** to have some basic *ou* rudimentary notions *ou* some basic knowledge of chemistry, have a rudimentary knowledge of chemistry; **avoir quelques ~s d'anglais** to have a smattering of English *ou* some basic knowledge of English; **nous n'en sommes qu'aux ~s** we're still on the basics; **on en est encore au stade des ~s** we're still at a rudimentary stage.

(b) (*Anat, Zool*) rudiment.

rudimentaire [rydimɑ̃tɛr] *adj* rudimentary.

rudoiement [rydwamɑ̃] *nm* rough *ou* harsh treatment.

rudoyer [rydwaje] (8) *vt* to treat harshly.

rue [ry] *nf* (*voie, habitants*) street. (*péj: populace*) **la ~** the mob; **~ à sens unique** one-way street; **scènes de la ~** street scenes; **élevé dans la ~** brought up in the street(s); **être à la ~** to be on the streets; **jeter qn à la ~** to put sb out *ou* throw sb out (into the street); *V* **chaussée, coin, combat** *etc.*

ruée [rɥe] *nf* rush; (*péj*) stampede. **à l'ouverture, ce fut la ~ vers l'entrée du magasin** when the shop opened, there was a (great) rush *ou* a stampede for the entrance, as soon as the doors opened there was a stampede *ou* a mad scramble to get into the shop; (*fig*) **dès que quelqu'un prend sa retraite ou démissionne, c'est la ~** the moment someone retires or resigns there's a scramble for the position; **dans la ~, il fut renversé** he was knocked over in the (on)rush *ou* stampede; **la ~ vers l'or** the gold rush.

ruelle [rɥɛl] *nf* (*rue*) alley(-way); (††) *[chambre]* ruelle††, space (between bed and wall); (*Hist, Littérat*) ruelle (*room used in 17th century to hold literary salons*).

ruer [rɥe] (1) **1** *vi [cheval]* to kick (out). **prenez garde, il rue** watch out — he kicks; (*fig*) **~ dans les brancards** to become rebellious, get unruly.

2 se ruer *vpr*: **se ~ sur** *personne, article en vente, nourriture* to pounce on; *emplois vacants* to fling o.s. *ou* pounce at; **se ~ vers** *sortie, porte* to dash *ou* rush for *ou* towards; **se ~ dans/hors de** *pièce, maison* to dash *ou* rush *ou* tear into/out of; **se ~ dans l'escalier** (*monter*) to tear *ou* dash up the stairs; (*descendre*) to tear down the stairs, hurl o.s. down the stairs; **se ~ à l'assaut** to hurl *ou* fling o.s. into the attack.

ruf(f)ian†† [ryfjɑ̃] *nm* ruffian.

rugby [rygbi] *nm* Rugby (football), rugger*. **~ à quinze** Rugby Union; **~ à treize** Rugby League.

rugbyman [rygbiman], *pl* **rugbymen** [rygbimɛn] *nm* rugby player.

rugir [ryʒir] (2) **1** *vi [fauve, mer, moteur]* to roar; *[vent, tempête]* to howl, roar. *[personne]* **~ de douleur** to howl *ou* roar with pain; **~ de colère** to bellow *ou* roar with anger. **2** *vt ordres, menaces* to roar *ou* bellow out.

rugissement [ryʒismɑ̃] *nm* (*V* **rugir**) roar; roaring (*U*); howl; howling (*U*). **~ de douleur** howl *ou* roar of pain; **~ de colère** roar of anger.

rugosité [rygozite] *nf* **(a)** (*U: V* **rugueux**) roughness; coarseness; ruggedness, bumpiness. **(b)** (*aspérité*) rough patch, bump.

rugueux, -euse [rygø, øz] *adj* (*gén*) rough; *peau, tissu* rough, coarse; *sol* rugged, rough, bumpy.

ruine [rɥin] *nf* **(a)** (*lit, fig: décombres, destruction*) ruin. **~s**

romaines Roman ruins; **acheter une ~ à la campagne** to buy a ruin in the country; (*péj*) **~ (humaine)** (human) wreck; **en ~** in ruin(s), ruined (*épith*); **causer la ~ de** *monarchie* to bring about the ruin *ou* downfall of; *réputation, carrière, santé* to ruin, bring about the ruin of; *banquier, firme* to ruin, bring ruin upon; **c'est la ~ de tous mes espoirs** that puts paid to *ou* that xans the ruin of all my hopes; **courir** *ou* **aller à sa ~** to be on the road to ruin, be heading for ruin; **menacer ~** to be threatening to collapse; **tomber en ruine** to fall in ruins.

(b) (*acquisition coûteuse*) **cette voiture est une vraie ~** that car will ruin me.

ruiner [ʀɥine] (1) **1** *vt* **(a)** *personne, pays* to ruin, cause the ruin of. **ça ne va pas te ~!*** it won't break* *ou* ruin you!

(b) *réputation* to ruin, wreck; *espoirs* to shatter, dash, ruin; *santé* to ruin.

2 se ruiner *vpr* (*dépenser tout son argent*) to ruin *ou* bankrupt o.s.; (*fig: dépenser trop*) to spend a fortune.

ruineux, -euse [ʀɥinø, øz] *adj goût* extravagant, ruinously expensive; *dépense* ruinous; *acquisition, voiture* (*prix élevé*) ruinous, ruinously expensive; (*entretien coûteux*) expensive to run (*ou* keep *etc*). **ce n'est pas ~!** it won't break* *ou* ruin us, it doesn't cost a fortune.

ruisseau, *pl* **~x** [ʀɥiso] *nm* **(a)** (*cours d'eau*) stream, brook. (*fig*) **des ~x de** *larmes* floods of; *lave, sang* streams of.

(b) (*caniveau*) gutter. (*fig*) **élevé dans le ~** brought up *ou* dragged up* in the gutter; (*fig*) **tirer qn du ~** to pull *ou* drag sb out of the gutter.

ruisselant, e [ʀɥislɑ̃, ɑ̃t] *adj mur* streaming, running with water; *visage* streaming; *personne* dripping wet, streaming.

ruisseler [ʀɥisle] (4) *vi* **(a)** (*couler*) *[lumière]* to stream; *[cheveux]* to flow, stream (*sur* over); *[liquide, pluie]* to stream, flow (*sur* down).

(b) (*être couvert d'eau*) **~ (d'eau)** *[mur]* to run with water, stream (with water); *[visage]* to stream (with water); **~ de lumière/larmes** to stream with light/tears; **~ de sueur** to drip *ou* stream with sweat; **le visage ruisselant de larmes** his face streaming with tears, with tears streaming down his face.

ruisselet [ʀɥislɛ] *nm* rivulet, brooklet.

ruissellement [ʀɥisɛlmɑ̃] **1** *nm*: **le ~ de la pluie/de l'eau sur le mur** the rain/water streaming *ou* running *ou* flowing down the wall; **le ~ de sa chevelure sur ses épaules** her hair flowing *ou* streaming over her shoulders; **un ~ de pierreries** a glistening *ou* glittering cascade of jewels; **ébloui par ce ~ de lumière** dazzled by this stream of light.

2: (*Géol*) **ruissellement pluvial** run-off.

rumba [ʀumba] *nf* rumba.

rumeur [ʀymœʀ] *nf* **(a)** (*nouvelle imprécise*) rumour. **selon certaines ~s, elle ...** rumour has it that she ..., it is rumoured that she ...; **si l'on en croit la ~ publique, il ...** if you believe what is publicly rumoured, he ...; **faire courir de fausses ~s** to spread rumours.

(b) (*son*) *[vagues, vent]* murmur(ing) (*U*); *[ville, rue, circulation]* hum (*U*), rumbling; *[émeute]* hubbub (*U*), rumbling; *[bureau, conversation]* buzz (*U*), rumbling, hubbub (*U*).

(c) (*protestation*) rumblings (*pl*). **~ de mécontentement** rumblings of discontent; **une ~ s'éleva** *ou* **des ~s s'élevèrent de la foule** rumblings rose up from the crowd.

ruminant [ʀyminɑ̃] *nm* (*Zool*) ruminant.

rumination [ʀyminasjɔ̃] *nf* (*Zool*) rumination.

ruminer [ʀymine] (1) **1** *vt* (*Zool*) to ruminate; (*fig*) *projet* to ruminate on *ou* over, chew over; *chagrin* to brood over; *vengeance* to ponder, meditate. **toujours dans son coin, à ~ (ses pensées)** always in his corner chewing the cud (*fig*) *ou* chewing things over *ou* pondering (things).

2 *vi* (*Zool*) to ruminate, chew the cud.

rumsteck [ʀɔmstɛk] *nm* = **romsteck.**

runes [ʀyn] *nfpl* runes.

runique [ʀynik] *adj* runic.

rupestre [ʀypɛstʀ(ə)] *adj* (*Bot*) rupestrine, rock (*épith*); (*Art*) rupestrian, rupestral, rock (*épith*).

rupin, e: [ʀypɛ̃, in] *adj appartement, quartier* ritzy:, plush(y)*; *personne* stinking *ou* filthy rich:. **c'est un ~** he's got money to burn*, he's stinking *ou* filthy rich: *ou* rolling in it*; **les ~s** the stinking *ou* filthy rich:.

rupture [ʀyptyʀ] **1** *nf* **(a)** (*annulation: action*) *[relations diplomatiques]* breaking off, severing, rupture; *[fiançailles, pourparlers]* breaking off. **la ~ du traité/contrat par ce pays** this country's breaking the treaty/contract, the breach of the treaty/contract by this country.

(b) (*annulation: résultat*) *[contrat, traité]* breach (*de* of); *[relations diplomatiques]* severance, rupture (*de* of); *[pourparlers]* breakdown (*de* of, in). **la ~ de leurs fiançailles l'a tué** their broken engagement killed him; **une ~ d'équilibre est à craindre entre ces nations** an upset in the balance of power *ou* an upset balance of power is to be feared among these states.

(c) (*séparation amoureuse*) break-up, split. **sa ~ (d')avec Louise** his split *ou* break-up with Louise; **~ passagère** temporary break-up; (*fig*) **être en ~ avec le monde/les idées de son temps** to be at odds with the world/the ideas of one's time.

(d) (*cassure, déchirure*) *[câble]* breaking, parting; *[poutre, branche, corde]* breaking; *[digue]* bursting, breach(ing); *[veine]* bursting, rupture; *[organe]* rupture; *[tendon]* rupture, tearing. **limite de ~** breaking point.

(e) (*solution de continuité*) break. **~ entre le passé et le présent** break between the past and the present; **~ de rythme** (sudden) break in (the) rhythm; **~ de ton** abrupt change in *ou* of tone.

2: (*Méd*) **rupture d'anévrisme** aneurysmal rupture; (*Jur*) **rupture de ban** *illegal return from banishment*; (*Jur*) **en rupture de ban** *illegally returning from banishment*; (*fig*) in defiance of the accepted code of conduct; **en rupture de ban avec la société** at odds with society; (*Élec*) **rupture de circuit** break in the circuit; (*Jur*) **rupture de contrat** breach of contract; (*Pol*) **rupture diplomatique** breaking off *ou* severing of diplomatic relations (*U*); **rupture de direction** steering failure; **rupture d'équilibre** (*lit*) loss of balance; (*fig*) upsetting of the balance; (*Aut*) **rupture d'essieu** broken axle; **rupture de pente** change of incline *ou* gradient.

rural, e, *mpl* **-aux** [ʀyʀal, o] **1** *adj* (*gén*) country (*épith*), rural; (*Admin*) rural. **2** *nm,f* country person, rustic. **les ruraux** country people, countryfolk; *V* **exode.**

ruse [ʀyz] *nf* **(a)** (*U*) (*pour gagner, obtenir un avantage*) cunning, craftiness, slyness; (*pour tromper*) trickery, guile. **obtenir qch par ~** to obtain sth by *ou* through trickery *ou* by guile.

(b) (*subterfuge*) trick, ruse. (*lit, fig, hum*) **~ de guerre** stratagem, tactics (*pl*); **avec des ~s de Sioux** with crafty tactics; **usant de ~s féminines** using her womanly wiles.

rusé, e [ʀyze] (*ptp de* **ruser**) *adj personne* cunning, crafty, sly, wily; *air* sly, wily. **~ comme un (vieux) renard** as sly *ou* cunning as a fox; **c'est un ~** he's a crafty *ou* sly one.

ruser [ʀyze] (1) *vi* (*V* **ruse**) to use cunning; to use trickery. **ne ruse pas avec moi!** don't try and be clever *ou* smart* with me!

russe [ʀys] **1** *adj* Russian. **œuf dur à la ~** œuf dur à la Russe; **boire à la ~** to drink (and cast one's glass aside) in the Russian style; *V* **montagne, roulette. 2** *nm* (*Ling*) Russian. **3** *nmf*: **R~** Russian; **R~ blanc(he)** White Russian.

Russie [ʀysi] *nf* Russia. **la ~ blanche** White Russia; **~ soviétique** Soviet Russia.

russification [ʀysifikasjɔ̃] *nf* russianization, russification.

russifier [ʀysifje] (7) *vt* to russianize, russify.

rustaud, e [ʀysto, od] **1** *adj* countrified, rustic.

2 *nm,f* country bumpkin, yokel, hillbilly (*US*).

rusticité [ʀystisite] *nf* **(a)** *[manières, personne]* rustic simplicity, rusticity (*frm*). **(b)** (*Agr*) hardiness.

rustine [ʀystin] *nf* ® rubber repair patch (*for bicycle tyre*).

rustique [ʀystik] **1** *adj* **(a)** *mobilier* rustic; *maçonnerie* rustic, rusticated. **bois ~** rustic wood.

(b) (*littér*) *maison* rustic (*épith*); *vie, manières* rustic, country (*épith*).

(c) (*Agr*) hardy.

2 *nm* (*style*) rustic style. **meubler une maison en ~** to furnish a house in the rustic style *ou* with rustic furniture.

rustre [ʀystʀ(ə)] **1** *nm* lout, boor. **2** *adj* brutish, boorish.

rut [ʀyt] *nm* (*état*) *[mâle]* rut; *[femelle]* heat; (*période*) rutting (period), heat period. **être en ~** to be rutting, be in *ou* on heat.

rutabaga [ʀytabaga] *nm* swede, rutabaga (*US*).

rutilant, e [ʀytilɑ̃, ɑ̃t] *adj* (*brillant*) brightly shining, gleaming; (*rare: rouge ardent*) rutilant (*rare*). **vêtu d'un uniforme ~** very spick and span *ou* very spruce in his (*ou* her) uniform.

rutilement [ʀytilmɑ̃] *nm* gleam.

rutiler [ʀytile] (1) *vi* to gleam, shine brightly.

rythme [ʀitm(ə)] *nm* **(a)** (*Art, Littérat, Mus*) rhythm. **marquer le ~** to beat time; (*Mus*) **au ~ de** to the beat *ou* rhythm of; **avoir le sens du ~** to have a sense of rhythm; (*Théât*) **pièce qui manque de ~** play which lacks tempo, slow-moving play.

(b) (*cadence*) *[respiration, cœur, saisons]* rhythm. **interrompant le ~ de sa respiration** interrupting the rhythm of his breathing.

(c) (*vitesse*) *[respiration]* rate; *[battements du cœur]* rate, speed; *[vie, travail]* tempo, pace; *[production]* rate. **~ cardiaque** (rate of) heartbeat; **à ce ~-là, il ne va plus en rester** at that rate, there won't be any left; **il n'arrive pas à suivre le ~** he can't keep up (the pace); **produire des voitures au ~ de 1.000 par jour** to produce cars at the rate of 1,000 a *ou* per day.

rythmé, e [ʀitme] (*ptp de* **rythmer**) *adj* rhythmic(al). **bien ~** highly rhythmic(al).

rythmer [ʀitme] (1) *vt* (*cadencer*) *prose, phrase, travail* to give rhythm to, give (a certain) rhythm to, punctuate. **leur marche rythmée par des chansons** their march, given rhythm by their songs; **les saisons rythmaient leur vie** the seasons gave (a certain) rhythm to their life *ou* punctuated their life.

rythmique [ʀitmik] **1** *adj* rhythmic(al); *V* **section. 2** *nf* (*Littérat*) rhythmics (*sg*). **la (danse) ~** rhythmics (*sg*).

S

S, s [ɛs] *nm* **(a)** (*lettre*) S, s. **(b)** (*figure*) zigzag; (*virages*) double bend, S bend, Z bend. **faire des s** to zigzag; **en s** *route* zigzagging (*épith*), winding; *barre* S-shaped.
s' [s] *V* **se, si¹**.
sa [sa] *adj poss V* **son¹**.
Saba [saba] *nf* Sheba.
sabayon [sabajɔ̃] *nm* zabaglione.
sabbat [saba] *nm* **(a)** (*Rel*) Sabbath. **(b)** (*: *bruit*) racket, row*. **(c)** *[sorcières]* (witches') sabbath.
sabbatique [sabatik] *adj* (*Rel, Univ*) sabbatical.
sabin, e [sabɛ̃, in] **1** *adj* Sabine. **2** *nm,f*: S~(e) Sabine.
sabir [sabiʀ] *nm* (*lit*) = pidgin; (**fig*) jargon.
sablage [sɑblaʒ] *nm [allée]* sanding; *[façade]* sandblasting.
sable¹ [sɑbl(ə)] **1** *nm* sand. **de ~** *dune, vent* sand (*épith*); *fond, plage* sandy; **~s mouvants** quicksand(s); **tempête de ~** sandstorm; (*fig*) **être sur le ~*** to be down-and-out; *V* **grain, marchand.**
2 *adj inv* sandy, sand-coloured.
sable² [sɑbl(ə)] *nm* (*Hér*) sable.
sablé, e [sɑble] (*ptp de* **sabler**) **1** *adj* **(a)** *gâteau* made with shortbread dough; *V* **pâte. (b)** *route* sandy, sanded. **2** *nm* shortbread biscuit (*Brit*) *ou* cookie (*US*), piece of shortbread.
sabler [sɑble] (1) *vt* **(a)** *route* to sand; *façade* to sandblast. **(b) ~ le champagne** to drink *ou* have champagne.
sableux, -euse [sɑblø, øz] **1** *adj* sandy. **2 sableuse** *nf* (*machine*) sandblast.
sablier [sɑblije] *nm* (*gén*) hourglass, sandglass; (*Culin*) egg timer.
sablière [sɑblijɛʀ] *nf* (*carrière*) sand quarry; (*Constr*) stringpiece; (*Rail*) sand-box.
sablonneux, -euse [sɑblɔnø, øz] *adj* sandy.
sablonnière [sɑblɔnjɛʀ] *nf* sand quarry.
sabord [sabɔʀ] *nm* scuttle (*Naut*).
sabordage [sabɔʀdaʒ] *nm,* **sabordement** [sabɔʀdəmɑ̃] *nm* (*Naut*) scuttling; (*fig*) *[entreprise]* winding up, shutting down.
saborder [sabɔʀde] (1) **1** *vt* (*Naut*) to scuttle; (*fig*) *entreprise* to wind up, shut down; *négociations, projet* to put paid to. **2 se saborder** *vpr* (*Naut*) to scuttle one's ship; (*fig*) to wind up, shut down.
sabot [sabo] *nm* **(a)** (*chaussure*) clog. (*fig*) **je le vois venir avec ses gros ~s** I can see just what he's after, I can see him coming a mile off (*fig*); *V* **baignoire.**
(b) (*Zool*) hoof.
(c) (**péj*) (*bateau*) old tub*, old wreck*; (*voiture*) old heap*, old crock*; (*machine, piano*) useless heap (of rubbish)*; (*personne*) useless twit* (*Brit*). **il travaille comme un ~** he's a shoddy worker, he's a real botcher; **il joue comme un ~** he's a hopeless *ou* pathetic* player.
(d) (*toupie*) (whipping) top.
(e) (*Tech*) *[pied de table, poteau]* ferrule. **~ de frein** brake shoe; **~ de Denver** Denver shoe.
sabotage [sabɔtaʒ] *nm* **(a)** (*action: Mil, Pol, fig*) sabotage; (*acte*) act of sabotage. **(b)** (*bâclage*) botching.
saboter [sabɔte] (1) *vt* **(a)** (*Mil, Pol, fig*) to sabotage. **(b)** (*bâcler*) to make a (proper) mess of, botch; (*abîmer*) to mess up, ruin.
saboterie [sabɔtʀi] *nf* clog factory.
saboteur, -euse [sabɔtœʀ, øz] *nm,f* (*Mil, Pol*) saboteur; (*bâcleur*) shoddy worker, botcher.
sabotier, -ière [sabɔtje, jɛʀ] *nm,f* (*fabricant*) clog-maker; (*marchand*) clog-seller.
sabre [sɑbʀ(ə)] *nm* sabre. **~ d'abordage** cutlass; **~ de cavalerie** riding sabre; **mettre ~ au clair** to draw one's sword; **charger ~ au clair** to charge with swords drawn; (*fig*) **le ~ et le goupillon** the Army and the Church.
sabrer [sɑbʀe] (1) *vt* **(a)** (*Mil*) to sabre, cut down.
(b) (*littér: marquer*) **la ride qui sabrait son front** the line that cut *ou* was scored across his brow; **visage sabré de cicatrices** face scored *ou* slashed with scars; **dessin sabré de coups de crayon rageurs** drawing scored *ou* plastered with angry strokes of the pencil.
(c) (*: *biffer*) *texte* to slash (great) chunks out of*; *passage, phrase* to cut out, scrub (out)*.
(d) (*) (*couler*) *étudiant* to give a hammering to‡; (*renvoyer*) *employé* to sack*, fire*. **se faire ~** *[étudiant]* to get a hammering‡; *[employé]* to get the sack*, get fired* *ou* sacked*.
(e) (*: *critiquer*) *devoir* to tear to pieces *ou* to shreds; *livre, pièce* to slam*, pan*.
(f) (*: *bâcler*) *travail* to knock off* (in a rush), belt through‡.
(g) (*: *saper*) *personne* to shatter*; *énergie* to drain. **cette nouvelle m'a sabré (le moral)** I was really shattered by the news*, the news really shattered me *ou* knocked me for six* (*Brit*) *ou* for a loop* (*US*).
sabretache [sɑbʀətaʃ] *nf* sabretache.
sabreur [sɑbʀœʀ] *nm* (*péj*) fighting cock (*péj*) (*soldier*).
sac¹ [sak] **1** *nm* **(a)** (*gén*) bag; (*de grande taille, en toile*) sack; (*cartable*) (school)bag; (*à bretelles*) satchel. **~ à charbon** coalsack; **mettre en ~(s)** to put in sacks, sack; *V* **course.**
(b) (*contenu*) bag, bagful; sack, sackful.
(c) (‡: *argent*) ten francs, ≃ quid* (*Brit*), two bucks* (*US*).
(d) (*loc*) **habillé comme un ~** dressed like a tramp; **mettre dans le même ~*** to lump together*; **l'affaire est** *ou* **c'est dans le ~*** it's in the bag*; **des gens de ~ et de corde**†† gallows birds; (*Rel*) **le ~ et la cendre** sackcloth and ashes; *V* **main, tour².**
2: sac de couchage sleeping bag; **sac à dos** rucksack, knapsack; **sac d'embrouilles*** web of intrigue; **sac à main** handbag; **sac à malice** bag of tricks; **sac de marin** kitbag; **sac de nœuds*** = **sac d'embrouilles***; **sac à ouvrage** workbag; **sac de plage** beach bag; **sac à provisions** shopping bag; (*en papier*) (paper) carrier (*Brit*), carrier-bag (*Brit*); **sac de sable** (*Constr, Mil*) sandbag; (*Boxe*) punchbag; (*arg Camping*) **sac à viande** sleeping bag sheet; **sac à vin*** (old) soak*, drunkard; **sac de voyage** overnight bag, travelling bag.
sac² [sak] *nm [ville]* sack, sacking. **mettre à ~** *ville* to sack; *maison, pièce* to ransack.
saccade [sakad] *nf* jerk. **avancer par ~s** to jerk forward *ou* along, move forward *ou* along in fits and starts *ou* jerkily; **parler par ~s** to speak haltingly *ou* in short bursts.
saccadé, e [sakade] *adj démarche, gestes, style* jerky; *débit, respiration* spasmodic, halting; *bruit* staccato; *sommeil* fitful.
saccage [sakaʒ] *nm [pièce]* havoc (*de* in); *[jardin]* havoc, devastation (*de* in).
saccager [sakaʒe] (3) *vt* **(a)** (*dévaster*) *pièce* to turn upside down, create havoc in; *jardin* to create havoc in, wreck, devastate. **ils ont tout saccagé dans la maison** they turned the whole house upside down; **les enfants saccagent tout** children wreck everything; **champ saccagé par la grêle** field devastated by the hail.
(b) (*piller*) *ville, pays* to sack, lay waste; *maison* to ransack.
saccageur, -euse [sakaʒœʀ, øz] *nm,f* (*dévastateur*) vandal; (*pillard*) pillager, plunderer.
saccharine [sakaʀin] *nf* saccharin(e).
saccharose [sakaʀoz] *nm* sucrose, saccharose.
sacerdoce [sasɛʀdɔs] *nm* (*Rel*) priesthood; (*fig*) calling, vocation.
sacerdotal, e, *mpl* **-aux** [sasɛʀdɔtal, o] *adj* priestly, sacerdotal.
sachem [saʃɛm] *nm* sachem.
sachet [saʃɛ] *nm [bonbons]* bag; *[lavande, poudre]* sachet. **~ de thé** tea bag.
sacoche [sakɔʃ] *nf* (*gén*) bag; (*pour outils*) toolbag; *[cycliste]* (*de selle*) saddlebag; (*de porte-bagages*) panier; *[écolier]* (school)bag; (*à bretelles*) satchel; *[encaisseur]* (money)bag; *[facteur]* (post-)bag.
sacquer* [sake] (1) *vt* **(a)** *employé* to kick out‡, give the sack* *ou* push‡ *ou* boot‡ to. **se faire ~** to get the sack* *ou* push‡ *ou* boot‡, get (o.s.) kicked out‡. **(b)** *élève* (*sanctionner*) to give a hammering to‡; (*recaler*) to plough* (*Brit*), fail.
sacral, e, *mpl* **-aux** [sakʀal, o] *adj* sacred.
sacralisation [sakʀalizɑsjɔ̃] *nf*: **la ~ des loisirs/de la famille** regarding leisure time/the family as sacred.
sacraliser [sakʀalize] (1) *vt* to regard as sacred. **~ la réussite sociale/la famille** to regard social success/the family as sacred.
sacramentel, -elle [sakʀamɑ̃tɛl] *adj* **(a)** (*fig: rituel*) ritual, ritualistic. **(b)** (*Rel*) *rite, formule* sacramental.
sacre [sakʀ(ə)] *nm [roi]* coronation; *[évêque]* consecration.
sacré, e¹ [sakʀe] (*ptp de* **sacrer**) **1** *adj* **(a)** (*après n: Rel*) *lieu, objet* sacred, holy; *art, musique* sacred; *horreur, terreur* holy. **la fête du S~-Cœur** the Feast of the Sacred Heart; **le S~ Collège** the Sacred College.
(b) (*après n: inviolable*) *droit, promesse* sacred. **son sommeil, c'est ~** his sleep is sacred.
(c) (*: *avant n: maudit*) blasted*, confounded*, damned‡. **~ nom de nom!‡** hell and damnation!‡
(d) (*: *avant n: considérable*) **un ~ ...** a *ou* one heck* *ou* hell‡ of a ..., a right* ...; **c'est un ~ imbécile/menteur** he's a right idiot/liar*, he's one heck* *ou* hell‡ of an idiot/a liar; **il a un ~ toupet** he's got a *ou* one heck* *ou* hell‡ of a cheek, he's got a right cheek*.
(e) (*: *avant n: admiration, surprise*) **~ farceur!** you old devil (you)!*; **ce ~ Paul a encore gagné aux courses** that devil Paul *ou* that blinking (*Brit*) Paul has gone and won on the horses again*.
2 *nm*: **le ~** the sacred.
sacré, e² [sakʀe] *adj* (*Anat*) sacral.
sacrebleu*†† [sakʀəblø] *excl* 'struth!* (*Brit*), confound it!*
sacrement [sakʀəmɑ̃] *nm* sacrament. **recevoir les derniers ~s** to receive the last sacraments; **il est mort, muni des ~s de l'Église** he died fortified with the (last) rites *ou* sacraments of the Church; *V* **saint.**
sacrément* [sakʀemɑ̃] *adv intéressant, laid, froid* jolly* (*Brit*), damned‡, ever so*. **j'ai eu ~ peur** I was jolly* (*Brit*) *ou* damned‡ *ou* ever so* scared; **ça m'a ~ plu** I liked it ever so much*.
sacrer [sakʀe] (1) **1** *vt roi* to crown; *évêque* to consecrate. (*fig*) **il fut sacré sauveur de la patrie** he was hailed as the saviour of the country. **2** *vi* (*††) to curse, swear.

sacrificateur, -trice [sakʀifikatœʀ, tʀis] *nm,f* sacrificer.
sacrificatoire [sakʀifikatwaʀ] *adj* sacrificial.
sacrifice [sakʀifis] *nm* (*Rel, fig*) sacrifice. **faire un ~/des ~s** to make a sacrifice/sacrifices; **faire le ~ de sa vie/d'une journée de vacances** to sacrifice one's life/a day's holiday; **offrir qch en ~ à** to offer sth as a sacrifice to; **~ de soi** self-sacrifice; *V* **saint.**
sacrificiel, -elle [sakʀifisjɛl] *adj* sacrificial.
sacrifié, e [sakʀifje] (*ptp de* **sacrifier**) *adj peuple, troupe* sacrificed. **les jeunes sont les ~s de notre société** the young are the sacrificial victims of our society; (*Comm*) **articles ~s** give-aways*, items given away at knockdown prices.
sacrifier [sakʀifje] (7) **1** *vt* (*gén*) to sacrifice (*à* to, *pour* for); (*Comm*) *marchandises* to give away (at a knockdown price). **~ sa vie pour sa patrie** to lay down *ou* sacrifice one's life for one's country; **~ sa carrière/une partie de son temps** to give up *ou* sacrifice one's career/part of one's time.
2 sacrifier à *vt indir préjugés, mode* to conform to.
3 se sacrifier *vpr* to sacrifice o.s. (*à* to, *pour* for).
sacrilège [sakʀilɛʒ] **1** *adj* (*Rel, fig*) sacrilegious. **2** *nm* (*Rel, fig*) sacrilege. **ce serait un ~ de** it would be (a) sacrilege to. **3** *nmf* sacrilegious person.
sacripant [sakʀipɑ̃] *nm* (††, *hum*) rogue, scoundrel.
sacristain [sakʀistɛ̃] *nm* (*Rel*) *[sacristie]* sacristan; *[église]* sexton.
sacristie [sakʀisti] *nf* (*catholique*) sacristy; (*protestante*) vestry; *V* **punaise.**
sacro-saint, e [sakʀɔsɛ̃, ɛ̃t] *adj* (*lit, iro*) sacrosanct.
sacrum [sakʀɔm] *nm* sacrum.
sadique [sadik] **1** *adj* sadistic. **2** *nmf* sadist.
sadiquement [sadikmɑ̃] *adv* sadistically.
sadisme [sadism(ə)] *nm* sadism.
sadomasochisme [sadɔmazɔʃism(ə)] *nm* sadomasochism.
sadomasochiste [sadɔmazɔʃist(ə)] **1** *adj* sadomasochistic. **2** *nmf* sadomasochist.
safari [safaʀi] *nm* safari. **faire un ~** to go on safari; **~-photo** photographic safari.
safran [safʀɑ̃] **1** *nm* **(a)** (*Bot, Culin, couleur*) saffron. **riz au ~** saffron rice. **(b)** (*Naut*) rudder blade. **2** *adj inv* saffron(-coloured), saffron (yellow).
safrané, e [safʀane] (*ptp de* **safraner**) *adj plat, couleur* saffron (*épith*); *tissu* saffron(-coloured), saffron (yellow).
safraner [safʀane] (1) *vt plat* to flavour *ou* season with saffron.
saga [saga] *nf* saga.
sagace [sagas] *adj* (*littér*) sagacious, shrewd.
sagacité [sagasite] *nf* sagacity, shrewdness. **avec ~** shrewdly.
sagaie [sagɛ] *nf* assegai, assagai.
sage [saʒ] **1** *adj* **(a)** (*avisé*) *conseil* wise, sound, sensible; *personne* wise; *action, démarche* wise, sensible. **il serait plus ~ de ...** it would be wiser *ou* more sensible to ..., you (*ou* he *etc*) would be better advised to ... .
(b) (*chaste*) *jeune fille* good, proper (*attrib*).
(c) (*docile*) *enfant, animal* good, well-behaved. **sois ~** be good, behave yourself, be a good boy (*ou* girl); **~ comme une image** (as) good as gold; **il a été très ~ chez son oncle** he was very well-behaved *ou* he behaved (himself) very well at his uncle's.
(d) (*modéré, décent*) *goûts* sober, moderate. **une petite robe bien ~** a sober little dress *ou* number*.
2 *nm* wise man; (*Antiq*) sage.
sage-femme, *pl* **sages-femmes** [saʒfam] *nf* midwife.
sagement [saʒmɑ̃] *adv* **(a)** (*avec bon sens*) *conseiller, agir* wisely, sensibly.
(b) (*chastement*) properly. **se conduire ~** to be good, behave o.s. (properly).
(c) (*docilement*) quietly. **il est resté ~ assis sans rien dire** he sat quietly *ou* he sat like a good child *ou* boy (*ou* girl) and said nothing; **va bien ~ te coucher** be a good boy (*ou* girl) and go to bed, off you go to bed like a good boy (*ou* girl).
(d) (*modérément*) wisely, moderately. **savoir user ~ de qch** to know how to use sth wisely *ou* in moderation *ou* moderately.
sagesse [saʒɛs] *nf* **(a)** (*bon sens*) *[personne]* wisdom, (good) sense; *[conseil]* soundness; *[action, démarche]* wisdom; (*expérience*) wisdom. **il a eu la ~ de** he had the wisdom *ou* (good) sense to, he was wise *ou* sensible enough to; **écouter la voix de la ~** to listen to the voice of wisdom; **la ~ des nations** popular wisdom.
(b) (*chasteté*) properness.
(c) (*docilité*) *[enfant]* good behaviour. **il est la ~ même** he is the model of a well-behaved child; *V* **dent.**
(d) (*modération*) moderation. **savoir utiliser qch avec ~** to know how to use sth wisely *ou* in moderation.
Sagittaire [saʒitɛʀ] *nm* (*Astron*) **le ~** Sagittarius, the Archer; **être (du) ~** to be Sagittarius *ou* a Sagittarian.
sagouin⁑ [sagwɛ̃] *nm* (*personne sale*) dirty *ou* filthy pig*; (*salopard*) swine⁑, slob⁑.
Sahara [saaʀa] *nm*: **le ~** the Sahara (desert).
saharien, -ienne [saaʀjɛ̃, jɛn] **1** *adj* (*du Sahara*) Saharan; (*très chaud*) tropical. **2 saharienne** *nf* safari jacket.
saignant, e [sɛɲɑ̃, ɑ̃t] *adj plaie* (*lit*) bleeding; (*fig*) raw; *entrecôte* rare, underdone; (⁑) *critique, mésaventure* bloody (*Brit*) *ou* damned nasty⁑. **je n'aime pas le ~** I don't like underdone meat.
saignée [seɲe] *nf* **(a)** (*Méd*) (*épanchement*) bleeding (*U*). (*opération*) blood letting (*U*), bleeding (*U*). **faire une ~ à qn** to bleed sb, let sb's blood.
(b) (*fig: perte*) *[budget]* savage cut (*à, dans* in). **les ~s que j'ai dû faire sur mon salaire/mes économies pour ...** the huge holes I had to make in my salary/savings to ...; **les ~s faites dans le pays par la guerre** the heavy losses imposed on the country by the war.
(c) (*Anat*) **la ~ du bras** the bend of the arm.
(d) (*sillon*) *[sol]* trench, ditch; *[mur]* groove.
saignement [sɛɲmɑ̃] *nm* bleeding (*U*). **~ de nez** nosebleed.
saigner [seɲe] (1) **1** *vi* **(a)** to bleed. **il saigne comme un bœuf** blood is gushing out of him; **il saignait du nez** he had (a) nosebleed, his nose was bleeding.
(b) (*fig littér*) *[orgueil, dignité]* to sting, bleed (*littér*). **mon cœur saigne** *ou* **le cœur me saigne encore** my heart is still bleeding (*littér*).
2 *vt* **(a)** *animal* to kill (*by bleeding*); *malade* to bleed.
(b) (*exploiter*) to bleed. **~ qn à blanc** to bleed sb white.
3 se saigner *vpr*: **se ~ (aux quatre veines) pour qn** to bleed o.s. white for sb, sacrifice o.s. for sb.
saillant, e [sajɑ̃, ɑ̃t] **1** *adj* **(a)** *menton* prominent, protruding (*épith*), jutting (*épith*); *front, muscle, veine* protruding (*épith*), prominent, protuberant; *pommette* prominent; *yeux* bulging (*épith*), protuberant, protruding (*épith*); *corniche* projecting (*épith*); *V* **angle.**
(b) *événement, trait, point* salient, outstanding.
2 *nm* (*avancée*) salient.
saillie [saji] *nf* **(a)** (*aspérité*) projection. **faire ~** to project, jut out; **qui forme ~, en ~** projecting, overhanging. **(b)** (*littér: boutade*) witticism. **(c)** (*Zool: accouplement*) covering, serving.
saillir [sajiʀ] (2) **1** *vi [balcon, corniche]* to jut out, stick out, project; *[menton]* to jut out, protrude; *[poitrine, pommette]* to be prominent; *[muscle, veine]* to protrude, stand out; *[yeux]* to bulge, protrude. **2** *vt* (*Zool*) to cover, serve.
sain, saine [sɛ̃, sɛn] *adj* **(a)** (*en bonne santé*) *personne* healthy; *constitution, dents* healthy, sound. **être/arriver ~ et sauf** to be/arrive safe and sound; **il est sorti ~ et sauf de l'accident** he escaped unharmed *ou* safe and sound from the accident; **~ de corps et d'esprit** sound in body and mind.
(b) (*salubre*) *climat, nourriture* healthy, wholesome. **il est ~ de se promener après le repas** it is good for you *ou* healthy to take a walk after meals; **il est ~ de rire de temps en temps** it's good (for one) to laugh from time to time.
(c) (*non abîmé*) *fruit* sound; *viande* good; *mur, fondations* sound; (*fig*) *gestion, affaire* healthy.
(d) (*moralement*) *personne* sane; *politique, jugement* sound, sane; *idées, goûts, humeur* healthy; *lectures* wholesome.
(e) (*Naut*) *rade* clear, safe.
saindoux [sɛ̃du] *nm* lard.
sainement [sɛnmɑ̃] *adv vivre* healthily; *manger* healthily, wholesomely; *juger* sanely; *raisonner* soundly. **être ~ logé** to have healthy accommodation.
sainfoin [sɛ̃fwɛ̃] *nm* sainfoin.
saint, e [sɛ̃, sɛ̃t] **1** *adj* **(a)** (*sacré*) *semaine, image* holy. **les ~es Écritures** the Holy Scriptures, Holy Scripture; **les ~es huiles** the holy oils; **la ~e Croix/Famille** the Holy Cross/Family; **le vendredi ~** Good Friday; **le jeudi ~** Maundy Thursday; **le mercredi/mardi ~** Wednesday/Tuesday before Easter, the Wednesday/Tuesday of Holy Week; *V* **guerre, semaine, terre.**
(b) (*devant prénom*) Saint. (*apôtre*) **~ Pierre/Paul** Saint Peter/Paul; (*église*) **S~-Pierre/-Paul** Saint Peter's/Paul's; (*fête*) **ils ont fêté la S~-Pierre** they celebrated the feast of Saint Peter; (*jour*) **le jour de la S~-Pierre, à la S~-Pierre** (on) Saint Peter's day.
(c) (*pieux*) *personne, pensée* saintly, godly; *vie, action* pious, saintly, holy.
(d) (**loc*) **toute la ~e journée** the whole blessed day*; **avoir une ~e terreur de qch** to have a holy terror of sth*; **il est arrivé avec tout son ~-frusquin** he has arrived with all his clobber* (*Brit*) *ou* gear*; **il y avait le frère, l'oncle, le chat et tout le ~-frusquin** there were the brother, the uncle, the cat — Old Uncle Tom Cobbly and all* (*Brit*); **à la ~-glinglin** never in a month of Sundays*; **il te le rendra à la ~-glinglin** he'll never give it back to you in a month of Sundays*; **jusqu'à la ~-glinglin** till the cows come home*; *V* **danse.**
2 *nm,f* (*lit, fig*) saint. **il veut se faire passer pour un (petit) ~** he wants to pass for a saint; **elle a la patience d'une ~e** she has the patience of a saint *ou* of Job; **un ~ de bois/pierre** a wooden/stone statue of a saint; *V* **prêcher.**
3: (*Hist*) **la Sainte-Alliance** the Holy Alliance; (*Hist*) **la Saint Barthélémy** St Bartholomew's Day Massacre; **saint-bernard** *nm inv* (*chien*) St Bernard; (*fig*) good Samaritan; **saint-cyrien** *nm, pl* **saint-cyriens** (military) cadet (*of the Saint-Cyr academy*); **Saint-Domingue** Santo Domingo; **le Saint-Empire romain germanique** the Holy Roman Empire; **le Saint-Esprit** the Holy Spirit *ou* Ghost (*V* **opération**); **les saints de glace** the 11th, 12th and 13th of May; **Sainte-Hélène** St Helena; **saint-honoré** *nm, pl* **saint-honoré(s)** Saint Honoré (gâteau); **la Saint-Jean** Midsummer('s) Day; **le Saint-Laurent** the St. Lawrence (river); **Saint-Marin** San Marino; (*péj*) **sainte nitouche** (pious) hypocrite; **c'est une sainte nitouche** she looks as if butter wouldn't melt in her mouth; **de sainte nitouche** *attitude, air* hypocritically pious; **le Saint-Office** the Holy Office; **saint patron** patron saint; **Saint-Père** Holy Father; **le saint sacrement** the Blessed Sacrament; **le saint sacrifice** the Holy Sacrifice of the Mass; **le Saint des Saints** the Holy of Holies; **le saint sépulcre** the Holy Sepulchre; **le Saint-Siège** the Holy See; **saint-simonien, -ienne** *adj, nm,f, mpl* **saint-simoniens** Saint-Simonian; **saint-simonisme** *nm* Saint-Simonism; **le Saint Suaire** the Holy Shroud; **la Saint-Sylvestre** New Year's Eve; **la Sainte Trinité** the Holy Trinity; **la Sainte Vierge** the Blessed Virgin.
saintement [sɛ̃tmɑ̃] *adv agir, mourir* like a saint. **vivre ~** to lead a saintly *ou* holy life, live like a saint.
sainteté [sɛ̃tte] *nf* **(a)** *[personne]* saintliness, godliness; *[Évangile, Vierge]* holiness; *[lieu]* holiness, sanctity; *[mariage]* sanctity; *V* **odeur. (b) Sa S~ (le pape)** His Holiness (the Pope).

saisi [sezi] *nm* (*Jur*) distrainee.

saisie [sezi] **1** *nf* **(a)** *[biens]* seizure, distraint (*T*), distress (*T*).
(b) *[publication, articles prohibés]* seizure, confiscation.
(c) (*capture*) capture.
2: saisie-arrêt *nf, pl* **saisies-arrêts** distraint, attachment; **saisie conservatoire** seizure of goods *(to prevent sale etc)*; **saisie-exécution** *nf, pl* **saisies-exécutions** distraint (*for sale by court order)*; **saisie immobilière** seizure of property.

saisir [seziʀ] (2) **1** *vt* **(a)** (*prendre*) to take hold of, catch hold of; (*s'emparer de*) to seize, grab (hold of). ~ **qn à la gorge** to grab *ou* seize sb by the throat; ~ **un ballon au vol** to catch a ball (in mid air); **il lui saisit le bras pour l'empêcher de sauter** he grabbed (hold of) *ou* seized his arm to stop him jumping; **ils le saisirent à bras le corps** they took hold of *ou* seized him bodily.
(b) (*fig*) *occasion* to seize; *prétexte* to seize (on). ~ **une occasion/la chance au vol** to jump at the opportunity/the chance; ~ **l'occasion par les cheveux*** to grasp the opportunity when it arises; ~ **la balle au bond** to jump at the opportunity (while the going is good).
(c) (*entendre*) *mot, nom* to catch, get*; (*comprendre*) *explications* to grasp, understand, get*. **il a saisi quelques noms au vol** he caught *ou* overheard various names in passing; **d'un coup d'œil, il saisit ce qui se passait** at a glance he understood what was going on; **tu saisis ce que je veux dire?*** do you get it?*, do you get what I mean?*
(d) *[peur]* to take hold of, seize, grip; *[colère, allégresse]* to take hold of, come over; *[malaise]* to come over. **le froid l'a saisi** *ou* **il a été saisi par le froid en sortant** he was struck by the sudden cold as he went out; **saisi de joie** overcome with joy; **saisi de peur** seized *ou* gripped by fear; **saisi de panique/d'horreur** panic-/horror-stricken.
(e) (*impressionner, surprendre*) ~ **qn** to bring sb up with a start; **la ressemblance entre les 2 sœurs le saisit** he was brought up short *ou* with a start by the resemblance between the 2 sisters; **être saisi par** *horreur* to be gripped by; *beauté, grâce* to be captivated by; **son air de franchise a saisi tout le monde** his apparent frankness struck everybody; **elle fut tellement saisie que ...** she was so overcome that ... .
(f) (*Jur*) (*procéder à la saisie de*) *personne, chose* to seize; (*porter devant*) *juridiction* to submit *ou* refer to. ~ **le Conseil de Sécurité d'une affaire** to submit *ou* refer a matter to the Security Council; **la Cour a été saisie de l'affaire** the case has been submitted *ou* referred to the Court.
(g) (*Culin*) *viande* to fry quickly, fry over a fierce heat.
2 se saisir *vpr*: **se** ~ **de qch/qn** to seize *ou* grab sth/sb.

saisissable [sezisabl(ə)] *adj* **(a)** *nuance, sensation* perceptible. **(b)** (*Jur*) distrainable.

saisissant, e [sezisɑ̃, ɑ̃t] **1** *adj* **(a)** *spectacle* gripping; *ressemblance, différence* startling, striking; *froid* biting, piercing. **(b)** (*Jur*) distraining. **2** *nm* (*Jur*) distrainer.

saisissement [sezismɑ̃] *nm* (*frisson de froid*) sudden chill; (*émotion*) (sudden) agitation, (rush of) emotion.

saison [sɛzɔ̃] *nf* **(a)** (*division de l'année*) season. **la belle/mauvaise** ~ the summer/winter months; (*littér*) **la** ~ **nouvelle** springtide (*littér*); **en cette** ~ at this time of year; **en toutes** ~**s** all (the) year round; **il fait un temps de** ~ the weather is right *ou* what one would expect for the time of year, the weather is seasonable.
(b) (*époque*) season. ~ **des amours/des fraises/théâtrale/touristique** mating/strawberry/theatre/tourist season; **la** ~ **des pluies** the rainy *ou* wet season; **la** ~ **des moissons/des vendanges** harvest/grape-harvest(ing) time; **les nouvelles toilettes de la** ~ the new fashions of the season; **nous faisons la** ~ **sur la côte d'Azur** we're working on the Côte d'Azur during the season; **en (haute)** ~ **les prix sont plus chers** at the height of the season prices are higher; *V* **marchand, mort**[2], **voiture.**
(c) (*cure*) stay (*at a spa*), cure.
(d) (*loc*) **hors** ~ *plante* out of season (*attrib*); *prix* off-season (*épith*), low-season (*épith*); **prendre ses vacances hors** ~ *ou* **en basse** ~ to go on holiday in the off season *ou* low season; **de** ~: **faire preuve d'un optimisme de** ~ to show fitting optimism; (*littér*) **vos plaisanteries ne sont pas de** ~ your jokes are totally out of place.

saisonnier, -ière [sɛzɔnje, jɛʀ] **1** *adj* seasonal. **2** *nm,f* seasonal worker.

salace [salas] *adj* (*littér*) salacious.

salacité [salasite] *nf* (*littér*) salaciousness, salacity.

salade [salad] *nf* **(a)** (*plante*) (*laitue*) lettuce; (*scarole*) endive. **la laitue est une** ~ lettuce is a salad vegetable.
(b) (*plat*) green salad. ~ **de tomates/de fruits/russe** tomato/fruit/Russian salad; ~ **niçoise** salade niçoise; **haricots en** ~ bean salad; *V* **panier.**
(c) (**fig: confusion*) tangle, muddle.
(d) (**fig: mensonges*) ~s stories*; **raconter des** ~**s** to spin yarns, tell stories*.
(e) *[armure]* sallet.

saladier [saladje] *nm* salad bowl.

salage [salaʒ] *nm* salting.

salaire [salɛʀ] *nm* **(a)** (*mensuel*) salary, pay; (*journalier, hebdomadaire*) wage(s), pay. **famille à** ~ **unique** single income family; ~ **de famine** *ou* **de misère** starvation wages; ~ **minimum** minimum wage; ~ **minimum interprofessionnel garanti** (index-linked) guaranteed minimum wage; *V* **bulletin.**
(b) (*fig: récompense*) reward (*de* for); (*châtiment*) reward, retribution, recompense (*de* for); *V* **tout.**

salaison [salɛzɔ̃] *nf* **(a)** (*procédé*) salting. **(b)** (*aliment*) (*viande*) salt meat; (*poisson*) salt fish.

salamalecs* [salamalɛk] *nmpl* (*péj*) exaggerated politeness. **faire des** ~ to be ridiculously overpolite.

salamandre [salamɑ̃dʀ(ə)] *nf* **(a)** (*Zool*) salamander.
(b) (*poêle*) slow-combustion stove.

salami [salami] *nm* salami.

salant [salɑ̃] *adj m V* **marais.**

salarial, e, *mpl* **-aux** [salaʀjal, o] *adj* (*V* **salaire**) salary (*épith*); pay (*épith*); wage(s) (*épith*); *V* **masse.**

salariat [salaʀja] *nm* **(a)** (*V* **salaire**) (*salariés*) salaried class; wage-earning class; (*mode de paiement*) payment by salary; payment by wages.
(b) (*condition*) (being in) employment. **être réduit au** ~ **après avoir été patron** to be reduced to the ranks of the employees *ou* of the salaried staff after having been one's own boss.

salarié, e [salaʀje] **1** *adj* **(a)** (*V* **salaire**) *travailleur* salaried (*épith*); wage-earning. **(b)** *travail* paid. **2** *nm,f* (*V* **salaire**) salaried employee; wage-earner.

salarisation [salaʀizɑsjɔ̃] *nf* putting on a regular salary.

salariser [salaʀize] (1) *vt* to put on a regular salary.

salaud‡ [salo] *nm* bastard∵, sod∵ (*Brit*), swine‡. **alors mon** ~, **tu ne t'en fais pas!** well you old bugger — you're not exactly overdoing it!∵; **10.000 F? ben, mon** ~! 10,000 francs, bugger me!∵; **tu es** ~ you're an absolute bastard∵ *ou* sod∵ (*Brit*) *ou* swine‡.

sale [sal] *adj* **(a)** (*crasseux*) dirty. **j'ai les mains/pieds** ~**s** I've got dirty hands/feet, my hands/feet are dirty; **blanc** ~ dirty white; ~ **comme un cochon** *ou* **un porc** *ou* **un peigne** filthy (dirty); **oh la** ~! you dirty girl!; *V* **laver.**
(b) (*ordurier*) *histoire* dirty, filthy.
(c) (*: *avant n: mauvais*) nasty. ~ **bête** nasty *ou* foul creature; ~ **gosse** horrible brat, nasty little brat; ~ **temps** filthy* *ou* foul *ou* lousy* weather; ~ **tour** dirty trick; ~ **type** foul *ou* nasty character, nasty piece of work; **avoir une** ~ **gueule‡** to have a nasty face; **faire une** ~ **gueule‡** to be bloody annoyed‡; **il m'est arrivé une** ~ **histoire** something really nasty *ou* rotten* happened to me; **il a un** ~ **caractère** he has a foul *ou* rotten* *ou* lousy* temper, he's foul-tempered.

salé, e [sale] **1** *adj* **(a)** (*contenant du sel*) *saveur, mer* salty; (*additionné de sel*) *amande, plat* salted; (*conservé au sel*) *poisson, viande* salt (*épith*); *beurre* salted; *V* **eau, petit, pré.**
(b) (*: *grivois*) spicy*, juicy*, fruity‡.
(c) (*: *sévère*) *punition* stiff*; *facture* steep*.
2 *nm* (*nourriture*) salty food; (*porc salé*) salt pork.
3 *adv*: **manger** ~ to like a lot of salt on one's food, like one's food well salted; **avec son régime, il ne peut pas manger trop** ~ with his diet he can't have his food too salty.

salement [salmɑ̃] *adv* **(a)** (*malproprement, bassement*) dirtily.
(b) (‡: *très*) *dur, embêtant* bloody‡ (*Brit*), damned‡. **j'ai** ~ **mal** it's bloody (*Brit*) *ou* damned painful‡, it hurts like mad*; **j'ai eu** ~ **peur** I had a *ou* one hell of a fright‡, I was bloody (*Brit*) *ou* damned scared‡.

saler [sale] (1) *vt* **(a)** *plat, soupe* to put salt in, salt; (*pour conserver*) to salt. **tu ne sales pas assez** you don't put enough salt in, you don't use enough salt. **(b)** (*) *client* to do*, fleece; *facture* to bump up*; *inculpé* to be tough on*.

saleté [salte] *nf* **(a)** (*malpropreté*) *[lieu, personne]* dirtiness.
(b) (*crasse*) dirt, filth. **murs couverts de** ~ walls covered in dirt *ou* filth; **vivre dans la** ~ to live in filth *ou* squalor; **le chauffage au charbon fait de la** ~ coal heating makes a lot of mess *ou* dirt, coal is a dirty *ou* messy way to heat; **tu as fait de la** ~ **en réparant le moteur** you've made a mess repairing the motor.
(c) (*ordure*) dirt (*U*). **il y a une** ~ **par terre/sur ta robe** there's some dirt *ou* muck* on the floor/your dress; **j'ai une** ~ **dans l'œil** I've got some dirt in my eye; **tu as fait des** ~**s partout en perçant le mur** you've made a mess all over the place *ou* you've dirtied everything drilling the wall; **enlève tes** ~**s de ma chambre** get your (old) rubbish out of my room; **le chat a fait des** ~**s** *ou* **ses** ~**s dans le salon** the cat has done its business *ou* made a mess in the lounge.
(d) (*: *chose sans valeur*) rubbish (*U*), junk (*U*). **ce réfrigérateur est une** ~ *ou* **de la vraie** ~ this fridge is a load of old rubbish*; **c'est une** ~ **qu'ils ont achetée en vacances** it's some (old) junk *ou* rubbish *ou* trash they bought on holiday*; **chez eux, il n'y a que des** ~**s** (*bibelots*) there's junk *ou* trash *ou* rubbishy stuff lying about all over their place*; (*meubles*) they've just got cheap and nasty stuff *ou* (cheap) rubbish *ou* junk at their place*; **on n'a qu'à acheter une** ~ **quelconque au gosse** we only need to get some rubbishy toy *ou* some bit of junk *ou* rubbish *ou* trash for the kid*; **il se bourre de** ~**s avant le repas** he stuffs himself with rubbish *ou* muck before meals*.
(e) (*: *maladie*) **je me demande où j'ai bien pu attraper cette** ~**-là** I wonder where on earth I could have caught this blasted thing* *ou* bug*; **cet enfant récolte toutes les** ~**s qui traînent** this child catches every blasted thing going*.
(f) (*: *obscénité*) dirty *ou* filthy thing (to say)*. **dire des** ~**s** to say filthy things*, talk filth*.
(g) (*: *méchanceté*) dirty *ou* filthy trick*. **faire une** ~ **à qn** to play a dirty *ou* filthy trick on sb*; **on en a vu, des** ~**s pendant la guerre** we saw plenty of disgusting things during the war.
(h) (*: *salaud*) nasty piece of work*, nasty character.

salicylate [salisilat] *nm* salicylate.

salicylique [salisilik] *adj*: **acide** ~ salicylic acid.

salière [saljɛʀ] *nf* (*récipient*), (*) *[clavicule]* saltcellar.

salification [salifikɑsjɔ̃] *nf* salification.

salifier [salifje] (7) *vt* to salify.

saligaud‡ [saligo] *nm* (*malpropre*) dirty *ou* filthy pig‡; (*salaud*) swine‡, bastard∵.

salin, e [salɛ̃, in] **1** *adj* saline. **2** *nm* salt marsh. **3 saline** *nf* (*entreprise*) saltworks; (*salin*) salt marsh.

salinité [salinite] *nf* salinity.

salique [salik] *adj* Salic, Salian. **loi** ~ Salic law.

salir [saliʀ] (2) **1** *vt* **(a)** *lieu* to (make) dirty, mess up*, make a mess in; *objet* to (make) dirty, soil. **le charbon salit** coal is messy *ou* dirty.

(b) *imagination* to corrupt, defile; *réputation* to sully, soil, tarnish. ~ **qn** to sully *ou* soil *ou* tarnish sb's reputation.

2 se salir *vpr* **(a)** *[tissu]* to get dirty *ou* soiled; *[personne]* to get dirty, dirty o.s. **le blanc se salit facilement** white shows the dirt (easily), white soils easily; *(lit, fig)* **se ~ les mains** to get one's hands dirty, dirty one's hands.

(b) *(se déshonorer)* to sully *ou* soil *ou* tarnish one's reputation.

salissant, e [salisɑ̃, ɑ̃t] *adj étoffe* which shows the dirt, which soils easily; *travail* dirty, messy.

salissure [salisyʀ] *nf (U)* dirt, filth; *(tache)* dirty mark.

salivaire [salivɛʀ] *adj* salivary.

salivation [salivɑsjɔ̃] *nf* salivation.

salive [saliv] *nf* saliva, spittle. *(fig)* **épargne** *ou* **ne gaspille pas ta ~** save your breath, don't waste your breath.

saliver [salive] (1) *vi* to salivate.

salle [sal] **1** *nf* **(a)** *[musée, café]* room; *[château]* hall; *[restaurant]* (dining) room; *[hôpital]* ward; *V* **fille, garçon.**

(b) *(Ciné, Théât) (auditorium)* auditorium, theatre; *(public)* audience; *(cinéma)* cinema *(Brit)*, movie theater *(US)*. **plusieurs ~s de quartier ont dû fermer** several local cinemas had to close down; **faire ~ comble** to have a full house.

2: salle d'armes arms room; **salle d'attente** waiting room; **salle d'audience** courtroom; **salle de bain(s)** bathroom; **salle de bal** ballroom; **salle de banquets** *[château]* banqueting hall; **salle de billard** billiard room; *(Rel)* **salle du chapitre** chapter house; **salle de cinéma** cinema *(Brit)*, movie theater *(US)*; **salle de classe** classroom; **salle commune** *[colonie de vacances etc]* commonroom; *[hôpital]* ward; **salle de concert** concert hall; **salle de conférences** lecture room; *(grande)* lecture hall *ou* theatre; **salle de douches** shower-room, showers; **salle d'eau** shower-room; **salle d'étude(s)** prep room; **salle des fêtes** village hall; **salle de garde** staff waiting room *(in hospital)*; **salle de jeu** *(pour enfants)* playroom; *[casino]* gaming room; **salle des machines** engine room; **salle à manger** *(pièce)* dining room; *(meubles)* dining room suite; **les salles obscures** the cinemas *(Brit)*, the movie theaters *(US)*; **salle d'opération** operating theatre; **salle des pas perdus** (waiting) hall; **salle de police** guardhouse, guardroom; **'salle pour noces et banquets'** 'functions catered for'; **salle des professeurs** commonroom, staff room; **salle de projection** film theatre; **salle de rédaction** (newspaper) office; **salle de séjour** living room; **salle de spectacle** theatre, cinema; **salle du trône** throne room; **salle des ventes** saleroom, auction room.

salmigondis [salmigɔ̃di] *nm (Culin, fig)* hotchpotch.

salmis [salmi] *nm* salmi. **~ de perdreaux** salmi of partridges.

saloir [salwaʀ] *nm* salting-tub.

Salomé [salɔme] *nf* Salome.

Salomon [salɔmɔ̃] *nm* Solomon.

salon [salɔ̃] **1** *nm* **(a)** *[appartement, maison]* lounge *(Brit)*, sitting room, living room; *[hôtel]* lounge; *[navire]* saloon, lounge.

(b) *(meubles)* lounge *(Brit) ou* living-room suite.

(c) *(exposition)* exhibition, show.

(d) *(cercle littéraire)* salon.

2: Salon des Arts ménagers ≈ Ideal Home *ou* Modern Homes Exhibition *(Brit)*; **salon d'attente** waiting room; **Salon de l'Auto** Motor Show; **salon de beauté** beauty salon *ou* parlour; **salon de coiffure** hairdressing salon; **salon d'essayage** fitting room; **salon particulier** private room; **salon-salle à manger** living (room) cum dining room, living-dining room; **salon de thé** tearoom.

salop‡ [salo] *nm* = **salaud**‡.

salopard‡ [salɔpaʀ] *nm* bastard‡, sod‡ *(Brit)*.

salope‡ [salɔp] *nf (méchante, déloyale)* bitch‡, cow‡ *(Brit)*; *(dévergondée)* tart‡; *(sale)* dirty cow‡ *(Brit)*.

saloper‡ [salɔpe] (1) *vt (bâcler)* to botch, bungle, make a mess of; *(salir)* to mess up*, muck up*.

saloperie‡ [salɔpʀi] *nf* **(a)** *(chose sans valeur)* trash* *(U)*, junk *(U)*, rubbish *(U)*. **ce transistor est une ~ *ou* de la vraie ~** this transistor is absolute trash *ou* rubbish; **ils n'achètent que des ~s** they only buy trash *ou* junk *ou* rubbish.

(b) *(mauvaise nourriture)* muck* *(U)*, rubbish* *(U)*. **ils nous ont fait manger de la ~ *ou* des ~s** they gave us awful muck *ou* rubbish to eat*; **c'est bon, ces petites ~s** these little bits and pieces are really good.

(c) *(maladie)* **il a dû attraper une ~ en vacances** he must have caught something *ou* a bug* on holiday; **il récolte toutes les ~s** he gets every blasted thing going*.

(d) *(ordure)* dirt *(U)*, mess *(U)*, muck* *(U)*. **le grenier est plein de ~s** the attic is full of junk *ou* rubbish *ou* muck*; **quand on ramone la cheminée ça fait des ~s *ou* de la ~ partout** when the chimney gets swept there's dirt *ou* muck* *ou* (a) mess everywhere; **va faire tes ~s ailleurs** go and make your mess somewhere else.

(e) *(action)* dirty trick*; *(parole)* bitchy remark*.

(f) *(obscénités)* **~s** dirty *ou* filthy things (to say)*; **dire des ~s** to talk filth*, say filthy things*.

(g) *(crasse)* filth.

salopette [salɔpɛt] *nf [ouvrier]* overall(s); *[femme, enfant]* dungarees *(pl)*; *(Ski)* salopette.

salpêtre [salpɛtʀ(ə)] *nm* saltpetre.

salpêtrer [salpetʀe] (1) *vt* **(a)** *(Agr) terre* to add saltpetre to. **(b)** *mur* to cover with saltpetre. **cave salpêtrée** cellar covered with saltpetre.

salsifis [salsifi] *nm* salsify, oyster-plant.

saltimbanque [saltɛ̃bɑ̃k] *nmf* (travelling) acrobat.

salubre [salybʀ(ə)] *adj* healthy, salubrious *(frm)*.

salubrité [salybʀite] *nf [lieu, région, climat]* healthiness, salubrity *(frm)*, salubriousness *(frm)*. **par mesure de ~** as a health measure; **~ publique** public health.

saluer [salɥe] (1) *vt* **(a)** *(dire bonjour)* to greet. **se découvrir/s'incliner pour ~ qn** to raise one's hat/bow to sb (in greeting); **~ qn de la main** to wave (one's hand) to sb (in greeting); **~ qn d'un signe de tête** to nod (a greeting) to sb; **~ qn à son arrivée** to greet sb on his arrival; **~ une dame dans sa loge** to pay one's respects to a lady in her box; **saluez-le de ma part** give him my regards.

(b) *(dire au revoir)* to take one's leave. **il nous salua et sortit** he took his leave (of us) and went out; **~ qn à son départ** to take one's leave of sb (as one goes); **acteur qui salue (le public)** actor who bows to the audience.

(c) *(Mil, Naut) supérieur, drapeau, navire* to salute.

(d) *(témoigner son respect) ennemi vaincu* to salute; *héroïsme* to bow to. **nous saluons en vous l'homme qui a sauvé tant de vies** we salute you as the man who has saved so many lives; **je salue le courage des sauveteurs** I bow to *ou* I salute the courage of the rescuers.

(e) *(célébrer, acclamer) décision, événement* to greet; *arrivée* to greet, hail. **~ qn comme roi** to acclaim *ou* hail sb (as) king; *(Rel)* **'je vous salue, Marie'** 'Hail, Mary'; **nous saluons la naissance d'un nouveau journal** we greet *ou* salute the birth of a new newspaper; *(hum)* **il/son arrivée fut salué(e) par des huées** he/his arrival was greeted with *ou* by booing.

salut [saly] **1** *nm* **(a)** *(de la main)* wave (of the hand); *(de la tête)* nod (of the head); *(du buste)* bow; *(Mil, Naut)* salute. **faire un ~** to wave (one's hand); to nod (one's head); to bow; **faire le ~ militaire** to give the military salute; **~ au drapeau** salute to the colours.

(b) *(sauvegarde) [personne]* (personal) safety; *[nation]* safety. **trouver son ~ dans la fuite** to find (one's) safety in flight; **mesures de ~ public** measures for the protection of the general public; **ancre *ou* planche de ~** sheet anchor *(fig)*.

(c) *(Rel: rédemption)* salvation; *V* **armée**[2], **hors.**

2 *excl* **(a)** (*) *(bonjour)* hi (there)!*, hello!; *(au revoir)* see you!*, bye!*, cheerio!* *(Brit)*. **~, les gars!** hi (there) lads!*

(b) *(littér)* (all) hail. **~ (à toi) puissant seigneur** (all) hail (to thee) mighty lord *(littér)*; **~, forêt de mon enfance** hail (to thee), o forest of my childhood *(littér)*.

salutaire [salytɛʀ] *adj* **(a)** *conseil* salutary *(épith)*, profitable *(épith)*; *choc, épreuve* salutary *(épith)*; *influence* healthy *(épith)*, salutary *(épith)*; *dégoût* healthy *(épith)*. **cette déception lui a été ~** that disappointment was good for him *ou* did him some good.

(b) *air* healthy, salubrious *(frm)*; *remède* beneficial. **ce petit repos m'a été ~** that little rest did me good *ou* was good for me.

salutairement [salytɛʀmɑ̃] *adv (littér) conseiller* profitably; *réagir* in a healthy way.

salutation [salytɑsjɔ̃] *nf* salutation, greeting. **veuillez agréer, Monsieur, mes ~s distinguées** yours faithfully *ou* truly.

salutiste [salytist(ə)] *adj, nmf* Salvationist.

salvateur, -trice [salvatœʀ, tʀis] *adj (littér)* saving *(épith)*.

salve [salv(ə)] *nf (Mil)* salvo; *[applaudissements]* salvo, volley.

Samarie [samaʀi] *nf* Samaria.

samaritain, e [samaʀitɛ̃, ɛn] **1** *adj* Samaritan. **2** *nm,f:* **S~(e)** Samaritan; *V* **bon**[1].

samba [sɑ̃mba] *nf* samba.

samedi [samdi] *nm* Saturday. **~ nous irons** on Saturday we'll go; **~ nous sommes allés ...** on Saturday *ou* last Saturday we went...; **~ prochain** next Saturday, Saturday next; **~ qui vient** this Saturday, next Saturday; **~ dernier** last Saturday; **le premier/dernier ~ du mois** the first/last Saturday of *ou* in the month; **un ~ sur deux** every other *ou* second Saturday; **nous sommes ~ (aujourd'hui)** it's Saturday (today); **~, le 18 décembre** Saturday December 18th; **le ~ 23 janvier** on Saturday January 23rd; **il y a huit/quinze jours ~ dernier** a week/a fortnight *ou* two weeks past on Saturday; **le ~ suivant** the following Saturday; **l'autre ~** the Saturday before last; **~ matin/après-midi** Saturday morning/afternoon; **~ soir** Saturday evening *ou* night; **la nuit de ~** Saturday night; **l'édition de ~ *ou* du ~** the Saturday edition; *V* **huit, quinze.**

samouraï [samuʀaj] *nm* samurai.

samovar [samɔvaʀ] *nm* samovar.

sampan(g) [sɑ̃pɑ̃] *nm* sampan.

samuraï [samuʀaj] *nm* = **samouraï.**

sana* [sana] *nm abrév de* **sanatorium.**

sanatorium [sanatɔʀjɔm] *nm* sanatorium *(Brit)*, sanitarium *(US)*.

sanctificateur, -trice [sɑ̃ktifikatœʀ, tʀis] **1** *adj* sanctifying *(épith)*. **2** *nm,f* sanctifier. **3** *nm:* **le S~** the Holy Spirit *ou* Ghost.

sanctification [sɑ̃ktifikɑsjɔ̃] *nf* sanctification.

sanctifier [sɑ̃ktifje] (7) *vt* to sanctify, hallow. **~ le dimanche** to observe the Sabbath; *(Rel)* **'que ton nom soit sanctifié'** 'hallowed be Thy name'.

sanction [sɑ̃ksjɔ̃] *nf* **(a)** *(condamnation)* sanction, penalty; *(Scol)* punishment; *(fig: conséquence)* penalty (*de* for). **~s économiques** economic sanctions; **prendre des ~s contre qn** to impose sanctions on sb.

(b) *(ratification)* sanction *(U)*, approval *(U)*. **recevoir la ~ de qn** to obtain sb's sanction *ou* approval.

sanctionner [sɑ̃ksjɔne] (1) *vt* **(a)** *(punir) faute, personne* to punish. **(b)** *(consacrer) (gén)* to sanction, approve; *loi* to sanction.

sanctuaire [sɑ̃ktɥɛʀ] *nm* **(a)** *(Rel) (lieu saint)* sanctuary, shrine; *[temple, église]* sanctuary. **(b)** *(fig littér)* sanctuary.

sanctus [sɑ̃ktys] *nm* sanctus.

sandale [sɑ̃dal] *nf* sandal.

sandalette [sɑ̃dalɛt] *nf* sandal.

sandow [sɑ̃do] *nm* ® *(attache)* luggage elastic; *(Aviat)* catapult.

sandwich, *pl* ~s *ou* ~es [sɑ̃dwitʃ] *nm* sandwich. **(pris) en ~ (entre)*** sandwiched (between); **les 2 voitures l'ont pris en ~*** he was sandwiched between the 2 cars; *V* **homme.**

sang [sɑ̃] **1** *nm* **(a)** (*lit, fig*) blood. **animal à ~ froid/chaud** cold-blooded/warm-blooded animal; **le ~ a coulé** blood has flowed; **verser** *ou* **faire couler le ~** to shed *ou* spill blood; (*fig*) **avoir du ~ sur les mains** to have blood on one's hands; **son ~ crie vengeance** his blood cries (for) vengeance; **être en ~** to be bleeding; **pincer qn (jusqu')au ~** to pinch sb till he bleeds *ou* till the blood comes; **payer son crime de son ~** to pay for one's crime with one's life; **donner son ~ pour sa patrie** to shed one's blood for one's country; *V* **bon¹, mauvais, pinte.**

(b) (*race, famille*) blood. **de ~ royal** of royal blood; **du même ~** of the same flesh and blood; **liens du ~** blood ties, ties of blood; *V* **voix.**

(c) (*loc*) **avoir le ~ chaud** (*s'emporter facilement*) to be hotheaded; (*être sensuel*) to be hot-blooded; **animaux à ~ chaud/froid** warm-/cold-blooded animals; **avoir du ~ dans les veines** to have courage; **il n'a pas de ~ dans les veines, il a du ~ de navet** *ou* **de poulet** (*manque de courage*) he's a spineless individual; (*manque d'énergie*) he's a lethargic individual; **il a le jeu/la passion de la musique dans le ~** he's got gambling/a passion for music in his blood; **avoir du ~ bleu** to have blue blood, be blue-blooded; **le ~ lui monta au visage** the blood rushed to his face; **avoir le ~ qui monte à la tête** to be about to burst out in anger; **mon ~ n'a fait qu'un tour** (*émotion, peur*) my heart missed *ou* skipped a beat; (*colère, indignation*) I saw red.

(d) se ronger *ou* **se manger les ~s** to worry (o.s.), fret; **tourner les ~s à qn** to shake sb up.

2: sang-froid *nm inv* sangfroid, cool*, calm; **garder/perdre son sang-froid** to keep/lose one's head *ou* one's cool*; **faire qch de sang-froid** to do sth in cold blood *ou* cold-bloodedly; **répondre avec sang-froid** to reply coolly *ou* calmly; **meurtre accompli de sang-froid** cold-blooded murder; **sang-mêlé** *nmf inv* half-caste.

sanglant, e [sɑ̃glɑ̃, ɑ̃t] *adj* **(a)** *couteau, plaie* bloody; *bandage, habits* blood-soaked, bloody; *mains, visage* covered in blood, bloody.

(b) *combat, guerre* bloody.

(c) *insulte, reproche* cruel, extremely hurtful; *défaite* cruel.

(d) (*littér: couleur*) blood-red.

sangle [sɑ̃gl(ə)] *nf* (*gén*) strap; *[selle]* girth. *[siège]* ~s webbing; *V* **lit.**

sangler [sɑ̃gle] (1) **1** *vt cheval* to girth; *colis, corps* to strap up. **sanglé dans son uniforme** done up *ou* strapped up tight in one's uniform. **2 se sangler** *vpr* to do one's belt up tight.

sanglier [sɑ̃glije] *nm* (wild) boar.

sanglot [sɑ̃glo] *nm* sob. **avoir des ~s dans la voix** to have a sob in one's voice; **elle répondit dans un ~ que ...** she answered with a sob that ...; *V* **éclater.**

sangloter [sɑ̃glɔte] (1) *vi* to sob.

sangria [sɑ̃gʀija] *nf* sangria, fruit punch.

sangsue [sɑ̃sy] *nf* (*lit, fig*) leech.

sanguin, e [sɑ̃gɛ̃, in] **1** *adj* **(a)** *caractère, homme* fiery, passionate; *visage* ruddy, sanguine (*frm*). **orange ~e** blood orange.

(b) (*Anat*) blood (*épith*).

2 sanguine *nf* **(a)** (*Bot*) blood orange.

(b) (*dessin*) red pencil drawing; (*crayon*) red pencil.

sanguinaire [sɑ̃ginɛʀ] *adj personne* bloodthirsty, sanguinary (*frm, littér*); *combat* bloody, sanguinary (*frm, littér*).

sanguinolent, e [sɑ̃ginɔlɑ̃, ɑ̃t] *adj crachat* streaked with blood. **plaie ~e** wound that is bleeding slightly *ou* from which blood is oozing.

sanitaire [sanitɛʀ] **1** *adj* **(a)** (*Méd*) *services, mesures* health (*épith*); *conditions* sanitary. **campagne ~** campaign to improve sanitary conditions; *V* **cordon, train.**

(b) (*Plomberie*) **l'installation ~ est défectueuse** the bathroom plumbing is faulty; **appareil ~** bathroom *ou* sanitary appliance.

2 *nm:* **le ~** bathroom installations (*pl*); **les ~s** (*lieu*) the bathroom (*sg*); (*appareils*) the bathroom (suite) (*sg*); (*plomberie*) the bathroom plumbing (*sg*).

sans [sɑ̃] **1** *prép* **(a)** (*privation, absence*) without. **ménage ~ enfant** childless couple; **~ père/mère** fatherless/motherless, with no father/mother; **il est ~ secrétaire en ce moment** he is without a secretary at the moment, he has no secretary at the moment; **ils sont ~ argent** *ou* **le sou** they have no money, they are penniless; **je suis sorti ~ chapeau ni manteau** I went out without (a) hat or coat *ou* with no hat or coat; **repas à 60 F ~ le vin** meal at 60 francs exclusive of wine *ou* not including wine.

(b) (*manière, caractérisationhu9 without.* **manger ~ fourchette** to eat without a fork; **boire ~ soif** to drink without being thirsty; **il est parti ~ même** *ou* **~ seulement un mot de remerciement** he left without even (so much as) *ou* without so much as a word of thanks; **la situation est ~ remède** the situation cannot be remedied *ou* is beyond *ou* past remedy; **l'histoire n'est pas ~ intérêt** the story is not devoid of interest *ou* is not without interest; **nous avons trouvé sa maison ~ mal** we found his house with no difficulty *ou* with no trouble *ou* without difficulty; **la situation n'est pas ~ nous inquiéter** the situation is somewhat disturbing; **il a accepté ~ hésitation** he accepted unhesitatingly *ou* without hesitation; **travailler ~ arrêt** *ou* (*littér*) **~ trêve** to work ceaselessly (*littér*) *ou* without a break *ou* relentlessly (*littér*); **marcher ~ chaussures** to walk barefoot; **marcher ~ but** to walk aimlessly; **promenade ~ but** aimless walk; **il est ~ scrupules** he is unscrupulous, he has no scruples, he is devoid of scruple(s); **il est ~ préjugés** he is unprejudiced *ou* unbiased *ou* free from prejudice(s); (*fig*) **objet ~ prix** priceless object; **robe ~ manches** sleeveless dress; **pièce ~ tapis** uncarpeted room; (*Scol*) **dictée ~ fautes** error-free dictation; **je le connais, ~ plus** I know him but no more than that; *V* **cesse, doute, effort** *etc.*

(c) (*cause ou condition négative*) but for. **~ cette réunion, il aurait pu partir ce soir** if it had not been for *ou* were it not for *ou* but for this meeting he could have left tonight; **~ sa présence d'esprit, il se tuait** had he not had such presence of mind *ou* without *ou* but for his presence of mind he would have killed himself.

(d) (*avec infin ou subj*) without. **vous n'êtes pas ~ savoir** you must be aware, you cannot but know (*frm*); **il est entré ~ faire de bruit** he came in without making a noise *ou* noiselessly; **il est entré ~ (même** *ou* **seulement) que je l'entende** he came in without my (even) hearing him; **je n'irai pas ~ être invité** I won't go without being invited; **~ que cela (ne) vous dérange** as long as *ou* provided that it doesn't put you out; **il lui écrivit ~ plus attendre** he wrote to her without further delay; **j'y crois ~ y croire** I believe it and I don't; **~ (même) que nous le sachions, il avait écrit** he had written without our (even) knowing; **je ne suis pas ~ avoir des doutes sur son honnêteté** I have my doubts *ou* I am not without some doubts as to his honesty; **il ne se passe pas de jour ~ qu'il lui écrive** not a day passes without his writing to him *ou* but that (*littér*) he writes to him; **il va ~ dire que** it goes without saying that; *V* **jamais.**

(e) non ~: non ~ peine *ou* **mal** *ou* **difficulté** not without difficulty; **l'incendie a été maîtrisé, non ~ que les pompiers aient dû intervenir** the fire was brought under control but not until the fire brigade were brought in *ou* but not without the fire brigade's being brought in.

(f) (*) **~ ça, ~ quoi** otherwise; **si on m'offre un bon prix je vends ma voiture, ~ ça** *ou* **~ quoi je la garde** I'll sell my car if I'm offered a good price for it but otherwise *ou* if not, I'll keep it; **sois sage, ~ ça ...!** be good or else...!, be good - otherwise ...!

2 *adv* (*) **votre parapluie! vous alliez partir ~** your umbrella! you were going to go off without it; **il a oublié ses lunettes et il ne peut pas conduire ~** he's forgotten his glasses, and he can't drive without them.

3: sans-abri *nmf inv* homeless person; **les sans-abri** the homeless; **sans-cœur** (*adj inv*) heartless; (*nmf inv*) heartless person; (*Hist*) **sans-culotte** *nm, pl* **sans-culottes** sans culotte; **sans faute** *loc adv* without fail; **sans-fil** *nf* wireless telegraphy; **sans-filiste** *nmf* wireless enthusiast; **sans-gêne** (*adj inv*) inconsiderate; (*nm inv*) lack of consideration (for others), inconsiderateness; (*nmf inv*) inconsiderate type; **sans-logis = sans-abri**; **sans-soin** (*adj inv*) careless; (*nmf inv*) careless person; **sans-le-sou** *nmf inv* pauper; **sans-souci** *adj inv* carefree; **sans-travail** *nmf inv* unemployed person; **les sans-travail** the jobless, the unemployed.

sanscrit, e, sanskrit, e [sɑ̃skʀi, it] *adj, nm* Sanskrit.

sansonnet [sɑ̃sɔnɛ] *nm* starling; *V* **roupie.**

santal [sɑ̃tal] *nm* **(bois de) ~** sandal(wood).

santé [sɑ̃te] *nf* **(a)** *[personne, esprit, pays]* health. **en bonne/mauvaise ~** in good/bad health; **c'est bon/mauvais pour la ~** it's good/bad for the health *ou* for you; **être en pleine ~** to be in perfect health; **avoir la ~** to be healthy, be in good health; **il n'a pas de ~, il a une petite ~** he's not a healthy type, he has poor health, he's not very strong; **avoir une ~ de fer** to have an iron constitution; **comment va la ~?*** how are you keeping?*; **meilleure ~** get well soon; *V* **maison.**

(b) (*Admin*) **la ~ publique** public health; (*Naut*) **la ~** the quarantine service; (*Admin*) **services de ~** health services; **ministre/ministère de la S~** Minister/Ministry of Health.

(c) (*en trinquant*) **à votre ~!, ~!*** cheers!*, (your) good health!; **à la ~ de Paul!** (here's to) Paul!; **boire à la ~ de qn** to drink (to) sb's health.

santon [sɑ̃tɔ̃] *nm* (ornamental) figure (*at a Christmas crib*).

saoul [su] = **soûl.**

saoulard, e‡ [sulaʀ, aʀd(ə)] *nm,f* = **soûlard**‡.

sapajou [sapaʒu] *nm* (*Zool*) sapajou.

sape [sap] *nf* **(a)** (*lit, fig: action*) undermining, sapping; (*tranchée*) approach *ou* sapping trench. **travail de ~** (*Mil*) sap; (*fig*) insidious undermining process *ou* work.

(b) (*habits*) **~s**‡ gear* (*U*), clobber‡ (*U: Brit*).

sapement [sapmɑ̃] *nm* (*rare*) undermining, sapping.

saper [sape] (1) **1** *vt* (*lit, fig*) to undermine, sap. **2 se saper**‡ *vpr* to do o.s. up*. **il s'était sapé pour aller danser** he had done *ou* got himself up to go dancing*.

saperlipopette [sapɛʀlipɔpɛt] *excl* († *hum*) gad!†, gadzooks! († *hum*).

sapeur [sapœʀ] **1** *nm* (*Mil*) sapper; *V* **fumer. 2: sapeur-pompier** *nm, pl* **sapeurs-pompiers** fireman.

saphique [safik] *adj, nm* (*Littérat*) Sapphic.

saphir [safiʀ] **1** *nm* (*pierre*) sapphire; (*aiguille*) sapphire, needle. **2** *adj inv* sapphire.

saphisme [safism(ə)] *nm* (*Littérat*) Sapphism.

sapide [sapid] *adj* sapid.

sapidité [sapidite] *nf* sapidity.

sapience [sapjɑ̃s] *nf* sapience (*frm*), wisdom.

sapin [sapɛ̃] *nm* (*arbre*) fir (tree); (*bois*) fir. **~ de Noël** Christmas tree; **costume en ~**‡ wooden overcoat‡; **une toux qui sent le ~**‡ a cough which sounds as though one hasn't long to go.

sapinière [sapinjɛʀ] *nf* fir plantation *ou* forest.

saponacé, e [sapɔnase] *adj* saponaceous.

saponification [sapɔnifikɑsjɔ̃] *nf* saponification.

saponifier [sapɔnifje] (7) *vt* to saponify.

sapristi*† [sapʀisti] *excl* (*colère*) for God's sake!*; (*surprise*) good grief!, great heavens!†

saquer* [sake] (1) *vt* = **sacquer*.**

sarabande [saʀabɑ̃d] *nf* (*danse*) saraband; (*: *tapage*) racket*, hullabaloo*; (*succession*) jumble. **faire la ~*** to make a racket* *ou* a hullabaloo*; **les souvenirs/chiffres qui dansent la ~ dans**

ma tête the memories/figures that are whirling around in my head.

sarbacane [saʀbakan] *nf* (*arme*) blowpipe, blowgun; (*jouet*) peashooter.

sarcasme [saʀkasm(ə)] *nm* (*ironie*) sarcasm; (*remarque*) sarcastic remark.

sarcastique [saʀkastik] *adj* sarcastic.

sarcastiquement [saʀkastikmɑ̃] *adv* sarcastically.

sarcelle [saʀsɛl] *nf* teal.

sarclage [saʀklaʒ] *nm* (*V* **sarcler**) weeding; pulling up.

sarcler [saʀkle] (1) *vt jardin, culture* to weed; *mauvaise herbe* to pull up.

sarcloir [saʀklwaʀ] *nm* spud, weeding hoe.

sarcophage [saʀkɔfaʒ] *nm* (*cercueil*) sarcophagus.

Sardaigne [saʀdɛɲ] *nf* Sardinia.

sarde [saʀd(ə)] **1** *adj* Sardinian. **2** *nm* (*Ling*) Sardinian. **3** *nmf:* **S~** Sardinian.

sardine [saʀdin] *nf* **(a)** sardine. **serrés** *ou* **tassés comme des ~s (en boîte)** packed *ou* squashed together like sardines (in a tin). **(b)** (*arg Mil*) stripe.

sardinerie [saʀdinʀi] *nf* sardine cannery.

sardinier, -ière [saʀdinje, jɛʀ] **1** *adj* sardine (*épith*). **2** *nm,f* (*ouvrier*) sardine canner. **3** *nm* (*bateau*) sardine boat; (*pêcheur*) sardine fisher.

sardonique [saʀdɔnik] *adj* sardonic.

sardoniquement [saʀdɔnikmɑ̃] *adv* sardonically.

sargasse [saʀgas] *nf* sargasso, gulfweed; *V* **mer.**

sari [saʀi] *nm* sari.

sarigue [saʀig] *nf* (o)possum.

sarment [saʀmɑ̃] *nm* (*tige*) twining *ou* climbing stem, bine (*T*). **~ (de vigne)** vine shoot.

sarmenteux, -euse [saʀmɑ̃tø, øz] *adj plante* climbing (*épith*); *tige* climbing (*épith*), twining (*épith*).

sarrasin[1], **e** [saʀazɛ̃, in] (*Hist*) **1** *adj* Saracen. **2** *nm,f:* **S~(e)** Saracen.

sarrasin[2] [saʀazɛ̃] *nm* (*Bot*) buckwheat.

sarrau [saʀo] *nm* smock.

Sarre [saʀ] *nf:* **la ~** the Saar.

sarriette [saʀjɛt] *nf* savory.

sarrois, e [saʀwa, waz] **1** *adj* Saar (*épith*). **2** *nm,f:* **S~(e)** inhabitant *ou* native of the Saar.

sas [sɑ] *nm* **(a)** (*Espace, Naut*) airlock; *[écluse]* lock. **(b)** (*tamis*) sieve, screen.

sassafras [sasafʀɑ] *nm* sassafras.

sasser [sɑse] (1) *vt farine* to sift, screen; *péniche* to pass through a lock.

Satan [satɑ̃] *nm* Satan.

satané, e* [satane] *adj* blasted*, confounded*.

satanique [satanik] *adj* (*de Satan*) satanic; (*fig*) *rire, plaisir, ruse* fiendish, satanic, wicked.

satanisme [satanism(ə)] *nm* (*culte*) Satanism; (*fig*) fiendishness, wickedness. (*fig*) **c'est du ~!** it's fiendish! *ou* wicked!

satellisation [satelizɑsjɔ̃] *nf* **(a)** *[fusée]* (launching and) putting into orbit. **programme de ~** satellite launching programme. **(b)** *[pays]* **la ~ de cet état est à craindre** it is to be feared that this state will become a satellite (state).

satelliser [satelize] (1) *vt fusée* to put into orbit (round the earth); *pays* to make a satellite of, make into a satellite.

satellite [satelit] *nm* **(a)** (*Astron, Espace, Pol*) satellite. **~ artificiel** artificial satellite; **pays/villes ~s** satellite countries/towns. **(b)** (*Tech*) **(pignon) ~** bevel pinion.

satiété [sasjete] *nf* satiety, satiation. **(jusqu')à ~** *manger, boire* to satiety *ou* satiation; *répéter* ad nauseam; **j'en ai à ~** I've more than enough, I've enough and to spare.

satin [satɛ̃] *nm* satin. **elle avait une peau de ~** her skin was (like) satin, she had satin(-smooth) skin; **~ de laine/de coton** wool/cotton satin.

satiné, e [satine] (*ptp de* **satiner**) **1** *adj tissu, aspect* satiny, satin-like; *peau* satin (*épith*), satin-smooth; *peinture, papier* with a silk finish. **2** *nm* satin(-like) *ou* satiny quality.

satiner [satine] (1) *vt étoffe* to put a satin finish on; *photo, papier* to give a silk finish to, put a silk finish on. **la lumière satinait sa peau** the light gave her skin a satin-like quality *ou* gloss, her skin shone like satin beneath the light.

satinette [satinɛt] *nf* (*en coton et soie*) satinet; (*en coton*) sateen.

satire [satiʀ] *nf* (*gén*) satire; (*écrite*) satire, lampoon. **faire la ~ de qch** to satirize sth, lampoon sth.

satirique [satiʀik] *adj* satirical, satiric.

satiriquement [satiʀikmɑ̃] *adv* satirically.

satiriser [satiʀize] (1) *vt* (*gén*) to satirize; (*par écrit*) to satirize, lampoon.

satisfaction [satisfaksjɔ̃] *nf* **(a)** (*assouvissement*) *[faim, passion]* satisfaction, appeasement; *[soif]* satisfaction, quenching; *[envie]* satisfaction; *[désir]* satisfaction, gratification.

(b) (*contentement*) satisfaction. **éprouver une certaine ~ à faire** to feel a certain satisfaction in doing, get a certain satisfaction out of doing *ou* from doing; **donner (toute** *ou* **entière) ~ à qn** to give (complete) satisfaction to sb, satisfy sb (completely); **je vois avec ~ que** I'm gratified to see that; **à la ~ générale** *ou* **de tous** to the general satisfaction, to everybody's satisfaction.

(c) une ~: c'est une ~ qu'il pourrait m'accorder he might grant me that satisfaction; **leur fils ne leur a donné que des ~s** their son has been a (source of) great satisfaction to them; **~ d'amour-propre** gratification (*U*) of one's self-esteem.

(d) (*gén, Rel: réparation, gain de cause*) satisfaction. **obtenir ~** to get *ou* obtain satisfaction; **donner ~ à qn** to give sb satisfaction; **j'aurai ~ de cette offense** I will have satisfaction for that insult.

satisfaire [satisfɛʀ] (60) **1** *vt personne, cœur, curiosité* to satisfy; *désir* to satisfy, gratify; *passion, faim* to satisfy, appease; *besoin* to satisfy, answer, gratify; *soif* to satisfy, quench; *demande* to satisfy, meet. **votre nouvel assistant vous satisfait-il?** are you satisfied with your new assistant?, is your new assistant satisfactory?, does your new assistant satisfy you?; **j'espère que cette solution vous satisfait** I hope you find this solution satisfactory, I hope this solution satisfies you, I hope you are satisfied *ou* happy with this solution; (*euph*) **~ un besoin pressant** to satisfy an urgent need, attend to the call of nature (*hum*); **~ l'attente de qn** to come up to sb's expectations.

2 satisfaire à *vt indir désir* to satisfy, gratify; *promesse, engagement* to fulfil; *demande, revendication* to meet, satisfy; *condition* to meet, fulfil, satisfy; *goût* to satisfy. **avez-vous satisfait à vos obligations militaires?** have you fulfilled the requirement for military service?; **cette installation ne satisfait pas aux normes** this installation does not comply with *ou* satisfy standard requirements.

3 se satisfaire *vpr* to be satisfied (*de* with); (*euph*) to relieve o.s.

satisfaisant, e [satisfəzɑ̃, ɑ̃t] *adj* (*acceptable*) satisfactory; (*qui fait plaisir*) satisfying.

satisfait, e [satisfɛ, ɛt] (*ptp de* **satisfaire**) *adj personne, air* satisfied. **être ~ de qn** to be satisfied with sb; **être ~ de** *solution, décision* to be satisfied with, be happy with *ou* about; *soirée* to be pleased with; **être ~ de soi** to be self-satisfied, be satisfied with o.s.; **il est ~ de son sort** he is satisfied *ou* happy with his lot.

satisfecit [satisfesit] *nm inv* (*Scol*) good report. (*fig*) **je lui donne un ~ pour la façon dont il a mené son affaire** I give him full marks for the way he conducted the business.

satrape [satʀap] *nm* satrap.

saturable [satyʀabl(ə)] *adj* saturable.

saturant, e [satyʀɑ̃, ɑ̃t] *adj* saturating. **vapeur ~e** saturated vapour.

saturateur [satyʀatœʀ] *nm [radiateur]* humidifier.

saturation [satyʀɑsjɔ̃] *nf* (*gén, Sci*) saturation. **être/arriver à ~** to be at/reach saturation point; **manger à ~** to eat till one reaches saturation point; **avoir de qch jusqu'à ~** to have as much as one can take of sth.

saturer [satyʀe] (1) *vt* (*gén, Sci*) to saturate (*de* with). (*fig*) **~ les électeurs de promesses** to swamp the electors with promises; **la terre est saturée d'eau après la pluie** the ground is saturated (with water) after the rain; **j'ai mangé tant de fraises que j'en suis saturé** I've eaten so many strawberries that I can't take any more *ou* that I've had as many as I can take.

saturnales [satyʀnal] *nfpl* (*lit*) Saturnalia; (*fig*) saturnalia.

Saturne [satyʀn(ə)] *nm* (*Astron, Myth*) Saturn. (*Pharm*) **extrait** *ou* **sel de s~** lead acetate.

saturnien, -ienne [satyʀnjɛ̃, jɛn] *adj* (*littér*) saturnine.

saturnin, e [satyʀnɛ̃, in] *adj* saturnine.

saturnisme [satyʀnism(ə)] *nm* lead poisoning, saturnism (*T*).

satyre [satiʀ] *nm* (*: *obsédé*) lecher*, sex maniac*; (*Myth, Zool*) satyr.

satyrique [satiʀik] *adj* satyric.

sauce [sos] *nf* **(a)** (*Culin*) sauce; *[salade]* dressing; (*jus de viande*) gravy. **viande en ~** meat cooked in a sauce; **~ blanche/piquant/tomate** white/piquant/tomato sauce; **~ béchamel/vinaigrette** béchamel/vinaigrette sauce; **~ à l'orange/aux câpres** orange/caper sauce; **~ chasseur/mousseline** sauce chasseur/mousseline; **~ madère/suprême** madeira/suprême sauce.

(b) (*) (*remplissage*) padding*. (*présentation*) **reprendre un vieux discours en changeant la ~** to dish up an old speech with a new slant*, take an old speech and dress it up; **il faudrait mettre un peu de ~ pour étoffer ce devoir** you'll have to pad out this piece of work, you'll have to put some padding* in this piece of work.

(c) (*loc*) **à quelle ~ allons-nous être mangés?** I wonder what Fate has in store for us; **mettre qn à toutes les ~s** to make sb do any job going*; **mettre un exemple à toutes les ~s** to turn *ou* adapt an example to fit any case; **recevoir la ~*** to get soaked *ou* drenched.

saucée* [sose] *nf* downpour. **recevoir** *ou* **prendre une ~** to get soaked *ou* drenched.

saucer [sose] (3) *vt* **(a)** *assiette* to wipe (the sauce off); *pain* to dip in the sauce. **(b) se faire ~*, être saucé*** to get soaked *ou* drenched.

saucier [sosje] *nm* sauce chef *ou* cook.

saucière [sosjɛʀ] *nf* sauceboat; *[jus de viande]* gravy boat.

saucisse [sosis] *nf* **(a)** (*Culin*) sausage. **~ de Strasbourg** (type of) beef sausage; **~ de Francfort** ≈ frankfurter; *V* **attacher, chair. (b)** (*Aviat*) sausage. **(c) (grande) ~*** nincompoop*, great ninny*.

saucisson [sosisɔ̃] *nm* **(a)** (*Culin*) (large) (slicing) sausage. **~ à l'ail** garlic sausage; **~ sec** (dry) pork and beef sausage; *V* **ficeler. (b)** (*pain*) (cylindrical) loaf.

saucissonné, e* [sosisɔne] **1** *ptp de* **saucissonner. 2** *adj* trussed up.

saucissonner* [sosisɔne] (1) *vi* to (have a) picnic.

sauf[1], **sauve** [sof, sov] *adj personne* unharmed, unhurt; *honneur* saved, intact; *V* **sain, vie.**

sauf[2] [sof] *prép* **(a)** (*à part*) except, but, save (*frm*). **tout le monde ~ lui** everyone except *ou* but *ou* save (*frm*) him; **nous sortons tout le temps ~ s'il/quand il pleut** we always go out except if/when it's raining; **le repas était excellent ~ le dessert** *ou* **~ pour ce qui est du dessert** the meal was excellent except for *ou* but for *ou* apart from the dessert; **~ que** except that, but that (*frm*).

(b) (*sous réserve de*) unless. **nous irons demain, ~ s'il pleut**

we'll go tomorrow unless it rains; ~ **avis contraire** unless you hear *ou* are told otherwise, unless you hear to the contrary; ~ **erreur de ma part** if I'm not mistaken; ~ **imprévu** barring the unexpected, unless anything unforeseen happens.

(c) (*loc*) (*littér*) **il accepte de nous aider,** ~ **à nous critiquer si nous échouons** he agrees to help us even if he does (reserve the right to) criticize us if we fail; (††, *hum*) ~ **le respect que je vous dois** with all due respect; (††, *hum*) ~ **votre respect** saving your presence (††, *hum*).

sauf-conduit, *pl* **sauf-conduits** [sofkɔ̃dɥi] *nm* safe-conduct.

sauge [soʒ] *nf* (*Culin*) sage; (*ornementale*) salvia.

saugrenu, e [sogʀəny] *adj* preposterous, ludicrous.

saulaie [solɛ] *nf* willow plantation.

saule [sol] *nm* willow (tree). ~ **pleureur** weeping willow.

saumâtre [somɑtʀ(ə)] *adj eau, goût* briny, unpleasantly salty; *plaisanterie, impression, humeur* nasty, unpleasant. **il l'a trouvée** ~**:** he found it a bit off* (*Brit*), he was not amused.

saumon [somɔ̃] **1** *nm* salmon. **2** *adj inv* salmon (pink).

saumoné, e [somɔne] *adj couleur* salmon (pink); *V* **truite.**

saumure [somyʀ] *nf* brine.

saumuré, e [somyʀe] *adj hareng* pickled (in brine).

sauna [sona] *nm* (*bain*) sauna (bath); (*établissement*) sauna.

saunier [sonje] *nm* (*ouvrier*) worker in a saltworks; (*exploitant*) salt merchant.

saupiquet [sopikɛ] *nm* (*sauce, ragoût*) *type of spicy sauce or stew.*

saupoudrage [sopudʀaʒ] *nm* (*V* **saupoudrer**) sprinkling; dredging, dusting.

saupoudrer [sopudʀe] (1) *vt* (*gén*) to sprinkle; (*Culin*) to dredge, dust, sprinkle (*de* with).

saupoudreuse [sopudʀøz] *nf* dredger.

saur [sɔʀ] *adj m V* **hareng.**

saurien [sɔʀjɛ̃] *nm* saurian. ~**s** Sauria (*T*), saurians.

saut [so] **1** *nm* **(a)** (*lit, fig: bond*) jump, leap. (*Sport*) ~ **avec/sans élan** running/standing jump; **faire un** ~ to (make a) jump *ou* leap; **faire un** ~ **dans l'inconnu/le vide** to (make a) leap into the unknown/the void; **le véhicule fit un** ~ **de 100 mètres dans le ravin** the vehicle fell *ou* dropped 100 metres into the ravine; **se lever d'un** ~ to jump *ou* leap up, jump *ou* leap to one's feet; **quittons Louis XIV et faisons un** ~ **d'un siècle** let us leave Louis XIV and jump a century; (*fig*) **progresser** *ou* **avancer par** ~**s** to go forward by *ou* in stages.

(b) (*Sport*) jumping. **épreuves de** ~ jumping events.

(c) (*Géog: cascade*) waterfall.

(d) (*loc*) **faire qch au** ~ **du lit** to do sth on getting up *ou* getting out of bed, do sth as soon as one gets up *ou* gets out of bed; **prendre qn au** ~ **du lit** to find sb just out of bed (when one calls); **faire le** ~ to take the plunge; **faire un** ~ **chez qn** to pop *ou* nip over *ou* round to sb's (place)*; **il a fait un** ~ **jusqu'à Bordeaux** he made a flying visit to Bordeaux.

2: (*Natation*) **saut de l'ange** swallow dive; **saut de carpe** jack-knife dive, pike; **saut en chute libre** (*sport*) free-fall parachuting; (*bond*) free-fall jump; **saut en ciseaux** scissors (jump); **saut à la corde** skipping (*with a rope*); **saut de haies** hurdling; **saut en hauteur** (*sport*) high jump; (*bond*) (high) jump; **saut-de-lit** *nm inv* negligée, housecoat; **saut en longueur** (*sport*) long jump; (*bond*) (long) jump; **saut-de-loup** *nm, pl* **sauts-de-loup** (wide) ditch; **saut de la mort** leap of death; **saut-de-mouton** *nm, pl* **sauts-de-mouton** flyover (*Brit*), overpass (*US*); **saut en parachute** (*sport*) parachuting, parachute jumping; (*bond*) parachute jump; **saut à la perche** (*sport*) pole vaulting; (*bond*) (pole) vault; **saut périlleux** somersault; **saut à pieds joints** standing jump; **saut de puce** step (*fig*); **saut en rouleau** western roll; **saut à skis** (*sport*) skijumping; (*bond*) jump.

saute [sot] *nf* sudden change. ~ **d'humeur** sudden change of mood; ~ **de température** jump in temperature; ~ **de vent** (sudden) change of wind direction.

saute- [sot] *préf V* **sauter.**

sauté, e [sote] (*ptp de* **sauter**) *adj, nm* sauté. ~ **de veau** sauté of veal.

sauter [sote] (1) **1** *vi* **(a)** [*personne*] to jump, leap (*dans* into, *par-dessus* over); (*vers le bas*) to jump *ou* leap (down); (*vers le haut*) to jump *ou* leap (up); [*oiseau*] to hop; [*insecte*] to jump, hop; [*kangourou*] to jump. ~ **à pieds joints** to jump with (the) feet together, make a standing jump; ~ **à cloche-pied** to hop; ~ **à la corde** to skip (*with a rope*); ~ **en parachute** to parachute, make a parachute jump; (*Sport*) ~ **en ciseaux** to do a scissors jump; **faire** ~ **un enfant sur ses genoux** to bounce *ou* dandle a child on one's knee; **les cahots faisaient** ~ **les passagers** the passengers jolted *ou* bounced along over the bumps; **il sauta de la table** he jumped *ou* leapt (down) off *ou* from the table; ~ **en l'air** to jump *ou* leap *ou* spring up, jump *ou* leap *ou* spring into the air; (*fig*) ~ **en l'air** *ou* **au plafond** (*de colère*) to hit the roof*; (*de joie*) to jump for joy; (*de surprise, de peur*) to jump (out of one's skin), start up; (*lit, fig*) ~ **de joie** to jump for joy.

(b) (*se précipiter*) ~ **(à bas) du lit** to jump *ou* leap *ou* spring out of bed; ~ **en selle** to jump *ou* leap *ou* spring into the saddle; ~ **à la gorge** *ou* **au collet de qn** to fly *ou* leap at sb's throat; ~ **au cou de qn** to fly into sb's arms; ~ **dans un taxi/un autobus** to jump *ou* leap *ou* spring into a taxi/onto a bus; ~ **d'un train en marche** to jump *ou* leap from a moving train; (*fig*) ~ **sur une occasion/une proposition** to jump *ou* leap at an opportunity/an offer; **il m'a sauté dessus** he pounced on me, he leaped at me; (*fig*) **saute-lui dessus* quand il sortira du bureau pour lui demander ...** grab him when he comes out of the office and ask him ...; **va faire tes devoirs, et que ça saute!*** go and do your homework and get a move on!* *ou* be quick about it!; **il est malade, cela saute aux yeux** he's ill – it sticks out a mile *ou* it's (quite) obvious, you can't miss the fact that he's ill; **sa malhonnêteté saute aux yeux** his dishonesty sticks out a mile *ou* is (quite) obvious.

(c) (*indiquant la discontinuité*) to jump, leap. ~ **d'un sujet à l'autre** to jump *ou* leap *ou* skip from one subject to another; (*Scol*) ~ **de 3e en 1ère** ≃ to go *ou* jump (straight) from the 5th form to the lower 6th.

(d) [*bouchon*] to pop *ou* fly out; [*bouton*] to fly *ou* pop off; [*chaîne de vélo*] to come off; (*) [*cours, classe*] to be cancelled. **faire** ~ **une crêpe** to toss a pancake; **faire** ~ **une serrure** to burst *ou* break open a lock.

(e) (*exploser*) [*bombe, pont, bâtiment*] to blow up, explode; (*Élec*) [*fil, circuit*] to fuse; [*fusible*] to blow. **faire** ~ *train, édifice* to blow up; (*Élec*) *plombs* to blow; **faire** ~ **une mine** (*pour la détruire*) to blow up a mine; (*pour détruire un bâtiment etc*) to set off a mine; **se faire** ~ **la cervelle*** *ou* **le caisson:** to blow one's brains out; (*Casino*) **faire** ~ **la banque** to break the bank.

(f) (*: *être renvoyé*) [*employé, ministère*] to get the sack* *ou* the boot:, get kicked out:. **faire** ~ **qn** to give sb the sack* *ou* the boot:, kick sb out:.

(g) (*Culin*) **faire** ~ to sauté, (shallow) fry.

2 *vt* **(a)** (*franchir*) *obstacle, mur* to jump (over), leap (over). **il saute 5 mètres** he can jump 5 metres; **il sauta le fossé d'un bond** he jumped *ou* cleared the ditch with one bound; (*fig*) ~ **le pas** *ou* **le fossé** to take the plunge.

(b) (*omettre*) *page, repas* to skip, miss (out). (*Scol*) ~ **une classe** to skip a class; **faire** ~ **un cours** to cancel a class *ou* a lecture; **on la saute ici!:** we're starving to death here!*

(c) (*: *avoir des rapports sexuels*) to lay:.

3: **saute-mouton** *nm* leapfrog; (*Hist*) **saute-ruisseau** *nm inv* errand boy, office boy (*in a lawyer's office*).

sauterelle [sotʀɛl] *nf* (*Zool*) grasshopper. (**fig*) **(grande)** ~ beanpole.

sauterie [sotʀi] *nf* party.

sauteur, -euse [sotœʀ, øz] **1** *adj insecte* jumping (*épith*); *oiseau* hopping (*épith*).

2 *nm,f* (*cheval, athlète*) jumper.

3 *nm* (*péj: homme*) unreliable type *ou* individual.

4 sauteuse *nf* **(a)** (*Culin*) shallow casserole, high-sided frying pan.

(b) (*:*péj: femme*) tart:, scrubber: (*Brit*). **c'est une petite** *ou* **une drôle de** ~**euse** she's an easy lay:, she's a right little tart: *ou* scrubber: (*Brit*).

5: **sauteur en hauteur/en longueur** high/long jumper; **sauteur à la perche** pole vaulter; **sauteur à skis** skijumper.

sautillant, e [sotijɑ̃, ɑ̃t] *adj* (*V* **sautiller**) *mouvement* hopping (*épith*), skipping (*épith*); *oiseau* hopping (*épith*); *enfant* skipping (*épith*); hopping (*épith*); *musique* bouncy, bouncing (*épith*); *style* jumpy, jerky.

sautillement [sotijmɑ̃] *nm* (*V* **sautiller**) hopping; skipping.

sautiller [sotije] (1) *vi* [*oiseau*] to hop; [*enfant*] to skip; (*sur un pied*) to hop.

sautoir [sotwaʀ] *nm* **(a)** (*Bijouterie*) chain. ~ **de perles** string of pearls; **porter qch en** ~ to wear sth (on a chain) round one's neck; **épées en** ~ crossed swords. **(b)** (*Sport*) jumping pit.

sauvage [sovaʒ] **1** *adj* **(a)** (*non civilisé*) *animal, plante, lieu* wild; *peuplade* savage. **vivre à l'état** ~ to live wild; *V* **soie**[1].

(b) (*farouche*) *animal* wild; *personne* unsociable.

(c) (*brutal*) *cri* wild; *conduite* savage, wild; *combat* savage.

(d) (*illégal*) *camping, vente* unauthorized; *concurrence* unfair; *crèche, école* unofficial; *V* **grève.**

2 *nmf* **(a)** (*solitaire*) unsociable type, recluse. **vivre en** ~ to live a secluded life, live as a recluse.

(b) (*brute*) brute, savage. **mœurs de** ~**s** brutal *ou* brutish *ou* savage ways.

(c) (*indigène*) savage.

sauvagement [sovaʒmɑ̃] *adv frapper* savagely, wildly; *tuer* savagely, brutally.

sauvageon, -onne [sovaʒɔ̃, ɔn] **1** *nm,f* little savage. **2** *nm* wild stock (*for grafting*).

sauvagerie [sovaʒʀi] *nf* (*cruauté*) savagery, savageness, brutality; (*insociabilité*) unsociability, unsociableness.

sauvagin, e [sovaʒɛ̃, in] **1** *adj odeur, goût* of wildfowl. **2 sauvagine** *nf* wildfowl. **chasse à la** ~**e** wildfowling.

sauve [sov] *adj f V* **sauf**[1].

sauvegarde [sovgaʀd(ə)] *nf* safeguard. **sous la** ~ **de** under the protection of; **être la** ~ **de** to safeguard, be the safeguard of; **clause de** ~ safety clause.

sauvegarder [sovgaʀde] (1) *vt* to safeguard.

sauve-qui-peut [sovkipø] *nm inv* (*cri*) (cry of) run for your life; (*panique*) stampede, mad rush.

sauver [sove] (1) **1** *vt* **(a)** (*épargner la mort, la faillite à*) to save; (*porter secours à, essayer de ramener etc*) to rescue. ~ **qn/une firme de** *danger, désastre* to save sb/a firm from, rescue sb/a firm from; **un mot de lui peut tout** ~ a word from him could save everything.

(b) (*sauvegarder*) *biens, cargaison, mobilier* to save, rescue; *honneur* to save. ~ **qch de** *incendie etc* to save *ou* rescue sth from.

(c) (*Rel*) *pécheurs* to save. **se** ~ to be saved.

(d) (*fig: racheter*) to save, redeem. **ce sont les illustrations qui sauvent le livre** it's the illustrations which save *ou* redeem the book, the illustrations are the redeeming feature *ou* the saving grace of the book.

(e) (*loc*) ~ **la vie à qn** to save sb's life; ~ **sa peau/tête** to save one's skin/head; (*fig*) ~ **les meubles** to salvage *ou* save something from the wreckage (*fig*); ~ **la mise** to retrieve the situation; ~ **les apparences** to keep up appearances.

2 se sauver *vpr* **(a)** **se** ~ **de** *danger, mauvais pas, désastre* to save o.s. from.

(b) (*s'enfuir*) to run away (*de* from); (*: *partir*) to be off*, get going*. **sauve-toi*, il est déjà 8 heures** you'd better be off* *ou* get going*, it's already 8 o'clock; **bon, je mon sauve*** right, I'm off* *ou* I'm on my way; **vite, le lait se sauve*** quick, the milk's boiling over.

(c) sauve qui peut! run for your life!; *V* **sauve-qui-peut.**

sauvetage [sovtaʒ] *nm* **(a)** *[personnes]* rescue; (*moral*) salvation; *[biens]* salvaging. **le ~ des naufragés** rescuing the shipwrecked, the rescue of the shipwrecked; **opérer le ~ de** *personnes* to rescue; *biens* to salvage; **bateau** *ou* **canot de ~** lifeboat; **~ en mer/montagne** sea-/mountain-rescue; *V* **bouée, ceinture** *etc.*

(b) (*technique*) **le ~** life-saving; **épreuve/cours de ~** life-saving competition/lessons.

sauveteur [sovtœʀ] *nm* rescuer.

sauvette* [sovɛt] *nf*: **à la ~** *se marier etc* hastily, hurriedly, double-quick*; **vente à la ~** (unauthorized) street hawking *ou* peddling; **vendre à la ~** to hawk *ou* peddle on the streets (*without authorization*).

sauveur [sovœʀ] *adj m, nm* saviour.

savamment [savamɑ̃] *adv* (*avec érudition*) learnedly; (*adroitement*) skilfully, cleverly. (*par expérience*) **j'en parle ~** I speak knowingly.

savane [savan] *nf* savannah; (*Can**) swamp.

savant, e [savɑ̃, ɑ̃t] **1** *adj* **(a)** (*érudit*) *personne* learned, scholarly; *édition* scholarly; *société, mot* learned. **être ~ en** to be learned in; (*hum*) **c'est trop ~ pour moi** *[livre, discussion]* it's too highbrow for me; *[problème]* it's too difficult *ou* complicated for me.

(b) (*habile*) *stratagème, dosage, arrangement* clever, skilful. **le ~ désordre de sa tenue** the studied untidiness of his clothing.

(c) *chien, puce* performing (*épith*).

2 *nm* (*sciences*) scientist; (*lettres*) scholar.

savarin [savaʀɛ̃] *nm* (*Culin*) savarin.

savate* [savat] *nf* **(a)** (*pantoufle*) worn-out old slipper; (*soulier*) worn-out old shoe; *V* **traîner. (b)** (*maladroit*) clumsy idiot *ou* oaf.

savetier†† [savtje] *nm* cobbler†.

saveur [savœʀ] *nf* (*lit: goût*) flavour; (*fig: piment*) savour.

Savoie [savwa] *nf* Savoy; *V* **biscuit.**

savoir [savwaʀ] (32) **1** *vt* **(a)** to know. **~ le nom/l'adresse de qn** to know sb's name/address; **c'est difficile à ~** it's difficult to ascertain *ou* know; **je ne savais quoi** *ou* **que dire/faire** I didn't know what to say/do; **oui, je (le) sais** yes I know; **je savais qu'elle était malade, je la savais malade** I knew (that) she was ill, I knew her to be ill; **on ne lui savait pas de parents/de fortune** we didn't know whether *ou* if he had any relatives/money; (*en fait il en a*) we didn't know (that) he had any relatives/money; **savez-vous quand/comment il vient?** do you know when/how he's coming?; **vous savez la nouvelle?** have you heard *ou* do you know the news?; **elle sait cela par** *ou* **de son boucher** she heard it from her butcher; **tout le village sut bientôt la catastrophe** the whole village soon knew *ou* heard *ou* learnt of *ou* about the disaster; **personne ne savait sur quel pied danser/où se mettre** nobody knew what to do/where to put themselves; **il ne savait pas s'il devait accepter** he didn't know whether to accept (or not) *ou* whether *ou* if he should accept (or not); **je crois savoir que** I believe *ou* understand that; **je n'en sais rien** I don't know, I have no idea; **il ment — qu'en savez-vous?** he is lying — how do you know? *ou* what do you know about it?; **il nous a fait ~ que** he informed us *ou* let us know that; **ça se saurait si c'était vrai** it would be known if it were true, if that were true people would know about it; **ça finira bien par se ~** it will surely end up getting out *ou* getting known.

(b) (*avoir des connaissances sur*) to know. **~ le grec/son rôle/sa leçon** to know Greek/one's part/one's lesson; **dites-nous ce que vous savez de l'affaire** tell us what you know about *ou* of the business; **il croit tout ~** he thinks he knows everything *ou* knows it all*; **tu en sais, des choses*** you certainly know a thing or two, don't you!*; **il ne sait ni A ni B, il ne sait rien de rien** he doesn't know a (single) thing.

(c) (*avec infin: être capable de*) to know how to. **elle sait lire et écrire** she can read and write, she knows how to read and write; **il ne sait pas nager** he can't swim, he isn't able to *ou* doesn't know how to swim; **~ plaire** to know how to please; **~ vivre** *[épicurien]* to know how to live; *[homme du monde]* to know how to behave; **il sait parler aux enfants** he's good at talking to children, he knows how to talk *ou* he can talk to children; **elle saura bien se défendre** she'll be quite able to look after herself *ou* quite capable of looking after herself, she'll know how to look after herself all right; **il a toujours su y faire** *ou* **s'y prendre** he's always known how to go about things (the right way); **il sait écouter** he's a good listener; **il faut ~ attendre/se contenter de peu** you have to learn to be patient *ou* to wait/be content with little; (*littér, hum*) **on ne saurait penser à tout** one can't think of everything; **je ne saurais vous exprimer toute ma gratitude** I shall never be able to *ou* I could never express my gratitude; **je ne saurais pas vous répondre/vous renseigner** I'm afraid I couldn't answer you *ou* give you an answer/give you any information; **ces explications out su éclairer et rassurer** these explanations proved both enlightening and reassuring.

(d) (*se rendre compte*) to know. **il ne sait plus ce qu'il dit** he doesn't know *ou* realize what he's saying, he isn't aware of what he's saying; **je ne sais plus ce que je dis** I no longer know what I'm saying; **il ne sait pas ce qu'il veut** he doesn't know what he wants, he doesn't know his own mind; **il se savait très malade** he knew he was very ill; **elle sait bien qu'il ment** she's well aware of the fact that *ou* she knows very well *ou* full well that he's lying; **sans le ~** (*sans s'en rendre compte*) without knowing *ou* realizing (it), unknowingly; (*sans le faire exprès*) unwittingly, unknowingly; **c'est un artiste sans le ~** he's an artist but he doesn't know it *ou* he isn't aware of the fact.

(e) (*loc*) **qui sait?** who knows?; **et que sais-je encore** and I don't know what else; **~ si ça va lui plaire!** how can we tell if he'll like it or not!, I don't know whether he's going to *ou* whether he'll like it (or not)!; **je sais ce que je sais** I know what I know; **et puis, tu sais, nous serons très heureux de t'aider** and then, you know, we'll be very happy to help you; **il nous a emmenés je ne sais où** he took us goodness knows where; **il y a je ne sais combien de temps qu'il ne l'a vue** it's *ou* it has been I don't know how long since he (last) saw her, I don't how long it is *ou* it has been since he(last) saw her; **elle ne sait pas quoi faire** *ou* **elle ne sait que faire pour l'aider/le consoler** she's at a loss to know how to help him/comfort him; **on ne sait pas par quel bout le prendre** you just don't know how to tackle him; **on ne sait jamais** you never know, you *ou* one can never tell, one never knows; **(pour autant) que je sache** as far as I know, to the best of my knowledge; **pas que je sache** not as far as I know, not to my knowledge; **je ne sache pas que je vous ai invité!** I'm not aware that *ou* I don't know that I invited you!; **sachez (bien) que jamais je n'accepterai!** I'll have you know *ou* you may be assured that I shall never accept; **oui, mais sachez qu'à l'origine, c'est elle-même qui ne le voulait pas** yes but you should know *ou* you may as well know that at the start it was she herself who didn't want to; **à ~** that is, namely, i.e.; (*hum*) **l'objet/la personne que vous savez sera là demain** you-know-what/you-know-who will be there tomorrow (*hum*); (*frm*) **vous n'êtes pas sans ~ que** you are not *ou* will not be unaware (of the fact) that (*frm*), you will not be ignorant of the fact that (*frm*); **il m'a su gré/il ne m'a su aucun gré de l'avoir averti** he was grateful to me/he wasn't in the least grateful to me for having warned him; **il ne savait à quel saint se vouer** he didn't know which way to turn; **si je savais, j'irais la chercher** if I knew (for sure) *ou* if I could be sure, I would go and look for her; **elle ne savait où donner de la tête** she didn't know whether she was coming or going *ou* what to do first; **si j'avais su** had I known, if I had known; *V* **dieu, qui** *etc.*

2 *nm* learning, knowledge.

3: savoir-faire *nm inv* savoir-faire, know-how*; **savoir-vivre** *nm inv* savoir-vivre, mannerliness; **il n'a aucun savoir-vivre** he has no savoir-vivre, he has no idea how to behave (in society).

savon [savɔ̃] *nm* **(a)** (*matière*) soap (*U*); (*morceau*) bar *ou* tablet *ou* cake of soap. **~ liquide/noir** liquid/soft soap; **~ à barbe/de toilette/de Marseille** shaving/toilet/household soap; **~ en paillettes/en poudre** soap flakes/powder; *V* **bulle, pain.**

(b) (*) **il m'a passé/j'ai reçu un (bon) ~** he gave me/I got a (good) ticking-off* (*Brit*) *ou* dressing-down*, he (really) tore a strip/I (really) got a strip torn off me* (*Brit*).

savonnage [savɔnaʒ] *nm* soaping (*U*).

savonner [savɔne] (1) *vt linge, enfant* to soap; *barbe* to lather, soap.

savonnerie [savɔnʀi] *nf* (*usine*) soap factory.

savonnette [savɔnɛt] *nf* bar *ou* tablet *ou* cake of (toilet) soap.

savonneux, -euse [savɔnø, øz] *adj* soapy.

savourer [savuʀe] (1) *vt plat, boisson, plaisanterie, triomphe* to savour.

savoureux, -euse [savuʀø, øz] *adj plat* tasty, flavoursome; *anecdote* juicy*, spicy.

savoyard, e [savwajaʀ, aʀd(ə)] **1** *adj* Savoyard. **2** *nm,f*: **S~(e)** Savoyard.

Saxe [saks(ə)] *nf* Saxony; *V* **porcelaine.**

saxe [saks(ə)] *nm* Dresden china (*U*); (*objet*) piece of Dresden china.

saxo* [sakso] **1** *nm* (*instrument*) sax*. **2** *nm* (*musicien*) sax player*.

saxon, -onne [saksɔ̃, ɔn] **1** *adj* Saxon. **2** *nm* (*Ling*) Saxon. **3** *nm,f*: **S~(ne)** Saxon.

saxophone [saksɔfɔn] *nm* saxophone.

saxophoniste [saksɔfɔnist(ə)] *nmf* saxophonist, saxophone player.

saynète [sɛnɛt] *nf* playlet.

sbire [sbiʀ] *nm* (*péj*) henchman (*péj*).

scabreux, -euse [skabʀø, øz] *adj* (*indécent*) improper, shocking; (*dangereux*) risky.

scalaire [skalɛʀ] *adj* (*Math*) scalar.

scalène [skalɛn] *adj* scalene.

scalp [skalp] *nm* (*action*) scalping; (*chevelure*) scalp.

scalpel [skalpɛl] *nm* scalpel.

scalper [skalpe] (1) *vt* to scalp.

scandale [skɑ̃dal] *nm* **(a)** (*fait choquant, affaire*) scandal. **~ financier/public** financial/public scandal; **c'est un ~!** it's scandalous! *ou* outrageous!, it's a scandal!; **sa tenue/ce livre a fait ~** his clothes/that book scandalized people, people found his clothes/that book scandalizing; **au grand ~ de mon père, j'ai voulu épouser un étranger** I wanted to marry a foreigner, which scandalized my father; **elle va crier au ~** she'll cry out in indignation; **les gens vont crier au ~** there'll be an outcry *ou* a public outcry; **à ~** *livre, couple* controversial, headline-hitting* (*épith*); **journal à ~** scandal sheet.

(b) (*scène, tapage*) scene, fuss. **faire un** *ou* **du ~** to make a scene, kick up a fuss*; **et pas de ~!** and don't make a fuss!; **condamné pour ~ sur la voie publique** fined for disturbing the peace *ou* for creating a public disturbance.

scandaleusement [skɑ̃daløzmɑ̃] *adv* scandalously, outrageously.

scandaleux, -euse [skɑ̃dalø, øz] *adj conduite, propos, prix* scandalous, outrageous, shocking; *littérature, chronique* outrageous, shocking. **vie ~euse** life of scandal, scandalous life.

scandaliser [skɑ̃dalize] (1) *vt* to scandalize, shock deeply. **se ~ de qch** to be deeply shocked at sth, be scandalized by sth.

scander [skɑ̃de] (1) *vt vers* to scan; *discours* to give emphasis to; *mots* to articulate separately; *nom, slogan* to chant.

scandinave [skɑ̃dinav] **1** *adj* Scandinavian. **2** *nmf*: **S~** Scandinavian.

Scandinavie [skɑ̃dinavi] *nf* Scandinavia.

scansion [skɑ̃sjɔ̃] *nf* scanning, scansion.

scaphandre [skafɑ̃dʀ(ə)] *nm [plongeur]* diving suit; *[cosmonaute]* space-suit. **~ autonome** aqualung.

scaphandrier [skafɑ̃dʀije] *nm* (underwater) diver.

scapulaire [skapylɛʀ] *adj, nm* (*Anat, Méd, Rel*) scapular.

scarabée [skaʀabe] *nm* beetle, scarab (*T*).

scarificateur [skaʀifikatœʀ] *nm* (*Méd*) scarificator; (*Agr*) scarifier.

scarification [skaʀifikɑsjɔ̃] *nf* scarification.

scarifier [skaʀifje] (7) *vt* (*Agr, Méd*) to scarify.

scarlatine [skaʀlatin] *nf* scarlet fever, scarlatina (*T*).

scarole [skaʀɔl] *nf* endive.

scatologie [skatɔlɔʒi] *nf* scatology.

scatologique [skatɔlɔʒik] *adj* scatological, lavatorial*.

sceau, *pl* **~x** [so] *nm* (*cachet, estampille*) seal; (*fig: marque*) stamp, mark. **mettre son ~ sur** to put one's seal to *ou* on; **apposer son ~ sur** to affix one's seal to; (*fig*) **porter le ~ du génie** to bear the stamp *ou* mark of genius; **sous le ~ du secret** under the seal of secrecy; *V* **garde**[2].

scélérat, e [seleʀa, at] **1** *adj* (*littér*, ††) villainous, blackguardly††; wicked. **2** *nm,f* (*littér*, ††: *criminel*) villain, blackguard††. **petit ~!*** (you) little rascal!

scélératesse [seleʀatɛs] *nf* (*littér*, ††) (*caractère*) villainy, wickedness; (*acte*) villainy, villainous *ou* wicked *ou* blackguardly†† deed.

scellement [sɛlmɑ̃] *nm* (*V* **sceller**) sealing; embedding (*U*).

sceller [sele] (1) *vt* **(a)** *pacte, document, sac* to seal. **(b)** (*Constr*) to embed.

scellés [sele] *nmpl* seals. **mettre les ~ sur une porte** to put the seals on a door, affix the seals to a door.

scénario [senaʀjo] *nm* (*Ciné, Théât: plan*) scenario; (*Ciné: découpage et dialogues*) screenplay, (film) script, scenario; (*en futurologie*) scenario. (*fig*) **ça s'est déroulé selon le ~ habituel** (*attentat*) it followed the usual pattern; (*conférence de presse*) it followed the usual ritual *ou* pattern; **c'est toujours le même ~*** it's always the same old ritual *ou* carry-on* (*Brit*).

scénariste [senaʀist(ə)] *nmf* (*Ciné*) scriptwriter.

scène [sɛn] *nf* **(a)** (*estrade*) stage. **~ tournante** revolving stage; **être en ~** to be on stage; **sortir de ~** to go offstage, exit; **en ~!** on stage!; **occuper le devant de la scène** to be in the foreground; *V* **entrée.**

(b) (*le théâtre*) **la ~** the stage; **les vedettes de la ~ et de l'écran** the stars of stage and screen; **à la ~ comme à la ville** (both) on stage and off, both on and off (the) stage; **porter une œuvre à la ~** to bring a work to the stage, stage a work; **adapter un film pour la ~** to adapt a film for the stage; **mettre en ~** (*Théât*) *personnage, histoire* to present, put on stage; *auteur, romancier* to stage; *pièce de théâtre* to stage, direct; (*Ciné*) *film* to direct; **ce chapitre met en ~/dans ce chapitre l'auteur met en ~ un nouveau personnage** this chapter presents/in this chapter the author presents a new character; *V* **metteur, mise**[2].

(c) (*Ciné, Théât: division*) scene. **dans la première ~** in the first *ou* opening scene, in scene one; **~ d'amour** love scene; (*fig*) **elle m'a joué la grande ~ du deux*** she put on a great act, she acted out a big scene*.

(d) (*décor*) scene. **la ~ représente un salon du 18e siècle** the scene represents an 18th-century drawing room; **changement de ~** scene change.

(e) (*lieu de l'action*) scene. (*Ciné, Théât*) **la ~ est** *ou* **se passe à Rome** the action takes place in Rome, the scene is set in Rome; (*gén*) **arrivé sur la ~ du crime/drame** having arrived at the scene of the crime/drama.

(f) (*spectacle*) scene. **le témoin a assisté à toute la ~** the witness was present at *ou* during the whole scene.

(g) (*confrontation, dispute*) scene. **une ~ de réconciliation** a scene of reconciliation; **j'ai assisté à une pénible ~ de rupture** I witnessed a distressing break-up scene; **faire une ~ d'indignation** to put on a great show of indignation; **~ de ménage** domestic fight *ou* scene; **faire une ~** to make a scene; **il m'a fait une ~ parce que j'avais oublié la clef** he made a scene because I had forgotten the key; **avoir une ~ (avec qn)** to have a scene (with sb).

(h) (*fig: domaine*) scene. **sur la ~ politique/universitaire/internationale** on the political/university/international scene.

(i) (*Art: tableau*) scene. **~ d'intérieur/mythologique** indoor/mythological scene.

scénique [senik] *adj* theatrical; *V* **indication.**

scéniquement [senikmɑ̃] *adv* (*Théât*) theatrically.

scepticisme [sɛptisism(ə)] *nm* scepticism.

sceptique [sɛptik] **1** *adj* sceptical, sceptic. **2** *nmf* sceptic; (*Philos*) Sceptic.

sceptiquement [sɛptikmɑ̃] *adv* sceptically.

sceptre [sɛptʀ(ə)] *nm* (*lit, fig*) sceptre.

schah [ʃa] *nm* = **shah.**

schako [ʃako] *nm* = **shako.**

schapska [ʃapska] *nm* = **chapska.**

scheik [ʃɛk] *nm* = **cheik.**

schelem [ʃlɛm] *nm* = **chelem.**

schelling [ʃeliŋ] *nm* = **schilling.**

schéma [ʃema] *nm* **(a)** (*diagramme*) diagram, sketch. **(b)** (*résumé*) outline. **faire le ~ de l'opération** to give an outline of the operation.

schématique [ʃematik] *adj dessin* diagrammatic(al), schematic; (*péj*) *interprétation, conception* oversimplified.

schématiquement [ʃematikmɑ̃] *adv représenter* diagrammatically, schematically. **il exposa l'affaire ~** he gave an outline of the affair, he outlined the affair.

schématisation [ʃematizɑsjɔ̃] *nf* schematization; (*péj*) (over)simplification.

schématiser [ʃematize] (1) *vt* to schematize; (*péj*) to (over)simplify.

schématisme [ʃematism(ə)] *nm* (*péj*) oversimplicity.

schème [ʃɛm] *nm* (*Psych*) schema; (*Art*) design, scheme.

scherzando [skɛʀtsando] *adv* scherzando.

scherzo [skɛʀtso] **1** *nm* scherzo. **2** *adv* scherzando.

schilling [ʃiliŋ] *nm* schilling.

schismatique [ʃismatik] *adj, nmf* schismatic.

schisme [ʃism(ə)] *nm* schism. **faire ~** to split away.

schiste [ʃist(ə)] *nm* schist.

schisteux, -euse [ʃistø, øz] *adj* schistose.

schizoïde [skizɔid] *adj, nmf* schizoid.

schizophrène [skizɔfʀɛn] *adj, nmf* (*Méd, fig*) schizophrenic.

schizophrénie [skizɔfʀeni] *nf* (*Méd, fig*) schizophrenia.

schlague [ʃlag] *nf* (*Mil Hist*) **la ~** drubbing, flogging; **ils n'obéissent qu'à la ~:** they only obey if you really lay into them: *ou* if you give them what-for:.

schlass: [ʃlas] **1** *adj inv* sozzled:, plastered:. **2** *nm* knife.

schlinguer: [ʃlɛ̃ge] (1) *vi* to pong:, stink to high heaven*.

schlittage [ʃlitaʒ] *nm* sledging (*of wood*).

schlitte [ʃlit] *nf* sledge (*for transporting wood*).

schlitter [ʃlite] (1) *vt* to sledge (*wood*).

schnaps [ʃnaps] *nm* schnap(p)s.

schnock:, schnoque: [ʃnɔk] *nm*: **(vieux) ~** (old) fathead!: *ou* blockhead!:; **eh! du ~** hey, fathead!: *ou* blockhead!:

schnouff† [ʃnuf] *nf* (*arg Drogue*) dope (*arg*), junk (*arg*).

schuss [ʃus] **1** *nm* schuss. **2** *adv*: **descendre (tout) ~** to schuss (down).

sciage [sjaʒ] *nm [bois, métal]* sawing.

sciatique [sjatik] **1** *nf* sciatica. **2** *adj* sciatic.

scie [si] *nf* **(a)** saw. **~ à bois** wood saw; **~ circulaire** circular saw; **~ à chantourner** *ou* **découper** fretsaw; (*mécanique*) jigsaw; **~ mécanique** power saw; **~ à métaux** hacksaw; **~ musicale** musical saw; **~ à ruban** bandsaw; **~ à tronçonner** chain-saw, cross-cut saw; *V* **dent, poisson.**

(b) (*péj*) (*chanson*) catch-tune; (*personne*) bore.

sciemment [sjamɑ̃] *adv* knowingly, wittingly.

science [sjɑ̃s] **1** *nf* **(a)** (*domaine scientifique*) science. **les ~s** (*gén*) the sciences; (*Scol*) science; **la ~ du beau/de l'être** the science of beauty/of being; **~s appliquées/humaines/occultes** applied/human/occult sciences; **~s sociales** social sciences; (*Scol*) **~s naturelles** biology, natural science†.

(b) (*art, habileté*) art. **la ~ de la guerre** the science *ou* art of war; **faire qch avec une ~ consommée** to do sth with consummate skill; **sa ~ des couleurs** his skill *ou* technique in the use of colour.

(c) (*érudition*) knowledge. **avoir la ~ infuse** to have innate knowledge; (*Rel*) **la ~ du bien et du mal** the knowledge of good and evil; **savoir de ~ certaine que** to know for a fact *ou* for certain that; *V* **puits.**

2: science-fiction *nf* science fiction; **film/livre de science-fiction** science fiction film/book; **œuvre de science-fiction** work of science fiction.

scientifique [sjɑ̃tifik] **1** *adj* scientific. **2** *nmf* scientist.

scientifiquement [sjɑ̃tifikmɑ̃] *adv* scientifically.

scientisme [sjɑ̃tism(ə)] *nm* scientism.

scientiste [sjɑ̃tist(ə)] **1** *nmf* adept of scientism. **2** *adj* scientistic.

scier [sje] (7) *vt* **(a)** (*gén*) *bois, métal* to saw; *bûche* to saw (up); *partie en trop* to saw off. **~ une branche pour faire des bûches** to saw (up) a branch into logs.

(b) (*: *stupéfier*) **ça m'a scié!** it bowled me over!*, it staggered me!*; **c'est vraiment sciant!** it's absolutely staggering!*

scierie [siʀi] *nf* sawmill.

scieur [sjœʀ] *nm* sawyer. **~ de long** pit sawyer.

Scilly [sili] *n*: **les îles ~** the Scilly Isles.

scinder [sɛ̃de] (1) **1** *vt* to split (up), divide (up) (*en* in, into). **2 se scinder** *vpr* to split (up) (*en* in, into).

scintillant, e [sɛ̃tijɑ̃, ɑ̃t] *adj* (*V* **scintiller**) sparkling; glittering; twinkling; scintillating; glistening.

scintillation [sɛ̃tijɑsjɔ̃] *nf* (*Astron, Phys*) scintillation. **compteur à ~s** scintillation counter.

scintillement [sɛ̃tijmɑ̃] *nm* (*V* **scintiller**) sparkling; glittering; twinkling; scintillating; glistening. **le ~ de son esprit** his scintillating mind.

scintiller [sɛ̃tije] (1) *vi [diamant]* to sparkle, glitter; *[étoile]* to twinkle, sparkle, scintillate; *[yeux]* to sparkle; *[lumières, firmament]* to glitter, sparkle; *[goutte d'eau]* to glisten; *[esprit]* to sparkle, scintillate.

scion [sjɔ̃] *nm* (*Bot*) (*gén*) twig; (*greffe*) scion; (*Pêche*) top piece.

Scipion [sipjɔ̃] *nm* Scipio.

scission [sisjɔ̃] *nf* **(a)** (*schisme*) split, scission (*frm*). **faire ~** to split away, secede. **(b)** (*Bot, Phys*) fission.

scissioniste [sisjɔnist(ə)] *adj, nmf* secessionist.

scissipare [sisipaʀ] *adj* fissiparous.

scissiparité [sisipaʀite] *nf* scissiparity, schizogenesis.

sciure [sjyʀ] *nf*: **~ (de bois)** sawdust; **acheter une bague dans la ~**† to buy a ring from a street hawker.

scléreux, -euse [skleʀø, øz] *adj* sclerotic.

sclérose [skleʀoz] *nf* **(a)** (*Méd*) sclerosis. **~ artérielle** hardening of the arteries, arteriosclerosis (*T*); **~ en plaques** multiple sclerosis. **(b)** (*fig*) ossification.

sclérosé, e [skleʀoze] (*ptp de* **se scléroser**) *adj* (*lit*) sclerosed, sclerotic; (*fig*) ossified.
scléroser (se) [skleʀoze] (1) *vpr* (*Méd*) to become sclerotic *ou* sclerosed, sclerose; (*fig*) to become ossified.
sclérotique [skleʀɔtik] *nf* sclera.
scolaire [skɔlɛʀ] *adj* **(a)** (*gén*) school (*épith*). **année ~** school *ou* academic year; **ses succès ~s** his success in *ou* at school, his scholastic achievements *ou* attainments; **enfant d'âge ~** child of school age; *V* **établissement, groupe, livret.**
(b) (*péj*) schoolish. **son livre est un peu ~ par endroits** his book is a bit schoolish in places.
scolairement [skɔlɛʀmɑ̃] *adv réciter* schoolishly.
scolarisation [skɔlaʀizɑsjɔ̃] *nf* [*enfant*] schooling. **la scolarisation d'une population/d'un pays** providing a population with schooling/country with schools.
scolariser [skɔlaʀize] (1) *vt enfant* to provide with schooling; *pays, région* to provide with schools *ou* schooling.
scolarité [skɔlaʀite] *nf* schooling. **la ~ a été prolongée** schooling has been extended, the school-leaving age has been raised; **pendant mes années de ~** during my school years *ou* years at school; **~ obligatoire** compulsory school attendance *ou* schooling; *V* **certificat, frais².**
scolastique [skɔlastik] **1** *adj* (*Philos, péj*) scholastic. **2** *nf* scholasticism. **3** *nm* (*Philos*) scholastic, schoolman; (*péj*) scholastic.
scoliose [skɔljoz] *nf* scoliosis.
scolopendre [skɔlɔpɑ̃dʀ(ə)] *nf* (*Zool*) centipede, scolopendra (*T*); (*Bot*) hart's-tongue, scolopendrium (*T*).
sconse [skɔ̃s] *nm* skunk (fur).
scooter [skutœʀ] *nm* (motor) scooter.
scopie* [skɔpi] *nf abrév de* **radioscopie.**
scorbut [skɔʀbyt] *nm* scurvy.
scorbutique [skɔʀbytik] *adj symptômes* of scurvy, scorbutic (*T*); *personne* suffering from scurvy, scorbutic (*T*).
score [skɔʀ] *nm* (*Sport*) score.
scorie [skɔʀi] *nf* (*gén pl*) (*Ind*) slag (*U*), scoria (*U*), clinker (*U*). (*Géol*) **~s (volcaniques)** (volcanic) scoria.
scorpion [skɔʀpjɔ̃] *nm* **(a)** (*Zool*) scorpion. **~ d'eau** water-scorpion; **~ de mer** scorpion-fish. **(b)** (*Astron*) **le S~** Scorpio, the Scorpion; **être (du) S~** to be Scorpio.
scotch [skɔtʃ] *nm* **(a)** (*boisson*) scotch (whisky). **(b)** ® sellotape ® (*Brit*), Scotchtape ® (*US*). **coller qch avec du ~** to sellotape (*Brit*) *ou* Scotchtape (*US*) sth, stick sth with sellotape (*Brit*) *ou* Scotchtape (*US*).
scout, e [skut] *adj, nm* (boy) scout.
scoutisme [skutism(ə)] *nm* (*mouvement*) (boy) scout movement; (*activités*) scouting.
scribe [skʀib] *nm* (*péj: bureaucrate*) penpusher (*péj*); (*Hist*) scribe.
scribouillard, e [skʀibujaʀ, aʀd(ə)] *nm,f* (*péj*) penpusher (*péj*).
script [skʀipt] **1** *nm* **(a)** (**écriture**) **~** printing; **apprendre le ~** to learn how to print (letters); **écrire en ~** to print. **(b)** (*Ciné*) (shooting) script. **2** *nf* = **script-girl.**
scriptes [skʀipt(ə)] *nfpl* (*Typ*) script.
scripteur [skʀiptœʀ] *nm* (*Ling*) writer.
script-girl, *pl* **script-girls** [skʀiptgœʀl] *nf* continuity girl.
scrofule [skʀɔfyl] *nf* (*Méd*) scrofula. (*Hist Méd*) **~s** scrofula, king's evil.
scrofuleux, -euse [skʀɔfylø, øz] *adj tumeur* scrofulous; *personne* scrofulous, suffering from scrofula.
scrotum [skʀɔtɔm] *nm* scrotum.
scrupule [skʀypyl] *nm* **(a)** scruple. **avoir des ~s** to have scruples; **avoir des ~s à** *ou* **se faire ~ de faire qch** to have scruples *ou* misgivings *ou* qualms about doing sth; **faire taire ses ~s** to silence one's qualms of conscience *ou* one's scruples; **je n'aurais aucun ~ à refuser** I wouldn't have any scruples *ou* qualms *ou* misgivings about refusing, I wouldn't scruple to refuse; **son honnêteté est poussée jusqu'au ~** his honesty is absolutely scrupulous; **il est denué de ~s** he has no scruples, he is completely unscrupulous; **sans ~s** *personne* unscrupulous, without scruples; *agir* without scruple, unscrupulously; **vos ~s vous honorent** your scrupulousness is *ou* your scruples are a credit to you; **je comprends votre ~** *ou* **vos ~s** I understand your scruples.
(b) (*souci de*) **~ de: dans un** *ou* **par un ~ d'honnêteté/d'exactitude historique** in scrupulous regard for honesty/historical exactness.
scrupuleusement [skʀypyløzmɑ̃] *adv* scrupulously.
scrupuleux, -euse [skʀypylø, øz] *adj personne, honnêteté* scrupulous. **peu ~** unscrupulous.
scrutateur, -trice [skʀytatœʀ, tʀis] **1** *adj* (*littér*) *regard, caractère* searching. **2** *nm* (*Pol*) scrutineer (*Brit*), canvasser (*US*).
scruter [skʀyte] (1) *vt horizon* to search, scrutinize, examine; *objet, personne* to scrutinize, examine; *pénombre* to peer into, search.
scrutin [skʀytɛ̃] *nm* **(a)** (*vote*) ballot. **par voie de ~** by ballot; **voter au ~ secret** to vote by secret ballot; **il a été élu au 3e tour de ~** he was elected on *ou* at the third ballot *ou* round; **dépouiller le ~** to count the votes.
(b) (*élection*) poll. **le jour du ~** (the) polling day.
(c) (*modalité*) **~ de liste** list system; **~ d'arrondissement** district election system; **~ majoritaire** election on a majority basis; **~ uninominal** uninominal system.
sculpter [skylte] (1) *vt statue, marbre* to sculpture, sculpt; *meuble* to carve, sculpture, sculpt; *bâton, bois* to carve (*dans* out of). **elle peint et sculpte** she paints and sculptures *ou* sculpts.
sculpteur [skyltœʀ] *nm* (*homme*) sculptor; (*femme*) sculptress. **~ sur bois** woodcarver.
sculptural, e, *mpl* **-aux** [skyltyʀal, o] *adj* (*Art*) sculptural; (*fig*) *beauté, femme* statuesque.
sculpture [skyltyʀ] *nf* (*art, objet*) sculpture. **~ sur bois** woodcarving.
Scylla [sila] *nf* Scylla; *V* **tomber.**
se [s(ə)] *pron* **(a)** (*valeur strictement réfléchie*) (*sg*) (*indéfini*) oneself; (*sujet humain mâle*) himself; (*sujet humain femelle*) herself; (*sujet non humain*) itself; (*pl*) themselves. **~ regarder dans la glace** to look at o.s. in the mirror; (*action le plus souvent réfléchie: forme parfois intransitive en anglais*) **~ raser/laver** to shave/wash; **~ mouiller/salir** to get wet/dirty; **~ brûler/couper** to burn/cut o.s.; *V* **écouter, faire.**
(b) (*réciproque*) each other, one another. **deux personnes qui s'aiment** two people who love each other *ou* one another; **des gens/3 frères qui ~ haïssent** people/3 brothers who hate one another *ou* each other.
(c) (*valeur possessive: se traduit par l'adjectif possessif*) **~ casser la jambe** to break one's leg; **il ~ lave les mains** he is washing his hands; **elle s'est coupé les cheveux** she has cut her hair.
(d) (*valeur passive: généralement rendu par une construction passive*) **cela ne ~ fait pas** that's not done; **cela ~ répare/recolle facilement** it can easily be repaired again/glued together again; **la vérité finira par ~ savoir** (the) truth will out (in the end), the truth will finally be found out; **l'anglais ~ parle dans le monde entier** English is spoken throughout the world; **cela ~ vend bien** it sells well; **les escargots ~ servent dans la coquille** snails are served in their shells *ou* the shell, one serves snails in the shell.
(e) (*en tournure impersonnelle*) **il ~ peut que** it may be that, it is possible that; **comment ~ fait-il que ...?** how is it that ...?
(f) (*autres emplois pronominaux*) (*exprime le devenir*) **s'améliorer** to get better; **s'élargir** to get wider; **~ développer** to develop; **~ transformer** to change; (*indique une action subie*) **~ boucher** to become *ou* get blocked; **~ casser** to break; **~ fendre** to crack; *pour tous ces cas, et les emplois purement pronominaux* (*à valeur intransitive*), *V le verbe en question.*
séance [seɑ̃s] *nf* **(a)** (*réunion*) [*conseil municipal*] meeting, session; [*tribunal, parlement*] session, sitting. **être en ~** to be in session, sit; **la ~ est levée** *ou* **close** the meeting is ended, the meeting is at an end; *V* **suspension.**
(b) (*période*) session. **~ de photographie/gymnastique** photographic *ou* photography/gymnastics session; **~ de pose** sitting.
(c) (*représentation*) (*Théât*) performance. **~ privée** private showing *ou* performance; **~ de cinéma** film show; (*Ciné*) **première/dernière ~** first/last showing.
(d) (*: *scène*) performance*. **faire une ~ à qn** to give sb a performance*.
(e) **~ tenante** forthwith; **nous partirons ~ tenante** we shall leave forthwith.
séant¹ [seɑ̃] *nm* (*hum: derrière*) posterior (*hum*). (*frm*) **se mettre sur son ~** to sit up (*from a lying position*).
séant², e [seɑ̃, ɑ̃t] *adj* (*littér: convenable*) seemly (*littér*), fitting (*littér*). **il n'est pas ~ de dire cela** it is unseemly *ou* unfitting to *ou* it is not seemly *ou* fitting to say that.
seau, *pl* **~x** [so] *nm* (*récipient*) bucket, pail; (*contenu*) bucket(ful), pail(ful). **il pleut à ~x, la pluie tombe à ~x** it's coming *ou* pouring down in buckets *ou* bucketfuls, it's raining buckets* *ou* cats and dogs*; **~ à champagne/glace** champagne/ice-bucket; **~ d'enfant** child's bucket *ou* pail; **~ hygiénique** slop pail.
sébacé, e [sebase] *adj* sebaceous.
Sébastien [sebastjɛ̃] *nm* Sebastian.
sébile [sebil] *nf* (small wooden) bowl.
séborrhée [sebɔʀe] *nf* seborrhoea.
sébum [sebɔm] *nm* sebum.
sec, sèche [sɛk, sɛʃ] **1** *adj* **(a)** *climat, temps, bois, linge, toux* dry; *raisins, figue* dried. **je n'ai plus un poil de ~*** I'm sweating like a pig*, I'm soaked through; **elle le regarda partir, l'œil ~** she watched him go, dry-eyed; (*fig*) **avoir la gorge sèche*,** (*fig*) **avoir le gosier ~*** to be parched *ou* dry; *V* **cale¹, cinq, cul** *etc.*
(b) (*sans graisse*) *épiderme, cheveu* dry; (*maigre*) *personne, bras* lean. **il est ~ comme un coup de trique*** *ou* **comme un hareng*** he's as thin as a rake.
(c) (*sans douceur*) *style, ton, vin, rire, bruit* dry; *personne* hard(-hearted), cold; *cœur* cold, hard; *réponse* curt; *tissu* harsh; *dessin* harsh, dry (*T*); *jeu* crisp. (*Sport*) **placage ~** hard tackle; **il lui a écrit une lettre très sèche** he wrote him a very dry letter; **se casser avec un bruit ~** to break with a sharp snap; *V* **coup.**
(d) (*sans eau*) *alcool* neat. **il prend son whisky ~** he takes *ou* drinks his whisky neat *ou* straight.
(e) (*Cartes*) **atout/valet ~** singleton trumps/jack; **son valet était ~** his jack was a singleton.
(f) (**loc*) **je l'ai eu ~** I was cut up (about it)*; **être** *ou* **rester ~** to be stumped*; **je suis ~ sur ce sujet** I draw a blank on that subject.
2 *adv frapper* hard. **boire ~** to drink hard, be a hard *ou* heavy drinker; **démarrer ~** (*sans douceur*) to start (up) with a jolt *ou* jerk; (*rapidement*) to tear off; (*fig*) **ça démarre ~ ce soir** it's getting off to a good start this evening; **aussi ~!*** pronto!*; **et lui, aussi ~*, a répondu que.** and he replied straight away that.
3 *nm:* **tenir qch au ~** to keep sth in a dry place; **rester au ~** to stay in the dry; **un puits à ~** a dry *ou* dried-up well; **être à ~** [*torrent, puits*] to be dry *ou* dried-up; (*: *sans argent*) [*personne*] to be broke* *ou* skint* (*Brit*); [*caisse*] to be empty; **mettre à ~ un étang** [*personne*] to drain; [*soleil*] to dry up; **mettre à ~ un joueur** to clean out a gambler*.
4 sèche* *nf* (*cigarette*) fag* (*Brit*).

sécable [sekabl(ə)] *adj* divisible.
sécant, e [sekɑ̃, ɑ̃t] *adj, nf* secant.
sécateur [sekatœʀ] *nm* (pair of) secateurs, (pair of) pruning shears.
sécession [sesesjɔ̃] *nf* secession. **faire ~** to secede; *V* **guerre.**
sécessionniste [sesesjɔnist(ə)] *adj, nmf* secessionist.
séchage [seʃaʒ] *nm* drying; *[bois]* seasoning.
sèche- [sɛʃ] *préf V* **sécher.**
sèchement [sɛʃmɑ̃] *adv* *disserter* drily, dryly; *répondre (froidement)* drily, dryly; *(brièvement)* curtly.
sécher [seʃe] (6) **1** *vt* **(a)** *(gén)* to dry; *cours d'eau, flaque* to dry (up). **sèche tes larmes** dry your tears *ou* eyes; **se ~ au soleil/avec une serviette** to dry o.s. in the sun/with a towel; **se ~ devant le feu** to dry o.s. *ou* dry (o.s.) off in front of the fire.
(b) *(arg Scol: manquer)* *cours* to skip*. **ce matin, je vais ~ (les cours)** this morning I'm going to skip classes*.
(c) (‡) **~ son verre** to drain one's glass; **~ son verre de bière** to down *ou* knock back *ou* drain one's glass of beer*.
2 *vi* **(a)** *[surface mouillée, peinture]* to dry (off); *[substance imbibée de liquide]* to dry (out); *[linge]* to dry. **faire** *ou* **laisser ~ qch** to leave sth to dry (off *ou* out); **mettre le linge à ~** to put out the washing to dry; **'faire ~ sans essorer'** 'do not spin (dry)'.
(b) *(se déshydrater)* *[bois]* to dry out; *[fleur]* to dry up *ou* out. **le caoutchouc a séché** the rubber has dried up *ou* gone dry; **~ sur pied** *[plante]* to wilt on the stalk; *(fig)* *[personne]* to languish; **faire ~** *fruits, viande, fleurs* to dry; *bois* to season.
(c) *(arg Scol: rester sec)* to be stumped*. **j'ai séché en maths** I drew a (complete) blank *ou* I dried up* completely in maths.
3: sèche-cheveux *nm inv* hair-drier; **sèche-linge** *nm inv* drying cabinet.
sécheresse [sɛʃʀɛs] *nf* **(a)** *[climat, sol, ton, style]* dryness; *[réponse]* curtness; *[cœur]* coldness, hardness; *[dessin]* harshness, dryness *(T)*. **(b)** *(absence de pluie)* drought.
séchoir [seʃwaʀ] *nm* *(local)* drying shed; *(appareil)* drier. **~ à linge** *(pliant)* clothes-horse; **~ à chanvre/à tabac** hemp/tobacco drying shed; **~ à cheveux** hair-drier.
second, e[1] [s(ə)gɔ̃, ɔ̃d] **1** *adj* **(a)** *(numériquement)* second. **en ~ lieu** second(ly), in the second place; **de ~e main** secondhand; **~ violon/ténor** second violin/tenor; *V* **noce.**
(b) *(hiérarchiquement)* second. **de ~ choix** *(de mauvaise qualité)* low-quality, low-grade; *(Comm: catégorie)* class two; **voyager en ~e classe** to travel second-class; **passer en ~** to come second; **commander en ~** to be second in command; **officier** *ou* **capitaine en ~** first mate; *V* **plan**[1].
(c) *(autre, nouveau)* second. **une ~e jeunesse** a second youth; **dans une ~e vie** in a second life; **cet écrivain est un ~ Hugo** this writer is a second Hugo; **chez lui, c'est une ~e nature** with him it's second nature; **doué de ~e vue** gifted with second sight; **trouver son ~ souffle** *(Sport)* to get one's second wind; *(fig)* to find a new lease of life; **être dans un état ~** to be in a sort of trance; *V* **habitude.**
(d) *(dérivé)* *cause* secondary.
2 *nm,f* second. **il a été reçu ~ (en maths)** he came *ou* was second (in maths); *(littér)* **sans ~** second to none, peerless *(littér)*.
3 *nm* **(a)** *(adjoint)* second in command; *(Naut)* first mate. **(b)** *(étage)* second floor *(Brit)*, third floor *(US)*. **la dame du ~** the lady on the second floor *(Brit)* *ou* the third floor *(US)*.
(c) *(dans une charade)* second. **mon ~ est un ...** my second is a ... *ou* is in ... .
4 seconde *nf* *(classe de transport)* second class; *(billet)* second-class ticket; *(Scol)* ≈ fifth form *(Brit)* *(in secondary school)*; *(Aut)* second (gear); *(Mus)* second; *(Escrime)* seconde. *(Rail)* **les ~es sont à l'avant** the second-class seats *ou* carriages are at the front *ou* in front; **voyager en ~e** to travel second-class.
secondaire [s(ə)gɔ̃dɛʀ] **1** *adj* *(gén, Chim, Scol)* secondary; *(Géol)* mesozoic, secondary††; *(Psych)* *caractère* tending not to relate to present events; *(Littérat)* **intrigue ~** subplot; *(gén, Méd)* **effets ~s** side effects; *V* **secteur.**
2 *nm* *(Géol)* **le ~** the Mesozoic, the Secondary Era††; *(Scol)* **le ~** secondary *(Brit)* *ou* high-school *(US)* education; **les professeurs du ~** secondary school *(Brit)* *ou* high-school *(US)* teachers; *(Élec)* **(enroulement) ~** secondary (winding); *(Écon)* **le (secteur) ~** secondary industry.
secondairement [s(ə)gɔ̃dɛʀmɑ̃] *adv* secondarily.
secondarité [s(ə)gɔ̃daʀite] *nf* persistent abstraction from present events.
seconde[2] [s(ə)gɔ̃d] *nf* *(Géom, Temps)* second. **(attends) une ~!** just a *ou* one second! *ou* sec!*
secondement [s(ə)gɔ̃dmɑ̃] *adv* second(ly).
seconder [s(ə)gɔ̃de] (1) *vt* *(lit, fig)* to assist, aid, help.
secouer [s(ə)kwe] (1) **1** *vt* **(a)** *arbre, salade* to shake; *poussière, miettes* to shake off; *paresse, oppression* to shake off; *tapis* to shake (out). **arrête de me ~ comme un prunier** stop shaking me up and down, stop shaking me like a rag doll; **~ la tête** *(pour dire oui)* to nod (one's head); *(pour dire non)* to shake one's head; **l'explosion secoua l'hôtel** the explosion shook *ou* rocked the hotel; **on est drôlement secoué** *(dans un autocar)* you're terribly shaken about; *(dans un bateau)* you're terribly tossed about; **le vent secouait le petit bateau** the wind tossed the little boat about.
(b) *(traumatiser)* to shake (up). **ce deuil l'a beaucoup secoué** this bereavement has really shaken him (up).
(c) *(fig)* *(bousculer)* to shake up. **cet élève ne travaille que lorsqu'on le secoue** this pupil only works if he's shaken up *ou* given a good shake*; **~ les puces à qn*** *(réprimander)* to tick* *(Brit)* *ou* tell sb off, give sb a ticking-off* *(Brit)* *ou* telling-off; *(stimuler)* to give sb a good shake(-up)*, shake sb up*; **secoue tes puces*** *ou* **ta graisse‡** shake yourself out of it*, shake yourself up*.
2 se secouer *vpr* *(lit)* to shake o.s.; *(*fig: faire un effort)* to shake o.s. out of it*, shake o.s. up*. **secouez-vous si vous voulez passer l'examen** you'll have to shake yourself out of it* *ou* shake yourself up* if you want to pass the exam.
secourable [s(ə)kuʀabl(ə)] *adj* *personne* helpful; *V* **main.**
secourir [s(ə)kuʀiʀ] (11) *vt* *blessé, pauvre* to help, succour *(littér)*, assist, aid; *misère* to help relieve *ou* ease.
secourisme [s(ə)kuʀism(ə)] *nm* first aid.
secouriste [s(ə)kuʀist(ə)] *nmf* first-aid worker.
secours [s(ə)kuʀ] *nm* **(a)** *(aide)* help, aid, assistance. **appeler qn à son ~** to call sb to one's aid *ou* assistance; **demander du ~** to ask for help *ou* assistance; **crier au ~** to shout *ou* call (out) for help; **au ~!** help!; **aller au ~ de qn** to go to sb's aid *ou* assistance; **porter ~ à qn** to give sb help *ou* assistance.
(b) *(aumône)* aid *(U)*. **distribuer/recevoir des ~** to distribute/receive aid; **société de ~ mutuel** mutual aid association.
(c) *(sauvetage)* aid *(U)*, assistance *(U)*. **porter ~ à un alpiniste** to bring help *ou* aid to a mountaineer; **~ aux blessés** aid *ou* assistance for the wounded; **~ d'urgence** emergency aid *ou* assistance; **le ~ en montagne/en mer** mountain/sea rescue; **équipe de ~** rescue party *ou* team; **quand les ~ arrivèrent** when help arrived; *V* **poste**[2], **premier.**
(d) *(Mil)* relief *(U)*. **la colonne de ~** the relief column; **les ~ sont attendus** relief is expected.
(e) *(Rel)* **mourir avec/sans les ~ de la religion** to die with/without the last rites.
(f) *(loc)* **cela m'a été/ne m'a pas été d'un grand ~** this has been a *ou* of great help/of little help to me; **une bonne nuit te serait de meilleur ~ que ces pilules** a good night's sleep would be more help to you than these pills; **de ~: éclairage/sortie de ~** emergency lighting/exit; **batterie/roue de ~** spare battery/wheel.
secousse [s(ə)kus] *nf* **(a)** *(cahot)* *[voiture, train]* jolt, bump; *[avion]* bump. **sans une ~** *s'arrêter* without a jolt, smoothly; *transporter* smoothly; **avancer par ~s** to move jerkily *ou* in jerks.
(b) *(choc moral)* jolt, shock; *(traction)* tug, pull. **~ (électrique)** (electric) shock; **donner des ~s à** *corde* to give a few tugs *ou* pulls to; *thermomètre* to give a few shakes to.
(c) ~ (tellurique *ou* **sismique)** (earth) tremor; *(fig)* **~ politique** political upheaval.
secret, -ète [səkʀɛ, ɛt] **1** *adj* **(a)** *document, rite* secret. **garder** *ou* **tenir qch ~** to keep sth secret *ou* (in the) dark*; *V* **agent, service.**
(b) *(caché)* *tiroir, porte, vie, pressentiment* secret. **nos plus secrètes pensées** our most secret *ou* our innermost thoughts; **un charme ~** a hidden charm.
(c) *(renfermé)* *personne* reticent, reserved.
2 *nm* **(a)** secret. **c'est son ~** it's his secret; **il a gardé le ~ de notre projet** he kept our plan secret; **ne pas avoir de ~ pour qn** *[personne]* to have no secrets from sb, keep nothing from sb; *[sujet]* to have *ou* hold no secrets for sb; **il n'en fait pas un ~** he makes no secret about it; **~ d'alcôve** intimate gossip *(U)*; **~ de fabrication** trade secret; **~ d'État** state secret; **c'est le ~ de Polichinelle** it's an open secret; **ce n'est un ~ pour personne que ...** it's no secret that ... .
(b) *(moyen, mécanisme)* secret. **~ de fabrication** trade secret; **le ~ du bonheur/de la réussite/de la bonne cuisine** the secret of happiness/of success/ of good cooking; **il a trouvé le ~ pour obtenir tout ce qu'il veut** he's found the secret for getting everything he wants; **une sauce/un tour de passe-passe dont il a le ~** a sauce/conjuring trick of which he (alone) has the secret; **il a le ~ de ces plaisanteries stupides** he's got the knack of telling these stupid jokes; **tiroir à ~** drawer with a secret lock.
(c) *(discrétion, silence)* secrecy. **demander/exiger/promettre le ~ (absolu)** to ask for/demand/promise (absolute) secrecy; **trahir le ~** to betray the oath of secrecy; **le ~ professionnel** professional secrecy; **le ~ d'État** official secrecy; **le ~ de la confession** the seal of the confessional; **le gouvernement a gardé le ~ sur les négociations** the government has maintained silence *ou* remained silent about the negotiations; *V* **sceau.**
(d) *(mystère)* secret. **les ~s de la nature** the secrets of nature, nature's secrets; **pénétrer dans le ~ des cœurs** to penetrate the secrets of the heart.
(e) *(loc)* **dans le ~** in secret *ou* secrecy, secretly; **négociations menées dans le plus grand ~** negotiations carried out in the strictest *ou* utmost secrecy; **mettre qn dans le ~** to let sb into *ou* in on the secret, let sb in on it*; **être dans le ~** to be in on the secret, be in on it*; **être dans le ~ des dieux** to share the secrets of the powers that be; **en ~** *(sans témoins)* in secret *ou* secrecy, secretly; *(intérieurement)* secretly; *(Prison)* **au ~** in solitary confinement, in solitary*.
3 secrète *nf* *(Police)* the secret police; *(Rel)* the Secret.
secrétaire [s(ə)kʀetɛʀ] **1** *nmf* *(gén)* secretary. **~ médicale/commerciale** medical/business *ou* commercial secretary.
2 *nm* *(meuble)* writing desk, secretaire *(Brit)*, secretary *(US)*.
3: secrétaire d'ambassade embassy secretary; **secrétaire de direction** private *ou* personal secretary *(to a director or directors)*, executive secretary; **secrétaire d'État** Secretary of State; **secrétaire général** Secretary-General; **secrétaire de mairie** ≈ town clerk *(in charge of records and legal business)*; **secrétaire de rédaction** sub-editor.
secrétariat [s(ə)kʀetaʀja] *nm* **(a)** *(fonction officielle)* secretaryship, post *ou* office of secretary; *(durée de fonction)*

secretaryship, term (of office) as secretary; (*bureau*) secretariat. ~ **d'État** post *ou* office of Secretary of State; (*bureau*) office of the Secretary of State; ~ **général des Nations Unies** post *ou* office of Secretary-General of the United Nations.
(b) (*profession, travail*) secretarial work; (*bureaux*) *[école]* (secretary's) office; *[usine, administration]* secretarial offices; *[organisation internationale]* secretariat; (*personnel*) secretarial staff. **école de** ~ secretarial college; ~ **de rédaction** editorial office.
secrète [səkʀɛt] *V* **secret.**
sécréter [sekʀete] (6) *vt* (*Bot, Physiol*) to secrete; (*fig*) *ennui* to exude.
sécréteur, -euse *ou* **-trice** [sekʀetœʀ, øz, tʀis] *adj* secretory.
sécrétion [sekʀesjɔ̃] *nf* secretion.
sécrétoire [sekʀetwaʀ] *adj* secretory.
sectaire [sɛktɛʀ] *adj, nmf* sectarian.
sectarisme [sɛktaʀism(ə)] *nm* sectarianism.
secte [sɛkt(ə)] *nf* sect.
secteur [sɛktœʀ] *nm* **(a)** (*Écon, Mil*) sector; (*Admin*) district; (*gén: zone*) area; (*fig*) (*domaine*) area; (*partie*) part. **dans le** ~* (*ici*) round here; (*là-bas*) round there; **changer de** ~* to move elsewhere; (*Écon*) ~ **primaire/secondaire/tertiaire** primary/secondary/tertiary industry; (*Écon*) ~ **public/privé** public/private sector.
(b) (*Élec*) (*zone*) local supply area. (*circuit*) **le** ~ the mains (supply); **panne de** ~ local supply breakdown; **fonctionne sur pile et** ~ battery or mains operated.
(c) (*Géom*) sector. ~ **sphérique** spherical sector, sector of sphere.
section [sɛksjɔ̃] *nf* **(a)** (*coupe*) section. **prenons un tube de** ~ **double** let's get a tube which is twice the bore; **dessiner la** ~ **d'un os/d'une tige/d'une cuisine** to draw the section of a bone/of a stem/of a kitchen, draw a bone/a stem/a kitchen in section; **la** ~ **(de ce câble) est toute rouillée** the end (of this cable) is all rusted.
(b) (*Admin*) section. ~ **du Conseil d'État** department of the Council of State; ~ **(du) contentieux** legal section *ou* department; ~ **électorale** ward; **mettre un élève en** ~ **littéraire/scientifique** to put a pupil into the literature/science section.
(c) (*partie*) *[ouvrage]* section; *[route, rivière, voie ferrée]* section; (*en autobus*) fare stage. **de la Porte d'Orléans à ma rue, il y a 2** ~**s** from the Porte d'Orléans to my street there are 2 fare stages; *V* **fin**[2].
(d) (*Mus*) section. ~ **mélodique/rythmique** melody/rhythm section.
(e) (*Mil*) platoon.
(f) (*Math*) section. ~ **conique/plane** conic/plane section.
sectionnement [sɛksjɔnmɑ̃] *nm* (*V* **sectionner**) severance; division (*into sections*).
sectionner [sɛksjɔne] (1) **1** *vt tube, fil, artère* to sever; *circonscription, groupe* to divide (up), split (up) (*en* into). **2 se sectionner** *vpr* to be severed; to divide *ou* split (up) (into sections).
sectoriel, -ielle [sɛktɔʀjɛl] *adj* sector-based.
séculaire [sekylɛʀ] *adj* (*très vieux*) *arbre, croyance* age-old; (*qui a lieu tous les cent ans*) *fête, jeux* secular. **ces forêts/maisons sont 4 fois** ~**s** these forests/houses are 4 centuries old; **année** ~ last year of the century.
sécularisation [sekylaʀizɑsjɔ̃] *nf* secularization.
séculariser [sekylaʀize] (1) *vt* to secularize.
séculier, -ière [sekylje, jɛʀ] **1** *adj clergé, autorité* secular; *V* **bras. 2** *nm* secular.
secundo [s(ə)gɔ̃do] *adv* second(ly), in the second place.
sécuriser [sekyʀize] (1) *vt* to give (a feeling of) security to.
sécurité [sekyʀite] **1** *nf* (*tranquillité d'esprit*) feeling *ou* sense of security; (*absence de danger*) safety; (*conditions d'ordre, absence de troubles*) security. **être/se sentir en** ~ to be/feel safe, be/feel secure; **une fausse impression de** ~ a false sense of security; **cette retraite représentait pour lui une** ~ this pension meant security for him; **la** ~ **de l'emploi** security of employment, job security; **assurer la** ~ **d'un personnage important/des ouvriers/des installations** to ensure the safety of an important person/of workers/of the equipment; **l'État assure la** ~ **des citoyens** the State looks after the security *ou* safety of its citizens; **des mesures de** ~ **très strictes avaient été prises** very strict security precautions *ou* measures had been taken, security was very tight; **de** ~ *dispositif* safety; *V* **ceinture, compagnie, conseil** *etc.*
2: la sécurité routière road safety; **la Sécurité sociale** ≃ (the) Social Security (*Brit*).
sédatif, -ive [sedatif, iv] *adj, nm* sedative.
sédentaire [sedɑ̃tɛʀ] *adj vie, travail, goûts, personne* sedentary; *population* settled, sedentary; (*Mil*) permanently garrisoned.
sédentairement [sedɑ̃tɛʀmɑ̃] *adv* sedentarily.
sédentarisation [sedɑ̃taʀizɑsjɔ̃] *nf* settling process.
sédentariser [sedɑ̃taʀize] (1) *vt* to settle. **population sédentarisée** settled population.
sédentarité [sedɑ̃taʀite] *nf* settled way of life.
sédiment [sedimɑ̃] *nm* (*Méd, fig*) sediment; (*Géol*) deposit, sediment.
sédimentaire [sedimɑ̃tɛʀ] *adj* sedimentary.
sédimentation [sedimɑ̃tɑsjɔ̃] *nf* sedimentation.
séditieux, -euse [sedisjø, øz] **1** *adj* (*en sédition*) *général, troupes* insurrectionary (*épith*), insurgent (*épith*); (*agitateur*) *esprit, propos, réunion* seditious. **2** *nm,f* insurrectionary, insurgent.
sédition [sedisjɔ̃] *nf* insurrection, sedition. **esprit de** ~ spirit of sedition *ou* insurrection *ou* revolt.
séducteur, -trice [sedyktœʀ, tʀis] **1** *adj* seductive. **2** *nm* (*débaucheur*) seducer; (*péj: Don Juan*) womanizer (*péj*). **3 séductrice** *nf* seductress.
séduction [sedyksjɔ̃] *nf* **(a)** (*V* **séduire**) seduction, seducing; charming; captivation; winning over. **scène de** ~ seduction scene.
(b) (*attirance*) appeal. **troublé par la** ~ **de sa jeunesse** disturbed by the charm *ou* seductiveness of her youth; **exercer une forte** ~ **sur** to exercise a strong attraction over, have a great deal of appeal for; **les** ~**s de la vie estudiantine** the attractions *ou* appeal of student life.
séduire [sedɥiʀ] (38) *vt* **(a)** (*abuser de*) to seduce.
(b) (*attirer, gagner*) *[femme, tenue]* to charm, captivate; *[négociateur, charlatan]* to win over, charm. **son but était de** ~ her aim was to charm *ou* captivate us (*ou* him *etc*); **ils ont essayé de nous** ~ **avec ces propositions** they tried to win us over *ou* charm us with these proposals.
(c) (*plaire*) *[tenue, style, qualité, projet]* to appeal to. **une des qualités qui me séduisent le plus** one of the qualities which most appeal to me *ou* which I find most appealing; **leur projet/genre de vie me séduit mais ...** their plan/life style does appeal to me but ..., their plan/life style appeals to me *ou* does have some attraction for me but ...; **leur projet m'a séduit** their plan tempted me *ou* appealed to me; **cette idée va-t-elle les** ~? is this idea going to tempt them? *ou* appeal to them?
séduisant, e [sedɥizɑ̃, ɑ̃t] *adj femme, beauté* enticing (*épith*), seductive; *homme, démarche, visage* (very) attractive; *tenue, projet, genre de vie, style* appealing, attractive.
segment [sɛgmɑ̃] *nm* (*gén*) segment. (*Aut*) ~ **de frein** brake shoe; (*Aut*) ~ **de piston** piston ring.
segmentation [sɛgmɑ̃tɑsjɔ̃] *nf* (*gén*) segmentation.
segmenter (se) [sɛgmɑ̃te] (1) *vpr* to segment.
ségrégation [segʀegɑsjɔ̃] *nf* segregation.
ségrégationnisme [segʀegɑsjɔnism(ə)] *nm* segregationism.
ségrégationniste [segʀegɑsjɔnist(ə)] **1** *adj manifestant* segregationist; *problème* of segregation; *troubles* due to segregation. **2** *nmf* segregationist.
seiche [sɛʃ] *nf* (*Zool*) cuttlefish; *V* **os.**
séide [seid] *nm* (fanatically devoted) henchman.
seigle [sɛgl(ə)] *nm* rye; *V* **pain.**
seigneur [sɛɲœʀ] *nm* **(a)** (*Hist: suzerain, noble*) lord; (*fig: maître*) overlord. (*hum*) **mon** ~ **et maître** my lord and master; *V* **à, grand. (b)** (*Rel*) **le S**~ the Lord; **Notre-S**~ **Jésus-Christ** Our Lord Jesus Christ; *V* **jour, vigne.**
seigneurial, e, *mpl* -aux [sɛɲœʀjal, o] *adj château, domaine* seigniorial; *allure, luxe* lordly, stately.
seigneurie [sɛɲœʀi] *nf* **(a) votre/sa S**~ your/his Lordship. **(b)** (*terre*) (lord's) domain, seigniory; (*droits féodaux*) seigniory.
sein [sɛ̃] *nm* **(a)** (*mamelle*) breast. **donner le** ~ **à un bébé** (*méthode*) to breast-feed (a baby), suckle† a baby; (*être en train d'allaiter*) to feed a baby (at the breast), suckle† a baby; (*présenter le sein*) to give a baby the breast; **prendre le** ~ to take the breast; *V* **faux**[2], **nourrir.**
(b) (*littér*) (*poitrine*) breast (*littér*), bosom (*littér*); (*matrice*) womb; (*fig: giron, milieu*) bosom. **pleurer dans le** ~ **d'un ami** to cry on a friend's breast *ou* bosom; **porter un enfant dans son** ~ to carry a child in one's womb; **dans le** ~ **de la terre/de l'église** in the bosom of the earth/of the church; *V* **réchauffer.**
(c) au ~ **de** (*parmi, dans*) *équipe, institution* within; (*littér*) *bonheur, flots* in the midst of.
Seine [sɛn] *nf* **la** ~ the Seine.
seing [sɛ̃] *nm* (††) signature. (*Jur*) **acte sous** ~ **privé** private agreement (*document not legally certified*).
séisme [seism(ə)] *nm* (*Géog*) earthquake, seism (*T*); (*fig*) upheaval.
séismique [seismik] *adj* = **sismique.**
séismographe [seismɔgʀaf] *nm* = **sismographe.**
séismologie [seismɔlɔʒi] *nf* = **sismologie.**
seize [sɛz] *adj inv, nm* sixteen; *pour loc V* **six.**
seizième [sɛzjɛm] *adj, nmf* sixteenth; (*Sport*) ~**s de finale** first round (*of 5-round knockout competition*); **le** ~ **(arrondissement)** the sixteenth arrondissement (*fashionable residential area in Paris*); *pour autres loc V* **sixième.**
seizièmement [sɛzjɛmmɑ̃] *adv* in the sixteenth place, sixteenth.
séjour [seʒuʀ] *nm* **(a)** (*arrêt*) stay, sojourn (*littér*). **faire un** ~ **de 3 semaines à Paris** to stay (for) 3 weeks in Paris, have a 3-week stay in Paris; **faire un** ~ **forcé à Calais** to have an enforced stay in Calais; *V* **interdit**[1], **permis, taxe.**
(b) (*salon*) living room, lounge (*Brit*). **un** ~ **double** a through lounge (*Brit*); *V* **salle.**
(c) (*littér: endroit*) abode (*littér*), dwelling place (*littér*); (*demeure temporaire*) sojourn (*littér*). **le** ~ **des dieux** the abode *ou* dwelling place of the gods.
séjourner [seʒuʀne] (1) *vi [personne]* to stay, sojourn (*littér*); *[neige, eau]* to lie.
sel [sɛl] **1** *nm* **(a)** (*gén, Chim*) salt. (*à respirer*) ~**s** smelling salts; *V* **esprit, gros, poivre.**
(b) (*fig*) (*humour*) wit; (*piquant*) spice. **la remarque ne manque pas de** ~ the remark has a certain wit; **c'est ce qui fait tout le** ~ **de l'aventure** that's what gives the adventure its spice; (*littér*) **ils sont le** ~ **de la terre** they are the salt of the earth; *V* **grain.**
2: sel attique Attic salt *ou* wit; **sels de bain** bath salts; **sel de céleri** celery salt; **sel de cuisine** cooking salt; **sel fin** = **sel de table**; **sel gemme** rock salt; **sel marin** sea salt; **sel de table** table salt.
select* [selɛkt] *adj inv*, **sélect, e*** [selɛkt, ɛkt(ə)] *adj personne* posh*, high-class; *clientèle, club, endroit* select, posh*.
sélecteur [selɛktœʀ] *nm [ordinateur, poste de TV, central téléphonique]* selector; *[motocyclette]* gear lever.

sélectif, -ive [selɛktif, iv] *adj* (*gén*) selective.

sélection [selɛksjɔ̃] *nf* **(a)** (*action*) choosing, selection, picking. **faire** *ou* **opérer** *ou* **effectuer une ~ parmi** to make a selection from among; (*Sport*) **comité de ~** selection committee; (*Élevage, Zool*) **la ~** selection; **épreuve de ~** (selection) trial; (*Bio*) **~ (naturelle)** natural selection; **~ professionnelle** professional recruitment.
(b) (*choix, gamme*) *[articles, produits, œuvres]* selection. **avant d'acheter, voyez notre ~ d'appareils ménagers** before buying, see our selection of household appliances.
(c) (*Sport*) selection. (*Ftbl, Rugby*) **avoir plus de 20 ~s (pour l'équipe nationale) à son actif** to have been capped (*Brit*) more than 20 times, have more than 20 caps (*Brit*) to one's credit, have been selected *ou* picked more than 20 times (to play for the national team).

sélectionné, e [selɛksjɔne] (*ptp de* **sélectionner**) **1** *adj* (*soigneusement choisi*) specially selected, choice (*épith*). **2** *nm,f* (*Ftbl etc*) selected player; (*Athlétisme*) selected competitor.

sélectionner [selɛksjɔne] (1) *vt athlètes, produits* to select, pick. (*Ftbl*) **3 fois sélectionné pour l'équipe nationale** capped (*Brit*) 3 times (to play for the national team), selected 3 times to play for the national team.

sélectionneur, -euse [selɛksjɔnœʀ, øz] *nm,f* (*Sport*) selector.

sélectivité [selɛktivite] *nf* (*Rad*) selectivity.

self* [sɛlf] *nm*, **self-service**, *pl* **self-services** [sɛlfsɛʀvis] *nm* self-service (restaurant), cafeteria.

selle [sɛl] *nf* **(a)** (*Cyclisme, Équitation*) saddle. **monter sans ~** to ride bareback; **se mettre en ~** to mount, get into the saddle; **mettre qn en ~** (*lit*) to put sb in the saddle; (*fig*) to give sb a leg-up; **se remettre en ~** (*lit*) to remount, get back into the saddle; (*fig*) to get back in the saddle; (*lit, fig*) **être bien en ~** to be firmly in the saddle; *V* **cheval**.
(b) (*Boucherie*) saddle.
(c) (*Méd*) **~s** stools, motions; **êtes-vous allé à la ~ aujourd'hui?** have you had *ou* passed a motion today?, have your bowels moved today?
(d) (*Art*) *[sculpteur]* turntable.

seller [sele] (1) *vt* to saddle.

sellerie [sɛlʀi] *nf* (*métier, articles, selles*) saddlery; (*lieu de rangement*) tack room, harness room, saddle room.

sellette [sɛlɛt] *nf* **(a) être/mettre qn sur la ~** to be/put sb on the carpet (*fig*). **(b)** (*Art*) (*pour sculpteur*) small turntable; (*pour statue, pot de fleur*) stand. **(c)** (*Constr*) cradle. **(d)** *[cheval de trait]* saddle.

sellier [selje] *nm* saddler.

selon [s(ə)lɔ̃] *prép* **(a)** (*conformément à*) in accordance with. **~ la volonté de qn** in accordance with sb's wishes.
(b) (*en proportion de, en fonction de*) according to. **vivre ~ ses moyens** to live according to one's means; **le nombre varie ~ la saison** the number varies (along) with the season, the number varies according to the season; **on répartit les enfants ~ l'âge** *ou* **leur âge/la taille** *ou* **leur taille** the children were grouped according to age/height; **c'est ~ le cas/les circonstances** it all depends on the individual case/on the circumstances; **c'est ~** it (all) depends; **il acceptera ou n'acceptera pas, ~ son humeur** he may or may not accept, depending on *ou* according to his mood *ou* how he feels.
(c) (*suivant l'opinion de*) according to. **~ les journaux, il aurait été assassiné** according to the papers, he was murdered; **~ moi/lui, elle devrait se plaindre** in my/his opinion *ou* to my mind/according to him, she should complain; **~ les prévisions de la radio, il fera beau demain** according to the radio forecast it will be fine tomorrow.
(d) (*loc*) **~ toute apparence** to all appearances; **~ toute vraisemblance** in all probability; **~ que** according to *ou* depending on whether, according as (*frm*).

Seltz [sɛls] *nf V* **eau**.

semailles [s(ə)mɑj] *nfpl* (*opération*) sowing (*U*); (*période*) seedtime; (*graine*) seed, seeds.

semaine [s(ə)mɛn] *nf* **(a)** (*gén*) week. **la première ~ de mai** the first week in *ou* of May; **en ~** during the week, on weekdays; **louer/travailler à la ~** to let/work by the week; **dans 2 ~s à partir d'aujourd'hui** 2 weeks *ou* a fortnight (*Brit*) (from) today; **la ~ de 40 heures** the 40-hour (working) week; *V* **courant, fin²**.
(b) (*salaire*) week's wages *ou* pay, weekly wage *ou* pay; (*argent de poche*) week's *ou* weekly pocket money.
(c) (*Publicité*) week. **~ publicitaire/commerciale** publicity/business week; **la ~ du livre/du bricolage** book/do-it-yourself week; **la ~ contre la faim** feed the hungry week; **la ~ contre la tuberculose** anti-tuberculosis week; (*hum*) **c'est sa ~ de bonté!*** it's charity *ou* do-gooders' week!* (*hum*).
(d) (*Bijouterie*) (*bracelet*) (seven-band) bracelet; (*bague*) (seven-band) ring.
(e) (*loc*) **la ~ sainte** Holy Week; **il te le rendra la ~ des quatre jeudis** he'll never give it back to you in a month of Sundays; **faire la ~ anglaise** to work *ou* do a five-day week; (*Mil*) **être de ~** to be on duty (*for the week*); **officier de ~** officer on duty (*for the week*), officer of the week; *V* **petit**.

semainier, -ière [s(ə)menje, mɛnjɛʀ] **1** *nm,f* (*personne*) person on duty (*for the week*). **2** *nm* (*agenda*) desk diary; (*meuble*) chest of (seven) drawers, semainier.

sémanticien, -ienne [semɑ̃tisjɛ̃, jɛn] *nm,f* semantician, semanticist.

sémantique [semɑ̃tik] **1** *adj* semantic. **2** *nf* semantics (*sg*).

sémaphore [semafɔʀ] *nm* (*Naut*) semaphore; (*Rail*) semaphore signal.

semblable [sɑ̃blabl(ə)] **1** *adj* **(a)** (*similaire*) similar. **~ à** like, similar to; **dans un cas ~, j'aurais refusé** in a similar case I should have refused; **je ne connais rien de ~** I don't know anything like that; **maison ~ à tant d'autres** house like so many others *ou* similar to so many others; **en cette circonstance, il a été ~ à lui-même** on this occasion he remained himself.
(b) (*avant n: tel*) such. **de ~s calomnies sont inacceptables** such calumnies *ou* calumnies of this kind are unacceptable.
(c) (*qui se ressemblent*) **~s** alike; **les deux frères étaient ~s (en tout)** the two brothers were alike (in everything); *V* **triangle**.
2 *nm* fellow creature, fellow man. **aimer son ~** to love one's fellow creatures *ou* fellow men; (*péj*) **toi et tes ~s** you and your kind (*péj*), you and people like you (*péj*).

semblablement [sɑ̃blabləmɑ̃] *adv* similarly.

semblant [sɑ̃blɑ̃] *nm* **(a) ~ de: un ~ de calme/de bonheur/de vie/de vérité** a semblance of calm/happiness/life/truth; **un ~ de réponse** some vague attempt at a reply; **un ~ de soleil** a glimmer of sun; **un ~ de sourire** the shadow of a smile; **nous avons un ~ de jardin** we've got the mere semblance of a garden; *V* **faux²**.
(b) faire ~ de: faire ~ de dormir/lire to pretend to be asleep/to read; **il fait ~** he's pretending; **il ne fait ~ de rien* mais il entend tout** he's pretending to take no notice but he can hear everything.

sembler [sɑ̃ble] (1) **1** *vb impers* **(a)** (*paraître*) **il semble** it seems; **il semble bon/inutile de faire** it seems a good idea/useless to do; **il semblerait qu'il ne soit pas venu** it would seem *ou* appear that he didn't come, it looks as though *ou* as if he didn't come.
(b) (*estimer*) **il me semble** it seems *ou* appears to me; **il peut te ~ démodé de ...** it may seem *ou* appear old-fashioned to you to ...; **il me semble que tu n'as pas le droit de ...** it seems *ou* appears to me (that) you don't have the right to ..., it looks to me as though *ou* as if you don't have the right to ...; **comme bon me/te semble** as I/you see fit, as I/you think best *ou* fit; **prenez qui/ce que bon vous semble** take whom/what you please *ou* wish.
(c) (*croire*) **il me semble que** I think (that); **il me semblait bien que je l'avais posé là** I really thought *ou* did think I had put it down here; **il me semble revoir mon grand-père** it's as though I see *ou* it's like seeing my grandfather again; **il me semble vous l'avoir déjà dit** I think *ou* I have a feeling I've already told you.
(d) (*loc*) **je vous connais ce me semble**† methinks I know you††, it seems to me that I know you; **je suis déjà venu ici me semble-t-il** it seems to me (that) I've been here before, I seem to have been here before; **à ce qu'il me semble, notre organisation est mauvaise** to my mind *ou* it seems to me (that) our organization is bad, our organization seems bad to me; (*frm, hum*) **que vous en semble?** what do you think (of it)?
2 *vi* to seem. **la maison lui sembla magnifique** the house seemed magnificent to him; **ce bain lui sembla bon après cette dure journée** that bath seemed good to him after that hard day; **il semblait content/nerveux** he seemed (to be) *ou* appeared happy/nervous; **oh! vous me semblez bien pessimiste!** you do sound *ou* seem very pessimistic!; **il ne semblait pas convaincu** he didn't seem (to be) *ou* didn't look *ou* sound convinced, it *ou* he didn't look *ou* sound as though he were convinced; **les frontières de la science semblent reculer** the frontiers of science seem *ou* appear to be retreating.

semé, e [s(ə)me] (*ptp de* **semer**) *adj*: **questions ~es de pièges** questions bristling with traps; **parcours ~ de difficultés** route plagued with difficulties; **robe ~e de diamants** diamond-spangled dress, dress studded with diamonds; **récit ~ d'anecdotes** story interspersed *ou* sprinkled with anecdotes; **campagne ~e d'arbres** countryside dotted with trees; **la vie est ~e de joies et de peines** life is strewn with joys and troubles.

semelle [s(ə)mɛl] *nf* **(a)** sole. **~s (intérieures)** insoles, inner soles; **~s compensées** platform soles; **chaussures à ~s compensées** platform shoes; **chaussettes à ~s renforcées** socks with reinforced soles; **leur viande était de la vraie ~*** their meat was as tough as old boots* (*Brit*) *ou* shoe leather (*US*), their meat was like leather; *V* **battre, crêpe²**.
(b) d'une ~*: il n'a pas avancé/reculé d'une ~ he hasn't advanced/moved back (so much as) a single inch *ou* an inch; **il ne m'a pas quitté d'une ~** he never left me by so much as a single inch *ou* an inch.
(c) (*Tech*) *[rail]* base plate pad; *[machine]* bedplate.

semence [s(ə)mɑ̃s] *nf* **(a)** (*Agr, fig*) seed. **blé/pommes de terre de ~** seed corn/potatoes.
(b) (*sperme*) semen, seed (*littér*).
(c) (*clou*) tack.
(d) (*Bijouterie*) **~ de diamants** diamond sparks; **~ de perles** seed pearls.

semer [s(ə)me] (5) *vt* **(a)** (*répandre*) *graines, mort, peur, discorde* to sow; *clous, confettis* to scatter, strew; *faux bruits* to spread, disseminate (*frm*), sow. **~ ses propos de platitudes** to intersperse *ou* sprinkle one's remarks with platitudes; *V* **qui**.
(b) (*: *perdre*) *mouchoir* to lose, shed*; *poursuivant* to lose, shake off.

semestre [s(ə)mɛstʀ(ə)] *nm* **(a)** (*période*) half-year, six-month period; (*Univ*) semester. **taxe payée par ~** tax paid half-yearly; **pendant le premier/second ~ (de l'année)** during the first/second half of the year, during the first/second six-month period (of the year).
(b) (*loyer*) half-yearly *ou* six months' rent. **je vous dois un ~** I owe you six months' *ou* half a year's rent.

semestriel, -elle [səmɛstʀijɛl] *adj* (*V* **semestre**) half-yearly, six-monthly; semestral.

semestriellement [səmɛstʀijɛlmɑ̃] *adv* (*V* **semestre**) half-yearly; every *ou* each semester.

semeur, -euse [s(ə)mœʀ, øz] *nm,f* sower. **~ de discorde** sower of discord; ~ **de faux bruits** sower *ou* disseminator (*frm*) *ou* spreader of false rumours.

semi- [səmi] **1** *préf* semi-.

2: semi-aride *adj* semiarid; **semi-automatique** *adj* semiautomatic; **semi-auxiliaire** (*adj*) semiauxiliary; (*nm*) semiauxiliary verb; **semi-circulaire** *adj* semicircular; **semi-conducteur, -trice,** *mpl* **semi-conducteurs** (*adj*) *propriétés, caractéristiques* semiconducting; (*nm*) semiconductor; **semi-consonne** *nf, pl* **semi-consonnes** semivowel, semiconsonant; **semi-final, e** *adj* semifinished; **semi-nomade,** *pl* **semi-nomades** (*adj*) seminomadic; (*nmf*) seminomad; **semi-nomadisme** *nm* seminomadism; **semi-perméable** *adj* semipermeable; **semi-précieux, -euse** *adj* semiprecious; (*Jur*) **semi-public, -ique** *adj* semipublic; **semi-remorque,** *pl* **semi-remorques** (*nf: remorque*) trailer (*Brit*), semitrailer (*US*); (*nm: camion*) articulated lorry *ou* truck (*Brit*), trailer truck (*US*); **semi-voyelle** *nf, pl* **semi-voyelles** semivowel.

sémillant, e [semijɑ̃, ɑ̃t] *adj* (*vif, alerte*) *personne* vivacious, spirited; *allure, esprit* vivacious; (*fringant*) dashing (*épith*), full of dash (*attrib*).

séminaire [seminɛʀ] *nm* (*Rel*) seminary; (*Univ*) seminar.

séminal, e, *mpl* **-aux** [seminal, o] *adj* (*Bio*) seminal.

séminariste [seminaʀist(ə)] *nm* seminarist.

sémiologie [semjɔlɔʒi] *nf* (*Ling, Méd*) semiology.

sémiologique [semjɔlɔʒik] *adj* semiological.

sémiotique [semjɔtik] **1** *adj* semiotic. **2** *nf* semiotics (*sg*).

sémique [semik] *adj* semic. **acte** ~ semic *ou* meaningful act.

semis [s(ə)mi] *nm* (*plante*) seedling; (*opération*) sowing; (*terrain*) seedbed, seed plot.

sémite [semit] **1** *adj* Semitic. **2** *nmf*: **S**~ Semite.

sémitisme [semitism(ə)] *nm* Semitism.

semoir [səmwaʀ] *nm* **(a)** (*machine*) seeder. ~ **à engrais** muck-spreader, manure spreader. **(b)** (*sac*) seed-bag, seed-lip.

semonce [səmɔ̃s] *nf* reprimand. (*Naut*) **coup de** ~ warning shot across the bows.

semoule [s(ə)mul] *nf* semolina; *V* **sucre.**

sempiternel, -elle [sɛ̃pitɛʀnɛl] *adj plaintes, reproches* eternal (*épith*), never-ending, never-ceasing.

sempiternellement [sɛ̃pitɛʀnɛlmɑ̃] *adv* eternally.

sénat [sena] *nm* senate.

sénateur [senatœʀ] *nm* senator.

sénatorial, e, *mpl* **-aux** [senatɔʀjal, o] *adj* senatorial.

sénatus-consulte, *pl* **sénatus-consultes** [senatyskɔ̃sylt(ə)] *nm* (*Hist: sous Napoléon, Antiq*) senatus consultum.

séné [sene] *nm* senna.

sénéchal, *pl* **-aux** [seneʃal, o] *nm* (*Hist*) seneschal.

sénéchaussée [seneʃose] *nf* (*Hist*) (*juridiction*) seneschalsy; (*tribunal*) seneschal's court.

Sénégal [senegal] *nm* Senegal.

sénégalais, e [senegalɛ, ɛz] **1** *adj* Senegalese. **2** *nm,f*: **S**~**(e)** Senegalese.

Sénèque [senɛk] *nm* Seneca.

sénescence [senesɑ̃s] *nf* senescence.

sénile [senil] *adj* (*péj, Méd*) senile.

sénilité [senilite] *nf* senility.

senior [senjɔʀ] *adj, nm* (*Sport*) senior.

sens [sɑ̃s] **1** *nm* **(a)** (*vue, goût etc*) sense. **les** ~ the senses; **avoir le** ~ **de l'odorat/de l'ouïe très développé** to have a highly developed *ou* a very keen sense of smell/hearing; **reprendre ses** ~ to regain consciousness; *V* **organe.**

(b) (*instinct*) sense. **avoir le** ~ **du rythme/de l'humour** to have a sense of rhythm/humour; **il n'a aucun** ~ **moral/pratique** he has no moral/practical sense; **avoir le** ~ **des réalités** to be a realist; **avoir le** ~ **de l'orientation** to have a (good) sense of direction.

(c) (*raison, avis*) sense. **ce qu'il dit est plein de** ~ what he is saying makes (good) sense *ou* is very sensible; **un homme de (bon)** ~ a man of (good) sense; **cela n'a pas de** ~ that doesn't make (any) sense, there's no sense in that; ~ **commun** common sense; **il a perdu le** ~ **(commun)** he's lost his *ou* all common sense; **à mon** ~ to my mind, to my way of thinking, in my opinion; *V* **dépit, sixième, tomber** *etc.*

(d) (*signification*) meaning. **au** ~ **propre/figuré** in the literal *ou* true/figurative sense *ou* meaning; **ce qui donne un** ~ **à la vie/à son action** what gives (a) meaning to life/to his action; **le** ~ **d'un geste** the meaning of a gesture; **qui n'a pas de** ~**, dépourvu de** ~ meaningless, which has no meaning; **en un (certain)** ~ in a (certain) sense; **en ce** ~ **que** in the sense that.

(e) (*direction*) direction. **aller** *ou* **être dans le bon/mauvais** ~ to go *ou* be in the right/wrong direction, go the right/wrong way; **mesurer/fendre qch dans le** ~ **de la longueur** to measure/split sth along its length *ou* lengthwise *ou* lengthways; **ça fait 10 mètres dans le** ~ **de la longueur** that's 10 metres in length *ou* lengthwise *ou* lengthways; **dans le** ~ **de la largeur** across its width, in width, widthwise; **dans le** ~ **(du bois/du tissu)** with the grain (of the wood/of the fabric); **dans le** ~ **contraire du courant** against the stream; **arriver/venir en** ~ **contraire** *ou* **inverse** to arrive/come from the opposite direction; **aller en** ~ **contraire** to go in the opposite direction; **dans le** ~ **des aiguilles d'une montre** clockwise; **dans le** ~ **contraire des aiguilles d'une montre** anticlockwise (*Brit*), counterclockwise (*US*); **dans le** ~ **de la marche** facing the front (of the train), facing the engine; **il retourna la boîte dans tous les** ~ **avant de l'ouvrir** he turned the box this way and that before opening it; **être/mettre** ~ **dessus dessous** (*lit*) to be/put *ou* turn upside down; (*fig*) to be/turn upside down; ~ **devant derrière** back to front, the wrong way round.

(f) (*ligne directrice*) **il a répondu/agi dans le même** ~ he replied/acted on *ou* along the same lines; **j'ai donné des directives dans ce** ~ I've given instructions to that effect *ou* end; **dans quel** ~ **allez-vous orienter votre action?** along what lines are you going to direct your action?

2: (*Aut*) **sens giratoire** roundabout (*Brit*), traffic circle (*US*); **la place est en sens giratoire** the square forms a roundabout; (*Aut*) **sens interdit** one-way street; **'sens interdit'** 'no entry'; **vous êtes en sens interdit** you are in a one-way street, you are going the wrong way (up a one-way street); (*Aut*) **sens unique** one-way street; **à sens unique** (*Aut*) one-way; (*fig: concession*) one-sided.

sensass* [sɑ̃sas] *adj* fantastic*, terrific*, sensational*.

sensation [sɑ̃sasjɔ̃] *nf* **(a)** (*perception*) sensation; (*impression*) feeling, sensation. **il eut une** ~ **d'étouffement** he had a feeling of suffocation, he had a suffocating feeling *ou* sensation; **j'ai la** ~ **de l'avoir déjà vu** I have a feeling I've seen him before; **quelle** ~ **cela te produit-il?** what do you feel?; what does it make you feel?; what kind of sensation does it give you?; **un amateur de** ~**s fortes** an enthusiast for sensational experiences *ou* big thrills.

(b) (*effet*) **faire** ~ to cause *ou* create a sensation; **roman à** ~ sensational novel; **la presse à** ~ the gutter press.

sensationnel, -elle [sɑ̃sasjɔnɛl] *adj* (*: *merveilleux*) fantastic*, terrific*, sensational*; (*qui fait sensation*) sensational.

sensé, e [sɑ̃se] *adj* sensible.

sensément [sɑ̃semɑ̃] *adv* sensibly.

sensibilisateur, -trice [sɑ̃sibilizatœʀ, tʀis] **1** *adj* sensitizing. **2** *nm* sensitizer.

sensibilisation [sɑ̃sibilizasjɔ̃] *nf* **(a)** (*fig*) **il s'agit d'éviter la** ~ **de l'opinion publique à ce problème par la presse** we must prevent public opinion from becoming sensitive *ou* alive to this problem through the press; **la** ~ **de l'opinion publique à ce problème est récente** public opinion has only become sensitive *ou* alive to this problem in recent years.

(b) (*Bio, Phot*) sensitization.

sensibilisé, e [sɑ̃sibilize] (*ptp de* **sensibiliser**) *adj*: ~ **à** *personne, public* sensitive *ou* alive to; ~ **aux problèmes politiques/sociaux** politically/socially aware.

sensibiliser [sɑ̃sibilize] (1) *vt* **(a)** ~ **qn** to make sb sensitive *ou* alive (*à* to). **(b)** (*Bio, Phot*) to sensitize.

sensibilité [sɑ̃sibilite] *nf* [*personne*] (*gén*) sensitivity, sensitiveness; (*de l'artiste*) sensibility, sensitivity; (*Tech*) [*pellicule, instrument, muscle*] sensitivity.

sensible [sɑ̃sibl(ə)] *adj* **(a)** (*impressionnable*) sensitive (*à* to). **pas recommandé aux personnes** ~**s** not recommended for people of (a) nervous disposition; **elle a le cœur** ~ she is tender-hearted, she has a tender heart; **être** ~ **aux attentions de qn/au charme de qch** to be sensitive to sb's attentions/to the charm of sth.

(b) (*tangible*) perceptible. **le vent était à peine** ~ the wind was scarcely *ou* hardly perceptible; ~ **à la vue/l'ouïe** perceptible to the eye/the ear.

(c) (*appréciable*) *progrès, changement, différence* appreciable, noticeable, palpable (*épith*). **la différence n'est pas** ~ the difference is hardly noticeable *ou* appreciable.

(d) (*Physiol*) *organe, blessure* sensitive. **avoir l'ouïe/l'odorat** ~ to have sensitive *ou* keen hearing/a keen sense of smell; ~ **au chaud/froid** sensitive to (the) heat/cold; **elle est** ~ **au froid** she feels the cold, she's sensitive to (the) cold; **être** ~ **de la bouche/gorge** to have a sensitive mouth/throat.

(e) (*Tech*) *papier, balance, baromètre* sensitive; *V* **corde.**

(f) (*Mus*) **(note)** ~ leading note.

(g) (*Philos*) **intuition** ~ sensory intuition; **être** ~ sentient being; **univers** ~ sensible universe.

sensiblement [sɑ̃sibləmɑ̃] *adv* **(a)** (*presque*) approximately, more or less. **être** ~ **du même âge/de la même taille** to be approximately *ou* more or less the same age/height. **(b)** (*notablement*) appreciably, noticeably.

sensiblerie [sɑ̃sibləʀi] *nf* (*sentimentalité*) sentimentality, mawkishness; (*impressionnabilité*) squeamishness.

sensitif, -ive [sɑ̃sitif, iv] **1** *adj* (*Anat*) *nerf* sensory; (*littér*) oversensitive. **2 sensitive** *nf* (*Bot: mimosa*) sensitive plant.

sensoriel, -elle [sɑ̃sɔʀjɛl] *adj* sensory, sensorial.

sensorimoteur, -trice [sɑ̃sɔʀimɔtœʀ, tʀis] *adj* sensorimotor.

sensualisme [sɑ̃sɥalism(ə)] *nm* (*Philos*) sensualism.

sensualiste [sɑ̃sɥalist(ə)] (*Philos*) **1** *adj* sensualist, sensualistic. **2** *nmf* sensualist.

sensualité [sɑ̃sɥalite] *nf* (*V* **sensuel**) sensuality; sensuousness.

sensuel, -elle [sɑ̃sɥɛl] *adj* (*porté à ou dénotant la volupté*) sensual; (*qui recherche et apprécie les sensations raffinées*) sensuous.

sensuellement [sɑ̃sɥɛlmɑ̃] *adv* (*V* **sensuel**) sensually; sensuously.

sente [sɑ̃t] *nf* (*littér*) (foot)path.

sentence [sɑ̃tɑ̃s] *nf* (*verdict*) sentence; (*adage*) maxim.

sentencieusement [sɑ̃tɑ̃sjøzmɑ̃] *adv* sententiously.

sentencieux, -euse [sɑ̃tɑ̃sjø, øz] *adj* sententious.

senteur [sɑ̃tœʀ] *nf* (*littér*) scent, perfume; *V* **pois.**

senti, e [sɑ̃ti] (*ptp de* **sentir**) *adj sentiment* heartfelt, sincere. **bien** ~: **quelques vérités bien** ~**es** a few home truths; **quelques mots bien** ~**s** (*bien choisis*) a few well-chosen *ou* well-expressed words; (*de blâme*) a few well-chosen words; **un discours bien** ~ a well-delivered *ou* heartfelt speech.

sentier [sɑ̃tje] *nm* (*lit*) (foot)path; (*fig*) path. (*lit, fig*) **suivre les/aller hors des** ~**s battus** to keep to/go off the *ou* stray from the beaten track; (*lit, fig*) **être sur le** ~ **de la guerre** to be on the warpath.

sentiment [sɑ̃timɑ̃] *nm* **(a)** (*émotion*) feeling. **un** ~ **de pitié/tendresse/haine** a feeling of pity/tenderness/hatred; ~ **de culpabilité** guilt *ou* guilty feeling; **avoir de bons/mauvais** ~**s à l'égard de qn** to have kind/ill feelings for sb; **bons** ~**s** finer feelings; **dans ce cas, il faut savoir oublier les ~s** in this case, we have to put sentiment to *ou* on one side *ou* to disregard our own feelings in the matter.

(b) (*sensibilité*) **le ~** feeling, emotion; (*péj*) sentiment; **être capable de ~** to be capable of emotion; **être dépourvu de ~** to be devoid of all feeling *ou* emotion; (*Théât etc*) **jouer/danser avec ~** to play/dance with feeling; **agir par ~** to let one's feelings guide *ou* determine one's actions; (*péj*) **faire du ~** to sentimentalize, be sentimental; **tu ne m'auras pas au *ou* par le ~*** sentimental appeals won't work with me.

(c) (*conscience*) **avoir le ~ de** to be aware of; **elle avait le ~ très vif de sa valeur** she was keenly aware of her worth, she had a keen sense of her worth; **avoir le ~ que quelque chose va arriver** to have a feeling that something is going to happen.

(d) (*formules de politesse*) **recevez, Monsieur, *ou* veuillez agréer, Monsieur, (l'expression de) mes ~s distingués *ou* respectueux** yours faithfully; **transmettez-lui nos meilleurs ~s** give him our best wishes.

(e) (*littér: opinion*) feeling.

sentimental, e, *mpl* **-aux** [sɑ̃timɑ̃tal, o] *adj* **(a)** (*tendre*) *personne* sentimental. **c'est un ~** he's sentimental, he's a sentimentalist.

(b) (*non raisonné*) *réaction, voyage* sentimental.

(c) (*amoureux*) *vie, aventure* love (*épith*). **il a des problèmes ~aux** he has problems with his love life.

(d) (*péj*) *personne, chanson, film* sentimental, soppy*. **ne sois pas si ~** don't be so soft *ou* soppy*.

sentimentalement [sɑ̃timɑ̃talmɑ̃] *adv* sentimentally, soppily*.

sentimentalisme [sɑ̃timɑ̃talism(ə)] *nm* sentimentalism.

sentimentalité [sɑ̃timɑ̃talite] *nf* sentimentality, soppiness*.

sentinelle [sɑ̃tinɛl] *nf* sentry, sentinel († *ou littér*). (*Mil*) **être en ~** to be on sentry duty, stand sentry; (*fig*) **mets-toi en ~ à la fenêtre** stand guard at the window.

sentir [sɑ̃tiʀ] (16) **1** *vt* **(a)** (*percevoir*) (*par l'odorat*) to smell; (*au goût*) to taste; (*au toucher, contact*) to feel. **~ un courant d'air** to feel a draught; **~ son cœur battre/ses yeux se fermer** to feel one's heart beating/one's eyes closing; **il ne peut pas ~ la différence entre le beurre et la margarine** he can't taste *ou* tell the difference between butter and margarine; **elle sentit une odeur de gaz/de brûlé** she smelt gas/burning; **on sent qu'il y a de l'ail dans ce plat** you can taste the garlic in this dish, you can tell there's garlic in this dish; **il ne sent jamais le froid/la fatigue** he never feels the cold/feels tired; **elle sentit qu'on lui tapait sur l'épaule** she felt somebody tapping her on the shoulder; **je suis enrhumé, je ne sens plus rien** I have a cold and can't smell anything *ou* and I've lost all sense of smell; (*fig: froid*) **je ne sens plus mes doigts** I have lost all sensation in my fingers, I can't feel my fingers any longer; (*fatigue*) **je ne sens plus mes jambes** my legs are dropping off*; (*fig*) **il ne peut pas le ~*** he can't stand *ou* bear (the sight of) him; (*fig*) **~ l'écurie** to get the smell *ou* scent of home in one's nostrils.

(b) (*avec attrib: dégager une certaine odeur*) to smell; (*avoir un certain goût*) to taste. **~ bon/mauvais** to smell good *ou* nice/bad; **~ des pieds/de la bouche** to have smelly feet/bad breath; **son manteau sent la fumée** his coat smells of smoke; **ce poisson commence à ~** this fish is beginning to smell; **ce thé sent le jasmin** (*goût*) this tea tastes of jasmine; (*odeur*) this tea smells of jasmine; **la pièce sent le renfermé/le moisi** the room smells stale/musty; **ça ne sent pas la rose!*** it's not a very nice smell, is it?

(c) (*fig: dénoter*) to be indicative of, reveal. **plaisanteries qui sentent la caserne** jokes with a whiff of the barrack room about them; **plaisanteries qui sentent le potache** jokes with a touch of the schoolboy about them; **une certaine arrogance qui sent la petite bourgeoisie** a certain arrogance indicative of *ou* which reveals a middle-class background.

(d) (*annoncer*) **une adolescence turbulente qui sent le pénitencier** a stormy adolescence which foreshadows the reformatory; **ça sent le fagot/l'autoritarisme** it smacks *ou* savours of heresy/authoritarianism; **ça sent le piège** there's a trap *ou* catch in it; **ça sent la pluie/la neige** it looks *ou* feels like rain/snow; **ça sent l'orage** there's a storm in the air; **ça sent le printemps** spring is in the air; **ça sent la punition** someone's in for a telling off*, someone's going to be punished; **ça sent le roussi*** there's going to be trouble; **cela sent la poudre** things could flare up.

(e) (*avoir conscience de*) *changement, fatigue* to feel, be aware *ou* conscious of; *importance de qch* to be aware *ou* conscious of; (*apprécier*) *beauté, élégance de qch* to appreciate; (*pressentir*) *danger, difficulté* to sense. **~ que** to feel *ou* be aware *ou* conscious that; (*pressentir*) to sense that; **il sentait la panique le gagner** he felt panic rising within him; **sentant le but proche ...** sensing the goal was at hand ...; **il ne sent pas sa force** he doesn't know *ou* realize his own strength; **elle sent maintenant le vide causé par son départ** now she is feeling the emptiness left by his departure; **sentez-vous la beauté de ce passage?** do you feel *ou* appreciate the beauty of this passage?; **le cheval sentait (venir) l'orage** the horse sensed the storm (coming); **il sentit qu'il ne reviendrait jamais** he sensed *ou* felt that he would never come back (again); **nul besoin de réfléchir, cela se sent** there's no need to think about it — you can feel *ou* sense it; **c'est sa façon de ~ (les choses)** that's his way of feeling (things), that's how he feels about things.

(f) faire ~: faire ~ son autorité to make one's authority felt; **essayez de faire ~ la beauté d'une œuvre d'art** try to bring out *ou* demonstrate *ou* show the beauty of a work of art; **les effets des restrictions commencent à se faire ~** the effects of the restrictions are beginning to be felt *ou* to make themselves felt.

2 se sentir *vpr* **(a) se ~ mal/mieux/fatigué** to feel ill/better/tired; **se ~ revivre/rajeunir** to feel o.s. coming alive again/growing young again; **il ne se sent pas la force/le courage de le lui dire** he doesn't feel strong/brave enough to say it to him.

(b) (*être perceptible*) *[effet]* to be felt, show. **cette amélioration/augmentation se sent** this improvement/increase can be felt *ou* shows; **les effets des grèves vont se ~ à la fin du mois** the effect of the strikes will be felt *ou* will show at the end of the month.

(c) (*loc*) **ne pas se ~ de joie** to be beside o.s. with joy; **il ne se sent plus!*** he's beside himself!; **non, mais tu ne te sens plus!*** really, have you taken leave of your senses!

seoir [swaʀ] (26) (*frm*) **1** *vi* (*convenir à*) **~ à qn** to become sb.

2 *vb impers*: **il sied de/que** it is proper *ou* fitting to/that; **comme il sied** as is proper *ou* fitting; **il lui sied/ne lui sied pas de faire** it befits *ou* becomes/ill befits *ou* ill becomes him to do.

sep [sɛp] *nm* = **cep.**

sépale [sepal] *nm* sepal.

séparable [sepaʀabl(ə)] *adj* separable (*de* from). **2 concepts difficilement ~s** 2 concepts which are difficult to separate.

séparateur, -trice [sepaʀatœʀ, tʀis] **1** *adj* separating (*épith*), separative. (*Opt*) **pouvoir ~ de l'œil/d'un instrument d'optique** resolving power of the eye/of an optical instrument. **2** *nm* (*Élec, Tech*) separator.

séparation [sepaʀɑsjɔ̃] *nf* **(a)** (*action: V* **séparer**) pulling off *ou* away; separation; separating out; parting; splitting, division; driving apart; pulling apart. **nous recommandons la ~ des filles et des garçons** we recommend separating the girls and the boys *ou* splitting up the girls and the boys *ou* the separation of the girls and he boys; **mur de ~** separating *ou* dividing wall.

(b) (*V* **se séparer**) parting; splitting off; separation; dispersal; breaking up; split-up*; split- *ou* break-up. (*Jur*) **~ de corps** legal separation; (*Jur*) **~ de fait *ou* à l'amiable** voluntary separation; **des ~s déchirantes** heartrending partings.

(c) (*absence*) *[amis, parents]* (period of) separation. **une longue ~ avait transformé leurs rapports** a long (period of) separation had changed their relationship.

(d) (*disjonction*) *[pouvoirs, notions, services]* separation. (*Pol*) **la ~ des pouvoirs** the separation of powers; (*Pol*) **la ~ de l'Église et de l'État** the separation of the Church and the State; (*Jur*) **le régime de la ~ de biens** separation *ou* division of property (*type of marriage settlement*).

(e) (*cloison*) division, partition; (*fig*) dividing line. **il faut faire une ~ très nette entre ces problèmes** you must draw a very clear dividing line between these problems.

séparatisme [sepaʀatism(ə)] *nm* (*Pol, Rel*) separatism.

séparatiste [sepaʀatist(ə)] *adj, nmf* (*Pol*) separatist; (*Hist US: sudiste*) secessionist.

séparé, e [sepaʀe] (*ptp de* **séparer**) *adj* **(a)** (*distinct*) *sons, notions* separate. **(b)** *personnes* (*Jur: désuni*) separated; (*gén: éloigné*) parted (*attrib*), apart (*attrib*). **vivre ~** to live apart, be separated (*de* from).

séparément [sepaʀemɑ̃] *adv* separately.

séparer [sepaʀe] (1) **1** *vt* **(a)** (*détacher*) *écorce, peau, enveloppe* to pull off, pull away (*de* from); (*extraire*) *éléments, gaz, liquides* to separate (out) (*de* from). **~ la tête du tronc** to sever the head from the trunk; **~ la noix de sa coquille** to separate the nut from its shell; **~ le grain du son** to separate the grain from the bran; **~ des gaz/liquides** to separate (out) gases/liquids; **~ un minerai de ses impuretés** to separate an ore from its impurities; (*Bible*) **~ le bon grain de l'ivraie** to separate the wheat from the chaff.

(b) (*diviser*) to part, split, divide. **~ les cheveux par une raie** to part one's hair; **~ un territoire (en deux) par une frontière** to split *ou* divide a territory (into two) by a frontier.

(c) (*désunir*) *amis, alliés* to part, drive apart; *adversaires, combattants* to separate, pull apart, part. **~ deux hommes qui se battent** to separate *ou* pull apart *ou* part two men who are fighting; **~ qn et *ou* de qn d'autre** to separate *ou* part sb from sb else; **dans cet hôpital, ils séparent les hommes et les femmes** in this hospital they separate the men from *ou* and the women; **ils avaient séparé l'enfant de sa mère** they had separated *ou* parted the child from its mother.

(d) *territoires, classes sociales, générations* to separate. **une barrière sépare les spectateurs des *ou* et les joueurs** a barrier separates the spectators from the players; **un simple grillage nous séparait des fauves** a simple wire fence was all that separated us from *ou* was all that was between us and the big cats; **une chaîne de montagnes sépare la France et *ou* de l'Espagne** a chain of mountains separates France from *ou* and Spain; **un seul obstacle le séparait encore du but** only one obstacle stood *ou* remained between him and his goal.

(e) (*différencier*) *questions, aspects* to distinguish between. **~ l'érudition de *ou* et l'intelligence** to distinguish *ou* differentiate between learning and intelligence.

2 se séparer *vpr* **(a)** (*se défaire de*) **se ~ de** *employé, objet personnel* to part with; **en voyage, ne vous séparez jamais de votre passeport** when travelling never part with *ou* be parted from your passport.

(b) (*s'écarter*) to divide, part (*de* from); (*se détacher*) to split off, separate off (*de* from). **écorce qui se sépare du tronc** bark which comes away from the trunk; **l'endroit où les branches se séparent du tronc** the place where the branches split *ou* separate off from the trunk; **le second étage de la fusée s'est séparé (de la base)** the second stage of the rocket has split off (from the base) *ou* separated (off) from the base; **à cet endroit, le fleuve se sépare en deux** at this place the river divides into two; **les routes/branches se séparent** the roads/branches divide *ou* part.

(c) (*se disperser*) *[adversaires]* to separate, break apart; *[manifestants, participants]* to disperse; *[assemblée]* to break up; *[convives]* to leave each other, part; *[époux]* to part, split up*, separate (*Jur*). **se ~ de son mari/sa femme** to part *ou* separate from one's husband/wife.

sépia [sepja] *nf* (*Zool: sécrétion*) cuttlefish ink, sepia; (*substance, couleur, dessin*) sepia. **(dessin à la) ~** sepia (drawing).

sept [sɛt] *adj, nm inv* seven. **les ~ péchés capitaux** the seven deadly sins; **les ~ merveilles du monde** the seven wonders of the world; *pour autres loc V* **six.**

septain [sɛtɛ̃] *nm seven-line stanza or poem.*

septante [sɛptɑ̃t] *adj inv* (††, *ou Belgique, Suisse*) seventy. (*Hist Rel*) **les S~** the Seventy; (*Bible*) **la version des S~** the Septuagint.

septembre [sɛptɑ̃bʀ(ə)] *nm* September. **le mois de ~** the month of September; **le premier/dix ~** (*nm*) the first/tenth of September; (*adv*) on the first/tenth of September; **en ~** in September; **au mois de ~** in (the month of) September; **au début (du mois) de ~, début ~** at the beginning of September; **au milieu (du mois) de ~, à la mi-~** in the middle of September, in mid-September; **à la fin (du mois) de ~, fin ~** at the end of September; **pendant le mois de ~** during September; **vers la fin de ~** late in September, in late September; **~ a été très froid** September was very cold; **~ prochain/dernier** next/last September.

septennal, e, *mpl* **-aux** [sɛptenal, o] *adj* (*durée*) *mandat, période* seven-year (*épith*); (*fréquence*) *festival* septennial.

septennat [sɛptena] *nm* seven-year term (of office); *[roi]* seven-year reign.

septentrion [sɛptɑ̃tʀijɔ̃] *nm* (††, *littér*) north.

septentrional, e, *mpl* **-aux** [sɛptɑ̃tʀijɔnal, o] *adj* northern.

septicémie [sɛptisemi] *nf* (*Méd*) blood poisoning, septicaemia (*T*).

septicémique [sɛptisemik] *adj* septicaemic.

septicité [sɛptisite] *nf* septicity.

septième [sɛtjɛm] **1** *adj, nm* seventh. **le ~ art** the cinema; **être au ~ ciel** to be in (the) seventh heaven; *pour autres loc V* **sixième. 2** *nf* (*Mus*) seventh.

septièmement [sɛtjɛmmɑ̃] *adv* seventhly; *pour loc V* **sixièmement.**

septique [sɛptik] *adj fièvre, bactérie* septic; *V* **fosse.**

septuagénaire [sɛptɥaʒenɛʀ] *adj, nmf* septuagenarian.

septuagésime [sɛptɥaʒezim] *nf* Septuagesima.

septuor [sɛptɥɔʀ] *nm* septet(te).

septuple [sɛptypl(ə)] **1** *adj* sevenfold, septuple (*rare*). **2** *nm*: **le ~ de 2** seven times 2.

septupler [sɛptyple] (1) **1** *vt*: **~ qch** to increase sth sevenfold. **2** *vi* to increase sevenfold.

sépulcral, e, *mpl* **-aux** [sepylkʀal, o] *adj atmosphère, voix* sepulchral; *salle* tomb-like.

sépulcre [sepylkʀ(ə)] *nm* sepulchre; *V* **saint.**

sépulture [sepyltyʀ] *nf* **(a)** (†, *littér: inhumation*) sepulture (*littér*), burial. **être privé de ~** to be refused burial. **(b)** (*tombeau*) burial place; *V* **violation.**

séquelles [sekɛl] *nfpl [maladie]* after-effects; *[guerre, révolution]* aftermath; *[décision]* consequences.

séquence [sekɑ̃s] *nf* (*Ciné, Ling, Mus, Rel*) sequence; (*Cartes*) run.

séquentiel, -ielle [sekɑ̃sjɛl] *adj programme, information* sequential. (*Ling*) **arrangement ~ de la langue** sequential ordering of language.

séquestration [sekɛstʀɑsjɔ̃] *nf* (*V* **séquestrer**) illegal confinement; impoundment.

séquestre [sekɛstʀ(ə)] *nm* (*Jur*) (*action*) impoundment; (*Pol*) *[biens ennemis]* confiscation, impoundment, sequestration; (*dépositaire*) depository. **placer des biens sous ~** to sequester goods.

séquestrer [sekɛstʀe] (1) *vt personne* to confine illegally; *biens* to impound (*pending decision over ownership*). (*littér*) **vivre séquestré du monde** to live sequestered from the world (*littér*).

sequin [səkɛ̃] *nm* (*Hist: pièce d'or*) sequin.

séquoia [sekɔja] *nm* sequoia.

sérac [seʀak] *nm* serac.

sérail [seʀaj] *nm* seraglio.

séraphin [seʀafɛ̃] *nm* seraph.

séraphique [seʀafik] *adj* (*Rel, fig*) seraphic.

serbe [sɛʀb(ə)] **1** *adj* Serbian. **2** *nm* (*Ling*) Serbian. **3** *nmf*: **S~** Serb.

Serbie [sɛʀbi] *nf* Serbia.

serbo-croate [sɛʀbɔkʀɔat] **1** *adj* Serbo-Croat(ian). **2** *nm* (*Ling*) Serbo-Croat.

Sercq [sɛʀk] *nm* Sark.

serein, e [səʀɛ̃, ɛn] *adj* **(a)** (*calme*) *ciel, nuit, jour* serene, clear; *âme, foi, visage* serene, calm. **(b)** (*impartial*) *jugement, critique* calm, dispassionate.

sereinement [səʀɛnmɑ̃] *adv* (*V* **serein**) serenely; clearly; calmly; dispassionately.

sérénade [seʀenad] *nf* **(a)** (*Mus: concert, pièce*) serenade. **donner une ~ à qn** to serenade sb. **(b)** (**hum: charivari*) racket*, hullabaloo*.

sérénissime [seʀenisim] *adj*: **Son Altesse ~** His (*ou* Her) Most Serene Highness.

sérénité [seʀenite] *nf* (*V* **serein**) serenity; clarity; calmness; dispassionateness.

séreux, -euse [seʀø, øz] *adj* serous.

serf, serve [sɛʀ(f), sɛʀv(ə)] **1** *adj personne* in serfdom (*attrib*). **condition serve** (state of) serfdom; **terre serve** land held in villein tenure. **2** *nm,f* serf.

serfouette [sɛʀfwɛt] *nf* hoe-fork.

serge [sɛʀʒ(ə)] *nf* serge.

sergent[1] [sɛʀʒɑ̃] *nm* (*Mil*) sergeant. **~-chef** staff sergeant; **~ de ville**†† policeman; **~-fourrier** quartermaster sergeant; **~ instructeur** drill sergeant; **~-major** ≃ quartermaster sergeant (*in charge of accounts etc*).

sergent[2] [sɛʀʒɑ̃] *nm* cramp, clamp.

séricicole [seʀisikɔl] *adj* silkworm-breeding (*épith*), sericultural (*T*).

sériciculteur [seʀisikyltœʀ] *nm* silkworm breeder, sericulturist (*T*).

sériciculture [seʀisikyltyʀ] *nf* silkworm breeding, sericulture (*T*).

série [seʀi] *nf* **(a)** (*suite*) *[timbres]* set, series; *[clefs, casseroles, volumes]* set; *[tests]* series, battery; *[ennuis, accidents, succès]* series, string*. (*beaucoup*) **(toute) une ~ de*...** a (whole) series *ou* string* of ... ; **(ouvrages de) ~ noire** crime thrillers; **ambiance/poursuite (de) ~ noire** crime-thriller atmosphere/chase; (*fig*) **c'est la ~ noire** it's one disaster following (on) another, it's one disaster after another, it's a run of bad luck.

(b) (*catégorie*) (*Naut*) class; (*Sport*) rank; (*épreuve de qualification*) qualifying heat *ou* round. **joueur de deuxième ~** player of the second rank.

(c) (*Comm, Ind*) **fabrication** *ou* **production en ~** (*lit, fig*) mass production; **article/véhicule de ~** standard article/vehicle; *V* **fin**[2], **hors.**

(d) (*Chim, Math, Mus*) series; (*Billard*) break. (*Élec*) **monté en ~** connected in series.

sériel, -elle [seʀjɛl] *adj ordre* serial. (*Mus*) **musique ~le** serial *ou* twelve-note *ou* dodecaphonic music.

sérier [seʀje] (7) *vt problèmes, questions* to classify, arrange.

sérieusement [seʀjøzmɑ̃] *adv* (*V* **sérieux**) seriously; responsibly; genuinely; considerably. **non, il l'a dit ~** no — he meant it seriously, no — he was in earnest when he said that.

sérieux, -euse [seʀjø, øz] **1** *adj* **(a)** (*grave, ne plaisantant pas*) *personne, air* serious, earnest, solemn. **~ comme un pape** solemn as a judge.

(b) (*digne de confiance*) *maison de commerce, tuteur* reliable, dependable; *employé, élève, apprenti* reliable, responsible; (*moralement*) *jeune homme, jeune fille* responsible, trustworthy. **partir skier pendant les examens, ce n'est vraiment pas ~!** it's not taking a very responsible *ou* serious attitude to go off skiing during the exams.

(c) (*fait consciencieusement, à fond*) *travail, études* serious.

(d) (*réfléchi*) *personne* serious, serious-minded.

(e) (*de bonne foi*) *acquéreur, promesses, raison* genuine, serious; *renseignements* genuine, reliable. **un client ~** (*hum: qui achète beaucoup*) a serious customer; **non, il était ~** no, he was serious *ou* he meant it; **c'est ~, ce que vous dites?** are you serious?, do you really mean that?; **ce n'est pas ~, il ne le fera jamais** he doesn't really mean it *ou* it isn't a genuine threat (*ou* promise) — he'll never do it!; **'pas ~ s'abstenir'** 'only genuine inquirers need apply'.

(f) (*digne d'attention*) *conversation, livre, projet* serious. **passons aux affaires** *ou* **choses ~euses** let us move on to more serious matters.

(g) (*important, grave*) *situation, affaire, maladie* serious.

(h) (*intensif*) *raison* good; *coup* serious; *somme, différence* considerable. **de ~euses chances de ...** a strong *ou* good chance of ... ; **de ~euses raisons de ...** good reasons to ... ; **ils ont une ~euse avance** they have a strong *ou* good lead.

2 *nm* (*V adj*) seriousness; earnestness; serious-mindedness. **garder son ~** to keep a straight face; **perdre son ~** to give way to laughter; **prendre au ~** to take seriously; **se prendre au ~** to take o.s. seriously.

sérigraphie [seʀigʀafi] *nf* silk-screen printing, serigraphy (*T*).

serin [s(ə)ʀɛ̃] *nm* (*Orn*) canary; († *péj: niais*) ninny*.

seriner [s(ə)ʀine] (1) *vt* **(a)** (*péj: rabâcher*) **~ qch à qn** to drum *ou* din sth into sb; **tais-toi, tu nous serines!*** oh, be quiet, you keep telling us the same thing over and over again! *ou* we're tired of hearing the same thing all the time!

(b) ~ (un air à) un oiseau to teach a bird a tune using a bird-organ.

seringue [s(ə)ʀɛ̃g] *nf* (*Méd*) syringe; *[jardinier]* garden syringe; *[pâtissier]* (icing) syringe. *[mécanicien]* **~ à graisse** grease gun.

serment [sɛʀmɑ̃] *nm* **(a)** (*solennel*) oath. **faire un ~** to take an oath; **~ sur l'honneur** solemn oath, word of honour; **sous ~** on *ou* under oath; **~ d'Hippocrate** Hippocratic oath; **~ professionnel** oath of office; *V* **prestation, prêter.**

(b) (*promesse*) pledge. **échanger des ~s (d'amour)** to exchange vows *ou* pledges of love; (*fig*) **~ d'ivrogne** empty vow, vain resolve; **je te fais le ~ de ne plus jouer** I (solemnly) swear to you *ou* I'll make (you) a solemn promise that I'll never gamble again; *V* **faux**[2].

sermon [sɛʀmɔ̃] *nm* (*Rel*) sermon; (*fig péj*) lecture, sermon.

sermonner [sɛʀmɔne] (1) *vt*: **~ qn** to lecture sb, give sb a talking-to.

sermonneur, -euse [sɛʀmɔnœʀ, øz] *nm,f* (*péj*) sermonizer, preacher.

sérologie [seʀɔlɔʒi] *nf* serology.

sérosité [seʀozite] *nf* serous fluid, serosity.

sérothérapie [seʀɔteʀapi] *nf* serotherapy.

serpe [sɛʀp(ə)] *nf* billhook, bill. (*fig*) **un visage taillé à la ~** *ou* **à coups de ~** a craggy *ou* rugged face.

serpent [sɛʀpɑ̃] **1** *nm* **(a)** (*Zool*) snake. (*Rel*) **le ~** the serpent; **une ruse/prudence de ~** snake-like cunning/caution; *V* **charmeur, réchauffer.**

(b) (*fig: ruban*) ribbon. **un ~ de fumée** a ribbon of smoke; **le ~ argenté du fleuve** the silvery ribbon of the river.

2: serpent d'eau grass snake; **serpent à lunettes** Indian cobra; (*hum Presse*) **serpent de mer** mythical monster, Loch Ness monster; (*Écon*) **le serpent (monétaire)** the snake; (*Myth*)

serpent à plumes plumed serpent; serpent à sonnettes rattlesnake.
serpentaire [sɛʀpɑ̃tɛʀ] *nm* (*Zool*) secretary bird, serpent-eater.
serpenteau, *pl* ~x [sɛʀpɑ̃to] *nm* (*Zool*) young snake; (*feu d'artifice*) serpent.
serpenter [sɛʀpɑ̃te] (1) *vi* [*rivière, chemin*] to snake, meander, wind; [*vallée*] to wind. **la route descendait en serpentant vers la plaine** the road snaked *ou* wound (its way) down to the plain.
serpentin, e [sɛʀpɑ̃tɛ̃, in] **1** *adj* (*gén*) serpentine. **2** *nm* (*ruban*) streamer; (*Chim*) coil. **3 serpentine** *nf* (*Minér*) serpentine.
serpette [sɛʀpɛt] *nf* pruning knife.
serpillière [sɛʀpijɛʀ] *nf* floorcloth.
serpolet [sɛʀpɔlɛ] *nm* mother-of-thyme, wild thyme.
serrage [sɛʀaʒ] *nm* (*gén, Tech*) [*vis, écrou*] tightening; [*joint*] clamping; [*nœud*] tightening, pulling tight; *V* **bague, collier, vis**[1].
serre[1] [sɛʀ] *nf* (*gén*) greenhouse, glasshouse; (*attenant à une maison*) conservatory. **pousser en ~** to grow under glass; **~ chaude** hothouse.
serre[2] [sɛʀ] *nf* (*griffe*) talon, claw.
serre- [sɛʀ] *préf V* **serrer.**
serré, e [seʀe] (*ptp de* **serrer**) **1** *adj* **(a)** *vêtement, soulier* tight.
(b) *passagers, spectateurs* (tightly) packed. **être ~s comme des harengs** *ou* **sardines** to be packed like sardines; **mettez-vous ailleurs, nous sommes trop ~s à cette table** sit somewhere else because we are too crowded at this table; *V* **rang.**
(c) *tissu* closely woven; *réseau* dense; *mailles, écriture* close; *herbe, blés, forêt* dense; (*fig*) *style* tight, concise. **un café (bien) ~** a (good) strong coffee; **pousser en touffes ~es** to grow in thick clumps.
(d) (*bloqué*) **trop ~** too tight; **pas assez ~** not tight enough; *V aussi* **serrer.**
(e) (*contracté*) **avoir le cœur ~** to feel a pang of anguish; **avoir la gorge ~e** to feel a tightening *ou* a lump in one's throat; **les poings ~s** with clenched fists; *V aussi* **serrer.**
(f) *discussion* closely conducted, closely argued; *jeu, lutte, match* tight, close-fought; *budget* tight. (*fig*) **la partie est ~e, nous jouons une partie ~e** it is a tight game, we're in a tight game; **un train de vie assez ~** a rather straitened life style.
2 *adv*: **écrire ~** to write one's letters close together, write a cramped hand; (*fig*) **jouer ~** to play it tight, play a tight game; **vivre ~** to live on a tight budget.
serrement [sɛʀmɑ̃] *nm* **(a) ~ de main** handshake; **~ de cœur** pang of anguish; **~ de gorge** *ou* **à la gorge** tightening in the throat. **(b)** (*Min*) dam.
serrer [seʀe] (1) **1** *vt* **(a)** (*maintenir, presser*) to grip, hold tight. **~ une pipe/un os entre ses dents** to have a pipe/a bone between one's teeth; **~ qn dans ses bras/contre son cœur** to clasp sb in one's arms/to one's chest; **~ la main à qn** (*la donner à qn*) to shake sb's hand, shake hands with sb; (*presser*) to squeeze *ou* press sb's hand; **se ~ la main** to shake hands; **~ qn à la gorge** to grab sb by the throat; *V* **kiki.**
(b) (*contracter*) **~ le poing/les mâchoires** to clench one's fist/jaws; **~ les lèvres** to set one's lips; **les mâchoires serrées** with set *ou* clenched jaws; **les lèvres serrées** with tight lips, tight-lipped; **avoir le cœur serré par l'émotion** to feel one's heart wrung by emotion; **avoir la gorge serrée par l'émotion** to be choked by emotion; **cela serre le cœur** *ou* **c'est à vous ~ le cœur de les voir si malheureux** it wrings your heart *ou* makes your heart bleed to see them so unhappy; **~ les dents** (*lit*) to clench *ou* set one's teeth; (*fig*) to grit one's teeth; (*fig*) **~ les fesses‡** to be scared stiff *ou* out of one's wits*.
(c) (*comprimer*) to be too tight; (*mouler*) to fit tightly. **mon pantalon me serre** my trousers are too tight (for me); **cette jupe me serre (à) la taille** this skirt is too tight round the *ou* my waist; **elle se serre la taille dans un corset pour paraître plus jeune** she wears a tight corset to make herself look younger; **ces chaussures me serrent (le pied)** these shoes are too tight; **son jersey lui serrait avantageusement le buste** the tight fit of her jersey showed her figure off to advantage.
(d) (*bloquer*) *vis, écrou* to tighten; *joint* to clamp; *robinet* to turn off tight; *nœud, lacet, ceinture* to tighten, pull tight; (*tendre*) *câble* to tauten, make taut, tighten. **~ le frein à main** to put on the handbrake; (*fig*) **~ la vis à qn*** to crack down harder on sb*.
(e) (*se tenir près de*) (*par derrière*) to keep close behind; (*latéralement*) *automobile, concurrent* to squeeze (*contre* up against). **~ qn de près** to follow close behind sb; **~ une femme de près** to force one's attentions on a woman; **~ de près l'ennemi** to pursue the enemy closely; **~ qn dans un coin** to wedge sb in a corner; **~ un cycliste contre le trottoir** to squeeze a cyclist against the pavement; **~ le trottoir** to hug the kerb; (*Aut*) **~ sa droite** to keep (well) to the right; **ne serre pas cette voiture de trop près** don't get too close to *ou* behind that car; (*fig*) **~ une question de plus près** to study a question more closely; (*fig*) **~ le texte** to follow the text closely, keep close to the text; (*Naut*) **~ la côte** to sail close to the shore, hug the shore; (*Naut*) **~ le vent** to hug the wind.
(f) (*rapprocher*) *objets alignés, mots, lignes* to close up, put close together. (*Mil*) **~ les rangs** to close ranks; **serrez!** close ranks!; **~ son style** to write concisely *ou* in a condensed *ou* concise style; **il faudra ~ les invités: la table est petite** we'll have to squeeze the guests up *ou* together since the table is small.
(g) (*dial*, †: *ranger*) to put away.
2 *vi* (*Aut: obliquer*) **~ à droite/gauche** to move in to the right-/left-hand lane; **'véhicules lents serrez à droite'** 'slow-moving vehicles keep to the right'.
3 se serrer *vpr* **(a)** (*se rapprocher*) **se ~ contre qn** to huddle (up) against sb; (*tendrement*) to cuddle up to sb; **se ~ autour de la table/du feu** to squeeze *ou* crowd round the table/fire; **se ~ pour faire de la place** to squeeze up to make room; **serrez-vous un peu** squeeze up a bit.
(b) (*se contracter*) **à cette vue, son cœur se serra** at the sight of this he felt a pang of anguish; **ses poings se serrèrent, presque malgré lui** his fists clenched *ou* he clenched his fists almost in spite of himself.
(c) (*loc*) **se ~ les coudes** to stick together, back one another up; **se ~ (la ceinture)** to tighten one's belt.
4: serre-file *nm, pl* **serre-files** (*Mil*) file closer; **serre-frein(s)** *nm inv* brakesman; **serre-joint(s)** *nm inv* clamp, cramp; **serre-livres** *nm inv* book end; **serre-tête** *nm inv* (*bandeau*) headband; (*bonnet*) [*cycliste, skieur*] skullcap; [*aviateur*] helmet.
serrure [seʀyʀ] *nf* [*poste, coffre-fort, valise*] lock. **~ de sûreté** safety lock; *V* **trou.**
serrurerie [seʀyʀʀi] *nf* (*métier*) locksmithing, locksmith's trade; (*travail*) ironwork. **~ d'art** ornamental *ou* wrought-iron work; **grosse ~** heavy ironwork.
serrurier [seʀyʀje] *nm* [*serrures, clefs*] locksmith; [*fer forgé*] ironsmith.
sertir [sɛʀtiʀ] (2) *vt* **(a)** *pierre précieuse* to set. **(b)** (*Tech*) *pièces de tôle* to crimp.
sertissage [sɛʀtisaʒ] *nm* (*V* **sertir**) setting; crimping.
sertisseur, -euse [sɛʀtisœʀ, øz] *nm,f* (*V* **sertir**) setter; crimper.
sertissure [sɛʀtisyʀ] *nf* [*pierre précieuse*] (*procédé*) setting; (*objet*) bezel.
sérum [seʀɔm] *nm* **(a)** (*Physiol*) **~ (sanguin)** (blood) serum; **~ artificiel** *ou* **physiologique** normal *ou* physiological salt solution.
(b) (*Méd*) serum. **~ antidiphtérique/antitétanique/antivenimeux** anti-diphtheric/antitetanus/snakebite serum; (*fig*) **~ de vérité** truth drug.
servage [sɛʀvaʒ] *nm* (*Hist*) serfdom; (*fig*) bondage, thraldom.
servant, e [sɛʀvɑ̃, ɑ̃t] **1** *adj*: **chevalier** *ou* **cavalier ~** escort.
2 *nm* (*Rel*) server; (*Mil*) [*pièce d'artillerie*] server; (*Tennis*) = **serveur.**
3 servante *nf* **(a)** (*domestique*) servant, maidservant.
(b) (*meuble*) dinner wagon, (dining-room) trolley; (*Tech: support*) adjustable support *ou* rest.
serve [sɛʀv(ə)] *V* **serf.**
serveur, -euse [sɛʀvœʀ, øz] **1** *nm* **(a)** [*restaurant*] waiter; [*bar*] barman. **(b)** (*ouvrier*) [*machine*] feeder. **(c)** (*Tennis*) server. **(d)** (*Cartes*) dealer. **2 serveuse** *nf* [*restaurant*] waitress; [*bar*] barmaid.
serviabilité [sɛʀvjabilite] *nf* obligingness, willingness to help.
serviable [sɛʀvjabl(ə)] *adj* obliging, willing to help.
service [sɛʀvis] **1** *nm* **(a)** (*travail, fonction*) duty. (*temps de travail*) **le ~** (period of) duty; **un ~ de surveillance/contrôle** surveillance/checking duties; (*Mil*) **~ intérieur** barracks duty; (*Mil*) **~ de jour/semaine** day/week duty; **quel ~ fait-il cette semaine?** what duty is he on this week?; **on ne fume pas pendant le ~** smoking is not allowed during duty hours; **être à cheval sur le ~** to be strict about the rules at work; **heures de ~** hours of duty; **il est très ~(-)~*** he's very hot *ou* keen on the rules and regulations* *ou* on doing the job properly*; **prendre son ~** to come on duty; **être de ~** to be on duty; **pompier/médecin de ~** duty fireman/doctor, fireman/doctor on duty; (*Admin, Mil*) **en ~ commandé** on an official assignment; **avoir 25 ans de ~** to have completed 25 years' service; *V* **note, règlement.**
(b) (*gén pl: prestation*) service. (*Écon*) **~s** services; **offrir ses ~s à qn** to offer sb one's services; **offre de ~** offer of service; **s'assurer les ~s de qn** to enlist sb's services; (*Écon*) **biens et ~s** goods and services.
(c) (*domesticité*) (domestic) service. **entrer/être en ~ chez qn** to go into/be in sb's service, go into/be in service with sb; **être au ~ de** *maître, Dieu* to be in the service of; **se mettre au ~ de** *maître* to enter the service of *ou* go into service with; *Dieu, nation, état* to place o.s. in the service of; **10 ans de ~ chez le même maître** 10 years in service with the same master; **escalier de ~** service *ou* servants' stairs; **entrée de ~** service *ou* tradesman's entrance.
(d) (*Mil*) **le ~ (militaire)** military *ou* national service; **le ~ civil pour les objecteurs de conscience** non-military national service for conscientious objectors; **bon pour le ~** fit for military service; **faire son ~** to do one's military *ou* national service; **~ armé** combatant service; *V* **état.**
(e) (*fonction, organisation d'intérêt public*) service; (*section, département*) department, section. **le ~ hospitalier/de la poste** the hospital/postal service; **les ~s de santé/postaux** health (care)/postal services; **~ du contentieux/des achats/de la publicité** legal/buying/publicity department; **les ~s d'un ministère** the departments of a ministry; **le ~ des urgences** the casualty department; *V* **chef**[1].
(f) (*Rel: office, messe*) service. **~ funèbre** funeral service.
(g) (*faveur, aide*) service. **rendre un petit ~ à qn** to do sb a favour, do sb a small service; **tous les ~s qu'il m'a rendus** all the favours *ou* services he has done me; **rendre ~ à qn** (*aider*) to do sb a good turn; (*s'avérer utile*) to come in useful *ou* handy for sb, be of use to sb; **il aime rendre ~** he likes to do good turns *ou* be helpful; (*fig*) **rendre un mauvais ~ à qn** to do sb a disservice; (*frm*) **qu'y-a-t-il pour votre ~?** how can I be of service to you? (*frm*); **je suis à votre ~** I am at your service (*frm*).
(h) (*à table, au restaurant*) service; (*pourboire*) service charge; (*série de repas*) sitting. **Jean fera le ~** John will serve (out); **la nourriture est bonne mais le ~ est exécrable** the food is good but the service is shocking; **laisse 10 F pour le ~** leave 10 francs for the service; **ils ont oublié de facturer le ~** they

have forgotten to include the service (charge) on the bill; ~ **compris/non compris** service included/not included, inclusive/exclusive of service; **premier/deuxième** ~ first/second sitting; *V* **libre, self.**

(i) (*assortiment*) *[couverts]* set; *[vaisselle, linge de table]* service, set. ~ **de table** set of table linen; ~ **à thé** tea set *ou* service; ~ **à liqueurs** set of liqueur glasses; ~ **à poisson** (*plats*) set of fish plates; (*couverts*) fish service; ~ **à fondue/asperges** fondue/asparagus set; ~ **à gâteaux** cake cutlery *ou* set; ~ **à fromage** set of cheese dishes; ~ **de 12 couteaux** set of 12 knives; **un beau** ~ **de Limoges** a beautiful service of Limoges china.

(j) *[machine, installation]* operation, working. **faire le** ~ **d'une pièce d'artillerie** to operate *ou* work a piece of artillery.

(k) (*fonctionnement, usage*) **mettre en** ~ *installation, usine* to put *ou* bring into service; **hors de** ~ out of order *ou* commission (*hum*); **machine/vêtement qui fait un long** ~ machine/garment which gives long service.

(l) (*transport*) service. **un** ~ **d'autocars dessert ces localités** there is a coach service to these districts; **assurer le** ~ **entre** to provide a service between; ~ **d'hiver/d'été** winter/summer service.

(m) (*Tennis*) service. **faire le** ~ to serve; **être au** ~ to have the service; **il a un excellent** ~ he has an excellent service *ou* serve*.

2: service après-vente after-sales service; **service d'ordre** (*policiers*) police contingent; (*manifestants*) team of stewards (responsible for crowd control *etc*); **pour assurer le service d'ordre** to maintain (good) order; **un important service d'ordre assurait le bon déroulement de la manifestation** a large police contingent ensured that the demonstration passed off smoothly; **service de presse** (*distribution*) distribution of review copies; (*ouvrage*) review copy; (*agence*) press relations department; **services secrets** secret service.

serviette [sɛʀvjɛt] **1** *nf* **(a)** (*en tissu*) ~ **(de toilette)** (hand) towel; ~ **(de table)** serviette, (table) napkin; *V* **rond.**

(b) (*cartable*) *[écolier, homme d'affaires]* briefcase.

2: serviette de bain bath towel; **serviette-éponge** *nf, pl* **serviettes-éponges** terry towel; **serviette hygiénique** *ou* **périodique** sanitary towel; **serviette en papier** paper serviette, paper (table) napkin.

servile [sɛʀvil] *adj* **(a)** (*soumis*) *homme, flatterie, obéissance* servile, cringing; *traduction, imitation* slavish. **(b)** (*littér: de serf*) *condition, travail* servile.

servilement [sɛʀvilmɑ̃] *adv* (*V* **servile**) servilely; cringingly; slavishly.

servilité [sɛʀvilite] *nf* (*V* **servile**) servility; slavishness.

servir [sɛʀviʀ] (14) **1** *vt* **(a)** (*être au service de*) *pays, Dieu, état, cause* to serve; (*emploi absolu: être soldat*) to serve. (*Rel*) ~ **le prêtre** to serve the priest; (*Rel*) ~ **la messe** to serve Mass.

(b) *[domestique] patron* to serve, wait on. **il sert comme chauffeur** he serves as a chauffeur; **elle aime se faire** ~ she likes to be waited on.

(c) (*aider*) *personne* to be of service to, aid. ~ **les ambitions/les intérêts de qn** to serve *ou* aid sb's ambitions/interests; **ceci nous sert** this serves our interests; **sa prudence l'a servi auprès des autorités** his caution served him well *ou* stood him in good stead in his dealings with the authorities; **il a été servi par les circonstances** he was aided by circumstances; **il a été servi par une bonne mémoire** he was well served *ou* aided by a good memory.

(d) (*dans un magasin*) *client* to serve, attend to; (*au restaurant*) *consommateur* to serve; *dîneur* to wait on; (*chez soi, à table*) to serve. **ce boucher nous sert depuis des années** this butcher has supplied us for years, we've been going to this butcher for years; **le boucher m'a bien servi** the butcher has given me good meat; **on vous sert, Madame?** are you being attended to? *ou* served?; ~ **qn d'un plat** to serve sb with a dish, serve a dish to sb; **il a faim, servez-le bien** he is hungry so give him a good helping; **prenez, n'attendez pas qu'on vous serve** help yourself — don't wait to be served; **'Madame est servie'** 'dinner is served'; **pour vous** ~† at your service; **des garçons en livrée servaient** waiters in livery waited *ou* served at table; **il sert dans un café** he is a waiter in a café; (*fig*) **les paysans voulaient la pluie, ils ont été servis!** the farmers wanted rain — now their wish has been granted! *ou* well, they've got what they wanted!; (*fig*) **en fait d'ennuis, elle a été servie** as regards troubles, she's had her share (and more); *V* **on.**

(e) (*Mil*) *pièce d'artillerie* to serve.

(f) (*donner*) *rafraîchissement, plat* to serve. ~ **qch à qn** to serve sb with sth, help sb to sth; ~ **le déjeuner/dîner** to serve (up) lunch/dinner; **le vin rouge doit se** ~ **chambré** red wine must be served at room temperature; **'~ frais'** 'serve cool'; ~ **à déjeuner/dîner** to serve lunch/dinner (*à qn* to sb); ~ **à boire** to serve a drink *ou* drinks; ~ **à boire à qn** to serve a drink to sb; **on nous a servi le petit déjeuner au lit** we were served (our) breakfast in bed; **à table, c'est servi!** come and sit down now, it's ready!; (*fig*) **il nous sert toujours les mêmes plaisanteries** he always trots out the same old jokes.

(g) (*procurer*) to pay. ~ **une rente/une pension/des intérêts à qn** to pay sb an income/a pension/interest.

(h) (*Cartes*) to deal.

(i) (*Tennis*) to serve. **à vous de** ~ your service, it's your turn to serve.

(j) (*être utile*) ~ **à** *personne* to be of use *ou* help to; *usage, opération* to be of use in, be useful for; ~ **à faire** to be used for doing; **ça m'a servi à réparer ce meuble** I used it to mend this piece of furniture; **cela ne sert à rien** *[objet]* this is no use, this is useless; *[démarche]* there is no point in it, it serves no (useful) purpose; **cela ne sert à rien de pleurer/réclamer** it's no use crying/complaining, crying/complaining doesn't help; **à quoi sert cet objet?** what is this object used for?; **à quoi servirait de réclamer?** what use would complaining be?, what would be the point of complaining?; **est-ce que cela pourrait vous** ~? could this be (of) any use to you?; **vos conseils lui ont bien servi** your advice has been very useful *ou* helpful to him; **ne jette pas cette boîte, cela peut toujours** ~ don't throw that box away — it may still come in handy *ou* still be of some use; **ces projecteurs servent à guider les avions** these floodlights are used to guide *ou* for guiding the planes; **cet instrument sert à beaucoup de choses** this implement has many uses *ou* is used for many things; **cela a servi à nous faire comprendre les difficultés** this served to make us understand the difficulties; *V* **rien.**

(k) ~ **de** *[personne]* to act as; *[ustensile, objet]* to serve as; **elle lui a servi d'interprète/de témoin** she acted as his interpreter/as a witness (for him); **cette pièce sert de chambre d'amis** this room serves as *ou* is used as a guest room; **cela pourrait te** ~ **de table** you could use that as a table, that would serve as a table for you; ~ **de leçon à qn** to be a lesson to sb; ~ **d'exemple à qn** to serve as an example to sb.

2 se servir *vpr* **(a)** (*à table, dans une distribution*) to help o.s. (*chez un fournisseur*) **se** ~ **chez X** to buy *ou* shop at X's; **se** ~ **en viande chez X** to buy one's meat at X's *ou* from X, go to X's for one's meat; **servez-vous donc de viande** do help yourself to meat; (*iro*) **je t'en prie, sers-toi** go ahead, help yourself.

(b) se ~ **de** *outil, mot, main-d'œuvre* to use; *personne* to use, make use of; **il sait bien se** ~ **de cet outil** he knows how to use this tool; **t'es-tu servi de ce vêtement?** have you used this garment?; **il se sert de sa voiture pour aller au bureau** he uses his car to go to the office; **se** ~ **de ses relations** to make use of *ou* use one's acquaintances.

serviteur [sɛʀvitœʀ] *nm* (*gén*) servant. (*hum*) **en ce qui concerne votre** ~ ... as far as yours truly is concerned ... (*hum*).

servitude [sɛʀvityd] *nf* **(a)** (*esclavage*) servitude. **(b)** (*gén pl: contrainte*) constraint. **(c)** (*Jur*) easement. ~ **de passage** right of way.

servocommande [sɛʀvɔkɔmɑ̃d] *nf* (*Tech*) servo-mechanism.

servofrein [sɛʀvɔfʀɛ̃] *nm* (*Tech*) servo(-assisted) brake.

servomécanisme [sɛʀvɔmekanism(ə)] *nm* (*Tech*) servo system.

servomoteur [sɛʀvɔmɔtœʀ] *nm* (*Tech*) servo-motor.

ses [se] *adj poss V* **son**[1].

sésame [sezam] *nm* (*Bot*) sesame. (*fig*) **(S)~-ouvre-toi** open sesame.

sessile [sesil] *adj* (*Bot*) sessile.

session [sesjɔ̃] *nf* (*Jur, Parl*) session. (*Univ*) ~ **(d'examen)** university exam session; **la** ~ **de juin** the June exams; **la** ~ **de septembre, la seconde** ~ the (September) resits (*Brit*).

sesterce [sɛstɛʀs(ə)] *nm* (*Hist*) sesterce, sestertius; (*mille unités*) sestertium.

set [sɛt] *nm* (*Tennis*) set; *V* **balle**[1].

sétacé, e [setase] *adj* setaceous.

setter [setɛʀ] *nm* setter.

seuil [sœj] *nm* **(a)** *[porte]* (*dalle etc*) door sill, doorstep; (*entrée*) doorway, threshold†; (*fig*) threshold. **se tenir sur le** ~ **de sa maison** to stand in the doorway of one's house; **il m'a reçu sur le** ~ he kept me on the doorstep *ou* at the door, he didn't ask me in; **avoir la campagne au** ~ **de sa maison** to have the country on one's doorstep; (*fig: début*) **le** ~ **de** *période* the threshold of; (*fig*) **au** ~ **de la mort** on the threshold of death, on the brink of the grave; (*fig*) **le** ~ **du désert** the edge of the desert.

(b) (*Géog, Tech*) sill.

(c) (*fig: limite*) threshold; (*Psych*) threshold, limen (*T*). ~ **auditif** auditory threshold; ~ **de rentabilité** break-even point.

seul, e [sœl] **1** *adj* **(a)** (*après n ou attrib*) *personne* (*sans compagnie, non accompagnée*) alone (*attrib*), on one's own (*attrib*), by oneself (*attrib*); (*isolé*) lonely; *objet, mot* alone (*attrib*), on its own (*attrib*), by itself (*attrib*). **être/rester** ~ to be/remain alone *ou* on one's own *ou* by oelf; **laissez-moi** ~ **quelques instants** leave me alone *ou* on my own *ou* by myself for a moment; ~ **avec qn/ses pensées/son chagrin** alone with sb/one's thoughts/one's grief; **ils se retrouvèrent enfin** ~**s** they were alone (together) *ou* on their own *ou* by themselves at last; **un homme** ~**/une femme** ~**e peut très bien se débrouiller** a man on his own/a woman on her own *ou* a single man/woman can manage perfectly well; **au bal, il y avait beaucoup d'hommes** ~**s** at the dance there were many men on their own; **salon pour dames** ~**es** lounge for unaccompanied ladies; **se sentir (très)** ~ to feel (very) lonely *ou* lonesome; ~ **au monde** alone in the world; **mot employé** ~ word used alone *ou* on its own *ou* by itself; **la lampe** ~**e ne suffit pas** the lamp alone *ou* on its own is not enough, the lamp is not enough on its own *ou* by itself; *V* **cavalier.**

(b) (*avant n: unique*) **un** ~ **homme/livre** (*et non plusieurs*) one man/book, a single man/book; (*à l'exception de tout autre*) only one man/book; **le** ~ **homme/livre** the one man/book, the only man/book, the sole man/book; **les** ~**es personnes/conditions** the only people/conditions; **un** ~ **livre suffit** one book *ou* a single book will do; **un** ~ **homme peut vous aider: Paul** only one man can help you — Paul; **pour cette** ~**e raison** for this reason alone *ou* only, for this one reason; **son** ~ **souci est de** ... his only *ou* sole *ou* one concern is to ...; **un** ~ **moment d'inattention** one *ou* a single moment's lapse of concentration; **il n'y a qu'un** ~ **Dieu** there is only one God, there is one God only *ou* alone; **une** ~**e fois** only once, once only.

(c) (*en apposition*) only, alone. ~ **le résultat compte** the result alone counts, only the result counts; ~**s les parents sont admis** only parents are admitted; ~**e Gabrielle peut le faire** only Gabrielle *ou* Gabrielle alone can do it; ~**e l'imprudence peut être la cause de cet accident** only carelessness can be the cause of this accident; **lui ~ est venu en voiture** he alone *ou* only he came by car; **à eux ~s, ils ont fait plus de dégâts que ...** they did more damage by themselves *ou* on their own than ...; **je l'ai fait à moi (tout) ~** I did it (all) on my own *ou* (all) by myself, I did it single-handed.

(d) (*loc*) **~ et unique** one and only; **c'est la ~e et même personne** it's one and the same person; **~ de son espèce** alone of its kind, the only one of its kind; **d'un ~ coup** (*subitement*) suddenly; (*ensemble, à la fois*) in *ou* at one blow; **d'un ~ tenant** *terrain* all in one piece, lying together; **vous êtes ~ juge** you alone are the judge *ou* can judge; **à ~e fin de** with the sole purpose of; **dans la ~e intention de** with the one *ou* sole intention of; **du ~ fait que ...** by the very fact that ...; **à la ~e pensée de ...** at the mere thought of ...; **la ~e pensée d'y retourner la remplissait de frayeur** the mere thought *ou* the thought alone of going back there filled her with fear; **parler à qn ~ à ~** to speak to sb in private *ou* privately *ou* alone; **se retrouver ~ à ~ avec qn** to find o.s. alone with sb; (*fig*) **comme un ~ homme** as one man.

2 *adv* **(a)** (*sans compagnie*) **parler/rire ~** to talk/laugh to oneself; **rire tout ~** to have a quiet laugh to oneself; **vivre/travailler ~** to live/work alone *ou* by oneself *ou* on one's own.

(b) (*sans aide*) by oneself, on one's own, unaided. **faire qch (tout) ~** to do sth (all) by oneself *ou* (all) on one's own, do sth unaided *ou* single-handed; *V* **tout**.

3 *nm,f*: **un ~ peut le faire** (*et non plusieurs*) one man can do it, a single man can do it; (*à l'exception de tout autre*) only one man can do it; **un ~ contre tous** one (man) against all; **le ~ que j'aime** the only one I love; **vous n'êtes pas la ~e à vous plaindre** you aren't the only one to complain, you aren't alone in complaining; **une ~e de ses peintures n'a pas été détruite dans l'incendie** only one of his paintings was not destroyed in the fire; **il n'en reste pas un ~** there isn't a single *ou* solitary one left.

seulement [sœlmɑ̃] *adv* **(a)** (*quantité: pas davantage*) only. **5 personnes ~ sont venues** only 5 people came; **nous serons ~ 4** there will be only 4 of us; **je pars pour 2 jours ~** I am going away for 2 days only, I'm only going away for 2 days.

(b) (*exclusivement*) only, alone, solely. **on ne vit pas ~ de pain** you can't live on bread alone *ou* only *ou* solely on bread; **ce n'est pas ~ sa maladie qui le déprime** it's not only *ou* just his illness that depresses him; **50 F, c'est ~ le prix de la chambre** 50 francs is the price for just the room *ou* is the price for the room only; **on leur permet de lire ~ le soir** they are allowed to read only at night *ou* at night only; **il fait cela ~ pour nous ennuyer** he does that only *ou* solely to annoy us, he only does that to annoy us.

(c) (*temps: pas avant*) only. **il vient ~ d'entrer** he's only just (now) come in; **ce fut ~ vers 10 heures qu'il arriva** it was not until about 10 o'clock that he arrived; **il est parti ~ ce matin** he left only this morning, he only left this morning.

(d) (*en tête de proposition: mais, toutefois*) only, but. **je connais un bon chirurgien, ~ il est cher** I know a good surgeon only *ou* but he is expensive.

(e) (*loc*) **non ~ il a plu, mais (encore) il a fait froid** it didn't only rain but it was cold too, it not only rained but it was also cold; **pas ~** (*même pas*): **on ne nous a pas ~ donné un verre d'eau** we were not even given a glass of water, we were not given so much as a glass of water; **il n'a pas ~ de quoi se payer un costume** he hasn't even enough to buy himself a suit; **il est parti sans ~ nous prévenir** he left without so much as *ou* without even warning us; **si ~** if only; *V* **si**[1].

seulet, -ette* [sœlɛ, ɛt] *adj* (*hum*) lonesome, lonely, all alone. **se sentir bien ~** to feel all alone *ou* very lonesome.

sève [sɛv] *nf* [*arbre*] sap; (*fig*) sap, life, vigour. **~ ascendante** *ou* **brute/descendante** *ou* **élaborée** rising *ou* crude/falling *ou* elaborated sap; **les arbres sont en pleine ~** the sap has risen in the trees; **la jeunesse est débordante de ~** young people are brimming with strength and vigour.

sévère [sevɛʀ] *adj* **(a)** *maître, juge, climat, règlement* severe, harsh; *parent, éducation* strict, severe, stern; *regard, ton* severe, stern; *critique, jugement* severe. **une morale ~** a stern *ou* severe code of morals.

(b) *style, architecture* severe; *tenue* severe, stern. **une beauté ~** a severe beauty.

(c) (*intensif*) *pertes, échec* severe, grave.

sévèrement [sevɛʀmɑ̃] *adv* (*V* **sévère**) severely; harshly; strictly; sternly. **un malade ~ atteint** a severely affected patient.

sévérité [seveʀite] *nf* (*V* **sévère**) severity; harshness; strictness; sternness; gravity.

sévices [sevis] *nmpl* (physical) cruelty (*U*), ill treatment (*U*). **exercer des ~ sur son enfant** to ill-treat one's child.

Séville [sevil] *n* Seville.

sévir [seviʀ] (2) *vi* **(a)** (*punir*) to act ruthlessly. **~ contre** *personne, abus, pratique* to deal ruthlessly with; **si vous continuez, je vais devoir ~** if you carry on, I shall have to deal severely with you *ou* use harsh measures.

(b) (*exercer ses ravages*) [*fléau, épidémie*] to rage, hold sway; (*iro*) [*doctrine, régime*] to rage, hold sway; [*orchestre, mode*] to cause misery. **la pauvreté sévissait** poverty was rampant *ou* rife.

sevrage [səvʀaʒ] *nm* (*V* **sevrer**) weaning; severing, sevrance.

sevrer [səvʀe] (5) *vt* **(a)** *nourrisson, jeune animal* to wean. **(b)** (*Horticulture*) to sever. **(c)** (*fig*) **~ qn de qch** to deprive sb of sth; **nous avons été sevrés de théâtre** we have been deprived of visits to the theatre.

sexagénaire [sɛgzaʒenɛʀ] *adj, nmf* sexagenarian.

sexagésimal, e, *mpl* **-aux** [sɛgzaʒezimal, o] *adj* sexagesimal.

sexagésime [sɛgzaʒezim] *nf* (*Rel*) Sexagesima (Sunday).

sex-appeal [sɛksapil] *nm* sex appeal.

sexe [sɛks(ə)] *nm* **(a)** (*catégorie*) sex. **enfant du ~ masculin/féminin** child of male/female sex, male/female child; **le ~ faible/fort** the weaker/stronger sex; **le (beau) ~** the fair sex.

(b) (*sexualité*) sex. **ce journal ne s'occupe que de ~** this paper is full of nothing but sex.

(c) (*organes génitaux*) genitals, sex organs; *V* **cacher**.

sexologie [sɛksɔlɔʒi] *nf* sexology.

sexologue [sɛksɔlɔg] *nmf* sexologist, sex specialist.

sextant [sɛkstɑ̃] *nm* (*instrument*) sextant; (*Math: arc*) sextant arc.

sextuor [sɛkstɥɔʀ] *nm* (*Mus*) sextet(te).

sextuple [sɛkstypl(ə)] **1** *adj* sixfold. **2** *nm*: **12 est le ~ de 2** 12 is six times 2; **ils en ont reçu le ~** they have had a sixfold return.

sextupler [sɛkstyple] (1) *vti* to increase six times *ou* sixfold.

sexualiser [sɛksɥalize] (1) *vt* to sexualize.

sexualité [sɛksɥalite] *nf* sexuality. **troubles de la ~** sexual problems.

sexué, e [sɛksɥe] *adj* *mammifères, plantes* sexed, sexual; *reproduction* sexual.

sexuel, -elle [sɛksɥɛl] *adj* *caractère, instinct, plaisir* sexual; *éducation, hormone, organe* sexual, sex (*épith*). **l'acte ~** the sex act; *V* **obsédé**.

sexuellement [sɛksɥɛlmɑ̃] *adv* sexually.

sexy* [sɛksi] *adj inv* sexy*.

seyant, e [sɛjɑ̃, ɑ̃t] *adj* *vêtement* becoming.

shah [ʃa] *nm* shah.

shake-hand [ʃɛkɑ̃d] *nm inv* (†, *hum*) handshake.

shakespearien, -ienne [ʃɛkspiʀjɛ̃, jɛn] *adj* Shakespearian.

shako [ʃako] *nm* shako.

shampooing [ʃɑ̃pwɛ̃] *nm* shampoo. **faire un ~ à qn** to give sb a shampoo, shampoo *ou* wash sb's hair; **~ colorant** rinse.

shérif [ʃeʀif] *nm* sheriff.

sherpa [ʃɛʀpa] *nmf* Sherpa.

sherry [ʃeʀi] *nm* sherry.

shimmy [ʃimi] *nm* (*Aut*) shimmy.

shintô [ʃɛ̃to] *nm*, **shintoïsme** [ʃɛ̃tɔism(ə)] *nm* Shinto, Shintoism.

shoot [ʃut] *nm* (*Ftbl*) shot.

shooter [ʃute] (1) **1** *vi* (*Ftbl*) to shoot, make a shot. **2** *vt*: **~ un penalty** to take a penalty (kick *ou* shot). **3 se shooter** *vpr* (*arg Drogue*) to fix (*arg*), shoot (up) (*arg*).

shopping [ʃɔpiŋ] *nm* shopping. **faire du ~** to go shopping.

short [ʃɔʀt] *nm*: **~(s)** pair of shorts, shorts (*pl*); **être en ~(s)** to be in shorts *ou* wearing shorts.

si[1] [si] **1** *conj* **(a)** (*éventualité, condition*) if. **s'il fait beau demain (et ~ j'en ai *ou* et que j'en aie le temps), je sortirai** if it is fine tomorrow (and (if) I have time), I will go out.

(b) (*hypothèse*) if. **~ j'avais de l'argent, j'achèterais une voiture** if I had any money *ou* had I any money I would buy a car; **même s'il s'excusait, je ne lui pardonnerais pas** even if he were to apologize, I should not forgive him; **~ nous n'avions pas été prévenus (et ~ nous avions attendu *ou* et que nous eussions attendu), nous serions arrivés *ou* nous arrivions trop tard** if we hadn't been warned (and (if) we had waited), we should have arrived too late; **il a déclaré que ~ on ne l'augmentait pas, il partirait *ou* il partait** he said that if he didn't get a rise he would leave *ou* he was leaving; *V* **comme**.

(c) (*répétition: toutes les fois que*) if, when. **s'il faisait beau, il allait se promener** if *ou* when it was nice, he used to go *ou* he would go for a walk; **~ je sors sans parapluie, il pleut** if *ou* whenever I go out without an umbrella, it always rains.

(d) (*opposition*) while, whilst (*surtout Brit*). **~ lui est aimable, sa femme (par contre) est arrogante** while *ou* whereas he is very pleasant, his wife (on the other hand) is arrogant.

(e) (*exposant un fait*) **s'il ne joue plus, c'est qu'il s'est cassé la jambe** if he doesn't play any more it's because he has broken his leg, the reason he no longer plays is that he has broken his leg; **c'est un miracle ~ la voiture n'a pas pris feu** it's a miracle (that) the car didn't catch fire; **excusez-nous *ou* pardonnez-nous ~ nous n'avons pas pu venir** please excuse *ou* forgive us for not being able to come.

(f) (*dans une interrogation indirecte*) if, whether. **il ignore/demande ~ elle viendra** he doesn't know/is asking whether *ou* if she will come; **il faut s'assurer ~ la voiture marche** we must make sure that *ou* if *ou* whether the car is working; **vous imaginez s'ils étaient fiers!** you can imagine how proud they were!; **~ je veux y aller! quelle question!** do I want to go! what a question!

(g) (*en corrélation avec proposition implicite*) if. **~ j'avais su!** if I had only known!, had I only *ou* but known!; **~ je le tenais!** if I could (only) lay my hands on him!; **et s'il refusait?** and what if he refused?, and what if he should refuse?, and supposing he refused?; **~ tu lui téléphonais?** how *ou* what about phoning him?, supposing you phoned him?; **~ nous allions nous promener?** what *ou* how about going for a walk?, what do you say to a walk?

(h) **~ ce n'est**: **qui peut le savoir, ~ ce n'est lui?** who will know if not him? *ou* apart from him?; **~ ce n'est elle, qui aurait osé?** who but her would have dared?; **~ ce n'était la crainte de les décourager** if it were not *ou* were it not for the fear of putting them off; **il n'avait rien emporté, ~ ce n'est quelques biscuits et une pomme** he had taken nothing with him apart from *ou* other than a few biscuits and an apple; **une des plus belles, ~ ce n'est la plus belle** one of the most beautiful, if not the most beautiful; **elle se porte bien, ~ ce n'est qu'elle est très fatiguée** she's quite well apart from the fact that she is very tired *ou* apart from feeling very tired.

(i) (*loc*) **~ tant est que** so long as, provided that, if ... (that is); **invite-les tous, ~ tant est que nous ayons assez de verres** invite them all, so long as we have enough glasses *ou* if we have enough glasses (that is); **s'il te** *ou* **vous plaît** please; ~ **je ne me trompe** *ou (frm, iro)* **ne m'abuse** if I am not mistaken *ou* under a misapprehension *(frm)*, unless I'm mistaken; *(frm, hum)* ~ **j'ose dire** if I may say so; *(frm)* ~ **je puis dire** if I may put it like that; ~ **l'on peut dire** so to speak; ~ **on veut**, ~ **l'on veut** as it were; ~ **j'ai bien compris/entendu** if I understood correctly/heard properly; ~ **seulement il venait/était venu** if only he was coming/had come; **brave homme s'il en fut** a fine man if ever there was one; ~ **c'est ça*, je m'en vais** if that's how it is, I'm off*.

2 *nm inv* if. **avec des ~ et des mais, on mettrait Paris dans une bouteille** if ifs and ands were pots and pans there'd be no need for tinkers.

si[2] [si] *adv* **(a)** *(affirmatif)* **vous ne venez pas? — ~/mais ~/que ~** aren't you coming? — yes I am/of course I am/indeed I am *ou* I certainly am; **vous n'avez rien mangé? — ~, une pomme** haven't you had anything to eat? — yes (I have), an apple; **~, ~, il faut venir** oh but you must come!; **il n'a pas voulu, moi ~** he didn't want to, but I did; **répondre que ~** to reply that one would *(ou* did, was *etc)*; **il n'a pas écrit? — il semble bien** *ou* **il paraît que ~** hasn't he written? — yes, it seems that he has (done); **~ fait**† indeed yes.

(b) *(intensif: tellement) (modifiant attrib, adv)* so. *(modifiant épith)* **un ami ~ gentil** such a kind friend, so kind a friend *(frm)*; **des amis ~ gentils, de ~ gentils amis** such kind friends; **il parle ~ bas qu'on ne l'entend pas** he speaks so low *ou* in such a low voice that you can't hear him; **j'ai ~ faim** I'm so hungry; **elle n'est pas ~ stupide qu'elle ne puisse comprendre ceci** she's not so stupid that she can't understand this; **je pensais qu'il ne viendrait pas, mais quand je lui en ai parlé il m'a répondu que ~** I thought he wouldn't come but when I mentioned it to him he told me he would; **je croyais qu'elle ne voulait pas venir, mais il m'a dit que ~** I thought she didn't want to come but he said she did.

(c) ~ bien que so that; *V* **tant**.

(d) *(concessif: aussi)* however. **~ bête soit-il** *ou* **qu'il soit, il comprendra** (as) stupid as he is *ou* however stupid he is he will understand; **~ rapidement qu'il progresse** however fast he's making progress, as fast as his progress is; **~ adroitement qu'il ait parlé, il n'a convaincu personne** for all that he spoke very cleverly *ou* however cleverly he may have spoken he didn't convince anyone; **~ beau qu'il fasse, il ne peut encore sortir** however good the weather is he cannot go out yet; **~ peu que ce soit** however little it may be, little as *ou* though it may be *(frm)*.

(e) *(égalité: aussi)* as, so. **elle n'est pas ~ timide que vous croyez** she's not so *ou* as shy as you think; **il ne travaille pas ~ lentement qu'il en a l'air** he doesn't work as slowly as he seems to.

si[3] [si] *nm inv (Mus)* B; *(en chantant la gamme)* si.

Siam [sjam] *nm* Siam.

siamois, e [sjamwa, waz] **1** *adj (Géog*†*), chat* Siamese. **frères/sœurs ~(es)** (boy/girl) Siamese twins. **2** *nm,f* **(a)** *(Géog* †*)* **S~(e)** Siamese. **(b)** *(pl: jumeaux)* Siamese twins. **3** *nm (chat)* Siamese.

Sibérie [sibeʀi] *nf* Siberia.

sibérien, -enne [sibeʀjɛ̃, ɛn] *adj (Géog, fig)* Siberian.

sibilant, e [sibilɑ̃, ɑ̃t] *adj (Méd)* sibilant.

sibylle [sibil] *nf* sibyl.

sibyllin, e [sibilɛ̃, in] *adj (Myth, fig)* sibylline.

sic [sik] *adv* sic.

siccatif, -ive [sikatif, iv] *adj, nm* siccative.

Sicile [sisil] *nf* Sicily.

sicilien, -enne [sisiljɛ̃, ɛn] **1** *adj* Sicilian. **2** *nm* **(a) S~** Sicilian. **(b)** *(dialecte)* Sicilian. **3 sicilienne** *nf* **(a) S~ne** Sicilian. **(b)** *(danse)* Siciliano, Sicilienne.

side-car, *pl* **side-cars** [sidkaʀ] *nm (habitacle)* sidecar; *(véhicule entier)* (motorcycle) combination.

sidéral, e, *mpl* **-aux** [sideʀal, o] *adj* sidereal.

sidérant, e* [sideʀɑ̃, ɑ̃t] *adj* staggering*, shattering*.

sidérer* [sideʀe] (6) *vt* to stagger*, shatter*.

sidérurgie [sideʀyʀʒi] *nf (fabrication)* iron and steel metallurgy; *(industrie)* iron and steel industry.

sidérurgique [sideʀyʀʒik] *adj procédé* (iron and) steel-making *(épith)*; *industrie* iron and steel *(épith)*.

sidérurgiste [sideʀyʀʒist(ə)] *nmf* (iron and) steel maker.

sidi [sidi] *nm (péj)* wog**:** *(péj) North African immigrant (resident in France)*.

siècle[1] [sjɛkl(ə)] *nm (période de cent ans, date)* century; *(époque, âge)* age, century. **au 3e ~ avant Jésus-Christ/après Jésus-Christ** *ou* **de notre ère** in the 3rd century B.C./A.D.; **être de son ~/d'un autre ~** to belong to one's age/to another age; **de ~ en ~** from age to age, through the ages; **le ~ de Périclès/d'Auguste** the age of Pericles/Augustus; **le S~ des lumières** (the Age of) the Enlightenment; **il y a un ~** *ou* **des ~s que nous ne nous sommes vus*** it has been *ou* it is years *ou* ages since we last saw each other; **cet arbre a/ces ruines ont des ~s** this tree is/these ruins are centuries old; *V* **consommation, grand, mal**.

siècle[2] [sjɛkl(ə)] *nm (Rel)* world. **les plaisirs du ~** worldly pleasures, the pleasures of the world.

siège[1] [sjɛʒ] *nm* **(a)** *(meuble, de W.-C.)* seat. **~ de jardin/de bureau** garden/office chair; **prenez un ~** take a seat; **Dupont, le spécialiste du ~ de bureau** Dupont, the specialist in office seating; *(Aut)* **~ avant/arrière** front/back seat; *(Aviat)* **~ éjectable** ejector seat; *(Aut)* **~ baquet** bucket seat.

(b) *(frm, Méd: postérieur)* seat; *V* **bain**.

(c) *(Pol: fonction)* seat.

(d) *(Jur) [magistrat]* bench; *V* **magistrature**.

(e) *(résidence principale) [firme]* head office; *[parti, organisation internationale]* headquarters; *[tribunal, assemblée]* seat. **~ social** registered office; **~ épiscopal/pontifical** episcopal/pontifical see; **cette organisation, dont le ~ est à Genève** this Geneva-based organization, this organization which is based in Geneva *ou* which has its headquarters in Geneva; *V* **saint**.

(f) *(fig: centre) [maladie, passions, rébellion]* seat; *(Physiol) [faculté, sensation]* centre.

siège[2] [sjɛʒ] *nm [place forte]* siege. **mettre le ~ devant** to besiege; *(lit, fig)* **faire le ~ de** to lay siege to; **lever le ~** *(lit)* to raise the siege; *(fig)* to get up and go; *V* **état**.

siéger [sjeʒe] (3 *et* 6) *vi [députés, tribunal, assemblée]* to sit; *(fig) [maladie]* to be located; *[faculté]* to have its centre; *[passion]* to have its seat. **voilà où siège le mal** that's where the trouble lies, that's the seat of the trouble.

sien, sienne [sjɛ̃, sjɛn] **1** *pron poss*: **le ~, la sienne, les ~s, les siennes** *[homme]* his (own); *[femme]* hers, her own; *[chose, animal]* its own; *[nation]* its own, hers, her own; *(indéf)* one's own; **ce sac/cette robe est le ~/la sienne** this bag/dress is hers, this is HER bag/dress; **il est parti avec une casquette qui n'est pas la sienne** he went away with a cap which isn't his (own); **le voisin est furieux parce que nos fleurs sont plus jolies que les siennes** our neighbour is furious because our flowers are nicer than his (own); **mes enfants sont sortis avec 2 des ~s/les 2 ~s** my children have gone out with 2 of hers/her (own) 2; **cet oiseau préfère les nids des autres au ~** this bird prefers other birds' nests to its own; **je préfère mes ciseaux, les ~s ne coupent pas** I prefer my scissors because hers don't cut; *(emphatique)* **la sienne de voiture est plus rapide*** HIS car is faster, HIS is a faster car; **de tous les pays, on préfère toujours le ~** of all countries one always prefers one's own.

2 *nm* **(a)** *(U)* **les choses s'arrangent depuis qu'il/elle y a mis du ~** things are beginning to sort themselves out since he/she began to pull his/her weight; **chacun doit être prêt à y mettre du ~** everyone must be prepared to pull his weight *ou* to make some effort.

(b) les ~s *(famille)* one's family, one's (own) folks*; *(partisans)* one's own people; **Dieu reconnaît les ~s** God knows his own *ou* his people.

3 *nf*: **il/elle a encore fait des siennes*** he/she has (gone and) done it again*; **le mal de mer commençait à faire des siennes parmi les passagers** seasickness was beginning to claim some victims among the passengers.

4 *adj poss (littér)* **un ~ cousin** a cousin of his *ou* hers; **il fait siennes toutes les opinions de son père** he adopts all his father's opinions.

sieste [sjɛst(ə)] *nf (gén)* nap, snooze*; *(en Espagne etc)* siesta. **faire la ~** to have *ou* take a nap; to have a siesta.

sieur [sjœʀ] *nm*: **le ~ X** *(*†† *ou Jur)* Mr X; *(péj hum)* Master X.

sifflant, e [siflɑ̃, ɑ̃t] *adj sonorité* whistling; *toux* wheezing; *prononciation* hissing, whistling. **(consonne) ~e** sibilant.

sifflement [sifləmɑ̃] *nm* **(a)** *(V* **siffler** *: volontaire)* whistling *(U)*; hissing *(U)*. **un ~** a whistle; a hiss; **un ~ d'admiration** a whistle of admiration; **un ~ mélodieux** a melodious whistle; **des ~s se firent entendre** one could hear whistling noises; **j'entendis le ~ aigu/les ~s de la locomotive** I heard the shrill whistle/the whistling of the locomotive.

(b) *(V* **siffler** *: involontaire)* hissing *(U)*; wheezing *(U)*; whistling *(U)*. **des ~s** whistling noises; hissing noises; **~ d'oreilles** whistling in the ears.

siffler [sifle] (1) **1** *vi* **(a)** *(volontairement) [personne]* to whistle; *(avec un sifflet)* to blow one's *ou* a whistle; *[oiseau, train]* to whistle; *[serpent]* to hiss.

(b) *(involontairement) [vapeur, gaz, machine à vapeur]* to hiss; *[voix, respiration]* to wheeze; *[vent]* to whistle; *[projectile]* to whistle, hiss. **la balle/l'obus siffla à ses oreilles** the bullet/shell whistled *ou* hissed past his ears; **il siffle en dormant/parlant** he whistles in his sleep/when he talks; **il siffle en respirant** he wheezes.

2 *vt* **(a)** *(appeler) chien, enfant* to whistle for; *fille* to whistle at; *automobiliste ou joueur en faute* to blow one's whistle at; *(signaler) départ, faute* to blow one's whistle for. *(Ftbl)* **~ la fin du match** to blow the final whistle, blow for time.

(b) *(huer)* **~ un acteur/une pièce** to whistle one's disapproval of an actor/a play, hiss *ou* boo an actor/a play.

(c) *(moduler) air, chanson* to whistle.

(d) *(*: *avaler)* to guzzle*, knock back:.

sifflet [siflɛ] *nm* **(a)** *(instrument, son)* whistle. **~ à roulette** whistle; **~ à vapeur** steam whistle; **~ d'alarme** alarm whistle; *V* **coup**. **(b) ~s** *(huées)* whistles of disapproval, hissing, booing, cat calls. **(c)** *(*: *gorge)* **serrer le ~ à qn** to throttle sb; *V* **couper**.

siffleur, -euse [siflœʀ, øz] **1** *adj merle* whistling; *serpent* hissing. **(canard) ~** widgeon. **2** *nm,f (qui sifflote)* whistler; *(qui hue)* hisser, booer.

siffleux [siflø] *nm (Can*)* groundhog, woodchuck, whistler *(US, Can)*.

sifflotement [siflɔtmɑ̃] *nm* whistling *(U)*.

siffloter [siflɔte] (1) **1** *vi* to whistle (a tune). **~ entre ses dents** to whistle under one's breath. **2** *vt air* to whistle.

sigillé, e [siʒile] *adj* sigillated.

sigle [sigl(ə)] *nm* (set of) initials, abbreviation.

sigma [sigma] *nm* sigma.

signal, *pl* **-aux** [siɲal, o] *nm* **(a)** *(signe convenu; Psych: stimulus)* signal; *(indice)* sign. **donner le ~ de** *(lit)* to give the signal for; *(fig: déclencher)* to be the signal *ou* sign for, signal; **cette émeute fut le ~ d'une véritable révolution** the riot was the signal for the start of *ou* signalled the outbreak of a virtual revolution; **à mon ~ tous se levèrent** when I gave the signal *ou* sign everyone got up; **donner le ~ du départ** *(gén)* to give the signal for departure; *(Sport)* to give the starting signal; **~ de détresse** distress signal.

(b) (*Naut, Rail: écriteau, avertisseur*) signal; (*Aut: écriteau*) (road)sign. (*feux*) **signaux (lumineux)** traffic signals *ou* lights; (*Rail*) ~ **d'alarme** alarm; **tirer le ~ d'alarme** to pull the alarm, pull the communication cord (*Brit*); ~ **sonore** *ou* **acoustique** sound *ou* acoustic signal; ~ **optique/lumineux** visual/light signal; (*Rail*) ~ **avancé** advance signal.

(c) (*Ling, Ordinateurs, Téléc*) signal. ~ **horaire** time signal.

signalé, e [siɲale] (*ptp de* **signaler**) *adj* (*rare, littér*) *service, récompense* signal (*littér*) (*épith*).

signalement [siɲalmɑ̃] *nm [personne, véhicule]* description, particulars.

signaler [siɲale] (1) **1** *vt* **(a)** (*être l'indice de*) to indicate, be a sign of. **ces changements signalent une évolution très nette** these changes are the sign of *ou* indicate a very definite development; **des empreintes qui signalent la présence de qn** footprints indicating sb's presence.

(b) *[sonnerie, écriteau]* to signal; *[personne]* (*faire un signe*) to signal; (*en mettant un écriteau ou une indication*) to indicate. **on signale l'arrivée d'un train au moyen d'une sonnerie** the arrival of a train is signalled by a bell ringing, a bell warns of *ou* signals the arrival of a train; **sur ma carte, ils signalent l'existence d'une source près du village** my map indicates that there's a spring near the village; **signalez que vous allez tourner à droite en tendant le bras droit** indicate *ou* signal that you are turning right by putting out your right arm.

(c) *erreur, détail* to indicate, point out; *fait nouveau, vol, perte* to report. **on signale la présence de l'ennemi** there are reports of the enemy's presence; **on signale l'arrivée du bateau** it has been reported *ou* there have been reports that the boat will arrive shortly; **rien à ~** nothing to report; **~ qn à l'attention de qn** to bring sb to sb's attention; **~ qn à la vindicte publique** to expose sb to public condemnation; **nous vous signalons en outre que ...** we would further point out to you that ... .

2 se signaler *vpr* **(a)** (*s'illustrer*) to distinguish o.s., stand out. **il se signale par sa bravoure** he distinguishes himself by his courage, his courage makes him stand out.

(b) (*attirer l'attention*) to draw attention to o.s. **se ~ à l'attention de qn** to attract sb's attention, bring o.s. to sb's attention.

signalétique [siɲaletik] *adj détail* identifying, descriptive. **fiche ~** identification sheet.

signalisation [siɲalizɑsjɔ̃] *nf* **(a)** (*action: V* **signaliser**) erection of (road)signs (and signals) (*de* on); laying out of runway markings and lights (*de* on); putting signals (*de* on). **erreur de ~** (*Aut*) signposting error; (*Rail*) signalling error; **panneau de ~** roadsign; **moyens de ~** means of signalling.

(b) (*signaux*) signals. **~ routière** roadsigns; **une bonne ~** a good signal system.

signaliser [siɲalize] (1) *vt route, réseau* to put up (road)signs on; *piste* to put runway markings and lights on; *voie* to put signals on. **bien signalisé** with good roadsigns; with good (runway) markings and lights; with good signals.

signataire [siɲatɛʀ] *nmf [traité, paix]* signatory. **les ~s** those signing, the signatories; **pays ~s** signatory countries.

signature [siɲatyʀ] *nf* **(a)** (*action*) signing; (*marque, nom*) signature. (*Comm*) **les fondés de pouvoir ont la ~** the senior executives may sign for the company; **le devoir d'honorer sa ~** the duty to honour one's signature.

(b) (*Typ*) signature (*mark*).

signe [siɲ] **1** *nm* **(a)** (*geste*) (*de la main*) sign, gesture; (*de l'expression*) sign. **s'exprimer par ~s** to use signs to communicate; **langage par ~s** sign language; **échanger des ~s d'intelligence** to exchange knowing looks; **faire un ~ à qn** to make a sign to sb, sign to sb; **un ~ de tête affirmatif/négatif** a nod/a shake of the head; **ils se faisaient des ~s** they were making signs to each other; **un ~ d'adieu/de refus** a sign of farewell/refusal.

(b) (*indice*) sign. **~ précurseur** portent, omen, forewarning; **c'est un ~ de pluie** it's a sign it's going to rain, it's a sign of rain; **c'est ~ qu'il va pleuvoir/qu'il est de retour** it shows *ou* it's a sign that it's going to rain/that he's back; **c'est bon/mauvais ~** it's a good/bad sign; (*lit, fig*) **ne pas donner ~ de vie** to give no sign of life; **c'est un ~ des temps** it's a sign of the times.

(c) (*trait*) mark. **'~s particuliers: néant'** 'special peculiarities: none'.

(d) (*symbole: gén, Ling, Math, Mus*) sign; (*Typ*) *[correcteurs]* mark. **le ~ moins/plus** the minus/plus sign.

(e) (*Astrol*) **~ du zodiaque** sign of the zodiac; **sous quel ~ es-tu né?** what sign were you born under?; (*fig*) **rencontre placée sous le ~ de l'amitié franco-britannique** meeting where the keynote was Franco-British friendship *ou* where the dominant theme was Franco-British friendship; **ministère qui a vécu sous le ~ du mécontentement** a term of office for the government where the dominant mood was one of discontent.

(f) (*loc*) **faire ~ à qn** (*lit*) to make a sign to sb; (*fig: contacter*) to get in touch with sb, contact sb; **faire ~ à qn d'entrer** to make a sign for sb to come in, sign to sb to come in; **il m'a fait ~ de la tête de ne pas bouger** he shook his head to tell me not to move; **faire ~ du doigt à qn** to beckon (to) sb with one's finger; **faire ~ que oui** to nod in agreement, nod that one will (*ou* did *etc*); **faire ~ que non** to shake one's head (in disagreement *ou* dissent); **en ~ de protestation** as a sign *ou* mark of protest; **en ~ de respect** as a sign *ou* mark *ou* token of respect; **en ~ de deuil** as a sign of mourning.

2: signe cabalistique cabalistic sign; **signe de la croix** sign of the cross; **faire le signe de la croix** *ou* **un signe de croix** to make the sign of the cross, cross o.s.; **signes extérieurs de richesse** outward signs of wealth; **signe de ponctuation** punctuation mark; **signe de ralliement** rallying symbol.

signer [siɲe] (1) **1** *vt* **(a)** *document, traité, œuvre d'art* to sign. **signez au bas de la page/en marge** sign at the bottom of the page/in the margin; **~ un chèque en blanc** to sign a blank cheque; **~ son nom** to sign one's name; **~ d'une croix/de son sang/de son vrai nom** to sign with a cross/with one's blood/with one's real name; **tableau non signé** unsigned painting; **cravate/carrosserie signée X** tie/coachwork by X; (*fig*) **c'est signé!*** it's written all over it!*; (*fig*) **c'est signé Louis!*** it has Louis written all over it!*; (*fig*) **il a signé son arrêt de mort** he has signed his own death warrant.

(b) (*Tech*) to hallmark.

2 se signer *vpr* (*Rel*) to cross o.s.

signet [siɲɛ] *nm* (book) marker, bookmark.

signifiant [siɲifjɑ̃] *nm* (*Ling*) signifier, signifiant.

significatif, -ive [siɲifikatif, iv] *adj* **(a)** (*révélateur*) *mot, sourire, geste* significant, revealing. **ces oublis sont ~s de son état d'esprit** his forgetfulness is indicative of his state of mind.

(b) (*expressif*) *symbole* meaningful, significant.

signification [siɲifikɑsjɔ̃] *nf* **(a)** (*sens*) *[fait]* significance (*U*), meaning; *[mot, symbole]* meaning. (*Ling*) **la ~** signification.

(b) (*U: Jur*) *[décision judiciaire]* notification.

signifié [siɲifje] *nm* (*Ling*) signified, signifié.

signifier [siɲifje] (7) *vt* **(a)** (*avoir pour sens*) to mean, signify. **que signifie ce mot/son silence?** what is the meaning of this word/his silence?, what does this word/his silence mean?; (*Sémantique*) **les symboles signifient** symbols convey meaning; **que signifie cette cérémonie?** what is the significance of this ceremony?, what does this ceremony signify?; **ses colères ne signifient rien** his tempers don't mean anything; **bonté ne signifie pas forcément faiblesse** kindness does not necessarily mean *ou* signify *ou* imply weakness *ou* is not necessarily synonymous with weakness; **l'envol des hirondelles signifie que l'automne est proche** the departure of the swallows means *ou* shows that autumn is near *ou* signifies the approach of autumn; **qu'est-ce que cela signifie?** (*indignation*) (*gén*) what's the meaning of this?; (*après remarque hostile*) what's that supposed to mean?

(b) (*frm: faire connaître*) to make known. **~ ses intentions/sa volonté à qn** to make one's intentions/wishes known to sb, inform sb of one's intentions/wishes; (*renvoyer*) **~ son congé à qn** to give sb notice of dismissal, give sb his notice; **son regard me signifiait tout son mépris** his look conveyed to me his utter scorn; **signifiez-lui qu'il doit se rendre à cette convocation** inform him that he is to answer this summons.

(c) (*Jur*) *exploit, décision judiciaire* to serve notice of (*à* on), notify (*à* to).

silence [silɑ̃s] *nm* **(a)** (*absence de bruits, de conversation*) silence. **garder le ~** to keep silent, say nothing; **faire ~** to be silent; **faire qch en ~** to do sth in silence; **il n'arrive pas à faire le ~ dans sa classe** he can't get silence in his class *ou* get his class to be silent; **sortez vos cahiers et en ~!** get out your books and no talking!; **(faites) ~!** silence!, no talking!; (*Ciné*) **~! on tourne** quiet everybody, action!; **il prononça son discours dans un ~ absolu** there was dead silence while he made his speech; *V* **minute, parole.**

(b) (*pause: dans la conversation, un récit*) pause; (*Mus*) rest. **récit entrecoupé de longs ~s** account broken by lengthy pauses; **il y eut un ~ gêné** there was an embarrassed silence; **à son entrée il y eut un ~** there was a hush when he came in.

(c) (*impossibilité ou refus de s'exprimer*) silence. **les journaux gardèrent le ~ sur cette grève** the newspapers kept silent *ou* were silent on this strike; **contraindre l'opposition au ~** to reduce the opposition to silence; **passer qch sous ~** to pass over sth in silence; **souffrir en ~** to suffer in silence; **surprise préparée dans le plus grand ~** surprise prepared in the greatest secrecy; *V* **loi.**

(d) (*paix*) silence, still(ness). **dans le grand ~ de la plaine** in the great silence *ou* stillness of the plain; **vivre dans la solitude et le ~** to live in solitary silence.

silencieusement [silɑ̃sjøzmɑ̃] *adv* (*V* **silencieux**) silently; quietly; noiselessly.

silencieux, -euse [silɑ̃sjø, øz] **1** *adj* **(a)** *mouvement, pas, élèves, auditeurs* silent, quiet; *moteur, machine* quiet, noiseless. **le voyage du retour fut ~** the return journey was quiet *ou* was a silent one; **rester ~** to remain silent.

(b) (*paisible*) *lieu, cloître* silent, still.

(c) (*peu communicatif*) quiet; (*qui ne veut ou ne peut s'exprimer*) silent.

2 *nm [arme à feu]* silencer; *[pot d'échappement]* silencer (*Brit*), muffler (*US*).

silex [silɛks] *nm* flint. (*Archéol*) **des (armes en) ~** flints.

silhouettage [silwɛtaʒ] *nm* (*Phot*) blocking out.

silhouette [silwɛt] *nf* **(a)** (*profil: vu à contre-jour etc*) outline, silhouette; (*lignes, galbe*) outline. **la ~ du château se détache sur le couchant** the outline *ou* silhouette of the château stands out *ou* the château is silhouetted against the sunset; **on le voyait en ~, à contre-jour** he could be seen in outline *ou* silhouetted against the light.

(b) (*allure*) figure. **une ~ un peu masculine** a slightly masculine figure.

(c) (*figure*) figure. **des ~s multicolores parsemaient la neige** the snow was dotted with colourful figures; **~s de tir** figure targets.

silhouetter [silwete] (1) **1** *vt* **(a)** (*Art*) to outline. **l'artiste silhouetta un corps de femme** the artist outlined *ou* drew an outline of a woman's body.

(b) (*Phot*) to block out.

2 se silhouetter *vpr* to be silhouetted. **le clocher se silhouette sur le ciel** the bell tower is silhouetted *ou* outlined against the sky.

silicate [silikat] *nm* silicate.

silice [silis] *nf* silica. **~ fondue** *ou* **vitreuse** silica glass.

siliceux, -euse [silisø, øz] *adj* siliceous, silicious.
silicium [silisjɔm] *nm* silicon.
silicone [silikon] *nf* silicone.
silicose [silikoz] *nf* silicosis.
sillage [sijaʒ] *nm* **(a)** *[embarcation]* wake; *[avion à réaction]* (vapour) trail; *(fig) [personne, animal, parfum]* trail. *(lit, fig)* **dans le ~ de qn** (following) in sb's wake; **aspiré dans son ~** pulled along in his wake. **(b)** *(Phys)* wake.
sillon [sijɔ̃] *nm* **(a)** *[champ]* furrow. *(littér)* **les ~s** the (ploughed) fields; *(fig littér)* **creuser son ~** to plough one's (own) furrow. **(b)** *(fig: ride, rayure)* furrow. **(c)** *(Anat)* fissure. **(d)** *[disque]* groove.
sillonner [sijɔne] (1) *vt* **(a)** *(traverser) [avion, bateau, routes]* to cut across, cross. **les canaux qui sillonnent la Hollande** the canals which cut across *ou* which criss-cross Holland; **région sillonnée de canaux/routes** region which is criss-crossed by canals/roads; **des avions ont sillonné le ciel toute la journée** planes have been droning backwards and forwards *ou* to and fro across the sky all day.
(b) *(creuser) [rides, ravins, crevasses]* to furrow. **visage sillonné de rides** face furrowed with wrinkles; **front sillonné d'une ride profonde** deeply furrowed brow.
silo [silo] *nm* *(Aviat, Mil)* silo. **~ à céréales/fourrages** grain/fodder silo; **mettre en ~** to put in a silo, silo.
silotage [silɔtaʒ] *nm* *(Tech)* ensilage.
silure [silyʀ] *nm* silurid.
simagrée [simagʀe] *nf (gén pl)* fuss *(U)*, playacting *(U)*. **elle a fait beaucoup de ~s avant d'accepter son cadeau** she made a great fuss (about it) *ou* she put on a great show of reluctance before she accepted his present.
simiesque [simjɛsk(ə)] *adj* *(V* **singe***)* monkey-like; ape-like.
similaire [similɛʀ] *adj* similar. **le rouge à lèvres, le fond de teint et produits ~s** lipstick, foundation cream and similar products *ou* products of a similar nature *ou* type.
simili [simili] **1** *préf* imitation *(épith)*, artificial. **~cuir** imitation leather, leatherette. **2** *nm* imitation. **bijoux en ~** imitation *ou* costume jewellery. **3** *nf* (*) *abrév de* **similigravure**.
similigravure [similigʀavyʀ] *nf* half-tone engraving.
similitude [similityd] *nf* **(a)** similarity. **il y a certaines ~s entre ces méthodes** there are certain likenesses *ou* similarities between these methods. **(b)** *(Géom)* similarity.
Simon [simɔ̃] *nm* Simon.
simonie [simɔni] *nf* simony.
simoun [simun] *nm* simoom, simoon.
simple [sɛ̃pl(ə)] **1** *adj* **(a)** *(non composé)* simple; *(non multiple)* single. **billet ~ (course)** single ticket; *V* **aller, partie², passé.**
(b) *(peu complexe)* simple; *(facile)* simple, straightforward. **réduit à sa plus ~ expression** reduced to a minimum; **~ comme bonjour*** *ou* **chou*** easy as falling off a log* *ou* as pie* *ou* as winking*; **dans ce cas, c'est bien ~: je m'en vais** in that case it's quite simple — I'm leaving, in that case I'm quite simply leaving; **ce serait trop ~!** that would be too easy! *ou* too simple!
(c) *(modeste) personne* plain *(épith)*, simple, unaffected; *vie, goûts* simple; *robe, repas, style* simple, plain. **il a su rester ~** he has managed to stay unaffected; **être ~ dans sa mise** to dress simply *ou* plainly; *(hum)* **dans le plus ~ appareil** in one's birthday suit, in the altogether* *(hum)*.
(d) *(naïf)* simple. **~ d'esprit** *(adj)* simple-minded; *(nmf)* simpleton, simple-minded person.
(e) *(valeur restrictive)* simple. **un ~ particulier/salarié** an ordinary citizen/wage earner; **un ~ soldat** a private; **une ~ formalité** a simple formality; **un ~ regard/une ~ remarque la déconcertait** just a *ou* (even) a mere look/comment would upset her; **d'un ~ geste de la main** with a simple movement of his hand; *V* **pur.**
2 *nm* **(a) passer du ~ au double** to double.
(b) *(Bot)* medicinal plant, simple†.
(c) *(Tennis)* singles. **~ messieurs/dames** men's/ladies' singles.
simplement [sɛ̃pləmɑ̃] *adv* **(a)** *(V* **simple***)* simply; straightforwardly; plainly; unaffectedly.
(b) *(seulement)* simply, merely, just. **je veux ~ dire que ...** I simply *ou* merely *ou* just want to say that ... ; **c'est (tout) ~ incroyable que tu ne l'aies pas vue** it's (just) simply incredible that you didn't see her; *V* **purement.**
simplet, -ette [sɛ̃plɛ, ɛt] *adj* **(a)** *personne* simple, ingenuous. **(b)** *raisonnement, question* simplistic, naïve; *roman, intrigue* simple, unsophisticated.
simplicité [sɛ̃plisite] *nf* **(a)** *(V* **simple***)* simplicity; straightforwardness; plainness; unaffectedness. **(b)** *(naïveté)* simpleness.
simplifiable [sɛ̃plifjabl(ə)] *adj* *(gén) méthode* that can be simplified; *(Math) fraction* reducible.
simplificateur, -trice [sɛ̃plifikatœʀ, tʀis] *adj* simplifying *(épith)*.
simplification [sɛ̃plifikɑsjɔ̃] *nf* simplification.
simplifier [sɛ̃plifje] (7) *vt* *(gén, Math)* to simplify. **pour ~ la vie/cette tâche** to simplify one's existence/this job, to make life/this job simpler; **il a le travers de trop ~** he tends to oversimplify.
simplisme [sɛ̃plism(ə)] *nm* *(péj)* simplism.
simpliste [sɛ̃plist(ə)] *adj* *(péj)* simplistic.
simulacre [simylakʀ(ə)] *nm* *(action simulée)* enactment. **les acteurs firent un ~ de sacrifice humain** the actors enacted a human sacrifice; *(péj: fausse apparence)* **un ~ de justice** a pretence of justice; **un ~ de gouvernement/procès** a sham government/trial, a mockery of a government/a trial.
simulateur, -trice [simylatœʀ, tʀis] **1** *nm,f* *(gén)* shammer, pretender; *(Mil: qui feint la maladie)* malingerer. **2** *nm* *(Tech)* **~ de vol** flight simulator.
simulation [simylɑsjɔ̃] *nf* *(V* **simuler***)* feigning, simulation. **il n'est pas malade, c'est de la ~** *(gén)* he isn't ill — it's all sham *ou* it's all put on; *(Mil)* he isn't ill — he's just malingering.
simulé, e [simyle] *(ptp de* **simuler***)* *adj* *(feint) attaque, retraite* feigned, sham *(épith)*; *amabilité, gravité* feigned, sham *(épith)*, simulated *(frm)*; *(imité) velours, colonnade* simulated; *(Tech: reproduit) conditions, situation* simulated.
simuler [simyle] (1) *vt* **(a)** *(feindre) sentiment, attaque* to feign, sham, simulate *(frm)*. **~ une maladie** to feign illness, pretend to be ill.
(b) *(avoir l'apparence de)* to simulate. **ce papier peint simule une boiserie** this wallpaper is made to look like *ou* simulates wood panelling.
(c) *(Tech: reproduire) conditions, situation* to simulate.
(d) *(Jur) contrat, vente* to effect fictitiously.
simultané, e [simyltane] *adj* simultaneous; *V* **traduction.**
simultanéisme [simyltaneism(ə)] *nm* *(Littérat: procédé narratif)* (use of) simultaneous action.
simultanéité [simyltaneite] *nf* simultaneousness, simultaneity.
simultanément [simyltanemɑ̃] *adv* simultaneously.
Sinaï [sinaj] *nm* Sinai.
sinapisé [sinapize] *adj*: **bain/cataplasme ~** mustard bath/poultice.
sinapisme [sinapism(ə)] *nm* mustard poultice *ou* plaster.
sincère [sɛ̃sɛʀ] *adj personne, aveu, paroles* sincere; *réponse, explication* sincere, honest; *repentir, amour, partisan, admiration* sincere, genuine, true *(épith)*; *élections, documents* genuine. **est-il ~ dans son amitié?** is he sincere in his friendship?, is his friendship sincere? *ou* genuine?; **un ami ~ des bêtes/arts** a true *ou* genuine friend of animals/of the arts; *(formule épistolaire)* **mes ~s condoléances** my sincere *ou* heartfelt condolences; **mes regrets les plus ~s** my sincerest regrets.
sincèrement [sɛ̃sɛʀmɑ̃] *adv* **(a)** *(V* **sincère***)* sincerely; honestly; truly; genuinely. **je suis ~ désolé que ...** I am sincerely *ou* truly sorry that ...
(b) *(pour parler franchement)* honestly, really. **~, vous feriez mieux de refuser** honestly *ou* really you would be better saying no.
sincérité [sɛ̃seʀite] *nf* *(V* **sincère***)* sincerity; honesty; genuineness. **en toute ~** in all sincerity.
sinécure [sinekyʀ] *nf* sinecure. **ce n'est pas une ~*** it's not exactly a rest cure.
sine die [sinedje] *adv* sine die.
sine qua non [sinekwanɔn] *adj*: **une condition ~** an indispensable condition, a sine qua non.
Singapour [sɛ̃gapuʀ] *nm* Singapore.
singe [sɛ̃ʒ] *nm* **(a)** *(Zool)* monkey; *(de grande taille)* ape. **les grands ~s** the big apes.
(b) *(fig) (personne laide)* horror; *(enfant espiègle)* monkey.
(c) *(arg Mil: corned beef)* bully beef *(arg Mil)*.
(d) *(† arg Typ etc: patron)* boss*.
(e) *(loc)* **faire le ~** to monkey about *(pulling faces etc)*; **être agile/malin comme un ~** to be as agile/crafty *ou* artful as a monkey; *V* **apprendre, monnaie.**
singer [sɛ̃ʒe] (3) *vt personne, démarche* to ape, mimic, take off*; *sentiments* to feign.
singerie [sɛ̃ʒʀi] *nf* **(a)** *(gén pl: grimaces et pitreries)* antics *(pl)*, clowning *(U)*. **faire des ~s** to clown about, play the fool. **(b)** *(simagrées)* **~s** airs and graces. **(c)** *(rare: cage)* monkey house.
singulariser [sɛ̃gylaʀize] (1) **1** *vt* to mark out, make conspicuous. **2 se singulariser** *vpr* to call attention to o.s., make o.s. conspicuous.
singularité [sɛ̃gylaʀite] *nf* **(a)** *(U: V* **singulier***)* remarkable nature; singularity; uncommon nature. **(b)** *(exception, anomalie)* peculiarity.
singulier, -ière [sɛ̃gylje, jɛʀ] **1** *adj* **(a)** *(étonnant)* remarkable, singular *(frm)*; *(littér: peu commun)* singular, remarkable, uncommon. **je trouve ~ qu'il n'ait pas jugé bon de ...** I find it (pretty) remarkable that he didn't see fit to ... .
(b) *(Ling)* singular.
(c) *V* **combat.**
2 *nm* *(Ling)* singular.
singulièrement [sɛ̃gyljɛʀmɑ̃] *adv* **(a)** *(étrangement)* in a peculiar way, oddly, strangely.
(b) *(beaucoup)* remarkably, singularly *(frm)*. *(très)* **~ intéressant/fort** uncommonly *ou* extremely interesting/strong; **ceci m'a ~ aiguisé l'appétit** this sharpened my appetite remarkably; **il me déplaît ~ de voir ...** I find it particularly unpleasant to see ... .
(c) *(en particulier)* particularly, especially.
sinistre [sinistʀ(ə)] **1** *adj bruit, endroit, projet* sinister. *(avant n: intensif)* **un ~ voyou/imbécile** an appalling lout/idiot.
2 *nm* *(catastrophe)* disaster; *(incendie)* blaze; *(Assurances: cas)* accident. **l'assuré doit déclarer le ~ dans les 24 heures** any (accident) claim must be notified within 24 hours; *(Assurances)* **évaluer l'importance d'un ~** to appraise the extent of the damage *ou* loss *etc.*
sinistré, e [sinistʀe] **1** *adj région, pays* (disaster-)stricken *(épith)*. **2** *nm,f* disaster victim.
sinistrement [sinistʀəmɑ̃] *adv* in a sinister way.
sino- [sinɔ] *préf* Sino-. **~soviétique** Sino-Soviet.
sinoc‡ [sinɔk] *adj* = **sinoque‡**.
sinologie [sinɔlɔʒi] *nf* sinology.
sinologue [sinɔlɔg] *nmf* sinologist, specialist in Chinese affairs, China watcher*.
sinon [sinɔ̃] *conj* **(a)** *(frm: sauf)* except, other than, save†. **on ne possède jamais rien, ~ soi-même** there is nothing one ever possesses, except (for) *ou* other than *ou* save† oneself; **à quoi peut**

bien servir cette manœuvre ~ à nous intimider? what can be the purpose of this manoeuvre other than to intimidate us?; **un homme courageux, ~ qu'il était un tant soit peu casse-cou†** a courageous man, save† for being a trifle reckless.

(b) (*de concession: si ce n'est*) if not. **il faut le faire, ~ pour le plaisir, du moins par devoir** it must be done, if not for pleasure, (then) at least out of duty; **il avait leur approbation, ~ leur enthousiasme** he had their approval, if not their enthusiasm; **je ne sais pas grand-chose, ~ qu'il a démissionné** I don't know much about it, only that he has resigned; (*frm*) **cette histoire est savoureuse, ~ très morale** this story is spicy if not very moral; (*frm*) **ils y étaient opposés, ~ hostiles** they were opposed, if not (actively) hostile, to it.

(c) (*autrement*) otherwise, or else. **fais-le, ~ nous aurons des ennuis** do it, otherwise *ou* or else we will be in trouble; **faites-le, vous vous exposerez ~ à des ennuis** do it – you will lay yourself open to trouble otherwise; **elle doit être malade, ~ elle serait déjà venue** she must be ill, otherwise *ou* or else she would have already come; (*pour indiquer la menace*) **fais-le, ~ ...** do it, or else ... .

sinophile [sinɔfil] *adj, nmf* sinophile.

sinoque‡ [sinɔk] *adj* batty*, daft*, loony‡.

sinueux, -euse [sinɥø, øz] *adj route* winding (*épith*); *rivière* winding (*épith*), meandering (*épith*); *ligne* sinuous; (*fig*) *pensée* tortuous.

sinuosité [sinɥozite] *nf* **(a)** (*gén pl: courbe*) *[route]* winding (*U*), curve; *[rivière]* winding (*U*), meandering (*U*), curve, loop. (*fig*) **les ~s de sa pensée** his tortuous train of thought.

(b) (*U: V* **sinueux**) winding; meandering; tortuousness.

sinus[1] [sinys] *nm inv* (*Anat*) sinus. **~ frontal/maxillaire** frontal/maxillary sinus.

sinus[2] [sinys] *nm* (*Math*) sine.

sinusite [sinyzit] *nf* (*Méd*) sinusitis.

sinusoïdal, e, *mpl* **-aux** [sinyzɔidal, o] *adj* sinusoidal.

sinusoïde [sinyzɔid] *nf* (*Math*) sinusoid.

sionisme [sjɔnism(ə)] *nm* Zionism.

sioniste [sjɔnist(ə)] *adj, nmf* Zionist.

sioux [sju] **1** *adj inv* Sioux. **2** *nm* (*Ling*) Sioux. **3** *nmf inv*: **S~** Sioux; *V* **ruse.**

siphon [sifɔ̃] *nm* (*tube, bouteille, Zool*) siphon; *[évier, W.-C.]* U-bend; (*Spéléologie*) sump.

siphonné, e‡ [sifɔne] **1** *ptp de* **siphonner**. **2** *adj* nutty‡, cracked‡.

siphonner [sifɔne] (1) *vt* to siphon.

sire [siʀ] *nm* **(a)** (*au roi*) **S~** Sire. **(b)** (*Hist: seigneur*) lord. **(c) un triste ~** an unsavoury individual; **un pauvre ~†** a poor *ou* penniless fellow.

sirène [siʀɛn] *nf* **(a)** (*Myth, fig*) siren, mermaid. (*fig*) **écouter le chant des ~s** to listen to the sirens' *ou* mermaids' song. **(b)** (*appareil*) *[bateau, ambulance]* siren; *[usine]* hooter. **~ d'alarme** (*en temps de guerre*) air-raid siren; (*en temps de paix*) fire alarm.

sirocco, siroco [siʀɔko] *nm* sirocco.

sirop [siʀo] *nm* (*pharmaceutique*) syrup, mixture; (*à diluer: pour une boisson*) syrup, cordial; (*boisson*) (fruit) cordial. **~ d'orgeat** barley water; **~ de groseille/d'ananas/de menthe** redcurrant/pineapple/mint cordial; **~ d'érable** maple syrup; **~ de maïs** corn syrup; **~ contre la toux** cough mixture *ou* syrup *ou* linctus.

siroter [siʀɔte] (1) *vt* to sip.

sirupeux, -euse [siʀypø, øz] *adj liquide* syrupy; (*fig péj*) *musique* syrupy.

sis, sise [si, siz] *adj* (*Admin, Jur*) located.

sisal [sizal] *nm* sisal.

sismal, e, *mpl* **-aux** [sismal, o] *adj* (*Géog*) **ligne ~e** path of an earthquake.

sismicité [sismisite] *nf* seismicity.

sismique [sismik] *adj* seismic; *V* **secousse.**

sismographe [sismɔgʀaf] *nm* seismograph.

sismographie [sismɔgʀafi] *nf* seismography.

sismologie [sismɔlɔʒi] *nf* seismology.

sismomètre [sismɔmɛtʀ(ə)] *nm* seismometer.

sistre [sistʀ(ə)] *nm* sistrum.

Sisyphe [sizif] *nm* Sisyphus; *V* **rocher.**

site [sit] **1** *nm* **(a)** (*environnement*) setting; (*endroit pittoresque*) beauty spot. **construire un château dans le ~ approprié** to build a château in the right setting; **dans un ~ merveilleux/très sauvage** in a marvellous/very wild setting; **~s naturels/historiques** natural/historic sites; **les ~s pittoresques d'une région** the beauty spots of an area; **la protection des ~s** the conservation of places of interest; **un ~ classé** a classified site; **'Beaumanoir, ses plages, ses hôtels, ses ~s'** 'Beaumanoir for beaches, hotels and places to visit *ou* places of interest'.

(b) (*emplacement*) site. **~ favorable à la construction d'un barrage** suitable site for the construction of a dam.

(c) (*Mil*) **(angle de) ~** (angle of) site; **ligne de ~** line of sight.

2: site archéologique archeological site; **site propre** bus lane.

sit-in [sitin] *nm inv* sit-in.

sitôt [sito] **1** *adv* **(a) ~ couchée, elle s'endormit** as soon as *ou* immediately she was in bed she fell asleep, she was no sooner in bed *ou* no sooner was she in bed than she fell asleep; **~ dit, ~ fait** no sooner said than done; **~ après avoir traversé la ville, ils se trouvèrent dans les collines** immediately on leaving the town *ou* straight after driving through the town they found themselves in the hills; **~ après la guerre** straight *ou* immediately after the war, immediately the war was over.

(b) (*avec nég*) **de ~: ce n'est pas de ~ qu'il reviendra** he won't be back for quite a while *ou* for (quite) some time, he won't be back in a hurry*; **il a été si bien puni qu'il ne recommencera pas de ~!** he was so severely punished that he won't be doing that again for a while! *ou* in a hurry!*

(c) ~ que, ~ après que as soon as, no sooner than; **~ (après) que le docteur fut parti, elle se sentit mieux** as soon as the doctor had left she felt better, the doctor had no sooner left than she felt better; **~ qu'il sera guéri, il reprendra le travail** as soon as he is better he'll go back to work.

2 *prép* (*littér*) **~ la rentrée des classes, il faudra que ...** as soon as school is back, we must ... ; **~ les vacances, elle partait** she would go *ou* went away as soon as the holidays started, the holidays had no sooner begun than she would go away.

situation [sitɥɑsjɔ̃] *nf* **(a)** (*emplacement*) situation, position, location. **la ~ de cette villa est excellente** this villa is excellently situated, the villa has an excellent situation.

(b) (*conjoncture, circonstances*) situation. (*Philos*) **étudier/montrer l'homme en ~** to study/show man in his situation; **être en ~ de faire** to be in a position to do; (*iro*) **elle est dans une ~ intéressante*** she is in an interesting condition (*iro*) *ou* in the family way*; **~ de fait** de facto situation; **~ de famille** marital status; *V* **comique.**

(c) (*emploi*) post, situation. **chercher une/perdre sa ~** to look for a/lose one's post; **se faire une belle ~** to work up to a good position.

(d) (*Fin: état*) statement of finances. **~ de trésorerie** cash flow statement.

situé, e [sitɥe] (*ptp de* **situer**) *adj* situated. **bien/mal ~** well/badly situated.

situer [sitɥe] (1) **1** *vt* **(a)** (*lit: placer, construire*) to site, situate, locate.

(b) (*par la pensée: localiser*) to set, place; (*: *catégoriser*) *personne* to place, pin down*.

2 se situer *vpr* **(a)** (*emploi réfléchi*) to place o.s. **essayer de se ~ par rapport à qn/qch** to try to place o.s. in relation to sb/sth.

(b) (*se trouver*) (*dans l'espace*) to be situated; (*dans le temps*) to come; (*par rapport à des notions*) to stand. **l'action/cette scène se situe à Paris** the action/this scene is set *ou* takes place in Paris.

six [sis], *devant n commençant par consonne* [si], *devant n commençant par voyelle ou h muet* [siz] **1** *adj cardinal inv* six. **il y avait ~ mille personnes** there were six thousand people; **ils sont ~ enfants** there are six children; **les ~ huitièmes de cette somme** six eighths of this sum; **il a ~ ans** he is six (years old); **un enfant de ~ ans** a six-year-old (child), a child of six; **objet de ~ F** a six-franc article; **polygone à ~ faces** six-sided polygon; **couper qch en ~ morceaux** to cut sth into six pieces; **j'en ai pris trois, il en reste ~** I've taken three (of them) and there are six (of them) left; **il est trois heures moins ~** it is six minutes to three; **par vingt voix contre ~** by twenty votes to six; **cinq jours/fois sur ~** five days/times out of six; **ils sont venus tous les ~** all six of them came; **ils ont porté la table à eux ~** the six of them carried the table; **ils ont mangé le jambon à eux ~** the six of them ate the ham, they ate the ham between the six of them; **partagez cela entre vous ~** share that among the six of you; **ils viennent à ~ pour déjeuner** there are six coming to lunch; **on peut s'asseoir à ~ autour de cette table** this table can seat six (people); **ils vivent à ~ dans une seule pièce** there are six of them living in one room; **se battre à ~ contre un/à un contre ~** to fight six against one/one against six; **entrer ~ par ~** to come in by sixes *ou* six at a time *ou* six by six; **se mettre en rangs par ~** to form rows of six.

2 *adj ordinal inv*: **arriver le ~ septembre** to arrive on the sixth of September *ou* (on) September the sixth *ou* (on) September sixth; **Louis ~** Louis the Sixth; **chapitre/page ~** chapter/page six; **le numéro ~ gagne un lot** number six wins a prize; **il habite au numéro ~ de la rue Arthur** he lives at number six (in) Rue Arthur; **il est ~ heures du soir** it's six in the evening.

3 *nm inv* **(a)** six. **trente-/quarante-~** thirty-/forty-six; **quatre et deux font ~** four and two are *ou* make six; **il fait mal ses ~** he writes his sixes badly; **c'est le ~ qui a gagné** (*numéro*) (number) six has won; (*coureur*) number six has won; **il habite au ~ (de la rue)** he lives at number six; **il habite ~ rue de Paris** he lives at six Rue de Paris; **nous sommes le ~ aujourd'hui** it's the sixth today; **il est venu le ~** he came on the sixth; **il est payé le ~ *ou* tous les ~ de chaque mois** he is paid on the sixth of each month; (*Cartes*) **le ~ de cœur** the six of hearts; (*Dominos*) **le ~ et deux** the six-two.

(b) (*Pol: jusqu'en 1973*) **les S~, l'Europe des S~** the Six, the Europe of the Six.

4: (*Mus*) **six-huit** *nm inv* six-eight (time); **mesure à six-huit** bar in six-eight (time); (*Sport*) **les Six Jours** *six-day cycling event*; (*Naut*) **six-mâts** *nm inv* six-master; **six quatre deux*** *nf*: **faire qch à la six quatre deux** to do sth in a slapdash way, do sth any old how* (*Brit*) *ou* way*.

sixain [sizɛ̃] *nm* = **sizain.**

sixième [sizjɛm] **1** *adj* sixth. **vingt-/trente-~** twenty-/thirty-sixth; **recevoir la ~ partie d'un héritage** to receive a sixth of a bequest; **demeurer dans le ~ (arrondissement)** to live in the sixth arrondissement (*in Paris*); **habiter au ~ (étage)** to live on the sixth floor.

2 *nmf* (*gén*) sixth (person). **se classer ~** to come sixth; **nous avons besoin d'un ~ pour compléter l'équipe** we need a sixth (person) to complete the team; **elle est arrivée (la) ~ dans la course** she came (in) sixth in the race.

3 *nm* (*portion*) sixth. **calculer le ~ d'un nombre** to work out the sixth of a number; **recevoir le ~ *ou* un ~ d'une somme** to receive a sixth of a sum; **(les) deux ~s du budget seront consacrés à ...** two sixths of the budget will be given over to ... .

4 *nf* (*Scol*) (*degré*) ≃ first year *ou* form (*Brit*); (*classe*) ≃ first form (*Brit*). **entrer en (classe de) ~** ≃ to go into the first form (*Brit*); **élève/professeur de ~** ≃ first form pupil/teacher.

sixièmement [sizjɛmmɑ̃] *adv* in the sixth place, sixthly.
sixte [sikst(ə)] *nf (Mus)* sixth; *(Escrime)* sixte.
sizain [sizɛ̃] *nm (Littérat)* six-line stanza; *(Cartes) packet of 6 packs of cards.*
skaï [skaj] *nm* ® Skai (fabric) ®, leatherette.
sketch, *pl* ~**es** [skɛtʃ] *nm* (variety) sketch.
ski [ski] **1** *nm (objet)* ski; *(sport)* skiing. **s'acheter des ~s** to buy o.s. a pair of skis *ou* some skis; **aller quelque part à** *ou* **en ~s** to go somewhere on skis, ski somewhere; **faire du ~** to ski, go skiing; **vacances/équipement de ~** ski(ing) holiday/equipment; **chaussures/moniteur/épreuve de ~** ski boots/instructor/race; *V* **piste.**
2: ski alpin Alpine skiing; **ski-bob** *nm* ski-bob; **ski court** short ski; **ski évolutif** short ski method, ski évolutif; **ski de fond** langlauf; **ski nautique** water-skiing; **ski nordique** Nordic skiing; **ski de piste** downhill skiing; **ski de randonnée** cross-country skiing.
skiable [skjabl(ə)] *adj* skiable.
skier [skje] (7) *vi* to ski.
skieur, -euse [skjœʀ, øz] *nm,f* skier; *(ski nautique)* water-skier.
skiff [skif] *nm* skiff.
slalom [slalɔm] *nm (épreuve, piste)* slalom; *(mouvement)* slalom movement; *(fig: entre divers obstacles)* zigzag. **faire du ~ (entre ... ou parmi ...)** to slalom (between ...); **descente en ~** slalom descent; **~ géant/spécial** giant/special slalom.
slalomer [slalɔme] (1) *vi (Ski)* to slalom; *(fig: entre divers obstacles)* to zigzag.
slalomeur, -euse [slalɔmœʀ, øz] *nm,f (Ski)* slalom skier *ou* specialist.
slave [slav] **1** *adj* Slav(onic), Slavic; *langue* Slavic, Slavonic. **le charme ~** Slavonic charm. **2** *nmf*: **S~** Slav.
slavisant, e [slavizɑ̃, ɑ̃t] *nm,f* Slavist.
slavophile [slavɔfil] *adj, nmf* Slavophile.
sleeping† [slipiŋ] *nm* sleeping car.
slip [slip] *nm* **(a)** *[homme]* briefs *(pl)*, (under)pants *(pl)*; *[femme]* pant(ie)s *(pl)*, briefs *(pl)*. **~ de bain** *[homme]* (bathing *ou* swimming) trunks *(pl)*; *(du bikini)* (bikini) briefs *(pl)*; **j'ai acheté 2 ~s** I bought 2 pairs of briefs *ou* pants.
(b) *(Naut)* slipway.
slogan [slɔgɑ̃] *nm* slogan.
slovaque [slɔvak] **1** *adj* Slovak. **2** *nmf*: **S~** Slovak.
Slovaquie [slɔvaki] *nf* Slovakia.
slovène [slɔvɛn] **1** *adj* Slovene. **2** *nm (Ling)* Slovene. **3** *nmf*: **S~** Slovene.
slow [slo] *nm (blues etc)* slow number; *(fox-trot)* slow fox trot.
smala* [smala] *nf (troupe)* tribe*.
smash [smaʃ] *nm (Tennis)* smash.
smasher [smaʃe] (1) *(Tennis)* **1** *vt* to smash. **2** *vi* to smash (the ball).
smic* [smik] *nm (d'après* **S.M.I.C.**) *index-linked minimum statutory wage.*
smicard, e* [smikaʀ, aʀd(ə)] *nm,f* minimum wage earner.
smig* [smig] *nm (d'après* **S.M.I.G.**) *guaranteed minimum wage (replaced by S.M.I.C.).*
smigard, e* [smigaʀ, aʀd(ə)] *nm,f* minimum wage earner.
smoking [smɔkiŋ] *nm (costume)* dinner suit, evening suit, dress suit; *(veston)* dinner jacket, DJ* *(Brit)*, tuxedo *(US)*.
snack [snak] *nm*, **snack-bar**, *pl* **snack-bars** [snakbaʀ] *nm* snack bar.
snob [snɔb] **1** *nmf* snob. **2** *adj* snobby, posh*.
snober [snɔbe] (1) *vt*: **~ qn** to snub sb, give sb the cold shoulder.
snobinard, e* [snɔbinaʀ, aʀd(ə)] *(péj)* **1** *adj* snooty*, stuck-up*, snobbish. **2** *nm,f* stuck-up thing*.
snobisme [snɔbism(ə)] *nm* snobbery. **~ à l'envers** inverted snobbery.
sobre [sɔbʀ(ə)] *adj personne* temperate, abstemious; *repas* abstemious, frugal; *style, éloquence* sober. **~ de gestes/paroles** sparing of gestures/words; **~ comme un chameau** as sober as a judge.
sobrement [sɔbʀəmɑ̃] *adv (V* **sobre**) temperately; abstemiously; frugally; soberly.
sobriété [sɔbʀijete] *nf (V* **sobre**) temperance; abstemiousness; frugality; sobriety. **~ de gestes/paroles** restraint in one's gestures/words.
sobriquet [sɔbʀikɛ] *nm* nickname.
soc [sɔk] *nm* ploughshare.
sociabilité [sɔsjabilite] *nf (V* **sociable**) social nature; sociability; hospitality.
sociable [sɔsjabl(ə)] *adj* **(a)** *(qui vit en groupe)* social. **(b)** *(ouvert, civil) personne, caractère* sociable; *milieu* hospitable.
social, e, *mpl* **-aux** [sɔsjal, o] **1** *adj* **(a)** *animal, créature* social.
(b) *rapports, phénomène, conventions* social. **le ~ et le sacré** matters social and matters sacred; *V* **science.**
(c) *classe, conflit, questions, loi, politique* social; *revendications* over social conditions. **la victoire électorale passe par le ~** elections are won and lost on social issues.
(d) *(Admin)* services **~aux** social services; **prestations ~es** social security benefits; **aide ~e** welfare; *(subsides)* social security (benefits); **assurances ~es** ≃ National Insurance *(Brit)*; *V* **assistant, avantage, sécurité.**
(e) *(Comm) V* **capital, raison, siège**[1].
2: social-démocrate *adj, nmf, mpl* **sociaux-démocrates** Social Democrat.
socialement [sɔsjalmɑ̃] *adv* socially.
socialisant, e [sɔsjalizɑ̃, ɑ̃t] *adj* with socialist leanings *ou* tendencies.
socialisation [sɔsjalizɑsjɔ̃] *nf* socialization.
socialiser [sɔsjalize] (1) *vt* to socialize.
socialisme [sɔsjalism(ə)] *nm* socialism. **~ utopique/scientifique/révolutionnaire** utopian/scientific/revolutionary socialism.
socialiste [sɔsjalist(ə)] *adj, nmf* socialist.
sociétaire [sɔsjetɛʀ] *nmf* member *(of a society)*. **~ de la Comédie-Française** (shareholding) member of the Comédie-Française.
société [sɔsjete] **1** *nf* **(a)** *(groupe, communauté)* society. **la ~** society; **la vie en ~** life in society; **~ sans classe** classless society.
(b) *(club) (littéraire, savante)* society; *(sportive)* club. **~ de pêche/tir** angling/shooting club; **~ secrète/savante** secret/learned society; **la S~ protectrice des animaux** ≃ the Royal Society for the Prevention of Cruelty to Animals.
(c) *(Comm)* company, firm. **~ immobilière/financière/d'assurance** property *(Brit) ou* real estate *(US)*/finance/insurance company; **~ immobilière** (property) development company; **~ de crédit immobilier** ≃ building society *(Brit)*.
(d) *(classes oisives)* **la ~** society; **la bonne ~** polite society; **la haute ~** high society.
(e) *(assemblée)* company, gathering. **il y venait une ~ assez mêlée/une ~ d'artistes et d'écrivains** a fairly mixed company *ou* gathering/a company *ou* gathering of artists and writers used to come; **toute la ~ se leva pour l'acclamer** the whole company rose to acclaim him.
(f) *(compagnie)* company, society *(frm, littér)*. **rechercher/priser la ~ de qn** to seek/esteem sb's company *ou* society *(frm, littér) ou* companionship; **dans la ~ de qn** in the company *ou* society *(frm, littér)* of sb; *V* **jeu, talent**[1].
2: société par actions joint stock company; **société anonyme** ≃ limited company *(surtout Brit)*; **société à capital variable** company with variable capital; **société en commandite** limited partnership; **la société de consommation** the consumer society; **société d'exploitation** development company; **société de Jésus** Society of Jesus; **société en nom collectif** general partnership; **société à responsabilité limitée** limited liability company *(surtout Brit)*; *(Hist Pol)* **la Société des Nations** the League of Nations; **société de tempérance** temperance society.
socioculturel, -elle [sɔsjɔkyltyʀɛl] *adj* sociocultural.
sociodrame [sɔsjɔdʀam] *nm* sociodrama.
socio-économique [sɔsjɔekɔnɔmik] *adj* socioeconomic.
socio-éducatif, -ive [sɔsjɔedykatif, iv] *adj* socioeducational.
socio-géographique [sɔsjɔʒeɔgʀafik] *adj* socio-geographic.
sociogramme [sɔsjɔgʀam] *nm* sociogram.
sociolinguistique [sɔsjɔlɛ̃gɥistik] *nf* socio-linguistics *(sg)*.
sociologie [sɔsjɔlɔʒi] *nf* sociology.
sociologique [sɔsjɔlɔʒik] *adj* sociological.
sociologiquement [sɔsjɔlɔʒikmɑ̃] *adv* sociologically.
sociologue [sɔsjɔlɔg] *nmf* sociologist.
sociométrie [sɔsjɔmetʀi] *nf* sociometry.
socio-professionnel, -elle [sɔsjɔpʀɔfɛsjɔnɛl] *adj* socio-professional.
socle [sɔkl(ə)] *nm* **(a)** *[statue, colonne]* plinth, pedestal, socle *(T)*; *[lampe, vase]* base. **(b)** *(Géog)* platform.
socque [sɔk] *nm (sabot)* clog.
socquette [sɔkɛt] *nf* ankle sock.
Socrate [sɔkʀat] *nm* Socrates.
socratique [sɔkʀatik] *adj* Socratic.
soda [sɔda] *nm* fizzy drink. **~ à l'orange** orangeade.
sodé, e [sɔde] *adj* sodium *(épith)*.
sodique [sɔdik] *adj* sodic.
sodium [sɔdjɔm] *nm* sodium.
sodomie [sɔdɔmi] *nf* sodomy.
sodomite [sɔdɔmit] *nm* sodomite.
sœur [sœʀ] *nf* **(a)** *(lit, fig)* sister. **avec un dévouement de ~** with a sister's *ou* with sisterly devotion; **et ta ~?**‡ go and take a running jump*, get lost‡; **la poésie, ~ de la musique** poetry, sister of *ou* to music; **peuplades/organisations ~s** sister peoples/organizations; *(hum)* **j'ai trouvé la ~ de cette commode chez un antiquaire** I found the partner to this chest of drawers in an antique shop; *V* **âme, lait.**
(b) *(Rel)* nun, sister; *(comme titre)* Sister. **~ Jeanne** Sister Jeanne; **élevée chez les ~s** convent educated; **on l'a mise en pension chez les ~s** she was sent to a convent (boarding) school; **les Petites ~s des pauvres** the Little Sisters of the Poor; **les ~s de la Charité** the Sisters of Charity; *V* **bon**[1].
sœurette* [sœʀɛt] *nf* little sister.
sofa [sɔfa] *nm* sofa.
soi [swa] **1** *pron pers* **(a)** *(gén)* one(self); *(fonction d'attribut)* oneself; *(avec il(s), elle(s) comme antécédent: gén frm,* †) himself; herself; itself. **n'aimer que ~** to love only oneself; **regarder devant/derrière ~** to look in front of/behind one; **malgré ~** in spite of oneself; **avoir confiance en ~** to have confidence in oneself.
(b) *(loc)* **aller de ~** to be self-evident, be obvious; **cela va de ~** it's obvious, it stands to reason, that goes without saying; **il va de ~ que ...** it goes without saying *ou* it stands to reason that ... ; **en ~** *(intrinsèquement)* in itself; **être/exister pour ~** to be/exist only for oneself; **dans un groupe, on peut se rendre service entre ~** in a group, people *ou* you* can help each other *ou* one another (out); *(frm)* **il n'agissait que pour ~** he was only acting for himself *ou* in his own interests; *(évite une ambiguïté)* **elle comprenait qu'il fût mécontent de ~** she understood his not being pleased with himself; **il allait droit devant ~** he was going straight ahead (of him); **être/rester ~** to be/remain oneself; *V* **chacun, hors, maître** *etc.*
(c) **~-même** oneself; **on le fait ~-même** you do it yourself, one does it oneself *(frm)*; **le respect de ~-même** self-respect; *(hum)* **Monsieur X? — ~-même!** Mr X? — in person! *ou* none other!; *pour autres loc V* **même.**

2 *nm* (*Philos, littér: personnalité, conscience*) self; (*Psych: inconscient*) id. **la conscience de ~** self-awareness, awareness of self; *V* **en-soi, pour-soi.**
soi-disant [swadizɑ̃] **1** *adj inv* so-called.
2 *adv* supposedly. **il était ~ parti à Rome** he had supposedly left for Rome, he was supposed to have left for Rome; **il était venu ~ pour discuter** he had come for a discussion – or so he said (anyway), he had come ostensibly for a discussion; **~ que*** ... it would appear that ... , apparently ... .
soie[1] [swa] *nf* **(a)** (*Tex*) silk. **~ sauvage** wild silk; **~ grège** raw silk; *V* **papier, ver.**
(b) (*poil*) *[sanglier etc]* bristle. **brosse en ~s de sanglier** (boar) bristle brush; **brosse à dents en ~s de nylon** nylon (bristle) brush, brush with nylon bristles.
soie[2] [swa] *nf* (*Tech*) *[lime, couteau]* tang.
soient [swa] *V* **être.**
soierie [swaʀi] *nf* (*tissu*) silk; (*industrie, commerce*) silk trade; (*filature*) silk mill.
soif [swaf] *nf* **(a)** (*lit*) thirst. **avoir ~** to be thirsty; *[plante, terre]* to be dry *ou* thirsty; **donner ~** to make one thirsty; **le sel donne ~** salt makes you thirsty, salt gives one a thirst; **jusqu'à plus ~** (*lit*) till one's thirst is quenched; (*fig*) till one can take no more; **rester sur sa ~** (*rare: lit*) to remain thirsty; (*fig*) to be left thirsting for more, be left unsatisfied; *V* **boire, garder, mourir.**
(b) (*fig: désir*) **~ de** *richesse, connaissances, vengeance* thirst *ou* craving for; **~ de faire qch** craving to do sth.
soiffard, e*† [swafaʀ, aʀd(ə)] (*péj*) **1** *adj* boozy*. **2** *nm,f* boozer*.
soigné, e [swaɲe] (*ptp de* **soigner**) *adj* **(a)** (*propre*) *personne, tenue, chevelure* well-groomed, neat; *ongles* well-groomed, well-kept; *mains* well-cared-for. **peu ~** *personne* untidy; *cheveux* unkempt, untidy; *ongles, mains* unkempt, neglected (-looking); **il est très ~ de sa personne** he is very well turned out *ou* well-groomed.
(b) (*consciencieux*) *travail, style, présentation* careful, meticulous; *vitrine* neat, carefully laid out; *jardin* well-kept; *repas* carefully prepared. **peu ~** careless; badly laid-out; badly kept; badly prepared.
(c) (*: *intensif*) *note* massive*, whopping* (*épith*); *punition* stiff*. **avoir un rhume (quelque chose de) ~** to have a real beauty* *ou* a whopper* of a cold; **la note était ~e** it was SOME bill* *ou* a massive* *ou* whopping* bill.
soigner [swaɲe] (1) *vt* **(a)** *patient, maladie [médecin]* to treat; *[infirmière, mère]* to look after, nurse; *blessé* to tend. **j'ai été très bien soigné dans cette clinique** I had very good treatment in this clinic, I was very well looked after in this clinic; **tu devrais te faire ~** you should have treatment *ou* see a doctor; **rentrez chez vous pour ~ votre grippe** go back home and look after *ou* nurse that cold (of yours); **soigne-toi bien** take good care of yourself, look after yourself properly; **je soigne mes rhumatismes avec des pilules** I'm taking pills for my rheumatism; **de nos jours, la tuberculose se soigne** these days tuberculosis can be treated.
(b) (*dorloter*) *chien, plantes, invité* to look after, take (good) care of; (*entretenir*) *ongles, chevelure* to look after, take care of; *tenue* to take care over; (*fignoler*) *travail, repas, style, présentation* to take care over. **elle se soigne avec coquetterie** she takes great care over her appearance, she is tremendously interested in her appearance; (*hum*) **ils se soignent: champagne, saumon, cigares etc!** they take good care of *ou* look after themselves (all right) – champagne, salmon, cigars, the lot!
(c) (**loc*) **(il) faut te faire ~!** you need your brains tested!* *ou* your head seen to!* (*surtout Brit*); **10 F le café: ils nous ont soignés!** 10 francs for a coffee — they've rooked us* (*Brit*) *ou* we've been had* *ou* done*; **ils lui sont tombés dessus à quatre: j'aime autant te dire qu'ils l'ont soigné** four of them laid into him – I can tell you they really let him have it*; **ça se soigne, tu sais!** there's a cure for that, you know!
soigneur [swaɲœʀ] *nm* (*Boxe*) second; (*Cyclisme, Ftbl*) trainer.
soigneusement [swaɲøzmɑ̃] *adv* (*V* **soigneux**) tidily; neatly, carefully; painstakingly; meticulously. **~ préparé** carefully prepared, prepared with care.
soigneux, -euse [swaɲø, øz] *adj* **(a)** (*propre, ordonné*) tidy, neat. **ce garçon n'est pas assez ~** this boy isn't tidy enough.
(b) (*diligent*) *travailleur* careful, painstaking; *travail* careful, meticulous. **être ~ dans son travail** to be careful in one's work, take care over one's work.
(c) ~ de: être ~ de sa santé to be careful about one's health; **être ~ de ses affaires** to be careful with one's belongings; **être ~ de sa personne** to be careful about *ou* take care over one's appearance; **être ~ de ses vêtements** to be careful with one's clothes, take care of *ou* look after one's clothes.
soi-même [swamɛm] *pron V* **même, soi.**
soin [swɛ̃] *nm* **(a)** (*application*) care; (*ordre et propreté*) tidiness, neatness. **sans ~** (*adj*) careless; untidy; (*adv*) carelessly; untidily; **faire qch avec (grand) ~** to do sth with (great) care *ou* (very) carefully; **il n'a aucun ~, il est sans ~** he is untidy; **il nous évite avec un certain ~, il met un certain ~ à nous éviter** he takes great care to avoid us, he is scrupulously avoiding us.
(b) (*charge, responsabilité*) care. **confier à qn le ~ de ses affaires** to entrust sb with the care of one's affairs; **confier à qn le ~ de faire** to entrust sb to do; **je vous laisse ce ~** I leave this to you, I leave you to take care of this; **son premier ~ fut de faire ...** his first concern was to do ...; (*littér*) **le ~ de son salut/avenir l'occupait tout entier** his thoughts were filled with the care of his salvation/future (*littér*).
(c) ~s (*entretien, hygiène*) care (*U*); (*attention*) care (and attention) (*U*); (*traitement*) attention (*U*), treatment (*U*); **les ~s du ménage** *ou* **domestiques** the care of the home; **l'enfant a besoin des ~s d'une mère** the child needs a mother's care (and attention); **~s de beauté** beauty care; **pour les ~s de la chevelure/des ongles utilisez ...** for hair-/nail-care use ...; **les ~s du visage** face-care, care of the complexion; **son état demande des ~s** his condition needs treatment *ou* (medical) attention; **le blessé a reçu les premiers ~s** the injured man has been given first aid; **confier qn/qch aux (bons) ~s de** to leave sb/sth in the hands *ou* care of; (*sur lettre: frm*) **aux bons ~s de** care of, c/o; **être aux petits ~s pour qn** to lavish attention upon sb, wait on sb hand and foot.
(d) (*loc*) **avoir** *ou* **prendre ~ de faire** to take care to do, make a point of doing; **avoir** *ou* **prendre ~ de qn/qch** to take care of *ou* look after sb/sth; **il prend bien ~/grand ~ de sa petite personne** he takes good care/great care of his little self; **ayez** *ou* **prenez ~ d'éteindre** take care *ou* be sure to turn out the lights, make sure you turn out the lights.
soir [swaʀ] *nm* **(a)** evening. **les ~s d'automne/d'hiver** autumn/winter evenings; **le ~ descend** evening is closing in; **le ~ où j'y suis allé** the evening I went; **viens nous voir un de ces ~s** come and see us one evening *ou* night; (*fig littér*) **au ~ de la/sa vie** in the evening of life/his life (*littér*).
(b) du ~: repas/journal du ~ evening meal/paper; **5 heures du ~** 5 (o'clock) in the afternoon *ou* evening, 5 p.m.; **8 heures du ~** 8 (o'clock) in the evening, 8 o'clock at night, 8 p.m.; **11 heures du ~** 11 (o'clock) at night, 11 p.m.; *V* **cours, robe.**
(c) (*loc: compléments de temps*) **le ~ je vais souvent les voir** in the evening I often go to see them, I often go to see them of an evening; **le ~, je suis allé les voir/il a plu** in the evening I went to see them/it rained; **il pleut assez souvent le ~** it quite often rains in the evening(s); **j'y vais ce ~** I'm going this evening *ou* tonight; **tous les ~s, chaque ~** every evening *ou* night; **hier ~** last night, yesterday evening; **demain ~** tomorrow evening *ou* night; **dimanche ~** Sunday evening *ou* night; **hier/la veille/le 17 au ~** in the evening (of) yesterday/of the next day/of the 17th.
soirée [swaʀe] *nf* **(a)** (*soir*) evening.
(b) (*réception*) party. **~ dansante** dance; *V* **tenu.**
(c) (*Ciné, Théât: séance*) evening performance. **donner un spectacle/une pièce en ~** to give an evening performance of a show/play.
soissons [swasɔ̃] *nmpl* (*haricots*) (variety of) dwarf beans.
soit [swa] **1** *adv* (*frm: oui*) very well, well and good, so be it (*frm*). **eh bien, ~, qu'il y aille!** very well then *ou* well and good then, let him go!; *V* **tant.**
2 *conj* **(a)** (*d'alternative*) **~ ... ~: ~ l'un ~ l'autre** (either) one or the other; **~ avant ~ après** (either) before or after; **~ timidité, ~ mépris** *ou* **~ timidité ou mépris, elle ne lui adressait jamais la parole** be it (out of) *ou* whether out of shyness or contempt she never spoke to him; **~ que** + *subj*: **~ qu'il soit fatigué, ~ qu'il en ait assez** whether he is tired or whether he has had enough; **~ qu'il n'entende pas, ou ne veuille pas entendre** whether he cannot hear or (whether) he does not wish to hear.
(b) (*à savoir*) that is to say. **des détails importants, ~ l'approvisionnement, le transport etc** important details, that is to say provisions, transport etc.
(c) (*Math: posons*) **~ un rectangle ABCD** let ABCD be a rectangle.
soixantaine [swasɑ̃tɛn] *nf* **(a)** (*environ soixante*) sixty or so, (round) about sixty, sixty-odd*. **il y avait une ~ de personnes/de livres** there were sixty or so *ou* (round) about sixty people/books, there were sixty-odd* people/books; **la ~ de spectateurs qui étaient là** the sixty or so *ou* the sixty-odd* people there; **ils étaient une bonne ~** there were a good sixty of them; **il y a une ~/une bonne ~ d'années** sixty or so *ou* sixty-odd*/a good sixty years ago; **ça doit coûter une ~ de mille (francs)** that must cost sixty thousand or so francs *ou* (round) about sixty thousand francs *ou* some sixty thousand francs.
(b) (*soixante unités*) sixty. **sa collection n'atteint pas encore/a dépassé la ~** his collection has not yet reached/has passed the sixty mark, there are not yet sixty/are now over sixty in his collection.
(c) (*âge*) sixty. **approcher de la/atteindre la ~** to near/reach sixty; **un homme dans la ~** a man in his sixties; **d'une ~ d'années** *personne* of about sixty; *arbre* sixty or so years old; **elle a la ~** she is sixtyish *ou* around sixty.
soixante [swasɑ̃t] *adj inv, nm inv* sixty. **à la page ~** on page sixty; **habiter au ~** to live at number sixty; **les années ~** the sixties, the 60s; **~ et un** sixty-one; **~ et unième** sixty-first; **~-dix** seventy; **~-dixième** seventieth; **~ mille** sixty thousand.
soixantième [swasɑ̃tjɛm] *adj, nm* sixtieth.
soja [sɔʒa] *nm* (*plante*) soya; (*graines*) soya beans (*pl*). **germes de ~** (soya) bean sprouts.
sol[1] [sɔl] **1** *nm* (*gén*) ground; (*plancher*) floor; (*revêtement*) floor, flooring (*U*); (*territoire, terrain: Agr, Géol*) soil. **étendu sur le ~** spread out on the ground; **la surface du ~** the floor surface; (*Constr*) **la pose des ~s** the laying of floors *ou* of flooring; **sur ~ français** on French soil; (*Aviat*) **essais/vitesse au ~** ground tests/speed; (*Sport*) **exercices au ~** floor exercises.
2: (*Mil*) **sol-air** *adj inv* ground-to-air; **sol-sol** *adj inv* ground-to-ground.
sol[2] [sɔl] *nm inv* (*Mus*) G; (*en chantant la gamme*) so(h); *V* **clef.**
sol[3] [sɔl] *nm* (*Chim*) sol.
solaire [sɔlɛʀ] *adj* **(a)** (*Astrol, Astron*) solar; *crème, filtre* sun (*attrib*); *V* **cadran, spectre, système. (b)** *V* **plexus.**
solarium [sɔlaʀjɔm] *nm* solarium.
soldanelle [sɔldanɛl] *nf* (*Bot*) (*primulacée*) soldanella; (*liseron*) sea bindweed.
soldat [sɔlda] *nm* (*gén*) soldier. **(simple) ~, ~ de 2e classe** (*Armée de terre*) private; (*Armée de l'air*) aircraftman (*Brit*),

airman basic (*US*); ~ de 1ère classe (*Armée de terre*) ≃ private (*Brit*), private first class (*US*); (*Armée de l'air*) leading aircraftman (*Brit*), airman first class (*US*); ~ d'infanterie infantryman; se faire ~ to join the army, enlist; le S~ inconnu the Unknown Soldier *ou* Warrior; (*fig littér*) ~ de la liberté/du Christ soldier of liberty/of Christ; ~ de plomb tin *ou* toy soldier; *V* fille.

soldatesque [sɔldatɛsk(ə)] (*péj*) 1 *nf* army rabble. 2 *adj* (*rare*, †) barrack-room (*épith*).

solde¹ [sɔld(ə)] *nf* (a) [*soldat, matelot*] pay. (b) (*péj*) être à la ~ de to be in the pay of; avoir qn à sa ~ to have sb in one's pay.

solde² [sɔld(ə)] *nm* (a) (*Comm: reliquat*) (*gén*) balance; (*reste à payer*) balance outstanding. il y a un ~ de 10 F en votre faveur there is a balance of 10 francs in your favour *ou* to your credit; ~ débiteur/créditeur debit/credit balance; pour ~ de (tout) compte in settlement.
(b) ~ (de marchandises) sale goods (*pl*); vente de ~s sale, sale of reduced items; ~ de lainages sale of woollens, woollen sale; mettre des marchandises en ~ to put goods in a sale; vendre/acheter qch en ~ to sell (off)/buy sth at sale price; article (vendu) en ~ sale(s) item *ou* article; les ~s (*parfois f*) the sales *ou* Sales; je l'ai acheté aux ~s I bought it in the sales; la saison des ~s the sales season.

solder [sɔlde] (1) 1 *vt* (a) *compte* (*arrêter*) to draw up; (*acquitter*) to pay (off) the balance of, settle, balance.
(b) *marchandises* to sell (off) at sale price. ils soldent ces pantalons à 30 F they are selling off these trousers at *ou* for 30 francs, they are selling these trousers in the sale at *ou* for 30 francs; je vous le solde à 10 F I'll let you have it for 10 francs, I'll knock it down* *ou* reduce it to 10 francs for you.
2 se solder *vpr*: se ~ par (*Comm*) [*exercice, budget*] to show; (*fig*) [*entreprise, opération*] to end in; les comptes se soldent par un bénéfice the accounts show a profit; l'exercice se solde par un déficit/boni de 50 millions the end-of-year figures show a loss/profit of 50 million; l'entreprise/la conférence s'est soldée par un échec the undertaking/conference ended in failure *ou* came to nothing.

sole¹ [sɔl] *nf* (*poisson*) sole.

sole² [sɔl] *nf* (*Tech*) [*four*] hearth; [*sabot, bateau*] sole.

solécisme [sɔlesism(ə)] *nm* solecism (*in language*).

soleil [sɔlɛj] *nm* (a) (*astre: gén, Astron, Myth*) sun. orienté au ~ levant/couchant facing the rising/setting sun; le ~ de minuit the midnight sun; (*littér*) les ~s pâles/brumeux de l'hiver the pale/misty sun of winter; (*fig*) tu es mon (rayon de) ~ you are the sunshine of my life; *V* coucher, lever, rayon *etc*.
(b) (*chaleur*) sun, sunshine; (*lumière*) sun, sunshine, sunlight. au ~ in the sun; être assis/se mettre au ~ to be sitting in/go into the sun(shine) *ou* sun(light); vivre au ~ to live in the sun; il y a du ~, il fait du ~, il fait ~* the sun is shining, it's sunny; il fait un beau ~ it's lovely and sunny; il fait un ~ de plomb the sun is blazing down, there's a blazing sun; être en plein ~ to be right in the sun; des jours sans ~ sunless days; se chercher un coin au ~ to look for a spot in the sun(shine) *ou* a sunny spot; chat qui cherche le ~ cat looking for a sunny spot; les pays du ~ the lands of the sun; *V* bain, coup, fondre.
(c) (*motif, ornement*) sun.
(d) (*feu d'artifice*) Catherine wheel.
(e) (*acrobatie*) grand circle. (*fig: culbute*) faire un ~ to turn *ou* do a somersault, somersault.
(f) (*fleur*) sunflower.
(g) (*loc*) se lever avec le ~ to rise with the sun, be up with the sun *ou* the lark; (*Prov*) le ~ brille pour tout le monde nature belongs to everyone; rien de nouveau *ou* neuf sous le ~ there's nothing new under the sun; avoir du bien au ~ to be the owner of property, have property; (*fig*) se faire/avoir une place au ~ to find oneself/have a place in the sun.

solennel, -elle [sɔlanɛl] *adj* (*gén*) solemn; *séance* ceremonial; *V* communion.

solennellement [sɔlanɛlmɑ̃] *adv* (*V* solennel) solemnly; ceremonially, in ceremony.

solenniser [sɔlanize] (1) *vt* to solemnize.

solennité [sɔlanite] *nf* (a) (*U*) solemnity. (b) (*fête*) grand occasion; (*Rel*) solemnity. (c) (*gén pl: formalité*) formality, solemnity.

solénoïde [sɔlenɔid] *nm* (*Élec*) solenoid.

soleret [sɔlʀɛ] *nm* (*Hist*) solleret.

solfège [sɔlfɛʒ] *nm* (*rudiments*) rudiments of music; (*livre*) book on the rudiments of music.

solfier [sɔlfje] (7) *vt* to solfa.

soli [sɔli] *nmpl de* solo.

solidaire [sɔlidɛʀ] *adj* (a) (*mutuellement liés*) être ~s to show solidarity, stand *ou* stick together; pendant les grèves les ouvriers sont ~s during strikes, workers stand *ou* stick together *ou* show solidarity; être ~ de to stand by, be behind; nous sommes ~s du gouvernement we stand by *ou* are behind *ou* are backing the government; être ~ des victimes d'un régime to show solidarity with *ou* stand by *ou* support the victims of a régime; ces pays se sentent ~s these countries feel they have each others' support *ou* feel solidarity with each other.
(b) (*interdépendant*) *mécanismes, pièces, systèmes* interdependent. (*dépendant de*) être ~ de to be bound up with, be dependent on.
(c) (*Jur*) *contrat, engagement* binding all parties; *débiteurs* jointly responsible.

solidairement [sɔlidɛʀmɑ̃] *adv* jointly, jointly and severally (*T*).

solidariser (se) [sɔlidaʀize] (1) *vpr*: se ~ avec to show solidarity with.

solidarité [sɔlidaʀite] *nf* (a) (*V* solidaire) solidarity; interdependence. ~ de classe/professionnelle class/professional solidarity; cesser le travail par ~ avec des grévustes to come out in sympathy *ou* stop work in sympathy with the strikers; *V* grève.
(b) (*Jur*) joint and several liability.

solide [sɔlid] 1 *adj* (a) (*non liquide*) *nourriture, état, corps* solid. ne lui donnez pas encore d'aliments ~s don't give him any solid food *ou* any solids yet.
(b) (*robuste*) *matériaux* solid, sturdy, tough; *outil* solid, strong; *construction* solid, sturdy. c'est du ~ it's solid stuff; être ~ sur ses jambes to be steady on one's legs; avoir une position ~ to have a secure position.
(c) (*fig: durable, sérieux*) *institutions, qualités* sound, solid; *bases* solid, firm, sound; *amitié, vertus* solid; *connaissances, raisons* sound. doué d'un ~ bon sens possessing sound common sense *ou* good solid common sense; ces opinions/raisonnements ne reposent sur rien de ~ these opinions/arguments have no solid *ou* sound foundation.
(d) (*fig*) *personne* (*vigoureux, en bonne santé*) sturdy, robust; (*sérieux, sûr*) reliable, solid; *poigne, jambes, bras* sturdy, solid; *santé, poumons, cœur* sound; *esprit, psychisme* sound. avoir la tête ~ (*lit*) to have a hard head; (*fig: équilibré*) to have a good head on one's shoulders; il n'a plus la tête bien ~ his mind's not what it was; *V* rein.
(e) (*intensif*) *coup de poing* (good) hefty*; *revenus* substantial; *engueulade* good, proper*. un ~ repas le remit d'aplomb a (good) solid meal set him up again.
(f) (*loc*) être ~ au poste (*Mil*) to be loyal to one's post; (*fig*) to be completely dependable *ou* reliable; ~ comme le Pont-Neuf† *personne* (as) strong as an ox.
2 *nm* (*Géom, Phys*) solid.

solidement [sɔlidmɑ̃] *adv* (a) (*lit*) *fixer, attacher, tenir* firmly; *fabriquer, construire* solidly. résister ~ to put up a solid *ou* firm resistance.
(b) (*fig*) *s'établir, s'installer* securely, firmly, solidly; *raisonner* soundly. rester ~ attaché aux traditions to remain firmly attached to traditions; être ~ attaché à qn/qch to be deeply *ou* profoundly attached to sb/sth; il l'a ~ engueulé* he gave him a good *ou* proper telling-off*, he told him off well and truly*.

solidification [sɔlidifikɑsjɔ̃] *nf* solidification.

solidifier *vt*, **se solidifier** *vpr* [sɔlidifje] (7) to solidify.

solidité [sɔlidite] *nf* (*V* solide) solidity; sturdiness; toughness; soundness; robustness; reliability.

soliloque [sɔlilɔk] *nm* soliloquy.

soliloquer [sɔlilɔke] (1) *vi* to soliloquize.

solipède [sɔlipɛd] *adj, nm* solidungulate.

solipsisme [sɔlipsism(ə)] *nm* solipsism.

soliste [sɔlist(ə)] *nmf* soloist.

solitaire [sɔlitɛʀ] 1 *adj* (a) (*isolé*) *passant* solitary (*épith*), lone (*épith*); *maison, arbre, rocher* solitary (*épith*), lonely (*épith*), isolated. là vivaient quelques chasseurs/bûcherons ~s there lived a few solitary *ou* lone hunters/woodcutters.
(b) (*désert*) *parc, demeure, chemin* lonely (*épith*), deserted, solitary (*épith*).
(c) (*sans compagnie*) *adolescent, vieillard, vie* solitary, lonely, lonesome (*US*); *passe-temps, caractère* solitary; *V* plaisir.
(d) *V* ver.
2 *nmf* (*ermite*) solitary, recluse; (*fig: ours*) lone wolf, loner. il préfère travailler en ~ he prefers to work on his own.
3 *nm* (a) (*sanglier*) old boar.
(b) (*diamant*) solitaire.
(c) (*jeu*) solitaire.

solitairement [sɔlitɛʀmɑ̃] *adv* *souffrir* alone. vivre ~ to lead a solitary life, live alone.

solitude [sɔlityd] *nf* [*personne*] (*tranquillité*) solitude; (*manque de compagnie*) loneliness; [*endroit*] loneliness. ~ morale moral solitude; cette ~ à deux que peut devenir le mariage this shared solitude which marriage may turn into; (*littér*) les ~s glacées du Grand Nord the icy solitudes of the far North (*littér*).

solive [sɔliv] *nf* joist.

sollicitation [sɔlisitɑsjɔ̃] *nf* (a) (*démarche*) entreaty, appeal.
(b) (*littér: gén pl: tentation*) solicitation (*littér*), enticement.
(c) (*action exercée sur qch*) prompting. l'engin répondait aux moindres ~s de son pilote the craft responded to the slightest promptings of its pilot.

solliciter [sɔlisite] (1) *vt* (a) (*frm: demander*) *poste* to seek, solicit (*frm*); *faveur, audience, explication* to seek, request, solicit (*frm*) (*de qn* from sb).
(b) (*frm: faire appel à*) *personne* to appeal to. ~ qn de faire to appeal to sb *ou* request sb to do; je l'ai déjà sollicité à plusieurs reprises à ce sujet I have already appealed to him *ou* approached him on several occasions over this matter; il est très sollicité there are many calls upon him, he's very much in demand.
(c) (*agir sur*) *curiosité, sens de qn* to appeal to; *attention* to attract, solicit (*frm*). les attractions qui sollicitent le touriste the attractions that are there to tempt the tourist; mille détails sollicitaient leur curiosité a thousand details appealed to their curiosity; le moteur répondait immédiatement lorsque le pilote le sollicitait the engine responded immediately when the pilot prompted it.

solliciteur, -euse [sɔlisitœʀ, øz] 1 *nm,f* supplicant. 2 *nm* (*Can*) ~ général Solicitor General.

sollicitude [sɔlisityd] *nf* concern (*U*), solicitude (*frm*). toutes leurs ~s finissaient par nous agacer we found their constant concern (for our welfare) *ou* their solicitude (*frm*) annoying in the end.

solo [sɔlo], *pl* ~s *ou* soli *adj inv, nm* solo. ~ de violon violin

solo; **violon ~** solo violin; **jouer/chanter en ~** to sing/play solo.
solstice [sɔlstis] *nm* solstice. **~ d'hiver/d'été** winter/summer solstice.
solubiliser [sɔlybilize] (1) *vt* to make soluble.
solubilité [sɔlybilite] *nf* solubility.
soluble [sɔlybl(ə)] *adj* **(a)** *substance* soluble. **(b)** *problème* soluble, solvable.
soluté [sɔlyte] *nm* (*Chim, Pharm*) solution.
solution [sɔlysjɔ̃] **1** *nf* **(a)** *[problème, énigme, équation]* (*action*) solution, solving (*de* of); (*résultat*) solution, answer (*de* to).
(b) *[difficulté, situation]* (*issue*) solution, answer (*de* to); (*moyens employés*) solution (*de* to). **c'est une ~ de facilité** that's an easy answer *ou* the easy way out; **ce n'est pas une ~ à la crise qu'ils traversent** that's no answer to *ou* no real way out of the crisis they're in, that's no real way to resolve the crisis they're in; **hâter la ~ d'une crise** to hasten the resolution *ou* settling of a crisis.
(c) (*Chim: action, mélange*) solution. **en ~** in solution.
2: (*frm*) **solution de continuité** solution of continuity (*frm*).
solutionner [sɔlysjɔne] (1) *vt* to solve.
solvabilité [sɔlvabilite] *nf* solvency.
solvable [sɔlvabl(ə)] *adj* (*Fin*) solvent.
solvant [sɔlvɑ̃] *nm* (*Chim*) solvent.
soma [sɔma] *nm* soma.
Somalie [sɔmali] *nf* Somaliland.
somatique [sɔmatik] *adj* (*Bio, Psych*) somatic.
sombre [sɔ̃bʀ(ə)] *adj* **(a)** (*peu éclairé, foncé*) dark. (*littér*) **de ~s abîmes** dark abysses; **il fait déjà ~** it's already dark; **bleu/vert ~** dark blue/green; *V* **coupe**².
(b) (*fig*) (*mélancolique*) sombre, gloomy, dismal; (*ténébreux, funeste*) dark, sombre. **de ~s pensées** sombre *ou* gloomy thoughts, dark *ou* black thoughts; **un ~ avenir** a dark *ou* gloomy *ou* dismal future; **les moments *ou* heures ~s de notre histoire** the dark *ou* sombre moments of our history.
(c) (*valeur intensive*) **~ idiot/brute** dreadful idiot/brute; **une ~ histoire d'enlèvement** a murky story of abduction.
sombrement [sɔ̃bʀ(ə)mɑ̃] *adv* (*V* **sombre**) darkly; sombrely; gloomily, dismally.
sombrer [sɔ̃bʀe] (1) *vi [bateau]* to sink, go down, founder; (*fig*) *[raison]* to give way; *[empire]* to founder; *[fortune]* to be swallowed up. **~ dans le désespoir/le sommeil** to sink into despair/sleep; **~ corps et biens** to go down with all hands.
sombrero [sɔ̃bʀeʀo] *nm* sombrero.
sommaire [sɔmɛʀ] **1** *adj exposé, explication* basic, summary (*épith*), brief; *réponse* brief, summary (*épith*); *examen* brief, cursory, perfunctory; *instruction, réparation, repas* basic; *tenue, décoration* scanty; *justice, procédure, exécution* summary (*épith*).
2 *nm* (*exposé*) summary; (*résumé de chapitre*) summary, argument.
sommairement [sɔmɛʀmɑ̃] *adv* (*V* **sommaire**) basically; summarily; briefly; cursorily; scantily. **il me l'a expliqué assez ~** he gave me a fairly basic explanation of it.
sommation [sɔmɑsjɔ̃] *nf* (*Jur*) summons; (*frm: injonction*) demand; (*avant de faire feu*) warning. (*Jur*) **recevoir ~ de payer une dette** to be served with notice to pay a debt *ou* with a demand for payment of a debt; (*Mil, Police*) **faire les ~s d'usage** to give the standard *ou* customary warnings.
somme¹ [sɔm] *nf V* **bête**.
somme² [sɔm] *nm* nap, snooze*. **faire un petit ~** to have a (short) nap *ou* a (little) snooze* *ou* forty winks*.
somme³ [sɔm] *nf* **(a)** (*Math*) sum; (*gén*) (*pluralité*) sum total; (*quantité*) amount. **~ algébrique** algebraic sum; **la ~ totale** the grand total, the total sum; **faire la ~ de** to add up; **la ~ des dégâts est considérable** the (total) amount of damage *ou* the total damage is considerable; **une ~ de travail énorme** an enormous amount of work.
(b) ~ (d'argent) sum *ou* amount (of money); (*intensif*) **c'est une ~!** it's quite a sum, it's quite a large amount.
(c) (*ouvrage de synthèse*) general survey. **une ~ littéraire/scientifique** a general survey of literature/of science.
(d) (*loc*) **en ~** (*tout bien considéré*) all in all; (*en résumé, après tout*) in sum, in short; **en ~, il ne s'agit que d'un incident sans importance** all in all, it's only an incident of minor importance; **en ~, vous n'en voulez plus?** in sum *ou* in short, you don't want any more?; (*frm*) **~ toute** when all's said and done.
sommeil [sɔmɛj] *nm* **(a)** (*état du dormeur, Physiol, Zool*) sleep; (*envie de dormir*) drowsiness, sleepiness. **avoir ~** to be *ou* feel sleepy; **tomber de ~** to be ready to drop (with tiredness *ou* sleep); **un ~ agréable l'envahissait** a pleasant drowsiness *ou* sleepiness *ou* desire to sleep was creeping over him; **8 heures de ~** 8 hours' sleep; **avoir le ~ léger** to be a light sleeper, sleep lightly; **dormir d'un ~ agité** to sleep restlessly; **un ~ de plomb** a heavy *ou* deep sleep; **premier ~** first hours of sleep; **nuit sans ~** sleepless night; *V* **cure**¹, **dormir, maladie.**
(b) (*fig: gén littér: inactivité*) **le ~ de la nature** nature's sleep (*littér*), the dormant state of nature; **affaires en ~** dormant affairs, affairs in abeyance; **laisser une affaire en ~** to leave a matter (lying) dormant, leave a matter in abeyance; **le ~ de la petite ville pendant l'hiver** the sleepiness of the little town during winter; (*littér*) **le ~ éternel, le dernier ~** eternal rest; **le ~ des morts** the sleep of the dead.
sommeiller [sɔmeje] (1) *vi [personne]* to doze; (*fig*) *[qualité, défaut, nature]* to lie dormant; *V* **cochon**¹.
sommelier [sɔməlje] *nm* wine waiter.
sommer¹ [sɔme] (1) *vt* (*frm: enjoindre*) **~ qn de faire** to charge *ou* enjoin sb to do (*frm*); (*Jur*) **~ qn de *ou* à comparaître** to summon sb to appear.
sommer² [sɔme] (1) *vt* (*additionner*) to sum.
sommet [sɔmɛ] *nm* **(a)** (*point culminant*) *[montagne]* summit, top; *[tour, arbre, toit, pente, hiérarchie]* top; *[vague]* crest; *[crâne]* crown, vertex (*T*); (*Géom, Math*) *[angle]* vertex; *[solide, figure, parabole]* vertex, apex. (*fig*) **les ~s de la gloire/des honneurs** the summits *ou* heights of fame/honour; (*littér, hum*) **redescendons de ces ~s** let us climb down from these lofty heights (*littér, hum*); *V* **conférence.**
(b) (*cime, montagne*) summit, mountain top. **l'air pur des ~s** the pure air of the summits *ou* the mountaintops.
sommier [sɔmje] *nm* **(a)** *[lit]* **~ (à ressorts)** (*s'encastrant dans le lit, fixé au lit*) springing (*U*) (*of bedstead*); (*avec pieds*) (interior-sprung) divan base; **~ (métallique)** mesh-springing; mesh-sprung divan base.
(b) (*Tech*) *[voûte]* impost, springer; *[clocher]* stock; *[porte, fenêtre]* transom; *[grille]* lower crossbar; *[orgue]* windchest.
sommité [sɔmite] *nf* **(a)** (*personne*) prominent person, leading light (*de* in). **(b)** (*Bot*) head.
somnambule [sɔmnɑ̃byl] **1** *nmf* sleepwalker, somnambulist (*T*). **marcher/agir comme un ~** to walk/act like a sleepwalker *ou* as if in a trance. **2** *adj*: être **~** to be a sleepwalker, sleepwalk.
somnambulisme [sɔmnɑ̃bylism(ə)] *nm* sleepwalking, somnambulism (*T*).
somnifère [sɔmnifɛʀ] **1** *nm* sleeping drug, soporific; (*pilule*) sleeping pill, sleeping tablet. **2** *adj* (*rare*) somniferous (*frm*), sleep-inducing, soporific.
somnolence [sɔmnɔlɑ̃s] *nf* sleepiness (*U*), drowsiness (*U*), somnolence (*U*) (*frm*); (*fig*) indolence, inertia.
somnolent, e [sɔmnɔlɑ̃, ɑ̃t] *adj* sleepy, drowsy, somnolent (*frm*); (*fig*) *vie, province* drowsy, languid; *faculté* dormant, inert.
somnoler [sɔmnɔle] (1) *vi* (*lit*) to doze; (*fig*) to lie dormant.
somptuaire [sɔ̃ptɥɛʀ] *adj* **(a)** *loi, réforme* sumptuary. **(b)** *dépense* **~** extravagant expenditure (*U*); **arts ~s** decorative arts.
somptueusement [sɔ̃ptɥøzmɑ̃] *adv* (*V* **somptueux**) sumptuously; magnificently; lavishly; handsomely.
somptueux, -euse [sɔ̃ptɥø, øz] *adj habit, résidence* sumptuous, magnificent; *train de vie* lavish; *cadeau* handsome (*épith*), sumptuous; *repas, festin* sumptuous, lavish.
somptuosité [sɔ̃ptɥozite] *nf* (*V* **somptueux**) sumptuousness (*U*); magnificence (*U*); lavishness (*U*); handsomeness (*U*).
son¹ [sɔ̃], **sa** [sa], **ses** [se] *adj poss* **(a)** *[homme]* his; (*emphatique*) his own; *[femme]* her; (*emphatique*) her own; *[nation]* its, her; (*emphatique*) its own, her own. **S~ Altesse Royale** (*prince*) His Royal Highness; (*princesse*) Her Royal Highness; **Sa Majesté** (*roi*) His Majesty; (*reine*) Her Majesty; **Sa Sainteté le pape** His Holiness the Pope; **ce n'est pas ~ genre** he *ou* she is not that sort, it's not like him *ou* her; **quand s'est passé ~ accident?** when did she *ou* he have her *ou* his accident?; **~ père et sa mère, ses père et mère** his (*ou* her) father and (his *ou* her) mother; (*emphatique*) **~ jardin à elle/lui est une vraie jungle** HIS *ou* his own/HER *ou* her own garden is a real jungle; **ses date et lieu de naissance** his (*ou* her) date and place of birth; **à sa vue, elle poussa un cri** she screamed at the sight of him (*ou* her) *ou* on seeing him (*ou* her); **un de ses amis** one of his (*ou* her) friends, a friend of his (*ou* hers); **~ idiote de sœur*** that stupid sister of hers (*ou* his).
(b) *[objet, abstraction]* its. **l'hôtel est réputé pour sa cuisine** the hotel is famous for its food; **pour comprendre ce crime il faut chercher ~ mobile** to understand this crime we must try to find the motivation for it; **ça a ~ importance** that has its *ou* a certain importance.
(c) (*à valeur d'indéfini*) one's; (*après chacun, personne etc*) his, her. **faire ses études** to study; **on ne connaît pas ~ bonheur** one never knows how fortunate one is; **être satisfait de sa situation** to be satisfied with one's situation; **chacun selon ses possibilités** each according to his (own) capabilities; **personne ne sait comment finira sa vie** no one knows how his life will end.
(d) (*: *valeur affective, ironique, intensive*) **il doit (bien) gagner ~ million par an** he must be (easily) earning a million a year; **avoir ~ samedi/dimanche** to have (one's) Saturday(s)/Sunday(s) off; **il a passé tout ~ dimanche à travailler** he spent the whole of *ou* all Sunday working; **~ M X ne me plaît pas du tout** I don't care for his Mr X at all; **avoir ses petites manies** to have one's little fads; **elle a ses jours!** she has her (good) days!; **il a sa crise de foie** he is having one of his liverish attacks; **cet enfant ne ferme jamais ses portes** that child will never shut doors *ou* a door behind him; *V* **sentir.**
son² [sɔ̃] *nm* **(a)** (*gén, Ling, Phys*) sound. **le timbre et la hauteur du ~ d'une cloche/d'un tambour/d'un avertisseur** the tone and pitch of the sound of a bell/a drum/an alarm; **réveillé par le ~ des cloches/tambours/klaxons** woken by the sound of bells/drums/hooters, woken by the ringing of bells/the beat of drums/the blare of hooters; **défiler au ~ d'une fanfare** to march past to the music of a band; (*fig*) **n'entendre qu'un/entendre un autre ~ de cloche** to hear only one/another side of the story; (*fig*) **annoncer *ou* proclamer qch à ~ de trompe** to blazon *ou* trumpet sth abroad; *V* **mur, qui.**
(b) (*Ciné, Rad, TV*) sound. **baisser le ~** to turn down the sound *ou* volume; **équipe/ingénieur du ~** sound team/engineer; **synchroniser le ~ et l'image** to synchronize the sound and the picture; **(spectacle) ~ et lumière** son et lumière (display); *V* **pris.**
son³ [sɔ̃] *nm* bran; **farine de ~** bran flour; *V* **tache.**
sonar [sɔnaʀ] *nm* sonar.
sonate [sɔnat] *nf* sonata; *V* **forme.**
sonatine [sɔnatin] *nf* sonatina.
sondage [sɔ̃daʒ] *nm* (*Tech: forage*) boring, drilling; (*Mét, Naut*) sounding; (*Méd*) probing (*U*), probe; (*pour évacuer*)

catheterization; (*fig*) sounding out of opinion (*U*). ~ **(d'opinion)** (opinion) poll, Gallup Poll.

sonde [sɔ̃d] *nf* **(a)** (*Naut*) (*instrument*) lead line, sounding line; (*relevé: gén pl*) soundings (*pl*). **naviguer à la** ~ to navigate by soundings; **jeter une** ~ to cast the lead.
(b) (*Tech: de forage*) borer, drill.
(c) (*Méd*) probe; (*à canal central*) catheter; (*d'alimentation*) feeding tube. **mettre une** ~ **à qn** to put a catheter in sb; **alimenter un malade avec une** ~ to feed a patient through a tube.
(d) (*Aviat, Mét*) sonde. ~ **atmosphérique** sonde; ~ **spatiale** probe; *V* **ballon.**
(e) (*de douanier: pour fouiller*) probe; (*Comm: pour prélever*) taster; (*à avalanche*) pole (*for locating victims*). ~ **à fromage** cheese taster.

sonder [sɔ̃de] (1) *vt* **(a)** (*Naut*) to sound; (*Mét*) to probe; (*Tech*) *terrain* to bore, drill; *bagages* to probe, search (with a probe); *avalanche* to probe; (*Méd*) *plaie* to probe; *vessie* to catheterize. (*littér*) **il sonda l'abîme du regard** his eyes probed the depths of the abyss (*littér*).
(b) (*fig*) *personne* to sound out; *conscience, avenir* to sound out, probe. ~ **les esprits** to sound out opinion; ~ **l'opinion** to make a survey of (public) opinion; *V* **terrain.**

sondeur [sɔ̃dœʀ] *nm* (*Tech*) sounder.

songe [sɔ̃ʒ] *nm* (*littér*) dream. **en** ~ in a dream; **faire un** ~ to have a dream.

songe-creux [sɔ̃ʒkʀø] *nm inv* (†, *littér*) visionary.

songer [sɔ̃ʒe] (3) **1** *vi* (*littér: rêver*) to dream.
2 *vt*: ~ **que** ... to reflect *ou* consider that ... ; **'ils pourraient refuser' songeait-il** 'they could refuse' he reflected *ou* mused; **songez que cela peut présenter de grands dangers** remember *ou* you must be aware that it can present great dangers; **il n'avait jamais songé qu'ils puissent réussir** he had never imagined they might be successful.
3 songer à *vt indir* (*évoquer*) to muse over *ou* upon, think over, reflect upon; (*considérer, penser à*) to consider, think over, reflect upon; (*envisager*) to contemplate, think of *ou* about; (*s'occuper de, prendre soin de*) to think of, have regard for. **songez-y** think it over, consider it; **il ne songe qu'à son avancement** he thinks only of *ou* he has regard only for his own advancement; ~ **à faire qch** to contemplate doing sth, think of *ou* about doing sth; **quand on songe à tout ce gaspillage** when you think of all this waste.

songerie [sɔ̃ʒʀi] *nf* (*littér*) reverie.

songeur, -euse [sɔ̃ʒœʀ, øz] **1** *adj* pensive. **cela me laisse** ~ I just don't know what to think. **2** *nm,f* dreamer.

sonique [sɔnik] *adj vitesse* sonic. **barrière** ~ sound barrier.

sonnant, e [sɔnɑ̃, ɑ̃t] *adj* **(a) à 4 heures** ~**(es)** on the stroke *ou* dot of 4, at 4 (o'clock) sharp. **(b)** *V* **espèce. (c)** *horloge* chiming, striking.

sonné, e [sɔne] (*ptp de* **sonner**) *adj* **(a) il est midi** ~ it's gone twelve; **avoir trente ans bien** ~**s*** to be on the wrong side of thirty*. **(b)** (*: *fou*) cracked*, off one's rocker* (*attrib*). **(c)** (*: *assommé*) groggy.

sonner [sɔne] (1) **1** *vt* **(a)** *cloche* to ring; *tocsin, glas* to sound, toll; *clairon* to sound. ~ **trois coups à la porte** to ring three times at the door; **se faire** ~ **les cloches*** to get a good ticking-off* (*Brit*) *ou* telling-off*.
(b) (*annoncer*) *messe, matines* to ring the bell for; *réveil, rassemblement, retraite* to sound. ~ **l'alarme** to sound the alarm; (*Mil*) ~ **la charge** to sound the charge; ~ **l'heure** to strike the hour; **la pendule sonne 3 heures** the clock strikes 3 (o'clock).
(c) (*appeler*) *portier, infirmière* to ring for. **on ne t'a pas sonné!*** nobody asked you!, who rang your bell?* (*surtout Brit*).
(d) (*: *étourdir*) *[chute]* to knock out; *[nouvelle]* to stagger*, take aback. **la nouvelle l'a un peu sonné** he was rather taken aback *ou* staggered* at *ou* by the news.
2 *vi* **(a)** *[cloches, téléphone]* to ring; *[réveil]* to ring, go off; *[clairon, trompette]* to sound; *[tocsin, glas]* to sound, toll. (*Scol etc*) **la cloche a sonné** the bell has gone *ou* rung; ~ **à toute volée** to peal (out); (*fig*) **les oreilles lui sonnent** his ears are ringing.
(b) (*son métallique*) *[marteau]* to ring; *[clefs, monnaie]* to jangle, jingle. ~ **clair** to give a clear ring; ~ **creux** (*lit*) to sound hollow; (*fig*) to ring hollow; ~ **faux** (*lit*) to sound out of tune; (*fig*) to ring false; (*fig*) ~ **bien/mal** to sound good/bad; **l'argent sonna sur le comptoir** the money jingled *ou* jangled onto the counter.
(c) (*être annoncé*) *[midi, minuit]* to strike. **3 heures venaient de** ~ 3 o'clock had just struck, it had just struck 3 o'clock; **la récréation a sonné** the bell has gone for break; **la messe sonne** the bell is ringing *ou* going for mass; *V* **heure.**
(d) (*actionner une sonnette*) to ring. **on a sonné** the bell has just gone, I just heard the bell, somebody just rang (the bell); ~ **chez qn** to ring at sb's door, ring sb's doorbell.
(e) (*Phonétique*) **faire** ~ to sound.
3 sonner de *vt indir clairon, cor* to sound.

sonnerie [sɔnʀi] *nf* **(a)** (*son*) *[sonnette, cloches]* ringing. **la** ~ **du clairon** the bugle call, the sound of the bugle; **j'ai entendu la** ~ **du téléphone** I heard the telephone ringing; **la** ~ **du téléphone l'a réveillé** he was woken by the telephone('s) ringing *ou* the telephone bell; ~ **d'alarme** alarm bell.
(b) (*Mil: air*) call. **la** ~ **du réveil** (the sounding of) reveille.
(c) (*mécanisme*) *[réveil]* alarm (mechanism), bell; *[pendule]* chimes (*pl*), chiming *ou* striking mechanism; (*sonnette*) bell. ~ **électrique/téléphonique** electric/telephone bell.

sonnet [sɔnɛ] *nm* sonnet.

sonnette [sɔnɛt] *nf* **(a)** (*électrique, de porte*) bell; (*clochette*) (hand)bell. ~ **de nuit** night-bell; ~ **d'alarme** alarm bell; *V* **coup, serpent.**
(b) (*Tech*) pile driver.

sonneur [sɔnœʀ] *nm* **(a)** ~ **(de cloches)** bell ringer. **(b)** pile driver operator.

sono* [sono] *nf* (*abrév de* **sonorisation**) P.A. (system).

sonore [sɔnɔʀ] **1** *adj* **(a)** *objet, surface en métal* resonant; *voix* ringing (*épith*), sonorous, resonant; *rire* ringing (*épith*), resounding (*épith*); *baiser, gifle* resounding (*épith*).
(b) *salle* resonant; *voûte* echoing.
(c) (*péj*) *paroles, mots* high-sounding, sonorous.
(d) (*Acoustique*) *vibrations* sound (*épith*). **onde** ~ sound wave; **fond** ~ background noise.
(e) (*Ciné*) **film** ~ sound film; **bande** *ou* **piste** ~ sound track; **effets** ~**s** sound effects.
(f) (*Ling*) voiced.
2 *nf* (*Ling*) voiced consonant.

sonorisation [sɔnɔʀizɑsjɔ̃] *nf* **(a)** (*Ciné*) adding the sound track (*de* to). **(b)** *[salle de conférences etc]* (*action*) fitting with a public address system; (*équipement*) public address system, P.A. (system). **(c)** (*Ling*) voicing.

sonoriser [sɔnɔʀize] (1) *vt* **(a)** *film* to add the sound track to; *salle de conférences* to fit with a public address system *ou* a P.A. (system). **(b)** (*Ling*) to voice.

sonorité [sɔnɔʀite] *nf* **(a)** (*timbre, son*) *[radio, instrument de musique]* tone; *[voix]* sonority, tone. ~**s** *[voix, instrument]* tones. **(b)** (*Ling*) voicing. **(c)** (*résonance*) *[air]* sonority, resonance; *[salle]* acoustics (*pl*); *[cirque rocheux, grotte]* resonance.

sonothèque [sɔnɔtɛk] *nf* sound (effects) library.

sont [sɔ̃] *V* **être.**

sophisme [sɔfism(ə)] *nm* sophism.

sophiste [sɔfist(ə)] *nmf* sophist.

sophistication [sɔfistikɑsjɔ̃] *nf* (*affectation*) sophistication; (†: *altération*) adulteration.

sophistique [sɔfistik] **1** *adj* sophistic. **2** *nf* sophistry.

sophistiqué, e [sɔfistike] *adj* (*gén*) sophisticated.

Sophocle [sɔfɔkl(ə)] *nm* Sophocles.

soporifique [sɔpɔʀifik] **1** *adj* (*lit*) soporific, sleep-inducing; (*fig péj*) soporific. **2** *nm* sleeping drug, soporific.

soprano [sɔpʀano], *pl* ~**s** *ou* **soprani** [sɔpʀani] **1** *nm* soprano (voice). **2** *nmf* soprano. ~ **dramatique/lyrique** dramatic/lyric soprano.

sorbet [sɔʀbɛ] *nm* water ice, sorbet.

sorbetière [sɔʀbətjɛʀ] *nf* ice cream churn.

sorbonnard, e [sɔʀbɔnaʀ, aʀd(ə)] (*péj*) **1** *adj* pedantic, worthy of the Sorbonne (*attrib*). **2** *nm,f student or teacher at the Sorbonne.*

sorcellerie [sɔʀsɛlʀi] *nf* witchcraft, sorcery. (*fig*) **c'est de la** ~**!** it's magic!

sorcier [sɔʀsje] *nm* (*lit*) sorcerer. (*fig*) **il ne faut pas être** ~ **pour** ... you don't have to be a wizard to ... ; (*fig*) **ce n'est pas** ~**!** you don't need witchcraft *ou* magic to do it (*ou* solve it *etc*)!; *V* **apprenti.**

sorcière [sɔʀsjɛʀ] *nf* witch, sorceress; (*fig péj*) (old) witch, (old) hag.

sordide [sɔʀdid] *adj ruelle, quartier* sordid, squalid; *action, mentalité* base, sordid; *gains* sordid.

sordidement [sɔʀdidmɑ̃] *adv* (*V* **sordide**) sordidly; squalidly; basely.

sordidité [sɔʀdidite] *nf* (*V* **sordide**) sordidness; squalidness; baseness.

sorgho [sɔʀgo] *nm* sorghum.

Sorlingues [sɔʀlɛ̃g] *nfpl*: **les (îles)** ~ the Scilly Isles, the Isles of Scilly.

sornettes† [sɔʀnɛt] *nfpl* twaddle†, balderdash†.

sort [sɔʀ] *nm* **(a)** (*situation, condition*) lot. **c'est le** ~ **des paresseux d'échouer** it's the lot of the lazy to fail; **améliorer le** ~ **des malheureux/handicapés** to improve the lot of the unfortunate/the handicapped; **envier le** ~ **de qn** to envy sb's lot.
(b) (*destinée*) fate. (*hum*) **abandonner qn à son triste** ~ to abandon sb to his sad fate; **sa proposition a eu** *ou* **subi le même** ~ **que les précédentes** his proposal met with the same fate as the previous ones; **faire un** ~ **à un plat/une bouteille*** to polish off a dish/a bottle*.
(c) (*désignation par le hasard*) **le** ~ **est tombé sur lui** he was chosen by fate, it fell to his lot; **le** ~ **en est jeté** the die is cast; **le** ~ **décidera** fate will decide; **tirer au** ~ to draw lots; **tirer qch au** ~ to draw lots for sth; *V* **tirage.**
(d) (*puissance, destin*) fate. **le** ~ **est aveugle** fate is blind; **pour essayer de conjurer le (mauvais)** ~ to try to ward off fate.
(e) (*sorcellerie*) curse, spell. **il y a un** ~ **sur** ... there is a curse on ... ; **jeter un** ~ **sur** to put a curse *ou* spell *ou* jinx* on.

sortable* [sɔʀtabl(ə)] *adj* (*gén nég*) *personne* presentable. **tu n'es pas** ~**!** we (*ou* I) can't take you anywhere!*

sortant, e [sɔʀtɑ̃, ɑ̃t] **1** *adj député etc* retiring (*épith*). **les numéros** ~**s** the numbers which come up. **2** *nm* (*personne: gén pl*) les ~**s** the outgoing crowd.

sorte [sɔʀt(ə)] *nf* **(a)** (*espèce*) sort, kind. **toutes** ~**s de gens/choses** all kinds *ou* sorts *ou* manner of people/things; **des vêtements de toutes (les)** ~**s** all kinds *ou* sorts *ou* manner of clothes; **nous avons 3** ~**s de fleurs** we have 3 kinds *ou* types *ou* sorts of flower(s); **des roches de même** ~ rocks of the same sort *ou* kind *ou* type.
(b) une ~ **de** a sort *ou* kind of; (*péj*) **une** ~ **de médecin/véhicule** a doctor/car of sorts; **robe taillée dans une** ~ **de satin** dress cut out of some sort *ou* kind of satin, dress cut out of a sort *ou* kind of satin.
(c) (*loc*) **de la** ~ (*de cette façon*) in that fashion *ou* way; **accoutré de la** ~ dressed in that fashion *ou* way; **il n'a rien fait de la** ~ he did nothing of the kind *ou* no such thing; **de** ~ **à** so as to, in order to; **en quelque** ~ in a way, as it were; **vous avouez l'avoir dit, en quelque** ~ you are in a way *ou* as it were admitting

to having said it; **en aucune ~**† not at all, not in the least; **de (telle) ~ que** (*de façon à ce que*) so that, in such a way that; (*si bien que*) so much so that; **faire en ~ de: faites en ~ d'avoir fini demain** see to it *ou* arrange it *ou* arrange things so that you will have finished tomorrow; **faire en ~ que** to see to it that; (†, *littér*) **en ~ que** (*de façon à ce que*) so that, in such a way that; (*si bien que*) so much so that.

sortie [sɔʀti] **1** *nf* **(a)** (*action, moment*) *[personne]* leaving; *[véhicule, bateau, armée occupante]* departure; (*Théât*) exit. **à sa ~, tous se sont tus** when he went out *ou* left everybody fell silent; **à sa ~ du salon** when he went out of *ou* left the lounge; **faire une ~ remarquée** to be noticed as one leaves; **faire une ~ discrète** to leave discreetly; **faire une ~** (*Aviat, Mil*) to make a sortie; *[gardien de but]* to leave the goal mouth; **la ~ des ouvriers/bureaux/théâtres** when the workers/offices/theatres come out; **attention! ~ d'usine/de camions** caution, factory/vehicle exit; **sa mère l'attend tous les jours à la ~ de l'école** his mother waits for him every day after school *ou* when school comes out *ou* finishes; **retrouvons-nous à la ~ (du concert)** let's meet at the end (of the concert); **elle attend la ~ des artistes** she's waiting for the performers to come out; **à sa ~ de prison** on his discharge from prison, when he comes (*ou* came) out of prison; **c'est sa première ~ depuis sa maladie** it's his first day *ou* time out since his illness; (*Théât*) **elle a manqué sa ~ à l'acte 2** she fluffed her exit in act 2; *V* **faux**[2].

(b) (*congé*) day off; (*promenade etc*) outing; (*le soir: au théâtre etc*) evening *ou* night out. **c'est le jour de ~ de la bonne** it's the maid's day off; **c'est le jour de ~ des pensionnaires** it's the boarders' day out; **il est de ~** *[soldat, domestique]* it's his day off; **ils viennent déjeuner le dimanche, cela leur fait une petite ~** they come to lunch on Sundays – it gives them a little outing *ou* it's a day out for them; **elle s'est acheté une robe du soir pour leurs ~s** she's bought herself an evening dress for when they go out *ou* have a night out.

(c) (*lieu*) exit. **~ de secours** emergency exit; **~ des artistes** stage door; **les ~s de Paris sont encombrées** the roads out of Paris are jammed; **par ici la ~!** this way out!; (*fig*) **trouver/se ménager une (porte de) ~** to find/arrange a way out.

(d) (*écoulement*) *[eau, gaz]* outflow. **cela empêche la ~ des gaz** that prevents the gases from coming out *ou* escaping.

(e) (*emportement, algarade*) outburst; (*remarque drôle*) sally; (*remarque incongrue*) peculiar *ou* odd remark. **elle est sujette à ce genre de ~** she's given to that kind of outburst; she's always coming out with that kind of sally; she's always coming up with that kind of odd remark; **faire une ~ à qn** to let fly at sb; **faire une ~ contre qch** to lash out against sth.

(f) (*Comm: mise en vente etc*) *[voiture, modèle]* launching; *[livre]* appearance, publication; *[disque, film]* release.

(g) (*Comm*) *[marchandises, devises]* export. **la ~ de l'or/des devises/de certains produits est contingentée** there are controls on gold/currency/certain products leaving the country *ou* on the export of gold/currency/certain products; **il y a eu d'importantes ~s de devises** large amounts of currency have been flowing out of *ou* leaving the country.

(h) (*Comm, Fin: somme dépensée*) item of expenditure. **il y a eu plus de ~s que de rentrées** there are more outgoings than receipts.

2: **sortie de bain** bathrobe.

sortilège [sɔʀtilɛʒ] *nm* (magic) spell.

sortir [sɔʀtiʀ] (16) **1** *vi* **(a)** (*lit*) (*gén*) (*aller*) to go out, leave; (*venir*) to come out, leave; (*à pied*) to walk out; (*en voiture*) to drive out, go *ou* come out; *[véhicule]* to drive out, go *ou* come out; (*Théât*) to exit, leave (the stage). **~ de pièce** to go *ou* come out of, leave; *région, pays* to leave; **~ de chez qn** to go *ou* come out of sb's (house *etc*), leave sb's (house *etc*); **~ en courant** to run out; **~ en boitant** to limp out; **faire ~ la voiture du garage** to take *ou* get the car out of the garage; **il sortit discrètement (de la pièce)** he went out (of the room) *ou* left (the room) discreetly, he slipped out (of the room); **faites ~ ces gens** make these people go *ou* leave, get these people out; **sors (d'ici)!** get out (of here)!; **~ par la porte de la cave/par la fenêtre** to go *ou* get out *ou* leave by the cellar door/the window; (*Théât*) **'la servante sort'** 'exit the maid'; (*Théât*) **'les 3 gardes sortent'** 'exeunt 3 guards'; **laisser ~ qn** to let sb out *ou* leave; **ne laissez ~ personne** don't let anybody out *ou* leave; **laisser ~ qn de** *pièce, pays* to let sb out of *ou* leave.

(b) *[objet, pièce]* to come out. **le curseur est sorti de la rainure** the runner has come out of the groove; **je n'arrive pas à faire ~ ces débris** I can't manage to get this mess out *ou* to clear this mess; **le joint est sorti de son logement** the joint has come out of its socket.

(c) (*quitter chez soi*) to go out. **~ faire des courses/prendre l'air** to go out shopping/for some fresh air; **~ acheter du pain** to go out to buy *ou* for some bread; **~ dîner/déjeuner** to go out for *ou* to dinner/lunch; **ils sortent beaucoup/ne sortent pas beaucoup** they go out a lot/don't go out much; **mes parents ne me laissent pas ~** my parents don't let me (go) out; **on lui permet de ~ maintenant qu'il va mieux** he is allowed (to go) out now that he is getting better; **c'est le soir que les moustiques sortent** it's at night-time that the mosquitoes come out; **il n'est jamais sorti de son village** he has never been out of *ou* gone outside his village.

(d) (*Comm*) *[marchandises, devises]* to leave. **tout ce qui sort (du pays) doit être déclaré** everything going out *ou* leaving (the country) must be declared.

(e) (*quitter*) to leave, come out. **~ du théâtre** to go out of *ou* leave the theatre; **~ de l'hôpital/de prison** to come out of hospital/prison; **quand sort-il?** (*de prison*) when does he come *ou* get out?; (*de l'hôpital*) when is he coming out? *ou* leaving?; **ils sortent à 11 heures** (*du théâtre*) they come out at 11 o'clock; **~ de l'eau** to come out of the water; **~ du lit** to get out of bed; *[fleuve]* **~ de son lit** to overflow its banks; (*Rail*) **~ des rails** to go off the rails; **il aura du mal à ~ de ce mauvais pas** he'll have a job getting out of this trouble; **~ de convalescence/d'un profond sommeil** to come out of convalescence/a deep sleep; **~ de son calme** to lose one's calm; **~ de son indifférence** to overcome one's indifference; **~ sain et sauf d'un accident** to come out of an accident unscathed; **il a trop de copies à corriger, il ne s'en sort pas** he has too many exercises to correct – there's no end to them.

(f) (*marquant le passé immédiat*) **on sortait de l'hiver** it was getting near the end of winter; **il sort d'ici** he's just left; **il sort du lit** he's just got up; **on ne croirait pas qu'elle sort de chez le coiffeur!** you'd never believe she'd just come out of the hairdresser's! *ou* just had her hair done!; **il sort de maladie*** *ou* **d'être malade*** he's just been ill; **il sort d'une période de cafard** he's just gone through *ou* had a spell of being fed up.

(g) **~ de** (*s'écarter de*): **~ du sujet/de la question** to go *ou* get off the subject/the point; **~ de la légalité** to overstep *ou* go outside *ou* go beyond the law; **~ du jeu** *[balle, ballon etc]* to go out; **~ des limites de** to go beyond the bounds of, overstep the limits of; **cela sort de mon domaine/ma compétence** that's outside my field/my authority; **vous sortez de votre rôle** that is not your responsibility *ou* part of your brief; **cela sort de l'ordinaire** that's out of the ordinary; **il n'y a pas à ~ de là, nous avons besoin de lui** there's no getting away from it — we need him; **il ne veut pas ~ de là** he won't budge.

(h) **~ de** (*être issu de*): **~ d'une bonne famille/du peuple** to come from a good family/from the working class; **il sort du Lycée X** he was (educated) at the Lycée X; **il sort de l'université de X** he was *ou* he studied at the University of X.

(i) (*dépasser*) to stick out; (*commencer à pousser*) *[blé, plante]* to come up; *[dent]* to come through. **les yeux lui sortaient de la tête** his eyes were popping *ou* starting out of his head.

(j) (*être fabriqué, publié etc*) to come out; *[disque, film]* to be released. **~ de** to come from; **tout ce qui sort de cette maison est de qualité** everything that comes from that firm is good quality; **une encyclopédie qui sort par fascicules** an encyclopaedia which comes out in parts; **sa robe sort de chez un grand couturier** her dress comes from one of the great couturier's.

(k) (*Jeu, Loterie*) *[numéro, couleur]* to come up *ou* out.

(l) **~ de** (*provenir de*) to come from; (*fig*) **sait-on ce qui sortira de ces entrevues!** who knows what'll come (out) of these talks! *ou* what these talks will lead to!; **des mots qui sortent du cœur** words which come from the heart; **une odeur de brûlé sortait de la cuisine** a smell of burning came from the kitchen; **une épaisse fumée sortait par les fenêtres** thick smoke was pouring out of the windows.

(m) (*loc*) **~ de ses gonds** (*lit*) to come off (of) its hinges; (*fig*) to fly off the handle; **je sors d'en prendre*** I've had quite enough thank you (*iro*); **il est sorti d'affaire** (*il a été malade*) he has pulled through; (*il a eu des ennuis*) he has got over it; **on n'est pas sorti de l'auberge*** we're not out of the wood (*Brit*) *ou* woods (*US*) yet; **se croire sorti de la cuisse de Jupiter*** to think a lot of o.s., think one is the cat's whiskers* (*Brit*) *ou* the bee's knees* (*Brit*); **tu te crois sorti de la cuisse de Jupiter!*** you think you're God's gift to mankind!; **cela lui est sorti de la mémoire** *ou* **de l'esprit** that slipped his memory *ou* his mind; **mais d'où sort-il (donc)?** (*il est tout sale*) where HAS he been!; (*il ne sait pas la nouvelle*) where has he been (all this time)?; (*il est mal élevé*) where was he brought up? (*iro*); (*il est bête*) where did they find him? (*iro*), some mothers do have 'em* (*surtout Brit*).

2 *vt* **(a)** (*mener dehors*) *personne, chien* to take out; (*expulser*) *personne* to throw out. **sortez-le!** throw him out!, get him out of here!

(b) (*retirer*) to take out; (*Aviat*) *train d'atterrissage* to lower. **~ des vêtements d'une armoire/des bijoux d'un coffret** to get *ou* take clothes out of a wardrobe/jewels out of a (jewel) box; **ils ont réussi à ~ les spéléologues de la grotte** they managed to get the potholers out of the cave; **il sortit de sa poche un paquet de bonbons** he took *ou* brought *ou* pulled a packet of sweets out of his pocket; **~ les mains de ses poches** to take one's hands out of one's pockets; **~ ses bras des manches** to take one's arms out of the sleeves; **les douaniers ont tout sorti de sa valise** the Customs men took everything out of his suitcase; **quand il fait beau, on sort les fauteuils dans le jardin** when the weather's nice we take the armchairs out into the garden; **soudain, il sortit un revolver de sa poche** suddenly he took *ou* brought *ou* pulled a revolver out of his pocket.

(c) (*Comm: plus gén* **faire ~**) *marchandises* (*par la douane*) to take out; (*en fraude*) to smuggle out.

(d) (*mettre en vente*) *voiture, modèle* to bring out; *livre* to bring out, publish; *disque, film [artiste]* to bring out; *[compagnie]* to release.

(e) (*: *dire*) to come out with*. **il vous sort de ces réflexions!** he really comes out with some incredible remarks!*; **elle en a sorti une bien bonne** she came out with a good one*; **qu'est-ce qu'il va encore nous ~?** what will he come out with next?*

3 se sortir *vpr* to go out. **s'en sortir: tu crois qu'il va s'en sortir?** (*il est malade*) do you think he'll pull through?; (*il est surchargé de travail*) do you think he'll ever get to *ou* see the end of it?; (*il est sur la sellette*) do you think he'll come through all right?

4 *nm* (*rare, littér*) **au ~ de l'hiver/de l'enfance** as winter/childhood draws (*ou* drew) to a close.

sosie [sozi] *nm* double (*person*).

sot, sotte [so, sɔt] **1** *adj* silly, foolish, stupid. (*Prov*) **il n'y a pas**

de ~ métier every trade has its value. **2** *nm,f* (†, *frm: niais*) fool; (*enfant*) (little) idiot; (*Hist Littérat: bouffon*) fool.
sotie [sɔti] *nf* (*Hist Littérat*) *satirical farce of 15th and 16th centuries.*
sottement [sɔtmɑ̃] *adv* foolishly, stupidly.
sottise [sɔtiz] *nf* **(a)** (*U*) stupidity, foolishness. **(b)** (*parole*) silly *ou* foolish thing *ou* remark; (*action*) silly *ou* foolish thing (to do), folly (†, *frm*). **dire des ~s** *[enfant]* to say silly *ou* stupid *ou* foolish things; (†, *frm*) *[philosophe, auteur]* to make foolish affirmations; **faire une ~** *[adulte]* to do a silly *ou* foolish thing, commit a folly (†, *frm*); **faire des ~s** *[enfant]* to misbehave, be naughty, do naughty things.
sottisier [sɔtizje] *nm* collection of foolish quotations.
sou [su] *nm* **(a)** (*monnaie*) (*Hist*) sou, ≃ shilling (*Brit*); (†, *Suisse: cinq centimes*) 5 centimes (*pl*); (*Can**) cent. (*Can*) **un trente ~s** a quarter (*US, Can*).
(b) (*loc*) **appareil** *ou* **machine à ~s** (*jeu*) one-armed bandit, fruit-machine; (*péj, hum: distributeur*) slot machine; **donner/compter/économiser ~ à** *ou* **par ~** to give/count/save penny by penny; **il n'a pas le ~** he hasn't got a penny *ou* a sou (to his name); **il est sans un** *ou* **le ~** he's penniless; **il n'a pas un ~ vaillant** he hasn't a penny to bless himself with; **dépenser jusqu'à son dernier ~** to spend every last penny; **il n'a pas pour un ~ de méchanceté/bon sens** he hasn't an ounce *ou* a pen-n'orth* (*Brit*) of unkindness/good sense (in him); **il n'est pas hypocrite/menteur pour un ~** he isn't at all *ou* the least bit hypocritical/untruthful; **propre/reluisant** *ou* **brillant comme un ~ neuf** (as) clean/bright as a new pin; *V* **gros, près, quatre.**
soubassement [subasmɑ̃] *nm* *[maison]* base; *[murs, fenêtre]* dado; *[colonne]* crepidoma; (*Géol*) bedrock.
soubresaut [subʀəso] *nm* **(a)** (*cahot*) jolt. **le véhicule fit un ~** the vehicle gave a jolt; **sa monture fit un ~** his mount gave a sudden start.
(b) (*tressaillement*) (*de peur*) start; (*d'agonie*) convulsive movement. **avoir un ~** to give a start, start (up); to make a convulsive movement.
soubrette [subʀɛt] *nf* (†, *hum: femme de chambre*) maid; (*Théât*) soubrette, maidservant.
souche [suʃ] *nf* **(a)** (*Bot*) *[arbre]* stump; *[vigne]* stock. **rester planté comme une ~** to stand stock-still; *V* **dormir.**
(b) *[famille, race]* founder. **faire ~** to found a line; **de vieille ~** of old stock.
(c) (*Ling*) root. **mot de ~ latine** word with a Latin root; **mot ~** root word.
(d) (*Bio*) *[microbes]* colony, clone.
(e) (*talon*) counterfoil, stub. **carnet à ~s** counterfoil book.
(f) (*Archit*) *[cheminée]* (chimney) stack.
souci[1] [susi] *nm*: **~ (des jardins)** marigold; **~ d'eau** *ou* **des marais** marsh marigold.
souci[2] [susi] *nm* **(a)** (*U: inquiétude*) worry. **se faire du ~** to worry; **être sans ~** to be free of worries *ou* care(s); **cela t'éviterait bien du ~** it would spare you a lot of worry; **cela lui donne (bien) du ~** it worries him (a lot), he worries (a great deal) over it.
(b) (*tracas*) worry. **vivre sans ~s** to live free of worries *ou* care(s); **~s d'argent** money worries, worries about money; **sa santé/mon fils est mon plus grand ~** his health/my son is my biggest worry.
(c) (*préoccupation*) concern (*de* for). **avoir ~ du bien-être de son prochain** to have concern for the well-being of one's neighbour; **sa carrière/le bien-être de ses enfants est son unique ~** his career/his children's well-being is his sole concern *ou* is all he worries about; **avoir le ~ de bien faire** to be concerned about doing things well; **dans le ~ de lui plaire** in his concern to please her; **c'est le moindre** *ou* **le cadet de mes ~s** that's the least of my worries.
soucier [susje] (7) **1 se soucier** *vpr*: **se ~ de** to care about; **se ~ des autres** to care about *ou* for others, show concern for others; **je ne m'en soucie guère** I am quite indifferent about it; **il s'en soucie comme de sa première chemise** *ou* **comme de l'an quarante*** he doesn't give *ou* care a fig (about it)*, he couldn't care less (about it)*; (*littér*) **il se soucie peu de plaire** he cares little *ou* he doesn't bother whether he is liked or not; **il se soucie fort de ce qu'ils pensent** he cares very much what they think; (*littér*) **se ~ que** + *subj* to care that.
2 *vt* (†, *littér*) to worry, trouble.
soucieux, -euse [susjø, øz] *adj* **(a)** (*inquiet*) *personne, air, ton* concerned, worried. **peu ~** unconcerned.
(b) être ~ de qch to be concerned with *ou* about sth; **~ de son seul intérêt** concerned solely with *ou* about his own interests; **être ~ de faire** to be anxious to do; (*frm*) **~ que** concerned *ou* anxious that; **peu ~ qu'on le voie** caring little *ou* unconcerned whether he be *ou* is seen or not.
soucoupe [sukup] *nf* saucer. **~ volante** flying saucer; *V* **œil.**
soudage [sudaʒ] *nm* (*avec brasure, fil à souder*) soldering; (*autogène*) welding.
soudain, e [sudɛ̃, ɛn] **1** *adj* (*gén*) sudden; *mort* sudden, unexpected. **2** *adv* (*tout à coup*) suddenly, all of a sudden. **~, il se mit à pleurer** all of a sudden he started to cry, he suddenly started to cry.
soudainement [sudɛnmɑ̃] *adv* suddenly.
soudaineté [sudɛnte] *nf* suddenness.
Soudan [sudɑ̃] *nm*: **le ~** (the) Sudan.
soudanais, e [sudanɛ, ɛz] **1** *adj* Sudanese, of *ou* from (the) Sudan.
2 *nm,f*: **S~(e)** Sudanese, inhabitant *ou* native of (the) Sudan.
soudard [sudaʀ] *nm* (*péj*) ruffianly *ou* roughneck soldier.
soude [sud] *nf* **(a)** (*industrielle*) soda. **~ caustique** caustic soda; *V* **bicarbonate. (b)** (*Bot*) saltwort. (*Chim*) **(cendre de) ~†** soda ash.
soudé, e [sude] (*ptp de* **souder**) *adj* **(a)** *organes, pétales* joined (together). **(b)** (*fig: rivé*) **~ au plancher/à la paroi** glued to the floor/wall.
souder [sude] (1) **1** *vt* **(a)** *métal* (*avec brasure, fil à souder*) to solder; (*soudure autogène*) to weld; **~ à chaud/froid** to hot/cold weld; *V* **fer, fil, lampe.**
(b) *os* to knit.
(c) (*fig: unir*) *choses, organismes* to fuse (together); (*littér*) *cœurs, êtres* to bind *ou* knit together (*littér*), unite.
2 se souder *vpr* *[os]* to knit together; (*littér: s'unir*) to be knit together (*littér*).
soudeur [sudœʀ] *nm* (*V* **souder**) solderer; welder.
soudoyer [sudwaje] (8) *vt* (*péj*) to bribe, buy over.
soudure [sudyʀ] *nf* **(a)** (*Tech: V* **souder**) (*opération*) soldering; welding; (*endroit*) soldered joint; weld; (*substance*) solder. **~ à l'arc** arc welding; **~ autogène** welding.
(b) *[os]* knitting; *[organes, pétales]* join; (*littér*) *[partis, cœurs]* binding *ou* knitting (*littér*) together, uniting.
(c) (*loc*) **faire la ~ (entre)** to bridge the gap (between).
soufflage [suflaʒ] *nm* **(a) ~ du verre** glass-blowing. **(b)** (*Métal*) blowing.
souffle [sufl(ə)] *nm* **(a)** (*expiration*) (*en soufflant*) blow, puff; (*en respirant*) breath. **éteindre une bougie d'un ~ (puissant)** to put out a candle with a (hard) puff *ou* blow *ou* by blowing (hard); **il murmura mon nom dans un ~** he breathed my name; **le dernier ~ d'un agonisant** the last breath of a dying man; **pour jouer d'un instrument à vent, il faut du ~** you need a lot of breath *ou* puff* (*Brit*) to play a wind instrument.
(b) (*respiration*) breathing. **le ~ régulier d'un dormeur** the regular breathing of someone asleep; **on entendait un ~ dans l'obscurité** we heard (someone) breathing in the darkness; **avoir du ~: il a du ~** (*lit*) he has a lot of breath *ou* puff* (*Brit*); (**fig*) (*culot, témérité*) he has some nerve*; **manquer de ~** to be short of breath; **avoir le ~ court** to be short-winded; **retenir son ~** to hold one's breath; **reprendre son ~** to get one's breath back; **n'avoir plus de ~, être à bout de ~** to be out of breath; (*lit*) **avoir le ~ coupé** to be winded; (*fig*) **il en a eu le ~ coupé** it (quite) took his breath away; *V* **second.**
(c) (*déplacement d'air*) *[incendie, ventilateur, explosion]* blast.
(d) (*vent*) puff *ou* breath of air, puff of wind. **le ~ du vent dans les feuilles** the wind blowing through the leaves, the leaves blowing in the wind; **un ~ d'air faisait bruire le feuillage** a slight breeze was rustling the leaves; **brin d'herbe agité au moindre ~ (d'air** *ou* **de vent)** blade of grass blown about by the slightest puff *ou* breath of air *ou* the slightest puff (of wind); **il n'y avait pas un ~ (d'air** *ou* **de vent)** there was not a breath of air.
(e) (*fig: force créatrice*) inspiration. **le ~ du génie** the inspiration born of genius; (*Rel*) **le ~ créateur** the breath of God.
(f) (*Méd*) **~ cardiaque** *ou* **au cœur** cardiac *ou* heart murmur.
soufflé, e [sufle] (*ptp de* **souffler**) **1** *adj* **(a)** (*Culin*) soufflé (*épith*). **(b)** (*) (*surpris*) flabbergasted*, staggered*. **2** *nm* (*Culin*) soufflé. **~ au fromage** cheese soufflé.
souffler [sufle] (1) **1** *vi* **(a)** *[vent, personne]* to blow. **~ sur le feu** to blow on the fire; **~ dans un instrument à vent** to blow (into) a wind instrument; **~ sur une bougie (pour l'éteindre)** to blow a candle (to put it out), blow out a candle; **~ sur sa soupe (pour la faire refroidir)** to blow (on) one's soup (to cool it); **~ sur ses doigts (pour les réchauffer)** to blow on one's fingers (to warm them up); (*lit, fig*) **observer** *ou* **regarder de quel côté le vent souffle** to see which way the wind is blowing; **le vent a soufflé si fort qu'il a abattu deux arbres** the wind was so strong *ou* blew so hard (that) it blew two trees down; **le vent soufflait en rafales** the wind was blowing in gusts; **le vent soufflait en tempête** it was blowing a gale, the wind was howling.
(b) (*respirer avec peine*) to puff (and blow). **il ne peut monter les escaliers sans ~** he can't go up the stairs without puffing (and blowing); **~ comme un bœuf** *ou* **un phoque*** to puff and blow like a grampus.
(c) (*se reposer*) **laisser ~ qn/un animal** to give sb/an animal a breather, let sb/an animal get his/its breath back (*fig*); **il ne prend jamais le temps de ~** he never lets up, he never stops to get his breath back; **donnez-lui un peu de temps pour ~** (*pour se reposer*) give him time to get his breath back, give him a breather; (*avant de payer*) give him a breather*.
2 *vt* **(a)** *bougie, feu* to blow out.
(b) ~ de la fumée au nez de qn to blow smoke in(to) sb's face; **~ des odeurs d'ail au visage de qn** to breathe garlic over sb *ou* into sb's face; **le ventilateur soufflait des odeurs de graillon** the fan was blowing greasy smells around; **le vent leur soufflait le sable dans les yeux** the wind was blowing the sand into their eyes; (*fig*) **~ le chaud et le froid** to lay down the law.
(c) (*: *prendre*) to pinch*, nick* (*Brit*) (*à qn* from sb). **il lui a soufflé sa petite amie/son poste** he has pinched his girlfriend/his job*.
(d) *[bombe, explosion]* **leur maison a été soufflée par une bombe** their house was destroyed by the blast from a bomb.
(e) (*dire*) *conseil, réponse, réplique* to whisper (*à qn* to sb). **~ sa leçon à qn** to whisper sb's lesson to him; (*Théât*) **~ son rôle à qn** to prompt sb, give sb a prompt, whisper sb's lines to him; (*Théât*) **qui est-ce qui souffle ce soir?** who's prompting this evening?; **~ qch à l'oreille de qn** to whisper sth in sb's ear; **ne pas ~ mot** not to breathe a word.
(f) (*: *étonner*) to flabbergast*, stagger*. **elle a été soufflée d'apprendre leur échec** she was flabbergasted* *ou* staggered* to hear of their failure; **leur toupet m'a soufflé** I was flabbergasted* *ou* staggered* at their cheek, their cheek flabbergasted* *ou* staggered* me.

(g) (*Tech*) ~ **le verre** to blow glass.

soufflerie [suflәʀi] *nf [orgue, forge]* bellows; (*Tech: d'aération etc*) ventilating fan; (*Ind*) blowing engine. (*Aviat*) ~ **(aérodynamique)** wind tunnel.

soufflet[1] [suflɛ] *nm* **(a)** *[forge]* bellows. **(b)** (*Rail*) vestibule; (*Couture*) gusset; *[sac, classeur]* extendible gusset; *[appareil photographique]* bellows.

soufflet[2] [suflɛ] *nm* (*gifle*) slap (in the face); (†, *littér*) slap in the face (*fig*).

souffleter [suflәte] (4) *vt* († *littér*) ~ **qn** (*gifler*) to slap sb (in the face), give sb a slap (in the face); (*fig: outrager*) to give sb a slap in the face.

souffleur, -euse [suflœʀ, øz] **1** *nm,f* (*Théât*) prompter. (*Tech*) ~ **de verre** glass-blower; *V* **trou**.

2 souffleuse *nf* (*Can*) snowblower.

souffrance [sufʀɑ̃s] *nf* **(a)** (*douleur*) suffering.

(b) (*fig*) **être en** ~ *[marchandises, colis]* to be awaiting delivery, be held up; *[affaire, dossier]* to be pending, be waiting to be dealt with.

souffrant, e [sufʀɑ̃, ɑ̃t] *adj* **(a)** (*malade*) *personne* unwell, poorly*. **(b)** (*littér*) **l'humanité ~e** suffering humanity; **l'Église ~e** the Church suffering.

souffre-douleur [sufʀәdulœʀ] *nmf inv* whipping boy, underdog. **être le ~ de qn/d'un groupe** to be sb's whipping boy/the underdog *ou* whipping boy of a group.

souffreteux, -euse [sufʀәtø, øz] *adj* sickly.

souffrir [sufʀiʀ] (18) **1** *vi* **(a)** (*physiquement*) to suffer. **la pauvre fille souffre beaucoup** the poor girl is in great pain *ou* is suffering a great deal; **où souffrez-vous?** where is the pain?, where are you in pain?, where does it hurt?; (*lit, fig*) ~ **en silence** to suffer in silence; ~ **comme un damné** to suffer torment(s); **faire ~ qn** *[personne, blessure]* to hurt sb; **mes cors me font ~** my corns are hurting (me) *ou* are painful; ~ **de la tête** to have a headache; (*habituellement*) to have headaches; ~ **de l'estomac/des reins** to have stomach/kidney trouble; **il souffre d'une grave maladie/de rhumatismes** he is suffering from a serious illness/from rheumatism; ~ **du froid/de la chaleur** to suffer from the cold/from the heat.

(b) (*moralement*) to suffer. **faire ~ qn** *[personne]* to make sb suffer; *[attitude, événement]* to cause sb pain; **il a beaucoup souffert d'avoir été chassé de son pays** he has suffered a great deal from being chased out of his country; **je souffre de le voir si affaibli** it pains *ou* grieves me to see him so weakened.

(c) (*pâtir*) to suffer. **les fraises souffrent de la chaleur** strawberries suffer in (the) heat; **les fraises ont souffert du gel tardif** the strawberries have suffered from *ou* have been hard hit by the late frost; **ils sont lents, et la productivité en souffre** they are slow and productivity is suffering; **ils souffrent d'un manque d'expérience certain** they suffer from a definite lack of experience; **la nation a souffert de la guerre** the nation has suffered from the war.

(d) (*) **on a fini par gagner, mais ils nous ont fait ~** *ou* **mais on a souffert** we won in the end but they gave us a rough time* *ou* they put us through it*; **les mathématiques m'ont toujours fait ~** maths has always given me trouble.

2 *vt* **(a)** (*éprouver*) *pertes* to endure, suffer; *tourments* to endure, undergo. ~ **le martyre** to go through agonies, go through hell on earth; **sa jambe lui fait ~ le martyre** his leg gives him agonies; ~ **mille morts** to go through agonies.

(b) (*supporter*) *affront, mépris* to suffer, endure. **je ne peux ~ de te voir malheureux** I cannot bear *ou* endure to see you unhappy, I cannot abide seeing you unhappy.

(c) ne pas pouvoir ~ qch: il ne peut pas ~ le mensonge/les épinards/cet individu he can't stand *ou* bear lies/spinach/that individual; **il ne peut pas ~ que ...** he cannot bear that ....

(d) (*littér: tolérer*) ~ **que** to allow *ou* permit that; **souffrez que je vous contredise** allow *ou* permit me to contradict you; **je ne souffrirai pas que mon fils en pâtisse** I will not allow my son to suffer from it.

(e) (*admettre*) **cette affaire ne peut ~ aucun retard** this matter admits of *ou* allows of no delay *ou* simply cannot be delayed; **la règle souffre quelques exceptions** the rule admits of *ou* allows of a few exceptions; **la règle ne peut ~ aucune exception** the rule admits of no exception.

soufrage [sufʀaʒ] *nm [vigne, laine]* sulphuration; *[allumettes]* sulphuring.

soufre [sufʀ(ә)] *nm* sulphur. **jaune ~** sulphur yellow; (*fig*) **sentir le ~** to smack of heresy.

soufrer [sufʀe] (1) *vt vigne* to (treat with) sulphur; *allumettes* to sulphur; *laine* to sulphurate.

souhait [swɛ] *nm* wish. **les ~s de bonne année** New Year greetings, good wishes for the New Year; **à tes ~s!** bless you!; **à ~: la viande était rôtie à ~** the meat was done to perfection; **le vin était fruité à ~** the wine was delightfully fruity *ou* as fruity as one could wish; **tout marchait à ~** everything went as well as one could wish *ou* went perfectly; **tout lui réussit à ~** everything works to perfection for him.

souhaitable [swɛtabl(ә)] *adj* desirable.

souhaiter [swete] (1) *vt* **(a)** *réussite, changements* to wish for. ~ **que** to hope that; **il est à ~ que** it is to be hoped that; **je souhaite qu'il réussisse** I hope he succeeds, I would like him to succeed; **je souhaite réussir** I hope to succeed; ~ **pouvoir** *ou* (*littér*) ~ **de pouvoir étudier/partir à l'étranger** to hope to be able to study/go abroad; (*littér*) **je le souhaitais mort/loin** I wished him dead/far away; **je souhaitais l'examen terminé** I wished the exam were over, I wished the exam (to be) over; **je souhaiterais vous aider** I wish I could help you.

(b) ~ à qn le bonheur/la réussite to wish sb happiness/success; **je vous souhaite bien des choses** all good wishes, every good wish; **~ à qn de réussir** to wish sb success; (*iro*) **je vous souhaite bien du plaisir!** I wish you joy! (*iro*); ~ **la bonne année/bonne chance à qn** to wish sb a happy New Year/(the best of) luck; **je vous la souhaite bonne et heureuse‡** here's hoping you have a really good New Year!*

souiller [suje] (1) *vt* (*littér*) (*lit*) *drap, vêtement* to soil, dirty; *atmosphère* to dirty; (*fig*) *réputation, pureté, âme* to sully, tarnish. **souillé de boue** spattered with mud; (*fig*) **le besoin de ~ qu'éprouve cet auteur** this author's need to defile everything; (*fig*) ~ **ses mains du sang des innocents** to stain one's hands with the blood of innocents; (*fig*) ~ **la couche nuptiale** to defile the conjugal bed.

souillon [sujɔ̃] *nf* slattern, slut.

souillure [sujyʀ] *nf* (*littér*) (*lit*) stain; (*fig*) blemish, stain. **la ~ du péché** the stain of sin.

soûl, soûle [su, sul] **1** *adj* **(a)** (*ivre*) drunk, drunken (*épith*). ~ **comme une bourrique** *ou* **un Polonais*** (as) drunk as a lord (*surtout Brit*).

(b) (*fig*) ~ **de: ~s de musique/poésie après 3 jours de festival** our (*ou* their) heads reeling with music/poetry after 3 days of festival; (*littér*) ~ **de plaisirs** surfeited *ou* satiated with pleasures.

2 *nm*: **tout son** (*ou* **mon** *etc*) **~: manger tout son ~** to eat one's fill, eat to one's heart's content; **chanter tout son ~** to sing to one's heart's content; **elle a ri/pleuré tout son ~** she laughed/cried till she could laugh/cry no more.

soulagement [sulaʒmɑ̃] *nm* relief. **ça a été un ~ d'apprendre que** it was a relief *ou* I was (*ou* we were *etc*) relieved to learn that.

soulager [sulaʒe] (3) **1** *vt* **(a)** *personne* (*physiquement*) to relieve; (*moralement*) to relieve, soothe; *douleur* to relieve, soothe; *maux* to relieve; *conscience* to ease. **ça le soulage de s'étendre** he finds relief in stretching out, it relieves him *ou* his pain to stretch out; **ça le soulage de prendre ces pilules** these pills bring him relief; **buvez, ça vous soulagera** drink this — it'll give you relief *ou* make you feel better; **être soulagé d'avoir fait qch** to be relieved to have done sth; **cet aveu l'a soulagé** this confession made him feel better *ou* eased his conscience *ou* took a weight off his mind; ~ **les pauvres/les déshérités** to bring relief to *ou* relieve the poor/the underprivileged; **il faut ~ la pauvreté** we must relieve poverty.

(b) (*décharger*) *personne* to relieve (**de** of); (*Archit*) *mur, poutre* to relieve the strain on. (*hum*) ~ **qn de son portefeuille** to relieve sb of his wallet (*hum*).

2 se soulager *vpr* **(a)** (*se décharger d'un souci*) to find relief, ease one's feelings; (*apaiser sa conscience*) to ease one's conscience. **elle se soulageait en lui prodiguant des insultes** she found relief in *ou* eased her feelings by throwing insults at him; **leurs consciences se soulagent à bon marché** their consciences can be eased at little expense.

(b) (*: *euph*) to relieve o.s.*.

soûlard, e‡ [sulaʀ, aʀd(ә)] *nm,f* drunkard.

soûlaud, e‡ [sulo, od] *nm,f* = **soûlard‡**.

soûler [sule] (1) **1** *vt* **(a)** (*rendre ivre*) ~ **qn** *[personne]* to get sb drunk; *[boisson]* to make sb drunk.

(b) (*fig*) ~ **qn** (*fatiguer*) to make sb's head spin *ou* reel; (*littér: griser*) *[parfum]* to go to sb's head, intoxicate sb; *[vent, vitesse, théories, visions]* to intoxicate *ou* inebriate sb, make sb's head spin *ou* reel.

(c) (*fig*) ~ **qn de** *théories, promesses* to intoxicate *ou* inebriate sb with, make sb's head spin *ou* reel with; *luxe, sensations* to intoxicate sb with.

2 se soûler *vpr* (*s'enivrer*) to get drunk. **se ~ la gueule‡** to get pissed‡ (*Brit*) *ou* stoned‡; (*fig*) **se ~ de** *bruit, vitesse, vent, parfums* to intoxicate o.s. with, get high on*; *théories, visions, sensations* to intoxicate o.s. with.

soûlerie [sulʀi] *nf* (*péj*) drunken binge.

soulèvement [sulɛvmɑ̃] *nm* **(a)** (*révolte*) uprising.

(b) (*Géol*) upthrust, upheaval.

soulever [sulve] (5) **1** *vt* **(a)** (*lever*) *fardeau, malade, couvercle, rideau* to lift (up). ~ **qn de terre** to lift sb (up) off the ground; (*fig*) **cela me soulève le cœur** *[odeur]* it makes me feel sick *ou* want to heave, it turns my stomach; *[attitude]* it makes me sick.

(b) (*remuer*) *poussière* to raise. **le véhicule soulevait des nuages de poussière** the vehicle made clouds of dust fly *ou* swirl up, the vehicle sent up *ou* raised clouds of dust; **le bateau soulevait de grosses vagues** the boat was sending up great waves; **le vent soulevait les vagues/le sable** the wind made the waves swell *ou* whipped up the waves/blew *ou* whipped up the sand.

(c) (*indigner*) to stir up; (*pousser à la révolte*) to stir up (to revolt); (*exalter*) to stir. ~ **l'opinion publique (contre qn)** to stir up *ou* rouse public opinion (against sb).

(d) (*provoquer*) *enthousiasme, colère* to arouse; *protestations, applaudissements* to raise; *difficultés, questions* to raise, bring up.

(e) (*évoquer*) *question, problème* to raise, bring up.

(f) (‡: *voler*) ~ **qch (à qn)** to pinch* *ou* swipe‡ sth (from sb).

2 se soulever *vpr* **(a)** (*se lever*) to lift o.s. up. **soulève-toi pour que je redresse ton oreiller** lift yourself up *ou* sit up a bit so that I can plump up your pillow.

(b) (*être levé*) *[véhicule, couvercle, rideau]* to lift; (*fig*) *[vagues, mer]* to swell (up). (*fig*) **à cette vue, le cœur se soulève** the sight of it makes one's stomach turn; (*fig*) **à cette vue, son cœur se souleva** his stomach turned at the sight.

(c) (*s'insurger*) to rise up.

soulier [sulje] *nm* shoe. **~s bas/plats** low-heeled/flat shoes; **~s montants** boots; **~s de marche** walking shoes; (*fig*) **être dans ses petits ~s** to feel awkward.

soulignage [suliɲaʒ] *nm*, **soulignement** [suliɲmɑ̃] *nm* (*rare*) underlining.

souligner [suliɲe] (1) *vt* **(a)** (*lit*) to underline; (*fig: accentuer*) to accentuate, emphasize. ~ **qch d'un trait double** to double underline sth, underline sth with a double line; ~ **qch en rouge** to underline sth in red; ~ **les yeux de noir** to accentuate one's eyes with (black) eye-liner; **ce tissu à rayures soulignait son embonpoint** that striped material emphasized *ou* accentuated his stoutness.
(b) (*faire remarquer*) to underline, stress, emphasize. **il souligna l'importance de cette rencontre** he underlined *ou* stressed *ou* emphasized the importance of this meeting.

soûlographie* [sulɔgʀafi] *nf* (*hum*) getting drunk, boozing*.

soumettre [sumɛtʀ(ə)] (56) **1** *vt* **(a)** (*dompter*) *pays, peuple* to subject, subjugate; *personne* to subject; *rebelles* to put down, subdue, subjugate.
(b) (*asservir*) ~ **qn à** *maître, passions, loi* to subject sb to.
(c) (*astreindre*) ~ **qn à** *traitement, formalité, régime, impôt* to subject sb to; ~ **qch à** *traitement, essai, taxe* to subject sth to; **tout citoyen/ce revenu est soumis à l'impôt** every citizen/this income is subject to tax(ation).
(d) (*présenter*) *idée, cas, manuscrit* to submit (*à* to). ~ **une idée/un projet/une question à qn** to submit an idea/a plan/a matter to sb, put an idea/a plan/a matter before sb.
2 se soumettre *vpr* **(a)** (*obéir*) to submit (*à* to).
(b) se ~ **à** *traitement, formalité* to submit to; *entraînement, régime* to submit o.s. to.

soumis, e [sumi, iz] (*ptp de* **soumettre**) *adj* (*docile*) *personne, air* submissive; *V* **fille.**

soumission [sumisjɔ̃] *nf* **(a)** (*obéissance*) submission (*à* to). **il est toujours d'une parfaite** ~ **à leur égard** he is always totally submissive to their wishes. **(b)** (*acte de reddition*) submission. **ils ont fait leur** ~ they have submitted. **(c)** (*Comm*) tender.

soumissionnaire [sumisjɔnɛʀ] *nmf* (*Comm*) tenderer.

soumissionner [sumisjɔne] (1) *vt* (*Comm*) to tender for.

soupape [supap] *nf* valve. (*lit, fig*) ~ **de sûreté** safety valve; (*Aut*) ~ **d'admission/d'échappement** inlet/exhaust valve; (*Aut*) ~**s en tête/en chapelle** *ou* **latérale** overhead/side valves.

soupçon [supsɔ̃] *nm* **(a)** (*suspicion*) suspicion. **conduite exempte de tout** ~ conduct free from all suspicion; **homme à l'abri de** *ou* **au-dessus de tout** ~ man free from *ou* man above all *ou* any suspicion; **sa femme eut bientôt des** ~**s** his wife soon had her suspicions *ou* became suspicious; **éveiller les** ~**s de qn** to arouse sb's suspicions; **avoir** ~ **de qch** to suspect sth; **des difficultés dont il n'avait pas** ~ difficulties of which he had no inkling *ou* no suspicion; **avoir** ~ **que** to suspect that, have an inkling that.
(b) (*petite quantité*) *[assaisonnement, vulgarité]* hint, touch, suggestion; *[vin, lait]* drop.

soupçonnable [supsɔnabl(ə)] *adj* (*gén nég*) that arouses suspicion(s).

soupçonner [supsɔne] (1) *vt* to suspect. **il est soupçonné de vol** he is suspected of theft; **on le soupçonne d'y avoir participé, on soupçonne qu'il y a participé** he is suspected of having taken part in it; **il soupçonnait un piège** he suspected a trap; **vous ne soupçonnez pas ce que ça demande comme travail** you haven't an inkling *ou* you've no idea how much work that involves.

soupçonneusement [supsɔnøzmɑ̃] *adv* with suspicion, suspiciously.

soupçonneux, -euse [supsɔnø, øz] *adj* suspicious.

soupe [sup] *nf* **(a)** (*Culin*) soup. ~ **à l'oignon/aux légumes/de poisson** onion/vegetable/fish soup; *V* **cheveu, marchand.**
(b) (‡: *nourriture*) grub‡, nosh‡. **à la** ~! grub up!‡, grub's up!‡.
(c) († *loc*) **avoir droit à la** ~ **à la grimace** to have to put up with sulking *ou* with stony silence (from one's wife); **il est (très)** ~ **au lait,** (*rare*) **c'est une** ~ **au lait** he flies off the handle easily, he's very quick-tempered; ~ **populaire** soup kitchen.

soupente [supɑ̃t] *nf* cupboard (*surtout Brit*) *ou* closet (*US*) (under the stairs).

souper [supe] **1** *nm* supper; (*Belgique, Can, Suisse: dîner*) dinner, supper.
2 *vi* (1) **(a)** to have supper; (*Belgique, Can, Suisse*) to have dinner *ou* supper. **après le spectacle, nous sommes allés** ~ after the play we went for supper.
(b) (*) **j'en ai soupé de ces histoires!** I'm sick and tired* *ou* I've had a bellyful‡ of all this fuss!

soupeser [supəze] (5) *vt* (*lit*) to weigh in one's hand(s), feel the weight of; (*fig*) to weigh up.

soupière [supjɛʀ] *nf* (soup) tureen.

soupir [supiʀ] *nm* **(a)** sigh. ~ **de soulagement** sigh of relief; **pousser un gros** ~ to let out *ou* give a heavy sigh, sigh heavily; (*littér*) **les** ~**s du vent** the sighing *ou* soughing (*littér*) of the wind; *V* **dernier.**
(b) (*Mus*) crotchet rest; *V* **demi-, quart.**

soupirail, *pl* **-aux** [supiʀaj, o] *nm* (small) basement window (*gen with bars*).

soupirant [supiʀɑ̃] *nm* († *ou hum*) suitor († *ou hum*), wooer († *ou hum*).

soupirer [supiʀe] (1) *vi* (*lit*) to sigh. ~ **d'aise** to sigh with contentment; (*littér*) ~ **après** *ou* **pour qch/qn** to sigh for sth/sb (*littér*), yearn for sth/sb; **'j'ai tout perdu' soupira-t-il** 'I've lost everything' he sighed; **... dit-il en soupirant ...** he said with a sigh.

souple [supl(ə)] *adj* **(a)** (*flexible*) *corps, membres, matériau* supple; *branche, tige* pliable, supple; ~ **comme un chat** *ou* **une chatte** as agile as a cat; *V* **échine.**
(b) (*fig: qui s'adapte*) *personne, caractère, esprit* flexible, adaptable; *discipline, forme d'expression, règlement* flexible.
(c) (*gracieux, fluide*) *corps, silhouette* lithe, lissom (*littér*); *démarche, taille* lithe, supple; *style* fluid, flowing (*épith*).

souplesse [suplɛs] *nf* (*V* **souple**) suppleness; pliability; flexibility; adaptability; litheness; lissomness (*littér*); fluidity.

souquenille [suknij] *nf* (*Hist*) smock.

souquer [suke] (1) *vi*: ~ **ferme** to pull hard (at the oars).

source [suʀs(ə)] *nf* **(a)** (*point d'eau*) spring. ~ **thermale/d'eau minérale** hot *ou* thermal/mineral spring; *V* **couler, eau.**
(b) (*foyer*) ~ **de chaleur/d'énergie** source of heat/energy; ~ **lumineuse** *ou* **de lumière** source of light, light source; ~ **sonore** source of sound.
(c) *[cours d'eau]* source. **cette rivière prend sa** ~ **dans le Massif central** this river has its source in *ou* springs up in the Massif Central.
(d) (*fig: origine*) source. ~ **de ridicule/profits** source of ridicule/profit; **l'argent est la** ~ **de tous nos maux** money is the root of all our ills; **de** ~ **sûre, de bonne** ~ from a reliable source, on good authority; **tenir qch de** ~ **sûre** to have sth on good authority, get sth from a reliable source; **de** ~ **généralement bien informée** from a usually well-informed *ou* accurate source; **de** ~ **autorisée** from an official source; *V* **retour.**

sourcier [suʀsje] *nm* water diviner; *V* **baguette.**

sourcil [suʀsi] *nm* (eye)brow. **aux** ~**s épais** heavy-browed, beetle-browed; *V* **froncer.**

sourcilier, -ière [suʀsilje, jɛʀ] *adj* superciliary; *V* **arcade.**

sourciller [suʀsije] (1) *vi*: **il n'a pas sourcillé** he didn't turn a hair *ou* bat an eyelid; **écoutant sans** ~ **mes reproches** listening to my reproaches without turning a hair *ou* batting an eyelid.

sourcilleux, -euse [suʀsijø, øz] *adj* (*pointilleux*) finicky; (*littér: hautain*) haughty.

sourd, e [suʀ, suʀd(ə)] **1** *adj* **(a)** *personne* deaf. ~ **d'une oreille** deaf in one ear; **être** ~ **comme un pot*** to be as deaf as a post; **faire la** ~**e oreille (à des supplications)** to turn a deaf ear (to entreaties); *V* **naissance.**
(b) ~ **à** *conseils, prières* deaf to; *vacarme, environnement* oblivious of *ou* to.
(c) *son* muffled, muted; *couleur* muted, toned-down, subdued; (*Phonétique*) *consonne* voiceless; *V* **lanterne.**
(d) (*vague*) *douleur* dull; *désir, angoisse, inquiétude* gnawing; *colère, hostilité* veiled, subdued.
(e) (*caché*) *lutte, menées* silent, hidden. **se livrer à de** ~**es manigances** to be engaged in silent manoeuvring.
2 *nm,f* deaf person. **les** ~**s** the deaf; ~**(e)-muet(te),** *mpl* ~**s-muets** (*adj*) deaf-and-dumb; (*nm,f*) deaf-mute; **taper** *ou* **frapper comme un** ~ to bang with all one's might; **crier** *ou* **hurler comme un** ~ to yell like a deaf man *ou* at the top of one's voice; *V* **dialogue, pire, tomber.**
3 sourde *nf* (*Phonétique*) voiceless consonant.

sourdement [suʀdəmɑ̃] *adv* (*avec un bruit assourdi*) dully; (*littér: souterrainement, secrètement*) silently. **le tonnerre grondait** ~ **au loin** there was a muffled rumble of thunder *ou* thunder rumbled dully in the distance.

sourdine [suʀdin] *nf* mute. **jouer en** ~ to play softly *ou* quietly; (*fig*) **faire qch en** ~ to do sth on the quiet; (*fig*) **mettre une** ~ **à** *enthousiasme, prétentions* to tone down.

sourdre [suʀdʀ(ə)] *vi* *[source]* to rise; *[eau]* to spring up, rise; (*fig, littér*) to well up, rise.

souriant, e [suʀjɑ̃, ɑ̃t] *adj* *visage* smiling; *personne* cheerful; (*fig*) *pensée, philosophie* benign, agreeable.

souriceau, *pl* ~**x** [suʀiso] *nm* young mouse.

souricière [suʀisjɛʀ] *nf* (*lit*) mousetrap; (*fig*) trap.

sourire [suʀiʀ] **1** *nm* smile. **le** ~ **aux lèvres** with a smile on his lips; **avec le** ~ (*accueillir qn*) with a smile; (*exécuter une tâche*) cheerfully; **gardez le** ~! keep smiling!; (*lit, fig*) **avoir le** ~ to have a smile on one's face; **faire un** ~ **à qn** to give sb a smile; **faire des** ~**s à qn** to keep smiling at sb; **un large** ~ (*chaleureux*) a broad smile; (*amusé*) a (broad) grin, a broad smile; *V* **coin.**
2 *vi* (36) **(a)** to smile (*à qn* at sb). ~ **à la vie** to delight in living; **faire** ~: (*lit*) **cette remarque les fit** ~ this remark made them smile *ou* brought a smile to their faces; (*fig*) **ce projet ridicule fait** ~ this ridiculous project is laughable.
(b) ~ **à** (*plaire à*) to appeal to; (*être favorable à*) to smile on, favour; **cette idée ne me sourit guère** that idea doesn't appeal to me, I don't fancy that idea*; **l'idée de faire cela ne me sourit pas** I don't relish the thought of doing that, the idea of doing that doesn't appeal to me; **la chance lui souriait** luck smiled on him.

souris[1] [suʀi] *nf* **(a)** (*Zool*) mouse. ~ **blanche** white mouse (*bred for experiments*); *V* **gris, jouer, trou. (b)** (‡: *femme*) bird* (*Brit*), broad* (*US*). **(c)** *[gigot]* knuckle-joint.

souris[2]†† [suʀi] *nm* smile.

sournois, e [suʀnwa, waz] *adj personne* deceitful, deep (*attrib*), underhand; *regard, air* shifty; *méthode, propos, attaque* underhand. **c'est un petit** ~ he's an underhand little devil*.

sournoisement [suʀnwazmɑ̃] *adv* (*V* **sournois**) deceitfully; in an underhand manner; shiftily. **il s'approcha** ~ **de lui** he stole *ou* crept stealthily up to him.

sournoiserie [suʀnwazʀi] *nf* (*V* **sournois:** *littér*) deceitfulness; underhand manner; shiftiness.

sous [su] **1** *prép* **(a)** (*position*) under, underneath, beneath; (*atmosphère*) in. **s'abriter** ~ **un arbre/un parapluie** to shelter under *ou* underneath *ou* beneath a tree/an umbrella; **porter son sac** ~ **son bras** to carry one's bag under one's arm; **se promener** ~ **la pluie/le soleil** to take a walk in the rain/in the sunshine; **le village est plus joli** ~ **le soleil/la lune/la clarté des étoiles** the village is prettier in the sunshine/in the *ou* by moonlight/by starlight; **le pays était** ~ **la neige** the country was covered with *ou* in snow; **l'Angleterre s'étendait** ~ **eux** England spread out beneath *ou* below them; **dormir** ~ **la tente** to sleep under canvas *ou* in a tent; **abri** ~ **roche** cliff-face *ou* rock-face shelter; **une mèche dépassait de** ~ **son chapeau** a lock of hair hung down from under her hat; ~ **terre** under the ground, underground; **rien de neuf** *ou* **nouveau** ~ **le soleil** there's nothing new under the sun; **ils ne veulent plus vivre** ~ **le même toit** they don't want to live under the same roof any longer; **cela s'est passé** ~ **nos yeux** it happened before *ou* under our very eyes; ~ **le canon** *ou* **le feu de l'ennemi** under enemy fire; (*fig*) **vous trouverez le renseignement** ~ **tel numéro/telle rubrique** you will find the information under such-and-such a number/heading; (*fig*) ~ **des dehors frustes/une apparence paisible** beneath *ou* behind his (*ou* her *etc*) rough exterior/his (*ou* her *etc*) peaceful exterior; *V* **manteau, prétexte** *etc.*

(b) (*temps*) (*à l'époque de*) under, during; (*dans un délai de*) within. ~ **le règne/le pontificat de** under *ou* during the reign/the pontificate of; ~ **Charles X** under Charles X; ~ **la Révolution/la VIe République** at the time of *ou* during the Revolution/the VIth Republic; ~ **peu** shortly, before long; ~ **huitaine/quinzaine** within the *ou* a week/two weeks *ou* the *ou* a fortnight (*Brit*).

(c) (*cause*) under. ~ **l'influence de qn/qch** under the influence of sb/sth; ~ **l'empire de la terreur** in the grip of terror; **le rocher s'est effrité** ~ **l'action du soleil/du gel** the rock has crumbled (away) due to *ou* under the action of the sun/the frost; **il a agi** ~ **l'effet** *ou* **le coup de la colère** his action was sparked off *ou* triggered off by anger; **plier** ~ **le poids de qch** to bend beneath *ou* under the weight of sth; *V* **faix.**

(d) (*manière*) **examiner une question** ~ **tous ses angles** *ou* **toutes ses faces** to examine every angle *ou* facet of a question, look at a question from every angle; ~ **un faux nom/une identité d'emprunt** under a false name/an assumed identity; ~ **certaines conditions j'accepte** I accept on certain conditions; **je ne le connaissais pas** ~ **ce jour-là** I didn't know him in that light, I didn't know that side *ou* aspect of him; ~ **ce rapport** on that score, in this *ou* that respect; **il a été peint** ~ **les traits d'un berger** he was painted as a shepherd *ou* in the guise of a shepherd; *V* **clef, enveloppe, garantie** *etc.*

(e) (*dépendance*) under. **être** ~ **les ordres/la protection/la garde de qn** to be under sb's orders/under *ou* in sb's protection/in sb's care; **se mettre** ~ **la protection/la garde de qn** to commit o.s. to *ou* into sb's protection/care; **se mettre** ~ **les ordres de qn** to submit (o.s.) to sb's orders; **l'affaire est** ~ **sa direction** he is running *ou* managing the affair, the affair is under his management; **l'affaire est** ~ **sa responsabilité** the affair is *ou* comes within his responsibility; *V* **auspice, charme, tutelle** *etc.*

(f) (*Méd*) ~ **anesthésie** under anaesthetic *ou* anaesthesia; **malade** ~ **perfusion** patient on the drip.

(g) (*Tech*) **câble** ~ **gaine** sheathed *ou* encased cable; **(emballé)** ~ **plastique** plastic-wrapped; ~ **tube** in (a) tube; **(emballé)** ~ **vide** vacuum-packed.

2 *préf* **(a)** (*infériorité*) **c'est du** ~**-art/du** ~**-Sartre/de la** ~**-littérature** it's pseudo-art/pseudo-Sartre/pseudo-literature; **il fait du** ~**-Giono** he's a sort of substandard Giono; ~**-homme** subhuman.

(b) (*subordination*) sub-. ~**-directeur/-bibliothécaire** *etc* assistant *ou* sub-manager/-librarian *etc*; ~**-classe/-catégorie** sub-class/-category; ~**-agence** sub-branch.

(c) (*insuffisance*) under..., insufficiently. ~**-alimentation** undernourishment, malnutrition; ~**-alimenté** undernourished, underfed; ~**-consommation** underconsumption; **la région est** ~**-équipée** the region is underequipped; ~**-équipement** lack of equipment; ~**-évaluer** to underestimate, underrate; ~**-industrialisé** underindustrialized; ~**-peuplé** underpopulated; ~**-production** underproduction; **les dangers de la** ~**-productivité** the dangers of underproductivity; ~**-rémunéré** underpaid; **la région est** ~**-scolarisée** the region is underequipped in schooling facilities; **la région est** ~**-urbanisée** the region is insufficiently urbanized.

3: sous-bois *nm inv* undergrowth; **sous-brigadier** *nm, pl* **sous-brigadiers** deputy sergeant; **sous-chef** *nm, pl* **sous-chefs** (*gén*) second-in-command; (*Admin*) **sous-chef de bureau** deputy chief clerk; **sous-chef de gare** deputy *ou* substationmaster; **sous-commission** *nf, pl* **sous-commissions** subcommittee; **sous-continent** *nm, pl* **sous-continents** subcontinent; **sous-cutané, e** *adj* subcutaneous; **sous-développé, e** *adj* underdeveloped; **les pays sous-développés** the underdeveloped *ou* developing *ou* emergent countries; **sous-développement** *nm* underdevelopment; (*Rel*) **sous-diacre** *nm, pl* **sous-diacres** sub-deacon; **sous-emploi** *nm* underemployment; **sous-ensemble** *nm, pl* **sous-ensembles** subset; **sous-entendre** *vt* to imply, infer; **il faut sous-entendre que** it is to be inferred *ou* understood that; **sous-entendu, e,** *mpl* **sous-entendus** (*adj*) implied, understood; (*nm*) innuendo, insinuation; **sous-estimer** *vt* to underestimate, underrate; **sous-exposer** *vt* to underexpose; **sous-exposition** *nf, pl* **sous-expositions** (*Phot*) under-exposure (*U*); **sous-fifre*** *nm, pl* **sous-fifres** underling; **sous-jacent, e** *adj* (*lit*) subjacent, underlying; (*fig*) underlying; (*Mil*) **sous-lieutenant** *nm, pl* **sous-lieutenants** sub-lieutenant; **sous-locataire** *nmf, pl* **sous-locataires** subtenant; **sous-location** *nf* subletting; **sous-louer** *vt* to sublet; **sous-main** *nm inv* desk blotter; (*fig*) **en sous-main** secretly; **sous-maîtresse** *nf, pl* **sous-maîtresses** brothel-keeper, madam; **sous-marin, e,** *mpl* **sous-marins** (*adj*) *pêche, chasse* underwater (*épith*); *végétation, faune* submarine (*épith*); (*nm*) submarine; **sous-marin de poche** pocket submarine; **sous-marinier** *nm, pl* **sous-mariniers** submariner; (*Comm*) **sous-marque** *nf, pl* **sous-marques** sub-brand; (*Can*) **sous-ministre** *nm, pl* **sous-ministres** deputy minister; (*Math*) **sous-multiple** *nm, pl* **sous-multiples** submultiple; **sous-nutrition** *nf* malnutrition; (*Mil*) **sous-off*** *nm, pl* **sous-offs** *abrév de* **sous-officier**; **sous-officier** *nm, pl* **sous-officiers** non-commissioned officer, N.C.O.; **sous-ordre** *nm, pl* **sous-ordres** (*Zool*) suborder; (*sous-fifre*) subordinate, underling; **sous-pied** *nm, pl* **sous-pieds** (under-)strap; **sous-préfecture** *nf, pl* **sous-préfectures** sub-prefecture; **sous-préfet** *nm, pl* **sous-préfets** sub-prefect; **sous-préfète** *nf, pl* **sous-préfètes** sub-prefect's wife; **sous-produit** *nm, pl* **sous-produits** (*lit*) by-product; (*fig*) pale imitation; **sous-prolétaire** *nmf, pl* **sous-prolétaires** (underprivileged) worker; **sous-prolétariat** *nm* underprivileged *ou* downtrodden class; **sous-secrétaire** *nm* (*pl* **sous-secrétaires**) **d'État** ≃ (Parliamentary) Under-Secretary; **sous-secrétariat** *nm, pl* **sous-secrétariats** post of Under-Secretary; **sous-sol** *nm, pl* **sous-sols** *[terre]* subsoil, substratum; *[magasin, maison]* basement; **sous-tendre** *vt* (*Géom*) to subtend; (*fig*) to underlie; **sous-titre** *nm, pl* **sous-titres** subtitle; **sous-titrer** *vt* to subtitle; **en version originale sous-titrée** in the original (version) with subtitles; **sous-traitance** *nf* subcontracting; **sous-traitant** *nm, pl* **sous-traitants** subcontractor; **sous-traiter** (*vi*) to become a subcontractor, be subcontracted; (*vt*) *affaire* to subcontract; **sous-ventrière** *nf, pl* **sous-ventrières** girth, bellyband; **sous-verre** *nm inv* (*encadrement*) glass mount; (*Phot*) photograph mounted under glass; **sous-vêtement** *nm, pl* **sous-vêtements** undergarment; **sous-vêtements** underwear, undergarments.

souscripteur, -trice [suskʀiptœʀ, tʀis] *nm,f [emprunt, publication]* subscriber (*de* to).

souscription [suskʀipsjɔ̃] *nf* (*action*) subscription; (*somme*) subscription, contribution. **ouvrir une** ~ **en faveur de ...** to start a fund in aid of ...; **livre en** ~ book sold on a subscription basis; **ce livre est offert en** ~ **jusqu'au 15 novembre, au prix de 75 F** this book is available to subscribers until November 15th at the prepublication price of 75 francs.

souscrire [suskʀiʀ] (39) **1 souscrire à** *vt indir* **(a)** *emprunt, publication* to subscribe to; ~ **à la construction de** to contribute *ou* subscribe to the construction of; **il a souscrit pour 100 F à la construction du monument** he contributed *ou* subscribed 100 francs to the construction of the monument.

(b) *idée, opinion, projet* to subscribe to. **c'est une excellente idée et j'y souscris** it's an excellent idea and I subscribe to it.

2 *vt* (*Comm*) *billet* to sign.

souscrit, e [suskʀi, it] (*ptp de* **souscrire**) *adj:* **capital** ~ subscribed capital.

soussigné, e [susiɲe] *adj, nm,f* undersigned. **je** ~ **Dupont Charles-Henri déclare que ...** I the undersigned certify that ...; **les (témoins)** ~**s** we the undersigned.

soustractif, -ive [sustʀaktif, iv] *adj* subtractive.

soustraction [sustʀaksjɔ̃] *nf* **(a)** (*Math*) subtraction. **faire la** ~ **de** *somme* to take away, subtract; **et il faut encore déduire les frais de réparation: faites la** ~ **vous-même** in addition you have to deduct repair costs — you can work it out for yourself.

(b) (*frm: vol*) removal, abstraction.

soustraire [sustʀɛʀ] (50) **1** *vt* **(a)** (*gén, Math: défalquer*) to subtract, take away (*de* from).

(b) (*frm: dérober*) to remove, abstract; (*cacher*) to conceal, shield (*à* from). ~ **qn à la justice/à la colère de qn** to shield sb from justice/from sb's anger.

2 se soustraire *vpr* (*frm*) **se** ~ **à** *devoir* to shirk; *obligation, corvée* to escape, shirk; *autorité* to elude, escape from; *curiosité* to conceal o.s. from, escape from; **se** ~ **à la justice** to elude justice; (*s'enfuir*) to abscond; **quelle corvée! comment m'y** ~**?** what drudgery! how shall I escape it? *ou* get out of it?

soutane [sutan] *nf* cassock, soutane. (*fig*) **prendre la** ~ to enter the Church.

soute [sut] *nf [navire]* hold. ~ **(à bagages)** *[bateau, avion]* baggage hold; ~ **à charbon** coal-bunker; ~ **à munitions** ammunition store; ~ **à mazout** oil-tank; ~ **à bombes** bomb bay.

soutenable [sutnabl(ə)] *adj opinion* tenable, defensible.

soutenance [sutnɑ̃s] *nf* (*Univ*) ~ **de thèse** ≃ viva, viva voce (examination).

soutènement [sutɛnmɑ̃] *nm:* **travaux de** ~ support(ing) works; **ouvrage de** ~ support(ing) structure; *V* **mur.**

souteneur [sutnœʀ] *nm* procurer.

soutenir [sutniʀ] (22) **1** *vt* **(a)** (*servir d'appui à*) *personne, toit, mur* to support, hold up; *[médicament etc]* to sustain. **on lui a fait une piqûre pour** ~ **le cœur** they gave him an injection to sustain his heart; **ses jambes peuvent à peine le** ~ his legs can hardly support him *ou* hold him up; **un fauteuil qui soutient bien le dos** an armchair which gives good support to the back *ou* which supports the back well; **prenez un peu d'alcool, cela soutient** have a little drink — it'll give you a lift* *ou* keep you going.

(b) (*aider*) *gouvernement, parti, candidat* to support, back; *famille* to support. **elle soutient les enfants contre leur père** she takes the children's part *ou* she stands up for the children against their father; **son amitié/il les a beaucoup soutenus dans leur épreuve** his friendship/he was a real prop to them in their time of trouble, his friendship was something/he was something *ou* someone for them to lean on in their time of trouble.

(c) (*faire durer*) *attention, conversation, effort* to keep up, sustain; *réputation* to keep up, maintain.

(d) (*résister à*) *assaut, combat* to stand up to, withstand; *regard* to bear, support. **il a bien soutenu le choc** he stood up well to the shock *ou* withstood the shock well; ~ **la comparaison avec** to bear *ou* stand comparison with, compare (favourably) with.

(e) (*affirmer*) *opinion, doctrine* to uphold, support; (*défendre*) *droits* to uphold, defend. (*Univ*) ~ **sa thèse** to attend *ou* have one's viva; **c'est une doctrine que je ne pourrai jamais** ~ it is a doctrine which I shall never be able to support *ou* uphold; **elle soutient toujours le contraire de ce qu'il dit** she always maintains the opposite of what he says; **il a soutenu jusqu'au bout qu'il était innocent** he maintained to the end that he was innocent.

2 se soutenir *vpr* **(a)** (*se maintenir*) (*sur ses jambes*) to hold o.s. up, support o.s.; (*dans l'eau*) to keep (o.s.) afloat *ou* up. **se ~ dans l'eau** to keep (o.s.) afloat *ou* up, hold *ou* keep o.s. above the water; **l'oiseau se soutient dans l'air grâce à ses ailes** birds hold *ou* keep themselves up (in the air) thanks to their wings; **il n'arrivait plus à se ~ sur ses jambes** his legs could no longer support him, he could no longer stand on his legs.

(b) (*fig*) **ça peut se ~** it's a tenable point of view; **un tel point de vue ne peut se ~** a point of view like that is indefensible *ou* untenable; **l'intérêt se soutient jusqu'à la fin** the interest is kept up *ou* sustained *ou* maintained right to the end.

(c) (*s'entraider*) to stand by each other. **dans la famille, ils se soutiennent tous** the family all stand by each other *ou* stick together.

soutenu, e [sutny] (*ptp de* **soutenir**) *adj* (*élevé, ferme*) *style* elevated; (*constant, assidu*) *attention, effort* sustained, unflagging; *travail* sustained; (*intense*) *couleur* strong.

souterrain, e [sutɛʀɛ̃, ɛn] **1** *adj* (*lit*) underground, subterranean; (*fig*) subterranean; *V* **passage**. **2** *nm* underground *ou* subterranean passage.

soutien [sutjɛ̃] *nm* **(a)** (*gén: étai, aide*) support. (*Mil*) **unité de ~** support *ou* reserve unit; (*Admin*) **~ de famille** breadwinner (*status entailing exemption from national service*).

(b) (*action*) *[voûte]* supporting. **~ des prix** price support.

soutien-gorge, *pl* **soutiens-gorge** [sutjɛ̃gɔʀʒ(ə)] *nm* bra.

soutier [sutje] *nm* (*Naut*) coal-trimmer.

soutirer [sutiʀe] (1) *vt* **(a)** (*prendre*) **~ qch à qn** to squeeze *ou* get sth out of sb, extract sth from sb. **(b)** *vin* to decant, rack.

souvenance [suvnɑ̃s] *nf* (*littér*) recollection. **avoir ~ de** to recollect, have a recollection of.

souvenir [suvniʀ] **1** *nm* **(a)** (*réminiscence*) memory, recollection. **elle a gardé de lui un bon/mauvais ~** she has good/bad memories of him; **ce n'est plus maintenant qu'un mauvais ~** it's just a bad memory now; **je n'ai qu'un vague ~ de l'incident/de l'avoir rencontré** I have only a vague recollection of the incident/of having met him *ou* of meeting him; **raconter des ~s d'enfance/de guerre** to recount memories of one's childhood/of the war.

(b) (*littér: fait de se souvenir*) recollection, remembrance (*frm, littér*). **avoir le ~ de qch** to have a memory of sth; **garder le ~ de qch** to retain the memory of sth; **perdre le ~ de qch** to lose all recollection of sth; (*frm*) **je n'ai pas ~ d'avoir ...** I have no recollection *ou* remembrance (*frm*) of having...; **en ~ de** in memory *ou* remembrance of; **évoquer le ~ de qn** to evoke the memory of sb.

(c) (*mémoire*) memory. **dans un coin de mon ~** in a corner of my memory.

(d) (*objet gardé pour le souvenir*) keepsake, memento; (*pour touristes*) souvenir; (*marque, témoignage d'un événement*) souvenir. **garder qch comme ~ (de qn)** to keep sth as a memento (of sb); **cette cicatrice est un ~ de la guerre** this scar is a souvenir from the war; **boutique** *ou* **magasin de ~s** souvenir shop.

(e) (*formules de politesse*) **amical** *ou* **affectueux ~** yours (ever); **mon bon ~ à X** remember me to X, (my) regards to X; **rappelez-moi au bon ~ de votre mère** remember me to your mother, give my (kind) regards to your mother; **croyez à mon fidèle ~** yours ever, yours sincerely.

2 se souvenir (22) *vpr*: **se ~ de qn** to remember sb; **se ~ de qch/d'avoir fait/que ...** to remember *ou* recall *ou* recollect sth/doing sth/that ...; **il a plu tout l'été, tu t'en souviens?** *ou* **tu te souviens?*** it rained all summer, do you remember? *ou* recall?, it rained all summer, remember?*; **elle lui a donné une leçon dont il se souviendra** she taught him a lesson he won't forget; **souvenez-vous qu'il est très puissant** bear in mind *ou* remember that he is very powerful; **souviens-toi de ta promesse!** remember your promise!; **tu m'as fait me ~ que ...,** (*littér*) **tu m'as fait ~ que ...** you have reminded me that ... .

3 *vb impers* (*littér*) **il me souvient d'avoir entendu raconter cette histoire** I recollect *ou* recall *ou* remember having heard *ou* hearing that story.

souvent [suvɑ̃] *adv* often. **le plus ~, cela marche bien** more often than not it works well; **faire qch plus ~ qu'à son** (*ou* **mon** *etc*) **tour** to have more than one's fair share of doing sth; **peu ~** seldom; (*Prov*) **~ femme varie (bien fol est qui s'y fie)** woman is fickle.

souventes fois††, souventefois†† [suvɑ̃tfwa] *adv* oft(times) (††, *littér*).

souverain, e [suvʀɛ̃, ɛn] **1** *adj* **(a)** (*Pol*) *état, puissance* sovereign; *assemblée, cour, juge* supreme. **le ~ pontife** the Supreme Pontiff.

(b) (*suprême*) **le ~ bien** the sovereign good; **remède ~ contre qch** sovereign remedy against sth.

(c) (*intensif*) supreme. **~ mépris/indifférence** supreme contempt/indifference.

2 *nm,f* **(a)** (*monarque*) sovereign, monarch. **~ absolu/constitutionnel** absolute/constitutional monarch; **la ~e britannique** the British sovereign.

(b) (*fig*) sovereign. **s'imposer en ~** to reign supreme; **la philosophie est la ~e des disciplines de l'esprit** philosophy is the most noble *ou* the highest of the mental disciplines.

3 *nm* **(a)** (*Jur, Pol*) **le ~** the sovereign power.

(b) (*Hist Brit: monnaie*) sovereign.

souverainement [suvʀɛnmɑ̃] *adv* **(a)** (*intensément*) supremely. **ça me déplaît ~** I dislike it intensely. **(b)** (*en tant que souverain*) with sovereign power.

souveraineté [suvʀɛnte] *nf* sovereignty.

soviet [sɔvjɛt] *nm* soviet.

soviétique [sɔvjetik] **1** *adj* Soviet. **2** *nmf*: **S~** Soviet citizen.

soviétiser [sovjetize] (1) *vt* to sovietize.

soya [sɔja] *nm* = **soja.**

soyeux, -euse [swajø, øz] **1** *adj* silky. **2** *nm* silk manufacturer (*of Lyons*), silk merchant (*of Lyons*).

spacieusement [spasjøzmɑ̃] *adv* spaciously. **~ aménagé** spaciously laid out; **nous sommes ~ logés** we have ample room in our accommodation *ou* where we are staying.

spacieux, -euse [spasjø, øz] *adj* spacious, roomy.

spadassin [spadasɛ̃] *nm* (*littér*, †: *mercenaire*) hired killer *ou* assassin; (†: *bretteur*) swordsman.

spaghetti [spageti] *nm* (*gén pl*) **~s** spaghetti; (*rare*) **un ~** a strand of spaghetti.

Spahi [spai] *nm* (*Hist Mil*) Spahi (*soldier of native cavalry corps of French army in North Africa*).

sparadrap [spaʀadʀa] *nm* adhesive *ou* sticking plaster.

sparring-partner [spaʀiŋpaʀtnɛʀ] *nm* sparring partner.

Sparte [spaʀt(ə)] *nf* Sparta.

spartiate [spaʀsjat] **1** *adj* Spartan. **2** *nmf* (*Hist*) **S~** Spartan. **3** *nf* (*chaussures*) **~s** Roman sandals.

spasme [spasm(ə)] *nm* spasm.

spasmodique [spasmɔdik] *adj* spasmodic.

spasmodiquement [spasmɔdikmɑ̃] *adv* spasmodically.

spath [spat] *nm* (*Minér*) spar.

spatial, e, *mpl* **-aux** [spasjal, o] *adj* (*opposé à temporel*) spatial; (*Espace*) space (*épith*).

spatialement [spasjalmɑ̃] *adv* spatially.

spatialisation [spasjalizasjɔ̃] *nf* spatialization.

spatialiser [spasjalize] (1) *vt* to spatialize.

spatio-temporel, -elle [spasjɔtɑ̃pɔʀɛl] *adj* spatiotemporal.

spatule [spatyl] *nf* **(a)** (*ustensile*) *[peintre, cuisinier]* spatula. **(b)** (*bout*) *[ski, manche de cuiller etc]* tip. **(c)** (*oiseau*) spoonbill.

speaker [spikœʀ] *nm* (*Rad, TV*) announcer.

speakerine [spikʀin] *nf* (*Rad, TV*) (woman) announcer.

spécial, e, *mpl* **-aux** [spesjal, o] *adj* (*gén*) special; (*bizarre*) peculiar. (*euph*) **il a des mœurs un peu ~es** he's a bit the other way inclined* (*euph*), he has certain tendencies (*euph*).

spécialement [spesjalmɑ̃] *adv* (*plus particulièrement*) especially, particularly; (*tout exprès*) specially. **pas ~ intéressant** not particularly *ou* especially interesting; **c'est très intéressant, ~ vers la fin** it is very interesting, especially *ou* particularly towards the end; **on l'a choisi ~ pour ce travail** he was specially chosen for this job; **~ construit pour cet usage** specially built for this use.

spécialisation [spesjalizasjɔ̃] *nf* specialization.

spécialisé, e [spesjalize] (*ptp de* **spécialiser**) *adj travail, personne* specialized. **être ~ dans** *[personne]* to be a specialist in; *[firme]* to specialize in; *V* **ouvrier.**

spécialiser [spesjalize] (1) **1 se spécialiser** *vpr* to specialize (*dans* in). **2** *vt* (*rare*) **~ qn** to make sb into a specialist.

spécialiste [spesjalist(ə)] *nmf* (*gén, Méd*) specialist.

spécialité [spesjalite] *nf* (*gén, Culin*) speciality; (*Univ etc: branche*) specialism, special field. **~ pharmaceutique** patent medicine; **il a la ~ de faire ...*** he has a special *ou* particular knack of doing ..., he specializes in doing ... .

spécieusement [spesjøzmɑ̃] *adv* speciously.

spécieux, -euse [spesjø, øz] *adj* specious.

spécification [spesifikasjɔ̃] *nf* specification.

spécificité [spesifisite] *nf* specificity.

spécifier [spesifje] (7) *vt* (*préciser son choix*) to specify, state; (*indiquer, mentionner*) to state. **veuillez ~ le modèle que vous désirez** please specify the model that you require *ou* desire; **en passant votre commande, n'oubliez pas de ~ votre numéro d'arrondissement** when placing your order, don't forget to state your district number; **a-t-il spécifié l'heure?** did he specify *ou* state the time?; **j'avais bien spécifié qu'il devait venir le matin** I had stated specifically that he should come in the morning.

spécifique [spesifik] *adj* specific.

spécifiquement [spesifikmɑ̃] *adv* (*tout exprès*) specifically; (*typiquement*) typically.

spécimen [spesimɛn] *nm* (*gén: échantillon, exemple*) specimen; (*exemplaire publicitaire*) specimen copy, sample copy. (**numéro**) **~** sample copy.

spectacle [spɛktakl(ə)] *nm* **(a)** (*vue, tableau*) sight; (*grandiose, magnifique*) sight, spectacle. **au ~ de** at the sight of; (*péj*) **se donner** *ou* **s'offrir en ~ (à qn)** to make a spectacle *ou* an exhibition of o.s. (in front of sb).

(b) (*représentation: Ciné, Théât etc*) show. (*branche*) **le ~** show business, entertainment, show biz*; (*rubrique*) '**~s**' 'entertainment'; **le ~ va commencer** the show is about to begin; **un ~ lyrique/dramatique** a musical/dramatic entertainment; **~ de variétés** variety show; **aller au ~** to go to a show; **l'industrie du ~** the entertainment(s) industry; *V* **grand, salle.**

spectaculaire [spɛktakylɛʀ] *adj* spectacular.

spectateur, -trice [spɛktatœʀ, tʀis] *nm,f* *[événement, accident]* onlooker, witness; (*Sport*) spectator; (*Ciné, Théât*) member of the audience. **les ~s** the audience; (*fig*) **traverser la vie en ~** to go through life as an onlooker *ou* a spectator.

spectral, e, *mpl* **-aux** [spɛktʀal, o] *adj* **(a)** (*fantomatique*) ghostly, spectral. **(b)** (*Phys*) spectral; *V* **analyse.**

spectre [spɛktʀ(ə)] *nm* **(a)** (*fig: fantôme*) spectre. **le ~ de la guerre se dressait à l'horizon** the spectre of war loomed on the horizon. **(b)** (*Phys*) spectrum. **les couleurs du ~** the colours of the spectrum; **~ solaire** solar spectrum; **~ de résonance** resonance spectrum.

spectrographe [spɛktʀɔgʀaf] *nm* spectrograph.

spéculateur, -trice [spekylatœʀ, tʀis] *nm,f* speculator.

spéculatif, -ive [spekylatif, iv] *adj* (*Fin, Philos*) speculative.

spéculation [spekylasjɔ̃] *nf* speculation.

spéculer [spekyle] (1) *vi* (*Philos*) to speculate (*sur* on, about);

(*Fin*) to speculate (*sur* in). (*fig: tabler sur*) ~ **sur** to bank on, rely on.

speech [spitʃ] *nm* († *ou**: *laïus*) speech (*after a dinner, toast etc*).

spéléo [speleo] *nf, nmf abrév de* **spéléologie, spéléologue.**

spéléologie [speleɔlɔʒi] *nf* (*étude*) speleology; (*exploration*) potholing, caving*.

spéléologique [speleɔlɔʒik] *adj* (*V* **spéléologie**) speleological; potholing (*épith*), caving* (*épith*).

spéléologue [speleɔlɔg] *nmf* (*V* **spéléologie**) speleologist; potholer, caver*.

spermatique [spɛʀmatik] *adj* spermatic.

spermatogénèse [spɛʀmatɔʒenɛz] *nf* spermatogenesis.

spermatozoïde [spɛʀmatɔzɔid] *nm* sperm, spermatozoon.

sperme [spɛʀm(ə)] *nm* semen, sperm.

sphère [sfɛʀ] *nf* (*Astron, fig*) sphere. **les hautes ~s de la politique** the higher realms of politics; ~ **d'influence/d'attributions/d'activité** sphere of influence/competence/activity.

sphéricité [sfeʀisite] *nf* sphericity.

sphérique [sfeʀik] *adj* spherical.

sphincter [sfɛ̃ktɛʀ] *nm* sphincter.

sphinx [sfɛ̃ks] *nm* (*Art, Myth, fig*) sphinx; (*Zool*) hawkmoth, sphinx-moth.

spinal, e, *mpl* **-aux** [spinal, o] *adj* spinal.

spiral, e, *mpl* **-aux** [spiʀal, o] **1** *adj* spiral. **2** *nm*: **(ressort)** ~ hairspring. **3 spirale** *nf* spiral. **s'élever/tomber en ~e** to spiral up(wards)/down(wards).

spiralé, e [spiʀale] *adj* spiral (*épith*).

spirante [spiʀɑ̃t] *adj f, nf*: **(consonne)** ~ spirant.

spire [spiʀ] *nf* [*hélice, spirale*] (single) turn; [*coquille*] whorl; [*ressort*] spiral.

spirite [spiʀit] **1** *adj* spiritualist(ic). **2** *nmf* spiritualist.

spiritisme [spiʀitism(ə)] *nm* spiritualism, spiritism.

spiritualiser [spiʀitɥalize] (1) *vt* to spiritualize.

spiritualisme [spiʀitɥalism(ə)] *nm* spiritualism.

spiritualiste [spiʀitɥalist(ə)] **1** *adj* spiritualist(ic). **2** *nmf* spiritualist.

spiritualité [spiʀitɥalite] *nf* spirituality.

spirituel, -elle [spiʀitɥɛl] *adj* **(a)** (*vif, fin*) witty. **(b)** (*Philos, Rel, gén*) spiritual. **musique ~le** sacred music; **concert** ~ concert of sacred music.

spirituellement [spiʀitɥɛlmɑ̃] *adv* (*V* **spirituel**) wittily; spiritually.

spiritueux, -euse [spiʀitɥø, øz] **1** *adj* (*rare*) spirituous (*rare*). **2** *nm* spirit. **les** ~ spirits.

spiroïdal, e, *mpl* **-aux** [spiʀɔidal, o] *adj* spiroid.

spleen [splin] *nm* († *ou littér*) spleen (*fig littér*).

splendeur [splɑ̃dœʀ] *nf* **(a)** [*paysage, réception, résidence*] splendour, magnificence. **ce tapis est une** ~ this carpet is quite magnificent; **les ~s de l'art africain** the splendours of African art.

(b) (*gloire*) glory, splendour. **du temps de sa** ~ in the days of its (*ou* his *etc*) glory *ou* splendour; (*iro*) **dans toute sa/leur** ~ in all its/their glory.

(c) (*littér: éclat, lumière*) brilliance, splendour.

splendide [splɑ̃did] *adj temps, journée* splendid; *réception, résidence, spectacle* splendid, magnificent; *femme, bébé* magnificent, splendid-looking.

splendidement [splɑ̃didmɑ̃] *adv* splendidly, magnificently.

splénétique [splenetik] *adj* († *littér*) splenetic.

spoliateur, -trice [spɔljatœʀ, tʀis] **1** *adj loi* spoliatory. **2** *nm,f* despoiler.

spoliation [spɔljɑsjɔ̃] *nf* despoilment (*de* of).

spolier [spɔlje] (7) *vt* to despoil.

spondaïque [spɔ̃daik] *adj* spondaic.

spondée [spɔ̃de] *nm* spondee.

spongieux, -euse [spɔ̃ʒjø, øz] *adj* (*gén, Anat*) spongy.

spontané, e [spɔ̃tane] *adj* (*gén*) spontaneous; *V* **génération.**

spontanéité [spɔ̃taneite] *nf* spontaneity.

spontanément [spɔ̃tanemɑ̃] *adv* spontaneously.

sporadicité [spɔʀadisite] *nf* sporadic nature *ou* occurrence.

sporadique [spɔʀadik] *adj* sporadic.

sporadiquement [spɔʀadikmɑ̃] *adv* sporadically.

sporange [spɔʀɑ̃ʒ] *nm* sporangium, spore case.

spore [spɔʀ] *nf* spore.

sport [spɔʀ] **1** *nm* **(a)** sport. **~s individuels/d'équipe** individual/team sports; **faire du ~ pour se maintenir en forme** to do sport in order to keep (o.s.) fit; **station de ~s d'hiver** winter sports resort; **aller aux ~s d'hiver** to go on a winter sports holiday, go winter sporting; **de** ~ *vêtement, terrain, voiture* sports (*épith*).

(b) (*) **il va y avoir du ~!** we'll see some fun!* *ou* action*; **faire ça, c'est vraiment du** ~ doing that is no picnic*.

2 *adj* **(a)** *vêtement, coupe* casual.

(b) (†: *chic, fair-play*) sporting, fair.

sportif, -ive [spɔʀtif, iv] **1** *adj* **(a)** *épreuve, journal, résultats* sports (*épith*); *pêche, marche* competitive (*épith*).

(b) *jeunesse* athletic, fond of sports (*attrib*); *allure, démarche* athletic.

(c) *attitude, mentalité, comportement* sporting, sportsmanlike. **faire preuve d'esprit** ~ to show sportsmanship.

2 *nm* sportsman.

3 sportive *nf* sportswoman.

sportivement [spɔʀtivmɑ̃] *adv* sportingly.

sportivité [spɔʀtivite] *nf* sportsmanship.

spot [spɔt] *nm* **(a)** (*Phys*) light spot; (*Élec*) scanning spot. **(b)** (*lampe: Théât etc*) spotlight, spot. **(c)** ~ **(publicitaire)** (*publicité*) commercial, advert*, ad*.

spoutnik [sputnik] *nm* sputnik.

sprat [spʀat] *nm* sprat.

spray [spʀɛ] *nm* (*aérosol*) spray, aerosol.

sprint [spʀint] *nm* (*de fin de course*) (final) sprint, final spurt; (*épreuve*) sprint. **battu au ~ (final)** beaten in the (final) sprint.

sprinter[1] [spʀintœʀ] *nm* sprinter; (*en fin de course*) fast finisher.

sprinter[2] [spʀinte] (1) *vi* to sprint; (*en fin de course*) to put on a final spurt.

squale [skwal] *nm* dogfish (shark).

squame [skwam] *nf* (*Méd*) scale, squama (*T*).

square [skwaʀ] *nm* public garden(s), square (with garden).

squatter [skwatœʀ] *nm* squatter.

squelette [skəlɛt] *nm* (*lit, fig*) skeleton. **après sa maladie, c'était un vrai** ~ after his illness he was just a bag of bones *ou* he was an absolute skeleton.

squelettique [skəletik] *adj personne, arbre* scrawny, skeleton-like; *exposé* sketchy, skimpy; (*Anat*) skeletal. **d'une maigreur** ~ all skin and bone; **il est** ~ he's scrawny, he's an absolute skeleton, he's mere skin and bone; **des effectifs ~s** a minimal staff.

stabilisateur, -trice [stabilizatœʀ, tʀis] **1** *adj* stabilizing. **2** *nm* (*Tech*) [*véhicule*] anti-roll device; [*navire*] stabilizer; [*avion*] (*horizontal*) tailplane; (*vertical*) fixed fin; (*Chim*) stabilizer.

stabilisation [stabilizɑsjɔ̃] *nf* stabilization.

stabiliser [stabilize] (1) **1** *vt* (*gén*) to stabilize; *terrain* to consolidate; *V* **accotement. 2 se stabiliser** *vpr* to stabilize, become stabilized.

stabilité [stabilite] *nf* stability.

stable [stabl(ə)] *adj monnaie, gouvernement, personne,* (*Chim*), (*Phys*) stable; *position, échelle* stable, steady.

stabulation [stabylɑsjɔ̃] *nf* [*bétail*] stalling; [*chevaux*] stabling; [*poissons*] storing in tanks.

staccato [stakato] **1** *adv* staccato. **2** *nm* staccato passage.

stade [stad] *nm* **(a)** (*sportif*) stadium. **(b)** (*période, étape*) stage. **il en est resté au ~ de l'adolescence** he never got beyond adolescence; (*Psych*) ~ **oral/anal** oral/anal stage.

staff [staf] *nm* staff (*building material*).

stage [staʒ] *nm* (*période*) training period; (*cours*) training course; [*avocat*] articles (*pl*). ~ **de perfectionnement** advanced training course; **il a fait son ~ chez Maître X** he did his articles in Mr X's practice *ou* under Mr X; **faire un** ~ to undergo a period of training, go on a (training) course.

stagiaire [staʒjɛʀ] **1** *nmf* trainee. **2** *adj* trainee (*épith*).

stagnant, e [stagnɑ̃, ɑ̃t] *adj* (*lit, fig*) stagnant.

stagnation [stagnɑsjɔ̃] *nf* (*lit, fig*) stagnation.

stagner [stagne] (1) *vi* (*lit, fig*) to stagnate.

stalactite [stalaktit] *nf* stalactite.

stalag [stalag] *nm* stalag.

stalagmite [stalagmit] *nf* stalagmite.

stalinien, -ienne [stalinjɛ̃, jɛn] *adj, nm,f* Stalinist.

stalinisme [stalinism(ə)] *nm* Stalinism.

stalle [stal] *nf* [*cheval*] stall, box; (*Rel*) stall.

stance [stɑ̃s] *nf* (†: *strophe*) stanza. (*poème*) **~s** *type of verse form* (*of lyrical poem*).

stand [stɑ̃d] *nm* [*exposition*] stand; [*foire*] stall. ~ **(de tir)** [*foire*], (*Sport*) shooting range; (*Mil*) firing range; (*Cyclisme etc*) ~ **de ravitaillement** pit.

standard[1] [stɑ̃daʀ] *nm* (*Téléc*) switchboard.

standard[2] [stɑ̃daʀ] **1** *nm*: ~ **de vie** standard of living. **2** *adj inv* (*Comm, Tech*) standard (*épith*).

standardisation [stɑ̃daʀdizɑsjɔ̃] *nf* standardization.

standardiser [stɑ̃daʀdize] (1) *vt* to standardize.

standardiste [stɑ̃daʀdist(ə)] *nmf* switchboard operator. **demandez à la** ~ ask the operator.

standing [stɑ̃diŋ] *nm* standing. (*Comm*) **immeuble de grand** ~ block of luxury flats (*Brit*) *ou* apartments (*US*).

staphylocoque [stafilɔkɔk] *nm* staphylococcus.

star [staʀ] *nf* (*Ciné*) star.

starlette, (*rare*) **starlet** [staʀlɛt] *nf* starlet.

starter [staʀtɛʀ] *nm* **(a)** (*Aut*) choke. **mettre le** ~ to pull the choke out; **marcher au** ~ to run with the choke out. **(b)** (*Sport*) starter.

station [stɑsjɔ̃] *nf* **(a)** (*lieu d'arrêt*) ~ **(de métro)** (underground (*Brit*) *ou* subway (*US*)) station; ~ **(d'autobus)** (bus) stop; ~ **(de chemin de fer)** halt; ~ **de taxis** taxi rank.

(b) (*poste, établissement*) station. ~ **d'observation/de recherches** observation/research station; ~ **agronomique/météorologique** agricultural research/meteorological station; ~ **géodésique** geodesic station; ~ **émettrice** transmitting station; ~ **(de) radar** radar tracking station; ~ **radiophonique** radio station; ~ **service** service *ou* petrol (*Brit*) *ou* filling station.

(c) (*site*) site; (*Bot, Zool*) station. ~ **préhistorique** prehistoric site; (*Bot*) **une ~ de gentianes** a gentian station.

(d) (*de vacances*) resort. ~ **balnéaire/climatique** sea *ou* seaside/health resort; ~ **de sports d'hiver** winter sports *ou* (winter) ski resort; ~ **thermale** thermal spa.

(e) (*posture*) posture, stance. **la ~ debout lui est pénible** standing upright is painful to him, an upright posture *ou* stance is painful to him.

(f) (*halte*) stop. **faire des ~s prolongées devant les vitrines** to make lengthy stops in front of the shop windows.

(g) (*Rel*) station. **les ~s de la Croix** the Stations of the Cross.

stationnaire [stasjɔnɛʀ] *adj* stationary.

stationnement [stasjɔnmɑ̃] *nm* (*Aut*) parking. ~ **alterné** parking on alternate sides; ~ **bilatéral/unilatéral** parking on both sides/on one side only; '~ **interdit**' 'no parking', 'no waiting'; (*sur autoroute*) 'no stopping'.

stationner [stasjɔne] (1) *vi* (*être garé*) to be parked; (*se garer*) to park.

statique [statik] 1 *adj* static. 2 *nf* statics (*sg*).

statiquement [statikmɑ̃] *adv* statically.

statisticien, -ienne [statistisjɛ̃, jɛn] *nm,f* statistician.

statistique [statistik] 1 *nf* (*science*) statistics (*sg*). (*données*) **des ~s** statistics (*pl*); **une ~** a statistic. 2 *adj* statistical.

statistiquement [statistikmɑ̃] *adv* statistically.

statuaire [statɥɛʀ] 1 *nf* statuary. 2 *adj* statuary. 3 *nm* (*littér*) statuary, sculptor.

statue [staty] *nf* statue. (*fig*) **elle était la ~ du désespoir** she was the picture of despair; (*fig*) **changé en ~ de sel** transfixed, rooted to the spot.

statuer [statɥe] (1) *vi*: **~ sur** to rule on, give a ruling on.

statuette [statɥɛt] *nf* statuette.

statufier [statyfje] (7) *vt* (*immortaliser*) to erect a statue to; (*pétrifier*) to transfix, root to the spot.

statu quo [statykwo] *nm* status quo.

stature [statyʀ] *nf* (*lit, fig: envergure*) stature. **de haute ~** of (great) stature.

statut [staty] *nm* (a) (*position*) status. (b) (*règlement*) **~s** statutes.

statutaire [statytɛʀ] *adj* statutory, statutable. **horaire ~** regulation *ou* statutory number of working hours.

statutairement [statytɛʀmɑ̃] *adv* in accordance with the statutes *ou* regulations.

steak [stɛk] *nm* steak. **~ au poivre** steak au poivre.

stéarine [steaʀin] *nf* stearin.

stéatite [steatit] *nf* steatite.

steeple [stipl(ə)] *nm* (*Athlétisme, Équitation*) steeplechase. **le 3.000 mètres ~** the 3,000 metres steeplechase.

stèle [stɛl] *nf* stela, stele.

stellaire [stelɛʀ] 1 *adj* stellar. 2 *nf* stitchwort.

stencil [stɛnsil] *nm* stencil.

stendhalien, -ienne [stɛ̃daljɛ̃, jɛn] *adj* Stendhalian.

sténo [steno] *nmf, nf abrév de* **sténographe, sténographie.**

sténodactylo[1] [stenɔdaktilo] *nf*, **sténodactylographe**† [stenɔdaktilɔgʀaf] *nf* shorthand typist.

sténodactylo[2] [stenɔdaktilo] *nf*, **sténodactylographie**† [stenɔdaktilɔgʀafi] *nf* shorthand typing.

sténographe† [stenɔgʀaf] *nmf* stenographer†.

sténographie [stenɔgʀafi] *nf* shorthand, stenography (*frm*, †).

sténographier [stenɔgʀafje] (7) *vt* to take down in shorthand.

sténographique [stenɔgʀafik] *adj* shorthand (*épith*), stenographic (*frm*, †).

sténotype [stenɔtip] *nf* stenotype.

sténotyper [stenɔtipe] (1) *vt* to stenotype.

sténotypie [stenɔtipi] *nf* stenotypy.

sténotypiste [stenɔtipist(ə)] *nmf* stenotypist.

stentor [stɑ̃tɔʀ] *nm*: **une voix de ~** a stentorian voice.

stéphanois, e [stefanwa, waz] 1 *adj* of *ou* from Saint-Étienne. 2 *nm,f*: **S~(e)** inhabitant *ou* native of Saint-Étienne.

steppe [stɛp] *nf* steppe.

stère [stɛʀ] *nm* stere.

stéréo [stereo] *nf, adj* (*abrév de* **stéréophonie, stéréophonique**) stereo.

stéréophonie [stereɔfɔni] *nf* stereophony.

stéréophonique [stereɔfɔnik] *adj* stereophonic.

stéréoscope [stereɔskɔp] *nm* stereoscope.

stéréoscopique [stereɔskɔpik] *adj* stereoscopic.

stéréotype [stereɔtip] *nm* (*lit, fig*) stereotype.

stéréotypé, e [stereɔtipe] *adj* stereotyped.

stérile [steril] *adj femme* infertile, sterile, barren; *homme, union* sterile; *milieu* sterile; *terre* barren; *sujet, réflexions, pensées* sterile; *discussion, effort* fruitless, futile.

stérilet [sterilɛ] *nm* coil, loop, intra-uterine device, I.U.D.

stérilisant, e [sterilizɑ̃, ɑ̃t] *adj* (*lit*) sterilizing; (*fig*) unproductive, fruitless.

stérilisateur [sterilizatœʀ] *nm* sterilizer.

stérilisation [sterilizɑsjɔ̃] *nf* sterilization.

stériliser [sterilize] (1) *vt* to sterilize.

stérilité [sterilite] *nf* (*U: V* **stérile**) infertility; sterility; barrenness; fruitlessness, futileness.

sternum [stɛʀnɔm] *nm* breastbone, sternum (*T*).

stéthoscope [stetɔskɔp] *nm* stethoscope.

steward [stiwaʀt] *nm* steward.

stewardesse† [stjuwaʀdɛs] *nf* stewardess.

stigmate [stigmat] *nm* (a) (*marque*) (*Méd*) mark, scar. (*Rel*) **~s** stigmata; (*fig*) **~s du vice/de la bêtise** marks of vice/folly. (b) (*orifice*) (*Zool*) stigma, spiracle; (*Bot*) stigma.

stigmatisation [stigmatizɑsjɔ̃] *nf* (*Rel*) stigmatization; (*rare: blâme*) condemnation, denunciation.

stigmatiser [stigmatize] (1) *vt* (*blâmer*) to denounce, condemn, stigmatize.

stimulant, e [stimylɑ̃, ɑ̃t] 1 *adj* stimulating. 2 *nm* (*physique*) stimulant; (*intellectuel*) stimulus, spur, incentive.

stimulation [stimylɑsjɔ̃] *nf* stimulation.

stimuler [stimyle] (1) *vt personne* to stimulate, spur on; *appétit, zèle* to stimulate.

stimulus [stimylys], *pl* **stimuli** [stimyli] *nm* (*Physiol, Psych*) stimulus.

stipendié, e [stipɑ̃dje] (*ptp de* **stipendier**) *adj* (*littér, péj*) hired.

stipendier [stipɑ̃dje] (7) *vt* (*littér, péj*) to hire, take into one's pay.

stipulation [stipylɑsjɔ̃] *nf* stipulation.

stipuler [stipyle] (1) *vt* to specify, state, stipulate.

stock [stɔk] *nm* (*Comm*) stock; (*fig*) stock, supply.

stockage [stɔkaʒ] *nm* stocking.

stocker [stɔke] (1) *vt* (*Comm*) to stock, keep in stock; (*péj: pour spéculer, amasser*) to stockpile.

Stockholm [stɔkɔlm] *n* Stockholm.

stockiste [stɔkist(ə)] *nmf* (*Comm*) stockist (*Brit*), dealer (*US*); (*Aut*) agent.

stoïcien, -ienne [stɔisjɛ̃, jɛn] *adj, nm,f* stoic.

stoïcisme [stɔisism(ə)] *nm* (*Philos*) Stoicism; (*fig*) stoicism.

stoïque [stɔik] *adj* stoical, stoic.

stoïquement [stɔikmɑ̃] *adv* stoically.

stomacal, e, *mpl* **-aux** [stɔmakal, o] *adj* stomach (*épith*), gastric.

stomatologie [stɔmatɔlɔʒi] *nf* stomatology.

stomatologiste [stɔmatɔlɔʒist(ə)] *nmf*, **stomatologue** [stɔmatɔlɔg] *nmf* stomatologist.

stop [stɔp] 1 *excl* (a) **~!** stop! (b) (*Téléc*) stop. 2 *nm* (a) (*Aut*) (*panneau*) stop sign; (*feu arrière*) brake-light. (b) (*) *abrév de* **auto-stop.**

stoppage [stɔpaʒ] *nm* invisible mending.

stopper [stɔpe] (1) 1 *vi* to halt, stop. 2 *vt* (a) (*arrêter*) to stop, halt. (b) (*Couture*) *bas* to stop from running. **faire ~ un vêtement** to get a garment (invisibly) mended.

stoppeur, -euse [stɔpœʀ, øz] *nm,f* invisible mender.

store [stɔʀ] *nm* (*en plastique, tissu*) blind, shade; *[magasin]* awning, shade. **~ vénitien** *ou* **à lamelles orientables** Venetian blind.

strabisme [stʀabism(ə)] *nm* squinting, strabismus (*T*). **il souffre d'un léger ~** he has a slight squint, he suffers from a slight strabismus (*T*).

stradivarius [stʀadivaʀjys] *nm* Stradivarius.

strangulation [stʀɑ̃gylɑsjɔ̃] *nf* strangulation.

strapontin [stʀapɔ̃tɛ̃] *nm* (*Aut, Théât*) jump seat, foldaway seat; (*fig: position subalterne*) minor role.

strasbourgeois, e [stʀasbuʀʒwa, waz] 1 *adj* of *ou* from Strasbourg. 2 *nm,f*: **S~(e)** inhabitant *ou* native of Strasbourg.

strass [stʀas] *nm* paste, strass.

stratagème [stʀataʒɛm] *nm* stratagem.

strate [stʀat] *nf* stratum.

stratège [stʀatɛʒ] *nm* (*Mil, fig*) strategist.

stratégie [stʀateʒi] *nf* (*Mil, fig*) strategy.

stratégique [stʀateʒik] *adj* strategic.

stratégiquement [stʀateʒikmɑ̃] *adv* strategically.

stratification [stʀatifikɑsjɔ̃] *nf* stratification.

stratifié, e [stʀatifje] (*ptp de* **stratifier**) *adj* stratified; (*Tech*) laminated.

stratifier [stʀatifje] (7) *vt* to stratify.

strato-cumulus [stʀatɔkymylys] *nm inv* stratocumulus.

stratosphère [stʀatɔsfɛʀ] *nf* stratosphere.

stratosphérique [stʀatɔsferik] *adj* stratospheric.

stratus [stʀatys] *nm* stratus.

streptocoque [stʀɛptɔkɔk] *nm* streptococcus.

streptomycine [stʀɛptɔmisin] *nf* streptomycin.

stress [stʀɛs] *nm* (*gén, Méd*) stress.

striation [stʀijɑsjɔ̃] *nf* striation.

strict, e [stʀikt(ə)] *adj discipline, maître, morale, obligation, sens* strict; *tenue, aménagement* plain; *interprétation* literal. **l'observation ~e du règlement** the strict observance of the rules; **c'est la ~e vérité** it is the plain *ou* simple truth; **c'est son droit le plus ~** it is his most basic right; **un uniforme/costume très ~** a very austere *ou* plain uniform/suit; **le ~ nécessaire/minimum** the bare essentials/minimum; **au sens ~ du terme** in the strict sense of the word; **dans la plus ~e intimité** strictly in private; **il est très ~ sur la ponctualité** he is a stickler for punctuality, he's very strict about punctuality; **il était très ~ avec nous** *ou* **à notre égard** he was very strict with us.

strictement [stʀiktəmɑ̃] *adv* (*V* **strict**) strictly; plainly.

strident, e [stʀidɑ̃, ɑ̃t] *adj* shrill, strident.

stridulation [stʀidylɑsjɔ̃] *nf* stridulation, chirring.

striduler [stʀidyle] (1) *vi* (*rare*) to stridulate, chirr.

strie [stʀi] *nf* (*de couleur*) streak; (*en relief*) ridge, groove; (*Anat, Géol*) stria.

strier [stʀije] (7) *vt* (*V* **strie**) to streak; to ridge, to groove; to striate.

strip-tease [stʀiptiz] *nm* striptease.

strip-teaseuse, *pl* **strip-teaseuses** [stʀiptizøz] *nf* stripper, striptease artist.

striure [stʀijyʀ] *nf [couleurs]* streaking (*U*). **la ~** *ou* **les ~s de la pierre** the ridges *ou* grooves in the stone.

stroboscope [stʀɔbɔskɔp] *nm* stroboscope.

strontium [stʀɔ̃sjɔm] *nm* strontium.

strophe [stʀɔf] *nf* (*Littérat*) verse, stanza; (*Théât grec*) strophe.

structural, e, *mpl* **-aux** [stʀyktyʀal, o] *adj* structural.

structuralement [stʀyktyʀalmɑ̃] *adv* structurally.

structuralisme [stʀyktyʀalism(ə)] *nm* structuralism.

structuraliste [stʀyktyʀalist(ə)] *adj, nmf* structuralist.

structuration [stʀyktyʀɑsjɔ̃] *nf* structuring.

structure [stʀyktyʀ] *nf* structure. **~s d'accueil** reception facilities.

structuré, e [stʀyktyʀe] (*ptp de* **structurer**) *adj* structured.

structurel, -elle [stʀyktyʀɛl] *adj* structural.

structurer [stʀyktyʀe] (1) *vt* to structure.

strychnine [stʀiknin] *nf* strychnine.

stuc [styk] *nm* stucco.

studieusement [stydjøzmɑ̃] *adv* studiously.

studieux, -euse [stydjø, øz] *adj personne* studious; *vacances, soirée* study (*épith*).

studio [stydjo] *nm* (*Ciné, TV: de prise de vues*) studio; (*salle de cinéma*) film theatre, arts cinema; (*d'artiste*) studio; (*d'habitation*) self-contained (one-roomed) flatlet (*Brit*) *ou* studio apartment (*US*). (*Ciné*) **tourner en ~** to film *ou* shoot in the studio.

stupéfaction [stypefaksjɔ̃] *nf* (*étonnement*) stupefaction, amazement.

stupéfaire [stypefɛʀ] (60) *vt* to stun, astound, dumbfound.

stupéfait, e [stypefɛ, ɛt] (*ptp de* **stupéfaire**) *adj* stunned, dumbfounded, astounded (*de qch* at sth). ~ **de voir que ...** astounded *ou* stunned to see that ... .

stupéfiant, e [stypefjɑ̃, ɑ̃t] **1** *adj* (*étonnant*) stunning, astounding, staggering*; (*Méd*) stupefying, stupefacient (*T*). **2** *nm* drug, narcotic, stupefacient (*T*); *V* **brigade.**

stupéfié, e [stypefje] (*ptp de* **stupéfier**) *adj* stunned, staggered, dumbfounded.

stupéfier [stypefje] (7) *vt* (*étonner*) to stun, stagger, astound; (*Méd, littér*) to stupefy.

stupeur [stypœʀ] *nf* (*étonnement*) astonishment, amazement; (*Méd*) stupor.

stupide [stypid] *adj* (*inepte*) stupid, silly, foolish; (*hébété*) stunned, bemused (*littér, frm*).

stupidement [stypidmɑ̃] *adv* stupidly.

stupidité [stypidite] *nf* (*U*) stupidity; (*parole, acte*) stupid *ou* silly *ou* foolish thing to say (*ou* do). **c'est une vraie** ~ *ou* **de la** ~ that's a really stupid *ou* silly *ou* foolish thing to say (*ou* do).

stupre [stypʀ(ə)] *nm* (†, *littér: U*) debauchery, depravity.

style [stil] **1** *nm* **(a)** (*gén, Art, Littérat, Sport*) style. **meubles/reliure de** ~ period furniture/binding; **meubles de** ~ **Directoire/Louis XVI** Directoire/Louis XVI furniture; **je reconnais là son** ~ **de grand seigneur** I recognize his lordly style in that; **cet athlète a du** ~ this athlete has style; **offensive/opération de grand** ~ full-scale *ou* large-scale offensive/operation; *V* **exercice.**

(b) (*Bot*) style; *[cylindre enregistreur]* stylus; *[cadran solaire]* style, gnomon; (*Hist: poinçon*) style, stylus.

2: (*Ling*) **style direct/indirect** direct/indirect speech; (*Ling*) **style indirect libre** indirect free speech; **style journalistique** journalistic style, journalese (*péj*); **style télégraphique** telegraphese (*U*); **style de vie** life style.

styler [stile] (1) *vt domestique etc* to train. **un domestique (bien) stylé** a well-trained servant.

stylet [stilɛ] *nm* (*poignard*) stiletto, stylet; (*Méd*) stylet; (*Zool*) proboscis, stylet.

stylisation [stilizɑsjɔ̃] *nf* stylization.

styliser [stilize] (1) *vt* to stylize. **colombe/fleur stylisée** stylized dove/flower.

stylisme [stilism(ə)] *nm* concern for style.

styliste [stilist(ə)] *nmf* (*dessinateur industriel*) designer; (*écrivain*) stylist.

stylisticien, -ienne [stilistisjɛ̃, jɛn] *nm,f* stylistician, specialist in stylistics.

stylistique [stilistik] **1** *nf* stylistics (*sg*). **2** *adj analyse, emploi* stylistic.

stylo [stilo] *nm* pen. ~**(-bille** *ou* **à bille)** biro ® (*Brit*), ball-point (pen); ~ **(à encre** *ou* **à réservoir)** (fountain) pen; ~**-feutre** felt-tip pen; ~ **à cartouche** cartridge pen.

stylographe† [stilɔgʀaf] *nm* fountain pen.

su [sy] (*ptp de* **savoir**) *nm*: **au** ~ **de** with the knowledge of; *V* **vu¹**.

suaire [sɥɛʀ] *nm* (*littér: linceul*) shroud, winding sheet; (*fig*) shroud; *V* **saint.**

suant, e [sɥɑ̃, ɑ̃t] *adj* (*en sueur*) sweaty; (*: *ennuyeux*) *film, cours* deadly (dull)*. **ce film est** ~ this film is a real drag: *ou* is deadly*; **ce qu'il est** ~**!** what a drag: *ou* a pain (in the neck)* he is!

suave [sɥav] *adj personne, manières, voix, regard* suave, smooth; *musique, parfum* sweet; *couleurs* mellow; *formes* smooth.

suavement [sɥavmɑ̃] *adv s'exprimer* suavely.

suavité [sɥavite] *nf* (*V* **suave**) suavity; smoothness; sweetness; mellowness.

subalterne [sybaltɛʀn(ə)] **1** *adj rôle* subordinate, subsidiary; *employé, poste* junior (*épith*). (*Mil*) **officier** ~ subaltern. **2** *nmf* subordinate, inferior.

subconscient, e [sypkɔ̃sjɑ̃, ɑ̃t] *adj, nm* subconscious.

subdélégué, e [sybdelege] (*ptp de* **subdéléguer**) *nm,f* subdelegate.

subdéléguer [sybdelege] (6) *vt* to subdelegate.

subdiviser [sybdivize] (1) **1** *vt* to subdivide (*en* into). **2 se subdiviser** *vpr* to be subdivided, be further divided (*en* into).

subdivision [sybdivizjɔ̃] *nf* subdivision.

subir [sybiʀ] (2) *vt* **(a)** (*être victime de*) *affront* to be subjected to, suffer; *violences, attaque, critique* to undergo, suffer, be subjected to; *perte, défaite, dégâts* to suffer, sustain. **faire** ~ **un affront/des tortures à qn** to subject sb to an insult/to torture; **faire** ~ **des pertes/une défaite à l'ennemi** to inflict losses/defeat upon the enemy.

(b) (*être soumis à*) *charme* to be subject to, be under the influence of; *influence* to be under; *peine de prison* to undergo, serve; *examen* to undergo, go through; *opération* to undergo. ~ **les effets de qch** to be affected by sth, experience the effects of sth; ~ **la loi du plus fort** to be subjected to the law of the strongest; ~ **les rigueurs de l'hiver** to undergo *ou* be subjected to the rigours of (the) winter; **faire** ~ **son influence à qn** to exert an influence over sb; **faire** ~ **un examen à qn** to put sb through *ou* subject sb to an examination, make sb undergo an examination.

(c) (*endurer*) to suffer, put up with, endure. **il faut** ~ **et se taire** you must suffer in silence; **il va falloir le** ~ **pendant toute la journée*** we're going to have to put up with him* *ou* endure him all day.

(d) (*recevoir*) *modification, transformation* to undergo, go through.

subit, e [sybi, it] *adj* sudden.

subitement [sybitmɑ̃] *adv* suddenly, all of a sudden.

subito (presto)* [sybito(pʀesto)] *adv* (*brusquement*) all of a sudden; (*immédiatement*) at once.

subjectif, -ive [sybʒɛktif, iv] *adj* subjective. **un danger** ~ a danger which one creates for oneself.

subjectivement [sybʒɛktivmɑ̃] *adv* subjectively.

subjectivisme [sybʒɛktivism(ə)] *nm* subjectivism.

subjectiviste [sybʒɛktivist(ə)] **1** *adj* subjectivistic. **2** *nmf* subjectivist.

subjectivité [sybʒɛktivite] *nf* subjectivity.

subjonctif, -ive [sybʒɔ̃ktif, iv] *adj, nm* subjunctive.

subjuguer [sybʒyge] (1) *vt auditoire* to captivate, enthrall; (*littér*) *esprits, personne malléable* to render powerless; (†) *peuple vaincu* to subjugate. **être subjugué par le charme/la personnalité de qn** to be captivated by sb's charm/personality.

sublimation [syblimɑsjɔ̃] *nf* (*Chim, Psych*) sublimation.

sublime [syblim] **1** *adj* (*littér*) sublime. ~ **de dévouement** sublimely dedicated. **2** *nm*: **le** ~ the sublime.

sublimé, e [syblime] (*ptp de* **sublimer**) **1** *adj* sublimate(d). **2** *nm* sublimate.

sublimement [syblimmɑ̃] *adv* sublimely.

sublimer [syblime] (1) *vt* (*Psych*) to sublimate; (*Chim*) to sublimate, sublime.

subliminal, e, *mpl* **-aux** [sybliminal, o] *adj* subliminal.

sublimité [syblimite] *nf* (*littér*) sublimeness (*U*), sublimity.

sublingual, e, *mpl* **-aux** [syblɛ̃gwal, o] *adj* sublingual. **comprimé** ~ tablet to be dissolved under the tongue.

submergé, e [sybmɛʀʒe] (*ptp de* **submerger**) *adj* **(a)** *terres, plaine* flooded, submerged; *récifs* submerged.

(b) (*fig: débordé, dépassé*) snowed under. ~ **de** *appels téléphoniques, commandes* snowed under *ou* swamped *ou* inundated with; *douleur, plaisir, inquiétudes* overwhelmed *ou* overcome with; **nous étions complètement** ~**s** we were completely snowed under, we were up to our eyes in it*; ~ **de travail** snowed under *ou* swamped with work, up to one's eyes in work*.

submerger [sybmɛʀʒe] (3) *vt* (*lit: inonder*) *terres, plaine* to flood, submerge; *barque* to submerge. (*fig*) ~ **qn** *[foule]* to engulf; *[ennemi]* to overwhelm; *[émotion]* to overcome, overwhelm; **les quelques agents furent submergés par la foule** the one or two police were engulfed in *ou* by the crowd; **ils nous submergeaient de travail** they swamped *ou* inundated us with work.

submersible [sybmɛʀsibl(ə)] *adj, nm* (*Naut*) submarine.

submersion [sybmɛʀsjɔ̃] *nf [terres]* flooding, submersion. (*Méd*) **mort par** ~ death by drowning.

subodorer [sybɔdɔʀe] (1) *vt* (*hum: soupçonner*) *irrégularité, malversation* to scent. **il subodora quelque chose de pas très catholique** he smelt a rat.

subordination [sybɔʀdinɑsjɔ̃] *nf* subordination. **je m'élève contre la** ~ **de cette décision à leurs plans** I object to this decision being subject to their plans; *V* **conjonction.**

subordonné, e [sybɔʀdɔne] (*ptp de* **subordonner**) **1** *adj* (*gén, Ling*) subordinate (*à* to). **2** *nm,f* subordinate. **3 subordonnée** *nf* (*Ling*) subordinate clause.

subordonner [sybɔʀdɔne] (1) *vt* **(a)** ~ **qn à** (*dans une hiérarchie*) to subordinate sb to; **accepter de se** ~ **à qn** to agree to subordinate o.s. to sb, accept a subordinate position under sb.

(b) ~ **qch à** (*placer au second rang*) to subordinate sth to; (*faire dépendre de*) **nous subordonnons notre décision à ses plans** our decision will be subject to his plans; **leur départ est subordonné au résultat des examens** their departure is subject to *ou* depends on the exam results.

subornation [sybɔʀnɑsjɔ̃] *nf* (*Jur*) bribing, subornation (*T*).

suborner [sybɔʀne] (1) *vt* (*Jur*) *témoins* to bribe, suborn (*T*); (*littér*) *jeune fille* to lead astray, seduce.

suborneur† [sybɔʀnœʀ] *nm* seducer.

subreptice [sybʀɛptis] *adj* surreptitious.

subrepticement [sybʀɛptismɑ̃] *adv* surreptitiously.

subrogation [sybʀɔgɑsjɔ̃] *nf* (*Jur*) subrogation.

subrogé, e [sybʀɔʒe] (*ptp de* **subroger**) *nm,f* (*Jur*) surrogate. ~**(-)tuteur** surrogate guardian.

subroger [sybʀɔʒe] (3) *vt* (*Jur*) to subrogate, substitute.

subséquemment [sypsekamɑ̃] *adv* (†, *Jur*) subsequently.

subséquent, e [sypsekɑ̃, ɑ̃t] *adj* (†, *Jur*) subsequent.

subside [sypsid] *nm* grant. **les modestes** ~**s qu'il recevait de son père** the small allowance he received from his father.

subsidiaire [sypsidjɛʀ] *adj raison, motif* subsidiary; *V* **question.**

subsidiairement [sypsidjɛʀmɑ̃] *adv* subsidiarily.

subsistance [sybzistɑ̃s] *nf* (*moyens d'existence*) subsistence. **assurer la** ~ **de sa famille/de qn** to support *ou* maintain *ou* keep one's family/sb; **assurer sa (propre)** ~ to keep *ou* support o.s.; **ma** ~ **était assurée, j'avais la** ~ **assurée** I had enough to live on; **pour toute** ~ *ou* **tous moyens de** ~**, ils n'avaient que 2 chèvres** their sole means of subsistence was 2 goats; **ils tirent leur** ~ **de certaines racines** they live on certain root crops; **elle contribue à la** ~ **du ménage** she contributes towards the maintenance of the family *ou* towards the housekeeping money.

subsistant, e [sybzistɑ̃, ɑ̃t] *adj* remaining (*épith*).

subsister [sybziste] (1) *vi [personne]* (*ne pas périr*) to live on, survive; (*se nourrir, gagner sa vie*) to live, stay alive; *[erreur, doute, vestiges]* to remain, subsist. **ils ont tout juste de quoi** ~ they have just enough to live on *ou* to keep body and soul together; **il subsiste quelques doutes quant à ...** there still remains *ou* exists some doubt as to ... , some doubt subsists *ou* remains as to ... .

substance [sypstɑ̃s] *nf* (*gén, Philos*) substance. **voilà, en** ~**, ce qu'ils ont dit** here is, in substance, what they said; **la** ~ **de notre discussion** the substance *ou* gist of our discussion; (*Anat*) ~ **blanche/grise** white/grey matter; **le lait est une** ~ **alimentaire** milk is a food.

substantialité [sypstɑ̃sjalite] *nf* substantiality.

substantiel, -elle [sypstɑ̃sjɛl] *adj* (*gén, Philos*) substantial.

substantiellement [sypstɑ̃sjɛlmɑ̃] *adv* substantially.

substantif, -ive [sypstɑ̃tif, iv] 1 *adj proposition* noun (*épith*); *emploi* nominal, substantival; *style* nominal. 2 *nm* noun, substantive.

substantifique [sypstɑ̃tifik] *adj* (*hum*) **la ~ moelle** the very substance.

substantivation [sypstɑ̃tivɑsjɔ̃] *nf* nominalization.

substantivement [sypstɑ̃tivmɑ̃] *adv* nominally, as a noun, substantively.

substantiver [sypstɑ̃tive] (1) *vt* to nominalize.

substituer [sypstitɥe] (1) 1 *vt*: **~ qch/qn à** to substitute sth/sb for. 2 **se substituer** *vpr*: **se ~ à qn** (*en évinçant*) to substitute o.s. for sb; (*en le représentant*) to substitute for sb, act as a substitute for sb; **l'adjoint s'est substitué au chef** the deputy is substituting for the boss.

substitut [sypstity] *nm* (*magistrat*) deputy public prosecutor; (*succédané*) substitute (*de* for).

substitution [sypstitysjɔ̃] *nf* (*gén, Chim*) (*intentionnelle*) substitution (*à* for); (*accidentelle*) *[vêtements, bébés]* mix-up (*de* of, in). **ils s'étaient aperçus trop tard qu'il y avait eu ~ d'enfants** they realized too late that the children had been mixed up *ou* that they had got the children mixed up.

substrat [sypstʀa] *nm*, **substratum**† [sypstʀatɔm] *nm* (*Géol, Ling, Philos*) substratum.

subsumer [sypsyme] (1) *vt* to subsume.

subterfuge [syptɛʀfyʒ] *nm* subterfuge.

subtil, e [syptil] *adj* (*sagace*) *personne, esprit* subtle, discerning; *réponse* subtle; (*raffiné*) *nuance, distinction* subtle, fine, nice (*littér*); *raisonnement* subtle.

subtilement [syptilmɑ̃] *adv* subtly, in a subtle way; *laisser comprendre* subtly.

subtilisation [syptilizɑsjɔ̃] *nf* spiriting away.

subtiliser [syptilize] (1) 1 *vt* (*dérober*) to spirit away (*hum*). **il s'est fait ~ sa valise** his suitcase has been spirited away. 2 *vi* (*rare, littér: raffiner*) to subtilize.

subtilité [syptilite] *nf* (*V* **subtil**) subtlety; nicety (*littér*). **des ~s** subtleties; niceties.

subtropical, e, *mpl* **-aux** [syptʀɔpikal, o] *adj* subtropical.

suburbain, e [sybyʀbɛ̃, ɛn] *adj* suburban.

subvenir [sybvəniʀ] (22) **subvenir à** *vt indir besoins* to provide for, meet; *frais* to meet, cover.

subvention [sybvɑ̃sjɔ̃] *nf* (*gén*) grant; (*aux agriculteurs*) subsidy; (*à un théâtre*) subsidy, grant.

subventionner [sybvɑ̃sjɔne] (1) *vt* (*V* **subvention**) to grant funds to; to subsidize. **école subventionnée** grant-aided school; **théâtre subventionné** subsidized theatre.

subversif, -ive [sybvɛʀsif, iv] *adj* subversive.

subversion [sybvɛʀsjɔ̃] *nf* subversion.

subversivement [sybvɛʀsivmɑ̃] *adv* subversively.

suc [syk] *nm [plante]* sap; *[viande, fleur, fruit]* juice; (*fig littér*) *[œuvre]* pith, meat. **~s digestifs** *ou* **gastriques** gastric juices.

succédané [syksedane] *nm* (*substitut, ersatz*) substitute (*de* for); (*médicament*) substitute, succedaneum (*T*).

succéder [syksede] (6) 1 **succéder à** *vt indir directeur, roi* to succeed; *jours, choses, personnes* to succeed, follow; (*Jur*) *titres, héritage* to inherit, succeed to. **~ à qn à la tête d'une entreprise** to succeed sb at the head of a firm; **des prés succédèrent aux champs de blé** cornfields were followed *ou* replaced by meadows, meadows followed (upon) cornfields; **le rire succéda à la peur** fear gave way to laughter; (*frm*) **~ à la couronne** to succeed to the throne.

2 **se succéder** *vpr* to follow one another, succeed one another. **ils se succédèrent de père en fils** son followed father; **3 gouvernements se sont succédé en 3 ans** 3 governments have succeeded *ou* followed one another *ou* have come one after the other in 3 years; **les mois se succédèrent** month followed month; **les échecs se succédèrent** failure followed (upon) failure.

succès [syksɛ] *nm* **(a)** (*réussite*) *[entreprise, roman]* success. **~ militaires/sportifs** military/sporting successes; **le ~ ne l'a pas changé** success hasn't changed him; **~ d'estime** succès d'estime, praise from the critics (*with poor sales*); **avoir du ~ auprès des femmes** to have success *ou* be successful with women.

(b) (*livre*) success, bestseller; (*chanson, disque*) success, hit*; (*film, pièce*) box-office success, hit*. **~ de librairie** bestseller; **tous ses livres ont été des ~** all his books were bestsellers *ou* a success.

(c) (*conquête amoureuse*) **~ (féminin)** conquest; **son charme lui vaut des ~ nombreux** his charm brings him many conquests *ou* much success with women.

(d) (*loc*) **avec ~** successfully; **avec un égal ~** equally successfully, with equal success; **sans ~** unsuccessfully, without success; **à ~** *auteur, livre* successful, bestselling; *film* successful, hit* (*épith*); **chanson/pièce à ~** hit*, successful song/play; **roman à ~** successful novel, bestseller; **avoir du ~, être un ~** to be successful, be a success; **cette pièce a eu un grand ~** *ou* **beaucoup de ~** this play was a great success *ou* was very successful *ou* was a big hit*.

successeur [syksesœʀ] *nm* (*gén*) successor.

successif, -ive [syksesif, iv] *adj* successive.

succession [syksesjɔ̃] *nf* **(a)** (*enchaînement, série*) succession. **la ~ des saisons** the succession *ou* sequence of the seasons; **toute une ~ de visiteurs/malheurs** a whole succession *ou* series of visitors/misfortunes.

(b) (*transmission de pouvoir*) succession; (*Jur*) (*transmission de biens*) succession; (*patrimoine*) estate, inheritance. **s'occuper d'une ~** to be occupied with a succession; **partager une ~** to share an estate *ou* an inheritance; (*Jur*) **la ~ est ouverte** = the will is going through probate; **par voie de ~** by right of inheritance *ou* succession; **prendre la ~ de** *ministre, directeur* to succeed, take over from; *roi* to succeed; *maison de commerce* to take over; *V* **droit**[3], **guerre**.

successivement [syksesivmɑ̃] *adv* successively.

succinct, e [syksɛ̃, ɛ̃t] *adj écrit* succinct; *repas* frugal.

succinctement [syksɛ̃tmɑ̃] *adv raconter* succinctly; *manger* frugally.

succion [syksjɔ̃] *nf* (*Phys, Tech*) suction; (*Méd*) *[plaie]* sucking. **bruit de ~** sucking noise.

succomber [sykɔ̃be] (1) *vi* **(a)** (*mourir*) to die, succumb (*littér*).

(b) (*être vaincu*) to succumb; (*par tentations*) to succumb, give way. **~ sous le nombre** to be overcome by numbers; **~ à** *tentation* to succumb *ou* yield to; *promesses* to succumb to; *fatigue, désespoir, sommeil* to give way to, succumb to; (*littér: lit, fig*) **~ sous le poids de** to yield *ou* give way beneath the weight of.

succulence [sykylɑ̃s] *nf* (*littér*) succulence.

succulent, e [sykylɑ̃, ɑ̃t] *adj* (*délicieux*) *fruit, rôti* succulent; *mets, repas* delicious; (††: *juteux*) succulent.

succursale [sykyʀsal] *nf [magasin, firme]* branch; *V* **magasin**.

sucer [syse] (3) *vt* (*lit*) to suck. **toujours à ~ des bonbons** always sucking (at) sweets; **ces pastilles se sucent** these tablets are to be sucked; **ce procès lui a sucé toutes ses économies**‡ this lawsuit has bled him of all his savings; **se ~ la poire**‡ to neck‡, kiss passionately.

sucette [sysɛt] *nf* (*bonbon*) lollipop, lolly (*Brit*); (*tétine*) dummy, comforter (*Brit*), pacifier (*US*).

suçon* [sysɔ̃] *nm mark made on the skin by sucking.* **elle lui fit un ~ au cou** she gave him a love bite* (on his neck).

suçoter [sysɔte] (1) *vt* to suck at.

sucrage [sykʀaʒ] *nm [vin]* sugaring, sweetening.

sucrant, e [sykʀɑ̃, ɑ̃t] *adj* sweetening. **c'est très ~** it makes things very sweet, it's very sweet.

sucre [sykʀ(ə)] 1 *nm* (*substance*) sugar; (*morceau*) lump of sugar, sugar lump, sugar cube. **fraises au ~** strawberries sprinkled with sugar; **cet enfant n'est pas en ~ quand même!** for goodness sake, the child won't break!; **être tout ~ tout miel** to be all sweetness and light; **mon petit trésor en ~** my little honey-bun *ou* sugarplum; **prendre 2 ~s dans son café** to take 2 lumps (of sugar) *ou* 2 sugars* in one's coffee; *V* **pain, pince** *etc.*

2: **sucre de betterave** beet sugar; **sucre brun** brown sugar; **sucre candi** candy sugar; **sucre de canne** cane sugar; **sucre cristallisé** coarse-grained sugar; (*Can**) **sucre d'érable** maple sugar; **sucre glace** icing sugar; **sucre en morceaux** lump sugar, cube sugar; **sucre d'orge** (*substance*) barley sugar; (*bâton*) stick of barley sugar; **sucre en poudre** granulated sugar (*fine*); **sucre roux = sucre brun**; **sucre semoule** granulated sugar; **sucre vanillé** vanilla sugar.

sucré, e [sykʀe] (*ptp de* **sucrer**) 1 *adj* **(a)** *fruit, saveur, vin* sweet; *jus de fruits, lait condensé* sweetened. **ce thé est trop ~** this tea is too sweet; **prenez-vous votre café ~?** do you take sugar (in your coffee)?; **tasse de thé bien ~e** well-sweetened cup of tea, cup of nice sweet tea*; **non ~** unsweetened; *V* **eau**.

(b) (*péj*) *ton* sugary, honeyed; *air* sickly-sweet. **faire le ~** to turn on the sweetness.

2 *nm*: **le ~ et le salé** sweet and savoury food; **je préfère le ~ au salé** I prefer sweets to savouries *ou* sweet things to savouries.

sucrer [sykʀe] (1) 1 *vt* **(a)** *boisson* to sugar, put sugar in, sweeten; *produit alimentaire* to sweeten. **le miel sucre autant que le sucre lui-même** honey sweetens as well as sugar, honey is as good a sweetener as sugar; **on peut ~ avec du miel** honey may be used as a sweetener *ou* may be used to sweeten things; **sucrez à volonté** sweeten *ou* add sugar to taste; (*fig*) **~ les fraises**‡ to have the shakes*.

(b) (‡: *supprimer*) **~ son argent de poche à qn** to stop sb's pocket money; **il s'est fait ~ ses heures supplémentaires** he's had his overtime money stopped.

2 **se sucrer** *vpr* **(a)** (*lit: prendre du sucre*) to help o.s. to sugar, have some sugar.

(b) (‡*fig: s'enrichir*) to line one's pocket(s)*.

sucrerie [sykʀəʀi] *nf* **(a)** **~s** sweets, sweet things; **aimer les ~s** to have a sweet tooth, like sweet things. **(b)** (*usine*) sugar house; (*raffinerie*) sugar refinery.

sucrier, -ière [sykʀije, ijɛʀ] 1 *adj industrie, betterave* sugar (*épith*); *région* sugar-producing. 2 *nm* **(a)** (*récipient*) sugar basin, sugar bowl. **~ (verseur)** sugar dispenser *ou* shaker.

(b) (*industriel*) sugar producer.

sud [syd] 1 *nm* **(a)** (*point cardinal*) south. **le vent du ~** the south wind; **un vent du ~** a south(erly) wind, a southerly (*Naut*); **le vent tourne/est au ~** the wind is veering south(wards) *ou* towards the south/is blowing from the south; **regarder vers le ~** *ou* **dans la direction du ~** to look south(wards) *ou* towards the south; **au ~** (*situation*) in the south; (*direction*) to the south, south(wards); **au ~ de** south of, to the south of; **l'appartement est (exposé) au ~/exposé plein ~** the flat faces (the) south *ou* southwards/due south, the flat looks south(wards)/due south; **l'Europe/l'Italie/la Bourgogne du ~** Southern Europe/Italy/Burgundy; *V* **Amérique, Corée, croix** *etc.*

(b) (*partie, régions australes*) south. **le S~ de la France, le S~** the South (of France).

2 *adj inv région, partie* southern; *entrée, paroi* south; *versant, côte* south(ern); *côté* south(ward); *direction* southward, southerly (*Mét*); *V* **hémisphère, pôle**.

3: **sud-africain, e** *adj* South African; **Sud-Africain, e** *nm,f*, *mpl* **Sud-Africains** South African; **sud-américain, e** *adj* South American; **Sud-Américain, e** *nm,f*, *mpl* **Sud-Américains** South American; **sud-coréen, -enne** *adj* South Korean; **Sud-Coréen, -enne** *nm,f*, *mpl* **Sud-Coréens** South Korean; **sud-est** *nm, adj* *inv* south-east; **sud-ouest** *nm, adj inv* south-west; **sud-sud-est** *nm, adj inv* south-south-east; **sud-sud-ouest** *nm, adj inv* south-south-west; **sud-vietnamien, -ienne** *adj* South Vietnamese; **Sud-Vietnamien, -ienne** *nm,f, mpl* **Sud-Vietnamiens** South Vietnamese.

sudation [sydasjɔ̃] *nf* sweating, sudation (*T*).

sudatoire [sydatwaʀ] *adj* sudatory.

sudiste [sydist(ə)] (*Hist US*) **1** *nmf* Southerner. **2** *adj* Southern.

sudorifère [sydɔʀifɛʀ] *adj* = **sudoripare.**

sudorifique [sydɔʀifik] *adj, nm* sudorific.

sudoripare [sydɔʀipaʀ] *adj* sudoriferous, sudoriparous.

Suède [sɥɛd] *nf* Sweden.

suède [sɥɛd] *nm* (*peau*) suede. **en** *ou* **de ~** suede.

suédine [sɥedin] *nf* suedette.

suédois, e [sɥedwa, waz] **1** *adj* Swedish; *V* **allumette, gymnastique. 2** *nm* (*Ling*) Swedish. **3** *nm,f*: **S~(e)** Swede.

suée* [sɥe] *nf* sweat. **prendre** *ou* **attraper une bonne ~** to work up a good sweat*; **à l'idée de cette épreuve, j'en avais la ~** I was in a (cold) sweat at the idea of the test*; **je dois aller le voir, quelle ~!** I've got to go and see him — what a drag!‡ *ou* pain!‡

suer [sɥe] (1) **1** *vi* **(a)** (*transpirer*) to sweat; (*fig: peiner*) to sweat* (*sur* over). **~ de peur** to sweat with fear, be in a cold sweat; **~ à grosses gouttes** to sweat profusely; **~ sur une dissertation** to sweat over an essay*.

(b) (*suinter*) *[murs]* to ooze, sweat (*de* with).

(c) (*Culin*) **faire ~** to sweat.

(d) (*loc*) **faire ~ qn** (*lit*) *[médicament]* to make sb sweat; (*péj*) **faire ~ le burnous‡** to use sweated labour, exploit native labour; **tu me fais ~‡** you're a pain (in the neck)‡ *ou* a drag‡; **on se fait ~ ici‡** what a drag it is here‡, we're getting really cheesed (off) here‡.

2 *vt* **(a)** *sueur, sang* to sweat. (*fig*) **~ sang et eau à** *ou* **pour faire qch** to sweat blood (over) doing sth *ou* to do sth.

(b) *humidité* to ooze.

(c) (*révéler, respirer*) *pauvreté, misère, avarice, lâcheté* to exude.

(d) (*danser*) **en ~ une‡** to shake a leg‡.

sueur [sɥœʀ] *nf* sweat (*U*). **en ~** in a sweat, sweating; **à la ~ de son front** by the sweat of one's brow; **donner des ~s froides à qn** to put sb in(to) a cold sweat; **j'en avais des ~s froides** I was in a cold sweat.

suffire [syfiʀ] (37) **1** *vi* **(a)** (*être assez*) *[somme, durée, quantité]* to be enough, be sufficient, suffice. **cette explication ne (me) suffit pas** this explanation isn't enough *ou* isn't sufficient (for me) *ou* won't do; **5 hommes me suffisent (pour ce travail)** 5 men will do me (for this job); **un rien suffirait pour** *ou* **à bouleverser nos plans** the smallest thing would be enough *ou* sufficient to upset our plans, it would only take the smallest thing to upset our plans; *V* **à.**

(b) (*arriver à, satisfaire, combler*) **~ à** *besoins* to meet; *personne* to be enough for; **ma femme me suffit** *ou* **suffit à mon bonheur, je suis heureux** my wife is all I need to make me happy, my wife is enough to make me happy; **il ne suffit pas aux besoins de la famille** he does not meet the needs of his family; **il ne peut ~ à tout** he can't manage (to do) everything, he can't cope with everything; **les week-ends, il ne suffisait plus à servir les clients** at weekends he could no longer manage to serve all the customers *ou* he could no longer cope (with serving) all the customers.

(c) (*loc*) **ça suffit** that's enough, that'll do; **(ça) suffit!** that's enough!, that will do!; **comme ennuis, ça suffit (comme ça)** we've had enough troubles thank you very much*; **ça suffit d'une fois** once is enough; **ça ne te suffit pas de l'avoir tourmentée?** isn't it enough for you to have tormented her?

2 *vb impers* **(a) il suffit de faire/de qch/que: il suffit de s'inscrire pour devenir membre** enrolling is enough *ou* sufficient to become a member; **il suffit de (la) faire réchauffer et la soupe est prête** just heat (up) the soup and it's ready (to serve); **il suffit que vous leur écriviez** it will be enough if you write to them, your writing to them will be enough *ou* will be sufficient *ou* will suffice (*frm*); **il suffit d'un accord verbal pour conclure l'affaire** a verbal agreement is sufficient *ou* is enough *ou* will suffice (*frm*) to conclude the matter.

(b) (*intensif*) **il suffit d'un rien pour l'inquiéter** it only takes the smallest thing to worry him, the smallest thing is enough to worry him; **il lui suffit d'un regard pour comprendre** a look was enough to make him understand, he needed only a look to understand; **il suffit qu'il ouvre la bouche pour que tout le monde se taise** he has *ou* needs only to open his mouth and everyone stops talking *ou* to make everyone stop talking; **il suffit d'une fois: on n'est jamais trop prudent** once is enough — you can never be too careful.

3 se suffire *vpr*: **se ~ (à soi-même)** *[pays, personne]* to be self-sufficient; **la beauté se suffit (à elle-même)** beauty is sufficient unto itself (*littér*); **ils se suffisent (l'un à l'autre)** they are enough for each other.

suffisamment [syfizamɑ̃] *adv* sufficiently, enough. **~ fort/clair** sufficiently strong/clear, strong/clear enough; **être ~ vêtu** to have sufficient *ou* enough clothes on, be adequately dressed; **lettre ~ affranchie** sufficiently *ou* adequately stamped letter; **~ de nourriture/d'argent** sufficient *ou* enough food/money; **y a-t-il ~ à boire?** is there enough *ou* sufficient to drink?

suffisance [syfizɑ̃s] *nf* **(a)** (*vanité*) self-importance, bumptiousness.

(b) (*littér*) **avoir sa ~ de qch†, avoir qch en ~** to have sth in plenty, have a sufficiency of sth; **il y en a en ~** there is sufficient of it; **des livres, il en a sa ~† *ou* à sa ~** he has books aplenty†.

suffisant, e [syfizɑ̃, ɑ̃t] *adj* **(a)** (*adéquat*) sufficient; (*Scol*) *résultats* satisfactory. **c'est ~ pour qu'il se mette en colère** it's enough to make him lose his temper; **je n'ai pas la place/la somme ~e** I haven't got sufficient *ou* enough room/money; *V* **condition, grâce.**

(b) (*prétentieux*) *personne, ton* self-important, bumptious.

suffixal, e, *mpl* **-aux** [syfiksal, o] *adj* suffixal.

suffixation [syfiksasjɔ̃] *nf* suffixation.

suffixe [syfiks(ə)] *nm* suffix.

suffixer [syfikse] (1) *vt* to add a suffix to.

suffocant, e [syfɔkɑ̃, ɑ̃t] *adj* **(a)** *fumée, chaleur* suffocating, stifling.

(b) (*étonnant*) staggering*.

suffocation [syfɔkasjɔ̃] *nf* (*action*) suffocation; (*sensation*) suffocating feeling. **il avait des ~s** he had fits of choking.

suffoquer [syfɔke] (1) **1** *vi* (*lit*) to choke, suffocate, stifle. (*fig*) **~ de** to choke with.

2 *vt* **(a)** *[fumée]* to suffocate, choke, stifle; *[colère, joie]* to choke. **les larmes la suffoquaient** she was choking with tears.

(b) (*étonner*) *[nouvelle, comportement de qn]* to stagger*. **la nouvelle nous a suffoqués** the news took our breath away, we were staggered* by the news.

suffrage [syfʀaʒ] **1** *nm* **(a)** (*Pol: voix*) vote. **~s exprimés** valid votes.

(b) (*fig*) *[public, critique]* approval (*U*), approbation (*U*). **accorder son ~ à qn/qch** to give one's approval *ou* approbation to sb/sth; **ce livre a remporté tous les ~s** this book met with universal approval *ou* approbation.

2: suffrage censitaire suffrage on the basis of property qualification; **suffrage direct** direct suffrage; **suffrage indirect** indirect suffrage; **suffrage restreint** restricted suffrage; **suffrage universel** universal suffrage *ou* franchise.

suffragette [syfʀaʒɛt] *nf* suffragette.

suggérer [sygʒeʀe] (6) *vt* (*gén*) to suggest; *solution, projet* to suggest, put forward. **~ une réponse à qn** to suggest a reply to sb; **je lui suggérai que c'était moins facile qu'il ne pensait** I suggested to him *ou* I put it to him that it was not as easy as he thought; **~ à qn une solution** to put forward *ou* suggest *ou* put a solution to sb; **j'ai suggéré d'aller au cinéma/que nous allions au cinéma** I suggested going to the cinema/that we went to the cinema; **elle lui a suggéré de voir un médecin** she suggested he should see a doctor.

suggestibilité [sygʒɛstibilite] *nf* suggestibility.

suggestible [sygʒɛstibl(ə)] *adj* suggestible.

suggestif, -ive [sygʒɛstif, iv] *adj* (*évocateur, indécent*) suggestive.

suggestion [sygʒɛstjɔ̃] *nf* suggestion.

suggestionner [sygʒɛstjɔne] (1) *vt* to influence by suggestion.

suggestivité [sygʒɛstivite] *nf* suggestiveness.

suicidaire [sɥisidɛʀ] **1** *adj* suicidal. **2** *nmf* person with suicidal tendencies.

suicide [sɥisid] *nm* (*lit, fig*) suicide. (*fig*) **c'est un** *ou* **du ~!** it's suicide!

suicidé, e [sɥiside] (*ptp de* **se suicider**) **1** *adj*: **personne ~e** person who has committed suicide. **2** *nm,f* suicide (*person*).

suicider (se) [sɥiside] (1) *vpr* to commit suicide. (*iro*) **on a suicidé le témoin gênant** they have had the embarrassing witness 'commit suicide'.

suie [sɥi] *nf* soot; *V* **noir.**

suif [sɥif] *nm* tallow. **~ de mouton** mutton suet.

sui generis [sɥiʒeneʀis] *loc adv* sui generis. **l'odeur ~ d'une prison** the distinctive *ou* peculiar smell of a prison.

suint [sɥɛ̃] *nm [laine]* suint.

suintement [sɥɛ̃tmɑ̃] *nm* (*V* **suinter**) oozing; sweating; weeping. **des ~s sur le mur** oozing moisture on the wall.

suinter [sɥɛ̃te] (1) *vi [eau]* to ooze; *[mur]* to ooze, sweat; *[plaie]* to weep, ooze.

Suisse [sɥis] *nf* (*pays*) Switzerland. **~ romande/allemande** *ou* **alémanique** French-speaking/German-speaking Switzerland.

suisse [sɥis] **1** *adj* Swiss. **~ romand** Swiss French; **~-allemand** Swiss German. **2** *nm* **(a) S~** Swiss; **S~ romand** French-speaking Swiss; **S~-allemand** German-speaking Swiss, Swiss German; *V* **boire, petit. (b)** (*bedeau*) ≃ verger. **(c)** (*Can*) chipmunk.

Suissesse [sɥisɛs] *nf* Swiss (woman).

suite [sɥit] *nf* **(a)** (*escorte*) retinue, suite.

(b) (*nouvel épisode*) continuation, following episode; (*second roman, film*) sequel; (*rebondissement d'une affaire*) follow-up; (*reste*) remainder, rest. **voici la ~ de notre feuilleton** here is the next episode in *ou* the continuation of our serial; **ce roman/film a une ~** there is a sequel to this novel/film; (*Presse*) **voici la ~ de l'affaire que nous évoquions hier** here is the follow-up to the item we mentioned yesterday; **la ~ du film/du repas/de la lettre était moins bonne** the remainder *ou* the rest of the film/meal/letter was not so good; **la ~ au prochain numéro** to be continued (in the next issue); **~ et fin** concluding *ou* final episode; **la ~ des événements devait lui donner raison** what followed was to prove him right; **attendons la ~** (*d'un repas*) let's wait for the next course; (*d'un discours*) let's see what comes next; (*d'un événement*) let's (wait and) see how it turns out; **lisez donc la ~** do read on, do read what follows.

(c) (*aboutissement*) result. (*prolongements*) **~s** *[maladie]* effects; *[accident]* results; *[affaire, incident]* consequences, repercussions; **la ~ logique de** the obvious *ou* logical result of; **il a succombé des ~s de ses blessures/sa maladie** he succumbed to the after-effects of his wounds/illness; **cet incident a eu des ~s fâcheuses/n'a pas eu de ~s** the incident has had annoying consequences *ou* repercussions/has had no repercussions.

(d) (*succession*) (*Math*) series. **~ de** *personnes, maisons* succession *ou* string *ou* series of; *événements* succession *ou* train of; (*Comm*) **article sans ~** discontinued line.

(e) (*frm: cohérence*) coherence. **il y a beaucoup de ~ dans son raisonnement/ses réponses** there is a good deal of coherence in his reasoning/his replies; **ses propos n'avaient guère de ~** what he said lacked coherence *ou* consistency; **travailler avec ~** to work steadily; **des propos sans ~** disjointed talk; **avoir de la ~ dans les idées** (*réfléchi, décidé*) to show great singleness of purpose; (*iro: entêté*) not to be easily put off; *V* **esprit**.

(f) (*appartement*) suite.

(g) (*Mus*) suite. **~ instrumentale/orchestrale** instrumental/orchestral suite.

(h) (*loc*) (*Comm*) **(comme) ~ à votre lettre/notre entretien** further to your letter/our conversation; **à la ~** (*successivement*) one after the other; (*derrière*) **mettez-vous à la ~** join on at the back, go to *ou* join the back of the queue (*Brit*) *ou* line (*US*); **à la ~ de** (*derrière*) behind; (*en conséquence de*) following; **entraîner qn à sa ~** (*lit*) to drag sb along behind one; (*fig*) **entraîner qn à sa ~ dans une affaire** to drag sb into an affair; **de ~** (*immédiatement*) at once; **je reviens de ~** I'll be straight *ou* right back; **boire 3 verres de ~** to drink 3 glasses in a row *ou* in succession *ou* one after the other; **pendant 3 jours de ~** (for) 3 days on end *ou* in succession; **il est venu 3 jours de ~** he came 3 days in a row *ou* 3 days running; **il n'arrive pas à dire trois mots de ~** he can't string three words together; (*à cause de*) **par ~ de** owing to, as a result of; (*par conséquent*) **par ~** consequently, therefore; (*ensuite*) **par la ~, dans la ~** afterwards, subsequently; **donner ~ à** *projet* to pursue, follow up; *demande, commande* to follow up; *lettre* to follow up; **ils n'ont pas donné ~ à notre lettre** they have taken no action concerning our letter, they have not followed up our letter; **faire ~ à** *événement* to follow (upon); *chapitre* to follow (after); *bâtiment* to adjoin; **prendre la ~ de** *firme, directeur* to succeed, take over from; *V* **ainsi, tout**.

suivant[1]**, e** [sɥivɑ̃, ɑ̃t] **1** *adj* **(a)** (*dans le temps*) following, next; (*dans une série*) next. **le mardi ~ je la revis** the following *ou* next Tuesday I saw her again; **vendredi et les jours ~s** Friday and the following days; **le malade ~ était très atteint** the next patient was very badly affected; **voir page ~e** see next page.

(b) (*ci-après*) following. **faites l'exercice ~** do the following exercise.

2 *nm,f* **(a)** (*prochain*) (*dans une série*) next (one); (*dans le temps*) following (one), next (one). **(au) ~!** next (please)!; **cette année fut mauvaise et les ~es ne le furent guère moins** that year was bad and the following ones *ou* next ones were scarcely less so; **je descends à la ~e*** I'm getting off at the next stop.

(b) (*littér: membre d'escorte*) attendant.

3 suivante *nf* (*Théât*) soubrette, lady's maid; (††) companion.

suivant[2] [sɥivɑ̃] *prép* (*selon*) according to. **~ son habitude** as is (*ou* was) his habit *ou* wont, in keeping with his habit; **~ l'usage** in keeping *ou* conformity with custom; **~ l'expression consacrée** as the saying goes, as they say; **~ les jours/les cas** according to *ou* depending on the day/the circumstances; **découper ~ le pointillé** cut (out) along the dotted line; **~ que** according to whether.

suiveur [sɥivœʀ] *nm* **(a)** [*course cycliste etc*] (official) follower (*of a race*).

(b) (†: *dragueur*) **elle se retourna, son ~ avait disparu** she turned round - the man who was following her had disappeared; **elle va me prendre pour un ~** she'll think I'm the sort (of fellow) who follows women.

suivi, e [sɥivi] (*ptp de* **suivre**) *adj* **(a)** (*régulier*) *travail* steady; *correspondance* regular; (*constant*) *qualité* consistent; *effort* consistent, sustained; (*Comm*) *demande* constant, steady; (*cohérent*) *conversation, histoire, raisonnement* coherent; *politique* consistent.

(b) (*Comm*) *article* in general production (*attrib*).

(c) très ~ *cours* well-attended; *mode, recommandation* widely adopted; *example, feuilleton* widely followed. **un match très ~** a match with a wide audience; **un cours peu ~** a poorly-attended course; **une mode peu ~e** a fashion which is not widely adopted; **un exemple peu ~** an example which is not widely followed; **un procès très ~** a trial that is being closely followed by the public; **un feuilleton très ~** a serial with a large following.

suivre [sɥivʀ(ə)] (40) **1** *vt* **(a)** (*gén: accompagner, marcher derrière, venir après*) to follow. **elle le suit comme un petit chien** she follows him (around) like a little dog; **il me suit comme mon ombre** he follows me about like my shadow; **vous marchez trop vite, je ne peux pas vous ~** you are walking too quickly, I can't keep up (with you); **partez sans moi, je vous suis** go on without me and I'll follow (on); **ils se suivaient sur l'étroit sentier** they were following one behind the other on the narrow path; **l'été suit le printemps** summer follows (after) spring; (*fig*) **son image me suit sans cesse** his image follows me everywhere *ou* is constantly with me; **il la suivit des yeux** he followed her with his eyes, his eyes followed her; (*iro*) **certains députés, suivez mon regard, ont ...** certain deputies, without mentioning any names *ou* no names mentioned, have ...; **suivre qn à la trace** to follow sb's tracks; (*iro*) **on peut le ~ à la trace!** there's no mistaking where he has been!; **faire ~ qn** to have sb followed; **suivez le guide!** this way, please!; *V* **qui**.

(b) (*dans une série*) to follow. **leurs enfants se suivent (de près)** their children come one after the other; **la maison qui suit la mienne** the house after mine *ou* following mine; **3 démissions qui se suivent** 3 resignations in a row *ou* coming one after the other, 3 resignations running *ou* in close succession; *V* **jour**.

(c) (*longer*) [*personne*] to follow, keep to; [*route, itinéraire*] to follow. **suivez la N7 sur 10 km** keep to *ou* go along *ou* follow the N7 (road) for 10 km; **~ une piste** to follow up a clue.

(d) (*se conformer à*) *personne, exemple, mode, conseil* to follow. **~ un traitement** to follow a course of treatment; **~ un régime** to be on a diet; **~ son instinct** to follow one's instinct *ou* one's nose*; **il se leva et chacun suivit son exemple** he stood up and everyone followed suit *ou* followed his lead *ou* example; **on n'a pas voulu le ~** we didn't want to follow his advice; **la maladie/l'enquête suit son cours** the illness/the inquiry is running *ou* taking its course; **il me fait ~ un régime sévère** he has put me on a strict diet; **~ le mouvement** to follow the crowd; *V* **marche**[1].

(e) (*Scol*) *classe, cours* (*être inscrit à*) to attend, go to; (*être attentif à*) to follow, attend to; (*assimiler*) *programme* to keep up with.

(f) (*observer l'évolution de*) *carrière de qn, affaire, match* to follow; *feuilleton* to follow, keep up with. **~ un malade/un élève** to follow the progress of a patient/pupil; **~ l'actualité** to keep up with *ou* follow the news; **c'est une affaire à ~** it's an affair worth following *ou* worth keeping an eye on; **il se fait ~** *ou* **il est suivi par un médecin** he's having treatment from a doctor, he is under the doctor*; **j'ai suivi ses articles avec intérêt** I've followed his articles with interest; **à ~** to be continued.

(g) (*Comm*) *article* to (continue to) stock.

(h) (*comprendre*) *argument, personne, exposé* to follow. **jusqu'ici je vous suis** I'm with you* *ou* I follow you so far; **il parlait si vite qu'on le suivait mal** he spoke so fast he was difficult to follow; **là, je ne vous suis pas très bien** I don't really follow you *ou* I'm not really with you* there.

2 *vi* **(a)** [*élève*] (*être attentif*) to attend, pay attention. **suivez avec votre voisin** *ou* **sur le livre de votre voisin** follow on your neighbour's book; **il ne suit jamais, en classe** he never attends *ou* never pays attention in class.

(b) [*élève*] (*assimiler le programme*) to keep up, follow. **va-t-il pouvoir ~ l'année prochaine?** will he be able to keep up *ou* follow next year?

(c) faire ~ son courrier to have one's mail forwarded; **'faire ~'** 'please forward'.

(d) (*venir après*) to follow. **lisez ce qui suit** read what follows; **les enfants suivent à pied** the children are following on foot.

3 *vb impers:* **il suit de ce que vous dites que ...** it follows from what you say that ...; **comme suit** as follows.

4 se suivre *vpr* **(a)** [*cartes, pages, nombres*] (*se succéder en bon ordre*) to be in (the right) order. **les pages ne se suivent pas** the pages are not in (the right) order, the pages are in the wrong order *ou* are out of order.

(b) (*être cohérent*) [*argument, pensée*] to be coherent, be consistent. **dans son roman, rien ne se suit** there's no coherence *ou* consistency in his novel.

sujet, -ette [syʒɛ, ɛt] **1** *adj:* **~ à** *vertige, mal de mer* liable to, subject to, prone to; *lubies, sautes d'humeur* subject to, prone to; **~ aux accidents** accident-prone; **il était ~ aux accidents les plus bizarres** he was prone *ou* subject to the strangest accidents; **il n'est pas ~ à faire des imprudences** he is not one to do anything imprudent; **~ à caution** *renseignement, nouvelle* unconfirmed; *moralité, vie privée, honnêteté* questionable; **je vous dis ça mais c'est ~ à caution** I'm telling you that but I can't guarantee it's true.

2 *nm,f* (*gouverné*) subject.

3 *nm* **(a)** (*matière, question*) subject (*de* for). **ce n'est pas un ~ de conversation** it's not a subject for conversation; **un excellent ~ de conversation** an excellent topic (of conversation) *ou* subject (for conversation); **c'était devenu un ~ de plaisanterie** it had become a standing joke *ou* something to joke about; **il y a des ~s qui ne se prêtent pas à la plaisanterie** there are a few subjects *ou* topics that do not lend themselves to joking; **chercher un ~ de dissertation/thèse** to look for a subject for an essay/a thesis; **~ d'examen** examination question; **à l'oral, quel ~ ont-ils donné?** what subject did they give you *ou* did they set in the oral?; **il a choisi les ~s d'examen cette année** he set the examination paper *ou* the examination questions this year; **ça ferait un bon ~ de comédie** that would be a good subject *ou* theme for a comedy; **bibliographie par ~s** bibliography arranged by subjects; *V* **vif**.

(b) (*motif, cause*) **~ de** cause for, ground(s) for; **~ de mécontentement/de dispute** cause *ou* grounds for dissatisfaction/for dispute; **il n'avait vraiment pas ~ de se mettre en colère/se plaindre** he really had no cause *ou* grounds for losing *ou* to lose his temper/for complaint; **ayant tout ~ de croire à sa bonne foi** having every reason to believe in his good faith; **protester/réclamer sans ~** to protest/complain without (good) cause *ou* groundlessly.

(c) (*individu*) subject. (*Ling*) **le ~ parlant** the speaker; **les rats qui servent de ~s (d'expérience)** the rats which serve as experimental subjects; **son frère est un brillant ~/un ~ d'élite** his brother is a brilliant/an exceptionally brilliant student; **un mauvais ~** (*enfant*) a bad boy; (*jeune homme*) a bad lot.

(d) (*Ling, Mus, Philos*) subject.

(e) (*à propos de*) **au ~ de** about, concerning; **que sais-tu à son ~?** what do you know about *ou* of him?; **au ~ de cette fille, je peux vous dire que ...** about *ou* concerning that girl *ou* with regard to that girl, I can tell you that ...; **à ce ~, je voulais vous dire que ...** on that subject *ou* about that*, I wanted to tell you that ... .

sujétion [syʒesjɔ̃] *nf* **(a)** (*asservissement*) subjection. **maintenir un peuple dans la ~** *ou* **sous sa ~** to keep a nation in subjection; **tomber sous la ~ de** to fall into sb's power *ou* under sb's sway; (*fig littér*) **~ aux passions/au désir** subjection to passions/desire.

(b) (*obligation, contrainte*) constraint. **les enfants étaient pour elle une ~** the children were a real constraint to her *ou* were like a yoke round her neck; **des habitudes qui deviennent des ~s** habits which become compulsions.

sulfamides [sylfamid] *nmpl* sulpha drugs, sulphonamides (*T*).

sulfatage [sylfataʒ] *nm [vigne]* spraying with copper sulphate.

sulfate [sylfat] *nm* sulphate. **~ de cuivre** copper sulphate.

sulfaté, e [sylfate] (*ptp de* **sulfater**) *adj* sulphated.

sulfater [sylfate] (1) *vt vigne* to spray with copper sulphate.

sulfateuse [sylfatøz] *nf* **(a)** (*Agr*) copper sulphate spraying machine.
(b) (*arg Crime: mitraillette*) machine gun, MG*.

sulfite [sylfit] *nm* sulphite.

sulfure [sylfyʀ] *nm* sulphide.

sulfuré, e [sylfyʀe] (*ptp de* **sulfurer**) *adj* sulphurated, sulphuretted. **hydrogène ~** hydrogen sulphide.

sulfurer [sylfyʀe] (1) *vt* to sulphurate, sulphurize.

sulfureux, -euse [sylfyʀø, øz] *adj* sulphurous. **anhydride** *ou* **gaz ~** sulphur dioxide.

sulfurique [sylfyʀik] *adj* sulphuric. **anhydride ~** sulphur trioxide.

sulfurisé, e [sylfyʀize] *adj*: **papier ~** greaseproof paper.

sultan [syltɑ̃] *nm* sultan.

sultanat [syltana] *nm* sultanate.

sultane [syltan] *nf* sultana (*sultan's wife*).

sumérien, -ienne [symeʀjɛ̃, jɛn] **1** *adj* Sumerian. **2** *nm* (*Ling*) Sumerian. **3** *nm,f*: **S~(ne)** Sumerian.

summum [sɔmɔm] *nm [gloire, civilisation]* acme, climax; *[bêtise, hypocrisie]* height.

super [sypɛʀ] **1** *nm* (*abrév de* **supercarburant**) super, four- *ou* five-star (petrol). **2** *préf* (*) **~ cher/chic** fantastically expensive/smart*; **~-bombe/-ordinateur** super-bomb/-computer*; (*Pol*) **les ~-grands** the super-powers. **3** *adj inv* (*) terrific*, great*.

superbe [sypɛʀb(ə)] **1** *adj* **(a)** (*splendide*) *temps, journée* superb, glorious; *femme, enfant* beautiful, gorgeous; *maison, cheval, corps, yeux* magnificent, beautiful; *résultat, salaire, performance* magnificent, superb. **revenu de vacances avec une mine ~** back from holiday looking wonderfully healthy; (*littér*) **~ d'indifférence** superbly indifferent.
(b) (†, *littér: orgueilleux*) arrogant, haughty.
2 *nf* (†, *littér*) arrogance, haughtiness.

superbement [sypɛʀbəmɑ̃] *adv* superbly, beautifully.

supercarburant [sypɛʀkaʀbyʀɑ̃] *nm* high-octane petrol (*Brit*), high-octane *ou* high-test gasoline (*US*).

supercherie [sypɛʀʃəʀi] *nf* trick, trickery (*U*). **il s'aperçut de la ~** he saw through the trickery *ou* trick; **user de ~s pour tromper qn** to trick sb, deceive sb with trickery; **~ littéraire** literary fabrication.

superfétation [sypɛʀfetɑsjɔ̃] *nf* (*littér*) superfluity.

superfétatoire [sypɛʀfetatwaʀ] *adj* (*littér*) superfluous, supererogatory (*littér*).

superficialité [sypɛʀfisjalite] *nf* superficiality.

superficie [sypɛʀfisi] *nf* (*aire*) (surface) area; (*littér: surface: lit, fig*) surface.

superficiel, -ielle [sypɛʀfisjɛl] *adj* (*gén*) superficial; *idées, esprit, personne* superficial, shallow; *beauté, sentiments, blessure* superficial, skin-deep (*attrib*); *V* **tension**.

superficiellement [sypɛʀfisjɛlmɑ̃] *adv* superficially.

superfin, e [sypɛʀfɛ̃, in] *adj* (*Comm*) *beurre, produit* superfine (*épith*), superquality (*épith*); *qualité* superfine (*épith*).

superflu, e [sypɛʀfly] **1** *adj* superfluous. **2** *nm* superfluity. **se débarrasser du ~** to get rid of the surplus; **le ~ est ce qui fait le charme de la vie** it is superfluity that gives life its charm.

superfluité [sypɛʀflyite] *nf* (*littér*) superfluity.

superforteresse [sypɛʀfɔʀtəʀɛs] *nf* (*Aviat*) superfort(ress).

supérieur, e [sypeʀjœʀ] **1** *adj* **(a)** (*du haut: dans l'espace*) (*gén*) upper (*épith*); *planètes* superior. **dans la partie ~e du clocher** in the highest *ou* upper *ou* top part of the belfry; **la partie ~e de l'objet** the top part of the object; **le feu a pris dans les étages ~s** fire broke out on the upper floors; **montez à l'étage ~** go to the next floor up *ou* to the floor above, go up to the next floor.
(b) (*du haut: dans une hiérarchie*) *classes sociales* upper (*épith*); *niveaux, échelons* upper (*épith*), topmost; *animaux, végétaux* higher (*épith*). (*Rel*) **Père ~** Father Superior; (*Rel*) **Mère ~e** Mother Superior; **à l'échelon ~** on the next rung up; *V* **cadre, mathématique, officier**[1].
(c) (*excellent, qui prévaut*) *intérêts, principe* higher (*épith*); *intelligence, esprit* superior. **produit de qualité ~e** product of superior quality; **des considérations d'ordre ~** considerations of the highest order *ou* a high order.
(d) (*hautain*) *air, ton, regard* superior.
(e) (*plus important, meilleur*) *qualité, poste* superior, higher; *nombre, vitesse* higher, greater; *quantité* greater, larger. **forces ~es en nombres** forces superior in number(s); **~ à** *nombre* greater *ou* higher than, above; *somme* greater than; *production* greater than, superior to; **intelligence/qualité ~e à la moyenne** above-average *ou* higher than average intelligence /quality; **parvenir à un niveau ~ à ...** to reach a higher level than ... *ou* a level higher than ...; **travail d'un niveau ~ à ...** work of a higher standard than ...; **roman/auteur ~ à un autre** novel/author superior to another; **être hiérarchiquement ~ à qn** to be higher (up) than sb *ou* be above sb in the hierarchy, be hierarchically superior to sb.
(f) (*fig: à la hauteur de*) **~ à sa tâche** more than equal to the task; **il a su se montrer ~ aux événements** he was able to rise above events; **restant ~ à la situation** remaining master of the situation.
2 *nm,f* (*Admin, Mil, Rel*) superior. **mon ~ hiérarchique** my immediate superior.

supérieurement [sypeʀjœʀmɑ̃] *adv exécuter qch, dessiner* exceptionally well. **~ doué/ennuyeux** exceptionally gifted/boring.

supériorité [sypeʀjɔʀite] *nf* **(a)** (*prééminence*) superiority. **nous avons la ~ du nombre** we outnumber them, we are superior in number(s); *V* **complexe**.
(b) (*condescendance*) superiority. **air de ~** superior air, air of superiority; **sourire de ~** superior smile.

superlatif, -ive [sypɛʀlatif, iv] **1** *adj* superlative. **2** *nm* superlative. **~ absolu/relatif** absolute/relative superlative.

superlativement [sypɛʀlativmɑ̃] *adv* superlatively.

supermarché [sypɛʀmaʀʃe] *nm* supermarket.

superphosphate [sypɛʀfɔsfat] *nm* superphosphate.

superposable [sypɛʀpozabl(ə)] *adj* (*gén*) that may be superimposed, superimposable (*à* on); (*éléments de mobilier*) stacking (*épith*).

superposé, e [sypɛʀpoze] (*ptp de* **superposer**) *adj couches, blocs* superposed; (*fig*) *visions, images* superimposed.

superposer [sypɛʀpoze] (1) **1** *vt* **(a)** (*empiler*) *couches, blocs* to superpose (*à* on); *éléments de mobilier* to stack. (*fig*) **~ les consignes aux consignes** to heap *ou* pile order upon order.
(b) (*faire chevaucher*) *cartes, clichés,* (*fig*) *visions* to superimpose; *figures géométriques* to superpose. **~ qch à** to superimpose sth on; to superpose sth on.
2 se superposer *vpr* **(a)** (*se recouvrir*) *[clichés photographiques, visions, images]* to be superimposed (on one another).
(b) (*s'ajouter*) *[couches, éléments]* to be superposed.

superposition [sypɛʀpozisjɔ̃] *nf* **(a)** (*action: V* **superposer**) superposing; superimposition.
(b) (*état*) superposition; (*Phot*) superimposition. **le ~ de ces couches** the fact that these strata are superposed; **une ~ de terrasses s'élevant à l'infini** a series of terraces (one on top of the other) rising infinitely upwards.

superpréfet [sypɛʀpʀefɛ] *nm* superprefect (*in charge of a region*).

superproduction [sypɛʀpʀɔdyksjɔ̃] *nf* (*Ciné*) spectacular.

supersonique [sypɛʀsɔnik] *adj* supersonic; *V* **bang**.

superstitieusement [sypɛʀstisjøzmɑ̃] *adv* superstitiously.

superstitieux, -euse [sypɛʀstisjø, øz] *adj* superstitious.

superstition [sypɛʀstisjɔ̃] *nf* superstition. **il a la ~ du chiffre 13** he's got a superstition about *ou* he's superstitious about the number 13.

superstrat [sypɛʀstʀa] *nm* (*Ling*) superstratum.

superstructure [sypɛʀstʀyktyʀ] *nf* (*gén*) superstructure.

superviser [sypɛʀvize] (1) *vt* to supervise.

supin [sypɛ̃] *nm* (*Ling*) supine.

supplanter [syplɑ̃te] (1) *vt* to supplant.

suppléance [sypleɑ̃s] *nf* (*remplacement*) (*poste*) supply post; (*action*) temporary replacement. **professeur chargé d'une ~ dans un village** teacher appointed to a supply post in a village; **elle faisait des ~s pour gagner sa vie** she took supply posts *ou* did supply teaching to earn her living.

suppléant, e [sypleɑ̃, ɑ̃t] **1** *adj* supply (*épith*); deputy (*épith*). **médecin ~** locum; (*Gram*) **verbe ~** substitute verb.
2 *nm,f* (*professeur*) supply teacher; (*juge*) deputy (judge); (*député*) deputy (M.P.); (*médecin*) locum. **pendant les vacances, on fait appel à des ~s** during the holidays we take on temporary staff.

suppléer [syplee] (1) *vt* **(a)** (*ajouter*) *mot manquant* to supply, provide; *somme complémentaire* to make up, supply.
(b) (*compenser*) *lacune* to fill in; *manque, défaut* to make up for.
(c) (*frm: remplacer*) *professeur* to stand in for, replace; *juge* to deputize for. (*littér*) **la machine a suppléé l'homme dans ce domaine** the machine has supplanted *ou* replaced man in this area.
(d) ~ à (*compenser*) *défaut, manque* to make up for; (*remplacer*) *qualité, faculté* to substitute for; **ils suppléaient aux machines par l'abondante main-d'œuvre** they substituted a large labour force for machines.

supplément [syplemɑ̃] *nm* **(a)** (*surcroît*) **un ~ de: un ~ de travail/salaire** extra *ou* additional work/pay; **avoir droit à un ~ de 100 F sur ses allocations familiales** to be allowed a supplement of 100 francs *ou* a 100-franc supplement on one's family allowance, be allowed an extra *ou* an additional 100 francs on one's family allowance; **un ~ d'information** supplementary *ou* additional information; **je voudrais un ~ (de viande), s'il vous plaît** I'd like an extra portion (of meat) please.
(b) *[journal, dictionnaire]* supplement. **~ illustré** illustrated supplement.
(c) (*à payer*) (*au théâtre, au restaurant*) extra charge, supplement; (*dans l'autobus*) excess fare, supplement. **~ de 1ère classe** excess fare *ou* supplement for travelling 1st class, 1st-class supplement; **payer un ~ pour excès de bagages** to pay extra for excess luggage, pay (for) excess luggage, pay excess on one's luggage.
(d) en ~ extra; **le fromage est en ~** cheese is extra, an additional charge is made for cheese; **le tableau de bord en bois est en ~** the wooden dashboard is an extra *ou* comes as an extra, there is extra to pay for the wooden dashboard.
(e) (*Math*) *[angle]* supplement.

supplémentaire [syplemɑ̃tɛʀ] *adj dépenses, crédits, retards* additional, further (*épith*); *travail, vérifications* additional, extra (*épith*); *trains, autobus* relief (*épith*); (*Géom*) *angle* supplementary. **accorder un délai ~** to grant an extension of time limit; *V* **heure**.

supplémenter [syplemɑ̃te] (1) *vt*: **~ le billet de qn** to issue sb with a supplementary ticket (*for an excess fare*).

suppliant, e [sypljɑ̃, ɑ̃t] **1** *adj regard, voix* beseeching, imploring; *personne* imploring. **2** *nm,f* suppliant, supplicant.

supplication [syplikɑsjɔ̃] *nf* (*gén*) plea, entreaty; (*Rel*) supplication.

supplice [syplis] **1** *nm* **(a)** (*peine corporelle*) form of torture, torture (*U*). (*peine capitale*) **le (dernier)** ~ execution, death; **le ~ de la roue** torture on the wheel; **le ~ du fouet** flogging, the lash.

(b) (*souffrance*) torture. **~s moraux** moral tortures *ou* torments; (*fig*) **éprouver le ~ de l'incertitude** to be tortured *ou* tormented by uncertainty, suffer the ordeal *ou* torture of uncertainty; (*fig*) **cette lecture est un (vrai) ~!** reading this book is (quite) an ordeal!

(c) (*loc*) **être au ~** (*appréhension*) to be in agonies *ou* on the rack; (*gêne, douleur*) to be in misery; **mettre qn au ~** to torture sb.

2: supplice chinois Chinese torture (*U*); (*Rel*) **le supplice de la Croix** the Crucifixion; (*lit*) **supplice de Tantale** torment of Tantalus; (*fig*) **soumis à un véritable supplice de Tantale** tortured *ou* suffering like Tantalus.

supplicié, e [syplisje] (*ptp de* **supplicier**) *nm,f* victim of torture, torture victim. **les corps/cris des ~s** the bodies/cries of the torture victims *ou* of the tortured.

supplicier [syplisje] (7) *vt* (*lit, fig*) to torture; (*à mort*) to torture to death.

supplier [syplije] (7) *vt* to beseech, implore, entreat (*de faire* to do). **~ qn à genoux** to beseech *ou* implore *ou* entreat sb on one's knees; **n'insistez pas, je vous en supplie** I beg of you not to insist.

supplique [syplik] *nf* petition. **présenter une ~ au roi** to petition the king, bring a petition before the king.

support [sypɔʀ] *nm* **(a)** (*gén: soutien*) support; (*béquille, pied*) prop, support; [*instruments de laboratoire, outils, livre*] stand.

(b) (*moyen*) medium; (*aide*) aid. **~ publicitaire** advertising medium; **conférence faite à l'aide d'un ~ écrit/magnétique/visuel** lecture given with the help of a written text/a tape/visual aids; **~ audio-visuel** audio-visual aid.

(c) (*Peinture*) [*dessin*] support; (*Ordinateurs*) [*information codée*] input medium. **le symbole est le ~ du concept** the symbol is the physical medium through which the concept is expressed.

supportable [sypɔʀtabl(ə)] *adj douleur* bearable; *conduite* tolerable; *température* bearable; (*: *passable, pas trop mauvais*) tolerable.

supporter[1] [sypɔʀte] (1) *vt* **(a)** (*servir de base à*) to support, hold up.

(b) (*subir*) *frais* to bear; *conséquences, affront, malheur* to suffer, endure. **il m'a fait ~ les conséquences de son acte** he made me suffer the consequences of his act.

(c) (*endurer*) *maladie, solitude, revers* to bear, endure, put up with; *douleur* to bear, endure; *conduite, ingratitude* to tolerate, put up with; *recommandations, personne* to put up with, bear. **maladie courageusement supportée** illness bravely borne; **il ne pouvait plus ~ la vie** he could endure *ou* bear life no longer; **supportant ces formalités avec impatience** impatiently putting up with these formalities; **la mort d'un être cher est difficile à ~** the death of a loved one is hard to bear; **il va falloir le ~ pendant toute la journée!** we're going to have to put up with him all day long!; **elle supporte tout d'eux, sans jamais rien dire** she puts up with *ou* she takes anything from them without a word; **je les supporte, sans plus** I can just about put up with them; **je ne supporte pas ce genre de comportement/qu'on me parle sur ce ton** I won't put up with *ou* stand for *ou* tolerate this sort of behaviour/being spoken to in that tone of voice; **je ne peux pas ~ l'hypocrisie** I can't bear *ou* abide hypocrisy; **je ne peux pas les ~** I can't bear *ou* stand them; **je ne supporte pas qu'elle fasse cela** I won't stand for *ou* tolerate her doing that; **je ne supporte pas de voir ça** I can't bear seeing *ou* to see that, I can't stand seeing that; **ils ne peuvent pas se ~** they can't bear *ou* stand each other.

(d) (*résister à*) *température, conditions atmosphériques, épreuve* to withstand. **verre qui supporte la chaleur** heatproof *ou* heat-resistant glass; **il a bien/mal supporté l'opération** he took the operation well/badly; **il ne supporte pas l'alcool/l'avion** he can't take alcohol/plane journeys; **elle ne supporte pas de voir le sang** *ou* **la vue du sang** she can't bear *ou* stand the sight of blood *ou* seeing blood; **il ne supporte pas la chaleur** heat doesn't agree *ou* disagrees with him, he can't take *ou* stand *ou* bear the heat; **je ne supporte pas les épinards** spinach doesn't agree *ou* disagrees with me; **lait facile à ~** easily-digested milk; **tu as de la chance de ~ l'ail** you're lucky to be able to take garlic; **il n'a pas supporté la fondue** the fondue didn't agree with him.

(e) (*) **on supporte un gilet, par ce temps** you can do with a cardigan in this weather*; **je pensais avoir trop chaud avec un pull, mais on le supporte** I thought I'd be too hot with a jumper but I can do with it after all*.

supporter[2] [sypɔʀtɛʀ] *nm* (*Sport*) supporter.

supposable [sypozabl(ə)] *adj* supposable.

supposé, e [sypoze] (*ptp de* **supposer**) *adj nombre, total* estimated; *auteur* supposed.

supposer [sypoze] (1) *vt* **(a)** (*à titre d'hypothèse*) to suppose. **supposons un conflit atomique** let's suppose *ou* if we suppose there to be an atomic conflict *ou* (that) an atomic conflict takes place; **en supposant que, à ~ que** supposing (that); (*Sci*) **pour les besoins de l'expérience, la pression est supposée constante** for the purposes of the experiment the pressure is taken to be *ou* assumed (to be) constant; (*Scol*) **supposons une ligne A-B** let's postulate a line A-B.

(b) (*présumer*) to suppose. **~ qn amoureux/jaloux** to imagine *ou* suppose sb to be in love/jealous; **je lui suppose une grande ambition** I imagine him to have great ambition; **je ne peux que le ~** I can only make a supposition; **cela laisse ~ que** it leads one to suppose that; **je suppose que tu es contre** I take it *ou* I assume *ou* I suppose you are against it.

(c) (*impliquer, présupposer*) to presuppose; (*suggérer, laisser deviner*) to imply. **la gestation suppose la fécondation** gestation presupposes fertilization; **ta réponse suppose que tu n'as rien compris** your reply implies that you haven't understood a thing.

supposition [sypozisjɔ̃] *nf* supposition. **une ~ que ...*** supposing ... .

suppositoire [sypozitwaʀ] *nm* suppository.

suppôt [sypo] *nm* (*littér*) henchman. **~ de Satan** hellhound.

suppression [sypʀesjɔ̃] *nf* (*V* **supprimer**) deletion; removal; cancellation; withdrawal; abolition; suppression. **faire des ~s dans un texte** to make some deletions in a text; **la ~ de la douleur/fatigue** the elimination of pain/fatigue.

supprimer [sypʀime] (1) **1** *vt* **(a)** (*enlever*) *mot, clause* to delete, remove (*de* from); *mur* to remove, knock down; *trains* to cancel; *permis de conduire* to withdraw, take away (*de* from). **~ qch à qn** to deprive sb of sth; **~ les sorties/les permissions aux soldats** to put a stop *ou* an end to the soldiers' outings/leave; **on lui a supprimé sa prime/sa pension** he's had his bonus/pension stopped, he has been deprived of his bonus/pension; **plusieurs emplois ont été supprimés dans cette usine** several jobs have been done away with in this factory.

(b) (*faire disparaître*) *loi* to do away with, abolish; *publication, document* to suppress; *obstacle* to remove; *témoin gênant* to do away with, suppress; *discrimination, (Comm) concurrence* to do away with, put an end to, abolish. **il est dangereux de ~ (les effets de) la fatigue** it is dangerous to suppress (the effects of) fatigue; **prenez ce fortifiant pour ~ la fatigue** take this tonic to eliminate *ou* banish tiredness; **ce médicament supprime la douleur** this medicine kills pain *ou* eliminates pain *ou* is a painkiller; **on ne parviendra jamais à ~ la douleur** we shall never succeed in doing away with *ou* in eliminating pain; **~ la discrimination raciale** to do away with *ou* put an end to *ou* abolish racial discrimination; **les grands ensembles suppriment l'individualisme** housing schemes put an end to *ou* destroy individualism; **l'avion supprime les distances** air travel does away with long distances; **cette technique supprime des opérations inutiles** this technique does away with *ou* cuts out some useless operations; **dans l'alimentation, il faut ~ les intermédiaires** in the food trade we must cut out *ou* do away with intermediaries.

2 se supprimer *vpr* to do away with o.s., take one's own life.

suppuration [sypyʀɑsjɔ̃] *nf* suppuration.

suppurer [sypyʀe] (1) *vi* to suppurate.

supputation [sypytɑsjɔ̃] *nf* **(a)** (*action: V* **supputer**) calculation; computation. **(b)** (*pronostic*) prognostication.

supputer [sypyte] (1) *vt dépenses, frais* to calculate, compute; *chances, possibilités* to calculate.

supra[1] ... [sypʀa] *préf* supra ... .

supra[2] [sypʀa] *adv* supra.

supranational, e, *mpl* **-aux** [sypʀanasjɔnal, o] *adj* supranational.

supraterrestre [sypʀatɛʀɛstʀ(ə)] *adj* superterrestrial.

suprématie [sypʀemasi] *nf* supremacy.

suprême [sypʀɛm] **1** *adj* (*gén*) supreme. **au ~ degré** to the highest degree. **2** *nm* (*Culin*) supreme; *V* **sauce.**

suprêmement [sypʀɛmmɑ̃] *adv* supremely.

sur[1] [syʀ] **1** *prép* **(a)** (*position*) on, upon; (*sur le haut de*) on top of, on; (*avec mouvement*) on, onto; (*dans*) on, in; (*par-dessus*) over; (*au-dessus*) above. **il y a un sac ~ la table/un tableau ~ le mur** there's a bag on the table/a picture on the wall; **mettre une annonce ~ le tableau** to put a notice (up) on the board; **il a laissé tous ses papiers ~ la table** he left all his papers (lying) on the table; **se promener ~ la rivière** to go boating on the river; **il y avait beaucoup de circulation ~ la route** there was a lot of traffic on the road; **~ ma route** *ou* **mon chemin** on my way; (*Rad*) **~ les grandes/petites ondes** on long/short wave; (*Géog*) **X-~-mer** X-upon-sea, X-on-sea; **elle rangea ses chapeaux ~ l'armoire** she put her hats away on top of the wardrobe; **pose ta valise ~ une chaise** put your case (down) on a chair; **elle a jeté son sac ~ la table** she threw her bag onto the table; **il grimpa ~ le toit** he climbed (up) onto the roof; **une chambre (qui donne) ~ la rue** a room that looks out onto the street; **il n'est jamais monté ~ un bateau** he's never been in *ou* on a boat; **~ la place (du marché)** in the (market) square; **la clef est restée ~ la porte** the key was left in the door; **lire qch ~ le journal*** to read sth in the paper; **un pont ~ la rivière** a bridge across *ou* on *ou* over the river; **il neige ~ Paris/~ toute l'Europe** snow is falling on *ou* in Paris/over the whole of Europe, it's snowing in Paris/all over Europe; **l'avion est passé ~ nos têtes** the aircraft flew over *ou* above our heads *ou* overhead; **mettre un linge ~ un plat/un couvercle ~ une casserole** to put a cloth over a dish/a lid on a saucepan; (*fig*) **s'endormir ~ un livre/son travail** to fall asleep over a book/over *ou* at one's work; **ne t'appuie pas ~ le mur** don't lean on *ou* against the wall; **retire tes livres de ~ la table** take your books (from) off the table; **je n'ai pas d'argent/la lettre ~ moi** I haven't (got) any money/the letter on *ou* with me; **elle a acheté des poires ~ le marché** she bought pears at the market; *V* **pied, piste, place** *etc.*

(b) (*direction*) to, towards. **tourner ~ la droite** to turn (to the) right; **l'église est ~ votre gauche** the church is on *ou* to your left; **diriger** *ou* **tourner ses regards/son attention ~ qch** to turn one's eyes/attention towards sth; **se jeter ~ qn** to throw *ou* hurl o.s. upon *ou* at sb; **tirer ~ qn** to shoot at sb; **fermez bien la porte ~ vous** be sure and close the door behind *ou* after you; *V* **loucher, sauter.**

(c) (*temps: proximité, approximation*) **il est arrivé ~ les 2 heures** he came (at) about *ou* (at) around 2; **il va ~ ses quinze**

ans/la quarantaine he's getting on for fifteen/forty; **l'acte s'achève** *ou* **se termine ~ une réconciliation** the act ends with a reconciliation; **il est ~ le** *ou* **son départ, il est ~ le point de partir** he's just going, he's (just) about to leave; **il a été pris ~ le fait** he was caught in the act *ou* red-handed; **~-le-champ, ~ l'heure** at once, straightaway; **~ le moment, je n'ai pas compris** at the time *ou* at first I didn't understand; **~ ce, il est sorti** whereupon *ou* upon which he went out; **~ ce, ~ ces mots** so saying, with this *ou* that; **~ ce, il faut que je vous quitte** and now I must leave you; **boire du café ~ de la bière** to drink coffee on top of beer; *V* **entrefait, parole, prendre** *etc.*

(d) *(cause)* on, by. **~ invitation/commande** by invitation/order; **nous l'avons nommé ~ la recommandation/les conseils de X** we appointed him on X's recommendation/advice; **croire qn ~ parole** to take sb's word for it; *V* **juger.**

(e) *(moyen, manière)* on. **ils vivent ~ son traitement/ses économies** they live on *ou* off* his salary/savings; **ne le prends pas ~ ce ton** don't take it like that; **prendre modèle ~ qn** to model o.s. on *ou* upon sb; **rester ~ la défensive/ses gardes** to stay on the defensive/one's guard; **chanter** *ou* **entonner qch ~ l'air de** to sing sth to the tune of; *(Mus)* **fantaisie** *etc* **~ un air de** fantasy *etc* on an air by *ou* from; *(Mus)* **~ le mode mineur** in the minor mode; *V* **mesure.**

(f) *(matière, sujet)* on, about. **causerie/conférence/renseignements ~ la Grèce/la drogue** talk/lecture/information on *ou* about Greece/drug addiction; **roman/film ~ Louis XIV** novel/film about Louis XIV; **questionner** *ou* **interroger qn ~ qch** to question sb about *ou* on sth; **gémir** *ou* **se lamenter ~ ses malheurs** to lament (over) *ou* bemoan one's misfortunes; **être ~ un travail** to be occupied with *ou* (in the process of) doing a job; **être ~ une bonne affaire/une piste/un coup*** to be on to a bargain/on a trail/on a job; *V* **réfléchir** *etc.*

(g) *(rapport de proportion etc)* out of, in; *(mesure)* by; *(accumulation)* after. **~ 12 verres, 6 sont ébréchés** out of 12 glasses 6 are chipped; **un homme ~ 10** one man in (every) *ou* out of 10; **9 fois ~ 10** 9 times out of 10; **il a 9 chances ~ 10 de réussir** he has 9 chances out of 10 of succeeding, his chances of success are 9 out of 10; *(Scol, Univ etc)* **il mérite 7 ~ 10** he deserves 7 out of 10; **la cuisine fait 2 mètres ~ 3** the kitchen is *ou* measures 2 metres by 3; **un jour/un vendredi ~ trois** every third day/Friday; **il vient un jour/mercredi ~ deux** he comes every other day/Wednesday; **faire faute ~ faute** to make one mistake after another; **il a eu rhume ~ rhume** he's had one cold after another *ou* the other, he's had cold after cold.

(h) *(influence, supériorité)* over, on. **avoir de l'influence/de l'effet ~ qn** to have influence on *ou* over/an effect on sb; **cela a influé ~ sa décision** that has influenced *ou* had an influence on his decision; **elle ne peut rien ~ lui** she can't control him, she has no control over him; **savoir prendre ~ soi** to keep a grip on o.s.; **prendre ~ soi de faire qch** to take it upon o.s. to do sth; *V* **emporter, régner** *etc.*

2 *préf:* **~excité** overexcited; **~production** overproduction; **~dosage** overdose; *V* **surabondance, surchauffer** *etc.*

3: sur-le-champ *adv* immediately; **sur-place** *nm:* **faire du sur-place** to mark time; **on a fait du sur-place jusqu'à Orly** it was stop-start all the way to Orly.

sur², e [syʀ] *adj (aigre)* sour.

sûr, e [syʀ] **1** *adj* **(a) ~ de** *résultats, succès* sure *ou* certain of; *allié, réflexes, moyens* sure of; *fait, diagnostic, affirmation* sure *ou* certain of *ou* about; **il avait le moral et était ~ du succès** he was in good spirits and was sure *ou* certain *ou* assured of success; **s'il s'entraîne régulièrement, il est ~ du succès** if he trains regularly he's sure of success; **il est ~ de son fait** he's sure of his facts, he's certain *ou* sure about it; **il est ~ de son fait** *ou* **coup*** he's sure *ou* confident he'll pull it off*; **~ de soi** self-assured, self-confident, sure of oneself *(péj)*; **elle n'est pas ~e d'elle(-même)** she's lacking in self-assurance *ou* self-confidence; **j'en étais ~!** I knew it!, just as I thought!; **j'en suis ~ et certain** I'm positive (about it), I'm absolutely certain (of it).

(b) *(certain)* certain, sure. **la chose est ~e** that's certain, that's for sure* *ou* certain*; **ce** *ou* **il n'est pas ~ qu'elle aille au Maroc** it's not definite *ou* certain that she's going to Morocco; **est-ce si ~ qu'il gagne?** is he so certain *ou* sure to win?; **c'est ~ et certain** that's absolutely certain; **ce n'est pas si ~*** it's not that certain*, don't be so sure; *V* **coup.**

(c) *(sans danger) quartier, rue* safe. **peu ~** *quartier etc* unsafe; **il est plus ~ de ne pas compter sur lui** it's safer not to rely on him; **le plus ~ est de mettre sa voiture au garage le soir** the safest thing is to put your car in the garage at night; **en lieu ~** in a safe place; **en mains ~es** in safe hands.

(d) *(digne de confiance) personne, firme* reliable, trustworthy; *renseignements, diagnostic* reliable; *valeurs morales, raisonnement* sound; *remède, moyen* safe, reliable, sure; *dispositif, arme, valeurs boursières* safe; *main, pied, œil* steady; *goût, instinct* reliable, sound. **le temps n'est pas assez ~ pour une ascension** the weather's not certain *ou* reliable enough to go climbing; **avoir la main ~e** to have a steady hand; **raisonner sur des bases peu ~es** to argue on unsound *ou* shaky premises; **nous apprenons de source ~e que ...** we have been informed by a reliable source that ...; **peu ~** *allié* unreliable, untrustworthy; *renseignements* unreliable; *moyen, méthode* unreliable, unsafe.

2 *adv* (*) **~ que: ~ qu'il y a quelque chose qui ne tourne pas rond** there must be *ou* there's definitely something wrong; *V* **bien, pour.**

surabondamment [syʀabɔ̃damɑ̃] *adv (littér) expliquer* in excessive detail. **~ décoré de** overabundantly decorated with.

surabondance [syʀabɔ̃dɑ̃s] *nf* overabundance, superabundance.

surabondant, e [syʀabɔ̃dɑ̃, ɑ̃t] *adj* overabundant, superabundant.

surabonder [syʀabɔ̃de] (1) *vi* **(a)** *[richesses, plantes, matière première]* to be overabundant, be superabundant, overabound. **une station où surabondent les touristes** a resort overflowing *ou* bursting with tourists; **des circulaires où surabondent les fautes d'impression** circulars littered with printing errors; **un port où surabondent les tavernes** a port with an inordinate number of taverns.

(b) *(littér)* **~ de: ~ de richesses** to have an overabundance of riches, have overabundant riches; **~ d'erreurs** to abound with errors.

suractivé, e [syʀaktive] *adj* superactivated.

suractivité [syʀaktivite] *nf* superactivity.

suraigu, -uë [syʀegy] *adj* very high-pitched, very shrill.

surajouter [syʀaʒute] (1) *vt* to add. **ornements surajoutés** superfluously added ornaments, superfluous ornaments; **raisons auxquelles se surajoutent celles-ci** reasons to which one might add the following.

suralimentation [syʀalimɑ̃tɑsjɔ̃] *nf* (*V* **suralimenter**) overfeeding; overeating.

suralimenter [syʀalimɑ̃te] (1) **1** *vt personne* to overfeed; *moteur* to give too much fuel to. **2 se suralimenter** *vpr* to overeat.

suranné, e [syʀane] *adj idées, mode* outmoded, outdated, antiquated; *beauté, tournure, style* outdated, outmoded.

surbaissé, e [syʀbese] (*ptp de* **surbaisser**) *adj plafond etc* lowered; *(Archit) voûte* surbased; *carrosserie, auto* low.

surbaissement [syʀbɛsmɑ̃] *nm (Archit)* surbasement.

surbaisser [syʀbese] (1) *vt plafond* to lower; *(Archit) voûte* to surbase; *(Aut) voiture, chassis* to make lower.

surboum†* [syʀbum] *nf* party.

surcharge [syʀʃaʀʒ(ə)] *nf* **(a)** *[véhicule]* overloading.

(b) *(poids en excédent)* extra load, excess load. **une tonne de ~** an extra *ou* excess load of a ton; **les passagers/marchandises en ~** the excess *ou* extra passengers/goods; **prendre des passagers en ~** to take on excess *ou* extra passengers; **payer un supplément pour une ~ de bagages** to pay extra for excess luggage, pay (for) excess luggage, pay excess on one's luggage.

(c) *(fig)* **cela me cause une ~ de travail/dépenses** this gives me extra work/expense; **il y a une ~ de détails/d'ornements** there is a surfeit *ou* an overabundance of detail/ornamentation.

(d) *(ajout) [document, chèque]* alteration; *[timbre-poste]* surcharge.

surcharger [syʀʃaʀʒe] (3) *vt voiture, cheval* to overload; *timbre* to surcharge. **~ qn de travail/d'impôts** to overload *ou* overburden sb with work/taxes; **un manuscrit surchargé de corrections** a manuscript covered *ou* littered with corrections.

surchauffe [syʀʃof] *nf (Écon)* overheating; *(Tech)* superheating; *(Phys)* superheat.

surchauffer [syʀʃofe] (1) *vt pièce* to overheat; *(Phys, Tech)* to superheat.

surchoix [syʀʃwa] *adj inv viande* prime *(épith)*, top-quality; *produit, fruit* top-quality.

surclasser [syʀklɑse] (1) *vt* to outclass.

surcompensation [syʀkɔ̃pɑ̃sɑsjɔ̃] *nf (Psych)* overcompensation.

surcomposé, e [syʀkɔ̃poze] *adj* double-compound.

surcompression [syʀkɔ̃pʀesjɔ̃] *nf [gaz]* supercharging.

surcomprimer [syʀkɔ̃pʀime] (1) *vt gaz* to supercharge.

surcontrer [syʀkɔ̃tʀe] (1) *vt (Cartes)* to redouble.

surcouper [syʀkupe] (1) *vt (Cartes)* to overtrump.

surcroît [syʀkʀwa] *nm* **(a) un ~ de: cela lui a donné un ~ de travail/d'inquiétudes** that gave him additional work/anxieties; **ça lui a valu un ~ de respect** this won him added *ou* increased respect; **par (un) ~ d'honnêteté/de scrupules** through an excess of honesty/scruples, through excessive honesty/scrupulousness; **pour ~ de bonheur/malheur il vient de ...** to add to his happiness/misfortune(s) he has just ... .

(b) *(de plus)* **de** *ou* **par ~** what is more, moreover; **avare et paresseux de** *ou* **par ~** miserly and idle to boot, miserly and — what's more — idle; **en ~** in addition.

surdi-mutité [syʀdimytite] *nf* deaf-and-dumbness.

surdité [syʀdite] *nf* deafness.

sureau, *pl* **~x** [syʀo] *nm* elder (tree). **les baies du ~** elderberries.

surélévation [syʀelevɑsjɔ̃] *nf (action)* raising, heightening; *(état)* extra height.

surélever [syʀɛlve] (5) *vt plafond, étage* to raise, heighten; *mur* to heighten. **~ une maison d'un étage** to heighten a house by one storey; **rez-de-chaussée surélevé** raised ground floor, ground floor higher than street level.

sûrement [syʀmɑ̃] *adv* **(a)** *(sans risques, efficacement) cacher qch, progresser* in safety; *attacher* securely; *fonctionner* safely. **l'expérience instruit plus ~ que les livres** experience is a surer teacher than books; *V* **lentement.**

(b) *(certainement)* certainly. **— ~!** (most) certainly!; **— ~ pas!** surely not!; **il viendra ~** he'll certainly come, he's sure to come; **~ qu'il a été retenu*** he must have been held up, he has surely been held up.

surenchère [syʀɑ̃ʃɛʀ] *nf* **(a)** (*Comm*) *(sur prix fixé)* overbid; (*enchère plus élevée*) higher bid. **faire une ~ (sur)** to make a higher bid (than); **une douzaine de ~s successives firent monter le prix de la potiche que je convoitais** a dozen bids one after the other put up the price of the vase I fancied; **faire une ~ de 10 F (sur)** to bid 10 francs more *ou* higher (than), bid 10 francs over the previous bid *ou* bidder.

(b) (*fig: exagération, excès*) **la presse, royaume de la ~ et**

de la sensation the press, domain of the overstatement and of sensationalism; **la ~ électorale** outbidding tactics of rival (political) parties; **une ~ de violence** an increasing build-up of violence.

surenchérir [syʀɑ̃ʃeʀiʀ] (2) *vi* (*offrir plus qu'un autre*) to bid higher (*sur* than); (*élever son offre*) to raise one's bid; (*fig: lors d'élections etc*) to try to outmatch *ou* outbid each other (*de* with). **~ sur une offre** to bid higher than an offer *ou* bid, top a bid*; **~ sur qn** to bid higher than sb, outbid *ou* overbid sb.

surentraînement [syʀɑ̃tʀɛnmɑ̃] *nm* (*Sport*) overtraining.

surentraîner *vt*, **se surentraîner** *vpr* [syʀɑ̃tʀene] (1) to overtrain.

suréquipement [syʀekipmɑ̃] *nm* overequipment.

suréquiper [syʀekipe] (1) *vt* to overequip.

surestimation [syʀɛstimɑsjɔ̃] *nf* (*V* **surestimer**) overestimation; overvaluation.

surestimer [syʀɛstime] (1) *vt importance, puissance, forces* to overestimate; *tableau, maison à vendre* to overvalue.

suret, -ette [syʀɛ, ɛt] *adj* sharp, tart.

sûreté [syʀte] *nf* **(a)** (*sécurité*) safety. **complot contre la ~ de l'état** plot against state security; **pour plus de ~** as an extra precaution, to be on the safe side; **être en ~** to be in safety, be safe; **mettre qn/qch en ~** to put sb/sth in a safe *ou* secure place; **serrure/verrou** *etc* **de ~** safety lock/bolt *etc*; **c'est une ~ supplémentaire** it's an extra precaution.

(b) (*exactitude, efficacité*) *[renseignements, méthode]* reliability; *V* **cour, prudence.**

(c) (*précision*) *[coup d'œil, geste]* steadiness; *[goût]* reliability, soundness; *[réflexe, diagnostic]* reliability. **il a une grande ~ de main** he has a very sure hand; **~ d'exécution** sureness of touch.

(d) (*dispositif*) safety device. **mettre une arme à la ~** to put the safety catch *ou* lock on a gun; *V* **cran.**

(e) (*garantie*) assurance, guarantee. **demander/donner des ~s à qn** to ask sb for/give sb assurances *ou* a guarantee; (*Jur*) **~ personnelle** guaranty; **~ réelle** security.

(f) (*Police*) **la S~ (nationale)** ≃ the CID (*Brit*), the Criminal Investigation Department (*Brit*), ≃ the FBI (*US*), the Federal Bureau of Investigation (*US*).

surévaluer [syʀevalɥe] (1) *vt* to overvalue.

surexcitable [syʀɛksitabl(ə)] *adj* overexcitable.

surexcitation [syʀɛksitɑsjɔ̃] *nf* overexcitement.

surexciter [syʀɛksite] (1) *vt* to overexcite.

surexposer [syʀɛkspoze] (1) *vt* (*Phot*) to overexpose.

surexposition [syʀɛkspozisjɔ̃] *nf* overexposure.

surface [syʀfas] **1** *nf* (*gén, Géom*) surface; (*aire*) *[champ, chambre]* surface area. **faire ~** to surface; **en ~** *nager, naviguer* at the surface, near the surface; (*fig*) *travailler, apprendre* superficially; **tout en ~** *personne* superficial, shallow; **ne voir que la ~ des choses** not to see below the surface of things, see only the surface of things; **l'appartement fait 100 mètres carrés de ~** the flat has a surface area of 100 square metres.

2: surface de chauffe heating-surface; (*Admin*) **surface corrigée** amended area (*calculated on the basis of amenities etc for assessing rent*); (*Aviat*) **surface porteuse** aerofoil; (*Ftbl*) **surface de réparation** penalty area; (*Aviat*) **surface de sustentation = surface porteuse.**

surfaire [syʀfɛʀ] (60) *vt réputation, auteur* to overrate; (*rare*) *marchandise* to overprice.

surfait, e [syʀfɛ, ɛt] (*ptp de* **surfaire**) *adj ouvrage, auteur* overrated.

surfilage [syʀfilaʒ] *nm* (*Couture*) overcasting.

surfiler [syʀfile] (1) *vt* (*Couture*) to overcast.

surfin, e [syʀfɛ̃, in] *adj beurre, produit* superfine (*épith*), superquality (*épith*); *qualité* superfine (*épith*).

surgelé, e [syʀʒəle] *adj* deep-frozen. **(aliments) ~s** (deep-) frozen food.

surgir [syʀʒiʀ] (2) *vi* **(a)** *[animal, véhicule en mouvement, spectre]* to appear suddenly; *[montagne, navire]* to loom up (suddenly); *[plante, immeuble]* to shoot up, spring up. **dans son délire, il faisait ~ en esprit les objets de ses désirs** in his delirious state he conjured up (in his mind) the objects of his desires.

(b) *[problèmes, difficultés]* to arise, crop up; *[dilemme]* to arise.

surgissement [syʀʒismɑ̃] *nm* (*littér: V* **surgir**) sudden appearance; sudden looming up; shooting up, springing up.

surhausser [syʀose] (1) *vt* (*gén, Archit*) to raise.

surhomme [syʀɔm] *nm* superman.

surhumain, e [syʀymɛ̃, ɛn] *adj* superhuman.

surimposé, e [syʀɛ̃poze] **1** *ptp de* **surimposer. 2** *adj* (*Géol*) superimposed.

surimposer [syʀɛ̃poze] (1) *vt* (*taxer*) to overtax.

surimposition [syʀɛ̃pozisjɔ̃] *nf* (*Fin*) overtaxation. **payer une ~** to pay too much tax.

surimpression [syʀɛ̃pʀesjɔ̃] *nf* (*Phot*) double exposure; (*fig*) *[idées, visions]* superimposition. **en ~** superimposed; **on voyait, en ~, apparaître le visage de la mère** the mother's face appeared superimposed (on it).

surintendance [syʀɛ̃tɑ̃dɑ̃s] *nf* (*Hist*) superintendency.

surintendant [syʀɛ̃tɑ̃dɑ̃] *nm* (*Hist*) superintendent.

surir [syʀiʀ] (2) *vi* to turn sour, (go) sour.

surjet [syʀʒɛ] *nm* overcast seam. **point de ~** overcast stitch.

surjeter [syʀʒəte] (4) *vt* (*Couture*) to overcast.

sur-le-champ [syʀləʃɑ̃] *adv V* **sur**[1].

surlendemain [syʀlɑ̃dmɛ̃] *nm*: **le ~ de son arrivée** two days after his arrival; **il est mort le ~** he died two days later; **il revint le lendemain et le ~** he came back the next day and the day after (that); **le ~ matin** two days later in the morning.

surmenage [syʀmənaʒ] *nm* **(a)** (*V* **surmener**) overworking. **éviter le ~ des élèves** to avoid overworking schoolchildren.

(b) (*V* **se surmener**) overwork(ing). **éviter à tout prix le ~** to avoid overwork(ing) at all costs.

(c) (*état maladif*) overwork. **souffrant de ~** suffering from (the effects of) overwork; **le ~ intellectuel** mental fatigue, brain-fag*.

surmener [syʀməne] (5) **1** *vt personne, animal* to overwork. **2 se surmener** *vpr* to overwork (o.s.).

sur-moi [syʀmwa] *nm* superego.

surmontable [syʀmɔ̃tabl(ə)] *adj* surmountable. **obstacle difficilement ~** obstacle that is difficult to surmount *ou* that can be surmounted only with difficulty.

surmonter [syʀmɔ̃te] (1) **1** *vt* **(a)** (*être au-dessus de*) to surmount, top. **surmonté d'un dôme/clocheton** surmounted *ou* topped by a dome/bell-turret; **un clocheton surmontait l'édifice** the building was surmounted *ou* topped by a bell-turret.

(b) (*vaincre*) *obstacle, difficultés* to overcome, get over, surmount; *dégoût, peur* to overcome, get the better of. **la peur peut se ~** fear can be overcome.

2 se surmonter *vpr* to master o.s., control o.s.

surmultiplié, e [syʀmyltiplije] *adj*: **vitesse ~e** overdrive.

surnager [syʀnaʒe] (3) *vi [huile, objet]* to float (on the surface); *[sentiment, souvenir]* to linger on.

surnaturel, -elle [syʀnatyʀɛl] **1** *adj* supernatural; (*ambiance inquiétante*) uncanny. **2** *nm*: **le ~** the supernatural, the occult.

surnom [syʀnɔ̃] *nm* nickname. **'le Courageux', ~ du roi Richard** 'the Brave', the name by which King Richard was known.

surnombre [syʀnɔ̃bʀ(ə)] *nm*: **en ~** *participants etc* too many; **plusieurs élèves en ~** several pupils too many; **nous étions en ~ et avons dû partir** there were too many of us and so we had to leave; **Marie, qui était arrivée à l'improviste, était en ~** Marie, who had turned up unexpectedly, was one too many.

surnommer [syʀnɔme] (1) *vt* **~ qn 'le gros'** to nickname sb 'fatty'; **~ un roi 'le Fort'** to give a king the name 'the Strong'; **cette infirmité l'avait fait ~ 'le Crapaud'** this disability had earned him the nickname of 'the Toad'; **le roi Richard surnommé 'le Courageux'** King Richard known as *ou* named 'the Brave'.

surnuméraire [syʀnymeʀɛʀ] *adj, nmf* supernumerary.

suroffre [syʀɔfʀ(ə)] *nf* (*Jur*) higher offer *ou* bid.

suroît [syʀwa] *nm* (*vent*) south-wester, sou'wester; (*chapeau*) sou'wester. **vent de ~** south-westerly wind.

surpassement [syʀpɑsmɑ̃] *nm* (*littér*) **~ de soi** surpassing (of) oneself.

surpasser [syʀpɑse] (1) **1** *vt* **(a)** (*l'emporter sur*) *concurrent, rival* to surpass, outdo. **~ qn en agilité/connaissances** to surpass sb in agility/knowledge; **sa gloire surpassait en éclat celle de Napoléon** his glory outshone that of Napoleon.

(b) (*dépasser*) to surpass. **le résultat surpasse toutes les espérances** the result surpasses *ou* is beyond all our hopes.

2 se surpasser *vpr* to surpass o.s. **le cuisinier s'est surpassé aujourd'hui** the cook has surpassed himself today; (*iro*) **encore un échec, décidément tu te surpasses!** another failure — you're really surpassing yourself!

surpayer [syʀpeje] (8) *vt employé* to overpay; *marchandise* to pay too much for.

surpeuplé, e [syʀpœple] *adj* overpopulated.

surpeuplement [syʀpœpləmɑ̃] *nm* overpopulation.

sur-place [syʀplas] *nm V* **sur**[1].

surplis [syʀpli] *nm* surplice.

surplomb [syʀplɔ̃] *nm* overhang. **en ~** overhanging.

surplomber [syʀplɔ̃be] (1) **1** *vi* (*Tech*) to be out of plumb. **2** *vt* to overhang.

surplus [syʀply] *nm* **(a)** (*excédent non écoulé*) surplus (*U*). **vendre le ~ de son stock** to sell off one's surplus stock; **avoir des marchandises en ~** to have surplus goods.

(b) (*reste non utilisé*) **il me reste un ~ de clous/de papier dont je ne me suis pas servi** I've got some nails/paper left over *ou* some surplus nails/paper that I didn't use; **avec le ~ (de bois), je vais essayer de me faire une cabane** with what's left over (of the wood) *ou* with the leftover *ou* surplus (wood) I'm going to try to build myself a hut; **ce sont des ~ qui restent de la guerre/de l'exposition** they're *ou* it's left over *ou* it's surplus from the war/exhibition; **~ américains** American army surplus.

(c) (*d'ailleurs*) **au ~** moreover, what is more.

surpopulation [syʀpɔpylɑsjɔ̃] *nf* overpopulation.

surprenant, e [syʀpʀənɑ̃, ɑ̃t] *adj* (*étonnant*) amazing, surprising; (*remarquable*) amazing, astonishing.

surprendre [syʀpʀɑ̃dʀ(ə)] (58) **1** *vt* **(a)** (*prendre sur le fait*) *voleur* to surprise, catch in the act.

(b) (*découvrir*) *secret, complot* to discover; *conversation* to overhear; *regard, sourire complice* to intercept. **je crus ~ en lui de la gêne** I thought that I detected some embarrassment in him.

(c) (*prendre au dépourvu*) (*par attaque*) *ennemi* to surprise; (*par visite inopinée*) *amis, voisins etc* to catch unawares, catch on the hop*. **~ des amis chez eux** to drop in unexpectedly on friends, pay a surprise visit to friends; **espérant la ~ au bain/au lit** hoping to catch her in the bath/in bed; **je vais aller le ~ au travail** I'm going to drop in (unexpectedly) on him at work, I'm going to catch him unawares at work.

(d) *[pluie, marée, nuit]* to catch out. **se laisser ~ par la marée** to be caught out by the tide; **se laisser ~ par la pluie** to be caught in the rain *ou* caught out by the rain; **se laisser ~ par la nuit** to be overtaken by nightfall.

(e) (*étonner*) *[nouvelle, conduite]* to amaze, surprise. **tu me surprends** you amaze me; **cela me surprendrait fort** that would greatly surprise me.

(f) (*littér*) ~ **la vigilance de qn** to catch sb out; ~ **la bonne foi de qn** to betray sb's good faith; ~ **la confiance de qn**† to win sb's trust fraudulently.

2 se surprendre *vpr:* se ~ **à faire qch** to catch *ou* find o.s. doing sth.

surpression [syʀpʀesjɔ̃] *nf* (*Tech*) superpressure.

surprime [syʀpʀim] *nf* (*Assurances*) additional premium.

surpris, e[1] [syʀpʀi, iz] (*ptp de* **surprendre**) *adj air, regard* surprised. ~ **de qch** surprised *ou* amazed at sth; ~ **de me voir là/que je sois encore là** surprised *ou* amazed at seeing me there *ou* to see me there/that I was still there.

surprise[2] [syʀpʀiz] **1** *nf* **(a)** (*étonnement*) surprise. **regarder qn avec** ~ to look at sb with surprise; **avoir la** ~ **de voir que** to be surprised to see that; **à ma grande** ~ much to my surprise, to my great surprise.

(b) (*cause d'étonnement, cadeau*) surprise. **voyage sans** ~**s** uneventful *ou* unremarkable journey; **prix sans** ~**s** (all-) inclusive price; **avec ça, pas de (mauvaises)** ~**s!** you'll have no nasty *ou* unpleasant surprises with this!; **il m'a apporté une petite** ~ he brought me a little surprise; *V* **pochette**.

(c) par ~ *attaquer* by surprise; **il m'a pris par** ~ he caught me off guard.

2: surprise-partie *nf, pl* **surprises-parties** party.

surproduction [syʀpʀɔdyksjɔ̃] *nf* overproduction.

surréalisme [syʀʀealism(ə)] *nm* surrealism.

surréaliste [syʀʀealist(ə)] **1** *adj écrivain, peintre* surrealist; *tableau, poème* surrealist, surrealistic; (*bizarre*) surrealistic, way-out*. **2** *nmf* surrealist.

surrénal, e, *mpl* **-aux** [syʀʀenal, o] **1** *adj* suprarenal. **2** *nfpl:* ~**es** suprarenals.

sursaut [syʀso] *nm* (*mouvement brusque*) start, jump. (*fig: élan, accès*) ~ **d'énergie/d'indignation** (sudden) burst *ou* fit of energy/indignation; **se réveiller en** ~ to wake up with a start; **avoir un** ~ to give a start, jump; **cela lui fit faire un** ~ it made him jump *ou* start.

sursauter [syʀsote] (1) *vi* to start, jump, give a start. **faire** ~ **qn** to make sb start *ou* jump, give sb a start.

surseoir [syʀswaʀ] (26) **surseoir à** *vt indir publication, délibération* to defer, postpone; (*Jur*) *poursuites, jugement, exécution* to stay. ~ **à l'exécution d'un condamné** to grant a reprieve to a condemned man.

sursis [syʀsi] *nm* **(a)** (*Jur*) *[condamnation à mort]* reprieve. **peine avec** ~ *ou* **assortie du** ~ suspended sentence; **il a eu le** ~**/2 ans avec** ~ he was given a suspended sentence/a 2-year suspended sentence; ~ **à exécution** *ou* **d'exécution** stay of execution.

(b) (*Mil*) ~ **(d'incorporation)** deferment.

(c) (*fig: temps de répit*) reprieve. **c'est un mort en** ~ he's a condemned man, he's living under a death sentence.

sursitaire [syʀsitɛʀ] **1** *adj* (*Mil*) deferred (*épith*); (*Jur*) with a suspended sentence. **2** *nm* (*Mil*) deferred conscript.

surtaxe [syʀtaks(ə)] *nf* surcharge; *[lettre mal affranchie]* surcharge; *[envoi exprès etc]* additional charge, surcharge. ~ **à l'importation** import surcharge.

surtaxer [syʀtakse] (1) *vt* to surcharge.

surtension [syʀtɑ̃sjɔ̃] *nf* (*Élec*) overvoltage.

surtout[1] [syʀtu] *adv* **(a)** (*avant tout, d'abord*) above all; (*spécialement*) especially, particularly. **rapide, efficace et** ~ **discret** quick, efficient and above all discreet; **il est assez timide,** ~ **avec les femmes** he's quite shy, especially *ou* particularly with women; **j'aime** ~ **les romans, mais je lis aussi de la poésie** I particularly like novels *ou* above all I like novels, but I also read poetry; **dernièrement, j'ai** ~ **lu des romans** I have read mostly *ou* mainly novels of late; **j'aime les romans,** ~ **les romans policiers** I like novels, especially *ou* particularly detective novels; **le poulet, je l'aime** ~ **à la basquaise** I like chicken best (when) cooked the Basque way.

(b) ~ **que*** especially as *ou* since.

(c) ~, **motus et bouche cousue!** don't forget, mum's the word!; ~ **pas maintenant** certainly not now; **je ne veux** ~ **pas vous déranger** the last thing I want is to disturb you, I certainly don't want to disturb you; ~ **pas!** certainly not!; ~ **ne vous mettez pas en frais** whatever you do, don't go to any expense.

surtout[2]† [syʀtu] *nm* (*manteau*) greatcoat†.

surveillance [syʀvɛjɑ̃s] *nf* (*action: V* **surveiller**) watch; supervision; invigilation. **exercer une** ~ **continuelle/une étroite** ~ **sur** to keep a constant/close watch over; **sous la** ~ **de la police** under police surveillance; **mission/service de** ~ surveillance mission/personnel; **déjouer** *ou* **tromper la** ~ **de ses gardiens** to slip by *ou* evade the guards on watch.

2: surveillance légale legal surveillance (*of impounded property*); **surveillance médicale** medical supervision; **surveillance policière** police surveillance; **la surveillance du territoire** ≃ the Intelligence Service.

surveillant, e [syʀvɛjɑ̃, ɑ̃t] **1** *nm,f [prison]* warder; *[usine, chantier]* supervisor, overseer; *[magasin]* shopwalker; (*Scol*) (*pion*) monitor (*adult employed for supervision*); (*aux examens*) invigilator.

2: (*Scol*) **surveillant d'étude**† study *ou* prep† monitor; (*Scol*) **surveillant général**† chief monitor, monitor in charge (*of discipline*); (*Scol*) **surveillant d'internat** supervisor of boarders, boarders' monitor; (*Méd*) **surveillant de salle** head nurse, ≃ sister.

surveillé, e [syʀveje] (*ptp de* **surveiller**) *adj V* **liberté**.

surveiller [syʀveje] (1) **1** *vt* **(a)** (*garder*) *enfant, élève, bagages* to watch, keep an eye on; *prisonnier* to keep watch over, keep (a) watch on; *malade* to watch over, keep watch over. **il faut voir comme elle le surveille!** you should see the way she watches him!; ~ **qn de près** to keep a close eye *ou* watch on sb.

(b) (*contrôler*) *éducation, études de qn* to supervise; *réparation, construction* to supervise, oversee; (*Scol*) *examen* to invigilate. **surveille la soupe une minute** keep an eye on the soup a minute, watch the soup a minute.

(c) (*défendre*) *locaux* to keep watch on; *territoire* to watch over, keep watch over.

(d) (*épier*) *personne, mouvements, proie* to watch; *adversaire* (*Mil*) to keep watch on; (*Sport*) to watch. **se sentant surveillé, il partit** feeling he was being watched, he left.

(e) (*fig*) ~ **son langage/sa ligne** to watch one's language/one's figure.

2 se surveiller *vpr* to keep a check *ou* a watch on o.s. **elle devrait se** ~, **elle grossit de plus en plus** she ought to keep a check *ou* watch on herself *ou* she ought to watch herself because she's getting fatter and fatter.

survenir [syʀvəniʀ] (22) *vi [événement]* to take place; *[incident, complications, retards]* to occur, arise; *[personne]* to appear, arrive (unexpectedly). **s'il survient des complications ...** should any complications arise ... .

survêtement [syʀvɛtmɑ̃] *nm* (*sportif*) tracksuit; *[alpiniste, skieur]* overgarments.

survie [syʀvi] *nf [malade, accidenté]* survival; (*Rel: dans l'au-delà*) afterlife; (*fig*) *[auteur, amitié, institution, mode]* survival. **ce médicament lui a donné quelques mois de** ~ this drug has given him a few more months of life *ou* to live; **une** ~ **de quelques jours, à quoi bon, dans son état?** what's the use of letting him survive *ou* live *ou* of prolonging his life for a few more days in his condition?

survireur, -euse [syʀviʀœʀ, øz] *adj* (*Aut*) **voiture** ~**euse** car which oversteers.

survivance [syʀvivɑ̃s] *nf* **(a)** (*vestige*) relic, survival. **(b)** (*littér*) *[âme]* survival. ~ **de l'âme** survival of the soul (after death), afterlife.

survivant, e [syʀvivɑ̃, ɑ̃t] **1** *adj* surviving. **2** *nm,f* (*rescapé, Jur*) survivor. **des sœurs, la** ~**e ...** the surviving sister ...; **un** ~ **d'un âge révolu** a survivor *ou* a survival from a past age.

survivre [syʀvivʀ(ə)] **1** *vi* **(a)** (*continuer à vivre: lit, fig*) to survive. (*après accident etc*) **va-t-il** ~**?** will he live? *ou* survive?; **il n'avait aucune chance de** ~ he had no chance of survival *ou* surviving; ~ **à** *accident, maladie, humiliation* to survive; (*fig*) **rien ne survivait de leurs anciennes coutumes** nothing survived of their old customs.

(b) (*vivre plus longtemps que*) ~ **à** *[personne]* to outlive; *[œuvre, idée]* to outlive, outlast.

2 se survivre *vpr* **(a)** (*se perpétuer*) **se** ~ **dans** *œuvre, enfant, souvenir* to live on in.

(b) (*péj*) *[auteur]* to outlive one's talent; *[aventurier]* to outlive one's time.

survol [syʀvɔl] *nm* (*V* **survoler**) **le** ~ **de** flying over; skimming through, skipping through; skimming over; **faire un** ~ **à basse altitude** to make a low flight.

survoler [syʀvɔle] (1) *vt* (*lit*) to fly over; (*fig*) *livre* to skim through, skip through; *question* to skim over.

survoltage [syʀvɔltaʒ] *nm* (*Élec*) boosting.

survolté, e [syʀvɔlte] *adj* **(a)** (*surexcité*) worked up, wrought up. **(b)** (*Élec*) stepped up, boosted.

sus [sy(s)] *adv* **(a)** (*Admin*) **en** ~ in addition; **en** ~ **de** in addition to, over and above. **(b)** (††, *hum*) ~ **à: courir** ~ **à l'ennemi** to rush upon the enemy; ~ **à l'ennemi!** at them!; ~ **au tyran!** at the tyrant!

susceptibilité [sysɛptibilite] *nf* touchiness (*U*), sensitiveness (*U*). **afin de ménager les** ~**s** so as not to offend people's susceptibilities *ou* sensibilities.

susceptible [sysɛptibl(ə)] *adj* **(a)** (*ombrageux*) touchy, thin-skinned, sensitive.

(b) ~ **de qch/d'être: ces axiomes ne sont pas** ~**s de démonstration** *ou* **d'être démontrés** these axioms are not susceptible of proof *ou* cannot be proved; **texte** ~ **d'être amélioré** *ou* **d'améliorations** text open to improvement *ou* that can be improved upon; **ces gens ne sont pas** ~**s d'éprouver du chagrin** these people are not susceptible to grief.

(c) ~ **de faire: il est** ~ **de gagner** he may well win, he is liable to win; **un second** ~ **lui aussi de prendre l'initiative des opérations** a second-in-command who is also in a position to *ou* who is also able to direct operations; **des conférences** ~**s de l'intéresser** lectures liable *ou* likely to be of interest to him *ou* that may well be of interest to him.

susciter [sysite] (1) *vt* **(a)** (*donner naissance à*) *admiration, intérêt* to arouse; *passions, jalousies, haine* to arouse, incite; *controverse, critiques, querelle* to give rise to, provoke; *obstacles* to give rise to, create.

(b) (*provoquer volontairement*) to create. ~ **des obstacles/ennuis à qn** to create obstacles/difficulties for sb; ~ **des ennemis à qn** to make enemies for sb.

suscription [syskʀipsjɔ̃] *nf* (*Admin*) address.

susdit, e [sysdi, dit] *adj* (*Jur*) foresaid (*Jur*).

susmentionné, e [sysmɑ̃sjɔne] *adj* (*Admin*) above-mentioned (*Admin, frm*).

susnommé, e [sysnɔme] *adj, nm,f* (*Admin, Jur*) above-named (*Admin, frm*).

suspect, e [syspɛ(kt), ɛkt(ə)] **1** *adj* **(a)** (*louche*) *individu, conduite, attitude* suspicious. **sa générosité m'est** *ou* **me paraît** ~**e** I find his generosity suspicious, his generosity seems suspicious to me.

(b) (*douteux*) *opinion, témoignage, citoyen* suspect. **individu** ~ **au régime** (individual) suspect in the eyes of the régime; **pensées** ~**es à la majorité conservatrice** thoughts which the conservative majority find suspect.

(c) ~ **de** suspected of; **ils sont** ~**s de collusion avec l'ennemi** they are suspected of collusion with the enemy; **X, pourtant, bien peu** ~ **de royalisme, a proposé que ...** X, hardly likely to be

suspected of royalism, did however propose that ... .
2 *nm,f* suspect.
suspecter [syspɛkte] (1) *vt personne* to suspect; *bonne foi, honnêteté* to have (one's) suspicions about, question. **~ qn de faire** to suspect sb of doing; **on le suspecte de sympathies gauchistes** he is suspected of having leftist sympathies.
suspendre [syspɑ̃dʀ(ə)] (41) **1** *vt* **(a)** (*accrocher*) *vêtements* to hang up. **~ qch à** *clou, crochet* to hang sth on.
(b) (*fixer*) *lampe, décoration* to hang, suspend (*à* from); *hamac* to sling (up). **~ un lustre au plafond par une chaîne** to hang *ou* suspend a chandelier from the ceiling on *ou* by *ou* with a chain; **~ un hamac à des crochets/à deux poteaux** to sling a hammock between some hooks/two posts.
(c) (*interrompre*) (*gén*) to suspend; *récit* to break off; *audience, séance* to adjourn.
(d) (*remettre*) *jugement* to suspend, defer; *décision* to postpone, defer.
(e) (*destituer*) *prélat, fonctionnaire, joueur* to suspend. **~ qn de ses fonctions** to suspend sb from office.
2 se suspendre *vpr:* se **~ à** *branche, barre* to hang from (*par* by).
suspendu, e [syspɑ̃dy] (*ptp de* **suspendre**) *adj* **(a)** (*accroché*) **~ à: vêtement** *etc* **~ à** garment *etc* hanging on; **lustre** *etc* **~ à** light *etc* hanging *ou* suspended from; **benne ~e à un câble/~e dans le vide** skip suspended by a cable/in mid air; **montre ~e à une chaîne** watch hanging on a chain; (*fig*) **être ~ aux lèvres de qn** to hang upon sb's every word; (*fig*) **chalets ~s au-dessus d'une gorge** chalets suspended over a gorge; *V* **jardin, pont.**
(b) (*Aut*) **voiture bien/mal ~e** car with good/poor suspension.
suspens [syspɑ̃] *nm* **(a)** (*sur une voie de garage*) **en ~** *affaire, projet, travail* in abeyance; **une question laissée en ~** a question that has been shelved; **laisser une affaire en ~** to leave an affair in abeyance.
(b) (*dans l'incertitude*) **en ~** in suspense; **tenir les lecteurs en ~** to keep the reader in suspense.
(c) (*en suspension*) **en ~** *poussière, flocons de neige* in suspension; **en ~ dans l'air** suspended in the air.
(d) (*littér: suspense*) suspense.
suspense [syspɑ̃s] *nm* suspense.
suspenseur [syspɑ̃sœʀ] **1** *adj m* suspensary. **2** *nm* suspensar.
suspensif, -ive [syspɑ̃sif, iv] *adj* (*Jur*) suspensive.
suspension [syspɑ̃sjɔ̃] **1** *nf* **(a)** (*action: V* **suspendre**) hanging; suspending; suspension; breaking off; adjournment; deferment; postponement. **prononcer la ~ de qn pour 2 ans** to suspend sb for 2 years; *V* **point**[1].
(b) (*Aut*) suspension. **~ à roues indépendantes/hydropneumatique** independent/hydropneumatic suspension; *V* **ressort**[1].
(c) (*lustre*) (pendent) light fitting.
(d) (*installation, système*) suspension.
(e) (*Chim*) suspension.
(f) en ~ *particule, poussière* in suspension, suspended; **en ~ dans l'air** *poussière* hanging on the air, suspended in the air; **en ~ dans l'air** *ou* **dans le vide** *personne, câble* suspended in mid air.
2: suspension d'armes suspension of fighting; **suspension d'audience** adjournment; **suspension des hostilités** suspension of hostilities; **suspension de paiement** suspension of payment(s); **suspension de séance** adjournment.
suspicieusement [syspisjøzmɑ̃] *adv* suspiciously.
suspicieux, -euse [syspisjø, øz] *adj* suspicious.
suspicion [syspisjɔ̃] *nf* suspicion. **avoir de la ~ à l'égard de qn** to be suspicious of sb, have one's suspicions about sb.
sustentateur, -trice [systɑ̃tatœʀ, tʀis] *adj* (*Aviat*) lifting. **surface ~trice** aerofoil.
sustentation [systɑ̃tɑsjɔ̃] *nf* (*Aviat*) lift. (*Aviat*) **plan de ~** aerofoil; (*Géom*) **polygone ou base de ~** base.
sustenter [systɑ̃te] (1) **1** *vt* (†: *nourrir*) to sustain. **2 se sustenter** *vpr* (*hum, frm*) to take sustenance (*hum, frm*).
susurrement [sysyʀmɑ̃] *nm* (*V* **susurrer**) whisper; whispering (*U*); murmuring.
susurrer [sysyʀe] (1) *vti [personne]* to whisper; *[eau]* to murmur.
susvisé, e [sysvize] *adj* (*Admin*) above-mentioned (*Admin*).
suture [sytyʀ] *nf* (*Anat, Bot, Méd*) suture; *V* **point**[2].
suturer [sytyʀe] (1) *vt* to suture (*Méd*), stitch up.
suzerain, e [syzʀɛ̃, ɛn] *adj, nm,f* suzerain.
suzeraineté [syzʀɛnte] *nf* suzerainty.
svelte [svɛlt(ə)] *adj personne* svelte, willowy; *édifice, silhouette* slender.
sveltesse [svɛltɛs] *nf* slenderness.
sweepstake [swipstɛk] *nm* sweepstake.
swiftien, -ienne [swiftjɛ̃, jɛn] *adj* Swiftian.
swing [swiŋ] *nm* swing.
swinguer* [swiŋge] (1) *vi* to swing*. **ça swingue!** they are really swinging it!*
sybarite [sibaʀit] *nmf* sybarite.
sybaritique [sibaʀitik] *adj* sybaritic.
sybaritisme [sibaʀitism(ə)] *nm* sybaritism.
sycomore [sikɔmɔʀ] *nm* sycamore (tree).
sycophante [sikɔfɑ̃t] *nm* (*littér: délateur*) informer.
syllabation [silabɑsjɔ̃] *nf* syllabication, syllabification.
syllabe [silab] *nf* syllable.
syllabique [silabik] *adj* syllabic.
syllabisme [silabism(ə)] *nm* syllabism.
syllogisme [silɔʒism(ə)] *nm* syllogism.
syllogistique [silɔʒistik] *adj* syllogistic.
sylphe [silf(ə)] *nm* sylph. **sa taille de ~** her sylphlike figure.
sylphide [silfid] *nf* sylphid; (*fig*) sylphlike creature. **sa taille de ~** her sylphlike figure.
sylvestre [silvɛstʀ(ə)] *adj* forest (*épith*), silvan (*littér*); *V* **pin.**
sylviculteur [silvikyltœʀ] *nm* forester.
sylviculture [silvikyltyʀ] *nf* forestry, silviculture (*T*).
symbiose [sɛ̃bjoz] *nf* symbiosis.
symbole [sɛ̃bɔl] *nm* (*gén*) symbol.
symbolique [sɛ̃bɔlik] **1** *adj* (*gén*) symbolic(al); (*fig: très modique*) *donation, augmentation, émolument, amende* token (*épith*), nominal; *cotisation, contribution, dommage-intérêts* nominal. **c'est un geste purement ~** it's a purely symbolic(al) gesture, it's just a token gesture.
2 *nf* (*science*) symbolics (*sg*); (*système de symboles*) symbolic system.
symboliquement [sɛ̃bɔlikmɑ̃] *adv* symbolically.
symbolisation [sɛ̃bɔlizɑsjɔ̃] *nf* symbolization.
symboliser [sɛ̃bɔlize] (1) *vt* to symbolize.
symbolisme [sɛ̃bɔlism(ə)] *nm* (*gén*) symbolism; (*Littérat*) Symbolism.
symboliste [sɛ̃bɔlist(ə)] *adj, nmf* Symbolist.
symétrie [simetʀi] *nf* (*gén*) symmetry. **centre/axe de ~** centre/axis of symmetry.
symétrique [simetʀik] **1** *adj* symmetrical (*de* to, *par rapport à* in relation to). **2** *nm [muscle]* symmetry. **3** *nf [figure plane]* symmetrical figure.
symétriquement [simetʀikmɑ̃] *adv* symmetrically.
sympa* [sɛ̃pa] *adj inv* (*abrév de* **sympathique**) *personne, soirée* nice; *endroit, ambiance* nice, friendly. **un type vachement ~** a nice *ou* good bloke* (*Brit*) *ou* guy*; **sois ~, prête-le-moi** be a pal* and lend it to me.
sympathie [sɛ̃pati] *nf* **(a)** (*inclination*) liking. **ressentir de la ~ à l'égard de qn** to (rather) like sb, have a liking for sb; **j'ai beaucoup de ~ pour lui** I have a great liking for him, I like him a great deal; **il inspire la ~** he's very likeable, he's a likeable sort; **n'ayant que peu de ~ pour cette nouvelle théorie** having little time for this new theory*, being unfavourable to(wards) this new theory; **accueillir une idée avec ~** to receive an idea favourably.
(b) (*affinité*) fellow feeling. **la ~ qui existe entre eux** the fellow feeling that exists between them, the affinity they feel for each other; **des relations de ~ les unissaient** they were united by a fellow feeling; **il n'y a guère de ~ entre ces factions/personnes** there's no love lost between these factions/people; (*rare*) **être en ~ avec qn** to be at one with sb (*frm*).
(c) (*frm*) sympathy. **croyez à notre ~** you have our deepest sympathy; **témoignages de ~** (*pour deuil*) expressions of sympathy.
sympathique [sɛ̃patik] **1** *adj* **(a)** (*agréable, aimable*) *personne* likeable, nice; *geste, accueil* friendly, kindly; *soirée, réunion, ambiance* pleasant, friendly; *plat* good, nice. **il m'est (très) ~, je le trouve (très) ~** I like him (very much), I find him (very) likeable; **il a une tête ~** he has a friendly face.
(b) (*Anat*) sympathetic.
(c) *V* **encre.**
2 *nm* (*Anat*) **le (grand) ~** the sympathetic nervous system.
sympathiquement [sɛ̃patikmɑ̃] *adv accueillir, traiter* in a friendly manner. **ils ont ~ offert de nous aider** they have kindly offered to help us; **ils nous ont ~ reçus** they gave us a friendly reception.
sympathisant, e [sɛ̃patizɑ̃, ɑ̃t] **1** *adj* (*Pol*) sympathizing (*épith*). **2** *nm,f* (*Pol*) sympathizer.
sympathiser [sɛ̃patize] (1) *vi* (*bien s'entendre*) to get on (well) (*avec* with); (*se prendre d'amitié*) to hit it off* (*avec* with). (*fréquenter*) **ils ne sympathisent pas avec les voisins** they don't have much contact with *ou* much to do with* the neighbours; **je suis heureux de voir qu'il sympathise avec Lucien** I'm pleased to see he gets on (well) with Lucien; **ils ont tout de suite sympathisé** they took to each other immediately, they hit it off* straight away.
symphonie [sɛ̃fɔni] *nf* (*Mus, fig*) symphony. **~ concertante** symphonia concertante.
symphonique [sɛ̃fɔnik] *adj* symphonic; *V* **orchestre, poème.**
symphoniste [sɛ̃fɔnist(ə)] *nmf* symphonist.
symposium [sɛ̃pozjɔm] *nm* symposium.
symptomatique [sɛ̃ptɔmatik] *adj* (*Méd*) symptomatic; (*révélateur*) significant. **~ de** symptomatic of.
symptomatiquement [sɛ̃ptɔmatikmɑ̃] *adv* symptomatically.
symptôme [sɛ̃ptom] *nm* (*Méd*) symptom; (*signe, indice*) sign, symptom.
synagogue [sinagɔg] *nf* synagogue.
synchrone [sɛ̃kʀɔn] *adj* synchronous.
synchronie [sɛ̃kʀɔni] *nf* synchronic level, synchrony.
synchronique [sɛ̃kʀɔnik] *adj* synchronic; *V* **tableau.**
synchronisation [sɛ̃kʀɔnizɑsjɔ̃] *nf* synchronization.
synchronisé, e [sɛ̃kʀɔnize] (*ptp de* **synchroniser**) *adj* synchronized.
synchroniser [sɛ̃kʀɔnize] (1) *vt* to synchronize.
synchroniseur [sɛ̃kʀɔnizœʀ] *nm* (*Élec*) synchronizer; (*Aut*) synchromesh.
synchroniseuse [sɛ̃kʀɔnizøz] *nf* (*Ciné*) synchronizer.
synchronisme [sɛ̃kʀɔnism(ə)] *nm [oscillations, dates]* synchronism; (*fig*) synchronization.
synclinal, e, *mpl* **-aux** [sɛ̃klinal, o] **1** *adj* synclinal. **2** *nm* syncline.
syncope [sɛ̃kɔp] *nf* **(a)** (*évanouissement*) blackout, fainting fit, syncope (*T*). **avoir une ~** to have a blackout, have a fainting fit; **tomber en ~** to faint, pass out. **(b)** (*Mus*) syncopation. **(c)** (*Ling*) syncope.
syncopé, e [sɛ̃kɔpe] *adj* **(a)** (*Littérat, Mus*) syncopated. **(b)** (*: *stupéfait*) staggered*, flabbergasted*.
syncrétisme [sɛ̃kʀetism(ə)] *nm* syncretism.
syndic [sɛ̃dik] *nm* (*Hist*) syndic; (*Jur*) receiver. **~ (d'im-**

meuble) managing agent.

syndical, e, *mpl* **-aux** [sɛ̃dikal, o] *adj* (trade-)union (*épith*); *V* **chambre, tarif.**

syndicalisme [sɛ̃dikalism(ə)] *nm* (*doctrine, mouvement*) trade unionism; (*activité*) union(ist) activities (*pl*). **collègue au ~ ardent** colleague with strongly unionist views; **faire du ~** to participate in unionist activities.

syndicaliste [sɛ̃dikalist(ə)] **1** *nmf* trade unionist.

2 *adj chef* trade-union (*épith*); *doctrine, idéal* unionist (*épith*).

syndicat [sɛ̃dika] **1** *nm* **(a)** *[travailleurs, employés]* (trade) union; *[employeurs]* union, syndicate; *[producteurs agricoles]* union. **~ de mineurs/de journalistes** miners'/journalists' union.

(b) (*non professionnel*) association; *V* **2.**

2: (*Admin*) **syndicat de communes** association of communes; **syndicat financier** syndicate of financiers; **syndicat d'initiative** tourist (information) office *ou* bureau; (*Admin*) **syndicat interdépartemental** association of regional authorities; **syndicat ouvrier** trade union; **syndicat patronal** employers' syndicate, federation of employers; **syndicat de propriétaires** association of property owners.

syndicataire [sɛ̃dikatɛʀ] **1** *adj* of a syndicate. **2** *nmf* syndicate member.

syndiqué, e [sɛ̃dike] (*ptp de* **syndiquer**) **1** *adj* belonging to a (trade) union. **ouvrier ~** union member; **est-il ~?** is he in a *ou* the union?, is he a union man *ou* member?; **les travailleurs non ~s** workers who are not members of a *ou* the union, non-union workers.

2 *nm,f* union member.

syndiquer [sɛ̃dike] (1) **1** *vt* to unionize. **2 se syndiquer** *vpr* (*se grouper*) to form a trade union; (*adhérer*) to join a trade union.

syndrome [sɛ̃dʀom] *nm* syndrome.

synecdoque [sinɛkdɔk] *nf* synecdoche.

synérèse [sineʀɛz] *nf* (*Ling*) synaeresis; (*Chim*) syneresis.

synesthésie [sinɛstezi] *nf* synaesthesia.

synode [sinɔd] *nm* synod.

synodique [sinɔdik] *adj* (*Astron*) synodic(al); (*Rel*) synodal.

synonyme [sinɔnim] **1** *adj* synonymous (*de* with). **2** *nm* synonym.

synonymie [sinɔnimi] *nf* synonymy.

synonymique [sinɔnimik] *adj* synonymic(al).

synopsis [sinɔpsis] *nf ou nm* (*Ciné*) synopsis.

synoptique [sinɔptik] *V* **évangile, tableau.**

synovie [sinɔvi] *nf* synovia; *V* **épanchement.**

synovite [sinɔvit] *nf* synovitis.

syntactique [sɛ̃taktik] *adj* = **syntaxique.**

syntagmatique [sɛ̃tagmatik] *adj* syntagmatic.

syntagme [sɛ̃tagm(ə)] *nm* (word) group, phrase, syntagm (*T*). **~ nominal** nominal group, noun phrase.

syntaxe [sɛ̃taks(ə)] *nf* syntax.

syntaxique [sɛ̃taksik] *adj* syntactic.

synthèse [sɛ̃tɛz] *nf* synthesis. **faire la ~ de qch** to synthesize sth; (*Chim*) **produit de ~** product of synthesis.

synthétique [sɛ̃tetik] *adj* synthetic.

synthétiquement [sɛ̃tetikmɑ̃] *adv* synthetically.

synthétiser [sɛ̃tetize] (1) *vt* to synthetize, synthesize.

syphilis [sifilis] *nf* syphilis.

syphilitique [sifilitik] *adj, nmf* syphilitic.

Syrie [siʀi] *nf* Syria.

syrien, -ienne [siʀjɛ̃, jɛn] **1** *adj* Syrian. **2** *nm,f*: **S~(ne)** Syrian.

systématique [sistematik] *adj soutien, aide* unconditional; *opposition* systematic; *classement, esprit* systematic. **opposer un refus ~ à qch** to refuse sth systematically; **avec l'intention ~ de nuire** systematically intending to harm; **il est trop ~** he's too narrow *ou* dogmatic, his views are too set.

systématiquement [sistematikmɑ̃] *adv* systematically.

systématisation [sistematizɑsjɔ̃] *nf* systematization.

systématiser [sistematize] (1) **1** *vt recherches, mesures* to systematize. **il n'a pas le sens de la nuance, il systématise (tout)** he has no sense of nuance — he systematizes everything. **2 se systématiser** *vpr* to become the rule.

système [sistɛm] **1** *nm* **(a)** (*gén: théorie, structure, méthode, dispositif, réseau*) system. **un ~ de vie** an approach to living; *V* **esprit.**

(b) (*moyen*) system. **il connaît un ~ pour entrer sans payer** he's got a system for getting in without paying; **il connaît le ~** he knows the trick *ou* system; **le meilleur ~, c'est de se relayer** the best plan *ou* system is to take turns.

(c) (*loc*) **par ~** *agir* in a systematic way; *contredire* systematically; **il me tape** *ou* **court** *ou* **porte sur le ~*** he gets on my wick* *ou* nerves*.

2: système D* resourcefulness; **système d'équations** system of equations; **système métrique** metric system; **système nerveux** nervous system; **système pileux** hair; **système solaire** solar system.

systématique [sistematik] *adj* systematic. (*péj*) **il est trop ~** he's too rigid in his thinking.

systématiquement [sistematikmɑ̃] *adv* systematically.

systole [sistɔl] *nf* systole.

syzygie [siziʒi] *nf* syzygy.

T

T, t [te] *nm* (*lettre*) T, t. **en T** *table, immeuble* T-shaped; **bandage/antenne en T** T-bandage/-aerial.

t' [t(ə)] *V* **te, tu.**

ta [ta] *adj poss V* **ton**[1].

tabac [taba] **1** *nm* **(a)** (*plante, produit*) tobacco; (*couleur*) tobacco brown; (*magasin*) tobacconist's (*surtout Brit*) (shop). **(café-)~** café (*with tobacco and stamp counter*); *V* **blague, bureau, débit.**

(b) (*loc*) **passer qn à ~** to beat sb up; (*arg Théât*) **faire un ~** to be a great hit *ou* a roaring success; **c'est toujours le même ~*** it's always the same old thing; **quelque chose du même ~*** something like that; *V* **coup, passage.**

2 *adj inv* buff.

3: tabac blond/brun light/dark tobacco; **tabac à chiquer** chewing tobacco; **tabac à priser** snuff.

tabagie [tabaʒi] *nf* smoke den.

tabassée* [tabɑse] *nf* (*passage à tabac*) belting*; (*bagarre*) punch-up* (*surtout Brit*), brawl.

tabasser* [tabɑse] (1) **1** *vt* (*passer à tabac*) **~ qn** to do sb over* (*Brit*), give sb a belting*. **2 se tabasser** *vpr* (*se bagarrer*) to have a punch-up* (*surtout Brit*) *ou* fight.

tabatière [tabatjɛʀ] *nf* **(a)** (*boîte*) snuffbox. **(b)** (*lucarne*) skylight; *V* **fenêtre.**

tabellion [tabeljɔ̃] *nm* (*hum péj: notaire*) lawyer, legal worthy (*hum péj*).

tabernacle [tabɛʀnakl(ə)] *nm* (*Rel*) tabernacle.

table [tabl(ə)] **1** *nf* **(a)** (*meuble*) table. **~ de salle à manger/de cuisine/de billard** dining-room/kitchen/billiard table; *V* **carte, tennis.**

(b) (*pour le repas*) **être à ~** to be having a meal, be eating, be at table; **à ~!** come and eat!, dinner (*ou* lunch *etc*) is ready!; **mettre** *ou* (*littér*) **dresser la ~** to lay *ou* set the table; **passer à** *ou* **se mettre à ~** to sit down to eat, sit down at the table; **se lever de ~** to get up *ou* rise (*frm*) from the table; **quitter la ~, sortir de ~** to leave the table; **~ de 12 couverts** table set for 12; **linge/vin/propos de ~** table linen/wine/talk.

(c) (*tablée*) table. **toute la ~ éclata de rire** the whole table burst out laughing; **une ~ de 4** a table for 4; **soldats et officiers mangeaient à la même ~** soldiers and officers ate at the same table.

(d) (*nourriture*) **une ~ frugale** frugal fare (*U*); **avoir une bonne ~** to keep a good table; **aimer (les plaisirs de) la ~** to enjoy one's food.

(e) (*tablette avec inscriptions*) **~ de marbre** marble tablet; **les T~s de la Loi** the tables of the law; *V* **douze.**

(f) (*liste*) table. **~ de logarithmes/de multiplication** log/multiplication table; **~ alphabétique** alphabetical table.

(g) (*Géol: plateau*) tableland, plateau.

(h) (*loc*) (*Philos*) **~ rase** tabula rasa; **faire ~ rase** to make a clean sweep (*de* of); (*arg Police*) **se mettre à ~** to talk, come clean; **tenir ~ ouverte** to keep open house.

2: table à abattants drop-leaf table; **table anglaise** gate-legged table; (*Rel*) **table d'autel** altar stone; **table basse** coffee table, occasional table; **table de bridge** card *ou* bridge table; **table de chevet** bedside table; (*Rel*) **table de communion** communion rail; **table de conférence** conference table; **table à dessin** drawing board; **table d'écoute** wire-tapping set; **tables gigognes** nest of tables; (*Mus*) **table d'harmonie** sounding board; **table d'honneur** top table; **table d'hôte: faire table d'hôte** *to serve a buffet supper for residents*; **table de malade** bedtable; **table des matières** (table of) contents; **table de nuit = table de chevet**; **table d'opération** operating table; **table d'orientation** viewpoint indicator; **table à ouvrage** worktable; **table à rallonges** extending table, pull-out table; **table à repasser** ironing board; (*lit, fig*) **table ronde** round table; **table roulante** trolley; (*Mil*) **tables de tir** range tables; **table de toilette** washstand; **table tournante** séance table; **table de travail** work table *ou* desk.

tableau, *pl* **~x** [tablo] **1** *nm* **(a)** (*peinture*) painting; (*reproduction, gravure*) picture; *V* **galerie.**

(b) (*fig: scène*) picture, scene. **le ~ l'émut au plus haut point** he was deeply moved by the scene; **un ~ tragique/idyllique** a tragic/an idyllic picture *ou* scene; **le ~ changeant de la vallée du Rhône** the changing picture of the Rhône valley.
(c) (*Théât*) scene.
(d) (*description*) picture. **un ~ de la guerre** a picture *ou* depiction of war; **il m'a fait un ~ très noir de la situation** he drew me a very black picture of the situation.
(e) (*Scol*) **~ (noir)** (black)board; **aller au ~** (*lit*) to go out *ou* up to the blackboard; (*se faire interroger*) to be asked questions (*on a school subject*).
(f) (*support mural*) *[sonneries]* board; *[fusibles]* box; *[clefs]* rack, board.
(g) (*panneau*) board; (*Rail*) train indicator. **~ des départs/arrivées** departure(s)/arrival(s) board; **~ des horaires** timetable.
(h) (*carte, graphique*) table, chart. **~ généalogique/chronologique** genealogical/chronological table *ou* chart; **~ des conjugaisons** conjugation table, table of conjugations.
(i) (*Admin: liste*) register, roll, list.
(j) (*loc*) **vous voyez (d'ici) le ~!** you can (just) picture it!; **pour compléter** *ou* **achever le ~** to cap it all, to put the finishing touches; (*fig*) **miser sur les deux ~x** to back both horses (*fig*); **il a gagné sur les deux/sur tous les ~x** he won (out) on both/all counts.
2: tableau d'affichage notice board; (*Admin*) **tableau d'avancement** promotion table; **tableau de bord** *[auto]* dashboard, instrument panel; *[avion, bateau]* instrument panel; (*lit, fig*) **tableau de chasse** tally; **tableau d'honneur** list of merit; **tableau de maître** masterpiece; **tableau de service** (*gén*) work notice board; (*horaire de service*) duty roster; **tableau synchronique** synchronic table of events *etc*; **tableau synoptique** synoptic table; (*Théât*) **tableau vivant** tableau (vivant).
tableautin [tablotɛ̃] *nm* (*rare*) little picture.
tablée [table] *nf* table (*of people*). **toute la ~ éclata de rire** the whole table burst out laughing; **il y avait au restaurant une ~ de provinciaux qui ...** at the restaurant there was a party of country people who ... .
tabler [table] (1) *vi*: **~ sur qch** to count *ou* reckon *ou* bank on sth; **il avait tablé sur une baisse des cours** he had counted *ou* reckoned *ou* banked on the rates going down; **table sur ton travail plutôt que sur la chance** rely on your work rather than on luck.
tablette [tablɛt] *nf* **(a)** (*plaquette*) *[chocolat]* bar; *[médicament]* tablet; *[chewing-gum]* stick; *[métal]* block.
(b) (*planchette, rayon*) *[lavabo, étagère, cheminée]* shelf; *[secrétaire]* flap; *[fenêtre]* sill. **~ à glissière** pull-out flap.
(c) (*Hist: pour écrire*) tablet. **~ de cire** wax tablet; (*hum*) **je vais le marquer sur mes ~s** I'll make a note of it; (*hum*) **ce n'est pas écrit sur mes ~s** I have no record of it.
tablier [tablije] *nm* **(a)** (*Habillement*) (*gén*) apron; *[ménagère]* apron, pinafore; *[écolier]* overall, smock; *V* **rendre, robe. (b)** *[pont]* roadway. **(c)** (*Tech: plaque protectrice*) *[cheminée]* (flue-)shutter; *[magasin]* (iron *ou* steel) shutter; *[laminoir]* guard; (*Aut: entre moteur et habitacle*) bulkhead.
tabou [tabu] **1** *nm* taboo. **2** *adj* (*sacré, frappé d'interdit*) taboo; (*fig: intouchable*) *employé, auteur* untouchable.
tabouret [tabuʀɛ] *nm* (*pour s'asseoir*) stool; (*pour les pieds*) footstool. **~ de piano/de bar** piano/bar stool.
tabulaire [tabylɛʀ] *adj* tabular.
tabulateur [tabylatœʀ] *nm* tabulator (*on typewriter*).
tabulatrice [tabylatʀis] *nf* tabulator (*for punched cards*).
tac [tak] *nm* **(a)** (*bruit*) tap. **le ~ ~ des mitrailleuses** the rat-a-tat(-tat) of the machine guns; *V* **tic-tac. (b) répondre** *ou* **riposter du ~ au ~** to give tit for tat.
tache [taʃ] **1** *nf* **(a)** (*moucheture*) *[fruit]* mark; *[léopard]* spot; *[plumage, pelage]* mark(ing), spot; *[peau]* blotch, mark. (*fig*) **faire ~** to jar, stick out like a sore thumb*; **les ~s des ongles** the white marks on the fingernails.
(b) (*salissure*) stain, mark. **~ de graisse** greasy mark, grease stain; **~ de brûlure/de suie** burn/sooty mark; **des draps couverts de ~s** sheets covered in stains; **sa robe n'avait pas une ~** her dress was spotless.
(c) (*littér: flétrissure*) blot, stain. **c'est une ~ à sa réputation** it's a blot *ou* stain on his reputation; **sans ~** *vie, conduite* spotless, unblemished; *naissance* untainted; *V* **agneau, pur.**
(d) (*impression visuelle*) **~ de couleur** spot *ou* patch of colour; **le soleil parsemait la campagne de ~s d'or** the sun scattered patches *ou* flecks *ou* spots of gold over the countryside; **des ~s d'ombre çà et là** spots *ou* patches of shadow here and there.
(e) (*Peinture*) spot, dot, blob.
2: tache d'encre ink stain; (*sur le papier*) (ink) blot *ou* blotch; **tache d'huile** oily mark, oil stain; (*fig*) **faire tache d'huile** to spread, gain ground; **tache jaune (de l'œil)** yellow spot (of the eye); (*Rel*) **tache originelle** stain of original sin; **tache de rousseur** freckle; **tache de sang** bloodstain; (*Astron*) **tache solaire** sunspot; **tache de son = tache de rousseur; tache de vin** (*sur la nappe*) wine stain; (*sur la peau: envie*) strawberry mark.
tâche [tɑʃ] *nf* **(a)** (*besogne*) task, work (*U*); (*mission*) task, job. **assigner une ~ à qn** to set sb a task, give sb a job to do; **mourir à la ~** to die in harness.
(b) (*loc*) **à la ~** *payer* by the piece; **ouvrier à la ~** pieceworker; **travail à la ~** piecework; **être à la ~** to be on piecework; (*fig*) **je ne suis pas à la ~*** I'll do it in my own good time; (†, *littér*) **prendre à ~ de faire qch** to set o.s. the task of doing sth, take it upon o.s. to do sth.
tachéomètre [takeɔmɛtʀ(ə)] *nm* tacheometer.
tachéométrie [takeɔmetʀi] *nf* tacheometry.
tacher [taʃe] (1) **1** *vt* **(a)** *[encre, vin]* to stain; *[graisse]* to mark, stain. **le café tache** coffee stains (badly) *ou* leaves a stain; **taché de sang** bloodstained.
(b) (*littér: colorer*) *pré, robe* to spot, dot; *peau, fourrure* to spot, mark. **pelage blanc taché de noir** white coat with black spots *ou* markings.
(c) (†: *souiller*) to stain, sully (*littér*, †).
2 se tacher *vpr* **(a)** (*se salir*) *[personne]* to get stains on one's clothes, get o.s. dirty; *[nappe, tissu]* to get stained *ou* marked. **c'est un tissu qui se tache facilement** this is a fabric that stains easily.
(b) (*s'abîmer*) *[fruits]* to become marked.
tâcher [tɑʃe] (1) *vi* (*essayer de*) **~ de faire** to try *ou* endeavour (*frm*) to do; **tâchez de venir avant samedi** try to *ou* try and come *ou* endeavour to (*frm*) come before Saturday; **et tâche de ne pas recommencer*** and mind it doesn't happen again; **tâche qu'il n'en sache rien*** see to it that he doesn't know anything about it.
tâcheron [tɑʃʀɔ̃] *nm* **(a)** (*péj*) drudge, toiler. **(b)** (*ouvrier*) (*dans le bâtiment*) jobber; (*agricole*) pieceworker.
tacheter [taʃte] (4) *vt peau, fourrure* to spot, speckle; *tissu, champ* to spot, dot, speckle. **pelage blanc tacheté de brun** white coat with brown spots *ou* markings.
tachisme [taʃism(ə)] *nm* (*art abstrait*) tachisme.
tachiste [taʃist(ə)] *nmf painter of the tachisme school.*
tachycardie [takikaʀdi] *nf* tachycardia.
tachygraphe [takigʀaf] *nm* tachograph, black box*.
tachymètre [takimɛtʀ(ə)] *nm* tachymeter, tachometer.
tacite [tasit] *adj* tacit. (*Jur*) **~ reconduction** renewal of contract by tacit agreement.
Tacite [tasit] *nm* Tacitus.
tacitement [tasitmɑ̃] *adv* tacitly.
taciturne [tasityʀn(ə)] *adj* taciturn, silent.
tacot* [tako] *nm* (*voiture*) banger*, crate*.
tact [takt] *nm* (*doigté, délicatesse*) tact. **avoir du ~** to have tact, be tactful; **un homme de ~** a tactful man; **avec ~** tactfully, with tact; **sans ~** (*adj*) tactless; (*adv*) tactlessly; **manquer de ~** to be tactless, be lacking in tact.
tacticien, -ienne [taktisjɛ̃, jɛn] *nm,f* tactician.
tactile [taktil] *adj* tactile.
tactique [taktik] **1** *adj* tactical. **2** *nf* (*gén*) tactics (*pl*). **changer de ~** to change (one's) tactics.
tænia [tenja] *nm* = **ténia.**
taffetas [tafta] *nm* (*Tex*) taffeta. **~ (gommé)** sticking plaster.
Tage [tɑʒ] *nm*: **le ~** the Tagus.
Tahiti [taiti] *nf* Tahiti.
tahitien, -ienne [taisjɛ̃, jɛn] **1** *adj* Tahitian. **2** *nm,f*: **T~(ne)** Tahitian.
taïaut† [tajo] *excl* tallyho!
taie [tɛ] *nf* **(a) ~ (d'oreiller)** pillowcase, pillowslip; **~ de traversin** bolster case. **(b)** (*Méd*) opaque spot, leucoma (*T*). (*fig littér*) **avoir une ~ sur l'œil** to be blinkered.
taïga [tajga] *nf* (*Géog*) taiga.
taillable [tɑjabl(ə)] *adj*: **~ et corvéable (à merci)** (*Hist*) subject to tallage; (*fig*) *bonne, ouvrier* there to do one's master's bidding.
taillader [tɑjade] (1) *vt* to slash, gash.
taillandier [tɑjɑ̃dje] *nm* edge-tool maker.
taille[1] [tɑj] *nf* **(a)** (*stature*) *[personne, cheval]* height. **homme de ~ moyenne** man of average height; **homme de petite ~** short man, man of small stature (*frm*); **homme de haute ~** tall man; **il doit faire 1 mètre 70 de ~** he must be 1 metre 70 (tall); **ils sont de la même ~** they are the same height; (*fig*) **de la ~ de César** of Caesar's stature.
(b) (*dimension générale*) size. **de petite/moyenne ~** small-/medium-sized; **ils ont un chien de belle ~!** they have a pretty big *ou* large dog!; **le paquet est de la ~ d'une boîte à chaussures** the parcel is the size of a shoebox.
(c) (*Comm: mesure*) size. **les grandes/petites ~s** the large/small sizes; **la ~ 40** size 40; **il lui faut la ~ en dessous/en dessus** he needs the next size down/up, he needs one *ou* a size smaller/larger; **2 ~s en dessous/en dessus** 2 sizes smaller/larger; **ce pantalon n'est pas à sa ~** these trousers aren't his size; **avez-vous quelque chose dans ma ~?** do you have anything in my size?; **si je trouvais quelqu'un de ma ~** if I found someone my size.
(d) (*loc*) **à la ~ de** in keeping with, in line with; **c'est un poste/sujet à la ~ de ses capacités** *ou* **à sa ~** it's a job/subject in keeping *ou* in line with his capabilities; **être de ~ à faire** to be up to doing, be quite capable of doing; **il n'est pas de ~** (*pour une tâche*) he isn't up to it; (*face à un concurrent, dans la vie*) he doesn't measure up; **de ~** *erreur, enjeu* considerable, sizeable; **la gaffe est de ~!** it's no small blunder!
(e) (*partie du corps, du vêtement*) waist. **elle n'a pas de ~** she has no waist(line), she doesn't go in at the waist; **avoir la ~ fine** to have a slim waist, be slim-waisted; **avoir une ~ de guêpe** to be wasp-waisted; **avoir la ~ mannequin** to have a perfect figure; **avoir la ~ bien prise** to have a neat waist(line); **prendre qn par la ~** to put one's arm round sb's waist; **ils se tenaient par la ~** they had their arms round each other's waist; **robe serrée à la ~** dress fitted at the waist; **robe à ~ basse/haute** low-/high-waisted dress; **pantalon (à) ~ basse** low-waisted trousers, hipsters; **robe sans ~** waistless dress; *V* **tour**[2].
taille[2] [tɑj] *nf* **(a)** (*V* **tailler**) cutting; hewing (*frm*); carving; sharpening; cutting out; pruning, cutting back; trimming; clipping. **diamant de ~ hexagonale/en étoile** diamond with a six-sided/star-shaped cut; *V* **pierre.**
(b) (*rare: taillis*) **~s** coppice.
(c) (*tranchant*) *[épée, sabre]* edge. **recevoir un coup de ~** to receive a blow from the edge of the sword; *V* **frapper.**
(d) (*Hist: redevance*) tallage, taille.
(e) (*Min: galerie*) tunnel.
taillé, e [tɑje] (*ptp de* **tailler**) *adj* **(a)** (*bâti*) *personne* **bien ~**

well-built; **il est ~ en athlète** he is built like an athlete, he has an athletic build.

(b) (*destiné à*) *personne* ~ **pour être/faire** cut out to be/do; ~ **pour qch** cut out for sth, tailor-made for sth.

(c) (*coupé*) *arbre* pruned; *haie* clipped, trimmed; *moustache, barbe* trimmed. **crayon ~ en pointe** pencil sharpened to a point; **il avait les cheveux ~s en brosse** he had a crew-cut; (*fig*) **visage ~ à la serpe** rough-hewn features; *V* **âge.**

taille-crayon(s) [tɑjkʀɛjɔ̃] *nm inv* pencil sharpener.

taille-douce, *pl* **tailles-douces** [tɑjdus] *nf* line engraving.

tailler [tɑje] (1) **1** *vt* **(a)** (*travailler*) *pierre précieuse* to cut; *pierre* to cut, hew (*frm*); *bois* to carve; *crayon* to sharpen; *tissu* to cut (out); *arbre, vigne* to prune, cut back; *haie* to trim, clip, cut; *barbe* to trim. **~ qch en biseau** to bevel sth; **~ qch en pointe** to cut sth to a point; **se ~ la moustache** to trim one's moustache.

(b) (*confectionner*) *vêtement* to make; *statue* to carve; *tartines* to cut, slice; (*Alpinisme*) *marche* to cut. (*fig*) **rôle taillé à sa mesure** tailor-made role.

(c) (*loc*) ~ **une bavette*** to have a natter* (*Brit*) *ou* a rap* (*US*); ~ **des croupières à qn**†† to make difficulties for sb; ~ **une armée en pièces** to hack an army to pieces.

2 *vi*: ~ **dans la chair** *ou* **dans le vif** to cut into the flesh.

3 se tailler *vpr* **(a)** (‡: *partir*) to beat it‡, clear off‡.

(b) (*loc*) **se ~ un franc succès** to be a great success; **se ~ la part du lion** to take the lion's share; **se ~ un empire/une place** to carve out an empire/a place for o.s.

tailleur [tɑjœʀ] **1** *nm* **(a)** (*couturier*) tailor. **~ pour dames** ladies' tailor.

(b) (*costume*) suit (*for women*).

(c) en ~ *assis, s'asseoir* cross-legged.

2: tailleur de diamants diamond-cutter; **tailleur à façon** bespoke tailor; **tailleur de pierre(s)** stone-cutter; **tailleur de vignes** vine pruner.

taillis [taji] *nm* copse, coppice. **dans les ~** in the copse *ou* coppice *ou* trees.

tain [tɛ̃] *nm* **(a)** *[miroir]* silvering. **glace sans ~** two-way mirror. **(b)** (*Tech: bain*) tin bath.

taire [tɛʀ] (54) **1 se taire** *vpr* **(a)** (*être silencieux*) *[personne]* to be silent *ou* quiet; (*fig littér*) *[nature, forêt]* to be silent, be still (*littér*); *[vent]* to be still (*littér*); *[bruit]* to disappear. **les élèves se taisaient** the pupils kept *ou* were quiet *ou* silent; **taisez-vous!** be quiet!, be silent! (*frm*); **ils ne voulaient pas se ~, malgré les injonctions répétées du maître** they (just) wouldn't stop talking *ou* be quiet *ou* keep quiet in spite of the master's repeated instructions; **les dîneurs se sont tus** the diners stopped talking *ou* went *ou* were silent; **l'orchestre s'était tu** the orchestra had fallen silent *ou* was silent.

(b) (*s'abstenir de s'exprimer*) to keep quiet, remain silent. **dans ces cas il vaut mieux se ~** in these cases it's best to keep quiet *ou* to remain silent *ou* to say nothing; **savoir souffrir et se ~** to know how to suffer in silence; **se ~ sur qch** to say nothing *ou* keep quiet about sth; **il a perdu une bonne occasion de se ~** he really said the wrong thing, him and his big mouth!*; **tais-toi!*** (*ne m'en parle pas*) don't talk to me about it!, I don't wish to hear about it!

2 *vt* **(a)** (*celer*) *nom, fait, vérité* to hush up, not to tell. **~ la vérité, c'est déjà mentir** not to tell *ou* not telling the truth *ou* to hush up *ou* hushing up the truth is as good as lying.

(b) (*refuser de dire*) *motifs, raisons* to conceal, say nothing about. **une personne dont je tairai le nom** a person who shall be *ou* remain nameless *ou* whose name I shan't mention.

(c) (*garder pour soi*) *douleur, chagrin, amertume* to stifle, keep to o.s.

3 *vi*: **faire ~** *témoin gênant, opposition, récriminations* to silence; **fais taire les enfants** make the children keep *ou* be quiet, make the children shut up*, do shut the children up*.

talc [talk] *nm [toilette]* talc, talcum powder; (*Chim*) talc(um).

talé, e [tale] (*ptp de* **taler**) *adj fruits* bruised.

talent[1] [talɑ̃] *nm* **(a)** (*disposition, aptitude*) talent. **il a des ~s dans tous les domaines** he has talents in all fields; **un ~ littéraire** a literary talent; **il n'a pas le métier d'un professionel mais un beau ~ d'amateur** he lacks professional expertise but has a fine amateur talent; **des ~s de société** society talents; (*hum*) **montrez-nous vos ~s*** show us what you can do; **décidément, vous avez tous les ~s!** what a talented young man (*ou* woman *etc*) you are!

(b) le ~ talent; **avoir du ~** to have talent, be talented; **avoir beaucoup de ~** to have a great deal of talent, be highly talented; **un auteur de (grand) ~** a (highly) talented author.

(c) (*personnes douées*) **~s** talent (*U*); **encourager les jeunes ~s** to encourage young talent; **faire appel aux ~s disponibles** to call on (all) the available talent.

(d) (*iro*) **il a le ~ de se faire des ennemis** he has a gift for making enemies (*iro*).

talent[2] [talɑ̃] *nm* (*monnaie*) talent.

talentueusement [talɑ̃tɥøzmɑ̃] *adv* with talent.

talentueux, -euse [talɑ̃tɥø, øz] *adj* talented.

taler [tale] (1) *vt fruits* to bruise.

talion [taljɔ̃] *nm V* **loi.**

talisman [talismɑ̃] *nm* talisman.

Talmud [talmyd] *nm* Talmud.

talmudique [talmydik] *adj* Talmudic.

talmudiste [talmydist(ə)] *nm* Talmudist.

taloche* [talɔʃ] *nf* clout*, cuff. **flanquer une ~ à qn** to clout* *ou* cuff sb, give sb a clout* *ou* cuff.

talocher* [talɔʃe] (1) *vt* to cuff.

talon [talɔ̃] **1** *nm* **(a)** (*Anat*) *[cheval, chaussure]* heel. **montrer** *ou* **tourner les ~s** to take to one's heels, show a clean pair of heels (*Brit*); **être sur les ~s de qn** to be at *ou* (hot) on sb's heels; *V* **estomac.**

(b) (*croûton, bout*) *[jambon, fromage]* heel; *[pain]* crust, heel.

(c) *[pipe]* spur.

(d) *[chèque]* stub, counterfoil; *[carnet à souche]* stub.

(e) (*Cartes*) talon.

(f) (*Mus*) *[archet]* heel.

2: talon d'Achille Achilles' heel; **talons aiguilles** stiletto heels; **talons bottier** medium heels; **talons hauts** high heels; **talons plats** flat heels.

talonner [talɔne] (1) *vt* **(a)** (*suivre*) *fugitifs, coureurs* to follow (hot) on the heels of. **talonné par qn** hotly pursued by sb. **(b)** (*harceler*) *débiteur, entrepreneur* to hound; *[faim]* to gnaw at. **(c)** (*frapper du talon*) *[cheval]* to kick, dig one's heels into, spur on. (*Rugby*) **~ (le ballon)** to heel (the ball).

talonnette [talɔnɛt] *nf [chaussures, pantalon]* heelpiece.

talonneur [talɔnœʀ] *nm* (*Rugby*) hooker.

talquer [talke] (1) *vt* to put talcum powder *ou* talc on.

talqueux, -euse [talkø, øz] *adj* talcose.

talus [taly] **1** *nm* **(a)** *[route, voie ferrée]* embankment; *[terrassement]* bank, embankment.

(b) (*Mil*) talus.

2: (*Géol*) **talus continental** continental slope; **talus de déblai** excavation slope; (*Géol*) **talus d'éboulis** scree; **talus de remblai** embankment slope.

talweg [talvɛg] *nm* = **thalweg.**

tamanoir [tamanwaʀ] *nm* ant bear.

tamarin [tamaʀɛ̃] *nm* **(a)** (*Zool*) tamarin. **(b)** (*fruit*) tamarind (fruit). **(c)** = **tamarinier. (d)** = **tamaris.**

tamarinier [tamaʀinje] *nm* tamarind (*tree*).

tamaris [tamaʀis] *nm* tamarisk.

tambouille* [tɑ̃buj] *nf* (*péj: nourriture, cuisine*) grub*. **faire la ~** to cook the grub*; **une bonne ~** some lovely grub*.

tambour [tɑ̃buʀ] **1** *nm* **(a)** (*instrument de musique*) drum; *V* **roulement.**

(b) (*musicien*) drummer.

(c) (*à broder*) embroidery hoop, tambour.

(d) (*porte*) (*sas*) tambour; (*à tourniquet*) revolving door(s).

(e) (*cylindre*) *[machine à laver, treuil, roue de loterie]* drum; *[moulinet]* spool; *[montre]* barrel; *V* **frein.**

(f) (*Archit*) *[colonne, coupole]* drum.

(g) (*loc*) **~ battant** briskly; **sans ~ ni trompette** without any fuss.

2: tambour de basque tambourine; **tambour d'église** tambour; **tambour de frein** brake drum; **tambour-major** *nm, pl* **tambours-majors** drum major; **tambour plat** side drum; **tambour de ville** ≃ town crier.

tambourin [tɑ̃buʀɛ̃] *nm* (*tambour de basque*) tambourine; (*tambour haut et étroit*) tambourin.

tambourinage [tɑ̃buʀinaʒ] *nm* drumming.

tambourinaire [tɑ̃buʀinɛʀ] *nm* (*rare: joueur de tambourin*) tambourin player.

tambourinement [tɑ̃buʀinmɑ̃] *nm* drumming (*U*).

tambouriner [tɑ̃buʀine] (1) **1** *vi* (*avec les doigts*) to drum. **~ contre** *ou* **à/sur** to drum (one's fingers) against *ou* at/on; (*fig*) **la pluie tambourinait sur le toit** the rain was beating down *ou* drumming on the roof.

2 *vt* **(a)** (*jouer*) *marche* to drum *ou* beat out.

(b) (†: *annoncer*) *nouvelle, décret* to cry (out). (*fig*) **~ une nouvelle** to blaze a piece of news abroad.

tamil [tamil] = **tamoul.**

tamis [tami] *nm* (*gén*) sieve; (*à sable*) riddle, sifter. **passer au ~** (*lit*) to sieve, sift; (*fig*) *campagne, bois* to comb, search, scour; *personnes* to check out thoroughly; *dossier* to sift *ou* search through.

tamisage [tamizaʒ] *nm* (*V* **tamiser**) sieving; sifting; riddling; filtering.

Tamise [tamiz] *nf*: **la ~** the Thames.

tamisé, e [tamize] (*ptp de* **tamiser**) *adj lumière* (*artificielle*) subdued; (*du jour*) soft, softened.

tamiser [tamize] (1) *vt farine, plâtre* to sieve, sift; *sable* to riddle, sift; (*fig*) *lumière* to filter.

tamoul [tamul] *adj, nm* Tamil.

tampon [tɑ̃pɔ̃] **1** *nm* **(a)** (*pour boucher*) (*gén*) stopper, plug; (*en bois*) plug, bung; (*en coton*) wad, plug; (*pour hémorragie, règles*) tampon; (*pour nettoyer une plaie*) swab; (*pour étendre un liquide*) pad. **rouler qch en ~** to roll sth (up) into a ball; *V* **vernir.**

(b) (*Menuiserie: cheville*) (wall-)plug.

(c) (*timbre*) (*instrument*) (rubber) stamp; (*cachet*) stamp. **le ~ de la poste** the postmark; **apposer** *ou* **mettre un ~ sur qch** to stamp sth, put a stamp on sth.

(d) (*Rail, fig: amortisseur*) buffer. **servir de ~ entre deux personnes** to act as a buffer between two people.

2 *adj inv*: **état/zone ~** buffer state/zone.

3: tampon buvard blotter; **tampon encreur** inking-pad; **tampon à nettoyer** cleaning pad; **tampon à récurer** scouring pad, scourer.

tamponnement [tɑ̃pɔnmɑ̃] *nm* **(a)** (*collision*) collision, crash. **(b)** (*Méd*) *[plaie]* tamponade, tamponage. **(c)** (*Tech*) *[mur]* plugging.

tamponner [tɑ̃pɔne] (1) **1** *vt* **(a)** (*essuyer*) *plaie* to mop up, dab; *yeux* to dab (at); *front* to mop, dab; *surface à sécher, vernir etc* to mop, dab.

(b) (*heurter: Rail*) to run *ou* ram into; (*entrer en collision avec*) *train, véhicule* to ram, ram *ou* crash into. **se ~** to crash into each other, ram each other.

(c) (*avec un timbre*) *document, lettre* to stamp.

(d) (*Tech: percer*) *mur* to plug, put (wall-)plugs in.

2 se tamponner‡ *vpr*: **s'en ~** not to give a damn‡; **se ~ de qch** not to give a damn about sth‡.

tamponneuse [tɑ̃pɔnøz] *adj f V* **auto.**
tam-tam, *pl* **tam-tams** [tamtam] *nm* **(a)** (*tambour*) tomtom. **(b)** (*fig: battage, tapage*) fuss. **faire du ~ autour de*** *affaire, événement* to make a lot of fuss *ou* a great ballyhoo* about.
tan [tɑ̃] *nm* tan (*for tanning*).
tancer [tɑ̃se] (3) *vt* (*littér*) to berate (*littér*), rebuke (*littér, frm*).
tanche [tɑ̃ʃ] *nf* tench.
tandem [tɑ̃dɛm] *nm* (*bicyclette*) tandem; (*fig: duo*) pair, duo.
tandis [tɑ̃di] *conj*: **~ que** (*simultanéité*) while, whilst (*frm*); (*marque le contraste, l'opposition*) whereas, while, whilst (*frm*).
tangage [tɑ̃gaʒ] *nm* (*V* **tanguer**) pitching (and tossing); reeling. (*Naut*) **il y a du ~** she's pitching.
tangence [tɑ̃ʒɑ̃s] *nf* tangency.
tangent, e [tɑ̃ʒɑ̃, ɑ̃t] **1** *adj* **(a)** (*Géom*) tangent, tangential. **~ à** tangent *ou* tangential to.
(b) (*: *serré, de justesse*) close, touch-and-go* (*attrib*). **on est passé de justesse mais c'était ~** we just made it but it was a near *ou* close thing *ou* it was touch-and-go*; **il était ~** he was a borderline case.
2 tangente *nf* (*Géom*) tangent. (*fig*) **prendre la ~e*** (*partir*) to make off*; (*éluder*) to dodge the issue, wriggle out*.
tangentiel, -ielle [tɑ̃ʒɑ̃sjɛl] *adj* tangential.
tangentiellement [tɑ̃ʒɑ̃sjɛlmɑ̃] *adv* tangentially.
Tanger [tɑ̃ʒe] *n* Tangier(s).
tangible [tɑ̃ʒibl(ə)] *adj* tangible.
tangiblement [tɑ̃ʒibləmɑ̃] *adv* tangibly.
tanguer [tɑ̃ge] (1) *vi* **(a)** *[navire, avion]* to pitch. **(b)** (*ballotter*) to pitch and toss, reel. **tout tanguait autour de lui** everything around him was reeling.
tanière [tanjɛʀ] *nf* *[animal]* den, lair; (*fig*) *[malfaiteur]* lair; *[poète, solitaire etc]* (*pièce*) den; (*maison*) hideaway, retreat.
tanin [tanɛ̃] *nm* tannin.
tank [tɑ̃k] *nm* (*char d'assaut, fig: voiture*) tank.
tanker [tɑ̃kɛʀ] *nm* tanker.
tannage [tanaʒ] *nm* tanning.
tannant, e [tanɑ̃, ɑ̃t] *adj* **(a)** (*: *ennuyeux*) maddening*, sickening*. **il est ~ avec ses remarques idiotes** he's maddening* *ou* he drives you mad* with his stupid remarks. **(b)** (*Tech*) tanning.
tanner [tane] (1) *vt* **(a)** *cuir* to tan; *visage* to weather. **visage tanné** weather-beaten face; **~ le cuir à qn**‡ to give sb a belting‡, tan sb's hide*.
(b) ~ qn* (*harceler*) to badger* *ou* pester sb; (*ennuyer*) to drive sb mad*, drive sb up the wall*.
tannerie [tanʀi] *nf* (*endroit*) tannery; (*activité*) tanning.
tanneur [tanœʀ] *nm* tanner.
tannin [tanɛ̃] *nm* = **tanin.**
tant [tɑ̃] *adv* **(a)** (*intensité: avec vb*) so much. **il mange ~!** he eats so much! *ou* such a lot!; **il l'aime ~!** he loves her so much!; **j'ai ~ marché que je suis épuisé** I've walked so much that I'm exhausted; (*littér*) **je n'aime rien ~ que l'odeur des sous-bois** there is nothing I love more than the scent of the undergrowth; **vous m'en direz ~!** is that really so!
(b) (*quantité*) **~ de** *temps, eau, argent* so much; *livres, arbres, gens* so many; *habileté, mauvaise foi* such, so much; **il y avait ~ de brouillard qu'il n'est pas parti** it was so foggy *ou* there was so much fog about that he did not go; **~ de fois** so many times, so often; **des gens comme il y en a ~** people of the kind you come across so often; **~ de précautions semblaient suspectes** so many precautions seemed suspicious; **fait avec ~ d'habileté** done with so much *ou* such skill; **elle a ~ de sensibilité** she has such sensitivity.
(c) (*avec adj, participe*) so. **il est rentré ~ le ciel était menaçant** he went home (because) the sky looked so overcast, the sky looked so overcast that he went home; **cet enfant ~ désiré** this child they had longed for so much; **~ il est vrai que ...** which only goes to show *ou* prove that ... ; **le jour ~ attendu arriva** the long-awaited day arrived.
(d) (*quantité imprécise*) so much. **gagner ~ par mois** to earn so much a month, earn such-and-such an amount a month; **il devrait donner ~ à l'un, ~ à l'autre** he should give so much to one, so much to the other; **~ pour cent** so many per cent.
(e) (*comparaison*) **ce n'est pas ~ leur maison qui me plaît que leur jardin** it's not so much their house that I like as their garden; **il criait ~ qu'il pouvait** he shouted as much as he could; **les enfants, ~ filles que garçons** the children, both girls and boys *ou* girls as well as boys *ou* (both) girls and boys alike; **ses œuvres ~ politiques que lyriques** his political as well as his poetic works, both his political and his poetic works.
(f) ~ que (*aussi longtemps que*) as long as; (*pendant que*) while; **~ qu'elle aura de la fièvre elle restera au lit** while *ou* as long as she has a temperature she'll stay in bed; **~ que tu n'auras pas fini tes devoirs tu resteras à la maison** until you've finished your homework you'll have to stay indoors; **~ que vous y êtes*, achetez les deux volumes** while you are about it *ou* at it, buy both volumes; **~ que vous êtes ici*, donnez-moi un coup de main** since *ou* seeing you are here, give me a hand.
(g) (*loc*) **(tout va bien) ~ qu'on la santé!** (you're all right) as long as you've got your health!; **~ bien que mal** *aller, marcher* so-so, as well as can be expected (*hum*); *réussir, s'efforcer* after a fashion, in a manner of speaking; **~ soit peu: il est un ~ soit peu prétentieux** he is ever so slightly *ou* he's a little bit pretentious; **s'il est ~ soit peu intelligent il saura s'en tirer** if he is (even) remotely intelligent *ou* if he has the slightest grain of intelligence he'll be able to get out of it; **si vous craignez ~ soit peu le froid, restez chez vous** if you feel the cold at all *ou* the slightest bit, stay at home; **~ mieux** (*à la bonne heure*) (that's) good *ou* fine *ou* great*; (*avec une certaine réserve*) so much the better, that's fine; **~ mieux pour lui** good for him; **~ pis** (*conciliant: ça ne fait rien*) never mind, (that's) too bad; (*peu importe, qu'à cela ne tienne*) (that's just) too bad; **~ pis pour lui** (that's just) too bad for him; **~ et si bien que** to such an extent that; **il a fait ~ et si bien qu'elle l'a quitté** he finally succeeded in making her leave him; **il y en a ~ et plus** (*eau, argent*) there is ever so much; (*objets, personnes*) there are ever so many; **il a protesté ~ et plus mais sans résultat** he protested for all he was worth *ou* over and over again but to no avail; **~ qu'à faire** might *ou* may as well; **~ qu'à faire, on va payer maintenant** we might *ou* may as well pay now; **~ qu'à faire, je préfère payer tout de suite** (since I have to pay) I might *ou* may as well pay straight away; **~ qu'à faire, faites-le bien** if you're going to do it, do it properly; **~ qu'à marcher, allons en forêt** if we have to walk *ou* if we ARE walking, let's go to the forest; **~ que ça?*** as much as that?; **pas ~ que ça*** not that much*; **tu la paies ~ que ça?*** do you pay her that much?* *ou* as much as that?; **je ne l'ai pas vu ~ que ça pendant les vacances*** I didn't see him (all) that much* during the holidays; **~ qu'à moi/lui/eux*** as for me/him/them; **~ s'en faut** not by a long way, far from it, not by a long chalk* (*Brit*) *ou* shot; **~ s'en faut qu'il ait l'intelligence de son frère** he's not nearly as *ou* nowhere near as *ou* nothing like as intelligent as his brother, he's not as intelligent as his brother – not by a long way *ou* chalk* (*Brit*) *ou* shot; (*Prov*) **~ va la cruche à l'eau qu'à la fin elle se casse** if you keep playing with fire you must expect to get burnt; *V* **en**[1], **si**[1], **tout.**
tantale [tɑ̃tal] *nm* **(a)** (*Myth*) **T~** Tantalus; *V* **supplice. (b)** (*Chim*) tantalum.
tante [tɑ̃t] *nf* (*parente*) aunt, aunty*; (‡: *homosexuel*) poof‡ (*Brit*), fairy‡, nancy-boy‡. **la ~ Jeanne** Aunt *ou* Aunty* Jean; (*mont de piété*) **ma ~*** uncle's‡, the pawnshop.
tantième [tɑ̃tjɛm] **1** *nm* percentage. **2** *adj*: **la ~ partie de qch** such (and such) a proportion of sth.
tantine [tɑ̃tin] *nf* (*langage enfantin*) aunty*.
tantinet [tɑ̃tinɛ] *adv*: **un ~ fatigant/ridicule** a tiny *ou* weeny* bit tiring/ridiculous.
tantôt [tɑ̃to] *adv* **(a)** (*cet après-midi*) this afternoon; (††: *tout à l'heure*) shortly. **mardi ~†*** on Tuesday afternoon. **(b)** (*parfois*) **~ à pied, ~ en voiture** sometimes on foot, sometimes by car; (*littér*) **~ riant, ~ pleurant** now laughing, now crying.
Tanzanie [tɑ̃zani] *nf* Tanzania.
taon [tɑ̃] *nm* horsefly, gadfly.
tapage [tapaʒ] **1** *nm* **(a)** (*vacarme*) din*, uproar, row*. **faire du ~** to create a din* *ou* an uproar, kick up *ou* make a row*.
(b) (*battage*) fuss, talk. **ils ont fait un tel ~ autour de cette affaire que ...** there was so much fuss made about *ou* so much talk over this affair that ... .
2: (*Jur*) **tapage nocturne** disturbance of the peace (*at night*).
tapageur, -euse [tapaʒœʀ, øz] *adj* **(a)** (*bruyant*) *enfant, hôtes* noisy, rowdy. **(b)** (*peu discret, voyant*) *publicité* obtrusive; *élégance, toilette* flashy, loud, showy.
tapant, e [tapɑ̃, ɑ̃t] *adj*: **à 8 heures ~(es)** at 8 (o'clock) sharp, on the stroke of 8, at 8 o'clock on the dot*.
tape [tap] *nf* (*coup*) slap.
tape- [tap] *préf V* **taper.**
tapé, e [tape] (*ptp de* **taper**) *adj* **(a)** *fruit* (*talé*) bruised; (*séché*) dried. **(b)** (*: *fou*) cracked*, bonkers‡ (*Brit*).
tapecul‡, tape-cul‡, *pl* **tape-culs** [tapky] *nm* (*voiture*) boneshaker.
taper [tape] (1) **1** *vt* **(a)** (*battre*) *tapis* to beat; (*) *enfant* to slap, clout*; (*claquer*) *porte* to bang, slam. **~ le carton*** to play cards.
(b) (*frapper*) **~ un coup/deux coups à la porte** to knock once/twice at the door, give a knock/two knocks at the door; (*péj*) **~ un air sur le piano** to bang out a tune on the piano.
(c) ~ (à la machine) *lettre* to type (out); **apprendre à ~ à la machine** to learn (how) to type; **elle tape bien** she types well, she's a good typist; **tapé à la machine** typed, typewritten.
(d) (‡: *emprunter à, solliciter*) **~ qn (de 10 F)** to touch sb* (for 10 francs), cadge (10 francs) off sb*.
2 *vi* **(a)** (*frapper, cogner*) **~ sur: ~ sur un clou** to hit a nail; **~ sur la table** to bang *ou* rap on the table; (*péj*) **~ sur un piano** to bang away at a piano; **~ sur qn*** to thump sb*; **~ sur la gueule de qn‡** to belt sb‡; (*fig*) **~ sur le ventre de** *ou* **à* qn** to be over-familiar with sb; **~ à: ~ à la porte/au mur** to knock on the door/wall; **il tapait comme un sourd** he was thumping away for all he was worth; **il tape (dur), le salaud‡** the swine's‡ hitting hard; **~ dans: ~ dans un ballon** to kick a ball about *ou* around.
(b) (*: *dire du mal de*) **~ sur qn** to run sb down*, have a go at sb* (behind his back).
(c) (*: *entamer*) **~ dans** *provisions, caisse* to dig into*.
(d) (*être fort, intense*) *[soleil]* to beat down; (*) *[vin]* to go to one's head.
(e) (‡: *sentir mauvais*) to stink*, pong*.
(f) (*loc*) **~ des pieds** to stamp one's feet; **~ des mains** to clap one's hands; (*fig*) **se faire ~ sur les doigts*** to be rapped over the knuckles; **il a tapé à côté*** he was wide of the mark; **~ sur les nerfs** *ou* **le système de qn*** to get on sb's nerves* *ou* wick‡; **~ dans l'œil de qn*** to take sb's fancy*; **~ dans le tas** (*bagarre*) to pitch into the crowd; (*repas*) to pitch in*, dig in*; *V* **mille**[1].
3 se taper *vpr* **(a)** (‡: *s'envoyer*) **se ~** *femme* to lay‡; *repas* to put away*; *corvée* to do; **on s'est tapé les 10 km à pied** we slogged it on foot for the (whole) 10 km*, we footed the whole 10 km.
(b) (*loc*) **se ~ (sur) les cuisses de contentement*** to slap one's thighs with satisfaction; **il y a de quoi se ~ le derrière*** *ou* **le cul‡ par terre** it's darned* *ou* bloody‡ (*Brit*) ridiculous; **c'est à se ~ la tête contre les murs** it's enough to drive you up the wall*; **se ~ la cloche*** to feed one's face*, have a blow-out‡; **il peut toujours se ~‡** he knows what he can do‡.
4: (*péj*) **tape-à-l'œil** *adj inv* *décoration, élégance* flashy, showy; **c'est du tape-à-l'œil** it's all show *ou* flash* (*Brit*).

tapette [tapɛt] *nf* **(a)** (*pour tapis*) carpet beater; (*pour mouches*) flyswatter. **(b)** (†*: *langue*) **elle a une (bonne) ~** *ou* **une de ces ~s** she's a real chatterbox*. **(c)** (‡: *homosexuel*) poof‡ (*Brit*), queer‡, fairy‡, nancy-boy‡.

tapeur, -euse* [tapœʀ, øz] *nm,f* (*emprunteur*) cadger*.

tapin‡ [tapɛ̃] *nm*: **faire le ~** to walk the streets (*for prostitution*).

tapinois [tapinwa] *nm*: **en ~** *s'approcher* furtively; *agir* on the sly.

tapioca [tapjɔka] *nm* tapioca.

tapir [tapiʀ] *nm* (*Zool*) tapir.

tapir (se) [tapiʀ] (2) *vpr* (*se blottir*) to crouch; (*se cacher*) to hide away; (*s'embusquer*) to lurk. **maison tapie au fond de la vallée** house hidden away at the bottom of the valley; **ce mal tapi en lui depuis des années** this sickness that for years had lurked within him.

tapis [tapi] **1** *nm* **(a)** *[sol]* (*gén*) carpet; (*petit*) rug; (*natte*) mat. **un carré de ~** a carpet square, a square of carpet(ing); *V* **marchand.**

(b) *[meuble, table]* cloth; *[table de jeu]* baize (*U*), cloth, covering. **le ~ vert des tables de conférence** the green baize *ou* covering of the conference tables.

(c) (*fig*) **~ de verdure/de neige** carpet of greenery/snow.

(d) (*loc*) **aller au ~** to go down for the count; (*lit, fig*) **envoyer qn au ~** to floor sb; **mettre** *ou* **porter sur le ~** *affaire, question* to lay on the table, bring up for discussion; **être/revenir sur le ~** to come up/come back up for discussion; *V* **amuser.**

2: **tapis de billard** billiard cloth; **tapis-brosse** *nm, pl* **tapis-brosses** doormat; **tapis de chœur** altar carpet; **tapis de couloir** runner; **tapis de haute laine** long-pile carpet; **tapis d'Orient** oriental carpet; **tapis persan** Persian carpet; **tapis de prière** prayer mat; **tapis ras** short-pile carpet; **tapis roulant** (*pour colis etc*) conveyor belt; (*pour piétons*) moving walkway, travelator; **tapis de sol** groundsheet; **tapis de table** table cover; **tapis volant** flying carpet.

tapissé, e [tapise] (*ptp de* **tapisser**) *adj*: **~ de**: **sol ~ de neige/mousse** ground carpeted with snow/moss; **mur ~ de photos/d'affiches** wall covered *ou* plastered with photos/posters; **~ de lierre/de mousse** ivy-/moss-clad; **~ de neige** snow-clad, covered in snow; **voiture ~e de cuir** car with leather trim *ou* upholstery.

tapisser [tapise] (1) *vt* **(a)** *[personne]* **~ (de papier peint)** to (wall)paper; **~ un mur/une pièce de tentures** to hang a wall/room with drapes, cover a wall/room with hangings; **~ un mur d'affiches/de photos** to plaster *ou* cover a wall with posters/photos.

(b) *[tenture, papier]* to cover, line; *[mousse, neige, lierre]* to carpet, cover; (*Anat, Bot*) *[membranes, tissus]* to line. **le lierre tapissait le mur** the wall was covered with ivy.

tapisserie [tapisʀi] *nf* **(a)** (*tenture*) tapestry; (*papier peint*) wallpaper; (*activité*) tapestry-making. **faire ~** *[subalterne]* to stand on the sidelines; *[danseur, danseuse]* to be a wallflower, sit out; **j'ai dû faire ~ pendant que mon mari dansait** I had to sit out *ou* I was a wallflower while my husband was dancing.

(b) (*broderie*) tapestry; (*activité*) tapestrywork. **fauteuil recouvert de ~** armchair upholstered with tapestry; **pantoufles en ~** embroidered slippers; *V* **point**².

tapissier, -ière [tapisje, jɛʀ] *nm,f* (*fabricant*) tapestry-maker; (*commerçant*) upholsterer; (*décorateur*) interior decorator.

tapon† [tapɔ̃] *nm*: **en ~** in a ball; **mettre en ~** to roll (up) into a ball.

tapotement [tapɔtmɑ̃] *nm* (*sur la table*) tapping (*U*); (*sur le piano*) plonking (*U*).

tapoter [tapɔte] (1) **1** *vt joue* to pat; *baromètre* to tap. **~ sa cigarette pour faire tomber la cendre** to flick (the ash off) one's cigarette; (*péj*) **~ une valse au piano** to plonk *ou* thump out a waltz at *ou* on the piano. **2** *vi*: **~ sur** *ou* **contre** to tap on.

taquet [takɛ] *nm* (*coin, cale*) wedge; (*cheville, butée*) peg; (*pour enrouler un cordage*) cleat.

taquin, e [takɛ̃, in] *adj caractère, personne* teasing (*épith*). **c'est un ~** he's a tease *ou* a teaser.

taquiner [takine] (1) *vt [personne]* to tease; *[fait, douleur]* to bother, worry. (*hum*) **~ le goujon** to do a bit of fishing; (*hum*) **~ la muse** to dabble in poetry, court the Muse (*hum*).

taquinerie [takinʀi] *nf* teasing (*U*). **agacé par ses ~s** annoyed by his teasing.

tarabiscoté, e [taʀabiskɔte] *adj meuble, style* (over-)ornate, fussy.

tarabuster [taʀabyste] (1) *vt [personne]* to badger, pester, chivvy; *[fait, idée]* to bother, worry.

taratata [taʀatata] *excl* (stuff and) nonsense!, rubbish!

taraud [taʀo] *nm* tap.

taraudage [taʀodaʒ] *nm* tapping. **~ à la machine/à la main** machine-/hand-tapping.

tarauder [taʀode] (1) *vt* (*Tech*) *plaque, écrou* to tap; *vis, boulon* to thread; (*fig*) *[insecte]* to bore into; *[remords, angoisse]* to pierce.

taraudeur, -euse [taʀodœʀ, øz] **1** *nm,f* (*ouvrier*) tapper. **2 taraudeuse** *nf* (*machine*) tapping-machine; (*à fileter*) threader.

tard [taʀ] **1** *adv* (*dans la journée, dans la saison*) late. **plus ~** later (on); **il est ~** it's late; **il se fait ~** it's getting late; **se coucher/travailler ~** to go to bed/work late; **travailler ~ dans la nuit** to work late (on) into the night; **il vint nous voir ~ dans la matinée/journée** he came to see us late in the morning *ou* in the late morning/late in the day; **il vous faut arriver jeudi au plus ~** you must come on Thursday at the latest; **pas plus ~ qu'hier** only yesterday; **remettre qch à plus ~** to put sth off till later (on); **il a attendu trop ~ pour s'inscrire** he left it too late to put his name down.

2 *nm*: **sur le ~** (*dans la vie*) late (on) in life, late in the day (*fig*); (*dans la journée*) late in the day; *V* **jamais, mieux, tôt.**

tarder [taʀde] (1) **1** *vi* **(a)** (*différer, traîner*) **~ à entreprendre qch** to put off *ou* delay starting sth; **ne tardez pas (à le faire)** don't be long doing it *ou* getting down to it; **~ en chemin** to loiter *ou* dawdle on the way; **sans (plus) ~** without (further) delay; **pourquoi tant ~?** why put it off so long?, why be so long about it?

(b) (*se faire attendre*) *[réaction, moment]* to be a long time coming; *[lettre]* to take a long time (coming), be a long time coming. **l'été tarde (à venir)** summer is a long time coming; **ce moment tant espéré avait tant tardé** this much hoped-for moment had taken so long to come *ou* had been so long (in) coming.

(c) (*loc nég*) **ne pas ~** (*se manifester promptement*): **ça ne va pas ~** it won't be long (coming); **ça n'a pas tardé** it wasn't long (in) coming; **leur réaction ne va pas ~** their reaction won't be long (in) coming; **il est 2 heures: ils ne vont pas ~** it's 2 o'clock – they won't be long (now); **ils n'ont pas tardé à être endettés** before long they were in debt, it wasn't long before they were in debt; **il n'a pas tardé à s'en apercevoir** it didn't take him long to notice, he noticed soon enough; **ils n'ont pas tardé à réagir, leur réaction n'a pas tardé** they weren't long (in) reacting, their reaction came soon enough.

(d) (*sembler long*) **le temps** *ou* **le moment me tarde d'être en vacances** I'm longing to be on holiday, I can't wait to be on holiday.

2 *vb impers* (*littér*) **il me tarde de le revoir/que ces travaux soient finis** I am longing *ou* I cannot wait to see him again/for this work to be finished.

tardif, -ive [taʀdif, iv] *adj apparition, maturité, rentrée, repas* late; *regrets, remords* belated, tardy (*frm*); *fruits* late.

tardivement [taʀdivmɑ̃] *adv* (*à une heure tardive*) *rentrer* late; (*après coup, trop tard*) *s'apercevoir de qch* belatedly, tardily (*frm*).

tare [taʀ] *nf* **(a)** (*contrepoids*) tare. **faire la ~** to allow for the tare.

(b) (*défaut*) *[personne, marchandise]* defect (*de* in, of); *[société, système]* flaw (*de* in), defect (*de* of). **c'est une ~ de ne pas avoir fait de maths** it's a weakness not to have done any maths.

taré, e [taʀe] **1** *adj régime, politicien* tainted, corrupt; *enfant, animal* with a defect. (*péj*) **il faut être ~ pour faire cela*** you have to be sick to do that*.

2 *nm,f* (*Méd*) degenerate. (*péj*) **regardez-moi ce ~*** look at that cretin*.

tarentelle [taʀɑ̃tɛl] *nf* tarantella.

tarentule [taʀɑ̃tyl] *nf* tarantula.

tarer [taʀe] (1) *vt* (*Comm*) to tare, allow for the tare.

targette [taʀʒɛt] *nf* bolt (*on a door*).

targuer (se) [taʀge] (1) *vpr* (*se vanter*) **se ~ de qch** to boast about sth, pride *ou* preen o.s. on sth; **se ~ de ce que ...** to boast that ... ; **se ~ d'avoir fait qch** to pride o.s. on having done sth; **se targuant d'y parvenir aisément ...** boasting (that) he would easily manage it ... .

tarière [taʀjɛʀ] *nf* **(a)** (*Tech*) (*pour le bois*) auger; (*pour le sol*) drill. **(b)** (*Zool*) drill, ovipositor (*T*).

tarif [taʀif] *nm* (*tableau*) price list, tariff (*Brit*); (*barème*) rate, rates (*pl*), tariff (*Brit*); (*prix*) rate. **consulter/afficher le ~ des consommations** to check/put up the price list for drinks *ou* the drinks tariff (*Brit*); **le ~ postal pour l'étranger/le ~ des taxis va augmenter** overseas postage rates/taxi fares are going up; **les ~s postaux/douaniers vont augmenter** postage/customs rates are going up; **payé au ~ syndical** paid according to union rates, paid the union rate *ou* on the union scale; **est-ce le ~ habituel?** is this the usual *ou* going rate?; **voyager à plein ~/à ~ réduit** to travel at full/reduced fare; (*hum*) **50 F d'amende/2 mois de prison, c'est le ~!*** a 50-franc fine/2 months' prison is what you get!

tarifaire [taʀifɛʀ] *adj* tariff (*épith*).

tarifer [taʀife] (1) *vt* to fix the price *ou* rate for. **marchandises tarifées** fixed-price goods.

tarin [taʀɛ̃] *nm* (‡: *nez*) conk‡; (*Orn*) siskin.

tarir [taʀiʀ] (2) **1** *vi* **(a)** *[cours d'eau, puits]* to run dry, dry up; *[larmes]* to dry (up); *[pitié, conversation]* to dry up; *[imagination, ressource]* to run dry, dry up.

(b) *[personne]* **il ne tarit pas sur ce sujet** he can't stop talking about that; **il ne tarit pas d'éloges sur elle** he never stops *ou* he can't stop praising her.

2 *vt* (*lit, fig*) to dry up. (*littér*) **~ les larmes de qn** to dry sb's tears.

3 se tarir *vpr [source, imagination]* to run dry, dry up.

tarissement [taʀismɑ̃] *nm* (*V* **tarir, se tarir**) drying up.

tarot [taʀo] *nm* (*paquet: aussi* **jeu de ~s**) tarot (pack); (*jeu*) tarot.

tarse [taʀs(ə)] *nm* (*Anat, Zool*) tarsus.

tarsien, -ienne [taʀsjɛ̃, jɛn] *adj* tarsal.

tartan [taʀtɑ̃] *nm* tartan.

tartane [taʀtan] *nf* tartan (*boat*).

tartare [taʀtaʀ] **1** *adj* **(a)** (*Hist*) Tartar. **(b)** (*Culin*) **sauce ~** tartar(e) sauce; **(steak) ~** steak tartare. **2** *nmf* (*Hist*) **T~** Tartar.

tartarin [taʀtaʀɛ̃] *nm* († *hum*) braggart†.

tarte [taʀt(ə)] **1** *nf* **(a)** (*Culin*) tart. **~ aux fruits/à la crème** fruit/cream tart; (*fig péj*) **~ à la crème** *comique, comédie* slapstick (*épith*), custard-pie (*épith*); **c'est pas de la ~‡** it's no joke*, it's no easy matter.

(b) (‡: *gifle*) clout*, clip round the ear*.

2 *adj inv* (*) daft*, stupid.

tartelette [taʀtəlɛt] *nf* tartlet, tart.

tartine [taʀtin] *nf* **(a)** (*beurrée*) slice of bread and butter; (*à la confiture*) slice of bread and jam; (*tranche prête à être tar-*

tinée) slice of bread. **le matin, on mange des ~s** in the morning we have bread and butter; **tu as déjà mangé 3 ~s, ça suffit** you've already had 3 slices, that's enough; **elle me beurra une ~** she buttered me a slice of bread; **couper des tranches de pain pour faire des ~s** to cut (slices of) bread for buttering; **~ au miel/à la confiture/au foie gras** slice *ou* piece of bread and honey/jam/liver pâté; **~ grillée et beurrée** piece of toast and butter; **as-tu du pain pour les ~s?** have you got any bread to slice?

(b) (**fig: lettre, article*) screed. **il en a mis une ~** he wrote reams *ou* a great screed*; **il y a une ~ dans la Gazette à propos de ...** there's a long screed in the Gazette about ... .

tartiner [taʀtine] (1) *vt pain* to spread (*de* with); *beurre* to spread. **foie gras/fromage à ~** liver/cheese spread; **~ du pain de beurre** to butter bread, spread bread with butter; *V* **fromage.**

tartre [taʀtʀ(ə)] *nm [dents]* tartar; *[chaudière, bouilloire]* fur; *[tonneau]* tartar.

tartrique [taʀtʀik] *adj*: **acide ~** tartaric acid.

tartu(f)fe [taʀtyf] *nm* (sanctimonious) hypocrite, tartuffe. **il est un peu ~** he's something of a hypocrite *ou* tartuffe.

tartu(f)ferie [taʀtyfʀi] *nf* hypocrisy.

tas [tɑ] **1** *nm* **(a)** (*amas*) pile, heap. **mettre en ~** to make a pile of, put into a heap, heap *ou* pile up.

(b) (*: *beaucoup de*) **un** *ou* **des ~ de** loads of*, heaps of*, lots of; **il connaît un ~ de choses/gens** he knows loads* *ou* heaps* *ou* lots of things/people; **il m'a raconté un ~ de mensonges** he told me a pack of lies; **~ de crétins*** you load of idiots!*

(c) (*loc*) **dans le ~** (*parmi eux*) in the crowd; (*dans la foule*) **tirer/taper dans le ~** to fire/pitch into the crowd; **foncer dans le ~** to charge in; **dans le ~, on en trouvera bien un qui sache conduire** you're bound to find one out of the whole crowd who can drive; **former qn sur le ~** to train sb on the job*; *V* **grève.**

2: (*Archit*) **tas de charge** tas de charge; **tas de fumier** dung *ou* manure heap.

Tasmanie [tasmani] *nf* Tasmania.

tasmanien, -ienne [tasmanjɛ̃, jɛn] **1** *adj* Tasmanian. **2** *nm,f*: **T~(ne)** Tasmanian.

tassage [tɑsaʒ] *nm* boxing in.

tasse [tɑs] *nf* cup. **~ de porcelaine** china cup; **~ à thé** teacup; **~ à café** coffee cup; **~ de thé** cup of tea; (*fig*) **boire une** *ou* **la ~*** to swallow *ou* get a mouthful (*when swimming*).

tassé, e [tɑse] (*ptp de* **tasser**) *adj* **(a)** (*affaissé*) *façade, mur* that has settled *ou* sunk; *vieillard* shrunken. **~ sur sa chaise** slumped on his chair. **(b)** (*serrés*) *spectateurs, passagers* packed (tight). **(c) bien ~*** (*corsé, fort*) *whisky* stiff (*épith*); *café* good strong (*épith*), good and strong (*attrib*); (*bien rempli*) *demi, ballon* well-filled, full to the brim (*attrib*).

tasseau, *pl* **~x** [tɑso] *nm* stake, stake anvil; (*support*) bracket.

tassement [tɑsmɑ̃] *nm* **(a)** *[sol, neige]* packing down. **(b)** *[mur, terrain]* settling. (*Méd*) **~ de la colonne (vertébrale)** compression of the spinal column.

tasser [tɑse] (1) **1** *vt* **(a)** (*comprimer*) *sol, neige* to pack down; *foin, paille* to pack. **~ le contenu d'une valise** to push *ou* ram down the contents of a case; **~ le tabac dans sa pipe** to pack down the tobacco in one's pipe; **~ les passagers dans un véhicule** to cram *ou* pack the passengers into a vehicle.

(b) (*Sport*) *concurrent* to box in.

2 se tasser *vpr* **(a)** (*s'affaisser*) *[façade, mur, terrain]* to settle, sink; (*fig*) *[vieillard, corps]* to shrink.

(b) (*se serrer*) to bunch up. **on s'est tassé à 10 dans la voiture** 10 of us crammed into the car; **tassez-vous, il y a encore de la place** bunch *ou* squeeze up, there's still room.

(c) (*: *s'arranger*) to settle down. **ne vous en faites pas, ça va se ~** don't worry — things will settle down *ou* iron themselves out*.

(d) (‡: *engloutir*) *petits fours, boissons* to down*, get through*.

taste-vin [tastəvɛ̃] *nm inv* (wine-)tasting cup.

tata [tata] *nf* (*langage enfantin: tante*) auntie*; (‡: *pédéraste*) poof‡ (*Brit*), queer‡, fairy‡.

tâter [tɑte] (1) **1** *vt* **(a)** (*palper*) *objet, étoffe, pouls* to feel. **~ qch du bout des doigts** to feel sth with one's fingertips; **marcher en tâtant les murs** to feel *ou* grope one's way along the walls.

(b) (*sonder*) *adversaire, concurrent* to try (out). **~ l'opinion** to sound out opinion; (*fig*) **~ le terrain** to find out *ou* see how the land lies, test the ground.

2 *vi* **(a)** (†, *littér: goûter à*) **~ de** *mets* to taste, try.

(b) (*essayer, passer par*) to sample, try out. **~ de la prison** to sample prison life, have a taste of prison; **il a tâté de tous les métiers** he has had a go* at *ou* he has tried his hand at all possible jobs.

3 se tâter *vpr* **(a)** (*après une chute*) to feel o.s. (*for injuries*); (*pensant avoir perdu qch*) to feel one's pocket(s). **il se releva, se tâta: rien de cassé** he got up and felt himself but (he had) nothing broken.

(b) (*: *hésiter*) to be in (*Brit*) *ou* of (*US*) two minds. **viendras-tu? — je ne sais pas, je me tâte** are you coming? — I don't know, I'm in (*Brit*) *ou* of (*US*) two minds (about it) *ou* I haven't made up my mind (about it).

tâte-vin [tɑtvɛ̃] *nm inv* = **taste-vin.**

tatillon, -onne [tatijɔ̃, ɔn] *adj* finicky, pernickety. **il est ~, c'est un ~** he's very finicky *ou* pernickety.

tâtonnement [tɑtɔnmɑ̃] *nm* (*gén pl: essai*) trial and error (*U*), experimentation (*U*). **après bien des ~s** after a good deal of experimentation *ou* of trial and error; **procéder par ~(s)** to move forward by trial and error.

tâtonner [tɑtɔne] (1) *vi* **(a)** (*pour se diriger*) to grope *ou* feel one's way (along), grope along; (*pour trouver qch*) to grope *ou* feel around *ou* about. **(b)** (*fig*) to grope around; (*par méthode*) to proceed by trial and error.

tâtons [tɑtɔ̃] *adv*: **à ~**: (*lit, fig*) **avancer à ~** to grope along, grope *ou* feel one's way along; (*lit, fig*) **chercher qch à ~** to grope *ou* feel around for sth.

tatou [tatu] *nm* armadillo.

tatouage [tatwaʒ] *nm* (*action*) tattooing; (*dessin*) tattoo.

tatouer [tatwe] (1) *vt* to tattoo.

tatoueur [tatwœʀ] *nm* tattooer.

taudis [todi] *nm* (*logement*) hovel, slum; (*pl: Admin, gén*) slums.

taule‡ [tol] *nf* **(a)** (*prison*) nick‡ (*Brit*), clink‡. **il a fait de la ~** he's done time *ou* a stretch*, he has been inside*; **il a eu 5 ans de ~** he has been given a 5-year stretch* *ou* 5 years in the nick‡ (*Brit*) *ou* in clink‡. **(b)** (*chambre*) room.

taulier, -ière‡ [tolje, jɛʀ] *nm,f* (hotel) boss*.

taupe [top] *nf* **(a)** (*animal*) mole; (*fourrure*) moleskin. (*fig péj*) **une vieille ~** an old crone *ou* hag (*péj*), an old bag‡ (*péj*); (*fig*) **ils vivent comme des ~s dans leurs grands immeubles** they live closeted away *ou* completely shut up in their high-rise flats, they never get out to see the light of day from their high-rise flats; *V* **myope.**

(b) (*arg Scol: classe*) advanced maths class (*preparing for the Grandes Écoles*).

taupin [topɛ̃] *nm* **(a)** (*Zool*) click beetle, elaterida (*T*). **(b)** (*Scol*) maths student (*V* **taupe**).

taupinière [topinjɛʀ] *nf* (*tas*) molehill; (*galeries, terrier*) mole tunnel; (*fig péj: immeuble, bureaux*) rabbit warren.

taureau, *pl* **~x** [tɔʀo] *nm* (*Zool*) bull. (*Astron*) **le T~** Taurus, the Bull; **~ de combat** fighting bull; **il avait une force de ~** he was as strong as an ox; **une encolure** *ou* **un cou de ~** a bull neck; (*fig*) **prendre le ~ par les cornes** to take the bull by the horns; **être (du) T~** to be Taurus *ou* a Taurean; *V* **course.**

taurillon [tɔʀijɔ̃] *nm* bull-calf.

taurin, e [tɔʀɛ̃, in] *adj* bullfighting (*épith*).

tauromachie [tɔʀɔmaʃi] *nf* bullfighting.

tauromachique [tɔʀɔmaʃik] *adj* bullfighting (*épith*).

tautologie [totɔlɔʒi] *nf* tautology.

tautologique [totɔlɔʒik] *adj* tautological.

taux [to] *nm* **(a)** (*gén, Fin, Statistique*) rate. **~ d'intérêt** interest rate, rate of interest; **~ des salaires** wage rate; **~ de change** exchange rate, rate of exchange; **~ de mortalité** mortality rate.

(b) (*niveau, degré*) *[infirmité]* degree; *[cholestérol, sucre]* level.

tavelé, e [tavle] (*ptp de* **taveler**) *adj fruit* marked. **visage ~ de taches de son** face speckled with *ou* covered in freckles; **visage ~ par la petite vérole** pockmarked face, face pitted with pockmarks.

taveler [tavle] (4) **1** *vt fruit* to mark; *visage* to speckle. **2 se taveler** *vpr [fruit]* to become marked.

tavelure [tavlyʀ] *nf [fruit]* mark; *[peau]* mark, spot.

taverne [tavɛʀn(ə)] *nf* (*Hist, rare*) inn, tavern; (*Can*) tavern, beer parlor (*Can*).

tavernier, -ière [tavɛʀnje, jɛʀ] *nm,f* (*Hist, hum*) innkeeper.

taxable [taksabl(ə)] *adj* taxable.

taxateur [taksatœʀ] *nm* (*Admin*) taxer; (*Jur*) taxing master. **juge ~** taxing master.

taxation [taksɑsjɔ̃] *nf* (*V* **taxer**) taxing, taxation; fixing (the rate); fixing the price; assessment. **~ d'office** estimation of tax(es).

taxe [taks(ə)] **1** *nf* **(a)** (*impôt, redevance*) tax; (*à la douane*) duty. **~s locales/municipales** local/municipal taxes; **toutes ~s comprises** inclusive of tax; *V* **hors.**

(b) (*Admin, Comm: tarif*) statutory price. **vendre des marchandises à la ~/plus cher que la ~** to sell goods at/for more than the statutory price.

(c) (*Jur*) *[dépens]* taxation, assessment.

2: taxe de luxe tax on luxury goods; **taxe de séjour** tourist tax; **taxe à** *ou* **sur la valeur ajoutée** value added tax, VAT.

taxer [takse] (1) **(a)** (*imposer*) *marchandises, service* to put *ou* impose a tax on, tax.

(b) *particuliers* to tax. **~ qn d'office** to assess sb to tax *ou* taxation.

(c) (*Admin, Comm*) *valeur* to fix (the rate of); *marchandise* to fix the price of; (*Jur*) *dépens* to tax, assess.

(d) ~ qn de qch (*qualifier de*) to call sb sth; (*accuser de*) to tax sb with sth (*frm, littér*), accuse sb of sth; **une méthode que l'on a taxée de charlatanisme** a method to which the term charlatanism has been applied; **il m'a taxé d'imbécile** he called me an idiot.

taxi [taksi] *nm* **(a)** (*voiture*) taxi, (taxi)cab; *V* **avion, chauffeur, station. (b)** (*: *chauffeur*) cabby*, taxi driver.

taxidermie [taksidɛʀmi] *nf* taxidermy.

taximètre [taksimɛtʀ(ə)] *nm* (taxi)meter.

taxinomie [taksinɔmi] *nf* taxonomy.

taxiphone [taksifɔn] *nm* pay phone, public (tele)phone.

taxonomie [taksɔnɔmi] *nf* = **taxinomie.**

tchécoslovaque [tʃekɔslɔvak] *adj* Czechoslovak(ian).

Tchécoslovaquie [tʃekɔslɔvaki] *nf* Czechoslovakia.

tchèque [tʃɛk] **1** *adj* Czech. **2** *nm* (*Ling*) Czech. **3** *nmf*: **T~** Czech.

te [t(ə)] *pron* (*objet direct ou indirect*) you; (*réfléchi*) yourself. **~ l'a-t-il dit?** did he tell you?, did he tell you about it?; **t'en a-t-il parlé?** did he speak to you about it?

té [te] *nm* T-square.

technicien, -ienne [tɛknisjɛ̃, jɛn] *nm,f* technician. **~ de (la) télévision** television technician; **c'est un ~ de la politique/finance** he's a political/financial expert *ou* wizard*; **c'est un ~ du roman** he's a practitioner *ou* practician (*Brit*) of the novel.

technicité [tɛknisite] *nf* technical nature.

technique [tɛknik] 1 *nf* **(a)** (*méthode, procédés*) *[peintre, art]* technique. **des ~s nouvelles** new techniques; **manquer de ~** to lack technique; **il n'a pas la ~*** he hasn't got the knack* *ou* technique.
(b) (*aire de la connaissance*) **la ~** technique.
2 *adj* technical; *V* **escale, incident.**

techniquement [tɛknikmɑ̃] *adv* technically.
technocrate [tɛknɔkʀat] *nmf* technocrat.
technocratie [tɛknɔkʀasi] *nf* technocracy.
technocratique [tɛknɔkʀatik] *adj* technocratic.
technologie [tɛknɔlɔʒi] *nf* technology.
technologique [tɛknɔlɔʒik] *adj* technological.
technologue [tɛknɔlɔg] *nmf* technologist.
teck [tɛk] *nm* teak.
teckel [tekɛl] *nm* dachshund.
tectonique [tɛktɔnik] 1 *adj* tectonic. 2 *nf* tectonics (*sg*).
Te Deum [tedeɔm] *nm inv* Te Deum.
tégument [tegymɑ̃] *nm* (*Bot, Zool*) integument.
teigne [tɛɲ] *nf* **(a)** (*Zool*) moth, tinea (*T*). **(b)** (*Méd*) ringworm, tinea (*T*). **(c)** (*fig péj*) (*homme*) foul character; (*femme*) shrew (*péj*), vixen (*péj*). **méchant comme une ~** as nasty as anything.
teigneux, -euse [tɛɲø, øz] *adj* suffering from ringworm. **il est ~** (*lit*) he has *ou* is suffering from ringworm; (*péj: pouilleux*) he's scabby*; (*péj: acariâtre*) he's a foul character.
teindre [tɛ̃dʀ(ə)] (52) 1 *vt vêtement, cheveux* to dye. **les myrtilles teignent les mains (de violet)** bilberries stain your hands (purple).
2 **se teindre** *vpr* **(a) se ~ (les cheveux)** to dye one's hair; **se ~ la barbe/la moustache** to dye one's beard/moustache.
(b) (*littér: se colorer*) **les montagnes se teignaient de pourpre** the mountains took on a purple hue *ou* tinge *ou* tint (*littér*).
teint, e [tɛ̃, tɛ̃t] (*ptp de* **teindre**) 1 *adj cheveux, laine* dyed. (*péj*) **elle est ~e** her hair is dyed, she has dyed her hair.
2 *nm* (*permanent*) complexion, colouring; (*momentané*) colour. **avoir le ~ jaune** to have a sallow complexion *ou* colouring; **il revint de vacances le ~ frais** he came back from his holidays with a fresh *ou* good colour; *V* **bon[1], fond, grand.**
3 **teinte** *nf* (*nuance*) shade, hue (*littér*), tint; (*couleur*) colour; (*fig*) tinge, hint. **pull aux ~es vives** brightly-coloured sweater; (*fig*) **avec une ~e de tristesse dans la voix** with a tinge *ou* hint of sadness in his voice; *V* **demi-.**
teinté, e [tɛ̃te] (*ptp de* **teinter**) *adj bois* stained; *verre* tinted. **table ~e acajou** mahogany-stained table; (*fig*) **discours ~ de puritanisme** speech tinged with puritanism.
teinter [tɛ̃te] (1) 1 *vt papier, verre* to tint; *meuble, bois* to stain. **un peu d'eau teintée de vin** a little water with a hint of wine *ou* just coloured with wine.
2 **se teinter** *vpr* (*littér*) **se ~ d'amertume** to become tinged with bitterness; **les sommets se teintèrent de pourpre** the peaks took on a purple tinge *ou* hue (*littér*).
teinture [tɛ̃tyʀ] *nf* **(a)** (*colorant*) dye; (*action*) dyeing. (*fig*) **une ~ de maths/de français** a smattering of maths/French, a nodding acquaintance with maths/French. **(b)** (*Pharm*) tincture. **~ d'arnica/d'iode** tincture of arnica/iodine.
teinturerie [tɛ̃tyʀʀi] *nf* (*métier, industrie*) dyeing; (*magasin*) (dry) cleaner's.
teinturier, -ière [tɛ̃tyʀje, jɛʀ] *nm,f* (*qui nettoie*) dry cleaner; (*qui teint*) dyer.
tek [tɛk] *nm* = **teck.**
tel, telle [tɛl] 1 *adj* **(a)** (*similitude*) (*sg: avec n concret*) such, like; (*avec n abstrait*) such; (*pl*) such. **une telle ignorance/réponse est inexcusable** such ignorance/such an answer is unpardonable; **~ père, ~ fils** like father like son; **nous n'avons pas de ~s orages en Europe** we don't get such storms *ou* storms like this in Europe; **as-tu jamais rien vu de ~?** have you ever seen such a thing?, have you ever seen the like? *ou* anything like it?; **s'il n'est pas menteur, il passe pour ~** perhaps he isn't a liar but he is taken for one *ou* but they say he is; **il a filé ~ un zèbre** he ran off as quick as an arrow *ou* a shot; **~s sont ces gens que vous croyiez honnêtes** such are those whom you believed (to be) honest; (*frm*) **prenez telles décisions qui vous sembleront nécessaires** take such decisions as you find necessary; **il est le patron, en tant que ~** *ou* **comme ~ il aurait dû agir** he is the boss and as such he ought to have taken action; **~ il était enfant, ~ je le retrouve** thus he was as a child, and thus he has remained; (*littér*) **le lac ~ un miroir** the lake like a mirror *ou* mirror-like (*littér*); *V* **rien.**
(b) (*valeur d'indéfini*) such-and-such. **~ et ~** such-and-such; **venez ~ jour/à telle heure** come on such-and-such a day/at such-and-such a time; **telle quantité d'arsenic peut tuer un homme et pas un autre** a given quantity of arsenic can kill one man and not another; **telle ou telle personne vous dira que** someone *ou* somebody or other will tell you that; **j'ai lu dans ~ et ~ article que** I read in some article or other that; **l'homme en général et non ~ homme** man in general and not any one *ou* particular *ou* given man; **~ enfant qui se croit menacé devient agressif** any child that feels (himself) threatened will become aggressive; **l'on sait ~ bureau où** there's *ou* I know a certain office *ou* one office where.
(c) ~ que like, (such *ou* the same *ou* just) as; (*énumération*) like, such as; **il est resté ~ que je le connaissais** he is still the same *ou* just as he used to be; **un homme ~ que lui doit comprendre** a man like him *ou* such a man as he (*frm*) must understand; **~ que je le connais, il ne viendra pas** if I know him, he won't come; **~ que vous me voyez, je reviens d'Afrique** I'm just (this minute) back from Africa; **~ que vous me voyez, j'ai 72 ans** you wouldn't think it to look at me but I'm 72; **restez ~ que vous êtes** stay (just) as you are; **là il se montre ~ qu'il est** now he's showing himself in his true colours *ou* as he really is; **les métaux ~s que l'or, l'argent et le platine** metals like *ou* such as gold, silver and platinum; (*littér*) **le ciel à l'occident ~ qu'un brasier** the western sky like a fiery furnace (*littér*).
(d) ~ quel, ~ que*: il a acheté la maison telle quelle *ou* **telle que*** he bought the house (just) as it was *ou* stood; **laissez tous ces dossiers ~s quels** *ou* **~s que*** leave all those files as they are *ou* as you find them; **il m'a dit: 'sortez d'ici ou je vous sors' ~ que!*** he said to me 'get out of here or I'll throw you out' — just like that!
(e) (*intensif*) (*sg: avec n concret*) such a; (*avec n abstrait*) such; (*pl*) such. **on n'a jamais vu (une) telle cohue** you've never seen such a mob; **c'est une telle joie de l'entendre!** what joy *ou* it's such a joy to hear him!
(f) (*avec conséquence*) **de telle façon** *ou* **manière** in such a way; **ils ont eu de ~s ennuis avec leur voiture qu'ils l'ont vendue** they had such (a lot of) trouble with their car that they sold it; **de telle sorte que** so that; **à telle(s) enseigne(s) que** so much so that, the proof being that, indeed; *V* **point[1].**
2 *pron indéf*: **~ vous dira qu'il faut voter oui, ~ autre ...** one will tell you you must vote yes, another ...; (*Prov*) **~ qui rit vendredi, dimanche pleurera** up one day, down the next; **si ~ ou ~ vous dit que** if somebody (or other) *ou* if anybody tells you that; (*Prov*) **~ est pris qui croyait prendre** (it's) the biter bitten; *V* **un.**
télé* [tele] *nf* (*abrév de* **télévision**) TV*, telly* (*Brit*).
télébenne [telebɛn] *nf*, **télécabine** [telekabin] *nf* cable-car.
télécommande [telekɔmɑ̃d] *nf* remote control.
télécommander [telekɔmɑ̃de] (1) *vt* (*Tech*) to operate by remote control. (*fig*) **~ des menées subversives/un complot de l'étranger** to mastermind subversive activity/a plot from abroad.
télécommunication [telekɔmynikasjɔ̃] *nf* (*gén pl*) telecommunication.
téléenseignement [teleɑ̃sɛɲmɑ̃] *nm* television teaching, teaching by television.
téléférique [telefeʀik] *nm* (*installation*) cableway; (*cabine*) cable-car.
télégénique [teleʒenik] *adj* who comes over well on television.
télégramme [telegʀam] *nm* telegram, wire, cable.
télégraphe [telegʀaf] *nm* telegraph.
télégraphie [telegʀafi] *nf* (*technique*) telegraphy. **~ optique** signalling; **~ sans fil**† wireless telegraphy†.
télégraphier [telegʀafje] (7) *vt message* to telegraph, wire, cable. **tu devrais lui ~** you should send him a telegram *ou* wire *ou* cable, you should wire (to) him *ou* cable him.
télégraphique [telegʀafik] *adj* **(a)** *poteau, fils* telegraph (*épith*); *alphabet, code* Morse (*épith*); *message* telegram (*épith*), telegraphed, telegraphic. **adresse ~** telegraphic address. **(b)** (*fig*) *style, langage* telegraphic.
télégraphiste [telegʀafist(ə)] *nmf* (*technicien*) telegrapher, telegraphist; (*messager*) telegraph boy.
téléguidage [telegidaʒ] *nm* radio control.
téléguider [telegide] (1) *vt* (*Tech*) to radio-control; (*fig*) to control (from a distance).
téléimprimeur [teleɛ̃pʀimœʀ] *nm* teleprinter.
Télémaque [telemak] *nm* Telemachus.
télémètre [telemɛtʀ(ə)] *nm* (*Mil, Phot*) rangefinder.
téléobjectif [teleɔbʒɛktif] *nm* telephoto lens.
téléologie [teleɔlɔʒi] *nf* teleology.
télépathe [telepat] 1 *nmf* telepathist. 2 *adj* telepathic.
télépathie [telepati] *nf* telepathy.
télépathique [telepatik] *adj* telepathic.
téléphérage [telefeʀaʒ] *nm* transport by cableway.
téléphérique [telefeʀik] *nm* = **téléférique.**
téléphone [telefɔn] 1 *nm* (*système*) telephone; (*appareil*) (tele)phone. (*Admin*) **les T~s** ≃ Post Office Telecommunications (*Brit*); **avoir le ~** to be on the (tele)phone; **demande-le-lui au** *ou* **par ~, ce sera plus simple** phone him (and ask about it) — it will be simpler; *V* **abonné, numéro** *etc.*
2: **téléphone arabe** bush telegraph; **téléphone automatique** automatic telephone system; **téléphone de brousse = téléphone arabe; téléphone interne** internal telephone; **téléphone à manivelle** magneto telephone; **téléphone manuel** manually-operated telephone system; **téléphone public** public (tele)phone; (*Pol*) **téléphone rouge** hot line.
téléphoner [telefɔne] (1) 1 *vt message* to (tele)phone; (*fig*) *coups, manœuvre* to telegraph. **il m'a téléphoné la nouvelle** he phoned me the news; **téléphone-lui de venir** phone him and tell him to come; (*fig*) **leur manœuvre était téléphonée*** you could see their move coming a mile off*.
2 *vi*: **~ à qn** to telephone sb, phone *ou* ring *ou* call sb (up); **où est Jean? — il téléphone** where's John? — he's on the phone *ou* he's phoning *ou* he's making a call; **j'étais en train de ~ à Jean** I was on the phone to John, I was busy phoning John; **je téléphone beaucoup, je n'aime pas écrire** I phone people a lot *ou* I use the phone a lot as I don't like writing.
téléphonie [telefɔni] *nf* telephony. **~ sans fil** wireless telephony, radiotelephony.
téléphonique [telefɔnik] *adj liaison, ligne, réseau* telephone (*épith*), telephonic (*frm*). **conversation ~** (tele)phone conversation; *V* **appel, cabine, communication.**
téléphoniste [telefɔnist(ə)] *nmf [poste]* telephonist (*surtout Brit*), (telephone) operator; *[entreprise]* switchboard operator.
téléphotographie [telefɔtɔgʀafi] *nf* telephotography.
télescopage [telɛskɔpaʒ] *nm [véhicules]* concertinaing (*U*); *[trains]* telescoping, concertinaing (up).
télescope [telɛskɔp] *nm* telescope.
télescoper [telɛskɔpe] (1) 1 *vt véhicule* to smash up. 2 **se télescoper** *vpr [véhicules]* to concertina; *[trains]* to telescope, concertina.
télescopique [telɛskɔpik] *adj* (*gén*) telescopic.
téléscripteur [teleskʀiptœʀ] *nm* teleprinter.

télésiège [telesjɛʒ] *nm* chairlift.
téléski [teleski] *nm* ski tow. ~ **à fourche** T-bar tow.
téléspectateur, -trice [telespɛktatœʀ, tʀis] *nm,f* (television *ou* TV) viewer.
télétype [teletip] *nm* teleprinter.
téléviser [televize] (1) *vt* to televise; *V* **journal.**
téléviseur [televizœʀ] *nm* television (set).
télévision [televizjɔ̃] *nf* (*gén*) television; (*appareil*) television (set). **à la** ~ on television.
télex [telɛks] *nm* telex.
tellement [tɛlmɑ̃] *adv* **(a)** (*si*) (*avec adj ou adv*) so; (*avec comp*) so much. **il est ~ gentil** he's so (very) nice; ~ **mieux/plus fort/plus beau** so much better/stronger/more beautiful; **j'étais ~ fatigué que je me suis couché immédiatement** I was so (very) tired (that) I went straight to bed; (*nég, avec subj: littér*) **il n'est pas ~ pauvre qu'il ne puisse ...** he's not so (very) poor that he cannot... .
(b) (*tant*) so much. (*tant de*) ~ **de gens** so many people; ~ **de temps** so much time, so long; **il a ~ insisté que ...** he insisted so much that ..., he was so insistent that ...; **il travaille ~ qu'il se rend malade** he works so much *ou* hard (that) he is making himself ill; (*nég, avec subj: littér*) **il ne travaille pas ~ qu'il ait besoin de repos** he does not work to such an extent *ou* so very much that he needs rest.
(c) (*introduisant une causale: tant*) **on ne le comprend pas,** ~ **il parle vite** he talks so quickly (that) you can't understand him; **il trouve à peine le temps de dormir,** ~ **il travaille** he hardly finds time to sleep, he works so much *ou* hard.
(d) (*avec nég: pas très, pas beaucoup*) **pas ~ fort/lentement** not (all) that strong/slowly, not so (very) strong/slowly; **il ne travaille pas** ~ he doesn't work (all) that much *ou* hard, he doesn't work so (very) much *ou* hard; **cet article n'est plus ~ demandé** this article is no longer (very) much in demand; **ce n'est plus ~ à la mode** it's not really *ou* all that fashionable any more; **cela ne se fait plus** ~ it's not done (very) much *ou* all that much any more; **tu aimes le cinéma? — pas** ~ do you like the cinema? — not (all) that much *ou* not particularly *ou* not especially; **y allez-vous toujours? — plus ~, maintenant qu'il y a le bébé** do you still go there? — not (very) much now (that) there's the baby; **on ne la voit plus** ~ we don't really see (very) much of her any more.
tellurique [telyʀik] *adj* telluric; *V* **secousse.**
téméraire [temeʀɛʀ] *adj action, entreprise* rash, reckless, foolhardy; *jugement* rash; *personne* reckless, foolhardy, rash. ~ **dans ses jugements** rash in his judgments.
témérairement [temeʀɛʀmɑ̃] *adv* (*V* **téméraire**) rashly; recklessly; foolhardily.
témérité [temeʀite] *nf* (*V* **téméraire**) rashness; recklessness; foolhardiness.
témoignage [temwaɲaʒ] *nm* **(a)** (*en justice*) (*déclaration*) testimony (*U*), evidence (*U*); (*faits relatés*) evidence (*U*). **d'après le ~ de M X** according to Mr X's testimony *ou* evidence, according to the evidence of *ou* given by Mr X; **j'étais présent lors de son** ~ I was present when he gave evidence *ou* gave his testimony; **ces ~s sont contradictoires** these are contradictory pieces of evidence; **appelé en** ~ called as a witness, called (upon) to give evidence *ou* to testify; *V* **faux**[2].
(b) (*récit, rapport*) account, testimony. **ce livre est un merveilleux ~ sur notre époque** this book gives a marvellous account of the age we live in; **invoquer le ~ d'un voyageur** to call upon a traveller to give his (eyewitness) account *ou* his testimony.
(c) (*attestation*) ~ **de probité/de bonne conduite** evidence (*U*) *ou* proof (*U*) of honesty/of good conduct; **invoquer le ~ de qn pour prouver sa bonne foi** to call on sb's evidence *ou* testimony to prove one's good faith.
(d) (*manifestation*) ~ **d'amitié/de reconnaissance** (*geste*) expression of friendship/gratitude; (*cadeau*) token *ou* mark *ou* sign of friendship/gratitude; **leurs ~s de sympathie nous ont touchés** we are touched by their expressions of sympathy; **en ~ de ma reconnaissance** as a token *ou* mark of my gratitude; **le ~ émouvant de leur confiance** the touching expression of their confidence.
témoigner [temwaɲe] (1) **1** *vi* (*Jur*) to testify. ~ **en faveur de/contre qn** to testify *ou* give evidence in sb's favour/against sb; ~ **en justice** to testify in court.
2 *vt* **(a)** (*attester que*) ~ **que** to testify that; **il a témoigné qu'il ne l'avait jamais vu** *ou* **ne l'avoir jamais vu** he testified that he had never seen him.
(b) (*faire preuve de, faire paraître*) to show, display; *goût, reconnaissance* to show, evince (*frm*). ~ **un goût pour qch** to show *ou* display a taste *ou* liking for sth; ~ **de l'aversion à qn** to show *ou* evince (*frm*) an aversion for *ou* from sb.
(c) (*démontrer*) ~ **que/de qch** to attest *ou* reveal that/sth; **son attitude témoigne de sa préoccupation** *ou* **qu'il est préoccupé** his attitude reveals his preoccupation *ou* that he is preoccupied; (*fig*) **sa mort témoigne qu'on ne peut vivre seul** his death testifies to the fact that one cannot live alone.
(d) (*manifester*) ~ **de** to bear witness to, attest, bespeak (*frm*); **ce livre témoigne d'une certaine originalité** this book bears witness to *ou* attests *ou* bespeaks (*frm*) a certain originality.
3 témoigner de *vt indir* (*confirmer*) to testify to, bear witness to; ~ **de Dieu** to bear witness to God; **je peux en** ~ I can testify *ou* bear witness to that.
témoin [temwɛ̃] **1** *nm* **(a)** (*gén, Jur: personne*) witness; [*duel*] second. ~ **auriculaire** earwitness; ~ **oculaire** eyewitness; ~ **direct/indirect** direct/indirect witness; ~ **de moralité** character reference (*person*); ~ **gênant** embarrassing witness; (*Jur*) **être ~ à charge/à décharge** to be (a) witness for the prosecution/for the defence; **être ~ de** [*spectateur*] **une scène** to witness, be a witness to; [*garant*] **la sincérité de qn** to vouch for; **prendre qn à ~ (de qch)** to call sb to witness (to *ou* of sth); **parler devant ~(s)** to speak in front of witnesses; **faire qch sans** ~ to do sth unwitnessed; **cela doit être signé devant** ~ this must be signed in front of a witness; **il a été mon ~ à notre mariage** he was (a) witness at our marriage ceremony; (*Rel*) **les T~s de Jéhovah** Jehovah's Witnesses; (*fig*) **ces lieux ~s de notre enfance** these places which saw *ou* witnessed our childhood; *V* **faux**[2].
(b) (*chose, personne: preuve*) evidence (*U*), testimony. **ces ruines sont le ~ de la férocité des combats** these ruins are (the) evidence of *ou* a testimony to the fierceness of the fighting; **ces aristocrates sont les ~s d'une époque révolue** these aristocrats are the surviving evidence of a bygone age; **la région est riche, ~ les constructions nouvelles qui se dressent partout** the region is rich — witness the new buildings going up everywhere.
(c) (*Sport*) baton. **passer le** ~ to hand on *ou* pass the baton.
(d) (*Géol*) outlier; [*excavations*] dumpling; *V* **butte.**
(e) (*Constr: posé sur une fente*) telltale.
2 *adj* (*après n*) control (*épith*). **des magasins(-)~s pour empêcher les abus** control *ou* check shops to prevent abuses; **animaux/sujets ~s** control animals/subjects; **appartement** ~ show-flat; **réalisation** ~ pilot *ou* test development; *V* **lampe.**
tempe [tɑ̃p] *nf* (*Anat*) temple. **avoir les ~s grisonnantes** to have greying temples, be going grey at the temples.
tempérament [tɑ̃peʀamɑ̃] *nm* **(a)** (*constitution*) constitution. ~ **robuste/faible** strong/weak constitution; **se tuer** *ou* **s'esquinter le ~*** to wreck one's health; ~ **sanguin/lymphatique** sanguine/lymphatic constitution; ~ **nerveux** nervous disposition.
(b) (*nature, caractère*) disposition, temperament, nature. **elle a un ~ actif/réservé** she is of *ou* has an active/a reserved disposition; ~ **romantique** romantic nature *ou* temperament; **moqueur par** ~ naturally given to *ou* disposed to mockery, mocking by nature; **c'est un** ~ he has a strong personality.
(c) (*sensualité*) sexual disposition. **être de ~ ardent/froid** to be of a passionate/sexually cold disposition; **avoir du** ~ to be hot-blooded *ou* highly sexed*.
(d) (*Comm*) **vente à** ~ sale on deferred (payment) terms; **achat à** ~ = hire purchase (*Brit*), H.P.* (*Brit*), installment plan (*US*); **trop d'achats à ~ l'avaient mis dans une situation difficile** too many hire purchase commitments (*Brit*) *ou* too many purchases on H.P.* (*Brit*) had got him into a difficult situation.
(e) (*Mus*) temperament.
tempérance [tɑ̃peʀɑ̃s] *nf* temperance; *V* **société.**
tempérant, e [tɑ̃peʀɑ̃, ɑ̃t] *adj* temperate.
température [tɑ̃peʀatyʀ] *nf* **(a)** (*Mét, Phys*) temperature. (*Phys*) ~ **d'ébullition/de fusion** boiling/melting point; (*Phys*) ~ **absolue** *ou* **en degrés absolus** absolute temperature.
(b) (*chaleur du corps*) temperature. **animaux à ~ fixe/variable** warm-blooded/cold-blooded animals; **avoir** *ou* **faire de la** ~ to have a temperature, be running a temperature; **prendre la ~ de** *malade* to take the temperature of; (*fig*) *auditoire, groupe public* to gauge the temperature of, test *ou* get the feeling of; *V* **feuille.**
tempéré, e [tɑ̃peʀe] (*ptp de* **tempérer**) *adj climat, zone* temperate; (*Mus*) tempered.
tempérer [tɑ̃peʀe] (16) *vt froid, rigueur du climat* to temper; (*littér*) *peine, douleur* to soothe, ease; (*littér*) *ardeur, sévérité* to temper.
tempête [tɑ̃pɛt] *nf* **(a)** (*lit*) storm, tempest (*littér*). ~ **de neige** snowstorm; ~ **de sable** sandstorm; *V* **lampe, qui, souffler.**
(b) (*fig: agitation*) storm. **une ~ dans un verre d'eau** a storm in a teacup (*Brit*), a tempest in a teapot (*US*); **cela va déchaîner des ~s** that's going to cause a storm; **il est resté calme dans la** ~ he remained calm in the midst of the storm *ou* while the storm raged all around him.
(c) (*déchaînement*) **une ~ d'applaudissements** a storm of applause, thunderous applause (*U*); **une ~ d'injures** a storm of abuse; **une ~ de rires** a storm of laughter, gales (*pl*) of laughter.
tempêter [tɑ̃pete] (1) *vi* to rant and rave, rage.
tempétueux, -euse [tɑ̃petɥø, øz] *adj* (*littér*) *région, côte* tempestuous (*littér*), stormy; (*fig*) *vie, époque* tempestuous, stormy, turbulent.
temple [tɑ̃pl(ə)] *nm* **(a)** (*Hist, littér*) temple. **(b)** (*Rel*) (Protestant) church. **(c) l'Ordre du ~, le T~** the Order of the Temple.
templier [tɑ̃plije] *nm* (Knight) Templar.
tempo [tɛmpo] *nm* (*Mus, fig*) tempo.
temporaire [tɑ̃pɔʀɛʀ] *adj personnel, employé, fonctions* temporary. **nomination à titre** ~ temporary appointment, appointment on a temporary basis.
temporairement [tɑ̃pɔʀɛʀmɑ̃] *adv* temporarily.
temporal, e, *mpl* **-aux** [tɑ̃pɔʀal, o] (*Anat*) **1** *adj* temporal.
2 *nm* temporal (bone).
temporalité [tɑ̃pɔʀalite] *nf* (*Ling, Philos*) temporality.
temporel, -elle [tɑ̃pɔʀɛl] *adj* **(a)** (*Rel*) (*non spirituel*) worldly, temporal; (*non éternel*) temporal. **biens ~s** temporal *ou* worldly goods, temporals. **(b)** (*Ling, Philos*) temporal.
temporellement [tɑ̃pɔʀɛlmɑ̃] *adv* temporally.
temporisateur, -trice [tɑ̃pɔʀizatœʀ, tʀis] **1** *adj* temporizing (*épith*), stalling (*épith*). **une stratégie de ~** temporizing *ou* stalling *ou* delaying tactics. **2** *nm,f* temporizer.
temporisation [tɑ̃pɔʀizasjɔ̃] *nf* temporization, stalling, playing for time*.
temporiser [tɑ̃pɔʀize] (1) *vi* to temporize, stall, play for time*.
temps[1] [tɑ̃] **1** *nm* **(a)** (*passage des ans*) **le** ~ time; (*personnifié*) **le T~** (Old) Father Time; **l'action du** ~ the action of time; *V* **tuer.**

(b) (*durée*) time. **cela prend trop de ~** it takes (up) too much time; **la blessure mettra du ~ à guérir** the wound will take (some) time to heal; **il a mis beaucoup de ~ à se préparer** he took a long time to get ready; **avec le ~, ça s'oubliera** it'll all be forgotten with *ou* in time; **la jeunesse n'a qu'un ~** youth will not endure; **travailler à plein ~/à ~ partiel** to work full-time/part-time; **peu de ~ avant/après** (*prép*) shortly before/after, a short while *ou* time before/after; (*adv*) shortly before/after(wards), a short while *ou* time before/after(wards); **dans peu de ~** before (very) long, presently (*Brit*); **dans quelque ~** before too long, in a (little) while; **pour un ~** for a time *ou* while; **durant** *ou* **pendant (tout) ce ~ (là)** all this time; **je ne le vois plus depuis quelque ~** I haven't seen him for a (little) while *ou* some (little) time; *V* **emploi, laps** *etc.*

(c) (*portion de temps*) time. **~ d'arrêt** pause, halt; **marquer un ~ d'arrêt** to pause momentarily; **s'accorder un ~ de réflexion** to give o.s. time for reflection; **la plupart du ~** most of the time; **avoir le ~ (de faire)** to have time (to do); **je n'ai pas le ~** I haven't time; **vous avez tout votre ~** you have all the time in the world *ou* plenty of time *ou* all the time you need; **il n'y a pas de ~ à perdre** there's no time to lose *ou* to be lost; **prenez donc votre ~** do take your time; **cela fait gagner beaucoup de ~** it saves a lot *ou* a great deal of time, it's very time-saving; **chercher à gagner du ~** to try to save time; **passer son ~ à la lecture** *ou* **à lire** to spend one's time reading; **il passe tout son ~ à ceci/faire ...** he's spending all his time on this/all his time doing ...; **donnez-moi le ~ de m'habiller et je suis à vous** just give me time to get dressed *ou* I'll just get dressed and I'll be with you; **je me suis arrêté en chemin juste le ~ de prendre un verre** I stopped on the way just long enough for a drink *ou* to have a drink; **le ~ perdu ne se rattrape jamais** time and tide wait for no man (*Prov*); **faire son ~** *[soldat]* to serve one's time (in the army); *[prisonnier]* to do *ou* serve one's time; (*fig*) **il a fait son ~** *[auteur]* he has had his day; *[objet]* it has had its day.

(d) (*moment précis*) time. **il est ~ de partir** it's time to go, it's time we left; **il est** *ou* **il serait (grand) ~ qu'il parte** it's (high) time he went, it's time for him to go; **le ~ est venu de supprimer les frontières** the time has come to abolish frontiers, it's time frontiers were abolished; **il était ~!** none too soon!, not before time!; **il n'est plus ~ de se lamenter** the time for bemoaning one's lot is past *ou* over.

(e) (*époque*) time, times (*pl*). **en ~ de guerre/paix** in wartime/peacetime; **en ~ de crise** in times of crisis; **par les ~ qui courent** these days, nowadays; **les ~ modernes** modern times; **dans les ~ anciens** in ancient times *ou* days; **en ces ~ troublés** in these troubled times; **les ~ sont bien changés** times have changed; **le ~ n'est plus où ...** gone are the days when ...; **c'était le bon ~** those were good times; **dans le ~** at one time, once upon a time; **dans le** *ou* **au bon vieux ~** in the good old days; **en ce ~ là** at that time; **en ~ normal** in normal circumstances; **les premiers ~** at the beginning, at first; **ces** *ou* **les derniers ~** *ou* **derniers ~** lately, latterly; *V* **nuit, signe.**

(f) (*époque délimitée*) time(s), day(s). **du ~ de Néron** in Nero's time *ou* day(s), at the time of Nero; **au ~ des Tudors** in Tudor times, in the days of the Tudors; **de mon ~** in MY day *ou* time; **dans mon jeune ~** in my younger days; **être de son ~** to move with the times; **quels ~ nous vivons!** what times we're living in!; **les ~ sont durs!** times are hard!; **les jeunes de notre ~** young people of our time *ou* (of) today, young people these days.

(g) (*saison*) **le ~ des moissons/des vacances** harvest/holiday time; **le ~ de la chasse** the hunting season.

(h) (*Mus*) beat; (*Gym*) *[exercice, mouvement]* stage. **~ fort/faible** strong/weak beat; (*fig*) **les ~ forts et les ~ faibles d'un roman** the powerful and the subdued moments of a novel; **à deux/trois ~** in duple/triple time; **~ de valse** waltz time.

(i) (*Ling*) *[verbe]* tense. **~ simple/composé** simple/compound tense; **~ surcomposé** double-compound tense; **adverbe/complément de ~** adverb/complement of time, temporal adverb/complement; *V* **concordance.**

(j) (*Tech: phase*) stroke. **moteur à 4 ~** 4-stroke engine; **un 2 ~** a 2-stroke.

(k) (*Sport*) *[coureur, concurrent]* time. **dans les meilleurs ~** among the best times.

(l) (*loc*) **à ~** in time; **en un ~ où** at a time when; **de ~ en ~, de ~ à autre** from time to time, now and again, every now and then; **de tout ~** from time immemorial; (*littér*) **du ~ que, du ~ où, dans le ~ où, au ~ où** in the days when, at the time when; **en ~ et lieu** in due course, at the proper time (and place); **en ~ opportun** at an appropriate time; **ce n'est ni le ~ ni le lieu de discuter** this is neither the time nor the place for discussions; **en ~ voulu** *ou* **utile** in due time *ou* course; **à ~ perdu** in one's spare time; **il faut bien passer le ~** you've got to pass the time somehow; **cela fait passer le ~** it passes the time; (*Prov*) **le ~ c'est de l'argent** time is money; *V* **juste, tout.**

2: (*Sci*) **temps astronomique** mean *ou* astronomical time; (*Phys*) **temps atomique** atomic time; **temps mort** (*Ftbl, Rugby*) injury time (*U*); (*fig*) (*dans le commerce, le travail*) slack period; (*dans la conversation*) lull; (*Ordinateurs*) **temps partagé** time-sharing; (*Ordinateurs*) **temps réel** real time; **temps solaire vrai** apparent *ou* real solar time.

temps² [tɑ̃] *nm* (*conditions atmosphériques*) weather. **quel ~ fait-il?** what's the weather like?; **il fait beau/mauvais ~** the weather's fine/bad; **le ~ s'est mis au beau** it has turned (out) fine; **par ~ pluvieux/mauvais ~** in wet/bad weather; **sortir par tous les ~** to go out in all weathers; **avec le ~ qu'il fait!** in this weather!, with the weather we are having!; **~ de chien*** rotten* *ou* lousy* weather; **il faisait un beau ~ sec** (*pendant une période*) it was beautiful dry weather; (*ce jour-là*) it was a lovely dry day; **le ~ est lourd aujourd'hui** it's close today; (*fig*) **prendre le ~ comme il vient** to take things as they come.

tenable [t(ə)nabl(ə)] *adj* (*gén nég*) *température, situation* bearable. **il fait trop chaud ici, ce n'est pas ~** it's too warm here, it's unbearable; **quand ils sont ensemble, ce n'est plus ~** when they're together it becomes *ou* they become unbearable.

tenace [tənas] *adj* **(a)** (*persistant*) *douleur, rhume* stubborn; *croyance, préjugés* deep-rooted, stubborn, deep-seated; *souvenir* persistent; *espoir, illusions* tenacious, stubborn; *odeur* lingering, persistent.

(b) (*têtu, obstiné*) *quémandeur* persistent; *chercheur* dogged, tenacious; *résistance, volonté* tenacious, stubborn.

(c) *colle* firmly adhesive, strong.

tenacement [tənasmɑ̃] *adv* (*V* **tenace**) stubbornly; persistently; tenaciously; doggedly.

ténacité [tenasite] *nf* (*V* **tenace**) stubbornness; deep-rooted nature; persistence; tenacity; doggedness.

tenaille [t(ə)nɑj] *nf* **(a)** (*gén pl*) *[menuisier, bricoleur]* pincers; *[forgeron]* tongs; *[cordonnier]* nippers, pincers.

(b) (*Mil*) *[fortification]* tenaille, tenail. (*manœuvre*) **prendre en ~** to catch in a pincer movement; **mouvement de ~** pincer movement.

tenailler [tənɑje] (1) *vt [remords, inquiétude]* to torture, torment. **la faim le tenaillait** he was gnawed by hunger; **le remords/l'inquiétude le tenaillait** he was racked *ou* tortured *ou* tormented by remorse/worry.

tenancier [tənɑ̃sje] *nm* **(a)** *[maison de jeu, hôtel, bar]* manager.

(b) *[ferme]* tenant farmer; (*Hist*) *[terre]* (feudal) tenant.

tenancière [tənɑ̃sjɛʀ] *nf [maison close]* brothel-keeper, madam; *[salon de jeu, hôtel, bar]* manageress.

tenant, e [tənɑ̃, ɑ̃t] **1** *adj:* **chemise à col ~** shirt with an attached collar *ou* with collar attached; *V* **séance.**

2 *nm* **(a)** (*gén pl: partisan*) *[doctrine]* supporter, upholder (*de* of), adherent (*de* to); *[homme politique]* supporter.

(b) (*Sport*) *[titre, coupe]* holder.

(c) (*loc*) (*fig*) **les ~s et (les) aboutissants d'une affaire** the ins and outs of a question; **d'un (seul) ~** *terrain* all in one piece, lying together; **100 hectares d'un seul ~** 100 unbroken *ou* uninterrupted hectares.

tendance [tɑ̃dɑ̃s] *nf* **(a)** (*inclination, Psych*) tendency. (*Psych*) **~s refoulées/inconscientes** repressed/unconscious tendencies; **la ~ principale de son caractère est l'égoïsme** the chief tendency in his character *ou* his chief tendency is egoism; **manifester des ~s homosexuelles** to show homosexual leanings *ou* tendencies; **~ à l'exagération/à s'enivrer** tendency to exaggerate *ou* for exaggeration/to get drunk.

(b) (*opinions*) *[parti, politicien]* leanings (*pl*), sympathies (*pl*); *[groupe artistique, artiste]* leanings (*pl*); *[livre]* drift, tenor. **il est de ~ gauchiste/surréaliste** he has leftist/surrealist leanings; **à quelle ~ (politique) appartient-il?** what are his (political) leanings? *ou* sympathies?

(c) (*évolution*) *[art, langage, système économique ou politique]* trend. **~s démographiques** population trends; **~ à la hausse/baisse** *[prix]* upward/downward trend, rising/falling trend; *[température]* upward/downward trend; **la récente ~ à la baisse des valeurs mobilières** the recent downward *ou* falling trend in stocks and shares; **les ~s actuelles de l'opinion publique** the current trends in public opinion.

(d) (*loc*) **avoir ~ à** *paresse, exagération* to have a tendency for, tend *ou* be inclined towards; **avoir ~ à s'enivrer/être impertinent** to have a tendency to get drunk/to be impertinent, tend *ou* be inclined to get drunk/to be impertinent; **cette roue a ~ à se bloquer** this wheel tends *ou* has a tendency *ou* is inclined to jam; **le temps a ~ à se gâter vers le soir** the weather tends to deteriorate towards the evening; **en période d'inflation les prix ont ~ à monter** in a period of inflation, prices tend *ou* have a tendency *ou* are inclined to go up.

tendancieusement [tɑ̃dɑ̃sjøzmɑ̃] *adv* tendentiously.

tendancieux, -ieuse [tɑ̃dɑ̃sjø, jøz] *adj* tendentious.

tender [tɑ̃dɛʀ] *nm* (*Rail*) tender.

tendeur [tɑ̃dœʀ] *nm* (*dispositif*) *[fil de fer]* wire-strainer; *[ficelle de tente]* runner; *[chaîne de bicyclette]* chain-adjuster; (*câble élastique*) elastic *ou* extensible strap. **~ de chaussures** shoe-stretcher.

tendineux, -euse [tɑ̃dinø, øz] *adj viande* stringy; (*Anat*) tendinous.

tendon [tɑ̃dɔ̃] *nm* tendon, sinew. **~ d'Achille** Achilles' tendon.

tendre¹ [tɑ̃dʀ(ə)] (41) **1** *vt* **(a)** (*raidir*) *corde, câble, corde de raquette* to tighten, tauten; *corde d'arc* to brace, draw tight; *arc* to bend, draw back; *ressort* to set; *muscles* to tense, brace; *pièce de tissu* to stretch, pull *ou* draw tight. **~ la peau d'un tambour** to brace a drum; **~ le jarret** to flex *ou* brace one's leg muscles; (*littér*) **~ son esprit vers ...** to bend one's mind to ... .

(b) (*installer, poser*) *tapisserie, tenture* to hang; *piège* to set. **~ une bâche sur une remorque** to pull a tarpaulin over a trailer; **~ une chaîne entre deux poteaux** to hang *ou* fasten a chain between two posts; **~ ses filets** (*lit*) to set one's nets; (*fig*) to set one's snares; (*fig*) **~ un piège/une embuscade (à qn)** to set a trap/an ambush (for sb).

(c) († *littér: tapisser*) **~ une pièce de tentures** to hang a room with draperies; **~ une pièce de soie bleue** to put blue silk hangings *ou* draperies in a room.

(d) (*avancer*) **~ le cou** to crane one's neck; **~ l'oreille** to prick up one's ears; **~ l'esprit (vers)** to bend one's mind (to); **~ la joue** to offer one's cheek; (*fig*) **~ l'autre joue** to turn the other cheek; (*fig*) **~ la gorge au couteau** to lay one's head on the block; **~ la main** to hold out one's hand; **~ le bras** to stretch out one's arm; **il me tendit la main** he held out his hand to me; **il me tendit les bras** he stretched out his arms to me; **~ une main secourable** to offer a helping hand; **~ le dos** (*aux coups*) to brace one's back.

(e) (*présenter, donner*) **~ qch à qn** (*briquet, objet demandé*) to hold sth out to *ou* for sb; (*cigarette offerte, bonbon*) to offer sth to sb; **il lui tendit un paquet de cigarettes/un bonbon** he held out a packet of cigarettes to him/offered him a sweet; (*fig*) ~ **la perche à qn** to throw sb a line.

2 se tendre *vpr [corde]* to become taut, tighten; *[rapports]* to become strained.

3 *vi* **(a)** (*aboutir à*) ~ **à qch/à faire** to tend towards sth/to do; **le langage tend à se simplifier sans cesse** language tends to become simpler all the time; (*sens affaibli*) **ceci tend à prouver/confirmer que ...** this tends to prove/confirm that ... .

(b) (*littér: viser à*) ~ **à qch/à faire** to aim at sth/to do; **cette mesure tend à faciliter les échanges** this measure aims to facilitate *ou* at facilitating exchanges; ~ **à** *ou* **vers la perfection** to strive towards *ou* aim at perfection.

(c) (*Math*) ~ **vers l'infini** to tend towards infinity.

tendre[2] [tɑ̃dʀ(ə)] *adj* **(a)** (*délicat*) *peau, pierre, bois* soft; *pain* fresh(ly made), new; *haricots, viande* tender. **avoir la bouche ~** *[cheval]* to be tender-mouthed; (*littér*) **couché dans l'herbe ~** lying in the sweet grass; (*littér*) **~s bourgeons/fleurettes** tender shoots/little flowers; **depuis sa plus ~ enfance** from his earliest days; (*hum*) **dans ma ~ enfance** in my innocent childhood days; **~ comme la rosée** as sweet as honey; *V* **âge.**

(b) (*affectueux*) *personne* tender, affectionate, loving; *amour, amitié, regard* fond, tender; **ne pas être ~ pour qn** to be hard on sb; **~ aveu** tender confession; *V* **cœur.**

(c) *couleurs* soft, delicate. **rose/vert/bleu ~** soft *ou* delicate pink/green/blue.

tendrement [tɑ̃dʀəmɑ̃] *adv* (*V* **tendre**[2]) tenderly; affectionately, lovingly; fondly. **époux ~ unis** partners joined by a tender love.

tendresse [tɑ̃dʀɛs] *nf* **(a)** (*U: V* **tendre**[2]) tenderness; fondness.

(b) la ~ tenderness; **privé de ~ maternelle** denied maternal affection; **un besoin de ~** a need for tenderness *ou* affection; **avoir de la ~ pour qn** to feel tenderness *ou* affection for sb.

(c) (*câlineries*) **~s** tokens of affection, tenderness (*U*); **combler qn de ~s** to overwhelm sb with tenderness *ou* with tokens of (one's) affection; **'mille ~s'** 'lots of love', 'much love'.

(d) (*littér: indulgence*) **n'avoir aucune ~ pour** to have no fondness for (*littér*); **il avait gardé des ~s royalistes** he had retained (his) royalist sympathies.

tendreté [tɑ̃dʀəte] *nf [viande]* tenderness; *[bois, métal]* softness.

tendron [tɑ̃dʀɔ̃] *nm* **(a)** (*Culin*) **~s de veau** tendrons of veal.

(b) (*pousse, bourgeon*) (tender) shoot. **(c)** († *hum: jeune fille*) young *ou* little girl.

tendu, e [tɑ̃dy] (*ptp de* **tendre**[1]) *adj* **(a)** (*raide*) *corde, toile* tight, taut; *muscles* tensed, braced. **la corde est trop ~e/bien ~e** the rope is too tight *ou* taut/taut; **la corde est mal ~e** the rope is slack *ou* isn't tight *ou* taut enough.

(b) (*empreint de nervosité*) *rapports, relations* strained; *personne* tense, strained; *situation* tense.

(c) les bras ~s with arms outstretched, with outstretched arms; **s'avancer la main ~e** to come forward with one's hand held out.

(d) (*tapissé de*) **~ de** *velours, soie* hung with; **chambre ~e de bleu/de soie bleue** bedroom with blue hangings/blue silk hangings.

ténèbres [tenɛbʀ(ə)] *nfpl* (*littér*) *[nuit, cachot]* darkness, gloom. **plongé dans les ~** plunged into darkness; **s'avançant à tâtons dans les ~** groping his way forward in the dark(ness) *ou* gloom; **les ~ de la mort** the shades of death (*littér*); (*littér*) **le prince/l'empire des ~** the prince/world of darkness; (*fig*) **les ~ de l'ignorance** the darkness of ignorance; (*fig*) **les ~ de l'inconscient** the dark regions *ou* murky depths of the unconscious; (*fig*) **une lueur au milieu des ~** a ray of light in the darkness *ou* amidst the gloom (*littér*).

ténébreux, -euse [tenebʀø, øz] *adj* **(a)** (*littér: obscur*) *prison, forêt* dark, gloomy, tenebrous (*littér*); (*fig*) *conscience, intrigue, desseins* dark (*épith*); (*fig*) *époque, temps* obscure; (*fig*) *affaire, philosophie* dark (*épith*), mysterious, tenebrous (*littér*).

(b) (*rare, littér*) *personne* saturnine; *V* **beau.**

teneur [tənœʀ] *nf* **(a)** *[traité]* terms (*pl*); *[lettre]* content, terms (*pl*); *[article]* content.

(b) *[minerai]* grade. **de haute/faible ~** high-/low-grade (*épith*); **~ en cuivre/fer** copper/iron content; **la forte ~ en fer d'un minerai** the high iron content of an ore, the high percentage of iron in an ore.

(c) *[substance, solution]* **~ en alcool/eau/fer** alcohol/water/iron content; **la ~ en hémoglobine du sang** the haemoglobin content of the blood.

tenez [təne] *excl V* **tenir.**

ténia [tenja] *nm* tape worm, taenia (*T*).

tenir [t(ə)niʀ] (22) **1** *vt* **(a)** (*lit: gén*) *[personne]* to hold. **ils se tenaient (par) la main** they were holding hands *ou* holding each other by the hand; **il se tenait le ventre de douleur** he was clutching *ou* holding his stomach in pain; *V* **compagnie, œil, rigueur** *etc.*

(b) († *littér*) **faire ~ qch à qn** *lettre etc* to transmit *ou* communicate sth to sb.

(c) (*maintenir dans un certain état*) to keep; (*dans une certaine position*) to hold, keep. **~ les yeux fermés/les bras levés** to keep one's eyes shut/one's arms raised *ou* up; **~ un plat au chaud** to keep a dish hot; **une robe qui tient chaud** a warm dress, a dress which keeps you warm; **le café le tient éveillé** coffee keeps him awake; **elle tient ses enfants très propres** she keeps her children very neat; **~ qch en place/en position** to hold *ou* keep sth in place/position; *V* **échec**[1]**, haleine, respect** *etc.*

(d) (*Mus: garder*) *note* to hold. **~ l'accord** to stay in tune.

(e) (*avoir, détenir*) *voleur,* (*:*) *rhume etc* to have, have got; *vérité, preuve* to hold, have. (*menace*) **si je le tenais!** if I could get my hands *ou* lay hands on him!; **nous le tenons** (*lit: nous l'avons attrapé*) we've got *ou* caught him; (*il ne peut se désister*) we've got him (where we want him); (*il est coincé, est à notre merci*) we've got him; **je tiens un de ces rhumes!:** I've got a stinking cold*; **nous tenons maintenant la preuve de son innocence** we now hold *ou* have proof of his innocence; **je tiens le mot de l'énigme/la clef du mystère** I've got the secret of the riddle/the key to the mystery; **nous tenons un bon filon** we're on to a good thing *ou* something good*, we've struck it rich*; **parfait, je tiens mon article/mon sujet** fine, now I have my article/my subject; (*Prov*) **un tiens vaut mieux que deux tu l'auras,** (*Prov*) **mieux vaut ~ que courir** a bird in the hand is worth two in the bush (*Prov*); *V* **main.**

(f) (*Comm: stocker*) *article, marchandise* to stock, keep.

(g) (*avoir de l'autorité sur*) *enfant, classe* to have under control, keep under control, control; *pays* to have under one's control. **il tient (bien) sa classe** he has *ou* keeps his class (well) under control, he controls his class well; **les enfants sont très tenus** the children are held very much in check *ou* are kept on a very tight rein.

(h) *hôtel, magasin* to run, keep; *comptes, registre* to keep; *emploi, poste* to hold; *V* **barre, orgue.**

(i) *séance, conférence* to hold.

(j) *maison, ménage* to keep; *V* **tenu.**

(k) (*avoir reçu*) **~ de qn** *renseignement* to have from sb; *meuble, bijou* to have got from sb; *trait physique, de caractère* to get from sb; **il tient cela de son père** he gets that from his father; **je tiens ce renseignement d'un voisin** I have *ou* I got this information from a neighbour; *V* **source.**

(l) (*occuper*) *place, largeur* to take up. **tu tiens trop de place!** you are taking up too much room!; **le camion tenait toute la largeur/la moitié de la chaussée** the lorry took up the whole width of/half the roadway; (*Aut*) **il ne tenait pas sa droite** he was not keeping to the right; (*fig*) **~ une place importante** to hold an important place; *V* **lieu, rang.**

(m) (*contenir*) *[récipient]* to hold.

(n) (*retenir, fixer*) to hold. **ses livres sont tenus par une courroie** his books are held (together) by a strap; **il m'a tenu la tête sous l'eau** he held my head under the water.

(o) (*résister à, bien se comporter*) *[souliers]* **~ l'eau** to keep out the water; **~ le vin*** to be able to hold *ou* take (*surtout Brit*) one's drink; (*Naut*) **~ la mer** *[bateau]* to be seaworthy; (*Aut*) **~ la route** to hold the road; **une tente qui tient la tempête** a tent which can withstand storms; *V* **coup.**

(p) (*immobiliser*) **cette maladie le tient depuis 2 mois** he has had this illness for 2 months (now); **il m'a tenu dans son bureau pendant une heure** he kept me in his office for an hour; **il est très tenu par ses affaires** he's very tied by his business; (*littér*) **la colère le tenait** anger gripped him; (*littér*) **l'envie me tenait de ...** I was filled *ou* gripped by the desire to ... ; *V* **jambe.**

(q) (*respecter*) *promesse* to keep; *pari* to keep to, honour; *V* **parole.**

(r) (*se livrer à*) *discours, raisonnement* to give; *propos* to say; *langage* to use. **il tenait un langage d'une rare grossièreté** the language he used *ou* employed (*frm*) was singularly coarse; **~ des propos désobligeants à l'égard de qn** to make *ou* pass offensive remarks about sb, say offensive things about sb; **elle me tenait des discours sans fin sur la morale** she gave me endless lectures on morality, she lectured me endlessly on morality; **il aime ~ de grands discours** he likes to hold forth.

(s) ~ qn/qch pour to regard sb/sth as, consider sb/sth (as), hold sb/sth to be (*frm*); **je le tenais pour un honnête homme** I regarded him as *ou* considered him (to be) *ou* held him to be (*frm*) an honest man; **~ pour certain que ...** to regard it as certain that ... , consider it certain that ... ; **tenez-vous-le pour dit** consider yourself told once and for all; *V* **estime, quitte.**

(t) en ~ pour qn: to fancy sb* (*surtout Brit*), be keen on sb*.

(u) tiens!, tenez! (*en donnant*) take this, here (you are); (*de surprise*) **tiens, voilà le facteur** ah *ou* hullo, there's the postman; **tiens, tiens*** well, well!, fancy that!; (*pour attirer l'attention*) **tenez, je vais vous expliquer** look, I'll explain to you; **tenez, ça m'écœure** you know, that sickens me.

2 *vi* **(a)** *[objet fixe, nœud]* to hold; *[objets empilés, échafaudage]* to stay up, hold (up). **croyez-vous que le clou tienne?** do you think the nail will hold?; **l'armoire tient au mur** the cupboard is held *ou* fixed to the wall; **ce chapeau ne tient pas sur ma tête** this hat won't stay on (my head); **la branche est cassée, mais elle tient encore bien à l'arbre** the branch is broken but it's still firmly attached to the tree; (*être contigu*) **le jardin tient à la ferme** the garden adjoins the farmhouse; **il n'y a pas de bal/match qui tienne** there's no question of going to any dance/match; **ça tient toujours, notre pique-nique de jeudi?*** is our picnic on Thursday still on?*, does our picnic on Thursday still stand?

(b) *[personne]* **~ debout** to stand up; **je ne tiens plus debout** I'm dropping* *ou* ready to drop*, I can hardly stand up any more; **il tient bien sur ses jambes** he is very steady on his legs; **cet enfant ne tient pas en place** this child cannot keep *ou* stay still.

(c) (*Mil, gén: résister*) to hold out. **~ bon** *ou* **ferme** to stand fast *ou* firm, hold out; **il fait trop chaud, on ne tient plus ici** it's too hot — we can't stand it any longer; **furieux, il n'a pas pu ~: il a protesté violemment** in a blazing fury he couldn't contain himself and he protested vehemently.

(d) (*être contenu dans*) **~ dans** *ou* **à** *ou* **en** to fit in(to); **ils ne tiendront pas dans la pièce/la voiture** the room/the car will not hold them, they will not fit into the room/the car; **nous tenons 4**

à cette table this table seats 4, we can get 4 round this table; **son discours tient en quelques pages** his speech takes up just a few pages, his speech is just a few pages long; **est-ce que la caisse tiendra en hauteur?** will the box fit in vertically?

(e) (*durer*) *[accord, beau temps]* to hold; *[couleur]* to be fast; *[mariage]* to last; *[fleurs]* to last (well); *[mise en plis]* to stay in.

3 tenir à *vt indir* **(a)** (*aimer, priser*) *réputation, opinion de qn* to value, care about; *objet aimé* to be attached to, be fond of; *personne* to be attached to, be fond of, care for; **il ne tenait plus à la vie** he felt no further attachment to life, he no longer cared about living; **voudriez-vous un peu de vin? — je n'y tiens pas** would you like some wine? — not really *ou* not particularly *ou* I'm not that keen*.

(b) (*vouloir*) ~ **à** + *infin*, ~ **à ce que** + *subj* to be anxious to, be anxious that; **il tient beaucoup à vous connaître** he is very anxious to meet you, he is very keen *ou* eager to meet you; **elle a tenu absolument à parler** she insisted on speaking; **il tient à ce que nous sachions ...** he insists *ou* is anxious that we should know ... ; **si vous y tenez** if you really want to; **tu viens avec nous? — si tu y tiens** are you coming with us? — if you really want me to *ou* if you insist.

(c) (*avoir pour cause*) to be due to, stem from.

4 tenir de *vt indir* (*ressembler à*) *parent* to take after; **il tient de son père** he takes after his father; **il a de qui** ~ it runs in the family; **sa réussite tient du prodige** his success is something of a miracle; **cela tient du comique et du tragique** there's something (both) comic and tragic about it.

5 *vb impers* to depend. **il ne tient qu'à vous de décider** it's up to you to decide, the decision rests with you; **il ne tient qu'à elle que cela se fasse** it's up to her whether it is done; **cela ne tient pas qu'à lui** it doesn't depend on him alone; **à quoi cela tient-il qu'il n'écrive pas?** how is it *ou* why is it that he doesn't write?; **qu'à cela ne tienne** never mind (that), that needn't matter, that's no problem.

6 se tenir *vpr* **(a) se** ~ **à qch** to hold on to sth.

(b) (*être dans une position ou un état ou un lieu*) **se** ~ **debout/couché/à genoux** to be standing (up)/lying (down)/kneeling (down) *ou* on one's knees; **tenez-vous prêts à partir** be ready to leave; **elle se tenait à sa fenêtre/dans un coin de la pièce** she was standing at her window/in a corner of the room; **tiens-toi tranquille** (*lit*) keep still; (*fig: ne pas agir*) lie low; **tiens-toi droit** (*debout*) stand up straight; (*assis*) sit up (straight).

(c) (*se conduire*) to behave. (*avertissement*) **vous n'avez plus qu'à bien vous** ~! you'd better behave yourself!, you just behave yourself!

(d) (*réunion etc: avoir lieu*) to be held. **le marché se tient là chaque semaine** the market is held there every week.

(e) (*être lié*) to hang *ou* hold together. **tous les faits se tiennent** all the facts hang *ou* hold together.

(f) (*se retenir: gén nég*) **il ne peut se** ~ **de rire/critiquer** he can't help laughing/criticizing; **il ne se tenait pas de joie** he couldn't contain his joy; **se** ~ **à quatre pour ne pas faire qch** to struggle to stop o.s. (from) doing sth, restrain o.s. forcibly from doing sth.

(g) s'en ~ **à qch** (*se limiter à*) to confine o.s. to, stick to*; (*se satisfaire de*) to content o.s. with; **nous nous en tiendrons là pour aujourd'hui** we'll leave it at that for today; **il aimerait savoir à quoi s'en** ~ he'd like to know where he stands.

tennis [tenis] **1** *nm* **(a)** (*Sport*) tennis. ~ **sur gazon** lawn tennis; ~ **sur terre battue** hard-court tennis; ~ **en salle** indoor tennis; ~ **de table** table tennis.

(b) (*terrain*) (tennis) court.

2 *nfpl* (*chaussures*) tennis shoes; (*par extension, chaussures de gym*) plimsolls, gym shoes, sneakers.

tennisman† [tenisman], *pl* **tennismen** [tenismɛn] *nm* tennis player.

tenon [tənɔ̃] *nm* (*Menuiserie*) tenon. **assemblage à** ~ **et mortaise** mortice and tenon joint.

ténor [tenɔʀ] **1** *nm* (*Mus*) tenor; (*fig*) (*Pol*) leading light, big name*; (*Sport*) star player, big name*. **2** *adj* tenor.

tenseur [tɑ̃sœʀ] **1** *nm* **(a)** (*Anat, Math*) tensor. **(b)** (*Tech: dispositif*) *[fil de fer]* wire-strainer; *[ficelle de tente]* runner; *[chaîne de bicyclette]* chain-adjuster.

2 *adj m*: **muscle** ~ tensor muscle.

tension [tɑ̃sjɔ̃] *nf* **(a)** (*état tendu*) *[ressort, cordes de piano, muscles]* tension; *[courroie]* tightness, tautness, tension. **chaîne à** ~ **réglable** adjustable tension chain; **corde de** ~ **d'une scie** tightening-cord of a saw.

(b) (*Phonétique*) (*phase d'articulation*) attack; (*état d'un phonème tendu*) tension, tenseness.

(c) (*Élec*) voltage, tension. ~ **de 110 volts** tension of 110 volts; **à haute/basse** ~ high-/low-voltage *ou* tension (*épith*); **sous** ~ (*lit*) live; (*fig*) under stress; **chute de** ~ voltage drop, drop in voltage.

(d) (*Méd*) ~ **(artérielle)** blood pressure; **avoir de la** ~ *ou* **trop de** ~ to have (high) blood pressure *ou* hypertension (*T*); **prendre la** ~ **de qn** to take sb's blood pressure.

(e) (*fig*) *[relations]* tension (*de* in); *[situation]* tenseness (*de* of). **dans un état de** ~ **nerveuse** in a state of nervous tension *ou* stress; ~ **entre deux pays/personnes/groupes** strained relationship between *ou* tension between two countries/people/groups.

(f) (*concentration, effort*) ~ **d'esprit** sustained mental effort; (*littér*) ~ **vers un but/idéal** striving towards a goal/an ideal.

(g) (*Phys*) *[liquide]* tension; *[vapeur]* pressure; (*Tech*) stress. ~ **superficielle** surface tension.

tentaculaire [tɑ̃takylɛʀ] *adj* (*Zool*) tentacular. (*fig*) **villes** ~**s** sprawling towns; **firmes** ~**s** monster (international) combines.

tentacule [tɑ̃takyl] *nm* (*Zool, fig*) tentacle.

tentant, e [tɑ̃tɑ̃, ɑ̃t] *adj plat* tempting, inviting, enticing; *offre* tempting, attractive, enticing; *projet* tempting, attractive.

tentateur, -trice [tɑ̃tatœʀ, tʀis] **1** *adj beauté* tempting, alluring, enticing; *propos* tempting, enticing. (*Rel*) **l'esprit** ~ the Tempter. **2** *nm* tempter. (*Rel*) **le T**~ the Tempter. **3 tentatrice** *nf* temptress.

tentation [tɑ̃tɑsjɔ̃] *nf* temptation.

tentative [tɑ̃tativ] *nf* (*gén*) attempt, endeavour; (*sportive, style journalistique*) bid, attempt. **de vaines** ~**s** vain attempts *ou* endeavours; ~ **d'évasion** attempt *ou* bid to escape, escape bid *ou* attempt; ~ **de meurtre/de suicide** murder/suicide attempt; (*Jur*) ~ **de meurtre/de vol** attempted murder/theft; (*Jur, Méd*) ~ **de suicide** attempted suicide; **faire une** ~ **auprès de qn (en vue de ...)** to approach sb (with a view to ...).

tente [tɑ̃t] **1** *nf* (*gén*) tent. ~ **de camping** (camping) tent; **coucher sous la** ~ to sleep under canvas; (*fig*) **se retirer sous sa** ~ to go and sulk in one's tent (*fig*). **2: tente-abri** *nf, pl* **tentes-abris** shelter tent; **tente de cirque** circus tent, marquee; (*Méd*) **tente à oxygène** oxygen tent; **tente de plage** beach tent.

tenté, e [tɑ̃te] (*ptp de* **tenter**) *adj*: **être** ~ **de faire/croire qch** to be tempted to do/believe sth.

tenter [tɑ̃te] (1) *vt* **(a)** (*chercher à séduire*) *personne* (*gén, Rel*) to tempt. ~ **qn (par une offre)** to tempt sb (with an offer); **ce n'était pas cher, elle s'est laissée** ~ it wasn't expensive and she yielded *ou* succumbed to the temptation; **c'est vraiment** ~ **le diable** it's really tempting fate *ou* Providence.

(b) (*risquer*) *expérience, démarche* to try, attempt. **on a tout tenté pour le sauver** they tried everything to save him; **on a tenté l'impossible pour le sauver** they attempted the impossible to save him; ~ **la** *ou* **sa chance** to try one's luck; ~ **le coup*** to have a go*, give it a try* *ou* a whirl*; **nous allons** ~ **l'expérience pour voir** we shall try the experiment to see.

(c) (*essayer*) ~ **de faire** to attempt *ou* try to do; **je vais** ~ **de le convaincre** I'll try *ou* attempt to convince him, I'll try and convince him.

tenture [tɑ̃tyʀ] *nf* **(a)** (*tapisserie*) hanging. **(b)** (*grands rideaux*) hanging, curtain; (*derrière une porte*) door curtain. **(c)** (*de deuil*) funeral hangings.

tenu, e [t(ə)ny] (*ptp de* **tenir**) **1** *adj* **(a)** (*entretenu*) **bien** ~ *enfant* well *ou* neatly turned out; *maison* well-kept, well looked after; **mal** ~ *enfant* poorly turned out, untidy; *maison* poorly kept, poorly looked after.

(b) (*strictement surveillé*) **leurs filles sont très** ~**es** their daughters are kept on a tight rein *ou* are held very much in check.

(c) (*obligé*) **être** ~ **de faire** to be obliged to do; **être** ~ **au secret professionnel** to be bound by professional secrecy; *V* **à**.

(d) (*Mus*) *note* held, sustained.

2 tenue *nf* **(a)** *[maison]* upkeep, running; *[magasin]* running; *[classe]* handling, control; *[séance]* holding; (*Mus*) *[note]* holding, sustaining. **la** ~**e des livres de comptes** the book-keeping; ~**e fautive de la plume** wrong way of holding one's pen.

(b) (*conduite*) (good) manners (*pl*), good behaviour. **bonne** ~**e en classe/à table** good behaviour in class/at (the) table; **avoir de la/manquer de** ~**e** to have/lack good manners, know/not know how to behave (o.s.); **allons! un peu de** ~**e!** come on, behave yourself!, come on, watch your manners!

(c) (*qualité*) *[journal]* standard, quality. **une publication qui a de la** ~**e** a publication of a high standard, a quality publication; **une publication de haute** ~**e** a quality publication.

(d) (*maintien*) posture. **mauvaise** ~**e d'un écolier** bad posture of a schoolboy.

(e) (*habillement, apparence*) dress, appearance; (*vêtements, uniforme*) dress. **leur** ~**e négligée** their sloppy dress *ou* appearance; **en** ~**e négligée** wearing *ou* in casual clothes; ~**e d'intérieur** indoor clothes; **en** ~**e légère** (*vêtements légers*) wearing *ou* in light clothing; (*tenue osée*) scantily dressed *ou* clad; **en petite** ~**e** *homme* scantily dressed *ou* clad; *femme* scantily dressed *ou* clad, in one's undies (*hum*); **en grande** ~**e** in full dress (uniform); (*Mil*) **être en** ~**e** to be in uniform; (*Mil*) ~ **camouflée/de campagne** camouflage/combat dress; **des touristes en** ~**e estivale/d'hiver** tourists in summer/winter clothes.

3: (*Mil*) **tenue de combat** battle dress; (*Aut*) **tenue de route** road holding; **tenue de service** uniform; **tenue de soirée** evening dress; **tenue de sport** sports clothes, sports gear; **tenue de ville** *[homme]* lounge suit; *[femme]* town dress *ou* suit; (*Aviat*) **tenue de vol** flying gear.

ténu, e [teny] *adj* (*littér*) *point, particule* fine; *fil* slender, fine; *brume* thin; *voix* thin; *raisons* tenuous, flimsy; *nuances, causes* tenuous, subtle.

ténuité [tenɥite] *nf* (*littér*) (*V* **ténu**) fineness; slenderness; thinness; tenuousness, tenuity; flimsiness; subtlety.

tenure [tənyʀ] *nf* (*Hist Jur*) tenure.

ter [tɛʀ] **1** *adj*: **il habite au 10** ~ he lives at (number) 10 B. **2** *adv* (*Mus*) three times, ter.

tératologie [teʀatɔlɔʒi] *nf* teratology.

tératologique [teʀatɔlɔʒik] *adj* teratological.

tercet [tɛʀsɛ] *nm* (*Poésie*) tercet, triplet.

térébenthine [teʀebɑ̃tin] *nf* turpentine. **nettoyer à l'essence de** ~ *ou* **à la** ~ to clean with turpentine *ou* turps*.

térébinthe [teʀebɛ̃t] *nm* terebinth.

tergal [tɛʀgal] *nm* ® Terylene ®.

tergiversations [tɛʀʒivɛʀsɑsjɔ̃] *nfpl* humming and hawing (*U*), shilly-shallying* (*U*).

tergiverser [tɛʀʒivɛʀse] (1) *vi* to hum and haw, shilly-shally*.

terme [tɛʀm(ə)] *nm* **(a)** (*mot, expression, Ling*) term; (*Math, Philos: élément*) term. (*formulation*) ~**s** terms; **aux** ~**s du contrat** according to the terms of the contract; **en** ~**s clairs/voilés/flatteurs** in clear/veiled/flattering terms; **en**

d'autres ~s in other words; **... et le ~ est faible ...** and that's putting it mildly; **~ de marine/de métier** nautical/professional term; *V* **acception, force, moyen.**

(b) (*date limite*) time limit, deadline; (*littér: fin*) *[vie, voyage, récit]* end, term (*littér*). **passé ce ~** after this date; **se fixer un ~ pour ...** to set o.s. a time limit *ou* a deadline for ...; **arriver à ~** *[délai]* to expire; *[opération]* to reach its *ou* a conclusion; *[paiement]* to fall due; **mettre un ~ à qch** to put an end *ou* a stop to sth; **mener qch à ~** to bring sth to completion, carry sth through (to completion); **arrivé au ~ de sa vie** having reached the end *ou* the term (*littér*) of his life; **prévisions/projets à court/long ~** short-term *ou* short-range/long-term *ou* long-range forecasts/plans.

(c) (*Méd*) **à ~** *accouchement* full-term; *naître* at term; **avant ~** *naître, accoucher* prematurely; **bébé né/naissance avant ~** premature baby/birth; **un bébé né 2 mois avant ~** a baby born 2 months premature, a 2-months premature baby.

(d) *[loyer]* (*date*) term, date for payment; (*période*) rental term *ou* period; (*somme*) (quarterly) rent (*U*). **payer à ~ échu** to pay at the end of the rental term, pay a term in arrears; **le (jour du) ~** the term *ou* date for payment; **il a un ~ de retard** he's one quarter *ou* one payment behind (with his rent); **devoir/payer son ~** to owe/pay one's rent.

(e) (*Bourse, Fin*) **à ~** forward; **transaction à ~** (*Bourse de marchandises*) forward transaction; (*Bourse de valeurs*) settlement bargain; **marché à ~** settlement market, forward market; **crédit/emprunt à court/long ~** short-term *ou* short-dated/long-term *ou* long-dated credit/loan, short/long credit/loan.

(f) (*relations*) **~s** terms; **être en bons/mauvais ~s avec qn** to be on good *ou* friendly/bad terms with sb; **ils sont dans les meilleurs ~s** they are on the best of terms.

terminaison [tɛʀminɛzɔ̃] *nf* (*Ling*) ending. (*Anat*) **~s nerveuses** nerve endings.

terminal, e, *mpl* **-aux** [tɛʀminal, o] *adj phase, élément* terminal, final. (*Scol*) **(classe) ~e** ≃ Upper Sixth.

terminer [tɛʀmine] (1) **1** *vt* **(a)** (*clore*) *débat, séance* to bring to an end *ou* to a close, terminate.

(b) (*achever*) *travail* to finish (off), complete; *repas, récit* to finish, end; *vacances, temps d'exil* to end, finish. **il termina en nous réprimandant** he finished (up *ou* off) *ou* he ended by giving us a reprimand; **j'ai terminé ainsi ma journée** and so I ended my day; **nous avons terminé la journée/soirée chez un ami/par une promenade** we finished off *ou* ended the day/evening at a friend's house/with a walk; **~ ses jours à la campagne/à l'hôpital** to end one's days in the country/in hospital; **~ un repas par un café** to finish off *ou* end a meal with a coffee; **~ un livre par quelques conseils pratiques** to end a book with a few pieces of practical advice; **en avoir terminé avec un travail** to be finished with a job; **j'en ai terminé avec eux** I am *ou* have finished with them, I have done with them.

(c) (*former le dernier élément*) **le café termina le repas** the meal concluded *ou* ended with coffee, coffee finished off *ou* concluded *ou* ended the meal; **un bourgeon termine la tige** the stalk ends in a bud.

2 se terminer *vpr* **(a)** (*prendre fin*) *[rue, domaine]* to end, terminate (*frm*); *[affaire, repas, vacances]* to (come to an) end. **les vacances se terminent demain** the holidays (come to an) end tomorrow; **le parc se termine ici** the park ends here; **ça s'est bien/mal terminé** it ended well/badly, it turned out well *ou* all right/badly (in the end).

(b) (*s'achever sur*) **~ par** to end with; **la thèse se termine par une bibliographie** the thesis ends with a bibliography; **la soirée se termina par un jeu** the evening ended with a game; **ces verbes se terminent par le suffixe 'ir'** these verbs end in the suffix 'ir'.

(c) (*finir en*) **se ~ en** to end in; **les mots qui se terminent en 'ation'** words which end in 'ation'; **cette comédie se termine en tragédie** this comedy ends in tragedy; **se ~ en pointe** to end in a point.

terminologie [tɛʀminɔlɔʒi] *nf* terminology.

terminus [tɛʀminys] *nm [autobus, train]* terminus. **~! tout le monde descend!** (last stop!) all change!

termite [tɛʀmit] *nm* termite, white ant.

termitière [tɛʀmitjɛʀ] *nf* ant-hill, termitary (*T*).

ternaire [tɛʀnɛʀ] *adj* compound.

terne [tɛʀn(ə)] *adj teint* colourless, lifeless; *regard* lifeless; *personne* dull, colourless, drab; *style, conversation* dull, drab, lacklustre; *couleur, journée, vie* dull, drab.

terni, e [tɛʀni] (*ptp de* **ternir**) *adj argenterie, métal, réputation* tarnished; *glace* dulled.

ternir [tɛʀniʀ] (2) **1** *vt* **(a)** (*lit*) *métal* to tarnish; *glace, meuble* to dull; *teint* to drain of colour.

(b) (*fig*) *mémoire, honneur, réputation* to tarnish, sully, besmirch.

2 se ternir *vpr [métal]* to tarnish, become tarnished; *[glace]* to (become) dull; *[réputation]* to become tarnished.

ternissement [tɛʀnismɑ̃] *nm [métal]* tarnishing; *[glace]* dulling.

ternissure [tɛʀnisyʀ] *nf* (*V* **terni**) (*aspect*) tarnish, tarnished condition; dullness; (*tache*) tarnished spot; dull spot.

terrain [tɛʀɛ̃] **1** *nm* **(a)** (*relief*) ground, terrain (*T, littér*); (*sol*) soil, ground. **~ caillouteux/vallonné** stony/hilly ground; **~ meuble/lourd** loose/heavy soil *ou* ground; **c'est un bon ~ pour la culture** it's (a) good soil for cultivation; *V* **accident, glissement** *etc.*

(b) (*Ftbl, Rugby*) pitch, field; (*avec les installations*) ground; (*Courses, Golf*) course. **~ de basket-ball** basketball court.

(c) (*Comm: étendue de terre*) (*U*) land; (*parcelle*) plot (of land), piece of land; (*à bâtir*) site. **~ à lotir** land for dividing into plots; **chercher un ~ convenable pour un bâtiment** to look for a suitable site for a building; **'~ à bâtir'** 'site *ou* building land for sale'; **une maison avec 2 hectares de ~** a house with 2 hectares of land; **le prix du ~ à Paris** the price of land in Paris.

(d) (*Géog, Géol: souvent pl*) formation. **les ~s primaires/glaciaires** primary/glacial formations.

(e) (*Mil*) (*lieu d'opérations*) terrain; (*gagné ou perdu*) ground. (*lit, fig*) **céder/gagner/perdre du ~** to give/gain/lose ground; **reconnaître le ~** (*lit*) to reconnoitre the terrain; (*fig*) to see how the land lies, get the lie of the land; (*fig*) **sonder** *ou* **tâter le ~** to test the ground, put out feelers; **avoir l'avantage du ~** (*lit*) to have territorial advantage; (*fig*) to have the advantage of being on (one's) home ground; **préparer/déblayer le ~** to prepare/clear the ground; **sur le ~** (*Sport*) on the field; (*Sociol etc*) in the field; *V* **céder, reconnaître** *etc.*

(f) (*fig: domaine, sujet*) ground. **être sur son ~** to be on home ground *ou* territory; **trouver un ~ d'entente** to find an area of agreement; **chercher un ~ favorable à la discussion** to seek an area conducive to (useful) discussion; **je ne le suivrai pas sur ce ~** I can't go along with him there *ou* on that; **être en** *ou* **sur un ~ mouvant** to be on uncertain ground; **être sur un ~ glissant** to be on slippery *ou* dangerous ground; **le journaliste s'aventura sur un ~ brûlant** the journalist ventured onto dangerous ground *ou* risked a highly sensitive *ou* ticklish issue; **l'épidémie a trouvé un ~ tout prêt chez les réfugiés** the epidemic found an ideal breeding ground amongst the refugees.

2: terrain d'atterrissage landing ground; **terrain d'aviation** airfield; **terrain de camping** campsite, camping ground; **terrain de chasse** hunting ground; **terrain d'exercice** training ground; **terrain de jeu** playing field, playground (*Scol*); **terrain militaire** army ground; **terrain de sport** sports ground; **terrain de tir** shooting *ou* firing range; **terrain vague** waste ground (*U*), wasteland (*U*).

terrasse [tɛʀas] *nf* **(a)** *[parc, jardin]* terrace. **cultures en ~s** terrace cultivation; (*Géog*) **~ fluviale** river terrace.

(b) *[appartement]* terrace; (*sur le toit*) terrace roof. **toiture en ~** flat roof.

(c) *[café]* pavement (area). **j'ai aperçu Charles attablé à la ~ du Café Royal** I saw Charles sitting outside the Café Royal; **à la ~** outside; **il refusa de me servir à la ~** he refused to serve me outside.

terrassement [tɛʀasmɑ̃] *nm* **(a)** (*action*) excavation. **travaux de ~** excavation works. **(b)** (*terres creusées*) **~s** earthworks; *[voie ferrée]* embankments.

terrasser [tɛʀase] (1) *vt* **(a)** *personne [adversaire]* to floor, bring down; (*fig*) *[fatigue]* to overcome; *[attaque]* to bring down; *[émotion, nouvelle]* to overwhelm; *[maladie]* to lay low. **cette maladie l'a terrassé** this illness laid him low.

(b) (*Tech*) to excavate, dig out; (*Agr*) to dig over.

terrassier [tɛʀasje] *nm* navvy (*Brit*).

terre [tɛʀ] **1** *nf* **(a)** (*planète*) earth; (*ensemble des lieux, populations*) earth, world; (*ici-bas, s'opposant à l'au-delà*) earth, world. **la planète T~** the planet Earth; **Dieu créa le Ciel et la T~** God created the Heavens and the Earth, God created Heaven and Earth; **il a parcouru la ~ entière** he has travelled the world over, he has travelled all over the globe; **prendre à témoin la ~ entière** to take the world as one's witness; **tant qu'il y aura des hommes sur la ~** as long as there are men on (the) earth; **être seul sur (la) ~** to be alone in (all) the world; **il ne faut pas s'attendre au bonheur sur (cette) ~** happiness is not to be expected in this world *ou* on this earth; (*fig*) **redescendre** *ou* **revenir sur ~** to come down *ou* back to earth; *V* **remuer, sel, ventre** *etc.*

(b) (*sol: surface*) ground, land; (*matière*) earth, soil; (*pour la poterie*) clay. **pipe/vase en ~** clay pipe/vase; **ne t'allonge pas par ~, la ~ est humide** don't lie on the ground – it's damp, don't lie down – the ground is damp; **une ~ fertile/aride** a fertile/an arid soil; **retourner/labourer la ~** to turn over/work the soil; **travailler la ~** to work the soil *ou* land; **poser qch à** *ou* **par ~** to put sth (down) on the ground; **jeter qch à** *ou* **par ~** to throw sth (down) on the ground, throw sth to the ground; **cela fiche** *ou* **flanque tous nos projets par ~*** that throws all our plans out of the window*, that really messes up all our plans*; **mettre qn en ~** to bury sb; **mettre qch en ~** to put sth into the soil; **5 mètres sous ~** 5 metres underground; (*fig*) **être à six pieds sous ~** to be six feet under, be pushing up the daisies*; *V* **chemin, motte, ver.**

(c) (*étendue, campagne*) land (*U*). **une bande** *ou* **langue de ~** a strip of land; **retourner à la/aimer la ~** to return to/love the land; **des ~s à blé** corn-growing land; **il a acheté un bout** *ou* **un lopin de ~** he's bought a piece *ou* patch *ou* plot of land; **~s en friche** *ou* **en jachère/incultes** fallow/uncultivated land.

(d) (*par opposition à mer*) land (*U*). **sur la ~ ferme** on dry land, on terra firma; **apercevoir la ~** to sight land; (*Naut*) **~!** land ho!; (*Naut*) **aller à ~** to go ashore; **dans les ~s** inland; **aller/voyager par (voie de) ~** to go/travel by land *ou* overland; *V* **toucher.**

(e) (*propriété, domaine*) land (*gén U*). **la ~** land; **une ~** an estate; **il a acheté une ~ en Normandie** he's bought an estate *ou* some land in Normandy; **vivre sur/de ses ~s** to live on/off one's lands *ou* estates; **la ~ est un excellent investissement** land is an excellent investment.

(f) (*pays, région*) land, country. **sa ~ natale** his native land *ou* country; **la France, ~ d'accueil** France, (the) land of welcome; **~s lointaines/australes** distant/southern lands; **la T~ promise** the Promised Land.

(g) (*Élec*) earth. **mettre** *ou* **relier à la ~** to earth; *V* **pris.**

2: terre battue hard-packed surface; (*Tennis*) **jouer sur terre battue** to play on a hard court; (*fig*) **terre brûlée: politique de la terre brûlée** scorched earth policy; **terre de bruyère**

heath-mould, heath-peat; terre cuite (*pour briques, tuiles*) baked clay; (*pour jattes, statuettes*) terracotta; objets en terre cuite, terres cuites terracotta ware (*U*); une terre cuite a terracotta (object); terre à foulon fuller's earth; terre glaise clay; terre-neuvas *nm, pl* terres-neuvas fishing boat (*for fishing off Newfoundland*); Terre-Neuve *nf* Newfoundland; terre-neuve *nm inv* (*chien*) Newfoundland; terre-neuvien, -ienne *adj* Newfoundland (*épith*); Terre-Neuvien(ne) *nm,f, mpl* Terre-Neuviens Newfoundlander; (*fig*) cet homme est un vrai terre-neuve that man's a real (good) Samaritan!; (*Géog*) terre noire chernozem; terre-plein *nm, pl* terre-pleins (*Mil*) terreplein; (*Constr*) platform; (*Chim*) terres rares rare earths; la Terre Sainte the Holy Land; terre de Sienne sienna; terre à terre, terre-à-terre *adj inv esprit* down-to-earth, matter-of-fact; *personne* down-to-earth, unimaginative, prosaic; *préoccupations* mundane, workaday, prosaic; terres vierges virgin lands.

terreau [tɛʀo] *nm* compost. ~ de feuilles leaf mould.

terrer [tɛʀe] (1) 1 se terrer *vpr* (a) *[personne poursuivie]* to flatten o.s., crouch down; *[criminel recherché]* to lie low, go to ground *ou* earth; *[personne peu sociable]* to hide (o.s.) away. terrés dans la cave, pendant les bombardements hidden (away) in the cellar during the bombings.
(b) *[lapin, renard]* (*dans son terrier*) to go to earth *ou* ground; (*contre terre*) to crouch down, flatten itself.
2 *vt* (*Agr*) *arbre* to earth round *ou* up; *pelouse* to spread with soil; *semis* to earth over; (*Tech*) *drap* to full.

terrestre [tɛʀɛstʀ(ə)] *adj* (a) *faune, flore, transports, habitat* land (*épith*); *surface, magnétisme* earth's (*épith*), terrestrial, of earth. (*Mil*) effectifs ~s land forces; *V* croûte, écorce, globe.
(b) (*d'ici-bas*) *biens, plaisirs, vie* earthly, terrestrial; *V* paradis.

terreur [tɛʀœʀ] *nf* (a) (*peur*) terror (*gén U*). avec ~ with dread; vaines ~s vain *ou* empty fears; le dentiste était ma grande ~ the dentist was my greatest fear, I was terrified of the dentist; il vivait dans la ~ d'être découvert/de la police he lived in terror of being discovered/of the police.
(b) (*terrorisme*) terror. (*Hist*) la T~ the (Reign of) Terror.
(c) (**hum: personne*) terror. jouer les ~s to play the tough guy*; c'est la ~ de la ville he's the terror of the town.

terreux, -euse [tɛʀø, øz] *adj* (a) *goût, odeur* earthy. (b) *sabots* muddy; *mains* grubby, soiled; *salade* gritty, dirty. (c) *teint* sallow; *ciel* muddy, leaden.

terri [tɛʀi] *nm* = terril.

terrible [tɛʀibl(ə)] 1 *adj* (a) (*effroyable*) *accident, maladie, châtiment* terrible, dreadful; *arme* terrible.
(b) (*terrifiant, féroce*) *guerrier, air, menaces* terrible, fearsome.
(c) (*intensif*) *vent, force, pression, bruit, colère* terrific, tremendous, fantastic. c'est un ~ menteur he's a terrible *ou* an awful liar; c'est ~ ce qu'il peut manger it's terrific *ou* fantastic what he can eat*.
(d) (*affligeant, pénible*) c'est ~ d'en arriver là it's terrible *ou* dreadful to have come to this; ce qu'elle a fait, c'est ~ what she has done is terrible *ou* dreadful *ou* awful; le ~ est qu'il refuse qu'on l'aide the awful *ou* dreadful part about it is that he refuses to be helped.
(e) (*casse-pieds, pénible*) il est ~, avec sa manie de toujours vous contredire he's awful *ou* dreadful, with his insistence on always contradicting; c'est ~ de devoir toujours tout répéter it's awful *ou* dreadful always having to repeat everything; *V* enfant.
(f) (*: *formidable*) *film, soirée, personne* terrific*, great*, tremendous*. ce film n'est pas ~ this film is nothing special *ou* marvellous.
2 *adv* (:) ça marche ~ it's working fantastically (well)* *ou* really great:.

terriblement [tɛʀibləmɑ̃] *adv* (a) (*extrêmement*) terribly, dreadfully, awfully. (b) (†: *affreusement*) terribly†.

terrien, -ienne [tɛʀjɛ̃, jɛn] 1 *adj* (a) landed (*épith*), landowning (*épith*). propriétaire ~ landowner, landed proprietor.
(b) vertus ~nes virtues of the soil *ou* land; avoir une vieille ascendance ~ne to come of old country stock.
2 *nm* (a) (*paysan*) man of the soil, countryman.
(b) (*habitant de la Terre*) Earthman, earthling.
(c) (*non-marin*) landsman.
3 terrienne *nf* (*V nm*) countrywoman; Earthwoman, earthling; landswoman.

terrier [tɛʀje] *nm* (a) (*tanière*) *[lapin, taupe]* burrow, hole; *[renard]* earth. (b) (*chien*) terrier.

terrifiant, e [tɛʀifjɑ̃, ɑ̃t] *adj* (a) (*effrayant*) terrifying.
(b) (*sens affaibli*) *progrès, appétit* fearsome, incredible. c'est ~ comme il a maigri/grandi! it's awful *ou* frightening how much weight he has lost/how tall he has grown!

terrifier [tɛʀifje] (7) *vt* to terrify.

terril [tɛʀi(l)] *nm* (coal)tip, slag heap.

terrine [tɛʀin] *nf* (*pot*) earthenware vessel, terrine; (*Culin*) (*récipient*) terrine; (*pâté*) pâté. ~ du chef chef's special pâté.

territoire [tɛʀitwaʀ] *nm* (*gén, Pol, Zool*) territory; *[département, commune]* area; (*Jur*) *[évêque]* jurisdiction, obedience; *[juge]* jurisdiction; *V* aménagement, surveillance.

territorial, e, *mpl* **-aux** [tɛʀitɔʀjal, o] 1 *adj* (a) *puissance* land (*épith*); *intégrité, modifications* territorial. eaux ~es territorial waters; armée ~e Territorial Army.
(b) (*Jur: opposé à personnel*) territorial.
2 *nm* (*Mil*) Territorial.
3 territoriale *nf* (*Mil*) Territorial Army.

territorialité [tɛʀitɔʀjalite] *nf* (*Jur*) territoriality.

terroir [tɛʀwaʀ] *nm* (a) (*Agr*) soil. vin qui a un goût de ~ wine which has a taste *ou* tang of its soil.
(b) (*fig: région rurale*) accent du ~ country *ou* rural accent, brogue; mots du ~ words with a rural flavour; il sent son ~ he is very much of his native heath *ou* soil; poète du ~ poet of the land.

terroriser [tɛʀɔʀize] (1) *vt* to terrorize.

terrorisme [tɛʀɔʀism(ə)] *nm* terrorism.

terroriste [tɛʀɔʀist(ə)] *adj, nmf* terrorist.

tertiaire [tɛʀsjɛʀ] 1 *adj* (*Géol, Méd*) tertiary. (*Écon*) (secteur) ~ service industries, tertiary sector (*T*), tertiary industry (*T*).
2 *nm* (*Géol*) Tertiary.

tertio [tɛʀsjo] *adv* third(ly).

tertre [tɛʀtʀ(ə)] *nm* (*monticule*) hillock, mound, knoll (*littér*); *[sépulture]* (burial) mound.

tes [te] *adj poss V* ton[1].

tesson [tesɔ̃] *nm*: ~ (de bouteille) piece of broken glass *ou* bottle.

test[1] [tɛst] 1 *nm* (*gén*) test. faire passer un ~ à qn to give sb a test; soumettre qn à des ~s to subject sb to tests, test sb; ~ d'orientation professionnelle vocational *ou* occupational test; ~ biologique biological test.
2 *adj*: conflit-/région-~ test conflict/area.

test[2] [tɛst] *nm* (*Zool*) test.

test[3] [tɛst] *nm* = têt.

testament [tɛstamɑ̃] 1 *nm* (a) (*Rel*) Ancien/Nouveau T~ Old/New Testament.
(b) (*Jur*) will, testament (*Jur*), last will and testament (*Jur, frm*). mourir sans ~ to die intestate (*Jur, frm*) *ou* without leaving a will; ceci est mon ~ this is my last will and testament; (*hum*) il peut faire son ~* he can *ou* he'd better make out his will* (*hum*); *V* coucher, léguer.
(c) (*fig*) *[homme politique, artiste]* testament.
2: testament par acte public, testament authentique *will dictated to notary in the presence of witnesses*; testament mystique *will written or dictated by testator, signed by him, and handed in sealed envelope, before witnesses, to notary*; testament olographe *will written, dated and signed by the testator*; testament secret = testament mystique.

testamentaire [tɛstamɑ̃tɛʀ] *adj*: dispositions ~s clauses *ou* provisions of a will, devises (*T*); donation ~ bequest, legacy; héritier ~ devisee; *V* exécuteur.

testateur, -trice [tɛstatœʀ, tʀis] 1 *nm* testator, devisor. 2 testatrice *nf* testatrix, devisor.

tester[1] [tɛste] (1) *vt* to test.

tester[2] [tɛste] (1) *vi* to make (out) one's will.

testicule [tɛstikyl] *nm* testicle, testis (*pl* testes) (*T*).

têt [tɛ] *nm* (*Chim*) ~ à rôtir roasting dish *ou* crucible; ~ à gaz beehive shelf.

tétanique [tetanik] *adj convulsions* tetanic; *patient* tetanus (*épith*), suffering from tetanus (*attrib*).

tétaniser [tetanize] (1) *vt* to tetanize.

tétanos [tetanos] *nm* tetanus, lockjaw. ~ musculaire *ou* physiologique tetanus (of a muscle).

têtard [tɛtaʀ] *nm* (*Zool*) tadpole.

tête [tɛt] 1 *nf* (a) (*gén*) *[homme, animal]* head. être ~ nue, n'avoir rien sur la ~ to be bareheaded, have nothing on one's head; avoir une ~ frisée to have curly hair, have a curly head of hair; avoir mal à la ~ to have a headache; j'ai la ~ lourde my head feels heavy; avoir la ~ sale/propre to have dirty/clean hair; de la ~ aux pieds from head to foot *ou* toe, from top to toe; (*lit*) entrer/marcher la ~ haute/basse to come in/walk with one's head held high/down; veau à deux ~s two-headed calf; se tenir la ~ à deux mains to hold one's head in one's hands; rester la ~ en bas to stay with one's head down; *V* fromage, hocher *etc.*
(b) (*fig: vie*) head, neck. réclamer la ~ de qn to demand sb's head; jurer sur la ~ de qn to swear on sb's life *ou* head; risquer sa ~ to risk one's neck; sauver sa ~ to save one's skin *ou* neck; il y va de sa ~ his neck is at stake.
(c) (*visage, expression*) face. il a une ~ sympathique he has a friendly face; il a une ~ sinistre he has a sinister look about him; il a une bonne ~ he looks a decent sort; quand il a appris la nouvelle il a fait une (drôle de) ~! you should have seen his face when he heard the news!; il en fait une ~! what a face!, just look at his face!; faire la ~ to sulk, have the sulks*; faire une ~ d'enterrement *ou* de six pieds de long to have a face as long as a fiddle; quelle (sale) ~ il a! he looks a nasty piece of work, he has a really nasty look about him; je connais cette ~-là! I know that face; mettre un nom sur une ~ to put a name to a face; il a *ou* c'est une ~ à claques* *ou* à gifles* he has got the sort of face you'd love to swipe* *ou* that just asks to be swiped*; *V* coup.
(d) (*personne*) head. ~ couronnée crowned head; (*animal*) 20 ~s de bétail 20 head of cattle; c'est une forte ~ he is self-willed; c'est une mauvaise ~ he's an awkward customer; une ~ chaude a hothead; une ~ brûlée a wild adventurer; les ~s vont tomber heads will roll; le repas coûtera 50 F par ~ *ou* par ~ de pipe: the meal will cost 50 francs a head *ou* 50 francs per person *ou* 50 francs apiece*; (*péj*) ~ de lard!: go on, you pigheaded oaf!: (*péj*).
(e) (*mesure*) head. il a une ~ de plus he is a head taller; (*Courses*) gagner d'une ~ to win by a head.
(f) *[clou, marteau]* head; *[arbre]* top. ~ d'ail head of garlic; ~ d'artichaut artichoke head; ~ d'épingle pinhead; à la ~ du lit at the head of the bed.
(g) (*partie antérieure*) *[train, procession]* front, head; (*Mil*) *[colonne, peloton]* head. (*Rail*) voiture de ~ front coach; on monte en ~ *ou* en queue? shall we get on at the front or (at) the back?; être en ~ to be in the lead *ou* in front; ils sont entrés dans la ville, musique en ~ they came into the town led *ou* headed by the band; tué à la ~ de ses troupes killed at the head of his troops; *V* soupape.

(h) *[page, liste, chapitre, classe]* top, head. (*Presse*) **article de ~** leading article, leader (column); **en ~ de phrase** at the head of the sentence; **être** *ou* **venir en ~ de liste** to head the list, come at the head *ou* top of the list; **être à la ~ d'un mouvement/d'une affaire** to be at the head of a movement/an affair, head a movement/an affair; **être la ~ d'un mouvement/d'une affaire** to be the brains *ou* the mastermind behind a movement/an affair.

(i) (*faculté(s) mentale(s)*) **avoir (toute) sa ~** to have (all) one's wits about one; **n'avoir rien dans la ~** to be empty-headed; **où ai-je la ~?** whatever am I thinking of?; **avoir une petite ~** to be dim-witted; **alors, petite ~!*** well, dimwit!*; **avoir** *ou* **être une ~ sans cervelle** *ou* **en l'air** *ou* **de linotte** to be scatterbrained, be a scatterbrain; **avoir de la ~** to have a good head on one's shoulders; **avoir la ~ sur les épaules** to be level-headed; **femme/homme de ~** level-headed *ou* capable woman/man; **calculer qch de ~** to work sth out in one's head; **je n'ai plus le chiffre/le nom en ~** the number/the name has gone (clean) out of my head; **chercher qch dans sa ~** to search one's memory for sth; **mettre** *ou* **fourrer* qch dans la ~ de qn** to put *ou* get *ou* stick* sth into sb's head; **se mettre dans la ~** *ou* **en ~ que** (*s'imaginer*) to get it into one's head that; **se mettre dans la** *ou* **en ~ de faire qch** (*se décider*) to take it into one's head to do sth; **j'ai la ~ vide** my mind is a blank *ou* has gone blank; **avoir la ~ à ce qu'on fait** to have one's mind on what one is doing; **avoir la ~ ailleurs** to have one's mind on other matters *ou* elsewhere; **se casser** *ou* **se creuser la ~** to rack one's brains; **il ne se sont pas cassé** *ou* **creusé la ~!** they didn't exactly put themselves out! *ou* overexert themselves!; **n'en faire qu'à sa ~** to do (exactly) as one pleases, please o.s., go one's own (sweet*) way; **(faire qch) à ~ reposée** (to do sth) in a more leisurely moment; *V* **idée, perdre** *etc.*

(j) (*tempérament*) **avoir la ~ chaude/froide** to be quick- *ou* fiery-tempered/cool-headed; **avoir la ~ dure** to be thick-(headed) *ou* a thickhead *ou* blockheaded* *ou* a blockhead*; **avoir** *ou* **être une ~ de mule** *ou* **de bois, être une ~ de pioche*** to be as stubborn as a mule, be mulish *ou* pigheaded; **avoir la ~ près du bonnet** to be quick-tempered; *V* **coup.**

(k) (*Ftbl*) header. **faire une ~** to head the ball.

(l) (*loc*) (*fig*) **aller** *ou* **marcher la ~ haute** to walk with one's head held high, carry one's head high; (*fig*) **avoir la ~ basse** to hang one's head; (*lit*) **courir** *ou* **foncer ~ baissée** to rush *ou* charge headlong; (*fig*) **y aller ~ baissée** to charge in blindly; (*fig*) **se jeter** *ou* **donner ~ baissée dans** *entreprise, piège* to rush headlong into; **tomber la ~ la première** to fall headfirst; **jeter** *ou* **lancer à la ~ de qn que ...** to hurl in sb's face that ... ; **en avoir par-dessus la ~** to be fed up to the teeth*; **j'en donnerais ma ~ à couper** I would stake my life on it; **ne plus savoir où donner de la ~** not to know which way to turn; **prendre la ~** to take the lead, take charge; **tenir ~ à** to stand up to; **mettre la ~ de qn à prix** to put a price on sb's head; **se trouver à la ~ d'une petite fortune/de 2 maisons** to find o.s. the possessor of a small fortune/2 houses; *V* **martel, payer, tourner** *etc.*

2: (*Théât*) **tête d'affiche** top of the bill; **être la tête d'affiche** to head the bill, be top of the bill; **tête-bêche** *adv* head to foot *ou* tail; **timbre tête-bêche** tête-bêche stamp; (*Aut*) **tête de bielle** big end; **tête chercheuse** homing device; **fusée à tête chercheuse** homing rocket; **tête de cuvée** tête de cuvée; (*Aut*) **tête de Delco** ® distributor head; (*Tech*) **tête d'injection** swivel; **tête de lecture** *[pick-up]* pickup head; *[magnétophone]* recording head; **tête de ligne** terminus, end of the line (*Rail*); (*Pol*) **tête de liste** chief candidate (*in list system of voting*); **tête-de-loup** *nf, pl* **têtes-de-loup** ceiling brush; **tête de mort** (*emblème*) death's-head; *[pavillon]* skull and crossbones, Jolly Roger; (*Zool*) death's-head moth; (*Culin*) Gouda cheese; **tête-de-nègre** *adj inv* nigger-brown (*Brit*); **tête nucléaire** nuclear warhead; **tête de pont** (*au-delà d'un fleuve*) bridgehead; (*au-delà de la mer*) beachhead; **tête-à-queue** *nm inv* spin; **faire un tête-à-queue** *[cheval]* to turn about; *[voiture]* to spin round; (*Tennis*) **tête de série** seeded player; **tête-à-tête** *nm inv* (*conversation*) tête-à-tête, private conversation; (*meuble*) tête-à-tête; (*service*) breakfast set for two; tea *ou* coffee set for two; **en tête-à-tête** alone together; **dîner en tête-à-tête** intimate dinner for two; **discussion en tête-à-tête** discussion in private; **tête de Turc** whipping boy, Aunt Sally.

tétée [tete] *nf* (*action*) sucking; (*repas, lait*) feed. **5 ~s par jour** 5 feeds a day; **l'heure de la ~** feeding time (*of baby*).

téter [tete] (6) *vt* **(a)** *lait* to suck; *biberon, sein* to suck at. **~ sa mère** to suck at one's mother's breast; **donner à ~ à un bébé** to feed a baby (at the breast), suckle a baby†. **(b)** (*) *pouce* to suck; *pipe* to suck at *ou* on.

têtière [tɛtjɛʀ] *nf* *[cheval]* headstall; *[divan]* antimacassar.

tétine [tetin] *nf* *[vache]* udder, dug (*T*); *[truie]* teat, dug (*T*); *[biberon]* teat; (*sucette*) dummy, comforter (*Brit*), pacifier (*US*).

téton‡ [tetɔ̃] *nm* breast, tit*.

tétracorde [tetʀakɔʀd(ə)] *nm* tetrachord.

tétraèdre [tetʀaɛdʀ(ə)] *nm* tetrahedron.

tétraédrique [tetʀaedʀik] *adj* tetrahedral.

tétralogie [tetʀalɔʒi] *nf* tetralogy.

tétramètre [tetʀamɛtʀ(ə)] *nm* tetrameter.

tétrarque [tetʀaʀk(ə)] *nm* tetrarch.

tétrasyllabe [tetʀasilab] **1** *adj* tetrasyllabic. **2** *nm* tetrasyllable.

tétrasyllabique [tetʀasilabik] *adj* tetrasyllabic.

têtu, e [tety] *adj* stubborn, mulish, pigheaded. **~ comme une mule** *ou* **bourrique** as stubborn *ou* obstinate as a mule.

teuf-teuf, *pl* **teufs-teufs** [tœftœf] *nm* **(a)** (*bruit*) *[train]* puff-puff, chuff-chuff; *[voiture]* chug-chug. **(b)** (*: *automobile*) bone-shaker; (*langage enfantin: train*) puff-puff.

teuton, -onne [tøtɔ̃, ɔn] **1** *adj* (*Hist, péj*) Teutonic. **2** *nm,f*: **T~(ne)** Teuton.

teutonique [tøtɔnik] *adj* (*Hist, péj*) Teutonic.

texan, e [tɛksɑ̃, an] **1** *adj* Texan. **2** *nm,f*: **T~(e)** Texan.

texte [tɛkst(ə)] *nm* **(a)** (*U*) *[loi, contrat, pièce de théâtre etc]* text. **lire Shakespeare/la Bible dans le ~ (original)** to read Shakespeare/the Bible in the original (text); (*iro*) **en français dans le ~** those were the very words used, to quote the words used; (*Théât*) **apprendre son ~** to learn one's lines; **les illustrations sont bonnes mais il y a trop de ~** the pictures are good but there is too much text.

(b) (*œuvre écrite*) text; (*fragment*) passage, piece. **~s choisis** selected passages; **expliquez ce ~ de Gide** comment on this passage *ou* piece from *ou* by Gide; **il y a des erreurs dans le ~** there are textual errors *ou* errors in the text; *V* **explication.**

(c) (*énoncé*) *[devoir, dissertation]* subject, topic; (*Rel*) text; *V* **cahier.**

textile [tɛkstil] **1** *nm* **(a)** (*matière*) textile. **~s artificiels** man-made fibres; **~s synthétiques** synthetic *ou* man-made fibres. **(b)** (*Ind*) **le ~** the textile industry, textiles (*pl*). **2** *adj* textile.

textuel, -elle [tɛkstɥɛl] *adj* (*conforme au texte*) *traduction* literal, word for word; *copie* exact; *citation* verbatim (*épith*), exact; (*tiré du texte*) textual. **elle m'a dit d'aller me faire cuire un œuf: ~, mon vieux!*** she told me to get lost — those were her very words!, she told me to get lost, and I quote!; **c'est ~** those were his (*ou* her *etc*) very *ou* exact words.

textuellement [tɛkstɥɛlmɑ̃] *adv* (*conformément aux paroles*) exactly, verbatim, word for word; (*conformément au texte: V* **textuel**) literally, word for word; exactly; verbatim. **alors il m'a dit, ~, que j'étais un imbécile** so he told me, in these very words *ou* and I quote, that I was stupid.

texture [tɛkstyʀ] *nf* (*lit, fig*) texture.

thaï [tai] **1** *nm* (*Ling*) Thai. **2** *adj inv* Thai.

thaïlandais, e [tailɑ̃dɛ, ɛz] **1** *adj* Thai. **2** *nm,f*: **T~(e)** Thai, Thailander.

Thaïlande [tailɑ̃d] *nf* Thailand.

thalamus [talamys] *nm* (*Anat*) thalamus.

thalassémie [talasemi] *nf* thalassemia.

thalassothérapie [talasɔteʀapi] *nf* sea water therapy.

thalle [tal] *nm* thallus.

thallium [taljɔm] *nm* thallium.

thallophytes [talɔfit] *nm ou nf* thallophyte, thallogen.

thalweg [talvɛg] *nm* thalweg.

thaumaturge [tomatyʀʒ(ə)] **1** *nm* miracle-worker, thaumaturge (*T*), thaumaturgist (*T*). **2** *adj* miracle-working (*épith*), thaumaturgic(al) (*T*).

thé [te] **1** *nm* **(a)** (*feuilles séchées, boisson*) tea. **~ de Chine** China tea; **les ~s de Ceylan** Ceylon teas; **~ au lait/nature** tea with milk/without milk; **~ au citron/à la menthe** lemon/mint tea; *V* **feuille, rose, salon.**

(b) (*arbre*) tea plant.

(c) (*réunion*) tea party. **~ dansant** early evening dance, thé-dansant (*rare*).

2 *adj inv*: **rose ~** tea rose.

théâtral, e, *mpl* **-aux** [teatʀal, o] *adj* **(a)** *œuvre, situation* theatrical, dramatic; *rubrique, chronique* stage (*épith*), theatre (*épith*); *saison* theatre (*épith*); *représentation* stage (*épith*), theatrical. **la censure ~e** stage censorship, censorship in the theatre.

(b) (*fig péj*) *air, attitude, personne* theatrical, histrionic, stagey*. **ses attitudes ~es m'agacent** his theatricals *ou* histrionics irritate me.

théâtralement [teatʀalmɑ̃] *adv* (*V* **théâtral**) theatrically, histrionically, stagily*.

théâtre [teatʀ(ə)] *nm* **(a)** (*U*) (*gén: comme genre artistique*) theatre; (*comme ensemble de techniques*) drama, theatre; (*comme activité, profession*) stage, theatre. **faire du ~** to be on the stage; **faire un peu de ~** to do a bit of acting; **s'intéresser au ~** to be interested in drama *ou* the theatre; **elle veut faire du ~, elle se destine au ~** she wants to go on the stage; **je préfère le ~ au cinéma** *[acteur]* I prefer the stage *ou* the theatre to films; *[spectateur]* I prefer the theatre to the cinema; **je n'aime pas le ~ à la télévision** I do not like stage productions on television; **c'est du ~ filmé** it's a filmed stage production; **ses pièces ne sont pas du bon ~** his plays are not good theatre *ou* drama, his plays do not stage well; **technique** *ou* **art du ~** stagecraft; **~ d'essai** experimental theatre *ou* drama; **il fait du ~ d'amateurs** he's involved in *ou* he does some amateur dramatics; **un roman adapté pour le ~** a novel adapted for the stage; *V* **coup, critique**[2].

(b) (*lieu, entreprise*) theatre. **~ de marionnettes/de verdure** puppet/open-air theatre; **il ne va jamais au ~** he never goes to the theatre, he is not a theatregoer; **à la sortie des ~s il est difficile de trouver un taxi** when the theatres come out, it's difficult to get a taxi; **le ~ est plein ce soir** it's a full house tonight; **~ d'ombres** shadow theatre; **~ de guignol** ≈ Punch and Judy show; *V* **agence, jumeau.**

(c) de ~ stage (*épith*), theatre (*épith*); **un homme/une femme de ~** a man/woman of the theatre *ou* stage; **les gens de ~** theatre *ou* stage people; **accessoires/costumes/décors/grimage de ~** stage props/costumes/sets/make-up; **artifices de ~** stage tricks; **directeur de ~** theatrical *ou* stage director; **troupe de ~** theatre *ou* stage *ou* drama company; **voix/gestes de ~** theatrical *ou* histrionic *ou* stagey* voice/gestures.

(d) (*genre littéraire*) drama, theatre; (*œuvres théâtrales*) plays (*pl*), dramatic works (*pl*), theatre. **le ~ de Sheridan** Sheridan's plays *ou* dramatic works, the theatre of Sheridan; **le ~ classique/élisabéthain** the classical/Elizabethan theatre, classical/Elizabethan drama; **le ~ antique** the theatre *ou* drama of

antiquity; **le ~ de caractères/de situation** the theatre of character/situation; **le ~ à thèse** didactic theatre; **le ~ de boulevard, le boulevard** light theatrical entertainment (*as performed in the theatres of the Paris Boulevards*); **le ~ burlesque** the theatre of burlesque, the burlesque theatre; *V* **pièce.**
(e) (*fig péj*) (*exagération*) theatricals (*pl*), histrionics (*pl*); (*simulation*) playacting. **il fait son ~** he's doing his theatricals; **c'est du ~** it's just playacting.
(f) *[événement, crime]* scene. **les Flandres ont été le ~ de combats sanglants** Flanders has been the scene of bloody fighting; (*Mil*) **le ~ des opérations** the theatre of operations.
thébaïde [tebaid] *nf* (*littér*) solitary retreat.
thébain, e [tebɛ̃, ɛn] **1** *adj* Theban. **2** *nm,f*: **T~(e)** Theban.
Thèbes [tɛb] *n* Thebes.
théière [tejɛʀ] *nf* teapot.
théine [tein] *nf* theine.
théisme [teism(ə)] *nm* theism.
théiste [teist(ə)] **1** *adj* theistic(al), theist. **2** *nmf* theist.
thématique [tematik] **1** *adj* (*gén*) thematic; (*Ling*) *voyelle* thematic. **2** *nf* set of themes.
thème [tɛm] *nm* **(a)** (*sujet: gén, Littérat, Mus*) theme. **~ de composition d'un peintre** a painter's theme; (*Mil*) **~ tactique** tactical ground plan; (*Psych*) **~s délirants** themes of delusion.
(b) (*Scol: traduction*) translation (*into the foreign language*), prose (composition). **~ et version** prose (composition) and unseen (translation); **~ allemand/espagnol** German/Spanish prose (composition), translation into German/Spanish; *V* **fort.**
(c) (*Ling*) stem, theme. **~ nominal/verbal** noun/verb stem *ou* theme.
(d) (*Astrol*) **~ astral** horoscope, birth chart.
théocratie [teɔkʀasi] *nf* theocracy.
théocratique [teɔkʀatik] *adj* theocratic.
Théocrite [teɔkʀit] *nm* Theocritus.
théodicée [teɔdise] *nf* theodicy.
théodolite [teɔdɔlit] *nm* theodolite.
Théodore [teɔdɔʀ] *nm* Theodore.
théologal, e, *mpl* **-aux** [teɔlɔgal, o] *adj* *V* **vertu.**
théologie [teɔlɔʒi] *nf* theology. **études de ~** theological studies; **faire sa ~** to study theology *ou* divinity.
théologien [teɔlɔʒjɛ̃] *nm* theologian.
théologique [teɔlɔʒik] *adj* (*Rel*) theological.
théologiquement [teɔlɔʒikmɑ̃] *adv* theologically.
Théophile [teɔfil] *nm* Theophilus.
Théophraste [teɔfʀast(ə)] *nm* Theophrastus.
théorème [teɔʀɛm] *nm* theorem.
théoricien, -ienne [teɔʀisjɛ̃, jɛn] *nm,f* theoretician, theorist.
théorie[1] [teɔʀi] *nf* (*doctrine, hypothèse*) theory. **la ~ et la pratique** theory and practice; **en ~** in theory, on paper* (*fig*); **la ~, c'est bien joli, mais ...** theory *ou* theorizing is all very well, but ... ; (*Math*) **la ~ des ensembles** set theory.
théorie[2] [teɔʀi] *nf* (*littér: procession*) procession, file.
théorique [teɔʀik] *adj* theoretical, theoretic (*rare*). **c'est une liberté toute ~** it's a purely theoretical freedom.
théoriquement [teɔʀikmɑ̃] *adv* theoretically. **~, c'est vrai** in theory *ou* theoretically it's true.
théosophe [teɔzɔf] *nmf* theosophist.
théosophie [teɔzɔfi] *nf* theosophy.
thérapeute [teʀapøt] *nmf* therapist, therapeutist (*Brit*).
thérapeutique [teʀapøtik] **1** *adj* therapeutic. **2** *nf* (*branche de la médecine*) therapeutics (*sg*); (*traitement*) therapy.
thérapie [teʀapi] *nf* = **thérapeutique.**
Thérèse [teʀɛz] *nf* Theresa, Teresa.
thermal, e, *mpl* **-aux** [tɛʀmal, o] *adj*: **cure ~e** water cure; **faire une cure ~e** to take the waters; **eaux ~es** hot (mineral) springs (*with curative properties*); **émanations ~es** thermal *ou* hot springs; **établissement ~** hydropathic *ou* water-cure establishment; **source ~e** thermal *ou* hot spring (*with curative properties*); **station ~e** spa.
thermalisme [tɛʀmalism(ə)] *nm* (*science*) balneology; (*pratique ou gérance des stations thermales*) management and organization of spas. **~ social** *government scheme in operation since 1945 to enable all classes of society to take advantage of water cures.*
thermes [tɛʀm(ə)] *nmpl* (*Hist*) thermae; (*établissement thermal*) hot *ou* thermal baths.
thermidor [tɛʀmidɔʀ] *nm* Thermidor (*11th month of French Republican calendar*).
thermie† [tɛʀmi] *nf* (*Phys*) therm.
thermique [tɛʀmik] *adj* *unité* thermal; *énergie* thermic. **moteur ~** heat engine; **carte ~** temperature map; **centrale ~** thermal power station; **ascendance ~** thermal, thermal current; **science ~** science of heat.
thermochimie [tɛʀmɔʃimi] *nf* thermochemistry.
thermocouple [tɛʀmɔkupl(ə)] *nm* (*Phys*) thermocouple, thermoelectric couple.
thermodynamique [tɛʀmɔdinamik] **1** *nf* thermodynamics (*sg*). **2** *adj* thermodynamic(al).
thermoélectricité [tɛʀmɔelɛktʀisite] *nf* thermoelectricity.
thermoélectrique [tɛʀmɔelɛktʀik] *adj* thermoelectric(al). **couple ~** thermoelectric couple, thermocouple; **effet ~** thermoelectric *ou* Seebeck effect; **pile ~** thermopile, thermoelectric pile.
thermogène [tɛʀmɔʒɛn] *adj* *V* **ouate.**
thermographe [tɛʀmɔgʀaf] *nm* thermograph.
thermomètre [tɛʀmɔmɛtʀ(ə)] *nm* thermometer. **le ~ indique 38°/monte** the thermometer stands at *ou* is standing at *ou* is showing 38°/is going up; **~ à mercure/à alcool** mercury/alcohol thermometer; **~ à maxima et minima** maximum and minimum thermometer; **~ médical** clinical thermometer; (*fig*) **le ~ de l'opinion publique** the barometer *ou* gauge of public opinion.
thermométrie [tɛʀmɔmetʀi] *nf* thermometry.
thermométrique [tɛʀmɔmetʀik] *adj* thermometric(al).
thermonucléaire [tɛʀmɔnykleɛʀ] *adj* thermonuclear.
thermopile [tɛʀmɔpil] *nf* thermopile.
thermoplastique [tɛʀmɔplastik] *adj* thermoplastic.
thermopropulsion [tɛʀmɔpʀɔpylsjɔ̃] *nf* thermal propulsion.
Thermopyles [tɛʀmɔpil] *nfpl* Thermopylae.
thermorégulation [tɛʀmɔʀegylɑsjɔ̃] *nf* thermotaxis, thermoregulation.
thermorésistant, e [tɛʀmɔʀezistɑ̃, ɑ̃t] *adj* thermosetting.
thermos [tɛʀmos] *nm ou nf* (®: *aussi* **bouteille ~**) vacuum *ou* Thermos ® flask.
thermostat [tɛʀmɔsta] *nm* thermostat.
thermothérapie [tɛʀmɔteʀapi] *nf* thermotherapy.
thésaurisation [tezɔʀizɑsjɔ̃] *nf* hoarding (*of money*); (*Écon*) building up of capital.
thésauriser [tezɔʀize] (1) **1** *vi* to hoard money. **2** *vt* (*rare*) to hoard (up).
thésauriseur, -euse [tezɔʀizœʀ, øz] *nm,f* (*rare*) hoarder (*of money*).
thèse [tɛz] *nf* **(a)** (*doctrine*) thesis, argument. (*Littérat*) **pièce/roman à ~** pièce/roman à thèse (*T*), play/novel expounding a philosophical *ou* social thesis. **(b)** (*Univ*) thesis. **~ d'État** ≃ Higher Doctoral thesis; **~ d'université** ≃ Ph.D. thesis, doctoral thesis; **~ de 3e cycle** ≃ M.A. *ou* M.Sc. thesis, Master's thesis; *V* **soutenance, soutenir. (c)** (*Philos*) thesis.
Thésée [teze] *nm* Theseus.
Thessalie [tɛsali] *nf* Thessaly.
thessalien, -ienne [tɛsaljɛ̃, jɛn] **1** *adj* Thessalian. **2** *nm,f*: **T~(ne)** Thessalian.
thêta [teta] *nm* theta.
thibaude [tibod] *nf* anti-slip undercarpeting (*U*).
Thibau(l)t [tibo] *nm* Theobald.
Thibet [tibɛ] *nm* = **Tibet.**
thibétain, e [tibetɛ̃, ɛn] = **tibétain.**
Thierry [tjeʀi] *nm* Terry.
Thomas [tɔmɑ] *nm* Thomas.
thomisme [tɔmism(ə)] *nm* Thomism.
thomiste [tɔmist(ə)] **1** *adj* Thomistic(al). **2** *nmf* Thomist.
thon [tɔ̃] *nm* (*Zool*) tunny (fish), tuna; (*en boîte*) tuna(-fish) (*U*).
thonier [tɔnje] *nm* tunny boat.
thoracique [tɔʀasik] *adj* *cavité, canal* thoracic. **cage ~** ribcage; **capacité ~** respiratory *ou* vital capacity.
thorax [tɔʀaks] *nm* thorax.
thrombose [tʀɔ̃boz] *nf* thrombosis.
Thucydide [tysidid] *nm* Thucydides.
Thulé [tyle] *nm* Thule.
thune‡†† [tyn] *nf* 5-franc piece.
thuriféraire [tyʀifeʀɛʀ] *nm* (*Rel*) thurifier; (*fig littér*) flatterer, sycophant.
thuya [tyja] *nm* thuja.
thym [tɛ̃] *nm* thyme. **~ sauvage** wild thyme.
thymique [timik] *adj* (*Méd, Psych*) thymic.
thymus [timys] *nm* thymus.
thyroïde [tiʀɔid] **1** *adj* thyroid (*épith*). **2** *nf*: **(glande) ~** thyroid (gland).
thyroïdien, -ienne [tiʀɔidjɛ̃, jɛn] *adj* thyroid (*épith*).
thyrse [tiʀs(ə)] *nm* (*Bot, Myth*) thyrsus.
tiare [tjaʀ] *nf* tiara.
Tibère [tibɛʀ] *nm* Tiberius.
Tibériade [tibeʀjad] *n*: **le lac de ~** the Sea of Tiberias.
Tibet [tibɛ] *nm* Tibet.
tibétain, e [tibetɛ̃, ɛn] **1** *adj* Tibetan. **2** *nm* (*Ling*) Tibetan. **3** *nm,f*: **T~(e)** Tibetan.
tibia [tibja] *nm* (*Anat: os*) tibia (*T*), shinbone; (*partie antérieure de la jambe*) shin. **donner un coup de pied dans les ~s à qn** to kick sb in the shins.
Tibre [tibʀ(ə)] *nm*: **le ~** the Tiber.
tic [tik] *nm* **(a)** (*mouvement convulsif*) (facial) twitch *ou* tic; (*du corps*) twitch, mannerism, tic; (*autre manie*) mannerism. **~ (nerveux)** nervous twitch *ou* tic; **~ de langage** (verbal) mannerism, verbal tic; **il a un ~ facial inquiétant** he has a worrying facial twitch *ou* tic; **il est plein de ~s** he is ridden with tics, he never stops twitching.
(b) (*Vét*) cribbing (*U*), crib-biting (*U*).
ticket [tikɛ] **1** *nm* **(a)** (*billet*) ticket. **~ de métro/consigne/vestiaire** underground/left-luggage/cloakroom ticket.
(b) (‡: *10F*) 10-franc note, ≃ quid* (*Brit*), ≃ greenback* (*US*).
(c) (‡) **avoir un** *ou* **le ~ (avec qn): j'ai le ~ avec sa sœur** I've made a hit with his sister*.
2: ticket modérateur patient's contribution (*towards cost of medical treatment*); **ticket de quai** platform ticket; **ticket de rationnement** (ration) coupon.
tic-tac [tiktak] *nm* ticking, tick-tock. **faire ~** to tick, go tick tock.
tictaquer [tiktake] (1) *vi* to tick (away).
tiédasse [tjedas] *adj* (*péj*) lukewarm, tepid.
tiède [tjɛd] **1** *adj* **(a)** *boisson, bain* lukewarm, tepid; *vent, saison* mild, warm; *atmosphère* balmy; (*fig littér: sécurisant, enveloppant*) warmly enveloping.
(b) (*péj*) *sentiment, foi, accueil* lukewarm, tepid; *chrétien, communiste* half-hearted, lukewarm.
2 *nmf* (*péj*) lukewarm *ou* half-hearted individual. **des mesures qui risquent d'effaroucher les ~s** measures likely to scare the half-hearted *ou* lukewarm.
3 *adv*: **boire ~: elle boit son café ~** she doesn't like her coffee too hot; **les Anglais boivent leur bière ~** the English drink their beer (luke)warm *ou* tepid; **qu'il se dépêche un peu, je n'aime pas boire ~** I wish he'd hurry up because I don't like drinking things cold.

tièdement [tjɛdmɑ̃] *adv (péj: V* **tiède**) in a lukewarm way; half-heartedly.

tiédeur [tjedœʀ] *nf* (*V* **tiède** *adj*) lukewarmness; tepidness; mildness, warmth; balminess; half-heartedness.

tiédir [tjediʀ] (2) **1** *vi* **(a)** (*devenir moins chaud*) to cool (down); (*se réchauffer*) to grow warm(er). **faire ~ de l'eau/une boisson** to warm *ou* heat up some water/a drink.
(b) (*fig*) *[sentiment, foi, ardeur]* to cool (off).
2 *vt [soleil, source de chaleur]* to warm (up); *[air frais]* to cool (down).

tiédissement [tjedismɑ̃] *nm* (*V* **tiédir**) cooling (down); warming up; cooling (off).

tien, tienne [tjɛ̃, tjɛn] **1** *pron poss:* **le ~, la tienne, les ~s, les tiennes** yours, your own, (††, *Rel*) thine; **ce sac n'est pas le ~** this bag is not yours, this is not YOUR bag; **mes fils/filles sont stupides comparé(e)s aux ~s/tiennes** my sons/daughters are stupid compared to yours *ou* your own; **à la tienne** your (good) health, cheers*; (*hum*) **à la tienne, Étienne*** here's mud in your eye!* (*hum*), bottoms up!* (*hum*); (*iro*) **tu vas faire ce travail tout seul? — à la tienne!*** are you going to do the job all by yourself? — good luck to you!* *ou* rather you than me!*; *pour autres exemples V* **sien.**
2 *nm* **(a)** (*U*) **il n'y a pas à distinguer le ~ du mien** what's mine is yours; *pour autres exemples V* **sien.**
(b) les ~s your family, your (own) folks*; **toi et tous les ~s** you and your whole set; *V* **sien.**
3 *adj poss* (*littér*) **un ~ cousin** a cousin of yours.

tiens [tjɛ̃] *excl V* **tenir**; (*Prov*) **un ~ vaut mieux que deux tu l'auras** a bird in the hand is worth two in the bush (*Prov*).

tierce[1] [tjɛʀs(ə)] **1** *nf* **(a)** (*Mus*) third. **~ majeure/mineure** major/minor third. **(b)** (*Cartes*) tierce. **~ majeure** tierce major. **(c)** (*Typ*) final proof. **(d)** (*Rel*) terce. **(e)** (*Escrime*) tierce. **2** *adj V* **tiers.**

tiercé, e [tjɛʀse] **1** *adj* (*Hér*) tiercé, tierced; *V* **rime.**
2 *nm French system of forecast betting.* **réussir le ~ dans l'ordre/dans le désordre** to win on the tiercé with the right placings/but without the right placings; **un beau ~** a good win on the tiercé; **toucher** *ou* **gagner le ~** to win the tiercé.

tierceron [tjɛʀsəʀɔ̃] *nm* tierceron.

tiers, tierce[2] [tjɛʀ, tjɛʀs(ə)] **1** *adj* (*rare*) third. (*Math*) **a tierce** a triple dash; **une tierce personne** a third party, an outsider; (*Typ*) **tierce épreuve final** proof; (*Jur*) **~ porteur** endorsee; (*Jur*) **tierce opposition** opposition by third party (*to outcome of litigation*).
2 *nm* **(a)** (*fraction*) third. **le premier ~/les deux premiers ~ de l'année** the first third/the first two thirds of the year; **j'ai lu un ~/les deux ~ du livre** I have read a third/two thirds of the book; **j'en suis au ~** I'm a third of the way through; **l'article est trop long d'un ~** the article is too long by a third.
(b) (*troisième personne*) third party *ou* person; (*étranger, inconnu*) outsider; (*Jur*) third party. **il a appris la nouvelle par un ~** he learnt the news through a third party; he learnt the news through an outsider; **l'assurance ne couvre pas les ~** the insurance does not cover third party risks; **il se moque du ~ comme du quart**† he doesn't care a fig for the rest of the world; *V* **assurance.**
3: tiers(-)arbitre *nm, pl* **tiers(-)arbitres** independent arbitrator; (*Hist*) **le Tiers-État** *nm* the third estate; (*Pol*) **le Tiers-Monde** *nm* the Third World; (*Rel*) **tiers ordre** third order; **tiers payant** direct payment by insurers (*for medical treatment*); **tiers-point** *nm, pl* **tiers-points** (*Archit*) crown; (*lime*) saw-file; **tiers provisionnel** provisional *ou* interim payment (*of tax*); (*Scol*) **Tiers Temps pédagogique** *system of primary education allowing time for non-curricular activities.*

tif: [tif] *nm* (*gén pl*) hair. **~s** hair.

tige [tiʒ] *nf* **(a)** (*Bot*) *[fleur, arbre]* stem; *[céréales, graminées]* stalk. **fleurs à longues ~s** long-stemmed flowers; **(arbre de) haute/basse ~** standard/half-standard tree; **~ aérienne/souterraine** overground/underground stem.
(b) (*plant*) sapling.
(c) (*fig*) *[colonne, plume, démarreur]* shaft; *[botte, chaussette, bas]* leg (part); *[chaussure]* ankle (part); *[clef, clou]* shank; *[pompe]* rod. **chaussures à ~** boots; **chaussures à ~ haute** knee-length boots; **chaussures à ~ basse** ankle(-length) boots; **~ de métal** metal rod.
(d) (†, *littér*) *[arbre généalogique]* stock. **faire ~** to found a line.

tignasse [tiɲas] *nf* (*chevelure mal peignée*) shock of hair, mop (of hair); (*: *cheveux*) hair.

tigre [tigʀ(ə)] *nm* (*Zool, fig*) tiger. **~ royal** Bengal tiger.

Tigre [tigʀ(ə)] *nm:* **le ~** the Tigris.

tigré, e [tigʀe] *adj* **(a)** (*tacheté*) spotted (*de* with); *cheval* piebald.
(b) (*rayé*) striped, streaked. **chat ~** tabby (cat).

tigresse [tigʀɛs] *nf* (*Zool, fig*) tigress.

tilbury [tilbyʀi] *nm* tilbury.

tilde [tild(ə)] *nm* tilde.

tillac [tijak] *nm* (*Hist Naut*) upper deck.

tilleul [tijœl] *nm* (*arbre*) lime (tree), linden (tree); (*infusion*) lime(-blossom) tea. **(vert) ~** lime green.

timbale [tɛ̃bal] *nf* **(a)** (*Mus*) kettledrum, timp*. **les ~s** the timpani, the timps*, the kettledrums.
(b) (*gobelet*) (metal) cup (*without handle*), (metal) tumbler.
(c) (*Culin*) (*moule*) timbale (mould). (*mets*) **~ de langouste** lobster timbale.

timbalier [tɛ̃balje] *nm* timpanist.

timbrage [tɛ̃bʀaʒ] *nm* (*V* **timbrer**) stamping; postmarking. **dispensé du ~** postage paid.

timbre [tɛ̃bʀ(ə)] **1** *nm* **(a)** (*vignette*) stamp. **~(-poste)** (postage) stamp; **~ neuf/oblitéré** new/used stamp; **marché** *ou* **bourse aux ~s** stamp market; **~s antituberculeux/anticancéreux** TB/cancer research stamps; *V* **collection.**
(b) (*marque*) stamp; (*cachet de la poste*) postmark. **mettre** *ou* **apposer** *ou* **imprimer son ~ sur** to put one's stamp on, affix one's stamp to; **~ sec/humide** embossed/ink(ed) stamp; *V* **droit**[3].
(c) (*instrument*) stamp. **~ de caoutchouc/cuivre** rubber/brass stamp.
(d) (*Mus*) *[tambour]* snares (*pl*).
(e) (*son, qualité d'un son*) *[instrument, voix]* timbre, tone; *[voyelle]* timbre. **avoir le ~ voilé** to have a muffled tone to one's voice; **une voix qui a du ~** a sonorous *ou* resonant voice; **une voix sans ~** a voice lacking in resonance.
(f) (*sonnette*) bell.
2: timbre d'escompte, timbre-escompte *nm, pl* **timbres-escompte** trading stamp; **timbre fiscal** excise stamp; **timbre horodateur** time and date stamp; **timbre de quittance, timbre-quittance** *nm, pl* **timbres-quittance** receipt stamp.

timbré, e [tɛ̃bʀe] (*ptp de* **timbrer**) *adj* **(a)** (*Admin, Jur*) *document, acte* stamped, bearing a stamp (*attrib*); *V* **papier.**
(b) *voix* resonant, sonorous; *sonorité* resonant. **une voix bien ~e** a beautifully resonant voice; **mal ~** lacking in resonance.
(c) (*: *fou*) cracked*, dotty*.

timbrer [tɛ̃bʀe] (1) *vt* (*apposer un cachet sur*) *document, acte* to stamp; *lettre, envoi* to postmark; (*affranchir*) *lettre, envoi* to stamp, put a stamp (*ou* stamps) on. **lettre timbrée de** *ou* **à Paris** letter with a Paris postmark, letter postmarked Paris.

timide [timid] *adj* **(a)** (*timoré*) *personne, critique, réponse* timid, timorous, unadventurous; *entreprise, style* timid, unadventurous; *tentative* timid, timorous.
(b) (*emprunté*) *personne, air, sourire, voix* shy, timid; *amoureux* shy, bashful, timid. **faussement ~** coy; **c'est un grand ~** he's awfully shy.

timidement [timidmɑ̃] *adv* (*V* **timide**) timidly; timorously; unadventurously; shyly; bashfully.

timidité [timidite] *nf* (*V* **timide**) timidity; timorousness; unadventurousness; shyness; bashfulness.

timon [timɔ̃] *nm [char]* shaft; *[charrue]* beam; *[embarcation]* tiller.

timonerie [timɔnʀi] *nf* **(a)** (*Naut*) (*poste, service*) wheelhouse; (*marins*) wheelhouse crew. **(b)** (*Aut*) steering and braking systems.

timonier [timɔnje] *nm* **(a)** (*Naut*) helmsman, steersman.
(b) (*cheval*) wheel-horse, wheeler.

timoré, e [timɔʀe] *adj* (*gén*) *caractère, personne* timorous, fearful, timid; (*Rel, littér*) *conscience* over-scrupulous.

Timothée [timɔte] *nm* Timothy.

tinctorial, e, *mpl* **-aux** [tɛ̃ktɔʀjal, o] *adj opération, produit* tinctorial (*T*), dyeing (*épith*). **matières ~es** dyestuffs; **plantes ~es** plants used in dyeing.

tinette [tinɛt] *nf* (*pour la vidange*) sanitary tub. (*arg Mil: toilettes*) **~s** latrines.

tintamarre [tɛ̃tamaʀ] *nm* din, racket*. **faire du ~** to make a din *ou* racket*.

tintement [tɛ̃tmɑ̃] *nm* (*V* **tinter**) ringing; chiming; tinkling; jingling; chinking. **~ d'oreilles** ringing in the ears, tinnitus (*T*).

tinter [tɛ̃te] (1) **1** *vi [cloche]* to ring, chime; *[clochette]* to tinkle, jingle; *[objets métalliques, pièces de monnaie]* to jingle, chink; *[verres entrechoqués]* to chink; *[verre frotté]* to ring. **faire ~** to ring; to make tinkle; to make jingle; to make chink; **trois coups tintèrent** the bell rang *ou* chimed three times; **les oreilles me tintent** my ears are ringing, there's a ringing in my ears; (*fig*) **les oreilles ont dû vous ~** your ears must have been burning.
2 *vt cloche, heure, angélus* to ring; *messe* to ring for.

tintin: [tɛ̃tɛ̃] *excl* nothing doing!*, no go!: **faire ~** to go without.

tintinnabuler [tɛ̃tinabyle] (1) *vi* (*littér*) to tinkle, tintinnabulate (*littér*).

tintouin* [tɛ̃twɛ̃] *nm* **(a)** (*fracas*) bother, worry. **donner du ~ à qn** to give sb a lot of bother; **se donner du ~** to go to a lot of bother. **(b)** (*bruit*) racket*, din.

tique [tik] *nf* tick (*Zool*).

tiquer [tike] (1) *vi* **(a)** *[personne]* to pull a face. **sans ~** without turning a hair *ou* batting an eyelid *ou* raising an eyebrow. **(b)** *[cheval]* to crib(-bite), suck wind.

tiqueté, e [tikte] *adj* (*rare, littér*) speckled, mottled.

tir [tiʀ] **1** *nm* **(a)** (*discipline sportive ou militaire*) shooting. **~ au pistolet/à la carabine** pistol/rifle shooting; *V* **stand.**
(b) (*action de tirer*) firing (*U*). **en position de ~** in firing position; **prêt au ~** ready for firing; **commander/déclencher le ~** to order/set off *ou* open the firing; **puissance/vitesse de ~ d'une arme** fire-power/firing speed of a gun; **des ~s d'exercice** practice rounds; **des ~s à blanc** firing blank rounds *ou* blanks.
(c) (*manière de tirer*) firing; (*trajectoire des projectiles*) fire. **arme à ~ automatique/rapide** automatic/rapid-firing gun; **régler/ajuster le ~** to regulate/adjust the fire; **arme à ~ courbe/tendu** gun with curved/flat trajectory fire; **~ groupé/direct** grouped/direct fire; **plan/angle/ligne de ~** plane/angle/line of fire; *V* **table.**
(d) (*feu, rafales*) fire (*U*). **stoppés par un ~ de mitrailleuses/d'artillerie** halted by machine-gun/artillery fire.
(e) (*Boules*) shot (*at another bowl*); (*Ftbl*) shot. **~ au but** shot at goal.
(f) (*stand*) **~ (forain)** shooting gallery, rifle range.
2: tir d'appui = tir de soutien; tir à l'arbalète crossbow archery; **tir à l'arc** archery; **tir de barrage** barrage fire; **tir au pigeon** clay pigeon shooting; **tir de soutien** support fire.

tirade [tiʀad] *nf* tirade.

tirage [tiʀaʒ] **1** *nm* **(a)** *[chèque]* drawing; *[vin]* drawing off; *[carte]* taking, drawing.
(b) (*Phot, Typ*) printing. **faire le ~ de clichés/d'une épreuve**

to print negatives/a proof; ~ **à la main** hand-printing; **un ~ sur papier glace** a print on glazed paper.

(c) *[journal]* circulation; *[livre]* (*nombre d'exemplaires*) (print-)run; (*édition*) edition. ~ **de luxe/limité** de luxe/limited edition; **cet auteur réalise de gros ~s** this author's works are printed in great numbers; **quel est le ~ de cet ouvrage?** how many copies of this work were printed? (*ou* are being printed?); **les gros ~s de la presse quotidienne** the high circulation figures of the daily press; ~ **de 2.000 exemplaires** run *ou* impression of 2,000 copies.

(d) *[cheminée]* draught.

(e) (*Loterie*) draw. **le ~ des numéros gagnants** the draw for the winning numbers.

(f) (*: *désaccord*) friction. **il y avait du ~ entre eux** there was some friction between them.

2: tirage à part off-print; **tirage au sort** drawing lots; **procéder par tirage au sort** to draw lots.

tiraillement [tiʀajmɑ̃] *nm* **(a)** (*sur une corde etc*) tugging (*U*), pulling (*U*). **ces ~s ont causé la rupture de la corde** all this pulling *ou* tugging caused the rope to break.

(b) (*douleur*) (*intestinal, stomacal*) gnawing *ou* crampy pain, gripey pain*; (*de la peau, musculaire, sur une plaie*) stabbing pain. **~s d'estomac** gnawing *ou* crampy pains in the stomach.

(c) (*fig*) (*doutes, hésitations*) agonizing indecision (*U*); (*conflits, friction*) friction (*U*), conflict (*U*). **~s (de la conscience) entre devoir et ambition** friction *ou* conflict (within one's conscience) between duty and ambition.

tirailler [tiʀaje] (1) **1** *vt* **(a)** *corde, moustache, manche* to pull at, tug at. **les enfants tiraillaient le pauvre vieux de droite et de gauche** the children were tugging the old man this way and that; ~ **qn par le bras** *ou* **la manche** to pull *ou* tug at sb's sleeve.

(b) *[douleurs]* to gnaw at, stab at. **des douleurs qui tiraillent l'estomac** gnawing *ou* crampy pains in the stomach; **des élancements lui tiraillaient l'épaule** shooting pains were stabbing at his shoulder.

(c) *[doutes, remords]* to tug at, plague, pester; *[choix, contradictions]* to beset, plague. **être tiraillé entre plusieurs possibilités** to be torn between several possibilities; **la crainte et l'ambition le tiraillaient** he was torn between fear and ambition.

2 *vi* (*en tous sens*) to shoot wild; (*Mil: tir de harcèlement*) to fire at random. **ça tiraillait de tous côtés dans le bois** there was firing on all sides in the wood.

tirailleur [tiʀajœʀ] *nm* **(a)** (*Mil, fig*) skirmisher. **se déployer/avancer en ~s** to be deployed/advance as a skirmish contingent. **(b)** (*Hist Mil: dans les colonies*) soldier, infantryman (*native*).

tirant [tiʀɑ̃] *nm* **(a)** (*cordon*) (draw)string; (*tirette*) *[botte]* (boot-)strap; (*partie de la tige*) *[chaussure]* facing.

(b) (*Constr*) *[arcades]* tie-rod; *[comble]* tie-beam.

(c) (*Naut*) ~ **(d'eau)** draught; ~ **avant/arrière** draught at the bows/stern; **avoir 6 mètres de ~ (d'eau)** to draw 6 metres of water.

tire[1]**:** [tiʀ] *nf* (*voiture*) wagon*, car.

tire[2] [tiʀ] *nf*: **vol à la ~** picking pockets; **voleur à la ~** pick-pocket.

tire[3] [tiʀ] *nf* (*Can*) toffee, taffy (*Can, US*); molasses, maple candy. ~ **d'érable** maple toffee *ou* taffy (*Can, US*); ~ **sur la neige** taffy-on-the-snow (*Can, US*).

tire- [tiʀ] *préf V* **tirer.**

tiré, e [tiʀe] (*ptp de* **tirer**) **1** *adj* **(a)** (*tendu*) *traits, visage* drawn, haggard. **avoir les traits ~s** to look drawn *ou* haggard; **les cheveux ~s en arrière** with one's hair drawn back; ~ **à quatre épingles** done up *ou* dressed up to the nines*, dressed fit to kill* (*hum*), done up like a dog's dinner*; (*fig*) ~ **par les cheveux** far-fetched.

(b) *V* **couteau.**

(c) (*Fin*) **la personne ~e** the drawee.

2 *nm* (*Fin*) drawee.

3 tirée* *nf* (*long trajet*) long haul*, long trek. (*: *quantité*) **une ~e de** a load* of, heaps* *ou* tons* of.

4: tiré à part *adj, nm* off-print.

tire-d'aile(s) [tiʀdɛl] *loc adv*: **à ~** *voler* swiftly; **passer à ~** to pass by in full flight; **s'envoler à ~** to take flight in a flurry of feathers; (*fig*) **partir à ~** to leave at top speed, take flight.

tirée [tiʀe] *V* **tiré.**

tirelire [tiʀliʀ] *nf* **(a)** moneybox; (*en forme de cochon*) piggy bank. **casser la ~** to break open the piggy bank. **(b)** (:) (*estomac, ventre*) belly:, gut(s):; (*tête*) nut*, bonce: (*Brit*); (*visage*) face.

tirer [tiʀe] (1) **1** *vt* **(a)** (*amener vers soi*) *pièce mobile, poignée, corde* to pull; *manche, robe* to pull down; *chaussette* to pull up. **ne tire pas, ça risque de tomber/ça va l'étrangler** don't pull or it'll fall/strangle him; ~ **les cheveux à qn** to pull sb's hair; ~ **l'aiguille** to ply the needle; **annonce qui tire l'œil** *ou* **le regard** advertisement which draws the eye; **de petits caractères qui tirent les yeux** small print which strains one's eyes; (*lit*) ~ **qch à soi** to pull sth to(wards) one; (*fig*) ~ **un texte/auteur à soi** to turn a text/an author round to suit one; *V* **couverture, diable, révérence** *etc.*

(b) *rideaux* (*fermer, rare: ouvrir*) to draw, pull; *verrou* (*fermer*) to slide to, shoot; (*rare: ouvrir*) to draw. **tire la porte** pull the door to; **il est tard: tire les rideaux** it's getting late so pull the curtains (to) *ou* draw the curtains; **as-tu tiré le verrou?** have you bolted the door?

(c) *personne* to pull. ~ **qn par le bras** to pull sb's arm, pull sb by the arm; ~ **qn par la manche** to tug *ou* pluck (*frm*) sb's sleeve; ~ **qn de côté** *ou* **à l'écart** to draw sb aside.

(d) (*haler, remorquer*) *véhicule, charge* to pull, draw; *navire, remorque* to tow; *charrue* to draw, pull. **une charrue tirée par un tracteur** a plough drawn *ou* pulled by a tractor, a tractor-drawn plough; **carrosse tiré par 8 chevaux** carriage drawn by 8 horses.

(e) (*retirer, extraire*) *épée, couteau* to draw, pull out; *vin, cidre* to draw; *carte, billet, numéro* to draw; (*fig*) *conclusions, morale, argument, idée, thème* to draw; (*fig*) *plaisir, satisfaction* to draw, derive (*de* from). ~ **une substance d'une matière première** to extract a substance from a raw material; ~ **le jus d'un citron** to extract the juice from a lemon, squeeze the juice from a lemon *ou* out of a lemon; ~ **un son d'un instrument** to get a sound out of *ou* draw a sound from an instrument; **cette pièce tire son jour** *ou* **sa lumière de cette lucarne** this room gets its light from *ou* is lit by this skylight; ~ **un objet d'un tiroir/d'un sac** to pull an object out of a drawer/bag; ~ **son chapeau/sa casquette à qn** to raise one's hat/cap to sb; ~ **de l'argent d'une activité/d'une terre** to make *ou* derive money from an activity/a piece of land; ~ **de l'argent de qn** to get money out of sb; ~ **qn du sommeil** to arouse sb from sleep; ~ **qn du lit** to get *ou* drag sb out of bed; ~ **qn de son travail** to take *ou* drag sb away from his work; **ce bruit le tira de sa rêverie** this noise brought him out of *ou* roused him from his daydream; ~ **qch de qn** to obtain sth from sb, get sth out of sb; **on ne peut rien en ~** you can't get anything out of him; ~ **des larmes/gémissements à qn** to draw tears/moans from sb; **savoir ~ qch de la vie/d'un moment** (to know how) to get sth out of life/a moment; (*à l'Épiphanie*) ~ **les rois** to cut the Twelfth Night cake; *V* **clair, épingle, parti**[1] *etc.*

(f) (*délivrer*) ~ **qn de prison/des décombres/d'une situation dangereuse** to get sb out of prison/the rubble/a dangerous situation; ~ **qn du doute** to remove *ou* dispel sb's doubts; ~ **qn de l'erreur** to disabuse sb; ~ **qn de la misère/de l'obscurité** to rescue sb from poverty/obscurity; **il faut le ~ de là** we'll have to help him out; *V* **affaire, embarras.**

(g) (*indiquant l'origine*) ~ **son origine/sa raison d'être de** to have as its origin/raison d'être; **mots tirés du latin** words taken from (the) Latin; ~ **son nom de** to take one's name from; **pièce tirée d'un roman** play taken from a novel; **on tire de l'huile des olives** oil is extracted from olives; **l'opium est tiré du pavot** opium is obtained from the poppy.

(h) (*choisir*) *billet, numéro* to draw; *carte* to take, draw; *loterie* to draw, carry out the draw for. (*fig*) **il a tiré un bon/mauvais numéro** he's been lucky/unlucky in the draw; *V* **carte, court**[1] *etc.*

(i) (*Phot, Typ*) to print. **on tire ce journal à 100.000 exemplaires** this paper has a circulation of 100,000; ~ **un roman à 8.000 exemplaires** to print 8,000 copies of a novel; **tirons quelques épreuves de ce texte** let's run off *ou* print a few proofs of the text; (*fig*) **tiré à des centaines d'exemplaires** turned out *ou* churned out by the hundred; *V* **bon**[2].

(j) (*tracer*) *ligne, trait* to draw; *plan* to draw up; *portrait* to do. **se faire ~ le portrait** (*croquer*) to have one's picture *ou* portrait drawn; (*photographier*) to have one's picture *ou* photograph taken.

(k) *coup de fusil, coup de canon, coup de feu, balle* to fire; *flèche* to shoot; *boule* to throw (*so as to hit another or the jack*); *feu d'artifice* to set off; *gibier* to shoot. **il a tiré plusieurs coups de revolver sur l'agent** he shot *ou* fired at the policeman several times; **il a tiré plusieurs coups de feu et s'est enfui** he fired several times *ou* several shots and ran off; ~ **le canon** to fire the cannon; **la balle a été tirée avec un gros calibre** the bullet was fired from a large-calibre gun; **il a tiré 2 bartavelles et un faisan** he shot 2 rock partridges and a pheasant; (*fig*) ~ **un coup**∵ to have a bang∵, have it off∵.

(l) *chèque, lettre de change* to draw.

(m) (*Naut*) ~ **6 mètres** to draw 6 metres of water; ~ **un bord** *ou* **une bordée** to tack.

(n) (*: *passer*) to get through. **encore une heure/un mois à ~** another hour/month to get through; ~ **2 ans de prison/service** to do 2 years in prison *ou* a 2-year stretch*/2 years in the army; **voilà une semaine de tirée** that's one week over with*.

2 *vi* **(a)** (*faire feu*) to fire. **il leur donna l'ordre de ~** he gave the order for them to fire; **le canon tirait sans arrêt** the cannon fired continuously; ~ **en l'air** to fire shots in the air; ~ **à vue** to shoot on sight; ~ **à balles/à blanc** to fire bullets/blanks; *V* **boulet, tas.**

(b) (*se servir d'une arme à feu, viser*) to shoot. **apprendre à ~** to learn to shoot; ~ **au but** to hit the target.

(c) (*Ftbl*) to shoot, take a shot; (*Boules*) to throw (*one 'boule' at another or at the jack*). ~ **au but** to take a shot at goal, shoot at goal.

(d) (*Presse*) ~ **à 10.000 exemplaires** to have a circulation of 10,000.

(e) *[cheminée, poêle]* to draw. **la cheminée tire bien** the chimney draws well.

(f) *[moteur, voiture]* to pull. **le moteur tire bien en côte** the engine pulls well on hills.

(g) *[points de suture, sparadrap]* to pull. **ma peau est très sèche et me tire** my skin is very dry and feels tight.

(h) (*loc*) ~ **au flanc*** *ou* **au cul:** to skive*; ~ **dans les jambes** *ou* **pattes* de qn** to make life difficult for sb.

3 tirer sur *vt indir* **(a)** *corde, poignée* to pull at *ou* on, tug at. ~ **sur les rênes** to pull in *ou* on the reins; **ne tire pas si fort** don't pull so hard; (*fig*) ~ **sur la ficelle*** *ou* **la corde*** to push one's luck*.

(b) (*approcher de*) *couleur* to border on, verge on. **il tire sur la soixantaine** he's getting on for sixty.

(c) (*faire feu sur*) to shoot at, fire (a shot *ou* shots) at. **il m'a tiré dessus** he shot *ou* fired at me; **se ~ dessus** (*lit*) to shoot *ou* fire at each other; (*fig: se critiquer, quereller*) to shoot each other down, snipe at one another.

(d) (*aspirer*) *pipe* to pull at, draw on; *cigarette, cigare* to puff at, draw on, take a drag at*.

4 tirer à *vt indir*: ~ **à sa fin** to be drawing to a close; ~ **à conséquence** to matter; **cela ne tire pas à conséquence** it's of no consequence, it doesn't matter.

5 se tirer *vpr* **(a)** (*s'échapper à*) se ~ **de** *danger, situation* to get (o.s.) out of; **s'en** ~*: **sa voiture était en mille morceaux mais lui s'en est tiré** his car was smashed to pieces but he escaped; **il est très malade mais je crois qu'il va s'en** ~ he's very ill but I think he'll pull through; **la première fois il a eu le sursis mais cette fois il ne va pas s'en** ~ **si facilement** the first time he got a suspended sentence but he won't get off so lightly this time; **il s'en est tiré avec une amende/une jambe cassée** he got off *ou* away with a fine/a broken leg; **il s'en est tiré à bon compte** he got off lightly; *V* **affaire, flûte, patte.**

(b) (*se débrouiller*) **bien/mal se** ~ **de qch** (*tâche, travail*) to manage *ou* handle sth well/badly, make a good/bad job of sth; **comment va-t-il se** ~ **de ce sujet/travail?** how will he get on with *ou* cope with this subject/job?; **s'en** ~: **les questions étaient difficiles mais il s'en est bien tiré** the questions were difficult but he managed *ou* handled them well *ou* coped very well with them; **on n'a pas beacoup d'argent mais on s'en tire** we haven't a lot of money but we get by *ou* we manage; **on s'en tire tout juste** we just scrape by, we just (about) get by.

(c) (‡: *déguerpir*) to push off‡, shove off‡, clear off‡. **allez, on se tire** come on — we'll be off*, come on — let's push off‡ *ou* clear off‡.

(d) (*: *toucher à sa fin*) *[période, travail]* to drag towards its close. **ça se tire** the end is (at last) in sight.

(e) (*être tendu*) *[traits, visage]* to become drawn.

6: tire-bonde *nm, pl* **tire-bondes** bung-drawer; **tire-botte** *nm, pl* **tire-bottes** (*pour se chausser*) boot-hook; (*pour se déchausser*) bootjack; **tire-bouchon** *nm, pl* **tire-bouchons** corkscrew; (*mèche de cheveux*) corkscrew curl; **en tire-bouchon** corkscrew (*épith*), in a corkscrew; **tire-bouchonner** (*vt*) *mèche* to twiddle, twirl; (*vi*) *[pantalons]* to crumple (up); **pantalons tire-bouchonnés** crumpled (up) trousers; **se tire-bouchonner‡** *vpr* to be creased up *ou* fall about laughing*, be in stitches*; **tire-au-cul‡** *nmf inv* = **tire-au-flanc; tire-fesses*** *nm inv* (*gén, à perche*) ski tow; (*à archet*) T-bar tow; **tire-au-flanc*** *nmf inv* skiver*; **tire-jus‡** *nm inv* snot-rag‡; **tire-laine††** *nm inv* footpad††; **tire-lait** *nm inv* breast-pump; **tire-larigot: à tire-larigot*** *loc adv* to one's heart's content; **tire-ligne** *nm, pl* **tire-lignes** drawing pen.

tiret [tiʀɛ] *nm* (*trait*) dash; (*en fin de ligne*, †: *trait d'union*) hyphen.

tirette [tiʀɛt] *nf* **(a)** *[bureau, table]* (*pour écrire*) (writing) leaf; (*pour ranger des crayons etc*) (pencil) tray; (*pour soutenir un abattant*) loper, support.

(b) *[fermeture éclair]* pull, tab.

(c) *[cheminée]* damper.

(d) (*cordon*) *[sonnette]* bell-pull; *[rideaux]* (curtain) cord *ou* pull.

tireur, -euse [tiʀœʀ, øz] **1** *nm* (*f rare*) **(a) c'est le fait d'un** ~ **isolé** it is the work of a lone gunman *ou* gunner; (*Mil*) ~ **d'élite** marksman, sharpshooter; **c'est un bon** ~ he is a good shot; **concours ouvert aux** ~**s débutants et entraînés** shooting competition open to beginners and advanced classes.

(b) (*Boules*) thrower.

(c) (*Phot*) printer.

2 *nm* (*Fin*) *[chèque, lettre de change]* drawer.

3 tireuse *nf* **(a)** ~**euse de cartes** fortuneteller (*using cards*).

(b) (*Tech*) (hand) pump (*for filling bottles, drawing beer*).

(c) (*Phot*) contact printer.

tiroir [tiʀwaʀ] **1** *nm* **(a)** *[table, commode]* drawer. (*fig*) **roman/pièce à** ~**s** novel/play made up of episodes, roman/pièce à tiroirs (*T*); *V* **fond, nom. (b)** (*Tech*) slide valve. **2: tiroir-caisse** *nm, pl* **tiroirs-caisses** till.

tisane [tizan] *nf* **(a)** (*boisson*) herb(al) tea. ~ **de tilleul/de menthe** lime(-blossom)/mint tea; (*hum*) **c'est de la** ~* it's pretty watery stuff*. **(b)** (‡: *correction*) belting‡, hiding*.

tison [tizɔ̃] *nm* brand; *V* **allumette.**

tisonner [tizɔne] (1) *vt* to poke.

tisonnier [tizɔnje] *nm* poker.

tissage [tisaʒ] *nm* weaving.

tisser [tise] (1) *vt* (*lit, fig*) to weave. **l'araignée tisse sa toile** the spider spins its web; *V* **métier.**

tisserand, e [tisʀɑ̃, ɑ̃d] *nm,f* weaver.

tisseur, -euse [tisœʀ, øz] *nm,f* weaver.

tissu[1] [tisy] **1** *nm* **(a)** (*Tex*) (*par opposition à autres substances*) cloth, fabric; (*vu dans son aspect, ses propriétés*) fabric, material; (*qu'on va acheter, travailler*) material, fabric. **les parois sont en** ~ **et non en bois** the walls are cloth not wood; **c'est un** ~ **très délicat** it's a very delicate fabric *ou* material; **acheter du** ~**/3 mètres de** ~ **pour faire une robe** to buy material *ou* fabric/3 metres of material *ou* fabric to make a dress; **choisir un** ~ **pour faire une robe** to choose material to make a dress, choose a dress fabric *ou* material; ~ **imprimé/à fleurs** printed/floral-patterned material *ou* fabric; ~ **synthétique/irrétrécissable** synthetic/shrinkproof material *ou* fabric; ~**s d'ameublement** soft furnishings; **étoffe à** ~ **lâche/serré** loosely-/finely-woven material *ou* fabric.

(b) (*fig péj*) **un** ~ **de mensonges/contradictions** a web *ou* tissue (*littér*) of lies/contradictions; **un** ~ **d'intrigues** a web of intrigue; **un** ~ **d'horreurs/d'obscénités/d'inepties** a farrago of horrors/obscenities/stupidities.

(c) (*Anat, Bot*) tissue. ~ **sanguin/osseux/cicatriciel** blood/bone/scar *ou* cicatricial (*T*) tissue.

2: tissu-éponge *nm, pl* **tissus-éponge** (terry) towelling (*U*).

tissu[2]**, e** [tisy] **1** (*rare*) *ptp de* **tisser. 2** *adj* (*littér: composé de*) ~ **de contradictions/ramifications** woven through with contradictions/complications.

Titan [titɑ̃] *nm* Titan. (*fig*) **œuvre/travail de** ~ titanic work/task.

titane [titan] *nm* titanium.

titanesque [titanɛsk(ə)] *adj*, **titanique** [titanik] *adj* titanic.

Tite-Live [titliv] *nm* Livy.

titi [titi] *nm*: ~ **(parisien)** (cocky) Parisian kid*.

Titien [tisjɛ̃] *nm* Titian.

titillation [titilɑsjɔ̃] *nf* (*littér, hum*) titillation.

titiller [titile] (1) *vt* (*littér, hum*) to titillate.

titrage [titʀaʒ] *nm* (*V* **titrer**) assaying; titration; titling.

titre [titʀ(ə)] **1** *nm* **(a)** *[livre, film, poème, tableau]* title; *[chapitre]* heading, title; (*Jur*) *[code]* title. (*Presse*) **les (gros)** ~**s** the headlines; (*Presse*) ~ **sur 5 colonnes à la une** 5-column front page headline; (*Typ*) ~ **courant** running head; (*Typ*) **(page de)** ~ title page; *V* **sous.**

(b) (*honorifique, de charge, de fonctions professionnelles*) title; (*appellation, formule de politesse*) form of address; (*littér: toute appellation ou qualificatif*) title, name. ~ **nobiliaire** *ou* **de noblesse** title; ~ **universitaire** academic title; **conférer à qn le** ~ **de maréchal/prince** to confer the title of marshal/prince on sb; **il ne mérite pas le** ~ **de citoyen/d'invité** he is unworthy of the name *ou* title of citizen/guest.

(c) (*Sport*) title.

(d) en ~ (*Admin*) titular; (*Comm*) *fournisseur* appointed; (*hum*) *maîtresse, victime* official, recognized.

(e) (*document*) title. ~ **de propriété** title deed; (*Admin*) ~ **de transport** ticket.

(f) (*Bourse, Fin*) security. **acheter/vendre des** ~**s** to buy/sell securities *ou* stock; ~ **de rente** government security *ou* bond; ~ **au porteur** bearer bond; ~**s nominatifs** registered securities.

(g) (*preuve de capacité, diplôme*) (*gén*) qualification; (*Univ*) degree, qualification. **nommer/recruter sur** ~**s** to appoint/recruit according to qualifications; **il a tous les** ~**s (nécessaires) pour enseigner** he is fully qualified *ou* he has all the necessary qualifications to teach.

(h) (*littér, gén pl: droit, prétentions*) **avoir des** ~**s à la reconnaissance de qn** to have a right to sb's gratitude; **ses** ~**s de gloire** his claims to fame.

(i) *[or, argent, monnaie]* fineness; *[solution]* titre. **or/argent au** ~ standard gold/silver; ~ **d'alcool** *ou* **alcoolique** alcohol content.

(j) (*loc*) **à ce** ~ (*en cette qualité*) as such; (*pour cette raison*) on this account, therefore; **à quel** ~**?** on what grounds?; **au même** ~ in the same way; **il y a droit au même** ~ **que les autres** he is entitled to it in the same way as the others; **à aucun** ~ on no account; **nous ne voulons de lui à aucun** ~ we don't want him on any account; **à des** ~**s divers, à plusieurs** ~**s** on several accounts; **à double** ~ on two accounts; **à** ~ **privé/personnel** in a private/personal capacity; **à** ~ **permanent/provisoire** on a permanent/temporary basis, permanently/provisionally; **à** ~ **exceptionnel** *ou* **d'exception** (*dans ce cas*) in this exceptional case; (*dans certains cas*) in exceptional cases; **à** ~ **d'ami/de client fidèle** as a friend/a faithful customer; **à** ~ **gratuit** freely, free of charge; **à** ~ **gracieux** free of *ou* without charge; **à** ~ **lucratif** for payment; **à** ~ **d'essai** on a trial basis; **à** ~ **d'exemple** as an example, by way of example; (*frm*) **à** ~ **onéreux** in return for payment; **à** ~ **indicatif** for information only; **il travaille à** ~ **de secrétaire** he works as a secretary; **à** ~ **consultatif** *collaborer* in an advisory *ou* a consultative capacity; **on vous donne 100 F à** ~ **d'indemnité** we are giving you 100 francs by way of indemnity *ou* as an indemnity; *V* **juste.**

2: titre-restaurant *nm, pl* **titres-restaurant** ≃ luncheon voucher (*surtout Brit*).

titré, e [titʀe] (*ptp de* **titrer**) *adj* **(a)** (*noble*) *personne* titled; *terres* carrying a title (*attrib*). **(b)** (*Tech*) *liqueur* standard.

titrer [titʀe] (1) *vt* **(a)** (*gén ptp: ennoblir*) to confer a title on.

(b) (*Chim*) *alliage* to assay; *solution* to titrate.

(c) (*Ciné*) to title.

(d) (*Presse*) to run as a headline. ~ **sur 2/5 colonnes: 'Défaite de la Gauche'** to run a 2/5-column headline: 'Defeat of the Left'.

(e) *[alcool, vin]* ~ **10°/38°** to be 10°/38° proof (*on the Gay Lussac scale*), ≃ to be 17°/66° proof.

titubant, e [titybɑ̃, ɑ̃t] *adj* (*V* **tituber**) staggering; reeling; unsteady.

tituber [titybe] (1) *vi* *[personne]* (*de faiblesse, fatigue*) to stagger (along); (*d'ivresse*) to stagger (along), reel (along); *[démarche]* to be unsteady. **il avançait vers nous/sortit de la cuisine en titubant** he came staggering *ou* stumbling *ou* tottering towards us/out of the kitchen, he staggered *ou* tottered towards us/out of the kitchen; **nous titubions de fatigue** we were so tired that we could hardly keep upright, we were staggering *ou* tottering *ou* stumbling along, so tired were we.

titulaire [titylɛʀ] **1** *adj* **(a)** (*Admin*) *professeur* with tenure. **rendre qn** ~ to give sb tenure; **être** ~ to have tenure; **être** ~ **de** (*Univ*) *chaire* to occupy, hold; (*Pol*) *portefeuille* to hold.

(b) (*Jur*) **(être)** ~ **de** *droit* (to be) entitled to; *permis, carte* (to be) the holder of.

(c) (*Rel*) *évêque* titular (*épith*). **saint/patron** ~ **d'une église** (titular) saint/patron of a church.

2 *nmf* (*Admin*) *[poste]* incumbent; (*Jur*) *[droit]* person entitled (*de* to); *[permis, carte]* holder; (*Rel*) *[église]* titular saint.

titularisation [titylaʀizɑsjɔ̃] *nf* granting of tenure (*de qn* to sb).

titulariser [titylaʀize] (1) *vt* to give tenure to.

toast [tost] *nm* **(a)** (*pain grillé*) slice *ou* piece of toast. **un** ~ **beurré** a slice *ou* piece of buttered toast. **(b)** (*discours*) toast. ~ **de bienvenue** welcoming toast; **porter un** ~ **en l'honneur de qn** to drink (a toast) to sb, toast sb.

toboggan [tɔbɔgɑ̃] *nm* **(a)** (*traîneau*) toboggan. **faire du ~** to go tobogganing; **piste de ~** toboggan run. **(b)** (*glissière*) (*jeu*) slide; *[piscine]* chute; (*Tech: pour manutention*) chute; (*Aut: viaduc*) flyover (*Brit*), overpass (*US*).

toc¹ [tɔk] **1** *excl* **(a)** (*bruit: gén ~ ~*) knock knock!, rat-a-tat (-tat)!

(b) (**: repartie*) et **~!** (*en s'adressant à qn*) so there!*; (*en racontant la réaction de qn*) and serves him (*ou* her *etc*) jolly (*Brit*) *ou* damned well right!*

2 *adj* (**: gén ~ ~: idiot*) cracked*, barmy*.

toc² [tɔk] **1** *nm*: **c'est du ~** (*imitation, faux*) it's fake; (*camelote*) it's rubbish *ou* trash* *ou* junk*; **en ~** *bijou, bracelet* imitation, fake; rubbishy, trashy*.

2 *adv, adj*: **ça fait ~, c'est ~** (*imité, tape-à-l'œil*) it's a gaudy imitation; (*camelote*) it looks cheap *ou* rubbishy, it's junk*.

tocante* [tɔkɑ̃t] *nf* ticker*, watch.

tocard, e‡ [tɔkaʀ, aʀd(ə)] **1** *adj meubles, décor* cheap and nasty, trashy*. **2** *nm* (*personne*) dead loss*, useless twit‡; (*cheval*) nag (*péj*).

toccata [tɔkata] *nf* toccata.

tocsin [tɔksɛ̃] *nm* alarm (bell), tocsin (*littér*). **sonner le ~** to ring the alarm, sound the tocsin (*littér*).

toge [tɔʒ] *nf* **(a)** (*Hist*) toga. **~ virile/prétexte** toga virilis/ praetexta. **(b)** (*Jur, Scol*) gown.

togolais, e [tɔgɔlɛ, ɛz] **1** *adj* of *ou* from Togo. **2** *nm,f*: **T~(e)** inhabitant *ou* native of Togo.

tohu-bohu [tɔybɔy] *nm* (*désordre*) jumble, confusion; (*agitation*) hustle (and bustle); (*tumulte*) hubbub, commotion.

toi [twa] *pron pers* **(a)** (*sujet, objet*) you, YOU. **~ et lui, vous êtes tous les deux aussi têtus** you and he are as stubborn the one as the other, the two of you are (both) equally stubborn; **si j'étais ~, j'irais** if I were you *ou* in your shoes I'd go; **il n'obéit qu'à ~** you are the only one he obeys, he obeys only you; **il a accepté, ~ non** *ou* **pas** he accepted but you didn't *ou* but not you; **c'est enfin ~!** here you are at last!; **qui l'a vu? ~?** who saw him? (did) you?; **~ mentir? ce n'est pas possible** YOU tell a lie? I can't believe it; **~ qui sais tout, explique-moi** you're the one who knows everything so explain to me; **marche devant** *ou* **va devant, c'est ~ qui connais le chemin** you go first (since) you know the way *ou* you are the one who knows the way; **~, tu n'as pas à te plaindre** YOU have no cause to complain; **pourquoi ne le ferais-je pas, tu l'as bien fait ~!** why shouldn't I do it? YOU did it, didn't you? *ou* you jolly (*Brit*) well did (it)!*; **tu l'as vu, ~?** did YOU see him?, have YOU seen him?; **t'épouser, ~? jamais!** marry YOU? never!; **~, je te connais** I know YOU; **aide-moi, ~!** you there *ou* hey you, give me a hand!; **~, tu m'agaces!, tu m'agaces, ~!** (oh) you get on my nerves!; **~, pauvre innocent, tu n'as rien compris** YOU, poor fool, haven't understood a thing, you poor fool — you haven't understood a thing!

(b) (*avec vpr: souvent non traduit*) **assieds-~** sit down!; **mets-~ là!** stand over there!; **toi, tais-~!** you be quiet!; **montre-~ un peu aimable!** be a bit more pleasant!

(c) (*avec prép*) you, yourself. **à ~ tout seul, tu ne peux pas le faire** you can't do it on your own; **cette maison est-elle à ~?** does this house belong to you?, is this house yours?; **tu n'as même pas une chambre à ~ tout seul?** you don't even have a room of your own? *ou* a room to yourself?, **tu ne penses qu'à ~** you only think of yourself, you think only of yourself; **je compte sur ~** I'm counting on you.

(d) (*dans comparaisons*) you. **il me connaît mieux que ~** (*qu'il ne te connaît*) he knows me better than (he knows) you; (*que tu ne me connais*) he knows me better than you (do); **il est plus/moins fort que ~** he is stronger than/not so strong as you; **il a fait comme ~** he did what you did, he did the same as you.

toile [twal] **1** *nf* **(a)** (*U: tissu*) (*gén*) cloth; (*grossière, de chanvre*) *[pneu]* canvas; (*de coton, lin etc*) cotton (*ou* linen *etc*); (*pièce*) piece of cloth. **grosse ~** (rough *ou* coarse) canvas; **~ de lin/coton** linen/cotton (cloth); **en ~, de ~** *draps* linen; *pantalon, blazer* (heavy) cotton; *sac* canvas; **en ~ tergal** in Terylene fabric; **~ caoutchoutée/plastifiée** rubberized/plastic-coated cloth; **relié ~** cloth bound; **~ d'amiante/métallique** asbestos/ metal cloth; **~ imprimée** printed cotton, cotton print; *V* **chanson, village.**

(b) (*Art*) (*support*) canvas; (*œuvre*) canvas, painting. **il expose ses ~s chez X** he exhibits his canvasses *ou* paintings at X's; **une ~ de maître** an old master; **gâcher** *ou* **barbouiller de la ~** to daub on canvas.

(c) (*) **les ~s** the sheets; **se mettre** *ou* **s'enfiler dans les ~s** to hit the hay* *ou* the sack*.

(d) (*Naut: ensemble des voiles*) sails. **faire de la/réduire la ~** to make/take in sail; **navire chargé de ~s** ship under canvas, ship under full sail.

(e) *[araignée]* web. **la ~ de l'araignée** the spider's web; **une belle ~ d'araignée** a beautiful spider's web; **grenier plein de ~s d'araignées** attic full of cobwebs.

2: toile d'avion aeroplane cloth *ou* linen; **toile à bâche** tarpaulin; **toile cirée** oilcloth; **toile émeri** emery cloth; **toile de fond** (*Théât*) backdrop, backcloth; (*fig*) backdrop; **toile de Jouy** ≃ Liberty print; **toile de jute** hessian; **toile à matelas** ticking; **toile à sac** sacking, sackcloth; **toile de tente** (*Camping*) canvas, tent (*excluding poles, flysheet etc*); (*Mil*) tent sheet; **toile à voile** sailcloth.

toilerie [twalʀi] *nf* (*fabrication*) textile manufacture (*of cotton, linen, canvas etc*); (*commerce*) cotton (*ou* linen *etc*) trade; (*atelier*) cotton (*ou* linen *etc*) mill.

toilettage [twalɛtaʒ] *nm* grooming (*of domestic animal*).

toilette [twalɛt] *nf* **(a)** (*ablutions*) wash; (*temps passé à se parer*) getting ready, toilet (*frm*). **faire sa ~** to have a wash, get washed; **être à sa ~** to be dressing, be getting ready; **faire une grande ~/une ~ rapide** *ou* **un brin de ~** to have a thorough/ quick wash; **faire une ~ de chat** to give o.s. a cat-lick *ou* a lick and a promise; **~ intime** personal hygiene; **elle passe des heures à sa ~** she spends hours getting ready *ou* washing and dressing *ou* at her toilet (*frm*); **la ~ des enfants prend toujours du temps** children always take a long time washing; **un délicieux savon pour la ~ matinale** an exquisite soap for morning skin care; **une lotion pour la ~ de bébé** a cleansing lotion for baby; **articles/nécessaire de ~** toilet articles/bag; **faire la ~ d'un mort** to lay out a corpse; **la ~ d'un condamné à mort** the washing of a prisoner before execution; *V* **cabinet, gant, trousse** *etc.*

(b) (*fig: nettoyage*) *[voiture]* cleaning, tarting up* (*hum: surtout Brit*); *[maison, monument]* facelift. **faire la ~ de** *voiture* to clean, tart up* (*hum*); *monument, maison* to give a facelift to, tart up* (*hum*).

(c) *[animal]* (*que fait le chat etc*) washing, preening; (*que fait le maître d'un chien, chat etc*) grooming. **le chat faisait une ~ minutieuse** the cat was washing itself carefully; **faire la ~ de son chien** to groom one's dog.

(d) (*meuble*) washstand.

(e) (*habillement, parure*) clothes (*pl*). **en ~ de bal** dressed for a dance, in a dance dress; **~ de mariée** wedding *ou* bridal dress *ou* gown; **être en grande ~** to be dressed (very) grandly; **parler ~** to talk (about) clothes; **aimer la ~** to like clothes; **elle porte bien la ~** she wears her clothes well; **elle prend beaucoup de soins/dépense beaucoup pour sa ~** she takes great care over/ spends a good deal on her clothes.

(f) (*costume*) outfit. **elle a changé 3 fois de ~!** she has changed her outfit *ou* clothes 3 times!; **'nos ~s d'été'** 'summer wear *ou* outfits'; **on voit déjà les ~s d'été** you can already see people in summer outfits *ou* clothes.

(g) (*W.-C.*) **~s** toilet; (*publiques*) public conveniences (*Brit*) *ou* lavatory, restroom (*US*); **aller aux ~s** to go to the toilet; (*dans un café etc*) **où sont les ~s** (*gén*) where is the toilet?; (*pour femmes*) where is the ladies?*; (*pour hommes*) where is the gents?*

(h) (†: *petite pièce de toile*) small piece of cloth.

toiletter [twalete] (1) *vt chien, chat* to groom.

toi-même [twamɛm] *pron V* **même.**

toise [twaz] *nf* **(a)** (*instrument*) height gauge. **passer à la ~** (*vt*) *recrues etc* to measure the height of; (*vi*) *[recrues etc]* to have one's height measured.

(b) (*Hist: mesure*) toise (= $6^1/_2$ *ft*).

toiser [twaze] (1) *vt* **(a)** (*regarder avec dédain*) to eye scornfully (up and down). **ils se toisèrent** they eyed each other scornfully (up and down). **(b)** (†, *littér: évaluer*) to estimate.

toison [twazɔ̃] *nf* **(a)** *[mouton]* fleece. **la T~ d'or** the Golden Fleece. **(b)** (*chevelure*) (*épaisse*) mop; (*longue*) mane. **(c)** (*poils*) abundant growth.

toit [twa] *nm* **(a)** (*gén*) roof. **~ de chaume/de tuiles/d'ardoises** thatched/tiled/slate roof; **~ plat** *ou* **en terrasse/en pente** flat/ sloping roof; **habiter sous le ~** *ou* **les ~s** to live under the eaves; (*fig*) **le ~ du monde** the roof of the world (*the Himalayas or Tibet*); (*fig*) **crier** *ou* **publier qch sur (tous) les ~s** to shout *ou* proclaim sth from the rooftops *ou* housetops; **voiture à ~ ouvrant** car with a sunshine roof.

(b) (*fig: maison*) **avoir un ~** to have a home; **être sans ~** to have no roof over one's head, have nowhere to call one's own; **sous le ~ de qn** under sb's roof, in sb's house; **vivre sous le même ~** to live under the same roof; **vivre sous le ~ paternel** to live in the paternal home.

toiture [twatyʀ] *nf* roof.

tokai, tokay [tɔkɛ] *nm*, **tokaï** [tɔkaj] *nm* Tokay.

tôle¹ [tol] *nf* (*matériau*) sheet metal; (*pièce*) steel (*ou* iron) sheet. **~ d'acier/d'aluminium** sheet steel/aluminium; **~ étamée** tinplate; **~ galvanisée/émaillée** galvanized/enamelled iron; **~ ondulée** corrugated iron; (*fig: route*) rugged dirt track.

tole²‡ [tol] *nf* = **taule‡.**

Tolède [tɔlɛd] *n* Toledo.

tôlée [tole] *adj f*: **neige ~** crusted snow.

tolérable [tɔleʀabl(ə)] *adj comportement, retard* tolerable; *douleur, attente* tolerable, bearable. **cette attitude n'est pas ~** this attitude is intolerable *ou* cannot be tolerated.

tolérance [tɔleʀɑ̃s] *nf* **(a)** (*compréhension, largeur d'esprit*) tolerance. **~ religieuse** religious tolerance *ou* toleration.

(b) (*liberté limitée*) **c'est une ~, pas un droit** it is tolerated *ou* sanctioned rather than allowed as of right; (*Comm: produits hors taxe*) **il y a une ~ de 2 litres de spiritueux/200 cigarettes** there's an allowance of 2 litres of spirits/200 cigarettes; **~ orthographique/grammaticale** permitted departure in spelling/grammar; *V* **maison.**

(c) (*Méd, Tech*) tolerance; *V* **marge.**

(d) (*Hist, Rel*) toleration.

tolérant, e [tɔleʀɑ̃, ɑ̃t] *adj* tolerant.

tolérantisme [tɔleʀɑ̃tism(ə)] *nm* (*Hist Rel*) tolerationism.

tolérer [tɔleʀe] (6) *vt* **(a)** (*ne pas sévir contre*) *culte, pratiques, abus, infractions* to tolerate; (*autoriser*) to allow. **ils tolèrent un excédent de bagages de 15 kg** they allow 15 kg (of) excess baggage.

(b) (*supporter*) *comportement, excentricités, personne* to put up with, tolerate; *douleur* to bear, endure, stand. **ils ne s'aimaient guère: disons qu'ils se toléraient** they did not like each other much — it was more that they put up with *ou* tolerated each other; **je ne tolérerai pas cette impertinence/ces retards** I shall not stand for *ou* put up with *ou* tolerate this impertinence/this constant lateness; **il tolérait qu'on l'appelle par son prénom** he tolerated being called by his first name, he allowed people to call him by his first name; **il ne tolère pas qu'on le contredise** he won't stand (for) *ou* tolerate being contradicted.

(c) (*Bio, Méd*) *[organisme]* to tolerate; (*Tech*) *[matériau, système]* to tolerate. **il ne tolère pas l'alcool** he can't tolerate alcohol.

tôlerie [tolʀi] *nf* **(a)** (*fabrication*) sheet metal manufacture; (*commerce*) sheet metal trade; (*atelier*) sheet metal workshop. **(b)** (*tôles*) *[auto]* panels (*pl*), coachwork; *[bateau, chaudière]* plates (*pl*), steel-work.

tolet [tɔlɛ] *nm* thole(pin).

tôlier[1] [tolje] *nm* sheet iron *ou* steel manufacturer. **(ouvrier-)~** sheet metal worker; **~ en voitures** panel beater; **~ de bâtiment** sheet metal worker (*in building industry*).

tôlier[2], **-ière**: [tolje, jɛʀ] *nm,f* = **taulier**:.

tollé [tɔle] *nm* general outcry *ou* protest. **ce fut un ~ (général)** there was a general outcry.

tomahawk [tɔmaok] *nm* tomahawk.

tomaison [tɔmɛzɔ̃] *nf* volume numbering.

tomate [tɔmat] *nf* (*plante*) tomato (plant); (*fruit*) tomato; *V* **rouge.**

tombal, e, *mpl* **~s** [tɔ̃bal] *adj dalle* funerary; (*littér: funèbre*) tomb-like, funereal (*épith*). **inscription ~e** tombstone inscription; *V* **pierre.**

tombant, e [tɔ̃bɑ̃, ɑ̃t] *adj draperies* hanging (*épith*); *épaules* sloping (*épith*), drooping (*épith*); *moustaches* drooping (*épith*); *V* **nuit.**

tombe [tɔ̃b] *nf* **(a)** (*gén*) grave; (*avec monument*) tomb; (*pierre*) gravestone, tombstone. **froid comme la ~** cold as the tomb; **silencieux comme la ~** silent as the grave *ou* tomb; *V* **muet, recueillir, retourner.**

(b) (*loc*) **suivre qn dans la ~** to follow sb to the grave; **avoir un pied dans la ~** to have one foot in the grave; (*littér*) **descendre dans la ~** to go to one's grave.

tombeau, *pl* **~x** [tɔ̃bo] *nm* **(a)** (*lit*) tomb. **mettre au ~** to entomb; **mise au ~** entombment.

(b) (*fig*) (*endroit lugubre ou solitaire*) grave, tomb; (*ruine*) *[espérances, amour]* death (*U*); (*lieu du trépas*) grave. (*trépas*) **jusqu'au ~** to the grave; **descendre au ~** to go to one's grave; **cette pièce est un ~** this room is like a grave *ou* tomb.

(c) à ~ ouvert at breakneck speed.

tombée [tɔ̃be] *nf* **(a) (à) la ~ de la nuit** (at) nightfall; **(à) la ~ du jour** (at) the close of the day.

(b) (*rare: littér*) *[neige, pluie]* fall.

tomber [tɔ̃be] (1) **1** *vi* **(a)** (*de la station debout*) to fall (over *ou* down). **il est tombé en courant et s'est cassé la jambe** he fell (over *ou* down) while running and broke his leg; **le chien l'a fait ~** the dog knocked him over *ou* down; **~ par terre** to fall down, fall to the ground; **~ raide mort** to fall down *ou* drop (down) dead; **~ à genoux** to fall on(to) one's knees; (*fig*) **~ aux pieds** *ou* **genoux de qn** to fall at sb's feet; (*fig*) **~ dans les bras de qn** to fall into sb's arms; **~ de tout son long** to fall headlong, go sprawling, measure one's length; **se laisser ~ dans un fauteuil** to drop *ou* fall into an armchair; (*fig*) **~ de fatigue** to drop from exhaustion; (*fig*) **~ de sommeil** to be falling asleep on one's feet; *V* **inanition, pomme, renverse.**

(b) (*de la position verticale*) *[arbre, bouteille, poteau]* to fall (over *ou* down); *[chaise, pile d'objets]* to fall (over); *[échafaudage, mur]* to fall down, collapse. **faire ~** to knock over; to knock down.

(c) (*d'un endroit élevé*) *[personne, objet]* to fall (down); *[avion]* to fall; (*fig littér: pécher*) to fall. **attention, tu vas ~** careful, you'll fall; (*fig*) **~ (bien) bas** to sink (very) low; (*fig littér*) **ne condamnez pas un homme qui est tombé** do not condemn a fallen man; **~ d'un arbre** to fall down from a tree, fall out of a tree; **~ dans** *ou* **à l'eau** to fall into the water; **~ de bicyclette/cheval** to fall off one's bicycle/from *ou* off one's horse; **~ à bas de son cheval** to fall down from one's horse; **il tombait des pierres** stones were falling.

(d) (*se détacher*) *[feuilles, fruits]* to fall; *[cheveux]* to fall (out). **ramasser des fruits tombés** to pick up fruit that has fallen, pick up windfalls; **le journal tombe (des presses) à 6 heures** the paper comes off the press at 6 o'clock; **un télex vient de ~** a telex has just come through; **la plume me tombe des mains** the pen is falling from my hand.

(e) *[eau, lumière]* to fall; *[neige, pluie]* to fall, come down; *[brouillard]* to come down. **il tombe de la neige** snow is falling; **qu'est-ce qu'il tombe!*** it isn't half coming down!*, it's coming down in buckets!*; **l'eau tombait en cascades** the water was cascading down; **il tombe quelques gouttes** there are a few drops of rain (falling), it's spotting (with rain); **la nuit tombe** night is falling; **la foudre est tombée deux fois/tout près** the lighting has struck twice/nearby.

(f) (*fig: être tué*) *[combattant]* to fall. **ils tombaient les uns après les autres** they were falling one after the other; **tombé au champ d'honneur** fallen on the field of honour; *V* **mouche.**

(g) (*fig*) *[ville, régime, garnison]* to fall. **faire ~ le gouvernement** to bring down the government, bring the government down; (*Cartes*) **l'as et le roi sont tombés** the ace and king have gone *ou* have been played; (*Cartes*) **faire ~ une carte** to drop.

(h) (*baisser*) *[température]* to drop, fall; *[vent, fièvre]* to drop; *[baromètre]* to fall; *[jour]* to draw to a close; *[voix]* to drop, fall away; *[prix, nombre]* to fall, drop; *[colère, conversation]* to die down; *[exaltation, assurance, enthousiasme]* to fall away. **faire ~** *température, vent, prix* to bring down. **laisser ~ sa voix à la fin d'une strophe** to let one's voice drop *ou* fall away *ou* drop one's voice at the end of a verse.

(i) (*disparaître*) *[obstacle, objection]* to disappear; *[plan, projet]* to fall through; *[droit, poursuites]* to lapse.

(j) (*pendre, descendre*) *[draperie, robe, chevelure]* to fall, hang; *[pantalon]* to hang; *[moustaches, épaules]* to droop. **ses cheveux lui tombaient sur les épaules** his hair fell *ou* hung onto his shoulders; **les lourds rideaux tombaient jusqu'au plancher** the heavy curtains hung down to the floor; **ce pantalon tombe bien** these trousers hang well.

(k) (*devenir: avec attribut, avec en: V aussi les noms et adjectifs en question*) **~ malade** to fall ill; **~ amoureux** to fall in love (*de* with); **~ d'accord** to reach agreement; **~ en disgrâce** to fall into disgrace; **~ en syncope** to fall into a faint; *V* **arrêt, désuétude** *etc.*

(l) (*avec dans, sous: se trouver: V aussi les noms en question*) **~ dans un piège/une embuscade** to fall into a trap/an ambush; **~ dans l'oubli** to fall into oblivion; **~ dans l'excès/le ridicule** to lapse into excess/the ridiculous; **~ d'un excès dans un autre** to go on from one excess to another; **~ sous la domination de** to fall *ou* come under the domination of; **~ en mains ennemies** to fall into enemy hands; *V* **coupe**[2]**, dent, main** *etc.*

(m) (*échoir*) *[date, choix, sort]* to fall. **Pâques tombe tard cette année** Easter falls late this year; **Noël tombe un mardi** Christmas falls on a Tuesday; **les deux concerts tombent le même jour** the two concerts fall on the same day; **le choix est tombé sur lui** the choice fell on him; **et il a fallu que ça tombe sur moi** it (just) had to be me.

(n) (*arriver inopinément*) **il est tombé en pleine réunion/scène de ménage** he walked straight into a meeting/a domestic row.

(o) laisser ~ *objet qu'on porte* to drop*; (*) *amis, activité* to drop*; **laissez ~!*, laisse ~!*** give it a rest!*; **il a laissé ~ le feu** he let the fire die down.

(p) (*loc*) **~ à l'eau** *[projets etc]* to fall through; **bien/mal ~** (*avoir de la chance*) to be lucky/unlucky; **il est vraiment bien/mal tombé avec son nouveau patron** he's really lucky/unlucky with his new boss; **bien/mal ~, ~ bien/mal** (*arriver, se produire au bon/mauvais moment*) to come at the right/wrong moment; **ça tombe bien** that's lucky *ou* fortunate; **ça tombe à point** *ou* **à pic*** that's perfect timing; **ça ne pouvait pas mieux ~** that couldn't have come at a better time; **~ de Charybde en Scylla** to jump out of the frying pan into the fire; **~ juste** (*en devinant*) to be (exactly) right; *[calculs]* to come out right; **~ de haut** to come down to earth (with a bump); **~ de son haut** to be brought down a peg or two; **il n'est pas tombé de la dernière pluie** *ou* **averse*** he wasn't born yesterday; **ce n'est pas tombé dans l'oreille d'un sourd** it didn't fall on deaf ears; **il est tombé sur la tête!*** he's got a screw loose*; **~ en quenouille** to pass into female hands; (*fig*) **~ de la lune** to have dropped in from another planet; (*fig*) **~ du ciel** to be a godsend, be heaven-sent; **~ des nues** to be completely taken aback; (*fig*) **~ à l'eau** *[projets, entreprise]* to fall through; **~ à plat** *[plaisanterie]* to fall flat; *[pièce de théâtre]* to be a flop; **cela tombe sous le sens** it's (perfectly) obvious, it stands to reason; *V* **bras, cul.**

2 tomber sur *vt indir* **(a)** (*rencontrer*) *connaissance* to run into, come across; *détail* to come across. **prenez cette rue, et vous tombez sur le boulevard** go along this street and you come out on the boulevard.

(b) (*se poser*) *[regard]* to fall *ou* light upon; *[conversation]* to come round to.

(c) (*) (*attaquer*) to set about*, go for*; (*critiquer*) to go for*. **il m'est tombé sur le râble**: *ou* **le paletot**: *ou* **le dos**: he set on me*, he went for me; *V* **bras.**

(d) (*: *s'inviter, survenir*) to land on*. **il nous est tombé dessus le jour de ton anniversaire** he landed on us on your birthday*.

3 *vt* **(a)** (*Sport*) **~ qn** to throw sb; **~ une femme**: to seduce *ou* have: a woman.

(b) ~ la veste* to slip off one's jacket.

tombereau, *pl* **~x** [tɔ̃bʀo] *nm* (*charrette*) tipcart; (*contenu*) cartload.

tombeur [tɔ̃bœʀ] *nm* (*lutteur*) thrower. (*fig*) **~ (de femmes)*** Casanova.

tombola [tɔ̃bɔla] *nf* tombola.

Tombouctou [tɔ̃buktu] *n* Timbuktoo.

tome [tɔm] *nm* (*division*) part, book; (*volume*) volume.

tomer [tɔme] (1) *vt ouvrage* to divide into parts *ou* books; *page, volume* to mark with the volume number.

tomette [tɔmɛt] *nf* = **tommette.**

tomme [tɔm] *nf* tomme (cheese).

tommette [tɔmɛt] *nf* (red, hexagonal) floor-tile.

ton[1] [tɔ̃], **ta** [ta], **tes** [te] *adj poss* **(a)** (*possession, relation*) your, (*emphatique*) your own; (†, *Rel*) thy. **~ fils et ta fille** your son and (your) daughter; (*Rel*) **que ta volonté soit faite** Thy will be done; *pour autres exemples V* **son**[1].

(b) (*valeur affective, ironique, intensive*) **je vois que tu connais tes classiques!** I can see that you know your classics!; **tu as de la chance d'avoir ~ samedi!*** you're lucky to have (your) Saturday(s) off!*; **~ Paris est devenu très bruyant** this Paris of yours is getting very noisy; **tu vas avoir ta crise de foie si tu manges ça** you'll have one of your liverish attacks *ou* you'll upset your liver if you eat that; **ferme donc ta porte!** shut the door behind you; *pour autres exemples V* **son**[1].

ton[2] [tɔ̃] *nm* **(a)** (*hauteur de la voix*) pitch; (*timbre*) tone; (*qualité de la voix*) tone (of voice). **~ aigu/grave** shrill/low pitch; **~ nasillard** nasal tone; **d'un ~ détaché/brusque/pédant** in a detached/an abrupt/a pedantic tone (of voice); **sur le ~ de la conversation/plaisanterie** in a conversational/joking tone (of voice); **hausser/baisser le ~** to raise/lower (the tone of) one's voice *ou* one's tone; (*fig*) **hausser le ~** to adopt an arrogant tone; (*fig*) **faire baisser le ~ à qn** to make sb change his tune, bring sb down a peg (or two); (*fig*) **il devra changer de ~/baisser le ~** he'll have to sing a different tune/change his tune; (*fig*) **ne le prenez pas sur ce ~** don't take it in that way *ou* like that; (*fig*) **alors là, si vous le prenez sur ce ~** well if that's the way you're going to take it; (*fig*) **dire/répéter sur tous les ~s** to say/repeat in every possible way.

(b) (*Mus*) (*intervalle*) tone; *[morceau]* key; *[instrument à* *vent]* crook; (*hauteur de la voix, d'un instrument*) pitch. **le ~ de si majeur** the key of B major; **passer d'un ~ à un autre** to change from one key to another; **il y a un ~ majeur entre do et ré** there is a whole *ou* full tone between doh and ray; **prendre le ~** to tune up (*de* to); **donner le ~** to give the pitch; **il/ce n'est pas dans le ~** he/it is not in tune; **le ~ est trop haut pour elle** it is set in too high a key for her, it is pitched too high for her.

(c) (*Ling, Phonétique*) tone. **langue à ~s** tone language.

(d) (*manière de s'exprimer, décrire*) tone. **le ~ précieux/soutenu de sa prose** the precious/elevated tone of his prose; **des plaisanteries** *ou* **remarques de bon ~** jokes *ou* remarks in good taste; **il est de bon ~ de faire** it is good form to do; **être dans le ~** to fit in; **il s'est vite mis dans le ~** he soon fitted in; **donner le ~** to set the tone; (*en matière de mode*) to set the fashion; *V* **bon**[1].

(e) (*couleur, nuance*) shade, tone. **être dans le ~** to tone in, match; **la ceinture n'est pas du même ~** *ou* **dans le même ~ que la robe** the belt does not match the dress; **des ~s chauds** warm tones *ou* shades; **des ~s dégradés** gradual shadings; **~ sur ~** in matching tones.

tonal, e, *mpl* **~s** [tɔnal] *adj* (*Ling, Mus*) tonal.

tonalité [tɔnalite] *nf* **(a)** (*Mus: système*) tonality; (*Mus: ton*) key; (*Phonétique*) *[voyelle]* tone. **(b)** (*fidélité*) *[poste, amplificateur]* tone. **(c)** (*timbre, qualité*) *[voix]* tone; (*fig*) *[texte, impression]* tone; *[couleurs]* tonality. **(d)** (*Téléc*) dialling tone. **je n'ai pas la ~** I'm not getting the dialling tone.

tondeur [tɔ̃dœʀ] *nm*: **~ de drap** cloth shearer; **~ de moutons** sheep shearer.

tondeuse [tɔ̃døz] *nf* (*à cheveux*) clippers (*pl*); (*pour les moutons*) shears (*pl*); (*Tex: pour les draps*) shears (*pl*). **~ (à gazon)** (lawn)mower; **~ à main/mécanique** hand-/motor-mower; **les cheveux coupés à la ~** with closely-cropped hair.

tondre [tɔ̃dʀ(ə)] (41) *vt* **(a)** *mouton, toison* to shear; *gazon* to mow; *haie* to clip, cut; *caniche, poil* to clip; *cheveux* to crop; *drap, feutre* to shear.

(b) (*) *personne* (*couper les cheveux*) to chop*; (*escroquer*) to fleece*. **je vais me faire ~** I'm going for a chop* (*surtout Brit*), I'm going to get my hair chopped*; **~ la laine sur le dos de qn**† to have the shirt off sb's back.

tondu, e [tɔ̃dy] (*ptp de* **tondre**) *adj cheveux, tête* (closely-) cropped; *personne* with closely-cropped hair, close-cropped; *pelouse*, (*fig*) *sommet* closely-cropped. (*péj: aux cheveux courts*) **regardez-moi ce ~** just look at that short back and sides; *V* **pelé**.

tonicité [tɔnisite] *nf* **(a)** (*Méd*) *[tissus]* tone, tonicity (*T*), tonus (*T*). **(b)** (*fig*) *[air, mer]* tonic *ou* bracing effect.

tonifiant, e [tɔnifjɑ̃, ɑ̃t] **1** *adj air* bracing, invigorating; *massage, lotion* tonic (*épith*), stimulating; *lecture, expérience* invigorating, stimulating. **2** *nm* tonic.

tonifier [tɔnifje] (7) *vt muscles, peau* to tone up; (*fig*) *esprit, personne* to invigorate, stimulate. **cela tonifie tout l'organisme** it tones up the whole system.

tonique [tɔnik] **1** *adj* **(a)** *médicament, vin, boisson* tonic (*épith*), fortifying; *lotion* toning (*épith*).

(b) (*fig*) *air, froid* invigorating, bracing; *idée, expérience* stimulating; *lecture* invigorating, stimulating.

(c) (*Ling*) *syllabe, voyelle* tonic, accented; *accent* tonic.

2 *nm* (*Méd, fig*) tonic; (*lotion*) toning lotion. **~ du cœur** heart tonic.

3 *nf* (*Mus*) tonic, keynote.

tonitruant, e [tɔnitʀyɑ̃, ɑ̃t] *adj voix* thundering (*épith*), booming (*épith*).

tonitruer [tɔnitʀye] (1) *vi* to thunder.

Tonkin [tɔ̃kɛ̃] *nm* Tonkin.

tonkinois, e [tɔ̃kinwa, waz] **1** *adj* Tonkinese. **2** *nm,f*: **T~(e)** Tonkinese.

tonnage [tɔnaʒ] *nm* tonnage, burden. **~ brut/net** gross/net tonnage; *[port, pays]* tonnage.

tonnant, e [tɔnɑ̃, ɑ̃t] *adj voix, acclamation* thunderous, thundering (*épith*).

tonne [tɔn] *nf* **(a)** (*unité de poids*) (metric) ton, tonne (*Brit*). **une ~ de bois** a ton *ou* tonne of wood; (*Statistique*) **~ kilométrique** ton kilometre; **un navire de 10.000 ~s** a 10,000-ton *ou* -tonne ship, a ship of 10,000 tons *ou* tonnes; **un (camion de) 5 ~s** a 5-ton lorry, a 5-tonner*.

(b) des ~s de* tons of*, loads of*.

(c) (*Tech: récipient*) tun; (*Naut: bouée*) nun-buoy.

tonneau, *pl* **~x** [tɔno] *nm* **(a)** (*récipient, contenu*) barrel. **vin au ~** wine from the barrel *ou* cask; (*fig*) **c'est le ~ des Danaïdes** it is a Sisyphean task; (*péj*) **être du même ~*** to be of the same kind; *V* **perce**.

(b) (*Aviat*) hesitation flick roll (*Brit*), hesitation snap roll (*US*); *V* **demi-**.

(c) (*Aut*) somersault. **faire un ~** to somersault, roll over.

(d) (*Naut*) ton. **un bateau de 1.500 ~x** a 1,500-ton ship.

tonnelet [tɔnlɛ] *nm* keg, (small) cask.

tonnelier [tɔnəlje] *nm* cooper.

tonnelle [tɔnɛl] *nf* (*abri*) bower, arbour; (*Archit*) barrel vault.

tonnellerie [tɔnɛlʀi] *nf* cooperage.

tonner [tɔne] (1) **1** *vi* **(a)** *[canons, artillerie]* to thunder, boom, roar.

(b) *[personne]* to thunder, rage (*contre* against).

2 *vb impers* to thunder. **il tonne** it is thundering; **il a tonné vers 2 heures** there was some thunder about 2 o'clock; **il tonnait sans discontinuer** it went on thundering without a break.

tonnerre [tɔnɛʀ] **1** *nm* **(a)** (*détonation*) thunder; (†: *foudre*) thunderbolt. **le ~ gronde** there is a rumble of thunder; **un bruit/une voix de ~** a noise/voice like thunder, a thunderous noise/voice; (*fig*) **un ~ d'applaudissements** thunderous applause, a thunder of applause; (*fig*) **le ~ des canons** the roar *ou* the thundering of the canons; *V* **coup**.

(b) (*: *valeur intensive*) **du ~** terrific*, fantastic*; **ça marchait le ~** it was going great guns*; **un livre du ~ de Dieu** one *ou* a hell of a book‡, a fantastic book*.

2 *excl*: **~!***† ye gods!*†; **mille ~s!***, **~ de Brest!*** shiver my timbers!* (†, *hum*); **~ de Dieu!‡** hell and damnation!‡; hell's bells!*

tonsure [tɔ̃syʀ] *nf* (*Rel*) tonsure; (*: *calvitie*) bald spot *ou* patch. **porter la ~** to wear the tonsure.

tonsuré, e [tɔ̃syʀe] (*ptp de* **tonsurer**) *adj* tonsured. (*péj*) **un ~** a monk.

tonsurer [tɔ̃syʀe] (1) *vt* to tonsure.

tonte [tɔ̃t] *nf* **(a)** (*action*) *[moutons]* shearing; *[haie]* clipping; *[gazon]* mowing. **(b)** (*laine*) fleece. **(c)** (*époque*) shearing-time.

tontine [tɔ̃tin] *nf* (*Hist Jur*) tontine.

tonton [tɔ̃tɔ̃] *nm* (*langage enfantin*) uncle.

tonus [tɔnys] *nm* **(a) ~ musculaire** muscular tone *ou* tonus (*T*); **~ nerveux** nerve tone. **(b)** (*fig: dynamisme*) energy, dynamism.

top [tɔp] **1** *nm* pip. (*Rad*) **au 4e ~ il sera midi** at the 4th stroke it will be twelve o'clock. **2** *adj*: **~ secret** top secret.

topaze [tɔpɑz] *nf* topaz.

tope [tɔp] *excl V* **toper**.

toper [tɔpe] (1) *vi*: **~ à qch** to shake on sth, agree to sth; **tope (-là), topez-là!** done!, you're on!*, it's a deal!*

topinambour [tɔpinɑ̃buʀ] *nm* Jerusalem artichoke.

topique [tɔpik] **1** *adj* (*rare, frm*) *argument, explication* pertinent; *citation* apposite; (*Méd*) *remède, médicament* topical, local. **2** *nm* (*Méd*) topical *ou* local remedy; (*Philos*) topic. **3** *nf* (*Philos*) topics (*sg*).

topo* [tɔpo] *nm* (*exposé, rapport*) rundown*; (*péj: laïus*) spiel*. **c'est toujours le même ~** it's always the same old story*.

topographe [tɔpɔgʀaf] *nm* topographer.

topographie [tɔpɔgʀafi] *nf* (*technique*) topography; (*configuration*) layout, topography; (†, *rare: description*) topographical description; (*croquis*) topographical plan.

topographique [tɔpɔgʀafik] *adj* topographic(al).

topographiquement [tɔpɔgʀafikmɑ̃] *adv* topographically.

topologie [tɔpɔlɔʒi] *nf* topology.

topologique [tɔpɔlɔʒik] *adj* topologic(al).

toponyme [tɔpɔnim] *nm* place-name, toponym (*T*).

toponymie [tɔpɔnimi] *nf* (*étude*) toponymy (*T*), study of place-names; (*noms de lieu*) toponymy (*T*), place-names (*pl*).

toponymique [tɔpɔnimik] *adj* toponymic.

toquade [tɔkad] *nf* (*péj*) (*pour qn*) infatuation; (*pour qch*) fad, craze. **avoir une ~ pour qn** to be infatuated with sb.

toquante‡ [tɔkɑ̃t] *nf* = **tocante‡**.

toquard, e‡ [tɔkaʀ, aʀd(ə)] = **tocard‡**.

toque [tɔk] *nf* *[femme]* fur hat; *[juge, jockey]* cap. **~ de cuisinier** chef's hat.

toqué, e* [tɔke] *adj* crazy*, cracked*, nuts* (*attrib*). **être ~ de qn** to be crazy *ou* mad *ou* nuts about sb*; **méfiez-vous de ce ~** watch that nutcase*.

toquer[1]* **(se)** [tɔke] (1) *vpr*: **se ~ d'une femme** to lose one's head over a woman, go crazy over a woman*.

toquer[2]* [tɔke] (1) *vi* to tap, rap. **~ (à la porte)** to tap *ou* rap at the door.

torche [tɔʀʃ(ə)] *nf* **(a)** (*flambeau*) torch. **~ électrique** (electric) torch; **être transformé en ~ vivante** to be turned into a human torch; (*Parachutisme*) **se mettre en ~** to candle.

(b) (*Ind: torchère*) flare.

torche-cul‡, *pl* **torche-culs** [tɔʀʃəky] *nm* bog-paper‡ ( ) (*Brit*); (*fig*, †: *écrit*) drivel (*U*).

torcher [tɔʀʃe] (1) **1** *vt* **(a)** (*) *assiette* to wipe (clean); *jus* to mop up.

(b) (‡) *bébé, derrière* to wipe.

(c) (*péj*) *travail, rapport* (*trousser, produire*) to toss off*; (*bâcler*) to make a mess of*, do a bad job on. **un rapport/article bien torché** a well-written report/article.

2 se torcher‡ *vpr*: **se ~ (le cul** *ou* **le derrière)** to wipe one's backside‡; (*fig*) **je m'en torche** I don't care *ou* give a damn‡.

torchère [tɔʀʃɛʀ] *nf* **(a)** (*Ind*) flare. **(b)** (*vase*) cresset; (*candélabre*) torchère; (*chandelier*) candelabrum.

torchis [tɔʀʃi] *nm* cob (*for walls*).

torchon [tɔʀʃɔ̃] *nm* **(a)** (*gén*) cloth; (*pour épousseter*) duster; (*à vaisselle*) tea towel, dish towel. **coup de ~** (*lit*) wipe with a (tea)cloth; dust; (*fig*) (*bagarre*) dust-up*, scrap; (*épuration*) clear-out; (*fig: épurer*) **donner un coup de ~** to have a clear-out; (*fig*) **le ~ brûle** there's a running battle (going on); *V* **mélanger**.

(b) (*péj*) (*devoir mal présenté*) mess (*U*); (*écrit sans valeur*) drivel (*U*), tripe* (*U*); (*mauvais journal*) rag. **ce devoir est un ~** this homework is a mess.

torchonner* [tɔʀʃɔne] (1) *vt* (*péj*) *travail* to do a rushed job on. **un devoir torchonné** a slipshod piece of homework.

tordant, e* [tɔʀdɑ̃, ɑ̃t] *adj* killing*, screamingly funny*. **il est ~** he's a scream* *ou* a kill*.

tord-boyaux*† [tɔʀbwajo] *nm inv* gut-rot‡.

tordre [tɔʀdʀ(ə)] (41) **1** *vt* **(a)** (*entre ses mains*) to wring; (*pour essorer*) to wring (out); *tresses* to wind; (*Tex*) *brins, laine* to twist; *bras, poignet* to twist. (*sur étiquette*) **ne pas ~** do not wring; **~ le cou à un poulet** to wring a chicken's neck; (*fig*) **je vais lui ~ le cou** I'll wring his neck (for him); **cet alcool vous tord les boyaux*** this drink rots your guts‡; **la peur lui tordit l'estomac** his stomach was turning over with fear, fear was churning his stomach.

(b) (*plier*) *barre de fer* to twist.

(c) (*déformer*) *traits, visage* to contort, twist. **une joie sadique lui tordait la bouche** his mouth was twisted into a sadistic smile; **la colère lui tordait le visage** his face was contorted with anger.

2 se tordre *vpr* **(a)** *[personne]* **se ~ de douleur** to be doubled up with pain; **se ~ (de rire)** to be doubled up *ou* creased up with laughter; **c'est à se ~ (de rire)** you'd die (laughing)*.

(b) *[barre, poteau]* to bend; *[roue]* to buckle, twist; (*littér: être contourné*) *[racine, tronc]* to twist round, writhe (*littér*).

(c) se ~ le bras/le poignet/la cheville to sprain *ou* twist one's arm/wrist/ankle; **se ~ les mains (de désespoir)** to wring one's hands (in despair).

tordu, e [tɔʀdy] (*ptp de* **tordre**) *adj nez* crooked; *jambes* bent, crooked; *tronc* twisted; *règle, barre* bent; *roue* bent, buckled, twisted. **avoir l'esprit ~** to have a warped *ou* weird mind; **être (complètement) ~‡** to be round the bend* (*Brit*) *ou* the twist‡; **un ~** (*péj: contrefait*) a misshapen creature; (‡: *fou*) a loony‡, a nut case*; **va donc, eh ~!‡** you (great) twit!‡.

tore [tɔʀ] *nm*: **~ magnétique** magnetic core.

toréador [tɔʀeadɔʀ] *nm* toreador.

toréer [tɔʀee] (1) *vi* to fight *ou* work a bull.

torero [tɔʀeʀo] *nm* bullfighter, torero.

torgnole* [tɔʀɲɔl] *nf* clout*, wallop*, swipe*.

toril [tɔʀil] *nm* bullpen.

tornade [tɔʀnad] *nf* tornado.

toron [tɔʀɔ̃] *nm* (*brin*) strand.

torontois, e [tɔʀɔ̃twa, waz] **1** *adj* Torontonian. **2** *nm,f*: **T~(e)** Torontonian.

torpédo [tɔʀpedo] *nf* open tourer.

torpeur [tɔʀpœʀ] *nf* torpor.

torpide [tɔʀpid] *adj* (*littér*) torpid.

torpillage [tɔʀpijaʒ] *nm* torpedoing.

torpille [tɔʀpij] *nf* **(a)** (*Mil*) (*sous-marine*) torpedo. (*bombe*) **~ (aérienne)** (aerial) torpedo; *V* **lancer. (b)** (*Zool*) torpedo.

torpiller [tɔʀpije] (1) *vt navire*, (*fig*) *plan* to torpedo.

torpilleur [tɔʀpijœʀ] *nm* torpedo boat; *V* **contre.**

torréfacteur [tɔʀefaktœʀ] *nm* (*V* **torréfier**) roaster; toasting machine.

torréfaction [tɔʀefaksjɔ̃] *nf* (*V* **torréfier**) roasting; toasting.

torréfier [tɔʀefje] (7) *vt café* to roast; *tabac* to toast.

torrent [tɔʀɑ̃] *nm* (*cours d'eau*) torrent. **~ de lave** torrent of lava; (*fig: pluie*) **des ~s d'eau** torrential rain; **il pleut à ~s** the rain is coming down in torrents; (*fig*) **un ~ de** *injures* a torrent *ou* stream of; *paroles* a torrent *ou* flood of; *musique* a flood of; (*fig*) **des ~s de** *fumée* a stream *ou* streams of; *larmes, lumière* a stream *ou* flood of, streams *ou* floods of.

torrentiel, -elle [tɔʀɑ̃sjɛl] *adj pluie*, (*Géog*) *eaux, régime* torrential.

torrentueux, -euse [tɔʀɑ̃tɥø, øz] *adj cours d'eau* torrential, onrushing (*épith*), surging (*épith*); (*fig*) *vie* hectic; *discours* onrushing (*épith*).

torride [tɔʀid] *adj région, climat* torrid; *journée, chaleur* scorching, torrid (*frm*).

tors, torse[1] [tɔʀ, tɔʀs(ə)] *ou* (*rare*) **torte** [tɔʀt(ə)] *adj fil* twisted; *colonne* wreathed; *pied de verre* twist (*épith*); *jambes* crooked, bent.

torsade [tɔʀsad] *nf [fils]* twist; (*Archit*) cable moulding. **~ de cheveux** twist *ou* coil of hair; **en ~** *embrasse, cheveux* twisted; **colonne à ~s** cabled column.

torsader [tɔʀsade] (1) *vt frange, corde, cheveux* to twist. **colonne torsadée** cabled column.

torse[2] [tɔʀs(ə)] *nm* (*gén*) chest; (*Anat, Sculp*) torso. **~ nu** stripped to the waist, bare-chested; *V* **bomber.**

torsion [tɔʀsjɔ̃] *nf* (*action*) twisting; (*Phys, Tech*) torsion. **exercer sur qn une ~ du bras** to twist sb's arm back; *V* **couple.**

tort [tɔʀ] *nm* **(a)** (*action, attitude blâmable*) fault. **il a un ~, c'est de trop parler** he has one fault and that's talking too much; **il a le ~ d'être trop jeune** his trouble is *ou* his fault is that he's too young; **il a eu le ~ d'être impoli un jour avec le patron** he made the mistake one day of being rude to the boss; **ils ont tous les ~s de leur côté** the fault *ou* wrong is entirely on their side; (*Jur*) **les ~s sont du côté du mari/cycliste** the fault is on the part of the husband/cyclist, the husband/cyclist is at fault; **avoir des ~s envers qn** to have wronged sb; **il n'a aucun ~** he's in no way in the wrong *ou* to blame; **reconnaître/regretter ses ~s** to acknowledge/be sorry for the wrong one has done *ou* for one's wrongs *ou* one's wrongdoings; **vous avez refusé? c'est un ~** did you refuse? – you were wrong (to do so) *ou* you shouldn't have (done so).

(b) (*dommage, préjudice*) wrong. **redresser un ~** to right a wrong; **causer** *ou* **faire du ~ à qn, faire ~ à qn** to harm sb, do sb harm; **ça ne fait de ~ à personne** it doesn't harm *ou* hurt anybody; **il s'est fait du ~** he has harmed himself, he has done himself no good; **cette mesure va faire du ~ aux produits laitiers** this measure will harm *ou* be harmful to *ou* be detrimental to the dairy industry; *V* **redresseur.**

(c) à ~ wrongly; **soupçonner/accuser qn à ~** to suspect/accuse sb wrongly; **c'est à ~ qu'on l'avait dit malade** he was wrongly *ou* mistakenly said to be ill; **à ~ ou à raison** rightly or wrongly; **à ~ et à travers: dépenser à ~ et à travers** to spend wildly, spend money here there and everywhere*; **il parle à ~ et à travers** he's blathering*, he's saying any old thing*.

(d) être/se mettre/se sentir dans son ~ to be/put o.s./feel o.s. in the wrong; **mettre qn dans son ~** to put sb in the wrong; **être en ~** to be in the wrong *ou* at fault.

(e) (*avec avoir, faire, donner*) **avoir ~** to be wrong; **il a ~ de se mettre en colère** he is wrong *ou* it is wrong of him to get angry; **il n'a pas tout à fait ~ de dire que** he is not altogether *ou* entirely wrong in saying that; **elle a grand** *ou* **bien ~ de le croire** she's very wrong to believe it; **tu aurais bien ~ de te gêner!** you'd be quite wrong to bother yourself!; *V* **absent.**

(f) donner ~: donner ~ à qn (*sujet nom de personne*) to lay the blame on sb, blame sb; (*sujet nom de chose*) to show sb to be wrong, prove sb wrong; **ils ont donné ~ au camionneur** they laid the blame on *ou* they blamed the lorry driver; **les statistiques donnent ~ à son rapport** statistics show *ou* prove his report to be wrong *ou* inaccurate; **les événements lui ont donné ~** events showed that he was wrong.

torte [tɔʀt(ə)] *adj f V* **tors.**

torticolis [tɔʀtikɔli] *nm* stiff neck, torticollis (*T*). **avoir/attraper le ~** to have/get a stiff neck.

tortillard [tɔʀtijaʀ] *nm* (*hum, péj: train*) local train.

tortillement [tɔʀtijmɑ̃] *nm* (*V* **se tortiller**) writhing; wriggling; squirming; fidgeting. **~ des hanches** wiggling of the hips.

tortiller [tɔʀtije] (1) **1** *vt corde, mouchoir* to twist; *cheveux, cravate* to twiddle (with); *moustache* to twirl; *doigts* to twiddle.

2 *vi*: **~ des hanches** to wiggle one's hips; (*fig*) **il n'y a pas à ~*** there's no wriggling round it.

3 se tortiller *vpr* **(a)** *[serpent]* to writhe; *[ver]* to wriggle, squirm; *[personne]* (*en dansant, en se débattant etc*) to wriggle; (*d'impatience*) to fidget, wriggle; (*par embarras, de douleur*) to squirm. **se ~ comme une anguille** *ou* **un ver** to wriggle like a worm *ou* an eel, squirm like an eel.

(b) *[fumée]* to curl upwards; *[racine, tige]* to curl, writhe.

tortillon* [tɔʀtijɔ̃] *nm* (*péj*) twist.

tortionnaire [tɔʀsjɔnɛʀ] *nm* torturer.

tortue [tɔʀty] *nf* **(a)** (*Zool*) tortoise; (*fig*) slowcoach. **~ de mer** turtle; **avancer comme une ~** *ou* **d'un pas de ~** to crawl along at a snail's pace. **(b)** (*Hist Mil*) testudo, tortoise.

tortueusement [tɔʀtɥøzmɑ̃] *adv* (*V* **tortueux**) windingly; tortuously; meanderingly; deviously.

tortueux, -euse [tɔʀtɥø, øz] *adj* **(a)** (*lit*) *chemin, escalier* winding, twisting, tortuous (*littér*); *rivière* winding, meandering. **(b)** (*fig péj*) *langage, discours, allure* tortuous; *manœuvres, conduite* devious.

torturant, e [tɔʀtyʀɑ̃, ɑ̃t] *adj* agonizing.

torture [tɔʀtyʀ] *nf* (*lit*) torture; (*fig*) torture, torment. **instruments de ~** instruments of torture; (*fig*) **mettre qn à la ~** to torture sb, make sb suffer; (*fig*) **les ~s de la passion** the torture *ou* torments of passion; **salle** *ou* **chambre des ~s** torture chamber.

torturer [tɔʀtyʀe] (1) **1** *vt* **(a)** (*lit*) *prisonnier, animal* to torture; (*fig*) *[faim, douleur, remords]* to rack, torment, torture; *[personne]* to torture.

(b) (*littér: dénaturer*) *texte* to distort, torture (*littér*). **visage torturé par le chagrin** face racked with grief; **la poésie torturée, déchirante de X** the tormented, heartrending poetry of X.

2 se torturer *vpr*: **se ~ le cerveau** *ou* **l'esprit** to cudgel one's brains.

torve [tɔʀv(ə)] *adj regard, œil* menacing, grim.

toscan, e [tɔskɑ̃, an] **1** *adj* Tuscan. **2** *nm* (*Ling*) Tuscan.

Toscane [tɔskan] *nf* Tuscany.

tôt [to] *adv* **(a)** (*au début d'une portion de temps*) early. **se lever/se coucher (très) ~** to get up/go to bed (very) early; **il se lève ~** he is an early riser, he gets up early; **venez ~ dans la matinée/soirée** come early (on) in the morning/evening *ou* in the early morning/evening; **~ dans l'année** early (on) in the year, in the early part of the year; **~ le matin, il n'est pas très lucide** he's not very clear-headed first thing (in the morning) *ou* early in the morning; **il n'est pas si ~ que je croyais** it's not as early as I thought; **Pâques est plus ~ cette année** Easter falls earlier (on) this year; **il arrive toujours ~ le jeudi** he is always early on Thursdays.

(b) (*au bout de peu de temps*) soon, early. **il est (encore) un peu (trop) ~ pour le juger** it's (still) a little too soon *ou* early *ou* it's (still) rather early to judge him; **~ ou tard il faudra qu'il se décide** sooner or later he will have to make up his mind; **il a eu ~ fait de s'en apercevoir!** he was quick *ou* it didn't take him long to notice it!, it wasn't long before he noticed it!; **il aura ~ fait de s'en apercevoir!** it won't be long before he notices it!, it won't take him long to notice it!; **si tu étais venu une heure plus ~, tu le rencontrais** if you had come an hour sooner *ou* earlier you would have met him; **si seulement vous me l'aviez dit plus ~!** if only you had told me sooner! *ou* earlier!; **ce n'est pas trop ~!** it's not a moment too soon!, it's not before time!, and about time too!*; **je ne m'attendais pas à le revoir si ~** I didn't expect to see him (again) so soon; **il n'était pas plus ~ parti que la voiture est tombée en panne** no sooner had he set off *ou* he had no sooner set off than the car broke down.

(c) le plus ~, au plus ~: venez le plus ~ possible come as early *ou* as soon as you can; **le plus ~ sera le mieux** the sooner the better; **il peut venir jeudi au plus ~** Thursday is the earliest *ou* soonest he can come; **c'est au plus ~ en mai qu'il prendra la décision** it'll be May at the earliest that he takes *ou* he'll take the decision, he'll decide in May at the earliest; **il faut qu'il vienne au plus ~** he must come as soon as possible.

total, e, *mpl* **-aux** [total, o] **1** *adj* **(a)** (*absolu*) *sacrifice, destruction, séparation* total, complete; *ruine, désespoir* utter (*épith*), total, complete; *liberté, confiance* complete, absolute; *silence* total, complete, absolute; *pardon* absolute; *éclipse* total; *V* **guerre.**

(b) (*global*) *hauteur, somme, revenu* total. **la somme ~e est plus élevée que nous ne pensions** the total is higher than we thought.

2 *adv* (*) (net) result, net outcome. **~, il a tout perdu** the net result *ou* outcome was he lost everything, net result – he lost everything*.

3 *nm* (*quantité globale*) total (number); (*résultat global*) total. **le ~ s'élève à 150 F** the total amounts to 150 francs; **le ~ de la population** the total (number of the) population; **faire le ~** to work out the total; (*fig*) **si on fait le ~, ils n'ont pas réalisé grand'chose** if you add it all up *ou* together they didn't achieve very much; **au ~** (*lit*) in total; (*fig*) on the whole, all things considered, all in all.

totalement [tɔtalmɑ̃] *adv* totally, completely. **c'est ~ faux** (*en entier*) it's totally *ou* completely *ou* wholly wrong; (*absolument*) it's totally *ou* completely *ou* utterly wrong.

totalisateur, -trice [tɔtalizatœʀ, tʀis] **1** *adj appareil, machine* adding (*épith*). **2** *nm* (*Comm*) adding machine; (*aux courses*) totalizator, tote*.

totaliser [tɔtalize] (1) *vt* **(a)** (*additionner*) to total, totalize.

(b) (*avoir au total*) to total, have a total of. **à eux deux ils totalisent 60 ans de service** between them they total *ou* have a total of 60 years' service; **le candidat qui totalise le plus grand nombre de points** the candidate with the highest total (number of points).

totalitaire [tɔtalitɛʀ] *adj* (*Pol*) *régime* totalitarian; (*Philos*) *conception* all-embracing, global.

totalitarisme [tɔtalitaʀism(ə)] *nm* totalitarianism.

totalité [tɔtalite] *nf* **(a)** (*gén*) **la ~ de** all of; **la ~ du sable/des livres** all (of) the sand/the books; **la ~ du livre/de la population** all the book/the population, the whole *ou* entire book/population; **la ~ de son salaire** his whole *ou* entire salary, all of his salary; **la ~ de ses biens** all of his possessions; **en ~: vendu en ~ aux États-Unis** all sold to the USA; **édité en ~ par X** published entirely by X; **pris dans sa ~** taken as a whole *ou* in its entirety; **j'en connais la quasi-~** I know virtually all of them *ou* just about all of them; **la presque ~ de la population** almost all the population, virtually *ou* almost the whole *ou* entire population.

(b) (*Philos*) totality.

totem [tɔtɛm] *nm* (*gén*) totem; (*poteau*) totem pole.

totémique [tɔtemik] *adj* totemic.

totémisme [tɔtemism(ə)] *nm* totemism.

toto‡ [toto] *nm* (*pou*) louse, cootie* (*US*).

toton [tɔtɔ̃] *nm* teetotum.

touareg [twaʀɛg] **1** *adj* Tuareg. **2** *nm* (*Ling*) Tuareg. **3** *nmf*: **T~** Tuareg.

toubib* [tubib] *nm* doctor. **il est ~** he's a doctor; **aller chez le ~** to go and see the doc* *ou* the quack*.

toucan [tukɑ̃] *nm* toucan.

touchant[1] [tuʃɑ̃] *prép* (†, *littér*) concerning, with regard to.

touchant[2], **e** [tuʃɑ̃, ɑ̃t] *adj* (*émouvant*) *histoire, lettre, situation, adieux* touching, moving; (*attendrissant*) *geste, reconnaissance, enthousiasme* touching. **~ de naïveté/d'ignorance** touchingly naïve/ignorant.

touche [tuʃ] *nf* **(a)** *[piano, machine à écrire]* key; *[instrument à corde]* fingerboard.

(b) (*Peinture: pose de la couleur*) touch, stroke; (*fig: style*) *[peintre, écrivain]* touch. **appliquer la couleur par petites ~s** to apply the colour with small strokes *ou* in small touches *ou* dabs, dab the colour on; **finesse de ~ d'un peintre/auteur** deftness of touch of a painter/an author; (*fig*) **une ~ exotique** an exotic touch; **une ~ de gaieté** a touch *ou* note of gaiety.

(c) (*Pêche*) bite. **faire une ~** to have a bite.

(d) (*Escrime*) hit.

(e) (*Ftbl, Rugby*) (*aussi* **ligne de ~**) touchline; (*sortie*) touch; (*remise en jeu*) (*Ftbl*) throw-in; (*Rugby*) line-out. **rentrée en ~** throw-in; line-out; **le ballon est sorti en ~** the ball has gone into touch (*Brit*), the ball is in touch (*Brit*); **rester sur la ~** to stay on the touch-lines (*Brit*); (*Ftbl*) **jouer la ~** to play for time (*by putting the ball repeatedly out of play*); *V* **juge**.

(f) (*: *allure*) **quelle drôle de ~!** what a sight!*, what DOES he (*ou* she *etc*) look like!*; **il a une de ces ~s!** he looks like nothing on earth!*; **il a la ~ de quelqu'un qui sort de prison** he looks like he just got out of prison*.

(g) (*loc*) (*fig*) **être mis/rester sur la ~** to be put/stay on the sidelines; **faire une ~*** to make a hit*; **avoir *ou* avoir fait une ~*** to have made a hit*; *V* **pierre**.

touche-à-tout [tuʃatu] *nmf inv* (*gén enfant*) (little) meddler; (*fig: chercheur, inventeur*) dabbler. **c'est un ~** (*lit*) he's a little meddler, his little fingers are into everything; (*fig*) he dabbles in everything.

toucher [tuʃe] (1) **1** *vt* **(a)** (*pour sentir, prendre*) (*gén*) to touch; (*pour palper*) *fruits, tissu, enflure* to feel. **~ qch du doigt/avec un bâton** to touch sth with one's finger/a stick; **~ la main à qn** to give sb a quick handshake; (*fig*) **il n'a pas touché un verre de vin depuis son accident** he hasn't touched a drop of wine since his accident; (*fig*) **je n'avais pas touché une raquette/une carte depuis 6 mois** I hadn't had a racket/a card in my hands for 6 months; (*fig*) **il n'a pas touché une balle pendant ce match** he didn't hit a single ball throughout the match; **il me toucha l'épaule** he touched *ou* tapped my shoulder; **'prière de ne pas ~'** 'please do not touch'.

(b) (*être ou entrer en contact avec*) to touch. **il ne faut pas que ça touche (le mur/le plafond)** it mustn't touch (the wall/ceiling); (*Lutte*) **il lui fit ~ le sol des épaules** he got his shoulders down on the floor; **~ le fond** to touch the bottom; **~ terre** to land; **l'avion toucha le sol et rebondit** the plane touched down and bounced up again; **les deux lignes se touchent** the two lines touch; **au football on ne doit pas ~ le ballon (de la main)** in football one mustn't touch the ball (with one's hand) *ou* one mustn't handle the ball.

(c) (*être proche de*) (*lit*) to adjoin; (*fig*) *[affaire]* to concern; *[personne]* to be a near relative of. **son jardin touche le nôtre** his garden (ad)joins ours *ou* is adjacent to ours; **nos deux jardins se touchent** our two gardens are adjacent (to each other) *ou* join each other; **les deux villes se sont tellement développées qu'elles se touchent presque** the two towns have been developed to such an extent that they almost meet.

(d) (*atteindre: lit, fig*) *adversaire, objectif* to hit. (*Boxe*) **il l'a touché au menton/foie** he hit him on the chin/stomach; **il s'affaissa, touché d'une balle en plein cœur** he slumped to the ground, hit by a bullet in the heart.

(e) (*contacter*) to reach, get in touch with, contact. **où peut-on le ~ par téléphone?** where can he be reached *ou* contacted by phone?, where can one get in touch with him by phone?

(f) (*faire escale à*) *port* to put in at, call at, touch.

(g) (*recevoir*) *pension, traitement* to draw, get; *prime* to get, receive; *chèque* to cash; (*Mil*) *ration, équipement* to draw; (*Scol*) *fournitures* to receive, get. **~ le tiercé/le gros lot** to win the tiercé/the first prize; **il touche une petite pension** he gets a small pension; **il touche sa pension le 10 du mois** he draws his pension on the 10th of the month; **il est allé à la poste ~ sa pension** he went to draw (out) his pension at the post office; **à partir du mois prochain, ils toucheront 1.000 F par mois/des primes** as from next month they'll get *ou* they'll be paid 1,000 francs a month/bonuses; **il a fini le travail mais n'a encore rien touché** he's finished the work but he hasn't had anything for it yet.

(h) (*émouvoir*) *[drame, deuil]* to affect; *[scène attendrissante]* to touch, move; *[critique, reproche]* to have an effect on. **cette tragédie les a beaucoup touchés** this tragedy affected them greatly; **votre reproche l'a touché au vif** your reproach touched *ou* cut him to the quick; **rien ne le touche** there is nothing that can move him; **votre cadeau/geste nous a vivement touchés** we were deeply touched by your gift/gesture; **un style qui touche** an affecting *ou* a moving style; *V* **corde**.

(i) (*concerner*) to affect. **ce problème ne nous touche pas** this problem does not affect *ou* concern us; **ils n'ont pas été touchés par la dévaluation** they haven't been affected *ou* hit* by the devaluation.

(j) (*loc*) **je vais lui en ~ un mot** I'll have a word with him *ou* a word in his ear about it, I'll mention it to him; **tu devrais ~ un mot de cette affaire au patron** you should have a word with the boss about this business; **touchons du bois!*** touch wood!*; **pas touche!*** hands off!*; **touché, coulé!*** touché.

2 se toucher* *vpr* (*euph*) (*se masturber*) to play with o.s.* (*euph*); (*se peloter etc*) to pet*.

3 toucher à *vt indir* **(a)** *objet dangereux, défendu* to touch; *capital, économies* to break into, touch. **n'y touche pas!** don't touch!; **prière de ne pas ~ aux objets exposés** please do not touch *ou* kindly refrain from handling the exhibits; **~ à tout** to be into everything; **elle n'a pas touché à son déjeuner/au fromage** she didn't touch her lunch/the cheese; **on n'a pas touché au fromage** we haven't touched the cheese, the cheese has been left untouched; **il n'a jamais touché à une raquette/un fusil** he has never handled a racket/rifle, he has never had a racket/rifle in his hand.

(b) (*malmener*) *enfant, jeune fille* to touch, lay a finger on; (*attaquer*) *réputation, légende* to question. **s'il touche à cet enfant/ma sœur, gare à lui!** if he lays a finger on *ou* touches that child/my sister, he'd better watch out!; **s'il touche à un cheveu de cet enfant, gare à lui!** if he so much as touches a hair of that child's head, he'd better watch out!; **personne n'ose ~ à cette légende** nobody dares question that legend.

(c) (*modifier*) *règlement, loi, tradition* to meddle with; *mécanisme* to tamper with; *monument, site classé* to touch. **quelqu'un a touché au moteur** someone has tampered with the engine; **on peut rénover sans ~ à la façade** it's possible to renovate without touching the façade.

(d) (*concerner*) *intérêts* to affect; *problème, question, domaine* to touch, have to do with; (*aborder*) *période, but* to near, approach; *sujet, question* to broach, come onto. **je touche ici à un problème d'ordre très général** here I am coming onto *ou* broaching a problem of a very general character; **vous touchez là à une question délicate** that is a very delicate matter you have broached; **il touchait à la cinquantaine/vieillesse** he was nearing *ou* approaching fifty/old age; **nous touchons au but** we're nearing our goal; **l'hiver/la guerre touche à sa fin** winter/the war is nearing its end; (*fig littér*) **~ au port** to be within sight of home.

(e) (*être en contact avec*) to touch, come up to; (*être contigu à*) to border on, adjoin; (*confiner à*) to verge on, border on. **l'armoire touchait presque au plafond** the wardrobe almost touched *ou* came up to the ceiling; **le jardin touche à la forêt** the garden adjoins the forest *ou* borders on the forest; **cela touche à la folie/pornographie** that verges *ou* borders on madness/pornography.

(f) (*loc*) **avec un air de ne pas y ~, sans avoir l'air d'y ~** looking as if butter would not melt in his (*ou* her *etc*) mouth, acting the innocent*.

4 *nm* **(a)** (*sens*) (sense of) touch.

(b) (*action, manière de toucher*) touch; (*impression produite*) feel. **doux au ~** soft to the touch; **cela a le ~ de la soie** it has the feel of silk (about it), it feels like silk; **s'habituer à reconnaître les objets au ~** to become used to recognizing objects by touch *ou* feel(ing); **on reconnaît la soie au ~** you can tell silk by the feel of it.

(c) (*Mus*) touch.

(d) (*Méd*) (internal) examination. **~ rectal/vaginal** rectal/vaginal examination.

touée [twe] *nf* (*Naut*) (*câble*) warp, cable; (*longueur de chaîne*) scope.

touer [twe] (1) *vt* (*Naut*) to warp, kedge.

toueur [twœʀ] *nm*: **(bateau) ~** warping tug.

touffe [tuf] *nf [herbe]* tuft, clump; *[arbres, buissons]* clump; *[cheveux, poils]* tuft; *[fleurs]* cluster, clump. **~ de lavande** lavender bush, clump of lavender.

touffeur [tufœʀ] *nf* (†, *littér*) suffocating *ou* sweltering heat.

touffu, e [tufy] *adj* **(a)** (*épais, dense*) *barbe, sourcils* bushy; *arbres* with dense foliage; *haie* thick, bushy; *bois, maquis, végétation* dense, thick.

(b) (*fig*) *roman, style* involved, complex.

touiller* [tuje] (1) *vt lessive* to stir round; *sauce, café* to stir.

toujours [tuʒuʀ] *adv* **(a)** (*continuité*) always; (*répétition: souvent péj*) forever, always, all the time. **je l'avais ~ cru célibataire** I (had) always thought he was a bachelor; **je t'aimerai ~** I shall always love you, I shall love you forever; **je déteste et détesterai ~ l'avion** I hate flying and always shall; **la vie se déroule ~ pareille** life goes on the same as ever *ou* forever the same; **il est ~ à** *ou* **en train de critiquer** he is always *ou* forever criticizing, he keeps on criticizing; **une rue ~ encombrée** a street (that is) always *ou* forever *ou* constantly jammed with traffic; **les saisons ~ pareilles** the never-changing seasons; **il n'est pas ~ très ponctuel** he's not always very punctual; **il est ~ à l'heure** he's always *ou* invariably on time; **il fut ~ modeste** he was ever (*littér*) modest; **les journaux sont ~ plus pessimistes** the newspapers are more and more pessimistic; **comme ~** as ever, as always; **ce sont des amis de ~** they are lifelong friends; **il est parti pour ~** he's gone forever *ou* for good; *V* **depuis.**

(b) (*prolongement de l'action = encore*) still. **bien qu'à la retraite il travaillait ~** although he had retired he was still working *ou* he had kept on working; **j'espère ~ qu'elle viendra** I keep hoping she'll come; **ils n'ont ~ pas répondu** they still haven't replied; **est-ce que X est rentré? — non il est ~ à Paris/non ~ pas** is X back? — no he is still in Paris/no not yet *ou* no he's still not back; **il est ~ le même/~ aussi désagréable** he is (still) the same as ever/(still) as unpleasant as ever.

(c) (*intensif*) anyway, anyhow. **écrivez ~, il vous répondra peut-être** write anyway *ou* anyhow *ou* you may as well write — he (just) might answer you; **il vient ~ un moment où** there must *ou* will (always *ou* inevitably) come a time when; **buvez ~ un verre avant de partir** have a drink at least *ou* anyway *ou* anyhow before you go; **c'est ~ pas toi qui l'auras*** at all events *ou* at any rate it won't be you that gets it*; **où est-elle? — pas chez moi ~!** where is she? — not at my place anyway! *ou* at any rate!; **je trouverai ~ (bien) une excuse** I can always think up an excuse; **passez à la gare, vous aurez ~ bien un train** go (along) to the station — you're sure *ou* bound to get a train *ou* there's bound to be a train; **tu peux ~ courir!*** you haven't a hope! *ou* a chance!, you've got some hope! (*iro*); **il aime donner des conseils mais ~ avec tact** he likes to give advice but he always does it tactfully; **vous pouvez ~ crier, il n'y a personne** shout as much as you like *ou* shout by all means — there's no one about; **~ est-il que** the fact remains that, that does not alter the fact that, be that as it may; **il était peut-être là, ~ est-il que je ne l'ai pas vu** he may well have been there, (but) the fact remains *ou* that does not alter the fact that I didn't see him; **cette politique semblait raisonnable, ~ est-il qu'elle a échoué** this policy seemed reasonable, (but) be that as it may *ou* but the fact remains it was a failure; **c'est ~ ça de pris*** that's something anyway, (well) at least that's something; **ça peut ~ servir** it'll come in handy some day, it'll always come in handy.

toulousain, e [tuluzɛ̃, ɛn] **1** *adj* of *ou* from Toulouse.
2 *nm,f*: **T~(e)** inhabitant *ou* native of Toulouse.

toundra [tundʀa] *nf* tundra.

toupet [tupɛ] *nm* **(a) ~ (de cheveux)** quiff. **(b)** (*: *culot*) sauce*, nerve, cheek. **avoir du ~** to have a nerve *ou* a cheek; **il ne manque pas d'un certain ~** he doesn't lack sauce* *ou* cheek.

toupie [tupi] *nf* **(a)** (*jouet*) (spinning) top. **~ à musique** humming-top; *V* **tourner.** **(b) vieille ~**‡ silly old trout‡. **(c)** (*Tech*) *[menuisier]* spindle moulding-machine; *[plombier]* turn-pin.

tour[1] [tuʀ] **1** *nf* **(a)** (*édifice*) tower; (*Hist: machine de guerre*) siege tower. **(immeuble) ~** tower block, high-rise block.
(b) (*Échecs*) castle, rook.
2: la tour de Babel the Tower of Babel; (*fig*) **c'est une tour de Babel** it's a real Tower of Babel *ou* a babel of tongues; (*Aviat*) **tour de contrôle** control tower; **la tour Eiffel** the Eiffel Tower; **tour de guet** watchtower, look-out tower; (*fig*) **tour d'ivoire** ivory tower; **la tour de Londres** the Tower of London; **la tour penchée de Pise** the Leaning Tower of Pisa.

tour[2] [tuʀ] **1** *nm* **(a)** (*parcours autour de*) **faire le ~ de** *parc, pays, circuit, montagne* to go round; (*fig*) *possibilités* to explore; *magasins* to go round, look round; *problème* to consider from all angles; *[aiguille, boule] cercle, cadran, circuit* to go round; **~ de ville** (*pour touristes*) city tour; **le ~ du parc prend bien une heure** it takes a good hour to walk round the park; **si on faisait le ~?** shall we go round (it)? *ou* walk (it)?; (*fig*) **faire le ~ du cadran** to sleep (right) round the clock; **faire le ~ du monde** to go round the world; **faire un ~ d'Europe** to go on a European tour, tour Europe; **faire un ~ d'Europe en auto-stop** to hitch-hike around Europe; **un ~ du monde en bateau** a boat trip (a)round the world, a round-the-world trip by boat; **la route fait (tout) le ~ de leur propriété** the road goes (right) round their estate; **faire le ~ des invités** to do the rounds of the guests; **la bouteille/plaisanterie a fait le ~ de la table** the bottle/joke went round the table.

(b) (*excursion*) trip, outing; (*balade*) (*à pied*) walk, stroll; (*en voiture*) run, drive. (*Sport*) **~ (de piste)** lap; (*Sport*) **~ d'honneur** lap of honour; **faire un ~ de manège** *ou* **de chevaux de bois** to have a ride on a merry-go-round; **faire un (petit) ~** (*à pied*) to go for a (short) walk *ou* stroll; (*en voiture*) to go for a (short) run *ou* drive; **faire un ~ en ville/ sur le marché** to go for a walk round town/round the market; **faire un ~ en Italie** to go for a trip round Italy; **un ~ de jardin/en voiture vous fera du bien** a walk *ou* stroll round the garden/a run *ou* drive (in the car) will do you good; **faire le ~ du propriétaire** to look *ou* go round *ou* over one's property; **je vais te faire faire le ~ du propriétaire** I'll show you over *ou* round the place; (*littér*) **la rivière fait des ~s et des détours** the river winds its way in and out, the river twists and turns (along its way).

(c) (*de succession*) turn. **c'est votre ~** it's your turn; **attendre/perdre son ~** to wait/miss one's turn; **parler à son ~** to speak in turn; **ils parleront chacun à leur ~** they will each speak in turn; **attends, tu parleras à ton ~** wait — you'll have your turn to speak; **chacun son ~** everyone will have his turn; **nous le faisons chacun à notre ~** (*deux personnes*) we do it in turn, we take turns at it, we do it turn and turn about*; (*plusieurs personnes*) we take turns at it, we do it by turns; **c'est au ~ de Marc de parler** it's Mark's turn to speak; **à qui le ~?** whose turn is it?, who is next?; **avoir un ~ de faveur** to get in ahead of one's turn; **mon prochain ~ de garde** *ou* **service est à 8 heures** my next spell *ou* turn of duty is at 8 o'clock; (*lit, fig*) **votre ~ viendra** your turn will come; *V* **souvent.**

(d) (*Pol*) **~ (de scrutin)** ballot; **au premier/second ~** in the first/second ballot *ou* round.

(e) (*circonférence*) *[partie du corps]* measurement; *[tronc, colonne]* girth; *[visage]* contour, outline; *[surface]* circumference. **~ de taille/tête** waist/head measurement; **~ de poitrine** *[homme]* chest measurement; *[femme]* bust measurement; **~ de hanches** hip measurement; **mesurer le ~ d'une table** to measure round a table, measure the circumference of a table; **la table fait 3 mètres de ~** the table measures 3 metres round (the edge); **le tronc fait 3 mètres de ~** the trunk measures 3 metres round *ou* has a girth of 3 metres.

(f) (*rotation*) *[roue, manivelle]* turn, revolution; *[axe, arbre]* revolution. **un ~ de vis** a (turn of a) screw; **l'hélice a fait deux ~s** the propeller turned *ou* revolved twice; (*Aut*) **régime de 2.000 ~s (minute)** speed of 2,000 revs *ou* revolutions per minute; **il suffit d'un ~ de clef/manivelle** it just needs one turn of the key/handle; **donne encore un ~ de vis** give it another screw *ou* turn, give another turn of the screw; **donner un ~ de clef** to turn the key, give the key a turn; (*Cyclisme*) **battre un concurrent d'un ~ de roue** to beat a competitor by a wheel's turn; **faire un ~/plusieurs ~s sur soi-même** to spin round once/several times (on oneself); **faire un ~ de valse** to waltz round the floor; **après quelques ~s de valse** after waltzing round the floor a few times; *V* **double, quart.**

(g) (*tournure*) *[situation, conversation]* turn. **la situation prend un ~ dramatique/désagréable** the situation is taking a dramatic/an unpleasant turn; **il a un ~ de phrase élégant** he has an elegant turn of phrase; **un certain ~ d'esprit** a certain turn *ou* cast of mind.

(h) (*expression*) **~ (de phrase)** turn of phrase.

(i) (*exercice*) *[acrobate]* feat, stunt; *[jongleur, prestidigitateur]* trick. **~ d'adresse** feat of skill, skilful trick; **~ de passe-passe** trick, sleight of hand (*U*); **elle a réussi cela par un simple ~ de passe-passe** she managed it by mere sleight of hand; **~s d'agilité** acrobatics; **~ de cartes** card trick; **et le ~ est joué!** and Bob's your uncle!*, and there you have it!; **c'est un ~ à prendre!** it's just a knack one picks up; **avoir plus d'un ~ dans son sac** to have more than one trick up one's sleeve.

(j) (*duperie*) trick. **faire** *ou* **jouer un ~ à qn** to play a trick on sb; **un ~ pendable** a rotten trick; **un ~ de cochon*** *ou* **de salaud**‡ a dirty *ou* lousy trick*, a mean trick; **je lui réserve un ~ à ma façon!** I'll pay him back in my own way!; *V* **jouer.**

(k) (*loc*) **à ~ de bras** *frapper, taper* with all one's strength *ou* might; (*fig*) *composer, produire* prolifically; **il écrit des chansons à ~ de bras** he writes songs by the dozen, he runs off *ou* churns out songs one after the other; **à ~ de rôle** in turn; **~ à ~** in turn; **elle se sentait ~ à ~ optimiste et désespérée** she felt optimistic and despairing by turns, she felt alternately optimistic and despairing.

2: tour de chant song recital; **tour de cou** (*gén*) choker; (*fourrure*) fur collar; **tour de force** (*lit*) feat of strength, tour de force; (*fig*) amazing feat; **Tour de France** (*course cycliste*) Tour de France; (*Hist*) *[compagnons]* Tour de France (*carried out by a journeyman completing his apprenticeship*); (*fig*) **tour d'horizon** (general) survey; **tour de lit** (bed) valance; **tour de main** (*mouvement*) knack; (*adresse*) dexterity; **avoir/acquérir un tour de main** to have/pick up a knack; **en un tour de main** in the twinkling of an eye, (as) quick as a flash; **tour de piste** (*Sport*) lap; (*cirque*) circuit (of the ring); **tour de reins: souffrir d'un tour de reins** to suffer from a sprained back; **se donner un tour de reins** to sprain one's back.

tour[3] [tuʀ] *nm* (*Tech*) lathe. **~ de potier** potter's wheel; **un objet fait au ~** an object turned on the lathe; **travail au ~** lathe-work; (*fig littér*) **des jambes/cuisses faites au ~** well-turned (†, *littér*) *ou* shapely legs/thighs.

tourangeau, -elle [tuʀɑ̃ʒo, ɛl] **1** *adj* of *ou* from Touraine *ou* Tours (*épith*), Touraine (*épith*) *ou* Tours (*épith*).
2 *nm,f*: **T~(-elle)** Tourangeau (*native or inhabitant of Tours or of Touraine*).

tourbe [tuʀb(ə)] *nf* peat. **~ limoneuse** alluvial peat.

tourbeux, -euse [tuʀbø, øz] *adj* **(a)** *terrain* (*qui contient de la tourbe*) peat (*épith*), peaty; (*de la nature de la tourbe*) peaty. **(b)** *plante* found in peat.

tourbière [tuʀbjɛʀ] *nf* peat bog.

tourbillon [tuʀbijɔ̃] *nm* **(a)** (*atmosphérique*) **~ (de vent)** whirlwind; **~ de fumée/sable/neige** swirl *ou* eddy of smoke/sand/snow; **le sable s'élevait en ~s** the sand was swirling up.
(b) (*dans l'eau*) whirlpool.
(c) (*Phys*) vortex.
(d) (*fig*) whirl. **~ de plaisirs** whirl of pleasure, giddy round of pleasure(s); **le ~ de la vie/des affaires** the hurly-burly *ou* hustle and bustle of life/business; **il regardait du balcon le ~ des danseurs** he looked down from the balcony upon the whirling *ou* swirling group of dancers.

tourbillonnant, e [tuʀbijɔnɑ̃, ɑ̃t] *adj vent, feuilles* whirling, swirling, eddying; *vie* whirlwind (*épith*); *jupes* swirling.
tourbillonnement [tuʀbijɔnmɑ̃] *nm* (*V* **tourbillonner**) whirling, swirling; eddying; twirling.
tourbillonner [tuʀbijɔne] (1) *vi [poussière, sable, feuilles mortes]* to whirl, swirl, eddy; *[danseurs]* to whirl (around), swirl (around), twirl (around); (*fig*) *[idées]* to swirl (round), whirl (round).
tourelle [tuʀɛl] *nf* **(a)** (*petite tour*) turret.
(b) (*Mil, Naut*) (gun) turret; *[caméra]* lens turret; *[sous-marin]* conning tower.
tourisme [tuʀism(ə)] *nm* (*phénomène social*) tourism; (*activité*) touring, sightseeing. (*industrie*) **le ~** tourism, the tourist industry *ou* trade; **le ~ français se porte bien** the French tourist industry *ou* trade is in good shape; **grâce au ~, l'exode rural a pu être stoppé dans cette région** thanks to tourism it has been possible to halt the exodus from the country in this region; **le ~ d'hiver s'y est beaucoup développé** the winter sports industry has greatly developed there; **~ d'hiver/d'été** winter/summer tourism, the winter/summer tourist trade; **avion/voiture de ~** private plane/car; **office du ~** tourist office; **agence de ~** tourist agency; **faire du ~/un peu de ~** to do some/a little sightseeing; *V* **grand.**
touriste [tuʀist(ə)] *nmf* tourist; *V* **classe.**
touristique [tuʀistik] *adj itinéraire, billet, activités, renseignements, guide* tourist (*épith*); *région, ville* popular with (the) tourists (*attrib*), touristic (*péj*). **le menu ~** the tourist *ou* cheap menu; **d'attrait ~ assez faible** with little to attract (the) tourists, with little tourist appeal.
tourment [tuʀmɑ̃] *nm* (*littér*) (*physique*) agony; (*moral*) agony, torment, torture. **les ~s de la jalousie** the torments *ou* agonies of jealousy; **les ~s de la maternité** the agonies of motherhood.
tourmente [tuʀmɑ̃t] *nf* (*tempête*) storm, tempest (*littér*); (*fig: sociale, politique*) upheaval, storm.
tourmenté, e [tuʀmɑ̃te] (*ptp de* **tourmenter**) *adj* **(a)** *personne* tormented, tortured; *expression, visage, esprit* anguished, tormented, tortured.
(b) *paysage, formes* tortured (*littér*); *style, art* tortured, anguished.
(c) (*littér*) *vie, mer* stormy, turbulent, tempestuous (*littér*).
tourmenter [tuʀmɑ̃te] (1) **1** *vt* **(a)** *[personne]* to torment. **ses créanciers continuaient à le ~** his creditors continued to harass him.
(b) *[douleur, rhumatismes]* to rack, torment; *[remords, doute]* to rack, torment, plague; *[ambition, envie, jalousie]* to torment. **ce doute le tourmente depuis longtemps** this doubt has been tormenting *ou* plaguing him for a long time.
2 se tourmenter *vpr* to fret, worry (o.s.). **ne vous tourmentez pas, ce n'était pas de votre faute** don't distress *ou* worry yourself — it wasn't your fault; **il se tourmente à cause de son fils** he is fretting *ou* worrying about his son.
tourmenteur, -euse [tuʀmɑ̃tœʀ, øz] *nm,f* (*littér: persécuteur*) tormentor.
tournage [tuʀnaʒ] *nm* **(a)** (*Ciné*) shooting. **(b)** (*Menuiserie*) turning. **le ~ sur bois/métal** wood-/metal-turning. **(c)** (*Naut*) belaying cleat.
tournant, e [tuʀnɑ̃, ɑ̃t] **1** *adj* **(a)** *fauteuil, dispositif* swivel (*épith*); *feu, scène* revolving (*épith*); *V* **grève, plaque, pont, table.**
(b) *mouvement, manœuvre* encircling (*épith*).
(c) *escalier* spiral (*épith*); (*littér*) *ruelle, couloir* winding, twisting.
2 *nm* **(a)** (*lit: virage*) bend. **~ en épingle à cheveux** hairpin bend; **prendre bien/mal son ~** to take a bend well/badly, corner well/badly.
(b) (*fig*) **~ décisif** watershed; **les ~s de l'histoire/de sa vie** the watersheds *ou* turning points in history/in his life; **rattraper** *ou* **avoir qn au ~*** to get one's own back on sb, get even with sb; **attendre qn au ~*** to wait for the chance to trip sb up.
tourné, e[1] [tuʀne] (*ptp de* **tourner**) *adj* **(a) bien ~** *personne* shapely, with a good figure; *jambes* shapely; *taille* neat, trim; (*fig*) *compliment, poème, expression* well-turned.
(b) mal ~ *article, lettre* badly expressed *ou* phrased; *expression* unfortunate; **avoir l'esprit mal ~** to have a nasty turn of mind.
(c) *lait, vin* sour.
(d) (*Menuiserie*) *pied, objet* turned.
tournebouler* [tuʀnəbule] (1) *vt personne* to put in a whirl. **~ la cervelle à qn** to turn sb's head *ou* brain, put sb's head in a whirl; **il en était tourneboulé** his head was in a whirl over it.
tournebroche [tuʀnəbʀɔʃ] *nm* roasting jack.
tourne-disque, *pl* **tourne-disques** [tuʀnədisk(ə)] *nm* record player.
tournedos [tuʀnədo] *nm* tournedos.
tournée[2] [tuʀne] *nf* **(a)** (*tour*) *[conférencier, artiste]* tour; *[inspecteur, livreur, représentant]* round. **partir/être en ~** to set off on/be on tour; to set off on/be on one's rounds; **~ de conférences/théâtrale** lecture/theatre tour; **faire une ~ électorale** to do an election tour; **~ d'inspection** round of inspection; **faire la ~ de** *magasins, musées, cafés* to do the rounds of, go round; **faire la ~ des grands ducs†** to go out on the town *ou* on a spree*.
(b) (*consommations*) round (of drinks). **payer une/sa ~** to buy *ou* stand a/one's round (of drinks); **c'est ma ~** it's my round.
(c) (*: *raclée*) hiding*, thrashing.
tournemain [tuʀnəmɛ̃] *nm*: **en un ~** in a trice, in the twinkling of an eye.
tourner [tuʀne] (1) **1** *vt* **(a)** *manivelle, clef, poignée* to turn; *sauce* to stir; *page* to turn (over). **tournez s.v.p., T.S.V.P.** please turn over, P.T.O.; **~ et retourner** *chose* to turn over and over; *pensée, problème* to turn over and over (in one's mind).
(b) (*diriger, orienter*) *appareil, tête, yeux* to turn. **elle tourna son regard** *ou* **les yeux vers la fenêtre** she turned her eyes towards the window; **~ la tête à droite/gauche/de côté** to turn one's head to the right/to the left/sideways; **quand il m'a vu, il a tourné la tête** when he saw me he looked away *ou* he turned his head away; **~ les pieds en dedans/en dehors** to turn one's toes *ou* feet in/out; **~ le dos à** (*lit, fig: se détourner de*) to turn one's back on; (*fig: ne pas faire face à*) to have one's back (turned) to; **tourne le tableau de l'autre côté/contre le mur** turn the picture the other way round/round to face the wall; **~ ses pensées/efforts vers** to turn one's thoughts/efforts towards *ou* to.
(c) (*contourner*) (*Naut*) *cap* to round; *armée* to turn, outflank; *obstacle* to round; (*fig: éluder*) *difficulté, règlement* to get round *ou* past. **~ la loi** to get round the law, find a loophole in the law; **il vient de ~ le coin de la rue** he has just turned the corner.
(d) (*frm: exprimer*) *phrase, compliment* to turn; *demande, lettre* to phrase, express.
(e) (*transformer*) **~ qch/qn en** to turn sth/sb into; **~ qn/qch en ridicule** *ou* **dérision** to ridicule sb/sth, hold sb/sth up to ridicule; **il a tourné l'incident en plaisanterie** he laughed off the incident, he made light of the incident, he made a joke out of the incident; **il tourne tout à son avantage** he turns everything to his (own) advantage.
(f) (*Ciné*) *scène [cinéaste]* to shoot, film; *[acteur]* to film, do; *film* (*faire les prises de vue*) to shoot; (*produire*) to make; (*jouer dans*) to make, do. **ils ont dû ~ en studio** they had to do the filming in the studio; *V* **silence.**
(g) (*Tech*) *bois, ivoire* to turn; *pot* to throw.
(h) (*loc*) **~ bride** (*lit*) to turn back; (*fig*) to do an about-turn; **~ casaque** (*lit*) to turn tail, flee; (*fig*) to turn one's coat, change sides; **~ le cœur** *ou* **l'estomac à qn** to turn sb's stomach, make sb heave; (*fig*) **~ la page** to turn the page; (*littér*) **~ ses pas vers** to wend one's way towards (*littér*); **se ~ les pouces** to twiddle one's thumbs; **~ le sang** *ou* **les sangs à qn** to shake sb up; **~ la tête à qn** *[vin]* to go to sb's head; *[succès]* to go to *ou* turn sb's head; *[femme]* to turn sb's head; *V* **talon.**
2 *vi* **(a)** *[manège, compteur, aiguille d'horloge etc]* to turn, go round; *[disque, cylindre, roue]* to turn, revolve; *[pièce sur un axe, clef, danseur]* to turn; *[toupie]* to spin; *[taximètre]* to tick away; *[usine, moteur]* to run. **~ (sur ses gonds)** *[porte]* to turn (on its hinges); **~ sur soi-même** to turn round on o.s.; (*très vite*) to spin round and round; **l'heure tourne** time is passing *ou* is going on; **la grande aiguille tourne plus vite que la petite** the big hand goes round faster than the small one; **tout d'un coup, j'ai vu tout ~** all of a sudden my head began to spin *ou* swim; **faire ~ le moteur** to run the engine; **~ au ralenti** to tick over; **~ à plein régime** to run at maximum revs; **~ à vide** *[moteur]* to run in neutral; *[engrenage, mécanisme]* to turn without gripping; **c'est lui qui va faire ~ l'affaire** he's the one who's going to keep the business going; **les éléphants tournent sur la piste** the elephants move round the ring.
(b) ~ autour de *[terre]* to revolve *ou* go round; *[chemin]* to wind *ou* go round; *[oiseau]* to wheel *ou* circle *ou* fly round; *[mouches]* to buzz *ou* fly round; **~ autour de la piste** to go round the track; **~ autour de qn** (*péj: importuner*) to hang round sb; (*pour courtiser*) to hang round sb; (*par curiosité*) to hover round sb; **un individu tourne autour de la maison depuis une heure** somebody has been hanging round outside the house for an hour; **~ autour de** *ou* **sur qch** to centre on; **l'enquête tourne autour de ces 3 suspects/de cet indice capital** the enquiry centres on these 3 suspects/this vital clue; **la conversation a tourné sur la politique** the conversation centred on politics.
(c) (*changer de direction*) *[vent, opinion]* to turn, shift, veer (round); *[chemin, promeneur]* to turn. **la chance a tourné** his (*on her etc*) luck has changed.
(d) (*évoluer*) **bien ~** to turn out well; **mal ~** *[farce, entreprise]* to go wrong, turn out badly; *[personne]* to turn out badly; **ça va mal ~*** no good will come of it, that'll lead to trouble; **si les choses avaient tourné autrement** if things had turned out *ou* gone differently; **~ à l'avantage de qn** to turn to sb's advantage; **la discussion a tourné en bagarre** the argument turned *ou* degenerated into a fight; **cela risque de faire ~ la discussion en bagarre** it might turn the argument into a fight; **sa bronchite a tourné en pneumonie** his bronchitis has turned *ou* developed into pneumonia; **le débat tournait à la politique** the debate was turning to *ou* moving on to politics; **le temps a tourné au froid/à la pluie** the weather has turned cold/rainy; **~ au vert/rouge** to turn *ou* go green/red; **~ au drame/au tragique** to take a dramatic/tragic turn.
(e) *[lait]* to turn (sour). **~ (au vinaigre)** *[vin]* to turn (vinegary); **faire ~** to turn sour.
(f) (*loc*) **~ à l'aigre** *ou* **au vinaigre** to turn sour; **~ court** *[entreprise, projet, débat]* to come to a sudden end; **~ de l'œil*** to pass out*, faint; **~ en rond** (*lit*) to walk round and round; (*fig*) to go round in circles; **~ rond** to run smoothly; **ça ne tourne pas rond chez elle*, elle ne tourne pas rond*** she's not quite with us*, she must be a bit touched*; **qu'est-ce qui ne tourne pas rond?*** what's the matter?, what's wrong?, what's up?*; (*fig*) **~ autour du pot** to beat about the bush; **la tête me tourne** my head is spinning; **faire ~ qn en bourrique** to drive sb round the bend* *ou* up the wall*.
3 se tourner *vpr*: **se ~ du côté de** *ou* **vers qn/qch** to turn towards sb/sth; **se ~ vers qn pour lui demander aide** to turn to sb for help; **se ~ vers une profession/la politique/une question** to turn to a profession/to politics/to a question; **se ~ contre qn** to turn against sb; **se ~ et se retourner dans son lit** to toss and turn in bed; **de quelque côté qu'on se tourne** whichever way one turns; **tourne-toi (de l'autre côté)** turn round *ou* the other way.

tournesol [tuRnəsɔl] *nm* **(a)** (*Bot*) sunflower; *V* **huile. (b)** (*Chim*) litmus.

tourneur [tuRnœR] **1** *nm* (*Tech*) turner. ~ **sur bois/métaux** wood/metal turner.
2 *adj V* **derviche.**

tournevis [tuRnəvis] *nm* screwdriver.

tournicoter* [tuRnikɔte] (1) *vi,* **tourniquer** [tuRnike] (1) *vi* (*péj*) to wander up and down.

tourniquet [tuRnikɛ] *nm* **(a)** (*barrière*) turnstile; (*porte*) revolving door.
(b) (*Tech*) ~ **hydraulique** reaction turbine; (*d'arrosage*) (lawn-)sprinkler.
(c) (*présentoir*) revolving stand.
(d) (*Méd*) tourniquet.
(e) (*arg Mil*) court-martial. **passer au** ~ to come up before a court-martial.

tournis [tuRni] *nm* **(a)** (*Vét*) sturdy. **(b)** (*) **avoir le** ~ to feel dizzy *ou* giddy; **cela/il me donne le** ~ that/he makes me (feel) dizzy *ou* giddy.

tournoi [tuRnwa] *nm* **(a)** (*Hist*) tournament, tourney. **(b)** (*Sport*) tournament. ~ **d'échecs/de tennis** chess/tennis tournament; (*fig littér*) **un** ~ **d'éloquence/d'adresse** a contest of eloquence/skill.

tournoiement [tuRnwamɑ̃] *nm* (*V* **tournoyer**) whirling, twirling; swirling; eddying; wheeling. **des** ~**s de feuilles** swirling *ou* eddying leaves; **les** ~**s des danseurs** the whirling (of the) dancers.

tournoyer [tuRnwaje] (8) *vi* **(a)** (*sur place*) *[danseur]* to whirl (round), twirl (round); *[eau, fumée]* to swirl, eddy. **faire** ~ **qch** to whirl *ou* twirl sth; **la fumée s'élevait en tournoyant** the smoke swirled up.
(b) (*en cercles*) *[oiseaux]* to wheel (round); *[feuilles mortes]* to swirl *ou* eddy around.

tournure [tuRnyR] *nf* **(a)** (*tour de phrase*) turn of phrase; (*forme*) form. ~ **négative/impersonnelle** negative/impersonal form; **la** ~ **précieuse de ses phrases** the precious phrasing of his sentences.
(b) (*apparence*) *[événements]* turn. **la** ~ **des événements** the turn of events; **la** ~ **que prenaient les événements** the way the situation was developing; **la situation a pris une mauvaise/meilleure** ~ the situation took a turn for the worse/for the better; **donner une autre** ~ **à une affaire** to put a matter in a different light, put a new face on a matter; **prendre** ~ to take shape.
(c) ~ **d'esprit** turn *ou* cast of mind.
(d) (†: *allure*) bearing. **il a belle** ~ he carries himself well.

tourte [tuRt(ə)] **1** *adj* (‡: *bête*) thick‡, dense*. **2** *nf* (*Culin*) pie. ~ **à la viande/au poisson** meat/fish pie.

tourteau[1], *pl* ~**x** [tuRto] *nm* (*Agr*) oilcake, cattle-cake.

tourteau[2], *pl* ~**x** [tuRto] *nm* (*Zool*) (sort of) (edible) crab.

tourtereau, *pl* ~**x** [tuRtəRo] *nm* (*Zool: rare*) young turtledove. (*fig*) ~**x** lovebirds.

tourterelle [tuRtəRɛl] *nf* turtledove.

tourtière [tuRtjɛR] *nf* (*à tourtes*) pie tin; (*à tartes*) pie dish *ou* plate.

tous [tu] *V* **tout.**

toussailler [tusaje] (1) *vi* to have a bit of a cough. **arrête de** ~! stop coughing and spluttering like that!

Toussaint [tusɛ̃] *nf* All Saints' Day.

tousser [tuse] (1) *vi* **(a)** *[personne]* (*lit, pour avertir etc*) to cough. **ne sors pas, tu tousses encore un peu** don't go out — you've still got a bit of a cough. **(b)** (*fig*) *[moteur]* to splutter, cough, hiccup.

toussoter [tusɔte] (1) *vi* (*lit*) to have a bit of a *ou* a slight cough; (*pour avertir, signaler*) to cough softly, give a little cough. **je l'entendais** ~ **dans la pièce à côté** I could hear him coughing a little in the next room; **cet enfant toussote: je vais lui faire prendre du sirop** this child has a bit of a *ou* a slight cough — I'm going to give him some cough mixture.

tout [tu], **toute** [tut], *mpl* **tous** [tu] (*adj*) *ou* [tus] (*pron*), *fpl* **toutes** [tut] **1** *adj* **(a)** (*avec déterminant: complet, entier*) ~ **le, toute la** all (the), the whole (of the); **il a plu toute la nuit** it rained the whole (of the) night *ou* all night (long) *ou* throughout the night; **il a plu toute cette nuit/toute une nuit** it rained all (of) last night/for a whole night; **pendant** ~ **le voyage** during the whole (of the) trip; ~ **le monde** everybody, everyone; ~ **le reste** (all) the rest; ~ **le temps** all the time; **il a** ~ **le temps/l'argent qu'il lui faut** he has all the time/money he needs; **avoir** ~ **son temps** to have all the time one needs, have all the time in the world; **il a dépensé** ~ **son argent** he has spent all (of) his money; **mange toute ta viande** eat up your meat, eat all (of) your meat; **il passé toutes ses vacances à lire** he spent the whole of *ou* all (of) his holidays reading; **toute la France regardait le match** the whole of *ou* all France was watching the match; **c'est toute une affaire** it's quite a business, it's a whole rigmarole*; **c'est** ~ **le portrait de son père** he is the dead spit of *ou* the spitting image of his father; **féliciter qn de** ~ **son cœur** to congratulate sb wholeheartedly; **il courait de toute la vitesse de ses petites jambes** he was running as fast as his little legs would carry him; *V* **somme**[3].
(b) (*intensif: tout à fait*) **c'est** ~ **le contraire** it's quite the opposite *ou* the very opposite; **lui** ~ **le premier** him *ou* he first of all; **c'est** ~ **autre chose** that's quite another matter.
(c) (*seul, unique*) **c'est** ~ **l'effet que cela lui fait** that's all the effect *ou* the only effect it has on him; **c'est là** ~ **le problème** that's the whole problem, that's just where the problem lies; ~ **le secret est dans la rapidité** the whole secret lies in speed; **cet enfant est toute ma joie** this child is my only *ou* sole joy, all my joy in life lies with this child; **pour toute réponse, il grogna** his only reply was a grunt *ou* was to grunt; **il avait une valise pour** ~ **bagage** one case was all the luggage he had *ou* all he had in the way of luggage, as luggage he had one single case; **ils avaient pour** ~ **domestique une bonne** one maid was all the servants they had, all they had in the way of servants was one maid.
(d) (*sans déterminant: complet, total*) all (of), the whole of. **donner toute satisfaction** to give complete satisfaction, be completely satisfactory; **il a lu** ~ **Balzac** he has read the whole of *ou* all (of) Balzac; **de toute beauté** most beautiful, of the utmost beauty; **elle a visité** ~ **Londres** she has been round the whole of London; **de** ~ **temps, de toute éternité** since time immemorial, since the beginning of time; **de** ~ **repos** easy; **ce n'est pas un travail de** ~ **repos** it's not an easy job; **à** ~ **prix** at all costs; **à toute allure** *ou* **vitesse** at full *ou* top speed; **il est parti à toute vitesse** he left like a shot; **il a une patience/un courage à toute épreuve** his patience/courage will stand any test, he has an inexhaustible supply of patience/courage; **selon toute apparence** to all appearances; **en toute simplicité/franchise** in all simplicity/sincerity.
(e) (*sans déterminant: n'importe quel, chaque*) any, all. **toute personne susceptible de nous aider** any person *ou* everyone likely to help us; **toute trace d'agitation a disparu** all *ou* any trace of agitation has gone; **à toute heure (du jour ou de la nuit)** at any time *ou* at all times (of the day or night); **à** ~ **instant** at any moment; **à** ~ **âge** at any age, at all ages; **'restauration à toute heure'** 'meals served all day'; ~ **autre (que lui) aurait deviné** anybody *ou* anyone (but him) would have guessed; **pour** ~ **renseignement, téléphoner ...** for all information, ring ... .
(f) (*en apposition: complètement*) **il était** ~ **à son travail** he was entirely taken up by *ou* absorbed in his work; **un manteau** ~ **en laine** an all wool coat; **habillé** ~ **en noir** dressed all in black; **un style** ~ **en nuances** a very subtle style; **un jeu** ~ **en douceur** a very delicate style of play.
(g) tous, toutes (*l'ensemble, la totalité*) all, every; **toutes les personnes que nous connaissons** all the people *ou* everyone *ou* everybody (that) we know; **tous les moyens lui sont bons** he will use any means to achieve his ends; **il avait toutes les raisons d'être mécontent** he had every reason to be *ou* for being displeased; **tous les hommes sont mortels** all men are mortal; **courir dans tous les sens** to run in all directions *ou* in every direction; **il roulait tous feux éteints** he was driving with all his lights out; **des individus de toutes tendances/tous bords** individuals of all tendencies/shades of opinion; **toutes sortes de** all sorts of, every kind of.
(h) (*de récapitulation: littér*) **le saut en hauteur, la course, le lancer du javelot, toutes disciplines qui exigent ...** the high jump, running, throwing the javelin, all (of them) disciplines requiring ... .
(i) tous *ou* **toutes les** (*chaque*) every; **tous les jours/ans/mois** every day/year/month; **venir tous les jours** to come every day *ou* daily; **tous les deux jours/mois** every other day/month, every two days/months; **tous les 10 mètres** every 10 metres; **il vient tous les combien?*** how often does he come?; **toutes les 3 heures** every 3 hours, at 3-hourly intervals; (*hum*) **tous les trente-six du mois** once in a blue moon.
(j) (*avec numéral: ensemble*) **tous (les) deux** both (of them), each (of them); **tous (les) 3/4** all 3/4 (of them); **tous les 5/6** *etc* all 5/6 *etc* (of them).
(k) (*loc*) **en** ~ **bien** ~ **honneur** with the most honourable (of) intentions; **à** ~ **bout de champ** = **à tout propos; en** ~ **cas** in any case, at any rate; ~ **un chacun** all and sundry, everybody and anybody; (*Prov*) **tous les chemins mènent à Rome** all roads lead to Rome; **de** ~ **côté, de tous côtés** *chercher, regarder* on all sides, everywhere; **à tous égards** in every respect; **en** ~ **état de cause** in any case; **de toute façon** in any case, anyway, anyhow; **à** ~ **instant** continually, constantly; **à toutes jambes** as fast as one's legs can carry one; **en tous lieux** everywhere; (*Prov*) **toute peine mérite salaire** the labourer is worthy of his hire; **faire** ~ **son possible** to do one's utmost; **pour** ~ **potage** all told, all in all, altogether; **toutes proportions gardées** relatively speaking, making due allowances; **à** ~ **propos** every other minute.
2 *pron indéf* **(a)** (*gén*) everything, all; (*sans discrimination*) anything. **il a** ~ **organisé** he organized everything, he organized it all; **ses enfants mangent (de)** ~ her children will eat anything; **il vend de** ~ he sells everything; **on ne peut pas** ~ **faire** one can't do everything; ~ **va bien** all's (going) well, everything's fine; **avec lui, c'est** ~ **ou rien** with him it's all or nothing; **être** ~ **pour qn** to be everything to sb; **son travail, ses enfants,** ~ **l'exaspère** his work, the children, everything annoys him; ~ **lui est bon** everything *ou* all is grist to his mill; ~ **ce qui ...** everything that ...; ~ **ce que ...** everything (that) ... .
(b) tous, toutes all; **tous/toutes tant qu'ils/qu'elles sont** all of them, every single one of them; **tous sont arrivés** they have all arrived; **il les déteste tous** *ou* **toutes** he hates them all *ou* all of them; **nous avons tous nos défauts** we all *ou* we each of us have our faults; **nous mourrons tous** we shall all die; **vous tous qui m'écoutez** all of you who are listening to me; **écoutez bien tous!** listen, all of you!; **il s'attaque à nous tous** he's attacking us all; **tous ensemble** all together.
(c) (*loc*) ~ **est bien qui finit bien** all's well that ends well; ~ **est pour le mieux dans le meilleur des mondes** everything is for the best in the best of all possible worlds; ~ **a une fin** there is an end to everything, everything comes to an end; **... et** ~ **et** ~***** ... and all that sort of thing, ... and so on and so on; ~ **finit par des chansons** things always turn out for the best; ~ **passe,** ~ **casse** nothing lasts for ever; (*fig*) ~ **est là** that's what matters *ou* counts; **c'est** ~ that's all; **c'est** ~ **dire** I need say no more; **ce sera** ~? will that be all?, (will there be) anything else?; **ce n'est pas** ~ **(que) d'en parler** there's more to it than just talking about

it; **ce n'est pas ~ de partir, il faut arriver** it's not enough to set off — one must arrive as well; **c'était ~ ce qu'il y a de chic** it was the last word in chic *ou* the ultimate in chic; **il y avait des gens ~ ce qu'il y a de plus distingué(s)** there were the most distinguished people there; **à ~ prendre, ~ bien considéré** all things considered, taking everything into consideration; (*Comm*) **~ compris** inclusive, all-in; **la formule du ~ compris** inclusive *ou* all-in terms; (*péj*) **avoir ~ d'un brigand/du clown** to be an absolute *ou* a real brigand/clown; **avoir ~ d'une intrigante** to be a real schemer; **en ~** in all; (*Prov*) **~ vient à point à qui sait attendre** everything comes to he who waits; (*Prov*) **~ ce qui brille n'est pas or** all that glitters is not gold (*Prov*); *V* **après, comme, malgré** *etc.*

3 *adv* **(a)** (*tout à fait*) **c'est ~ neuf** (*objet*) it's brand new; (*littér*) **son bonheur ~ neuf** his new-found happiness; **il/elle est ~ étonné(e)** he/she is very *ou* most surprised; **les toutes premières années** the very first *ou* early years; **c'est une ~ autre histoire** that's quite another story; **elles étaient ~ heureuses/toutes contentes** they were most *ou* extremely happy/pleased; **il a mangé sa viande toute crue** he ate his meat quite *ou* completely raw; **c'est ~ naturel** it's perfectly *ou* quite natural; **la ville ~ entière** the whole town; **~(e) nu(e)** stark naked; **~ enfant** *ou* **toute petite elle aimait la campagne** as a (very) small child she liked the country; **il est ~ seul** he's all alone; **il l'a fait ~ seul** he did it (all) on his own; **cette tasse ne s'est pas cassée toute seule!** this cup didn't break all by itself!; **cela va ~ seul** it all goes smoothly.

(b) (*concession: quoique*) **~ médecin qu'il soit** even though *ou* although he is a doctor, I don't care if he IS a doctor; **toute malade qu'elle se dise** however ill *ou* no matter how ill she says she is; **~ grand que soit leur appartement** however large *ou* no matter how large their flat (is).

(c) (*intensif*) **~ près** *ou* **à côté** very near *ou* close; **~ au loin** far away, right *ou* far in the distance; **~ là-bas** right over there; **~ simplement** *ou* **bonnement** quite simply; **je vois cela ~ autrement** I see it quite differently; **~ en bas de la colline** right at the bottom of the hill; **~ dans le fond/au bout** right at the bottom/at the end; **~ court: il répondit ~ court que non** he just answered no (and that was all); **ne m'appelez pas Dupont de la Motte, pour les amis c'est Dupont ~ court** don't call me Dupont de la Motte, it's plain Dupont to my friends; **parler ~ bas** to speak very low *ou* quietly; **il était ~ en sueur** he was running with sweat; **elle était ~ en larmes** she was in floods of tears; **le jardin est ~ en fleurs** the garden is a mass of flowers.

(d) ~ en+*participe présent*: **~ en marchant/travaillant** as *ou* while you walk/work, while walking/working; **elle tricotait ~ en regardant la télévision** she used to knit while watching the television.

(e) (*avec n*) **être ~ yeux/oreilles** to be all eyes/ears; (*hum*) **je suis ~ ouïe** I am all ears!; **être ~ sucre ~ miel** to be all sweetness and light; **~ laine/coton** all wool/cotton; **être ~ feu ~ flammes** to be fired with enthusiasm.

(f) (*loc*) **~ au plus** at the (very) most; **~ au moins** at (the very) least; **~ d'abord** first of all, in the first place; **~ de même** (*en dépit de cela*) all the same, for all that; **~ de même!** well really!; **c'est ~ de même agaçant** it IS annoying, it's really most annoying; **des idées/formules toutes faites** ready-made ideas/phrases; **~ cuit: vendu ~ cuit** sold ready-cooked; (*fig*) **c'est du ~ cuit*** it's a cinch* *ou* a pushover*; **dire qch ~ à trac** to say sth right out of the blue; **~ plein*: il est gentil/mignon ~ plein*** he is really very *ou* really awfully* nice/sweet; **~ nouveau ~ beau** (just) wait till the novelty wears off; **c'est ~ comme*** it comes to the same thing really; **c'est ~ un** it's one and the same thing; **être ~ d'une pièce** to be as straight as a die; **c'est ~ vu*** that's the top and bottom of it*, that's all there is to it.

4 *nm* **(a)** whole. **tous ces éléments forment un ~** all these elements make up a whole; **acheter/vendre/prendre le ~** to buy/sell/take the (whole) lot *ou* all of it (*ou* them); (*charade*) **mon ~** my whole *ou* all.

(b) (*loc*) **le ~ est qu'il arrive à temps** the main *ou* most important thing is that he arrives in time; **du ~ au ~** completely, utterly, entirely; **ce n'est pas le ~*** this is no good, this isn't good enough; **ce n'est pas le ~ de s'amuser, il faut travailler** we can't keep on enjoying ourselves like this — we must get down to work; **du ~** at all; **pas du ~** not at all; **il n'y a pas de pain du ~** there's no bread at all; **il n'y a plus du ~ de pain** there's no bread left at all; **je n'entends rien du ~** I can't hear a thing, I can't hear anything at all; *V* **comme.**

5: tous azimuts *adj inv* (*Mil*) *défense* omnidirectional, on all fronts (*attrib*); (*fig*) *concurrence, opération* omnidirectional; **tout à coup** all of a sudden, suddenly, all at once; **tout-à-l'égout** *nm inv* mains drainage; **tout à fait** quite, entirely, altogether; **tout-fou*** *adj m, pl* **tout-fous** over-excited; **tout de go** *dire* straight out*; *entrer* straight; **tout-en-un** *adv inv*: **collant tout-en-un** body stocking; **tout à l'heure** (*futur*) presently (*Brit*), in a moment; (*passé*) just now, a moment ago; **le tout-Paris** all Paris; **tout-petit** *nm, pl* **tout-petits** little one; **un jeu pour les tout-petits** a game for tiny tots *ou* for the very young; **toute-puissance** *nf* omnipotence; **tout-puissant, e** *adj* almighty, omnipotent, all-powerful; **tous risques** *adj inv assurance etc* all-risks; **tout de suite** straightaway, at once, immediately; **tout terrain** (*adj inv*) *véhicule, pneus* all-roads (*épith*); (*nm inv: véhicule*) all-purpose *ou* all-roads vehicle; **tout-venant** *nm* (*charbon*) raw coal; (*péj*) **le tout-venant** (*personnes*) the rag tag and bobtail, the hoi-polloi; (*articles, marchandises*) the ragbag.

toutefois [tutfwa] *adv* however. **sans ~ que cela les retarde** without that delaying them however; **si ~ il est d'accord** if he agrees however *ou* nonetheless.

toutou [tutu] *nm* (*langage enfantin*) doggie, bow-wow (*langage enfantin*). (*fig*) **suivre qn/obéir à qn comme un ~** to follow sb about/obey sb as meekly as a lamb.

toux [tu] *nf* cough. **~ grasse/sèche/nerveuse** loose/dry/nervous cough; *V* **quinte**[2].

toxémie [tɔksemi] *nf* blood poisoning, toxaemia.

toxicité [tɔksisite] *nf* toxicity.

toxicologie [tɔksikɔlɔʒi] *nf* toxicology.

toxicologique [tɔksikɔlɔʒik] *adj* toxicological.

toxicologue [tɔksikɔlɔg] *nmf* toxicologist.

toxicomane [tɔksikɔman] *nmf* drug addict.

toxicomanie [tɔksikɔmani] *nf* drug addiction.

toxine [tɔksin] *nf* toxin.

toxique [tɔksik] **1** *adj* toxic, poisonous. **2** *nm* toxin, poison.

trac[1] [tʀak] *nm* (*Théât, en public*) stage fright; (*aux examens etc*) nerves (*pl*). **avoir le ~** to have *ou* get stage fright; to get (an attack *ou* fit of) nerves; **ficher le ~ à qn*** to put the wind up sb*, give sb a fright.

trac[2] [tʀak] *nm*: **tout à ~** *dire, demander* right out of the blue.

traçage [tʀasaʒ] *nm* (*Tech*) scribing.

traçant, e [tʀasɑ̃, ɑ̃t] *adj* **(a)** (*Bot*) *racine* running, creeping. **(b)** (*Mil*) *obus, balle* tracer.

tracas [tʀaka] **1** *nm* (*littér* †: *embarras*) bother, upset. **se donner bien du ~** to give o.s. a great deal of trouble. **2** *nmpl* (*soucis, ennuis*) worries.

tracasser [tʀakase] (1) **1** *vt* to worry, bother. **2 se tracasser** *vpr* (*se faire du souci*) to worry, fret. **ne te tracasse pas pour si peu!** don't worry *ou* fret over a little thing like that!

tracasserie [tʀakasʀi] *nf* (*gén pl*) harassment.

tracassier, -ière [tʀakasje, jɛʀ] *adj* irksome, pestering (*épith*).

trace [tʀas] *nf* **(a)** (*empreinte*) *[animal, fugitif, pneu]* tracks (*pl*). **la ~ du renard diffère de celle de la belette** the fox's tracks differ from those of the weasel; **suivre une ~ de blaireau** to follow some badger tracks; **~s de pas** footprints; **~s de pneus** tyre tracks; **il n'y avait pas ~ des documents volés/du fugitif dans l'appartement** there was no trace of the stolen documents/of the fugitive in the flat; **on ne trouve pas ~ de cet événement dans les journaux** there's no trace of this event to be found in the papers.

(b) (*chemin frayé*) track, path. **s'ouvrir une ~ dans la brousse** to open up a track *ou* path through the undergrowth; (*Alpinisme, Ski*) **faire la ~** to be the first to ski (*ou* walk *etc*) on new snow; **on voyait leur ~ dans la face nord** we could see their tracks on the north face.

(c) (*marque*) *[sang]* trace; *[brûlure, encre]* mark; *[outil]* mark; *[blessure, maladie]* mark. **~s de freinage** brake marks; **~s de doigt** (*sur disque, meuble*) finger marks; **~s d'effraction** signs of a break-in; (*littér*) **les ~s de la souffrance** the marks of suffering; **des ~s de fatigue se lisaient sur son visage** his face showed signs of fatigue *ou* bore the marks of fatigue; **cet incident avait laissé une ~ durable/profonde sur son esprit** the incident had left an indelible/a definite mark on his mind.

(d) (*vestige: gén pl*) *[bataille, civilisation]* trace; (*indice: gén pl*) *[bagarre, passage]* sign. **on y voyait les ~s d'une orgie/d'un passage récent** you could see the signs of an orgy/that somebody had recently passed by; **retrouver les ~s d'une civilisation disparue** to rediscover the traces of a lost civilisation.

(e) (*quantité minime*) *[poison, substance]* trace. **on y a trouvé de l'albumine à l'état de ~** traces of albumen have been found; (*fig*) **il ne montrait nulle ~ de repentir/de chagrin** he showed no sign(s) of being sorry/of grief; **sans une ~ d'accent étranger** without a *ou* any trace of a foreign accent.

(f) (*loc*) **disparaître sans laisser de ~s** to disappear without trace; **suivre à la ~** *animal, fugitif* to track; (*fig*) **on peut le suivre à la ~** you can always tell when HE has been here; **être sur la ~ de** *fugitif* to be on the track *ou* trail of; *complot, document* to be on the track of; **perdre la ~ d'un fugitif** to lose track of *ou* lose the trail of a fugitive; **retrouver la ~ d'un fugitif** to pick up the trail of a fugitive again; (*fig*) **marcher sur** *ou* **suivre les ~s de qn** to follow in sb's footsteps.

tracé [tʀase] *nm* **(a)** (*plan*) *[réseau routier ou ferroviaire, installations]* layout, plan.

(b) (*parcours*) *[ligne de chemin de fer, autoroute]* route; *[rivière]* line, course; *[itinéraire]* course; (*contour*) *[côte, crête]* line.

(c) (*graphisme*) *[dessin, écriture]* line.

tracer [tʀase] (3) **1** *vt* **(a)** (*dessiner*) *ligne, triangle, plan* to draw; (*écrire*) *chiffre, mot* to trace. (*fig*) **~ le tableau d'une époque** to draw *ou* paint the picture of a period.

(b) *route, piste* (*frayer*) to open up; (*baliser*) to mark out. (*fig*) **~ le chemin** *ou* **la voie à qn** to show sb the way.

2 *vi* (‡: *courir*) to get a move on*, shift* (*Brit*).

traceur, -euse [tʀasœʀ, øz] **1** *adj* (*Sci*) *substance* tracer (*épith*). **2** *nm [appareil enregistreur]* pen; (*Sci: isotope*) tracer.

trachéal, e, *mpl* **-aux** [tʀakeal, o] *adj* tracheal.

trachée [tʀaʃe] *nf* **(a)** (*Anat*) **~(-artère)** windpipe, trachea. **(b)** (*Zool*) trachea.

trachéen, -enne [tʀakeɛ̃, ɛn] *adj* (*Zool*) tracheal.

trachéite [tʀakeit] *nf* tracheitis.

trachéotomie [tʀakeɔtɔmi] *nf* tracheotomy.

traçoir [tʀaswaʀ] *nm [dessinateur, graveur]* scriber; *[jardinier]* drill marker.

tract [tʀakt] *nm* tract, pamphlet.

tractations [tʀaktɑsjɔ̃] *nfpl* (*gén péj*) dealings (*pl*), bargaining (*U*).

tracté, e [tʀakte] *adj* tractor-drawn (*Mil*).

tracteur [tʀaktœʀ] *nm* tractor.

traction [tʀaksjɔ̃] *nf* **(a)** (*Sci, gén: action, mouvement*) traction. (*Sci*) **résistance à la/effort de ~** tensile strength/stress; **faire des ~s** to do pull-ups; (*au sol*) to do press-ups *ou* push-ups.

(b) (*mode d'entraînement d'un véhicule*) traction, haulage;

T-Z

(*Rail*) traction. ~ animale/mécanique animal/mechanical traction *ou* haulage; à ~ animale drawn by animals; à ~ mécanique mechanically drawn; ~ à vapeur/électrique steam/electric traction; (*Aut*) ~ arrière rear-wheel drive; (*Aut*) ~ avant (*dispositif*) front-wheel drive; (*automobile*) car with front-wheel drive.
(c) (*Rail*) la ~ the engine and driver section; service du matériel et de la ~ mechanical and electrical engineer's department.

tractus [tʀaktys] *nm* tract.

tradition [tʀadisjɔ̃] *nf* (a) (*gén*) tradition. (*Rel*) la T~ Tradition; (*Littérat*) la ~ manuscrite d'une œuvre the manuscript tradition of a work; de ~ traditional; fidèle à la ~ true to tradition; c'était bien dans la ~ française it was very much in the French tradition; il est de ~ *ou* c'est la ~ que/de faire it is a tradition *ou* traditional that/to do.
(b) (*Jur*) tradition, transfer.

traditionalisme [tʀadisjɔnalism(ə)] *nm* traditionalism.

traditionaliste [tʀadisjɔnalist(ə)] 1 *adj* traditionalist(ic). 2 *nmf* traditionalist.

traditionnel, -elle [tʀadisjɔnɛl] *adj pratique, interprétation, opinion* traditional; (*: *habituel*) good old* (*épith*), usual. sa ~le robe noire* her good old* *ou* usual black dress.

traditionnellement [tʀadisjɔnɛlmɑ̃] *adv* traditionally; (*: *habituellement*) as always, as usual. ~ vêtue de noir* dressed in black as always *ou* as is (*ou* was) her wont (*hum*).

traducteur, -trice [tʀadyktœʀ, tʀis] *nm,f* translator. ~-interprète translator-interpreter.

traduction [tʀadyksjɔ̃] *nf* (a) (*action, opération, technique*) translation, translating (*dans, en* into); (*phrase, texte, Scol: exercice*) translation. la ~ en arabe pose de nombreux problèmes translation *ou* translating into Arabic presents many problems; la ~ de ce texte a pris 3 semaines the translation of *ou* translating this text took 3 weeks; c'est une ~ assez libre it's a fairly free translation *ou* rendering; une excellente ~ de Proust an excellent translation of Proust; la ~ automatique machine *ou* automatic translation; la ~ simultanée simultaneous translation.
(b) (*fig: interprétation*) rendering, expression.

traduire [tʀadɥiʀ] (38) *vt* (a) *mot, texte, auteur* to translate (*en, dans* into). traduit de l'allemand translated from (the) German.
(b) (*exprimer*) to convey, render, express; (*rendre manifeste*) to be the expression of. les mots traduisent la pensée words convey *ou* render *ou* express thought; ce tableau traduit un sentiment de désespoir this picture conveys *ou* expresses a feeling of despair; sa peur se traduisait par une grande volubilité his fear found expression in great volubility.
(c) (*Jur*) ~ qn en justice to bring sb before the courts; ~ qn en correctionnelle to bring sb before the criminal court.

traduisible [tʀadɥizibl(ə)] *adj* translatable.

Trafalgar [tʀafalgaʀ] *nm* Trafalgar; *V* coup.

trafic [tʀafik] *nm* (a) (*péj*) (*commerce clandestin*) traffic; (*activité*) trafficking; (†: *commerce*) trade (*de* in). ~ d'armes arms dealing, gunrunning; faire le ~ d'armes to be engaged in arms dealing *ou* gunrunning; ~ des stupéfiants *ou* de la drogue drug traffic, drug trafficking; faire le ~ des stupéfiants *ou* de la drogue to traffic in drugs; le ~ des vins/cuirs† the wine/leather trade.
(b) (*fig: activités suspectes*) dealings (*pl*); (*: *micmac*) funny business*, goings-on* (*pl*). (*Hist*) ~ des bénéfices selling of benefices; (*Jur*) ~ d'influence trading of favours; (*fig péj*) faire ~ de son honneur to trade in one's honour; (*fig hum*) faire (le) ~ de ses charmes to offer one's charms for sale; il se fait ici un drôle de ~* there's some funny business going on here*, there are some strange goings-on here*.
(c) (*Aut, Aviat, Rail*) traffic. ~ maritime/routier/aérien/ferroviaire sea/road/air/rail traffic; ligne à fort ~ line carrying dense *ou* heavy traffic; ~ (de) marchandises/(de) voyageurs *ou* passagers goods/passenger traffic.

trafiquant, e [tʀafikɑ̃, ɑ̃t] *nm,f* (*péj*) trafficker. ~ de drogues drug trafficker; ~ d'armes arms dealer, gunrunner.

trafiquer [tʀafike] (1) 1 *vi* (*péj*) to traffic, trade (illicitly). ~ de qch to traffic in sth, trade illicitly in sth; ~ de son influence/ses charmes to offer one's influence/charms for sale.
2 *vt* (*:*péj*) *moteur, voiture, vin* to doctor*.

tragédie [tʀaʒedi] *nf* (*gén, Théât*) tragedy.

tragédien [tʀaʒedjɛ̃] *nm* tragedian, tragic actor.

tragédienne [tʀaʒedjɛn] *nf* tragedienne, tragic actress.

tragi-comédie, *pl* **tragi-comédies** [tʀaʒikɔmedi] *nf* (*Théât, fig*) tragi-comedy.

tragi-comique [tʀaʒikɔmik] *adj* (*Théât, fig*) tragi-comic.

tragique [tʀaʒik] 1 *adj* (*Théât, fig*) tragic. ce n'est pas ~* it's not the end of the world*.
2 *nm* (a) (*auteur*) tragedian, tragic author.
(b) (*genre*) tragedy.
(c) (*caractère dramatique*) *[situation]* tragedy. la situation tourne au ~ the situation is taking a tragic turn; prendre qch au ~ to act as if sth were a tragedy, make a tragedy out of sth.

tragiquement [tʀaʒikmɑ̃] *adv* tragically.

trahir [tʀaiʀ] (2) *vt* (a) *ami, patrie, cause,* (†) *femme* to betray. ~ la confiance/les intérêts de qn to betray sb's confidence/interests; (*fig*) ses sens le trahirent: pour une fois il se trompa his senses betrayed *ou* deceived him — for once he was mistaken.
(b) (*révéler, manifester*) *secret, émotion* to betray, give away. ~ sa pensée to betray one's thoughts; son intonation trahissait sa colère his intonation betrayed his anger; sa peur se trahissait par une grande volubilité his fear betrayed itself in a great flow of words.
(c) (*lâcher*) *[forces, santé]* to fail. ses forces l'ont trahi his strength failed him; ses nerfs l'ont trahi his nerves let him down *ou* failed him.
(d) (*mal exprimer*) to misrepresent. ces mots ont trahi ma pensée those words misrepresented what I had in mind; ce traducteur/cet interprète a trahi ma pièce this translator/performer has given a totally false rendering of my play.

trahison [tʀaizɔ̃] *nf* (*gén*) betrayal; (*Jur, Mil: crime*) treason. il est capable des pires ~s he is capable of the worst treachery.

traille [tʀɑj] *nf* (*câble*) ferry-cable; (*bac*) (cable) ferry.

train [tʀɛ̃] 1 *nm* (a) (*Rail*) train. ~ omnibus/express/rapide slow *ou* stopping/fast/express train; ~ direct fast *ou* non-stop *ou* express train; ~ à vapeur/électrique steam/electric train; ~ de marchandises/voyageurs goods/passenger train; ~ auto-couchettes car-sleeper train; ~s supplémentaires extra trains; le ~ de Paris/Lyon the Paris/Lyons train; les ~s de neige the winter-sports trains; voyager par *ou* prendre le ~ to travel by rail *ou* train, take the train; monter dans *ou* prendre le ~ en marche (*lit*) to get on the moving train; (*fig*) to jump on *ou* climb onto the bandwagon; la Grande-Bretagne a pris le ~ du Marché commun en marche Great Britain has jumped on *ou* climbed onto the Common Market bandwagon.
(b) (*allure*) pace. ralentir/accélérer le ~ to slow down/speed up, slow/quicken the pace; aller son ~ to carry along; aller son petit ~ to go along at one's own pace; l'affaire va son petit ~ things are chugging *ou* jogging along (nicely); aller bon ~ *[affaire, travaux]* to make good progress; *[voiture]* to go at a good pace, make good progress; aller grand ~ to make brisk progress, move along briskly; les langues des commères allaient bon ~ the old wives' tongues were wagging away *ou* were going nineteen to the dozen; mener/suivre le ~ to set/follow the pace; il allait à un ~ d'enfer he was going at a furious pace *ou* hell for leather; au ~ où il travaille (at) the rate he is working; au *ou* du ~ où vont les choses the rate things are going, at THIS rate; *V* fond.
(c) être en ~ (*en action*) to be under way; (*de bonne humeur*) to be in good spirits; mettre qn en ~ (*l'égayer*) to put sb in good spirits; mettre un travail en ~ to get a job under way *ou* started off; mise en ~ *[travail]* starting (up), start; (*Typ*) make-ready; (*exercices de gym*) warm-up; être/se sentir en ~ to be/feel in good form; elle ne se sent pas très en ~ she doesn't feel too good *ou* too bright*.
(d) être en ~ de faire qch to be doing sth; être en ~ de manger/regarder la télévision to be (busy) eating/watching television; j'étais juste en ~ de manger I was (right) in the middle of eating, I was just eating; on l'a pris en ~ de voler he was caught stealing.
(e) (*file*) *[bateaux, mulets, chevaux]* train, line. (*Mil*) le ~ (des équipages) ≈ the (Army) Service Corps; ~ de bois (de flottage) timber raft; (*Espace*) ~ spatial space train.
(f) (*Tech: jeu*) ~ d'engrenages train of gears; ~ de pneus set of (four) tyres.
(g) (*Admin: série*) un ~ d'arrêtés/de mesures a batch of decrees/measures; un premier ~ de réformes a first batch *ou* set of reforms.
(h) (*de locomotion*) (*Aut*) ~ avant/arrière front/rear wheel-axle unit; *[animal]* ~ de devant forequarters (*pl*); ~ de derrière hindquarters (*pl*).
(i) (*: *derrière*) backside*, rear (end)*; *V* filer, magner.
2: (*Aviat*) train d'atterrissage undercarriage, landing gear; train électrique (*jouet*) electric train; train de maison (†: *domestiques*) household, retainers (†: *pl*); (*dépenses, ménage*) (household) establishment; (*Phys*) train d'ondes wave train; (*Mil*) train sanitaire hospital train; train de vie style of living.

traînailler [tʀɛnɑje] (1) *vi* (a) (*être lent*) to dawdle.
(b) (*vagabonder*) to loaf around, loiter.

traînant, e [tʀɛnɑ̃, ɑ̃t] *adj voix, accent* drawling (*épith*); *robe, aile* trailing (*épith*); *démarche* lingering (*épith*).

traînard, e [tʀɛnaʀ, ɑʀd(ə)] *nm,f* (*en marchant*) straggler; (*: *au travail*) slowcoach* (*Brit*), slowpoke* (*US*).

traînasser [tʀɛnase] (1) *vi* = traînailler.

traîne [tʀɛn] *nf* (a) *[robe]* train. (b) (*Pêche*) dragnet. pêche à la ~ dragnet fishing. (c) (*fig*) être à la ~ (*en remorque*) to be in tow; (*: *en retard, en arrière*) to lag behind.

traîneau, *pl* ~x [tʀɛno] *nm* (a) (*véhicule*) sleigh, sledge (*Brit*), sled (*US*). promenade en ~ sleigh ride. (b) (*Pêche*) dragnet.

traînée [tʀene] *nf* (a) (*laissée par un véhicule, un animal etc*) trail, tracks (*pl*); (*sur un mur: d'humidité, de sang etc*) streak; (*bande, raie: dans le ciel, un tableau*) streak. ~s de brouillard wisps *ou* streaks of fog; ~ de poudre powder trail; se répandre comme une ~ de poudre to spread like wildfire.
(b) (*péj: femme de mauvaise vie*) slut, hussy†.
(c) (*Tech: force*) drag.

traîne-lattes* [tʀɛnlat] *nm inv* = traîne-savates*.

traînement [tʀɛnmɑ̃] *nm [jambes, pieds]* trailing, dragging; *[voix]* drawl.

traîne-misère [tʀɛnmizɛʀ] *nm inv* wretch.

traîne-patins* [tʀɛnpatɛ̃] *nm inv* = traîne-savates*.

traîner [tʀene] (1) 1 *vt* (a) (*tirer*) *sac, objet lourd, personne* to pull, drag; *wagon* to pull, haul; *charrette* to draw, pull. ~ un meuble à travers une pièce to pull *ou* drag a piece of furniture across a room; ~ qn par les pieds to drag sb along by the feet; ~ les pieds to drag one's feet, shuffle along; ~ la jambe *ou* la patte* to limp, hobble; elle traînait sa poupée dans la poussière she was trailing *ou* dragging her doll through the dust; (*fig*) ~ ses guêtres* to mooch around*; (*fig*) ~ la savate* to bum around*; (*fig*) ~ qn dans la boue *ou* fange to drag sb *ou* sb's name through the mud; (*fig*) ~ un boulet to have a millstone round one's neck.
(b) (*emmener: péj*) to drag (with one). il traîne sa femme à

toutes les réunions he drags his wife along (with him) to all the meetings; **elle est obligée de ~ ses enfants partout** she has to trail *ou* drag her children round (with her) everywhere; **il traîne toujours une vieille valise avec lui** he is always dragging *ou* lugging* an old case around with him; (*fig*) **~ de vieilles idées/des conceptions surannées** to cling to old ideas/outdated conceptions.

(c) (*subir*) **elle traîne cette bronchite depuis janvier** this bronchitis has been with her *ou* plaguing her since January; **elle traîne un mauvais rhume** she has a bad cold she can't get rid of; **~ une existence misérable** to drag out a wretched existence; **cette mélancolie qu'il traîna sans pouvoir s'en défaire** this melancholy which oppressed him and would not be dispelled.

(d) (*faire durer*) to drag out, draw out. **(faire) ~ les choses en longueur** to drag things out.

(e) (faire) ~ *mots* to drawl; *fin de phrase* to drag out, drawl. **(faire) ~ sa voix** to drawl.

2 *vi* **(a)** *[personne]* (*rester en arrière*) to lag *ou* trail behind; (*aller lentement*) to dawdle, hang about; (*péj: errer*) to hang about. **~ en chemin** to dawdle on the way; **~ (dans) les rues** to roam the streets, hang about the streets; **elle laisse ses enfants ~ dans la rue** she lets her children hang about the street(s); **on est en retard, il ne s'agit plus de ~** we're late — we must stop hanging about *ou* dawdling; **~ dans les cafés** to hang around the cafés; **après sa maladie, il a encore traîné 2 ans** after his illness he lingered on for 2 years.

(b) *[chose]* (*être éparpillé*) to lie about *ou* around. **ses livres traînent sur toutes les chaises** his books are lying about on all the chairs; **ne laisse pas ~ ton argent/tes affaires** don't leave your money/things lying about *ou* around; **des histoires/idées qui traînent partout** stories/ideas that float around everywhere.

(c) (*durer trop longtemps*) to drag on; (*subsister*) to cling (*dans* to), hang on (*dans* in). **un procès qui traîne** a case which is dragging on; **une maladie qui traîne** a lingering illness, an illness which drags on; **la discussion a traîné en longueur** the discussion dragged on for ages *ou* dragged on and on; **ça n'a pas traîné!*** that wasn't long coming!; **il n'a pas traîné (à répondre)*** he didn't hang about* (— he replied straight away); **ça ne traînera pas, il vous/les mettra tous à la porte*** he'll throw you/them all out before you/they know what's happening *ou* where you/they are*; **faire ~ qch** to drag sth out; **doctrine où traînent des relents de fascisme** doctrine to which the smell of fascism still clings.

(d) *[robe, manteau]* to trail. **ta ceinture/ton lacet traîne par terre** your belt/shoelace is trailing *ou* hanging *ou* dragging on the ground; **des effilochures de brume qui traînent dans le ciel** wisps of mist which trail across the sky.

3 se traîner *vpr* **(a)** *[personne fatiguée]* to drag o.s. **se ~ par terre** to crawl on the ground; **avec cette chaleur, on se traîne** it's all one can do to drag oneself around in this heat; **elle a pu se ~ jusqu'à son fauteuil** she managed to drag herself (over) to her chair; **je ne peux même plus me ~** I can't even drag myself about any more; (*fig*) **se ~ aux pieds de qn** to grovel at sb's feet.

(b) *[conversation, journée, hiver]* to drag on.

traîne-savates* [tʀɛnsavat] *nm inv* (*vagabond*) tramp, bum:.

traîneur, -euse [tʀɛnœʀ, øz] *nm,f* (*rare: péj*) **c'est un ~ de cafés/de rues** he's always hanging about the cafés/streets.

train-train, traintrain [tʀɛ̃tʀɛ̃] *nm* humdrum routine. **le ~ de la vie quotidienne** the humdrum routine of everyday life, the daily round.

traire [tʀɛʀ] (50) *vt vache* to milk; *lait* to draw. **machine à ~** milking machine; **à l'heure de ~** at milking time.

trait [tʀɛ] **1** *nm* **(a)** (*ligne*) (*en dessinant*) stroke; (*en soulignant, dans un graphique*) line. **faire *ou* tirer *ou* tracer un ~** to draw a line; **dessin au ~** (*technique, œuvre*) line drawing; (*Art*) **le ~ est ferme** the line is firm; (*lit, fig*) **d'un ~ de plume** with one stroke of the pen; **~ de repère** reference mark; **biffer qch d'un ~** to score *ou* cross sth out; **copier *ou* reproduire qch ~ pour ~** to copy sth line by line, make a line for line copy of sth; **les ~s d'un dessin/portrait** the lines of a drawing/portrait; **dessiner qch à grands ~s** to sketch sth roughly, make a rough sketch of sth; (*fig*) **décrire qch à grands ~s** to describe sth in broad outline; (*fig*) **il l'a décrit en ~s vifs et émouvants** he drew a vivid and moving picture of it (*fig*).

(b) (*élément caractéristique*) feature, trait. **c'est un ~ de cet auteur** this is a (characteristic) trait *ou* feature of this author; **les ~s dominants d'une époque/œuvre** the dominant features of an age/a work; **avoir des ~s de ressemblance avec** to have certain features in common with; **il tient ce ~ de caractère de son père** this trait (of character) comes to him from his father, he gets this characteristic from his father.

(c) (*acte révélateur*) **~ de générosité/courage/perfidie** act of generosity/courage/wickedness.

(d) ~s (*physionomie*) features; **avoir des ~s fins/réguliers** to have delicate/regular features; **avoir les ~s tirés/creusés** to have drawn/sunken features.

(e) (†: *projectile*) arrow, dart; (*littér: attaque malveillante*) taunt, gibe. **filer *ou* partir comme un ~** to be off like an arrow *ou* a shot; **il l'anéantit de ce ~ mordant** he crushed him with this biting taunt; **un ~ satirique/d'ironie** a shaft of satire/irony (*littér*); (*fig*) **les ~s de la calomnie** the darts of slander (*littér*).

(f) (*courroie*) trace.

(g) (*traction*) **animal *ou* bête/cheval de ~** draught animal/horse.

(h) (*Mus*) virtuosic passage.

(i) (*Rel*) tract.

(j) (*gorgée*) draught (*frm*), gulp. **d'un ~** in one breath, at one go; **à longs ~s** in long draughts; **à grands ~s** in great gulps.

(k) (*loc*) **avoir ~ à** to relate to, have to do with, concern; **tout ce qui a ~ à cette affaire** everything relating to *ou* (having) to do with *ou* concerning this matter; **d'un ~** *avaler, boire* in one gulp, at one go; *dormir* uninterruptedly, without waking.

2: trait (d'esprit) flash *ou* shaft of wit, witticism; **trait de génie** brainwave, flash of inspiration *ou* genius; **trait de lumière** (*lit*) shaft *ou* ray of light; (*fig*) flash of inspiration, sudden revelation (*U*); **trait de scie** cutting-line; **trait d'union** (*Typ*) hyphen; (*fig*) link.

traitable [tʀɛtabl(ə)] *adj* **(a)** (*littér*) *personne* accommodating, tractable (*frm*). **(b)** *sujet, matière* manageable.

traitant [tʀɛtɑ̃] *adj m V* **médecin.**

traite [tʀɛt] *nf* **(a)** (*trafic*) **~ des Noirs** slave trade; **~ des blanches** white slave trade.

(b) (*Comm: billet*) draft, bill. **tirer/escompter une ~** to draw/discount a draft.

(c) (*parcours*) stretch. **d'une (seule) ~** (*lit*) at a stretch, without stopping on the way; (*fig*) at a stretch, in one go.

(d) *[vache]* milking. **~ mécanique** machine milking; **l'heure de la ~** milking time.

traité [tʀete] *nm* **(a)** (*livre*) treatise. **(b)** (*convention*) treaty. **~ de paix** peace treaty.

traitement [tʀɛtmɑ̃] *nm* **(a)** (*manière d'agir*) treatment. **mauvais ~s** ill-treatment (*U*); **~ de faveur** special *ou* preferential treatment.

(b) (*Méd*) treatment. **suivre/prescrire un ~ douloureux** to undergo/prescribe painful treatment *ou* a painful course of treatment.

(c) (*rémunération*) salary.

(d) (*Tech*) *[matières premières]* processing, treating. **le ~ de l'information *ou* des données** data processing.

traiter [tʀete] (1) **1** *vt* **(a)** *personne, animal* to treat; (*Méd: soigner*) *malade, maladie* to treat; (†) *invités* to entertain. **~ qn bien/mal/comme un chien** to treat sb well/badly/like a dog; **~ qn d'égal à égal** to treat sb as an equal; **~ qn en enfant/malade** to treat sb as *ou* like a child/an invalid; **ils traitent leurs enfants/domestiques durement** they are hard with *ou* on their children/servants; **les congressistes ont été magnifiquement traités** the conference members were entertained magnificently; **se faire ~ pour une affection pulmonaire** to undergo treatment for *ou* be treated for lung trouble.

(b) (*qualifier*) **~ qn de fou/menteur** to call sb a fool/a liar; **~ qn de tous les noms** to call sb all the names imaginable *ou* all the names under the sun; **ils se sont traités de voleur(s)** they called each other thieves.

(c) (*examiner, s'occuper de*) *question* to treat, deal with; (*Art*) *thème, sujet* to treat; (*Comm*) *affaire* to handle, deal with. **il n'a pas traité le sujet** he has not dealt with the subject.

(d) (*Tech*) *cuir, minerai, pétrole* to treat, process. **laine non traitée** untreated wool.

2 traiter de *vt indir* to deal with, treat of (*frm*). **le livre/romancier traite des problèmes de la drogue** the book-/novelist deals with *ou* treats of (*frm*) the problems of drugs.

3 *vi* (*négocier, parlementer*) to deal, have dealings. **~ avec qn** to deal with sb, have dealings with sb; **les pays doivent ~ entre eux** countries must deal *ou* have dealings with each other.

traiteur [tʀɛtœʀ] *nm* caterer. **épicier-~** grocer and caterer.

traître, traîtresse [tʀɛtʀ(ə), tʀɛtʀɛs] **1** *adj* **(a)** *personne* treacherous, traitorous; *allure* treacherous; *douceur, paroles* perfidious, treacherous. **être ~ à une cause/à sa patrie** to be a traitor to a cause/one's country, betray a cause/one's country.

(b) (*fig: dangereux*) *animal* vicious; *vin* deceptive; *escalier, virage* treacherous.

(c) (*loc*) **ne pas dire un ~ mot** not to breathe a (single) word.

2 *nm* **(a)** (*gén*) traitor; (*Théât*) villain.

(b) (†: *perfide*) scoundrel†.

(c) en ~: prendre/attaquer qn en ~ to play an underhand trick/make an insidious attack on sb.

3 traîtresse *nf* traitress.

traîtreusement [tʀɛtʀøzmɑ̃] *adv* treacherously.

traîtrise [tʀɛtʀiz] *nf* **(a)** (*U*) treachery, treacherousness. **(b)** (*acte*) (piece of) treachery; (*danger*) treacherousness (*U*), peril.

trajectoire [tʀaʒɛktwaʀ] *nf* (*gén*) trajectory; *[projectile]* path, trajectory (*T*).

trajet [tʀaʒɛ] *nm* **(a)** (*distance à parcourir*) distance; (*itinéraire*) route; (*parcours, voyage*) journey; (*par mer*) voyage. **un ~ de 8 km** a distance of 8 km; **choisir le ~ le plus long** to choose the longest route *ou* way; **elle fait à pied le court ~ de son bureau à la gare** she walks the short distance from her office to the station; **le ~ aller/retour** the outward/return journey; **faire le ~ de Paris à Lyon en voiture/train** to do the journey from Paris to Lyons by car/train; **le ~ par mer est plus intéressant** the sea voyage *ou* crossing is more interesting; (*fig*) **quel ~ il a parcouru depuis son dernier roman!** what a long way he has come since his last novel!

(b) (*Anat*) *[nerf, artère]* course; (*Méd*) *[projectile]* path. **le ~ de la balle passe très près du cœur** the path taken by the bullet passes very close to the heart.

tralala* [tʀalala] *nm* (*luxe, apprêts*) fuss (*U*), frills*; (*accessoires*) fripperies. **faire du ~** to make a lot of fuss; **en grand ~** with all the works*, with a great deal of fuss; **avec tout le ~** with all the frills* *ou* trimmings.

tram [tʀam] *nm* = **tramway.**

tramail [tʀamaj] *nm* trammel (net).

trame [tʀam] *nf* **(a)** *[tissu]* weft, woof. **usé jusqu'à la ~** threadbare. **(b)** (*fig*) *[roman]* framework; *[vie]* web, texture. **(c)** (*Typ: quadrillage*) screen; (*TV: lignes*) frame.

tramer [tʀame] (1) *vt* **(a)** *évasion, coup d'État* to plot; *complot* to hatch, weave (*littér*). **il se trame quelque chose** there's something brewing. **(b)** (*Tex*) to weave. **(c)** (*Typ*) to screen.

tramontane [tʀamɔ̃tan] *nf* tramontana. **perdre la ~**† to go off one's head, lose one's wits.

tramp [tʀɑ̃p] *nm* tramp (*ship*).

tramway [tʀamwɛ] *nm* (*moyen de transport*) tram(way); (*voiture*) tram(car).

tranchant, e [tʀɑ̃ʃɑ̃, ɑ̃t] **1** *adj* **(a)** *couteau, arête* sharp. **du côté ~/non ~** with the cutting/blunt edge.
(b) (*fig*) *personne, ton* assertive, peremptory.
2 *nm* **(a)** *[couteau]* cutting edge. **avec le ~ de la main** with the edge of one's hand; *V* **double.**
(b) (*instrument*) *[apiculteur]* scraper; *[tanneur]* fleshing knife.
(c) (*fig*) *[argument, réprimande]* force, impact.

tranche [tʀɑ̃ʃ] *nf* **(a)** (*portion*) *[pain, jambon, rôti]* slice; *[bacon]* rasher. **~ de bœuf** beefsteak; **~ de veau** veal cutlet; **~ de saumon** salmon steak; **~ napolitaine** neapolitan slice; **en ~s** sliced, in slices; **couper en ~s** to slice, cut into slices.
(b) (*bord*) *[livre, pièce de monnaie, planche]* edge; *V* **doré.**
(c) (*section*) (*gén*) section; (*Fin*) *[actions, bons]* block; (*Admin*) *[revenus]* bracket. (*Loterie*) **~ (d'émission)** issue; (*Admin*) **~ d'âge/de salaires** age/wage bracket.
(d) (*Boucherie: morceau*) **~ grasse** silverside; **bifteck dans la ~** ≈ piece of braising steak.

tranché, e[1] [tʀɑ̃ʃe] *adj couleurs* clear, distinct; *opinion, limite* clear-cut, definite.

tranchée[2] [tʀɑ̃ʃe] *nf* **(a)** (*gén, Mil: fossé*) trench; *V* **guerre. (b)** (*Sylviculture*) cutting.

tranchées [tʀɑ̃ʃe] *nfpl* (*Méd*) colic, gripes, tormina (*T*). **~ utérines** after-pains.

tranchefile [tʀɑ̃ʃfil] *nf [reliure]* headband.

trancher [tʀɑ̃ʃe] (1) **1** *vt* **(a)** (*couper*) *corde, nœud, lien* to cut, sever. **~ le cou** *ou* **la tête à** *ou* **de qn** to cut off *ou* sever sb's head; **~ la gorge à qn** to cut *ou* slit sb's throat; (*fig*) **la mort** *ou* **la Parque tranche le fil des jours** death severs *ou* the Fates sever the thread of our days; *V* **nœud.**
(b) (†, *frm: mettre fin à*) *discussion* to conclude, bring to a close. **~ court** *ou* **net** to bring to a firm conclusion; **tranchons là!** let's close the matter there.
(c) (*résoudre*) *question, difficulté* to settle, decide, resolve; (*emploi absolu: décider*) to take a decision. **~ un différend** to settle a difference; **le juge a dû ~/a tranché que** the judge had to make a ruling/ruled that; **il ne faut pas avoir peur de ~** one must not be afraid of taking decisions.
2 *vi* **(a)** (*couper*) (*Méd*) **~ dans le vif** to cut into the flesh; (*fig*) to take drastic action.
(b) (*former contraste avec*) *[couleur]* to stand out clearly (*sur, avec* against); *[trait, qualité]* to contrast strongly *ou* sharply (*sur, avec* with). **cette vallée sombre tranche sur le paysage environnant** this dark valley stands out against the surrounding countryside; **la journée du dimanche a tranché sur une semaine très agitée** Sunday formed a sharp contrast to a very busy week.

tranchet [tʀɑ̃ʃɛ] *nm [bourrelier, sellier]* leather knife; *[plombier]* hacking knife.

tranchoir [tʀɑ̃ʃwaʀ] *nm* **(a)** (*Culin*) (*plateau*) trencher†, platter; (*couteau*) chopper.
(b) (*Zool*) zanclus.

tranquille [tʀɑ̃kil] *adj* **(a)** (*calme*) *eau, mer, air* quiet, tranquil (*littér*); *sommeil* gentle, peaceful, tranquil (*littér*); *vie, journée, vacances* peaceful, tranquil (*littér*), quiet; *endroit* quiet, peaceful, tranquil (*littér*). **un ~ bien-être l'envahissait** a feeling of quiet *ou* calm well-being was creeping over him; **c'est l'heure la plus ~ de la journée** it's the quietest *ou* most peaceful time of day; **aller/entrer d'un pas ~** to walk/enter calmly.
(b) (*assuré*) *courage, conviction,* quiet. **avec une ~ assurance** with quiet assurance.
(c) (*paisible*) *tempérament, personne* quiet, placid; *voisins, enfants, élèves* quiet. (*non affairé, dérangé*) **être ~** to have some peace; **rester/se tenir ~** to stay/be quiet; **pour une fois qu'il est ~** when he's quiet for once; **nous étions bien ~s et il a fallu qu'il nous dérange** we were having a nice quiet time and he had to come and disturb us; **ferme la porte, j'aime être ~ après le repas** close the door — I like (to have) some peace after my meal; **laisser qn ~** to leave sb alone, to leave sb in peace, give sb a bit of peace; **laisser qch ~** to leave sth alone; **laisse-le donc ~, tu vois bien qu'il travaille/qu'il est moins fort que toi** leave him alone *ou* let him be* — you can see he's working/not as strong as you are; **laissez-moi ~ avec vos questions** stop bothering me with your questions; *V* **père.**
(d) (*rassuré*) **être ~** to feel *ou* be easy in one's mind; **tu peux être ~** you needn't worry, you can set your mind at rest; **il a l'esprit ~** his mind is at rest, he has an easy mind; **pour avoir l'esprit ~** to set my (*ou* his *etc*) mind at rest; **avoir la conscience ~** to be at peace with one's conscience, have an easy conscience; **pouvoir dormir ~** to be able to sleep easy (in one's bed); **comme cela, nous serons ~s** that way our minds will be at rest; **soyez ~, tout ira bien** set your mind at rest *ou* don't worry — everything will be all right; **maintenant je peux mourir ~** now I can die in peace *ou* with an easy conscience.
(e) (*: *certain*) **être ~ (que ...)** to be sure (that ...); (*iro*) **soyez ~, je me vengerai** don't (you) worry *ou* rest assured — I shall have my revenge; **il n'ira pas, je suis ~** he won't go, I'm sure of it; **tu peux être ~ que ...** you may be sure that ..., rest assured that ... .
(f) (*Pharm*) **baume ~** soothing balm.

tranquillement [tʀɑ̃kilmɑ̃] *adv* (*V* **tranquille**) quietly; tranquilly; gently; peacefully; placidly. **il vivait ~ dans la plus grande abjection** he lived quietly *ou* at peace in the most utter abjection; **on peut y aller ~: ça ne risque plus rien*** we can go ahead safely — there's no risk now.

tranquillisant, e [tʀɑ̃kilizɑ̃, ɑ̃t] **1** *adj nouvelle* reassuring; *effet, produit* soothing, tranquillizing. **2** *nm* (*Méd*) tranquillizer.

tranquilliser [tʀɑ̃kilize] (1) *vt*: **~ qn** to reassure sb, set sb's mind at rest; **se ~** to set one's mind at rest.

tranquillité [tʀɑ̃kilite] *nf* **(a)** (*calme: V* **tranquille**) quietness; tranquillity; gentleness; peacefulness. **en toute ~** without being bothered *ou* disturbed; **troubler la ~ publique** to disturb the peace.
(b) (*sérénité*) peace, tranquillity.
(c) (*absence d'agitation, ordre*) peace. **travailler dans la ~** to work in peace (and quiet).
(d) (*absence de souci*) **~ (d'esprit)** peace of mind; **~ matérielle** material security; **en toute ~** with complete peace of mind, free from all anxiety.

trans ... [tʀɑ̃z] *préf* trans ... .

transaction [tʀɑ̃zaksjɔ̃] *nf* **(a)** (*Comm*) transaction. **(b)** (*Jur: compromis*) settlement, compromise (*out of court*).

transactionnel, -elle [tʀɑ̃zaksjɔnɛl] *adj* (*Jur*) compromise (*épith*), settlement (*épith*). **formule ~le** compromise formula; **règlement ~** compromise settlement.

transafricain, e [tʀɑ̃zafʀikɛ̃, ɛn] *adj* transafrican.

transalpin, e [tʀɑ̃zalpɛ̃, in] *adj* transalpine.

transaméricain, e [tʀɑ̃zameʀikɛ̃, ɛn] *adj* transamerican (*épith*).

transat [tʀɑ̃zat] *nm abrév de* **transatlantique.**

transatlantique [tʀɑ̃zatlɑ̃tik] **1** *adj* transatlantic. **2** *nm* (*paquebot*) transatlantic liner; (*fauteuil*) deckchair.

transbahuter* [tʀɑ̃zbayte] (1) **1** *vt* to shift, hump along*, lug along*. **2 se transbahuter** *vpr* to trapes along*, lug o.s. along*.

transbordement [tʀɑ̃sbɔʀdəmɑ̃] *nm* (*V* **transborder**) tran(s)shipment; transfer.

transborder [tʀɑ̃sbɔʀde] (1) *vt* (*Naut*) to tran(s)ship; (*Rail*) to transfer.

transbordeur [tʀɑ̃sbɔʀdœʀ] *nm*: **(pont) ~** transporter bridge.

transcanadien, -ienne [tʀɑ̃skanadjɛ̃, jɛn] *adj* Trans-Canada (*épith*).

transcendance [tʀɑ̃sɑ̃dɑ̃s] *nf* (*Philos*) transcendence, transcendency; (*littér*, †: *excellence*) transcendence (*littér*); (*fait de se surpasser*) self-transcendence (*littér*).

transcendant, e [tʀɑ̃sɑ̃dɑ̃, ɑ̃t] *adj* **(a)** (*littér: sublime*) *génie, mérite* transcendent (*littér*). **(b)** (*Philos*) transcendent(al). **être ~ à** to transcend. **(c)** (*Math*) transcendental.

transcendantal, e, mpl -aux [tʀɑ̃sɑ̃dɑ̃tal, o] *adj* transcendental.

transcendantalisme [tʀɑ̃sɑ̃dɑ̃talism(ə)] *nm* transcendentalism.

transcender [tʀɑ̃sɑ̃de] (1) **1** *vt* to transcend. **2 se transcender** *vpr* to transcend o.s.

transcodage [tʀɑ̃skɔdaʒ] *nm* (code) conversion.

transcoder [tʀɑ̃skɔde] (1) *vt* (*Ordinateurs*) *programme* to convert.

transcontinental, e, mpl -aux [tʀɑ̃skɔ̃tinɑ̃tal, o] *adj* transcontinental.

transcripteur [tʀɑ̃skʀiptœʀ] *nm* transcriber.

transcription [tʀɑ̃skʀipsjɔ̃] *nf* **(a)** (*U: V* **transcrire**) copying out; transcription; transliteration. **(b)** (*copie*) copy; (*translittération*) transcript; (*Mus*) transcription. **~ phonétique** phonetic transcription.

transcrire [tʀɑ̃skʀiʀ] (39) *vt* **(a)** (*copier*) to copy out, transcribe (*frm*). **(b)** (*translittérer*) to transcribe, transliterate. **(c)** (*Mus*) to transcribe.

transe [tʀɑ̃s] *nf* **(a)** (*état second*) trance. **être en ~** to be in a trance; **entrer en ~** (*lit*) to go into a trance; (*fig: s'énerver*) to go into a rage, see red*.
(b) (*affres*) **~s** agony; **être dans les ~s** to be in *ou* suffer agony, go through agony; **être dans les ~s de l'attente/des examens** to be in agonies of anticipation/over the exams.

transept [tʀɑ̃sɛpt] *nm* transept.

transfèrement [tʀɑ̃sfɛʀmɑ̃] *nm [prisonnier]* transfer. **~ cellulaire** transfer by prison van.

transférer [tʀɑ̃sfeʀe] (6) *vt* **(a)** *fonctionnaire, assemblée, bureaux* to transfer, move; *prisonnier,* (*Sport*) *joueur* to transfer; *dépouille mortelle, reliques, évêque* to transfer, translate (*frm, littér*).
(b) *capitaux* to transfer, move; *propriété, droit* to transfer, convey (*T*); (*Comptabilité: par virement etc*) to transfer.
(c) (*fig, Psych*) to transfer. **~ des sentiments sur qn** to transfer feelings onto sb.

transfert [tʀɑ̃sfɛʀ] *nm* **(a)** (*V* **transférer**) transfer; translation; conveyance. **(b)** (*Psych*) transference.

transfiguration [tʀɑ̃sfigyʀɑsjɔ̃] *nf* transfiguration.

transfigurer [tʀɑ̃sfigyʀe] (1) *vt* (*transformer*) to transform, transfigure (*frm*); (*Rel*) to transfigure.

transfo* [tʀɑ̃sfo] *nm abrév de* **transformateur.**

transformable [tʀɑ̃sfɔʀmabl(ə)] *adj structure, canapé* convertible; *aspect* transformable; (*Rugby*) *essai* convertible.

transformateur, -trice [tʀɑ̃sfɔʀmatœʀ, tʀis] **1** *adj processus* transformation (*épith*); *action* transforming (*épith*). **pouvoir ~** power to transform. **2** *nm* transformer.

transformation [tʀɑ̃sfɔʀmɑsjɔ̃] *nf* **(a)** (*action, résultat: V* **transformer**) change; alteration; conversion; transformation. **travaux de ~, ~s** conversion work; **depuis son mariage, nous assistons chez lui à une véritable ~** since he married we have seen a real transformation in him *ou* a complete change come over him; *V* **industrie.**
(b) (*Rugby*) conversion.

(c) (*Géom, Math*) transformation.
transformationnel, -elle [tʀɑ̃sfɔʀmasjɔnɛl] *adj* transformational.
transformer [tʀɑ̃sfɔʀme] (1) **1** *vt* **(a)** (*modifier*) *personne, caractère* to change, alter; *maison, magasin, matière première* to convert; *vêtement* to alter, remake; (*changer radicalement, améliorer*) *personne, caractère, pays* to transform. **le bonheur/son séjour à la montagne l'a transformé** happiness/his holiday in the mountains has transformed him *ou* made a new man of him; **rêver de ~ la société/les hommes** to dream of transforming society/men; **depuis qu'il va à l'école, il est transformé** since he's been at school he has been a different child.
(b) ~ qn/qch en to turn sb/sth into; **~ la houille en énergie** to convert coal into energy; **~ du plomb en or** to turn *ou* change *ou* transmute lead into gold; **on a transformé la grange en atelier** the barn has been converted into a studio; **elle a fait ~ son manteau en jaquette** she's had her coat made into a jacket; **elle a transformé leur pavillon en palais** she has transformed their house into a palace.
(c) (*Rugby*) *essai* to convert.
(d) (*Géom, Math*) to transform.
2 se tranformer *vpr* (*Bot, Zool*) *[larve, embryon]* to be transformed, transform itself; (*Chim, Phys*) *[énergie, matière]* to be converted; *[personne, pays]* to change, alter; (*radicalement*) to be transformed. **se ~ en** to be transformed into; to be converted into; to change *ou* turn into; **la chenille se transforme en papillon** the caterpillar transforms itself *ou* turns into a butterfly; **il s'est transformé en agneau** he has turned *ou* been transformed into a lamb; **la ville s'est étonnamment transformée en 2 ans** the town has changed astonishingly in 2 years *ou* has undergone astonishing changes in 2 years; **il s'est bien transformé depuis qu'il a ce poste** there's been a real transformation *ou* change in him *ou* a real change has come over him since he has had this job.
transformisme [tʀɑ̃sfɔʀmism(ə)] *nm* transformism.
transformiste [tʀɑ̃sfɔʀmist(ə)] *adj, nmf* transformist.
transfuge [tʀɑ̃sfyʒ] *nmf* (*Mil, Pol*) renegade.
transfuser [tʀɑ̃sfyze] (1) *vt sang, liquide* to transfuse; (*fig littér*) to transfuse (*littér*) (*à* into), instil (*à* into), impart (*à* to).
transfusion [tʀɑ̃sfyzjɔ̃] *nf*: **~ (sanguine)** (blood) transfusion.
transgresser [tʀɑ̃sgʀese] (1) *vt règle, code* to infringe, contravene, transgress (*littér*); *ordre* to disobey, go against, contravene.
transgresseur [tʀɑ̃sgʀesœʀ] *nm* (*littér*) transgressor (*littér*).
transgression [tʀɑ̃sgʀesjɔ̃] *nf* (*V* **transgresser**) infringement; contravention; transgression; disobedience.
transhumance [tʀɑ̃zymɑ̃s] *nf* transhumance.
transhumant, e [tʀɑ̃zymɑ̃, ɑ̃t] *adj* transhumant.
transhumer [tʀɑ̃zyme] (1) *vti* to move to new pastures (for the summer).
transi, e [tʀɑ̃zi] (*ptp de* **transir**) *adj*: **être ~ (de froid)** to be numb with cold *ou* chilled to the bone *ou* frozen to the marrow; **être ~ de peur** to be paralyzed by fear, be transfixed *ou* numbed with fear; *V* **amoureux.**
transiger [tʀɑ̃ziʒe] (3) *vi* **(a)** (*Jur, gén: dans un différend*) to compromise, come to terms *ou* an agreement.
(b) (*fig*) **~ avec/sur qch: ~ avec sa conscience** to come to a compromise *ou* make a deal with one's conscience; **~ avec le devoir** to come to a compromise with duty; **ne pas ~ sur l'honneur/le devoir** to make no compromise in matters of honour/duty; **je me refuse à ~ sur ce point** I refuse to compromise on this point, I am adamant on this point.
transir [tʀɑ̃ziʀ] (2) *vt* (*littér*) *[froid]* to chill to the bone, numb, freeze to the marrow; *[peur]* to paralyze, transfix, numb.
transistor [tʀɑ̃zistɔʀ] *nm* (*élément, poste de radio*) transistor.
transistorisé, e [tʀɑ̃zistɔʀize] *adj* transistorized.
transit [tʀɑ̃zit] *nm* transit. **en ~** *marchandises, voyageurs* in transit; **de ~** *document, port* transit (*épith*).
transitaire [tʀɑ̃zitɛʀ] **1** *adj pays* of transit; *commerce* which is done in transit. **2** *nmf* forwarding agent.
transiter [tʀɑ̃zite] (1) **1** *vt marchandises* to pass *ou* convey in transit. **2** *vi* to pass in transit.
transitif, -ive [tʀɑ̃zitif, iv] *adj* (*Ling, Philos*) transitive.
transition [tʀɑ̃zisjɔ̃] *nf* (*gén, Art, Ciné, Mus, Sci*) transition. **de ~** *période, mesure* transitional; **sans ~** without any transition.
transitivement [tʀɑ̃zitivmɑ̃] *adv* transitively.
transitivité [tʀɑ̃zitivite] *nf* (*Ling, Philos*) transitivity.
transitoire [tʀɑ̃zitwaʀ] *adj* **(a)** (*fugitif*) transitory, transient. **(b)** (*de transition*) *régime, mesures* transitional, provisional; *fonction* interim (*épith*), provisional.
transitoirement [tʀɑ̃zitwaʀmɑ̃] *adv* (*V* **transitoire**) transitorily; transiently; provisionally.
Transjordanie [tʀɑ̃sʒɔʀdani] *nf* Transjordania, Transjordan.
translation [tʀɑ̃slɑsjɔ̃] *nf* **(a)** (*Admin*) *[tribunal, évêque]* translation (*frm*), transfer; (*Jur*) *[droit, propriété]* transfer, conveyance; (*littér*) *[dépouille, cendres]* translation (*frm, littér*); (*Rel*) *[fête]* transfer, translation (*frm*).
(b) (*Géom, Sci*) translation. **mouvement de ~** translatory movement.
translit(t)ération [tʀɑ̃sliteʀɑsjɔ̃] *nf* transliteration.
translit(t)érer [tʀɑ̃sliteʀe] (6) *vt* to transliterate.
translucide [tʀɑ̃slysid] *adj* translucent.
translucidité [tʀɑ̃slysidite] *nf* translucence, translucency.
transmetteur [tʀɑ̃smɛtœʀ] *nm* (*Téléc*) transmitter. (*Naut*) **~ d'ondes** speaking tube.
transmettre [tʀɑ̃smɛtʀ(ə)] (56) *vt* **(a)** (*léguer*) *biens, secret, tradition, autorité* to hand down, pass on; *qualité* to pass on; (*transférer*) *biens, titre, autorité* to pass on, hand over, transmit (*frm*); (*communiquer*) *secret, recette* to pass on. **sa mère lui avait transmis le goût de la nature** his mother had passed her love of nature on to him.
(b) *message, ordre, renseignement* to pass on, convey; *lettre, colis* to send on, forward; (*Téléc*) *signal* to transmit; (*Rad, TV*) *émission, discours* to broadcast. **~ sur ondes courtes** (*Téléc*) to transmit on short wave; (*Rad, TV*) to broadcast on short wave; **veuillez ~ mes amitiés à Paul** kindly pass on *ou* convey my best wishes to Paul; **veuillez ~ mon meilleur souvenir à Paul** kindly remember me to Paul.
(c) (*Sport*) *ballon* to pass; *témoin, flambeau* to hand over, pass on.
(d) (*Sci*) *énergie, impulsion* to transmit; (*Méd*) *maladie* to pass on, transmit (*T*); (*Bio*) *microbe* to transmit. **une maladie qui se transmet par contact** an illness passed on *ou* transmitted by contact; **il risque de ~ son rhume aux autres** he's likely to pass on *ou* transmit (*T*) his cold to others.
transmigration [tʀɑ̃smigʀɑsjɔ̃] *nf* transmigration.
transmigrer [tʀɑ̃smigʀe] (1) *vi* to transmigrate.
transmissibilité [tʀɑ̃smisibilite] *nf* transmissibility.
transmissible [tʀɑ̃smisibl(ə)] *adj patrimoine, droit, caractère* transmissible, transmittable.
transmission [tʀɑ̃smisjɔ̃] *nf* **(a)** (*U: V* **transmettre**) handing down; passing on; handing over; transmission; conveying; sending on, forwarding; broadcasting; passing. (*Aut, Tech*) **les organes de ~, la ~** the parts of the transmission system, the transmission; (*Pol*) **~ des pouvoirs** handing over *ou* transfer of power; *V* **arbre, courroie.**
(b) (*Mil: service*) **~s** = Signals (corps).
(c) ~ de pensée thought transfer, telepathy.
transmuer [tʀɑ̃smɥe] (1) *vt* (*Chim, littér*) to transmute.
transmutabilité [tʀɑ̃smytabilite] *nf* transmutability.
transmutation [tʀɑ̃smytɑsjɔ̃] *nf* (*Chim, Phys, littér*) transmutation.
transmuter [tʀɑ̃smyte] (1) *vt* = **transmuer.**
transnational, e, *mpl* **-aux** [tʀɑ̃snasjɔnal, o] *adj* transnational.
transocéanien, -ienne [tʀɑ̃zɔseanjɛ̃, jɛn] *adj*, **transocéanique** [tʀɑ̃zɔseanik] *adj* transoceanic.
transparaître [tʀɑ̃spaʀɛtʀ(ə)] (57) *vi* to show (through).
transparence [tʀɑ̃spaʀɑ̃s] *nf* **(a)** (*V* **transparent**) transparency, transparence; limpidity; clearness. **regarder qch par ~** to look at sth against the light; **voir qch par ~** to see sth showing through; **éclairé par ~** with the light shining through.
(b) (*Ciné*) back projection.
transparent, e [tʀɑ̃spaʀɑ̃, ɑ̃t] **1** *adj* **(a)** (*lit*) *verre, porcelaine* transparent; *papier, tissu* transparent, see-through*.
(b) (*diaphane*) *eau, ciel* transparent, limpid; *teint, âme, personne* transparent; *regard, yeux* transparent, limpid, clear.
(c) (*fig: évident*) *allusion, sentiment, intentions* transparent, evident.
2 *nm* **(a)** (*écran*) transparent screen (*lit from behind, for decoration*).
(b) (*Archit*) openwork motif (*to be seen against the light*).
(c) (*feuille réglée*) ruled sheet (*placed under writing paper*).
transpercer [tʀɑ̃spɛʀse] (3) *vt* **(a)** (*d'un coup d'épée*) to run through, transfix; (*d'un coup de couteau*) to stab; *[épée, lame]* to pierce; *[balle]* to go through. (*fig*) **transpercé de douleur** pierced by sorrow; (*fig*) **~ qn du regard** to give sb a piercing look.
(b) *[froid, pluie]* to go through, pierce. **malgré nos chandails, le froid nous transperçait** despite our jumpers, the cold was going *ou* cutting straight through us; **la pluie avait finalement transpercé ma pèlerine/la toile de tente** the rain had finally come through *ou* penetrated my cape/the tent roof.
transpiration [tʀɑ̃spiʀɑsjɔ̃] *nf* (*processus*) perspiration, perspiring; (*Bot*) transpiration; (*sueur*) perspiration, sweat. **être en ~** to be perspiring *ou* sweating *ou* in a sweat.
transpirer [tʀɑ̃spiʀe] (1) *vi* **(a)** (*lit*) to perspire, sweat; (*Bot*) to transpire; (*: *travailler dur*) to sweat over sth*. **il transpire des mains/pieds** his hands/feet perspire *ou* sweat, he has sweaty hands/feet; **~ à grosses gouttes** to be running *ou* streaming with sweat; **~ sur un devoir*** to sweat over an exercise*.
(b) (*fig*) *[secret, projet, détails]* to come to light, leak out. **rien n'a transpiré** nothing came to light, nothing leaked out.
transplant [tʀɑ̃splɑ̃] *nm* (*Bio*) transplant.
transplantable [tʀɑ̃splɑ̃tabl(ə)] *adj* transplantable.
transplantation [tʀɑ̃splɑ̃tɑsjɔ̃] *nf [arbre, peuple, traditions]* transplantation, transplanting; (*Méd*) (*technique*) transplantation; (*intervention*) transplant. **~ cardiaque/du rein** heart/kidney transplant.
transplantement [tʀɑ̃splɑ̃tmɑ̃] *nm* (*rare*, †) = **transplantation.**
transplanter [tʀɑ̃splɑ̃te] (1) *vt* (*Bot, Méd, fig*) to transplant. **se ~ dans un pays lointain** to uproot o.s. and move to a faraway country.
transport [tʀɑ̃spɔʀ] **1** *nm* **(a)** (*U: V* **transporter**) carrying; moving; transport(ation), conveying; conveyance; bringing; carrying over, transposition. (*Rail*) **~ de voyageurs/marchandises** passenger/goods transportation, conveyance *ou* transport of passengers/goods; **un car se chargera du ~ des bagages** the luggage will be taken by coach; **pour faciliter le ~ des blessés** to facilitate the transport of the injured, to enable the injured to be moved more easily; **le ~ des blessés graves pose de nombreux problèmes** transporting *ou* moving seriously injured people poses many problems; **endommagé pendant le ~** damaged in transit; **~ maritime** *ou* **par mer** sea transport(ation), transport(ation) by sea; **~ par train** *ou* **rail** rail transport(ation), transport(ation) by rail; **~ par air** *ou* **avion** air transport(ation); (*Mil*) **~ de troupes** (*action*) troop transportation; (*navire, train*) troop transport; **entreprise de ~(s)** transport business; **matériel/frais de ~** transportation equipment/costs; *V* **avion, moyen.**

(b) les ~s transport; **~s publics** *ou* **en commun** public transport; **~s urbains** city *ou* urban transport; **~s fluviaux** transport by inland waterway; **~(s) routier(s)** road haulage *ou* transport; **~s aériens/maritimes** air/sea transport.

(c) (*littér, hum: manifestation d'émotion*) transport. **(avec) des ~s de joie/d'enthousiasme** (with) transports of delight/enthusiasm; **~ de colère** fit of rage *ou* anger; **~ au cerveau** seizure, stroke; **~s amoureux** amorous transports.

2: (*Jur*) **transport de justice, transport sur les lieux** *visit by public prosecutor's department to scene of crime etc.*

transportable [tʀɑ̃spɔʀtabl(ə)] *adj marchandise* transportable; *blessé, malade* fit to be moved (*attrib*).

transporter [tʀɑ̃spɔʀte] (1) **1** *vt* **(a)** (*à la main, à dos*) to carry, move; (*avec un véhicule*) *marchandises, voyageurs* to transport, carry, convey; (*Tech*) *énergie, son* to carry. **le car transportait les écoliers/touristes** the coach was carrying schoolchildren/tourists, the coach had schoolchildren/tourists on board; **le camion a transporté les soldats/le matériel au camp de base** the lorry took *ou* conveyed the soldiers/the equipment to base camp; **on a transporté le blessé à l'hôpital** the injured man was taken *ou* transported to hospital; **on l'a transporté d'urgence à l'hôpital** he was rushed to hospital; **~ des marchandises par terre/mer** to transport *ou* carry *ou* convey goods by land/sea; **~ des marchandises par train/avion** to transport *ou* convey goods by train/plane; **ils ont dû ~ tout le matériel à bras** they had to move all the equipment by hand; **le sable/vin est transporté par péniche** the sand/wine is transported *ou* carried by barge; **elle transportait une forte somme d'argent** she was carrying a large sum of money; (*fig*) **cette musique nous transporte dans un autre monde/siècle** this music transports us into another world/century.

(b) (*transférer*) *traditions, conflit* to carry, bring; *thème, idée* to carry over, transpose. **~ la guerre/la maladie dans un autre pays** to carry *ou* spread war/disease into another country; **~ un fait divers à l'écran** to bring a news item to the screen; **~ une somme d'un compte à un autre** to transfer a sum of money from one account to another; **dans sa traduction, il transporte la scène à Moscou** in his translation, he shifts the scene to Moscow.

(c) (*littér: agiter, exalter*) to carry away, send into raptures (*littér*). **~ qn de joie/d'enthousiasme** to send sb into raptures *ou* transports (*hum, littér*) of delight/enthusiasm; **être** *ou* **se sentir transporté de joie/d'admiration** to be in transports (*hum, littér*) of delight/admiration, be carried away with delight/admiration; **transporté de fureur** beside o.s. with fury; **cette musique m'a transporté** this music carried me away *ou* sent me into raptures.

2 se transporter *vpr* (*se déplacer*) to betake o.s. (*frm*), repair (*frm*). (*Jur*) **le parquet s'est transporté sur les lieux** the public prosecutor's office visited the scene; **se ~ quelque part par la pensée** to transport o.s. somewhere in imagination, let one's imagination carry one away somewhere.

transporteur [tʀɑ̃spɔʀtœʀ] *nm* **(a)** (*entrepreneur*) haulier (*Brit*), haulage contractor, carrier; (*Jur: partie contractante*) carrier. **(b)** (*Tech: appareil*) conveyor.

transposable [tʀɑ̃spozabl(ə)] *adj* transposable.

transposer [tʀɑ̃spoze] (1) *vt* to transpose.

transposition [tʀɑ̃spozisjɔ̃] *nf* transposition.

transrhénan, e [tʀɑ̃sʀenɑ̃, an] *adj* transrhenane.

transsaharien, -ienne [tʀɑ̃ssaaʀjɛ̃, jɛn] *adj* trans-Saharan.

transsibérien, -enne [tʀɑ̃ssibeʀjɛ̃, ɛn] *adj* trans-Siberian. **le ~** the Trans-Siberian Railway.

transsubstantiation [tʀɑ̃ssypstɑ̃sjasjɔ̃] *nf* transubstantiation.

transvasement [tʀɑ̃svazmɑ̃] *nm* decanting.

transvaser [tʀɑ̃svaze] (1) *vt* to decant.

transversal, e, mpl -aux [tʀɑ̃svɛʀsal, o] *adj coupe, fibre, pièce, barre* cross (*épith*), transverse (*T*); *mur, chemin, rue* which runs across *ou* at right angles; *vallée* transverse. (*Aut, Transport*) **axe ~, liaison ~e** cross-country trunk road (*Brit*) *ou* highway (*US*), cross-country link.

transversalement [tʀɑ̃svɛʀsalmɑ̃] *adv* across, crosswise, transversely (*T*).

transverse [tʀɑ̃svɛʀs(ə)] *adj* (*Anat*) transverse.

transvestisme [tʀɑ̃svɛstism(ə)] *nm* = **travestisme.**

trapèze [tʀapɛz] *nm* **(a)** (*Géom*) trapezium (*Brit*), trapezoid (*US*). **(b)** (*Sport*) trapeze. **~ volant** flying trapeze; **faire du ~** to perform on the trapeze. **(c)** (*Anat*) **(muscle) ~** trapezius (muscle).

trapéziste [tʀapezist(ə)] *nmf* trapeze artist.

trapézoïdal, e, mpl -aux [tʀapezɔidal, o] *adj* trapezoidal.

trappe [tʀap] *nf* **(a)** (*dans le plancher*) trap door; (*Tech: d'accès, d'évacuation*) hatch; (*Théât*) trap door; (*Aviat: pour parachute*) exit door. **(b)** (*piège*) trap.

Trappe [tʀap] *nf* (*couvent*) Trappist monastery; (*ordre*) Trappist order.

trappeur [tʀapœʀ] *nm* trapper, fur trader.

trappiste [tʀapist(ə)] *nm* Trappist (monk).

trapu, e [tʀapy] *adj* **(a)** *personne* squat, stocky, thickset; *maison* squat. **(b)** (*arg Scol: calé*) *élève* brainy*, terrific*; *question, problème* rough, tough. **une question ~e** a stinker* of a question, a really tough question, a poser*; **il est ~ en latin** he's terrific* at Latin.

traquenard [tʀaknaʀ] *nm* (*piège*) trap; (*fig*) *[grammaire, loi]* pitfall, trap.

traquer [tʀake] (1) *vt gibier* to track (down); *fugitif* to track down, run to earth, hunt down; (*fig littér*) *abus, injustice* to hunt down; (*harceler*) *[journalistes, percepteur etc]* to hound, pursue. **air/regard de bête traquée** look/gaze of a hunted animal; **c'était maintenant un homme traqué, aux abois** he was now at bay, a hunted man.

trauma [tʀoma] *nm* (*Méd, Psych*) trauma.

traumatique [tʀomatik] *adj* traumatic.

traumatisant, e [tʀomatizɑ̃, ɑ̃t] *adj* traumatizing.

traumatiser [tʀomatize] (1) *vt* to traumatize.

traumatisme [tʀomatism(ə)] *nm* traumatism. **~ crânien** cranial traumatism.

traumatologie [tʀomatɔlɔʒi] *nf* traumatology.

traumatologique [tʀomatɔlɔʒik] *adj* traumatological.

travail[1], *pl* **-aux** [tʀavaj, o] **1** *nm* **(a)** (*U: labeur, tâches à accomplir*) work. **~ intellectuel** brainwork, intellectual work; **~ manuel** manual work; **~ musculaire** heavy labour; **fatigue due au ~ scolaire** tiredness due to school work; **je n'y touche pas: c'est le ~ de l'électricien** I'm not touching it — that's the electrician's job; **observer qn au ~** to watch sb at work *ou* working; **séance/déjeuner de ~** working session/lunch; **ce mouvement demande des semaines de ~** it takes weeks of work to perfect this movement; **avoir du ~/beaucoup de ~** to have (some) work/a lot of work to do; **se mettre au ~** to set to *ou* get down to work; **j'ai un ~ fou en ce moment*** I've got a load of work on at the moment*, I'm up to my eyes in work at the moment*; *V* **cabinet, table.**

(b) (*tâche*) work (*U*), job; (*ouvrage*) work (*U*). **c'est un ~ de spécialiste** (*difficile à faire*) it's work for a specialist, it's a specialist's job; (*bien fait*) it's the work of a specialist; **commencer/achever/interrompre un ~** to start/complete/interrupt a piece of work *ou* a job; **ce n'est pas du ~** that's not work!, (do you) call that work!*; **~aux scientifiques/de recherche** scientific/research work; **~aux sur bois** woodwork; **~aux sur métal** metalwork; **il est l'auteur d'un gros ~ sur le romantisme** he is the author of a sizeable work on romanticism; (*Mil*) **~aux d'approche/de siège** sapping *ou* approach/siege works; **~aux de réfection/de réparation/de construction** renovation/repair/building work; **faire faire des ~aux dans la maison** to have some work *ou* some jobs done in the house; **~aux de plomberie** plumbing work; **~aux d'aménagement** alterations, alteration work; **les ~aux de la ferme** farm work; **les ~aux pénibles, les gros ~aux** the heavy work *ou* tasks; **entreprendre de grands ~aux d'assainissement/d'irrigation** to undertake large-scale sanitation/irrigation work; **'pendant les ~aux, le magasin restera ouvert'** 'business as usual during alterations', 'the shop will remain open (as usual) during alterations'; **attention! ~aux!** caution! work in progress!; (*sur la route*) road works ahead! (*Brit*).

(c) (*métier, profession*) job, occupation; (*situation*) work (*U*), job, situation. (*activité rétribuée*) **le ~** work (*U*); **avoir un ~ intéressant/lucratif** to have an interesting/a highly paid occupation *ou* job; **apprendre un ~** to learn a job; **être sans ~, ne pas avoir de ~** to be out of work *ou* without a job *ou* unemployed; **~ à mi-/plein temps** part-/full-time work; (*Ind*) **accident/conflit/législation du ~** industrial accident/dispute/legislation; **~ de bureau/d'équipe** office/team work; **~ en usine** factory work, work in a factory; **~ en atelier** work in a workshop; **~ à la pièce** *ou* **aux pièces** piecework; **~ à domicile** outwork (*Brit*), homework; **elle a un ~ à domicile/au dehors** she has a job at home/outside, she works at home/goes out to work; (*Ind*) **cesser le ~** to stop work, down tools; **reprendre le ~** to go back to work; *V* **bleu.**

(d) (*Écon: opposé au capital*) labour. **l'exploitation du ~** the exploitation of labour; **association capital-~** cooperation between workers and management *ou* workers and the bosses*; *V* **division.**

(e) (*facture*) work (*U*). **dentelle d'un ~ très fin** finely-worked lace; **sculpture d'un ~ délicat** finely-wrought sculpture; **c'est un très joli ~** it's a very nice piece of craftsmanship *ou* work.

(f) (*façonnage*) *[bois, cuir, fer]* working. (*Peinture*) **le ~ de la pâte** working the paste; **le ~ du marbre requiert une grande habileté** working with marble requires great skill.

(g) *[machine, organe]* (*fonctionnement spécifique*) working(s); (*tâche spécifique*) work, operation. (*Physiol*) **~ musculaire** muscular effort, work of the muscles.

(h) (*effet*) *[gel, érosion, eaux]* work; (*évolution*) *[bois]* warp, warping; *[vin, cidre]* working. **le ~ de l'imagination/l'inconscient** the workings of the imagination/the unconsciorle **~ du temps** the work of time.

(i) (*Phys*) work. **unité de ~** unit of work.

(j) (*Méd*) *[femme]* labour. **femme en ~** woman in labour; **entrer en ~** to go into *ou* start labour; **salle de ~** labour ward.

2: travaux agricoles agricultural *ou* farm work; **travaux d'aiguille** needlework; (*fig*) **travaux d'approche** manoeuvres, manoeuvring; **faire des travaux d'approche** to manoeuvre; (*fig*) **un travail de Bénédictin** a painstaking task; **travail à la chaîne** assembly line *ou* production line work; **travaux des champs = travaux agricoles; travaux de dame** handwork; (*Scol, Univ*) **travaux dirigés** supervised practical work; (*fig*) **un travail de forçat** hard labour (*fig*); **travaux forcés** hard labour; **les travaux d'Hercule** the labours of Hercules; (*Scol*) **travaux manuels** handicrafts; **travaux ménagers** housework; **travail noir** moonlighting; (*Scol, Univ*) **travaux pratiques** practical work; **travaux préparatoires** *[projet de loi]* preliminary documents; **travaux publics** public works; (*administration*) public works department; **un travail de Romain** a Herculean task.

travail[2] [tʀavaj] *nm* (*appareil*) trave.

travaillé, e [tʀavaje] (*ptp de* **travailler**) *adj* **(a)** (*façonné*) *bois, cuivre* worked, wrought.

(b) (*fignolé*) *style, phrases* polished, studied; *meuble, ornement* intricate, finely-worked.

(c) (*tourmenté*) **~ par le remords/la peur/la jalousie** tormented *ou* distracted by remorse/fear/jealousy.

travailler [tʀavaje] (1) **1** *vi* **(a)** (*faire sa besogne*) to work. **~**

dur/d'arrache-pied to work hard/flat out*; ~ **comme un forçat/une bête de somme** to work like a galley slave/a horse *ou* a Trojan; **il aime ~ au jardin** he likes working in the garden; **je vais ~ un peu à la bibliothèque** I'm going to do some work in the library; **faire ~ sa tête** *ou* **sa matière grise** to set one's mind *ou* the grey matter to work; **faire ~ ses bras** to exercise one's arms; ~ **du chapeau*** to be slightly dotty*; **va ~** (go and) get on with your work.

(b) (*exercer un métier*) to work. ~ **en usine** to work in a factory; ~ **à domicile** to work at home; ~ **aux pièces** to do piece work; **tu pourras te l'offrir quand tu travailleras** you'll be able to buy *ou* afford it once you start work; **il a commencé à ~ chez X hier** he started work *ou* he went to work at X's yesterday; **sa femme travaille** his wife goes out to work, his wife works; **on finit de ~ à 17 heures** we finish *ou* stop work at 5 o'clock.

(c) (*s'exercer*) *[artiste, acrobate]* to practise, train; *[boxeur]* to have a workout, train; *[musicien]* to practise. ~ **sans filet** (*lit*) to work without a safety net; (*fig*) to be out on one's own, risk one's neck.

(d) (*agir, fonctionner*) *[firme, argent]* to work. **l'industrie travaille pour le pays** industry works for the country; ~ **à perte** to work *ou* be working at a loss; **faire ~ l'argent** to make one's money work for one; **le temps travaille pour/contre eux** time is on their side/against them.

(e) *[métal, bois]* to warp; *[vin, cidre]* to work, ferment; *[pâte]* to work, rise; (*fig*) *[imagination]* to work.

2 *vt* **(a)** (*façonner*) *matière, verre, fer* to work, shape. ~ **la terre** to work *ou* cultivate the land; ~ **la pâte** (*Culin*) to knead *ou* work the dough; (*Peinture*) to work the paste.

(b) (*potasser*) *branche, discipline* to work at *ou* on; *morceau de musique* to work on, practise; (*fignoler*) *style, phrase* to polish up, work on; (*Sport*) *mouvement, coup* to work on. ~ **le chant/piano** to practise singing/the piano; ~ **son piano/violon** to do one's piano/violin practice; (*Tennis*) ~ **une balle** to put some spin on a ball.

(c) (*agir sur*) *personne* to work on. ~ **l'opinion/les esprits** to work on public opinion/people's minds; (*Boxe*) ~ **qn au corps** to punch sb around the body.

(d) (*faire s'exercer*) *taureau, cheval* to work.

(e) (*préoccuper*) *[doutes, faits]* to distract, worry; (*tourmenter*) *[douleur, fièvre]* to distract, torment. **cette idée/ce projet le travaille** this idea/plan is on his mind *ou* is preying on his mind.

3 travailler à *vt indir livre, projet* to work on; *cause, but* to work for; (*s'efforcer d'obtenir*) to work towards. ~ **à la perte de qn** to work towards sb's downfall, endeavour to bring about sb's downfall; ~ **à nuire à qn** to endeavour to harm sb.

travailleur, -euse [travajœr, øz] **1** *adj* (*consciencieux*) hard-working.

2 *nm,f* **(a)** (*gén*) worker. **un bon/mauvais ~, une bonne/mauvaise ~euse** a good/bad worker.

(b) (*personne consciencieuse*) (hard) worker.

3 *nm* (*personne exerçant un métier, une profession*) worker. **les ~s** the workers, working people; **les revendications des ~s** the claims made by the workers; **il avait loué sa ferme à des ~s étrangers** he had rented his farm to immigrant workers; **le problème des ~s étrangers** the problem of immigrant labour *ou* workers.

4: travailleur agricole agricultural *ou* farm worker; **travailleur à domicile** homeworker; **travailleuse familiale** home help; **travailleur de force** labourer; **travailleur indépendant** self-employed person; **travailleur intellectuel** intellectual worker; **travailleur manuel** manual worker.

travaillisme [travajism(ə)] *nm* Labour philosophy, Labour brand of socialism.

travailliste [travajist(ə)] **1** *adj* Labour. **2** *nmf* Labour Party member. **il est ~** he is Labour, he supports Labour; **les ~s** Labour.

travée [trave] *nf* **(a)** (*section*) *[mur, voûte, rayon, nef]* bay; *[pont]* span.

(b) (*Tech: portée*) span.

(c) (*rangée*) *[église, amphithéâtre]* row (of benches); *[théâtre]* row (of seats). **les ~s du fond manifestèrent leur mécontentement** the back rows showed their annoyance.

travelling [travliŋ] *nm* (*Ciné*) (*dispositif*) dolly, travelling platform; (*mouvement*) tracking. ~ **avant/arrière/latéral** tracking in/out/sideways; ~ **optique** zoom shots (*pl*).

travers[1] [travɛr] *nm* (*défaut*) failing, fault, shortcoming. **chacun a ses petits ~** everyone has his little failings *ou* faults.

travers[2] [travɛr] *nm* **(a)** (*sens diagonal, transversal*) **en ~** across, crosswise; **en ~ de** across; **couper/scier en ~** to cut/saw across; **pose la planche en ~** lay the plank across *ou* crosswise; **un arbre était en ~ de la route** a tree was lying across the road; **le véhicule dérapa et se mit en ~ (de la route)** the vehicle skidded and stopped sideways on *ou* stopped across the road; (*fig*) **se mettre en ~ (des projets de qn)** to stand in the way (of sb's plans); *V* **tort**.

(b) (*Naut*) *navire* **en ~, par le ~** abeam, on the beam; **vent de ~** wind on the beam; **mettre un navire en ~** to heave to; **se mettre en ~** to heave to; **s'échouer en ~** to run aground on the beam.

(c) au ~ through; **au ~ de** through; **la palissade est délabrée: on voit au ~/le vent passe au ~** the fence is falling down and you can see (right) through/the wind comes (right) through; **au ~ de ses mensonges, on devine sa peur** through his lies, you can tell he's frightened; (*fig*) **passer au ~** to get away (with it).

(d) de ~ (*pas droit*) crooked, askew; (*fig: à côté*) **répondre de ~** to give a silly answer; **comprendre de ~** to misunderstand; (*fig: mal*) **aller** *ou* **marcher de ~** to be going wrong; **avoir la bouche/le nez de ~** to have a crooked mouth/nose; **marcher de ~** to totter along; **il répond toujours de ~** he never gives a proper answer; **il raisonne toujours de ~** his reasoning is always unsound; **se mettre de ~** *[véhicule etc]* to stop sideways on; **elle a mis son chapeau de ~** she has put her hat on crooked, her hat is not on straight; **il a l'esprit un peu de ~** he's slightly odd; **il lui a jeté un regard** *ou* **il l'a regardé de ~** he looked askance at him, he gave him a funny look; **il a avalé sa soupe de ~, sa soupe est passée de ~** his soup has gone down the wrong way; **tout va de ~ chez eux en ce moment** everything is going wrong *ou* nothing is going right for them at the moment; **prendre qch de ~** to take sth the wrong way; **il prend tout de ~** he takes everything the wrong way *ou* amiss (*frm*).

(e) à ~ *vitre, maille, trou, foule* through; *campagne, bois* across, through; **voir qn à ~ la vitre** to see sb through the window; **ce n'est pas opaque, on voit à ~** it's not opaque — you can see through (it); **le renard est passé à ~ le grillage** the fox went through the fence; **sentir le froid à ~ un manteau** to feel the cold through a coat; **juger qn à ~ son œuvre** to judge sb through his work; **à ~ les siècles** through the centuries; **à ~ les divers rapports, on entrevoit la vérité** through the various reports, we can get some idea of the truth; **passer à ~ champs/bois** to go (*ou* run *etc*) through *ou* across fields/through woods; **la couche de glace est mince, tu risques de passer à ~** the layer of ice is thin — you could fall through.

traversable [travɛrsabl(ə)] *adj* which can be crossed, traversable (*frm*). **rivière ~ à gué** fordable river.

traverse [travɛrs(ə)] *nf* **(a)** (*Rail*) sleeper. **(b)** (*pièce, barre transversale*) strut, crosspiece. **(c) chemin de ~, ~†** road which cuts across, shortcut.

traversée [travɛrse] **1** *nf* **(a)** *[rue, mer, pont etc]* crossing; *[ville, forêt, tunnel etc]* going through. **la ~ des Alpes/de l'Atlantique en avion** the crossing of the Alps/of the Atlantic by plane; **la ~ de la ville en voiture peut prendre 2 heures** driving through *ou* crossing the town can take 2 hours by car; **faire la ~ d'un fleuve à la nage** to swim across a river.

(b) (*Naut: trajet*) crossing.

(c) (*Alpinisme*) (*course*) through-route; (*passage*) traverse.

2: (*fig Pol*) **traversée du désert** time (spent) in the wilderness.

traverser [travɛrse] (1) *vt* **(a)** *[personne, véhicule] rue, pont* to cross; *chaîne de montagnes, mer* to cross, traverse (*littér*); *ville, forêt, tunnel* to go through. ~ **une rivière à la nage** to swim across a river; ~ **une rivière en bac** to take a ferry across a river, cross a river by ferry; **il traversa le salon à grands pas** he strode across the living room; **avant de ~, assurez-vous que la chaussée est libre** before crossing, see that the road is clear.

(b) *[pont, route]* to cross, run across; *[tunnel]* to cross under; *[barre, trait]* to run across. **le fleuve/cette route traverse tout le pays** the river/this road runs *ou* cuts right across the country; **ce tunnel traverse les Alpes** this tunnel crosses under the Alps; **un pont traverse le Rhône en amont de Valence** a bridge crosses *ou* there is a bridge across the Rhone upstream from Valence; **une cicatrice lui traversait le front** he had a scar (right) across his forehead, a scar ran right across his forehead.

(c) (*percer*) *[projectile, infiltration]* to go *ou* come through. ~ **qch de part en part** to go right through sth; **les clous ont traversé la semelle** the nails have come through the sole; **la pluie a traversé la tente** the rain has come through the tent; **une balle lui traversa la tête** a bullet went through his head; **il s'effondra, la cuisse traversée d'une balle** he collapsed, shot through the thigh; **une douleur lui traversa le poignet** a pain shot through his wrist; **une idée lui traversa l'esprit** an idea passed through his mind *ou* occurred to him; **la joue traversée d'une cicatrice** with a scar across his cheek.

(d) (*passer à travers*) ~ **la foule** to make one's way through the crowd.

(e) (*fig: dans le temps*) *période* to go *ou* live through; *crise* to pass *ou* go through, undergo. **sa gloire a traversé les siècles** his glory travelled down the ages.

traversier, -ière [travɛrsje, jɛr] **1** *adj* **(a)** *rue* which runs across. **(b)** (*Naut*) *navire* cutting across the bows. **(c)** *V* **flûte**.

2 *nm* (*Can*) ferryboat.

traversin [travɛrsɛ̃] *nm [lit]* bolster.

travesti, e [travɛsti] (*ptp de* **travestir**) **1** *adj* (*gén: déguisé*) disguised; (*Théât*) *acteur* playing a female role; *rôle* female (*played by man*); *V* **bal**.

2 *nm* **(a)** (*Théât: acteur*) actor playing a female role; (*artiste de cabaret*) female impersonator, drag artist; (*Psych: déséquilibré*) transvestite. **numéro de ~** drag act.

(b) (*déguisement*) fancy dress. **en ~** in fancy dress.

travestir [travɛstir] (2) **1** *vt* **(a)** (*déguiser*) *personne* to dress up; *acteur* to cast in a female role. ~ **un homme en femme** to dress a man up as a woman.

(b) (*fig*) *vérité, paroles* to travesty, misrepresent.

2 se travestir *vpr* (*pour un bal*) to put on fancy dress; (*Théât*) to put on a woman's costume; (*pour un numéro de cabaret*) to put on drag; (*Psych*) to dress as a woman. **se ~ en Arlequin** to dress up as Harlequin.

travestisme [travɛstism(ə)] *nm* (*Psych*) transvestism.

travestissement [travɛstismɑ̃] *nm* **(a)** (*U: V* **travestir**) dressing up; casting in a female role; travesty, misrepresentation; putting on fancy dress; putting on female costume; putting on drag; dressing as a woman.

(b) (*déguisement*) fancy dress (*U*).

traviole* [travjɔl] *adv*: **de ~** skew-whiff*, crooked.

trayeur, -euse [trɛjœr, øz] **1** *nm,f* milker. **2 trayeuse** *nf* (*machine*) milking machine.

trébuchant, e [trebyʃɑ̃, ɑ̃t] *adj* (*chancelant*) *démarche, ivrogne* tottering (*épith*), staggering (*épith*); (*fig*) *diction, voix* halting (*épith*), quavering (*épith*); *V* **espèce.**

trébucher [tʀebyʃe] (1) *vi* (*lit, fig*) to stumble. **faire ~ qn** to trip sb up; **~ sur** *ou* **contre** *racine, pierre* to stumble over, trip against; *mot, morceau difficile* to stumble over.

trébuchet [tʀebyʃɛ] *nm* **(a)** (*piège*) bird-trap. **(b)** (*balance*) assay balance.

tréfilage [tʀefilaʒ] *nm* wiredrawing.

tréfiler [tʀefile] (1) *vt* to wiredraw.

tréfilerie [tʀefilʀi] *nf* wireworks.

trèfle [tʀɛfl(ə)] *nm* **(a)** (*Bot*) clover. **~ à quatre (feuilles)** four-leaf clover; **~ blanc** white clover.
(b) (*Cartes*) clubs. **jouer ~** to play a club *ou* clubs.
(c) (*Aut*) **(carrefour en) ~** cloverleaf (junction *ou* intersection).
(d) (*Archit*) trefoil.
(e) (*‡: argent*) lolly‡ (*Brit*), dough‡.

tréflière [tʀeflijɛʀ] *nf* field of clover.

tréfonds [tʀefɔ̃] *nm* (*littér*) **le ~ de** the inmost depths of; **ébranlé jusqu'au ~** profoundly shaken, shaken to the core; **dans le ~ de mon cœur** deep down in my heart; **le ~ de l'homme** the inmost depths of man; **dans le ~ de son âme** deep down, in the depths of his soul (*littér*).

treillage [tʀɛjaʒ] *nm* (*sur un mur*) lattice work, trellis(work); (*clôture*) trellis fence.

treillager [tʀɛjaʒe] (3) *vt mur* to trellis, lattice; *fenêtre* to lattice. **panneau treillagé de ruban, pour y déposer lettres et messages** board criss-crossed with tape for letters and messages.

treille [tʀɛj] *nf* (*tonnelle*) vine arbour; (*vigne*) climbing vine; *V* **jus.**

treillis[1] [tʀeji] *nm* (*en bois*) trellis; (*en métal*) wire-mesh; (*Constr*) lattice work.

treillis[2] [tʀeji] *nm* (*Tex*) canvas; (*Mil: tenue*) combat uniform.

treize [tʀɛz] *adj inv, nm inv* thirteen. **~ à la douzaine** baker's dozen; *pour autres loc V* **six.**

treizième [tʀɛzjɛm] *adj, nm* thirteenth; **~ mois** (*de salaire*) (bonus) thirteenth month's salary; *pour loc V* **sixième.**

treizièmement [tʀɛzjɛmmɑ̃] *adv* in the thirteenth place.

tréma [tʀema] *nm* dieresis. **i ~** i dieresis.

trémail [tʀemaj] *nm* = **tramail.**

tremblant, e [tʀɑ̃blɑ̃, ɑ̃t] *adj personne, membre, main* trembling, shaking; *voix* trembling, tremulous, quavering (*épith*); *lumière* trembling (*épith*), quivering (*épith*), flickering (*épith*). **il se présenta ~ devant son chef** he appeared shaking before his boss.

tremble [tʀɑ̃bl(ə)] *nm* aspen.

tremblé, e [tʀɑ̃ble] (*ptp de* **trembler**) *adj* **(a)** *écriture, dessin* shaky; *voix* shaky, tremulous, quavering (*épith*); *note* quavering (*épith*). **(b)** (*Typ*) **(filet) ~** wavy *ou* waved rule.

tremblement [tʀɑ̃bləmɑ̃] **1** *nm* **(a)** (*V* **trembler**) shiver; trembling (*U*); shaking (*U*); fluttering (*U*); flickering (*U*); quivering (*U*); wavering (*U*); vibration. **un ~ le parcourut** a shiver went through him; **il fut saisi d'un ~ convulsif** he was seized with a violent fit of shivering; **avec des ~s dans la voix** with a trembling *ou* quavering voice.
(b) (*loc*) **tout le ~*** (*les autres choses ou personnes*) the whole outfit*, the whole caboodle*; (*tout le reste*) all that jazz* *ou* guff‡.
2: tremblement de terre earthquake.

trembler [tʀɑ̃ble] (1) *vi* **(a)** *[personne]* (*de froid, de fièvre*) to shiver, tremble (*de* with); (*de peur, d'indignation, de colère*) to tremble, shake (*de* with). **il tremblait de tout son corps** *ou* **de tous ses membres** he was shaking *ou* trembling all over; **~ comme une feuille** to shake *ou* tremble like a leaf.
(b) *[feuille]* to tremble, flutter; *[lumière]* to tremble, flicker, quiver; *[flamme]* to tremble, flicker, waver; *[voix]* to tremble, shake, quaver; *[son]* to tremble, quaver; *[main]* to tremble, shake.
(c) *[bâtiment, fenêtre]* to shake; *[plancher]* to tremble, vibrate; *[terre]* to shake, quake. **faire ~ le sol** to make the ground tremble, shake the ground; **la terre a tremblé** there has been an earth tremor.
(d) (*fig: avoir peur*) to tremble. **~ pour qn/qch** to fear for *ou* tremble for (*frm*) sb/sth, be anxious over sb/sth; **~ à la pensée de qch** to tremble at the (very) thought of sth; **il tremble de l'avoir perdu** he is afraid *ou* he fears that he has lost it; **je tremble qu'elle ne s'en remette pas** I fear that she may not recover; **il vint me trouver, tremblant** he came looking for me in fear and trembling; **il fait ~ ses subordonnés** he strikes fear into those under him, his subordinates live in dread of him.

tremblotant, e [tʀɑ̃blɔtɑ̃, ɑ̃t] *adj personne* trembling, shaking; *voix* quavering (*épith*), tremulous; *lumière* trembling (*épith*), flickering (*épith*).

tremblote* [tʀɑ̃blɔt] *nf*: **avoir la ~** (*froid*) to have the shivers*; (*peur*) to have the jitters*.

tremblotement [tʀɑ̃blɔtmɑ̃] *nm* (*V* **trembloter**) trembling (*U*); shaking (*U*); quavering (*U*); flickering (*U*). **avec un ~ dans sa voix** with a tremble in his voice.

trembloter [tʀɑ̃blɔte] (1) *vi [personne, mains]* to tremble *ou* shake (slightly); *[voix]* to quaver, tremble; *[lumière]* to tremble, flicker.

trémie [tʀemi] *nf* **(a)** (*Tech: entonnoir*) *[concasseur, broyeur, trieuse]* hopper. **(b)** (*mangeoire*) feedbox. **(c)** (*Constr: pour l'âtre*) space for a hearth.

trémière [tʀemjɛʀ] *adj f V* **rose.**

trémolo [tʀemɔlo] *nm [instrument]* tremolo; *[voix]* quaver. **avec des ~s dans la voix** with a tremor in one's voice.

trémoussement [tʀemusmɑ̃] *nm* jigging about (*U*), wiggling (*U*).

trémousser (se) [tʀemuse] (1) *vpr* to jig about, wiggle. **se ~ sur sa chaise** to wriggle *ou* jig about on one's chair; **marcher en se trémoussant** to wiggle as one walks.

trempage [tʀɑ̃paʒ] *nm [linge, graines, semences]* soaking; *[papier]* damping, wetting.

trempe [tʀɑ̃p] *nf* **(a)** (*Tech*) *[acier]* (*processus*) quenching; (*qualité*) temper. **de bonne ~** well-tempered.
(b) (*fig*) *[personne, âme]* calibre. **un homme de sa ~** a man of his calibre *ou* of his moral fibre.
(c) (*Tech: trempage*) *[papier]* damping, wetting; *[peaux]* soaking.
(d) (*‡: correction*) walloping‡, hiding*.

trempé, e [tʀɑ̃pe] (*ptp de* **tremper**) *adj* **(a)** (*mouillé*) *vêtement, personne* soaked, drenched. **~ de sueur** bathed *ou* soaked in *ou* streaming with perspiration; **~ jusqu'aux os** *ou* **comme une soupe*** wet through, soaked to the skin, absolutely drenched, like a drowned rat; **joues/visage ~(es) de pleurs** cheeks/face bathed in tears.
(b) (*Tech*) *acier, verre* tempered. (*fig*) **caractère bien ~** sturdy character.

tremper [tʀɑ̃pe] (1) **1** *vt* **(a)** (*mouiller*) to soak, drench; (*gén* **faire ~**) *linge, graines* to soak; *aliments* to soak, steep; *papier* to damp, wet; *tiges de fleurs* to stand in water. **la pluie a trempé sa veste/le tapis** the rain has soaked *ou* drenched his jacket/the carpet.
(b) (*plonger*) *mouchoir, plume* to dip (*dans* into, in); *pain, biscuit* to dip, dunk (*dans* in). **~ sa main dans l'eau** to dip one's hand in the water; **~ ses lèvres dans une boisson** to take just a sip of a drink; **il n'aime pas qu'on lui trempe la tête dans l'eau** he doesn't like having his head ducked in the water; **~ la soupe**† to pour soup onto bread.
(c) (*Tech*) *métal, lame* to quench.
(d) (*littér: aguerrir, fortifier*) *personne, caractère, âme* to steel, strengthen.
2 *vi* **(a)** *[tige de fleur]* to stand in water; *[linge, graines, semences]* to soak. **faire ~ le linge, mettre le linge à ~** to soak the washing, put the washing to soak.
(b) (*fig péj: participer*) **~ dans** *crime, affaire, complot* to take part in, have a hand in, be involved in.
3 se tremper *vpr* (*prendre un bain rapide*) to have a quick dip; (*se mouiller*) to get (o.s.) soaked *ou* soaking wet, get drenched. **je ne fais que me ~** I'm just going for a quick dip.

trempette [tʀɑ̃pɛt] *nf* **(a)** (*pain trempé*) piece of bread (*for dunking*); (*sucre trempé*) sugar lump (*for dunking*). **faire ~** to dunk one's bread; to dunk one's sugar. **(b)** (*baignade*) (quick) dip. **faire ~** to have a (quick) dip.

tremplin [tʀɑ̃plɛ̃] *nm* **(a)** (*lit*) *[piscine]* diving-board, springboard; *[gymnase]* springboard; *[ski]* ski-jump. **(b)** (*fig*) springboard. **servir de ~ à qn** to be a springboard for sb.

trémulation [tʀemylasjɔ̃] *nf* (*Méd*) tremor.

trentaine [tʀɑ̃tɛn] *nf* (*âge, nombre*) about thirty, thirty or so; *pour loc V* **soixantaine.**

trente [tʀɑ̃t] **1** *adj inv, nm inv* thirty; *pour loc V* **six, soixante.**
2: (*Jeu***) trente-et-quarante** *nm inv* trente et quarante; **trente-six** (*lit*) thirty-six; (**fig: beaucoup*) umpteen*; **il y en a trente-six modèles** there are umpteen* models; **il n'y a pas trente-six possibilités** there aren't all that many choices; **j'ai trente-six mille choses à faire** I've a thousand and one things to do; **voir trente-six chandelles** to see stars; **dans le trente-sixième dessous*** right down in the dumps*; **trente et un** *nm* (*lit, Cartes*) thirty-one; (*fig*) **être/se mettre sur son trente et un** to be wearing/put on one's Sunday best *ou* one's glad rags*.

trentième [tʀɑ̃tjɛm] *adj, nm* thirtieth; *pour loc V* **sixième, soixantième.**

trépan [tʀepɑ̃] *nm* (*Méd*) trephine, trepan; (*Tech*) trepan.

trépanation [tʀepanasjɔ̃] *nf* (*Méd*) trephination, trepanation.

trépaner [tʀepane] (1) *vt* (*Méd*) to trephine, trepan.

trépas [tʀepa] *nm* (*littér*) demise, death; *V* **vie.**

trépassé, e [tʀepase] (*ptp de* **trépasser**) *adj* (*littér*) deceased, dead. **les ~s** the departed; (*Rel*) **le jour** *ou* **la fête des T~s** All Souls' (day).

trépasser [tʀepase] (1) *vi* (*littér*) to pass away, depart this life.

trépidant, e [tʀepidɑ̃, ɑ̃t] *adj machine, plancher* vibrating, quivering; *rythme* pulsating (*épith*), thrilling (*épith*); *vie* hectic, busy.

trépidation [tʀepidasjɔ̃] *nf* vibration, reverberation; (*fig*) *[vie]* flurry (*U*), whirl (*U*).

trépider [tʀepide] (1) *vi [machine, plancher]* to vibrate, reverberate.

trépied [tʀepje] *nm* (*gén*) tripod; (*dans l'âtre*) trivet.

trépignement [tʀepiɲmɑ̃] *nm* stamping (of feet) (*U*).

trépigner [tʀepiɲe] (1) **1** *vi* to stamp one's feet. **~ d'impatience/d'enthousiasme** to stamp (one's feet) with impatience/enthusiasm; **~ de colère** to stamp one's feet with rage, be hopping mad*. **2** *vt* to stamp *ou* trample on.

trépointe [tʀepwɛ̃t] *nf* welt.

tréponème [tʀepɔnɛm] *nm* treponema.

très [tʀɛ] *adv* (*avec adj*) very, awfully* (*surtout Brit*), terribly*, most; (*avec adv*) very; (*devant certains ptp etc*) (very) much, greatly, highly. **~ intelligent/difficile** very *ou* awfully* (*surtout Brit*) *ou* most intelligent/difficult; **~ admiré** greatly *ou* highly *ou* (very) much admired; **~ industrialisé/automatisé** highly industrialized/automatized; **il est ~ conscient de** he is very much aware of; **c'est ~ bien écrit/fait** it's very *ou* awfully* (*surtout Brit*) well written/done; **~ peu de gens** very few people; **c'est un garçon ~ travailleur** he is a very *ou* most hard-working lad, he's a very *ou* an awfully* (*surtout Brit*) hard worker; **elle est ~ grande dame** she is very much the great lady *ou* every bit a great lady; **avoir ~ peur** to be very much afraid *ou* very *ou* terribly* frightened; **avoir ~ faim** to be very *ou* terribly* hungry; **elle a été vraiment ~ aimable** she was really most *ou* awfully* (*surtout Brit*) kind; **c'est ~ nécessaire** it's most essential; **ils sont ~ amis/~ liés** they are great friends/very close (friends); **je suis ~, ~ content** I'm very, very *ou* terribly, terribly* pleased; **j'ai ~ envie de le rencontrer** I would very much like to meet him, I am very *ou* most anxious to meet him; **il est ~ en avant/arrière** (*sur le chemin*) he is well *ou* a long way ahead/behind; (*dans une salle*) he is well forward *ou* a long way to the front/well back *ou* a long way back; **être ~ à la page*** *ou* **dans le vent*** to be very *ou* terribly with-it*; **je ne suis jamais ~ à mon aise avec lui** I never feel very *ou* particularly *ou* terribly* comfortable with him; **êtes-vous fatigué?** — **~/pas ~** are you tired? — very *ou* terribly*/not very *ou* not terribly*; **~ bien, si vous insistez** all right *ou* very well, if you insist; **~ bien, je vais le lui expliquer** all right *ou* fine* *ou* very good *ou* O.K.*, I'll explain to him; **travailler le samedi? ~ peu pour moi!** work on Saturday? not likely!* *ou* not me!; *V* **peu.**

trésor [tʀezɔʀ] *nm* **(a)** (*richesses enfouies*) treasure (*U*); (*Jur: trouvé*) treasure-trove (*U*); (*fig: chose, personne, vertu précieuse*) treasure. **course** *ou* **chasse au/chercheur de ~** treasure hunt/hunter.

(b) (*petit musée*) treasure-house, treasury. **le ~ de Notre-Dame** the treasure-house of Notre-Dame.

(c) (*gén pl: richesses*) treasure. **les ~s du Louvre/de l'océan** the treasures *ou* riches of the Louvre/the ocean; (*hum*) **je vais chercher dans mes ~s** I'll look through my treasures *ou* precious possessions.

(d) (*source*) **un ~ de conseils/renseignements** a mine *ou* store of advice/information; (*quantité*) **des ~s de dévouement/de patience** a wealth of devotion/patience, boundless devotion/patience; **dépenser des ~s d'ingéniosité** to expend boundless ingenuity.

(e) (*ouvrage*) treasury.

(f) (*Admin, Fin: ressources*) *[roi, état]* exchequer, finances; *[organisation secrète]* finances, funds. (*service*) **T~ (public)** public revenue department; *V* **bon**[2].

(g) (*affectif*) **mon (petit) ~** my (little) treasure, my precious; **tu es un ~ de m'avoir acheté ce disque** you're a (real) treasure for buying me this record.

trésorerie [tʀezɔʀʀi] *nf* **(a)** (*bureaux*) *[Trésor public]* public revenue office; *[firme]* accounts department.

(b) (*gestion*) accounts. **leur ~ est bien/mal tenue** their accounts are well/badly kept; *V* **moyen.**

(c) (*argent disponible*) finances, funds. **difficultés de ~** cash shortage, cash (flow) problems, shortage of funds.

(d) (*fonction*) treasurership.

trésorier, -ière [tʀezɔʀje, jɛʀ] *nm,f* (*gén*) *[club, association]* treasurer. (*Admin*) **~-payeur général** paymaster (*for a département*).

tressage [tʀɛsaʒ] *nm* (*V* **tresser**) plaiting; braiding; weaving; twisting.

tressaillement [tʀesajmɑ̃] *nm* (*V* **tressaillir**) thrill, quiver, quivering (*U*); shudder, shuddering (*U*); wince; start; twitch, twitching (*U*); shaking (*U*), vibration.

tressaillir [tʀesajiʀ] (13) *vi* **(a)** (*frémir*) (*de plaisir*) to thrill, quiver; (*de peur*) to shudder, shiver; (*de douleur*) to wince. **son cœur tressaillait** his heart was fluttering.

(b) (*sursauter*) to start, give a start. **faire ~ qn** to startle sb.

(c) (*s'agiter*) *[personne, animal, nerf]* to quiver, twitch; *[plancher, véhicule]* to shake, vibrate.

tressautement [tʀesotmɑ̃] *nm* (*V* **tressauter**) start; jump, jumping (*U*); jolt, jolting (*U*), tossing (*U*); shaking (*U*).

tressauter [tʀesote] (1) *vi* **(a)** (*sursauter*) to start, jump. **faire ~ qn** to give sb a start, make sb jump.

(b) (*être secoué*) *[voyageurs]* to be jolted *ou* tossed about; *[objets]* to shake about, jump about. **faire ~ les voyageurs** to toss the passengers about; **les tasses tressautent sur le plateau** the cups are shaking *ou* jumping about on the tray.

tresse [tʀɛs] *nf* **(a)** (*cheveux*) plait, braid. **(b)** (*cordon*) braid. **(c)** (*Archit: motif*) strapwork.

tresser [tʀese] (1) *vt* **(a)** *cheveux, rubans* to plait, braid; *paille* to plait. **(b)** *panier, guirlande* to weave; *câble, corde, cordon* to twist. (*fig*) **~ des couronnes à qn** to laud sb to the skies, sing sb's praises.

tréteau, *pl* **~x** [tʀeto] *nm* **(a)** trestle. **(b)** (*Théât fig*) **les ~x** the boards, the stage; **monter sur les ~x** to go on the boards *ou* the stage.

treuil [tʀœj] *nm* winch, windlass.

treuiller [tʀœje] (1) *vt* to winch up.

trêve [tʀɛv] *nf* **(a)** (*Mil, Pol*) truce. (*Hist*) **~ de Dieu** truce of God; (*hum*) **~ des confiseurs** Christmas *ou* New Year (political) truce.

(b) (*fig: répit*) respite, rest. **s'accorder une ~** to allow o.s. a (moment's) respite *ou* a rest; (*littér*) **faire ~ à** *disputes, travaux* to rest from.

(c) ~ de (*assez de*): **~ de plaisanteries/d'atermoiement** enough of this joking/procrastination.

(d) sans ~ (*sans cesse*) unremittingly, unceasingly, relentlessly.

tri [tʀi] *nm* **(a)** (*U: V* **trier**) sorting out; sorting; marshalling; grading; selection; picking over; sifting. **faire le ~ de** to sort out; to sort; to marshal; to grade; to select, pick; to pick over; to sift; **on a procédé à des ~s successifs pour sélectionner les meilleurs candidats** they used several selection procedures to sift out the best candidates.

(b) (*Poste*) sorting. **le (bureau de) ~** the sorting office.

tri ... [tʀi] *préf* tri ... .

triacide [tʀiasid] *nm* triacid.

triade [tʀijad] *nf* (*littér*) triad.

triage [tʀijaʒ] *nm* **(a)** (*U: V* **trier**) sorting out; sorting; marshalling; grading; selection; picking over; sifting. **ils ont procédé à des ~s successifs pour sélectionner les meilleurs candidats** they used several selection procedures to sift out the best candidates.

(b) (*Rail*) (*opération*) shunting; (*endroit*) marshalling yard. **manœuvres de ~** shunting manœuvres; *V* **gare**[1].

triangle [tʀijɑ̃gl(ə)] *nm* (*Géom, Mus*) triangle. **en ~** in a triangle; **~ isocèle/équilatéral/rectangle/scalène** isosceles/equilateral/right-angled/scalene triangle; **~s semblables/égaux** similar/equal triangles; **~ quelconque** ordinary triangle; **soit un ~ quelconque ABC** let ABC be any triangle.

triangulaire [tʀijɑ̃gylɛʀ] *adj section, voile, prisme* triangular; *débat, élection, tournoi* three-cornered.

triangulation [tʀijɑ̃gylɑsjɔ̃] *nf* triangulation.

trianguler [tʀijɑ̃gyle] (1) *vt* to triangulate.

trias [tʀijɑs] *nm* (*terrain*) trias; (*période*) Triassic, Trias.

triasique [tʀijɑzik] *adj* Triassic.

triatomique [tʀiatɔmik] *adj* triatomic.

tribal, e, *mpl* **-aux** [tʀibal, o] *adj* tribal.

tribalisme [tʀibalism(ə)] *nm* (*littér*) tribalism.

tribo-électricité [tʀibɔelɛktʀisite] *nf* tribo-electricity.

tribo-luminescence [tʀibɔlyminesɑ̃s] *nf* tribo-luminescence.

tribord [tʀibɔʀ] *nm* starboard. **à ~** to starboard, on the starboard side.

tribu [tʀiby] *nf* (*Ethnologie, Hist, fig*) tribe.

tribulations [tʀibylɑsjɔ̃] *nfpl* (*mésaventures*) tribulations, trials, troubles.

tribun [tʀibœ̃] *nm* (*Hist romaine*) tribune; (*littér: défenseur*) tribune (*littér*).

tribunal, *pl* **-aux** [tʀibynal, o] **1** *nm* **(a)** court. **~ administratif/judiciaire/d'exception** administrative/judicial/special court; **~ révolutionnaire/militaire** revolutionary/military tribunal; **porter une affaire devant les ~aux** to bring a case before the courts; **affaire renvoyée d'un ~ à l'autre** case referred from one court to another.

(b) (*fig*) **le ~ des hommes** the justice of men; **être jugé par le ~ suprême** *ou* **de Dieu** to appear before the judgment seat of God; **être condamné par le ~ de l'histoire** to be condemned by the judgment of history, be judged and condemned by history; **s'ériger en ~ du goût/des mœurs** to set o.s. up as an arbiter of (good) taste/morals.

2: tribunal des conflits jurisdictional court; **tribunal pour enfants** juvenile court; **tribunal de grande instance** Departmental court, ≃ high court; **tribunal d'instance** ≃ magistrates' court; **tribunal de police** police court; **tribunal de première instance** court of first instance.

tribune [tʀibyn] **1** *nf* **(a)** (*pour le public*) *[église, assemblée, tribunal]* gallery; (*gén pl*) *[stade, champ de courses]* stand. **~ d'honneur** grandstand; **les ~s du public/de la presse** public/press gallery; **les applaudissements des ~s** applause from the stands; **il avait une ~** he had a seat in the stand.

(b) (*pour un orateur*) platform, tribune (*frm*), rostrum (*frm*). **monter à la ~** to mount the platform *ou* rostrum, stand up to speak; (*Parl*) to address the House.

(c) (*fig: débat*) forum. **~ radiophonique** radio forum; **offrir une ~ à la contestation** to offer a forum *ou* platform for protest; **~ libre d'un journal** opinion column in *ou* of a newspaper; **organiser une ~ sur un sujet d'actualité** to organize an open forum *ou* a free discussion on a topic of the day.

2: tribune d'orgue organ loft.

tribut [tʀiby] *nm* (*lit, fig*) tribute. **payer ~ au vainqueur** to pay tribute to the conqueror (*money etc*); **rendre** *ou* **payer un ~ d'admiration/de respect à qn** to give sb the admiration/respect due to him; (*fig littér*) **payer ~ à la nature** to go the way of all flesh, pay the debt of nature.

tributaire [tʀibytɛʀ] *adj* **(a)** (*dépendant*) **être ~ de** to be dependant *ou* reliant on.

(b) (*Géog*) **être ~ de** to be a tributary of, flow into.

(c) (*Hist*) tributary. **être ~ de qn** to be a tributary of sb, pay tribute to sb.

tricentenaire [tʀisɑ̃tnɛʀ] **1** *adj* three-hundred-year-old (*épith*).

2 *nm* tercentenary, tricentennial.

tricéphale [tʀisefal] *adj* (*littér*) three-headed.

triceps [tʀisɛps] *adj, nm*: **(muscle) ~** triceps (muscle).

triche* [tʀiʃ] *nf* cheating.

tricher [tʀiʃe] (1) *vi* (*gén*) to cheat. **~ sur son âge** to lie about *ou* cheat over one's age; **~ sur le poids/la longueur** to cheat over *ou* on the weight/the length, give short weight/short measure; **~ sur les prix** to cheat over the price, overcharge; **~ en affaires/en amour** to cheat *ou* not to play fair in business/love; **on a dû ~ un peu: un des murs est en contre-plaqué** we had to cheat a bit — one of the walls is plywood.

tricherie [tʀiʃʀi] *nf* (*astucieuse*) **on s'en tire avec une petite ~** we'll get round it by using a little trick to fix it, we'll cheat a bit to fix it.

tricheur, -euse [tʀiʃœʀ, øz] *nm,f* (*gén*) cheater, cheat*; (*en affaires*) swindler, trickster, cheat*.

trichrome [tʀikʀom] *adj* (*Tech*) three-colour (*épith*), trichromatic.

trichromie [tʀikʀɔmi] *nf* (*Tech*) three-colour process.

tricolore [tʀikɔlɔʀ] *adj* (*gén*) three-coloured, tricolour(ed) (*frm*); (*aux couleurs françaises*) red, white and blue. **le drapeau ~** the (French) tricolour; (*fig*) **le chauvinisme ~** French *ou* Gallic chauvinism; (*Sport*) **l'équipe ~*, les ~s*** the French team.

tricorne [tʀikɔʀn(ə)] *nm* three-cornered hat, tricorn(e).

tricot [tʀiko] *nm* **(a)** (*vêtement*) jumper (*Brit*), sweater, jersey. **~ de corps** vest (*Brit*), undershirt (*US*).

(b) (*technique, ouvrage*) knitting (*U*). **faire du ~** to knit, do some knitting; **~ jacquard** Jacquard knitwear; *V* **point**[2].

(c) (*tissu*) knitted fabric. **en ~** knitted; **~ plat** ordinary knitting, knitting on 2 needles; **~ rond** knitting on 4 needles; **vêtements de ~** knitwear.

tricotage [tʀikɔtaʒ] *nm* knitting.

tricoter [tʀikɔte] (1) **1** *vt vêtement, maille* to knit.

2 *vi* **(a)** to knit; *V* **aiguille, laine, machine**[3].

(b) (*) *[cycliste]* to twiddle*, pedal like mad*; *[danseur]* to prance about *ou* jig about like a mad thing*. **~ des jambes** *[fugitif]* to run like mad*; *[danseur]* to prance about *ou* jig about madly*.

tricoteur [tʀikɔtœʀ] *nm* (*rare*) knitter; (*: *cycliste*) hard pedaller. **~ de filets** netmaker.

tricoteuse [tʀikɔtøz] *nf* (*personne*) knitter; (*machine*) knitting machine; (*meuble*) tricoteuse.

trictrac [tʀiktʀak] *nm* (*jeu*) backgammon; (*partie*) game of backgammon; (*damier*) backgammon board.

tricycle [tʀisikl(ə)] *nm [enfant]* tricycle; *[livreur]* delivery tricycle.

trident [tʀidɑ̃] *nm* (*Myth*) trident; (*Pêche*) trident, fish-spear; (*Agr*) three-pronged fork.

tridimensionnel, -elle [tʀidimɑ̃sjɔnɛl] *adj* three-dimensional.

trièdre [tʀiɛdʀ(ə)] **1** *adj* trihedral. **2** *nm* trihedron.

triennal, e, *mpl* **-aux** [tʀiɛnal, o] *adj prix, foire, élection* triennial, three-yearly; *charge, mandat, plan* three-year (*épith*); *magistrat, président* elected *ou* appointed for three years. (*Agr*) **assolement ~** 3-year rotation of crops.

triennat [tʀiɛna] *nm* three-year period of office. **X, durant son ~** X, during his three years in office.

trier [tʀije] (7) *vt* **(a)** (*classer*) (*gén*) to sort out; *lettres, fiches* to sort; *wagons* to marshal; *fruits* to sort; (*en calibrant*) to grade.

(b) (*sélectionner*) *grains, visiteurs* to sort out; *volontaires* to select, pick; *lentilles* to pick over; (*en tamisant*) to sift. (*fig*) **triés sur le volet** hand-picked.

trieur, -euse [tʀijœʀ, øz] **1** *nm,f* (*V* **trier:** *personne*) sorter; grader. **2** *nm* (*machine*) sorter. **~ de grains** grain sorter; **~-calibreur** *[fruits]* sorter; *[œufs]* grader, grading machine.

trifluvien, -ienne [tʀiflyvjɛ̃, jɛn] **1** *adj* of *ou* from Three Rivers. **2** *nm,f*: **T~(ne)** inhabitant *ou* native of Three Rivers.

trilogie [tʀilɔʒi] *nf* trilogy.

trimarder‡ [tʀimaʀde] (1) *vi* (*vagabonder*) to walk the roads, be on the road.

trimardeur, -euse‡ [tʀimaʀdœʀ, øz] *nm,f* (*vagabond*) tramp (*Brit*), hobo (*US*).

trimbal(l)age [tʀɛ̃balaʒ] *nm,* **trimbal(l)ement** [tʀɛ̃balmɑ̃] *nm [bagages, marchandises]* carting around*. **on en a bien pour 3 à 4 heures de ~** we'll be carting this stuff around for 3 or 4 hours*.

trimbal(l)er [tʀɛ̃bale] (1) **1** *vt* (*) *bagages, marchandises* to lug* *ou* cart* around; (*péj*) *personne* to trail along*. **qu'est-ce qu'il (se) trimballe!**‡ (*bêtise*) he's as thick as they come‡; (*ivresse*) he's had a skinful*, he's loaded to the eyeballs‡.

2 se trimbal(l)er‡ *vpr* to trail along*. **on a dû se ~ en voiture jusque chez eux** we had to trail over to their place in the car*.

trimer* [tʀime] (1) *vi* to slave away. **faire ~ qn** to keep sb's nose to the grindstone, drive sb hard, keep sb hard at it*.

trimestre [tʀimɛstʀ(ə)] *nm* **(a)** (*période*) (*gén, Comm*) quarter; (*Scol*) term. (*Scol*) **premier/second/troisième ~** Autumn/Winter/Summer term.

(b) (*somme*) (*loyer*) quarter, quarter's rent; (*frais de scolarité*) term's fees; (*salaire*) quarter's income.

trimestriel, -elle [tʀimɛstʀijɛl] *adj publication* quarterly; *paiement* three-monthly, quarterly; *fonction, charge* three-month (*épith*), for three months (*attrib*); (*Scol*) *bulletin, examen* end-of-term (*épith*), termly.

trimestriellement [tʀimɛstʀijɛlmɑ̃] *adv payer* on a quarterly *ou* three-monthly basis, every quarter, every three months; *publier* quarterly; (*Scol*) once a term.

trimètre [tʀimɛtʀ(ə)] *nm* trimeter.

trimoteur [tʀimɔtœʀ] *nm* three-engined aircraft (*U*).

tringle [tʀɛ̃gl(ə)] *nf* **(a)** (*Tech*) rod. **~ d'escalier/à rideaux** stair/curtain rod. **(b)** (*Archit: moulure*) tenia. **(c) se mettre la ~**‡ to tighten one's belt.

trinitaire [tʀinitɛʀ] *adj, nmf* (*Rel*) Trinitarian.

trinité [tʀinite] *nf* (*triade*) trinity. **la T~** (*dogme*) the Trinity; (*fête*) Trinity Sunday; **à la T~** on Trinity Sunday; *V* **Pâques, saint.**

trinitrotoluène [tʀinitʀɔtɔlɥɛn] *nm* trinitrotoluene, trinitrotoluol.

trinôme [tʀinom] *nm* (*Math*) trinomial.

trinquer [tʀɛ̃ke] (1) *vi* **(a)** (*porter un toast*) to clink glasses. **~ à qch/qn** to drink to sth/sb.

(b) (*: *écoper*) to cop it‡.

(c) (†*: *trop boire*) to booze*.

(d) (†: *se heurter*) to knock *ou* bump into one another.

trinquet [tʀɛ̃kɛ] *nm* (*Naut*) foremast.

trinquette [tʀɛ̃kɛt] *nf* (*Naut*) fore(-topmast) staysail.

trio [tʀijo] *nm* (*Mus*) trio; (*groupe*) threesome, trio.

triode [tʀiɔd] *nf* triode.

triolet [tʀijɔlɛ] *nm* (*Mus*) triplet; (*Hist Littérat*) triolet.

triomphal, e, *mpl* **-aux** [tʀijɔ̃fal, o] *adj succès, élection* triumphal; *entrée, accueil, geste, air* triumphant; (*Hist romaine*) triumphal.

triomphalement [tʀijɔ̃falmɑ̃] *adv accueillir, saluer* in triumph; *annoncer* triumphantly.

triomphant, e [tʀijɔ̃fɑ̃, ɑ̃t] *adj* triumphant.

triomphateur, -trice [tʀijɔ̃fatœʀ, tʀis] **1** *adj parti, nation* triumphant. **2** *nm,f* (*vainqueur*) triumphant victor. **3** *nm* (*Hist romaine*) triumphant *ou* triumphing general.

triomphe [tʀijɔ̃f] *nm* **(a)** (*Mil, Pol, Sport, gén*) triumph; *[maladie, mode]* victory. **cet acquittement représente le ~ de la justice/du bon sens** this acquittal represents the triumph of *ou* is a triumph for justice/common sense.

(b) (*Hist romaine, gén: honneurs*) triumph. **en ~** in triumph; **porter qn en ~** to bear *ou* carry sb in triumph, carry sb shoulder-high (in triumph); *V* **arc.**

(c) (*exultation*) triumph. **air/cri de ~** air/cry of triumph, triumphant air/cry; **leur ~ fut de courte durée** their triumph was short-lived.

(d) (*succès*) triumph. **cette pièce/cet artiste a remporté un ~** this play/artist has been *ou* had a triumphant success.

triompher [tʀijɔ̃fe] (1) **1** *vi* **(a)** (*militairement*) to triumph; (*aux élections, en sport, gén*) to triumph, win; *[cause, raison]* to prevail, be triumphant; *[maladie]* to claim its victory; *[mode]* to win *ou* achieve success *ou* popularity. **faire ~ une cause/une mode** to bring *ou* give victory to a cause/to a fashion; *V* **vaincre.**

(b) (*crier victoire*) to exult, rejoice.

(c) (*exceller*) to triumph, excel.

2 triompher de *vt indir ennemi* to triumph over, vanquish; *concurrent, rival* to triumph over, overcome; *obstacle, difficulté* to triumph over, surmount, overcome; *peur, timidité* to conquer.

tripaille‡ [tʀipaj] *nf* (*péj*) guts*, innards.

triparti, e [tʀipaʀti] *adj* (*Bot, Pol: à trois éléments*) tripartite; (*Pol: à trois partis*) three-party (*épith*).

tripartisme [tʀipaʀtism(ə)] *nm* three-party government.

tripartite [tʀipaʀtit] *adj* = **triparti.**

tripatouillage* [tʀipatujaʒ] *nm* (*péj: U: V* **tripatouiller**) fiddling about*; fiddling*; messing about*; (*opération malhonnête*) fiddle*. **~ électoral** election fiddle*, electoral jiggery-pokery* (*U: surtout Brit*).

tripatouiller* [tʀipatuje] (1) *vt* (*péj*) **(a)** (*remanier*) *texte* to fiddle about with*; *comptes, résultats électoraux* to fiddle*, tamper with. **(b)** (*manier*) to fiddle *ou* mess about with*; *femme* to paw*.

tripatouilleur, -euse* [tʀipatujœʀ, øz] *nm,f* (*péj*) (*touche-à-tout*) fiddler*; (*affairiste*) grafter* (*péj*).

tripe [tʀip] *nf* **(a)** (*Culin*) **~s** tripe; **~s à la mode de Caen/à la lyonnaise** tripe à la mode de Caen/à la Lyonnaise.

(b) (*: *intestins*) **~s** guts*; **cela vous prend aux ~s** that gets you in the guts* *ou* right there*; **rendre ~s et boyaux** to be as sick as a dog*.

(c) (**fig: fibre*) **avoir la ~ républicaine/royaliste** to be a republican/a royalist through and through *ou* to the core.

triperie [tʀipʀi] *nf* (*boutique*) tripe shop; (*commerce*) tripe trade.

tripette* [tʀipɛt] *nf*: **ça ne vaut pas ~** that's not worth tuppence* (*Brit*) *ou* a wooden nickel* (*US*).

triphasé, e [tʀifɑze] *adj* three-phase.

triphtongue [tʀiftɔ̃g] *nf* triphthong.

tripier, -ière [tʀipje, jɛʀ] *nm,f* tripe seller, tripe butcher.

triplace [tʀiplas] *adj* three-seater.

triplan [tʀiplɑ̃] *nm* triplane.

triple [tʀipl(ə)] **1** *adj* **(a)** (*à trois éléments ou aspects*) triple; (*trois fois plus grand*) treble. **au ~ galop** hell for leather*; **le prix est ~ de ce qu'il était** the price is three times what it was, the price has trebled; **faire qch en ~ exemplaire** to make three copies of sth, do sth in triplicate; **il faut que l'épaisseur soit ~** three thicknesses are needed, a treble thickness is needed; **avec ~ couture** triple stitched; **avec ~ semelle** with a three-layer sole; **les murs sont ~s** there are three thicknesses of wall, the wall is in three sections; **l'inconvénient en est ~** there are three disadvantages, the disadvantages are threefold; **~ naissance** birth of triplets; **prendre une ~ dose (de)** to take three times the dose (of), take a triple dose (of).

(b) (*intensif*) **~ idiot/sot** prize idiot/fool.

2 *nm*: **manger/gagner le ~ (de qn)** to eat/earn three times as much (as sb *ou* as sb does); **celui-ci pèse le ~ de l'autre** this one weighs three times as much as the other *ou* is three times *ou* treble the weight of the other; **9 est le ~ de 3** 9 is three times 3; **c'est le ~ du prix normal/de la distance Paris-Londres** it's three times *ou* treble the normal price/the distance between Paris and London; **on a mis le ~ de temps à le faire** it took three times as long *ou* treble the time to do it.

3: (*Mus*) **triple croche** *nf* demi-semiquaver (*Brit*), thirty-second note (*US*); (*Hist Pol*) **Triple Entente** *nf* Triple Alliance; (*péj*) **triple menton** *nm* row of chins; (*Sport*) **triple saut** *nm* triple jump.

triplé, e [tʀiple] (*ptp de* **tripler**) **1** *nm* (*Sport*) treble. **2 triplés** *nmpl* (*bébés*) triplets; (*mâles*) boy triplets. **3 triplées** *nfpl* girl triplets.

triplement [tʀipləmɑ̃] **1** *adv* (*pour trois raisons*) in three ways; (*à un degré triple, valeur intensive*) trebly, three times over. **2** *nm* (*V* **tripler**) trebling (*de* of), tripling (*de* of); threefold increase (*de* in).

tripler [tʀiple] (1) **1** *vt* to treble, triple. **il tripla la dose** he made the dose three times as big, he trebled the dose; **~ la longueur/l'épaisseur de qch** to treble *ou* triple the length/thickness of sth, make sth three times as long/thick; **~ la couche protectrice** to put on three protective coats, give three layers of protective coating; **~ le service d'autobus/la garnison** to make the bus service three times as frequent/the garrison three times as large, treble the frequency of the bus service/the size of the garrison; **~ sa mise** to treble one's stake.

2 *vi* to triple, treble, increase threefold. **~ de valeur/de poids** to treble in value/in weight.

triplette [tʀiplɛt] *nf* (*Boules*) threesome.

triplex [tʀiplɛks] *nm* ® (*verre*) Triplex ®.

triporteur [tʀipɔʀtœʀ] *nm* delivery tricycle.
tripot [tʀipo] *nm* (*péj*) dive*, joint*.
tripotage* [tʀipɔtaʒ] *nm* (*péj: U: V* **tripoter**) playing (*de* with); speculating (*de* with); fingering; fiddling (*de* with); pawing; (*manigances*) jiggery-pokery* (*U: surtout Brit*). ~**s électoraux** election fiddles*, electoral jiggery-pokery* (*surtout Brit*).
tripotée: [tʀipɔte] *nf* **(a)** (*correction*) belting:, hiding*. **(b)** (*grand nombre*) **une ~ de...** loads* of...; lots of...; **avoir toute une ~ d'enfants** to have a whole string of children*.
tripoter* [tʀipɔte] (1) (*péj*) **1** *vt* **(a)** *fonds* to play with, speculate with.
(b) *objet, fruits* to fiddle with, finger; (*machinalement*) *montre, stylo, bouton* to fiddle with, play with, toy with. **se ~ le nez/la barbe** to fiddle with one's nose/beard.
(c) (:) *femme, partie du corps* to paw*.
2 *vi* **(a)** (*fouiller*) to root about*, rummage about*. **~ dans les affaires de qn/dans un tiroir** to root about* *ou* rummage about* in sb's things/in a drawer.
(b) (*trafiquer*) **~ en Bourse/dans l'immobilier** to be *ou* get involved in some shady business on the Stock Market/in property; **il a tripoté dans diverses affaires assez louches** he has had a hand in a few fairly shady affairs.
tripoteur, -euse* [tʀipɔtœʀ, øz] *nm,f* (*péj*) (*affairiste*) shark*, shady dealer*; (:: *peloteur*) feeler:, groper:.
triptyque [tʀiptik] *nm* **(a)** (*Art, Littérat*) triptych. **(b)** (*Admin: classement*) triptyque.
trique [tʀik] *nf* cudgel. **mener qn à la ~** to bully sb along; **donner des coups de ~** to cudgel, thrash; **maigre** *ou* **sec comme un coup de ~** as skinny as a rake.
trirectangle [tʀiʀɛktɑ̃gl(ə)] *adj* trirectangular.
trirème [tʀiʀɛm] *nf* trireme.
trisaïeul, *pl* **~s** *ou* **-eux** [tʀizajœl, ø] *nm* great-great-grandfather. **les ~eux** the great-great-grandparents.
trisaïeule [tʀizajœl] *nf* great-great-grandmother.
trisannuel, -elle [tʀizanɥɛl] *adj fête, plante* triennial.
trisection [tʀisɛksjɔ̃] *nf* (*Géom*) trisection.
trisser (se): [tʀise] (1) *vpr* (*partir*) to clear off*, skedaddle*.
trissyllabe [tʀisilab] = **trisyllabe.**
trissyllabique [tʀisilabik] *adj* = **trisyllabique.**
Tristan [tʀistɑ̃] *nm* Tristan, Tristram.
triste [tʀist(ə)] *adj* **(a)** (*malheureux, affligé*) *personne* sad, unhappy; *regard, sourire* sad, sorrowful. **d'un air ~** sadly, with a sad look; **d'une voix ~** sadly, in a sad voice; **un enfant à l'air ~** a sad-looking *ou* an unhappy-looking child; **les animaux en cage ont l'air ~** caged animals look sad *ou* miserable; **être ~ à l'idée** *ou* **à la pensée de partir** to be sad at the idea *ou* thought of leaving; **elle était ~ de voir partir ses enfants** she was sad to see her children go.
(b) (*sombre, maussade*) *personne, pensée* sad, gloomy; *couleur, temps, journée* dreary, dismal, miserable; *paysage* sad, bleak, dreary. **il aime les chansons ~s** he likes sad *ou* melancholy songs; **~ à pleurer** hopelessly miserable; **il est ~ comme une porte de prison** *ou* **un bonnet de nuit** he's as miserable as sin; **faire (une) ~ figure** to look downcast, look sorry for o.s.; **faire ~ mine** *ou* **figure à** to give a cool reception to, greet unenthusiastically; **avoir** *ou* **faire ~ mine, avoir** *ou* **faire ~ figure** to cut a sorry figure, look a sorry sight; *V* **vin.**
(c) (*attristant, pénible*) *nouvelle, épreuve, destin* sad. **depuis ces ~s événements** since these sad events took place; **c'est une ~ nécessité** it is a painful necessity, it is sadly necessary; **il se lamente toujours sur son ~ sort** he is always bewailing his unhappy *ou* sad fate; **ce furent des mois bien ~s** these were very sad *ou* unhappy months; **il est de mon ~ devoir de vous dire que ...** it is my painful duty to have to tell you that ...; **~ chose que il est à sorry** *ou* sad state of affairs when; **depuis son accident, il est dans un ~ état** (ever) since his accident he has been in a sad *ou* sorry state.
(d) (*avant n: péj: lamentable*) **quelle ~ affaire/personne/époque** what a dreadful business/person/age; **une ~ réputation** a sorry reputation; **un ~ sire** *ou* **personnage** an unsavoury individual; **ses ~s résultats à l'examen** his wretched *ou* deplorable exam results.
tristement [tʀistəmɑ̃] *adv* **(a)** (*d'un air triste*) sadly, sorrowfully.
(b) (*de façon lugubre*) sadly, gloomily.
(c) (*valeur intensive, péjorative*) sadly, regrettably. **il est ~ célèbre** he is regrettably well-known; **c'est ~ vrai** sadly it is only too true, it is sadly true.
tristesse [tʀistɛs] *nf* **(a)** (*U: caractère, état*) *[personne, pensée]* sadness, gloominess; *[couleur, temps, journée]* dreariness, *[paysage]* sadness, bleakness, dreariness. **il sourit toujours avec une certaine ~** there is always a certain sadness in his smile; **enclin à la ~** given to melancholy, inclined to be gloomy *ou* sad.
(b) (*chagrin*) sadness (*U*), sorrow. **avoir un accès de ~** to be overcome by sadness; **les ~s de la vie** life's sorrows, the sorrows of life; **c'est avec une grande ~ que nous apprenons son décès** it is with deep sadness *ou* sorrow that we have learned of his death.
trisyllabe [tʀisilab] **1** *adj* trisyllabic. **2** *nm* trisyllable.
trisyllabique [tʀisilabik] *adj* trisyllabic.
tritium [tʀitjɔm] *nm* (*Phys*) tritium.
triton[1] [tʀitɔ̃] *nm* (*Zool*) triton. (*Myth*) **T~** Triton.
triton[2] [tʀitɔ̃] *nm* (*Mus*) tritone, augmented fourth.
trituration [tʀityʀasjɔ̃] *nf* (*V* **triturer**) grinding up, trituration (*T*); pummelling, kneading; manipulation.
triturer [tʀityʀe] (1) *vt* **(a)** (*broyer*) *sel, médicament, fibres* to grind up, triturate (*T*).
(b) (*malaxer*) *pâte* to pummel, knead; (*fig: manipuler*) *objet, clef, poignée* to manipulate. **ce masseur vous triture les chairs** this masseur pummels your flesh; **il s'agit non plus d'influencer, mais véritablement de ~ l'opinion** it's no longer a matter of influencing public opinion but of bludgeoning *ou* coercing it into changing.
(c) se ~ la cervelle* *ou* **les méninges*** to rack one's brains*.
triumvir [tʀijɔmviʀ] *nm* triumvir.
triumviral, e, *mpl* **-aux** [tʀijɔmviʀal, o] *adj* triumviral.
triumvirat [tʀijɔmviʀa] *nm* triumvirate.
trivalence [tʀivalɑ̃s] *nf* trivalence, trivalency.
trivalent, e [tʀivalɑ̃, ɑ̃t] *adj* trivalent.
trivalve [tʀivalv(ə)] *adj* trivalve.
trivial, e, *mpl* **-aux** [tʀivjal, o] *adj* **(a)** (*vulgaire*) *langage, plaisanterie* coarse, crude.
(b) (*littér: ordinaire*) *objets, actes* mundane, commonplace; *détail* mundane, trivial; (†: *rebattu*) trite, commonplace. **le style ~** the commonplace style; **le genre ~** the commonplace.
trivialement [tʀivjalmɑ̃] *adv* (*V* **trivial**) coarsely, crudely; in a mundane way; in a commonplace way; trivially; tritely.
trivialité [tʀivjalite] *nf* **(a)** (*U: V* **trivial**) coarseness, crudeness; mundane nature; commonplace nature; triviality; triteness.
(b) (*remarque: V* **trivial**) coarse *ou* crude remark; commonplace *ou* trite remark; (*détail: V* **trivial**) coarse *ou* crude detail; mundane *ou* trivial detail.
troc [tʀɔk] *nm* (*échange*) exchange; (*système*) barter. **faire un ~ avec qn** to make an exchange with sb; **faire le ~ de qch avec qch d'autre** to barter *ou* exchange sth for sth else.
trochaïque [tʀɔkaik] *adj* trochaic.
trochée [tʀɔʃe] *nf* trochee.
troène [tʀɔɛn] *nm* privet.
troglodyte [tʀɔglɔdit] *nm* (*Ethnologie*) troglodyte (*T*), cave dweller; (*fig*) troglodyte; (*Orn*) wren.
troglodytique [tʀɔglɔditik] *adj* (*Ethnologie*) troglodytic (*T*), cave-dwelling (*épith*). **habitation ~** cave dwelling, cave-dweller's settlement.
trogne* [tʀɔɲ] *nf* (*péj: visage*) mug: (*péj*), face.
trognon [tʀɔɲɔ̃] *nm [fruit]* core; *[chou]* stalk. **~ de pomme** apple core; **jusqu'au ~**: well and truly; **mon petit ~*** sweetie pie*.
Troie [tʀwa] *n* Troy. **la guerre/le cheval de ~** the Trojan War/Horse.
troïka [tʀɔika] *nf* (*lit, Pol*) troika.
trois [tʀwa] **1** *adj inv* **(a)** three; (*troisième*) third. **ils habitent** *ou* **vivent à ~ dans une seule pièce** there are three of them living in (the) one room; **volume/acte ~** volume/act three; **le ~ (janvier)** the third (of January); **Henri III** Henry the Third; *pour autres loc V* **six** *et* **fois, ménage** *etc.*
(b) (*approximation*) **achète deux ou ~** *ou* **~ ou quatre citrons** buy a couple of lemons; **je pars dans ~ minutes** I'm off in a couple of *ou* a few minutes; **il n'a pas dit ~ mots** he hardly opened his mouth *ou* said a word; **en ~ coups de cuiller à pot*** in two shakes of a lamb's tail*, in a jiffy*.
2 *nm inv* three; (*troisième*) third; (*Cartes, Dés*) three; *pour loc V* **six.**
3: (*Théât*) **les trois coups** *mpl* the three knocks (*announcing beginning of play*); (*Mus*) **trois-deux** *nm* three-two time; (*Phys*) **les trois dimensions** *fpl* the three dimensions; **à trois dimensions** three-dimensional; **trois étoiles** (*adj*) *cognac, restaurant* three-star (*épith*); (*nm*) (*restaurant*) three-star restaurant; (*hôtel*) three-star hotel; (*Myth*) **les trois Grâces** *fpl* the three Graces; (*Mus*) **trois-huit** *nm* three-eight (time); (*Naut*) **trois-mâts** *nm inv* three-master; **les trois Mousquetaires** *mpl* the Three Musketeers; (*Hist*) **les trois ordres** *mpl* the three estates; **trois-pièces** *nm inv* (*complet*) three-piece suit; (*appartement*) three-room flat; **trois-quarts**[1] *nmpl* three-quarters; **portrait de trois-quarts** three-quarter(s) portrait; **manteau trois-quarts** three-quarter (length) coat; **j'ai fait les trois-quarts du travail** I've done three-quarters of the work; **les trois-quarts des gens l'ignorent** the great majority of people *ou* most people don't know this; **aux trois-quarts détruit** almost totally destroyed; **trois-quarts**[2] *nm inv* (*violon*) three-quarter violin; (*Rugby*) three-quarter; **il joue trois-quarts aile** he plays wing three-quarter; (*Mus*) **trois-quatre** *nm* three-four time; (*Mus*) **trois temps** three beats to the bar; **à trois temps** in triple time.
troisième [tʀwazjɛm] *adj, nmf* third. **le ~ degré** (*torture*) the third degree; **le ~ sexe** the third sex; **le ~ âge** (*période*) the years of retirement; (*groupe social*) senior citizens; **être** *ou* **faire le ~ larron dans cette affaire** to take advantage of the other two quarrelling over this business; (*Aut*) **en ~** in third (gear); *pour autres loc V* **sixième.**
troisièmement [tʀwazjɛmmɑ̃] *adv* third(ly), in the third place.
trolley [tʀɔlɛ] *nm* (*dispositif*) trolley(-wheel); (*: *bus*) trolley bus.
trolleybus [tʀɔlɛbys] *nm* trolley bus.
trombe [tʀɔ̃b] *nf* **(a)** (*Mét*) waterspout. (*fig: pluie*) **une ~ d'eau, des ~s d'eau** a cloudburst *ou* downpour; (*fig*) **des ~s de lave/débris** streams *ou* torrents of lava/debris. **(b) entrer/sortir/passer en ~** to sweep in/out/by like a whirlwind.
trombine: [tʀɔ̃bin] *nf* (*visage*) face, mug: (*péj*); (*tête*) nut*.
tromblon [tʀɔ̃blɔ̃] *nm* **(a)** (*Mil*) (*Hist*) blunderbuss; *[fusil lance-roquettes]* grenade launcher.
(b) (:: *chapeau*) headgear* (*U*).
trombone [tʀɔ̃bɔn] *nm* **(a)** (*Mus*) (*instrument*) trombone; (*tromboniste*) trombonist, trombone (player). **~ à coulisse/à pistons** slide/valve trombone. **(b)** (*agrafe*) paper clip.
tromboniste [tʀɔ̃bɔnist(ə)] *nmf* trombonist, trombone (player).
trompe [tʀɔ̃p] **1** *nf* **(a)** (*Mus*) trumpet, horn; (†: *avertisseur, sirène*) horn. **~ de chasse** hunting horn; **~ de brume** fog horn; *V* **son**[2].

(b) (*Zool*) *[éléphant]* trunk, proboscis (*T*); *[insecte]* proboscis; *[tapir]* snout, proboscis (*T*).
(c) (*Tech*) ~ **à eau/mercure** water/mercury pump.
(d) (*Archit*) squinch.
2: (*Anat*) **trompe d'Eustache** Eustachian tube; (*Anat*) **trompe de Fallope** *ou* **utérine** Fallopian tube.

trompe-la-mort [tʀɔ̃plamɔʀ] *nmf inv* death-dodger.

trompe-l'œil [tʀɔ̃plœj] *nm inv* **(a)** trompe-l'œil. **peinture en ~** trompe-l'œil painting; **décor en ~** decor done in trompe-l'œil; **peint en ~ sur un mur** painted in trompe-l'œil on a wall. **(b)** (*fig*) eyewash*. **c'est du ~** it's all eyewash*.

tromper [tʀɔ̃pe] (1) **1** *vt* **(a)** (*duper*) to deceive; (*être infidèle à*) *époux* to be unfaithful to, deceive. **~ qn sur qch** to deceive *ou* mislead sb about *ou* over sth; **~ sa femme avec une autre** to deceive one's wife *ou* be unfaithful to one's wife with another woman; **un mari trompé** a husband who has been deceived; **cela ne trompe personne** that doesn't fool anybody.
(b) (*induire en erreur par accident*) to mislead; *[symptômes etc] docteur, expert* to deceive, mislead. **les apparences trompent** appearances are deceptive; **c'est ce qui vous trompe** that's where you are mistaken *ou* wrong.
(c) (*déjouer*) *poursuivants [personne]* to elude, trick, escape from; *[manœuvre]* to fool, trick; *vigilance* to elude. **il a trompé la surveillance de ses gardes et s'est enfui** he evaded *ou* eluded the guards and made his escape.
(d) (*décevoir*) **~ l'attente/l'espoir de qn** to fall short of *ou* fail to come up to *ou* deceive (*frm*) sb's expectations/hopes; **être trompé dans son attente/ses espoirs** to be disappointed *ou* deceived (*frm*) in one's expectations/hopes; **~ la faim/la soif** to stave off one's hunger/thirst; **pour ~ leur longue attente** to while away *ou* beguile (*frm*) their long wait.
2 se tromper *vpr* **(a)** to make a mistake, be mistaken. **se ~ de 5 F dans un calcul** to be 5 francs out in one's reckoning; **tout le monde peut se ~** anybody can make a mistake; **se ~ sur les intentions de qn** to be mistaken regarding sb's intentions, misjudge sb's intentions; **on pourrait s'y ~, c'est à s'y ~** you'd hardly know the difference; **ne vous y trompez pas, il arrivera à ses fins** make no mistake — he will obtain his ends; **si je ne me trompe** if I am not mistaken, unless I'm very much mistaken.
(b) se ~ de route/de chapeau to take the wrong road/hat; **se ~ d'adresse** to get the wrong address; (*fig*) **tu te trompes d'adresse** *ou* **de porte** you've come to the wrong place, you've got the wrong person; **se ~ de jour/date** to get the day/date wrong, make a mistake about the day/date.

tromperie [tʀɔ̃pʀi] *nf* **(a)** (*duperie*) deception, deceit, trickery (*U*). **(b)** (*littér: illusion*) illusion.

trompeter [tʀɔ̃p(ə)te] (4) *vt* (*péj*) *nouvelle* to trumpet abroad, shout from the housetops.

trompette [tʀɔ̃pɛt] **1** *nf* **(a)** (*Mus*) trumpet. **~ de cavalerie** bugle; **~ d'harmonie** *ou* **à pistons** *ou* **chromatique** orchestral *ou* valve *ou* chromatic trumpet; **~ basse/bouchée** bass/muted trumpet; (*Bible*) **la ~ du Jugement dernier** the last Trump; (*littér*) **la ~ de la Renommée** the Trumpet of Fame; *V* **nez, tambour.**
(b) (*Bot*) **~ de la mort** horn of plenty.
(c) (*coquillage*) trumpet shell.
2 *nm* (*trompettiste*) trumpeter, trumpet (player).

trompettiste [tʀɔ̃petist(ə)] *nmf* trumpet player, trumpeter.

trompeur, -euse [tʀɔ̃pœʀ, øz] **1** *adj* **(a)** *personne* deceitful, deceiving (*épith*); *paroles, discours* deceitful.
(b) *apparences* deceptive, misleading; *distance, profondeur* deceptive. **les apparences sont ~euses** appearances are deceptive.
2 *nm,f* deceiver. (*Prov*) **à ~, ~ et demi** every rogue has his match.

trompeusement [tʀɔ̃pøzmɑ̃] *adv* (*V* **trompeur**) deceitfully; deceptively.

tronc [tʀɔ̃] **1** *nm* **(a)** *[arbre]* trunk; *[colonne]* shaft, trunk; (*Géom*) *[cône, pyramide]* frustum; (*Anat*) *[nerf, vaisseau]* trunk, mainstem. **~ d'arbre** tree trunk; **~ de cône/pyramide** truncated cone/pyramid.
(b) (*Anat: thorax et abdomen*) trunk; *[cadavre mutilé]* torso.
(c) (*boîte*) (collection) box. **le ~ des pauvres** the poorbox.
2: (*Scol*) **tronc commun** common-core syllabus.

tronche: [tʀɔ̃ʃ] *nf* (*visage*) mug: (*péj*), face; (*tête*) nut*.

tronçon [tʀɔ̃sɔ̃] *nm* **(a)** *[tube, colonne, serpent]* section. **(b)** *[route, voie]* section, stretch; *[convoi, colonne]* section; *[phrase, texte]* part.

tronconique [tʀɔ̃kɔnik] *adj* like a flattened cone *ou* a sawn-off cone.

tronçonnage [tʀɔ̃sɔnaʒ] *nm*, **tronçonnement** [tʀɔ̃sɔnmɑ̃] *nm* (*V* **tronçonner**) sawing *ou* cutting up; cutting into sections.

tronçonner [tʀɔ̃sɔne] (1) *vt tronc* to saw *ou* cut up; *tube, barre* to cut into sections.

tronçonneuse [tʀɔ̃sɔnøz] *nf* chain saw.

trône [tʀon] *nm* **(a)** (*siège, fonction*) throne. **~ pontifical** papal throne; **placer qn/monter sur le ~** to put sb on/come to *ou* ascend the throne; **chasser du ~** to dethrone, remove from the throne; **le ~ et l'autel** King and Church.
(b) (*:hum: des W.-C.*) throne* (*hum*). **être sur le ~** to be on the throne.

trôner [tʀone] (1) *vi* **(a)** *[roi, divinité]* to sit enthroned, sit on the throne. **(b)** (*avoir la place d'honneur*) *[personne]* to sit enthroned; *[chose]* to sit imposingly; (*péj: faire l'important*) to lord it.

tronquer [tʀɔ̃ke] (1) *vt* **(a)** *colonne, statue* to truncate.
(b) (*fig*) *citation, texte* to truncate, curtail, cut down; *détails, faits* to abbreviate, cut out.

trop [tʀo] **1** *adv* **(a)** (*avec vb: à l'excès*) too much; (*devant adv, adj*) too. **beaucoup** *ou* **bien ~** *manger etc* far *ou* much too much; **beaucoup** *ou* **bien** *ou* (*littér*) **par ~** (*avec adj*) far too, much too; **il a ~ mangé/bu** he has had too much to eat/drink, he has eaten/drunk too much; **je suis exténué d'avoir ~ marché** I'm exhausted from having walked too far *ou* too much; **il a ~ travaillé** he has worked too hard *ou* has overworked; **la pièce est ~ chauffée** the room is overheated; **la maison est ~ grande/loin pour eux** the house is too large/far for them; **un ~ grand effort l'épuiserait** too great an effort would exhaust him; **des restrictions ~ sévères aggraveraient la situation économique** too severe restrictions would aggravate the economic situation; **elle en a déjà bien ~ dit** she has said far *ou* much too much already; **il ne faut pas ~ demander/insister** one mustn't be too greedy/pressing, one mustn't be overdemanding/overinsistent; **tu as conduit ~ vite/lentement** you drove too fast/slowly; **tu as ~ conduit** you drove for too long, you have been driving (for) too long; **il ne faut pas ~ aller le voir** we must not go to visit him too often; **vous êtes ~ (nombreux)/~ peu (nombreux)** there are too many/too few of you; **une ~ forte dose** an overdose.
(b) ~ de (*quantité*) too much; (*nombre*) too many; **j'ai acheté ~ de pain/d'oranges** I've bought too much bread/too many oranges; **n'apportez pas de pain, il y en a déjà ~** don't bring any bread — there is too much already; **n'apportez pas de verres, il y en a déjà ~** don't bring any glasses — there are too many already; **s'il te reste ~ de dollars, vends-les moi** if you have dollars left over *ou* to spare, sell me them; **nous avons ~ de personnel** we are overstaffed; **il y a ~ de monde dans la salle** the hall is overcrowded *ou* overfull, there are too many people in the hall; **j'ai ~ de travail** I'm overworked, I have too much work (to do); **ils ne seront pas ~ de deux pour ce travail** this job will need the two of them (on it); **~ de bonté/d'égoïsme** excessive kindness/selfishness.
(c) (*avec conséquence*) too much; (*devant adj, adv*) too. **il mange beaucoup ~ pour maigrir** he eats far too much to lose any weight; **le village est ~ loin pour qu'il puisse y aller à pied** the village is too far for him to walk there; **elle a ~ de travail pour qu'on lui permette de sortir tôt** she has too much work (to do) for her to be allowed out early; **il est bien ~ idiot pour comprendre** he is far too stupid *ou* too much of an idiot to understand; **c'est ~ beau pour être vrai!** it's too good to be true!
(d) (*superl, intensif*) too, so (very). **j'ai oublié mes papiers, c'est vraiment ~ bête** how stupid (of me) *ou* it's too stupid for words — I've forgotten my papers; **il y a vraiment par ~ de gens égoïstes** there are far too many selfish people about; **c'est par ~ injuste** it's too unfair for words; **c'est ~ drôle!** it's too funny for words!, how funny!; **il n'est pas ~ satisfait/mécontent du résultat** he's not over-pleased *ou* too satisfied *ou* too pleased/not too unhappy *ou* dissatisfied with the result; **nous n'avons pas ~ de place chez nous** we haven't got (so) very much room *ou* (all) that much* room at our place; **vous êtes ~ aimable** you are too *ou* most kind; **je ne sais ~ que faire** I am not too *ou* quite sure what to do *ou* what I should do, I don't really know what to do; **il n'aime pas ~ ça*** he isn't too keen *ou* overkeen (on it), he doesn't like it overmuch *ou* (all) that much*; **cela n'a que ~ duré** it's gone on (far) too long already; **je ne le sais que ~** I know only too well, I am only too well aware; **je n'ai pas ~ confiance en lui** I haven't much *ou* all that much* confidence in him; **c'est ~!, c'en est ~!, ~ c'est ~!** that's going too far!, enough is enough!; **cela ne va pas ~ bien** things are not going so *ou* terribly well; **je n'en sais ~ rien** I don't really know; *V* **tôt.**
(e) de ~, en ~: il y a une personne/2 personnes de ~ *ou* **en ~ dans l'ascenseur** there is one person/there are 2 persons too many in the lift; **s'il y a du pain en ~, j'en emporterai** if there is any bread (left) over *ou* any bread extra I'll take some away; **il m'a rendu 2 F de ~** *ou* **en ~** he gave me back 2 francs too much; **ces 5 F sont de ~** that's 5 francs too much; **l'argent versé en ~** the excess payment; **il pèse 3 kg de ~** he is 3 kg overweight; **si je suis de ~, je peux m'en aller!** if I'm in the way *ou* not welcome I can always leave!; **cette remarque est de ~** that remark is uncalled-for; **il a bu un verre** *ou* **un coup* de ~** he's had a drink *ou* one* too many; **tu manges/bois de ~*** you eat/drink too much.
2 *nm* excess. **le ~ d'importance accordé à** the excessive importance attributed to; **que faire du ~ qui reste?** what is to be done with what is left (over)? *ou* with the extra?

trope [tʀɔp] *nm* (*Littérat*) trope.

trophée [tʀɔfe] *nm* trophy. **~ de chasse** hunting trophy.

tropical, e, *mpl* **-aux** [tʀɔpikal, o] *adj* tropical.

tropique [tʀɔpik] **1** *adj année* tropical. **2** *nm* **(a)** (*Géog: ligne*) tropic. **~ du cancer/capricorne** tropic of Cancer/Capricorn. **(b)** (*zone*) **les ~s** the tropics; **le soleil des ~s** the tropical sun.

tropisme [tʀɔpism(ə)] *nm* (*Bio*) tropism.

troposphère [tʀɔpɔsfɛʀ] *nf* troposphere.

trop-perçu, *pl* **trop-perçus** [tʀopɛʀsy] *nm* (*Admin, Comm*) excess (tax) payment, overpayment (of tax).

trop-plein, *pl* **trop-pleins** [tʀoplɛ̃] *nm* **(a)** (*excès d'eau*) *[réservoir, barrage]* overflow; *[vase]* excess water; (*tuyau d'évacuation*) overflow (pipe); (*déversoir*) overflow outlet.
(b) (*excès de contenu: grains etc*) excess.
(c) (*fig*) **~ d'amour/d'amitié** overflowing love/friendship; **~ de vie** *ou* **d'énergie** surplus *ou* boundless energy; **déverser le ~ de son cœur/âme** to pour out one's heart/soul *ou* all one's pent-up feelings.

troquer [tʀɔke] (1) *vt:* **~ qch contre qch d'autre** to barter *ou* trade sth for sth else; (*fig: remplacer*) to trade *ou* swap sth for sth else.

troquet: [tʀɔkɛ] *nm* small café.

trot [tʀo] *nm [cheval]* trot. **petit/grand ~** jog/full trot; **~ de manège** dressage trot; **~ assis/enlevé** close/rising trot; **course de ~ attelé** trotting race; **course de ~ monté** *trotting race* *under saddle*; (*lit*) **aller au** ~ to trot along; (*fig*) **au** ~* at the double; (*lit*, **fig*) **partir au** ~ to set off at a trot; **prendre le** ~ to break into a trot.

trotskyste [tʀɔtskist(ə)] *adj, nmf* trotskyist, trotskyite (*péj*).

trotte* [tʀɔt] *nf*: **il y a** *ou* **ça fait une** ~ **(d'ici au village)** it's a fair distance (from here to the village); **on a fait une (jolie)** ~ we've come a good way*, we covered a good distance.

trotter [tʀɔte] (1) **1** *vi* **(a)** *[cheval, cavalier]* to trot.

(b) (*fig*) *[personne]* (*marcher à petits pas*) to trot about (*ou* along *etc*); (*marcher beaucoup*) to run around, run hither and thither; *[souris, enfants]* to scurry (about), scamper (about). **un air/une idée qui vous trotte dans** *ou* **par la tête** *ou* **la cervelle** a tune/an idea which keeps running around in *ou* through your head; **cela fait** ~ **l'imagination** that gets the imagination going.

2 se trotter* *vpr* (*se sauver*) to dash (off)*.

trotteur, -euse [tʀɔtœʀ, øz] **1** *nm,f* (*cheval*) trotter, trotting horse. **2 trotteuse** *nf* (*aiguille*) (sweep) second hand.

trottin†† [tʀɔtɛ̃] *nm* (dressmaker's) errand girl.

trottinement [tʀɔtinmɑ̃] *nm* (*V* **trottiner**) jogging; trotting; scurrying, scampering.

trottiner [tʀɔtine] (1) *vi [cheval]* to jog along; *[personne]* to trot along; *[souris]* to scurry *ou* scamper about *ou* along.

trottinette [tʀɔtinɛt] *nf* (child's) scooter.

trottoir [tʀɔtwaʀ] *nm* **(a)** pavement (*Brit*), sidewalk (*US*). ~ **roulant** moving walkway, travellator (*Brit*). **(b)** (*péj*) **faire le** ~* to walk the streets, be a streetwalker.

trou [tʀu] **1** *nm* **(a)** (*gén, Golf*) hole; (*terrier*) hole, burrow; *[flûte etc]* (finger-)hole; *[aiguille]* eye. **par le** ~ **de la serrure** through the keyhole; (*Théât*) **le** ~ **du souffleur** the prompt box; **faire un** ~ (*dans le sol*) to dig *ou* make a hole; (*dans une haie*) to make a hole *ou* a gap; (*dans un mur avec une vrille etc*) to bore *ou* make a hole; (*en perforant: dans le cuir, papier*) to punch *ou* make a hole; (*avec des ciseaux, un couteau*) to cut a hole; (*en usant, frottant*) to wear a hole; (*Golf*) **faire un** ~ **en un** to get a hole in one; **il a fait un** ~ **à son pantalon** (*usure*) he has (worn) a hole in his trousers; (*brûlure, acide*) he has burnt a hole in his trousers; (*déchirure*) he has torn a hole in his trousers; **ses chaussettes sont pleines de** ~**s** *ou* **ont des** ~**s partout** his socks are in holes *ou* are full of holes; **sol/rocher creusé** *ou* **piqué de** ~**s** ground/rock pitted with holes; (*fig*) **une œuvre qui a des** ~**s** a work with certain weaknesses *ou* weak parts.

(b) (*fig*) (*moment de libre*) gap; (*déficit*) deficit; (*Sport: trouée*) gap, space. **un** ~ **(de 10 millions) dans la comptabilité** a deficit (of 10 million) in the accounts; (*Sport*) **faire le** ~ to break *ou* burst through; **cela a fait un gros** ~ **dans ses économies** it made quite a hole in his savings; **j'ai un** ~ **dans la matinée, venez me voir** I have a gap in my schedule during the morning so come and see me; **avoir un** ~ **(de mémoire)** to have a lapse of memory.

(c) (*Anat*) foramen. ~ **optique** optic foramen; ~**s intervertébraux** intervertebral foramina; *V* **œil**.

(d) (*péj: localité*) place, hole* (*péj*). **ce village est un** ~ this village is a real hole* (*péj*) *ou* dump* (*péj*); **il n'est jamais sorti de son** ~ he has never been out of his own backyard; **chercher un petit** ~ **pas cher** to look for a little place that's not too dear; **un** ~ **perdu** *ou* **paumé*** a dead-and-alive (little) hole* (*péj*).

(e) (*loc*) (*fig*) **(se) faire son** ~* to make a niche for o.s.; (*fig*) **vivre tranquille dans son** ~ to live quietly in one's little hidey-hole* *ou* hideaway; (*prison*) **être au** ~* to be in (the) nick‡ *ou* in clink‡; (*fig*) **quand on sera dans le** ~* when we're dead and buried *ou* dead and gone, when we're six feet under*; *V* **boire**.

2: **trou d'aération** airhole, (air) vent; (*Aviat*) **trou d'air** air pocket; **trou de balle**∵ arse-hole∵ (*Brit*), asshole∵ (*US*); (*fig: imbécile*) berk‡ (*Brit*), twat∵; (*Naut*) **trou du chat** lubber's hole; **trou du cul**∵ = **trou de balle**∵; **trou d'homme** manhole; **trou-madame** *nm, pl* **trous-madame** troll-madam (*type of bagatelle*); **trou du milieu** = **trou normand**; **trou de nez**‡ nose-hole‡; (*Astron*) **trou noir** black hole; **trou normand** *glass of spirits, often Calvados, drunk between courses of meal*; **trou d'obus** shell-hole *ou* -crater; **trou de souris** mousehole; **d'embarrassement, elle serait rentrée dans un trou de souris** she was so embarrassed that she would have liked the ground to swallow her up; (*Couture*) **trou-trou** *nm, pl* **trou-trous** *lace trimming through which ribbon is passed*.

troubadour [tʀubaduʀ] *nm* troubadour.

troublant, e [tʀublɑ̃, ɑ̃t] *adj* (*déconcertant*) disturbing, disquieting, unsettling; (*sexuellement provocant*) disturbing, arousing.

trouble[1] [tʀubl(ə)] **1** *adj* **(a)** *eau, vin* unclear, cloudy, turbid (*littér*); *regard* misty, dull; *image* blurred, misty, indistinct. **avoir la vue** ~ to have blurred vision; *V* **pêcher**[1].

(b) (*fig*) (*impur, équivoque*) *affaire* shady, murky; *désir* dark (*épith*); *joie perverse* (*épith*); (*vague, pas franc*) *regard* shifty, uneasy.

2 *adv*: **voir** ~ to have blurred vision, see things dimly *ou* as if through a mist.

trouble[2] [tʀubl(ə)] *nm* **(a)** (*agitation, remue-ménage*) tumult, turmoil; (*zizanie, désunion*) discord, trouble. **semer** *ou* **répandre le** ~ **(parmi)** to sow discord (among), cause trouble (among).

(b) (*émeute*) ~**s** disturbances, troubles; ~**s politiques/sociaux** political/social unrest (*U*) *ou* disturbances; **des** ~**s sanglants** disturbances *ou* troubles causing bloodshed; *V* **fauteur**.

(c) (*émoi affectif ou sensuel*) (inner) turmoil, agitation; (*inquiétude, désarroi*) distress; (*gêne, perplexité*) confusion, embarrassment. **le** ~ **étrange qui s'empara d'elle** the strange inner turmoil *ou* agitation which overcame her; **le** ~ **profond causé par ces événements traumatisants** the profound distress caused by these traumatic events; (*littér*) **le** ~ **de son âme/cœur** the tumult *ou* turmoil in his soul/heart; **le** ~ **de son esprit** the agitation in his mind, the turmoil his mind was in; **dominer/se laisser trahir par son** ~ to overcome/give o.s. away by one's confusion *ou* embarrassment.

(d) (*gén pl: Méd*) trouble (*U*), disorder. ~**s physiologiques/psychiques** physiological/psychological trouble *ou* disorders; ~**s de la vision** trouble with one's (eye)sight *ou* vision; ~**s de la personnalité** personality problems *ou* disorders; **ce n'est qu'un** ~ **passager** it's only a passing disorder.

trouble-fête [tʀubləfɛt] *nmf inv* spoilsport.

troubler [tʀuble] (1) **1** *vt* **(a)** (*perturber*) *ordre* to disturb, disrupt; *sommeil, tranquillité, silence* to disturb; *représentation, réunion* to disrupt; *jugement, raison, esprit* to cloud. ~ **l'ordre public** to disturb public order, cause a breach of public order; **en ces temps troublés** in these troubled times.

(b) *personne* (*démonter, impressionner*) to disturb, disconcert; (*inquiéter*) to trouble, perturb; (*gêner, embrouiller*) to bother, confuse; (*d'émoi amoureux*) to disturb, agitate, arouse. **ce film/cet événement l'a profondément troublé** this film/event has disturbed him deeply; **la perspective d'un échec ne le trouble pas du tout** the prospect of failure doesn't perturb *ou* trouble him in the slightest; **il y a quand même un détail qui me trouble** there's still a detail which is bothering *ou* confusing me; **cesse de parler, tu me troubles (dans mes calculs)** stop talking — you are disturbing me (in my calculations); ~ **un candidat** to disconcert a candidate, put a candidate off; ~ **(les sens de) qn** to disturb *ou* agitate sb.

(c) (*brouiller*) *eau* to make cloudy *ou* turbid (*littér*); *vin* to cloud, make cloudy; *atmosphère* to cloud; *ciel* to darken, cloud; (*TV*) *image* to upset, disturb. **les larmes lui troublaient la vue** tears clouded *ou* blurred her vision.

2 se troubler *vpr* **(a)** (*devenir trouble*) *[eau]* to cloud, become cloudy *ou* turbid (*littér*).

(b) (*perdre contenance*) to become flustered. **il se trouble facilement aux examens/lorsqu'il a à parler** he is easily flustered *ou* disconcerted in exams/when he has to speak; **il répondit sans se** ~ he replied unperturbed.

troué, e [tʀue] (*ptp de* **trouer**) **1** *adj*: **bas/sac** ~ stocking/bag with a hole *ou* with holes in it; **avoir un bas (de)** ~ to have a hole in one's stocking, have a stocking with a hole in it; **ce sac est** ~ this bag has a hole *ou* holes (in it); **une veste toute** ~**e** a jacket that is full of holes; **ses chaussettes sont toutes** ~**es** his socks are full of holes; **le rocher était** ~ **comme une éponge** the rock was pitted like a sponge; **ce seau est** ~ **comme une passoire** *ou* **écumoire** this bucket has a bottom like a sieve *ou* colander, this bucket has as many holes in it as a sieve *ou* colander; **son gant** ~ **laissait passer son pouce** his thumb stuck *ou* poked out through a hole in his glove.

2 trouée *nf* **(a)** *[haie, forêt, nuages]* gap, break (*de* in).

(b) (*Mil*) breach. **faire une** ~**e** to make a breach, break through.

(c) (*Géog: défilé*) gap. **la** ~**e de Belfort** the Belfort Gap.

trouer [tʀue] (1) *vt* **(a)** *vêtement* to make *ou* wear a hole in; *ticket* to punch (a hole in). **il a troué son pantalon** (*avec une cigarette*) he's burnt a hole in his trousers; (*dans les ronces*) he's torn *ou* ripped a hole in his trousers; (*par usure*) he's worn a hole in his trousers; **ces chaussettes se sont trouées très vite** these socks soon got holes in them *ou* soon went into holes; **la poitrine trouée d'une balle** his chest pierced by a bullet; ~ **la peau à qn**‡ to put a bullet into sb*; **se faire** ~ **la peau**‡ to get o.s. shot up*, get a bullet in one's hide*.

(b) (*fig: traverser*) *silence, nuit* to pierce. **une fusée troua l'obscurité** a rocket pierced the darkness; **un cri troua l'air** a shout rent *ou* pierced the air; **des élancements lui trouaient la tête** sharp pains shot through his head.

(c) (*fig: parsemer: gén ptp*) to dot. **la plaine trouée d'ombres** the plain dotted with shadows; **des rochers troués de lichen/de mousse** rocks dotted with lichen/moss.

troufignon‡† [tʀufiɲɔ̃] *nm* backside‡, arse∵.

troufion* [tʀufjɔ̃] *nm* soldier.

trouillard, e‡ [tʀujaʀ, aʀd(ə)] (*péj*) **1** *adj* yellow*, chicken* (*attrib*), yellow-bellied‡. **2** *nm,f* yellowbelly‡.

trouille‡ [tʀuj] *nf*: **avoir la** ~ to be in a (blue) funk‡, have the wind up*; **flanquer** *ou* **ficher la** ~ **à qn** to put the wind up sb*, scare the pants off sb‡.

trouillomètre‡ [tʀujɔmɛtʀ(ə)] *nm*: **avoir le** ~ **à zéro** to be in a blue funk‡, be scared stiff*.

troupe [tʀup] *nf* **(a)** (*Mil, Scoutisme*) troop. (*Mil*) **la** ~ (*l'armée*) the army; (*les simples soldats*) the troops (*pl*); **les** ~**s** the troops; ~**s de choc/de débarquement** shock/landing troops; **lever des** ~**s** to raise troops; **faire intervenir la** ~ to call *ou* bring in the army; **réservé à la** ~ reserved for the troops; **il y avait de la** ~ **cantonnée au village** there were some army units billeted in the village; *V* **enfant, homme**.

(b) *[chanteurs, danseurs]* troupe. *[acteurs]* ~ **(de théâtre)** (theatrical) company.

(c) *[gens, animaux]* band, group, troop. **se déplacer en** ~ to go about in a band *ou* group *ou* troop.

troupeau, *pl* ~**x** [tʀupo] *nm [bœufs, chevaux]* (*dans un pré*) herd; (*transhumant*) drove; *[moutons, chèvres]* flock; *[oies]* gaggle; (*péj*) *[touristes, prisonniers]* herd (*péj*), hoard (*péj*). (*Rel*) **le** ~ **du Seigneur** the Lord's flock.

troupier [tʀupje] **1** *nm* (†) private. **boire comme un** ~ to drink like a fish; **fumer comme un** ~ to smoke like a chimney; **jurer comme un** ~ to swear like a trooper. **2** *adj V* **comique**.

trousse [tʀus] *nf* **(a)** (*étui*) (*gén*) case, kit; *[médecin, chirurgien]* instrument case; *[écolier]* pencil case *ou* wallet. ~ **à aiguilles** needle case; ~ **à couture** sewing case *ou* kit; ~ **de maquillage**

vanity case *ou* bag; ~ **à outils** toolkit; ~ **à ongles** nail kit, manicure set; ~ **de toilette** *ou* **de voyage** (*sac*) toilet bag, sponge bag; (*mallette*) travelling case.

(b) (*loc*) **aux** ~**s de** (hot) on the heels of, on the tail of; **les créanciers/policiers étaient à ses** ~**s** the creditors/policemen were on his tail *ou* (hot) on his heels; **avoir la police aux** ~**s** to have the police on one's tail *ou* (hot) on one's heels.

trousseau, *pl* ~**x** [tʀuso] *nm* **(a)** ~ **de clefs** bunch of keys. **(b)** (*vêtements, linge*) *[mariée]* trousseau; *[écolier]* outfit.

troussequin [tʀuskɛ̃] *nm* = **trusquin.**

trousser [tʀuse] (1) *vt* **(a)** (*Culin*) *volaille* to truss. **(b)** (†: *retrousser*) *robe, jupes* to pick *ou* tuck up. **se** ~ to pick *ou* tuck up one's skirts. **(c)** (†, *hum*) *femme* to tumble†. **(d)** (†: *expédier*) *poème, article, discours* to dash off, throw together.

trousseur [tʀusœʀ] *nm* (†, *hum*) ~ **de jupons** womanizer, ladykiller.

trouvaille [tʀuvɑj] *nf* (*objet*) find; (*fig: idée, métaphore, procédé*) stroke of inspiration.

trouver [tʀuve] (1) **1** *vt* **(a)** (*en cherchant*) *objet, emploi, main-d'œuvre, renseignement* to find. **je ne le trouve pas** I can't find it; **où peut-on le** ~**?** where can he be found?, where is he to be found?; **on lui a trouvé une place dans un lycée** he was found a place in a lycée, they found him a place *ou* a place for him in a lycée; **est-ce qu'ils trouveront le chemin?** will they find the way? *ou* their way?; ~ **le temps/l'énergie/le courage de faire qch** to find (the) time/the energy/the courage to do sth; ~ **refuge/faveur auprès de qn** to find refuge/favour with sb; **comment avez-vous trouvé un secrétaire si compétent?** how did you come by *ou* find such a competent secretary?; **elle a trouvé en lui un ami sûr/un associé compétent** she has found in him a faithful friend/a competent partner; **on ne lui trouve que des qualités** he has only virtues *ou* good qualities; **ça ne se trouve pas dans** *ou* **sous les pas d'un cheval** you don't find that at every street corner; *V* **chercher, enfant, objet.**

(b) (*rendre visite*) **aller/venir** ~ **qn** to go/come and see sb.

(c) (*rencontrer par hasard*) *document, information, personne* to find, come upon, come across; *difficultés* to meet with, come across, come up against. **on trouve cette plante** *ou* **cette plante se trouve sous tous les climats humides** this plant is found *ou* is to be found in all damp climates.

(d) (*imaginer, inventer*) *solution, prétexte, cause, moyen* to find. **j'ai trouvé!** I've got it!*; **c'est tout trouvé** that solves the problem, that's the answer; **formule bien trouvée** clever *ou* happy phrase; (*iro*) **tu as trouvé ça tout seul!** did you think it out all by yourself? (*iro*); **où est-il allé** ~ **ça?** where (on earth) did he get that idea from?, whatever gave him that idea?

(e) (*avec à + infin*) ~ **à redire (à tout)** to find something to criticize (in everything); ~ **à manger/à boire** to find something to eat/to drink; **elle trouve toujours à faire dans la maison** she can always find something to do in the house; ~ **à se distraire/à s'occuper** to find a way to amuse/occupy o.s., find something to amuse/occupy o.s. with; **ils trouveront bien à les loger quelque part** they will surely find a way to put them up somewhere, they will surely find somewhere to put them up.

(f) (*éprouver*) ~ **du plaisir à qch/à faire qch** to take pleasure in sth/in doing sth; ~ **un malin plaisir à taquiner qn** to get a malicious pleasure out of teasing sb, take a malicious pleasure in teasing sb, derive a malicious pleasure from teasing sb; ~ **de la difficulté à faire** to find *ou* have difficulty in doing; ~ **une consolation dans le travail** to find consolation in work *ou* in working.

(g) (*avec attribut du complément*) (*découvrir*) to find. ~ **qch cassé/vide** to find sth broken/empty; (*estimer, juger*) ~ **qch à son goût/trop cher** to find sth to one's liking/too expensive; (*fig*) **j'ai trouvé les oiseaux envolés** I found the birds had flown (away); ~ **porte close** to find nobody at home *ou* in; ~ **que** to find *ou* think that; **je trouve cela trop sucré/lourd** I find it too sweet/heavy, it's too sweet/heavy for me; **elle trouve qu'il fait trop chaud ici** she finds it too hot (in) here; **je le trouve fatigué** I think he looks tired, I find him tired-looking, I find him looking tired; **tu lui trouves bonne mine?** do you think he's looking well?; **comment l'as-tu trouvé?** what did you think of him?, how did you find him?; **vous la trouvez sympathique?** do you like her?, do you think she's nice?, do you find her a nice person?; **trouvez-vous cela normal?** do you think that's as it should be?; **tu trouves ça drôle!** *ou* **que c'est drôle!** so you think that's funny!, so you find that funny!; **vous trouvez?** (do) ynu think so?; **il a trouvé bon de nous écrire** he thought *ou* saw fit to write to us; ~ **le temps court/long** to find that time passes quickly *ou* races on/passes slowly *ou* hangs heavy *ou* heavily on one's hands.

(h) (*loc*) ~ **grâce auprès de qn** to find favour with sb; ~ **à qui parler** to meet one's match; ~ **son maître** to find one's master; **cet objet n'avait pas trouvé d'amateur** no one had expressed *ou* shown any interest in the object; **cet objet n'avait pas trouvé preneur** the object had had no takers; ~ **la mort (dans un accident)** to meet one's death (in an accident); **je la trouve mauvaise!*** *ou* **saumâtre!*** I think it's a bit off* (*Brit*), I don't like it at all; (*hum*) ~ **son bonheur** *ou* **sa vie dans qch** to find exactly what one is after *ou* what one is looking for in sth; ~ **le sommeil** to get to sleep, fall asleep; ~ **chaussure à son pied** to find a suitable match; (*fig*) ~ **le joint*** to come up with the (right) answer* (*fig*); ~ **son compte à faire qch** to be better (off) doing sth; **il a trouvé son compte dans cette affaire** he got something out of this bit of business; (*lit*) ~ **le moyen de faire** to find some means of doing; (*fig hum*) **il a trouvé le moyen de s'égarer** he managed *ou* contrived to get (himself) lost.

2 se trouver *vpr* **(a)** (*être soudain dans une situation, un endroit*) *[personne]* to find o.s.; *[chose]* to be. **il se trouva nez à nez avec Paul** he found himself face to face with Paul; **la question se trouva reléguée au second plan** the question was relegated to the background; **le camion se trouva coincé entre ...** the lorry was jammed between ... ; **je me suis trouvé dans l'impossibilité de répondre** I found myself unable to reply; (*iro*) **je me suis trouvé fin!** a fine *ou* right* fool I looked!

(b) (*être placé dans une situation, être situé*) *[personne]* to be; *[chose]* to be, be situated. **ça ne se trouve pas sur la carte** it isn't *ou* doesn't appear on the map; **son nom ne se trouve pas sur la liste** his name is not on *ou* does not appear on the list; **je me trouvais près de l'entrée** I was (standing *ou* sitting *etc*) near the entrance; **nous nous trouvons dans une situation délicate** we are in a delicate situation; **il se trouve dans l'impossibilité de venir** he is unable to come, he is not in a position to come; **il se trouve dans l'obligation de partir** he has to *ou* is compelled to leave; **il ne fait pas bon se** ~ **dehors par ce froid** it's not pleasant to be out in this cold; **la maison se trouve au coin de la rue** the house is (situated) *ou* stands on the corner of the street; **où se trouve la poste?** where is the post office?; **les toilettes se trouvent près de l'entrée** the toilets are (situated) near the entrance.

(c) (*se sentir*) to feel. **se** ~ **bien** (*dans un fauteuil etc*) to feel comfortable; (*santé*) to feel well; **il se trouve mieux en montagne** he feels better in the mountains; **elle se trouvait bien dans ce pays** she was happy in this country; **se** ~ **mal** to faint, pass out; **se** ~ **bien/mal d'avoir fait qch** to have reason to be glad/to regret having done sth; **il s'en est bien trouvé** he benefited from it; **il s'en est mal trouvé** he lived to regret it.

(d) (*avec infin: exprime la coïncidence*) **se** ~ **être/avoir ...** to happen to be/have ... ; **elles se trouvaient avoir le même chapeau** it turned out that they had *ou* they happened to have the same hat.

(e) (*en méditant etc*) **essayer de se** ~ to try to find o.s.

3 *vpr impers* **(a)** (*le fait est*) **il se trouve que c'est moi** it happens to be me, it's me as it happens; **il se trouvait qu'elle avait menti** it turned out that she had been lying; **comme il se trouve parfois/souvent** as is sometimes/often the case, as sometimes/often happens; **et s'il se trouve qu'elles ne viennent pas?** and what if (it happens that) they don't come?

(b) (*il y a*) **il se trouve toujours des gens qui disent ...** *ou* **pour dire ...** there are always people *ou* you'll always find people who will say ... .

(c) (*) **ils sont sortis, si ça se trouve** they may well be out, they're probably out.

trouvère [tʀuvɛʀ] *nm* trouvère.

troyen, -enne [tʀwajɛ̃, ɛn] **1** *adj* Trojan. **2** *nm,f*: **T**~**(ne)** Trojan.

truand, e [tʀyɑ̃, ɑ̃d] **1** *nm,f* (†) beggar. **2** *nm* villain, crook.

truander: [tʀyɑ̃de] (1) *vt* to swindle, do:.

trublion [tʀyblijɔ̃] *nm* troublemaker, agitator.

truc[1] [tʀyk] *nm* **(a)** (*) (*moyen, combine*) way; (*dispositif*) thingummy*, whatsit*. **trouver le** ~ **(pour faire)** to get *ou* find the knack (of doing); **avoir le** ~ to have the knack; **cherche un** ~ **pour venir me voir** try to wangle coming to see me*, try to find some way of coming to see me; **c'est connu leur** ~***, on le connaît leur** ~ ***** we know what they're up to* *ou* playing at*, we're onto their little game*; **les** ~**s du métier** the tricks of the trade.

(b) (*tour*) *[prestidigitateur]* trick; (*trucage: Ciné etc*) trick, effect. **c'est impressionnant mais ce n'est qu'un** ~ it's impressive but it's only a trick *ou* an effect.

(c) (*: *chose, idée*) thing. **on m'a raconté un** ~ **extraordinaire** I've been told an extraordinary thing; **j'ai pensé (à) un** ~ I've thought of something, I've had a thought; **il y a un tas de** ~**s à faire** there's a heap of things to do*; **il n'y a pas un** ~ **de vrai là-dedans** there's not a word of truth in it.

(d) (*: *machin*) (*dont le nom échappe*) thingumajig*, thingummy*, whatsit*; (*inconnu, jamais vu*) contraption, thing, thingumajig*; (*tableau, statue bizarre*) thing. **méfie-toi de ces** ~**s-là** be careful of *ou* beware of those things.

(e) (:: *personne*) **T**~**(-chouette), Machin-**~ what's-his-(*ou* her) name*, what-d'you-call-him* (*ou* her), thingummybob*.

truc[2] [tʀyk] *nm* (*Rail*) truck, waggon.

trucage [tʀykaʒ] *nm* = **truquage.**

truchement [tʀyʃmɑ̃] *nm* **(a) par le** ~ **de qn** through (the intervention of) sb; **par le** ~ **de qch** with the aid of sth. **(b)** (††, *littér: moyen d'expression, intermédiaire*) medium, means of expression.

trucider: [tʀyside] (1) *vt* (*hum*) to knock off:, bump off:.

truck [tʀyk] *nm* = **truc**[2].

trucmuche: [tʀykmyʃ] *nm* thingumajig*, thingummybob*, whatsit*.

truculence [tʀykylɑ̃s] *nf* (*V* **truculent**) vividness; colourfulness; raciness.

truculent, e [tʀykylɑ̃, ɑ̃t] *adj langage* vivid, colourful, racy; *personnage* colourful, larger-than-life (*épith*), larger than life (*attrib*).

truelle [tʀyɛl] *nf [maçon]* trowel. (*Culin*) ~ **à poisson** fish slice.

truffe [tʀyf] *nf* **(a)** (*Bot*) truffle. **(b)** (*Culin*) ~**s (au chocolat)** (chocolate) truffles. **(c)** (*nez du chien*) nose. **(d)** (*: *idiot*) nitwit*, twit*.

truffer [tʀyfe] (1) *vt* **(a)** (*Culin*) to garnish with truffles. **(b)** (*fig: remplir*) ~ **qch de** to pepper sth with; **truffé de citations** peppered *ou* larded with quotations; **truffé de pièges** bristling with traps.

truie [tʀɥi] *nf* (*Zool*) sow.

truisme [tʀyism(ə)] *nm* (*littér*) truism.

truite [tʀɥit] *nf* trout. ~ **saumonée** salmon trout; ~ **de mer** sea trout; ~ **arc-en-ciel** rainbow trout; (*Culin*) ~ **meunière** truite *ou* trout meunière.

truité, e [tʀɥite] *adj* **(a)** (*tacheté*) *cheval* mottled, speckled;

chien spotted, speckled. **(b)** (*craquelé*) *porcelaine* crackled.
trumeau, *pl* **~x** [tʀymo] *nm* **(a)** (*pilier*) pier; (*entre portes, fenêtres*) pier; (*panneau ou glace*) pier glass; *[cheminée]* overmantel. **(b)** (*Culin*) shin of beef.
truquage [tʀykaʒ] *nm* **(a)** (*U: V* **truquer**) rigging; fixing*; adapting; doctoring*; fiddling*; faking. (*Ciné*) **le ~ d'une scène** using trick effects in a scene.
(b) (*Ciné*) **un ~ très réussi** a very successful effect; **~s optiques** optical effects *ou* illusions; **~s de laboratoire** lab effects.
truqué, e [tʀyke] (*ptp de* **truquer**) *adj élections* rigged; *combat* fixed*; *cartes, dés* fixed*. (*Ciné*) **une scène ~e** a scene involving trick effects.
truquer [tʀyke] (1) *vt* **(a)** *élections* to rig, fix*; (*gén ptp*) *combat* to fix. (*Ciné*) **~ une scène** to use trick effects in a scene.
(b) *serrure, verrou* to adapt, fix*; *cartes, dés* to fix*.
(c) (†: *falsifier*) *dossier* to doctor*; *comptes* to fiddle*; *œuvre d'art, meuble* to fake.
trusquin [tʀyskɛ̃] *nm* marking gauge.
trust [tʀœst] *nm* (*Écon: cartel*) trust; (*toute grande entreprise*) corporation; *V* **antitrust**.
truster [tʀœste] (1) *vt* (*Écon*) *secteur du marché* to monopolize, corner; *produit* to have the monopoly of, monopolize; (*: *accaparer*) to monopolize.
trypanosome [tʀipanozɔm] *nm* trypanosome.
tsar [dzaʀ] *nm* tsar, czar, tzar.
tsarévitch [dzaʀevitʃ] *nm* tsarevich, czarevich, tzarevich.
tsarine [dzaʀin] *nf* tsarina, czarina, tzarina.
tsarisme [dzaʀism(ə)] *nm* tsarism, czarism, tzarism.
tsariste [dzaʀist(ə)] *adj* tsarist, czarist, tzarist.
tsé-tsé [tsetse] *nf*: **(mouche) ~** tsetse fly.
tsigane [tsigan] **1** *adj* (Hungarian) gypsy *ou* gipsy, tzigane. **violoniste/musique ~** (Hungarian) gypsy violinist/music. **2** *nmf*: **T~** (Hungarian) Gypsy *ou* Gipsy, Tzigane.
tsoin-tsoin‡, tsouin-tsouin‡ [tswɛ̃tswɛ̃] *excl* boom-boom!
tss-tss [tsstss] *excl* tut-tut!
tu, t'* [ty, t] **1** *pron pers* you (*as opposed to 'vous': familiar form of address*); (*Rel*) thou. **t'as* de la chance** you're lucky.
2 *nm*: **employer le ~** to use the 'tu' form; **dire ~ à qn** to address sb as 'tu'; **être à ~ et à toi avec qn** to be on first-name terms with sb, be a great pal of sb*.
tuant, e [tɥɑ̃, ɑ̃t] *adj* (*fatigant*) killing, exhausting; (*énervant*) exasperating, tiresome.
tub [tœb] *nm* (*bassin*) (bath)tub; (*bain*) bath.
tuba [tyba] *nm* (*Mus*) tuba; (*Sport*) snorkel, breathing tube.
tubard, e‡ [tybaʀ, aʀd(ə)] (*abrév péj de* **tuberculeux**) **1** *adj* suffering from TB. **2** *nm,f* TB case.
tube [tyb] *nm* **(a)** (*tuyau*) (*gén, de mesure, en verre*) tube; (*de canalisation, tubulure, métallique*) pipe. **~ capillaire** capillary tube; **~ compte-gouttes** pipette; **~ à injection** hypodermic syringe; (*Mil*) **~ lance-torpilles** torpedo tube; (*Élec*) **~ au néon** neon tube; (*Élec*) **~ redresseur** vacuum diode; **~ régulateur de potentiel** triode; (*Élec*) **~ à rayons cathodiques** cathode ray tube; *V* **plein.**
(b) (*emballage*) *[aspirine, comprimés, dentifrice etc]* tube. **~ de rouge (à lèvres)** lipstick.
(c) (*Anat, Bot: conduit*) **~ digestif** digestive tract, alimentary canal; **~s urinifères** uriniferous tubules; **~ pollinique** pollen tube.
(d) (*: *chanson à succès*) hit song *ou* record.
(e) (‡: *téléphone*) **donner un coup de ~ à qn** to give sb a buzz* *ou* a tinkle*.
(f) (†*: *haut-de-forme*) topper*.
tubercule [tybɛʀkyl] *nm* (*Anat, Méd*) tubercle; (*Bot*) tuber.
tuberculeux, -euse [tybɛʀkylø, øz] **1** *adj* **(a)** (*Méd*) tuberculous, tubercular. **être ~** to suffer from tuberculosis *ou* TB, have tuberculosis *ou* TB. **(b)** (*Bot*) tuberous, tuberose. **2** *nm,f* tuberculosis *ou* tubercular *ou* TB patient.
tuberculine [tybɛʀkylin] *nf* tuberculin.
tuberculose [tybɛʀkyloz] *nf* tuberculosis. **~ pulmonaire** pulmonary tuberculosis; **~ osseuse** tuberculosis of the bones.
tubéreuse [tybeʀøz] *nf* (*Bot*) tuberose.
tubulaire [tybylɛʀ] *adj* tubular.
tubulé, e [tybyle] *adj plante* tubulate; *flacon* tubulated.
tubuleux, -euse [tybylø, øz] *adj* tubulous, tubulate.
tubulure [tybylyʀ] *nf* **(a)** (*tube*) pipe. **(b)** (*Tech: ouverture*) tubulure. (*tubes*) **~s** piping; (*Aut*) **~ d'échappement/d'admission** exhaust/inlet manifold; **~ d'alimentation** feed *ou* supply pipe.
tudieu†† [tydjø] *excl* zounds!††, 'sdeath!††.
tué, e [tɥe] (*ptp de* **tuer**) *nm,f* (*dans un accident, au combat*) person killed. **les ~s** the dead, those killed; **il y a eu 5 ~s et 4 blessés** there were 5 (people) killed *ou* 5 dead and 4 injured.
tue-mouche [tymuʃ] **1** *nm inv* (*Bot*) **(amanite) ~** fly agaric. **2** *adj*: **papier** *ou* **ruban ~(s)** flypaper.
tuer [tɥe] (1) **1** *vt* **(a)** *personne, animal* to kill; (*à la chasse*) to shoot. (*Bible*) **tu ne tueras point** thou shalt not kill; **~ qn à coups de pierre/de couteau** to stone/stab *ou* knife sb to death; **~ qn d'une balle** to shoot sb dead; **l'alcool tue** alcohol can kill *ou* is a killer; **la route tue** the highway is deadly *ou* is a killer; **cet enfant me tuera** this child will be the death of me; **la honte/le déshonneur la tuerait** shame/dishonour would kill her (*fig*); (*fig*) **il est à ~!** you (*ou* I) could kill him!; **il n'a jamais tué personne!** he wouldn't hurt a fly, he's quite harmless; **quelle odeur! ça tue les mouches à 15 pas!*** what a stink!* it would kill a man at 15 paces!; (*fig*) **un coup** *ou* **une gifle à ~ un bœuf** a blow to fell an ox; **~ la poule aux œufs d'or/le veau gras** to kill the goose that lays the golden eggs/the fatted calf.
(b) (*ruiner*) to kill; (*exténuer*) to exhaust, wear out. **la bureaucratie tue toute initiative** bureaucracy kills (off) all initiative; **les supermarchés n'ont pas tué le petit commerce** supermarkets have not killed off small traders; **ce rouge tue tout leur décor** this red kills (the effect of) their whole decor; **ces escaliers/ces querelles me tuent** these stairs/quarrels will be the death of me; **~ qch dans l'œuf** to nip sth in the bud; **~ le temps** to kill time.
2 se tuer *vpr* **(a)** (*accident*) to be killed. **il s'est tué en montagne/en voiture** he was killed in a mountaineering/car accident.
(b) (*suicide*) to kill o.s. **il s'est tué d'une balle dans la tête** he put a bullet through his head, he killed himself with a bullet through his *ou* the head.
(c) (*fig*) **se ~ à la peine** to work o.s. to death; **se ~ de travail** to work o.s. to death, kill o.s. with work; **se ~ à répéter/à essayer de faire comprendre qch à qn** to wear o.s. out repeating sth to sb/trying to make sb understand sth.
tuerie [tyʀi] *nf* (*carnage*) slaughter, carnage.
tue-tête [tytɛt] *adv*: **à ~: crier/chanter à ~** to shout/sing at the top of one's voice, shout/sing one's head off*.
tueur, -euse [tɥœʀ, øz] **1** *nm,f* **(a)** (*assassin*) killer. **~ (à gages)** hired *ou* professional killer. **(b)** (*chasseur*) **~ de lions/d'éléphants** lion-/elephant-killer. **2** *nm* (*d'abattoir*) slaughterman, slaughterer.
tuf [tyf] *nm* (*Géol*) tuff.
tuile [tɥil] *nf* **(a)** (*lit*) tile. **~ creuse** *ou* **romaine** *ou* **ronde** curved tile; **~ faîtière** ridge tile; **~s mécaniques** industrial *ou* interlocking tiles; **couvrir un toit de ~s** to tile a roof; **~s de pierre/d'ardoise** stone/slate tiles; **nous préférons la ~ à l'ardoise** we prefer tiles to slate. **(b)** (*: *coup de malchance*) blow. **quelle ~!** what a blow! **(c)** (*Culin*) (sort of) biscuit.
tuilerie [tɥilʀi] *nf* (*fabrique*) tilery; (*four*) tilery, tile-kiln.
tulipe [tylip] *nf* (*Bot*) tulip; (*ornement*) tulip-shaped glass (*ou* lamp *etc*).
tulle [tyl] *nm* tulle.
tuméfaction [tymefaksjɔ̃] *nf* (*U*) swelling *ou* puffing up, tumefaction (*T*); (*partie tuméfiée*) swelling.
tuméfier [tymefje] (7) **1** *vt* to cause to swell, tumefy (*T*). **visage/œil tuméfié** puffed-up *ou* swollen face/eye. **2 se tuméfier** *vpr* to swell *ou* puff up, tumefy (*T*).
tumescence [tymesɑ̃s] *nf* tumescence.
tumescent, e [tymesɑ̃, ɑ̃t] *adj* tumescent.
tumeur [tymœʀ] *nf* tumour (*de* of), growth (*de* in). **~ bénigne/maligne** benign/malignant tumour; **~ au cerveau** brain tumour.
tumoral, e, *mpl* **-aux** [tymɔʀal, o] *adj* tumorous, tumoral.
tumulte [tymylt(ə)] *nm* **(a)** (*bruit*) *[foule]* commotion; *[voix]* hubbub; *[acclamations]* thunder, tumult. **un ~ d'applaudissements** thunderous applause, a thunder of applause; (*littér*) **le ~ des flots/de l'orage** the tumult of the waves/of the storm.
(b) (*agitation*) *[affaires]* hurly-burly; *[passions]* turmoil, tumult; *[rue, ville]* hustle and bustle (*de* in, of), commotion (*de* in).
tumultueusement [tymyltɥøzmɑ̃] *adv* (*V* **tumultueux**) stormily; turbulently; tumultuously.
tumultueux, -euse [tymyltɥø, øz] *adj séance* stormy, turbulent, tumultuous; *foule* turbulent, agitated; (*littér*) *flots, bouillonnement* turbulent; *vie, période* stormy, turbulent; *passion* tumultuous, turbulent.
tumulus [tymylys] *nm* burial mound, tumulus (*T*), barrow (*T*).
tungstène [tœ̃kstɛn] *nm* tungsten, wolfram.
tunique [tynik] *nf* **(a)** (*romaine, d'uniforme scolaire ou militaire*) tunic; (*de prêtre*) tunicle, tunic; (*de femme*) (*droite*) tunic; (*à forme ample*) smock; (*longue*) gown; (*d'écolière*) gym-slip.
(b) (*Anat*) tunic, tunica; (*Bot*) tunic. **~ de l'œil** tunica albuginea of the eye.
Tunis [tynis] *n* Tunis.
Tunisie [tynizi] *nf* Tunisia.
tunisien, -enne [tynizjɛ̃, ɛn] **1** *adj* Tunisian. **2** *nmf*: **T~(ne)** Tunisian.
tunnel [tynɛl] *nm* **(a)** (*lit, gén*) tunnel. **~ routier** road tunnel; **~ aérodynamique** wind tunnel.
(b) (*fig*) tunnel. **arriver au bout du ~** to come to the end of the tunnel.
tuque [tyk] *nf* (*Can*) woollen cap, tuque (*Can*).
turban [tyʀbɑ̃] *nm* turban.
turbin‡ [tyʀbɛ̃] *nm* (*emploi*) job. **aller au ~** to go off to the daily grind*; **se remettre au ~** to get back to the slog* *ou* the grind*.
turbine [tyʀbin] *nf* turbine. **~ hydraulique** water *ou* hydraulic turbine; **~ à réaction/à impulsion** reaction/impulse turbine; **~ à vapeur/à gaz** steam/gas turbine.
turbiner‡ [tyʀbine] (1) *vi* to graft (away)‡, slog away‡.
turbocompresseur [tyʀbɔkɔ̃pʀesœʀ] *nm* turbo-compressor.
turbomoteur [tyʀbɔmɔtœʀ] *nm* turbine engine.
turbopompe [tyʀbɔpɔ̃p] *nf* turbopump, turbine-pump.
turbopropulseur [tyʀbɔpʀɔpylsœʀ] *nm* turboprop.
turboréacteur [tyʀbɔʀeaktœʀ] *nm* turbojet.
turbot [tyʀbo] *nm* turbot.
turbotrain [tyʀbɔtʀɛ̃] *nm* turbotrain.
turbulence [tyʀbylɑ̃s] *nf* **(a)** (*agitation*) excitement; (*V* **turbulent**) boisterousness; turbulence; unruliness; (*vivacité*) boisterousness.
(b) (*Sci: remous*) turbulence (*U*). (*Aviat*) **il y a des ~s** there is turbulence.
turbulent, e [tyʀbylɑ̃, ɑ̃t] *adj* **(a)** (*vif*) boisterous, turbulent; (*agité*) unruly, turbulent. **(b)** (*littér: tumultueux*) *passion* turbulent, stormy; (*Sci*) turbulent.
turc, turque [tyʀk(ə)] **1** *adj* Turkish. **à la turque** (*accroupi, assis*) cross-legged; *cabinets* seatless; (*Mus*) alla turca; *V* **bain, café, tête.**
2 *nm* **(a)** (*personne*) **T~** Turk; (*fig*) **les jeunes T~s d'un parti**

the Young Turks of a party. **(b)** (*Ling*) Turkish.
3 *nf*: **Turque** Turkish woman.
turf [tyRf] *nm* (*terrain*) racecourse. (*activité*) **le ~** racing, the turf.
turfiste [tyRfist(ə)] *nmf* racegoer.
turgescence [tyRʒesɑ̃s] *nf* turgescence.
turgescent, e [tyRʒesɑ̃, ɑ̃t] *adj* turgescent.
turgide [tyRʒid] *adj* (*littér*) swollen.
turlupiner* [tyRlypine] (1) *vt* to bother, worry.
turne [tyRn(ə)] *nf* **(a)** († *péj: logement*) digs*. **(b)** (*Scol: chambre*) room.
turpitude [tyRpityd] *nf* **(a)** (*U*) turpitude. **(b)** (*acte: gén pl*) base act.
turque [tyRk] *V* **turc.**
Turquie [tyRki] *nf* Turkey.
turquoise [tyRkwaz] *nf, adj inv* turquoise.
tutélaire [tyteleR] *adj* (*littér: protecteur*) tutelary, protecting (*épith*); (*Jur: de la tutelle*) tutelary.
tutelle [tytel] *nf* **(a)** (*Jur*) guardianship; (*Pol*) trusteeship. **~ administrative** administrative supervision (by government over local authorities); **avoir la ~ de qn, avoir qn en ~** to have the guardianship of sb; **mettre qn en ~** to put sb in the care of a guardian; **enfant en ~** child under guardianship; **territoires sous ~** trust territories.
(b) (*dépendance*) supervision; (*protection*) tutelage, protection. **sous la ~ américaine** under American supervision; **mettre sous ~** to put under supervision; **être sous la ~ de qn** (*dépendant*) to be under sb's supervision; (*protégé*) to be in sb's tutelage; **prendre qn sous sa ~** to take sb under one's wing.
tuteur, -trice [tytœR, tRis] **1** *nm,f* (*Jur, fig littér: protecteur*) guardian. **~ légal/testamentaire** legal/testamentary guardian; **~ ad hoc** *specially appointed guardian.* **2** *nm* (*Agr*) stake, support, prop.
tutoiement [tytwamɑ̃] *nm* use of (the familiar) 'tu' (*instead of 'vous'*).
tutoyer [tytwaje] (8) *vt* **(a)** (*lit*) **~ qn** to use (the familiar) 'tu' when speaking to sb, address sb as 'tu' (*instead of 'vous'*). **(b)** (*fig littér*) to be on familiar *ou* intimate terms with.
tutti quanti [tutikwɑ̃ti] *nmpl*: **et ~** and all the rest (of them), and all that lot* *ou* crowd*.
tutu [tyty] *nm* tutu, ballet skirt.
tuyau, *pl* **~x** [tɥijo] **1** *nm* **(a)** (*gén, rigide*) pipe, length of piping; (*flexible, en caoutchouc, vendu au mètre*) length of rubber tubing, rubber tubing (*U*); *[pipe]* stem. (*fig*) **dans le ~ de l'oreille*** in somebody's ear.
(b) (*Habillement: pli*) flute.
(c) (*) (*gén: conseil*) tip; (*mise au courant*) gen* (*U*). **quelques ~x pour le bricoleur** a few tips for the do-it-yourself enthusiast; **il nous a donné des ~x sur leurs activités/projets** he gave us some gen* on their activities/plans.
2: tuyau d'alimentation feeder pipe; **tuyau d'arrosage** hosepipe, garden hose; **tuyau de cheminée** chimney pipe; **tuyau de descente** (*pluvial*) downpipe, fall pipe; *[lavabo, W.-C.]* wastepipe; **tuyau d'échappement** exhaust (pipe); **tuyau d'orgue** (*Géol, Mus*) organ pipe; **tuyau de poêle** stovepipe; (*†*fig*) **(chapeau en) tuyau de poêle** stovepipe hat; **tuyau de pompe** pump pipe.
tuyautage [tɥijotaʒ] *nm* **(a)** *[linge]* fluting, goffering. **(b)** (*: *V* **tuyauter**) giving of a tip; putting in the know*.
tuyauter [tɥijote] (1) *vt* **(a)** *linge* to flute, goffer. **un tuyauté** a fluted frill. **(b)** (*) **~ qn** (*conseiller*) to give sb a tip; (*mettre au courant*) to give sb some gen*, put sb in the know*.
tuyauterie [tɥijotRi] *nf [machines, canalisations]* piping (*U*); *[orgue]* pipes.
tuyère [tyjeR] *nf [turbine]* nozzle; *[four, haut fourneau]* tuyère, twyer. **~ d'éjection** exhaust *ou* propulsion nozzle.
tweed [twid] *nm* tweed.
twist [twist] *nm* twist (*dance*).
tympan [tɛ̃pɑ̃] *nm* **(a)** (*Anat*) eardrum, tympanum (*T*). **bruit à vous déchirer *ou* crever les ~s** earsplitting noise; *V* **caisse. (b)** (*Archit*) tympan(um). **(c)** (*Tech: pignon*) pinion.
tympanique [tɛ̃panik] *adj* (*Anat*) tympanic.
tympanon [tɛ̃panɔ̃] *nm* (*Mus*) dulcimer.
type [tip] **1** *nm* **(a)** (*modèle: Ethnologie etc: ensemble de caractères*) type. **il y a plusieurs ~s de bicyclettes** there are several types of bicycle; **une pompe du ~ B5** a pump of type B5, a type B5 pump; **une pompe du ~ réglementaire** a regulation-type pump; **une voiture (de) ~ break** an estate-type car; **des savanes (du) ~ jungle** jungle-type savannas; **certains ~s humains** certain human types; **avoir le ~ oriental/nordique** to be Oriental-/Nordic-looking, have Oriental/Nordic looks; **un beau ~ de femme/d'homme** a fine specimen of womanhood/manhood; **c'est le ~ d'homme à faire cela** he's the type *ou* sort of man who would do that; **ce *ou* il/elle n'est pas mon ~*** he/she is not my type *ou* sort.
(b) (*personne, chose: représentant*) classic example. **c'est le ~ (parfait) de l'intellectuel/du vieux garçon** he's the typical *ou* classic intellectual/old bachelor, he's a perfect *ou* classic example of the intellectual/old bachelor; **il s'était efforcé de créer un ~ de beauté** he had striven to create an ideal type of beauty; **c'est le ~ même de la machination politique** it's a classic example of political intrigue.
(c) (*: *individu*) chap*, bloke* (*Brit*), guy*; (†: *individu remarquable*) character. **quel sale ~!** what a nasty piece of work (that chap* *ou* bloke* (*Brit*) is)!; **c'est vraiment un ~!**† he's quite a character!
(d) (*Typ*) (*pièce, ensemble des caractères*) type; (*empreinte*) typeface; (*Numismatique*) type.
2 *adj inv* typical, classic; (*Statistique*) standard. **l'erreur/le politicien ~** the typical *ou* classic mistake/politician; (*Statistique*) **l'écart/l'erreur ~** the standard deviation/error; **l'exemple/la situation ~** the typical *ou* classic example/situation; **un portrait ~ du Français** a picture of the classic *ou* typical Frenchman.
typer [tipe] (1) *vt* **(a)** (*caractériser*) **auteur/acteur qui type son personnage** author/actor who brings out the features of the character well; **un personnage bien typé** a character well rendered as a type. **(b)** (*Tech*) to stamp, mark.
typesse [tipɛs] *nf* (*: *péj*) female* (*péj*).
typhique [tifik] *adj* (*du typhus*) typhous; (*de la typhoïde*) typhic. **bacille ~** typhoid bacillus.
typhoïde [tifɔid] *adj* typhoid. **la (fièvre) ~** typhoid (fever).
typhoïdique [tifɔidik] *adj* typhic.
typhon [tifɔ̃] *nm* typhoon.
typhus [tifys] *nm* typhus (fever).
typique [tipik] *adj* (*gén*) typical; (*Bio*) true to type. **~ de ...** typical of ... ; **sa réaction est ~** his reaction is typical (of him) *ou* true to type; **un cas ~ de ...** a typical case of ... . **musique.**
typiquement [tipikmɑ̃] *adv* typically.
typo* [tipɔ] *nm* (*abrév de* **typographe**) typo*.
typographe [tipɔgRaf] *nmf* (*gén*) typographer; (*compositeur à la main*) hand compositor.
typographie [tipɔgRafi] *nf* **(a)** (*procédé d'impression*) letterpress (printing); (*opérations de composition, art*) typography. **(b)** (*aspect*) typography.
typographique [tipɔgRafik] *adj procédé, impression* letterpress (*épith*); *opérations, art* typographic(al). **erreur *ou* faute ~** typographic(al) *ou* printer's error, misprint; **argot ~** typographers' jargon; **cet ouvrage est une réussite ~** this work is a success typographically *ou* as regards typography.
typographiquement [tipɔgRafikmɑ̃] *adv imprimer* by letterpress. **livre ~ réussi** book that is a success typographically *ou* successful as regards typography.
typolithographie [tipɔlitɔgRafi] *nf* typolithography.
typologie [tipɔlɔʒi] *nf* typology.
typologique [tipɔlɔʒik] *adj* typological.
tyran [tiRɑ̃] *nm* (*lit, fig*) tyrant.
tyranneau, *pl* **~x** [tiRano] *nm* (*hum, péj*) petty tyrant.
tyrannie [tiRani] *nf* (*lit, fig*) tyranny. **la ~ de la mode/d'un mari** the tyranny of fashion/of a husband; **exercer sa ~ sur qn** to tyrannize sb, wield one's tyrannical powers over sb.
tyrannique [tiRanik] *adj* tyrannical, tyrannous.
tyranniquement [tiRanikmɑ̃] *adv* tyrannically.
tyranniser [tiRanize] (1) *vt* (*lit, fig*) to tyrannize.
Tyrol [tiRɔl] *nm*: **le ~** the Tyrol.
tyrolien, -ienne [tiRɔljɛ̃, jɛn] **1** *adj* Tyrolean; *V* **chapeau. 2** *nm,f*: **T~(ne)** Tyrolean. **3 tyrolienne** *nf* (*chant*) Tyrolienne.
tzar [dzaR] *nm*, **tzarévitch** [dzaRevitʃ] *nm*, **tzarine** [dzaRin] *nf* = **tsar, tsarévitch, tsarine.**
tzigane [dzigan] = **tsigane.**

U

U, u [y] *nm* (*lettre*) U, u. **poutre en U** U(-shaped) beam; **vallée en U** U-shaped valley.
ubac [ybak] *nm* (*Géog*) north(-facing) side, ubac (*T*).
ubiquité [ybikɥite] *nf* ubiquity; (*Rel*) Ubiquity. **avoir le don d'~** to be ubiquitous, be everywhere at once (*hum*).
ubuesque [ybyɛsk(ə)] *adj* (*grotesque*) grotesque; (*Littérat*) Ubuesque.
uhlan [ylɑ̃] *nm* uhlan.
ukase [ykɑz] *nm* (*Hist, fig*) ukase.
Ukraine [ykʀɛn] *nf* Ukraine.
ukrainien, -ienne [ykʀɛnjɛ̃, jɛn] **1** *adj* Ukrainian. **2** *nm* (*Ling*) Ukrainian. **3** *nm,f*: **U~(ne)** Ukrainian.
ulcération [ylseʀɑsjɔ̃] *nf* ulceration.
ulcère [ylsɛʀ] *nm* ulcer. **~ à l'estomac** stomach ulcer.
ulcérer [ylseʀe] (6) *vt* **(a)** (*révolter*) to sicken, appal. **(b)** (*Méd*) to ulcerate. **blessure qui s'ulcère** wound that ulcerates *ou* festers.
ulcéreux, -euse [ylseʀø, øz] *adj* ulcerated, ulcerous.
ultérieur, e [ylteʀjœʀ] *adj* later, subsequent, ulterior. **à une date ~e** at a later date; (*Comm*) **commandes ~es** further orders.
ultérieurement [ylteʀjœʀmɑ̃] *adv* later.
ultimatum [yltimatɔm] *nm* ultimatum.
ultime [yltim] *adj* ultimate, final.
ultra [yltʀa] **1** *nm* (*réactionnaire*) extreme reactionary; (*extrémiste*) extremist. (*Hist*) **U~(-royaliste)** ultra(-royalist).
2 *préf*: **~-chic/-rapide/-long** ultra-fashionable/-fast/-long; **crème ~-pénétrante** deep-cleansing cream.
3: **ultra-court** (*gén*) ultra-short; (*Rad*) **ondes ultra-courtes** ultra-high frequency; **ultra-microscopique** ultramicroscopic; **ultra-moderne, ultramoderne** ultramodern; **ultra-sensible** *surface, balance* ultra-sensitive; **film** *ou* **pellicule ultra-sensible** high-speed film; **ultra-son, ultrason** ultrasonic sound; **les ultra-sons** ultrasonic sounds, ultrasonics; **ultra-sonique, ultrasonique** ultrasonic; **ultra-violet, ultraviolet** (*adj*) ultraviolet; (*nm*) ultraviolet ray.
ultramicroscope [yltʀamikʀɔskɔp] *nm* ultramicroscope.
ultramontain, e [yltʀamɔ̃tɛ̃, ɛn] *adj* (*Hist*) ultramontane.
ultravirus [yltʀaviʀys] *nm* ultravirus.
ululation [ylylɑsjɔ̃] *nf* = **hululement.**
ululement [ylylmɑ̃] *nm* = **hululement.**
ululer [ylyle] (1) *vi* = **hululer.**
Ulysse [ylis] *nm* Ulysses.
un, une [œ̃, yn] **1** *art indéf* **(a)** a, an (*devant voyelle*); (*un, une quelconque*) some. **ne venez pas ~ dimanche** don't come on a Sunday; **le témoignage d'~ enfant n'est pas valable** a child's evidence *ou* the evidence of a child is not valid; **c'est l'œuvre d'~ poète** it's the work of a poet; **retrouvons-nous dans ~ café** let's meet in a café *ou* in some café (or other); **~ jour/soir il partit** one day/evening he went away; **une fois, il est venu avec ~ ami et ...** once he came with a friend and ... ; **passez ~ soir** drop in one *ou* some evening; **~ jour, tu comprendras** one day *ou* some day you'll understand; *V* **fois.**
(b) (*avec noms abstraits*) **avec une grande sagesse/violence** with great wisdom/violence, very wisely/violently; **des hommes d'~ courage sans égal** men of unparalleled courage; *V* **certain.**
(c) (*avec nom propre*) a, an. **ce n'est pas ~ Picasso** (*hum: personne*) he's no Picasso, he's not exactly (a) Picasso; (*tableau*) it's not a Picasso; **on a élu ~ (nommé)** *ou* **~ (certain) Dupont** a certain Dupont has been appointed, they've appointed a man called Dupont; **Monsieur Un tel** Mr so-and-so; **Madame Une telle** Mrs so-and-so; **c'est encore ~ Kennedy qui fait parler de lui** that's yet another Kennedy in the news; **il a le talent d'~ Hugo** he has the talent of a Hugo; **cet enfant sera ~ Paganini** this child will be another Paganini.
(d) (*intensif*) **elle a fait une scène!** *ou* **une de ces scènes!** she made a dreadful scene! *ou* such a scene!, what a scene she made!; **j'ai une faim/une soif!** *ou* **une de ces faims/une de ces soifs!** I'm so hungry/thirsty, I'm starving/terribly thirsty; **il est d'~ sale!** *ou* **d'une saleté!** he's so dirty!, he's filthy!; *V* **besoin, comble, monde.**
(e) (*loc*) **~ autre** another, another one; **~ certain M X** a (certain) Mr X, one Mr X; **~ (petit) peu** a little; *V* **pas¹, rien.**
2 *pron* **(a)** one. **prêtez-moi ~ de vos livres** lend me one of your books; **prêtez-m'en ~** lend me one (of them); **il est ~ des rares qui m'ont écrit** he's one of the few (people) who wrote to me; **j'en connais ~ qui sera content!** I know someone *ou* somebody *ou* ONE person who'll be pleased!; **il est ~ de ces enfants qui s'ennuient partout** he's the kind of child *ou* one of those children who gets bored wherever he goes; **j'en ai vu ~ très joli de chapeau*** I've seen a very nice hat; **~ à qui je voudrais parler c'est Jean** there's someone *ou* ONE person I'd like to speak to and that is John, someone *ou* ONE person I'd like to speak to is John.
(b) (*avec art déf*) **l'~** one; **les ~s** some; **l'une des meilleures chanteuses** one of the best singers; **l'~ ... l'autre** (the) one ... the other; **les ~s disent ... les autres ...** some say ... others ... ; **prenez l'~ ou l'autre** take one or the other; **l'une et l'autre solution sont acceptables** either solution is acceptable, both solutions are acceptable; **elles étaient assises en face l'une de l'autre** they were sitting opposite one another *ou* each other; **ils se regardaient l'~ l'autre** they looked at one another *ou* at each other; (*à tout prendre*) **l'~ dans l'autre** on balance, by and large; **l'~ dans l'autre, cela fera dans les 2.000 F** (what) with one thing and another it will work out at some 2,000 francs.
3 *adj inv* **(a)** (*cardinal*) one. **vingt-et-~** twenty-one; **il n'en reste qu'~** there's only one left; **nous sommes six contre ~** we are six against one; **~ seul** one only, only one; **pas ~ (seul)** not one; (*emphatique*) not a single one; **il n'y en a pas eu ~ pour m'aider** not a soul *ou* nobody lifted a finger to help me; **je suis resté une heure/~ jour** I stayed one hour/one day; **~ à ~, ~ par ~** one by one; **(l')~ des trois a dû mentir** one of the three must have been lying; **sans ~ (sou)*** penniless, broke*; **le cavalier ne faisait qu'~ avec son cheval** horse and rider were as one; **les deux frères ne font qu'~** the two brothers are like one person; (*Prov*) **une de perdue, dix de retrouvées** win a few – lose a few, there are plenty more fish in the sea; *V* **fois, moins, tout.**
(b) (*chiffre*) one. **~ et ~ font deux** one and one are two; **j'ai tiré le (numéro) ~** I picked (number) one; **et d'~ (de fait)** that's one done *ou* finished *ou* out of the way; **et d'une!*** for a start!; **personne ne t'a forcé de venir, et d'une!** no one forced you to come — that's the first thing!, one — no one forced you to come; **il n'a fait ni une ni deux, il a accepté** he accepted without a second's hesitation *ou* like a shot.
(c) (*ordinal*) **page/chapitre ~** page/chapter one; (*Presse*) **la une** the front page, page one; **il est une heure** it's one o'clock.
4 *adj* (*formant un tout*) **le Dieu ~ et indivisible** the one and indivisible God.
unanime [ynanim] *adj témoins, sentiment, vote* unanimous. **~s à penser que** unanimous in thinking that.
unanimement [ynanimmɑ̃] *adv* unanimously.
unanimité [ynanimite] *nf* unanimity. **vote acquis à l'~** unanimous vote; **ils ont voté à l'~ pour** they voted unanimously for; **élu/voté à l'~** elected/voted unanimously; **élu à l'~ moins une voix** elected with only one vote against; **cette décision a fait l'~** this decision was approved unanimously.
uni, e [yni] (*ptp de* **unir**) *adj* **(a)** (*sans ornements*) *tissu, jupe* plain, self-coloured; *couleur* plain. **tissu de couleur ~e** self-coloured *ou* plain fabric; **l'imprimé et l'~** printed and plain *ou* self-coloured fabrics *ou* material.
(b) (*soudé*) *couple, amis* close; *famille* close(-knit). **ils sont ~s comme les deux doigts de la main, ils sont très ~s** they are very close; **présenter un front ~ contre l'adversaire** to present a united front to the enemy.
(c) (*uniforme, lisse*) *surface* smooth, even; *mer* calm, unruffled. (*littér*) **une vie ~e et sans nuages** a serene untroubled life.
unicellulaire [yniselylɛʀ] *adj* unicellular.
unicité [ynisite] *nf* uniqueness, unicity (*T*).
unicolore [ynikɔlɔʀ] *adj* self-coloured.
unidirectionnel, -elle [ynidiʀɛksjɔnɛl] *adj* unidirectional.
unième [ynjɛm] *adj*: **vingt/trente et ~** twenty-/thirty-first.
unièmement [ynjɛmmɑ̃] *adv*: **vingt/trente et ~** twenty-/thirty-first.
unificateur, -trice [ynifikatœʀ, tʀis] *adj* unifying.
unification [ynifikɑsjɔ̃] *nf* (*V* **unifier**) unification; standardization.
unifier [ynifje] (7) *vt pays, systèmes* to unify; *parti* to unify, unite; (*Comm*) *tarifs etc* to standardize, unify. **des pays qui s'unifient lentement** countries that slowly become unified.
uniforme [ynifɔʀm(ə)] **1** *adj* (*gén*) uniform; *vitesse, mouvement* regular, uniform; *terrain, surface* even; *style* uniform, unvarying; *vie, conduite* unchanging, uniform.
2 *nm* (*lit, fig*) (*vêtement*) uniform. **en (grand) ~** in (dress) uniform; **endosser/quitter l'~** to join/leave the forces; **il y avait beaucoup d'~s à ce dîner** there were a great many officers at the dinner.
uniformément [ynifɔʀmemɑ̃] *adv* (*V* **uniforme**) uniformly; regularly; evenly; unvaryingly; unchangingly. **le temps s'écoule ~** time passes at a steady *ou* an unchanging pace *ou* rate, time goes steadily by; (*Phys*) **vitesse ~ accélérée** uniform (rate of) change of speed.
uniformisation [ynifɔʀmizɑsjɔ̃] *nf* standardization.
uniformiser [ynifɔʀmize] (1) *vt paysage, mœurs, tarifs* to standardize; *teinte* to make uniform.
uniformité [ynifɔʀmite] *nf* (*V* **uniforme**) uniformity; regularity; evenness.
unijambiste [yniʒɑ̃bist(ə)] **1** *adj* one-legged. **2** *nmf* one-legged man (*ou* woman).
unilatéral, e, *mpl* **-aux** [ynilateʀal, o] *adj* (*gén, Bot, Jur*) unilateral; *V* **stationnement.**
unilatéralement [ynilateʀalmɑ̃] *adv* unilaterally.
unilingue [ynilɛ̃g] *adj* unilingual.
uniment [ynimɑ̃] *adv* (*littér: uniformément*) smoothly. (†: *simplement*) **(tout) ~** (quite) plainly.
uninominal, e, *mpl* **-aux** [yninɔminal, o] *adj vote* uninom-

inal (*rare*), for a single member (*attrib*).
union [ynjɔ̃] **1** *nf* **(a)** (*alliance*) *[états, partis, fortunes]* union. **en ~ avec** in union with; (*Prov*) **l'~ fait la force** strength through unity (*Prov*).
(b) (*mariage*) union.
(c) (*juxtaposition*) *[éléments, couleurs]* combination, blending; *V* **trait.**
(d) (*groupe*) association, union.
2: union charnelle union of the flesh; **union conjugale** marital union; **union de consommateurs** consumers' association; **union douanière** customs union; **l'union libre** free love; (*Rel*) **union mystique** mystic union; **Union des Républiques Socialistes Soviétiques** Union of Soviet Socialist Republics; **l'Union Soviétique** the Soviet Union.
unionisme [ynjɔnism(ə)] *nm* (*gén*) unionism; (*Hist*) Unionism.
unioniste [ynjɔnist(ə)] *adj, nmf* (*gén*) unionist; (*Hist*) Unionist.
unipare [ynipaʀ] *adj* uniparous.
unipolaire [ynipɔlɛʀ] *adj* unipolar.
unique [ynik] *adj* **(a)** (*seul*) only. **mon ~ souci/espoir** my only *ou* sole (*frm*) *ou* one concern/hope; **fils/fille ~** only son/daughter; (*Pol*) **système à parti ~** one-party system; **route à voie ~** single-lane road; **tiré par un cheval ~** drawn by only one *ou* by a single horse; **~ en France/en Europe** the only one of its kind in France/in Europe; **deux aspects d'un même et ~ problème** two aspects of one and the same problem; *V* **salaire, seul.**
(b) (*après n: exceptionnel*) *livre, talent* unique. **~ en son genre** unique of its kind; **un paysage ~ au monde** an absolutely unique landscape.
(c) (*: *impayable*) priceless*. **il est ~ ce gars-là!** that fellow's priceless!*
uniquement [ynikmɑ̃] *adv* **(a)** (*exclusivement*) only, solely, exclusively. **ne fais-tu que du classement? — pas ~** are you only doing the sorting out? — not only *ou* not just that; **il était venu ~ pour me voir** he had come solely to see me, he had come for the sole purpose of seeing me; **il pense ~ à l'argent** he thinks only of money; **si ~ dévoué à son maître** so exclusively devoted to his master.
(b) (*simplement*) only, merely, just. **c'était ~ par curiosité** it was only *ou* just *ou* merely out of curiosity.
unir [yniʀ] (2) **1** *vt* **(a)** (*associer*) *états, partis, fortunes* to unite (*à* with). **~ ses forces** to combine one's forces; **ces noms unis dans notre mémoire** these names linked in our memory; **le sentiment commun qui les unit** the common feeling which binds them together *ou* unites them.
(b) (*marier*) to unite, join together. **~ en mariage** to unite *ou* join in marriage.
(c) (*juxtaposer, combiner*) *couleurs, qualités* to combine (*à* with). **il unit l'intelligence au courage** he combines intelligence with courage.
(d) (*relier*) *continents, villes* to link, join up.
2 s'unir *vpr* **(a)** (*s'associer*) *[pays, partis, fortunes]* to unite (*à, avec* with). **s'~ contre un ennemi commun** to unite against a common enemy.
(b) (*se marier*) to be joined (together) in marriage. **des jeunes gens qui vont s'~** a young couple who are going to be joined (together) in marriage.
(c) (*s'accoupler*) **s'~ dans une étreinte fougueuse** to come together in a passionate embrace.
(d) (*se combiner*) *[mots, formes, couleurs, qualités]* to combine (*à, avec* with).
unisexe [ynisɛks] *adj inv* unisex.
unisexué, e [ynisɛksɥe] *adj* (*Bio, Bot*) unisexual.
unisson [ynisɔ̃] *nm*: **à l'~** in unison.
unitaire [ynitɛʀ] **1** *adj* (*Comm, Math, Phys*) unitary; (*Pol*) unitarian; (*Rel*) Unitarian.
2 *nmf* (*Rel*) Unitarian.
unitarien, -ienne [ynitaʀjɛ̃, jɛn] *adj, nm,f* (*Pol*) unitarian; (*Rel*) Unitarian.
unitarisme [ynitaʀism(ə)] *nm* (*Pol*) unitarianism; (*Rel*) Unitarianism.
unité [ynite] *nf* **(a)** (*cohésion*) unity. **~ de vues** unity of views; (*Littérat*) **les trois ~s** the three unities.
(b) (*Comm, Math: élément*) unit. **la colonne des ~s** the units column; **~ de mesure** unit of measure; **antibiotique à 100.000 ~s** antibiotic with 100,000 units; (*Comm*) **prix de vente à l'~** unit selling price; (*Univ*) **~ de valeur** credit.
(c) (*Mil*) (*troupe*) unit; (*navire*) (war)ship; *V* **choc.**
(d) (*: *10.000 F*) ten thousand (new) francs.
univers [ynivɛʀ] *nm* (*gén*) universe; (*milieu, domaine*) world, universe. **son ~ se borne à son travail** his work is his whole universe *ou* world; (*Ling*) **l'~ du discours** the universe of discourse.
universalisation [ynivɛʀsalizɑsjɔ̃] *nf* universalization.
universaliser [ynivɛʀsalize] (1) *vt* to universalize.
universalisme [ynivɛʀsalism(ə)] *nm* (*Rel*) Universalism; (*Philos*) universalism.
universaliste [ynivɛʀsalist(ə)] *adj, nmf* (*Rel*) Universalist; (*Philos*) universalist.
universalité [ynivɛʀsalite] *nf* universality.
universaux [ynivɛʀso] *nmpl* (*Philos*) universals.
universel, -elle [ynivɛʀsɛl] *adj* **(a)** (*gén*) universal; *réputation* world-wide, universal. **c'est un esprit ~** he has an all-embracing mind; **c'est un homme ~** he is a man of vast *ou* universal knowledge; *V* **légataire, suffrage.**
(b) (*aux applications multiples*) *outil, appareil* universal, all-purpose (*épith*). **clef ~le** adjustable spanner; **remède ~** universal remedy.
universellement [ynivɛʀsɛlmɑ̃] *adv* universally.
universitaire [ynivɛʀsitɛʀ] **1** *adj vie étudiante, restaurant* university (*épith*); *études, milieux, carrière, diplôme* university (*épith*), academic; *V* **année, centre, cité.**
2 *nmf* academic. **une famille d'~s** a family of academics.
université [ynivɛʀsite] *nf* university. **l'U~ s'oppose à ...** the Universities are against ... .
univocité [ynivɔsite] *nf* (*Math, Philos*) univocity.
univoque [ynivɔk] *adj mot* univocal; *relation* one-to-one.
Untel [œ̃tɛl] *n*: **Monsieur/Madame ~** Mr/Mrs so-and-so; **les ~** the so-and-sos.
uppercut [ypɛʀkyt] *nm* uppercut.
uranifère [yʀanifɛʀ] *adj* uranium-bearing.
uranium [yʀanjɔm] *nm* uranium. **~ enrichi** enriched uranium.
Uranus [yʀanys] *nf* Uranus.
urbain, e [yʀbɛ̃, ɛn] *adj* **(a)** (*de la ville*) (*gén*) urban; *transports* city (*épith*), urban. **(b)** (*littér: poli*) urbane.
urbanisation [yʀbanizɑsjɔ̃] *nf* urbanization.
urbaniser [yʀbanize] (1) *vt* to urbanize. **la campagne environnante s'urbanise rapidement** the surrounding countryside is quickly becoming urbanized *ou* is being quickly built up; *V* **zone.**
urbanisme [yʀbanism(ə)] *nm* town planning.
urbaniste [yʀbanist(ə)] **1** *nmf* town planner. **2** *adj* = **urbanistique.**
urbanistique [yʀbanistik] *adj réglementation, impératifs* urbanistic. **nouvelles conceptions ~s** new concepts in town planning.
urbanité [yʀbanite] *nf* urbanity.
urée [yʀe] *nf* urea.
urémie [yʀemi] *nf* uraemia.
urémique [yʀemik] *adj* uraemic.
uretère [yʀtɛʀ] *nm* ureter.
urètre [yʀɛtʀ(ə)] *nm* urethra.
urgence [yʀʒɑ̃s] *nf* **(a)** *[décision, départ, situation]* urgency. **il y a ~** it's urgent, it's a matter of (great) urgency; **y a-t-il ~ à ce que nous fassions ... ?** is it urgent for us to do ...?; **d'~** *mesures, situation* emergency (*épith*); **faire qch d'~/de toute** *ou* **d'extrême ~** to do sth as a matter of urgency/with the utmost urgency; **transporté d'~ à l'hôpital** rushed to hospital; **à envoyer d'~** to be sent immediately; **convoquer d'~ les actionnaires** to call an emergency meeting of the shareholders; *V* **cas, état.**
(b) (*cas urgent*) emergency. **service/salle des ~s** emergency section/ward.
urgent, e [yʀʒɑ̃, ɑ̃t] *adj* (*pressant*) urgent. **rien d'~** nothing urgent; **l'~ est de** the most urgent thing is to; **il est ~ de réparer le toit** the roof needs urgent repair.
urger* [yʀʒe] (3) *vi*: **ça urge!** it's urgent!
urinaire [yʀinɛʀ] *adj* urinary.
urinal, *pl* **-aux** [yʀinal, o] *nm* (bed) urinal.
urine [yʀin] *nf* urine (*U*). **sucre dans les ~s** sugar in the urine.
uriner [yʀine] (1) *vi* to urinate, pass *ou* make water (*T*).
urinoir [yʀinwaʀ] *nm* (public) urinal.
urique [yʀik] *adj* uric.
urne [yʀn(ə)] *nf* **(a)** (*Pol*) **~ (électorale)** ballot box; **aller aux ~s** to vote, go to the polls. **(b)** (*vase*) urn. **~ funéraire** funeral urn.
urogénital, e, *mpl* **-aux** [yʀɔʒenital, o] *adj* urogenital.
urologie [yʀɔlɔʒi] *nf* urology.
urologue [yʀɔlɔg] *nmf* urologist.
urticaire [yʀtikɛʀ] *nf* nettle rash, hives, urticaria (*T*).
uruguayen, -enne [yʀygwajɛ̃, ɛn] **1** *adj* Uruguayan. **2** *nm,f*: **U~(ne)** Uruguayan.
us [ys] *nmpl* (††) customs. **~ et coutumes** (habits and) customs.
usage [yzaʒ] *nm* **(a)** (*utilisation*) *[appareil, méthode]* use. **apprendre l'~ de la boussole** to learn how to use a compass; **il fait un ~ immodéré d'eau de toilette** he uses (far) too much *ou* an excessive amount of toilet water; **abîmé par l'~** damaged through constant use; **elle nous laisse l'~ de son jardin** she lets us use her garden, she gives us *ou* allows us the use of her garden; *V* **garanti.**
(b) (*exercice, pratique*) *[membre, langue]* use; *[faculté]* use, power. (*littér*) **il n'a pas l'~ du monde** he lacks savoir-faire *ou* the social graces.
(c) (*fonction, application*) *[instrument]* use. **outil à ~s multiples** multi-purpose tool; (*Méd*) **à ~ externe/interne** for external/internal use; **servir à divers ~s** to have several uses, serve several purposes; *V* **valeur.**
(d) (*coutume, habitude*) custom. **un ~ qui se perd** a vanishing custom, a custom which is dying out; **c'est l'~** it's the custom, it's what's done, it's the way things are done; **ce n'est pas l'~ (de)** it's not done (to), it's not the custom (to); **entrer dans l'~ (courant)** *[objet, mot]* to come into common *ou* current use; *[mœurs]* to become common practice; **contraire aux ~s** contrary to common practice *ou* to custom; **il n'est pas dans les ~s de la compagnie de faire cela** the company is not in the habit of doing that, it is not the usual policy of the company to do that *ou* customary for the company to do that; **il était d'~** *ou* **c'était un ~ de** it was customary *ou* a custom *ou* usual to; **formule d'~** set formula; **après les compliments/recommandations d'~** after the usual *ou* customary compliments/recommendations.
(e) (*Ling*) **l'~** usage; **expression consacrée par l'~** expression fixed by usage; **l'~ écrit/oral** written/spoken usage; **l'~ décide** (common) usage decides; *V aussi* **bon**[1].
(f) (*littér: politesse*) **avoir de l'~** to have breeding; **manquer d'~** to lack breeding, be lacking in the social graces.
(g) (*loc*) **faire ~ de** *pouvoir, droit* to exercise; *permission, avantage* to make use of; *violence, force, procédé* to use, employ; *expression* to use; *objet, thème* to make use of; **faire (un) bon/mauvais ~ de qch** to put sth to good/bad use, make good/bad use of sth; **avoir l'~ de qch** (*droit d'utiliser*) to have the use of sth; (*occasion d'utiliser*) **en aurez-vous l'~?** will you have any use for it?; **ces souliers ont fait de l'~** these shoes

have lasted a long time, I've (*ou* we've *etc*) had good use out of these shoes; **vous verrez à l'~ comme c'est utile** you'll see when you use it how useful it is; **ça s'assouplira à l'~** it will soften with use; **son français s'améliorera à l'~** his French will improve with practice; **à l'~ de** for use of, for; **à son ~ personnel, pour son propre ~** for (one's) personal use; **notice à l'~ de** notice for (the attention of); **à l'~ des écoles** *émission* for schools; *manuel* for use in schools; **en ~** *dispositif, mot* in use; *V* **hors.**

usagé, e [yzaʒe] *adj* (*qui a beaucoup servi*) *pneu, habits* worn, old; (*d'occasion*) used, secondhand. **quelques ustensiles ~s** some old utensils.

usager, -ère [yzaʒe, ɛʀ] *nm,f* user. **~ de la route** roaduser.

usant, e* [yzɑ̃, ɑ̃t] *adj* (*fatigant*) *travail* exhausting, wearing; *personne* tiresome. **il est ~ avec ses discours** he wears *ou* tires you out with his talking.

usé, e [yze] (*ptp de* **user**) *adj* **(a)** (*détérioré*) *objet* worn; *vêtement, tapis* worn, worn-out; (*fig*) *personne* worn-out (*in health or age*). **~ jusqu'à la corde** threadbare; *V* **eau.**

(b) (*banal*) *thème, expression* hackneyed, trite; *plaisanterie* well-worn, stale, corny*.

user [yze] (1) **1** *vt* **(a)** (*détériorer*) *outil, roches* to wear away; *vêtements* to wear out. **~ un manteau jusqu'à la corde** to wear out a coat, wear a coat threadbare; (*hum*) **ils ont usé leurs fonds de culottes sur les mêmes bancs** they were at school together.

(b) (*fig: épuiser*) *personne, forces* to wear out; *nerfs* to wear down; *influence* to weaken, sap. **la maladie l'avait usé** illness had worn him out.

(c) (*consommer*) *essence, charbon* to use, burn; *papier, huile, eau* to use. **ce poêle use trop de charbon** this stove uses *ou* burns too much coal; **il use 2 paires de chaussures par mois** he goes through 2 pairs of shoes (in) a month.

2 *vi* (*littér: se comporter*): **en ~ mal avec** *ou* **à l'égard de qn** to treat *ou* use sb badly, deal badly by sb; **en ~ bien avec** *ou* **à l'égard de qn** to treat sb well, deal well by sb.

3 user de *vt indir* (*utiliser*) *pouvoir, patience, droit* to exercise; *permission, avantage* to make use of; *violence, force, procédé* to use, employ; *expression, mot* to use; (*littér*) *objet, thème* to make use of. **usant de douceur** using gentle means; **il en a usé et abusé** he has used and abused it.

4 s'user *vpr* [*tissu, vêtement*] to wear out. **mon manteau s'use** my coat is showing signs of wear; **elle s'use les yeux à trop lire** she's straining her eyes by reading too muct; **elle s'est usée au travail** she wore herself out with work.

usinage [yzinaʒ] *nm* (*V* **usiner**) machining; manufacturing.

usine [yzin] **1** *nf* factory. **un copain de l'~** *ou* **d'~** a mate from the works *ou* factory; **travailler en ~** to work in a factory; **travail en ~** factory work; (*fig*) **ce bureau est une vraie ~*** this office is like a factory!; *V* **cheminée.**

2: usine atomique atomic energy station, atomic plant; **usine d'automobiles** car factory *ou* plant; **usine à gaz** gasworks; **usine métallurgique** ironworks; **usine de pâte à papier** paper mill; **usine sidérurgique** steelworks, steel mill; **usine textile** textile plant *ou* factory, mill; **usine de traitement des ordures** sewage works *ou* farm *ou* plant.

usiner [yzine] (1) *vt* (*travailler, traiter*) to machine; (*fabriquer*) to manufacture. (*travailler dur*) **ça usine dans le coin!*** they're hard at it round here!*

usité, e [yzite] *adj* in common use, common. **un temps très/peu ~** a very commonly-used/a rarely-used tense; **le moins ~** the least (commonly) used; **ce mot n'est plus ~** this word is no longer used *ou* in use.

ustensile [ystɑ̃sil] *nm* (*gén: outil, instrument*) implement. **~s*** implements, tackle, gear; **~ (de cuisine)** (kitchen) utensil; **~s de ménage** household cleaning stuff *ou* things; **~s de jardinage** gardening tools *ou* implements; **qu'est-ce que c'est que cet ~?*** what's that gadget? *ou* contraption?*

usuel, -elle [yzɥɛl] **1** *adj objet* everyday (*épith*), ordinary; *mot, expression, vocabulaire* everyday (*épith*). **dénomination ~le d'une plante** common name for *ou* of a plant; **il est ~ de faire** it is usual to do, it is common practice to do.

2 *nm* (*livre*) book on the open shelf. **c'est un ~** it's on the open shelves.

usuellement [yzɥɛlmɑ̃] *adv* ordinarily, commonly.

usufruit [yzyfʀɥi] *nm* usufruct.

usufruitier, -ière [yzyfʀɥitje, jɛʀ] *adj, nm,f* usufructuary.

usuraire [yzyʀɛʀ] *adj taux, prêt* usurious.

usure[1] [yzyʀ] *nf* **(a)** (*processus*) [*vêtement*] wear (and tear); [*objet*] wear; [*terrain, roche*] wearing away; [*forces, énergie*] wearing out; (*Ling*) [*mot*] weakening. **~ normale** fair wear and tear; **résiste à l'~** resists wear, wears well; **subir l'~ du temps** to be worn away by time; **on l'aura à l'~** we'll wear him down in the end; *V* **guerre.**

(b) (*état*) [*objet, vêtement*] worn state.

usure[2] [yzyʀ] *nf* (*intérêt*) usury. **prêter à ~** to lend at usurious rates of interest; (*fig littér*) **je te le rendrai avec ~** I will get my own back (on you) with interest.

usurier, -ière [yzyʀje, jɛʀ] *nm,f* usurer.

usurpateur, -trice [yzyʀpatœʀ, tʀis] **1** *adj tendance, pouvoir* usurping (*épith*).

2 *nm,f* usurper.

usurpation [yzyʀpɑsjɔ̃] *nf* (*V* **usurper**) usurpation; encroachment.

usurpatoire [yzyʀpatwaʀ] *adj* usurpatory.

usurper [yzyʀpe] (1) **1** *vt pouvoir, honneur* to usurp. **il a usurpé le titre de docteur en médecine** he wrongfully took *ou* assumed the title of Doctor of Medicine; **réputation usurpée** usurped reputation.

2 *vi* (*littér: empiéter*) **~ sur** to encroach (up)on.

ut [yt] *nm* (*Mus*) (the note) C; *V* **clef.**

utérin, e [yteʀɛ̃, in] *adj* uterine.

utérus [yteʀys] *nm* womb; *V* **col.**

utile [ytil] *adj* **(a)** *objet, appareil, action* useful; *aide, conseil* useful, helpful (*à qn* to *ou* for sb). **livre ~ à lire** useful book to read; **cela vous sera certainement ~** that'll certainly be of use to you; **ton parapluie m'a été bien ~ ce matin** your umbrella came in very handy (for me) this morning; **ne considérer que l'~** to be only concerned with what's useful; **est-il vraiment ~ que j'y aille?** do I really need to go?; *V* **charge, temps[1].**

(b) *collaborateur, relation* useful. **il adore se rendre ~** he loves to make himself useful; **puis-je vous être ~?** can I be of help?, can I do anything for you?

utilement [ytilmɑ̃] *adv* (*avec profit*) profitably, usefully. **conseiller ~ qn** to give sb useful advice.

utilisable [ytilizabl(ə)] *adj* usable. **est-ce encore ~?** [*cahier, vêtement*] can it still be used?, is it still usable?; [*appareil*] is it still usable? *ou* working?

utilisateur, -trice [ytilizatœʀ, tʀis] *nm,f* [*appareil*] user.

utilisation [ytilizɑsjɔ̃] *nf* (*gén*) use; (*Culin*) [*restes*] using (up).

utiliser [ytilize] (1) *vt* **(a)** (*employer*) *appareil, système* to use, utilize; *outil, produit, mot* to use; *force, moyen* to use, employ; *droit* to use; *avantage* to make use of. **savoir ~ les compétences** to know how to make the most of *ou* make use of people's abilities.

(b) (*tirer parti de*) *personne, incident* to make use of; (*Culin*) *restes* to use (up).

utilitaire [ytiliteʀ] *adj* utilitarian; *V* **véhicule.**

utilitarisme [ytilitaʀism(ə)] *nm* utilitarianism.

utilitariste [ytilitaʀist(ə)] *adj, nmf* (*Philos*) utilitarian.

utilité [ytilite] *nf* usefulness; use. **je ne conteste pas l'~ de cet appareil** I don't deny the usefulness of this apparatus; **cet outil a son ~** this tool has its uses; **cet outil peut avoir son ~** this tool might come in handy *ou* useful; **d'une grande ~** very useful, of great use *ou* usefulness *ou* help (*attrib*); **ce livre ne m'est pas d'une grande ~** this book isn't much use *ou* a great deal of use to me; **de peu d'~** of little use *ou* help (*attrib*); **d'aucune ~** (of) no use (*attrib*) *ou* help; **sans ~** useless; **auras-tu l'~ de cet objet?** will you have any use for this object?; **de quelle ~ est-ce que cela peut (bien) vous être?** what earthly use is it to you?, what on earth can you use it for?; (*Jur*) **reconnu** *ou* **déclaré d'~ publique** state-approved; **jouer les ~s** (*Théât*) to play small *ou* bit parts; (*fig*) to play second fiddle.

utopie [ytɔpi] *nf* **(a)** (*genre, ouvrage, idéal politique*) utopia, Utopia. **(b)** (*idée, plan chimérique*) utopian view *ou* idea *etc.* **~s** utopianism, utopian views *ou* ideas; **ceci est une véritable ~** that's sheer utopianism.

utopique [ytɔpik] *adj* utopian, Utopian; *V* **socialisme.**

utopiste [ytɔpist(ə)] *nmf* utopian, Utopian.

uvulaire [yvylɛʀ] *adj* uvular.

uvule [yvyl] *nf* (*rare: luette*) uvula.

V

V, v [ve] *nm* (*lettre*) V, v. **en V** V-shaped; **moteur en V** V-engine; **encolure en V** V-neck; **décolleté en V** plunging (V-)neckline; **le V de la victoire** the victory sign, the V for victory.
va [va] *V* **aller.**
vacance [vakɑ̃s] **1** *nf* **(a)** (*Admin: poste*) vacancy.
(b) (*Jur*) **~ de succession** abeyance of succession.
(c) (*littér: disponibilité*) unencumbered state (*littér*). **en état de ~** unencumbered (*littér*).
2 vacances *nfpl* **(a)** (*gén: repos*) holiday (*Brit*), vacation (*US*); (*Scol*) holiday(s); (*Univ*) vacation; *[salariés]* holiday(s). **les ~s de Noël** the Christmas holidays; **partir en ~s** to go away on holiday; **au moment de partir en ~s** at the time of setting off on (our) holiday *ou* on our holidays; **il n'a jamais pris de ~s** he has never taken a holiday; **avoir droit à 4 semaines de ~s** to be entitled to 4 weeks' holiday(s); **prendre ses ~s en une fois** to take (all) one's holiday(s) at once; **être en ~s** to be on holiday; **j'ai besoin de ~s/de quelques jours de ~s** I need a holiday *ou* vacation/a few days' holiday *ou* vacation; **~s de neige** winter sports holiday; **pays/lieu de ~s** holiday country/place; **la ville est déserte pendant les ~s** the town is deserted during the holidays; *V* **colonie, devoir, grand.**
(b) (*Jur*) **~s judiciaires** recess, vacation.
vacancier, -ière [vakɑ̃sje, jɛʀ] *nm,f* holiday-maker (*Brit*), vacationist (*US*).
vacant, e [vakɑ̃, ɑ̃t] *adj* **(a)** *poste, siège* vacant; *appartement* unoccupied, vacant.
(b) (*Jur*) *biens, succession* in abeyance (*attrib*).
(c) (*fig littér*) **l'air ~** with a vacant air; **un cœur/esprit ~** unencumbered heart/mind (*littér*).
vacarme [vakaʀm(ə)] *nm* din, racket*, row*. **faire du ~** to make a din *ou* racket* *ou* row*; **un ~ de klaxons** the blaring of hooters; **un ~ continuel de camions/de coups de marteau** a constant roaring of lorries/thumping of hammers.
vacation [vakɑsjɔ̃] *nf* (*Jur*) *[expert, notaire]* (*temps de travail*) session, sitting; (*honoraires*) fee. (*Jur: vacances*) **~s** recess, vacation.
vaccin [vaksɛ̃] *nm* (*substance*) vaccine; (*vaccination*) vaccination. **faire un ~ à qn** to give sb a vaccination; (*fig*) **un ~ contre qch** a safeguard against sth.
vaccinable [vaksinabl(ə)] *adj* able to be vaccinated, that can be vaccinated.
vaccinal, e, *mpl* **-aux** [vaksinal, o] *adj* vaccinal.
vaccinateur, -trice [vaksinatœʀ, tʀis] **1** *adj* vaccinating (*épith*).
2 *nm,f* vaccinator.
vaccination [vaksinɑsjɔ̃] *nf* vaccination.
vaccine [vaksin] *nf* (*maladie*) cowpox, vaccinia (*T*); (†: *inoculation*) inoculation of cowpox. **fausse ~** vacinella, false vaccinia.
vacciner [vaksine] (1) *vt* (*Méd*) to vaccinate (*contre* against). **se faire ~** to have a vaccination, get vaccinated; (*fig*) **être vacciné contre qch*** to have become immune to sth.
vachard, e: [vaʃaʀ, aʀd(ə)] *adj* (*méchant*) nasty, rotten*, mean.
vache [vaʃ] **1** *nf* **(a)** (*Zool*) cow; (*cuir*) cowhide; *V* **lait, plancher**[1].
(b) (*:péj: police*) **les ~s** the fuzz:, the bulls: (*US*); (*hum*) **~ à roulette** motorbike cop*.
(c) (*: personne méchante*) (*femme*) bitch:, cow:; (*homme*) swine:; *V* **peau.**
(d) (*loc*) **comme une ~ qui regarde passer les trains** phlegmatically, with a gormless* *ou* vacant air; **il parle français comme une ~ espagnole** he absolutely murders the French language; **manger de la ~ enragée** to go through hard *ou* lean times; **en ~:: donner des coups de pied en ~ à qn** to kick sb slyly; **faire un coup en ~ à qn** to pull a fast one on sb*, do the dirty on sb: (*Brit*); **ah! les ~!:** the swine(s)!:; **ah la ~!:** (*surprise, admiration*) blimey!: (*Brit*), I'll be jiggered!*; (*douleur, indignation*) hell!:, damn (me)!:; (*intensif*) **une ~ de: ...** a *ou* one hell of a: ... ; **une ~ de surprise/bagnole:** a *ou* one hell of a surprise/car:.
2 *adj* (*: méchant, sévère*) rotten*, mean*. **il est ~** he's a (rotten) swine:, he's really rotten* *ou* mean; **elle est ~** she's a (mean *ou* rotten) cow: *ou* bitch:, she's really rotten* *ou* mean; **c'est ~ pour eux** it's really rotten for them*.
3: vache à eau (canvas) water bag; (*fig*) **vaches grasses** fat years, prosperous times; (*péj*) **vache à lait*** mug* (*person*) (*péj*); (*fig*) **vaches maigres** lean years *ou* times.
vachement: [vaʃmɑ̃] *adv* **(a)** (*très*) **~ bon/difficile** damned: *ou* bloody: (*Brit*) good/hard; **on s'est ~ dépêchés** we rushed like hell:; **on s'est ~ trompés** we made one *ou* a hell of a mistake:; **il pleut ~** it's raining damned: *ou* bloody: (*Brit*) hard.
(b) (*méchamment*) in a rotten* *ou* mean way.
vacher [vaʃe] *nm* cowherd.
vachère [vaʃɛʀ] *nf* cowgirl.
vacherie [vaʃʀi] *nf* **(a)** (*étable*) cowshed, (cow) byre.
(b) (*: méchanceté*) (*U*) rottenness*, meanness; (*action*) dirty trick*; (*remarque*) nasty *ou* bitchy: remark.
(c) (*: intensif*) **cette ~ d'appareil ne veut pas marcher** this damned: *ou* bloody: (*Brit*) machine refuses to go; **quelle ~ de temps!** what damned: *ou* bloody: (*Brit*) awful weather!
vacherin [vaʃʀɛ̃] *nm* (*Culin*) vacherin.
vachette [vaʃɛt] *nf* **(a)** (*jeune vache*) young cow. **(b)** (*cuir*) calfskin.
vacillant, e [vasijɑ̃, ɑ̃t] *adj* **(a)** (*lit*) *jambes, démarche* unsteady, shaky, wobbly; *lueur, flamme* flickering (*épith*).
(b) (*fig*) *santé, mémoire* shaky, failing; *raison* failing; *caractère* indecisive, wavering (*épith*).
vacillation [vasijasjɔ̃] *nf* (*rare*) *[démarche]* unsteadiness, shakiness; *[flamme]* flickering. **les ~s de la flamme** the flickering of the flame; **les ~s de son esprit/sa raison** the wavering of his mind/reason, his wavering *ou* failing mind/reason.
vacillement [vasijmɑ̃] *nm* (*V* **vaciller**) swaying; wobbling; faltering, wavering. **ses ~s m'inquiétaient: je craignais qu'elle ne fût malade** her unsteadiness *ou* shakiness worried me and I feared that she might be ill.
vaciller [vasije] (1) *vi* **(a)** (*lit*) *[personne]* to sway (to and fro); *[bébé]* to wobble; *[mur, poteau]* to sway (to and fro); *[meuble]* to wobble. **~ sur ses jambes** to stand unsteadily on one's legs, sway to and fro (on one's legs); **il s'avança en vacillant vers la porte** he tottered towards the door.
(b) *[flamme, lumière]* to flicker.
(c) (*fig*) *[voix]* to shake; *[résolution, courage]* to falter, waver, vacillate (*frm*); *[raison, intelligence]* to fail; *[santé, mémoire]* to be shaky, be failing. **il vacillait dans ses résolutions** he wavered *ou* vacillated in his resolution.
va-comme-je-te-pousse [vakɔmʒtəpus] *adv*: **à la ~** in a slap-dash manner, any old how* (*Brit*) *ou* way.
vacuité [vakɥite] *nf* (*littér: vide*) vacuity (*littér*), emptiness; (*intellectuelle, spirituelle*) vacuity, vacuousness.
vade-mecum [vademekɔm] *nm inv* pocketbook, vade mecum.
vadrouille* [vadʀuj] *nf* ramble, rove-around*. **être en ~** to be on the rove.
vadrouiller* [vadʀuje] (1) *vi* to rove around *ou* about. **~ dans les rues de Paris** to knock* *ou* loaf* *ou* rove about the streets of Paris.
va-et-vient [vaevjɛ̃] *nm inv* **(a)** *[personnes, véhicules]* comings and goings (*pl*), to-ings and fro-ings (*pl*); *[rue, bureau, café]* comings and goings (*pl*) (*de* in), to-ings and fro-ings (*pl*) (*de* in).
(b) *[piston, pièce]* (*gén*) to and fro (motion), backwards and forwards motion; (*verticalement*) up-and-down movement. **faire le ~ entre** *[bateau, train]* to go to and fro between, ply between; *[pièce de mécanisme]* to go to and fro between.
(c) (*gond*) helical hinge. **porte à ~** swing door.
(d) (*bac*) (small) ferryboat.
(e) (*téléphérage*) jig-back.
(f) (*Élec*) **(interrupteur de) ~** two-way switch; **circuit de ~** two-way wiring (*U*) *ou* wiring system.
vagabond, e [vagabɔ̃, ɔ̃d] **1** *adj* (*littér*) *peuple, vie* wandering (*épith*); *imagination* roaming (*épith*), roving (*épith*), restless. **avoir l'humeur ~e** to be in a restless mood. **2** *nm,f* (*péj: rôdeur*) tramp, vagrant, vagabond; (*littér: aventurier*) wanderer.
vagabondage [vagabɔ̃daʒ] *nm* (*errance*) wandering, roaming; (*Jur, péj: vie sans domicile fixe*) vagrancy. **leurs ~s à travers l'Europe** their wanderings *ou* roamings across Europe; **après une longue période de ~ il échoua en prison** after a long period of vagrancy he ended up in prison.
vagabonder [vagabɔ̃de] (1) *vi* *[personne]* to roam, wander; (*fig*) *[imagination, esprit]* to roam, rove, wander. **~ à travers l'Europe** to roam the length and breadth of Europe, wander across Europe.
vagin [vaʒɛ̃] *nm* vagina.
vaginal, e, *mpl* **-aux** [vaʒinal, o] *adj* vaginal.
vagir [vaʒiʀ] (2) *vi* to cry (*of newborn baby*).
vagissant, e [vaʒisɑ̃, ɑ̃t] *adj* crying (*of newborn baby*).
vagissement [vaʒismɑ̃] *nm* cry (*of newborn baby*).
vague[1] [vag] **1** *adj* (*imprécis*) *renseignement, geste* vague; *notion, idée* vague, hazy; *sentiment, forme* vague, indistinct; (*distrait*) *air, regard* faraway (*épith*), abstracted (*épith*); (*ample*) *robe, manteau* loose(-fitting). **d'un air ~** with a faraway look, with an abstracted expression; **il y avait rencontré une ~ parente** there he had met someone vaguely related to him *ou* some distant relation or other; *V* **terrain.**
2 *nm* **(a)** (*littér*) *[forme]* vagueness, indistinctness; *[passions, sentiments]* vagueness.
(b) le ~ vagueness; **j'ai horreur du ~** I can't bear vagueness; **nous sommes dans le ~** things are rather unclear to us; **il est resté dans le ~** he kept it all rather vague; **regarder dans le ~** to gaze (vacantly) into space *ou* into the blue; **les yeux perdus dans le ~** with a faraway look in his eyes.
(c) ~ à l'âme vague melancholy; **avoir du** *ou* **le ~ à l'âme** to feel vaguely melancholic.
vague[2] [vag] *nf* **(a)** (*lit*) wave. **~ de fond** (*lit*) ground swell (*U*); (*fig*) surge of opinion; (*littér*) **le gonflement de la ~** the swelling of the waves.
(b) (*fig: déferlement*) wave. **~ d'enthousiasme/de tendresse**

wave *ou* surge of enthusiasm/tenderness; ~ **d'applaudissements/de protestations** wave of applause/protest(s); **premières ~s d'arrivées** first waves of arrivals; **premières ~s de touristes/d'immigrants** first influxes of tourists/immigrants; (*Mil*) ~ **d'assaut** wave of assault; (*Mét*) ~ **de chaleur** heatwave; (*Mét*) ~ **de froid** cold spell *ou* snap; *V* **nouveau.**

(c) *[émanations]* wave. **une ~ de gaz se propagea jusqu'à nous** a smell of gas drifted *ou* wafted up to us.

(d) (*fig: ondulation*) (*Archit*) waved motif; *[chevelure]* wave; (*littér*) *[blés, fougères etc]* wave, undulation (*littér*).

vaguelette [vaglɛt] *nf* wavelet, ripple.

vaguement [vagmɑ̃] *adv* vaguely. **un geste ~ surpris/incrédule** a gesture of vague surprise/incredulity, a vaguely surprised/incredulous gesture.

vaguemestre [vagmɛstʀ(ə)] *nm* (*Mil, Naut*) *officer responsible for the delivery of mail.*

vaguer [vage] (1) *vi* (*littér*) to wander, roam.

vahiné [vaine] *nf* vahine.

vaillamment [vajamɑ̃] *adv* (*V* **vaillant**) bravely, courageously; valiantly, gallantly.

vaillance [vajɑ̃s] *nf* (*courage*) courage, bravery; (*au combat*) valour, gallantry, valiance.

vaillant, e [vajɑ̃, ɑ̃t] *adj* **(a)** (*courageux*) brave, courageous; (*au combat*) valiant, gallant; *V* **à, sou.**

(b) (*vigoureux, plein de santé*) vigorous, hale and hearty, robust. **je ne me sens pas très ~** I'm feeling (a bit) under the weather, I don't feel particularly great today*.

vaille que vaille [vajkəvaj] *loc adv* whatever happens, come what may.

vain, e [vɛ̃, vɛn] **1** *adj* **(a)** (*futile*) *paroles, promesse* empty, hollow, vain (*épith*); *craintes, espoir, plaisirs* vain (*épith*), empty. **des gens pour qui la loyauté n'est pas un ~ mot** people for whom loyalty is not an empty word, people for whom the word loyalty really means something.

(b) (*frivole*) *personne, peuple* shallow, superficial.

(c) (*infructueux*) *effort, tentative, attente* vain (*épith*), in vain (*attrib*), futile, fruitless; (*stérile*) *regrets, discussion* vain (*épith*), useless, idle (*épith*). **son sacrifice n'aura pas été ~** his sacrifice will not have been in vain; **il est ~ d'essayer de ...** it is futile to try to ... .

(d) (*littér: vaniteux*) vain (*de* of).

(e) (*loc*) **en ~** in vain; **elle essaya en ~ de s'en souvenir** she tried vainly *ou* in vain to remember; **ce ne fut pas en ~ que ...** it was not in vain that ... ; **je ressayai, mais en ~** I tried again, but in vain *ou* but to no avail; (*frm*) **invoquer le nom de Dieu en ~** to take the name of God in vain.

2: (*Jur*) **vaine pâture** common grazing land.

vaincre [vɛ̃kʀ(ə)] (42) *vt* **(a)** *rival, concurrent* to defeat; *armée, ennemi* to defeat, vanquish (*littér*), conquer. **les meilleurs ont fini par ~** the best men finally won; **sachons ~ ou sachons périr!** do or die!; (*Prov*) **à ~ sans péril, on triomphe sans gloire** triumph without peril brings no glory.

(b) *obstacle* to overcome; *difficulté* to overcome, triumph over, conquer; *instincts, timidité, sentiment* to triumph over, conquer, overcome; *maladie* to triumph over, conquer; *résistance* to overcome, defeat.

vaincu, e [vɛ̃ky] (*ptp de* **vaincre**) **1** *adj* defeated, vanquished (*littér*). **s'avouer ~** to admit defeat; **être ~ d'avance** to be beaten *ou* defeated before one begins.

2 *nm,f* defeated man (*ou* woman). **les ~s** the vanquished (*littér*), the defeated; **malheur aux ~s!** woe to the vanquished! (*littér*); **mentalité/attitude de ~** defeatist mentality/attitude.

vainement [vɛnmɑ̃] *adv* vainly, unavailingly.

vainqueur [vɛ̃kœʀ] **1** *nm* (*à la guerre*) conqueror, victor; (*en sport*) winner. **le ~ de l'Everest** the conqueror of Everest; **les ~s de cette équipe** the conquerors of this team; **les ~s de cette compétition** the winners in *ou* of this competition; **sortir ~ d'une épreuve** to emerge (as) the winner of a contest; **arriver quelque part en ~** to arrive somewhere as conqueror.

2 *adj m* victorious, triumphant.

vair [vɛʀ] *nm* vair.

vairon [vɛʀɔ̃] **1** *nm* (*Zool*) minnow.

2 *adj m* **yeux ~s** wall-eyes.

vaisseau, *pl* **~x** [vɛso] *nm* **(a)** (*Naut*) vessel (*frm*), ship. **~ amiral** flagship; **~ de guerre** warship; **le ~ fantôme** the Flying Dutchman; (*Aviat*) **~ spatial** spaceship; *V* **brûler, capitaine, lieutenant.**

(b) (*Anat*) vessel. **~ sanguin/lymphatique/capillaire** blood/lymphatic/capillary vessel.

(c) (*Bot*) vessel. **plante à ~x** vascular plant.

(d) (*Archit*) nave.

vaisselier [vɛsəlje] *nm* dresser (*cupboard*).

vaisselle [vɛsɛl] *nf* (*plats*) crockery; (*plats à laver*) dishes (*pl*), crockery; (*lavage*) washing-up (*Brit*), dishes (*pl*). **~ de porcelaine/faïence** china/earthenware crockery; **~ plate** (gold *ou* silver) plate; **faire la ~** to wash up, do the washing-up (*Brit*) *ou* the dishes; **la ~ était faite en deux minutes** the washing-up (*Brit*) was *ou* the dishes were done in two minutes; *V* **eau, essuyer, laver.**

val, *pl* **~s** *ou* **vaux** [val, vo] *nm* (*gén dans noms de lieux*) valley. **le V~ de Loire** the Val de Loire (*part of the Loire Valley*); *V* **mont.**

valable [valabl(ə)] *adj* **(a)** (*utilisable, légitime*) *contrat, passeport,* (*Jur*) valid; *excuse, raison* valid, legitimate, good (*épith*); *loi, critère, théorie, motif* valid. **elle n'a aucune raison ~ de le faire** she has no good *ou* valid reason for doing so; **ce n'est ~ que dans certains cas** it is only valid *ou* it only holds *ou* applies in certain cases.

(b) (*qui a du mérite*) *œuvre, solution, commentaire* really good, worthwhile; *équipements* decent, worthwhile; *concurrent, auteur* really good, worth his (*ou* her) salt (*attrib*); *V* **interlocuteur.**

valablement [valabləmɑ̃] *adv* **(a)** (*légitimement: V* **valable**) validly; legitimately. **ce billet ne peut pas être ~ utilisé** this ticket is not valid; **ne pouvant ~ soutenir que ...** not being able to uphold legitimately that ... .

(b) (*de façon satisfaisante*) **pour en parler ~, il faut des connaissances en linguistique** to be able to say anything worthwhile *ou* worth saying *ou* valid about it one would have to know something about linguistics.

valdinguer* [valdɛ̃ge] (1) *vi*: **aller ~** *[personne]* to go flat on one's face*, go sprawling; **les boîtes ont failli ~ (par terre)** the tins nearly came crashing down; (*fig*) **envoyer ~ qn** to tell sb to clear off* *ou* buzz off*, send sb packing*; **envoyer ~ qch** to send sth flying*.

Valence [valɑ̃s] *n* (*en Espagne*) Valencia; (*en France*) Valence.

valence [valɑ̃s] *nf* (*Phys*) valency. **~-gramme** gramme-equivalent.

valenciennes [valɑ̃sjɛn] *nf inv* Valenciennes lace.

valériane [valeʀjan] *nf* valerian.

valet [valɛ] **1** *nm* **(a)** (*domestique*) (man)servant; (*Hist*) *[seigneur]* valet; (*péj Pol*) lackey (*péj*). **premier ~ de chambre du roi** king's first valet; (*Théât*) **~ de comédie** manservant (part *ou* role); (*Théât*) **jouer les ~s** to play servant parts *ou* roles.

(b) (*Cartes*) jack, knave.

(c) (*cintre*) **~ (de nuit)** valet.

(d) (*Tech*) **~ (de menuisier)** (woodworker's) clamp.

2: valet de chambre manservant, valet; **valet d'écurie** groom, stableboy, stable lad; **valet de ferme** farmhand; **valet de pied** footman.

valetaille [valtɑj] *nf* (†*ou péj*) menials (*pl*), flunkeys† (*pl*).

valétudinaire [valetydinɛʀ] *adj, nmf* (*littér*) valetudinarian.

valeur [valœʀ] *nf* **(a)** (*U: commerciale*) value, worth; (*Fin*) *[devise, action]* value, price. (*Écon*) **~ d'usage/d'échange** usage *ou* practical/exchange value; (*Comm*) **~ marchande** market value; **~ vénale** monetary value; **vu la ~ de ces objets il faudra les faire assurer** in view of the value of these things they will have to be insured; **quelle est la ~ de cet objet?** what is this thing worth?, what is the value of this thing?; **prendre/perdre de la ~** to go up/down in value, lose/gain in value; **la ~ intrinsèque de qch** the intrinsic value *ou* worth of sth; **fixer la ~ d'une devise** to fix the price of a currency; **quelle est la ~ de la livre en ce moment?** what is the pound worth *ou* what is the value of the pound at the moment?; (*jugement subjectif*) **la livre/le franc/cette pièce n'a plus de ~** the pound/franc/this coin is worthless; **estimer la ~ d'un terrain/tableau à 2.000 F** to value a piece of land/a picture at 2,000 francs, put the value *ou* estimate the value of a piece of land/of a picture at 2,000 francs; **ces tableaux sont de même ~ ou ont la même ~** these pictures are of equal value *ou* have the same value; (*Poste*) **en ~ déclarée** value declared; *V* **taxe.**

(b) (*Bourse: gén pl: titre*) security. (*Bourse*) **~s** securities, stocks and shares; (*Comm: effet*) bill (of exchange). **~s (mobilières)** transferable securities; (*Comm*) **~ en compte** value in account; *V* **bourse.**

(c) (*U: qualité*) *[personne, auteur]* worth, merit; *[roman, tableau]* value, merit; *[science, théorie]* value. **un homme de (grande) ~** a man of great personal worth *ou* merit; **professeur/acteur de ~** a teacher/an actor of considerable merit; **la ~ de cette méthode/découverte reste à prouver** the value of this method/discovery is still to be proved; **estimer** *ou* **juger qn/qch à sa (juste) ~** to estimate *ou* judge sb/sth at his/its true value; **son œuvre n'est pas sans ~** his work is not without value *ou* merit; **je doute de la ~ de cette méthode** I am doubtful as to the value *ou* merit(s) of this method *ou* as to how valuable this method is; **ce meuble n'a qu'une ~ sentimentale** this piece of furniture has only sentimental value; **accorder** *ou* **attacher de la ~ à qch** to value sth, place value on sth; *V* **jugement, juste.**

(d) ~s (morales/intellectuelles) (moral/intellectual) values; **échelle** *ou* **hiérarchie des ~s** scale of values.

(e) (*idée de mesure, de délimitation*) *[couleur, terme, carte à jouer]* value; (*Math*) *[fonction]* value; (*Mus*) *[note]* value, length. **la ~ affective/poétique d'un mot** the emotive/poetic value of a word; (*Math*) **~ absolue** absolute value; **~ relative/absolue d'un terme** relative/absolute value of a term; **en ~ absolue/relative l'ouvrier américain gagne plus que son homologue français** in absolute/relative terms American workmen earn more than their French counterparts; (*Mus*) **la ~ d'une blanche est deux noires** one minim is equivalent to *ou* equals two crochets, one minim is worth two crochets; **donnez-lui la ~ d'un verre à liqueur/d'une cuiller à café** give him the equivalent of a liqueur glass/a teaspoonful, give him a liqueur glass's worth/a teaspoon's worth.

(f) (*loc*) **de ~** *bijou, meuble* valuable, of value; **objets de ~** valuables, articles of value; **sans ~** *objet* valueless, worthless; *témoignage* invalid, valueless; **mettre en ~** *bien, terrain* to exploit; *capitaux* to exploit, turn to good account; (*fig*) *détail, caractéristique* to bring out, highlight; *objet décoratif* to set off, show (off) to advantage, highlight; **mettre qn en ~** *[conversation, esprit]* to bring out sb's personal qualities; **ce chapeau te met en ~** that hat (of yours) is very flattering *ou* becoming; *V* **mise²**.

valeureusement [valœʀøzmɑ̃] *adv* (*littér*) valorously.

valeureux, -euse [valœʀø, øz] *adj* (*littér*) valorous.

validation [validɑsjɔ̃] *nf* (*V* **valider**) validation; authentication; ratification.

valide [valid] *adj* **(a)** *personne* (*non blessé ou handicapé*) able-bodied; (*en bonne santé*) fit, well (*attrib*); *membre* good (*épith*). **la population ~** the able-bodied population; **se sentir assez ~**

pour faire to feel fit *ou* well enough to do, feel up to doing.
(b) *billet, carte d'identité* valid.

validement [validmɑ̃] *adv* validly.

valider [valide] (1) *vt passeport, billet* to validate; *document* to authenticate; *décision* to ratify.

validité [validite] *nf* validity. **durée de ~ d'un billet** (period of) validity of a ticket.

valise [valiz] *nf* (suit)case. **faire sa ~/ses ~s** to pack one's (suit)case/(suit)cases *ou* bags, pack; (*fig*) **faire ses ~s** *ou* **sa ~** to pack one's bags; **la ~ (diplomatique)** the diplomatic bag; *V* **boucler.**

vallée [vale] *nf* (*Géog*) valley. **les gens de la ~** the lowland people; **~ suspendue/glaciaire** hanging/U-shaped *ou* glaciated valley; (*fig littér*) **la vie est une ~ de larmes** life is a vale *ou* valley of tears (*littér*).

vallon [valɔ̃] *nm* small valley.

vallonné, e [valɔne] *adj* undulating, cut by valleys (*attrib*).

vallonnement [valɔnmɑ̃] *nm* undulation.

valoir [valwaʀ] (29) **1** *vi* **(a)** *[propriété, bijou]* **~ (un certain prix/une certaine somme)** to be worth (a certain price/amount); **~ de l'argent** to be worth money; **ça vaut bien 10 F** (*estimation*) it must be worth 10 francs; (*jugement*) it is well worth (the) 10 francs; **~ cher/encore plus cher** to be worth a lot/still more; **cette montre vaut-elle plus cher que l'autre? — elles se valent à peu près** is this watch worth more than the other one? — they are worth about the same (amount); *V* **pesant.**

(b) (*avoir certaines qualités*) **que vaut cet auteur/cette pièce/le nouveau maire?** is this author/this play/the new mayor any good?; **sa dernière pièce ne valait pas grand-chose** his last play wasn't particularly good, his last play wasn't up to much*; **ils ne valent pas mieux l'un que l'autre** there's nothing to choose between them, they are two of a kind; **leur fils ne vaut pas cher!** their son isn't much good *ou* isn't up to much*; **tissu/marchandise qui ne vaut rien** material/article which is no good, rubbishy *ou* trashy material/article; **il a conscience de ce qu'il vaut** he is aware of his worth, he knows his worth *ou* what he's worth; **ce climat ne vaut rien pour les rhumatismes** this climate is no good (at all) for rheumatism; **l'inaction ne lui vaut rien** inactivity does not suit him *ou* isn't (any) good for him; **ça ne lui a rien valu** that didn't do him any good; **votre argument ne vaut rien** your argument is worthless; **cet outil ne vaut rien** this tool is useless *ou* no good *ou* no use.

(c) (*être valable*) to hold, apply, be valid. **ceci ne vaut que dans certains cas** this only holds *ou* applies *ou* is only valid in certain cases; **la décision vaut pour tout le monde** the decision goes for* *ou* applies to everyone; **cette pièce/cet auteur vaut surtout par son originalité** this play's/author's merit *ou* worth lies chiefly in its/his originality; *V aussi* **vaille.**

(d) (*équivaloir à*) **la campagne vaut bien la mer** the countryside is just as good *ou* is every bit as good as the seaside; (*Mus*) **une blanche vaut deux noires** one minim is equivalent to *ou* equals two crochets, one minim is worth (the same as) two crochets; **il vaut largement son frère** he is every bit as good as his brother *ou* quite the equal of his brother; **ce nouveau médicament/traitement ne vaut pas le précédent** this new medicine/treatment is not as good as *ou* isn't up to* *ou* isn't a patch on* the previous one; **tout cela ne vaut pas la mer/la liberté** this is all very well but it's not like the seaside/having one's freedom *ou* but give me the seaside/freedom any day!; **ces deux candidats/méthodes se valent** there's nothing to choose between these two applicants/methods, these two applicants/methods are of equal merit; **cette méthode en vaut une autre** it's as good a method as any (other); (*en mal*) **ces deux frères se valent** these two brothers are two of a kind; **ça se vaut*** it's six of one and half a dozen of the other*, it's all one, it's all the same; *V* **homme.**

(e) (*justifier*) to be worth. **Lyon vaut (bien) une visite/le déplacement** Lyons is (well) worth a visit/the journey; **le musée valait le détour** the museum was worth the detour; **cela vaut la peine** it's worth it, it's worth the trouble; **le film vaut (la peine) d'être vu** *ou* **qu'on le voie** the film is worth seeing; **cela valait la peine d'essayer** it was worth trying *ou* a try; **ça vaut la peine qu'il y aille** it's worth it for him to go, it's worth his while going; **cela ne vaut pas la peine d'en parler** (*c'est trop mauvais*) it's not worth wasting one's breath over, it's not worth talking about; (*c'est insignifiant*) it's hardly *ou* not worth mentioning.

(f) (*Comm*) **à ~** to be deducted; **paiement/acompte à ~ sur ...** payment/deposit to be deducted from ... ; **j'ai 20 F à ~ dans ce grand magasin** I've 20 francs' credit at this store.

(g) faire ~ *domaine* to exploit; *titres, capitaux* to exploit, turn to (good) account, invest profitably; *droits* to assert; *fait, argument* to emphasize; (*mettre en vedette*) *caractéristique* to highlight, bring out; *personne* to show off to advantage; **je lui fis ~ que ...** I impressed upon him that ... ; **se faire ~** to push o.s. forward, get o.s. noticed; **il ne sait pas se faire ~** he doesn't know how to show himself off to best advantage.

(h) (*loc*) **cette nouvelle machine ne vaut pas un clou*** this new machine is no use to man nor beast* *ou* is no earthly use*; **ne faire/n'écrire rien qui vaille** to do/write nothing useful *ou* worthwhile *ou* of any use; **cela ne me dit rien qui vaille** it doesn't appeal to me in the least *ou* slightest; **ça vaut le coup*** it's worth a go* *ou* a bash*; **ça ne vaut pas le coup de partir pour 2 jours*** it's not worth going (just) for 2 days; **il vaut mieux refuser, mieux vaut refuser** it is better to refuse; **il vaudrait mieux que vous refusiez** you had better refuse, you would do better *ou* best to refuse, you had best refuse; **avertis-le: ça vaut mieux** I would tell him if I were you, it would be better if you told him; **il vaut mieux le prévenir** we (*ou* you *etc*) had better tell him; **mieux vaut trop de travail que pas assez** too much work is better than not enough; *V* **mieux.**

2 *vt* (*causer, coûter*) **~ qch à qn** to earn sb sth; **ceci lui a valu des louanges/des reproches** this earned *ou* brought him praise/reproaches *ou* brought praise/reproaches upon him; **les soucis/les ennuis que nous a valus cette affaire!** the worry/trouble that this business has cost *ou* brought us!; **qu'est-ce qui nous vaut l'honneur de cette visite?** to what do we owe the honour of this visit?; **l'incident lui a valu d'être accusé d'imprudence** the incident earned him the accusation of carelessness; **un bon rhume, c'est tout ce que cela lui a valu de sortir sous la pluie** a bad cold is all he gained *ou* got for going out in the rain.

valorisation [valɔʀizasjɔ̃] *nf* (*V* **valoriser**) (economic) development; valorization; self-actualization.

valoriser [valɔʀize] (1) *vt* **(a)** (*Écon*) *région* to develop (the economy of); *produit* to valorize. **(b)** (*Psych*) *conduite, personne* to increase the standing of, actualize (*T*). **se ~** to increase one's standing, self-actualize (*T*).

valse [vals(ə)] *nf* **(a)** (*danse, air*) waltz. **~ lente/viennoise** slow/Viennese waltz; **~ musette** waltz (*to accordion accompaniment*).

(b) (*fig: carrousel*) musical chairs. **la ~ des ministres** *ou* **des portefeuilles** the ministerial musical chairs; **~ hésitation** pussyfooting* (*U*).

valser [valse] (1) *vi* **(a)** (*danser*) to waltz.

(b) (**fig*) **envoyer ~ qch/qn** (*en heurtant*) to send sth/sb flying; **envoyer ~ qn** (*rembarrer*) to send sb packing*; **il est allé ~ contre le mur** he went flying against the wall; **faire ~ l'argent** to spend money like water, throw money around; **faire ~ les chiffres** to dazzle people with figures; **faire ~ les ministres/les employés** to juggle the ministers/the staff around.

valseur, -euse [valsœʀ, øz] *nm,f* waltzer.

valve [valv(ə)] *nf* (*Bot, Élec, Tech, Zool*) valve.

valvulaire [valvylɛʀ] *adj* (*Anat, Méd*) valvular.

valvule [valvyl] *nf* (*Anat*) valve; (*Bot*) valvule; (*Tech*) valve.

vamp [vɑ̃p] *nf* vamp.

vamper* [vɑ̃pe] (1) *vt* to vamp.

vampire [vɑ̃piʀ] *nm* **(a)** (*fantôme*) vampire. **(b)** (*fig*) (†: *criminel*) vampire; (*escroc, requin*) vulture, vampire, bloodsucker. **(c)** (*Zool*) vampire bat.

vampirisme [vɑ̃piʀism(ə)] *nm* (*Psych*) necrophilia; (*fig: rapacité*) vampirism.

van[1] [vɑ̃] *nm* (*panier*) winnowing basket.

van[2] [vɑ̃] *nm* (*véhicule*) horse-box.

vanadium [vanadjɔm] *nm* vanadium.

vandale [vɑ̃dal] **1** *nmf* vandal; (*Hist*) Vandal. **2** *adj* vandal (*épith*); (*Hist*) Vandalic.

vandalisme [vɑ̃dalism(ə)] *nm* vandalism.

vandoise [vɑ̃dwaz] *nf* dace.

vanille [vanij] *nf* (*Bot, Culin*) vanilla. **crème/glace à la ~** vanilla cream/ice cream.

vanillé, e [vanije] *adj* vanilla (*épith*), vanilla-flavoured.

vanillier [vanije] *nm* vanilla plant.

vanité [vanite] *nf* **(a)** (*amour-propre*) vanity, conceit. **il avait des petites ~s d'artiste** he had the little conceits of an artist; **sans ~** without false modesty; **tirer ~ de** to pride o.s. on; **flatter/blesser qn dans sa ~** to flatter/wound sb's pride.

(b) (*littér: futilité: V* **vain**) emptiness; hollowness; vanity; shallowness, superficiality; futility, fruitlessness; uselessness, idleness.

vaniteusement [vanitøzmɑ̃] *adv* vainly, conceitedly.

vaniteux, -euse [vanitø, øz] **1** *adj* vain, conceited. **2** *nm,f* vain *ou* conceited person.

vannage [vanaʒ] *nm* winnowing.

vanne [van] *nf* **(a)** *[écluse]* (lock) gate, sluice (gate); *[barrage, digue]* floodgate, (sluice) gate; *[moulin]* (weir) hatch; *[canalisation]* gate. **(b)** (**:** *remarque*) dig*, jibe. **envoyer une ~ à qn** to have a dig at sb*, jibe at sb.

vanneau, *pl* **~x** [vano] *nm* peewit, lapwing.

vanner [vane] (1) *vt* **(a)** (*Agr*) to winnow. **(b)** (**:** *fatiguer*) to fag out* (*Brit*), do in*, knacker**:** (*Brit*). **je suis vanné** I'm dead-beat* *ou* fagged out* (*Brit*) *ou* knackered**:** (*Brit*).

vannerie [vanʀi] *nf* (*métier*) basketry, basketwork; (*objets*) wickerwork, basketwork.

vanneur, -euse [vanœʀ, øz] *nm,f* winnower.

vannier [vanje] *nm* basket maker, basket worker.

vantail, *pl* **-aux** [vɑ̃taj, o] *nm [porte]* leaf; *[armoire]* door. **porte à double ~** *ou* **à (deux) vantaux** Dutch door.

vantard, e [vɑ̃taʀ, aʀd(ə)] **1** *adj* boastful, bragging (*épith*), boasting (*épith*). **2** *nm,f* braggart, boaster.

vantardise [vɑ̃taʀdiz] *nf* (*caractère*) boastfulness; (*propos*) boast, boasting (*U*), bragging (*U*).

vanter [vɑ̃te] (1) **1** *vt* (*recommander, préconiser*) *auteur, endroit* to speak highly of, speak in praise of; *qualités* to vaunt (*frm*), praise, speak highly of, speak in praise of; *méthode, avantages, marchandises* to vaunt; (*frm: louer*) *personne, qualités* to extol (*frm*), laud (*frm*).

2 se vanter *vpr* **(a)** (*fanfaronner*) to boast, brag. **sans (vouloir) me ~** without false modesty, without wishing to boast *ou* brag.

(b) (*se targuer*) **se ~ de** to pride o.s. on. **se ~ d'avoir fait qch** to pride o.s. on having done sth; **se ~ de (pouvoir) faire ...** to boast one can *ou* will do ... ; (*iro*) **il ne s'en est pas vanté** he kept quiet about it; **il n'y a pas de quoi se ~** there's nothing to be proud of *ou* to boast about; **et il s'en vante!** and he's proud of it!

va-nu-pieds [vanypje] *nmf inv* (*péj*) tramp, beggar.

vapes: [vap] *nfpl*: **tomber dans les ~** to fall into a dead faint*; **être dans les ~** (*distrait*) to have one's head in the clouds; (*évanoui*) to be out for the count* *ou* out cold*; (*drogué, après un choc*) to be woozy* *ou* in a daze.

vapeur [vapœʀ] *nf* **(a)** (*littér: brouillard*) haze (*U*), vapour (*U*). **(b) ~ (d'eau)** steam, (water) vapour; **~ atmosphérique**

atmospheric vapour; (*Tech*) **à ~** steam (*épith*); **bateau à ~** steamship; **repassage à la ~** steam-ironing; (*Culin*) **(cuit à la) ~** steamed.

(c) (*émanation: Chim, Phys*) vapour. **~ d'essence** petrol vapour; **~ saturante** saturated vapour; **~ sèche** dry steam.

(d) (†: *gén pl: malaises*) **~s** vapours†.

(e) (*gén pl: griserie*) **les ~s de l'ivresse/de la gloire** the heady fumes of intoxication/of glory.

(f) (*loc*) **aller à toute ~** *[navire]* to sail full steam ahead; (**fig*) to go at full speed, go full steam ahead (*fig*); **renverser la ~** (*lit*) to reverse engines; (*fig*) to go into reverse.

vaporeux, -euse [vapɔʀø, øz] *adj tissu, robe* filmy, gossamer (*épith, littér*), diaphanous; (*littér*) *lumière, atmosphère* hazy, misty, vaporous; *nuage, cheveux* gossamer (*épith, littér*). (*Art*) **lointain ~** sfumato background.

vaporisateur [vapɔʀizatœʀ] *nm* (*à parfum*) spray, atomizer; (*Agr*) spray; (*Tech*) vaporizer.

vaporisation [vapɔʀizɑsjɔ̃] *nf* (*V* **vaporiser**) spraying; vaporization.

vaporiser [vapɔʀize] (1) **1** *vt* **(a)** *parfum, insecticide, surface* to spray. **(b)** (*Phys*) to vaporize, turn to vapour. **2 se vaporiser** *vpr* (*Phys*) to vaporize.

vaquer [vake] (1) **1 vaquer à** *vt indir* (*s'occuper de*) to attend to, see to. **~ à ses occupations** to attend to one's affairs, go about one's business. **2** *vi* **(a)** (†: *être vacant*) to stand *ou* be vacant. **(b)** (*Admin: être en vacances*) to be on vacation.

varappe [vaʀap] *nf* (*sport*) rock climbing; (*ascension*) (rock) climb.

varappeur [vaʀapœʀ] *nm* (rock) climber, cragsman.

varappeuse [vaʀapøz] *nf* (rock) climber.

varech [vaʀɛk] *nm* wrack, varec.

vareuse [vaʀøz] *nf [pêcheur, marin]* pea jacket; (*d'uniforme*) tunic; (*de ville*) (sports) jacket.

variabilité [vaʀjabilite] *nf* **(a)** *[temps, humeur]* changeableness, variableness. **(b)** (*Math, Sci*) variability.

variable [vaʀjabl(ə)] **1** *adj* **(a)** (*incertain*) *temps* variable, changeable, unsettled; *humeur* changeable, variable; (*Mét*) *vent* variable. **le baromètre est au ~** the barometer is at *ou* reads 'change'; **le temps est au ~** the weather is variable *ou* changeable *ou* unsettled.

(b) (*susceptible de changements*) *montant, allocation, part* variable; *dimensions, modalités, formes* adaptable, variable; (*Math, Sci*) *grandeur, quantité, facteur* variable; (*Ling*) *forme, mot* inflectional, inflected (*épith*). (*Fin*) **à revenu ~** variable yield (*épith*); **la récolte est ~: parfois bonne, parfois maigre** the harvest is variable *ou* varies: sometimes good, sometimes poor; **mot ~ en genre** word that is inflected *ou* marked for gender; *V* **foyer, géométrie**.

(c) (*au pl: varié*) *résultats, réactions* varied, various, varying (*épith*). **les réactions sont très ~s: certains sont pour, d'autres sont contre** reactions are very varied *ou* vary greatly: some are for and others are against.

2 *nf* (*Chim, Math, Phys, Statistique*) variable.

variance [vaʀjɑ̃s] *nf* variance.

variante [vaʀjɑ̃t] *nf* (*gén*) variant (*de* of), variation (*de* on); (*Ling, Littérat*) variant (*de* of). **une variante (d'itinéraire)** an alternative route.

variateur [vaʀjatœʀ] *nm*: **~ de vitesse** speed variator.

variation [vaʀjɑsjɔ̃] *nf* **(a)** (*U: V* **varier**) variation, varying; change, changing.

(b) (*écart, changement, Sci*) variation (*de* in); (*transformation*) change (*de* in). **les ~s de la température** the variations in (the) temperature, the temperature variations; **les ~s du mode de vie au cours des siècles** the changes in life-style through the centuries; **les ~s orthographiques/phonétiques au cours des siècles/selon les régions** orthographic/phonetic variations *ou* variants throughout the centuries/from region to region.

(c) (*Mus*) variation. (*fig hum*) **~s sur un thème connu** variations on the same old theme *ou* on a well-worn theme.

varice [vaʀis] *nf* (*Méd*) varicose vein, varix (*T*).

varicelle [vaʀisɛl] *nf* chickenpox, varicella (*T*).

varié, e [vaʀje] (*ptp de* **varier**) *adj* **(a)** (*non monotone*) *style, existence* varied, varying (*épith*); *paysage* varied, varying (*épith*); *programme, menu* (*qu'on change souvent*) varying (*épith*); (*diversifié*) varied. **un travail très ~** a very varied job; (*Mil*) **en terrain ~** on irregular terrain; (*Mus*) **air ~** theme with *ou* and variations; *V* **musique**.

(b) (*littér: non uni*) *tissu, couleur* variegated.

(c) (*divers*) *résultats, opinions* various, varying (*épith*), varied, divers (*épith*); *produits, sujets, objets* various, divers (*épith*). **hors-d'œuvre ~s** selection of hors d'œuvres, hors d'œuvres variés; **ayant recours à des arguments ~s** having recourse to various *ou* divers arguments.

varier [vaʀje] (7) **1** *vi* **(a)** (*changer*) to vary, change. (*Math*) **faire ~ une fonction** to vary a function; *V* **souvent**.

(b) (*différer, présenter divers aspects ou degrés, Sci*) to vary; (*Ling*) *[mot, forme]* to be inflected. **les professeurs varient souvent dans leurs opinions au sujet de ...** teachers' opinions often vary on the subject of ... .

2 *vt* **(a)** *style, menu, vie* (*changer*) to vary; (*rendre moins monotone*) to vary, lend *ou* give variety to. (*iro*) **pour ~ les plaisirs** just for a pleasant change (*iro*); **ils ne font que ~ la sauce*** they only dress it up differently*; **elle variait souvent sa coiffure/le menu** she often varied her hair style/the menu *ou* rang the changes on her hair style/the menu.

(b) *problèmes, thèmes, produits* to vary, diversify.

variété [vaʀjete] *nf* **(a)** (*U: V* **varié**) variety; diversity. **étonné par la grande ~ des produits/opinions** surprised at the great variety *ou* wide range of products/opinions; **aimer la ~** to like variety.

(b) (*type, espèce*) variety; (*aspect, forme*) variety, type. **il cultive exclusivement cette ~ de rose** he cultivates exclusively this variety of rose; **on y rencontrait toutes les ~s de criminels/de costumes** there you could find every possible variety *ou* type of criminal/costume.

(c) **~s** (*Littérat*) miscellanies; (*Music hall*) variety show; (*Rad, TV: musique*) light music (*U*); **émission/spectacle/théâtre de ~s** variety programme/show/hall.

variole [vaʀjɔl] *nf* smallpox, variola (*T*).

variolé, e [vaʀjɔle] *adj* pockmarked.

varioleux, -euse [vaʀjɔlø, øz] **1** *adj* suffering from smallpox, variolous (*T*). **2** *nm* (*gén pl*) smallpox case, patient suffering from smallpox.

variolique [vaʀjɔlik] *adj* smallpox (*épith*), variolous (*T*).

variqueux, -euse [vaʀikø, øz] *adj* varicose.

varlope [vaʀlɔp] *nf* trying-plane.

varloper [vaʀlɔpe] (1) *vt* to plane (down).

Varsovie [vaʀsɔvi] *n* Warsaw.

vasculaire [vaskylɛʀ] *adj* (*Anat, Bot*) vascular. **système ~ sanguin** blood-vascular system.

vascularisation [vaskylaʀizɑsjɔ̃] *nf* (*processus*) vascularization; (*réseau*) vascularity.

vascularisé, e [vaskylaʀize] *adj* vascular.

vase[1] [vɑz] **1** *nm* (*à fleurs, décoratif*) vase. (*fig*) **en ~ clos** *vivre, croître* in isolation, cut off from the world, in seclusion; *étudier, discuter* behind closed doors, in seclusion; (*Horticulture*) **taillé en ~** cut in the shape of a vase, vase-shaped; *V* **goutte**.

2: **vases communicants** communicating vessels; **vase de nuit** chamber(pot); (*Rel*) **vases sacrés** sacred vessels.

vase[2] [vɑz] *nf* silt, mud, sludge (*on riverbed*).

vaseline [vazlin] *nf* vaseline, petroleum jelly.

vaseux, -euse [vɑzø, øz] *adj* **(a)** (*) (*fatigué*) washed out* (*attrib*), off-colour* (*attrib*), under the weather* (*attrib*); (*confus*) woolly*, hazy. **(b)** (*boueux*) silty, muddy, sludgy.

vasistas [vazistɑs] *nm [porte]* (opening) window, fanlight; *[fenêtre]* fanlight.

vaso-constricteur, *pl* **vaso-constricteurs** [vazɔkɔ̃stʀiktœʀ] **1** *adj m* vasoconstrictor (*épith*). **2** *nm* vasoconstrictor (nerve).

vaso-dilatateur, *pl* **vaso-dilatateurs** [vazɔdilatatœʀ] **1** *adj m* vasodilator (*épith*). **2** *nm* vasodilator (nerve).

vaso-dilatation [vazɔdilatɑsjɔ̃] *nf* vasodilatation.

vaso-moteur, -trice [vazɔmɔtœʀ, tʀis] *adj* vasomotor (*épith*).

vasouillard, e* [vazujaʀ, aʀd(ə)] *adj personne* woolly-minded*, muddle-headed; *explication, raisonnement* woolly*, muddled.

vasouiller* [vazuje] (1) *vi [personne]* to flounder, struggle, fumble about; *[opération, affaire]* to struggle along, limp along; *[argument, article]* to go haywire*.

vasque [vask(ə)] *nf* (*bassin*) basin; (*coupe*) bowl.

vassal, e, *mpl* **-aux** [vasal, o] *nm,f* (*Hist, fig*) vassal.

vassalité [vasalite] *nf*, **vasselage** [vaslaʒ] *nm* (*Hist, fig*) vassalage.

vaste [vast(ə)] *adj* **(a)** *surface, étendue* vast, immense; *édifice, salle* vast, immense, enormous, huge; *vêtement* huge, enormous; *organisation, groupement* vast, huge. **à la tête d'un ~ empire industriel** at the head of a vast *ou* huge industrial empire; **de par le ~ monde** throughout the whole wide world.

(b) (*fig*) *connaissances, érudition* vast, immense, far-reaching; *génie, culture* immense, enormous; *ambitions* vast, enormous, immense; *domaine, sujet* wide(-ranging), huge, vast; *problème* wide-ranging, far-reaching. **un homme d'une ~ culture** a man of immense *ou* enormous culture, a highly cultured man; **ce sujet est trop ~** this subject is far too wide (-ranging) *ou* vast.

(c) (*: *intensif*) **une ~ rigolade** a great laugh*; **c'est une ~ plaisanterie/fumisterie** it's a huge *ou* an enormous joke/hoax.

Vatican [vatikɑ̃] *nm*: **le ~** the Vatican.

Vaticane [vatikan] *adj f*: **la (bibliothèque) ~** the Vatican Library.

vaticinateur, -trice [vatisinatœʀ, tʀis] *nm,f* (*littér*) vaticinator (*frm, littér*).

vaticination [vatisinɑsjɔ̃] *nf* (*littér*) vaticination (*frm, littér*). (*péj*) **~s** pompous predictions *ou* prophecies.

vaticiner [vatisine] (1) *vi* (*littér: prophétiser*) to vaticinate (*frm, littér*); (*péj*) to make pompous predictions *ou* prophecies.

va-tout [vatu] *nm*: **jouer son ~** to stake *ou* risk one's all.

vaudeville [vodvil] *nm* vaudeville, light comedy.

vaudevillesque [vodvilɛsk(ə)] *adj* vaudeville (*épith*).

vaudevilliste [vodvilist(ə)] *nm* writer of vaudeville.

vaudois, e [vodwa, waz] **1** *adj* (*Hist*) Waldensian; (*Géog*) Vaudois, of *ou* from the canton of Vaud. **2** *nm,f* (*Hist*) Waldensian. (*Géog*) **V~(e)** Vaudois.

vaudou [vodu] **1** *nm*: **le (culte du) ~** voodoo. **2** *adj inv* voodoo (*épith*).

vau-l'eau [volo] *adv*: **à ~** (*lit*) with the stream *ou* current; (*fig*) **aller** *ou* **s'en aller à ~** to be on the road to ruin; **voilà tous mes projets à ~** there are all my plans in ruins! *ou* down the drain!*

vaurien, -enne [voʀjɛ̃, ɛn] **1** *nm,f* (*voyou*) good-for-nothing; (*garnement*) little devil*. **petit ~!** little devil!* **2** *nm* (*Naut*) small sloop.

vaut [vo] *V* **valoir**.

vautour [votuʀ] *nm* (*Zool, fig*) vulture.

vautrer (se) [votʀe] (1) *vpr*: **se ~ dans** *boue, (fig) vice, obscénité, oisiveté* to wallow in; *fauteuil* to loll in; **se ~ sur** *tapis, canapé* to sprawl on; **vautré à plat ventre** *ou* **par terre** sprawling *ou* sprawled (flat) on the ground; **vautré dans l'herbe/sur le tapis** sprawling *ou* sprawled in the grass/on the carpet; (*fig littér*) **se ~ dans la fange** to wallow in the mire.

vauvert [vovɛʀ] *V* **diable**.

vaux [vo] *nmpl V* **val.**
va-vite* [vavit] *adv*: **à la ~** in a rush *ou* hurry; **faire qch à la ~** to rush sth, do sth in a rush *ou* hurry.
veau, *pl* **~x** [vo] *nm* **(a)** (*Zool*) calf. (*Bible*) **le V~ d'or** the golden calf; **adorer le V~ d'or** to worship Mammon; **tuer le ~ gras** to kill the fatted calf; *V* **crier, pleurer.**
(b) (*Culin*) veal. **escalope/côte/paupiettes de ~** veal escalope/chop/olives; **foie/pied/tête de ~** calf's liver/foot/head; **rôti de ~** roast veal; **~ marengo** veal marengo; *V* **blanquette.**
(c) (*cuir*) calfskin.
(d) (**péj*) (*personne*) clod* (*péj*), lump* (*péj*); (*cheval*) nag (*péj*); (*automobile*) tank* (*péj*).
vecteur [vɛktœʀ] **1** *adj m* (*Astron, Géom*) **rayon ~** radius vector. **2** *nm* (*Bio, Math*) vector; (*Mil: véhicule*) carrier.
vectoriel, -elle [vɛktɔʀjɛl] *adj* (*Math*) vectorial. **calcul ~** vector analysis.
vécu, e [veky] (*ptp de* **vivre**) **1** *adj histoire, aventure* real(-life) (*épith*), factual; *roman* real-life (*épith*), based on fact (*attrib*); (*Philos*) *temps, durée* lived.
2 *nm* (*Philos*) **le ~** that which has been lived; **ce que le lecteur veut, c'est du ~** what the reader wants is real-life *ou* factual experience.
vedettariat [vədɛtaʀja] *nm* (*état*) stardom; (*vedettes*) stars (*pl*).
vedette [vədɛt] *nf* **(a)** (*artiste, fig: personnage en vue*) star. **les ~s de l'écran/du cinéma** screen/film stars; **une ~ de la diplomatie/de la politique** a leading light *ou* figure in diplomacy/politics; (*fig*) **produit/station-~** leading product/station.
(b) (*Ciné, Théât: première place*) **avoir la ~** to top the bill, have star billing; (*fig*) **avoir** *ou* **tenir la ~ (de l'actualité)** to be in the spotlight, make the headlines; (*fig*) **pendant toute la soirée il a eu la ~** he was in the limelight *ou* was the centre of attraction all evening; **partager la ~ avec qn** to share star billing with sb, top the bill alongside sb; **mettre qn en ~** (*Ciné*) to give sb star billing; (*fig*) to push sb into the limelight, put the spotlight on sb; **en ~ américaine** as a special guest star.
(c) (*embarcation*) launch; (*Mil*) patrol boat.
(d) (*Mil††: guetteur*) sentinel.
vedettisation [vədetizɑsjɔ̃] *nf*: **la ~ de qn** pushing sb into the limelight, putting the spotlight on sb.
védique [vedik] *adj* Vedic.
védisme [vedism(ə)] *nm* vedaism.
végétal, e, *mpl* **-aux** [veʒetal, o] **1** *adj graisses, teintures, huiles* vegetable (*épith*); *biologie, histologie, fibres, cellules* plant (*épith*); *sol* rich in humus; *ornementation* plant-like; *V* **règne. 2** *nm* vegetable, plant.
végétalisme [veʒetalism(ə)] *nm* veganism.
végétarien, -ienne [veʒetaʀjɛ̃, jɛn] *adj, nm,f* vegetarian.
végétarisme [veʒetaʀism(ə)] *nm* vegetarianism.
végétatif, -ive [veʒetatif, iv] *adj* **(a)** (*Bot, Physiol*) vegetative. **(b)** (*fig péj*) vegetative, vegetable (*épith*).
végétation [veʒetɑsjɔ̃] *nf* **(a)** (*Bot*) vegetation. **(b)** (*Méd*) **~s (adénoïdes)** adenoids.
végéter [veʒete] (6) *vi* (*péj*) *[personne]* to vegetate; *[affaire]* to stagnate; (*†: pousser*) to grow, vegetate.
véhémence [veemɑ̃s] *nf* (*littér*) vehemence. **protester avec ~** to protest vehemently.
véhément, e [veemɑ̃, ɑ̃t] *adj* (*littér*) vehement.
véhémentement [veemɑ̃tmɑ̃] *adv* (*littér*) vehemently.
véhiculaire [veikylɛʀ] *adj* (*Ling*) **langue ~** lingua franca, common language.
véhicule [veikyl] *nm* **(a)** (*moyen de transport, agent de transmission*) vehicle. **~ automobile/utilitaire** motor/commercial vehicle. **(b)** (*fig*) vehicle, medium. **le langage est le ~ de la pensée** language is the vehicle *ou* medium of thought.
véhiculer [veikyle] (1) *vt marchandises, troupes* to convey, transport; (*fig*) *substance, idées* to convey, serve as a vehicle for.
veille [vɛj] *nf* **(a)** (*état*) wakefulness; (*période*) period of wakefulness. **en état de ~** in the waking state, awake; **entre la ~ et le sommeil** between waking and sleeping.
(b) (*garde*) (night) watch. **homme de ~** (night) watch; **prendre la ~** to take one's turn on watch.
(c) (*jour précédent*) **la ~** the day before; **la ~ au soir** the previous evening, the night *ou* evening before; **la ~ de Pâques/de cet examen** the day before Easter/that exam; **la ~ de Noël/du jour de l'an** Christmas/New Year's Eve; **la ~ de sa mort** on the eve of his death, on the day before his death; *V* **demain.**
(d) (*fig*) **à la ~ de** *guerre, révolution* on the eve of; **être à la ~ de commettre une grave injustice/une grosse erreur** to be on the brink *ou* verge of committing a grave injustice/of making a big mistake; **ils étaient à la ~ d'être renvoyés/de manquer de vivres** they were on the point of being dismissed/of running out of supplies.
veillée [veje] *nf* **(a)** (*soirée: période*) evening (*spent in company*). **passer la ~ à jouer aux cartes** to spend the evening playing cards; (*réunion*) **il se souvient de ces ~s d'hiver** he remembers those winter evening gatherings; **~ d'armes** (*Hist*) knightly vigil; (*fig*) night before combat (*fig*).
(b) ~ (funèbre) watch.
veiller [veje] (1) **1** *vi* **(a)** (*rester éveillé*) to stay up, sit up. **~ au chevet d'un malade** to sit up at the bed of a sick person; **~ auprès du mort** to keep watch over the body.
(b) (*être de garde*) to be on watch; (*rester vigilant*) to be watchful, be vigilant.
(c) (*être en état de veille*) to be awake.
(d) (*faire la veillée*) to spend the evening in company.
2 *vt mort, malade* to watch over, sit up with.
3 *vt indir* **(a) veiller à** *intérêts, approvisionnement* to attend to, see to, look after; *bon fonctionnement, bonne marche de qch* to attend to, see to. **~ au bon fonctionnement d'une machine** to see to it that a machine is working properly, attend *ou* see to the proper working of a machine; **~ au bon ordre** to see to it that order is maintained; **~ à ce que ...** to see to it that ..., make sure that ...; (*fig*) **~ au grain** to keep an eye open for trouble *ou* problems, look out for squalls (*fig*).
(b) (*surveiller*) **veiller sur** *personne, santé, bonheur de qn* to watch over, keep a watchful eye on.
veilleur [vɛjœʀ] *nm* **(a) ~ (de nuit)** (night) watchman. **(b)** (*Mil*) look-out.
veilleuse [vɛjøz] *nf* **(a)** (*lampe*) night light; (*Aut*) sidelight. **mettre en ~** *lampe* to dim; (*fig*) **mettre qch en ~** to shelve sth, put sth into abeyance; **se mettre en ~** to slacken off; **mets-la en ~!:** cool it!: **(b)** (*flamme*) pilot light.
veinard, e* [vɛnaʀ, aʀd(ə)] **1** *adj* lucky, jammy: (*Brit*). **2** *nm,f* lucky devil* *ou* dog*, jammy so-and-so: (*Brit*).
veine [vɛn] *nf* **(a)** (*Anat*) vein. **~ coronaire/pulmonaire** coronary/pulmonary vein; **~ cave** vena cava; **~ porte** portal vein; (*fig*) **avoir du feu dans les ~s** to have fire in one's veins; *V* **ouvrir, saigner.**
(b) (*nervure*) vein; (*filon*) *[houille]* seam, vein; *[minerai non ferreux]* vein; *[minerai de fer]* lode, vein.
(c) (*fig: inspiration*) **~ poétique/dramatique** poetic/dramatic inspiration; **sa ~ est tarie** his inspiration has dried up; **de la même ~** in the same vein; **être en ~** to be inspired, have a fit of inspiration; **être en ~ de patience/bonté** to be in a patient/benevolent mood *ou* frame of mind.
(d) (**: chance*) luck. **c'est une ~** that's a bit of luck, what a bit of luck; **un coup de ~** a stroke of luck; **pas de ~!** hard *ou* bad *ou* rotten* luck!; **avoir de la ~** to be lucky; **ce type a de la ~** that fellow's a lucky devil* *ou* dog*; **avoir une ~ de cocu:** *ou* **pendu*** to have the luck of the devil*; **il a eu de la ~ aux examens** he was lucky *ou* in luck at the exams, his luck was in at the exams; **il n'a pas eu de ~ aux examens** his luck was out at the exams; (*iro*) **c'est bien ma ~** that's just my (rotten*) luck.
veiné, e [vene] (*ptp de* **veiner**) *adj* **(a)** *bras, peau* veined, veiny. **bras à la peau ~e** arm with the veins apparent on the skin.
(b) (*fig*) *bois* grained; *marbre* veined. **marbre ~ de vert** marble with green veins, green-veined marble.
veiner [vene] (1) *vt* (*pour donner l'aspect du bois*) to grain; (*pour donner l'aspect du marbre*) to vein. **les stries qui veinent une dalle de marbre** the streaks veining the surface of a marble slab; **les nervures qui veinent une feuille** the veins that appear on the surface of a leaf.
veineux, -euse [vɛnø, øz] *adj* **(a)** *système, sang* venous. **(b)** *bois* grainy; *marbre* veined.
veinule [venyl] *nf* (*Anat*) veinlet, venule (*T*); (*Bot*) venule.
veinure [venyʀ] *nf* (*V* **veiner**) graining; veining. **admirant la ~ du marbre** admiring the veins *ou* veining of the marble.
vêlage [vɛlaʒ] *nm* (*Géog, Zool*) calving.
vélaire [velɛʀ] *adj, nf*: **(consonne/voyelle) ~** velar (consonant/vowel).
vélarisation [velaʀizɑsjɔ̃] *nf* velarization.
vêlement [vɛlmɑ̃] *nm* = **vêlage.**
vêler [vele] (1) *vi* to calve.
vélin [velɛ̃] *nm* (*peau*) vellum. **(papier) ~** vellum (paper).
vélite [velit] *nm* (*Hist*) velites (*pl*).
velléitaire [veleitɛʀ] **1** *adj* irresolute, indecisive, wavering (*épith*). **2** *nmf* waverer.
velléité [veleite] *nf* vague desire, vague impulse. **leurs ~s révolutionnaires ne m'effrayaient guère** I was scarcely alarmed by their vague desire for revolution *ou* their vague revolutionary impulses; **une ~ de sourire/menace** a hint of a smile/threat.
vélo* [velo] *nm* bike, cycle. **~ de course** racing cycle; **être à ~** *ou* **en ~** to be on a bike; **venir à** *ou* **en ~** to come by bike *ou* on a bike; **faire du ~: je fais beaucoup de ~** I cycle a lot, I do a lot of cycling; **on va faire un peu de ~** we're going out (for a ride) on our bikes; **aller à ~: à 5 ans il allait déjà à ~** he could already ride a bike at 5; **on y va à ~?** shall we go by bike? *ou* on our bikes?
véloce [velɔs] *adj* (*littér*) swift, fleet (*littér*).
vélocement [velɔsmɑ̃] *adv* (*littér*) swiftly, fleetly (*littér*).
vélocipède†† [velɔsipɛd] *nm* velocipede.
vélocité [velɔsite] *nf* **(a)** (*Mus*) nimbleness, swiftness. **exercices de ~** exercises for the agility of the fingers. **(b)** (*littér: vitesse*) swiftness, fleetness (*littér*).
vélodrome [velɔdʀom] *nm* velodrome.
vélomoteur [velɔmɔtœʀ] *nm* light motorcycle.
vélomotoriste [velɔmɔtɔʀist(ə)] *nmf* rider of light motorcycle.
velours [v(ə)luʀ] *nm* **(a)** (*tissu*) velvet. **~ de coton/de laine** cotton/wool velvet; **~ côtelé** corduroy, cord; **~ uni** velvet; *V* **jouer, main.**
(b) (*velouté*) velvet. **le ~ de la pêche** the bloom of the peach; **le ~ de sa joue** the velvety texture of her cheek, her velvet(y) cheek; **peau/yeux de ~** velvet(y) skin/eyes; (*fig*) **faire des yeux de ~ à qn** to make sheep's eyes at sb; **ce potage/cette crème est un vrai ~** this soup/cream dessert is velvety-smooth; **elle avait des yeux de ~** she had velvety eyes; *V* **œil, patte.**
velouté, e [vəlute] (*ptp de* **velouter**) **1** *adj* **(a)** (*Tex*) brushed; (*à motifs*) with a raised velvet pattern.
(b) (*fig: doux*) *joues* velvet (*épith*), velvety, velvet-smooth; *pêche* velvety, downy; *crème, potage* velvety, smooth; *vin* smooth, velvety; *lumière, regard* soft, mellow; *voix* velvet-smooth, mellow.
2 *nm* **(a)** (*douceur: V adj*) velvet-softness; velvetiness; velvety-smoothness, smoothness; downiness; softness; mellowness.

(b) (*Culin*) (*sauce*) velouté sauce; (*potage*) velouté. **~ de tomates/d'asperges** cream of tomato/asparagus soup.

velouter [vəlute] (1) **1** *vt* **(a)** *papier* to put a velvety finish on. (*fig*) **le duvet qui veloutait ses joues** the down that gave a velvet softness to her cheeks.

(b) *joues, pêche* to give a velvet(y) texture to; *vin, crème, potage* to make smooth; *lumière, regard* to soften, mellow; *voix* to mellow.

2 se velouter *vpr* (*V* **velouter**) to take on a velvety texture; to become smooth; to soften; to mellow.

velouteux, -euse [vəlutø, øz] *adj* velvet-like, velvety.

Velpeau [vɛlpo] *nm V* **bande**[1].

velu, e [vəly] *adj main* hairy; *plante* hairy, villous (*T*).

velum, vélum [velɔm] *nm* canopy.

venaison [vənɛzɔ̃] *nf* venison.

vénal, e, *mpl* **-aux** [venal, o] *adj* **(a)** *personne* venal, mercenary; *activité, affection* venal. **(b)** (*Hist*) *office* venal; *V* **valeur.**

vénalement [venalmɑ̃] *adv* venally.

vénalité [venalite] *nf* venality.

venant [v(ə)nɑ̃] *nm V* **tout.**

vendable [vɑ̃dabl(ə)] *adj* saleable, marketable.

vendange [vɑ̃dɑ̃ʒ] *nf* (*parfois pl: récolte*) wine harvest, grape harvest, vintage; (*raisins récoltés*) grapes (harvested), grape crop; (*gén pl: période*) grape harvest (time), vintage. **pendant les ~s** during grape harvest (time), during the vintage; **faire la ~** *ou* **les ~s** to harvest the grapes.

vendanger [vɑ̃dɑ̃ʒe] (3) **1** *vt vigne* to gather *ou* harvest grapes from; *raisins* to harvest, vintage (*rare*). **2** *vi* (*faire la vendange*) to harvest the grapes; (*presser le raisin*) to press the grapes.

vendangeur, -euse [vɑ̃dɑ̃ʒœʀ, øz] **1** *nm,f* grape-picker, vintager (*rare*). **2** *nf* (*fleur*) aster.

vendéen, -enne [vɑ̃deɛ̃, ɛn] **1** *adj* of *ou* from the Vendée. **2** *nm,f*: **V~(ne)** inhabitant *ou* native of the Vendée.

vendémiaire [vɑ̃demjɛʀ] *nm* Vendémiaire (*1st month of French Republican calendar*).

vendetta [vɑ̃deta] *nf* vendetta.

vendeur [vɑ̃dœʀ] *nm* **(a)** (*dans un magasin*) shop assistant; *[grand magasin]* shop *ou* sales assistant, salesman. **'cherchons 2 ~s, rayon librairie'** '2 sales assistants required for our book department'.

(b) (*marchand*) seller, salesman. **~ ambulant** itinerant *ou* travelling salesman; **~ à la sauvette** street hawker; **~ de journaux** newspaper seller.

(c) (*Comm: chargé des ventes*) salesman. (*fig*) **c'est un excellent ~** he is an excellent salesman, he has a flair for selling.

(d) (*Jur*) vendor, seller; (*Écon*) seller. **cette responsabilité incombe au ~** this responsibility falls on the vendor *ou* seller; **je ne suis pas ~** I'm not selling; **les pays ~s de cacao** the cocoa-selling countries.

vendeuse [vɑ̃døz] *nf* **(a)** (*dans un magasin*) shop assistant; *[grand magasin]* shop *ou* sales assistant, saleswoman; (*jeune*) salesgirl.

(b) (*marchande*) seller, saleswoman. **~ de poissons/légumes** fish/vegetable seller *ou* saleswoman.

vendre [vɑ̃dʀ(ə)] (41) **1** *vt* **(a)** *marchandise, valeurs* to sell (*à* to). **~ qch à qn** to sell sb sth *ou* sth to sb; **elle vend des foulards à 10 F** she sells scarves for *ou* at 10 francs; **il m'a vendu un tableau 500 F** he sold me a picture for 500 francs; **l'art de ~** the art of selling; **elle vend cher** she is expensive *ou* dear, her prices are high; (*Comm*) **ces affiches publicitaires font ~** these advertising posters get things sold *ou* are boosting sales; **~ qch aux enchères** to sell sth by auction; **~ sa part d'une affaire** to sell (out) one's share of a business; **(maison/terrain) à ~** (house/land) for sale; **~ son droit d'aînesse pour un plat de lentilles** to sell one's birthright for a mess of potage; *V* **crédit, prix** etc.

(b) (*péj*) *droit, honneur, charge* to sell. **~ son âme/honneur** to sell one's soul/honour; **~ son silence** to be paid for one's silence; **il vendrait (ses) père et mère** he would sell his father and mother.

(c) (*fig: faire payer*) **ils nous ont vendu très cher ce droit/cet avantage** they made us pay dear *ou* dearly for this right/advantage; **~ chèrement sa vie** *ou* **sa peau*** to sell one's life *ou* one's skin dearly.

(d) (*: *trahir*) *personne, complice* to sell, sell out*.

(e) (*loc*) **~ la peau de l'ours (avant de l'avoir tué)** to count one's chickens (before they are hatched); **~ la mèche*** (*volontairement*) to give the game away*; (*involontairement*) to let the cat out of the bag*, give the game away*.

2 se vendre *vpr* **(a)** *[marchandise]* to sell, be sold. **se ~ à la pièce/douzaine** to be sold singly/by the dozen; **ça se vend bien/comme des petits pains** that sells well/like hot cakes; **un ouvrage/auteur qui se vend bien** a work/an author that sells well.

(b) (*péj: se laisser corrompre*) to sell o.s. **se ~ à un parti/l'ennemi** to sell oneself to a party/the enemy.

(c) (*se trahir*) to give o.s. away.

vendredi [vɑ̃dʀədi] *nm* Friday. **~ saint** Good Friday; *pour autres loc V* **samedi.**

vendu, e [vɑ̃dy] (*ptp de* **vendre**) **1** *adj fonctionnaire, juge* bribed, who has sold himself for money; *V* **adjuger. 2** *nm* mercenary traitor.

venelle [vənɛl] *nf* alley.

vénéneux, -euse [venenø, øz] *adj* (*lit*) poisonous; (*fig littér*) pernicious, harmful.

vénérable [veneʀabl(ə)] **1** *adj* (*littér, hum: respectable*) venerable; (*hum: très vieux*) *personne* ancient, venerable; *chose* ancient. **une automobile d'un âge ~** a motorcar of venerable age, an ancient motorcar. **2** *nm* (*Rel*) Venerable; (*Franc-Maçonnerie*) Worshipful Master.

vénération [veneʀɑsjɔ̃] *nf* (*Rel*) veneration; (*gén: grande estime*) veneration, reverence.

vénérer [veneʀe] (6) *vt* (*Rel*) to venerate; (*gén*) to venerate, revere.

vénerie [vɛnʀi] *nf* **(a)** (*art*) venery (*T*), hunting. **petite ~** small game hunting; **grande ~** hunting of larger animals. **(b)** (*administration*) **la ~** the Hunt.

vénérien, -ienne [veneʀjɛ̃, jɛn] **1** *adj* **(a)** (*Méd*) venereal. **maladies ~nes** venereal diseases, V.D.

(b) (††: *sexuel*) venereal††, sexual.

2 *nm* (*gén pl: malade*) V.D. patient, person with V.D. *ou* venereal disease.

vénér(é)ologiste [veneʀ(e)ɔlɔʒist(ə)] *nmf* specialist in venereal diseases, V.D. specialist.

veneur [vənœʀ] *nm* (*Hist*) huntsman, venerer††; *V* **grand.**

Venezuela [venezɥela] *nm* Venezuela.

vénézuélien, -ienne [venezɥeljɛ̃, jɛn] **1** *adj* Venezuelan. **2** *nm,f*: **V~(ne)** Venezuelan.

vengeance [vɑ̃ʒɑ̃s] *nf* (*V* **se venger**) vengeance; revenge. **tirer ~ de** to be avenged for; to be revenged for; **exercer sa ~ sur** to take (one's) revenge on, wreak vengeance upon (*littér*); **ce forfait crie** *ou* **demande ~** this crime cries out for *ou* demands revenge; **agir par ~** to act out of revenge; **de petites ~s** little acts of vengeance; little acts of revenge; **une ~ cruelle** cruel vengeance; cruel revenge; **la ~ divine** divine vengeance; (*Prov*) **la ~ est un plat qui se mange froid** never take revenge in the heat of the moment.

venger [vɑ̃ʒe] (3) **1** *vt* **(a)** *personne, honneur, mémoire* to avenge (*de* for). **ceci m'a vengé de lui** that was my revenge on him.

(b) *injustice, affront* to avenge. **rien ne vengera cette injustice** nothing will avenge this injustice, there is no revenge for this injustice.

2 se venger *vpr* (*chercher réparation*) to avenge o.s., be avenged; (*assouvir sa rancune*) to take (one's) revenge *ou* vengeance, be revenged. **se ~ de qn** to take revenge on *ou* wreak vengeance upon sb (*littér*); **se ~ de qn sur sa famille** to take revenge on sb through his family; **se ~ de qch** to avenge o.s. for sth; to take one's revenge for sth; **je me vengerai** I shall be avenged; I shall get *ou* have *ou* take my revenge; (*fig*) **il se vengeait par son éclatante santé de la préférence accordée à ses sœurs** his radiant health more than avenged him *ou* compensated for the preference shown for his sisters.

vengeur, -geresse [vɑ̃ʒœʀ, ʒʀɛs] **1** *adj personne* (re)vengeful; *bras, lettre, pamphlet* avenging (*épith*). **2** *nm,f* avenger.

véniel, -elle [venjɛl] *adj faute, oubli* venial (*littér*), pardonable, excusable; *V* **péché.**

véniellement [venjɛlmɑ̃] *adv* venially.

venimeux, -euse [vənimø, øz] *adj* **(a)** (*lit*) *serpent, piqûre* venomous, poisonous. **(b)** (*fig*) *personne, voix* venomous, vicious; *remarque, haine* venomous, envenomed, vicious. **une langue ~euse** a poisonous *ou* venomous *ou* vicious tongue.

venimosité [vənimozite] *nf* (*rare*) venomousness, venom.

venin [vənɛ̃] *nm* **(a)** (*lit*) venom, poison. **~ de serpent** snake venom; **crochets à ~** poison fangs; **sérum contre les ~s** antivenom serum.

(b) (*fig*) venom, viciousness. **jeter** *ou* **cracher son ~** to spit out one's venom; **répandre son ~ contre qn** to pour out one's venom against sb; **paroles pleines de ~** venomous *ou* envenomed words, words full of venom *ou* viciousness.

venir [v(ə)niʀ] (22) **1** *vi* **(a)** (*gén*) to come. **ils viennent de Lyon** they are coming from Lyons; **les victimes venaient de Lyon** the casualties were on their way *ou* were coming from Lyons; **ils sont venus en voiture** they came by car, they drove (here); **ils sont venus par le train** they came by train; **ils sont venus en avion** they came by air, they flew (here); **je viens!** I'm coming!, I'm on my way!*; **je viens dans un instant** I'll be there in a moment; **il venait sur nous sans nous voir/l'air furieux** he advanced upon us without seeing us/looking furious; (*s'adresser à*) **il est venu à nous plutôt qu'à son supérieur** he came to us rather than (to) his superior; **il vient chez nous tous les jeudis** he comes (round) to our house *ou* to us every Thursday; **il ne vient jamais aux réunions** he never comes to meetings; **je viens de la part de Jules** I've come *ou* I'm here on behalf of Jules; **de la part de qui venez-vous?** who asked you to come?, who sent you?, who had you come?; *V* **aller.**

(b) faire ~ *médecin, plombier* to call, send for; **tu nous as fait ~ pour rien: la réunion n'a pas eu lieu** you got us to come *ou* you made us come for nothing – the meeting didn't take place; **faire ~ son vin de Provence/ses robes de Paris** to get one's wine sent from Provence/one's dresses sent from Paris, send to Provence for one's wine/to Paris for one's dresses.

(c) (*fig*) *[idées, bruit]* to come. **mot qui vient sur les lèvres/sous la plume** word that comes to the tongue/pen; **les idées ne viennent pas** the ideas aren't coming; **le bruit est venu jusqu'à nous que ...** word has reached us *ou* come to us that ...; **l'idée lui est venue de ...** the idea came *ou* occurred to him to ..., it occurred to him to ...; **ça ne me serait pas venu à l'idée** that would never have occurred to me *ou* entered my head, I should never have thought of that.

(d) (*survenir*) to come. **quand l'aube vint** when dawn came; **la nuit vient vite** night is coming (on) fast; **ceci vient à point/mal à propos** this comes (along) just at the right/wrong moment; *V* **voir.**

(e) (*dans le temps, dans une série*) to come. **ça vient avant/après** that comes before/after; **le moment viendra où ...** the time will come when ...; **la semaine/l'année qui vient** the coming week/year; *V* **venu.**

(f) (*se développer*) *[plante]* to come along. **cette plante vient bien** this plant is coming along *ou* is doing well *ou* nicely.

(g) ~ **de** (*provenance, cause*) to come from; **ils viennent de Paris** they come *ou* are from Paris; **ce produit vient du Maroc** this product comes from Morocco; **l'épée lui vient de son oncle** the sword has been passed down to him by his uncle; **ces troubles viennent du foie** this trouble comes from the liver; **ceci vient de son imprudence** this is the result of his carelessness, this comes from his carelessness; **d'où vient que ...?** how is it that ...?, what is the reason that ...?; **de là vient que ...** the result of this is that ...; **d'où vient cette hâte soudaine?** what's the reason for this sudden haste?, how come* *ou* why this sudden haste?; **ça vient de ce que ...** it comes *ou* results from the fact that ... .

(h) (*atteindre*) ~ **à** (*vers le haut*) to come up to, reach (up to); (*vers le bas*) to come down to, reach (down to); (*en longueur, en superficie*) to come out to, reach; **l'eau nous vient aux genoux** the water comes up to *ou* reaches (up to) our knees; **il me vient à l'épaule** he comes up to my shoulder; **sa jupe lui vient aux genoux** her skirt comes down to *ou* reaches her knees; **la forêt vient jusqu'à la route** the forest comes (right) out to *ou* reaches the road.

(i) en ~ **à: j'en viens maintenant à votre question/à cet aspect du problème** I shall now come *ou* turn to your question/that aspect of the problem; **venons-en au fait** let's get to the point; **j'en viens à la conclusion que ...** I have come to *ou* reached the conclusion that ..., I'm coming to the conclusion that ...; **j'en viens à leur avis** I'm coming round to their opinion; **j'en viens à me demander si ...** I'm beginning to wonder if ...; **il faudra bien en** ~ **là** we'll have to come *ou* resort to that in the end, that's what it'll come to in the end; **il en est venu à mendier** he was reduced to begging, he had to resort to begging; **il en est venu à haïr ses parents** he has got to the stage of loathing his parents; **comment les choses en sont-elles venues là?** how did things come to this? *ou* get to this stage? *ou* get into this state?; **en** ~ **aux mains** *ou* **coups** to come to blows; **où voulez-vous en** ~? what are you getting *ou* driving at?

(j) y ~**: j'y viens, mais ne me brusquez pas** I'm coming round to it *ou* to the idea, but don't hustle me; **il faudra bien qu'il y vienne** he'll just have to come round to it.

(k) (*loc*) ~ **au monde** to come into the world, be born; **s'en aller** *ou* **retourner comme on est venu** to leave as one came; (*menace*) **viens-y!** just (you) come here!; (*menace*) **qu'il y vienne!** just let him come!; (*impatience*) **ça vient?** well, when are we getting it?, come on!; **alors ce dossier ça vient?** well, when am I (*ou* are we) getting this file?; **à** ~**: les années/générations à** ~ the years/generations to come, future years/generations; ~ **à bout de** *travail* to get through, get to the end of; *adversaire* to get the better of, overcome; *repas, gâteau* to get through; **je n'en viendrai jamais à bout** I'll never manage it, I'll never get through it.

2 *vb aux* **(a)** (*se déplacer pour*) **je suis venu travailler** I have come to work; **il va** ~ **la voir** he's going to come to see her; **viens m'aider** come and help me; **après cela ne viens pas te plaindre!** and don't (you) come and complain *ou* come complaining afterwards!

(b) (*passé récent*) ~ **de faire** to have just done; **il vient d'arriver** he has just arrived; **elle venait de se lever** she had just got up.

(c) (*éventualité*) ~ **à faire: s'il venait à mourir** if he were to die *ou* if he should (happen to) die; **vint à passer un officier** an officer happened to pass by; **s'il venait à passer par là** if he should (happen to) go that way.

3 *vb impers* **(a) il vient beaucoup d'enfants** a lot of children are coming, there are a lot of children coming; **il lui est venu des boutons** he came out in spots; **il ne lui viendrait pas à l'idée** *ou* **à l'esprit que ...** it wouldn't occur to him that ..., it wouldn't enter his head that ... .

(b) il vient un temps/une heure où ... the time/the hour is coming when ... .

(c) (*éventualité*) **s'il vient à pleuvoir/neiger** if it should (happen to) rain/snow.

4 s'en venir *vpr* (*littér*, †) to come, approach. **il s'en venait tranquillement** he was coming along *ou* approaching unhurriedly; **il s'en vint nous voir** he came to see us.

Venise [vəniz] *n* Venice.

vénitien, -ienne [venisjɛ̃, jɛn] **1** *adj* Venetian; *V* **lanterne, store.**

2 *nm,f*: **V~(ne)** Venetian.

vent [vɑ̃] **1** *nm* **(a)** wind. ~ **du nord/d'ouest** North/West wind; (*Astron*) ~ **solaire** solar wind; (*Naut*) ~ **contraire** headwind; **il y a** *ou* **il fait du** ~ it is windy, there's a wind blowing; (*lit, fig*) **le** ~ **tourne** the wind is turning; **un** ~ **d'orage** a stormy wind; **un** ~ **à décorner les bœufs** a fierce gale, a howling wind; **un coup** *ou* **une rafale de** ~ **a emporté son chapeau** a gust of wind carried *ou* blew his hat off; **flotter au** ~ to flutter in the wind; (*lit, fig*) **observer d'où vient le** ~ to see how the wind blows; **être en plein** ~ to be exposed to the wind; *V* **coup, moulin, quatre** *etc.*

(b) (*fig: tendance*) **le** ~ **est à l'optimisme** there is a feeling of optimism, there is optimism in the air; **un** ~ **de révolte/contestation soufflait** a wind of revolt/protest was blowing.

(c) (*euph*, †: *gaz intestinal*) wind (*U*). **il a des** ~**s** he has wind; **lâcher un** ~ to break wind.

(d) (*loc: Chasse, Naut*) **au** ~ **(de)** to windward (of); **sous le** ~ **(de)** to leeward (of); **avoir bon** ~ to have a fair wind; **prendre le** ~ (*lit*) to test the wind; (*fig*) to find out *ou* see how the wind blows *ou* which way the wind is blowing *ou* how the land lies; **venir au** ~ to turn into the wind; ~ **arrière/debout** rear/head wind; **avoir le** ~ **debout** to head into the wind; **avoir le** ~ **arrière** *ou* **en poupe** to have the wind astern, sail *ou* run before the wind; (*fig*) **il a le** ~ **en poupe** he has the wind in his sails; **aller contre le** ~ to go into the wind; **chasser au** ~ *ou* **dans le** ~ to hunt upwind.

(e) (*autres loc*) **à tous les** ~**s** *ou* **aux quatre** ~**s** to the four winds (of heaven), to all (four) points of the compass; **être dans le** ~* to be with it*, be trendy*; **une jeune fille/robe dans le** ~* a trendy girl/dress*; (*péj*) **c'est du** ~* it's all wind *ou* hot air*; **avoir** ~ **de** to get wind of; **ayant eu** ~ **de sa nomination** having got wind of his nomination; (*gén hum*) **quel bon** ~ **vous amène?** to what do I (*ou* we) owe the pleasure (of seeing you *ou* of your visit)? (*hum*); **contre** ~**s et marées: elle l'a fait contre** ~**s et marées** she did it against all the odds *ou* despite all the obstacles; **je le ferai contre** ~**s et marées** I'll do it come hell or high water; **faire du** ~ *[éventail]* to create a breeze; (*sur le feu*) to fan the flame, blow up the fire; (*fig péj*) *[personne]* to throw one's weight about; **avoir du** ~ **dans les voiles*** to be half-seas over*, be under the influence*, be tiddly*; **rapide comme le** ~ swift as the wind.

2: vent coulis draught.

ventail, *pl* **-aux** [vɑ̃taj, o] *nm* ventail.

vente [vɑ̃t] **1** *nf* **(a)** (*action*) sale. **la** ~ **de cet article est interdite** the sale of this article is forbidden; **bureau de** ~ sales office; **être en** ~ **libre** (*gén*) to be freely sold, have no sales restrictions; (*sans ordonnance*) to be sold without prescription; **en** ~ **dès demain** available *ou* on sale as from tomorrow; **en** ~ **dans toutes les pharmacies/chez votre libraire** available *ou* on sale at all chemists/at your local bookshop; **tous les articles exposés sont en** ~ all (the) goods on show are for sale; **mettre en** ~ *produit* to put on sale; *maison, objet personnel* to put up for sale; **les articles en** ~ **dans ce magasin** the goods on sale in this store; **nous n'en avons pas la** ~ we have no demand *ou* sale for that, we can't sell that; **contrat/promesse de** ~ sales contract/agreement; *V* **crédit, point**[1]**, sauvette** *etc.*

(b) (*Comm*) (*transaction*) sale. **la** ~ (*service*) sales (*pl*); (*technique*) selling; **avoir l'expérience de la** ~ to have sales experience, have experience in selling; **s'occuper de la** ~ (*dans une affaire*) to deal with the sales; **il a un pourcentage sur les** ~**s** he gets a percentage on sales; **directeur/direction/service des** ~**s** sales director/management/department.

(c) ~ **(aux enchères)** (auction) sale, auction; **courir les** ~**s** to do the rounds of the sales *ou* auctions; *V* **hôtel, salle.**

(d) (*Bourse*) selling. **la livre vaut 10 F à la** ~ the selling rate for (the pound) sterling is 10 francs.

2: vente par adjudication sale by auction; **vente de charité** charity sale *ou* bazaar, jumble sale, sale of work; **vente judiciaire** auction by order of the court; **vente paroissiale** church sale *ou* bazaar; **vente publique** public sale.

venté, e [vɑ̃te] (*ptp de* **venter**) *adj* windswept, windy.

venter [vɑ̃te] (1) *vb impers* (*littér*) **il vente** the wind blows; *V* **pleuvoir.**

venteux, -euse [vɑ̃tø, øz] *adj* windswept, windy.

ventilateur [vɑ̃tilatœʀ] *nm* (*gén*) fan; (*dans un mur, une fenêtre*) ventilator, fan. ~ **électrique** electric fan; ~ **à hélice** blade fan; ~ **à turbine** turbine ventilator; *V* **courroie.**

ventilation [vɑ̃tilɑsjɔ̃] *nf* **(a)** (*aération*) ventilation. **il y a une bonne** ~ **dans cette pièce** this room is well ventilated, this room has good ventilation. **(b)** (*V* **ventiler b**) breaking down; separate valuation. **voici la** ~ **des ventes pour l'année 1976** here is the breakdown of sales for (the year) 1976.

ventiler [vɑ̃tile] (1) *vt* **(a)** (*aérer*) *pièce, tunnel* to ventilate. **pièce bien/mal ventilée** well/poorly ventilated room. **(b)** (*décomposer*) *total, chiffre, somme* to break down; (*Jur*) *produit d'une vente* to value separately.

ventôse [vɑ̃toz] *nm* Ventôse (*6th month of French Republican calendar*).

ventouse [vɑ̃tuz] *nf* **(a)** (*Méd*) cupping glass. **poser des** ~**s à qn** to place cupping glasses on sb, cup sb.

(b) (*Zool*) sucker.

(c) (*dispositif adhésif*) suction disc, suction pad. **faire** ~ to cling, adhere; **porte-savon à** ~ suction-grip soap holder, self-adhering soap holder.

(d) (*Tech: ouverture*) airhole, air-vent.

ventral, e, *mpl* **-aux** [vɑ̃tʀal, o] *adj* ventral; *V* **parachute, rouleau.**

ventre [vɑ̃tʀ(ə)] *nm* **(a)** (*abdomen*) stomach, tummy* (*gén langage enfantin*), belly‡. **dormir/être étendu sur le** ~ to sleep/be lying on one's stomach *ou* front; **avoir/prendre du** ~ to have/be getting rather a paunch, have/be getting a bit of a tummy* *ou* belly‡; **rentrer le** ~ to hold *ou* pull in one's stomach; (*fig*) **passer sur le** ~ **de qn** to ride roughshod over sb, walk over sb; *V* **bas**[1]**, danse, plat**[1]**.**

(b) (*estomac*) stomach. **avoir le ventre creux** to have an empty stomach; **avoir le** ~ **plein** to be full; **avoir mal au** ~, **avoir des maux de** ~ to have stomach ache *ou* (a) tummy ache*; (*fig*) **ça me ferait mal au** ~ it would sicken me, it would make me sick; (*fig*) **ouvrir sa montre pour voir ce qu'elle a dans le** ~* to open (up) one's watch to see what it has got inside *ou* what's inside it; (*Prov*) ~ **affamé n'a point d'oreilles** words are wasted on a starving man; *V* **œil, reconnaissance.**

(c) (*utérus*) womb; *V* **bas**[1]**.**

(d) *[animal]* (under)belly.

(e) *[cruche, vase]* bulb, bulbous part; *[bateau]* belly, bilge; *[avion]* belly; *V* **atterrissage.**

(f) (*Tech*) **faire** ~ *[mur]* to bulge; *[plafond]* to sag, bulge.

(g) (*Phys*) *[onde]* antinode.

(h) (*loc*) **courir** *ou* **aller** ~ **à terre** to go flat out* (*Brit*) *ou* at top speed *ou* hell for leather*; **avoir quelque chose dans le** ~***: nous allons voir s'il a quelque chose dans le** ~ we'll see if he has guts*; **il n'a rien dans le** ~ he has no guts*, he's spineless; **chercher à savoir ce que qn a dans le** ~ to try and find out what is (going on) in sb's mind; *V* **cœur.**

ventrebleu†† [vɑ̃tʀəblø] *excl* gadzooks!††, zounds!††.
ventrée† [vɑ̃tʀe] *nf (repas)* stuffing* (*U*). **une ~ de pâtes** a good stuffing* *ou* a bellyful* of pasta.
ventre-saint-gris†† [vɑ̃tʀəsɛ̃gʀi] *excl* gadzooks!††, zounds!††
ventriculaire [vɑ̃tʀikylɛʀ] *adj* ventricular.
ventricule [vɑ̃tʀikyl] *nm* ventricle.
ventrière [vɑ̃tʀijɛʀ] *nf* **(a)** (*sangle*) girth; (*toile de transport*) sling. **(b)** (*Constr*) purlin; (*Naut*) bilge block.
ventriloque [vɑ̃tʀilɔk] *nmf* ventriloquist. **il est ~** he can throw his voice; (*de profession*) he's a ventriloquist.
ventriloquie [vɑ̃tʀilɔki] *nf* ventriloquy, ventriloquism.
ventripotent, e [vɑ̃tʀipɔtɑ̃, ɑ̃t] *adj* potbellied.
ventru, e [vɑ̃tʀy] *adj personne* potbellied; *pot, commode* bulbous.
venu, e [v(ə)ny] (*ptp de* **venir**) **1** *adj* **(a)** (*fondé, placé*) **être bien ~ de** *ou* **à faire** to have (good) grounds for doing; **être mal ~ de** *ou* **à faire** to have no grounds for doing, be in no position to do; **il serait mal ~ de** *ou* **à se plaindre/refuser** he is in no position to complain/refuse, he should be the last to complain-/refuse.

(b) (*à propos*) **bien ~** *événement, question, remarque* timely, apposite; **mal ~** *événement, question, remarque* untimely, inapposite, out of place (*attrib*), out-of-place (*épith*); **un empressement mal ~** unseemly *ou* unfitting haste; **il serait mal ~ de lui poser cette question** it would not be fitting to ask him.

(c) (*développé*) **bien ~** *enfant* sturdy, sturdily built; *plante, arbre* well-developed, fine; *pièce, œuvre* well-written; **mal ~** *enfant* stunted.

(d) (*arrivé*) **tard ~** late; **tôt ~** early; *V* **dernier, nouveau, premier.**

2 venue *nf* **(a)** [*personne*] coming. **à l'occasion de sa ~e nous irons ...** when he comes we'll go ... ; *V* **allée.**

(b) (*littér: avènement*) coming. **la ~e du printemps/du Christ** the coming of spring/of Christ; **lors de ma ~e au monde** when I came into the world.

(c) (*loc: littér*) **d'une seule ~e, tout d'une ~e** *arbre* straight-growing (*épith*); **d'une belle ~e** finely developed.
Vénus [venys] *nf* (*Astron, Myth*) Venus; (*Zool*) venus. (*fig: femme*) **une ~** a venus, a great beauty; *V* **mont.**
vêpres [vɛpʀ(ə)] *nfpl* vespers. **sonner les ~** to ring the vespers bell.
ver [vɛʀ] **1** *nm* (*gén*) worm; (*larve*) grub; [*viande, fruits, fromage*] maggot; [*bois*] woodworm (*U*). **mangé** *ou* **rongé aux ~s** worm-eaten; (*Méd*) **avoir des ~s** to have worms; (*fig*) **le ~ est dans le fruit** the rot has already set in; **tirer les ~s du nez à qn*** to worm information out of sb*; *V* **nu, piqué.**

2: ver d'eau caddis worm; **ver luisant** glow-worm; **ver de sable** sea slug; **ver à soie** silkworm; **ver solitaire** tapeworm; **ver de terre** earthworm; (*fig péj*) worm.
véracité [veʀasite] *nf* [*rapport, récit, témoin*] veracity (*frm*), truthfulness; [*déclaration, fait*] truth, veracity (*frm*). **raconter qch avec ~** to tell sth truthfully.
véranda [veʀɑ̃da] *nf* veranda(h).
verbal, e, *mpl* **-aux** [vɛʀbal, o] *adj* **(a)** (*oral*) verbal; *V* **procès, rapport. (b)** (*Ling*) *adjectif, locution* verbal; *système, forme, terminaison* verb (*épith*), verbal.
verbalement [vɛʀbalmɑ̃] *adv dire, faire savoir* verbally, by word of mouth; *approuver, donner son accord* verbally.
verbalisateur [vɛʀbalizatœʀ] *adj m*: **l'agent ~ devra toujours ...** an officer reporting a minor offence must always ... ; **l'agent ~ a oublié de ...** the officer who booked* *ou* reported me (*ou* him *etc*) forgot to ... .
verbalisation [vɛʀbalizasjɔ̃] *nf reporting (by an officer) of a minor offence.*
verbaliser [vɛʀbalize] (1) *vi*: **l'agent a dû ~** the officer had to book* *ou* report him (*ou* me *etc*).
verbalisme [vɛʀbalism(ə)] *nm* verbalism.
verbe [vɛʀb(ə)] *nm* **(a)** (*Gram*) verb. **~ défectif/impersonnel** defective/impersonal verb; **~ transitif/intransitif** transitive/intransitive verb; **~ actif/passif** active/passive verb, verb in the active/passive (voice); **~ d'action/d'état** verb of action/state; **~ fort** strong verb.

(b) (*Rel*) **le V~** the Word; **le V~ s'est fait chair** the Word was made flesh.

(c) (*littér: mots, langage*) language, word. **la magie du ~** the magic of language *ou* the word.

(d) (*littér: ton de voix*) tone (of voice). **avoir le ~ haut** to speak in a high and mighty tone, sound high and mighty.
verbeux, -euse [vɛʀbø, øz] *adj* verbose, wordy, prolix.
verbiage [vɛʀbjaʒ] *nm* verbiage.
verbosité [vɛʀbozite] *nf* verbosity, wordiness, prolixity.
verdâtre [vɛʀdɑtʀ(ə)] *adj* greenish.
verdeur [vɛʀdœʀ] *nf* **(a)** (*jeunesse*) vigour, vitality. **(b)** [*fruit*] tartness, sharpness; [*vin*] acidity. **(c)** [*langage*] forthrightness.
verdict [vɛʀdik(t)] *nm* (*Jur, gén*) verdict. (*Jur*) **~ de culpabilité/d'acquittement** verdict of guilty/of not guilty; **rendre un ~** to give a verdict, return a verdict (*Jur*).
verdier [vɛʀdje] *nm* greenfinch.
verdir [vɛʀdiʀ] (2) **1** *vi* to turn *ou* go green. **2** *vt* to turn green.
verdoiement [vɛʀdwamɑ̃] *nm* (*état*) verdancy (*littér*), greenness. (*action*) **le ~ des prés au printemps** the verdant hue taken on by the meadows in spring (*littér*).
verdoyant, e [vɛʀdwajɑ̃, ɑ̃t] *adj* verdant (*littér*), green.
verdoyer [vɛʀdwaje] (8) *vi* (*être vert*) to be verdant (*littér*) *ou* green; (*devenir vert*) to become verdant (*littér*) *ou* green.
verduniser [vɛʀdynize] (1) *vt* to chlorinate.
verdure [vɛʀdyʀ] *nf* **(a)** (*végétation*) greenery (*U*), verdure (*U*) (*littér*). **tapis de ~** greensward (*littér*); **rideau de ~** curtain of greenery *ou* verdure (*littér*); **tapisserie de ~** *ou* **à ~s** verdure (*tapestry*); **je vous mets un peu de ~?** (*pour un bouquet*) shall I put some greenery in for you?; *V* **théâtre.**

(b) (*littér: couleur*) verdure (*littér*), greenness.

(c) (*légumes verts*) green vegetable, greenstuff (*U*).
véreux, -euse [veʀø, øz] *adj* **(a)** (*lit*) *aliment* maggoty, worm-eaten. **(b)** (*fig*) *agent, financier* dubious, shady*; *affaire* dubious, fishy*, shady*.
verge [vɛʀʒ(ə)] *nf* **(a)** (†: *baguette*) stick, cane, rod. (*pour fouetter*) **~s** birch(-rod). **(b)** (*Hist: insigne d'autorité*) [*huissier*] wand; [*bedeau*] rod. **(c)** (*Anat*) penis. **(d)** (*Tech: tringle*) shank. **(e)** (*Can*) yard (*0,914 m*).
vergé, e [vɛʀʒe] *adj, nm*: **(papier) ~** laid paper.
verger [vɛʀʒe] *nm* orchard.
vergeté, e [vɛʀʒəte] *adj* streaked.
vergeture [vɛʀʒətyʀ] *nf* stretch mark, stria (*T*).
verglacé, e [vɛʀglase] *adj* icy, iced-over.
verglas [vɛʀgla] *nm* (black) ice (*on road etc*).
vergogne [vɛʀgɔɲ] *nf*: **sans ~** (*adj*) shameless; (*adv*) shamelessly.
vergue [vɛʀg(ə)] *nf* (*Naut*) yard. **grand ~** main yard; **~ de misaine** foreyard; **~ de hune** topsail yard.
véridique [veʀidik] *adj récit, témoignage* truthful, true, veracious (*frm*); *témoin* truthful, veracious (*frm*); *repentir, douleur* genuine, authentic.
véridiquement [veʀidikmɑ̃] *adv* truthfully, veraciously (*frm*).
vérifiable [veʀifjabl(ə)] *adj* verifiable. **c'est aisément ~** it can easily be checked.
vérificateur, -trice [veʀifikatœʀ, tʀis] **1** *adj appareil, système* checking (*épith*), verifying (*épith*). **employé ~** controller, checker.

2 *nm,f* controller, checker. **~ des douanes** Customs inspector; (*Fin*) **~ des comptes** auditor; (*Can*) **~ général** Auditor General.
vérificatif, -ive [veʀifikatif, iv] *adj* checking (*épith*).
vérification [veʀifikasjɔ̃] *nf* **(a)** (*comparaison: V* **vérifier**) checking; verifying; verification; ascertaining; auditing. (*opération*) **une ou plusieurs ~s** one or several checks; **~ faite, il se trouve que ...** on checking, we find that ... ; (*Police*) **~ d'identité** identity check; (*Jur*) **~ d'écritures** authentication of handwriting; (*Pol*) **~ du scrutin** *ou* **des votes** scrutiny of votes.

(b) (*preuve: V* **vérifier**) establishing; confirming; proving (to be true).

(c) (*confirmation*) [*soupçons, conjecture*] confirmation; [*hypothèse, théorie*] proof, confirmation.
vérifier [veʀifje] (7) **1** *vt* **(a)** (*comparer à la réalité*) *affirmation, fait, récit* to check, verify; *adresse, renseignement* to check; *véracité, authenticité* to ascertain, verify, check; (*Fin*) *comptes* to audit. **~ si/que ...** to check if/that ... .

(b) (*comparer à la norme*) *poids, mesure, classement* to check. **ne vous faites pas de souci, cela a été vérifié et revérifié** don't worry – it has been checked and double-checked *ou* cross-checked.

(c) (*établir la véracité de, prouver*) *affirmation, fait* to establish the truth of, confirm (the truth of), prove to be true; *axiome* to establish *ou* confirm the truth of; *témoignage* to establish the veracity of, confirm (the veracity of); *authenticité, véracité* to establish, confirm, prove.

(d) (*confirmer*) *soupçons, conjecture* to bear out, confirm; *hypothèse, théorie* to bear out, confirm, prove. **cet accident a vérifié mes craintes** this accident has borne out *ou* confirmed my fears.

2 se vérifier *vpr* (*V* **vérifier d**) to be borne out; to be confirmed; to be proved.
vérin [veʀɛ̃] *nm* jack. **~ hydraulique/pneumatique** hydraulic/ pneumatic jack.
véritable [veʀitabl(ə)] *adj* **(a)** (*authentique*) *cuir, perles, larmes, colère* real, genuine; *argent, or* real; *ami, artiste, vocation* real (*épith*), genuine, true (*épith*). **l'art/l'amour ~ se reconnaît d'emblée** true art/love is immediately recognizable.

(b) (*épith: vrai, réel*) *identité, raisons* true, real; *nom* real. **la ~ religion/joie** true religion/joy; **sous son jour ~** in its (*ou* his *etc*) true light; **ça n'a pas de ~ fondement** that has no real foundation.

(c) (*intensif: qui mérite bien son nom*) **un ~ coquin** an absolute *ou* a real *ou* a downright rogue; **c'est une ~ folie** it's absolute madness, it's a veritable (*frm*) *ou* an absolute folly; **c'est une ~ expédition/révolution** it's a real *ou* veritable (*frm*) expedition/revolution.
véritablement [veʀitabləmɑ̃] *adv* really. **est-il ~ fatigué/diplômé?** is he really *ou* truly tired/qualified?; **il l'a ~ fait/rencontré** he actually *ou* really did it/met him; **ce n'est pas truqué: ils traversent ~ les flammes** it isn't fixed – they really *ou* genuinely do go through the flames; **ce n'est pas ~ un roman/dictionnaire** it's not really a novel/dictionary, it's not a real novel/dictionary; (*intensif*) **c'est ~ délicieux** it's absolutely *ou* positively *ou* really delicious.
vérité [veʀite] *nf* **(a) la ~** (*connaissance du vrai*) truth; (*conformité aux faits*) the truth; **nul n'est dépositaire de la ~** no one has a monopoly of truth; **la ~ d'un fait/principe** the truth of a fact/principle; **c'est l'entière ~** it is the whole truth; **c'est la ~ vraie*** it's the honest truth*; **la ~ toute nue** the naked truth; **son souci de (la) ~** his desire for (the) truth; **dire la ~** to tell *ou* speak the truth; (*Jur, hum*) **jurez de dire la ~, toute la ~, rien que la ~** do you swear to tell the truth, the whole truth and nothing but the truth?; **la ~, c'est qu'il est paresseux** the truth (of the matter) is, he's lazy, truth is* *ou* truth to tell, he's lazy; **la ~ historique/matérielle** historical/material truth; (*Prov*) **la ~ sort de la bouche des enfants** out of the mouths of babes and sucklings (comes forth truth) (*Prov*); (*Prov*) **la ~ n'est pas toujours bonne à dire** the truth is sometimes best left unsaid.

(b) (*vraisemblance, ressemblance au réel*) [*portrait*] lifelikeness, trueness to life; [tableau, personnage] trueness to life. s'efforcer à la ~ en art to strive to be true to life in art; le désespoir de ce peintre était de ne pouvoir rendre la ~ de certains objets it was the despair of this painter that he was unable to depict the true nature of certain objects; (la réalité) la ~ dépasse souvent ce qu'on imagine (the) truth often surpasses one's imaginings.

(c) (sincérité, authenticité) truthfulness, sincerity. un air/accent de ~ an air/a note of sincerity ou truthfulness, a truthful look/note; ce jeune auteur s'exprime avec une ~ rafraîchissante this young author expresses himself with refreshing sincerity ou truthfulness.

(d) (fait vrai, évidence) truth. une ~ bien sentie a heartfelt truth; ~s éternelles/premières eternal/first truths ou verities (frm); V quatre.

(e) (loc) en ~ (en fait) really, actually; c'est peu de chose, en ~ it's really ou actually nothing very much; (Bible) 'en ~ je vous le dis' 'verily I say unto you'; (frm) à la ~, en ~ (à dire vrai) to tell the truth, truth to tell (frm), to be honest; (frm) à la ~ ou en ~ il préfère s'amuser que de travailler to tell the truth ou truth to tell (frm) ou to be honest he prefers to enjoy himself rather than work; c'est bien peu de chose en ~ it's actually ou really nothing very much; plus qu'il n'en faut, en ~, pour en causer la ruine in fact ou indeed more than enough to cause its downfall; j'étais à la ~ loin de m'en douter to tell the truth ou truth to tell (frm) I was far from suspecting; la ~, c'est que je n'en sais rien (the) truth is that ou to tell the truth I know nothing about it.

verjus [vɛʀʒy] nm verjuice.

vermeil, -eille [vɛʀmɛj] 1 adj tissu, objet vermilion, bright red; bouche ruby (épith), cherry (épith), ruby- ou cherry-red; teint rosy. 2 nm vermeil.

vermicelle [vɛʀmisɛl] nm (souvent pl: pâtes) ~(s) vermicelli; (potage au) ~(s) vermicelli soup.

vermiculaire [vɛʀmikylɛʀ] adj (Anat) vermicular, vermiform. appendice ~ vermiform appendix; éminence ~ vermis; contraction ~ peristalsis (U).

vermiculé, e [vɛʀmikyle] adj vermiculated.

vermiculure [vɛʀmikylyʀ] nf (gén pl) vermiculation (U).

vermifuge [vɛʀmifyʒ] adj, nm vermifuge.

vermillon [vɛʀmijɔ̃] 1 nm (poudre) vermilion, cinnabar. (couleur) (rouge) ~ vermilion, scarlet. 2 adj inv vermilion, scarlet.

vermine [vɛʀmin] nf (a) (parasites) vermin. couvert de ~ crawling with vermin, lice-ridden. (b) (littér péj: racaille) vermin; († péj: vaurien) knave (†, littér), cur (†, littér).

vermisseau, pl ~x [vɛʀmiso] nm (ver) small worm, vermicule (T). (fig) un ~ a mere worm, dirt (U).

vermoulu, e [vɛʀmuly] adj bois full of woodworm, worm-eaten. cette commode est ~e there is woodworm in this chest, this chest is full of woodworm ou is worm-eaten.

vermoulure [vɛʀmulyʀ] nf (traces) woodworm (U), worm holes (pl).

vermout(h) [vɛʀmut] nm vermouth.

vernaculaire [vɛʀnakylɛʀ] adj vernacular.

vernal, e, mpl **-aux** [vɛʀnal, o] adj (littér) vernal (littér).

verni, e [vɛʀni] (ptp de vernir) adj (a) bois varnished; (fig: luisant) feuilles shiny, glossy. cuir ~ patent leather; souliers ~s patent (leather) shoes; terre ~e glazed earthenware.

(b) (*: chanceux) lucky, jammy‡ (Brit). il est ~, c'est un ~ he's lucky ou jammy‡ (Brit), he's a lucky devil* ou dog*.

vernier [vɛʀnje] nm vernier (scale).

vernir [vɛʀniʀ] (2) vt bois, tableau, ongles, cuir to varnish; poterie to glaze. (Ébénisterie) ~ au tampon to French polish.

vernis [vɛʀni] nm (a) [bois, tableau, mur] varnish; [poterie] glaze. ~ (à ongles) nail varnish ou polish; ~ cellulosique/synthétique cellulose/synthetic varnish.

(b) (éclat) shine, gloss. des chaussures d'un ~ éclatant shoes with a brilliant shine ou a high gloss (on them).

(c) (fig) veneer (fig). ~ de culture veneer of culture.

vernissage [vɛʀnisaʒ] nm (a) (U: V vernir) varnishing; glazing; (V vernisser) glazing. (b) (exposition) preview (at art gallery).

vernissé, e [vɛʀnise] (ptp de vernisser) adj poterie, tuile glazed; (fig: luisant) feuillage shiny, glossy.

vernisser [vɛʀnise] (1) vt to glaze.

vernisseur, -euse [vɛʀnisœʀ, øz] nm,f (V vernir) varnisher; glazer.

vérole [veʀɔl] nf (a) (variole) V petit. (b) (‡: syphilis) pox‡. il a/il a attrapé la ~ he's got/he has caught the pox‡.

vérolé, e‡ [veʀɔle] adj: il est ~ he has the pox‡.

véronal [veʀɔnal] nm (Pharm) veronal.

Vérone [veʀɔn] n Verona.

véronique [veʀɔnik] nf (Bot) speedwell, veronica; (Tauromachie) veronica.

verrat [vɛʀa] nm boar.

verre [vɛʀ] 1 nm (a) (substance) glass. ~ moulé/étiré/coulé pressed/cast/drawn glass; ~ de sécurité safety glass; ~ sandwich laminated glass; ~ trempé toughened glass; cela se casse ou se brise comme du ~ it's as brittle as glass; V laine, papier, pâte.

(b) (objet) [vitre, cadre] glass; [lunettes] lens. mettre qch sous ~ to put sth under glass; ~ grossissant/déformant magnifying/distorting glass; (Opt) ~s correcteurs (de la vue) corrective lenses; porter des ~s to wear glasses; V sous.

(c) (récipient, contenu) glass. ~ à bière/liqueur beer/liqueur glass; (pour une recette) ajouter un ~ à liqueur de .../un ~ de lait ≃ add two tablespoons of .../one cup of milk; un ~ d'eau/de bière a glass of water/beer; V casser, noyer², tempête.

(d) (boisson alcoolique) drink. payer un ~ à qn to buy ou offer sb a drink; boire ou prendre un ~ to have a drink; videz vos ~s! drink up!; un petit ~* a quick one*, a dram*; il est toujours entre deux ~s* he's always on the bottle*; avoir bu un ~ de trop*, avoir un ~ dans le nez* to have had one too many*, have had a drop too much*, have had one over the eight*.

2: verre armé wired glass; verre ballon balloon glass, brandy glass; verre blanc plain glass; verre cathédrale cathedral glass; verres de contact contact lenses; verre à ou de dégustation wine-tasting glass; verre à dents tooth mug ou glass; verre dépoli frosted glass; verres fumés tinted lenses; verre de lampe lamp glass, (lamp) chimney; verre de montre watch glass; verre à moutarde (glass) mustard jar; verre à pied stemmed glass; verre à vin wineglass; verre à vitre window glass; verre à whisky whisky glass ou tumbler.

verrerie [vɛʀʀi] nf (usine) glassworks, glass factory; (fabrication du verre) glass-making; (manufacture d'objets) glass-working; (objets) glassware; (commerce) glass trade ou industry.

verrier [vɛʀje] nm (ouvrier) glassworker; (artiste) glass artist, artist in glass.

verrière [vɛʀjɛʀ] nf (a) (fenêtre) [église, édifice] window. (b) (toit vitré) glass roof. (c) (paroi vitrée) glass wall. (d) (Aviat) canopy.

verroterie [vɛʀɔtʀi] nf: un collier de ~ a necklace of glass beads; bijoux en ~ glass jewellery.

verrou [vɛʀu] nm (a) [porte] bolt. tire/pousse le ~ unbolt/bolt the door; as-tu mis le ~? have you bolted the door?; (fig) sous les ~s: mettre qn sous les ~s to put sb under lock and key; être sous les ~s to be behind bars.

(b) (Tech) [aiguillage] facing point lock; [culasse] bolt.

(c) (Géol) constriction.

(d) (Mil) stopper (in breach).

verrouillage [vɛʀujaʒ] nm (a) (action: V verrouiller) bolting; locking; closing. (b) (dispositif) locking mechanism.

verrouiller [vɛʀuje] (1) vt porte to bolt; culasse to lock; (Mil) brèche to close. (fig) se ~ chez soi to shut o.s. away at home.

verrue [vɛʀy] nf (lit) wart, verruca (T); (fig) eyesore. cette usine est une ~ au milieu du paysage this factory is a blot on the landscape ou an eyesore in the middle of the countryside.

verruqueux, -euse [vɛʀykø, øz] adj warty, verrucose (T).

vers¹ [vɛʀ] prép (a) (direction) toward(s), to. en allant ~ Aix/la gare going to ou toward(s) Aix/the station; le lieu ~ lequel il nous menait the place he was leading us to ou to which he was leading us; la foule se dirigeait ~ la plage the crowd was making for the beach; '~ la plage' 'to the beach'; '~ les bateaux' 'to the boats'; elle fit un pas ~ la fenêtre she took a step toward(s) the window; notre chambre regarde ~ le sud/la colline our bedroom faces ou looks south/faces the hills ou looks toward(s) the hills; il tendit la main ~ la bouteille he reached out for the bottle, he stretched out his hand toward(s) the bottle; le pays se dirige droit ~ l'abîme the country is heading straight for disaster; c'est un pas ~ la paix/la vérité it's a step toward(s) (establishing) peace/(finding out) the truth; 'V~ une Sémantique de l'anglais' 'Towards a Semantics of English'.

(b) (position: du côté de) c'est ~ Aix que nous avons eu une panne it was (somewhere) near Aix ou round about Aix that we broke down; ~ la droite, la brume se levait to ou toward(s) the right the mist was rising; ~ 2.000 mètres l'air est frais at around the 2,000 metres mark ou at about 2,000 metres the air is cool.

(c) (temps: approximation) (at) about, (at) around. ~ quelle heure doit-il venir? (at) around ou (at) about what time is he due?; elle a commencé à lire ~ 6 ans she started reading at about 6 ou around 6; il était ~ (les) 3 heures quand je suis rentré it was about ou around 3 when I came home; ~ la fin de la soirée/de l'année toward(s) ou going on for* the end of the evening/the year; ~ 1900/le début du siècle toward(s) ou about 1900/the turn of the century; ~ ce temps-là at about that time.

vers² [vɛʀ] nm (a) (sg: ligne) line, verse (rare). au 3e ~ in line 3, in the 3rd line; ~ de dix syllabes, ~ décasyllabe line of ten syllables, decasyllabic line; ~ blancs/libres blank/free verse; un ~ boiteux a short line, a hypometric line (T); je me souviens d'un ~ de Virgile I recall a line by Virgil; réciter quelques ~ to recite a few lines of poetry.

(b) (pl: poésie) verse (U). ~ de circonstance occasional verse; traduction en ~ verse translation; faire des ~ to write verse, versify (péj); mettre en ~ to put into verse; il fait des ~ de temps en temps he writes a little verse from time to time.

versant [vɛʀsɑ̃] nm [vallée] side; [massif] slopes (pl). les Pyrénées ont un ~ français et un ~ espagnol the Pyrenees have a French side and a Spanish side; le ~ nord/français de ce massif the northern/French slopes of this range.

versatile [vɛʀsatil] adj fickle, changeable, capricious.

versatilité [vɛʀsatilite] nf fickleness, changeability, capriciousness.

verse [vɛʀs(ə)] adv: à ~ in torrents; il pleut à ~ it is pouring down, it's coming down in torrents ou in buckets*.

versé, e [vɛʀse] (ptp de verser) adj: ~ dans: ~/peu ~ dans l'histoire ancienne (well-)versed/ill-versed in ancient history; ~/peu ~ dans l'art de l'escrime (highly) skilled ou accomplished/unaccomplished in the art of fencing; l'homme le plus ~ de France dans l'art chaldéen the most learned man in France in the field of Chaldean art.

Verseau [vɛʀso] nm (Astron) le ~ Aquarius, the Water-carrier. être (du) ~ to be Aquarius ou an Aquarian.

versement [vɛʀsəmɑ̃] nm payment; (échelonné) instalment. le ~ d'une somme sur un compte the payment of a sum into an account; ~ par chèque/virement payment by cheque/credit transfer; en ~s (échelonnés) in ou by instalments.

verser [vɛʀse] (1) **1** *vt* **(a)** *liquide, grains* to pour, tip (*dans* into, *sur* onto); (*servir*) *thé, café, vin* to pour (out) (*dans* into). ~ **le café dans les tasses** to pour the coffee into the cups; ~ **des haricots (d'un sac) dans un bocal** to pour *ou* tip beans (from a bag) into a jar; ~ **du vin à qn** to pour sb some wine; ~ **un verre de vin à qn** to pour sb a glass of wine, pour a glass of wine for sb; **verse-lui/-toi à boire** pour him/yourself a drink; **veux-tu** ~ **à boire/le vin s'il te plaît?** will you pour (out) *ou* serve the drinks/the wine please?; *V* **huile.**

(b) (*répandre*) *larmes, sang,* (*littér*) *clarté* to shed; (*déverser*) to pour out, scatter (*sur* onto); (*littér: apporter*) *apaisement etc* to dispense, pour forth (*à qn* to sb). (*tuer*) ~ **le sang** to shed *ou* spill blood; (*littér, hum*) ~ **un pleur/quelques pleurs** to shed a tear/a few tears; **ils versaient des brouettées de fleurs devant la procession** they scattered barrowfuls of flowers in front of the procession; **drogue qui verse l'oubli** drug which brings oblivion.

(c) (*classer*) ~ **une pièce à un dossier** to add an item to a file.

(d) (*payer: gén, Fin*) to pay. ~ **une somme à un compte** to pay a sum of money into an account; ~ **des intérêts à qn** to pay sb interest; ~ **des arrhes** to put down *ou* pay a deposit; ~ **une rente à qn** to pay sb a pension.

(e) (*affecter, incorporer*) ~ **qn dans** to assign *ou* attach sb to; **se faire** ~ **dans l'infanterie** to get o.s. assigned *ou* attached to the infantry.

(f) (*renverser: plus gén* **faire** ~) *voiture* to overturn; (*rare: coucher*) *blés, plantes* to flatten. **le chauffeur les a versés dans la rivière** the driver tipped them into the river.

2 *vi* **(a)** (*basculer*) *[véhicule]* to overturn. **il va nous faire** ~ **dans le fossé** he'll tip us into the ditch, we'll end up in the ditch because of him; **il a déjà versé deux fois** he has already overturned twice.

(b) (*tomber dans*) ~ **dans** to lapse into; ~ **dans la sentimentalité** to lapse into sentimentality.

verset [vɛʀsɛ] *nm* (*Rel*) (*passage de la Bible*) verse; (*prière*) versicle; (*Littérat*) verse.

verseur, -euse [vɛʀsœʀ, øz] **1** *adj*: **bec** ~ (pouring) lip; **bouchon** ~ pour-through stopper; **sucrier** ~ sugar dispenser. **2** *nm* (*dispositif*) pourer. **3 verseuse** *nf* (*cafetière*) coffeepot.

versificateur [vɛʀsifikatœʀ] *nm* writer of verse, versifier (*péj*), rhymester (*péj*).

versification [vɛʀsifikɑsjɔ̃] *nf* versification.

versifier [vɛʀsifje] (7) **1** *vt* to put into verse. **une œuvre versifiée** a work put into verse. **2** *vi* to write verse, versify (*péj*).

version [vɛʀsjɔ̃] *nf* **(a)** (*Scol: traduction*) translation (*into the mother tongue*), unseen (translation). ~ **grecque/anglaise** Greek/English unseen (translation), translation from Greek/English. **(b)** (*variante*) *[œuvre, texte]* version. **film en** ~ **originale** film in the original language *ou* version; **film italien en** ~ **française** Italian film dubbed in French. **(c)** (*interprétation*) *[incident, faits]* version.

verso [vɛʀso] *nm* back. **au** ~ on the back (of the page); **'voir au** ~**'** 'see over(leaf)'.

verste [vɛʀst(ə)] *nf* verst.

vert, verte [vɛʀ, vɛʀt(ə)] **1** *adj* **(a)** (*couleur*) green. ~ **de peur** green with fear; *V* **feu**[1], **haricot, tapis** *etc.*

(b) (*pas mûr*) *céréale, fruit* unripe, green; *vin* young; (*frais, non séché*) *foin, bois* green. **être au régime** ~ to be on a green-vegetable diet *ou* a diet of green vegetables; *V* **cuir.**

(c) (*fig*) *vieillard* vigorous, sprightly, spry. **au temps de sa verte jeunesse** in the first bloom of his youth.

(d) (†: *sévère*) *réprimande* sharp, stiff.

(e) *propos, histoire* spicy, saucy*. **elle en a vu des vertes et des pas mûres*** she has been through it*, she has had a hard time (of it); **il en a dit des vertes (et des pas mûres)*** he said some pretty spicy *ou* saucy* things; *V* **langue.**

2 *nm* (*couleur*) green. ~ **olive/pistache/émeraude** olive/pistachio/emerald(-green); ~ **pomme/d'eau/bouteille** apple-/sea-/bottle-green; **mettre un cheval au** ~ to put a horse out to grass *ou* to pasture; (*fig*) **se mettre au** ~ to take a rest *ou* a refreshing break in the country; *V* **tendre.**

3 verte *nf* (†*: *absinthe*) absinth(e).

4: vert-de-gris (*nm inv*) verdigris; (*adj inv*) grey(ish)-green; **vert-de-grisé, e** *adj, mpl* **vert-de-grisés** coated with verdigris; (*fig*) grey(ish)-green.

vertébral, e, *mpl* **-aux** [vɛʀtebʀal, o] *adj* vertebral; *V* **colonne.**

vertèbre [vɛʀtɛbʀ(ə)] *nf* vertebra. **se déplacer une** ~ to slip a disc, dislocate a vertebra (*T*).

vertébré, e [vɛʀtebʀe] *adj, nm* vertebrate.

vertement [vɛʀtəmɑ̃] *adv réprimander, répliquer* sharply, in no uncertain terms.

vertical, e, *mpl* **-aux** [vɛʀtikal, o] **1** *adj* (*gén*) *ligne, plan, éclairage* vertical; *position, station* vertical, upright; *V* **concentration.**

2 verticale *nf* **(a) la** ~**e** the vertical; **à la** ~**e** *s'élever, tomber* vertically; **falaise à la** ~**e** vertical *ou* sheer cliff; **écarté de la** ~**e** off the vertical.

(b) (*ligne, Archit*) vertical line.

3 *nm* (*Astron*) vertical circle.

verticalement [vɛʀtikalmɑ̃] *adv monter* vertically, straight up; *descendre* vertically, straight down.

verticalité [vɛʀtikalite] *nf* verticalness, verticality.

vertige [vɛʀtiʒ] *nm* **(a)** (*peur du vide*) **le** ~ vertigo; **avoir le** ~ to suffer from vertigo, get dizzy; **il eut soudain le** ~ *ou* **fut pris soudain de** ~ he was suddenly overcome by vertigo *ou* dizziness *ou* giddiness, he suddenly felt dizzy *ou* giddy, he had a sudden fit of vertigo *ou* dizziness *ou* giddiness; **un précipice à donner le** ~ a precipice that would make you (feel) dizzy *ou* giddy; **cela me donne le** ~ it makes me feel dizzy *ou* giddy, it gives me vertigo.

(b) (*étourdissement*) dizzy *ou* giddy spell, dizziness (*U*), giddiness (*U*). **avoir un** ~ to have a dizzy *ou* giddy spell *ou* turn*.

(c) (*fig: égarement*) fever. **les spéculateurs étaient gagnés par ce** ~ the speculators had caught this fever; **le** ~ **de la gloire** the intoxication of glory; **d'autres, gagnés eux aussi par le** ~ **de l'expansion ...** others, who had also been bitten by the expansion bug ... *ou* who had also caught the expansion fever ... .

vertigineusement [vɛʀtiʒinøzmɑ̃] *adv*: ~ **haut** breathtakingly high, of a dizzy height; **se lancer** ~ **dans la descente** to plunge into a breathtaking descent; **les prix montent** ~ prices are rising at a dizzy *ou* breathtaking rate, prices are rocketing; **les cours se sont effondrés** ~ stock market prices have dropped at a dizzy *ou* breathtaking rate.

vertigineux, -euse [vɛʀtiʒinø, øz] *adj* **(a)** *plongée, descente* breathtaking; *précipice* breathtakingly high; *vitesse, hauteur* breathtaking, dizzy (*épith*), giddy (*épith*). **nous descendions par un sentier** ~ we came down by a path at a dizzy *ou* giddy height.

(b) (*fig: très rapide*) breathtaking. **une hausse/baisse de prix** ~**euse** a breathtaking rise/drop in price.

(c) (*Méd*) vertiginous.

vertigo [vɛʀtigo] *nm* (*Vét*) (blind) staggers.

vertu [vɛʀty] *nf* **(a)** (*gén: morale*) virtue. **à la** ~ **farouche** of fierce virtue; (*fig: personne*) **ce n'est pas une** ~ she's no saint *ou* angel, she's no paragon of virtue; **les** ~**s bourgeoises** the bourgeois virtues; **les (quatre)** ~**s cardinales** the (four) cardinal virtues; ~ **théologales** theological virtues; *V* **femme, nécessité, prix.**

(b) (*littér: pouvoir*) virtue (†, *littér*), power. ~ **magique** magic power; ~ **curative** healing virtue.

(c) en ~ **de** in accordance with.

vertueusement [vɛʀtɥøzmɑ̃] *adv* virtuously.

vertueux, -euse [vɛʀtɥø, øz] *adj* virtuous.

vertugadin [vɛʀtygadɛ̃] *nm* (*Hist: vêtement*) farthingale.

verve [vɛʀv(ə)] *nf* **(a)** (*esprit, éloquence*) witty eloquence. **être en** ~ to be in brilliant form. **(b)** (*littér: fougue, entrain*) verve, vigour, zest. **la** ~ **de son style** the verve *ou* vigour of his style.

verveine [vɛʀvɛn] *nf* (*plante*) vervain, verbena; (*boisson*) verbena tea.

vésical, e, *mpl* **-aux** [vezikal, o] *adj* vesical.

vésicant, e [vezikɑ̃, ɑ̃t] *adj* vesicant, vesicatory.

vésicatoire [vezikatwaʀ] **1** *adj* vesicatory. **2** *nm* (*Méd*) vesicatory.

vésiculaire [vezikylɛʀ] *adj* vesicular.

vésicule [vezikyl] *nf* vesicle. **la** ~ **(biliaire)** the gall-bladder.

vésiculeux, -euse [vezikylø, øz] *adj* = **vésiculaire.**

vespasienne [vɛspazjɛn] *nf* urinal.

vespéral, e, *mpl* **-aux** [vɛspeʀal, o] **1** *adj* (*littér*) evening (*épith*). **2** *nm* (*Rel*) vesperal.

vesse [vɛs] *nf*(†) silent fart‡. (*Bot*) ~**-de-loup** puffball.

vessie [vesi] *nf* (*Anat*) bladder, vesica (*T*); (*animale: utilisée comme sac*) bladder. ~ **natatoire** swim bladder; **elle veut nous faire prendre des** ~**s pour des lanternes** she would have us believe that the moon is made of green cheese, she's trying to pull the wool over our eyes.

vestale [vɛstal] *nf* (*Hist*) vestal; (*fig littér*) vestal, vestal virgin.

veste [vɛst(ə)] *nf* **(a)** jacket. ~ **droite/croisée** single-/double-breasted jacket; ~ **de pyjama** pyjama jacket *ou* top; ~ **d'intérieur** smoking jacket.

(b) (**loc*) **retourner sa** ~ to turn one's coat, change one's colours; **ramasser** *ou* **prendre une** ~ to come a cropper*; *V* **tomber.**

vestiaire [vɛstjɛʀ] *nm* **(a)** *[théâtre, restaurant]* cloakroom; *[stade, piscine]* changing-room. **réclamer son** ~ to get one's belongings out of the cloakroom; **au** ~**! au** ~**!*** get off!

(b) (*meuble*) coat stand, hat stand. (*métallique*) **(armoire-)**~ locker.

(c) (*rare: garde-robe*) wardrobe. **un** ~ **bien fourni** a well-stocked wardrobe.

vestibule [vɛstibyl] *nm* **(a)** *[maison]* hall; *[hôtel]* hall, vestibule; *[église]* vestibule. **(b)** (*Anat*) vestibule.

vestige [vɛstiʒ] *nm* (*objet*) relic; (*fragment*) trace; (*abstrait*) *[coutume, splendeur, gloire]* vestige, remnant, relic. ~**s** *[ville]* remains, vestiges; *[civilisation, passé]* vestiges, remnants, relics; **il avait gardé un** ~ **de son ancienne arrogance** he had retained a trace *ou* vestige of his former arrogance; **les** ~**s de leur armée décimée** the remnants of their decimated army; **des** ~**s de la guerre** the vestiges of war.

vestimentaire [vɛstimɑ̃tɛʀ] *adj*: **dépenses** ~**s** clothing expenditure, expenditure on clothing; **élégance** ~ sartorial elegance; **ces fantaisies** ~**s n'étaient pas de son goût** these eccentricities of dress were not to his taste; **il se préoccupait beaucoup de détails** ~**s** he was very preoccupied with the details of his dress.

veston [vɛstɔ̃] *nm* jacket; *V* **complet.**

Vésuve [vezyv] *nm* Vesuvius.

vêtement [vɛtmɑ̃] *nm* **(a)** (*article d'habillement*) garment, item *ou* article of clothing; (*ensemble, combinaison*) set of clothes, clothing (*U*), clothes (*pl*); (*frm: de dessus: manteau, veste*) coat. (*Comm: industrie*) **le** ~ the clothing industry, the rag trade*; **c'est un** ~ **très pratique** it's a very practical garment *ou* item of clothing *ou* article of clothing; **le** ~ **anti-g des astronautes** astronauts' anti-gravity clothing *ou* clothes.

(b) ~**s** clothes; **où ai-je mis mes** ~**s?** where did I put my clothes? *ou* things?*; **emporte des** ~**s chauds** take (some) warm clothes *ou* clothing; ~ **de sport/de ville** (*comme catégorie commerciale*) sportswear/town wear (*U*), sports/town garments *ou* clothes; (*personnels*) sports/town clothes, sports/town gear*; ~ **de bébé** babywear, baby garments *ou* clothes;

~s de travail working clothes; **~s de deuil** mourning clothes; **~s du dimanche** Sunday clothes, Sunday best (*parfois hum ou péj*); **~s de dessous** underwear (*U*), underclothes.

(c) (*parure*) garment (*fig*). le style est le **~ de la pensée** style is what clothes thought.

vétéran [veteʀɑ̃] *nm* (*Mil*) veteran; (*fig*) veteran, old hand*. **un ~ de l'enseignement primaire** a veteran of *ou* an old hand* at primary teaching.

vétérinaire [veteʀinɛʀ] **1** *nm* vet, veterinary surgeon (*frm*). **2** *adj* veterinary.

vétille [vetij] *nf* trifle, triviality. **ergoter sur des ~s** to quibble over trifles *ou* trivia *ou* trivialities.

vétilleux, -euse [vetijø, øz] *adj* punctilious.

vêtir [vetiʀ] (20) **1** *vt* (*frm*) (*habiller*) to clothe, dress; (*revêtir*) to don (*frm*), put on.

2 se vêtir *vpr* to dress (o.s.). (*littér*) **les monts se vêtaient de pourpre** the mountains were clothed *ou* clad in purple (*littér*).

veto [veto] *nm* (*Pol, gén*) veto. **opposer son ~ à qch** to veto sth.

vêtu, e [vety] (*ptp de* **vêtir**) *adj* dressed. **bien/mal ~** well-/badly-dressed; **court ~e** short-skirted; **à demi-~** half-dressed; **~ de** dressed in, wearing; (*littér*) **colline ~e des ors de l'automne** hill clad *ou* clothed in the golden hues of autumn (*littér*).

vétuste [vetyst(ə)] *adj* ancient, timeworn.

vétusté [vetyste] *nf* (great) age. **branlant de ~** wobbly with age.

veuf, veuve [vœf, vœv] **1** *adj* **(a)** widowed. **il est deux fois ~** he has been twice widowed, he is a widower twice over; **rester ~/veuve de qn** to be left sb's widower/widow; (*fig*) **ce soir je suis ~** I'm a bachelor tonight.

(b) (*fig littér*) **~ de** bereft of.

2 *nm* widower.

3 veuve *nf* (*gén*) widow. **défenseur de la veuve et de l'orphelin** defender of the weak and of the oppressed.

veule [vøl] *adj personne, air* spineless.

veulerie [vølʀi] *nf* spinelessness.

veuvage [vœvaʒ] *nm* widowhood.

veuve [vœv] *V* **veuf.**

vexant, e [vɛksɑ̃, ɑ̃t] *adj* **(a)** (*contrariant*) annoying, vexing. **c'est ~ de ne pas pouvoir profiter de l'occasion** it's annoying *ou* vexing *ou* a nuisance not to be able to take advantage of the situation. **(b)** (*blessant*) hurtful.

vexation [vɛksɑsjɔ̃] *nf* **(a)** (*humiliation*) (little) humiliation. **essuyer des ~s** to suffer (little) humiliations. **(b)** (*littér,* †: *exaction*) harassment.

vexatoire [vɛksatwaʀ] *adj*: **mesures ~s** harassment.

vexer [vɛkse] (1) **1** *vt* (*offenser*) to hurt, upset, vex. **être vexé par qch** to be hurt by sth, be upset *ou* vexed at sth.

2 se vexer *vpr* to be hurt (*de* by), be *ou* get upset (*de* at), be *ou* get vexed (*de* at). **se ~ d'un rien** to be easily hurt *ou* upset *ou* vexed.

via [vja] *prép* via, by way of.

viabilisé, e [vjabilize] *adj terrain* with services (laid on).

viabilité [vjabilite] *nf* **(a)** *[chemin]* practicability. **avec/sans ~** *terrain* with/without services (laid on). **(b)** *[organisme, entreprise]* viability.

viable [vjabl(ə)] *adj* (*gén*) viable.

viaduc [vjadyk] *nm* viaduct.

viager, -ère [vjaʒe, ɛʀ] **1** *adj* (*Jur*) *rente, revenus* life (*épith*), for life (*attrib*). **à titre ~** for as long as one lives, for the duration of one's life.

2 *nm* (*rente*) life income; (*bien*) *property mortgaged for a life income.* **mettre/acheter un bien en ~** *to sell/buy a property in return for a life income, the property reverting to the purchaser on the seller's death.*

viande [vjɑ̃d] *nf* **(a)** meat. **~ rouge/blanche** red/white meat; **~ de boucherie** (butcher's) meat; (*charcuterie*) **~s froides** cold meat(s); *V* **plat**[2]. **(b)** (:) **montrer sa ~** to bare one's flesh; **amène ta ~!** shift your carcass over here:; *V* **sac.**

viatique [vjatik] *nm* (*argent*) money (for the journey); (*provisions*) provisions (*pl*) (for the journey); (*Rel: communion*) viaticum; (*littér: soutien*) (precious) asset. **la culture est un ~** culture is a precious asset; **l'ayant muni de ce ~, elle l'embrassa et le regarda partir** having give him these provisions (for the journey), she kissed him and watched him set off.

vibrant, e [vibʀɑ̃, ɑ̃t] *adj* **(a)** (*lit*) *corde, membrane* vibrating.

(b) *son, voix* vibrant, resonant; (*Phonétique*) *consonne* lateral, vibrant. **voix ~e d'émotion** voice vibrant with emotion.

(c) *discours* (powerfully) emotive; *nature* emotive. **~ d'émotion contenue** vibrant with suppressed emotion.

vibraphone [vibʀafɔn] *nm* vibraphone, vibes* (*pl*).

vibraphoniste [vibʀafɔnist(ə)] *nmf* vibraphone player, vibes player*.

vibratile [vibʀatil] *adj* vibratile.

vibration [vibʀɑsjɔ̃] *nf* (*gén, Phys*) vibration. **la ~ de sa voix** the vibration *ou* resonance of his voice; **la ~ de l'air (due à la chaleur)** the quivering *ou* shimmering of the air (due to the heat).

vibrato [vibʀato] *nm* vibrato.

vibratoire [vibʀatwaʀ] *adj* vibratory.

vibrer [vibʀe] (1) **1** *vi* **(a)** (*gén, Phys*) to vibrate. **faire ~ qch** to cause sth to vibrate, vibrate sth.

(b) (*d'émotion*) *[voix]* to quiver, be vibrant; *[passion]* to be stirred; *[personne, âme]* to thrill (*de* with). **~ en écoutant Beethoven** to be stirred when listening to a piece by Beethoven; **faire ~ qn/un auditoire** to stir *ou* thrill sb/an audience, send a thrill through sb/an audience; **~ d'enthousiasme** to be vibrant with enthusiasm; **des accents qui font ~ l'âme** accents which stir *ou* thrill the soul.

2 *vt* (*Tech*) *béton* to vibrate.

vibreur [vibʀœʀ] *nm* vibrator.

vibrion [vibʀijɔ̃] *nm* vibrio.

vibromasseur [vibʀɔmasœʀ] *nm* vibrator.

vicaire [vikɛʀ] *nm [paroisse]* curate. *[évêque]* **grand ~, ~ général** vicar-general; *[pape]* **~ apostolique** vicar apostolic; **le ~ de Jésus-Christ** the vicar of Christ.

vicariat [vikaʀja] *nm* curacy.

vice [vis] *nm* **(a)** (*défaut moral, mauvais penchant*) vice. (*mal, débauche*) **le ~** vice; (*hum*) **le tabac est mon ~** tobacco is my vice (*hum*); **elle travaille 15 heures par jour: c'est du ~!*** it's perverted *ou* it's sheer perversion the way she works 15 hours a day like that!; **vivre dans le ~** to live a life of vice; *V* **oisiveté, pauvreté.**

(b) (*défectuosité*) fault, defect. **~ de prononciation** fault in pronunciation; **~ de conformation** congenital malformation; **~ de construction** construction fault *ou* defect, fault *ou* defect in construction; (*Jur*) **~ rédhibitoire** redhibitory defect; (*Jur*) **~ de forme** legal flaw *ou* irregularity.

vice- [vis] **1** *préf* vice-.

2: vice-amiral *nm, pl* **vice-amiraux** vice-admiral; **vice-chancelier** *nm, pl* **vice-chanceliers** vice-chancellor; **vice-consul** *nm, pl* **vice-consuls** vice-consul; **vice-consulat** *nm, pl* **vice-consulats** vice-consulate; **vice-légat** *nm, pl* **vice-légats** vice-legate; **vice-légation** *nf, pl* **vice-légations** vice-legateship; **vice-présidence** *nf, pl* **vice-présidences** vice-presidency, vice-chairmanship; **vice-président, e** *nm,f, mpl* **vice-présidents** vice-president, vice-chairman; (*Univ*) **vice-recteur** *nm, pl* **vice-recteurs** vice-rector; **vice-reine** *nf, pl* **vice-reines** lady viceroy, vicereine; **vice-roi** *nm, pl* **vice-rois** viceroy; **vice-royauté** *nf, pl* **vice-royautés** viceroyalty.

vicennal, e, *mpl* **-aux** [visenal, o] *adj* (*rare*) vicennial.

vicésimal, e, *mpl* **-aux** [visezimal, o] *adj* vigesimal, vicenary.

vice versa [viseveʀsa] *adv* vice versa.

vichy [viʃi] *nm* **(a)** (*Tex*) gingham. **(b) (eau de) ~** vichy *ou* Vichy water; **~ fraise** strawberry syrup in vichy water.

viciation [visjɑsjɔ̃] *nf* (*V* **vicier**) pollution; tainting; vitiation (*frm*); contamination.

vicié, e [visje] (*ptp de* **vicier**) *adj air* polluted, tainted, vitiated (*frm*).

vicier [visje] (7) *vt* **(a)** *atmosphère* to pollute, taint, vitiate (*frm*); *sang* to contaminate, taint, vitiate (*frm*).

(b) (*fig*) *rapports* to taint; *esprit, atmosphère* to taint, pollute.

(c) (*Jur*) *élection* to invalidate; *acte juridique* to vitiate, invalidate.

vicieusement [visjøzmɑ̃] *adv* (*V* **vicieux**) licentiously; lecherously; nastily*; incorrectly; wrongly.

vicieux, -euse [visjø, øz] *adj* **(a)** (*pervers*) *personne, penchant* licentious, dissolute, lecherous. **c'est un petit ~** he's a little lecher.

(b) (*littér: pourri de vices*) vicious (*littér*), depraved, vice-ridden.

(c) (*rétif*) *cheval* restive, unruly.

(d) (*trompeur, pas franc*) *attaque, balle* well-disguised, nasty*; *V* **cercle.**

(e) (*fautif*) *prononciation, expression* incorrect, wrong.

vicinal, e, *mpl* **-aux** [visinal, o] *adj* (*Admin*) **chemin ~** by-road, byway.

vicissitudes [visisityd] *nfpl* (*infortunes*) tribulations, trials, trials and tribulations; (*littér: variations, événements*) vicissitudes, vagaries.

vicomte [vikɔ̃t] *nm* viscount.

vicomté [vikɔ̃te] *nf* viscountcy, viscounty.

vicomtesse [vikɔ̃tɛs] *nf* viscountess.

victime [viktim] *nf* (*gén*) victim; *[accident, catastrophe]* casualty, victim. **la ~ du sacrifice** the sacrificial victim; **cet arbre fut la première ~ du froid** this tree was the first casualty *ou* victim of the cold; **entreprise ~ de la concurrence** business which was a victim of competition; **~ de son imprudence/imprévoyance** victim of his own imprudence/lack of foresight; **être ~ de** *escroc, crise cardiaque, calomnie* to be the victim of.

victoire [viktwaʀ] *nf* (*gén*) victory; (*Sport*) win, victory. (*Boxe*) **~ aux points** win on points; **~ à la Pyrrhus** Pyrrhic victory; **crier** *ou* **chanter ~** to crow (over one's victory).

Victor [viktɔʀ] *nm* Victor.

victoria [viktɔʀja] *nf* (*Bot, Hist: voiture*) victoria.

victorien, -ienne [viktɔʀjɛ̃, jɛn] *adj* Victorian.

victorieusement [viktɔʀjøzmɑ̃] *adv* (*V* **victorieux**) victoriously; triumphantly.

victorieux, -euse [viktɔʀjø, øz] *adj général, campagne, armée* victorious; *équipe* winning (*épith*), victorious; *parti* victorious; *air, sourire* triumphant.

victuailles [viktɥɑj] *nfpl* provisions, victuals (*rare*).

vidage [vidaʒ] *nm* **(a)** (*rare*) *[récipient]* emptying. **(b)** (*: *expulsion*) kicking out*, chucking out*.

vidame [vidam] *nm* (*Hist*) vidame.

vidange [vidɑ̃ʒ] *nf* **(a)** *[fosse, tonneau, réservoir, fosse d'aisance]* emptying; (*Aut*) oil change. **entreprise de ~** sewage disposal business; (*Aut*) **faire la ~** to change the oil, do an *ou* the oil change.

(b) (*matières*) **~s** sewage.

(c) (*dispositif*) *[lavabo]* waste outlet.

vidanger [vidɑ̃ʒe] (3) *vt* **(a)** *réservoir, fosse d'aisance* to empty. **(b)** *huile, eau* to drain (off), empty out.

vidangeur [vidɑ̃ʒœʀ] *nm* cesspool emptier.

vide [vid] **1** *adj* **(a)** (*lit*) (*gén*) empty; (*disponible*) *appartement, siège* empty, vacant. **avoir l'estomac** *ou* **le ventre ~** to have an empty stomach; **ne partez pas le ventre ~** don't leave on an empty stomach; (*Comm*) **bouteilles/caisses ~s** empty bottles/cases, empties*; *V* **case, main.**

(b) (*fig*) (*sans intérêt, creux*) *journée, heures* empty; (*stérile*) *discussion, paroles, style* empty, vacuous. **sa vie était ~** his life was empty *ou* a void; **passer une journée** ~ to spend a day with nothing to do, spend an empty day; *V* **tête.**

(c) ~ **de** empty *ou* (de)void of; ~ **de sens** *mot, expression* meaningless, empty *ou* (de)void of (all) meaning; *paroles* meaningless, empty; **les rues** ~**s de voitures** the streets empty *ou* devoid of cars; **elle se sentait** ~ **de tout sentiment** she felt (de)void *ou* empty of all feeling.

2 *nm* **(a)** (*ressenti comme absence d'appui, verticalité*) drop; (*perçu, autour de soi, vacuité*) emptiness (*U*); (*espace sans air*) vacuum. (*l'espace*) **le** ~ the void; **être au-dessus du** ~ to be over *ou* above a drop; **avoir/n'avoir pas peur du** ~ to be/not to be afraid of heights, have no head/a head for heights; **faire le** ~ **dans** to create a vacuum in; **sous** ~ under vacuum; **emballé sous** ~ vacuum-packed; **emballage sous** ~ vacuum packing; **regarder dans le** ~ to gaze *ou* stare into space *ou* emptiness; **ce lieu n'est que** ~ **et silence** this place is nothing but emptiness and silence; *V* **nature.**

(b) (*creux, trou*) (*entre deux objets*) gap, (empty) space; (*Archit*) void. **un** ~ **de mémoire** a gap in one's memory; **un** ~ **douloureux dans son cœur** an aching void in one's heart; **son départ fait un grand** ~ his departure leaves a big empty space; (*Constr*) ~ **sanitaire** underfloor space.

(c) (*fig*) *[existence, journées oisives]* emptiness. **le** ~ **de l'existence** the emptiness of existence.

(d) (*loc*) **à** ~ empty; **le car est reparti à** ~ the coach went off again empty; **faire le** ~ **autour de qn** to keep (right) away from sb, leave sb on his own; **faire le** ~ **dans son esprit** to make one's mind a blank; **parler dans le** ~ (*sans objet*) to talk vacuously; (*personne n'écoute*) to talk to a brick wall, waste one's breath; *V* **nettoyage, passage, tourner.**

vide- [vid] *préf V* **vider.**

vidé, e [vide] (*ptp de* **vider**) *adj* (*) *personne* worn out.

vidéocassette [videokasɛt] *nf* video-cassette.

vidéogramme [videogʀam] *nm* video-recording (*cassette etc*).

vidéophone [videɔfɔn] *nm* videophone.

vider [vide] (1) **1** *vt* **(a)** *récipient, réservoir, meuble, pièce* to empty; *étang, citerne* to empty, drain. ~ **un appartement de ses meubles** to empty *ou* clear a flat of its furniture; ~ **un étang de ses poissons** to empty *ou* clear a pond of its fish; ~ **un tiroir sur la table/dans une corbeille** to empty a drawer (out) onto the table/into a wastebasket; (*en consommant*) **ils ont vidé 3 bouteilles** they emptied *ou* drained 3 bottles; **il vida son verre et partit** he emptied *ou* drained his glass and left; (*en emportant*) **ils ont vidé tous les tiroirs** they cleaned out *ou* emptied all the drawers.

(b) *contenu* to empty (out). ~ **l'eau d'un bassin** to empty the water out of a basin; **va** ~ **les ordures** go and empty (out) the rubbish; ~ **des déchets dans une poubelle** to empty waste into a dustbin.

(c) (*faire évacuer*) *lieu* to empty, clear. **la pluie a vidé les rues** the rain emptied *ou* cleared the streets.

(d) (*quitter*) *endroit, logement* to quit, vacate. ~ **les lieux** to quit *ou* vacate the premises.

(e) (*évider*) *poisson, poulet* to gut, clean out; *pomme* to core.

(f) (†; *régler*) *querelle, affaire* to settle.

(g) (*Équitation*) *cavalier* to throw. ~ **les arçons/les étriers** to leave the saddle/the stirrups.

(h) (*: *expulser*) *trouble-fête, indésirable* to throw out*, chuck out*. ~ **qn d'une réunion/d'un bistro** to throw *ou* chuck sb out of a meeting/café*.

(i) (*épuiser*) to wear out. **ce travail m'a vidé*** this piece of work has worn me out; **travail qui vous vide l'esprit** occupation that leaves you mentally drained *ou* exhausted.

(j) (*loc*) ~ **son sac*** to come out with it*; ~ **l'abcès** to root out the evil; ~ **son cœur** to pour out one's heart.

2 se vider *vpr [récipient, réservoir, bassin]* to empty. **les eaux sales se vident dans l'égout** the dirty water empties *ou* drains into the sewer; **ce réservoir se vide dans un canal** this reservoir empties into a canal; **en août, la ville se vide (de ses habitants)** in August, the town empties (of its inhabitants).

3: vide-ordures *nm inv* (rubbish) chute; **vide-poches** *nm inv* tidy; (*Aut*) glove compartment; **vide-pomme** *nm, pl* **vide-pommes** apple-corer.

videur, -euse [vidœʀ, øz] *nm,f* (*de boîte de nuit*) bouncer*.

viduité [vidɥite] *nf* (*Jur*) widowhood, viduity (*T*). **délai de** ~ minimum legal period of widowhood.

vie [vi] *nf* **(a)** (*gén, Bio, fig*) life. **la** ~ life; (*Rel*) **la V**~ the Life; **être en** ~ to be alive; **être bien en** ~ to be well and truly alive, be alive and kicking*; **donner la** ~ to give birth; **donner/risquer sa** ~ **pour** to give/risk one's life for; **rappeler qn à/revenir à la** ~ to bring sb back/come back to life; **tôt/tard dans la** ~ early/late in life; **attends de connaître la** ~ **pour juger** wait until you know (something) about life before you pass judgment; ~ **intra-utérine** life in the womb, intra-uterine life (*T*); ~ **végétative** vegetable existence.

(b) (*animation*) life. **être plein de** ~ to be full of life; **donner la** ~ **à** to liven up, enliven, bring life to; **sa présence met de la** ~ **dans la maison** he brings some life *ou* a bit of life into the house.

(c) (*activités*) life. **dans la** ~ **courante** in everyday life; **(mode de)** ~ way of life, life style; **avoir/mener une** ~ **facile/dure** to have/lead an easy/a hard life; **mener une** ~ **sédentaire** to have a sedentary way of life *ou* a sedentary life style, lead a sedentary life; **mener joyeuse** ~ to have a gay life, lead a gay *ou* lively existence; **la** ~ **intellectuelle à Paris** the intellectual life of Paris, intellectual life in Paris; ~ **sentimentale/conjugale/professionnelle** love/married/professional life; ~ **de garçon** bachelor's life *ou* existence (*V* **enterrer**); **la** ~ **militaire** life in the services; **la** ~ **d'un professeur n'est pas toujours drôle** a teacher's life *ou* the life of a teacher isn't always much fun; **la** ~ **des animaux/des plantes** animal/plant life; **il poursuivit sa petite** ~ he carried on with his day-to-day existence *ou* his daily affairs; **la** ~ **(à l')américaine** the American way of life; ~ **de bohème/de patachon*** bohemian/disorderly way of life *ou* life style; ~ **de château** life of luxury; *V* **certificat, vivre** *etc.*

(d) (*moyens matériels*) living. **(le coût de) la** ~ the cost of living; **la** ~ **augmente** the cost of living is rising *ou* going up; **la** ~ **chère est la cause du mécontentement** the high cost of living is the cause of discontent; *V* **coût, gagner, niveau.**

(e) (*durée*) life(time). **il a habité ici toute sa** ~ he lived here all his life; **des habits qui durent une** ~ clothes that last a lifetime; **faire qch une fois dans sa** ~ to do sth once in one's life(time); **une telle occasion arrive une seule fois dans la** ~ such an opportunity occurs only once in a lifetime.

(f) (*biographie*) life (story). **écrire/lire une** ~ **de qn** to write/read a life of sb; **j'ai lu la** ~ **de Hitler** I read Hitler's life story *ou* the story of Hitler's life; **elle m'a raconté toute sa** ~ she told me her whole life story, she told me the story of her life.

(g) (*loc*) (*nommer qn etc*) **à** ~ for life; **il est nommé à** ~ he is appointed for life, he has a life appointment; **directeur nommé à** ~ life director, director for life; **à la** ~ **à la mort** *amitié, fidélité* undying (*épith*); **amis à la** ~ **à la mort** lifelong friends, friends for life; **rester fidèle à qn à la** ~ **à la mort** to remain faithful to sb to one's dying day; **pour la** ~: **il est infirme pour la** ~ he is an invalid for life; **amis pour la** ~ friends for life, lifelong friends; **passer de** ~ **à trépas** to pass on; **faire passer qn de** ~ **à trépas** to dispatch sb into the next world; **une question de** ~ **et de mort** a matter of life and death; **de ma** ~ **je n'ai jamais vu de telles idioties** never (in my life) have I seen such stupidity, I have never (in my life) seen such stupidity; **c'est la belle** ~**!** this is the life!; **ce n'est pas une** ~**!** it's a rotten* *ou* hard life!; ~ **de bâton de chaise** riotous existence; **c'est une** ~ **de chien!*** it's a dog's life!*; **c'est la** ~**!** that's life!; **la** ~ **est ainsi faite!** such is life!, that's life!; **jamais de la** ~ **je n'y retournerai** I shall never go back there in my life, I shall never go there again, I shall never ever go back there; **jamais de la** ~**!** never!, not on your life!*; **être entre la** ~ **et la mort** to be at death's door; **avoir la** ~ **dure** *[personne, animal]* to have nine lives; *[superstitions]* to die hard; **mener la** ~ **dure à qn** to give sb a hard time of it, make life hard for sb; **sans** ~ *personne* (*mort*) lifeless; (*évanoui*) insensible; (*amorphe*) lifeless, listless; *regard* lifeless, listless; **faire sa** ~ to live (one's life) as one pleases *ou* sees fit; **faire la** ~ (*se débaucher*) to lead a life of pleasure; (*: *faire une scène*) to kick up a fuss* *ou* a row*, make a scene; **chaque fois, elle me fait la** ~ she goes on (and on) at me every time; **il en a fait une** ~ **lorsque ...** he kicked up a real row* *ou* fuss* *ou* made a real scene when ... ; **faire une** ~ **impossible à qn** to make sb's life intolerable *ou* impossible (for him); **laisser la** ~ **sauve à qn** to spare sb's life; **il dut à sa franchise d'avoir la** ~ **sauve** he owed his life to his frankness, it was thanks to his frankness that his life was spared; **voir la** ~ **en rose** to see life through rose-tinted *ou* rose-coloured glasses, take a rosy view of life; **ce roman montre la** ~ **en rose** this novel gives a rosy picture *ou* view of life.

vieil [vjɛj] *V* **vieux.**

vieillard [vjɛjaʀ] *nm* old man. **les** ~**s** the elderly, old people *ou* men.

vieille [vjɛj] *V* **vieux.**

vieillerie [vjɛjʀi] *nf* **(a)** (*objet*) old-fashioned thing; (*rare: idée, œuvre*) old *ou* worn-out *ou* stale idea. **aimer les** ~**s** to like old *ou* old-fashioned things *ou* stuff. **(b)** (*littér: cachet suranné*) outdatedness, old-fashionedness.

vieillesse [vjɛjɛs] *nf* **(a)** (*période*) old age; (*fait d'être vieux*) (old) age. **mourir de** ~ to die of old age; *V* **bâton. (b)** (*vieillards*) **la** ~ the old, the elderly, the aged; **aide à la** ~ help for the old *ou* the elderly *ou* the aged; *V* **jeunesse. (c)** *[choses]* age, oldness.

vieilli, e [vjeji] (*ptp de* **vieillir**) *adj* (*marqué par l'âge*) aged, grown old (*attrib*); (*suranné*) dated. **vin** ~ **dans la cave** wine aged in the cellar; ~ **dans la profession** grown old in the profession; **une ville** ~**e** a town which has aged *ou* grown old.

vieillir [vjejiʀ] (2) **1** *vi* **(a)** (*prendre de l'âge*) *[personne, maison, organe]* to grow old; *[population]* to age. ~ **dans un métier** to grow old in a job; **savoir** ~ to grow old gracefully; **l'art de** ~ the art of growing old (gracefully).

(b) (*paraître plus vieux*) to age. **il a vieilli de 10 ans en quelques jours** he aged (by) 10 years in a few days; **je la trouve très vieillie** I find she has aged a lot; **il ne vieillit pas** he doesn't get any older.

(c) (*fig: passer de mode*) *[auteur, mot, doctrine]* to become (out)dated.

(d) (*Culin*) *[vin, fromage]* to age.

2 *vt* **(a)** *[coiffure, maladie]* to age, put years on. **cette coiffure vous vieillit** that hair style ages you *ou* puts years on you.

(b) (*par fausse estimation*) ~ **qn** to make sb older than he (really) is; **vous me vieillissez de 5 ans** you're making me 5 years older than I (really) am.

3 se vieillir *vpr* to make o.s. older. **il se vieillit à plaisir** he makes himself older when it suits him.

vieillissant, e [vjejisɑ̃, ɑ̃t] *adj personne* ageing, who is growing old; *œuvre* ageing, which is becoming (out)dated.

vieillissement [vjejismɑ̃] *nm* **(a)** *[personne, population, maison, institution]* ageing. **le** ~ **fait perdre à la peau son élasticité** ageing *ou* the ageing process makes the skin lose its elasticity.

(b) *[mot, doctrine, œuvre]* becoming (out)dated. **le** ~ **prématuré d'un auteur** an author's becoming dated before his time.

(c) *[vin, fromage]* ageing. ~ **forcé** artificial ageing.

vieillot, -otte [vjɛjo, ɔt] *adj* **(a)** (*démodé*) antiquated, quaint.

(b) (*rare: vieux*) old-looking.

vielle [vjɛl] *nf* hurdy-gurdy.

Vienne [vjɛn] *n* Vienna.

viennois, e [vjɛnwa, waz] 1 *adj* Viennese. 2 *nm,f*: **V~(e)** Viennese.

vierge [vjɛʀʒ(ə)] 1 *nf* (a) (*pucelle*) virgin.
(b) (*Rel*) **la (Sainte) V~** the (Blessed) Virgin; *V* **fil**.
(c) (*Astron*) **la V~** Virgo, the Virgin; **être de la V~** to be Virgo *ou* a Virgoan.
2 *adj* (a) *personne* virgin (*épith*). **rester/être ~** to remain/be a virgin.
(b) *ovule* unfertilized.
(c) (*fig*) *feuille de papier* blank, virgin (*épith*); *film* unexposed; *casier judiciaire* clean; *terre, neige* virgin (*épith*); *V* **huile, laine, vigne** *etc.*
(d) (*littér: exempt*) **~ de** free from, unsullied by; **~ de tout reproche** free from (all) reproach.

Viet-Nam [vjɛtnam] *nm* Vietnam. **~ du Nord/du Sud** North/South Vietnam.

vietnamien, -ienne [vjɛtnamjɛ̃, jɛn] 1 *adj* Vietnamese. 2 *nm* (*Ling*) Vietnamese. 3 *nm,f*: **V~(ne)** Vietnamese; **V~(ne) du Nord/Sud** North/South Vietnamese.

vieux [vjø], **vieille** [vjɛj], **vieil** [vjɛj] *devant nm commençant par une voyelle ou h muet, mpl* **vieux** [vjø] 1 *adj* (a) (*âgé*) old. **très ~** ancient (*hum*), very old; **un vieil homme** an old man; **une vieille femme** an old woman; **c'est un homme déjà ~** he's already an old man; **les vieilles gens** old people, old folk*, the aged *ou* elderly; **il est plus ~ que moi** he is older than I am; **~ comme Hérode** *ou* **Mathusalem** as old as Methuselah; **~ comme le monde** as old as the hills; **il commence à se faire ~** he is getting on (in years), he's beginning to grow old; **il est ~ avant l'âge** he is old before his time; **sur ses ~ jours, il était devenu sourd** he had gone deaf in his old age; **un ~ retraité** an old pensioner; **il n'a pas fait de ~ os** he didn't last *ou* live long; **il n'a pas fait de ~ os dans cette entreprise** he didn't last long in that firm; *V* **retraite, vivre**.
(b) (*ancien: idée de valeur*) *demeure, bijoux, meuble* old; (*expérimenté*) *marin, guide* old. **une belle vieille demeure** a fine old house; **un vin ~** an old wine; **vieilles danses** old dances; **~ français** Old French; **vieil anglais** Old English.
(c) (*usé*) *objet, maison, habits* old. **ce pull est très ~** this sweater is ancient *ou* very old; **~ papiers** waste paper; **~ journaux** old (news)papers; **de vieilles nouvelles** old news.
(d) (*avant n: de longue date*) *ami, habitude, amitié* old, long-standing; (*passé*) *coutumes* old, ancient. **un vieil ami** a long-standing friend, a friend of long standing; **de vieille race** *ou* **souche** of ancient lineage; **vieille famille** ancient family; **de vieille date** long-standing; **connaître qn de vieille date** to have known sb for a very long time; **c'est une vieille histoire** it's an old story; **nous avons beaucoup de ~ souvenirs en commun** we have a lot of old memories in common; **alors, c'est la vieille question/le ~ problème** it's the same old question/problem; **traîner un ~ rhume** to have a cold that is dragging on.
(e) (*avant n: de naguère*) old; (*précédent*) old, former, previous. **la vieille génération** the older generation; **mon vieil enthousiasme** my old *ou* former *ou* previous enthusiasm; **ma vieille voiture était plus rapide que la nouvelle** my old *ou* former *ou* previous car was quicker than the new one; **le ~ Paris/Lyon** old Paris/Lyons; **la vieille France/Angleterre** the France/England of bygone days; **il est de la vieille école** he belongs to *ou* is (one) of the old school; **ses vieilles craintes se réveillaient** his old fears were aroused once more.
(f) (*intensif*) **vieille bique*** old bag‡; (*péj*) **~ jeton*** *ou* **shnock‡** old misery*; **vieille noix*** (silly) old twit* *ou* fathead‡; **espèce de ~ crétin!*** stupid twit!*; **c'est un ~ gâteux*** he's an old dodderer*; **n'importe quel ~ bout de papier fera l'affaire** any old bit of paper will do*; *V* **bon**[1].
2 *nm* (a) old man. **les ~** the old *ou* aged *ou* elderly, old people, old folk*; **un ~ de la vieille*** one of the old brigade; (*père*) **le ~‡** my *ou* the old man‡; (*parents*) **ses ~‡** his folks*, his old man and woman‡; **mon (petit) ~*, tu vas m'expliquer ça** listen you, you're going to give me an explanation; **alors, (mon) ~*, tu viens?** are you coming then, old man?* *ou* old chap?* *ou* old boy?*; **comment ça va, mon ~?*** how are you, old boy?*; **tu fais partie des ~ maintenant** you're one of the old folks now; *V* **petit**.
(b) **préférer le ~ au neuf** to prefer old things to new; **faire du neuf avec du ~** to turn old into new; *V* **coup**.
3 **vieille** *nf* old woman. (*mère*) **la vieille‡** my *ou* the old woman‡ *ou* lady‡; **alors, ma vieille*, tu viens?** are you coming then, old girl?*; (*hum: à un homme*) are you coming then, old man?* *ou* old chap?* *ou* old boy?*; **comment ça va, ma vieille?*** how are you, old girl?*; *V aussi* **vieux** *et* **petit**.
4 *adv* **vivre** to an old age, to a ripe old age; *s'habiller* old. **elle s'habille trop ~** she dresses too old (for herself); **ce manteau fait ~** this coat makes you (look) old.
5: (*péj*) **vieux beau** ageing beau; († *hum fig*) **vieille branche** old fruit* (*Brit*) *ou* bean* (*hum*); **la vieille école: de la vieille école** old-fashioned, traditional; **vieille fille** spinster, old maid; **elle est très vieille fille** she is very old-maidish; **vieille France** *adj inv personne, politesse* old-world, old(e)-world(e) (*hum*); **vieux garçon** bachelor; **des habitudes de vieux garçon** bachelor ways; **la vieille garde** the old guard; **vieux jeu** *adj inv idées* old-hat (*attrib*), outmoded; *personne* behind the times (*attrib*), old-fashioned, old hat (*attrib*); *vêtement* old-fashioned, out-of-date (*épith*), out of date (*attrib*); **vieilles lunes** olden days; **le Vieux Monde** the Old World; **vieil or** *n, adj inv* old gold; **vieux rose** *adj inv* old rose; **vieux routier** old stager.

vif, vive[1] [vif, viv] 1 *adj* (a) (*plein de vie*) *enfant, personne* lively, vivacious; *mouvement, rythme, style* lively, animated, brisk; (*alerte*) sharp, quick (*attrib*); *imagination* lively, keen; *intelligence* keen, quick. **il a l'œil** *ou* **le regard ~** he has a sharp *ou* keen eye; **à l'esprit ~** quick-witted.
(b) (*brusque, emporté*) *personne* sharp, brusque, quick-tempered; *ton, propos, attitude* sharp, brusque. **il s'est montré un peu ~ avec elle** he was rather sharp *ou* brusque *ou* quick-tempered with her; **le débat prit un tour assez ~** the discussion took on a rather acrimonious tone.
(c) (*profond, intense*) *émotion* keen (*épith*), intense; *souvenirs* vivid; *impression* vivid, intense; *plaisirs, désir* intense, keen (*épith*); *déception* acute, keen (*épith*), intense. **j'ai le sentiment très ~ de l'avoir vexé** I have the distinct feeling that I have offended him, I'm keenly aware of having offended him.
(d) (*gén avant n: intensif: fort, grand*) *goût* strong, distinct; *chagrin, regret, satisfaction* deep, great. **une vive satisfaction** a great *ou* deep feeling of satisfaction, deep *ou* great satisfaction; **une vive impatience** great impatience; **un ~ penchant pour ...** a strong liking *ou* inclination for ... ; **à vive allure** at a brisk pace; (*formules de politesse*) **avec mes plus ~s remerciements** with my most profound thanks; **c'est avec un ~ plaisir que ...** it is with very great pleasure that ... .
(e) (*aux sens: tranché, mordant*) *lumière, éclat* bright, brilliant; *couleur* vivid, brilliant; *froid* biting, bitter; *douleur* sharp; *vent* keen; *ongles, arête* sharp. **le teint ~** with a high complexion; **l'air ~ les revigorait** the bracing air gave them new life; **rouge ~** vivid *ou* brilliant red; **il faisait un froid très ~** it was bitterly cold.
(f) (*à nu*) *pierre* bare; *joints* dry.
(g) (†: *vivant*) alive. **brûler/enterrer ~ qn** to burn/bury sb alive; **de vive voix** *renseigner, communiquer* by word of mouth; *remercier* personally, in person; **eau vive** running water; *V* **chaux, mort**[2], **œuvre** *etc.*
2 *nm* (a) (*loc*) **à ~** *chair* bared; *plaie* open; **avoir les nerfs à ~** to have frayed nerves, be on edge; **avoir la sensibilité à ~** to be highly strung; **être atteint** *ou* **touché** *ou* **piqué au ~** to be cut *ou* hurt to the quick; **tailler** *ou* **couper** *ou* **trancher dans le ~** (*lit*) to cut into the living flesh; (*fig*) to strike at the very root of the evil; **entrer dans le ~ du sujet** to get to the heart of the matter; **sur le ~** *peindre, décrire* from life; **prendre qn (en photo) sur le ~** to photograph sb in a real-life situation.
(b) (*Pêche*) **pêcher au ~** to fish with live bait.
(c) (*Jur: personne vivante*) living person. **donation entre ~s** donation inter vivos; *V* **mort**[2].
3: (*Chim*††) **vif-argent** *nm inv* quicksilver; (*fig*) **il a du vif-argent dans les veines, c'est du vif-argent** he is a live wire.

vigie [viʒi] *nf* (a) (*Naut*) (*matelot*) look-out, watch; (*poste*) [*mât*] look-out post, crow's-nest; [*proue*] look-out post. **être en ~** to be on watch. (b) (*Rail*) **~ de frein** brake cabin.

vigilance [viʒilɑ̃s] *nf* (*V* **vigilant**) vigilance; watchfulness.

vigilant, e [viʒilɑ̃, ɑ̃t] *adj personne, œil* vigilant, watchful; *attention, soins* vigilant.

vigile[1] [viʒil] *nf* (*Rel*) vigil.

vigile[2] [viʒil] *nm* (*Hist*) watch; (*veilleur de nuit*) (night) watchman.

vigne [viɲ] 1 *nf* (a) (*plante*) vine. (†) **être dans les ~s du Seigneur** to be in one's cups †; *V* **cep, pied**. (b) (*vignoble*) vineyard; *V* **pêche**[1]. 2: **vigne vierge** Virginia creeper.

vigneau, *pl* **~x** [viɲo] *nm* winkle.

vigneron, -onne [viɲʀɔ̃, ɔn] *nm,f* (*f rare*) wine grower.

vignette [viɲɛt] *nf* (a) (*Art: motif*) vignette.
(b) (†: *illustration*) illustration.
(c) (*Comm: timbre*) (manufacturer's) label *ou* seal. (*Aut*) **la ~ (de l'impôt)** ≃ the (road) tax disc; **~ de la Sécurité sociale** *price label on medicines for reimbursement by Social Security.*

vignoble [viɲɔbl(ə)] *nm* vineyard. (*ensemble de vignobles*) **le ~ français/bordelais** the vineyards of France/Bordeaux.

vignot [viɲo] *nm* = **vigneau**.

vigogne [vigɔɲ] *nf* (*Zool*) vicuna; (*Tex*) vicuna (wool).

vigoureusement [viguʀøzmɑ̃] *adv taper, frotter* vigorously, energetically; *protester, résister* vigorously; *peindre, écrire* vigorously, with vigour. **plante qui pousse ~** plant that grows vigorously *ou* sturdily.

vigoureux, -euse [viguʀø, øz] *adj* (a) (*robuste*) *personne* vigorous; *corps* robust, vigorous; *bras* sturdy, strong; *mains* strong, powerful; *santé* robust; *plante* vigorous, sturdy, robust. **manier la hache d'un bras ~** to wield the axe with vigour, wield the axe vigorously; **il est encore ~ pour son âge** he's still hale and hearty *ou* still vigorous for his age.
(b) (*fig*) *esprit* vigorous; *style, dessin* vigorous, energetic; *sentiment, passion* violent; *résistance* vigorous, strenuous.

vigueur [vigœʀ] *nf* (a) (*robustesse: V* **vigoureux**) vigour; robustness; sturdiness; strength. **sans ~** without vigour; **dans toute la ~ de la jeunesse** in the full vigour of youth; **se débattre avec ~** to defend o.s. vigorously *ou* with vigour; **donner de la ~ à** to invigorate.
(b) (*spirituelle, morale*) vigour, strength; [*réaction, protestation*] vigour, vigorousness. **~ intellectuelle** intellectual vigour; **s'exprimer/protester avec ~** to express o.s./protest vigorously.
(c) (*fermeté*) [*coloris, style*] vigour, energy.
(d) **en ~** *loi, dispositions* in force; *terminologie, formule* current, in use; **entrer en ~** to come into force *ou* effect; **faire entrer en ~** to bring into force *ou* effect *ou* operation; **cesser d'être en ~** to cease to apply.

Viking [vikiŋ] *nm* Viking.

vil, e [vil] *adj* (a) (*littér: méprisable*) vile, base. (b) (††: *non noble*) low(ly). (c) (††: *sans valeur*) *marchandises* worthless, cheap. **métaux ~s** base metals. (d) **à ~ prix** at a very low price.

vilain, e [vilɛ̃, ɛn] **1** *adj* **(a)** (*laid à voir*) *personne, visage, vêtement* ugly(-looking); *couleur* nasty. **elle n'est pas ~e** she's not bad-looking, she's not unattractive.
(b) (*mauvais*) *temps* nasty, bad, lousy*; *odeur* nasty, bad. **il a fait ~ toute la semaine*** it has been nasty *ou* lousy* (weather) all week.
(c) (*grave, dangereux*) *blessure, affaire* nasty. **jouer un ~ tour à qn** to play a nasty *ou* mean trick on sb; *V* **drap.**
(d) (*moralement laid*) *action, pensée* wicked. (*langage des parents*) **~s mots** naughty *ou* wicked words; **c'est un ~ monsieur** *ou* **coco*** he's a nasty customer *ou* piece of work* (*Brit*).
(e) (*langage des parents: pas sage*) *enfant, conduite* naughty. **oh le ~!** what a naughty boy (you are)!
2 *nm* **(a)** (*Hist*) villein, villain.
(b) (*) **il va y avoir du ~, ça va tourner au ~** it's going to turn nasty.
vilainement [vilɛnmɑ̃] *adv* wickedly.
vilebrequin [vilbʀəkɛ̃] *nm* (*outil*) (bit-)brace; (*Aut*) crankshaft.
vilement [vilmɑ̃] *adv* (*littér*) vilely, basely.
vilenie [vilni] *nf* (*littér*) (*U*) vileness, baseness; (*acte*) villainy, vile *ou* base deed.
vilipender [vilipɑ̃de] (1) *vt* (*littér*) to revile, vilify, inveigh against.
villa [villa] *nf* (detached) house.
village [vilaʒ] *nm* (*bourg, habitants*) village. **~ de toile** tent village, holiday encampment; **il est bien de son ~** he's a real country cousin; *V* **idiot.**
villageois, e [vilaʒwa, waz] **1** *adj atmosphère, coutumes* village (*épith*), rustic (*épith*). **un air ~** a rustic air. **2** *nm* (*résident*) villager, village resident; (†: *campagnard*) countryman. **3 villageoise** *nf* villager, village resident; countrywoman.
ville [vil] **1** *nf* **(a)** (*cité, ses habitants*) town; (*plus importante*) city. **en ~, à la ~** in town, in the city; **aller en ~** to go into town; **habiter la ~** to live in a town *ou* city; **sa ~ d'attache était Genève** the town he had most links with was Geneva, Geneva was his home-base; *V* **centre, hôtel, sergent**[1].
(b) (*quartier*) **~ basse/haute** lower/upper (part of the) town; **vieille ~** old (part of) town; **~ arabe/européenne** Arab/European quarter.
(c) (*municipalité*) ≃ local authority, (town) council. **dépenses assumées par la ~** local authority spending *ou* expenditure.
(d) (*vie urbaine*) **la ~** city life, the city; **aimer la ~** to like city life *ou* the city; **les gens de la ~** townspeople *ou* folk, city folk; **vêtements de ~** town wear *ou* clothes.
2: ville champignon mushroom town; **ville d'eaux** spa (town); **la Ville éternelle** the Eternal City; **ville forte** fortified town; **la Ville lumière** the City of Light, Paris; **Ville sainte** Holy City; **ville satellite** satellite town.
villégiature [vileʒjatyʀ] *nf* **(a)** (*séjour*) holiday (*Brit*), vacation (*US*). **être en ~ quelque part** to be on holiday (*Brit*) *ou* vacation (*US*) *ou* to be holidaying (*Brit*) *ou* vacationing (*US*) somewhere; **aller en ~ quelque part/dans sa maison de campagne** to go for a holiday (*Brit*) *ou* vacation (*US*) *ou* to holiday (*Brit*) *ou* vacation (*US*) somewhere/in one's country house.
(b) (*lieu*) (holiday) resort.
villosité [vilozite] *nf* villosity.
vin [vɛ̃] *nm* **(a)** wine. **~ blanc/rouge/rosé** white/red/rosé wine; **~ mousseux/de liqueur/de coupage** sparkling/fortified/blended wine; **~ ordinaire** *ou* **de table/de messe** ordinary *ou* table/mass wine; **~ nouveau** new wine; **grand/petit ~** vintage/local wine; **~ chaud** mulled wine; **~ cuit** cooked wine; *V* **lie, quand** *etc.*
(b) (*réunion*) **~ d'honneur** reception (*where wine is served*).
(c) (*liqueur*) **~ de palme/de canne** palm/cane wine.
(d) (*loc*) **être entre deux ~s** to be tipsy; **avoir le ~ gai/triste/mauvais** to get happy/get depressed/turn nasty when one has had a drink *ou* after a few glasses (of wine *etc*).
vinaigre [vinɛgʀ(ə)] *nm* vinegar. **~ de vin/d'alcool** wine/spirit vinegar; (*fig*) **tourner au ~** to turn sour; *V* **mère, mouche.**
vinaigrer [vinegʀe] (1) *vt* to season with vinegar. **salade trop vinaigrée** salad with too much vinegar (on it).
vinaigrerie [vinɛgʀəʀi] *nf* (*fabrication*) vinegar-making; (*usine*) vinegar factory.
vinaigrette [vinɛgʀɛt] *nf* French dressing, vinaigrette, oil and vinegar dressing. **tomates (en** *ou* **à la) ~** tomatoes in French dressing *ou* in oil and vinegar dressing, tomatoes (in) vinaigrette.
vinaigrier [vinɛgʀije] *nm* **(a)** (*fabricant*) vinegar-maker; (*commerçant*) vinegar dealer. **(b)** (*flacon*) vinegar cruet *ou* bottle.
vinasse [vinas] *nf* (*péj*) plonk* (*Brit péj*), cheap wine; (*Tech*) vinasse.
Vincent [vɛ̃sɑ̃] *nm* Vincent.
vindicatif, -ive [vɛ̃dikatif, iv] *adj* vindictive.
vindicte [vɛ̃dikt(ə)] *nf* (*Jur*) **~ publique** prosecution and conviction; **désigner qn à la ~ publique** to expose sb to public condemnation.
vineux, -euse [vinø, øz] *adj* **(a)** *couleur, odeur, goût* win(e)y, of wine; *pêche* wine-flavoured, that tastes win(e)y; *haleine* wine-laden (*épith*), that smells of wine; *teint* (cherry-)red. **d'une couleur ~euse** wine-coloured, win(e)y-coloured, the colour of wine; **rouge ~** wine-red, win(e)y red.
(b) (*Tech*) full-bodied.
(c) (†: *riche en vin*) **coteaux ~** vine-covered hills; **une région ~euse** a rich wine-growing area.
vingt [vɛ̃] ([vɛ̃t] *en liaison et dans les nombres de 22 à 29*) **1** *adj inv, nm inv* twenty. **je te l'ai dit ~ fois** I've told you a hundred times; **il n'avait plus son cœur/ses jambes de ~ ans** he no longer had the legs/heart of a young man *ou* of a twenty-year-old; **~ dieux!** ye gods!; *pour autres loc V* **six, soixante.**
2: vingt-deux *adj inv, nm inv* twenty-two; **vingt-deux (voilà) les flics!‡** watch out! it's the fuzz!‡; **vingt-deux!*** watch out!; **vingt-quatre heures** twenty-four hours; **vingt-quatre heures sur vingt-quatre** round the clock, twenty-four hours a day.
vingtaine [vɛ̃tɛn] *nf*: **une ~** about twenty, twenty or so, (about) a score; **une ~ de personnes** (about) a score of people, twenty people or so, about twenty people; **un jeune homme d'une ~ d'années** a young man of around *ou* about twenty *ou* of twenty or so.
vingtième [vɛ̃tjɛm] **1** *adj* twentieth. **la ~ partie** the twentieth part; **au ~ siècle** in the twentieth century. **2** *nm* twentieth, twentieth part.
vingtièmement [vɛ̃tjɛmmɑ̃] *adv* in the twentieth place.
vinicole [vinikɔl] *adj industrie* wine (*épith*); *région* wine-growing (*épith*), wine-producing; *établissement* wine-making (*épith*).
vinifère [vinifɛʀ] *adj* viniferous.
vinification [vinifikɑsjɔ̃] *nf [raisin]* wine-making (process), wine production; *[sucres]* vinification.
vinifier [vinifje] (7) *vt moût* to convert into wine.
vinyle [vinil] *nm* vinyl.
vioc‡ [vjɔk] *nmf* = **vioque‡.**
viol [vjɔl] *nm [femme]* rape; *[temple]* violation, desecration.
violacé, e [vjɔlase] (*ptp de* **violacer**) **1** *adj* purplish, mauvish. **2 violacée** *nfpl* (*Bot*) **les ~es** the violaceae.
violacer [vjɔlase] (3) **1** *vt* to make *ou* turn purple *ou* mauve. **2 se violacer** *vpr* to turn *ou* become purple *ou* mauve, take on a purple hue (*littér*).
violateur, -trice [vjɔlatœʀ, tʀis] *nm,f* **(a)** (*profanateur*) *[tombeau]* violator, desecrator; *[lois]* transgressor. **(b)** (††) *[femme]* ravisher (*littér*).
violation [vjɔlɑsjɔ̃] *nf* (*V* **violer**) violation; breaking; transgression; infringement; desecration. (*Jur*) **~ de domicile** forcible entry (*into a person's home*); (*Jur*) **~ du secret professionnel** breach *ou* violation of professional secrecy; (*Jur*) **~ de sépulture** violation *ou* desecration of graves.
violâtre [vjɔlɑtʀ(ə)] *adj* purplish, mauvish.
viole [vjɔl] *nf* viol. **~ d'amour** viola d'amore; **~ de gambe** viola da gamba, bass viol.
violemment [vjɔlamɑ̃] *adv* violently.
violence [vjɔlɑ̃s] *nf* **(a)** (*U: V* **violent**) violence; pungency; fierceness; strenuousness; drastic nature.
(b) (*force brutale*) violence; (*acte*) violence (*U*), act of violence. **mouvement de ~** violent impulse; **répondre à la ~ par la ~** to meet violence with violence; **commettre des ~s contre qn** to commit acts of violence against sb; *V* **non.**
(c) (*contrainte*) violence, coercion. **avoir recours à la ~** to have recourse to violence *ou* coercion; **faire ~ à qn** to do violence to sb; **faire ~ à une femme**† to use a woman violently††; **se faire ~** to force o.s.; **faire ~ à** *texte, sentiments* to do violence to; *V* **doux.**
violent, e [vjɔlɑ̃, ɑ̃t] *adj* **(a)** (*gén*) violent; *odeur* pungent; *orage, vent* violent, fierce; *exercice, effort* violent, strenuous; *remède* drastic. **c'est un ~** he is a violent man; **~ besoin de s'affirmer** intense *ou* urgent need to assert o.s.; **saisi d'une peur ~e** seized by a violent *ou* rabid fear; *V* **mort**[1], **révolution. (b)** (*: *excessif*) **c'est un peu ~!** it's a bit much!*, that's going a bit far!*
violenter [vjɔlɑ̃te] (1) *vt* **(a)** *femme* to assault (sexually). **(b)** (*littér*) *texte, désir, inclination* to do violence to.
violer [vjɔle] (1) *vt* **(a)** *traité* to violate, break; *loi* to violate, transgress, break; *droit* to violate, infringe; *promesse* to break.
(b) *sépulture, temple* to violate, desecrate; *frontières, territoire* to violate. **~ le domicile de qn** to force an entry into sb's home.
(c) *consciences* to violate.
(d) *femme* to rape, ravish (†, *littér*), violate (*littér*).
violet, -ette [vjɔlɛ, ɛt] **1** *adj* purple, violet.
2 *nm* (*couleur*) purple. **le ~ lui va bien** purple suits him (well); **porter du ~** to wear purple; **peindre qch en ~** to paint sth purple; (*Peinture*) **un tube de ~** a tube of purple; **robe d'un ~ assez pâle** dress in a rather pale shade of purple *ou* violet, dress in (a) rather pale purple *ou* violet.
3 violette *nf* (*Bot*) violet. **~te odorante** sweet violet; **~te de Parme** Parma violet.
violine [vjɔlin] *adj* dark purple, deep purple.
violon [vjɔlɔ̃] *nm* **(a)** (*instrument d'orchestre*) violin, fiddle*; (*de violoneux*) fiddle; *V* **accorder.**
(b) (*musicien d'orchestre*) violin, fiddle*. **premier ~** *[orchestre]* leader; *[quatuor]* first violin *ou* fiddle*; **second ~** second violin *ou* fiddle*; *V* **vite.**
(c) (*: *prison*) lock-up*, jug‡, nick‡ (*Brit*). **au ~** in the lock-up* *ou* the jug‡ *ou* the nick‡ (*Brit*).
(d) ~ d'Ingres (artistic) hobby.
violoncelle [vjɔlɔ̃sɛl] *nm* cello, violoncello (*T*).
violoncelliste [vjɔlɔ̃selist(ə)] *nmf* cellist, cello-player, violoncellist (*T*).
violoneux [vjɔlɔnø] *nm* (*de village, péj*) fiddler.
violoniste [vjɔlɔnist(ə)] *nmf* violonist, violin-player, fiddler*.
vioque‡ [vjɔk] *nmf* (*père, mère*) **le ~** my *ou* the old man‡; **la ~** my *ou* the old woman‡ *ou* lady‡.
viorne [vjɔʀn(ə)] *nf* (*Bot*) viburnum.
vipère [vipɛʀ] *nf* adder, viper. **~ aspic** asp; **cette femme est une ~** that woman is a (real) viper; **elle a une langue de ~** she's got a viper's tongue *ou* a poisonous *ou* venomous tongue; *V* **nœud.**
vipereau, *pl* **~x** [vipʀo] *nm* young viper.
vipérin, e [vipeʀɛ̃, in] **1** *adj* (*Zool*) viperine. **2 vipérine** *nf* **(a)** (*Bot*) viper's bugloss. **(b)** (*Zool*) **(couleuvre) ~** viperine snake, grass snake.

virage [viʀaʒ] *nm* **(a)** (*action*) *[avion, véhicule, coureur]* turn. (*Aviat*) **faire un ~ sur l'aile** to bank; (*Aut*) **prendre un ~ sur les chapeaux de roues** to take a bend on two wheels *ou* on one's hub caps; **prendre un ~ à la corde** to hug the bend.

(b) (*Aut: tournant*) bend. **~ en épingle à cheveux** hairpin bend; **~ en S** S-bend; '**~ sur 3 km**' 'bends for 3 km'; **~ relevé** banked corner; **cette voiture prend bien les ~s** this car corners well, this car takes bends *ou* corners well; **il a pris son ~ trop vite** he went into *ou* took the bend too fast; **accélérer dans les ~s** to accelerate round the bends *ou* corners.

(c) (*fig*) change in policy *ou* direction. **le ~ européen du gouvernement britannique** the British government's change of policy *ou* direction over Europe, the change in the British government's European policy; **amorcer un ~ à droite** to take a turn to the right.

(d) (*transformation*) (*Chim*) *[papier de tournesol]* change in colour. (*Phot*) **~ à l'or/au cuivre** gold/copper toning; (*Méd*) **~ d'une cuti-réaction** positive reaction of a skin test.

virago [viʀago] *nf* virago.

viral, e, *mpl* **-aux** [viʀal, o] *adj* viral.

vire [viʀ] *nf* ledge (*on slope, rock face*).

virée [viʀe] *nf* (*en voiture*) drive, run, trip; (*de plusieurs jours*) trip; (*à pied*) walk; (*de plusieurs jours*) walking *ou* hiking tour; (*en vélo*) run, trip; (*de plusieurs jours*) trip; (*dans les cafés etc*) tour. **faire une ~** to go for a run (*ou* walk, drive *etc*); **faire une belle ~ (à vélo) dans la campagne** to go for a nice (bicycle) run in the country, go for a nice run *ou* trip in the country (on one's bicycle); **faire une ~ en voiture** to go for a drive, go for a run *ou* trip in the car; **cette ~ dans les cafés de la région s'est mal terminée** this tour of the cafés of the district had an unhappy ending.

virelai [viʀlɛ] *nm* (*Littérat*) virelay.

virement [viʀmɑ̃] *nm* **(a)** (*Fin*) **~ (bancaire)** credit transfer; **~ postal** ≃ (National) Giro transfer; **faire un ~ (d'un compte sur un autre)** to make a (credit) transfer (from one account to another); **~ budgétaire** reallocation of funds.

(b) (*Naut*) **~ de bord** tacking.

virer [viʀe] (1) **1** *vi* **(a)** (*changer de direction*) *[véhicule, avion, bateau]* to turn. (*Aviat*) **~ sur l'aile** to bank.

(b) (*Naut*) **~ de bord** to tack; **~ vent devant** to go about; **~ vent arrière** to wear; **~ sur ses amarres** to turn at anchor; **~ au cabestan** to heave at the capstan.

(c) (*tourner sur soi*) to turn round and round. (*littér*, †) **~ à tout vent** to be as changeable as a weathercock.

(d) (*changer de couleur, d'aspect*) *[couleur]* to turn, change; (*Phot*) *[épreuves]* to tone; (*Méd*) *[cuti-réaction]* to come up positive. **bleu qui vire au violet** blue which is turning purple, blue which is changing to purple; **~ à l'aigre** to turn sour.

2 *vt* **(a)** (*Fin*) to transfer (*à un compte* (in)to an account).

(b) (*) (*expulser*) to kick out*, chuck out*; (*renvoyer*) to sack, kick out*, chuck out*. **~ qn d'une réunion** to kick *ou* chuck sb out of a meeting*; **se faire ~** to get (o.s.) kicked out *ou* chucked out (of one's job)*, get the sack.

(c) (*Phot*) *épreuve* to tone. (*Méd*) **il a viré sa cuti(-réaction)*** he gave a positive skin test, his skin test came up positive; (*fig*) **~ sa cuti*** to throw off the fetters (*fig*).

vireux, -euse [viʀø, øz] *adj* (*littér*) noxious. **amanite ~euse** amanita virosa.

virevolte [viʀvɔlt(ə)] *nf* *[danseuse]* twirl; *[cheval]* demivolt; (*fig: volte-face*) about-turn, volte-face. **les ~s élégantes de la danseuse** the elegant twirling of the dancer.

virevolter [viʀvɔlte] (1) *vi* *[danseuse]* to twirl around; *[cheval]* to do a demivolt; (*fig littér*) to make a complete about-turn.

Virgile [viʀʒil] *nm* Virgil.

virginal, e, *mpl* **-aux** [viʀʒinal, o] **1** *adj* (*littér*) virginal, maidenly (*littér*). **blanc ~** virgin white. **2** *nm* virginal, virginals (*pl*).

Virginie [viʀʒini] *nf* Virginia.

virginité [viʀʒinite] *nf* **(a)** (*lit*) virginity, maidenhood (*littér*). **refaire une ~ à qn** to restore sb's image.

(b) (*fig littér*) *[neige, aube, âme]* purity. **il voulait rendre à ce lieu sa ~** he wished to give back to this place its untouched *ou* virgin quality.

virgule [viʀgyl] *nf* **(a)** (*de ponctuation*) comma. **mettre une ~** to put a comma; (*fig*) **sans y changer une ~** without changing a (single) thing, without touching a single comma; (*fig*) **moustaches en ~** curled moustache; *V* **point**[1].

(b) (*Math*) (decimal) point. **(arrondi à) 3 chiffres après la ~** (correct to) 3 decimal places; **5 ~ 2** (*5,2*) 5 point 2, 5·2; **~ flottante** floating decimal.

viril, e [viʀil] *adj attributs, apparence, formes* male, masculine; *attitude, courage, langage, traits* manly, virile; *prouesses, amant* virile. **force ~e** virile strength; *V* **âge, membre, toge.**

virilement [viʀilmɑ̃] *adv* in a manly *ou* virile way.

virilisant, e [viʀilizɑ̃, ɑ̃t] *adj médicament* that provokes male characteristics.

virilisation [viʀilizɑsjɔ̃] *nf* virilism.

viriliser [viʀilize] (1) *vt* (*Bio*) to give male characteristics to; (*en apparence*) *femme* to make appear mannish *ou* masculine; *homme* to make (appear) more manly *ou* masculine.

virilité [viʀilite] *nf* (*V* **viril**) masculinity; manliness; virility.

virole [viʀɔl] *nf* **(a)** (*bague*) ferrule. **(b)** (*Tech: moule*) collar (*mould*).

viroler [viʀɔle] (1) *vt* **(a)** *couteau, parapluie* to ferrule, fit with a ferrule. **(b)** (*Tech*) to place in a collar.

virtualité [viʀtɥalite] *nf* (*V* **virtuel**) potentiality; virtuality.

virtuel, -elle [viʀtɥɛl] *adj* (*gén*), *sens, revenu* potential; (*Philos, Phys*) virtual; *V* **image.**

virtuellement [viʀtɥɛlmɑ̃] *adv* **(a)** (*littér: en puissance*) potentially. **(b)** (*pratiquement*) virtually, to all intents and purposes. **c'était ~ fini** it was virtually over, to all intents and purposes it was over.

virtuose [viʀtɥoz] **1** *nmf* (*Mus*) virtuoso; (*fig: artiste*) master. **~ du violon** violin virtuoso; **~ de la plume** master of the pen, virtuosic writer; **~ du pinceau** master of the brush, virtuosic painter. **2** *adj* virtuoso.

virtuosité [viʀtɥozite] *nf* virtuosity. (*Mus*) **exercices de ~** exercises in virtuosity.

virulence [viʀylɑ̃s] *nf* virulence, viciousness. **critiquer avec ~** to criticize virulently *ou* viciously.

virulent, e [viʀylɑ̃, ɑ̃t] *adj* virulent, vicious.

virus [viʀys] *nm* (*lit*) virus. **~ de la rage** rabies virus; (*fig*) **le ~ de la danse/du jeu** the dancing/gambling bug.

vis[1] [vis] **1** *nf* **(a)** (*à bois etc*) screw. **~ à bois** wood screw; **~ à métaux** metal screw; **~ à tête plate/à tête ronde** flat-headed/round-headed screw; **~ à ailettes** wing nut; **il faudra donner un tour de ~** you'll have to give the screw a turn *ou* tighten the screw a little; *V* **pas**[1], **serrer.**

(b) **escalier à ~, ~**† spiral staircase.

2: vis d'Archimède Archimedes' screw; **vis sans fin** worm, endless screw; **vis micrométrique** micrometer screw; (*Aut*) **vis platinées** (contact) points; **vis de pressoir** press screw; **vis de serrage** binding *ou* clamping screw.

vis[2] [vi] *V* **vivre, voir.**

visa [viza] *nm* (*gén*) stamp; *[passeport]* visa. **~ de censure** (censor's) certificate; (*fig*) **~ pour ...** passport to ... .

visage [vizaʒ] **1** *nm* **(a)** (*figure, fig: expression, personne, aspect*) face. **au ~ pâle/joufflu** pale-/chubby-faced; **un ~ connu/ami** a known/friendly face; **je lui trouve bon ~** (to me) she is looking well; **sans ~** faceless; **le vrai ~ de ...** the true face of ... ; **un homme à deux ~s** a two-faced man; *V* **soin.**

(b) (*loc*) **agir/parler à ~ découvert** to act/speak openly; **elle changea de ~** her face *ou* expression changed; **faire bon ~** to put a good face on it; **faire bon ~ à qn** to put on a show of friendliness *ou* amiability (*frm*) for sb.

2: Visage pâle paleface.

visagiste [vizaʒist(ə)] *nmf* beautician.

vis-à-vis [vizavi] **1** *prép* **(a)** (*en face de*) **~ (de) la place** opposite *ou* vis-à-vis the square.

(b) (*comparé à*) **~ de** beside, vis-à-vis, next to; **mon savoir est nul ~ du sien** my knowledge is nothing next to *ou* beside *ou* vis-à-vis his.

(c) **~ de** (*envers*) towards, vis-à-vis; (*à l'égard de*) vis-à-vis; **être sincère ~ de soi-même** to be frank with oneself; **être méfiant ~ de la littérature** to be mistrustful towards literature; **j'en ai honte ~ de lui** I'm ashamed of it in front of *ou* before him.

2 *adv* (*face à face*) face to face. **leurs maisons se font ~** their houses are facing *ou* opposite each other.

3 *nm inv* **(a)** (*position*) **en ~** facing *ou* opposite each other; **des immeubles en ~** buildings facing *ou* opposite each other; **assis en ~** sitting facing *ou* opposite each other, sitting face to face.

(b) (*tête-à-tête*) encounter, meeting. **un ~ ennuyeux** a tiresome encounter *ou* meeting.

(c) (*personne faisant face*) person opposite; (*aux cartes: partenaire*) partner; (*homologue*) opposite number, counterpart.

(d) (*immeuble etc*) **immeuble sans ~** building with an open *ou* unimpeded outlook; **avoir une école pour ~** to have a school opposite, look out at *ou* on a school.

(e) (*canapé*) tête-à-tête.

viscéral, e, *mpl* **-aux** [viseʀal, o] *adj* **(a)** (*Anat*) visceral. **(b)** (*fig*) *haine, peur* deep-seated, deep-rooted.

viscère [visɛʀ] *nm* (*gén pl*) **~s** intestines, entrails, viscera (*T*).

viscosité [viskozite] *nf* *[liquide]* viscosity; *[surface gluante]* stickiness, viscosity.

visée [vize] *nf* **(a)** (*avec une arme*) taking aim (*U*), aiming (*U*); (*Arpentage*) sighting. **pour faciliter la ~, ce fusil comporte un dispositif spécial** to help you to (take) aim *ou* to help your aim, this rifle comes equipped with a special device; *V* **ligne**[1].

(b) (*gén pl: dessein*) aims, designs. **avoir des ~s sur qn/qch** to have designs on sb/sth.

viser[1] [vize] (1) **1** *vt* **(a)** *objectif* to aim at *ou* for; *cible* to aim at.

(b) (*ambitionner*) *effet* to aim at; *carrière* to aim at, set one's sights on.

(c) (*concerner*) *[mesure, remarque]* to be aimed at, be directed at. **être/se sentir visé** to feel one is being got at*.

(d) (:: *regarder*) to have a dekko: (*Brit*) at, take a look at. **vise un peu ça!** just have a dekko: (*Brit*) *ou* take a look at that!

2 *vi* **(a)** *[tireur]* to aim, take aim. **~ juste/trop haut/trop bas** to aim accurately/(too) high/(too) low; **~ à la tête/au cœur** to aim for the head/heart.

(b) (*fig: ambitionner*) **~ haut/plus haut** to set one's sights high/higher, aim high/higher.

3 viser à *vt indir* (*avoir pour but de*) **~ à qch/à faire** to aim at sth/at doing *ou* to do; **scène qui vise à provoquer le rire** scene which sets out to provoke *ou* which aims at provoking laughter; **mesures qui visent à la réunification de la majorité** measures which are aimed at reuniting *ou* which aim to reunite the majority.

viser[2] [vize] (1) *vt* (*Admin*) *passeport* to visa; *document* to stamp. **faire ~ un passeport** to have a passport visaed.

viseur [vizœʀ] *nm* **(a)** *[arme]* sights (*pl*); *[caméra]* viewfinder. **(b)** (*Astron: lunette*) telescopic sight.

visibilité [vizibilite] *nf* (*gén, Sci*) visibility. **bonne/mauvaise ~** good/bad visibility; **~ nulle** nil *ou* zero visibility; **ce pare-brise permet une très bonne ~** this windscreen gives excellent visibility; **sans ~** *pilotage, virage* blind (*épith*).

visible [vizibl(ə)] *adj* **(a)** (*lit*) visible.

(b) (*fig: évident, net*) *embarras, surprise* obvious, evident, visible; *amélioration, progrès* clear, visible, perceptible; *réparation, reprise* obvious. **son embarras était ~** his embarrassment was obvious *ou* evident *ou* visible, you could see his embarrassment *ou* that he was embarrassed; **il ne le veut pas, c'est ~** he doesn't want to, that's obvious *ou* apparent *ou* clear; **il est ~ que ...** it is obvious *ou* apparent *ou* clear that ... .

(c) (*en état de recevoir*) **Monsieur est-il ~?** is Mr X (*ou* Lord X *etc*) able to receive (visitors)?, is Mr X (*ou* Lord X *etc*) receiving (visitors)?; **elle n'est pas ~ le matin** she's not at home to visitors *ou* not in to visitors in the morning.

visiblement [viziblәmɑ̃] *adv* (a) (*manifestement*) obviously, clearly. **il était ~ inquiet** he was obviously *ou* clearly worried; **~, c'est une erreur** obviously *ou* clearly it's a mistake.

(b) (*rare: de façon perceptible à l'œil*) visibly, perceptibly.

visière [vizjɛʀ] *nf* (a) *[casquette plate, képi etc]* peak; (*pour le soleil, en celluloïd*) eyeshade. **mettre sa main en ~** to shade one's eyes with one's hand. (b) *[armure]* visor; *V* **rompre.**

vision [vizjɔ̃] *nf* (a) (*action de voir qch*) **la ~ de ce film l'avait bouleversé** seeing this film had really upset him; (*Ciné*) **première ~ européenne** first European showing, European première.

(b) (*faculté de percevoir*) (eye)sight, vision (*frm, T*); (*opération de la perception*) vision, sight. **une ~ défectueuse** defective (eye)sight *ou* vision; **le mécanisme de la ~** the mechanism of vision *ou* sight; **champ de ~** field of view *ou* vision; **pour faciliter la ~** to aid (eye)sight *ou* vision; **~ nette/floue** clear/hazy vision; **porter des lunettes pour la ~ de loin** to wear glasses for seeing distances *ou* for seeing at a distance.

(c) (*conception*) vision. **la ~ romantique de ce peintre** this painter's romantic vision.

(d) (*image, apparition, mirage*) vision. **tu as des ~s*** you're seeing things.

visionnaire [vizjɔnɛʀ] *adj, nmf* visionary.

visionner [vizjɔne] (1) *vt* to view.

visionneuse [vizjɔnøz] *nf* viewer (*for transparencies or film*).

visiophone [vizjɔfɔn] *nm* = **vidéophone.**

Visitation [vizitɑsjɔ̃] *nf*: **la ~** the Visitation.

visite [vizit] **1** *nf* (a) (*U: V* **visiter**) visiting; going round; examination, inspection; going over, searching; going through; calling on. (*à la prison, l'hôpital*) **heures/jour de ~** *ou* **des ~s** visiting hours/day; **la ~ (du château) a duré 2 heures** it took 2 hours to go round (the castle); *V* **droit**[3].

(b) (*tournée, inspection*) visit. **au programme il y a des ~s de musée** there are museum visits on the programme; **~ accompagnée** *ou* **guidée** guided tour; **ces ~s nocturnes au garde-manger** these nocturnal visits *ou* trips to the pantry; **il redoutait les ~s de l'inspecteur** he feared the inspector's visits.

(c) (*chez une connaissance etc*) visit. **une courte ~** a short visit, a call; **une ~ de politesse/de remerciements** a courtesy/thank you call *ou* visit; **être en ~ chez qn** to be paying sb a visit, be on a visit to sb; **rendre ~ à qn** to pay sb a visit, call on sb, visit sb; **je vais lui faire une petite ~, cela lui fera plaisir** I'm going to pay him a call *ou* a short visit *ou* I'm going to call on him – that will please him; **rendre à qn sa ~** to return sb's visit, pay sb a return visit; **avoir** *ou* **recevoir la ~ de qn** to have a visit from sb; *V* **carte.**

(d) (*visiteur*) visitor. **nous avons des ~s** we've got visitors *ou* company *ou* guests; **j'ai une ~ dans le salon** I have a visitor *ou* I have company in the lounge; **nous attendons de la ~** *ou* **des ~s** we are expecting visitors *ou* company *ou* guests; (*hum*) **tiens, nous avons de la ~*** hey, we've got company *ou* guests*.

(e) (*officielle*) *[chef d'État]* visit. **en ~ officielle dans les pays de l'Est** on an official visit to the countries of the east.

(f) (*médicale*) **~ (à domicile)** (house)call, visit; **~ de contrôle** follow-up visit; **la ~** (*chez le médecin*) (medical) consultations (*pl*); (*Mil*) (*quotidienne*) sick parade; (*d'entrée*) medicals (*pl*), medical examinations (*pl*); **aller à la ~** to go to the surgery (for a consultation); **l'heure de la ~** surgery hours (*pl*); (*Mil*) **passer la ~** (*d'entrée*) to have one's medical.

(g) (*Comm*) visit, call; (*d'expert*) inspection. **j'ai reçu la ~ d'un représentant** I received a visit *ou* call from a representative, a representative called (on me).

2: (*Rel*) **visite du diocèse = visite épiscopale**; (*Jur*) **visite domiciliaire** house search, domiciliary visit (*frm*); **visite de douane** customs inspection *ou* examination; (*Rel*) **visite épiscopale** pastoral visitation.

visiter [vizite] (1) *vt* (a) (*en touriste, curieux*) *pays, ville* to visit; *château, musée* to go round, visit. **~ une maison** (*à vendre*) to go over *ou* view a house, look a house over, look over a house; **il me fit ~ son appartement/laboratoire** he showed me round his flat/laboratory; **il nous a fait ~ la maison que nous envisagions d'acheter** he showed us round *ou* over the house we were thinking of buying.

(b) (*en cherchant qch*) *bagages* to examine, inspect; *boutiques* to go over, search; *recoins* to search (in), examine; *armoire* to go through, search (in); (*Admin*) *navire* to inspect; (*hum*) *coffre-fort* to visit (*hum*), pay a visit to (*hum*).

(c) (*par charité*) *malades, prisonniers* to visit.

(d) *[médecin, représentant, inspecteur]* to visit, call on.

(e) (*Rel*) to visit.

(f) (*rare: fréquenter*) *voisins, connaissances* to visit, call on.

visiteur, -euse [vizitœʀ, øz] **1** *nm,f* (*gén: touriste, à l'hôpital*) visitor. (*représentant*) **~ en bonneterie/pharmacie** millinery/pharmaceutical *ou* drugs representative *ou* rep*; *V* **infirmière.**

2: **visiteur des douanes** customs inspector; **visiteur médical** medical representative *ou* rep*.

vison [vizɔ̃] *nm* (*animal, fourrure*) mink; (*manteau*) mink (coat).

visonnière [vizɔnjɛʀ] *nf* (*Can*) mink farm, minkery (*Can*).

visqueux, -euse [viskø, øz] *adj* (a) *liquide* viscous, thick; *pâte* sticky, viscous; (*péj*) *surface, objet* sticky, goo(e)y*, viscous.

(b) (*fig péj*) *personne, manière* smarmy, slimy.

vissage [visaʒ] *nm* screwing (on *ou* down).

visser [vise] (1) *vt* (a) (*au moyen de vis*) *plaque, serrure* to screw on; *couvercle* to screw down *ou* on. **ce n'est pas bien vissé** it's not screwed down *ou* up properly; **~ un objet sur qch** to screw an object on to sth; (*fig*) **rester vissé sur sa chaise** to be *ou* sit glued to one's chair; (*fig*) **rester vissé devant qn** to be rooted to the spot before sb.

(b) (*en tournant*) *couvercle, bouchon, écrou* to screw on. **ce couvercle se visse** this is a screw-on lid, this lid screws on; **ce n'est pas bien vissé** *[bouchon]* it's not screwed on *ou* down properly; *[écrou]* it's not screwed down *ou* up properly.

(c) (*Sport: donner de l'effet à*) *balle* to put a spin on.

(d) (*‡: surveiller*) *élève, employé* to keep a tight rein on, crack down on*. **depuis la fugue du petit Marcel, ils les vissent** ever since little Marcel ran off they keep a tight rein on them *ou* they have really cracked down on them*.

visu [vizy] *adv*: **de ~** with one's own eyes; **s'assurer de qch de ~** to check sth with one's own eyes *ou* for oneself.

visualisation [vizɥalizɑsjɔ̃] *nf* (*V* **visualiser**) visualization; making visual.

visualiser [vizɥalize] (1) *vt* (*Tech: par fluorescence etc*) *courant de particules etc* to make visible, visualize; (*audio-visuel*) *concept, idée* to make visual.

visuel, -elle [vizɥɛl] *adj* (*gén*) visual. **troubles ~s** eye trouble (*U*); **cet écrivain est un ~** this author favours visual techniques, visual images predominate in the writings of this author; *V* **audio-, champ.**

visuellement [vizɥɛlmɑ̃] *adv* visually.

vit [vi] *V* **vivre, voir.**

vital, e, mpl -aux [vital, o] *adj* (*Bio, gén*) vital; *V* **centre, espace, minimum.**

vitalisme [vitalism(ә)] *nm* (*Philos*) vitalism.

vitalité [vitalite] *nf [personne]* energy, vitality; *[institution, terme]* vitality. **il est plein de ~** he's full of energy *ou* go* *ou* vitality; **la ~ de ces enfants est incroyable** the energy of these children is unbelievable.

vitamine [vitamin] *nf* vitamin; *V* **carence.**

vitaminé, e [vitamine] *adj* with added vitamins.

vitaminique [vitaminik] *adj* vitamin (*épith*).

vite [vit] **1** *adv* (a) (*à vive allure*) *rouler, marcher* fast, quickly; *progresser, avancer* quickly, rapidly, swiftly.

(b) (*rapidement*) *travailler, se dérouler, se passer* quickly, fast; (*en hâte*) *faire un travail* quickly, in a rush *ou* hurry. **ça s'est passé si ~, je n'ai rien vu** it happened so quickly *ou* fast I didn't see a thing; **il travaille ~ et bien** he works quickly *ou* fast and well; **c'est trop ~ fait** it was done too quickly *ou* in too much of a rush *ou* hurry; **inutile d'essayer de faire cela ~: ce sera du mauvais travail** there's no point in trying to do that quickly *ou* in a hurry *ou* rush — it will just be a bad piece of work; **c'est ~ fait** it doesn't take long, it doesn't take a moment *ou* a second; **ça ne va pas ~** it's slow work; **fais ~!** be quick about it!, look sharp!*; **le temps passe ~** time flies; (*fig*) **aller ~ en besogne*** to be a fast worker*, not to waste any time (getting down to it)*; **aller plus ~ que les violons** *ou* **la musique** to jump the gun; *V* **aller.**

(c) (*sous peu, tôt*) soon, in no time. **on a ~ fait de dire que ...** it's easy to say that ...; **il eut ~ fait de découvrir que...** he soon *ou* quickly discovered that ..., in no time he discovered that ...; **ce sera ~ fait** it won't take long, it won't take a moment *ou* a second; **elle sera ~ arrivée/guérie** she'll soon be here/better, she'll be here/better in no time.

(d) (*sans délai: toute de suite*) quick. **lève-toi ~!** get up quick!; **va ~ voir!** go and see quick!; **au plus ~** as quick as possible; **faites-moi ça, et ~!** do this for me and be quick about it; **eh, pas si ~!** hey, not so fast!, hey, hold on (a minute)!; **~! un médecin** quick! a doctor; **et plus ~ que ça!** and get a move on!*, and be quick about it!; **là il (y) va un peu ~** he's being a bit hasty.

2 *adj* (*style journalistique: Sport*) fast.

vitesse [vitɛs] **1** *nf* (a) (*promptitude, hâte*) speed, quickness, rapidity. **surpris de la ~ avec laquelle ils ont fait ce travail/répondu** surprised at the speed *ou* quickness *ou* rapidity with which they did this piece of work/replied; **en ~** (*rapidement*) quickly; (*en hâte*) in a hurry *ou* rush; **faites-moi ça en ~** do this for me quickly; **faites-moi ça, et en ~!** do this for me and be quick about it!; **on va prendre un verre en ~** we'll go for a quick drink; **écrire un petit mot en ~** to scribble a hasty note; **j'ai préparé le déjeuner/cette conférence un peu en ~** I prepared lunch/this lecture in a bit of a hurry *ou* rush; **à toute ~, en quatrième ~** at full *ou* top speed; **(à la nouvelle) il est arrivé en quatrième ~** *ou* **à toute ~** (on hearing the news) he came like a shot.

(b) *[véhicule, projectile, courant, processus]* speed. **aimer la ~** to love speed; **à la ~ de 60 km/h** at (a speed of) 60 km/h; **à quelle ~ allait-il, quelle ~ faisait-il?** what speed was he going at? *ou* doing?; **faire de la ~** to go *ou* drive fast; **faire une ~ (moyenne) de 60** to do an average (speed) of 60; **prendre de la ~** to gather *ou* increase speed, pick up speed; **gagner** *ou* **prendre qn de ~** (*lit*) to beat sb, outstrip sb; (*fig*) to beat sb to it, pip sb at the post*; **~ acquise moyenne/maximale** average/maximum speed; **~ de propagation/de réaction/de rotation** speed of propagation/reaction/rotation; *V* **course, excès, perte.**

(c) (*Rail*) **grande/petite ~** fast/slow goods service; **expédier un colis en petite ~** to send a parcel by slow goods service; **expédier un colis en grande ~** to express a parcel, send a parcel express *ou* by fast goods service.

(d) (*Aut*) gear. **changer de ~** to change gear; **en 2e/4e ~** in

2nd/4th gear; **passer les ~s** to go *ou* run through the gears; *V* **boîte.**

2: vitesse acquise momentum; **vitesse de croisière** cruising speed; **vitesse initiale** muzzle velocity; **vitesse de libération** escape velocity *ou* speed; **vitesse de pointe** maximum *ou* top speed; **vitesse du son** speed of sound; **vitesse de sustentation** minimum flying speed.

viticole [vitikɔl] *adj industrie* wine (*épith*); *région, établissement* wine-growing (*épith*), wine-producing. **culture ~** wine growing, viticulture (*T*).

viticulteur [vitikyltœʀ] *nm* wine grower, viticulturist (*T*).

viticulture [vitikyltyʀ] *nf* wine growing, viticulture (*T*).

vitrage [vitʀaʒ] *nm* **(a)** (*U: V* **vitrer**) glazing. **(b)** (*vitres*) windows (*pl*); (*cloison*) glass partition; (*toit*) glass roof. **(c)** (*rideau*) net curtain; (*tissu*) net curtaining.

vitrail, *pl* -aux [vitʀaj, o] *nm* stained-glass window. **l'art du ~, le ~** the art of stained-glass window making.

vitre [vitʀ(ə)] *nf* **(a)** *[fenêtre, vitrine]* (window) pane, pane (of glass); *[voiture]* window. **poser/mastiquer une ~** to put in/putty a window pane *ou* a pane of glass; **verre à ~** window glass; **laver les ~s** to wash the windows; **appuyer son front à la ~** to press one's forehead against the window (pane); **les camions font trembler les ~s** the lorries make the window panes *ou* the windows rattle; **casser une ~** to break a window (pane).

(b) (*fenêtre*) **~s** windows; **fermer les ~s** to close the windows.

vitré, e [vitʀe] (*ptp de* **vitrer**) *adj* **(a)** *porte, cloison* glass (*épith*); *V* **baie. (b)** (*Anat*) **corps ~** vitreous body; **humeur ~e** vitreous humour.

vitrer [vitʀe] (1) *vt fenêtre* to glaze, put glass in; *véranda, porte* to put windows in, put glass in.

vitrerie [vitʀəʀi] *nf* (*activité*) glaziery, glazing; (*marchandise*) glass.

vitreux, -euse [vitʀø, øz] *adj* **(a)** (*Anat*) *humeur* vitreous. **(b)** (*Géol*) vitreous; *V* **porcelaine. (c)** (*péj: terne, glauque*) *yeux* glassy, dull; *regard* glassy, glazed, lacklustre (*épith*); *surface, eau* dull.

vitrier [vitʀije] *nm* glazier.

vitrification [vitʀifikɑsjɔ̃] *nf* (*V* **vitrifier**) vitrification; glazing.

vitrifier [vitʀifje] (7) **1** *vt* (*par fusion*) to vitrify; (*par enduit*) to glaze, put a glaze on. (*fig*) **les couloirs de neige vitrifiés par le gel** the snow gullies that the frost had made like glass. **2 se vitrifier** *vpr* to vitrify.

vitrine [vitʀin] *nf* **(a)** (*devanture*) (shop) window. **en ~** in the window; **la ~ du boucher/de la pâtisserie** the butcher's/cake shop window; **faire les ~s** to dress the windows; **~ publicitaire** display case, showcase; *V* **lécher.**

(b) (*armoire*) (*chez soi*) display cabinet; (*au musée etc*) showcase, display cabinet.

vitriol [vitʀijɔl] *nm* (*Hist Chim*) vitriol. **huile de ~** oil of vitriol; (*fig*) **une critique/un style au ~** a vitriolic review/style; († *fig*) **un alcool au ~, du ~** firewater.

vitriolage [vitʀijɔlaʒ] *nm* (*Tech*) vitriolization.

vitrioler [vitʀijɔle] (1) *vt* **(a)** (*Tech*) to vitriolize, treat with vitriol *ou* (concentrated) sulphuric acid. **(b)** *victime d'agression* to throw vitriol at.

vitupération [vitypeʀɑsjɔ̃] *nf* (*propos*) **~s** rantings and ravings, vituperations (*frm*).

vitupérer [vitypeʀe] (6) **1** *vi* to rant and rave. **~ contre qn/qch** to rail against sb/sth, rant and rave about sb/sth. **2** *vt* (*littér*) to vituperate, revile.

vivable [vivabl(ə)] *adj* **(a)** (*) *personne* livable-with*. **il n'est pas ~** he's not livable-with*, he's impossible to live with. **(b)** *milieu, monde* fit to live in. **cette maison n'est pas ~** this house is not fit to live in.

vivace¹ [vivas] *adj* **(a)** *arbre* hardy. **plante ~** (hardy) perennial. **(b)** *préjugé* inveterate, indestructible; *haine* indestructible, inveterate, undying; *foi* steadfast, undying.

vivace² [vivatʃe] *adv, adj* (*Mus*) vivace.

vivacité [vivasite] *nf* **(a)** (*vie: V* **vif**) liveliness, vivacity; briskness; sharpness, quickness; keenness. **~ d'esprit** quick-wittedness; **avoir de la ~** to be lively *ou* vivacious.

(b) (*brusquerie*) sharpness, brusqueness. **~ d'humeur** brusqueness, quick-temperedness.

(c) (*caractère tranché, mordant: V* **vif**) brightness, brilliance; vividness; bitterness; sharpness; keenness.

(d) (*littér: intensité: V* **vif**) keenness, intensity; vividness.

vivandière [vivɑ̃djɛʀ] *nf* (*Hist*) vivandière.

vivant, e [vivɑ̃, ɑ̃t] **1** *adj* **(a)** (*en vie*) living, alive (*attrib*), live (*épith*). **né ~** born alive; **il est encore ~** he's still alive *ou* living; **il n'en sortira pas ~** he won't come out of it alive; **expériences sur des animaux ~s** experiments on live *ou* living animals, live animal experiments; (*fig*) **c'est un cadavre/squelette ~** he's a living corpse/skeleton.

(b) (*plein de vie*) *regard, visage, enfant* lively; *ville, quartier, rue* lively, full of life (*attrib*); *portrait* lifelike, true to life (*attrib*); *dialogue, récit, film* lively; (*fig*) *personnage* lifelike.

(c) (*doué de vie*) *matière, organisme* living; *V* **être.**

(d) (*constitué par des êtres vivants*) *machine, témoignage, preuve* living. **c'est le portrait ~ de sa mère** he's the (living) image of his mother; *V* **tableau.**

(e) (*en usage*) *expression, croyance, influence* living. **une expression encore très ~e** an expression which is still very much alive; *V* **langue.**

(f) (*Rel*) **le pain ~** the bread of life; **le Dieu ~** the living God.

2 *nm* **(a)** (*personne*) (*Rel*) **les ~s** the living; **les ~s et les morts** (*gén*) the living and the dead; (*Rel*) the quick and the dead (*Bible*); **rayer qn du nombre des ~s** to strike sb's name from the number of the living; *V* **bon¹.**

(b) (*vie*) **du ~ de qn: de son ~** in his lifetime, while he was alive; **du ~ de ma mère, mon père ne buvait pas beaucoup** in my mother's lifetime *ou* while my mother was alive, my father didn't drink much.

vivarium [vivaʀjɔm] *nm* vivarium.

vivat [viva] *nm* (*gén pl*) **~s** cheers.

vive² [viv] **1** *V* **vif, vivre. 2** *excl:* **~ le roi/la France/l'amour!** long live the king/France/love!; **~(nt) les vacances/la mariée!** three cheers for *ou* hurrah for the holidays/the bride.

vivement [vivmɑ̃] *adv* **(a)** (*avec brusquerie*) sharply, brusquely.

(b) (*beaucoup*) *regretter* deeply, greatly; *désirer* keenly, greatly; *affecter, ressentir, intéresser* deeply, keenly. **s'intéresser ~ à** to take a keen *ou* deep interest in, be keenly *ou* deeply interested in.

(c) (*avec éclat*) *colorer* brilliantly, vividly; *briller* brightly, brilliantly.

(d) (*littér: rapidement*) *agir, se mouvoir* in a lively manner.

(e) (*marque un souhait*) **~ les vacances!** roll on the holidays!* (*Brit*); **~ que ce soit fini!** I'll be glad when it's all over!, roll on the end!* (*Brit*).

viveur [vivœʀ] *nm* high liver, pleasure-seeker.

vivier [vivje] *nm* (*étang*) fishpond; (*réservoir*) fish-tank.

vivifiant, e [vivifjɑ̃, ɑ̃t] *adj air, brise* invigorating, enlivening, bracing; *joie, ambiance* invigorating, enlivening, vivifying; *V* **grâce.**

vivifier [vivifje] (7) *vt* **(a)** *personne* to invigorate, enliven; *sang, plante* to invigorate; (*fig littér*) *âme* to vitalize, quicken (*littér*); *race* to vitalize, give life to.

(b) (*Rel, littér*) *[foi, force]* to give life, quicken (*Rel, littér*). **l'esprit vivifie** the spirit gives life.

vivipare [vivipaʀ] *adj* viviparous. **~s** vivipara.

viviparité [vivipaʀite] *nf* viviparity.

vivisection [vivisɛksjɔ̃] *nf* vivisection.

vivoter [vivɔte] (1) *vi [personne]* to rub *ou* get along (somehow); *[affaire]* to struggle along.

vivre [vivʀ(ə)] (46) **1** *vi* **(a)** (*être vivant*) to live, be alive. **il n'a vécu que quelques jours** he lived only a few days; **je ne savais pas qu'il vivait encore** I did not know he was still alive *ou* living; **quand l'ambulance est arrivée, il vivait encore** he was still alive when the ambulance arrived; **quand elle arriva, il avait cessé de ~** he was dead when she arrived; **~ vieux** to live to a ripe old age, live to a great age; **il vivra centenaire** he'll live to be a hundred; **le peu de temps qu'il lui reste à ~** the little time he has left (to live); **le colonialisme a vécu** colonialism is a thing of the past; **ce manteau a vécu*** this coat is finished *ou* has had its day; **il fait bon ~** it's good to be alive, it's a good life; *V* **âme, qui.**

(b) (*habiter, passer sa vie*) to live. **~ à Londres/en France** to live in London/in France; **~ avec qn** to live with sb; **~ dans le passé/dans ses livres/dans la crainte** to live in the past/in one's books/in fear; **se laisser ~** to take life as it comes.

(c) (*exister, se comporter*) to live. **~ bien** to live well, have a good life; **~ saintement** to lead a saintly life, live like a saint; **se laisser ~** to live for the day; **être facile/difficile à ~** to be easy/difficult to live with *ou* to get on with; **ces gens-là savent ~** those people (really) know how to live; **c'est un homme qui a beaucoup vécu** he's a man who has seen a lot of life; (*fig*) **elle ne vit plus depuis que son fils est pilote** she lives on her nerves since her son became a pilot; **il ne vit que pour sa famille** he lives only for his family; **ils vivent ensemble/comme mari et femme** they live together/as man and wife; *V* **art, joie, savoir.**

(d) (*subsister*) to live (*de* on). **~ de laitages/de son traitement/de rentes** to live on dairy produce/one's salary/one's (private) income; (*Bible*) **l'homme ne vit pas seulement de pain** man shall not live by bread alone; **~ au jour le jour** to live from day to day *ou* from hand to mouth; **~ largement** to live well; **avoir (juste) de quoi ~** to have (just) enough to live on; **travailler/écrire pour ~** to work/write for a living; **faire ~ qn** to provide (a living) for sb, support sb; **~ de l'air du temps** to live on air; **~ d'amour et d'eau fraîche** to live on love alone; **il faut bien ~!** a man (*ou* woman) has got to live!, you have to live!; *V* **crochet.**

(e) (*fig*) *[portrait, idée, rue, paysage]* to be alive. **un portrait qui vit** a lifelike portrait, a portrait which seems alive; **sa gloire vivra longtemps** his glory will live on *ou* will endure; **les plantes et les roches vivent comme les hommes** plants and rocks are alive *ou* have a life of their own — just like men.

2 *vt* **(a)** (*passer*) to live, spend. **~ des jours heureux/des heures joyeuses** to live through *ou* spend happy days/hours; **il vivait un beau roman d'amour** his life was a love story come true; **la vie ne vaut pas la peine d'être vécue** life is not worth living.

(b) (*être mêlé à*) *événement, guerre* to live through. **nous vivons des temps troublés** we are living in *ou* through troubled times; **le pays vit une période de crise** the country is going through a period of crisis.

(c) (*éprouver intensément*) **~ sa vie** to live one's own life; **~ sa foi/son art** to live out one's faith/one's art; **~ l'instant/le présent** to live for the moment/the present; **~ son époque intensément** to be intensely involved in the period one lives in.

3 *nm* (*littér*) **le ~ et le couvert** bed and board; **le ~ et le logement** board and lodging; **~s** supplies, provisions; *V* **couper.**

vivrier, -ière [vivʀije, ijɛʀ] *adj* (*rare*) food-producing (*épith*).

vizir [viziʀ] *nm* vizier.

v'là [vla] *prép* (*abrév de* **voilà**) **~ le facteur** here's the postman.

vlan, v'lan [vlɑ̃] *excl* wham!, bang! **et ~! dans la figure** smack *ou* slap-bang in the face; **et ~! il est parti en claquant la porte** wham! *ou* bang! he slammed the door and left.

vocable [vɔkabl(ə)] *nm* **(a)** (*mot*) term. **(b)** (*Rel*) **église sous le ~ de saint Pierre** church dedicated to St Peter.

vocabulaire [vɔkabylɛʀ] *nm* **(a)** (*dictionnaire*) vocabulary, word list. **~ français-anglais** French-English vocabulary; **~ de la photographie** dictionary *ou* lexicon of photographic terms.
(b) (*d'un individu, d'un groupe; terminologie*) vocabulary. **enrichir son ~** to enrich one's vocabulary; **il avait un ~ exact** he had a very precise vocabulary; **quel ~!** what language!; **~ technique/médical** technical/medical vocabulary.

vocal, e, *mpl* -aux [vɔkal, o] *adj organe, musique* vocal; *V* **corde**.

vocalement [vɔkalmɑ̃] *adv* vocally.

vocalique [vɔkalik] *adj* vowel (*épith*), vocalic.

vocalisation [vɔkalizɑsjɔ̃] *nf* (*Ling*) vocalization; (*Mus*) singing exercise.

vocalise [vɔkaliz] *nf* singing exercise. **faire des ~s** to practise (one's) singing exercises.

vocaliser [vɔkalize] (1) **1** *vt* (*Ling*) to vocalize. **2** *vi* (*Mus*) to practise (one's) singing exercises. **3 se vocaliser** *vpr* (*Ling*) to become vocalized.

vocalisme [vɔkalism(ə)] *nm* (*Ling*) (*théorie*) vocalism; (*système vocalique*) vowel system; *[mot]* vowel pattern.

vocatif [vɔkatif] *nm* vocative (case).

vocation [vɔkɑsjɔ̃] *nf* **(a)** (*Rel*) vocation, calling, call; (*pour un métier, une activité*) vocation, calling. **~ contrariée** frustrated vocation; **avoir/ne pas avoir la ~** to have/lack a vocation, have/not have a calling for it; **avoir la ~ de l'enseignement/du théâtre** to be cut out to be a teacher *ou* for teaching/for acting *ou* the theatre; **~ artistique** artistic calling; **rater sa ~** to miss one's vocation; (*hum*) **il a la ~** it's a real vocation for him.
(b) (*destin*) vocation, calling. **la ~ maternelle de la femme** woman's maternal vocation *ou* calling; **la ~ industrielle du Japon** the industrial calling of Japan.
(c) (*Admin*) **avoir ~ à *ou* pour** to have authority to.

vocifération [vɔsifeʀɑsjɔ̃] *nf* cry of rage, vociferation.

vociférer [vɔsifeʀe] (6) **1** *vi* to utter cries of rage, vociferate. **~ contre qn** to shout angrily at sb, scream at sb. **2** *vt insulte, ordre* to shout (out), scream. **~ des injures** to hurl abuse, shout (out) *ou* scream insults.

vodka [vɔdka] *nf* vodka.

vœu, *pl* ~x [vø] *nm* **(a)** (*Rel, gén: promesse*) vow. **faire (le) ~ de faire** to vow to do, make a vow to do; **~x de religion** religious vows; **~x de célibat** vows of celibacy; **~ de chasteté** vow of chastity; **faire ~ de pauvreté** to take a vow of poverty.
(b) (*gén, Pol: souhait*) wish. **faire un ~** to make a wish; **nous formons des ~x pour votre santé** we send our good wishes for your recovery; **l'assemblée a émis le ~ que ...** the assembly expressed the wish *ou* its desire that ...; **je fais le ~ qu'il me pardonne** I pray (that) he may forgive me.
(c) (*formule épistolaire*) **~x** best wishes; **tous nos ~x (de bonheur)** all good wishes *ou* every good wish for your happiness; **(nos) meilleurs ~x pour Noël et la nouvelle année** (our) best wishes for Christmas and the New Year.

vogue [vɔg] *nf* **(a)** (*popularité*) fashion, vogue. **connaître une ~ extraordinaire** to be extremely fashionable *ou* popular, be tremendously in vogue; **être en ~** to be in fashion *ou* vogue, be fashionable; **la ~ de la mini-jupe est en baisse** miniskirts are going out of fashion, the fashion *ou* vogue for miniskirts is on the way out; **c'est la grande ~ maintenant** it's all the rage now.
(b) (*dial: foire*) fair.

voguer [vɔge] (1) *vi* (*littér*) *[embarcation, vaisseau spatial]* to sail; (*fig*) *[pensées]* to drift, wander. **nous voguions vers l'Amérique** we were sailing towards America; **l'embarcation voguait au fil de l'eau** the boat was drifting *ou* floating along on *ou* with the current; (*fig*) **nous voguons, frêles esquifs, au gré du hasard** we drift (along), frail vessels on the waters of fate (*littér*); (*hum*) **vogue la galère!** come what may!

voici [vwasi] *prép* **(a)** (*pour désigner: s'opposant à voilà*) here is, here are, this is, these are. **~ mon bureau et voilà le vôtre** here is *ou* this is my office and there is *ou* that is yours; **~ mon frère et voilà sa femme** this is *ou* here is my brother and there is *ou* that is his wife.
(b) (*pour désigner: même valeur que voilà*) here is, here are, this is, these are. **~ mon frère** this is my brother; **~ le livre que vous cherchiez** here's the book you were looking for; **l'homme/la maison que ~** this (particular) man/house; **M Dupont, que ~** M Dupont here; **il m'a raconté l'histoire que ~** he told me the following story.
(c) (*pour annoncer, introduire*) here is, here are, this is, these are. **~ le printemps/la pluie** here comes spring/the rain; **~ la fin de l'hiver** the end of winter is here; **me/nous/le *etc* ~** here I am/we are/he is *etc*; **les ~ prêts à partir** they're ready to leave, that's them ready to leave*; **nous ~ arrivés** here we are, we've arrived; **le ~ qui se plaint encore** there he goes, complaining again, that's him complaining again*; **me ~ à me ronger les sangs pendant que lui ...** (*au présent*) here am I *ou* here's me* in a terrible state while he ...; (*au passé*) there was I *ou* there was me* in a terrible state while he ...; **vous voulez des preuves, en ~** you want proof, well here you are then; **nous y ~** (*lieu*) here we are; (*question délicate etc*) now we're getting there *ou* near it *ou* near the truth; **~ qui va vous surprendre** here's something that'll surprise you; **~ qu'il se met à pleuvoir maintenant** and now it's starting to rain; **~ ce que je compte faire** this is what I'm hoping to do; **~ ce qu'il m'a dit/ce dont il s'agit** this is what he told me/what it's all about; **~ comment il faut faire** this is how it's done; **~ pourquoi je l'ai fait** this *ou* that was why I did it; **~ pourquoi je l'avais supprimé** that was why I'd eliminated it; **~ que tombe la nuit** night is falling, it is getting dark.
(d) (*il y a*) **~ 5 ans que je ne l'ai pas vu** it's 5 years (now) since I last saw him, I haven't seen him for the past 5 years; **il est parti ~ une heure** he left an hour ago, it's an hour since he left; **~ bientôt 20 ans que nous sommes mariés** it'll soon be 20 years since we got married, we'll have been married 20 years soon.

voie [vwa] **1** *nf* **(a)** (*route, chemin*) way; (*Admin: route*) road; (*moyen de transport*) route. (*Hist*) **~ romaine/sacrée** Roman/sacred way; **par la ~ des airs** by air; **emprunter la ~ maritime** to go by sea, use the sea route; **~s de communication** communication routes; **~s navigables** waterways; **~ sans issue** no through road, cul-de-sac; **~ privée** private road.
(b) (*partie d'une route*) lane. **'travaux — passage à ~ unique'** 'roadworks — single-lane traffic'; **route à ~ unique** single-lane road, single-track road; **route à 3/4 ~s** 3-/4-lane road.
(c) (*Rail*) track, (railway) line. **ligne à ~ unique/à 2 ~s** single-/double-track line; **ligne à ~ étroite** narrow-gauge line; **on répare les ~s** the line *ou* track is under repair; **~ montante/descendante** up/down line; **le train est annoncé sur la ~ 2** the train will arrive at platform 2.
(d) (*Anat*) **~s digestives/respiratoires/urinaires** digestive/respiratory/urinary tract; **par ~ buccale *ou* orale** orally.
(e) (*fig*) way. **la ~ du bien/mal** the path of good/evil; **la ~ de l'honneur** the honourable course; **entrer dans la ~ des aveux** to make a confession; **ouvrir/tracer/montrer la ~** to open up/mark out/show the way; **préparer la ~ à qn/qch** to prepare *ou* pave the way for sb/sth; **continuez sur cette ~** continue in this way; **il est sur la bonne ~** he's on the right track; **l'affaire est en bonne ~** the matter is shaping *ou* going well; **mettre qn sur la ~** to put sb on the right track; **trouver sa ~** to find one's way (in life); **la ~ est libre** the way is clear *ou* open.
(f) (*filière, moyen*) **par des ~s détournées** by devious *ou* roundabout means; **par la ~ hiérarchique/diplomatique** through official/diplomatic channels; **par ~ de conséquence** in consequence, as a result.
(g) en ~ de: en ~ de réorganisation in the process of reorganization, undergoing reorganization; **en ~ d'exécution** in (the) process of being carried out, being carried out; **pays en ~ de développement** developing country; **en ~ de guérison** getting better, regaining one's health; **en ~ de cicatrisation** (well) on the way to healing over; **en ~ d'achèvement** (well) on the way to completion, nearing completion, being completed; **il est en ~ de perdre sa situation** he is on the way to losing his job, he's heading for dismissal.
2: voie d'accès acces road; **voie de dégagement urbain** urban relief road; **les voies de Dieu, les voies divines** the ways of God *ou* Providence; **les voies de Dieu sont insondables** the ways of God are unfathomable; **voie d'eau** leak; (*Jur*) **voies de fait** assault (*U*); **se livrer à des voies de fait sur qn** to assault sb, commit an assault on sb; (*Rail*) **voie ferrée** railway line; (*Rail*) **voie de garage** siding; (*fig*) **mettre sur une voie de garage** *affaire* to shelve; *personne* to shunt to one side; **la voie lactée** the Milky Way; (*Admin*) **voies et moyens** ways and means; **voie de passage** major route; **les voies de la Providence = les voies de Dieu**; (*Admin*) **la voie publique** the public highway; **voie de raccordement** slip road; (*Admin*) **voie vicinale** local road.

voilà [vwala] **1** *prép* **(a)** (*pour désigner: s'opposant à voici*) there is, there are, that is, those are. **voici mon bureau et ~ le vôtre** here's *ou* this is my office and there's *ou* and that's yours; **voici mon frère et ~ sa femme** this is *ou* here is my brother and that is *ou* there is his wife.
(b) (*pour désigner: même valeur que voici*) there is, there are, that is, those are. **~ mon frère** this is *ou* here is my brother; **~ le livre que vous cherchiez** there's *ou* here's the book you were looking for; **l'homme/la maison que ~** that man/house (there); **M Dupont que ~** M Dupont there; **il m'a raconté l'histoire que ~** he told me the following story.
(c) (*pour annoncer, introduire*) there is, there are, that is, those are. **~ le printemps/la pluie** here comes spring/the rain; **~ la fin de l'hiver** the end of winter is here; **le ~, c'est lui** there he is, that's him; **le ~ prêt à partir** he's ready to leave, that's him ready to leave*; **le ~ que se plaint encore** there he goes, complaining again, that's him complaining again*; **me ~ à me ronger les sangs pendant que lui ...** (*au présent*) there am I *ou* here's me* in a terrible state while he ...; (*au passé*) there was I *ou* there was me* in a terrible state while he ...; **~ ce que je compte faire** this is what I'm hoping to do; **~ ce qu'il m'a dit/ce dont il s'agit** that's *ou* this is what he told me/what it's all about; **~ comment il faut faire** that's how it's done; **~ pourquoi je l'ai fait** that's why I did it; **~ que tombe la nuit** night is falling, it's getting dark; **~ qu'il se met à pleuvoir maintenant** and now it's starting to rain; **~ où je veux en venir** that's what I'm getting at, that's my point; **nous y ~** (*lieu*) here we are; (*question délicate etc*) now, we're getting there *ou* near it *ou* near the truth.
(d) (*pour résumer*) **... et ~ pourquoi je n'ai pas pu le faire** and that's why *ou* that's the reason I wasn't able to do it; **~ ce qui fait que c'est impossible** that's what makes it impossible; **~ qui est louche** that's a bit odd *ou* suspicious; **~ qui s'appelle parler** that's what I call talking, that's something like talking*.
(e) (*il y a*) **~ une heure que je l'attends** I've been waiting for him for an hour now, that's a whole hour I've been waiting for him now; **~ 5 ans que je ne l'ai pas vu** it's 5 years since I last saw him, I haven't seen him for the past 5 years; **il est parti ~ une heure** he left an hour ago, it's an hour since he left; **~ bientôt 20 ans que nous sommes mariés** it'll soon be 20 years since we got married, we'll have been married 20 years soon.
(f) (*loc*) **en ~ une histoire/blague!** what a story/joke!, that's some story/joke!*; **en ~ un imbécile!** there's an idiot for you!, what a fool!; **en ~ assez!** that's enough!, that'll do!; **veux-tu de l'argent? — en ~** do you want some money? — here's some *ou* here you are; **vous voulez des preuves, en ~** you want proof, well here you are then; **~ le hic** that's the snag *ou* catch, there's *ou* that's the hitch; **~ tout** that's all; **et ~ tout** and that's all

there is to it *ou* all there is to say, and that's the top and bottom of it*; ~ **bien les Français!** how like the French!, isn't that just like the French!, that's the French all over!*; **(et) ne ~-t-il pas qu'il s'avise de se déshabiller** lo and behold, he suddenly decides to get undressed!, I'm blest if he doesn't suddenly decide to get undressed!; **nous ~ frais!** now we're in a mess! *ou* a nice pickle!*, that's a fine mess *ou* pickle we're in!*

2 *excl*: **~! j'arrive!** here I come!, there — I'm coming!; **ah! ~! je comprends!** oh, (so) that's it, I understand!, oh, I SEE!; **je n'ai pas pu le faire, et ~!** I couldn't do it and that's all there was to it! *ou* so there!*; **~, je m'appelle M Dupont et je suis votre nouvel instituteur** right (then), my name is M Dupont and I'm your new teacher.

voilage [vwalaʒ] *nm* (*rideau*) net curtain; (*tissu*) net (*U*), veiling (*U*); *[chapeau, vêtement]* gauze (*U*), veiling (*U*).

voile[1] [vwal] *nf* **(a)** *[bateau]* sail. **~ carrée/latine** square/lateen sail; **faire ~ vers** to sail towards; **mettre à la ~** to make way under sail; (*lit*) **(mettre) toutes ~s dehors** to crowd *ou* cram on all sail; (* *fig*) **mettre les ~s** to clear off‡, push off‡.

(b) (*gén littér: embarcation*) sail (*inv: littér*), vessel.

(c) (*navigation, sport*) sailing. **faire de la ~** to sail, go sailing; **demain on va faire de la ~** we're going sailing tomorrow.

voile[2] [vwal] *nm* **(a)** (*gén: coiffure, vêtement*) veil. **~ de deuil** (mourning) veil; **les musulmanes portent le ~** Moslem women wear the veil; (*Rel*) **prendre le ~** to take the veil.

(b) *[statue, plaque commémorative]* veil.

(c) (*tissu*) net (*U*). **~ de coton/de tergal ®** cotton/Terylene ® net.

(d) (*fig: qui cache*) veil. **le ~ de l'oubli** the veil of oblivion; **sous le ~ de la franchise** under the veil *ou* a pretence of candour; **jeter/tirer un ~ sur qch** to cast/draw a veil over sth; **lever le ~ de** to unveil, lift the veil from; **enlever un coin du ~** to lift a corner of the veil.

(e) (*fig: qui rend flou*) **~ de brume** veil of mist, veiling mist; **un ~ de cheveux blonds** a fringe of fair hair; **avoir un ~ devant les yeux** to have a film before one's eyes.

(f) (*Phot*) fog (*U*).

(g) (*Méd*) **~ au poumon** shadow on the lung; **le ~ noir/gris/rouge/des aviateurs** blackout/greyout/redout.

(h) (*Anat*) **~ du palais** soft palate, velum.

(i) (*Bot*) *[champignon]* veil.

voilé, e[1] [vwale] (*ptp de* **voiler[1]**) *adj* **(a)** *femme, statue* veiled.

(b) *termes, allusion, sens* veiled. **il fit une allusion peu ~e à** he made a broad hint *ou* a thinly veiled hint at.

(c) (*flou*) *lumière, ciel* hazy; *éclat* dimmed; *regard* misty; *contour* hazy, misty; *photo* fogged. **les yeux ~s de larmes** his eyes misty *ou* misted (over) *ou* blurred with tears; **sa voix était un peu ~e** his voice was slightly husky *ou* veiled.

voilé, e[2] [vwale] (*ptp de* **voiler[2]**) *adj* (*tordu*) *roue* buckled; *planche* warped.

voilement [vwalmɑ̃] *nm* (*Tech*) *[roue]* buckle; *[planche]* warp.

voiler[1] [vwale] (1) **1** *vt* (*lit, fig: littér*) to veil. **les larmes voilaient ses yeux** tears dimmed his eyes, his eyes were misty with tears; **un brouillard voilait les sommets** the peaks were veiled by *ou* shrouded in fog.

2 se voiler *vpr* **(a) se ~ le visage** *[musulmane]* to wear a veil; (*fig*) **se ~ la face** to hide one's face, look away, avert one's gaze.

(b) (*devenir flou*) *[horizon, soleil]* to mist over; *[ciel]* to grow hazy *ou* misty; *[regard, yeux]* to mist over, become glazed; *[voix]* to become husky *ou* veiled.

voiler[2] [vwale] (1) **1 se voiler** *vpr [roue]* to buckle; *[planche]* to warp. **2** *vt* to buckle; to warp.

voilerie [vwalʀi] *nf* sail-loft.

voilette [vwalɛt] *nf* (hat) veil.

voilier [valje] *nm* **(a)** (*navire à voiles*) sailing ship; (*de plaisance*) sailing boat. **(b)** (*métier*) sail maker. **(c)** (*Zool*) long-flight bird.

voilure[1] [vwalyʀ] *nf* **(a)** *[bateau]* sails. **réduire la ~** to shorten sail; **une ~ de 1,000m²** $1,000m^2$ of sail. **(b)** *[planeur]* aerofoils.

(c) *[parachute]* canopy.

voilure[2] [vwalyʀ] *nf* = **voilement.**

voir [vwaʀ] (30) **1** *vt* **(a)** to see. **je l'ai vu de mes yeux** I saw it with my own eyes; **on n'y voit rien** you can't see a thing; **~ double** (*être ivre*) to see double; **c'est un film à ~** it's a film worth seeing; **il a vu du pays** he has seen the world; **nous les avons vus sauter** we saw them jump; **on a vu le voleur entrer** the thief was seen entering; **j'ai vu bâtir ces maisons** I saw these houses being built; **il faut le ~ pour le croire** it has to be seen to be believed; **as-tu jamais vu pareille impolitesse?** have you ever seen *ou* did you ever see such rudeness?; **je voudrais la ~ travailler avec plus d'enthousiasme** I'd like to see her work more enthusiastically; **je voudrais t'y ~!** I'd like to see how you'd do it!, I'd like to see you try!; **je l'ai vu naître!** I've known him since he was born *ou* since he was a baby; **le pays qui l'a vu naître** the land of his birth, his native country; **il a vu deux guerres** he has lived through *ou* seen two wars; **cette maison a vu bien des drames** this house has known *ou* seen many a drama.

(b) (*imaginer, se représenter*) to see, imagine. **je ne le vois pas** *ou* **je le vois mal habitant la banlieue** I (somehow) can't see *ou* imagine him living in the suburbs; **nous ne voyons pas qu'il ait de quoi s'inquiéter** we can't see that he has any reason for worrying; **ne ~ que par qn** to see only *ou* see everything through sb's eyes; **je le/me verrais bien dans ce rôle** I could just see him/myself in this role; **elle se voyait déjà célèbre** she imagined herself already famous; **voyez-vous une solution?** can you see a solution?; **il ne s'est pas vu mourir** death took him unawares; **~ la vie en rose** to look at life through rose-coloured glasses, take a rosy view of life; **~ les choses en noir** to take a black view of things; **~ loin** to see ahead; **~ le problème sous un autre jour** to see *ou* view the problem in a different light; **je ne vois pas comment ils auraient pu gagner** I don't see how they could have won; **je ne vois pas d'inconvénient** I can't see any drawback; **on n'en voit pas le bout** *ou* **la fin** there seems to be no end to it.

(c) (*examiner, étudier*) *problème, dossier* to look at; *leçon* to go over; *circulaire* to see, read. **il faudra ~ la question de plus près** we'll have to look at *ou* into the question more closely, the question requires closer examination; **il faut** *ou* **il faudra ~** we'll have to see; **je verrai (ce que je dois faire)** I'll have to see, I'll think about it *ou* think what to do; **il a encore 3 malades à ~** he still has 3 patients to see.

(d) (*juger, concevoir*) to see. **c'est à vous de ~ s'il est compétent** it's up to you to see *ou* decide whether he is competent; **voici comment on peut ~ les choses** you can look at things this way; **se faire mal ~ (de qn)** to be frowned on (by sb); **se faire bien ~ (de qn)** to (try to) make o.s. popular (with sb); **nous ne voyons pas le problème de la même façon** we don't see *ou* view the problem in the same way; **façon de ~** view of things, outlook; **il a vu petit/grand** he planned things on a small/grand *ou* big scale, he thought small/big*; **ne ~ aucun mal à** to see no harm in; **ne ~ que son intérêt** to consider only one's own interest.

(e) (*découvrir, constater*) to see, find (out). **aller ~ s'il y a quelqu'un** to go and see *ou* go and find out if there is anybody there; **vous verrez que ce n'est pas leur faute** you will see *ou* find that they are not to blame; **il ne fera plus cette erreur — c'est à ~** he won't make the same mistake again — that remains to be seen; **nous allons bien ~!** we'll soon find out!, we'll see soon enough!; **voyez si elle accepte** see if she'll agree; **des meubles comme on en voit dans tous les appartements bourgeois** the sort of furniture you find in any middle-class home.

(f) (*recevoir, rendre visite à*) *médecin, avocat* to see. **il voit le directeur ce soir** he is seeing the manager tonight; **on ne vous voit plus!** we never see you these days, you've become quite a stranger; **nous essayerons de nous ~ à Londres** we shall try to see each other *ou* to meet in London; **le ministre doit ~ les délégués** the minister is to see *ou* meet the delegates; **ils se voient beaucoup** they see a lot of each other; **passez me ~ quand vous serez à Paris** look me up *ou* call in and see me (*Brit*) when you're in Paris; **aller ~** *docteur, avocat* to go and see; *connaissance* to go and see, call on, visit; **aller ~ qn à l'hôpital** to visit sb *ou* go and see sb in hospital.

(g) (*faire l'expérience de*) **il en a vu (de dures** *ou* **de toutes les couleurs** *ou* **des vertes et des pas mûres*)** he has been through the mill *ou* through it, he has taken some hard knocks; **en faire ~ (de dures** *ou* **de toutes les couleurs) à qn** to give sb a hard time, lead sb a merry dance; **j'en ai vu d'autres!** I've been through *ou* seen worse!; **a-t-on jamais vu ça?, on n'a jamais vu ça!** did you ever see *ou* hear the like?; **on aura tout vu!** I've seen everything now!; **vous n'avez encore rien vu!** you haven't seen anything yet!

(h) (*comprendre*) to see. **il ne voit pas ce que vous voulez dire** he doesn't see *ou* grasp what you mean; **elle ne voyait pas le côté drôle de l'aventure** she could not see *ou* appreciate the funny side of what happened; **vous aurez du mal à lui faire ~ que ...** you will find it difficult to make him see *ou* realize that ... ; **je ne vois pas comment il a pu oublier** I don't see how he could forget; **~ clair dans un problème/une affaire** to have a clear understanding of a problem/matter, grasp a problem/matter clearly.

(i) (*avec faire, laisser, pouvoir*) **laisser ~** (*révéler*) to show, reveal; **il a bien laissé ~ sa déception** he couldn't help showing his disappointment *ou* making his disappointment plain; **faire ~** (*montrer*) to show; **faites-moi ~ ce dessin** let me see *ou* show me this picture; **elle ne peut pas le ~*** she can't stand (the sight of) him.

(j) ~ venir to wait and see; **~ venir (les événements)** to wait and see (what happens); **on t'a vu venir*** they saw you coming!*; **je te vois venir*** I can see what you're leading up to *ou* getting at*.

(k) (*loc*) **tu vois, vois-tu, voyez-vous** you see; **voyons** let's see now; **tu vois ça d'ici** you can just imagine; **un peu de charité, voyons!** come (on) now, let's be charitable; **mais voyons, il n'a jamais dit cela!** come, come, he never said that; **dites ~, vous connaissez la nouvelle?** tell me, have you heard the news?; **dis-moi ~** tell me; **essaie ~!*** just try it and see!, just you try it!; **regarde ~ ce qu'il a fait*** just look what he has done!; **histoire de ~, pour ~** just to see; (*menace*) **essaie un peu, pour ~!** just you try!; **son travail est fait (il) faut ~ (comme)!‡** you should just see the state of the work he has done!; **c'est tout vu** that's all there is to it, that's the top and bottom of it*; **qu'il aille se faire ~!‡** he can go to hell!‡; **il ferait beau ~ qu'il ...** it would be a fine thing if he ... ; **va ~ ailleurs si j'y suis‡** get lost‡; **allez donc ~ si c'est vrai!** just try and find out if it's true!; **je n'ai rien à ~ dans cette affaire** this matter has nothing to do with me *ou* is no concern of mine; **cela n'a rien à ~ avec ...** this has got nothing to do with ... ; **n'y ~ que du feu** to be completely hoodwinked *ou* taken in*; **~ trente-six chandelles** to see stars; **ne pas ~ plus loin que le bout de son nez** to see no further than the end of one's nose; **je l'ai vu comme je vous vois** I saw him as plainly as I see you now.

2 voir à *vt indir* (*littér: veiller à*) **nous verrons à vous contenter** we shall do our best *ou* our utmost to please you; **il faudra ~ à ce qu'il obéisse** we must see *ou* make sure that he obeys; **voyez à être à l'heure** see that you are on time *ou* are prompt; (*menace*) **il faudrait ~ à ne pas nous ennuyer** you had better make sure not to *ou* better not cause us any trouble.

3 se voir *vpr* **(a)** (*se trouver*) **se ~ forcé de** to find o.s. forced to; je me vois dans la triste obligation de sadly, I find myself obliged to; se ~ soudain dans la misère to find o.s. suddenly in poverty.

(b) (*être visible, évident*) *[tache, couleur, sentiments]* to show. cette reprise/tache ne se voit pas this alteration/stain doesn't show; cela se voit! that's obvious!

(c) (*se produire*) cela se voit tous les jours it happens every day, it's an everyday occurrence; cela ne s'est jamais vu! it's unheard of!; une attitude qui ne se voit que trop fréquemment an all-too-common attitude; des attitudes/préjugés qui se voient encore chez ... attitudes/prejudices which are still commonplace *ou* encountered in ... .

(d) (*simple fonction passive*) ils se sont vu interdire l'accès du musée they found themselves refused admission to the museum; ces outils se sont vus relégués au grenier these tools have been put away in the attic.

voire [vwaʀ] *adv* (a) (*frm: et même*) indeed, nay (†, *littér*). (b) (†, *hum: j'en doute*) indeed? (†, *hum*).

voirie [vwaʀi] *nf* (a) (*enlèvement des ordures*) refuse collection; (*dépotoir*) refuse dump. (b) (*entretien des routes etc*) highway maintenance; (*service administratif*) highways department; (*voie publique*) (public) highways.

voisé, e [vwaze] *adj* (*Phonétique*) voiced.

voisement [vwazmɑ̃] *nm* (*Phonétique*) voicing.

voisin, e [vwazɛ̃, in] 1 *adj* (a) (*proche*) neighbouring; (*le plus proche, adjacent*) next. les maisons/rues ~es the neighbouring houses/streets; il habite la maison/rue ~e he lives in the next house/street; 2 maisons ~es (*l'une de l'autre*) 2 adjoining houses, 2 houses next to each other; une maison ~e de l'église a house next to *ou* adjoining the church; les pays ~s de la Suisse the countries bordering on *ou* adjoining Switzerland; les années ~es de 1870 the years around 1870.

(b) (*fig*) *idées, espèces, cas* connected. ~ de akin to, related to; un animal ~ du chat an animal akin to *ou* related to the cat; dans un état ~ de la folie in a state bordering on *ou* akin to madness.

2 *nm,f* (a) (*gén: personne; fig: état*) neighbour. nos ~s d'à-côté our next-door neighbours; nos ~s de palier our neighbours across the landing; un de mes ~s de table one of the people next to me at table, one of my neighbours at table; je demandai à mon ~ de me passer le sel I asked the person (sitting) next to me *ou* my neighbour to pass me the salt; (*en classe*) qui est ta ~e cette année? who is sitting next to you this year?; mon voisin de dortoir/de salle the person in the next bed to mine (in the dormitory/ward).

(b) (*rare fig: prochain*) fellow (*rare*).

voisinage [vwazinaʒ] *nm* (a) (*voisins*) neighbourhood. ameuter tout le ~ to rouse the whole neighbourhood; être connu de tout le ~ to be known throughout the neighbourhood.

(b) (*relations*) être en bon ~ avec qn, entretenir des relations de bon ~ avec qn to be on neighbourly terms with sb.

(c) (*environs*) vicinity. les villages du ~ the villages in the vicinity, the villages round about; se trouver dans le ~ to be in the vicinity.

(d) (*proximité*) proximity, closeness. le ~ de la montagne the proximity *ou* closeness of the mountains; il n'était pas enchanté du ~ de cette usine he wasn't very happy at having the factory so close *ou* on his doorstep; le ~ du printemps the closeness *ou* nearness of spring.

(e) (*Math*) *[point]* neighbourhood.

voisiner [vwazine] (1) *vi* (*être près de*) ~ avec qch to be (placed) side by side with sth.

voiture [vwatyʀ] 1 *nf* (a) (*automobile*) (motor)car. ~ de location hired *ou* rented car; ~ de sport sportscar; ~ de tourisme saloon, private car.

(b) (*wagon*) carriage, coach. ~ de tête/queue front/back carriage *ou* coach; ~-restaurant dining car; en ~! all aboard!

(c) (*véhicule attelé, poussé*) (*pour marchandises*) cart; (*pour voyageurs*) carriage, coach; *V* petit.

2: voiture à bras handcart; voiture cellulaire prison van; voiture d'enfant pram, perambulator (*frm*); voiture d'infirme invalid carriage; voiture pie ≈ panda car (*Brit*); (*Hist*) voiture de poste mail coach, stagecoach; voiture des quatre saisons costermonger's barrow.

voiturée† [vwatyʀe] *nf* *[choses]* cartload; *[personnes]* carriageful, coachload.

voiturer [vwatyʀe] (1) *vt* (†, *hum*) (*sur un chariot*) to wheel in; (*: *en voiture*) to take in the car.

voiturette [vwatyʀɛt] *nf* (*d'infirme*) carriage; (*petite auto*) little *ou* small car.

voiturier [vwatyʀje] *nm* (†, *Jur*) carrier, carter.

voix [vwa] *nf* (a) voice. à ~ basse/haute in a low *ou* hushed/loud voice; ils parlaient à ~ basse they were talking in hushed *ou* low voices *ou* in undertones; ~ de crécelle/de fausset rasping/falsetto voice; d'une ~ blanche in a toneless *ou* flat voice; à haute et intelligible ~ loud and clear; avoir de la ~ to have a good (singing) voice; être *ou* rester sans ~ to be speechless; de la ~ et du geste by word and gesture, with words and gestures; une ~ lui cria de monter a voice shouted to him to come up; donner de la ~ (*aboyer*) to bay, give tongue; (*: *crier*) to bawl*; la ~ des violons the voice of the violins; *V* élever, gros, portée[2] *etc.*

(b) (*conseil, avertissement*) ~ de la conscience/raison voice of conscience/reason; se fier à la ~ d'un ami to rely on *ou* trust to a friend's advice; la ~ du sang the ties of blood, the call of the blood; c'est la ~ du sang qui parle he must heed the call of his blood.

(c) (*opinion*) voice; (*Pol: suffrage*) vote. la ~ du peuple the voice of the people, vox populi; avoir ~ consultative to have consultative powers *ou* a consultative voice; donner sa ~ à un candidat to give a candidate one's vote, vote for a candidate; avoir ~ au chapitre to have a say in the matter.

(d) (*Mus*) voice. chanter à 2/3 ~ to sing in 2/3 parts; fugue à 3 ~ fugue in 3 voices; ~ de basse/ténor bass/tenor (voice); chanter d'une ~ fausse/juste to sing out of tune/in tune; ~ de tête/de poitrine head/chest voice; être/ne pas être en ~ to be/not to be in good voice; la ~ humaine/céleste de l'orgue the vox humana/voix céleste on the organ.

(e) (*Ling*) voice.

vol[1] [vɔl] 1 *nm* (a) *[oiseau, avion]* (*gén*) flight. (*Zool*) ~ ramé/plané flapping/gliding flight; (*Aviat*) ~ d'essai/de nuit trial/night flight; il y a 8 heures de ~ entre ... it's an 8-hour flight between ... ; heures/conditions de ~ flying hours/conditions; *V* haut, ravitaillement.

(b) (*Zool: formation*) flock, flight. un ~ de perdrix a covey *ou* flock of partridges; un ~ de moucherons a cloud of gnats.

(c) (*loc*) en (plein) ~ in (full) flight; prendre son ~ to take wing, fly off *ou* away; au ~: attraper au ~ *autobus* to leap onto as it moves off; *ballon, objet lancé* to catch as it flies past; saisir une occasion au ~ to leap at *ou* seize an opportunity; saisir *ou* cueillir une remarque/une impression au ~ to catch a chance *ou* passing remark/impression; à ~ d'oiseau as the crow flies; tirer un oiseau au ~ to shoot (at) a bird on the wing.

2: vol sur aile delta, vol libre hang-gliding; vol à voile gliding.

vol[2] [vɔl] 1 *nm* (*délit*) theft. (*Jur*) ~ simple/qualifié common/aggravated *ou* compound theft; ~s de voiture car thefts; (*fig*) c'est du ~! it's daylight robbery!; (*fig*) c'est du ~ organisé it's a racket.

2: (*Jur*) vol domestique *theft committed by an employee*; (*Jur*) vol avec effraction robbery *ou* theft with breaking and entering; vol à l'étalage shoplifting (*U*); (*Jur*) vol à main armée armed robbery; vol à la tire pickpocketing (*U*).

volage [vɔlaʒ] *adj* *époux, cœur* flighty, fickle, inconstant.

volaille [vɔlɑj] *nf* (*Culin, Zool*) une ~ a fowl; la ~ poultry; les ~s cancanaient dans la basse-cour the poultry *ou* fowls were cackling in the farmyard; ~ rôtie roast poultry (*U*) *ou* fowl (*U*).

volailler [vɔlɑje] *nm* poulterer.

volant[1] [vɔlɑ̃] 1 *nm* (a) (*Aut*) steering wheel. prendre le ~, se mettre au ~ to take the wheel; un brusque coup de ~ a sharp turn of the wheel; as du ~ crack *ou* ace driver.

(b) (*Tech: roue*) (*régulateur*) flywheel; (*de commande*) (hand)wheel.

(c) *[rideau, robe]* flounce. jupe à ~s flounced skirt, skirt with flounces.

(d) (*objet lancé*) shuttlecock; (*jeu*) battledore and shuttlecock.

(e) *[carnet à souches]* tear-off portion.

2: volant magnétique magneto; volant de sécurité safeguard.

volant[2], **e** [vɔlɑ̃, ɑ̃t] *adj* (a) (*gén, Aviat: qui vole*) flying. (*Aviat*) le personnel ~, les ~s the flight *ou* flying staff; *V* poisson, soucoupe, tapis *etc.*

(b) (*littér: fugace*) *ombre, forme* fleeting.

(c) (*mobile, transportable*) *pont, camp, personnel* flying; *V* feuille.

volatil, e[1] [vɔlatil] *adj* (*Chim*) volatile; (*fig littér*) evanescent, ephemeral; *V* alcali.

volatile[2] [vɔlatil] *nm* (*gén hum*) (*volaille*) fowl; (*tout oiseau*) winged *ou* feathered creature.

volatilisable [vɔlatilizabl(ə)] *adj* volatilizable.

volatiliser [vɔlatilize] (1) 1 *vt* (*Chim*) to volatilize; (*fig*) to extinguish, obliterate. 2 **se volatiliser** *vpr* (*Chim*) to volatilize; (*fig*) to vanish (into thin air).

volatilité [vɔlatilite] *nf* volatility.

vol-au-vent [vɔlovɑ̃] *nm inv* vol-au-vent.

volcan [vɔlkɑ̃] *nm* (a) (*Géog*) volcano. ~ en activité/éteint active/extinct volcano. (b) (*fig*) (*personne*) spitfire; (*situation*) powder keg.

volcanique [vɔlkanik] *adj* (*lit, fig*) volcanic.

volcanisme [vɔlkanism(ə)] *nm* volcanism.

volcanologie [vɔlkanɔlɔʒi] *nf* (*littér*) vulcanology.

volcanologue [vɔlkanɔlɔg] *nmf* vulcanologist.

volée [vɔle] *nf* (a) *[oiseaux]* (*envol, distance*) flight. (*groupe*) une ~ de moineaux/corbeaux a flock *ou* flight of sparrows/crows; (*fig*) une ~ d'enfants a swarm of children; prendre sa ~ (*lit*) to take wing, fly off *ou* away; (*fig: s'affranchir*) to spread one's wings; *V* haut.

(b) (*décharge, tir*) ~ de flèches flight *ou* volley of arrows; ~ d'obus volley of shells.

(c) (*suite de coups*) volley. une ~ de coups a volley of blows; une ~ de coups de bâton a volley *ou* flurry of blows; administrer/recevoir une bonne ~ to give/get a sound thrashing *ou* beating.

(d) (*Ftbl, Tennis*) volley. de ~ on the volley; *V* demi-.

(e) ~ d'escalier flight of stairs.

(f) (*loc*) à la ~: jeter qch à la ~ to fling sth about; semer à la ~ to sow broadcast, broadcast; attraper la balle à la ~ to catch the ball in mid air; saisir une allusion à la ~ to pick up a passing allusion; à la ~, à toute ~ *gifler, lancer* vigorously, with full force; les cloches sonnaient à toute ~ the bells were pealing out; il referma la porte/fenêtre à la ~ *ou* à toute ~ he slammed the door/window shut.

voler[1] [vɔle] (1) *vi* (a) *[oiseau, avion, pilote]* to fly. vouloir ~ avant d'avoir des ailes to want to run before one can walk; ~ de ses propres ailes to stand on one's own two feet, fend for o.s.; *V* entendre.

(b) (*fig*) *[flèche, pierres, insultes]* to fly. ~ en éclats to fly into pieces; ~ au vent *[neige, voile, feuille]* to fly in the wind, float on the wind; ~ de bouche en bouche *[nouvelles]* to fly from mouth to mouth.

(c) (*s'élancer*) ~ **vers qn/dans les bras de qn** to fly to sb/into sb's arms; ~ **au secours de qn** to fly to sb's assistance.

(d) (*littér: passer, aller très vite*) *[temps]* to fly; *[embarcation, véhicule]* to fly (along). **son cheval volait/semblait** ~ his horse flew (along)/seemed to fly (along).

voler² [vɔle] (1) *vt* **(a)** ~ **de l'argent/une idée** *etc* **à qn** to steal money/an idea *etc* from sb; ~ **par nécessité** to steal out of necessity; **se faire** ~ **ses bagages** to have one's luggage stolen; (*fig*) **il ne l'a pas volé!** he asked for it!; *V* **qui.**

(b) ~ **qn** (*dérober son argent*) to rob sb; ~ **les clients** to rob *ou* cheat customers; ~ **les clients sur le poids/la quantité** to cheat customers over (the) weight/quantity, give customers short measure; ~ **qn lors d'un partage** to cheat sb when sharing out; **se sentir volé** (*spectacle interrompu etc*) to feel cheated *ou* robbed; **on n'est pas volé*** you get your money's worth all right*.

volet [vɔlɛ] *nm* **(a)** *[fenêtre, hublot]* shutter.

(b) (*Aviat*) flap. ~ **d'intrados/de freinage** split/brake flap; ~ **de courbure** *[parachute]* flap.

(c) (*Aut: panneau articulé*) bonnet flap; (*Tech*) *[roue à aube]* paddle. ~ **de carburateur** throttle valve, butterfly valve.

(d) *[triptyque]* volet, wing; *[feuillet, carte]* section; *V* **trier.**

voleter [vɔlte] (4) *vi [oiseau]* to flutter about, flit about; *[rubans, flocons]* to flutter.

voleur, -euse [vɔlœʀ, øz] **1** *adj personne* thieving (*épith*); *commerçant* swindling (*épith*), dishonest. ~ **comme une pie** thievish as a magpie.

2 *nm,f* (*malfaiteur*) thief; (*escroc, fig: qui exploite le client etc*) swindler. ~ **de grand chemin** highwayman; ~ **à l'étalage** shoplifter; ~ **à la tire†** pickpocket; ~ **d'enfants†** kidnapper; **au** ~! stop thief!

volière [vɔljɛʀ] *nf* (*cage*) aviary. (*fig*) **ce bureau est une** ~ this office is a proper henhouse* (*hum*).

volige [vɔliʒ] *nf* lath.

volitif, -ive [vɔlitif, iv] *adj* volitional, volitive.

volition [vɔlisjɔ̃] *nf* volition.

volley-ball [vɔlɛbol] *nm* volleyball.

volleyeur, -euse [vɔlɛjœʀ, øz] *nm,f* (*Volley-ball*) volleyball player; (*Tennis*) volleyer.

volontaire [vɔlɔ̃tɛʀ] **1** *adj* **(a)** (*voulu*) *acte, enrôlement, prisonnier* voluntary; *oubli* intentional; *V* **engagé. (b)** (*décidé*) *personne* self-willed, wilful, headstrong; *expression, menton* determined. **2** *nmf* (*Mil, gén*) volunteer.

volontairement [vɔlɔ̃tɛʀmɑ̃] *adv* **(a)** (*de son plein gré*) voluntarily, of one's own free will; (*Jur: facultativement*) voluntarily. **(b)** (*exprès*) intentionally, deliberately. **(c)** (*d'une manière décidée*) determinedly.

volontariat [vɔlɔ̃taʀja] *nm* (*Mil*) voluntary service.

volonté [vɔlɔ̃te] *nf* **(a)** (*faculté*) will; (*souhait, intention*) wish, will (*frm*). **manifester sa** ~ **de faire qch** to show one's intention of doing sth; **accomplir/respecter la** ~ **de qn** to carry out/respect sb's wishes; **la** ~ **nationale** the will of the nation; **la** ~ **générale** the general will; ~ **de puissance** will for power; ~ **de guérir/réussir** will to recover/succeed; *V* **dernier, indépendant, quatre.**

(b) (*disposition*) **bonne** ~ goodwill, willingness; **mauvaise** ~ lack of goodwill, unwillingness; **il a beaucoup de bonne** ~ **mais peu d'aptitude** he has a lot of goodwill but not much aptitude, he shows great willingness but not much aptitude; **il met de la bonne/mauvaise** ~ **à faire son travail** he goes about his work with goodwill/grudgingly, he does his work willingly/unwillingly *ou* with a good/bad grace; **il y met de la mauvaise** ~ he's grudging about it, he does it unwillingly *ou* with a bad grace; **avec la meilleure** ~ **du monde** with the best will in the world.

(c) (*caractère, énergie*) willpower, will. **faire un effort de** ~ to make an effort of will(power); **avoir de la** ~ to have willpower; **cet homme a une** ~ **de fer** this man has an iron will *ou* a will of iron; **réussir à force de** ~ to succeed through sheer will(power) *ou* determination; **échouer par manque de** ~ to fail through lack of will(power) *ou* determination; **faire acte de** ~ to display willpower.

(d) (*loc*) **à** ~ at will; **servez-vous de pain à** ~ take as much bread as you like; **'sucrer à** ~' 'sweeten to taste'; **vous pouvez le prendre ou le laisser à** ~ you can take it or leave it as you wish *ou* just as you like; (*Comm*) **billet payable à** ~ promissory note payable on demand; **fais-en à ta** ~ do as you wish *ou* please; *V* **feu**¹.

volontiers [vɔlɔ̃tje] *adv* **(a)** (*de bonne grâce*) with pleasure, gladly, willingly. **je l'aiderais** ~ I would gladly *ou* willingly help him; **voulez-vous dîner chez nous?** — ~ would you like to eat with us? — I'd love to *ou* with pleasure.

(b) (*naturellement*) readily, willingly. **il lit** ~ **pendant des heures** he will happily *ou* willingly read for hours on end; **on croit** ~ **que ...** people readily believe that ... , people are apt *ou* quite ready to believe that ... ; **il est** ~ **pessimiste** he is given to pessimism, he is pessimistic by nature.

volt [vɔlt] *nm* volt.

voltage [vɔltaʒ] *nm* voltage.

voltaïque [vɔltaik] *adj* voltaic, galvanic.

voltaire [vɔltɛʀ] *nm* Voltaire chair.

voltairien, -ienne [vɔltɛʀjɛ̃, jɛn] *adj* Voltairian, Voltairean.

volte [vɔlt(ə)] *nf* (*Équitation*) volte.

volte-face [vɔltəfas] *nf inv* **(a)** (*lit*) **faire** ~ to turn round. **(b)** (*fig*) volte-face, about-turn. **faire une** ~ to make a volte-face, do *ou* make an about-turn.

volter [vɔlte] (1) *vi* (*Équitation*) **faire** ~ **un cheval** to make a horse circle.

voltige [vɔltiʒ] *nf* (*Équitation*) trick riding; (*Aviat*) (aerial) acrobatics. (*Gym*) **(haute)** ~ acrobatics; **c'est de la (haute)** ~ **intellectuelle** it's mental gymnastics.

voltiger [vɔltiʒe] (3) *vi [oiseaux]* to flit about, flutter about; *[objet léger]* to flutter about.

voltigeur [vɔltiʒœʀ] *nm* **(a)** (*acrobate*) acrobat. **(b)** (*Hist Mil*) light infantryman.

voltmètre [vɔltmɛtʀ(ə)] *nm* voltmeter.

volubile [vɔlybil] *adj* **(a)** *personne, éloquence* voluble. **(b)** (*Bot*) voluble.

volubilis [vɔlybilis] *nm* convolvulus, morning glory.

volubilité [vɔlybilite] *nf* volubility.

volume [vɔlym] *nm* **(a)** (*livre, tome*) volume. (*fig*) **écrire des** ~**s à qn*** to write reams to sb*.

(b) (*gén, Art, Géom, Sci: espace, quantité*) volume. ~ **moléculaire/atomique** molecular/atomic volume; ~ **d'eau d'un fleuve** volume of water in a river; **eau oxygénée à 20** ~**s** 20-volume hydrogen peroxide; **le** ~ **des importations** the volume of imports; **faire du** ~ *[gros objets]* to be bulky, take up space.

(c) (*intensité*) *[son]* volume. ~ **de la voix/la radio** volume of the voice/radio; ~ **sonore** sound volume.

volumétrique [vɔlymetʀik] *adj* volumetric.

volumineux, -euse [vɔlyminø, øz] *adj* voluminous, bulky.

volupté [vɔlypte] *nf* (*sensuelle*) sensual delight, sensual *ou* voluptuous pleasure; (*morale, intellectuelle*) exquisite delight *ou* pleasure.

voluptueusement [vɔlyptɥøzmɑ̃] *adv* voluptuously.

voluptueux, -euse [vɔlyptɥø, øz] *adj* voluptuous.

volute [vɔlyt] *nf* **(a)** *[colonne, grille, escalier]* volute; *[fumée]* curl, wreath (*littér*); *[vague]* curl. **en** ~ voluted, volute. **(b)** (*Zool*) volute.

volve [vɔlv(ə)] *nf* volva.

vomi [vɔmi] *nm* vomit.

vomique [vɔmik] *adj f V* **noix.**

vomiquier [vɔmikje] *nm* nux vomica (*tree*).

vomir [vɔmiʀ] (2) *vt* **(a)** *aliments* to vomit, bring up; *sang* to spit, bring up. **avoir envie de** ~ to want to be sick; (*fig*) **cela donne envie de** ~, **c'est à** ~ it makes you *ou* it's enough to make you sick, it's nauseating.

(b) (*fig*) *lave, flammes* to belch forth, spew forth; *injures, haine* to spew out.

(c) (*fig: détester*) to loathe, abhor. **il vomit les intellectuels** he has a loathing for *ou* loathes intellectuals.

vomissement [vɔmismɑ̃] *nm* **(a)** (*action*) vomiting (*U*). **il fut pris de** ~**s** he (suddenly) started vomiting. **(b)** (*matières*) vomit (*U*).

vomissure [vɔmisyʀ] *nf* vomit (*U*).

vomitif, -ive [vɔmitif, iv] *adj, nm* (*Pharm*) emetic, vomitory.

vorace [vɔʀas] *adj animal, personne, curiosité* voracious. **appétit** ~ voracious *ou* ravenous appetite; **plantes** ~**s** plants which deplete the soil.

voracement [vɔʀasmɑ̃] *adv* voraciously.

voracité [vɔʀasite] *nf* voracity, voraciousness.

vortex [vɔʀtɛks] *nm* (*littér*) vortex.

vos [vo] *adj poss V* **votre.**

vosgien, -ienne [voʒjɛ̃, jɛn] **1** *adj* Vosges (*épith*), of *ou* from the Vosges. **2** *nm,f*: **V**~**(ne)** inhabitant *ou* native of the Vosges.

votant, e [vɔtɑ̃, ɑ̃t] *nm,f* voter.

vote [vɔt] *nm* **(a)** (*U*) *[projet de loi]* vote (*de* for); *[loi, réforme]* passing; *[crédits]* voting.

(b) (*suffrage, acte, opération*) vote. ~ **de confiance** vote of confidence; **procéder au** ~ to proceed to a vote; ~ **à main levée** vote by a show of hands; ~ **secret/par correspondance/par procuration** secret/postal/proxy vote; ~ **direct/indirect** direct/indirect vote; *V* **bulletin, bureau, droit**³.

voter [vɔte] (1) **1** *vi* to vote. ~ **à main levé** to vote by a show of hands; ~ **à droite/pour X** to vote for the Right/for X. **2** *vt* (*adopter*) *projet de loi* to vote for; *loi, réforme* to pass; *crédits* to vote. ~ **libéral** to vote Liberal.

votif, -ive [vɔtif, iv] *adj* votive.

votre [vɔtʀ(ə)], *pl* **vos** [vo] *adj poss* your; (*emphatique*) your own; (†, *Rel*) thy. **laissez** ~ **manteau et vos gants au vestiaire** (*à une personne*) leave your coat and gloves in the cloakroom; (*à plusieurs personnes*) leave your coats and gloves in the cloakroom; (†, *Rel*) **que** ~ **volonté soit faite** Thy will be done (†); **V**~ **Excellence/Majesté** Your Excellency/Majesty; *pour autres loc V* **son**¹, **ton**¹.

vôtre [votʀ(ə)] **1** *pron poss*: **le** ~, **la** ~, **les** ~**s** yours, your own; **ce sac n'est pas le** ~ this bag is not yours, this is not YOUR bag; **nos enfants sont sortis avec les** ~**s** our children are out with yours *ou* your own; **à la (bonne)** ~**!** your (good) health!, cheers!; *pour autres loc V* **sien.**

2 *nmf* **(a)** (*U*) **j'espère que vous y mettrez du** ~ I hope you'll pull your weight *ou* do your bit*; *V aussi* **sien.**

(b) les ~**s** your family, your (own) folks*; **vous et tous les** ~**s** you and all those like you; **bonne année à vous et à tous les** ~**s** Happy New Year to you and yours; **nous pourrons être des** ~**s ce soir** we shall be able to join your party *ou* join you tonight; *V* **sien.**

3 *adj poss* (*littér*) yours. **son cœur est** ~ **depuis toujours** his heart has always been yours; *V* **sien.**

vouer [vwe] (1) *vt* **(a)** (*Rel*) ~ **qn à Dieu/à la Vierge** to dedicate sb to God/to the Virgin Mary; *V* **savoir.**

(b) (*promettre*) to vow. **il lui a voué un amour éternel** he vowed his undying love to her.

(c) (*consacrer*) to devote. ~ **son temps à ses études** to devote one's time to one's studies; **se** ~ **à une cause** to dedicate o.s. *ou* devote o.s. to a cause.

(d) (*gén ptp: condamner*) to doom. **projet voué à l'échec** plan doomed to *ou* destined for failure; **famille vouée à la misère** family doomed to poverty.

vouloir [vulwaʀ] (31) **1** *vt* **(a)** (*sens fort: exiger*) *objet, augmentation, changement* to want. ~ **faire** to want to do; ~

que qn fasse/qch se fasse to want sb to do/sth to be done; qu'il le veuille ou non whether he likes *ou* wants it or not; il veut absolument ce jouet/venir/qu'elle parte he is set on this toy/coming/her leaving, he is determined to have this toy/to come/(that) she should leave; il a voulu partir avant la nuit he wanted to leave before dark; il ne veut pas y aller/qu'elle y aille he doesn't want to go/her to go; (*Prov*) ~, c'est pouvoir where there's a will there's a way (*Prov*); qu'est-ce qu'ils veulent maintenant? what do they want now?; il sait ce qu'il veut he knows what he wants.

(b) (*sens affaibli: gén dans une interrogation, une négation*) voulez-vous à boire/manger? would you like something to drink/eat?; tu veux (*ou* vous voulez) quelque chose à boire?* would you like *ou* do you want something to drink?; comment voulez-vous votre poisson, frit ou poché? how would you like your fish — fried or poached?; je ne veux pas qu'il se croie obligé de ... I shouldn't like *ou* I don't want him to feel obliged to ... ; il ne voulait pas vous blesser he didn't want to hurt you; ça va comme tu veux (*ou* vous voulez)?* is everything going all right *ou* O.K. (for you)?*; ~ du bien/mal à qn to wish sb well/ill *ou* harm, be well-/ill-disposed towards sb; je ne lui veux pas de mal I don't wish him any harm; (*iro*) un ami qui vous veut du bien a well-wisher (*iro*); que lui voulez-vous? what do you want with him?

(c) (*au conditionnel: désirer, souhaiter*) je voudrais ceci/faire ceci/qu'il fasse cela I would like this/to do this/him to do this; je voudrais une livre de beurre I would like a pound of butter; il aurait voulu être docteur mais ... he would have liked to be a doctor *ou* he'd like to have been a doctor but ... ; je voudrais/j'aurais voulu que vous voyiez sa tête! I wish you could see/could have seen his face!; je voudrais qu'il soit plus énergique, (*frm*) je lui voudrais plus d'énergie I wish he showed *ou* would show more energy.

(d) (*avec si, comme*) si tu veux (*ou* vous voulez) if you like; s'il voulait, il pourrait être ministre if he wanted (to), he could be a minister, he could be a minister if he so desired; s'il voulait (bien) nous aider, cela gagnerait du temps if he'd help us *ou* if he felt like helping us, it would save time; comme tu veux (*ou* vous voulez) as you like *ou* wish *ou* please; bon, comme tu voudras all right, have it your own way *ou* as you like; comme vous voulez, moi ça m'est égal just as you like *ou* please *ou* wish, it makes no difference to me; oui, si on veut (*dans un sens, d'un côté*) yes, if you like; s'ils veulent garder leur avance, ils ne peuvent se permettre de relâcher leur effort if they are *ou* intend to keep their lead they can't afford to reduce their efforts.

(e) (*escompter, demander*) ~ qch de qn to want sth from sb; je veux de vous plus de fermeté/une promesse I want more firmness/a promise from you; ~ un certain prix de qch to want a certain price for sth; j'en veux 10 F I want 10 francs for it.

(f) bien ~: je veux bien le faire/qu'il vienne (*très volontiers*) I'm happy *ou* I'll be happy to do it/for him to come; (*il n'y a pas d'inconvénient*) I'm quite happy to do it/for him to come; (*s'il le faut vraiment*) I don't mind doing it/if he comes; moi je veux bien le croire mais ... I'll take his word for it but ... , I'm quite prepared to believe him but ... ; je voudrais bien y aller I'd really like *ou* I'd love to go; si tu voulais bien le faire, ça nous rendrait service if you'd care *ou* be willing to do it, you'd be doing us a favour; moi je veux bien, mais ... fair enough*, but ... .

(g) (*consentir*) ils ne voulurent pas nous recevoir they wouldn't see us, they weren't willing to see us; le moteur ne veut pas partir the engine won't start; le feu n'a pas voulu prendre the fire wouldn't catch; il joue bien quand il veut he plays well when he wants to *ou* has a mind (to)*.

(h) [*choses*] (*requérir*) to want, require. ces plantes veulent de l'eau these plants want *ou* need water; l'usage veut que ... custom requires that ... .

(i) (*ordre*) veux-tu (bien) te taire!, voulez-vous (bien) vous taire! will you be quiet!; veuillez quitter la pièce immédiatement please leave the room at once.

(j) [*destin, sort etc*] le hasard voulut que ... chance decreed that ... , as fate would have it ... .

(k) (*chercher à, essayer*) to try. elle voulut se lever mais elle retomba she tried to get up but she fell back; il veut se faire remarquer he wants to make himself noticed, he's out to be noticed*.

(l) (*s'attendre à*) to expect. comment voulez-vous que je sache? how do you expect me to know?, how should I know?; il a tout, pourquoi voudriez-vous qu'il réclame? he has everything so why should he complain?; qu'est-ce que vous voulez que j'y fasse? what do you expect *ou* want me to do about it?; et dans ces conditions, vous voudriez que nous acceptions? and under these conditions you expect us to agree? *ou* you would have us agree?

(m) (*formules de politesse*) voulez-vous bien leur dire que ... would you please tell them that ... ; voudriez-vous avoir l'obligeance *ou* l'amabilité de would you be so kind as to; veuillez croire à toute ma sympathie please accept my deepest sympathy; voulez-vous me prêter ce livre? will you lend me this book?; *V* agréer.

(n) (*prétendre*) to claim. une philosophie qui veut que l'homme soit ... a philosophy which claims that man is ... ; il veut que les hommes soient égaux: je ne suis pas d'accord avec lui he'd have it that *ou* he makes out that men are equal but I don't agree with him.

(o) en ~ à: en ~ à qn to have sth against sb, have a grudge against sb; en ~ à qn de qch to hold sth against sb; il m'en veut beaucoup d'avoir fait cela he holds a tremendous grudge against me for having done that; il m'en veut d'avoir fait rater ce projet he holds it against me that I made the plan fail, he has a grudge against me for making the plan fail; il m'en veut de mon incompréhension he holds my lack of understanding against me, he resents my failure to understand; ne m'en voulez pas, (*frm*) ne m'en veuillez pas don't hold it against me; tu ne m'en veux pas? no hard feelings?; en ~ à qch to be after sth; il en veut à son argent he is after her money.

(p) ~ dire (*signifier*) to mean; qu'est-ce que cela veut dire? (*mot etc*) what does that mean?; (*attitude de qn*) what does that imply? *ou* mean?

(q) (*loc*) que voulez-vous! (*ou* que veux-tu!), qu'est-ce que vous voulez! what can we do?, it can't be helped!, what can you expect!; je voudrais bien vous y voir! I'd like to see how you'd do it! *ou* you doing it!; je veux être pendu si ... I'll be hanged *ou* damned if ... ; qu'est-ce que vous voulez qu'on y fasse? what can anyone do about it?, what can be done about it?, what do you expect us (*ou* them *etc*) to do?; sans le ~ unintentionally, involuntarily, inadvertently; tu l'as voulu you asked for it; tu l'auras voulu it'll have been your own fault, you'll have brought it on yourself; il veut sans ~ he only half wants to; il y a eu des discours en veux-tu en voilà there were speeches galore; elle fait de lui ce qu'elle veut she does what she likes with him, she twists him round her little finger.

2 vouloir de *vt indir* (*gén nég, interrog*) ~ de qn/qch to want sb/sth; on ne veut plus de lui au bureau they don't want him *ou* won't have him in the office any more; je ne veux pas de lui comme chauffeur I don't want him *ou* won't have him as a driver; voudront-ils de moi dans leur nouvelle maison? will they want me in their new house?; elle ne veut plus de ce chapeau she doesn't want this hat any more.

3 *nm* **(a)** (*littér: volonté*) will.

(b) bon ~ goodwill; mauvais ~ ill will; selon le bon ~ de according to the pleasure of; avec un mauvais ~ évident with obvious malice *ou* ill will; attendre le bon ~ de qn to wait on sb's pleasure.

voulu, e [vuly] (*ptp de* vouloir) *adj* **(a)** (*requis*) required, requisite. il n'avait pas l'argent ~ he didn't have the required *ou* requisite money *ou* the money required; le temps ~ the time required.

(b) (*volontaire*) deliberate, intentional. c'est ~* it's done on purpose, it's intentional.

vous [vu] **1** *pron pers* **(a)** (*sujet, objet*) you; (*sg: tu*) you. ~ avez bien répondu tous les deux you both answered well, the two of you answered well; vous et lui, ~ êtes aussi têtus l'un que l'autre you and he are as stubborn (the) one as the other, you are both equally stubborn; si j'étais ~, j'accepterais if I were you *ou* in your shoes I'd accept; eux ont accepté, ~ pas *ou* pas ~ they accepted but you didn't, they accepted but not you; ~ parti(s), je pourrai travailler once you've gone *ou* with you out of the way, I'll be able to work; c'est enfin ~, ~ voilà enfin here you are at last; qui l'a vu?, ~? who saw him?, (did) you? *ou* was it you?; je ~ ai demandé de m'aider I asked you to help me; elle n'obéit qu'à ~ you're the only one *ou* ones she obeys.

(b) (*emphatique: insistance, apostrophe*) (*sujet*) you, yourself (*sg*), you yourselves (*pl*); (*objet*) you. ~ tous écoutez-moi listen to me all of you *ou* the lot of you*; ~ vous n'avez pas à vous plaindre you have no cause to complain; vous ne le connaissez pas ~ you don't know him; pourquoi je ne le ferais pas: vous l'avez bien fait, ~! why shouldn't I do it — YOU did (it)! *ou* you yourself *ou* you yourselves did it!; ~ mentir?, ce n'est pas possible you tell a lie?, I can't believe it; alors ~ vous ne partez pas? so what about you — aren't you going?; ~ aidez-moi! you (there) *ou* hey you, give me a hand!; je vous demande à ~ parce que je vous connais I'm asking you because I know you; je vous connais ~! I know you; ~ vous m'agacez!, vous m'agacez ~! (oh) you're getting on my nerves!; ~ je vois que vous n'êtes pas bien it's obvious to me that you are not well.

(c) (*emphatique avec qui, que*) c'est ~ qui avez raison it's you who is *ou* are right; ~ tous qui m'écoutez all of you listening to me; et ~ qui détestiez le cinéma, vous avez bien changé and (to think) you're the one who hated the cinema — well you've changed a lot!

(d) (*avec prép*) you. à ~ 4 vous pourrez le porter with 4 of you *ou* between (the) 4 of you you'll be able to carry it; cette maison est-elle à ~? does this house belong to you?, is this house yours? *ou* your own?; vous n'avez même pas une chambre à ~ tout seul/tout seuls? you don't even have a room of your own? *ou* a room to yourself/yourselves?; c'est à ~ de décider (*sg*) it's up to you *ou* to yourself to decide; (*pl*) it's up to you *ou* to yourselves to decide; l'un de ~ *ou* d'entre ~ doit le savoir one of you must know; vous ne pensez qu'à ~ you think only of yourself *ou* yourselves.

(e) (*dans comparaisons*) you. il me connaît mieux que ~ (*mieux qu'il ne vous connaît*) he knows me better than (he knows) you; (*mieux que vous ne me connaissez*) he knows me better than you do; il est plus/moins fort que ~ he is stronger than you/not as strong as you (are); il a fait comme ~ he did as *ou* what you did, he did like you* *ou* the same as you.

(f) (*avec vpr: souvent non traduit*) ~ êtes-vous bien amusé(s)? did you have a good time?; je crois que vous ~ connaissez I believe you know each other; servez-~ donc do help yourself *ou* yourselves; ne ~ disputez pas don't fight; asseyez-~ donc do sit down.

2 *nm*: dire ~ à qn to call sb 'vous'; le ~ est de moins en moins employé (the form of address) 'vous' *ou* the 'vous' form is used less and less frequently.

vous-même, *pl* **vous-mêmes** [vumɛm] *pron V* même.

voussoir [vuswaʀ] *nm* voussoir.

voussoyer [vuswaje] (8) *vt* = vouvoyer.

voussure [vusyʀ] *nf* (*courbure*) arching; (*partie cintrée*) arch; (*Archit: archivolte*) archivolt.

voûte [vut] 1 nf (Archit) vault. ~ en plein cintre/d'arête semicircular/groined vault; ~ en ogive/en berceau ribbed/barrel vault; ~ en éventail fan-vaulting (U); en ~ vaulted; (fig) la ~ d'une caverne the vault of a cave; (fig) une ~ d'arbres an archway of trees; V clef.

2: la voûte céleste the vault ou canopy of heaven; voûte crânienne dome of the skull, vault of the cranium (T); la voûte étoilée the starry vault ou dome; voûte du palais ou palatine roof of the mouth; voûte plantaire arch (of the foot).

voûté, e [vute] (ptp de voûter) adj (a) cave, plafond vaulted, arched. (b) dos bent; personne stooped. être ~, avoir le dos ~ to be stooped, have a stoop.

voûter [vute] (1) vt (a) (Archit) to arch, vault. (b) personne, dos to make stooped. la vieillesse l'a voûté age has given him a stoop; il s'est voûté avec l'âge he has become stooped with age.

vouvoiement [vuvwamɑ̃] nm addressing sb as 'vous'.

vouvoyer [vuvwaje] (8) vt: ~ qn to address sb as 'vous'.

voyage [vwajaʒ] nm (a) journey, trip. le ~, les ~s travelling; il aime les ~s he likes travel ou travelling; le ~ le fatigue travelling tires him; le ~ l'a fatigué the journey tired him; j'ai fait un beau ~ I had a very nice trip; les ~s de Christophe Colomb the voyages ou journeys of Christopher Columbus; il revient de ~ he's just come back from a journey ou a trip; les fatigues du ~ the strain of the journey; il est en ~ he's away; il est absent — il est parti en ~ he's away — he has gone off on a trip ou a journey; au moment de partir en ~ just as he (ou I etc) was setting off on his (ou my etc) journey ou travels; il reste 3 jours de ~ there are still 3 days' travelling left, the journey will take another 3 days (to do); lors de notre ~ en Espagne on our trip to Spain, during ou on our travels in Spain; frais/souvenirs de ~ travel expenses/souvenirs; ~ d'affaires/d'agrément/d'études business/pleasure/study trip; ~ d'information fact-finding trip; ~ de noces honeymoon; ~ organisé package tour; (Prov) les ~s forment la jeunesse travel broadens the mind; V agence, bon[1].

(b) (course) trip. faire 2 ~s pour transporter qch to make 2 trips to transport sth; j'ai dû faire le ~ de Grenoble une seconde fois I had to make the trip to Grenoble a second time; un ~ de charbon devrait suffire one load of coal should be enough.

(c) (Drogue) trip.

voyager [vwajaʒe] (3) vi (a) (faire des voyages) to travel. comment as-tu voyagé? how did you travel?; j'ai voyagé en avion/par mer/en 1ère classe I travelled by air/by sea/1st class; aimer ~ to be fond of travelling; il a beaucoup voyagé he has travelled widely ou a great deal, he has done a lot of travelling.

(b) (Comm) to travel. ~ pour un quotidien parisien to travel for a Paris daily paper.

(c) [chose] to travel. cette malle a beaucoup voyagé this trunk has travelled a great deal ou has done a lot of travelling; ces vins/ces denrées voyagent mal/bien these wines/goods travel badly/well; ce paquet s'est abîmé en voyageant this package has been damaged in transit.

voyageur, -euse [vwajaʒœʀ, øz] 1 adj (littér) humeur, tempérament wayfaring (littér); V commis, pigeon. 2 nm,f (explorateur, Comm) traveller; (passager) traveller, passenger. ~ de commerce commercial traveller.

voyance [vwajɑ̃s] nf clairvoyance.

voyant, e [vwajɑ̃, ɑ̃t] 1 adj couleurs loud, gaudy, garish.

2 nm,f (illuminé) visionary, seer; (personne qui voit) sighted person.

3 voyante nf (cartomancienne etc) ~e (extra-lucide) clairvoyant.

4 nm (a) (signal) light. ~ d'essence/d'huile petrol/oil warning light.

(b) (de l'arpenteur) levelling rod ou staff.

voyelle [vwajɛl] nf vowel. ~ orale/nasale oral/nasal vowel.

voyeur, -euse [vwajœʀ, øz] nm,f (f rare) peeping Tom, voyeur (T).

voyeurisme [vwajœʀism(ə)] nm voyeurism.

voyou [vwaju] 1 nm (enfant) street urchin, guttersnipe; (adulte) lout, hoodlum, hooligan, yobbo: (Brit). 2 adj (gén inv, f rare: voyoute) loutish. un air ~ a loutish manner.

vrac [vʀak] adv: en ~ (au poids, sans emballage) (au détail) loose; (en gros) in bulk; (fig: en désordre) in a jumble, higgledy-piggledy.

vrai, vraie [vʀɛ] 1 adj (a) (après n: exact) récit, fait true; (Art, Littérat) couleurs, personnage true. ce que tu dis est ~ what you say is true ou right; c'est dangereux, c'est ou (frm) il est ~, mais ... it's dangerous, it's true ou certainly, but ... ; le tableau, tristement ~, que peint de notre société cet auteur the picture, sadly only too true (to life), which this author paints of our society; pas ~?* right?*, aren't (ou won't etc) we (ou you etc)?; c'est pas ~!* oh no!; V trop, vérité.

(b) (gén avant n: réel) real. ce sont ses ~s cheveux that's his real ou own hair; une vraie blonde a real ou genuine blonde; un ~ Picasso a real ou genuine Picasso; son ~ nom c'est Charles his real ou true name is Charles; des bijoux en or ~ jewellery in real gold; lui c'est un cheik, un ~ de ~* he's a sheik — the real thing ou the genuine article; un ~ socialiste a true socialist.

(c) (avant n: intensif) real. c'est un ~ fou! he's really mad!, he's downright mad!; c'est un ~ communiste! he's a real communist!; c'est une vraie mère pour moi she's a real mother to me; un ~ chef d'œuvre/héros a real masterpiece/hero.

(d) (avant n: bon) real. c'est le ~ moyen de le faire that's the real way to do it.

(e) (Sci) le temps solaire/le jour ~ real solar time/time.

2 nm (a) (la vérité) le ~ the truth; il y a du ~ dans ce qu'il dit there's some truth ou there's an element of truth in what he says; distinguer le ~ du faux to distinguish truth from falsehood ou the true from the false; être dans le ~ to be right; V plaider.

(b) (loc) il dit ~ he's right (in what he says), it's true what he says; à dire ~, à ~ dire, à dire le ~ to tell (you) the truth, in (actual) fact; (gén langage enfantin) pour de ~* for real*, really, seriously; c'est pour de ~?* is it for real?*, do you (ou they etc) really mean it?; au ~†, de ~† in (actual) fact.

3 adv: faire ~ [décor, perruque] to look real ou like the real thing; [peintre, artiste] to strive for realism, paint (ou draw etc) realistically; ~†, quelle honte! oh really, how shameful!

vraiment [vʀɛmɑ̃] adv (a) (véritablement) really. s'aiment-ils ~? do they really (and truly) love each other?; nous voulons ~ la paix we really (and truly) want peace.

(b) (intensif) really. il est ~ idiot he's a real idiot; ~, il exagère! really, he's going too far!; je ne sais ~ pas quoi faire I really ou honestly don't know what to do; oui ~, c'est dommage yes, it's a real shame.

(c) (de doute) — ~? really?, is that so?; il est parti — ~? he has gone — (has he) really?

vraisemblable [vʀɛsɑ̃blabl(ə)] adj hypothèse, interprétation likely; situation, intrigue plausible, convincing. peu ~ excuse, histoire improbable, unlikely; il est (très) ~ que it's (highly) ou (very) likely ou probable that; un auteur qui s'efforce au ~ an author who strives to be true to life.

vraisemblablement [vʀɛsɑ̃blabləmɑ̃] adv in all likelihood, very likely*. la fin, ~ proche, des hostilités the likelihood of an imminent end to the hostilities.

vraisemblance [vʀɛsɑ̃blɑ̃s] nf [hypothèse, interprétation] likelihood; [situation romanesque] verisimilitude, plausibility. selon toute ~ in all likelihood, in all probability.

vrille [vʀij] nf (a) (Bot) tendril.

(b) (Tech) gimlet.

(c) (spirale) spiral; (Aviat) spin, tailspin. escalier en ~ spiral staircase; (Aviat) descente en ~ spiral dive; (Aviat) descendre en ~ to spiral downwards, come down in a spin; (Aviat) se mettre en ~ to go into a tailspin.

vrillé, e [vʀije] (ptp de vriller) adj tige tendrilled; fil twisted.

vriller [vʀije] (1) 1 vt to bore into, pierce. 2 vi (Aviat) to spiral, spin; [fil] to become twisted.

vrombir [vʀɔ̃biʀ] (2) vi to hum.

vrombissement [vʀɔ̃bismɑ̃] nm humming (U).

vu[1], vue[1] [vy] (ptp de voir) 1 adj (a) (*: compris) c'est ~? all right?, got it?*, understood?; c'est bien ~? all clear?*, is that quite clear?; ~? O.K.?*, right?*; c'est tout ~ that's all there is to it, that's the top and bottom of it*; V ni.

(b) (Sport) une balle/passe bien vue a well-judged ball/pass.

(c) (considéré) bien ~ personne well thought of, highly regarded; chose good form (attrib); mal ~ personne poorly thought of; chose bad form (attrib); il est mal ~ du patron the boss thinks poorly of him ou has a poor opinion of him; ici c'est bien ~ de porter une cravate it's good form round here to wear a tie.

2 nm: au ~ et au su de tous openly and publicly.

vu[2] [vy] 1 prép (gén, Jur) in view of. ~ la situation, cela valait mieux it was better, in view of ou seeing the situation.

2 conj (*) ~ que in view of the fact that, seeing that; ~ qu'il était tard, nous avons abandonné la partie seeing how late it was, we abandoned the game.

vue[2] [vy] nf (a) (sens) sight, eyesight. perdre la ~ to lose one's (eye)sight; troubles de la ~ sight trouble, disorders of vision (frm); il a la ~ basse ou courte he is short-sighted.

(b) (regard) détourner la ~ to look away, avert one's gaze (littér); (littér) porter la ~ sur qn/qch to cast one's eyes over sb/sth, look in sb's direction/in the direction of sth; s'offrir à la ~ de tous to present o.s. for all to see; il l'a fait à la ~ de tous he did it in full view of everybody; (lit, fig) perdre de ~ to lose sight of; il lui en a mis plein la ~* he put on quite a show for her.

(c) (panorama) view. de cette colline, on a une très belle ~ de la ville there's a very fine view of the town from this hill; d'ici il y a de la ~ you get a good ou fine view from here; avec ~ imprenable with an open ou unimpeded ou unobstructed view ou outlook (no future building plans); ces immeubles nous bouchent la ~ those buildings block our view; cette pièce a ~ sur la mer this room looks out onto the sea; de là, on avait une ~ de profil de la cathédrale from there you had a side view of the cathedral; V perte, point[1].

(d) (spectacle) sight. la ~ du sang l'a fait s'évanouir the sight of the blood made him faint; à sa ~ elle s'est mise à rougir when she saw him she began to blush.

(e) (image) view. ~ photographique photographic view, shot; ils nous ont montré des ~s prises lors de leurs vacances they showed us some photos they'd taken on their holidays; ~ de la ville sous la neige view of the town in the snow.

(f) (opinion) ~s views; présenter ses ~s sur un sujet to present one's views on a subject; de courtes ~s short-sighted views; V échange.

(g) (conception) view. il a une ~ pessimiste de la situation he has a pessimistic view of the situation; donner une ~ d'ensemble to give an overall view; don de seconde ou double ~ gift of second sight; c'est une ~ de l'esprit that's a purely theoretical view; V point[1].

(h) (projet) ~s plans; (sur qn ou ses biens) designs; il a des ~s sur la fortune de cette femme he has designs on ou he has his eye on that woman's fortune; elle a des ~s sur lui (pour un projet, pour l'épouser) she has her eye on him.

(i) (Jur: fenêtre) window.

(j) (loc) de ~ by sight; je le connais de ~ I know him by sight; à ~ payable etc at sight; (Aviat) piloter, atterrir visually; atterrissage visual; à ~ d'œil (rapidement) before one's very eyes; (*par une estimation rapide*) at a quick glance; il maigrit à ~ **d'œil** he seems to be getting thinner before our very eyes *ou* by the minute*; **à ~ de nez**‡ roughly*, at a rough guess; **en ~** (*lit, fig: proche*) in sight; (*en évidence*) **(bien) en ~** conspicuous; (*célèbre*) **très/assez en ~** very much/much in the public eye; **il a mis sa pancarte bien en ~** he put his placard in a prominent *ou* a conspicuous position *ou* where everyone could see it; **c'est un des politiciens les plus en ~** he's one of the most prominent *ou* best-known men in politics; **avoir qch/qn en ~**: **avoir un poste en ~** to have one's sights on a job; **avoir un collaborateur en ~** to have an associate in mind; **avoir en ~ de faire** to have it in mind to do, plan to do; **en ~ de**: **il a acheté une maison en ~ de son mariage** he has bought a house with his marriage in mind; **il s'entraîne en ~ de la course de dimanche/de devenir champion du monde** he's training with a view to the race on Sunday/becoming world champion; **il a dit cela en ~ de le décourager** he said that with the idea of discouraging him; *V* **changement, garder, tirer.**

vulcain [vylkɛ̃] *nm* red admiral.

vulcanisation [vylkanizɑsjɔ̃] *nf* vulcanization.

vulcaniser [vylkanize] (1) *vt* to vulcanize.

vulgaire [vylgɛʀ] **1** *adj* **(a)** (*grossier*) *langage, personne* vulgar, coarse; *genre, décor* vulgar, crude.

(b) (*prosaïque*) *réalités, problèmes* commonplace, everyday (*épith*), mundane.

(c) (*usuel, banal*) common, popular. **nom ~** common *ou* popular name; **langues ~s** common languages; *V* **latin.**

(d) (*littér,*†: *du peuple*) common. **esprit ~** common mind; **l'opinion ~** the common opinion.

(e) (*avant n: quelconque*) common, ordinary. **~ escroc** common swindler; **de la ~ matière plastique** ordinary *ou* common or garden plastic.

2 *nm* (†, *hum: peuple*) **le ~** the common herd; (*la vulgarité*) **tomber dans le ~** to lapse into vulgarity.

vulgairement [vylgɛʀmɑ̃] *adv* **(a)** (*grossièrement*) vulgarly, coarsely.

(b) (*couramment*) *dénommer* popularly, commonly. **le fruit de l'églantier, ~ appelé** *ou* **que l'on appelle ~ gratte-cul** the fruit of the wild rose, commonly known as *ou* called haws.

vulgarisateur, -trice [vylgaʀizatœʀ, tʀis] *nm,f* popularizer.

vulgarisation [vylgaʀizɑsjɔ̃] *nf* popularization. **~ scientifique** scientific popularization; **ouvrage de ~** popularizing work; **ouvrage de ~ scientifique** popular scientific work.

vulgariser [vylgaʀize] (1) *vt* **(a)** *ouvrage* to popularize. **(b)** (*littér: rendre vulgaire*) to coarsen. **cet accent la vulgarise** this accent makes her sound coarse.

vulgarisme [vylgaʀism(ə)] *nm* vulgarism.

vulgarité [vylgaʀite] *nf* **(a)** (*grossièreté*) vulgarity, coarseness (*U*). **des ~s** vulgarities. **(b)** (*littér: terre à terre*) commonplaceness, ordinariness.

vulgate [vylgat] *nf* vulgate.

vulnérabilité [vylneʀabilite] *nf* vulnerability.

vulnérable [vylneʀabl(ə)] *adj* (*gén, Cartes*) vulnerable.

vulvaire [vylvɛʀ] **1** *adj* (*Anat*) vulvar. **2** *nf* (*Bot*) stinking goosefoot.

vulve [vylv(ə)] *nf* vulva.

W

W, w [dubləve] *nm* (*lettre*) W, w.

wagnérien, -ienne [vagneʀjɛ̃, jɛn] **1** *adj* Wagnerian. **2** *nm,f* Wagnerian, Wagnerite.

wagon [vagɔ̃] **1** *nm* **(a)** (*Rail: véhicule*) (*de marchandises*) truck, wagon, freight car (*US*); (*de voyageurs*) carriage, car (*US*). **(b)** (*contenu*) truckload, wagonload. **un plein ~ de marchandises** a truckful *ou* truckload of goods; **il y en a tout un ~*** there are stacks of them*, there's a whole pile of them*.

2: wagon à bestiaux cattle truck *ou* wagon; **wagon-citerne** *nm, pl* **wagons-citernes** tanker, tank wagon; **wagon-foudre** *nm, pl* **wagons-foudres** (wine) tanker *ou* tank wagon; **wagon frigorifique** refrigerated van; **wagon-lit** *nm, pl* **wagons-lits** sleeping car, sleeper; **wagon de marchandises** goods truck, freight car (*US*); **wagon-poste** *nm, pl* **wagons-postes** mail van; **wagon-réservoir** *nm, pl* **wagons-réservoir** = **wagon-citerne**; **wagon-restaurant** *nm, pl* **wagons-restaurants** restaurant *ou* dining car; **wagon de voyageurs** passenger carriage *ou* car (*US*).

wagonnet [vagɔnɛ] *nm* small truck.

walkyrie [valkiʀi] *nf* Valkyrie.

wallon, -onne [walɔ̃, ɔn] **1** *adj* Walloon. **2** *nm* (*Ling*) Walloon. **3** *nm,f*: **W~(ne)** Walloon.

wapiti [wapiti] *nm* wapiti.

water-closet(s) [watɛʀklozɛt] *nmpl* (*rare*) = **waters.**

water-polo [watɛʀpɔlo] *nm* water polo.

waters [watɛʀ] *nmpl* toilet, lavatory, loo*.

watt [wat] *nm* watt.

watt-heure, *pl* **watts-heures** [watœʀ] *nm* watt hour.

wattman† [watman] *nm* tram driver.

week-end, *pl* **week-ends** [wikɛnd] *nm* weekend. **partir** *ou* **aller en ~** to go away for the weekend.

western [wɛstɛʀn] *nm* western. **~-spaghetti** spaghetti western.

Westphalie [vɛsfali] *nf* Westphalia.

whisky, *pl* **whiskies** [wiski] *nm* whisky; (*irlandais*) whiskey.

whist [wist] *nm* whist.

wigwam [wigwam] *nm* wigwam.

wisigoth, e [vizigo, ɔt] **1** *adj* Visigothic. **2** *nm,f*: **W~(e)** Visigoth.

wisigothique [vizigɔtik] *adj* Visigothic.

X

X, x [iks] *nm* **(a)** (*lettre*) X, x; (*Math*) x. (*Math*) **l'axe des x** the x axis; **croisés en X** forming an x; **ça fait x temps que je ne l'ai pas vu*** I haven't seen him for n months*, it's months since I (last) saw him; (*Jur*) **plainte contre X** action against person or persons unknown; *V* **rayon.**

(b) (*arg Univ*) **l'X** the École Polytechnique; **un X** a student of the École Polytechnique.

xénon [ksenɔ̃] *nm* xenon.

xénophobe [ksenɔfɔb] **1** *adj* xenophobic. **2** *nmf* xenophobe.

xénophobie [ksenɔfɔbi] *nf* xenophobia.

xérès [gzeʀɛs] **1** *nm* (*vin*) sherry. **2** *n*: **X~** (*ville*) Jerez.

xylographe [ksilɔgʀaf] *nm* xylographer.

xylographie [ksilɔgʀafi] *nf* (*technique*) xylography; (*gravure*) xylograph.

xylographique [ksilɔgʀafik] *adj* xylographic.

xylophone [ksilɔfɔn] *nm* xylophone.

Y

Y, y[1] [igʀɛk] *nm* (*lettre*) Y, y. (*Math*) **l'axe des y** the y axis.
y[2] [i] **1** *adv* (*indiquant le lieu*) there. **restez-~** stay there; **nous ~ avons passé 2 jours** we spent 2 days there; **il avait une feuille de papier et il ~ dessinait un bateau** he had a sheet of paper and he was drawing a ship on it; **avez-vous vu le film? — j'~ vais demain** have you seen the film? — I'm going (to see it) tomorrow; **les maisons étaient neuves, personne n'~ avait habité** the houses were new and nobody had lived in them; **la pièce est sombre, quand on ~ entre, on n'~ voit rien** the room is dark and when you go in you can't see a thing; **j'~ suis, j'~ reste** here I am and here I stay; **vous ~ allez, à ce dîner?*** are you going to this dinner then?; **je suis passé le voir mais il n'~ était pas** I called in to see him but he wasn't there.

2 *pron pers* **(a)** (*gén se rapportant à des choses*) it. **vous serez là? — n'~ comptez pas** you'll be there? — out of the question; **n'~ pensez plus** forget (about) it, don't think about it; **à votre place, je ne m'~ fierais pas** if I were you I wouldn't trust it; **il a plu alors que personne ne s'~ attendait** it rained when no one was expecting it (to); **il ~ trouve du plaisir** he finds pleasure in it, he gets enjoyment out of it.

(b) (*loc*) **elle s'~ connaît** she knows all about it, she's an expert; **il faudra vous ~ faire** you'll just have to get used to it; **je n'~ suis pour rien** it is nothing to do with me, I had no part in it; **ça ~ est pour quelque chose** it has something to do with it; *V* **avoir, comprendre, voir** *etc.*

(c) (*: *il*) (*aussi iro*) **c'est-~ pas gentil?** isn't it nice?; **~ en a qui exagèrent** some people *ou* folk* go too far; **du pain? ~ en a pas** bread? there's none.
yacht [jɔt] *nm* yacht.
yachting† [jɔtiŋ] *nm* yachting.
yacht(s)man† [jɔtman], *pl* **yacht(s)men** [jɔtmɛn] *nm* yacht(s)man.
ya(c)k [jak] *nm* yak.
yaourt [jauʀ(t)] *nm* yog(h)urt.
yatagan [jatagɑ̃] *nm* yataghan.
yeux [jø] *nmpl de* **œil**.
yé-yé*, *pl* **yé-yés** [jeje] **1** *adj*: **musique ~** pop music (*of the early 1960s*); (*fig*) **il veut faire ~** he wants to look with-it*. **2** *nmf pop singer or teenage fan of the early 1960s.*
yiddish [(j)idiʃ] *adj, nm* Yiddish.
yod [jɔd] *nm* yod.
yoga [jɔga] *nm* yoga.
yoghourt [jɔguʀ(t)] *nm* = **yaourt.**
yogi [jɔgi] *nm* yogi.
yole [jɔl] *nf* skiff.
yougoslave [jugɔslav] **1** *adj* Yugoslav, Yugoslavian. **2** *nmf*: **Y~** Yugoslav, Yugoslavian.
Yougoslavie [jugɔslavi] *nf* Yugoslavia.
youpin, e [jupɛ̃, in] *nm,f* (*péj*) Yid (*péj*).
yourte [juʀt(ə)] *nf* yurt.
youyou [juju] *nm* dinghy.
yo-yo [jojo] *nm inv* yo-yo.
ypérite [ipeʀit] *nf* mustard gas, yperite (*T*).
yucca [juka] *nm* yucca.

Z

Z, z [zɛd] *nm* (*lettre*) Z, z; *V* **A.**
Zacharie [zakaʀi] *nm* Zachariah.
zagaie [sagɛ] *nf* = **sagaie.**
Zambèze [zɑ̃bɛz] *nm*: **le ~** the Zambezi.
zazou [zazu] *nm* (*parfois péj*) ≃ hepcat*.
zèbre [zɛbʀ(ə)] *nm* (*Zool*) zebra; (*: *individu*) bloke* (*Brit*), guy*. **un drôle de ~** a queer fish*, an odd bod* (*Brit*); **filer** *ou* **courir comme un ~** to run like a hare *ou* the wind.
zébrer [zebʀe] (6) *vt* to stripe, streak (*de* with).
zébrure [zebʀyʀ] *nf* stripe, streak; *[coup de fouet]* weal.
zébu [zeby] *nm* zebu.
Zélande [zelɑ̃d] *nf* Zealand; *V* **nouveau.**
zélateur, -trice [zelatœʀ, tʀis] *nm,f* (*gén*) champion, partisan (*péj*), zealot (*péj*); (*Rel*) Zealot.
zèle [zɛl] *nm* zeal. **avec ~** zealously, with zeal; (*péj*) **faire du ~** to be over-zealous, overdo it; **pas de ~!** don't overdo it!; *V* **grève.**
zélé, e [zele] *adj* zealous.
zélote [zelɔt] *nm* Zealot.
zénith [zenit] *nm* (*lit, fig*) zenith. **le soleil est au ~** *ou* **à son ~** the sun is at its zenith *ou* height; **au ~ de la gloire** at the zenith *ou* peak of glory.
zénithal, e, *mpl* **-aux** [zenital, o] *adj* zenithal.
Zénon [zenɔ̃] *nm* Zeno.
zéphyr [zefiʀ] *nm* (*vent*) zephyr. (*Myth*) **Z~** Zephyr(us).
zéphyrien, -ienne [zefiʀjɛ̃, jɛn] *adj* (*littér*) zephyr-like (*littér*).
zeppelin [zɛplɛ̃] *nm* zeppelin.
zéro [zeʀo] **1** *nm* **(a)** (*gén, Math*) zero, nought; (*dans un numéro de téléphone*) O. **remettre un compteur à ~** to reset a meter at *ou* to zero; **tout ça, pour moi, c'est ~, je veux des preuves*** as far as I'm concerned that's worthless *ou* a waste of time — I want some proof; **les avoir à ~**‡ to be scared out of one's wits*, be scared stiff*; **repartir de ~, recommencer à ~** to start from scratch *ou* rock-bottom again, go back to square one; *V* **moral, partir**[1], **réduire.**

(b) (*température*) freezing (point), zero (*Centigrade*). **3 degrés au-dessus de ~** 3 degrees above freezing (point) *ou* above zero; **3 degrés au-dessous de ~** 3 degrees below freezing (point) *ou* below zero, 3 degrees below*, minus 3 (degrees Centigrade); **~ absolu** absolute zero.

(c) (*Ftbl*) nil; (*Tennis*) love. (*Tennis*) **mener par 2 jeux/sets à ~** to lead (by) 2 games/sets to love.

(d) (*Scol*) zero, nought. **~ de conduite** bad mark for behaviour *ou* conduct; **~ pointé** nought (out of ten *ou* twenty *etc*); (*fig*) **mais en cuisine, ~ (pour la question)*** but as far as cooking goes he's (*ou* she's) useless* *ou* a dead loss*.

(e) (*: *personne*) nonentity.

2 *adj*: **~ heure (~)** zero hour; **~ heure trente** zero thirty hours; **il a fait ~ faute** he didn't make any mistakes, he didn't make a single mistake; **j'ai eu ~ point** I got no marks (at all), I got zero; **ça m'a coûté ~ franc ~ centime*** I got it for precisely *ou* exactly nothing.
zeste [zɛst(ə)] *nm* *[citron, orange]* peel (*U*); (*en cuisine*) zest (*U*), peel (*U*). **avec un ~ de citron** with a piece of lemon peel.
zêta [dzeta] *nm* zeta.
zeugma [zøgma] *nm* zeugma.
Zeus [zøs] *nm* Zeus.
zézaiement [zezɛmɑ̃] *nm* lisp.
zézayer [zezeje] (8) *vi* to lisp.
zibeline [ziblin] *nf* sable.
zieuter‡ [zjøte] (1) *vt* (*longuement*) to eye; (*rapidement*) to have a dekko at‡ (*Brit*), have a squint at*.
zig*† [zig] *nm*, **zigomar***† [zigɔmaʀ] *nm*, **zigoto***† [zigɔto] *nm* bloke* (*Brit*), chap*, geezer*† (*Brit*). **c'est un drôle de ~** he's a queer fish*, he's a strange geezer*† (*Brit*).
zigouiller* [ziguje] (1) *vt* to do in*.
zigue*† [zig] *nm* = **zig***†.
zigzag [zigzag] *nm* zigzag. **route en ~** windy *ou* zigzagging road; **faire des ~s** *[route]* to zigzag; *[personne]* to zigzag along.
zigzaguer [zigzage] (1) *vi* to zigzag (along).
zinc [zɛ̃g] *nm* **(a)** (*métal*) zinc. **(b)** (*: *avion*) plane. **(c)** (*: *comptoir*) bar, counter. **boire un coup sur** *ou* **devant le ~** to have a drink (up) at the bar *ou* counter.
zingueur [zɛ̃gœʀ] *nm* zinc worker.
zinnia [zinja] *nm* zinnia.
zinzin* [zɛ̃zɛ̃] **1** *adj* cracked*, nuts*, barmy*. **2** *nm* thingummy(jig)*, what's-it*.
zippé, e [zipe] (*ptp de* **zipper**) *adj* zip-up (*épith*), with a zip.
zipper [zipe] (1) *vt* to zip up.
zircon [ziʀkɔ̃] *nm* zircon.
zizanie [zizani] *nf* ill-feeling. **mettre** *ou* **semer la ~ dans une famille** to set a family at loggerheads, stir up ill-feeling in a family.
zizi* [zizi] *nm* (*hum*) willy* (*hum, langage enfantin*).

zodiacal, e, *mpl* **-aux** [zɔdjakal, o] *adj constellation, signe* of the zodiac; *lumière* zodiacal.
zodiaque [zɔdjak] *nm* zodiac.
zona [zona] *nm* shingles (*sg*), herpes zoster (*T*).
zone [zon] **1** *nf* **(a)** (*gén, Sci*) zone, area. (*Agr*) ~ **d'élevage** *etc* cattle-breeding *etc* area; ~ **d'influence (d'un pays)** sphere *ou* zone of influence (of a country); ~ **franc/sterling** franc/sterling area; (*fig*) **de deuxième/troisième** ~ second-/third-rate.
(b) (*bidonville*) **la** ~ the slum belt.
2: la zone des armées the war zone; **zone bleue** ≃ restricted parking zone *ou* area; **zone dangereuse** danger zone; (*Mét*) **zone de dépression** trough of low pressure; **zone franche** free zone; **zone de salaires** salary weighting; (*Admin*) **zone à urbaniser en priorité** *zone scheduled for priority housing development.*
zoning [zoniŋ] *nm* zoning.
zoo [zoo] *nm* zoo.
zoologie [zɔɔlɔʒi] *nf* zoology.
zoologique [zɔɔlɔʒik] *adj* zoological.
zoologiste [zɔɔlɔʒist(ə)] *nmf*, **zoologue** [zɔɔlɔg] *nmf* zoologist.
zoom [zum] *nm* (*objectif*) zoom lens; (*effet*) zoom.
Zoroastre [zɔʀɔastʀ(ə)] *nm* Zoroaster, Zarathustra.
zou [zu] *excl:* **(allez)** ~! (*partez*) off with you!, shoo!*; (*dépêchez-vous*) get a move on!*; **et** ~**, les voilà partis!** zoom, off they go!*
zouave [zwav] *nm* Zouave, zouave. **faire le** ~* to play the fool, fool around.
Zoulou [zulu] *nm* Zulu.
zozo*† [zozo] *nm* nit(wit)*, ninny*.
zozoter [zɔzɔte] (1) *vi* to lisp.
zut* [zyt] *excl* (*c'est embêtant*) dash (it)!*, darn (it)!*, drat (it)!*; (*tais-toi*) (do) shut up!*
zygote [zigɔt] *nm* zygote.

ENGLISH-FRENCH DICTIONARY
DICTIONNAIRE ANGLAIS-FRANÇAIS

A

A, a[1] [eɪ] **1** *n* **(a)** (*letter*) A, a *m*. **to know sth from A to Z** connaître qch à fond *or* par cœur; **he doesn't know A from B** il est ignare; (*in house numbers*) **24a** 24 bis; (*Brit Aut*) **on the A4** sur la (route) A4, ≃ sur la RN4 *or* la nationale 4.
(b) (*Mus*) la *m*.
2 *cpd*: **A-1**, (*US*) **A no. 1** de première qualité, parfait, champion*; **ABC** *V* **ABC**; **A-bomb** bombe *f* atomique; (*Brit Scol*) **A-levels** ≃ baccalauréat *m*; **A-line dress** robe *f* trapèze *inv*.
a[2] [eɪ, ə] *indef art* (*before vowel or mute h*: **an**) **(a)** un, une. ~ **tree** un arbre; **an apple** une pomme; **such** ~ **hat** un tel *or* pareil chapeau; **so large** ~ **country** un si grand pays.
(b) (*def art in French*) le, la, les. **to have** ~ **good ear** avoir l'oreille juste; **he smokes** ~ **pipe** il fume la pipe; **to set an example** donner l'exemple; **I have read** ~ **third of the book** j'ai lu le tiers du livre; **we haven't** ~ **penny** nous n'avons pas le sou; ~ **woman hates violence** les femmes détestent la violence.
(c) (*absent in French*) **she was** ~ **doctor** elle était médecin; **as** ~ **soldier** en tant que soldat; **my uncle,** ~ **sailor** mon oncle, qui est marin; **what** ~ **pleasure!** quel plaisir!; **to make** ~ **fortune** faire fortune.
(d) un(e) certain(e). **I have heard of** ~ **Mr X** j'ai entendu parler d'un certain M X.
(e) le *or* la même. **they are much of an age** ils sont du même âge; **they are of** ~ **size** ils sont de la même grandeur.
(f) (*a single*) un(e) seul(e). **to empty a glass at** ~ **draught** vider un verre d'un trait; **at** ~ **blow** d'un seul coup.
(g) (*with abstract nouns*) du, de la, des. **to make** ~ **noise/**~ **fuss** faire du bruit/des histoires.
(h) ~ **few survivors** quelques survivants; ~ **lot of** *or* ~ **great many flowers** beaucoup de fleurs.
(i) (*distributive use*) **£4** ~ **person/head** 4 livres par personne/par tête; **3 francs** ~ **kilo** 3 F le kilo; **twice** ~ **month** deux fois par mois; **twice** ~ **year** deux fois l'an *or* par an; **80 km an hour** 80 km/h, 80 kilomètres-heure, 80 kilomètres à l'heure.
Aachen ['ɑːxən] *n* Aix-la-Chapelle.
aback [ə'bæk] *adv*: **to be taken** ~ être interloqué *or* décontenancé, en rester tout interdit *or* déconcerté.
abacus ['æbəkəs] *n, pl* **abaci** ['æbəsaɪ] **(a)** boulier *m* (compteur), abaque *m*. **(b)** (*Archit*) abaque *m*.
abaft [ə'bɑːft] (*Naut*) **1** *adv* sur *or* vers l'arrière. **2** *prep* en arrière de, sur l'arrière de.
abandon [ə'bændən] **1** *vt* **(a)** (*forsake*) *person* abandonner, quitter, délaisser. (*fig*) **to** ~ **o.s.** to se livrer à, s'abandonner à, se laisser aller à.
(b) (*Jur etc: give up*) *property, right* renoncer à; *action* se désister de.
(c) (*Naut*) *ship* évacuer; (*Jur*) *cargo* faire (acte de) délaissement de.
2 *n* (*U*) laisser-aller *m*, abandon *m*, relâchement *m*. **with (gay)** ~ avec (une belle) désinvolture.
abandoned [ə'bændənd] *adj* **(a)** (*forsaken*) *person* abandonné, délaissé; *place* abandonné. **(b)** (*dissolute*) débauché.
abandonment [ə'bændənmənt] *n* (*lit, fig*) abandon *m*; (*Jur*) *[action]* désistement *m*; *[property, right]* cession *f*; *[cargo]* délaissement *m*.
abase [ə'beɪs] *vt* (*humiliate*) *person* mortifier, humilier; (*degrade*) *person* abaisser, avilir; *person's qualities, actions* rabaisser, ravaler. **to** ~ **o.s. so far as to do** s'abaisser *or* s'humilier jusqu'à faire.
abasement [ə'beɪsmənt] *n* (*U*) (*moral decay*) dégradation *f*, avilissement *m*; (*humiliation*) humiliation *f*, mortification *f*.
abash [ə'bæʃ] *vt* confondre, décontenancer. **to feel** ~**ed** être confus.
abate [ə'beɪt] **1** *vi [storm, emotions, pain]* s'apaiser, se calmer; *[flood]* baisser; *[fever]* baisser, décroître; *[wind]* tomber; (*Naut*) mollir; *[courage]* faiblir, s'affaiblir, diminuer; *[rent]* baisser.
2 *vt* **(a)** (*lessen*) affaiblir; *noise, pollution* réduire; (*remove*) supprimer; *rent, tax* baisser.
(b) (*Jur: abolish*) *writ* annuler; *sentence* remettre; *corruption* faire cesser, mettre fin à.
abatement [ə'beɪtmənt] *n* (*U*) (*reduction, lessening*) diminution *f*, réduction *f*; *[noise, pollution]* suppression *f*, réduction; (*Med*) *[illness]* régression *f*; (*Jur*) *[legacy]* réduction; *[punishment]* atténuation *f*; *[fine]* annulation *f*, levée *f*.
abattoir ['æbətwɑːʳ] *n* abattoir *m*.
abbess ['æbɪs] *n* abbesse *f*.
abbey ['æbɪ] *n* (*monastery*) abbaye *f*; (*church*) (église *f*) abbatiale *f*. **Westminster A**~ l'Abbaye de Westminster.
abbot ['æbət] *n* abbé *m*, (Père *m*) supérieur *m*.
abbreviate [ə'briːvɪeɪt] *vt* abréger, raccourcir.
abbreviation [əˌbriːvɪ'eɪʃən] *n* abréviation *f*.
ABC ['eɪbiː'siː] *n* abc *m*, alphabet *m*. (*Brit Rail*) **the** ~ **(guide)** l'indicateur *m* des chemins de fer; **it's as easy** *or* **simple as** ~ * c'est simple comme bonjour, rien de plus simple.
abdicate ['æbdɪkeɪt] **1** *vt right* renoncer à, abdiquer; *function* se démettre de. **to** ~ **the throne** renoncer à la couronne, abdiquer. **2** *vi* abdiquer.
abdication [ˌæbdɪ'keɪʃən] *n [king]* abdication *f*, renonciation *f*; *[mandate etc]* démission *f* (*of* de); *[right]* renonciation (*of* à), désistement *m* (*of* de).
abdomen ['æbdəmen, (*Med*) æb'dəʊmen] *n* abdomen *m*.
abdominal [æb'dɒmɪnl] *adj* abdominal.
abduct [æb'dʌkt] *vt* enlever (*un enfant etc*).
abduction [æb'dʌkʃən] *n* **(a)** (*Jur etc*) enlèvement *m*, rapt *m*. **(b)** (*Logic*) abduction *f*.
abductor [æb'dʌktəʳ] *n* **(a)** (*person*) ravisseur *m*, -euse *f*. **(b)** (*Anat*) abducteur *m*.
abed† [ə'bed] *adv* (*liter*) au lit, couché. **to lie** ~ être couché.
aberrant [ə'berənt] *adj* (*Bio, fig*) aberrant, anormal.
aberration [ˌæbə'reɪʃən] *n* **(a)** (*U: lit, fig*) aberration *f*, égarement *m*. **in a moment of** ~ dans un moment d'aberration.
(b) (*instance of this*) anomalie *f*, idée *or* action aberrante, aberration *f*.
(c) (*Astron, Opt*) aberration *f*.
abet [ə'bet] *vt* encourager, soutenir. **to** ~ **sb in a crime** encourager *or* aider qn à commettre un crime; *V* **aid 2**.
abetter, abettor [ə'betəʳ] *n* instigateur *m*, -trice *f* d'un crime.
abeyance [ə'beɪəns] *n* suspension *f* temporaire, interruption *f* provisoire. *[law, custom]* **to fall into** ~ tomber en désuétude; **the question is in** ~ la question reste en suspens.
abhor [əb'hɔːʳ] *vt* abhorrer, avoir en horreur, exécrer; *V* **nature**.
abhorrence [əb'hɒrəns] *n* horreur *f*, aversion *f* (*of* de), répulsion *f*. **to hold in** ~ avoir horreur de, avoir en horreur.
abhorrent [əb'hɒrənt] *adj* odieux, exécrable, répugnant (*to* à).
abide [ə'baɪd] **1** *vt* **(a)** (*neg only: tolerate*) endurer, supporter, souffrir. **I can't** ~ **her** je ne peux pas la supporter *or* la souffrir *or* la sentir*.
(b) (*liter: await*) attendre.
2 *vi* (†: *endure*) subsister, durer, se maintenir; (*live*) demeurer, habiter.
abide by *vt fus rule, decision* se soumettre à, se conformer à, respecter; *consequences* accepter, supporter; *promise* rester *or* demeurer fidèle à; *resolve* maintenir, s'en tenir à.
abiding [ə'baɪdɪŋ] *adj* (*liter*) constant, éternel; *V* **law** *etc*.
ability [ə'bɪlɪtɪ] *n* **(a)** (*U: power, proficiency*) aptitude *f* (*to do* à faire), capacité *f* (*to do* pour faire), compétence *f* (*in* en, *to do* pour faire). **to the best of one's** ~ de son mieux.
(b) (*U: cleverness*) habileté *f*, talent *m*. **a person of great** ~ une personne très douée; **he has a certain artistic** ~ il a un certain don *or* talent artistique.
(c) (*mental powers*) **abilities** talents *mpl*, dons intellectuels.
abject ['æbdʒekt] *adj person, action* abject, vil, méprisable; *state, condition* misérable, pitoyable; *apology* servile. **in** ~ **poverty** dans la misère noire.
abjectly ['æbdʒektlɪ] *adv* (*V* **abject**) abjectement; misérablement; avec servilité.
abjure [əb'dʒʊəʳ] *vt one's rights* renoncer (publiquement *or* par serment) à. **to** ~ **one's religion** abjurer sa religion, apostasier.
ablative ['æblətɪv] **1** *n* ablatif *m*. **in the** ~ à l'ablatif; ~ **absolute** ablatif absolu. **2** *adj* ablatif.
ablaze [ə'bleɪz] *adv, adj* (*lit*) en feu, en flammes. **to set** ~ embraser (*liter*); **to be** ~ flamber; (*fig*) ~ **with anger** enflammé de colère; (*fig*) ~ **with light** resplendissant de lumière.
able ['eɪbl] **1** *adj* **(a)** (*'to be* ~ *' sert d'infinitif à l'auxiliaire de mode 'can/could' dans quelques-uns des sens de cet auxiliaire*) **to be** ~ **to do** (*have means or opportunity*) pouvoir faire; (*know how to*) savoir faire; (*be capable of*) être à même de *or* en mesure de faire; **I ran fast and so was** ~ **to catch the bus** en courant vite j'ai réussi à attraper l'autobus (*NB 'could' ne peut être employé dans ce contexte*); *V* **can**[1] **b**.
(b) (*having power, means, opportunity*) capable, en état (*to do* de faire), apte, propre (*to do* à faire). ~ **to pay** en mesure de payer; **you are better** ~ **to do it than he is** (*it's easier for you*) vous êtes mieux à même de le faire *or* plus en état de le faire que lui; (*you're better qualified*) vous êtes plus propre à le faire *or* mieux désigné pour le faire que lui.
(c) (*clever*) capable, compétent, de talent. **an** ~ **man** un homme de talent.

(d) (*Med: healthy*) sain. (*Jur*) ~ **in body and mind** sain de corps et d'esprit.

2 *cpd*: **able-bodied** robuste, fort, solide; (*Mil*) *recruit* bon pour le service; (*Naut*) **able(-bodied) seaman** matelot breveté *or* de deuxième classe; **able-minded** intelligent.

ablution [əˈbluːʃən] *n* (*Rel*) ablution *f*.

ably [ˈeɪblɪ] *adv* habilement, avec adresse, avec talent.

abnegate [ˈæbnɪgeɪt] *vt responsibility* renier, répudier, rejeter; *one's rights* renoncer à; *one's religion* abjurer.

abnegation [ˌæbnɪˈgeɪʃən] *n* (*denial*) reniement *m*, désaveu *m*; (*renunciation*) renoncement *m*. **self-**~ abnégation *f*.

abnormal [æbˈnɔːməl] *adj* anormal, exceptionnel; (*Med*) anormal.

abnormality [ˌæbnɔːˈmælɪtɪ] *n* **(a)** (*U*) caractère anormal *or* exceptionnel. **(b)** (*instance of this, also Bio, Psych*) anomalie *f*; (*Med*) difformité *f*, malformation *f*.

abnormally [æbˈnɔːməlɪ] *adv* anormalement, d'une manière anormale, exceptionnellement.

aboard [əˈbɔːd] **1** *adv* **(a)** (*Aviat, Naut*) à bord. **to go** ~ (s')embarquer, monter à bord; **to take** ~ embarquer; **all** ~! (*Rail*) en voiture!; (*Naut*) tout le monde à bord!

(b) (*Naut*) le long du bord. **close** ~ bord à bord.

2 *prep* (*Aviat, Naut*) à bord de. ~ **the train/bus** dans le train/le bus.

abode [əˈbəʊd] *n* (*liter*) demeure *f*; (*Jur*) domicile *m*. **to take up one's** ~ élire domicile; *V* **fixed**.

abolish [əˈbɒlɪʃ] *vt practice, custom* supprimer; *death penalty* abolir; *law* abroger, abolir.

abolishment [əˈbɒlɪʃmənt] *n*, **abolition** [ˌæbəʊˈlɪʃən] *n* (*V* **abolish**) suppression *f*; abolition *f*; abrogation *f*.

abolitionist [ˌæbəʊˈlɪʃənɪst] *n* (*Hist*) abolitionniste *mf*, anti-esclavagiste *mf*.

abominable [əˈbɒmɪnəbl] *adj* (*hateful*) abominable, odieux, détestable; (*unpleasant*) abominable, affreux, horrible. **the** ~ **snowman** l'abominable homme *m* des neiges.

abominably [əˈbɒmɪnəblɪ] *adv* **(a)** abominablement, odieusement. **(b) it's** ~ **cold** il fait abominablement froid, il fait un froid abominable.

abominate [əˈbɒmɪneɪt] *vt* abhorrer, exécrer, abominer.

abomination [əˌbɒmɪˈneɪʃən] *n* **(a)** (*U*) abomination *f*. **I hold him in** ~ je l'ai en abomination *or* en horreur, il me remplit d'horreur. **(b)** (*loathsome thing, act*) abomination *f*, objet *m* d'horreur, acte *m* abominable. **this coffee is an** ~* ce café est abominable *or* est une abomination*.

aboriginal [ˌæbəˈrɪdʒənl] *adj*, *n person* autochtone (*mf*), aborigène (*mf*); *plant, animal* aborigène.

aborigine [ˌæbəˈrɪdʒɪnɪ] *n* aborigène *mf*.

abort [əˈbɔːt] **1** *vi* (*Med, fig*) avorter; (*Mil, Space*) échouer. **2** *vt* (*Med, fig*) faire avorter; (*Space*) *mission, operation* abandonner *or* interrompre (pour raison de sécurité).

abortion [əˈbɔːʃən] *n* **(a)** (*Med*) avortement *m*, interruption *f* (volontaire) de grossesse. **spontaneous** ~ avortement spontané, interruption de grossesse; **to have an** ~ avorter; **to get an** ~ se faire avorter; ~ **law reform** réforme *f* de la loi sur l'avortement.

(b) (*fig*) *[plans etc]* avortement *m*.

(c) (*Med: creature*) avorton *m*.

abortionist [əˈbɔːʃənɪst] *n* avorteur *m*, -euse *f*. **backstreet** ~ faiseuse *f* d'anges.

abortive [əˈbɔːtɪv] *adj* **(a)** (*unsuccessful*) *plan* manqué, raté, qui a échoué. **it was an** ~ **effort** c'était un coup manqué *or* raté; **he made an** ~ **attempt to speak** il a fait une tentative infructueuse pour parler. **(b)** (*Med*) *method, medicine* abortif.

abound [əˈbaʊnd] *vi [fish, resources etc]* abonder; *[river, town, area etc]* abonder (*in* en), regorger (*in* de).

about [əˈbaʊt] (*phr vb elem*) **1** *adv* **(a)** (*approximately*) vers, à peu près, environ. ~ **11 o'clock** vers 11 heures, sur les 11 heures; **it's** ~ **11 o'clock** il est environ *or* à peu près 11 heures; (*emphatic*) **it's** ~ **time!** il est (bien) temps!; **it's** ~ **time to go** il est presque temps de partir; **there were** ~ **25 and now there are** ~ **30** il y en avait environ 25 *or* dans les 25 et à présent il y en a une trentaine; **she's** ~ **as old as you** elle est à peu près de votre âge; **I've had** ~ **enough!*** je commence à en avoir marre!* *or* en avoir jusque là!* *or* en avoir ras le bol!‡

(b) (*here and there*) çà *or* ici et là, de tous côtés. **shoes lying** ~ des chaussures dans tous les coins *or* traînant çà et là; **to throw one's arms** ~ gesticuler, agiter les bras en tous sens.

(c) (*near*) près, par ici, par là. **there was nobody** ~ il n'y avait personne; **there is a rumour** ~ **that...** le bruit court que..., on dit que...; **he's somewhere** ~ il n'est pas loin, il est par ici quelque part, il est (quelque part) dans les parages; **there's a lot of flu** ~ il y a beaucoup de grippes en ce moment.

(d) (*all round*) autour, à la ronde. **all** ~ tout autour; **to glance** ~ jeter un coup d'œil autour de soi.

(e) (*opposite direction*) à l'envers, à rebours. (*fig*) **it's the other way** ~ c'est tout le contraire; (*Mil*) ~ **turn!**, ~ **face!** demi-tour, marche!; (*Naut*) **to go** *or* **put** ~ virer de bord vent debout *or* vent devant; *V* **ready, right**.

(f) (*in phrases*) **to be** ~ **to do** être sur le point de faire, aller faire; **she's up and** ~ **again** elle est de nouveau sur pied; **you should be out and** ~! ne restez donc pas enfermé!; *V* **bring about, come about, turn about** *etc*.

2 *prep* **(a)** (*concerning*) au sujet de, concernant, à propos de. **I heard nothing** ~ **it** je n'en ai pas entendu parler; **what is it** ~? de quoi s'agit-il?; **I know what it's all** ~ je sais de quoi il retourne; **to speak** ~ **sth** parler de qch; **well, what** ~ **it?*** (*does it matter?*) et alors?*; (*what do you think?*) alors qu'est-ce que tu en penses?; **what** ~ **me?*** et moi alors?*; **how** ~ *or* **what** ~ **going to the pictures?*** si on allait au cinéma?; **what** ~ **a coffee?** si on prenait un café?, est-ce que tu veux un café?

(b) (*near to*) vers, dans le voisinage de; (*somewhere in*) en, dans. **I dropped it** ~ **here** je l'ai laissé tomber par ici *or* près d'ici; **round** ~ **the Arctic Circle** près du Cercle polaire; ~ **the house** quelque part dans la maison; **to wander** ~ **the town/the streets** errer dans la ville/par les rues.

(c) (*occupied with*) occupé à. **what are you** ~? que faites-vous?, qu'est-ce que vous fabriquez là?*; **while we're** ~ **it** pendant que nous y sommes; **I don't know what he's** ~ je ne sais pas ce qu'il fabrique*; **mind what you're** ~! faites (un peu) attention!; **how does one go** ~ **it?** comment est-ce qu'on s'y prend?; **to go** ~ **one's business** s'occuper de ses (propres) affaires; **to send sb** ~ **his business** envoyer promener* qn.

(d) (*with, on*) **I've got it** ~ **me somewhere** je l'ai quelque part sur moi; **there is something horrible** ~ **him** il y a quelque chose d'horrible en lui; **there is something interesting** ~ **him** il a un côté intéressant; **there is something charming** ~ **him** il a un certain charme.

(e) (*round*) autour de. **the trees (round)** ~ **the pond** les arbres qui entourent l'étang; **the countryside (round)** ~ **Edinburgh** la campagne autour d'Édimbourg.

about face [əˈbaʊtˈfeɪs], **about turn** [əˈbaʊtˈtɜːn] **1** *excl* (*Mil*) demi-tour, marche!

2 about-face, about-turn *vi* (*Mil*) faire un demi-tour; (*fig*) faire volte-face.

3 *n* (*Mil*) demi-tour *m*; (*fig*) volte-face *f*. **to do an** ~ faire un demi-tour; (*fig*) faire volte-face.

above [əˈbʌv] (*phr vb elem*) **1** *adv* **(a)** (*overhead, higher up*) au-dessus, en haut, en l'air. **from** ~ d'en haut; **view from** ~ vue plongeante; **the flat** ~ l'appartement au-dessus *or* du dessus; **the powers** ~ (*of higher rank*) les autorités supérieures; (*in heaven*) les puissances célestes; (*fig*) **a warning from** ~ un avertissement (venu) d'en haut.

(b) (*more*) **boys of 16 and** ~ les garçons à partir de 16 ans; **seats at 10 francs and** ~ places à partir de 10 F; *V* **over**.

(c) (*earlier: in book etc*) ci-dessus, plus haut. **as** ~ comme ci-dessus, comme plus haut; **the address as** ~ l'adresse ci-dessus.

(d) (*upstream*) en amont, plus haut.

2 *prep* **(a)** (*higher than, superior to*) au-dessus de, plus haut que. ~ **the horizon** au-dessus de l'horizon; ~ **average** au-dessus de la moyenne, supérieur à la moyenne; ~ **all** par-dessus tout, surtout.

(b) (*more than*) plus de. **children** ~ **7 years of age** les enfants de plus de 7 ans *or* au-dessus de 7 ans; **it will cost** ~ **£10** ça coûtera plus de 10 livres; **over and** ~ **(the cost of)** ... en plus de (ce que coûte) ... .

(c) (*beyond*) au-delà de. **to get** ~ **o.s.** avoir des idées de grandeur; **to live** ~ **one's means** vivre au-delà de *or* au-dessus de ses moyens; **that is quite** ~ **me*** ceci me dépasse; **this book is** ~ **me*** ce livre est trop compliqué pour moi; *V* **head**.

(d) (*too proud, honest etc for*) **he is** ~ **such behaviour** il est au-dessus d'une pareille conduite; **he's not** ~ **stealing/theft** il irait jusqu'à voler/jusqu'au vol; **he's not** ~ **playing with the children** il ne dédaigne pas de jouer avec les enfants.

(e) (*upstream from*) en amont de, plus haut que.

(f) (*north of*) au nord de, au-dessus de.

3 *adj* ci-dessus mentionné, précité. **the** ~ **decree** le décret précité.

4 *cpd*: **aboveboard** (*adj*) *person* franc (*f* franche), loyal, ouvert; *action, decision* loyal; (*adv*) cartes sur table, ouvertement; **aboveground** (*lit*) au-dessus du sol, à la surface; (*Tech*) extérieur; **above-mentioned** mentionné ci-dessus, susmentionné, précité; **above-named** susnommé.

abracadabra [ˌæbrəkəˈdæbrə] **1** *excl* abracadabra! **2** *n* (*in spells*) formule *f* magique; (*gibberish*) charabia *m*, baragouin *m*.

abrade [əˈbreɪd] *vt* user en frottant *or* par le frottement; *skin etc* écorcher, érafler; (*Geol*) éroder.

Abraham [ˈeɪbrəhæm] *n* Abraham *m*.

abrasion [əˈbreɪʒən] *n* (*V* **abrade**) frottement *m*; (*Med*) écorchure *f*; érosion *f*; (*Tech*) abrasion *f*.

abrasive [əˈbreɪsɪv] **1** *adj* abrasif; (*fig*) *voice* caustique; *wit* corrosif. **2** *n* abrasif *m*.

abreast [əˈbrest] *adv* **(a)** *[horses, vehicles, ships]* de front; *[persons]* de front, l'un(e) à côté de l'autre, côte à côte. **to walk 3** ~ marcher 3 de front; (*Naut*) **(in) line** ~ en ligne de front.

(b) ~ **of** à la hauteur de, parallèlement à, en ligne avec; (*Naut*) **to be** ~ **of a ship** être à la hauteur *or* par le travers d'un navire; (*fig*) **to be** ~ **of the times** marcher avec son temps; (*fig*) **to keep** ~ **of** suivre (les progrès de), se maintenir *or* se tenir au courant de.

abridge [əˈbrɪdʒ] *vt book* abréger; *article, speech* raccourcir, abréger; *interview* écourter; *text* réduire. ~**d edition** édition abrégée.

abridgement [əˈbrɪdʒmənt] *n* **(a)** (*shortened version*) résumé *m*, abrégé *m*. **(b)** (*U*) diminution *f*, réduction *f*; *[rights]* privation *f*.

abroad [əˈbrɔːd] *adv* **(a)** (*in foreign land*) à l'étranger. **to go/be** ~ aller/être à l'étranger; **news from** ~ nouvelles de l'étranger; *V* **home**.

(b) (*far and wide*) au loin; (*in all directions*) de tous côtés, dans toutes les directions. **scattered** ~ éparpillé de tous côtés *or* aux quatre vents; **there is a rumour** ~ **that ...** le bruit circule *or* court que ...; *V* **noise**.

(c) (†: *out of doors*) (au) dehors, hors de chez soi.

abrogate [ˈæbrəʊgeɪt] *vt* abroger, abolir.

abrogation [ˌæbrəʊˈgeɪʃən] *n* abrogation *f*.

abrupt [əˈbrʌpt] *adj turn* soudain; *question, dismissal* brusque; *departure* précipité; *person, conduct* bourru, brusque; *style, speech* heurté; *slope* abrupt, raide.

abruptly [əˈbrʌptlɪ] *adv turn, move* brusquement, tout à coup;

speak, behave avec brusquerie, sans cérémonie, abruptement; *rise* en pente raide, à pic.

abruptness [əˈbrʌptnɪs] *n* (*V* **abrupt**) (*suddenness*) soudaineté *f*; (*haste*) précipitation *f*; *[style]* décousu *m*; *[person, behaviour]* brusquerie *f*, rudesse *f*; (*steepness*) raideur *f*.

abscess [ˈæbsɪs] *n* abcès *m*.

abscond [əbˈskɒnd] *vi* s'enfuir, prendre la fuite, se sauver (*from* de).

absconder [əbˈskɒndəʳ] *n* fugitif *m*, -ive *f*; (*from prison*) évadé(e) *m(f)*.

absconding [əbˈskɒndɪŋ] **1** *adj* en fuite. **2** *n* fuite *f*; *[prisoner]* évasion *f*.

abseil [ˈæpsaɪl] **1** *vi* descendre en rappel. **2** *n* (descente *f* en) rappel *m*.

absence [ˈæbsəns] *n* **(a)** (*U*) (*being away*) absence *f*, éloignement *m*; (*Jur*) non-comparution *f*, défaut *m*. **during the ~ of sb** pendant *or* en l'absence de qn; (*Jur*) **sentenced in his ~** condamné par contumace; *V* **leave**.

(b) (*instance of this*) absence *f*. (*Scol*) **many ~s** de nombreuses périodes d'absence; **an ~ of 3 months** une absence de 3 mois.

(c) (*U: lack*) manque *m*, défaut *m*. **in the ~ of information** faute de renseignements.

(d) ~ of mind distraction *f*, absence *f*.

absent [ˈæbsənt] **1** *adj* **(a)** (*away*) absent. (*Mil*) **~ without leave** absent sans permission.

(b) (*absent-minded*) distrait.

(c) (*lacking*) absent. **sympathy was noticeably ~ from his manner** son attitude révélait clairement un manque de sympathie.

2 *cpd*: **absent-minded** *person* distrait, préoccupé; *air, manner* absent, distrait; **absent-mindedly** distraitement, d'un air distrait *or* absent, d'un ton préoccupé; **absent-mindedness** distraction *f*, absence *f*.

3 [æbˈsent] *vt*: **to ~ o.s.** s'absenter (*from* de).

absentee [ˌæbsənˈtiː] **1** *n* absent(e) *m(f)*, manquant(e) *m(f)*; (*habitual*) absentéiste *mf*. **2** *cpd*: **absentee landlord** (propriétaire *mf*) absentéiste *mf*; **absentee voter** électeur *m*, -trice *f* par correspondance.

absenteeism [ˌæbsənˈtiːɪzəm] *n* absentéisme *m*.

absently [ˈæbsəntlɪ] *adv* distraitement, en pensant à autre chose.

absinth(e) [ˈæbsɪnθ] *n* absinthe *f*.

absolute [ˈæbsəluːt] **1** *adj* **(a)** (*whole, undeniable*) absolu, total, complet (*f* -ète); (*Chem*) *alcohol* absolu, anhydre. **~ necessity** force majeure, nécessité absolue; **~ distress** misère complète, totale indigence; (*Jur*) **the divorce was made ~** le (jugement en) divorce a été prononcé; **it's an ~ scandal*** c'est un véritable scandale; **~ idiot*** parfait crétin*; **it's an ~ fact that ...** c'est un fait indiscutable que ... .

(b) (*unlimited*) *power* absolu, illimité, souverain; *monarch* absolu.

(c) (*unqualified*) *refusal, command* absolu, formel; (*Jur*) *proof* irréfutable, formel. **~ veto** véto formel; *V* **ablative**.

2 *n* absolu *m*.

absolutely [ˈæbsəluːtlɪ] *adv* **(a)** (*completely*) absolument, complètement, tout à fait.

(b) (*unconditionally*) *refuse* absolument, formellement.

(c) (*certainly*) absolument. **oh ~!** mais bien sûr!

(d) (*Gram*) **verb used ~** verbe employé absolument *or* dans un sens absolu.

absolution [ˌæbsəˈluːʃən] *n* absolution *f*, remise *f* des péchés; (*in liturgy*) absoute *f*.

absolutism [ˈæbsəluːtɪzəm] *n* (*Pol*) absolutisme *m*; (*Rel*) prédestination *f*.

absolve [əbˈzɒlv] *vt* (*from sin, of crime*) absoudre (*from, of* de); (*Jur*) acquitter (*of* de); (*from obligation, oath*) décharger, délier (*from* de).

absorb [əbˈsɔːb] *vt* **(a)** (*lit, fig*) absorber; *sound, shock* amortir. **to ~ surplus stocks** absorber les surplus.

(b) (*gen pass*) **to become ~ed in one's work/in a book** s'absorber dans son travail/dans la lecture d'un livre; **to be ~ed in a book** être plongé dans un livre; **to be completely ~ed in one's work** être tout entier à son travail.

absorbency [əbˈsɔːbənsɪ] *n* pouvoir absorbant; (*Chem, Phys*) absorptivité *f*.

absorbent [əbˈsɔːbənt] **1** *adj* absorbant. (*US*) **~ cotton** coton *m* hydrophile. **2** *n* absorbant *m*.

absorbing [əbˈsɔːbɪŋ] *adj* (*lit*) absorbant; (*fig*) *book, film* passionnant, captivant; *work* absorbant.

absorption [əbˈsɔːpʃən] *n* **(a)** (*Phys, Physiol*) absorption *f*; (*Aut*) *[shocks]* amortissement *m*; (*fig*) *[person into group etc]* absorption, intégration *f*.

(b) (*fig*) concentration *f* (d'esprit). **his ~ in his studies prevented him from ...** ses études l'absorbaient à tel point qu'elles l'empêchaient de ... .

abstain [əbˈsteɪn] *vi* **(a)** s'abstenir (*from* de, *from doing* de faire). **(b)** (*be teetotaller*) s'abstenir complètement (de l'usage) des boissons alcoolisées.

abstainer [əbˈsteɪnəʳ] *n* **(a)** (*also* **total ~**) personne *f* qui s'abstient de toute boisson alcoolisée *or* qui ne boit pas d'alcool. **(b)** (*Pol*) abstentionniste *mf*.

abstemious [əbˈstiːmɪəs] *adj person* sobre, frugal; *meal* frugal.

abstemiousness [əbˈstiːmɪəsnɪs] *n* (*V* **abstemious**) sobriété *f*; frugalité *f*.

abstention [əbˈstenʃən] *n* (*from voting*) abstention *f*; (*from drinking*) abstinence *f*. (*Parl etc*) **400 votes with 3 ~s** 400 voix et 3 abstentions.

abstinence [ˈæbstɪnəns] *n* (*also Rel*) abstinence *f* (*from* de). **(total) ~** abstention *f* de toute boisson alcoolisée.

abstinent [ˈæbstɪnənt] *adj* sobre, tempérant; (*Rel*) abstinent.

abstract [ˈæbstrækt] **1** *adj idea, number, art, artist* abstrait.

2 *n* **(a)** (*Philos*) abstrait *m*. **in the ~** dans l'abstrait.

(b) (*summary*) résumé *m*, abrégé *m*.

(c) (*work of art*) œuvre abstraite.

3 [æbˈstrækt] *vt* **(a)** (*also Chem: remove*) dégager, isoler (*from* de).

(b) (*steal*) soustraire, dérober (*sth from sb* qch à qn).

(c) *ideas* faire abstraction de.

(d) (*summarize*) *book* résumer.

abstracted [æbˈstræktɪd] *adj person* (*absent-minded*) distrait; (*preoccupied*) préoccupé, absorbé.

abstraction [æbˈstrækʃən] *n* **(a)** (*act of removing*) extraction *f*; (*: *stealing*) appropriation *f*.

(b) (*absent-mindedness*) distraction *f*. **with an air of ~** d'un air distrait *or* préoccupé.

(c) (*concept*) idée abstraite, abstraction *f*.

abstruse [æbˈstruːs] *adj* abstrus (*liter*).

abstruseness [æbˈstruːsnɪs] *n* complexité *f*, caractère abstrus (*liter*).

absurd [əbˈsɜːd] **1** *adj* déraisonnable, absurde. **it's ~!** c'est idiot!, c'est insensé!, c'est absurde! **2** *n* (*Philos*) absurde *m*.

absurdity [əbˈsɜːdɪtɪ] *n* absurdité *f*.

absurdly [əbˈsɜːdlɪ] *adv* absurdement, ridiculement.

abundance [əˈbʌndəns] *n* (*U*) **(a)** (*plenty*) abondance *f*, profusion *f*. **in ~** en abondance, à foison, à profusion. **(b)** (*wealth*) abondance *f*, aisance *f*. **to live in ~** vivre dans l'abondance.

abundant [əˈbʌndənt] *adj* riche (*in* en), abondant. **there is ~ proof that he is guilty** les preuves de sa culpabilité abondent.

abundantly [əˈbʌndəntlɪ] *adv* abondamment, copieusement. **to grow ~** pousser à foison; **it was ~ clear that ...** il était tout à fait clair que ...; **he made it ~ clear to me that ...** il m'a bien fait comprendre *or* m'a bien précisé que ... .

abuse [əˈbjuːz] **1** *vt* **(a)** (*misuse*) *privilege* abuser de.

(b) *person* (*speak unkindly of*) injurier, insulter; (*ill-treat*) maltraiter, malmener.

2 [əˈbjuːs] *n* **(a)** *[power, authority]* abus *m*; *[language]* emploi abusif.

(b) (*unjust practice*) abus *m*. **to remedy ~s** réprimer les abus.

(c) (*U: curses, insults*) insultes *fpl*, injures *fpl*.

abusive [əbˈjuːsɪv] *adj* **(a)** (*offensive*) injurieux, offensant, grossier. **to use ~ language to sb** injurier qn. **(b)** (*wrongly used*) abusif, mauvais.

abut [əˈbʌt] *vi*: **to ~ on** confiner à, être contigu (*f* -guë) à.

abutment [əˈbʌtmənt] *n* (*Archit*) contrefort *m*, piédroit *m*; (*esp on bridge*) butée *f*.

abysmal [əˈbɪzməl] *adj* insondable, sans fond. (*fig*) **~ ignorance** ignorance crasse *or* sans bornes; **his work was quite ~** son travail était tout à fait exécrable.

abysmally [əˈbɪzməlɪ] *adv* abominablement, atrocement. **~ ignorant** d'une ignorance crasse *or* sans bornes; **his work is ~ bad** son travail est atrocement *or* abominablement mauvais, il travaille atrocement *or* abominablement mal.

abyss [əˈbɪs] *n* (*lit, fig*) abîme *m*, gouffre *m*; (*in sea*) abysse *m*.

Abyssinia [ˌæbɪˈsɪnɪə] *n* Abyssinie *f*.

Abyssinian [ˌæbɪˈsɪnɪən] **1** *adj* abyssinien, abyssin (*rare*).

2 *n* Abyssinien(ne) *m(f)*, Abyssin(e) *m(f)* (*rare*). **the ~ Empire** l'empire *m* d'Éthiopie.

acacia [əˈkeɪʃə] *n* acacia *m*.

academic [ˌækəˈdemɪk] **1** *adj* **(a)** (*of studying, colleges*) universitaire, scolaire. **~ gown** toge *f* de professeur *or* d'étudiant; **~ freedom** liberté *f* de l'enseignement; (*Univ*) **~ year** année *f* universitaire.

(b) (*theoretical*) théorique, spéculatif. **~ debate** discussion sans portée pratique *or* toute théorique.

(c) (*scholarly*) *style, approach* intellectuel.

(d) (*of an academy*) académique.

(e) *art, portrait* académique.

2 *n* (*university teacher*) universitaire *mf*.

academicals [ˌækəˈdemɪkəlz] *npl* toge *f* (, épitoge *f*) et bonnet *m* universitaires.

academician [əˌkædəˈmɪʃən] *n* académicien(ne) *m(f)*; *V* **academy b**.

academy [əˈkædəmɪ] *n* **(a)** (*private college*) école privée, collège *m*, pensionnat *m*. **military/naval ~** école militaire/navale; (*Brit*) **~ of music** conservatoire *m*; (*Brit*) **secretarial ~** école de commerce et de secrétariat.

(b) (*society*) académie *f*, société *f*. **the (Royal) A~** l'Académie Royale (*de Londres*); *V* **French**.

acanthus [əˈkænθəs] *n* acanthe *f*.

accede [ækˈsiːd] *vi* **(a) to ~ to a request** agréer une demande, donner suite à une demande; **to ~ to a suggestion** agréer *or* accepter une proposition.

(b) (*gain position*) entrer en possession (*to an office* d'une charge). **to ~ to the throne** monter sur le trône.

(c) (*join*) adhérer, se joindre (*to a party* à un parti).

accelerate [ækˈseləreɪt] **1** *vt movement* accélérer; *work* activer; *events* précipiter, hâter. **2** *vi* (*esp Aut*) accélérer.

acceleration [ækˌseləˈreɪʃən] *n* accélération *f*; (*Aut*) accélération, reprises *fpl*.

accelerator [ækˈseləreɪtəʳ] *n* (*esp Aut*) accélérateur *m*. **to step on the ~** appuyer sur l'accélérateur *or* le champignon*.

accent [ˈæksənt] **1** *n* **(a)** (*stress on part of word*) accent *m* (tonique).

(b) (*intonation, pronunciation*) accent *m*. **to speak French without an ~** parler français sans accent.

(c) (*written mark*) accent *m*; *V* **acute** *etc*.

(d) (*way of speaking*) **~s** accents *mpl*, paroles *fpl*; **in ~s of rage** avec des accents de rage (dans la voix).

2 [æk'sent] *vt* **(a)** (*emphasize*) *word* accentuer, mettre l'accent sur; *syllable* accentuer, appuyer sur.
(b) (*fig: make prominent*) accentuer, mettre en valeur.

accentuate [æk'sentjʊeɪt] *vt* (*emphasize*) accentuer, faire ressortir, souligner; (*draw attention to*) attirer l'attention sur.

accentuation [æk,sentjʊ'eɪʃən] *n* accentuation *f*.

accept [ək'sept] *vt* **(a)** *gift, invitation, apology* accepter; *goods* prendre livraison de; *excuse, fact, report, findings* admettre, accepter; *one's duty* se soumettre à; *one's fate* accepter, se résigner à; *task* se charger de, accepter; (*Comm*) *bill* accepter. **I ~ that ...** je conviens que ... .
(b) (*allow*) *action, behaviour* admettre, accepter.

acceptable [ək'septəbl] *adj* **(a)** (*worth accepting*) *offer, suggestion* acceptable. **(b)** (*welcome*) bienvenu, opportun. **the money was most ~** l'argent est arrivé fort à propos.

acceptance [ək'septəns] *n* **(a)** *[invitation, gift]* acceptation *f*; *[proposal]* consentement *m* (*of* à); (*Comm*) *[bill]* acceptation.
(b) (*approval*) réception *f* favorable, approbation *f*. **the idea met with general ~** l'idée a reçu l'approbation générale *or* a remporté tous les suffrages.

acceptation [,æksep'teɪʃən] *n* **(a)** (*meaning*) acceptation *f*, signification *f*. **(b)** (*approval*) approbation *f*.

accepted [ək'septɪd] *adj* accepté; *fact* reconnu; *idea* reçu; *behaviour, pronunciation* admis.

acceptor [ək'septə^r] *n* (*Comm*) accepteur *m*.

access ['ækses] **1** *n* (*U*) **(a)** (*way of approach*) accès *m*, abord *m*; (*Jur*) droit *m* de passage. **easy of ~** d'accès facile, facilement accessible; **~ to his room is by a staircase** on accède à sa chambre par un escalier; *[road, gate]* **to give ~ to** donner accès à, commander l'accès à.
(b) (*permission to see, use*) accès *m*; (*Jur: in divorce*) droit *m* de visite. **to have ~ to sb** avoir accès auprès de qn, avoir ses entrées chez qn; **to have ~ to a book/papers** avoir accès à un livre/à des documents.
(c) (*sudden outburst*) *[anger, remorse]* accès *m*; *[generosity]* élan *m*; *[illness]* accès, attaque *f*, crise *f*.
2 *cpd*: **access road** route *f* d'accès; *[motorway]* bretelle *f* d'accès *or* de raccordement; (*to motorway*) **there is an access road for Melun** Melun est raccordé (à l'autoroute).

accessary [æk'sesərɪ] (*Jur*) **1** *n* complice *mf*. **~ before the fact/after the fact** complice par instigation/par assistance. **2** *adj* complice (*to* de).

accessibility [æk,sesɪ'bɪlɪtɪ] *n* *[place]* accessibilité *f*, facilité *f* d'accès. (*fig*) **the president's ~ was widely known** tout le monde savait que le président était très accessible.

accessible [æk'sesəbl] *adj* **(a)** *place* accessible, d'accès facile; *knowledge* à la portée de tous, accessible; *person* accessible, approchable, d'un abord facile.
(b) (*able to be influenced*) ouvert, accessible (*to* à). **she is not ~ to reason** elle n'est pas accessible à la raison, avec elle on ne peut pas raisonner.

accession [æk'seʃən] *n* **(a)** (*gaining of position*) accession *f* (*to* à); (*to fortune, property*) accession (*to* à), entrée *f* en possession (*to* de). **~ (to the throne)** avènement *m*.
(b) (*addition, increase*) accroissement *m*, augmentation *f*. **the ~ of new members to the party** l'adhésion *f* de membres nouveaux au parti.
(c) (*consent*) accord *m*, assentiment *m*; (*Jur, Pol: to a treaty etc*) adhésion *f*.

accessory [æk'sesərɪ] **1** *adj* **(a)** (*additional*) accessoire, auxiliaire.
(b) (*Jur*) = **accessary 2**.
2 *n* **(a)** (*gen pl: Dress, Theat etc*) accessoire(s) *m(pl)*; (*Tech*) appareillage *m*; (*Comm*) accessoire. **car accessories** accessoires d'automobile; **toilet accessories** objets *mpl* de toilette.
(b) (*Jur*) = **accessary 1**.

accidence ['æksɪdəns] *n* (*Ling*) morphologie flexionnelle; (*Philos*) accident *m*.

accident ['æksɪdənt] **1** *n* **(a)** (*mishap, disaster*) accident *m*, malheur *m*. **to meet with** *or* **have an ~** avoir un accident; **road ~** accident de la route *or* de la circulation.
(b) (*unforeseen event*) événement fortuit, accident *m*; (*chance*) hasard *m*, chance *f*. **by ~** accidentellement, par hasard.
(c) (*Philos*) accident *m*.
2 *cpd*: **(road) accident figures/statistics** chiffres *mpl*/statistiques *fpl* des accidents de la route; **accident insurance** assurance *f* (contre les) accidents; (*Aut*) **accident prevention** prévention *or* sécurité routière; **to be accident-prone** être prédisposé(e) *or* sujet(te) aux accidents, attirer les accidents; (*Aut*) **accident protection** protection routière.

accidental [,æksɪ'dentl] **1** *adj* **(a)** (*happening by chance*) *death* accidentel; *meeting* fortuit. **(b)** (*of secondary importance*) *effect, benefit* secondaire, accessoire. **(c)** (*Mus, Philos*) accidentel. **2** *n* (*Mus*) accident *m*.

accidentally [,æksɪ'dentəlɪ] *adv* (*by chance*) par hasard, fortuitement; (*not deliberately*) accidentellement. **it was done quite ~** on ne l'a pas fait exprès.

acclaim [ə'kleɪm] **1** *vt* (*applaud*) acclamer. **to ~ sb king** proclamer qn roi. **2** *n* acclamation *f*. **it met with great public/critical ~** cela a été salué unanimement par le public/les critiques.

acclamation [,æklə'meɪʃən] *n* acclamation *f*.

acclimate [ə'klaɪmət] *vt* (*US*) = **acclimatize**.

acclimatization [ə,klaɪmətaɪ'zeɪʃən] *n*, (*US*) **acclimation** [,æklaɪ'meɪʃən] *n* (*lit*) acclimatation *f*; (*fig: to new situation etc*) accoutumance *f* (*to* à).

acclimatize [ə'klaɪmətaɪz], (*US*) **acclimate** [ə'klaɪmət] **1** *vt* (*lit, fig*) acclimater (*to* à). **2** *vi* (*lit, fig: also* **become ~d**) s'acclimater (*to* à).

acclivity [ə'klɪvɪtɪ] *n* montée *f*.

accolade ['ækəʊleɪd] *n* accolade *f*; (*fig*) marque *f* d'approbation.

accommodate [ə'kɒmədeɪt] *vt* **(a)** (*provide lodging for*) *person* loger, recevoir; (*contain*) *[car]* contenir; *[house]* contenir, recevoir. **the hotel can ~ 60 people** l'hôtel peut recevoir *or* accueillir 60 personnes.
(b) (*supply*) équiper (*sb with sth* qn de qch), fournir (*sb with sth* qch à qn). **to ~ sb with a loan** consentir un prêt à qn.
(c) (*adapt*) *plans, wishes* accommoder, adapter (*to* à). **to ~ o.s. to** s'adapter à, s'accommoder à.

accommodating [ə'kɒmədeɪtɪŋ] *adj* (*obliging*) obligeant; (*easy to deal with*) accommodant, conciliant.

accommodation [ə,kɒmə'deɪʃən] **1** *n* **(a)** (*space for people*) place *f*. (*US*) **~s** logement *m*, hébergement *m*; **'~ (to let)'** 'appartements *mpl* *or* chambres *fpl* à louer'; **we have no ~ (available)** nous n'avons pas de place, c'est complet; **there is no ~ for children** on n'accepte pas les enfants; *V* **seating**.
(b) (*adjustment*) arrangement *m*, compromis *m*. **to come to an ~ with sb** arriver à un compromis avec qn.
(c) (*Anat, Psych*) accommodation *f*.
2 *cpd*: **accommodation address** adresse *f*, boîte *f* aux lettres (*utilisée simplement pour la correspondance*); (*Comm*) **accommodation bill** billet *m* *or* effet *m* de complaisance; **accommodation bureau** agence *f* de logement; (*Naut*) **accommodation ladder** échelle *f* de coupée; **accommodation road** route *f* à usage restreint; (*US Rail*) **accommodation train** (train *m*) omnibus *m*.

accompaniment [ə'kʌmpənɪmənt] *n* accompagnement *m*, complément *m*; (*Mus*) accompagnement; (*Culin*) accompagnement, garniture *f*.

accompanist [ə'kʌmpənɪst] *n* (*Mus*) accompagnateur *m*, -trice *f*.

accompany [ə'kʌmpənɪ] *vt* **(a)** (*escort*) accompagner, suivre. **accompanied by** accompagné de *or* par. **(b)** (*fig*) accompagner. **cold accompanied by shivering** rhume accompagné de frissons. **(c)** (*Mus*) accompagner (*on* à).

accomplice [ə'kʌmplɪs] *n* complice *mf*. **to be an ~ to** *or* **in a crime** tremper dans un crime, être complice d'un crime.

accomplish [ə'kʌmplɪʃ] *vt* accomplir, exécuter; *task* accomplir, achever; *desire* réaliser; *journey* effectuer. **to ~ one's object** arriver à ses fins.

accomplished [ə'kʌmplɪʃt] *adj* *person* doué, accompli, qui possède tous les talents; *performance* accompli, parfait.

accomplishment [ə'kʌmplɪʃmənt] *n* **(a)** (*achievement*) œuvre accomplie, projet réalisé. **(b)** (*skill: gen pl*) **~s** talents *mpl*. **(c)** (*U: completion*) réalisation *f*, accomplissement *m*.

accord [ə'kɔːd] **1** *vt* *favour* accorder, concéder (*to* à).
2 *vi* s'accorder, concorder (*with* avec).
3 *n* **(a)** (*U: agreement*) consentement *m*, accord *m*. **of his own ~** de son plein gré, de lui-même, de son propre chef; **with one ~** d'un commun accord; **to be in ~ with** être d'accord avec.
(b) (*treaty*) traité *m*, pacte *m*.

accordance [ə'kɔːdəns] *n* accord *m* (*with* avec), conformité (*with* à). **in ~ with** conformément à, suivant, en accord avec.

according [ə'kɔːdɪŋ] *adv* **(a) ~ to** conformément à, selon, suivant. **everything went ~ to plan** tout s'est passé comme prévu *or* sans anicroches; **~ to what he says** d'après ce qu'il dit, à en juger par ce qu'il dit; **~ to him they've gone** selon lui *or* d'après lui ils sont partis.
(b) ~ as dans la mesure où, selon que, suivant que +*indic*.

accordingly [ə'kɔːdɪŋlɪ] *adv* **(a)** (*therefore*) en conséquence, par conséquent. **(b)** (*in accordance with circumstances*) en conséquence.

accordion [ə'kɔːdɪən] *n* accordéon *m*. **~ pleat** pli *m* (en) accordéon *inv*.

accordionist [ə'kɔːdɪənɪst] *n* accordéoniste *mf*.

accost [ə'kɒst] *vt* accoster, aborder; (*Jur*) accoster.

account [ə'kaʊnt] **1** *n* **(a)** (*Comm, Fin*) compte *m*, note *f*. **to open an ~** ouvrir un compte; **put it on my ~** (*in shop*) vous le mettrez à *or* sur mon compte; (*in hotel*) vous le mettrez sur mon compte *or* sur ma note; **in ~ with** en compte avec; **~ payable** dettes passives; **~ rendered** facture non payée; **on ~** à compte; **payment on ~** acompte *m*, à-valoir *m*, paiement *m* à compte; **to pay £50 on ~** verser un acompte de 50 livres; (*Advertising*) **they have the Michelin ~** c'est eux qui détiennent la publicité (de) Michelin; *V* **bank**[2], **current, settle**[2] *etc*.
(b) (*calculation*) compte *m*, calcul *m*. **to keep the ~s** tenir la comptabilité *or* les comptes.
(c) (*U: benefit*) profit *m*, avantage *m*. **to turn sth to ~** mettre qch à profit, tirer parti de qch.
(d) (*explanation*) compte rendu, explication *f*. **to call sb to ~ for having done** demander des comptes à qn pour avoir fait; **he gave a good ~ of himself** il s'en est bien tiré, il a fait bonne impression.
(e) (*report*) compte rendu, exposé *m*, récit *m*. **by all ~s** d'après l'opinion générale, au dire de tous; **to give an ~ of** faire le compte rendu de *or* un exposé sur; **by her own ~** d'après ce qu'elle dit, d'après ses dires.
(f) (*importance, consideration*) importance *f*, valeur *f*. **man of no ~** homme sans importance; **your statement is of no ~ to them** ils n'attachent aucune importance *or* valeur à votre déclaration; **to take sth into ~** prendre qch en considération, tenir compte de qch, avoir égard à qch; **these facts must be taken into ~** ces faits doivent entrer en ligne de compte; **to leave sth out of ~, to take no ~ of sth** ne pas tenir compte de qch; **to take little ~ of** faire peu de cas de.
(g) on ~ of à cause de; **on no ~** en aucun cas, sous aucun prétexte; **on her ~** à cause d'elle, par égard pour elle.
2 *cpd*: **account book** livre *m* de comptes; (*Comm, Fin*) **account day** terme *m*, jour *m* de liquidation; **accounts department** (service *m* de) comptabilité *f*.

3 *vt* estimer, juger. **to ~ o.s. lucky** s'estimer heureux; **to ~ sb (to be) innocent** considérer qn comme innocent.
account for *vt fus* **(a)** (*explain, justify*) *expenses* rendre compte de, justifier de; *one's conduct* justifier; *circumstances* expliquer. **there's no accounting for tastes** des goûts et des couleurs on ne dispute pas (*Prov*), chacun son goût; **everyone is accounted for** on n'a oublié personne; (*after accident etc*) **3 people have not yet been accounted for** 3 personnes n'ont pas encore été retrouvées.
(b) (*Hunting etc: kill*) tuer.
accountable [əˈkaʊntəbl] *adj* responsable (*for* de). **to be ~ to sb for sth** être responsable de qch *or* répondre de qch devant qn; **he is not ~ for his actions** (*need not account for*) il n'a pas à répondre de ses actes; (*is not responsible for*) il n'est pas responsable de ses actes.
accountancy [əˈkaʊntənsɪ] *n* (*subject*) comptabilité *f*; (*profession*) profession *f* de comptable. **to study ~** faire des études de comptable *or* de comptabilité.
accountant [əˈkaʊntənt] *n* comptable *mf*. **~'s office** agence *f* comptable.
accounting [əˈkaʊntɪŋ] *n* comptabilité *f*. **~ machine** machine *f* comptable.
accoutred [əˈkuːtəd] *adj* (*esp Mil*) équipé (*with* de).
accoutrements [əˈkuːtrəmənts], (*US*) **accouterments** [əˈkuːtərments] *npl* (*Mil*) équipement *m*.
accredit [əˈkredɪt] *vt* **(a)** (*credit*) *rumour* accréditer. **to ~ sth to sb** attribuer qch à qn; **to be ~ed with having done** être censé avoir fait. **(b)** *representative* accréditer (*to* auprès de); *ambassador* accréditer (*to* près).
accredited [əˈkredɪtɪd] *adj person* accrédité, autorisé; *opinion, belief* admis, accepté. **~ representative** représentant accrédité (*to* auprès de).
accretion [əˈkriːʃən] *n* **(a)** (*increase, growth*) accroissement *m* (organique). **(b)** (*result of growth: Geol etc*) concrétion *f*, addition *f*; *[wealth etc]* accroissement *m*, accumulation *f*.
accrue [əˈkruː] *vi* **(a)** *[money, advantages]* revenir (*to* à). **(b)** (*Fin*) *[interest]* courir, s'accroître, s'accumuler. **~d interest** intérêt couru; **~d income** revenu accumulé.
accumulate [əˈkjuːmjʊleɪt] **1** *vt* accumuler, amasser, amonceler. **2** *vi* s'accumuler, s'amasser.
accumulation [əˌkjuːmjʊˈleɪʃən] *n* **(a)** (*U*) accumulation *f*, amoncellement *m*; (*Fin*) *[capital]* accroissement *m*. **(b)** (*material accumulated*) amas *m*, tas *m*, monceau *m*.
accumulative [əˈkjuːmjʊlətɪv] *adj* qui s'accumule; (*Fin*) cumulatif.
accumulator [əˈkjuːmjʊleɪtəʳ] *n* (*Brit*) accumulateur *m*, accus* *mpl*.
accuracy [ˈækjʊrəsɪ] *n [figures, clock]* exactitude *f*; *[story, report]* précision *f*; *[translation]* exactitude, fidélité *f*; *[judgment, assessment]* justesse *f*.
accurate [ˈækjʊrɪt] *adj* (*V* **accuracy**) exact, précis, juste; *memory, translation* fidèle. **to take ~ aim** viser juste, bien viser.
accurately [ˈækjʊrɪtlɪ] *adv* (*V* **accuracy**) avec précision, fidèlement, exactement.
accursed, accurst [əˈkɜːst] *adj* (*liter*) (*damned*) maudit; (*hateful*) détestable, exécrable.
accusal [əˈkjuːzl] *n* accusation *f*.
accusation [ˌækjʊˈzeɪʃən] *n* accusation *f*; (*Jur*) accusation, plainte *f*. (*Jur*) **to bring an ~ against sb** porter plainte *or* déposer (une) plainte contre qn.
accusative [əˈkjuːzətɪv] **1** *n* accusatif *m*. **in the ~** à l'accusatif. **2** *adj* accusatif.
accuse [əˈkjuːz] *vt* accuser (*sb of sth* qn de qch, *sb of doing* qn de faire).
accused [əˈkjuːzd] *n* (*Jur*) accusé(e) *m(f)*, inculpé(e) *m(f)*.
accuser [əˈkjuːzəʳ] *n* accusateur *m*, -trice *f*.
accusing [əˈkjuːzɪŋ] *adj* accusateur (*f* -trice).
accusingly [əˈkjuːzɪŋlɪ] *adv* d'une manière accusatrice.
accustom [əˈkʌstəm] *vt* habituer, accoutumer (*sb to sth* qn à qch, *sb to doing* qn à faire). **to ~ o.s. to** s'habituer à, s'accoutumer à.
accustomed [əˈkʌstəmd] *adj* **(a)** (*used*) habitué, accoutumé (*to* à, *to do, to doing* à faire). **to become** *or* **get ~ to sth/to doing** s'habituer *or* s'accoutumer à qch/à faire; **I am not ~ to such treatment** je n'ai pas l'habitude qu'on me traite (*subj*) de cette façon. **(b)** (*usual*) habituel, coutumier, familier.
ace [eɪs] *n* **(a)** (*Cards, Dice, Dominoes*) as *m*. **~ of diamonds** as de carreau; (*fig*) **to keep an ~ up one's sleeve** avoir un atout dans sa manche; (*fig*) **to play one's ~** jouer sa meilleure carte; (*fig*) **within an ~ of sth** à deux doigts de qch; (*Tennis*) **to serve an ~** passer une balle de service irrattrapable, servir un as; *V* **clean**. **(b)** (*pilot, racing driver etc*) as *m*.
acerbity [əˈsɜːbɪtɪ] *n* âpreté *f*, aigreur *f*.
acetate [ˈæsɪteɪt] *n* acétate *m*.
acetic [əˈsiːtɪk] *adj* acétique. **~ acid** acide *m* acétique.
acetone [ˈæsɪtəʊn] *n* acétone *f*.
acetylene [əˈsetɪliːn] **1** *n* acétylène *m*.
2 *cpd*: **acetylene burner** chalumeau *m* à acétylène; **acetylene lamp** lampe *f* à acétylène; **acetylene torch = acetylene burner; acetylene welding** soudure *f* autogène.
ache [eɪk] **1** *vi* faire mal, être douloureux. **my head ~s** j'ai mal à la tête; **to be aching all over** (*after exercise*) être courbaturé; (*from illness*) avoir mal partout; **it makes my heart ~** cela me brise *or* me fend le cœur; (*fig*) **to be aching** *or* **to ~ to do** mourir d'envie de faire, brûler de faire.
2 *n* **(a)** (*physical*) douleur *f*, souffrance *f*. **all his ~s and pains** toutes ses douleurs, tous ses maux; **he's always complaining of ~s and pains** il se plaint toujours d'avoir mal partout; *V* **tooth** *etc*.
(b) (*fig*) peine *f*; *V* **heart**.
achieve [əˈtʃiːv] *vt task* accomplir, exécuter, réaliser; *aim* atteindre, arriver à; *success* obtenir; *fame* parvenir à; *victory* remporter.
achievement [əˈtʃiːvmənt] *n* **(a)** (*success, feat*) exploit *m*, réussite *f*, haut fait. **(b)** (*U: completion*) exécution *f*, accomplissement *m*, réalisation *f*.
Achilles [əˈkɪliːz] *n* Achille *m*. (*fig*) **~' heel** talon *m* d'Achille; (*Anat*) **~' tendon** tendon *m* d'Achille.
aching [ˈeɪkɪŋ] *adj* douloureux, endolori. (*fig*) **to have an ~ heart** avoir le cœur gros.
acid [ˈæsɪd] **1** *n* **(a)** acide *m*.
(b) (*Drugs sl*) acide : *m*, D : *m*.
2 *cpd*: **acid-proof** résistant aux acides; (*fig*) **acid test** épreuve décisive; (*fig*) **to stand the acid test** être à toute épreuve.
3 *adj* **(a)** (*sour*) acide. (*Brit*) **~ drops** bonbons acidulés.
(b) (*fig: sharp*) *person* revêche; *voice* aigre; *remark* mordant, acide.
acidify [əˈsɪdɪfaɪ] *vt* acidifier.
acidity [əˈsɪdɪtɪ] *n* (*Chem, fig*) acidité *f*.
acidulous [əˈsɪdjʊləs] *adj* acidulé.
ack-ack [ˈækˈæk] *n* défense *f* contre avions, D.C.A. *f*. **~ fire** tir *m* de D.C.A.; **~ guns** canons antiaériens *or* de D.C.A.
acknowledge [əkˈnɒlɪdʒ] *vt* **(a)** (*admit*) *error* reconnaître, avouer, confesser. **to ~ sb as leader** reconnaître qn pour chef; **to ~ o.s. beaten** s'avouer battu.
(b) (*confirm receipt of*) *greeting* répondre à; (*also* **~ receipt of**) *letter, parcel* accuser réception de. **to ~ a gift from sb** remercier qn pour *or* d'un cadeau.
(c) (*express thanks for*) *person's action, services, help* manifester sa gratitude pour, se montrer reconnaissant de; *applause, cheers* saluer pour répondre à.
(d) (*indicate recognition of*) faire attention à. **I smiled at him but he didn't even ~ me** je lui ai souri mais il n'a même pas fait mine d'y répondre *or* mais il a fait comme s'il ne me voyait pas; **he didn't even ~ my presence** il a fait comme si je n'étais pas là; (*Jur*) **to ~ a child** reconnaître un enfant.
acknowledged [əkˈnɒlɪdʒd] *adj leader, expert etc* reconnu (de tous); *child* reconnu; *letter* dont on a accusé réception.
acknowledgement [əkˈnɒlɪdʒmənt] *n* **(a)** (*U*) reconnaissance *f*; *[one's error etc]* aveu *m*. **in ~ of your help** en reconnaissance *or* en remerciement de votre aide.
(b) *[money]* reçu *m*, récépissé *m*, quittance *f*; *[letter]* accusé *m* de réception; (*in preface etc*) remerciements *mpl*. **to quote without ~** faire une citation sans mentionner la source.
acme [ˈækmɪ] *n* point culminant, faîte *m*, apogée *m*.
acne [ˈæknɪ] *n* acné *f*.
acolyte [ˈækəʊlaɪt] *n* acolyte *m*.
aconite [ˈækənaɪt] *n* aconit *m*.
acorn [ˈeɪkɔːn] *n* (*Bot*) gland *m*. **~ cup** cupule *f*.
acoustic [əˈkuːstɪk] *adj* acoustique.
acoustics [əˈkuːstɪks] *n* **(a)** (*Phys: +sg vb*) acoustique *f*. **(b)** *[room etc]* (*+pl vb*) acoustique *f*.
acquaint [əˈkweɪnt] *vt* **(a)** (*inform*) aviser, avertir, instruire (*sb with sth* qn de qch), renseigner (*sb with sth* qn sur qch). **to ~ sb with the situation** mettre qn au courant *or* au fait de la situation.
(b) to be ~ed with *person, subject* connaître; *fact* savoir, être au courant de; **to become ~ed with sb** faire la connaissance de qn; **to become ~ed with the facts** prendre connaissance des faits.
acquaintance [əˈkweɪntəns] *n* **(a)** (*U*) connaissance *f*. **to make sb's ~** faire la connaissance de qn, faire connaissance avec qn; **to improve upon ~** gagner à être connu; **to have some ~ with French** avoir une certaine connaissance du français, savoir un peu le français; *V* **claim**.
(b) (*person*) relation *f*. **she's an ~ of mine** je la connais un peu, c'est une de mes relations; **old ~s** de vieilles connaissances.
acquaintanceship [əˈkweɪntənsʃɪp] *n* relations *fpl*, cercle *m* de connaissances. **a wide ~** de nombreuses relations.
acquiesce [ˌækwɪˈes] *vi* acquiescer, consentir. **to ~ in an opinion** se ranger à une opinion *or* à un avis; **to ~ in a proposal** donner son accord *or* son assentiment à une proposition.
acquiescence [ˌækwɪˈesns] *n* consentement *m*, assentiment *m*, acquiescement *m* (*in* à).
acquiescent [ˌækwɪˈesnt] *adj* consentant.
acquire [əˈkwaɪəʳ] *vt knowledge, money, fame, experience* acquérir; *language* apprendre; *habit* prendre, contracter; *reputation* se faire. **to ~ a taste for** prendre goût à.
acquired [əˈkwaɪəd] *adj*: **~ characteristic** caractère acquis; **~ taste** goût *m* qui s'acquiert; **it's an ~ taste** on finit par aimer ça, c'est un goût qui s'acquiert.
acquirement [əˈkwaɪəmənt] *n* **(a)** (*U*) acquisition *f* (*of* de). **(b)** (*skill*) talent *m* (acquis), connaissance *f*.
acquisition [ˌækwɪˈzɪʃən] *n* acquisition *f*; (*: *person*) recrue *f* (*to* pour).
acquisitive [əˈkwɪzɪtɪv] *adj* (*for money*) âpre au gain, thésauriseur (*liter*); (*greedy*) avide (*of* de). **~ instinct** instinct *m* de possession; **to have an ~ nature** avoir l'instinct de possession très développé.
acquisitiveness [əˈkwɪzɪtɪvnɪs] *n* instinct *m* de possession, goût *m* de la propriété.
acquit [əˈkwɪt] *vt* **(a)** (*Jur*) acquitter, décharger (*of* de).
(b) to ~ o.s. well in battle bien se conduire *or* se comporter au combat; **it was a difficult job but he ~ted himself well** c'était une tâche difficile mais il s'en est bien tiré.
(c) *debt* régler, s'acquitter de.
acquittal [əˈkwɪtl] *n* **(a)** (*Jur*) acquittement *m*. **(b)** *[duty]* accomplissement *m*. **(c)** *[debt]* acquittement *m*.

acre ['eɪkəʳ] *n* ≃ demi-hectare *m*, arpent† *m*, acre *f*. **he owns a few ~s (of land) in Sussex** il possède quelques hectares (de terrain) *or* un terrain de quelques hectares dans le Sussex; (*fig*) **the rolling ~s of the estate** la vaste étendue du domaine; (*fig*) **~s of*** des hectares de, des kilomètres et des kilomètres de; *V* **god.**

acreage ['eɪkərɪdʒ] *n* aire *f*, superficie *f*. **what ~ have you?** combien avez-vous d'hectares?; **to farm a large ~** cultiver *or* exploiter de grandes superficies.

acrid ['ækrɪd] *adj* (*lit*) âcre; (*fig*) *remark, style* acerbe, mordant.

Acrilan ['ækrɪlæn] *n* ® Acrilan *m* ®.

acrimonious [ˌækrɪ'məʊnɪəs] *adj* acrimonieux, aigre.

acrimony ['ækrɪmənɪ] *n* acrimonie *f*, aigreur *f*.

acrobat ['ækrəbæt] *n* acrobate *mf*.

acrobatic [ˌækrəʊ'bætɪk] *adj* acrobatique.

acrobatics [ˌækrəʊ'bætɪks] *npl* acrobatie *f*. **to do ~** faire des acrobaties *or* de l'acrobatie.

acronym ['ækrənɪm] *n* sigle *m*, acronyme *m*.

across [ə'krɒs] (*phr vb elem*) **1** *prep* **(a)** (*from one side to other of*) d'un côté à l'autre de. **bridge ~ the river** pont *m* sur le fleuve; **to walk ~ the road** traverser la route.

(b) (*on other side of*) de l'autre côté de. **he lives ~ the street** il habite en face; **the shop ~ the road** le magasin d'en face, le magasin de l'autre côté de la rue; **lands ~ the sea** terres *fpl* d'outre-mer; **from ~ the Channel** de l'autre côté de la Manche, d'outre-Manche.

(c) (*crosswise over*) en travers de, à travers. **to go ~ the fields** *or* **~ country** aller *or* prendre à travers champs; **plank ~ a door** planche *f* en travers d'une porte; **with his arms folded ~ his chest** les bras croisés sur la poitrine.

2 *adv* (*from one side to other*) **the river is 5 km ~** le fleuve a 5 km de large; **to help sb ~** aider qn à traverser; (*fig*) **to get sth ~*** faire comprendre *or* apprécier qch, faire passer la rampe à qch; **~ from** en face de.

acrostic [ə'krɒstɪk] *n* acrostiche *m*.

acrylic [ə'krɪlɪk] *adj* acrylique.

act [ækt] **1** *n* **(a)** (*deed*) action *f*, acte *m*. **in the ~ of doing** en train de faire; **caught in the ~** pris sur le fait *or* en flagrant délit; (*on insurance policy*) **~ of God** désastre naturel, fléau *m* de la nature; **~ of faith** acte de foi; (*Rel*) **A~s of the Apostles** Actes des Apôtres.

(b) (*Jur*) loi *f*. (*Brit*) **A~ of Parliament** loi adoptée par le Parlement.

(c) (*Theat*) acte *m*; (*circus etc*) numéro *m*. (*fig*) **he's just putting on an ~** il joue la comédie; (*fig*) **to get in on the ~*** (parvenir à) participer aux opérations.

2 *vi* **(a)** (*do sth*) agir. **the government must ~ now** le gouvernement doit agir immédiatement; **you have ~ed very generously** vous avez été très généreux, vous avez agi avec beaucoup de générosité; **to ~ for the best** faire pour le mieux; **to ~ on sb's behalf** agir au nom de qn, représenter qn.

(b) (*behave*) agir, se comporter, se conduire. **to ~ like a fool** agir *or* se comporter comme un imbécile.

(c) (*machine etc*) fonctionner, marcher.

(d) (*Theat*) jouer. **have you ever ~ed before?** avez-vous déjà fait du théâtre (*or* du cinéma)?; **she's not crying, she's only ~ing** elle ne pleure pas, elle fait seulement semblant *or* elle joue la comédie.

(e) (*serve*) servir, faire office, faire fonction (*as* de). **the table ~s as a desk** la table sert de bureau.

(f) *[medicine, chemical]* (*have an effect*) agir (*on* sur).

3 *vt* (*Theat*) *part* jouer, tenir. **to ~ Hamlet** jouer *or* tenir le rôle d'Hamlet, incarner Hamlet; (*fig*) **to ~ the fool*** faire l'idiot *or* le pitre; (*Theat, fig*) **to ~ the part of** tenir le rôle de.

act out *vt sep* faire un récit mimé de.

act up *vi* **(a)** (*) *[person]* se conduire mal. **the car has started acting up** la voiture s'est mise à faire des caprices *or* à faire des siennes*.

(b) to act up to one's principles mettre ses principes en pratique.

act (up)on *vt fus advice, suggestion* suivre, se conformer à; *order* exécuter. **I acted (up)on your letter at once** j'ai fait le nécessaire *or* pris toutes mesures utiles dès que j'ai reçu votre lettre.

actable ['æktəbl] *adj play* jouable.

acting ['æktɪŋ] **1** *adj* suppléant, provisoire, par intérim. **~ headmaster** directeur suppléant; **~ head of department** chef *m* de section par intérim.

2 *n* (*Cine, Theat: performance*) jeu *m*, interprétation *f*. **his ~ is very good** il joue très bien; **I like his ~** j'aime son jeu; **he has done some ~** il a fait du théâtre (*or* du cinéma).

actinic [æk'tɪnɪk] *adj* actinique.

action ['ækʃən] **1** *n* **(a)** (*U*) action *f*, effet *m*. **to put into ~** *plan* mettre à exécution; *one's principles, a suggestion* mettre en action *or* en pratique; *machine* mettre en marche; **the time has come for ~** il est temps d'agir; **to take ~** prendre une initiative *or* des mesures, agir; **to go into ~** entrer en action, passer à l'action *or* à l'acte (*V* 1f); **telephone out of ~** appareil *m* en dérangement; **his illness put him out of ~ for 6 weeks** sa maladie l'a mis hors de combat pendant 6 semaines.

(b) (*deed*) acte *m*, action *f*. **to judge sb by his ~s** juger qn sur ses actes; **to suit the ~ to the word** joindre le geste à la parole; **~s speak louder than words** les actes sont plus éloquents que les paroles.

(c) (*Theat*) *[play]* intrigue *f*, action *f*; *[actor]* jeu *m*.

(d) (*Jur*) procès *m*, action *f* en justice. **to bring an ~ against sb** intenter une action *or* un procès contre qn, poursuivre qn en justice, actionner qn.

(e) (*Tech*) mécanisme *m*, marche *f*; *[clock etc]* mécanique *f*. (*lit, fig*) **to put sth out of ~** mettre qch hors d'usage *or* hors de service; **machine out of ~** machine hors d'usage *or* détraquée.

(f) (*Mil*) combat *m*, engagement *m*, action *f*. **to go into ~** *[unit, person]* aller *or* marcher au combat; *[army]* engager le combat; **killed in ~** tué à l'ennemi *or* au combat, tombé au champ d'honneur (*frm*); **he saw (some) ~ in North Africa** il a combattu *or* il a vu le feu en Afrique du Nord; *V* **enemy.**

2 *cpd*: **action painting** tachisme *m*; (*Brit: TV Sport*) **action replay** *répétition immédiate d'une séquence*; (*Mil*) **action stations** postes *mpl* de combat; (*Mil, fig*) **action stations!** à vos postes!

actionable ['ækʃnəbl] *adj* (*Jur*) sujet à procès, donnant matière à procès.

activate ['æktɪveɪt] *vt* (*also Chem, Tech*) activer; (*Phys*) rendre radioactif.

active ['æktɪv] *adj* **(a)** *person* actif, leste, agile; *life* actif; *mind, imagination* vif, actif; *file, case* en cours. **~ volcano** volcan *m* en activité; **to take an ~ part in** prendre une part active à, avoir un rôle positif dans; **to give ~ consideration to sth** soumettre qch à une étude attentive; **we're giving ~ consideration to the idea of doing** nous examinons sérieusement la possibilité *or* le projet de faire; **in ~ employment** en activité.

(b) (*Mil*) **on ~ service** en campagne; **he saw ~ service in Italy and Germany** il a fait campagne *or* il a servi en Italie et en Allemagne; **the ~ list** l'armée active; **to be on the ~ list** être en activité (de service).

(c) (*Gram*) **~ voice** voix active, actif *m*; **in the ~ (voice)** à l'actif.

actively ['æktɪvlɪ] *adv* activement.

activist ['æktɪvɪst] *n* activiste *mf*.

activity [æk'tɪvɪtɪ] *n* **(a)** (*U*) *[person]* activité *f*; *[town, port]* mouvement *m*. **(b) activities** activités *fpl*, occupations *fpl*; **business activities** activités professionnelles.

actor ['æktəʳ] *n* acteur *m*, comédien *m*.

actress ['æktrɪs] *n* actrice *f*, comédienne *f*.

actual ['æktjʊəl] *adj* (*real*) réel, véritable; (*factual*) concret, positif. **the ~ figures** les chiffres exacts; **the ~ result** le résultat même *or* véritable; **to take an ~ example** prendre un exemple concret; **an ~ fact** un fait positif; **in ~ fact** en fait; **his ~ words were ...** il a dit très exactement ...

actuality [ˌæktjʊ'ælɪtɪ] *n* **(a)** (*U*) réalité *f*. **(b) actualities** réalités *fpl*, conditions réelles *or* actuelles.

actualize ['æktjʊəlaɪz] *vt* réaliser; (*Philos*) actualiser.

actually ['æktjʊəlɪ] *adv* **(a)** (*really*) effectivement, réellement, véritablement, en *or* de fait. **~ present** bel et bien présent, effectivement présent; **he's ~ a liar** en fait *or* de fait c'est un menteur; **the person ~ in charge is ...** la personne véritablement responsable *or* responsable en fait, c'est ...; **what did he ~ say?** qu'est-ce qu'il a dit exactement? *or* au juste?

(b) (*even*) même. **he ~ beat her** il est (même) allé jusqu'à la battre.

(c) (*truth to tell*) à vrai dire, pour tout dire, en fait. **~ I don't know him** à vrai dire *or* en fait, je ne le connais pas.

actuary ['æktjʊərɪ] *n* actuaire *mf*.

actuate ['æktjʊeɪt] *vt person* faire agir, inciter, pousser. **~d by** animé de, mû par, poussé par.

acuity [ə'kju:ɪtɪ] *n* acuité *f*.

acumen ['ækjʊmen] *n* perspicacité *f*, finesse *f*, pénétration *f*. **business ~** sens aigu des affaires.

acupuncture ['ækjʊpʌŋktʃəʳ] *n* acupuncture *f*.

acute [ə'kju:t] *adj* **(a)** *person, mind* pénétrant, perspicace, avisé. **to have an ~ sense of smell/~ hearing** avoir l'odorat fin/l'oreille fine.

(b) (*Med*) aigu (*f* -guë); (*fig*) *remorse, anxiety* vif; *pain* aigu, vif; *shortage, situation* critique, grave. **an ~ scarcity** un manque aigu, une grave pénurie.

(c) (*Math*) **~ angle** angle aigu; **~-angled** acutangle.

(d) (*Gram*) **~ accent** accent aigu.

acutely [ə'kju:tlɪ] *adv* **(a)** (*intensely*) *suffer* vivement, intensément. **I am ~ aware that** je suis profondément conscient que.

(b) (*shrewdly*) *observe* avec perspicacité.

acuteness [ə'kju:tnɪs] *n* **(a)** (*Med*) *[disease]* violence *f*; *[pain]* violence, intensité *f*. **(b)** (*Math*) *[angle]* acuité *f*. **(c)** *[person]* perspicacité *f*, finesse *f*, pénétration *f*; *[senses]* finesse.

ad* [æd] *n* (*abbr of* **advertisement**) (*announcement*) annonce *f*; (*Comm*) réclame *f*; *V* **small.**

adage ['ædɪdʒ] *n* adage *m*.

Adam ['ædəm] *n* Adam *m*. **~'s apple** pomme *f* d'Adam; (*fig*) **I don't know him from ~*** je ne le connais ni d'Ève ni d'Adam.

adamant ['ædəmənt] *adj* inflexible. **~ to their prayers** insensible *or* sourd à leurs prières.

adapt [ə'dæpt] **1** *vt* adapter, approprier, ajuster (*sth to sth* qch à qch). **to ~ o.s.** s'adapter, s'accommoder, se faire (*to* à); **to ~ a novel for television** adapter un roman pour la télévision.

2 *vi* s'adapter. **she's very willing to ~** elle est très accommodante *or* très conciliante.

adaptability [əˌdæptə'bɪlɪtɪ] *n* *[person]* faculté *f* d'adaptation. **~ of a play to television** possibilité *f* qu'il y a d'adapter une pièce pour la télévision.

adaptable [ə'dæptəbl] *adj* adaptable.

adaptation [ˌædæp'teɪʃən] *n* **(a)** adaptation *f* (*of* de, *to* à). **(b)** *[novel for screen etc]* adaptation *f*.

adapter, adaptor [ə'dæptəʳ] *n* **(a)** (*person*) adaptateur *m*, -trice *f*. **(b)** (*device*) adaptateur *m*; (*Brit Elec*) prise *f* *or* fiche *f* multiple.

add [æd] *vt* **(a)** ajouter (*to* à). **~ some more pepper** ajoutez encore *or* rajoutez un peu de poivre; **to ~ insult to injury** porter l'insulte à son comble; **~ed to which ...** ajoutez à cela que ...

(b) (*Math*) *figures* additionner. **~ing machine** calculatrice *f*, machine *f* à calculer.

(c) (*say besides*) ajouter (*that* que). **there is nothing to ~** c'est tout dire, il n'y a rien à ajouter.

add in *vt sep details* inclure, ajouter; *considerations* faire entrer en ligne de compte.

add to *vt fus* augmenter, accroître, ajouter à. **this only adds to our anxiety** ceci ne fait qu'ajouter à *or* qu'accroître notre inquiétude.

add together *vt sep figures, advantages, drawbacks* additionner.

add up 1 *vi* (*Math*) **these figures don't add up (right) or won't add up** ces chiffres ne font pas le compte (exact); (*fig*) **it all adds up*** tout cela concorde, tout s'explique; (*fig*) **it doesn't add up*** cela ne rime à rien, il y a quelque chose qui cloche.

2 *vt sep* **(a)** *figures* additionner. **to add up a column of figures** totaliser une colonne de chiffres.

(b) (*fig*) *advantages, reasons* faire la somme de.

add up to *vt fus [figures]* s'élever à, se monter à; (* *fig: mean*) signifier, se résumer à.

addendum [ə'dendəm] *n, pl* **addenda** [ə'dendə] addendum *m.*

adder ['ædəʳ] *n* vipère *f.*

addict ['ædɪkt] **1** *n* (*Med*) intoxiqué(e) *m(f)*; (*fig*) fanatique *mf.* **he's a yoga ~*** c'est un fanatique *or* un mordu* *or* un fana* du yoga; *V* **drug, heroin** *etc.* **2** [ə'dɪkt] *vt*: **to ~ o.s. to** s'adonner à.

addicted [ə'dɪktɪd] *adj* adonné (*to* à). **to become ~ to** s'adonner à; **~ to drink/drugs** adonné à la boisson/aux stupéfiants; **he's ~ to drugs** c'est un drogué *or* toxicomane; **he's ~ to smoking** c'est un fumeur invétéré; (*fig*) **to be ~ to football/films*** se passionner pour le football/le cinéma, être un mordu* *or* un fana* du football/du cinéma.

addiction [ə'dɪkʃən] *n* penchant *m or* goût *m* très fort (*to* pour); (*Med*) dépendance *f* (*to* à). **this drug produces ~** cette drogue crée une dépendance; *V* **drug.**

addictive [ə'dɪktɪv] *adj* qui crée une dépendance.

addition [ə'dɪʃən] *n* **(a)** (*Math etc*) addition *f.*

(b) (*increase*) augmentation *f* (*to* de); (*to tax, income, profit*) surcroît *m* (*to* de); (*fact of adding*) adjonction *f.* **in ~** de plus, de surcroît, en sus; **in ~ to** en plus de, en sus de; **there's been an ~ to the family** la famille s'est agrandie; **he is a welcome ~ to our team** son arrivée enrichit notre équipe; **this is a welcome ~ to the series/collection** *etc* ceci enrichit la série/la collection *etc.*

additional [ə'dɪʃənl] *adj* additionnel, supplémentaire.

additionally [ə'dɪʃənlɪ] *adv* en plus, en outre, en sus.

additive ['ædɪtɪv] *adj, n* additif (*m*).

addled ['ædld] *adj* (*fig*) *brain* fumeux, brouillon; (*lit*) *egg* pourri.

addle-headed ['ædl'hedɪd] *adj* écervelé, brouillon.

address [ə'dres] **1** *n* **(a)** *[person] (on letter etc)* adresse *f.* **to change one's ~** changer d'adresse; *V* **name.**

(b) (*talk*) discours *m,* allocution *f*; *V* **public.**

(c) (*way of speaking*) conversation *f*; (*way of behaving*) abord *m.*

(d) form *or* **manner of ~** titre *m* (*à employer en s'adressant à qn*).

(e) (†, *liter*) **~es** cour *f,* galanterie *f*; **to pay one's ~es to a lady** faire la cour à une dame.

2 *vt* **(a)** (*direct*) *speech, writing* adresser (*to* à). **this is ~ed to you** ceci s'adresse à vous (*V also* **2c**); **~ your complaints to ...** adressez vos réclamations à ...; **to ~ o.s. to a task** s'attaquer *or* se mettre à une tâche.

(b) (*speak to*) s'adresser à; *crowd* haranguer; (*write to*) adresser un écrit à; **he ~ed the meeting** il a pris la parole devant l'assistance; **don't ~ me as 'Colonel'** ne m'appelez pas 'Colonel'; *V* **chair.**

(c) *letter, parcel* adresser (*to sb* à qn), mettre *or* écrire l'adresse sur. **this is ~ed to you** ceci vous est adressé.

addressee [,ædre'siː] *n* destinataire *mf.*

Addressograph [ə'dresəʊgrɑːf] *n* ® machine *f* à adresser, adressographe *m.*

adduce [ə'djuːs] *vt proof, reason* apporter, fournir; *authority* invoquer, citer.

adenoidal ['ædɪnɔɪdl] *adj* adénoïde.

adenoids ['ædɪnɔɪdz] *npl* végétations* *fpl* (adénoïdes).

adept ['ædept] **1** *n* expert *m* (*in, at* en). **2** [ə'dept] *adj* expert (*in, at* à, en, dans, *at doing* à faire), versé (*in* en, dans).

adequacy ['ædɪkwəsɪ] *n [reward, punishment, description]* à-propos *m*; *[person]* compétence *f,* capacité *f.*

adequate ['ædɪkwɪt] *adj amount, supply* suffisant, adéquat (*for sth* pour qch, *to do* pour faire); *tool etc* adapté, qui convient (*to* à); *essay, performance* satisfaisant, acceptable. **to feel ~ to the task** se sentir à la hauteur de la tâche.

adequately ['ædɪkwɪtlɪ] *adv* suffisamment, de façon adéquate, convenablement.

adhere [əd'hɪəʳ] *vi* **(a)** (*stick*) adhérer, coller (*to* à). **(b)** (*be faithful to*) **to ~ to** *party* adhérer à, donner son adhésion à; *rule* obéir à; *resolve* persister dans, maintenir.

adherence [əd'hɪərəns] *n* adhésion *f* (*to* à).

adherent [əd'hɪərənt] *n* adhérent(e) *m(f),* partisan(e) *m(f)*; *[religion, doctrine]* adepte *mf.*

adhesion [əd'hiːʒən] *n* (*lit, Med, Tech*) adhérence *f*; (*fig: support*) adhésion *f.*

adhesive [əd'hiːzɪv] **1** *adj paper etc* adhésif, collant; *envelope* gommé. **~ plaster** sparadrap *m*; **~ tape** ruban adhésif, Scotch *m* ®. **2** *n* adhésif *m.*

adieu [ə'djuː] *n, excl* adieu *m.* († *frm*) **to bid sb ~** faire ses adieux à qn.

ad infinitum [,ædɪnfɪ'naɪtəm] *adv* à l'infini.

ad interim ['æd'ɪntərɪm] **1** *adv* par intérim. **2** *adj* (*Jur*) *judgment* provisoire.

adipose ['ædɪpəʊs] *adj* adipeux.

adiposity [,ædɪ'pɒsɪtɪ] *n* adiposité *f.*

adjacent [ə'dʒeɪsənt] *adj* adjacent (*to* à); *room, house* voisin (*to* de), contigu (*f* -guë) (*to* à); *building* qui jouxte, jouxtant; *territory* limitrophe.

adjectival [,ædʒek'taɪvəl] *adj* adjectif, adjectival.

adjective ['ædʒektɪv] *n* adjectif *m.*

adjoin [ə'dʒɔɪn] **1** *vt* être contigu (*f* -guë) à, toucher à. **2** *vi* se toucher, être contigu.

adjoining [ə'dʒɔɪnɪŋ] *adj* voisin de, attenant à, adjacent à. **in the ~ room** dans la pièce voisine *or* à côté.

adjourn [ə'dʒɜːn] **1** *vt* ajourner, renvoyer, remettre, reporter (*to* à). **to ~ sth until the next day** ajourner *or* renvoyer *or* remettre *or* reporter qch au lendemain; **to ~ sth for a week** remettre qch à huitaine; **to ~ sth for a month** ajourner qch à un mois; **to ~ a meeting** (*break off*) suspendre la séance; (*close*) lever la séance; **the meeting is** *or* **stands ~ed** la séance est levée.

2 *vi* **(a)** (*break off*) suspendre la séance; (*close*) lever la séance. **the meeting ~ed** on a suspendu *or* levé la séance; **Parliament ~ed** (*concluded debate*) la séance de la Chambre a été levée; (*interrupted debate*) la Chambre a suspendu *or* interrompu la séance; (*recess*) la Chambre s'est ajournée jusqu'à la rentrée.

(b) (*move*) se retirer (*to* dans, à), passer (*to* à). **to ~ to the drawing room** passer au salon.

adjournment [ə'dʒɜːnmənt] *n [meeting]* suspension *f,* ajournement *m*; (*Jur*) *[case]* remise *f,* renvoi *m.* (*Parl*) **to move the ~** demander la clôture.

adjudge [ə'dʒʌdʒ] *vt* **(a)** (*Jur*) juger, prononcer. **to ~ sb guilty** prononcer *or* déclarer qn coupable. **(b)** (*award*) décerner, adjuger, attribuer. **he was ~d the winner** il a été déclaré gagnant.

adjudicate [ə'dʒuːdɪkeɪt] **1** *vt* **(a)** (*judge*) *competition* juger; *claim* décider.

(b) (*award*) *prize* adjuger, attribuer (*to* à).

(c) (*Jur: declare*) déclarer. **to ~ sb bankrupt** déclarer qn en faillite.

2 *vi* se prononcer (*on* sur).

adjudication [ə,dʒuːdɪ'keɪʃən] *n* **(a)** jugement *m,* arrêt *m,* décision *f* (*du juge etc*). **(b)** (*Jur*) **~ of bankruptcy** déclaration *f* de faillite.

adjudicator [ə'dʒuːdɪkeɪtəʳ] *n* juge *m* (*d'une compétition etc*).

adjunct ['ædʒʌŋkt] **1** *n* **(a)** (*thing*) accessoire *m*; (*person*) adjoint(e) *m(f),* auxiliaire *mf.*

(b) (*Gram*) mot *m* accessoire, complément *m.*

2 *adj* **(a)** (*added, connected*) accessoire, complémentaire.

(b) (*subordinate*) *person* subordonné, auxiliaire, subalterne.

adjure [ə'dʒʊəʳ] *vt* adjurer, supplier (*sb to do* qn de faire).

adjust [ə'dʒʌst] **1** *vt* (*adapt*) ajuster, adapter (*to* à); (*Tech*) ajuster, régler, mettre au point; *differences* régler; (*Naut*) *compass* rectifier, régler; *tie, picture* arranger; *dress, glasses* rajuster. **to ~ o.s. to a new situation** s'adapter à une nouvelle situation; **to ~ one's hair** se recoiffer, arranger sa coiffure; **to ~ one's clothes** mettre de l'ordre dans sa tenue; (*Insurance*) **to ~ a claim** ajuster une demande d'indemnité.

2 *vi* s'adapter (*to* à).

adjustable [ə'dʒʌstəbl] *adj* qui peut s'ajuster; *tool, fastening* réglable. **~ spanner** clef *f* à molette; **the dates/hours are ~** les dates/les heures sont flexibles; (*Scol, Univ*) **~ timetable** horaire aménagé.

adjustment [ə'dʒʌstmənt] *n* **(a)** (*Opt, Tech*) réglage *m,* ajustage *m,* mise *f* au point; (*Naut*)*[compass]* réglage; *[prices, wages etc]* rajustement *m.* **'exchange flat for house: cash ~'** 'échangerais appartement contre maison: règlement (de la différence) comptant'. **(b)** *[person]* adaptation *f.* **social ~** adaptation au niveau social.

adjutant ['ædʒətənt] *n* **(a)** (*Mil*) adjudant-major *m.* **(b)** (*also* **~ bird**) marabout *m.*

ad lib [æd'lɪb] **1** *adv continue* à volonté. **there was food/drink ~** il y avait à manger/à boire à discrétion.

2 *n* (*Theat*) improvisation(s) *f(pl),* paroles improvisées; (*witticism*) mot *m* d'esprit impromptu.

3 ad-lib *adj speech, performance* improvisé, spontané, impromptu.

4 *vi* (*Theat etc*) improviser.

5 *vt* (*: *gen, also Theat*) *speech, joke* improviser.

adman* ['ædmæn] *n* publicitaire *mf,* spécialiste *mf* de la publicité.

admass ['ædmæs] **1** *n* masse(s) *f(pl).* **2** *cpd culture, life* de masse, de grande consommation.

admin* ['ædmɪn] *n* (*Brit*) *abbr of* **administration a.**

administer [əd'mɪnɪstəʳ] **1** *vt* **(a)** (*manage*) *business* gérer, administrer; *property* régir; *public affairs* administrer. **to ~ the affairs of a minor** gérer les biens d'un mineur.

(b) (*dispense etc*) *alms* distribuer (*to* à); *justice* rendre, dispenser; *punishment, sacraments, medicine* administrer (*to* à). **to ~ an oath to sb** faire prêter serment à qn; **the oath has been ~ed to the witness** le témoin a prêté serment.

2 *vi*: **to ~ to sb's needs** subvenir *or* pourvoir aux besoins de qn.

administration [əd,mɪnɪs'treɪʃən] *n* **(a)** (*U: management*) *[business etc]* administration *f,* gestion *f,* direction *f*; *[public affairs]* administration; (*Jur*) *[estate, inheritance]* curatelle *f.*

(b) (*Pol*) (*government*) gouvernement *m*; (*ministry*) ministère *m.* **under previous ~s** sous des gouvernements précédents.

(c) (*U*) *[justice, remedy, sacrament]* administration *f*; *[oath]* prestation *f.*

administrative [əd'mɪnɪstrətɪv] *adj* administratif.

administrator [əd'mɪnɪstreɪtəʳ] *n [business, public affairs etc]* administrateur *m,* -trice *f*; (*Jur*) *[estate, inheritance]* curateur *m,* -trice *f.*

admirable [ˈædmərəbl] *adj* admirable, excellent.
admirably [ˈædmərəblɪ] *adv* admirablement.
admiral [ˈædmərəl] *n* **(a)** (*Naut*) amiral *m* (d'escadre). **A~ of the Fleet** amiral (à cinq étoiles). **(b)** (*butterfly*) vanesse *f*, paon-de-jour *m*; *V* **red.**
Admiralty [ˈædmərəltɪ] *n* (*Brit: since 1964* ~ **Board**) ≃ ministère *m* de la Marine; *V* **lord.**
admiration [ˌædməˈreɪʃən] *n* admiration *f* (*of, for* pour). **to be the ~ of** faire l'admiration de.
admire [ədˈmaɪəʳ] *vt* admirer; exprimer son admiration de *or* pour.
admirer [ədˈmaɪərəʳ] *n* **(a)** admirateur *m*, -trice *f*. **(b)** (†: *lover*) soupirant† *m*.
admiring [ədˈmaɪərɪŋ] *adj* admiratif.
admiringly [ədˈmaɪərɪŋlɪ] *adv* avec admiration.
admissibility [ədˌmɪsəˈbɪlɪtɪ] *n* admissibilité *f*.
admissible [ədˈmɪsəbl] *adj idea, plan* acceptable, admissible; (*Jur*) *appeal, evidence, witness* recevable; *document* valable.
admission [ədˈmɪʃən] *n* **(a)** (*entry*) admission *f*, entrée *f*, accès *m* (*to* à). ~ **free** entrée gratuite; ~ **to a school** admission à une école; **to gain ~ to sb** trouver accès auprès de qn; **to gain ~ to a school/club** être admis dans une école/un club.
(b) (*person admitted*) entrée *f*.
(c) (*Jur*) *[evidence etc]* acceptation *f*, admission *f*.
(d) (*confession*) aveu *m*. **by one's own ~** de son propre aveu.
admit [ədˈmɪt] *vt* **(a)** (*let in*) *person* laisser entrer, faire entrer; *light, air* laisser passer, laisser entrer. **children not ~ted** entrée interdite aux enfants; **this ticket ~s 2** ce billet est valable pour 2 personnes.
(b) (*have space for*) *[halls, harbours etc]* contenir, (pouvoir) recevoir.
(c) (*acknowledge*) reconnaître, admettre, convenir de. **I must ~ that ...** je dois avouer *or* admettre *or* convenir que ...; **I must ~ I was wrong, I was wrong I ~** j'ai eu tort, j'en conviens; **to ~ one's guilt** reconnaître sa culpabilité, s'avouer coupable.
(d) *claim* faire droit à. (*Jur*) **to ~ sb's evidence** admettre comme valable le témoignage de qn, prendre en considération les preuves fournies par qn.
admit of *vt fus* admettre, permettre. **it admits of no delay** cela n'admet *or* ne peut souffrir aucun retard; *V* **excuse.**
admit to *vt fus* reconnaître. **to admit to a feeling of ...** avouer avoir un sentiment de ... .
admittance [ədˈmɪtəns] *n* droit *m* d'entrée, admission *f*, accès *m* (*to* auprès de). **I gained ~ to the hall** on m'a laissé entrer dans la salle; **I was denied ~** on m'a refusé l'entrée; **no ~** accès interdit au public; **no ~ except on business** accès interdit à toute personne étrangère au service.
admittedly [ədˈmɪtɪdlɪ] *adv* de l'aveu général, de l'aveu de tous. ~ **this is true** je reconnais que c'est vrai, il faut reconnaître *or* convenir que c'est vrai.
admixture [ədˈmɪkstʃəʳ] *n* mélange *m*, incorporation *f*. **X with an ~ of Y** X additionné de Y, Y mélangé à X.
admonish [ədˈmɒnɪʃ] *vt* **(a)** (*reprove*) admonester, réprimander (*for doing* pour avoir fait, *about, for* pour, à propos de).
(b) (*warn*) avertir, prévenir (*against doing* de ne pas faire), mettre en garde (*against* contre); (*Jur*) avertir.
(c) (*exhort*) exhorter, engager (*to do* à faire).
(d) (†, *liter: remind*) **to ~ sb of a duty** rappeler qn à un devoir.
admonition [ˌædməʊˈnɪʃən] *n* **(a)** (*rebuke*) remontrance *f*, réprimande *f*, admonestation *f*. **(b)** (*warning*) avertissement *m*, admonition *f*; (*Jur*) avertissement.
ad nauseam [ˌædˈnɔːsɪæm] *adv repeat* à satiété; *do* jusqu'à saturation, à satiété. **to talk ~ about sth** raconter des histoires à n'en plus finir sur qch.
ado [əˈduː] *n* agitation *f*, embarras *m*, affairement *m*. **much ~ about nothing** beaucoup de bruit pour rien; **without more ~** sans plus de cérémonies *or* d'histoires*.
adobe [əˈdəʊbɪ] *n* adobe *m*. ~ **wall** mur *m* d'adobe.
adolescence [ˌædəʊˈlesns] *n* adolescence *f*.
adolescent [ˌædəʊˈlesnt] *adj, n* adolescent(e) *m(f)*.
Adonis [əˈdəʊnɪs] *n* (*Myth, fig*) Adonis *m*.
adopt [əˈdɒpt] *vt* **(a)** *child* adopter. **(b)** *idea, method* adopter, choisir, suivre; (*Pol*) *motion* adopter; *candidate* choisir.
adopted [əˈdɒptɪd] *adj child* adopté; *country* d'adoption, adoptif. ~ **son** fils adoptif; ~ **daughter** fille adoptive.
adoption [əˈdɒpʃən] *n [child, country, law, idea]* adoption *f*; *[career, method]* choix *m*.
adoptive [əˈdɒptɪv] *adj parent, child* adoptif; *country* d'adoption.
adorable [əˈdɔːrəbl] *adj* adorable.
adoration [ˌædəˈreɪʃən] *n* adoration *f*.
adore [əˈdɔːʳ] *vt* adorer.
adoringly [əˈdɔːrɪŋlɪ] *adv* avec adoration.
adorn [əˈdɔːn] *vt* orner, parer (*with* de). **to ~ o.s.** se parer.
adornment [əˈdɔːnmənt] *n* **(a)** (*in room*) ornement *m*; (*on dress*) parure *f*. **(b)** (*U*) décoration *f*.
adrenal [əˈdriːnl] **1** *adj* surrénal. **2** *n* (*also* ~ **gland**) surrénale *f*.
adrenalin [əˈdrenəlɪn] *n* (*Brit*) adrénaline *f*. (*fig*) **he felt the ~ rising** il a senti son pouls s'emballer.
Adriatic (Sea) [ˌeɪdrɪˈætɪk(ˈsiː)] *n* (mer *f*) Adriatique *f*.
adrift [əˈdrɪft] *adv, adj* (*Naut*) à la dérive; (*fig*) à l'abandon. *[ship]* **to go ~** aller à la dérive; (*fig*) **to be (all) ~** divaguer, dérailler*; (*fig*) **to turn sb ~** mettre qn à la porte, laisser qn se débrouiller tout seul; (*fig*) **to come ~*** *[wire etc]* se détacher; *[plans]* tomber à l'eau.
adroit [əˈdrɔɪt] *adj* adroit, habile.
adroitly [əˈdrɔɪtlɪ] *adv* adroitement, habilement.
adroitness [əˈdrɔɪtnɪs] *n* adresse *f*, dextérité *f*.
adulate [ˈædjʊleɪt] *vt* aduler, flagorner.
adulation [ˌædjʊˈleɪʃən] *n* adulation *f*, flagornerie *f*.
adult [ˈædʌlt] **1** *n* adulte *mf*. (*Cine etc*) **~s only** interdit aux moins de 18 ans.
2 *adj* **(a)** *person, animal* adulte.
(b) *film, book* pour adultes. ~ **classes** cours *m* pour *or* d'adultes; ~ **education** enseignement *m* de promotion sociale, enseignement post-scolaire.
adulterate [əˈdʌltəreɪt] **1** *vt* frelater, falsifier, adultérer. **~d milk** lait falsifié. **2** *adj* **(a)** *goods, wine* falsifié, frelaté. **(b)** (*Jur*) *spouse* adultère; *child* adultérin.
adulteration [əˌdʌltəˈreɪʃən] *n* altération *f*, frelatage *m*, falsification *f*.
adulterer [əˈdʌltərəʳ] *n* adultère *m* (*personne*).
adulteress [əˈdʌltərɪs] *n* adultère *f*.
adulterous [əˈdʌltərəs] *adj* adultère.
adultery [əˈdʌltərɪ] *n* adultère *m*.
adumbrate [ˈædʌmbreɪt] *vt* esquisser, ébaucher; *event* faire pressentir, préfigurer.
advance [ədˈvɑːns] **1** *n* **(a)** (*progress, movement forward*) avance *f*, marche *f* en avant; (*Mil*) avance, progression *f*. **to make ~s in technology** faire des progrès *mpl* en technologie.
(b) (*U*) **in ~** en avance, par avance, d'avance; **to be in ~ of one's time** être en avance sur *or* devancer son époque; **to book in ~** retenir *or* louer à l'avance; **a week in ~** une semaine à l'avance; (*Rail*) **luggage in ~** bagages enregistrés.
(c) (*in prices, wages*) hausse *f*, augmentation *f* (*in* de).
(d) (*sum of money*) avance *f* (*on* sur), prêt *m*.
(e) (*overtures of friendship*) **~s** avances *fpl*; **to make ~s to sb** faire des avances à qn.
2 *cpd*: **advance booking office** (guichet *m* de) location *f*; **advance copy** *[book]* exemplaire *m* de lancement; *[speech]* texte distribué à l'avance (à la presse); (*Mil*) **advance guard** avant-garde *f*; **advance notice** préavis *m*, avertissement *m*; (*Mil*) **advance party** pointe *f* d'avant-garde; (*Fin*) **advance payment** paiement anticipé *or* par anticipation; (*Mil*) **advance post** poste avancé.
3 *vt* **(a)** (*move forward*) *date, time* avancer; (*Mil*) *troops* avancer; *work* faire progresser *or* avancer; (*promote*) *person* élever, promouvoir (*to* à).
(b) (*suggest, propose*) *reason, explanation* avancer; *opinion* avancer, émettre.
(c) (*lend*) *money* avancer, prêter, faire une avance de.
(d) (*raise*) *prices* augmenter, faire monter, hausser.
4 *vi* **(a)** (*go forward*) avancer, s'avancer, marcher (*on, towards* vers); *[troops]* se porter en avant. **he ~d upon me** il est venu vers *or* a marché sur moi.
(b) (*progress*) *[work, civilization, mankind]* progresser, faire des progrès; *[person]* (*in rank*) recevoir de l'avancement; (*Mil*) monter en grade.
(c) (*rise*) *[prices]* monter, augmenter, être en hausse.
advanced [ədˈvɑːnst] *adj ideas, age, pupil, child* avancé; *studies, class* supérieur; *work* poussé. ~ **mathematics** hautes études mathématiques; **the season is well ~** la saison est bien avancée; ~ **in years** d'un âge avancé.
advancement [ədˈvɑːnsmənt] *n* **(a)** (*improvement*) progrès *m*, avancement *m*. **(b)** (*promotion*) avancement *m*, promotion *f*.
advantage [ədˈvɑːntɪdʒ] **1** *n* **(a)** avantage *m*, supériorité *f*. **to have an ~ over sb, to have the ~ of sb** avoir un avantage sur qn; **that gives you an ~ over me** cela vous donne un avantage sur moi; **to have the ~ of numbers** avoir l'avantage du nombre (*over* sur); **to take ~ of sb** profiter *or* abuser de qn; **I took ~ of the opportunity** j'ai profité de l'occasion; **to turn sth to ~** tirer parti de qch, tourner qch à son avantage; **I find it to my ~** j'y trouve mon compte; **it is to his ~ to do it** cela l'arrange *or* c'est son intérêt de le faire, il a tout intérêt à le faire; **to the best ~** le plus avantageusement possible; **this dress shows her off to ~** cette robe l'avantage, elle est à son avantage dans cette robe.
(b) (*Tennis*) avantage *m*.
2 *vt* avantager.
advantageous [ˌædvənˈteɪdʒəs] *adj* avantageux (*to* pour), favorable, profitable (*to* à).
advent [ˈædvənt] *n* **(a)** venue *f*, avènement *m*. **(b)** (*Rel*) **A~** Avent *m*.
adventitious [ˌædvenˈtɪʃəs] *adj* fortuit, accidentel; (*Bot, Med*) adventice.
adventure [ədˈventʃəʳ] **1** *n* aventure *f*. **to have an ~** avoir une aventure. **2** *vt* aventurer, risquer, hasarder. **3** *vi* s'aventurer, se risquer (*on* dans). **4** *cpd story, film* d'aventures.
adventurer [ədˈventʃərəʳ] *n* aventurier *m*.
adventuress [ədˈventʃərɪs] *n* aventurière *f*.
adventurous [ədˈventʃərəs] *adj person* aventureux, audacieux; *journey* aventureux, hasardeux.
adverb [ˈædvɜːb] *n* adverbe *m*.
adverbial [ədˈvɜːbɪəl] *adj* adverbial.
adversary [ˈædvəsərɪ] *n* adversaire *mf*.
adverse [ˈædvɜːs] *adj factor, report, opinion* défavorable, hostile; *wind* contraire, debout. *[person]* **in ~ circumstances** dans l'adversité; ~ **to** hostile à, contraire à.
adversity [ədˈvɜːsɪtɪ] *n* **(a)** (*U*) adversité *f*. **in ~** dans l'adversité. **(b)** (*event*) malheur *m*.
advert[1] [ədˈvɜːt] *vi* se reporter, faire allusion, se référer (*to* à).
advert[2]* [ˈædvɜːt] *n* (*Brit abbr of* **advertisement**) (*announcement*) annonce *f* (publicitaire); (*Comm*) réclame *f*.
advertise [ˈædvətaɪz] **1** *vt* **(a)** (*Comm etc*) *goods* faire de la publicité *or* de la réclame pour. **to ~ sth on television/in the press** faire de la publicité *or* de la réclame pour qch à la télévision/dans les journaux; **I've seen that soap ~d on television** j'ai vu une publicité pour ce savon à la télévision.
(b) (*in newspaper etc*) **to ~ a flat (for sale)** mettre *or* insérer une annonce pour vendre un appartement.

(c) (*make conspicuous*) afficher. **don't ~ your ignorance!** inutile d'afficher votre ignorance!
2 *vi* **(a)** faire de la publicité *or* de la réclame. **it pays to ~** la publicité paie.
(b) chercher par voie d'annonce. **to ~ for a flat/a secretary** faire paraître une annonce pour trouver un appartement/une secrétaire.
advertisement [əd'vɜ:tɪsmənt] *n* **(a)** (*Comm*) réclame *f*, publicité *f*; (*TV*) spot *m* publicitaire. (*Cine, Press, Rad, TV*) **~s** publicité; **I saw an ~ for that soap in the papers** j'ai vu une réclame *or* une publicité pour ce savon dans les journaux; **I made tea during the ~s** j'ai fait le thé pendant que passait la publicité; **he's not a good ~** *or* **an ~ for his school** il ne constitue pas une bonne réclame pour son école.
(b) (*announcement*) annonce *f*. **~ column** petites annonces; **to put an ~ in a paper** mettre une annonce dans un journal; *V* **classified, small.**
(c) (*U*) réclame *f*, publicité *f*. (*fig*) **his arrival received no ~** son arrivée n'a pas été annoncée; *V* **self.**
advertiser ['ædvətaɪzə^{r}] *n* annonceur *m* (publicitaire).
advertising ['ædvətaɪzɪŋ] **1** *n* publicité *f*, réclame *f*.
2 *cpd firm, work* publicitaire. **advertising agency** agence *f* de publicité; **advertising campaign** campagne *f* publicitaire; **advertising medium** organe *m* de publicité; **advertising rates** tarifs *mpl* publicitaires; *V* **jingle.**
advice [əd'vaɪs] *n* **(a)** (*U*) avis *m*, conseils *mpl*. **a piece of ~** un avis, un conseil; **to seek ~ from sb** demander conseil à qn; **to take medical/legal ~** consulter un médecin/un avocat; **to take** *or* **follow sb's ~** suivre le(s) conseil(s) de qn.
(b) (*Comm: notification*) avis *m*. **as per ~ of** *or* **from** suivant avis de; **~ note** avis; *V* **legal.**
advisability [əd,vaɪzə'bɪlɪtɪ] *n* opportunité *f* (*of sth* de qch, *of doing* de faire).
advisable [əd'vaɪzəbl] *adj* recommandable, opportun, judicieux. **it is ~ to be vaccinated** il est conseillé de se faire vacciner; **I do not think it ~ for you to come** je ne vous conseille pas de venir.
advise [əd'vaɪz] *vt* **(a)** (*give advice to*) conseiller, donner des conseils à (*sb on/about sth* qn sur/à propos de qch). **to ~ sb to do** conseiller à qn de faire, recommander à qn de faire, engager qn à faire; **to ~ sb against sth** déconseiller qch à qn; **to ~ sb against doing** conseiller à qn de ne pas faire.
(b) (*recommend*) *course of action* recommander. **I shouldn't ~ your going to see him** je ne vous conseillerais *or* recommanderais pas d'aller le voir.
(c) (*Comm: inform*) **to ~ sb of sth** aviser *or* informer qn de qch, faire part à qn de qch.
advised† [əd'vaɪzd] *adj plan, act* réfléchi, délibéré, judicieux; *V* **ill.**
advisedly [əd'vaɪzɪdlɪ] *adv* délibérément, en (toute) connaissance de cause, après mûre réflexion.
adviser [əd'vaɪzə^{r}] *n* conseiller *m*, -ère *f*; *V* **legal, spiritual.**
advisory [əd'vaɪzərɪ] *adj* consultatif. **~ board** conseil consultatif; **in an ~ capacity** à titre consultatif.
advocacy ['ædvəkəsɪ] *n [cause etc]* plaidoyer *m* (*of* en faveur de).
advocate ['ædvəkɪt] **1** *n* **(a)** (*upholder*) *[cause etc]* défenseur *m*, avocat(e) *m(f)*. **to be an ~ of** être partisan(e) de; **to become the ~ of** se faire le champion (*or* la championne) de; *V* **devil.**
(b) (*Scot Jur*) avocat *m* (plaidant); *V* **lord.**
2 ['ædvəkeɪt] *vt* recommander, préconiser, prôner.
adz(e) [ædz] *n* herminette *f*, doloire *f*.
Aegean (Sea) [i:'dʒi:ən('si:)] *n* (mer *f*) Égée *f*.
aegis ['i:dʒɪs] *n* égide *f*, protection *f*. **under the ~ of** sous l'égide de.
aeolian [i:'əʊlɪən] *adj* éolien. **~ harp** harpe éolienne.
aeon ['i:ən] *n* temps infini, période *f* incommensurable. **through ~s of time** à travers des éternités.
aerate ['ɛəreɪt] *vt liquid* gazéifier; *blood* oxygéner; *soil* retourner. **~d water** eau gazeuse.
aerial ['ɛərɪəl] **1** *adj* **(a)** (*in the air*) aérien. **~ cableway** téléphérique *m*; **~ camera** appareil *m* de photo pour prises de vues aériennes; (*US*) **~ ladder** échelle pivotante; **~ photograph** photographie aérienne; **~ railway** téléphérique; **~ survey** prise *f* de vue aérienne.
(b) (*immaterial*) irréel, imaginaire.
2 *n* (*esp Brit: Telec etc*) antenne *f*; *V* **indoor.**
3 *cpd*: **aerial input** puissance reçue par l'antenne; **aerial mast** mât *m* d'antenne.
aerie ['ɛərɪ] *n* (*esp US*) aire *f* (*d'aigle etc*).
aero ... ['ɛərəʊ] *pref* aéro ... .
aerobatics ['ɛərəʊ'bætɪks] *npl* acrobatie(s) aérienne(s).
aerodrome ['ɛərədrəʊm] *n* (*Brit*) aérodrome *m*.
aerodynamic ['ɛərəʊdaɪ'næmɪk] *adj* aérodynamique.
aerodynamics ['ɛərəʊdaɪ'næmɪks] *n* (*U*) aérodynamique *f*.
aero-engine ['ɛərəʊ,endʒɪn] *n* aéromoteur *m*.
aerogram ['ɛərəʊgræm] *n* radiotélégramme *m*.
aerograph ['ɛərəʊgræf] *n* météorographe *m*.
aerolite ['ɛərəlaɪt] *n* aérolithe *m*.
aeromodelling ['ɛərəʊ'mɒdlɪŋ] *n* aéromodélisme *m*.
aeronaut ['ɛərənɔ:t] *n* aéronaute *mf*.
aeronautic(al) [,ɛərə'nɔ:tɪk(əl)] *adj* aéronautique. **~ engineering** aéronautique *f*.
aeronautics [,ɛərə'nɔ:tɪks] *n* (*U*) aéronautique *f*.
aeroplane ['ɛərəpleɪn] *n* (*Brit*) avion *m*, aéroplane† *m*.
aerosol ['ɛərəsɒl] **1** *n* **(a)** (*system*) aérosol *m*. **(b)** (*spray*) (*small*) atomiseur *m*; (*larger*) bombe *f*. **2** *cpd insecticide, paint* en aérosol, en bombe; *perfume* en atomiseur.
aerospace ['ɛərəʊspeɪs] *adj*: **~ industry** industrie aérospatiale.
Aesop ['i:sɒp] *n* Ésope *m*. **~'s Fables** les fables *fpl* d'Ésope.
aesthete, (*US*) **esthete** ['i:sθi:t] *n* esthète *mf*.
aesthetic(al), (*US*) **esthetic(al)** [i:s'θetɪk(əl)] *adj* esthétique.
aesthetically, (*US*) **esthetically** [i:s'θetɪkəlɪ] *adv* esthétiquement.
aestheticism, (*US*) **estheticism** [i:s'θetɪsɪzəm] *n* esthétisme *m*.
aesthetics, (*US*) **esthetics** [i:s'θetɪks] *n* (*U*) esthétique *f*.
afar [ə'fɑ:^{r}] *adv* (au) loin, à distance. **from ~** de loin.
affability [,æfə'bɪlɪtɪ] *n* affabilité *f*, amabilité *f*.
affable ['æfəbl] *adj* affable, aimable.
affably ['æfəblɪ] *adv* avec affabilité, affablement, aimablement.
affair [ə'fɛə^{r}] *n* **(a)** (*event*) affaire *f*, événement *m*. **it was a scandalous ~** ce fut un scandale; **~ of honour** affaire d'honneur; **the Suez ~** l'affaire de Suez.
(b) (*concern*) affaire *f*. **this is not her ~** ce n'est pas son affaire, cela ne la regarde pas.
(c) (*business of any kind*) **~s** affaires *fpl*, questions *fpl*; **in the present state of ~s** les choses étant ce qu'elles sont, étant donné les circonstances actuelles; **it was a dreadful state of ~s** la situation était épouvantable; **~s of state** affaires d'État; **to put one's ~s in order** (*business*) mettre de l'ordre dans ses affaires; (*belongings*) mettre ses affaires en ordre; *V* **current, foreign.**
(d) (*love ~*) liaison *f*, affaire *f* de cœur, aventure *f* (amoureuse). **to have an ~ with sb** avoir une liaison avec qn.
(e) (**: material object*) affaire *f*, chose *f*.
affect[1] [ə'fekt] *vt* **(a)** (*have effect on, concern*) affecter, avoir un effet sur, toucher; *one's feelings, emotions* émouvoir, affecter, toucher. **his decision does not ~ me personally** sa décision ne me touche pas personnellement.
(b) (*attack*) *[disease]* affecter, attaquer, agir sur.
affect[2] [ə'fekt] *vt* **(a)** (*feign*) *ignorance, indifference* affecter, feindre.
(b) (*have a liking for*) aimer, affectionner. **she ~s bright colours** elle a une prédilection pour *or* elle aime *or* elle affectionne les couleurs vives.
affectation [,æfek'teɪʃən] *n* **(a)** (*pretence*) affectation *f*, simulation *f*. **an ~ of interest/indifference** une affectation d'intérêt/d'indifférence.
(b) (*artificiality*) affectation *f*, manque *m* de naturel. **her ~s annoy me** ses manières affectées *or* ses poses *fpl* m'agacent.
affected [ə'fektɪd] *adj* **(a)** (*insincere*) *person, behaviour* affecté, maniéré; *accent, clothes* affecté. *[person]* **to be ~** poser. **(b)** (*moved emotionally*) touché, ému.
affectedly [ə'fektɪdlɪ] *adv* avec affectation, d'une manière affectée.
affecting [ə'fektɪŋ] *adj* touchant, émouvant.
affection [ə'fekʃən] *n* **(a)** (*U: fondness*) affection *f*, tendresse *f* (*for, towards* pour). **to win sb's ~(s)** se faire aimer de qn, gagner l'affection *or* le cœur de qn; **I have a great ~ for her** j'ai beaucoup d'affection pour elle.
(b) (*Med*) affection *f*, maladie *f*.
affectionate [ə'fekʃənɪt] *adj* affectueux, tendre, aimant. (*letter-ending*) **your ~ daughter** votre fille affectionnée.
affectionately [ə'fekʃənɪtlɪ] *adv* affectueusement. (*letter-ending*) **yours ~** (bien) affectueusement (à vous).
affective [ə'fektɪv] *adj* affectif.
affidavit [,æfɪ'deɪvɪt] *n* (*Jur*) déclaration *f* sous serment. **to swear an ~ (to the effect that)** déclarer sous serment (que).
affiliate [ə'fɪlɪeɪt] *vt* affilier (*to, with* à). **to ~ o.s., to be ~d** s'affilier (*to, with* à); (*Comm*) **~d company** filiale *f*.
affiliation [ə,fɪlɪ'eɪʃən] *n* **(a)** (*Comm etc*) affiliation *f*. **(b)** (*Jur*) attribution *f* de paternité. **~ order** jugement *m* en constatation de paternité.
affinity [ə'fɪnɪtɪ] *n* **(a)** (*gen, Bio, Chem, Ling, Math, Philos*) affinité *f* (*with, to* avec, *between* entre); (*connection, resemblance*) ressemblance *f*, rapport *m*. **the ~ of one thing to another** la ressemblance d'une chose avec une autre.
(b) (*Jur: relationship*) affinité *f* (*to, with* avec).
(c) (*liking*) attrait *m*, attraction *f* (*with, for* pour). **there is a certain ~ between them** ils ont des affinités.
affirm [ə'fɜ:m] *vt* affirmer, soutenir (*that* que). **to ~ sth to sb** assurer qn de la vérité de qch.
affirmation [,æfə'meɪʃən] *n* affirmation *f*, assertion *f*.
affirmative [ə'fɜ:mətɪv] **1** *n* (*Gram*) affirmatif *m*. **in the ~** à l'affirmatif; (*gen*) **to answer in the ~** répondre affirmativement *or* par l'affirmative, répondre que oui.
2 *adj* affirmatif. **if the answer is ~** si la réponse est affirmative, si la réponse est oui *or* dans l'affirmative.
affirmatively [ə'fɜ:mətɪvlɪ] *adv* affirmativement.
affix[1] [ə'fɪks] *vt seal, signature* apposer, ajouter (*to* à); *stamp* coller (*to* à).
affix[2] ['æfɪks] *n* (*Gram*) affixe *m*.
afflict [ə'flɪkt] *vt* **(a)** (*physically*) affliger. **to be ~ed with gout** être affligé *or* souffrir de la goutte. **(b)** (*emotionally*) affliger, désoler.
affliction [ə'flɪkʃən] *n* **(a)** (*U*) affliction *f*, détresse *f*. **people in ~** les gens dans la détresse. **(b)** infirmité *f*. **the ~s of old age** les infirmités de la vieillesse.
affluence ['æflʊəns] *n* (*plenty*) abondance *f*; (*wealth*) richesse *f*. **to rise to ~** parvenir à la fortune.
affluent[1] ['æflʊənt] *adj* (*plentiful*) abondant; (*wealthy*) riche. **to be ~** vivre dans l'aisance; **the ~ society** la société d'abondance.
affluent[2] ['æflʊənt] *n* (*Geog*) affluent *m*.
afflux ['æflʌks] *n* **(a)** (*Med*) afflux *m*. **(b)** *[people etc]* affluence *f*, afflux *m*.
afford [ə'fɔ:d] *vt* **(a)** (*following can, could, be able to*) **to be able to ~ to buy sth** avoir les moyens d'acheter qch; **I can't ~ a new hat** je ne peux pas m'offrir *or* me payer* un nouveau chapeau;

he can well ~ a new car il a tout à fait les moyens *or* ses moyens lui permettent de s'acheter une nouvelle voiture; (*fig*) he can't ~ (to make) a mistake il ne peut pas se permettre (de faire) une erreur; I can't ~ the time to do it je n'ai pas le temps de le faire; *V* ill.

(b) (*provide*) fournir, offrir, procurer. to ~ sb great pleasure procurer un grand plaisir à qn; this will ~ me an opportunity to say ceci me fournira l'occasion de dire.

afforest [æ'fɒrɪst] *vt* reboiser.

afforestation [æ,fɒrɪs'teɪʃən] *n* reboisement *m*. ~ policy politique *f* de reboisement.

affranchise [æ'fræntʃaɪz] *vt* affranchir.

affray [ə'freɪ] *n* bagarre *f*, échauffourée *f*, rixe *f*.

affright [ə'fraɪt] (†, *liter*) 1 *vt* effrayer, terrifier. 2 *n* effroi *m*, épouvante *f*, terreur *f*.

affront [ə'frʌnt] 1 *vt* (a) (*insult*) insulter, faire un affront à, offenser. (b) (*face*) affronter, braver. 2 *n* affront *m*, insulte *f*.

Afghan ['æfgæn] 1 *n* (a) Afghan(e) *m(f)*. (b) (*Ling*) afghan *m*. (c) (*also* ~ hound) lévrier afghan. 2 *adj* afghan.

Afghanistan [æf'gænɪstæn] *n* Afghanistan *m*.

afield [ə'fi:ld] *adv* au loin. countries further ~ pays plus lointains; very far ~ très loin; too far ~ trop loin; to explore farther ~ pousser plus loin l'exploration; (*fig*) to go farther ~ for help/support chercher plus loin de l'aide/un soutien.

afire [ə'faɪəʳ] *adj, adv* (*liter*) (*lit*) en feu, embrasé (*liter*); (*fig*) enflammé (*with* de).

aflame [ə'fleɪm] *adj, adv* en flammes, en feu, embrasé (*liter*). (*fig*) to be ~ with colour briller de vives couleurs, rutiler; (*fig*) ~ with anger enflammé de colère.

afloat [ə'fləʊt] *adv* (a) (*on water*) à flot, sur l'eau. to set a boat ~ mettre un bateau à l'eau *or* à flot; to stay ~ [*person*] garder la tête hors de l'eau, surnager; [*thing*] flotter, surnager; (*fig*) to get a business ~ lancer une affaire; (*fig*) to keep a business ~ maintenir une affaire à flot.

(b) (*Naut: on board ship*) en mer, à la mer. service ~ service *m* à bord; to serve ~ servir en mer.

(c) (*fig: of rumour etc*) en circulation, qui court *or* se répand. there is a rumour ~ that ... le bruit court que ... + *indic or cond.*

afoot [ə'fʊt] *adv* (a) (*in progress*) there is something ~ il se prépare *or* se trame quelque chose; there is a plan ~ to do on a formé le projet *or* on envisage de faire.

(b) (†, *liter*) à pied. to be ~ être sur pied; early ~ debout *or* sur pied de bonne heure.

aforementioned [ə,fɔ:'menʃənd] *adj*, **aforenamed** [ə'fɔ:neɪmd] *adj*, **aforesaid** [ə'fɔ:sed] *adj* (*Jur etc*) susdit, susmentionné, précité.

aforethought [ə'fɔ:θɔ:t] *adj* prémédité; *V* malice.

afoul [ə'faʊl] *adv* (*esp US*) to run ~ of sb se mettre qn à dos, s'attirer le mécontentement de qn; to run ~ of a ship entrer en collision avec un bateau.

afraid [ə'freɪd] *adj* (a) (*frightened*) *person, animal* effrayé, qui a peur. to be ~ of sb/sth avoir peur de qn/qch, craindre qn/qch; don't be ~! n'ayez pas peur!, ne craignez rien!; I am ~ of hurting him *or* that I might hurt him j'ai peur *or* je crains de lui faire mal; I am ~ he will *or* might hurt me, (*liter*) I am ~ lest he (might) hurt me je crains *or* j'ai peur qu'il (ne) me fasse mal; I am ~ to go *or* of going je n'ose pas y aller, j'ai peur d'y aller; he is ~ of work il n'aime pas beaucoup travailler; he is not ~ of work le travail ne lui fait pas peur *or* ne le rebute pas.

(b) (*expressing polite regret*) I'm ~ I can't do it je regrette *or* je suis désolé, (mais) je ne pourrai pas le faire; I'm ~ that ... je regrette de vous dire que ...; I am ~ I shall not be able to come je suis désolé de ne pouvoir venir, je crains de ne pas pouvoir venir; are you going? — I'm ~ not/I'm ~ so vous y allez? — hélas non/hélas oui; |here are too many people, I'm ~ je regrette, mais il y a trop de monde.

afresh [ə'freʃ] *adv* de nouveau, de plus belle. to start ~ recommencer.

Africa ['æfrɪkə] *n* Afrique *f*.

African ['æfrɪkən] 1 *n* Africain(e) *m(f)*. 2 *adj* africain. ~ elephant éléphant *m* d'Afrique; ~ violet saintpaulia *f*.

Afrikaaner [,æfrɪ'kɑ:nəʳ] *n* Afrikander *mf*.

Afrikaans [,æfrɪ'kɑ:ns] *n* (*Ling*) afrikaans *m*.

Afrikander [,æfrɪ'kændəʳ] *n* = **Afrikaaner.**

afro ['æfrəʊ] *adj*: to go ~* s'africaniser; ~ hair style coiffure *f* afro*.

Afro-Asian ['æfrəʊ'eɪʃən] *adj* afro-asiatique.

aft [ɑ:ft] *adv* (*Naut*) sur *or* à *or* vers l'arrière *m*. wind dead ~ vent en poupe, vent arrière.

after ['ɑ:ftəʳ] (*phr vb elem*) 1 *prep* (a) (*time*) après. ~ dinner après le dîner; the day ~ tomorrow après-demain *m*; ~ this date passé cette date; shortly ~ 10 o'clock peu après 10 heures; it was ~ 2 o'clock il était plus de 2 heures; (*US*) it was 20 ~ 3 il était 3h 20; ~ hours* après la fermeture, après le travail; ~ seeing her après l'avoir vue; ~ which he sat down après quoi il s'est assis; ~ what has happened après ce qui s'est passé.

(b) (*order*) après. the noun comes ~ the verb le substantif vient a) rès le verbe; ~ you, sir après vous, Monsieur; ~ you with the salt passez-moi le sel s'il vous plaît.

(c) (*place*) après. to run ~ sb courir après qn; he shut the door ~ her il a refermé la porte sur elle; come in and shut the door ~ you entrez et (re)fermez la porte (derrière vous); to shout ~ sb crier à qn.

(d) (*in spite of*) ~ all après tout; to succeed ~ all réussir malgré *or* après tout; ~ all I said to him après tout ce que je lui ai dit.

(e) (*succession*) day ~ day jour après jour, tous les jours; kilometre ~ kilometre sur des kilomètres et des kilomètres; kilometre ~ kilometre of forest des kilomètres et des kilomètres de forêt; you tell me lie ~ lie tu me racontes mensonge sur mensonge; time ~ time maintes (et maintes) fois; they went out one ~ the other (*individually*) ils sont sortis les uns après les autres; (*in a line*) ils sont sortis à la file.

(f) (*manner: according to*) ~ El Greco d'après Le Gréco; ~ the old style à la vieille mode, à l'ancienne; she takes ~ her mother elle tient de sa mère; a young man ~ your own heart un jeune homme comme tu les aimes; to name a child ~ sb donner à un enfant le nom de qn.

(g) (*pursuit, inquiry*) to be ~ sb chercher qn, être en quête de qn; the police are ~ him for this robbery il est recherché par la police *or* la police est à ses trousses pour ce vol; to be ~ sth rechercher qch, être à la recherche de qch; she's ~ a green hat elle cherche un chapeau vert; what are you ~? (*want*) qu'est-ce que vous voulez? *or* désirez?; (*have in mind*) qu'avez-vous en tête?; I see what he's ~ je vois où il veut en venir; (*fig*) she's always ~ her children* elle est toujours après ses enfants*; she inquired ~ you elle a demandé de vos nouvelles.

2 *adv* (*place, order, time*) après, ensuite. for years ~ pendant des années après cela; soon ~ bientôt après; the week ~ la semaine d'après, la semaine suivante; what comes ~? qu'est-ce qui vient ensuite?, et ensuite?

3 *conj* après. ~ he had closed the door, she spoke après qu'il eut fermé la porte, elle parla; ~ he had closed the door, he spoke après avoir fermé la porte, il a parlé.

4 *adj*: in ~ life *or* ~ years *or* ~ days plus tard (dans la vie), par *or* dans la suite.

5 *npl* (*Brit: dessert*) ~s* dessert *m*.

6 *cpd*: (*Med*) afterbirth délivre *m*, arrière-faix *m*; afterburner, afterburning postcombustion *f*; aftercare [*convalescent*] post-cure *f*; [*ex-prisoner*] surveillance *f* (après libération); (*Naut*) afterdeck arrière-pont *m*, pont *m* arrière; after-dinner drink digestif *m*; after-dinner speaker orateur *m* (de fin de banquet); he's a good after-dinner speaker il fait de très bonnes allocutions *or* de très bons discours (de fin de dîner); after-effect [*events etc*] suite *f*, répercussion *f*; [*treatment*] réaction *f*; [*illness*] séquelle *f*; (*Psych*) after-effect *m*; afterglow [*setting sun*] dernières lueurs, derniers reflets; [*person*] (*after exercise*) réaction *f* agréable; afterlife vie future (*V* 4); to have an after-lunch nap faire la sieste; aftermath suites *fpl*, conséquences *fpl*, séquelles *fpl*; the aftermath of war le contrecoup *or* les conséquences de la guerre; afternoon *V* afternoon; (*Comm*) after-sales service service *m* après-vente; after-shave lotion *f* après-rasage, after-shave *m*; (*lit, fig*) aftertaste arrière-goût *m*; afterthought *V* afterthought; after-treatment (*Med etc*) soins *mpl*; (*Tex*) apprêt *m*, fixage *m*.

afternoon ['ɑ:ftə'nu:n] 1 *n* après-midi *m or f*. in the ~, (*US*) ~s l'après-midi; at 3 o'clock in the ~ à 3 heures de l'après-midi; on Sunday ~(s) le dimanche après-midi; every ~ l'après-midi, chaque après-midi; on the ~ of December 2nd l'après-midi du 2 décembre, le 2 décembre dans l'après-midi; he will go this ~ il ira cet après-midi *or* tantôt; good ~! (*on meeting sb*) bonjour!; (*on leaving sb*) bon après-midi!

2 *cpd lecture, class, train, meeting* (de) l'après-midi. afternoon performance matinée *f*; afternoon tea thé *m* (de cinq heures).

afterthought ['ɑ:ftəθɔ:t] *n* pensée *f* après coup. I had an ~ cela m'est venu après coup; I had ~s *or* an ~ about my decision j'ai eu après coup des doutes sur ma décision; the window was added as an ~ la fenêtre a été ajoutée après coup.

afterwards ['ɑ:ftəwədz] *adv* après, ensuite, plus tard, par la suite.

again [ə'gen] (*phr vb elem*) *adv* (a) (*once more*) de nouveau, encore une fois, une fois de plus. here we are ~! nous revoilà!; ~ and ~, time and ~ à plusieurs reprises, maintes et maintes fois; I've told you ~ and ~ je te l'ai dit et répété (je ne sais combien de fois); he was soon well ~ il s'est vite remis; she is home ~ elle est rentrée chez elle, elle est de retour chez elle; what's his name ~? comment s'appelle-t-il déjà?; to begin ~ recommencer; to see ~ revoir; *V* now.

(b) (*with neg*) not ... ~ ne ... plus; I won't do it ~ je ne le ferai plus; never ~ jamais plus, plus jamais; I won't do it ever ~ je ne le ferai plus jamais; (*excl*) never ~! c'est bien la dernière fois!; (*iro*) not ~! encore!

(c) as much ~ deux fois autant; he is as old ~ as Mary il a deux fois l'âge de Marie.

(d) (*emphatic: besides, moreover*) de plus, d'ailleurs, en outre. then ~ ..., and ~ ... d'autre part ..., d'un autre côté ...; ~ it is not certain that ... et d'ailleurs *or* et encore il n'est pas sûr que ... .

against [ə'genst] (*phr vb elem*) *prep* (a) (*indicating opposition, protest*) contre, en opposition à, à l'encontre de. ~ the law (*adj*) contraire à la loi; (*adv*) contrairement à la loi; (*lit, fig*) there's no law ~ it il n'y a pas de loi qui s'y oppose, il n'y a pas de loi contre; conditions are ~ us les conditions nous sont défavorables *or* sont contre nous; ~ that, it might be said ... en revanche *or* par contre on pourrait dire ...; to be ~ capital punishment être contre la peine de mort; I'm ~ helping him at all je ne suis pas d'avis qu'on l'aide (*subj*); to be dead ~ sth s'opposer absolument à qch; (*Pol*) to run ~ sb se présenter contre qn; ~ all comers envers et contre tous; now we're up ~ it! nous voici au pied du mur!, c'est maintenant qu'on va s'amuser!*; ~ my will (*despite myself*) malgré moi, à contre-cœur; (*despite my opposition*) malgré moi, contre ma volonté; to work ~ time *or* the clock travailler contre la montre, faire la course contre la montre (*fig*); *V* grain, hair, odds.

(b) (*indicating collision, impact*) contre, sur. to hit one's head ~ the mantelpiece se cogner la tête contre la cheminée; the truck ran ~ a tree le camion s'est jeté sur *or* a percuté un arbre.

(c) (*in contrast to*) contre, sur. **~ the light** à contre-jour; **the trees stood out ~ the sunset** les arbres se détachaient sur le (soleil) couchant.

(d) (*in preparation for*) en vue de, en prévision de, pour. **preparations ~ sb's return** préparatifs pour le retour *or* en prévision du retour de qn; **to have the roof repaired ~ the rainy season** faire réparer le toit en vue de la saison des pluies.

(e) (*indicating support*) contre. **to lean ~ a wall** s'appuyer contre un mur *or* au mur.

(f) (as) ~ contre, en comparaison de; **3 prizes for her (as) ~ 6 for him** 3 prix pour elle contre 6 pour lui.

(g) numbered tickets are available ~ this voucher on peut obtenir des billets numérotés contre remise de ce bon; *V* **over.**

agape [əˈgeɪp] *adj, adv* bouche bée.

agar-agar [ˌeɪgəˈeɪgəʳ] *n* agar-agar *m*, gélose *f.*

agate [ˈægət] *n* agate *f.*

agave [əˈgeɪvɪ] *n* agavé *m.*

age [eɪdʒ] **1** *n* **(a)** (*length of life*) âge *m.* **what's her ~?, what ~ is she?** quel âge a-t-elle?; **he is 10 years of ~** il a 10 ans; **you don't look your ~** vous ne faites pas votre âge; **we are of an ~** nous sommes du même âge; (*Jur etc*) **to come of ~** atteindre sa majorité; **to be of ~** être majeur; *V* **middle, under** *etc.*

(b) (*latter part of life*) vieillesse *f*, âge *m.* **the infirmities of ~** les infirmités de la vieillesse *or* de l'âge; *V* **old.**

(c) (*Geol, Myth*) âge *m*; (*Hist, Literat*) époque *f*, siècle *m*; *V* **enlightenment, stone** *etc.*

(d) (*: *gen pl: long time*) **I haven't seen him for ~s** il y a un siècle que je ne le vois plus, il y a une éternité que je ne l'ai vu; **she stayed for ~s** elle est restée (là) pendant une éternité *or* un temps fou.

2 *vi* vieillir, prendre de l'âge. **she had ~d beyond her years** elle paraissait *or* faisait maintenant plus que son âge; **to ~ well** *[wine]* s'améliorer en vieillissant; *[person]* vieillir bien.

3 *vt* **(a)** vieillir. **this dress ~s you** cette robe vous vieillit.

(b) *wine etc* laisser vieillir.

4 *cpd* d'âge. **the 40-50 age group** le groupe *or* la tranche d'âge de 40 à 50 ans, les 40 à 50 ans; **age limit** limite *f* d'âge; **age-old** séculaire, antique.

aged [eɪdʒd] **1** *adj* **(a)** âgé de. **a boy ~ 10** un garçon (âgé) de 10 ans. **(b)** [ˈeɪdʒɪd] âgé, vieux (*f* vieille). **2** *npl*: **the ~** les vieillards *mpl*; **the ~ and infirm** les gens âgés et infirmes.

ageing [ˈeɪdʒɪŋ] **1** *adj person* vieillissant; *person, thing* qui se fait vieux (*f* vieille). **2** *n* vieillissement *m.*

ageless [ˈeɪdʒlɪs] *adj person* sans âge. **~ beauty** beauté *f* toujours jeune.

agency [ˈeɪdʒənsɪ] *n* **(a)** (*Comm*) agence *f*, bureau *m.* **this garage has the Citroën ~** ce garage est le concessionnaire Citroën; *V* **advertising, news, tourist** *etc.*

(b) (*means*) action *f*, intermédiaire *m*, entremise *f.* **through** *or* **by the ~ of friends** par l'intermédiaire *or* l'entremise d'amis, grâce à des amis; **through the ~ of water** par l'action de l'eau.

agenda [əˈdʒendə] *n* ordre *m* du jour, programme *m.* **on the ~** à l'ordre du jour.

agent [ˈeɪdʒənt] *n* **(a)** *[firm etc]* agent(e) *m(f)*, représentant(e) *m(f)* (*of, for* de); *V* **foreign, free, law, special** *etc.* **(b)** (*thing, person: producing effect*) agent *m*; *V* **chemical** *etc.*

agglomerate [əˈglɒməreɪt] **1** *vt* agglomérer. **2** *vi* s'agglomérer. **3** *adj* aggloméré.

agglomeration [əˌglɒməˈreɪʃən] *n* agglomération *f.*

agglutinate [əˈgluːtɪneɪt] **1** *vt* agglutiner. **2** *vi* s'agglutiner. **3** *adj* agglutiné; (*Ling*) agglutinant.

agglutination [əˌgluːtɪˈneɪʃən] *n* agglutination *f.*

agglutinative [əˈgluːtɪnətɪv] *adj substance, language* agglutinant.

aggrandize [əˈgrændaɪz] *vt* agrandir, grandir.

aggrandizement [əˈgrændɪzmənt] *n* agrandissement *m*; *[influence]* accroissement *m.*

aggravate [ˈægrəveɪt] *vt* **(a)** *illness* aggraver, (faire) empirer; *quarrel, situation* envenimer; *pain* augmenter. **(b)** (*annoy*) exaspérer, agacer, porter *or* taper sur les nerfs de*.

aggravating [ˈægrəveɪtɪŋ] *adj* **(a)** (*worsening*) *circumstances* aggravant. **(b)** (*annoying*) exaspérant, agaçant.

aggravation [ˌægrəˈveɪʃən] *n* (*V* **aggravate**) **(a)** aggravation *f*; envenimement *m.* **(b)** exaspération *f*, agacement *m*, irritation *f.*

aggregate [ˈægrɪgɪt] **1** *n* **(a)** ensemble *m*, total *m.* **in the ~** dans l'ensemble, en somme.

(b) (*Constr, Geol*) agrégat *m.*

2 *adj* collectif, global, total. **~ value** valeur collective.

3 [ˈægrɪgeɪt] *vt* **(a)** (*gather together*) agréger, rassembler.

(b) (*amount to*) s'élever à, former un total de.

4 *vi* s'agréger, s'unir en un tout.

aggression [əˈgreʃən] *n* (*also Psych*) agression *f*; *V* **non-aggression.**

aggressive [əˈgresɪv] *adj person, sales technique, behaviour, speech* agressif; (*Mil etc*) *tactics, action* offensif; (*Psych*) agressif.

aggressively [əˈgresɪvlɪ] *adv* d'une manière agressive, agressivement.

aggressiveness [əˈgresɪvnɪs] *n* agressivité *f.*

aggressor [əˈgresəʳ] *n* agresseur *m.*

aggrieved [əˈgriːvd] *adj* chagriné, blessé, affligé (*at, by* par).

aggro* [ˈægrəʊ] *n* (*abbr of* **aggression**) (*emotion*) agressivité *f*; (*physical violence*) grabuge* *m.*

aghast [əˈgɑːst] *adj* atterré (*at* de), frappé d'horreur.

agile [ˈædʒaɪl] *adj* agile, leste.

agility [əˈdʒɪlɪtɪ] *n* agilité *f*, souplesse *f.*

aging [ˈeɪdʒɪŋ] = **ageing.**

agitate [ˈædʒɪteɪt] **1** *vt* **(a)** *liquid* agiter, remuer.

(b) (*excite, upset*) émouvoir, troubler, tourmenter.

2 *vi* exciter l'opinion publique, faire de l'agitation. **to ~ for/against sth** faire campagne *or* mener une campagne en faveur de/contre qch.

agitated [ˈædʒɪteɪtɪd] *adj* inquiet (*f* -ète), agité. **to be very ~** être dans tous ses états.

agitation [ˌædʒɪˈteɪʃən] *n* **(a)** *[mind]* émotion *f*, trouble *m*, agitation *f.* **in a state of ~** agité.

(b) (*social unrest*) agitation *f*, troubles *mpl*; (*deliberate stirring up*) campagne *f* (*for* pour, *against* contre).

(c) *[liquid]* agitation *f*, mouvement *m.*

agitator [ˈædʒɪteɪtəʳ] *n* **(a)** (*person*) agitateur *m*, -trice *f*, fauteur *m* (de troubles), trublion *m.* **(b)** (*device*) agitateur *m.*

aglow [əˈgləʊ] *adj sky* embrasé (*liter*); *fire* rougeoyant, incandescent. **the sun sets the mountain ~** le soleil embrase la montagne; (*fig*) **~ with pleasure/health** rayonnant de plaisir/de santé.

agnostic [ægˈnɒstɪk] *adj, n* agnostique (*mf*).

agnosticism [ægˈnɒstɪsɪzəm] *n* agnosticisme *m.*

ago [əˈgəʊ] *adv* il y a. **a week ~** il y a huit jours; **how long ~?** il y a combien de temps (de cela)?; **a little while ~** tout à l'heure, il y a peu de temps; **he left 10 minutes ~** il est sorti il y a 10 minutes *or* depuis 10 minutes; **as long ~ as 1950** déjà en 1950, dès 1950; **no longer ~ than yesterday** pas plus tard qu'hier.

agog [əˈgɒg] *adj, adv* en émoi. **to be (all) ~ (with excitement) about sth** être en émoi à cause de qch; **to set ~** mettre en émoi; **to be ~ to do** griller d'envie *or* être impatient de faire, brûler de faire; **~ for news** impatient d'avoir des nouvelles.

agonized [ˈægənaɪzd] *adj* atroce, d'angoisse, déchirant.

agonizing [ˈægənaɪzɪŋ] *adj situation* angoissant; *cry* déchirant. **~ reappraisal** réévaluation *or* révision déchirante.

agony [ˈægənɪ] **1** *n* (*mental pain*) angoisse *f*, supplice *m*; (*physical pain*) paroxysme *m*; (*also* **death ~**) agonie *f.* **to suffer agonies** souffrir le martyre *or* mille morts; **to be in an ~* of impatience** se mourir d'impatience; **to be in ~*** souffrir le martyre; *V* **pile. 2** *cpd*: (*Brit Press*) **agony column** annonces personnelles, messages personnels.

agrarian [əˈgreərɪən] **1** *adj reform, laws* agraire. **A~ Revolution** réforme(s) *f(pl)* agraire(s). **2** *n* (*Pol Hist*) agrarien(ne) *m(f).*

agree [əˈgriː] **1** *vt* **(a)** (*consent*) consentir (*to do* à faire), accepter (*to do* de faire). **he ~d to do it** il a consenti à *or* accepté de le faire, il a bien voulu le faire.

(b) (*admit*) avouer. **I ~ (that) I was wrong** je reconnais *or* conviens que je me suis trompé, j'avoue *or* je reconnais mon erreur.

(c) (*have same opinion*) convenir (*to do* de faire), se mettre d'accord (*to do* pour faire). **everyone ~s that we should stay** tout le monde s'accorde à reconnaître que *or* tout le monde est unanime pour reconnaître que nous devrions rester, de l'avis de tous nous devrions rester; **they ~d (amongst themselves) to do it** ils ont convenu de le faire, ils se sont mis d'accord *or* se sont accordés pour le faire; **it was ~d** c'était convenu; **to ~ to differ** rester sur ses positions, garder chacun son opinion.

(d) *statement, report* accepter *or* reconnaître la véracité de; *price* se mettre d'accord sur, convenir de.

2 *vi* **(a)** (*hold same opinion*) être d'accord (*with* avec), être du même avis (*with* que). **they all ~d in finding the play dull** tous ont été d'accord pour trouver la pièce ennuyeuse, tous ont été d'avis que la pièce était ennuyeuse; **she ~s with me that it is unfair** elle est d'accord avec moi pour dire *or* elle trouve comme moi que c'est injuste; **he entirely ~s with me** il est tout à fait d'accord *or* en plein accord avec moi; **I can't ~ with you there** je ne suis absolument pas d'accord avec vous sur ce point; **I don't ~ with children smoking*** je n'admets pas que les enfants fument (*subj*).

(b) (*come to terms*) se mettre d'accord (*with* avec); (*get on well*) s'entendre (bien), s'accorder (bien). **to ~ about** *or* **on sth** se mettre d'accord sur qch, convenir de qch; **we haven't ~d about the price/about where to go** nous ne nous sommes pas mis d'accord sur le prix/sur l'endroit où aller, nous n'avons pas convenu du prix/de l'endroit où aller; **they ~ d as to how to do it/as to what it should cost** ils sont tombés *or* se sont mis d'accord sur la manière de le faire/sur le prix que cela devrait coûter; *V* **agreed.**

(c) to ~ to a proposal accepter une proposition, donner son consentement *or* son adhésion à une proposition; **I ~ to your marriage/your marrying her** je consens à votre mariage/à ce que vous l'épousiez; **he ~d to the project** il a donné son adhésion au projet.

(d) *[ideas, stories, assessments]* concorder, coïncider (*with* avec), correspondre (*with* à). **his explanation ~s with what I know** son explication correspond à ce que je sais; **these statements do not ~ with each other** ces affirmations ne concordent pas.

(e) (*Gram*) s'accorder (*with* avec).

(f) (*suit the health of*) **sea air ~s with invalids** l'air marin est bon pour les malades *or* réussit aux malades; **the heat does not ~ with her** la chaleur l'incommode; **onions don't ~ with me** les oignons ne me réussissent pas.

agreeable [əˈgriːəbl] *adj* **(a)** (*pleasant*) *person* agréable, aimable; *thing* agréable.

(b) (*willing*) consentant. **to be ~ to (doing) sth** consentir volontiers à (faire) qch; **I am quite ~** volontiers, je veux bien; **I am quite ~ to doing it** je ne demande pas mieux que de le faire, je veux bien le faire.

agreeably [əˈgriːəblɪ] *adv* agréablement.

agreed [əˈgriːd] *adj* **(a)** d'accord. **we are ~** nous sommes d'accord (*about* au sujet de, à propos de, *on* sur); **the ministers were ~** un accord est intervenu entre les ministres, les ministres sont tombés d'accord.

(b) *time, place, amount* convenu. **it's all ~** c'est tout décidé *or* convenu; **as ~** comme convenu; **it's ~ that** il est convenu que+*indic*; **(is that) ~?** entendu?, d'accord?; **~!** entendu!, d'accord!

agreement [əˈgriːmənt] *n* **(a)** (*mutual understanding*) accord *m*, harmonie *f*. **to be in ~ on a subject** être d'accord sur un sujet. **(b)** (*arrangement, contract*) accord *m*, accommodement *m*; (*Pol, frm*) pacte *m*. **to come to an ~** parvenir à une entente *or* un accommodement, tomber d'accord; **to sign an ~** signer un accord; **by mutual ~** (*both thinking same*) d'un commun accord; (*without quarrelling*) à l'amiable; *V* **gentleman.**
(c) (*Gram*) accord *m*.

agricultural [ˌægrɪˈkʌltʃərəl] *adj worker, produce, country* agricole; *tool* aratoire, agricole. **~ expert** expert *m* agronome; **~ college** école *f* d'agriculture; **~ show** exposition *f* agricole, salon *m* de l'agriculture; (*local*) comice *m* agricole.

agriculture [ˈægrɪkʌltʃəʳ] *n* agriculture *f*. (*Brit*) **Minister/Ministry of A~**, (*US*) **Secretary/Department of A~** ministre *m*/ministère *m* de l'Agriculture.

agricultur(al)ist [ˌægrɪˈkʌltʃər(əl)ɪst] *n* agronome *mf*; (*farmer*) agriculteur *m*.

agronomist [əˈgrɒnəmɪst] *n* agronome *mf*.

agronomy [əˈgrɒnəmɪ] *n* agronomie *f*.

aground [əˈgraʊnd] *adv, adj ship* échoué. **to be ~** toucher le fond; **to be fast ~** être bien échoué; **to run ~** s'échouer.

ague†† [ˈeɪgjuː] *n* (*Med*) fièvre *f*.

ah [ɑː] *excl* ah!

aha [ɑːˈhɑː] *excl* ah, ah!

ahead [əˈhed] (*phr vb elem*) *adv* **(a)** (*in space*) en avant, devant. **to draw ~** gagner de l'avant; **stay here, I'll go on ~** restez ici, moi je vais en avant; (*lit, fig*) **to get ~** prendre de l'avance; (*Naut, also fig*) **full speed ~!** en avant toute!; *V* **fire, go, look.**
(b) (*in time*) en avance. **~ of time** avant l'heure, en avance; **2 hours ~ of the next car** en avance de 2 heures sur la voiture suivante; **he's 2 hours ~ of you** il a 2 heures d'avance sur vous; **clocks here are 2 hours ~ of clocks over there** les pendules d'ici ont 2 heures d'avance sur celles de là-bas *or* avancent de 2 heures sur celles de là-bas; (*fig*) **to be ~ of one's time** être en avance sur son époque; **to plan ~** faire des projets à l'avance; **to think ~** prévoir, penser à l'avenir, anticiper.

ahoy [əˈhɔɪ] *excl* (*Naut*) ohé!, holà! **ship ~!** ohé du navire!

aid [eɪd] **1** *n* **(a)** (*U*) (*help*) aide *f*, assistance *f*, secours *m*; (*international*) aide. **by** *or* **with the ~ of sb** avec l'aide de qn; **by** *or* **with the ~ of sth** à l'aide de qch; **sale in ~ of the blind** vente *f* (de charité) au profit des aveugles; (*Brit fig*) **what is the meeting in ~ of?*** c'est dans quel but cette réunion?, à quoi rime cette réunion? (*pej*); **Marshall A~** le plan Marshall; *V* **first aid, mutual.**
(b) (*helper*) aide *mf*, assistant(e) *m(f)*; (*gen pl: equipment, apparatus*) aide *f*. **audio-visual ~s** support audio-visuel, moyens audio-visuels; *V* **deaf.**
2 *vt person* aider, assister, secourir, venir en aide à; *progress, recovery* contribuer à. **to ~ one another** s'entraider, s'aider les uns les autres; **to ~ sb to do** aider qn à faire; (*Jur*) **to ~ and abet (sb)** être complice (de qn).

aide [eɪd] *n* aide *mf*, assistant(e) *m(f)*. **~-de-camp** aide *m* de camp; **~-mémoire** mémorandum *m*.

ail [eɪl] **1** *vt*: **what ~s you?** qu'avez-vous?; **what's ~ing them?** qu'est-ce qui leur prend?*, quelle mouche les a piqués? **2** *vi* souffrir, être souffrant.

aileron [ˈeɪlərɒn] *n* (*Aviat*) aileron *m*.

ailing [ˈeɪlɪŋ] *adj* en mauvaise santé, souffrant. **she is always ~** elle est de santé fragile, elle a une petite santé.

ailment [ˈeɪlmənt] *n* indisposition *f*. **all his (little) ~s** tous ses maux.

aim [eɪm] **1** *n* **(a) to miss one's ~** manquer son coup *or* son but; **to take ~** viser; **to take ~ at sb/sth** viser qn/qch; **his ~ is bad** il vise mal.
(b) (*fig: purpose*) but *m*, objet *m*, visées *fpl*. **with the ~ of doing** dans le but de faire; **her ~ is to do** elle a pour but de faire, elle vise à faire; **his ~s are open to suspicion** ses visées ambitieuses *or* ses ambitions sont suspectes.
2 *vt* **(a)** (*direct*) *gun* braquer (*at* sur); *blow* allonger, décocher (*at* à); *remark* diriger (*at* contre). **to ~ a gun at sb** braquer un revolver sur qn, viser qn avec un revolver; **to ~ a stone at sb** lancer une pierre sur *or* à qn; (*fig*) **his remarks are ~ed at his father** ses remarques visent son père.
(b) (*intend*) viser, aspirer (*to do, at doing* à faire).
3 *vi* viser. **to ~ at** (*lit*) viser; (*fig*) viser, aspirer à; *V* **high.**

aimless [ˈeɪmlɪs] *adj person, way of life* sans but, désœuvré; *pursuit* sans objet, qui ne mène à rien, futile.

aimlessly [ˈeɪmlɪslɪ] *adv wander* sans but, à l'aventure. **to talk ~** parler de tout et de rien, parler à bâtons rompus.

ain't‡ [eɪnt] = **am not, is not, are not, has not, have not;** *V* **be, have.**

air [ɛəʳ] **1** *n* **(a)** air *m*. **in the open ~** en plein air; **a change of ~** un changement d'air; **I need some ~!** j'ai besoin d'air!; **to go out for a breath of (fresh) ~** sortir prendre l'air *or* le frais; **to take the ~**† prendre le frais; **to transport by ~** transporter par avion; **to go by ~** aller en *or* voyager par avion; **to throw sth (up) into the ~** jeter qch en l'air; **the balloon rose up into the ~** le ballon s'est élevé (dans les airs).
(b) (*fig phrases*) **there's sth in the ~** il se prépare qch, il se trame qch; **it's still all in the ~** ce ne sont encore que des projets en l'air *or* de vagues projets; **all her plans were up in the ~** (*vague*) tous ses projets étaient vagues *or* flous; **all her plans have gone up in the ~** (*destroyed*) tous ses projets sont tombés à l'eau; **there's a rumour in the ~ that ...** le bruit court que ...; **to give sb the ~**‡ envoyer promener qn; **he went up in the ~* when he heard the news** (*in anger*) il a bondi en apprenant la nouvelle; (*in excitement*) il a sauté d'enthousiasme en apprenant la nouvelle; **to be up in the ~ about*** (*angry*) être très monté *or* très en colère à l'idée de; (*excited*) être tout en émoi *or* très excité à l'idée de; **I can't live on ~** je ne peux pas vivre de l'air du temps; **to walk** *or* **tread on ~** être aux anges, ne pas se sentir de joie; *V* **castle, hot, mid**[1]**, thin.**
(c) on the ~ (*Rad*) à la radio, sur les ondes, à l'antenne; (*TV*) à l'antenne; **you're on the ~** vous avez l'antenne; **he's on the ~ every day** il parle à la radio tous les jours; **the station is on the ~** la station émet; **the programme goes** *or* **is put on the ~ every week** l'émission passe (sur l'antenne) *or* est diffusée toutes les semaines; **to go off the ~** quitter l'antenne.
(d) (*breeze*) brise *f*, léger souffle.
(e) (*manner*) aspect *m*, mine *f*, air *m*. **with an ~ of bewilderment** d'un air perplexe; **with a proud ~** d'un air fier, avec une mine hautaine; **she has an ~ about her** elle a de l'allure, elle a un certain chic; **to put on ~s, to give o.s. ~s** se donner de grands airs; **~s and graces** minauderies *fpl*; **to put on ~s and graces** minauder.
(f) (*Mus*) air *m*.
2 *vt* **(a)** *clothes, linen* aérer, sécher; *room, bed* aérer. **to put clothes out to ~** mettre des vêtements à l'air *or* à aérer.
(b) *anger* exhaler; *opinions* faire connaître.
3 *cpd flow, current* atmosphérique; (*Mil*) *superiority* aérien. **air base** base aérienne; (*Brit*) **air bed** matelas *m* pneumatique; **airborne troops** troupes aéroportées; **the plane was airborne** l'avion avait décollé; **air brake** (*on truck*) frein *m* à air comprimé; (*Aviat*) frein aérodynamique, aérofrein *m*; (*Constr*) **air brick** brique évidée *or* creuse; **air bubble** (*in liquids*) bulle *f* d'air; (*in glass, metal*) soufflure *f*; **airbus** aérobus *m*, airbus *m*; (*Aut, Physiol*) **air chamber** chambre *f* à air; (*Brit*) **Air Chief Marshal** général *m* d'armée aérienne; (*Brit*) **Air Commodore** général *m* de brigade aérienne; **air-conditioned** climatisé; **air conditioner** climatiseur *m*; **air conditioning** climatisation *f*; **air-cooled** *engine* à refroidissement par air; (*US**) *room* climatisé; **aircraft** (*pl inv*) avion *m*; **aircraft carrier** porte-avions *m inv*; (*Brit*) **aircraft(s)man** soldat *m* de deuxième classe (de l'armée de l'air); **aircrew** équipage *m* (*d'un avion*); **air cushion** coussin *m* pneumatique; (*Tech*) matelas *m or* coussin *m* d'air; **air display** fête *f* aéronautique, meeting *m* d'aviation; (*US*) **airdrome** = **aerodrome; airdrop** (*vt*) parachuter; (*n*) parachutage *m*; (*Tech*) **air duct** conduit *m* d'air *or* d'aération; **air ferry** avion transbordeur; **airfield** terrain *m* d'aviation, (petit) aérodrome *m*; **air force** armée *f* de l'air, aviation *f* militaire; **airframe** cellule *f* (d'avion); **airframe industry** industrie *f* de la construction des cellules aéronautiques; **air freight** transport *m* par avion, fret aérien; **to send by air freight** expédier par voie aérienne; **airgun** fusil *m or* carabine *f* à air comprimé; **air hole** prise *f* d'air, soupirail *m*; **air hostess** hôtesse *f* de l'air; **air intake** entrée *f* d'air, prise *f* d'air; **air lane** couloir aérien *or* de navigation aérienne; **air letter** lettre *f* par avion; **airlift** pont aérien; **airline** (*Aviat*) ligne aérienne, compagnie *f* d'aviation; (*diver's*) voie *f* d'air; **airliner** avion *m* de ligne, (avion) long-courrier *m or* moyen-courrier *m*; **airlock** (*in spacecraft, caisson etc*) sas *m*; (*in pipe*) bouchon *m or* bulle *f* d'air; **airmail** *V* **airmail; airman** aviateur *m*; (*in Air Force*) soldat *m* (de l'armée de l'air); **Air Marshal** général *m* de corps aérien; (*Met*) **air mass** masse *f* d'air; **air mattress** matelas *m* pneumatique; (*US*) **airplane** = **aeroplane; air pocket** trou *m or* poche *f* d'air; **airport** aéroport *m*; **air pressure** pression *f* atmosphérique; **air pump** compresseur *m*, machine *f* pneumatique; **air purifier** purificateur *m* d'air; **air raid** attaque aérienne, raid aérien; **air-raid precautions** défense passive; **air-raid shelter** abri antiaérien; **air-raid warden** préposé(e) *m(f)* à la défense passive; **air-raid warning** alerte *f* (aérienne); (*Brit*) **airscrew** hélice *f* (*d'avion*); **air-sea base** base aéronavale; **air-sea rescue** sauvetage *m* en mer (*par hélicoptère etc*); **air shaft** (*Min*) puits *m* d'aérage; (*Naut*) manche *f* à vent; **airshed** hangar *m* (d'aviation); **airship** (ballon *m*) dirigeable *m*; **air show** (*trade exhibition*) salon *m* de l'aéronautique; (*flying display*) meeting *m or* rallye *m* d'aviation; **to be airsick** avoir le mal de l'air; **airsickness** mal *m* de l'air; (*Aviat*) **airspeed** vitesse relative; **airspeed indicator** badin *m*; **airstrip** piste *f* d'atterrissage; **air terminal** aérogare *f*; **airtight** hermétique, étanche (à l'air); (*Mil*) **air-to-air** avion-avion *inv*; (*Mil*) **air-to-ground, air-to-surface** air-sol *inv*; **air traffic control** contrôle *m* du trafic; **air traffic controller** contrôleur *m*, -euse *f* de la navigation aérienne, aiguilleur *m* du ciel; **air vent** trou *m* d'aération; (*Brit*) **Air Vice Marshal** général *m* de division aérienne; **airway** (*route*) voie aérienne; (*airline company*) compagnie *f* d'aviation; (*ventilator shaft*) conduit *m* d'air; **airwoman** aviatrice *f*; (*in Air Force*) (femme *f*) auxiliaire *f* (de l'armée de l'air); **airworthiness** navigabilité *f* (*V* **certificate a**); **airworthy** en état de navigation.

airily [ˈɛərɪlɪ] *adj* légèrement, d'un ton dégagé, avec désinvolture *or* insouciance.

airiness [ˈɛərɪnɪs] *n* [*room*] aération *f*, (bonne) ventilation *f*; (*fig*) [*manner*] désinvolture *f*, insouciance *f*.

airing [ˈɛərɪŋ] **1** *n* [*linen*] aération *f*. (*fig*) **to go for** *or* **take an ~*** (aller) prendre l'air, faire un petit tour; (*fig*) **to give an idea an ~** mettre une idée en discussion *or* sur le tapis. **2** *cpd*: (*Brit*) **airing cupboard** placard-séchoir *m*.

airless [ˈɛəlɪs] *adj* **(a)** *room* privé d'air. **it is ~ in here** il n'y a pas d'air ici, cela sent le renfermé ici. **(b)** (*Met*) calme, tranquille. **(c)** *space* sans air.

airmail [ˈɛəmeɪl] **1** *n* poste aérienne. **by ~** par avion.
2 *vt letter, parcel* expédier par avion.
3 *cpd*: **airmail edition** édition *f* par avion; **airmail letter** lettre *f* par avion; (*of newspaper*) **airmail paper** papier *m* pelure; **airmail stamp, airmail sticker** étiquette *f* 'par avion'.

airy [ˈɛərɪ] **1** *adj* **(a)** *room* bien aéré. **(b)** (*immaterial*) léger, impalpable, éthéré. **(c)** (*casual*) *manner* léger, désinvolte, dégagé. ~ **promises** promesses *fpl* en l'air *or* vaines. **2** *cpd*: (*Brit*) **airy-fairy*** *idea, person* farfelu.

aisle [aɪl] *n* **(a)** *[church]* bas-côté *m*, nef latérale; (*between pews*) allée centrale. **to take a girl up the** ~ mener une jeune fille à l'autel. **(b)** *[theatre]* passage *m*; *[train, coach]* couloir *m* (central).

aitch [eɪtʃ] *n* (*letter*) H, h *m or f*. (*Culin*) ~ **bone** culotte *f* (de bœuf); *V* **drop**.

ajar [əˈdʒɑːʳ] *adj, adv* entr'ouvert, entrebâillé.

akimbo [əˈkɪmbəʊ] *adj*: **with arms** ~ les poings sur les hanches.

akin [əˈkɪn] *adj*: ~ **to** (*similar*) qui tient de, qui ressemble à; (*of same family as*) parent de, apparenté à.

alabaster [ˈæləbɑːstəʳ] **1** *n* albâtre *m*. **2** *cpd* (*lit, fig*) d'albâtre.

alacrity [əˈlækrɪtɪ] *n* empressement *m*, promptitude *f*, alacrité *f*.

Aladdin [əˈlædɪn] *n* Aladin *m*.

alarm [əˈlɑːm] **1** *n* **(a)** (*warning*) alarme *f*, alerte *f*. **to raise the** ~ donner l'alarme *or* l'éveil; ~**s and excursions** (*Theat*) bruits *mpl* de bataille en coulisse; (*fig*) branlebas *m* de combat; *V* **burglar, false.**

(b) (*U: fear*) inquiétude *f*, alarme *f*. **to cause sb** ~ mettre qn dans l'inquiétude, alarmer qn.

(c) = ~ **clock;** *V* **3.**

2 *vt* **(a)** (*frighten*) *person* alarmer, éveiller des craintes chez; *animal, bird* effaroucher, faire peur à. **to become** ~**ed** *[person]* prendre peur, s'alarmer; *[animal]* prendre peur, s'effaroucher.

(b) (*warn*) alerter, alarmer.

3 *cpd call* d'alarme. **alarm bell** sonnerie *f* d'alarme; **alarm clock** réveil *m*, réveille-matin *m inv*; **alarm signal** signal *m* d'alarme.

alarming [əˈlɑːmɪŋ] *adj* alarmant.

alarmingly [əˈlɑːmɪŋlɪ] *adv* d'une manière alarmante.

alarmist [əˈlɑːmɪst] *adj, n* alarmiste (*mf*).

alas [əˈlæs] *excl* hélas!

Alaska [əˈlæskə] *n* Alaska *m*; *V* **bake.**

alb [ælb] *n* aube *f* (*d'un prêtre*).

Albania [ælˈbeɪnɪə] *n* Albanie *f*.

Albanian [ælˈbeɪnɪən] **1** *adj* albanais. **2** *n* **(a)** Albanais(e) *m(f)*. **(b)** (*Ling*) albanais *m*.

albatross [ˈælbətrɒs] *n* albatros *m*.

albeit [ɔːlˈbiːɪt] *conj* (*liter*) encore que + *subj*, bien que + *subj*, quoique + *subj*.

albinism [ˈælbɪnɪzəm] *n* albinisme *m*.

albino [ælˈbiːnəʊ] *n* albinos *mf*. ~ **rabbit** lapin *m* albinos.

Albion [ˈælbɪən] *n* Albion *f*.

album [ˈælbəm] *n* (*book, long-playing record*) album *m*.

albumen, albumin [ˈælbjʊmɪn] *n* (*egg white*) albumen *m*, blanc *m* de l'œuf; (*Bot*) albumen; (*Physiol*) albumine *f*.

albuminous [ælˈbjuːmɪnəs] *adj* albumineux.

alchemist [ˈælkɪmɪst] *n* alchimiste *m*.

alchemy [ˈælkɪmɪ] *n* (*lit, fig*) alchimie *f*.

alcohol [ˈælkəhɒl] *n* alcool *m*.

alcoholic [ˌælkəˈhɒlɪk] **1** *adj person* alcoolique; *drink* alcoolisé, alcoolique. **2** *n* alcoolique *mf*. **A**~**s Anonymous** société *f* d'entraide des alcooliques, alcooliques *mpl* anonymes.

alcoholism [ˈælkəhɒlɪzəm] *n* alcoolisme *m*.

alcove [ˈælkəʊv] *n* (*in room*) alcôve *f*; (*in wall*) niche *f*; (*in garden*) tonnelle *f*, berceau *m*.

alder [ˈɔːldəʳ] *n* aulne *m or* aune *m*.

alderman [ˈɔːldəmən] *n* alderman *m*, conseiller *m*, -ère *f* municipal(e); (*Hist*) échevin *m*.

ale [eɪl] *n* bière *f*, ale *f*; *V* **brown, light², pale¹.**

Alec [ˈælɪk] *n* (*dim of* **Alexander**) Alex *m*; *V* **smart.**

alert [əˈlɜːt] **1** *n* alerte *f*. **to give the** ~ donner l'alerte; **on the** ~ sur le qui-vive; **to put troops on the** ~ mettre les troupes en état d'alerte.

2 *adj* (*watchful*) vigilant; (*acute*) éveillé; (*brisk*) alerte, vif.

3 *vt* alerter; *troops* mettre en état d'alerte; (*fig*) éveiller l'attention de (*to* sur). **we are now** ~**ed to the possible dangers** notre attention est maintenant éveillée sur les dangers possibles, nous sommes maintenant sensibilisés aux dangers possibles.

alertness [əˈlɜːtnɪs] *n* (*V* **alert 2**) vigilance *f*; esprit éveillé; vivacité *f*.

Alexander [ˌælɪgˈzɑːndəʳ] *n* Alexandre *m*.

Alexandria [ˌælɪgˈzɑːndrɪə] *n* Alexandrie.

alexandrine [ˌælɪgˈzændraɪn] *adj, n* alexandrin (*m*).

alfalfa [ælˈfælfə] *n* luzerne *f*.

alfresco [ælˈfreskəʊ] *adj, adv* en plein air.

alga [ˈælgə] *n, pl* **algae** [ˈældʒiː] (*gen pl*) algue(s) *f(pl)*.

algebra [ˈældʒɪbrə] *n* algèbre *f*.

algebraic [ˌældʒɪˈbreɪɪk] *adj* algébrique.

Algeria [ælˈdʒɪərɪə] *n* Algérie *f*.

Algerian [ælˈdʒɪərɪən] **1** *n* Algérien(ne) *m(f)*. **2** *adj* algérien.

Algiers [ælˈdʒɪəz] *n* Alger.

ALGOL [ˈælgɒl] *n* (*Computers*) ALGOL *m*.

alias [ˈeɪlɪæs] **1** *adv* alias. **2** *n* faux nom, nom d'emprunt; *[writer]* nom de guerre.

alibi [ˈælɪbaɪ] *n* alibi *m*.

Alice [ˈælɪs] *n* Alice *f*. ~ **band** bandeau *m* (*pour les cheveux*); ~ **in Wonderland** Alice au pays des merveilles.

alien [ˈeɪlɪən] **1** *n* étranger *m*, -ère *f*.

2 *adj* **(a)** (*foreign*) étranger.

(b) (*different*) ~ **from** étranger à, éloigné de; ~ **to** contraire à, opposé à; **cruelty is** ~ **to him** il ne sait pas ce que c'est que la cruauté *or* que d'être cruel, la cruauté est contraire à sa nature.

alienate [ˈeɪlɪəneɪt] *vt* (*also Jur*) aliéner. **this has** ~**d all his friends** ceci a aliéné tous ses amis; **she has** ~**d all her friends** elle s'est aliéné tous ses amis (*by doing* en faisant).

alienation [ˌeɪlɪəˈneɪʃən] *n* **(a)** (*estrangement*) désaffection *f*, éloignement *m* (*from* de). **(b)** (*Jur*) aliénation *f*. **(c)** (*Med, Psych*) aliénation *f* (mentale).

alienist [ˈeɪlɪənɪst] *n* aliéniste *mf*.

alight¹ [əˈlaɪt] *vi [person]* descendre (*from* de), mettre pied à terre; *[bird]* se poser (*on* sur).

alight on *vt fus fact* apprendre par hasard; *idea* tomber sur.

alight² [əˈlaɪt] *adj* allumé, en feu, embrasé (*liter*). **keep the fire** ~ ne laissez pas éteindre le feu; **to set sth** ~ mettre le feu à qch; (*fig*) **her face was** ~ **with pleasure** son visage rayonnait de joie.

align [əˈlaɪn] **1** *vt* **(a)** aligner, mettre en ligne; (*Tech*) dégauchir.

(b) (*Fin, Pol*) aligner (*on* sur). **to** ~ **o.s. with sb** s'aligner sur qn; **the non-**~**ed countries** les pays non-alignés *or* neutralistes.

2 *vi [persons]* s'aligner; *[objects]* être alignés.

alignment [əˈlaɪnmənt] *n* (*lit, fig*) alignement *m*; *V* **non-alignment.**

alike [əˈlaɪk] **1** *adj* semblable, pareil, égal. *[people]* **to be** ~ se ressembler, être semblable; **it's all** ~ **to me** cela m'est tout à fait égal, je n'ai pas de préférence.

2 *adv* pareillement, de la même manière, de même. **winter and summer** ~ été comme hiver; **they always think** ~ ils sont toujours du même avis; **to dress** ~ s'habiller de la même façon *or* de façon identique.

alimentary [ˌælɪˈmentərɪ] *adj* alimentaire. ~ **canal** tube digestif.

alimony [ˈælɪmənɪ] *n* (*Jur*) pension *f* alimentaire.

alive [əˈlaɪv] *adj* **(a)** (*living*) vivant, en vie, vif; (*in existence*) au monde. **to burn** ~ brûler vif; **while** ~**, he was always ...** de son vivant, il était toujours ...; **it's good to be** ~ il fait bon vivre; **no man** ~ personne au monde; **to do sth as well as anyone** ~ faire qch aussi bien que n'importe qui; **to keep** ~ (*lit*) *person* maintenir en vie; (*fig*) *tradition* préserver; *memory* garder; **to stay** ~ rester en vie, survivre.

(b) ~ **to** sensible à; **I am very** ~ **to the honour you do me** je suis très sensible à l'honneur que vous me faites; **to be** ~ **to one's interests** veiller à ses intérêts; **to be** ~ **to a danger** être conscient d'un danger.

(c) (*alert*) alerte, vif; (*active*) actif, plein de vie. **to be** ~ **and kicking*** (*living*) être bien en vie; (*full of energy*) être plein de vie; **look** ~**!*** allons, remuez-vous!

(d) ~ **with insects** grouillant d'insectes.

alkali [ˈælkəlaɪ] *n* alcali *m*.

alkaline [ˈælkəlaɪn] *adj* alcalin.

alkaloid [ˈælkəlɔɪd] *n* alcaloïde *m*.

all [ɔːl] **1** *adj* **(a)** (*every one of, the whole*) tout *m*, toute *f*, tous (les) *mpl*, toutes (les) *fpl*. ~ **the country** tout le pays, le pays tout entier; ~ **my life** toute ma vie; **people of** ~ **countries** les gens de tous les pays; ~ **the others** tous (*or* toutes) les autres; ~ **you boys** vous (tous) les garçons; ~ **three** tous (*or* toutes) les trois; ~ **(the) day** toute la journée; **to dislike** ~ **sport** détester le sport *or* tout (genre de) sport; ~ **that** tout cela; **for** ~ **that** malgré tout, en dépit de tout cela; ~ **kinds of,** ~ **sorts of,** ~ **manner of** toutes sortes de; ~ **mod cons** tout confort (moderne); **it is beyond** ~ **doubt** c'est indéniable *or* incontestable; **why ask me of** ~ **people?** pourquoi me le demander à moi?

(b) (*the utmost*) tout, le plus possible. **with** ~ **haste** en toute hâte; **with** ~ **(possible) care** avec tout le soin possible.

2 *pron* **(a)** (*sg: the whole amount, everything*) tout. ~ **is well** tout va bien; **that is** ~ c'est tout, voilà tout; **if that's** ~ **then it's not important** s'il n'y a que cela *or* si ce n'est que cela alors ce n'est pas important; ~ **in good time** chaque chose en son temps; **when** ~ **is said and done** somme toute, en fin de compte, tout compte fait; **and I don't know what** ~***** et je ne sais quoi encore; **what with the snow and** ~**: we didn't go** avec la neige et (tout) le reste* nous n'y sommes pas allés; ~ **of the house was destroyed** toute la maison a été détruite; ~ **of it was lost** (le) tout a été perdu; **he drank** ~ **of it** il a tout bu, il l'a bu en entier; ~ **of Paris** Paris tout entier; **that is** ~ **he said** c'est tout ce qu'il a dit; ~ **I want is to sleep** tout ce que je veux c'est dormir; **he saw** ~ **there was to see** il a vu tout ce qu'il y avait à voir; ~ **that is in the box is yours** tout ce qui est dans la boîte est à vous; **bring it** ~ apportez le tout.

(b) (*pl*) tous *mpl*, toutes *fpl*. **we** ~ **sat down** nous nous sommes tous assis (*or* toutes assises); **the girls** ~ **knew that ...** les jeunes filles savaient toutes que ...; ~ **of them failed** ils ont tous échoué, tous ont échoué; ~ **of the boys came** tous les garçons sont venus, les garçons sont tous venus; **they were** ~ **broken** ils étaient tous cassés; **one and** ~ tous sans exception; ~ **who knew him loved him** tous ceux qui l'ont connu l'ont aimé; ~ **(whom) I saw said that it was true** tous ceux que j'ai vus ont dit que c'était vrai; **the score was two** ~ (*Tennis*) le score était deux partout; (*other sports*) le score était deux à deux; *V* **each, sundry.**

(c) (*in phrases*) **if she comes at** ~ si tant est qu'elle vienne; **do you think she will come at** ~**?** croyez-vous seulement qu'elle vienne?; **very rarely if at** ~ très rarement si tant est, très rarement et encore; **I don't know at** ~ je n'en sais rien (du tout); **if you study this author at** ~ pour peu que vous étudiiez cet auteur; **if there is any water at** ~ si seulement il y a de l'eau; **if at** ~ **possible** dans la mesure du possible; **are you going? — not at** ~ vous y allez? — pas du tout; **thank you! — not at** ~**!** merci! — je vous en prie *or* (il n'y a) pas de quoi *or* de rien*; **it was** ~ **I could do to stop him from leaving** c'est à peine *or* tout juste si j'ai pu l'empêcher de s'en aller; **it was** ~ **I could do not to laugh** c'est à peine *or* tout juste si j'ai pu m'empêcher de rire, j'ai eu toutes les peines du monde à m'empêcher de rire; **it's not as bad as** ~ **that** ce n'est pas (vraiment) si mal que ça; **it isn't** ~ **that expensive!*** ce n'est pas si cher que ça!; **that's** ~ **very well but ...** tout cela est bien beau *or* joli mais ...; **taking it** ~ **in** ~ à tout prendre; **she is ~ in ~ to him** elle est tout pour lui; **~ but** presque, à peu de choses près; **he ~ but lost it** c'est tout juste s'il ne l'a pas perdu, il a bien failli le perdre; **the film was ~ but over** le film touchait à sa fin; **for ~ I know** autant que je sache; **for ~ his wealth he was unhappy** toute sa fortune ne l'empêchait pas d'être malheureux, malgré sa fortune il était malheureux; **for ~ he may say** quoi qu'il en dise; **once and for ~** une fois pour toutes; **most of ~** surtout; **it would be best of ~ if he resigned, the best of ~ would be for him to resign** le mieux serait qu'il donne (*subj*) sa démission.

3 *adv* **(a)** (*quite, entirely*) tout, tout à fait, complètement. **~ of a sudden** tout à coup, tout d'un coup, soudain, subitement; **~ too soon it was time to go** malheureusement il a bientôt fallu partir; **the evening passed ~ too quickly** la soirée n'est passée que trop rapidement; **dressed ~ in white** habillé tout en blanc, tout habillé de blanc; **she was ~ ears** elle était tout oreilles; **~ along the road** tout le long de la route; **I feared that ~ along** je l'ai craint depuis le début; **he won the race ~ the same** il a néanmoins *or* tout de même gagné la course; **it's ~ the same to me** cela m'est tout à fait égal, peu m'importe; **it's ~ one to them** cela leur est entièrement égal; **~ over** (*everywhere*) partout, d'un bout à l'autre; (*finished*) fini; **covered ~ over with dust** tout couvert de poussière; **the match was ~ over before ...** le match était fini *or* terminé avant ...; **to be ~ for sth*** être tout à fait en faveur de qch; **to be ~ for doing*** ne demander qu'à faire, vouloir à toute force faire; **~ in one piece** tout d'une pièce; **to be ~ in*** être éreinté, n'en pouvoir plus, être à bout*; **to be ~ there*** être sain d'esprit, avoir toute sa tête; **she's not quite ~ there*** il lui manque une case*; **it is ~ up with him*** il est fichu*; **~ at one go** d'un seul coup; *V* **all right, square.**

(b) (*with comps*) **~ the better!** tant mieux!; **~ the more ... as** d'autant plus ... que; **~ the more so since ...** d'autant plus que ... .

4 *n*: **I would give my ~ to see him** je donnerais tout ce que j'ai pour le voir; **to stake one's ~** risquer le tout pour le tout; **she had staked her ~ on his coming** elle avait tout misé sur sa venue.

5 *cpd*: **all-American** cent pour cent américain; (*US*) **all-around = all-round; all clear!** fin d'alerte!; **all clear (signal)** (signal *m* de) fin *f* d'alerte; **all-day** qui dure toute la journée; **all-embracing** qui embrasse tout, compréhensif; **All Fools' Day** le premier avril; **on all fours** à quatre pattes; **All Hallows** la Toussaint; **all-important** de la plus haute importance, capital; (*Brit*) **all-in** *price* net, tout compris; *insurance policy* tous risques; (*Comm*) *tariff* inclusif; (*Brit*) **the holiday cost £80 all-in** les vacances ont coûté 80 livres tout compris; **all-in wrestling** lutte *f* libre; (*Aut*) **all-metal body** carrosserie toute en tôle; (*Mil*) **all-night pass** permission *f* de nuit; (*Comm etc*) **all-night service** permanence *f* de nuit, service *m* de nuit; (*Cine*) **all-night showing** spectacle *m* de nuit; **to go all-out** aller à la limite de ses forces, y mettre toutes ses forces; **all-out effort** effort *m* maximum; **allover** (qui est) sur toute la surface; **allover pattern** dessin *m* *or* motif *m* qui recouvre toute une surface; **all-powerful** tout-puissant; **all-purpose** qui répond à tous les besoins; *knife, spanner* universel; **all right** *V* **all right; all-round** *sportsman* complet (*f* -ète); *improvement* général, sur toute la ligne; **to be a good all-rounder** être solide en tout *or* bon en tout; **All Saints' Day** (le jour de) la Toussaint; **All Souls' Day** le jour *or* la fête des Morts; **allspice** poivre *m* de la Jamaïque; (*Theat*) **all-star performance, show with an all-star cast** plateau *m* de vedettes; **all-time** *V* **all-time; all-weather** de toute saison, tous temps; **all-weather court** (terrain *m* en) quick *m* ®; **all-the-year-round** *sport* que l'on pratique toute l'année; *resort* ouvert toute l'année.

Allah ['ælə] *n* Allah *m*.

allay [ə'leɪ] *vt fears* modérer, apaiser; *pain, thirst* soulager, apaiser. **to ~ suspicion** dissiper les soupçons.

allegation [ˌælɪ'geɪʃən] *n* allégation *f*.

allege [ə'ledʒ] *vt* alléguer, prétendre (*that* que). **to ~ illness** prétexter *or* alléguer une maladie; **he is ~d to have said that ...** il aurait dit que ..., on prétend qu'il a dit que ... .

alleged [ə'ledʒd] *adj reason* allégué, prétendu; *thief, author* présumé.

allegedly [ə'ledʒɪdlɪ] *adv* à ce que l'on prétend, paraît-il, prétend-on.

allegiance [ə'liːdʒəns] *n* fidélité *f*, obéissance *f*. **oath of ~** serment *m* de fidélité; serment d'allégeance (*au souverain*).

allegoric(al) [ˌælɪ'gɒrɪk(əl)] *adj* allégorique.

allegorically [ˌælɪ'gɒrɪkəlɪ] *adv* sous forme d'allégorie, allégoriquement.

allegory ['ælɪgərɪ] *n* allégorie *f*.

alleluia [ˌælɪ'luːjə] *excl* alléluia!

allergic [ə'lɜːdʒɪk] *adj* (*Med*, **fig*) allergique (*to* à).

allergy ['ælədʒɪ] *n* allergie *f* (*to* à).

alleviate [ə'liːvɪeɪt] *vt pain* alléger, soulager, calmer; *sorrow* adoucir; *thirst* apaiser, calmer.

alleviation [əˌliːvɪ'eɪʃən] *n* (*V* **alleviate**) allègement *m*, soulagement *m*; adoucissement *m*; apaisement *m*.

alley[1] ['ælɪ] **1** *n* (*between buildings*) ruelle *f*; (*in garden*) allée *f*; (*US: between counters*) passage *m*. (*fig*) **this is right up my ~*** c'est ce que je fais le mieux, c'est tout à fait mon rayon; *V* **blind, bowling.**

2 *cpd*: **alley cat** chat *m* de gouttière; **she's got the morals of an alley cat‡** elle couche à droite et à gauche*; **alleyway** ruelle *f*.

alley[2] ['ælɪ] *n* (*Sport*) (grosse) bille *f*, callot *m*.

alliance [ə'laɪəns] *n* [*states*] alliance *f*, pacte *m*, union *f*; [*persons*] alliance. **to enter into an ~ with** s'allier avec.

allied ['ælaɪd] *adj* **(a)** allié, apparenté (*to* à, *with* avec). **~ nations** nations alliées *or* coalisées. **(b)** (*Bio*) de la même famille *or* espèce. (*fig*) **history and ~ subjects** l'histoire et sujets connexes *or* apparentés.

alligator ['ælɪgeɪtəʳ] *n* alligator *m*. **~(-skin) bag** sac *m* en alligator.

alliteration [əˌlɪtə'reɪʃən] *n* allitération *f*.

alliterative [ə'lɪtərətɪv] *adj* allitératif.

allocate ['æləʊkeɪt] *vt* **(a)** (*allot*) *money, task* allouer, attribuer (*to* à); *money* affecter (*to a certain use* à un certain usage). **(b)** (*apportion*) répartir, distribuer (*among* parmi).

allocation [ˌæləʊ'keɪʃən] *n* **(a)** (*allotting*) affectation *f*, allocation *f*; (*to individual*) attribution *f*. **(b)** (*apportioning among group*) répartition *f*. **(c)** (*sum of money allocated*) part *f*, somme assignée.

allot [ə'lɒt] *vt* **(a)** attribuer, assigner (*sth to sb* qch à qn). **everyone was ~ted a piece of land** chacun a reçu un terrain en lot; **to do sth in the time ~ted to one** faire qch dans le temps qui (vous) est imparti *or* assigné; **to ~ sth to a certain use** affecter *or* destiner qch à un certain usage.

(b) (*share among group*) répartir, distribuer.

allotment [ə'lɒtmənt] *n* **(a)** (*Brit: ground for cultivation*) parcelle *f* *or* lopin *m* de terre (*loué pour la culture*), lotissement *m*.

(b) (*division of shares*) partage *m*, lotissement *m*; (*distribution of shares*) distribution *f*, part *f*.

(c) (*Mil etc: from pay*) délégation *f* de solde.

allow [ə'laʊ] *vt* **(a)** (*permit*) permettre, autoriser; (*tolerate*) tolérer, souffrir. **to ~ sb sth** permettre qch à qn; **to ~ sb to do** permettre à qn de faire, autoriser qn à faire; **to ~ sb in/out/past** *etc* permettre à qn d'entrer/de sortir/de passer *etc*; **to ~ sth to happen** laisser se produire qch; **to ~ o.s. to be persuaded** se laisser persuader; **~ us to help you** permettez que nous vous aidions, permettez-nous de vous aider; **we are not ~ed much freedom** on nous accorde peu de liberté; **smoking is not ~ed** il est interdit *or* défendu de fumer; **no children/dogs ~ed** interdit aux enfants/chiens; **I will not ~ such behaviour** je ne tolérerai *or* souffrirai pas une telle conduite.

(b) (*grant*) *money* accorder, allouer. **to ~ sb £30 a month** allouer à qn 30 livres par mois; (*Jur*) **to ~ sb a thousand pounds damages** accorder à qn mille livres de dommages et intérêts; **to ~ space for** prévoir *or* ménager de la place pour; (*Comm*) **to ~ sb a discount** faire bénéficier qn d'une remise, consentir une remise à qn; **~ (yourself) an hour to cross the city** comptez une heure pour traverser la ville; **~ 5 cm for shrinkage** prévoyez 5 cm (de plus) pour le cas où le tissu rétrécirait.

(c) (*agree as possible*) *claim* admettre. **I ~ this to be true** je conviens que ceci est exact.

(d) (*concede*) admettre, reconnaître, convenir (*that* que). **~ing that ...** en admettant que ... + *subj*.

allow for *vt fus* tenir compte de; *money spent, funds allocated* (*by deduction*) déduire pour; (*by addition*) ajouter pour. **allowing for the circumstances** compte tenu des circonstances; **after allowing for his expenses** déduction faite de *or* en tenant compte de ses dépenses; **we must allow for the cost of the wood** il faut compter (avec) le prix du bois; **allowing for the shrinking of the material** en tenant compte du rétrécissement du tissu *or* du fait que le tissu rétrécit; **to allow for all possibilities** parer à toute éventualité.

allow of *vt fus* admettre, tolérer, souffrir. **the situation allows of no delay** la situation ne souffre *or* n'admet aucun retard.

allowable [ə'laʊəbl] *adj* permis, admissible, légitime. (*Tax*) **~ expenses** dépenses *fpl* déductibles.

allowance [ə'laʊəns] *n* **(a)** (*money given to sb*) allocation *f*, rente *f*; (*for lodgings, food etc*) indemnité *f*; (*from separated husband*) pension *f* alimentaire; (*salary*) appointements *mpl*; (*food*) ration *f*. **he makes his mother an ~** il verse une rente *or* une pension à sa mère; **his father gives him an ~ of £100 per month** son père lui alloue 100 livres par mois *or* lui verse une mensualité de 100 livres; **rent ~** allocation de logement; **~ in kind** prestation *f* en nature; (*Mil*) **~ for quarters** indemnité de logement; *V* **car, clothing, family** *etc*.

(b) (*Comm, Fin: discount*) réduction *f*, rabais *m*, concession *f*. **tax ~s** sommes *fpl* déductibles.

(c) you must learn to make ~s tu dois apprendre à faire la part des choses; (*excuse*) **to make ~(s) for sb** se montrer indulgent envers qn, essayer de comprendre qn; (*allow for*) **to make ~(s) for sth** tenir compte de qch, prendre qch en considération.

alloy ['ælɔɪ] **1** *n* alliage *m*; [*gold*] carature *f*. **~ steel** acier allié *or* spécial. **2** [ə'lɔɪ] *vt* (*Metal*) allier, faire un alliage de; (*fig*) altérer, diminuer la valeur de, corrompre.

all right ['ɔːl'raɪt] **1** *adj* **(a)** (*satisfactory*) (très) bien. **it's ~** ça va*, tout va bien; **he's ~*** (*doubtfully*) il n'est pas mal*; (*approvingly*) c'est un brave type*, c'est un type bien*; *V* **bit**[2].

(b) (*safe, well*) en bonne santé. **to be ~** (*healthy*) aller bien, être en bonne santé; (*safe*) être sain et sauf; **she's ~ again** elle est tout à fait remise, la revoilà d'aplomb; **I'm ~ Jack‡** moi je suis peinard‡, moi, ça va* (= *tant pis pour vous*).

(c) (*well-provided with money*) **we're ~ for the rest of our lives** nous sommes tranquilles *or* nous avons tout ce qu'il nous faut pour le restant de nos jours.

2 *excl* (*in approval*) ça y est!, ça va!*; (*in agreement*) entendu!, c'est ça!; (*in exasperation*) ça va!*

all-time ['ɔːl'taɪm] *adj* sans précédent, inouï, de tous les temps. **~ record** record *m* sans précédent; **an ~ low*** un record de médiocrité; **the pound has reached an ~ low** la livre est tombée au taux le plus bas jamais atteint.

allude [ə'luːd] *vi* [*person*] faire allusion (*to* à); [*letter etc*] avoir trait à, se rapporter à.

allure [ə'ljʊəʳ] **1** *vt* (*attract*) attirer; (*entice*) séduire. **2** *n* attirance *f*, charme *m*, attrait *m*.

alluring [ə'ljʊərɪŋ] *adj* attrayant, séduisant.

allusion [ə'luːʒən] *n* allusion *f*.

allusive [ə'luːsɪv] *adj* allusif, qui contient une allusion.

allusively [ə'luːsɪvlɪ] *adv* par allusion.

alluvial [əˈluːvɪəl] *adj ground* alluvial; *deposit* alluvionnaire.
alluvium [əˈluːvɪəm] *n* alluvion *f.*
ally[1] [əˈlaɪ] **1** *vt* allier, unir (*with* avec). **to ~ o.s. with** s'allier avec. **2** [ˈælaɪ] *n* (*gen*) allié(e) *m(f)*; (*Pol*) allié(e), coalisé(e) *m(f)*. **the Allies** les Alliés.
ally[2] [ˈælɪ] *n* = **alley**[2].
almanac [ˈɔːlmənæk] *n* almanach *m*, annuaire *m*; *V* **nautical.**
almighty [ɔːlˈmaɪtɪ] **1** *adj* **(a)** tout-puissant, omnipotent. **A~ God** Dieu Tout-Puissant.
(b) (*) très grand, extrême, fameux. **he is an ~ fool** c'est un fameux *or* sacré* imbécile; **they're making an ~ din** ils font un vacarme du diable *or* de tous les diables.
2 *n*: **the A~** le Tout-Puissant.
3 *adv* (*) extrêmement, énormément, fameusement.
almond [ˈɑːmənd] **1** *n* amande *f*, (*also* **~ tree**) amandier *m*; *V* **burnt, sugar** *etc.* **2** *cpd oil, paste* d'amande. **almond-eyed** aux yeux en amande; **almond-shaped** en amande.
almoner† [ˈɑːmənə^r] *n* (*Brit*) **(lady) ~** assistante sociale (*attachée à un hôpital*).
almost [ˈɔːlməʊst] *adv* presque, à peu près. **it is ~ midnight** il est presque *or* bientôt minuit; **~ always** presque *or* à peu près toujours; **he ~ fell** il a failli tomber; **you are ~ there** vous y êtes presque; **I can ~ do it** j'arrive presque à le faire; **his work is ~ finished** son travail est presque *or* à peu près terminé.
alms [ɑːmz] *n* aumône *f*. **to give ~** faire l'aumône *or* la charité; **~ box** tronc *m* des *or* pour les pauvres; (*Hist*) **~ house** hospice *m*.
aloe [ˈæləʊ] *n* aloès *m*; *V* **bitter.**
aloft [əˈlɒft] *adv* (*also* **up ~**) en haut, en l'air; (*Naut*) dans la mâture; (*hum*) au ciel.
alone [əˈləʊn] *adj, adv* **(a)** (*by o.s.*) seul. **all ~** tout(e) seul(e); **quite ~** tout à fait seul(e); **you can't do it ~** vous ne pouvez pas le faire seul; **leave them ~ together** laissez-les seuls ensemble.
(b) (*the only one*) seul. **he ~ could tell you** lui seul pourrait vous le dire; **you ~ can do it** vous êtes le seul à pouvoir le faire; **we are not ~ in thinking** nous ne sommes pas les seuls à penser, il n'y a pas que nous à penser *or* qui pensions; **he lives on bread ~** il ne vit que de pain, il vit uniquement de pain; **this book is mine ~** ce livre est à moi seul; **that charm which is hers ~** ce charme qui lui est propre *or* qui n'appartient qu'à elle.
(c) (*fig*) **to let** *or* **leave sb ~** laisser qn tranquille, laisser la paix à qn; **leave** *or* **let me ~!** laisse-moi tranquille!, fiche-moi la paix!*; **leave** *or* **let him ~ to do it** laisse-le faire tout seul; **leave** *or* **let the book ~!** ne touche pas au livre!, laisse le livre tranquille!*; **I advise you to leave the whole business ~** je vous conseille de ne pas vous mêler de l'affaire; (*Prov*) **let well ~** le mieux est l'ennemi du bien (*Prov*).
(d) (*as conj*) **let ~** sans parler de; **he can't read, let ~ write** il ne sait pas lire, encore moins écrire; **he can't afford food, let ~ clothes** il n'a pas de quoi s'acheter de la nourriture, sans parler de vêtements *or* encore moins des vêtements.
along [əˈlɒŋ] (*phr vb elem*) **1** *adv* **(a)** en avant. **come ~!** allez venez!, venez donc!; **I'll be ~ in a moment** j'arrive tout de suite; **she'll be ~ tomorrow** elle viendra demain; **how is he getting ~?** (*in health*) comment va-t-il?; (*in business etc*) comment vont ses affaires?; (*Scol*) comment vont ses études?; *V* **move along** *etc.*
(b) come ~ with me venez avec moi; **he came ~ with 6 others** il est venu accompagné de 6 autres; **bring your friend ~** amène ton camarade (avec toi); **~ here** dans cette direction-ci, par là, de ce côté-ci; (*fig*) **get ~ with you!*** (*go away*) fiche le camp!*, décampe!*; (*you can't mean it*) allons donc!, sans blague!*.
(c) all ~ (*space*) d'un bout à l'autre; (*time*) du début à la fin; **I could see all ~ that he would refuse** je voyais depuis le début qu'il allait refuser.
2 *prep* le long de. **to walk ~ the beach** se promener le long de la plage; **the railway runs ~ the beach** la ligne de chemin de fer longe la plage; **the trees ~ the road** les arbres qui sont au bord de la route *or* qui bordent la route; **all ~ the street** tout le long de *or* d'un bout à l'autre de la rue; **somewhere ~ the way he lost a glove** quelque part en chemin il a perdu un gant; (*fig*) **somewhere ~ the way** *or* **somewhere ~ the line* someone made a mistake** à un moment donné quelqu'un a fait une erreur; **to proceed ~ the lines suggested** agir *or* procéder conformément à la ligne d'action proposée.
alongside [əˈlɒŋˈsaɪd] **1** *prep* (*along: also Naut*) le long de; (*beside*) à côté de, près de. (*Naut*) **to make fast ~** (*quayside*) s'amarrer à *or* au quai; (*another vessel*) s'amarrer bord à bord, s'amarrer à *or* en couple; (*Naut*) **to come ~ the quay** accoster le quai; *[vehicle]* **to stop ~ the kerb** s'arrêter au bord du trottoir *or* le long du trottoir; **the car drew up ~ me** la voiture s'est arrêtée à côté de moi *or* à ma hauteur.
2 *adv* (*Naut*) *[ships]* (*beside one another*) bord à bord, à couple. **to come ~** accoster; **to pass ~ of a ship** longer un navire.
aloof [əˈluːf] **1** *adj person, character* distant. **he was very ~ with me** il s'est montré très distant à mon égard; **she kept very (much) ~** elle s'est montrée très distante, elle a gardé *or* conservé ses distances.
2 *adv* à distance, à l'écart. **to remain** *or* **stay** *or* **stand** *or* **keep ~ from a group** se tenir à l'écart *or* à distance d'un groupe; **to remain** *or* **stay** *or* **stand** *or* **keep ~ from arguments** ne pas se mêler aux discussions, ne jamais se mêler à la discussion.
aloofness [əˈluːfnɪs] *n* réserve *f*, attitude distante.
alopecia [ˌæləʊˈpiːʃə] *n* alopécie *f.*
aloud [əˈlaʊd] *adv read* à haute voix, à voix haute, tout haut; *think, wonder* tout haut.
alp [ælp] *n* (*peak*) pic *m*; (*mountain*) montagne *f*; (*pasture*) alpe *f*. **the A~s** les Alpes.
alpaca [ælˈpækə] *n* alpaga *m.*
alpenhorn [ˈælpɪnˌhɔːn] *n* cor *m* des Alpes.
alpenstock [ˈælpɪnstɒk] *n* alpenstock *m.*
alpha [ˈælfə] *n* **(a)** (*letter*) alpha *m*. **~ particle** particule *f* alpha. **(b)** (*Brit: Scol, Univ*) ≃ très bonne note. **~ plus** ≃ excellente note.
alphabet [ˈælfəbet] *n* alphabet *m*; *V* **deaf, finger.**
alphabetic(al) [ˌælfəˈbetɪk(əl)] *adj* alphabétique. **in alphabetical order** par ordre alphabétique, dans l'ordre alphabétique.
alphabetically [ˌælfəˈbetɪkəlɪ] *adv* alphabétiquement, par ordre alphabétique.
alphabetize [ˈælfəbətaɪz] *vt* mettre en *or* classer par ordre alphabétique.
alpine [ˈælpaɪn] *adj* des Alpes; *climate, scenery* alpestre; *club, troops* alpin. **~ hut** (chalet-)refuge *m*; **~ range** chaîne alpine; **~ plants** (*on lower slopes*) plantes *fpl* alpestres, (*on higher slopes*) plantes alpines.
alpinist [ˈælpɪnɪst] *n* alpiniste *mf.*
already [ɔːlˈredɪ] *adv* déjà.
alright [ˈɔːlˌraɪt] = **all right.**
Alsace [ˈælsæs] *n* Alsace *f.*
Alsace-Lorraine [ˈælsæsləˈreɪn] *n* Alsace-Lorraine *f.*
Alsatian [ælˈseɪʃən] **1** *n* **(a)** Alsacien(ne) *m(f)*. **(b)** (*Brit: also* **~ dog**) chien *m* loup, berger allemand. **2** *adj* alsacien, d'Alsace; *wine* d'Alsace.
also [ˈɔːlsəʊ] **1** *adv* **(a)** (*too*) aussi, également. **her cousin ~ came** son cousin aussi est venu *or* est venu également.
(b) (*moreover*) de plus, en outre, également. **~ I must explain that ...** de plus *or* en outre, je dois expliquer que ..., je dois également expliquer que ... .
2 *cpd*: **also-ran** (*Sport*) autre concurrent *m* (*n'ayant pas pu se classer*); (*Horse-racing*) cheval non classé; (*: *person*) perdant(e) *m(f)*.
altar [ˈɒltə^r] **1** *n* (*Rel*) autel *m*. **high ~** maître-autel *m*; (*fig*) **he was sacrificed on the ~ of productivity** il a été immolé sur l'autel de la productivité.
2 *cpd*: **altar boy** enfant *m* de chœur; **altar cloth** nappe *f* d'autel; **altar piece** retable *m*; **altar rail(s)** clôture *f or* balustre *m* (du chœur); (*Rel*) table *f* de communion.
alter [ˈɒltə^r] **1** *vt* **(a)** (*gen*) changer, modifier, (*stronger*) transformer; (*adapt*) adapter, ajuster; *painting, poem, speech etc* retoucher, (*stronger*) remanier; *garment* retoucher, (*stronger*) transformer. **to ~ one's plans** changer de projets, modifier *or* transformer ses projets; **to ~ one's attitude** changer d'attitude (*to* envers); **that ~s the case** voilà qui est différent *or* qui change tout; (*Naut*) **to ~ course** changer de cap *or* de route; **to ~ sth for the better** changer qch en mieux, améliorer qch; **to ~ sth for the worse** changer qch en mal, altérer qch.
(b) (*falsify*) *date, evidence* falsifier, fausser; *text* altérer.
(c) (*US: castrate*) châtrer, castrer.
2 *vi* changer. **to ~ for the better** *[circumstances]* s'améliorer; *[person, character]* changer en mieux; **to ~ for the worse** *[circumstances]* empirer, s'aggraver; *[person, character]* changer en mal.
alteration [ˌɒltəˈreɪʃən] *n* **(a)** (*U: V* **alter**: *act of altering*) changement *m*, modification *f*; transformation *f*; retouchage *m*, remaniement *m*. **programme/timetable subject to ~** programme/horaire sujet à des changements *or* modifications.
(b) (*to plan, rules etc*) modification *f*, changement *m* (*to, in* apporté à); (*to painting, poem, essay etc*) retouche *f*, (*major*) remaniement *m*; (*to garment*) retouche, (*major*) transformation *f*. (*Archit*) **~s** transformations *fpl* (*to* apportées à); **they're having ~s made to their house** ils font des travaux dans leur maison; **he made several ~s to his canvas/manuscript** en peignant/en écrivant il a eu plusieurs repentirs; (*Naut*) **~ of route** (*deliberate*) changement *m* de route; (*involuntary*) déroutement *m*.
altercation [ˌɒltəˈkeɪʃən] *n* altercation *f*. **to have an ~** se disputer, avoir une altercation.
alter ego [ˈæltərˈiːɡəʊ] *n* alter ego *m*. **he is my ~** c'est un autre moi-même, c'est mon alter ego.
alternate [ɒlˈtɜːnɪt] **1** *adj* **(a)** (*by turns*) alternatif, alterné; (*Bot, Math*) *leaves, angle* alterné. **~ motion** mouvement alternatif; **~ action of tranquillizers and stimulants** action alternée des tranquillisants et des stimulants; (*Poetry*) **~ rhymes** rimes croisées *or* alternées; **chairs in ~ rows** chaises *fpl* (disposées) en quinconce.
(b) (*every second*) tous les deux. **on ~ days** tous les deux jours, un jour sur deux; **they work on ~ days** ils travaillent un jour sur deux à tour de rôle, l'un travaille un jour et l'autre le lendemain.
(c) (*US*) = **alternative 1.**
2 *n* (*US*) remplaçant(e) *m(f)*, suppléant(e) *m(f)*.
3 [ˈɒltɜːneɪt] *vt* faire alterner, employer alternativement *or* tour à tour. **to ~ crops** alterner les cultures, pratiquer l'assolement.
4 *vi* alterner (*with* avec), se succéder (*tour à tour*).
alternately [ɒlˈtɜːnɪtlɪ] *adv* alternativement, tour à tour. **~ with** en alternance avec.
alternating [ˈɒltɜːneɪtɪŋ] *adj* alternant. (*Math*) **~ series** série alternée; (*Elec*) **~ current** courant alternatif.
alternation [ˌɒltɜːˈneɪʃən] *n* alternance *f*; *[emotions etc]* alternatives *fpl.*
alternative [ɒlˈtɜːnətɪv] **1** *adj possibility, answer* autre; (*Philos*) *proposition* alternatif; (*Mil*) *position* de repli; (*Tech*) de rechange. **~ proposal** contre-proposition *f*; **the only ~ method** la seule autre méthode, la seule méthode de rechange; (*Aut*) **~ route** itinéraire *m* de délestage.
2 *n* (*choice*) (*between two*) alternative *f*, choix *m*; (*between several*) choix; (*solution*) (*only one*) alternative, seule autre solution, solution unique de rechange; (*one of several*) autre

solution, solution de rechange; (*Philos*) terme *m* d'une alternative *or* d'un dilemme. **she had no ~ but to accept** elle n'avait pas d'autre solution que d'accepter, force lui a été d'accepter.

alternatively [ɒl'tɜːnətɪvlɪ] *adv* comme alternative, sinon. **or ~** ou bien.

alternator ['ɒltɜːneɪtəʳ] *n* (*Elec*) alternateur *m*.

although [ɔːl'ðəʊ] *conj* bien que + *subj*, quoique + *subj*, malgré le fait que + *subj*, encore que + *subj*. **~ it's raining there are 20 people here already** bien qu'il pleuve *or* malgré la pluie il y a déjà 20 personnes; **I'll do it ~ I don't want to** je le ferai bien que *or* quoique *or* encore que je n'en aie pas envie; **I'm sorry for her ~ I can't help her** je la plains bien que *or* quoique *or* encore que je ne puisse l'aider en rien; **~ poor they were honest** ils étaient honnêtes bien que *or* quoique *or* encore que pauvres; **~ young he knew that ...** bien qu'il *or* quoiqu'il *or* encore qu'il fût jeune, il savait que ..., malgré sa jeunesse il savait que ...; **(even) ~ he might agree to go** quand bien même il accepterait d'y aller; **I will do it ~ I (should) die in the attempt** je le ferai dussé-je y laisser la vie.

altimeter ['æltɪmiːtəʳ] *n* altimètre *m*.

altitude ['æltɪtjuːd] *n* (*height above sea level*) altitude *f*; (*building*) hauteur *f*. (*gen pl: high place*) **~s** hauteur(s), altitude; **it is difficult to breathe at these ~s** *or* **at this ~** il est difficile de respirer à cette altitude; **~ sickness** mal *m* d'altitude *or* des montagnes.

alto ['æltəʊ] *n* **(a)** (*female voice*) contralto *m*; (*male voice*) haute-contre *f*. **to sing the ~ part** chanter la partie de contralto/haute-contre. **(b)** (*instrument*) alto *m*. **~ saxophone** saxophone *m* alto.

altogether [ˌɔːltə'geðəʳ] **1** *adv* **(a)** (*wholly*) entièrement, tout à fait, complètement. **it is ~ out of the question** il n'en est absolument pas question.

(b) (*on the whole*) somme toute, tout compte fait, au total. **~ it wasn't very pleasant** somme toute ce n'était pas très agréable.

(c) (*with everything included*) en tout. **what do I owe you ~?** je vous dois combien en tout?, combien vous dois-je au total?; **taken ~** à tout prendre.

2 *n* (*hum*) **in the ~*** tout nu, dans le plus simple appareil (*hum*), en costume d'Adam (*or* d'Ève)*.

altruism ['æltrʊɪzəm] *n* altruisme *m*.

altruist ['æltrʊɪst] *n* altruiste *mf*.

altruistic [ˌæltrʊ'ɪstɪk] *adj* altruiste.

alum ['æləm] *n* alun *m*.

aluminium [ˌæljʊ'mɪnɪəm], (*US*) **aluminum** [ə'luːmɪnəm] **1** *n* aluminium *m*. **2** *cpd pot, pan etc* en *or* d'aluminium. **~ bronze** bronze *m* d'aluminium.

alumnus [ə'lʌmnəs] *nm*, *pl* **alumni** [ə'lʌmnaɪ], **alumna** [ə'lʌmnə] *nf*, *pl* **alumnae** [ə'lʌmniː] (*US*) (*Scol*) ancien(ne) élève *mf*; (*Univ*) ancien(ne) étudiant(e) *m(f)*.

alveolar [æl'vɪələʳ] *adj* alvéolaire.

always ['ɔːlweɪz] *adv* toujours. **as/for/nearly ~** comme/pour/presque toujours; **office ~ open** (bureau *m* ouvert en) permanence *f*; *V* **excepting.**

am [æm] *V* **be.**

amalgam [ə'mælgəm] *n* amalgame *m*.

amalgamate [ə'mælgəmeɪt] **1** *vt metals* amalgamer; *companies, shares* (faire) fusionner, unifier. **2** *vi [metals]* s'amalgamer; *[companies]* fusionner, s'unifier; *[ethnic groups]* se mélanger.

amalgamation [əˌmælgə'meɪʃən] *n* (*V* **amalgamate**) amalgamation *f*; fusion *f*, fusionnement *m*, unification *f*; *[ethnic groups]* mélange *m*, métissage *m*.

amanuensis [əˌmænjʊ'ensɪs] *n*, *pl* **amanuenses** [əˌmænjʊ'ensiːz] (*secretary, assistant*) secrétaire *mf*; (*copyist*) copiste *mf*.

amaryllis [ˌæmə'rɪlɪs] *n* amaryllis *f*.

amass [ə'mæs] *vt objects* amasser, accumuler, amonceler; *fortune* amasser, réunir.

amateur ['æmətəʳ] **1** *n* (*also Sport*) amateur *m*.

2 *cpd painter, footballer, football* amateur; *photography, sports* d'amateur. **amateur dramatics** théâtre *m* amateur; **to have an amateur interest in sth** s'intéresser à qch en amateur; (*pej*) **amateur work** travail *m* d'amateur *or* de dilettante (*gen pej*).

amateurish ['æmətərɪʃ] *adj* (*pej*) d'amateur, de dilettante. **~ efforts/work** efforts/travail peu sérieux.

amateurism ['æmətərɪzəm] *n* amateurisme *m* (*also pej*), dilettantisme *m*.

amatory ['æmətərɪ] *adj* (*frm, liter*) *feelings* amoureux; *poetry* galant; *letter* d'amour.

amaze [ə'meɪz] *vt* stupéfier, frapper de stupeur, ébahir. **to be ~d at (seeing) sth** être stupéfait *or* stupéfié de (voir) qch; (*iro*) **you ~ me!** pas possible!, c'est pas vrai!* (*iro*).

amazement [ə'meɪzmənt] *n* stupéfaction *f*, stupeur *f*, ébahissement *m*.

amazing [ə'meɪzɪŋ] *adj* stupéfiant, ahurissant, renversant*. **it's ~!** c'est ahurissant!, je n'en reviens pas!; (*Comm*) **'~ new offer'** 'offre sensationnelle'.

amazingly [ə'meɪzɪŋlɪ] *adv* étonnamment. **~ (enough), he got it right first time** chose étonnante, il a réussi du premier coup; **~, he survived** par miracle il en a réchappé; **she is ~ courageous** elle est d'un courage extraordinaire *or* étonnant.

Amazon ['æməzən] *n* **(a)** (*river*) Amazone *m*. **(b)** (*Myth*) Amazone *f*. (*fig*) **she's a real ~** c'est une véritable athlète.

ambassador [æm'bæsədəʳ] *n* (*lit, fig*) ambassadeur *m*. **French ~** ambassadeur de France; **~-at-large** ambassadeur extraordinaire *or* chargé de mission(s).

ambassadorial [æmˌbæsə'dɔːrɪəl] *adj* d'ambassadeur.

ambassadorship [æm'bæsədəʃɪp] *n* fonction *f* d'ambassadeur, ambassade *f*.

ambassadress [æm'bæsɪdrɪs] *n* (*lit, fig*) ambassadrice *f*.

amber ['æmbəʳ] **1** *n* ambre *m*. **2** *adj jewellery* d'ambre. **~-coloured** ambré; (*Brit Aut*) **~ light** feu *m* orange.

ambergris ['æmbəgriːs] *n* ambre gris.

ambi ... ['æmbɪ] *pref* ambi ... .

ambidextrous [ˌæmbɪ'dekstrəs] *adj* ambidextre.

ambient ['æmbɪənt] *adj* ambiant.

ambiguity [ˌæmbɪ'gjʊɪtɪ] *n* **(a)** (*U*) *[word, phrase]* ambiguïté *f*, équivoque *f*; (*in thought, speech: lack of clarity*) ambiguïté, obscurité *f*. **(b)** (*ambiguous phrase etc*) ambiguïté *f*, expression ambiguë.

ambiguous [æm'bɪgjʊəs] *adj word, phrase* ambigu (*f* -guë), équivoque; *thought* obscur; *past* douteux, équivoque.

ambit ['æmbɪt] *n [town, land]* limites *fpl*; *[country]* confins *mpl*; (*fig*) *[authority etc]* étendue *f*, portée *f*.

ambition [æm'bɪʃən] *n* ambition *f*. **it is my ~ to do** mon ambition est de faire, j'ai l'ambition de faire.

ambitious [æm'bɪʃəs] *adj person, plan* ambitieux. **to be ~ to do** ambitionner de faire; **to be ~ of** *or* **for fame** briguer la gloire.

ambitiously [æm'bɪʃəslɪ] *adv* ambitieusement.

ambivalence [æm'bɪvələns] *n* ambivalence *f*.

ambivalent [æm'bɪvələnt] *adj* ambivalent.

amble ['æmbl] **1** *vi [horse]* aller l'amble, ambler; *[person]* aller *or* marcher d'un pas tranquille. **to ~ in/out** *etc* entrer/sortir *etc* d'un pas tranquille; *[person]* **to ~ along** se promener *or* aller sans se presser; **he ~d up to me** il s'est avancé vers moi sans se presser; **the train ~s through the valley** le train traverse lentement la vallée.

2 *n [horse]* amble *m*; *[person]* pas *m or* allure *f* tranquille, démarche lente.

ambrosia [æm'brəʊzɪə] *n* ambroisie *f*.

ambrosial [æm'brəʊzɪəl] *adj* (au parfum *or* au goût) d'ambroisie.

ambulance ['æmbjʊləns] **1** *n* **(a)** ambulance *f*; *V* **flying.**

(b) (*Mil* †) ambulance *f*.

2 *cpd:* **ambulance driver** ambulancier *m*, -ière *f*; **ambulance man** (*driver*) ambulancier *m*; (*inside*) infirmier *m* (d'ambulance); (*carrying stretcher*) brancardier *m*; **ambulance nurse** infirmière *f* (d'ambulance); **ambulance train** train *m* sanitaire.

ambush ['æmbʊʃ] **1** *n* embuscade *f*, guet-apens *m*. **troops in ~** troupes embusquées; **to be** *or* **lie in ~** se tenir en embuscade; **to be** *or* **lie in ~ for sb** tendre une embuscade à qn; *V* **fall.** **2** *vt* attirer *or* faire tomber dans une embuscade.

ameba [ə'miːbə] *n* = **amoeba.**

ameliorate [ə'miːlɪəreɪt] **1** *vt* améliorer. **2** *vi* s'améliorer.

amelioration [əˌmiːlɪə'reɪʃən] *n* amélioration *f*.

amen ['ɑː'men] **1** *excl* (*Rel*) amen, ainsi soit-il. **2** *n* amen *m inv*. (*Rel, fig*) **to say ~ to, to give one's ~ to** dire amen à.

amenable [ə'miːnəbl] *adj* **(a)** (*answerable*) *person* responsable (*to sb* envers qn, *for sth* de qch). **~ to the law** responsable devant la loi.

(b) (*tractable, responsive*) *person* maniable, souple. **he is ~ to argument** c'est un homme qui est prêt à se laisser convaincre; **~ to discipline** disciplinable; **~ to kindness** sensible à la douceur; **~ to reason** raisonnable, disposé à entendre raison; (*Med*) **~ to treatment** curable, guérissable.

(c) (*within the scope of*) **~ to** qui relève de, relevant de, du ressort de.

amend [ə'mend] **1** *vt rule* amender, modifier; (*Parl*) amender; *wording* modifier; *mistake* rectifier, corriger; *habits* réformer. **2** *vi* s'amender.

amendment [ə'mendmənt] *n* (*V* **amend**) amendement *m*, modification *f*, rectification *f*; (*Parl*) amendement.

amends [ə'mendz] *npl* compensation *f*, réparation *f*, dédommagement *m*. **to make ~** faire amende honorable; **to make ~ to sb for sth** dédommager qn de qch, faire réparation à qn de qch, donner satisfaction à qn de qch; **to make ~ for an injury** (*with money*) compenser un dommage; (*with kindness*) réparer un tort; **I'll try to make ~** j'essaierai de réparer mes torts *or* de me racheter.

amenity [ə'miːnɪtɪ] **1** *n* **(a)** (*U: pleasantness*) *[district, climate, situation]* charme *m*, agrément *m*.

(b) (*gen pl: pleasant features*) **amenities** commodités *fpl*, agréments *mpl*.

(c) (*pl: courtesies*) **amenities** civilités *fpl*, politesses *fpl*.

2 *cpd:* (*Brit Med*) **amenity bed** lit 'privé' (dans un hôpital); **amenity society** association *f* pour la sauvegarde de l'environnement.

America [ə'merɪkə] *n* Amérique *f*; *V* **north** *etc.*

American [ə'merɪkən] **1** *adj* (*of America*) américain, d'Amérique; (*of USA*) américain, des États-Unis. **~ English** anglais américain; **~ Indian** Indien(ne) *m(f)* d'Amérique; (*US: in hotels*) **~ plan** (chambre avec) pension complète.

2 *n* **(a)** Américain(e) *m(f)*.

(b) (*Ling*) américain *m*.

americanism [ə'merɪkənɪzəm] *n* américanisme *m*.

americanize [ə'merɪkənaɪz] *vt* américaniser.

Amerind ['æmərɪnd] *n* **(a)** Indien(ne) *m(f)* d'Amérique. **(b)** (*Ling*) langue amérindienne.

Amerindian [æmə'rɪndɪən] **1** *n* = **Amerind.** **2** *adj* amérindien.

amethyst ['æmɪθɪst] **1** *n* améthyste *f*. **2** *cpd jewellery* d'améthyste; *colour* violet d'améthyste *inv*.

amiability [ˌeɪmɪə'bɪlɪtɪ] *n* amabilité *f*, gentillesse *f* (*to, towards* envers).

amiable ['eɪmɪəbl] *adj* aimable, gentil.

amiably ['eɪmɪəblɪ] *adv* aimablement, avec amabilité, avec gentillesse.

amicable ['æmɪkəbl] *adj feeling* amical; *relationship* amical, d'amitié. (*Jur*) **~ settlement** arrangement *m* à l'amiable.

amicably ['æmɪkəblɪ] *adv* amicalement; (*Jur*) à l'amiable.

amidships [ə'mɪdʃɪps] *adv* (*Naut*) au milieu *or* par le milieu du navire.

amid(st) [ə'mɪd(st)] *prep* parmi, au milieu de.

amino acid [ə'mi:nəʊ'æsɪd] *n* acide aminé, amino-acide *m*.

amiss [ə'mɪs] **1** *adv* (*wrongly*) mal, de travers; (*at wrong place, time etc*) mal à propos. **to take sth ~** prendre qch de travers *or* en mauvaise part; **don't take it ~** ne le prenez pas mal, ne vous en offensez pas; **to speak ~ of** parler mal de; **nothing comes ~ to him** il tire parti de tout, il s'arrange de tout; **a drink wouldn't come ~*** je ne refuserais pas un verre; **a little courtesy on his part wouldn't come ~** un peu de politesse ne lui ferait pas de mal.

2 *adj* (*wrongly worded, timed etc*) mal à propos. **something is ~ in your calculations** il y a quelque chose qui ne va pas *or* qui cloche dans tes calculs; **what's ~ with you?** qu'est-ce qui ne va pas?, qu'est-ce qui te tracasse?; **there's something ~** il y a quelque chose qui ne va pas *or* qui cloche; **to say something ~** dire quelque chose mal à propos.

amity ['æmɪtɪ] *n* amitié *f*, bonne intelligence; (*between two countries*) concorde *f*, bons rapports, bonnes relations.

ammeter ['æmɪtə^r] *n* ampèremètre *m*.

ammo ['æməʊ] *n* (*Mil sl abbr of* **ammunition**) munitions *fpl*.

ammonia [ə'məʊnɪə] *n* (gaz *m*) ammoniac *m*; *V* **household, liquid.**

ammunition [ˌæmjʊ'nɪʃən] **1** *n* munitions *fpl*. **2** *cpd*: **ammunition belt** ceinturon *m*; **ammunition dump** dépôt *m or* parc *m* de munitions; **ammunition pouch** cartouchière *f*.

amnesia [æm'ni:zɪə] *n* amnésie *f*.

amnesty ['æmnɪstɪ] **1** *n* amnistie *f*. **under an ~** en vertu d'une amnistie; **A~ International** Amnesty International. **2** *vt* amnistier.

amoeba [ə'mi:bə] *n* amibe *f*.

amoebic [ə'mi:bɪk] *adj* amibien. **~ dysentery** dysenterie amibienne.

amok [ə'mɒk] *adv* = **amuck.**

among(st) [ə'mʌŋ(st)] *prep* parmi, entre. **divide the chocolates ~ you** partagez-vous les chocolats; **~ the lambs is one black one** un des agneaux est noir; **this is ~ the things we must do** ceci fait partie des choses que nous avons à faire; **settle it ~ yourselves** arrangez cela entre vous; **don't quarrel ~ yourselves** ne vous disputez pas, pas de disputes entre vous; **he is ~ those who know** il est de ces gens qui savent, il fait partie de ceux qui savent; **~ other things** entre autres (choses); **~ the French** chez les Français; **to count sb ~ one's friends** compter qn parmi *or* au nombre de ses amis; **to be ~ friends** être entre amis; **one ~ a thousand** un entre mille; **to be sitting ~ the audience** être assis au milieu des *or* parmi les spectateurs.

amoral [æ'mɒrəl] *adj* amoral.

amorous ['æmərəs] *adj* amoureux. **to make ~ advances to** faire des avances à (*connotations sexuelles*).

amorously ['æmərəslɪ] *adv* amoureusement.

amorphous [ə'mɔ:fəs] *adj* (*also Miner*) amorphe; (*fig*) *personality* amorphe; *style, ideas* informe, sans forme.

amortization [əˌmɔ:taɪ'zeɪʃən] *n* amortissement *m*.

amortize [ə'mɔ:taɪz] *vt debt* amortir.

amortizement [ə'mɔ:tɪzmənt] *n* = **amortization.**

amount [ə'maʊnt] *n* **(a)** (*total*) montant *m*, total *m*; (*sum of money*) somme *f*. **the ~ of a bill** le montant d'une facture; **debts to the ~ of £20** dettes qui se montent à 20 livres; **there is a small ~ still to pay** il reste une petite somme à payer.

(b) (*quantity*) quantité *f*. **I have an enormous ~ of work** j'ai énormément de travail; **quite an ~ of** beaucoup de; **any ~ of** quantité de, énormément de; **she's got any ~ of friends** elle a énormément *or* des quantités d'amis; **I've got any ~ of time** j'ai tout le temps (qu'il me) faut, j'ai tout mon temps.

(c) (*U: value, importance*) importance *f*, signification *f*. **the information is of little ~** ce renseignement n'a pas grande importance.

amount to *vt fus* **(a)** (*Math etc*) *[sums, figures, debts]* s'élever à, monter à, se chiffrer à.

(b) (*be equivalent to*) équivaloir à, se ramener à, se réduire à. **it amounts to the same thing** cela revient au même; **it amounts to stealing/a change in policy** cela revient *or* équivaut à du vol/un changement de politique; **this amounts to very little** cela ne représente pas grand-chose; **he will never amount to much** il ne fera jamais grand-chose; **one day he will amount to something** un jour il sera quelqu'un.

amour [ə'mʊə^r] **1** *n* intrigue amoureuse, liaison *f*. **2** *cpd*: **amour-propre** amour-propre *m*.

amp(ère) ['æmp(εə^r)] **1** *n* ampère *m*. **2** *cpd*: **ampère-hour** ampère-heure *m*; **a 13-amp plug** une fiche de 13 ampères.

ampersand ['æmpəsænd] *n* esperluète *f*.

amphetamine [æm'fetəmi:n] *n* amphétamine *f*.

amphibia [æm'fɪbɪə] *npl* batraciens *mpl*, amphibiens *mpl*.

amphibian [æm'fɪbɪən] **1** *adj animal, vehicle, tank* amphibie. **2** *n* (*Zool*) amphibie *m*; (*car*) voiture *f* amphibie; (*aircraft*) avion *m* amphibie; (*tank*) char *m* amphibie.

amphibious [æm'fɪbɪəs] *adj* amphibie.

amphitheatre, (*US*) **amphitheater** ['æmfɪˌθɪətə^r] *n* (*Hist, Theat, gen*) amphithéâtre *m*; (*in mountains*) cirque *m*.

amphora ['æmfərə] *n, pl* **amphorae** ['æmfəˌri:] amphore *f*.

ample ['æmpl] *adj* **(a)** (*more than enough of*) bien *or* largement assez de. **~ grounds for divorce** de solides motifs de divorce; **to have ~ means** avoir de gros moyens *or* une grosse fortune; **to have ~ reason to believe that ...** avoir de fortes *or* de solides raisons de croire que ...; **there is ~ room for** il y a largement la place pour; (*fig*) **there is ~ room for improvement** il y a encore bien du chemin *or* bien des progrès à faire; **to have ~ time** avoir grandement *or* largement le temps (*to do* de *or* pour faire).

(b) (*large*) *garment* ample.

amplifier ['æmplɪfaɪə^r] *n* amplificateur *m*, ampli* *m*.

amplify ['æmplɪfaɪ] *vt sound* amplifier; *statement, idea* développer; *story* amplifier.

amplitude ['æmplɪtju:d] *n* (*Astron, Phys*) amplitude *f*; *[style, thought]* ampleur *f*.

amply ['æmplɪ] *adv* amplement, grandement, largement.

ampoule ['æmpu:l] *n* ampoule *f* (*pour seringue*).

amputate ['æmpjʊteɪt] *vt* amputer. **to ~ sb's leg** amputer qn de la jambe.

amputation [ˌæmpjʊ'teɪʃən] *n* amputation *f*. **to carry out the ~ of a limb** pratiquer l'amputation d'un membre.

Amsterdam ['æmstədæm] *n* Amsterdam.

amuck [ə'mʌk] *adv*: **to run ~** (*lit*) être pris d'un accès *or* d'une crise de folie meurtrière *or* furieuse; (*in Far East*) s'abandonner à l'amok; (**fig*) *[person]* perdre tout contrôle de soi-même; (*fig*) *[crowd]* se déchaîner.

amulet ['æmjʊlɪt] *n* amulette *f*.

amuse [ə'mju:z] *vt* **(a)** (*cause mirth to*) amuser, divertir, faire rire. **it ~d us** cela nous a fait rire; **to be ~d at** *or* **by** s'amuser de; **he was not ~d** il n'a pas trouvé ça drôle; **an ~d expression** un air amusé.

(b) (*entertain*) distraire, divertir, amuser. **to ~ o.s. by doing** s'amuser à faire; **to ~ o.s. with sth/sb** s'amuser avec qch/aux dépens de qn; **you'll have to ~ yourselves for a while** il va vous falloir trouver de quoi vous distraire *or* de quoi vous occuper pendant quelque temps.

amusement [ə'mju:zmənt] **1** *n* **(a)** (*U*) amusement *m*, divertissement *m*. **look of ~** regard amusé; **to hide one's ~** dissimuler son envie de rire; **to do sth for ~** faire qch pour se distraire; **(much) to my ~** à mon grand amusement; **there was general ~ at this** ceci a fait rire tout le monde.

(b) (*diversion, pastime*) distraction *f*, jeu *m*, amusement *m*. **a town with plenty of ~s** une ville qui offre beaucoup de distractions.

2 *cpd*: **amusement arcade** ≈ luna-park *m*; **amusement park** (*fairground*) parc *m* d'attractions; (*playground*) parc.

amusing [ə'mju:zɪŋ] *adj* amusant, drôle, divertissant. **highly ~** divertissant au possible, très drôle.

amusingly [ə'mju:zɪŋlɪ] *adv* d'une manière amusante, drôlement.

an [æn, ən, n] **1** *indef art V* **a²**. **2** *conj* (††) si.

Anabaptist [ˌænə'bæptɪst] *n* anabaptiste *mf*.

anachronism [ə'nækrənɪzəm] *n* anachronisme *m*.

anachronistic [əˌnækrə'nɪstɪk] *adj* anachronique.

anaconda [ˌænə'kɒndə] *n* eunecte *m*, anaconda *m*.

anacreontic [əˌnækrɪ'ɒntɪk] **1** *adj* anacréontique. **2** *n* poème *m* anacréontique.

anaemia [ə'ni:mɪə] *n* anémie *f*; *V* **pernicious.**

anaemic [ə'ni:mɪk] *adj* (*Med, fig*) anémique. **to become ~** s'anémier.

anaesthesia [ˌænɪs'θi:zɪə] *n* anesthésie *f*.

anaesthetic [ˌænɪs'θetɪk] **1** *n* anesthésique *m*. **under the ~** sous anesthésie; **to give sb an ~** anesthésier qn. **2** *adj* anesthésique.

anaesthetist [æ'ni:sθɪtɪst] *n* anesthésiste *mf*.

anaesthetize [æ'ni:sθɪtaɪz] *vt* (*by anaesthetic*) anesthésier; (*by other methods*) insensibiliser.

anagram ['ænəgræm] *n* anagramme *f*.

anal ['eɪnəl] *adj* anal.

analgesia [ˌænæl'dʒi:zɪə] *n* analgésie *f*.

analgesic [ˌænæl'dʒi:sɪk] *adj, n* analgésique (*m*).

analog ['ænəlɒg] *n* (*US*) = **analogue. ~ computer** calculateur *m* analogique.

analogic(al) [ˌænə'lɒdʒɪk(əl)] *adj* analogique.

analogous [ə'næləgəs] *adj* analogue (*to, with* à).

analogue ['ænəlɒg] *n* analogue *m*.

analogy [ə'nælədʒɪ] *n* analogie *f* (*between* entre, *with* avec). **to argue from ~** raisonner par analogie; **by ~ with** par analogie avec.

analyse, (*US*) **analyze** ['ænəlaɪz] *vt* **(a)** analyser, faire l'analyse de; (*Gram*) *sentence* faire l'analyse logique de. **(b)** (*US*) psychanalyser.

analysis [ə'næləsɪs] *n, pl* **analyses** [ə'nælɪsi:z] **(a)** analyse *f*; (*Gram*) *[sentence]* analyse logique. (*fig*) **in the ultimate** *or* **last** *or* **final ~** en dernière analyse, finalement. **(b)** (*US*) psychanalyse *f*.

analyst ['ænəlɪst] *n* **(a)** (*Chem etc*) analyste *m*. **(b)** (*US*) (psych)analyste *mf*.

analytic(al) [ˌænə'lɪtɪk(əl)] *adj* analytique.

analyze ['ænəlaɪz] *vt* (*US*) = **analyse.**

anapaest, (*US*) **anapest** ['ænəpi:st] *n* anapeste *m*.

anarchic(al) [æ'nɑ:kɪk(əl)] *adj* anarchique.

anarchism ['ænəkɪzəm] *n* anarchisme *m*.

anarchist ['ænəkɪst] *n* anarchiste *mf*.

anarchy ['ænəkɪ] *n* anarchie *f*.

anathema [ə'næθɪmə] *n* (*Rel, fig*) anathème *m*. (*fig*) **the whole idea of exploiting people was ~ to him** il avait en abomination l'idée d'exploiter les gens.

anathematize [ə'næθɪmətaɪz] *vt* frapper d'anathème, jeter l'anathème sur.

anatomical [ˌænə'tɒmɪkəl] *adj* anatomique.

anatomist [ə'nætəmɪst] *n* anatomiste *mf*.

anatomize [ə'nætəmaɪz] *vt* disséquer.

anatomy [ə'nætəmɪ] *n* (*Med, Sci*) anatomie *f*; (*fig*) *[country etc]* structure *f*. **he had spots all over his ~** il avait des boutons partout, il était couvert de boutons.

ancestor ['ænsɪstə^r] *n* (*lit*) ancêtre *m*, aïeul *m*; (*fig*) ancêtre.

ancestral [æn'sestrəl] *adj* ancestral. **~ home** château ancestral.

ancestress ['ænsɪstrɪs] *n* aïeule *f*.

A-B

ancestry [ˈænsɪstrɪ] *n* **(a)** (*lineage*) ascendance *f*. **(b)** (*collective n*) ancêtres *mpl*, aïeux *mpl*, ascendants *mpl*.

anchor [ˈæŋkəʳ] **1** *n* ancre *f*. **to be at ~** être à l'ancre; **to come to ~** jeter l'ancre, mouiller; *V* **cast, ride, weigh** *etc*.
2 *vt* (*Naut*) mettre à l'ancre; (*fig*) ancrer, enraciner.
3 *vi* (*Naut*) mouiller, jeter l'ancre, se mettre à l'ancre.
4 *cpd*: **anchor ice** glaces *fpl* de fond; **anchor man** (*Rad, TV*) présentateur-réalisateur *m*; (*fig: in team, organization*) pilier *m*, pivot *m*.

anchorage [ˈæŋkərɪdʒ] *n* (*Naut*) mouillage *m*, ancrage *m*. **~ dues** droits *mpl* de mouillage *or* d'ancrage.

anchorite [ˈæŋkəraɪt] *n* anachorète *m*.

anchovy [ˈæntʃəvɪ] *n* anchois *m*. **~ paste** pâte *f* d'anchois (*vendue toute préparée*); **~ sauce** sauce *f* aux anchois.

ancient [ˈeɪnʃənt] **1** *adj* **(a)** *world, painting* antique; *document, custom* ancien. **in ~ days** il y a très longtemps; **~ history** histoire ancienne; **it's ~ history*** c'est de l'histoire ancienne; (*Brit*) **(scheduled as an) ~ monument** (classé) monument historique; **~ Rome** la Rome antique; **~ rocks** de vieilles roches.
(b) (*: *gen hum*) *person* très vieux (*f* vieille); *clothes, object* antique, très vieux, antédiluvien*. **this is positively ~** cela remonte à Mathusalem *or* au déluge; **a really ~ car** une antique guimbarde; **he's getting pretty ~** il se fait vieux, il prend de la bouteille*.
2 *n* **(a)** (*people of long ago*) **the ~s** les anciens *mpl*.
(b) (*hum*) vieillard *m*, patriarche *m*.

ancillary [ænˈsɪlərɪ] *adj service, help, forces* auxiliaire. **~ to** subordonné à; **(hospital) ~ workers** personnel *m* des services auxiliaires (des hôpitaux *or* hospitaliers).

and [ænd, ənd, nd, ən] *conj* **(a)** et. **a man ~ a woman** un homme et une femme; **his table ~ chair** sa table et sa chaise; **~ how!*** et comment!*; **~?** et alors?; **on Saturday ~/or Sunday** (*Admin*) samedi et/ou dimanche; (*gen*) samedi ou dimanche ou les deux.
(b) (*in numbers*) **three hundred ~ ten** trois cent dix; **two thousand ~ eight** deux mille huit; **two pounds ~ six pence** deux livres (et) six pence; **an hour ~ twenty minutes** une heure vingt (minutes); **five ~ three quarters** cinq trois quarts.
(c) (*+infin vb*) **try ~ come** tâchez de venir; **remember ~ bring flowers** n'oubliez pas d'apporter des fleurs; **he went ~ opened the door** il est allé ouvrir la porte; **wait ~ see** on verra bien, attendez voir.
(d) (*repetition, continuation*) **better ~ better** de mieux en mieux; **now ~ then** de temps en temps; **for hours ~ hours** pendant des heures et des heures; **I rang ~ rang** j'ai sonné et resonné; **he talked ~ talked/waited ~ waited** il a parlé/attendu pendant des heures; **~ so on, ~ so forth** et ainsi de suite; **he goes on ~ on*** quand il commence il n'y a plus moyen de l'arrêter *or* il n'en finit plus.
(e) (*with comp adj*) **uglier ~ uglier** de plus en plus laid; **more ~ more difficult** de plus en plus difficile.
(f) (*with neg or implied neg*) ni. **to go out without a hat ~ coat** sortir sans chapeau ni manteau; **you can't buy ~ sell here** on ne peut ni acheter ni vendre ici.
(g) (*phrases*) **eggs ~ bacon** œufs au bacon; **summer ~ winter (alike)** été comme hiver; **a carriage ~ pair** une voiture à deux chevaux.
(h) (*implying cond*) **flee ~ you are lost** fuyez et vous êtes perdu, si vous fuyez vous êtes perdu.

Andean [ˈændɪən] *adj* des Andes.

Andes [ˈændiːz] *n* Andes *fpl*.

andiron [ˈændaɪən] *n* chenet *m*.

Andrew [ˈændruː] *n* André *m*.

anecdote [ˈænɪkdəʊt] *n* anecdote *f*.

anemia [əˈniːmɪə] *n* = **anaemia.**

anemic [əˈniːmɪk] *adj* = **anaemic.**

anemone [əˈnemənɪ] *n* anémone *f*; *V* **sea.**

anent [əˈnent] *prep* (*Scot*) concernant, à propos de.

aneroid [ˈænərɔɪd] *adj* anéroïde. **~ (barometer)** baromètre *m* anéroïde.

anesthesia [ˌænɪsˈθiːzɪə] *n* = **anaesthesia.**

anesthetic [ˌænɪsˈθetɪk] = **anaesthetic.**

anesthetist [æˈniːsθɪtɪst] *n* = **anaesthetist.**

anesthetize [æˈniːsθɪtaɪz] *vt* = **anaesthetize.**

aneurism [ˈænjʊrɪzəm] *n* anévrisme *m*.

anew [əˈnjuː] *adv* (*again*) de nouveau, encore; (*in a new way*) à nouveau. **to begin ~** recommencer.

angel [ˈeɪndʒəl] **1** *n* ange *m*; (*: *person*) ange, amour *m*. **~ of Darkness** ange des Ténèbres; **be an ~ and fetch me my gloves** apporte-moi mes gants tu seras un ange; **speak** *or* **talk of ~s!*** quand on parle du loup (on en voit la queue)!; *V* **guardian.**
2 *cpd*: **angel cake** ≈ gâteau *m* de Savoie; **angelfish** (*shark*) ange *m*; (*tropical fish*) chétodon *m*.

angelica [ænˈdʒelɪkə] *n* angélique *f*.

angelic(al) [ænˈdʒelɪk(əl)] *adj* angélique.

angelus [ˈændʒɪləs] *n* (*prayer, bell*) angélus *m*.

anger [ˈæŋgəʳ] **1** *n* colère *f*; (*violent*) fureur *f*, courroux *m* (*liter*). **to act in ~** agir sous l'empire *or* sous le coup de la colère, agir avec emportement; **words spoken in ~** mots prononcés sous l'empire *or* sous le coup de la colère; **to move sb to ~** mettre qn en colère; **his ~ knew no bounds** sa colère *or* son emportement ne connut plus de bornes; **in great ~** furieux, courroucé (*liter*).
2 *vt* mettre en colère, irriter; (*greatly*) courroucer (*liter*). **to be easily ~ed** se mettre facilement en colère, s'emporter facilement.

angina [ænˈdʒaɪnə] *n* angine *f*. **~ (pectoris)** angine de poitrine.

angle¹ [ˈæŋgl] **1** *n* **(a)** (*also Math*) angle *m*. **at an ~ of** formant un angle de; **at an ~** en biais; **cut at an ~** *pipe, edge* coupé en biseau; **the building stands at an ~ to the street** le bâtiment fait angle avec la rue; (*Aviat*) **~ of climb** angle d'ascension; (*Constr*) **~ iron** fer *m*, équerre *f*; *V* **acute, right.**
(b) (*fig: aspect, point of view*) angle *m*, aspect *m*. **the various ~s of a topic** les divers aspects d'un sujet; **to study a topic from every ~** étudier un sujet sous toutes ses faces *or* sous tous les angles; **from the parents' ~** du point de vue des parents; **let's have your ~ on it*** dites-nous votre point de vue là-dessus, dites-nous comment vous voyez ça*.
2 *vt* **(a)** (*) *information, report* présenter sous un certain angle. **he ~d his article towards middle-class readers** il a rédigé son article à l'intention des classes moyennes *or* de façon à plaire au lecteur bourgeois.
(b) (*Tennis*) **to ~ a shot** croiser sa balle, jouer la diagonale.
(c) *lamp etc* régler à l'angle voulu. **she ~d the lamp towards her desk** elle a dirigé la lumière (de la lampe) sur son bureau.
3 *vi*: **the road ~s (to the) right** la route fait un virage à droite.

angle² [ˈæŋgl] *vi* **(a)** (*lit*) pêcher à la ligne. **to ~ for trout** pêcher la truite.
(b) (*fig*) **to ~ for sb's attention** chercher à attirer l'attention de qn; **to ~ for compliments** chercher *or* quêter des compliments; **to ~ for a rise in salary/for an invitation** chercher à se faire augmenter/à se faire inviter; **she's angling for a husband** elle fait la chasse au mari.

angler [ˈæŋgləʳ] *n* pêcheur *m*, -euse *f* (à la ligne).

Angles [ˈæŋglz] *npl* (*Hist*) Angles *mpl*.

Anglican [ˈæŋglɪkən] *adj, n* anglican(e) *m(f)*.

Anglicanism [ˈæŋglɪkənɪzəm] *n* anglicanisme *m*.

anglicism [ˈæŋglɪsɪzəm] *n* anglicisme *m*.

anglicist [ˈæŋglɪsɪst] *n* angliciste *mf*.

anglicize [ˈæŋglɪsaɪz] *vt* angliciser.

angling [ˈæŋglɪŋ] *n* pêche *f* (à la ligne).

Anglo- [ˈæŋgləʊ] *pref* anglo-. **~French** anglo-français, franco-britannique, franco-anglais.

Anglo-Catholic [ˈæŋgləʊˈkæθəlɪk] **1** *n* anglican(e) *m(f)* (proche du catholicisme). **2** *adj* des anglicans (proches du catholicisme).

Anglo-Indian [ˈæŋgləʊˈɪndɪən] *n* (*English person in India*) Anglais(e) *m(f)* des Indes; (*person of English and Indian descent*) métis(se) *m(f)* d'Anglais(e) et d'Indien(ne).

anglophile [ˈæŋgləʊfaɪl] *adj, n* anglophile (*mf*).

anglophobe [ˈæŋgləʊfəʊb] *adj, n* anglophobe (*mf*).

Anglo-Saxon [ˈæŋgləʊˈsæksən] **1** *adj* anglo-saxon. **2** *n* **(a)** Anglo-Saxon(ne) *m(f)*. **(b)** (*Ling*) anglo-saxon *m*.

angora [æŋˈgɔːrə] **1** *n* **(a)** (*cat/rabbit*) (chat *m*/lapin *m*) angora *m*; (*goat*) chèvre *f* angora. **(b)** (*wool*) laine *f* angora, angora *m*.
2 *adj cat, rabbit etc* angora *inv*; *sweater* (en) angora.

angostura [æŋgəˈstjʊərə] *n* angusture *f*. ® **~ bitters** bitter *m* à base d'angusture.

angrily [ˈæŋgrɪlɪ] *adv leave* en colère; *talk* avec colère, avec emportement.

angry [ˈæŋgrɪ] *adj* **(a)** *person* en colère (*with sb* contre qn, *at sth* à cause de qch, *about sth* à propos de qch); (*furious*) furieux (*with sb* contre qn, *at sth* de qch, *about sth* à cause de qch); (*annoyed*) irrité (*with sb* contre qn, *at sth* de qch, *about sth* à cause de qch); *look* irrité, furieux, courroucé (*liter*); *reply* plein *or* vibrant de colère; (*fig*) *sea* mauvais, démonté. **to get ~** se fâcher, se mettre en colère; **to make sb ~** mettre qn en colère; **he was ~ at being dismissed** il était furieux d'avoir été renvoyé *or* qu'on l'ait renvoyé; **in an ~ voice** sur le ton de la colère; **you won't be ~ if I tell you?** vous n'allez pas vous fâcher si je vous le dis?; **this sort of thing makes me ~** ce genre de chose me met hors de moi; (*Brit Literat*) **~ young man** jeune homme *m* en colère.
(b) (*inflamed*) *wound* enflammé, irrité; (*painful*) douloureux. **the blow left an ~ mark on his forehead** le coup lui a laissé une vilaine meurtrissure au front.

anguish [ˈæŋgwɪʃ] *n* (*mental*) angoisse *f*, anxiété *f*; (*physical*) supplice *m*. **to be in ~** (*mentally*) être dans l'angoisse *or* angoissé; (*physically*) être au supplice, souffrir le martyre.

anguished [ˈæŋgwɪʃt] *adj* (*mentally*) angoissé; (*physically*) plein de souffrance.

angular [ˈæŋgjʊləʳ] *adj* anguleux; *face* anguleux, osseux, maigre; *features* anguleux; *movement* dégingandé, saccadé.

aniline [ˈænɪliːn] *n* aniline *f*. **~ dyes** colorants *mpl* à base d'aniline.

animal [ˈænɪməl] **1** *n* (*lit*) animal *m*; (**pej: person*) brute *f*. **2** *adj fats, oil, instinct* animal. **~ husbandry** élevage *m*; **~ kingdom** règne animal; **~ spirits** entrain *m*, vivacité *f*; **full of ~ spirits** plein d'entrain *or* de vivacité *or* de vie.

animate [ˈænɪmɪt] **1** *adj* (*living*) vivant, animé; (*lively*) animé, vivant, vivace.
2 [ˈænɪmeɪt] *vt* **(a)** (*lit*) animer, vivifier (*liter*).
(b) (*fig*) *discussion* animer, rendre vivant, aviver; *courage* stimuler, exciter. **to ~ sb to do** pousser qn à faire.

animated [ˈænɪmeɪtɪd] *adj* animé. **to become ~** s'animer; **the talk was growing ~** la conversation s'animait *or* s'échauffait; (*Cine*) **(~) cartoon** dessin(s) animé(s), film *m* d'animation.

animatedly [ˈænɪmeɪtɪdlɪ] *adv talk* d'un ton animé, avec animation; *behave* avec entrain, avec vivacité.

animation [ˌænɪˈmeɪʃən] *n [person]* vivacité *f*, entrain *m*; *[face]* animation *f*; *[scene, street etc]* activité *f*, animation; (*Cine*) animation; *V* **suspend.**

animator [ˈænɪmeɪtəʳ] *n* (*Cine*) animateur *m*, -trice *f*.

animosity [ˌænɪˈmɒsɪtɪ] *n* animosité *f* (*against, towards* contre), hostilité *f* (*against, towards* envers), antipathie *f* (*against, towards* pour).

animus [ˈænɪməs] *n* (*U*) = **animosity.**

anise [ˈænɪs] *n* anis *m*.

aniseed [ˈænɪsiːd] **1** *n* graine *f* d'anis. **2** *cpd flavour* à l'anis. **aniseed ball** bonbon *m* à l'anis.

anisette [ˌænɪ'zet] *n* anisette *f*.
ankle ['æŋkl] **1** *n* cheville *f*.
2 *cpd*: **anklebone** astragale *m*; **he was ankle-deep in water** l'eau lui montait (jusqu')à la cheville, il avait de l'eau (jusqu')à la cheville; **the water is ankle-deep** l'eau monte *or* vient (jusqu')à la cheville; (*Brit*) **ankle sock** socquette *f*; **ankle strap** bride *f*.
anklet ['æŋklɪt] *n* bracelet *m or* anneau *m* de cheville; (*US*) socquette *f*.
Ann [æn] *n* Anne *f*.
annalist ['ænəlɪst] *n* annaliste *m*.
annals ['ænəlz] *npl* annales *fpl*.
Anne [æn] *n* Anne *f*; *V* **queen.**
anneal [ə'ni:l] *vt glass, metal* recuire.
annex [ə'neks] **1** *vt* annexer. **2** ['æneks] *n* (*building, document*) annexe *f*.
annexation [ˌænek'seɪʃən] *n* (*act*) annexion *f* (*of* de); (*territory*) territoire *m* annexe.
annexe ['æneks] *n* = **annex 2.**
annihilate [ə'naɪəleɪt] *vt army, fleet* anéantir; (*fig*) *space, time* annihiler, supprimer; *effect* annihiler.
annihilation [əˌnaɪə'leɪʃən] *n* (*Mil*) anéantissement *m*; (*fig*) suppression *f*.
anniversary [ˌænɪ'vɜ:sərɪ] **1** *n* anniversaire *m* (*d'une date, d'un événement*); *V* **wedding. 2** *cpd*: **anniversary dinner** dîner commémoratif *or* anniversaire.
Anno Domini ['ænəʊ'dɒmɪnaɪ] *n* **(a)** l'an *m* de notre ère, après Jésus-Christ, ap. J.-C., l'an de grâce (*liter*). **in 53 ~** en 53 après Jésus-Christ *or* ap. J.-C., en l'an 53 de notre ère; **the 2nd century ~** le 2e siècle de notre ère.
(b) (*) vieillesse *f*, le poids des ans (*hum*). **he is showing signs of ~** il commence à prendre de l'âge *or* à se faire vieux.
annotate ['ænəʊteɪt] *vt* annoter.
annotation [ˌænəʊ'teɪʃən] *n* annotation *f*, note *f*.
announce [ə'naʊns] *vt fact, piece of news, decision* annoncer, faire connaître; *guest* annoncer. **to ~ the birth/death of** faire part de la naissance de/du décès de; **'I won't' he ~d** 'je ne le ferai pas' annonça-t-il; **it is ~d from London** on apprend de Londres.
announcement [ə'naʊnsmənt] *n* (*gen*) annonce *f*; (*esp Admin*) avis *m*; (*newspaper entry: about birth, marriage, death*) avis, faire-part *m*; (*letter, card*) faire-part.
announcer [ə'naʊnsə^r] *n* (*Rad, TV*) (*linking programmes*) speaker(ine) *m(f)*, annonceur *m*, -euse *f*; (*within a programme*) présentateur *m*, -trice *f*; (*newsreader*) journaliste *mf*.
annoy [ə'nɔɪ] *vt* (*vex*) ennuyer, agacer, contrarier; (*deliberately irritate*) *person, animal* agacer, énerver, embêter*; (*inconvenience*) importuner, ennuyer. **to be/get ~ed with sb** être/se mettre en colère contre qn; **to be ~ed about** *or* **over an event** être contrarié par un événement; **to be ~ed about** *or* **over a decision** être mécontent d'une décision; **to be ~ed with sb about sth** être mécontent de qn à propos de qch, savoir mauvais gré à qn de qch (*frm*); **to get ~ed with a machine** se mettre en colère *or* s'énerver* contre une machine; **don't get ~ed!** ne vous fâchez pas!; **I am very ~ed that he hasn't come** je suis très ennuyé *or* contrarié qu'il ne soit pas venu; **I am very ~ed with him for not coming** je suis très mécontent qu'il ne soit pas venu.
annoyance [ə'nɔɪəns] *n* **(a)** (*displeasure*) mécontentement *m*, déplaisir *m*, contrariété *f*. **with a look of ~** d'un air contrarié *or* ennuyé; **he found to his great ~ that ...** il s'est aperçu à son grand mécontentement *or* déplaisir que ... .
(b) (*cause of ~*) tracas *m*, ennui *m*, désagrément *m*.
annoying [ə'nɔɪɪŋ] *adj* (*slightly irritating*) agaçant, énervant, embêtant*; (*very irritating*) ennuyeux, fâcheux. **the ~ thing about it is that ...** ce qui est agaçant *or* ennuyeux dans cette histoire c'est que ...; **how ~!** que c'est agaçant! *or* ennuyeux!
annoyingly [ə'nɔɪɪŋlɪ] *adv* d'une façon agaçante. **the sound was ~ loud** le son était si fort que ç'en était gênant.
annual ['ænjʊəl] **1** *adj* annuel. (*Comm etc*) **~ general meeting** assemblée générale annuelle. **2** *n* **(a)** (*Bot*) plante annuelle; *V* **hardy. (b)** (*book*) publication annuelle; (*children's comic book*) album *m*.
annually ['ænjʊəlɪ] *adv* annuellement, tous les ans. **£5,000 ~** 5.000 livres par an.
annuity [ə'nju:ɪtɪ] *n* (*regular income*) rente *f*; (*for life*) rente viagère, viager *m*; (*investment*) viager. **to invest money in an ~** placer de l'argent en viager; *V* **defer¹, life.**
annul [ə'nʌl] *vt law* abroger, abolir; *decision, judgment* casser, annuler, infirmer; *marriage* annuler.
annulment [ə'nʌlmənt] *n* (*V* **annul**) abrogation *f*, abolition *f*; cassation *f*, annulation *f*, infirmation *f*.
Annunciation [əˌnʌnsɪ'eɪʃən] *n* Annonciation *f*.
anode ['ænəʊd] *n* anode *f*.
anodyne ['ænəʊdaɪn] **1** *n* (*Med*) analgésique *m*, calmant *m*; (*fig liter*) baume *m*. **2** *adj* (*Med*) antalgique, analgésique, calmant; (*fig liter*) apaisant.
anoint [ə'nɔɪnt] *vt* oindre (*with* de), consacrer *or* bénir par l'onction. **to ~ sb king** sacrer qn, faire qn roi par la cérémonie du sacre; **to be ~ed*** avoir une veine de pendu*.
anomalous [ə'nɒmələs] *adj* (*Gram, Med*) anormal, irrégulier; (*fig*) anormal.
anomaly [ə'nɒməlɪ] *n* anomalie *f*.
anon¹ [ə'nɒn] *adv* († *or hum*) tout à l'heure, bientôt, sous peu; *V* **ever.**
anon² [ə'nɒn] *adj* (*abbr of* **anonymous**) anonyme. (*at end of text*) **'A~'** 'anonyme', 'auteur inconnu'.
anonymity [ˌænə'nɪmɪtɪ] *n* anonymat *m*.
anonymous [ə'nɒnɪməs] *adj author, letter* anonyme. **to remain ~** garder l'anonymat.
anonymously [ə'nɒnɪməslɪ] *adv publish* anonymement, sans nom d'auteur; *donate* anonymement, en gardant l'anonymat, sous le couvert de l'anonymat.
anorak ['ænəræk] *n* anorak *m*.
anorexia [ænə'reksɪə] *n* anorexie *f*.
another [ə'nʌðə^r] **1** *adj* **(a)** (*one more*) un ... de plus, encore un. **take ~ 10** prenez-en encore 10; **to wait ~ hour** attendre une heure de plus *or* encore une heure; **I shan't wait ~ minute!** je n'attendrai pas une minute de plus!; **without ~ word** sans ajouter un mot, sans un mot de plus; **~ glass?** vous reprendrez bien un verre?; **in ~ 20 years** dans 20 ans d'ici.
(b) (*similar*) un autre, un second. **there is not ~ book like it, there is not ~ such book** il n'y a pas d'autre livre qui lui ressemble (*subj*), ce livre est unique dans son genre; **he will be ~ Hitler** ce sera un second *or* nouvel Hitler.
(c) (*different*) un autre. **that's quite ~ matter** c'est une tout autre question, c'est tout autre chose; **do it ~ time** remettez cela à plus tard, vous le ferez une autre fois.
2 *pron* **(a)** un(e) autre, encore un(e). **many ~** bien d'autres, beaucoup d'autres, maint(e) autre (*liter*); **taking one with ~** l'un dans l'autre, en moyenne; **between** *or* **what with* one thing and ~** en fin de compte.
(b) one ~ = each other; *V* **each.**
answer ['ɑ:nsə^r] **1** *n* **(a)** réponse *f*; (*sharp*) réplique *f*, riposte *f*; (*to criticism, objection*) réponse, réfutation *f*. **to get an ~** obtenir une réponse; **to write sb an ~** répondre à qn (par écrit); **his only ~ was to shrug his shoulders** pour toute réponse il a haussé les épaules, il a répondu par un haussement d'épaules; (*Telec*) **there's no ~** ça ne répond pas; **I knocked but there was no ~** j'ai frappé mais sans réponse *or* mais on ne m'a pas répondu; (*Comm*) **in ~ to your letter** suite à *or* en réponse à votre lettre; **I could find no ~** je n'ai rien trouvé à répondre; **she's always got an ~** elle a réponse à tout; (*Jur*) **~ to a charge** réponse à une accusation; (*hum*) **it's the ~ to a maiden's prayer*** c'est ce dont j'ai toujours rêvé; (*hum*) **for her he was the ~ to a maiden's prayer*** c'était l'homme de ses rêves; **there is no ~ to that** que voulez-vous répondre à ça?; (*Rel*) **the ~ to my prayer** l'exaucement *m* de ma prière; **it's the poor man's ~ to caviar** c'est le caviar du pauvre; *V* **know.**
(b) (*solution to problem*) solution *f*. **~ to the riddle** mot *m* de l'énigme; (*fig*) **there is no easy ~** c'est un problème difficile à résoudre; **there must be an ~** il doit y avoir une explication *or* une solution, cela doit pouvoir s'expliquer.
2 *vt* **(a)** *letter, telephone, question* répondre à; *criticism* répondre à, (*sharply*) répliquer à. **~ me** répondez-moi; **to ~ the bell** *or* **door** aller *or* venir ouvrir (la porte), aller voir qui est à la porte *or* qui est là; *[servant summoned]* **to ~ the bell** répondre au coup de sonnette; **I didn't ~ a word** je n'ai rien répondu, je n'ai pas soufflé mot.
(b) (*fulfil; solve*) *description* répondre à, correspondre à; *prayer* exaucer; *problem* résoudre; *need* répondre à, satisfaire. **it ~s the purpose** cela fait l'affaire; **this machine ~s several purposes** cet appareil a plusieurs utilisations.
(c) (*Jur*) **to ~ a charge** répondre à *or* réfuter une accusation.
(d) (*Naut*) **to ~ the helm** obéir à la barre.
3 *vi* **(a)** (*say, write in reply*) répondre, donner une réponse.
(b) (*succeed*) *[plan etc]* faire l'affaire, réussir.
(c) he ~s to the name of il répond au nom de, il s'appelle; **he ~s to that description** il répond à cette description.
answer back *vt sep* répondre (avec impertinence) (*to* à). (*to child*) **don't answer back!** ne réponds pas!
answer for *vt fus sb's safety etc* répondre de, se porter garant de, être responsable de. **to answer for the truth of sth** garantir l'exactitude de qch; **he has a lot to answer for** il a bien des comptes à rendre, il a une lourde responsabilité.
answerable ['ɑ:nsərəbl] *adj* **(a)** *question* susceptible de réponse, qui admet une réponse; *charge, argument* réfutable; *problem* soluble.
(b) (*responsible*) responsable (*to sb* devant qn, *for sth* de qch), garant (*to sb* envers qn, *for sth* de qch), comptable (*to sb* à qn, *for sth* de qch). **I am ~ to no one** je n'ai de comptes à rendre à personne.
ant [ænt] *n* fourmi *f*. **~eater** fourmilier *m*; **~-heap, ~hill** fourmilière *f*.
antacid ['ænt'æsɪd] **1** *adj* alcalin, antiacide. **2** *n* (médicament *m*) alcalin *m*, antiacide *m*.
antagonism [æn'tægənɪzəm] *n* antagonisme *m* (*between* entre), opposition *f* (*to* à). **the ~ which existed between them** l'antagonisme qui existait entre eux; **to show ~ to an idea** se montrer hostile à une idée.
antagonist [æn'tægənɪst] *n* antagoniste *mf*, adversaire *mf*.
antagonistic [ænˌtægə'nɪstɪk] *adj force, interest* opposé, contraire. **to be ~ to sth** être opposé *or* hostile à qch; **to be ~ to sb** être en opposition avec qn; **two ~ ideas/decisions** deux idées/décisions antagonistes *or* opposées.
antagonize [æn'tægənaɪz] *vt person* éveiller l'hostilité de, contrarier. **I don't want to ~ him** je ne veux pas le contrarier *or* me le mettre à dos.
Antarctic [ænt'ɑ:ktɪk] **1** *n* régions antarctiques *or* australes, Antarctique *m*. **2** *adj* antarctique, austral. **~ Circle** cercle *m* Antarctique; **~ (Ocean)** océan *m* Antarctique *or* Austral.
Antarctica [ænt'ɑ:ktɪkə] *n* Antarctique *m*, continent *m* antarctique, Terres Australes.
ante ['æntɪ] *n* (*Cards: in poker*) première mise.
ante ... ['æntɪ] *pref* anté ..., anti ... .
antecedent [ˌæntɪ'si:dənt] **1** *adj* antérieur (*to* à), précédent. **2** *n* **(a)** (*Gram, Math, Philos*) antécédent *m*. **(b) the ~s of sb** les antécédents *or* le passé de qn.
antechamber ['æntɪˌtʃeɪmbə^r] *n* antichambre *f*.
antedate ['æntɪ'deɪt] *vt* **(a)** (*give earlier date to*) *document* antidater. **(b)** (*come before*) *event* précéder, dater d'avant.

antediluvian ['æntɪdɪ'lu:vɪən] *adj* antédiluvien; (**hum*) *person, hat* antédiluvien* (*hum*).

antelope ['æntɪləʊp] *n* antilope *f*.

antenatal ['æntɪ'neɪtl] *adj* prénatal. ~ **clinic** service *m* de consultation prénatale; **to attend an** ~ **clinic** aller à la visite prénatale.

antenna [æn'tenə] *n, pl* **antennae** [æn'teni:] (*Rad, Telec, TV, Zool*) antenne *f*.

antepenultimate ['æntɪpɪ'nʌltɪmɪt] *adj* antépénultième.

anterior [æn'tɪərɪəʳ] *adj* antérieur (*to* à).

anteroom ['æntɪrʊm] *n* antichambre *f*, vestibule *m*.

anthem ['ænθəm] *n* motet *m*; *V* **national.**

anther ['ænθəʳ] *n* anthère *f*.

anthologist [æn'θɒlədʒɪst] *n* anthologiste *mf*.

anthology [æn'θɒlədʒɪ] *n* anthologie *f*.

Anthony ['æntənɪ] *n* Antoine *m*.

anthracite ['ænθrəsaɪt] **1** *n* anthracite *m*. **2** *adj*: ~ **(grey)** (gris) anthracite *inv*.

anthrax ['ænθræks] *n* (*Med, Vet: disease*) charbon *m*; (*Med: boil*) anthrax *m*.

anthrop(o) ... ['ænθrəʊp(ɒ)] *pref* anthropo ... .

anthropoid ['ænθrəʊpɔɪd] *adj, n* anthropoïde (*m*).

anthropological [,ænθrəpə'lɒdʒɪkəl] *adj* anthropologique.

anthropologist [,ænθrə'pɒlədʒɪst] *n* anthropologiste *mf*, anthropologue *mf*.

anthropology [,ænθrə'pɒlədʒɪ] *n* anthropologie *f*.

anthropometry [,ænθrə'pɒmɪtrɪ] *n* anthropométrie *f*.

anthropomorphism [,ænθrəʊpə'mɔ:fɪzəm] *n* anthropomorphisme *m*.

anthropomorphous [,ænθrəʊpə'mɔ:fəs] *adj* anthropomorphe.

anthropophagi [,ænθrəʊ'pɒfəgaɪ] *npl* anthropophages *mpl*, cannibales *mpl*.

anthropophagous [,ænθrəʊ'pɒfəgəs] *adj* anthropophage, cannibale.

anthropophagy [,ænθrəʊ'pɒfədʒɪ] *n* anthropophagie *f*, cannibalisme *m*.

anti ... ['æntɪ] *pref* anti ..., contre ... . **he's rather** ~* il est plutôt contre.

anti-aircraft ['æntɪ'ɛəkrɑ:ft] *adj gun* antiaérien. ~ **defence** défense *f* contre avions, D.C.A. *f*.

antibiotic ['æntɪbaɪ'ɒtɪk] *adj, n* antibiotique (*m*).

antibody ['æntɪ,bɒdɪ] *n* anticorps *m*.

antic ['æntɪk] *n* (*gen pl*) *[child, animal]* cabriole *f*, gambade *f*; *[clown]* bouffonnerie *f*, singerie *f*. (*pej: behaviour*) **all his** ~**s** tout le cinéma* *or* le cirque* qu'il a fait; **he's up to his** ~**s again** il fait de nouveau des siennes*.

Antichrist ['æntɪkraɪst] *n* Antéchrist *m*.

anticipate [æn'tɪsɪpeɪt] *vt* **(a)** (*expect, foresee*) prévoir, s'attendre à. **we don't** ~ **any trouble** nous ne prévoyons pas d'ennuis; **I** ~ **that he will come** je m'attends à ce qu'il vienne; **do you** ~ **that it will be easy?** pensez-vous que ce sera facile?; **they** ~**d great pleasure from this visit** ils se sont promis beaucoup de joie de cette visite; **I** ~ **seeing him tomorrow** je pense le voir demain; **the attendance is larger than I** ~**d** je ne m'attendais pas à ce que l'assistance soit aussi nombreuse; **as** ~**d** comme prévu.

(b) (*use, deal with or get before due time*) *pleasure* savourer à l'avance; *grief, pain* souffrir à l'avance; *success* escompter; *wishes, objections, command, request* aller au devant de, prévenir, devancer; *needs* aller au devant de. **to** ~ **one's income/profits** anticiper sur son revenu/sur ses bénéfices; **to** ~ **an event** anticiper sur un événement; **to** ~ **a question/a blow/an attack** prévoir une question/un coup/une attaque.

(c) (*forestall*) **to** ~ **sb's doing sth** faire qch avant qn; **they** ~**d Columbus' discovery of America** *or* ~**d Columbus in discovering America** ils ont découvert l'Amérique avant Christophe Colomb.

anticipation [æn,tɪsɪ'peɪʃən] *n* **(a)** (*expectation, foreseeing*) attente *f*.

(b) (*experiencing etc in advance*) *[pleasure]* attente *f*; *[grief, pain]* appréhension *f*; *[profits, income]* jouissance anticipée. ~ **of sb's wishes** *etc* empressement *m* à aller au-devant des désirs *etc* de qn.

(c) in ~ par anticipation, à l'avance; (*Comm*) **thanking you in** ~ en vous remerciant d'avance, avec mes remerciements anticipés; **in** ~ **of a fine week** en prévision d'une semaine de beau temps; **we wait with growing** ~ nous attendons avec une impatience grandissante.

anticlerical ['æntɪ'klerɪkl] *adj, n* anticlérical(e) *m(f)*.

anticlericalism ['æntɪ'klerɪkəlɪzəm] *n* anticléricalisme *m*.

anticlimax ['æntɪ'klaɪmæks] *n [style, thought]* chute *f* (*dans le trivial*). **the ceremony was an** ~ la cérémonie a été une déception par contraste à l'attente *or* n'a pas répondu à l'attente; **what an** ~! quelle retombée!, quelle douche froide!

anticline ['æntɪklaɪn] *n* anticlinal *m*.

anticlockwise ['æntɪ'klɒkwaɪz] *adv* (*Brit*) dans le sens inverse des aiguilles d'une montre.

anticoagulant ['æntɪkəʊ'ægjʊlənt] *adj, n* anticoagulant (*m*).

anticorrosive ['æntɪkə'rəʊsɪv] *adj, n* anticorrosif (*m*).

anticyclone ['æntɪ'saɪkləʊn] *n* anticyclone *m*.

anti-dazzle ['æntɪ'dæzl] *adj* antiaveuglant. (*Aut*) ~ **headlights** phares anti-éblouissants.

antidote ['æntɪdəʊt] *n* (*Med, fig*) antidote *m* (*for, to* à, contre), contrepoison *m* (*for, to* de).

antifreeze ['æntɪ'fri:z] *n* antigel *m*.

anti-friction ['æntɪ'frɪkʃən] *adj* antifriction *inv*.

antigen ['æntɪdʒən] *n* antigène *m*.

anti-glare ['æntɪ'glɛəʳ] *adj* = **anti-dazzle.**

antihistamine [,æntɪ'hɪstəmɪn] *n* (produit *m*) antihistaminique *m*.

anti-knock ['æntɪ'nɒk] *n* antidétonant *m*.

Antilles [æn'tɪli:z] *npl* Antilles *fpl*. **Greater/Lesser** ~ Grandes/Petites Antilles.

antilogarithm [,æntɪ'lɒgərɪθəm] *n* antilogarithme *m*.

antimacassar ['æntɪmə'kæsəʳ] *n* têtière *f*, appui-tête *m*.

antimagnetic [,æntɪmæg'netɪk] *adj* antimagnétique.

antimissile ['æntɪ'mɪsaɪl] *adj* antimissile.

antimony ['æntɪmənɪ] *n* antimoine *m*.

antipathetic [,æntɪpə'θetɪk] *adj* antipathique (*to* à).

antipathy [æn'tɪpəθɪ] *n* antipathie *f*, aversion *f* (*against, to* pour).

antiphony [æn'tɪfənɪ] *n* (*Mus*) antienne *f*.

antipodes [æn'tɪpədi:z] *npl* antipodes *mpl*.

antiquarian [,æntɪ'kwɛərɪən] **1** *adj* d'antiquaire. ~ **bookseller** libraire *mf* spécialisé(e) dans le livre ancien; ~ **collection** collection *f* d'antiquités.

2 *n* **(a)** amateur *m* d'antiquités.

(b) (*Comm*) antiquaire *mf*. ~**'s shop** magasin *m* d'antiquités.

antiquary ['æntɪkwərɪ] *n* (*collector*) collectionneur *m*, -euse *f* d'antiquités; (*student*) archéologue *mf*; (*Comm*) antiquaire *mf*.

antiquated ['æntɪkweɪtɪd] *adj* vieilli, vieillot; *ideas, manners* vieillot, suranné; *person* vieux jeu *inv*; *building* vétuste.

antique [æn'ti:k] **1** *adj* (*very old*) ancien; (*pre-medieval*) antique; (*) antédiluvien*. ~ **furniture** meubles anciens.

2 *n* (*sculpture, ornament etc*) objet *m* d'art (ancien); (*furniture*) meuble ancien. **it's a genuine** ~ c'est un objet (*or* un meuble) d'époque.

3 *cpd*: **antique dealer** antiquaire *mf*; **antique shop** magasin *m* d'antiquités.

antiquity [æn'tɪkwɪtɪ] *n* **(a)** (*U: old times*) antiquité *f*. **(b) antiquities** (*buildings*) monuments *mpl* antiques; (*works of art*) objets *mpl* d'art antiques, antiquités *fpl*.

anti-roll bar ['æntɪ'rəʊlbɑ:ʳ] *n* (*suspension*) barre *f* anti-roulis, stabilisateur *m*.

antirrhinum [,æntɪ'raɪnəm] *n* muflier *m*, gueule-de-loup *f*.

anti-rust ['æntɪ'rʌst] *adj* antirouille *inv*.

anti-semite ['æntɪ'si:maɪt] *n* antisémite *mf*.

anti-semitic ['æntɪsɪ'mɪtɪk] *adj* antisémite, antisémitique.

anti-semitism ['æntɪ'semɪtɪzəm] *n* antisémitisme *m*.

antisepsis [,æntɪ'sepsɪs] *n* antisepsie *f*.

antiseptic [,æntɪ'septɪk] *adj, n* antiseptique (*m*).

anti-skid ['æntɪ'skɪd] *adj* antidérapant.

antislavery ['æntɪ'sleɪvərɪ] *adj* antiesclavagiste.

antisocial ['æntɪ'səʊʃəl] *adj tendency, behaviour* antisocial. **don't be** ~*, **come and join us** ne sois pas si sauvage, viens nous rejoindre.

anti-tank ['æntɪ'tæŋk] *adj* antichar. ~ **mines** mines *fpl* antichars.

anti-theft ['æntɪ'θeft] *adj*: ~ **device** (*Aut*) antivol *m*; (*gen*) dispositif *m* contre le vol, dispositif antivol.

antithesis [æn'tɪθɪsɪs] *n, pl* **antitheses** [æn'tɪθɪsi:z] **(a)** (*direct opposite*) opposé *m*, contraire *m* (*to, of* de).

(b) (*contrast*) *[ideas etc]* antithèse *f* (*between* entre, *of one thing to another* d'une chose avec une autre), contraste *m*, opposition *f* (*between* entre).

(c) (*Literat*) antithèse *f*.

antithetic(al) [,æntɪ'θetɪk(əl)] *adj* antithétique.

antithetically [,æntɪ'θetɪkəlɪ] *adv* par antithèse.

anti-trust law ['æntɪ'trʌst,lɔ:] *n* loi *f* antitrust *inv*.

antivivisectionist ['æntɪ,vɪvɪ'sekʃənɪst] *n* adversaire *mf* de la vivisection.

antler ['æntləʳ] *n* merrain *m*. **the** ~**s** les bois *mpl*, la ramure (*U*).

Antony ['æntənɪ] *n* Antoine *m*.

antonym ['æntənɪm] *n* antonyme *m*.

Antwerp ['æntwɜ:p] *n* Anvers.

anus ['eɪnəs] *n* anus *m*.

anvil ['ænvɪl] *n* enclume *f*.

anxiety [æŋ'zaɪətɪ] *n* **(a)** (*concern*) anxiété *f*, grande inquiétude, appréhension *f*; (*Psych*) anxiété. **deep** ~ angoisse *f*; **it is a great** ~ **to me** ceci m'inquiète énormément, ceci me donne énormément de soucis; **in his** ~ **to be gone he left his pen behind** il était si préoccupé de partir qu'il en a oublié son stylo, dans son souci de partir au plus vite il a oublié son stylo; (*Psych*) ~ **neurosis** anxiété névrotique.

(b) (*keen desire*) grand désir, désir ardent, fièvre *f*. ~ **to do well** grand désir de réussir.

anxious ['æŋkʃəs] *adj* **(a)** (*troubled*) anxieux, angoissé, (très) inquiet (*f* -ète). **very** ~ **about** très inquiet de; **with an** ~ **glance** jetant un regard anxieux *or* angoissé; **to be over** ~ être d'une anxiété maladive; **she is** ~ **about my health** mon état de santé la préoccupe *or* l'inquiète beaucoup.

(b) (*causing anxiety*) inquiétant, alarmant, angoissant. **an** ~ **moment** un moment d'anxiété *or* de grande inquiétude; ~ **hours** des heures sombres.

(c) (*strongly desirous*) anxieux, impatient, très désireux (*for* de). ~ **for praise** avide de louanges; ~ **to start** pressé *or* impatient de partir; **he is** ~ **to see you before you go** il tient beaucoup à *or* désirerait beaucoup vous voir avant votre départ; **I am** ~ **that he should do it** je tiens beaucoup à ce qu'il le fasse; **I am** ~ **for her return** *or* **for her to come back** il me tarde qu'elle revienne, j'attends son retour avec impatience; **not to be very** ~ **to do** avoir peu envie de faire.

anxiously ['æŋkʃəslɪ] *adv* **(a)** (*with concern*) avec inquiétude, anxieusement. **(b)** (*eagerly*) avec impatience.

anxiousness ['æŋkʃəsnɪs] *n* = **anxiety.**

any ['enɪ] **1** *adj* **(a)** (*with neg and implied neg* = *some*) **I haven't** ~ **money/books** je n'ai pas d'argent/de livres; **you haven't** ~ **excuse** vous n'avez aucune excuse; **this pan hasn't** ~ **lid** cette casserole n'a pas de couvercle; **there isn't** ~ **sign of life** il n'y a pas le moindre signe de vie; **without** ~ **difficulty sans la**

moindre difficulté; **the impossibility of giving them ~ money/advice** l'impossibilité de leur donner de l'argent/aucun conseil; **I have hardly ~ money left** il ne me reste presque plus d'argent.

(b) (*in interrog sentences, clauses of cond and hypotheses* = some) **have you ~ butter?** avez-vous du beurre?; **can you see ~ birds in this tree?** voyez-vous des oiseaux dans cet arbre?; **are there ~ others?** y en a-t-il d'autres?; **is it ~ use trying?** est-ce que cela vaut la peine d'essayer?; **have you ~ complaints?** avez-vous quelque sujet de vous plaindre?, avez-vous à vous plaindre de quelque chose?; **is there ~ man who will help me?** y a-t-il quelqu'un qui pourrait m'aider?; **he can do it if ~ man can** si quelqu'un peut le faire c'est bien lui; **if it is in ~ way inconvenient to you** si cela vous cause un dérangement quel qu'il soit, si cela vous cause le moindre dérangement; **if you see ~ children** si vous voyez des enfants; **if you have ~ money** si vous avez de l'argent.

(c) (*in affirmative sentences: no matter which*) n'importe quel, quelconque; (*each and every*) tout. **take ~ two points** prenez deux points quelconques; **take ~ dress you like** prenez n'importe quelle robe, prenez la robe que vous voulez, prenez n'importe laquelle de ces robes; **come at ~ time** venez à n'importe quelle heure; **he should arrive ~ day/minute now** il devrait arriver d'un jour à l'autre/d'une minute à l'autre; **at ~ moment** *or* **~ minute now war might begin** la guerre pourrait éclater à tout moment *or* d'une minute à l'autre *or* d'un instant à l'autre; **~ day now the rains will start** la saison des pluies va commencer incessamment; **at ~ hour of the day (or night)** à toute heure du jour (ou de la nuit); **~ amount** *or* **number of** n'importe quelle quantité de (*V also* **1d**); **~ person who breaks the rules will be punished** toute personne qui enfreindra le règlement *or* toute infraction (au règlement) sera punie.

(d) (*phrases*) **in ~ case** de toute façon; **at ~ rate** en tout cas; **we have ~ amount of time/money** nous avons tout le temps/tout l'argent qu'il nous faut; **there are ~ number of ways to do it** il y a des quantités de façons *or* il y a mille façons de le faire.

2 *pron* **(a)** (*with neg and implied neg*) **she has 2 brothers and I haven't ~** elle a 2 frères alors que moi je n'en ai pas (un seul); **I don't believe ~ of them has done it** je ne crois pas qu'aucun d'eux l'ait fait; **I have hardly ~ left** il ne m'en reste presque plus; **I haven't ~ gloves and I can't go out without ~** je ne peux pas sortir sans gants et je n'en ai pas, je n'ai pas de gants et je ne peux pas sortir sans*.

(b) (*in interrog, cond, hypothetical constructions*) **have you got ~?** en avez-vous?; **if ~ of you can sing** si l'un (quelconque) d'entre vous *or* si quelqu'un parmi vous sait chanter; **if ~ of them should come out** si l'un (quelconque) d'entre eux sortait; **few, if ~, will come** il viendra peu de gens, si tant est qu'il en vienne *or* (et) peut-être même personne.

(c) (*in affirmative sentences*) **~ of those books will do** n'importe lequel de ces livres fera l'affaire; **~ but him would have been afraid** tout autre que lui aurait eu peur.

3 *adv* **(a)** (*in neg sentences, gen with comps*) nullement, en aucune façon, aucunement. **she is not ~ more intelligent than her sister** elle n'est nullement *or* en aucune façon *or* aucunement plus intelligente que sa sœur; **I can't hear him ~ more** je ne l'entends plus; **don't do it ~ more!** ne recommence pas!; **we can't go ~ further** nous ne pouvons pas aller plus loin; **I shan't wait ~ longer** je n'attendrai pas plus longtemps; **they didn't behave ~ too well** ils ne se sont pas tellement bien conduits; **without ~ more discussion they left** ils sont partis sans ajouter un mot.

(b) (*in interrog, cond and hypothetical constructions, gen with comps*) un peu, si peu que ce soit. **are you feeling ~ better?** vous sentez-vous un peu mieux?; **do you want ~ more soup?** voulez-vous encore de la soupe? *or* encore un peu de soupe?; **if you see ~ more beautiful flower than this** si vous voyez jamais plus belle fleur que celle-ci; **I couldn't do that ~ more than I could fly** je ne serais pas plus capable de faire cela que de voler.

(c) (*) **the rope didn't help them ~** la corde ne leur a pas servi à grand-chose *or* ne leur a servi à rien du tout.

anybody ['enɪbɒdɪ] *pron* **(a)** (*with neg and implied neg* = somebody) **I can't see ~** je ne vois personne; **there is hardly ~ there** il n'y a presque personne là; **without ~ seeing him** sans que personne le voie; **it's impossible for ~ to see him today** personne ne peut le voir aujourd'hui.

(b) (*in interrog, cond and hypothetical constructions* = somebody) quelqu'un. **was there ~ there?** est-ce qu'il y avait quelqu'un (là)?; **did ~ see you?** est-ce que quelqu'un t'a vu?, est-ce qu'on t'a vu?; **~ want my sandwich?*** quelqu'un veut mon sandwich?*; **if ~ touches that** si quelqu'un touche à cela; **if ~ can do it, he can** si quelqu'un peut le faire c'est bien lui.

(c) (*in affirmative sentences: no matter who*) **~ who wants to do it should say so now** si quelqu'un veut le faire qu'il le dise tout de suite; **~ could tell you** n'importe qui pourrait vous le dire; **~ would have thought he had lost** on aurait pu croire *or* on aurait cru qu'il avait perdu; **bring ~ you like** amenez qui vous voudrez; **~ who had heard him speak would agree** quiconque l'a entendu parler serait d'accord; **~ with any sense would know that!** le premier venu saurait cela pourvu qu'il ait un minimum de bon sens!; **~ but Robert** n'importe qui d'autre que *or* tout autre que Robert; **~ else** n'importe qui d'autre, toute autre personne; **~ else would have cried but not he** un autre aurait pleuré, lui non; **bring ~ else you like** amenez n'importe qui d'autre; **is there ~ else I can talk to?** est-ce qu'il y a quelqu'un d'autre à qui je puisse parler?; **bring somebody to help us, ~ will do** amenez quelqu'un pour nous aider, n'importe qui *or* le premier venu fera l'affaire; **it's ~'s guess!*** vous en savez autant que moi!, allez donc savoir!*; **it's ~'s guess* how many will come** impossible de prévoir combien viendront.

(d) (*person of importance*) quelqu'un (d'important *or* de bien *or* de connu); (*person of no importance*) n'importe qui. **work harder if you want to be ~** il faut travailler plus si vous voulez devenir quelqu'un; **he's not just ~, he's the boss** ce n'est pas n'importe qui, c'est le patron.

anyhow ['enɪhaʊ] *adv* **(a)** (*in any way whatever*) n'importe comment. **do it ~ you like but you must do it** faites-le comme vous voulez mais il faut le faire; **the house was closed and I couldn't get in ~** la maison était fermée et je n'avais aucun moyen d'entrer; **~ I do it, it always fails** de quelque façon que je m'y prenne ça ne réussit jamais.

(b) (*carelessly, haphazardly: also* **any old how***) n'importe comment, tant bien que mal. **I came in late and finished my essay ~** je suis rentré tard et j'ai bâclé* la fin de ma dissertation; **the books were all ~ on the floor** les livres étaient tous en désordre *or* en vrac *or* n'importe comment par terre.

(c) (*in any case, at all events*) en tout cas, dans tous les cas, de toute façon. **whatever you say, they'll do it ~** vous pouvez dire ce que vous voulez, ils le feront de toute façon *or* quand même; **~ he eventually did it** toujours est-il qu'il a fini par le faire, il a quand même fini par le faire.

anyone ['enɪwʌn] *pron* = **anybody.**

anyplace* ['enɪpleɪs] *adv* (*US*) = **anywhere.**

anything ['enɪθɪŋ] *pron* **(a)** (*with neg and implied neg* = *something*) **there wasn't ~ to be done** il n'y avait rien à faire; **there isn't ~ in the box** il n'y a rien dans la boîte; **we haven't seen ~** nous n'avons rien vu; **hardly ~** presque rien; **without ~ happening** sans qu'il se passe (*subj*) rien; **this is ~ but pleasant** ceci n'a vraiment rien d'agréable; (*reply to question*) **~ but!** pas du tout!, pas le moins du monde!, tout *or* bien au contraire!

(b) (*in interrog, cond and hypothetical constructions* = *something*) **was there ~ in the room?** est-ce qu'il y avait quelque chose dans la pièce?; **did you see ~?** avez-vous vu quelque chose?; **are you doing ~ tonight?** faites-vous *or* vous faites* quelque chose ce soir?, avez-vous quelque chose de prévu pour ce soir?; **is there ~ in this idea?** peut-on tirer quoi que ce soit de cette idée?; **can ~ be done?** y a-t-il quelque chose à faire?, peut-on faire quelque chose?; **can't ~ be done?** n'y a-t-il rien à faire?, ne peut-on faire quelque chose?; **~ else?** (*Comm*) et avec ça?*, c'est tout ce qu'il vous faut?, ce sera tout?; (*have you anything more to tell me, give me etc*) c'est tout?, il y a quelque chose d'autre?; **have you heard ~ of her?** avez-vous de ses nouvelles?; **is there ~ more tiring than ...?** y a-t-il rien de plus fatigant que ...?; **if ~ should happen to me** s'il m'arrivait quelque chose *or* quoi que ce soit; **if I see ~ I'll tell you** si je vois quelque chose je te le dirai; **he must have ~ between 15 and 20 apple trees** il doit avoir quelque chose comme 15 ou 20 pommiers; **if ~ it's an improvement** ce serait plutôt une amélioration.

(c) (*in affirmative sentences: no matter what*) **say ~ (at all)** dites n'importe quoi; **take ~ you like** prenez ce que vous voudrez; **~ else would disappoint her** s'il en était autrement elle serait déçue; **~ else is impossible** il n'y a pas d'autre possibilité; **I'll try ~ else** j'essaierai n'importe quoi d'autre; **I'd give ~ to know the secret** je donnerais n'importe quoi pour connaître le secret; **they eat ~** (*they're not fussy*) ils mangent de tout; (*also* **they eat any old thing***) ils mangent n'importe quoi.

(d) (*: *intensive adv phrases*) **he ran like ~** il s'est mis à courir comme un dératé *or* fou; **she cried like ~** elle a pleuré comme une Madeleine*; **we laughed like ~** on a ri comme des fous, ce qu'on a pu rire!; **they worked like ~** ils ont travaillé comme des nègres *or* des dingues‡; **it's raining like ~** ce qu'il peut pleuvoir!, il pleut *or* tombe des cordes; **it's as big as ~** c'est très très grand; **it was as silly as ~** c'était idiot comme tout*.

anytime ['enɪtaɪm] *adv* = **any time;** *V* **time.**

anyway ['enɪweɪ] *adv* = **anyhow.**

anywhere ['enɪwɛəʳ] *adv* **(a)** (*in affirmative sentences*) n'importe où, partout. **I'm not going to live just ~** je ne veux pas habiter n'importe où; **put it down ~** pose-le n'importe où; **you can find that soap ~** ce savon se trouve partout; **go ~ you like** va où tu veux; **~ you go it's the same** où que vous alliez c'est la même chose, c'est partout pareil; **~ else** partout ailleurs; **the books were all ~* on the shelves** les livres étaient rangés *or* placés n'importe comment sur les rayons.

(b) (*in neg sentences*) nulle part, en aucun endroit, en aucun lieu. **they didn't go ~** ils ne sont allés nulle part; **not ~ else** nulle part ailleurs; **not ~ special** nulle part en particulier; (*fig: in guessing etc*) **you aren't ~ near it!** vous n'y êtes pas du tout!; (*fig*) **it won't get you ~** cela ne vous mènera à rien; (*Sport etc*) **he came first and the rest didn't come ~*** il est arrivé très loin en tête des autres.

(c) (*in interrog sentences*) quelque part. **have you seen it ~?** l'avez-vous vu quelque part?; **~ else** ailleurs.

aorist ['ɛəɒrɪst] *n* aoriste *m.*

aorta [eɪ'ɔːtə] *n* aorte *f.*

apace [ə'peɪs] *adv* rapidement, vite.

Apache [ə'pætʃɪ] *n* Apache *mf.*

apart [ə'pɑːt] (*phr vb elem*) **1** *adv* **(a)** (*separated*) à distance. **houses a long way ~** maisons (fort) éloignées l'une de l'autre *or* à une grande distance l'une de l'autre; **set equally ~** espacés à intervalles réguliers; **their birthdays were 2 days ~** leurs anniversaires étaient à 2 jours d'intervalle; **to stand with one's feet ~** se tenir les jambes écartées.

(b) (*on one side*) à part, de côté, à l'écart. **to hold o.s. ~** se tenir à l'écart (*from* de); **joking ~** plaisanterie à part; **that ~** à part cela, cela mis à part; **~ from these difficulties** en dehors de *or* à part ces difficultés, ces difficultés mises à part; **~ from the fact that** outre que, hormis que.

(c) (*separately, distinctly*) séparément. **they are living ~ now** ils sont séparés maintenant; **he lives ~ from his wife** il est séparé de sa femme, il n'habite plus avec sa femme; **you can't tell the twins ~** on ne peut distinguer les jumeaux l'un de l'autre; **we'll have to keep those boys ~** il va falloir séparer ces garçons.

(d) (*into pieces*) en pièces, en morceaux. **to come ~** *[two objects]* se séparer, se détacher; *[one object]* se défaire, se désagréger; **it came ~ in my hands** cela m'est resté dans les mains; **to take ~** démonter, désassembler; *V* **fall apart** *etc.*

2 *adj* (*following n*) **they are in a class ~** ils sont tout à fait à part; **this is something quite ~** c'est quelque chose de tout à fait différent *or* à part.

apartheid [əˈpɑːteɪt] *n* apartheid *m*.

apartment [əˈpɑːtmənt] *n* **(a)** (*Brit*) (*room*) pièce *f*; (*bedroom*) chambre *f*. **a 5-~ house** une maison de 5 pièces; **~s** appartement *m*, logement *m*; **furnished ~s** meublé *m*.

(b) (*US*) appartement *m*, logement *m*. **~ building, ~ house** (*block*) immeuble *m* (*de résidence*); (*divided house*) maison *f* (*divisée en appartements*).

apathetic [ˌæpəˈθetɪk] *adj* apathique, indifférent, sans réaction.

apathy [ˈæpəθɪ] *n* apathie *f*, indifférence *f*.

ape [eɪp] **1** *n* (*Zool*) (grand) singe *m*, anthropoïde *m*. (*pej*: *person*) **big ~*** grande brute. **2** *vt* singer.

Apennines [ˈæpənaɪnz] *npl* Apennins *mpl*.

aperient [əˈpɪərɪənt] *adj*, *n* laxatif (*m*).

aperitif [əˈperɪtɪv] *n* apéritif *m*.

aperture [ˈæpətʃjʊəʳ] *n* (*hole*) orifice *m*, trou *m*, ouverture *f*; (*gap*) brèche *f*, trouée *f*; (*Phot*) ouverture (du diaphragme).

apex [ˈeɪpeks] *n*, *pl* **apices** [ˈeɪpɪsiːz] (*Geom*, *Med*) sommet *m*; (*fig*) sommet, point culminant; *V* **base**[1].

aphasia [æˈfeɪzɪə] *n* aphasie *f*.

aphis [ˈeɪfɪs] *n*, *pl* **aphides** [ˈeɪfɪdiːz] aphis *m*.

aphorism [ˈæfərɪzəm] *n* aphorisme *m*.

aphrodisiac [ˌæfrəʊˈdɪzɪæk] *adj*, *n* aphrodisiaque (*m*).

apiary [ˈeɪpɪərɪ] *n* rucher *m*.

apiece [əˈpiːs] *adv* (*each person*) chacun(e), par personne, par tête; (*each thing*) chacun(e), (la) pièce.

aplomb [əˈplɒm] *n* sang-froid *m*, assurance *f*, aplomb *m* (*pej*).

Apocalypse [əˈpɒkəlɪps] *n* Apocalypse *f*.

apocalyptic [əˌpɒkəˈlɪptɪk] *adj* apocalyptique.

apocopate [əˈpɒkəpeɪt] *vt* raccourcir par apocope.

apocope [əˈpɒkəpɪ] *n* apocope *f*.

Apocrypha [əˈpɒkrɪfə] *npl* apocryphes *mpl*.

apocryphal [əˈpɒkrɪfəl] *adj* apocryphe.

apogee [ˈæpəʊdʒiː] *n* apogée *m*.

apolitical [ˌeɪpəˈlɪtɪkəl] *adj* apolitique.

Apollo [əˈpɒləʊ] *n* Apollon *m*.

apologetic [əˌpɒləˈdʒetɪk] *adj smile, look, gesture* d'excuse. **an ~ air** un air de s'excuser; **he was very ~ for not coming** il s'est confondu *or* s'est répandu en excuses de n'être pas venu; **she was very ~ about her mistake** elle s'est beaucoup excusée de son erreur.

apologetically [əˌpɒləˈdʒetɪkəlɪ] *adv* en s'excusant, pour s'excuser.

apologetics [əˌpɒləˈdʒetɪks] *n* (*U*) apologétique *f*.

apologize [əˈpɒlədʒaɪz] *vi* s'excuser. **to ~ to sb for sth** s'excuser de qch auprès de qn, faire *or* présenter des excuses à qn pour qch; **she ~d to them for her son** elle leur a demandé d'excuser la conduite de son fils; **to ~ profusely** se confondre *or* se répandre en excuses.

apology [əˈpɒlədʒɪ] *n* **(a)** (*expression of regret*) excuses *fpl*. **a letter of ~** une lettre d'excuses; **to make an ~ for sth/for having done** s'excuser de qch/d'avoir fait, faire *or* présenter ses excuses pour qch/pour avoir fait; (*for absence at meeting*) **there are apologies from X** X vous prie d'excuser son absence; **to send one's apologies** envoyer une lettre d'excuse; (*more informally*) envoyer un mot d'excuse.

(b) (*defence*: *for beliefs etc*) apologie *f*, justification *f* (*for* de).

(c) (*pej*) **it was an ~ for a bed/speech** en fait de *or* comme lit/discours c'était plutôt minable*; **he gave me an ~ for a smile** il m'a gratifié d'une sorte de grimace qui se voulait être un sourire; **we were given an ~ for a lunch** on nous a servi un casse-croûte minable pompeusement appelé déjeuner, on nous a servi un déjeuner absolument minable*.

apoplectic [ˌæpəˈplektɪk] **1** *adj* apoplectique. (*Med*, *fig*) **~ fit** attaque *f* d'apoplexie. **2** *n* apoplectique *mf*.

apoplexy [ˈæpəpleksɪ] *n* apoplexie *f*.

apostasy [əˈpɒstəsɪ] *n* apostasie *f*.

apostate [əˈpɒstɪt] *adj*, *n* apostat(e) *m(f)*.

apostatize [əˈpɒstətaɪz] *vi* apostasier.

apostle [əˈpɒsl] *n* apôtre *m*. **A~s' Creed** symbole *m* des apôtres, Credo *m*; **to say the A~s' Creed** dire le Credo; **~ spoon** petite cuiller (*décorée d'une figure d'apôtre*).

apostolic [ˌæpəsˈtɒlɪk] *adj* apostolique.

apostrophe [əˈpɒstrəfɪ] *n* (*Gram*, *Literat*) apostrophe *f*.

apostrophize [əˈpɒstrəfaɪz] *vt* apostropher.

apothecary†† [əˈpɒθɪkərɪ] *n* apothicaire†† *m*.

apotheosis [əˌpɒθɪˈəʊsɪs] *n* apothéose *f*.

appal, (*US*) **appall** [əˈpɔːl] *vt* consterner; (*frighten*) épouvanter. **I am ~led at your behaviour** ta conduite me consterne.

Appalachian [ˌæpəˈleɪʃən] *adj*, *n*: **the ~ Mountains, the ~s** les (monts) Appalaches *mpl*.

appalling [əˈpɔːlɪŋ] *adj destruction* épouvantable, effroyable; *ignorance* consternant, navrant.

appallingly [əˈpɔːlɪŋlɪ] *adv* épouvantablement, effroyablement.

apparatus [ˌæpəˈreɪtəs] *n* **(a)** (*equipment*) appareil *m*, dispositif *m*, mécanisme *m*. **camping ~** équipement *m* de camping; **heating ~** appareil de chauffage.

(b) (*Anat*) appareil *m*.

(c) (*Literat*) **critical ~** appareil *m or* apparat *m* critique.

apparel† [əˈpærəl] (*liter*) **1** *n* (*U*) habillement *m*. **2** *vt* vêtir, revêtir.

apparent [əˈpærənt] *adj* **(a)** (*obvious*) évident, apparent, manifeste. **to become ~** apparaître; *V* **heir**. **(b)** (*not real*) apparent, de surface. **in spite of his ~ weakness** malgré son air de faiblesse; **more ~ than real** plus apparent que réel.

apparently [əˈpærəntlɪ] *adv* apparemment, en apparence. **this is ~ the case** il semble que ce soit le cas, c'est paraît-il *or* apparemment le cas.

apparition [ˌæpəˈrɪʃən] *n* (*spirit*, *appearance*) apparition *f*.

appeal [əˈpiːl] **1** *vi* **(a)** (*request publicly*) lancer un appel (*on behalf of* en faveur de, *for sth* pour obtenir qch). **to ~ for the blind** lancer un appel au profit des *or* pour les aveugles; **to ~ for calm** faire un appel au calme; (*Fin*) **to ~ for funds** faire un appel de fonds; **he ~ed for silence** il a demandé le silence; **he ~ed for tolerance** il a demandé à ses auditeurs d'être tolérants; (*Pol*) **to ~ to the country** en appeler au pays.

(b) (*beg*) faire appel *m* (*to* à). **she ~ed to his generosity** elle a fait appel à sa générosité; **to ~ to sb for money/help** demander de l'argent/des secours à qn; **I ~ to you!** je vous le demande instamment!, je vous en supplie!

(c) (*Jur*) interjeter appel, se pourvoir en appel. **to ~ to the supreme court** se pourvoir en cassation; **to ~ against a judgment** appeler d'un jugement; **to ~ against a decision** faire opposition à une décision.

(d) (*attract*) **to ~ to** *[object, idea]* plaire à, attirer, tenter; *[person]* plaire à. **it doesn't ~ to me** cela ne m'intéresse pas, cela ne me dit rien*; **the idea ~ed to him** l'idée l'a séduit; **it ~s to the imagination** cela parle à l'imagination.

2 *n* **(a)** (*public call*) appel *m*. **~ to arms** appel aux armes; (*Comm*, *Fin*) **~ for funds** appel de fonds; **he made a public ~ for the blind** il a lancé un appel au profit des aveugles.

(b) (*supplication*) prière *f*, supplication *f*, appel *m*. **with a look of ~** d'un air suppliant *or* implorant; **~ for help** appel au secours.

(c) (*Jur*) appel *m*, pourvoi *m*. **notice of ~** infirmation *f*; **act of ~** acte *m* d'appel; **with no right of ~** sans appel; **acquitted on ~** acquitté en seconde instance; *V* **lodge, lord**.

(d) (*attraction*) *[person, object]* attrait *m*, charme *m*; *[plan, idea]* intérêt *m*.

3 *cpd*: (*Jur*) **Appeal Court** cour *f* d'appel.

appealing [əˈpiːlɪŋ] *adj* (*moving*) émouvant, attendrissant; *look* pathétique; (*begging*) suppliant, implorant; (*attractive*) attirant, attachant.

appealingly [əˈpiːlɪŋlɪ] *adv* (*V* **appealing**) de façon émouvante; d'un air suppliant; (*charmingly*) avec beaucoup de charme.

appear [əˈpɪəʳ] *vi* **(a)** (*become visible*) *[person, sun etc]* apparaître, se montrer; *[ghost, vision]* apparaître, se manifester (*to sb* à qn).

(b) (*arrive*) arriver, se présenter, faire son apparition (*hum*). **he ~ed from nowhere*** il est apparu comme par miracle *or* comme par un coup de baguette magique.

(c) (*Jur etc*) comparaître. **to ~ before a court** comparaître devant un tribunal; **to ~ on a charge of** être jugé pour; **to ~ for sb** plaider pour qn, représenter qn; **to ~ for the defence/for the accused** plaider pour la défense/pour l'accusé; *V* **fail, failure**.

(d) (*Theat*) **to ~ in 'Hamlet'** jouer dans 'Hamlet'; **to ~ as Hamlet** jouer Hamlet; **to ~ on TV** passer à la télévision.

(e) *[publication]* paraître, sortir, être publié.

(f) (*physical aspect*) paraître, avoir l'air. **they ~ (to be) ill** ils ont l'air malades.

(g) (*on evidence*) paraître (*that* que + *indic*). **he came then? — so it ~s** *or* **so it would ~** il est donc venu? — il paraît que oui; **it ~s that he did say that** il paraît qu'il a bien dit cela (*V also* **h**); **he got the job or so it ~s** *or* **so it would ~** il a eu le poste à ce qu'il paraît, il paraît qu'il a eu le poste; **as will presently ~** comme il paraîtra par la suite, comme on verra bientôt; (*iro*) **it's raining! — so it ~s!** il pleut! — on dirait! (*iro*).

(h) (*by surmise*) sembler (*that* que *gen* + *subj*), sembler bien (*that* que + *indic*), sembler à qn (*that* que + *indic*). **there ~s to be a mistake** il semble qu'il y ait une erreur; **it ~s he did say that** il semble avoir bien dit cela, il semble qu'il ait bien dit cela; **it ~s to me they are mistaken** il me semble qu'ils ont tort; **how does it ~ to you?** qu'en pensez-vous?, que vous en semble-t-il?

appearance [əˈpɪərəns] *n* **(a)** (*act*) apparition *f*, arrivée *f*, entrée *f*. **to make an ~** faire son apparition, se montrer, se présenter; **to make a personal ~** apparaître en personne; **to put in an ~** faire acte de présence.

(b) (*Jur*) **~ before a court** comparution *f* devant un tribunal.

(c) (*Theat*) **since his ~ in 'Hamlet'** depuis qu'il a joué dans 'Hamlet'; **in order of ~** par ordre d'entrée en scène; **his ~ on TV** son passage à la télévision.

(d) *[publication]* parution *f*.

(e) (*look*, *aspect*) apparence *f*, aspect *m*. **to have a good ~** *[object, house]* avoir bon air; *[person]* faire bonne figure; **at first ~** au premier abord, à première vue; **the ~ of the houses** l'aspect des maisons; **his ~ worried us** la mine qu'il avait nous a inquiétés; **~s are deceptive** *or* **deceiving** il ne faut pas se fier aux apparences, les apparences peuvent être trompeuses; **you shouldn't go by ~s** il ne faut pas juger sur l'apparence; **for ~s' sake, (in order) to keep up ~s** pour sauver les apparences, pour la forme; **to put on an ~ of disgust** faire semblant d'être dégoûté; **to all ~s** selon toute apparence.

appease [əˈpiːz] *vt person* calmer, apaiser, rasséréner; *anger* apaiser, calmer; *hunger, thirst* apaiser, assouvir, calmer.

appeasement [əˈpiːzmənt] *n* (*V* **appease**) apaisement *m*, assouvissement *m*; (*Pol*) apaisement, conciliation *f*.

appellant [əˈpelənt] **1** *n* partie appelante, appelant(e) *m(f)*. **2** *adj* appelant.

appellation [ˌæpeˈleɪʃən] *n* appellation *f*, désignation *f*.

append [əˈpend] *vt notes* joindre, ajouter; *document* joindre, annexer; *signature* apposer.

appendage [əˈpendɪdʒ] *n* appendice *m*, prolongement *m*; (*Bio*) appendice.

appendectomy [ˌæpenˈdektəmɪ] *n*, **appendicectomy** [ˌæpendɪˈsektəmɪ] *n* appendicectomie *f*.

appendicitis [əˌpendɪˈsaɪtɪs] *n* appendicite *f*. **was it ~?** c'était une appendicite?

appendix [əˈpendɪks] *n, pl* **appendices** [əˈpendɪsiːz] **(a)** (*Anat*) appendice *m*. **to have one's ~ out** se faire opérer de l'appendicite. **(b)** *[book]* appendice *m*; *[document]* annexe *f*.

appertain [ˌæpəˈteɪn] *vi* (*belong*) appartenir (*to* à); (*form part*) faire partie (*to* de); (*relate*) se rapporter (*to* à), relever (*to* de).

appetite [ˈæpɪtaɪt] *n* appétit *m*. **he has no ~** il n'a pas d'appétit, il n'a jamais faim; **to have a good ~** avoir bon appétit; **to eat with (an) ~** manger de bon appétit; **skiing gives one an ~** le ski ouvre l'appétit; (*fig*) **I have no ~ for this sort of book** je n'ai pas de goût pour ce genre de livre; *V* **spoil**.

appetizer [ˈæpɪtaɪzəʳ] *n* (*drink*) apéritif *m*; (*food*) amuse-gueule* *m inv*.

appetizing [ˈæpɪtaɪzɪŋ] *adj* (*lit, fig*) appétissant.

Appian [ˈæpɪən] *adj*: **~ Way** voie Appienne.

applaud [əˈplɔːd] *vt person, thing* applaudir; (*fig*) *decision, efforts* applaudir à, approuver.

applause [əˈplɔːz] *n* (*U*) applaudissements *mpl*, acclamation *f*. **to win the ~ of** être applaudi *or* acclamé par; **there was loud ~** les applaudissements ont crépité.

apple [ˈæpl] **1** *n* pomme *f*; (*also* **~ tree**) pommier *m*. **he's/it's the ~ of my eye** je tiens à lui/j'y tiens comme à la prunelle de mes yeux; **~ of discord** pomme de discorde; *V* **Adam, cooking, eating**.

2 *cpd*: **apple blossom** fleur *f* de pommier; **apple brandy** eau-de-vie *f* de pommes; (*from Normandy*) calvados *m*; **applecart** voiture *f* de *or* des quatre-saisons (*V* **upset 1a**); **applecore** trognon *m* de pomme; **apple dumpling** pomme *f* au four (*enrobée de pâte brisée*); **apple fritter** beignet *m* aux pommes; (*US*) **applejack** = **apple brandy**; **apple orchard** champ *m* de pommiers, pommeraie *f*; **apple pie** tourte *f* aux pommes (*recouverte de pâte*); (*Brit*) **apple-pie bed** lit *m* en portefeuille; **in apple-pie order** en ordre parfait; **apple sauce** (*Culin*) compote *f* de pommes; (*US**) bobards* *mpl*; **apple turnover** chausson *m* aux pommes.

appliance [əˈplaɪəns] *n* **(a)** appareil *m*; (*smaller*) dispositif *m*, instrument *m*. **electrical ~s** appareils électriques. **(b)** (*Brit: fire engine*) autopompe *f*.

applicability [ˌæplɪkəˈbɪlɪtɪ] *n* applicabilité *f*.

applicable [əˈplɪkəbl] *adj* applicable (*to* à).

applicant [ˈæplɪkənt] *n* (*for job*) candidat(e) *m(f)* (*for a post* à un poste), postulant(e) *m(f)*; (*Jur*) requérant(e) *m(f)*; (*Admin: for money, assistance etc*) demandeur *m*, -euse *f*.

application [ˌæplɪˈkeɪʃən] **1** *n* **(a)** (*request*) demande *f*. **~ for a job** demande d'emploi, candidature *f* à un poste; **on ~** sur demande; **to make ~ to sb for sth** s'adresser à qn pour obtenir qch; **to submit an ~** faire une demande; **details may be had on ~ to X** s'adresser à X pour tous renseignements.

(b) (*putting into effect*) *[law, theory, discovery, treatment etc]* application *f*. **the ~ of a new technique to ...** l'application d'une technique nouvelle à ... .

(c) (*Med, Pharm, Tech etc*) (*act of applying*) application *f*; (*substance applied*) enduit *m*. **the ~ of the ointment was painful** l'application de la pommade a été douloureuse; (*Pharm*) **for external ~ only** réservé à l'usage externe, pour usage externe.

(d) (*diligence*) application *f*, attention *f*.

(e) (*relevancy*) portée *f*, pertinence *f*. **his arguments have no ~ to the present case** ses arguments ne s'appliquent pas au cas présent.

2 *cpd*: **application form** formulaire *m* de demande.

applicator [ˈæplɪkeɪtəʳ] *n* applicateur *m*.

applied [əˈplaɪd] *adj* (*gen, Ling, Math, Sci etc*) appliqué. **~ arts** arts décoratifs; **~ sciences** sciences appliquées.

appliqué [æˈpliːkeɪ] **1** *vt* coudre (*en application*). **2** *n* (*ornament*) application *f*; (*end product; also* **~ work**) travail *m* d'application.

apply [əˈplaɪ] **1** *vt* **(a)** *paint, ointment, dressing* appliquer, mettre (*to* sur). **to ~ heat to sth** (*Tech*) exposer qch à la chaleur; (*Med*) échauffer qch; **to ~ a match to sth** mettre le feu à qch avec une allumette, allumer qch avec une allumette.

(b) *theory* appliquer (*to* à), mettre en pratique *or* en application; *rule, law* appliquer (*to* à). **we can't ~ this rule to you** nous ne pouvons pas appliquer cette règle à votre cas.

(c) to ~ pressure on sth exercer une pression sur qch; **to ~ pressure on sb** faire pression sur qn; (*Aut, Tech*) **to ~ the brakes** actionner les freins, freiner.

(d) to ~ one's mind *or* **o.s. to (doing) sth** s'appliquer à (faire) qch; **to ~ one's attention to** porter *or* fixer son attention sur.

2 *vi* s'adresser, avoir recours (*to sb for sth* à qn pour obtenir qch). **~ at the office/to the manager** adressez-vous au bureau/au directeur; (*on notice*) s'adresser au bureau/au directeur.

apply for *vt fus scholarship, grant, money, assistance* demander. **to apply for a job** faire une demande d'emploi (*to sb* auprès de qn), poser sa candidature pour *or* être candidat à un poste; (*Jur*) **to apply for a divorce** formuler une demande en divorce; *V* **patent**.

apply to *vt fus* s'appliquer à, se rapporter à, se référer à. **this does not apply to you** ceci ne s'applique pas à vous, ceci ne vous concerne pas.

appoint [əˈpɔɪnt] *vt* **(a)** (*fix, decide*) *date, place* fixer, désigner. **at the ~ed time** à l'heure dite *or* convenue; **~ed agent** agent attitré.

(b) (*nominate*) nommer, désigner (*sb to a post* qn à un poste). **to ~ sb manager** nommer qn directeur; **to ~ a new secretary** engager une nouvelle secrétaire.

(c) (†: *order*) prescrire, ordonner (*that* que +*subj*), décider (*that* que +*indic*).

(d) a well-~ed house une maison bien aménagée *or* installée.

appointment [əˈpɔɪntmənt] *n* **(a)** (*arrangement to meet*) rendez-vous *m*; (*meeting*) entrevue *f*. **to make an ~ with sb** donner rendez-vous à qn, prendre rendez-vous avec qn; *[2 people]* **to make an ~** se donner rendez-vous; **to keep an ~** aller à un rendez-vous; **I have an ~ at 10 o'clock** j'ai (un) rendez-vous à 10 heures; (*to caller*) **have you an ~?** avez-vous pris rendez-vous?; **to meet sb by ~** rencontrer qn sur rendez-vous; *V* **break**.

(b) (*selection, nomination*) nomination *f*, désignation *f* (*to a post* à un emploi); (*office assigned*) emploi *m*; poste *m*. **there are still several ~s to be made** il y a encore plusieurs postes à pourvoir; (*Comm*) **'By ~ to Her Majesty the Queen'** 'fournisseur *m* de S.M. la Reine'; (*Press*) **'~s (vacant)'** 'offres *fpl* d'emploi'; **~s bureau** *or* **office** agence *f* *or* bureau *m* de placement.

apportion [əˈpɔːʃən] *vt money* répartir, partager; *land, property* lotir; *blame* répartir. **to ~ sth to sb** assigner qch à qn.

apposite [ˈæpəzɪt] *adj* juste, à propos, pertinent.

apposition [ˌæpəˈzɪʃən] *n* apposition *f*.

appraisal [əˈpreɪzəl] *n* évaluation *f*, estimation *f*, appréciation *f*.

appraise [əˈpreɪz] *vt property, jewellery* évaluer, estimer (la valeur *or* le coût de); *importance* évaluer, estimer; *worth* estimer.

appreciable [əˈpriːʃəbl] *adj* appréciable, sensible.

appreciably [əˈpriːʃəblɪ] *adv* sensiblement, de façon appréciable.

appreciate [əˈpriːʃɪeɪt] **1** *vt* **(a)** (*assess, be aware of*) *object, difficulty* évaluer, estimer; *fact, sb's attitude* se rendre compte de, être conscient de. **to ~ sth at its true value** estimer qch à sa juste valeur; **yes, I ~ that** oui, je sais bien *or* je comprends bien *or* je m'en rends bien compte; **I fully ~ the fact that** je me rends parfaitement compte du fait que; **they did not ~ the danger** ils ne se sont pas rendu compte du danger.

(b) (*value, esteem, like*) *help* apprécier; *music, painting, books* apprécier, goûter; *person* apprécier (à sa juste valeur), faire (grand) cas de.

(c) (*be grateful for*) être sensible à, être reconnaissant de. **we do ~ your kindness/your work/what you have done** nous vous sommes très reconnaissants de votre gentillesse/du travail que vous avez fait/de ce que vous avez fait; **we deeply ~ this honour** nous sommes profondément sensibles à cet honneur; **he felt that nobody ~d him** il ne se sentait pas apprécié à sa juste valeur, il avait le sentiment que personne ne l'appréciait à sa juste valeur.

(d) (*raise in value*) hausser la valeur de.

2 *vi* (*Fin etc*) *[currency]* monter; *[object, property]* prendre de la valeur.

appreciation [əˌpriːʃɪˈeɪʃən] *n* **(a)** (*judgment, estimation*) appréciation *f*, évaluation *f*, estimation *f*; (*Art, Literat, Mus*) critique *f*.

(b) (*gratitude*) reconnaissance *f*. **she smiled her ~** elle a remercié d'un sourire.

(c) (*Fin*) hausse *f*, augmentation *f*, valorisation *f*.

appreciative [əˈpriːʃɪətɪv] *adj person* sensible (*of* à); *comment* élogieux. **to be ~ of good food** apprécier la bonne cuisine; **to cast an ~ glance at a woman** jeter un regard connaisseur *or* admiratif sur une femme.

apprehend [ˌæprɪˈhend] *vt* **(a)** (*arrest*) appréhender, arrêter. **(b)** (*understand*) comprendre, percevoir, concevoir. **(c)** (*fear*) craindre, redouter, appréhender.

apprehension [ˌæprɪˈhenʃən] *n* **(a)** (*fear*) appréhension *f*, inquiétude *f*, crainte *f*. **(b)** (*arrest*) arrestation *f*. **(c)** (*understanding*) compréhension *f*, entendement *m*.

apprehensive [ˌæprɪˈhensɪv] *adj* inquiet (*f* -ète), appréhensif, craintif. **to be ~ for sb's safety** craindre pour la sécurité de qn; **to be ~ of danger** appréhender *or* craindre *or* redouter le danger.

apprehensively [ˌæprɪˈhensɪvlɪ] *adv* avec appréhension, craintivement.

apprentice [əˈprentɪs] **1** *n* apprenti(e) *m(f)*; (*Archit, Mus etc*) élève *mf*. **to place sb as an ~ to** mettre qn en apprentissage chez; **plumber's/joiner's ~** apprenti plombier/menuisier.

2 *vt* mettre *or* placer en apprentissage (*to* chez), placer comme élève (*to* chez). **he is ~d to a joiner** il est en apprentissage chez un menuisier; **he is ~d to an architect** c'est l'élève d'un architecte.

3 *cpd*: **apprentice pilot** élève *mf* pilote; **apprentice plumber** apprenti *m* plombier.

apprenticeship [əˈprentɪʃɪp] *n* apprentissage *m*.

apprise [əˈpraɪz] *vt* informer, instruire, prévenir (*sb of sth* qn de qch), apprendre (*sb of sth* qch à qn). **to be ~d of sth** prendre connaissance de qch.

appro* [ˈæprəʊ] *n* (*Comm abbr of* **approval**) **on ~** à *or* sous condition, à l'essai.

approach [əˈprəʊtʃ] **1** *vi* *[person, vehicle]* (s')approcher; *[date, season, death, war]* approcher, être proche.

2 *vt* **(a)** *place* (s')approcher de, s'avancer vers.

(b) (*fig*) **to ~ a subject** aborder une question; **it all depends on how one ~es it** tout dépend de la façon dont on s'y prend.

(c) to ~ sb about sth s'adresser à qn à propos de qch, parler de qch à qn; **have you ~ed him already?** est-ce que vous lui avez déjà parlé?; **a man ~ed me in the street** un homme m'a abordé dans la rue; **I saw him ~ing me** je l'ai vu qui venait vers moi;

(*fig*) **he is easy/difficult to ~** il est d'un abord facile/difficile, il est d'approche aisée/difficile.

(d) (*approximate to, be near to*) approcher de. **she is ~ing 30** elle approche de la trentaine, elle va sur ses 30 ans; **it was ~ing midnight** il était près de *or* presque minuit; **this ~es perfection** ceci atteint presque à la perfection; **a colour ~ing red** une couleur qui touche au rouge *or* voisine du rouge.

3 *n* **(a)** *[person, vehicle]* approche *f*, arrivée *f*. **the cat fled at his ~** le chat s'est enfui à son approche; **we watched his ~** nous l'avons regardé arriver.

(b) *[date, season, death etc]* approche(s) *f(pl)*. **at the ~ of Easter** à l'approche *or* aux approches de Pâques.

(c) (*fig*) **his ~ to the problem** sa façon d'aborder le problème; **I like his ~ (to it)** j'aime sa façon de s'y prendre; **a new ~ to teaching French** une nouvelle façon d'enseigner le français; **to make ~es to sb** (*Comm etc, gen*) faire des avances *fpl or* des ouvertures *fpl* à qn, faire des démarches *fpl* auprès de qn; (*amorous*) faire des avances à qn; (*Comm, gen*) **to make an ~ to sb** faire une proposition à qn; **he is easy/not easy of ~** il est d'un abord facile/difficile, il est d'approche aisée/difficile; *V also* **3d**.

(d) (*access route*) approche *f*, abord *m*, voie *f* d'accès. **all the ~s to the town were guarded** tous les abords *or* toutes les approches *or* toutes les voies d'accès de la ville étaient gardé(e)s; **a town easy/not easy of ~** une ville d'accès facile/difficile, **the ~ to the top of the hill** le chemin qui mène au sommet de la colline; **the station ~** les abords de la gare.

(e) (*approximation*) ressemblance *f* (*to* à), apparence *f* (*to* de). **some ~ to gaiety** une certaine apparence de gaieté; **it is an ~ to perfection** cela touche à la perfection.

4 *cpd*: (*Aviat*) **approach light** balise *f*; (*Aviat*) **approach lights** balisage *m*; **approach road** (*to city*) voie *f* de dégagement urbain; (*to motorway*) route *f* d'accès, voie *f* de raccordement, bretelle *f*; (*Golf*) **approach shot** approche *f*; (*Aviat*) **approach stage** phase *f* d'approche.

approachable [əˈprəʊtʃəbl] *adj place* accessible, approchable; *person* abordable, approchable, accessible.

approaching [əˈprəʊtʃɪŋ] *adj date, event* prochain, qui (s')approche. **the ~ vehicle** le véhicule venant en sens inverse.

approbation [ˌæprəˈbeɪʃən] *n* approbation *f*. **a nod of ~** un signe de tête approbateur.

appropriate [əˈprəʊprɪɪt] **1** *adj moment, decision, ruling* opportun; *remark* bien venu, opportun, juste; *word* juste, propre; *name* bien choisi; *authority, department* compétent. **~ for** *or* **to** propre à, approprié à; **words/behaviour/a speech ~ to the occasion** paroles/conduite/un discours de circonstance; **it would not be ~ for me to comment** ce n'est pas à moi de faire des commentaires; **he is the ~ person to ask** c'est à lui qu'il faut le demander.

2 [əˈprəʊprɪeɪt] *vt* **(a)** (*take for one's own use*) s'approprier, s'attribuer, s'emparer de.

(b) (*set aside for special use*) *funds* affecter (*to, for* à).

appropriately [əˈprəʊprɪɪtlɪ] *adv speak, comment* avec à-propos, pertinemment; *decide* à juste titre; *design* convenablement. **~ situated** situé au bon endroit, situé où il faut; **~ named** (le) bien nommé, au nom bien choisi.

appropriateness [əˈprəʊprɪɪtnɪs] *n [moment, decision]* opportunité *f*; *[remark]* justesse *f*, à-propos *m*, opportunité; *[word]* justesse.

appropriation [əˌprəʊprɪˈeɪʃən] *n* (*act: also Jur*) appropriation *f*; (*funds assigned*) dotation *f*; (*US Pol*) crédit *m* budgétaire. (*US Pol*) **~ bill** loi *f* de finances.

approval [əˈpruːvəl] *n* approbation *f*, assentiment *m*. (*Comm*) **on ~** à *or* sous condition, à l'essai; **a nod of ~** un signe de tête approbateur; **does it meet with your ~?, has it got your ~?** l'approuvez-vous?, y consentez-vous?, cela a-t-il votre approbation?

approve [əˈpruːv] *vt action, publication, medicine, drug* approuver; *decision* ratifier, homologuer; *request* agréer. **to be ~d by** recueillir *or* avoir l'approbation de; **read and ~d** lu et approuvé; (*Brit* †) **~d school** centre *m* d'éducation surveillée.

approve of *vt fus behaviour, idea* approuver, être partisan de; *person* avoir bonne opinion de. **I don't approve of his conduct** je n'approuve pas sa conduite; **men don't always approve of Women's Lib** les hommes n'approuvent pas toujours le M.L.F.; **I don't approve of this marriage** je suis contre ce mariage; **I don't approve of your decision** je ne peux pas approuver *or* je désapprouve la décision que vous avez prise; **she doesn't approve of smoking/drinking** elle n'approuve pas qu'on fume(*subj*)/boive ; **he approves of being punctual** il est partisan de la ponctualité; **he doesn't approve of me** il n'a pas bonne opinion de moi, il n'approuve pas *or* il désapprouve ma façon d'être; **we approve of our new neighbours** nos nouveaux voisins nous plaisent.

approving [əˈpruːvɪŋ] *adj* approbateur (*f* -trice), approbatif.

approvingly [əˈpruːvɪŋlɪ] *adv* d'un air *or* d'un ton approbateur.

approximate [əˈprɒksɪmɪt] **1** *adj time, date, heat, amount, calculation* approximatif. **a sum ~ to what is needed** une somme voisine *or* proche de celle qui est requise; **figures ~ to the nearest franc** chiffres arrondis au franc près.

2 [əˈprɒksɪmeɪt] *vi* s'approcher, se rapprocher (*to* de). **his account ~s to the truth** son compte rendu est proche de la vérité *or* est à peu près véridique.

approximately [əˈprɒksɪmətlɪ] *adv* approximativement, à peu près, environ.

approximation [əˌprɒksɪˈmeɪʃən] *n* **(a)** (*guess, estimate: also Math, Phys*) approximation *f*. **(b)** (*closeness*) proximité *f* (*to* de).

appurtenance [əˈpɜːtɪnəns] *n* (*gen pl*) installations *fpl*, accessoires *mpl*. **the house and its ~s** (*its outhouses etc*) l'immeuble avec ses dépendances *fpl*; (*Jur: its rights, privileges etc*) l'immeuble avec ses circonstances et dépendances *or* ses appartenances.

apricot [ˈeɪprɪkɒt] **1** *n* abricot *m*; (*also* **~ tree**) abricotier *m*. **2** *cpd*: **apricot jam** confiture *f* d'abricots; **apricot tart** tarte *f* aux abricots.

April [ˈeɪprəl] **1** *n* avril *m*; *for phrases V* **September. 2** *cpd*: **April fool** (*person*) victime *f* d'un poisson d'avril; (*joke*) poisson d'avril; **to make an April fool of sb** faire un poisson d'avril à qn; **April Fools' Day** le premier avril; **April showers** ≃ giboulées *fpl* de mars.

apron [ˈeɪprən] *n* **(a)** (*garment*) tablier *m*. (*fig*) **tied to his mother's ~ strings** pendu aux jupes de sa mère. **(b)** (*Aviat*) aire *f* de stationnement. **(c)** (*Tech*) tablier *m*. **(d)** (*Theat: also* **~ stage**) avant-scène *f*.

apropos [ˌæprəˈpəʊ] **1** *adv* à propos, opportunément. **~ of** à propos de. **2** *adj* opportun, (fait) à propos.

apse [æps] *n* abside *f*.

apt [æpt] *adj* **(a)** (*inclined, tending*) *thing* susceptible (*to do* de faire), sujet (*to sth* à qch); *person* enclin, porté, disposé (*to sth* à qch, *to do* à faire). **he is ~ to be late** (*usually is*) il a tendance à être en retard, (*preferably is*) il est enclin *or* porté *or* disposé à être en retard; **one is ~ to believe that ...** on croit volontiers que ..., on a tendance à croire que ... .

(b) (*likely*) **am I ~ to find him in at this time?** ai-je une chance de le trouver chez lui à cette heure-ci?; **he's ~ to be out in the afternoons** il a tendance à ne pas être chez lui l'après-midi, il lui arrive souvent d'être sorti l'après-midi.

(c) (*appropriate*) *remark, comment, reply* approprié, juste, pertinent.

(d) (*gifted*) *pupil* doué, intelligent.

aptitude [ˈæptɪtjuːd] *n* aptitude *f* (*for* à), disposition *f* (*for* pour). **to have an ~ for learning** avoir des dispositions pour l'étude; **he shows great ~** il promet beaucoup; **~ test** test *m* (d'aptitude).

aptly [ˈæptlɪ] *adv answer* pertinemment, avec justesse; *behave* avec propos, à propos. **~ enough, he arrived just then** il est arrivé, fort à propos, juste à ce moment-là; (*iro*) comme par hasard, il est arrivé juste à ce moment-là (*iro*).

aptness [ˈæptnɪs] *n* **(a)** (*suitability*) *[remark etc]* à-propos *m*, justesse *f*. **(b)** (*giftedness*) = **aptitude.**

aqualung [ˈækwəlʌŋ] *n* scaphandre *m* autonome.

aquamarine [ˌækwəməˈriːn] **1** *n* (*stone*) aigue-marine *f*; (*colour*) bleu-vert *m inv*. **2** *adj* bleu-vert *inv*.

aquanaut [ˈækwənɔːt] *n* scaphandrier *m*, plongeur *m*.

aquaplane [ˈækwəpleɪn] **1** *n* aquaplane *m*. **2** *vi* **(a)** (*Sport*) faire de l'aquaplane. **(b)** (*Aut*) faire de l'aquaplaning *m*.

aquarium [əˈkwɛərɪəm] *n* aquarium *m*.

Aquarius [əˈkwɛərɪəs] *n* (*Astron*) le Verseau.

aquatic [əˈkwætɪk] *adj animal, plant* aquatique; (*Sport*) nautique.

aquatint [ˈækwətɪnt] *n* aquatinte *f*.

aqueduct [ˈækwɪdʌkt] *n* aqueduc *m*.

aqueous [ˈeɪkwɪəs] *adj* aqueux.

aquiline [ˈækwɪlaɪn] *adj nose* aquilin, en bec d'aigle; *profile* aquilin.

Aquinas [əˈkwaɪnəs] *n*: **St Thomas ~** saint Thomas d'Aquin.

Arab [ˈærəb] **1** *n* **(a)** Arabe *mf*; *V* **street. (b)** (*also* **~ horse**) (cheval *m*) arabe *m*. **2** *adj* arabe.

arabesque [ˌærəˈbesk] *n* arabesque *f*.

Arabia [əˈreɪbɪə] *n* Arabie *f*.

Arabian [əˈreɪbɪən] *adj* arabe, d'Arabie. **~ Desert** désert *m* d'Arabie; **~ Gulf** golfe *m* Arabique; **the ~ Nights** les Mille et Une Nuits; **~ Sea** mer *f* d'Arabie.

Arabic [ˈærəbɪk] **1** *n* (*Ling*) arabe *m*. **2** *adj* arabe. **~ numerals** chiffres *mpl* arabes; *V* **gum**[2].

Arabist [ˈærəbɪst] *n* arabisant(e) *m(f)*.

arable [ˈærəbl] *adj* arable, cultivable. **~ farming** culture *f*.

arachnid [əˈræknɪd] *n*: **~s** arachnides *mpl*.

arbiter [ˈɑːbɪtəʳ] *n* arbitre *m*, médiateur *m*, -trice *f*.

arbitrarily [ˈɑːbɪtrərəlɪ] *adv* arbitrairement.

arbitrary [ˈɑːbɪtrərɪ] *adj* arbitraire.

arbitrate [ˈɑːbɪtreɪt] **1** *vt* arbitrer, juger, trancher. **2** *vi* décider en qualité d'arbitre, arbitrer.

arbitration [ˌɑːbɪˈtreɪʃən] *n* (*also Ind*) arbitrage *m*. **to go to ~** recourir à l'arbitrage; **~ tribunal** instance chargée d'arbitrer les conflits sociaux; *V* **refer.**

arbitrator [ˈɑːbɪtreɪtəʳ] *n* arbitre *m*, médiateur *m*, -trice *f*.

arboreal [ɑːˈbɔːrɪəl] *adj shape* arborescent; *animal, technique* arboricole.

arbour, (*US*) **arbor** [ˈɑːbəʳ] *n* tonnelle *f*, charmille† *f*.

arc [ɑːk] **1** *n* arc *m*.

2 *cpd*: **arc lamp, arc light** lampe *f* à arc; (*Cine, TV*) sunlight *m*; **arc welding** soudure *f* à l'arc voltaïque.

3 *vi* décrire un arc (de cercle). **the rocket ~ed down into the sea** la fusée a décrit un arc avant de retomber dans la mer.

arcade [ɑːˈkeɪd] *n* (*series of arches*) arcade *f*, galerie *f*; (*shopping precinct*) passage *m*, galerie marchande.

Arcadia [ɑːˈkeɪdɪə] *n* Arcadie *f*.

Arcadian [ɑːˈkeɪdɪən] **1** *adj* arcadien, d'Arcadie. **2** *n* Arcadien(ne) *m(f)*.

Arcady [ˈɑːkədɪ] *n* Arcadie *f*.

arch[1] [ɑːtʃ] **1** *n* **(a)** (*Archit*) (*in church etc*) arc *m*, cintre *m*, voûte *f*; *[bridge etc]* arche *f*. **~way** voûte (d'entrée), porche *m*, (*longer*) passage voûté.

(b) (*Anat*) arcade *f*; *[foot]* cambrure *f*, voûte *f* plantaire; *V* **fallen.**

2 *vi* former voûte, être en forme d'arche, s'arquer. **~ed window** fenêtre cintrée.

3 *vt* arquer, cambrer. **~ed foot/back** pied/dos cambré; **the cat ~es his back** le chat fait le gros dos.

arch[2] [ɑːtʃ] *adj glance, person* malicieux, coquin.
arch[3] [ɑːtʃ] *pref* archi ... . **~-enemy** ennemi *m* par excellence, ennemi numéro un; **the A~-enemy** Satan *m*; **~ hypocrite** grand hypocrite; **~ liar** fieffé menteur; **~-priest** archiprêtre *m*; **~ traitor** traître *m* insigne; **~ villain** scélérat achevé, parfait scélérat; **the ~ villain** le principal scélérat.
archaeological, (*US*) **archeological** [ˌɑːkɪəˈlɒdʒɪkəl] *adj* archéologique.
archaeologist, (*US*) **archeologist** [ˌɑːkɪˈɒlədʒɪst] *n* archéologue *mf.*
archaeology, (*US*) **archeology** [ˌɑːkɪˈɒlədʒɪ] *n* archéologie *f.*
archaic [ɑːˈkeɪɪk] *adj* archaïque.
archaism [ˈɑːkeɪɪzəm] *n* archaïsme *m.*
archangel [ˈɑːkˌeɪndʒəl] *n* archange *m.* **the A~ Michael** l'archange Michel, saint Michel archange.
archbishop [ˈɑːtʃˈbɪʃəp] *n* archevêque *m.*
archbishopric [ɑːtʃˈbɪʃəprɪk] *n* archevêché *m.*
archdeacon [ˈɑːtʃˈdiːkən] *n* archidiacre *m.*
archdiocese [ˈɑːtʃˈdaɪəsɪs] *n* archidiocèse *m.*
archduchess [ˈɑːtʃˈdʌtʃɪs] *n* archiduchesse *f.*
archduchy [ˈɑːtʃˈdʌtʃɪ] *n* archiduché *m.*
archduke [ˈɑːtʃˈdjuːk] *n* archiduc *m.*
archeological [ˌɑːkɪəˈlɒdʒɪkəl] *adj* (*US*) = **archaeological.**
archeologist [ˌɑːkɪˈɒlədʒɪst] *n* (*US*) = **archaeologist.**
archeology [ˌɑːkɪˈɒlədʒɪ] *n* (*US*) = **archaeology.**
archer [ˈɑːtʃəʳ] *n* archer *m.*
archery [ˈɑːtʃərɪ] *n* tir *m* à l'arc.
archetypal [ˈɑːkɪtaɪpəl] *adj* archétype.
archetype [ˈɑːkɪtaɪp] *n* archétype *m.*
Archimedes [ˌɑːkɪˈmiːdiːz] *n* Archimède *m.*
archipelago [ˌɑːkɪˈpelɪgəʊ] *n, pl* **~s** *or* **~es (a)** archipel *m.* **(b)** (*Geog*) **the A~** la mer Égée.
archiphoneme [ˌɑːkɪˈfəʊniːm] *n* archiphonème *m.*
architect [ˈɑːkɪtekt] *n* architecte *m*; (*fig*) architecte, artisan *m*; *V* **naval.**
architectural [ˌɑːkɪˈtektʃərəl] *adj* architectural.
architecture [ˈɑːkɪtektʃəʳ] *n* architecture *f.*
architrave [ˈɑːkɪtreɪv] *n* (*Archit*) architrave *f*; *[door, window]* encadrement *m.*
archives [ˈɑːkaɪvz] *npl* archives *fpl.*
archivist [ˈɑːkɪvɪst] *n* archiviste *mf.*
archness [ˈɑːtʃnɪs] *n* malice *f.*
arctic [ˈɑːktɪk] **1** *adj* (*Geog*) **A~** arctique; (*fig: very cold*) glacial. **2** *n*: **the A~** les régions *fpl* arctiques, l'Arctique *m.* **3** *cpd*: **Arctic Circle** cercle *m* Arctique; **Arctic Ocean** océan *m or* mer *f* Arctique.
ardent [ˈɑːdənt] *adj* ardent, passionné, fervent. **to be an ~ admirer of** être un fervent admirateur de.
ardently [ˈɑːdəntlɪ] *adv* ardemment, avec ardeur, avec ferveur.
ardour, (*US*) **ardor** [ˈɑːdəʳ] *n* ardeur *f*, ferveur *f.*
arduous [ˈɑːdjʊəs] *adj work* ardu, difficile, laborieux; *road* ardu, raide; *hill* raide, escarpé.
arduously [ˈɑːdjʊəslɪ] *adv* péniblement, laborieusement.
arduousness [ˈɑːdjʊəsnɪs] *n* difficulté *f*, dureté *f.*
are [ɑːʳ, əʳ] *V* **be.**
area [ˈɛərɪə] **1** *n* **(a)** (*surface measure*) aire *f*, superficie *f.* **this field has an ~ of 800 square metres** ce champ a une superficie de 800 m^2 *or* a 800 m^2 de superficie, l'aire de ce champ est de 800 m^2.
(b) (*region*) région *f*; (*Mil, Pol*) (*large*) territoire *m*; (*smaller*) secteur *m*, zone *f.* **the London ~** la région londonienne *or* de Londres; **in the whole ~** dans toute l'étendue du pays *or* de la région; *V* **sterling.**
(c) (*fig*) *[knowledge, enquiry]* domaine *m*, champ *m.* **the ~s of disagreement** les zones *fpl* de désaccord; **in this ~** à ce propos.
(d) (*Brit, also* (*US*) **~way**: *courtyard*) courette *f* en contrebas (*sur la rue*).
(e) (*part of room*) **dining ~** coin *m* salle-à-manger; **sleeping ~** coin chambre.
2 *cpd*: **area manager** directeur régional; **area office** agence régionale.
arena [əˈriːnə] *n* arène *f.* (*fig*) **to enter the ~** descendre dans l'arène, entrer en lice; (*fig*) **the political ~** l'arène politique.
aren't [ɑːnt] = **are not, am not;** *V* **be.**
Argentina [ˌɑːdʒənˈtiːnə] *n* Argentine *f.*
Argentine [ˈɑːdʒəntaɪn] **1** *n* **(a)** (*Geog*) **the ~** l'Argentine *f.* **(b)** = **Argentinian. 2** *adj* argentin.
Argentinian [ˌɑːdʒənˈtɪnɪən] **1** *n* Argentin(e) *m(f).* **2** *adj* argentin.
argon [ˈɑːgɒn] *n* argon *m.*
Argonaut [ˈɑːgənɔːt] *n* Argonaute *m.*
argosy [ˈɑːgəsɪ] *n* (*liter*) galion *m* (*de commerce*).
arguable [ˈɑːgjʊəbl] *adj* discutable, contestable. **it is ~ that** on peut soutenir que.
arguably [ˈɑːgjʊəblɪ] *adv*: **he is ~ the worst president ever known** on peut soutenir que c'est le pire président qu'on ait jamais vu.
argue [ˈɑːgjuː] **1** *vi* **(a)** (*dispute, quarrel*) se disputer (*with sb* avec qn, *about sth* au sujet *or* à propos de qch). **they are always arguing** ils se disputent tout le temps; **don't ~!** pas de discussion!; (*to children*) **stop arguing!** arrêtez de vous disputer!
(b) (*reason, debate*) raisonner, argumenter. **to ~ against sb** argumenter contre qn; **he ~d against going** il a donné les raisons qu'il avait de ne pas vouloir y aller; **to ~ about sth** argumenter sur qch; **to ~ from sth** tirer argument de qch.
(c) (*Jur etc*) *[fact, evidence]* parler. **it ~s in favour of** c'est un argument *or* cela témoigne en faveur de; **it ~s well for him** cela parle en sa faveur.
2 *vt* **(a) to ~ sb into/out of doing** persuader/dissuader qn de faire; **to ~ sb into/out of a scheme** persuader/dissuader qn d'adopter un projet; **they ~d me into believing it** à force d'arguments ils sont arrivés à me le faire croire.
(b) (*debate*) *case* discuter, débattre. **a well- ~d case** un cas étayé de bons arguments; **to ~ one's way out of a situation** se sortir d'une situation à force d'argumentation *or* d'arguments; **to ~ the toss*** discuter le coup*.
(c) (*show evidence of*) dénoter, indiquer. **it ~s a certain lack of feeling** cela dénote *or* indique une certaine insensibilité.
(d) (*maintain*) soutenir, affirmer (*that* que).
argue out *vt sep problem* discuter *or* débattre (à fond).
argument [ˈɑːgjʊmənt] *n* **(a)** (*debate*) discussion *f*, controverse *f*, débat *m.* **it is beyond ~** c'est indiscutable; **you've only heard one side of the ~** tu n'as entendu qu'une seule version de l'affaire *or* de l'histoire; **for ~'s sake** par exemple, à titre d'exemple; **he is open to ~** il est prêt à écouter les arguments; **the decision is open to ~** la décision est sujette à discussion; **it is open to ~ that** on peut soutenir que.
(b) (*dispute*) dispute *f*, discussion *f.* **they have had an ~** ils se sont disputés; (*hum*) **he has had an ~ with a tree** il s'est bagarré* avec un arbre (*hum*).
(c) (*reasons advanced*) argument *m.* **his ~ is that ...** il soutient que ...; **there is a strong ~ in favour of** *or* **for doing** il y a de bonnes raisons pour faire; **there is a strong ~ in favour of his resignation** il y a de bonnes raisons pour qu'il démissionne (*subj*); *V* **line**[1].
(d) (*synopsis*) sommaire *m*, argument *m.*
argumentation [ˌɑːgjʊmənˈteɪʃən] *n* argumentation *f.*
argumentative [ˌɑːgjʊˈmentətɪv] *adj person* raisonneur, ergoteur (*pej*); *book* qui prête à controverse.
argy-bargy* [ˈɑːdʒɪˈbɑːdʒɪ] *n* (*Brit*) discutailleries* *fpl.* **to get caught up in an ~** se laisser entraîner dans des discussions sans fin.
aria [ˈɑːrɪə] *n* aria *f.*
Arian [ˈɛərɪən] **1** *n* Arien(ne) *m(f).* **2** *adj* arien.
Arianism [ˈɛərɪənɪzəm] *n* arianisme *m.*
arid [ˈærɪd] *adj* (*lit*) aride, desséché; (*fig*) aride, ingrat.
aridity [əˈrɪdɪtɪ] *n* (*lit, fig*) aridité *f.*
Aries [ˈɛəriːz] *n* (*Astron*) le Bélier.
aright [əˈraɪt] *adv* bien, correctement, juste. **to set things ~** mettre bon ordre à l'affaire.
arise [əˈraɪz] *pret* **arose,** *ptp* **arisen** [əˈrɪzn] *vi* **(a)** *[difficulty]* survenir, surgir; *[question]* se présenter, se poser; *[cry]* s'élever. **if the question ~s** le cas échéant; **should the need ~** en cas de besoin, si le besoin s'en fait sentir, si besoin il y a; **should the occasion ~** si l'occasion se présente; **a doubt arose** un doute s'est fait jour.
(b) (*result*) résulter, provenir (*from* de). **arising from this, can you say that** à partir de ceci, pouvez-vous dire que.
(c) (†, *liter*) *[person]* se lever; *[sun]* se lever, paraître, poindre (*liter*).
aristocracy [ˌærɪsˈtɒkrəsɪ] *n* aristocratie *f.*
aristocrat [ˈærɪstəkræt] *n* aristocrate *mf.*
aristocratic [ˌærɪstəˈkrætɪk] *adj* aristocratique.
Aristophanes [ˌærɪsˈtɒfəniːz] *n* Aristophane *m.*
Aristotelian [ˌærɪstəˈtiːlɪən] *adj* aristotélicien.
Aristotle [ˈærɪstɒtl] *n* Aristote *m.*
arithmetic [əˈrɪθmətɪk] **1** *n* arithmétique *f.* **2** [ˌærɪθˈmetɪk] *adj* arithmétique.
arithmetical [ˌærɪθˈmetɪkəl] *adj* arithmétique.
arithmetician [əˌrɪθməˈtɪʃən] *n* arithméticien(ne) *m(f).*
ark [ɑːk] *n* (*Hist*) arche *f.* (*Rel*) **A~ of the Covenant** arche d'alliance; (*fig*) **it's out of the ~*** ça date du déluge, c'est antédiluvien*; *V* **Noah.**
arm[1] [ɑːm] **1** *n* **(a)** (*Anat*) bras *m.* **to hold sth/sb in one's ~s** tenir qch/qn dans ses bras; **he had a coat over his ~** il avait un manteau sur le bras; **take my ~** prenez mon bras; **to give one's ~ to sb** donner *or* offrir le bras à qn; (†, *liter*) **to have sb on one's ~** avoir qn à son bras; **on her husband's ~** au bras de son mari; **to take sb in one's ~s** prendre qn dans ses bras; **to put one's ~ round sb** passer son bras autour des épaules de qn; **~ in ~** bras dessus bras dessous; **with ~s wide apart** les bras écartés *or* en croix; **within ~'s reach** à portée de la main; **with folded ~s** les bras croisés; **at ~'s length** à bout de bras; (*fig*) **to keep sb at ~'s length** tenir qn à distance; **with open ~s** à bras ouverts; (*liter*) **in the ~s of Morpheus** dans les bras de Morphée; **the (long) ~ of the law** le bras de la loi; (*fig*) **to have a long ~** avoir le bras long; *V* **babe, chance, open.**
(b) *[river, crane, pick-up]* bras *m*; *[coat etc]* manche *f*; *[armchair]* bras, accoudoir *m.* **~ of the sea** bras de mer.
2 *cpd*: **armband** brassard *m*; (*mourning*) brassard de deuil, crêpe *m*; **armchair** fauteuil *m*; **armchair general** *etc* général *m etc* en chambre; **armhole** emmanchure *f*; **armlet** *V* **armlet; armpit** aisselle *f*; **armrest** accoudoir *m.*
arm[2] [ɑːm] **1** *n* **(a)** (*weapon*) arme *f.* **under ~s** sous les armes; **in ~s** armé; **to ~s!** aux armes!; (*lit, fig*) **to take up ~s against sb/sth** s'insurger contre qn/qch (*lit, fig*); (*fig*) **to be up in ~s against sb/the authorities** être en rébellion ouverte contre qn/les autorités; **to be up in ~s against a decision/the cost of living** *etc* s'élever contre *or* partir en guerre contre une décision/le coût de la vie *etc*; **she was up in ~s about his selfishness** son égoïsme la faisait sortir de ses gonds *or* la mettait hors d'elle-même; **no need to get up in ~s over such a small thing!** pas la peine de te monter *or* t'emballer pour si peu!; *V* **man.**
(b) (*branch of military service*) arme *f*; *V* **fleet**[1].
(c) (*Her*) **~s** armes *fpl*, armoiries *fpl*; *V* **coat.**
2 *cpd*: **arms factory** fabrique *f* d'armes; (*Comm*) **arms manufacturer** fabricant *m* d'armes, armurier *m*; **arms race** course *f* aux armements.

3 *vt* **(a)** *person, nation* armer. (*fig*) **to ~ o.s. with patience** s'armer de patience.

(b) *missile* munir d'une (tête d')ogive; *weapon* armer.

4 *vi* (s')armer, prendre les armes (*against* contre).

Armada [ɑːˈmɑːdə] *n* Armada *f.*

armadillo [ˌɑːməˈdɪləʊ] *n* tatou *m.*

Armageddon [ˌɑːməˈgedn] *n* (*lit*) Armageddon *m*; (*fig*) Armageddon, lutte *f* suprême.

armament [ˈɑːməmənt] *n* **(a)** (*gen pl: fighting strength*) force *f* de frappe. **(b)** (*gen pl: weapons*) **~s** armement *m*, matériel *m* de guerre; **~s race** course *f* aux armements. **(c)** (*U: preparation for war*) armement *m.*

armature [ˈɑːmətjʊəʳ] *n* (*Mil*) (*armour*) armure *f*; (*armour-plating*) blindage *m*; (*Zool*) carapace *f*; (*Elec, Phys*) armature *f*; (*Sculp etc: framework*) armature.

armed [ɑːmd] *adj* (*lit, fig*) armé (*with* de); *missile* muni d'une (tête d') ogive. **~ to the teeth** armé jusqu'aux dents; **~ conflict** conflit armé; **the ~ forces** les (forces) armées *fpl*; **~ neutrality** neutralité armée; **~ robbery** vol *m or* attaque *f* à main armée.

-armed [ɑːmd] *adj ending in cpds*: **long-/short-armed** aux bras longs/courts.

Armenia [ɑːˈmiːnɪə] *n* Arménie *f.*

Armenian [ɑːˈmiːnɪən] **1** *adj* arménien. **2** *n* **(a)** Arménien(ne) *m(f).* **(b)** (*Ling*) arménien *m.*

armful [ˈɑːmfʊl] *n* brassée *f.* **in ~s** à pleins bras; **to have ~s of** avoir plein les bras de.

armistice [ˈɑːmɪstɪs] *n* armistice *m.* (*Brit*) **A~ Day** le onze novembre.

armlet [ˈɑːmlɪt] *n* (*armband*) brassard *m*; (*bracelet*) bracelet *m.*

armorial [ɑːˈmɔːrɪəl] **1** *adj* armorial. **~ bearings** armoiries *fpl.* **2** *n* armorial *m.*

armour, (*US*) **armor** [ˈɑːməʳ] **1** *n* **(a)** (*U*) armure *f.* **in full ~** armé de pied en cap; *V* **suit.**

(b) (*Mil*) (*U: ~-plating*) blindage *m*; (*collective n*) (*vehicles*) blindés *mpl*; (*forces*) forces blindées.

2 *cpd*: **armour-clad** (*Mil*) blindé; (*Naut*) cuirassé, blindé; **armour-piercing** (*Mil*) *mine, gun* antichar; *shell, bullet* perforant; **armour-plate, armour-plating** (*Mil*) blindage *m*; (*Naut*) cuirasse *f*; **armour-plated = armour-clad.**

armourer, (*US*) **armorer** [ˈɑːmərəʳ] *n* armurier *m.*

armoury, (*US*) **armory** [ˈɑːmərɪ] *n* dépôt *m* d'armes, arsenal *m*; (*US: arms factory*) fabrique *f* d'armes, armurerie *f.*

army [ˈɑːmɪ] **1** *n* **(a)** armée *f* (de terre). **to be in the ~** être dans l'armée, être militaire; **to join the ~** s'engager; **to go into the ~** *[professional]* devenir militaire *m* de carrière; *[conscript]* partir au service; *V* **occupation, slang, territorial.**

(b) (*fig*) foule *f*, multitude *f*, armée *f.*

2 *cpd life, nurse, uniform* militaire. **army corps** corps *m* d'armée; **Army List** annuaire *m* militaire, annuaire des officiers de carrière (*armée de Terre*); **army officer** officier *m* (*de l'armée de terre*).

aroma [əˈrəʊmə] *n* arôme *m.*

aromatic [ˌærəʊˈmætɪk] **1** *adj* aromatique. **2** *n* aromate *m.*

arose [əˈrəʊz] *pret of* **arise.**

around [əˈraʊnd] (*phr vb elem*) **1** *adv* **(a)** autour. **all ~** tout autour, de tous côtés; **for miles ~** sur un rayon de plusieurs kilomètres, des kilomètres à l'entour; **for 8 km ~** dans un rayon de 8 km.

(b) (*nearby*) autour, alentour, dans les parages. **he is somewhere ~** il est dans les parages; **to stroll ~** se promener (quelque part) par là; **she'll be ~ soon** elle sera bientôt là *or* ici; **is he ~?*** (est-ce qu')il est là?; **there's a lot of flu ~** il y a beaucoup de grippes en ce moment; **he's been ~*** (*travelled*) il a pas mal roulé sa bosse*; (*experienced*) il n'est pas né d'hier *or* de la dernière pluie.

2 *prep* (*esp US*) **(a)** (*round*) autour de. **to go ~ an obstacle** faire le tour d'un *or* contourner un obstacle; **the country ~ the town** les environs *mpl or* alentours *mpl* de la ville; **the first building ~ the corner** le premier immeuble après le coin; **it's just ~ the corner** (*lit*) c'est juste après le coin; (*fig: very near*) c'est à deux pas (d'ici).

(b) (*about*) **to wander ~ the city** errer dans *or* par toute la ville; **they are somewhere ~ the house** ils sont quelque part dans la maison.

(c) (*approximately*) environ, à peu près. **~ 2 kilos** environ *or* à peu près 2 kilos, 2 kilos environ; **~ 1800** vers *or* aux alentours de 1800; **~ 10 o'clock** vers 10 heures, vers *or* sur les 10 heures.

arouse [əˈraʊz] *vt* **(a)** (*awaken*) *person* réveiller, éveiller. **to ~ sb from his sleep** tirer qn du sommeil.

(b) (*cause*) *suspicion, curiosity etc* éveiller, susciter; *anger* exciter, provoquer; *contempt* appeler.

(c) (*stimulate*) stimuler, réveiller*. **that ~d him to protest** cela l'a poussé à protester; **to ~ sb to an effort** obtenir un effort de qn.

arrack [ˈærək] *n* arac(k) *m.*

arraign [əˈreɪn] *vt* **(a)** *person* (*Jur*) poursuivre en justice, traduire devant un tribunal; (*fig*) accuser, mettre en cause. **(b)** *statement, opinion* attaquer, critiquer, blâmer.

arraignment [əˈreɪnmənt] *n* attaque *f*, critique *f* sévère; (*Jur*) assignation *f.*

arrange [əˈreɪndʒ] **1** *vt* **(a)** (*put in order*) *room* arranger, aménager; *clothing* arranger; *books, objects* ranger, mettre en ordre; *flowers* arranger, disposer. **to ~ one's hair** arranger sa coiffure; **flower arranging** *or* **arrangement** art *m* de faire des bouquets, décoration florale.

(b) (*decide on*) *meeting* arranger, organiser, fixer; *date* fixer; *plans, programme* arrêter, convenir de, s'entendre sur. **to ~ to do** s'arranger pour faire; **it was ~d that** il a été arrangé *or* décidé *or* convenu que +*cond*; **I have something ~d for tonight** j'ai quelque chose de prévu pour ce soir; **to ~ a marriage** faire un mariage; (*Press*) **a marriage has been ~d between X and Y** on nous prie d'annoncer le mariage de X avec *or* et de Y.

(c) (†: *settle*) *dispute* régler, arranger.

(d) (*Mus*) arranger, adapter. **to ~ sth for violin and piano** arranger qch pour violon et piano.

2 *vi* **(a)** (*fix details*) s'arranger, prendre des *or* ses dispositions (*for sb to do* pour que qn fasse). **to ~ for sb's luggage to be sent up** faire monter les bagages de qn.

(b) (*come to agreement*) s'arranger (*with sb about sth* avec qn au sujet de qch), s'entendre (*with sb about sth* avec qn sur qch). **to ~ with sb to do** décider avec qn de faire, s'entendre avec qn pour faire.

arrangement [əˈreɪndʒmənt] *n* **(a)** *[room]* aménagement *m*; *[furniture]* arrangement *m*, disposition *f*; *[flowers, hair clothing]* arrangement; *V* **flower.**

(b) (*agreement*) règlement *m*, arrangement *m.* **to do sth by ~ with sb** s'entendre *or* s'arranger avec qn pour faire qch; **larger sizes by ~** tailles supérieures sur demande; **price by ~** prix *m* à débattre; **to come to an ~ with sb** passer un arrangement *or* faire un compromis avec qn, s'arranger *or* s'entendre avec qn (*to do* pour faire); **by ~ with Covent Garden** avec l'autorisation *f* de Covent Garden.

(c) (*plans, preparations*) **~s** mesures *fpl*, préparatifs *mpl*, dispositions *fpl*; **to make ~s for a holiday** faire des préparatifs pour des vacances, organiser des vacances (à l'avance); **to make ~s for sth to be done** prendre des mesures *or* dispositions pour faire faire qch; **can you make ~s to come tomorrow?** pouvez-vous vous arranger pour venir demain?

(d) (*Mus*) adaptation *f*, arrangement *m.*

arrant [ˈærənt] *adj fool* fini; *liar* fieffé.

array [əˈreɪ] **1** *vt* **(a)** (*Mil*) *troops* déployer, ranger, disposer.

(b) (*liter: clothe*) *person* revêtir (*in* de).

2 *n* **(a)** (*Mil*) rang *m*, ordre *m.* **in battle ~** en ordre de bataille.

(b) (*display*) *[objects]* ensemble impressionnant, collection *f*, étalage *m.*

(c) (*Math etc*) tableau *m.* **~ of figures** tableau de nombres.

(d) (*ceremonial dress*) habit *m* d'apparat; (*fine clothes*) parure *f*, atours *mpl* (*iro*).

arrears [əˈrɪəz] *n* arriéré *m.* **rent in ~** (loyer) arriéré; **to get into ~** s'arriérer; **to be/get in ~ with one's correspondence** avoir/prendre du retard dans sa correspondance.

arrest [əˈrest] **1** *vt* **(a)** *[police etc] suspect* arrêter, appréhender.

(b) *person's attention, interest* retenir, attirer.

(c) *growth, development, progress* (*stop*) arrêter; (*hinder*) entraver; (*retard*) retarder. **measures to ~ inflation** des mesures pour arrêter l'inflation; (*Med*) **to ~ (the course of) a disease** enrayer une maladie; (*Med*) **~ed development** atrophie *f*; (*Psych*) atrophie de la personnalité.

2 *n* **(a)** *[person]* arrestation *f.* **under ~** en état d'arrestation; (*Mil*) aux arrêts; **to put sb under ~** arrêter qn; (*Mil*) mettre qn aux arrêts; **to make an ~** procéder à une arrestation; (*Mil*) **open/close ~** ≃ arrêts *mpl* simples/de rigueur.

(b) (*Jur*) **~ of judgment** suspension *f* d'exécution d'un jugement.

arresting [əˈrestɪŋ] *adj* frappant, saisissant.

arrival [əˈraɪvəl] *n* **(a)** (*U*) *[person, vehicle, letter, parcel]* arrivée *f*; (*Comm*) *[goods in bulk]* arrivage *m.* **on ~** à l'arrivée; (*Rail etc*) **~s and departures** arrivées et départs; **~ platform** quai *m* d'arrivée.

(b) (*person*) arrivant(e) *m(f).* **who was the first ~?** qui est arrivé le premier?; **a new ~** un nouveau venu, une nouvelle venue; (*: *baby*) un(e) nouveau-né(e); **the latest ~** le dernier arrivé.

arrive [əˈraɪv] *vi* **(a)** *[person, vehicle, letter, goods]* arriver. **to ~ at a town** arriver à *or* atteindre une ville; **as soon as he ~s** dès son arrivée; **to ~ (up)on the scene** survenir; **the moment has ~d when we must go** le moment est venu pour nous de partir.

(b) (*succeed in business etc*) arriver, réussir.

arrive at *vt fus decision, solution* aboutir à, parvenir à; *perfection* atteindre. **to arrive at a price** *[one person]* fixer un prix; *[2 people]* se mettre d'accord sur un prix; **they finally arrived at the idea of doing** ils en sont finalement venus à l'idée de faire.

arrogance [ˈærəgəns] *n* arrogance *f*, morgue *f.*

arrogant [ˈærəgənt] *adj* arrogant, plein de morgue.

arrogate [ˈærəʊgeɪt] *vt* **(a)** (*claim unjustly*) *authority, right* revendiquer à tort, s'arroger; *victory* s'attribuer. **to ~ sth to o.s.** s'arroger *or* s'attribuer qch. **(b)** (*attribute unjustly*) attribuer injustement (*sth to sb* qch à qn).

arrow [ˈærəʊ] **1** *n* (*weapon, directional sign*) flèche *f.*

2 *vt item on list etc* cocher; *route, direction* flécher. (*insert*) **to ~ (in)** ajouter (*en marge etc*).

3 *vi [rocket etc]* monter en flèche.

4 *cpd*: **arrowhead** fer *m*, pointe *f* (de flèche); **arrowroot** (*Culin*) arrow-root *m*; (*Bot*) marante *f.*

arse✱ [ɑːs] *n* (*esp Brit*) cul✱ *m.*

arse about✱, **arse around**✱ *vi* déconner✱.

arsenal [ˈɑːsɪnl] *n* arsenal *m.*

arsenic [ˈɑːsnɪk] *n* arsenic *m.* **~ poisoning** empoisonnement *m* à l'arsenic.

arsenical [ɑːˈsenɪkəl] *adj substance* arsenical. **~ poisoning** empoisonnement *m* à l'arsenic.

arson [ˈɑːsn] *n* incendie volontaire *or* criminel.

arsonist [ˈɑːsənɪst] *n* incendiaire *mf.*

art[1] [ɑːt] **1** *n* **(a)** (*U*) art *m.* **~ for ~'s sake** l'art pour l'art; **to study ~** (*gen*) faire des études d'art; (*Univ*) faire les beaux-arts; *V* **work.**

(b) (*human skill*) art *m*, habileté *f.* **the ~ of**

embroidering/embroidery l'art de broder/de la broderie; **to do sth with ~** faire qch avec art *or* habileté; **~s and crafts** artisanat *m*; *V* **black, fine[1], liberal** *etc.*

(c) (*Univ*) **Faculty of A~s** faculté *f* des Lettres (et Sciences Humaines); *V* **bachelor, master.**

(d) (*cunning*) artifice *m*, ruse *f*; (*trick*) stratagème *m*, artifice, ruse. **to use every ~ in order to do** user de tous les artifices pour faire.

2 *cpd*: **art collection** collection *f* de tableaux; **art exhibition** exposition *f* (de peinture *or* de sculpture); **art form** moyen *m* d'expression artistique; **art gallery** (*museum*) musée *m* d'art; (*shop*) galerie *f* (de tableaux *or* d'art); **art paper** papier couché; **art school** école *f* des beaux-arts; (*Univ*) **Arts degree** licence *f* ès lettres; **art student** étudiant(e) *m(f)* des *or* en beaux-arts.

art[2] [ɑːt] (††, *liter*) **thou ~ = you are** *V* **be.**

artefact [ˈɑːtɪfækt] *n* objet fabriqué.

arterial [ɑːˈtɪərɪəl] *adj* **(a)** (*Anat*) artériel. **(b)** (*Rail*) **~ line** grande ligne; (*Aut*) **~ road** route *f* or voie *f* à grande circulation.

arteriosclerosis [ɑːˈtɪərɪəʊsklɪˈrəʊsɪs] *n* artériosclérose *f*.

artery [ˈɑːtərɪ] *n* (*Anat*) artère *f*; (*fig: road*) artère, route *f* or voie *f* à grande circulation.

artesian [ɑːˈtiːzɪən] *n*: **~ well** puits artésien.

artful [ˈɑːtfʊl] *adj* rusé, malin (*f* -igne), astucieux. **he's an ~ one*** c'est un petit malin*; **~ dodger** roublard(e)* *m(f)*.

artfully [ˈɑːtfəlɪ] *adv* (*cunningly*) astucieusement, avec astuce; (*skilfully*) avec adresse, habilement.

artfulness [ˈɑːtfʊlnɪs] *n* (*cunning*) astuce *f*, ruse *f*; (*skill*) adresse *f*, habileté *f*.

arthritic [ɑːˈθrɪtɪk] *adj* arthritique.

arthritis [ɑːˈθraɪtɪs] *n* arthrite *f*; *V* **rheumatoid.**

arthropoda [ɑːˈθrɒpədə] *npl* arthropodes *mpl*.

Arthur [ˈɑːθəʳ] *n* Arthur *m*.

Arthurian [ɑːˈθjʊərɪən] *adj* du roi Arthur, d'Arthur.

artichoke [ˈɑːtɪtʃəʊk] *n* artichaut *m*; *V* **globe, Jerusalem.**

article [ˈɑːtɪkl] **1** *n* **(a)** (*object*) objet *m*; (*Comm*) article *m*, marchandise *f*. **~ of clothing** pièce *f* d'habillement; **~s of clothing** vêtements *mpl*; **~ of food** produit *m* or denrée *f* (alimentaire); **~s of value** objets de valeur.

(b) (*Press*) article *m*; *V* **leading.**

(c) (*Jur etc*) [*treaty, document*] article *m*. **~s of apprenticeship** contrat *m* d'apprentissage; **~ of faith** article de foi; (*Rel*) **the Thirty-Nine A~s** *les trente-neuf articles de foi de l'Église anglicane*; (*US Mil*) **~s of war** code *m* de justice militaire.

(d) (*Gram*) article *m*; *V* **definite.**

2 *vt* **(a)** *apprentice* (*to trade*) mettre en apprentissage (*to* chez); (*to profession*) mettre en stage (*to* chez, auprès de).

(b) (*Jur*) stipuler.

articulate [ɑːˈtɪkjʊlɪt] **1** *adj* **(a)** *speech* bien articulé, net, distinct; *thought* clair, net.

(b) *person* qui s'exprime bien. **to be (very) ~** s'exprimer avec facilité *or* aisance.

(c) (*Anat, Bot*) *limb* articulé.

2 [ɑːˈtɪkjʊleɪt] *vt* **(a)** *word, sentence* articuler.

(b) (*Anat, Bot*) articuler. (*Brit*) **~d lorry** semi-remorque *m*.

3 *vi* articuler.

articulately [ɑːˈtɪkjʊlɪtlɪ] *adv* avec facilité, avec aisance.

articulation [ɑːˌtɪkjʊˈleɪʃən] *n* articulation *f*.

artifact [ˈɑːtɪfækt] *n* = **artefact.**

artifice [ˈɑːtɪfɪs] *n* **(a)** (*will, stratagem*) artifice *m*, ruse *f*, stratagème *m*. **(b)** (*U: cunning*) adresse *f*, art *m*. **(c)** (†: *contrivance*) stratagème *m*.

artificial [ˌɑːtɪˈfɪʃəl] *adj* **(a)** (*synthetic*) *light, flowers* artificiel; (*Comm*) *leather, jewel* synthétique, artificiel. **~ hair** cheveux *mpl* postiches; **~ insemination** insémination artificielle; **~ leg** jambe artificielle; **~ limb** prothèse *f*, membre artificiel; **~ manure** engrais *mpl* chimiques; **~ respiration** respiration artificielle; **~ silk** rayonne *f*, soie artificielle; **~ teeth** fausses dents, prothèse *f* dentaire.

(b) (*affected*) *manner* factice, étudié, artificiel; *tears* feint, factice; *smile* forcé; *person* affecté. **it was a very ~ situation** la situation manquait de spontanéité *or* de naturel.

artificiality [ˌɑːtɪfɪʃɪˈælɪtɪ] *n* manque *m* de naturel.

artificially [ˌɑːtɪˈfɪʃəlɪ] *adv* artificiellement.

artillery [ɑːˈtɪlərɪ] *n* artillerie *f*. **~ man** artilleur *m*; **light ~** artillerie légère; *V* **heavy.**

artisan [ˈɑːtɪzæn] *n* artisan *m*. (*collectively*) **the ~s** l'artisanat *m*.

artist [ˈɑːtɪst] *n* **(a)** (*Art etc, also fig*) artiste *mf*. **(b)** = **artiste.**

artiste [ɑːˈtiːst] *n* (*Cine, Theat, TV*) artiste *mf*; *V* **variety.**

artistic [ɑːˈtɪstɪk] *adj arrangement, activity, sense* artistique; *temperament* artiste. **she is very ~** elle a un sens artistique très développé.

artistically [ɑːˈtɪstɪkəlɪ] *adv* artistiquement, artistement, avec art.

artistry [ˈɑːtɪstrɪ] *n* (*U*) art *m*, talent *m or* goût *m or* génie *m* artistique.

artless [ˈɑːtlɪs] *adj* **(a)** (*without guile*) *person* naturel, ingénu. **~ beauty** beauté naturelle; **~ charm** charme ingénu. **(b)** (*slightly pej: crude*) *object* grossier; *translation* mal fait, lourd.

artlessly [ˈɑːtlɪslɪ] *adv* ingénument.

artlessness [ˈɑːtlɪsnɪs] *n* (*V* **artless**) ingénuité *f*; naturel *m*; grossièreté *f* (d'exécution), lourdeur *f*.

arty* [ˈɑːtɪ] *adj person* qui a le genre artiste *or* bohème; *clothes* de style bohème; *decoration, style* (d'un art) apprêté.

arty-crafty [ˈɑːtɪˈkrɑːftɪ] *adj*, (*US*) **artsy-craftsy** [ˈɑːtsɪˈkrɑːftsɪ] *adj* (*pej*) *object, style* (exagérément) artisanal; *person* qui affiche un genre artiste *or* bohème.

Aryan [ˈɛərɪən] **1** *n* Aryen(ne) *m(f)*. **2** *adj* aryen.

as [æz, əz] **1** *conj* **(a)** (*when, while*) comme, alors que, tandis que, pendant que. **~ she was resting she heard it** tandis qu'elle *or* comme elle se reposait elle l'entendit; **I saw him ~ he came out** je l'ai vu au moment où *or* comme il sortait; **~ a child, she was obedient** (étant) enfant, elle était obéissante; **he got deafer ~ he got older** il devenait plus sourd à mesure qu'il vieillissait *or* en vieillissant.

(b) (*since*) puisque, étant donné que, comme. **~ he has not come, we cannot leave** puisqu'il *or* comme il *or* étant donné qu'il n'est pas arrivé, nous ne pouvons pas partir.

(c) (*in comparisons of equality*) **as ... ~** aussi ... que; **not as** *or* **not so ... ~** pas aussi *or* si ... que; **I am as tall ~ you** je suis aussi grand que vous; **I am not so** *or* **not as tall ~ you** je ne suis pas aussi *or* pas si grand que vous; **is it as difficult ~ that?** est-ce si *or* aussi difficile que ça?; **it's not so** *or* **not as good ~ all that** ce n'est pas si bon que cela; **you hate it as much ~ I do** vous en avez autant horreur que moi; **she is twice as rich ~ her sister** elle est deux fois plus riche que sa sœur; **by day (as well) ~ by night** de jour comme de nuit, le jour comme la nuit; (*frm*) **be so good/kind ~ to help me** soyez assez bon/assez gentil pour m'aider, ayez la bonté/la gentillesse de m'aider; *V* **far, good, long[1], many, much, soon, well[2].**

(d) (*concessive*). **big ~ the box is, it won't hold them all** si grande que soit la boîte elle ne pourra pas les contenir tous; **important ~ the president is ...** pour *or* si important que soit le président ...; **try ~ he would, he couldn't do it** il a eu beau essayer, il n'y est pas arrivé; **be that ~ it may** quoi qu'il en soit.

(e) (*manner*) comme, de même que, ainsi (que). **do ~ you like** faites comme vous voudrez; **a woman dressed ~ a man** une femme vêtue comme un homme *or* habillée en homme; **disguised ~ a woman** déguisé en femme; **m ~ in Marcel** m comme Marcel; **she left ~ (she had) promised** elle est partie comme (elle l'avait) promis; **he came ~ (had been) agreed** il est venu comme (cela avait été) entendu *or* prévu; **~ (is) usual** comme d'habitude, comme à l'ordinaire; **~ often happens** comme il arrive souvent; **the village, nestling ~ it does in the valley** le village, ainsi blotti dans la vallée; (*liter*) **~ the father does, so will the son do** de même que fait le père ainsi fera le fils (*liter*); **knowing him ~ I do** le connaissant comme je le connais; **she is very gifted, ~ is her brother** elle est très douée, comme son frère *or* ainsi que son frère *or* de même que son frère; **France, ~ you know, is ...** la France, comme *or* ainsi que vous le savez, est ...; **~ it were** pour ainsi dire; **~ it is, I can't come** les choses étant ce qu'elles sont, je ne peux pas venir; **leave it ~ it is** laisse ça tel quel *or* tel que*.

(f) (*in the capacity of*) en tant que, en qualité de, comme. **sold ~ a slave** vendu comme esclave; **~ a bachelor he cannot comment** étant donné qu'il est *or* en tant que célibataire il ne peut rien dire là-dessus; (*Theat*) **Olivier ~ Hamlet** Olivier dans le rôle de Hamlet; **Napoleon, ~ a statesman but not ~ a soldier, decided ...** Napoléon, en homme d'État mais pas en soldat, décida ...; **think of her ~ a mother, not ~ a teacher** considère-la comme une mère et non comme un professeur; **~ such** (*in that capacity*) à ce titre, comme tel (*f* telle), en tant que tel; (*in itself*) en soi; **the soldier, ~ such, deserves respect** tout soldat, comme tel, mérite le respect; **the work ~ such is boring but the pay is good** le travail en soi est ennuyeux mais le salaire est bon.

(g) (*after certain vbs*) **to treat sb ~ a child** traiter qn comme un enfant *or* en enfant; **to acknowledge sb ~ leader** reconnaître qn pour chef; *V* **regard, represent** *etc.*

(h) (*in rel clauses following 'same' and 'such'*) **such people ~ knew him** les gens qui le connaissaient; **such a book ~ you gave him** un livre comme celui que tu lui as donné; **the same day ~ last year** le même jour que l'année dernière; **the same woman ~ spoke to me** la femme *or* celle qui m'a parlé; **the same girl ~ I saw yesterday** la même fille que j'ai vue hier; **such a man ~ he is, a man such ~ he is** un homme tel que lui, un homme comme lui; **animals such ~ cats, such animals ~ cats** les animaux tels que les chats, les animaux comme (par exemple) les chats.

(i) ~ if, ~ though comme si, comme; **he walks ~ if he's been drinking** il marche comme s'il avait bu *or* comme quelqu'un qui aurait bu; **he rose ~ if to go out** il s'est levé comme pour sortir; **it was ~ if** *or* **though he had not died** c'était comme s'il n'était pas mort; **it's ~ if** *or* **~ though we were at war** les choses se passent comme si nous étions en guerre.

(j) ~ for, ~ to, ~ regards quant à; **~ for her mother ...** quant à sa mère ...; **to question sb ~ to his intentions** interroger qn sur ses intentions.

(k) so ~ to + *infin* pour, de façon à, afin de + *infin*; **he stood up so ~ to see better** il s'est levé pour mieux voir; **she put it down gently so ~ not to break it** elle l'a posé doucement pour ne pas le casser.

2 *adv* aussi, si. **I am ~ tall as you** je suis aussi grand que vous; **I am not ~ tall as you** je ne suis pas si *or* pas aussi grand que vous; **~ distinct from** contrairement à; *V* **yet.**

asbestos [æzˈbestəs] *n* amiante *f*, asbeste *m*. **~ mat** plaque *f* d'amiante.

asbestosis [ˌæzbesˈtəʊsɪs] *n* asbestose *f*.

ascend [əˈsend] **1** *vi* monter, s'élever (*to* à, jusqu'à); (*in time*) remonter (*to* à). **2** *vt ladder* monter à; *mountain* gravir, faire l'ascension de; *river* remonter; *staircase* monter. **to ~ the throne** monter sur le trône.

ascendancy [əˈsendənsɪ] *n* ascendant *m*, influence *f*, empire *m* (*over* sur).

ascendant [əˈsendənt] **1** *n* (*Astrol, fig*) ascendant *m*. (*Astrol*) **to be in the ~** être à l'ascendant; (*fig*) **his fortunes are in the ~** tout lui sourit (actuellement); (*fig*) **a politician in the ~** un homme politique qui monte.

2 *adj person* dominant; (*Astrol*) ascendant.

ascension [əˈsenʃən] *n* ascension *f*. (*Rel*) **the A~** l'Ascension; **A~ Day** (jour *m or* fête *f* de) l'Ascension.

ascent [ə'sent] *n [mountain etc]* ascension *f*; (*fig: in time*) retour *m*; (*in rank*) montée *f*, avancement *m*.
ascertain [ˌæsə'teɪn] *vt truth* établir; *what happened* établir, s'assurer de, se rendre compte de; *person's age, name, address etc* vérifier. **to ~ that sth is true** s'assurer *or* vérifier que qch est vrai; **when the facts were ~ed** quand les faits ont été vérifiés *or* avérés.
ascertainable [ˌæsə'teɪnəbl] *adj* vérifiable.
ascertainment [ˌæsə'teɪnmənt] *n* constatation *f*, vérification *f*.
ascetic [ə'setɪk] **1** *adj* ascétique. **2** *n* ascète *mf*.
asceticism [ə'setɪsɪzəm] *n* ascétisme *m*.
ascribable [ə'skraɪbəbl] *adj* (*V* **ascribe**) attribuable, imputable (*to* à).
ascribe [ə'skraɪb] *vt virtue, piece of work* attribuer (*to* à); *fault, blame* imputer (*to* à).
ascription [ə'skrɪpʃən] *n* (*V* **ascribe**) attribution *f*, imputation *f* (*to* à).
asdic ['æzdɪk] *n* (*Brit Mil*) asdic *m*.
aseptic [eɪ'septɪk] *adj* aseptique. (*Space*) **~ tank** cuve *f* W.-C.
asexual [eɪ'seksjʊəl] *adj* (*Bot, fig*) asexué.
ash[1] [æʃ] *n* (*Bot: also* **~ tree**) frêne *m*; *V* **mountain** *etc*.
ash[2] [æʃ] **1** *n [fire, coal, cigarette]* cendre *f*. (*of the dead*) **~es** cendres; **to reduce sth to ~es** mettre *or* réduire qch en cendres; (*Rel*) **~es to ~es, dust to dust** tu es poussière et tu retourneras en poussière; (*Cricket*) **the A~es** *trophée fictif des matches Australie-Angleterre*; *V* **sack**[2].
2 *cpd*: **ash-bin** (*for ashes*) cendrier *m* (*d'un four etc*); (*for rubbish*) boîte *f* à ordures, poubelle *f*; **ash blond(e)** blond cendré; **ashcan** = **ash-bin**; **ash-coloured** gris cendré *inv*; **ash pan** cendrier *m* (*de poêle etc*); **ashtray** cendrier *m*; (*Rel*) **Ash Wednesday** mercredi *m* des Cendres.
ashamed [ə'ʃeɪmd] *adj* honteux, confus. **to be** *or* **feel ~, to be ~ of o.s.** avoir honte; **to be ~ of** avoir honte de, rougir de; **I am ~ of her** j'ai honte d'elle, elle me fait honte; **you ought to be ~ (of yourself)** vous devriez avoir honte; **I am ~ to say (that)** à ma honte je dois dire (que); **he was ~ to ask for money** il était embarrassé d'avoir à demander de l'argent.
ashen ['æʃn] *adj* **(a)** (*pale*) *face* terreux, cendreux, plombé; (*greyish*) cendré, couleur de cendre. **(b)** (*of ashwood*) en (bois de) frêne.
ashlar ['æʃləʳ] *n* pierre *f* de taille (*équarrie*); (*smaller*) moellon *m*.
ashore [ə'ʃɔːʳ] *adv* **(a)** (*on land*) à terre. **to go ~** débarquer, descendre à terre; **to set** *or* **put sb ~** débarquer qn. **(b)** (*aground*) échoué, à la côte. **to run ~** s'échouer.
ashy ['æʃɪ] *adj* **(a)** (*ash-coloured*) cendré, couleur de cendre; (*pale*) terreux, cendreux, plombé. **(b)** (*covered with ashes*) couvert de cendres.
Asia ['eɪʃə] *n* Asie *f*. **~ Minor** Asie mineure.
Asian ['eɪʃn], **Asiatic** [ˌeɪsɪ'ætɪk] **1** *adj* asiatique. (*Med*) **Asian flu** grippe *f* asiatique. **2** *n* Asiatique *mf*.
aside [ə'saɪd] (*phr vb elem*) **1** *adv* de côté, à l'écart, à part. **to put sth ~** mettre qch de côté; **can you put it ~ for me?** pouvez-vous me le réserver? *or* me le mettre de côté?; **to turn ~** se détourner (*from* de); **to stand ~** se tenir à l'écart; **to step ~** s'écarter, faire un pas de côté; **to take sb ~** prendre qn à part; (*Jur*) **to set ~ a verdict** casser un jugement; **joking ~** plaisanterie *or* blague* à part; **~ from** à part.
2 *n* (*esp Theat*) aparté *m*. **to say sth in an ~** dire qch en aparté.
asinine ['æsɪnaɪn] *adj* (*pej*) sot (*f* sotte), stupide, idiot.
ask [ɑːsk] **1** *vt* **(a)** (*inquire*) demander. **to ~ sb sth** demander qch à qn; **to ~ sb about sth** interroger *or* questionner *or* poser des questions à qn au sujet de qch, s'informer de qch auprès de qn; **to ~ (sb) a question** poser une question (à qn); **I don't know, ~ your father** je ne sais pas, demande(-le) à ton père; **~ him if he has seen her** demande-lui s'il l'a vue; **don't ~ me!*** allez savoir!*, est-ce que je sais (moi)!*; (*in exasperation*) **I ~ you!*** je vous demande un peu!*; (*keep quiet*) **I'm not ~ing you!*** je ne te demande rien (à toi)!*, je ne te demande pas l'heure qu'il est.*
(b) (*request*) demander, solliciter; (*Comm*) *price* demander. **to ~ sb to do** demander à qn de faire, prier qn de faire; **to ~ that sth be done** demander que qch soit fait; **to ~ sb for sth** demander qch à qn; **to ~ sb a favour, to ~ a favour of sb** demander une faveur à qn, solliciter une faveur de qn; **he ~ed to go on the picnic** il a demandé à se joindre *or* s'il pouvait se joindre au pique-nique; **I don't ~ much from you** je ne t'en demande pas beaucoup; **that's ~ing a lot/too much!** c'est beaucoup/trop (en) demander!; **that's ~ing the impossible** c'est demander l'impossible; (*Comm*) **how much are they ~ing for it?** ils en demandent *or* veulent combien?; (*Comm*) **he is ~ing £20,000 for the house** il demande 20.000 livres *or* veut 20.000 livres pour la maison; (*Comm*) **~ing price** prix *m* de départ, prix demandé au départ.
(c) (*invite*) inviter. **to ~ sb to go to the theatre** inviter qn (à aller) au théâtre; **to ~ sb to lunch** inviter qn à déjeuner; **I was ~ed into the drawing room** on m'a prié d'entrer au salon; **how about ~ing him?** et si on l'invitait?, et si on lui demandait de venir?; **to ~ sb in/out/up** *etc* demander à qn *or* prier qn d'entrer/de sortir/de monter *etc*.
2 *vi* demander. **to ~ about sth** s'informer de qch, se renseigner sur qch; **it's there for the ~ing** il suffit de le demander (pour l'obtenir), on l'a comme on veut.
ask after *vt fus person* demander des nouvelles de. **to ask after sb's health** s'informer de la santé de qn.
ask along *vt sep* inviter; (*to one's home*) inviter (à la maison).
ask back *vt sep* **(a)** (*for a second visit*) réinviter.
(b) (*on a reciprocal visit*) **to ask sb back** rendre son invitation à qn.
ask for *vt fus help, permission, money* demander; *person* demander à voir. **he asked for his pen back** il a demandé qu'on lui rende son stylo; **to ask for the moon** *or* **the sky** demander la lune; **they are asking for trouble*** ils cherchent les ennuis *or* les embêtements*; **she was asking for it!*** elle l'a bien cherché!*, elle ne l'a pas volé!*.
ask in *vt sep* inviter à entrer. **to ask sb in for a drink** inviter qn à (entrer) prendre un verre.
ask out *vt sep* inviter à sortir. **he asked her out to dinner/to see a film** il l'a invitée (à dîner) au restaurant/au cinéma.
askance [ə'skɑːns] *adv* **(a)** (*fig: disapprovingly*) **to look ~ at sb** jeter un coup d'œil désapprobateur *or* un regard torve à qn, regarder qn de travers*; **to look ~ at sb's hat/work** *etc* regarder le chapeau/le travail *etc* de qn d'un œil désapprobateur; **to look ~ at a suggestion** se formaliser d'une suggestion.
(b) (*lit: look sideways at*) **to look ~ at sb/sth** regarder qn/qch de côté.
askew [ə'skjuː] *adv* obliquement, de travers, de guingois*, de traviole*.
aslant [ə'slɑːnt] **1** *adv* de travers, de *or* en biais, obliquement. **2** *prep* en travers de.
asleep [ə'sliːp] **1** *adj* **(a)** (*sleeping*) endormi. **to be ~** dormir, être endormi; **to be fast** *or* **sound ~** dormir profondément *or* d'un sommeil profond *or* à poings fermés. **(b)** (*numb*) *finger etc* engourdi. **2** *adv*: **to fall** *or* **drop ~** s'endormir.
asp[1] [æsp] *n* (*Zool*) aspic *m*.
asp[2] [æsp] *n* (*Bot*) = **aspen.**
asparagus [əs'pærəgəs] *n* (*U*) asperge *f*. **to eat ~** manger des asperges; **~ fern** asparagus *m*.
aspect ['æspekt] *n* **(a)** (*appearance*) aspect *m*, air *m*, mine *f*. **of fierce ~** à la mine *or* à l'aspect féroce.
(b) *[question, subject etc]* aspect *m*, angle *m*, face *f*. **to study every ~ of a question** étudier une question sous toutes ses faces *or* tous ses aspects; **seen from this ~** vu sous cet angle.
(c) *[building etc]* exposition *f*, orientation *f*. **the house has a southerly ~** la maison est exposée *or* orientée au midi.
(d) (*Gram*) aspect *m*.
aspen ['æspən] *n* (*Bot*) tremble *m*. **to shake** *or* **tremble like an ~** trembler comme une feuille.
asperity [æs'perɪtɪ] *n* **(a)** (*U*) *[manner, style, voice]* aspérité *f*; *[person]* rudesse *f*. **(b)** (*gen pl*) *[climate, weather]* rigueur(s) *f(pl)*.
aspersion [əs'pɜːʃən] *n* (*untruthful*) calomnie *f*; (*truthful*) médisance *f*; *V* **cast.**
asphalt ['æsfælt] **1** *n* asphalte *m*. **2** *vt* asphalter. **3** *cpd road* asphalté. **asphalt jungle** jungle asphaltée *or* de béton.
asphyxia [æs'fɪksɪə] *n* asphyxie *f*.
asphyxiate [æs'fɪksɪeɪt] **1** *vt* asphyxier. **2** *vi* s'asphyxier.
asphyxiation [æsˌfɪksɪ'eɪʃən] *n* asphyxie *f*.
aspic ['æspɪk] *n* (*Culin*) gelée *f* (*pour hors d'œuvre*). **chicken in ~** aspic *m* de volaille.
aspidistra [ˌæspɪ'dɪstrə] *n* aspidistra *m*.
aspirant ['æspɪrənt] *n* aspirant(e) *m(f)*, candidat(e) *m(f)* (*to, after* à).
aspirate ['æspərɪt] **1** *n* aspirée *f*. **2** *adj* aspiré. **~ h** h aspiré(e). **3** ['æspəreɪt] *vt* aspirer.
aspiration [ˌæspə'reɪʃən] *n* aspiration *f*.
aspire [əs'paɪəʳ] *vi*: **to ~ after** *or* **to sth** aspirer *or* viser à qch, ambitionner qch; **to ~ to do** aspirer à faire; **to ~ to fame** briguer la célébrité; **to ~ to a second car** ambitionner (d'avoir) une deuxième voiture; **we can't ~ to that*** nos prétentions ne vont pas jusque-là.
aspirin ['æsprɪn] *n* (*substance*) aspirine *f*; (*tablet*) (comprimé *m* d')aspirine.
aspiring [əs'paɪərɪŋ] *adj* ambitieux.
ass[1] [æs] *n* **(a)** âne *m*. **she-~** ânesse *f*; **~'s foal** ânon *m*.
(b) (**pej*) idiot(e) *m(f)*, imbécile *mf*. **he is a perfect ~** il est bête comme ses pieds*; **to make an ~ of o.s.** se rendre ridicule, se conduire comme un idiot *or* imbécile; **don't be an ~!** (*action*) ne fais pas l'imbécile!; (*speech*) ne dis pas de sottises!
ass[2]✱ [æs] *n* (*US*) = **arse.**
assail [ə'seɪl] *vt* (*lit*) attaquer, assaillir; (*fig: with questions etc*) assaillir, accabler, harceler (*with* de); (*gen pass*) *[doubts etc]* assaillir.
assailant [ə'seɪlənt] *n* agresseur *m*, assaillant(e) *m(f)*.
assassin [ə'sæsɪn] *n* (*Pol*) assassin *m*.
assassinate [ə'sæsɪneɪt] *vt* (*Pol*) assassiner.
assassination [əˌsæsɪ'neɪʃən] *n* (*Pol*) assassinat *m*.
assault [ə'sɔːlt] **1** *n* **(a)** (*Mil*) assaut *m*. **taken by ~** emporté *or* pris d'assaut; **to make an ~ on** donner l'assaut à, aller *or* monter à l'assaut de.
(b) (*Jur*) agression *f*. **~ and battery** coups *mpl* et blessures *fpl*, voies *fpl* de fait; (*fig*) **~ on sb's good name** atteinte *f* à la réputation de qn; *V* **indecent.**
2 *vt* **(a)** (*Jur: attack*) se livrer à des voies de fait sur; (*attack sexually*) se livrer à des violences sexuelles sur, violenter. (*fig*) **to ~ people's sensibilities** blesser la sensibilité (des gens).
(b) (*Mil*) attaquer, donner l'assaut à.
3 *cpd*: (*Mil*) **assault course** parcours *m* du combattant.
assay [ə'seɪ] **1** *n* essai *m* (*d'un métal précieux etc*). **2** *vt* **(a)** *mineral, ore* essayer. **(b)** (*††: try*) essayer, tenter (*to do* de faire).
assemblage [ə'semblɪdʒ] *n* **(a)** (*Tech: putting together*) assemblage *m*, montage *m*. **(b)** (*collection*) *[things]* collection *f*, ensemble *m*; *[people]* réunion *f*.
assemble [ə'sembl] **1** *vt objects, ideas* assembler; *people* rassembler, réunir; (*Tech*) *machine* monter, assembler; (*Pol*) *parliament* convoquer. **2** *vi* s'assembler, se réunir, se rassembler.
assembly [ə'semblɪ] **1** *n* **(a)** (*meeting*) assemblée *f*, réunion *f*; (*Scol*) rassemblement *m* des élèves. **in open ~** en séance publique; *V* **unlawful.**

(b) (*Tech: assembling of framework, machine*) assemblage *m*, montage *m*; (*whole unit*) assemblage. **the engine ~** le bloc moteur; *V* **tail.**
(c) (*Mil: call*) rassemblement *m* (*sonnerie*).
(d) (*Pol*) assemblée *f*.
2 *cpd*: **assembly line** chaîne *f* de montage; (*US*) **assemblyman** membre *m* d'une assemblée législative; **assembly room(s)** salle *f* de réunion; *[town hall]* salle des fêtes; **assembly shop** atelier *m* de montage.
assent [ə'sent] **1** *n* assentiment *m*, consentement *m*, acquiescement *m*. **with one ~** d'un commun accord, (*of more than two people*) à l'unanimité; *V* **nod, royal. 2** *vi* consentir, donner son assentiment, acquiescer (*to* à).
assert [ə'sɜːt] *vt* **(a)** (*declare*) affirmer, soutenir; *one's innocence* protester de. **(b)** (*maintain*) *claim* défendre; *one's due* revendiquer. **to ~ o.s.** *or* **one's rights** faire valoir ses droits.
assertion [ə'sɜːʃən] *n* **(a)** (*statement*) affirmation *f*, assertion *f*; *V* **self. (b)** (*U*) défense *f*, revendication *f*.
assertive [ə'sɜːtɪv] *adj tone, manner* assuré; (*pej*) péremptoire.
assess [ə'ses] *vt* **(a)** (*estimate*) estimer, évaluer.
(b) *payment* fixer *or* déterminer le montant de; *income tax* établir; *property* calculer la valeur imposable de; *damages* fixer.
(c) (*fig: evaluate*) *situation* évaluer; *time, amount* estimer, évaluer; *candidate* juger (la valeur de).
assessable [ə'sesəbl] *adj* imposable. (*Fin*) **~ income** (*or* **profits** *etc*) assiette *f* de l'impôt.
assessment [ə'sesmənt] *n* (*V* **assess**) **(a)** estimation *f*, évaluation *f*. **(b)** détermination *f* (du montant), établissement *m* (de l'impôt), calcul *m* (de la valeur imposable). **(c)** (*fig*) évaluation *f*; estimation *f*; *[candidate]* jugement *m* (*of* sur), opinion *f* qu'on se fait (*of* de). **what is his ~ of the situation?** comment voit-il *or* juge-t-il la situation?
assessor [ə'sesəʳ] *n* **(a)** (*Jur*) (juge *m*) assesseur *m*. **(b)** *[property]* expert *m*. (*US*) **~ of taxes** contrôleur *m*, -euse *f* des contributions directes.
asset ['æset] **1** *n* **(a) ~s** biens *mpl*, avoir *m*, capital *m*; (*Comm, Fin, Jur*) actif *m*; **~s and liabilities** actif et passif *m*; **their ~s amount to £1M** ils ont un million de livres à leur actif, leur actif est d'un million de livres; *V* **liquid.**
(b) (*advantage*) avantage *m*, atout *m*. **he is one of our greatest ~s** il constitue un de nos meilleurs atouts.
2 *cpd*: (*Fin*) **asset-stripping** cannibalisation *f* (d'une compagnie).
asseverate [ə'sevəreɪt] *vt* affirmer solennellement; *one's innocence, loyalty* protester de.
asseveration [əˌsevə'reɪʃən] *n* (*V* **asseverate**) affirmation *f* (solennelle), protestation *f*.
assiduity [ˌæsɪ'djuːɪtɪ] *n* assiduité *f*, zèle *m*.
assiduous [ə'sɪdjuəs] *adj* assidu.
assiduously [ə'sɪdjuəslɪ] *adv* assidûment.
assign [ə'saɪn] **1** *vt* **(a)** (*allot*) *task, office* assigner; *date* assigner, fixer; *room* attribuer, affecter, consacrer (*to a purpose* à un usage); *meaning* donner, attribuer, attacher (*to* à). **to ~ a reason for sth** donner la raison de qch; **the event is ~ed to the year 1600** on fait remonter cet événement à 1600.
(b) (*appoint*) *person* nommer, affecter, désigner (*to* à).
(c) (*Jur*) *property, right* céder *or* faire cession de (*to sb* à qn). **she ~ed her whole property to her niece** elle a transféré tous ses biens sur la tête *or* au nom de sa nièce.
2 *n* (†, *frm*) = **assignee.**
assignation [ˌæsɪg'neɪʃən] *n* **(a)** (*appointment*) rendez-vous *m* (*souvent galant*). **(b)** (*allocation*) attribution *f*; *[money]* allocation *f*; *[person, room]* affectation *f*. **(c)** (*Jur*) cession *f*, transfert *m* (de biens).
assignee [ˌæsaɪ'niː] *n* (*Jur*) cessionnaire *mf*.
assignment [ə'saɪnmənt] *n* **(a)** (*task*) mission *f*; (*Scol etc*) devoir *m*, dissertation *f*. **(b)** (*U*) (*allocation*) attribution *f*; *[money]* allocation *f*; *[person, room]* affectation *f*.
assimilate [ə'sɪmɪleɪt] **1** *vt* **(a)** (*absorb*) *food, knowledge* assimiler. **(b)** (*compare*) comparer, assimiler (*to* à), rapprocher (*to* de). **2** *vi* s'assimiler, être assimilé.
assimilation [əˌsɪmɪ'leɪʃən] *n* (*absorption*) assimilation *f*; (*comparison*) assimilation (*to* à), comparaison *f*, rapprochement *m* (*to* avec).
assist [ə'sɪst] **1** *vt* aider, assister (*to do, in doing* à faire), prêter son assistance à (*to do, in doing* pour faire). **to ~ sb in/out** *etc* aider qn à entrer/sortir *etc*; **to ~ one another** s'entr'aider; **~ed by** avec le concours de; (*Travel*) **~ed passage** billet subventionné.
2 *vi* **(a)** (*help*) aider, prêter secours. **to ~ in (doing) sth** aider à (faire) qch.
(b) (*frm*, †: *be present*) assister (*at* à).
assistance [ə'sɪstəns] *n* aide *f*, secours *m*, assistance *f*. **to give ~ to sb** prêter secours à qn; **to come to sb's ~** venir à l'aide *or* au secours de qn, secourir qn; **can I be of ~?** puis-je vous aider?, puis-je vous être utile?
assistant [ə'sɪstənt] **1** *n* aide *mf*, auxiliaire *mf*; (*Scol, US Univ*) assistant(e) *m(f)*; *V* **laboratory, shop** *etc*.
2 *cpd* adjoint, sous-. **assistant librarian** bibliothécaire *mf* adjoint(e), sous-bibliothécaire *mf*; **assistant manager** sous-directeur *m*, directeur adjoint; (*Scol*) **assistant master, assistant mistress** professeur *m* (*de lycée etc*); **assistant priest** vicaire *m*; (*US Univ*) **assistant professor** ≃ maître assistant; **assistant secretary** secrétaire *mf* adjoint(e), sous-secrétaire *mf*; **assistant teacher** instituteur *m*, -trice *f*.
assizes [ə'saɪzɪz] *npl* (*Brit Jur*) assises *fpl*.
associate [ə'səʊʃɪɪt] **1** *adj* uni, associé, allié. (*Jur*) **~ judge** juge *m* assesseur; (*US Univ*) **~ professor** ≃ maître *m* de conférences.
2 *n* **(a)** (*fellow worker*) associé(e) *m(f)*, collègue *mf*; (*Jur: also* **~ in crime**) complice *mf*. **to be ~s in an undertaking** participer conjointement à une entreprise.
(b) *[a society]* membre *m*, associé *m*; *[learned body]* (membre) correspondant *m*.
3 [ə'səʊʃɪeɪt] *vt* **(a)** *ideas, things* associer (*one thing with another* une chose à *or* avec une autre).
(b) to be ~d with sth être associé à qch; **to ~ o.s.** *or* **be ~d with sb in an undertaking** s'associer à *or* avec qn dans une entreprise; **to be ~d with a plot** tremper dans un complot; **I should like to ~ myself with what has been said** je voudrais me faire l'écho de cette opinion; **I don't wish to be ~d with it** je préfère que mon nom ne soit pas mêlé à ceci.
4 *vi [people]* se fréquenter. **to ~ with sb** fréquenter qn, être en relations avec qn.
association [əˌsəʊsɪ'eɪʃən] **1** *n* **(a)** (*U*) association *f* (*with* avec), fréquentation *f* (*with* de).
(b) (*organization*) association *f*, union *f*, société *f*, club *m*. **to form an ~** constituer une société.
(c) (*connection*) *[ideas]* association *f*. **by ~ of ideas** par (une) association d'idées; **full of historic ~s** riche en souvenirs historiques; **this word has nasty ~s** ce mot a des connotations *fpl* désagréables.
2 *cpd*: (*Brit*) **association football** football *m* (*association*).
assonance ['æsənəns] *n* assonance *f*.
assort [ə'sɔːt] **1** *vt* **(a)** (*match*) assortir (*with* à). **(b)** (*classify*) ranger, classer, classifier. **2** *vi [colours etc]* s'assortir, aller bien (*with* avec); *[people]* s'entendre *or* s'accorder (*with* avec).
assorted [ə'sɔːtɪd] *adj* assorti. (*Comm*) **in ~ sizes** dans toutes les tailles; *V* **ill.**
assortment [ə'sɔːtmənt] *n [objects]* collection *f*, assortiment *m*; *[people]* mélange *m*. **this shop has a good ~** ce magasin a un grand choix *or* a une bonne sélection; **an ~ of people/guests** des gens/des invités (très) divers.
assuage [ə'sweɪdʒ] *vt hunger, desire* satisfaire, assouvir; *thirst* étancher, assouvir, calmer; *anger, pain* soulager, apaiser, calmer; *person* apaiser, calmer.
assume [ə'sjuːm] *vt* **(a)** (*accept, presume, suppose*) supposer, présumer, admettre. **assuming this to be true** en admettant *or* supposant que ceci est *or* soit vrai; **~d innocent** présumé innocent; **let us ~ that** admettons que, supposons que +*subj*; **you resigned, I ~** vous avez démissionné, je suppose *or* présume; **you are assuming a lot** vous faites bien des suppositions.
(b) (*take upon o.s.*) *responsibility, burden* assumer, endosser; *power, importance, possession* prendre; *title, right, authority* s'arroger, s'approprier, s'attribuer; *name* adopter, prendre; *air, attitude* adopter, se donner. **to ~ control of** prendre en main la direction de; **to ~ the role of arbiter** assumer le rôle d'arbitre; **to ~ a look of innocence** affecter un air d'innocence; **~d name** nom *m* d'emprunt, pseudonyme *m*; **to go under an ~d name** se servir d'un pseudonyme.
assumption [ə'sʌmpʃən] *n* **(a)** (*supposition*) supposition *f*, hypothèse *f*. **on the ~ that** en supposant que +*subj*; **to go on the ~ that ...** présumer que ... .
(b) *[power etc]* appropriation *f*; *[indifference]* affectation *f*.
(c) (*Rel*) **the A~** l'Assomption *f*; (*public holiday*) le 15 août; **A~ Day** (jour *m or* fête *f* de) l'Assomption.
assurance [ə'ʃʊərəns] *n* **(a)** (*certainty*) assurance *f*, conviction *f*. **in the ~ that** avec la conviction *or* l'assurance que.
(b) (*self-confidence*) confiance *f* en soi, assurance *f*; (*overconfidence*) audace *f*.
(c) (*promise*) garantie *f*, promesse formelle, assurance *f* ferme. **you have my ~ that** je vous promets formellement que.
(d) (*Brit: insurance*) assurance *f*; *V* **life.**
assure [ə'ʃʊəʳ] *vt* **(a)** (*state positively*) affirmer, assurer, certifier; (*convince, reassure*) convaincre, assurer (*sb of sth* qn de qch). **it is so, I (can) ~ you** c'est vrai, je vous assure; *V* **rest.**
(b) (*make certain*) *happiness, success* garantir, assurer.
(c) (*Brit: insure*) assurer.
assured [ə'ʃʊəd] *adj, n* assuré(e) *m(f)* (*of* de).
assuredly [ə'ʃʊərɪdlɪ] *adv* assurément, certainement, sans aucun *or* le moindre doute.
aster ['æstəʳ] *n* aster *m*.
asterisk ['æstərɪsk] **1** *n* astérisque *m*. **2** *vt* marquer d'un astérisque.
astern [ə'stɜːn] *adv* (*Naut*) à *or* sur l'arrière, en poupe. **to go** *or* **come ~** faire machine arrière, battre en arrière, culer; **~ of** à *or* sur l'arrière de.
asteroid ['æstərɔɪd] *n* astéroïde *m*.
asthma ['æsmə] *n* asthme *m*.
asthmatic [æs'mætɪk] *adj, n* asthmatique *(mf)*.
astigmatic [ˌæstɪg'mætɪk] *adj, n* astigmate *(mf)*.
astigmatism [æs'tɪgmətɪzəm] *n* astigmatisme *m*.
astir [ə'stɜːʳ] *adj, adv* (*excited*) agité, en émoi; (*out of bed*) debout *inv*, levé.
astonish [ə'stɒnɪʃ] *vt* étonner; (*stronger*) ahurir, ébahir, stupéfier. **I am ~ed that** cela m'étonne *or* m'ahurit *etc* que +*subj*; (*iro*) **you ~ me!** non! pas possible!, ce n'est pas vrai! (*iro*).
astonishing [ə'stɒnɪʃɪŋ] *adj* étonnant; (*stronger*) ahurissant, stupéfiant. **that is ~, coming from them** venant d'eux, c'est ahurissant *or* étonnant; **with an ~ lack of discretion** avec un incroyable manque de discrétion.
astonishingly [ə'stɒnɪʃɪŋlɪ] *adv* incroyablement. **~ enough** pour étonnant *or* stupéfiant que cela paraisse.
astonishment [ə'stɒnɪʃmənt] *n* étonnement *m*, surprise *f*; (*stronger*) ahurissement *m*, stupéfaction *f*. **look of ~** regard stupéfait; **to my ~** à mon grand étonnement, à ma stupéfaction.
astound [ə'staʊnd] *vt* stupéfier, confondre, abasourdir, ébahir.

I am ~ed j'en reste abasourdi, je n'en crois pas mes yeux *or* mes oreilles, j'en suis sidéré*.

astounding [əˈstaʊndɪŋ] *adj* stupéfiant, ahurissant, époustouflant*.

astrakhan [ˌæstrəˈkæn] **1** *n* astrakan *m.* **2** *cpd coat* d'astrakan.

astral [ˈæstrəl] *adj* astral.

astray [əˈstreɪ] *adv* (*lit, fig*) **to go ~** s'égarer; *V* **lead¹**.

astride [əˈstraɪd] **1** *adj, adv* à califourchon, à cheval. **to ride ~** monter à califourchon. **2** *prep* à califourchon sur, à cheval sur, chevauchant.

astringent [əsˈtrɪndʒənt] **1** *adj* (*Med*) astringent; (*fig*) dur, sévère. **~ lotion** lotion astringente. **2** *n* (*Med*) astringent *m.*

astro ... [ˈæstrəʊ] *pref* astro ... .

astrologer [əsˈtrɒlədʒəʳ] *n* astrologue *m.*

astrological [ˌæstrəˈlɒdʒɪkəl] *adj* astrologique.

astrology [əsˈtrɒlədʒɪ] *n* astrologie *f.*

astronaut [ˈæstrənɔːt] *n* astronaute *mf.*

astronautic(al) [ˌæstrəʊˈnɔːtɪk(əl)] *adj* astronautique.

astronautics [ˌæstrəʊˈnɔːtɪks] *n* (*U*) astronautique *f.*

astronomer [əsˈtrɒnəməʳ] *n* astronome *m.*

astronomic(al) [ˌæstrəˈnɒmɪk(əl)] *adj* (*lit, fig*) astronomique.

astronomy [əsˈtrɒnəmɪ] *n* astronomie *f.*

astrophysics [ˈæstrəʊˈfɪzɪks] *n* (*U*) astrophysique *f.*

astute [əsˈtjuːt] *adj* fin, astucieux, malin (*f* -igne), rusé (*pej*). **how very ~ of you!** quelle finesse! (*also iro*).

astutely [əsˈtjuːtlɪ] *adv* (*shrewdly*) avec finesse, astucieusement; (*pej*) par la ruse.

astuteness [əsˈtjuːtnɪs] *n* (*U*) finesse *f*, sagacité *f*, astuce *f*, ruse *f* (*pej*).

asunder [əˈsʌndəʳ] *adv* (*liter*) (*apart*) écartés, éloignés (*l'un de l'autre*); (*in pieces*) en morceaux.

asylum [əˈsaɪləm] *n* **(a)** (*U*) asile *m*, refuge *m.* **political ~** asile politique. **(b)** (†: *also* **lunatic ~**) asile *m* (d'aliénés)†.

asymmetric(al) [ˌeɪsɪˈmetrɪk(əl)] *adj* asymétrique.

at [æt] (*phr vb elem*) **1** *prep* **(a)** (*place, position*) à, chez. **~ my brother's** chez mon frère; **~ home** à la maison, chez soi; **to dry o.s. ~ the fire** se sécher devant le feu; **to stand ~ the window** se tenir à *or* devant la fenêtre; **~ her heels** sur ses talons; **to come in ~ the door** entrer par la porte; **to find a gap to go in ~** trouver une brèche par où passer *or* entrer; *V* **hand, sea** *etc.*

(b) (*direction*) vers, dans la direction de, sur. **look ~ them** regardez-les; **to aim ~ sb** viser qn; **an attempt ~ escape** une tentative d'évasion; *V* **jump at, laugh at** *etc.*

(c) (*arrival*) à. **to arrive ~ the house** arriver à la maison; (*fig*) **to get ~ the truth** parvenir à la vérité.

(d) (*time, frequency, order*) à. **~ 10 o'clock** à 10 heures; **~ night** la nuit; **3 ~ a time** 3 par 3, 3 à la fois, (*stairs, steps*) 3 à 3; **~ times** de temps en temps, parfois; **~ once** (*immediately*) immédiatement, tout de suite; (*at the same time*) en même temps, à la fois; **~ a time like this** à un moment pareil; **~ my time of life** à mon âge.

(e) (*activity*) en train de, occupé à. **to play ~ football** jouer au football; **pupils ~ play** élèves en récréation; **while we are ~ it*** pendant que nous y sommes *or* qu'on y est*; **let me see you ~ it again!*** que je t'y reprenne!*; **they are ~ it again!*** les voilà qui recommencent!, voilà qu'ils remettent ça!*; **they are ~ it all day*** ils font ça toute la journée.

(f) (*state, condition*) en. **good ~ languages** bon en langues; **~ war** en guerre; *V* **best** *etc.*

(g) (*manner*) **~ full speed** à toute allure; **~ 80 km/h** à 80 km/h; **he drove ~ 80 km/h** il faisait du 80 (à l'heure).

(h) (*cause*) (à cause) de, à propos de. **to be surprised ~ sth** être étonné de qch; **annoyed ~** contrarié par; **angry ~** en colère contre; **~ the request of** à *or* sur la demande *or* la requête de.

(i) (*rate, value, degree*) à, dans, en. **~ best** au mieux; **~ best I cannot arrive before ten** c'est tout au plus si je pourrai arriver à dix heures; **~ first** d'abord; **nothing ~ all** rien du tout; **~ all costs** à tout prix; **~ the rate of** à raison de; **~ any rate** de toute façon; **he sells them ~ 2 francs a kilo** il les vend 2 F le kilo; **let's leave it ~ that** restons-en là!; **~ that rate** à ce compte-là, dans ce cas; **~ a stroke** d'un seul coup; **he's only a teacher and a poor one ~ that** ce n'est qu'un professeur et encore assez piètre.

(j) she's been ~ me the whole day* (*annoying me*) elle m'a harcelé *or* tanné* toute la journée, elle m'a cassé les pieds* toute la journée; **she was (on) ~ her husband to buy a new car*** elle a harcelé son mari pour qu'il achète (*subj*) une nouvelle voiture; **he's always (on) ~ me*** (*nagging me*) il est toujours après moi*.

2 *cpd*: **at-home** réception *f* (*chez soi*).

atavism [ˈætəvɪzəm] *n* atavisme *m.*

atavistic [ˌætəˈvɪstɪk] *adj* atavique.

ataxia [əˈtæksɪə] *n* ataxie *f.*

ataxic [əˈtæksɪk] *adj* ataxique.

ate [et, (*US*) eit] *pret of* **eat**.

atheism [ˈeɪθɪɪzəm] *n* athéisme *m.*

atheist [ˈeɪθɪɪst] *n* athée *mf.*

atheistic(al) [ˌeɪθɪˈɪstɪk(əl)] *adj* athée.

Athenian [əˈθiːnɪən] **1** *n* Athénien(ne) *m(f).* **2** *adj* athénien.

Athens [ˈæθɪnz] *n* Athènes.

athirst [əˈθɜːst] *adj* (*liter: lit, fig*) altéré, assoiffé (*for* de).

athlete [ˈæθliːt] *n* (*in competitions*) athlète *mf.* (*gen*) **he's a fine ~** il est très sportif, c'est un sportif; (*Med*) **~'s foot** mycose *f.*

athletic [æθˈletɪk] *adj activity* athlétique; *meeting* sportif, d'athlétisme; (*gen*) *person* sportif, athlétique. **~ sports** athlétisme *m*; (*US*) **~ supporter** suspensoir *m.*

athletics [æθˈletɪks] *n* (*U*) (*Brit*) athlétisme *m*; (*US*) sport *m.*

athwart [əˈθwɔːt] **1** *adv* en travers; (*Naut*) par le travers. **2** *prep* en travers de; (*Naut*) par le travers de.

Atlantic [ətˈlæntɪk] *adj* atlantique. **the ~ (Ocean)** l'Atlantique *m*, l'océan Atlantique; **~ Charter** Pacte *m* atlantique; **~ liner** transatlantique *m*; (*Can*) **the ~ Provinces** les Provinces *fpl* Atlantiques; *V* **north** *etc.*

Atlantis [ətˈlæntɪs] *n* Atlantide *f.*

atlas [ˈætləs] *n* **(a)** atlas *m.* **(b)** (*Myth*) **A~** Atlas *m*; **A~ Mountains** (monts *mpl* de l')Atlas *m.*

atmosphere [ˈætməsfɪəʳ] *n* (*lit, Phys*) atmosphère *f*; (*fig*) atmosphère, ambiance *f.*

atmospheric [ˌætməsˈferɪk] *adj* atmosphérique.

atmospherics [ˌætməsˈferɪks] *n* (*U: Rad, Telec*) parasites *mpl.*

atoll [ˈætɒl] *n* atoll *m.*

atom [ˈætəm] **1** *n* atome *m*; (*fig*) atome, grain *m*, brin *m*, parcelle *f.* **smashed to ~s** réduit en miettes; **not an ~ of truth** pas l'ombre *f* de la vérité, pas un brin *or* pas un grain de vérité; **if you had an ~ of sense** si tu avais une parcelle *or* un grain *or* un atome de bon sens.

2 *cpd*: **atom-bomb** (*n*) bombe *f* atomique; (*vt*) attaquer à la bombe atomique.

atomic [əˈtɒmɪk] **1** *adj* atomique.

2 *cpd*: **the atomic age** l'ère *f* atomique; **atomic bomb** bombe *f* atomique; **atomic clock** horloge *f* atomique; **atomic energy** énergie *f* atomique *or* nucléaire; **atomic number** nombre *m or* numéro *m* atomique; **atomic physicist/physics** physicien(ne) *m(f)*/physique *f* atomique; **atomic pile** pile *f* atomique; **atomic-powered** (fonctionnant à l'énergie) atomique; **atomic power station** centrale *f* nucléaire; **atomic warfare** guerre *f* nucléaire *or* atomique; **atomic weight** poids *m or* masse *f* atomique.

atomize [ˈætəmaɪz] *vt liquid* pulvériser, atomiser, vaporiser; *solid* pulvériser, atomiser.

atomizer [ˈætəmaɪzəʳ] *n* atomiseur *m.*

atonal [æˈtəʊnl] *adj* atonal.

atone [əˈtəʊn] *vi*: **to ~ for** *sin* expier; *mistake* racheter, réparer.

atonement [əˈtəʊnmənt] *n* (*V* **atone**) expiation *f*; réparation *f.* **to make ~ for a sin** expier un péché; **to make ~ for a mistake** réparer une erreur.

atonic [æˈtɒnɪk] *adj syllable* atone; *muscle* atonique.

atop [əˈtɒp] **1** *adv* en haut, au sommet. **2** *prep* en haut de, au sommet de.

atrocious [əˈtrəʊʃəs] *adj crime* atroce; (*: *very bad*) affreux, horrible, atroce.

atrocity [əˈtrɒsɪtɪ] *n* atrocité *f.*

atrophy [ˈætrəfɪ] **1** *n* atrophie *f.* **2** *vt* atrophier. **3** *vi* s'atrophier.

attach [əˈtætʃ] **1** *vt* **(a)** (*join*) attacher, lier, joindre (*to* à). **document ~ed to a letter** document joint à une lettre; **the ~ed letter** la lettre ci-jointe; **to ~ o.s. to a group** se joindre à un groupe, entrer dans un groupe; (*fig: be fond of*) **to be ~ed to sb/sth** être attaché à qn/qch; **he's ~ed*** (*married etc*) il n'est pas libre.

(b) (*attribute*) *value* attacher, attribuer (*to* à). **to ~ credence to** ajouter foi à; *V* **importance**.

(c) (*Jur*) *person* arrêter, appréhender; *goods, salary* saisir.

(d) (*Mil etc*) *troops* affecter (*to* à). **he is ~ed to the Foreign Office** il est attaché au ministère des Affaires étrangères.

2 *vi* (*rare, frm*) être attribué, être imputé (*to* à). **no blame ~es to you** le blâme ne repose nullement sur vous; **salary ~ing to a post** salaire afférent à un emploi (*frm*), salaire qui s'attache à un emploi.

attaché [əˈtæʃeɪ] *n* attaché(e) *m(f).* **~ case** mallette *f*, attaché-case *m.*

attachment [əˈtætʃmənt] *n* **(a)** (*U*) fixation *f.*

(b) (*for tool etc: accessory*) accessoire *m.*

(c) (*fig: affection*) attachement *m* (*to* à), affection *f* (*to* pour).

(d) (*Jur*) (*on person*) arrestation *f*; (*on goods, salary*) saisie *f* (*on* de).

(e) (*period of practical work, temporary transfer*) stage *m.* **to be on ~** faire un stage (*to* à, auprès de, chez).

attack [əˈtæk] **1** *n* **(a)** (*Mil, fig*) attaque *f* (*on* contre). **to return to the ~** revenir à la charge; **~ on sb's life** attentat *m* contre qn; (*Jur*) attentat à la vie de qn; **to leave o.s. open to ~** prêter le flanc à la critique; **~ is the best form of defence** le meilleur moyen de défense c'est l'attaque; **to be under ~** (*Mil*) être attaqué (*from* par); (*fig*) être en butte aux attaques (*from* de).

(b) (*Med etc*) crise *f*, attaque *f.* **~ of fever** accès *m* de fièvre; **~ of nerves** crise *f* de nerfs; **the repeated ~s of a disease** les assauts répétés d'une maladie *or* d'un mal; *V* **heart**.

2 *vt* **(a)** (*lit, fig*) *person* attaquer; (*Mil*) *enemy* attaquer, assaillir. (*fig*) **to be ~ed by doubts** être assailli par des doutes, être rongé de doutes.

(b) *task, problem* s'attaquer à. **we must ~ poverty** nous devons combattre la pauvreté.

(c) (*Chem*) *metal* attaquer, corroder, ronger. (*fig*) **this idea ~s the whole structure of society** cette idée menace toute la structure de la société.

attackable [əˈtækəbl] *adj* attaquable.

attacker [əˈtækəʳ] *n* attaquant *m*, agresseur *m.*

attain [əˈteɪn] **1** *vt aim, rank, age* atteindre, parvenir à, arriver à; *knowledge* acquérir; *happiness* atteindre à; *one's hopes* réaliser. **2** *vi* (*to perfection etc*) atteindre, toucher (*to* à); (*to power, prosperity*) parvenir (*to* à).

attainable [əˈteɪnəbl] *adj* accessible (*by* à), à la portée (*by* de).

attainment [əˈteɪnmənt] *n* **(a)** (*U*) *[knowledge]* acquisition *f*; *[happiness]* conquête *f*; *[one's hopes]* réalisation *f.* **difficult of ~** difficile à acquérir *or* conquérir, difficile à réaliser.

(b) (*gen pl: achievement*) travail *m*, résultats *mpl* (obtenus).

attempt [əˈtempt] **1** *vt* essayer, tenter (*to do* de faire); *task* entreprendre, s'attaquer à. **~ed escape/murder/theft** *etc* tentative *f* d'évasion/de meurtre/de vol *etc*; **to ~ suicide** essayer *or* tenter de se suicider.

2 *n* **(a)** tentative *f*, entreprise *f*, effort *m*; (*unsuccessful*) essai *m.* **to make one's first ~** faire son coup d'essai, essayer pour la première fois; **to make an ~ at doing** essayer de faire,

s'essayer à faire; **to be successful at the first ~** réussir du premier coup; **he had to give up the ~** il lui a fallu (y) renoncer; **he made no ~ to help us** il n'a rien fait pour *or* il n'a pas essayé de nous aider; **to make an ~ on the record** essayer de battre le record; **he made two ~s at it** il a essayé par deux fois de le faire; **it was a good ~ on his part but ...** il a vraiment essayé mais ... .
(b) (*attack*) attentat *m* (*upon a person's life* contre qn), attaque *f*.

attend [ə'tend] **1** *vt* **(a)** *meeting, lecture* assister à, être à; *classes, course of studies* suivre; *church, school* aller à. **the meeting was well ~ed** il y avait beaucoup de monde à la réunion.
(b) (*serve, accompany*) servir, être au service de; accompagner. *[doctor]* **to ~ a patient** soigner un malade; **~ed by a maid** servi par une *or* accompagné d'une femme de chambre; (*fig*) **method ~ed by great risks** méthode qui comporte de grands risques.
2 *vi* **(a)** (*pay attention*) faire attention.
(b) (*be present*) être présent *or* là. **will you ~?** tu viendras?

attend to *vt fus advice* prêter attention à, être attentif à; *one's task, one's business* s'occuper de. **to attend to a customer** s'occuper d'un client, servir un client; (*in shop*) **are you being attended to?** est-ce qu'on s'occupe de vous?

attend (up)on† *vt fus person* être au service de.

attendance [ə'tendəns] **1** *n* **(a)** service *m*. **he was in ~ on the queen** il escortait la reine, il faisait partie de la suite de la reine; **to be in ~** être de service; (*Med*) **~ on a patient** visites *fpl* à un malade; *V* **dance**.
(b) (*being present*) présence *f*. **regular ~ at** assiduité *f* à; **is my ~ necessary?** est-il nécessaire que je sois présent? *or* là?
(c) (*number of people present*) assistance *f*. **a large ~** une nombreuse assistance; **what was the ~ at the meeting?** combien de gens y avait-il à la réunion?
2 *cpd*: (*Scol*) **attendance officer** ≃ inspecteur *m* (chargé de faire respecter l'obligation scolaire); **attendance record** registre *m* de(s) présence(s).

attendant [ə'tendənt] **1** *n* **(a)** (*servant*) serviteur† *m*, domestique *mf*; *[museum etc]* gardien(ne) *m(f)*.
(b) (†*Med*) médecin *m* (de famille).
(c) (*gen pl: companions, escort*) **~s** membres *mpl* de la suite (*on* de); **the prince and his ~s** le prince et sa suite.
2 *adj* **(a)** (*accompanying*) qui suit *or* accompagne. **the ~ crowd** la foule qui était présente; **the ~ circumstances** les circonstances concomitantes; **old age and its ~ ills** la vieillesse et les infirmités qui l'accompagnent.
(b) (*serving*) au service (*on sb* de qn).

attention [ə'tenʃən] **1** *n* **(a)** (*U: consideration, notice, observation*) attention *f*. **may I have your ~?** puis-je avoir votre attention?; **give me your ~ for a moment** accordez-moi votre attention un instant; **to pay ~ to** faire *or* prêter attention à; **to pay special ~ to** faire tout particulièrement attention à, prêter une attention toute particulière à; **no ~ has been paid to my advice** on n'a fait aucun cas de *or* tenu aucun compte de *or* prêté aucune attention à mes conseils; **it has come to my ~ that** je me suis aperçu que; **for the ~ of X** à l'attention de X; **it needs daily ~** il faut s'en occuper tous les jours; (*Comm etc*) **it shall have my earliest ~** je m'en occuperai dès que possible; **I was all ~*** j'étais tout oreilles; *V* **attract, call, catch, hold.**
(b) (*kindnesses*) **~s** attentions *fpl*, soins *mpl*, prévenances *fpl*; **to show ~s to** avoir des égards pour; **to pay one's ~s to a woman** faire la cour à *or* courtiser une femme.
(c) (*Mil*) garde-à-vous *m*. **to stand at/come to ~** être/se mettre au garde-à-vous; **~!** garde-à-vous!
2 *cpd*: **attention-seeking** destiné à se faire remarquer; **his attention span is too short** il ne peut pas se concentrer assez longtemps.

attentive [ə'tentɪv] *adj* **(a)** prévenant (*to sb* envers qn), empressé (*to sb* auprès de qn). **~ to sb's interests** soucieux des intérêts de qn; **~ to sb's advice** attentif aux conseils de qn; **~ to detail** soucieux du détail, méticuleux.
(b) *audience, spectator* attentif.

attentively [ə'tentɪvlɪ] *adv* attentivement, avec attention. **to listen ~** écouter de toutes ses oreilles *or* attentivement.

attentiveness [ə'tentɪvnɪs] *n* attention *f*, prévenance *f*.

attenuate [ə'tenjʊeɪt] **1** *vt statement* atténuer, modérer; *gas* raréfier; *thread, line* affiner, amincir. **attenuating circumstances** circonstances atténuantes.
2 *vi* s'atténuer, diminuer.
3 *adj* atténué, diminué; (*fig: refined*) adouci, émoussé.

attenuation [əˌtenjʊ'eɪʃən] *n* atténuation *f*, diminution *f*.

attest [ə'test] **1** *vt* **(a)** (*certify*) attester, assurer; (*prove*) démontrer, témoigner de, prouver; (*Jur*) *signature* légaliser. (*Brit Agr*) **~ed herd** cheptel certifié (*comme ayant été tuberculinisé*).
(b) (*put on oath*) faire prêter serment à.
2 *vi* prêter serment; affirmer sous serment (*that* que). **to ~ to sth** se porter garant de qch, témoigner de qch.

attestation [ˌætes'teɪʃən] *n* (*V* **attest**) attestation *f* (*that* que); (*Jur*) attestation, témoignage *m*; *[signature]* légalisation *f*; (*taking oath*) assermentation *f*, prestation *f* de serment.

attic ['ætɪk] *n* grenier *m*. **~ room** mansarde *f*.

Attila ['ætɪlə] *n* Attila *m*.

attire [ə'taɪəʳ] **1** *vt* vêtir, parer (*in* de). **to ~ o.s. in** se parer de. **2** *n* (*U*) vêtements *mpl*, habits *mpl*; (*ceremonial*) tenue *f*; (*hum*) atours *mpl* (*hum*).

attitude ['ætɪtjuːd] *n* **(a)** (*way of standing*) attitude *f*, position *f*. **to strike an ~** poser, prendre une pose affectée *or* théâtrale.
(b) (*way of thinking*) disposition *f*, attitude *f*. **~ of mind** état *m or* disposition d'esprit; **his ~ towards me** son attitude envers moi *or* à mon égard; **I don't like your ~** je n'aime pas l'attitude que vous prenez; **if that's your ~** si c'est ainsi *or* si c'est comme ça* que tu le prends.

attitudinize [ˌætɪ'tjuːdɪnaɪz] *vi* se donner des attitudes, poser, prendre un air *or* un style affecté.

attorney [ə'tɜːnɪ] *n* **(a)** (*Comm, Jur*) mandataire *m*, représentant *m*; *V* **power.** **(b)** (*US: also* **~-at-law**) avoué *m*. **(c)** **A~ General**; *V* **district.** (*Brit*) ≃ Procureur Général; (*US*) ≃ Garde *m* des Sceaux, Ministre *m* de la Justice.

attract [ə'trækt] *vt* **(a)** *[magnet etc]* attirer. (*fig*) **to ~ sb's interest/attention** susciter *or* éveiller *or* attirer l'intérêt/l'attention de qn. **(b)** (*charm, interest*) *[person, subject, quality]* attirer, séduire, exercer une attraction sur. **I am not ~ed to her** elle ne me plaît pas, elle ne m'attire pas.

attraction [ə'trækʃən] *n* **(a)** (*U: Phys, fig*) attraction *f*. **~ of gravity** attraction universelle.
(b) (*often pl: pleasant things*) attractions(s) *f(pl)*, séductions *fpl*, attrait(s) *m(pl)*. **the chief ~ of the party** le clou de la fête; **the chief ~ of this plan** l'attrait principal de ce projet; **one of the ~s of family life** un des charmes de la vie de famille.

attractive [ə'træktɪv] *adj* **(a)** *person, manner* attrayant, séduisant, attirant; *price, sum, idea, plan* intéressant; *prospect, offer* attrayant, intéressant. **a most ~ old house** une très belle vieille maison. **(b)** (*Phys*) attractif.

attractively [ə'træktɪvlɪ] *adv* d'une manière attrayante *or* séduisante. **~ designed garden** jardin agréablement dessiné; **~ dressed woman** femme élégamment habillée.

attributable [ə'trɪbjʊtəbl] *adj* attribuable, imputable (*to* à).

attribute [ə'trɪbjuːt] **1** *vt* attribuer (*sth to sb* qch à qn); *feelings, words* prêter, attribuer (*to sb* à qn); *crime, fault* imputer (*to sb* à qn). **they ~ his failure to his laziness** ils attribuent son échec à sa paresse, ils mettent son échec sur le compte de sa paresse. **2** ['ætrɪbjuːt] *n* **(a)** attribut *m*. **(b)** (*Gram*) épithète *f*.

attribution [ˌætrɪ'bjuːʃən] *n* **(a)** (*U*) attribution *f*, imputation *f*. **~ of sth to a purpose** affectation *f* de qch à un but. **(b) ~s** attributions *fpl*.

attributive [ə'trɪbjʊtɪv] **1** *adj* attributif; (*Gram*) qualificatif. **2** *n* attribut *m*; (*Gram*) épithète *f*.

attrition [ə'trɪʃən] *n* **(a)** usure *f* (*par frottement*). **(b)** (*Rel*) attrition *f*.

attune [ə'tjuːn] *vt* (*lit, fig*) harmoniser, mettre à l'unisson, accorder (*to* avec). **tastes ~d to mine** des goûts en accord avec les miens; **to ~ o.s. to (doing) sth** s'habituer à (faire) qch.

atypical [ˌeɪ'tɪpɪkəl] *adj* atypique.

aubergine ['əʊbəʒiːn] *n* (*esp Brit*) aubergine *f*.

auburn ['ɔːbən] *adj* auburn *inv*.

auction ['ɔːkʃən] **1** *n* (vente *f* aux) enchères *fpl*, (vente à la) criée *f*. **to sell by ~** vendre aux enchères *or* à la criée; **to put sth up for ~** mettre qch dans une vente aux enchères; *V* **Dutch.**
2 *vt* (*also* **~ off**) vendre aux enchères *or* à la criée.
3 *cpd*: **auction bridge** bridge *m* aux enchères; **auction room** salle *f* des ventes; **auction sale** (vente *f* aux) enchères *fpl*, vente à la criée.

audacious [ɔː'deɪʃəs] *adj* (*bold*) audacieux, hardi, intrépide; (*impudent*) effronté, insolent, impudent.

audacity [ɔː'dæsɪtɪ] *n* (*V* **audacious**) audace *f*, hardiesse *f*, intrépidité *f*; effronterie *f*, insolence *f*, impudence *f*. **to have the ~ to say** avoir l'effronterie *or* l'audace de dire.

audibility [ˌɔːdɪ'bɪlɪtɪ] *n* audibilité *f*.

audible ['ɔːdɪbl] *adj sound* audible, perceptible; *voice* intelligible, distinct. **she was hardly ~** on l'entendait à peine; **there was ~ laughter** des rires se firent entendre.

audibly ['ɔːdɪblɪ] *adv* distinctement, clairement.

audience ['ɔːdɪəns] **1** *n* **(a)** (*U*) (*Theat*) spectateurs *mpl*, public *m*; (*of speaker*) auditoire *m*, assistance *f*; (*Mus, Rad*) auditeurs *mpl*; (*TV*) téléspectateurs *mpl*. (*Theat*) **the whole ~ applauded** toute la salle a applaudi; **those in the ~** les gens dans la salle, les membres de l'assistance *or* du public; **there was a big ~** les spectateurs étaient nombreux.
(b) (*formal interview*) audience *f*. **to grant an ~ to** donner *or* accorder audience à; **to receive sb in ~** recevoir qn en audience.
2 *cpd*: **audience chamber** salle *f* d'audience; **audience participation** participation *f* de l'assistance (*à ce qui se passe sur scène*); (*Rad, TV*) **audience rating** indice *m* d'audience; (*Rad, TV*) **audience research** études *fpl* d'opinion.

audio ['ɔːdɪəʊ] *pref* audio-.

audio-visual [ˌɔːdɪəʊ'vɪzjʊəl] *adj* audio-visuel. **~ aids** support audio-visuel, moyens audio-visuels.

audit ['ɔːdɪt] **1** *n* vérification *f* or apurement *m* des comptes. **2** *vt* **(a)** *accounts* vérifier, apurer. **(b)** (*US Univ*) **to ~ a lecture course** assister (à un cours) comme auditeur libre.

audition [ɔː'dɪʃən] **1** *n* **(a)** (*Theat etc*) audition *f*; (*Cine, TV*) (séance *f* d')essai *m*. **to give sb an ~** (*Theat*) auditionner qn; (*Cine*) faire faire un essai à qn.
(b) (*U: power of hearing*) ouïe *f*, audition *f*.
2 *vt* auditionner. **he was ~ed for the part** on lui a fait passer une audition *or* fait faire un essai pour le rôle.
3 *vi* (*Theat*) auditionner. **he ~ed for (the part of) Hamlet** (*Theat*) il a auditionné pour le rôle de Hamlet; (*Cine, TV*) on lui a fait faire un essai pour le rôle de Hamlet.

auditor ['ɔːdɪtəʳ] *n* **(a)** (*listener*) auditeur *m*, -trice *f*. **(b)** (*Comm*) expert-comptable *m*, vérificateur *m* (de comptes). **(c)** (*US Univ*) auditeur *m* libre.

auditorium [ˌɔːdɪ'tɔːrɪəm] *n* salle *f*.

auditory ['ɔːdɪtərɪ] *adj* (*Physiol etc*) auditif.

Augean [ɔː'dʒiːən] *adj*: **the ~ Stables** les écuries *fpl* d'Augias.

auger ['ɔːgəʳ] *n [carpenter]* vrille *f*; (*Tech*) foreuse *f*.

aught [ɔːt] *n* (††, *liter*) quoi que ce soit *m*, quelque chose *m*. **for ~ I know** (pour) autant que je sache; **for ~ I care** pour ce que cela me fait.

augment [ɔːgˈment] **1** *vt* augmenter, accroître; (*Mus*) augmenter. **2** *vi* augmenter, s'accroître, grandir.

augmentation [ˌɔːgmenˈteɪʃən] *n* augmentation *f*, accroissement *m*.

augmentative [ɔːgˈmentətɪv] *adj* augmentatif.

augur [ˈɔːgəʳ] **1** *n* augure *m*. **2** *vi*: **to ~ well/ill (for)** être de bon/de mauvais augure (pour). **3** *vt* (*foretell*) prédire, prévoir; (*be an omen of*) présager. **it ~s no good** cela ne présage *or* n'annonce rien de bon.

augury [ˈɔːgjʊrɪ] *n* (*omen, sign*) augure *m*, présage *m*; (*forecast*) prédiction *f*. **to take the auguries** consulter les augures.

August [ˈɔːgəst] *n* août *m*; *for phrases V* **September**.

august [ɔːˈgʌst] *adj* auguste, imposant, majestueux.

Augustan [ɔːˈgʌstən] *adj* **(a)** d'Auguste. **the ~ Age** (*Latin Literat*) le siècle d'Auguste; (*English Literat*) l'époque *f* néoclassique. **(b) ~ Confession** Confession *f* d'Augsbourg.

Augustine [ɔːˈgʌstɪn] *adj* de l'ordre de saint Augustin, augustinien.

Augustinian [ˌɔːgəsˈtɪnɪən] **1** *adj* augustinien, de (l'ordre de) saint Augustin. **2** *n* augustin(e) *m(f)*.

Augustus [ɔːˈgʌstəs] *n* Auguste *m*.

aunt [ɑːnt] *n* tante *f*. **yes ~** oui ma tante; (*Brit*) **A~ Sally** (*game*) jeu *m* de massacre; (*fig: person*) tête *f* de Turc.

auntie*, aunty* [ˈɑːntɪ] *n* tata*** *f*, tantine*** *f*, tatie*** *f*. (*Brit hum*) **A~** la B.B.C.

au pair [ˈəʊˈpɛə] **1** *adj*: **~ girl** jeune fille *f* au pair. **2** *n, pl* **au pairs** = **~ girl**. **3** *adv* au pair.

aura [ˈɔːrə] *n* (*emanating from a person*) aura *f*, émanation *f*; (*surrounding a place*) atmosphère *f*, ambiance *f*.

aural [ˈɔːrəl] *adj* (*Anat*) auriculaire (*des oreilles*).

auricle [ˈɔːrɪkl] *n* (*Med*) *[ear]* pavillon *m* auriculaire, oreille *f* externe; *[heart]* oreillette *f*.

aurochs [ˈɔːrɒks] *n* aurochs *m*.

aurora borealis [ɔːˈrɔːrəbɔːrɪˈeɪlɪs] *n* aurore boréale.

auscultate [ˈɔːskəlteɪt] *vt* ausculter.

auscultation [ˌɔːskəlˈteɪʃən] *n* auscultation *f*.

auspices [ˈɔːspɪsɪz] *npl* **(a)** (*sponsorship*) auspices *mpl*. **under the ~ of** sous les auspices de. **(b)** (*auguries*) auspices *mpl*. **under favourable ~** sous d'heureux auspices.

auspicious [ɔːsˈpɪʃəs] *adj sign* de bon augure; *occasion, wind* propice, favorable. **to make an ~ start** prendre un bon départ, bien partir.

auspiciously [ɔːsˈpɪʃəslɪ] *adv* favorablement, sous d'heureux auspices. **to start ~** bien partir.

Aussie* [ˈɒzɪ] = **Australian.**

austere [ɒsˈtɪəʳ] *adj person, place* austère, sévère; *thing* austère, dépouillé, sévère.

austerely [ɒsˈtɪəlɪ] *adv* avec austérité, austèrement.

austerity [ɒsˈterɪtɪ] *n* **(a)** (*U*) austérité *f*, sévérité *f*. **days** *or* **years of ~** temps *m* de restrictions. **(b) austerities** austérités *fpl*.

Australasia [ˌɔːstrəˈleɪsjə] *n* Australasie *f*.

Australia [ɒsˈtreɪlɪə] *n* Australie *f*.

Australian [ɒsˈtreɪlɪən] **1** *n* Australien(ne) *m(f)*. **2** *adj* australien.

Austria [ˈɒstrɪə] *n* Autriche *f*.

Austrian [ˈɒstrɪən] **1** *n* Autrichien(ne) *m(f)*. **2** *adj* autrichien.

authentic [ɔːˈθentɪk] *adj* authentique.

authenticate [ɔːˈθentɪkeɪt] *vt* vérifier *or* établir l'authenticité de; *signature* certifier.

authenticity [ˌɔːθenˈtɪsɪtɪ] *n* authenticité *f*.

author [ˈɔːθəʳ] *n* **(a)** (*writer*) écrivain *m*, auteur *m*. **~'s copy** manuscrit *m* de l'auteur. **(b)** *[any work of art]* auteur *m*, créateur *m*; *[plan, trouble etc]* auteur.

authoress [ˈɔːθərɪs] *n* femme *f* auteur *or* écrivain, auteur *m*, écrivain *m*.

authoritarian [ˌɔːθɒrɪˈtɛərɪən] **1** *adj* autoritaire. **2** *n* partisan(e) *m(f)* de l'autorité.

authoritative [ɔːˈθɒrɪtətɪv] *adj opinion, statement, source* autorisé; *person* autoritaire, impérieux; *treatise, edition* qui fait autorité.

authority [ɔːˈθɒrɪtɪ] *n* **(a)** (*power to give orders*) autorité *f*, pouvoir *m*. **I'm in ~ here** c'est moi qui commande ici; **to be in ~ over sb** avoir autorité sur qn; **those in ~** ceux qui nous gouvernent.

(b) (*right*) autorisation *f* (formelle), mandat *m*, pouvoir *m*. **to give sb ~ to do** autoriser qn à faire; **to do sth without ~** faire qch sans autorisation; **she had no ~ to do it** elle n'avait pas qualité pour le faire; **on her own ~** de son propre chef, de sa propre autorité.

(c) (*competence*) **to speak with ~** parler avec compétence *or* autorité.

(d) (*gen pl: person or group*) **authorities** autorités *fpl*, corps constitués, administration *f*; **apply to the proper authorities** adressez-vous à qui de droit *or* aux autorités compétentes; **the health authorities** les services *mpl* de la santé publique; **the public/local/district authorities** les autorités publiques/locales/régionales.

(e) (*person with special knowledge*) autorité *f* (*on* en matière de), expert *m* (*on* en); (*book*) autorité, source *f* (autorisée). *[person, book]* **to be an ~** faire autorité (*on* en matière de); **to consult an ~** consulter un avis autorisé; **I have it on good ~ that ...** je tiens *or* sais de source sûre *or* de bonne source que ...; **what is your ~?** sur quoi vous appuyez-vous (pour dire cela)?; **to say sth on the ~ of Plato** dire qch en invoquant l'autorité de Platon.

authorization [ˌɔːθəraɪˈzeɪʃən] *n* **(a)** (*giving of authority*) autorisation *f* (*of, for* pour, *to do* de faire). **(b)** (*legal right*) pouvoir *m*, mandat *m* (*to do* de faire).

authorize [ˈɔːθəraɪz] *vt action, plan* autoriser; *person* donner pouvoir *or* mandat (*sb to do* à qn de faire), autoriser (*sb to do* qn à faire). **to be ~d to do** avoir qualité pour faire, être autorisé à faire; **~d by custom** sanctionné par l'usage; (*Rel*) **the A~d Version** la Bible de 1611.

authorship [ˈɔːθəʃɪp] *n* **(a)** (*U: origin*) *[book, idea etc]* paternité *f*. **to establish the ~ of a book** identifier l'auteur d'un livre, établir la paternité littéraire d'un ouvrage. **(b)** (*occupation*) profession *f or* métier *m* d'écrivain.

autism [ˈɔːtɪzəm] *n* autisme *m*.

autistic [ɔːˈtɪstɪk] *adj* autistique.

auto [ˈɔːtəʊ] *n* (*US*) voiture *f*, auto *f*.

auto ... [ˈɔːtəʊ] *pref* auto ... .

autobiographic(al) [ˈɔːtəʊˌbaɪəʊˈgræfɪk(əl)] *adj* autobiographique.

autobiography [ˌɔːtəʊbaɪˈɒgrəfɪ] *n* autobiographie *f*.

autocade [ˈɔːtəʊkeɪd] *n* (*US*) cortège *m or* procession *f* d'automobiles.

autocracy [ɔːˈtɒkrəsɪ] *n* autocratie *f*.

autocrat [ˈɔːtəʊkræt] *n* autocrate *m*.

autocratic [ˌɔːtəʊˈkrætɪk] *adj* autocratique.

autocross [ˈɔːtəʊkrɒs] *n* auto-cross *m*.

autocue [ˈɔːtəʊkjuː] *n* (*Brit TV*) autocue *m or f*.

autocycle [ˈɔːtəʊsaɪkl] *n* (*small*) cyclomoteur *m*; (*more powerful*) vélomoteur *m*.

auto-da-fe [ˈɔːtəʊdɑːˈfeɪ] *n, pl* **autos-da-fe** autodafé *m*.

autogiro [ˈɔːtəʊˈdʒaɪərəʊ] *n* autogire *m*.

autograph [ˈɔːtəgrɑːf] **1** *n* autographe *m*. **~ album** livre *m or* album *m* d'autographes. **2** *vt book* dédicacer, autographier, signer.

automat [ˈɔːtəmæt] *n* cafétéria *f* automatique (*munie exclusivement de distributeurs*).

automate [ˈɔːtəmeɪt] *vt* rendre automatique, automatiser.

automatic [ˌɔːtəˈmætɪk] **1** *adj* (*lit, fig*) automatique. (*Aviat*) **on ~ pilot** en pilotage automatique; (*fig*) **to work/drive on ~ pilot*** travailler/conduire comme un automate.

2 *n* (*gun*) automatique *m*; (*Brit Aut*) voiture *f* (à transmission) automatique.

automatically [ˌɔːtəˈmætɪkəlɪ] *adv* (*lit, fig*) automatiquement.

automation [ˌɔːtəˈmeɪʃən] *n* (*technique, system, action*) automatisation *f*; (*state of being automated*) automation *f*.

automaton [ɔːˈtɒmətən] *n, pl* **automata** [ɔːˈtɒmətə] automate *m*.

automobile [ˈɔːtəməbiːl] *n* automobile *f*, auto *f*.

automotive [ˌɔːtəˈməʊtɪv] *adj* **(a)** (*Aut*) *industry, design* (de l')automobile. **(b)** (*self-propelled*) automoteur.

autonomous [ɔːˈtɒnəməs] *adj* autonome.

autonomy [ɔːˈtɒnəmɪ] *n* autonomie *f*.

autopsy [ˈɔːtɒpsɪ] *n* autopsie *f*.

autosuggestion [ˈɔːtəʊsəˈdʒestʃən] *n* autosuggestion *f*.

autumn [ˈɔːtəm] **1** *n* automne *m*. **in ~** en automne. **2** *cpd* d'automne, automnal (*liter*). **autumn leaves** (*dead*) feuilles mortes; (*on tree*) feuilles d'automne.

autumnal [ɔːˈtʌmnəl] *adj* d'automne, automnal (*liter*).

auxiliary [ɔːgˈzɪlɪərɪ] **1** *adj* subsidiaire (*to* à), auxiliaire. (*Aviat*) **~ tank** réservoir *m* supplémentaire; **~ verb** verbe *m* auxiliaire. **2** *n* **(a)** auxiliaire *mf*. **nursing ~** infirmier *m*, -ière *f* auxiliaire, aide-soignant(e) *m(f)*; (*Mil*) **auxiliaries** auxiliaires *mpl*. **(b)** (*Gram*) (verbe *m*) auxiliaire *m*.

avail [əˈveɪl] **1** *vt*: **to ~ o.s. of an opportunity** saisir une occasion, profiter d'une occasion; **to ~ o.s. of a right** user d'un *or* se prévaloir d'un droit; **to ~ o.s. of a service** utiliser un service.

2 *vi* († *liter*) être efficace, servir. **nought ~ed** rien n'y faisait; **it ~ed him nothing** cela ne lui a servi à rien.

3 *n*: **to no ~** sans résultat; **your advice was of no ~** vos conseils n'ont eu aucun effet; **it is of no ~ to complain** il ne sert à rien de protester; **it is of little ~** cela ne sert pas à grand-chose.

availability [əˌveɪləˈbɪlɪtɪ] *n* **(a)** *[material, people]* disponibilité *f*. **(b)** (*US: validity*) validité *f*.

available [əˈveɪləbl] *adj* **(a)** *personnel* disponible; *thing* disponible, utilisable. **to make sth ~ to sb** mettre qch à la disposition de qn; **to try every ~ means** essayer (par) tous les moyens (possibles); **he is not ~ just now** il n'est pas libre en ce moment; (*Press*) **he is not ~ for comment** il se refuse à toute déclaration.

(b) (*US: valid*) valable, valide (*for* pour).

avalanche [ˈævəlɑːnʃ] **1** *n* (*lit, fig*) avalanche *f*. **2** *cpd*: **avalanche precautions** mesures *fpl* de sécurité anti-avalanche; **avalanche warning** alerte *f* aux avalanches; (*on sign*) 'attention (aux) avalanches'. **3** *vi* tomber en avalanche.

avant-garde [ˈævɑ̃ŋˈgɑːd] **1** *n* (*Mil, fig*) avant-garde *f*. **2** *cpd* (*fig*) *dress, style* d'avant-garde, ultramoderne.

avarice [ˈævərɪs] *n* avarice *f*, cupidité *f*.

avaricious [ˌævəˈrɪʃəs] *adj* avare, cupide (*liter*).

Ave Maria [ˈɑːveɪməˈrɪə] *n* avé Maria *m inv*.

avenge [əˈvendʒ] *vt person, thing* venger. **to ~ o.s. on sb** prendre sa revanche sur qn, exercer sa vengeance sur qn.

avenger [əˈvendʒəʳ] *n* vengeur *m*, -eresse *f*.

avenging [əˈvendʒɪŋ] *adj* vengeur (*f* -eresse) (*liter*).

avenue [ˈævənjuː] *n* (*private road with trees*) avenue *f*, allée bordée d'arbres; (*wide road in town*) avenue, boulevard *m*; (*fig*) route *f*. (*fig*) **to explore every ~** considérer toutes les possibilités.

aver [əˈvɜːʳ] *vt* affirmer, déclarer.

average [ˈævərɪdʒ] **1** *n* moyenne *f*. **on ~** en moyenne; **a rough ~** une moyenne approximative; **to take an ~ of results** prendre la moyenne des résultats; **above/below ~** au-dessus/en-dessous de la moyenne; **to do an ~ of 70 km/h** rouler à *or* faire une moyenne de 70 km/h, faire du 70 de moyenne*.

2 *adj* **(a)** *price, figure, height, size* moyen.

(b) (*fig*) moyen. **an ~ pupil** un élève moyen; **the ~ Frenchman** le Français moyen; **a man of ~ abilities** un homme de capacités moyennes.

3 *vt* **(a)** (*find the* ~ *of*) établir *or* faire la moyenne de.
(b) (*reach an* ~ *of*) atteindre la moyenne de. **we** ~ **8 hours' work a day** nous travaillons en moyenne 8 heures par jour; **the sales** ~ **200 copies a month** la vente moyenne est de 200 exemplaires par mois, il se vend en moyenne 200 exemplaires par mois; **we** ~**d 50 the whole way** nous avons fait (du) 50 de moyenne* pendant tout le trajet.

average out 1 *vi*: **our working hours average out at 8 per day** nous travaillons en moyenne 8 heures par jour.
2 *vt sep* faire la moyenne de.

averse [ə'vɜːs] *adj* adversaire, ennemi (*to* de), peu disposé (*to* à). **to be** ~ **to doing** répugner à faire; **he is** ~ **to getting up early** il a horreur de se lever tôt; **I am not** ~ **to an occasional drink** je ne refuse pas un verre de temps en temps, je ne suis pas opposé à un verre de temps à autre.

aversion [ə'vɜːʃən] *n* **(a)** (*U: strong dislike*) aversion *f*, dégoût *m*, répugnance *f*. **he has a strong** ~ **to work** il a horreur de travailler; **he has a strong** ~ **to me** il ne peut pas me souffrir; **I took an** ~ **to it** je me suis mis à détester cela; **I have an** ~ **to X** X m'est antipathique.
(b) (*object of* ~) objet *m* d'aversion; *V* **pet**[1].

avert [ə'vɜːt] *vt danger, accident* prévenir, éviter; *blow* détourner, parer; *suspicion* écarter; *one's eyes, one's thoughts* détourner (*from* de).

aviary ['eɪvɪərɪ] *n* volière *f*.

aviation [ˌeɪvɪ'eɪʃən] *n* aviation *f*. ~ **fuel** kérosène *m*; ~ **industry** aéronautique *f*.

aviator ['eɪvɪeɪtə[r]] *n* aviateur *m*, -trice *f*.

avid ['ævɪd] *adj* avide (*for* de).

avidity [ə'vɪdɪtɪ] *n* avidité *f* (*for* de).

avidly ['ævɪdlɪ] *adv* avidement, avec avidité.

avocado [ˌævə'kɑːdəʊ] *n* (*also* ~ **pear**) avocat *m*; (*tree*) avocatier *m*.

avocation [ˌævəʊ'keɪʃən] *n* **(a)** (*employment*) métier *m*, profession *f*. **(b)** (*minor occupation*) activité *f* de loisir, passe-temps *m* (habituel), violon *m* d'Ingres.

avoid [ə'vɔɪd] *vt person, obstacle* éviter; *danger* échapper à, éviter, esquiver. **to** ~ **tax** (*legally*) se soustraire à l'impôt; (*illegally*) frauder le fisc; **to** ~ **doing** éviter de faire; ~ **being seen** évitez qu'on ne vous voie; **to** ~ **sb's eye** fuir le regard de qn; **to** ~ **notice** échapper aux regards; **I can't** ~ **going now** je ne peux plus faire autrement que d'y aller, je ne peux plus me dispenser d'y aller; **this way we** ~ **London** en passant par ici nous évitons Londres; **it is to be** ~**ed like the plague** il faut fuir cela comme la peste.

avoidable [ə'vɔɪdəbl] *adj* évitable.

avoidance [ə'vɔɪdəns] *n*: **his** ~ **of me** le soin qu'il met à m'éviter; **his** ~ **of his duty** ses manquements *mpl* au devoir; **tax** ~ évasion fiscale.

avoirdupois [ˌævədə'pɔɪz] **1** *n* **(a)** (*lit*) poids commercial (*système britannique des poids et mesures*).
(b) (*: *overweight*) excès *m* de poids. **he suffers from** ~ il souffre d'embonpoint, il est trop gros, il a des kilos en trop *or* à perdre.
2 *cpd conforme aux poids et mesures officiellement établis.* **an avoirdupois pound** une livre (*453,6 grammes*).

avow [ə'vaʊ] *vt* avouer, confesser, admettre. **to** ~ **o.s. beaten** s'avouer *or* se déclarer battu; **he is an** ~**ed atheist** il avoue être athée; ~**ed enemy** ennemi déclaré.

avowal [ə'vaʊəl] *n* aveu *m*.

avowedly [ə'vaʊɪdlɪ] *adv* (*by one's own admission*) de son propre aveu; (*clearly*) manifestement, nettement.

avuncular [ə'vʌŋkjʊlə[r]] *adj* avunculaire.

await [ə'weɪt] *vt* **(a)** (*wait for*) *object, event* attendre, être dans l'attente de; *person* attendre. **parcels** ~**ing delivery** colis en souffrance; **long-**~**ed event** événement longtemps attendu.
(b) (*be in store for*) être réservé à, être préparé pour, attendre. **the fate that** ~**s us** le sort qui nous attend *or* qui nous est réservé.

awake [ə'weɪk] *pret* **awoke** *or* **awaked,** *ptp* **awoken** *or* **awaked 1** *vi* s'éveiller, se réveiller. **to** ~ **from sleep** sortir du sommeil, s'éveiller, se réveiller; (*fig*) **to** ~ **to one's responsibilities** s'éveiller à *or* prendre conscience de *or* se rendre compte de ses responsabilités; (*fig*) **to** ~ **to the fact that** s'apercevoir du fait que; (*fig*) **to** ~ **from one's illusions** revenir de ses illusions.
2 *vt* **(a)** (*wake*) *person* éveiller, réveiller.
(b) (*fig: arouse*) *suspicion* éveiller; *hope, curiosity* éveiller, faire naître; *memories* réveiller.
3 *adj* **(a)** (*not asleep*) éveillé, réveillé. **he was** ~ il était réveillé, il ne dormait pas; **he was still** ~ il ne s'était pas encore endormi; **to lie** ~ être au lit sans (pouvoir) dormir; **to stay** ~ **all night** (*deliberately*) veiller toute la nuit; (*involuntarily*) passer une nuit blanche; **it kept me** ~ cela m'a empêché de dormir.
(b) (*alert*) en éveil, vigilant. **to be** ~ **to** être conscient de, avoir conscience de.

awaken [ə'weɪkən] *vti* = **awake.**

awakening [ə'weɪknɪŋ] **1** *n* (*lit, fig*) réveil *m*. (*lit, fig*) **a rude** ~ un réveil brutal. **2** *adj interest, passion* naissant.

award [ə'wɔːd] **1** *vt prize etc* décerner, attribuer (*to* à); *sum of money* allouer, attribuer (*to* à); *dignity, honour* conférer (*to* à); *damages* accorder (*to* à).
2 *n* **(a)** (*prize*) récompense *f*, prix *m*; (*scholarship*) bourse *f*.
(b) (*Jur: judgment*) décision *f*, sentence arbitrale.

aware [ə'wɛə[r]] *adj* **(a)** (*conscious*) conscient (*of* de); (*informed*) au courant, averti (*of* de). **to become** ~ **of sth/that sth is happening** prendre conscience *or* se rendre compte de qch/que qch se passe; **to be** ~ **of sth** être conscient de qch, avoir conscience de qch; **to be** ~ **that something is happening** être conscient *or* avoir conscience que quelque chose se passe; **I am quite** ~ **of it** je le sais, je ne l'ignore pas, je m'en rends bien compte; **as far as I am** ~ autant que je sache; **not that I am** ~ **of** pas que je sache; **to make sb** ~ **of sth** rendre qn conscient de qch.
(b) (*knowledgeable*) informé, avisé. **politically** ~ politisé; **socially** ~ au courant des problèmes sociaux.

awareness [ə'wɛənɪs] *n* (*U*) conscience *f* (*of* de).

awash [ə'wɒʃ] *adj* (*Naut*) à fleur d'eau, qui affleure; (*flooded*) inondé (*with* de).

away [ə'weɪ] (*phr vb elem*) **1** *adv* **(a)** (*to or at a distance*) au loin, loin. **far** ~ au loin, très loin; **the lake is 3 km** ~ le lac est à 3 km de distance *or* à une distance de 3 km; ~ **back in the distance** très loin derrière (dans le lointain); ~ **back in prehistoric times** dans les temps reculés de la préhistoire; ~ **back in 1600** il y a bien longtemps en 1600; ~ **back in the 40s** il y a longtemps déjà dans les années 40; **keep the child** ~ **from the fire** tenez l'enfant loin *or* éloigné du feu; ~ **over there** là-bas au loin *or* dans le lointain, loin là-bas.
(b) (*absent*) ~! hors d'ici!; ~ **with you!** allez-vous-en!; **to be** ~ être absent *or* parti, ne pas être là; **he is** ~ **in London** il est (parti) à Londres; **when I have to be** ~ lorsque je dois m'absenter; **she was** ~ **before I could speak** elle était partie avant que j'aie pu parler; **don't look** ~ ne détournez pas les yeux; ~ **with kings!** à bas les rois!; *V* **brush away, go away** *etc.*
(c) (*continuously*) sans arrêt *or* interruption, continuellement. **to talk** ~ parler sans arrêt; **to work** ~ travailler sans arrêt.
(d) (*expressing loss, lessening, exhaustion*) **to die** ~ s'éteindre, s'évanouir, se dissiper; **to gamble** ~ **one's money** perdre son argent au jeu; **the snow has melted** ~ la neige a fondu complètement; *V* **boil away, get away.**
(e) (*phrases*) **now she's** ~ **with the idea that*...** la voilà partie avec l'idée que ...; **he's really** ~ **with the whole scheme*** il est vraiment emballé* par le projet; *V* **far, out, right** *etc.*
2 *adj* (*Sport*) ~ **match** match *m* à l'extérieur; ~ **team** (équipe *f* des) visiteurs *mpl*, équipe jouant à l'extérieur.

awe [ɔː] **1** *n* crainte révérentielle, effroi mêlé de respect *or* d'admiration. **to be** *or* **stand in** ~ **of sb** être intimidé par qn, être rempli du plus grand respect pour qn.
2 *vt* inspirer un respect mêlé de crainte à. **in an** ~**d voice** d'une voix (à la fois) respectueuse et intimidée.
3 *cpd*: **awe-inspiring, awesome** (*impressive*) impressionnant, imposant; (*frightening*) terrifiant; **awe-struck** (*frightened*) frappé de terreur; (*astounded*) stupéfait.

awful ['ɔːfəl] *adj* **(a)** affreux, terrible, atroce. **he's an** ~ **bore** il est assommant*; **what** ~ **weather!** quel temps de chien!*; **he's got an** ~ **cheek!** il a un de ces culots!*; *or* un fameux culot!*; **how** ~! comme c'est affreux!, quelle chose affreuse!; **it was simply** ~ c'était affreux vous ne pouvez pas savoir*; **his English is** ~ il parle anglais comme une vache espagnole; **there were an** ~ **lot of people/cars** il y avait un monde fou/un nombre incroyable de voitures.
(b) (*dreadful*) épouvantable, terrifiant, effrayant; (*impressive*) imposant, impressionnant.

awfully ['ɔːflɪ] *adv* vraiment, très, terriblement. **he is** ~ **nice** il est absolument charmant *or* gentil comme tout*; **thanks** ~ merci infiniment; **I am** ~ **glad** je suis rudement* content; **I am** ~ **sorry** je suis vraiment désolé; **an** ~ **big house** une très grande maison.

awfulness ['ɔːfʊlnɪs] *n* [*situation etc*] horreur *f*. **the** ~ **of it** ce qu'il y a d'affreux *or* de terrible dans cette affaire, ce que cette affaire a d'affreux *or* de terrible.

awhile [ə'waɪl] *adv* un instant, un moment, (pendant) quelque temps. **wait** ~ attendez un peu; **not yet** ~ pas de sitôt.

awkward ['ɔːkwəd] *adj* **(a)** (*inconvenient, difficult, embarrassing*) *tool* peu commode, peu maniable, mal conçu; *path* difficile, malaisé; (*Aut*) *bend* difficile *or* malaisé à négocier; *problem, task* délicat; *question* gênant, embarrassant; *silence* gêné, embarrassé; *situation* délicat, gênant. **at an** ~ **time** au mauvais moment; **an** ~ **moment** (*inconvenient*) un moment inopportun *or* mal à propos; (*embarrassing*) un moment gênant *or* de gêne; **he's an** ~ **customer*** c'est un type pas commode *or* pas facile*; **an** ~ **shape** une forme malcommode; **can you come tomorrow? — it's a bit** ~ pouvez-vous venir demain? — ce n'est pas très commode; **it's** ~ **for me** cela m'est assez difficile, cela ne m'est pas très facile; **he's being** ~ **about it** il ne se montre pas très coopératif à ce sujet; **it's all a bit** ~ tout ceci est un peu ennuyeux *or* gênant.
(b) (*clumsy*) *person* gauche, maladroit, empoté*; *movement, gesture* maladroit, peu élégant; *style* gauche, lourd, peu élégant. **the** ~ **age** l'âge ingrat.

awkwardly ['ɔːkwədlɪ] *adv* **(a)** *speak* d'un ton embarrassé *or* gêné.
(b) *behave, handle* gauchement, maladroitement; *move, walk* maladroitement, peu élégamment. ~ **placed** placé à un endroit difficile *or* gênant; ~ **expressed** gauchement exprimé, mal dit.

awkwardness ['ɔːkwədnɪs] *n* **(a)** (*clumsiness*) gaucherie *f*, maladresse *f*. **(b)** [*situation*] côté gênant *or* embarrassant. **(c)** (*discomfort*) embarras *m*, gêne *f*.

awl [ɔːl] *n* alêne *f*, poinçon *m*.

awning ['ɔːnɪŋ] *n* (*Naut*) taud *m or* taude *f*, tente *f*; [*shop*] banne *f*, store *m*; [*hotel door*] marquise *f*; [*tent*] auvent *m*.

awoke [ə'wəʊk] *pret of* **awake.**

awoken [ə'wəʊkən] *ptp of* **awake.**

awry [ə'raɪ] *adj, adv* **(a)** (*askew*) de travers, de guingois*. **(b)** (*wrong*) de travers. **to go** ~ [*plan etc*] s'en aller à vau-l'eau; [*undertaking*] mal tourner.

ax (*US*), **axe** [æks] **1** *n* hache *f*; (*fig: in expenditure etc*) coupe *f* sombre. (*fig*) **to have an** ~ **to grind** prêcher pour son saint (*fig*); (*fig*) **I've no** ~ **to grind** ce n'est pas un but personnel que je poursuis, ce n'est pas mon intérêt personnel que j'ai en vue, je ne prêche pas pour mon saint; (*fig*) **when the ~ fell** quand le coup fut porté.

2 *vt* (*fig*) **to ~ expenditure** réduire les dépenses, faire *or* opérer des coupes sombres dans le budget; **to ~ sb** mettre qn à la porte.

axial [ˈæksɪəl] *adj* axial.

axiom [ˈæksɪəm] *n* axiome *m.*

axiomatic [ˌæksɪəʊˈmætɪk] *adj* axiomatique; (*clear*) évident.

axis [ˈæksɪs] *n, pl* **axes** [ˈæksiːz] axe *m.* (*Hist*) **the A~ (Powers)** les puissances *fpl* de l'Axe.

axle [ˈæksl] **1** *n [wheel]* axe *m*; (*Aut:* **~-tree**) essieu *m.* **front/rear axle** essieu avant/arrière.

2 *cpd:* (*Rail*) **axle-box** boîte *f* d'essieu; **axle cap** chapeau *m* de roue *or* de moyeu; **axle grease** graisse *f* à essieux; **axle-pin** esse *f*, clavette *f* d'essieu.

ay(e) [aɪ] **1** *excl, adv* (*esp Scot, N Engl*) oui. (*Naut*) **~, ~ sir!** oui, commandant (*or* capitaine *etc*).

2 *n* oui *m.* (*in voting*) **the ~s and noes** les voix *fpl* pour et contre; **90 ~s and 2 noes** 90 pour et 2 contre; **the ~s have it** les oui l'emportent.

aye† [eɪ] *adv* (*Scot*) toujours.

azalea [əˈzeɪlɪə] *n* azalée *f.*

Azores [əˈzɔːz] *npl* Açores *fpl.*

Aztec [ˈæztek] **1** *n* Aztèque *mf.* **2** *adj* aztèque.

azure [ˈeɪʒə^{r}] **1** *n* azur *m.* **2** *adj* azuré, d'azur, bleu ciel *inv.*

B

B, b [biː] *n* **(a)** (*letter*) B, b *m.* (*in house numbers*) **number 1b** numéro *m* 1 ter. **(b)** (*Mus*) si *m.*

baa [bɑː] **1** *n* bêlement *m.* **~!** bê!; **~-lamb** (*mot enfantin désignant un*) petit agneau. **2** *vi* bêler.

babble [ˈbæbl] **1** *n [voices]* rumeur *f*; *[baby]* babil *m*, babillage *m*; *[stream]* gazouillement *m.*

2 *vi* (*hastily, indistinctly*) bredouiller, bafouiller*; (*foolishly*) bavarder; *[baby]* gazouiller, babiller; *[stream]* jaser, gazouiller.

3 *vt* (*also* **~ out**) (*hastily, indistinctly*) bredouiller; (*foolishly*) raconter. **to ~ (out) a secret** laisser échapper un secret.

babble away, babble on *vi* babiller *or* jaser sans arrêt.

babbler [ˈbæblə^{r}] *n* bavard(e) *m(f).*

babbling [ˈbæblɪŋ] **1** *adj person, baby, stream* babillard. **2** *n* = **babble (1).**

babe [beɪb] *n* **(a)** (*liter, also* *) enfant *mf* (en bas âge), petit(e) enfant. **~ in arms** enfant au berceau *or* qui vient de naître.

(b) (*: *inexperienced person*) innocent(e) *m(f).*

(c) (*US*‡: *girl*) pépée‡ *f*, minette* *f*, nana‡ *f.* **come on ~!** viens ma belle!

babel [ˈbeɪbəl] *n* (*noise*) brouhaha *m*; (*confusion*) tohu-bohu *m*; *V* **tower.**

baboon [bəˈbuːn] *n* babouin *m.*

baby [ˈbeɪbɪ] **1** *n* **(a)** bébé *m.* **the ~ of the family** le petit dernier, la petite dernière, le benjamin, la benjamine; **I have known him since he was a ~** je l'ai connu tout petit *or* tout bébé; (*pej*) **don't be such a ~* (about it)!** ne fais pas l'enfant!; (*fig*) **he was left holding the ~*** tout lui est retombé dessus, il est resté avec l'affaire sur les bras*; (*fig*) **to throw out the ~ with the bathwater** jeter l'enfant avec l'eau du bain; *V* **have.**

(b) (*US*‡) (*girlfriend*) copine* *f*, petite amie, nana‡ *f*; (*man, person*) mec‡ *m.* **come on ~!** (*to woman*) viens ma belle!; (*to man*) viens mon gars!*

(c) (*: *special responsibility*) **the new system is his ~** le nouveau système est son affaire, il est le père du nouveau système; **that's not my ~** je n'ai rien à voir là-dedans.

2 *vt* (*) *person* dorloter, cajoler.

3 *cpd clothes etc* de bébé; *tiger, wolf* bébé-. **baby-batterer** bourreau *m* d'enfants; **baby-battering** mauvais traitements infligés aux enfants; **baby boy** petit garçon; (*US*) **baby carriage** voiture *f* d'enfant; **baby-doll pyjamas** baby-doll *m*; **baby elephant** éléphanteau *m*; **baby face** visage poupin; **baby girl** petite fille; **baby grand (piano)** (piano *m*) demi-queue *m*; **baby linen** layette *f*; **baby-minder** nourrice *f* (*qui garde les enfants pendant que leurs mères travaillent*); **baby-scales** pèse-bébé *m*; **baby-sit** garder les bébés *or* les enfants; **baby-sitter** baby-sitter *m*; **baby-sitting** garde *f* d'enfants, baby-sitting *m*; **to go baby-sitting** faire du baby-sitting; **baby-snatcher** ravisseur *m*, -euse *f* d'enfants (au berceau); (*fig*) **he/she is a baby-snatcher!*** il/elle les prend au berceau!*; **baby-snatching** enlèvement *m or* rapt *m* d'enfant; (* *fig*) détournement *m* de mineur (*iro*); **baby talk** langage enfantin *or* de bébé; **baby-walker** trotte-bébé *m inv.*

babyhood [ˈbeɪbɪhʊd] *n* petite enfance.

babyish [ˈbeɪbɪɪʃ] *adj* (*slightly pej*) *clothes* de bébé; *behaviour, speech* puéril, enfantin.

Babylon [ˈbæbɪlən] *n* (*Geog, fig*) Babylone.

baccalaureate [ˌbækəˈlɔːrɪɪt] *n* (*US Univ*) licence *f.*

baccara(t) [ˈbækərɑː] *n* baccara *m.*

bacchanal [ˈbækənæl] **1** *adj* bachique. **2** *n* (*worshipper*) adorateur *m*, -trice *f* de Bacchus; (*reveller*) noceur* *m*, -euse* *f*; (*orgy*) orgie *f.*

bacchanalia [ˌbækəˈneɪlɪə] *n* (*festival*) bacchanales *fpl*; (*orgy*) orgie *f.*

bacchanalian [ˌbækəˈneɪlɪən] *adj*, **bacchic** [ˈbækɪk] *adj* bachique.

Bacchus [ˈbækəs] *n* Bacchus *m.*

baccy‡ [ˈbækɪ] *n* (*abbr of* **tobacco**) tabac *m.*

bachelor [ˈbætʃələ^{r}] **1** *n* **(a)** (*unmarried man*) célibataire *m*, vieux garçon; *V* **confirmed.**

(b) (*Univ*) **B~ of Arts/of Science/of Law** licencié(e) *m(f)* ès lettres/ès sciences/en droit.

(c) (*Hist*) bachelier *m.*

2 *cpd:* **bachelor flat** garçonnière *f*, studio *m*; **bachelor girl** célibataire *f.*

bachelorhood [ˈbætʃələhʊd] *n* vie *f* de garçon, célibat *m* (*hommes seulement*).

bacillary [bəˈsɪlərɪ] *adj* bacillaire.

bacillus [bəˈsɪləs] *n, pl* **bacilli** [bəˈsɪlaɪ] bacille *m.*

back [bæk] (*phr vb elem*) **1** *n* **(a)** *[person, animal]* dos *m.* **to be on one's ~** (*lit*) être (étendu) sur le dos; (*: *be ill*) être au lit; **to fall on one's ~** tomber à la renverse; **to carry sth/sb on one's ~** porter qn/qch sur son dos; (*fig*) **he did it behind his mother's ~** il l'a fait derrière le dos de sa mère *or* en cachette de sa mère; (*fig*) **he went behind his teacher's ~ to the headmaster** il est allé voir le directeur derrière le dos du professeur *or* en cachette du professeur; (*lit, fig*) **~ to ~** dos à dos (*V also* **4**); **with one's ~ to the light** le dos à la lumière; **he had his ~ to the houses** il tournait le dos aux maisons; **to stand** *or* **sit with one's ~ to sb/sth** tourner le dos à qn/qch; (*Rail*) **to sit with one's ~ to the engine** être assis dans le sens contraire à la marche; **he stood with his ~ (up) against the wall** il était adossé au mur; (*fig*) **to have one's ~ to the wall** être au pied du mur (*fig*); **to put one's ~ into doing sth** mettre toute son énergie à faire qch; (*fig*) **put your ~ into it!*** allons, un peu de nerf!*; **to put** *or* **get sb's ~ up** braquer qn; **to get off sb's ~** laisser qn en paix, cesser de harceler qn; (*fig*) **he's at the ~ of* all this trouble** il est à l'origine de tous ces ennuis; (*fig*) **I was late and on the ~ of that* the car broke down** j'étais en retard et par-dessus le marché *or* et en plus la voiture est tombée en panne; *V* **break, broad, see[1], stab** *etc.*

(b) *[chair]* dossier *m*; *[book]* dos *m.* (*Naut*) **the ship broke its ~** le navire s'est cassé en deux; *V* **hard** *etc.*

(c) (*as opposed to front*) (*gen*) dos *m*, derrière *m*; *[hand, hill, medal]* revers *m*; *[record]* deuxième face *f*; *[dress]* dos; *[head, house]* derrière; *[page, cheque]* verso *m*; *[material]* envers *m.* **you've got it on ~ to front** tu l'as mis devant derrière; **the index is at the ~ of the book** l'index se trouve à la fin du livre; **to have an idea at the ~ of one's mind** avoir une idée derrière la tête; **to sit in the ~ (of a car)** être à l'arrière (d'une voiture); **I know Paris like the ~ of my hand** je connais Paris comme ma poche.

(d) (*furthest from the front*) *[cupboard, garden, hall, stage]* fond *m.* **at the very ~** tout au fond; (*fig*) **at the ~ of beyond*** au diable (vert*), en plein bled*.

(e) (*Ftbl etc*) arrière *m.*

(f) (*vat*) bac *m.*

2 *adj* **(a)** (*not front*) arrière *inv*, de derrière. **~ door** porte *f* de derrière; (*fig*) **to enter a profession through the ~ door** entrer dans une profession par la petite porte; **~ garden** jardin *m* de derrière; **~ room** chambre *f* sur le derrière *or* du fond (*V also* **4**); **~ seat** siège *m* de derrière, siège *or* banquette *f* arrière; (*fig*) **to take a ~ seat*** passer au second plan; (*fig*) **he's a ~seat driver*** il est toujours à donner des conseils au conducteur; (*Aut*) **in the ~ seat** sur le siège arrière; (*Sport*) **~ straight** ligne droite opposée; **~ street** rue écartée; (*pej*) rue mal fréquentée *or* mal famée (*V* **abortionist**); **he grew up in the ~ streets of Leeds** il a grandi dans les quartiers pauvres de Leeds; **~ tooth** molaire *f*; (*Ling*) **~ vowel** voyelle postérieure; **~ wheel** roue *f* arrière.

(b) (*overdue*) *taxes* arriéré. **to make up ~ payments** solder l'arriéré; **~ interest** intérêts courus; **to owe ~ rent** devoir un arriéré de loyer.

3 *adv* **(a)** (*to the rear*) en arrière, à *or* vers l'arrière. **(stand) ~!** rangez-vous!, reculez!; **far ~** loin derrière; **the house stands ~ from the road** la maison est en retrait rapport à la route; ~ **and forth,** ~ **and forward** en allant et venant, dans *or* par un mouvement de va-et-vient *V* **keep back, look back** *etc.*

(b) (*in return*) **to give** ~ rendre; **to answer** ~ répondre; *V* **pay back** *etc.*

(c) (*again: often re-+vb in French*) **to come** ~ revenir; **to go** ~ retourner; **to go** ~ **home** rentrer (chez soi); **to be** ~ être de retour, être rentré; **he's not** ~ **yet** il n'est pas encore rentré *or* revenu; **I'll be** ~ **at 6** je serai de retour *or* je rentrerai à 6 heures; **as soon as I'm** ~ dès mon retour; **he went to Lyons and then** ~ **to Paris** il est allé à Lyon et puis est rentré à Paris; **he went to Paris and** ~ il a fait le voyage de Paris aller et retour, il a fait Paris et retour*; **the journey there and** ~ le trajet aller et retour; **you can go there and** ~ **in a day** tu peux faire l'aller et retour en une journée.

(d) (*in time phrases*) **as far** ~ **as 1800** en remontant jusqu'en 1800, déjà en 1800; **far** ~ **in the past** à une époque reculée (du passé); **a week** ~* il y a une semaine.

4 *cpd*: **backache** mal *m* de *or* aux reins; (*Brit Parl*) **backbench** banc *m* des membres sans portefeuille (*de la majorité ou de l'opposition*); **backbencher** membre *m* du Parlement sans portefeuille (*dans la majorité comme dans l'opposition*); **the backbenchers** le gros des députés; **backbite** médire de, débiner*; **backbiting** médisance *f*; (*Brit*) **back boiler** (petite) chaudière *f* (*à l'arrière d'une cheminée*); **backbone** *V* **backbone; back-breaking work** (*physical*) travail *m* à vous casser les reins; (*mental*) travail éreintant; **backchat** (**U*) impertinence *f*; (*Theat*) échange *m* de plaisanteries (*sur scène*); (*Brit: Theat, fig*) **back-cloth** toile *f* de fond; (*Brit*) **back-comb** *hair* crêper; **backdate** *cheque, letter* antidater; **increase backdated to January** augmentation *f* avec rappel à compter de janvier; **backdrop** = **back-cloth;** *[bus, train]* **back-end** arrière *m*; (*Brit*) **back-end of the year** arrière-saison *f*; **backfire** *V* **backfire;** (*Ling*) **back-formation** dérivation régressive; **backgammon** trictrac *m*, jacquet *m*; **background** *V* **background; backhand** (*adj*) *blow* en revers; *writing* penché à gauche; (*n*) (*Tennis: also* **backhanded stroke**) revers *m*; (*fig*) **backhanded** *action* déloyal; *compliment* équivoque; (*Brit*) **backhander** (*blow*) revers *m*; (**:reproof*) réprimande *f*, semonce *f*; (*: *bribe*) pot-de-vin *m*; **back-kitchen** arrière-cuisine *f*; **backlash** (*Tech*) secousse *f*, saccade *f*; *[explosion]* contre-coup *m*, répercussion *f*; (*Pol, fig: hostile reaction*) réaction brutale, répercussions *fpl*; **backlog*** (*of rent etc*) arriéré *m* (de loyers); (*of work*) arriéré de travail, accumulation *f* de travail (en retard); *[newspaper etc]* **back number** vieux numéro; *[person]* **to be a back number** être vieux jeu, ne plus être à la page; **back-pack** (*Space*) appareil dorsal de survie; (*Sport*) sac *m* à dos *or* de montagne; **to go back-packing** faire de la randonnée (en emportant son matériel de couchage); **back pay** rappel *m* de salaire *or* de traitement; (*Mil, Naut*) rappel *or* arriéré *m* de solde; **back-pedal** rétropédaler, pédaler en arrière; (*fig: retreat*) faire marche arrière; (*Cine*) **back-projection** surimpression *f*; **backrest** dossier *m*; (*fig*) **back-room boy*** expert *m* (*qui travaille dans l'ombre*); (*boffin*) chercheur *m* scientifique (*anonyme*); (*fig*) **the backroom boys*** ceux qui restent dans la coulisse; **backshift** (*period*) poste *m* du soir; (*workers*) équipe *f* du soir; **to be on the backshift** faire le (poste du) soir; **back-shop** arrière-boutique *f*; **backside** (*back part*) arrière *m*, (*: *buttocks*) derrière *m*, postérieur* *m*; **back sight** *[rifle]* cran *m* de mire; (*Surv*) rétrovisée *f*; (*fig*) **backslapping*** (grandes) démonstrations *fpl* d'amitié; (*fig*) **backslide** retomber dans l'erreur, retomber dans le vice; *[ex-prisoner]* récidiver; (*Rel*) être relaps; **backslider** récidiviste *mf*; (*Rel*) relaps(e) *m(f)*; (*Typ*) **backspace** rappeler le chariot; (*Typ*) **backspacer** rappel *m* de chariot, rappel arrière; **backstage** (*adv*) derrière la scène, dans la *or* les coulisse(s); (*n*) coulisse(s) *f(pl)*; **to go backstage** aller dans la coulisse; **backstair(s)** *V* **backstair(s); backstitch** point *m* arrière; (*Swimming*) **backstroke** dos crawlé, nage *f* sur le dos; (*Brit*) **a row of back-to-back houses** une rangée de maisons adossées les unes aux autres; **backtrack** faire marche arrière *or* machine arrière (*fig*); (*US*) **to backtrack home*** retourner chez soi; **back-up** (*n: support*) appui *m*, soutien *m*; (*adj*) *aircraft, coach* supplémentaire, de réserve; *pilot etc* remplaçant; (*Naut, fig*) **backwash** remous *m* (*from* provoqué par); **backwater** (*pool*) eau stagnante; *[river]* bras mort; (*fig: backward place*) trou perdu; (*fig: peaceful spot*) (petit) coin *m* tranquille; **to live in a backwater** habiter un petit coin tranquille; (*pej*) habiter en plein bled* (*pej*); **backwoods** région (forestière) inexploitée; (*fig pej*) **to live in the backwoods** vivre en plein bled* (*pej*); **backwoodsman** pionnier *m*; (*fig pej*) rustre *m*; **backyard** arrière-cour *f*.

5 *vt* **(a)** (*strengthen, support*) *wall* renforcer; *map* entoiler, renforcer; *book* endosser; *picture* maroufler; (*fig*) *singer* accompagner; (*encourage, support*) *person* soutenir, appuyer; *candidate* pistonner*; (*finance*) *person, enterprise* financer, commanditer. (*Fin*) **to** ~ **a bill** endosser *or* avaliser un effet.

(b) (*bet on*) *horse* parier sur, miser sur, jouer. **the horse was heavily** ~**ed** le cheval était bien coté; **to** ~ **a horse each way** jouer un cheval gagnant et placé; **to** ~ **a loser** (*Sport*) parier *or* miser sur un (cheval) perdant; (*Comm*) mal placer son argent; (*fig*) soutenir une cause perdue d'avance.

(c) (*reverse*) *car, horse, cart* faire reculer; *train* refouler. (*Naut*) **to** ~ **water** *or* **the oars** (nager à) culer.

6 *vi* **(a)** (*move backwards*) *[person, animal]* reculer; *[vehicle]* faire marche arrière. **to** ~ **in/out** *etc* *[vehicle]* entrer/sortir *etc* en marche arrière; *[person]* entrer/sortir *etc* à reculons.

(b) *[wind]* tourner en sens inverse des aiguilles d'une montre.

back away *vi* (se) reculer.

back down *vi* (*lit*) descendre à reculons; (*fig*) se dérober, se dégonfler*.

back on to *vt fus [house etc]* donner par derrière sur.

back out 1 *vi* (*lit*) *[person]* sortir à reculons; *[car etc]* sortir en marche arrière (*of* de); (*fig*) se dédire, se retirer (*of* de), se dérober (*of* à). **to back out of an argument/a duty** se soustraire *or* se dérober à une discussion/à un devoir; **to back out of a bargain** se dégager d'un marché.

2 *vt sep vehicle* sortir en marche arrière.

back up 1 *vi* (*Aut*) faire marche arrière.

2 *vt sep* **(a)** (*support*) appuyer, soutenir, épauler.

(b) (*reverse*) *vehicle* faire reculer.

3 back-up *V* **back 4.**

backbone ['bækbəʊn] *n* **(a)** *[person, animal]* épine dorsale, colonne vertébrale; *[fish]* arête centrale. **English to the** ~ anglais jusqu'à la moelle (des os).

(b) (*main part, axis*) point *m* d'appui, pivot *m*. **to be the** ~ **of an organization** être *or* former le pivot d'une organisation.

(c) (*strength of character*) énergie *f*, fermeté *f*, caractère *m*. **he's got no** ~ c'est un mollusque.

-backed [bækt] *adj ending in cpds* **(a)** à dossier. **low-backed chair** chaise *f* à dossier bas. **(b)** doublé de. **rubber-backed carpet** tapis doublé de caoutchouc.

backer ['bækəʳ] *n* (*supporter*) partisan(e) *m(f)*; (*Betting*) parieur *m*, -euse *f*; (*Fin*) *[bill]* avaliseur *m*; *[firm, play, film]* commanditaire *m*.

backfire ['bæk'faɪəʳ] **1** *n* (*Aut*) (*explosion*) raté *m* (d'allumage); (*noise*) pétarade *f*. **2** *vi* (*Aut*) pétarader, avoir un raté (d'allumage); (*miscarry*) *[plan etc]* échouer, foirer*:.

background ['bækgraʊnd] **1** *n* **(a)** (*Art*) *[fabric]* fond *m*; *[photograph]* arrière-plan *m*; (*Theat*) arrière *m* du décor. **in the** ~ dans le fond, à l'arrière-plan; **on a blue** ~ sur fond bleu.

(b) (*fig*) arrière-plan *m*, second plan. **to remain in the** ~ s'effacer, rester dans l'ombre; **to keep sb in the** ~ tenir qn à l'écart.

(c) (*circumstances etc*) antécédents *mpl*; (*Soc*) milieu socioculturel, cadre *m* de vie; (*Pol*) climat *m* politique; (*basic knowledge*) données *fpl or* éléments *mpl* de base; (*experience*) fonds *m*, acquis *m*, formation *f*. **he has a good professional** ~ il a de l'acquis *or* une bonne formation; **family/working-class** ~ milieu familial/ouvrier; **what is his** ~? (*social*) de quel milieu est-il?; (*professional*) qu'est-ce qu'il a comme formation?

(d) (*relevant information*) documentation *f*. **to fill in the** ~ compléter la documentation; **what is the** ~ **to these events?** quel est le contexte dans lequel se sont déroulés ces événements?

2 *cpd*: (*Rad, Theat, TV etc*) **background music** musique *f* de fond; **to play sth as background music** passer qch en fond sonore; **background noise** bruit *m* de fond, fond *m* sonore; **background reading** lectures générales (autour du sujet); (*Press*) **background story** papier *m* d'ambiance; **background studies** (études *fpl* de) culture générale.

backing ['bækɪŋ] *n* **(a)** (*lit*) renforcement *m*, support *m*; *[book]* endossure *f*; *[picture]* entoilage *m*; (*fig*) (*Fin, Pol*) soutien *m*; (*Mus*) accompagnement *m*. **(b)** (*Betting*) paris *mpl*. **(c)** (*movement*) *[horse, cart etc]* recul *m*; *[boat]* nage *f* à culer; *[wind]* changement *m* de direction en sens inverse des aiguilles d'une montre.

backstair(s) ['bæk'steə(z)] *n* escalier *m* de service; (*secret*) escalier dérobé. ~ **gossip** propos *mpl* d'antichambre; ~ **intrigue** menées *fpl*, manigances *fpl*.

backward ['bækwəd] **1** *adj* **(a)** (*to the rear*) *look, step* en arrière; (*fig*) *step, move* rétrograde, en arrière. ~ **and forward movement** mouvement *m* de va-et-vient; ~ **flow** contre-courant *m*.

(b) (*retarded*) *district, nation, culture* arriéré, peu avancé; (*Med*) *child* arriéré.

(c) (*reluctant*) lent, peu disposé (*in doing* à faire), hésitant. **he was not** ~ **in taking the money** il ne s'est pas fait prier pour prendre l'argent.

2 *adv* = **backwards.**

3 *cpd*: **a backward-looking project** un projet rétrograde.

backwardness ['bækwədnɪs] *n* (*Psych*) arriération mentale; (*Econ*) état arriéré; (*reluctance, shyness*) manque *m* d'empressement, lenteur *f* (*in doing* à faire).

backward(s) ['bækwəd(z)] (*phr vb elem*) *adv* **(a)** (*towards the back*) en arrière. **to fall** ~ tomber à la renverse; **to flow** ~ aller *or* couler à contre-courant; **to walk** ~ **and forwards** marcher de long en large, aller et venir; **to go** ~ **and forwards between two places** aller et venir *or* faire la navette entre deux endroits; *V* **lean over.**

(b) (*back foremost*) à rebours. **to go/walk** ~ aller/marcher à reculons *or* à rebours; **the car moved** ~ **a little** la voiture a reculé un peu.

(c) (*in reverse of usual way*) à l'envers, en commençant par la fin. **I know the poem** ~* je sais le poème sur le bout des doigts; **I know this road** ~* je connais cette route comme ma poche; **to stroke a cat** ~ caresser un chat à rebrousse-poil.

(d) (*fig: in time*) en arrière, vers le passé. **to look** ~ jeter un regard en arrière, remonter dans le passé; **to reckon** ~ **to a date** remonter jusqu'à une date.

(e) (*retrogressively*) en rétrogradant.

bacon ['beɪkən] *n* lard *m*; (*in rashers*) bacon *m*. ~ **and eggs** œufs *mpl* au jambon; **a** ~ **rasher** une tranche de bacon; ~**-slicer** machine *f* à débiter le bacon en tranches; (*fig*) **to bring home the** ~* décrocher la timbale*; *V* **boil**[1], **save**[1], **streaky.**

bacteria [bæk'tɪərɪə] *npl of* **bacterium.**

bacterial [bæk'tɪərɪəl] *adj* bactérien.

bacteriological [bæk,tɪərɪə'lɒdʒɪkəl] *adj* bactériologique.

bacteriologist [bæk,tɪərɪ'ɒlədʒɪst] *n* bactériologiste *mf*.

bacteriology [bæk,tɪərɪ'ɒlədʒɪ] *n* bactériologie *f*.

bacterium [bæk'tɪərɪəm] *n, pl* **bacteria** bactérie *f*.

bad [bæd] **1** *adj, comp* **worse,** *superl* **worst (a)** (*wicked*) *action, habit* mauvais; *person* méchant; *behaviour* mauvais, détestable. ~ language grossièretés fpl, gros mots; he's a ~ lot* c'est un mauvais sujet or un sale type*; it was a ~ thing to do/to say ce n'était pas bien de faire cela/de dire cela; it was very ~ of him to frighten the children ce n'était vraiment pas bien de sa part de faire peur aux enfants; you ~ boy! vilain!, méchant!; ~ dog! vilain chien!

(b) (inferior) workmanship mauvais, de mauvaise qualité; (decayed) food mauvais, gâté; tooth carié; (false) coin, money faux (f fausse); (unfavourable) report mauvais; opinion mauvais, triste; result mauvais, malheureux; (unpleasant) news, weather, smell mauvais; (serious) mistake, accident, wound grave. it is not so ~ ce n'est pas si mal; it is not ~ at all ce n'est pas mal du tout; (that's) too ~! (indignant) c'est un peu fort!; (sympathetic) quel dommage!; it's too ~ of you ce n'est vraiment pas bien de votre part; she's ill? that's very ~ elle est malade? c'est bien ennuyeux; how is he? — (he's) not so ~ comment va-t-il? — (il ne va) pas trop mal; I did not know she was so ~ je ne la savais pas si malade; that is ~ for the health/the eyes cela ne vaut rien or c'est mauvais pour la santé/les yeux; this is ~ for you cela ne vous vaut rien; it's ~ for him to eat fatty foods les aliments gras sont mauvais pour lui; (Med) to feel ~ se sentir mal; (fig) I feel very ~ about it* ça m'embête*; things are going from ~ to worse tout va or les choses vont de mal en pis; business is ~ les affaires vont mal; she speaks ~ English elle parle un mauvais anglais; to go ~ [food] se gâter, pourrir; [milk] tourner; [bread etc] moisir; [teeth] se gâter, se carier; this will cause ~ blood between them ceci va créer de l'animosité entre eux; (Brit) I am in his ~ books*, I am in ~ with him‡ je ne suis pas dans ses petits papiers*, il ne m'a pas à la bonne‡; it's a ~ business (sad) c'est une triste affaire; (unpleasant) c'est une mauvaise histoire; (Insurance) ~ claim réclamation mal fondée; a ~ cold un gros or sale* rhume; ~ debt créance douteuse, mauvaise créance; to come to a ~ end mal finir; a ~ error of judgment une grossière erreur de jugement; in ~ faith de mauvaise foi; it is (in) ~ form to do† il est de mauvais ton de faire; I've got a ~ head j'ai mal à la tête; ~ headache violent mal de tête; her ~ leg sa mauvaise jambe, sa jambe malade; to be in a ~ mood or temper être de mauvaise humeur; to have a ~ name avoir (une) mauvaise réputation; ~ quality food/material etc aliments mpl/tissu m etc de qualité inférieure or de mauvaise qualité; (Ling) in a ~ sense dans un sens péjoratif; there is a ~ smell in this room ça sent mauvais dans cette pièce; to be on ~ terms with sb être en mauvais termes avec qn; it wouldn't be a ~ thing (to do) ça ne ferait pas de mal (de faire), ce ne serait pas une mauvaise idée (de faire); to have a ~ time of it (poverty) manger de la vache enragée; (pain) avoir très mal, en baver‡; (in difficult situation) être dans une mauvaise passe; to be in a ~ way (in a fix) être dans de mauvais draps or dans le pétrin; (very ill) être très mal, filer un mauvais coton; V blood, penny, shot etc.

2 n (U) mal m, mauvais m. to take the good with the ~ prendre le bon avec le mauvais; he's gone to the ~* il a mal tourné; I am 50p to the ~* j'en suis de 50 pence*.

3 adv (is obsessed by) he's got it ~* (about hobby etc) c'est une marotte chez lui; (about person) il l'a dans la peau‡.

4 cpd: (US) badlands bad-lands mpl; bad-mannered mal élevé; to be bad-tempered avoir mauvais caractère, être grincheux or acariâtre.

baddie‡ ['bædɪ] n méchant m.

baddish ['bædɪʃ] adj pas fameux, pas brillant.

bade [beɪd] pret of bid.

badge [bædʒ] n [team, association] insigne m; [an order, police] plaque f; (Mil) insigne; (sew-on, stick-on: for jeans etc) badge m; (Scouting) badge; (fig: symbol) symbole m, signe m (distinctif). his ~ of office l'insigne de sa fonction.

badger ['bædʒəʳ] 1 n (animal, brush) blaireau m. 2 vt harceler, importuner (with de). to ~ sth out of sb soutirer qch à qn à force de le harceler.

badly ['bædlɪ] adv, comp worse, superl worst (a) mal. ~ dressed mal habillé; (in interview, exam etc) he did ~ il a mal réussi, ça a mal marché (pour lui); you did ~ (out of it), you came off ~ tu n'as pas été gâté; I came off ~ in that transaction c'est moi qui ai fait les frais de cette transaction; (Comm, Fin) to be doing ~ faire de mauvaises affaires; things are going ~ les choses vont or tournent mal; he took it very ~ il a très mal pris la chose; [machine etc] to work ~ mal fonctionner; to be ~ off être dans la gêne; he is ~ off for space il manque de place.

(b) (seriously) grièvement, gravement, sérieusement. ~ beaten battu à plate couture; the ~ disabled les grands infirmes, les grands invalides; ~ wounded grièvement blessé.

(c) (very much) to want sth ~ avoir grande envie de qch; I need it ~ j'en ai absolument besoin, il me le faut absolument; he ~ needs a beating* il a sérieusement besoin d'une correction.

badminton ['bædmɪntən] n badminton m.

badness ['bædnɪs] n (U) (a) (poor quality) mauvaise qualité, mauvais état. (b) (wickedness) méchanceté f.

baffle ['bæfl] 1 vt person déconcerter, dérouter; pursuers semer; plot déjouer; hope, expectation décevoir, tromper; description, explanation échapper à, défier.

2 n (Tech) déflecteur m; (Acoustics) baffle m.

3 cpd: baffle-board écran m; baffle-plate (Tech) déflecteur m; (Acoustics) baffle m.

baffling ['bæflɪŋ] adj déconcertant, déroutant.

bag [bæg] 1 n sac m; (luggage) valise f; (Zool) sac, poche f. ~s (luggage) bagages mpl, valises fpl; (Brit‡: trousers) falzar‡ m; (Brit) ~s of‡ des masses de*; paper ~ sac en papier; she's got ~s under the eyes* elle a des poches or valises‡ sous les yeux; with ~ and baggage avec armes et bagages; to pack up ~ and baggage plier bagage, prendre ses cliques et ses claques*; the whole ~ of tricks tout le bataclan*, tout le fourbi*; (Hunting) to get a good ~ faire bonne chasse, faire un beau tableau; it's in the ~‡ c'est dans le sac* or dans la poche*; (US) to be left holding the ~* payer les pots cassés*; (pej) she's an old ~‡ (ugly) c'est un vieux tableau*; (grumpy) c'est une vieille teigne; V cat, money etc.

2 vt (a) (Hunting) animal tuer; (*: get) empocher, mettre le grappin sur*; (*: steal) faucher*, piquer‡. (Brit) ~s I, I ~s (that)!‡ à moi!

(b) (also ~ up) flour, goods mettre en sac, ensacher.

3 vi (also ~ out) (se) gonfler, s'enfler; [garment] goder.

4 cpd: bagpiper joueur m de cornemuse, joueur de biniou; bagpipe(s) [Scotland] cornemuse f; [Brittany] biniou m, cornemuse; to be accused of bag-snatching être accusé d'avoir arraché son sac à quelqu'un.

bagatelle [ˌbægə'tel] n (trifle) bagatelle f; (Mus) divertissement m; (Billiards) billard anglais, billard à blouses.

bagful ['bægfʊl] n sac plein, plein sac.

baggage ['bægɪdʒ] 1 n (a) (luggage) bagages mpl; (Mil) équipement m; V bag.

(b) (*†) (pert girl) coquine† f, friponne† f; (prostitute) traînée‡ f.

2 cpd: (esp US) baggage car fourgon m; baggage check bulletin m de consigne; baggage handler bagagiste m; baggage room consigne f; (Mil) baggage train train m des équipages; baggage wagon = baggage car.

bagging ['bægɪŋ] n (Tex) toile f à sac.

baggy ['bægɪ] adj (a) (puffy) gonflé, bouffant. (b) jacket, coat trop ample, flottant. trousers ~ at the knees pantalon m qui fait des poches aux genoux.

Bahama [bə'hɑːmə] adj, n: the ~ Islands, the ~s les Bahamas fpl.

bail¹ [beɪl] 1 n (Jur) (sum) caution f; (person) caution, répondant m. on ~ sous caution; to free sb on ~ mettre qn en liberté provisoire sous caution; to go or stand ~ for sb se porter or se rendre garant de qn; to find ~ for sb fournir une caution pour qn (pour sa mise en liberté provisoire); to ask for/grant/refuse ~ demander/accorder/refuser la mise en liberté sous caution; V jump.

2 vt (a) (Jur) (also ~ out) faire mettre en liberté provisoire sous caution.

(b) goods mettre en dépôt.

bail out vt sep (a) = bail¹ 2a.

(b) (fig) sortir d'affaire.

bail² [beɪl] n (Cricket) bâtonnet m.

bail³ [beɪl] 1 vt (also ~ out) boat écoper; water vider. 2 n écope f.

bailey ['beɪlɪ] n (wall) mur m d'enceinte; (courtyard) cour intérieure. B~ bridge pont m Bailey; V old.

bailiff ['beɪlɪf] n (Jur) huissier m; (Brit) [estate, lands] régisseur m, intendant m; (Hist) bailli m, gouverneur m.

bairn [bɛən] n (Scot, N Engl) enfant mf.

bait [beɪt] 1 n (Fishing, Hunting) amorce f, appât m; (fig) appât, leurre m. (lit, fig) to take or rise to or swallow the ~ mordre à l'hameçon.

2 vt (a) hook, trap amorcer, appâter, garnir.

(b) (torment) animal tourmenter; person harceler, tourmenter; V bear².

baize [beɪz] n serge f, reps m. (green) ~ door porte matelassée.

bake [beɪk] 1 vt (a) (Culin) (faire) cuire au four. she ~s her own bread elle fait son pain elle-même; to ~ a cake (faire) cuire un gâteau; ~d apples/potatoes pommes fpl/pommes de terre au four; ~d Alaska omelette norvégienne; ~d beans haricots blancs à la sauce tomate; V half.

(b) pottery, bricks cuire (au four). earth ~d by the sun sol desséché or cuit par le soleil.

2 vi (a) [bread, cakes] cuire (au four).

(b) she ~s every Tuesday (makes bread) elle fait du pain le mardi; (bakes cakes) elle fait de la pâtisserie tous les mardis.

(c) [pottery etc] cuire. (fig) we are baking in this heat* on cuit* or on grille* par cette chaleur; it's baking (hot) today!* il fait une de ces chaleurs aujourd'hui!

3 cpd: bakehouse = bakery.

Bakelite ['beɪkəlaɪt] n ® Bakélite f ®.

baker ['beɪkəʳ] n boulanger m, -ère f. ~'s shop boulangerie f; (fig) ~'s dozen treize à la douzaine; I've got a ~'s dozen j'en ai treize pour le prix de douze.

bakery ['beɪkərɪ] n (shop, workplace) boulangerie(-pâtisserie) f.

baking ['beɪkɪŋ] 1 n (a) (U) (Culin) cuisson f; [earthenware] cuisson, cuite f. the bread is our own ~ nous faisons le pain nous-mêmes.

(b) [bread] fournée f; [bricks etc] cuisson f.

2 cpd: baking dish plat m allant au four; baking powder levure f (chimique), ≈ levure alsacienne; baking sheet = baking tray; baking soda bicarbonate m de soude; baking tin [cakes] moule m (à gâteaux); [tarts] tourtière f; baking tray plaque f à gâteaux or de four.

baksheesh ['bækʃiːʃ] n bakchich m.

Balaclava [ˌbælə'klɑːvə] n (Geog) Balaklava; (Brit: also ~ helmet) passe-montagne m.

balalaika [ˌbælə'laɪkə] n balalaïka f.

balance ['bæləns] 1 n (a) (scales) balance f. (Astron) the B~ la Balance; (fig) to be or hang in the ~ être en balance; (fig) to hold the ~ faire pencher la balance; V spring.

(b) (counterpoise) contrepoids m, compensation f.

(c) (U: equilibrium) équilibre m, aplomb m. (lit, fig) to keep/lose one's ~ garder/perdre son équilibre; (lit, fig) off ~ mal équilibré; to throw sb off ~ (lit) faire perdre l'équilibre à qn; (fig) couper le souffle à qn; the ~ of power la balance or l'équilibre des forces; the ~ of power in Europe l'équilibre

européen; (*Jur*) **when the ~ of his mind was disturbed** alors qu'il n'était pas responsable de ses actes.
(d) (*U*) (*Art etc*) équilibre *m*, juste mesure *f*. **he has no sense of ~** il n'a aucun sens des proportions *or* de la mesure; **a nice ~ of humour and pathos** un délicat dosage d'humour et de pathétique.
(e) (*Comm, Fin*) (*equality of sides*) balance *f*; (*difference of one side over other*) solde *m*. **credit/debit ~** solde créditeur/débiteur; **~ in hand** solde créditeur; **~ carried forward** solde reporté *or* à reporter; **~ due** solde débiteur; **to pay off the ~ of an account** solder un compte; (*Econ*) **~ of trade** balance commerciale; **~ of payments** balance des paiements; **sterling ~s** balances sterling; (*fig*) **to strike a ~** trouver le juste milieu; (*fig*) **on ~** à tout prendre, tout compte fait.
(f) (*larger amount*) excédent *m*, surplus *m*. **the ~ of the blame is yours** c'est vous qui portez la plus lourde part de responsabilité.
(g) (*remainder*) reste *m*.
(h) *[clock, watch]* régulateur *m*, balancier *m*.
2 *cpd*: **balance sheet** bilan *m*, compte *m*; **balance weight** contrepoids *m*.
3 *vt* **(a)** (*maintain equilibrium of*) tenir en équilibre, mettre en équilibre; (*fig*) équilibrer, compenser. **to ~ o.s. on one foot** se tenir en équilibre sur un (seul) pied; **a ~d diet** un régime (alimentaire) bien équilibré; **~d personality** personnalité équilibrée; **~d views** vues judicieuses; **he is a very ~d person** il est très équilibré.
(b) (*weigh in the mind*) balancer, peser; *two arguments, two solutions* comparer. **this must be ~d against that** il faut peser le pour et le contre.
(c) (*equal, make up for*) équilibrer, compenser, contrebalancer.
(d) (*Comm, Fin*) *account* balancer, solder. **to ~ the budget** équilibrer le budget; **to ~ the books** clôturer les comptes, dresser le bilan; **to ~ the cash** faire la caisse.
4 *vi* **(a)** (*be in equilibrium*) se faire contrepoids; *[scales]* être en équilibre.
(b) (*Comm, Fin*) *[accounts]* s'équilibrer, être en équilibre.
(c) (*waver*) hésiter, balancer.
balance out *vt sep* (*fig*) contrebalancer, compenser, équilibrer.
balancing ['bælənsɪŋ] *n* **(a)** (*oscillation*) balancement *m*; (*fig: wavering*) hésitation *f*.
(b) (*equilibrium*) mise *f* en équilibre, stabilisation *f*. **to do a ~ act** (*Theat*) faire de l'équilibrisme; (*fig*) jongler.
(c) (*Comm, Fin*) **~ of accounts** règlement *m or* solde *m* des comptes; (*Comm, Fin*) **~ of the books** balances *fpl* (mensuelles).
balcony ['bælkənɪ] *n* **(a)** balcon *m*. **(b)** (*Theat*) fauteuils *mpl or* stalles *fpl* de deuxième balcon.
bald [bɔːld] **1** *adj* **(a)** *person, head* chauve; *bird* à tête blanche; *tyre* lisse. **~ as a coot* or an egg*** chauve comme une boule de billard* *or* comme un œuf*; **to be going ~** perdre ses cheveux, devenir chauve, se déplumer*; **~ patch** *[person]* (petite) tonsure *f*; *[animal]* place dépourvue de poils; *[carpet etc]* coin *m or* zone *f* dégarni(e) *or* pelé(e).
(b) *style* plat, sec. **a ~ statement** une simple exposition de faits; **a ~ lie** un mensonge flagrant *or* non déguisé.
2 *cpd*: **bald-headed** chauve, à (la) tête chauve.
baldachin ['bɔːldəkən] *n*, **baldachino** [ˌbældə'kiːnəʊ] *n* baldaquin *m*.
balderdash ['bɔːldədæʃ] *n* bêtises *fpl*, balivernes *fpl*.
baldly ['bɔːldlɪ] *adv* abruptement.
baldness ['bɔːldnɪs] *n* (*V* **bald**) *[person]* calvitie *f*; *[mountains etc]* nudité *f*; *[style]* platitude *f*, pauvreté *f*.
bale[1] [beɪl] **1** *n* (*Comm*) ballot *m*; *[cotton, hay]* balle *f*. **2** *vt* emballotter; emballer.
bale[2] [beɪl] *vt* (*Naut*) = **bail**[3] **1.**
bale out 1 *vi* (*Aviat*) sauter (en parachute).
2 *vt sep* = **bail out**; *V* **bail**[3] **1.**
Balearic [ˌbælɪ'ærɪk] *adj*: **the ~ Islands** les (îles *fpl*) Baléares *fpl*.
baleful ['beɪlfʊl] *adj* sinistre, funeste, maléfique. **to give sb/sth a ~ look** regarder qn/qch d'un œil torve.
balefully ['beɪlfəlɪ] *adv* sinistrement, d'un air sinistre; *look* d'un œil torve; *say* d'un ton menaçant.
balk [bɔːk] **1** *n* (*Agr*) terre non labourée; (*Constr*) (*on ceiling*) solive *f*; (*building timber*) bille *f*; (*fig: hindrance*) pierre *f* d'achoppement, obstacle *m*.
2 *vt* *[person]* contrarier, contrecarrer; *plan* déjouer, contrecarrer.
3 *vi* *[person]* s'arrêter, reculer, hésiter (*at* devant), regimber (*at* contre); *[horse]* se dérober (*at* devant).
Balkan ['bɔːlkən] *adj, n*: **the ~ Mountains** le (mont) Balkan; **the ~ States, the ~s** les États *mpl* balkaniques, les Balkans *mpl*; **the ~ Peninsula** la péninsule balkanique.
ball[1] [bɔːl] **1** *n* **(a)** (*gen, Cricket, Golf, Hockey, Tennis*) balle *f*; (*inflated: Ftbl etc*) ballon *m*; (*Billiards*) bille *f*, boule *f*; (*Croquet*) boule. **as round as a ~** rond comme une boule *or* bille; **cat curled up in a ~** chat couché en rond *or* pelotonné (en boule); **tennis/golf** *etc* **~** balle de tennis/de golf *etc*; **croquet ~** boule de croquet; **to knock the ~s about** (*Tennis etc*) faire des balles; (*Billiards*) caramboler; (*fig*) **to keep the ~ rolling** (*maintain conversation*) continuer *or* soutenir la conversation; (*maintain activity*) continuer à faire marcher la machine*, assurer la continuité; (*maintain interest*) soutenir l'intérêt; (*fig*) **to start *or* set the ~ rolling*** faire démarrer une affaire (*or* une conversation *etc*); (*Brit fig*) **the ~ is with you *or* in your court** (c'est) à vous de jouer; (*fig*) **to be on the ~*** (*competent*) être à la hauteur (de la situation *or* des circonstances); (*alert*) ouvrir l'œil et le bon*; (*Met*) **~ of fire, ~ lightning** globe *m* de feu, éclair *m* en boule; (*fig*) **he's a real ~ of fire*** il est débordant d'activité; *V* **eye, play, tennis** *etc*.
(b) *[rifle etc]* balle *f*. (*lit, fig*) **~ and chain** boulet *m*; *V* **cannon.**
(c) *[wool, string]* pelote *f*, peloton *m*. **to wind up into a ~** mettre en pelote.
(d) (*Culin*) *[meat, fish]* boulette *f*; *[potato]* croquette *f*.
(e) (*Tech*) bille *f* (de roulement).
(f) (*Anat*) **~ of the foot** (partie antérieure de la) plante *f* du pied; **~ of the thumb** (partie charnue du) pouce *m*; *V* **eye.**
(g) (*US: also* **~ game**) = **baseball**; *V* **base**[1] **3.**
(h) **~s**∵ (*Anat*) couilles∵ *fpl*; (*Brit: nonsense*) conneries∵ *fpl*, couillonnades∵ *fpl*; (*excl*) **~s!**∵ quelles conneries!∵
2 *cpd*: **ball-and-socket joint** (joint *m* à) rotule *f*; **ball bearings** roulement *m* à billes; (*Tennis*) **ballboy** ramasseur *m* de balles; **ball cartridge** cartouche *f* à balle; **ballcock** robinet *m* à flotteur; (*US*) **ballpark** stade *m* de base-ball; **ball-point (pen)** stylo *m* (à) bille, (pointe *f*) Bic *m* ®; **ball-shaped** sphérique; (*Brit*) **he made a balls-up‡ of the job** il a salopé le boulot‡; (*Brit*) **the meeting was a balls-up‡** la réunion a été bordélique‡ *or* un vrai bordel‡; (*US*) **ball-up‡** = **balls-up‡.**
3 *vt* *wool etc* mettre en pelote, pelotonner.
4 *vi* s'agglomérer.
ball(s) up∵ **1** *vt sep* semer la pagaïe dans*, foutre la merde dans∵. **to be/get ball(s)ed up** être/se retrouver en pleine pagaïe* *or* dans la merde jusqu'au cou‡.
2 ball(s)-up‡ *n* *V* **ball**[1] **2.**
ball[2] [bɔːl] **1** *n* (*dance*) bal *m*. (*lit, fig*) **to open the ~** ouvrir le bal; **to have a ~‡** se fendre la gueule‡, prendre son pied‡; *V* **fancy** *etc*. **2** *cpd*: **ballroom** *[hotel]* salle *f* de danse; *[mansion]* salle de bal; (*U*) **ballroom dancing** danse *f* (de salon).
ballad ['bæləd] *n* (*Mus*) romance *f*; (*Literat*) ballade *f*.
ballast ['bæləst] **1** *n* (*U*) **(a)** (*Aviat, Naut*) lest *m*. **ship in ~** vaisseau *m* en lest; **to sail in ~** être sur lest; (*fig*) **he's got no ~** il n'a pas de plomb dans la cervelle, il n'a rien dans la tête.
(b) (*stone, clinker*) pierraille *f*; (*Rail*) ballast *m*.
2 *vt* **(a)** (*Aviat, Naut*) lester.
(b) (*Tech*) empierrer, caillouter; (*Rail*) ballaster.
ballerina [ˌbælə'riːnə] *n* ballerine *f*.
ballet ['bæleɪ] **1** *n* ballet *m*. **2** *cpd*: **ballet dancer** danseur *m*, -euse *f* de ballet; **ballet shoe** chausson *m* de danse; **ballet skirt** tutu *m*.
ballistic [bə'lɪstɪk] *adj* balistique. **~ missile** engin *m* balistique.
ballistics [bə'lɪstɪks] *n* (*U*) balistique *f*.
balloon [bə'luːn] **1** *n* **(a)** (*Aviat*) ballon *m*, aérostat *m*. **navigable/captive ~** ballon dirigeable/captif; **to go up in a ~** monter en ballon; **the ~ went up*** l'affaire a éclaté; (*Met*) (**meteorological** *or* **weather**) **~** ballon-sonde *m*; *V* **barrage** *etc*.
(b) (*toy*) ballon *m*.
(c) (*for brandy: also* **~ glass**) verre *m* ballon *inv*; (*Chem: also* **~ flask**) ballon *m*.
(d) (*in drawings, comics*) bulle *f*.
2 *vi* **(a)** **to go ~ing** faire une *or* des ascension(s) en ballon.
(b) (*swell out*) gonfler, être ballonné.
3 *cpd*: **balloon tyre** pneu *m* ballon.
balloonist [bə'luːnɪst] *n* aéronaute *mf*.
ballot ['bælət] **1** *n* **(a)** (*Pol etc*) (*paper*) bulletin *m* de vote; (*method of voting*) scrutin *m*; (*round of voting*) (tour *m* de) scrutin. **to vote by ~** voter par scrutin; **first/second ~** premier/second tour de scrutin; **to take a ~** procéder à un scrutin *or* à un vote.
(b) (*drawing of lots*) tirage *m* au sort.
2 *vi* **(a)** (*Pol etc*) voter au scrutin secret.
(b) (*draw lots*) tirer au sort. **to ~ for a place** tirer au sort pour avoir une place.
3 *cpd*: **ballot box** urne *f* (électorale); **ballot paper** bulletin *m* de vote.
bally*† ['bælɪ] *adj* (*Brit*) sacré*, satané.
ballyhoo* [ˌbælɪ'huː] *n* (*pej*) (*publicity*) battage* *m*, bourrage *m* de crâne*; (*nonsense*) balivernes *fpl*.
balm [bɑːm] *n* **(a)** (*lit, fig*) baume *m*. **(b)** (*Bot*) mélisse officinale; (*lemon* **~**) citronelle *f*.
balmy ['bɑːmɪ] *adj* **(a)** (*liter*) (*fragrant*) embaumé, parfumé; (*mild*) doux (*f* douce), adoucissant. **(b)** (*Bot*) balsamique. **(c)** (*Brit*‡†) timbré*, maboul‡.
baloney‡ [bə'ləʊnɪ] *n* (*U*) foutaise‡ *f*, idiotie(s) *f(pl)*, balivernes *fpl*.
balsa ['bɔːlsə] *n* (*also* **~ wood**) balsa *m*.
balsam ['bɔːlsəm] *n* **(a)** baume *m*. **~ fir** sapin *m* baumier. **(b)** (*Bot*) **garden ~, yellow ~** balsamine *f*. **(c)** (*Chem*) oléorésine *f*.
Baltic ['bɔːltɪk] *adj, n*: **the ~ (Sea)** la (mer) Baltique; **~ trade** commerce *m* de la Baltique; **~ timber** bois *m* du nord; **~ port** port *m* de la Baltique; **the ~ States** les pays *mpl* baltes.
baluster ['bæləstə^r] *n* balustre *m*. **~s** = **bannisters.**
balustrade [ˌbæləs'treɪd] *n* balustrade *f*.
bamboo [bæm'buː] **1** *n* bambou *m*. **2** *cpd* *chair, fence* de *or* en bambou. (*Pol*) **the Bamboo Curtain** le rideau de bambou.
bamboozle [bæm'buːzl] *vt* **(a)** (*deceive*) avoir*, mettre dedans*, embobiner*. **he was ~d into writing the letter** en l'embobinant on est parvenu à lui faire écrire la lettre. **(b)** (*perplex*) déboussoler*. **she was quite ~d** elle ne savait plus où elle en était, elle était complètement perdue *or* déboussolée*.
ban [bæn] **1** *n* **(a)** (*prohibition*) **to put a ~ on sth/sb's doing** interdire qch/à qn de faire.
(b) (*condemnation*) proscription *f*; (*Rel, fig*) interdit *m*.
2 *vt* (*prohibit*) interdire (*sth/sb from doing* qch/à qn de faire); *person* exclure (*from* de); *action* rejeter, interdire; *book, film* interdire. **B~ the Bomb Campaign** campagne *f* contre la bombe atomique; (*Rel*) **to ~ a book/a film** mettre un livre/un film à l'index.

banal [bə'nɑːl] *adj* banal, ordinaire.
banality [bə'nælɪtɪ] *n* banalité *f*.
banana [bə'nɑːnə] 1 *n* (*fruit*) banane *f*; (*tree*) bananier *m*. 2 *cpd*: **banana-boat** bananier *m* (*cargo*); (*pej*) **banana republic** république bananière; **banana skin** peau *f* de banane.
band[1] [bænd] *n* [*barrel*] cercle *m*; [*metal wheel*] bandage *m*; (*iron*) lien *m*; (*cloth, paper*) bande *f*; (*stripe*) bande, (*narrow*) bandelette *f*; (*leather*) lanière *f*; [*cigar*] bague *f*; [*hat*] ruban *m*; (*Rad*) bande; (*magnetic tape*) bande (magnétique); [*gramophone record*] plage *f*; (*Tech*) bande *or* courroie *f* de transmission. (*Opt*) **~s of the spectrum** bandes du spectre; **metal ~** bande métallique; **elastic** *or* **rubber ~** élastique *m*; (*Tech*) **~-saw** scie *f* à ruban; *V* **frequency, waist, wave** *etc*.
band[2] [bænd] 1 *n* (a) (*group*) bande *f*, troupe *f*.
(b) (*Mus*) orchestre *m*; (*Mil etc*) clique *f*, fanfare *f*, musique *f*. **members of the ~** musiciens *mpl*; *V* **brass, one-man** *etc*.
2 *cpd*: **bandmaster** chef *m* d'orchestre, (*Mil etc*) chef de musique *or* de fanfare; **bandsman** musicien *m*; **bandstand** kiosque *m* (à musique); (*US*) **bandwagon** char *m* des musiciens (en tête de la cavalcade); (*fig*) **to jump** *or* **climb on the bandwagon** suivre le mouvement, prendre le train en marche*, se mettre du côté du manche*.
band together *vi* former une bande.
bandage ['bændɪdʒ] 1 *n* (*strip of cloth*) bande *f*; (*dressing*) bandage *m*, pansement *m*; [*blindfolding*] bandeau *m*. **head swathed in ~s** tête enveloppée de linges *or* de pansements; *V* **crêpe**.
2 *vt* (*also* **~ up**) *broken limb* bander; *wound* mettre un pansement *or* un bandage sur; *person* mettre un pansement *or* un bandage à.
bandan(n)a [bæn'dænə] *n* foulard *m* (*à pois*).
bandbox ['bændbɒks] *n* carton *m* à chapeau(x).
banderol(e) ['bændərɒl] *n* (*Archit, Her, Naut*) banderole *f*.
bandit ['bændɪt] *n* (*lit, fig*) bandit *m*; *V* **one**.
banditry ['bændɪtrɪ] *n* (*U*) banditisme *m*, vol *m* à main armée.
bandolier [ˌbændə'lɪəʳ] *n* cartouchière *f*.
bandy[1] ['bændɪ] *vt ball, reproaches* se renvoyer. **to ~ blows (with sb)** échanger des coups (avec qn); **to ~ words** discuter, avoir des mots* (avec qn).
bandy about *vt sep story, report* faire circuler. **to bandy sb's name about** parler de qn; **to have one's name bandied about** faire parler de soi.
bandy[2] ['bændɪ] *adj* (a) *leg* arqué, bancal. (b) (*also* **~-legged**) *person* bancal; *horse* arqué. **to be ~-legged** avoir les jambes arquées.
bane [beɪn] *n* (a) fléau *m*, peste *f*. **he's/it's the ~ of my life*** il/cela m'empoisonne la vie, il est/c'est le fléau de mon existence. (b) (*poison*) poison *m*.
baneful ['beɪnfʊl] *adj* funeste, fatal; *poison* mortel.
banefully ['beɪnfəlɪ] *adv* (*V* **baneful**) funestement; mortellement.
bang[1] [bæŋ] 1 *n* (a) (*noise*) [*gun, explosives*] détonation *f*, fracas *m*; (*Aviat*) bang *m* (supersonique); [*door*] claquement *m*. **the door closed with a ~** la porte a claqué; **to go off with a ~** [*fireworks*] détoner, éclater; (‡: *succeed*) être une réussite sensationnelle *or* du tonnerre‡.
(b) (*blow*) coup *m* (violent).
2 *adv, adj* (*) **to go ~** éclater; **~ in the middle** au beau milieu, en plein milieu; **~ against the wall** tout contre le mur; **I ran ~ into the worst traffic** je suis tombé en plein dans le pire embouteillage; **he came ~ up against fierce opposition** il s'est brusquement trouvé face à une opposition farouche; (*Brit*) **to hit the target ~ on** frapper en plein dans la cible *or* le mille; (*Brit*) **his answer was ~ on** sa réponse est tombée pile; (*Brit*) **she came ~ on time** elle est arrivée à l'heure pile.
3 *excl* pan!, vlan!, boum! **~ went a £10 note!‡** et pan, voilà un billet de 10 livres de parti!*
4 *vt* frapper violemment. **to ~ one's fist on the table** cogner du poing sur la table, frapper la table du poing; **to ~ one's head against** *or* **on sth** se cogner la tête à *or* contre qch; (*fig*) **you're ~ing your head against a brick wall when you argue with him*** autant cracher en l'air* que d'essayer de discuter avec lui; **to ~ the door** (faire) claquer la porte; **he ~ed the window shut** il a claqué la fenêtre.
5 *vi* (a) [*door*] claquer, battre; [*fireworks*] éclater; [*gun*] détoner.
(b) **to ~ on** *or* **at the door** donner de grands coups dans la porte.
bang about*, bang around* 1 *vi* faire du bruit *or* du potin*.
2 *vt sep books, boxes, chairs* cogner les uns contre les autres.
bang away *vi* [*guns*] tonner; [*person*] (*keep firing*) tirer sans arrêt (*at* sur); [*workman etc*] faire du vacarme.
bang down *vt sep* poser *or* jeter brusquement. **to bang down the lid** rabattre violemment le couvercle; (*Telec*) **to bang down the receiver** raccrocher brutalement.
bang into *vt fus* (a) (*collide with*) se cogner contre, heurter. **the car banged into a tree** la voiture a heurté un arbre *or* est rentrée* dans un arbre.
(b) (‡: *meet*) tomber sur, se trouver nez à nez avec.
bang out *vt sep*: **to bang out a tune on the piano** taper un air au piano.
bang together *vt sep objects* cogner l'un(e) contre l'autre. **I could have banged their heads together!*** j'en aurais pris un pour taper sur l'autre!
bang up against *vt fus* = **bang into**.
bang[2] [bæŋ] *n* [*hair*] frange *f*.
banger‡ ['bæŋəʳ] *n* (*Brit*) (a) (*sausage*) saucisse *f*. **~s and mash** saucisses à la purée. (b) (*old car*) (vieux) tacot* *m*, (vieille) guimbarde *f*.
Bangladesh [ˈbæŋglə'deʃ] *n* Bangladesh *m or* Bangla Desh *m*.
bangle ['bæŋgl] *n* [*arm, ankle*] bracelet *m*, (*rigid*) jonc *m*.
banish ['bænɪʃ] *vt person* exiler (*from* de, *to* en, à), bannir (*from* de), proscrire; *cares, fear* bannir, chasser.
banishment ['bænɪʃmənt] *n* bannissement *m*, exil *m*, proscription *f*.
banister ['bænɪstəʳ] *n* = **bannister**.
banjo ['bændʒəʊ] *n, pl* **~es**, (*US*) **~s** banjo *m*.
bank[1] [bæŋk] 1 *n* (a) [*earth, snow, flowers*] talus *m*; (*Rail*) remblai *m*; [*racecourse*] banquette *f* (irlandaise); (*Min: coal face*) front *m* de taille; (*pithead*) carreau *m*; [*sand, sea, river*] banc *m*. **a ~ of clouds** un rideau de nuages.
(b) (*edge*) [*river, lake*] bord *m*, rive *f*; (*above water level*) berge *f*; [*canal*] bord; (*at bend in road*) bord relevé. [*river, lake*] **the ~s** le rivage; [*Paris*] **the left/right ~** la rive gauche/droite.
(c) (*Aviat*) virage incliné *or* sur l'aile.
2 *vt* (a) (*also* **~ up**) *road* relever (*dans un virage*); *river* endiguer; *earth* amonceler. **to ~ the fire** couvrir le feu.
(b) **to ~ an aircraft** faire faire à un avion un virage sur l'aile.
3 *vi* (a) [*snow, clouds etc*] s'entasser, s'accumuler, s'amonceler.
(b) (*Aviat*) [*pilot, aircraft*] virer (sur l'aile).
bank[2] [bæŋk] 1 *n* (a) (*institution*) banque *f*; (*office*) (bureau *m* de) banque. **the B~ of France** la Banque de France; (*fig*) **it is as safe as the B~ of England** ça ne court aucun risque, c'est de tout repos, c'est de l'or en barre; *V* **saving**.
(b) (*Betting*) banque *f*. **to break the ~** faire sauter la banque.
(c) (*Med*) banque *f*; *V* **blood, eye** *etc*.
2 *cpd*: **bank account** compte *m* en banque; (*US*) **bank bill** billet *m* de banque; **bank-book** livret *m or* carnet *m* de banque; **bank card** carte *f* d'identité bancaire; **bank charges** frais *mpl* de banque; (*Brit*) **bank clerk** employé(e) *m(f)* de banque; (*Brit*) **bank holiday** jour férié; (*Brit*) **banknote** billet *m* de banque; **bank rate** taux *m* d'escompte; **bank statement** relevé *m* de compte.
3 *vt money* mettre *or* déposer en banque; (*Med*) *blood* entreposer, conserver.
4 *vi*: **to ~ with Lloyds** avoir un compte à la Lloyds; **where do you ~?** quelle est votre banque?
bank (up)on *vt fus* (*fig*) compter sur. **you mustn't bank (up)on it** il ne faut pas compter là-dessus.
bank[3] [bæŋk] *n* (a) (*row, tier*) [*organ*] clavier *m*; [*typewriter*] rang *m*; (*Elec*) [*switches*] rangée *f*. **~ of oars** rangée d'avirons. (b) (*rowers' bench*) banc *m* (de rameurs).
bankable ['bæŋkəbl] *adj* bancable, négociable en banque.
banker ['bæŋkəʳ] *n* (*Betting, Fin*) banquier *m*. **~'s card** carte *f* d'identité bancaire; (*Brit*) **~'s order** ordre *m* de virement bancaire (*pour paiements réguliers*).
banking[1] ['bæŋkɪŋ] *n* (a) [*road*] (*embankment*) remblai *m*; (*action*) remblayage *m*. (b) (*Aviat*) virage *m* sur l'aile.
banking[2] ['bæŋkɪŋ] 1 *n* (*Fin*) (*transaction*) opérations *fpl* de banque *or* bancaires; (*profession*) profession *f* de banquier, la banque. **to study ~** faire des études bancaires.
2 *cpd*: **banking account** compte *m* en banque; **banking hours** heures *fpl* d'ouverture des banques; **banking house** banque *f*, établissement *m* bancaire; **the big banking houses** la haute banque, les grandes banques.
bankrupt ['bæŋkrʌpt] 1 *n* (*Jur*) failli(e) *m(f)*; (**fig: penniless person*) fauché(e)* *m(f)*. **~'s certificate** concordat *m*; **~'s estate** actif *m* de la faillite.
2 *adj* (*Jur*) failli; (**fig: penniless*) fauché‡. (*fig*) **~ of ideas** *etc* dépourvu *or* dénué d'idées *etc*; [*person, business*] **to go ~** faire faillite; [*person*] **to be ~** être en faillite; **to be declared ~** être déclaré *or* mis en faillite.
3 *vt person* mettre en faillite; (*) ruiner.
bankruptcy ['bæŋkrəptsɪ] *n* (*Jur*) faillite *f*; (**fig*) ruine *f*. (*Brit*) **B~ Court** ≈ tribunal *m* de commerce; **~ proceedings** procédure *f* de faillite.
banner ['bænəʳ] *n* bannière *f*, étendard *m*; (*Rel, fig*) bannière. (*Press*) **~ headlines** manchette *f*.
ban(n)ister ['bænɪstəʳ] *n* rampe *f* (d'escalier). **to slide down the ~(s)** descendre sur la rampe.
banns [bænz] *npl* bans *mpl* (*de mariage*).
banquet ['bæŋkwɪt] 1 *n* (*ceremonial dinner*) banquet *m*; (*lavish feast*) festin *m*. 2 *vt* (*ceremoniously*) offrir un banquet à; (*more lavishly*) offrir un festin à, régaler. 3 *vi* faire un banquet, festoyer. 4 *cpd*: **banquet(ing) hall** salle *f* de(s) banquet(s); (*Hist*) salle des festins.
banshee ['bæn'ʃiː] *n* (a) (*Ir Myth*) fée *f* (*dont les cris présagent la mort*). (b) (‡: *siren*) sirène *f*.
bantam ['bæntəm] *n* coq nain, poule naine (*de Bantam*). (*Boxing*) **~-weight** poids *m* coq.
banter ['bæntəʳ] 1 *n* badinage *m*, plaisanterie *f*. 2 *vt* plaisanter. 3 *vi* badiner, plaisanter.
bantering ['bæntərɪŋ] *adj* plaisantin, badin.
banyan ['bænɪən] *n* banian *m*.
baptism ['bæptɪzəm] *n* baptême *m*. (*fig*) **~ of fire** baptême du feu.
baptismal [bæp'tɪzməl] *adj* de baptême, baptismal. **~ font** fonts baptismaux; **~ name** nom *m* de baptême; **~ vows** vœux *mpl* du baptême.
baptist ['bæptɪst] 1 *n* (a) baptiste *m*. **(Saint) John the B~** saint Jean-Baptiste. (b) (*Rel*) **B~** baptiste *mf*; **the B~ Church** l'Église *f* baptiste. 2 *adj* (*Rel*) **B~** baptiste.
baptize [bæp'taɪz] *vt* (*Rel, also* *) baptiser.
bar[1] [bɑːʳ] 1 *n* (a) (*slab*) [*metal*] barre *f*; [*wood*] planche *f*; [*gold*] lingot *m*; [*chocolate*] tablette *f*. **~ of soap** savonnette *f*, pain *m* de savon; **~ of gold** lingot (d'or).
(b) (*rod*) [*window, cage*] barreau *m*; [*grate*] barre *f*; [*door*] barre, bâcle *f*; (*Sport*) barre. **to be/put sb behind (prison) ~s** être/mettre qn sous les verrous; *V* **parallel** *etc*.
(c) [*river, harbour*] barre *f*.

(d) (*fig: obstacle*) obstacle *m.* **to be a ~ to progress** *etc.* empêcher le progrès *etc,* faire obstacle au progrès *etc*; *V* **colour.**

(e) *[light]* raie *f*; *[colour]* bande *f.*

(f) (*U: Jur*) (*profession*) barreau *m*; (*in court*) barre *f.* (*Brit*) **to call to the ~,** (*US*) **to admit to the ~** inscrire au barreau; (*Brit*) **to be called to the ~,** (*US*) **to be admitted to the ~** s'inscrire au barreau; **to read for the ~** préparer le barreau; **the prisoner at the ~** l'accusé(e) *m(f)*; (*fig*) **the ~ of public opinion/of conscience** le tribunal de l'opinion publique/de la conscience.

(g) (*public house*) café *m,* bar *m,* bistro(t)* *m*; *[hotel, theatre]* bar; *[station]* café, bar; (*at open-air shows etc*) buvette *f*; *V* **coffee, public.**

(h) (*counter*) (*for drinks*) comptoir *m.* **at the ~** au comptoir, sur le zinc‡; (*Comm*) **stocking/hat ~** rayon *m* des bas/des chapeaux.

(i) (*Mus*) mesure *f*; (*also* **~ line**) barre *f* de mesure. **the opening ~s** les premières mesures; *V* **double.**

(j) (*Brit Mil*) barrette *f* (*portée sur le ruban d'une médaille*), ≈ palme *f*; (*US Mil*) galon *m.*

(k) (*Her*) burelle *f.* **~ sinister** barre *f* de bâtardise.

(l) (*Met*) bar *m.*

2 *cpd*: **barmaid** serveuse *f* (*de bar*), barmaid *f*; **barman, bartender** barman *m.*

3 *vt* **(a)** (*obstruct*) *road* barrer. **to ~ sb's way** barrer le passage à qn, couper la route à qn; **to ~ the way to progress** faire obstacle au progrès.

(b) (*put bars on*) *window* griller, munir de barreaux. **to ~ the door** mettre la barre à la porte; (*lit, fig*) **to ~ the door against sb** barrer la porte à qn.

(c) (*exclude, prohibit*) *person* exclure (*from* de); *action, thing* défendre. **to ~ sb from a career** barrer une carrière à qn; **she ~s smoking in her house** elle défend qu'on fume (*subj*) chez elle; *V* **hold.**

(d) (*stripe*) rayer, barrer.

bar² [bɑːʳ] *prep* excepté, sauf, à l'exception de, à part. **~ accidents** sauf accident, à moins d'accident(s), sauf imprévu; **~ none** sans exception; **~ one** sauf un(e); *V also* **barring, shouting.**

barb¹ [bɑːb] **1** *n* **(a)** *[fish hook]* barbillon *m*; *[arrow]* barbelure *f*; *[feather]* barbe *f*; (*fig*) *[wit etc]* trait *m.* **the ~s of criticism** les traits acérés de la critique; **~ wire = barbed wire;** *V* **barbed 2.**

(b) (*Dress*) barbette *f.*

2 *vt arrow* garnir de barbelures, barbeler; *fish hook* garnir de barbillons.

barb² [bɑːb] *n* (*horse*) (cheval *m*) barbe *m.*

Barbados [bɑːˈbeɪdɒs] *n* Barbade *f.*

barbarian [bɑːˈbɛərɪən] *adj, n* (*Hist, fig*) barbare (*mf*).

barbaric [bɑːˈbærɪk] *adj* (*Hist, fig*) barbare, de barbare.

barbarism [ˈbɑːbərɪzəm] *n* **(a)** (*U: state*) barbarie *f.* **(b)** (*Ling*) barbarisme *m.*

barbarity [bɑːˈbærɪtɪ] *n* barbarie *f,* cruauté *f,* inhumanité *f.* **the barbarities of modern warfare** la barbarie *or* les atrocités *fpl* de la guerre moderne.

barbarize [ˈbɑːbəraɪz] *vt* **(a)** *people* ramener à l'état barbare. **(b)** *language* corrompre.

barbarous [ˈbɑːbərəs] *adj* (*Hist, Ling, fig*) barbare.

barbarously [ˈbɑːbərəslɪ] *adv* cruellement, inhumainement.

Barbary [ˈbɑːbərɪ] **1** *n* Barbarie *f,* États *mpl* barbaresques. **2** *cpd*: **Barbary ape** singe *m* de Barbarie; **Barbary duck** canard *m* de Barbarie; **Barbary horse** (cheval *m*) barbe *m.*

barbecue [ˈbɑːbɪkjuː] (*vb*: *prp* **barbecuing**) **1** *n* (*grid*) barbecue *m,* gril *m*; (*occasion*) barbecue; (*animal*) animal rôti entier. **2** *vt steak* griller au charbon de bois; *animal* rôtir tout entier.

barbed [bɑːbd] **1** *adj arrow* barbelé; (*fig*) *words, wit* acéré. **2** *cpd*: **barbed wire** fil *m* de fer barbelé; **barbed-wire entanglements** (réseau *m* de) barbelés *mpl*; **barbed-wire fence** haie barbelée, haie de barbelés.

barbel [ˈbɑːbəl] *n* (*fish*) barbeau *m*; (*filament*) barbillon *m,* barbe *f.*

barber [ˈbɑːbəʳ] *n* coiffeur *m* (pour hommes). **~'s pole** enseigne *f* de coiffeur.

barbican [ˈbɑːbɪkən] *n* barbacane *f.*

barbitone [ˈbɑːbɪtəʊn] *n* véronal *m.*

barbiturate [bɑːˈbɪtjʊrɪt] *n* barbiturique *m.*

barbituric [ˌbɑːbɪˈtjʊərɪk] *adj* barbiturique.

barcarol(l)e [ˌbɑːkəˈrəʊl] *n* barcarolle *f.*

bard¹ [bɑːd] *n* (*minstrel*) (*esp Celtic*) barde *m*; *[Ancient Greece]* aède *m*; (*Poetry, also hum: poet*) poète *m.* **the B~ of Avon** le chantre d'Avon (*Shakespeare*).

bard² [bɑːd] (*Culin*) **1** *n* barde *f* (de lard). **2** *vt* barder.

bardic [ˈbɑːdɪk] *adj* (*esp Celtic*) *poetry etc* du barde, des bardes.

bare [bɛəʳ] **1** *adj* **(a)** (*naked, uncovered*) *person, skin, sword, floor etc* nu; *hill, summit* pelé; *countryside, tree* dénudé, dépouillé; (*Elec*) *wire* dénudé, à nu. **~ to the waist** nu jusqu'à la ceinture; **in his ~ skin** tout nu; **he killed the wolf with his ~ hands** il a tué le loup à mains nues; (*Boxing*) **to fight with ~ hands** boxer à main nue; (*Golf*) **~ patch** place dénudée (d'herbe), place pelée; **the dog had a few ~ patches on his back** le chien avait la peau du dos pelée par endroits; **with his head ~** nu-tête *inv*; **to sleep on ~ boards** coucher sur la dure; **to lay ~ one's heart** montrer *or* mettre son cœur à nu; **to lay ~ a secret** révéler *or* dévoiler un secret; (*Cards*) **ace/king ~** as/roi sec.

(b) (*empty, unadorned*) *garden* dépouillé de sa végétation; *wall* nu; *style* dépouillé. **room ~ of furniture** pièce *f* vide; **~ cupboard** placard *m* vide *or* dégarni; **~ statement of facts** simple énoncé *m* des faits.

(c) (*just enough*) **the ~ necessities of life** le strict nécessaire; **to earn a ~ living** gagner tout juste *or* à peine de quoi vivre; **~ majority** faible majorité *f*; **it's a ~ possibility** c'est tout juste possible; **a ~ thank you** un merci tout sec.

2 *vt* mettre à nu, découvrir; *sword* dégainer, mettre à nu, tirer du fourreau; (*Elec*) *wire* dénuder, mettre à nu. *[person, animal]* **to ~ one's teeth** montrer les dents (*at* à); **to ~ one's head** se découvrir (la tête); **he ~d his teeth in a smile** il sourit de toutes ses dents.

3 *cpd*: **bareback** *ride* à nu, à cru; **bareback rider** cavalier *m,* -ière *f* qui monte à cru; **barefaced** *lie, liar* éhonté, impudent, effronté; **it is barefaced robbery** c'est un *or* du vol manifeste; **barefooted** (*adv*) nu-pieds, (les) pieds nus; (*adj*) aux pieds nus; **bareheaded** (*adv*) nu-tête *inv,* (la) tête nue; (*adj*) nu-tête *inv*; *woman* en cheveux; **barelegged** (*adv*) nu-jambes, (les) jambes nues; (*adj*) aux jambes nues.

barely [ˈbɛəlɪ] *adv* **(a)** (*scarcely*) à peine, tout juste. **he can ~ read** c'est tout juste *or* à peine s'il sait lire, il sait tout juste *or* à peine lire.

(b) **a ~ furnished room** une pièce pauvrement meublée.

(c) (*plainly*) sans détails. **to state a fact ~** donner un fait sans détails *or* tout sec.

bareness [ˈbɛənɪs] *n [person]* nudité *f*; *[room]* dénuement *m*; *[furniture]* pauvreté *f*; *[style]* (*poverty*) sécheresse *f,* pauvreté; (*simplicity*) dépouillé *m.*

bargain [ˈbɑːgɪn] **1** *n* **(a)** (*transaction*) marché *m,* affaire *f.* **to make** *or* **strike** *or* **drive a ~** conclure un marché (*with* avec); **it's a ~!*** c'est convenu! *or* entendu!; **a bad/good ~** une mauvaise/bonne affaire, une affaire désavantageuse/avantageuse; **a ~'s a ~** marché conclu reste conclu; (*fig*) **into the ~** par-dessus le marché, par surcroît, en plus; *V* **best, drive** *etc.*

(b) (*cheap offer*) occasion *f.* **it's a (real) ~!** c'est une véritable occasion! *or* affaire!

2 *cpd*: **bargain basement** coin *m* des (bonnes) affaires; **bargain-hunter** chercheur *m,* -euse *f* d'occasions; **bargain-hunting** chasse *f* aux (bonnes) occasions; (*Comm*) **bargain offer** offre avantageuse; **bargain price** prix avantageux; **bargain sale** soldes *mpl.*

3 *vi* **(a)** (*haggle*) **to ~ with sb** marchander avec qn; **to ~ over an article** marchander un article.

(b) (*negotiate*) négocier, entrer en négociation (*with* avec). **to ~ with sb for sth** négocier qch avec qn.

(c) (*fig*) **to ~ for sth** s'attendre à qch; **I did not ~ for that** je ne m'attendais pas à cela; **I got more than I ~ed for** je ne m'attendais pas à un coup pareil, j'ai eu du fil à retordre.

bargaining [ˈbɑːgənɪŋ] *n* marchandage *m.* **that gives us more ~ power** ceci nous donne une position de force *or* plus d'atouts dans les négociations; *V* **collective.**

barge [bɑːdʒ] **1** *n* (*on river, canal*) chaland *m*; (*large*) péniche *f*; (*with sail*) barge *f.* **the admiral's ~** la vedette de l'amiral; **motor ~** chaland automoteur, péniche automotrice; **state ~** barque *f* de cérémonie.

2 *cpd*: **bargeman** batelier *m,* marinier *m*; **barge pole** gaffe *f*; (*Brit*) **I wouldn't touch it with a barge pole*** (*revolting*) je n'y toucherais pas avec des pincettes; (*risky*) je ne m'y frotterais pas.

3 *vi* (*) **to ~ into a room** faire irruption dans une pièce, entrer sans façons dans une pièce; **he ~d through the crowd** il bousculait les gens pour passer.

barge about*, barge around* *vi* aller et venir comme un troupeau d'éléphants*.

barge in* *vi* (*enter*) faire irruption; (*interrupt*) se mêler à la conversation (sans y être invité); (*interfere*) se mêler de ce qui ne vous regarde pas.

barge into* *vt fus* (*knock against*) *person* rentrer dans*; *thing* donner *or* se cogner contre; (*interfere in*) *discussion, affair* intervenir mal à propos dans, se mêler de, mettre son nez dans.

barge through* *vi* traverser comme un ouragan.

bargee [bɑːˈdʒiː] *n* (*Brit*) batelier *m,* marinier *m.* **to swear like a ~** jurer comme un charretier.

baritone [ˈbærɪtəʊn] **1** *n* (*voice, singer, instrument*) baryton *m.* **2** *cpd voice, part* de baryton.

barium [ˈbɛərɪəm] *n* baryum *m.* (*Med*) **~ meal** (bouillie *f* de) sulfate *m* de baryum.

bark¹ [bɑːk] **1** *n [tree]* écorce *f.* **to strip the ~ off a tree** écorcer un arbre. **2** *vt tree* écorcer. **to ~ one's shins** s'écorcher *or* s'égratigner les jambes.

bark² [bɑːk] **1** *n [dog]* aboiement *m,* aboi *m*; *[fox]* glapissement *m*; (*: *cough*) toux sèche. **the ~ of a gun** un coup de canon; **to let out a ~** (*lit*) aboyer, pousser un aboiement; (*cough*) tousser; **his ~ is worse than his bite** il fait plus de bruit que de mal, tous les chiens qui aboient ne mordent pas (*Prov*).

2 *vi [dog]* aboyer (*at* après); *[fox]* glapir; *[gun]* aboyer, tonner; (*speak sharply*) crier, vociférer, aboyer; (*cough*) tousser. **to ~ at sb** aboyer après qn; (*fig*) **to ~ up the wrong tree** faire fausse route, se tromper d'adresse, être sur une fausse piste.

bark out *vt sep order* glapir.

bark³ [bɑːk] *n* (*Poetry*) barque *f*; (*Naut*) trois-mâts *or* quatre-mâts carré.

barker [ˈbɑːkəʳ] *n [fairground]* bonimenteur *m,* aboyeur† *m.*

barley [ˈbɑːlɪ] **1** *n* orge *f.* **pearl ~** orge perlé (*note gender*); **Scotch ~** orge mondé (*note gender*).

2 *cpd*: **barley beer** cervoise *f*; **barleycorn** grain *m* d'orge; **barley field** champ *m* d'orge; **barley sugar** sucre *m* d'orge; (*esp Brit*) **barley water** boisson orgée, orgeat *m.*

3 *excl* (*N Engl, Scot: in games*) pouce!

barm [bɑːm] *n* levure *f* (de bière).

barmy‡† [ˈbɑːmɪ] *adj* (*Brit*) timbré*, maboul‡.

barn [bɑːn] **1** *n* **(a)** grange *f.* **it's a great ~ of a house*** c'est une énorme bâtisse.

(b) (*US*) *[horses]* écurie *f*; *[cattle]* étable *f.*

2 *cpd*: **barn dance** danses campagnardes *or* paysannes *or* folkloriques; **it's as big as a barndoor** c'est gros comme une maison; **barn owl** effraie *f*, chouette *f* des clochers; **barnstorm** (*Theat*) jouer sur les tréteaux; (*US Pol*) faire une tournée électorale (dans les circonscriptions rurales); **barnstormer** (*Theat*) acteur ambulant; (*US Pol*) orateur électoral; **barnyard** basse-cour *f*; **barnyard fowls** volaille *f*.

barnacle ['bɑːnəkl] *n* **(a)** (*shellfish*) bernache *f*, anatife *m*; (*pej: person*) crampon* *m*; (‡: *old sailor*) vieux loup de mer*. **(b)** (*Orn: also* ~ **goose**) bernache *f*, bernacle *f*.

barogram ['bærəʊgræm] *n* barogramme *m*.

barograph ['bærəʊgrɑːf] *n* barographe *m*.

barometer [bə'rɒmɪtəʳ] *n* (*lit, fig*) baromètre *m*. **the ~ is showing set fair** le baromètre est au beau fixe; *V* **aneroid** *etc*.

barometric [ˌbærəʊ'metrɪk] *adj* barométrique.

baron ['bærən] *n* **(a)** baron *m*. (*fig*) **industrial** ~ magnat *m* de l'industrie, gros industriel. **(b)** ~ **of beef** double aloyau *m* de bœuf.

baroness ['bærənɪs] *n* baronne *f*.

baronet ['bærənɪt] *n* baronnet *m*.

baronial [bə'rəʊnɪəl] *adj* (*lit, fig*) baronnial, de baron, seigneurial. ~ **hall** demeure seigneuriale.

barony ['bærənɪ] *n* baronnie *f*.

baroque [bə'rɒk] *adj, n* (*Archit, Art, Mus*) baroque (*m*).

barque [bɑːk] *n* = **bark**[3].

barrack ['bærək] **1** *n* (*gen pl, often with sg vb*) (*Mil*) caserne *f*, quartier *m*. **cavalry** ~ quartier de cavalerie; **in ~s** à la caserne, au quartier; (*Brit*) **it's a (great) ~(s) of a place*** c'est une (vraie) caserne*; *V* **confine, naval** *etc*.

2 *cpd*: **barrack life** vie *f* de caserne; **barrack room** chambrée *f*; **barrack-room joke/language** plaisanterie *f*/propos *mpl* de caserne *or* de corps de garde; (*fig*) **to be a barrack-room lawyer** se promener toujours avec le code sous le bras; (*US*) **barracks bag** sac *m* (*de soldat*); **barrack square** cour *f* (de caserne).

3 *vt soldiers* caserner.

barracuda [ˌbærə'kjuːdə] *n* barracuda *m*.

barrage ['bærɑːʒ] *n* **(a)** *[river]* barrage *m*. **(b)** (*Mil*) tir *m* de barrage; (*fig*) *[questions, reproaches]* pluie *f*; *[words]* flot *m*, déluge *m*. ~ **balloon** ballon *m* de barrage, ballon de D.C.A.; *V* **creeping**.

-barred [bɑːd] *adj ending in cpds*: **five-barred gate** barrière *f* à cinq barreaux.

barrel ['bærəl] **1** *n* **(a)** (*cask*) *[wine]* tonneau *m*, barrique *f*, fût *m*; *[cider]* futaille *f*; *[herring]* caque *f*; *[oil]* baril *m*; *[tar]* gonne *f*; (*small*) baril; *V* **biscuit**.

(b) *[firearm]* canon *m*; *[fountain pen]* corps *m*; *[key]* canon; *[lock, clock]* barillet *m*. **to give sb both ~s*** lâcher ses deux coups sur qn*.

(c) *[horse etc]* tronc *m*.

2 *vt wine etc* mettre en fût *etc*.

3 *cpd*: **barrel organ** orgue *m* de Barbarie; **barrel-shaped** en forme de barrique *or* de tonneau; *person* gros comme une barrique; **barrel vault** voûte *f* en berceau.

barren ['bærən] **1** *adj land* stérile, improductif; (*dry*) aride; *tree, plant, woman* stérile; (*fig*) (*lacking content*) stérile; (*lacking interest*) ingrat, aride; *discussion* stérile; *style* aride, sec (*f* sèche). **2** *n* (*esp US: gen pl*) ~**(s)** lande(s) *f(pl)*; **B~ Grounds** toundra canadienne.

barrenness ['bærənnɪs] *n* (*V* **barren**) stérilité *f*; aridité *f*; sécheresse *f*.

barricade [ˌbærɪ'keɪd] **1** *n* barricade *f*; (*fig*) barrière *f*. **2** *vt street* barricader; (*also* ~ **in**) *person* barricader. **to ~ o.s. (in)** se barricader.

barrier ['bærɪəʳ] *n* barrière *f*; (*Rail: also* **ticket** ~) portillon *m* (d'accès); (*fig*) barrière, obstacle *m*. ~ **to progress** obstacle au progrès; ~ **cream** crème isolante *or* protectrice; *V* **great, sound**[1] *etc*.

barring ['bɑːrɪŋ] *prep* excepté, sauf. ~ **accidents** sauf accident, à moins d'accident(s), sauf imprévu; *V also* **bar**[2].

barrister ['bærɪstəʳ] *n* (*Brit: also* ~**-at-law**) avocat *m*.

barrow[1] ['bærəʊ] **1** *n* (*also* **wheel**~) brouette *f*; (*also* **coster's** ~) voiture *f* des quatre saisons; (*Rail: also* **luggage** ~) diable *m*; (*also* **hand** ~) civière *f*, (*without wheels*) brancard *m*; (*Min*) wagonnet *m*. **to wheel sth in a** ~ brouetter qch.

2 *cpd*: **barrow-boy** marchand *m* des quatre saisons.

barrow[2] ['bærəʊ] *n* (*Archeol*) tumulus *m*; (*Geog*) colline *f*.

Bart [bɑːt] *n abbr of* **baronet**.

barter ['bɑːtəʳ] **1** *n* échange *m*, troc *m*. **2** *vt* échanger, troquer (*for* contre). **3** *vi* faire un échange *or* un troc.

barter away *vt rights, liberty* vendre (*for* pour); *one's honour* faire trafic de.

Bartholomew [bɑː'θɒləmjuː] *n* Barthélemy *m*. (*Hist*) **the Massacre of St** ~ (le massacre de) la Saint-Barthélemy.

barytone ['bærɪtəʊn] *n* (*Mus*) baryton *m* (*instrument*).

basal ['beɪsl] *adj* (*lit, fig*) fondamental; (*Physiol*) basal.

basalt ['bæsɔːlt] *n* basalte *m*.

bascule ['bæskjuːl] *n* bascule *f*. ~ **bridge** pont *m* à bascule.

base[1] [beɪs] **1** *n* **(a)** (*main ingredient*) base *f*; (*starting point*) base, point *m* de départ; (*Chem, Math*) base; (*lowest part*) base, partie inférieure; *[column]* base, pied *m*; *[building]* soubassement *m*; *[cartridge, electric lamp]* culot *m*; *[tree]* pied. ~ **over apex** cul par-dessus tête.

(b) (*Mil etc*) base *f*; *V* **air** *etc*.

(c) (*Baseball*) base *f*.

2 *vt* (*fig*) *reasoning, belief, opinion* baser, fonder (*on* sur). (*Mil etc*) **to be ~d on York** être basé à York; **the post will be ~d on London but will involve considerable travel** le poste sera centré sur Londres mais il exigera de nombreux déplacements; **I am ~d on Glasgow now** j'opère maintenant à partir de Glasgow.

3 *cpd*: **baseball** base-ball *m*; (*US Constr*) **baseboard** plinthe *f*; *[paint]* **base coat** première couche; **base line** (*Baseball*) ligne *f* des bases; (*Surv*) base *f*; *[diagram]* ligne zéro; (*Tennis*) ligne de fond; (*Art*) ligne de fuite.

base[2] [beɪs] *adj* **(a)** *action, motive, thoughts* bas (*f* basse), abject, indigne; *behaviour* ignoble; *ingratitude, mind* bas; *birth, descent* bas; *task* bas, servile; *coin* faux (*f* fausse). ~ **metal** métal vil. **(b)** (*US*) = **bass**[1] **2**.

-based [beɪst] *adj ending in cpds*: **London-based** dont le centre d'opérations est Londres.

Basel ['bɑːzəl] *n* Bâle.

baseless ['beɪslɪs] *adj accusation etc* sans fondement; *suspicion* sans fondement, injustifié.

basely ['beɪslɪ] *adv* bassement, vilement, lâchement.

basement ['beɪsmənt] *n* sous-sol *m*. **in the** ~ au sous-sol; ~ **flat** (appartement *m* en) sous-sol (*also pej*), rez-de-jardin *m*.

baseness ['beɪsnɪs] *n* (*V* **base**[2]) bassesse *f*, indignité *f*; ignominie *f*; fausseté *f*.

bash* [bæʃ] **1** *n* coup *m*, coup de poing. **to give sb a ~ on the nose** donner un coup de poing sur le nez de qn; **the car bumper has had a** ~ le pare-choc est cabossé *or* bosselé; **I'll have a ~ (at it)‡** je vais essayer un coup*; **have a ~!‡** vas-y, essaie toujours!

2 *vt* frapper, cogner. (*lit, fig*) **to ~ one's head against a wall** se cogner la tête contre le mur; **to ~ sb on the head** assommer qn.

bash about*, bash around* *vt sep person* (*hit*) tabasser‡, flanquer* des coups à; (*ill-treat*) maltraiter, rudoyer; *car* malmener.

bash in* *vt sep door* enfoncer; *hat, car* cabosser, défoncer; *lid, cover* défoncer. **to bash sb's head in** défoncer le crâne de qn*.

bash up* *vt sep car* bousiller*; (*Brit*) *person* tabasser‡.

-basher* ['bæʃəʳ] *n ending in cpds*: **he's a queer-basher** il déblatère toujours contre les pédés‡.

bashful ['bæʃfʊl] *adj* (*shy*) timide, intimidé; (*modest*) pudique; (*shamefaced*) honteux.

bashfully ['bæʃfəlɪ] *adv* (*V* **bashful**) timidement, avec timidité; pudiquement; avec honte.

bashfulness ['bæʃfʊlnɪs] *n* (*V* **bashful**) timidité *f*; modestie *f*, pudeur *f*; honte *f*.

bashing‡ ['bæʃɪŋ] *n* rossée* *f*, raclée* *f*. **to take a** ~ *[team, regiment]* prendre une raclée* *or* une dérouillée‡; *[car, carpet etc]* en prendre un (vieux *or* sacré) coup*.

basic ['beɪsɪk] **1** *adj* **(a)** (*fundamental*) *difficulty, principle, problem, essentials* fondamental. (*Math*) **the four ~ operations** les quatre opérations fondamentales; ~ **French** le français fondamental *or* de base; ~ **vocabulary** vocabulaire *m* de base; **B~ English** l'anglais fondamental.

(b) (*forming starting point*) *salary, working hours* de base. **a ~ suit to which one can add accessories** un petit tailleur neutre auquel on peut ajouter des accessoires; **a ~ black dress** une petite robe noire.

(c) (*Chem*) basique. ~ **salt** sel *m* basique; ~ **slag** scorie *f* de déphosphoration.

2 *n* (*) **the ~s** l'essentiel *m*; **to get down to the ~s** en venir à l'essentiel.

basically ['beɪsɪklɪ] *adv* fondamentalement, à la base.

basil ['bæzl] *n* (*Bot*) basilic *m*.

basilica [bə'zɪlɪkə] *n* basilique *f*.

basilisk ['bæzɪlɪsk] *n* (*Myth, Zool*) basilic *m*.

basin ['beɪsn] *n* **(a)** (*gen*) cuvette *f*, bassine *f*; (*for food*) bol *m*; (*wide: for cream etc*) jatte *f*; (*also* **wash~, wash-hand** ~) cuvette; (*plumbed in*) lavabo *m*; *[lavatory]* cuvette; *[fountain]* vasque *f*; *V* **sugar** *etc*.

(b) (*Geog*) *[river]* bassin *m*; (*valley*) cuvette *f*; (*harbour*) bassin; *V* **catchment, tidal** *etc*.

basinful ['beɪsnfʊl] *n* *[milk]* bolée *f*; *[water]* pleine cuvette. **I've had a ~‡** j'en ai par-dessus la tête* *or* ras le bol‡ (*of* de).

basis ['beɪsɪs] *n, pl* **bases** ['beɪsiːz] (*lit, fig*) base *f*. **on that** ~ dans ces conditions; **on the ~ of what you've told me** par suite de ce que vous m'avez dit.

bask [bɑːsk] *vi*: **to ~ in the sun** se dorer au soleil; **to ~ in sb's favour** jouir de la faveur de qn; **~ing shark** (requin *m*) pèlerin *m*.

basket ['bɑːskɪt] **1** *n* (*shopping* ~) (*one-handled*) panier *m*; (*deeper, two-handled*) cabas *m*; (*clothes* ~) (*wide, two-handled*) corbeille *f* (à linge); (*dirty linen* ~) corbeille *or* panier (à linge sale); (*for flowers, fruit, bread*) corbeille; (*wastepaper* ~) corbeille (à papier); (*on person's back*) hotte *f*; (*on donkey*) panier; (*for game*) bourriche *f*; (*for fish, oysters*) bourriche, cloyère *f*; (*Basketball*) panier. **a ~(ful) of eggs** un panier d'œufs; *V* **laundry, luncheon, work** *etc*.

2 *cpd handle etc* de panier. **basketball** basket(-ball) *m*; **basketball player** basketteur *m*, -euse *f*; **basket chair** chaise *f* en osier; **basket maker** vannier *m*; **basketwork** vannerie *f*.

Basque [bæsk] **1** *n* **(a)** Basque *m*, Basquaise *f*. **(b)** (*Ling*) basque *m*. **2** *adj* basque. ~ **Country** Pays *m* basque; ~ **Provinces** provinces *fpl* basques.

bas-relief ['bæsrɪˌliːf] *n* bas-relief *m*.

bass[1] [beɪs] (*Mus*) **1** *n* (*part, singer*) basse *f*; *V* **double** *etc*.

2 *adj voice, note* bas (*f* basse), de basse; (*low-sounding*) bas, grave. ~ **tones** sons *mpl* graves.

3 *cpd*: **bass-baritone** basse chantante; **bass clarinet** clarinette basse; **bass clef** clef *f* de fa; **bass drum** grosse caisse; **bass-relief** = **bas-relief**; **bass strings** basses *fpl*; **bass viol** viole *f* de gambe.

bass[2] [bæs] *n* (*fibre*) teille *f*, tille *f*.

bass[3] [bæs] *n* (*fish*) (*freshwater*) perche *f*; (*sea*) bar *m*, loup *m*.

basset ['bæsɪt] *n* (*also* ~ **hound**) (chien *m*) basset *m*.

bassoon [bə'suːn] *n* basson *m*; *V* **double**.

basso profundo [ˌbæsəʊprə'fʊndəʊ] *n* (*singer, voice*) basse profonde.

bastard ['bɑːstəd] **1** *n* **(a)** bâtard(e) *m(f)*, enfant naturel(le) *m(f)*.
(b) (*‡pej: unpleasant person*) salaud‡ *m*, saligaud‡ *m*.
(c) (‡) **poor** ~ pauvre type*; **silly** ~ quel corniaud!‡
2 *adj child* naturel, bâtard; *language, dialect* corrompu, abâtardi; (*Typ*) *character* d'un autre œil. ~ **title** faux-titre *m*.
bastardy ['bɑːstədɪ] **1** *n* bâtardise *f*. **2** *cpd*: (*Jur*) **bastardy order** jugement *m* en constatation de paternité (*d'enfant illégitime*).
baste[1] [beɪst] *vt* (*Sewing*) bâtir, faufiler.
baste[2] [beɪst] *vt* (*Culin*) arroser.
bastion ['bæstɪən] *n* bastion *m*.
bat[1] [bæt] *n* (*Zool*) chauve-souris *f*. (*fig*) **to have ~s in the belfry*** avoir une araignée au plafond*; **to flee like a ~ out of hell*** s'enfuir comme si l'on avait le diable à ses trousses; (*Brit Mil*) **~man** ordonnance *f*; *V* **blind**.
bat[2] [bæt] (*Sport etc*) **1** *n* **(a)** (*Baseball, Cricket*) batte *f*; (*Table Tennis*) raquette *f*. (*fig*) **off one's own** ~ de sa propre initiative, de son propre chef; (*US*) **right off the** ~ sur-le-champ; (*Sport*) **he's a good** ~ il manie bien la batte; *V* **brick**.
(b) (*: *blow*) coup *m*, gnon‡ *m*.
2 *vi* (*Baseball, Cricket*) manier la batte.
3 *vt* **(a)** *ball* frapper (*avec une batte, raquette etc*).
(b) (‡: *hit*) cogner*, flanquer un coup à*.
bat[3] [bæt] *vt*: **he didn't ~ an eyelid** il n'a pas sourcillé *or* bronché; **without ~ting an eyelid** sans sourciller *or* broncher.
bat[4]‡ [bæt] *n* **(a)** (*Brit: speed*) allure *f*. **(b)** (*US: spree*) fête *f*, bombe* *f*, bringue‡ *f*. **to go off on a** ~ (aller) faire la fête *or* la bombe* *or* la bringue‡.
batch [bætʃ] *n [loaves]* fournée *f*; *[people]* groupe *m*; *[prisoners]* convoi *m*; *[recruits]* contingent *m*, fournée; *[letters]* paquet *m*, liasse *f*, tas *m*; (*Comm*) *[goods]* lot *m*; *[concrete]* gâchée *f*.
bate [beɪt] *vti* diminuer. **with ~d breath** en retenant son souffle.
bath [bɑːθ] **1** *n*, *pl* **~s** [bɑːðz] **(a)** bain *m*; (*~tub*) baignoire *f*. **to take** *or* **have a** ~ prendre un bain; **to give sb a** ~ baigner qn, faire prendre un bain à qn; **while I was in my** *or* **the** ~ pendant que j'étais dans *or* que je prenais mon bain; *[hotel]* **room with (private)** ~ chambre *f* avec salle de bain (particulière); *V* **blood, eye, order, Turkish** *etc*.
(b) **~s** (*washing*) (établissement *m* de) bains(-douches) *mpl*; (*swimming*) piscine *f*; (*Hist*) thermes *mpl*.
(c) (*Chem, Phot, Tech*) bain *m*; (*Phot: container*) cuvette *f*.
2 *vt* (*Brit*) baigner, donner un bain à.
3 *vi* (*Brit*) prendre un bain.
4 *cpd*: (*Brit*) **Bath bun** pain *m* aux raisins; **bathchair** fauteuil roulant, voiture *f* de malade; **bathmat** tapis *m* de bain; **bathrobe** peignoir *m* de bain; **bathroom** *V* **bathroom**; **bath salts** sels *mpl* de bain; **bath sheet/towel** drap *m*/serviette *f* de bain; **bathtub** baignoire *f*; (*round*) tub *m*; **bathwater** eau *f* du bain.
bathe [beɪð] **1** *vt* **(a)** baigner; *wound* laver. **to ~ one's eyes** se baigner *or* se bassiner les yeux; **to ~ one's feet** prendre un bain de pieds; **~d in tears** baigné de larmes; **to be ~d in sweat** être en nage, ruisseler (de sueur); (*US*) **to ~ the baby** baigner l'enfant.
(b) (*fig*) *[light etc]* baigner. **countryside ~d in light** paysage baigné de lumière.
(c) (*liter*) *[sea etc]* baigner.
2 *vi* se baigner, prendre un bain (*de mer, de rivière*); (*US*) prendre un bain (*dans une baignoire*).
3 *n* bain *m* (*de mer, de rivière*). **an enjoyable** ~ une baignade agréable; **to take** *or* **have a** ~ se baigner; **let's go for a** ~ allons nous baigner.
bather ['beɪðəʳ] *n* baigneur *m*, -euse *f*.
bathing ['beɪðɪŋ] **1** *n* bains *mpl*, baignade(s) *f(pl)*. ~ **prohibited** défense de se baigner, baignade interdite; **safe** ~ baignade sans (aucun) danger; *V* **sea**.
2 *cpd*: **bathing beauty** belle baigneuse; **bathing cap** bonnet *m* de bain; **bathing costume** maillot *m* (de bain); **bathing hut** cabine *f* (de bains); **bathing machine** cabine de bains roulante; **bathing suit** = **bathing costume**; **bathing trunks** maillot *m or* slip *m* de bain, caleçon *m* de bain; **bathing wrap** peignoir *m or* sortie *f* de bain.
bathos ['beɪθɒs] *n* (*Literat*) chute *f* du sublime au ridicule.
bathroom ['bɑːθrʊm] **1** *n* salle *f* de bains.
2 *cpd*: **bathroom cabinet** armoire *f* de toilette; **bathroom fittings** (*main fixtures*) appareils *mpl or* installations *fpl* sanitaires; (*accessories*) accessoires *mpl* (de salle de bains); **bathroom scales** balance *f*, pèse-personne *m inv*.
bathysphere ['bæθɪsfɪəʳ] *n* bathysphère *f*.
batiste [bæ'tiːst] *n* batiste *f*.
baton ['bætən] *n* (*Mil, Mus*) bâton *m*, baguette *f*; (*Brit*) *[policeman]* matraque *f*; *[French traffic policeman]* bâton; *[relay race]* témoin *m*. ~ **charge** charge *f* (*de police etc*) à la matraque.
bats‡ [bæts] *adj* toqué*, timbré*.
battalion [bə'tælɪən] *n* (*Mil, fig*) bataillon *m*.
batten[1] ['bætn] **1** *n* (*Carpentry*) latte *f*; *[roofing]* volige *f*; *[flooring]* latte, planche *f* (de parquet); (*Naut*) latte (de voile); (*Theat*) herse *f*. **2** *vt* latter; *roof* voliger; *floor* planchéier.
batten down *vt sep* (*Naut*) **to batten down the hatches** fermer les écoutilles, condamner les panneaux.
batten[2] ['bætn] *vi* (*prosper illegitimately*) s'engraisser (*on sb* aux dépens de qn, *on sth* de qch); (*feed greedily*) se gorger, se gaver, se bourrer (*on* de).
batter[1] ['bætəʳ] *n* **(a)** (*Culin*) (*for frying*) pâte *f* à frire; (*for pancakes*) pâte à crêpes. **fried fish in** ~ poisson frit (enrobé de pâte à frire).
(b) (*Typ*) (*damaged type*) caractère écrasé *or* défectueux; (*defect in print*) écrasement *m*.
batter[2] ['bætəʳ] **1** *vt* **(a)** (*strike repeatedly*) battre, frapper; *baby* maltraiter, martyriser. **ship ~ed by the waves** navire battu par les vagues; **town ~ed by bombing** ville ravagée *or* éventrée par les bombardements.
(b) (*Typ*) *type* endommager.
2 *vi*: **to ~ at the door** cogner *or* frapper à la porte à coups redoublés.
batter about *vt sep*: **to batter sb about** rouer qn de coups, rosser qn.
batter down *vt wall* démolir, abattre; (*Mil*) battre en brèche.
batter in *vt sep door* enfoncer, défoncer; *skull* défoncer.
battered ['bætəd] *adj hat, pan* cabossé, bosselé; *furniture, house* délabré. (*Med*) ~ **babies** enfants martyrs; ~ **face** visage meurtri; **a ~ old car** un vieux tacot cabossé*.
battering ['bætərɪŋ] *n*: **the town took a dreadful ~ during the war** la ville a été terriblement éprouvée pendant la guerre; **he got such a** ~ on l'a roué de coups, on l'a rossé; (*Mil*) ~ **ram** bélier *m*; *V* **baby**.
battery ['bætərɪ] **1** *n* **(a)** (*Mil, Naut*) batterie *f*.
(b) (*Elec*) *[torch, radio]* pile *f*; *[vehicle]* batterie *f*, accumulateurs *mpl*, accus* *mpl*.
(c) (*number of similar objects*) batterie *f*. **a ~ of questions** une pluie de questions.
(d) (*Agr*) éleveuse *f*.
(e) (*Jur*) voie *f* de fait; *V* **assault**.
2 *cpd*: (*Elec*) **battery charger** chargeur *m*; (*Agr*) **battery farming** élevage intensif *or* en batterie (de poulets); (*Mil*) **battery fire** tir *m* par salves; (*Agr*) **battery hen** poulet *m* de batterie; (*Rad*) **battery set** poste *m* à piles.
battle ['bætl] **1** *n* (*lit, fig*) bataille *f*, combat *m*. **to fight a** ~ se battre, lutter (*against* contre); **the B~ of Britain** la bataille d'Angleterre; (*Mil*) **killed in** ~ tué à l'ennemi; **to have a ~ of wits** jouer au plus fin; **life is a continual** ~ la vie est un combat perpétuel *or* une lutte perpétuelle; (*fig*) **to do ~ for/against** lutter pour/contre; (*fig*) **to fight sb's ~s** se battre pour qn; (*fig*) **we are fighting the same** ~ nous nous battons pour la même cause; (*fig*) **that's half the ~*** c'est déjà pas mal*; (*fig*) ~ **for control of sth/to control sth** lutte *or* combat pour obtenir le contrôle de qch/pour contrôler qch; *V* **join, losing** *etc*.
2 *cpd*: **in battle array** en bataille; **battle-axe** (*weapon*) hache *f* d'armes; (**pej: woman*) virago *f*; **battle cruiser** croiseur cuirassé; **battle cry** cri *m* de guerre; (*Mil*) **battle dress** tenue *f* de campagne *or* de combat; (*Mil, fig*) **battlefield, battleground** champ *m* de bataille; **in battle order** = **in battle array**; **battle royal** (*quarrel*) bataille *f* en règle; **battle-scarred** (*lit*) *troops, country* touché *or* marqué par la guerre; (*fig*) *person* marqué par la vie; (**hum*) *furniture* endommagé, abîmé; **battleship** cuirassé *m*; **battle zone** zone *f* de combat.
3 *vi* (*lit, fig*) se battre, lutter (*against* contre, *to do* pour faire), batailler (*to do* pour faire). (*fig*) **to ~ for breath** chercher son souffle.
battledore ['bætldɔːʳ] *n* (*Sport*) raquette *f*. ~ **and shuttlecock** (jeu *m* de) volant *m*.
battlements ['bætlmənts] *npl* (*wall*) remparts *mpl*; (*crenellation*) créneaux *mpl*.
batty‡ ['bætɪ] *adj* = **bats‡**.
bauble ['bɔːbl] *n* babiole *f*, colifichet *m*; *[jester]* marotte *f*.
baulk [bɔːlk] = **balk**.
bauxite ['bɔːksaɪt] *n* bauxite *f*.
Bavaria [bə'vɛərɪə] *n* Bavière *f*.
Bavarian [bə'vɛərɪən] **1** *n* Bavarois(e) *m(f)*. **2** *adj* bavarois. (*Culin*) ~ **cream** bavaroise *f*.
bawbee† [bɔː'biː] *n* (*Scot*) sou† *m*.
bawd† [bɔːd] *n* (*prostitute*) catin† *f*; (*brothel-keeper*) tenancière *f* de maison close; (*procurer*) entremetteuse *f*.
bawdiness ['bɔːdɪnɪs] *n* paillardise *f*.
bawdy ['bɔːdɪ] *adj* paillard. **~house** maison close, bordel‡ *m*.
bawl [bɔːl] **1** *vi* **(a)** brailler, gueuler‡, beugler* (*at* contre). **(b)** (‡: *weep*) brailler, beugler*. **2** *vt song, order* brailler, hurler, beugler*.
bawl out *vt sep* **(a)** = **bawl 2**.
(b) (‡: *scold*) engueuler‡.
bay[1] [beɪ] *n* (*Geog*) baie *f*, (*small*) anse *f*. **the B~ of Biscay** le golfe de Gascogne; (*US*) **the B~ State** le Massachusetts.
bay[2] [beɪ] **1** *n* (*Bot: also* **~ tree, sweet ~**) laurier(-sauce) *m*; (*fig*) lauriers *mpl*, honneurs *mpl*. ~ **wreath, ~s** couronne *f* de laurier. **2** *cpd*: **bay leaf** feuille *f* de laurier; **bay rum** lotion *f* capillaire.
bay[3] [beɪ] *n* **(a)** (*Archit*) travée *f*; *[window]* baie *f*. ~ **window** fenêtre *f* en saillie. **(b)** (*Rail*) voie *f* d'arrêt, quai *m* subsidiaire; *V* **bomb, loading, sick** *etc*.
bay[4] [beɪ] **1** *n [dog]* aboiement *m*, aboi *m*; *[pack]* abois. (*Hunting, fig*) **to be at** ~ être aux abois; (*Hunting, fig*) **to bring to** ~ acculer; (*fig*) **to keep** *or* **hold sb/sth at** ~ tenir qn/qch à distance *or* en échec.
2 *vi* aboyer (*at* à, après), donner de la voix. **to ~ (at) the moon** aboyer *or* hurler à la lune.
bay[5] [beɪ] **1** *adj horse* bai. **2** *n* cheval bai. (*horse*) **red** ~ alezan *m*.
bayonet ['beɪənɪt] **1** *n* baïonnette *f*. **the ~s** l'infanterie *f*; **2,000 ~s** 2.000 fantassins *mpl*; *V* **fix** *etc*.
2 *vt* passer à la baïonnette.
3 *cpd*: **bayonet charge** charge *f* à la baïonnette; **at bayonet point** à (la pointe de) la baïonnette; **bayonet practice** exercices *mpl* de baïonnette; (*Elec*) **bayonet socket** douille *f* à baïonnette.
bazaar [bə'zɑːʳ] *n* (*in East*) bazar *m*; (*large shop*) bazar; (*sale of work*) vente *f* de charité.
bazooka [bə'zuːkə] *n* bazooka *m*.
be [biː] *pres* **am, is, are**, *pret* **was, were, wast†, wert†**, *ptp* **been 1** *copulative vb* **(a)** (*joining subject and predicate*) être. **the sky is blue** le ciel est bleu; ~ **good!** sois sage!; **my coffee is**

cold mon café est froid; **he is lucky** il a de la chance; **he is a soldier** il est soldat; **he wants to ~ a doctor** il veut être médecin; **she is an Englishwoman** c'est une Anglaise; **who is that? — it's me!** qui est-ce? — c'est moi!

(b) (*health*) aller, se porter. **how are you?** comment allez-vous?, comment vous portez-vous? (*frm*); **I am better now** je vais mieux maintenant; **she is none too well** elle ne va pas trop *or* très bien.

(c) (*physical or mental state*) to ~ **cold/hot/hungry/thirsty/ashamed/right/wrong** avoir froid/chaud/faim/soif/honte/raison/tort; **my feet are cold** j'ai froid aux pieds; **my hands are frozen** j'ai les mains gelées, mes mains sont gelées; **I am worried** je suis inquiet.

(d) (*age*) **how old is he?** quel âge a-t-il?; **he will ~ 3 next week** il aura 3 ans la semaine prochaine; **I would take her to ~ 40** je lui donnerais 40 ans.

(e) (*measurement*) être. **the road is 1 km from the house** la route est à 1 km de la maison; **how far is London from here?** Londres est à quelle distance d'ici?, combien y-a-t-il d'ici à Londres?; **the door is 3 metres high** la porte a 3 mètres de haut; **how tall are you?** combien mesurez-vous?; **how long/wide is the table?** quelle est la longueur/la largeur de la table?, combien la table fait-elle de long/de large?

(f) (*cost*) coûter, faire. **how much is that?** combien cela fait-il? *or* coûte-t-il? *or* vaut-il?; **the book is 10 francs** le livre coûte 10 F; **it is cheap at the price** c'est bon marché à ce prix-là; **it is cheaper in the long run** cela revient moins cher à la longue.

(g) (*Math*) faire. **2 and 2 are 4** 2 et 2 font 4; **3 times 2 is 6** 3 fois 2 font 6.

(h) (+*poss pron*) être, appartenir. **that book is mine** ce livre m'appartient *or* est à moi; **it's his** c'est à lui, c'est le sien.

2 *aux vb* **(a)** (+*prp* = *continuous tense*) être en train de +*infin*. **what are you doing? — I am reading a book** qu'est-ce que vous faites? — je lis *or* je suis en train de lire un livre; **what have you been doing this week?** qu'avez-vous fait cette semaine?; **I have just been packing my case** je viens de faire ma valise; **I have been waiting for you for an hour** je vous attends depuis une heure; **the bus is stopping** l'autobus s'arrête; **so you aren't coming with us? — but I AM coming!** alors, vous ne venez pas avec nous? — mais si je viens avec vous!; **she is always complaining** elle se plaint toujours, elle est toujours en train de se plaindre; **will you ~ seeing her tomorrow?** est-ce que vous allez la voir demain?, comptez-vous la voir demain?; **what's been keeping you?** qu'est-ce qui t'a retenu?

(b) (+*ptp* = *pass*) être. **he was killed** il a été tué; **the door was shut in his face** on lui a fermé la porte au nez; **there is nothing left** il ne reste plus rien; **he is to ~ pitied** il est à plaindre; **the car is to ~ sold** la voiture doit être vendue; **peaches are sold by the kilo** les pêches se vendent au kilo; **let it ~ done at once** qu'on le fasse tout de suite; **it is said that** on dit que; **not to ~ confused with** à ne pas confondre avec; **is it to ~ wondered at if ...?** faut-il s'étonner si ...?

(c) (*in tag questions, short answers*) **he's always late, isn't he? — yes, he is** il est toujours en retard, n'est-ce pas? — oui, toujours; **she is pretty — no, she isn't** elle est jolie — non, elle n'est pas jolie; **you are not ill, are you?** tu n'es pas malade j'espère?; **it's all done, is it?** tout est fait, alors?; **was he pleased to hear it!*** il a été rudement* content de l'apprendre!; **but wasn't she glad when*...** mais n'empêche qu'elle a été contente quand*... .

(d) (+*to* +*infin*) **he is to do it** (*from duty, destiny, prearrangement*) il doit le faire; (*intention*) il va le faire; **I am to look after my mother** je dois m'occuper de ma mère; **they are shortly to ~ married** ils vont bientôt se marier; **when is the president to arrive?** quand le président doit-il arriver?; **she was never to return** elle ne devait jamais revenir; **the telegram was to warn us of the delay** le télégramme était pour nous avertir du retard.

(e) (+*neg* +*infin* = *prohibition*) **you are not to touch that** tu ne dois pas y toucher; **I am not to speak to him** on m'a défendu de lui parler; **I wasn't to tell you his name** je ne devais pas vous dire son nom; **this door is not to ~ opened** il est interdit *or* défendu d'ouvrir cette porte.

(f) (*modal 'were': possibility, supposition*) **if we were** *or* (*frm*) **were we in London now** si nous étions à Londres maintenant; **if I were** *or* (*frm*) **were I to tell him, what could he do?** et à supposer même que je le lui dise *or* et quand bien même je le lui dirais, que pourrait-il faire?; **if I were you I should refuse** à votre place *or* si j'étais vous je refuserais.

3 *vi* **(a)** (*exist, live, occur, remain, be situated*) être, exister. **to ~ or not to ~** être ou ne pas être; **the powers that ~** les autorités (constituées); **the best artist that ever was** le meilleur peintre qui ait jamais existé *or* qui fût jamais; **that may ~** cela se peut, peut-être; **~ that as it may** quoi qu'il en soit; **how is it that ...?** comment se fait-il que? +*indic or subj*; **let me ~** laissez-moi tranquille; **leave it as it is** laissez-le tel quel; **don't ~ too long in coming** ne tardez pas trop à venir; **I won't ~ long** je n'en ai pas pour longtemps; **to ~ in danger** être *or* se trouver en danger; **Christmas Day is on a Monday this year** Noël tombe un lundi cette année; **the match is tomorrow** le match a lieu demain; **he is there just now but he won't ~ (there) much longer** il est là en ce moment mais il ne va plus y être (pour) très longtemps.

(b) there is, there are il y a, il est (*liter*); **there is a mouse in the room** il y a une souris dans la pièce; **there was once a castle here** il y avait autrefois un château ici; **there will ~ dancing** on dansera; **there were three of us** nous étions trois; **there is nothing more beautiful** il n'y a *or* il n'est rien de plus beau; **there is no knowing what may happen** il est impossible de savoir ce qui va se passer; **he's a rogue if ever there was one** voilà un filou si jamais il en fut; **let there ~ light and there was light** que la lumière soit et la lumière fut; **there ~ing no alternative solution** comme il n'y a aucune autre solution.

(c) (*presenting, pointing out*) **here is a book** voici un livre; **here are 2 books** voici 2 livres; **there is the church** voilà l'église; **there are the 2 churches** voilà les 2 églises; **here you are!** (*I've found you*) ah vous voici!; (*take this*) tenez!; **there he was, sitting at the table** il était là, assis à la table.

(d) (*come, go: esp in perfect tense*) aller, être. **I have been to see my aunt** je suis allé voir ma tante; **I have already been to Paris** j'ai déjà été *or* je suis déjà allé à Paris; **the postman has already been** le facteur est déjà passé; **has anyone been while I was out?** il est venu quelqu'un *or* il n'est venu personne pendant que je n'étais pas là?; **he has been and gone** il est venu et reparti; **now you've been and done it!**‡ eh bien tu as fait du joli! (*iro*); **I've just been and broken it!**‡ (ça y est) voilà que je l'ai cassé!

(e) the bride-/mother-to-~ la future mariée/maman; **a would-~ poet** un soi-disant poète.

4 *impers vb* **(a)** (*weather etc*) faire. **it is fine/cold/dark** il fait beau/froid/nuit; **it is windy/foggy** il fait du vent/du brouillard.

(b) (*time*) être. **it is morning** c'est le matin; **it is 6 o'clock** il est 6 heures; **tomorrow is Friday** demain c'est vendredi; **it is the 14th June today** nous sommes (aujourd'hui) *or* c'est aujourd'hui le 14 juin; **it is a long time since I last saw you** il y a longtemps que je ne vous ai vu; **it was early** il était de bonne heure, il était tôt.

(c) (*distance*) **it is 5 km to the nearest town** la ville la plus proche est à 5 km.

(d) (*emphatic*) **it is he who did it** c'est lui qui l'a fait; **it is they who are responsible** ce sont eux les responsables; **it is us* who found it** c'est nous qui l'avons trouvé.

(e) (*supposition, probability*) **were it not that** si ce n'était que; **were it not for my friendship for him** si ce n'était mon amitié pour lui, sans mon amitié pour lui; **had it not been for him we should all be dead** sans lui nous serions tous morts; **as it were** pour ainsi dire; **and even if it were so** et quand bien même ce serait vrai.

5 *cpd*: **the be-all and end-all** le but suprême (*of* de), la fin des fins.

beach [biːtʃ] **1** *n* [*sea*] plage *f*; (*shore*) grève *f*; [*lake*] rivage *m*. **private/sandy ~** plage privée/de sable.

2 *vt boat* échouer.

3 *cpd*: **beach ball** ballon *m* de plage; **beach buggy** buggy *m*; **beachcomber** (*person*) (*lit*) ramasseur *m* d'épaves; (*fig: idler*) propre *m* à rien; (*wave*) vague déferlante; **beachhead** tête *f* de pont; **beach umbrella** parasol *m*; **beachwear** tenue *f* de plage.

beacon ['biːkən] **1** *n* **(a)** (*danger signal*) fanal *m* (d'un phare), phare *m*, signal lumineux; (*Naut*) balise *f*; (*Aviat*) balise, phare; (*fig*) phare, guide *m*, flambeau *m*; *V* **Belisha beacon, radio.**

(b) (*Hist: on hills*) feu *m* (d'alarme).

(c) (*hill: gen in place-names*) colline *f*.

2 *cpd*: **beacon light** balise lumineuse.

bead [biːd] *n* **(a)** (*of glass, coral, amber etc*) perle *f*; [*rosary*] grain *m*. **(string of) ~s** collier *m*; *V* **tell** *etc*.

(b) (*drop*) [*dew*] perle *f*; [*sweat*] goutte *f*; (*bubble*) bulle *f*. **his forehead was covered in ~s of sweat** la sueur lui perlait au front.

(c) [*gun*] guidon *m*. **to draw a ~ on** ajuster, viser.

beading ['biːdɪŋ] *n* (*Carpentry*) baguette *f*; (*Archit*) chapelet *m*; (*Dress*) broderie perlée, garniture *f* de perles.

beadle ['biːdl] *n* (*Brit Univ*) appariteur *m*, huissier *m*; (*Rel*) bedeau *m*.

beady ['biːdɪ] *adj*: **to watch sth with ~ eyes** regarder qch avec des yeux de fouine; **~-eyed** aux yeux en boutons de bottines.

beagle ['biːgl] **1** *n* beagle *m*. **2** *vi* chasser avec des beagles.

beak [biːk] *n* **(a)** [*bird, turtle etc*] bec *m*; (‡: *also* **~ed nose**) nez crochu. **(b)** (*Brit*‡) juge *m*; († *Brit Scol sl: headmaster*) protal *m* (*sl*).

beaker ['biːkəʳ] *n* gobelet *m*; (*wide*) coupe *f*; (*Chem etc*) vase *m* à bec.

beam [biːm] **1** *n* **(a)** (*Archit*) poutre *f*, solive *f*; (*thick*) madrier *m*; (*small*) poutrelle *f*, soliveau *m*; *V* **cross** *etc*.

(b) (*Naut*) (*transverse member*) barrot *m*; (*greatest width*) largeur *f*. **on the ~** par le travers; (*Naut*) **on the port ~** à bâbord; **on the starboard ~** à tribord; *V* **broad** *etc*.

(c) (*Tech*) [*scales*] fléau *m*; [*engine*] balancier *m*; [*plough*] age *m*; [*loom*] rouleau *m*.

(d) [*light, sunlight*] rayon *m*, trait *m*; [*lighthouse, headlight, searchlight*] faisceau *m* (lumineux); (*Phys*) faisceau; (*Aviat, Naut*) chenal *m* de radio-guidage. (*US*) **to be on/be off (the) ~** être/ne pas être dans le chenal de radio-guidage; (*fig*) **to be on (the) ~*** être sur la bonne voie; (*fig*) **to be off (the) ~***, (*US*) **to be off the ~*** dérailler*; *V* **electron** *etc*.

(e) (*smile*) sourire épanoui.

2 *vi* **(a)** [*sun*] rayonner, darder ses rayons. **to ~ forth** apparaître.

(b) she ~ed son visage s'est épanoui en un large sourire; **at the sight of the money she ~ed at me** elle a levé vers moi un visage épanoui *or* rayonnant en voyant l'argent; **her face was ~ing with joy** son visage rayonnait de joie.

3 *vt* (*Rad, Telec*) *message* transmettre par émission dirigée. **to ~ a programme to the Arab-speaking countries** diffuser un programme à l'intention des pays de langue arabe.

4 *cpd* (*Naut*) *sea, wind* de travers. **beam balance** balance *f* à fléau; **beam compass** compas *m* à verge; (*Naut*) **on her beam-ends** couché sur le côté *or* le flanc; (*fig*) **to be on one's beam-ends*** être dans la gêne, se trouver sans ressources.

beaming ['biːmɪŋ] **1** *adj sun* radieux, resplendissant; *smile, face* rayonnant, radieux, épanoui. **2** *n* (*Phys*) transmission *f* par ondes dirigées.

bean [biːn] **1** *n* (*Bot, Culin*) haricot *m*; (*green* ~) haricot (vert); (*broad* ~) fève *f*; *[coffee]* grain *m*. (*Brit*) **to be full of** ~**s*** être en pleine forme, péter le feu*; (*Brit*) **he hasn't a** ~**:** il n'a pas le sou *or* un radis:; **hullo, old** ~**!:** salut mon pote!:; *V* **bake, kidney, spill**[1] *etc.*

2 *cpd*: (*Brit*) **beanfeast***, (*Brit*) **beano:** (*meal*) gueuleton: *m*; (*spree*) bombe* *f*, nouba* *f*; (*Culin*) **beanshoots, beansprouts** germes *mpl* de soja; **beanstalk** tige *f* de haricot.

bear[1] [bɛə^{r}] *pret* **bore**, *ptp* **borne 1** *vt* **(a)** (*carry*) *burden, arms, message* porter. **music borne on the wind** musique portée par le vent; **to** ~ **away** emporter; **to** ~ **back** rapporter; *V* **mind.**

(b) (*show*) *inscription, mark, traces* porter. **this document** ~**s your signature** ce document porte votre signature; **to** ~ **some resemblance to** ressembler à, offrir une ressemblance avec; **to** ~ **no relation to** être sans rapport avec, n'avoir aucun rapport avec.

(c) (*be known by*) *name* porter.

(d) he bore himself like a soldier (*carried himself*) il avait une allure militaire *or* de soldat; (*conducted himself*) il se comportait en soldat.

(e) (*feel*) avoir en soi, porter. **the love/hatred he bore her** l'amour/la haine qu'il lui portait *or* qu'il avait à son égard; **to** ~ **sb a grudge, to** ~ **a grudge against sb** garder rancune à qn, en vouloir à qn (*for sth* de qch); **to** ~ **sb ill will** en avoir contre qn.

(f) (*bring, provide*) apporter, fournir. **to** ~ **witness to sth** attester *or* certifier qch; **to** ~ **false witness** porter un faux témoignage; **to** ~ **sb company**† tenir compagnie à qn.

(g) (*sustain, support*) soutenir, supporter. **to** ~ **the weight of** supporter le poids de; **to** ~ **comparison with** soutenir la comparaison avec; **to** ~ **the expense of sth** prendre les frais de qch à sa charge; **to** ~ **the responsibility for sth** assumer la responsabilité de qch.

(h) (*endure*) supporter, tolérer, souffrir. **I cannot** ~ **(the sight of) that man** je ne peux pas souffrir *or* voir cet homme; **he can't** ~ **the smell of cooking** il ne peut pas supporter les odeurs de cuisine; **she cannot** ~ **being laughed at** elle ne supporte pas qu'on se moque (*subj*) d'elle; **his language will not** ~ **repeating** ses propos sont trop grossiers pour être rapportés; *V* **brunt, grin.**

(i) (*produce, yield*) porter, produire, rapporter. (*lit, fig*) **to** ~ **fruit** porter des fruits; (*Fin*) **investment which** ~**s 5%** placement *m* qui rapporte 5%; (*Fin*) **to** ~ **interest at 5%** produire *or* rapporter un intérêt de 5%.

(j) (*give birth to*) donner naissance à, mettre au monde. **she has borne him 3 daughters** elle lui a donné 3 filles; *V* **born.**

(k) (*push, press*) entraîner, pousser, porter. **he was borne along by the crowd** il s'est trouvé entraîné *or* emporté par la foule.

2 *vi* **(a)** (*move*) se diriger. **to** ~ **right/left** prendre sur la droite/la gauche *or* à droite/à gauche; ~ **towards the church** allez vers l'église; ~ **north at the windmill** prenez la direction nord au moulin; (*Naut*) **to** ~ **away** arriver, laisser porter; (*Naut*) **to** ~ **off** prendre le large; (*Naut*) **to** ~ **up for** faire route vers.

(b) *[ice etc]* porter, supporter.

(c) *[fruit tree etc]* donner, produire.

(d) (*lean, press*) porter, appuyer (*on* sur). **he bore heavily on his stick** il s'appuyait lourdement sur sa canne; (*fig*) **these taxes** ~ **most heavily on the poor** ces impôts pèsent le plus lourdement sur les pauvres.

(e) (*phrases with 'bring'*) **to bring one's energies to** ~ **on sth** consacrer *or* mettre toute son énergie à qch; **to bring one's mind to** ~ **on sth** porter son attention sur qch; **to bring pressure to** ~ **on sth** exercer une pression sur qch; (*fig*) **to bring pressure to** ~ **on sb** faire pression sur qn; **to bring a telescope to** ~ **on** braquer une lunette sur; **to bring a gun to** ~ **on a target** pointer un canon sur un objectif.

bear down 1 *vi* **(a)** (*Naut*) *[ship]* venir (*on* sur); (*fig*) *[person]* foncer (*on* sur).

(b) (*press*) appuyer fermement, peser (*on* sur).

2 *vt sep* abattre, vaincre. **borne down by adversity** abattu par l'adversité.

bear in (up)on *vt fus* (*pass only*) **to be borne in upon sb** apparaître de plus en plus évident aux yeux de qn; **it was gradually borne in upon me that** la conviction s'est faite peu à peu en moi que, il est apparu de plus en plus évident à mes yeux que.

bear on *vt fus* = **bear upon.**

bear out *vt sep* confirmer, corroborer. **to bear sb out, to bear out what sb says** corroborer les dires de qn, corroborer ce que qn dit; **the result bears out our suspicions** le résultat confirme nos soupçons; **you will bear me out that ...** vous serez d'accord avec moi (pour dire) que ... .

bear up *vi* ne pas se laisser abattre *or* décourager; (*) tenir le coup*. **he bore up well under *or* against the death of his father** il a supporté courageusement la mort de son père; **bear up!*** courage!; **how are you? — bearing up!*** comment ça va? — ça se maintient: *or* on tient le coup* *or* on fait aller*; *V* **bear**[1] **2a.**

bear upon *vt fus* (*be relevant to*) se rapporter à, être relatif à, avoir trait à; (*concern*) intéresser, concerner.

bear with *vt fus person, sb's moods etc* supporter patiemment. **bear with me a little longer** je vous demande encore un peu de patience.

bear[2] [bɛə^{r}] **1** *n* **(a)** ours(e) *m(f)*. (*fig*) **he's like a** ~ **with a sore head*** il est d'une humeur massacrante *or* de dogue, il n'est pas à prendre avec des pincettes; (*Astron*) **the Great/the Little B**~ la Grande/ la Petite Ourse; *V* **grizzly, koala, polar** *etc.*

(b) (*pej: person*) ours *m* (*pej*).

(c) (*St Ex*) baissier *m*.

2 *vt* (*St Ex*) chercher à faire baisser.

3 *vi* (*St Ex*) jouer à la baisse.

4 *cpd*: **bear-baiting** combat *m* d'ours et de chiens; **bear cub** ourson *m*; **bear garden** (*lit*) arène *f* (pour combats d'ours); (*fig*) pétaudière *f*; **to turn a place into a bear garden** mettre un endroit sens dessus dessous, faire d'un endroit une pétaudière; (*St Ex*) **bear market** marché *m* en baisse; **bear pit** fosse *f* aux ours; (*Mil Dress*) **bearskin** bonnet *m* à poil; *V* **hug.**

bearable ['bɛərəbl] *adj* supportable, tolérable, tenable.

beard [bɪəd] **1** *n* **(a)** barbe *f*; (*small, pointed*) barbiche *f*, bouc *m*. **to have a** ~ porter la barbe; **to wear a full** ~ porter un collier de barbe *or* une barbe de sapeur; **a man with a** ~ un homme barbu *or* à barbe, un barbu; **a week's (growth of)** ~ une barbe de huit jours.

(b) *[fish, oyster]* barbe *f*; *[goat]* barbiche *f*; *[grain]* barbe, arête *f*; *[hook etc]* barbe, barbelure *f*; (*Typ*) talus *m*.

2 *vt* (*defy*) défier, narguer; (*face up to*) braver. (*fig*) **to** ~ **the lion in his den** aller braver le lion dans sa tanière.

bearded ['bɪədɪd] *adj man, animal* barbu; *arrow* barbelé; *comet* chevelu. **a** ~ **man** un barbu; **the** ~ **lady** la femme à barbe; ~ **wheat** blé barbu.

beardless ['bɪədlɪs] *adj* imberbe, sans barbe. (*fig*) ~ **youth** (petit) jeunet.

bearer ['bɛərə^{r}] **1** *n* **(a)** *[letter, news, burden]* porteur *m*, -euse *f*; (*at funeral*) porteur; (*servant*) serviteur *m*.

(b) *[name, title]* porteur *m*; *[passport]* titulaire *mf*; *[cheque]* porteur.

(c) (*Bot*) **a good** ~ un arbre qui donne bien.

(d) (*Constr, Tech*) support *m*.

2 *cpd*: **bearer bond** titre *m* au porteur; **bearer cheque** chèque *m* au porteur.

bearing ['bɛərɪŋ] *n* **(a)** (*posture, behaviour*) maintien *m*, port *m*, allure *f*. **soldierly** ~ allure martiale; **noble** ~ maintien noble; **queenly** ~ port de reine.

(b) (*relation, aspect*) relation *f*, rapport *m*. **to examine a question in all its** ~**s** examiner une question sous tous ses aspects; **to have no** ~ **on the subject** n'avoir aucun rapport avec le sujet.

(c) it is beyond (all) ~ c'est absolument insupportable.

(d) (*Naut: direction*) position *f*, relèvement *m*. **to take a compass** ~ prendre un relèvement au compas; **to take a ship's** ~**s** faire le point; **to take one's** ~**s** s'orienter, se repérer; (*fig*) **to lose one's** ~**s** être désorienté, perdre le nord.

(e) (*Tech*) palier *m*, coussinet *m*; *V* **ball**[1], **main** *etc.*

(f) (*Her*) *V* **armorial.**

bearish ['bɛərɪʃ] *adj* **(a)** *behaviour* d'ours; *person* bourru. **rather** ~ un peu ours *inv*, peu sociable. **(b)** (*St Ex*) ~ **tendency** tendance *f* à la baisse.

beast [biːst] *n* **(a)** bête *f*, animal *m*; (*as opposed to birds, fish*) quadrupède *m*. (*Rel*) **the B**~ l'Antéchrist *m*, la grande Bête de l'Apocalypse; **the king of the** ~**s** le roi des animaux; ~ **of burden** bête de somme *or* de charge; (*Agr*) ~**s** bétail *m*, bestiaux *mpl*; *V* **brute, wild.**

(b) (*pej: person*) (*cruel*) brute *f*, vache* *f*; (*: *disagreeable*) chameau* *m*. **what a** ~**!*** quelle (sale) rosse!*, quelle vache!*; *[greedy person]* **to make a** ~ **of o.s.** se goinfrer.

beastliness ['biːstlɪnɪs] *n* (*U*) (*act, quality*) bestialité *f*; *[language]* obscénité *f*; (*: *unpleasantness*) méchanceté *f*, rosserie* *f*.

beastly ['biːstlɪ] **1** *adj* (*bestial*) *person, conduct* bestial, brutal; (*disgusting*) *food, sight* dégoûtant, répugnant; (*Brit**: *unpleasant, disagreeable*) abominable, infect*, dégueulasse:; *child, trick* sale, vilain. **what** ~ **weather!*** quel temps infect!*, quel temps de chien!* *or* de cochon!*, quel sale temps!; **it's a** ~ **business*** c'est une sale affaire.

2 *adv* (*Brit**) terriblement, vachement:.

beat [biːt] (*vb: pret* **beat**, *ptp* **beaten**) **1** *n* **(a)** *[heart, pulse]* battement *m*, pulsation *f*; *[drums]* battement, roulement *m*; (*Acoustics*) battement. **to march to the** ~ **of the drum** marcher au (son du) tambour; *V also* **drum.**

(b) (*Mus*) mesure *f*; *[conductor's baton]* battement *m* (de la mesure); (*Jazz*) rythme *m*. **strong/weak** ~ temps fort/faible.

(c) *[policeman, sentry]* ronde *f*. (*fig*) **that's off my** ~ cela n'est pas de mon domaine *or* de mon rayon*; *V* **off.**

(d) (*Hunting*) battue *f*.

(e) (:) = **beatnik.**

2 *adj* **(a)** (*: *also* **dead-**~) éreinté, claqué*, crevé*.

(b) (:) beatnik *inv*. **the** ~ **generation** la génération beatnik *or* des beatniks.

3 *cpd*: **beat-up*** déglingué:, bousillé*.

4 *vt* **(a)** (*strike*) *person, animal* battre, frapper; *carpet* battre; *eggs, cream* fouetter, battre; *metal* battre. **to** ~ **sth flat** aplatir qch; **to** ~ **sb with a stick** donner des coups de bâton à qn; **to** ~ **sb black and blue** rouer qn de coups, battre qn comme plâtre; **to** ~ **a drum** battre du tambour; (*Mil*) **to** ~ **the retreat** battre la retraite; (*Mil, fig*) **to** ~ **a retreat** battre en retraite; ~ **it!:** fiche le camp!*, fous le camp!:, file!*; (*liter*) **to** ~ **one's breast** se frapper la poitrine; **to** ~ **a way through sth** se frayer un passage *or* un chemin à travers qch; (*Hunting*) **to** ~ **the forest/the moors** battre les bois/les landes; ~**ing the air with its wings** battant l'air de ses ailes; **the bird** ~**s its wings** l'oiseau bat des ailes; **to** ~ **time** battre la mesure; *V* **living, tattoo.**

(b) (*defeat*) vaincre, battre, triompher de. **the army was** ~**en** l'armée a été battue; **to** ~ **sb to the top of a hill** arriver au sommet d'une colline avant qn; (*fig*) **to** ~ **sb to it*** couper l'herbe sous le pied à qn, devancer qn; **to** ~ **sb at chess** battre qn aux échecs; **to** ~ **sb hollow *or* into a cocked hat** battre qn à plate(s) couture(s); **to** ~ **the record** battre le record; (*fig*) **coffee** ~**s tea any day*** le café vaut tout le thé du monde; **the police confess themselves** ~**en** la police s'avoue vaincue; **the problem has got me** ~**en *or*** ~* le problème me dépasse complètement; (*fig*) **that** ~**s everything!*, that takes some**

~ing!* ça, c'est le comble!, c'est le bouquet!; (*fig*) **his behaviour takes some ~ing*** sa conduite dépasse tout; (*fig*) **that ~s me*** cela me dépasse; (*fig*) **it ~s me how you can speak to her*** je ne comprends pas *or* ça me dépasse* que tu lui adresses (*subj*) la parole; **can you ~ it!*** tu as déjà vu ça toi!*, faut le faire!*

5 *vi* **(a)** *[rain, wind]* battre; *[sun]* (*also* **~ down**) taper*, darder ses rayons. **to ~ at the door** cogner à la porte; **the rain was ~ing against the window** la pluie battait contre la vitre; **the waves ~ against the cliff** les vagues battent la falaise; (*fig*) **he doesn't ~ about the bush** il n'y va pas par quatre chemins, il ne tourne pas autour du pot*.

(b) *[heart, pulse, drum]* battre. **her heart was ~ing with joy** son cœur battait *or* palpitait de joie; **with ~ing heart** le cœur battant; **his pulse began to ~ quicker** son pouls s'est mis à battre plus fort; **they heard the drums ~ing** ils entendaient le roulement des tambours.

(c) (*Naut*) **to ~ (to windward)** louvoyer au plus près.

beat back *vt sep enemy, flames* repousser.

beat down 1 *vi*: **the rain was beating down** il pleuvait à verse *or* à seaux *or* à torrents; *V also* **beat 5a.**

2 *vt sep* **(a)** (*reduce*) rabattre, baisser, faire baisser; *prices* faire baisser; *person* faire baisser ses prix à. **I beat him down to £2** je l'ai fait descendre à 2 livres.

(b) the rain has beaten down the wheat la pluie a couché les blés.

beat in *vt sep door* défoncer. **to beat sb's brains in** défoncer le crâne à qn.

beat off *vt sep attack, attacker* repousser.

beat out *vt sep* **(a)** *fire* étouffer.

(b) *metal* marteler, étaler *or* amincir au marteau.

(c) to beat out the rhythm marquer le rythme, battre la mesure.

beat up 1 *vt sep* **(a)** *eggs, cream* fouetter, battre; (**fig*) *person* passer à tabac, tabasser‡. (*fig*) **to beat it up‡** faire la bombe*.

(b) *recruits, volunteers, customers* racoler, recruter. **he beat up all the help he could** il a battu le rappel.

2 beat-up* *adj V* **beat 3.**

3 beating-up *n V* **beating 2.**

beaten [ˈbiːtn] **1** *ptp of* **beat.**

2 *adj* **(a)** *metal* battu, martelé; *earth, path* battu. **~ track** chemin *or* sentier battu; (*lit, fig*) **off the ~ track** hors des sentiers battus.

(b) (*defeated*) battu, vaincu.

(c) (*exhausted*) éreinté, claqué*, crevé*.

beater [ˈbiːtəʳ] *n* **(a)** (*gadget*) *[carpet]* tapette *f*; *[eggs]* (*whisk*) fouet *m*; (*rotary*) batteur *m*; (*Tex*) peigne *m*. **(b)** (*Hunting*) rabatteur *m*, traqueur *m*.

beatific [ˌbiːəˈtɪfɪk] *adj* béatifique. **to wear a ~ smile** sourire aux anges, arborer un sourire béat.

beatification [biːˌætɪfɪˈkeɪʃən] *n* béatification *f*.

beatify [biːˈætɪfaɪ] *vt* béatifier.

beating [ˈbiːtɪŋ] **1** *n* **(a)** (*series of blows*) correction *f*, raclée* *f*, rossée* *f*. **to give sb a ~** flanquer une correction *or* une rossée* *or* une raclée* à qn; **to get a ~** recevoir une correction *or* une rossée* *or* une volée*.

(b) (*U*) *[metal]* batte *f*; *[drums]* battement *m*, roulement *m*; *[carpet]* battage *m*.

(c) (*defeat*) défaite *f*. (*Sport, also**) **to take a ~** se faire battre à plate(s) couture(s), se faire piler*; **the car takes a ~ on that road*** la voiture en voit de dures sur cette route; *V* **beat 4b.**

(d) *[wings, heart etc]* battement *m*.

(e) (*Hunting*) rabattage *m*, rabat *m*.

2 *cpd*: **beating-up*** passage *m* à tabac, raclée* *f*.

beatitude [biːˈætɪtjuːd] *n* béatitude *f*. **the B~s** les béatitudes.

beatnik [ˈbiːtnɪk] *n, adj* beatnik (*mf*).

beau† [bəʊ] *n* (*dandy*) élégant *m*, dandy *m*; (*suitor*) galant *m*, prétendant *m*.

beauteous [ˈbjuːtɪəs] *adj* (*liter*) = **beautiful 1.**

beautician [bjuːˈtɪʃən] *n* esthéticien(ne) *m(f)*, visagiste *mf*.

beautiful [ˈbjuːtɪfʊl] **1** *adj person, music, picture, clothes* beau (*f* belle); *weather* superbe, splendide, magnifique; *dinner* magnifique. **really ~** de toute beauté. **2** *n*: **the ~** le beau.

beautifully [ˈbjuːtɪflɪ] *adv* admirablement, à la perfection, on ne peut mieux. **she sews ~** elle coud à la perfection *or* on ne peut mieux; **that will do ~** cela convient parfaitement, c'est tout à fait ce qu'il faut; **the sea was ~ calm** la mer était merveilleusement *or* parfaitement calme.

beautify [ˈbjuːtɪfaɪ] *vt* embellir, orner. **to ~ o.s.** se faire une beauté*.

beauty [ˈbjuːtɪ] **1** *n* **(a)** (*U*) beauté *f*. **to mar *or* spoil *or* ruin the ~ of sth** déparer qch; (*Prov*) **~ is only skin-deep** la beauté n'est pas tout; (*Prov*) **~ is in the eye of the beholder** il n'y a pas de laides amours; (*fig*) **the ~ of it is that*** ... le plus beau, c'est que ...; (*fig*) **that's the ~ of it** c'est ça qui est formidable*, c'est ce qu'il y a de formidable là-dedans*.

(b) beauté *f*. **she is a ~** elle est d'une grande beauté, c'est une beauté; **she is no ~*** ce n'est pas une beauté; **B~ and the Beast** la Belle et la Bête; **isn't this car/this apple** *etc* **a ~!*** quelle merveille que cette voiture/cette pomme! *etc.*

2 *cpd*: **beauty competition, beauty contest** concours *m* de beauté; **beauty cream** crème *f* de beauté; **beauty parlour** institut *m or* salon *m* de beauté; **beauty preparations** produits *mpl* de beauté; **beauty queen** reine *f* de beauté; **beauty salon** = **beauty parlour; off you go to bed now, you need your beauty sleep** va te coucher maintenant pour être tout frais demain matin; **beauty specialist** esthéticien(ne) *m(f)*, visagiste *mf*; **beauty spot** *[skin]* (*natural*) grain *m* de beauté; (*applied*) mouche *f*; *[countryside]* site naturel *or* touristique; **it's a real beauty spot** c'est vraiment un site merveilleux; **we visited all the beauty spots** nous avons visité tous les sites naturels *or* touristiques; **beauty treatment** soins *mpl* de beauté.

beaver [ˈbiːvəʳ] **1** *n* (*Zool*) castor *m*; (*fur*) (fourrure *f* de) castor; (*hat*) (chapeau *m* de) castor. **to work like a ~** travailler d'arrache-pied; *V* **eager.**

2 *cpd coat, hat* (en poil) de castor. (*Constr*) **beaverboard** ® aggloméré *m* (*bois*).

becalm [bɪˈkɑːm] *vt* (*gen pass*) **to be ~ed** être encalminé.

became [bɪˈkeɪm] *pret of* **become.**

because [bɪˈkɒz] **1** *conj* parce que. **I did it ~ you asked me to** je l'ai fait parce que tu me l'as demandé; **I shan't go out ~ it's raining** je ne sortirai pas à cause de la pluie; **it is the more surprising ~ we were not expecting it** c'est d'autant plus surprenant que nous ne nous y attendions pas; **if I did it, it was ~ it had to be done** si je l'ai fait, c'est qu'il fallait le faire; **~ he lied, he was punished** il a été puni pour avoir menti *or* parce qu'il avait menti; **we are annoyed ~ the weather is bad** nous sommes contrariés parce qu'il fait mauvais *or* de ce qu'il fait mauvais; **not ~ he was offended but ~ he was angry** non qu'il fût offusqué mais parce qu'il était furieux; **~ he was leaving** à cause de son départ.

2 *prep*: **~ of** à cause de, en raison de, vu; **~ of his age** en raison de son âge, vu son âge.

beck[1] [bek] *n* signe *m* (de tête *or* de la main). **to be at sb's ~ and call** obéir à qn au doigt et à l'œil; **he is at her ~ and call** elle le fait marcher au doigt et à l'œil; **to have sb at one's ~ and call** faire marcher qn à la baguette *or* au doigt et à l'œil.

beck[2] [bek] *n* (*N Engl*) ruisseau *m*, ru *m*.

beckon [ˈbekən] *vti* faire signe (à). **he ~ed (to) her to follow him** il lui a fait signe de le suivre; **he ~ed me in/back/over** *etc* il m'a fait signe d'entrer/de revenir/d'approcher *etc.*

become [bɪˈkʌm] *pret* **became,** *ptp* **become 1** *vi* **(a)** (*grow to be*) devenir, se faire. **to ~ famous** devenir célèbre; **to ~ old** vieillir, se faire vieux; **to ~ thin** maigrir; **to ~ fat** grossir; **to ~ accustomed (to)** s'accoutumer (à), s'habituer (à); **to ~ interested (in)** commencer à s'intéresser (à); *[person]* **to ~ known** commencer à être connu, se faire connaître.

(b) (*acquire position of*) devenir, se faire. **to ~ king** devenir roi; **to ~ a doctor** devenir *or* se faire médecin.

2 *impers vb*: **what has ~ of him?** qu'est-il devenu?; **I don't know what will ~ of her** je ne sais pas ce qu'elle va devenir.

3 *vt* (*liter, frm*) **(a)** (*suit*) aller à. **her hat does not ~ her** son chapeau ne lui va pas *or* ne l'avantage pas *or* ne lui sied pas (*frm*).

(b) (*befit*) convenir à, être digne de. **it does not ~ him to speak thus** il lui sied mal de parler ainsi.

becoming [bɪˈkʌmɪŋ] *adj behaviour, speech* convenable, bienséant; *clothes* seyant, qui va bien. **a ~ hair style** une coiffure seyante; **her hat is not ~** son chapeau ne lui va pas *or* ne l'avantage pas.

bed [bed] **1** *n* **(a)** (*furniture*) lit *m*, couche†† *f* (*liter*). **room with 2 ~s** chambre *f* à 2 lits; **to go to ~** se coucher; (*euph*) **to go to ~ with sb*** coucher avec qn*; **to get into ~** se coucher, se mettre au lit; **to get out of ~** se lever; **to get out of ~ on the wrong side***, (*US*) **to get up on the wrong side of the ~*** se lever du pied gauche; **to get sb to ~** mettre qn au lit; **to put sb to ~** coucher qn; **to make the ~** faire le lit; **to turn down the ~** préparer le lit (*en repliant le haut des draps*), faire la couverture; **to be in ~** être couché; (*through illness*) être alité, garder le lit; **to go home to ~** rentrer se coucher; **to sleep in separate ~s** faire lit à part; **before ~** avant de se coucher; (*frm, hum*) **~ of sickness** lit de douleur; **'~ and breakfast'** 'chambres' (*avec petit déjeuner*); **to book in (at a hotel) for ~ and breakfast** prendre une chambre avec le petit déjeuner (à l'hôtel); **we stayed at ~-and-breakfast places** nous avons pris pension *or* pris une chambre chez des particuliers; **~ and board** le gîte *or* le vivre et le couvert; *[hotel etc]* pension complète; (*Prov*) **as you make your ~ so you must lie on it** comme on fait son lit on se couche; (*fig*) **life is not a ~ of roses** la vie n'est pas une partie de plaisir; (*fig*) **my job isn't exactly a ~ of roses*** mon travail n'est pas exactement une sinécure; († *liter*) **she was brought to ~ of a boy** elle accoucha d'un garçon; (*Press*) **to put a paper to ~** boucler un journal; (*Press*) **the paper has gone to ~** le journal est bouclé; *V* **camp**[1], **death, feather** *etc.*

(b) (*layer*) (*Geol*) *[coal]* couche *f*, gisement *m*; *[clay]* couche, lit *m*; *[coral]* banc *m*; *[ore]* gisement; (*Constr*) *[mortar]* bain *m* (de mortier); (*Zool*) *[oysters]* banc.

(c) (*base*) (*Tech*) *[engine]* berceau *m*; *[lathe]* banc *m*; *[machine]* base *f*, bâti *m*; (*Archit*) *[building]* assises *fpl*.

(d) (*bottom*) *[sea]* fond *m*; *[river]* lit *m*.

(e) (*Horticulture*) *[vegetables]* planche *f*; (*square*) carré *m*; *[flowers]* parterre *m*, massif *m*; (*strip*) plate-bande *f*; (*oval, circular*) corbeille *f*.

2 *cpd*: **bed bath** (grande) toilette *f* (d'un malade); **bedbug** punaise *f*; **bedclothes** couvertures *fpl* et draps *mpl* (de lit), literie *f*; **bedcover** couvre-lit *m*, dessus-de-lit *m inv*; (*lit*) **they were bedfellows for a night** ils ont partagé le même lit une nuit; (*fig*) **they are queer bedfellows** ils font une drôle d'association; **bedhead** tête *f* de lit, chevet *m*; **bed jacket** liseuse *f*; **bed linen** draps *mpl* de lit (et taies *fpl* d'oreillers); **bed of nails** lit *m* à clous; **bedpan** bassin *m* (hygiénique); **bedpost** colonne *f* de lit; **bedridden** alité, cloué au lit, (*permanently*) grabataire; **bedrock** (*Geol*) soubassement *m*; (*fig*) base *f*; **bedroom** *V* **bedroom; bed-settee** divan-lit *m*; **bedside** *V* **bedside;** (*Brit*) **bed-sitter,** (*Brit*) **bed-sitting room,** (*Brit*) **bedsit‡** chambre meublée, studio *m*; **bedsocks** chaussettes *fpl* (de lit); **bedsore** escarre *f*; **bedspread** dessus-de-lit *m inv*, couvre-lit *m*; **bedstead** châlit *m*, bois *m* de lit; (*Bot*) **bedstraw** gaillet *m*; **bedtime** *V* **bedtime;** (*Med*) **bedwetting** incontinence *f* nocturne.

3 *vt* **(a)** (*Horticulture*) **to ~ (out) plants** repiquer des plantes.

(b) (*Tech*) *foundations* asseoir. **to ~ stones in mortar** cimenter *or* sceller des pierres.
(c) (:) *woman* coucher avec*.
bed down *vi* (aller) se coucher.
bedaub [bɪ'dɔ:b] *vt* barbouiller, enduire (*with* de).
-bedded ['bedɪd] *adj ending in cpds*: **twin-bedded room** chambre *f* à deux lits.
bedding ['bedɪŋ] *n* **(a)** literie *f*; (*Mil*) (matériel *m* de) couchage *m*; *[animals]* litière *f*. **(b)** (*Horticulture*) ~ **out** repiquage *m*.
bedeck [bɪ'dek] *vt* parer, orner (*with* de); (*slightly pej*) attifer* (*with* de).
bedevil [bɪ'devl] *vt* (*confuse*) mêler, brouiller, embrouiller; (*torment*) tourmenter, harceler.
bedevilment [bɪ'devlmənt] *n* (*confusion*) confusion *f*; (*torment*) tourment *m*, harcèlement *m*.
bedlam ['bedləm] *n* **(a)** (*uproar*) ramdam* *m*, chahut* *m*, chambard: *m*. **the class was a regular ~** la classe faisait un chahut terrible*. **(b)** (*Hist*) maison *f* de fous.
Bedouin ['bedʊɪn] **1** *n*, *pl* **~s**, *collectively* ~ **(a)** Bédouin(e) *m(f)*. **(b)** (*nomad*) **b~** nomade *mf*. **2** *adj* **(a)** bédouin. **(b) b~** nomade.
bedraggled [bɪ'drægld] *adj clothes* en désordre, débraillé; *person* dépenaillé*, débraillé; *hair* embroussaillé.
bedroom ['bedrʊm] **1** *n* chambre *f* (à coucher); *V* **spare**. **2** *cpd*: (*Theat*) **bedroom farce** comédie *f* de boulevard; **bedroom slipper** pantoufle *f*; **bedroom suite** chambre *f* à coucher (*mobilier*).
bedside ['bedsaɪd] **1** *n* chevet *m*. **at his ~** à son chevet.
2 *cpd book, lamp* de chevet. **bedside rug** descente *f* de lit; **bedside table** table *f* de chevet *or* de nuit; *[doctor]* **bedside manner** comportement *m* envers les malades; **he has a good bedside manner** il sait parler à ses malades.
bedtime ['bedtaɪm] **1** *n* heure *f* du coucher. **it is ~** il est l'heure d'aller se coucher *or* d'aller au lit; **it's past your ~** tu devrais être déjà couché.
2 *cpd*: **to tell a child a bedtime story** raconter une histoire à un enfant avant qu'il s'endorme.
bee [bi:] **1** *n* **(a)** abeille *f*. (*fig*) **to have a ~ in one's bonnet*** avoir une idée fixe, avoir une marotte; **they crowded round him like ~s round a honeypot** ils se pressaient autour de lui comme des mouches sur un pot de confiture; *V* **bumblebee, busy, queen** *etc*.
(b) (*esp US: meeting*) réunion active *or* de travail; (*competition*) concours *m*. **they have a sewing ~ on Thursdays** elles se réunissent pour coudre le jeudi; *V* **spelling**.
2 *cpd*: (*Orn*) **bee eater** guêpier *m*; (*lit, fig*) **beehive** ruche *f*; **beehive hair style** coiffure *f* en casque de Minerve *or* toute en hauteur; **beekeeper** apiculteur *m*, -trice *f*; **in a beeline** à vol d'oiseau, en ligne droite; **to make a beeline for** (*go straight to*) se diriger tout droit *or* en droite ligne vers; (*rush towards*) se ruer sur, filer droit sur; **beeswax** (*n*) cire *f* d'abeille; (*vt*) *floor etc* cirer, encaustiquer.
beech [bi:tʃ] **1** *n* (*also* **~ tree**) hêtre *m*; (*wood*) (bois *m* de) hêtre; *V* **copper**.
2 *cpd hedge, chair* de hêtre. **beechmast** faînes *fpl* (tombées); **beechnut** faîne *f*; **beechwood** (*material*) (bois *m* de) hêtre *m*; (*group of trees*) bois *m* de hêtres, hêtraie *f*.
beef [bi:f] **1** *n* (*U*) bœuf *m*. **roast ~** rôti *m* de bœuf, rosbif *m*; **there's too much ~ on him**: il a trop de viande:, il est trop gros; *V* **bully, corned** *etc*.
2 *cpd*: **beef cattle** bœufs *mpl* de boucherie; **beefeater** hallebardier *m* (*de la tour de Londres*); **beef olive** paupiette *f* (de bœuf); **beef sausage** saucisse *f* (*contenant du bœuf*); **beefsteak** bifteck *m*, steak *m*; **beef tea** bouillon *m* (de viande).
3 *vi* (:: *complain*) rouspéter*, râler* (*about* contre).
beefy* ['bi:fɪ] *adj* (*strong*) robuste, solide, costaud*; (*fat*) bien en chair.
been [bi:n] *ptp of* **be**.
beer [bɪəʳ] **1** *n* bière *f*. (*Brit*) **life's not all ~ and skittles** tout n'est pas qu'une partie de rigolade* en ce monde; *V* **draught, ginger, small** *etc*.
2 *cpd*: **beer barrel** tonneau *m* à bière; **beer bottle** canette *f*; **beer can** boîte *f* de bière; **beer engine** pompe *f* à bière; **beer glass** bock *m*, chope *f*; **beer pump = beer engine**.
beery ['bɪərɪ] *adj atmosphere, room* qui sent la bière; *party* où la bière coule à flots; *person* un peu éméché*, parti*. **~ face** trogne *f* d'ivrogne*.
beet [bi:t] **1** *n* betterave *f*. (*US*) **red ~** betterave (potagère); *V* **sugar** *etc*. **2** *cpd*: (*Brit*) **beetroot** betterave *f* (potagère); **beet sugar** sucre *m* de betterave.
beetle[1] ['bi:tl] **1** *n* (*Zool*) coléoptère *m*; (*also* **black ~**) cafard *m*, blatte *f*; (*scarab*) scarabée *m*. **there's a huge ~ in the bath!** il y a un énorme cafard dans la baignoire!; *V* **Colorado, death** *etc*.
2 *vi* (:) **to ~ in/out/through** *etc* entrer/sortir/traverser *etc* (en vitesse).
beetle off: *vi* décamper, ficher le camp*. **I must beetle off** il faut que je me sauve* (*subj*).
beetle[2] ['bi:tl] *cpd*: **beetle-browed** aux sourcils broussailleux; **beetling brow** front proéminent; **beetling cliffs** falaises surplombantes.
beetle[3] ['bi:tl] *n* (*mallet*) maillet *m*; (*big*) mailloche *f*; *[paving, pile driving]* mouton *m*.
befall [bɪ'fɔ:l] *pret* **befell**, *ptp* **befallen** (*liter: only infin and 3rd person*) **1** *vi* arriver, advenir, survenir. **whatever may ~** quoi qu'il puisse arriver, quoi qu'il advienne; **it befell that ...** il advint que ... .
2 *vt* arriver à, échoir à. **a misfortune befell him** il lui arriva un malheur.
befallen [bɪ'fɔ:lən] *ptp of* **befall**.
befell [bɪ'fel] *pret of* **befall**.
befit [bɪ'fɪt] *vt* (*frm: only infin and 3rd person*) convenir à. **it ill ~s him to speak thus** il lui convient *or* il lui sied (*frm*) mal de parler ainsi.
befitting [bɪ'fɪtɪŋ] *adj* convenable, seyant. **with ~ humility** avec l'humilité qui convient *or* qui sied (*frm*).
befog [bɪ'fɒg] *vt* (*puzzle*) brouiller, embrouiller; (*obscure*) *origin, meaning* obscurcir. **she was quite ~ged** elle était dans le brouillard (le plus complet).
before [bɪ'fɔ:ʳ] (*phr vb elem*) **1** *prep* **(a)** *[time]* avant. **~ Christ** avant Jésus-Christ; **the day ~ yesterday** avant-hier *m*; **he came the year ~ last** il est venu il y a deux ans; **the year ~ last was his centenary** son centenaire a eu lieu il y a deux ans; **the day ~ their departure** la veille de leur départ; **two days ~ Christmas** l'avant-veille *f* de Noël; **I got there ~ you** je suis arrivé avant vous, je vous ai devancé; **that was ~ my time** (*before I was here*) je n'étais pas encore là; (*before I was born*) je n'étais pas encore né; **I cannot do it ~ next week** je ne peux pas le faire avant la semaine prochaine; **~ now, ~ then** avant, auparavant; **you should have done it ~ now** vous devriez l'avoir déjà fait; **~ long** avant peu, sous peu, d'ici peu, avant longtemps, bientôt; **~ doing** avant de faire.
(b) *[order, rank]* avant. **ladies ~ gentlemen** les dames avant les messieurs; **~ everything** avant tout; **to come ~ sb/sth** précéder qn/qch.
(c) *[place, position]* devant. **he stood ~ me** il était (là) devant moi; **~ my (very) eyes** sous mes (propres) yeux; **the question ~ us** la question qui nous occupe; **the task ~ him** la tâche qu'il a devant lui *or* qui l'attend; **he fled ~ the enemy** il s'est enfui à l'approche de *or* devant l'ennemi; (*Naut*) **to sail ~ the mast** servir comme simple matelot; (*Naut*) **to sail ~ the wind** aller *or* avoir vent arrière; *V* **carry**.
(d) (*in presence of*) devant, en présence de. **he said it ~ us all** il l'a dit en notre présence *or* devant nous tous; **~ a lawyer** par-devant notaire; **to appear ~ a court/a judge** comparaître devant un tribunal/un juge; **he brought the case ~ the court** il a saisi le tribunal de l'affaire.
(e) (*rather than*) plutôt que. **to put death ~ dishonour** préférer la mort au déshonneur; **he would die ~ betraying his country** il mourrait plutôt que de trahir sa patrie.
2 *adv* **(a)** (*time*) avant, auparavant. **the day ~** la veille; **the evening ~** la veille au soir; **the week/year ~** la semaine/l'année d'avant *or* précédente; **two days ~** l'avant-veille, deux jours avant *or* auparavant; **I have read that book ~** j'ai déjà lu ce livre; **I had read it ~** je l'avais déjà lu, je l'avais lu auparavant; **she has never met him ~** c'est la première fois qu'elle le rencontre, elle ne l'a jamais encore rencontré; **it has never happened ~** cela n'est jamais arrivé jusqu'ici; **it had never happened ~** cela n'était jamais arrivé jusqu'alors; **long ~** longtemps auparavant; **to continue as ~** faire comme par le passé; **he should have told me ~** il aurait dû me le dire avant *or* plus tôt *or* auparavant.
(b) (*place*) en avant, devant.
(c) (*order*) avant. **that chapter and the one ~** ce chapitre et le précédent *or* et celui d'avant.
3 *conj* **(a)** (*time*) avant de + *infin*, avant que (+ne) + *subj*. **I did it ~ going out** je l'ai fait avant de sortir; **go and see him ~ he goes** allez le voir avant qu'il (ne) parte; **~ I come/go/return** avant mon arrivée/mon départ/mon retour; **we will need a year ~ it is finished** il nous faudra un an pour l'achever; **it will be a long time ~ he comes again** il ne reviendra pas de *or* d'ici longtemps; **it will be 6 weeks ~ the boat returns** le bateau ne reviendra pas avant 6 semaines; (*fig*) **~ you could say Jack Robinson** en moins de rien, en moins de deux, en moins de temps qu'il n'en faut pour le dire; **~ I forget, your mother phoned** avant que je n'oublie, votre mère a téléphoné.
(b) (*rather than*) plutôt que de + *infin*. **he will die ~ he surrenders** il mourra plutôt que de se rendre.
beforehand [bɪ'fɔ:hænd] *adv* d'avance, par avance, à l'avance, avant, au préalable, préalablement. **you must tell me ~** il faut me le dire à l'avance, il faut me prévenir avant *or* au préalable; **to make preparations well ~** faire des préparatifs bien à l'avance.
befoul [bɪ'faʊl] *vt* (*liter: lit, fig*) souiller (*liter*), salir.
befriend [bɪ'frend] *vt* (*help*) venir en aide à, aider; (*be friend to*) traiter en ami, donner son amitié à.
befuddle [bɪ'fʌdl] *vt* (*confuse*) brouiller l'esprit *or* les idées de; (*make tipsy*) griser, émécher. **~d with drink** éméché*.
beg [beg] **1** *vt* **(a)** *money, alms* mendier.
(b) *favour* solliciter, quémander. **to ~ sb's pardon** demander pardon à qn; **(I) ~ your pardon** (*apologizing*) je vous demande pardon; (*not having heard*) pardon?, vous disiez?; (*frm*) **I ~ to state that** je me permets de (vous) faire remarquer que, qu'il me soit permis de faire remarquer que; **I ~ to differ** permettez-moi d'être d'un autre avis, je me permets de ne pas partager cet avis; (*frm*) **I ~ to inform you that** je tiens à *or* j'ai l'honneur (*frm*) de vous faire savoir que; (*frm*) **to ~ leave to do** solliciter l'autorisation de faire.
(c) (*entreat*) supplier. **to ~ (of) sb to do** supplier qn de faire; **I ~ (of) you!** je vous en supplie!, de grâce!
(d) to ~ the question présumer vrai ce qui est en question; **this ~s the question** c'est présumer la question résolue.
2 *vi* **(a)** mendier, demander la charité. **to ~ for money** mendier; **to ~ for food** mendier de la nourriture; **to live by ~ging** vivre de charité *or* d'aumône; *[dog]* **to sit up and ~** faire le beau; (*fig*) **goods that go ~ging*** des marchandises dont personne ne veut *or* qui ne trouvent pas d'amateurs; (*fig*) **I'll have that sausage if it's going ~ging*** donne-moi *or* je vais m'adjuger cette saucisse s'il n'y a pas d'amateurs.
(b) (*entreat*) supplier. **to ~ for mercy/help** demander grâce/de l'aide; *V also* **1c**.

beg off* *vi* se faire excuser (*from* de).
began [bɪˈgæn] *pret of* **begin.**
beget [bɪˈget] *pret* **begot,** *ptp* **begotten** *vt* **(a)** (††) engendrer. **the only begotten Son of the Father** le Fils unique engendré par le Père.
(b) (*fig*) *difficulties etc* causer, créer, susciter. **poverty ~s crime** la misère conduit au crime *or* engendre le crime.
beggar [ˈbegəʳ] **1** *n* **(a)** (*also* **~ man, ~ woman**) mendiant(e) *m(f)*, mendigot(e)* *m(f)*; (*fig: very poor person*) indigent(e) *m(f)*, pauvre(sse)† *m(f)*. (*Prov*) **~s can't be choosers** nécessité fait loi (*Prov*); **~'s opera** opéra *m* de quat' sous.
(b) (*) **poor ~!** pauvre diable!*; **a lucky ~** un veinard*; **a queer little ~** un drôle de petit bonhomme.
2 *vt* (*lit*) réduire à la mendicité; (*fig: ruin*) mettre sur la paille, ruiner. (*fig*) **to ~ description** défier toute description.
3 *cpd:* (*Cards*) **beggar-my-neighbour** bataille *f*.
beggarly [ˈbegəlɪ] *adj amount* piètre, misérable; *existence* misérable, sordide; *meal* maigre, piètre, pauvre; *wage* dérisoire, de famine.
beggary [ˈbegərɪ] *n* mendicité *f*.
begin [bɪˈgɪn] *pret* **began,** *ptp* **begun 1** *vt* **(a)** (*start*) commencer (*to do, doing* à faire, de faire), se mettre (*to do, doing* à faire); *work* commencer, se mettre à; *task* entreprendre; *song* commencer (à chanter), entonner; *attack* déclencher; *bottle* commencer, entamer, déboucher; *book, letter [writer]* commencer (à écrire); *[reader]* commencer (à lire). **to ~ a cheque book/a page** commencer *or* prendre un nouveau carnet de chèques/une nouvelle page; **to ~ a journey** partir en voyage; **he began the day with a glass of milk** il a bu un verre de lait pour bien commencer la journée; **to ~ the day right** bien commencer la journée, se lever du pied droit; **to ~ life as** débuter dans la vie comme; **that doesn't (even) ~ to compare with ...** cela est loin d'être comparable à ..., cela n'a rien de comparable avec ...; **it soon began to rain** il n'a pas tardé à pleuvoir; **I'd begun to think you were not coming** je commençais à croire que tu ne viendrais pas; **to ~ again** *or* **afresh** recommencer (*to do* à faire), recommencer à zéro*; **'it's late' he began** 'il est tard' commença-t-il.
(b) (*originate, initiate*) *discussion* commencer, ouvrir; *conversation* amorcer, engager; *quarrel, argument, dispute* faire naître; *reform, movement, series of events* déclencher; *fashion* lancer; *custom, policy* inaugurer; *war* causer; *rumour* faire naître.
2 *vi* **(a)** *[person]* commencer, s'y mettre; *[speech, programme, meeting, ceremony]* commencer (*with* par). **let's ~!** commençons!, allons-y!, on s'y met!*; **we must ~ at once** il faut commencer *or* nous y mettre immédiatement; **well, to ~ at the beginning** eh bien! pour commencer par le commencement; **it's ~ning rather well/badly** cela s'annonce plutôt bien/mal; **to ~ in business** se lancer dans les affaires; **just where the hair ~s** à la naissance des cheveux; **before October ~s** avant le début d'octobre; **to ~ again** *or* **afresh** recommencer (à zéro*); **classes ~ on Monday** les cours commencent *or* reprennent lundi; **the classes ~ again soon** les cours reprennent bientôt, c'est bientôt la rentrée; **~ning from Monday** à partir de lundi; **he began in the sales department/as a clerk** il a débuté dans le service des ventes/comme employé; **he began as a Marxist** il a commencé par être marxiste, au début *or* au départ il a été marxiste; **he began with the intention of writing a thesis** au début son intention était *or* il avait l'intention d'écrire une thèse; **to ~ by doing** commencer par faire; **~ by putting everything away** commence par tout ranger; **to ~ with sth** commencer *or* débuter par qch; **~ with me!** commencez par moi!; **to ~ with, there were only 3 of them but later ...** (tout) d'abord, ils n'étaient que 3 mais plus tard ...; **this is false to ~ with** pour commencer *or* d'abord c'est faux; **we only had 100 francs to ~ with** nous n'avions que 100 F pour commencer *or* au début; **~ on a new page** prenez une nouvelle page.
(b) (*broach*) **to ~ on a book** commencer (à écrire *or* à lire) un livre; **to ~ on a course of study** commencer *or* entreprendre un programme d'études; **they had begun on a new bottle** ils avaient commencé *or* débouché *or* entamé une nouvelle bouteille; **I began on the job last week** j'ai commencé à travailler *or* j'ai débuté dans mon travail la semaine dernière.
(c) *[music, noise, guns]* commencer, retentir; *[fire]* commencer, prendre; *[river]* prendre sa source; *[road]* partir (*at* de); *[political party, movement, custom]* commencer, naître. **that's when the trouble ~s** c'est alors *or* là que les ennuis commencent; **it all began when he refused to pay** toute cette histoire a commencé *or* tout a commencé quand il a refusé de payer; **since the world began** depuis le commencement du monde, depuis que le monde est monde.
beginner [bɪˈgɪnəʳ] *n* **(a)** (*novice*) débutant(e) *m(f)*, novice *mf*. **it's just ~'s luck** aux innocents les mains pleines (*Prov*). **(b)** (*originator*) auteur *m*, cause *f*.
beginning [bɪˈgɪnɪŋ] *n* **(a)** *[speech, book, film, career etc]* commencement *m*, début *m*. **to make a ~** commencer, débuter; **the ~ of the academic year** la rentrée (universitaire *or* scolaire); **the ~ of the world** le commencement *or* l'origine *f* du monde; **in the ~** au commencement, au début; **from the ~** dès le début, dès le commencement; **since the ~ of time** depuis le commencement du monde, depuis que le monde est monde; **from ~ to end** du début *or* du commencement à la fin, de bout en bout, d'un bout à l'autre; **to start again at** *or* **from the ~** recommencer au commencement; **the ~ of negotiations** l'amorce *f or* l'ouverture *f* des négociations; **it was the ~ of the end for him** pour lui ce fut le commencement de la fin; **they taught him the ~s of science** ils lui ont enseigné les rudiments de la science.
(b) (*origin*) origine *f*, commencement *m*. **the shooting was the ~ of the rebellion** la fusillade a été à l'origine de la révolte; **fascism had its ~s in Italy** le fascisme prit naissance en Italie.
begone [bɪˈgɒn] *vi* (*liter,††: imper and infin only*) **~!** allez-vous-en!, partez!, hors d'ici! (*liter*); (*frm*) **they bade him ~** on lui intima l'ordre de partir.
begonia [bɪˈgəʊnɪə] *n* bégonia *m*.
begot [bɪˈgɒt] *pret of* **beget.**
begotten [bɪˈgɒtn] *ptp of* **beget.**
begrime [bɪˈgraɪm] *vt* noircir, souiller (*liter*); *face* barbouiller (*with* de).
begrudge [bɪˈgrʌdʒ] *vt* (*envy*) envier (*sb sth* qch à qn); (*give unwillingly*) mesurer, donner à contre-cœur, n'accorder qu'à regret. **I shan't ~ you £5** je te donne tes 5 livres sans regret, je ne vais pas te refuser 5 livres!; **to ~ sb his food** mesurer *or* reprocher* la nourriture à qn; **to ~ doing** faire à contre-cœur, rechigner à faire.
beguile [bɪˈgaɪl] *vt* **(a)** tromper, duper. **to ~ sb with promises** bercer qn de promesses, endormir qn avec des promesses; **to ~ sb into doing sth** amener *or* entraîner qn par supercherie à faire qch; **to ~ the time (doing)** faire passer le temps (à faire), tromper son ennui (en faisant).
(b) (*charm*) *person* distraire, amuser.
beguiling [bɪˈgaɪlɪŋ] *adj* séduisant, ensorcelant.
begum [ˈbeɪgəm] *n* bégum *f*.
begun [bɪˈgʌn] *ptp of* **begin.**
behalf [bɪˈhɑːf] *n*: **on ~ of** (*as representing*) de la part de, au nom de, pour; (*in the interest of*) en faveur de, dans l'intérêt de, pour; **to come on sb's ~** venir de la part de qn; **to act on sb's ~** agir pour qn *or* pour le compte de qn; **he spoke on my ~** il a parlé pour moi *or* en mon nom; **to plead on sb's ~** plaider en faveur de qn; **he was worried on my ~** il s'inquiétait pour moi *or* à mon sujet.
behave [bɪˈheɪv] *vi* (*also* **~ o.s.**) **(a)** (*conduct o.s.*) se conduire, se comporter. **to ~ (o.s.) well/badly** se conduire *or* se comporter bien/mal; **to ~ well towards sb** se comporter bien à l'égard de *or* envers qn, bien agir envers qn; **to ~ wisely** agir sagement; **to ~ like an honest man** se comporter *or* se conduire en honnête homme.
(b) (*conduct o.s. well*) bien se tenir; *[child]* être sage. **he knows how to ~ in society** il sait se tenir dans le monde; **~ yourself!** sois sage!, tiens-toi bien!
(c) *[machines etc]* marcher, fonctionner. **the ship ~s well at sea** le navire tient bien la mer.
behaviour, (*US*) **behavior** [bɪˈheɪvjəʳ] *n* **(a)** (*manner, bearing*) conduite *f*, comportement *m*. **to be on one's best ~** se conduire de son mieux; *[child]* se montrer d'une sagesse exemplaire.
(b) (*conduct towards others*) conduite *f*, comportement *m*, façon *f* d'agir *or* de se comporter (*to, towards sb* envers, à l'égard de qn).
(c) *[machines]* fonctionnement *m*.
behavioural, (*US*) **behavioral** [bɪˈheɪvjərəl] *adj* **(a)** *sciences, studies* behavioriste. **(b)** *problem, pattern* de comportement.
behaviourism, (*US*) **behaviorism** [bɪˈheɪvjərɪzəm] *n* behaviorisme *m*.
behaviourist, (*US*) **behaviorist** [bɪˈheɪvjərɪst] *adj, n* behavioriste (*mf*).
behead [bɪˈhed] *vt* décapiter.
beheld [bɪˈheld] *pret, ptp of* **behold.**
behest [bɪˈhest] *n* (*liter*) commandement *m*, ordre *m*. **at the ~ of** sur l'ordre de.
behind [bɪˈhaɪnd] (*phr vb elem*) **1** *adv* **(a)** (*in or at the rear*) derrière, par derrière, en arrière. **to stay ~** rester derrière les autres *or* en arrière; **to look ~** regarder en arrière; (*lit, fig*) **to leave ~** laisser derrière soi; **to come ~** suivre, venir derrière; *V* **fall behind** *etc*.
(b) (*late*) en retard. **to be ~ with one's studies/payments** être en retard dans ses études/ses paiements; **to be ~ with one's work** avoir du travail en retard, être en retard dans son travail; **I'm too far ~ to catch up now** j'ai pris trop de retard pour me remettre à flot *or* me rattraper maintenant.
2 *prep* **(a)** (*lit, fig: at the back of*) derrière. **~ the table** derrière la table; **come out from ~ the door** sortez de derrière la porte; **walk close ~ me** suivez-moi de près; **~ my back** (*lit*) derrière mon dos; (*fig*) derrière mon dos, à mon insu; (*fig*) **to put sth ~ one** oublier qch, refuser de penser à qch; (*Theat, fig*) **~ the scenes** dans les coulisses; (*fig*) **he has the Communists ~ him** il a les communistes derrière lui; (*fig*) **what is ~ this?** qu'y a-t-il là-dessous?
(b) (*more backward than*) en arrière de, en retard sur. **her son is ~ the other pupils** son fils est en retard sur les autres élèves.
(c) (*time*) **~ time** en retard; (*fig*) **to be ~ the times** être en retard sur son temps, ne pas être de son époque; **their youth is far ~ them** leur jeunesse est loin derrière eux.
3 *n* (*: buttocks*) derrière *m*, postérieur* *m*.
behindhand [bɪˈhaɪndhænd] *adv, adj* **(a)** (*late*) en retard. **(b)** (*in arrears*) en retard. **he is ~ with his work** il a du travail en retard, il est en retard dans son travail.
behold [bɪˈhəʊld] *pret, ptp* **beheld** *vt* (*liter*) voir, apercevoir. **~!** voici!, tenez!, regardez!; **~ thy servant** voici ton serviteur; **and ~ I am with you** et voici que je suis avec vous; *V* **lo.**
beholden [bɪˈhəʊldən] *adj* (*frm*) **to be ~** être redevable (*to sb for sth* à qn de qch).
behove [bɪˈhəʊv], (*US*) **behoove** [bɪˈhuːv] *impers vt* (*frm*) incomber, appartenir (*sb to do* à qn de faire), être du devoir *or* de l'intérêt (*sb to do* de qn de faire).
beige [beɪʒ] *adj, n* beige (*m*).
being [ˈbiːɪŋ] *n* **(a)** (*U: existence*) existence *f*. **to come into ~** prendre naissance; **the world came into ~** le monde fut créé; **to bring** *or* **call into ~** faire naître, susciter; **to bring a plan into ~**

exécuter *or* réaliser un plan; **then in ~** qui existait alors.
(b) être *m*, créature *f*. **human ~s** êtres humains; *V* **supreme.**
(c) (*essential nature*) être *m*, essence *f*. **all my ~ revolts at the idea** tout mon être se révolte à cette idée.
bejewelled, (*US*) **bejeweled** [bɪ'dʒuːəld] *adj* couvert *or* paré de bijoux.
belabour, (*US*) **belabor** [bɪ'leɪbəʳ] *vt* rouer de coups; (*fig: with words*) invectiver.
belated [bɪ'leɪtɪd] *adj apology, greetings, measures* tardif.
belay [bɪ'leɪ] *vt* (*Naut*) amarrer. **~ing pin** cabillot *m* (d'amarrage).
belch [beltʃ] **1** *vi [person]* faire un renvoi, roter. **2** *vt* (*also* **~ forth** *or* **out**) *[volcano, gun] smoke, flames* vomir, cracher. **3** *n* renvoi *m*, rot *m*.
beleaguered [bɪ'liːgəd] *adj city* assiégé, investi, cerné; *army* cerné.
belfry ['belfrɪ] *n* beffroi *m*; *[church]* clocher *m*, beffroi; *V* **bat**[1].
Belgian ['beldʒən] **1** *n* Belge *mf*. **2** *adj* belge, de Belgique.
Belgium ['beldʒəm] *n* Belgique *f*.
Belgrade [bel'greɪd] *n* Belgrade.
belie [bɪ'laɪ] *vt* (*fail to justify*) *hopes* démentir, tromper; (*prove false*) *words* donner le démenti à, démentir; *proverb* faire mentir; (*misrepresent*) *facts* donner une fausse impression *or* idée de.
belief [bɪ'liːf] *n* **(a)** (*U: acceptance as true*) croyance *f* (*in* en, à). **~ in ghosts** croyance aux revenants; **~ in God** croyance en Dieu; **he has lost his ~ in God** il ne croit plus en Dieu, il a perdu la foi (en Dieu); **worthy of ~** digne de foi; **it is beyond** *or* **past (all) ~** c'est incroyable, c'est à ne pas (y) croire; **wealthy beyond ~** incroyablement riche.
(b) (*Rel*) (*faith*) foi *f*; (*doctrine*) credo *m*.
(c) (*conviction*) opinion *f*, conviction *f*. **in the ~ that** persuadé que, convaincu que; **it is my ~ that** je suis convaincu *or* persuadé que, j'ai la conviction que; **to the best of my ~** autant que je sache; **to entertain the ~ that** être convaincu que, croire que; *V* **strong.**
(d) (*U: trust*) confiance *f*, foi *f* (*in* en). **he has no ~ in doctors** il n'a aucune confiance dans les médecins; **he has no ~ in the future** il ne fait pas confiance à l'avenir.
believable [bɪ'liːvəbl] *adj* croyable.
believe [bɪ'liːv] **1** *vt* **(a)** (*accept truth of*) *statement, account, evidence* croire, donner *or* ajouter foi à; *person* croire. **to ~ what sb says** croire ce que dit qn; **I don't ~ a word of it** je n'en crois rien *or* pas un mot; **don't you ~ it!*** ne va pas croire ça!*, crois-le et bois de l'eau (fraîche)*; **he could hardly ~ his eyes/ears** il en croyait à peine ses yeux/ses oreilles; **if he is to be ~d** à l'en croire, s'il faut l'en croire; **I ~ you, thousands wouldn't*** moi, je te crois, mais je dois être le seul!
(b) (*think*) croire, estimer. **I ~ I'm right** je crois avoir raison; **I don't ~ he will come** je ne crois pas qu'il viendra *or* qu'il vienne; **he is ~d to be ill** on le croit malade; **he is ~d to have a chance of succeeding** on lui donne des chances de succès; **that is ~d to be true** cela passe pour vrai; **I have every reason to ~ that ...** j'ai tout lieu de croire que ...; **I ~ so** je crois que oui, je le crois; **I ~ not** je crois que non, je ne (le) crois pas; **I don't know what to ~** je ne sais que croire *or* à quoi m'en tenir; *V* **make.**
2 *vi* croire; (*Rel*) croire, avoir la foi. **to ~ in** *God* croire en; *ghosts, promises, antibiotics etc* croire à; **to ~ in sb** croire en qn, avoir confiance en qn; **to ~ in a method** être partisan d'une méthode; **I don't ~ in doctors** je n'ai pas confiance dans les médecins, je ne crois pas aux médecins; **I don't ~ in letting children do what they want** je ne suis pas d'avis qu'il faille laisser les enfants faire ce qu'ils veulent.
believer [bɪ'liːvəʳ] *n* **(a)** partisan(e) *m(f)*, adepte *mf*. **~ in capital punishment** partisan de la peine capitale; **he is a great ~ in it** il est très partisan de. **(b)** (*Rel*) croyant(e) *m(f)*. **to be a ~ in ghosts/in astrology** croire aux revenants/à l'astrologie.
Belisha beacon [bɪ'liːʃə'biːkən] *n* lampadaire *m* (*à globe orange marquant un passage clouté*).
belittle [bɪ'lɪtl] *vt person, action, object* déprécier, rabaisser. **to ~ o.s.** se déprécier.
bell[1] [bel] **1** *n* **(a)** *[church, school]* cloche *f*; (*hand~*) clochette *f*; *[toys, animal's collar etc]* grelot *m*; *[cows]* cloche, clarine *f*; *[goats, sheep]* clochette; *[cats etc]* clochette, grelot; *[door]* sonnette *f*; (*electric*) sonnerie *f*; *[cycle, typewriter]* timbre *m*; *[telephone]* sonnerie. **great ~** bourdon *m*, grosse cloche; **the first ~ for mass was ringing** le premier coup de la messe sonnait; **there's the ~!** *[door]* on sonne!, ça sonne!*; *[telephone]* le téléphone (sonne)!; (*Naut*) **~s** coups *mpl* de cloche; **eight ~s** huit coups piqués; **to sound four/six/eight ~s** piquer quatre/six/huit (coups); *V* **answer, chime, ring**[2] *etc.*
(b) *[flower]* calice *m*, clochette *f*; *[trumpet, loudspeaker]* pavillon *m*.
2 *vt* mettre une cloche à. (*fig*) **to ~ the cat** attacher le grelot (*fig*).
3 *cpd*: **bell-bottomed trousers** pantalon *m* à pattes d'éléphant; (*Naut*) pantalon de marine; **bellboy** groom *m*, chasseur *m*; **bell glass** cloche *f* (en verre); **bell heather** bruyère cendrée; (*US*) **bellhop** = **bellboy**; **bell pull** *[door]* poignée *f* de sonnette; *[room]* cordon *m* de sonnette; **bell push** bouton *m* de sonnette; **bell ringer** sonneur *m*, carillonneur *m*; **bell rope** *[belfry]* corde *f* de cloche; *[room]* cordon *m* de sonnette; **bell-shaped** en forme de cloche *or* de clochette; **bell tent** tente *f* conique; **bell tower** clocher *m*.
bell[2] [bel] **1** *n [stag]* bramement *m*. **2** *vi* bramer.
belladonna [ˌbelə'dɒnə] *n* (*Bot, Med*) belladone *f*.
belle [bel] *n* beauté *f*, belle *f*. **the ~ of the ball** la reine du bal.
bellicose ['belɪkəʊs] *adj* belliqueux, guerrier.
bellicosity [ˌbelɪ'kɒsɪtɪ] *n* humeur belliqueuse, caractère belliqueux.
belligerence [bɪ'lɪdʒərəns] *n*, **belligerency** [bɪ'lɪdʒərənsɪ] *n* belligérance *f*.
belligerent [bɪ'lɪdʒərənt] *adj, n* belligérant(e) *m(f)*.
bellow ['beləʊ] **1** *vi [animals]* mugir; *[esp cow, bull]* beugler, meugler; *[person]* brailler, beugler*, gueuler‡ (*with* de); *[wind, ocean]* mugir.
2 *vt* (*also* **~ out**) *song, order* brailler, beugler*, hurler; *blasphemies* vociférer.
3 *n [animal]* mugissement *m*; *[esp cow, bull]* beuglement *m*, meuglement *m*; *[person]* hurlement *m*, beuglement*; *[storm, ocean]* mugissement.
bellows ['beləʊz] *npl [forge, organ]* soufflerie *f*; *[fire]* soufflet *m*. **a pair of ~** un soufflet.
belly ['belɪ] **1** n **(a)** (*abdomen*) ventre *m*, estomac *m*; (*big*) panse* *f*, bedaine* *f*; (*fig: appetite*) ventre, estomac. **his eyes were bigger than his ~‡** il a eu les yeux plus grands que le ventre.
(b) (*womb*) ventre *m*, sein *m* (*fig*).
(c) *[container]* panse *f*, ventre *m*; *[stone]* renflement *m*; *[violin]* table *f* harmonique; *[guitar]* table harmonique, ventre; *[ship]* ventre; *[sail]* creux *m*.
2 *vt* gonfler, enfler.
3 *vi* (*also* **~ out**) se gonfler, s'enfler.
4 *cpd*: **bellyache** (*n*) mal *m* de *or* au ventre; (*vi*:‡) ronchonner*, bougonner*; **to have a bellyache** avoir mal au ventre; **bellyaching‡** ronchonnement* *m*, bougonnement* *m*; **belly-band** sous-ventrière *f*; **belly button*** nombril *m*; **belly dance** danse *f* du ventre; **belly dancer** danseuse orientale, almée *f*; (*Swimming*) **to do a bellyflop** faire un plat-ventre; (*Aviat*) **belly-landing** atterrissage *m* sur le ventre; (*Aviat*) **to make a belly-landing** atterrir *or* se poser sur le ventre; **belly laugh** gros rire (gras); (*Aviat*) **belly tank** réservoir *m* de secours.
bellyful ['belɪfʊl] *n [food]* ventre plein. **he had had a ~‡** il en avait plein le dos*, il en avait ras le bol‡.
belong [bɪ'lɒŋ] *vi* **(a)** (*be the property*) appartenir, être (*to* à). **this book ~s to me** ce livre m'appartient, ce livre est à moi; **lands which ~ to the Crown** terres qui appartiennent à la Couronne; **the lid ~s to this box** le couvercle va avec cette boîte, c'est le couvercle de cette boîte.
(b) (*be member, inhabitant etc*) **to ~ to a society** faire partie *or* être membre d'une société; **to ~ to a town** *[native]* être originaire *or* natif d'une ville; *[inhabitant]* habiter une ville.
(c) (*be in right place*) être à sa place. **to feel that one doesn't ~** se sentir étranger; **to ~ together** aller ensemble; **stockings that don't ~ (together)** des bas qui ne font pas la paire; **the book ~s on this shelf** le livre va sur ce rayon; **put it back where it ~s** remets-le à sa place; **murder ~s under the heading of capital crimes** le meurtre rentre dans la catégorie des crimes capitaux.
(d) (*be the concern*) appartenir (*to* à), relever, être l'affaire, dépendre (*to* de). **that does not ~ to my duties** cela ne relève pas de mes fonctions; (*Jur*) **this case ~ed to the Appeal Court** ce procès ressortissait à la cour d'appel.
belongings [bɪ'lɒŋɪŋz] *npl* affaires *fpl*, possessions *fpl*. **personal ~** objets personnels.
beloved [bɪ'lʌvɪd] **1** *adj* (bien) aimé (*by, of* de), chéri. **~ by all** aimé de tous; **dearly ~ brethren** mes bien chers frères. **2** *n* bien-aimé(e) *m(f)*.
below [bɪ'ləʊ] (*phr vb elem*) **1** *prep* **(a)** (*lower than*) sous, au-dessous de, plus bas que. **~ the bed** sous le lit; **on the bed and ~ it** sur le lit et en dessous; **her skirt is well ~ her knees** sa jupe est bien au-dessous du genou; **~ average/sea level** au-dessous de la moyenne/du niveau de la mer; (*St Ex*) **~ par** au-dessous du pair; (*fig*) **he feels ~ par** il ne se sent pas en forme; **~ freezing point** au-dessous de zéro; **~ the horizon** au-dessous de l'horizon; **~ the surface** sous la surface; **to be ~ sb in rank** occuper un rang inférieur à qn, être au-dessous de qn; (*lit, fig*) **to hit ~ the belt** porter un coup bas; **that was ~ the belt!** ça c'était un coup bas! *or* un coup en traître!; **~ one's breath** à voix basse, à mi-voix; (*Naut*) **~ decks** sous le pont, en bas.
(b) *[river]* en aval de. **the Thames ~ London** la Tamise en aval de Londres.
(c) (*unworthy of*) **it would be ~ my dignity to speak to him** je m'abaisserais en lui parlant.
2 *adv* **(a)** (*lower down*) en bas, en dessous, plus bas; (*Naut*) en bas. **the tenants ~** les locataires du *or* d'en dessous; **they live 2 floors ~** ils habitent 2 étages en dessous; **~, we could see the valley** en bas *or* plus bas *or* en dessous nous apercevions la vallée; **voices from ~** des voix venant d'en bas; **the road ~** la route en contre-bas; (*on earth*) **here ~** ici-bas; (*in hell*) **down ~** en enfer; *V* **go below** *etc.*
(b) *[documents]* **see ~** voir plus bas *or* ci-dessous; **as stated ~** comme indiqué ci-dessous.
belt [belt] **1** *n* **(a)** (*Dress, Judo, fig*) ceinture *f*; (*Mil etc*) ceinturon *m*, ceinture; (*corset*) gaine *f*. **(shoulder) ~** baudrier *m*; (*lit, fig*) **blow below the ~** coup bas; (*fig*) **to pull in** *or* **tighten one's ~** se mettre *or* se serrer la ceinture*; (*Judo*) **to be a Black B~** être ceinture noire; (*Scol*) **to give sb the ~** punir qn à coups d'étrivière; *V* **safety** *etc.*
(b) (*tract of land*) (*Geog*) zone *f*; (*Agr*) région *f*. **industrial ~** zone industrielle; **the cotton ~** la région de culture du coton; *V* **green.**
(c) (*Tech*) courroie *f*. **~ pulley** poulie *f* de courroie; *V* **conveyor** *etc.*
(d) (*US: road*) route *f* de ceinture.
2 *vt* (*thrash*) administrer une correction à, donner une raclée* à; (‡: *hit*) flanquer *or* coller un gnon‡ à. **she ~ed him one in the eye‡** elle lui a flanqué *or* collé un gnon‡ dans l'œil.
3 *vi* (‡: *rush*) filer (à toutes jambes), se carapater‡. **to ~ in/out/across** *etc* entrer/sortir/traverser *etc* à toutes jambes *or*

à toute blinde**:**; **he ~ed down the street** il a descendu *or* dévalé la rue à fond de train *or* à fond la caisse**:**.

belt out* *vt sep*: **to belt out a song** chanter une chanson de tout son cœur *or* à pleins poumons.

belt up: *vi* (*Brit*) la boucler**:**, la fermer**:**. **belt up!** la ferme!**:**, boucle-la!**:**

belvedere [ˌbelvɪˈdɪəʳ] *n* belvédère *m*.

bemoan [bɪˈməʊn] *vt* pleurer, déplorer.

bemuse [bɪˈmjuːz] *vt* stupéfier, hébéter.

Ben [ben] *n* (*dim of* **Benjamin**) Benjamin *m*; *V* **big.**

ben [ben] *n* (*Scot*) mont *m*, sommet *m*.

bench [bentʃ] **1** *n* **(a)** (*seat*) (*gen, Parl*) banc *m*; (*in tiers*) gradin *m*; (*padded*) banquette *f*; *V* **back, opposition** *etc*.

(b) (*Jur*) **the B~** (*court*) la cour, le tribunal; (*judges collectively*) la magistrature. **to be raised to the ~** être nommé juge; **to be on the ~** (*permanent office*) être juge (*or* magistrat); (*when in court*) siéger au tribunal; **to appear before the ~** comparaître devant le tribunal; **the B~ has ruled that** la cour a décrété que; *V* **king.**

(c) *[laboratory, factory, workshop]* établi *m*; *V* **test.**

2 *cpd*: **bench lathe** tour *m* à banc; (*Surv*) **bench mark** repère *m* de nivellement; **bench vice** étau *m* d'établi.

bencher [ˈbentʃəʳ] *n* (*Brit Jur*) ≃ membre *m* de l'ordre des avocats; *V* **back.**

bend [bend] (*vb: pret, ptp* **bent**) **1** *n [river]* coude *m*, détour *m*; *[tube, pipe]* coude; *[arm]* pli *m*, saignée *f*; *[knee]* pli; *[road]* courbe *f*, coude, virage *m*; (*Naut: knot*) nœud *m* de jonction. **there is a ~ in the road** la route fait un coude *or* un virage; (*Aut*) **~s for 8 km** virages sur 8 km; *[car]* **to take a ~** prendre un virage *or* un tournant; (*fig*) **to get sth on the ~:** obtenir qch par la bande; (*Brit*) **round the ~:** tombé sur la tête*, cinglé**:**; (*Med*) **the ~s*** la maladie des caissons; (*Her*) **~ sinister** barre *f* de bâtardise; *V* **double, hair** *etc*.

2 *vt* **(a)** *back, body* courber; *leg, arm* plier; *knee, leg* fléchir, plier; *head* baisser, pencher, courber; *branch* courber, faire ployer; *light ray* réfracter; *rail, pipe, rod, beam* tordre, courber; *bow* bander; (*Naut*) *cable* étalinguer; *sail* enverguer. **to ~ lightly** infléchir, arquer; **to ~ at right angles** couder; **to ~ out of shape** fausser, gauchir; **with head bent over a book** la tête penchée *or* courbée sur un livre; **on ~ed knee(s)** à genoux; **to go down on ~ed knee** s'agenouiller, se mettre à genoux; (*fig*) **to ~ o.s. to sb's will** se plier à la volonté de qn; (*fig*) **to ~ sb to one's will** mettre qn sous son joug; *V also* **bent**[1].

(b) (*direct*) **to ~ one's steps towards** se diriger vers, porter ses pas vers; **all eyes were bent on him** tous les yeux *or* les regards étaient fixés *or* braqués sur lui; **to ~ one's efforts towards changing sth** diriger ses efforts vers la transformation de qch.

(c) (*pass only*) **to be bent on doing** être résolu *or* décidé à faire, vouloir absolument faire; **he is bent on seeing me** il veut absolument me voir; **he is bent on pleasure** il ne recherche que son plaisir.

3 *vi [person]* se courber, être courbé; *[branch, instrument etc]* être courbé, plier; *[river, road]* faire un coude, tourner; (*fig: submit*) se soumettre, céder (*to* à). **to ~ under a burden** ployer sous un fardeau; **to ~ backward/forward** se pencher en arrière/en avant; *V* **catch.**

bend back 1 *vi [wire etc]* se recourber; *[person]* se pencher en arrière.

2 *vt sep* replier, recourber.

bend down 1 *vi [person]* se courber, se baisser; *[tree, branch]* ployer, plier, se courber.

2 *vt sep wire* replier, recourber; *branch* faire ployer.

bend over 1 *vi [person]* se pencher. (*fig*) **to bend over backwards to help sb*** se mettre en quatre pour aider qn.

2 *vt sep* replier.

bender [ˈbendəʳ] *n* **(a)** (*Tech*) cintreuse *f*. **(b) to go on a ~:** aller se cuiter*.

beneath [bɪˈniːθ] **1** *prep* **(a)** (*under*) sous. **~ the table** sous la table; **to bend ~ a burden** ployer sous un fardeau.

(b) (*lower than*) au-dessous de, sous. **town ~ the castle** ville (située) au-dessous du château.

(c) (*unworthy of*) indigne de. **it is ~ my notice** cela ne mérite pas mon attention *or* que je m'y arrête (*subj*); **it is ~ her to interfere** il est indigne d'elle d'intervenir, elle ne daigne pas intervenir (*liter*); **to marry ~ one** faire une mésalliance.

2 *adv* dessous, au-dessous, en bas. **the flat ~** l'appartement *m* au-dessous *or* du dessous.

Benedictine [ˌbenɪˈdɪktɪn] **1** *n* **(a)** (*Rel*) bénédictin(e) *m(f)*. **(b) b~** [ˌbenɪˈdɪktiːn] (*liqueur*) bénédictine *f*. **2** *adj* bénédictin.

benediction [ˌbenɪˈdɪkʃən] *n* (*blessing*) bénédiction *f*; (*at table*) bénédicité *m*; (*Rel: office*) salut *m*; bénédiction.

benefaction [ˌbenɪˈfækʃən] *n* (*good deed*) bienfait *m*; (*gift*) donation *f*, don *m*.

benefactor [ˈbenɪfæktəʳ] *n* bienfaiteur *m*.

benefactress [ˈbenɪfæktrɪs] *n* bienfaitrice *f*.

benefice [ˈbenɪfɪs] *n* bénéfice *m* (*Rel*).

beneficence [bɪˈnefɪsəns] *n* **(a)** (*U*) bienfaisance *f*. **(b)** (*act*) acte *m or* œuvre *f* de bienfaisance.

beneficent [bɪˈnefɪsənt] *adj person* bienfaisant; *thing* salutaire.

beneficial [ˌbenɪˈfɪʃəl] *adj* salutaire, avantageux (*to* pour), favorable (*to* à). **~ to the health** bon pour la santé; **the change will be ~ to you** le changement vous fera du bien *or* vous sera salutaire; (*Jur*) **~ owner** usufruitier *m*, -ière *f*.

beneficiary [ˌbenɪˈfɪʃərɪ] *n [will etc]* bénéficiaire *mf*; (*Rel*) bénéficier *m*.

benefit [ˈbenɪfɪt] **1** *n* **(a)** (*advantage*) avantage *m*, profit *m*. **to have the ~ of** profiter de; **for the ~ of your health** dans l'intérêt de votre santé; **it is for his ~ that this was done** c'est pour son bien que cela a été fait; **to be to the ~ of sb** être dans l'intérêt de qn; (*fig*) **he's not really hurt, he's just crying for your ~*** il ne s'est pas vraiment fait mal, il pleure pour se faire remarquer (par vous); **to give sb/get the ~ of the doubt** laisser à qn/avoir le bénéfice du doute; **the ~s of a good education** les bienfaits *mpl or* les avantages *mpl* d'une bonne éducation.

(b) (*allowance of money*) allocation *f*, prestation *f*. **unemployment ~** allocations (de) chômage; *V* **sickness.**

(c) ~ of clergy (*privileges*) privilège *m* du clergé; (*rites*) rites *mpl* de l'Église, rites religieux; **marriage without ~ of clergy** mariage non béni par l'Église.

2 *vt* faire du bien à, profiter à.

3 *vi* se trouver bien (*from, by* de), gagner (*from, by doing* à faire). **he will ~ by** *or* **from a holiday** des vacances lui feront du bien.

4 *cpd*: **benefit club** assurance mutuelle, caisse *f* de secours mutuel; (*Sport*) **benefit match** match *m* au profit d'un joueur; **benefit performance** représentation *f* de bienfaisance; **benefit society** association *f* de secours mutuel *or* d'entraide.

Benelux [ˈbenɪlʌks] *n* Bénélux *m*. **the ~ countries** les pays du Bénélux.

benevolence [bɪˈnevələns] *n* **(a)** (*U*) (*kindness*) bienveillance *f*; (*generosity*) bienfaisance *f*, générosité *f*. **(b)** (*gift, act*) bienfait *m*. **(c)** (*Hist*) don forcé (*au souverain*).

benevolent [bɪˈnevələnt] *adj* **(a)** (*kind*) bienveillant (*to* envers). **~ smile** sourire bienveillant *or* plein de bonté. **(b)** (*charitable*) bienfaisant, charitable (*to* envers). **~ society** association *f* de secours mutuel *or* de bienfaisance.

Bengal [beŋˈgɔːl] **1** *n* Bengale *m*. **2** *cpd*: **Bengal light** feu *m* de Bengale; **Bengal tiger** tigre *m* du Bengale.

Bengali [beŋˈgɔːlɪ] **1** *n* **(a)** Bengali *mf*. **(b)** (*Ling*) bengali *m*. **2** *adj* bengali (*f inv*).

benighted [bɪˈnaɪtɪd] *adj* **(a)** (*fig*) *person* plongé dans (les ténèbres de) l'ignorance; *policy etc* à courte vue, aveugle. **(b)** († *lit*) surpris par la nuit.

benign [bɪˈnaɪn] *adj*, **benignant** [bɪˈnɪgnənt] *adj* **(a)** (*kindly*) bienveillant, affable; (*beneficial*) bienfaisant, salutaire; *climate* doux (*f* douce). **(b)** (*Med*) *tumour* bénin (*f* -igne).

benison [ˈbenɪzn] *n* bénédiction *f*.

Benjamin [ˈbendʒəmɪn] *n* Benjamin *m*.

bent[1] [bent] **1** *pret, ptp of* **bend. 2** *adj wire, pipe* tordu; (**:** *dishonest*) véreux**:**. (*homosexual*) **to be ~** être homosexuel(le); *V* **bend.**

bent[2] [bent] *n* **(a)** (*aptitude*) disposition *f*, aptitude *f* (*for* pour). **to have a ~ for languages** avoir des dispositions pour les langues.

(b) (*liking*) penchant *m*, goût *m*. **to have a ~ for** *or* **towards sth** avoir du goût *or* un penchant pour qch; **to follow one's ~** suivre son inclination *f*; **of literary ~** tourné vers les lettres.

bent[3] [bent] *n* (*grass, rushes*) agrostide *f*; (*land*) lande *f*.

bentwood [ˈbentwʊd] *adj furniture* en bois courbé. **~ chair** chaise *f* de bistro *or* de style bistro.

benumb [bɪˈnʌm] *vt* **(a)** *limb* engourdir, endormir. **fingers ~ed with cold** doigts engourdis par le froid, doigts gourds; **he was ~ed with cold** il était transi (de froid); **~ed with fright** glacé *or* transi de peur.

(b) (*fig*) *the mind* paralyser, engourdir.

Benzedrine [ˈbenzɪdriːn] *n* ® benzédrine *f*.

benzene [ˈbenziːn] *n* benzène *m*.

benzine [ˈbenziːn] *n* benzine *f*.

benzoin[1] [ˈbenzəʊɪn] *n* (*resin*) benjoin *m*; (*shrub*) styrax *m* (benjoin).

benzoin[2] [ˈbenzəʊɪn] *n* (*Chem*) benzoïne *f*.

bequeath [bɪˈkwiːð] *vt* (*in will*) léguer (*to* à); (*fig*) *tradition* transmettre, léguer (*to* à).

bequest [bɪˈkwest] *n* legs *m*.

berate [bɪˈreɪt] *vt* (*liter*) admonester (*liter*), réprimander.

Berber [ˈbɜːbəʳ] **1** *n* **(a)** Berbère *mf*. **(b)** (*Ling*) berbère *m*. **2** *adj* berbère.

bereave [bɪˈriːv] *vt* **(a)** *pret, ptp* **bereft** (*deprive*) priver, dépouiller, déposséder (*of* de). **bereft of hope** désespéré; **he is bereft of reason** il a perdu la raison. **(b)** *pret, ptp gen* **bereaved** (*by death*) ravir (*sb of sb* qn à qn).

bereaved [bɪˈriːvd] **1** *adj* endeuillé, affligé. **2** *n*: **the ~** la famille du disparu.

bereavement [bɪˈriːvmənt] *n* (*loss*) perte *f*; (*state*) deuil *m*. **a sad ~** une perte cruelle; **in his ~** dans son deuil; **owing to a recent ~** en raison d'un deuil récent.

bereft [bɪˈreft] *pret, ptp of* **bereave a.**

beret [ˈbereɪ] *n* béret *m*.

berg [bɜːg] *n abbr of* **iceberg.**

bergamot [ˈbɜːgəmɒt] *n* bergamote *f*.

beriberi [ˈberɪˈberɪ] *n* béribéri *m*.

Bering [ˈbeɪrɪŋ] *adj*: **~ Sea/Strait** mer *f*/détroit *m* de Béring *or* Behring.

Berlin [bɜːˈlɪn] **1** *n* **(a)** (*Geog*) Berlin. **East/West ~** Berlin Est/Ouest. **(b)** (*carriage*) **b~** berline *f*. **2** *cpd*: **the Berlin Wall** le mur de Berlin; **Berlin wool** laine *f* à broder.

Berliner [bɜːˈlɪnəʳ] *n* Berlinois(e) *m(f)*.

Bermuda [bɜːˈmjuːdə] **1** *n* Bermudes *fpl*. **2** *cpd*: **Bermuda shorts** bermuda *m*.

Berne [bɜːn] *n* Berne.

berry [ˈberɪ] **1** *n* baie *f*; *V* **brown. 2** *vi*: **to go ~ing** aller cueillir des baies.

berserk [bəˈsɜːk] **1** *adj* fou furieux (*f* folle furieuse). **to go ~** (*lit*) devenir fou furieux; (*fig: with anger*) se mettre en rage; (**:** *be reckless*) devenir fou *or* dingue**:**. **2** *n* (*Myth: also* **~er, baresark**) *guerrier m nordique combattant avec furie.*

berth [bɜːθ] **1** *n* **(a)** *[plane, train, ship]* couchette *f*. (*easy job*) **to find a soft ~:** trouver une bonne planque**:**.

(b) (*Naut: place for ship*) mouillage *m*, poste *m* d'amarrage. **to give a wide ~ to a ship** passer au large d'un navire; (*fig*) **to give sb a wide ~** éviter qn, se tenir à une distance respectueuse de qn; (*fig*) **you should give him a wide ~** vous devriez l'éviter à tout prix.

2 *vi* (*at anchor*) mouiller; (*alongside*) venir à quai, accoster.

3 *vt* **(a) to ~ a ship** (*assign place*) donner *or* assigner un poste d'amarrage à un navire; (*perform action*) amarrer un navire, faire accoster un navire.

(b) *person* donner *or* assigner une couchette à.

beryl ['berɪl] *n* béryl *m*.

beryllium [be'rɪljəm] *n* béryllium *m*.

beseech [bɪ'siːtʃ] *pret, ptp* **besought** *vt* (*liter*) **(a)** (*ask for*) *permission* demander instamment, solliciter; *pardon* implorer.

(b) (*entreat*) supplier, implorer, conjurer (*sb to do* qn de faire).

beseeching [bɪ'siːtʃɪŋ] **1** *adj voice, look* suppliant, implorant; *tone* suppliant, pressant. **2** *n* supplications *fpl*.

beseechingly [bɪ'siːtʃɪŋlɪ] *adv* d'un air *or* d'un ton suppliant *or* implorant.

beset [bɪ'set] *pret, ptp* **beset** *vt* **(a)** (*surround*) entourer, environner; (*assail*) assaillir. **path ~ with obstacles** chemin semé d'obstacles; **problem ~ with difficulties** problème hérissé de difficultés; **he is ~ with difficulties** les difficultés l'assaillent (de toutes parts); **~ with** *or* **by doubts** rongé *or* assailli par le doute.

(b) (*besiege*) cerner, encercler; *town* assiéger, investir.

besetting [bɪ'setɪŋ] *adj* habituel; *temptation* harcelant. **his ~ sin** son grand défaut.

beside [bɪ'saɪd] *prep* **(a)** (*at the side of*) à côté de, auprès de. **she sat down ~ him** elle s'est assise à côté de lui *or* à ses côtés (*frm*).

(b) (*compared with*) en comparaison de, auprès de, à côté de, comparé à, par rapport à.

(c) (*phrases*) **that's ~ the point** *or* **the mark** cela n'a rien à voir; **it's quite ~ the point to suggest that ...** il est tout à fait inutile de suggérer que...; **this is ~ the question** ceci n'a rien à voir avec la question; **to be ~ o.s. (with anger)** être hors de soi; **he was quite ~ himself (with excitement)** il ne se possédait plus; **he is ~ himself with joy** il est fou *or* transporté de joie, il ne se sent pas de joie.

besides [bɪ'saɪdz] **1** *adv* **(a)** (*in addition*) en outre, en plus, de plus. **many more ~** bien d'autres encore; **he wrote a novel and several short stories ~** il a écrit un roman et aussi plusieurs nouvelles.

(b) (*else*) de plus, d'autre. **there is nothing ~** il n'y a rien de plus *or* d'autre.

(c) (*moreover*) d'ailleurs, du reste, en outre.

2 *prep* **(a)** (*in addition to*) en plus de, en dehors de, outre. **others ~ ourselves** d'autres que nous; **there were 3 of us ~ Mary** nous étions 3 sans compter Marie; **~ this book I bought others** outre ce livre, j'en ai acheté d'autres; **~ which he was unwell** sans compter qu'il était souffrant, et par-dessus le marché il était souffrant.

(b) (*except*) excepté, hormis, en dehors de. **no one ~ you** personne en dehors de vous *or* excepté vous, personne d'autre que vous; **who ~ them** qui si ce n'est eux, qui à part eux *or* hormis eux.

besiege [bɪ'siːdʒ] *vt* **(a)** *town* assiéger, mettre le siège devant.

(b) (*fig: surround*) assaillir, entourer, se presser autour de. **~d by journalists** assailli par des journalistes.

(c) (*fig: pester*) assaillir, harceler (*with* de). **~d with questions** assailli de questions.

besieger [bɪ'siːdʒəʳ] *n* assiégeant(e) *m(f)*.

besmear [bɪ'smɪəʳ] *vt* (*lit*) barbouiller (*with* de); (*fig*) salir, souiller (*liter*).

besmirch [bɪ'smɜːtʃ] *vt* (*fig*) ternir, entacher; (*lit*) salir, souiller (*liter*).

besom ['biːzəm] *n* balai *m* de bouleau.

besotted [bɪ'sɒtɪd] *adj* **(a)** (*drunk*) abruti, hébété (*with* de). **(b)** (*infatuated*) entiché, fou (*f* folle) (*with* de). **(c)** (*foolish*) idiot, imbécile.

besought [bɪ'sɔːt] *pret, ptp of* **beseech**.

bespatter [bɪ'spætəʳ] *vt* éclabousser (*with* de).

bespeak [bɪ'spiːk] *pret* **bespoke**, *ptp* **bespoken** *or* **bespoke** *vt* **(a)** (*order*) *goods* commander; *room, place* retenir, réserver.

(b) (*indicate*) annoncer, témoigner de, prouver; *weakness, fault* accuser.

(c) (††: *forebode*) faire prévoir, laisser présager.

(d) (*liter: speak to*) parler à, s'adresser à.

bespectacled [bɪ'spektɪkld] *adj* à lunettes.

bespoke [bɪ'spəʊk] **1** *pret, ptp of* **bespeak**. **2** *adj* (*Brit*) *goods, garment* fait sur commande, fait sur mesure; *tailor etc* à façon.

bespoken [bɪ'spəʊkən] *ptp of* **bespeak**.

besprinkle [bɪ'sprɪŋkl] *vt* (*with liquid*) arroser, asperger (*with* de); (*with powder*) saupoudrer (*with* de); (*dot with*) parsemer (*with* de).

Bess [bes] *n* (*dim of* **Elizabeth**) Lisette, Babette. (*Hist*) **good Queen ~** la bonne reine Élisabeth (1ère).

best [best] **1** *adj, superl of* **good** le meilleur, la meilleure. **the ~ pupil in the class** le meilleur élève de la classe; **the ~ route to Paris** la route la meilleure *or* la plus directe pour Paris; **the ~ thing about her is ...** ce qu'il y a de meilleur chez elle c'est ...; **the ~ thing to do is to wait** le mieux c'est d'attendre; **the ~ years of one's life** les plus belles années de sa vie; **in one's ~ clothes** vêtu de ses plus beaux vêtements, sur son trente et un; **may the ~ man win!** que le meilleur gagne!; **to put one's ~ foot** *or* **leg forward** (*in walking*) allonger le pas; (*do one's best*) faire de son mieux; (*Cards*) **to have the ~ diamond** être maître à carreau; **she is her ~ friend** c'est sa meilleure amie; **she's his ~ girl**‡ c'est sa petite amie *or* sa nana‡; (*fig*) **the ~ part of** la plus grande partie de; **for the ~ part of an hour/month** pendant près d'une heure/d'un mois; *V* **behaviour, second-best, wish** *etc.*

2 *n* le mieux, le meilleur, ce qu'il y a de mieux. **to do one's (level) ~ (to win)** faire de son mieux (pour gagner), faire tout son possible (pour gagner); **do the ~ you can!** faites de votre mieux, faites pour le mieux; **to get the ~ out of sb** tirer le maximum de qn; **to get the ~ of the bargain** *or* **of it** l'emporter, avoir le dessus; **he wants the ~ of both worlds** il veut gagner sur les deux tableaux, il veut tout avoir; **to make the ~ of sth** s'accommoder de qch (du mieux que l'on peut); **to make the ~ of a bad job** *or* **a bad business** *or* **a bad bargain** faire contre mauvaise fortune bon cœur; **to make the ~ of one's opportunities** profiter au maximum des occasions qui se présentent; **the ~ of it** *or* **the ~ of the matter is that ...** le plus beau de l'affaire c'est que ...; **to be the ~ of friends** être les meilleurs amis (du monde); **it's all for the ~** c'est pour le mieux; **to do sth for the ~** faire qch dans les meilleures intentions; **to the ~ of my ability/knowledge/recollection** *etc* autant que je puisse/que je sache/que je me souvienne *etc*; **in one's (Sunday) ~*** endimanché, sur son trente et un; **to look one's ~** être resplendissant; *[woman]* être en beauté; (*on form*) **to be at one's ~** être en pleine forme* *or* en train; **the roses are at their ~ just now** les roses sont de toute beauté en ce moment; **that is Racine at his ~** voilà du meilleur Racine; **even at the ~ of times** même dans les circonstances les plus favorables; **even at the ~ of times he's not very patient but ...** il n'est jamais particulièrement patient mais ...; **at ~** au mieux; **even the ~ of us can make mistakes** tout le monde peut se tromper; **the ~ of plans can go astray** les meilleurs plans peuvent échouer; **he can sing with the ~ of them** il sait chanter comme pas un*; (*iro*) **and the ~ of (British) luck!**‡ je te souhaite bien du plaisir!* (*iro*).

3 *adv, superl of* **well** le mieux, le plus. **the ~ dressed man** l'homme le mieux habillé; **the ~ loved actor** l'acteur le plus aimé; **I like strawberries ~** je préfère les fraises à n'importe quoi *or* à tout; **that is the hat which suits her ~** voilà le chapeau qui lui va le mieux; **I helped him as ~ I could** je l'ai aidé de mon mieux *or* du mieux que j'ai pu; **to think it ~ to do** juger à propos de faire, trouver sage de faire; **do as you think ~** faites comme bon vous semble, faites à votre idée *or* pour le mieux; **you know ~** vous savez mieux que personne, c'est vous le mieux placé pour en juger, vous êtes (le) meilleur juge en la matière; **you had ~ go at once** tu ferais mieux de t'en aller tout de suite.

4 *vt* battre, l'emporter sur.

5 *cpd*: *[wedding]* **best man** garçon *m* d'honneur, témoin *m*; **bestseller** (*book*) best-seller *m*, (livre à) succès *m* de librairie; (*Comm: other article*) article *m* de grosse vente, best-seller *m*; (*author*) auteur *m* à succès.

bestial ['bestɪəl] *adj* (*lit, fig*) bestial.

bestiality [ˌbestɪ'ælɪtɪ] *n* **(a)** (*U*) bestialité *f*. **(b)** (*act*) acte bestial.

bestiary ['bestɪərɪ] *n* bestiaire *m* (*recueil*).

bestir [bɪ'stɜːʳ] *vt*: **to ~ o.s.** se remuer, se démener, s'activer.

bestow [bɪ'stəʊ] *vt* **(a)** (*grant*) *favour* accorder (*on, upon* à); *title* conférer (*on, upon* à). **to ~ the hand of one's daughter** accorder la main de sa fille.

(b) (*devote*) *energy* consacrer, employer (*upon* à); *admiration* accorder. **to ~ friendship on sb** prendre qn en amitié; **the attention ~ed on this boy** l'attention dont ce garçon est l'objet.

(c) (*place*) poser, déposer.

bestowal [bɪ'stəʊəl] *n* **(a)** (*U*) octroi *m*. **(b)** (*gift*) don *m*.

bestraddle [bɪ'strædl] *vt horse, bicycle* enfourcher; *wall* chevaucher; *chair* se mettre à califourchon sur.

bestrew [bɪ'struː] *pret* **bestrewed**, *ptp* **bestrewed** *or* **bestrewn** *vt* (*liter*) parsemer, joncher (*with* de).

bestride [bɪ'straɪd] *pret* **bestrode** [bɪ'strəʊd], *ptp* **bestridden** [bɪ'strɪdn] *vt* **(a)** *chair* être à cheval *or* à califourchon sur; *horse, bicycle* enfourcher. **(b)** *brook, ditch* enjamber.

bet [bet] **1** *vti* parier (*against* contre, *on* sur, *with* avec). **to ~ 10 to 1** parier (à) 10 contre 1; **to ~ on horses** parier *or* jouer aux courses; **to ~ on a horse** jouer un cheval; (*fig*) **I ~ he'll come!*** je te parie qu'il vient!* *or* qu'il viendra!; **I'll ~ you anything (you like)*** je te parie tout ce que tu veux; **~ you won't do it**‡ (je te parie que) t'es pas cap(able) de le faire‡; **you ~!**‡ un peu!‡, tu parles!‡; **~ you can't!**‡ chiche*!; **you can ~ your boots*** *or* **your bottom dollar*** *or* **your life*** **that ...** tu peux parier tout ce que tu veux *or* parier ta chemise que ... .

2 *n* pari *m*. **to make** *or* **lay a ~ (on)** parier (sur), faire un pari (sur); **to accept** *or* **take (on) a ~** accepter un pari; **to win a ~** gagner un pari; *V* **hedge, lay**[1].

beta ['biːtə] *n* bêta *m*.

betake [bɪ'teɪk] *pret* **betook**, *ptp* **betaken** [bɪ'teɪkən] *vt*: **to ~ o.s. to** (s'en) aller à, se rendre à.

betel ['biːtəl] *n* bétel *m*.

bethink [bɪ'θɪŋk] *pret, ptp* **bethought** *vt*: **to ~ o.s.** réfléchir, considérer; **to ~ o.s. of sth/to do/that ...** s'aviser de qch/de faire/que ... .

Bethlehem ['beθlɪhem] *n* Bethléem.

bethought [bɪ'θɔːt] *pret, ptp of* **bethink**.

betide [bɪ'taɪd] *vti*: **whatever (may) ~** quoi qu'il advienne *or* arrive (*subj*); *V* **woe**.

betimes [bɪ'taɪmz] *adv* (*liter*) (*early*) de bonne heure, tôt; (*quickly*) promptement, vite; (*in good time*) à temps, assez tôt.

betoken [bɪ'təʊkən] *vt* (*forecast*) présager, annoncer; (*indicate*) dénoter, être signe de.

betook [bɪ'tʊk] *pret of* **betake**.

betray [bɪ'treɪ] *vt* **(a)** (*be disloyal to*) *one's country* trahir, être traître à; *friends* trahir; *woman* tromper, trahir; (*fig*) *hope etc* trahir, tromper, décevoir. **he has ~ed our trust** il a trahi notre confiance, il a commis un abus de confiance.

(b) (*give up treacherously*) *person, secret* livrer (*to* à), trahir. **to ~ sb into enemy hands** livrer qn à l'ennemi *or* aux mains de l'ennemi.

(c) (*disclose*) *age, fears, intentions, facts, truth* trahir, révéler. **to ~ o.s.** se trahir; **his speech ~ed the fact that he had been drinking** on devinait à l'écouter qu'il avait bu.

betrayal [bɪ'treɪəl] *n* (*V* **betray**) **(a)** (*U*) *[country, woman, ally etc]* trahison *f*; *[age, secret, plan]* divulgation *f*; *[fears, intentions]* manifestation *f* (involontaire); *[facts, truth]* révélation *f*. **~ of trust** abus *m* de confiance.

(b) (*deed*) (acte *m* de) trahison *f*. **the ~ of Christ** la trahison envers le Christ.

betrayer [bɪ'treɪəʳ] *n [country]* traître(sse) *m(f)* (*of* à, envers); *[friend]* dénonciateur *m*, -trice *f* (*of* de). **she killed her ~** elle a tué celui qui l'avait trahie.

betroth [bɪ'trəʊð] *vt* (*liter*,††) fiancer (*to* à, avec), promettre en mariage (*to* à).

betrothal [bɪ'trəʊðəl] *n* (*liter*) fiançailles *fpl* (*to* avec).

betrothed [bɪ'trəʊðd] *adj, n* (*liter or hum*) fiancé(e) *m(f)*.

better[1] ['betəʳ] **1** *adj, comp of* **good** meilleur. **that book is ~ than this one** ce livre-là est meilleur que celui-ci; **she is a ~ dancer than her sister, she is ~ at dancing than her sister** elle danse mieux que sa sœur; **she is ~ at dancing than at singing** elle danse mieux qu'elle ne chante; **he's a ~ man than his brother** il est mieux que son frère; **you're a ~ man than I am!*** vous êtes plus doué que moi!*; **he's no ~ than a thief** c'est un voleur ni plus ni moins; **he's no ~ than he should be!*** ce n'est pas l'honnêteté qui l'étouffe!*; **she's no ~ than she should be!** ce n'est pas la vertu qui l'étouffe!*; (*Med*) **he is much ~ now** il va *or* se porte bien mieux maintenant; (*Med*) **how are you? — much ~** comment allez-vous? — bien mieux; (*Med*) **he got ~ very quickly after his illness** il s'est très vite remis de sa maladie; **the weather is getting ~** le temps s'améliore; **this book gets ~ towards the end** ce livre s'améliore vers la fin; **his technique got ~ as he grew older** sa technique s'est affirmée avec l'âge; **his writing is ~ since he got a new pen** son écriture est meilleure depuis qu'il a un nouveau stylo; **(it's getting) ~ and ~!** (ça va) de mieux en mieux!; **that's ~!** voilà qui est mieux!; **it couldn't be ~, nothing could be ~!** ça ne pourrait pas mieux tomber! *or* mieux se trouver!; **it would be ~ to stay at home** il vaudrait mieux rester à la maison; **wouldn't it be ~ to refuse?** ne vaudrait-il pas mieux refuser?; **it is ~ not to promise anything than to let him down** il vaut mieux ne rien promettre que de le décevoir; **a ~ class of hotel** un hôtel de catégorie supérieure; **he has seen ~ days** il a connu des jours meilleurs; **this hat has seen ~ days** ce chapeau n'est plus de la première fraîcheur; (*hum*) **his ~ half*** sa moitié* (*hum*); **his ~ nature stopped him from ...** ses bons sentiments, reprenant le dessus, l'ont empêché de ...; **to go one ~ than sb** damer le pion à qn; **the ~ part of a year/of 200 km** *etc* près d'un an/de 200 km *etc*; **to hope for ~ things** espérer mieux.

2 *adv, comp of* **well** mieux. **he sings ~ than you** il chante mieux que toi; **he sings ~ than he dances** il chante mieux qu'il ne danse; **the ~ I know him the more I admire him** mieux je le connais plus je l'admire; **I like it ~ than I used to** je l'aime mieux qu'autrefois *or* que je ne l'aimais autrefois; **all the ~, so much the ~** tant mieux (*for* pour); **he was all the ~ for it** il s'en est trouvé mieux; **it would be all the ~ for a drop of paint** un petit coup de peinture ne lui ferait pas de mal; **they are ~ off than we are** (*richer*) ils ont plus d'argent que nous; (*more fortunate*) ils sont dans une meilleure position que nous; **he is ~ off at his sister's than living alone** il est mieux chez sa sœur que s'il vivait tout seul; **I had ~ go** il faut que je m'en aille, il vaut mieux que je m'en aille; **hadn't you ~ speak to him?** ne vaudrait-il pas mieux que tu lui parles?; **write to her, or ~ still go and see her** écris-lui, ou mieux encore va la voir; **~ dressed** mieux habillé; **~ known** plus *or* mieux connu; (*Prov*) **~ late than never** mieux vaut tard que jamais (*Prov*); *V* **know, think** *etc*.

3 *n* **(a)** mieux *m*. **it's a change for the ~** c'est une amélioration, c'est un changement en mieux; **for ~ or (for) worse** pour le meilleur ou pour le pire; **to get the ~ of sb** triompher de qn; **to get the ~ of sth** venir à bout de qch.

(b) one's ~s ses supérieurs *mpl*.

4 *vt sb's achievements* dépasser; *record, score* améliorer. **to ~ o.s.** améliorer sa condition.

better[2] ['betəʳ] *n* parieur *m*, -euse *f*; (*at races*) turfiste *mf* (*qui parie sur les chevaux*).

betterment ['betəmənt] *n* amélioration *f*; (*Jur*) *[property]* plus-value *f*.

betting ['betɪŋ] **1** *n* pari(s) *m(pl)*. **the ~ was brisk** les paris allaient bon train; **the ~ was 2 to 1 on ...** la cote était 2 contre 1 sur..., on pariait à 2 contre 1 sur ...; **what is the ~ on his horse?** quelle cote fait son cheval?; **the ~ is he won't succeed** il y a peu de chances (pour) qu'il réussisse.

2 *cpd*: **if I were a betting man I'd say that ...** si j'avais l'habitude de faire des paris je dirais que ...; **betting news** résultats *mpl* des courses; (*Brit*) **betting shop** bureau *m* de paris (*appartenant à un bookmaker*); (*Brit*) **betting slip** bulletin *m* de pari individuel (= P.M.U.).

bettor ['betəʳ] *n* = **better**[2].

Betty ['betɪ] *n* (*dim of* **Elizabeth**) Élisabeth *f*, Babette *f*.

between [bɪ'twiːn] (*phr vb elem*) **1** *prep* **(a)** (*of place*) entre. **sit ~ those two boys** asseyez-vous entre ces deux garçons; **Switzerland lies ~ France, Italy, Germany and Austria** la Suisse est située entre la France, l'Italie, l'Allemagne et l'Autriche.

(b) (*of order, rank*) entre. **F comes ~ E and G** (la lettre) F se trouve *or* vient entre E et G; **a captain comes ~ a lieutenant and a major** un capitaine a un rang intermédiaire entre un lieutenant et un commandant.

(c) (*of time*) entre. **come ~ 5 and 6 o'clock** venez entre 5 et 6 heures; **he was born ~ the wars** il est né entre les deux guerres.

(d) (*of distance, amount*) entre. **~ 6 and 7 km/litres** *etc* entre 6 et 7 km/litres *etc*; **she is ~ 25 and 30** elle a entre 25 et 30 ans.

(e) (*to and from*) entre. **the ferry goes ~ Dover and Calais** le ferry(-boat) fait la navette entre Douvres et Calais.

(f) (*from one to other*) entre. **you will have time to rest ~ planes** vous aurez le temps de vous reposer entre les deux avions; **~ London and Birmingham there are several large towns** entre Londres et Birmingham il y a plusieurs grandes villes; **the train does not stop ~ here and London** le train est direct d'ici (à) Londres; **~ now and next week we must ...** d'ici la semaine prochaine nous devons ... .

(g) (*connection, relationship*) entre. **the friendship ~ Paul and Robert** l'amitié entre Paul et Robert; **after all there has been ~ us** après tout ce qu'il y a eu entre nous; **to choose ~ 2 hats** choisir entre 2 chapeaux; **the difference ~ them** la différence entre eux; **the match ~ A and B** le match qui oppose (*or* opposait *etc*) A à B; **the war ~ the 2 countries** la guerre entre les 2 pays; **a comparison ~ the 2 books** une comparaison entre les 2 livres, une comparaison des 2 livres; **the distance ~ them** la distance qui les sépare (l'un de l'autre), la distance entre eux.

(h) (*sharing*) entre. **divide the sweets ~ the 2 children** partagez les bonbons entre les 2 enfants; **the 4 boys have 5 oranges ~ them** les 4 garçons ont 5 oranges en tout *or* à eux tous; **~ ourselves,** *or* **~ you and me, he is not very clever** entre nous, il n'est pas très intelligent.

(i) (*combination, cooperation*) **the boys managed to lift the box ~ (the two of) them** à eux deux les garçons sont arrivés à soulever la caisse; **we got the letter written ~ us** à nous tous nous avons réussi à écrire la lettre.

(j) (*combined effect*) entre. **~ housework and study I have no time for going out** entre le ménage et mes études je n'ai pas le temps de sortir; **~ rage and alarm she could hardly think properly** prise entre la colère et l'inquiétude elle avait du mal à mettre de l'ordre dans ses pensées.

2 *adv* au milieu, dans l'intervalle. **her visits are few and far ~** ses visites sont très espacées *or* très rares; **rows of trees with grass in ~** des rangées d'arbres séparées par de l'herbe.

3 *cpd*: (*Naut*) **between decks** (*n*) entrepont *m*; (*adv*) dans l'entrepont.

betwixt [bɪ'twɪkst] **1** *prep* (††, *liter, dial*) = **between 1. 2** *adv*: **~ and between** entre les deux, ni l'un ni l'autre.

bevel ['bevəl] **1** *n* (*surface*) surface *f* oblique; (*also* **~ edge**) biseau *m*; (*tool: also* **~ square**) fausse équerre.

2 *cpd* en biseau. **bevel gear** engrenage *m* conique; **bevel wheel** roue dentée conique.

3 *vt* biseauter, tailler de biais *or* en biseau. **~led edge** bord biseauté; **~led mirror** glace biseautée.

beverage ['bevərɪdʒ] *n* boisson *f*; (*liter, hum*) breuvage *m*.

bevy ['bevɪ] *n [girls]* essaim *m*; *[people]* bande *f*, troupe *f*; *[larks, quails]* volée *f*; *[roe deer]* harde *f*.

bewail [bɪ'weɪl] *vt one's lot* se lamenter sur, déplorer; *sb's death* pleurer.

beware [bɪ'wɛəʳ] *vti* (*only in imper and infin*) **to ~ (of)** prendre garde (*sb/sth* à qn/à qch), se garder (*doing* de faire); se méfier (*sth* de qch); **~ of falling** prenez garde de tomber; **~ of being deceived,** (*frm*) **~ lest you are** *or* **lest you be deceived** prenez garde qu'on ne vous trompe (*subj*); **~ of listening to him** gardez-vous de l'écouter; **~ (of) how you speak** faites attention à ce que vous dites, surveillez vos paroles; **'~ of the dog!'** '(attention) chien méchant'; **'~ of pickpockets!'** 'attention aux pickpockets!'; **'trespassers ~!'** 'défense d'entrer!'; (*Comm*) **'~ of imitations'** 'se méfier des contrefaçons'.

bewilder [bɪ'wɪldəʳ] *vt* désorienter, dérouter; (*stronger*) abasourdir, confondre.

bewildering [bɪ'wɪldərɪŋ] *adj* déroutant, déconcertant; (*stronger*) ahurissant.

bewilderingly [bɪ'wɪldərɪŋlɪ] *adv* d'une façon déroutante *or* déconcertante *or* (*stronger*) ahurissante. **it is ~ complicated** c'est d'un compliqué déconcertant.

bewilderment [bɪ'wɪldəmənt] *n* confusion *f*, perplexité *f*; (*stronger*) ahurissement *m*, abasourdissement *m*, désorientation *f*.

bewitch [bɪ'wɪtʃ] *vt* ensorceler, enchanter; (*fig*) charmer, enchanter.

bewitching [bɪ'wɪtʃɪŋ] *adj look, smile* enchanteur (*f* -teresse), charmant, charmeur; *face, person* séduisant, charmant.

bewitchingly [bɪ'wɪtʃɪŋlɪ] *adv* d'une façon séduisante *or* enchanteresse, avec un charme enchanteur. **~ beautiful** belle à ravir, belle comme le jour.

bey [beɪ] *n* bey *m*.

beyond [bɪ'jɒnd] (*phr vb elem*) **1** *prep* **(a)** (*in space*) au-delà de, de l'autre côté de, plus loin que. **~ the Pyrenees** au-delà des Pyrénées; **you can't go ~ the barrier** vous ne pouvez pas aller au-delà de la barrière, vous ne pouvez pas dépasser la barrière; **~ the convent walls** en dehors des *or* par-delà les murs du couvent; **the countries ~ the sea** les pays au-delà des mers, les pays d'outre-mer.

(b) (*in time*) plus de. **she won't stay much ~ a month** elle ne restera pas beaucoup plus d'un mois; **it was ~ the middle of June** on avait dépassé la mi-juin; **~ bedtime** passé l'heure du coucher.

(c) (*surpassing, exceeding*) au-dessus de. **a task ~ her abilities** une tâche au-dessus de ses capacités; **this work is quite ~ him** ce travail le dépasse complètement; **it was ~ her to pass the exam** réussir à l'examen était au-dessus de ses forces; **maths is quite ~ me** les maths, ça me dépasse*; **it's ~ me why he hasn't left her*** je ne comprends pas *or* ça me dépasse* qu'il ne l'ait pas quittée; **~ belief** incroyable, à ne pas croire; **~ my**

reach hors de ma portée; ~ **doubt** hors de doute, indubitable; **that is** ~ **human understanding** cela dépasse l'entendement humain; **he is** ~ **caring** il ne s'en fait plus du tout; ~ **repair** irréparable; ~ **the pale** (*person*) infréquentable; (*behaviour*) totalement inacceptable; **that's going** ~ **a joke** cela dépasse les bornes (de la plaisanterie); **he lives** ~ **his means** il vit au-dessus de ses moyens; *V* **compare, grave**[1], **help** *etc.*

(d) (*with neg or interrog*) sauf, excepté. **he gave her no answer** ~ **a grunt** il ne lui a répondu que par un grognement, pour toute réponse il a émis un grognement.

2 *adv* au-delà, plus loin, là-bas. **the room** ~ la pièce (d')à côté; **the lands** ~ les terres lointaines.

3 *n* au-delà *m*. **the great B**~ l'au-delà; *V* **back.**

bezant ['bezənt] *n* besant *m.*

bezel ['bezl] 1 *n [chisel]* biseau *m*; *[gem]* facette *f*; (*holding gem*) chaton *m*; (*holding watch glass*) portée *f*. 2 *vt* tailler en biseau.

bezique [bɪ'ziːk] *n* bésigue *m.*

bi... [baɪ] *pref* bi... .

biannual [baɪ'ænjʊəl] 1 *adj* (*twice a year*) semestriel; (*every alternate year*) biennal, bisannuel. 2 *n* = **biennial 2.**

bias ['baɪəs] 1 *n* **(a)** (*inclination*) tendance *f*, inclination *f* (*towards* à), penchant *m* (*towards* pour); (*prejudice*) préjugé *m*, parti pris (*towards* pour, *against* contre), prévention *f* (*towards* en faveur de, *against* contre). **strong** ~ **towards** penchant marqué pour; **he is without** ~ il n'a aucun parti pris, il est sans préjugés.

(b) (*Sewing*) biais *m*. **cut on the** ~ coupé dans le biais; ~ **binding** biais (*ruban*).

(c) (*Sport*) *[bowls]* (*weight*) *poids placé à l'intérieur d'une boule;* (*swerve*) déviation *f*.

2 *vt* (*give inclination*) influencer (*towards* en faveur de, *against* contre); (*prejudice*) prévenir (*towards* en faveur de, *against* contre). **to be** ~**(s)ed towards/against** avoir un *or* des préjugé(s) en faveur de/contre; ~**(s)ed** partial.

bib [bɪb] *n* **(a)** *[child]* bavoir *m*. **(b)** *[apron]* bavette *f*. (*fig*) **in her best** ~ **and tucker*** sur son trente et un.

Bible ['baɪbl] 1 *n* (*lit*) Bible *f*; (*fig*) bible, évangile *m*; *V* **holy.**

2 *cpd*: **Bible class** (*Scol*) classe *f* d'instruction religieuse; (*Rel*) catéchisme *m*; **Bible oath** serment *m* (prêté) sur la Bible; **Bible stories** histoires tirées de la Bible; (*pej*) **Bible thumper*** évangéliste *m* de carrefour.

biblical ['bɪblɪkəl] *adj* biblique.

biblio... ['bɪblɪəʊ] *pref* biblio... .

bibliographer [ˌbɪblɪ'ɒgrəfəʳ] *n* bibliographe *mf.*

bibliographic(al) [ˌbɪblɪəʊ'græfɪk(əl)] *adj* bibliographique.

bibliography [ˌbɪblɪ'ɒgrəfɪ] *n* bibliographie *f.*

bibliomania [ˌbɪblɪəʊ'meɪnɪə] *n* bibliomanie *f.*

bibliomaniac [ˌbɪblɪəʊ'meɪnɪæk] *n* bibliomane *mf.*

bibliophile ['bɪblɪəʊfaɪl] *n* bibliophile *mf.*

bibulous ['bɪbjʊləs] *adj* adonné à la boisson; *look* aviné; *evening, party* bien arrosé.

bicameral [baɪ'kæmərəl] *adj* bicaméral. ~ **system** bicamérisme *m.*

bicarbonate [baɪ'kɑːbənɪt] *n* bicarbonate *m*. ~ **of soda** bicarbonate de soude.

bicentenary [ˌbaɪsen'tiːnərɪ] *adj, n* bicentenaire (*m*).

bicephalous [baɪ'sefələs] *adj* bicéphale.

biceps ['baɪseps] *n* biceps *m.*

bichloride ['baɪ'klɔːraɪd] *n* bichlorure *m.*

bichromate ['baɪ'krəʊmɪt] *n* bichromate *m.*

bicker ['bɪkəʳ] *vi* **(a)** (*quarrel*) se chamailler. **they are always** ~**ing** ils sont toujours à se chamailler *or* toujours en bisbille*. **(b)** *[stream]* murmurer; *[flame]* trembloter, vaciller.

bickering ['bɪkərɪŋ] 1 *n* chamailleries *fpl.* 2 *adj* **(a)** *person* querelleur. **(b)** *stream* murmurant; *flame* tremblotant, vacillant.

bicuspid [baɪ'kʌspɪd] 1 *adj* bicuspidé. 2 *n* (dent *f*) prémolaire *f.*

bicycle ['baɪsɪkl] 1 *n* bicyclette *f*, vélo *m*. **to ride a** ~ faire de la bicyclette *or* du vélo; *V* **racing** *etc.*

2 *vi* faire de la bicyclette *or* du vélo, aller à *or* en* bicyclette.

3 *cpd*: **bicycle bell** sonnette *f or* timbre *m* de bicyclette; **bicycle chain** chaîne *f* de bicyclette; **bicycle pump** pompe *f* à bicyclette; **bicycle rack** râtelier *m* à bicyclettes, porte-vélos *m inv*; **bicycle rickshaw** vélo-pousse *m*; **bicycle track** piste *f* cyclable.

bid [bɪd] *pret* **bade** *or* **bid,** *ptp* **bidden** *or* **bid** 1 *vt* **(a)** (*command*) ordonner, commander, enjoindre (*sb to do* à qn de faire). **he was** ~**den to come** on lui a ordonné de venir; **do what I** ~ **you** fais ce que je te dis *or* t'ordonne.

(b) (*say*) dire. **to** ~ **sb good morning** dire bonjour à qn; **to** ~ **sb farewell** dire au revoir à qn; **to** ~ **sb welcome** souhaiter la bienvenue à qn.

(c) (††: *invite*) inviter, convier.

(d) (*offer*) *amount* offrir, faire une offre de; (*at auction*) faire une enchère de. **he is** ~**ding 200 francs for the painting** il fait une offre *or* une enchère de 200 F pour le tableau; **I did not** ~ **(high) enough** je n'ai pas offert assez; **the one that** ~**s most** le plus offrant.

(e) (*Cards*) demander. **he** ~ **3 spades** il a demandé 3 piques.

2 *vi* **(a)** (*make an offer*) faire une offre, offrir, proposer un prix (*for* pour). **to** ~ **for sth** faire une offre pour qch; (*at auction*) faire une enchère pour qch; **to** ~ **against sb** renchérir sur qn.

(b) (*phrases*) **to** ~ **for power/fame** viser *or* ambitionner le pouvoir/la gloire; **to** ~ **fair to do** sembler devoir faire, promettre de faire; **everything** ~**s fair to be successful** tout semble annoncer *or* promettre le succès.

3 *n* **(a)** (*Comm*) offre *f*, enchère *f*. **to make a** ~ **for** faire une offre pour; (*at auction*) faire une enchère pour; **a high** ~ une forte enchère; **a higher** ~ une surenchère; **to make a higher** ~ surenchérir.

(b) (*Cards*) demande *f*, annonce *f*. **to raise the** ~ monter; (*Bridge*) **to make no** ~ passer parole; **'no** ~**'** 'parole', 'passe'.

(c) (*attempt*) tentative *f*. **suicide** ~ tentative de suicide; **to make a** ~ **for power** tenter de s'emparer du pouvoir; **to make a** ~ **for freedom** tenter de s'évader; **to make a** ~ **to do** tenter de faire.

biddable ['bɪdəbl] *adj* **(a)** *child* docile, obéissant. **(b)** (*Cards*) ~ **suit** couleur *f* demandable.

bidden ['bɪdn] *ptp of* **bid.**

bidder ['bɪdəʳ] *n* enchérisseur *m*, offrant *m*. **to sell to the highest** ~ vendre au plus offrant; **there were no** ~**s** personne n'a fait d'offre.

bidding ['bɪdɪŋ] *n* **(a)** (*at sale*) enchère(s) *f(pl)*. ~ **was brisk** les enchères étaient vives; **the** ~ **is closed** l'enchère est faite, c'est adjugé.

(b) (*Cards*) enchères *fpl.*

(c) (*order*) ordre *m*, commandement *m*. **at whose** ~? sur l'ordre de qui?; **I did his** ~ j'ai fait ce qu'il m'a dit, j'ai exécuté ses ordres; **he needed no second** ~ il ne se l'est pas fait dire deux fois.

bide [baɪd] (†, *liter, dial*) 1 *vi* = **abide 2.** 2 *vt* **(a)** (*still used*) **to** ~ **one's time** se réserver, attendre son heure *or* le bon moment, attendre le moment d'agir. **(b)** = **abide 1.**

bidet ['biːdeɪ] *n* bidet *m.*

biennial [baɪ'enɪəl] 1 *adj* **(a)** (*happening every two years*) biennal, bisannuel. **(b)** (*lasting two years*) biennal. 2 *n* (*Bot*) ~ **(plant)** (plante *f*) bisannuelle *f.*

bier [bɪəʳ] *n* (*for coffin*) brancards *mpl* (de cercueil); (*for corpse*) bière *f.*

biff* [bɪf] 1 *n* coup *m* de poing, baffe‡ *f*. 2 *excl* vlan!, pan! 3 *vt* cogner sur, flanquer une baffe à‡. **to** ~ **sb on the nose** flanquer* son poing dans *or* sur la figure de qn.

bifocal ['baɪ'fəʊkəl] 1 *adj* bifocal, à double foyer. 2 *npl*: ~**s** verres *mpl* à double foyer, lunettes bifocales.

bifurcate ['baɪfɜːkeɪt] 1 *vi* bifurquer. 2 *vt* faire bifurquer. 3 *adj* à deux branches.

bifurcation [ˌbaɪfɜː'keɪʃən] *n* bifurcation *f*, embranchement *m.*

big [bɪg] 1 *adj* **(a)** (*in height*) *person, building, tree* grand. **a** ~ **fellow** un grand gaillard; **a** ~ **man** un homme grand et fort; **to grow** ~ *or* ~**ger** grandir; *V also* **1b.**

(b) (*in bulk, amount*) *fruit, parcel, book* gros (*f* grosse). **to earn** ~ **money** gagner gros; **the deal involves** ~ **money** de grosses sommes sont en jeu dans cette transaction; **to grow** ~ *or* ~**ger** grossir; **a** ~ **stick** un gros bâton (*V also* **stick**); ~ **toe** gros orteil; ~ **with child** grosse, enceinte; *V* **drum** *etc.*

(c) (*in age*) grand, aîné. **my** ~ **brother** mon grand frère, mon frère aîné; **I am** ~ **enough to know** je suis assez grand pour savoir.

(d) (*important*) grand, important, marquant, remarquable. **a** ~ **man** un grand homme, un homme marquant *or* remarquable *or* important; **to look** ~ faire l'important; ~ **bug‡,** ~ **noise*,** ~ **shot*** huile‡ *f*, grosse légume‡, gros bonnet; ~ **business** les grosses affaires; **a** ~ **event** un fait marquant; **to have** ~ **ideas** voir grand; (*fig*) **what's the** ~ **idea?‡** ça (ne) va pas, non?‡; **a** ~ **lie** un gros mensonge; (*person*) **he's a** ~ **name in politics*** c'est un grand nom de la politique; **to do things in a** ~ **way** faire les choses en grand; **a tragedy? that's rather a** ~ **word** une tragédie? c'est un bien grand mot.

(e) (*conceited*) *person* prétentieux; *words* ambitieux. ~ **talk** fanfaronnades *fpl*, vantardise *f*; **he's too** ~ **for his boots** il a des prétentions; **he's got a** ~ **head*** il est crâneur*; **he's got a** ~ **mouth*** il ne sait pas se taire; **why can't you keep your** ~ **mouth shut!*** pas moyen que tu te taises!*, tu aurais mieux fait de la boucler!‡; **to make the** ~ **time‡** arriver, réussir; *V also* **3.**

(f) (*generous*) grand, généreux. **a heart as** ~ **as yours** un cœur aussi grand *or* aussi généreux que le vôtre; (*iro*) ~ **deal!‡** tu parles!‡; (*iro*) **that's** ~ **of you!*** quelle générosité! (*iro*).

2 *adv*: **to talk** ~* fanfaronner, se faire mousser*; **to go over** ~‡ avoir un succès fou *or* monstre*; **his speech went down** ~ **with his audience‡** ses auditeurs ont été emballés* par son discours.

3 *cpd*: (*Brit*) **Big Ben** Big Ben *m*; **big-boned** bien *or* fortement charpenté; (*Astron*) **the Big Dipper** la Grande Ourse; *[fairground]* **big dipper** montagnes *fpl* russes; (*Aut*) **big end** tête *f* de bielle; (*Pol*) **the Big Four** les Quatre (Grands); (*Brit*) **big game** gros gibier; **big game hunter** chasseur *m* de gros gibier; **big game hunting** chasse *f* au gros gibier; **bighead*** crâneur* *m*, -euse* *f*; **bigheaded*** crâneur*; **big-hearted** au grand cœur; **to be big-hearted** avoir bon cœur, avoir du cœur; **a big-hearted fellow** un homme de cœur; **bigmouth*** gueulard(e)‡ *m(f)*, hâbleur *m*, -euse *f*; **he is just a bigmouth** il ne sait jamais la boucler‡; **big-sounding** *idea, plan etc* prometteur; *name* ronflant, pompeux; **big-time*** *politician, industrialist* de première catégorie; *part, role* de premier plan; *farming* sur une grande échelle; **big-time gambler** flambeur‡ *m*; **big top** (*circus*) cirque *m*; (*main tent of it*) grand chapiteau; **bigwig‡** grosse légume‡, huile‡ *f.*

bigamist ['bɪgəmɪst] *n* bigame *mf.*

bigamous ['bɪgəməs] *adj* bigame.

bigamy ['bɪgəmɪ] *n* bigamie *f.*

bight [baɪt] *n* **(a)** (*Geog*) baie *f*, anse *f*; (*larger*) golfe *m*. **(b)** *[rope]* boucle *f.*

bigot ['bɪgət] *n* (*Philos, Pol, Rel*) fanatique *mf*, sectaire *mf*. **(religious)** ~ bigot(e) *m(f).*

bigoted ['bɪgətɪd] *adj* (*Rel*) bigot; (*Pol etc*) *person* fanatique, sectaire; *attitude, devotion* fanatique.

bigotry ['bɪgətrɪ] *n* (*U*) (*Rel*) bigoterie *f*, (*Philos, Pol etc*) fanatisme *m*, sectarisme *m.*

bijou ['bi:ʒu:] *adj* (*Brit*) '~ **residence for sale**' 'maison à vendre, véritable petit bijou'.
bike [baɪk] 1 *n* (*) vélo *m*, bécane* *f*. 2 *vi* (‡) aller *or* venir à vélo.
bikini [bɪ'ki:nɪ] *n* bikini *m*.
bilabial [baɪ'leɪbjəl] 1 *adj* bilabial. 2 *n* bilabiale *f*.
bilateral [baɪ'lætərəl] *adj* bilatéral.
bilberry ['bɪlbərɪ] *n* myrtille *f*, airelle *f*.
bile [baɪl] *n* **(a)** (*Anat*) bile *f*. ~ **stone** calcul *m* biliaire. **(b)** (*fig: anger*) mauvaise humeur. **(c)** (*Hist: choler*) bile *f*.
bilge [bɪldʒ] *n* **(a)** (*Naut*) (*rounded part of hull*) bouchain *m*, renflement *m*; (*bottom of hold*) fond *m* de cale, sentine *f*; (*also* ~ **water**) eau *f* de cale *or* de sentine.
(b) (‡: *nonsense*) idioties *fpl*, foutaises‡ *fpl*. **to talk** ~ raconter des foutaises‡, débloquer‡, déconner*.
bilharzia [bɪl'hɑ:zɪə] *n*, **bilharziasis** [,bɪlhɑ:'zaɪəsɪs] *n* (*disease*) bilharziose *f*.
bilingual [baɪ'lɪŋgwəl] *adj person, district, document* bilingue.
bilingualism [baɪ'lɪŋgwəlɪzəm] *n* bilinguisme *m*.
bilious ['bɪlɪəs] *adj* **(a)** (*Med*) bilieux. ~ **attack** crise *f* de foie. **(b)** (*fig*) maussade, irritable.
biliousness ['bɪlɪəsnɪs] *n* (*U*) (*Med*) affection *f* hépatique; (*fig*) tempérament bilieux *or* atrabilaire (*liter*).
bilk [bɪlk] *vt creditor* filouter, blouser*. **to** ~ **sb's efforts** mettre des bâtons dans les roues à qn.
bill[1] [bɪl] 1 *n* **(a)** (*account*) note *f*, facture *f*; (*esp Brit*) *[restaurant]* addition *f*; *[hotel]* note. **have you paid the milk** ~? as-tu payé le lait?; **a pile of** ~**s in the post** une pile de factures dans le courrier; **may I have the** ~ **please** l'addition *or* la note s'il vous plaît; **the factory has a high wages** ~ l'usine a d'importantes sorties en salaires, le poste salaires est élevé dans l'entreprise; *V* **foot, pay, settle**[2] *etc*.
(b) (*written statement*) état *m*, liste *f*. ~ **of fare** menu *m*, carte *f* (du jour); ~ **of costs** état des frais; (*Naut*) ~ **of health** patente *f* (de santé) (*V* **clean**); ~ **of lading** connaissement *m*; (*Constr*) ~ **of quantities** métré *m* (*devis*); (*Hist*) **B**~ **of Rights** déclaration *f* des droits; (*fig*) ~ **of rights** déclaration des droits (*d'un peuple*).
(c) (*Comm, Fin etc*) effet *m*, traite *f*. **to meet a** ~ faire honneur à un effet; **to draw a** ~ **on** tirer une traite sur, faire traite sur; ~ **of exchange** lettre *f or* effet de change; ~ **of sale** acte *m or* contrat *m* de vente; **exchequer** ~ bon *m* du Trésor; **foreign** ~ devise étrangère; *V* **endorse** *etc*.
(d) (*US: banknote*) billet *m* (de banque). **5-dollar** ~ billet de 5 dollars.
(e) (*Parl*) projet *m* de loi. **to propose/pass/throw out a** ~ présenter/voter/rejeter un projet de loi; (*Brit*) **the** ~ **passed the Commons** le projet de loi a été voté par la Chambre des Communes.
(f) (*Jur*) plainte *f*, requête *f*. ~ **of indictment** acte *m* d'accusation; ~ **of attainder** décret *m* de confiscation de biens et de mort civile.
(g) (*poster, advertisement*) (*Theat etc*) affiche *f*; *[house for sale]* écriteau *m*; (*public notice*) placard *m*. **to head** *or* **top the** ~ être en vedette, être en tête d'affiche; *V* **fill, hand, stick** *etc*.
2 *vt* **(a)** *goods* facturer. **to** ~ **sb for sth** envoyer la facture de qch à qn.
(b) *play* mettre à l'affiche, annoncer. **he is** ~**ed to play Hamlet** il est à l'affiche dans le rôle de Hamlet.
3 *cpd*: **billboard** panneau *m* d'affichage; (*US*) **billfold** portefeuille *m*; **billposter, billsticker** colleur *m* d'affiches, afficheur *m*.
bill[2] [bɪl] 1 *n* **(a)** *[bird]* bec *m*. **long-**~**ed bird** oiseau *m* à long bec; *V* **scissor** *etc*. **(b)** (*Geog*) promontoire *m*, cap *m*, bec *m*. **Portland B**~ le Bec de Portland. 2 *vi [birds]* se becqueter. (*lit, fig*) **to** ~ **and coo** roucouler.
bill[3] [bɪl] *n* **(a)** (*tool*) serpe *f*. ~**hook** serpette *f*. **(b)** (*Hist: weapon*) hache *f* d'armes.
Bill [bɪl] *n* (*dim of* **William**) Guillaume *m*.
billet[1] ['bɪlɪt] 1 *n* (*Mil*) (*document*) billet *m* de logement; (*accommodation*) cantonnement *m* (chez l'habitant). **a cushy** ~‡ un fromage*, une planque*. 2 *vt* (*Mil*) *soldier* loger, cantonner (*on sb* chez qn). **we had soldiers** ~**ed on us** des soldats étaient cantonnés chez nous; **troops were** ~**ed on our town** des troupes étaient cantonnées dans notre ville.
billet[2] ['bɪlɪt] *n [wood]* billette *f*, bûche *f*; *[metal]* billette; (*Archit*) billette.
billeting ['bɪlɪtɪŋ] *n* (*Mil*) cantonnement *m*. ~ **officer** chef *m* de cantonnement.
billiard ['bɪljəd] 1 *n* (*U*) ~**s** (jeu *m* de) billard *m*; **to have a game of** ~**s** faire une partie de billard.
2 *cpd*: **billiard ball** boule *f* de billard; **billiard cue** queue *f* de billard; (*Brit*) **billiard(s) saloon** (salle *f* de *or* café-)billard *m*; **billiard table** (table *f* de) billard *m*.
billing[1] ['bɪlɪŋ] *n* (*Theat*) **to get top/second** ~ figurer en tête d'affiche/en deuxième place à l'affiche.
billing[2] ['bɪlɪŋ] *n* (*lit, fig*) ~ **and cooing** roucoulements *mpl* (d'amoureux).
Billingsgate ['bɪlɪŋzgɪt] *n* **(a)** marché *m* au poisson (*de Londres*). **(b)** (*foul language*) **to talk** ~ *[man]* parler comme un charretier; *[woman]* parler comme une poissonnière.
billion ['bɪljən] *n* (*Brit*) billion *m*; (*US*) milliard *m*.
billow ['bɪləʊ] 1 *n* (*gen pl*) **(a)** *[water]* flot *m*; (*in the sea*) rouleau *m*, lame *f*. (*liter*) **the** ~**s** les flots (*liter*).
(b) *[cloth etc]* flot *m*; *[smoke]* flot, tourbillon *m*, volutes *fpl*; *[sail]* gonflement *m*.
2 *vi [sea]* se soulever; *[sail]* se gonfler; *[cloth]* onduler; *[smoke]* s'élever en tourbillons *or* en volutes, tournoyer.
billow out *vi [sail etc]* se gonfler.
billowy ['bɪləʊɪ] *adj sea* houleux, agité; *waves* gros (*f* grosse); *sail* gonflé (par le vent); *smoke* en (grosses) volutes.
Billy ['bɪlɪ] *n* (*dim of* **William**) Guillaume *m*.
billy[1] ['bɪlɪ] *n* (*US*) matraque *f*.
billy[2]**(can)** ['bɪlɪ(kæn)] *n* gamelle *f*.
billy goat ['bɪlɪgəʊt] 1 *n* bouc *m*. 2 *cpd*: **billy-goat beard** bouc *m* (*barbe*).
billy-ho*, billy-o* ['bɪlɪhəʊ] *n*: **like** ~ très fort; **to laugh like** ~ rire très fort, rire bruyamment; **it was raining like** ~ il tombait des cordes, il pleuvait à seaux; **he ran like** ~ il a couru comme un dératé *or* à toutes jambes.
bimetallic [,baɪmɪ'tælɪk] *adj* bimétallique.
bimetallism [baɪ'metəlɪzəm] *n* bimétallisme *m*.
bimonthly ['baɪ'mʌnθlɪ] 1 *adj* (*twice a month*) bimensuel; (*every two months*) bimestriel. 2 *adv* deux fois par mois; tous les deux mois.
bin [bɪn] 1 *n* **(a)** *[coal, corn]* coffre *m*; *[bread]* boîte *f*; (*in the country*) huche *f*.
(b) (*Brit*) *[wine]* casier *m* (à bouteilles). ~ **end** fin *f* de série.
(c) (*Brit: also* **dust**~, **rubbish** ~) boîte *f* à ordures, poubelle *f*.
2 *vt coal, corn* mettre dans un coffre.
binary ['baɪnərɪ] *adj* binaire. (*Chem*) ~ **compound** composé *m* binaire; (*Mus*) ~ **form/measure** forme *f*/rythme *m* binaire; (*Math*) ~ **notation/number/system** numération *f*/nombre *m*/système *m* binaire.
bind [baɪnd] *pret, ptp* **bound** 1 *vt* **(a)** (*fasten*) *thing* attacher; *2 or more things* attacher, lier; *person, animal* lier, attacher (*to* à); *prisoner* ligoter. **he bound the sticks (together) with string** il a attaché *or* lié les baguettes avec une ficelle; **bound hand and foot** pieds et poings liés; (*fig*) **bound by gratitude to sb** attaché à qn par la reconnaissance.
(b) (*encircle*) entourer (*with* de), ceindre (*with* de) (*liter*); (*Med*) *artery* ligaturer; *wound* panser, bander.
(c) (*secure edge of*) *material, hem* border (*with* de).
(d) *book* relier. **bound in calf** relié (en) veau.
(e) (*oblige, pledge*) obliger, contraindre (*sb to do* qn à faire). **to** ~ **o.s. to sth/to do sth** s'engager à qch/à faire qch; **to** ~ **sb to a promise** astreindre qn à tenir une promesse; **to** ~ **by an oath** lier par (un) serment; **to** ~ **sb as an apprentice (to)** mettre qn en apprentissage (chez); *V* **bound**[3].
(f) (*stick together*) lier, cimenter, donner de la cohésion à; (*Med*) *bowels* resserrer. (*Culin*) ~ **the mixture with an egg** lier la préparation avec un œuf; *V* **ice** *etc*.
2 *vi [rule]* être obligatoire; *[agreement]* engager; *[machinery]* se coincer, (se) gripper; (‡: *complain*) rouspéter*, geindre* (*about* à propos de).
3 *n* **(a)** (*Mus*) liaison *f*.
(b) (‡) (*person*) crampon* *m*, casse-pieds* *mf inv*, scie* *f*; (*thing*) scie*. **what a** ~ **that woman is!** quelle scie, cette bonne femme!*; **what a** ~ **you've got to go** quelle barbe* que tu aies à partir; **that meeting is a terrible** ~ cette réunion me casse les pieds* *or* me barbe*.
4 *cpd*: **bindweed** liseron *m*.
bind down *vt sep* (*fig*) obliger, contraindre, astreindre (*sb to do* qn à faire). **to be bound down (to do)** être obligé *or* contraint (de faire), être astreint (à faire).
bind on *vt sep* attacher (*avec une corde etc*).
bind over *vt sep* (*Jur*) mettre en liberté conditionnelle. **to bind sb over to keep the peace** relaxer qn sous condition qu'il ne trouble (*subj*) pas l'ordre public; **he was bound over for six months** on l'a relaxé sous peine de comparaître en cas de récidive dans les six mois.
bind together *vt sep* (*lit*) *sticks* lier; (*fig*) *people* unir.
bind up *vt sep wound* panser, bander; (*fig*) lier, attacher. **your life is bound up in hers** votre existence est étroitement liée à la sienne; **to be totally bound up with sb** se dévouer entièrement à qn; **to be totally bound up with one's work** se donner corps et âme à son travail; **question closely bound up with another** question étroitement liée à une autre; **it's all bound up with whether he comes or not** tout dépend s'il va venir ou pas*.
binder ['baɪndər] *n* **(a)** (*Agr*) (*machine*) lieuse *f*; (*person*) lieur *m*, -euse *f*; *V* **book**. **(b)** (*for papers*) classeur *m*; *V* **spring**. **(c)** (*Med etc*) bandage *m*. **(d)** (*Constr*) (*cement, mortar*) liant *m*, aggloméraant *m*; (*joist*) entrait *m*.
bindery ['baɪndərɪ] *n* atelier *m* de reliure.
binding ['baɪndɪŋ] 1 *n* **(a)** *[book]* reliure *f*; *V* **cloth, half**.
(b) *[tape]* extra-fort *m*; *V* **bias**.
(c) *[skis]* fixation *f*.
2 *adj* **(a)** *rule* obligatoire; *agreement, promise* qui lie, qui engage. **to be** ~ **on sb** être obligatoire pour qn, lier qn, engager qn; **a promise is** ~ on est lié par une promesse, chose promise chose due (*Prov*).
(b) (*Med*) *food etc* constipant; (*Constr*) agglomérant.
binge‡ [bɪndʒ] *n* bombe* *f*. **to go on a** ~, **to have a** ~ faire la bombe*, (aller) faire la bombe* *or* la bringue‡.
bingo ['bɪŋgəʊ] *n* (jeu *m* de) loto *m* (*joué pour de l'argent*).
binnacle ['bɪnəkl] *n* (*Naut*) habitacle *m*.
binocular [bɪ'nɒkjʊlər] 1 *adj* binoculaire. 2 *npl*: ~**s** jumelle(s) *f(pl)*.
binomial [baɪ'nəʊmɪəl] *adj*, *n* (*Math*) binôme (*m*). **the** ~ **theorem** le théorème (de binôme) de Newton.
bint‡ [bɪnt] *n* nana‡ *f*.
binuclear [baɪ'nju:klɪər] *adj* binucléaire.
bio... ['baɪəʊ] *pref* bio... .
biochemical ['baɪəʊ'kemɪkəl] 1 *adj* biochimique. 2 *n* substance *f* biochimique.
biochemist ['baɪəʊ'kemɪst] *n* biochimiste *mf*.
biochemistry ['baɪəʊ'kemɪstrɪ] *n* biochimie *f*.
biodegradable ['baɪəʊdɪ'greɪdəbl] *adj* biodégradable.
biogenesis ['baɪəʊ'dʒenɪsɪs] *n* biogénèse *f*.
biographer [baɪ'ɒgrəfər] *n* biographe *mf*.
biographic(al) [,baɪəʊ'græfɪk(əl)] *adj* biographique.

biography [baɪ'ɒgrəfɪ] *n* biographie *f*.
biological [ˌbaɪə'lɒdʒɪkəl] *adj warfare etc* biologique. ~ **soap powder** lessive *f* aux enzymes.
biologist [baɪ'ɒlədʒɪst] *n* biologiste *mf*.
biology [baɪ'ɒlədʒɪ] *n* biologie *f*.
biometrics [baɪə'metrɪks] *n*, **biometry** [baɪ'ɒmɪtrɪ] *n* (*U*) biométrie *f*.
biophysics [ˌbaɪəʊ'fɪzɪks] *n* (*U*) biophysique *f*.
biopsy ['baɪɒpsɪ] *n* biopsie *f*.
biotic [baɪ'ɒtɪk] *adj* biotique.
bipartisan [ˌbaɪ'pɑːtɪzæn] *adj* biparti *or* bipartite.
bipartite [baɪ'pɑːtaɪt] *adj* (*Bio, Pol*) biparti *or* bipartite; (*Jur*) *document* rédigé en double.
biped ['baɪped] *adj, n* bipède (*m*).
biplane ['baɪpleɪn] *n* (avion *m*) biplan *m*.
bipolar [baɪ'pəʊlə^r] *adj* bipolaire.
birch [bɜːtʃ] **1** *n* (*also* ~ **tree**) bouleau *m*; (*also* ~ **wood**) (bois *m* de) bouleau; (*for whipping*) verge *f*, fouet *m*; *V* **silver. 2** *vt* fouetter. **3** *cpd* de bouleau. **birch plantation** boulaie *f*, plantation *f* de bouleaux.
birching ['bɜːtʃɪŋ] *n* peine *f* du fouet (avec les verges).
bird [bɜːd] **1** *n* **(a)** oiseau *m*; (*game*) gibier *m* (à plume); (*Culin*) volaille *f*. **young** *or* **little** ~ petit oiseau, oisillon *m*; (*liter*) ~ **of ill omen** oiseau de mauvais augure *or* de malheur; (*lit, fig*) ~ **of passage** oiseau de passage; ~ **of prey** oiseau de proie; (*Prov*) **a** ~ **in the hand is worth two in the bush** un tiens vaut mieux que deux tu l'auras (*Prov*); (*Prov*) ~**s of a feather flock together** qui se ressemble s'assemble (*Prov*); **they're** ~**s of a feather** ils sont à mettre dans le même sac; **a little** ~ **told me*** mon petit doigt me l'a dit; (*fig*) **the** ~ **has flown** l'oiseau s'est envolé; (*fig*) **to give sb the** ~**:** envoyer paître* *or* bouler* qn; (*Theat sl*) huer, siffler; (*Theat sl*) **to get the** ~ se faire siffler *or* huer; **that's strictly for the** ~**s:** ça c'est bon pour les imbéciles; **he'll have to be told about the** ~**s and the bees** il va falloir lui expliquer comment font les petits oiseaux *or* que les bébés ne naissent pas dans les choux; *V* **early, jail, kill** *etc*.
(b) (:) (*fellow*) individu *m*, type* *m*; (*girl*) fille *f*, nana: *f*, pépée: *f*. **he's a queer** ~ c'est un drôle d'oiseau *or* de numéro*; **he's a cunning old** ~ c'est un vieux singe *or* rusé.
2 *cpd*: **bird bath** vasque *f* pour *or* où peuvent s'ébattre les oiseaux; (*pej*) **bird brain:** étourneau *m*, tête *f* de linotte; **birdcage** cage *f* à oiseaux; (*large*) volière *f*; **bird call** cri *m* d'oiseau; **bird fancier** (*breeder*) aviculteur *m*, -trice *f*; (*seller*) oiselier *m*, -ière *f*; **birdlime** glu *f*; **to go bird nesting** aller dénicher les oiseaux; **bird sanctuary** refuge *m* d'oiseaux, réserve *f* d'oiseaux; **birdseed** millet *m*, graine *f* pour les oiseaux; (*Bot*) **bird's eye** petit chêne; (*lit*) **a bird's-eye view of Paris** Paris (vu) à vol d'oiseau; (*fig*) **bird's-eye view** vue *f* d'ensemble, vue générale; (*Bot*) **bird's foot** pied-de-poule *m*; **bird's nest** nid *m* d'oiseau(x); (*Culin*) **bird's nest soup** soupe *f* aux nids d'hirondelles; **bird watcher** ornithologue *mf* amateur; **to go bird watching** aller observer les oiseaux.
birdie ['bɜːdɪ] *n* **(a)** (*baby talk*) (gentil) petit oiseau. **(b)** (*Golf*) birdie *m*.
biretta [bɪ'retə] *n* barrette *f*.
Biro ['baɪərəʊ] *n* ® (*Brit*) stylo *m* (à) bille, (pointe *f*) Bic *m* ®.
birth [bɜːθ] **1** *n* **(a)** (*being born*) naissance *f*; (*childbirth*) accouchement *m*, couches *fpl*; *[animal]* mise *f* bas. **during the** ~ pendant l'accouchement; **to give** ~ **to** *[woman]* donner naissance à; *[animal]* mettre bas; **blind/orphan from** ~ aveugle/orphelin de naissance; *V* **child, place, premature.**
(b) (*parentage*) naissance *f*, extraction *f*. **Scottish by** ~ écossais de naissance; **of good** ~ bien né, de bonne famille; **of humble** ~ de basse extraction.
(c) (*fig*) *[movement, idea]* naissance *f*, éclosion *f*; *[new era]* naissance, commencement *m*; *[trend, project]* naissance, lancement *m*; *[phenomenon]* apparition *f*.
2 *cpd*: **birth certificate** acte *m or* extrait *m* de naissance; **birth control** contrôle *m or* limitation *f* des naissances; **birthday** *V* **birthday; birthmark** tache *f* de vin; (*Med*) **birth pill** pilule *f* (anticonceptionnelle); **birthplace** (*gen, Admin*) lieu *m* de naissance; (*house*) maison natale; **the birthplace of civilization** le berceau de la civilisation; **birth rate** (taux *m* de) natalité *f*; **it is the birthright of every Englishman** c'est un droit que chaque Anglais a *or* acquiert en naissant; **birthstone** pierre *f* porte-bonheur (*selon le jour de naissance*).
birthday ['bɜːθdeɪ] **1** *n* anniversaire *m*. **what did you get for your** ~**?** qu'est-ce que tu as eu pour ton anniversaire?; *V* **happy.**
2 *cpd*: **birthday cake** gâteau *m* d'anniversaire; **birthday card** carte *f* d'anniversaire; (*Brit*) **Birthday Honours** *V* **honour 2; she is having a birthday party** on a organisé une petite fête *or* une soirée pour son anniversaire; **birthday present** cadeau *m* d'anniversaire; (*hum*) **in one's birthday suit** dans le costume d'Adam (*or* d'Ève)*, dans le plus simple appareil (*hum*).
biscuit ['bɪskɪt] **1** *n* **(a)** (*Brit*) petit gâteau sec, biscuit *m*. **that takes the** ~**!:** ça c'est le bouquet!*; **he takes the** ~**!:** il est marrant ce gars-là!:; *V* **digestive, ship, water** *etc*.
(b) (*US*) petit pain au lait.
2 *cpd*: **biscuit barrel** boîte *f* à biscuits; (*Pottery*) **biscuit-firing** dégourdi *m*; (*Pottery*) **biscuit ware** biscuit *m*.
3 *adj* (*also* ~**-coloured**) (couleur) biscuit *inv*, beige.
bisect [baɪ'sekt] **1** *vt* couper *or* diviser en deux; (*Math*) *line* couper en deux parties égales; *angle* bissecter. **2** *vi [road etc]* bifurquer.
bisection [baɪ'sekʃən] *n* (*Math*) division *f* en deux parties égales; *[angle]* bissection *f*.
bisector [baɪ'sektə^r] *n* (*Math*) bissectrice *f*.
bisexual ['baɪ'seksjʊəl] *adj* (*Bio, Zool*) bis(s)exué; (*Psych*) (sexuellement) ambivalent.

bishop ['bɪʃəp] *n* (*Rel*) évêque *m*; (*Chess*) fou *m*.
bishopric ['bɪʃəprɪk] *n* (*diocese*) évêché *m*; (*function*) épiscopat *m*.
bismuth ['bɪzməθ] *n* bismuth *m*.
bison ['baɪsn] *n* bison *m*.
bisque [bɪsk] *n* (*Culin: soup, also Sport*) bisque *f*; (*Pottery*) biscuit *m*.
bissextile [bɪ'sekstaɪl] **1** *n* année *f* bissextile. **2** *adj* bissextile.
bistoury ['bɪstʊrɪ] *n* bistouri *m*.
bistre ['bɪstə^r] *adj, n* bistre (*m*).
bit[1] [bɪt] *n* **(a)** *[horse]* mors *m*. (*lit, fig*) **to take the** ~ **between one's teeth** prendre le mors aux dents; *V* **champ**[1]. **(b)** (*tool*) mèche *f*; *V* **brace, centre.**
bit[2] [bɪt] **1** *n* **(a)** (*piece*) *[bread]* morceau *m*; *[paper, string]* bout *m*; *[book, talk etc]* passage *m*; (*tiny amount*) brin *m*. **a** ~ **of garden** un bout de jardin, un tout petit jardin; **a tiny little** ~ un tout petit peu; **there's a** ~ **of vanity in him** il a un brin de vanité; **a** ~ **of advice** un petit conseil; **a** ~ **of news** une nouvelle; **a** ~ **of luck** une chance; **what a** ~ **of luck!** quelle chance! *or* veine!*; (*euph*) **he's got a** ~ **on the side:** il a une poule* quelque part.
(b) (*phrases*) **a** ~ un peu*; **a good** ~ très, beaucoup; **I'm a** ~**/a little** ~**/a good** ~ **late** je suis un peu/un petit peu/très en retard; **it's a good** ~ **further than we thought** c'est bien *or* beaucoup plus loin que nous ne pensions; **a good** ~ **bigger** bien *or* beaucoup plus grand; **every** ~ **as good as** tout aussi bon que; **every** ~ **of the wall** le mur tout entier; **he's every** ~ **a soldier** il est militaire jusqu'à la moelle; **I'm a** ~ **of a socialist*** je suis un peu socialiste sur les bords*; **she's a** ~ **of a liar** elle est un brin *or* un tantinet menteuse; **it was a** ~ **of a shock** ça (nous) a plutôt fait un choc; **that's a** ~ **of all right:** c'est terrible: *or* chouette*; **that's a** ~ **thick!*** ça c'est un peu fort* *or* violent*; **not a** ~ pas du tout; **not a** ~ **of it!** pas du tout!, pas le moins du monde!; **don't believe a (single)** ~ **of it** n'en croyez pas un mot; **it's not a** ~ **of use** cela ne sert strictement *or* absolument à rien; **he wasn't a** ~ **the wiser** *or* **the better for it** il n'en était pas plus avancé; **in** ~**s and pieces** (*broken*) en morceaux, en miettes; (*dismantled*) en pièces détachées; (*fig*) *plan, scheme* en ruines; **bring all your** ~**s and pieces** apporte toutes tes petites affaires; **to come to** ~**s** (*break*) s'en aller *or* tomber en morceaux; (*dismantle*) se démonter; **he went to** ~**s*** il a craqué*; ~ **by** ~ petit à petit; **and a** ~ **over** et même un peu plus; **to do one's** ~ fournir sa part d'effort; **when it comes to the** ~ en fin de compte, quand tout est dit.
(c) (*of time*) un bout de temps, un instant, un peu. **after a good** ~ après un bon bout de temps*; **wait a** ~ attendez un instant *or* un peu.
(d) (*of money*) somme *f*. **to pay a good** ~ **for** payer pas mal pour.
(e) (*coin*) pièce *f*. **threepenny** ~ pièce de trois (anciens) pennies.
(f) (*Computers*) bit *m*.
2 *adj* (*Theat*) ~ **part** petit rôle, panne *f* (*Theat sl*).
bit[3] [bɪt] *pret of* **bite.**
bitch [bɪtʃ] **1** *n* **(a)** *[dog]* chienne *f*; *[canines generally]* femelle *f*; *[fox]* renarde *f*; *[wolf]* louve *f*. **terrier** ~ terrier *m* femelle.
(b) (*:pej: woman*) garce: *f*. **she's a** ~ elle est rosse*, c'est une garce:; **that** ~ **of a car:** cette garce de bagnole:; **that** ~ **of a job:** cette saloperie de boulot:.
2 *vi* (*: complain*) rouspéter*, râler* (*about* contre).
bitchy: ['bɪtʃɪ] *adj* (*ill-tempered*) *person* rouspéteur*, râleur*; (*spiteful, mean*) *person, action* rosse*, vache:. **that was a** ~ **thing to do** c'était vraiment une vacherie: *or* un coup (en) vache: (de faire cela).
bite [baɪt] (*vb: pret* **bit,** *ptp* **bitten**) **1** *n* **(a)** *[dog etc]* morsure *f*; *[insect]* piqûre *f*. **face covered in (insect)** ~**s** visage couvert de piqûres d'insectes; *V* **bark**[2], **flea** *etc*.
(b) (*piece bitten off*) bouchée *f*; (*something to eat*) morceau *m*, quelque chose (à manger). **in two** ~**s** en deux bouchées; **chew each** ~ **carefully** mâchez bien chaque bouchée; **she grudged him every** ~ elle lui reprochait chaque bouchée; **I'll get a** ~ **on the train** je mangerai un morceau dans le train; **there's not a** ~ **to eat** il n'y a rien à manger, il n'y a rien à se mettre sous la dent; **come and have a** ~ venez manger un morceau.
(c) (*Fishing*) touche *f*. **I haven't had a** ~ **all day** je n'ai pas eu une seule touche aujourd'hui; **got a** ~**?*** ça a mordu?
(d) *[sauce etc]* piquant *m*. (*fig*) **there's a** ~ **in the air** l'air est piquant; **his speech hadn't much** ~ son discours manquait de mordant.
2 *vt* **(a)** *[person, animal]* mordre. **to** ~ **one's nails** se ronger les ongles; **to** ~ **one's tongue/lips/fingers** se mordre la langue/les lèvres/les doigts; **to** ~ **in two** couper en deux d'un coup de dents; (*lit, fig*) **to** ~ **the dust** mordre la poussière; (*fig*) **to** ~ **the hand that feeds you** être d'une ingratitude monstrueuse; (*Prov*) **once bitten twice shy** chat échaudé craint l'eau froide (*Prov*); **to be bitten with* the desire to do** mourir d'envie de faire; (*be cheated*) **to get bitten:** se faire avoir*, se faire rouler*; **I've been bitten!:** j'ai été fait (comme un rat); *V* **biter.**
(b) *[snake, insect]* piquer, mordre. **what's biting you?:** qu'est-ce que tu as à râler?*
(c) *[cold, frost]* pincer, mordre; *[cold wind]* couper; *V* **frost.**
(d) *[file, acid, wheel]* mordre.
3 *vi [dog]* mordre; *[fish]* mordre (à l'hameçon); *[insect]* piquer; *[bird]* donner un *or* des coup(s) de bec; *[cold, frost, wind]* mordre, piquer, pincer; *[cogs]* s'engrener; *[anchor, screw]* mordre. **to** ~ **into sth** *[person]* mordre (dans) qch; *[acid]* mordre sur qch.
bite off *vt sep* arracher d'un coup de dent(s). **she bit off a piece of apple** elle a mordu dans la pomme; (*fig*) **he has bitten off more than he can chew** il a eu les yeux plus grands que le

ventre, il a visé trop haut; **to bite sb's head off*** rembarrer qn (brutalement).
bite on *vt fus* mordre, trouver prise sur.
bite through *vt fus tongue, lip* mordre (de part en part); *string, thread* couper *or* casser avec les dents.
biter ['baɪtəʳ] *n* (*loc*) **the ~ bit** tel est pris qui croyait prendre (*Prov*).
biting ['baɪtɪŋ] *adj cold* âpre, perçant, mordant; *winter* dur, rude; *wind* piquant, cinglant; (*fig*) *style, wit, remarks* mordant, caustique, cinglant. **~ irony** ironie mordante *or* cinglante; **~ sarcasm** sarcasme *m* acerbe *or* mordant.
bitingly ['baɪtɪŋlɪ] *adv speak* d'un ton mordant *or* caustique.
bitten ['bɪtn] *ptp of* **bite.**
bitter ['bɪtəʳ] **1** *adj* **(a)** *taste* amer, âpre. (*fig*) **it was a ~ pill to swallow** la pilule était amère.
(b) *cold, weather, wind* glacial, cinglant; *winter* rude, rigoureux.
(c) *person* amer; *critic, criticism* acerbe; *disappointment, reproach, tears* amer; *fate, sorrow* pénible, cruel; *hatred* acharné, profond; *opposition, protest* violent; *remorse* cuisant; *sight, look* amer, plein d'amertume; *suffering* âpre, cruel; *tone* âpre, amer, dur. (*fig*) **to the ~ end** jusqu'au bout; **his ~ enemy** son ennemi acharné; **he was always a ~ enemy of corruption** il a toujours été un adversaire acharné de la corruption; **I feel (very) ~ about the whole business** toute cette histoire m'a laissé un goût d'amertume.
2 *n* **(a)** (*Brit: beer*) bière anglaise (*pression*).
(b) (*Pharm*) amer *m*. **~s** bitter *m*, amer *m*; **gin and ~s** cocktail *m* au gin et au bitter.
3 *cpd*: **bitter aloes** aloès *m* (médicinal); **bitter lemon** Schweppes *m* ® au citron; **bitter orange** orange amère, bigarade *f*; **bittersweet** (*adj: lit, fig*) aigre-doux (*f* -douce); (*n*) (*Bot*) douce-amère *f*; (*fig*) amère douceur.
bitterly ['bɪtəlɪ] *adv* **(a)** *speak, complain* amèrement, avec amertume; *criticize, reproach* âprement; *weep* amèrement; *oppose, resist* avec acharnement. **(b)** *disappointed* cruellement; *jealous* profondément, horriblement. (*Met*) **it was ~ cold** il faisait un froid sibérien *or* de loup.
bittern ['bɪtɜːn] *n* butor *m* (*oiseau*).
bitterness ['bɪtənɪs] *n* (*U*) *[taste etc]* amertume *f*; *[weather]* rigueur *f*; *[person, attitude]* amertume; *[tone]* amertume, âpreté *f*; *[opposition etc]* violence *f*.
bitty* ['bɪtɪ] *adj* (*Brit*) décousu.
bitumen ['bɪtjʊmɪn] *n* bitume *m*.
bituminous [bɪ'tjuːmɪnəs] *adj* bitumineux.
bivalent ['baɪ'veɪlənt] *adj* (*Bio, Chem*) bivalent.
bivalve ['baɪvælv] *adj, n* bivalve (*m*).
bivouac ['bɪvʊæk] **1** *n* bivouac *m*. **2** *vi* bivouaquer.
bi-weekly ['baɪ'wiːklɪ] **1** *adj* (*twice in a week*) bihebdomadaire; (*fortnightly*) bimensuel. **2** *adv* (*twice a week*) deux fois par semaine; (*fortnightly*) tous les quinze jours.
biz‡ [bɪz] *n abbr of* **business**; *V* **show 2.**
bizarre [bɪ'zɑːʳ] *adj* bizarre.
blab [blæb] **1** *vi* **(a)** (*tell secret*) manger le morceau‡. **(b)** (*chatter*) jaser. **2** *vt* (*also* **~ out**) *secret* laisser échapper, aller raconter.
black [blæk] **1** *adj* **(a)** *hair, bread, clouds, coffee etc* noir. **eyes as ~ as sloes** des yeux noirs comme (du) jais, des yeux de jais; (*fig*) **~ and blue** couvert de bleus; **to beat sb ~ and blue** battre qn comme plâtre, rouer qn de coups; *V also* **3** *and* **belt, coal, jet², pot** *etc.*
(b) (*Negro*) noir, nègre. **~ man** Noir *m*; **~ woman** Noire *f*; **the ~ races** les races noires; **the ~ Americans** les Américains noirs; **'~ is beautiful'** ≃ nous sommes fiers d'être noirs; *V also* **3.**
(c) (*dark*) obscur, noir, sans lumière. **it is as ~ as pitch** il fait nuit noire, il fait noir comme dans un four.
(d) (*dirty*) noir, sale. **his hands were ~** il avait les mains noires; **he was as ~ as a sweep** il était noir de la tête aux pieds.
(e) (*fig*) (*wicked*) *crime, action* noir; *thought* mauvais; (*gloomy*) *thoughts, prospects* noir; *grief* intense, violent; *rage* noir; *despair* sombre; (*angry*) sombre, menaçant. **he looked as ~ as thunder** il avait l'air furibond; **to look ~** avoir l'air sombre; **to give sb a ~ look** jeter un regard noir à qn; **none of your ~ looks at me!** inutile de me lancer ces regards noirs! *or* meurtriers!; (*fig*) **~ in the face** noir de fureur; **you can scream till you're ~ in the face but ...** tu peux toujours t'égosiller *or* t'époumoner mais ...; **a ~ deed** un crime, un forfait (*liter*); **he painted their conduct in the ~est colours** il a présenté leur conduite sous les couleurs les plus noires; **it's a ~ outlook, things are looking ~** les choses se présentent très mal; **it's a ~ outlook** *or* **things are looking ~ for him** ses affaires se présentent très mal; **a ~ day on the roads** une sombre journée sur les routes; **it's a ~ day for England** c'est un jour (bien) triste pour l'Angleterre, (*stronger*) c'est un jour de deuil pour l'Angleterre; (*Brit Ind: during strike*) **to declare a cargo** *etc* **~** boycotter une cargaison *etc*; (*Ind*) **~ goods** marchandises boycottées.
2 *n* **(a)** (*colour*) noir *m*, couleur noire; (*mourning*) noir, deuil *m*; (*Roulette etc*) noir. **dressed in ~** habillé de noir; **to wear ~ for sb** porter le deuil de qn; **there it is in ~ and white** c'est écrit noir sur blanc; (*Art*) **~ and white** dessin *m* en noir et blanc; **~ and white artist** artiste *m* qui travaille en noir et blanc; (*fig*) **two ~s don't make a white** la faute de l'un n'excuse pas (celle de) l'autre; **to swear that ~ is white** *[obstinate person]* se refuser à l'évidence, nier l'évidence; *[liar]* mentir effrontément; *V* **lamp.**
(b) (*Negro*) Noir(e) *m(f)*.
(c) (*darkness*) ténèbres *fpl*, obscurité *f*; (*outdoors only*) nuit noire.

3 *cpd*: **black art(s)** magie noire, sciences *fpl* occultes; **blackball** (*n*) vote *m* contraire; (*vt*) blackbouler; **black beetle** cafard *m*, cancrelat *m*; **blackberry** mûre *f*; **blackberry bush** mûrier *m*; **to go blackberrying** aller cueillir les *or* des mûres; **blackbird** merle *m*; **blackboard** tableau *m* (noir); **blackboard duster** chiffon *m*; **the blackboard jungle** la loi de la jungle (dans les classes); **blackboard rubber** frottoir *m*; **she was in his black books** elle n'était pas dans ses petits papiers*, elle était mal vue (de lui); (*Aviat*) **black box** boîte noire *or* enregistreuse; **black cap** (*Orn*) fauvette *f* à tête noire; (*Brit Hist Jur*) bonnet noir (*que mettait un juge avant de prononcer la peine de mort*); (*fig*) **black-coated worker** (*in office*) employé(e) *m(f)* de bureau; (*in shop*) commis *m*, employé de magasin; **blackcock** coq *m* de bruyère (*noir*); **Black Country** Pays Noir (*de l'Angleterre*); (*fruit, bush*) **blackcurrant** cassis *m*; (*Hist*) **Black Death** peste noire; **black eye** œil poché *or* au beurre noir*; **to give sb a black eye** pocher l'œil à qn; **blackfriar** frère prêcheur; **Black Friday** (*Rel*) Vendredi saint; (*fig*) (vendredi) jour *m* néfaste; **black frost** gel *m*; **black grouse** = **blackcock**; **blackguard** *V* **blackguard; blackhead** point noir; **black-hearted** mauvais, malfaisant; (*Brit Hist*) **the Black Hole of Calcutta** le cachot de Calcutta; **black ice** verglas *m*; **blackjack** (*n*) (*flag*) pavillon noir (*des pirates*); (*drinking vessel*) pichet *m*; (*Min*) blende *f*; (*US: weapon*) matraque *f*; (*Cards*) vingt-et-un *m*; (*vt*) (*beat*) matraquer; (*coerce*) contraindre sous la menace (*sb into doing* qn à faire); **black lead** mine *f* de plomb, graphite *m*; **black-lead** *stove* frotter à la mine de plomb; **blackleg** *V* **blackleg; blacklist** (*n*) liste noire; (*vt*) *person* mettre sur la liste noire; *book* mettre à l'index; **black magic** magie noire; **blackmail** *V* **blackmail; Black Maria*** panier *m* à salade*; **black market** marché noir; **on the black market** au marché noir; **black marketeer** profiteur *m*, -euse *f* (*vendant au marché noir*); **black mass** messe noire; **Black Muslim** Musulman(e) Noir(e) *m(f)*, Black Muslim *mf*; **blackout** *V* **blackout**; (*Pol*) **Black Panthers** Panthères Noires; **Black Power (movement)** Black Power *m*, Pouvoir Noir; (*Brit Hist*) **the Black Prince** le Prince Noir; (*Brit*) **black pudding** boudin *m*; (*Brit Parl*) **Black Rod** Huissier *m* à verge noire (*de la chambre des Lords*); **Black Sea** mer Noire; (*fig*) **black sheep (of the family)** brebis galeuse (de la famille); (*Pol*) **blackshirt** chemise noire (*fasciste*); **blacksmith** (*shoes horses*) maréchal-ferrant *m*; (*forges iron*) forgeron *m*; (*Brit*) **(accident) black spot** point noir; (*Bot*) **blackthorn** épine noire, prunellier *m*; **black tie** (*on invitation*) 'smoking', 'cravate noire'; **black-tie** *dinner, function* habillé, en smoking; **black velvet** cocktail *m* (*de champagne et de stout*); (*Brit Mil*) **Black Watch** Black Watch *mpl* (*régiment écossais*).
4 *vt* **(a)** noircir; *shoes* cirer. **to ~ one's face** se noircir le visage; **to ~ sb's eye (for him)** pocher l'œil à qn.
(b) (*Brit Ind*) *cargo, firm, goods* boycotter.
black out **1** *vi* (*Med**) tomber dans les pommes*, tourner de l'œil*.
2 *vt sep* (*in wartime*) *town, building* faire le black-out dans. (*in peacetime*) **a power cut blacked out the building** une panne d'électricité a plongé l'immeuble dans l'obscurité (totale); (*Theat*) **to black out the stage** faire l'obscurité sur scène.
3 blackout *n V* **blackout.**
blackamoor†† ['blækəmʊəʳ] *n* nègre *m* (*pej*), moricaud* *m* (*slightly pej*).
blacken ['blækən] **1** *vt* **(a)** (*with dirt, soot, dust*) noircir, salir. **hands ~ed with filth** des mains noires de crasse.
(b) (*with paint, cosmetics etc*) noircir, barbouiller de noir.
(c) (*with smoke, by fire*) noircir. **~ed remains** restes calcinés; **there were ~ed pots on the open fire** il y avait dans la cheminée des marmites noircies.
(d) (*fig: discredit*) salir, noircir, ternir.
2 *vi* *[sky]* noircir, s'assombrir; *[furniture]* noircir, devenir noir.
blackguard ['blægɑːd] *n* canaille *f*, fripouille *f*.
blackguardly ['blægɑːdlɪ] *adj deed, person* infâme, ignoble.
blacking ['blækɪŋ] *n [shoes]* cirage *m* (noir); *[stoves]* pâte *f* à noircir.
blackish ['blækɪʃ] *adj* tirant sur le noir, noirâtre (*pej*).
blackleg ['blækleg] (*Brit Ind*) **1** *n* jaune *m*, briseur *m* de grève. **2** *vi* briser la grève. **3** *vt striker* prendre la place de; *fellow workers, union* se désolidariser de.
blackmail ['blækmeɪl] **1** *n* chantage *m*. **2** *vt* faire chanter, faire du chantage auprès de. **to ~ sb into doing** forcer qn par le chantage à faire.
blackmailer ['blækmeɪləʳ] *n* maître-chanteur *m*.
blackness ['blæknɪs] *n [colour, substance]* couleur *or* teinte noire, noirceur *f* (*liter*); *[night]* obscurité *f*, ténèbres *fpl*; *[hands, face]* saleté *f*, crasse *f*; *[crime etc]* atrocité *f*, noirceur *f* (*liter*).
blackout ['blækaʊt] *n* **(a)** (*Med**) (*amnesia*) trou *m* de mémoire; (*fainting*) étourdissement *m*, évanouissement *m*. **to have a ~** avoir un étourdissement, s'évanouir.
(b) *[lights]* panne *f* d'électricité; (*during war*) black-out *m*; (*Theat*) obscurcissement *m* de la scène.
bladder ['blædəʳ] **1** *n* (*Anat*) vessie *f*; (*Bot*) vésicule *f*; (*Ftbl etc*) vessie (*de ballon*); *V* **gall¹. 2** *cpd*: **bladder kelp** raisins *mpl* de mer; **bladderwort** utriculaire *f*; **bladder wrack** = **bladder kelp.**
blade [bleɪd] *n* **(a)** *[knife, tool, weapon, razor]* lame *f*; *[chopper, guillotine]* couperet *m*; *[tongue]* plat *m*; *[oar]* plat, pale *f*; *[spade]* fer *m*; *[turbine motor]* aube *f*; *[propeller]* pale, aile *f*; *[windscreen wiper]* caoutchouc *m*; *[grass, mace]* brin *m*; *[cereal]* pousse *f*; *[leaf]* limbe *m*. **wheat in the ~** blé *m* en herbe; *V* **shoulder. (b)** (*liter: sword*) lame *f*. **(c)** (*: *gallant*) gaillard *m*.
-bladed ['bleɪdɪd] *adj ending in cpds*: **two-bladed knife** canif *m* à deux lames.
blaeberry ['bleɪbərɪ] *n* myrtille *f*, airelle *f*.
blah‡ [blɑː] *n* boniment *m*, blablabla* *m*.

blamable ['bleɪməbl] *adj* blâmable.

blame [bleɪm] **1** *vt* **(a)** (*fix responsibility on*) **to ~ sb for sth, to ~ sth on sb*** rejeter la responsabilité de qch sur qn, mettre qch sur le dos de qn*; **I'm not to** ~ ce n'est pas ma faute; **you have only yourself to** ~ tu ne peux t'en prendre qu'à toi-même; **whom/what are we to ~ for this accident?** à qui/à quoi attribuer cet accident?; *V* **workman.**

(b) (*censure*) condamner, blâmer. **to ~ sb for doing** reprocher à qn de faire; **to ~ sb for sth** reprocher qch à qn; **to ~ o.s. for sth/for having done** se reprocher qch/d'avoir fait; **he was greatly to ~ for doing that** il a eu grand tort de faire cela.

2 *n* **(a)** (*responsibility*) faute *f*, responsabilité *f*. **to put** *or* **lay** *or* **throw the ~ for sth on sb** rejeter la responsabilité de qch sur qn; **to bear the** ~ supporter la responsabilité.

(b) (*censure*) blâme *m*, reproches *mpl*. **without** ~ exempt de blâme, irréprochable.

3 *cpd*: **blameworthy** répréhensible, blâmable.

blameless ['bleɪmlɪs] *adj* irréprochable, sans reproche, exempt de blâme.

blamelessly ['bleɪmlɪslɪ] *adv* d'une manière irréprochable, irréprochablement.

blanch [blɑːntʃ] **1** *vt* (*gen, Agr, Culin*) blanchir. **2** *vi* [*hair*] blanchir; (*with fear, rage*) blêmir.

blancmange [blə'mɒnʒ] *n* blanc-manger *m*.

bland [blænd] *adj* (*suave*) *manner* affable; *expression* aimable; (*ingratiating*) doucereux, mielleux; (*ironic*) légèrement moqueur *or* narquois; (*mild*) *air, flavour* doux (*f* douce).

blandish ['blændɪʃ] *vt* flatter, cajoler.

blandishment ['blændɪʃmənt] *n* (*gen pl*) flatterie(s) *f(pl)*.

blandly ['blændlɪ] *adv* (*V* **bland**) avec affabilité, affablement; aimablement; d'un air mielleux; d'un air un peu narquois, d'un ton légèrement moqueur *or* narquois.

blank [blæŋk] **1** *adj* **(a)** (*not written on*) *paper* blanc (*f* blanche); *page* blanc, vierge; *map* muet; *cheque* en blanc. (*fig*) **to give sb a ~ cheque (to do)** donner à qn carte blanche (pour faire); **~ space** blanc *m*, (espace *m*) vide *m*; **~ form** formulaire *m*, imprimé *m* (à remplir); (*on form*) **please leave** ~ laisser en blanc s.v.p.

(b) (*unrelieved*) *wall* aveugle; *silence, darkness* profond; *refusal, denial* absolu, net; (*empty*) *life etc* dépourvu d'intérêt, vide; (*expressionless*) *face* sans expression; *look* sans expression, vide; (*puzzled*) déconcerté, dérouté. **to look** ~ (*expressionless*) être sans expression; (*puzzled*) avoir l'air interdit; **a look of ~ astonishment** un regard ébahi; **his mind went** ~ il a eu un passage à vide *or* un trou; **~ cartridge** cartouche *f* à blanc.

(c) (*Poetry*) **~ verse** vers blancs *or* non rimés.

2 *adv fire* à blanc; *V* **point-blank.**

3 *n* **(a)** (*void*) blanc *m*, (espace *m*) vide *m*; (*fig: gap*) lacune *f*, trou *m*. **she left several ~s in her answers** elle a laissé plusieurs de ses réponses en blanc; **your departure has left a** ~ votre départ a laissé un vide; **my mind was a** ~ j'avais la tête vide, j'ai eu un passage à vide*.

(b) (*form*) formulaire *m*, imprimé *m*, fiche *f*. **telegraph** ~ formule *f* de télégramme.

(c) [*target*] but *m*; (*Dominoes*) blanc *m*; [*coin, medal, record*] flan *m*; (*cartridge*) cartouche *f* à blanc. (*fig*) **to draw (a)** ~ échouer, faire chou blanc; (*Dominoes*) **double** ~ double blanc.

blanket ['blæŋkɪt] **1** *n* couverture *f*; [*snow etc*] couche *f*; [*fog*] manteau *m*, nappe *f*; [*smoke*] nuage *m*. **born on the wrong side of the** ~ (de naissance) illégitime, adultérin; *V* **electric, wet.**

2 *cpd statement, condemnation etc* général, global. **this insurance policy gives blanket cover** cette police d'assurances couvre tous les risques *or* est tous risques; **blanket stitch** point *m* de feston; **blanket-stitch** border au point de feston.

3 *vt* **(a)** [*snow*] recouvrir; [*smoke*] recouvrir, envelopper.

(b) *sounds* étouffer, assourdir.

(c) (*Naut*) déventer.

blanket out *vt* noyer.

blanketing ['blæŋkɪtɪŋ] *n* **(a)** (*material*) laine *f* *or* lainage *m* à couvertures. **(b)** (*bedclothes*) couvertures *fpl*. **(c)** (*tossing in a blanket*) épreuve *f* de la couverture.

blankety-blank* ['blæŋkɪtɪ'blæŋk] *adj* (*euph*) = **blinking 1.**

blankly ['blæŋklɪ] *adv* (*V* **blank 1b**) *look* (*expressionlessly*) avec des yeux vides; (*puzzledly*) d'un air interdit *or* ébahi; *say, announce* positivement, carrément. **to look ~ at sb/sth** (*expressionlessly*) jeter sur qn/qch un regard dénué de toute expression; (*without understanding*) regarder qn/qch sans comprendre.

blare [blɛəʳ] **1** *n* (*gen*) vacarme *m*; [*hooter, car horn*] bruit strident; [*radio, music*] beuglement *m*; [*trumpet*] sonnerie *f*.

2 *vi* [*music, horn etc*] retentir; [*loud voice*] trompeter, claironner; [*radio*] beugler.

blare out **1** *vi* = **blare 2.**

2 *vt sep noise, music* faire retentir; (*fig*) *news* claironner, trompeter.

blarney* ['blɑːnɪ] **1** *n* boniment* *m*, bobards* *mpl*. (*loc*) **he's kissed the B~ stone** il sait faire du boniment*. **2** *vt person* enjôler, embobeliner*. **3** *vi* manier la flatterie, passer de la pommade.

blaspheme [blæs'fiːm] *vti* blasphémer (*against* contre).

blasphemer [blæs'fiːməʳ] *n* blasphémateur *m*, -trice *f*.

blasphemous ['blæsfɪməs] *adj person* blasphémateur (*f* -trice); *words* blasphématoire.

blasphemously ['blæsfɪməslɪ] *adv* d'une façon impie, avec impiété. **to speak** ~ blasphémer.

blasphemy ['blæsfɪmɪ] *n* blasphème *m*. **to utter** ~ blasphémer, dire des blasphèmes; **it is ~ to say that** c'est blasphémer que de dire cela.

blast [blɑːst] **1** *n* **(a)** (*sound*) [*bomb*] explosion *f*; [*space rocket*] grondement *m*, rugissement *m*; [*trumpets etc*] fanfare *f*, sonnerie *f* (de trompette); (*Min*) coup *m* de mine. **~ on the siren** coup de sirène; **to blow a ~ on the bugle** donner un coup de clairon; **the radio was going at full** ~ la radio marchait à plein volume.

(b) (*shock wave*) [*bomb etc*] souffle *m*; (*gust*) [*furnace*] souffle (d'air chaud). (*lit, fig*) **at full** ~ à pleine puissance; **~ of air/steam** jet *m* d'air/de vapeur; **~ of wind** coup *m* de vent, rafale *f*.

(c) (*liter: wind*) souffle *m*. **the icy** ~ le souffle glacé (du vent).

2 *cpd*: **blast effect** effet *m* de souffle; **blast furnace** haut fourneau; (*Space*) **blast-off** lancement *m*, mise *f* à feu (*d'une fusée spatiale*).

3 *vt* [*lightning*] *tree* foudroyer; (*with powder*) *rocks* faire sauter; (*blight*) *plant* détruire; (*fig*) *reputation, hopes, future* anéantir, détruire, briser; (*with words*) maudire.

4 *excl* (*Brit**) la barbe!* **~ him!** il est embêtant!* *or* empoisonnant!*

blast off **1** *vi* [*rocket etc*] être mis à feu.

2 **blast-off** *n V* **blast 2.**

blasted ['blɑːstɪd] *adj* **(a)** *heath* désolé, desséché; *tree* foudroyé, frappé par la foudre; (*fig*) *hopes* anéanti.

(b) (*: *annoying*) fichu* (*before n*), satané (*before n*), maudit (*before n*). **he's a ~ nuisance** c'est un enquiquineur*, il nous enquiquine*.

blasting ['blɑːstɪŋ] *n* (*Tech*) minage *m*. **'~ in progress'** 'attention, tir de mines'.

blastoderm ['blæstəʊdɜːm] *n* blastoderme *m*.

blatancy ['bleɪtənsɪ] *n* (*flagrance*) caractère flagrant, évidence *f*; (*showiness*) aspect criard *or* voyant.

blatant ['bleɪtənt] *adj* **(a)** (*very obvious*) *injustice, lie etc* criant, flagrant; *bully, social climber* éhonté; *coward, thief* fieffé. **a ~ liar** un menteur éhonté, un fieffé menteur. **(b)** (*showy*) *colour, dress* criard, voyant.

blatantly ['bleɪtəntlɪ] *adv* d'une manière flagrante, effrontément.

blather ['blæðəʳ] **1** *vi* raconter *or* débiter des bêtises, parler à tort et à travers. **2** *vt* raconter. **3** *n* bêtises *fpl*, idioties *fpl*, blablabla* *m*. **she's a ~*** elle dit n'importe quoi, elle dit tout ce qui lui passe par la tête.

blaze[1] [bleɪz] **1** *n* **(a)** (*fire*) feu *m*, flamme *f*, flambée *f*; (*conflagration*) incendie *m*, brasier *m*; (*light from fire*) lueur *f* des flammes *or* du brasier. **forest** ~ incendie de forêt; **all in a** ~ en flammes.

(b) [*gems, beauty etc*] éclat *m*, splendeur *f*. **~ of day** éclat du jour; **~ of light** torrent *m* de lumière; **~ of colour** flamboiement *m* de couleur(s).

(c) (*bursting forth*) [*fire, sun*] flamboiement *m*; [*rage*] explosion *f*. **in a ~ of anger he killed her** dans le feu de la colère *or* dans une explosion de colère il l'a tuée.

(d) (*) **go to ~s!** va te faire voir!*; **what the ~s!** qu'est-ce que ça peut bien fiche!*; **how the ~s!** comment diable!; **what the ~s have you done now?** qu'est-ce que tu as encore fichu?*; **like ~s** comme un fou *or* dingue*, furieusement; **he ran like ~s** il a filé comme un zèbre; **he worked like ~s** il a travaillé comme une brute *or* un dingue*.

2 *vi* **(a)** [*fire*] flamber; [*sun*] flamboyer, darder ses rayons.

(b) [*colour*] flamboyer; [*jewel, light*] resplendir, jeter un vif éclat; [*anger*] éclater; (*fig*) resplendir (*with* de). **garden blazing with colour** jardin resplendissant de couleur.

blaze abroad *vt sep* (*liter*) *news etc* crier sur tous les toits.

blaze away *vi* [*fire etc*] flamber (toujours); [*soldiers, guns*] maintenir un feu nourri (*at* contre).

blaze down *vi* [*sun*] flamboyer, darder ses rayons.

blaze forth *vi* (*liter*) [*sun*] apparaître soudain (dans tout son éclat); [*anger*] éclater.

blaze out *vi* [*fire*] se déclencher, s'embraser, éclater; [*sun*] apparaître soudain; [*light*] ruisseler; [*anger, hatred*] éclater.

blaze up *vi* [*fire*] s'enflammer, s'embraser (*liter*); (*fig*) [*person*] éclater, s'emporter; [*anger*] éclater.

blaze[2] [bleɪz] **1** *n* (*mark*) [*horse etc*] étoile *f*; [*tree*] marque *f*, encoche *f*. **2** *vt tree* marquer. **to ~ a trail** (*lit*) frayer un *or* le chemin; (*fig*) montrer la voie, faire un travail de pionnier(s).

blazer ['bleɪzəʳ] *n* blazer *m* (*à écusson*).

blazing ['bleɪzɪŋ] *adj* **(a)** *building etc* en feu, en flammes, embrasé; *torch* enflammé; *sun* éclatant, ardent; (*fig*) *eyes* flamboyant, qui jette des éclairs; *jewel* étincelant; *colour* criard. **(b)** (*: *also ~* **angry**) furibond, furibard*. **(c)** (*fig*) *indiscretion, lie* manifeste, flagrant.

blazon ['bleɪzn] **1** *n* (*Her*) blason *m*. **2** *vt* (*Her*) blasonner; (*fig: also* **~ abroad, ~ forth**) *virtues, story* proclamer, claironner.

bleach [bliːtʃ] **1** *n* décolorant *m*; (*liquid*) eau oxygénée. **(household)** ~ eau de Javel.

2 *vt* **(a)** *linen, bones etc* blanchir. **~ing agent** produit *m* à blanchir, décolorant *m*; **~ing powder** (chlorure *m*) décolorant.

(b) *hair* décolorer, oxygéner. **to ~ one's hair** se décolorer (les cheveux); **~ed hair** cheveux décolorés *or* oxygénés.

(c) (*Phot*) *image* blanchir.

3 *vi* blanchir.

bleach out *vt sep colour* enlever.

bleachers ['bliːtʃəz] *n* (*US*) gradins *mpl* (*de stade en plein soleil*).

bleak [bliːk] *adj country, landscape* exposé au vent, morne, désolé; *room* nu, austère; *weather, wind* froid, glacial; (*fig*) *existence* sombre, désolé; *prospect* triste, morne, lugubre; *smile* pâle. **it looks** *or* **things look rather ~ for him** les choses se présentent plutôt mal pour lui.

bleakly ['bliːklɪ] *adv look* d'un air désolé, sombrement; *speak* d'un ton morne, sombrement.

bleakness ['bli:knɪs] *n [landscape]* aspect morne *or* désolé; *[room, furnishings]* austérité *f*; *[weather]* froid *m*, rigueurs *fpl*; *[prospects, future]* aspect sombre *or* décourageant; *[smile, look]* tristesse *f*.

bleary ['blɪərɪ] *adj* **(a)** *eyes* (*from sleep, fatigue*) trouble, voilé; (*from illness*) chassieux; (*from tears, wind etc*) larmoyant. **~-eyed** aux yeux troubles (*or* chassieux *or* larmoyants). **(b)** *outline* indécis, vague.

bleat [bli:t] **1** *vi* **(a)** *[sheep]* bêler; *[goat]* bêler, chevroter.
(b) *[person, voice]* bêler, chevroter; (*: *talk nonsense*) débiter des idioties, débloquer‡; (‡: *complain*) se plaindre (*about* de), bêler*. **what are you ~ing about?‡** qu'est-ce que tu as à te lamenter?
2 *vt* (*also* **~ out**) dire d'une voix bêlante, chevroter. **to ~ out a protest** protester d'une voix bêlante *or* chevrotante.
3 *n* **(a)** *[sheep]* bêlement *m*; *[voice, goat]* bêlement, chevrotement *m*.
(b) (‡: **complaint**) lamentation *f*, jérémiade* *f*.

bleb [bleb] *n [skin]* cloque *f*, ampoule *f*; *[glass, water]* bulle *f*.

bled [bled] *pret, ptp of* **bleed.**

bleed [bli:d] *pret, ptp* **bled 1** *vi* **(a)** saigner, perdre du sang. **his nose is ~ing** il saigne du nez; **he is ~ing to death** il perd tout son sang; **the wound bled profusely** la plaie saignait copieusement; (*liter*) **his heart is ~ing** son cœur saigne; (*gen iro*) **my heart ~s for you** tu me fends le cœur (*iro*), tu vas me faire pleurer (*iro*).
(b) *[plant]* pleurer, perdre sa sève.
2 *vt* **(a)** (*lit*) *person* saigner, faire une saignée à.
(b) (*) tirer de l'argent à, faire casquer‡. **to ~ sb white** saigner qn à blanc.
3 *n* saignement *m*; *V* **nose.**

bleeder ['bli:dəʳ] *n* **(a)** (*Med**) hémophile *mf*. **(b)** (*Brit***) salaud‡ *m*, saligaud‡ *m*.

bleeding ['bli:dɪŋ] **1** *n* **(a)** (*taking blood from*) saignée *f*; (*losing blood*) saignement *m*, hémorragie *f*. **~ from the nose** saignement de nez; **to stop the ~** arrêter l'hémorragie.
(b) *[plant]* écoulement *m* de sève.
2 *adj* **(a)** *wound* saignant; *person* sanglant, ensanglanté; (*fig*) *heart* blessé, brisé.
(b) (**: *bloody*) foutu‡ (*before n*), maudit (*before n*); *V* **bloody.**
3 *adv* (**: *bloody*) vachement‡, foutrement**; *V* **bloody.**

bleep [bli:p] **1** *n* (*Rad, TV*) top *m*; (*in hospital etc*) bip *m*. **2** *vi [transmitter]* émettre des signaux. **3** *vt* (*in hospital etc*) biper.

bleeper ['bli:pəʳ] *n* bip *m*.

blemish ['blemɪʃ] **1** *n* (*defect*) défaut *m*, imperfection *f*; (*on fruit*) tache *f*; (*fig*) (*moral*) souillure *f* (*liter*), tare *f*; (*inborn*) défaut. **there's a ~ in this cup** cette tasse a un défaut; **to find a ~ in sth** trouver à redire à qch; **a ~ on his reputation** une tache *or* une souillure (*liter*) à sa réputation; **without (a) ~** (*lit*) sans imperfection; (*fig*) sans tache, sans souillure (*liter*).
2 *vt beauty etc* gâter; *reputation, honour* ternir, flétrir.

blench [blentʃ] *vi* **(a)** (*flinch*) sursauter. **without ~ing** sans sourciller, sans broncher. **(b)** (*turn pale*) pâlir *or* blêmir (de peur).

blend [blend] **1** *n* (*mixture*) *[tea, paint, whisky etc]* mélange *m*; *[qualities]* alliance *f*, mélange, fusion *f*. **excellent ~ of tea** thé *m* d'excellente qualité; *[coffee]* **Brazilian ~** café *m* du Brésil; **'our own ~'** 'mélange (spécial de la) maison'.
2 *vt* (*also* **~ in**) mélanger, mêler (*with* à, avec), faire un mélange (*sth with sth* de qch avec qch); *teas, coffees etc* mélanger, faire un mélange de; *wines* couper, mélanger; *qualities* joindre, unir (*with* à); *ideas, people* fusionner; *colours, styles* fondre, mêler.
3 *vi* (*also* **~ in**) se mêler, se mélanger (*with* à, avec), former un mélange (*with* avec); se confondre (*into* en); *[voices, perfumes]* se confondre, se mêler, se mélanger; *[styles]* se marier, s'allier; *[ideas, political parties, races]* fusionner; *[colours]* (*shade into one another*) se fondre; (*go well together*) s'allier, se marier. **the colours ~ (in) well** les couleurs vont bien ensemble.

blender ['blendəʳ] *n* (*machine*) (*Tech*) malaxeur *m*; (*Culin*) mixer *m*.

bless [bles] *pret, ptp* **blessed** *or* **blest** *vt [God, priest, person, fate]* bénir. **God ~ the king!** Dieu bénisse le roi!; **to be ~ed with** avoir le bonheur de posséder; **God did not ~ them with ...** Dieu ne leur accorda pas le bonheur d'avoir ...; **Nature ~ed him with ...** la Nature l'a doué de ...; **I was never ~ed with children** je n'ai jamais connu le bonheur d'avoir des enfants; (*iro*) **she'll ~ you for this!** elle va te bénir!*; **~ you!** mille fois merci!, vous êtes un ange!; (*sneezing*) à vos souhaits!; **and Paul, ~ his heart, had no idea that ...** et ce brave Paul (dans son innocence) ne savait pas que ...; **~ his little heart!** qu'il est mignon!; **~ my soul!*†** Mon Dieu!, Seigneur!†; **well, I'm blest!*** par exemple!, ça alors!*; **I'm** *or* **I'll be blest if I remember!*** c'est bien le diable* si je m'en souviens.

blessed ['blesɪd] **1** *adj* **(a)** (*Rel*) (*holy*) béni, saint, sanctifié; (*beatified*) bienheureux. **B~ Virgin** Sainte Vierge; **B~ Sacrament** Saint Sacrement; **~ be God!** (que) Dieu soit béni!; **the B~ John X** le bienheureux Jean X.
(b) (*Rel, liter: happy*) bienheureux, heureux. **~ are the pure in heart** bienheureux *or* heureux ceux qui ont le cœur pur; **of ~ memory** d'heureuse mémoire.
(c) (*liter: giving joy*) *thing* béni; *person* cher.
(d) (**euph: cursed*) sacré* (*before n*), fichu* (*before n*), satané (*before n*). **that child is a ~ nuisance!** cet enfant, quelle peste! *or* quel poison!*; **the whole ~ day** toute la sainte journée; **every ~ evening** tous les soirs que le bon Dieu fait*.
2 *npl*: **the B~** les bienheureux *mpl*.

blessedness ['blesɪdnɪs] *n* (*Rel*) béatitude *f*; (*happiness*) bonheur *m*, félicité *f*.

blessing ['blesɪŋ] *n* **(a)** (*divine favour*) grâce *f*, faveur *f*; (*prayer*) bénédiction *f*; (*at meal*) bénédicité *m*. **with God's ~ we shall succeed** nous réussirons par la grâce de Dieu; **the priest pronounced the ~** le prêtre a donné la bénédiction; (*at meal*) **to ask a ~** dire le bénédicité.
(b) (*benefit*) bien *m*, bienfait *m*, bénédiction *f*. **the ~s of civilization** les bienfaits *or* les avantages *mpl* de la civilisation; **what a ~ that ...!*** quelle chance que ...! + *subj*, heureusement que ...; **this rain has been a real ~*** cette pluie a été une vraie bénédiction*; **it was a ~ in disguise** c'était malgré les apparences un bien, à quelque chose malheur est bon (*Prov*); **the plan had his ~*** il avait donné sa bénédiction à ce projet*; *V* **count**[1].

blest [blest] (*liter*) **1** *pret, ptp of* **bless. 2** *adj* heureux. **3** *npl* = **blessed 2.**

blether ['bleðəʳ] = **blather.**

blew [blu:] *pret of* **blow**[1].

blight [blaɪt] **1** *n [cereals, plants]* rouille *f*, mildiou *m*, charbon *m*; *[fruit trees]* cloque *f*. **this marriage was a ~ on his happiness** ce mariage a terni son bonheur; **she's been a ~ on his life** elle a gâché son existence; **what a ~ that woman is!‡** cette femme est un vrai fléau! *or* une véritable plaie!*
2 *vt [disease] plants* rouiller; *wheat etc* nieller; *[wind]* saccager; (*fig*) *hopes* anéantir, détruire; *career, life* gâcher, briser; *future* gâcher.

blighter* ['blaɪtəʳ] *n* (*Brit*) type* *m*, bonne femme. **a funny ~** un drôle de numéro*; **silly ~** crétin(e)* *m(f)*, imbécile *mf*; **lucky ~!** quel(le) veinard(e)*!; **you ~!** espèce de chameau!*

Blighty ['blaɪtɪ] *n* (*Brit Mil sl:*†) l'Angleterre *f*, 'le pays'.

blimey‡ ['blaɪmɪ] *excl* (*Brit*) mince alors!*, merde alors!‡

blimp [blɪmp] *n* **(a)** (*Brit*) **a (Colonel) B~*** une (vieille) culotte de peau (*pej*). **(b)** (*Aviat*) petit dirigeable de reconnaissance.

blind [blaɪnd] **1** *adj* **(a)** *person, passion, obedience* aveugle. **a ~ man/woman** un/une aveugle; **a ~ boy** un jeune aveugle; **~ in one eye** borgne; **she is as ~ as a bat** elle est myope comme une taupe; **~ spot** (*Med*) point *m* aveugle; (*Aut, Aviat*) angle *m* mort; (*fig*) **that was his ~ spot** sur ce point il avait un bandeau sur les yeux *or* il refusait d'y voir clair; **she was ~ to his faults** elle ne voyait pas ses défauts; **I am not ~ to that consideration** cette considération ne m'échappe pas; (*fig*) **to turn a ~ eye to** fermer les yeux sur; **~ with passion** aveuglé par la passion; *V* **colour.**
(b) (*fig*) *corner, flying, landing* sans visibilité; *passage* sans issue; *door, window* faux (*f* fausse). (*Aut, Aviat*) **it was approaching on his ~ side** cela approchait dans son angle mort; (*lit, fig*) **~ alley** impasse *f*, cul-de-sac *m*; (*fig*) **a ~-alley job** une situation sans avenir; **~ date** (*meeting*) rendez-vous *m* (avec quelqu'un qu'on ne connaît pas); (*person*) inconnu(e) *m(f)* (avec qui on a rendez-vous); **not a ~ bit of use‡** qui ne sert strictement à rien.
2 *vt* aveugler, rendre aveugle; *[sun, light]* aveugler, éblouir; (*fig*) aveugler, empêcher de voir. **the war ~ed** les aveugles *mpl* de guerre; **her love ~ed her to his faults** son amour l'aveuglait sur ses défauts.
3 *n* **(a) the ~** les aveugles *mpl*; (*fig*) **it's the ~ leading the ~** c'est comme l'aveugle qui conduit l'aveugle.
(b) *[window]* store *m*, jalousie† *f*; *V* **Venetian.**
(c) (*pretence*) feinte *f*, faux prétexte, masque *m*. **this action is only a ~** cette action n'est qu'une feinte *or* qu'un masque.
(d) to go on a ~‡ (aller) se soûler la gueule‡.
4 *adv* (*Aviat*) **to fly ~** voler sans visibilité; **~ drunk‡** bourré‡, bituré‡, (complètement) rond‡.
5 *cpd*: **blind man's buff** colin-maillard *m*; **blind-stitch** (*n*) point perdu; (*vi*) coudre à points perdus; **blindworm** orvet *m*.

blinder ['blaɪndəʳ] *n* (*US*) œillère *f*.

blindfold ['blaɪndfəʊld] **1** *vt* bander les yeux à *or* de.
2 *n* bandeau *m*.
3 *adj* aux yeux bandés.
4 *adv* **(a)** (*lit*) les yeux bandés. **it's so easy I could do it ~** (c'est si facile que) je le ferais les yeux bandés.
(b) (*fig*) aveuglément, sans réfléchir.

blinding ['blaɪndɪŋ] *adj* aveuglant.

blindly ['blaɪndlɪ] *adv* (*lit*) en aveugle, comme un aveugle; (*fig*) *obey, follow* aveuglément.

blindness ['blaɪndnɪs] *n* cécité *f*; (*fig*) aveuglement *m* (*to* devant, à l'égard de). **~ to the truth** refus *m* de voir la vérité; *V* **colour.**

blink [blɪŋk] **1** *n [eyes]* clignotement *m* (des yeux), battement *m* des paupières; *[sun]* (petit) rayon *m*; *[hope]* lueur *f*; (*glimpse*) coup *m* d'œil. **my telly's on the ~*** ma télé est détraquée.
2 *vi* **(a)** cligner des yeux; (*half-close eyes*) plisser les yeux.
(b) *[light]* vaciller.
3 *vt*: **to ~ one's eyes** cligner des yeux; **to ~ back the tears** refouler les larmes (d'un battement de paupières).

blinker ['blɪŋkəʳ] *n* **(a)** (*Brit*) **~s** œillères *fpl*; (*fig*) **to wear ~s** avoir des œillères. **(b)** (*also* **~ light**) (feu *m*) clignotant *m*.

blinking ['blɪŋkɪŋ] **1** *adj* (*) sacré* (*before n*), fichu* (*before n*), satané (*before n*). **~ idiot** espèce *f* d'idiot. **2** *n [eyes]* clignement *m* (d'yeux); *[light]* vacillement *m*.

bliss [blɪs] *n* **(a)** (*Rel*) béatitude *f*; (*gen*) félicité *f*, bonheur suprême *or* absolu.
(b) (*) **what ~ to collapse into a chair!** quelle volupté de se laisser tomber dans un fauteuil!; **the concert was ~** le concert était divin; **isn't he ~!** c'est un ange!; **it's ~!** c'est merveilleux!, c'est divin!

blissful ['blɪsfʊl] *adj* (*Rel, gen*) bienheureux; (*) divin, merveilleux.

blissfully ['blɪsfəlɪ] *adv* heureusement. **~ happy** merveilleusement heureux; (*iro*) **~ unaware that ...** parfaitement inconscient du *or* dans l'ignorance béate du fait que ... .

blister ['blɪstəʳ] **1** *n [skin]* ampoule *f*, cloque *f*; *[paintwork]* boursouflure *f*; *[metal, glass]* soufflure *f*; *[glass]* bulle *f*; (‡ *pej: person*) fléau *m*, poison* *m*, plaie* *f*.
2 *cpd*: (*Comm*) **blister-pack** plaquette *f*, blister-pack *m*.
3 *vi [skin]* se couvrir d'ampoules; *[paintwork]* se boursoufler; *[metal, glass]* former des soufflures.
4 *vt paint* se boursoufler.
blistering ['blɪstərɪŋ] **1** *n [skin]* formation *f* d'ampoules; *[paint]* boursouflage *m*. **2** *adj heat* étouffant; *sun* brûlant; *(fig) attack, condemnation* cinglant, virulent, impitoyable. **a ~ day** un jour de canicule.
blithe [blaɪð] *adj* (*liter*) joyeux, gai, allègre.
blithely ['blaɪðlɪ] *adv* gaiement, joyeusement, avec allégresse.
blithering ['blɪðərɪŋ] *adj*: **~ idiot** crétin fini*; (*excl*) **you ~ idiot!** espèce d'idiot!
blithesome ['blaɪðsəm] *adj* = **blithe.**
blitz [blɪts] **1** *n* (*Mil*) attaque *f* éclair *inv*; (*Aviat*) bombardement *m* (aérien). **the B~** le Blitz; (*fig*) **to have a ~ on sth** s'attaquer à qch.
2 *cpd*: **blitzkrieg** la guerre-éclair.
3 *vt* bombarder. **~ed houses** maisons bombardées *or* sinistrées (*par un bombardement*).
blizzard ['blɪzəd] *n* tempête *f* de neige; (*in the Arctic*) blizzard *m*.
bloated ['bləʊtɪd] *adj* gonflé, boursouflé, bouffi; *face* bouffi, boursouflé; *stomach* gonflé, ballonné; (*fig: with pride etc*) bouffi, gonflé (*with* de); *style* bouffi.
bloater ['bləʊtəʳ] *n* hareng saur.
blob [blɒb] *n [water]* (grosse) goutte *f*; *[honey, glue]* goutte; *[ink]* pâté *m*, tache *f*; *[colour, paint]* tache.
bloc [blɒk] *n* **(a)** (*Pol*) bloc *m*. **(b) en ~** en bloc, en gros.
block [blɒk] **1** *n* **(a)** *[stone]* bloc *m*; *[wood]* billot *m*, bille *f*; (*anvil ~*) billot. (*toys*) **~s** (jeu *m* de) cubes *mpl*, jeu de construction; (*fig*) **he's a chip off the old ~** c'est bien le fils de son père; **butcher's ~** billot de boucher; **to die on the ~** périr sur le billot *or* l'échafaud.
(b) *[buildings]* pâté *m* (de maisons). (*Brit*) **a ~ of flats** un immeuble; **to take a stroll round the ~** faire le tour du pâté de maisons, faire un tour dans le coin; (*US*) **she lived 3 ~s away** elle habitait 3 rues plus loin.
(c) (*obstruction*) *[traffic]* embouteillage *m*, encombrement *m*; *[pipe]* obstruction *f*; (*Med*) blocage *m*; (*mental*) blocage; *V* **road.**
(d) (*large quantity*) section *f*. **~ of shares** tranche *f* d'actions; **~ of seats** groupe *m* de sièges.
(e) (*Brit Typ*) cliché *m* (*plaque*).
(f) (*also* **~ and tackle**) palan *m*, moufles *mpl*.
(g) (‡: *head*) caboche* *f*, ciboulot‡ *m*; *V* **knock.**
(h) (*Brit: writing pad*) bloc *m*.
2 *cpd*: **blockbuster*** bombe *f* de gros calibre; (*film, TV series*) superproduction *f*; (*argument*) argument *m* massue *inv*; **he's a real blockbuster*** il est d'une efficacité à tout casser; **in block capitals** = **in block letters**; (*pej*) **blockhead*** imbécile *mf*, crétin(e)* *m(f)*; (*Mil*) **blockhouse** blockhaus *m*; **in block letters** en (caractères) majuscules d'imprimerie; (*Rail*) **block system** bloc-système *m*, bloc *m* automatique à signaux lumineux.
3 *vt pipe etc* boucher, bloquer, obstruer; *road* bloquer, barrer; *harbour, wheel* bloquer; *progress, traffic* entraver, gêner; (*Ftbl*) *opponent* gêner; *transaction, credit, negotiations* bloquer. **the leaves ~ed the drain** les feuilles mortes ont bouché *or* bloqué le puisard; **to ~ sb's way** barrer le chemin à qn; (*Ftbl etc*) **to ~ the ball** bloquer (la balle).
4 *vi [wheel]* (se) bloquer.
block off *vt sep part of road etc* interdire, condamner; (*accidentally*) obstruer.
block out *vt sep* **(a)** (*obscure*) *view* boucher.
(b) (*sketch roughly*) *scheme, design* ébaucher.
(c) (*censor*) caviarder; (*delete*) caviarder, rayer, raturer.
block up *vt sep gangway* encombrer; *pipe* bloquer, obstruer; *window, entrance* murer, condamner; *hole* boucher, bloquer.
blockade [blɒ'keɪd] **1** *n* (*Mil*) blocus *m*; (*fig*) barrage *m*. **under ~** en état de blocus; **to break/raise the ~** forcer/lever le blocus.
2 *cpd*: **blockade runner** briseur *m* de blocus.
3 *vt* **(a)** (*Mil*) *town, port* bloquer, faire le blocus de; (*fig*) bloquer, obstruer.
(b) (*US*) *traffic* bloquer; *street* encombrer.
blockage ['blɒkɪdʒ] *n* (*gen*) obstruction *f*; (*Med*) obstruction, blocage *m*; (*mental*) blocage; (*fig*) bouchon *m*.
bloke* [bləʊk] *n* (*Brit*) type* *m*, mec‡ *m*.
blond(e) [blɒnd] *adj, n person* blond(e) *m(f)*; *V* **ash², platinum.**
blood [blʌd] **1** *n* **(a)** (*U*) sang *m*. **till the ~ comes** jusqu'au sang; **it's like trying to get ~ out of a stone** c'est comme si on parlait à un mur; **bad ~** désaccord *m*; **there is bad ~ between them** le torchon brûle (entre eux); (*liter*) **his ~ will be on your head** vous aurez sa mort sur la conscience; (*fig*) **there is ~ on his hands** il a la mort de quelqu'un sur la conscience, il a du sang sur les mains; **the ~ rushed to his face** le sang lui est monté au visage; **it makes my ~ boil** cela me fait bouillir; **my ~ was boiling** je bouillais (de rage); **his ~ is up** il est très monté; **he's out for ~*** il cherche quelqu'un sur qui passer sa colère; **she is out for his ~*** elle veut sa peau*; **you make my ~ run cold** vous me donnez le frisson; **his ~ ran cold** son sang s'est figé *or* s'est glacé dans ses veines; **the ties of ~** les liens du sang; (*Prov*) **~ is thicker than water** la voix du sang est la plus forte; **it's in his ~** il a cela dans le sang; **of Irish ~** de sang irlandais; (*fig*) **this firm needs new ~** cette maison a besoin d'un *or* de sang nouveau; *V* **blue, cold, flesh** *etc.*
(b) (†: *dandy*) petit-maître† *m*.
2 *vt* (*Hunting*) *hounds* acharner, donner le goût du sang à; (*fig*) *troops* donner le baptême du feu à.
3 *cpd*: **a blood-and-thunder film** *V* **a blood-and-thunder play; blood-and-thunder novel** roman *m* à sensation; **a blood-and-thunder play** un sombre mélodrame; (*Med*) **blood bank** banque *f* du sang; (*fig*) **blood bath** bain *m* de sang, massacre *m*; **blood blister** pinçon *m*; **blood brother** frère *m* de sang; **blood cell** globule *m* (sanguin); (*Med*) **blood count** numération *f* globulaire; **bloodcurdling** à (vous) figer *or* tourner* le sang, qui (vous) fige le sang; **blood donor** donneur *m*, -euse *f* de sang; **blood feud** vendetta *f*; (*Med*) **blood group** groupe sanguin; (*Med*) **blood grouping** recherche *f* du groupe sanguin; **blood heat** température *f* du sang; **bloodhound** (*Zool*) limier *m*; (*: *detective*) détective *m*, limier; (*Med*) **bloodletting** saignée *f*; **blood lust** soif *f* de sang; **blood money** prix *m* du sang; **blood orange** (orange *f*) sanguine *f*; **blood plasma** plasma sanguin; **blood poisoning** empoisonnement *m* du sang; **blood pressure** *V* **blood pressure**; (*US*) **blood pudding** boudin *m*; **blood-red** rouge (*m*) sang *inv*; **blood relation** parent(e) *m(f)* par le sang; (*US*) **blood sausage** = **blood pudding**; **bloodshed** effusion *f* de sang, carnage *m*; **without bloodshed** sans verser de sang, sans effusion de sang; **bloodshot eyes** yeux injectés (de sang); **to become bloodshot** s'injecter; **blood sports** sports *mpl* sanguinaires; **bloodstain** tache *f* de sang; **bloodstained** taché de sang, souillé (*liter*) de sang, ensanglanté; **bloodstock** bêtes *fpl* de race (pure) *or* de sang; **bloodstone** héliotrope *m* (*pierre*); **bloodstream** sang *m*, système sanguin; (*Zool, also* **pej*) **bloodsucker** sangsue *f*; (*Med*) **blood test** analyse *f* de sang, examen *m* du sang; **bloodthirstiness** *[person, animal]* soif *f* de sang; *[book, story]* cruauté *f*, caractère *m* sanguinaire; **bloodthirsty** *person, animal* altéré *or* assoiffé de sang, sanguinaire; *disposition, tale* sanguinaire; **blood transfusion** transfusion sanguine *or* de sang; **blood vessel** vaisseau sanguin; *V* **burst.**
bloodiness ['blʌdɪnɪs] *n* **(a)** (*lit*) état sanglant. **(b)** (∵) saloperie‡ *f*.
bloodless ['blʌdlɪs] *adj* (*without blood*) exsangue; *complexion* anémié, pâle; *victory* sans effusion de sang, pacifique.
bloodlessly ['blʌdlɪslɪ] *adv* sans effusion de sang, pacifiquement.
blood pressure ['blʌdpreʃəʳ] *n* tension *f* (artérielle). **to have high/low ~** faire de l'hypertension/hypotension; **to take sb's ~** prendre la tension de qn; (*Med*) **his ~ went up/down** sa tension a monté/a baissé; (*fig*) **his ~ rose at the news** il a failli avoir une attaque en apprenant la nouvelle.
bloody ['blʌdɪ] **1** *adj* **(a)** (*lit*) sanglant, taché de sang, ensanglanté; *battle* sanglant, sanguinaire; (*blood-coloured*) rouge, rouge sang *inv*. **a ~ nose** un nez en sang; **with ~ hands** les mains couvertes de sang *or* ensanglantées; **a ~ sun** un soleil rouge sang *or* couleur de sang; **~ mary** vodka *f* (au) jus de tomate, bloody mary *m*.
(b) (*Brit*∵) foutu‡ (*before n*), sacré* (*before n*). **this ~ machine won't start!** cette bon Dieu‡ de machine *or* cette foutue‡ machine ne veut pas démarrer!; **shut the ~ door!** (mais) nom de Dieu∵ veux-tu fermer la porte!; **it's a ~ nuisance** ce que c'est emmerdant‡; **you ~ fool!** espèce de con!∵; **you've got a ~ cheek!** *or* **nerve!** tu charries!‡; **those ~ doctors!** ces bon Dieu‡ de médecins, ces foutus‡ médecins; **~ hell!** merde alors!‡; **it's a ~ miracle he wasn't killed!** c'est un sacré* miracle qu'il n'ait pas été tué; **we had a perfectly ~ evening with them** ils nous ont fait passer une soirée (drôlement) emmerdante‡.
2 *adv* (*Brit*∵) vachement‡. **not ~ likely!** tu te fous de moi!‡, tu te fous de ma gueule!‡
3 *cpd*: (*Brit*) **bloody-minded‡** mauvais coucheur; **he's being bloody-minded‡** il le fait pour emmerder le monde‡; **out of sheer bloody-mindedness‡** (rien que) pour emmerder le monde‡, par pur sadisme.
4 *vt* ensanglanter, souiller de sang (*liter*).
bloom [bluːm] **1** *n* **(a)** fleur *f*.
(b) (*U*) (*lit*) floraison *f*; (*fig*) épanouissement *m*, floraison. **in ~** fleuri, éclos; **in full ~** en pleine floraison, épanoui; **to burst** *or* **come into ~** fleurir, s'épanouir; (*fig*) **in the ~ of her youth** dans la fleur de sa jeunesse, en pleine jeunesse.
(c) *[fruit, skin]* velouté *m*; *[flower]* épanouissement *m*. (*liter*) **the ~ had gone from her cheek** ses joues avaient perdu leurs fraîches couleurs.
2 *vi* (*lit*) fleurir, être en fleur, s'épanouir; (*fig*) être florissant, être heureux. **she was ~ing with health** elle était resplendissante de santé.
bloomer ['bluːməʳ] *n* **(a)** (‡) bévue *f*, gaffe* *f*. **to make a ~** faire une gaffe*, se foutre dedans‡, mettre les pieds dans le plat. **(b)** (*Dress*) **~s** culotte bouffante, short bouffant.
blooming ['bluːmɪŋ] *adj* **(a)** *tree* en fleur, fleuri; *looks, health* florissant. **(b)** (*) = **blinking 1.**
blossom ['blɒsəm] **1** *n* **(a)** (*U*) floraison *f*, fleur(s) *f(pl)*. **a spray of ~** une petite branche fleurie, un rameau en fleur(s); **tree in ~** arbre *m* en fleur(s); **pear trees in full ~** poiriers *mpl* en pleine floraison; **to come into ~** fleurir, s'épanouir; **peach ~** fleur de pêcher; *V* **orange.**
(b) fleur *f*.
2 *vi* fleurir, être en fleur(s), se couvrir de fleurs; *[person]* s'épanouir. (*fig*) **to ~ (out) into** devenir.
blot [blɒt] **1** *n [ink]* tache *f*, pâté *m*; (*fig*) tache, souillure *f* (*liter*). **a ~ on his character** *or* **on his escutcheon** une tache à sa réputation; **to be a ~ on the landscape** déparer le paysage (*also fig hum*).
2 *vt* **(a)** (*spot with ink*) tacher, faire des pâtés sur, barbouiller. (*Brit fig*) **to ~ one's copybook** faire un accroc à sa réputation.
(b) (*dry*) *ink, page* sécher.
3 *vi [blotting paper]* boire (l'encre).

blot out *vt sep* **(a)** *words* biffer, rayer; *memories* effacer; *[fog etc] view* voiler, masquer.
(b) *(destroy) nation* exterminer, liquider*; *city* annihiler, rayer de la carte.
blotch [blɒtʃ] **1** *n* **(a)** *(on skin) (mark)* tache *f*, marbrure *f*; *(spot)* bouton *m*. **(b)** *[ink, colour]* tache *f*. **2** *vt paper, written work* tacher, barbouiller, faire des taches sur.
blotchy [ˈblɒtʃɪ] *adj skin, complexion* couperosé, couvert de taches *or* de marbrures; *drawing, written work* couvert de taches, barbouillé.
blotter [ˈblɒtəʳ] *n* **(a)** *(block)* (bloc *m*) buvard *m*; *(sheet)* buvard; *(hand ~)* tampon *m* buvard; *(large, flat)* sous-main *m inv*. **(b)** *(US: notebook)* registre *m*.
blotting [ˈblɒtɪŋ] *cpd*: **blotting pad** (bloc *m*) buvard *m*; **blotting paper** (papier *m*) buvard *m*.
blotto‡ [ˈblɒtəʊ] *adj* bourré‡, bituré‡. **to be ~** être rond comme une barrique‡, être bourré‡.
blouse [blaʊz] *n [woman]* corsage *m*, chemisier *m*; *[workman, artist, peasant]* blouse *f*, sarrau *m*; *(US Mil)* vareuse *f*.
blow¹ [bləʊ] (*vb: pret* **blew**, *ptp* **blown**) **1** *n* **(a) to give a ~** *(through mouth)* souffler; *(through nose)* se moucher.
(b) *(wind)* coup *m* de vent, bourrasque *f*. **to go out for a ~** sortir prendre l'air *or* le frais.
2 *cpd*: **blowfly** mouche *f* à viande; *(US)* **blowgun** sarbacane *f*; **blowhole** *[whale]* évent *m*; *(Tech)* évent, bouche *f* d'aération; *(Metal)* **blowholes** soufflures *fpl*; *(Brit)* **blowlamp** lampe *f* à souder, chalumeau *m*; **blow-out** *V* **blow-out**; **blowpipe** *(weapon)* sarbacane *f*; *(Chem, Ind)* chalumeau *m*; *(Glass-making)* canne *f* (de souffleur), fêle *f*; *(US)* **blowtorch** lampe *f* à souder, chalumeau *m*; **blow-up** (‡: *quarrel*) engueulade‡ *f*, prise *f* de bec*, dispute *f*; *(Phot*)* agrandissement *m*.
3 *vt* **(a)** *[wind] ship* pousser; *leaves* chasser, faire voler. **the wind blew the ship off course** le vent a fait dévier le navire (de sa route) *or* a dérouté le navire; **a gust of wind blew her hat off** un coup de vent a fait s'envoler son chapeau; **the wind blew the chimney down** le vent a fait tomber *or* a renversé la cheminée; **the wind blew away the clouds** le vent a chassé *or* dispersé les nuages; **the wind blew the door open/shut** un coup de vent a ouvert/fermé la porte; *V* **ill**.
(b) *(drive air into) fire* souffler sur; *bellows* faire marcher. **to ~ one's nose** se moucher; **to ~ an egg** vider un œuf *(en soufflant dedans)*.
(c) *(make by blowing) bubbles* faire; *glass* souffler. **to ~ a kiss** envoyer un baiser.
(d) *trumpet, horn* jouer de, souffler dans. **the referee blew his whistle** l'arbitre a sifflé; *(fig)* **to ~ one's own trumpet** chanter ses propres louanges, se faire mousser*.
(e) *(destroy) fuse, safe* faire sauter. *(Aut)* **to ~ a gasket** griller* *or* faire sauter un joint de culasse; *(fig)* **the whole plan has been ~n sky-high** tout le projet a sauté.
(f) (‡: *spend extravagantly*) *wages, money* claquer‡, manger, bouffer‡. **I blew £5 on a new hat** j'ai claqué (un billet de) 5 livres pour un nouveau chapeau.
(g) *(phrases)* **to ~ one's top‡** piquer une colère*, se mettre en rogne*; **to ~ the gaff‡** vendre la mèche; **to ~ the gaff on sb‡** dénoncer *or* vendre qn; **he realized he was ~n‡** il a compris qu'il était brûlé; **~ the expense!*** tant pis pour la dépense!, au diable la dépense!; **well, I'm ~ed!*** ça alors!*, par exemple!; **I'll be ~ed if I'll do it!*** pas question que je le fasse!, je veux être pendu si je le fais!*; **~ it!*** la barbe!*, zut!*
4 *vi* **(a)** *[wind]* souffler. **the wind was ~ing hard** le vent soufflait très fort, il faisait grand vent; **it was ~ing a gale** le vent soufflait une tempête; **it's ~ing great guns*** il fait un vent à décorner les bœufs*; **the wind was ~ing from the south** le vent soufflait du sud; *(fig)* **to see which way the wind ~s** regarder *or* voir de quel côté souffle le vent, voir venir les choses; **she ~s hot and cold with me** avec moi elle souffle le chaud et le froid; **her enthusiasm ~s hot and cold** son enthousiasme a des hauts et des bas.
(b) *(move with wind)* **the door blew open/shut** un coup de vent a ouvert/a fermé la porte; **his hat blew out of the window** son chapeau s'est envolé par la fenêtre.
(c) *[trumpet]* sonner; *[whistle]* siffler; *[foghorn]* mugir. **when the whistle ~s** au coup de sifflet.
(d) *(breathe out hard)* souffler; *(breathe hard) [person]* souffler, être à bout de souffle; *[animal]* souffler. **to ~ on one's fingers** souffler dans ses doigts; **to ~ on one's soup** souffler sur sa soupe; *V* **puff**.
(e) *[whale]* souffler (par les évents).
(f) *[fuse, light bulb]* sauter, griller*; *[tyre]* éclater.
blow down 1 *vi [tree etc]* être abattu par le vent, se renverser, tomber.
2 *vt sep* abattre (en soufflant).
blow in 1 *vi* (*) s'amener‡, débarquer*; *(unexpectedly)* arriver *or* débarquer* à l'improviste.
2 *vt sep door, window* enfoncer. **look what the wind's blown in!*** regardez qui s'amène!*
blow off 1 *vi [hat]* s'envoler.
2 *vt sep* **(a)** *hat* emporter. *(fig)* **that blew the lid off the whole business*** c'est cela qui a fait découvrir le pot aux roses.
(b) *air* laisser échapper, lâcher. **to blow off steam*** se défouler*, dire ce qu'on a sur le cœur (*about* au sujet de).
blow out 1 *vi [light]* s'éteindre; *[tyre]* éclater; *[fuse]* sauter.
2 *vt sep* **(a)** *light* éteindre; *candle* souffler.
(b) *(puff out) one's cheeks* gonfler.
(c) to blow one's brains out se faire sauter *or* se brûler la cervelle.
3 blow-out *n V* **blow-out**.
blow over 1 *vi [storm, dispute]* se calmer, s'apaiser, passer.
2 *vt sep tree* renverser, abattre.
blow up 1 *vi* **(a)** *[bomb]* exploser, sauter. *(fig)* **the whole thing has blown up** tout a été fichu en l'air*.
(b) *[wind]* se lever; *[storm]* se préparer.
(c) (‡) *[person] (be angry)* se mettre en boule*; *(be indignant)* sauter au plafond*.
2 *vt sep* **(a)** *mine* (faire) exploser, faire sauter; *building, bridge* faire sauter.
(b) *tyre* gonfler. *(fig)* **blown up with pride** gonflé *or* bouffi d'orgueil.
(c) *photo* agrandir; *event* exagérer.
(d) (‡: *reprimand*) *person* passer un (bon) savon à*.
3 blow-up *n V* **blow¹ 2.**
blow² [bləʊ] *n* **(a)** *(lit)* coup *m*; *(with fist)* coup de poing. **to come to ~s** en venir aux mains; **at one ~** du premier coup; *(fig)* **he gave me a ~-by-~ account** il ne m'a fait grâce d'aucun détail; *V* **strike** *etc*.
(b) *(fig: sudden misfortune)* coup *m*, malheur *m*. **it was a terrible ~ for them** cela a été un coup terrible pour eux.
blow³ [bləʊ] *vi* (††, *liter*) fleurir, s'épanouir.
blower [ˈbləʊəʳ] *n [grate]* tablier *m or* rideau *m* de cheminée; *[ventilation]* ventilateur *m* (soufflant), machine *f* à vent; *(Min)* jet *m* de grisou; *(whale)* baleine *f*; (‡: *loudspeaker*) haut-parleur *m*; (*Brit*‡: *telephone*) bigophone‡ *m*. **to get on the ~‡ to sb** passer un coup de bigophone‡ à qn; *V* **glass**.
-blown [bləʊn] *adj ending in cpds V* **fly¹, wind¹**.
blow-out [ˈbləʊaʊt] *n* **(a)** *[tyre]* éclatement *m*. **(b)** *(Elec)* **there's been a ~** les plombs *mpl* ont sauté. **(c)** (‡: *meal*) gueuleton‡ *m*. **to have a ~** faire un gueuleton‡, gueuletonner‡.
blowy [ˈbləʊɪ] *adj* éventé, venteux (*rare*).
blowzed [ˈblaʊzd] *adj*, **blowzy** [ˈblaʊzɪ] *adj hair* mal peigné; *woman* échevelé.
blubber [ˈblʌbəʳ] **1** *n* **(a)** *[whale]* blanc *m* de baleine. **~-lipped** lippu. **(b) to have a ~** pleurer *or* chialer‡ un (bon) coup. **2** *vi (weep)* pleurer comme un veau*.
blubbery [ˈblʌbərɪ] *adj (fat)* plein de graisse. **~ lips** grosses lèvres molles.
bludgeon [ˈblʌdʒən] **1** *n* gourdin *m*, matraque *f*. **2** *vt* matraquer, assener un coup de gourdin *or* de matraque à. *(fig)* **he ~ed me into doing it** il m'a forcé la main (pour que je le fasse).
blue [bluː] **1** *adj* **(a)** bleu. **~ with cold** violet *or* bleu de froid; **you may talk till you are ~ in the face*** tu peux toujours parler; **I've told you till I'm ~ in the face*** je me tue à te le dire; **once in a ~ moon** tous les trente-six du mois; **like a ~ streak*** comme une flèche, au triple galop; **to have a ~ fit‡** piquer une crise*; *V also* **4** *and* **black, murder, true.**
(b) (*: *miserable*) cafardeux*, triste. **to feel ~** broyer du noir, avoir le cafard*; **to be in a ~ funk** avoir la frousse* *or* la trouille‡.
(c) *(fig: obscene) talk* grivois, gaulois; *book, film* porno* *inv*.
2 *n* **(a)** *(colour)* bleu *m*, azur *m*; *V* **navy, Prussian, sky** *etc*.
(b) *(sky)* azur *m (liter)*, ciel *m*. *(fig)* **to come out of the ~** tomber du ciel; **to go off into the ~** *(into the unknown)* partir à l'aventure; *(out of touch)* disparaître de la circulation*; *V* **bolt**.
(c) *(liter: sea)* **the ~** la mer, les flots *mpl*.
(d) *(depression)* **the ~s** le cafard*; **to have the ~s** broyer du noir, avoir le cafard*, avoir des idées noires; *(Mus)* **the ~s** le blues.
(e) *(Brit Univ)* **Dark/Light B~s** équipe *f* d'Oxford/de Cambridge; **he's got his ~ for rugby, he is a rugby ~** il a représenté son université au rugby (*gén Oxford ou Cambridge*).
(f) *(in washing)* bleu *m*.
3 *vt* (*Brit*‡: *squander*) manger, gaspiller; *money* claquer‡.
4 *cpd*: **blue baby** enfant bleu; **Bluebeard** Barbe-bleue *m*; **bluebell** jacinthe *f* des bois; *(Scot: harebell)* campanule *f*; **blueberry** myrtille *f*, airelle *f*; **bluebird** *(Orn)* oiseau bleu; *(fig)* oiseau bleu (du bonheur); **blue blood** sang bleu *or* noble; **blue-blooded** de sang noble, aristocratique; *(Brit Parl)* **blue book** livre bleu; **bluebottle** mouche *f* à vers *or* à viande; *(Bot)* bleuet *m*; (‡†: *policeman*) poulet* *m*; **blue cheese** (fromage *m*) bleu *m*; **blue collar worker** col bleu; **blue-eyed** aux yeux bleus; *(Brit fig)* **the blue-eyed boy** le chouchou*, le chéri; **blue jeans** blue-jean(s) *m(pl)*; *(Naut)* **Blue Peter** pavillon *m* de partance; **blueprint** *(print, process)* bleu *m (tirage)*; *(fig)* plan *m*, projet *m*, schéma directeur (*for* de); *(fig)* **bluestocking** bas-bleu *m*; **blue tit** mésange bleue.
blueness [ˈbluːnɪs] *n* bleu *m*.
bluey [ˈbluːɪ] *adj* bleuté.
bluff¹ [blʌf] **1** *adj* **(a)** *person* carré, direct. **(b)** *cliff, coast* à pic, escarpé. **2** *n (headland)* falaise avancée, cap *m*, promontoire *m*.
bluff² [blʌf] **1** *vi (also Cards)* bluffer*.
2 *vt* **(a)** *person* bluffer*, donner le change à. **we ~ed him into believing ...** nous l'avons si bien bluffé* qu'il a cru ...
(b) *(Cards) opponent* bluffer*.
3 *n (esp Cards)* bluff *m*; *V* **call**.
bluffer [ˈblʌfəʳ] *n* bluffeur *m*, -euse *f*.
bluish [ˈbluːɪʃ] *adj* bleuâtre, tirant sur le bleu.
blunder [ˈblʌndəʳ] **1** *n (gaffe)* bévue *f*, impair *m*, gaffe* *f*; *(error)* faute *f*, bourde *f*. **to make a ~** faire une gaffe* *or* une bévue *or* un impair; **social ~** impair.
2 *vi* **(a)** *(make mistake)* faire une bévue *or* une gaffe*. **we ~ed through to victory** de bévue en bévue nous sommes parvenus à la victoire.
(b) *(move clumsily)* avancer à l'aveuglette, tâtonner. **to ~ in/out** *etc* entrer/sortir *etc* à l'aveuglette; **to ~ against** *or* **into sth** buter *or* se cogner contre qch.
3 *vt affair, business* gâcher, saboter.
blunderbuss [ˈblʌndəbʌs] *n* tromblon *m*, espingole *f*.
blunderer [ˈblʌndərəʳ] *n* gaffeur* *m*, -euse* *f*.

blundering [ˈblʌndərɪŋ] **1** *adj person* gaffeur*, maladroit; *words, act* maladroit, malavisé. **2** *n* maladresse *f*.

blunt [blʌnt] **1** *adj* **(a)** *blade, knife* émoussé, qui ne coupe plus, peu tranchant; *pencil* mal taillé, épointé; *point, needle* émoussé, épointé. (*Jur, Police*) **with a ~ instrument** avec un instrument contondant.
(b) (*fig: outspoken*) *person, speech* brusque, carré; *fact* brutal. **he was very ~** il n'a pas mâché ses mots.
2 *vt blade, knife, point, sword* émousser; *pencil, needle* épointer; (*fig*) *palate, feelings* blaser, lasser.

bluntly [ˈblʌntlɪ] *adv speak* carrément, sans ménagements, sans mettre de gants*.

bluntness [ˈblʌntnɪs] *n* (*V* **blunt**) manque *m* de tranchant, état émoussé; absence *f* de pointe; (*outspokenness*) brusquerie *f*. **~ of speech** franc-parler *m*.

blur [blɜːʳ] **1** *n* **(a)** (*smear, blot*) tache *f*; *[ink]* pâté *m*, bavure *f*.
(b) (*vague form*) masse confuse, tache floue *or* indistincte.
(c) (*mist: on mirror etc*) buée *f*.
2 *vt* **(a)** *shining surface* embuer, troubler; *writing, inscription* estomper, effacer; *view, outline* estomper. **to become ~red** s'estomper; (*Phot*) **~red negative** cliché flou; (*TV*) **~red picture** image floue.
(b) *sight, judgment* troubler, brouiller. **eyes ~red with tears** yeux voilés de larmes.
(c) (*fig*) *reputation* ternir, tacher.

blurb [blɜːb] *n* baratin* *m* publicitaire.

blurt [blɜːt] *vt* (*also* **~ out**) *word* lâcher, jeter; *information, secrets* laisser échapper, lâcher étourdiment *or* à l'étourdie.

blush [blʌʃ] **1** *vi* **(a)** rougir, devenir rouge (*with* de). **to ~ deeply** rougir très fort, devenir tout rouge, piquer un fard*; **to ~ up to the ears** rougir jusqu'aux oreilles; **~ing** (*with shame*) le rouge au front; (*from embarrassment*) le rouge aux joues; (*hum*) **the ~ing bride** la mariée rougissante.
(b) (*fig: be ashamed*) rougir, avoir honte. **I ~ for him** j'ai honte pour lui; **I ~ to say so** je rougis de le dire.
2 *n* rougeur *f*. **with a ~** en rougissant; **without a ~** sans rougir; (*liter*) **the first ~ of dawn** les premières rougeurs de l'aube; (*liter*) **the ~ of the rose** l'incarnat *m* de la rose (*liter*); **at the first ~** au premier aspect, de prime abord; *V* **spare**.

bluster [ˈblʌstəʳ] **1** *vi* **(a)** *[wind]* faire rage, souffler violemment *or* en rafales; *[storm]* faire rage, se déchaîner. **~ing waves** vagues déchaînées *or* en fureur.
(b) (*fig*) *[person]* (*rage*) tempêter, fulminer (*at sb* contre qn); (*swagger*) faire le fanfaron *or* le bravache.
2 *n* **(a)** *[wind]* hurlements *mpl*, mugissement *m*; *[storm]* fracas *m*, vacarme *m*.
(b) (*fig: swagger*) air *m* bravache, fanfaronnade(s) *f(pl)*.

blusterer [ˈblʌstərəʳ] *n* fanfaron(ne) *m(f)*, bravache *m*.

blustering [ˈblʌstərɪŋ] **1** *adj* fanfaron. **2** *n* fanfaronnades *fpl*.

blustery [ˈblʌstərɪ] *adj wind* de tempête, qui souffle en rafales; *weather, day* venteux, à bourrasques.

boa [ˈbəʊə] *n* (*snake; fur or feather wrap*) boa *m*. **~ constrictor** (boa) constricteur *m*.

boar [bɔːʳ] **1** *n* (*wild*) sanglier *m*; (*male pig*) verrat *m*. **young (wild) ~** marcassin *m*; (*Culin*) **~'s head** hure *f* (de sanglier). **2** *cpd*: **boarhound** vautre *m*; **pack of boarhounds** vautrait *m*; **boar-hunting** chasse *f* au sanglier.

board [bɔːd] **1** *n* **(a)** (*piece of wood*) planche *f*; († *or hum*: *table*) table *f*. (*Theat*) **the ~s** les planches, la scène; (*fig*) **it is all quite above ~** c'est tout ce qu'il y a de plus régulier, c'est tout à fait dans les règles; (*fig*) **across the ~** (*adv*) systématiquement; (*adj*) général, de portée générale; *V* **bread, chess, diving** *etc*.
(b) (*U: provision of meals*) pension *f*. **~ and lodging** (chambre *f* avec) pension; **full ~** pension complète; *V* **bed**.
(c) (*group of officials, council*) conseil *m*, comité *m*, commission *f*. **~ of directors** conseil d'administration; (*Fin, Ind*) **he is on the ~, he has a seat on the ~** il siège au conseil d'administration; (*Brit*) **B~ of Trade** ministère *m* du Commerce; (*US*) **~ of trade** chambre *f* de commerce; **medical ~** commission médicale; (*Mil*) conseil de révision; **~ of inquiry** commission d'enquête; **~ of examiners** jury *m*, commission d'examen.
(d) (*U: Aviat, Naut*) bord *m*. **to go on ~** monter à bord, (s')embarquer; **to take goods on ~** embarquer des marchandises; **on ~ the Queen Elizabeth** à bord du Queen Elizabeth; **on ~ ship** à bord; **to go by the ~** (*lit*) être emporté (par-dessus bord); (*fig*) échouer; **she allowed her business to go by the ~** elle a laissé ses affaires aller à vau-l'eau.
(e) (*U: cardboard*) carton *m* (*U*).
2 *cpd*: **board game** jeu *m* de société (*se jouant sur un tableau*); **board room** salle *f* du conseil; (*Hist*) **Board school** école communale; (*US*) **boardwalk** passage *m* en bois, trottoir *m* en planches; (*on beach*) promenade *f* (en planches).
3 *vt* **(a)** (*go on to*) *ship, plane* monter à bord de; (*Naut*) (*in attack*) monter à l'abordage de, prendre à l'abordage; (*for inspection*) arraisonner; *train, bus* monter dans.
(b) (*cover with boards*) couvrir *or* garnir de planches, planchéier.
(c) (*feed, lodge*) prendre en pension *or* comme pensionnaire.
4 *vi* (*lodge*) **to ~ with sb** être en pension chez qn.

board out *vt sep person* mettre en pension (*with* chez).

board up *vt sep door, window* boucher, clouer des planches en travers de.

boarder [ˈbɔːdəʳ] *n* **(a)** pensionnaire *mf*. **to take in ~s** prendre des pensionnaires. **(b)** (*Brit Scol*) interne *mf*, pensionnaire *mf*; *V* **day**.

boarding [ˈbɔːdɪŋ] **1** *n* **(a)** *[floor]* planchéiage *m*; *[fence]* planches *fpl*.
(b) *[ship, plane]* embarquement *m*; (*Naut*) (*in attack*) abordage *m*; (*for inspection*) arraisonnement *m*.
2 *cpd*: (*Aviat, Naut*) **boarding card** carte *f* d'embarquement; **boarding house** pension *f* (de famille); (*Scol*) internat *m*; **to live at a boarding house** vivre dans une *or* en pension; **boarding officer** officier chargé de l'arraisonnement; **boarding pass = boarding card**; **boarding school** pension *f*, pensionnat *m*, internat *m*; **to send a child to boarding school** mettre un enfant en pension, mettre un enfant comme interne *or* pensionnaire (au lycée *etc*).

boast [bəʊst] **1** *n* rodomontade *f*, fanfaronnade *f*. **it is their ~ that they succeeded** ils se vantent *or* ils s'enorgueillissent d'avoir réussi.
2 *vi* se vanter (*about, of* de). **without ~ing** *or* **without wishing to ~, I may say ...** sans (vouloir) me vanter, je peux dire ... .
3 *vt* être fier de posséder, se glorifier d'avoir. **the church ~s a fine organ** l'église est fière de posséder un bel orgue.

boaster [ˈbəʊstəʳ] *n* vantard(e) *m(f)*, fanfaron(ne) *m(f)*, hâbleur *m*, -euse *f*.

boastful [ˈbəʊstfʊl] *adj person, words* fanfaron, vantard.

boastfully [ˈbəʊstfəlɪ] *adv* en se vantant, avec forfanterie.

boasting [ˈbəʊstɪŋ] *n* vantardise *f*, fanfaronnade(s) *f(pl)*.

boat [bəʊt] **1** *n* **(a)** (*gen*) bateau *m*; (*small light ~*) embarcation *f*; (*ship*) navire *m*, bâtiment *m*; (*vessel*) vaisseau *m*; (*liner*) paquebot *m*; (*rowing ~*) barque *f*, canot *m*; (*ship's ~*) canot, chaloupe *f*; (*sailing ~*) voilier *m*; (*barge*) chaland *m*, péniche *f*. **to go by ~** prendre le bateau; **to cross the ocean by ~** traverser l'océan en bateau *or* en paquebot; **to take the ~ at Dover** s'embarquer à *or* prendre le bateau à Douvres; (*fig*) **we're all in the same ~** nous sommes tous logés à la même enseigne, nous sommes tous dans la même galère; *V* **burn**[1], **life, miss**[1] *etc*.
(b) (*dish*) *V* **sauce** *etc*.
2 *vi*: **to go ~ing** aller faire une partie de canot; **to ~ up/down the river** remonter/descendre la rivière en bateau.
3 *cpd*: **boatbuilder** constructeur naval *or* (*smaller*) de bateaux; **boatbuilding** construction navale *or* (*smaller*) de bateaux; **boat deck** pont *m* des embarcations; **boat hook** gaffe *f*; **boathouse** hangar *m or* abri *m* à bateaux; **boatload** *[goods etc]* cargaison *f*; *[people]* plein bateau, cargaison (*hum*); **boatman** (*boat-hire proprietor*) loueur *m* de canots; (*rower*) passeur *m*; **boat race** course *f* d'aviron, régates *fpl*; **the Boat Race** la course d'aviron (*entre les Universités d'Oxford et de Cambridge*); **boat-shaped** en forme de bateau; **boat train** train *m* (*qui assure la correspondance avec le bateau*); **boatyard** chantier *m* de construction de bateaux.

boater [ˈbəʊtəʳ] *n* (*hat*) canotier *m*.

boatful [ˈbəʊtfʊl] *n [goods]* cargaison *f*; *[people]* plein bateau, cargaison (*hum*).

boating [ˈbəʊtɪŋ] **1** *n* canotage *m*. **2** *cpd club, accident* de canotage. **boating holiday/trip** vacances *fpl*/excursion *f* en bateau.

boatswain [ˈbəʊsn] *n* maître *m* d'équipage. **~'s chair** sellette *f*; **~'s mate** second maître; **~'s pipe** sifflet *m*.

Bob [bɒb] *n* (*dim of* **Robert**) Bob *m*. (*Brit*) **~'s your uncle!*** ce n'est pas plus difficile que cela!, c'est simple comme bonjour!

bob[1] [bɒb] **1** *vi* **(a)** se balancer, monter et descendre, s'agiter, sautiller; (*in the air*) pendiller. **to ~ (up and down) in** *or* **on the water** danser sur l'eau; **to ~ for apples** *essayer d'attraper avec les dents des pommes flottant sur l'eau.*
(b) (*curtsy*) faire une (petite) révérence.
2 *n* (*curtsy*) (petite) révérence *f*; (*nod*) (bref) salut *m* de tête; (*jerky movement*) petite secousse, petit coup.

bob down *vi* **(a)** (*duck*) baisser la tête; (*straight*) se baisser subitement.
(b) (*: be quiet*) la fermer*.

bob up *vi* remonter brusquement. (*fig*) **he bobbed up again in London** il s'est repointé* à Londres.

bob[2]* [bɒb] *n, pl inv* (*Brit*) shilling *m*.

bob[3] [bɒb] **1** *n* (*curl*) boucle *f*, mèche courte; (*haircut*) coiffure courte; (*straight*) coiffure à la Jeanne d'Arc; (*horse's tail*) queue écourtée; (*weight*) *[pendulum]* poids *m*; *[plumbline]* plomb *m*; *[ribbons]* nœud *m*; (*float*) bouchon *m*; (*bait*) paquet *m* de vers.
2 *vt hair* couper court; *horse's tail* écourter.
3 *vi* (*Fishing*) pêcher à la ligne flottante.
4 *cpd*: (*US*) **bobcat** lynx *m*; **bobtail** (*tail*) queue écourtée (*V* **rag**[1]); (*horse/dog*) cheval/chien écourté; **bobtailed** à (la) queue écourtée.

bob[4] [bɒb] *n* (*sleigh: also* **~sled, ~sleigh**) bobsleigh *m*; (*runner*) patin *m*.

bobbin [ˈbɒbɪn] *n [thread, wire]* bobine *f*; *[sewing machine]* bobine *f*; *[lace]* fuseau *m*. **~ lace** dentelle *f* aux fuseaux.

Bobby [ˈbɒbɪ] *n* (*dim of* **Robert**) Bobby *m*.

bobby* [ˈbɒbɪ] *n* flic* *m*.

bobby pin [ˈbɒbɪpɪn] *n* (*esp US*) pince *f* à cheveux, barrette *f*.

bobbysocks* [ˈbɒbɪsɒks] *n* (*US*) socquettes *fpl* (*portées par les filles*).

bobbysoxer* [ˈbɒbɪsɒksəʳ] *n* (*US*) minette* *f*.

Boccaccio [bɒˈkætʃɪəʊ] *n* Boccace *m*.

Boche* [bɒʃ] (*pej*) **1** *n* Boche* *m* (*pej*). **2** *adj* boche* (*pej*).

bock [bɒk] *n* **(a)** (*U*) bière allemande. **(b)** (*glass of beer*) bock *m*.

bod* [bɒd] *n* (*Brit*) type* *m*; *V* **odd**.

bode [bəʊd] **1** *vi*: **to ~ well** être de bon augure (*for* pour); **it ~s ill (for)** cela est de mauvais augure (pour), cela ne présage rien de bon (pour). **2** *vt* présager, annoncer, augurer.

bodice [ˈbɒdɪs] *n* **(a)** *[dress]* corsage *m*; *[peasant's dress]* corselet *m*. **(b)** (*vest*) cache-corset *m*.

-bodied [ˈbɒdɪd] *adj ending in cpds V* **able, full** *etc*.

bodiless [ˈbɒdɪlɪs] *adj* (*lit*) sans corps; (*insubstantial*) incorporel.

bodily ['bɒdɪlɪ] **1** *adv* **(a)** (*in the flesh*) physiquement, corporellement. **they were carried ~ to the door** ils ont été portés à bras-le-corps jusqu'à la porte.
(b) (*in person*) en personne. **he appeared ~** il apparut en personne.
(c) (*all together*) tout entier, en masse.
2 *adj* (*physical*) physique, corporel, matériel; *pain* physique. **~ illness** troubles *mpl* physiques; **~ needs** *or* **wants** besoins matériels; **~ harm** blessure *f*.
bodkin ['bɒdkɪn] *n* (*for threading tape*) passe-lacet *m*; (*for leather*) poinçon *m*; (††: *hairpin*) épingle *f* à cheveux.
body ['bɒdɪ] **1** *n* **(a)** *[man, animal]* corps *m*. **just enough to keep ~ and soul together** juste assez pour subsister; **to belong to sb ~ and soul** appartenir à qn corps et âme; *V* **sound**[2].
(b) (*corpse*) corps *m*, cadavre *m*.
(c) (*main part of structure*) *[dress]* corsage *m*, corps *m* (de robe); *[car]* carrosserie *f*; *[plane]* fuselage *m*; *[ship]* coque *f*; *[church]* nef *f*; *[speech, document]* fond *m*, corps. (*Brit Parl*) **in the ~ of the House** au centre de la Chambre.
(d) (*group, mass*) masse *f*, ensemble *m*, corps *m*. **~ of troops** corps de troupes; **the main ~ of the army** le gros de l'armée; **the great ~ of readers** la masse des lecteurs; **a large ~ of people** une masse de gens, une foule nombreuse; **in a ~** en masse; **taken in a ~** pris ensemble, dans leur ensemble; **the ~ politic** le corps politique; **legislative ~** corps législatif; **a large ~ of water** une grande masse d'eau; **a strong ~ of evidence** une forte accumulation de preuves.
(e) (*) (*man*) bonhomme* *m*; (*woman*) bonne femme*. **an inquisitive old ~** une vieille fouine; **a pleasant little ~** une gentille petite dame.
(f) (*Chem etc: piece of matter*) corps *m*. **heavenly ~** corps céleste; *V* **foreign.**
(g) (*U*) *[wine, paper]* corps *m*. **this wine has not enough ~** ce vin n'a pas assez de corps; **to give one's hair ~** donner du volume à ses cheveux.
2 *cpd*: **bodybuilder** (*Aut*) carrossier *m*; (*food*) aliment *m* énergétique; (*apparatus*) extenseur *m*; **body-building** culturisme *m*; **body-building exercises** exercices *mpl* de culturisme *or* de musculation; **bodyguard** garde *m* du corps; **body repairs** travaux *mpl* de carrosserie; **body (repair) shop** atelier *m* de carrosserie; (*Hist*) **body snatcher** déterreur *m* de cadavres; (*Space*) **body-waste disposal** évacuation *f* des matières organiques; (*Aut*) **bodywork** carrosserie *f*.
Boer ['bəʊəʳ] **1** *n* Boer *mf*. **the ~ War** la guerre des Boers. **2** *adj* boer (*f inv*).
boffin‡ ['bɒfɪn] *n* (*Brit*) chercheur *m* (*scientifique ou technique*).
bog [bɒg] **1** *n* **(a)** marais *m*, marécage *m*; *[peat]* tourbière *f*.
(b) (*Brit*‡) goguenot‡ *m*.
2 *vt* (*also* **~ down**: *gen pass*) *cart etc* embourber, enliser. (*lit, fig*) **to be** *or* **get ~ged down** s'embourber, s'enliser (*in* dans).
3 *cpd*: **bog oak** chêne *m* des marais.
bogey[1] ['bəʊgɪ] *n* (*bugbear*) bête noire; (*spectre, goblin*) spectre *m*, démon *m*. **~man** croque-mitaine *m*, père fouettard.
bogey[2] ['bəʊgɪ] *n* (*Golf*) bogey *m*, bogée *m*.
bogey[3] ['bəʊgɪ] *n* (*Rail*) bogie *m*; (*trolley*) diable *m*.
boggle ['bɒgl] *vi* **(a)** (*be alarmed, amazed*) être ahuri. **the mind ~s!** on croit rêver!; **his mind ~d when he heard the news** la nouvelle l'a plongé dans l'ahurissement. **(b)** (*hesitate*) hésiter (*at* à), reculer (*at* devant).
boggy ['bɒgɪ] *adj ground* marécageux, bourbeux, tourbeux.
bogie ['bəʊgɪ] *n* = **bogey**[3].
bogus ['bəʊgəs] *adj* faux (*f* fausse), bidon‡ *inv*, simulé. **~ transaction** transaction *f or* affaire *f* bidon‡ *inv or* à la gomme‡.
bogy ['bəʊgɪ] *n* = **bogey**[1], **bogey**[3].
Bohemia [bəʊ'hi:mɪə] *n* Bohême *f*.
Bohemian [bəʊ'hi:mɪən] **1** *n* (*Geog*) Bohémien(ne) *m(f)*; (*gipsy*) bohémien(ne); (*artist, writer etc*) bohème *mf*. **2** *adj* (*Geog*) bohémien; (*gipsy*) bohémien; *artist, surroundings* bohème. **~ life** (vie *f* de) bohème *f*.
bohemianism [bəʊ'hi:mɪənɪzəm] *n* (vie *f* de) bohème *f*.
boil[1] [bɔɪl] **1** *vi* **(a)** *[water etc]* bouillir. **the kettle is ~ing** l'eau bout (dans la bouilloire); **to begin to ~** se mettre à bouillir, entrer en ébullition; **to ~ fast/gently** bouillir à gros bouillons/à petits bouillons; **to let the kettle ~ dry** laisser s'évaporer complètement l'eau de la bouilloire; (*Culin*) **the potatoes were ~ing** les pommes de terre bouillaient; *V* **pot.**
(b) *[sea]* bouillonner; *[feelings]* bouillir (*with* de). **he was ~ing with rage** il bouillait (de rage); *V* **blood, boiling.**
2 *vt* **(a)** *water* faire bouillir, amener à ébullition.
(b) *food* (cuire à l'eau, (faire) bouillir. **~ed bacon** lard bouilli; **~ed beef** bœuf bouilli, pot-au-feu *m*; **~ed egg** œuf *m* à la coque; **~ed ham** jambon cuit (à l'eau); **~ed peas** pois cuits à l'eau; **~ed potatoes** pommes *fpl* à l'anglaise *or* à l'eau; (*Brit*) **~ed sweet** bonbon *m* à sucer; *V* **hard, soft.**
(c) (*wash*) **to ~ the whites** faire bouillir le (linge) blanc; **~ed shirt*** chemise empesée.
3 *n*: **on the ~** bouillant, qui bout; **off the ~** qui ne bout plus.
boil away *vi* **(a)** (*go on boiling*) bouillir très fort.
(b) (*evaporate completely*) s'évaporer, se réduire (par ébullition).
boil down **1** *vi [jam etc]* se réduire; (*fig*) se ramener, revenir (*to* à). **all the arguments boil down to this** tous les arguments se résument *or* reviennent *or* se ramènent à ceci; **it all boils down to the same thing** tout cela revient absolument au même.
2 *vt sep sauce etc* faire réduire (par ébullition).
boil over *vi* **(a)** *[water]* déborder; *[milk]* se sauver, déborder. **the kettle boiled over** (l'eau dans) la bouilloire a débordé.
(b) (*: *with rage*) bouillir (*with* de).
boil up *vi* (*lit*) *[milk]* monter. (*fig*) **anger was boiling up in him** la moutarde lui montait au nez; **they are boiling up* for a real row!** le torchon brûle!
boil[2] [bɔɪl] *n* (*Med*) furoncle *m*, clou *m*.
boiler ['bɔɪləʳ] **1** *n* **(a)** (*for hot water, steam*) chaudière *f*; (*Brit*: *for washing clothes*) lessiveuse *f*; (*pan*) casserole *f*; *V* **double, pot.**
(b) (*fowl*) poule *f* à faire au pot.
2 *cpd*: **boiler house** salle *f or* bâtiment *m* des chaudières; **boilermaker** chaudronnier *m*; **boilermaking** grosse chaudronnerie; (*Tech*) **boilerman** chauffeur *m*; **boiler room** (*Naut*) chaufferie *f*, chambre *f* de chauffe; (*gen*) = **boiler house**; (*Brit*) **boiler suit** bleu(s) *m(pl)* (de travail *or* de chauffe).
boiling ['bɔɪlɪŋ] **1** *n [water etc]* ébullition *f*, bouillonnement *m*.
2 *adj* **(a)** *water, oil* bouillant. (*Brit fig*) **the whole ~‡ lot** tout le bataclan*, tout le bazar*; **it's ~ (hot) today** il fait une chaleur terrible aujourd'hui; **I'm ~ (hot)*** je meurs de chaleur!
(b) (**fig: angry*) bouillant de colère, en rage. **he is ~** il bout de colère.
(c) (*Culin*) *beef* pour pot-au-feu. **~ fowl** poule *f* à faire au pot.
3 *adv*: **~ hot** (*lit*) tout bouillant; (*fig*) *V* **2.**
4 *cpd*: **boiling point** point *m* d'ébullition; (*fig*) **at boiling point** à ébullition.
boisterous ['bɔɪstərəs] *adj* **(a)** (*rough*) *sea* tumultueux, houleux, agité; *wind* furieux, violent. **(b)** (*exuberant*) *person* tapageur, bruyant, turbulent; *meeting* houleux. **~ spirits** gaieté bruyante *or* débordante.
boisterously ['bɔɪstərəslɪ] *adv* tumultueusement, bruyamment, impétueusement.
bold [bəʊld] *adj* **(a)** (*brave*) *person, action* hardi, audacieux, intrépide. **to grow ~** s'enhardir; **a ~ step** une démarche osée *or* audacieuse; *V* **face.**
(b) (*impudent, forward*) hardi, effronté, impudent. **to be** *or* **make so ~ as to do** avoir l'audace de faire, oser faire; **to make ~ with sth** prendre la liberté de se servir de qch; **if I may make so ~ ...** si je peux me permettre de faire remarquer ...; **as ~ as brass** d'une impudence peu commune, culotté*.
(c) (*Art, Literat: striking*) hardi, vigoureux. **to bring out in ~ relief** faire ressortir vigoureusement; **to paint in ~ strokes** avoir une touche puissante.
(d) (*Typ*) en grasse *or* mi-grasse. **~ type** caractères gras *or* mi-gras.
(e) *cliff, coastline* escarpé, abrupt.
boldly ['bəʊldlɪ] *adv* (*V* **bold**) hardiment, audacieusement, avec audace; effrontément, avec impudence; avec vigueur, vigoureusement.
boldness ['bəʊldnɪs] *n* (*V* **bold**) hardiesse *f*, audace *f*, intrépidité *f*; impudence *f*, effronterie *f*; vigueur *f*, hardiesse; escarpement *m*.
bole [bəʊl] *n* fût *m*, tronc *m* (d'arbre).
bolero [bə'lɛərəʊ] *n* (*all senses*) boléro *m*.
bolide ['bəʊlaɪd] *n* (*Astron*) bolide *m*.
Bolivia [bə'lɪvɪə] *n* Bolivie *f*.
Bolivian [bə'lɪvɪən] **1** *n* Bolivien(ne) *m(f)*. **2** *adj* bolivien.
boll [bəʊl] *n* graine *f* (*du cotonnier, du lin*). **~ weevil** anthonome *m* (*du cotonnier*).
bollard ['bɒləd] *n* *[quay]* bollard *m*; (*Brit*) *[road]* borne *f* (lumineuse).
bollix‡ ['bɒlɪks] *vt* (*US: also* **~ up**) = **ball(s) up 1.**
bollocks‡ ['bɒləks] *n* (*Brit*) = **balls**‡; *V* **ball**[1] **1h.**
boloney‡ [bə'ləʊnɪ] *n* idioties *fpl*, foutaises‡ *fpl*.
Bolshevik ['bɒlʃəvɪk] **1** *n* Bolchevik *mf*. **2** *adj* bolchevique.
Bolshevism ['bɒlʃəvɪzəm] *n* bolchevisme *m*.
Bolshevist ['bɒlʃəvɪst] = **Bolshevik.**
bolshie*, bolshy* ['bɒlʃɪ] (*pej*) **1** *n* (*Pol*) rouge *mf*. **2** *adj*: **he's very ~** il ne pense qu'à enquiquiner le monde*, c'est un mauvais coucheur; **he turned ~** il a commencé à râler*.
bolster ['bəʊlstəʳ] **1** *n* **(a)** *[bed]* traversin *m*. **(b)** (*Constr*) racinal *m*, sous-poutre *f*. **2** *vt* (*also* **~ up**) *person, morale* soutenir (*with* par).
bolt [bəʊlt] **1** *n* **(a)** *[door, window]* verrou *m*; *[lock]* pêne *m*; (*Tech: for nut*) boulon *m*; *[crossbow]* carreau *m*; *[rifle]* culasse *f* mobile; *[cloth]* rouleau *m*; (*lightning*) éclair *m*. (*fig*) **a ~ from the blue** un coup de tonnerre dans un ciel bleu; *V* **shoot.**
(b) (*dash*) fuite soudaine, départ *m* brusque. **he made a ~ for the door** il a fait un bond *or* a bondi vers la porte; (*fig*) **to make a ~ for it*** filer* *or* se sauver à toutes jambes.
2 *adv*: **~ upright** tout droit, droit comme un piquet *or* comme un i.
3 *cpd*: **bolt-hole** *[animal]* terrier *m*, trou *m*; *[person]* abri *m*, refuge *m*.
4 *vi* **(a)** (*run away*) *[horse]* s'emballer; *[person]* filer*, se sauver.
(b) (*move quickly*) se précipiter, foncer*. **he ~ed along the corridor** il a enfilé le couloir à toutes jambes.
5 *vt* **(a)** *food* engouffrer, engloutir.
(b) *door, window* verrouiller, fermer au verrou. **~ the door!** mettez *or* poussez le(s) verrou(s)!
(c) (*Tech*) *beams* boulonner.
bolt in **1** *vi* (*rush in*) entrer comme un ouragan.
2 *vt sep* (*lock in*) enfermer au verrou.
bolt on *vt sep* (*Tech*) boulonner.
bolt out **1** *vi* (*rush out*) sortir comme un ouragan.
2 *vt sep* (*lock out*) fermer la porte contre, mettre le(s) verrou(s) contre.
bolus ['bəʊləs] *n* (*Med*) bol *m*.
bomb [bɒm] **1** *n* bombe *f*. **letter/parcel ~** lettre *f*/paquet *m* piégé(e); (*Brit fig*) **his party went like a ~‡** sa réception a été (un succès) du tonnerre*; (*Brit fig*) **this car goes like a ~‡** elle file, cette bagnole*; (*Brit fig*) **the car cost a ~‡** la bagnole* a coûté les yeux de la tête; *V* **A, H** *etc.*

2 *cpd*: (*Aviat*) **bomb aimer** bombardier *m* (*aviateur*); **bomb bay** soute *f* à bombes; **bomb crater** entonnoir *m*; **bomb disposal** désamorçage *m*; **bomb disposal squad** *or* **unit** équipe *f* de désamorçage; **bombproof** blindé; **bombshell** *V* **bombshell**; **bomb shelter** abri *m* (anti-aérien); **bombsight** viseur *m* de bombardement; **bomb site** lieu bombardé.

3 *vt town* bombarder; *V* **dive**.

bomb out *vt sep house* détruire par un bombardement. **the family was bombed out** la famille a dû abandonner sa maison bombardée; **bombed out families** familles sinistrées (*par bombardement*).

bombard [bɒm'bɑːd] *vt* (*Mil, Phys, fig*) bombarder (*with* de).

bombardier [ˌbɒmbə'dɪəʳ] *n* (*Mil*) caporal *m* d'artillerie; (*Aviat*) bombardier *m* (*aviateur*).

bombardment [bɒm'bɑːdmənt] *n* (*Mil, Phys, fig*) bombardement *m*.

bombasine ['bɒmbəsiːn] *n* bombasin *m*.

bombast ['bɒmbæst] *n* grandiloquence *f*, emphase *f*, boursouflure *f*.

bombastic [bɒm'bæstɪk] *adj style* ampoulé, grandiloquent, pompeux; *person* grandiloquent, pompeux.

bombastically [bɒm'bæstɪkəlɪ] *adv speak* avec grandiloquence, avec emphase; *write* dans un style ampoulé.

Bombay [bɒm'beɪ] *n* Bombay. (*Culin*) ~ **duck** poisson salé (*pour accompagner un curry*).

bombazine ['bɒmbəziːn] *n* = **bombasine.**

bomber ['bɒməʳ] 1 *n* **(a)** (*aircraft*) bombardier *m*. **(b)** (*person*) plastiqueur *m*. 2 *cpd*: **bomber command** aviation *f* de bombardement; **bomber pilot** pilote *m* de bombardier.

bombing ['bɒmɪŋ] 1 *n* bombardement *m*; *V* **dive.** 2 *adj raid, mission, plane* de bombardement.

bombshell ['bɒmʃel] *n* **(a)** (*Mil*) obus *m*. (*fig*) **to come like a ~** éclater comme une bombe, faire l'effet d'une bombe; **this news was a ~ to them** cette nouvelle leur est tombée dessus comme une bombe.

(b) she's a real ~! c'est une fille sensass!ː

bona fide ['bəʊnə'faɪdɪ] 1 *adj traveller* de bonne foi; *offer* sérieux. 2 *adv* de bonne foi.

bona fides ['bəʊnə'faɪdɪz] *n* bonne foi.

bonanza [bə'nænzə] *n* (*fig*) aubaine *f*, filon *m*, mine *f* d'or; (*US Min*) riche filon.

Bonaparte ['bəʊnəpɑːt] *n* Bonaparte *m*.

bond [bɒnd] 1 *n* **(a)** (*agreement*) engagement *m*, obligation *f*, contrat *m*. **to enter into a ~** s'engager (*to do* à faire).

(b) (*link*) lien(s) *m(pl)*, attachement *m*. **to break a ~ with the past** rompre les liens avec le passé; **~s** (*chains*) fers *mpl*, chaînes *fpl*; (*fig*: *ties*) liens; **marriage ~s** liens conjugaux.

(c) (*Comm, Fin*) bon *m*, titre *m*.

(d) (*U*: *Comm*: *custody of goods*) entreposage *m* (*en attendant le paiement de la taxe*). **to put sth into ~** entreposer qch en douane.

(e) (*adhesion between surfaces*) adhérence *f*.

(f) (*Constr*) appareil *m*.

(g) (*Chem*) liaison *f*.

2 *vt* **(a)** (*Comm*) *goods* entreposer. **~ed warehouse** entrepôt *m* des douanes.

(b) (*Constr*) *bricks* liaisonner.

(c) (*Fin*) lier (par une garantie financière).

3 *cpd*: (*Fin*) **bondholder** porteur *m* d'obligations *or* de bons; (*Hist*) **bondman, bondsman** serf *m*, esclave *m*.

bondage ['bɒndɪdʒ] *n* **(a)** (*lit*) esclavage *m*, servage *m*. (*Hist*) **to be in ~ to** être le serf de. **(b)** (*fig*) esclavage *m*, asservissement *m*.

bonding ['bɒndɪŋ] *n* (*Constr*) liaison *f*; *[wood, plastic etc]* collage *m* (*à la résine synthétique*); (*Elec*) système *or* circuit régulateur de tension.

bone [bəʊn] 1 *n* **(a)** os *m*; *[fish]* arête *f*. **~s** *[the dead]* ossements *mpl*, os *mpl*, restes *mpl*; (*Mus*) castagnettes *fpl*; (ː: *dice*) dés *mpl* (à jouer); **chilled to the ~** transi de froid, glacé jusqu'à la moelle (des os); (*hum*) **my old ~s** mes vieux os, ma vieille carcasse*; (*fig*) **I feel it in my ~s** j'en ai le pressentiment, quelque chose me le dit; **~ of contention** pomme *f* de discorde; (*fig*) **to have a ~ to pick with sb** avoir un compte à régler avec qn; **he made no ~s about saying what he thought** il n'a pas hésité à dire ce qu'il pensait; **he made no ~s about it** il n'y est pas allé avec le dos de la cuiller* *or* par quatre chemins, il y est allé carrément; **there are no ~s broken** (*lit*) il n'y a rien de cassé; (*fig*) il y a plus de peur que de mal, il n'y a rien de grave; *V* **ankle, skin, wish** *etc.*

(b) (*U: substance*) os *m*. **handle (made) of ~** manche *m* en os.

(c) *[corset]* baleine *f*.

2 *cpd buttons etc* en os. **bone china** porcelaine *f* tendre; **bone-dry** absolument sec (*f* sèche); **boneheadː** crétin(e)* *m(f)*, abruti(e)* *m(f)*; **boneheadedː** idiot; **bone-idle*** fainéant *or* paresseux comme un loir *or* comme une couleuvre; **bone meal** engrais *m* (de cendres d'os); **bone-shakerː** (*car*) vieille guimbarde, tacot* *m*; (†: *cycle*) vélocipède† *m* (*sans pneus*).

3 *vt* **(a)** *meat, fowl* désosser; *fish* ôter les arêtes de.

(b) (ː: *steal*) piquerː, barboterː.

4 *vi* (ː) gaffer*.

bone upː *vt sep* (*also* **bone up on**) *subject* bûcher*, potasser*, bosserː.

boned [bəʊnd] *adj* **(a)** *meat* désossé; *fish* sans arêtes. **(b)** *corset* baleiné.

boneless ['bəʊnlɪs] *adj* **(a)** *meat* désossé, sans os; *fish* sans arêtes. **(b)** (*fig: weak*) mou (*f* molle), amorphe.

bonerː ['bəʊnəʳ] *n* (*US*) gaffe* *f*, bourde *f*. **to pull a ~** faire une gaffe*, mettre les pieds dans le plat.

bonfire ['bɒnfaɪəʳ] *n* feu *m* (de joie); (*for rubbish*) feu (de jardin).

bongo drum ['bɒŋgəʊdrʌm] *n* (tambour *m*) bongo *m*.

bonhomie ['bɒnɒmiː] *n* bonhomie *f*.

bonkersː ['bɒŋkəz] *adj* (*Brit*) cinglé*, dingueː.

bonnet ['bɒnɪt] *n* **(a)** (*hat*) *[woman]* capote *f*, bonnet *m*, chapeau *m* à brides; *[child]* béguin *m*, bonnet; (*Scot dial*) *[man]* béret *m*, bonnet; *V* **bee, sun** *etc.*

(b) (*Brit Aut*) capot *m*.

(c) (*Archit*) auvent *m*; *[chimney]* capuchon *m*.

(d) (*Naut*) bonnette *f*.

bonny ['bɒnɪ] *adj* (*esp Scot*) joli, beau (*f* belle).

bonus ['bəʊnəs] *n* gratification *f*, prime *f*; (*Comm*) prime; (*Brit Fin*) dividende exceptionnel. **~ of 500 francs** 500 F de prime; (*fig*) **as a ~** en prime; (*Fin*) **~ issue** émission *f* d'actions gratuites; *V* **incentive, no** *etc.*

bony ['bəʊnɪ] *adj* **(a)** (*Anat*) *tissue* osseux; (*fig*) *knee, person* anguleux, maigre, décharné. **(b)** *fish* plein d'arêtes; *meat* plein d'os.

boo [buː] 1 *excl* hou!, peuh! **he wouldn't say ~ to a goose*** il n'ose jamais ouvrir le bec*.

2 *vt actor, play* huer, siffler, conspuer. **to be ~ed off the stage** sortir de scène sous les huées *or* les sifflets.

3 *vi* huer.

4 *n* huée *f*.

boobː [buːb] 1 *n* **(a)** (*mistake*) gaffe* *f*; (*silly person*) ballot* *m*, nigaud(e) *m(f)*. **(b)** (*breast*) sein *m*, nichonː *m*. 2 *vi* (*Brit*) gaffer*.

booby ['buːbɪ] 1 *n* nigaud(e) *m(f)*, bêta* *m*. 2 *cpd*: (*Naut*) **booby hatch** écoutillon *m*; **booby prize** prix *m* de consolation (*décerné au dernier*); **booby trap** traquenard *m*; (*Mil*) objet piégé.

boodleː† ['buːdl] *n* (*money*) oseilleː *f*, pèzeː *m*.

boogie-woogie ['buːgɪˌwuːgɪ] *n* boogie-woogie *m*.

booing ['buːɪŋ] *n* huées *fpl*.

book [bʊk] 1 *n* **(a)** livre *m*, bouquin* *m*. **the (Good) B~** la Bible; *V* **bank²**, **telephone, text** *etc.*

(b) (*division*) *[Bible etc]* livre *m*; *[poem]* chant *m*.

(c) (*also* **exercise ~**) cahier *m*; *V* **note.**

(d) *[tickets etc]* carnet *m*. **~ of matches** pochette *f* d'allumettes; *V* **cheque, pass.**

(e) (*Comm, Fin*) **(account) ~s** livre *m* de comptes; **to keep the ~s of a firm** tenir les livres *or* la comptabilité *or* les comptes *mpl* d'une firme.

(f) *[club, society]* registre *m*. **to be on the ~s of an organization** être inscrit à une organisation; **to take one's name off the ~s** donner sa démission.

(g) (*Betting*) **to make (a) ~** inscrire les paris; (*bet*) parier.

(h) (*libretto*) *[opera etc]* livret *m*.

(i) (*Comm*) **~ of samples** album *m or* jeu *m* d'échantillons.

(j) (*phrases*) **to bring sb to ~** obliger qn à rendre des comptes; **by the ~** selon les règles; **to go by the ~, to stick to the ~** se conformer à la règle; **I am in his good ~s** je suis dans ses petits papiers*, il m'a à la bonneː; **to be in sb's bad ~s** être mal vu de qn; (*fig*) **in my ~* he's unreliable** à mon avis on ne peut pas se fier à lui; **he knew the district like a ~** il connaissait la région comme sa poche; **that's one for the ~!*** c'est à marquer d'une pierre blanche!, il faut faire une croix à la cheminée!; *V* **suit, throw.**

2 *cpd*: **bookbinder** relieur *m*, -euse *f*; **bookbinding** reliure *f* (*U*); **bookcase** bibliothèque *f* (*meuble*); **book club** cercle *m* de lecture, club *m* du livre; **book ends** serre-livres *m inv*, presse-livres *m inv*; **book jacket** jaquette *f*; **book-keeper** comptable *mf*; **book-keeping** comptabilité *f*; **book knowledge, book learning** connaissances *fpl* livresques; **book lover** bibliophile *mf*; **bookmaker** bookmaker *m*; **bookmark** marque *f*, signet *m*; (*US*) **bookmobile** bibliothèque circulante; **bookplate** ex-libris *m inv*; **book post** tarif *m* imprimés *inv*; **bookrest** support *m* à livres; **bookseller** libraire *mf* (*V* **secondhand**); **bookshelf** rayon *m* (de bibliothèque), étagère *f* (à livres); **bookshop** librairie *f*; **secondhand bookshop** boutique *f* de livres d'occasion; (*Brit*) **bookstall** *[station etc]* kiosque *m* à journaux; *[secondhand books]* étalage *m* de bouquiniste; **bookstore** librairie *f*; (*Brit*) **book token** bon-cadeau *m* (*négociable en librairie*), chèque-livre *m*; (*fig*) **bookworm** rat *m* de bibliothèque.

3 *vt* **(a)** *seat* louer; *room, sleeper* retenir, réserver; *ticket* prendre. **to ~ one's seat in advance** louer sa place à l'avance *or* d'avance; (*Theat*) **tonight's performance is ~ed up** *or* **fully ~ed** on joue à bureaux fermés *or* à guichets fermés ce soir; **the hotel is ~ed up** *or* **fully ~ed** l'hôtel est complet; **I'm ~ed for tomorrow lunch*** je suis pris demain à déjeuner; (*Rail*) **to ~ sb through to Birmingham** assurer à qn une réservation jusqu'à Birmingham.

(b) (*Comm, Fin*) *order* inscrire, enregistrer. **to ~ goods to sb's account** inscrire des marchandises au compte de qn.

(c) (*Police*) *driver etc* donner *or* mettre un procès-verbal *or* P.-V.* à; (*Ftbl*) *player* prendre le nom de. **to be ~ed for speeding** attraper une contravention *or* une contredanse* pour excès de vitesse.

book in 1 *vi* (*at hotel etc*) prendre une chambre.

2 *vt sep person* réserver une chambre à.

book up 1 *vi* louer.

2 *vt sep* (*gen pass*) retenir, réserver. **the school booked up all the seats on the coach** l'école a réservé toutes les places dans le car; **the tour is booked up** on ne prend plus d'inscriptions pour l'excursion; **the hotel is booked up until September** l'hôtel est complet jusqu'en septembre; **I'm very booked up*** je suis très pris; *V also* **book 3a.**

bookable ['bʊkəbl] *adj seat etc* qu'on peut retenir *or* réserver *or* louer. **seats ~ in advance** on peut retenir ses places (à l'avance); **seats ~ from 6th June** location (des places) ouverte dès le 6 juin.

bookie* ['bʊkɪ] *n* book: *m*, bookmaker *m*.

booking ['bʊkɪŋ] **1** *n* **(a)** (*esp Brit*) réservaion *f*. **to make a ~** louer, réserver, faire une réservation.
(b) (*Ftbl*) **there were 3 ~s at the game** l'arbitre a dû prendre le nom de 3 joueurs durant le match.
2 *cpd*: (*Brit*) (*Rail etc*) **booking clerk** préposé(e) *m(f)* aux réservations; (*Rail, Theat*) **booking office** (bureau *m* de) location *f*.

bookish ['bʊkɪʃ] *adj* qui aime les livres *or* la lecture, studieux; *word, phrase* livresque.

booklet ['bʊklɪt] *n* petit livre, brochure *f*, opuscule *m*, plaquette *f*.

boom[1] [buːm] *n* **(a)** (*barrier: across river etc*) barrage *m* (*de radeaux, de chaînes etc*). **(b)** (*Naut: spar*) gui *m*; (*Tech: also* **derrick ~**) bras *m*; (*jib of crane*) flèche *f*; *[microphone, camera]* perche *f*, girafe *f*.

boom[2] [buːm] **1** *n* (*sound*) *[sea, waves]* grondement *m*, mugissement *m*; *[wind]* mugissement, hurlements *mpl*; *[guns, thunder]* grondement; *[storm]* rugissement *m*; *[organ]* ronflement *m*; *[voices]* rugissement, grondement. (*Aviat*) **sonic ~** bang *m* supersonique.
2 *vi* **(a)** *[sea]* gronder, mugir; *[wind]* hurler, mugir (sourdement); *[thunder]* gronder, rouler.
(b) (*also* **~ out**) *[organ]* ronfler; *[guns]* tonner, gronder; *[voice]* retentir, résonner, tonner; *[person]* tonner, tonitruer.

boom out 1 *vi V* **boom**[2] **2b.**
2 *vt sep [person] words, speech* faire retentir.

boom[3] [buːm] **1** *vi* **(a)** (*Comm*) *[trade]* être en expansion *or* en hausse, prospérer. **business is ~ing** le commerce marche très bien *or* est en plein essor; **his books are ~ing** ses livres marchent très bien *or* se vendent comme des petits pains.
(b) (*Comm, Fin, St Ex*) *[prices]* être en forte hausse, monter en flèche.
2 *n* (*Comm*) *[business, transactions, firm]* montée *f* en flèche, forte hausse; *[product]* popularité *f*, vogue *f*, boom *m*; *[sales]* progression *f*, accroissement *m*; (*Comm, Fin, St Ex*) *[prices, shares]* brusque *or* très forte hausse; (*Econ: period of economic growth*) (vague *f* de) prospérité *f*, boom. **~ town** ville *f* en plein développement, ville champignon *inv*.

boomerang ['buːməræŋ] **1** *n* (*lit, fig*) boomerang *m*. **2** *vi* (*fig*) *[words, actions]* faire boomerang.

booming ['buːmɪŋ] **1** *adj sound* retentissant; *voice* tonitruant. **2** *n* = **boom**[2] **1.**

boon [buːn] **1** *n* **(a)** (*blessing*) bénédiction* *f*, aubaine *f*. **it would be a ~ if he went** quelle aubaine s'il s'en allait; **this new machine is a great ~** cette nouvelle machine est une bénédiction*; **my au pair girl is a ~ to me** ma jeune fille au pair m'est très précieuse.
(b) (††: *favour*) faveur *f*.
2 *adj*: **~ companion** joyeux compère.

boondocks ['buːndɒks] *npl* (*US*) **the ~** le bled* (*pej*).

boor [bʊəʳ] *n* (*coarse*) rustre *m*; (*ill-mannered*) malotru(e) *m(f)*, butor *m*.

boorish ['bʊərɪʃ] *adj* rustre, grossier, malappris.

boorishly ['bʊərɪʃlɪ] *adv* (*V* **boor**) *behave* en rustre; *speak* grossièrement.

boorishness ['bʊərɪʃnɪs] *n* rudesse *f*, manque *m* d'éducation *or* de savoir-vivre, goujaterie *f*.

boost [buːst] **1** *n*: **to give sb a ~ (up)** (*lit*) soulever qn par derrière *or* par en dessous; (*fig*) (*also* **give a ~ to sb's morale**) remonter le moral à qn; (*do publicity for*) **to give sb/a product a ~** faire de la réclame *or* du battage* pour qn/un produit.
2 *vt* **(a)** (*Elec*) survolter; (*Aut*) *engine* suralimenter. **the rockets ~ed the spacecraft** les fusées ont propulsé le vaisseau spatial.
(b) (*Comm, Ind etc: increase*) *price* hausser, faire monter; *output, productivity* accroître, développer; *sales* promouvoir, faire monter en flèche; *confidence etc* renforcer. (*Econ*) **to ~ the economy** donner du tonus à l'économie.
(c) (*do publicity for*) *person, product* faire de la réclame *or* du battage* pour.

booster ['buːstəʳ] *n* (*Elec*) survolteur *m*; (*Rad*) amplificateur *m*; (*Rail*) booster *m*; (*Space: also* **~ rocket**) fusée *f* de lancement, booster; (*Med: also* **~ shot, ~ dose**) (piqûre *f* de) rappel *m*.

boot[1] [buːt] **1** *n* **(a)** (*gen*) botte *f*; (*ankle ~*) bottillon *m*; (*wellington ~*) botte (en caoutchouc); (*lady's button ~*) bottine *f*; (*jack~, riding ~*) botte à l'écuyère; *[soldier]* brodequin *m*; *[workman etc]* grosse chaussure (montante), brodequin. (*fig*) **the ~ is on the other foot** les rôles sont renversés, c'est le monde à l'envers; (*fig*) **to give sb (the order of) the ~:** flanquer* qn à la porte, sacquer qn*; **to get the ~:** être flanqué* à la porte, être sacqué*; (*Brit*) **B~s** garçon *m* d'hôtel; *V* **bet, big, die**[1], **lick** *etc*.
(b) (*Brit*) *[car etc]* coffre *m*, malle *f* (arrière).
(c) (*Hist: for torture*) brodequin *m*.
2 *vt* donner *or* flanquer* des coups de pied à. (*lit and *fig*) **to ~ sb out** flanquer* qn à la porte.
3 *cpd*: **bootblack** cireur *m* (de chaussures); **bootlace** lacet *m* (de chaussure); (*US*) **bootleg:** (*vi*) faire la contrebande de l'alcool *or* des boissons alcooliques; (*vt*) vendre *or* importer en contrebande, fabriquer illicitement; (*adj*) *spirits* de contrebande; (*US*) **bootlegger:** bootlegger *m*; **bootlicker** lécheur* *m*, -euse* *f*, lèche-bottes* *mf inv*; **bootmaker** bottier *m*; **boot-polish** cirage *m*; **boot scraper** décrottoir *m*; **to pull o.s. up by one's (own) bootstraps** s'élever à la force du poignet.

boot[2] [buːt] **1** *n*: **to ~** par-dessus le marché, en plus, de plus, par surcroît; **and his insolence to ~** sans parler de son insolence. **2** *vt*: **what ~s it that ...?**†† qu'importe que ...? + *subj*.

bootee [buː'tiː] *n [baby]* petit chausson (*tricoté*); *[woman]* bottillon *m*.

booth [buːð] *n [fair]* baraque *f* (foraine); *[cinema, language laboratory, telephone etc]* cabine *f*; (*voting ~*) isoloir *m*.

bootless ['buːtlɪs] *adj* **(a)** (*without boots*) sans bottes. **(b)** (*liter: to no avail*) infructueux.

booty ['buːtɪ] *n* butin *m*.

booze: [buːz] **1** *n* (*U*) boisson(s) *f(pl)* (alcoolisée(s)). **I'm going to buy some ~** je vais acheter à boire; **to go on the ~** picoler:; **he's on the ~ just now** il picole: *or* biberonne* pas mal ces temps-ci; **he's off the ~** il ne boit plus.
2 *vi* biberonner*, lever le coude*.
3 *cpd*: (*Brit*) **booze-up:** beuverie *f*; **a good excuse for a booze-up** une bonne excuse pour aller boire un coup.

boozed: [buːzd] *adj* bourré:, bituré:.

boozer: ['buːzəʳ] *n* **(a)** (*drunkard*) pochard(e): *m(f)*, poivrot(e): *m(f)*, soûlard(e): *m(f)*. **(b)** (*Brit: pub*) bistro* *m*.

boozy: ['buːzɪ] *adj person* qui a la dalle en pente:, pochard:, soûlard:. **~ party** (partie *f* de) soûlographie* *f*.

bop [bɒp] *n*, *adj*, *n* bop (*m*).

bo-peep [bəʊ'piːp] *n* cache-cache *m*. **Little Bo-Peep** la petite bergère (*chanson enfantine*).

boracic [bə'ræsɪk] *adj* borique.

borage ['bɒrɪdʒ] *n* bourrache *f*.

borax ['bɔːræks] *n* borax *m*.

Bordeaux [bɔː'dəʊ] *n* **(a)** (*Geog*) Bordeaux. **native of ~** Bordelais(e) *m(f)*. **(b)** (*wine*) bordeaux *m*.

border ['bɔːdəʳ] **1** *n* **(a)** (*edge, side*) *[lake]* bord *m*, rive *f*; *[woods, field]* lisière *f*, limite *f*, bordure *f*.
(b) (*boundary, frontier*) frontière *f*, limite *f*. **within the ~s of** dans les limites *or* frontières de, à l'intérieur des frontières de; **to escape over the ~** s'enfuir en passant la frontière; **on the ~s of France** aux frontières françaises; (*Brit Geog*) **the B~s** la région frontière (*entre l'Écosse et l'Angleterre*).
(c) *[garden]* bordure *f*, plate-bande *f*; *V* **herbaceous.**
(d) (*edging*) *[carpet, dress]* bord *m*; *[picture]* bordure *f*, encadrement *m*, cadre *m*. *[notepaper]* **black ~** liseré noir.
2 *cpd*: **border dispute** différend *m* sur une question de frontière(s); **border incident** incident *m* de frontière; **borderland** pays *m* frontière, région *f* limitrophe; (*fig*) **on the borderland of sleep** aux frontières du sommeil et de la veille; **borderline** *V* **borderline**; **border raid** incursion *f*; **border town** ville *f* frontière.
3 *vt* **(a)** *[trees etc]* (*line edges of*) border; (*surround*) entourer, encadrer.
(b) France ~s Germany la France touche à l'Allemagne, la France et l'Allemagne ont une frontière commune; **~ing countries** pays avoisinants *or* limitrophes.

border (up)on *vt fus* **(a)** *[esp country]* être limitrophe de, avoisiner. **the two countries border (up)on one another** les deux pays ont une frontière commune *or* se touchent; **his estate borders (up)on mine** sa propriété et la mienne se touchent.
(b) (*fig: come near to being*) être voisin *or* proche de, frôler. **to border (up)on insanity** être voisin de *or* frôler la folie; **it borders (up)on fanaticism** cela touche au fanatisme, cela frise le fanatisme; **with a boldness bordering (up)on insolence** avec une hardiesse qui frisait l'insolence.

borderer ['bɔːdərəʳ] *n* frontalier *m*, -ière *f*; (*Brit*) Écossais(e) *m(f)* *or* Anglais(e) *m(f)* frontalier (*f* -ière).

borderline ['bɔːdəlaɪn] **1** *n [states, districts]* frontière *f*; (*fig*) *[categories, classes]* ligne *f* de démarcation. **2** *cpd* (*lit*) *territory* frontalier, limitrophe. **borderline case** cas *m* limite.

bore[1] [bɔːʳ] **1** *vt* **(a)** *hole* percer; *well* forer, creuser; *tunnel* creuser, percer.
(b) *rock* forer. **to ~ one's way through** se frayer un chemin en creusant *or* en forant à travers.
2 *vi* forer, sonder. **to ~ for oil** forer (le sous-sol) pour extraire du pétrole, rechercher du pétrole par sondage *or* forage.
3 *n* **(a)** (*also* **~hole**) trou *m* de sonde.
(b) *[tube, pipe, shot, gun, cannon]* calibre *m*. **a 12-~ shotgun** un fusil de (calibre) 12.

bore[2] [bɔːʳ] **1** *n* (*person*) raseur* *m*, -euse* *f*, casse-pieds* *mf inv*, importun(e) *m(f)*; (*event, situation*) ennui *m*, corvée *f*, scie* *f*. **what a ~ he is!** ce qu'il peut être ennuyeux! *or* raseur!* *or* casse-pieds!*; **it's a frightful ~ to have to do that** quel ennui *or* quelle barbe* *or* quelle scie* d'avoir à faire cela; **what a ~ this meeting is!** quelle corvée cette réunion!
2 *vt* ennuyer, assommer, raser*, casser les pieds* à. **to ~ sb stiff** *or* **to death** *or* **to tears, to ~ the pants off sb:** ennuyer qn à mourir *or* mortellement; **to be ~d stiff** *or* **to death** *or* **to tears** s'ennuyer ferme *or* à mourir, se casser les pieds*; **to be ~d (with doing)** s'ennuyer (à faire); **I am ~d with this work/this book/this film** ce travail/ce livre/ce film m'ennuie *or* m'assomme *or* me rase*; **he was ~d with reading** il en avait assez de lire.

bore[3] [bɔːʳ] *pret of* **bear**[1].

bore[4] [bɔːʳ] *n* (*tidal wave*) mascaret *m*.

boredom ['bɔːdəm] *n* ennui *m*. **his ~ with the whole proceedings** l'ennui que lui inspirait toute cette cérémonie.

borer ['bɔːrəʳ] *n* **(a)** (*Tech: tool*) (*for wood*) vrille *f*, perforatrice *f*, foret *m*; (*for metal cylinders*) alésoir *m*; (*for a well, mine*) foret, sonde *f*; (*person*) foreur *m*, perceur *m*. **(b)** (*Zool: insect*) insecte térébrant.

boric ['bɔːrɪk] *adj* borique.

boring[1] ['bɔːrɪŋ] (*Tech*) **1** *n* (*V* **borer a**) perforation *f*, forage *m*; alésage *m*; sondage *m*. **2** *adj*: **~ machine** (*gen*) perforatrice *f*; (*for metal cylinders*) alésoir *m*.

boring[2] ['bɔːrɪŋ] *adj* (*tedious*) ennuyeux, assommant, rasant*.

born [bɔːn] **1** *ptp of* **bear**[1]**1j.**
2 *adj* **(a)** né. **to be ~** naître; **to be ~ again** renaître; **~ in Paris**

né à Paris; **the town where he was ~** la ville où il est né, sa ville natale; **Napoleon was ~ in 1769** Napoléon naquit en 1769; **3 sons ~ to her** 3 fils nés d'elle; **every baby ~ into the world** tout enfant qui vient au monde; **when he was ~** quand il est né; **~ and bred** né et élevé; **a Parisian ~ and bred** un vrai Parisien de Paris; (*fig*) **he wasn't ~ yesterday‡** il n'est pas né d'hier *or* de la dernière pluie, il n'est pas tombé de la dernière averse; **in all my ~ days*** de toute ma vie; **high/low~** de haute/de basse extraction; **~ of poor parents** né de parents pauvres; **people ~ to riches** ceux qui naissent riches; **poets are ~, not made** on naît poète, on ne le devient pas; **qualities ~ in him** qualités innées (en lui); (*fig*) **misfortunes ~ of war** malheurs dûs à la guerre; *V* **first, new, silver, still^{2}** *etc.*

(b) (*innate*) **a ~ poet** un poète né; **~ fool** parfait idiot; *V* **loser.**

3 -born *adj ending in cpds* natif de+*n*, originaire de+*n*, d'origine+*adj*. **Chicago-born** natif *or* originaire de Chicago, né à Chicago; **Australian-born** d'origine australienne.

borne [bɔːn] *ptp of* **bear^{1}.**

Borneo ['bɔːnɪəʊ] *n* Bornéo *m.*

borough ['bʌrə] *n* (*also* **municipal ~**) municipalité *f*; (*in London*) arrondissement *m*; (*Brit Parl*) circonscription électorale urbaine.

borrow ['bɒrəʊ] *vt* **(a)** *money, word, book* emprunter (*from* à); (*fig*) *idea etc* emprunter (*from* à), adapter (*from* de). **a ~ed word** un mot d'emprunt; (*US*) **to ~ trouble** voir toujours tout en noir. **(b)**(*Math: in subtraction*) poser.

borrower ['bɒrəʊəʳ] *n* emprunteur *m*, -euse *f.*

borrowing ['bɒrəʊɪŋ] *n* emprunt *m.*

Borstal ['bɔːstl] *n* (*Brit Jur*) maison *f* de redressement. **~ boy** jeune délinquant (*qui est ou a été en maison de redressement*).

borzoi ['bɔːzɔɪ] *n* (lévrier *m*) barzoï *m.*

bosh‡ [bɒʃ] *n* blague(s)* *f(pl)*, bêtises *fpl*, foutaises‡ *fpl.*

bosk [bɒsk] *n*, **bosket** ['bɒskɪt] *n* (*plantation*) bosquet *m*; (*thicket*) fourré *m.*

bos'n ['bəʊsn] *n* = **boatswain.**

bosom ['bʊzəm] *n* [*person*] poitrine *f*, seins *mpl*; [*dress*] corsage *m*; (*fig*) sein, milieu *m*, fond *m*. **in the ~ of the family** au sein de la famille; (*liter*) **the ~ of the earth** les entrailles *fpl* (*liter*) de la terre; **~ friend** ami(e) *m(f)* intime *or* de cœur.

Bosphorus ['bɒsfərəs] *n*: **the ~** le Bosphore.

bosquet ['bɒskɪt] *n* = **bosk.**

boss^{1}* [bɒs] **1** *n* patron(ne) *m(f)*, chef *m*; [*gang etc*] caïd‡ *m*; (*US Pol*) chef (du parti). **it's his wife who is the ~** c'est sa femme qui porte la culotte*. **2** *vt person* mener, régenter; *organization* mener, diriger, faire marcher.

boss about*, boss around* *vt sep person* mener à la baguette, régenter.

boss^{2} [bɒs] **1** *n* (*knob*) [*shield*] ombon *m*; (*Archit*) bossage *m*; (*Tech*) mamelon *m*, bossage; [*propeller*] moyeu *m*. **2** *cpd*: **to be boss-eyed*** loucher.

bossy* ['bɒsɪ] *adj* autoritaire, tyrannique. **she's very ~** elle aime mener tout le monde à la baguette, c'est un vrai gendarme*.

Boston ['bɒstən] *n* Boston. (*US*) **~ ivy** vigne *f* vierge.

bosun ['bəʊsn] *n* = **boatswain.**

botanic(al) [bə'tænɪk(əl)] *adj* botanique. **~ garden** jardin *m* botanique.

botanist ['bɒtənɪst] *n* botaniste *mf.*

botanize ['bɒtənaɪz] *vi* herboriser.

botany ['bɒtənɪ] *n* (*U*) botanique *f.*

botch [bɒtʃ] **1** *vt* (*also* **~ up**) (*repair*) rafistoler*; (*bungle*) saboter, bousiller*, cochonner‡.

2 *n*: **to make a ~ of sth** bousiller* *or* saboter qch.

both [bəʊθ] **1** *adj* les deux, l'un(e) et l'autre. **~ books are his** les deux livres sont à lui, les livres sont à lui tous les deux; **on ~ sides** des deux côtés, de part et d'autre; **to hold sth in ~ hands** tenir qch à *or* des deux mains; (*fig*) **you can't have it ~ ways*** il faut choisir.

2 *pron* tous (les) deux *m*, toutes (les) deux *f*, l'un(e) et l'autre *m(f)*. **~ (of them) were there, they were ~ there** ils étaient là tous les deux; **~ of us** nous deux; **~ of us agree** nous sommes d'accord tous les deux; **~ alike** l'un comme l'autre.

3 *adv*: **~ this and that** non seulement ceci mais aussi cela, aussi bien ceci que cela; **~ you and I saw him** nous l'avons vu vous et moi, vous et moi (nous) l'avons vu; **~ Paul and I came** Paul et moi sommes venus tous les deux; **she was ~ laughing and crying** elle riait et pleurait à la fois.

bother ['bɒðəʳ] **1** *vt* (*annoy*) ennuyer, raser*, embêter*; (*pester*) harceler; (*worry*) inquiéter, ennuyer. **don't ~ me!** laisse-moi tranquille!, fiche-moi la paix!*, ne viens pas m'embêter!*; **don't ~ him with your problems** ne l'embête pas* *or* ne l'ennuie pas avec tes problèmes; **I'm sorry to ~ you** je m'excuse de vous déranger; **does it ~ you if I smoke?** ça vous ennuie *or* dérange que je fume? (*subj*) *or* si je fume?; **to ~ o.s.** *or* **one's head about sth** se tracasser au sujet de qch, se mettre martel en tête au sujet de qch; **to get (all hot and) ~ed*** se mettre dans tous ses états (*about* au sujet de); **I can't be ~ed going out** *or* **to go out** je n'ai pas le courage de sortir; **are you going? — I can't be ~ed** tu y vas? — non, je n'en ai pas envie *or* non, ça me casse les pieds*; **his leg ~s him a lot** sa jambe le fait pas mal souffrir.

2 *vi* se donner la peine (*to do* de faire). **please don't ~ to get up!** ne vous donnez pas la peine de vous lever!; **you needn't ~ to come** ce n'est pas la peine de venir; **don't ~ about me/about my lunch** ne vous occupez pas de moi/de mon déjeuner, ne vous tracassez pas pour moi/pour mon déjeuner; **I'll do it — please don't ~** je vais le faire — non ce n'est pas la peine *or* ne vous donnez pas cette peine.

3 *n* **(a)** ennui *m*, barbe* *f*, scie* *f*. **what a ~ it all is!** quel ennui *or* quelle barbe* que tout cela!

(b) (*U*) ennui *m*, embêtement* *m*. **she's having** *or* **in a spot of ~** elle a des ennuis *or* des embêtements* en ce moment; **we had a spot** *or* **bit of ~ with the car** on a eu un petit embêtement* avec la voiture.

4 *excl* (*: *esp Brit*) zut!*, flûte!*, la barbe!* **~ that child!** quelle barbe ce gosse!*

botheration* [ˌbɒðə'reɪʃən] *excl* zut!*, flûte!*, la barbe!*

bothersome ['bɒðəsəm] *adj* ennuyeux, gênant.

Botswana [ˌbɒts'wɑːnə] *n* Botswana *m.*

bottle ['bɒtl] **1** *n* (*container, contents*) bouteille *f*; (*perfume ~*) flacon *m*; (*medicine ~*) flacon, fiole *f*; (*wide-mouthed*) bocal *m*; (*goatskin*) outre *f*; (*of stone*) cruche *f*, cruchon *m*; (*for beer*) canette *f*; (*baby ~*) biberon *m*. **wine ~** bouteille à vin; **to drink a ~ of wine** boire une bouteille de vin; **we'll discuss it over a ~** nous en discuterons en prenant un verre; **he is too fond of the ~*** il aime trop la bouteille*; **to take to the ~*** se mettre à boire *or* picoler‡; **her husband's on the ~‡** son mari lève le coude*; **child brought up on the ~** enfant élevé *or* nourri au biberon; *V* **hot, ink** *etc.*

2 *cpd*: **bottlebrush** rince-bouteilles *m inv*; **bottle-fed** nourri au biberon; **bottle glass** verre *m* à bouteilles; **bottle-green** vert (*m*) bouteille *inv*; **bottleneck** (*lit*) goulot *m*; (*fig*) [*road*] rétrécissement *m* de la chaussée; [*traffic*] embouteillage *m*, bouchon *m*; [*production etc*] goulet *m* d'étranglement; **bottle-opener** décapsuleur *m*, ouvre-bouteille(s) *m*; **bottle party** surprise-party *f* (*où chacun apporte une bouteille*); **bottle rack** porte-bouteilles *m inv*, casier *m* à bouteilles; **bottlewasher** laveur *m*, -euse *f* de bouteilles, plongeur *m*, -euse *f* (*V* **cook**).

3 *vt wine* mettre en bouteille(s); *fruit* mettre en bocal *or* en conserve. **~d beer** bière *f* en canette; **~d wine** vin *m* en bouteille(s); **~d fruit** fruits *mpl* en bocal *or* en conserve.

bottle up *vt sep* (*fig*) *feelings etc* contenir, ravaler, refouler.

bottom ['bɒtəm] **1** *n* [*box, glass, well*] fond *m*; [*dress, heap, page*] bas *m*; [*tree, hill*] pied *m*; [*sea, lake, river*] fond; [*garden*] fond, bas; [*chair*] siège *m*, fond; [*ship*] carène *f*; (*buttocks*) derrière *m*, postérieur* *m*; (*fig: origin, foundation*) base *f*, origine *f*, fondement *m*. **at the ~ of page 10** en *or* au bas de la page 10; **at the ~ of the hill** au pied *or* au bas de la colline; **the name at the ~ of the list** le nom en bas de la liste; (*fig*) **he's at the ~ of the list** il est en queue de liste; **to be (at the) ~ of the class** être le dernier de la classe; **~s up!‡** cul sec!; **from the ~ of my heart** du fond de mon cœur; **at ~** au fond; **to knock the ~ out of an argument** démolir un argument; **the ~ fell out of his world*** son monde s'est effondré *or* a basculé (sous ses pieds); **at the ~ of the table** en bout de table, au bout de la table; **the ship went to the ~** le navire a coulé; **the ship touched the ~** le navire a touché le fond; **the ship was floating ~ up** le navire flottait la quille en l'air; **to be at the ~ of sth** être à l'origine de qch; **to get to the ~ of a mystery** aller jusqu'au fond d'un mystère; **we can't get to the ~ of it** impossible de découvrir le fin fond de cette histoire *or* affaire.

2 *cpd shelf* du bas, inférieur; *part of garden etc* du fond. **bottom dollar** dernier dollar (*V* **bet**); (*Brit*) **to put sth away in one's bottom drawer** mettre qch de côté pour son trousseau; [*building*] **bottom floor** rez-de-chaussée *m*; (*Aut*) **bottom gear** première *f* (vitesse); **bottom half** [*box*] partie inférieure; [*class, list*] deuxième moitié *f*; (*US*) **bottom lands** plaine alluviale; **bottommost** le plus bas; (*Comm, Fin*) **bottom price** prix le plus bas; **bottom step** première marche; *V* **rock-bottom.**

bottomless ['bɒtəmlɪs] *adj pit, well* sans fond, insondable; *mystery* insondable; *supply* inépuisable.

botulism ['bɒtjʊlɪzəm] *n* botulisme *m.*

bouclé [buː'kleɪ] **1** *n* (laine *f or* tissu *m*) bouclette *f*. **2** *adj* en laine *or* en tissu bouclette.

boudoir ['buːdwɑːʳ] *n* boudoir *m.*

bougainvillaea [ˌbuːgən'vɪlɪə] *n* bougainvillée *f*, bougainvillier *m.*

bough [baʊ] *n* (*liter*) rameau *m*, branche *f.*

bought [bɔːt] *pret, ptp of* **buy.**

bouillon ['buːjɔ̃ːŋ] *n* bouillon *m*, consommé *m*. **~ cube** bouillon cube *m.*

boulder ['bəʊldəʳ] *n* rocher *m* (rond), grosse pierre; (*smaller*) (gros) galet *m*. (*Geol*) **~ clay** dépôt *m* (argileux) erratique.

boulevard ['buːləvɑːʳ] *n* boulevard *m.*

bounce [baʊns] **1** *vi* **(a)** [*ball*] rebondir; [*person*] bondir, sauter, se précipiter (*into* dans, *out of* hors de). **to ~ in/out** *etc* entrer/sortir *etc* d'un bond; **the child ~d up and down on the bed** l'enfant faisait des bonds sur le lit; **the car ~d along the bad road** la voiture faisait des bonds sur la route défoncée; **the ball ~d down the stairs** la balle a rebondi de marche en marche.

(b) (*) [*cheque*] être sans provision, être refusé pour non-provision.

2 *vt* **(a)** *ball* faire rebondir.

(b) (‡: *eject*) vider‡, flanquer* à la porte.

(c) (*) *cheque* refuser.

3 *n* **(a)** (*rebound*) [*ball*] bond *m*, rebond *m.*

(b) (*U*) **this ball hasn't much ~ left** cette balle ne rebondit plus beaucoup; (*fig*) **he's got plenty of ~*** il a beaucoup d'allant, il est très dynamique.

bouncer‡ ['baʊnsəʳ] *n* (*at pub, dance hall etc*) videur‡ *m.*

bouncing ['baʊnsɪŋ] *adj* rebondi, dodu, potelé. **~ baby** beau bébé (florissant de santé).

bouncy ['baʊnsɪ] *adj ball, mattress* élastique; *hair* vigoureux; *person* dynamique, plein d'allant.

bound^{1} [baʊnd] **1** *n* (*lit, fig*) **~s** limite(s) *f(pl)*, bornes *fpl*; **his ambition knows no ~s** son ambition est sans bornes; **to keep within ~s** (*fig*) rester dans la juste mesure, user de modération; (*lit*) rester dans les limites; **within the ~s of probability** dans les limites du probable; **within the ~s of possibility** dans la

limite du possible; out of ~s *place etc* dont l'accès est interdit; (*Sport*) hors du terrain, sorti; *V* **break.**
2 *vt* (*gen pass*) *country* borner. ~ed by borné *or* limité par.

bound[2] [baʊnd] **1** *n* bond *m*, saut *m*. at a ~ d'un saut, d'un bond; *V* **leap.**
2 *vi* [*person*] bondir, sauter; [*horse*] bondir, faire un bond *or* des bonds. to ~ in/away/back *etc* entrer/partir/revenir *etc* en bondissant *or* d'un bond; the horse ~ed over the fence le cheval sauta la barrière (d'un bond).

bound[3] [baʊnd] **1** *pret, ptp of* **bind.**
2 *adj* (a) lié, attaché; *V* **earth, ice, spell**[1] *etc.*
(b) *book* relié. ~ in boards cartonné.
(c) (*fig*) (*obliged*) obligé, tenu; (*sure*) sûr, certain. you are not ~ to do it vous n'êtes pas obligé de le faire; I am ~ to confess je suis forcé d'avouer; you're ~ to do it (*obliged to*) vous êtes tenu *or* obligé de le faire; (*sure to*) vous le ferez sûrement; he's ~ to say so (*obliged to*) il est de son devoir de le dire, il doit le dire; (*sure to*) il le dira sûrement, il ne manquera pas de le dire; it is ~ to rain il va sûrement pleuvoir, il ne peut pas manquer de pleuvoir; it was ~ to happen cela devait arriver, c'était à prévoir; *V* **duty, honour** *etc.*
(d) (*destined*) ~ for *person* en route pour; *parcel* à destination de; *train* en direction de, à destination de; *ship, plane* à destination de, en route pour, (*about to leave*) en partance pour; where are you ~ for? où allez-vous?

-bound [baʊnd] *adj ending in cpds*: Australia-bound à destination de l'Australie; *V* **north, outward** *etc.*

boundary ['baʊndərɪ] **1** *n* limite *f*, frontière *f*. (*Cricket*) to score a ~ envoyer une balle jusqu'aux limites du terrain.
2 *cpd*: boundary (line) ligne *f* frontière *inv or* de démarcation; (*Sport*) limites *fpl* du terrain; boundary-stone borne *f*, pierre *f* de bornage.

bounden ['baʊndən] *adj*: ~ duty devoir impérieux.

bounder* ['baʊndə'] *n* (*esp Brit*) butor *m*, goujat *m*.

boundless ['baʊndlɪs] *adj space* infini; *trust* illimité; *ambition, devotion* sans bornes.

bounteous ['baʊntɪəs] *adj*, **bountiful** ['baʊntɪfʊl] *adj harvest* abondant; *rain* bienfaisant; *person* généreux, libéral, prodigue; *V* **lady.**

bounty ['baʊntɪ] *n* (a) (*U: generosity*) générosité *f*, libéralité *f*. (b) (*gift*) don *m*; (*Comm, Mil*) prime *f*.

bouquet ['bʊkeɪ] *n* (a) [*flowers*] bouquet *m*. (*Culin*) ~ garni bouquet garni. (b) [*wine*] bouquet *m*.

Bourbon ['bʊəbən] *n* (a) (*Hist*) Bourbon. (b) ['bɜːbən] (*US*) b~ (whisky) bourbon *m*.

bourgeois ['bʊəʒwɑː] *adj, n* bourgeois(e) *m(f)*.

bourgeoisie [ˌbʊəʒwɑː'ziː] *n* bourgeoisie *f*.

bout [baʊt] *n* (a) (*period*) période *f*; [*malaria etc*] attaque *f*, accès *m*. ~ of rheumatism crise *f* de rhumatisme; ~ of fever accès de fièvre; a ~ of bronchitis une bronchite; a ~ of flu une grippe; he's had several ~s of illness il a été malade plusieurs fois; a ~ of work(ing) une période de travail intensif; drinking ~ beuverie *f*.
(b) (*Boxing, Wrestling*) combat *m*; (*Fencing*) assaut *m*.

boutique [buː'tiːk] *n* boutique *f* (*de mode ou d'objets 'dans le vent'*).

bovine ['bəʊvaɪn] *adj* (*lit, fig*) bovin.

bow[1] [bəʊ] **1** *n* (a) (*weapon etc*) arc *m*. to draw the ~ tirer à l'arc; *V* **cross, long**[1], **string** *etc.*
(b) (*Mus*) archet *m*.
(c) (*curve*) [*rainbow etc*] arc *m*; *V* **saddle.**
(d) (*knot*) [*ribbon etc*] nœud *m*.
2 *vi* (*Mus*) manier l'archet.
3 *cpd*: bow compass compas *m* à balustre; bow-legged aux jambes arquées; bowlegs jambes arquées; (*Archery*) bowman archer *m*; (*Archery, Mus*) bowstring corde *f*; bow tie nœud *m* papillon; bow window fenêtre *f* en saillie, bow-window *m*.

bow[2] [baʊ] **1** *n* (*with head*) salut *m*; (*with body*) révérence *f*. to make a (deep) ~ saluer (bas); to give sb a gracious ~ adresser un gracieux salut à qn; (*fig*) to make one's ~ (as a pianist *etc*) faire ses débuts (de pianiste *etc*); to take a ~ saluer.
2 *vi* (a) (*in greeting*) saluer, incliner la tête. to ~ to sb saluer qn; to ~ and scrape faire des courbettes; ~ing and scraping salamalecs *mpl*, courbettes *fpl*.
(b) (*bend*) [*branch etc*] ployer, fléchir, se courber; [*person*] se courber.
(c) (*fig: submit*) s'incliner (*before, to* devant, *under* sous), se soumettre (*before, to* à, *under* sous). to ~ before the storm laisser passer l'orage; we must ~ to your greater knowledge nous devons nous incliner devant vos très grandes connaissances; to ~ to sb's opinion se soumettre à l'opinion de qn; to ~ to the inevitable s'incliner devant les faits *or* devant l'inévitable; to ~ to the majority s'incliner devant la majorité.
3 *vt* courber. to ~ one's back courber le dos; to ~ one's knee fléchir le genou; to ~ one's head pencher *or* courber la tête; his head was ~ed in thought il méditait la tête penchée; to ~ one's consent signifier son consentement par une inclination de tête; to ~ sb in/out faire entrer/faire sortir qn en saluant; to ~ o.s. out saluer pour prendre congé.

bow down 1 *vi* (*lit, fig*) s'incliner (*to sb* devant qn).
2 *vt sep* (*lit*) faire plier, courber; (*fig*) écraser, briser.

bow out *vi* (*fig*) tirer sa révérence (*fig*); *V also* **bow**[2] **3.**

bow[3] [baʊ] **1** *n* (a) (*often pl*) [*ship*] avant *m*, proue *f*. in the ~s à l'avant, en proue; on the port ~ par bâbord devant; on the starboard ~ par tribord devant. (b) (*oarsman*) nageur *m* de l'avant. **2** *cpd*: bowsprit beaupré *m*.

Bow bells ['bəʊ'belz] *npl* les cloches *fpl* de l'église de St-Mary-le-Bow (*à Londres*). born within the sound of ~ né en plein cœur de Londres.

bowdlerize ['baʊdləraɪz] *vt book* expurger.

bowel ['baʊəl] *n* (*Anat: gen pl*) [*person*] intestin(s) *m(pl)*; [*animal*] boyau(x) *m(pl)*, intestin(s). (*fig*) ~s entrailles *fpl*; ~s of the earth entrailles de la terre; (*liter*) ~s of compassion tendresse *f*, pitié *f*.

bower ['baʊə'] *n* (*arbour*) berceau *m* de verdure, tonnelle *f*, retraite ombragée; (††, *liter: cottage*) chaumière *f*, petite maison (à la campagne); [*lady*] boudoir *m*.

bowing[1] ['bəʊɪŋ] *n* (*Mus*) maniement *m* de l'archet, coup *m* d'archet. his ~ was sensitive il avait un coup d'archet délicat; to mark the ~ indiquer *or* introduire les coups d'archet.

bowing[2] ['baʊɪŋ] *n V* **bow**[2] **2a.**

bowl[1] [bəʊl] *n* (a) (*container*) bol *m*, jatte *f*; (*for water*) cuvette *f*; (*of crystal*) coupe *f*; [*beggar*] sébile *f*. a ~ of milk un bol de lait; a ~ of water une cuvette d'eau; a ~ of punch un bol *or* un saladier de punch; *V* **finger, salad, sugar** *etc.*
(b) [*wineglass*] coupe *f*; [*pipe*] fourneau *m*; [*spoon*] creux *m*; [*lamp*] globe *m*; [*lavatory, sink*] cuvette *f*.
(c) (*Geog*) bassin *m*, cuvette *f*.

bowl[2] [bəʊl] **1** *n* (*Sport*) boule *f*. (game of) ~s (*Brit*) (jeu *m* de) boules; (*in Provence*) pétanque *f*, boules; (*US: skittles*) bowling *m*.
2 *vi* (a) (*Brit*) jouer aux boules; (*US*) jouer au bowling; (*Provence*) jouer à la pétanque; (*Cricket*) lancer (la balle) (*to* à).
(b) [*person, car*] to ~ down the street descendre la rue à bonne allure; [*car*] to ~ along, to go ~ing along rouler bon train.
3 *vt* (a) (*roll*) *bowl, ball* lancer, faire rouler; *hoop* faire rouler.
(b) (*Cricket*) *ball* servir; *batsman* (*also* ~ out) mettre hors jeu.

bowl down* *vt sep* renverser.

bowl over *vt sep* (a) *ninepins* renverser, faire tomber.
(b) (*fig*) stupéfier, renverser, sidérer*. to be bowled over (by) (*surprise*) rester stupéfait *or* abasourdi *or* sidéré* (devant); (*emotion*) être bouleversé (par).

bowler[1] ['bəʊlə'] *n* (*Brit*) joueur *m*, -euse *f* de boules; (*US*) joueur de bowling; (*Provence*) joueur de pétanque, bouliste *mf*, pétanquiste *mf*; (*Cricket*) lanceur *m*, -euse *f* (de la balle).

bowler[2] ['bəʊlə'] *n* (*Brit: also* ~ hat) (chapeau *m*) melon *m*.

bowline ['bəʊlɪn] *n* (*knot*) nœud *m* de chaise; (*rope*) bouline *f*.

bowling ['bəʊlɪŋ] **1** *n* (*Brit*) jeu *m* de boules; (*US*) bowling *m*; (*Provence*) pétanque *f*.
2 *cpd*: bowling alley bowling *m*; bowling green terrain *m* de boules (*sur gazon*); bowling match (*Brit*) concours *m* de boules; (*US*) concours de bowling; (*Provence*) concours de pétanque.

bow-wow ['baʊwaʊ] (*baby talk*) **1** *n* toutou *m*. **2** ['baʊ'waʊ] *excl* oua, oua!

box[1] [bɒks] **1** *n* (a) boîte *f*; (*large*) caisse *f*; (*cardboard* ~) (boîte en) carton *m*; (*casket*) coffret *m*; (†: *trunk*) malle *f*. a ~ of matches/chocolates une boîte d'allumettes/de chocolats; (*Brit: television*) (on) the ~* (à) la télé*; *V* **ice, letter, tool** *etc.*
(b) [*money*] caisse *f*; (*Rel*) tronc *m*; [*child*] tirelire *f*; *V* **strong** *etc.*
(c) (*Aut, Tech*) [*axle, steering*] carter *m*; *V* **axle, gear** *etc.*
(d) (*Theat*) loge *f*; [*coachman*] siège *m* (du cocher); (*Jur*) [*jury, press*] banc *m*; [*witness*] barre *f*; [*stable*] stalle *f*, box *m*; *V* **horse, sentry, signal** *etc.*
(e) (*Brit: road junction*) zone *f* (de carrefour) d'accès réglementé.
2 *cpd*: boxboard carton compact; box calf box(-calf) *m*; box camera appareil *m* (photographique) petit format; (*Rail*) boxcar wagon *m* (de marchandises) couvert; (*Constr*) box girder poutre-caisson *f*; (*Brit*) box junction = **box**[1] **1e**; (*Post*) box-number boîte postale; box office *V* **box office**; (*Sewing*) box pleat pli creux; (*Brit*) box room (cabinet *m* de) débarras *m*; (*US*) box stall box *m*.
3 *vt* (a) mettre en boîte *or* en caisse *etc.*
(b) (*Naut*) to ~ the compass réciter les aires du vent.

box in *vt sep bath, sink* encastrer. (*fig*) to feel boxed in se sentir confiné *or* à l'étroit.

box off *vt sep* compartimenter.

box up *vt sep* mettre en boîte; (*fig*) enfermer.

box[2] [bɒks] **1** *vi* (*Sport*) boxer, faire de la boxe. **2** *vt* (a) (*Sport*) boxer avec, boxer*. (b) to ~ sb's ears gifler *or* claquer qn, flanquer* une claque *or* une gifle à qn. **3** *n*: a ~ on the ear une claque, une gifle.

box[3] [bɒks] **1** *n* (*Bot*) buis *m*. **2** *cpd* en *or* de buis. boxwood buis *m*.

boxer[1] ['bɒksə'] *n* (*Sport*) boxeur *m*. ~ shorts boxer-short *m*.

boxer[2] ['bɒksə'] *n* (*dog*) boxer *m*.

boxing ['bɒksɪŋ] **1** *n* boxe *f*. **2** *cpd*: boxing gloves/match gants *mpl*/match *m* de boxe; boxing ring ring *m*.

Boxing Day ['bɒksɪŋdeɪ] *n* (*Brit*) le lendemain de Noël.

box office ['bɒksɒfɪs] (*Theat*) **1** *n* (*office*) bureau *m* de location; (*window*) guichet *m* (de location). this show will be good ~ ce spectacle fera recette.
2 *cpd*: box-office attraction spectacle *m* à (grand) succès; box-office receipts recette *f*; box-office success pièce *f etc* qui fait courir les foules *or* qui fait recette.

boy [bɔɪ] **1** *n* (a) (*child*) garçon *m*, enfant *m*; (*young man*) jeune *m* (homme *m*), garçon; (*son*) fils *m*, garçon; (*Scol*) élève *m*, garçon. little ~ petit garçon, garçonnet *m*; beggar ~ petit mendiant; English ~ jeune Anglais; come here, my ~ viens ici mon petit *or* mon grand; bad ~!, naughty ~! vilain!; the Jones ~ le petit Jones; I lived here as a ~ j'habitais ici quand j'étais petit *or* enfant; he knew me from a ~ il me connaissait depuis mon (*or* son) enfance, il me connaissait depuis tout petit; ~s will be ~s! les garçons, on ne les changera jamais!; he was as much a ~ as ever il était toujours aussi gamin; (*Brit Scol*) an old ~ un ancien élève; (*Scol*) sit down, ~s (*to small boys*) asseyez-vous

mes enfants; (*to sixth formers etc*) asseyez-vous messieurs *or* mes amis; *V* **choir, day, page**[2] *etc.*
(b) (*: *fellow*) **my dear ~** mon cher (ami); **old ~** mon vieux; **the old ~** (*boss*) le patron; (*father*) le paternel*; **a night out with the ~s** une sortie avec les copains; *V* **wide.**
(c) (*native servant*) boy *m.*
2 *cpd*: **boyfriend** petit ami; **boy scout**† (*Catholic*) scout *m*; (*non-Catholic*) éclaireur *m*; **boy soprano** soprano *m.*
3 *excl* (*) bigre!*
boycott ['bɔɪkɒt] **1** *vt person, product, place* boycotter. **2** *n* boycottage *m.*
boyhood ['bɔɪhʊd] *n* enfance *f*, adolescence *f.*
boyish ['bɔɪɪʃ] *adj behaviour* d'enfant, de garçon; *smile* gamin; (*pej*) enfantin, puéril; (*tomboyish*) *girl* garçonnier; *behaviour* garçonnier, de garçon. **he looks very ~** il fait très gamin.
bra [brɑː] *n* (*abbr of* **brassière**) soutien-gorge *m.*
brace [breɪs] **1** *n* **(a)** attache *f*, agrafe *f*; (*Med*) appareil *m* orthopédique; (*dental*) appareil (dentaire); (*Constr*) entretoise *f*, étrésillon *m.* (*Brit Dress*) **~s** bretelles *fpl*; (*Tech*) **~ (and bit)** vilebrequin *m* (*à main*).
(b) (*pl inv: pair*) *[animals, pistols]* paire *f.*
(c) (*Mus, Typ: also* **~ bracket**) accolade *f.*
2 *vt* **(a)** (*support, strengthen*) attacher, lier; (*prop up*) soutenir, consolider, étayer; *structure* entretoiser, étrésillonner; *beam* armer (*with* de), soutenir.
(b) to ~ o.s. (*lit*) s'arc-bouter; (*fig*) se préparer mentalement (*to do* à faire), fortifier son âme (*to do* pour faire); **~ yourself for the news!** tenez-vous bien que je vous raconte la nouvelle *or* que je vous en dise une bien bonne*.
(c) *[climate etc]* fortifier, tonifier.
brace up *vt sep person* retremper, revigorer, remonter. **to brace o.s. up** rassembler ses forces (*to do* pour faire); (*by having a drink*) reprendre des forces (*hum*); (*excl*) **brace up!** du courage!
bracelet ['breɪslɪt] *n* **(a)** bracelet *m.* **(b)** (*handcuffs*) **~s‡** menottes *fpl*, bracelets *mpl* (*hum*).
bracer‡ ['breɪsəʳ] *n* (*drink*) remontant *m.*
bracing ['breɪsɪŋ] *adj air, climate* fortifiant, tonifiant. **a ~ wind** un vent vivifiant.
bracken ['brækən] *n* (*U*) fougère *f.*
bracket ['brækɪt] **1** *n* **(a)** (*angled support*) support *m*; *[shelf]* tasseau *m*, gousset *m*, potence *f*; (*Archit*) support, console *f*, corbeau *m.*
(b) *[lamp]* fixation *f.* **~ lamp** applique *f.*
(c) (*small shelf*) rayon *m*, étagère *f.*
(d) (*Typ*) (*round*) parenthèse *f*; (*square*) crochet *m*; (*Mus, Typ: also* **brace ~**) accolade *f.* **in ~s** entre parenthèses.
(e) (*fig: group*) classe *f*, groupe *m*, tranche *f.* **the lower income ~** la tranche des petits revenus; **he's in the £10,000 a year ~** il est dans la tranche (de revenus) des 10.000 livres par an.
2 *vt* **(a)** (*Typ*) mettre entre parenthèses *or* entre crochets; (*Mus*) réunir par une accolade.
(b) (*fig: also* **~ together**) *names, persons* mettre dans le même groupe *or* dans la même catégorie; *candidates etc* mettre ex aequo, accoler. (*Scol, Sport etc*) **~ed first** premiers ex aequo.
(c) (*Mil*) *target* encadrer.
brackish ['brækɪʃ] *adj water, taste* saumâtre.
brad [bræd] *n* semence *f*, clou *m* de tapissier. **~awl** poinçon *m.*
brae [breɪ] *n* (*Scot*) pente *f*, côte *f.*
brag [bræg] **1** *vi* se vanter, se glorifier, se targuer (*about, of* de, *about or of doing* de faire).
2 *vt*: **to ~ that one has done sth** se vanter d'avoir fait qch.
3 *n* **(a)** (*boast*) vanterie *f*, fanfaronnades *fpl.*
(b) = **braggart.**
(c) (*Cards*) *jeu de cartes semblable au poker.*
braggart ['brægət] *n* vantard(e) *m(f)*, fanfaron(ne) *m(f).*
Brahman ['brɑːmən] *n*, **Brahmin** ['brɑːmɪn] *n* brahmane *m.*
braid [breɪd] **1** *vt* **(a)** (*plait*) tresser, natter; (*interweave*) entrelacer (*with* avec).
(b) (*trim with ~*) *clothing, material* soutacher, galonner, passementer.
2 *n* **(a)** (*plait of hair*) tresse *f*, natte *f.*
(b) (*U: trimming*) soutache *f*, ganse *f*, galon *m*; (*Mil*) galon. **gold ~** galon d'or *or* doré.
Braille [breɪl] **1** *n* braille *m.* **2** *adj* braille *inv.*
brain [breɪn] **1** *n* **(a)** (*Anat*) cerveau *m*; (*fig*) cerveau, tête *f.* (*Anat, Culin*) **~s** cervelle *f*; (*fig*) **he's got that on the ~*** il ne pense qu'à ça!, ça le tient!*; (*fig*) **he's got politics on the ~*** il n'a que la politique en tête; **his ~ reeled** la tête lui a tourné; **to blow sb's ~s out** brûler la cervelle à qn; (*Culin*) **calves' ~** cervelle de veau; *V* **pick, rack**[2] *etc.*
(b) (*fig: gen pl: intelligence*) **~s** intelligence *f*; **he's got ~s** il est intelligent; **he's the ~s of the family** c'est le cerveau de la famille.
2 *vt* (‡) *person* assommer.
3 *cpd* (*Med*) *disease, operation* cérébral. **brain-child** idée personnelle, invention personnelle; **it's his brain-child** c'est lui qui l'a inventé; **brain drain** drainage *m* des cerveaux, émigration *f* des chercheurs (européens); **brain fever** fièvre cérébrale; **brain pan** boîte crânienne; **brainstorm** (*Med*) congestion cérébrale; (*Brit fig*) idée géniale; **brainstorming** remue-méninges *m* (*hum*), brain-storming *m*; (*US: advisory experts*) **brain trust** brain-trust *m*; **brainwash** faire un lavage de cerveau à; **he was brainwashed into believing that ...** on a réussi à lui faire croire *or* à lui mettre dans la tête que ...; **brainwashing** *[prisoners etc]* lavage *m* de cerveau; (*) *[the public etc]* bourrage* *m* de crâne; **brainwave** idée géniale, inspiration *f*; **brainwork** travail intellectuel.
brainless ['breɪnlɪs] *adj* sans cervelle, stupide. **to be ~** n'avoir rien dans la tête.
brainy* ['breɪnɪ] *adj* intelligent, doué.
braise [breɪz] *vt* (*Culin*) braiser.
brake[1] [breɪk] *n* (*Bot*) (*bracken*) fougère *f*; (*thicket*) fourré *m.*
brake[2] [breɪk] *n* (*vehicle*) break *m.*
brake[3] [breɪk] **1** *n* (*Aut etc*) frein *m.* **to put on** *or* **apply the ~s** freiner; (*fig*) **to act as a ~ on sb's activities** mettre un frein aux activités de qn; *V* **hand, slam on** *etc.*
2 *vi* freiner.
3 *cpd*: **brake band** ruban *m* de frein; **brake block** sabot *m or* patin *m* de frein; **brake drum** tambour *m* de frein; **brake fluid** liquide *m* pour freins (hydrauliques); **brake horse power** puissance *f* au frein; **brake lever** frein *m* (à main); **brake light** feu *m* rouge (*des freins*), stop *m*; **brake lining** garniture *f* de frein; (*US Rail*) **brakeman** = **brakesman; brake pedal** pédale *f* de frein; **brake shoe** mâchoire *f* de frein; (*Brit Rail*) **brakesman** garde-frein *m*, serre-frein *m*; (*Brit Rail*) **brake-van** fourgon *m* à frein.
braking ['breɪkɪŋ] **1** *n* freinage *m.* **2** *cpd*: **braking distance/power** distance *f*/puissance *f* de freinage.
bramble ['bræmbl] *n* **(a)** (*thorny shrub*) roncier *m*, roncière *f.*
(b) (*blackberry*) (*bush*) ronce *f* des haies, mûrier *m* sauvage; (*berry*) mûre *f* (sauvage).
bran [bræn] *n* son *m* (*de blé*). **~ mash** bran *or* son mouillé; (*Brit*) **~ tub** pêche miraculeuse.
branch [brɑːntʃ] **1** *n* **(a)** *[candelabra, tree]* branche *f*; *[river]* branche, bras *m*; *[mountain chain]* ramification *f*; *[road]* embranchement *m*; *[railway]* bifurcation *f*, raccordement *m*; *[pipe]* branchement *m*; *[family, race]* ramification, branche; (*Ling*) famille *f*; (*fig*) *[subject, science etc]* branche; (*Admin*) division *f*, section *f.* (*Mil*) **he did not belong to their ~ of the service** il n'appartenait pas à leur arme; *V* **olive, root** *etc.*
(b) (*Comm*) *[store, company]* succursale *f*, filiale *f*, branche *f*; (*provincial*) branche régionale; *[bank]* succursale. **main ~** maison *f* mère.
2 *cpd*: (*Comm*) **branch depot** dépôt *m* auxiliaire; (*Rail*) **branch line** ligne *f* secondaire; **branch-office** succursale *f* (locale), agence *f* (*ne se dit pas des magasins*).
3 *vi* **(a)** *[tree]* se ramifier.
(b) *[river, road etc]* bifurquer, se ramifier. **the river ~es at ...** le fleuve se divise en plusieurs bras à ... .
branch off *vi [road]* bifurquer. **the road branches off the main road at ...** la route quitte la grand-route à ... .
branch out *vi [businessman, company]* étendre ses services *or* ses activités. **the firm is branching out into the knitwear business** la compagnie étend la sphère de ses activités à *or* se lance dans la bonneterie.
brand [brænd] **1** *n* **(a)** (*Comm: trademark: also* **~ name**) marque *f* (de fabrique). **that rum is an excellent ~** c'est une excellente marque de rhum, ce rhum est de très bonne marque.
(b) (*mark*) *[cattle, property]* marque *f*; *[prisoner]* flétrissure *f*; (*fig: stigma*) marque, stigmate *m.*
(c) (*also* **~ing-iron**) fer *m* à marquer.
(d) (*burning wood*) tison *m*, brandon *m*, flambeau *m* (*liter*); *V* **fire.**
(e) (*liter*, †: *sword*) glaive *m* (*liter*), épée *f.*
2 *vt* **(a)** (*Comm*) *goods* donner une marque à. **~ed goods** produits *mpl* de marque.
(b) *cattle, property* marquer (au fer rouge). **~ed** marqué (au fer rouge); (*fig*) **to ~ sth on sb's memory** graver qch dans la mémoire de qn.
(c) (*stigmatize*) *person* flétrir, stigmatiser (*with* par).
3 *cpd*: **brand image** image *f* de marque; **branding-iron** fer *m* à marquer; **brand-new** tout neuf (*f* toute neuve), flambant neuf (*f* flambant neuve).
brandish ['brændɪʃ] *vt* brandir.
brandy ['brændɪ] *n* cognac *m*, fine *f* (champagne). **~ and soda** fine à l'eau; **plum ~** eau-de-vie *f* de prune *or* de quetsche; (*Culin*) **~ snap** cornet croquant.
brash [bræʃ] *adj* (*reckless*) impétueux, fougueux; (*impudent*) impertinent, effronté; (*tactless*) indiscret (*f* -ète); *colour* criard.
brass [brɑːs] **1** *n* **(a)** (*U*) cuivre *m* (jaune), laiton *m*, airain *m* (†, *liter*); *V* **bold.**
(b) (*memorial tablet*) plaque commémorative (en cuivre).
(c) (*object/ornament of ~*) objet *m*/ornement *m* en cuivre. **to do/clean the ~(es)** faire/astiquer les cuivres; (*Mus*) **the ~** les cuivres *mpl.*
(d) (‡:*U*) (*impudence*) toupet *m*, culot* *m*; (*Brit: money*) pognon‡ *m.* (*Mil sl*) **the (top) ~** les huiles‡ *fpl.*
2 *cpd ornament etc* en *or* de cuivre. **brass band** fanfare *f*, orchestre *m* de cuivres; **it's not worth a brass farthing*** cela ne vaut pas un clou *or* un pet de lapin‡ (*V* **care**); **brass foundry** fonderie *f* de cuivre; (*Mil sl*) **brass hat** huile‡ *f*; **brass knuckles** coup de poing américain; **he's got a brass neck‡** il a du toupet* *or* du culot*; **brass plate** plaque *f* de cuivre; *[church]* plaque mortuaire *or* commémorative; **brass rubbing** technique *f* de décalque et frottement; **to get down to brass tacks*** en venir aux faits *or* aux choses sérieuses; **brassware** chaudronnerie *f* d'art, dinanderie *f.*
brassie ['brɑːsɪ] *n* (*Golf*) = **brassy 2.**
brassière ['bræsɪəʳ] *n* soutien-gorge *m*; (*strapless*) bustier *m.*
brassy ['brɑːsɪ] **1** *adj colour etc* cuivré; *sound* cuivré, claironnant; (*: *impudent*) *person* culotté*. **2** *n* (*Golf*) brassie *m.*
brat [bræt] *n* (*pej*) moutard‡ *m*, môme* *mf*, gosse* *mf.* **all these ~s** toute cette marmaille*; **one of his ~s** un de ses lardons‡.
bravado [brəˈvɑːdəʊ] *n* bravade *f.*
brave [breɪv] **1** *adj* **(a)** *person* courageux, brave, vaillant; *smile, attempt, action* courageux, brave. **to be as ~ as a lion** être courageux comme un lion, être intrépide; **be ~!** du

courage!; **be ~ and tell her** prends ton courage à deux mains et va lui dire; *V* **face.**
(b) (*liter: fine*) beau (*f* belle), élégant. (*iro*) **it's a ~ new world!** on n'arrête pas le progrès! (*iro*).
2 *n* guerrier indien, brave *m*.
3 *vt death, danger, sb's anger* braver, affronter.
brave out *vt sep*: **to brave it out** faire face à la situation.
bravely [ˈbreɪvlɪ] *adv fight, answer* bravement, courageusement, vaillamment. **the flag was flying ~** le drapeau flottait splendidement.
bravery [ˈbreɪvərɪ] *m* (*U*) courage *m*, vaillance *f*, bravoure *f*.
bravo [ˈbrɑːˈvəʊ] *excl, n, pl* **~es** *or* **~s** bravo (*m*).
bravura [brəˈvʊərə] *n* (*also Mus*) bravoure *f*.
brawl [brɔːl] **1** *vi* se bagarrer*, se quereller. **2** *n* rixe *f*, bagarre *f*. **drunken ~** querelle *f* d'ivrognes.
brawling [ˈbrɔːlɪŋ] **1** *adj* bagarreur*, querelleur. **2** *n* rixe *f*, bagarre *f*.
brawn [brɔːn] *n* **(a)** (*Brit Culin*) fromage *m* de tête. **(b)** (*muscle*) muscle(s) *m(pl)*; (*strength*) muscle. **to have plenty of ~** être bien musclé, avoir du muscle.
brawny [ˈbrɔːnɪ] *adj arm* musculeux, fort; *person* musclé, vigoureux, costaud*.
bray [breɪ] **1** *n [ass]* braiement *m*; *[trumpet]* fanfare *f*, son éclatant. **2** *vi [ass]* braire; *[trumpet]* résonner, éclater.
braze [breɪz] *vt* souder (au laiton).
brazen [ˈbreɪzn] **1** *adj* (*brass*) de cuivre (jaune), de laiton; *sound* cuivré; (*fig: also* **~-faced**) impudent, effronté. **~ lie** mensonge effronté. **2** *vt*: **to ~ it out** payer d'effronterie, crâner*.
brazenly [ˈbreɪznlɪ] *adv* impudemment, effrontément.
brazier[1] [ˈbreɪzɪəʳ] *n [fire]* brasero *m*.
brazier[2] [ˈbreɪzɪəʳ] *n* (*craftsman*) chaudronnier *m*.
Brazil [brəˈzɪl] *n* Brésil *m*. **~ nut** noix *f* du Brésil.
Brazilian [brəˈzɪlɪən] **1** *n* Brésilien(ne) *m(f)*. **2** *adj* brésilien, du Brésil.
breach [briːtʃ] **1** *n* **(a)** (*Jur etc: violation*) infraction *f* (*of* à), manquement *m* (*of* à, aux devoirs de); *[rules, order, discipline]* infraction; *[friendship, good manners]* manquement (*of* à); *[law]* violation *f*. **~ of contract** rupture *f* de contrat; **a ~ of decorum** une inconvenance; **~ of faith** déloyauté *f*; **~ of the peace** attentat *m* à l'ordre public; **~ of promise** violation de promesse de mariage; **action for ~ of promise** ≈ action *f* en dommages-intérêts (*pour promesse de mariage*); **~ of professional secrecy** violation du secret professionnel; **~ of trust** abus *m* de confiance.
(b) (*estrangement*) brouille *f*, mésintelligence *f*.
(c) (*gap*) *[wall etc]* brèche *f*, trou *m*. (*Mil*) **to make a ~ in the enemy's lines** percer les lignes ennemies.
2 *vt wall* ouvrir une brèche dans, faire une trouée dans; (*Mil*) *enemy lines, defences* percer.
bread [bred] **1** *n* **(a)** pain *m*. **loaf of ~** pain, miche *f*; **new ~** pain frais; **~ fresh from the oven** du pain sortant du four; **~ and milk** soupe *f* au lait, panade *f*; **~ and butter** (*lit*) tartine *f* (beurrée *or* de beurre); (*fig*) gagne-pain *m inv*, moyens *mpl* de subsistance, croûte‡ *f*; (*fig*) **writing is his ~ and butter** sa plume est son gagne-pain, il vit de sa plume; **to put sb on (dry) ~ and water** mettre qn au pain (sec) et à l'eau; (*fig*) **he knows which side his ~ is buttered** il sait où est son intérêt; (*fig*) **to throw** *or* **cast one's ~ upon the water(s)** agir de façon désintéressée; (*Rel*) **the ~ and wine** les (deux) espèces *fpl*; (*Rel*) **to break ~** *[congregation]* recevoir la communion; *[priest]* administrer la communion; *V* **brown, dry, ginger** *etc*.
(b) (*food generally, livelihood*) pain *m*. **daily ~** pain quotidien; **to earn one's ~** gagner son pain *or* sa vie *or* sa croûte‡; **to take the ~ out of sb's mouth** retirer à qn le pain de la bouche.
(c) (‡: *money*) fric‡ *m*, oseille‡ *f*.
2 *cpd*: **bread-and-butter letter** lettre *f* de château, lettre de remerciements (*pour hospitalité reçue*); **breadbasket** corbeille *f* à pain; (‡: *stomach*) brioche* *f*, bedaine* *f*; **breadbin** boîte *f* à pain; (*in the country*) huche *f* à pain; **breadboard** planche *f* à pain; (*US*) **breadbox** = **breadbin**; **breadcrumb** miette *f* de pain; (*Culin*) **breadcrumbs** chapelure *f*; **fried in breadcrumbs** pané; **with breadcrumbs** gratiné (*à la chapelure*); **breadfruit** (*tree*) arbre *m* à pain; (*fruit*) fruit *m* de l'arbre à pain; **breadknife** couteau *m* à pain; (*US*) **bread line** *queue f de gens qui attendent pour toucher les bons de pain*; (*Brit*) **to be on the bread line*** être sans le sou *or* dans la purée*; **bread poultice** cataplasme *m* à la mie de pain; **bread sauce** sauce *f* à la mie de pain; **breadwinner** soutien *m* (de famille).
breadth [bretθ] *n* **(a)** (*width*) largeur *f*. **this field is 100 metres in ~** ce champ a 100 mètres de large; **~wise** dans la *or* en largeur; *V* **hairbreadth** *etc*.
(b) (*fig*) *[mind, thought]* largeur *f*; (*style*) ampleur *f*; (*Art*) largeur d'exécution; (*Mus*) jeu *m* large. (*Mus*) **~ of tone** ampleur du son.
break [breɪk] (*vb: pret* **broke,** *ptp* **broken**) **1** *n* **(a)** (*fracture*) (*lit*) cassure *f*, rupture *f*; (*fig*) *[relationship]* rupture, brouille *f*.
(b) (*gap*) *[wall]* trouée *f*, brèche *f*; *[rock]* faille *f*; *[line]* interruption *f*, rupture *f*.
(c) (*interruption, interval*) *[conversation]* interruption *f*, pause *f*; *[journey]* arrêt *m*; (*Brit Scol*) récréation *f*; (*Gram, Typ*) points *mpl* de suspension. **I need a ~** (*few minutes*) il faut que je m'arrête (*subj*) cinq minutes; (*holiday*) j'ai besoin de vacances; (*change*) j'ai besoin de me changer les idées; **to take a ~** s'arrêter cinq minutes; prendre des vacances; se changer les idées; **6 hours without a ~** 6 heures de suite, 6 heures sans discontinuer; (*Rad*) **~ in transmission** interruption (due à un incident technique); (*Elec*) **~ in circuit** rupture *f* de circuit; **a ~ in the clouds** une éclaircie; **a ~ in the weather** un changement de temps; **with a ~ in her voice** d'une voix entrecoupée.
(d) (*liter*) **at ~ of day** au point du jour, à l'aube.
(e) (*: *escape: also* **~out**) évasion *f*, fuite *f*, cavale‡ *f*. **to make a ~ for it** prendre la fuite, s'évader.
(f) (*: *luck, opportunity*) chance *f*, veine *f*. **to have a good/bad ~** avoir une période de veine/de déveine*; **he's had all the ~s** il a eu toutes les veines*; **give me a ~!** donnez-moi ma chance!
(g) (*esp Brit: Billiards*) série *f*.
(h) (*vehicle*) break *m*.
2 *cpd*: **breakaway** (*n*) (*separating*) *[people]* séparation *f*; *[group, movement]* rupture *f*; (*Sport*) échappée *f*; (*Boxing*) dégagement *m*; (*adj*) *group, movement* séparatiste, dissident; (*Pol*) **breakaway state** état dissident; **breakdown** *V* **breakdown**; **break-in** effraction *f*; **at breakneck speed** à une allure folle, à fond de train, à tombeau ouvert; **breakout** évasion *f* (*de prison*); **breakthrough** (*Mil*) percée *f*; *[research etc]* découverte sensationnelle; **break-up** *[ship]* bris *m*; *[ice]* débâcle *f*; *[friendship]* rupture *f*; *[empire]* démembrement *m*; *[political party]* débâcle *f*; **breaking-up** *[school, college]* début *m* des vacances, fin *f* des classes; *[meeting etc]* clôture *f*, levée *f*; **breakwater** brise-lames *m inv*, digue *f*.
3 *vt* **(a)** (*smash, fracture, tear*) *cup, chair* casser, briser; *shoelace* casser; *stick* casser, briser, rompre; *bone* casser, fracturer; *skin* entamer, écorcher. **the child has broken all his toys** l'enfant a cassé *or* brisé *or* démoli tous ses jouets; **to ~ one's neck** se rompre *or* se casser le cou (*V also* **2**); (*fig*) **I'll ~ his neck‡ if I catch him doing that again** si je l'y reprends je lui tords le cou*; **to ~ one's leg** se casser *or* se fracturer la jambe; **the bone is not broken** il n'y a pas de fracture; **his skin is not broken** il ne s'est pas écorché; **to ~ open** *door* enfoncer, forcer; *packet* ouvrir; *lock, safe* fracturer, forcer; (*fig*) **to ~ new** *or* **fresh ground** innover, faire œuvre de pionnier; (*Aviat*) **to ~ the sound barrier** franchir le mur du son; (*Sport etc*) **to ~ a record** battre un record; **to ~ one's back** se casser la colonne vertébrale; **he almost broke his back trying to lift the stone** il s'est donné un tour de reins en essayant de soulever la pierre; (*Brit fig*) **to ~ the back of a task** faire le plus dur *or* le plus gros d'une tâche; **to ~ one's heart over sth** avoir le cœur brisé par qch; **to ~ sb's heart** briser le cœur à *or* de qn; **to ~ the ice** (*lit, also in conversation etc*) briser *or* rompre la glace; (*broach tricky matter*) entamer le sujet (*délicat*); **to ~ surface** *[submarine]* revenir en surface; *[diver]* réapparaître; *V* **bone, bread.**
(b) (*fig: fail to observe*) *promise* manquer à, violer; *treaty* violer; *commandment* désobéir à. (*Mil*) **to ~ bounds** violer la consigne; **to ~ faith with sb** manquer de parole à qn; **to ~ the law** violer la loi; **to ~ parole** (*gen*)manquer à sa parole; (*Jur*) *se rendre coupable d'un délit durant la liberté conditionnelle*; **to ~ the sabbath** violer le sabbat; **to ~ a vow** rompre un serment, transgresser un vœu; **to ~ an appointment with sb** faire faux bond à qn.
(c) (*weaken, vanquish*) *health* abîmer, détériorer; *strike, rebellion* mater, briser; *courage, spirit* abattre, briser; *horse* dresser; (*Mil*) *officer* casser. **to ~ sb** (*morally*) causer la perte de qn; (*financially*) ruiner qn; **this will make or ~ him** (*financially*) cela fera sa fortune ou sa ruine; (*morally*) cela sera son salut ou sa perte; **to ~ sb of a habit** faire perdre une habitude à qn; **to ~ a habit** se débarrasser *or* se défaire d'une habitude; (*Betting*) **to ~ the bank** faire sauter la banque.
(d) (*interrupt*) *silence, spell, fast* rompre; *journey* arrêter, interrompre; (*Elec*) *current, circuit* couper. (*Tennis*) **to ~ sb's service** prendre à qn son service; **to ~ the thread of a story** couper le fil d'un récit.
(e) (*leave*) **to ~ jail** s'évader (de prison); **to ~ cover** *[fox, hare]* débusquer; *[stag]* débucher; *[hunted person]* sortir à découvert; (*Mil*) *[soldiers]* **to ~ ranks** rompre les rangs; **to ~ camp** lever le camp.
(f) (*soften*) *fall, blow* amortir, adoucir. **the wall ~s the force of the wind** le mur coupe le vent.
(g) *news* révéler, annoncer. **try to ~ it to her gently** essayez de le lui annoncer avec ménagements.
(h) (*Naut*) *flag, signal* déferler.
4 *vi* **(a)** (*fracture, fall apart*) (*gen*) (se) casser, se briser; *[stick, rope]* se casser, se rompre; *[bone]* se casser, se fracturer; *[wave]* déferler; *[clouds]* se disperser, se dissiper; *[troops]* rompre les rangs; *[ranks]* se rompre; (*fig*) *[heart]* se briser. (*Med*) **her waters broke** elle a perdu ses eaux.
(b) (*escape*) se libérer (*from* de). **to ~ free** se libérer, se dégager; **to ~ loose** *[person, animal]* s'échapper (*from* de); *[ship]* rompre ses amarres, partir à la dérive.
(c) *[news, story]* éclater, se répandre; *[storm]* éclater, se déchaîner.
(d) (*weaken, change*)*[health]* s'altérer, se détériorer; *[voice]* (*boy's*) muer; (*in emotion*) s'altérer, se briser, s'étrangler (*with* de); *[weather]* se gâter, s'altérer. **the heatwave was ~ing** la vague de chaleur touchait à sa fin; **he broke under torture** il a craqué sous la torture; **his courage** *or* **spirit broke** son courage l'a abandonné.
(e) (*Boxing*) se dégager. (*fig*) **to ~ with a friend** rompre avec un ami.
(f) *[dawn]* poindre; *[day]* se lever, poindre.
(g) (*Fin*) *[person]* faire faillite; *[bank]* sauter. **to ~ even** s'y retrouver.
(h) (*Ling*) *[vowel]* se diphtonguer.
(i) (*Sport*) *[ball]* dévier.
break away 1 *vi* **(a)** *[piece of cliff, railway coach]* se détacher (*from* de); *[boat]* rompre ses amarres, partir à la dérive. **to break away from a group** se détacher d'un groupe; **to break away from routine** sortir de la routine.
(b) (*Ftbl*) s'échapper; (*Racing*) s'échapper, se détacher du peloton.
2 *vt sep* (*lit, fig*) détacher (*from* de).
3 breakaway *adj, n V* **break 2.**

break down 1 *vi* **(a)** (*fail, cease to function*) *[vehicle, machine]* tomber en panne; *[health]* se détériorer; *[argument]* s'effondrer; *[resistance]* céder; *[negotiations, plan]* échouer.
(b) (*weep*) fondre en larmes, éclater en sanglots.
2 *vt sep* **(a)** (*demolish*) mettre en morceaux; (*fig*) *opposition* briser.
(b) (*analyse*) *accounts* détailler; (*Chem*) *substance* décomposer. **he broke down his argument into 3 points** il a décomposé son raisonnement en 3 points.
3 breakdown *n, cpd V* **breakdown.**
break forth *vi* (*liter*) *[light, water]* jaillir; *[storm]* éclater. **to break forth into song** se mettre à chanter, entonner un chant.
break in 1 *vi* **(a)** (*interrupt, intrude*) interrompre. **to break in (up)on sb/sth** interrompre qn/qch.
(b) (*enter illegally*) entrer par effraction.
2 *vt sep* **(a)** *door* enfoncer; *cask* défoncer.
(b) (*tame, train*) *horse* dresser. **it will take you 6 months before you're broken in* to the job** vous mettrez 6 mois à vous faire au métier *or* à vous roder*.
3 break-in *n V* **break 2.**
break into *vt fus* **(a)** (*enter illegally*) *house* entrer par effraction dans. **to break into a safe** fracturer *or* forcer un coffre-fort; **to break into the cashbox** forcer la caisse.
(b) (*use part of*) *savings* entamer. **to break into a new box of sth** entamer une nouvelle boîte de qch.
(c) (*begin suddenly*) commencer à, se mettre à. **to break into song** se mettre à chanter; **he broke into a long explanation** il s'est lancé dans une longue explication; **to break into a trot** *[horse]* prendre le trot; *[person]* se mettre à trotter.
break off 1 *vi* **(a)** se détacher net, se casser net.
(b) (*stop*) s'arrêter (*doing* de faire). **to break off from work** prendre un moment de répit *or* de récréation, interrompre le travail, faire la pause.
(c) (*end relationship*) rompre (*with sb* avec qn).
2 *vt sep* **(a)** *piece of rock, chocolate etc* casser, détacher.
(b) (*end, interrupt*) *engagement, negotiations* rompre; *habit* rompre avec, se défaire de; *work* interrompre, cesser.
break out 1 *vi* **(a)** *[epidemic, fire]* éclater, se déclarer; *[storm, war]* éclater. **to break out in(to) spots** se couvrir de boutons; **to break out into a sweat** prendre une suée*; **he broke out into a stream of insults** il a sorti un chapelet d'injures.
(b) (*escape*) s'échapper, s'évader (*of* de).
2 breakout *n V* **break 2.**
break through 1 *vi* (*Mil*) faire une percée; *[sun]* percer (les nuages).
2 *vt fus defences, obstacles* enfoncer, percer. **to break through sb's reserve** percer la réserve de qn; **to break through the crowd** se frayer un passage à travers la foule; (*Aviat*) **to break through the sound barrier** franchir le mur du son.
3 breakthrough *n V* **break 2.**
break up 1 *vi* **(a)** *[ice]* craquer, se fêler; *[road]* être défoncé; *[ship in storm]* se disloquer; *[partnership]* cesser, prendre fin; *[health]* se détériorer, se délabrer. **the weather is breaking up** le temps se gâte; **their marriage is breaking up** leur mariage est en train de se briser *or* est à vau-l'eau.
(b) (*disperse*) *[clouds, crowd]* se disperser; *[group]* se disperser, se séparer; *[meeting]* se disperser; *[friends]* se quitter, se séparer; (*Brit*) *[school, college]* entrer en vacances. **the schools break up tomorrow** les vacances (scolaires) commencent demain.
2 *vt sep* **(a)** (*lit*) mettre en morceaux, morceler; *house* démolir; *ground* ameublir; *road* défoncer. **to break sth up into 3 pieces** mettre *or* casser qch en 3 morceaux.
(b) (*fig*) *coalition* briser, rompre; *empire* démembrer. **to break up a marriage/a home** désunir un ménage/une famille.
(c) (*disperse*) *crowd, meeting* disperser.
3 break(ing)-up *n V* **break 2.**
breakable ['breɪkəbl] **1** *adj* cassable, fragile. **2** *n*: **~s** objets *mpl* fragiles.
breakage ['breɪkɪdʒ] *n* (*in chain*) rupture *f*; *[glass, china]* casse *f*, bris *m*. **to pay for ~s** payer la casse.
breakdown ['breɪkdaʊn] **1** *n* **(a)** *[machine, vehicle]* panne *f*.
(b) *[communications etc]* rupture *f*. *[railway system etc]* interruption *f* (subite) de service.
(c) (*Med*) (*mental*) dépression nerveuse; (*physical*) effondrement *m*.
(d) (*into categories etc*) analyse *f*.
2 *cpd*: (*Aut*) **breakdown gang/service** équipe *f*/service *m* de dépannage; (*Brit*) **breakdown van** *or* **truck** dépanneuse *f*.
breaker ['breɪkə^{r}] *n* **(a)** (*wave*) brisant *m*. **(b)** (*person*) briseur *m*, casseur *m*. **to send to the ~'s** *ship* envoyer à la démolition; *car* envoyer à la casse; *V* **house, law** *etc.* **(c)** (*machine*) concasseur *m*, broyeur *m*; *V* **ice** *etc.*
breakfast ['brekfəst] **1** *n* petit déjeuner *m*. **to have ~** déjeuner, prendre le (petit) déjeuner; *V* **wedding** *etc.*
2 *vi* déjeuner (*off, on* de).
3 *cpd*: **breakfast cereals** céréales *fpl* (*flocons mpl d'avoine, de maïs etc*); **breakfast cloth** nappe *f* (ordinaire); **breakfast cup** déjeuner *m* (*tasse*); **breakfast room** petite salle à manger; **breakfast set** service *m* à petit déjeuner.
breaking ['breɪkɪŋ] **1** *n [cup, chair]* bris *m*; *[bone, limb]* fracture *f*; (*Jur*) *[window, seals]* bris; *[promise]* manquement *m* (*of* à), violation *f* (*of* de); *[treaty, law]* violation (*of* de); *[commandment]* désobéissance *f* (*of* à); *[silence, spell]* rupture *f*; *[journey]* interruption *f* (*of* de).
2 *cpd*: (*Jur*) **breaking and entering** effraction *f*; (*Tech*) **breaking-point** point *m* de rupture; **to try sb's patience to breaking-point** pousser à bout la patience de qn; **she has reached breaking-point** elle est à bout, elle n'en peut plus; (*Pol etc*) **the situation has reached breaking-point** on est au point de rupture; (*Tech*) **breaking strain** point *m* de rupture; **breaking strength** module *m* de résistance; **breaking stress = breaking strain.**
bream [bri:m] *n* brème *f*.
breast [brest] **1** *n* **(a)** (*chest*) *[man, woman]* poitrine *f*; *[animal]* poitrine, poitrail *m*; (*Culin*) *[chicken etc]* blanc *m*; *V* **beat.**
(b) *[woman]* sein *m*, mamelle *f* (†, *liter*); *[man]* sein. **baby at the ~** enfant *mf* au sein.
(c) (*fig, liter*) cœur *m*, sein *m*, conscience *f*; *V* **clean.**
(d) (*Min*) front *m* de taille; *V* **chimney.**
2 *vt* **(a)** (*face*) *waves, storm, danger* affronter.
(b) *hill* atteindre le sommet de. (*Sport*) **to ~ the tape** franchir la ligne d'arrivée (le premier).
3 *cpd*: **breastbone** sternum *m*; *[bird]* bréchet *m*; **breast-fed** nourri au sein; **breast-feed** allaiter, donner le sein à; **breast-feeding** allaitement maternel *or* au sein; **breastplate** *[priest]* pectoral *m*; *[armour]* plastron *m* (de cuirasse); **breast-pocket** poche *f* de poitrine; **breast-stroke** brasse *f*; **to swim breast-stroke** nager la brasse; **breastwork** (*Mil*) parapet *m*; (*Naut*) rambarde *f*.
breath [breθ] **1** *n* **(a)** haleine *f*, souffle *m*, respiration *f*. **bad ~** mauvaise haleine; **to get one's ~ back** reprendre haleine, retrouver son souffle; **out of ~** à bout de souffle, essoufflé, hors d'haleine; **to take ~** respirer, reprendre haleine; **to take a deep ~** respirer à fond; (*fig*) **to take sb's ~ away** couper le souffle à qn; **save your ~!** inutile de gaspiller ta salive!; **to be short of ~** avoir le souffle court; **to gasp for ~** haleter; **to stop for ~** s'arrêter pour reprendre haleine; **to swear under one's ~** jurer tout bas; **she contradicted herself in the same ~** elle s'est contredite dans la même seconde; **to say sth (all) in one ~** dire qch tout d'un trait; (*fig*) **it was the ~ of life to him** c'était (toute) sa vie, cela lui était aussi précieux que la vie même; **his last ~** son dernier soupir; **with one's dying ~** en mourant; (*liter*) **to draw one's last ~** rendre l'âme, rendre le dernier soupir; *V* **catch, hold, waste** *etc.*
(b) (*air in movement*) souffle *m*. **there wasn't a ~ of air** il n'y avait pas un souffle d'air; **to go out for a ~ of air** sortir prendre l'air; **a little ~ of wind** un (léger) souffle d'air; (*fig*) **not a ~ of scandal** pas le moindre soupçon de scandale.
2 *cpd*: **breathtaking** stupéfiant, à vous couper le souffle.
breathalyse ['breθəlaɪz] *vt* faire subir l'alcootest à.
Breathalyser, (*US*) **Breathalyzer** ['breθəlaɪzə^{r}] *n* alcootest *m*.
breathe [bri:ð] **1** *vi* respirer. **to ~ deeply, to ~ heavily** (*after running etc*) haleter, souffler (fort); (*in illness*) respirer péniblement; **to ~ hard** souffler (fort), haleter; (*fig*) **to ~ freely, to ~ again** (pouvoir) respirer; (*be alive*) **she is still breathing** elle vit encore, elle est toujours en vie.
2 *vt* **(a)** *air* respirer. **to ~ one's last (breath)** rendre le dernier soupir; **to ~ air into sth** insuffler de l'air *or* souffler dans qch; **to ~ new life into sb** redonner goût à la vie *or* du courage à qn.
(b) (*utter*) *sigh* exhaler, laisser échapper, pousser; *prayer* murmurer. **to ~ a sigh of relief** pousser un soupir de soulagement; **don't ~ a word (about it)!** n'en dis rien à personne!, motus!
(c) (*Ling*) aspirer.
breathe in *vi, vt sep* aspirer, inspirer.
breathe out *vi, vt sep* expirer.
breather* ['bri:ðə^{r}] *n* **(a)** (*short rest*) moment *m* de repos *or* répit. **to give sb a ~** laisser souffler qn. **(b)** (*fresh air*) **let's go (out) for a ~** sortons prendre l'air.
breathing ['bri:ðɪŋ] **1** *n* **(a)** respiration *f*, souffle *m*. **heavy ~** respiration bruyante. **(b)** (*Ling*) aspiration *f*. (*Greek Gram*) **rough/smooth ~** esprit rude/doux. **2** *cpd*: **breathing apparatus** appareil *m* respiratoire; (*fig*) **a breathing space** le temps de souffler, un moment de répit.
breathless ['breθlɪs] *adj* (*from exertion*) hors d'haleine, haletant; (*through illness*) oppressé, qui a de la peine à respirer. **~ with excitement** le souffle coupé par l'émotion; **a ~ silence** un silence ému; **in ~ terror** le souffle coupé par la terreur.
breathlessly ['breθlɪslɪ] *adv* (en) haletant; (*fig*) en grande hâte.
bred [bred] **1** *pret, ptp of* **breed. 2** *adj ending in cpds*: **well-bred** bien élevé; *V* **country, ill.**
breech [bri:tʃ] **1** *n* **(a)** *[gun]* culasse *f*.
(b) (*Med*) **~ birth, ~ delivery** accouchement *m* par le siège; **he** *or* **she was a ~*** c'était un siège.
2 *vt gun* munir d'une culasse.
3 *cpd*: **breechblock** bloc *m* de culasse; (*Mil*) **breechloader** arme *f* qui se charge par la culasse.
breeches ['brɪtʃɪz] **1** *npl*: **(pair of) ~** (*knee* **~**) haut-de-chausses *m*; (*riding* **~**) culotte *f* (de cheval); **his wife wears the ~** c'est sa femme qui porte la culotte. **2** ['bri:tʃɪz] *cpd*: (*Naut*) **breeches buoy** bouée-culotte *f*.
breed [bri:d] *pret, ptp* **bred 1** *vt animals* élever, faire l'élevage de; (††) *children* élever; (*fig: give rise to*) faire naître, donner naissance à, engendrer. **he ~s horses** il fait l'élevage des chevaux; **to ~ in/out a characteristic** faire acquérir/faire perdre une caractéristique (*par la sélection*); *V* **born, cross, familiarity.**
2 *vi [animals]* se reproduire, se multiplier. **they ~ like rabbits** ils se multiplient comme des lapins.
3 *n* (*Zool*) (*race*) race *f*, espèce *f*; (*within race*) type *m*; (*fig*) sorte *f*, espèce; *V* **cross, half.**
breeder ['bri:də^{r}] *n* **(a)** (*Phys: also* **~ reactor**) générateur *m* *or* réacteur *m* nucléaire, pile autorégénératrice. **(b)** (*person*) éleveur *m*; *V* **cattle, stock** *etc.*
breeding ['bri:dɪŋ] *n* **(a)** (*reproduction*) reproduction *f*, procréation *f*. **~ season** *[animals]* saison *f* des accouplements; *[birds]* saison des nids.
(b) (*Agr: raising*) élevage *m*; *V* **cattle** *etc.*

(c) (*upbringing*) **(good)** ~ (bonne) éducation *f*, bonnes manières, savoir-vivre *m*; **to lack** ~ manquer de savoir-vivre.
(d) (*Phys*) production *f* d'énergie atomique.
breeks [bri:ks] *npl* (*Scot*) pantalon *m*.
breeze[1] [bri:z] **1** *n* (*wind*) brise *f*. **gentle** ~ petite brise, souffle *m* de vent; **stiff** ~ vent frais; **there is quite a** ~ cela souffle; *V* **sea** *etc*.
2 *vi*: **to** ~ **in/out** *etc* (*jauntily*) entrer/sortir *etc* d'un air dégagé; (*briskly*) entrer/sortir *etc* en coup de vent.
breeze[2] [bri:z] *n* (*cinders*) cendres *fpl* (de charbon). (*Brit*) ~ **block** parpaing *m*.
breezily [ˈbri:zɪlɪ] *adv* (*jauntily*) avec désinvolture, d'un air dégagé; (*joyfully*) gaiement, jovialement.
breezy [ˈbri:zɪ] *adj weather, day* frais (*f* fraîche); *corner, spot* éventé; (*fig*) (*jaunty*) désinvolte, dégagé; (*joyful*) gai, jovial.
Bren [bren] *n* (*Mil*) ~ **gun** fusil mitrailleur; ~ **(gun) carrier** chenillette *f* (pour fusil mitrailleur).
brethren [ˈbreðrɪn] *npl* **(a)** (††, *Rel*) frères *mpl*. **(b)** (*fellow members*) *[trade etc]* confrères *mpl*.
Breton [ˈbretən] **1** *adj* breton. **2** *n* **(a)** Breton(ne) *m(f)*. **(b)** (*Ling*) breton *m*.
breve [bri:v] *n* (*Typ*) brève *f*; (*Mus*) ronde *f*, carrée† *f*.
brevet [ˈbrevɪt] *n* (*esp Mil*) brevet *m*.
breviary [ˈbri:vɪərɪ] *n* bréviaire *m*.
brevity [ˈbrevɪtɪ] *n* (*shortness*) brièveté *f*; (*conciseness*) concision *f*. (*Prov*) ~ **is the soul of wit** les plaisanteries les plus courtes sont les meilleures.
brew [bru:] **1** *n* **(a)** *[beer]* brassage *m*; (*amount brewed*) brassin *m*; *V* **home**.
(b) *[tea]* infusion *f*; *[herbs]* tisane *f*. **witch's** ~ brouet *m* de sorcière (†, *hum*); (*Brit*) **let's have a** ~**-up**‡ on va se faire du *or* un thé.
2 *vt beer* brasser; *tea* faire infuser, préparer; *punch* préparer, mélanger; (*fig*) *scheme, mischief, plot* préparer, tramer, mijoter*.
3 *vi* **(a)** (*make beer*) brasser, faire de la bière.
(b) *[beer]* fermenter; *[tea]* infuser; (*fig*) *[storm]* couver, se préparer; *[plot]* se tramer, (se) mijoter*. **there's trouble** ~**ing** il y a de l'orage dans l'air, ça va barder‡, il va y avoir du grabuge*; **something's** ~**ing** il se trame quelque chose.
brew up *vi* **(a)** (*: *make tea*) faire du thé. **(b)** *[storm, dispute]* se préparer.
brewer [ˈbru:əʳ] *n* brasseur *m*.
brewery [ˈbru:ərɪ] *n* brasserie *f* (*fabrique*).
briar [ˈbraɪəʳ] *n* = **brier**.
bribe [braɪb] **1** *n* pot-de-vin *m*. **to take a** ~ *or* ~**s** se laisser corrompre *or* acheter, accepter un pot-de-vin; **to offer a** ~ faire une tentative de corruption, offrir un pot-de-vin; **I'll give the child a sweet as a** ~ **to be good** je donnerai un bonbon à l'enfant pour qu'il se tienne tranquille.
2 *vt* suborner, acheter (la conscience de), soudoyer; *witness* suborner. **to** ~ **sb into silence** acheter le silence de qn; **to** ~ **sb to do sth** soudoyer *or* corrompre qn pour qu'il fasse qch; **to let o.s. be** ~**d** se laisser soudoyer.
bribery [ˈbraɪbərɪ] *n* corruption *f*; (*Jur*) *[witness]* subornation *f*; (*Pol*) corruption électorale. (*Jur*) ~ **and corruption** corruption; **open to** ~ corruptible.
bric-à-brac [ˈbrɪkəbræk] *n* (*U*) bric-à-brac *m*. ~ **dealer** brocanteur *m*.
brick [brɪk] **1** *n* **(a)** (*Constr*) brique *f*. (*Prov*) **you can't make** ~**s without straw** à l'impossible nul n'est tenu (*Prov*); (*fig*) **he came down on me like a ton of** ~**s*** il m'a passé un de ces savons!*; (*fig*) **you might as well talk to a** ~ **wall*** autant (vaut) parler à un mur, autant cracher en l'air*; (*fig*) **to run one's head against** *or* **come up against a** ~ **wall** se heurter à un mur; *V* **cat, drop.**
(b) (*Brit: toy*) cube *m* (*de construction*). **box of** ~**s** jeu *m or* boîte *f* de construction.
(c) **a** ~ **of ice cream** une glace (*empaquetée*).
(d) (*†: *person*) type *m* sympa*, fille *f* sympa*. **be a** ~**!** sois sympa!* *or* chic!
2 *cpd* (*also* **brick-built**) *house* en brique(s). **brickbat** (*lit*) morceau *m* de brique; (**fig*) critique *f*; **brick-kiln** four *m* à briques; **bricklayer** maçon *m*; **brick red** (rouge) brique *inv*; **brickwork** briquetage *m*, brique *f*; **brickworks** briqueterie *f*.
brick in, brick up *vt sep door, window* murer.
bridal [ˈbraɪdl] *adj feast* de noce; *bed, chamber, procession* nuptial; *veil, gown* de mariée. ~ **suite** suite réservée aux jeunes mariés.
bride [braɪd] **1** *n* (jeune) mariée *f*; (*before wedding*) (future) mariée. **the** ~ **and** (~)**groom** les (jeunes) mariés; (*Rel*) **the** ~ **of Christ** l'épouse *f* du Christ.
2 *cpd*: **bridegroom** (*just married*) (jeune) marié *m*; (*about to be married*) (futur) marié; **bridesmaid** demoiselle *f* d'honneur.
bridge[1] [brɪdʒ] **1** *n* **(a)** pont *m*. **to build/throw a** ~ **across a river** construire/jeter un pont sur un fleuve; *V* **cross, draw, foot** *etc*.
(b) (*Naut*) passerelle *f* (de commandement).
(c) *[nose]* arête *f*, dos *m*; *[spectacles]* arcade *f*; *[violin]* chevalet *m*.
(d) (*Dentistry*) bridge *m*.
2 *vt river* construire *or* jeter un pont sur. (*fig*) **to** ~ **a gap** établir un *or* des contact(s) (*between* entre); (*Fin*) **bridging loan** crédit m de relais *or* de soudure.
3 *cpd*: **bridge-building** (*Mil*) pontage *m*; (*fig*) efforts *mpl* de rapprochement; (*Mil*) **bridgehead** tête *f* de pont.
bridge[2] [brɪdʒ] **1** *n* (*Cards*) bridge *m*. **to play** ~ bridger, jouer au bridge; *V* **auction, contract**[1]. **2** *cpd*: **bridge party** soirée *f or* réunion *f* de bridge; **bridge player** bridgeur *m*, -euse *f*; **bridge roll** petit pain (brioché).
bridle [ˈbraɪdl] **1** *n [horse]* bride *f*; (*fig*) frein *m*, contrainte *f*. ~ **path** sentier *m*.
2 *vt horse* brider; *one's emotions* refréner, mettre la bride à. **to** ~ **one's tongue** se taire, tenir sa langue.
3 *vi* (*in anger*) regimber, se rebiffer; (*in scorn*) lever le menton (*de mépris*).
brief [bri:f] **1** *adj* **(a)** (*short*) *life, meeting* bref; *stay* court, de courte durée, passager. **for a** ~ **period** pendant un temps très court; ~ **interval** court intervalle.
(b) (*concise*) *speech etc* bref, concis. ~ **account** exposé *m* sommaire; **in** ~ en deux mots, en résumé; **to be** ~**, he didn't come** bref *or* pour vous dire la chose en deux mots, il n'est pas venu.
(c) (*curt, abrupt*) *speech, reply* laconique; *manner* brusque.
2 *n* **(a)** (*Jur*) dossier *m*, cause *f*, affaire *f*. (*Jur*) **to hold a** ~ **for sb** représenter qn en justice; (*fig*) **I hold no** ~ **for those who ...** je ne me fais pas l'avocat *or* le défenseur de ceux qui ...; (*fig*) **I hold no** ~ **for him** je ne prends pas sa défense; **to have a watching** ~ **for** veiller (en justice) aux intérêts de; (*Jur*) **to take a** ~ accepter de plaider une cause.
(b) (*Mil: instructions*) briefing *m*; (*fig*) tâche *f*.
(c) (*Dress*) ~**s** slip *m*.
3 *vt* **(a)** (*Jur*) *barrister* confier une cause à.
(b) (*Mil*) *pilots, soldiers* donner des instructions à; (*) *person* mettre au fait, donner des tuyaux* à (*on sth* sur qch). (*Mil*) **the pilots were** ~**ed** les pilotes ont reçu leurs (dernières) instructions.
4 *cpd*: **briefcase** serviette *f*, porte-documents *m inv*.
briefing [ˈbri:fɪŋ] *n* (*Aviat, Mil*) instructions *fpl*; (*gen*) briefing *m*.
briefly [ˈbri:flɪ] *adv visit* en coup de vent; *reply* laconiquement, en peu de mots; *speak* brièvement.
briefness [ˈbri:fnɪs] *n* (*V* **brief**) brièveté *f*; concision *f*; laconisme *m*; brusquerie *f*.
brier [ˈbraɪəʳ] *n* **(a)** (*wood*) (racine *f* de) bruyère *f*; (*also* ~ **pipe**) pipe *f* de bruyère. **(b)** (*wild rose*) églantier *m*; (*thorny bush*) ronces *fpl*; (*thorn*) épine *f*. ~ **rose** églantine *f*.
brig [brɪg] *n* (*Naut*) brick *m*.
brigade [brɪˈgeɪd] *n* (*Mil, fig*) brigade *f*. (*fig*) **one of the old** ~ un vétéran, un vieux de la vieille; *V* **fire.**
brigadier [ˌbrɪgəˈdɪəʳ] *n* (*also* ~ **general**) général *m* de brigade.
brigand [ˈbrɪgənd] *n* brigand *m*, bandit *m*.
brigandage [ˈbrɪgəndɪdʒ] *n* brigandage *m*.
bright [braɪt] *adj* **(a)** (*shining*) *eyes* brillant, vif; *star, gem* brillant; *light* vif; *fire* vif, clair; *weather* clair, radieux; *sunshine* éclatant; *day, room* clair; *colour* vif, éclatant, lumineux; *metal* poli, luisant. ~**-eyed** aux yeux brillants; (*Met*) **to become** ~**er** s'éclaircir; (*Met*) ~ **intervals** *or* **periods** éclaircies *fpl*; **the outlook is** ~**er** (*Met*) on prévoit une amélioration (du temps); (*fig*) l'avenir se présente mieux *or* sous des couleurs plus favorables; (*fig*) **the** ~ **lights*** la vie à la ville.
(b) (*cheerful*) gai, joyeux; (*vivacious*) vif, animé; *face, smile, expression* rayonnant, radieux (*with* de); *look* radieux, brillant (*with* de); *prospects, future* brillant, splendide; *example, period of history* glorieux. ~**er days** des jours plus heureux; **as** ~ **as a button** gai comme un pinson; ~ **and early** de bon matin; (*fig*) **we must look on the** ~ **side** nous devons essayer d'être optimistes.
(c) (*intelligent*) *person* intelligent, doué, brillant; *child* éveillé. **he's a** ~ **spark*** il est vraiment futé, il est plein d'idées.
Bright [braɪt] *n*: ~**'s disease** mal *m* de Bright, néphrite *f* chronique.
brighten [ˈbraɪtn] (*also* ~ **up**) **1** *vt* **(a)** (*make cheerful*) *room, spirits, person* égayer; *conversation* égayer, animer; *prospects, situation, future* améliorer.
(b) (*make shine*) faire briller, rendre (plus) brillant; *metal* faire reluire; *colour* aviver.
2 *vi* **(a)** *[weather, sky]* s'éclaircir, se dégager.
(b) *[eyes]* s'éclairer, s'allumer; *[expression]* s'éclairer, s'épanouir; *[person]* s'égayer, s'animer; *[prospects, future]* s'améliorer, se présenter sous un meilleur jour.
brightly [ˈbraɪtlɪ] *adv* (*V* **bright**) **(a)** avec éclat, brillamment. **the sun shone** ~ le soleil brillait d'un vif éclat, le soleil flamboyait; **the fire burnt** ~ un feu clair flambait.
(b) gaiement, joyeusement; radieusement.
(c) intelligemment, brillamment.
brightness [ˈbraɪtnɪs] *n* (*V* **bright**) **(a)** éclat *m*, brillant *m*; *[light]* intensité *f*. **(b)** gaieté *f or* gaîté *f*, joie *f*; vivacité *f*. **(c)** intelligence *f*.
brill [brɪl] *n* barbue *f*.
brilliance [ˈbrɪljəns] *n*, **brilliancy** [ˈbrɪljənsɪ] *n* **(a)** (*splendour: lit, fig*) éclat *m*, brillant *m*. **(b)** (*great intelligence*) intelligence supérieure.
brilliant [ˈbrɪljənt] *adj* **(a)** *sunshine, light* éclatant. **(b)** *person, book, style, wit* brillant.
brilliantine [ˌbrɪljənˈti:n] *n* brillantine *f*.
brilliantly [ˈbrɪljəntlɪ] *adv* (*V* **brilliant**) avec éclat; brillamment.
brim [brɪm] **1** *n [cup, hat, lake]* bord *m*. **2** *vi* (être plein à) déborder (*with* de).
brim over *vi* (*lit, fig*) déborder (*with* de).
brimful [ˈbrɪmˈfʊl] *adj* (*lit*) plein à déborder (*with* de); (*fig*) débordant (*with* de).
brimstone [ˈbrɪmstəʊn] *n* soufre *m*; *V* **fire.**
brindle(d) [ˈbrɪndl(d)] *adj* moucheté, tavelé.
brine [braɪn] *n* **(a)** (*salt water*) eau salée; (*Culin*) saumure *f*. **(b)** (*liter*) (*sea*) mer *f*, océan *m*; (*sea water*) eau *f* de mer.
bring [brɪŋ] *pret, ptp* **brought 1** *vt* **(a)** *person, animal, vehicle* amener; *object, news, information* apporter. **to** ~ **sb up/down/across** *etc* faire monter/faire descendre/faire traverser *etc* qn (avec soi); **to** ~ **sth up/down** monter/descendre qch; **I brought him up his breakfast** je lui ai monté son petit déjeuner; *V* **bacon, bed.**

(b) (*cause*) amener, entraîner, causer; (*produce*) produire. **his books brought him a good income** ses livres lui rapportaient bien *or* lui étaient d'un bon rapport; **the hot weather ~s storms** le temps chaud provoque *or* amène des orages; **to ~ good/bad luck** porter bonheur/malheur; **to ~ a blush to sb's cheeks** faire rougir qn, faire monter le rouge aux joues de qn; **to ~ tears to sb's eyes** faire venir les larmes aux yeux de qn; **that brought him to the verge of insanity** cela l'a mené *or* amené au bord de la folie; **to ~ sth (up)on o.s.** s'attirer qch; **to ~ sb to book** faire rendre des comptes à qn; **to ~ sth to a close** *or* **end** faire aboutir qch, mettre fin à qch; **to ~ sb to his feet** faire lever qn; **to ~ sb to justice** traduire qn en justice; (*fig*) **to ~ sth to light** mettre qch en lumière; **to ~ sb low** abaisser qn; **to ~ sth to sb's knowledge** signaler qch à qn, porter qch à la connaissance de qn (*frm*); **to ~ sth to sb's mind** rappeler qch à qn; **to ~ to nothing** faire échouer, faire avorter; (*liter*) **to ~ sth to pass** causer qch; **to ~ to perfection** porter à la perfection; **to ~ sth into play** *or* **into line** faire jouer *or* agir qch; **to ~ sb to his senses** ramener qn à la raison; **to ~ into the world** mettre au monde; *V* **bear[1], head.**

(c) (+*infin: persuade*) amener, pousser, persuader (*sb to do* qn à faire). **he brought him to understand that** ... il l'a amené à comprendre que ...; **I cannot ~ myself to speak to him** je ne peux me résoudre à lui parler.

(d) (*Jur*) **to ~ an action against sb** intenter un procès à qn; **to ~ a charge against sb** porter une accusation contre qn; **the case was brought before Lord X** la cause fut entendue par Lord X; **to ~ evidence** avancer *or* fournir des preuves.

2 *cpd*: (*Brit*) **bring-and-buy sale** vente *f* de charité *or* de bienfaisance.

bring about *vt sep* **(a)** *reforms, review* amener, provoquer; *war* causer, provoquer; *accident* faire arriver, provoquer, occasionner; *sb's ruin* entraîner, amener.

(b) *boat* faire virer de bord.

bring along *vt sep*: **to bring sth along (with one)** apporter qch (avec soi); **to bring sb along (with one)** amener qn (avec soi); **may I bring along a friend?** puis-je amener un ami?

bring back *vt sep* **(a)** *person* ramener; *object* rapporter. **to bring a spacecraft back to earth** récupérer un vaisseau spatial; **her holiday brought back her health** ses vacances lui ont rendu la santé; **a rest will bring him back to normal** du repos le remettra d'aplomb.

(b) (*call to mind*) rappeler (à la mémoire).

bring down *vt sep* **(a)** *kite etc* ramener au sol; (*Hunting*) *animal, bird* descendre; *plane* faire atterrir; (*Mil*) *enemy plane* abattre, descendre; *tree, one's enemy* abattre.

(b) *dictator, government* faire tomber; *temperature, prices, cost of living* faire baisser; *swelling* réduire; (*Math*) *figure* abaisser. **his action brought down everyone's wrath upon him** son action lui a attiré *or* lui a valu la colère de tout le monde; **the play brought the house down*** la pièce a fait crouler la salle sous les applaudissements.

bring forth *vt sep* (*liter*) *fruit* produire; *child* mettre au monde; *animal* mettre bas; (*fig*) *protests, criticism* provoquer.

bring forward *vt sep* **(a)** *person* faire avancer; *chair etc* avancer; *witness* produire; *evidence, proof, argument* avancer.

(b) (*advance time of*) *meeting* avancer.

(c) (*Book-keeping*) *figure, amount* reporter.

bring in *vt sep* **(a)** *person* faire entrer; *object* rentrer.

(b) (*introduce*) *fashion* lancer; *custom* introduire. **to bring in the police/the troops** faire intervenir la police/l'armée.

(c) (*Fin*) *income* rapporter. **to bring in interest** rapporter des intérêts.

(d) (*Jur*) *[jury]* **to bring in a verdict** rendre un verdict; **to bring in a verdict of guilty, to bring sb in guilty** déclarer qn coupable; (*Parl*) **to bring in a bill** présenter *or* déposer un projet de loi.

bring off *vt sep* **(a)** *people from wreck* sauver.

(b) *plan, aim* réaliser; *deal* mener à bien, conclure; *attack, hoax* réussir. **he didn't manage to bring it off** il n'a pas réussi son coup.

bring on *vt sep* **(a)** (*cause*) *illness, quarrel* provoquer, causer. **to bring on sb's cold** enrhumer qn.

(b) (*Agr etc*) *crops, flowers* faire pousser.

(c) (*Theat*) *person* amener; *thing* apporter sur (la) scène.

bring out *vt sep* **(a)** *person* faire sortir; *object* sortir; (*fig*) *meaning* faire ressortir, mettre en évidence; *colour* faire ressortir; *qualities* faire valoir, mettre en valeur.

(b) *book* publier, faire paraître; *actress, new product* lancer.

bring over *vt sep* **(a)** *person* amener; *object* apporter.

(b) (*convert*) *person* convertir, gagner (*to* à).

bring round *vt sep* **(a)** (*to one's house etc*) *person* amener, faire venir; *object* apporter. (*fig*) **to bring the conversation round to football** ramener la conversation sur le football.

(b) *unconscious person* ranimer.

(c) (*convert*) *person* convertir, gagner (*to* à).

bring through *vt* (*always separate*) *sick person* sauver.

bring to *vt sep* **(a)** (*Naut*) mettre en panne.

(b) *unconscious person* ranimer.

bring together *vt sep* **(a)** (*put in touch*) mettre en contact, faire se rencontrer.

(b) (*end quarrel between*) réconcilier.

bring under *vt sep* (*fig*) assujettir, soumettre.

bring up *vt sep* **(a)** *person* faire monter; *object* monter.

(b) *child, animal* élever. **well/badly brought-up child** enfant bien/mal élevé.

(c) (*vomit*) vomir, rendre.

(d) (*call attention to*) *fact, allegation, problem* mentionner; *question* soulever.

(e) (*stop*) *person, vehicle* (faire) arrêter. **the question brought him up short** la question l'a arrêté net.

(f) (*Jur*) **to bring sb up before a court** citer *or* faire comparaître qn devant un tribunal.

(g) (*Mil, fig*) **to bring up the rear** fermer la marche.

(h) **to bring sth up to date** mettre qch à jour; **to bring sb up to date on sth** mettre qn au courant (des derniers développements) de qch.

brink [brɪŋk] *n* (*lit, fig*) bord *m*. **on the ~ of sth** à deux doigts de qch, au bord de qch; **on the ~ of doing** à deux doigts de faire, sur le point de faire.

brinkmanship* ['brɪŋkmənʃɪp] *n* stratégie *f* du bord de l'abîme.

briny ['braɪnɪ] **1** *adj* saumâtre, salé. **2** *n* (†, *hum*) **the ~** la grande bleue (†, *hum*).

briquette, briquet [brɪ'ket] *n* briquette *f*.

brisk [brɪsk] *adj* **(a)** (*lively*) vif, animé; (*abrupt in manner*) brusque.

(b) *movement* vif, rapide. **~ pace** allure (très) vive; **to take a ~ walk** marcher *or* se promener d'un bon pas; (*fig*) **at a ~ trot** au trot allongé.

(c) *attack* vigoureux, vivement mené; *trade* actif, florissant; *market* animé; *demand* important. **business is ~** les affaires marchent (bien); (*St Ex*) **trading was ~** le marché était actif; **the betting was ~** les paris allaient bon train.

(d) *beer* mousseux; *champagne, cider* pétillant.

(e) *air, weather* vivifiant, vif, frais (*f* fraîche).

brisket ['brɪskɪt] *n* poitrine *f* de bœuf.

briskly ['brɪsklɪ] *adv move* vivement; *walk* d'un bon pas; *speak* brusquement; *act* sans tarder. (*Comm etc*) **these goods are selling ~** ces articles se vendent (très) bien.

briskness ['brɪsknɪs] *n* (*V* **brisk**) *[person]* vivacité *f*, animation *f*; brusquerie *f*; *[movement]* rapidité *f*; *[trade]* activité *f*; *[market etc]* animation; *[air]* fraîcheur *f*.

brisling ['brɪzlɪŋ] *n* sprat *m*.

bristle ['brɪsl] **1** *n [beard, brush]* poil *m*; *[boar etc]* soie *f*; *[plant]* poil, soie. **brush with nylon ~s** brosse en nylon.

2 *cpd*: (*Comm*) **(pure) bristle brush** brosse *f* pur sanglier *inv*.

3 *vi* **(a)** *[animal hair]* se hérisser. (*fig*) **shirt bristling with pins** chemise hérissée d'épingles; **bristling with difficulties** hérissé de difficultés; **town bristling with police** ville grouillante de policiers.

(b) (*fig*) *[person]* s'irriter (*at* de), se hérisser. **he ~d at the suggestion** il s'est hérissé à cette suggestion.

bristly ['brɪslɪ] *adj animal, chin* au(x) poil(s) raide(s) *or* dur(s); *hair, beard* hérissé.

Bristol board ['brɪstəlbɔːd] *n* (*Art, Comm*) bristol *m*.

Britain ['brɪtən] *n* (*also* **Great ~**) Grande-Bretagne *f*.

Britannia [brɪ'tænɪə] *n* Britannia *f*. **~ metal** métal anglais.

Britannic [brɪ'tænɪk] *adj*: **Her ~ Majesty** sa Majesté Britannique.

briticism ['brɪtɪsɪzəm] *n* (*US*) anglicisme *m*.

British ['brɪtɪʃ] **1** *adj* britannique, anglais. **~ ambassador/embassy** ambassadeur *m*/ambassade *f* de Grande-Bretagne; **~ Columbia** Colombie *f* britannique; **the ~ Broadcasting Corporation** la BBC; **the ~ Commonwealth** le Commonwealth; (*US*) **~ English** l'anglais d'Angleterre; **~ Honduras** Honduras *m* britannique; **~ Isles** Îles *fpl* Britanniques; **the ~ nation** la nation britannique; **~ thermal unit** b.t.u. *f* (*unité de mesure calorifique*). **2** *n*: **the ~** les Britanniques *mpl*, les Anglais *mpl*.

Britisher ['brɪtɪʃə[r]] *n* (*US*) Britannique *mf*, Anglais (e) *m(f)*.

Briton ['brɪtən] *n* **(a)** Britannique *mf*, Anglais (e) *m(f)*. **(b)** (*Hist*) Breton(ne) *m(f)* (d'Angleterre).

Brittany ['brɪtənɪ] *n* Bretagne *f*.

brittle ['brɪtl] *adj* cassant, fragile; (*Culin*) friable. (*fig*) **in a ~ voice** d'une voix crispée.

broach [brəʊtʃ] **1** *vt barrel* mettre en perce; *box, supplies* entamer; *subject, topic* entamer, aborder. **2** *n* (*Culin*) broche *f*; (*tool*) perçoir *m*, foret *m* .

broad [brɔːd] **1** *adj* **(a)** (*wide*) *road, smile* large; (*extensive*) *ocean, estates* vaste, immense. **to grow ~er** s'élargir; **to make ~er** élargir; **to be ~ in the shoulder** être large d'épaules; (*fig*) **he's got a ~ back** il a bon dos; **the lake is 200 metres ~** le lac a 200 mètres de largeur *or* de large; (*fig*) **it's as ~ as it is long** c'est du pareil au même*, c'est bonnet blanc et blanc bonnet; **~ in the beam** *ship* ventru; (**pej*) *person* fort de l'arrière-train*; **in ~ daylight** (*lit*) en plein jour, au grand jour; (*fig*) au vu et au su de tous; **it was ~ daylight** il faisait grand jour; **~ hint** allusion transparente *or* à peine voilée; *V* **gauge.**

(b) (*not detailed*) grand, général. **these are the ~ outlines** voilà les grandes lignes *or* les données générales; **as a ~ rule** en règle générale; **in the ~est sense** au sens le plus large.

(c) (*liberal*) *mind, ideas* large, libéral.

(d) (*strongly marked*) *accent* prononcé. **he speaks ~ Scots** il parle avec un accent écossais à couper au couteau*.

(e) (*coarse*) grossier, vulgaire. **~ humour** humour grivois, gauloiserie *f*; **~ joke** plaisanterie grasse.

2 *n* **(a)** (*widest part*) **the ~ of the back** le milieu du dos; (*Geog*) **the (Norfolk) B~s** les Broads *or* les lacs *mpl* et estuaires *mpl* du Norfolk.

(b) (*US‡*) (*woman*) nana‡ *f*; (*prostitute*) putain‡ *f*.

3 *cpd*: **broad bean** fève *f*; **broad-brimmed** *hat* à larges bords; **broadcast** *V* **broadcast**; **broadcloth** fin drap noir (*en grande largeur*); (*US Sport*) **broad jump** saut *m* en longueur; (*carpet*) **broadloom** en grande largeur; **he is broad-minded** il a les idées (très) larges; **broad-mindedness** largeur *f* d'esprit, tolérance *f*; (*Hist, Typ*) **broadsheet** placard *m*; **broad-shouldered** large d'épaules; **broadside** *V* **broadside; broadsword** épée *f* à deux tranchants, glaive†† *m*; **broadways, broadwise** en largeur, dans le sens de la largeur.

broadcast ['brɔːdkɑːst] *pret, ptp* **broadcast 1** *vt* **(a)** *news, speech, programme* (*Rad*) (radio)diffuser, émettre; (*TV*) télé-

viser, émettre; (*fig*) *news, rumour etc* diffuser, répandre, raconter partout. (*fig*) **don't ~ it!*** ne va pas le crier sur les toits!
(b) (*Agr*) *seed* semer (à la volée).
2 *vi* (*Rad, TV*) *[station]* émettre; *[actor, interviewee]* participer à une émission; *[interviewer]* faire une émission. **X ~s by permission of** ... X participe à cette émission avec l'accord de ....
3 *n* (*Rad, TV*) émission *f*. **live/recorded ~** émission en direct/en différé; **repeat ~** reprise *f*, rediffusion *f*.
4 *adj* (*Rad*) (radio)diffusé; (*TV*) télévisé. **~ account of a match** (*Rad*) reportage radiodiffusé d'un match; (*TV*) reportage télévisé d'un match.
5 *adv sow* à la volée.

broadcaster [ˈbrɔːdkɑːstəʳ] *n* (*Rad, TV*) personnalité *f* de la radio *or* de la télévision.

broadcasting [ˈbrɔːdkɑːstɪŋ] **1** *n* (*Rad*) radiodiffusion *f*; (*TV*) télévision *f*. **that is the end of ~ for tonight** ainsi prennent fin nos émissions de la journée.
2 *cpd*: **broadcasting station** station *f* de radio, poste émetteur; *V* **British.**

broaden [ˈbrɔːdn] (*also* **~ out:** *lit, fig*) **1** *vt* élargir. **2** *vi* s'élargir.

broadly [ˈbrɔːdlɪ] *adv* (*fig*) dans les grandes lignes, en gros, généralement. **~ speaking** en gros, généralement parlant.

broadness [ˈbrɔːdnɪs] *n* *[road]* largeur *f*; *[joke, story]* grossièreté *f*, vulgarité *f*; *[accent]* caractère prononcé.

broadside [ˈbrɔːdsaɪd] *n* **(a)** (*Naut*) *[ship]* flanc *m*. (*Naut*) **~ on** (se présentant) par le travers; **he** *or* **his car hit me ~ on** il m'est rentré dans le flanc, il m'a heurté par le travers.
(b) (*Naut*) bordée *f*; (*fig: insults*) bordée d'injures *or* d'invectives. (*Naut*) **to fire a ~** lâcher une bordée; (*fig*) **he let him have a ~** il l'a incendié‡, il l'a descendu en flammes*.

brocade [brəʊˈkeɪd] **1** *n* brocart *m*. **2** *cpd* de brocart.

broccoli [ˈbrɒkəlɪ] *n* brocoli *m*.

brochure [ˈbrəʊʃjʊəʳ] *n* *[college, vacation course]* prospectus *m*; *[hotel, travel agent]* brochure *f*, dépliant *m* touristique.

brock [brɒk] *n* (*Brit: Zool, rare*) blaireau *m*.

brogue[1] [brəʊg] *n* (*shoe*) chaussure *f* de marche.

brogue[2] [brəʊg] *n* (*accent*) (*Irish*) accent irlandais; (*gen*) accent de terroir.

broil [brɔɪl] **1** *vt* (*Culin*) griller, faire cuire sur le gril; (*fig*) griller*. **~ing sun** soleil brûlant. **2** *vi* (*also fig*) griller.

broiler [ˈbrɔɪləʳ] *n* **(a)** (*fowl*) poulet *m* (à rôtir). **~ house** éleveuse *f*. **(b)** (*grill*) rôtisserie *f*, gril *m*.

broke [brəʊk] **1** *pret of* **break. 2** *adj* (‡) à sec*, fauché*. **to be dead** *or* **stony ~** être fauché (commes les blés)*, être (complètement) à sec*.

broken [ˈbrəʊkən] **1** *ptp of* **break.**
2 *adj* **(a)** (*lit*) cassé, brisé; *window* cassé; *neck, leg* fracturé, cassé; *rib* cassé, enfoncé; (*fig*) *promise* rompu, violé; *appointment* manqué; (*Ling*) *vowel* diphtongué. **~ bones** fractures *fpl* (d'os); (*Mus*) **~ chord** arpège *m*; **~ heart** cœur brisé; **she died of a ~ heart** elle est morte de chagrin *or* morte le cœur brisé; **~ home** foyer brisé; (*Comm*) **~ lots** articles dépareillés; **~ marriage** mariage brisé, ménage désuni; (*Math*) **~ numbers** fractions *fpl*; **he is a ~ reed** on ne peut jamais compter sur lui; **a ~ spell of weather** un temps variable.
(b) (*uneven*) *ground* accidenté; *road* défoncé; *surface* raboteux; *line* brisé; *coastline* dentelé; *V* **check**[3]**.**
(c) (*interrupted*) *journey* interrompu; *sleep* (*disturbed*) interrompu; (*restless*) agité; *sounds, gestures* incohérent; *voice* entrecoupé, brisé; *words* haché. **to speak ~ English** parler un mauvais anglais, baragouiner* l'anglais; **in ~ English** en mauvais anglais; **I've had several ~ nights** j'ai eu plusieurs mauvaises nuits.
(d) (*spoilt, ruined*) *health* délabré, affaibli; *spirit* abattu. **he is a ~ man** (*no spirit left*) il est brisé; (*financially*) il est ruiné; (*reputation-wise*) il est perdu de réputation *or* brûlé.
3 *cpd*: **broken-down** *car* en panne; *machine* détraqué; *horse* fourbu; *house* délabré, en ruines; **broken-hearted** au cœur brisé; **broken-winded** poussif.

brokenly [ˈbrəʊkənlɪ] *adv say* d'une voix entrecoupée; *sob* par à-coups; *speak a language* incorrectement, mal.

broker [ˈbrəʊkəʳ] *n* **(a)** (*St Ex*) ≈ courtier *m* (en bourse), agent *m* de change. **(b)** (*Comm*) courtier *m*; (*Naut*) courtier maritime. **wine ~** courtier en vins. **(c)** (*secondhand dealer*) brocanteur *m*; *V* **pawn**[2] *etc.*

brokerage [ˈbrəʊkərɪdʒ] *n*, **broking** [ˈbrəʊkɪŋ] *n* (*trade, commission*) courtage *m*.

brolly* [ˈbrɒlɪ] *n* (*Brit*) pépin* *m*, riflard* *m*.

bromide [ˈbrəʊmaɪd] *n* **(a)** (*Chem*) bromure *m*; (*Med**) bromure (de potassium). **~ paper** papier *m* au (gelatino-)bromure d'argent. **(b)** (*fig*) (*platitude*) banalité *or* platitude euphorisante; (*person*) raseur* *m*, -euse* *f*.

bronchial [ˈbrɒŋkɪəl] *adj infection* des bronches, bronchique. **~ tubes** bronches *fpl*.

bronchitis [brɒŋˈkaɪtɪs] *n* (*U*) bronchite *f*.

bronchopneumonia [ˌbrɒŋkəʊnjuːˈməʊnɪə] *n* (*U*) bronchopneumonie *f*.

bronco [ˈbrɒŋkəʊ] *n* cheval *m* semi-sauvage (de l'Ouest américain). (*US*) **~buster‡** cowboy *m* (*qui dompte les chevaux sauvages*).

brontosaurus [ˌbrɒntəˈsɔːrəs] *n* brontosaure *m*.

bronze [brɒnz] **1** *n* (*metal, colour, work of art*) bronze *m*. **2** *vi* se bronzer, brunir. **3** *vt metal* bronzer; *skin* brunir, faire bronzer.
4 *cpd* en bronze; (*colour*) (couleur *f* de) bronze *inv*. **Bronze Age** âge *m* du bronze.

bronzed [brɒnzd] *adj skin, person* bronzé, basané.

brooch [brəʊtʃ] *n* broche *f* (*bijou*).

brood [bruːd] **1** *n* *[birds]* couvée *f*, nichée *f*; *[mice]* nichée; *[children]* progéniture *f*, nichée (*hum*); *[vipers, scoundrels]* engeance *f*. **she has a great ~ of children** elle a une nombreuse progéniture; **I'm going to take my ~ home*** je vais remmener ma progéniture *or* ma nichée à la maison.
2 *cpd*: **brood hen** couveuse *f*; **brood mare** (jument *f*) poulinière *f*.
3 *vi* *[bird]* couver; *[storm, danger]* couver, menacer; *[person]* broyer du noir, ruminer. *[person]* **to ~ on** *misfortune* méditer sur; *plan* ruminer; *the past* ressasser; **to ~ over sth** *[night etc]* planer sur qch; *[storm]* couver sur qch; (*oppressively*) peser sur qch.

broody [ˈbruːdɪ] *adj* **(a) ~ hen** (poule *f*) couveuse *f*. **(b)** (*) *person* rêveur, distrait.

brook[1] [brʊk] *n* ruisseau *m*.

brook[2] [brʊk] *vt* (*liter*) *contradiction* souffrir, supporter, tolérer; *delay, reply* admettre, souffrir.

brooklet [ˈbrʊklɪt] *n* ruisselet *m*, petit ruisseau.

broom [brʊm] *n* **(a)** (*Bot*) genêt *m*.
(b) (*brush*) balai *m*; (*small*) balayette *f*. (*Prov*) **a new ~ sweeps clean** tout nouveau tout beau (*Prov*); **this firm needs a new ~** cette compagnie a besoin d'un bon coup de balai *or* a besoin de sang nouveau; **~stick** manche *m* à balai.

broth [brɒθ] *n* bouillon *m* de viande et de légumes.

brothel [ˈbrɒθl] *n* bordel* *m*, maison *f* de tolérance.

brother [ˈbrʌðəʳ] **1** *n* **(a)** (*gen, Rel*) frère *m*. **older/younger ~** frère aîné/cadet; **B~ Francis** Frère François; *V* **lay**[4]. **(b)** (*in trade unions*) camarade *m*. **2** *cpd*: **brother-in-law** beau-frère *m*; **his brother officers** ses compagnons *mpl* d'armes.

brotherhood [ˈbrʌðəhʊd] *n* **(a)** (*U: lit*) fraternité *f*; (*fig*) fraternité, confraternité *f*. **~ of man** fraternité des hommes. **(b)** (*association: esp Rel*) confrérie *f*; (*US*) corporation *f*.

brotherly [ˈbrʌðəlɪ] *adj* fraternel. **~ love** l'amour fraternel.

brougham [ˈbruːəm] *n* coupé *m* de ville.

brought [brɔːt] *pret, ptp of* **bring.**

brouhaha* [ˈbruːhɑːhɑː] *n* histoires* *fpl*.

brow [braʊ] *n* **(a)** (*forehead*) front *m*; (*arch above eye*) arcade sourcilière; (*eyebrow*) sourcil *m*; *V* **beetle**[2]**, high, knit, sweat** *etc.* **(b)** *[hill]* sommet *m*; *[cliff]* bord *m*; (*Min*) tour *f* d'extraction.

browbeat [ˈbraʊbiːt] *vt* intimider, rudoyer, brusquer. **to ~ sb into doing sth** forcer qn à faire qch par l'intimidation.

brown [braʊn] **1** *adj* **(a)** brun, marron *inv*; *hair* châtain; *boots, shoes, leather* marron. **light ~ hair** cheveux *mpl* châtain clair *inv*; **light ~ material** étoffe *f* marron clair; **~ ale** bière brune; **~ bread** pain bis; **~ bear** ours brun; **~ owl** (*Orn*) chat-huant *m*; *[Brownie Guides]* cheftaine *f*; **~ paper** papier *m* d'emballage; (*fig*) **in a ~ study** plongé dans ses pensées *or* méditations; **~ sugar** cassonade *f*, sucre brun; **to turn ~** *[person]* brunir; *[leaves]* roussir; *V* **nut.**
(b) (*tanned*) *person, skin* bronzé, bruni, hâlé. **as ~ as a berry** tout bronzé.
(c) (*dusky-skinned*) brun de peau.
2 *n* brun *m*, marron *m*. **her hair was a rich, deep ~** ses cheveux étaient d'un beau brun foncé.
3 *cpd*: (*US*) **brownout** (*Mil*) camouflage partiel des lumières; (*Elec*) panne partielle; (*US*) **brownstone** (*material*) grès brun; (*house*) bâtiment *m* de grès brun.
4 *vt* **(a)** *[sun]* *skin, person* bronzer, brunir, hâler.
(b) (*Culin*) *meat, fish, potatoes* faire dorer; *sauce* faire roussir.
(c) (*Brit*) **he is ~ed off‡** il en a marre* *or* ras le bol‡, il n'a plus le moral*.
5 *vi* **(a)** *[leaves]* roussir.
(b) *[person, skin]* brunir.
(c) (*Culin*) dorer.

brownie [ˈbraʊnɪ] *n* **(a)** (*fairy*) lutin *m*, farfadet *m*. **(b) B~ (Guide)** jeannette *f*. **(c)** ® (*camera*) brownie *m* kodak ®. **(d)** (*US: cake*) gâteau *m* au chocolat et aux noix.

browning [ˈbraʊnɪŋ] *n* (*Brit Culin*) produit préparé pour roux brun.

brownish [ˈbraʊnɪʃ] *adj* qui tire sur le brun, brunâtre (*slightly pej*).

browse [braʊz] **1** *vi* *[animal]* brouter, paître. (*fig*) **to ~ among books** feuilleter les livres (*d'une librairie, d'une bibliothèque*); **to ~ through a book** feuilleter *or* parcourir un livre.
2 *vt animals* brouter, paître.

brucellosis [ˌbruːsəˈləʊsɪs] *n* brucellose *f*.

bruise [bruːz] **1** *vt* **(a)** *person, part of body* faire un bleu à, contusionner; *finger* faire un pinçon à; *fruit* abîmer, taler; *lettuce* froisser. **to ~ one's foot** se faire un bleu au pied; **to be ~d all over** avoir le corps *or* être couvert de bleus.
(b) (*crush*) écraser, piler. (*liter*) **~d heart** cœur meurtri *or* blessé; (*liter*) **~d spirit** esprit meurtri.
2 *vi* *[fruit]* se taler, s'abîmer. **peaches ~ easily** les pêches se talent facilement; **he ~s easily** il se fait facilement des bleus.
3 *n* *[person]* bleu *m*, contusion *f*, ecchymose *f*, meurtrissure *f*; *[fruit]* meurtrissure, talure *f*. **body covered with ~s** corps couvert d'ecchymoses *or* de meurtrissures.

bruiser‡ [ˈbruːzəʳ] *n* malabar‡ *m*, cogneur‡ *m*.

brunch [brʌntʃ] *n* (grand) petit déjeuner *m* (*pris comme déjeuner*).

brunette [bruːˈnet] **1** *n* (femme *f*) brune *f*, brunette *f*.
2 *adj person, skin* brun; *eyes* marron *inv*; *hair* châtain.

brunt [brʌnt] *n*: **the ~** *[attack, blow]* le (plus gros du) choc; *[argument, displeasure]* le poids; **to bear the ~ of the assault** soutenir *or* essuyer le plus fort de l'attaque; **to bear the ~ of the work** faire le (plus) gros du travail; **to bear the ~ of the expense** payer le (plus) gros des frais; **he bore the ~ of it all** c'est lui qui a porté le poids de l'affaire.

brush [brʌʃ] **1** *n* **(a)** brosse *f*; (*paint ~*) pinceau *m*, brosse; (*broom*) balai *m*; (*short-handled: hearth ~ etc*) balayette *f*;

(*scrubbing* ~) brosse (dure); (*bottle* ~) rince-bouteilles *m inv*; (*shaving* ~) blaireau *m*. **hair/nail/shoe/tooth~** brosse à cheveux/à ongles/à chaussures/à dents; **clothes/hat** ~ brosse à habits/à chapeau; *V* **pastry, tar**[1] *etc*.
(b) coup *m* de brosse. **give your coat a** ~ donne un coup de brosse à ton manteau.
(c) (*light touch*) effleurement *m*.
(d) *[fox]* queue *f*.
(e) (*U: undergrowth*) broussailles *fpl*, taillis *m*.
(f) (*skirmish*) accrochage *m*, escarmouche *f*. **a** ~ **with the law** des ennuis avec la police; (*quarrel*) **to have a** ~ **with sb** avoir un accrochage *or* une prise de bec* avec qn.
(g) (*Elec*) *[commutator]* balai *m*; *[dynamo]* frottoir *m*; (*discharge*) décharge *f*.
2 *cpd*: **brush maker** (*manufacturer*) fabricant *m* de brosses; (*employee*) brossier *m*, -ière *f*; **to give sb the brush-off**‡ envoyer promener *or* bouler* *or* balader* qn; **to get the brush-off**‡ se faire envoyer sur les roses* *or* balader* *or* bouler*; **brush-stroke** coup *m or* trait *m* de pinceau; **brush-up** coup *m* de brosse (*V* **wash**); **to give one's English a brush-up*** rafraîchir ses notions d'anglais*; **brushwood** (*undergrowth*) broussailles *fpl*, taillis *m*; (*cuttings*) menu bois, brindilles *fpl*; (*Art*) **brushwork** facture *f*.
3 *vt* **(a)** *carpet* balayer; *clothes, hair etc* brosser, donner un coup de brosse à. **to** ~ **one's teeth** se laver les dents; **to** ~ **one's hair** se brosser les cheveux; **hair ~ed back** cheveux ramenés *or* rejetés en arrière.
(b) (*touch lightly*) frôler, effleurer; *the ground* raser.
(c) *wool* gratter.
4 *vi*: **to** ~ **against sb/sth** effleurer *or* frôler qn/qch; **to** ~ **past sb/sth** frôler qn/qch en passant.
brush aside *vt sep obstacle, objection* écarter, balayer.
brush away *vt sep tears* essuyer; *mud, dust* (*on clothes*) essuyer, brosser; (*on floor*) balayer; *insects* chasser.
brush down *vt sep person, garment* donner un coup de brosse à; *horse* brosser.
brush off 1 *vi*: **the mud brushes off easily** avec un coup de brosse la boue s'enlève facilement.
2 *vt sep mud, snow* enlever (à la brosse *or* à coups de balai); *insect* balayer, écarter d'un geste; *fluff on coat* enlever à la brosse *or* à la main.
3 **brush-off**‡ *n V* **brush 2**.
brush up 1 *vt sep* **(a)** *crumbs, dirt* ramasser avec une brosse *or* à la balayette.
(b) *wool* gratter.
(c) (*: *revise, improve*) se remettre à, revoir, réviser. **to brush up (on) one's English** se remettre à l'anglais.
2 **brush-up** *n V* **brush 2**, *also* **wash.**
brusque [bru:sk] *adj person, tone, manner* brusque, bourru, brutal.
brusquely ['bru:sklɪ] *adv behave, speak* avec brusquerie, avec rudesse.
brusqueness ['bru:sknɪs] *n* brusquerie *f*, rudesse *f*.
Brussels ['brʌslz] **1** *n* Bruxelles. **2** *cpd lace* de Bruxelles. **Brussels sprouts** choux *mpl* de Bruxelles.
brutal ['bru:tl] *adj* **(a)** *person, behaviour, reply* brutal, cruel. **(b)** (*lit*) brutal; *instincts* animal, de brute.
brutality [bru:'tælɪtɪ] *n* brutalité *f*, sauvagerie *f*.
brutally ['bru:təlɪ] *adv* brutalement, sauvagement, cruellement.
brute [bru:t] **1** *n* (*animal*) brute *f*, bête *f*; (*person*) (*cruel*) brute, brutal *m*; (*coarse*) brute (épaisse). **this machine is a ~!*** quelle vache que cette machine!‡
2 *adj* **(a)** (*animal-like*) de brute, animal, bestial. **the** ~ **beast** la brute.
(b) *strength, passion* brutal; *matter* brut. **by (sheer)** ~ **force** par la force.
brutish ['bru:tɪʃ] *adj* (*animal-like*) de brute, animal, bestial; (*unfeeling*) grossier, brutal; (*uncultured*) inculte, ignare.
bubble ['bʌbl] **1** *n* **(a)** bulle *f*. **to blow ~s** faire des bulles; **soap** ~ bulle de savon.
(b) (*pocket of gas*) bulle *f*; (*in liquid*) bouillon *m*; (*in glass*) bulle, soufflure *f*; (*in metal*) soufflure, boursouflement *m*. **air** ~ bulle d'air.
(c) (*fig*) chimère *f*; (*Comm*) affaire pourrie.
(d) (*sound*) glouglou *m*.
2 *cpd*: (*Brit*) **bubble and squeak** purée *f* aux choux et à la viande hachée; **bubble bath** bain *m* de mousse; (*Brit*) **bubble-car** petite voiture (*à toit transparent*), cloche *f* à fromage*; (*Comm, Fin*) **bubble company** compagnie véreuse; **bubble gum** chewing-gum *m* (qui fait des bulles).
3 *vi [liquid]* bouillonner, dégager des bulles; *[champagne]* pétiller; *[gas]* barboter; (*gurgle*) faire glouglou, gouglouter.
bubble out *vi [liquid]* sortir à gros bouillons.
bubble over *vi* (*lit, fig*) déborder. **to bubble over with joy** déborder de joie.
bubble up *vi [liquid]* monter en bouillonnant.
bubbly ['bʌblɪ] **1** *adj* pétillant, plein de bulles. **2** *n* (‡: *U*) champagne *m*.
bubonic [bju:'bɒnɪk] *adj* bubonique. ~ **plague** peste *f* bubonique.
buccaneer [ˌbʌkə'nɪəʳ] *n* (*Hist*) boucanier *m*; (*fig*) flibustier *m*, pirate *m*.
buck [bʌk] **1** *n* **(a)** (*male of deer, rabbit, hare etc*) mâle *m*.
(b) (†: *dandy*) élégant *m*, dandy *m*.
(c) (*US*‡: *dollar*) dollar *m*. **to be down to one's last** ~ être sur la paille; **to make a few ~s on the side** se faire un peu de pognon‡ à côté, se faire un petit à-côté*; (*at sb's expense*) se sucrer en douce*.
(d) to pass the ~ refiler* la responsabilité aux autres; **the** ~ **stops here*** il n'y a plus personne sur qui rejeter la responsabilité.
(e) (*sawhorse*) chevalet *m*, baudet *m*; (*Gymnastics*) cheval *m* d'arçons.
(f) the horse gave a ~ le cheval a lancé une ruade.
2 *cpd*: **buck rabbit** lapin *m* mâle; **buckshot** chevrotine(s) *f(pl)*; **buckskin** peau *f* de daim; **buckthorn** nerprun *m*, bourdaine *f*; **buck-tooth** dent proéminente; **to be buck-toothed** avoir des dents de lapin; **buckwheat** sarrasin *m*, blé noir.
3 *vi* **(a)** *[horse]* lancer *or* décocher une ruade.
(b) (*object to*) **to** ~ **at sth**‡ regimber devant qch.
buck up* 1 *vi* **(a)** (*hurry up*) se grouiller‡, se magner‡; (*exert o.s.*) se remuer*, se magner‡. **buck up!** remue-toi!*, grouille-toi!‡, active un peu!*
(b) (*cheer up*) reprendre de l'entrain, être ravigoté*.
2 *vt sep person* remonter le moral de, ravigoter*.
bucked‡ [bʌkt] *adj* ravigoté*.
bucket ['bʌkɪt] **1** *n* **(a)** seau *m*. ~ **of water** seau d'eau; **to weep ~s*** pleurer toutes les larmes de son corps; *V* **kick, rain.**
(b) (*Tech*) *[dredger, grain elevator]* godet *m*; *[pump]* piston *m*; *[wheel]* auget *m*. **chain of ~s** pompe *f* à chapelet, chapelet *m* hydraulique.
2 *vi*: **it's ~ing**‡, **the rain is ~ing (down)**‡ il pleut à seaux, il tombe des cordes *or* des hallebardes.
3 *cpd*: (*Tech*) **bucket elevator** noria *f*; **bucket seat** (siège-)baquet *m*; (*Fin*) **bucket shop** bureau *m or* maison *f* de contrepartie, bureau de courtier marron.
bucketful ['bʌkɪtfʊl] *n* plein seau. **I've had a ~**‡ **of him/his nonsense** j'en ai ras le bol‡ *or* par-dessus la tête de lui/de ses idioties.
buckle ['bʌkl] **1** *n* **(a)** *[shoe, belt]* boucle *f*.
(b) (*distortion*) *[wheel]* voilure *f*; *[metal]* gauchissement *m*, flambage *m*.
2 *vt* **(a)** *belt* boucler, attacher.
(b) *wheel* voiler; *metal* gauchir, fausser.
3 *vi* **(a)** *[belt, shoe]* se boucler, s'attacher.
(b) *[metal]* gauchir, se déformer; *[wheel]* se voiler.
buckle down* *vi* se coller au boulot*. **to buckle down to a job** s'atteler à un boulot*; **buckle down to it!** au boulot!
buckle on *vt sep armour* revêtir, endosser; *sword* ceindre.
buckle to* *vi* s'y mettre, s'y coller*.
buckram ['bʌkrəm] *n* bougran *m*.
bucksheе‡ [bʌk'ʃi:] *adj, adv* (*Brit*) gratis *inv*, à l'œil*.
bucolic [bju:'kɒlɪk] **1** *adj* bucolique, pastoral. **2** *n* (*Literat*) **the B~s** les Bucoliques *fpl*.
bud[1] [bʌd] **1** *n* **(a)** *[tree, plant]* bourgeon *m*, œil *m*; *[grafting]* écusson *m*. **to be in** ~ bourgeonner: (*fig*) **poet** *etc* **in the** ~ poète *m etc* en herbe; *V* **nip** *etc*. **(b)** *[flower]* bouton *m*. **in** ~ en bouton; *V* **rose**[2]. **(c)** (*Anat*) papille *f*; *V* **taste. 2** *vi [tree, plant]* bourgeonner, se couvrir de bourgeons; *[flower]* (commencer à) éclore; *[horns]* (commencer à) poindre *or* percer; *[talent etc]* (commencer à) percer. **3** *vt* (*Horticulture*) *tree* greffer, écussonner.
bud[2]‡ [bʌd] *n* (*US*) = **buddy***.
Buddha ['bʊdə] *n* Bouddha *m*.
Buddhism ['bʊdɪzəm] *n* bouddhisme *m*.
Buddhist ['bʊdɪst] **1** *n* Bouddhiste *mf*. **2** *adj monk* bouddhiste; *art, dogma* bouddhique.
budding ['bʌdɪŋ] *adj plant* bourgeonnant; *flower* en bouton; (*fig*) *poet etc* en herbe; *passion* naissant.
buddy* ['bʌdɪ] *n* (*US*) copain *m*, pote‡ *m*. **hi there, ~!** salut, mon pote!‡
budge [bʌdʒ] **1** *vi* (*move*) bouger; (*fig*) changer d'avis. **I will not** ~ **an inch** (*lit*) je ne bougerai pas d'ici; (*fig*) rien ne me fera changer d'avis.
2 *vt* (*lit*) faire bouger. (*fig*) **you can't** ~ **him** il reste inébranlable, vous ne le ferez pas changer d'avis.
budge over*, budge up* *vi* se pousser.
budgerigar ['bʌdʒərɪgɑ:ʳ] *n* perruche *f*.
budget ['bʌdʒɪt] **1** *n* (*gen, Fin*) budget *m*; (*Parl*) budget, loi *f* des finances. **my** ~ **won't run to steak nowadays** mon budget ne me permet plus d'acheter de bifteck.
2 *cpd*: (*Comm*) **budget account** compte-crédit *m*; (*Parl*) **budget day** jour *m* de la présentation du budget; (*US*) **budget plan** système *m* de crédit; (*Parl*) **budget speech** discours *m* de présentation du budget.
3 *vi* dresser *or* préparer un budget. **to** ~ **for sth** (*Econ*) inscrire *or* porter qch au budget, budgétiser qch; (*gen*) inscrire qch à son budget, prévoir des frais de qch.
4 *vt* budgétiser.
budgetary ['bʌdʒɪtrɪ] *adj* budgétaire. ~ **year** exercice *m* budgétaire.
budgie* ['bʌdʒɪ] *n abbr of* **budgerigar.**
buff[1] [bʌf] **1** *n* **(a)** (*leather*) (peau *f* de) buffle *m*; (*colour*) (couleur *f*) chamois *m*. **in the ~**‡ à poil‡. **(b)** (*polishing disc*) polissoir *m*. **2** *adj* **(a)** (de peau) de buffle, en buffle. **(b)** (*also* **~-coloured**) (couleur) chamois *inv*.
3 *vt metal* polir.
buff[2] [bʌf] *n* (*: *enthusiast*) mordu(e)* *m(f)*.
buffalo ['bʌfələʊ] *n, pl* ~ *or* **~es** (*wild ox*) buffle *m*, bufflesse *f*; (*esp in US*) bison *m*; *V* **water.**
buffer[1] ['bʌfəʳ] **1** *n* (*lit, fig*) tampon *m*; (*Rail*) (*on train*) tampon; (*at terminus*) butoir *m*; (*US Aut*) pare-chocs *m inv*. **2** *cpd*: (*Pol*) **buffer state** état *m* tampon.
buffer[2] ['bʌfəʳ] *n* (*for polishing*) polissoir *m*.
buffer[3]‡ ['bʌfəʳ] *n* (*Brit*) vieux fossile*.
buffet[1] ['bʌfɪt] **1** *n* (*blow*) (*with hand*) gifle *f*, soufflet *m*; (*with fist*) coup *m* de poing. (*fig*) **the ~s of fate** les coups du sort.
2 *vt* (*with hand*) frapper, souffleter; (*with fist*) donner un coup de poing à. **~ed by the waves** battu *or* ballotté par les

vagues; ~**ed by the wind** secoué par le vent; ~**ing wind** vent violent.

buffet[2] ['bʊfeɪ] **1** *n* (*refreshment bar, sideboard*) buffet *m.* (*in menu*) **cold** ~ viandes froides. **2** *cpd*: (*Brit Rail*) **buffet car** voiture-buffet *f*, buffet *m*; **buffet lunch** lunch *m*; **buffet supper** souper-buffet *m.*

buffeting ['bʌfɪtɪŋ] *n [person, object]* bourrades *fpl*, coups *mpl*; *[wind, rain etc]* assaut *m.* **to get a ~ from the waves** être ballotté (de tous côtés) par les vagues.

buffing ['bʌfɪŋ] *n* polissage *m.*

buffoon [bə'fu:n] *n* bouffon *m*, pitre *m*, clown *m.*

buffoonery [bə'fu:nərɪ] *n* bouffonnerie(s) *f(pl).*

bug [bʌg] **1** *n* **(a)** punaise *f*; (*: *any insect*) insecte *m*, bestiole* *f.* (*important person*) **big** ~‡ grosse légume‡, huile‡ *f*; *V* **fire.**

(b) (*: *germ*) microbe *m.* **he picked up a ~ on holiday** il a attrapé un microbe pendant ses vacances; **the flu ~** le virus de la grippe.

(c) (*US*‡: *defect, snag*) défaut *m*, inconvénient *m.*

(d) (*: *hidden microphone*) micro *m.*

2 *vt* **(a)** (*) *phone etc* brancher sur table d'écoute; *room etc* poser *or* installer des micros dans.

(b) (*US*‡: *annoy*) embêter*, casser les pieds à*.

3 *cpd*: **bugbear** épouvantail *m* (*fig*), cauchemar *m*; **bug-eyed‡** aux yeux à fleur de tête; **bughouse‡** (*US: asylum*) cabanon* *m*, maison *f* de dingues‡; (*Brit: cinema*) cinoche‡ *m*; **bug-hunter‡** entomologiste *mf*, chasseur *m* de petites bestioles*; **bug-ridden** infesté de punaises.

bugaboo ['bʌgəbu:] *n* **(a)** croque-mitaine *m*, loup-garou *m.* **(b)** (*US**: *nonsense*) balivernes *fpl.*

bugger ['bʌgəʳ] **1** *n* **(a)** (*Jur*) pédéraste *m.*

(b) (*∗∗*: *fellow*) con∗∗ *m*, couillon∗∗ *m*, corniaud‡ *m*; (*child*) mouflet* *m.* **silly ~▼** pauvre con∗∗; **poor little ~▼** pauvre petit bonhomme*.

2 *excl*: **~ (it)!▼** merde alors!‡

3 *vt* **(a)** (*Jur*) se livrer à la pédérastie avec.

(b) it's got me ~ed▼ je suis bien baisé∗∗.

bugger off▼ *vi* (*Brit*) foutre le camp‡.

bugging ['bʌgɪŋ] *n* utilisation *f* d'appareils d'écoute. **~ device** appareil *m* d'écoute (*clandestine*).

buggy ['bʌgɪ] *n* (*horse-drawn*) boghei *m*; (*for beach*) buggy *m*; (*for moon*) jeep *f* lunaire; (‡: *car*) bagnole* *f*; (*US: perambulator*) voi ure *f* d'enfant.

bugle ['bju:gl] *n* clairon *m.* **~ call** sonnerie *f* de clairon.

bugler ['bju:gləʳ] *n* (joueur *m* de) clairon *m.*

build [bɪld] (*vb: pret, ptp* **built**) **1** *n* carrure *f*, charpente *f.* **man of strong ~** homme solidement bâti *or* charpenté; **of the same ~ as ...** de même carrure que ... .

2 *vt house, town* bâtir, construire; *bridge, ship, machine* construire; *temple* bâtir, édifier; *nest* faire, bâtir; (*fig*) *theory, plan* bâtir, construire, édifier; *empire* fonder, bâtir; (*Games*) *words* former. **the house is being built** la maison se bâtit; **the architect who built the palace** l'architecte qui a bâti *or* qui a fait bâtir le palais; (*fig*) **to ~ castles in the air** faire des châteaux en Espagne; **to ~ a mirror into a wall** encastrer un miroir dans un mur.

3 *vi* bâtir; *[edifice]* se bâtir. **the house is ~ing** la maison se bâtit *or* est en construction; **to ~ upon a piece of land** bâtir sur un terrain; (*lit, fig*) **to ~ upon sand** bâtir sur le sable; (*frm*, †) **to ~ upon sb/a promise** faire fond sur qn/une promesse.

build in 1 *vt sep* (*lit*) *wardrobe* encastrer (*into* dans); (*fig*) *safeguards* intégrer (*into* à).

2 built-in *adj V* **built 3.**

build on *vt sep* ajouter (*to* à).

build up 1 *vi [business connection etc]* se développer; *[pressure]* s'accumuler; *[tension, excitement]* monter, augmenter.

2 *vt sep* **(a)** (*establish*) *reputation* édifier, bâtir; *business* créer, monter; *theory* échafauder; (*increase*) *production, forces* accroître, augmenter; *pressure* accumuler; *tension, excitement* augmenter, faire monter. **to build up one's strength** prendre des forces.

(b) (*cover with houses*) *area, land* urbaniser.

(c) (*fig: publicize*) *person, reputation* faire de la publicité pour, faire du battage* autour de.

3 build-up *n V* **build-up.**

4 built-up *adj V* **built 3.**

builder ['bɪldəʳ] *n* **(a)** *[houses etc]* entrepreneur *m*; *[ships, machines]* constructeur *m.* **~'s labourer** ouvrier *m* du bâtiment; *V* **organ. (b)** (*fig*) fondateur *m*, -trice *f*, créateur *m*, -trice *f*; *V* **empire.**

building ['bɪldɪŋ] **1** *n* **(a)** bâtiment *m*, construction *f*; (*imposing*) édifice *m*; (*habitation or offices*) immeuble *m*; *V* **public.**

(b) (*U*) construction *f.* **the ~ of the church took 7 years** la construction de l'église a demandé 7 ans, il a fallu 7 ans pour construire *or* édifier l'église; *V* **body, empire.**

2 *cpd*: **building contractor** entrepreneur *m* (de bâtiment *or* de construction); **building industry** (industrie *f* du) bâtiment *m*; **building labourer** ouvrier *m* du bâtiment; **building land** terrain *m* à bâtir; **building materials** matériaux *mpl* de construction; **building permit** permis *m* de construire; **building plot** (petit) terrain *m* à bâtir; **building site** chantier *m* (de construction); (*Brit*) **building society** société immobilière; **building trade** = **building industry**; **the building trades** les métiers du bâtiment.

build-up ['bɪldʌp] *n* **(a)** *[pressure]* intensification *f*; *[gas]* accumulation *f*; (*Mil*) *[troops]* rassemblement *m*; *[production]* accroissement *m*; *[tension, excitement]* montée *f.*

(b) (*fig*) présentation *f* publicitaire, battage* *m.* **to give sb/sth a good ~** faire une bonne publicité pour qn/qch.

built [bɪlt] **1** *pret, ptp of* **build.**

2 *adj house* bâti, construit (*of* de, en). *[person]* **to be solidly ~** avoir la charpente solide, être puissamment charpenté; *V* **well**[2].

3 *cpd*: **built-in** *bookcase, wardrobe, mirror, beam* encastré; (*fig*) *desire etc* inné, ancré (*V also* **obsolescence**); **built-in cupboard** placard *m* (encastré); (*Dress*) **built-up** *shoulders* rehaussé; *shoes* à semelle compensée; **built-up area** agglomération (urbaine).

4 -built *adj ending in cpds*: **pine-built house** maison *f* (construite) en bois de pin; **French-built ship** navire *m* de construction française.

bulb [bʌlb] *n* **(a)** *[plant]* bulbe *m*, oignon *m.* **~ of garlic** tête *f* d'ail. **(b)** (*Elec*) ampoule *f.* **(c)** (*Chem*) ballon *m*; *[thermometer]* cuvette *f.*

bulbous ['bʌlbəs] *adj plant* bulbeux; *nose* gros (*f* grosse), bulbeux.

Bulgaria [bʌl'gɛərɪə] *n* Bulgarie *f.*

Bulgarian [bʌl'gɛərɪən] **1** *adj* bulgare. **2** *n* **(a)** Bulgare *mf.* **(b)** (*Ling*) bulgare *m.*

bulge [bʌldʒ] **1** *n* **(a)** *[surface, metal]* bombement *m*; *[cheek]* gonflement *m*; *[column]* renflement *m*; *[jug, bottle]* panse *f*, ventre *m*; *[plaster]* bosse *f*; *[tyre]* soufflure *f*, hernie *f*; *[pocket, jacket, column]* renflement; (*Brit Mil*) saillant *m.* (*Hist*) **the Battle of the B~** la contre-offensive *or* la bataille des Ardennes (*1944*).

(b) (*increase*) *[numbers]* augmentation *f* temporaire; *[sales, prices, profits]* hausse *f*, poussée *f*; *[birth rate]* poussée. **the postwar ~** l'explosion *f* démographique de l'après-guerre.

2 *vi* (*also* **~ out**) (*swell*) se renfler, bomber; (*stick out*) faire *or* former saillie; *[plaster]* être bosselé; *[pocket, sack, cheek]* être gonflé (*with* de).

bulging ['bʌldʒɪŋ] *adj forehead, wall* bombé; *stomach* ballonné, protubérant; *furniture* pansu, ventru; *eyes* protubérant, globuleux, exorbité; *pockets, suitcase* bourré, plein à craquer.

bulk [bʌlk] **1** *n* **(a)** (*great size*) *[thing]* grosseur *f*, grandeur *f*; *[person]* corpulence *f*; (*large volume*) masse *f*, volume *m.* **a ship of great ~** un navire de fort tonnage.

(b) (*main part*) **the ~** la majeure partie, la plus grande partie, le (plus) gros (*of* de); **the ~ of the working community** la plus grande partie *or* l'ensemble *m* de la population ouvrière; **the ~ of the work is done** le plus gros du travail est fait.

(c) (*Comm*) **in ~** (*in large quantities*) en gros; (*not prepacked*) en vrac.

(d) (*Naut*) cargaison *f* (en cale).

2 *cpd*: **bulk-buying** achat *m* en gros; **bulk carrier** transporteur *m* de vrac; (*Naut*) **bulkhead** cloison *f*; **bulk transport** transport *m* en vrac.

3 *vi*: **to ~ large** occuper une large place *or* une place importante (*in sb's eyes* aux yeux de qn, *in sb's thoughts* dans la pensée *or* l'esprit de qn).

bulkiness ['bʌlkɪnɪs] *n [parcel, luggage]* grosseur *f*, volume *m*; *[person]* corpulence *f.*

bulky ['bʌlkɪ] *adj parcel, suitcase* volumineux, encombrant; *book* épais (*f* -aisse); *person* gros (*f* grosse), corpulent.

bull[1] [bʊl] **1** *n* **(a)** taureau *m.* (*fig*) **to take** *or* **seize** *or* **grasp the ~ by the horns** prendre *or* saisir le taureau par les cornes; **like a ~ in a china shop*** comme un éléphant dans un magasin de porcelaine; **to him this word is like a red rag to a ~** c'est un mot qui lui fait monter la moutarde au nez; **to go at it like a ~ at a gate*** foncer tête baissée; (*Astron*) **the B~** le Taureau; *V* **bull's-eye, cock, John.**

(b) (*male of elephant, whale etc*) mâle *m.*

(c) (*St Ex*) haussier *m.*

(d) (*Mil sl: cleaning, polishing*) fourbissage *m*; (‡: *claptrap*) foutaise(s)‡ *f(pl)*, connerie(s)∗∗ *f(pl).*

2 *cpd elephant etc* mâle; (*St Ex*) à la hausse. **bull calf** jeune taureau *m*, taurillon *m*; **bulldog** *V* **bulldog; bulldoze** *V* **bulldoze; bull's-eye** *V* **bull's-eye; bullfight** course *f* de taureaux, corrida *f*; **bullfighter** matador *m*, torero *m*, toréador *m*; **bullfighting** courses *fpl* de taureaux; (*art*) tauromachie *f*; **bullfinch** bouvreuil *m*; **bullfrog** grosse grenouille (d'Amérique); **bull neck** cou *m* de taureau; **bull-necked** au cou de taureau, épais d'encolure; **bullring** arène *f* (*pour courses de taureaux*); **bullshit▼** foutaise(s)‡ *f(pl)*, connerie(s)∗∗ *f(pl)*; **bullterrier** bull-terrier *m.*

3 *vt* (*St Ex*) *stocks, shares* pousser à la hausse. **to ~ the market** pousser les cours à la hausse.

bull[2] [bʊl] *n* (*Rel*) bulle *f.*

bulldog ['bʊldɒg] **1** *n* bouledogue *m.* **2** *cpd tenacity etc* acharné. (*fig*) **he is one of the bulldog breed** il est d'une ténacité à toute épreuve; (*Brit*) **bulldog clip** pince *f* (à dessin).

bulldoze ['bʊldəʊz] *vt* (*Constr*) passer au bulldozer. (*fig*) **to ~ sb into doing sth*** employer les grands moyens pour faire faire qch à qn; **he ~d his way into the meeting*** il a réussi à participer à cette réunion à la force du poignet (*fig*).

bulldozer ['bʊldəʊzəʳ] *n* bulldozer *m.*

bullet ['bʊlɪt] **1** *n* balle *f.* **2** *cpd*: **bulletheaded** à (la) tête ronde; **bullet hole** trou *m* de balle; **bulletproof** *(adj) garment etc* pare-balles *inv*; *car etc* blindé; (*vt*) blinder; **bullet-wound** blessure *f* par balle.

bulletin ['bʊlɪtɪn] *n* bulletin *m*, communiqué *m.* **health ~** bulletin de santé; **~ board** tableau *m* d'affichage; *V* **news.**

bullhorn ['bʊlhɔ:n] *n* (*US*) porte-voix *m inv*, mégaphone *m.*

bullion[1] ['bʊljən] *n* (*U*) encaisse-or *f*; (*gold ~*) or *m* en barre *or* en lingot(s); (*silver ~*) argent *m* en lingot(s).

bullion[2] ['bʊljən] *n* (*fringe*) frange *f* de cannetille.

bullock ['bʊlək] *n* bœuf *m*; (*young*) bouvillon *m.* **~ cart** char *m* à bœufs.

bull's-eye ['bʊlzaɪ] *n* **(a)** *[target]* centre *m*, noir *m* (de la cible),

mille *m.* (*lit, fig*) **to get a ~, to hit the ~** faire mouche, tirer *or* mettre dans le mille.
(b) (*sweet*) gros bonbon à la menthe.
(c) (*window*) œil-de-bœuf *m*, oculus *m*; (*in glass*) boudine *f*.

bully[1] ['bʊlɪ] **1** *n* **(a)** tyran *m*; (*esp Scol*) (petite) brute *f*, brutal *m*.
(b) (*Brit Hockey: also* **~-off**) engagement *m* (du jeu).
2 *vt* (*persecute*) tyranniser, persécuter; (*treat cruelly*) malmener, brutaliser; (*frighten*) intimider; (*Scol*) brutaliser, brimer. **to ~ sb into doing sth** contraindre qn par la menace à faire qch.
3 *vi* être une brute.

bully off *vi* (*Brit*) mettre la balle en jeu, engager (le jeu).

bully[2]‡ ['bʊlɪ] **1** *adj* (†) épatant†. **2** *excl*: **~ for you!** tu es un chef!‡

bully[3]* ['bʊlɪ] *n* (*Mil: also* **~ beef**) corned-beef *m*, singe‡ *m*.

bullying ['bʊlɪɪŋ] **1** *adj person, manner* tyrannique, brutal. **2** *n* brimade(s) *f(pl)*, intimidation *f*, brutalité(s) *f(pl)*.

bulrush ['bʊlrʌʃ] *n* jonc *m*.

bulwark ['bʊlwək] *n* (*rampart*) rempart *m*, fortification *f*; (*breakwater*) brise-lames *m inv*; (*fig: defence*) rempart; (*Naut*) bastingage *m*.

bum[1]‡ [bʌm] (*esp US*) **1** *n* (*vagrant*) clochard *m*, clodo‡ *m*; (*good-for-nothing*) bon à rien *m*.
2 *adj* moche*, minable*, de camelote*.
3 *vi* **(a)** (*scrounge*) taper* les autres.
(b) (*loaf: also* **~ about** *or* **around**) fainéanter, être clochard *or* clodo‡.
4 *vt money, food* écornifler*. **to ~ a meal off sb** taper qn d'un repas*.
5 *cpd*: (*Brit*) **bumbailiff** recors *m*; **bumboat** canot *m* d'approvisionnement.

bum[2]‡ [bʌm] *n* (*Brit: bottom*) derrière *m*, arrière-train* *m*.

bumblebee ['bʌmblbi:] *n* (*Zool*) bourdon *m*.

bumf‡ [bʌmf] *n* (*Brit*) (*pej: forms etc*) paperasses *fpl*, paperasserie *f*; (*toilet paper*) papier *m* cul*∴.

bump [bʌmp] **1** *n* **(a)** (*blow*) choc *m*, heurt *m*, coup *m*; (*jolt*) cahot *m*, secousse *f*; (*Boat-racing*) heurt.
(b) *[road]* bosse *f*, inégalité *f*; *[head, knee etc]* bosse. **~ of locality*** sens *m* de l'orientation.
(c) (*Aviat: rising air current*) (soudain) courant ascendant.
2 *vt [car] another car* heurter, tamponner; *boat* heurter. **to ~ one's head/knee** se cogner la tête/le genou (*against* contre); *[fairground]* **~ing cars** autos tamponneuses.
3 *vi*: **to ~ along** cahoter, bringuebaler; **to ~ down** (*sit*) s'asseoir brusquement.
4 *adv*: **the car ran ~ into a tree** la voiture est entrée de plein fouet *or* en plein dans un arbre.
5 *excl* boum!, pan!

bump into *vt fus* **(a)** *[person]* butter contre, se cogner contre; *[vehicle]* entrer en collision avec, tamponner, rentrer dans*.
(b) (*: *meet*) rencontrer par hasard, tomber sur.

bump off‡ *vt sep* liquider*, supprimer; (*with gun*) descendre‡.

bump up 1 *vi*: **the car bumped up onto the pavement** la voiture a grimpé sur le trottoir. **2** *vt sep* (*: *increase sharply*) *prices, sales, statistics* faire grimper*.

bump up against *vt fus* = **bump into.**

bumper ['bʌmpəʳ] **1** *n* **(a)** *[car]* pare-chocs *m inv*. **(b)** (*full glass*) rasade *f*, plein verre. **2** *adj crop, issue* exceptionnel, sensationnel.

bumph‡ [bʌmf] *n* = **bumf**‡.

bumpkin ['bʌmpkɪn] *n* (*also* **country ~**) rustre *m*, péquenaud‡ *m*, paysan *m* (*pej*).

bumptious ['bʌmpʃəs] *adj* suffisant, prétentieux.

bumpy ['bʌmpɪ] *adj road* bosselé, défoncé, inégal; *forehead* couvert de bosses; *ride* cahoteux; *crossing* agité. **we had a ~ flight/drive/crossing** nous avons été très secoués *or* chahutés* pendant le vol/sur la route/pendant la traversée.

bun [bʌn] **1** *n* **(a)** (*Culin*) petit pain au lait. **to have a ~ in the oven**‡ attendre famille, avoir un polichinelle dans le tiroir‡. **(b)** *[hair]* chignon *m*. **2** *cpd*: **bun-fight**‡ thé *m* (*servi pour un grand nombre de gens*).

bunch [bʌntʃ] **1** *n* **(a)** *[bananas]* régime *m*; *[roses, tulips]* bouquet *m*; *[feathers]* touffe *f*; *[hair]* touffe, houppe *f*; *[radishes, asparagus]* botte *f*; *[twigs]* poignée *f*, paquet *m*; *[keys]* trousseau *m*; *[ribbons]* nœud *m*, flot *m*. **~ of flowers** bouquet (de fleurs); **~ of grapes** grappe *f* de raisins; (*Brit*) **to wear one's hair in ~es** porter des couettes; (*fig*) **the pick of the ~** le dessus du panier.
(b) *[people]* groupe *m*, bande *f*, équipe* *f*; (*Sport*) *[runners]* peloton *m*. **the best of the ~** le meilleur de la bande *or* de l'équipe*; **the best of a bad ~*** le *or* les moins médiocre(s); **what a ~!** quelle équipe!*
2 *vt flowers* mettre en bouquets; *vegetables, straw* botteler, mettre en bottes.

bunch together 1 *vi* se serrer (en foule), se grouper.
2 *vt sep people, things* grouper, concentrer.

bunch up *vt sep* **(a)** *dress, skirt* retrousser, trousser.
(b) they sat bunched up on the bench ils étaient (assis) serrés sur le banc; **don't bunch up so much, space out!** ne vous entassez pas les uns sur les autres, desserrez-vous!

bundle ['bʌndl] **1** *n* **(a)** *[clothes]* paquet *m*, ballot *m*, balluchon* *m*; *[goods]* paquet, ballot; *[hay]* botte *f*; *[letters, papers]* liasse *f*; *[linen]* paquet; *[firewood]* fagot *m*; *[rods, sticks]* faisceau *m*, poignée *f*, paquet. **he is a ~ of nerves** c'est un paquet de nerfs; **that child is a ~ of mischief** cet enfant est un sac à malices.
(b) (‡: *money*) **a ~** beaucoup d'argent, un matelas‡; **to make a ~** faire son beurre*.
2 *vt* **(a)** (*also* **~ up**) empaqueter, mettre en paquet; *clothes* faire un ballot de; *hay* botteler; *papers, banknotes* mettre en liasse; *letters* mettre en paquet; *sticks* mettre en faisceau.
(b) (*put hastily*) **to ~ sth into a corner** fourrer *or* entasser qch dans un coin; **to ~ sb into the house** pousser *or* faire entrer qn dans la maison à la hâte *or* sans cérémonie.

bundle off *vt sep person* faire sortir (en toute hâte), pousser dehors (sans façons). **he was bundled off to Australia** on l'a expédié en Australie.

bundle out *vt sep* pousser dehors (sans façons), faire sortir (en toute hâte).

bundle up *vt sep* **(a)** = **bundle 2a.**
(b) (*US*) emmitoufler*.

bung [bʌŋ] **1** *n [cask]* bondon *m*, bonde *f*. **~hole** bonde.
2 *vt* **(a)** (*also* **~ up**) *cask* boucher; *pipe etc* boucher, obstruer. **his eyes were/his nose was ~ed up*** il avait les yeux tout bouffis/le nez bouché *or* pris; **I'm all ~ed up*** j'ai un gros rhume (de cerveau).
(b) (*Brit*‡: *throw*) flanquer*, envoyer*.

bung in‡ *vt sep* (*include*) rajouter (par-dessus le marché).

bung out‡ *vt sep* flanquer* à la porte; *rubbish* jeter.

bung up *vt sep V* **bung 2a.**

bungaloid ['bʌŋgəlɔɪd] *adj* (*pej*) de bungalow, genre *or* style bungalow. **~ growth** extension *f* d'habitations genre bungalow, extension pavillonnaire.

bungalow ['bʌŋgələʊ] *n* (petit) pavillon *m* (*en rez-de-chaussée*), bungalow *m*; (*in East*) bungalow.

bungle ['bʌŋgl] **1** *vt* gâcher, bâcler*, saboter. **it was a ~d job** c'était (du travail) bâclé*. **2** *vi* s'y prendre mal, faire les choses n'importe comment.

bungler ['bʌŋgləʳ] *n*: **he is a ~** il est incompétent.

bungling ['bʌŋglɪŋ] **1** *adj person* maladroit; *attempt* maladroit, gauche. **2** *n* (*U*) gâchis *m*, bâclage* *m*; maladresse *f*.

bunion ['bʌnjən] *n* (*Med*) oignon *m*.

bunk [bʌŋk] **1** *n* **(a)** (*Naut, Rail etc*) couchette *f*.
(b) (*Brit*) **to do a ~**‡ mettre les bouts‡ *or* les voiles*.
(c) (‡) *abbr of* **bunkum.**
2 *vi* **(a)** (*: *also* **~ down**) coucher, camper (*dans un lit de fortune*).
(b) (‡: *also* **~ off**) mettre les bouts‡ *or* les voiles*.
3 *cpd*: **to give sb a bunk-up*** soulever qn par derrière *or* par en dessous.

bunker ['bʌŋkəʳ] **1** *n* **(a)** *[coal]* coffre *m*; (*Naut*) soute *f* (à charbon *or* à mazout).
(b) (*Golf*) bunker *m*; (*fig*) obstacle *m*.
(c) (*Mil*) blockhaus *m*, bunker *m*.
2 *vt* **(a)** (*Naut*) *coal, oil* mettre en soute. (*Naut*) **to ~ a ship** mettre du charbon *or* du mazout en soute.
(b) to be ~ed (*Golf*) se trouver dans un bunker; (‡*fig*) se trouver face à un obstacle, se trouver dans une impasse.
3 *vi* (*Naut*) charbonner, mazouter.

bunkum‡ ['bʌŋkəm] *n* blague(s)* *f(pl)*, foutaise(s)‡ *f(pl)*, histoires *fpl*. **to talk ~** dire *or* débiter des balivernes *or* des foutaises‡; **that's all ~** tout ça c'est de la blague!*

bunny ['bʌnɪ] *n* **(a)** (*also* **~ rabbit**) Jeannot *m* lapin. **(b)** (*also* **~ girl**) hôtesse *f* (*du Club Playboy*).

Bunsen ['bʌnsn] *n*: **~ burner** bec *m* Bunsen.

bunting[1] ['bʌntɪŋ] *n* (*Orn*) bruant *m*; *V* **reed** *etc*.

bunting[2] ['bʌntɪŋ] *n* (*U*) (*material*) étamine *f* (à pavillon); (*flags etc*) drapeaux *mpl*, banderoles *fpl*, pavoisement *m*.

buoy [bɔɪ] **1** *n* bouée *f*, balise flottante. **to put down a ~** mouiller une bouée; **~ rope** orin *m*; *V* **life, mooring** *etc*. **2** *vt waterway* baliser; *net* liéger.

buoy up *vt sep* (*lit*) faire flotter, maintenir à flot; (*fig*) soutenir, épauler.

buoyancy ['bɔɪənsɪ] *n* **(a)** *[ship, object]* flottabilité *f*; *[liquid]* poussée *f*. **~ aid** gilet *m* de sauvetage; (*Naut*) **~ chamber** *or* **tank** caisson *m* étanche. **(b)** (*lightheartedness*) gaieté *f*, entrain *m*. **(c)** (*Fin*) fermeté *f*, tendance *f* à la hausse.

buoyant ['bɔɪənt] *adj* **(a)** *ship, object* capable de flotter, flottable; *liquid* dans lequel les objets flottent. **fresh water is not so ~ as salt** l'eau douce ne porte pas si bien que l'eau salée.
(b) (*lighthearted*) *person* enjoué, plein d'entrain *or* d'allant; *mood* gai, optimiste; *step* léger, élastique.
(c) (*Fin*) *market* soutenu, ferme.

buoyantly ['bɔɪəntlɪ] *adv walk, float* légèrement; (*fig*) gaiement *or* gaîment, avec entrain, avec optimisme.

bur[1] [bɜ:ʳ] *n* (*Bot*) bardane *f*; (‡*pej: person*) crampon* *m* (*pej*). **chestnut ~** bogue *f*.

bur[2] [bɜ:ʳ] **1** *n* (*Ling*) grasseyement *m*. **to speak with a ~** grasseyer. **2** *vti*: **to ~ (one's Rs)** prononcer les R grasseyés.

burble ['bɜ:bl] **1** *vi [stream]* murmurer; *[person]* marmonner. **what's he burbling (on) about?** qu'est-ce qu'il marmonne (dans sa barbe)? **2** *n [stream]* murmure *m*.

burbling ['bɜ:blɪŋ] *n* (*U*) *[stream]* murmure *m*; *[person]* marmonnement *m*.

burden ['bɜ:dn] **1** *n* **(a)** (*lit*) fardeau *m*, charge *f*, faix *m*; *V* **beast.**
(b) (*fig*) fardeau *m*, charge *f*; *[taxes, years]* poids *m*; *[debts]* fardeau. **to be a ~ to** être un fardeau pour, être à la charge de; **to make sb's life a ~** rendre la vie intenable à qn; **the ~ of the expense** les frais *mpl* à charge; (*Jur*) **~ of proof** charge *or* fardeau de la preuve; **the ~ of proof lies** *or* **rests with him** la charge de la preuve lui incombe, il lui incombe d'en fournir la preuve.
(c) (*Naut*) port *m*, tonnage *m*. **ship of 4,000 tons' ~** navire *m* qui jauge 4.000 tonneaux.
(d) (*chorus*) refrain *m*.
(e) (*chief theme*) substance *f*, fond *m*, essentiel *m*. **the ~ of their complaint** leur principal grief *or* sujet de plainte.
2 *vt* (*place* **~** *on*) charger (*with* de); (*oppress*) accabler (*with* de). **to ~ the people with taxes** grever le peuple d'impôts; **to ~ one's memory with facts** se (sur)charger la mémoire de faits.

burdensome ['bɜːdnsəm] *adj load* lourd, pesant, écrasant; *task, restriction* pénible.
burdock ['bɜːdɒk] *n* bardane *f*.
bureau [bjʊə'rəʊ] *n* **(a)** (*esp Brit: writing desk*) bureau *m*, secrétaire *m*. **(b)** (*US: chest of drawers*) commode *f*. **(c)** (*office*) bureau *m*; *V* **information, travel** *etc*. **(d)** (*government department*) service *m* (gouvernemental). (*US*) **federal ~** bureau fédéral.
bureaucracy [bjʊə'rɒkrəsɪ] *n* bureaucratie *f*.
bureaucrat ['bjʊərəʊkræt] *n* bureaucrate *mf*, rond-de-cuir *m* (*pej*).
bureaucratic [ˌbjʊərəʊ'krætɪk] *adj* bureaucratique.
burette [bjʊə'ret] *n* éprouvette graduée.
burgeon ['bɜːdʒən] *vi* (*liter*) *[flower]* (commencer à) éclore; *[plant]* bourgeonner, se couvrir de bourgeons; *[talent]* naître.
burgess ['bɜːdʒɪs] *n* **(a)** (*Brit Hist*) (*citizen*) bourgeois *m*, citoyen *m*; (*Parl*) député *m*, représentant *m* (au Parlement) d'un bourg *or* d'une circonscription universitaire. **(b)** (*US Hist*) député *m*.
burgh ['bʌrə] *n* (*Scot*) ville *f* (*possédant une charte*).
burglar ['bɜːgləʳ] **1** *n* cambrioleur *m*, -euse *f*; *V* **cat**. **2** *cpd*: **burglar alarm** sonnerie *f* d'alarme, sonnerie antivol; **burglar-proof** *house* muni d'un dispositif antivol; *lock* incrochetable.
burglarize ['bɜːgləraɪz] *vt* (*US*) cambrioler.
burglary ['bɜːglərɪ] *n* cambriolage *m*.
burgle ['bɜːgl] **1** *vt* cambrioler, dévaliser. **2** *vi* cambrioler.
burgomaster ['bɜːgəˌmɑːstəʳ] *n* bourgmestre *m*.
Burgundian [bɜː'gʌndɪən] **1** *adj* bourguignon, de Bourgogne. **2** *n* Bourguignon(ne) *m(f)*.
Burgundy ['bɜːgəndɪ] *n* (*Geog*) Bourgogne *f*. (*wine*) **b~** le bourgogne, le vin de Bourgogne.
burial ['berɪəl] **1** *n* (*interment*) enterrement *m*, inhumation *f*, ensevelissement *m* (*liter*); (*religious*) sépulture *f*; (*ceremony*) funérailles *fpl*, obsèques *fpl*; *[hopes etc]* mort *f*, fin *f*. **Christian ~** sépulture ecclésiastique *or* chrétienne.
2 *cpd*: **burial ground** cimetière *m*; **burial mound** tumulus *m*; **burial place** lieu *m* de sépulture; **burial service** office *m* des morts, service *m* funèbre; **burial vault** tombeau *m*.
burin ['bjʊərɪn] *n* burin *m* (à graver).
burke [bɜːk] *vt* (*suppress*) *scandal* étouffer; (*shelve*) *question* escamoter.
burlap ['bɜːlæp] *n* toile *f* d'emballage, toile à sac.
burlesque [bɜː'lesk] **1** *n* **(a)** (*parody*) *[book, poem etc]* parodie *f*; *[society, way of life]* caricature *f*.
(b) (*U: Literat*) (genre *m*) burlesque *m*.
(c) (*US Theat*) revue *f*.
2 *adj poem etc* burlesque; *description* caricatural.
3 *vt* (*make ridiculous*) tourner en ridicule; (*parody*) *book, author* parodier.
burly ['bɜːlɪ] *adj* de forte carrure, solidement charpenté. **a big ~ fellow** un grand costaud*; **a ~ policeman** un grand gaillard d'agent.
Burma ['bɜːmə] *n* Birmanie *f*.
Burmese [bɜː'miːz] **1** *adj* birman, de Birmanie. **the ~ Empire** l'Empire birman; **~ cat** chat(te) *m(f)* de Birmanie. **2** *n* **(a)** Birman(e) *m(f)*. **(b)** (*Ling*) birman *m*.
burn[1] [bɜːn] (*vb: pret, ptp* **burned** *or* **burnt**) **1** *n* **(a)** (*also Med*) brûlure *f*. **cigarette ~** brûlure de cigarette; *V* **degree**.
(b) (*Space*) *[rocket]* mise *f* à feu.
2 *vt* **(a)** *coal, electricity, rubbish* brûler; *town, building* incendier, mettre le feu à, faire brûler. **to ~ to a cinder** carboniser, calciner; **to be ~t to death** être brûlé vif, mourir carbonisé; **to be ~t alive** *or* **at the stake** être brûlé vif; **to ~ o.s.** se brûler; **to ~ one's finger** se brûler le doigt; **he ~t a hole in his coat with a cigarette** il a fait un trou à son manteau avec une cigarette; (*fig*) **you could ~ your fingers over this** vous risquez de vous brûler les doigts dans cette affaire; (*fig*) **money ~s a hole in my pocket** l'argent me fond dans les mains; (*fig*) **to ~ one's boats/one's bridges** brûler ses vaisseaux/les ponts; (*fig*) **to ~ the candle at both ends** brûler la chandelle par les deux bouts; *V* **midnight** *etc*.
(b) (*Culin*) *meat, toast, cakes* laisser brûler; *sauce, milk* laisser attacher.
(c) *[acid]* brûler, ronger; *[sun] person, skin* brûler. **his skin was ~t black by the sun** il était noir d'avoir été brûlé par le soleil.
3 *vi* **(a)** *[wood, meat, cakes etc]* brûler; *[milk, sauce]* attacher. **you left all the lights ~ing** vous avez laissé toutes les lumières allumées; **her skin ~s easily** elle a la peau facilement brûlée par le soleil, elle attrape facilement des coups de soleil; **my head is ~ing** j'ai la tête brûlante; **the wound was ~ing** la blessure cuisait; (*fig*) **a ~ing question** une question brûlante.
(b) *[person]* (*lit*) être brûlé vif; (*fig*) brûler (*with* de). **he was ~ing to get his revenge** *or* **~ing for revenge** il brûlait (du désir) de se venger.
(c) acid ~s into metal l'acide ronge le métal; (*fig*) **the date ~ed into his memory** la date se grava dans sa mémoire.
(d) (*Space*) *[rocket]* brûler.
burn away 1 *vi* **(a)** (*go on burning*) **the fire was burning away** le feu flambait *or* brûlait bien.
(b) se consumer.
2 *vt sep* détruire (par le feu); *paint* brûler au chalumeau.
burn down 1 *vi* **(a)** *[house etc]* brûler complètement, être réduit en cendres.
(b) *[fire, candle]* baisser.
2 *vt sep building* incendier. **the house was burnt down** la maison a été réduite en cendres *or* calcinée.
burn off *vt sep paint etc* brûler (au chalumeau).
burn out 1 *vi [fire, candle]* s'éteindre; *[light bulb]* griller, sauter.
2 *vt sep* **(a)** *candle* laisser brûler jusqu'au bout; *lamp* griller. **the candle burnt itself out** la bougie est morte; (*fig*) **he burnt himself out** il s'est usé (à force de travail).
(b) (*force out by fire*) *enemy troops etc* forcer à sortir en mettant le feu. **they were burnt out of house and home** un incendie a détruit leur maison avec tout ce qu'ils possédaient.
burn up 1 *vi* **(a)** *[fire etc]* flamber, monter.
(b) *[rocket etc in atmosphere]* se volatiliser, se désintégrer.
2 *vt sep* **(a)** *rubbish* brûler.
(b) burned up with envy dévoré d'envie.
burn[2] [bɜːn] *n* (*Scot*) ruisseau *m*.
burner ['bɜːnəʳ] *n [gas cooker]* brûleur *m*; *[lamp]* bec *m* (de gaz); *V* **Bunsen, charcoal** *etc*.
burning ['bɜːnɪŋ] **1** *adj* **(a)** (*on fire*) *town, forest* en flammes, embrasé (*liter*), incendié; *fire, candle* allumé; *coals* embrasé (*liter*); *feeling* cuisant. **the ~ bush** le buisson ardent; **with a ~ face** (*shame*) le rouge au front; (*embarrassment*) le rouge aux joues.
(b) (*fig*) *thirst, fever* brûlant; *faith* ardent, intense; *indignation* violent; *words* véhément, passionné; *question, topic* brûlant, passionnant. **it's a ~ shame that ...*** c'est une honte *or* un scandale que ... .
2 *n* **(a)** (*Culin*) brûlé *m*. **there is a smell of ~** ça sent le brûlé *or* le roussi; **I could smell ~** je sentais une odeur de brûlé.
(b) (*setting on fire*) incendie *m*, embrasement *m*. **they ordered the ~ of the town** ils ont ordonné l'incendie de la ville, ils ont ordonné qu'on mette le feu à la ville.
burnish ['bɜːnɪʃ] *vt metal* brunir, polir. **~ed hair** (beaux) cheveux brillants.
burnisher ['bɜːnɪʃəʳ] *n* (*person*) brunisseur *m*, -euse *f*; (*tool*) brunissoir *m*.
burnt [bɜːnt] **1** *pret, ptp of* **burn**[1].
2 *adj* brûlé, carbonisé. (*Prov*) **a ~ child dreads the fire** chat échaudé craint l'eau froide (*Prov*); **~ almond** amande grillée, praline *f*; **~ lime** chaux vive; **~ offering, ~ sacrifice** holocaus e *m*; **~ orange** orange foncé *inv*; **~ sienna, ~ umber** terre *f* de sienne *or* d'ombre brûlée; **~ smell/taste** odeur *f*/goût *m* de brûlé; **~ sugar** caramel *m*.
burp* [bɜːp] **1** *vi* roter*, faire un renvoi. **2** *vt*: **to ~ a baby** faire faire son rot* *or* son renvoi à un bébé. **3** *n* rot* *m*, renvoi *m*.
burr[1] [bɜːʳ] *n* = **bur**[1].
burr[2] [bɜːʳ] = **bur**[2].
burrow ['bʌrəʊ] **1** *n* terrier *m*. **2** *vi [rabbits etc]* creuser un terrier; *[dog, person]* fouir la terre, creuser (la terre). (*fig*) **to ~ into the past** fouiller dans le passé. **3** *vt* creuser. **to ~ one's way underground** (se) creuser (un chemin) sous terre.
bursar ['bɜːsəʳ] *n* **(a)** (*in school, small institution*) économe *mf*, intendant(e) *m(f)*; (*in university, large institution*) administrateur *m*, -trice *f*. **(b)** (*Brit: student*) (élève *mf*) boursier *m*, -ière *f*.
bursary ['bɜːsərɪ] *n* bourse *f* (d'études).
bursitis [bɜː'saɪtɪs] *n* hygroma *m*.
burst [bɜːst] (*vb: pret, ptp* **burst**) **1** *n [shell etc]* explosion *f*, éclatement *m*; *[anger, indignation]* explosion; *[anger, laughter]* éclat *m*; *[affection, eloquence]* élan *m*, transport *m*; *[activity]* vague *f*; *[enthusiasm]* accès *m*, montée *f*; *[thunder]* coup *m*; *[applause]* salve *f*; *[flames]* jaillissement *m*, jet *m*. **~ of rain** averse *f*; **to put on a ~ of speed** faire une pointe de vitesse; **~ of gunfire** rafale *f* (de tir); **~ of weeping** crise *f* de larmes.
2 *vi* **(a)** *[bomb, shell]* éclater, faire explosion; *[boiler]* éclater, sauter; *[bubble, balloon, tyre, abscess]* crever; *[bud]* éclore. (*fig*) **to ~ open** *[door]* s'ouvrir violemment; *[container]* s'éventrer.
(b) *[sack etc]* **to be ~ing** être plein à crever, regorger (*with* de); **to fill a sack to ~ing point** remplir un sac à craquer; (*fig*) **to be ~ing with health** déborder de santé; **to be ~ing with impatience** brûler d'impatience; **to be ~ing with pride** éclater d'orgueil; **to be ~ing with joy** déborder de joie; **I was ~ing to tell you*** je mourais d'envie de vous le dire.
(c) (*move etc suddenly*) se précipiter, se jeter (*into* dans, *out of* hors de). **the horse ~ into a gallop** le cheval a pris le galop; **he suddenly ~ into speech/song** il s'est mis tout d'un coup à parler/chanter; **the truth ~ (in) upon him** la vérité lui a soudain sauté aux yeux; **the applause ~ upon our ears** les applaudissements ont éclaté à nos oreilles; **to ~ into tears** fondre en larmes; *[flower]* **to ~ into bloom** s'épanouir (soudain); **to ~ into flames** prendre feu (soudain); **the sun ~ through the clouds** le soleil a percé les nuages; **the oil ~ from the well** le pétrole a jailli du puits.
3 *vt balloon, bubble, tyre* crever; *boiler* faire sauter. **to ~ open** *door* ouvrir violemment; *container* éventrer; **the river has ~ its banks** le fleuve a rompu ses digues; **to ~ one's sides with laughter*** se tordre de rire; (*Med*) **to ~ a blood vessel** (se) faire éclater une veine, (se) rompre un vaisseau; (*with anger etc*) **he almost ~ a blood vessel*** il a failli (en) prendre un coup de sang* *or* (en) avoir une attaque*.
burst forth *vi* (*liter*) *[person]* sortir précipitamment; *[sun]* surgir.
burst in 1 *vi* entrer en trombe *or* en coup de vent, faire irruption. **he burst in on us** il a fait irruption chez nous; **to burst in on a conversation** interrompre brutalement une conversation.
2 *vt sep door* enfoncer.
burst out *vi* **(a) to burst out of a room** se précipiter hors d'une pièce, sortir d'une pièce en trombe.
(b) she's bursting out of that dress elle éclate de partout *or* elle est très boudinée dans cette robe.
(c) (*in speech*) s'exclamer, s'écrier. **to burst out into explanations/threats** *etc* se répandre en explications/menaces *etc*.

(d) to burst out laughing éclater de rire; to burst out crying fondre en larmes; to burst out singing se mettre tout d'un coup à chanter.

burthen†† ['bɜːðən] = **burden**.

burton ['bɜːtn] *n*: he's gone for a ~‡ il a eu son compte*, il est fichu* *or* foutu‡; (*Aviat*) il s'est fait descendre*.

bury ['berɪ] *vt* **(a)** *person* enterrer, ensevelir, inhumer; *animal* enterrer. to ~ sb alive enterrer qn vivant; he was buried at sea son corps fut immergé (en haute mer); buried by an avalanche enseveli par une avalanche; *V* dead.

(b) *treasure* enterrer, enfouir; (*fig*) *quarrel* enterrer, oublier. the dog buried a bone le chien a enterré un os; (*fig*) to ~ one's head in the sand se cacher la tête dans le sable, pratiquer la politique de l'autruche; (*fig*) to ~ the hatchet *or* (*US*) the tomahawk enterrer la hache de guerre.

(c) (*conceal*) enfouir, cacher. to ~ o.s. under the blankets s'enfouir sous les couvertures; to ~ one's face in one's hands se couvrir *or* se cacher la figure de ses mains; a village buried in the country un village enfoui *or* caché *or* perdu en pleine campagne; she buried herself in the country elle est allée s'enterrer à la campagne.

(d) (*engross: gen ptp*) plonger. to ~ o.s. in one's studies se plonger dans ses études; buried in one's work plongé *or* absorbé dans son travail; buried in thought plongé dans une rêverie *or* dans ses pensées.

(e) (*plunge*) *hands, knife* enfoncer, plonger (*in* dans).

bus [bʌs] **1** *n, pl* ~es, (*US*) ~es *or* ~ses **(a)** autobus *m*, bus* *m*; (*long-distance*) autocar *m*, car *m*. all ~es stop here arrêt *m* fixe *or* obligatoire; *V* double, miss[1], trolley *etc*.

(b) (‡) (*car*) bagnole* *f*; (*plane*) (vieux) coucou* *m*.

2 *vi* (*) prendre l'autobus *or* le car.

3 *vt* (*esp US*) to ~ children to school transporter des enfants à l'école en car (*V* bussing).

4 *cpd*: (*US*) busboy aide-serveur *m*; bus conductor receveur *m* d'autobus; bus depot dépôt *m* d'autobus; bus driver conducteur *m* d'autobus; a busload of children un autobus (plein) d'enfants, un car entier *or* tout un autobus d'enfants; they came by the busload *or* in busloads ils sont venus par cars entiers; busman (*driver*) conducteur *m* d'autobus; (*conductor*) receveur *m*; (*fig*) to take a busman's holiday passer ses vacances à travailler; the busmen's strike la grève des employés des autobus; the house is/is not on a bus route la maison est/n'est pas sur un trajet d'autobus; bus service réseau *m or* service *m* d'autobus; bus shelter abri-bus *m*; bus station gare *f* d'autobus; [*coaches*] gare routière *or* des cars; bus stop arrêt *m* d'autobus; bus ticket ticket *m* d'autobus.

busby ['bʌzbɪ] *n* bonnet *m* à poil (*de soldat*).

bush[1] [bʊʃ] **1** *n* **(a)** (*shrub*) buisson *m*. (*fig*) he had a great ~ of hair il avait une épaisse tignasse; *V* beat, burning, rose[2] *etc*.

(b) (*thicket*) taillis *m*, fourré *m*; (*U: brushwood*) broussailles *fpl*. [*Africa, Australia*] the ~ la brousse; to take to the ~ partir *or* se réfugier dans la brousse; [*Corsica*] prendre le maquis.

2 *cpd*: bushfighting guérilla *f*; bushfire feu *m* de brousse; [*South Africa*] Bushman Boschiman *m*; [*Australia*] bushman broussard* *m*; bushranger [*Australia*] forçat réfugié dans la brousse, broussard* *m*; [*Can, US*] trappeur *m*; bush telegraph (*lit*) téléphone *m* de brousse; (* *fig*) téléphone arabe; (*US*) bushwhack (*vi*) se frayer un chemin à travers la brousse; (*vt: ambush*) tendre une embuscade à; bushwhacker (*frontiersman*) colon *m* de la brousse; (*guerilla soldier*) guérillero *m*; (*bandit*) bandit *m* de la brousse; [*Australia*] (*lumberjack*) bûcheron *m*; (*US*) bushwhacking = bushfighting.

bush[2] [bʊʃ] *n* (*Tech*) bague *f*.

bushed [bʊʃt] *adj* **(a)** (‡) (*puzzled*) ahuri, ébaubi*; (*exhausted*) flapi*, claqué*. **(b)** (*Australia*) perdu en brousse.

bushel ['bʊʃl] *n* (*measure*) boisseau *m*; *V* hide[1].

bushing ['bʊʃɪŋ] *n* (*Tech: esp US*) bague *f*.

bushy ['bʊʃɪ] *adj land, ground* broussailleux, couvert de buissons; *shrub* épais (*f* -aisse); *tree* touffu; *beard, eyebrows, hair* touffu, broussailleux.

busily ['bɪzɪlɪ] *adv* (*actively, eagerly*) activement; (*pej: officiously*) avec trop de zèle. to be ~ engaged in sth/in doing être très occupé *or* activement occupé à qch/à faire.

business ['bɪznɪs] **1** *n* **(a)** (*U*) (*commerce*) affaires *fpl*. to be in ~ être dans les affaires; to be in the grocery ~ être dans l'épicerie *or* l'alimentation; to be in ~ for o.s. travailler pour son propre compte; to set up in ~ as a butcher *etc* s'établir boucher *etc*; to do ~ with sb faire des affaires avec qn, travailler avec qn; ~ is looking up les affaires reprennent; ~ is ~ les affaires sont les affaires; to go to Paris on ~ aller à Paris pour affaires; to be away on ~ être en déplacement pour affaires; his ~ is cattle rearing il a une affaire d'élevage de bestiaux; his line of ~ sa partie; what's his line of ~?* qu'est-ce qu'il fait (dans la vie)?; to know one's ~ connaître son affaire, s'y connaître; (*fig*) to get down to ~ passer aux choses sérieuses, en venir au cœur du sujet; (*fig*) now we're in ~!* tout devient possible!; he means ~* il ne plaisante pas; to mix ~ with pleasure joindre l'utile à l'agréable.

(b) (*U: volume of trade*) our ~ has doubled in the last year notre chiffre d'affaires a doublé par rapport à l'année dernière, nous travaillons deux fois plus que l'année dernière; most of the shop's ~ comes from women la clientèle de la boutique est pour la plupart féminine; he gets a lot of ~ from the Americans il travaille beaucoup avec les Américains.

(c) (*commercial enterprise*) commerce *m*. he has a little ~ in the country il tient un petit commerce *or* il a une petite affaire à la campagne; he owns a grocery ~ il a un commerce d'alimentation.

(d) (*task, duty*) affaire *f*, devoir *m*. the ~ of the day l'ordre du jour; it's all part of the day's ~ cela fait partie de la routine journalière; to make it one's ~ to do sth se charger de faire qch; that's none of his ~ ce n'est pas son affaire, cela ne le regarde pas; it's your ~ to do it c'est à vous de le faire; you've no ~ to do that ce n'est pas à vous de faire cela; that's my ~ and none of yours c'est mon affaire et non la vôtre; mind your own ~ mêlez-vous de vos affaires *or* de ce qui vous regarde; I know my own ~ je ne veux pas me mêler de ce qui ne me regarde pas; *V* send.

(e) (*difficult job*) finding a flat is quite a ~ c'est toute une affaire de trouver un appartement; she made a (terrible) ~ of helping him elle a fait toute une histoire* pour l'aider.

(f) (*pej*) affaire *f*, histoire *f*. it's a bad ~ c'est une sale affaire *or* histoire; (*pej*) I am tired of this protest ~ j'en ai assez de cette histoire de contestation; there's some funny ~ going on il se passe quelque chose de louche *or* de pas catholique*.

2 *cpd lunch, meeting* d'affaires. his business address l'adresse *f* de son travail *or* de son bureau; business centre centre *m* des affaires; business college école *f* de commerce; (*fig*) the business end of a knife le côté opérant *or* la partie coupante d'un couteau; business expenses frais généraux; business girl (jeune) femme *f* d'affaires; businessman homme *m* d'affaires; big businessman brasseur *m* d'affaires; he's a good businessman il est très homme d'affaires; business manager (*Comm, Ind*) directeur commercial; (*Cine, Sport, Theat*) manager *m*; business school = business college; to have business sense avoir du flair pour les affaires; business suit complet *m* (veston); business trip voyage *m* d'affaires; businesswoman femme *f* d'affaires.

businesslike ['bɪznɪslaɪk] *adj person* pratique, méthodique, efficace; *firm, transaction* sérieux, régulier; *manner* sérieux, carré; *method* net, pratique, efficace; *style* net, précis; *appearance* sérieux. this is a very ~ knife!* ça c'est un couteau (sérieux)!*

busk [bʌsk] *vi* (*Brit*) jouer (*or* chanter) dans la rue.

busker ['bʌskəʳ] *n* (*Brit*) musicien ambulant *or* des rues.

bussing ['bʌsɪŋ] *n* ramassage *m* scolaire (*surtout aux U.S.A. comme mesure de déségrégation*).

bust[1] [bʌst] *n* **(a)** (*Sculp*) buste *m*. **(b)** (*Anat*) buste *m*, poitrine *f*. ~ measurement tour *m* de poitrine.

bust[2] [bʌst] **1** *adj* **(a)** (*: *broken*) fichu*, foutu‡.

(b) (‡: *bankrupt*) to go ~ faire faillite; to be ~ être fauché*, être à sec*.

2 *n* (‡: *spree*) bombe* *f*, bringue* *f*. to go on the ~, to have a ~ faire la bombe* *or* la bringue*.

3 *cpd*: bust-up‡ engueulade‡ *f*; to have a bust-up with sb‡ s'engueuler avec qn‡ (*et rompre*).

4 *vt* **(a)** (*) = burst 3.

(b) (‡) *criminal* choper*.

5 *vi*(‡) = burst 2.

bust up‡ **1** *vi* [*friends*] se brouiller, rompre après une engueulade‡.

2 *vt sep* (*fig*) *marriage, friendship* flanquer en l'air*.

3 bust-up‡: *n V* bust[2] 3.

bustard ['bʌstəd] *n* outarde *f*.

bustle[1] ['bʌsl] **1** *vi* s'affairer, se démener, s'agiter. to ~ about s'affairer; to ~ in/out *etc* entrer/sortir *etc* d'un air affairé. **2** *n* affairement *m*, remue-ménage *m*.

bustle[2] ['bʌsl] *n* (*Dress*) tournure *f*.

bustling ['bʌslɪŋ] **1** *adj person* actif, empressé, affairé; *place* bruyant, agité. ~ with life plein de vie, plein d'animation, trépidant. **2** *n* = bustle[1] 2.

busty ['bʌstɪ] *adj* (*) *woman* à la poitrine plantureuse. she's rather ~‡ il y a du monde au balcon‡, elle a une poitrine de nourrice*.

busy ['bɪzɪ] **1** *adj* **(a)** (*occupied*) *person* occupé (*doing* à faire, *with sth* à qch). she's ~ cooking elle est en train de faire la cuisine; he's ~ playing with the children il est occupé à jouer avec les enfants; to be ~ with the housework vaquer aux soins du ménage; too ~ to do sth trop occupé pour faire qch; he was ~ at his work il était tout entier à *or* absorbé dans son travail.

(b) (*active*) *person* affairé, diligent, actif; *person, manner* énergique; *day* chargé, de grande activité; *place* mouvementé, plein de mouvement; *street* passant, animé; *town* animé, grouillant d'activité. as ~ as a bee très occupé; she's a real ~ bee* elle est toujours à s'activer, elle est débordante d'activité; to keep o.s. ~ trouver à s'occuper; to get ~ s'y mettre; a ~ time une période de grande activité; the shop is at its busiest in summer c'est en été qu'il y a le plus d'affluence dans le magasin.

(c) (*Telec*) *line* occupé. (*US*) ~ signal tonalité *f* occupé *inv*.

2 *vt*: to ~ o.s. s'appliquer, s'occuper (*doing* à faire, *with sth* à qch).

3 *n* (‡: *detective*) flic* *m*.

4 *cpd*: busybody mouche *f* du coche, officieux *m*, -euse *f*; to be a busybody faire la mouche du coche.

but [bʌt] **1** *conj* **(a)** (*coordinating*) mais. I should like to do it ~ I have no money j'aimerais le faire mais je n'ai pas d'argent; she was poor ~ she was honest elle était pauvre mais honnête.

(b) (*contradicting*) mais. he's not English ~ Irish il n'est pas anglais mais irlandais; he wasn't singing, ~ he was shouting il ne chantait pas, il criait.

(c) (*subordinating*) I never eat asparagus ~ I remember that evening je ne mange jamais d'asperges sans me souvenir de cette soirée; never a week passes ~ she is ill il ne se passe jamais une semaine qu'elle ne soit malade; (*fig*) it never rains ~ it pours un malheur n'arrive jamais seul.

2 *adv* seulement, ne ... que. (*liter*) she's ~ a child ce n'est qu'une enfant; I cannot (help) ~ think je suis bien obligé de penser, je ne peux m'empêcher de penser; you can ~ try vous pouvez toujours essayer; (*liter*) if I could ~ tell you why si je pouvais seulement vous dire pourquoi; (*liter*) **she left ~ a few minutes ago** il n'y a que quelques minutes qu'elle est partie.

3 *prep* sauf, excepté; sinon. **no one ~ me could do it** personne sauf moi ne pourrait le faire, je suis le seul à pouvoir *or* qui puisse le faire; **they've all gone ~ me** ils sont tous partis sauf *or* excepté moi; **who could do it ~ me?** qui pourrait le faire sinon moi?; **no one ~ him** personne d'autre que lui; **anything ~ that** tout mais pas ça; **there was nothing for it ~ to jump** il n'y avait plus qu'à sauter; **the last house ~ one** l'avant-dernière maison; **the next house ~ one** la seconde maison à partir d'ici; **~ for you/~ for that I would be dead** sans vous/sans cela je serais mort.

4 *n*: **no ~s about it!** il n'y a pas de mais (qui tienne)!; *V* **if.**

butane ['bju:teɪn] *n* butane *m*. **~ gas** gaz *m* butane, butagaz *m* ®.

butch‡ [bʊtʃ] *n* gouine‡ *f*.

butcher ['bʊtʃəʳ] **1** *n* (*lit, fig*) boucher *m*. **at the ~'s** chez le boucher; **~'s boy** garçon *m* boucher, livreur *m* (*du boucher*); **~ meat** viande *f* de boucherie; **~'s shop** boucherie *f*; **~'s wife** bouchère *f*; (*Brit*) **to have a ~'s (hook)**‡ regarder, zieuter‡; *V* **pork** *etc*.

2 *vt animal* tuer, abattre; *person* égorger, massacrer; (*fig*) massacrer.

butchery ['bʊtʃərɪ] *n* **(a)** (*U*) (*lit*) abattage *m*; (*fig*) boucherie *f*, massacre *m*, carnage *m*. **(b)** (*slaughterhouse*) abattoir *m*.

butler ['bʌtləʳ] *n* maître *m* d'hôtel, majordome *m*. **~'s pantry** office *f*; **~'s tray** (*petit*) plateau *m* (*de service*).

butt[1] [bʌt] *n* [*wine, rainwater etc*] (gros) tonneau *m*.

butt[2] [bʌt] *n* (*end*) (gros) bout *m*; [*rifle*] crosse *f*; [*cigarette*] mégot *m*, bout; (*US*‡: *bottom*) derrière *m*, arrière-train* *m*.

butt[3] [bʌt] *n* (*target*) cible *f*; (*earth mound*) butte *f* (de tir). **the ~s** le champ de tir, le polygone (de tir); (*fig*) **to be a ~ for ridicule** être un objet de risée, être en butte au ridicule; **the ~ of a practical joker** la victime d'un farceur.

butt[4] [bʌt] **1** *n* coup *m* de tête; [*goat etc*] coup de corne. **2** *vt* **(a)** [*goat*] donner un coup de corne à; [*person*] donner un coup de tête à. **(b)** (*Tech*) abouter.

butt in *vi* (*fig*) s'immiscer dans les affaires des autres, intervenir; (*speaking*) dire son mot, mettre son grain de sel*. **I don't want to butt in** je ne veux pas m'immiscer dans la conversation.

butt into *vt fus meeting, conversation* intervenir dans, s'immiscer dans.

butter ['bʌtəʳ] **1** *n* beurre *m*. **she looks as if ~ wouldn't melt in her mouth** elle fait la sainte nitouche; **he looks as if ~ wouldn't melt in his mouth** il a un air sucré; *V* **bread, peanut** *etc*.

2 *cpd*: **butter bean** (gros) haricot blanc; **butter cloth** mousseline *f* à beurre, étamine *f*; **butter cooler** pot *m* à (rafraîchir le) beurre; (*Bot*) **buttercup** bouton *m* d'or, renoncule *f* des champs; **butter dish** beurrier *m*; **he is butter-fingered, he's a butter-fingers** tout lui glisse des mains *or* des doigts; **butterfingers** maladroit(e) *m(f)*, empoté(e)* *m(f)*; (*excl*) **butterfingers!** espèce d'empoté!*; **butterfly** *V* **butterfly; butter icing** glaçage *m* au beurre; **butter knife** couteau *m* à beurre; **buttermilk** babeurre *m*; **butter muslin** mousseline *f* à beurre, étamine *f*; (*dress material*) mousseline; **butter paper** papier *m* à beurre, papier sulfurisé; **butterscotch** caramel dur (au beurre).

3 *vt bread etc* beurrer.

butter up* *vt sep* (*fig*) passer de la pommade à.

butterfly ['bʌtəflaɪ] **1** *n* (*Zool, also fig*) papillon *m*. **to have butterflies in the stomach*** avoir le trac*.

2 *cpd*: **butterfly knot** nœud *m* papillon; **butterfly net** filet *m* à papillons; **butterfly nut** papillon *m*, écrou *m* à ailettes; **butterfly-stroke** brasse *f* papillon *inv*.

buttery ['bʌtərɪ] **1** *adj taste* de beurre; (*spread with butter*) beurré, couvert de beurre. **2** *n* [*college, school*] dépense *f*, office *f*.

buttock ['bʌtək] *n* fesse *f*. **~s** [*person*] fesses; [*animal*] croupe *f*.

button ['bʌtn] **1** *n* **(a)** [*garment, door, bell, lamp, fencing foil*] bouton *m*. **chocolate ~s** pastilles *fpl* de chocolat; (*esp Brit*) [*hotel*] **B~s*** groom *m*, chasseur *m*.

(b) (*Bot*) bouton *m*.

2 *vt* (*also* **~ up**) *garment* boutonner.

3 *vi* [*garment*] se boutonner.

4 *cpd*: **button-down collar** col boutonné; **buttonhook** tire-bouton *m*; **button mushroom** (petit) champignon *m* de couche *or* de Paris; **button-through dress** robe *f* chemisier.

buttonhole ['bʌtnhəʊl] **1** *n* **(a)** [*garment*] boutonnière *f*. **~ stitch** point *m* de boutonnière.

(b) (*Brit: flower*) fleur *f* (*portée à la boutonnière*). **to wear a ~** avoir *or* porter une fleur à sa boutonnière.

2 *vt* **(a)** (*fig*) *person* accrocher*.

(b) (*Sewing*) faire du point de boutonnière sur.

buttress ['bʌtrɪs] **1** *n* (*Archit*) contrefort *m*, éperon *m*; (*arch-shaped*) arc-boutant *m*; (*fig*) pilier *m*, soutien *m*, appui *m*; *V* **flying.** **2** *vt* (*Archit*) arc-bouter, soutenir, étayer; (*fig*) *argument* étayer, soutenir.

buxom ['bʌksəm] *adj* bien en chair, rondelet, aux formes généreuses.

buy [baɪ] *pret, ptp* **bought** **1** *vt* **(a)** (*purchase*) acheter (*sth from sb* qch à qn, *sth for sb* qch pour *or* à qn). **the things that money cannot ~** les choses qui ne s'achètent pas; **to ~ petrol** prendre de l'essence; **to ~ a train ticket** prendre un billet de chemin de fer; **to ~ a theatre ticket** louer *or* retenir *or* prendre une place de théâtre; **to ~ and sell goods** acheter et revendre des marchandises; **to ~ a pig in a poke*** acheter chat en poche; **to ~ sth cheap** acheter qch bon marché *or* pour une bouchée de pain; (*fig*) **the victory was dearly bought** la victoire fut chèrement payée.

(b) (*bribe*) *person* acheter, corrompre. **to ~ one's way into a business** avoir recours à la corruption pour entrer dans une affaire.

(c) (*: *believe*) croire. **he won't ~ that explanation** il n'est pas question qu'il avale* (*subj*) cette explication; **they bought the whole story** ils ont avalé* *or* gobé* toute l'histoire; **all right, I'll ~ it** (bon,) d'accord *or* je marche*.

(d) (‡: *die*) **he's bought it** il y est resté*.

2 *n* affaire *f*. **that house is a good/bad ~** cette maison est une bonne/mauvaise affaire.

buy back *vt sep* racheter.

buy in *vt sep goods* s'approvisionner en, stocker; (*St Ex*) acquérir, acheter.

buy off *vt sep* (*bribe*) *person* acheter le silence de; *claim* étouffer (par la corruption).

buy out *vt sep* (*Fin*) *person* désintéresser. (*Mil*) **to buy o.s. out** se racheter (*d'un engagement dans l'armée*).

buy over *vt sep* (*bribe*) corrompre, acheter.

buy up *vt sep* acheter en bloc, rafler*.

buyer ['baɪəʳ] *n* **(a)** (*gen*) acheteur *m*, -euse *f*, acquéreur *m*. **~'s market** marché acheteur *or* à la hausse; **house~** acheteur *or* acquéreur d'une propriété.

(b) (*for business firm, shop etc*) acheteur *m*, -euse *f* (professionnel(le)).

buzz [bʌz] **1** *n* **(a)** [*insect*] bourdonnement *m*, vrombissement *m*.

(b) [*conversation*] bourdonnement *m*, brouhaha *m*. **~ of approval** murmure *m* d'approbation.

(c) (*: *telephone call*) coup *m* de fil*. **to give sb a ~** donner *or* passer un coup de fil* à qn.

(d) (*Rad, Telec etc: extraneous noise*) friture *f*.

2 *cpd*: **buzz bomb** V1 *m*; **buzz saw** scie *f* mécanique *or* circulaire.

3 *vi* **(a)** [*insect*] bourdonner, vrombir.

(b) [*ears*] tinter, bourdonner. **my head is ~ing** j'ai des bourdonnements (dans la tête).

(c) [*hall, town*] être (tout) bourdonnant (*with* de).

4 *vt* **(a)** (*call by buzzer*) *person* appeler (par interphone); (*US**: *telephone*) donner *or* passer un coup de fil* à.

(b) (*Aviat*) *plane, building* raser.

buzz about*, buzz around* *vi* s'affairer, s'agiter, s'activer.

buzz off‡ *vi* (*Brit*) filer*, décamper*, foutre le camp‡.

buzzard ['bʌzəd] *n* (*falcon*) buse *f*, busard *m*; (*vulture*) urubu *m*.

buzzer ['bʌzəʳ] *n* **(a)** (*in office*) interphone *m*. **(b)** (*factory hooter*) sirène *f*, sifflet *m*.

buzzing ['bʌzɪŋ] **1** *n* **(a)** = **buzz 1a, 1b.** **(b)** (*in ears*) tintement *m*, bourdonnement *m*. **2** *adj insect* bourdonnant, vrombissant; *sound* confus, sourd.

by [baɪ] (*phr vb elem*) **1** *adv* **(a)** (*near*) près. **close** *or* **hard ~** tout près; *V* **stand by** *etc*.

(b) (*past*) **to go** *or* **pass ~** passer; **time goes ~** le temps passe; **he'll be ~ any minute** il sera là dans un instant; **it'll be difficult but we'll get ~** cela sera difficile mais on y arrivera; *V* **come by** *etc*.

(c) (*in reserve*) **to put** *or* **lay ~** mettre de côté; **I had £10 ~ for a rainy day** j'avais mis 10 livres de côté pour les mauvais jours.

(d) (*phrases*) **~ and ~** bientôt, (un peu) plus tard; **~ and large** généralement parlant; **taking it ~ and large** à tout prendre.

2 *prep* **(a)** (*close to*) à côté de, près de. **sitting ~ the fire** assis près du feu; **the house ~ the church** la maison à côté de l'église; **a holiday ~ the sea** des vacances au bord de la mer; **I've got it ~ me** je l'ai sous la main; **he is all ~ himself** il est (tout) seul; **he did it ~ himself** il l'a fait tout seul.

(b) (*direction: through, across, along*) par. **to come ~ the forest path** venir par le chemin de la forêt; **I went ~ Dover** j'y suis allé par Douvres; **he came in ~ the window** il est entré par la fenêtre; **to meet sb ~ the way** rencontrer qn en route; (*fig*) **~ the way, ~ the by(e)** à propos, au fait, soit dit en passant; (*Mil*) **'~ the right, march!'** 'à droite, droite!'

(c) (*direction: past*) auprès de, le long de, à côté de, devant. **I go ~ the church every day** je passe devant l'église tous les jours; **he rushed ~ me without seeing me** dans sa précipitation il est passé à côté de moi sans me voir.

(d) (*time: during*) **~ day** le jour, de jour; **~ night** la nuit, de nuit.

(e) (*time: not later than*) avant, pas plus tard que. **can you do it ~ tomorrow?** pouvez-vous le faire avant demain?; **I'll be back ~ midnight** je rentrerai avant minuit *or* pas plus tard que minuit; **~ tomorrow I'll be in France** d'ici demain je serai en France; **~ the time I got there he had gone** lorsque je suis arrivé *or* le temps que j'arrive (*subj*) il était parti; **~ 30th September we had paid out £500** au 30 septembre nous avions payé 500 livres; **~ yesterday I had realized that** dès hier je m'étais rendu compte que; **he ought to be here ~ now** il devrait être déjà ici; **~ then I knew he wasn't coming** à ce moment-là je savais déjà qu'il ne viendrait pas.

(f) (*amount*) à. **to sell ~ the metre/the kilo** vendre au mètre/au kilo; **to pay ~ the hour** payer à l'heure; **to rent a house ~ the month** louer une maison au mois; **to count ~ tens** compter par dix *or* par dizaines; **~ degrees** par degrés, graduellement; **one ~ one** un à un; **little ~ little** petit à petit, peu à peu.

(g) (*agent, cause*) par, de. **he was killed ~ lightning** il a été tué par la foudre; **a painting ~ Van Gogh** un tableau de Van Gogh; **surrounded ~ soldiers** entouré de soldats; **he was warned ~ his neighbour** il a été prévenu par son voisin.

(h) (*method, means, manner*) par. **~ land and (~) sea** par terre et par mer; **~ bus/car** en autobus/voiture; **~ bicycle** à bicyclette; **~ rail, ~ train** par le train, en train; **~ moonlight** au clair de lune; **~ electric light** à la lumière électrique; **~ return of post** par retour du courrier; **to know ~ heart** savoir par cœur; **to know sb ~ name/~ sight** connaître qn de nom/de vue; **he goes ~ the name of** il est connu sous le nom de; **~ chance** par hasard; ~ **mistake** par (suite d'une) erreur; **made ~ hand/~ machine** fait à la main/à la machine; **to lead ~ the hand** conduire par la main; **to pay ~ cheque** payer par chèque; **he had a daughter ~ his first wife** il a eu une fille de sa première femme; ~ **means of** au moyen de, par; ~ **saving hard he managed to buy it** à force d'économies *or* de faire des économies il est arrivé à l'acheter; **he succeeded ~ working hard** il a réussi grâce à un travail acharné; ~ **nature** par nature; ~ **birth** de naissance; **French ~ birth** français de naissance.

(i) (*according to*) d'après, suivant, selon. ~ **what he says** d'après *or* selon ce qu'il dit; **if we can go ~ what he says** si nous pouvons tabler sur ce qu'il dit; **to judge ~ appearances** juger sur les *or* d'après les apparences; ~ **right** de droit; ~ **rights** en toute *or* bonne justice; ~ **my watch it is 9 o'clock** il est 9 heures à ma montre *or* d'après ma montre; ~ **the rule** selon les règles; **to do one's duty ~ sb** remplir son devoir envers qn; ~ **your leave** avec votre permission; ~ **the terms of Article 1** aux termes de l'article 1; **to call sth ~ its proper name** appeler qch de son vrai nom; **it's all right ~ me*** je veux bien, je n'ai rien contre*.

(j) (*measuring difference*) de. **broader ~ a metre** plus large d'un mètre; **to win ~ a head** gagner d'une tête; **it missed me ~ 10 centimetres** cela m'a manqué de 10 centimètres; **he's too clever ~ half*** il est beaucoup trop malin; **better ~ far** (*adv*) beaucoup mieux; (*adj*) bien meilleur; ~ **far the best/dearest** de loin le meilleur/le plus cher.

(k) (*Math, Measure*) **to divide ~** diviser par; **a room 3 metres ~ 4** une pièce de 3 mètres sur 4.

(l) (*points of compass*) **south ~ south west** sud quart sud-ouest; **south-west ~ south** sud-ouest quart sud.

(m) (*in oaths*) par. **I swear ~ all I hold sacred** je jure par tout ce que j'ai de plus sacré; (*Jur*) **'I swear ~ Almighty God'** ≃ 'je le jure'; ~ **God I'll get you for this!‡** nom d'un chien‡ *or* nom de Dieu‡ je te le ferai payer!; **he swears ~ this remedy*** il ne jure que par ce remède.

by(e) [baɪ] **1** *n*: **by the ~** à propos, au fait, soit dit en passant.

2 *cpd*: **by-election** élection (législative) partielle; **by-law, bye-law** arrêté *m* (municipal); **bypass** *V* **bypass**; (*Theat*) **by-play** jeu *m* de scène secondaire; **by-product** (*Ind etc*) sous-produit *m*, dérivé *m*; (*fig*) conséquence *f* (secondaire); **by-road** chemin détourné, chemin de traverse; **byway** chemin *m* (écarté); (*fig*) *[subject]* à-côté *m* (*V* **highway**); **he** *or* **his name was a byword for meanness** son nom était devenu synonyme d'avarice.

bye* [baɪ] *excl* (*abbr of* **goodbye**) au revoir!, salut!* ~ **for now!** à tout à l'heure!

bye-bye* ['baɪ'baɪ] **1** *excl* au revoir!, salut!* **2** *n* (*baby talk*) **to go to ~s** aller au dodo*, aller faire dodo*.

bygone ['baɪgɒn] **1** *adj* passé, d'autrefois. **in ~ days** dans l'ancien temps, jadis. **2** *n* (*loc*) **let ~s be ~s** oublions le passé, passons l'éponge (là-dessus).

bypass ['baɪpɑːs] **1** *n* **(a)** (*road*) route *f or* bretelle *f* de contournement *m*. **the Carlisle ~** la route qui contourne Carlisle.

(b) (*Tech: pipe etc*) conduit *m* de dérivation.

(c) (*Elec*) dérivation *f*.

2 *vt* **(a)** *town, village* contourner, éviter.

(b) *fluid, gas* amener (en dérivation).

(c) (*fig*) **he ~ed his foreman and went straight to see the manager** il est allé trouver le directeur sans passer par le contremaître.

byre ['baɪəʳ] *n* (*Brit*) étable *f* (à vaches).

bystander ['baɪˌstændəʳ] *n* spectateur *m*, -trice *f*, assistant(e) *m(f)*.

Byzantine [baɪ'zæntaɪn] *adj* byzantin, de Byzance.

Byzantium [baɪ'zæntɪəm] *n* Byzance.

C

C, c [siː] *n* **(a)** (*letter*) C, c *m*. **(b)** (*Mus*) do *m*, ut *m*.

cab [kæb] **1** *n* **(a)** (*taxi*) taxi *m*; (*horse-drawn*) fiacre *m*. **by ~** en taxi, en fiacre. **(b)** (*Aut, Rail: driver's ~*) cabine *f*. **2** *cpd*: **cab-driver, cabman** = **cabby***; **cab rank, cab stand** station *f* de taxis.

cabal [kə'bæl] *n* (*intrigue*) cabale *f*, intrigue *f*; (*group*) cabale, clique *f*.

cabaret ['kæbəreɪ] *n* cabaret *m*; (*Brit: floor show*) spectacle *m* (de cabaret).

cabbage ['kæbɪdʒ] **1** *n* chou *m*. (*fig pej*) **she's just a ~*** elle végète. **2** *cpd*: **cabbage lettuce** laitue pommée; **cabbage rose** rose *f* cent-feuilles; **cabbage tree** palmiste *m*; **cabbage white (butterfly)** piéride *f* du chou.

cab(b)ala [kə'bɑːlə] *n* cabale *f* (*juive*).

cab(b)alistic [ˌkæbə'lɪstɪk] *adj* cabalistique.

cabby* ['kæbɪ] *n [taxi]* chauffeur *m* (de taxi), taxi* *m*; *[horse-drawn cab]* cocher *m* (de fiacre).

caber ['keɪbəʳ] *n* (*Sport*) tronc *m*. **to toss the ~** lancer le tronc; **tossing the ~** le lancement du tronc.

cabin ['kæbɪn] **1** *n* (*hut*) cabane *f*, hutte *f*; (*in Africa etc*) case *f*; (*Naut*) cabine *f*; (*Rail: signal box*) cabine d'aiguillage; (*Aut, Rail: driver's ~*) cabine; *V* **log**[1]. **2** *cpd*: (*Naut*) **cabin boy** mousse *m*; **cabin class** deuxième classe *f*; **cabin cruiser** yacht *m* de croisière (à moteur); **cabin trunk** malle-cabine *f*.

cabinet ['kæbɪnɪt] **1** *n* meuble *m* (de rangement); (*glass-fronted*) vitrine *f*; (*filing ~*) classeur *m*; (*Parl*) cabinet *m*; *V* **medicine**.

2 *cpd* (*Parl*) *crisis, decision* ministériel. (*Carpentry*) **cabinet-maker** ébéniste *m*; (*Carpentry*) **cabinetmaking** ébénisterie *f*; (*Parl*) **cabinet minister** ministre *m*, membre *m* du cabinet; *V* **reshuffle**.

cable ['keɪbl] **1** *n* (*Elec, Telec, gen*) câble *m*; (*Naut: measure*) encablure *f*. (*Telec*) **by ~** par câble; *V* **overhead**.

2 *vt* câbler, télégraphier (*sth to sb* qch à qn).

3 *cpd*: **cablecar** téléphérique *m*; (*on rail*) funiculaire *m*; **cablegram** câblogramme *m*; **cable-laying** pose *f* de câbles; **cable(-laying) ship** câblier *m*; **cable railway** funiculaire *m*; (*Knitting*) **cable stitch** point *m* de torsade; **cable television** télédistribution *f*; **cableway** benne suspendue.

caboodle‡ [kə'buːdl] *n*: **the whole ~** (et) tout le tremblement*, (et) tout le saint-frusquin*.

caboose [kə'buːs] *n* (*Naut*) cambuse *f*; (*US Rail*) fourgon *m* de queue.

ca'canny* ['kɔː'kænɪ] *excl* (*Scot*) doucement!

cacao [kə'kɑːəʊ] *n* (*bean*) cacao *m*; (*tree*) cacaoyer *m*.

cache [kæʃ] **1** *n* (*place*) cachette *f*. **a ~ of guns** des fusils cachés. **2** *vt* mettre dans une cachette.

cachet ['kæʃeɪ] *n* (*all senses*) cachet *m*.

cackle ['kækl] **1** *n [hen]* caquet *m*; *[people]* (*laugh*) gloussement *m*; (*talking*) caquetage *m*, jacasserie *f*; *V* **cut**. **2** *vi [hens]* caqueter; *[people]* (*laugh*) glousser; (*talk*) caqueter, jacasser.

cacophonous [kæ'kɒfənəs] *adj* cacophonique, discordant.

cacophony [kæ'kɒfənɪ] *n* cacophonie *f*.

cactus ['kæktəs] *n*, *pl* **cacti** ['kæktaɪ] cactus *m*.

cad*† [kæd] *n* (*Brit*) goujat *m*, malotru *m*, mufle *m*.

cadaver [kə'deɪvəʳ] *n* cadavre *m*.

cadaverous [kə'dævərəs] *adj* (*lit, fig*) *complexion* cadavéreux; *appearance* cadavérique.

caddie ['kædɪ] *n* caddie *m*.

caddish*† ['kædɪʃ] *adj person* grossier, mufle. **a ~ thing to do** une muflerie.

caddy ['kædɪ] *n* (*also* **tea ~**) boîte *f* à thé.

cadence ['keɪdəns] *n* (*intonation*) modulation *f* (de la voix); (*rhythm*) cadence *f*, rythme *m*; (*Mus*) cadence.

cadenza [kə'denzə] *n* (*Mus*) cadence *f*.

cadet [kə'det] **1** *n* **(a)** (*Mil etc*) élève *m* officier (*d'une école militaire ou navale*); (*Scol*) *collégien qui poursuit une préparation militaire*. ~ **school** école *f* militaire. **(b)** (*younger son*) cadet *m*. **2** *adj* cadet.

cadge [kædʒ] *vt*: **to ~ 10 francs from** *or* **off sb** taper* qn de 10 F; **to ~ lunch from** *or* **off sb** se faire inviter *or* se faire payer* à manger par qn; **to ~ a lift from** *or* **off sb** se faire emmener en voiture par qn; **he's always cadging** il est toujours à quémander quelque chose *or* à mendier.

cadger ['kædʒəʳ] *n* parasite *m*; *[money]* tapeur* *m*, -euse* *f*; *[meals]* pique-assiette *mf inv*.

Cadiz [kə'dɪz] *n* Cadix.

cadmium ['kædmɪəm] *n* cadmium *m*.

cadre ['kædrɪ] *n* (*Mil, fig*) cadre *m*.

caecum, (*US*) **cecum** ['siːkəm] *n* caecum *m*.

Caesar ['siːzəʳ] *n* César *m*.

Caesarean, Caesarian [siː'zɛərɪən] *adj* césarien. (*Med*) ~ **(operation** *or* **section)** césarienne *f*.

caesura [sɪ'zjʊərə] *n* césure *f*.

café ['kæfeɪ] *n* café(-restaurant) *m* (*Brit: sans boissons alcoolisées*).

cafeteria [ˌkæfɪ'tɪərɪə] *n* cafétéria *f*.

caffein(e) ['kæfiːn] *n* caféine *f*. **~-free** décaféiné.

caftan ['kæftæn] *n* caftan *m*.

cage [keɪdʒ] **1** *n* cage *f*; *[elevator]* cabine *f*; (*Min*) cage; (*fig*) prison *f* (*fig*). ~ **bird** oiseau *m* de volière *or* d'appartement. **2** *vt* (*also* **~ up**) mettre en cage, encager. **~d bird** oiseau *m* en cage.

cagey* ['keɪdʒɪ] *adj* **(a)** (*secretive*) peu communicatif; (*pej*) dissimulé. **she is ~ about her age** elle n'aime pas avouer son âge. **(b)** (*cautious*) prudent, qui ne veut pas se mouiller*.

cahoot(s)* [kəˈhuːt(s)] *n*: **to be in ~ (with)** être de mèche (avec)*.

caiman [ˈkeɪmən] *n* caïman *m*.

Cain [keɪn] *n* Caïn *m*. **to raise ~*** (*noise*) faire un boucan de tous les diables‡; (*fuss*) faire tout un scandale (*about* à propos de).

cairn [kɛən] *n* (*pile of stones*) cairn *m*; (*dog*) cairn.

cairngorm [ˈkɛəngɔːm] *n* quartz fumé.

Cairo [ˈkaɪərəʊ] *n* Le Caire.

caisson [ˈkeɪsən] *n* (*Mil, Naut*) caisson *m*.

cajole [kəˈdʒəʊl] *vt* cajoler. **to ~ sb into doing sth** faire faire qch à qn à force de cajoleries.

cajolery [kəˈdʒəʊlərɪ] *n* cajolerie *f*.

cake [keɪk] **1** *n* **(a)** (*large*) gâteau *m*; (*small*) pâtisserie *f*, gâteau; (*fruit ~ etc*) cake *m*; (*sponge ~ etc*) génoise *f*, gâteau de Savoie. (*fig*) **~s and ale** plaisirs *mpl*; **it's selling *or* going like hot ~s*** cela se vend comme des petits pains; **it's a piece of ~*** c'est du gâteau*, c'est de la tarte*; **he takes the ~*** à lui le pompon*; **that takes the ~!*** ça, c'est le bouquet!* *or* le comble!; *V* **Christmas, fish** *etc*.

(b) *[chocolate]* tablette *f*; *[wax, tobacco]* pain *m*. **~ of soap** savonnette *f*, (pain de) savon *m*.

2 *cpd*: **cake mix** préparation instantanée (pour gâteaux); **cake shop** pâtisserie *f* (*magasin*); **cake stand** assiette montée *or* à pied, (*tiered*) serviteur *m*; (*in shop*) présentoir *m* (à gâteaux).

3 *vt*: **~d** *blood* coagulé; *mud* séché; **his clothes were ~d with mud/blood** ses vêtements étaient raidis par la boue/le sang.

4 *vi* *[mud]* durcir, faire croûte; *[blood]* se coaguler.

calabash [ˈkæləbæʃ] *n* (*fruit*) calebasse *f*, gourde *f*; (*tree*) calebassier *m*; (*Mus*) calebasse (*utilisée comme bongo ou maraca*).

calaboose* [ˈkæləbuːs] *n* (*US*) taule‡ *f*.

calamine [ˈkæləmaɪn] *n* calamine *f*. **~ lotion** lotion calmante à la calamine.

calamitous [kəˈlæmɪtəs] *adj* *event, decision* catastrophique, désastreux; *person* infortuné.

calamity [kəˈlæmɪtɪ] *n* calamité *f*, désastre *m*.

calcareous [kælˈkɛərɪəs] *adj* calcaire.

calcification [ˌkælsɪfɪˈkeɪʃən] *n* calcification *f*.

calcify [ˈkælsɪfaɪ] **1** *vt* calcifier. **2** *vi* se calcifier.

calcination [ˌkælsɪˈneɪʃən] *n* calcination *f*.

calcine [ˈkælsaɪn] **1** *vt* (*Ind*) calciner. **2** *vi* (*Ind*) se calciner.

calcium [ˈkælsɪəm] *n* calcium *m*.

calculable [ˈkælkjʊləbl] *adj* calculable.

calculate [ˈkælkjʊleɪt] **1** *vt* (*Math etc*) calculer; (*reckon, judge*) évaluer; (*US: suppose*) supposer, estimer. **to ~ the cost of** calculer le prix de; **to ~ one's chances of escape** évaluer les chances qu'on a de s'évader; (*fig*) **this was not ~d to reassure me** cela n'était pas fait pour me rassurer.

2 *vi* (*Math*) calculer, faire des calculs. (*fig*) **to ~ for sth** prévoir qch.

calculate (up)on *vt fus* compter sur. **to calculate (up)on having good weather** compter sur le beau temps.

calculated [ˈkælkjʊleɪtɪd] *adj* *action, decision* délibéré, réfléchi; *insult* délibéré, prémédité; *gamble, risk* pris en toute connaissance de cause. **~ indiscretion** indiscrétion voulue *or* délibérée.

calculating [ˈkælkjʊleɪtɪŋ] *adj* **(a)** (*scheming, unemotional*) calculateur (*f* -trice), intéressé; (*cautious*) prudent, prévoyant. **(b) ~ machine = calculator b.**

calculation [ˌkælkjʊˈleɪʃən] *n* (*Math, fig*) calcul *m*. **to make a ~** faire *or* effectuer un calcul; **by my ~s** d'après mes calculs; **after much ~ they decided** après avoir fait beaucoup de calculs ils ont décidé; **it upset his ~s** cela a perturbé ses calculs.

calculator [ˈkælkjʊleɪtəʳ] *n* **(a)** (*person*) calculateur *m*, -trice *f*. **(b)** (*machine*) machine *f* à calculer, calculatrice *f*. **(c)** (*table of figures*) table *f*.

calculus [ˈkælkjʊləs] *n* (*Math, Med*) calcul *m*; *V* **differential, integral.**

Calcutta [kælˈkʌtə] *n* Calcutta.

calendar [ˈkæləndəʳ] **1** *n* **(a)** calendrier *m*.

(b) (*directory*) annuaire *m*. (*Brit*) **university ~** ≃ guide *m* de l'étudiant.

(c) (*Jur*) rôle *m*.

2 *cpd*: **calendar month** mois *m* (de calendrier); **calendar year** année civile.

3 *vt* (*index*) classer (*par ordre de date*); (*record*) inscrire sur un calendrier.

calends [ˈkæləndz] *npl* calendes *fpl*. (*fig*) **at the Greek ~** aux calendes grecques.

calf[1] [kɑːf] **1** *n, pl* **calves (a)** (*young cow or bull*) veau *m*. **a cow in *or* with ~** une vache pleine; *V* **fat.**

(b) (*also* **~skin**) (cuir *m* de) veau *m*, vachette *f*; (*for shoes, bags*) box(-calf) *m*.

(c) *[elephant]* éléphanteau *m*; *[deer]* faon *m*; *[whale]* baleineau *m*; *[buffalo]* buffletin *m*.

2 *cpd*: (*fig*) **calf love** amour *m* juvénile.

calf[2] [kɑːf] *n, pl* **calves** (*Anat*) mollet *m*.

caliber [ˈkælɪbəʳ] *n* (*US*) = **calibre.**

calibrate [ˈkælɪbreɪt] *vt* étalonner, calibrer.

calibration [ˌkælɪˈbreɪʃən] *n* étalonnage *m*, calibrage *m*.

calibre, (*US*) **caliber** [ˈkælɪbəʳ] *n* (*lit, fig*) calibre *m*. **a man of his ~** un homme de son envergure *or* de son calibre*.

calico [ˈkælɪkəʊ] *n* calicot *m*; (*US*) indienne *f*.

California [ˌkælɪˈfɔːnɪə] *n* Californie *f*.

calipers [ˈkælɪpəz] *npl* **(a)** (*Math*) compas *m*. **(b)** (*Med*) (*for limb*) gouttière *f*; (*for foot*) étrier *m*; (*leg-irons*) appareil *m* orthopédique.

caliph [ˈkeɪlɪf] *n* calife *m*.

calisthenics [ˌkælɪsˈθenɪks] *n* (*U*) gymnastique *f* (suédoise).

calk[1] [kɔːk] **1** *vt* *shoe, horseshoe* munir de crampons. **2** *n* *[shoe, horseshoe]* crampon *m*.

calk[2] [kɔːk] *vt* *drawing, design* décalquer, calquer.

call [kɔːl] **1** *n* **(a)** (*shout*) appel *m*, cri *m*. **within ~** à portée de (la) voix; **a ~ for help** un appel au secours; *V* **roll.**

(b) *[bird]* cri *m*; *[bugle, trumpet]* sonnerie *f*; *[drum]* batterie *f*.

(c) (*Telec*) appel *m*; (*also* **telephone ~**) coup *m* de téléphone, coup de fil*. **to make a ~** téléphoner, donner *or* passer un coup de fil*; *V* **local, long**[1]**, trunk.**

(d) (*summons, invitation*) *[duty]* appel *m*; *[justice]* exigence *f*; *[conscience]* voix *f*; (*Theat*) rappel *m*; (*vocation*) vocation *f*; (*Rel: in Presbyterian church*) nomination *f* (de pasteur). (*Rel*) **to have *or* receive a ~ to** être nommé pasteur à; **to give sb an early morning ~** réveiller qn de bonne heure; **I'd like a ~ at 7 a.m.** j'aimerais qu'on me réveille (*subj*) à 7 heures; *[doctor etc]* **to be on ~** être de garde; **the ~ of the unknown** l'attrait *m* de l'inconnu; **the ~ of the sea** l'appel du large.

(e) (*short visit: also Med*) visite *f*. **to make *or* pay a ~ on sb** rendre visite à qn, aller voir qn; **I have several ~s to make** j'ai plusieurs visites à faire; (*Naut*) **place *or* port of ~** (port *m* d') escale *f*; *V* **pay.**

(f) (*phrases*) (*Comm*) **there's not much ~ for these articles** ces articles ne sont pas très demandés; (*Comm*) **money repayable at *or* on ~/ at 3 months' ~** argent remboursable sur demande/à 3 mois; **I have many ~s on my time** je suis très pris *or* très occupé; **I have many ~s on my purse** j'ai beaucoup de dépenses *or* de frais; **there is no ~ for you to worry** vous n'avez pas besoin de *or* il n'y a pas lieu de vous inquiéter; **there was *or* you had no ~ to say that** vous n'aviez aucune raison de dire cela, vous n'aviez pas à dire cela.

(g) (*Bridge*) annonce *f*; (*Solo Whist*) demande *f*. **whose ~ is it?** à qui de parler? *or* d'annoncer?

2 *cpd*: **callbox** (*Brit*) cabine *f* (téléphonique); (*US*) téléphone *m* de police-secours; **callboy** (*Theat*) avertisseur *m*; *[hotel]* chasseur *m*, groom *m*; **call girl** prostituée *f* (*qu'on appelle par téléphone*), call-girl *f*; (*US Rad*) **call-in** programme *m* à ligne ouverte; (*US Telec*) **call letters** indicatif *m* (d'appel); (*Fin*) **call money** emprunt *m* remboursable sur demande; **call-over** appel nominal; (*Mil*) appel; (*Telec*) **call sign** indicatif *m* (d'appel); (*Mil*) **call-up** (*military service*) appel *m* (sous les drapeaux), convocation *f*; (*in wartime*) mobilisation générale, levée *f* en masse; **call-up papers** feuille *f* de route.

3 *vt* **(a)** *person* appeler, (*from afar*) héler; *sb's name* appeler, crier. **to ~ sb in/out/up** *etc* crier à qn d'entrer/de sortir/de monter *etc*.

(b) (*give name to*) appeler. **to be ~ed** s'appeler; **what are you ~ed?** comment vous appelez-vous?; **he is ~ed after his father** on lui a donné *or* il porte le nom de son père; **he ~s himself a colonel** il se prétend colonel; (*fig*) **to ~ a spade a spade** appeler un chat un chat, ne pas avoir peur des mots; **are you ~ing me a liar?** dites (tout de suite) que je suis un menteur; **he ~ed her a liar** il l'a traitée de menteuse; *V* **name, own, so.**

(c) (*consider*) trouver, considérer. **would you ~ French a difficult language?** diriez-vous que le français est difficile?; **I ~ that a shame** j'estime que c'est une honte; (*agreeing on price*) **shall we ~ it £1?** disons 1 livre?

(d) (*summon*) appeler, convoquer; (*waken*) réveiller. **to ~ a doctor** appeler *or* faire venir un médecin; **~ me at eight** réveillez-moi à huit heures; (*Rad*) **London ~ing** ici Londres; **the fire brigade was ~ed** on a appelé les pompiers; **~ me a taxi!** appelez-moi *or* faites venir un taxi!; **duty ~s (me)** le devoir m'appelle; **to ~ a meeting** convoquer une assemblée; (*Jur*) **his case was ~ed today** son affaire est venue aujourd'hui devant le tribunal; **to ~ sb as a witness** (*Jur*) avoir qn comme témoin; (*fig*) prendre qn à témoin (*to* de).

(e) (*Bridge*) **to ~ 3 spades** annoncer *or* demander 3 piques; **to ~ game** demander la sortie.

(f) (*phrases*) **to ~ sb to account** demander des comptes à qn; (*Parl*) **to ~ a division** passer au vote; (*Mil*) **to ~ to arms** *[rebel leader]* appeler aux armes; *[government]* appeler sous les drapeaux; **to ~ (sb's) attention to sth** attirer l'attention (de qn) sur qch; (*Rel*) **to ~ the banns** publier les bans; (*Brit Jur*) **to be ~ed to the bar** être inscrit au barreau; **to ~ sth into being** faire naître qch, créer qch; **he ~ed my bluff** il a prouvé que je bluffais*, il m'a coincé*; **let's ~ his bluff** on va essayer de prouver qu'il bluffe*; **let's ~ it a day!*** ça suffira pour aujourd'hui!*; **we ~ed it a day* at 3 o'clock** à 3 heures on a décidé de s'en tenir là; **to ~ a halt to sth** mettre fin à qch; **I haven't a minute to ~ my own*** je n'ai pas une minute à moi; (*fig*) **to ~ sth into play** mettre qch en jeu; **to ~ sth in(to) question** mettre qch en doute; **to ~ the roll** faire l'appel; **to ~ a strike** lancer un ordre de grève; **to ~ a truce** demander une trêve; *V* **mind** *etc*.

4 *vi* **(a)** *[person]* appeler, crier; *[birds]* pousser un cri. **I have been ~ing for 5 minutes** cela fait 5 minutes que j'appelle; **to ~ (out) to sb** appeler qn, (*from afar*) héler qn.

(b) (*visit: also* **~ in**) passer. **she ~ed (in) to see her mother** elle est passée voir sa mère; **he was out when I ~ed (in)** il n'était pas là quand je suis passé chez lui; **will you ~ (in) at the grocer's?** voulez-vous passer *or* vous arrêter chez l'épicier?; (*Naut*) **to ~ (in) at a port/at Dover** faire escale dans un port/à Douvres.

call aside *vt sep* *person* prendre à part, tirer à l'écart.

call away *vt sep*: **to be called away on business** être obligé de s'absenter pour affaires; **to be called away from a meeting** devoir quitter une réunion (*pour affaires plus pressantes*).

call back (*Telec*) **1** *vi* rappeler.

2 *vt sep* rappeler.

call down *vt sep* **(a)** *curses* appeler (*on sb* sur la tête de qn). **(b)** (*US*: scold*) enguirlander*, attraper.

call for *vt fus* **(a)** (*summon*) *person* appeler; *food, drink* demander, commander; (*fig*) *courage* demander, exiger, nécessiter. **to call for measures against** demander que des mesures soient prises contre; **the situation calls for a new approach** il est nécessaire d'envisager la situation d'une autre manière; **such rudeness was not called for** une telle grossièreté n'était pas justifiée.

(b) (*collect*) **I'll call for you at 6 o'clock** je passerai vous prendre à 6 heures; **he called for the books** il est passé chercher les livres.

call forth *vt sep* (*liter*) *protest* soulever, provoquer; *remark* provoquer.

call in 1 *vi* = **call 4b.**

2 *vt sep* **(a)** *doctor* faire venir, appeler; *police* appeler. **he was called in to arbitrate** on a fait appel à lui pour arbitrer.

(b) *money, library books* faire rentrer; *banknotes* retirer de la circulation; *faulty machines etc* rappeler.

call off 1 *vi* se décommander.

2 *vt sep* **(a)** *appointment* annuler; *agreement* rompre, résilier. **to call off a deal** résilier *or* annuler un marché; **to call off a strike** annuler un ordre de grève.

(b) *dog* rappeler.

call out 1 *vi* pousser un *or* des cri(s). **to call out for sth** demander qch à haute voix.

2 *vt sep* **(a)** *doctor* appeler; *troops, fire brigade* appeler, faire appel à. **to call workers out (on strike)** donner la consigne de grève.

(b) (*for duel*) appeler sur le terrain.

call over 1 *vt sep* **(a)** *list of names* faire l'appel de.

(b) he called me over to see the book il m'a appelé pour que je vienne voir le livre.

2 call-over *n V* **call 2.**

call round *vi*: **to call round to see sb** passer voir qn; **I'll call round in the morning** je passerai dans la matinée.

call up 1 *vt sep* **(a)** (*Mil*) *reinforcements, troops* appeler, mobiliser. **he's been called up** il a été appelé *or* mobilisé.

(b) (*esp US: Telec*) appeler (au téléphone), téléphoner à.

(c) (*recall*) *memories* évoquer.

2 call-up *n, adj V* **call 2.**

call (up)on *vt fus* **(a)** (*visit*) *person* rendre visite à, aller *or* passer voir.

(b) to call (up)on sb to do (*invite*) inviter qn à faire, prier qn de faire; (*demand*) sommer qn de faire, mettre qn en demeure de faire; **I now call (up)on Mr X to speak** je laisse maintenant la parole à M X; **to call (up)on sb for sth** demander *or* réclamer qch à qn; **to call (up)on God** invoquer le nom de Dieu.

caller ['kɔːləʳ] *n* (*visitor*) visiteur *m*, -euse *f*; (*Brit Telec*) demandeur *m*, -euse *f*.

calligraphic [ˌkælɪ'græfɪk] *adj* calligraphique.

calligraphy [kə'lɪgrəfɪ] *n* calligraphie *f*.

calling ['kɔːlɪŋ] **1** *n* **(a)** (†) (*occupation*) métier *m*, état† *m*; (*vocation*) vocation *f*. **by ~** de son état. **(b)** (*U*) *[meeting etc]* convocation *f*. **2** *cpd*: (*US*) **calling card** carte *f* de visite.

callipers ['kælɪpəz] *npl* = **calipers.**

callisthenics [ˌkælɪs'θenɪks] *n* = **calisthenics.**

callosity [kæ'lɒsɪtɪ] *n* callosité *f*.

callous ['kæləs] *adj* **(a)** (*fig*) dur, sans cœur, sans pitié. **~ to** insensible à. **(b)** (*Med*) calleux.

callously ['kæləslɪ] *adv act* sans pitié, durement; *speak* avec dureté, durement; *decide, suggest* cyniquement.

callousness ['kæləsnɪs] *n* (*V* **callous**) dureté *f*, manque *m* de cœur *or* de pitié, insensibilité *f*.

callow ['kæləʊ] *adj* inexpérimenté, novice. **a ~ youth** un blanc-bec; **~ youth** la folle jeunesse.

callus ['kæləs] *n* cal *m*, durillon *m*.

calm [kɑːm] **1** *adj sea, day* calme, paisible, tranquille; *person* calme; *attitude, behaviour* calme, tranquille. **the sea was dead ~** la mer était d'huile *or* était plate; **the weather is ~** le temps est au calme; **keep ~!** du calme!, calmez-vous!; **to grow ~** se calmer; (*fig*) **~ and collected** maître(sse) *m(f)* de soi.

2 *n* période *f* de calme *or* de tranquillité; (*after movement, agitation*) accalmie *f*. (*Naut*) **a dead ~** un calme plat; (*lit, fig*) **the ~ before the storm** le calme qui précède la tempête.

3 *vt* calmer, apaiser.

calm down 1 *vi* se calmer, s'apaiser. **calm down!** du calme!, ne t'énerve pas!

2 *vt sep person* calmer, apaiser.

calming ['kɑːmɪŋ] *adj* calmant, apaisant.

calmly ['kɑːmlɪ] *adv speak, act* calmement, avec calme. **she ~ told me that she wouldn't help me** elle m'a dit sans sourciller qu'elle ne m'aiderait pas.

calmness ['kɑːmnɪs] *n [person]* calme *m*; (*under stress*) sang-froid *m*; *[sea, elements]* calme.

Calor ['kæləʳ] *n* ® (*Brit*) **~ gas** butane *m*, butagaz *m* ®.

caloric ['kælərɪk] **1** *adj* thermique. **~ energy** énergie *f* thermique. **2** *n* chaleur *f*.

calorie ['kælərɪ] *n* calorie *f*. **she's too ~-conscious* to eat potatoes** elle a trop la hantise des calories *or* de sa ligne pour manger des pommes de terre; *V* **low[1].**

calorific [ˌkælə'rɪfɪk] *adj* calorifique.

calque [kælk] *n* calque *m*.

calumniate [kə'lʌmnɪeɪt] *vt* calomnier.

calumny ['kæləmnɪ] *n* calomnie *f*; (*Jur*) diffamation *f*.

calvary ['kælvərɪ] *n* (*monument*) calvaire *m*. **C~** le Calvaire.

calve [kɑːv] *vi* vêler, mettre bas.

calves [kɑːvz] *npl of* **calf[1], calf[2].**

Calvin ['kælvɪn] *n* Calvin *m*.

Calvinism ['kælvɪnɪzəm] *n* calvinisme *m*.

Calvinist ['kælvɪnɪst] *adj, n* calviniste (*mf*).

Calvinistic [ˌkælvɪ'nɪstɪk] *adj* calviniste.

calypso [kə'lɪpsəʊ] *n* calypso *m*.

calyx ['keɪlɪks] *n, pl* **calyces** ['keɪlɪsiːz] (*Bot*) calice *m*.

cam [kæm] *n* came *f*. (*Aut*) **~shaft** arbre *m* à cames.

camaraderie [ˌkæmə'rɑːdərɪ] *n* camaraderie *f*.

camber ['kæmbəʳ] **1** *n [road]* bombement *m*; (*Archit*) cambre *f*, cambrure *f*, courbure *f*; (*Aviat*) courbure; (*Naut*) *[deck]* tonture *f*.

2 *vt road* bomber; *beam* cambrer; (*Naut*) *deck* donner une tonture à.

3 *vi [beam]* être cambré; *[road]* bomber, être bombé.

Cambodia [kæm'bəʊdɪə] *n* Cambodge *m*.

Cambodian [kæm'bəʊdɪən] **1** *adj* cambodgien. **2** *n* **(a)** Cambodgien(ne) *m(f)*. **(b)** (*Ling*) cambodgien *m*.

cambric ['keɪmbrɪk] *n*, (*US*) **chambray** *n* batiste *f*.

came [keɪm] *pret of* **come.**

camel ['kæməl] **1** *n* (*gen*) chameau *m*; (*she-~*) chamelle *f*; (*dromedary*) dromadaire *m*; (*racing ~*) méhari *m*; *V* **straw.**

2 *cpd* (*colour*) *coat* (de couleur) fauve *inv*. (*Mil*) **the Camel Corps** les méharistes *mpl*; **camel hair** poil *m* de chameau; (*Art*) **camel-hair brush** pinceau *m* en poil de chameau; **camel-hair coat** manteau *m* en poil de chameau; (*imitation*) manteau en imitation de poil de chameau; **camel's-hair** = **camel-hair**; **camel train** caravane *f* de chameaux.

camellia [kə'miːlɪə] *n* camélia *m*.

cameo ['kæmɪəʊ] *n* camée *m*.

camera ['kæmərə] **1** *n* **(a)** appareil *m* (photographique), appareil-photo *m*; (*Cine, TV*) caméra *f*; *V* **aerial, colour, film.**

(b) (*Jur*) **in ~** à huis clos, en privé.

2 *cpd*: (*Cine, TV*) **cameraman** caméraman *m or* cameraman *m*; (*on credits*) 'prise *f* de vues'; **camera obscura** chambre noire (*appareil*); **camerawork** prise *f* de vues.

Cameroon [ˌkæmə'ruːn] *n* Cameroun *m*.

camisole ['kæmɪsəʊl] *n* camisole *f*.

camomile ['kæməʊmaɪl] *n* camomille *f*. **~ tea** (infusion *f* de) camomille.

camouflage ['kæməflɑːʒ] (*Mil, fig*) **1** *n* camouflage *m*. **2** *vt* camoufler.

camp[1] [kæmp] **1** *n* camp *m*, (*less permanent*) campement *m*; (*fig*) camp, parti *m*. **to be in ~** camper; **to go to ~** partir camper; (*fig*) **in the same ~** du même bord; **to have a foot in both ~s** avoir un pied dans chaque camp; *V* **concentration, holiday, pitch[1]** *etc*.

2 *cpd*: (*Brit*) **campbed** lit *m* de camp; **campfire** feu *m* de camp; **camp follower** (*fig*) sympathisant(e) *m(f)*; (*Mil*†: *prostitute*) prostituée *f*; (*Mil*†: *civilian worker*) civil *m accompagnant une armée*; **camp(ing) chair** chaise pliante (de camping); **camp(ing) ground, camp(ing) site** (*commercialized*) (terrain *m* de) camping *m*; (*clearing etc*) endroit *m* où camper, emplacement *m* de camping; (*with tent on it*) camp *m*; **camp(ing) stool** pliant *m*; **camp(ing) stove** réchaud *m* de camping.

3 *vi* camper. **to go ~ing** (aller) faire du camping.

camp out *vi* camper, vivre sous la tente. (*fig*) **we'll have to camp out in the kitchen*** il va falloir que nous campions (*subj*) dans la cuisine.

camp[2] [kæmp] **1** *adj* (*) (*affected*) affecté, maniéré, étudié; (*over-dramatic*) cabotin; (*effeminate*) efféminé; (*homosexual*) *man* (qui fait) pédé‡ *or* tapette‡; *manners, clothes* de pédé‡, de tapette‡; (*affecting delight in bad taste*) qui fait parade de vulgarité *or* de mauvais goût; (*sentimental and old-fashioned*) suranné.

2 *vt*: **to ~ it up‡** cabotiner*.

campaign [kæm'peɪn] **1** *n* (*Mil, fig*) campagne *f*. **to lead** *or* **conduct** *or* **run a ~ for/against** mener une campagne *or* faire campagne pour/contre; *V* **advertising, election.**

2 *vi* (*Mil*) faire campagne; (*fig*) mener une *or* faire campagne (*for* pour, *against* contre).

campaigner [kæm'peɪnəʳ] *n* (*Mil*) **(old) ~** vétéran *m*; (*fig*) **~ for/against apartheid** militant(e) *m(f)* pour/contre l'apartheid.

campanile [ˌkæmpə'niːlɪ] *n* campanile *m*.

camper ['kæmpəʳ] *n* campeur *m*, -euse *f*.

camphor ['kæmfəʳ] *n* camphre *m*.

camphorated ['kæmfəreɪtɪd] *adj* camphré. **~ oil** huile camphrée.

camping ['kæmpɪŋ] **1** *n* camping *m* (*activité*); *V* **camp[1]. 2** *cpd V* **camp[1] 2.**

campus ['kæmpəs] *n* (*esp US*) (*quadrangle*) campus *m*; (*building complex*) campus, ensemble *m* universitaire (*terrain, unités d'enseignement, résidence*); (*fig*) monde *m* universitaire.

campy‡ ['kæmpɪ] *adj* = **camp[2] 1.**

can[1] [kæn] *modal aux vb*: *neg* **cannot**; *cond and pret* **could.**

(a) (*indicating possibility; in neg improbability*) **the situation can change from day to day** la situation peut changer d'un jour à l'autre; **it could be true** cela pourrait être vrai, il se peut que cela soit vrai; **she could still decide to go** elle pourrait encore décider d'y aller; **you could be making a big mistake** tu fais peut-être *or* tu es peut-être en train de faire une grosse erreur; **can he have done it already?** est-il possible qu'il l'ait déjà fait?; **could he have done it without being seen?** est-ce qu'il aurait pu le faire *or* lui aurait-il été possible de le faire sans être vu?; **can** *or* **could you be hiding something from us?** est-il possible *or* se peut-il que vous nous cachiez (*subj*) quelque chose?; **he could have changed his mind without telling you** il aurait pu changer d'avis sans vous le dire; **(perhaps) he could have forgotten** il a peut-être oublié; **it could have been you who got hurt** cela aurait aussi bien pu être vous le blessé; **you can't be serious!** (ce n'est pas possible,) vous ne parlez pas sérieusement!; **he can't have known about it until you told him** (il est) impossible qu'il l'ait su avant que vous (ne) lui en ayez parlé; **she can't be very clever if she failed this exam** elle ne doit pas être très intelligente pour avoir été refusée à cet examen; **things can't be as**

bad as you say they are la situation n'est sûrement pas aussi mauvaise que tu le dis; **that cannot be!**† c'est impossible!; (*stressed, expressing astonishment*) **he CAN'T be dead!** ce n'est pas possible, il n'est pas mort!; **how CAN you say that?** comment pouvez-vous *or* osez-vous dire ça?; **where CAN he be?** où peut-il bien être?; **what CAN it be?** qu'est-ce que cela peut bien être?; **what COULD she have done with it?** qu'est-ce qu'elle a bien pu en faire?; (*phrases*) **as big/pretty** *etc* **as can** *or* **could be** aussi grand/joli *etc* que possible; **as soon as can** *or* **could be** aussitôt *or* dès que possible, le plus vite possible.

(b) (*am etc able to*) **he can lift the suitcase if he tries hard** il peut soulever la valise s'il fait l'effort nécessaire; **help me if you can** aidez-moi si vous (le) pouvez; **he will do what he can** il fera ce qu'il pourra, il fera son possible; **he will help you all he can** il vous aidera de son mieux; **can you come tomorrow?** pouvez-vous venir demain?; **he couldn't speak because he had a bad cold** il ne pouvait pas parler parce qu'il était très enrhumé; **I could have done that 20 years ago but can't now** il y a 20 ans j'aurais pu le faire mais (je ne peux) plus maintenant; **he could have helped us if he'd wanted to** il aurait pu nous aider s'il l'avait voulu; **he could have described it but he refused to do so** il aurait pu *or* su le décrire mais il a refusé (de le faire).

(c) (*know how to*) **he can read and write** il sait lire et écrire; **he can speak Italian** il parle italien, il sait l'italien; **she could not swim** elle ne savait pas nager.

(d) (*with verbs of perception*) **I can see you** je vous vois; **they could hear him speak** ils l'entendaient parler; **can you smell it?** tu le sens?; **I could see them coming in** je les voyais entrer *or* qui entraient; **he could hear her shouting** il l'entendait crier.

(e) (*have the right to, have permission to*) **you can go** vous pouvez partir; **can I have some milk? — yes, you can** puis-je avoir du lait?—(mais oui,) bien sûr; **could I have a word with you?—yes, you could** est-ce que je pourrais vous parler un instant (s'il vous plaît)?—oui bien sûr *or* certainement *or* mais naturellement; **I could have left earlier but decided to stay** j'aurais pu partir plus tôt, mais j'ai décidé de rester; **I can't go out** je n'ai pas le droit de sortir; **I couldn't leave until the meeting ended** il m'était impossible de partir *or* je ne pouvais pas partir avant la fin de la réunion.

(f) (*indicating suggestion*) **you could try telephoning him** tu pourrais (toujours) lui téléphoner; (*indicating reproach*) **you could have been a little more polite** tu aurais pu être un peu plus poli; **you could have told me before** tu aurais pu me le dire avant *or* plus tôt.

(g) (*be occasionally capable of*) **she can/could be very unpleasant** elle peut *or* sait/pouvait *or* savait (parfois) être très désagréable; **it can be very cold here** il arrive qu'il fasse très froid ici.

(h) (*: **could** = *want to*) **I could smack him!** je le giflerais!, je pourrais le gifler!; **I could have smacked him** je l'aurais giflé; **I could have wept** j'en aurais pleuré.

can[2] [kæn] **1** *n* **(a)** *[milk, oil, water]* bidon *m*; *[garbage]* boîte *f* à ordures, poubelle *f*; *V* **carry.**

(b) (*esp US*) boîte *f* (de conserve). **a ~ of fruit** une boîte de fruits (en conserve); **a ~ of beer** une boîte de bière; **meat in ~s** de la viande en boîte *or* en conserve.

(c) (*Cine*) *[film]* boîte *f*. **that film's in the ~**‡ ce film est prêt à sortir; (*after a take*) le film est dans la boîte.

2 *cpd*: **can opener** ouvre-boîtes *m inv*.

3 vt *food* mettre en boîte(s) *or* en conserve. **~ned fruit/salmon** fruits *mpl*/saumon *m* en boîte *or* en conserve; **~ned food, ~ned goods** conserves *fpl*; (*US*) **~ned heat** méta *m* ®; (*fig*) **~ned music*** musique *f* en conserve* *or* enregistrée; (*fig: drunk*) **to be ~ned**‡ être rétamé* *or* rond‡; (*US*) **~ it!**‡ ferme-la!‡, la ferme!‡

Canada [ˈkænədə] *n* Canada *m*.

Canadian [kəˈneɪdɪən] **1** *adj* canadien. **~ elk** orignal *m*. **2** *n* Canadien(ne) *m(f)*; *V* **French.**

canal [kəˈnæl] *n* **(a)** canal *m*. **~ barge** chaland *m*, péniche *f*. **(b)** (*Anat*) conduit *m*, canal *m*; *V* **alimentary.**

canalization [ˌkænəlaɪˈzeɪʃən] *n* canalisation *f*.

canalize [ˈkænəlaɪz] *vt* canaliser.

canapé [ˈkænəpeɪ] *n* (*Culin*) canapé *m*.

canard [kæˈnɑːd] *n* canard* *m*, bobard* *m*.

canary [kəˈnɛərɪ] **1** *n* **(a)** (*bird*) canari *m*, serin *m*.

(b) (*wine*) vin *m* des Canaries.

2 *cpd* (*also* **canary yellow**) (de couleur) jaune serin *inv*, jaune canari *inv*. (*Bot*) **canary grass** alpiste *m*; (*Geog*) **Canary Isles, Canaries** (îles *fpl*) Canaries *fpl*; (*Bot*) **canary seed** millet *m*.

canasta [kəˈnæstə] *n* canasta *f*.

cancan [ˈkænkæn] *n* (*also* **French ~**) cancan *m*.

cancel [ˈkænsəl] *vt* **(a)** (*cross out, delete*) barrer, rayer, biffer.

(b) (*annul, revoke*) *agreement, contract* résilier; *order, arrangement, meeting* annuler; *cheque* faire opposition à; *taxi, coach or car ordered, appointment, party* décommander; *stamp* oblitérer; *mortgage* lever; *decree, will* révoquer; *debt* régler, annuler; *train* supprimer; *candidature* retirer; *ticket* (*punch*) poinçonner; (*stamp*) oblitérer.

(c) (*Math*) *figures, amounts* éliminer.

cancel out *vt sep* (*Math*) *noughts* barrer; *[amounts etc]* annuler, éliminer; (*fig*) neutraliser. **they cancel each other out** (*Math*) ils s'annulent, ils s'éliminent; (*fig*) ils se neutralisent.

cancellation [ˌkænsəˈleɪʃən] *n* (*V* **cancel**) biffage *m*; résiliation *f*; annulation *f*; oblitération *f*; levée *f*; révocation *f*; règlement *m*; suppression *f*; retrait *m*; (*Math*) élimination *f*. **~s will not be accepted after ...** (*travel, hotel*) les réservations ne peuvent être annulées après ...; (*Theat*) les locations ne peuvent être annulées après ...; **I have 2 ~s for tomorrow** j'ai 2 personnes qui se sont décommandées pour demain, j'ai 2 réservations qui ont été annulées pour demain.

cancer [ˈkænsəʳ] **1** *n* (*Med*) cancer *m*; (*Astron, Geog*) **C~** Cancer *m*.

2 *cpd*: **cancer-causing** cancérigène; **cancer patient** cancéreux *m*, -euse *f*; **cancer-producing** = **cancer-causing**; **cancer research** cancérologie *f*, (*in appeals, funds, charities*) la lutte contre le cancer; **cancer specialist** cancérologue *mf*.

cancerous [ˈkænsərəs] *adj* cancéreux.

candelabra [ˌkændɪˈlɑːbrə] *n* candélabre *m*.

candid [ˈkændɪd] *adj* franc (*f* franche), sincère. **he gave me his ~ opinion of it** il m'a dit franchement ce qu'il en pensait.

candidacy [ˈkændɪdəsɪ] *n* (*esp US*) candidature *f*.

candidate [ˈkændɪdeɪt] *n* candidat(e) *m(f)*. **to stand as/be a ~** se porter/être candidat.

candidature [ˈkændɪdətʃəʳ] *n* (*Brit*) candidature *f*.

candidly [ˈkændɪdlɪ] *adv* franchement, sincèrement.

candidness [ˈkændɪdnɪs] *n* franchise *f*, sincérité *f*.

candied [ˈkændɪd] *adj* (*Culin*) *whole fruit* glacé, confit; *cherries, angelica etc* confit. **~ peel** écorce d'orange *or* de citron *etc* confite.

candle [ˈkændl] **1** *n* **(a)** *[wax]* bougie *f*; *[tallow]* chandelle *f*; *[church]* cierge *m*. **the game is not worth the ~** le jeu n'en vaut pas la chandelle; *V* **burn**[1]**, hold, Roman.**

(b) = **candle-power**; *V* 2.

2 *cpd*: **candle grease** suif *m*; **candlelight** lumière *f* de bougie *or* de chandelle; **by candlelight** à la lumière *or* à la lueur d'une bougie; **candlelight dinner** dîner *m* aux chandelles; (*US*) **candle pin** quille *f*; (*US: game*) **candle pins** jeu *m* de quilles; (*Elec*) **a 20 candle-power lamp** une (lampe de) 20 bougies; **candlestick** (*flat*) bougeoir *m*; (*tall*) chandelier *m*; **candlewick bedspread** dessus-de-lit *m* en chenille (de coton).

Candlemas [ˈkændlmæs] *n* la Chandeleur.

candour, (US) candor [ˈkændəʳ] *n* franchise *f*, sincérité *f*.

candy [ˈkændɪ] **1** *n* sucre candi; (*US*) bonbon(s) *m(pl)*.

2 *vt sugar* faire candir; *fruit* glacer, confire.

3 *vi* se candir, se cristalliser.

4 *cpd*: (*Brit*) **candy-floss** barbe *f* à papa; (*US*) **candy store** confiserie *f*; **candy-striped** à rayures multicolores.

cane [keɪn] **1** *n* **(a)** *[bamboo etc]* canne *f*; (*in basket- and furniture-making*) rotin *m*, jonc *m*; *V* **sugar.**

(b) (*walking stick*) canne *f*; (*stick*) badine *f*, jonc *m*; *[punishment]* trique *f*; (*Scol*) verge *f*, baguette *f*. **the schoolboy got the ~** l'écolier a été fouetté *or* a reçu le fouet.

2 *vt person* administrer *or* donner des coups de trique *or* de bâton à; (*Scol*) fouetter; (*fig*) taper sur les doigts de.

3 *cpd*: **cane chair** chaise cannée; **cane sugar** sucre *m* de canne.

canine [ˈkænaɪn] *adj* canin. (*Anat*) **~ (tooth)** canine *f*.

caning [ˈkeɪnɪŋ] *n*: **to get a ~** (*lit*) recevoir la trique; (*Scol*) recevoir le fouet, être fouetté; (*fig*) se faire taper sur les doigts; **to give sb a ~** = **to cane sb**; *V* **cane.**

canister [ˈkænɪstəʳ] *n* boîte *f* (*gén en métal*).

canker [ˈkæŋkəʳ] **1** *n* (*Med*) ulcère *m*, (*gen syphilitic*) chancre *m*; (*Bot, fig*) chancre. **~-worm** ver *m*. **2** *vt* (*Med*) ronger.

cankerous [ˈkæŋkərəs] *adj sore* rongeur; *tissue* chancreux.

cannabis [ˈkænəbɪs] *n* **(a)** (*plant*) chanvre indien. **(b)** (*resin*) cannabine *f*. **(c)** (*drug*) cannabis *m*.

cannery [ˈkænərɪ] *n* (*US*) fabrique *f* de conserves, conserverie *f*.

cannibal [ˈkænɪbəl] *adj, n* cannibale (*mf*), anthropophage (*mf*).

cannibalism [ˈkænɪbəlɪzəm] *n* cannibalisme *m*, anthropophagie *f*.

cannibalize [ˈkænɪbəlaɪz] *vt* (*Tech*) *machine, car* démonter pour en réutiliser les pièces.

canning [ˈkænɪŋ] *n* mise *f* en conserve *or* en boîte. **~ factory** fabrique *f* de conserves, conserverie *f*; **~ industry** industrie *f* de la conserve, conserverie.

cannon [ˈkænən] **1** *n* **(a)** (*Mil: pl* **~** *or* **~s**) canon *m*; *V* **water.**

(b) (*Tech*) canon *m*.

(c) (*Brit Billiards*) carambolage *m*.

2 *cpd*: **cannonball** boulet *m* de canon; **cannon fodder*** chair *f* à canon*; **within cannon-shot** à portée de canon.

3 *vi* (*Brit Billiards*) caramboler. **to ~ off the red** caramboler la rouge; (*fig*) **to ~ into** *or* **against sth** percuter qch; (*fig*) **to ~ into** *or* **against sb** se heurter contre qn.

cannonade [ˌkænəˈneɪd] *n* canonnade *f*.

cannot [ˈkænɒt] *neg of* **can**[1].

canny [ˈkænɪ] *adj* (*cautious*) prudent, circonspect; (*shrewd*) malin (*f* -igne), rusé, futé; (*careful with money*) regardant* (*pej*), économe. **~ answer** réponse *f* de Normand; *V* **ca'canny.**

canoe [kəˈnuː] **1** *n* canoë *m*; (*African*) pirogue *f*; (*single-seated river* **~**) canoë monoplace; (*Sport*) kayac *m*; *V* **paddle. 2** *vi* (*V* 1) faire du canoë; (*Sport*) faire du kayac; aller en pirogue.

canoeing [kəˈnuːɪŋ] *n* (*Sport*) (sport *m* du) canoë *m*.

canoeist [kəˈnuːɪst] *n* canoéiste *mf*.

canon [ˈkænən] *n* **(a)** (*Mus, Rel, Tech*) canon *m*; (*fig*) canon, critère *m*. (*Rel*) **~ of the mass** canon de la messe; (*Rel*) **~ law** droit *m* canon. **(b)** (*Rel: chapter member*) chanoine *m*.

cañon [ˈkænjən] *n* (*US*) = **canyon.**

canonical [kəˈnɒnɪkəl] *adj* (*Rel*) canonique, conforme aux canons de l'église; (*Mus*) en canon; (*fig*) autorisé, qui fait autorité. (*Rel*) **~ dress, ~s** vêtements sacerdotaux.

canonization [ˌkænənaɪˈzeɪʃən] *n* (*Rel*) canonisation *f*.

canonize [ˈkænənaɪz] *vt* (*Rel, fig*) canoniser.

canoodle‡† [kəˈnuːdl] *vi* se faire des mamours*.

canopy [ˈkænəpɪ] *n* *[bed]* baldaquin *m*, ciel *m* de lit; *[throne etc]* dais *m*; (*Archit*) baldaquin; *[parachute]* voilure *f*; *[cockpit]* verrière *f*; (*fig*) *[sky, heavens, foliage]* voûte *f*.

cant[1] [kænt] **1** *n* (*pej*) **(a)** (*insincere talk*) langage *m* de convention, phrases toutes faites; (*pious hypocrisy*) tartuferie *f*, affectation *f* de piété *or* de moralité. ~ **phrases** lieux communs, clichés *mpl*, expressions stéréotypées.

(b) (*jargon*) jargon *m*, argot *m* de métier. **lawyers' ~** jargon juridique; *V* **thief.**

2 *vi* parler avec hypocrisie *or* affectation.

cant[2] [kænt] **1** *n* **(a)** (*slope, steepness*) pente *f*, déclivité *f*; (*sloping surface*) plan incliné, surface *f* oblique. **this wall has a definite ~** ce mur penche très nettement.

(b) (*jolt*) secousse *f*, cahot *m*, à-coup *m*.

2 *vi* (*tilt*) pencher, s'incliner; (*Naut: change direction*) prendre une direction oblique.

3 *vt* (*tilt*) incliner, pencher; (*overturn*) renverser *or* retourner d'une saccade, retourner d'un coup sec.

can't [kɑːnt] *abbr of* **cannot**; *V* **can**[1].

cantaloup(e) ['kæntəluːp] *n* cantaloup *m*.

cantankerous [kæn'tæŋkərəs] *adj* (*ill-tempered*) acariâtre, revêche; (*aggressive*) hargneux; (*quarrelsome*) querelleur.

cantata [kæn'tɑːtə] *n* cantate *f*.

canteen [kæn'tiːn] *n* **(a)** (*restaurant*) cantine *f*. **(b)** (*Mil*) (*flask*) bidon *m*; (*mess tin*) gamelle *f*. **(c) a ~ of cutlery** une ménagère (*couverts de table*).

canter ['kæntə^r] **1** *n* petit galop (*très rassemblé*). **to go for a ~** aller faire une promenade à cheval (*au petit galop*); (*Brit fig*) **to win in** *or* **at a ~*** gagner haut la main, arriver dans un fauteuil*.

2 *vi* aller au petit galop.

3 *vt* mener *or* faire aller au petit galop.

Canterbury ['kæntəbərɪ] *n* Cantorbéry. (*Bot*) **~ bell** campanule *f*; (*Literat*) **~ Tales** les Contes *mpl* de Cantorbéry.

cantharides [kæn'θærɪdiːz] *npl* cantharides *fpl*.

canticle ['kæntɪkl] *n* cantique *m*, hymne *m*. **the C~s** le cantique des cantiques.

cantilever ['kæntɪliːvə^r] **1** *n* (*Tech*) cantilever *m*; (*Archit*) corbeau *m*, console *f*. **2** *cpd*: **cantilever beam** poutre *f* en console; **cantilever bridge** pont *m* cantilever.

canting ['kæntɪŋ] *adj* (*whining*) pleurnicheur, pleurard; (*hypocritical*) hypocrite, tartufe.

canto ['kæntəʊ] *n* chant *m* (*d'un poème*).

canton ['kæntɒn] **1** *n* (*Admin*) canton *m*. **2** *vt* **(a)** *land* diviser en cantons. **(b)** (*Mil*) *soldiers* cantonner.

cantonal ['kæntənl] *adj* cantonal.

Cantonese [ˌkæntə'niːz] **1** *adj* cantonais. **2** *n* **(a)** (*pl inv*) Cantonais(e) *m(f)*. **(b)** (*Ling*) cantonais *m*.

cantonment [kən'tuːnmənt] *n* cantonnement *m*.

cantor ['kæntɔː^r] *n* (*Rel*) chantre *m*.

Canuck* [kə'nʊk] *n* Canadien(ne) français(e) *m(f)*.

canvas ['kænvəs] **1** *n* **(a)** (*U*) (*Art, Naut*) *[tent]* toile *f*; (*Embroidery*) canevas *m*. **under ~** *[tent]* sous la tente; (*Naut*) sous voiles.

(b) (*painting*) toile *f*, tableau *m*.

2 *cpd* en *or* de toile. **canvas chair** chaise pliante (*de toile*); **canvas shoes** (*rope-soled*) espadrilles *fpl*; (*gen*) chaussures *fpl* de toile.

canvass ['kænvəs] **1** *vt* **(a)** (*Pol*) *district* faire du démarchage électoral dans; *person* solliciter la voix *or* le suffrage de.

(b) (*Comm*) *customers* solliciter des commandes de; *district* prospecter.

(c) *matter, question* débattre, examiner à fond.

2 *vi* **(a)** (*Pol*) *[candidate]* solliciter des suffrages *or* des voix. **to ~ for sb** (*Pol*) solliciter des voix pour qn; (*gen*) faire campagne pour qn.

(b) (*Comm*) visiter la clientèle faire la place; (*door to door*) faire du démarchage.

3 *n* = **canvassing.**

canvasser ['kænvəsə^r] *n* **(a)** (*Pol*) agent électoral (*qui sollicite les voix des électeurs*). **(b)** (*Comm*) placier *m*; (*door to door*) démarcheur *m*. **'no ~s'** 'accès interdit aux colporteurs'.

canvassing ['kænvəsɪŋ] *n* (*Pol*) démarchage électoral (*pour solliciter les suffrages*); (*when applying for job, membership etc*) visites *fpl* de candidature. (*Admin etc*) **no ~ allowed** ≃ s'abstenir de toute démarche personnelle.

canyon ['kænjən] *n* cañon *m*, gorge *f*.

cap [kæp] **1** *n* **(a)** (*headgear*) *[man, woman, boy, jockey]* casquette *f*; (*for women: regional*) coiffe *f*; *[judge]* toque *f*; *[baby, sailor]* bonnet *m*; *[officer]* képi *m*; *[soldier]* calot *m*; (*skull~*) calotte *f*; *[cardinal]* barrette *f*. (*Univ*) **~ and gown** costume *m* universitaire; (*fig*) **~ in hand** chapeau bas, humblement; (*fig*) **if the ~ fits, put it on** *or* **wear it** qui se sent morveux (qu'il) se mouche; *[woman]* **to set one's ~ at**† jeter son dévolu sur; **~ and bells** marotte *f* (de bouffon); (*Brit Sport*) **he's got his ~ for England, he's an England ~** il a été sélectionné pour l'équipe d'Angleterre, il joue pour l'Angleterre; *V* **black, feather, night, thinking.**

(b) (*lid, cover*) *[bottle]* capsule *f*; *[fountain pen]* capuchon *m*; (*Mil: on shell*) fusée *f*; (*Aut: of radiator, tyre-valve*) bouchon *m*; (*Naut: of mast*) chouque *m* *or* chouquet *m*; (*Archit*) chapiteau *m*, couronnement *m*; *[mushroom]* chapeau *m*; *V* **axle, knee, toe** *etc*.

(c) (*percussion ~*) capsule fulminante; (*for toy gun*) amorce *f*.

2 *vt* **(a)** (*V* 1b: *put cover on*) (*gen*) couvrir d'une capsule, d'un capuchon *etc*; *bottle etc* capsuler; (*Mil*) *shell* visser la fusée de; *V* **snow.**

(b) *person* coiffer; (*Univ*) conférer un grade universitaire à. (*Sport*) **he was ~ped 4 times for England** il a joué 4 fois dans l'équipe d'Angleterre.

(c) (*surpass, improve on*) *sb's words* renchérir sur; *achievements* surpasser. **he ~ped this story/quotation** il a trouvé une histoire/une citation encore meilleure que celle-ci; **to ~ it all*** pour couronner le tout, pour comble; **that ~s it all!*** ça, c'est le bouquet!* *or* le comble!

capability [ˌkeɪpə'bɪlətɪ] *n* **(a)** (*U*) aptitude *f* (*to do, of doing* à faire), capacité *f* (*to do, for doing* de faire). **he has the ~ to do it** il est capable de le faire, il en a la capacité, il a l'aptitude nécessaire.

(b) capabilities moyens *mpl*; **this child has capabilities** cet enfant a des moyens *or* est assez doué.

capable ['keɪpəbl] *adj* **(a)** *person* capable; *event, situation* susceptible (*of* de). **he is ~ of great anger/of getting angry very quickly** il est capable de se mettre très en colère/de s'emporter très vite; **the situation is ~ of review** *or* **of being reviewed** la situation est susceptible d'être reconsidérée.

(b) (*competent*) *child* capable; *worker* capable, compétent.

capably ['keɪpəblɪ] *adv* habilement, avec compétence.

capacious [kə'peɪʃəs] *adj hall, hotel* vaste, d'une grande capacité; *container* d'une grande contenance *or* capacité.

capacity [kə'pæsɪtɪ] **1** *n* **(a)** (*ability to hold, cubic content etc*) *[container]* contenance *f*, capacité *f*; *[hall, hotel]* capacité. **filled to ~** *jug* plein; *box, suitcase* plein, bourré; *hall, bus etc* plein, comble *inv*, bondé; **the hall has a seating ~ of 400** la salle peut contenir 400 personnes, la salle a 400 places assises; **the tank has a ~ of 100 litres** le réservoir a une capacité *or* une contenance de 100 litres.

(b) (*Elec, Phys*) capacité *f*; *[machine, factory]* rendement *m*. **to work at full ~** produire à plein rendement.

(c) (*mental ability: also* **capacities**) aptitude *f*, capacité(s) *f(pl)*, moyens *mpl*. **~ to do sth** aptitude à faire qch; **to the extent of my ~** dans la mesure de mes moyens; **this book is within the ~ of children** ce livre est à la portée des enfants; **he had lost all ~ for happiness** il avait perdu toute aptitude au bonheur *or* à être heureux; **his ~ for hard work** sa grande aptitude au travail.

(d) (*position, status*) qualité *f*, titre *m*. **in my ~ as a doctor** en ma qualité de médecin; **in his official ~** dans l'exercice de ses fonctions; **we must not employ him in any ~ whatsoever** il ne faut pas l'employer à quelque titre que ce soit.

(e) (*legal power*) pouvoir légal (*to do* de faire). **to have the ~ to do** avoir qualité pour faire.

2 *cpd*: (*Theat etc*) **there was a capacity attendance** c'était plein; **there was capacity booking** toutes les places étaient louées *or* retenues, on jouait à guichets fermés; **there was a capacity crowd** il n'y avait plus une place (de) libre; (*Sport*) le stade était comble.

caparison [kə'pærɪsn] (*liter*) **1** *n* caparaçon *m*. **2** *vt horse* caparaçonner.

cape[1] [keɪp] *n* (*full length*) cape *f*; (*half length*) pèlerine *f*; (*policeman's, cyclist's*) pèlerine.

cape[2] [keɪp] **1** *n* (*Geog*) cap *m*; (*high ~*) promontoire *m*.

2 *cpd*: (*in South Africa*) **Cape Coloureds** métis sud-africains; **Cape Horn** le cap Horn; **Cape of Good Hope** le cap de Bonne Espérance; **Cape Town** Le Cap; **Cape Verde Islands** îles *fpl* du Cap-Vert.

caper[1] ['keɪpə^r] **1** *vi* *[child, elf]* (*also* **~ about**) gambader, faire des gambades *or* des cabrioles. (*fool around*) **to ~ about*** faire l'idiot.

2 *n* **(a)** (*leap, jump*) cabriole *f*, gambade *f*. (*fig, gen pl: pranks*) **~s** farces *fpl*.

(b) (*) **that was quite a ~** ça a été une vraie rigolade*; (*hum, slightly pej*) **how did your French ~ go?** comment s'est passée votre petite virée* en France?

caper[2] ['keɪpə^r] *n* (*Culin*) câpre *f*; (*shrub*) câprier *m*. **~ sauce** sauce *f* aux câpres.

capercailzie [ˌkæpə'keɪlɪ] *n* grand tétras, grand coq de bruyère.

capeskin ['keɪpskɪn] *n* (*US*) peau *f* souple pour ganterie.

capful ['kæpfʊl] *n* (*measure of liquid*) **one ~ to 4 litres of water** une capsule (pleine) pour 4 litres d'eau.

capillary [kə'pɪlərɪ] *adj, n* (*Bio, Bot*) capillaire (*m*).

capital ['kæpɪtl] **1** *adj* **(a)** (*Jur*) capital. **~ offence** crime capital; **~ punishment** peine capitale, peine de mort; **~ sentence** condamnation *f* à mort.

(b) (*essential, important*) capital, fondamental, essentiel. **of ~ importance** d'une importance capitale.

(c) (*chief, principal*) capital, principal. **~ city** *V* 2a; **~ letter** *V* 2b; (*Naut*) **~ ship** grosse unité de guerre.

(d) (*†) épatant*, fameux*.

2 *n* **(a)** (*also* **~ city**) capitale *f*.

(b) (*Typ: also* **~ letter**) majuscule *f*, capitale *f*. **~ A, B** *etc* A, B *etc* majuscule.

(c) (*U: Comm, Fin*) (*money and property*) capital *m* (en espèces et en nature); (*money only*) capital, capitaux *mpl*, fonds *mpl*. **~ invested** mise *f* de fonds; **~ and labour** le capital et la main d'œuvre; (*fig*) **to make ~ out of** tirer parti *or* profit de; *V* **working.**

(d) (*Archit*) chapiteau *m*.

3 *cpd*: (*Fin*) **capital expenditure** dépenses *fpl* en capital; **capital gains** augmentation *f* de capital, plus-values *fpl* (en capital); **capital gains tax** impôt *m* sur les plus-values (en capital); **capital goods** biens *mpl* d'équipement *or* de production; **capital levy** prélèvement *m* *or* impôt *m* sur le capital; **capital reserves** réserves *fpl* et provisions *fpl*; **capital sum** capital *m*.

capitalism ['kæpɪtəlɪzəm] *n* capitalisme *m*.

capitalist ['kæpɪtəlɪst] *adj, n* capitaliste (*mf*).

capitalistic [ˌkæpɪtə'lɪstɪk] *adj* capitaliste.

capitalization [kəˌpɪtəlaɪ'zeɪʃən] *n* capitalisation *f*.

capitalize [kə'pɪtəlaɪz] **1** *vt* **(a)** (*Fin*) *property, plant* capitaliser; *company* constituer le capital social de (*par émission d'actions*); (*fig*) tirer profit *or* parti de. (*Fin*) **over-/under-~d** sur-/sous-capitalisé.

(b) (*Typ*) *word* mettre une majuscule à.

2 *vi* (*fig*) **to ~ on** *circumstances, information* tirer profit *or* parti de; *talents* tirer parti de; (*financially*) monnayer.

capitation [ˌkæpɪ'teɪʃən] *n* impôt *m* par tête.
Capitol ['kæpɪtl] *n* (*Hist*) **the ~** le Capitole.
capitulate [kə'pɪtjʊleɪt] *vi* (*Mil, fig*) capituler.
capitulation [kəˌpɪtjʊ'leɪʃən] *n* **(a)** (*Mil, fig*) capitulation *f.* **(b)** (*summary*) récapitulation *f,* sommaire *m.* **(c)** (*Jur*) **~s** capitulation *f.*
capon ['keɪpən] *n* chapon *m.*
caprice [kə'pri:s] *n* **(a)** saute *f* d'humeur. **(b)** (*Mus*) capriccio *m.*
capricious [kə'prɪʃəs] *adj* capricieux, fantasque.
capriciously [kə'prɪʃəslɪ] *adv* capricieusement.
Capricorn ['kæprɪkɔ:n] *n* (*Astron, Geog*) Capricorne *m.*
capsicum ['kæpsɪkəm] *n* (*plant, fruit*) (*sweet*) piment doux, poivron *m;* (*hot*) piment.
capsize [kæp'saɪz] **1** *vi* se renverser; (*Naut*) chavirer. **2** *vt* renverser; (*Naut*) faire chavirer.
capstan ['kæpstən] *n* (*Naut*) cabestan *m.* (*Brit*) **~ lathe** tour *m* revolver.
capsule ['kæpsju:l] *n* (*all senses*) capsule *f.*
captain ['kæptɪn] **1** *n* chef *m,* capitaine *m;* (*Mil*) capitaine; (*Navy*) capitaine (de vaisseau); (*Merchant Navy*) capitaine; (*Sport*) capitaine (d'équipe). (*Brit*) **(school) ~** *élève (des classes terminales) élu(e) pour faire la discipline;* **~ of industry** capitaine d'industrie.
2 *vt* (*Sport*) *team* être le capitaine de; (*Mil, Naut*) commander; (*fig*) diriger.
captaincy ['kæptənsɪ] *n* (*Mil*) grade *m* de capitaine; (*Sport*) poste *m* de capitaine. (*Mil*) **to get one's ~** être promu *or* passer capitaine; (*Sport*) **during his ~** quand il était capitaine (de l'équipe).
caption ['kæpʃən] **1** *n* **(a)** (*Press*) (*heading*) sous-titre *m;* (*under illustration*) légende *f.* **(b)** (*Cine*) sous-titre *m.* **2** *vt illustration* mettre une légende à; (*Cine*) sous-titrer.
captious ['kæpʃəs] *adj person* chicanier, vétilleux, qui trouve toujours à redire; *remark* critique.
captivate ['kæptɪveɪt] *vt* captiver, fasciner, tenir sous le charme.
captivating ['kæptɪveɪtɪŋ] *adj* captivant.
captive ['kæptɪv] **1** *n* captif *m,* -ive *f.* **to take sb ~** faire qn prisonnier; **to hold sb ~** garder qn en captivité; (*fig*) captiver qn, tenir qn sous le charme.
2 *adj person* captif, prisonnier; *balloon* captif. **she had a ~ audience** son auditoire était bien obligé de l'écouter.
captivity [kæp'tɪvɪtɪ] *n* captivité *f.* **in ~** en captivité.
captor ['kæptəʳ] *n* (*unlawful*) ravisseur *m;* (*lawful*) personne *f* qui capture.
capture ['kæptʃəʳ] **1** *vt animal, soldier* prendre, capturer; *escapee* reprendre; *city* prendre, s'emparer de; (*fig*) *attention* capter, captiver; *interest* gagner; (*Art*) reproduire, rendre. **2** *n [town, treasure, escapee]* capture *f.*
capuchin ['kæpjʊʃɪn] *n* **(a)** cape *f* (*avec capuchon*). **(b)** (*Rel*) **C~** capucin(e) *m(f).*
car [kɑ:ʳ] **1** *n* **(a)** (*Aut*) voiture *f,* automobile *f,* auto *f; V* **racing, saloon, sport** *etc.*
(b) (*US Rail*) wagon *m,* voiture *f; V* **dining car, freight** *etc.*
(c) (*tramcar*) (voiture *f* de) tramway *m,* tram *m.*
(d) (*US: of elevator*) cabine *f* (d'ascenseur).
(e) (*Aviat*) nacelle *f* (*de dirigeable*).
2 *cpd:* **car allowance** indemnité *f* de déplacements (*en voiture*); **car-ferry** *[sea]* ferry(-boat) *m; [river, small channel]* bac *m* (pour voitures), ferry *m;* (*US*) **carhop** serveur *m,* -euse *f* (*qui apporte à manger aux automobilistes dans leur voiture*); **car journey** voyage *m* en voiture; (*shorter*) trajet *m* en voiture; (*Brit*) **car park** parking *m,* parc *m* de stationnement; **carport** auvent *m* (pour voiture(s)); **to be car sick** être malade en voiture, avoir le mal de la route; **car sickness** mal *m* de la route; **car transporter** (*Aut*) camion *m or* (*Rail*) wagon *m* pour transport d'automobiles; **car wash** (*action*) lavage *m* de voitures; (*place*) lave-auto *m,* tunnel *m* de lavage; (*Ind*) **car-worker** ouvrier *m,* -ière *f* de l'industrie automobile.
carafe [kə'ræf] *n* carafe *f;* (*small*) carafon *m.*
caramel ['kærəməl] *n* (*Culin*) caramel *m.* **~ custard** *or* **cream** crème *f* (au) caramel.
caramelize ['kærəməlaɪz] **1** *vt* caraméliser. **2** *vi* se caraméliser.
carapace ['kærəpeɪs] *n* carapace *f.*
carat ['kærət] *n* carat *m.* **22 ~ gold** or *m* à 22 carats.
caravan ['kærəvæn] *n* (*Brit Aut*) caravane *f; [gipsy]* roulotte *f;* (*group: in desert etc*) caravane. **~ site** *[tourists]* camping *m* pour caravanes; *[gipsies]* campement *m.*
caravanette [ˌkærəvə'net] *n* (*Brit*) auto-camping *f,* voiture-camping *f.*
caravel [kærə'vel] *n* (*Naut*) caravelle *f.*
caraway ['kærəweɪ] *n* cumin *m,* carvi *m.* **~ seeds** graines *fpl* de cumin *or* de carvi.
carbide ['kɑ:baɪd] *n* carbure *m.*
carbine ['kɑ:baɪn] *n* carabine *f.*
carbohydrate ['kɑ:bəʊ'haɪdreɪt] *n* hydrate *m* de carbone; (*in diets etc*) **~s** farineux *mpl,* féculents *mpl.*
carbolic [kɑ:'bɒlɪk] *adj* phéniqué. **~ acid** phénol *m.*
carbon ['kɑ:bən] **1** *n* (*Chem*) carbone *m;* (*Art, Elec*) charbon *m;* (*paper, copy*) carbone.
2 *cpd:* **carbon copy** *[typing etc]* carbone *m;* (*fig*) réplique *f;* (*Archeol*) **carbon dating** datation *f* au carbone; **carbon dioxide** gaz *m* carbonique; **carbon monoxide** oxyde *m* de carbone; **carbon paper** (*Typ*) (papier *m*) carbone *m;* (*Phot: also* **carbon tissue**) papier *m* au charbon.
carbonaceous [ˌkɑ:bə'neɪʃəs] *adj* charbonneux; (*Chem*) carboné.
carbonate ['kɑ:bənɪt] *n* carbonate *m.*
carbonic [kɑ:'bɒnɪk] *adj* carbonique.
carboniferous [ˌkɑ:bə'nɪfərəs] *adj* carbonifère.
carbonization [ˌkɑ:bənaɪ'zeɪʃən] *n* carbonisation *f.*
carbonize ['kɑ:bənaɪz] *vt* carboniser.
carborundum [ˌkɑ:bə'rʌndəm] *n* ® carborundum *m* ®, siliciure *m* de carbone.
carboy ['kɑ:bɔɪ] *n* bonbonne *f.*
carbuncle ['kɑ:bʌŋkl] *n* **(a)** (*jewel*) escarboucle *f.* **(b)** (*Med*) furoncle *m.*
carburettor, (*US*) **carburetor** [ˌkɑ:bjʊ'retəʳ] *n* carburateur *m.*
carcass ['kɑ:kəs] *n* **(a)** *[animal]* carcasse *f,* cadavre *m;* (*Butchery*) carcasse; (*human corpse*) cadavre; (*: hum, iro: body*) carcasse. (*Culin*) **chicken ~** os *mpl or* carcasse de poulet. **(b)** (*Aut, Naut, Tech*) charpente *f,* carcasse *f.*
carcinogen [kɑ:'sɪnədʒən] *n* substance *f* cancérigène *or* cancérogène.
carcinogenic [ˌkɑ:sɪnə'dʒenɪk] **1** *n* = **carcinogen. 2** *adj* cancérigène *or* cancérogène.
carcinoma ['kɑ:sɪ'nəʊmə] *n* carcinome *m.*
card[1] [kɑ:d] **1** *n* **(a)** (*gen*) carte *f;* (*playing* **~**) carte; (*visiting* **~**) carte (de visite); (*invitation* **~**) carton *m or* carte d'invitation; (*post***~**) carte (postale); (*index* **~**) fiche *f;* (*member's* **~**) carte de membre *or* d'adhérent; (*press* **~**) carte de presse; (*library* **~**) carte (d'abonnement); (*at dance, races*) programme *m;* (*piece of cardboard*) (morceau *m* de) carton *m.* **identity ~** carte d'identité; **game of ~s** partie *f* de cartes; **to play ~s** jouer aux cartes; **high/low~** haute/basse carte; *V* **court, face, score, trump** *etc.*
(b) (*fig phrases*) **to play one's ~s well** bien mener son jeu *or* sa barque; **if you play your ~s properly** si vous manœuvrez habilement; **to play one's best/last ~** jouer sa meilleure/dernière carte; **to hold all the ~s** avoir tous les atouts (dans son jeu *or* en main); **to put** *or* **lay one's ~s on the table** jouer cartes sur table; **to have a ~ up one's sleeve** avoir un atout dans sa manche; **to throw in the ~s** abandonner la partie (*fig*); **it's (quite) on the ~s** *or* (*US*) **in the ~s that*...** il y a de grandes chances (pour) que ... + *subj;* (*Brit Ind etc*) **to get one's ~s** être mis à la porte, être licencié; (*Brit Ind etc*) **to ask for one's ~s** plaquer* *or* quitter son travail; **he's (quite) a ~!*†** c'est un rigolo!*
2 *cpd:* **cardboard** (*n*) carton *m* (*U*); (*adj*) *bookcover* cartonné; *doll* de *or* en carton; **cardboard box** (boîte *f* en) carton *m;* **card-carrying member** membre *m,* adhérent(e) *m(f);* **card catalogue** catalogue *m or* fichier *m* (*de bibliothèque*); **card game** (*e.g. bridge, whist etc*) jeu *m* de cartes; (*game of cards*) partie *f* de cartes; **card holder** *[political party, organization etc]* adhérent(e) *m(f); [library]* abonné(e) *m(f); [restaurant etc]* habitué(e) *m(f);* **card index** fichier *m;* **card-index** ficher, mettre sur fiches; **card sharp(er)** tricheur *m,* -euse *f* (*professionnel*); **card table** table *m* de jeu *or* à jouer; **card trick** tour *m* de cartes.
3 *vt* ficher, mettre sur fiches.
card[2] [kɑ:d] (*Tech*) **1** *n* carde *f.* **2** *vt wool, cotton* carder.
cardamom ['kɑ:dəməm] *n* cardamome *f.*
cardiac ['kɑ:dɪæk] *adj* cardiaque. **~ arrest** arrêt *m* du cœur.
cardigan ['kɑ:dɪgən] *n* cardigan *m,* gilet *m* (de laine).
cardinal ['kɑ:dɪnl] **1** *adj number, point* cardinal. **the four ~ virtues** les quatre vertus cardinales. **2** *n* (*Rel*) cardinal *m.* **~ red** rouge cardinal *inv,* pourpre.
cardiograph ['kɑ:dɪəgræf] *n* cardiographe *m.*
cardiological [ˌkɑ:dɪə'lɒdʒɪkəl] *adj* cardiologique.
cardiologist [ˌkɑ:dɪ'ɒlədʒɪst] *n* cardiologue *mf.*
cardiology [ˌkɑ:dɪ'ɒlədʒɪ] *n* cardiologie *f.*
care [kɛəʳ] **1** *n* **(a)** (*U: attention, heed*) attention *f,* soin *m;* (*charge, responsibility*) soins *mpl,* charge *f,* garde *f.* **with the greatest ~** avec le plus grand soin; (*on parcels*) **'with ~'** 'fragile'; **to take ~** faire attention; **it got broken despite all our ~** ça s'est cassé bien que nous y ayons fait très attention; **take ~ not to catch cold** *or* **that you don't catch cold** faites attention de *or* à ne pas prendre froid; **take ~** (fais) attention; (*as good wishes*) fais bien attention (à toi); **have a ~!†** prenez garde!; **you should take more ~ with** *or* **give more ~ to your work** vous devriez apporter plus d'attention *or* plus de soin à votre travail; **you should take more ~ of yourself** tu devrais faire plus attention (à ta santé); (*Jur*) **convicted of driving without due ~ and attention** condamné pour conduite négligente; **he took ~ to explain why ...** il a pris soin d'expliquer pourquoi ...; **to take ~ of** *book, details, arrangements* s'occuper de, se charger de; *valuables* garder; *person, animal* prendre soin de, s'occuper de; **to take good ~ of sb** bien s'occuper de qn; **to take good ~ of sth** prendre grand soin de qch; (*: *threateningly*) **I'll take ~ of him!** je vais m'occuper de lui!; **I'll take ~ of that** je vais m'en occuper; **he can take ~ of himself** il peut *or* sait se débrouiller* tout seul; **that can take ~ of itself** cela s'arrangera tout seul; **let the car take ~ of itself for a moment!*** laisse la voiture tranquille cinq minutes!; **I leave** *or* **put it in your ~** je le confie à vos soins, je vous le confie; (*on letters*) **~ of** (*abbr* **c/o**) aux bons soins de, chez, c/o; **he was left in his aunt's ~** on l'a laissé à la garde de sa tante; (*frm*) **to be in ~ of sb** être sous la garde *or* la surveillance de qn; **he is in the ~ of Dr X** c'est le docteur X qui le soigne.
(b) (*anxiety*) souci *m.* **he hasn't a ~ in the world** il n'a pas le moindre souci; **full of ~s** accablé de soucis; **the ~s of State** les responsabilités *fpl* de l'État.
2 *cpd:* **carefree** sans souci, insouciant; **caretaker** gardien(ne) *m(f),* concierge *mf;* (*Pol*) **caretaker government** gouvernement *m* intérimaire; **careworn** rongé par les soucis.
3 vi **(a)** (*feel interest, anxiety, sorrow*) se soucier (*about* de), s'intéresser (*about* à). **money is all he ~s about** il n'y a que l'ar-

gent qui l'intéresse (*subj*); **to ~ deeply about sth** être profondément concerné par qch; **to ~ deeply about sb** être profondément attaché à qn; **not to ~ about** se soucier peu de, se moquer de, se ficher de*; **he really ~s (about this)** c'est vraiment important pour lui; **I don't ~!, as if I ~d!** ça m'est égal!, je m'en moque!, je m'en fiche!*; **what do I ~?** qu'est-ce que cela me fait? *or* peut me faire?; **for all I ~** pour ce que cela me fait; **I couldn't ~ less what people say*** je me fiche pas mal* de ce que les gens peuvent dire; **shall we go to the pictures or not? — I don't ~ either way*** on va au cinéma ou non? — (l'un ou l'autre,) ça m'est égal; **he doesn't ~ a (brass) farthing*** *or* **a hang‡** *or* **two hoots‡** *or* **a damn‡** il s'en fiche* comme de l'an quarante *or* de sa première chemise; **who ~s!** qu'est-ce que cela peut bien faire!, on s'en moque!, on s'en fiche!*; *V* **naught.**

(b) (*like*) aimer. **would you ~ to take off your coat?** voulez-vous vous débarrasser de votre manteau?; **I shouldn't ~ to meet him** je n'aimerais pas le rencontrer, ça ne me dirait rien de le rencontrer; **I don't much ~ for it** cela ne me dit pas grand-chose; **I don't ~ for him** il ne me plaît pas tellement *or* beaucoup; **would you ~ for a cup of tea?** voulez-vous (prendre) une tasse de thé?; **would you ~ for a walk?** voulez-vous faire une promenade?

care for *vt fus invalid* soigner; *child* s'occuper de. **well-cared for** *invalid* qu'on soigne bien; *child* dont on s'occupe bien; *hands, hair* soigné; *garden* bien entretenu; *house* bien tenu.

careen [kə'riːn] **1** *vt* (*Naut*) *ship* caréner, mettre *or* abattre en carène. **2** *vi* (*Naut*) donner de la bande (*de façon dangereuse*).

career [kə'rɪəʳ] **1** *n* **(a)** (*profession, occupation*) carrière *f*, profession *f*. **journalism is his ~** il fait carrière dans le journalisme; **he is making a ~ (for himself) in advertising** il est en train de faire carrière dans la publicité.

(b) (*life, development, progress*) vie *f*, carrière *f*. **he studied the ~s of the great** il a étudié la vie des grands hommes.

(c) (*movement*) **in full ~** en pleine course.

2 *cpd soldier, diplomat* de carrière. **career girl** *jeune fille qui veut faire une carrière*; **careers guidance** orientation professionnelle; **careers officer** conseiller *m*, -ère *f* d'orientation professionnelle.

3 *vi* (*also* **~ along**) aller à toute vitesse *or* à toute allure. **to ~ up/down** *etc* monter/descendre *etc* à toute allure.

careerist [kə'rɪərɪst] *n* (*pej*) carriériste *mf* (*pej*).

careful ['kɛəfʊl] *adj* **(a)** (*painstaking*) *writer, worker* consciencieux, soigneux; *work* soigné.

(b) (*cautious*) prudent, circonspect; (*acting with care*) soigneux, soucieux (*of, with* de), attentif (*of, with* à). **(be) ~!** (fais) attention!; **be ~ with the glasses** fais attention aux verres; **be ~ not to let it fall, be ~ (that) you don't let it fall** faites attention à ne pas le laisser tomber; **be ~ of the dog** (faites) attention au chien; **be ~ what you do** faites attention à ce que vous faites; **be ~ (that) he doesn't hear you** faites attention à ce qu'il ne vous entende pas, prenez garde qu'il ne vous entende; **he was ~ to point out that** il a pris soin de faire remarquer que; **you can't be too ~*** (*gen*) on n'est jamais trop prudent, prudence est mère de sûreté (*Prov*); (*when double-checking sth*) deux précautions valent mieux qu'une.

(c) (*rather miserly*) parcimonieux; (**pej*) regardant. **he is very ~ with (his) money** il regarde à la dépense, il est très regardant.

carefully ['kɛəfəlɪ] *adv* **(a)** (*painstakingly*) soigneusement, avec soin. **(b)** (*cautiously*) prudemment, avec précaution. (*fig*) **we must go ~ here** il faut nous montrer prudents là-dessus; **he replied ~** il a répondu avec circonspection.

carefulness ['kɛəfʊlnɪs] *n* soin *m*, attention *f*.

careless ['kɛəlɪs] *adj* **(a)** (*taking little care*) négligent, qui manque de soin; (*unconcerned*) inattentif (*of* à), insouciant (*of* de); (*done without care*) *action* inconsidéré, irréfléchi; *work* peu soigné. **~ driver** conducteur négligent; **convicted of ~ driving** condamné pour conduite négligente; **~ mistake** faute *f* d'inattention; **this work is too ~** ce travail n'est pas assez soigné. **(b)** (*carefree*) sans souci, insouciant.

carelessly ['kɛəlɪslɪ] *adv* **(a)** (*inattentively, thoughtlessly*) négligemment, sans faire attention. **(b)** (*in carefree way*) avec insouciance.

carelessness ['kɛəlɪsnɪs] *n* (*V* **careless**) négligence *f*, manque *m* de soin; manque d'attention, insouciance *f*. **the ~ of his work** le peu de soin qu'il apporte à son travail.

caress [kə'res] **1** *n* caresse *f*. **2** *vt* (*fondle*) caresser; (*kiss*) embrasser.

caret ['kærət] *n* (*Typ*) lambda *m* (*signe d'insertion*).

cargo ['kɑːgəʊ] *n, pl* **~es** *or* **~s** cargaison *f*, chargement *m*. **~ boat** cargo *m*.

Caribbean [ˌkærɪ'biːən] *adj* caraïbe, des Caraïbes. **the ~ (Sea)** la mer des Antilles *or* des Caraïbes.

caribou ['kærɪbuː] *n* caribou *m*.

caricature ['kærɪkətjʊəʳ] **1** *n* **(a)** (*Art, fig*) caricature *f*. **(b)** (*U*) art *m* de la caricature. **2** *vt* (*Art, fig*) caricaturer.

caricaturist [ˌkærɪkə'tjʊərɪst] *n* caricaturiste *mf*.

caries ['kɛəriiːz] *n* carie *f*.

carillon [kə'rɪljən] *n* carillon *m*.

caring ['kɛərɪŋ] *adj parent* aimant; *teacher* bienveillant. **a ~ society** une société humanitaire; **a child needs a ~ environment** un enfant a besoin d'être entouré d'affection.

carious ['kɛərɪəs] *adj* carié, gâté.

Carmelite ['kɑːməlaɪt] *adj, n* carmélite (*f*).

carmine ['kɑːmaɪn] *adj, n* carmin (*m*).

carnage ['kɑːnɪdʒ] *n* carnage *m*.

carnal ['kɑːnl] *adj* (*of the flesh*) charnel; (*sensual*) sensuel; (*worldly*) *pleasure* matériel; *person* matérialiste; (*sexual*) sexuel. (*Jur*) **to have ~ knowledge of sb** avoir des relations sexuelles avec qn.

carnation [kɑː'neɪʃən] **1** *n* (*Bot*) œillet *m*. **2** *adj* (*pink*) rose; (*red*) incarnat.

carnival ['kɑːnɪvəl] **1** *n* carnaval *m*; (*US: fair*) fête *f* (foraine). **2** *cpd hat, procession* de carnaval.

carnivora [kɑː'nɪvərə] *npl* (*Zool*) carnivores *mpl*.

carnivore ['kɑːnɪvɔːʳ] *n* carnivore *m*, carnassier *m*.

carnivorous [kɑː'nɪvərəs] *adj* carnivore, carnassier.

carol ['kærəl] **1** *n* **(a)** (*song*) chant joyeux. **(Christmas) ~** chant de Noël. **(b)** *[birds]* ramage *m*; *[small birds]* gazouillis *m*. **2** *vi* chanter joyeusement; *[birds]* chanter; *[small birds]* gazouiller. **3** *vt* chanter, célébrer (par des chants).

caroller ['kærələʳ] *n* chanteur *m*, -euse *f*.

carom ['kærəm] (*Billiards*) **1** *n* carambolage *m*. **2** *vi* caramboler.

carotid [kə'rɒtɪd] **1** *n* carotide *f*. **2** *adj* carotidien.

carousal [kə'raʊzəl] *n* beuverie *f*, soûlerie* *f*.

carouse [kə'raʊz] *vi* faire la bombe*. **they ~d all night** ils ont passé la nuit en beuverie.

carousel [ˌkæruː'sel] *n* manège *m* (*de chevaux de bois etc*).

carp[1] [kɑːp] *n* (*fish*) carpe *f*.

carp[2] [kɑːp] *vi* critiquer. **to ~ at** *person* critiquer, blâmer; *thing, action* trouver à redire à *or* dans.

Carpathians [kɑː'peɪθɪənz] *npl*: **the ~** les Carpates *fpl*.

carpenter ['kɑːpɪntəʳ] **1** *n* charpentier *m*; (*joiner*) menuisier *m*. **2** *vi* faire de la charpenterie, faire de la menuiserie.

carpentry ['kɑːpɪntrɪ] *n* (*V* **carpenter 1**) charpenterie *f*; menuiserie *f*.

carpet ['kɑːpɪt] **1** *n* tapis *m*. (*fig*) **to be on the ~*** *[subject]* être sur le tapis; *[person scolded]* être sur la sellette; *V* **fitted, red, sweep.**

2 *vt* **(a)** *floor* recouvrir d'un tapis; (*with fitted carpet*) recouvrir d'une moquette, moquetter; (*fig*) tapisser.

(b) (*†: *scold*) *person* houspiller.

3 *cpd*: (*US*) **carpetbagger*** profiteur *m*, -euse *f* (*qui s'installe quelque part pour y faire fortune*); (*Hist*) *profiteur nordiste installé dans le Sud des États-Unis après la guerre de Sécession;* **carpet slippers** pantoufles *fpl*; **carpet sweeper** (*mechanical*) balai *m* mécanique; (*vacuum cleaner*) aspirateur *m*.

carpeting ['kɑːpɪtɪŋ] *n* (*U*) moquette *f*; *V* **wall.**

carping ['kɑːpɪŋ] **1** *adj person* chicanier, qui trouve à redire à tout; *manner* chicanier; *criticism* mesquin; *voice* malveillant. **2** *n* chicanerie *f*, critique *f* (malveillante).

carriage ['kærɪdʒ] **1** *n* **(a)** (*horse-drawn*) voiture *f* (de maître), équipage *m*. **~ and pair/and four** voiture *or* équipage *or* attelage *m* à deux chevaux/à quatre chevaux.

(b) (*Brit Rail*) voiture *f*, wagon *m* (de voyageurs).

(c) (*U: Brit Comm: conveyance of goods*) transport *m*, factage *m*. **~ forward** (en) port dû; **~ free** franco de port; **~ paid** (en) port payé.

(d) *[typewriter]* chariot *m*; *[printing press]* train *m*; (*Mil: also* **gun-~**) affût *m*.

(e) *[person]* (*bearing*) maintien *m*, port *m*.

2 *cpd*: **carriage drive** allée *f* (pour voitures), grande allée; (*US Comm*) **carriage trade** clientèle *f* riche, grosse clientèle; **carriageway** chaussée *f*; *V* **dual.**

carrier ['kærɪəʳ] **1** *n* **(a)** (*Comm*) (*company*) entreprise *f* de transports; (*truck owner etc*) entrepreneur *m* de transports, transporteur *m*, camionneur *m*. **by ~** (*Aut*) par la route, par camion; (*Rail*) par chemin de fer; **express ~** messageries *fpl*.

(b) (*basket etc: on car, cycle etc*) porte-bagages *m inv*; (*bag*) sac *m* (en plastique).

(c) (*Med*) porteur *m*, -euse *f*.

(d) (*aircraft ~*) porte-avions *m inv*; (*troop ~*) (*plane*) appareil transporteur (de troupes); (*ship*) transport *m*.

2 *cpd*: (*Brit*) **carrier-bag** sac *m* (en plastique); **carrier-pigeon** pigeon voyageur.

carrion ['kærɪən] **1** *n* (*U*) charogne *f*. **2** *cpd*: **carrion crow** corneille *f*, corbeau *m*; **carrion feeder** (*vulture*) charognard *m*; (*other*) *animal qui se nourrit de charognes*; **carrion flesh** charogne *f*.

carrot ['kærət] *n* (*lit, fig*) carotte *f*.

carroty ['kærətɪ] *adj hair* carotte *inv*, roux (*f* rousse). **to have ~ hair** être rouquin* *or* poil-de-carotte *inv*.

carrousel [ˌkæruː'sel] *n* (*US*) = **carousel.**

carry ['kærɪ] **1** *vt* **(a)** (*bear, transport*) *[person]* porter; *[vehicle]* transporter; *goods, heavy loads* transporter; *message, news* porter. **she was ~ing the child in her arms** elle portait l'enfant dans ses bras; **this ship carries coal/passengers** ce bateau transporte du charbon/des passagers; **this coach carries 30 people** ce car contient 30 personnes; **they carried enormous sacks of apples all day** ils ont transporté d'énormes sacs de pommes toute la journée; **as fast as his legs could ~ him** à toutes jambes; **the sea carried the boat westward** la mer a emporté le bateau vers l'ouest; (*fig*) **he carried his audience with him** il a enthousiasmé son auditoire, il a emporté la conviction de son auditoire; (*fig*) **to ~ coals to Newcastle** porter de l'eau à la rivière; (*fig*) **(to be left) to ~ the can*** (devoir) payer les pots cassés; **he carries his life in his hands** il risque sa vie; **£5 won't ~ you far these days** de nos jours on ne va pas loin avec 5 livres; **enough food to ~ us through the winter** assez de provisions pour nous durer *or* nous faire* tout l'hiver; **he's had one or two drinks more than he can ~*** il a bu un ou deux verres de trop; (*US*) **to ~ a torch for sb*** avoir le béguin pour qn*.

(b) (*have on one's person*) *identity card, documents* porter *or* avoir (sur soi); *matches, cigarettes, money* avoir (sur soi); *umbrella, gun, sword* porter. **to ~ in one's head** retenir dans sa tête.

(c) (*involve, lead to, entail*) avoir comme conséquence(s), produire; *consequences* entraîner. **to ~ conviction** être convaincant; (*Fin*) **to ~ interest** rapporter *or* produire des intérêts; **to ~ a mortgage** être grevé d'une hypothèque; **this job carries a lot of responsibility** ce travail implique *or* comporte de grandes responsabilités; **it also carries extra pay** cela comporte aussi un salaire supplémentaire; **this offence carries a penalty of £100** ce délit est passible d'une amende de 100 livres; **to ~ a crop** donner *or* produire une récolte; (*fig*) **to ~ weight** compter, avoir de l'importance; **to ~ authority** faire autorité.

(d) (*support*) *[pillar etc]* supporter, soutenir, porter. (*Naut fig*) **the ship was ~ing too much canvas** *or* **sail** le navire portait trop de toile.

(e) (*Comm*) *goods, stock* stocker, vendre. **we don't ~ that article** nous ne faisons pas cet article.

(f) (*Tech*) *[pipe] water, oil* amener; *[wire] sound* conduire.

(g) (*extend*) faire passer. **they carried the pipes under the street** ils ont fait passer les tuyaux sous la rue; (*fig*) **to ~ sth too far** *or* **to excess** pousser qch trop loin; **they carried the war into the enemy camp** ils ont porté la guerre sur le territoire de l'ennemi; **this basic theme is carried through the book** ce thème fondamental se retrouve tout au long du livre.

(h) (*bear successfully, win*) gagner, remporter; *fortress* enlever; *enemy's position* emporter d'assaut. **to ~ the day** (*fig*) gagner (la partie), l'emporter; (*Mil*) être vainqueur; **to ~ all** *or* **everything before one** marcher en vainqueur, l'emporter sur tous les tableaux; **he carried his point** il a eu gain de cause; **the motion/bill was carried** la motion/le projet de loi a été voté(e).

(i) to ~ o.s. se tenir, se comporter, se conduire; **she carries herself very well** elle se tient très droite; **he carries himself like a soldier** il a le port d'un militaire; **he carries himself with dignity** (*stands, walks*) il a un maintien fort digne; (*frm: behave*) il se comporte avec dignité; **he carried his head erect** il tenait la tête bien droite.

(j) *[newspaper etc] story, details* rapporter. **all the papers carried (the story of) the murder** l'histoire du meurtre était dans tous les journaux, tous les journaux ont parlé du meurtre.

(k) (*Math*) retenir. **... and ~ three** ... et je retiens trois.

(l) (*Med*) *child* attendre. **when she was ~ing her third son** quand elle était enceinte de *or* quand elle attendait son troisième fils.

2 *vi [voice, sound]* porter.

3 *cpd*: (*US*) **carryall** fourre-tout *m inv* (*sac*); **carrycot** porte-bébé *m*; (*wicker*) moïse *m*; (*pej*) **carry-on*** histoires *fpl*; **what a carry-on about nothing!*** que d'histoires pour rien!

carry away *vt sep* **(a)** (*lit*) *person* emporter; *thing* emporter, enlever; *[tide, wind]* emporter.

(b) (*fig*) transporter. **he was carried away by his friend's enthusiasm** il a été transporté par l'enthousiasme de son ami; **to get carried away by sth*** s'emballer* *or* s'enthousiasmer pour qch; **don't get carried away!*** ne t'emballe pas!*, du calme!; **I got carried away*** je me suis laissé entraîner, je n'ai pas su me retenir.

carry back *vt sep* (*lit*) *things* rapporter; *person* ramener; (*fig*) reporter; (*Fin*) reporter (*sur comptes antérieurs*). (*fig*) **the music carried me back to my youth** la musique m'a reporté à l'époque de ma jeunesse.

carry forward *vt sep* (*Book-keeping, gen*) reporter (*to* à).

carry off *vt sep* **(a)** (*lit*) *thing* emporter, enlever; (*kidnap*) enlever, ravir.

(b) (*fig*) *prizes, honours* remporter. **to carry it off well** s'en tirer à son honneur; **to carry it off*** réussir (son coup).

(c) (*euph: kill*) emporter. **he was carried off by pneumonia** il a été emporté par une pneumonie.

carry on 1 *vi* **(a)** continuer (*doing* à *or* de faire). **carry on!** continuez!; **carry on with your work!** continuez votre travail!; **if you carry on like that** si tu continues comme ça.

(b) (*: *make a scene*) faire une scène, faire des histoires. **you do carry on!** tu en fais des histoires!; **don't carry on so!** ne fais (donc) pas tant d'histoires! *or* toute une scène!

(c) (*: *have an affair*) **to carry on with sb** avoir une liaison avec qn.

2 *vt sep* **(a)** (*conduct*) *business, trade* faire marcher, diriger; *correspondence* entretenir; *conversation* soutenir; *negotiations* mener.

(b) (*continue*) *business, conversation* continuer, poursuivre; *tradition* poursuivre, entretenir, continuer.

3 carry-on* *n V* **carry 3.**

4 carrying-on *n V* **carrying-on.**

carry out *vt sep* **(a)** (*lit*) *thing, person, meal* emporter.

(b) (*fig: put into action*) *plan* exécuter, mener à bonne fin, réaliser; *order* exécuter; *idea* mettre à exécution, donner suite à; *one's duty* faire, accomplir, s'acquitter de; *obligation* s'acquitter de; *experiment* se livrer à, effectuer; *search, investigation, inquiry* mener, procéder à, conduire; *reform* effectuer, opérer; *the law, regulations* appliquer. **to carry out a promise** respecter *or* tenir une promesse.

carry over *vt sep* **(a)** (*lit*) faire passer du côté opposé, faire traverser.

(b) (*from one page to the other*) reporter (d'une page à l'autre); (*Book-keeping, St Ex*) reporter. (*Comm*) **to carry over stock from one season to the next** stocker des marchandises d'une saison sur l'autre.

carry through *vt sep plan* mener à bonne fin, exécuter, réaliser; *person* soutenir dans l'épreuve. **his courage carried him through** son courage lui a permis de surmonter l'épreuve.

carry up *vt sep* monter.

carrying-on ['kærɪɪŋ'ɒn] *n* **(a)** (*U*) *[work, business etc]* continuation *f*. **(b)** (*pej: often pl*) **carryings-on** façons *fpl* de se conduire *or* de faire.

cart [kɑːt] **1** *n* (*horse-drawn*) charrette *f*; (*tip-~*) tombereau *m*; (*hand ~*) voiture *f* à bras. (*fig*) **to put the ~ before the horse** mettre la charrue devant *or* avant les bœufs; (*fig*) **to be in the ~*** être dans le pétrin; *V* **dog.**

2 *cpd*: **cart-horse** cheval *m* de trait; **cartload** (*V* **1**) charretée *f*, tombereau *m*, voiturée *f*; **cart-track** chemin rural *or* de terre; (*lit*) **cartwheel** roue *f* de charrette; (*fig*) **to do** *or* **turn a cartwheel** faire la roue (*en gymnastique etc*); **cartwright** charron *m*.

3 *vt goods* (*in van, truck*) transporter (par camion), camionner; (*in cart*) charroyer, charrier; (*: *also* **~ about, ~ around**) *shopping, books* trimballer*, coltiner.

cart away *vt sep goods* emporter; *garbage* ramasser.

cartage ['kɑːtɪdʒ] *n* (*in van, truck*) camionnage *m*, transport *m*; (*in cart*) charroi *m*.

cartel [kɑː'tel] *n* (*Comm*) cartel *m*.

carter ['kɑːtə^{r}] *n* (*with lorry*) camionneur *m*; (*with cart*) charretier *m*.

Cartesian [kɑː'tiːzɪən] *adj, n* cartésien(ne) *m(f)*.

Carthage ['kɑːθɪdʒ] *n* Carthage.

Carthusian [kɑː'θjuːzɪən] **1** *adj* de(s) chartreux. **a ~ monk** un chartreux. **2** *n* chartreux *m*, -euse *f*.

cartilage ['kɑːtɪlɪdʒ] *n* cartilage *m*.

cartographer [kɑː'tɒgrəfə^{r}] *n* cartographe *mf*.

cartography [kɑː'tɒgrəfɪ] *n* cartographie *f*.

carton ['kɑːtən] *n* (*for yogurt, cream*) pot *m* (en carton); (*for milk, squash*) carton *m*; (*for ice cream*) boîte *f* (*en carton*); (*for cigarettes*) cartouche *f*.

cartoon [kɑː'tuːn] **1** *n [newspaper etc]* dessin *m* (humoristique); (*Cine, TV*) dessin animé; (*Art: sketch*) carton *m*. **2** *vt* caricaturer, ridiculiser (*par un dessin humoristique*).

cartoonist [ˌkɑː'tuːnɪst] *n [newspaper etc]* caricaturiste *mf*, dessinateur *m*, -trice *f* humoristique; (*Cine, TV*) dessinateur, -trice de dessins animés, animateur *m*, -trice *f*.

cartridge ['kɑːtrɪdʒ] **1** *n [rifle etc]* cartouche *f*; *[cannon]* gargousse *f*; *[record player]* cellule *f*; *[recording tape]* cartouche; *[camera]* chargeur *m*; *[pen]* cartouche.

2 *cpd*: **cartridge belt** (*belt*) (ceinture-) cartouchière *f*; (*strip*) bande *f* (de mitrailleuse); **cartridge case** *[rifle]* douille *f*, étui *m* (de cartouche); *[cannon]* douille; **cartridge paper** papier *m* à cartouche, papier fort; **cartridge player** lecteur *m* de cartouche.

carve [kɑːv] **1** *vt* tailler (*in, out of* dans); (*sculpt*) sculpter (*in, out of* dans); (*chisel*) ciseler (*in, out of* dans); (*Culin*) découper. **to ~ one's initials on** graver ses initiales sur *or* dans; **to ~ one's way through sth** se frayer un chemin à travers qch à coups de hache (*or* d'épée *etc*).

2 *cpd*: (*fig*) **carve-up*** *[inheritance]* partage *m*; *[estate, country]* morcellement *m*.

carve out *vt sep piece of wood* découper (*from* dans); *piece of land* prendre (*from* à); *statue, figure* sculpter, tailler (*of* dans); *tool* tailler. (*fig*) **to carve out a career for o.s.** faire carrière, se tailler une carrière.

carve up 1 *vt sep* **(a)** *meat* découper; (*fig*) *country* morceler; (*) *person* amocher‡ à coups de couteau; (*) *sb's face* taillader, balafrer.

(b) (‡*fig*) *play, performer* massacrer*, éreinter; *candidate, opponent* massacrer*.

2 carve-up* *n V* **carve 2.**

carver ['kɑːvə^{r}] *n* **(a)** (*Culin: knife*) couteau *m* à découper. **~s** service *m* à découper. **(b)** (*person*) personne *f* qui découpe.

carving ['kɑːvɪŋ] *n* **(a)** (*Art*) sculpture *f*. **(b)** (*U: Culin*) découpage *m*. **~ knife** couteau *m* à découper.

caryatid [ˌkærɪ'ætɪd] *n* cariatide *f*.

cascade [kæs'keɪd] **1** *n* cascade *f*; (*fig*) *[ribbons, silks, lace]* flot *m*; *[sparks]* pluie *f*. **2** *vi* tomber en cascade.

cascara [kæs'kɑːrə] *n* (*Pharm*) cascara sagrada *f*.

case[1] [keɪs] **1** *n* **(a)** cas *m*. **is it the ~ that ...?** est-il vrai que ...?; **that's not the ~** ce n'est pas le cas, il n'en est pas ainsi; **if that's the ~** en ce cas, dans ce cas-là; **as is the ~ here** comme c'est le cas ici; **such being the ~**, **in such a ~** en tel cas, en pareil cas; **if such is the ~** (*now*) si tel est le cas; (*if it happens*) le cas échéant, en tel *or* pareil cas; **put the ~ that ...** admettons que ... + *subj*; **as the ~ may be** selon le cas; **it's a clear ~ of lying** c'est un exemple manifeste de mensonge; **in ~ he comes** au cas où *or* pour le cas où il viendrait; **in ~ of** en cas de; **(just) in ~** à tout hasard, pour le cas où*; **in any ~** en tout cas, dans tous les cas; **in this ~** dans *or* en ce cas; **in that ~** dans ce cas-là; **in no ~** en aucun cas; **in the present ~** dans le cas présent; **as in the ~ of** comme dans le cas de; **in the ~ in point** en l'occurrence; **here is a ~ in point** en voici un bon exemple *or* un exemple pertinent; **in your ~** en ce qui vous concerne, dans votre cas; **in most ~s** dans la plupart des cas; **in nine ~s out of ten** neuf fois sur dix; **that alters the (whole) ~** cela change tout; **a difficult ~** un cas difficile.

(b) (*Med*) cas *m*; (*Soc*) cas social. **6 ~s of pneumonia** 6 cas de pneumonie; **the most serious ~s were sent to hospital** les cas les plus graves *or* les malades les plus atteints ont été envoyés à l'hôpital; (*fig: person*) **he's a hard ~** c'est un dur*; **she's a real ~!** c'est un cas* *or* un numéro* (,celle-là)!

(c) (*Jur*) affaire *f*, procès *m*, cause *f*. **to try a ~** juger une affaire; **to win one's ~** (*Jur*) gagner son procès; (*fig*) avoir gain de cause; **the ~ for the defendant** les arguments en faveur de l'accusé; **there is no ~ against ...** il n'y a pas lieu à poursuites contre ...; **he's working on the Smith ~** il s'occupe de l'affaire Smith.

(d) (*argument, reasoning*) arguments *mpl*. **to make out one's ~** expliquer ses raisons, présenter ses arguments, établir le bien-fondé de ce qu'on avance; **to make out a good ~ for sth** réunir *or* présenter de bons arguments en faveur de qch; **to make out a good ~ for doing** bien expliquer pourquoi il faudrait faire; **there is a strong ~ for/against compulsory vaccination** il y a *or* aurait beaucoup à dire en faveur de la/contre la vaccination obligatoire; **that is my ~** voilà mes arguments; **a ~ of conscience** un cas de conscience; **to have a good/strong ~** avoir de bons/solides arguments.

(e) (*Gram*) cas *m*.

(f) (*Bookbinding*) couverture *f*.

2 *cpd*: (*Soc*) **casebook** comptes rendus *mpl or* rapports *mpl* de cas sociaux (*réunis dans un registre*); (*Jur, Med, Soc*) **case file** dossier *m*; (*fig*) **case-hardened** endurci (*V also* **case**[2]); **case history** (*Soc*) évolution *f* du cas social; (*Med*) (*past facts*) antécédents médicaux; (*past and present development*) évolution *f* de la maladie; (*Soc*) **to have a heavy case load** avoir beaucoup de dossiers (sur les bras); (*Jur, Med, Soc*) **case notes** (notes *fpl* pour l'établissement d'un) dossier *m*; (*Jur, Med, Soc*) **case papers** pièces *fpl* de dossier; (*Soc*) **case work** travail *m* avec des cas (sociaux) individuels; (*Soc*) **case worker** ≃ assistante sociale.

case[2] [keɪs] **1** *n* **(a)** (*suitcase*) valise *f*; (*packing ~*) caisse *f*; (*crate: for bottles etc*) caisse; (*for peaches, lettuce, oysters etc*) cageot *m*; (*box*) boîte *f*; (*chest*) coffre *m*; (*for goods on display*) vitrine *f*; (*for jewels*) coffret *m*; (*for watch, pen, necklace etc*) écrin *m*; (*for camera, binoculars, umbrella, violin etc*) étui *m*; (*covering*) enveloppe *f*; (*Tech*) boîte; (*Aut*) carter *m*; *V* **book, pillow** *etc*.

(b) (*Typ*) casse *f*; *V* **lower**[1], **upper.**

2 *vt* **(a)** (*V* **1a**) mettre dans une caisse *or* un cageot *etc*; mettre en boîte.

(b) (‡) [*burglars etc*] *house, bank* se rancarder sur‡. **to ~ the joint** se rancarder sur la boîte‡ (*avant un mauvais coup*).

3 *cpd*: (*Metal*) **caseharden** cémenter; (*US*) **case knife** couteau *m* à gaine.

casement ['keɪsmənt] *n* (*window*) fenêtre *f* (à battants), croisée *f*; (*frame*) battant *m* de fenêtre; (*liter*) fenêtre *f*.

cash [kæʃ] **1** *n* (*U*) **(a)** (*notes and coins*) espèces *fpl*, argent *m*. **how much ~ is there in the till?** combien d'argent y a-t-il dans la caisse?; **I want to be paid in ~ and not by cheque** je veux être payé en espèces et non pas par chèque; **to pay in ~** payer en argent comptant *or* en espèces; **to take the ~ to the bank** porter l'argent à la banque; **ready ~** (argent *m*) liquide *m*; **how much do you have in (ready) ~?** combien avez-vous en liquide?; *V* **hard, petty, spot.**

(b) (*immediate payment*) **~ down** argent comptant; **to pay ~ (down)** payer comptant *or* cash*; **discount for ~** escompte *m or* remise *f* au comptant; **~ with order** payable à la commande; **~ on delivery** paiement *m* à la livraison, livraison contre espèces *or* contre remboursement.

(c) (*: *money in general*) argent *m*, sous* *mpl*. **how much ~ have you got?** combien d'argent as-tu?, qu'est-ce que tu as comme argent *or* comme sous?*; **I have no ~** je n'ai pas un sou *or* un rond*; **to be short of ~** être à court (d'argent); **I am out of ~** je suis à sec*, je suis sans le rond*.

2 *cpd*: **cash-and-carry** (*n*) supermarché *m* de gros et demi-gros; (*adj*) *goods, business* de gros et demi-gros, de cash-and-carry; **cashbook** livre *m* de caisse; **cashbox** caisse *f*; (*US*) **cash crop** récolte destinée à la vente; **cashdesk** [*shop, restaurant*] caisse *f*; [*cinema, theatre*] guichet *m*; **cash discount** escompte *m or* remise *f* au comptant; **cash flow** cash-flow *m*; **cash in hand** espèces *fpl* en caisse, encaisse *f*; **cash offer** offre *f* d'achat avec paiement comptant; **he made me a cash offer** il m'a proposé de payer comptant; **cash payment** paiement *m* comptant, versement *m* en espèces; **cash price** prix *m* (au) comptant; **cash prize** prix *m* en espèces; **cash receipts** recettes *fpl* de caisse; **cash reduction** = **cash discount**; **cash register** caisse *f* (enregistreuse); **cash sale** vente *f* (au) comptant; **cash terms** conditions *fpl* au comptant; **cash transaction** affaire *f or* opération *f* au comptant.

3 *vt cheque* encaisser, toucher; *banknote* changer, faire la monnaie de. **to ~ sb a cheque** donner à qn de l'argent contre un chèque; [*bank*] payer un chèque à qn; **to ~ a bill** encaisser une facture.

cash in *vt sep bonds, savings certificates* réaliser, se faire rembourser.

cash in on* *vt fus* tirer profit de.

cashew [kæ'ʃuː] *n* anacardier *m*; (*also* **~ nut**) noix *f* de cajou.

cashier[1] [kæ'ʃɪəʳ] *n* (*Comm, Fin*) caissier *m*.

cashier[2] [kæ'ʃɪəʳ] *vt* (*Mil*) casser; (*gen*) renvoyer, congédier.

cashmere [kæʃ'mɪəʳ] **1** *n* (*Tex*) cachemire *m*. **2** *cpd* de *or* en cachemire.

casing ['keɪsɪŋ] *n* (*gen*) revêtement *m*, enveloppe *f*; [*door, window*] chambranle *m*; [*tyre*] enveloppe extérieure; [*oil well*] cuvelage *m*.

casino [kə'siːnəʊ] *n* casino *m*.

cask [kɑːsk] *n* (*gen*) tonneau *m*, fût *m*; (*large*) pièce *f*, barrique *f*; (*small*) baril *m*. **wine in ~** vin *m* en fût.

casket ['kɑːskɪt] *n* [*jewels etc*] coffret *m*, boîte *f*; (*esp US: coffin*) cercueil *m*.

Caspian ['kæspɪən] *n*: **the ~ Sea** la mer Caspienne.

Cassandra [kə'sændrə] *n* (*Myth*) Cassandre *f*; (*fig*) oiseau *m* de malheur.

cassava [kə'sɑːvə] *n* (*Bot*) manioc *m*; (*Culin*) farine *f* de manioc.

casserole ['kæsərəʊl] **1** *n* (*Culin: utensil*) cocotte *f*; (*food*) ragoût *m* en cocotte. **2** *vt meat* (faire) cuire en *or* à la cocotte.

cassette [kæ'set] **1** *n* (*Sound Recording*) cassette *f*; (*Phot*) pellicule *f* (*en bobine*), recharge *f*. **2** *cpd*: **cassette deck** platine *f* à cassettes; **cassette player** lecteur *m* de cassettes; **cassette recorder** magnétophone *m* à cassettes.

cassock ['kæsək] *n* soutane *f*.

cassowary ['kæsəweərɪ] *n* casoar *m*.

cast [kɑːst] (*vb: pret, ptp* **cast**) **1** *n* **(a)** (*throw*) [*dice, net*] coup *m*; (*Fishing*) lancer *m*.

(b) (*Art, Tech*) (*act of ~ing metal*) coulage *m*, coulée *f*.

(c) (*mould*) moule *m*; (*in plaster, metal etc*) moulage *m*; [*medallion etc*] empreinte *f*. (*Med*) **to have one's leg in a ~** avoir une jambe dans le plâtre; (*fig*) **~ of features** traits *mpl*; **~ of mind** mentalité *f*, tournure *f* d'esprit; **a man of quite a different ~** un homme d'un tout autre genre; *V* **plaster** *etc*.

(d) (*Theat*) (*actors*) troupe *f*, acteurs *mpl*; (*list on programme etc*) distribution *f*.

(e) [*snake*] dépouille *f*; [*worm*] déjections *fpl*.

(f) (*Med: squint*) strabisme *m*. **to have a ~ in one eye** avoir un œil qui louche, loucher d'un œil.

2 *cpd*: **castaway** naufragé(e) *m(f)*; (*fig: from society etc*) réprouvé(e) *m(f)*; **cast-iron** (*n*) fonte *f*; (*adj*) de *or* en fonte; (*fig*) *will, constitution* de fer; *excuse, alibi* inattaquable, irréfutable; *case* solide; **cast-off clothes, cast-offs** vêtements *mpl* dont on ne veut plus, (*pej*) vieilles nippes* *or* frusques*; (*fig*) **the cast-offs from society** les laissés *mpl* pour compte (de la société).

3 *vt* **(a)** (*throw*) *dice* jeter; *net, fishing line, stone* lancer, jeter. (*Naut*) **to ~ anchor** jeter l'ancre, mouiller (l'ancre); **to ~ into jail** jeter en prison; (*fig*) **to ~ light on sth** faire la lumière sur qch; **to ~ sb's horoscope** tirer l'horoscope de qn; **to ~ lots** tirer au sort; **to ~ in one's lot with sb** partager le sort de qn; (*liter*) **to ~ o.s. on sb's mercy** s'en remettre à la clémence de qn (*liter*), remettre son sort entre les mains de qn; (*fig*) **to ~ pearls before swine** jeter des perles aux pourceaux, donner la confiture aux cochons; **to ~ a vote** voter; *V* **die**[2].

(b) (*fig*) jeter; *light* (pro)jeter. **to ~ aspersions on sth/sb** dénigrer qch/qn; **to ~ the blame on** rejeter le blâme sur; **to ~ doubt on** émettre des doutes sur; **to ~ a look at** jeter un regard sur; **to ~ a shadow on** (*lit*) projeter une ombre sur; (*fig*) jeter une ombre sur; **to ~ one's eye(s) round a room** promener ses regards *or* ses yeux sur une pièce, balayer une pièce du regard; **to ~ one's eye(s) in the direction of** porter ses regards du côté de; *V* **spell**[1] *etc*.

(c) (*shed*) se dépouiller de, se débarrasser de, perdre. [*snake*] **to ~ its skin** muer; [*horse*] **to ~ a shoe** perdre un fer; [*animal*] **to ~ its young** mettre bas (un petit) avant terme.

(d) (*Art, Tech*) *plaster* couler; *metal* couler, fondre; *statue* mouler; *V* **mould**[1].

(e) (*Theat*) *play* distribuer les rôles de. **he was ~ as Hamlet** *or* **for the part of Hamlet** on lui a donné le rôle de Hamlet.

cast about, cast around *vi*: **to cast about for sth** chercher qch; **to cast about for how to do/how to reply** chercher le moyen de faire/la façon de répondre.

cast aside *vt sep* rejeter, mettre de côté; (*fig*) rejeter, abandonner, se défaire de.

cast away 1 *vt sep* rejeter; (*fig*) se défaire de. (*Naut*) **to be cast away** être naufragé.

2 castaway *n V* **cast 2.**

cast back 1 *vi* (*fig, liter*) revenir (*to* à).

2 *vt sep*: **to cast one's thoughts back** se reporter en arrière.

cast down *vt sep object* jeter par terre, jeter vers le bas; *eyes* baisser; *weapons* déposer, mettre bas. (*fig, liter*) **to be cast down** être abattu *or* découragé *or* démoralisé.

cast in *vi, vt sep*: **to cast in (one's lot) with sb** partager le sort de qn.

cast off 1 *vi* (*Naut*) larguer les amarres, appareiller; (*Knitting*) arrêter (les mailles).

2 *vt sep* (*Naut*) larguer *or* lâcher les amarres de; (*Knitting*) arrêter; *bonds, chains* (*lit*) se défaire de, se libérer de; (*fig*) s'affranchir de.

3 cast-off *n, adj V* **cast 2.**

cast on (*Knitting*) **1** *vi* monter les mailles.

2 *vt sep stitch, sleeve* monter.

cast out *vt sep* (*liter*) renvoyer, chasser, expulser.

cast up *vt sep* **(a)** (*lit*) lancer en l'air. (*fig*) **to cast one's eyes up** lever les yeux au ciel.

(b) (*Math*) calculer, faire l'addition de.

(c) (*fig: reproach*) **to cast sth up to** *or* **at sb** reprocher qch à qn.

castanets [ˌkæstə'nets] *npl* castagnettes *fpl*.

caste [kɑːst] **1** *n* caste *f*, classe sociale. **to lose ~** déroger, déchoir. **2** *cpd*: **caste mark** (*in India*) signe *m* de (la) caste; (*fig*) signe distinctif (d'un groupe); **caste system** système *m* de caste(s).

castellated ['kæstəleɪtɪd] *adj* (*Archit*) crénelé, de style féodal. (*Tech*) **~ nut** écrou crénelé.

caster ['kɑːstəʳ] *n* **(a)** (*sifter*) saupoudroir *m*. (*Brit*) **~ sugar** sucre *m* en poudre. **(b)** (*wheel*) roulette *f*.

castigate ['kæstɪgeɪt] *vt person* châtier (*liter*), corriger, punir; *book etc* critiquer sévèrement; *theory, vice* fustiger (*liter*).

castigation [ˌkæstɪ'geɪʃən] *n* [*person*] châtiment *m*, correction *f*, punition *f*; [*book*] critique *f* sévère.

Castilian [kæs'tɪlɪən] **1** *adj* castillan. **2** *n* **(a)** Castillan(e) *m(f)*. **(b)** (*Ling*) espagnol *m*, castillan *m*.

casting ['kɑːstɪŋ] **1** *n* (*U: act of throwing*) jet *m*, lancer *m*, lancement *m*; (*Tech*) (*act*) fonte *f*, coulée *f*; (*object*) pièce fondue; (*Art*) moulage *m*; (*Theat*) distribution *f*.

2 *cpd*: **casting vote** voix prépondérante; **to have a casting vote** avoir voix prépondérante.

castle ['kɑːsl] **1** *n* **(a)** château *m* (fort). (*fig*) **~s in the air** châteaux en Espagne. **(b)** (*Chess*) tour *f*. **2** *vi* (*Chess*) roquer.

castling ['kɑːslɪŋ] *n* (*Chess*) roque *f*.

castor[1] ['kɑːstəʳ] *n* = **caster.**

castor[2] ['kɑːstəʳ] *n* **(a)** (*beaver*) castor *m*. **(b)** (*Med*) castoréum *m*. **~ oil** huile *f* de ricin.

castrate [kæs'treɪt] *vt animal, man* châtrer, castrer, émasculer; (*fig*) *personality* émasculer; *text, film, book* expurger.

castration [kæs'treɪʃən] *n* castration *f*.

castrato [kæs'trɑːtəʊ] *n, pl* **castrati** [kæs'trɑːtiː] castrat *m*.

casual ['kæʒjʊl] 1 adj (a) (happening by chance) fortuit, accidentel, fait par hasard; meeting de hasard; walk, stroll sans but précis; caller venu par hasard; remark fait au hasard or en passant. a ~ acquaintance (of mine) quelqu'un que je connais un peu; ~ glance coup m d'œil (jeté) au hasard; a ~ (love) affair une passade, une aventure; to have ~ sex faire l'amour au hasard d'une rencontre; I don't approve of ~ sex je n'approuve pas les rapports sexuels de rencontre.
(b) (careless) person, manners sans-gêne inv, désinvolte; clothes sport inv. he tried to sound ~ il a essayé de parler avec désinvolture; he was very ~ about it il ne semblait pas y attacher beaucoup d'importance; she was very ~ about the whole business elle a pris tout ça avec beaucoup de désinvolture.
(c) work intermittent; worker temporaire. ~ conversation conversation f à bâtons rompus; ~ labourer (on building sites) ouvrier m sans travail fixe; (on a farm) journalier m, -ière f.
2 n (a) (shoes) ~s chaussures fpl de sport.
(b) (worker) (in office) employé(e) m(f) temporaire; (in factory) ouvrier m, -ière f temporaire.

casually ['kæʒjʊlɪ] adv (by chance) par hasard, fortuitement; (informally, carelessly) avec sans-gêne, avec désinvolture; (intermittently) par intermittence, irrégulièrement. he said it (quite) ~ il l'a dit sans insister or en passant.

casualty ['kæʒjʊltɪ] 1 n (a) (Mil) (dead) mort(e) m(f); (wounded) blessé(e) m(f). casualties les morts mpl et blessés mpl; (dead) pertes fpl.
(b) (accident victim) accidenté(e) m(f), victime f; (accident) accident m.
2 cpd: casualty list (Mil) état m des pertes; (Aviat, gen) liste f des victimes; casualty ward salle f de traumatologie or des accidentés.

casuist ['kæzjʊɪst] n casuiste mf.

casuistry ['kæzjʊɪstrɪ] n (U) casuistique f; (instance of this) arguments mpl de casuiste.

cat [kæt] 1 n (a) chat(te) m(f); (species) félin m; (*pej: woman) rosse* f; V tabby, tom.
(b) = cat-o'nine-tails; V 2.
(c) (phrases) to let the ~ out of the bag vendre la mèche; the ~'s out of the bag ce n'est plus un secret maintenant; to wait for the ~ to jump, to wait to see which way the ~ jumps attendre pour voir la tournure prise par les événements or voir d'où vient le vent; to fight like ~ and dog (lit) se battre comme des chiffonniers; (fig) être or s'entendre or vivre comme chien et chat; to lead a ~ and dog life être or s'entendre or vivre comme chien et chat; (Prov) a ~ may look at a king un chien regarde bien un évêque; to be or jump around like a ~ on hot bricks être sur des charbons ardents; (Prov) when the ~'s away the mice will play quand le chat n'est pas là les souris dansent; that set the ~ among the pigeons ça a été le pavé dans la mare*; V bell[1], grin, rain, room.
2 cpd: (fig) to play (at) cat-and-mouse with sb, to play a cat-and-mouse game with sb jouer avec qn comme un chat avec une souris; cat-basket (for carrying) panier m pour chat; (for sleeping) corbeille f de chat; cat burglar monte-en-l'air* m inv; (Theat) catcall (n) sifflet m; (vi) siffler; catfish poisson-chat m; catgut (Mus, Sport) boyau m (de chat); (Med) catgut m; (US) cathouse‡ bordel‡ m; cat-lick* toilette f de chat, brin m de toilette; to give o.s. a cat-lick faire une toilette de chat or un brin de toilette; catlike (adj) félin; (adv) comme un chat; catmint herbe f aux chats; catnap (vi) sommeiller, faire un (petit) somme; (n) (petit) somme m; to take a catnap sommeiller, faire un (petit) somme; (US) catnip = catmint; cat-o'nine-tails martinet m, chat-à-neuf-queues m; cat's-cradle (jeu m des) figures fpl (que l'on forme entre ses doigts avec de la ficelle); (Brit Aut) cat's eyes clous mpl à catadioptre, catadioptres mpl, cataphotes mpl; cat's-paw dupe f (qui tire les marrons du feu); catsuit combinaison-pantalon f; (Rad) cat's-whisker chercheur m (de détecteur à galène); (Constr, Theat) catwalk passerelle f (gén courant le long d'une construction).

cataclysm ['kætəklɪzəm] n cataclysme m.

catacombs ['kætəku:mz] npl catacombes fpl.

catafalque ['kætəfælk] n catafalque m.

catalepsy ['kætəlepsɪ] n catalepsie f.

cataleptic [ˌkætə'leptɪk] adj cataleptique.

catalogue, (US) **catalog** ['kætəlɒg] 1 n catalogue m. 2 vt cataloguer.

catalysis [kə'tæləsɪs] n catalyse f.

catalyst ['kætəlɪst] n catalyseur m.

catalytic [ˌkætə'lɪtɪk] adj catalytique.

catamaran [ˌkætəmə'ræn] n catamaran m.

catapult ['kætəpʌlt] 1 n (slingshot) lance-pierre(s) m inv; (Aviat, Mil) catapulte f. (Aviat) ~-launched catapulté; (Aviat) ~ launching catapultage m. 2 vt (gen, Aviat, fig) catapulter.

cataract ['kætərækt] n (a) (waterfall) cataracte f. ~ of words déluge m de paroles. (b) (Med) cataracte f.

catarrh [kə'tɑ:ʳ] n rhume m (chronique), catarrhe m.

catarrhal [kə'tɑ:rəl] adj catarrheux.

catastrophe [kə'tæstrəfɪ] n catastrophe f.

catastrophic [ˌkætə'strɒfɪk] adj catastrophique (lit, *fig).

catch [kætʃ] (vb: pret, ptp caught) 1 n (a) (act, thing caught) prise f, capture f; (person caught) capture; (Fishing) pêche f, prise, capture (Comm). the fisherman lost his whole ~ le pêcheur a perdu toute sa pêche or prise; (as husband) he's a good ~* c'est un beau parti.
(b) (concealed drawback) attrape f, entourloupette* f. there must be a ~ in it somewhere il doit y avoir une entourloupette* or attrape là-dessous; where's the ~? qu'est-ce qui se cache là-dessous?
(c) [buckle] ardillon m; [door] loquet m; [latch] mentonnet m; [wheel] cliquet m; [window] loqueteau m.
(d) (fig) with a ~ in one's voice d'une voix entrecoupée.
(e) (Mus) canon m.
(f) (Sport) good ~! bien rattrapé!
2 cpd: it's a catch 22 situation* il n'y a pas moyen de s'en sortir, à tous les coups on perd; catch-as-catch-can catch m; catch phrase (constantly repeated) rengaine f, scie f; (vivid, striking phrase) slogan accrocheur; catch question colle* f; (US) catchup = ketchup; catchword (slogan) slogan m; (Pol) mot m d'ordre, slogan; (Printing) mot-souche m; [foot of page] réclame f; [top of page] mot-vedette m; (Theat: cue) réplique f.
3 vt (a) ball attraper; object attraper, saisir, prendre; fish, mice, thief prendre, attraper. to ~ sb by the arm prendre or saisir qn par le bras; you can usually ~ me (in) around noon* en général on peut m'avoir* or me trouver vers midi; (Rowing) to ~ a crab plonger la rame trop profond.
(b) (take by surprise) surprendre, prendre, attraper. to ~ sb doing sth surprendre qn à faire qch; if I ~ them at it!* si je les y prends!; if I ~ you at it again!* que je t'y reprenne!; (you won't) ~ me doing that again!* (il n'y a) pas de danger que je recommence! (subj), c'est bien la dernière fois que je le fais!; caught in the act pris sur le fait, pris en flagrant délit; we were caught in a storm nous avons été pris dans or surpris par un orage; to get caught by sb se faire or se laisser attraper par qn.
(c) (be in time for) prendre, ne pas manquer. he didn't ~ his train il a manqué son train; to ~ the post arriver à temps pour la levée.
(d) (become entangled in) [branch, thorns, nail] accrocher. to ~ one's foot in se prendre le pied dans.
(e) (understand, hear) saisir, comprendre. to ~ the meaning of saisir le sens de; I didn't ~ what he said je n'ai pas saisi or compris ce qu'il a dit.
(f) flavour sentir, discerner; tune attraper. to ~ the sound of sth percevoir le bruit de qch.
(g) (Med) disease attraper. to ~ a cold attraper un rhume; to ~ cold attraper or prendre froid; to ~ one's death of cold*, to ~ one's death‡ attraper la crève‡, prendre la mort*.
(h) (phrases) to ~ sb's attention attirer l'attention de qn; to ~ sb's eye attirer l'attention de qn; to ~ the chairman's eye, (Brit Parl) to ~ the Speaker's eye obtenir or se faire accorder or se faire donner la parole; to ~ sb a blow donner un coup à qn; she caught him one on the nose* elle lui a flanqué* un (bon) coup sur le nez; to ~ one's breath retenir son souffle (un instant); to ~ fire prendre feu; her dress caught fire le feu a pris à sa robe, sa robe s'est enflammée or a pris feu; (Art, Phot) to ~ a likeness saisir une ressemblance; to ~ sight of sb/sth apercevoir qn/qch; you'll ~ it!* tu vas écoper!*, tu vas prendre quelque chose!*; he caught it all right!* qu'est-ce qu'il a pris!*; to ~ sb on the wrong foot, to ~ sb off balance (lit) prendre qn à contre-pied; (fig) prendre qn au dépourvu; to ~ sb napping or bending prendre qn en défaut.
4 vi (a) [fire, wood, ice] prendre; (Culin) attacher.
(b) [lock] fermer; [key] mordre. her dress caught in the door/on a nail sa robe s'est prise dans la porte/s'est accrochée à un clou.

catch at vt fus object (essayer d')attraper. to catch at an opportunity sauter sur une occasion.

catch on vi (a) (become popular) [fashion] prendre; [song] devenir populaire, marcher.
(b) (understand) saisir, comprendre, piger‡ (to sth qch).

catch out vt sep (esp Brit) (catch sb napping) prendre en défaut; (catch sb in the act) prendre sur le fait. to catch sb out in a lie surprendre qn en train de mentir, prendre qn à mentir; he'll get caught out some day un beau jour il se fera prendre.

catch up 1 vi se rattraper, combler son retard; (with studies) se rattraper, se remettre au niveau; (with news, gossip) se remettre au courant. to catch up on or with one's work se (re)mettre à jour dans son travail; to catch up on or with sb (going in the same direction) rattraper qn, rejoindre qn; (in work etc) rattraper qn.
2 vt sep (a) person rattraper.
(b) (interrupt) person interrompre, couper la parole à.
(c) (pick up quickly) ramasser vivement.
(d) hair relever; curtain retenir.

catcher ['kætʃəʳ] n (a) (Baseball) joueur m qui doit attraper la balle.
(b) V mole[1], rat etc.

catching ['kætʃɪŋ] adj (Med) contagieux; (*fig) laughter, enthusiasm contagieux, communicatif; habit, mannerism contagieux.

catchment ['kætʃmənt] n captage m. ~ area (Geog: also ~ basin) bassin m hydrographique; [hospital] circonscription hospitalière; [school] aire f de recrutement.

catchpenny ['kætʃˌpenɪ] adj destiné à faire vendre. ~ title titre m attrape-nigaud inv.

catchy ['kætʃɪ] adj tune facile à retenir, entraînant.

catechism ['kætɪkɪzəm] n catéchisme m.

catechist ['kætɪkɪst] n catéchiste mf.

catechize ['kætɪkaɪz] vt (Rel) catéchiser; (fig) (teach) instruire (par questions et réponses); (examine) interroger, questionner.

categoric(al) [ˌkætɪ'gɒrɪk(əl)] adj catégorique.

categorically [ˌkætɪ'gɒrɪkəlɪ] adv catégoriquement.

categorize ['kætɪgəraɪz] vt classer par catégories.

category ['kætɪgərɪ] n catégorie f.

cater ['keɪtəʳ] vi (provide food) s'occuper de la nourriture, préparer un or des repas (for pour). (fig) to ~ for sb's needs pourvoir à; sb's tastes satisfaire; this magazine ~s for all ages ce

magazine s'adresse à tous les âges; (*expect*) **I didn't ~ for that*** je n'avais pas prévu cela.
cater-cornered [ˈkeɪtəˈkɔːnəd] *adj* (*US*) diagonal.
caterer [ˈkeɪtərəʳ] *n* fournisseur *m* (*en alimentation*); *[high-quality food]* traiteur *m.*
catering [ˈkeɪtərɪŋ] **1** *n* (*providing supplies*) approvisionnement *m*, ravitaillement *m*; (*providing meals*) restauration *f.* **the ~ for our reception was done by X** le buffet de notre réception a été confié à X *or* aux soins de X, le traiteur pour notre réception était X. **2** *cpd*: **catering industry** industrie *f* de la restauration; **catering trade** restauration *f.*
caterpillar [ˈkætəpɪləʳ] **1** *n* (*Tech, Zool*) chenille *f.* **2** *cpd vehicle, wheel* à chenilles. (*Tech*) **caterpillar track** chenille *f*; **caterpillar tractor** autochenille *f.*
caterwaul [ˈkætəwɔːl] **1** *vi [cat]* miauler; (*) *[person]* brailler, pousser des braillements. **2** *n [cat]* miaulement *m.*
caterwauling [ˈkætəwɔːlɪŋ] *n [cat]* miaulement *m*; *[music]* cacophonie *f*; *[person]* braillements *mpl*, hurlements *mpl.*
catharsis [kəˈθɑːsɪs] *n* (*Literat, Psych*) catharsis *f.*
cathartic [kəˈθɑːtɪk] **1** *adj* (*Literat, Med, Psych*) cathartique. **2** *n* (*Med*) purgatif *m*, cathartique *m.*
cathedral [kəˈθiːdrəl] **1** *n* cathédrale *f.* **2** *cpd*: **cathedral church** cathédrale *f*; **cathedral city** évêché *m*, ville épiscopale.
Catherine [ˈkæθərɪn] *n* Catherine *f.* (*firework*) **~ wheel** soleil *m.*
catheter [ˈkæθɪtəʳ] *n* cathéter *m*, sonde creuse.
cathode [ˈkæθəʊd] **1** *n* cathode *f.* **2** *cpd ray* cathodique. **cathode ray tube** tube *m* cathodique.
catholic [ˈkæθəlɪk] **1** *adj* **(a)** (*Rel*) **C~** catholique; **the C~ Church** l'Église *f* catholique.
(b) (*varied, all-embracing*) *taste(s), person* éclectique; (*universal*) universel; (*broadminded*) *views, person* libéral. **to be ~ in one's tastes** avoir des goûts éclectiques; **to be ~ in one's views** avoir des opinions libérales.
2 *n*: **C~** catholique *mf.*
Catholicism [kəˈθɒlɪsɪzəm] *n* catholicisme *m.*
cation [ˈkætaɪən] *n* (*Chem*) cation *m.*
catkin [ˈkætkɪn] *n* (*Bot*) chaton *m.*
catsup [ˈkætsəp] *n* (*US*) = **ketchup.**
cattiness* [ˈkætɪnɪs] *n* méchanceté *f*, rosserie* *f.*
cattle [ˈkætl] **1** *collective n* bovins *mpl*, bétail *m*, bestiaux *mpl.* **the prisoners were herded like ~** les prisonniers étaient parqués comme du bétail; *V* **head.**
2 *cpd*: **cattle breeder** éleveur *m* (de bestiaux); **cattle breeding** élevage *m* (du bétail); **'cattle crossing'** 'passage *m* de troupeaux'; (*Brit*) **cattle grid** *grille f à même la route permettant aux voitures mais non au bétail de passer*; **cattleman** vacher *m*, bouvier *m*; **cattle market** foire *f or* marché *m* aux bestiaux; **cattle plague** peste bovine; **cattle raising** = **cattle breeding**; **cattle shed** étable *f*; **cattle show** concours *m* agricole (où l'on présente du bétail); **cattle truck** (*Aut*) fourgon *m* à bestiaux; (*Brit Rail*) fourgon *or* wagon *m* à bestiaux.
catty* [ˈkætɪ] *adj* (*pej*) *person, gossip, criticism* méchant, rosse*, vache*. **~ remark** rosserie* *f*, vacherie* *f*; **to be ~ about sb/sth** dire des rosseries* *or* vacheries* de qn/qch.
Caucasian [kɔːˈkeɪzɪən] **1** *adj* (*Geog*) caucasien; (*Ethnology*) de race blanche. **2** *n* (*Geog*) Caucasien(ne) *m(f)*; (*Ethnology*) blanc *m*, blanche *f.*
caucasoid [ˈkɔːkəsɔɪd] **1** *adj* de race blanche. **2** *n* blanc *m*, blanche *f.*
Caucasus [ˈkɔːkəsəs] *n* Caucase *m.*
caucus [ˈkɔːkəs] *n* (*US*) (*committee*) comité électoral; (*meeting*) réunion *f* du comité électoral; (*Brit pej*) coterie *f* politique.
caudal [ˈkɔːdl] *adj* caudal.
caught [kɔːt] *pret, ptp of* **catch.**
caul [kɔːl] *n* (*Anat*) coiffe *f.*
cauldron [ˈkɔːldrən] *n* chaudron *m.*
cauliflower [ˈkɒlɪflaʊəʳ] **1** *n* chou-fleur *m.* **2** *cpd*: (*Culin*) **cauliflower cheese** chou-fleur *m* au gratin; (*fig*) **~ ear** oreille *f* en chou-fleur *or* en feuille de chou.
caulk [kɔːk] *vt* (*Naut*) calfater.
causal [ˈkɔːzəl] *adj* causal; (*Gram*) causal, causatif.
causality [kɔːˈzælɪtɪ] *n* causalité *f.*
causation [kɔːˈzeɪʃən] *n* (*causing*) causalité *f*; (*cause-effect relation*) relation *f* de cause à effet.
causative [ˈkɔːzətɪv] **1** *adj* causal; (*Gram*) causal, causatif. (*frm*) **~ of** (qui est) cause de. **2** *n* (*Gram*) mot causal *or* causatif.
cause [kɔːz] **1** *n* **(a)** (*gen, also Philos*) cause *f.* **~ and effect** la cause et l'effet *m*; **the relation of ~ and effect** la relation de cause à effet; **the ~ of his failure** la cause de son échec; **to be the ~ of** être cause de, causer.
(b) (*reason*) cause *f*, raison *f*, motif *m.* **she has no ~ to be angry** elle n'a aucune raison de se fâcher; **there's no ~ for anxiety** il n'y a pas lieu de s'inquiéter *or* de raison de s'inquiéter *or* de quoi s'inquiéter; **with (good) ~** à juste titre, de façon très justifiée; **without ~** sans cause *or* raison *or* motif; **without good ~** sans raison *or* cause *or* motif valable; **~ for complaint** sujet *m* de plainte.
(c) (*purpose*) cause *f*, parti *m.* **to make common ~ with** faire cause commune avec; **in the ~ of justice** pour (la cause de) la justice; **to work in a good ~** travailler pour la *or* une bonne cause; **it's all in a good ~*** c'est pour le bien de la communauté (*hum*); *V* **lost.**
(d) (*Jur*) cause *f.* **to plead sb's ~** plaider la cause de qn.
2 *vt* causer, occasionner, produire. **to ~ damage/an accident** causer des dégâts/un accident; **to ~ grief to sb** causer du chagrin à qn; **to ~ trouble** semer la perturbation; **to ~ trouble to sb** créer des ennuis à qn; **I don't want to ~ you any trouble** je ne veux en rien vous déranger; **to ~ sb to do sth** faire faire qch à qn; **to ~ sth to be done** faire faire qch.
causeway [ˈkɔːzweɪ] *n* chaussée *f.*
caustic [ˈkɔːstɪk] **1** *adj* (*Chem, fig*) caustique. **~ soda** soude *f* caustique; **~ remark** remarque *f* caustique. **2** *n* substance *f* caustique, caustique *m.*
cauterize [ˈkɔːtəraɪz] *vt* cautériser.
cautery [ˈkɔːtərɪ] *n* cautère *m.*
caution [ˈkɔːʃən] **1** *n* **(a)** (*U: circumspection*) prudence *f*, circonspection *f.* **proceed with ~** (*gen*) agissez avec prudence *or* circonspection; (*Aut*) avancez lentement.
(b) (*warning*) avertissement *m*; (*rebuke*) réprimande *f.* **he got off with a ~** il s'en est tiré avec une réprimande; (*Jur*) **~ money** cautionnement *m.*
(c) (*†: *rascal*) numéro* *m*, phénomène* *m.*
2 *vt* avertir, donner un avertissement à; (*Police: on charging suspect*) informer qn de ses droits. **to ~ sb against sth** mettre qn en garde contre qch; **to ~ sb against doing sth** prévenir qn de ce qui se passera s'il fait qch, déconseiller à qn de faire qch.
cautionary [ˈkɔːʃənərɪ] *adj* (servant) d'avertissement; (*Jur*) donné en garantie. **a ~ tale** un récit édifiant.
cautious [ˈkɔːʃəs] *adj* prudent, circonspect. **to be ~ about doing sth** longuement réfléchir avant de faire qch.
cautiously [ˈkɔːʃəslɪ] *adv* prudemment, avec prudence *or* circonspection.
cautiousness [ˈkɔːʃəsnɪs] *n* prudence *f*, circonspection *f.*
cavalcade [ˌkævəlˈkeɪd] *n* cavalcade *f.*
cavalier [ˌkævəˈlɪəʳ] **1** *n* (*gen, Mil*) cavalier *m*; (*Brit Hist*) royaliste *m* (*partisan de Charles Ier et de Charles II*).
2 *adj* **(a)** (*Brit Hist*) royaliste.
(b) (*slightly pej*) *person, manners* (*free and easy*) cavalier, désinvolte; (*supercilious*) arrogant, orgueilleux.
cavalierly [ˌkævəˈlɪəlɪ] *adv* cavalièrement.
cavalry [ˈkævəlrɪ] **1** *n* cavalerie *f*; *V* **household. 2** *cpd*: **cavalry charge** charge *f* de cavalerie; **cavalryman** cavalier *m* (*soldat*); **cavalry officer** officier *m* de cavalerie; (*Tex*) **cavalry twill** drap *m* sergé pour culotte de cheval, tricotine *f.*
cave[1] [keɪv] **1** *n* caverne *f*, grotte *f.*
2 *cpd*: (*Hist*) **cave dweller** (*in prehistory*) homme *m* des cavernes; *[primitive tribes]* troglodyte *mf*; **cave-in** *[floor, building]* effondrement *m*, affaissement *m*; (*: *defeat, surrender*) effondrement, dégonflage* *m*; (*Hist*) **caveman** homme *m* des cavernes; **cave painting** peinture *f* rupestre; **caving-in** = **cave-in.**
3 *vi*: **to go caving** faire de la spéléologie.
cave in 1 *vi* **(a)** *[floor, building]* s'effondrer, s'affaisser; *[wall, beam]* céder.
(b) (*: *yield*) se dégonfler*, caner*.
2 cave-in, caving-in *n V* **cave**[1] **2.**
cave[2] [ˈkeɪvɪ] *excl* (*Brit Scol sl†*) **~!** pet pet!*, vingt-deux!‡; **to keep ~** faire le guet.
caveat [ˈkævɪæt] *n* (*gen*) avertissement *m*; (*Jur*) notification *f* d'opposition.
cavern [ˈkævən] *n* caverne *f.*
cavernous [ˈkævənəs] *adj* **(a)** (*fig*) **~ darkness** ténèbres épaisses; **~ eyes** yeux *mpl* caves; **~ voice** voix caverneuse; **~ yawn** bâillement profond. **(b)** *mountain* plein de cavernes.
caviar(e) [ˈkævɪɑːʳ] *n* caviar *m.*
cavil [ˈkævɪl] *vi* ergoter, chicaner (*about, at* sur).
caving [ˈkeɪvɪŋ] *n* spéléologie *f.*
cavity [ˈkævɪtɪ] **1** *n [wood, metal, earth]* cavité *f*, creux *m*; *[bone, tooth]* cavité. **2** *cpd*: **cavity wall** mur creux; **cavity wall insulation** isolation *f* des murs creux.
cavort* [kəˈvɔːt] *vi* cabrioler, faire des cabrioles *or* des gambades.
cavy [ˈkeɪvɪ] *n* (*Zool*) cobaye *m*, cochon *m* d'Inde.
caw [kɔː] **1** *vi* croasser. **2** *n* croassement *m.*
cawing [ˈkɔːɪŋ] *n* (*U*) croassement *m.*
cay [keɪ] *n* (*sandbank*) banc *m* de sable; (*coral reef*) récif *m or* banc de corail.
cayenne [ˈkeɪen] *n* (*also* **~ pepper**) (poivre *m* de) cayenne *m.*
cayman [ˈkeɪmən] *n* caïman *m.*
cease [siːs] **1** *vi [activity, noise etc]* cesser, s'arrêter. (†, *liter*) **to ~ from work** cesser le travail; (†, *liter*) **to ~ from doing** cesser *or* s'arrêter de faire.
2 *vt work, activity* cesser, arrêter. **to ~ doing** cesser *or* arrêter de faire; (*Mil*) **to ~ fire** cesser le feu.
3 *n*: **without ~** sans cesse.
4 *cpd*: (*Mil*) **ceasefire** cessez-le-feu *m inv.*
ceaseless [ˈsiːslɪs] *adj* incessant, continuel.
ceaselessly [ˈsiːslɪslɪ] *adv* sans cesse, sans arrêt, continuellement.
cecum [ˈsiːkəm] *n* (*US*) = **caecum.**
cedar [ˈsiːdəʳ] **1** *n* cèdre *m.* **~ of Lebanon** cèdre du Liban. **2** *cpd* de *or* en cèdre. **cedar wood** (bois *m* de) cèdre *m.*
cede [siːd] *vt* céder.
cedilla [sɪˈdɪlə] *n* cédille *f.*
ceiling [ˈsiːlɪŋ] **1** *n* (*gen, Aviat, fig*) plafond *m.* **to fix a ~ for** *or* **put a ~ on prices/wages** fixer un plafond pour les prix/salaires; **to hit the ~** (‡: *get angry*) sortir de ses gonds, piquer une crise*; *[prices]* crever le plafond; **prices have reached their ~ at X** les prix plafonnent à X.
2 *cpd lamp, covering* de plafond; (*fig*) *rate, charge* plafond *inv.* **ceiling decoration** décoration *f* de plafond; **ceiling price** prix *m* plafond *inv.*
celandine [ˈseləndaɪn] *n* chélidoine *f.*
celebrant [ˈselɪbrənt] *n* célébrant *m*, officiant *m.*
celebrate [ˈselɪbreɪt] **1** *vt person* célébrer, glorifier; *event* célébrer, fêter; *anniversary* commémorer. (*Rel*) **to ~ mass** célébrer la messe. **2** *vi* **(a)** (*Rel*) célébrer (l'office). **(b)** (*) **let's ~!** il faut fêter ça!; (*with drink*) il faut arroser ça!*
celebrated [ˈselɪbreɪtɪd] *adj* célèbre.

celebration [ˌselɪˈbreɪʃən] *n* **(a)** (*occasion*) fêtes *fpl*, festivités *fpl*, cérémonie *f*; (*act*) célébration *f*. **(b)** (*U*) *[person, virtues etc]* louange *f*, éloge *m*.
celebrity [sɪˈlebrɪtɪ] *n* (*fame; person*) célébrité *f*.
celeriac [səˈlerɪæk] *n* céleri(-rave) *m*.
celerity [sɪˈlerɪtɪ] *n* célérité *f*, rapidité *f*, promptitude *f*.
celery [ˈselərɪ] **1** *n* céleri *m* (ordinaire *or* à côtes). **a bunch** *or* **head of** ~ un pied de céleri; **a stick of** ~ une côte de céleri. **2** *cpd seeds, salt* de céleri.
celestial [sɪˈlestɪəl] *adj* (*lit, fig*) céleste.
celibacy [ˈselɪbəsɪ] *n* célibat *m*.
celibate [ˈselɪbɪt] *adj, n* célibataire (*mf*).
cell [sel] *n* (*Bio, Bot, Jur, Mil, Phot, Pol, Zool*) cellule *f*; (*Elec*) élément *m* (*de pile*). (*Pol*) **to form a** ~ créer une cellule; *V* **condemn, death** *etc*.
cellar [ˈseləʳ] *n [wine]* cave *f*; *[wine, food etc]* cellier *m*. **he keeps an excellent** ~ il a une excellente cave; *V* **coal** *etc*.
cellist [ˈtʃelɪst] *n* violoncelliste *mf*.
cello [ˈtʃeləʊ] *n* violoncelle *m*.
cellophane [ˈseləfeɪn] *n* ® cellophane *f* ®.
cellular [ˈseljʊləʳ] *adj* **(a)** (*Anat, Bio etc*) cellulaire. **(b)** (*Tex*) *blanket* en cellular.
Celluloid [ˈseljʊlɔɪd] **1** *n* ® celluloïd *m* ®. **2** *cpd* en celluloïd.
cellulose [ˈseljʊləʊs] **1** *n* cellulose *f*. **2** *adj* cellulosique, en *or* de cellulose. ~ **acetate** acétate *m* de cellulose; ~ **varnish** vernis *m* cellulosique.
Celsius [ˈselsɪəs] *adj* Celsius *inv*.
Celt [kelt, selt] *n* Celte *mf*.
Celtic [ˈkeltɪk, ˈseltɪk] **1** *adj* celtique, celte. **2** *n* (*Ling*) celtique *m*.
cement [səˈment] **1** *n* (*Constr, fig*) ciment *m*; (*Chem, Dentistry*) amalgame *m*. **2** *vt* (*Constr, fig*) cimenter; (*Chem*) cémenter; (*Dentistry*) obturer. **3** *cpd*: **cement mixer** bétonnière *f*.
cementation [ˌsiːmenˈteɪʃən] *n* (*Constr, fig*) cimentation *f*; (*Tech*) cémentation *f*.
cemetery [ˈsemɪtrɪ] *n* cimetière *m*.
cenotaph [ˈsenətɑːf] *n* cénotaphe *m*.
censer [ˈsensəʳ] *n* encensoir *m*.
censor [ˈsensəʳ] **1** *n* censeur *m*. **2** *vt* censurer.
censorious [senˈsɔːrɪəs] *adj person, comments* hypercritique, sévère.
censorship [ˈsensəʃɪp] *n* (*U*) (*censoring*) censure *f*; (*function of censor*) censorat *m*.
censurable [ˈsenʃərəbl] *adj* blâmable, critiquable.
censure [ˈsenʃəʳ] **1** *vt* blâmer, critiquer. **2** *n* critique *f*, blâme *m*; *V* **vote**.
census [ˈsensəs] *n* recensement *m*. **to take a** ~ **of the population** faire le recensement de la population; (*Brit*) ~ **enumerator**, (*US*) ~ **taker** agent *m* recenseur.
cent [sent] *n* **(a) per** ~ pour cent. **(b)** (*Can, US: coin*) cent *m*. **I haven't a** ~* je n'ai pas un sou *or* rond*.
centaur [ˈsentɔːʳ] *n* centaure *m*.
centenarian [ˌsentɪˈnɛərɪən] *adj, n* centenaire (*mf*).
centenary [senˈtiːnərɪ] **1** *adj* centenaire. ~ **celebrations** fêtes *fpl* du centenaire. **2** *n* (*anniversary*) centenaire *m*; (*century*) siècle *m*. **he has just passed his** ~ il vient de fêter son centième anniversaire *or* son centenaire.
centennial [senˈtenɪəl] **1** *adj* (*100 years old*) centenaire, séculaire; (*every 100 years*) séculaire (*frm*). **2** *n* centenaire *m*, centième anniversaire *m*.
center [ˈsentəʳ] *n* (*US*) = **centre.**
centesimal [senˈtesɪməl] *adj* centésimal.
cent(i)... [ˈsent(ɪ)] *pref* centi...
centigrade [ˈsentɪgreɪd] *adj thermometer, scale* centigrade; *degree* centigrade, Celsius *inv*.
centigramme, (*US*) **centigram** [ˈsentɪgræm] *n* centigramme *m*.
centilitre, (*US*) **centiliter** [ˈsentɪˌliːtəʳ] *n* centilitre *m*.
centimetre, (*US*) **centimeter** [ˈsentɪˌmiːtəʳ] *n* centimètre *m*.
centipede [ˈsentɪpiːd] *n* mille-pattes *m inv*.
central [ˈsentrəl] **1** *adj* central. **C**~ **America** Amérique centrale; **C**~ **American** (*adj*) de l'Amérique centrale; (*n*) habitant(e) *m(f)* de l'Amérique centrale; **C**~ **Europe** Europe centrale; **C**~ **European** (*adj*) de l'Europe centrale; (*n*) habitant(e) *m(f)* de l'Europe centrale; ~ **heating** chauffage central; (*Physiol*) ~ **nervous system** système nerveux central; (*Brit Aut*) ~ **reservation** bande médiane; (*Can, US*) ~ **standard time** heure normale du centre.
2 *n* (*US*) central *m* téléphonique.
centralization [ˌsentrəlaɪˈzeɪʃən] *n* centralisation *f*.
centralize [ˈsentrəlaɪz] **1** *vt* centraliser. **2** *vi* se centraliser, être centralisé.
centre, (*US*) **center** [ˈsentəʳ] **1** *n* centre *m*. **the** ~ **of the target** le centre de la cible, le mille; **in the** ~ au centre; ~ **of gravity** centre de gravité; ~ **of attraction** (*lit*) centre d'attraction; (*fig*) point *m* de mire; **city** ~ centre de la ville; ~ **of commerce** centre commercial (*ville*); *V* **civic, community, nerve** *etc*.
2 *cpd*: (*Tech*) **centre bit** mèche *f* (*d'une vrille*), foret *m*, mèche anglaise; (*Naut*) **centre-board** dérive *f* (*d'un bateau*); **centre fold** double page *f* (détachable); (*Sport*) **centre-forward** avant-centre *m*; (*Sport*) **centre-half** demi-centre *m*; (*Pol*) **centre parties** partis *mpl* du centre; *[table]* **centre-piece** milieu *m* de table.
3 *vt* centrer. (*Ftbl*) **to** ~ **the ball** centrer.
4 *vi* **(a)** *[thoughts, hatred]* se concentrer (*on, in* sur); *[problem, talk etc]* tourner (*on* autour de).
(b) (*Archery*) frapper au centre.
centrifugal [senˈtrɪfjʊgəl] *adj* centrifuge. ~ **force** force *f* centrifuge.
centrifuge [ˈsentrɪfjuːʒ] *n* (*Tech*) centrifugeur *m*, centrifugeuse *f*.
centripetal [senˈtrɪpɪtl] *adj* centripète. ~ **force** force *f* centripète.
centurion [senˈtjʊərɪən] *n* centurion *m*.
century [ˈsentjʊrɪ] **1** *n* **(a)** siècle *m*. **several centuries ago** il y a plusieurs siècles; **in the twentieth** ~ au vingtième siècle.
(b) (*Mil Hist*) centurie *f*.
(c) (*Sport*) *centaine f de points*.
2 *cpd*: **centuries-old** séculaire, vieux (*f* vieille) de plusieurs siècles, plusieurs fois centenaire; (*US*) **century note**: billet *m* de cent dollars.
cephalic [sɪˈfælɪk] *adj* céphalique.
ceramic [sɪˈræmɪk] **1** *adj art* céramique; *cup, vase* en céramique. **2** *n* **(a)** (*U*) ~**s** la céramique. **(b)** (objet *m* en) céramique *f*.
cereal [ˈsɪərɪəl] **1** *n* (*plant*) céréale *f*; (*grain*) grain *m* (*de céréale*). **baby** ~ blédine *f* ®; **breakfast** ~ céréale *f*. **2** *adj* de céréale(s).
cerebellum [ˌserɪˈbeləm] *n* cervelet *m*.
cerebral [ˈserɪbrəl] *adj* cérébral. ~ **palsy** paralysie cérébrale.
cerebration [ˌserɪˈbreɪʃən] *n* cogitation *f*, méditation *f*; (*: *hard thinking*) cogitation (*iro*).
cerebrum [ˈserəbrəm] *n* (*Anat*) cerveau *m*.
ceremonial [ˌserɪˈməʊnɪəl] **1** *adj rite* cérémoniel; *dress* de cérémonie. **2** *n* cérémonial *m* (*U*); (*Rel*) cérémonial, rituel *m*.
ceremonially [ˌserɪˈməʊnɪəlɪ] *adv* avec cérémonie, selon le cérémonial d'usage.
ceremonious [ˌserɪˈməʊnɪəs] *adj* solennel; (*slightly pej*) cérémonieux.
ceremoniously [ˌserɪˈməʊnɪəslɪ] *adv* solennellement; (*slightly pej*) cérémonieusement.
ceremony [ˈserɪmənɪ] *n* **(a)** (*event*) cérémonie *f*; *V* **master. (b)** (*U*) cérémonies *fpl*, façons *fpl*. **to stand on** ~ faire des cérémonies, faire des façons; **with/without** ~ cérémonieusement/ sans cérémonie(s).
cerise [səˈriːz] *adj* (de) couleur cerise, cerise *inv*.
cert: [sɜːt] *n* (*Brit*) certitude *f*. **it's a dead** ~ ça ne fait pas un pli*, c'est couru*; **he's a** ~ **for the job** il est sûr et certain de décrocher le poste*.
certain [ˈsɜːtən] *adj* **(a)** (*definite, indisputable*) certain, sûr, indiscutable; *death, success* certain, inévitable; *remedy, cure* infaillible. **he is** ~ **to come** il viendra sans aucun doute; **it is** ~ **that he will go** il est certain qu'il ira; **that's for** ~* c'est sûr et certain*, il n'y a pas de doute; **he'll do it for** ~ il est certain qu'il le fera; **I cannot say for** ~ **that ...** je ne peux pas affirmer que ...; **I don't know for** ~ je n'en suis pas sûr.
(b) (*sure*) *person* certain, convaincu, sûr. **I am** ~ **he didn't do it** je suis certain qu'il n'a pas fait cela; **are you** ~ **of** *or* **about that?** en êtes-vous sûr *or* certain?; **be** ~ **to go** allez-y sans faute, ne manquez pas d'y aller; **you can be** ~ **of success** vous êtes sûr *or* assuré de réussir; **you don't sound very** ~ tu n'as pas l'air très convaincu *or* sûr; **to make** ~ **of sth** (*get facts about*) s'assurer de qch; (*be sure of getting*) s'assurer qch; **you should make** ~ **of your facts** vous devriez vérifier les faits que vous avancez; **I must make** ~ **of a seat** il faut que je m'assure (*subj*) d'avoir une place; **to make** ~ **that** s'assurer que.
(c) (*particular*) certain (*before n*), particulier; (*specific*) certain (*before n*), déterminé, précis. **a** ~ **gentleman** un certain monsieur; **on a** ~ **day in spring** un certain jour de printemps; **at a** ~ **hour** à une heure bien précise *or* déterminée; **there is a** ~ **way of doing it** il existe une façon particulière de le faire; **in** ~ **countries** dans certains pays.
(d) (*some*) certain (*before n*), quelque. **he had a** ~ **courage all the same** il avait tout de même un certain *or* du courage; **a** ~ **difficulty** une certaine difficulté, quelque difficulté; **to a** ~ **extent** dans une certaine mesure.
certainly [ˈsɜːtənlɪ] *adv* certainement, assurément, sans aucun doute. **will you do this? —** ~! voulez-vous faire cela? — bien sûr! *or* volontiers!; ~ **not!** certainement pas!, sûrement pas!; **this meat is** ~ **tough** il n'y a pas de doute, cette viande est dure; **it is** ~ **true that** on ne peut pas nier que + *subj or indic*; **I shall** ~ **be there** j'y serai sans faute, je ne manquerai pas d'y être; **you may** ~ **leave tomorrow** vous pouvez partir demain bien sûr; ~, **madam!** (mais) certainement *or* tout de suite, madame!
certainty [ˈsɜːtəntɪ] *n* **(a)** (*fact, quality*) certitude *f*, fait *or* événement certain. **for a** ~ à coup sûr, sans aucun doute; **to a** ~ certainement; **to be on a** ~ parier à coup sûr; **his success is a** ~ son succès est certain *or* ne fait aucun doute; **it is a moral** ~ c'est une certitude morale; **faced with the** ~ **of disaster** voyant le désastre inévitable.
(b) (*U: conviction*) certitude *f*, conviction *f*.
certifiable [ˌsɜːtɪˈfaɪəbl] *adj* **(a)** *fact, statement* qu'on peut certifier. **(b)** (*: *mad*) bon à enfermer.
certificate [səˈtɪfɪkɪt] *n* **(a)** (*legal document*) certificat *m*, acte *m*. ~ **of airworthiness** *or* **seaworthiness** certificat de navigabilité; ~ **of baptism** extrait *m* de baptême; **birth** ~ acte *or* extrait de naissance; *V* **death, marriage.**
(b) (*academic document*) diplôme *m*; *V* **teacher.**
certificated [səˈtɪfɪkeɪtɪd] *adj* diplômé.
certification [ˌsɜːtɪfɪˈkeɪʃən] *n* **(a)** (*U*) certification *f*, authentification *f*. **(b)** (*document*) certificat *m*.
certify [ˈsɜːtɪfaɪ] **1** *vt* **(a)** certifier, assurer, attester (*that* que). (*Jur*) **certified as a true copy** certifié conforme; (*Psych*) **to** ~ **sb (insane)** déclarer qn atteint d'aliénation mentale; (*Jur*) **certified lunatic** aliéné interdit *or* incapable.
(b) (*Fin*) *cheque* certifier. **certified cheque** chèque certifié; (*US*) **certified public accountant** expert-comptable *m*, comptable agréé (*Can*).
(c) (*Comm*) *goods* garantir. (*US Post*) **to send by certified**

mail ≃ envoyer en recommandé *or* avec avis de réception; (*US*) **certified milk** *lait soumis aux contrôles d'hygiène réglementaires.*
2 *vi*: **to ~ to sth** attester qch.
certitude [ˈsɜːtɪtjuːd] *n* certitude *f*, conviction absolue.
cerulean [ˌsɜːruːˈljən] *adj* (*liter*) bleu ciel *inv*, azuré.
cervical [ˈsɜːvɪkəl] *adj* cervical. **~ cancer** cancer *m* du col de l'utérus; **~ smear** frottis vaginal.
cervix [ˈsɜːvɪks] *n* col *m* de l'utérus.
cessation [seˈseɪʃən] *n* cessation *f*, arrêt *m*, interruption *f*, suspension *f*. **~ of hostilities** cessation des hostilités.
cession [ˈseʃən] *n* cession *f*. **act of ~** acte *m* de cession.
cesspit [ˈsespɪt] *n* fosse *f* à purin.
cesspool [ˈsespuːl] *n* fosse *f* d'aisance; (*fig*) cloaque *m*.
cetacean [sɪˈteɪʃɪən] *adj, n* cétacé (*m*).
Ceylon [sɪˈlɒn] *n* Ceylan *m*.
Ceylonese [sɪlɒˈniːz] **1** *adj* cingalais, ceylanais. **2** *n* **(a)** Cingalais(e) *m(f)*, Ceylanais(e) *m(f)*. **(b)** (*Ling*) cingalais *m*.
chafe [tʃeɪf] **1** *vt* **(a)** (*rub*) frotter, frictionner. **she ~d the child's hands to warm them** elle a frictionné les mains de l'enfant pour les réchauffer.
(b) (*rub against, irritate*) frotter contre, irriter, gratter. **his shirt ~d his neck** sa chemise frottait contre son cou *or* lui irritait le cou *or* lui grattait le cou; **~d lips/hands** lèvres/mains gercées.
(c) (*wear*) *collar, cuffs, rope* user (en frottant); (*Naut*) raguer.
2 *vi* s'user; *[rope]* raguer; (*fig*) s'impatienter, s'irriter (*at* de). **he ~d against these restrictions** ces restrictions l'irritaient; (*liter*) **they ~d under the yoke of tyranny** ils rongeaient leur frein sous la tyrannie.
3 *n* irritation *f*.
chaff[1] [tʃɑːf] **1** *n* (*U: Agr*) *[grain]* balle *f*; (*cut straw*) menue paille; *V* **wheat. 2** *vt straw* hacher.
chaff[2] [tʃɑːf] **1** *n* (*U: banter*) taquinerie *f*. **2** *vt* taquiner, blaguer*.
chaffinch [ˈtʃæfɪntʃ] *n* pinson *m*.
chafing dish [ˈtʃeɪfɪŋdɪʃ] *n* chauffe-plats *m inv*.
chagrin [ˈʃægrɪn] **1** *n* contrariété *f*, (vive) déception *f*. **much to my ~** à mon vif dépit. **2** *vt* contrarier, décevoir.
chain [tʃeɪn] **1** *n* **(a)** (*gen, also ornamental*) chaîne *f*. (*fetters*) **~s** chaînes, entraves *fpl*, fers *mpl*; *[mayor]* **~ of office** chaîne (*insigne de la fonction de maire*); **to keep a dog on a ~** tenir un chien à l'attache; **in ~s** enchaîné; (*Aut*) **~s** chaînes; *[lavatory]* **to pull the ~** tirer la chasse (d'eau); *V* **ball, bicycle** *etc*.
(b) *[mountains, atoms etc]* chaîne *f*; (*fig*) *[ideas]* enchaînement *m*; *[events]* série *f*, suite *f*. (*Comm*) **~ of shops** chaîne de magasins; *[people]* **to make a ~** faire la chaîne; *V* **bucket.**
(c) (*Tech*) (*for measuring*) chaîne *f* d'arpenteur; (*measure*) chaînée *f*.
2 *cpd*: **chain gang** chaîne *f* de forçats; **chain letter** lettre *f* faisant partie d'une chaîne; **chain letters** chaîne *f* (de lettres); **chain lightning** éclairs *mpl* en zigzag; (*U*) **chain mail** cotte *f* de mailles; **chain pump** pompe *f* à chapelet; (*Phys, fig*) **(to set up) a chain reaction** (provoquer) une réaction en chaîne; **chain smoke** fumer cigarette sur cigarette; **chain smoker** fumeur *m*, -euse *f* invétéré(e) (*qui fume sans discontinuer*); (*Sewing*) **chain stitch** point *m* de chaînette; **chain store** grand magasin (à succursales multiples).
3 *vt* (*lit, fig*) enchaîner; *door* mettre la chaîne à. **he was ~ed to the wall** il était enchaîné au mur.
chain down *vt sep* enchaîner.
chain up *vt sep animal* mettre à l'attache.
chair [tʃɛəʳ] **1** *n* **(a)** chaise *f*; (*armchair*) fauteuil *m*; (*seat*) siège *m*; (*Univ*) chaire *f*; (*sedan ~*) chaise à porteurs; (*wheel ~*) fauteuil roulant; (*US: electric ~*) chaise électrique. **to take a ~** s'asseoir; **dentist's ~** fauteuil de dentiste; (*Univ*) **to hold the ~ of French** être titulaire de *or* avoir la chaire de français; (*US*) **to go to the ~** passer à la chaise électrique; *V* **deck, easy, high** *etc*.
(b) (*Admin etc: function*) fauteuil présidentiel, présidence *f*. **to take the ~, to be in the ~** prendre la présidence, présider; **to address the ~** s'adresser au president; **~! ~!** à l'ordre!
2 *cpd*: **chair back** dossier *m* (de chaise); **chairlift** télésiège *m*; **chairman** *V* **chairman; chairperson*** président(e) *m(f)*.
3 *vt* **(a)** (*Admin*) *meeting* présider.
(b) *hero* porter en triomphe.
chairman [ˈtʃɛəmən] *n* président *m* (*d'un comité etc*). **Mr C~** Monsieur le Président; **Madam C~** Madame la Présidente.
chairmanship [ˈtʃɛəmənʃɪp] *n* présidence *f* (*d'un comité etc*). **under the ~ of** sous la présidence de.
chaise [ʃeɪz] *n* cabriolet *m*.
chalet [ˈʃæleɪ] *n* (*gen*) chalet *m*; *[motel]* bungalow *m*.
chalice [ˈtʃælɪs] *n* (*Rel*) calice *m*; (*liter: wine cup*) coupe *f*.
chalk [tʃɔːk] **1** *n* (*U*) craie *f*. **a (piece of) ~** une craie, un morceau de craie; (*Brit*) **they're as different as ~ from cheese** (*persons*) ils sont comme le jour et la nuit; (*things*) ce sont deux choses qui n'ont rien en commun, c'est le jour et la nuit; (*Brit fig*) **by a long ~** de beaucoup, de loin; **did he win? — not by a long ~** est-ce qu'il a gagné? — non, loin de là *or* il s'en faut de beaucoup; *V* **French.**
2 *cpd*: (*US*) **chalk board** tableau *m* (noir); **chalkpit** carrière *f* de craie.
3 *vt* (*write with ~*) écrire à la craie; (*rub with ~*) frotter de craie; *luggage* marquer à la craie.
chalk out *vt sep* (*lit*) *pattern* esquisser, tracer (à la craie); (*fig*) *project* esquisser; *plan of action* tracer.
chalk up *vt sep* **(a) chalk it up** mettez-le sur mon compte; **he chalked it up to experience** il l'a mis au compte de l'expérience.
(b) *achievement, victory* remporter.
chalky [ˈtʃɔːkɪ] *adj soil* crayeux, calcaire; *water* calcaire; *complexion* crayeux, blafard.
challenge [ˈtʃælɪndʒ] **1** *n* **(a)** défi *m*. **to issue** *or* **put out a ~** lancer un défi; **to take up the ~** relever le défi; (*fig*) **the ~ of new ideas** la stimulation qu'offrent de nouvelles idées; **the ~ of the 20th century** le défi du 20e siècle; **Smith's ~ for leadership** la tentative qu'a faite Smith pour s'emparer du pouvoir; **this is a ~ to us all** c'est un défi qui s'adresse à nous tous; **the job was a great ~ to him** il a pris cette tâche comme une gageure; **action that is a ~ to authority** action qui défie l'autorité; **it was a ~ to his skill** c'était un défi à son savoir-faire.
(b) (*Mil: by sentry*) sommation *f*.
(c) (*Jur: of juror, jury*) récusation *f*.
2 *vt* **(a)** (*summon, call*) défier (*sb to do* qn de faire); (*Sport*) inviter (*sb to a game* qn à faire une partie). **to ~ sb to a duel** provoquer qn en duel.
(b) (*call into question*) *statement* mettre en question, contester, révoquer en doute (*frm*). **to ~ sb's authority to do** contester à qn le droit de faire; **to ~ the wisdom of a plan** mettre en question la sagesse d'un projet.
(c) (*Mil*) *[sentry]* faire une sommation à.
(d) (*Jur*) *juror, jury* récuser.
challenger [ˈtʃælɪndʒəʳ] *n* provocateur *m*, -trice *f*; (*Sport*) challenger *m*.
challenging [ˈtʃælɪndʒɪŋ] *adj remark, speech* provocateur *m* (*f* -trice); *look, tone* de défi; *book* stimulant. **he found himself in a ~ situation** il s'est trouvé là devant une gageure; **this is a very ~ situation** cette situation est une véritable gageure.
chamber [ˈtʃeɪmbəʳ] **1** *n* **(a)** (†, *frm*) (*room*) salle *f*, pièce *f*; (*also* **bed~**) chambre *f*.
(b) (*Brit*) (*lodgings*) **~s** logement *m*, appartement *m*; *[bachelor]* garçonnière *f*; *[barrister, judge, magistrate]* cabinet *m*; *[solicitor]* étude *f*. (*Jur*) **to hear a case in ~s** ≃ juger un cas en référé.
(c) (*hall*) chambre *f*. **C~ of Commerce** Chambre *f* de commerce; **the C~ of Deputies** la Chambre des députés; (*Parl*) **the Upper/Lower C~** la Chambre haute/basse; **the C~ of Horrors** la Chambre d'épouvante; *V* **audience, second**[1].
(d) *[revolver]* chambre *f*; (*Anat*) cavité *f*. **the ~s of the eye** les chambres de l'œil.
(e) (†,*) = **chamber pot**; *V* **2.**
2 *cpd*: **chambermaid** femme *f* de chambre (*dans un hôtel*); **chamber music** musique *f* de chambre; **chamberpot** pot *m* de chambre, vase *m* de nuit†.
chamberlain [ˈtʃeɪmbəlɪn] *n* chambellan *m*.
chambray [ˈtʃæmbreɪ] *n* (*US*) = **cambric.**
chameleon [kəˈmiːlɪən] *n* (*Zool, fig*) caméléon *m*.
chamfer [ˈtʃæmfəʳ] (*Tech*) **1** *n* (*bevel*) chanfrein *m*; (*groove*) cannelure *f*. **2** *vt* chanfreiner; canneler.
chamois [ˈʃæmwɑː] *n* **(a)** (*Zool*) chamois *m*. **(b)** [ˈʃæmɪ] (*also* **~ cloth**) chamois *m*. **~ leather** peau *f* de chamois.
champ[1] [tʃæmp] **1** *vi* mâchonner. (*lit, fig*) **to ~ at the bit** ronger son frein. **2** *vt* mâchonner.
champ[2]* [tʃæmp] *n abbr of* **champion 1b.**
champagne [ʃæmˈpeɪn] **1** *n* (*wine*) champagne *m*. **2** *cpd* (*also* **champagne-coloured**) champagne *inv*. **champagne cup** cocktail *m* au champagne; **champagne glass** verre *m* à champagne; (*wide*) coupe *f* à champagne; (*tall and narrow*) flûte *f* à champagne.
champion [ˈtʃæmpjən] **1** *n* **(a)** champion *m*. **the ~ of free speech** le champion de la liberté d'expression.
(b) (*Sport: person, animal*) champion(ne) *m(f)*. **world ~** champion(ne) du monde; **boxing ~** champion de boxe; **skiing ~** champion(ne) de ski.
2 *adj* **(a)** sans rival, de première classe, maître; *show animal* champion. **~ swimmer** champion(ne) *m(f)* de natation.
(b) (*: *excellent*) *meal, holiday, film* du tonnerre*. **that's ~!** bravo!, chapeau!*, c'est champion!*
3 *vt person* prendre fait et cause pour; *action, cause* se faire le champion de, défendre.
championship [ˈtʃæmpjənʃɪp] *n* **(a)** (*Sport*) championnat *m*. **world ~** championnat du monde; **boxing ~** championnat de boxe. **(b)** (*U*) *[cause etc]* défense *f*.
chance [tʃɑːns] **1** *n* **(a)** (*luck*) hasard *m*. **by (sheer) ~** tout à fait par hasard, par (pur) hasard; (*by good luck*) par (pure) chance, par un coup de chance; **have you a pen on you by (any) ~?** auriez-vous par hasard un stylo sur vous?; **it was not ~ that he came** s'il est venu ce n'est pas par hasard, ce n'est pas par hasard qu'il est venu; **to trust to ~** s'en remettre au hasard; **a game of ~** un jeu de hasard; **to leave things to ~** laisser faire le hasard; **he left nothing to ~** il n'a rien laissé au hasard.
(b) (*possibility*) chance(s) *f(pl)*, possibilité *f*. **he hasn't much ~ of winning** il n'a pas beaucoup de chances de gagner; **on the ~ of your returning** dans le cas où vous reviendriez; **I went there on the ~ of seeing him** j'y suis allé dans l'espoir de le voir; **the ~s are that** il y a de grandes chances que + *subj*, il est très possible que + *subj*; **the ~s are against that happening** il y a peu de chances pour que cela arrive (*subj*); **the ~s are against him** il y a peu de chances pour qu'il réussisse; **there is little ~ of his coming** il est peu probable qu'il vienne; **you'll have to take a ~ on his coming** on verra bien s'il vient ou non; **he's taking no ~s*** il ne veut rien laisser au hasard, il ne veut prendre aucun risque; **that's a ~ we'll have to take** c'est un risque que nous allons devoir prendre *or* que nous avons à courir; *V* **long**[1]**, off.**
(c) (*opportunity*) occasion *f*, chance *f*. **I had the ~ to go** *or* **of going** j'ai eu l'occasion d'y aller, l'occasion m'a été donnée d'y aller; **if there's a ~ of buying it** s'il y a une possibilité d'achat; **to lose a ~** laisser passer une occasion; **to stand a good** *or* **fair ~** avoir des chances de réussir; **she was waiting for her ~** elle attendait son heure; **she was waiting for her ~ to speak** elle

attendait *or* guettait l'occasion de parler; **now's your ~!** vas-y!, saute sur l'occasion!, à toi de jouer!; **this is his big ~** c'est le grand moment pour lui; **give him another ~** laisse-lui encore sa chance; **he has had every ~** il a eu toutes les chances; **he never had a ~ in life** il n'a jamais eu sa chance dans la vie; **give me a ~ to show you what I can do** donnez-moi la possibilité de vous montrer ce que je sais faire; *V* **eye.**

2 *adj* fortuit, de hasard, accidentel. **a ~ companion** un compagnon rencontré par hasard; **a ~ discovery** une découverte accidentelle; **~ meeting** rencontre fortuite *or* de hasard.

3 *vi*: **it ~d that I was there** il s'est trouvé que j'étais là.

4 *vt* **(a)** (*happen*) **to ~ to do** faire par hasard, venir à faire (*frm*); **I ~d to hear his name** j'ai entendu son nom par hasard, il s'est trouvé que j'ai entendu son nom.

(b) (*risk*) **to ~ doing** se risquer à faire, prendre le risque de faire; **I'll go round without phoning and ~ finding him there** je vais passer chez lui sans téléphoner en espérant l'y trouver *or* avec l'espoir de l'y trouver; **I want to see her alone and I'll have to ~ finding her husband there** je voudrais la voir seule, mais il faut que je prenne le risque d'y trouver son mari; **I'll ~ it!*** je vais risquer *or* je risque le coup!*; **to ~ one's arm*** risquer le tout (pour le tout); **to ~ one's luck** tenter *or* courir sa chance.

chance upon *vt fus* (*frm*) *person* rencontrer par hasard; *thing* trouver par hasard.

chancel [ˈtʃɑːnsəl] *n* chœur *m* (*d'une église*). **~ screen** clôture *f* du chœur, jubé *m*.

chancellery [ˈtʃɑːnsələrɪ] *n* chancellerie *f*.

chancellor [ˈtʃɑːnsələʳ] *n* (*Hist, Jur, Pol*) chancelier *m*; (*Brit Univ*) recteur *m* honoraire. (*Brit*) **C~ of the Exchequer** Chancelier *m* de l'Échiquier, ≃ ministre *m* des Finances; *V* **lord.**

chancellorship [ˈtʃɑːnsələʃɪp] *n* fonctions *fpl* de chancelier.

chancery [ˈtʃɑːnsərɪ] *n* **(a)** (*Brit, Jur*) cour *f* de la chancellerie (*une des 5 divisions de la Haute Cour de justice anglaise*). **ward in ~** pupille *mf* (*sous tutelle judiciaire*).

(b) (*US*) = **chancellery.**

(c) (*US: also* **court of ~**) ≃ cour *f* d'équité *or* de la chancellerie.

chancre [ˈʃæŋkəʳ] *n* (*Med*) chancre *m*.

chancy* [ˈtʃɑːnsɪ] *adj* (*risky*) risqué, hasardeux; (*doubtful*) aléatoire, problématique.

chandelier [ˌʃændəˈlɪəʳ] *n* lustre *m*.

chandler [ˈtʃɑːndləʳ] *n* marchand *m* de couleurs, droguiste *m*. **ship's ~** shipchandler *m*, marchand de fournitures pour bateaux.

change [tʃeɪndʒ] **1** *n* **(a)** (*alteration*) changement *m* (*from* de, *into* en); (*slight*) modification *f*. **a ~ for the better** un changement en mieux, une amélioration; **a ~ for the worse** un changement en pire *or* en plus mal; **~ in the weather** changement de temps; **(just) for a ~** pour changer un peu; **by way of a ~** histoire de changer*; **to make a ~ in sth** changer qch, modifier qch; (*fig*) **to have a ~ of heart** changer d'avis; **it makes a ~*** ça change un peu*; **it will be a nice ~** cela nous fera un changement, voilà qui nous changera agréablement!; (*iro*) ça nous changera! (*iro*); (*Med*) **the ~ of life*** le retour d'âge.

(b) (*substitution*) changement *m*, substitution *f*. **~ of address** changement d'adresse; **~ of air** changement d'air; **he brought a ~ of clothes** il a apporté des vêtements de rechange; **I need a ~ of clothes** il faut que je me change (*subj*); **~ of scene** (*Theat*) changement de décor; (*fig*) changement *m* d'air; **~ of horses** relais *m*; **~ of job** changement de travail *or* de poste.

(c) (*U*) changement *m*, variété *f*. **she likes ~** elle aime le changement *or* la variété.

(d) (*U: money*) monnaie *f*. **small ~** petite monnaie; **can you give me ~ for this note/of £1?** pouvez-vous me faire la monnaie de ce billet/d'une livre?; **keep the ~** gardez la monnaie; (*notice*) **'no ~ given'** 'on est tenu de faire l'appoint'; **you don't get much ~ from a fiver these days** aujourd'hui il ne reste jamais grand-chose d'un billet de cinq livres; **you won't get much ~ out of him*** tu perds ton temps avec lui.

(e) (*St Ex*) **the C~** la Bourse; **on the C~** en Bourse.

2 *cpd*: **changeover** changement *m*, passage *m* (*from one thing to another* d'une chose à une autre); (*U: Mil*) *[guard]* relève *f*.

3 *vt* **(a)** (*by substitution*) changer de. **to ~ (one's) clothes** changer de vêtements, se changer; **to ~ one's address** changer d'adresse; **to ~ colour** changer de couleur; **to ~ hands** (*one's grip*) changer de main; *[goods, property]* changer de main *or* de propriétaire; (*) *[money]* (*between several people*) circuler de main en main; (*from one person to another*) passer en d'autres mains; (*Mil*) **to ~ (the) guard** faire la relève de la garde; (*Theat*) **to ~ the scene** changer le décor; **let's ~ the subject** changeons de sujet, parlons d'autre chose; **to ~ one's tune** changer de ton; **to ~ trains/stations/buses** changer de train/de gare/d'autobus; **to ~ one's name/seat** changer de nom/place; **to ~ one's opinion** *or* **mind** changer d'avis; (*Aut*) **to ~ gear** changer de vitesse; (*Aut*) **to ~ a wheel** changer une roue.

(b) (*exchange*) échanger, troquer (*sth for sth else* qch contre qch d'autre). (*lit*) **to ~ places (with sb)** changer de place (avec qn); (*fig*) **I wouldn't like to ~ places with you** je n'aimerais pas être à votre place; **to ~ sides** *or* **ends** (*Tennis*) changer de côté; (*Ftbl etc*) changer de camp; (*fig: in argument etc*) **to ~ sides** changer de camp; **they ~d hats (with one another)** ils ont échangé leurs chapeaux.

(c) *banknote, coin* faire la monnaie de, changer; *foreign currency* changer, convertir (*into* en).

(d) (*alter, modify, transform*) changer, modifier, transformer (*sth into sth else* qch en qch d'autre). **the witch ~d him into a cat** la sorcière l'a changé en chat; **his wife's death ~d him suddenly from a young man into an old one** la mort de sa femme a fait du jeune homme qu'il était un vieillard, il a vieilli tout d'un coup après la mort de sa femme; **this has ~d my ideas** ceci a modifié mes idées; **success has greatly ~d her** la réussite l'a complètement transformée.

4 *vi* **(a)** (*become different*) changer, se transformer. **you've ~d a lot!** tu as beaucoup changé!; **he will never ~** il ne changera jamais, on ne le changera pas; **the prince ~d into a swan** le prince s'est changé en cygne.

(b) (**~ clothes**) se changer. **I must ~ at once** je dois me changer tout de suite; **she ~d into an old skirt** elle s'est changée et a mis une vieille jupe.

(c) (*Rail etc*) changer. **you must ~ at Edinburgh** vous devez changer à Édimbourg; **all ~!** tout le monde descend!

(d) *[moon]* entrer dans une nouvelle phase.

change down *vi* (*Aut*) rétrograder.

change over 1 *vi* passer (*from* de, *to* à).

2 changeover *n V* **change 2.**

change up *vi* (*Aut*) monter les vitesses.

changeability [ˌtʃeɪndʒəˈbɪlɪtɪ] *n* *[circumstances, weather]* variabilité *f*.

changeable [ˈtʃeɪndʒəbl] *adj person* changeant, inconstant; *character* versatile, changeant; *colour* changeant; *weather, wind, circumstances* variable.

changeless [ˈtʃeɪndʒlɪs] *adj rite* immuable, invariable; *person* constant; *character* inaltérable.

changeling [ˈtʃeɪndʒlɪŋ] *n* enfant *mf* changé(e) (*substitué(e) à un(e) enfant volé(e)*).

changing [ˈtʃeɪndʒɪŋ] **1** *adj wind* variable, changeant; *expression* mobile. **2** *n* (*U*) acte *m* de (se) changer, changement *m*. **the ~ of the guard** la relève de la garde; (*Sport*) **~-room** vestiaire *m*.

channel [ˈtʃænl] **1** *n* **(a)** (*bed of river etc*) lit *m*; (*navigable passage*) chenal *m*; (*between two land masses*) bras *m* de mer; *[irrigation]* (*small*) rigole *f*, (*wider*) canal *m*; (*in street*) caniveau *m*; (*duct*) conduit *m*. (*Geog*) **the (English) C~** la Manche.

(b) (*groove in surface*) rainure *f*; (*Archit*) cannelure *f*.

(c) (*TV*) chaîne *f*.

(d) (*fig*) direction *f*. **he directed the conversation into a new ~** il a fait prendre à la conversation une nouvelle direction; **~ of communication** voie *f* de communication; (*Admin*) **to go through the usual ~s** suivre la filière (habituelle).

2 *cpd*: (*Geog*) **the Channel Isles** *or* **Islands** les îles Anglo-Normandes, les îles de la Manche; **the Channel tunnel** le tunnel sous la Manche.

3 *vt* **(a)** (*V* 1a) (*make* **~s** *in*) creuser des rigoles *or* des canaux dans; *street* pourvoir d'un *or* de caniveau(x). **the river ~led its way towards ...** la rivière a creusé son lit vers ... .

(b) (*fig*) *crowd* canaliser (*into* vers); *energies, efforts* canaliser, diriger, orienter (*towards, into* vers); *information* canaliser (*towards* vers), concentrer (*towards* dans).

(c) (*Archit*) canneler.

channel off *vt sep* (*lit*) *water* capter; (*fig*) *energy, resources* canaliser.

chant [tʃɑːnt] **1** *n* (*Mus*) chant *m* (lent), mélopée *f*; (*Rel Mus*) psalmodie *f*; *[crowd, demonstrators, audience etc]* chant scandé.

2 *vt* (*sing*) chanter; (*recite*) réciter; (*speak rhythmically*) entonner *or* chanter sur l'air des lampions; (*Rel*) psalmodier; *[crowd, demonstrators etc]* scander.

3 *vi* chanter; (*Rel*) psalmodier; *[crowd, demonstrators etc]* scander des slogans.

chantey [ˈʃæntɪ] *n* (*US*) chanson *f* de marin.

chaos [ˈkeɪɒs] *n* (*lit, fig*) chaos *m*.

chaotic [keɪˈɒtɪk] *adj* chaotique.

chap[1] [tʃæp] **1** *n* (*Med*) gerçure *f*, crevasse *f*. **2** *vi* se gercer, se crevasser. **3** *vt* gercer, crevasser.

chap[2] [tʃæp] *n* = **chop**[2].

chap[3]***** [tʃæp] *n* (*man*) type* *m*. (*term of address*) **old ~** mon vieux*; **he was a young ~** c'était un jeune homme; **a nice ~** un chic type*; **the poor old ~** le pauvre vieux*; **poor little ~** pauvre petit, pauvre bonhomme; **he's very deaf, poor ~** pauvre garçon *or* pauvre vieux*, il est très sourd; **be a good ~ and say nothing** sois gentil (et) ne dis rien.

chapel [ˈtʃæpəl] *n* **(a)** *[church, school, castle etc]* chapelle *f*; *[house]* oratoire *m*. **~ of ease** (église *f*) succursale *f*; *V* **lady. (b)** (*nonconformist church*) église *f*, temple *m*. **(c)** (*Ind*) *[printers etc]* association *f*.

chaperon [ˈʃæpərəʊn] **1** *n* chaperon *m*. **she was the ~** elle faisait office de chaperon. **2** *vt* chaperonner.

chaplain [ˈtʃæplɪn] *n* *[armed forces, prison, school, hospital etc]* aumônier *m*; (*Rel*) chapelain *m*.

chaplaincy [ˈtʃæplənsɪ] *n* (*V* **chaplain**) aumônerie *f*; chapellenie *f*.

chaplet [ˈtʃæplɪt] *n* *[flowers etc]* guirlande *f*; (*Archit, Rel*) chapelet *m*.

chappy‡ [ˈtʃæpɪ] *n* = **chap**[3].

chaps [tʃæps] *npl* (*US*) jambières *fpl* de cuir (*portées par les cowboys*).

chapter [ˈtʃæptəʳ] **1** *n* **(a)** *[book]* chapitre *m*. **in ~ 4** au chapitre 4; (*fig*) **to give** *or* **quote ~ and verse** citer ses références *or* ses autorités.

(b) (*Rel*) chapitre *m*.

(c) (*fig: period of one's life etc*) chapitre *m*, épisode *m*. **a ~ of accidents** une succession de mésaventures, une kyrielle de malheurs.

2 *cpd*: (*Rel*) **chapter room** salle *f* du chapitre *or* capitulaire.

char[1] [tʃɑːʳ] **1** *vt* (*burn black*) carboniser. **2** *vi* être carbonisé.

char[2]***** [tʃɑːʳ] (*Brit*) **1** *n* (*charwoman*) femme *f* de ménage. **2** *vi* (*also* **go out ~ring**) faire des ménages.

char[3] [tʃɑːʳ] *n* (*fish*) omble *m* (chevalier).

char[4]**‡** [tʃɑːʳ] *n* (*Brit: tea*) thé *m*.

char-à-banc† ['ʃærəbæŋ] *n* (auto)car *m* (*décapotable*).

character ['kærɪktəʳ] **1** *n* **(a)** (*temperament, disposition*) *[person]* caractère *m*, tempérament *m*. **he has the same ~ as his brother** il a le même caractère que son frère; **it's very much in ~ (for him)** c'est bien de lui, cela lui ressemble tout à fait; **that was not in ~ (for him)** cela ne lui ressemble pas, ce n'est pas dans son caractère.

(b) (*U*) *[country, village]* caractère *m*; *[book, film]* caractère, nature *f*.

(c) (*U: strength, energy, determination etc*) caractère *m*, détermination *f*, volonté *f*. **it takes ~ to say such a thing** il faut avoir du caractère pour dire une chose pareille.

(d) (*outstanding individual*) personnage *m*; (*: *original person*) numéro* *m*, phénomène* *m*. **he's quite a ~!*** c'est un numéro!* *or* un phénomène!*; **he's a queer** *or* **odd ~** c'est un type* curieux *or* un curieux personnage.

(e) réputation *f*. **of good/bad ~** qui a une bonne/qui a mauvaise réputation.

(f) (*testimonial*) références *fpl*.

(g) (*Literat*) personnage *m*; (*Theat*) personnage, rôle *m*. **one of Shakespeare's ~s** un des personnages de Shakespeare; **he played the ~ of Hamlet** il a joué (le rôle de) Hamlet.

(h) (*Typ*) caractère *m*, lettre *f*. **Gothic ~s** caractères gothiques.

2 *cpd*: (*Theat*) **character actor/actress** acteur *m*/actrice *f* de genre; **character comedy** comédie *f* de caractère; **character part** rôle *m* de composition.

characteristic [ˌkærɪktə'rɪstɪk] **1** *adj* caractéristique, typique. **with (his) ~ enthusiasm** avec l'enthousiasme qui le caractérise. **2** *n* caractéristique *f*, trait distinctif; (*Math*) caractéristique.

characteristically [ˌkærɪktə'rɪstɪkəlɪ] *adv* d'une façon caractéristique, typiquement.

characterization [ˌkærɪktəraɪ'zeɪʃən] *n* caractérisation *f*; (*Theat*) représentation *f* (des caractères); (*Literat*) peinture *f* des caractères. **~ in Dickens** la peinture des caractères chez Dickens, l'art du portrait chez Dickens.

characterize ['kærɪktəraɪz] *vt* caractériser, être caractéristique de; (*Literat*) caractériser, décrire *or* peindre le caractère de.

characterless ['kærɪktəlɪs] *adj* sans caractère, fade.

charade [ʃə'rɑːd] *n* charade *f*.

charcoal ['tʃɑːkəʊl] **1** *n* charbon *m* de bois. **2** *cpd drawing, sketch* au charbon; (*colour: also* **charcoal-grey**) gris foncé *inv*, (gris) anthracite *inv*. **charcoal burner** (*person*) charbonnier *m*; (*stove*) réchaud *m* à charbon de bois.

charge [tʃɑːdʒ] **1** *n* **(a)** (*Jur etc: accusation*) accusation *f*. **to repudiate a ~** repousser une accusation; **to lay** *or* **bring a ~ against sb** porter plainte *or* déposer une plainte contre qn; **he was arrested on a ~ of murder** il a été arrêté sous l'inculpation de meurtre.

(b) (*Mil: attack*) charge *f*, attaque *f*.

(c) (*cost*) **the hotel ~ was very reasonable** le prix de l'hôtel était très raisonnable; **to make a ~ for sth** faire payer qch; **is there a ~?** faut-il payer?, y a-t-il quelque chose à payer?; **free of ~** gratuit; **at a ~ of ...** moyennant ...; **extra ~** supplément *m*; **~ for admission** droit *m* d'entrée; **~ for delivery** (frais *mpl* de) port *m*; **'no ~ for admission'** 'entrée libre'; *V* **reverse** *etc*.

(d) (*responsibility*) charge *f*, responsabilité *f*. **he took ~** (*gen*) il a assumé la responsabilité (*or* les fonctions *etc*); (*Mil*) il a pris le commandement; **who takes ~ when ...?** qui est-ce qui est responsable quand ...?; **to take ~ of** se charger de; **to be in ~ of sb** avoir la charge de qn; **to have ~ of sth** être responsable de qch; **the children were placed in their aunt's ~** les enfants ont été confiés aux soins de *or* à la garde de leur tante; **who is in ~?** qui est le responsable?; **the man in ~** le responsable.

(e) (*person or thing cared for*) personne *f* *or* chose *f* à charge; (*burden, responsibility*) charge *f*, fardeau *m* (*on* pour); (*Rel: priest's flock*) ouailles *fpl*; (*parish*) cure *f*. **the nurse took her ~s for a walk** l'infirmière a fait faire une promenade aux malades dont elle a la charge *or* à ses malades; **to be a ~ on** être à (la) charge de.

(f) (*instructions*) recommandation *f*, instruction *f*. **to have strict ~ to do** avoir reçu l'ordre formel de faire; (*Jur*) **the judge's ~ to the jury** les recommandations données aux jurés par le juge.

(g) *[firearm, battery etc]* charge *f*; *V* **depth**.

(h) (*Her*) meuble *m*.

2 *cpd*: (*Comm*) **charge account** compte *m*; (*Brit Ind*) **chargehand** chef *m* d'équipe.

3 *vt* **(a)** (*Jur*) inculper. **to ~ sb with sth** (*Jur*) inculper *or* accuser qn de qch; (*gen*) accuser qn de qch.

(b) (*Mil: attack*) charger.

(c) (*in payment*) *person* faire payer; *amount* prendre, demander (*for* pour). **to ~ a commission** prélever une commission *or* un pourcentage; **I ~d him £2 for this table** je lui ai fait payer cette table 2 livres; **how much do you ~ for mending shoes?** combien prenez-vous pour réparer des chaussures?; **to ~ sb too much for sth** compter *or* faire payer qch trop cher à qn.

(d) (*record as debt: also* **~ up**) mettre sur le compte, porter au compte *or* au débit (*to sb* de qn). **~ all these purchases (up) to my account** mettez tous ces achats sur mon compte.

(e) *firearm, battery* charger. (*fig*) **~d with emotion** empreint d'émotion.

(f) (*command etc*) **to ~ sb to do** ordonner *or* commander *or* enjoindre (*liter*) à qn de faire, sommer qn de faire; **to ~ sb with sth** confier qch à qn, charger qn de qch; **to ~ o.s. with sth** se charger de qch.

4 *vi* **(a)** (*) se précipiter, foncer*. **to ~ in/out** entrer/sortir en coup de vent; **to ~ up/down** grimper/descendre à toute vitesse; **to ~ through** foncer à travers*.

(b) (*Mil*) **to ~ (down) on the enemy** fondre *or* foncer* sur l'ennemi.

(c) *[battery]* se charger, être en charge.

charge up *vt sep* = **charge 3d.**

chargeable ['tʃɑːdʒəbl] *adj* **(a)** (*Jur*) *person* **~ with** passible de poursuites pour. **(b) ~ to** à mettre aux frais de, à porter au compte de.

charger ['tʃɑːdʒəʳ] *n* **(a)** *[battery, firearm]* chargeur *m*. **(b)** (*Mil: horse*) cheval *m* (de bataille).

charily ['tʃɛərɪlɪ] *adv* prudemment, avec prudence *or* circonspection.

chariot ['tʃærɪət] *n* char *m*.

charioteer [ˌtʃærɪə'tɪəʳ] *n* conducteur *m* de char, aurige *m*.

charisma [kæ'rɪzmə] *n* charisme *m*.

charismatic [ˌkærɪz'mætɪk] *adj* charismatique.

charitable ['tʃærɪtəbl] *adj person, thought* charitable, généreux; *deed* de charité, charitable. **~ institution** fondation *f* charitable.

charitably ['tʃærɪtəblɪ] *adv* charitablement.

charity ['tʃærɪtɪ] *n* **(a)** (*U*) (*Christian virtue*) charité *f*; (*kindness*) charité, amour *m* du prochain. **for ~'s sake, out of ~** par (pure) charité; (*Prov*) **~ begins at home** charité bien ordonnée commence par soi-même (*Prov*); (*Rel*) **sister of C~** sœur *f* de charité; *V* **cold, faith.**

(b) (*charitable action*) acte *m* de charité, action *f* charitable.

(c) (*U: alms*) charité *f*, aumône *f*. **to live on ~** vivre d'aumônes; **~ sale** vente *f* de charité *or* de bienfaisance; **to collect for ~** faire une collecte pour une œuvre (charitable); **the proceeds go to ~** les fonds recueillis sont versés à des œuvres.

(d) (*charitable society*) fondation *f* *or* institution *f* charitable, œuvre *f* de bienfaisance.

charlady ['tʃɑːleɪdɪ] *n* (*Brit*) femme *f* de ménage.

charlatan ['ʃɑːlətən] **1** *n* charlatan *m*. **2** *adj* charlatanesque.

Charlemagne ['ʃɑːləmeɪn] *n* Charlemagne *m*.

Charles [tʃɑːlz] *n* Charles *m*.

charleston ['tʃɑːlstən] *n* charleston *m*.

charley horse* ['tʃɑːlɪhɔːs] *n* (*US*) crampe *f*, spasme *m*.

Charlie ['tʃɑːlɪ] *n* Charlot *m*. (*Brit:*) **he must have looked a proper ~!** il a dû avoir l'air fin! *or* malin!*

charlotte ['ʃɑːlət] *n* (*Culin*) charlotte *f*. **apple ~** charlotte aux pommes.

charm [tʃɑːm] **1** *n* **(a)** (*attractiveness*) charme *m*, attrait *m*. **a lady's ~s** les charmes d'une dame; **to have a lot of ~** avoir beaucoup de charme; **to fall victim to the ~s of** se rendre aux charmes de.

(b) (*spell*) charme *m*, enchantement *m*, sortilège *m*. **to hold sb under a ~** tenir qn sous le charme; **like a ~*** à merveille.

(c) (*amulet*) charme *m*, fétiche *m*, amulette *f*; (*trinket*) breloque *f*.

2 *cpd*: **charm bracelet** bracelet *m* à breloques; **charm school** cours *m* de maintien.

3 *vt* (*attract, please*) charmer, enchanter; (*cast spell on*) enchanter, ensorceler; *snakes* charmer. **to lead a ~ed life** être béni des dieux; **to ~ sth out of sb** obtenir qch de qn par le charme *or* en lui faisant du charme.

charm away *vt sep* faire disparaître comme par enchantement *or* par magie. **to charm away sb's cares** dissiper les soucis de qn comme par enchantement *or* par magie.

charmer ['tʃɑːməʳ] *n* charmeur *m*, -euse *f*; *V* **snake.**

charming ['tʃɑːmɪŋ] *adj* charmant.

charmingly ['tʃɑːmɪŋlɪ] *adv* d'une façon charmante, avec (beaucoup de) charme. **a ~ simple dress** une robe d'une simplicité charmante.

charnel-house ['tʃɑːnlhaʊs] *n* ossuaire *m*, charnier *m*.

chart [tʃɑːt] **1** *n* **(a)** (*map*) carte *f* (marine).

(b) (*graphs etc*) graphique *m*, diagramme *m*, tableau *m*; (*Med*) courbe *f*. **temperature ~** (*sheet*) feuille *f* de température; (*line*) courbe *f* de température; **(pop) ~s** hit-parade *m*, palmarès *m*.

2 *vt* **(a)** (*draw on map*) *route, journey* porter sur la carte.

(b) (*on graph*) *sales, profits, results* faire le graphique *or* la courbe de. **this graph ~s the progress made last year** ce graphique montre les progrès accomplis l'an dernier.

charter ['tʃɑːtəʳ] **1** *n* **(a)** (*document*) charte *f*; *[society, organization]* statuts *mpl*.

(b) (*U*) *[boat, plane, coach, train etc]* affrètement *m*. **on ~** sous contrat d'affrètement.

2 *cpd*: **charter flight** (vol *m* en) charter *m*; **to take a charter flight to Rome** aller à Rome en charter; (*US*) **charter member** membre fondateur; **charter party** charte-partie *f*; **charter plane** charter *m*.

3 *vt* **(a)** accorder une charte à, accorder un privilège (par une charte) à.

(b) *plane etc* affréter.

chartered ['tʃɑːtəd] *adj* (*Brit, Can*) **~ accountant** expert-comptable *m*, comptable agréé (*Can*); **~ company** société privilégiée; **~ society** compagnie *f* à charte; **~ surveyor** expert immobilier.

charwoman ['tʃɑːˌwʊmən] *n* femme *f* de ménage.

chary ['tʃɛərɪ] *adj* **(a)** (*cautious*) prudent, circonspect, avisé.

(b) (*stingy*) économe, avare, peu prodigue (*of* de). **he is ~ of giving praise** il est avare de compliments.

chase[1] [tʃeɪs] **1** *n* **(a)** (*action*) chasse *f*, poursuite *f*. **to give ~ to** faire *or* donner la chasse à, poursuivre; **in ~ of** à la poursuite de; **the ~** (*Sport*) la chasse (à courre); (*huntsmen*) la chasse, les chasseurs *mpl*; *V* **paper, steeple, wild** *etc*.

(b) (*game*) gibier *m*; (*enemy hunted*) ennemi *m* (poursuivi).

2 *vt* chasser, poursuivre, faire *or* donner la chasse à. **he ~d**

him down the hill il l'a poursuivi jusqu'au bas de la colline; **go and ~ yourself!‡** va te faire voir!‡

3 *vi* (*) cavaler‡. **to ~ up/down/out** *etc* monter/descendre/sortir *etc* au grand galop; (*lit, fig*) **to ~ after sb** courir après qn.

chase away, chase off 1 *vi* (*) filer*, se trotter‡.

2 *vt sep person, animal* chasser, faire partir.

chase up *vt sep information* rechercher, aller à la recherche de. **to chase sb up for sth** rappeler à qn de donner qch; **to chase sth up** réclamer qch (*à quelqu'un qui l'a emprunté ou promis*); **I'll chase it up for you** je vais essayer d'activer les choses (pour vous l'avoir); **I'll chase him up** je vais le presser, je vais lui dire de se dépêcher.

chase[2] [tʃeɪs] *vt* (*Tech*) *diamond* enchâsser (*in* dans); *silver* ciseler; *metal* repousser; *screw* fileter.

chaser ['tʃeɪsəʳ] *n* **(a)** *[person, ship, plane]* chasseur *m*. **(b)** (*Tech*) graveur *m* sur métaux; *[screw]* peigne *m* (à fileter). **(c)** (*: *drink*) *verre pris pour en faire descendre un autre*.

chasm ['kæzəm] *n* (*Geol*) gouffre *m*, abîme *m*; (*fig*) (*breach of relations*) gouffre, abîme; (*gap*) vide *m*, lacune *f*.

chassis ['ʃæsɪ] *n* (*Aut*) châssis *m*; (*Rad*) platine *f*, châssis; (*Aviat*) train *m* d'atterrissage; (*US*‡: *body*) châssis‡.

chaste [tʃeɪst] *adj person* chaste, pur; *style* sobre, simple, pur.

chastely ['tʃeɪstlɪ] *adv* (*V* **chaste**) chastement; avec sobriété, simplement.

chasten ['tʃeɪsn] *vt* (*punish*) châtier, corriger; (*subdue*) assagir, calmer; *style* châtier, épurer, corriger.

chastened ['tʃeɪsnd] *adj person* assagi, calmé; *style* châtié.

chasteness ['tʃeɪstnɪs] *n* (*V* **chaste**) chasteté *f*, pureté *f*; sobriété *f*, simplicité *f*.

chastening ['tʃeɪsnɪŋ] *adj thought* qui fait réfléchir (à deux fois). **the accident had a very ~ effect on him** l'accident l'a fait réfléchir *or* l'a assagi.

chastise [tʃæs'taɪz] *vt* (*punish*) punir, châtier; (*beat*) battre, corriger.

chastisement ['tʃæstɪzmənt] *n* (*V* **chastise**) punition *f*, châtiment *m*; correction *f*.

chastity ['tʃæstɪtɪ] *n* chasteté *f*, pudeur *f*. **~ belt** ceinture *f* de chasteté.

chasuble ['tʃæzjʊbl] *n* chasuble *f*.

chat [tʃæt] **1** *n* causette *f*, brin *m* de conversation *or* de causette. **to have a ~** bavarder, causer, faire un brin de causette (*with, to* avec); **we had a long ~** nous avons parlé *or* bavardé longtemps; (*Rad/TV*) **~ show** causerie *f or* tête-à-tête *m or* entretien *m* (radiodiffusé(e)/télévisé(e)).

2 *vi* bavarder, causer (*with* avec).

chat up‡ *vt sep* (*Brit*) *girl* baratiner‡.

chattels ['tʃætlz] *npl* (*gen*) biens *mpl*, possessions *fpl*; (*Jur*) biens meubles. **with all his goods and ~** avec tout ce qu'il possède (*or* possédait *etc*).

chatter ['tʃætəʳ] **1** *vi* **(a)** *[person]* bavarder, causer; *[women]* papoter, jacasser; *[children, monkeys]* jacasser; *[birds]* jacasser, jaser.

(b) *[engines]* cogner; *[tools]* brouter. **his teeth were ~ing** il claquait des dents.

2 *n [person]* bavardage *m*, papotage *m*; *[birds, children, monkeys]* jacassement *m*; *[engines]* cognement *m*; *[tools]* broutement *m*; *[teeth]* claquement *m*.

3 *cpd*: **chatterbox** moulin *m* à paroles*, bavard(e) *m(f)*; **to be a chatterbox** avoir la langue bien pendue, être bavard comme une pie *or* une pipelette*.

chatty* ['tʃætɪ] *adj person* papoteur* (*f* -euse), bavard; *style* familier, qui reste au niveau du bavardage; *letter* plein de bavardages.

chauffeur ['ʃəʊfəʳ] *n* chauffeur *m* (de maître).

chauvinism ['ʃəʊvɪnɪzəm] *n* chauvinisme *m*.

chauvinist ['ʃəʊvɪnɪst] *n* chauvin(e) *m(f)*; *V* **male**.

chauvinistic [,ʃəʊvɪ'nɪstɪk] *adj* chauvin.

chaw [tʃɔː] (*dial*) = **chew**.

cheap [tʃiːp] **1** *adj* **(a)** (*inexpensive*) bon marché *inv*, peu cher (*f* peu chère); *tickets* à prix réduit; *fare* réduit; *money* déprécié. **on the ~** au rabais; **he furnished the flat on the ~** il a meublé l'appartement en faisant un minimum de dépenses; (*Comm*) **to come ~er** revenir *or* coûter moins cher; **it's ~ at the price** (*Comm*) c'est une occasion à ce prix-là; (*fig*) les choses auraient pu être pires; **a ~er coat** un manteau meilleur marché *or* moins cher; **the ~est coat** le manteau le meilleur marché *or* le moins cher; (*Printing*) **~ edition** édition *f* populaire *or* bon marché; *V* **dirt**.

(b) (*pej: of poor quality*) de mauvaise qualité, de pacotille. **this stuff is ~ and nasty** c'est de la camelote*.

(c) (*fig pej: worthless*) *success, joke* facile. **his behaviour was very ~** il s'est très mal conduit; *[woman]* **to make o.s. ~** être facile; **to feel ~** avoir honte (*about* de).

2 *adv*: **to buy sth ~** (*not expensive*) acheter qch bon marché; (*cut-price*) acheter qch au rabais.

cheapen ['tʃiːpən] **1** *vt* baisser le prix de; (*fig*) déprécier. **to ~ o.s.** *[woman]* être facile; (*gen*) se déconsidérer. **2** *vi* baisser, devenir moins cher.

cheaply ['tʃiːplɪ] *adv* à bon marché, à bas prix, pour pas cher. (*fig*) **to get off ~*** s'en tirer à bon compte.

cheapness ['tʃiːpnɪs] *n* (*lit*) bas prix *m*; (*fig*) médiocrité *f*; *[style]* faux éclat *m*.

cheapskate‡ ['tʃiːpskeɪt] *n* (*US*) grigou* *m*, radin *mf*, avare *mf*.

cheat [tʃiːt] **1** *vt* (*deceive*) tromper, duper; (*defraud*) frauder; (*swindle*) escroquer; (*fig*) *time etc* tromper. **to ~ sb at cards** tromper qn aux cartes; **to ~ sb out of sth** escroquer qch à qn; **to ~ sb into doing sth** faire faire qch à qn en le trompant.

2 *vi* (*at cards, games*) tricher (*at* à); (*defraud*) frauder.

3 *n* **(a)** (*person*) (*at cards, games*) tricheur *m*, -euse *f*; (*deceiver*) fourbe *mf*; (*crook*) escroc *m*.

(b) (*trick*) (*at cards, games*) tricherie *f*; (*deceitful act*) tromperie *f*; (*fraud*) fraude *f*; (*swindle*) escroquerie *f*.

cheating ['tʃiːtɪŋ] **1** *n* = **cheat 3b**. **2** *adj* (*V* **cheat 3a**) tricheur; fourbe; d'escroc.

check[1] [tʃek] *n* (*US*) = **cheque**.

check[2] [tʃek] **1** *n* **(a)** (*setback*) *[movement]* arrêt *m* brusque; *[plans etc]* empêchement *m*; (*Mil*) échec *m*, revers *m*; (*pause, restraint*) arrêt momentané, pause *f*, interruption *f*. **to hold or keep in ~** tenir en échec; **to put a ~ on** mettre un frein à; **to act as a ~ upon** freiner.

(b) (*examination*) *[papers, passport, ticket]* contrôle *m*; *[luggage]* vérification *f*; (*at factory door*) pointage *m*; (*mark*) marque *f* de contrôle. **to make a ~ on** contrôler, vérifier, pointer; **to keep a ~ on** surveiller.

(c) (*Chess*) échec *m*. **in ~** en échec; (*excl*) **~!** échec au roi!

(d) (*US: receipt*) *[left luggage]* bulletin *m* de consigne; (*Theat*) contremarque *f*; (*Brit, US*) *[restaurant]* addition *f* (*dans un restaurant*).

2 *cpd*: (*US*) **checkbook** carnet *m* de chèques, chéquier *m*; (*Aviat*) **check-in** enregistrement *m*; (*Aviat*) **your check-in time is half-an-hour before departure** présentez-vous à l'enregistrement des bagages une demi-heure avant le départ; (*US*) **checking account** compte courant; (*Aviat*) **checklist** check-list *f*, liste *f* de contrôle; **checkmate** (*n*) (*Chess*) échec et mat *m*; (*fig*) échec total, fiasco *m*; (*vt*) (*Chess*) faire échec et mat à; (*fig*) *person* mettre en déconfiture*; *plans etc* déjouer; (*Comm*) **check-out** caisse *f* (*dans un libre-service*); (*Aut, Mil, Sport*) **checkpoint** contrôle *m*; **checkroom** (*US: cloakroom*) vestiaire *m*; **checkup** (*gen*) contrôle *m*, vérification *f*; (*Med*) examen *m* médical, bilan *m* de santé, check-up *m*; (*Med*) **to go for** *or* **have a checkup** se faire faire un bilan (de santé).

3 *vt* **(a)** (*examine, verify*) *accounts, figures, statement, quality etc* vérifier; *tickets, passports* contrôler; (*mark off*) pointer, faire le pointage de; (*tick off*) cocher. **to ~ a copy against the original** vérifier une copie sur *or* en se référant à l'original, collationner une copie avec l'original.

(b) (*stop*) *enemy* arrêter; *advance* enrayer; (*restrain*) refréner, contenir, maîtriser. **he ~ed his anger** il a maîtrisé sa colère.

(c) (*rebuke*) réprimander.

(d) (*Chess*) faire échec à.

(e) (*US*) *coats (in cloakroom)* mettre au vestiaire; *(Rail) luggage* (*register*) faire enregistrer; (*left luggage*) mettre à la consigne.

4 *vi* s'arrêter (*momentanément*).

check in 1 *vi* (*in hotel*) (*arrive*) arriver; (*register*) remplir une fiche (d'hôtel); (*Aviat*) se présenter à l'enregistrement.

2 *vt sep* faire remplir une fiche (d'hôtel) à; (*Aviat*) enregistrer.

3 check-in *n, adj V* **check[2] 2**.

check off *vt sep* pointer, cocher.

check on *vt fus* vérifier.

check out 1 *vi* **(a)** (*from hotel*) régler sa note.

(b) (‡*euph: die*) passer l'arme à gauche* (*euph*).

2 *vt sep luggage* retirer; *person* contrôler la sortie de; *hotel guest* faire payer sa note à.

3 check-out *n V* **check[2] 2**.

check over *vt sep* examiner, vérifier.

check up 1 *vi* se renseigner, vérifier. **to check up on sth** vérifier qch; **to check up on sb** se renseigner sur qn.

2 checkup *n V* **check[2] 2**.

check[3] [tʃek] **1** *n* (*gen pl*) **~s** (*pattern*) (étoffe *f* à) carreaux *mpl*, damier *m*; (*cloth*) tissu *m* à carreaux; **broken ~** pied-de-poule *m*. **2** *cpd* = **checked**.

checked [tʃekt] *adj tablecloth, suit, pattern* à carreaux.

checker ['tʃekəʳ] *n* (*V* **check[2] 3a**) vérificateur *m*, -trice *f*; contrôleur *m*, -euse *f*; (*US: in supermarket*) caissier *m*, -ière *f*; (*US: in cloakroom*) préposé(e) *m(f)* au vestiaire.

checkerboard ['tʃekəbɔːd] *n* (*US*) (*Chess*) échiquier *m*; (*Checkers*) damier *m*. **~ pattern** motif *m* à damiers.

checkered ['tʃekəd] *adj* (*US*) = **chequered**.

checkers ['tʃekəz] *npl* (*US*) jeu *m* de dames.

cheddar ['tʃedəʳ] *n* (fromage *m* de) cheddar *m*.

cheek [tʃiːk] **1** *n* **(a)** (*Anat*) joue *f*. **~ by jowl** côte à côte; **~ by jowl with** tout près de; **to dance ~ to ~** danser joue contre joue; **~bone** pommette *f*; *V* **tongue, turn**.

(b) (*: *impudence*) toupet* *m*, culot* *m*. **to have the ~ to do** avoir le toupet* *or* le culot* de faire; **what (a) ~!, of all the ~!** quel culot!*, quel toupet!*

2 *vt* (*Brit**: *also* **~ up**) *person* être insolent avec, narguer.

cheekily ['tʃiːkɪlɪ] *adv* effrontément, avec insolence.

cheekiness ['tʃiːkɪnɪs] *n* effronterie *f*, toupet* *m*, culot* *m*.

cheeky ['tʃiːkɪ] *adj child* effronté, insolent, culotté*; *remark* impertinent. **~ child** petit(e) effronté(e) *m(f)*; **you ~ monkey!***, **you ~ thing!*** quel toupet!*

cheep [tʃiːp] **1** *n [bird]* piaulement *m*; *[mouse]* couinement *m*. **2** *vi [bird]* piauler; *[mouse]* couiner. **3** *vt [person]* couiner*.

cheer [tʃɪəʳ] **1** *n* **(a) ~s** acclamations *fpl*, applaudissements *mpl*, hourras *mpl*, bravos *mpl*; **to give three ~s for** acclamer; **three ~s for ...!** un ban pour ...!, hourra pour ...!; **three ~s!** hourra!; **the children gave a loud ~** les enfants ont poussé des acclamations; (*esp Brit: when drinking*) **~s!*** à la vôtre!*, à la bonne vôtre!*

(b) (†: *cheerfulness*) gaieté *f*, joie *f*. **words of ~** paroles *fpl* d'encouragement; **be of good ~!** prenez courage!

(c) (†: *food etc*) chère *f*. **good ~** bonne chère.

2 *cpd*: (*Sport*) **cheer leader** meneur *m* (qui rythme les cris des supporters).

3 *vt* **(a)** (*also* ~ **up**) (*gladden*) égayer, dérider, réjouir; (*comfort*) consoler, réconforter, donner du courage à.
(b) (*applaud*) acclamer, applaudir.
4 *vi* applaudir, pousser des vivats *or* des hourras.
cheer on *vt sep person, team* encourager (*par des cris, des applaudissements*).
cheer up 1 *vi* (*be gladdened*) s'égayer, se dérider; (*be comforted*) prendre courage, prendre espoir. **cheer up!** courage!
2 *vt sep* = **cheer 3a.**
cheerful [ˈtʃɪəfʊl] *adj person, smile, conversation* joyeux, gai, enjoué, plein d'entrain; *place, appearance, colour* gai, riant; *prospect* attrayant; *news* réconfortant, réjouissant, qui réjouit le cœur. (*iro*) **that's ~!** c'est réjouissant! (*iro*).
cheerfully [ˈtʃɪəfʊlɪ] *adv* gaiement, joyeusement, avec entrain.
cheerfulness [ˈtʃɪəfʊlnɪs] *n [person]* bonne humeur *f*, gaieté *f*, entrain *m*; *[smile, conversation]* gaieté; *[place]* gaieté, aspect riant *or* réjouissant.
cheerily [ˈtʃɪərɪlɪ] *adv* gaiement, joyeusement, avec entrain.
cheering [ˈtʃɪərɪŋ] **1** *n(U)* applaudissements *mpl*, acclamations *fpl*, hourras *mpl*. **2** *adj news, sight* réconfortant, réjouissant, qui remonte le moral.
cheerio* [ˈtʃɪərɪˈəʊ] *excl* (*esp Brit*) **(a)** (*goodbye*) au revoir!, salut!* **(b)** (*your health*) à la vôtre!*
cheerless [ˈtʃɪəlɪs] *adj person, thing* morne, sombre, triste.
cheery [ˈtʃɪərɪ] *adj* gai, joyeux.
cheese [tʃiːz] **1** *n* fromage *m*. **Dutch ~** fromage de Hollande; (*for photograph*) **'say ~'** 'un petit sourire'; *V* **cottage, cream.**
2 *vi* (*Brit*) **to be ~d (off)‡** en avoir marre*; **to be ~d off with sth‡** en avoir marre de qch*.
3 *vt* (*US*) **~ it!‡** (*look out*) vingt-deux!‡; (*run away*) tire-toi!‡
4 *cpd sandwich* au fromage. **cheese board** plateau *m* à fromage(s); **cheeseburger** ≃ croque-monsieur *m* (*à la viande hachée*); (*U*) **cheesecake** (*Culin*) flan *m* au fromage blanc; (*: *fig*) (photo *f* de) pin-up *f*; **cheesecloth** (*for cheese*) étamine *f*, mousseline *f* à fromage; (*for clothes*) toile *f* à beurre; **cheese dip** (*genre de*) fondue *f*; **cheese dish** = **cheese board**; **cheeseparing** (*n*) économie(s) *f(pl)* de bouts de chandelles; (*adj*) *person* pingre, qui fait des économies de bouts de chandelles; *attitude, action* (de) rapiat*, pingre.
cheesy [ˈtʃiːzɪ] *n* **(a)** (*lit*) qui a un goût de fromage, qui sent le fromage. **(b)** (*US‡: pej*) moche*.
cheetah [ˈtʃiːtə] *n* guépard *m*.
chef [ʃef] *n* chef *m* (de cuisine).
cheiromancer [ˈkaɪərəmænsəʳ] *n* = **chiromancer.**
cheiromancy [ˈkaɪərəmænsɪ] *n* = **chiromancy.**
chemical [ˈkemɪkəl] **1** *adj* chimique. **~ agent** agent *m* chimique; **~ engineer** ingénieur *m* chimiste; **~ warfare** guerre *f* chimique. **2** *n* (*gen pl*) produit *m* chimique.
chemically [ˈkemɪkəlɪ] *adv* chimiquement.
chemise [ʃəˈmiːz] *n* (††: *undergarment*) chemise *f* (*de femme*); (*dress*) robe-chemisier *f*.
chemist [ˈkemɪst] *n* **(a)** (*researcher etc*) chimiste *mf*. **(b)** (*Brit: pharmacist*) pharmacien(ne) *m(f)*. **~'s shop** pharmacie *f*.
chemistry [ˈkemɪstrɪ] **1** *n* chimie *f*. (*fig*) **they work so well together because the ~ is right** ils travaillent très bien ensemble parce qu'ils ont des atomes crochus*. **2** *cpd*: **chemistry set** panoplie *f* de chimiste.
chenille [ʃəˈniːl] *n* (*Tex*) chenille *f*.
cheque, (*US*) **check** [tʃek] *n* chèque *m*. **~ for £10** chèque de 10 livres; **bad** *or* **dud ~** chèque sans provision *or* en bois*; **~ book** carnet *m* de chèques, chéquier *m*; **~ card** carte *f* d'identité bancaire; *V* **traveller** *etc*.
chequered, (*US*) **checkered** [ˈtʃekəd] *adj* (*lit*) à carreaux, à damier; (*fig*) varié. **he had a ~ career** sa carrière a connu des hauts et des bas.
cherish [ˈtʃerɪʃ] *vt person* chérir, aimer; *feelings, opinion* entretenir; *hope, illusions* nourrir, caresser; *memory* chérir. **one of his ~ed dreams** l'un de ses rêves les plus chers.
cheroot [ʃəˈruːt] *n* petit cigare (*à bouts coupés*), cigarillo *m*.
cherry [ˈtʃerɪ] **1** *n* (*fruit*) cerise *f*; (*also* **~ tree**) cerisier *m*. **wild ~** (*fruit*) merise *f*; (*tree*) merisier *m*.
2 *cpd* (*colour*) (rouge) cerise *inv*; (*liter*) *lips* vermeil; (*Culin*) *pie, tart* aux cerises. **cherry brandy** cherry-brandy *m*; **cherry orchard** cerisaie *f*; **cherry-red** (rouge) cerise *inv*.
cherub [ˈtʃerəb] *n* **(a)** *pl* **~s** chérubin *m*, petit amour, petit ange. **(b)** (*Rel*) *pl* **~im** chérubin *m*.
cherubic [tʃeˈruːbɪk] *adj face* de chérubin; *child, smile* angélique.
chervil [ˈtʃɜːvɪl] *n* cerfeuil *m*.
chess [tʃes] **1** *n* échecs *mpl*. **2** *cpd*: **chessboard** échiquier *m*; **chessman** pièce *f* (de jeu d'échecs); **chessplayer** joueur *m*, -euse *f* d'échecs.
chest[1] [tʃest] *n* (*box*) coffre *m*, caisse *f*; (*for tea*) caisse *f*. **~ of drawers** commode *f*; *V* **medicine, tea, tool** *etc*.
chest[2] [tʃest] **1** *n* (*Anat*) poitrine *f*; (*Med*) cage *f* thoracique. **to get something off one's ~*** déballer* ce qu'on a sur le cœur. **2** *cpd*: **chest cold** rhume *m* de poitrine; **chest specialist** spécialiste *mf* des voies respiratoires.
chesterfield [ˈtʃestəfiːld] *n* (*Can*) sofa *m*; (*Brit*) canapé *m*, sofa *m*.
chestnut [ˈtʃesnʌt] **1** *n* **(a)** châtaigne *f*; (*Culin*) châtaigne, marron *m*. (*fig*) **to pull sb's ~s out of the fire** tirer les marrons du feu pour qn; *V* **horse, Spanish, sweet.**
(b) (*also* **~ tree**) châtaignier *m*, marronnier *m*.
(c) (*horse*) alezan *m*.
(d) (**pej: old story*) vieille histoire rabâchée, vieille blague* usée.
2 *adj*: **~ hair** cheveux châtains; **~ horse** (cheval *m*) alezan *m*.
chesty [ˈtʃestɪ] *adj* (*Brit*) *person* fragile de la poitrine; *cough* de poitrine.

cheval glass [ʃəˈvælglɑːs] *n* psyché *f* (*glace*).
chevron [ˈʃevrən] *n* chevron *m*.
chew [tʃuː] **1** *vt* mâcher, mastiquer. **to ~ tobacco** chiquer; (*lit, fig*) **to ~ the cud** ruminer; **to ~ the fat‡** *or* **the rag‡** tailler une bavette*; **~ing gum** chewing-gum *m*. **2** *n* mâchement *m*, mastication *f*; *[tobacco]* chique *f*.
chew on *vt fus*, **chew over** *vt sep* (*fig*) *facts, problem* ruminer, ressasser, remâcher.
chew up *vt sep* mâchonner, mâchouiller*.
chiaroscuro [kɪˌɑːrəsˈkʊərəʊ] *n* clair-obscur *m*.
chic [ʃiːk] **1** *adj* chic *inv*, élégant. **2** *n* chic *m*, élégance *f*.
chicanery [ʃɪˈkeɪnərɪ] *n* (*legal trickery*) chicane *f*; (*false argument*) chicane, chicanerie *f*.
chick [tʃɪk] **1** *n* **(a)** (*chicken*) poussin *m*; (*nestling*) oisillon *m* (*qui vient d'éclore*); *V* **day.**
(b) (‡: *child*) poulet* *m*, coco* *m*. **come here ~!** viens ici mon coco! *or* mon petit poulet!
(c) (*US*‡: *girl*) pépée‡ *f*, poulette‡ *f*.
2 *cpd*: **chick pea** pois *m* chiche; **chickweed** mouron blanc *or* des oiseaux.
chicken [ˈtʃɪkɪn] **1** *n* **(a)** poulet(te) *m(f)*; (*very young*) poussin *m*; (*Culin*) poulet. (*pej*) **she's no ~!*** elle n'est plus toute jeune *or* de la première jeunesse; *V* **count[1]**.
(b) (**pej: coward*) trouillard(e)‡ *m(f)*, froussard(e)‡ *m(f)*.
2 *cpd*: **chicken farmer** éleveur *m* avicole *or* de volailles, volailleur *m*; **chicken farming** élevage *m* avicole *or* de volailles; **chicken feed** (*lit*) nourriture *f* pour volaille; (**pej: insignificant sum*) somme *f* dérisoire, bagatelle *f*; **chicken-hearted** froussard‡, trouillard‡, dégonflé*; **chicken liver** foie(s) *m(pl)* de volaille; **chickenpox** varicelle *f*; **chicken run** poulailler *m*; **chicken wire** grillage *m*.
chicken out‡ *vi* se dégonfler*.
chicory [ˈtʃɪkərɪ] *n [coffee]* chicorée *f*; *[salads]* endive *f*.
chide [tʃaɪd] *pret* **chid** [tʃɪd] *or* **chided,** *ptp* **chidden** [ˈtʃɪdn] *or* **chided** *vt* gronder, réprimander.
chief [tʃiːf] **1** *n* **(a)** (*gen, Her*) chef *m*. (*principally*) **in ~** principalement, surtout; (*Mil*) **~ of staff** chef d'état-major; **~ of state** chef d'État; *V* **commander, lord.**
(b) (*: *boss*) patron *m*. **yes, ~!** oui, chef! *or* patron!
2 *adj* principal, en chef. **~ assistant** premier assistant; (*Police*) **C~ Constable** ≃ chef *m* de la police départementale *etc*, Préfet *m* de police; (*Naut*) **~ engineer** ingénieur *m* en chef; **~ inspector** inspecteur principal *or* en chef; (*Naut*) **~ petty officer** ≃ premier maître, maître principal; **~ priest** archiprêtre *m*; **~ rabbi** grand rabbin; **~ town** chef-lieu *m*; *V* **justice.**
chiefly [ˈtʃiːflɪ] *adv* principalement, surtout.
chieftain [ˈtʃiːftən] *n* chef *m* (*de clan, de tribu*).
chiffon [ˈʃɪfɒn] **1** *n* mousseline *f* de soie. **2** *adj dress* en mousseline (de soie).
chignon [ˈʃiːnjɔ̃ːŋ] *n* chignon *m*.
chilblain [ˈtʃɪlbleɪn] *n* engelure *f*.
child [tʃaɪld] *pl* **children 1** *n* **(a)** enfant *mf*. **when still a ~, he ...** tout enfant, il ...; **don't be such a ~** ne fais pas l'enfant; **she has 3 children** elle a 3 enfants; **to be with ~** être enceinte.
(b) (*fig*) produit *m*, fruit *m*. **the ~ of his imagination** le produit *or* le fruit de son imagination; *V* **brain.**
2 *cpd labour* des enfants; *psychology, psychiatry* de l'enfant, infantile; *psychologist, psychiatrist* pour enfants. (*U*) **childbearing** maternité *f*; **constant childbearing** accouchements répétés, grossesses répétées; **of childbearing age** en âge d'avoir des enfants; **in childbed** en couches; **childbirth** accouchement *m*; **in childbirth** en couches; **child care** protection *f* infantile *or* de l'enfance, assistance *f* à l'enfance; **child guidance** hygiène sociale de l'enfance; **child guidance centre** *or* **clinic** centre *m* psycho-pédagogique; **childlike** d'enfant, innocent, pur; (*Brit*) **child minder** gardienne *f* d'enfants; **child prodigy** enfant *mf* prodige; (*fig*) **it's child's play** c'est enfantin, c'est un jeu d'enfant (*to sb* pour qn); **child welfare** protection *f* de l'enfance; **Child Welfare Centre** centre *m* *or* service *m* de protection de l'enfance.
childhood [ˈtʃaɪldhʊd] *n* enfance *f*. **in his ~ he ...** tout enfant il ...; *V* **second.**
childish [ˈtʃaɪldɪʃ] *adj* **(a)** (*slightly pej*) *behaviour* puéril (*pej*), d'enfant, enfantin. **~ reaction** réaction puérile; **don't be so ~** ne fais pas l'enfant; **he was very ~ about it** il s'est montré très puéril à ce sujet.
(b) *ailment, disease* infantile. **~ games** jeux *mpl* d'enfants.
childishly [ˈtʃaɪldɪʃlɪ] *adj think, say* comme un enfant, puérilement; *behave* en enfant, comme un enfant.
childishness [ˈtʃaɪldɪʃnɪs] *n* (*slightly pej*) puérilité *f*, enfantillage *m*.
childless [ˈtʃaɪldlɪs] *adj* sans enfants.
children [ˈtʃɪldrən] *npl of* **child.**
Chile [ˈtʃɪlɪ] *n* Chili *m*.
Chilean [ˈtʃɪlɪən] **1** *adj* chilien. **2** *n* Chilien(ne) *m(f)*.
chili [ˈtʃɪlɪ] *n* piment *m* (rouge). **~ con carne** bœuf haché aux piments et haricots rouges.
chill [tʃɪl] **1** *n* **(a)** fraîcheur *f*, froid *m*. **there's a ~ in the air** il fait assez frais *or* un peu froid; **to take the ~ off** *wine* chambrer; *water* dégourdir; *room* réchauffer un peu.
(b) (*fig*) froid *m*, froideur *f*. **to cast a ~ over** jeter un froid sur; **there was a certain ~ in the way she looked at me** il y avait une certaine froideur dans sa façon de me regarder; **he felt a certain ~ as he remembered ...** il a eu un *or* le frisson en se rappelant ...
(c) (*Med*) refroidissement *m*, coup *m* de froid. **to catch a ~** prendre froid, prendre un refroidissement.
2 *adj* frais, froid; (*fig*) froid, glacial, glacé.
3 *vt* **(a)** (*lit*) *person* faire frissonner, donner froid à; *wine*,

melon (faire) rafraîchir; *champagne* frapper; *meat* frigorifier, réfrigérer; *dessert* mettre au frais; *plant* geler; (*Tech*) tremper en coquille. **to be ~ed to the bone** *or* **marrow** être transi jusqu'aux os *or* jusqu'à la moelle.

(b) (*fig*) *enthusiasm* refroidir. **to ~ sb's blood** glacer le sang de qn; *V* **spine.**

4 *vi [wine]* rafraîchir.

chill(i)ness ['tʃɪl(ɪ)nɪs] *n* (*cold*) froid *m*; (*coolness*) fraîcheur *f*; (*fig*) froideur *f*.

chilling ['tʃɪlɪŋ] *adj wind* frais, froid; *look* froid, glacial, glacé; *thought* qui donne le frisson.

chilly ['tʃɪlɪ] *adj person* frileux; *weather, wind* froid, très frais (*f* fraîche); *manner, look, smile* glacé, froid. *[person]* **to feel ~** avoir froid; **it's rather ~** il fait frais *or* frisquet*.

chime [tʃaɪm] **1** *n* carillon *m*. **to ring the ~s** carillonner; **a ~ of bells** un carillon.

2 *vi [bells, voices]* carillonner.

3 *vt bells, hours* sonner.

chime in *vi* (*fig*) *[person]* faire chorus. **he chimed in with another complaint** il a fait chorus pour se plaindre à son tour.

chimera [kaɪ'mɪərə] *n* chimère *f*.

chimerical [kaɪ'merɪkəl] *adj* chimérique.

chimney ['tʃɪmnɪ] **1** *n* (*Archit, Geog, Naut, Sport*) cheminée *f*; *[lamp]* verre *m*.

2 *cpd*: **chimney breast** manteau *m* de (la) cheminée; **chimney corner** coin *m* du feu; **chimney pot** tuyau *m* de cheminée; **chimney-pot hat*** tuyau *m* de poêle*; **chimney stack** (*group of chimneys*) souche *f* de cheminée; *[factory]* tuyau *m* de cheminée (d'usine); **chimney sweep** ramoneur *m*.

chimpanzee [ˌtʃɪmpæn'ziː] *n* chimpanzé *m*.

chin [tʃɪn] **1** *n* menton *m*. **to keep one's ~ up*** tenir bon, tenir le coup*; **(keep your) ~ up!*** courage!, du cran!*; *V* **double. 2** *cpd*: **chinwag‡** causerie *f*; **to have a chinwag‡** tailler une bavette*, papoter.

China ['tʃaɪnə] **1** *n* Chine *f*. **2** *cpd*: (*pej in US*) **Chinaman** Chinois *m*, Chin(e)toque‡ *m* (*pej*); **China tea** thé *m* de Chine; **Chinatown** le quartier chinois (*d'une ville*).

china ['tʃaɪnə] **1** *n* (*U: material, dishes*) porcelaine *f*. **a piece of ~** une porcelaine; *V* **bone. 2** *cpd cup, figure* de *or* en porcelaine. **china clay** kaolin *m*; **china industry** industrie *f* de la porcelaine; (*U*) **chinaware** (objets *mpl* de) porcelaine *f*.

chinchilla [tʃɪn'tʃɪlə] *n* chinchilla *m*. **~ coat** manteau *m* de chinchilla.

Chinese ['tʃaɪ'niːz] **1** *adj* chinois. **~ lantern** lanterne vénitienne; **~ puzzle** casse-tête *m inv* chinois; **~ white** blanc *m* de zinc.

2 *n* **(a)** (*pl inv*) Chinois(e) *m(f)*. **(b)** (*Ling*) chinois *m*.

chink[1] [tʃɪŋk] *n* (*slit, hole*) *[wall]* fente *f*, fissure *f*; *[door]* entrebâillement *m*. (*fig*) **the ~ in the armour** le défaut de la cuirasse, le point faible *or* sensible.

chink[2] [tʃɪŋk] **1** *n* (*sound*) tintement *m* (*de verres, de pièces de monnaie*). **2** *vt* faire tinter. **3** *vi* tinter.

Chink‡ [tʃɪŋk] *n* (*pej*) Chin(e)toque‡ *mf* (*pej*).

chintz [tʃɪnts] *n* (*Tex*) chintz *m*. **~ curtains** rideaux *mpl* de chintz.

chip [tʃɪp] **1** *n* **(a)** (*gen*) fragment *m*; *[wood]* copeau *m*, éclat *m*; *[glass, stone]* éclat; (*Electronics*) microplaquette *f*. **he's a ~ off the old block*** c'est bien le fils de son père; **to have a ~ on one's shoulder** être aigri; **to have a ~ on one's shoulder because ...** n'avoir jamais digéré le fait que*...; (*Naut sl*) **C~s** charpentier *m*; *V* **polystyrene.**

(b) (*Culin*) **~s** (*Brit*) (pommes *fpl* de terre) frites *fpl*; (*US*) (pommes) chips *fpl*.

(c) (*break*) *[stone, crockery, glass]* ébréchure *f*; *[furniture]* écornure *f*. **this cup has a ~** cette tasse est ébréchée.

(d) (*Poker etc*) jeton *m*, fiche *f*. (*fig*) **to pass** *or* **hand in** *or* **have one's ~s*** passer l'arme à gauche*; **he's had his ~s‡** il est cuit* *or* fichu*; **when the ~s are down*** dans les moments cruciaux; (*US*) **in the ~s‡** plein aux as‡.

(e) (*Golf*) (coup *m* d')approche *f*.

2 *cpd*: **chipboard** (*US*) carton *m*; (*Brit*) bois aggloméré, panneau *m* de copeaux.

3 *vt* **(a)** (*damage*) *cup, plate* ébrécher; *furniture* écorner; *varnish, paint* écailler; *stone* écorner, enlever un éclat de. **to ~ wood** faire des copeaux; **the chicken ~ped the shell open** le poussin a cassé sa coquille.

(b) (*Brit*) *vegetables* couper en lamelles. **~ped potatoes** (pommes *fpl* de terre) frites *fpl*.

(c) (*cut deliberately*) tailler.

(d) (*Golf*) **to ~ the ball** jouer un coup (court) d'approche (du green).

4 *vi* (*V* 3) s'ébrécher; s'écorner; s'écailler.

chip at *vt fus* **(a)** *stone etc* enlever des éclats de. **(b)** (*: *make fun of*) se ficher de*.

chip away 1 *vi [paint etc]* s'écailler.

2 *vt sep paint etc* enlever *or* décaper petit à petit (*au couteau etc*).

chip in *vi* **(a)** (*: *interrupt*) dire son mot, mettre son grain de sel*.

(b) (*: *contribute*) contribuer, souscrire (*à une collecte etc*). **he chipped in with 10 francs** il y est allé de (ses) 10 F*.

chip off = **chip away.**

chipmunk ['tʃɪpmʌŋk] *n* tamia *m*, suisse *m* (*Can*).

chipolata [tʃɪpə'lɑːtə] *n* (*Brit*) chipolata *f*.

chippings ['tʃɪpɪŋz] *npl* gravillons *mpl*. **'loose ~'** 'attention gravillons'.

chiromancer ['kaɪərəmænsə[r]] *n* chiromancien(ne) *m(f)*.

chiromancy ['kaɪərəmænsɪ] *n* chiromancie *f*.

chiropodist [kɪ'rɒpədɪst] *n* pédicure *mf*.

chiropody [kɪ'rɒpədɪ] *n* (*science*) podologie *f*; (*treatment*) soins *mpl* du pied, traitement *m* des maladies des pieds.

chiropractic ['kaɪərəpræktɪk] *n* (*U*) chiropraxie *f*.

chiropractor ['kaɪərəpræktə[r]] *n* chiropracteur *m*.

chirp [tʃɜːp] **1** *vi* **(a)** *[birds]* pépier, gazouiller; *[crickets]* chanter, striduler (*liter*). **(b)** (*: *slightly pej*) *[person]* pépier, couiner* (*pej*). **2** *n [birds]* pépiement *m*, gazouillis *m*; *[crickets]* chant *m*, stridulation *f*; *[person]* murmure *m*. **not a ~ from you!‡** je ne veux pas t'entendre!, je ne veux pas entendre un seul murmure!

chirpy* ['tʃɜːpɪ] *adj person* gai, de bonne humeur; *voice, mood* gai.

chirrup ['tʃɪrəp] = **chirp.**

chisel ['tʃɪzl] **1** *n* (*Tech*) ciseau *m*; (*for engraving*) burin *m*; (*blunt ~*) matoir *m*; (*cold ~*) ciseau à froid, burin; (*hollow ~*) gouge *f*; (*mortise ~*) bédane *m*; (*roughing-out ~*) ébauchoir *m*.

2 *vt* **(a)** ciseler; (*Engraving*) buriner. **~led features** traits burinés; **finely ~led features** traits finement ciselés.

(b) (‡: *swindle*) *thing* resquiller; *person* rouler*, posséder‡. **to ~ sb out of sth** carotter* qch à qn.

chiseller‡ ['tʃɪzlə[r]] *n* escroc *m*, filou *m*.

chit[1] [tʃɪt] *n*: **she's a mere ~ of a girl** ce n'est qu'une gosse* *or* une gamine* *or* une mioche*.

chit[2] [tʃɪt] *n* note *f*, petit billet, mot* *m*.

chitchat ['tʃɪttʃæt] *n* bavardage *m*, papotage *m*.

chitterlings ['tʃɪtəlɪŋz] *npl* tripes *fpl* (de porc).

chitty ['tʃɪtɪ] *n* = **chit**[2].

chivalresque [ʃɪvəl'resk] *adj*, **chivalric** [ʃɪ'vælrɪk] *adj* chevaleresque.

chivalrous ['ʃɪvəlrəs] *adj* (*courteous*) chevaleresque; (*gallant*) galant.

chivalrously ['ʃɪvəlrəslɪ] *adv* (*V* **chivalrous**) de façon chevaleresque, galamment.

chivalry ['ʃɪvəlrɪ] *n* **(a)** chevalerie *f*. **the rules/the age of ~** les règles *fpl*/l'âge *m* de la chevalerie. **(b)** (*quality*) qualités *fpl* chevaleresques. **(c)** (*collective: Hist: knights*) chevalerie *f*.

chive [tʃaɪv] *n* (*gen pl*) ciboulette *f*, civette *f*.

chivvy* ['tʃɪvɪ] *vt* (*Brit*) **(a)** (*also* **~ along**) *person, animal* chasser, pourchasser. **(b)** (*pester*) ne pas laisser la paix à. **she chivvied him into writing the letter** elle l'a harcelé jusqu'à ce qu'il écrive la lettre.

chivvy about* *vt sep person* harceler, tarabuster.

chivvy up* *vt sep person* faire activer.

chloral ['klɔːrəl] *n* chloral *m*.

chlorate ['klɔːreɪt] *n* chlorate *m*.

chloric ['klɔːrɪk] *adj* chlorique. **~ acid** acide *m* chlorique.

chloride ['klɔːraɪd] *n* chlorure *m*. **~ of lime** chlorure de chaux.

chlorinate ['klɒrɪneɪt] *vt water* javelliser; (*Chem*) chlorurer.

chlorination [klɒrɪ'neɪʃən] *n [water]* javellisation *f*.

chlorine ['klɔːriːn] *n* chlore *m*.

chloroform ['klɒrəfɔːm] **1** *n* chloroforme *m*. **2** *vt* chloroformer.

chlorophyll ['klɒrəfɪl] *n* chlorophylle *f*.

choc* [tʃɒk] *n* (*abbr of* **chocolate**) choco‡ *m*. **~-ice** esquimau *m*.

chock [tʃɒk] **1** *n [wheel]* cale *f*; *[barrel]* cale, chantier *m*; (*Naut*) chantier, cale.

2 *vt wheel* caler; (*Naut*) mettre sur le chantier *or* sur cales.

3 *cpd*: **chock-a-block, chock-full** *basket, pan, box* plein à déborder (*of* de); *room* plein à craquer (*of* de), comble.

chocolate ['tʃɒklɪt] **1** *n* chocolat *m*. **(drinking) ~** chocolat; **a ~** un chocolat, une crotte au chocolat; *V* **dessert, milk, plain** *etc.*

2 *cpd* (*made of ~*) de chocolat; (*with ~ in it, flavoured with ~*) au chocolat, chocolaté; (*colour*) chocolat *inv*. **chocolate biscuit** biscuit *or* petit gâteau au chocolat; **chocolate eclair** éclair *m* au chocolat.

choice [tʃɔɪs] **1** *n* **(a)** (*act or possibility of choosing*) choix *m*. **to make a ~** faire un choix, choisir; **to take one's ~** faire son choix; **to have no ~** ne pas avoir le choix; **be careful in your ~** faites attention en choisissant; **he didn't have a free ~** il n'a pas été libre de choisir; **to have a very wide ~** avoir l'embarras du choix; **he had no ~ but to obey** il ne pouvait qu'obéir; **it's Hobson's ~** c'est à prendre ou à laisser; **from** *or* **for ~** de *or* par préférence; **he did it from ~** il l'a fait de son propre choix, il a choisi de le faire; **the house/girl of his (own) ~** la maison/fille de son (propre) choix.

(b) (*thing or person chosen*) choix *m*. **this book would be my ~** c'est ce livre que je choisirais.

(c) (*Comm etc: variety to choose from*) choix *m*, variété *f*. **a wide ~ of dresses** un grand choix de robes.

2 *adj* **(a)** (*Comm*) *goods, fruit* de choix. **~st** de premier choix.

(b) *word, phrase* bien choisi, approprié.

choir ['kwaɪə[r]] **1** *n* **(a)** (*Mus*) chœur *m*, chorale *f*; (*Rel*) chœur, maîtrise *f*. **to sing in the ~** faire partie du chœur *or* de la chorale, chanter dans la maîtrise.

(b) (*Archit, Rel*) chœur *m*.

2 *vti* chanter en chœur.

3 *cpd*: **choirboy** jeune choriste *m*, petit chanteur; **choir master** (*Mus*) chef *m* de(s) chœur(s); (*Rel*) maître *m* de chapelle; **choir organ** petit orgue; (*keyboard*) positif *m*; **choirstall** stalle *f* (du chœur).

choke [tʃəʊk] **1** *vt* **(a)** *person, voice, breathing* étrangler. **to ~ the life out of sb** étrangler qn; **in a voice ~d with sobs** d'une voix étranglée par les sanglots.

(b) (*fig*) *fire* étouffer; *pipe, tube* boucher, obstruer, engorger. **flowers ~d by weeds** fleurs étouffées par les mauvaises herbes; **street ~d with traffic** rue engorgée *or* embouteillée.

2 *vi* étouffer, s'étrangler. **she ~d with anger** la rage l'étouffait, elle étouffait de rage; **he was choking with laughter** il s'étranglait de rire.

3 *n* (*Aut*) starter *m*; (*Rad*) bobine *f* de réactance, inductance *f* de protection.

choke back *vt sep feelings* réprimer, étouffer, contenir; *words* contenir.
choke down *vt sep rage* contenir; *sobs* ravaler, étouffer.
choke off* *vt sep (fig) suggestions etc* étouffer (dans l'œuf); *discussion* empêcher; *person* envoyer promener*.
choke up 1 *vi* s'engorger, se boucher.
2 *vt sep pipe, drain* engorger, obstruer, boucher.
choker ['tʃəʊkəʳ] *n* **(a)** (*scarf*) foulard *m*, écharpe *f*; (*necktie*) cravate *f*; (*collar*) col droit; (*necklace*) collier *m* (de chien). **(b)** (‡) argument *m* massue. **that's a ~!** ça vous la boucle!‡
cholera ['kɒlərə] *n* choléra *m*.
choleric ['kɒlərɪk] *adj* colérique, coléreux.
choose [tʃuːz] *pret* **chose**, *ptp* **chosen 1** *vt* **(a)** (*select*) choisir, faire choix de; (*elect*) élire. **which will you ~?** lequel choisirez-vous?; **they chose a president** ils ont élu un président; **he was chosen leader** ils l'ont pris pour chef; **the chosen (people)** les élus *mpl*; **there is nothing to ~ between them** ils se valent; (*pej*) ils ne valent pas mieux l'un que l'autre; **in a few (well-)chosen words** en quelques mots choisis.
(b) décider, juger bon (*to do* de faire), vouloir (*to do* faire). **he chose not to speak** il a jugé bon de se taire, il a préféré se taire; **I cannot ~ but obey** je ne peux faire autrement que d'obéir, je ne peux qu'obéir.
2 *vi* choisir. **as you ~** comme vous l'entendez, à votre gré; **if you ~** si cela vous dit; **he'll do it when he ~s** il le fera quand il voudra *or* quand ça lui plaira; **to ~ between/among** faire un choix entre/parmi; **there's not much to ~ from** il n'y a pas tellement de choix.
choos(e)y* ['tʃuːzɪ] *adj person* difficile (à satisfaire). **I'm not ~** ça m'est égal; **you can't be ~ in your position** votre situation ne vous permet pas de faire le difficile; **I'm ~ about the people I go out with** je ne sors pas avec n'importe qui.
chop¹ [tʃɒp] **1** *n* **(a)** (*Culin*) côtelette *f*. **mutton/pork ~** côtelette de mouton/de porc; *V* **loin.**
(b) (*blow*) coup *m* (de hache *etc*). **to get the ~‡** se faire sacquer*.
2 *cpd*: **chop-chop‡** (*adv*) en moins de deux*; (*excl*) au trot!*, et que ça saute!*; **chophouse** (petit) restaurant *m*, gargote *f* (*pej*); **chopping block** billot *m*; **chopping board** planche *f* à hacher; **chopping knife** hachoir *m* (*couteau*); **chopsticks** baguettes *fpl*.
3 *vt* **(a)** trancher, couper (*à la hache*). **to ~ wood** couper *or* casser du bois (*à la hache*); **to ~ one's way through** se frayer un chemin à coups de hache à travers.
(b) (*Culin*) *meat, vegetables* hacher.
(c) (*Sport*) *ball* couper.
chop at *vt fus person etc* essayer de frapper; (*with axe*) *wood* taillader (*à la hache*).
chop down *vt sep tree* abattre.
chop off *vt sep* trancher, couper. **they chopped off his head** on lui a tranché la tête.
chop up *vt sep* hacher, couper en morceaux; (*Culin*) hacher menu.
chop² [tʃɒp] *n* (*Culin*) *[pork]* joue *f*. **~s** (*jaws of animals*) mâchoires *fpl*; (*cheeks*) joues; *[animals]* bajoues *fpl*; (*Tech*) *[vice]* mâchoires; **to lick one's ~s** se lécher *or* se pourlécher les babines.
chop³ [tʃɒp] **1** *vi* **(a)** (*Naut*) *[wind]* varier; *[waves]* clapoter.
(b) (*fig*) **to ~ and change** changer constamment d'avis; **he's always ~ping and changing** c'est une vraie girouette, il ne sait pas ce qu'il veut. **2** *vt* (*pej*) **to ~ logic** ergoter, discutailler.
chop⁴‡ [tʃɒp] *n* repas *m*, nourriture *f*, bouffe‡ *f*.
chopper ['tʃɒpəʳ] *n* **(a)** couperet *m*; hachoir *m*; (*Agr*) coupe-racines *m inv*. **(b)** (*Aviat*: helicopter*) hélicoptère *m*, batteur *m* à mayonnaise‡, banane‡ *f*.
choppy ['tʃɒpɪ] *adj lake* clapoteux; *sea* un peu agité; *wind* variable.
chopsuey [tʃɒp'suːɪ] *n* ragoût *m* (à la chinoise).
choral ['kɔːrəl] *adj* choral, chanté en chœur. **~ society** chorale *f*.
chorale [kɒ'rɑːl] *n* choral *m*.
chord [kɔːd] *n* (*Anat, Geom: also of harp etc*) corde *f*; (*Mus*) accord *m*. (*fig*) **to touch the right ~** toucher la corde sensible; *V* **vocal.**
chore [tʃɔːʳ] *n* (*everyday*) travail *m* de routine; (*unpleasant*) corvée *f*. **the ~s** les travaux du ménage; **to do the ~s** faire le ménage.
choreographer [ˌkɒrɪ'ɒgrəfəʳ] *n* chorégraphe *mf*.
choreographic [ˌkɒrɪəʊ'græfɪk] *adj* chorégraphique.
choreography [ˌkɒrɪ'ɒgrəfɪ] *n* chorégraphie *f*.
chorister ['kɒrɪstəʳ] *n* (*Rel*) choriste *m*.
chortle* ['tʃɔːtl] **1** *vi* glousser, rire (*about* de). **he was chortling over the newspaper** la lecture du journal le faisait glousser. **2** *n* gloussement *m*.
chorus ['kɔːrəs] **1** *n* **(a)** (*Mus, Theat: song, singers, speakers*) chœur *m*. **in ~** en chœur; **she's in the ~** (*at concert*) elle chante dans les chœurs; (*Theat*) elle fait partie de la troupe; (*Theat*) **~ girl** girl *f*; (*fig*) **a ~ of praise/objections** un concert de louanges/protestations.
(b) (*part of song*) refrain *m*. **to join in the ~** *[one person]* reprendre le refrain; *[several people]* reprendre le refrain en chœur.
2 *vt song* chanter *or* réciter en chœur; *verse* réciter en chœur.
chose [tʃəʊz] *pret of* **choose.**
chosen ['tʃəʊzn] **1** *ptp of* **choose;** *V* **choose 1a. 2** *npl*: **the ~** les élus *mpl*.
chough [tʃʌf] *n* crave *m* à bec rouge.
chow¹ [tʃaʊ] *n* (*dog*) chow-chow *m*.
chow²‡ [tʃaʊ] *n* (*food*) bouffe‡ *f*, boustifaille‡ *f*.
chowder ['tʃaʊdəʳ] *n* (*US*) (*stew*) ragoût *m* de poissons; (*soup*) bouillabaisse américaine; *V* **clam.**
Christ [kraɪst] **1** *n* (le) Christ, Jésus-Christ.
2 *excl* **~!**** merde (alors)!‡, Bon Dieu (de Bon Dieu)!‡
3 *cpd*: **the Christ Child** l'enfant Jésus; **Christlike** qui ressemble *or* semblable au Christ; **he had a Christlike forbearance** il avait la patience du Christ *or* une patience d'ange.
christen ['krɪsn] *vt* (*Rel, also Naut*) baptiser; (*gen: name*) appeler, nommer; (*nickname*) surnommer. **to ~ sb after** donner à qn le nom de; **he was ~ed Robert but everyone calls him Bob** son nom de baptême est Robert mais tout le monde l'appelle Bob.
Christendom ['krɪsndəm] *n* chrétienté *f*.
christening ['krɪsnɪŋ] *n* baptême *m*.
Christian ['krɪstɪən] **1** *adj* (*lit*) chrétien; (*fig*) charitable, compatissant. **the ~ era** l'ère chrétienne; **~ name** nom *m* de baptême, prénom *m*; **my ~ name is Mary** je m'appelle Marie, mon prénom est Marie; **~ Science** scientisme chrétien; **~ scientist** scientiste *mf* chrétien(ne).
2 *n* chrétien(ne) *m(f)*. **to become a ~** se faire chrétien.
Christianity [ˌkrɪstɪ'ænɪtɪ] *n* (*faith, religion*) christianisme *m*; (*character*) caractère *m or* qualité *f* du chrétien. **his ~ did not prevent him from ...** le fait d'être chrétien ne l'a pas empêché de ... .
Christianize ['krɪstɪənaɪz] *vt* christianiser.
Christmas ['krɪsməs] **1** *n* Noël *m*. **at ~** à (la) Noël; *V* **father, happy, merry.**
2 *cpd* de Noël. (*Brit*) **Christmas box** étrennes *fpl* (*offertes à Noël*); **Christmas cake** gâteau *m* de Noël (*gros cake décoré au sucre glace*); **Christmas card** carte *f* de Noël; **Christmas carol** chant *m* de Noël, noël *m*; (*Rel*) cantique *m* de Noël; **Christmas Day** le jour de Noël; **Christmas Eve** la veille de Noël; **Christmas party** fête *f or* arbre *m* de Noël; **Christmas present** cadeau *m* de Noël; **Christmas rose** rose *f* de Noël; **I got it in my Christmas stocking** ≃ je l'ai trouvé dans mon soulier *or* dans la cheminée *or* sous l'arbre (de Noël); **Christmas time** période *f* de Noël *or* des fêtes; **at Christmas time** à Noël; **Christmas tree** arbre *m* de Noël.
Christopher ['krɪstəfəʳ] *n* Christophe *m*.
chromatic [krə'mætɪk] *adj* (*Art, Mus*) chromatique. **~ printing** impression *f* polychrome; **~ scale** gamme *f* chromatique.
chrome [krəʊm] **1** *n* chrome *m*. **2** *cpd*: **chrome lacquer** laque *f or* peinture laquée (à base de chrome); **chrome steel** acier chromé; **chrome yellow** jaune *m* de chrome.
chromium ['krəʊmɪəm] **1** *n* chrome *m*. **2** *cpd*: **chromium-plated** chromé; **chromium-plating** chromage *m*.
chromosome ['krəʊməsəʊm] *n* chromosome *m*.
chronic ['krɒnɪk] *adj* (*Med*) *disease, state* chronique; (*fig*) *liar, smoker etc* invétéré; (‡) affreux, atroce*. **what ~ weather!** quel temps affreux! *or* atroce!*; **he's chronic!** il est imbuvable!
chronicle ['krɒnɪkl] **1** *n* chronique *f*. (*Rel*) **C~s** (livre *m* des) chroniques *fpl*; (*fig*) **a ~ of disasters** une succession de catastrophes. **2** *vt* faire la chronique de, enregistrer au jour le jour.
chronicler ['krɒnɪkləʳ] *n* chroniqueur *m*.
chronological [ˌkrɒnə'lɒdʒɪkəl] *adj* chronologique. **in ~ order** par ordre chronologique.
chronologically [ˌkrɒnə'lɒdʒɪkəlɪ] *adv* chronologiquement.
chronology [krə'nɒlədʒɪ] *n* chronologie *f*.
chronometer [krə'nɒmɪtəʳ] *n* chronomètre *m*.
chrysalis ['krɪsəlɪs] *n, pl* **chrysalises** ['krɪsəlɪsɪz] chrysalide *f*.
chrysanthemum [krɪ'sænθəməm] *n also abbr* **chrysanth*** [krɪ'sænt] chrysanthème *m*.
chub [tʃʌb] *n* chevesne *m*.
chubby ['tʃʌbɪ] *adj person, arm* potelé. **~-cheeked, ~-faced** joufflu.
chuck¹ [tʃʌk] **1** *vt* **(a)** (**: throw*) lancer, jeter, envoyer.
(b) (‡: *give up*) *job, hobby* lâcher, laisser tomber*; *girlfriend* plaquer‡, laisser tomber*. **~ it!** assez!, ça va!*, laisse tomber!*
(c) he ~ed her under the chin il lui a pris *or* caressé le menton.
2 *n* **(a) to give sb a ~ under the chin** prendre *or* caresser le menton à qn.
(b) to give sb the ~‡ balancer qn*; **he got the ~‡** il s'est fait balancer* *or* vider*.
chuck away* *vt sep* (*throw out*) *old clothes, books* balancer*; (*waste*) *money* jeter par les fenêtres; *opportunity* laisser passer.
chuck in‡ *vt sep* = **chuck up.**
chuck out* *vt sep useless article* balancer*; *person* vider*, sortir*.
chuck up‡ *vt sep job, hobby* lâcher, laisser tomber*.
chuck² [tʃʌk] **1** *n* (*Tech*) mandrin *m*. **2** *vt* (*Tech*) fixer sur un mandrin.
chuck³ [tʃʌk] *n* **(a)** (*also* **~ steak**) morceau *m* dans le paleron.
(b) (*US*‡) bouffe‡ *f*, graille‡ *f*. **~ wagon** chariot *m* garde-manger (*des pionniers*).
chucker-out‡ ['tʃʌkər'aʊt] *n* (*Brit*) videur* *m*.
chuckle ['tʃʌkl] **1** *n* gloussement *m*, petit rire. **we had a good ~ over it** ça nous a bien fait rire. **2** *vi* rire (*over, at* de), glousser.
chuffed‡ [tʃʌft] *adj* (*Brit*) tout content (*about* de), jouasse‡. **he was quite ~ about it** il était tout content.
chug [tʃʌg] **1** *n [machine]* souffle *m*; *[car, railway engine]* teuf-teuf *m*. **2** *vi [machine]* souffler; *[car]* faire teuf-teuf.
chug along *vi [car, train]* avancer en haletant *or* en faisant teuf-teuf.
chum* [tʃʌm] (*slightly*†) **1** *n* copain* *m*, copine* *f*. **2** *vi* (*share lodgings*) crécher ensemble‡.
chum up *vi* fraterniser (*with* avec).
chummy‡ ['tʃʌmɪ] *adj* sociable, (très) liant. **she is very ~ with him** elle est très copine avec lui*.
chump [tʃʌmp] *n* **(a)** (*) ballot* *m*, crétin(e)* *m(f)*. **(b)** (‡: *head*)

boule* *f*, caboche* *f*. **he's off his ~** il est timbré* *or* toqué*, il a perdu la boule*. **(c)** (*Culin*) **~ chop** côte *f* de mouton.
chunk [tʃʌŋk] *n [wood, metal, dough etc]* gros morceau; *[bread]* quignon *m*.
chunky ['tʃʌŋkɪ] *adj person* trapu; *knitwear* de grosse laine.
church [tʃɜ:tʃ] **1** *n* **(a)** (*building*) église *f*; *[French Protestants]* église, temple *m*. **he is inside the ~ now** il est maintenant dans l'église *or* dans le temple.
(b) (*U*) **to go to ~** aller à l'église *f*; *[Catholics]* aller à la messe; **to be in ~** être à l'église; *[Catholics]* être à la messe; **after ~** après l'office; (*for Catholics*) après la messe.
(c) (*whole body of Christians*) **the C~** l'Église *f*; **the C~ Militant** l'Église militante.
(d) (*denomination*) **the C~ of England** l'Église anglicane; **the C~ of Rome** l'Église catholique; *V* **high** *etc*.
(e) (*religious orders*) **C~** ordres *mpl*; **he has gone into the C~** il est entré dans les ordres.
2 *cpd*: **Church Fathers** Pères *mpl* de l'Église; **churchgoer** pratiquant(e) *m(f)*; **church hall** salle paroissiale; **he is/is not a good churchman** il est/n'est pas pratiquant; **church owl** chouette *f* des clochers, effraie *f*; **churchwarden** (*person*) bedeau *m*, marguillier *m*; (*pipe*) longue pipe (en terre); **churchyard** cimetière *m* (*autour d'une église*).
3 *vt* (*Rel*) faire assister à une messe.
churching ['tʃɜ:tʃɪŋ] *n* (*Rel*) **the ~ of women** la messe de relevailles.
churchy* ['tʃɜ:tʃɪ] *adj* (*pej*) *person* bigot, calotin* (*pej*). **a ~ person** une grenouille de bénitier* (*pej*).
churl [tʃɜ:l] *n* **(a)** (*ill-mannered person*) rustre *m*, malotru *m*; (*bad-tempered person*) ronchon *m*, personne *f* revêche. **(b)** (*Hist*) manant† *m*.
churlish ['tʃɜ:lɪʃ] *adj* (*ill-mannered*) fruste, grossier; (*bad-tempered*) hargneux, revêche. **it would be ~ not to thank him** il serait grossier *or* impoli de ne pas le remercier.
churlishly ['tʃɜ:lɪʃlɪ] *adv* (*V* **churlish**) grossièrement; avec hargne.
churlishness ['tʃɜ:lɪʃnɪs] *n* (*bad manners*) grossièreté *f*; (*bad temper*) mauvaise humeur *f*.
churn [tʃɜ:n] **1** *n* baratte *f*; (*Brit: milk can*) bidon *m*. **2** *vt* **(a)** (*Culin*) *butter* baratter. **(b)** (*also* **~ up**) *water* battre, fouetter, faire bouillonner. **(c)** (*Aut*) *engine* faire tourner. **3** *vi [sea etc]* bouillonner.
churn out *vt sep objects* débiter; *essays, letters, books* pondre en série*.
churn up *vt sep* = **churn 2b**.
chute [ʃu:t] *n* **(a)** glissière *f*; *V* **coal, refuse**[2]. **(b)** (*in river*) rapide *m*. **(c)** (*) = **parachute**. **(d)** (*Sport, for toboggans*) piste *f*; (*Brit: children's slide*) toboggan *m*.
chutney ['tʃʌtnɪ] *n* condiment *m* (*à base de fruits*). **apple/tomato ~** condiment à la pomme/à la tomate.
cicada [sɪ'kɑ:də] *n* cigale *f*.
cicatrice ['sɪkətrɪs] *n* cicatrice *f*.
Cicero ['sɪsərəʊ] *n* Cicéron *m*.
cicerone [ˌtʃɪtʃə'rəʊnɪ] *n* cicérone *m*.
cider ['saɪdə[r]] **1** *n* cidre *m*. **2** *cpd*: **cider-apple** pomme *f* à cidre; **cider-press** pressoir *m* à cidre; **cider vinegar** vinaigre *m* de cidre.
cigar [sɪ'gɑ:[r]] **1** *n* cigare *m*. **2** *cpd box etc* à cigares. **cigar case** étui *m* à cigares; **cigar holder** fume-cigare *m inv*; (*Aut*) **cigar lighter** allume-cigare *m inv*; **cigar-shaped** en forme de cigare.
cigarette [ˌsɪgə'ret] **1** *n* cigarette *f*.
2 *cpd box etc* à cigarettes. **cigarette ash** cendre *f* de cigarette; **cigarette case** étui *m* à cigarettes, porte-cigarettes *m inv*; **cigarette end** mégot *m*; **cigarette holder** fume-cigarette *m inv*; **cigarette lighter** briquet *m*; **cigarette paper** papier *m* à cigarettes.
cinch [sɪntʃ] **1** *n* **(a)** (*US: saddle girth*) sous-ventrière *f*, sangle *f* (de selle).
(b) it's a ~‡ (*certain*) c'est du tout cuit*, c'est du gâteau*; (*easy*) c'est l'enfance de l'art.
2 *vt* **(a)** *horse* sangler; *saddle* attacher par une sangle (de selle).
(b) (*fig*) *success* rendre sûr, assurer.
cinder ['sɪndə[r]] **1** *n* cendre *f*. **~s** (*burnt coal*) cendres *fpl* (de charbon); *[furnace, volcano]* scories *fpl*; **to rake out the ~s** racler les cendres (du foyer); **burnt to a ~** réduit en cendres.
2 *cpd*: (*US*) **cinder block** parpaing *m*; **cinder track** (piste *f*) cendrée *f*.
Cinderella [ˌsɪndə'relə] *n* Cendrillon *f*.
cine-camera ['sɪnɪ'kæmərə] *n* (*Brit*) caméra *f*.
cine-film ['sɪnɪfɪlm] *n* (*Brit*) film *m*.
cinema ['sɪnəmə] *n* cinéma *m*.
Cinemascope ['sɪnəməskəʊp] *n* ® cinémascope *m* ®.
cinematograph [ˌsɪnɪ'mætəgrɑ:f] *n* (*Brit*) cinématographe *m*.
cine-projector [ˌsɪnɪprə'dʒektə[r]] *n* (*Brit*) projecteur *m* de cinéma.
Cinerama [ˌsɪnə'rɑ:mə] *n* ® cinérama *m* ®.
cinerary ['sɪnərərɪ] *adj* cinéraire.
cinnabar ['sɪnəbɑ:[r]] *n* cinabre *m*.
cinnamon ['sɪnəmən] **1** *n* cannelle *f*. **2** *cpd cake, biscuit* à la cannelle; (*colour*) cannelle *inv*.
cipher ['saɪfə[r]] **1** *n* **(a)** (*Arabic numeral*) chiffre *m* (*arabe*); (*zero*) zéro *m*. (*fig*) **he's a mere ~** c'est un zéro *or* une nullité.
(b) (*secret writing*) chiffre *m*, code secret. **in ~** en chiffre, en code.
(c) (*monogram*) chiffre *m*, monogramme *m*.
2 *vt calculations, communications* chiffrer.
circle ['sɜ:kl] **1** *n* cercle *m*; *[hills, houses, vehicles]* cercle; *[mountains]* cirque *m*; (*round eyes*) cerne *m*; (*Gymnastics*) soleil *m*; (*Astron: orbit*) orbite *f*; (*Brit: Theat*) balcon *m*; *[knowledge]* cercle, sphère *f*; (*group of persons*) cercle, groupe *m*; *[underground railway]* ligne *f* de ceinture. **to stand in a ~** faire (un) cercle, se tenir en cercle; **to draw a ~** tracer un cercle; (*Math*) tracer une circonférence *or* un cercle; **an inner ~ of advisers** un groupe de proches conseillers; **in political ~s** dans les milieux *mpl* politiques; **to come full ~** revenir à son point de départ.
2 *vt* (*surround*) encercler, entourer; (*move round*) faire le tour de, tourner autour de.
3 *vi [birds]* faire *or* décrire des cercles; *[aircraft]* tourner (en rond). **the cyclists ~d round him** les cyclistes ont tourné autour de lui.
circle about, circle around, circle round *vi* faire *or* décrire des cercles, tourner.
circlet ['sɜ:klɪt] *n* petit cercle *m*; *[hair]* bandeau *m*; *[arm]* brassard *m*; *[finger]* anneau *m*.
circuit ['sɜ:kɪt] **1** *n* **(a)** (*journey around*) tour *m*, circuit *m*. **to make a ~ of** faire le tour de; **to make a wide ~ round a town** faire un grand détour autour d'une ville.
(b) (*Brit Jur*) (*journey*) tournée *f* (*des juges d'assises*); (*district*) circonscription *f* (judiciaire). **he is on the eastern ~** il fait la tournée de l'est.
(c) (*Cine, Theat: houses visited by same company*) tournée *f*; (*houses owned by same owner*) groupe *m*.
(d) (*Elec*) circuit *m*; *V* **closed, short**.
(e) (*Sport*) circuit *m*, parcours *m*.
2 *cpd*: (*Elec*) **circuit-breaker** disjoncteur *m*.
circuitous [sɜ:'kjʊɪtəs] *adj road, route* indirect, qui fait un détour; (*fig*) *means* détourné; *method* indirect.
circuitously [sɜ:'kjʊɪtəslɪ] *adv* (*lit*) en faisant un détour; (*fig*) de façon détournée *or* indirecte, indirectement.
circular ['sɜ:kjʊlə[r]] **1** *adj outline, saw, ticket* circulaire. **~ letter** circulaire *f*; **~ tour** voyage *m* circulaire, circuit *m*. **2** *n* (*letter*) circulaire *f*; (*printed advertisement etc*) prospectus *m*.
circularize ['sɜ:kjʊləraɪz] *vt person, firm* envoyer des circulaires *or* des prospectus à.
circulate ['sɜ:kjʊleɪt] **1** *vi* (*all senses*) circuler. **2** *vt object, bottle* faire circuler; *news* propager. (*Math*) **circulating decimal** fraction *f* périodique; **circulating library** bibliothèque *f* de prêt; (*Fin*) **circulating medium** monnaie *f* d'échange.
circulation [ˌsɜ:kjʊ'leɪʃən] **1** *n* (*U*) (*Anat, Bot, Fin, Med*) circulation *f*; *[news, rumour]* propagation *f*; *[newspaper etc]* tirage *m*. (*Med*) **he has poor ~** il a une mauvaise circulation; (*Fin*) **to put into ~** mettre en circulation; (*Fin*) **to take out of** *or* **withdraw from ~** retirer de la circulation; (*Fin*) **in ~** en circulation; **he's now back in ~*** il est à nouveau dans le circuit*.
2 *cpd*: (*Press*) **circulation manager** directeur *m* du service de la diffusion.
circulatory [ˌsɜ:kjʊ'leɪtərɪ] *adj* circulatoire.
circum ... ['sɜ:kəm] *pref* circon ... .
circumcise ['sɜ:kəmsaɪz] *vt* (*Med*) circoncire; (*fig*) purifier.
circumcision [ˌsɜ:kəm'sɪʒən] *n* circoncision *f*. (*Rel*) **the C~** (la fête de) la Circoncision.
circumference [sə'kʌmfərəns] *n* circonférence *f*.
circumflex ['sɜ:kəmfleks] **1** *adj* circonflexe. **2** *n* accent *m* circonflexe.
circumlocution [ˌsɜ:kəmlə'kju:ʃən] *n* circonlocution *f*.
circumlunar [ˌsɜ:kəm'lu:nə[r]] *adj* autour de la lune. **~ flight** vol *m* autour de la lune.
circumnavigate [ˌsɜ:kəm'nævɪgeɪt] *vt cape* doubler, contourner. **to ~ the globe** faire le tour du monde en bateau, naviguer tout autour du globe.
circumnavigation ['sɜ:kəmˌnævɪ'geɪʃən] *n* circumnavigation *f*.
circumscribe ['sɜ:kəmskraɪb] *vt* entourer d'une ligne; (*Math, fig*) circonscrire.
circumspect ['sɜ:kəmspekt] *adj* circonspect.
circumspection [ˌsɜ:kəm'spekʃən] *n* circonspection *f*.
circumspectly ['sɜ:kəmspektlɪ] *adv* avec circonspection, de façon circonspecte.
circumstance ['sɜ:kəmstəns] *n* **(a)** (*gen pl*) circonstance *f*, état *m* de choses; (*fact, detail*) circonstance *f*, détail *m*. **in** *or* **under the present ~s** dans les circonstances actuelles, vu l'état des choses; **in** *or* **under no ~s** en aucun cas; **under similar ~s** en pareil cas; **to take the ~s into account** tenir compte des *or* faire la part des circonstances; *V* **attenuate, extenuate, pomp**.
(b) (*financial condition*) **~s** moyens *mpl*, situation financière *or* pécuniaire; **in easy ~s** dans l'aisance, à l'aise; **in poor ~s** gêné, dans la gêne; **what are his ~s?** quelle est sa situation financière *or* pécuniaire?; **if our ~s allow it** si nos moyens nous le permettent.
circumstantial [ˌsɜ:kəm'stænʃəl] *adj* **(a)** (*detailed*) *report, statement* circonstancié, détaillé. **(b)** (*indirect*) *knowledge* indirect. (*Jur*) **~ evidence** preuve indirecte. **(c)** (*not essential*) accessoire, subsidiaire.
circumstantiate [ˌsɜ:kəm'stænʃɪeɪt] *vt evidence* confirmer en donnant des détails sur; *event* donner des détails circonstanciés sur.
circumvent [ˌsɜ:kəm'vent] *vt person* circonvenir; *law, regulations, rule* tourner; *sb's plan, project* faire échouer.
circumvention [ˌsɜ:kəm'venʃən] *n [plan, project]* mise *f* en échec. **the ~ of the guard/rule proved easy** circonvenir le garde/tourner le règlement s'avéra facile.
circus ['sɜ:kəs] **1** *n* (*Hist, Theat*) cirque *m*; (*in town*) rond-point *m*. **2** *cpd animal, clown* de cirque.
cirrhosis [sɪ'rəʊsɪs] *n* cirrhose *f*.
cirrus ['sɪrəs] *n, pl* **cirri** ['sɪraɪ] **(a)** (*cloud*) cirrus *m*. **(b)** (*Bot*) vrille *f*.
cissy ['sɪsɪ] *n* = **sissy**.

Cistercian [sɪs'tɜːʃən] 1 *n* cistercien(ne) *m(f)*. 2 *adj* cistercien. ~ **Order** ordre *m* de Cîteaux; **a** ~ **monk** un cistercien.
cistern ['sɪstən] *n* citerne *f*; *[WC]* chasse *f* d'eau; *[barometer]* cuvette *f*.
citadel ['sɪtədl] *n* citadelle *f*.
citation [saɪ'teɪʃən] *n* (*gen, Jur, Mil*) citation *f*.
cite [saɪt] *vt* (*gen, Jur, Mil*) citer. **to** ~ **as an example** citer en exemple; (*Jur*) **to** ~ **sb to appear** citer qn; *V* **dispatch**.
citizen ['sɪtɪzn] *n [town]* habitant(e) *m(f)*; *[state]* citoyen(ne) *m(f)*; (*Hist*) bourgeois(e) *m(f)*; (*townsman*) citadin(e) *m(f)*. **the** ~**s of Paris** les habitants de Paris, les Parisiens *mpl*; **French** ~ citoyen français; ~ **of the world** citoyen du monde; *V* **fellow**.
citizenry ['sɪtɪznrɪ] *n*: **the** ~ l'ensemble *m* des habitants (*d'une ville etc*).
citizenship ['sɪtɪznʃɪp] *n* citoyenneté *f*.
citrate ['sɪtreɪt] *n* citrate *m*.
citric ['sɪtrɪk] *adj* citrique. ~ **acid** acide *m* citrique.
citron ['sɪtrən] *n* (*fruit*) cédrat *m*; (*tree*) cédratier *m*.
citrus ['sɪtrəs] *n* citrus *mpl*. ~ **fruits** agrumes *mpl*.
city ['sɪtɪ] 1 *n* **(a)** (grande) ville *f*, cité *f*.
(b) (*Brit*) **the C**~ la Cité (de Londres), le centre des affaires; **he's (something) in the C**~* il est dans les affaires, il travaille dans la Cité (de Londres).
2 *cpd* (*Brit Press*) *editor, page, news* financier. (*Brit, US*) **city centre** centre *m* (de la) ville; **city dweller** citadin(e) *m(f)*; (*US*) **city editor** rédacteur en chef (pour les nouvelles locales); **the city fathers** les élus locaux (*d'une ville*); (*esp US*) **city hall** hôtel *m* de ville; (*US*) **city planner** urbaniste *mf*; (*US*) **city planning** urbanisme *m*; (*pej*) **city slicker*** bêcheur *m*, -euse *f* (*bien habillé venu de la ville*); **city state** cité *f*.
civet ['sɪvɪt] *n* (*cat, substance*) civette *f*.
civic ['sɪvɪk] *adj rights, virtues* civique; *guard, authorities* municipal. (*Brit*) ~ **centre** centre administratif (municipal); ~ **restaurant** restaurant *m* communautaire.
civics ['sɪvɪks] *n* instruction *f* civique.
civies* ['sɪvɪz] *npl* (*US*) = **civvies**, *V* **civvy 2.**
civil ['sɪvl] *adj* **(a)** (*of a community; also non-military*) civil. ~ **commotion** émeute *f*; ~ **defence** défense passive; ~ **disobedience** résistance passive (à la loi); ~ **disobedience campaign** campagne *f* de résistance passive; ~ **engineer** ingénieur *m* des travaux publics; ~ **engineering** travaux publics; ~ **law** (*system*) code civil; (*study*) droit civil; ~ **liberties** libertés *fpl* civiques; (*Brit*) ~ **list** liste civile (*allouée à la famille royale*); ~ **rights** droits *mpl* civiques; ~ **rights campaign**, ~ **rights movement** campagne pour les droits civiques; ~ **servant** fonctionnaire *mf*; ~ **service** fonction publique, administration *f*; ~ **service examination** concours *m* d'entrée dans la fonction publique; ~ **service recruitment** recrutement *m* de(s) fonctionnaires; ~ **war** guerre civile; ~ **wedding** mariage civil; **to have a** ~ **wedding** se marier à la mairie.
(b) (*polite*) civil, poli. **that's very** ~ **of you** vous êtes bien aimable; *V* **tongue.**
civilian [sɪ'vɪlɪən] 1 *n* civil(e) *m(f)* (*opposé à militaire*). 2 *adj* civil.
civility [sɪ'vɪlɪtɪ] *n* politesse *f*, courtoisie *f*, civilité *f*.
civilization [ˌsɪvɪlaɪ'zeɪʃən] *n* civilisation *f*.
civilize ['sɪvɪlaɪz] *vt* civiliser.
civilized ['sɪvɪlaɪzd] *adj* civilisé. **to become** ~ se civiliser.
civilly ['sɪvɪlɪ] *adv* poliment.
civism ['sɪvɪzəm] *n* civisme *m*.
civvy* ['sɪvɪ] (*abbr of* **civilian**) 1 *adj* (*Brit*) ~ **street** vie civile; **to be in** ~ **street** être civil *or* pékin*. 2 *npl*: **civvies** vêtements civils; **in civvies** (habillé) en civil *or* en bourgeois*.
clack [klæk] 1 *n* claquement *m*; *[pump etc]* clapet *m*; (*fig: talk*) jacasserie *f*, caquet *m*. 2 *vi* claquer; (*fig*) jacasser. **this will set tongues** ~**ing** cela va faire jaser (les gens).
clad [klæd] *adj* habillé, vêtu (*in* de).
claim [kleɪm] 1 *vt* **(a)** (*demand as one's due*) revendiquer, réclamer (*from sb* à qn); *property, prize, right* revendiquer. **to** ~ **diplomatic immunity** réclamer l'immunité diplomatique; **to** ~ **the right to decide** revendiquer le droit de décider; **to** ~ **damages** réclamer des dommages et intérêts.
(b) (*profess, contend, maintain*) prétendre, déclarer. **to** ~ **acquaintance with sb** prétendre connaître qn; **he** ~**s to have seen you** il prétend *or* déclare vous avoir vu, il déclare qu'il vous a vu; **both armies** ~**ed the victory** les deux armées ont revendiqué la victoire.
(c) (*demand*) *sb's attention* demander, solliciter; *sb's sympathy* solliciter.
2 *n* **(a)** (*act of claiming, instance of this*) revendication *f*, réclamation *f*; (*Insurance*) ≈ déclaration *f* de sinistre, demande *f* d'indemnité. **to lay** ~ **to** prétendre à, avoir des prétentions à; **there are many** ~**s on my time** mon temps est très pris; **there are many** ~**s on my purse** on fait beaucoup appel à ma bourse; **that's a big** ~ **to make!** la *or* cette prétention est de taille!; **his** ~ **that he acted legally** son affirmation d'avoir agi d'une manière licite; **to put in a** ~ (*gen*) faire une réclamation; (*Insurance*) faire une déclaration de sinistre *or* une demande d'indemnité; (*Ind*) **they put in a** ~ **for £1 per hour more** ils ont demandé une augmentation d' une livre de l'heure; (*Insurance*) **the** ~**s were all paid** les dommages ont été intégralement payés *or* réglés; (*Ind*) **a** ~ **for an extra £5 per week** une demande d'augmentation de 5 livres par semaine.
(b) (*right*) droit *m*, titre *m*. ~ **to ownership** droit à la propriété; ~ **to the throne** titre à la couronne; ~**s to sb's friendship** droits à l'amitié de qn.
(c) (*Min etc*) concession *f*; *V* **stake.**
claimant ['kleɪmənt] *n [throne]* prétendant(e) *m(f)* (*to* à); *[social benefits]* demandeur *m*, -eresse *f*; (*Jur*) requérant(e) *m(f)*.
clairvoyance [klɛə'vɔɪəns] *n* voyance *f*, (don *m* de) seconde vue.
clairvoyant(e) [klɛə'vɔɪənt] 1 *n* voyant(e) *m(f)*. 2 *adj* doué de seconde vue.
clam [klæm] *n* (*Zool*) clam *m*, (grosse) praire *f*. (*US Culin*) ~ **chowder** soupe *f* aux praires.
clam up‡ *vi* la boucler‡, la fermer‡. **to be clammed up like an oyster** être muet comme une carpe *or* comme la tombe; **he clammed up on me** il l'a bouclée‡, il ne m'a plus dit un mot là-dessus.
clamber ['klæmbəʳ] 1 *vi* grimper (*en s'aidant des mains ou en rampant*), se hisser (avec difficulté). **to** ~ **up a hill** gravir péniblement une colline; **to** ~ **over a wall** escalader un mur. 2 *n* escalade *f*.
clammy ['klæmɪ] *adj hand, touch* moite (et froid); *wall* suintant.
clamorous ['klæmərəs] *adj crowd* vociférant, bruyant; (*fig*) *demand* impérieux, criant.
clamour, (*US*) **clamor** ['klæməʳ] 1 *n* (*shouts*) clameur *f*, vociférations *fpl*, cris *mpl*; (*demands*) revendication *or* réclamation bruyante.
2 *vi* vociférer, pousser des cris. **to** ~ **against sth/sb** vociférer contre qch/qn; **to** ~ **for sth/sb** demander qch/qn à grands cris, réclamer qch/qn à cor et à cri.
clamp[1] [klæmp] 1 *n* (*gen*) attache *f*, pince *f*; (*bigger*) crampon *m*; (*Med*) clamp *m*; (*also* **ring** ~) collier *m* de serrage; (*Carpentry*) valet *m* (d'établi); (*Archit*) agrafe *f*; *[china]* agrafe; (*Elec*) serre-fils *m inv*; (*Naut*) serre-cables *m inv*.
2 *vt* serrer, cramponner; *stones, china* agrafer.
clamp down on* *vt fus person* serrer la vis à, visser*; *expenditure* mettre un frein à, freiner, restreindre; *information* supprimer, censurer; *the press, the opposition* bâillonner.
clamp[2] [klæmp] 1 *n [bricks]* tas *m*, pile *f* (*de briques séchées*); *[potatoes]* silo *m* (*de pommes de terre sous paille etc*). 2 *vt* entasser.
clamp[3] [klæmp] (*thump*) 1 *n* pas lourd *or* pesant. 2 *vi* marcher d'un pas pesant.
clan [klæn] *n* clan *m*.
clandestine [klæn'destɪn] *adj* clandestin.
clang [klæŋ] 1 *n* (*also* ~**ing noise**) bruit *m or* son *m* métallique; (*louder*) fracas *m* métallique. 2 *vi* émettre un son métallique. **the gate** ~**ed shut** la grille s'est refermée bruyamment *or* avec un bruit métallique.
clanger‡ ['klæŋəʳ] *n* (*Brit*) gaffe *f*. **to drop a** ~ faire une gaffe, gaffer lourdement.
clangorous ['klæŋgərəs] *adj noise* métallique.
clangour, (*US*) **clangor** ['klæŋgəʳ] *n* son *m or* bruit *m or* fracas *m* métallique.
clank [klæŋk] 1 *n* cliquetis *m*, bruit *m* métallique (*de chaînes etc*). 2 *vi* cliqueter, émettre un son métallique. 3 *vt* faire cliqueter.
clannish ['klænɪʃ] *adj* (*slightly pej: exclusive, unwelcoming*) *group* fermé; *person* qui a l'esprit de clan *or* de clique.
clap[1] [klæp] 1 *n* (*sound*) claquement *m*, bruit sec; *[hands]* battement *m*; (*action*) tape *f*; (*applause*) applaudissement *m*. **a** ~ **on the back** une tape dans le dos; **to give the dog a** ~ donner une tape amicale au chien; **a** ~ **of thunder** un coup de tonnerre; **he got a good** ~ il a été très applaudi.
2 *cpd*: **clapboard** bardeau *m*; **claptrap*** boniment* *m*, baratin* *m*.
3 *vt* **(a)** battre, frapper, taper; (*applaud*) applaudir. **to** ~ **one's hands** battre des mains; **to** ~ **sb on the back** donner à qn une tape dans le dos; **to** ~ **a dog** donner des tapes amicales à un chien; **he** ~**ped his hand over my mouth** il a mis *or* collé* sa main sur ma bouche.
(b) flanquer*, fourrer*. **to** ~ **sb in irons** jeter qn aux fers; **to** ~ **sb into prison*** fourrer* qn en prison; **to** ~ **eyes on** voir.
4 *vi* applaudir.
clap on *vt sep*: **to clap on one's hat** enfoncer son chapeau sur sa tête; (*Naut*) **to clap on sail** mettre toutes voiles dehors; (*Aut*) **to clap on the brakes** freiner brusquement, donner un coup de frein brutal.
clap to *vti* claquer.
clap[2]** [klæp] *n* chaude-pisse** *f*.
clapped-out‡ ['klæptaʊt] *adj person* crevé*, flapi*; *horse* fourbu; *car* crevé*.
clapper ['klæpəʳ] *n [bell]* battant *m*. (*Brit*) **to go like the** ~**s**‡ aller à toute blinde‡.
clapping ['klæpɪŋ] *n* applaudissements *mpl*.
claque [klæk] *n* (*Theat*) claque *f*.
claret ['klærət] 1 *n* (vin *m* de) bordeaux *m* (rouge). 2 *adj* (*also* ~**-coloured**) bordeaux *inv*.
clarification [ˌklærɪfɪ'keɪʃən] *n* clarification *f*; *[wine]* collage *m*.
clarify ['klærɪfaɪ] 1 *vt sugar, fat* clarifier; *wine* coller; (*fig*) *situation* éclaircir, clarifier. 2 *vi* se clarifier; (*fig*) s'éclaircir.
clarinet [ˌklærɪ'net] *n* clarinette *f*.
clarinet(t)ist [ˌklærɪ'netɪst] *n* clarinettiste *mf*.
clarion ['klærɪən] (*liter*) 1 *n* clairon *m*. **a** ~ **call** un appel de clairon. 2 *vt*: **to** ~ **(forth)** claironner.
clarity ['klærɪtɪ] *n* clarté *f*, précision *f*.
clash [klæʃ] 1 *vi* **(a)** (*bang noisily*) *[swords, metallic objects]* s'entrechoquer; *[cymbals]* résonner.
(b) (*be in dispute*) *[armies]* se heurter. **the 2 parties** ~ **over the question of** les 2 partis sont en désaccord total en ce qui concerne.
(c) (*conflict*) *[interests]* se heurter, être incompatible *or* en contradiction (*with* avec); *[personalities]* être incompatible (*with* avec); *[colours]* jurer, détonner (*with* avec).
(d) (*coincide*) *[two events, invitations etc]* tomber en même temps (*or* le même jour *etc*).

2 *vt metallic objects* heurter *or* choquer *or* entrechoquer bruyamment; *cymbals* faire résonner. (*Aut*) **to ~ the gears** faire grincer les vitesses.

3 *n* **(a)** (*sound*) choc *m or* fracas *m* métallique.

(b) *[armies, weapons]* choc *m*, heurt *m*; (*between people, parties*) accrochage* *m*; (*with police, troops*) accrochage, escarmouche *f*, échauffourée *f*. **during a ~ with the police** au cours d'une échauffourée avec la police; **I don't want a ~ with him about it** je ne veux pas me disputer avec lui à ce sujet; **to have a (verbal) ~ with sb** avoir un accrochage* *or* une algarade avec qn.

(c) *[interests]* conflit *m*. **a ~ of personalities** une incompatibilité de caractères.

(d) *[colours]* discordance *f*, heurt *m*.

(e) *[dates, events, invitations]* coïncidence *f* (fâcheuse).

clasp [klɑːsp] **1** *n* **(a)** *[brooch, necklace, purse]* fermoir *m*; *[belt]* boucle *f*.

(b) (*U: in one's arms, of a hand*) étreinte *f*.

2 *cpd*: **clasp knife** grand couteau pliant, eustache*† *m*.

3 *vt* étreindre, serrer. **to ~ sb's hand** serrer la main de qn; **to ~ one's hands (together)** joindre les mains; **with ~ed hands** les mains jointes; **to ~ sb in one's arms/to one's heart** serrer qn dans ses bras/sur son cœur.

4 *vi* s'agrafer, s'attacher, se fermer.

class [klɑːs] **1** *n* **(a)** (*group, division*) catégorie *f*, classe *f*; (*Bot, Mil, Soc, Zool etc*) classe; (*Naut: of ship*) type *m*; (*in Lloyd's Register*) cote *f*. (*fig*) **he's not in the same ~ as his brother** il n'arrive pas à la cheville de son frère; **these books are just not in the same ~** il n'y a pas de comparaison (possible) entre ces livres; **in a ~ by itself** hors concours, unique; **a good ~ (of) hotel** un très bon hôtel, un hôtel de très bonne classe; **the ruling ~** la classe dirigeante; (*Brit Univ*) **what ~ of degree did he get?** quelle mention a-t-il eue (à sa licence)?; **first ~ honours in history** ≃ licence *f* d'histoire avec mention très bien; *V* **middle, working** *etc*.

(b) (*Scol, Univ*) (*lesson*) classe *f*, cours *m*; (*students*) classe; (*US: year*) promotion *f* scolaire. **to give** *or* **take a ~** faire un cours; **to attend a ~** suivre un cours; **the French ~** la classe *or* le cours de français; **an evening ~** un cours du soir; (*US*) **the ~ of 1970** la promotion de 1970.

(c) (**U*) classe *f*, distinction *f*. **to have ~** avoir de la classe.

2 *vt* classer, classifier; (*Naut Insurance*) coter. **he was ~ed with the servants** il était assimilé aux domestiques.

3 *cpd*: **class-conscious** *person* conscient des distinctions sociales; (*pej: snobbish*) *person, attitude* snob *inv*; **class consciousness** conscience *f* de classe *or* des distinctions sociales; **class distinction** distinction sociale; **classmate** camarade *mf* de classe; **classroom** (salle *f* de) classe *f*; **class struggle, class war(fare)** lutte *f* des classes.

classic [ˈklæsɪk] **1** *adj* (*lit, fig*) classique. **it was ~!*** c'était le coup classique!* **2** *n* (*author, work*) classique *m*; (*Racing*) classique *f*. **to study ~s** étudier les humanités; (*fig*) **it is a ~ of its kind** c'est un classique du genre.

classical [ˈklæsɪkəl] *adj* classique. **~ Latin** latin *m* classique; **~ scholar** humaniste *mf*.

classicism [ˈklæsɪsɪzəm] *n* classicisme *m*.

classifiable [ˈklæsɪfaɪəbl] *adj* qu'on peut classifier.

classification [ˌklæsɪfɪˈkeɪʃən] *n* classification *f*.

classified [ˈklæsɪfaɪd] *adj* **(a)** classifié. (*Press*) **~ advertisement** petite annonce. **(b)** (*Admin: secret etc*) *document* classé secret (*f* classée secrète). **~ information** renseignements secrets.

classify [ˈklæsɪfaɪ] *vt* **(a)** classer, classifier. **(b)** (*Admin: restrict circulation*) classer secret.

classy‡ [ˈklɑːsɪ] *adj car, apartment, hotel* chic *inv*, de luxe; *person* ultra-chic *inv*, superchic* *inv*. **~ clothes** des vêtements tout ce qu'il y a de chic.

clatter [ˈklætəʳ] **1** *n* (*noise*) cliquetis *m*, (*louder*) fracas *m*. **the ~ of cutlery** le bruit *or* cliquetis de couverts entrechoqués.

2 *vi* (*rattle*) *[heels, keys, typewriter, chains]* cliqueter; (*bang*) *[large falling object, cymbals]* résonner. **to ~ in/out/away** *etc* entrer/sortir/partir *etc* bruyamment.

3 *vt* choquer *or* entrechoquer bruyamment.

clause [klɔːz] *n* **(a)** (*Gram*) membre *m* de phrase, proposition *f*. **principal/subordinate ~** proposition principale/subordonnée. **(b)** (*Jur*) *[contract, law, treaty]* clause *f*; *[will]* disposition *f*; *V* **saving**.

claustrophobia [ˌklɔːstrəˈfəʊbɪə] *n* claustrophobie *f*.

claustrophobic [ˌklɔːstrəˈfəʊbɪk] **1** *adj person* claustrophobe; *feeling* de claustrophobie; *situation, atmosphere* claustrophobique. **2** *n* claustrophobe *mf*.

clavichord [ˈklævɪkɔːd] *n* clavicorde *m*.

clavicle [ˈklævɪkl] *n* clavicule *f*.

claw [klɔː] **1** *n* **(a)** *[cat, lion, small bird etc]* griffe *f*; *[bird of prey]* serre *f*; *[lobster etc]* pince *f*; (‡: *hand*) patte* *f*. **to get one's ~s into sb** tenir qn dans ses griffes; **to get one's ~s on*** mettre le grappin sur*; **get your ~s off (that)!**‡ bas les pattes!*

(b) (*Tech*) *[bench]* valet *m*; *[hammer]* pied-de-biche *m*.

2 *cpd*: **claw-hammer** marteau fendu, marteau à pied-de-biche.

3 *vt* (*scratch*) griffer; (*rip*) déchirer *or* labourer avec ses griffes *or* ses serres; (*clutch*) agripper, serrer.

claw at *vt fus object* essayer de s'agripper à; *person* essayer de griffer.

clay [kleɪ] **1** *n* argile *f*, (terre *f*) glaise *f*. **potter's ~** argile (à potier); *V* **china**. **2** *cpd*: **clay pigeon** pigeon *m* d'argile *or* de ball-trap; **clay pigeon shooting** tir *m* au pigeon; **clay pipe** pipe *f* en terre; **clay pit** argilière *f*, glaisière *f*.

clayey [ˈkleɪɪ] *adj* argileux, glaiseux.

clean [kliːn] **1** *adj* **(a)** (*not dirty*) *clothes, plates, hands, house, car* propre, net; (*having clean habits*) *person, animal* propre. **to have ~ hands** avoir les mains propres; (*fig*) avoir les mains nettes *or* la conscience nette; **a ~ piece of paper** une feuille blanche; (*fig*) **a ~ bomb** une bombe propre *or* sans retombées (radio-actives); **to wipe sth ~** essuyer qch; **keep it ~** ne le salissez pas, tenez-le propre; **as ~ as a new pin** propre comme un sou neuf; (*fig*) **to make a ~ breast of it** décharger sa conscience, dire ce qu'on a sur la conscience; **to make a ~ sweep** faire table rase (*of* de).

(b) (*pure etc*) *reputation* net, sans tache; *joke, story* qui n'a rien de choquant; *contest, game* loyal. **~ living** une *or* la vie saine; (*Jur*) **a ~ record** *or* **sheet** un casier (judiciaire) vierge; **a ~ driving licence** un permis de conduire où n'est portée aucune contravention; (*fig*) **let's keep the party ~!*** pas d'inconvenances!, pas de grossièretés!; **~ player** joueur *m*, -euse *f* fair-play *inv*; **the doctor gave him a ~ bill of health** le médecin l'a trouvé en parfait état de santé.

(c) (*elegant etc*) *shape* fin, net, bien proportionné; *line, stroke* net; *profile* pur. **~ outlines** des contours nets *or* dégagés; **a ~ ship** un navire aux lignes élégantes; **this car has very ~ lines** cette voiture a une belle ligne; **a ~ cut** une coupure nette *or* franche; **~ leap** saut *m* sans toucher (l'obstacle); (*Tennis*) **~ ace!** as!

(d) (‡) **he's ~** (*unarmed*) il n'est pas armé, il n'a rien sur lui; (*innocent*) il n'a rien fait; (*no incriminating material in it*) **his room was quite ~** il n'y avait rien dans sa chambre, on n'a rien trouvé dans sa chambre.

2 *adv* entièrement, complètement, tout à fait. **I ~ forgot** j'ai complètement oublié; **he got ~ away** il a décampé sans laisser de traces; **to cut ~ through sth** couper qch de part en part; **he jumped ~ over the fence** il a sauté la barrière sans la toucher; **the car went ~ through the hedge** la voiture est carrément passée à travers la haie; **the fish jumped ~ out of the net** le poisson a sauté carrément hors du filet; **to break off ~** casser net; (*fig*) **to come ~**‡ se mettre à table‡; **to come ~ about sth**‡ révéler qch.

3 *n*: **to give sth a good ~(up)** bien nettoyer qch.

4 *cpd*: **clean-cut** bien délimité, net, clair; **clean-limbed** bien proportionné, bien découplé; **clean-living** décent, honnête; **clean-out** nettoyage *m* à fond; **clean-shaven** (*well-shaved*) *face* rasé de près, glabre; *head* rasé; **to be clean-shaven** n'avoir ni barbe ni moustache, être glabre; **cleanup** *V* **cleanup**.

5 *vt clothes, room* nettoyer; *vegetables* laver; *blackboard* essuyer. **to ~ one's teeth** se laver *or* se brosser les dents; **to ~ one's nails** se curer *or* se brosser les ongles; **to ~ one's face** se débarbouiller, se laver la figure; **to ~ the windows** faire les vitres; *V* **dry**.

6 *vi* se nettoyer. **that floor ~s easily** ce plancher se nettoie facilement *or* est facile à nettoyer.

clean off *vt sep writing* (*on blackboard*) essuyer; (*on wall*) enlever.

clean out **1** *vt sep drawer, box* nettoyer à fond; *cupboard, room* nettoyer *or* faire à fond; (**fig: leave penniless etc*) *person* nettoyer*. **the hotel bill cleaned me out*** la note de l'hôtel m'a nettoyé* *or* m'a mis à sec*; **he was cleaned out*** il était fauché *or* à sec*; **the burglars had cleaned out the whole house*** les cambrioleurs avaient complètement vidé la maison.

2 **clean-out** *n V* **clean 4**.

clean up **1** *vi* **(a)** tout nettoyer, mettre de l'ordre. **she had to clean up after the children's visit** elle a dû tout remettre en ordre après la visite des enfants.

(b) (**fig: make profit*) faire son beurre*. **he cleaned up on that sale** cette vente lui a rapporté gros, il a touché un joli paquet sur cette vente.

2 *vt* **(a)** *room* nettoyer. **to clean o.s. up** se laver, se débarbouiller.

(b) (*fig*) (re)mettre de l'ordre dans (les affaires de), épurer. **the new mayor cleaned up the city** le nouveau maire a épuré la ville *or* a remis de l'ordre dans la ville; **they are trying to clean up television** ils essaient d'épurer la télévision.

3 **cleanup** *n V* **cleanup**.

cleaner [ˈkliːnəʳ] *n* (*Comm*) teinturier *m*, -ière *f*; (*charwoman*) femme *f* de ménage; (*device*) appareil *m* de nettoyage; (*stain-remover*) détachant *m*. **the ~'s shop** la teinturerie; **he took his coat to the ~'s** il a donné son pardessus à nettoyer *or* au teinturier; (*fig*) **to take sb to the ~'s**‡ nettoyer* qn, soutirer le maximum à qn; *V* **dry, vacuum** *etc*.

cleaning [ˈkliːnɪŋ] **1** *n* nettoyage *m*; (*housework*) ménage *m*; *V* **spring**. **2** *cpd*: **cleaning fluid** détachant *m*; **cleaning woman** femme *f* de ménage.

cleanliness [ˈklenlɪnɪs] *n* propreté *f*, habitude *f* de la propreté. (*Prov*) **~ is next to godliness** la propreté du corps est parente de la propreté de l'âme.

cleanly[1] [ˈkliːnlɪ] *adv* proprement, nettement.

cleanly[2] [ˈklenlɪ] *adj person, animal* propre.

cleanness [ˈkliːnnɪs] *n* propreté *f*.

cleanse [klenz] *vt* nettoyer; *ditch, drain etc* curer; (*Bible: cure*) guérir; (*fig*) *person* laver (*of* de); (*Rel*) *soul etc* purifier. (*Med*) **to ~ the blood** dépurer le sang.

cleanser [ˈklenzəʳ] *n* (*detergent*) détersif *m*, détergent *m*; (*for complexion*) démaquillant *m*.

cleansing [ˈklenzɪŋ] **1** *adj* (*for complexion*) démaquillant; (*fig*) purifiant. **~ cream/lotion** crème/lotion démaquillante; **~ department** service *m* de voirie. **2** *n* nettoyage *m*.

cleanup [ˈkliːnʌp] *n* **(a)** *[room]* nettoyage *m*; *[person]* débarbouillage *m*; (*fig*) épuration *f*, assainissement *m*. **to give o.s. a ~** se laver, se débarbouiller; *V also* **clean 3**.

(b) (**fig*) profit *m*. **he made a good ~ from that business** il a fait son beurre dans cette affaire*, cette affaire lui a rapporté gros.

clear [klɪəʳ] **1** *adj* **(a)** (*not opaque, cloudy, indistinct*) *piece of glass, plastic* transparent; *water* clair, limpide, transparent; *lake, stream* limpide, transparent; *sky* clair, sans nuages; *weather* clair, serein; *photograph* net; *outline* clair, net, distinct; *complexion* clair, lumineux, transparent. **on a ~ day** par temps clair; **~ honey** miel *m* liquide; **~ red** rouge vif; **~ soup** bouillon *m*; (*made with meat*) bouillon (gras), consommé *m*; **he left with a ~ conscience** il est parti la conscience tranquille.

(b) (*easily heard*) *sound* clair, distinct, qui s'entend nettement. **his words were quite ~** ses paroles étaient tout à fait distinctes *or* s'entendaient très nettement; **you're not very ~** je ne vous entends pas bien.

(c) (*keen, discerning, lucid*) *explanation, account* clair, intelligible; *reasoning* clair, lucide; *intelligence* clair, pénétrant; *style* clair, net. **~ mind** *or* **thinker** esprit *m* lucide; **I want to be quite ~ on this point** (*understand clearly*) je veux savoir exactement ce qu'il en est; (*explain unambiguously*) je veux bien me faire comprendre; **he is not quite ~ about what he must do** il n'a pas bien compris *or* saisi ce qu'il doit faire; **to be quite ~ about sth, to get sth ~** bien comprendre qch.

(d) (*obvious, indisputable*) *proof, sign, consequence* évident, clair, manifeste; *motive* compréhensible. **~ indication** signe manifeste *or* certain; **it was a ~ case of murder** c'était un cas d'assassinat manifeste, il s'agissait manifestement d'un assassinat; **to make o.s.** *or* **one's meaning ~** se faire bien comprendre, bien préciser ce que l'on veut dire; **do I make myself quite ~?** est-ce que c'est bien clair?, vous me comprenez?; **to make it ~ to sb that** faire comprendre à qn que; **I wish to make it ~ that** je tiens à préciser que; **as ~ as day** clair comme le jour *or* comme de l'eau de roche; (*iro*) **as ~ as mud**: clair comme de l'encre; **it is ~ that he knows about such things** il est clair *or* évident qu'il s'y connaît; **it is ~ to me that** il me paraît hors de doute que; *V* **crystal.**

(e) (*free of obstacles etc*) *road, path etc* libre, dégagé; *route* sans obstacles, sans dangers. **the road is ~** la route est dégagée *or* libre; **~ space** espace *m* libre; **all ~!** fin d'alerte!; (*fig*) la voie est libre; **we had a ~ view** rien ne gênait la vue; **after this traffic holdup we had a ~ run home** une fois ce bouchon passé la route était dégagée jusqu'à la maison; **we were ~ of the town** nous étions hors de *or* sortis de l'agglomération; **~ of** (*free of*) débarrassé de, libre de, libéré de; **~ of debts** libre de dettes; **a ~ profit** un bénéfice net; **a ~ loss** une perte sèche; **three ~ days** trois jours pleins *or* entiers; **a ~ majority** une nette majorité; *V* **coast.**

2 *n*: **to send a message in ~** envoyer un message en clair; **to be in the ~*** (*above suspicion*) être au-dessus de tout soupçon; (*no longer suspected*) n'être plus soupçonné, être blanchi de tout soupçon; (*out of debt*) être libre de toutes dettes; (*out of danger*) être hors de danger.

3 *adv* **(a)** distinctement, nettement. **loud and ~** très distinctement.

(b) entièrement, complètement. **the thief got ~ away** le voleur a disparu sans laisser de traces, on n'a jamais revu le voleur.

(c) ~ of à l'écart de, à distance de; (*Naut*) **to steer ~ of** passer au large de; **to steer** *or* **keep ~ of sth/sb** éviter qch/qn; **to stand ~** s'écarter, se tenir à distance; **stand ~ of the doors!** dégagez les portes!; **to get ~ of** (*go away from*) s'éloigner *or* s'écarter de; (*rid o.s. of*) se débarrasser de; **it will be easier once we get ~ of winter** cela sera plus facile une fois l'hiver passé.

4 *cpd*: **clear-cut** net, précis, nettement défini; **clear-cut features** traits nets *or* bien dessinés; **clear-headed** lucide, perspicace; **clear-headedness** perspicacité *f*, lucidité *f*; **clear-sighted** (*lit*) qui a bonne vue; (*fig*) clairvoyant, qui voit juste; **clear-sightedness** (*lit*) bonne vue; (*fig*) clairvoyance *f*; (*Brit*) **clearway** route *f* à stationnement interdit.

5 *vt* **(a)** (*clarify*) *liquid* clarifier; *wine* coller; (*Med*) *blood* dépurer; *bowels* purger, dégager; (*fig*) *situation, account* éclaircir, clarifier. **to ~ the air** aérer; (*fig*) détendre l'atmosphère; **to ~ one's throat** s'éclaircir la voix; **to take sth to ~ one's head** prendre qch pour se dégager le cerveau.

(b) (*remove obstacles etc from*) *canal, path, road, railway line* débarrasser, dégager, déblayer; *pipe* déboucher; *land* défricher. **to ~ the table** débarrasser la table, desservir; **to ~ the decks (for action)** mettre en branle-bas (de combat); (*fig*) tout déblayer; **to ~ sth of rubbish** déblayer qch; (*lit*) **to ~ the way for** faire place à, libérer le passage pour; (*fig*) **to ~ the way for further discussions** préparer le terrain pour *or* ouvrir la voie à des négociations ultérieures; **~ the way!** circulez!, dégagez!*; **to ~ a way** *or* **a path through** (se) frayer un passage à travers; **to ~ a room** (*of people*) faire évacuer une salle; (*of things*) débarrasser une salle; (*Jur*) **to ~ the court** faire évacuer la salle; (*fig*) **to ~ the ground** déblayer le terrain; (*Post*) **the box is ~ed twice a day** la levée a lieu deux fois par jour; (*Ftbl*) **to ~ the ball** dégager le ballon.

(c) (*find innocent, acceptable etc*) *person* innocenter, disculper (*of* de). **he was ~ed of the murder charge** il a été disculpé de l'accusation d'assassinat; **he will easily ~ himself** il se disculpera facilement, il prouvera facilement son innocence; **to ~ sb of suspicion** laver qn de tout soupçon; **you will have to be ~ed by our security department** il faudra que nos services de sécurité donnent (*subj*) le feu vert en ce qui vous concerne; **we've ~ed it with him before beginning*** nous avons obtenu son accord avant de commencer; **you must ~ the project with the manager** il faut que le directeur donne (*subj*) le feu vert à votre projet.

(d) (*get past or over*) sauter, franchir, sauter *or* passer pardessus (sans toucher); *obstacle* éviter; (*Naut*) *rocks* éviter; *harbour* quitter. **the horse ~ed the gate by 10 cm** le cheval a sauté *or* a franchi la barrière avec 10 cm de reste *or* de marge; **the car ~ed the lamppost** la voiture a évité le réverbère de justesse; **raise the car till the wheel ~s the ground** soulevez la voiture jusqu'à ce que la roue ne touche (*subj*) plus le sol; **the boat just ~ed the bottom** le bateau a réussi à passer sans toucher le fond.

(e) *cheque* compenser; *account* solder, liquider; *debt* s'acquitter de; *profit* gagner net; (*Comm*) *goods* liquider; (*Customs*) *goods* dédouaner; *port dues* acquitter; *ship* expédier; (*fig*) *one's conscience* décharger; *doubts* dissiper. (*Comm*) **'half price to ~'** 'solde à moitié prix pour liquider'; **you must ~ your homework before you go out** il faut que tu te débarrasses (*subj*) de *or* que tu finisses tes devoirs avant de sortir; **I've ~ed £100 on this business** cette affaire me rapporte 100 livres net *or* tous frais payés; **I didn't even ~ my expenses** je ne suis même pas rentré dans mes frais.

6 *vi [weather]* s'éclaircir; *[sky]* se dégager; *[fog]* se dissiper; *[face, expression]* s'éclairer; (*Naut*) *[ship]* prendre la mer. **his brow ~ed** son visage s'est éclairé.

clear away 1 *vi* **(a)** *[mist etc]* se dissiper.

(b) (*clear the table*) desservir.

2 *vt sep* enlever, emporter, ôter. **to clear away the dishes** desservir *or* débarrasser (la table).

clear off 1 *vi*(*) filer*, décamper. **clear off!** fichez le camp!*, filez!*

2 *vt sep* se débarrasser de; *debts* s'acquitter de; (*Comm*) *stock* liquider; *goods* solder. **to clear off arrears of work** rattraper le retard dans son travail.

clear out 1 *vi*(*) = **clear off 1.**

2 *vt sep cupboard* vider; *room* nettoyer, débarrasser; *unwanted objects* enlever, jeter. **he cleared (everyone out of) the room** il a fait évacuer la pièce.

clear up 1 *vi* **(a)** *[weather]* s'éclaircir, se lever. **I think it will clear up** je pense que ça va se lever.

(b) (*tidy*) ranger, faire des rangements.

2 *vt sep* **(a)** *mystery* éclaircir, résoudre; *matter, subject* éclaircir, tirer au clair.

(b) (*tidy*) ranger, mettre en ordre.

clearance [ˈklɪərəns] **1** *n* **(a)** (*U*) *[road, path]* déblaiement *m*, dégagement *m*; *[land, bombsite]* déblaiement; *[room, court]* évacuation *f*; *[litter, objects, rubbish]* enlèvement *m*; (*Comm*) soldes *mpl*, liquidation *f* (du stock).

(b) *[boat, car etc]* dégagement *m*, espace *m* libre. **2 metre ~** espace de 2 mètres; **how much ~ is there between my car and yours?** je suis à combien de votre voiture?

(c) *[cheque]* compensation *f*; (*Customs*) dédouanement *m*; (*permission etc*) autorisation *f*, permis *m* (*de publier etc*). (*Naut*) **~ outwards/inwards** permis de sortie/d'entrée; **the despatch was sent to the Foreign Office for ~** la dépêche a été soumise au ministère des Affaires étrangères pour contrôle; (*Aviat*) **to give (sb) ~ for takeoff** donner (à qn) l'autorisation de décoller.

2 *cpd*: (*Naut*) **clearance certificate** congé *m* de navigation, lettre *f* de mer; (*Comm*) **clearance sale** soldes *mpl*.

clearing [ˈklɪərɪŋ] **1** *n* **(a)** (*in forest*) clairière *f*.

(b) (*U*) *[liquid]* clarification *f*; *[wine]* collage *m*; (*Med*) *[bowels]* purge *f*; *[blood]* dépuration *f*.

(c) (*U: tidying, unblocking*) *[room, cupboard, passage]* dégagement *m*, désencombrement *m*; *[rubbish]* ramassage *m*, déblaiement *m*; *[objects]* enlèvement *m*; *[land]* défrichement *m*; *[pipe etc]* débouchage *m*; *[road]* dégagement, déblaiement; *[room, court]* évacuation *f*.

(d) (*Jur*) *[accused]* disculpation *f*.

(e) (*Fin*) *[cheque]* compensation *f*; *[account]* liquidation *f*; *[debt]* acquittement *m*.

2 *cpd*: (*Brit*) **clearing bank** banque *f* (appartenant à une chambre de compensation); **clearing house** (*Banking*) chambre *f* de compensation; (*fig: for documents etc*) bureau *or* office central.

clearly [ˈklɪəlɪ] *adv* **(a)** (*distinctly*) *see, state* clairement, nettement; *hear* distinctement, nettement; *understand* bien, clairement. **(b)** (*obviously*) manifestement, évidemment.

clearness [ˈklɪənɪs] *n* **(a)** *[air, liquid]* transparence *f*, limpidité *f*; *[glass]* transparence. **(b)** *[sound, sight, print, thought etc]* clarté *f*, netteté *f*.

cleat [kliːt] *n* (*Carpentry*) tasseau *m*; (*Naut*) taquet *m*; (*on shoe*) clou *m*.

cleavage [ˈkliːvɪdʒ] *n* (*lit*) (*Chem, Geol*) clivage *m*; (*Bio*) *[cell]* division *f*; (*fig*) *[opinion]* division, clivage. **a dress which showed her ~*** une robe qui laissait voir la naissance des seins.

cleave[1] [kliːv] *pret* **cleft** *or* **clove**, *ptp* **cleft** *or* **cloven 1** *vt* (*gen liter*) fendre; (*Chem, Geol*) cliver; (*Bio*) diviser; (*fig*) diviser, séparer, désunir. **2** *vi* se fendre; (*Chem, Geol*) se cliver; (*Bio*) se diviser. **to ~ through the waves** fendre les vagues.

cleave[2] [kliːv] *pret, ptp* **cleaved** *vi* (*liter*) (*stick*) coller, adhérer (*to* à); (*fig*) s'attacher, rester attaché *or* fidèle (*to* à).

cleaver [ˈkliːvəʳ] *n* fendoir *m*, couperet *m*.

clef [klef] *n* (*Mus*) clef *f* *or* clé *f* (*signe*); *V* **bass**[1], **treble.**

cleft [kleft] **1** *pret, ptp of* **cleave**[1]. **2** *adj* fendu; *stick* fourchu. (*fig*) **to be in a ~ stick** se trouver *or* être dans une impasse; (*Anat*) **~ palate** palais fendu. **3** *n* (*in rock*) crevasse *f*, fissure *f*.

clematis [ˈklemətɪs] *n* clématite *f*.

clemency [ˈklemənsɪ] *n [person]* clémence *f* (*towards* envers); *[weather etc]* douceur *f*, clémence.

clement [ˈklemənt] *adj person* clément (*towards* envers); *weather* doux (*f* douce), clément.

clementine [ˈkleməntaɪn] *n* clémentine *f*.

clench [klentʃ] **1** *vt* **(a) to ~ sth (in one's hands)** empoigner *or* serrer qch dans ses mains; **to ~ one's fists/teeth** serrer les poings/les dents. **(b)** = **clinch 1. 2** *n* = **clinch 3a.**

Cleopatra [ˌkliːəˈpætrə] *n* Cléopâtre *f.* **~'s needle** l'obélisque *m* de Cléopâtre.
clerestory [ˈklɪəstɔːrɪ] *n* (*Archit*) claire-voie *f*, clair-étage *m.*
clergy [ˈklɜːdʒɪ] *collective n* (membres *mpl* du) clergé *m.* **~man** ecclésiastique *m*; (*Protestant*) pasteur *m*; (*Roman Catholic*) prêtre *m*, curé *m.*
cleric [ˈklerɪk] *n* ecclésiastique *m.*
clerical [ˈklerɪkəl] *adj* **(a)** (*Rel*) clérical, du clergé; *collar* de pasteur.
(b) (*Comm, Fin, Jur*) *job, position* de commis, d'employé; *work, worker, staff* de bureau. **~ error** (*in book-keeping*) erreur *f* d'écriture (commise par un employé); (*in manuscripts*) faute *f* de copiste.
clericalism [ˈklerɪkəlɪzəm] *n* cléricalisme *m.*
clerihew [ˈklerɪhjuː] *n* petit poème humoristique (*pseudo-biographique*).
clerk [klɑːk, (*US*) klɜːrk] *n* **(a)** (*in office*) employé(e) *m(f)* (*de bureau, de commerce*), commis *m*; (*Jur*) clerc *m.* **bank ~** employé(e) de banque; (*in hotel*) **desk ~** réceptionniste *mf*; (*Jur*) **C~ of the Court** greffier *m* (du tribunal); *V* **head, town.**
(b) (††) (*Rel*) ecclésiastique *m*; (*scholar*) clerc†† *m*, savant *m.*
(c) (*US: shop assistant*) vendeur *m*, -euse *f.*
(d) (*Brit Constr*) **~ of works** conducteur *m* de travaux.
clerkship [ˈklɑːkʃɪp, (*US*) ˈklɜːrkʃɪp] *n* fonctions *fpl* d'employé de bureau, emploi *m* de commis; (*Med*) stage *m.*
clever [ˈklevəʳ] **1** *adj* **(a)** (*intelligent*) *person* intelligent, à l'esprit éveillé, astucieux; *book* intelligemment écrit, ingénieux; *play, film* intelligemment *or* bien fait, intelligent; *machine, invention, explanation* ingénieux; *idea* astucieux, intelligent; *joke* fin, astucieux; *story* bien conduit, astucieux. **~ pupil** élève doué; **to be ~ at French** être fort en français.
(b) (*skilful*) *person* habile, adroit; *thing* bien fait. **a ~ workman** un ouvrier habile; **to be ~ at doing sth** être habile à faire qch; **to be ~ with one's hands** être adroit de ses mains; **he's very ~ with cars** il s'y connaît en voitures.
(c) (*smart*) *person* astucieux, malin (*f* -igne); *action* ingénieux, astucieux. **a ~ trick** un tour ingénieux *or* astucieux; **he was too ~ for me** il m'a roulé*, il m'a eu*; (*pej*) **~ Dick** petit *or* gros malin; *V* **half.**
2 *cpd*: (*pej*) **clever-clever*** un peu trop futé.
cleverly [ˈklevəlɪ] *adv* (*V* **clever**) intelligemment; astucieusement; ingénieusement; habilement, adroitement.
cleverness [ˈklevənɪs] *n* (*V* **clever**) intelligence *f*; astuce *f*, ingéniosité *f*; habileté *f*, adresse *f* (*at* à).
clew [kluː] *n* (*US*) = **clue.**
cliché [ˈkliːʃeɪ] *n* cliché *m*, expression *or* phrase toute faite.
click [klɪk] **1** *n* déclic *m*, petit bruit sec; *[tongue]* claquement *m*; *[wheel]* cliquet *m.*
2 *vi* faire un bruit sec, cliqueter. **the door ~ed shut** la porte s'est refermée avec un déclic; **the part ~ed into place** la pièce s'est mise en place *or* s'est enclenchée avec un déclic; (*fig*) **suddenly it ~ed‡** j'ai pigé‡ tout à coup; (*fig*) **to ~ with sb*** se découvrir des atomes crochus* avec qn; *(sexually)* taper dans l'œil à qn*.
3 *vt*: **to ~ one's heels** claquer des talons; **to ~ one's tongue** faire claquer sa langue, clapper de la langue; **she ~ed the shelf back into place** elle a remis l'étagère en place avec un déclic.
clicking [ˈklɪkɪŋ] *n* cliquetis *m.*
client [ˈklaɪənt] *n* client(e) *m(f).*
clientele [ˌkliːɑ̃ːnˈtel] *n* (*Comm*) clientèle *f*; (*Theat*) habitués *mpl.*
cliff [klɪf] **1** *n [seashore]* falaise *f*; *[mountains]* escarpement *m.*
2 *cpd*: **cliff-dweller** (*lit*) troglodyte *mf*; (*US*) habitant(e) *m(f)* de gratte-ciel; **cliff-hanger*** récit *m* (*or* situation *f etc*) à suspense; **cliff-hanging*** tendu, à suspense; **cliff-hanging vote*** vote *m* à suspense.
climacteric [klaɪˈmæktərɪk] **1** *n* climatère *m*; (*Med, esp US*) ménopause *f.* **2** *adj* climatérique; (*fig*) crucial, dangereux.
climactic [klaɪˈmæktɪk] *adj* à son *or* au point culminant, à son apogée.
climate [ˈklaɪmɪt] *n* (*Met, fig*) climat *m.* **the ~ of opinion** (les courants *mpl* de) l'opinion *f.*
climatic [klaɪˈmætɪk] *adj* climatique, climatérique.
climatology [ˌklaɪməˈtɒlədʒɪ] *n* climatologie *f.*
climax [ˈklaɪmæks] **1** *n* point culminant, apogée *m*; (*sexual*) orgasme *m*; (*Rhetoric*) gradation *f.* **the ~ of his political career** l'apogée de sa vie politique; **this brought matters to a ~** cela a porté l'affaire à son point culminant; (*fig*) **to come to a ~** atteindre son point culminant; (*fig*) **to work up to a ~** *[story, events]* tendre vers son point culminant, s'intensifier; *[speaker]* amener le point culminant.
2 *vt* amener *or* porter à son point culminant *or* au point culminant.
3 *vi* atteindre son *or* le point culminant.
climb [klaɪm] **1** *vt* (*also* **~ up**) *stairs, steps, slope* monter, grimper; *hill* grimper, escalader; *tree, ladder* grimper *or* monter sur *or* à; *rope* monter à; *cliff, wall* escalader; *mountain* gravir, faire l'ascension de.
2 *vi* **(a)** (*lit, fig: also* **~ up**) s'élever, monter; *[persons, plants]* grimper; *[road]* monter; *[aircraft, rocket]* monter, prendre de l'altitude; *[sun]* monter.
(b) to ~ down a tree descendre d'un arbre; **to ~ down a mountain** descendre d'une montagne, effectuer la descente d'une montagne; **to ~ over a wall/an obstacle** escalader un mur/un obstacle; **to ~ over a low wall** enjamber un mur bas; **to ~ into an aircraft/a boat** monter *or* grimper à bord d'un avion/bateau; **to ~ out of a hole** se hisser hors d'un trou; (*Sport*) **to go ~ing** faire de l'alpinisme; (*fig*) **to ~ to power** s'élever (jusqu') au pouvoir.
3 *n [hill]* montée *f*, côte *f*; (*Alpinism*) ascension *f*, *[aircraft]* montée, ascension.
4 *cpd*: **climb-down*** reculade *f*, dérobade *f.*
climb down 1 *vi* **(a)** (*lit*) (*from tree, wall*) descendre; (*Alpinism*) descendre, effectuer une descente.
(b) (*: *abandon one's position*) en rabattre.
2 climb-down* *n V* **climb 4.**
climb up *V* **climb 1, 2a.**
climber [ˈklaɪməʳ] *n* (*person*) grimpeur *m*, -euse *f*; (*mountaineer*) alpiniste *mf*, ascensionniste *mf*; (*fig pej*) arriviste *mf* (*pej*); (*plant*) plante grimpante; (*bird*) grimpeur *m.*
climbing [ˈklaɪmɪŋ] **1** *adj person, bird* grimpeur; (*Bot*) grimpant; (*Astron, Aviat*) ascendant.
2 *n* montée *f*, escalade *f*; (*Sport*) alpinisme *m*; (*fig*) arrivisme *m* (*pej*).
3 *cpd*: **climbing irons** crampons *mpl*; (*Aviat*) **climbing speed** vitesse ascensionnelle.
clinch [klɪntʃ] **1** *vt* (*also* **clench**) (*Tech*) *nail, rivet* river; (*Naut*) étalinguer; (*fig*) *argument* consolider, confirmer; *bargain* conclure. **to ~ the deal** conclure l'affaire; **to ~ an agreement** sceller un pacte; **that ~es it** comme ça c'est réglé, ça coupe court à tout*.
2 *vi* (*Boxing*) s'accrocher.
3 *n* **(a)** (*also* **clench**) (*Tech*) rivetage *m*; (*Naut*) étalingure *f.*
(b) (*Boxing*) accrochage *m.* **to get into a ~** s'accrocher.
(c) (‡: *embrace*) étreinte *f*, enlacement *m.* **in a ~** enlacés.
cling [klɪŋ] *pret, ptp* **clung** *vi* **(a)** (*hold tight*) se cramponner, s'accrocher (*to* à). **to ~ together, to ~ to one another** se tenir étroitement enlacés; (*fig*) **despite the opposition of all he clung to his opinion** il s'est cramponné à *or* a maintenu son opinion envers et contre tous; (*fig*) **to ~ to a belief** se raccrocher à une croyance; **to ~ to the belief that** se raccrocher à la notion que.
(b) (*stick*) adhérer, (se) coller, s'attacher (*to* à); *[clothes]* coller. **to ~ together, to ~ to one another** rester *or* être collés l'un à l'autre.
clinging [ˈklɪŋɪŋ] *adj garment* collant, qui moule le corps; *odour* tenace; (*pej*) *person* crampon* *inv*, collant*.
clinic [ˈklɪnɪk] *n* (*private nursing home, consultant's teaching session*) clinique *f*; (*health centre*) centre médico-social *or* d'hygiène sociale; (*also* **outpatients' ~**) service *m* de consultation (externe), dispensaire *m* (municipal).
clinical [ˈklɪnɪkəl] *adj* **(a)** (*Med*) *conditions, lecture* clinique. **~ thermometer** thermomètre médical. **(b)** (*fig*) *attitude, approach* objectif, impartial.
clink[1] [klɪŋk] **1** *vt* faire tinter *or* résonner *or* sonner. **to ~ glasses with sb** trinquer avec qn. **2** *vi* tinter, résonner. **3** *n* tintement *m* (*de verres etc*).
clink[2] [klɪŋk] *n* (*Prison sl*) taule‡ *f or* tôle‡ *f*, bloc* *m.*
clinker [ˈklɪŋkəʳ] *n* mâchefer *m*, scories *fpl.* (*Naut*) **~-built** (bordé) à clin(s).
clip[1] [klɪp] **1** *n* (*for papers*) attache *f*, trombone *m*; (*for tube*) collier *m*, bague *f*; (*also* **cartridge ~**) chargeur *m*; (*brooch*) clip *m.* **2** *vt papers* attacher (avec un trombone). **to ~ a brooch on one's dress** fixer une broche sur sa robe.
clip on *vt sep brooch* fixer; *document etc* attacher (avec un trombone).
clip together *vt sep* attacher.
clip[2] [klɪp] **1** *vt* **(a)** (*cut, snip*) couper (avec des ciseaux); *hedge* tailler; *sheep, dog* tondre; *ticket* poinçonner; *article from newspaper* découper; *hair* couper; *wings* rogner, couper. (*fig*) **to ~ sb's wings** rogner les ailes à qn; (*fig*) **he has a ~ped way of speaking** il avale ses mots *or* les syllabes (en parlant); (*fig*) **in a ~ped voice** d'un ton sec.
(b) (*: *hit*) flanquer une taloche à*. **I ~ped him on the jaw*** je lui ai flanqué un marron‡ à travers la figure.
2 *n* **(a) to give sth a ~ = to clip sth**; *V* **1a.**
(b) (*Cine*) extrait *m.*
(c) (*: *blow*) taloche* *f*, marron‡ *m.* **he gave him a ~ on the head** *or* **round the ear** il lui a flanqué une bonne taloche*.
3 *cpd*: (*pej*) **clip joint‡** boîte *f* où l'on se fait tondre *or* fusiller*; **that's a real clip joint** c'est vraiment le coup de fusil dans cette boîte*.
clipper [ˈklɪpəʳ] *n* **(a)** (*Aviat, Naut*) clipper *m.* **(b) ~s** (*tool*) tondeuse *f*; *V* **hair, hedge, nail.**
clippie‡ [ˈklɪpɪ] *n* (*Brit: conductress*) receveuse *f.*
clipping [ˈklɪpɪŋ] *n [newspaper etc]* coupure *f* de presse *or* de journal.
clique [kliːk] *n* (*slightly pej*) clique *f*, coterie *f*, chapelle *f.*
cliquey [ˈkliːkɪ] *adj*, **cliquish** [ˈkliːkɪʃ] *adj* (*slightly pej*) exclusif, qui a l'esprit de clique *or* de (petite) chapelle.
cliquishness [ˈkliːkɪʃnɪs] *n* (*slightly pej*) esprit *m* de clique *or* de chapelle.
clitoris [ˈklɪtərɪs] *n* clitoris *m.*
cloak [kləʊk] **1** *n* (*Dress*) grande cape; *[shepherd etc]* houppelande *f*; (*fig*) manteau *m*, voile *m.* (*fig*) **as a ~ for sth** pour cacher *or* masquer qch; **under the ~ of darkness** sous le manteau *or* le voile de la nuit.
2 *vt* (*fig*) masquer, déguiser, cacher; (*Dress*) revêtir d'un manteau. (*fig*) **~ed with respectability/mystery** empreint de respectabilité/de mystère.
3 *cpd*: **cloak-and-dagger** clandestin; **the cloak-and-dagger boys*** les membres *mpl* du service secret, les barbouzes‡ *mpl*; **a cloak-and-dagger story** un roman d'espionnage.
cloakroom [ˈkləʊkrʊm] *n* **(a)** *[coats etc]* vestiaire *m*; (*Brit: left luggage*) consigne *f.* **to put** *or* **leave in the ~** *clothes* mettre *or* déposer au vestiaire; *luggage* mettre à la consigne; **~ ticket** *[clothes]* numéro *m* de vestiaire; *[luggage]* bulletin *m* de consigne.
(b) (*Brit euph: toilet*) (*public*) toilettes *fpl*; (*in house*) cabinets *mpl.*

clobber‡ ['klɒbəʳ] **1** *n* (*U: Brit: belongings*) barda‡ *m*. **2** *vt* (*hit*) tabasser‡; (*fig*) mettre à plat*, démolir*.
cloche [klɒʃ] *n* (*Agr, Dress*) cloche *f*.
clock [klɒk] **1** *n* **(a)** (*large*) horloge *f*; (*smaller*) pendule *f*. **it's midday by the church ~** il est midi au clocher de l'église; **2 hours by the ~** 2 heures d'horloge; **to work round the ~** travailler vingt-quatre heures d'affilée *or* vingt-quatre heures sur vingt-quatre; (*fig*) travailler sans relâche; **to work against the ~** travailler contre la montre; **to put the ~ back/forward** retarder/avancer l'horloge; (*fig*) **you can't put the ~ back** ce qui est fait est fait; **this decision will put** *or* **set the ~ back 50 years** cette décision va nous ramener 50 ans en arrière; *V* **grand, o'clock, sleep** *etc*.
(b) *[taxi]* compteur *m*, taximètre *m*; (*Aut**: *milometer*) = compteur (kilométrique). (*Aut*) **there were 50.000 miles on the ~** la voiture avait 50.000 milles au compteur.
2 *cpd*: **clock-golf** jeu *m* de l'horloge; **clockmaker** horloger *m*; **clock-radio** radio-réveil *m*; **clock repairer** horloger réparateur; **clock-tower** clocher *m*; (*pej*) **he's a terrible clock-watcher** il ne fait que guetter l'heure de sortie, il a les yeux fixés sur la pendule; **to be guilty of clock-watching** passer son temps à surveiller les aiguilles de la pendule.
3 *vt* **(a)** (*Sport*) *runner* chronométrer. **he ~ed 4 minutes for the mile** il a fait le mille en 4 minutes.
(b) (*Brit‡: hit*) **he ~ed him one** il lui a flanqué un ramponneau‡ *or* un marron‡.
clock in 1 *vi* (*Ind*) pointer (à l'arrivée).
2 *vt sep*: **he clocked in 3 hours' work** il a fait 3 heures de travail.
clock off *vi* (*Ind*) pointer (à la sortie).
clock on *vi* = **clock in 1.**
clock out = **clock off.**
clock up *vt sep* **(a)** = **clock in 2.**
(b) (*Aut*) **he clocked up 250 miles** il a fait 250 milles au compteur.
clockwise ['klɒkwaɪz] *adv, adj* dans le sens des aiguilles d'une montre.
clockwork ['klɒkwɜːk] **1** *n* (*mechanism*) *[clock]* mouvement *m* (d'horloge); *[toy etc]* mécanisme *m*, rouages *mpl*. (*fig*) **to go like ~** aller comme sur des roulettes; *V* **regular.**
2 *cpd toy, tram, car* mécanique; (*fig*) précis, régulier. **with clockwork precision** avec la précision d'une horloge.
clod [klɒd] **1** *n* **(a)** *[earth etc]* motte *f* (de terre *etc*). **(b)** (*‡pej: person*) = **clodhopper‡**. **2** *cpd*: (*pej*) **clodhopper‡** (*person*) lourdaud *m*, balourd *m*; (*shoe*) godillot‡ *m*.
clog [klɒg] **1** *n* (*shoe*) (*wooden*) sabot *m*; (*with wooden soles*) socque *m*, galoche† *f*.
2 *vt* (*also* **~ up**) *pipe* boucher, encrasser; *wheel* bloquer; *passage* boucher, bloquer, obstruer; (*fig*) entraver, gêner.
3 *vi* (*also* **~ up**) *[pipe etc]* se boucher, s'encrasser.
cloister ['klɔɪstəʳ] **1** *n* (*Archit, Rel*) cloître *m*. **2** *vt* (*Rel*) cloîtrer. (*fig*) **to lead a ~ed life** mener une vie monacale *or* de cloître.
close¹ [kləʊs] **1** *adj* **(a)** (*near*) proche (*to* de), voisin (*to* de); (*fig*) proche, intime. **the house is ~ to the shops** la maison est près *or* proche des magasins; **sit here ~ to me** asseyez-vous ici près de moi; **his birthday is ~ to mine** son anniversaire est proche du mien; **to be ~ to tears** être au bord des larmes; **in ~ proximity to** dans le voisinage immédiat de, tout près de; **at ~ quarters** (*fig*) tout près (*with* de); (*Mil: hand to hand*) corps à corps; **~ connection between** rapport étroit entre; **~ contact** contact direct; **a ~ friendship** une amitié intime; **a ~ relative** un parent proche; **~ resemblance** ressemblance exacte *or* fidèle; **to bear a ~ resemblance to** ressembler beaucoup à; (*lit*) **to have a ~ shave** se (faire) raser de près; (*fig*) **to have a ~ call*** *or* **shave*** l'échapper belle, y échapper de justesse; **that was a ~ call!*** *or* **shave!*** il était moins une!*, on l'a échappé belle!; **she was very ~ to her brother** (*in age*) son frère et elle étaient d'âges très rapprochés *or* se suivaient de près; (*in friendship*) elle était très proche de son frère; **they were very ~ (friends)** ils étaient intimes; **a ~ circle of friends** un petit cercle d'amis intimes; *V* **comfort.**
(b) (*compact*) *handwriting, texture, rain, order, rank* serré; *grain* fin, dense; *account* près *or* proche de la vérité; *argument* concis, précis; *reasoning* serré. (*Aviat, Mil*) **in ~ formation** *or* **order** en ordre serré.
(c) (*strict*) *control, surveillance* étroit, qui ne se relâche pas; (*thorough*) *questioning, checking* serré, minutieux, attentif; *examination, study* attentif, rigoureux; *attention* soutenu; *translation* serré, fidèle; *silence* impénétrable; *investigation, enquiry* minutieux, détaillé. **to keep a ~ watch on sb/sth** surveiller qn/qch de près; **in ~ confinement** en détention surveillée.
(d) (*airless*) *room* mal aéré, qui manque de ventilation *or* d'air; *atmosphere* lourd, étouffant; *air* (*in a room*) renfermé. **it's very ~ in here** on ne respire pas ici, il n'y a pas d'air ici; **a ~ smell** une odeur de renfermé; **~ weather** temps lourd *or* étouffant; (*Met*) **it's ~ today** il fait lourd aujourd'hui.
(e) (*almost equal*) serré. **~ contest** lutte très serrée; **~ finish** arrivée serrée; **~ election** élection extrêmement serrée; **the two candidates were very ~** les deux candidats étaient presque à égalité.
(f) (*Ling*) *vowel* fermé.
(g) (*secretive*) *person* renfermé, secret, peu communicatif.
(h) (*Sport*) **~ season** chasse *or* pêche fermée.
2 *adv* étroitement, de près. **to hold sb ~** serrer qn dans ses bras, tenir qn tout contre soi; **~ by** tout près; **~ by** *or* **to the bridge** (tout) près du pont; **~ to the surface of the water** à fleur d'eau; **~ to the ground** au ras du sol; **~ by us** tout à côté de nous; **~ at hand** tout près; **~ (up)on** tout près de; **he is ~ on 60** il a près de 60 ans, il frise la soixantaine; **it's ~ on midnight** il est près de minuit; **he followed ~ behind me** il me suivait de près; **~ against the wall** tout contre le mur; **~ together** serrés les uns contre les autres; **to come ~r together** se rapprocher; **shut ~, ~ shut** hermétiquement fermé *or* clos; **to sail ~ to the wind** (*Naut*) naviguer au plus près; (*fig: nearly break law*) friser l'illégalité; (*fig: in jokes etc*) friser la vulgarité.
3 *cpd*: **close combat** corps à corps *m*; **close-cropped** *hair* (coupé) ras; *grass* ras; **close-fisted** avare, grippe-sou *inv*, pingre; **close-fitting** *clothes* ajusté, près du corps; **close-grained** *wood* au grain serré; **close-harmony singing** chant *m* dans une tessiture restreinte *or* rapprochée *or* réduite; (*fig*) **close-knit** très uni; (*fig*) **close-mouthed** taciturne, peu bavard; **close-run race** course très disputée; **close-set eyes** yeux rapprochés; **close-shaven** rasé de près; (*Cine, TV*) **close-up** (*photo, shot*) gros plan, détail *m* (grossi); **in close-up** en gros plan.
4 *n* (*enclosure*) clos *m*; *[cathedral]* enceinte *f*; (*Scot: alleyway*) passage *m*, couloir *m*.
close² [kləʊz] **1** *n* (*end*) fin *f*, conclusion *f*. **to come to a ~** arriver à sa fin, se terminer, prendre fin; **to draw to a ~** tirer à sa fin, approcher de sa conclusion; **to draw sth** *or* **bring sth to a ~** mettre fin à qch; (*liter*) **the ~ of (the) day** la tombée *or* la chute du jour; **towards the ~ of the century** vers la fin du siècle.
2 *cpd*: **close-down** *[shop, business etc]* fermeture *f* (définitive); (*Brit: Rad, TV*) fin *f* des émissions.
3 *vt* **(a)** (*shut*) fermer, clore; *eyes, door, factory, shop* fermer; *pipe, tube, opening* boucher; *road* barrer. **road ~d to traffic** route interdite à la circulation; **the shop is ~d** le magasin est fermé; **the shop is ~d on Sundays** le magasin ferme le dimanche; (*fig*) **to ~ one's mind to new ideas** fermer son esprit à toute idée nouvelle; *V* **ear¹, eye** *etc*.
(b) (*bring to an end*) *proceedings, discussion* achever, terminer, mettre fin à, clore; (*Fin*) *account* arrêter, clore; *bargain* conclure. **to ~ the meeting** lever la séance.
(c) (*bring together*) serrer, rapprocher. **to ~ a gap between 2 objects** réduire l'intervalle qui sépare 2 objets; (*Mil, also fig*) **to ~ ranks** serrer les rangs.
(d) (*Elec*) *circuit* fermer.
4 *vi* **(a)** *[door, box, lid, drawer]* fermer, se fermer; *[museum, theatre, shop]* fermer. **the door ~d** la porte s'est fermée; **the door/box ~s badly** la porte/la boîte ferme mal; **the shop ~s on Sundays/at 6 o'clock** le magasin ferme le dimanche/à 6 heures; **his eyes ~d** ses yeux se fermèrent; **his fingers ~d around the pencil** ses doigts se sont refermés sur le crayon.
(b) (*end*) (se) terminer, prendre fin, finir. **the meeting ~d abruptly** la séance a pris fin *or* s'est terminée brusquement; **he ~d with an appeal to their generosity** il a terminé par un appel à leur générosité; (*St Ex*) **shares ~d at 120p** les actions étaient cotées à 120 pence en clôture.
close down 1 *vi [business, shop]* fermer (définitivement); (*Brit: Rad, TV*) terminer les émissions.
2 *vt sep shop, business* fermer (définitivement).
3 close-down *n V* **close² 2.**
close in 1 *vi [hunters etc]* se rapprocher, approcher; *[evening, night]* approcher, descendre, tomber; *[darkness, fog]* descendre. **the days are closing in** les jours raccourcissent (de plus en plus); **to close in on sb** s'approcher *or* se rapprocher de qn, envelopper qn, cerner qn; (*Mil*) cerner qn de près.
2 *vt sep* clôturer, enclore.
close up 1 *vi [people in line etc]* se rapprocher, se serrer; (*Mil*) serrer les rangs; *[wound]* se refermer.
2 *vt sep house, shop* fermer (complètement); *pipe, tube, opening* fermer, obturer, boucher; *wound* refermer, recoudre.
close with *vt fus* **(a)** (*strike bargain with*) conclure un marché avec, tomber d'accord avec.
(b) (*agree to*) *offer, conditions* accepter.
(c) (*grapple with*) se prendre corps à corps avec.
closed [kləʊzd] *adj door, eyes* fermé, clos; *road* barré; *pipe, opening etc* bouché, obturé. (*Theat*) **'~'** 'relâche'; (*lit, fig*) **to find the door ~** trouver porte close; (*Jur*) **~ session** huis clos; **maths are a ~ book to me*** je suis complètement rebelle aux maths *or* bouché* en maths; **~-circuit television** télévision *f* en circuit fermé; (*Ind*) **~ shop** atelier *m or* organisation *f* qui n'admet que des travailleurs syndiqués; (*Ind*) **the unions insisted on a ~-shop policy** les syndicats ont exigé l'exclusion des travailleurs non syndiqués.
closely ['kləʊslɪ] *adv guard* étroitement; *grasp* en serrant fort; *watch, follow* de près; (*attentively*) *study* de près, minutieusement; attentivement; *listen* attentivement. **he held her ~ to him** il la serrait *or* la tenait serrée (tout) contre lui; **a ~ contested match** un match très serré *or* disputé; **they are ~ related** ils sont proches parents; **a matter ~ connected with ...** une affaire en relation directe avec *or* étroitement liée à ....
closeness ['kləʊsnɪs] *n* **(a)** *[cloth, weave]* texture *or* contexture serrée; *[friendship]* intimité *f*; *[resemblance, translation, reproduction]* fidélité *f*; *[examination, interrogation, study]* minutie *f*, rigueur *f*; *[reasoning]* logique *f*; *[pursuit]* vigueur *f*; *[pursuers]* proximité *f*. **~ of blood relationship** proche degré *m* de parenté.
(b) (*proximity*) proximité *f*.
(c) *[weather, atmosphere]* lourdeur *f*; *[room]* manque *m* d'air.
(d) (*stinginess*) avarice *f*.
closet ['klɒzɪt] **1** *n* **(a)** (*cupboard*) armoire *f*, placard *m*; (*for hanging clothes*) penderie *f*.
(b) (*small room*) cabinet *m* (de travail), (petit) bureau *m*.
(c) ((*also* **water ~**) cabinets *mpl*, waters *mpl*.
2 *vt* (*gen pass*) enfermer (*dans un cabinet de travail etc*). **he was ~ed with his father for several hours** son père et lui sont restés plusieurs heures enfermés à discuter.
closing ['kləʊzɪŋ] **1** *n* (*U*) *[factory, house, shop]* fermeture *f*; *[meeting]* clôture *f*; (*Fin*) clôture.

2 *adj* **(a)** final, dernier. ~ **remarks** observations finales; ~ **speech** discours *m* de clôture.

(b) de fermeture. (*Brit*) ~ **time** heure *f* de fermeture (*d'un magasin, d'un café etc*); **when is ~ time?** à quelle heure est-ce qu'on ferme?; '~ **time!'** 'on ferme!'; (*St Ex*) ~ **price** cours *m* en clôture; *V* **early.**

closure [ˈkləʊʒəʳ] *n* (*U: act, condition*) *[factory, business]* fermeture *f*; (*Parl*) clôture *f*. (*Parl*) **to move the ~** demander la clôture.

clot [klɒt] 1 *n* **(a)** *[blood, milk]* caillot *m*. **(b)** (*Brit*: *pej: person*) ballot* *m*, balourd *m*, gourde* *f*. 2 *vt blood* coaguler. (*Brit*) **~ted cream** crème *f* en grumeaux. 3 *vi [blood]* (se) coaguler.

cloth [klɒθ] 1 *n* **(a)** (*U*) tissu *m*, étoffe *f*; *[linen, cotton]* toile *f*; *[wool]* drap *m*; (*Bookbinding*) toile; (*Naut*) toile, voile *f*. **book bound in ~** livre relié toile; ~ **of gold** drap d'or; *V* **oil.**

(b) (*tablecloth*) nappe *f*; (*duster*) chiffon *m*, linge *m*; *V* **dish, tea** *etc.*

(c) (*Rel*) (*collective*) **the ~** le clergé; **out of respect for his ~** par respect pour son sacerdoce.

2 *cpd*: *[books]* **cloth-binding** reliure *f* en toile; **cloth-bound book** livre relié toile; (*Brit*) **cloth cap** casquette *f* (d'ouvrier).

clothe [kləʊð] *vt* habiller, vêtir (*in, with* de); (*fig*) revêtir, couvrir (*in, with* de).

clothes [kləʊðz] 1 *npl* **(a)** vêtements *mpl*, habits *mpl*. **with one's ~ on** (tout) habillé; **with one's ~ off** déshabillé, (tout) nu; **to put on/take off one's ~** s'habiller/se déshabiller; *[baby]* **in long ~** au *or* en maillot; *V* **plain.**

(b) (*also* **bed~**) draps *mpl* et couvertures *fpl*.

2 *cpd*: **clothes basket** panier *m* à linge; **clothes brush** brosse *f* à habits; **clothes hanger** cintre *m*; **clothes horse** séchoir *m* (à linge); **clothes line** corde *f* (à linge); **clothes moth** mite *f*; (*Brit*) **clothes peg,** (*US, Scot*) **clothespin** pince *f* à linge; **clothespole, clothes prop** perche *f or* support *m* pour corde à linge; **clothes rope = clothes line; clothes shop** magasin *m* d'habillement *or* de confection; (*US*) **clothes tree** portemanteau *m*.

clothier [ˈkləʊðɪəʳ] *n* (*clothes seller*) marchand *m* (de vêtements) de confection; (*cloth dealer, maker*) drapier *m*.

clothing [ˈkləʊðɪŋ] *n* (*U*) **(a)** (*clothes*) vêtements *mpl*. **an article of ~** un vêtement, une pièce d'habillement; ~ **allowance** indemnité *f* vestimentaire. **(b)** (*act of ~*) habillage *m*; *[monks, nuns]* prise *f* d'habit; (*providing with clothes*) habillement *m*.

cloud [klaʊd] 1 *n* **(a)** (*Met*) nuage *m*, nuée *f* (*liter*); *[smoke, dust etc]* nuage; *[insects, arrows etc]* nuée; *[gas]* nappe *f*. **to have one's head in the ~s** être dans les nuages *or* dans la lune; **to be on ~ nine**: être aux anges; (*fig*) **under a ~** (*under suspicion*) en butte aux soupçons; (*in disgrace*) en disgrâce; *V* **silver.**

(b) (*cloudiness*) *[liquid]* nuage *m*; *[mirror]* buée *f*; *[marble]* tache noire.

2 *vt liquid* rendre trouble; *mirror* embuer; *face, expression* assombrir, attrister; *mind* obscurcir, obnubiler; *reputation* ternir. **a ~ed sky** un ciel couvert *or* nuageux; **a ~ed expression** un air sombre *or* attristé; **to ~ the issue** brouiller les cartes (*fig*).

3 *vi* (*also* **~ over**) *[sky]* se couvrir (de nuages), s'obscurcir; (*fig*) *[face, expression]* s'assombrir, se rembrunir.

4 *cpd*: **cloudberry** (*berry*) (variété *f* de) framboise *f*; (*bush*) (variété de) framboisier *m*; **cloudburst** trombe(s) *f(pl)* (d'eau), déluge *m* (de pluie); (*liter*) **cloud-capped** couronné de nuages (*liter*); **she lives in cloud-cuckoo land** elle plane complètement, elle n'a pas les pieds sur terre.

cloudiness [ˈklaʊdɪnɪs] *n [sky]* état *or* aspect nuageux; *[liquid]* aspect trouble; *[mirror]* buée *f*.

cloudless [ˈklaʊdlɪs] *adj* sans nuages, immaculé.

cloudy [ˈklaʊdɪ] *adj sky* nuageux, couvert; *liquid* trouble; *diamond etc* taché, nuageux; *fabric* chiné, moiré; *leather* marbré. (*Met*) **it was ~** le temps était couvert.

clout [klaʊt] 1 *n* **(a)** (*blow*) coup *m* de poing (*or* de canne *etc*). **(b)** (*dial*) (*cloth*) chiffon *m*; (*garment*) vêtement *m*. 2 *vt object* frapper; *person* donner un coup de poing (*or* de canne *etc*) à.

clove[1] [kləʊv] *n* clou *m* de girofle. **oil of ~s** essence *f* de girofle; **~ of garlic** gousse *f* d'ail.

clove[2] [kləʊv] 1 *pret of* **cleave**[1]. 2 *cpd*: **clove hitch** (*knot*) demi-clef *f*.

cloven [ˈkləʊvn] 1 *ptp of* **cleave**[1]. 2 *cpd*: **clovenfooted** *animal* au(x) sabot(s) fendu(s); *devil* au(x) pied(s) fourchu(s); **cloven hoof** *[animal]* sabot fendu; *[devil]* pied fourchu.

clover [ˈkləʊvəʳ] *n* trèfle *m*. (*fig*) **to be in ~*** être *or* vivre comme un coq en pâte; **~leaf** (*Bot*) feuille *f* de trèfle; (*road intersection*) (croisement *m* en) trèfle; *V* **four.**

clown [klaʊn] 1 *n [circus etc]* clown *m*; (†, *Theat*) bouffon *m*, paillasse *m*; (*fig*) clown, pitre *m*. 2 *vi* (*fig: also* **~ about, ~ around**) faire le clown *or* le pitre *or* le singe.

clowning [ˈklaʊnɪŋ] *n* (*U*) pitreries *fpl*, singeries *fpl*.

cloy [klɔɪ] 1 *vt* rassasier (*with* de), écœurer. 2 *vi* perdre son charme.

cloying [ˈklɔɪɪŋ] *adj* (*lit, fig*) écœurant.

club [klʌb] 1 *n* **(a)** (*weapon*) massue *f*, matraque *f*, gourdin *m*; (*also* **golf ~**) club *m*; *V* **Indian.**

(b) (*Cards*) **~s** trèfles *mpl*; **the ace of ~s** l'as *m* de trèfle; **the six of ~s** le six de trèfle; **one ~** un trèfle; **he played a ~** il a joué trèfle; **~s are trumps** atout trèfle.

(c) (*circle, society*) club *m*, cercle *m*. **tennis ~** club de tennis; **he is dining at his ~** il dîne à son club *or* à son cercle; (*fig*) **join the ~!*** tu n'es pas le *or* la seul(e)!; *V* **benefit, youth** *etc.*

2 *vt person* matraquer, frapper avec un gourdin *or* une massue. **to ~ sb with a rifle** assommer qn d'un coup de crosse.

3 *cpd*: **he is the club bore** c'est le raseur* du club; **club chair** fauteuil *m* club *inv*; **club-foot** pied-bot *m*; **club-footed** pied-bot *inv*; (*Sport*) **clubhouse** pavillon *m*; **clubman** membre *m* d'un club; (*man about town*) homme *m* du monde, mondain *m*; **he is not a clubman** il n'est pas homme à fréquenter les clubs *or* les cercles; **he is a club member** il est membre du club; **clubroom** salle *f* de club *or* de réunion; **club sandwich** sandwich *m* mixte (à deux étages); **club subscription** cotisation *f*.

club together *vi* se cotiser (*to buy* pour acheter).

clubbable* [ˈklʌbəbl] *adj* sociable.

cluck [klʌk] 1 *vi [hens, people]* glousser. 2 *n* gloussement *m*.

clue, (*US*) **clew** [kluː] *n* indice *m*, indication *f*, fil directeur; *[crosswords]* définition *f*. **to find the ~ to sth** découvrir *or* trouver la clef de qch; (*lit*) **to have a ~** être sur une piste; (*fig*) **I haven't a ~!*** je n'en ai pas la moindre idée!, aucune idée!*

clue in: *vt sep* mettre au courant *or* au parfum*.

clue up: *vt sep* (*gen pass*) renseigner (*on* sur), mettre au courant (*on* de), affranchir:. **to get clued up about** *or* **on sth** se faire renseigner sur qch; **he's very clued up on politics** il est très calé* en politique.

clueless* [ˈkluːlɪs] *adj* (*Brit*) sans *or* qui n'a pas la moindre idée, qui ne sait rien de rien*.

clump[1] [klʌmp] *n [shrubs]* massif *m*; *[trees]* bouquet *m*; *[flowers]* touffe *f*, (*larger*) massif; *[grass]* touffe.

clump[2] [klʌmp] 1 *n* (*noise*) bruit *m* de pas lourd(s) *or* pesant(s). 2 *vi* (*also* **~ about**) marcher d'un pas lourd *or* pesant.

clumsily [ˈklʌmzɪlɪ] *adv* (*inelegantly*) gauchement, maladroitement; (*tactlessly*) sans tact.

clumsiness [ˈklʌmzɪnɪs] *n [person, action]* gaucherie *f*, maladresse *f*; *[tool etc]* incommodité *f*, caractère *m* peu pratique; *[shape, form]* lourdeur *f*; (*fig: tactlessness*) *[person, remark]* gaucherie, manque *m* de tact *or* de discrétion.

clumsy [ˈklʌmzɪ] *adj person, action* gauche, maladroit; *tool etc* malcommode, peu maniable; *shape, form* lourd, disgracieux; *painting, forgery* maladroit; (*fig: tactless*) *person, remark* gauche, maladroit, sans tact; *apology, style* gauche, lourd, inélégant.

clung [klʌŋ] *pret, ptp of* **cling.**

Cluniac [ˈkluːnɪæk] *adj, n* clunisien (*m*).

cluster [ˈklʌstəʳ] 1 *n [flowers, blossom, fruit]* grappe *f*; *[bananas]* régime *m*; *[trees]* bouquet *m*; *[bees]* essaim *m*; *[persons]* (petit) groupe *m*, rassemblement *m*; (*Ling*), *[houses, islands]* groupe; *[stars]* amas *m*; *[diamonds]* entourage *m*.

2 *vi [people]* se rassembler, se grouper (*around* autour de); *[things]* (*V* 1) former un groupe *or* une grappe *or* un bouquet *etc* (*around* autour de).

clutch [klʌtʃ] 1 *n* **(a)** (*action*) étreinte *f*, prise *f*.

(b) (*Aut*) embrayage *m*; (*also* **~ pedal**) pédale *f* d'embrayage. **to let in/out the ~** embrayer/débrayer; **~ plate** disque *m* d'embrayage.

(c) *[chickens, eggs]* couvée *f*.

(d) (*fig*) **to fall into sb's ~es** tomber sous les griffes *fpl or* sous la patte* de qn; **to get out of sb's ~es** se tirer des griffes de qn.

2 *vt* (*grasp*) empoigner, se saisir de, saisir, agripper; (*hold tightly*) étreindre, serrer fort; (*hold on to*) se cramponner à.

3 *vi*: **to ~ at** (*lit*) se cramponner à, s'agripper à; (*fig*) se cramponner à, se raccrocher à; (*fig*) **to ~ at a straw** se raccrocher à n'importe quoi.

clutter [ˈklʌtəʳ] 1 *n* **(a)** (*U: disorder, confusion*) désordre *m*, pagaie* *f*. **in a ~** en désordre, en pagaïe*.

(b) (*objects lying about*) désordre *m*, fouillis *m*.

2 *vt* (*also* **~ up**) (*lit*) mettre en désordre, mettre le désordre dans (*à force de laisser traîner des objets divers*); (*lit, fig*) encombrer (*with* de).

co ... [kəʊ] *pref* co ...

coach [kəʊtʃ] 1 *n* **(a)** (*Rail*) voiture *f*, wagon *m*; (*motor ~*) car *m*, autocar *m*; (*horse-drawn*) carrosse *m*; (*stagecoach*) diligence *f*, coche *m*. **~ and four** carrosse à quatre chevaux.

(b) (*tutor*) répétiteur *m*, -trice *f*; (*Sport*) entraîneur *m*.

2 *vt* donner des leçons particulières à; (*Sport*) entraîner. **to ~ sb for an exam** préparer qn à un examen; **he had been ~ed in what to say** on lui avait fait répéter ce qu'il aurait à dire.

3 *cpd*: (*Brit Aut*) **coachbuilder** carrossier *m*; (*Brit*) **coach building** carrosserie *f* (*construction*); **coachman** cocher *m*; **coach trip** excursion *f* en car; (*Brit Aut*) **coachwork** carrosserie *f* (*caisse d'une automobile*).

coadjutant [kəʊˈædʒʊtənt] *n* assistant(e) *m(f)*, aide *mf*.

coagulant [kəʊˈægjʊlənt] *n* coagulant *m*.

coagulate [kəʊˈægjʊleɪt] 1 *vt* coaguler. 2 *vi* se coaguler.

coagulation [kəʊˌægjʊˈleɪʃən] *n* coagulation *f*.

coal [kəʊl] 1 *n* charbon *m*; (*Ind*) houille f. **piece of ~** morceau *m* de charbon; **soft ~** houille grasse; (*fig*) **to be on hot ~s** être sur des charbons ardents; *V* **carry.**

2 *vt* fournir *or* ravitailler en charbon. (*Naut*) **to ~ ship** charbonner.

3 *vi* (*Naut*) charbonner.

4 *cpd fire* de charbon; *box, shed* à charbon. **coal basin** bassin houiller; **coal-black** noir comme du charbon; **coal-burning** à charbon, qui marche au charbon; **coal cellar** cave *f* à charbon; **coal chute** glissière *f* à charbon; **coal cutter** haveur *m*; **coal depot** dépôt *m* de charbon; **coaldust** poussier *m*, poussière *f* de charbon; **coal face** front *m* de taille; **coalfield** bassin houiller; **coalgas** gaz *m* (de houille); **coal hod** seau *m* à charbon; **coal industry** industrie houillère, charbonnages *mpl*; **coaling station** dépôt *m* de charbon; **coalman** (*also* **coal merchant**) charbonnier *m*, marchand *m* de charbon; (*delivery man*) charbonnier; (*Geol*) **coal measures** gisements houillers; **coalmine** houillère *f*, mine *f* de charbon; **coalminer** mineur *m*; **coalmining** charbonnage *m*; **coalpit = coalmine; coal scuttle** seau *m* à charbon; **coal shed** réserve *f* de charbon; **coal tar** coaltar *m*, goudron *m* de houille; (*Orn*) **coal tit** mésange noire; **coal yard** dépôt *m* de charbon.

coalesce [ˌkəʊəˈles] *vi* (*lit, fig*) s'unir (*en une masse, en un groupe etc*), se fondre (ensemble), se grouper.

coalescence [ˌkəʊəˈlesəns] *n* (*lit, fig*) fusion *f*, combinaison *f*, union *f*.

coalition [ˌkəʊəˈlɪʃən] *n* coalition *f*. (*Pol*) ~ **government** gouvernement *m* de coalition.

coarse [kɔːs] **1** *adj* **(a)** (*in texture*) *material* rude, grossier. ~ **cloth** drap grossier; ~ **linen** grosse toile; ~ **salt** gros sel; ~ **sand** sable *m* à gros grains, gros sable; ~ **sandpaper** papier *m* de verre à gros grain; ~ **skin** peau *f* rude; ~ **weave** texture grossière.
(b) (*common*) commun, ordinaire, grossier. ~ **food** nourriture *f* fruste; ~ **red wine** gros rouge.
(c) (*pej*) (*uncouth*) *manners* grossier, vulgaire; (*indecent*) *language, joke* grossier, indécent, cru; *laugh* gros, gras; *accent* commun, vulgaire.
2 *cpd*: **coarse-grained** à gros grain.

coarsely [ˈkɔːslɪ] *adv* (*V* **coarse**) grossièrement, vulgairement; indécemment, crûment; grassement. ~ **woven cloth** tissu *m* de texture grossière.

coarsen [ˈkɔːsn] (*V* **coarse**) **1** *vt* rendre grossier *or* vulgaire *etc*. **2** *vi* devenir rude *or* grossier *or* vulgaire *etc*.

coarseness [ˈkɔːsnɪs] *n* (*V* **coarse**) rudesse *f*; caractère *m* vulgaire *or* grossier; vulgarité *f*, grossièreté *f*.

coast [kəʊst] **1** *n* côte *f*; (*also* ~**line**) littoral *m*. (*fig*) **the** ~ **is clear** la voie *or* le champ est libre.
2 *vi* **(a)** (*Naut*: *also* ~ **along**) caboter.
(b) (*also* ~ **down**) (*Aut, Cycling*) descendre en roue libre; (*tobogganing*) descendre en luge.
3 *cpd*: **coastguard** garde *m* maritime; (*US*) douanier *m* garde-côte; **coastguard station** station *f* de garde-côte(s); **coastguard vessel** garde-côte *m*.

coastal [ˈkəʊstəl] *adj defence, state* côtier. ~ **navigation** navigation côtière; ~ **traffic** navigation côtière, cabotage *m*.

coaster [ˈkəʊstəʳ] *n* **(a)** (*Naut*) caboteur *m*. **(b)** (*drip mat*) dessous *m* de verre *or* de bouteille; (*wine tray*) présentoir *m* à bouteilles (*parfois roulant*). **(c) roller** ~ *V* **roller**.

coat [kəʊt] **1** *n* **(a)** *[man, woman]* manteau *m*; *[man]* (*also* **over**~, **top**~) pardessus *m*. (*fig*) **to turn one's** ~ retourner sa veste*; **a** ~ **and skirt** un ensemble manteau et jupe coordonnés; (*Her*) ~ **of arms** blason *m*, armoiries *fpl*, écu *m*; ~ **of mail** cotte *f* de maille; *V* **house, morning, sport** *etc*.
(b) *[animal]* pelage *m*, poil *m*; *[horse]* robe *f*.
(c) (*covering*) *[paint, tar etc]* couche *f*; *[plastic]* enveloppe *f*; *V* **base**[1], **top** *etc*.
2 *vt* enduire, couvrir, revêtir (*with* de); (*Elec*) armer; (*Culin*) (*with chocolate*) enrober; (*with egg*) dorer. **to** ~ **the wall with paint** passer une couche de peinture sur le mur; (*Med*) **his tongue was** ~**ed** il avait la langue chargée; (*fig*) **(in order) to** ~ **the pill** (pour) dorer la pilule.
3 *cpd*: **coat hanger** cintre *m*; **coatstand** portemanteau *m*; **coattails** queue *f* de pie (*habit*); (*fig*) **to be at sb's coattails** être pendu aux basques de qn; (*US Pol*) **to ride on sb's coattails** se faire élire dans le sillage *or* à la traîne (*pej*) de qn.

coating [ˈkəʊtɪŋ] *n* couche *f*.

co-author [ˈkəʊˌɔːθəʳ] *n* co-auteur *m*.

coax [kəʊks] *vt* cajoler *or* câliner (*pour amadouer*). **to** ~ **sb into doing** amener qn à force de cajoleries *or* de câlineries à faire; **to** ~ **sth out of sb** obtenir *or* tirer qch de qn par des cajoleries *or* des câlineries.

coaxing [ˈkəʊksɪŋ] **1** *n* câlineries *fpl*, cajolerie(s) *f(pl)*. **2** *adj* enjôleur, câlin.

coaxingly [ˈkəʊksɪŋlɪ] *adv speak, ask* d'une manière câline, d'un ton enjôleur; *look* d'un air câlin *or* enjôleur.

cob [kɒb] *n* (*swan*) cygne *m* mâle; (*horse*) cob *m*; (*also* ~**-nut**) grosse noisette; *[maize]* épi *m* (de maïs); *V* **corn**[1].

cobalt [ˈkəʊbɒlt] *n* cobalt *m*. ~ **60** cobalt 60, cobalt radio-actif; ~ **blue** bleu *m* de cobalt.

cobber‡ [ˈkɒbəʳ] *n* (*Australian*) pote‡ *m*.

cobble [ˈkɒbl] *vti* rapetasser*, rafistoler* (*surtout des chaussures*).

cobbled [ˈkɒbld] *adj*: ~ **street** rue pavée (*de pavés ronds*).

cobbler [ˈkɒbləʳ] *n* **(a)** cordonnier *m*. ~**'s wax** poix *f* de cordonnier. **(b)** (*US Culin*) tourte *f* aux fruits. **(c)** (*US: drink*) (sorte *f* de) punch *m* (glacé).

cobbles [ˈkɒblz] *npl*, **cobblestones** [ˈkɒblstəʊnz] *npl* pavés ronds.

COBOL [ˈkəʊbɔːl] *n* (*Computers*) COBOL *m*.

cobra [ˈkəʊbrə] *n* cobra *m*.

cobweb [ˈkɒbweb] *n* toile *f* d'araignée.

cocaine [kəˈkeɪn] *n* cocaïne *f*.

coccus [ˈkɒkəs] *n* coccidie *f*.

cochineal [ˈkɒtʃɪniːl] *n* (*insect*) cochenille *f*; (*colouring*) colorant *m* rouge.

cock [kɒk] **1** *n* **(a)** (*rooster*) coq *m*; (*male bird*) (oiseau *m*) mâle *m*. (*fig*) **the** ~ **of the walk** le roi (*fig*); *V* **fighting, game, weather** *etc*.
(b) (*tap*) robinet *m*.
(c) *[rifle]* chien *m*. **at full** ~ armé; **at half** ~ au cran de repos.
(d) *[hay]* meulon *m*; *[corn, oats]* moyette *f*.
(e) (*‡*) bitte*‡ *f*.
2 *vt* **(a)** *gun* armer.
(b) to ~ **one's ears** (*lit*) dresser les oreilles; (*fig*) dresser l'oreille; **to** ~ **one's eye at** glisser un coup d'œil à; (*lit*) **to** ~ **a snook (at)*** faire un pied de nez (à); (*fig*) **to** ~ **a snook at*** faire fi de.
3 *cpd bird* mâle. **cock-a-doodle-doo** cocorico *m*; **cock-a-hoop** (*adj*) fier comme Artaban; (*adv*) d'un air de triomphe; (*pej*) **cock-and-bull story** histoire *f* à dormir debout; **cockchafer** hanneton *m*; **at cockcrow** au premier chant du coq, à l'aube; **cock-eyed** (*: *cross-eyed*) qui louche; (*: *crooked*) de travers, de traviole*; (*: *mad, absurd*) absurde, qui ne tient pas debout, dingue‡; (‡: *drunk*) soûl*, schlass‡ *inv*; **cockfight** combat *m* de coqs; **cockfighting** combats *mpl* de coqs; **cock lobster** homard *m* (mâle); **cockpit** *[aircraft]* poste *m* de pilotage, cockpit *m*; *[yacht]* cockpit; *[racing car]* poste du pilote; (*Cockfighting*) arène *f* (*pour combats de coqs*); (*fig*) arènes; **cockroach** cafard *m*, blatte *f*, cancrelat *m*; **cockscomb** (*Orn*) crête *f* (*de coq*); (*Bot*) crête-de-coq *f* (*V* **coxcomb**); **cock sparrow** moineau *m* (*mâle*); (*pej*) **cocksure** (trop) sûr de soi, outrecuidant; **cocktail** *V* **cocktail**; **he made a cock-up of the job**‡ il a salopé le boulot‡; **the meeting was a cock-up**‡ la réunion a été bordélique‡ *or* un vrai bordel‡.

cockade [kɒˈkeɪd] *n* cocarde *f*.

cockatoo [ˌkɒkəˈtuː] *n* cacatoès *m*.

cocked [kɒkt] *adj*: ~ **hat** chapeau *m* à cornes; (*two points*) bicorne *m*; (*three points*) tricorne *m*; **to knock sb into a** ~ **hat**‡ battre qn à plate(s) couture(s).

cocker [ˈkɒkəʳ] *n* (*also* ~ **spaniel**) cocker *m*.

cockerel [ˈkɒkərəl] *n* jeune coq *m*.

cockiness [ˈkɒkɪnɪs] *n* impudence *f*, outrecuidance *f*, impertinence *f*.

cockle [ˈkɒkl] **1** *n* **(a)** (*shellfish*) coque *f*. (*fig*) **it warmed the** ~**s of his heart** cela lui a réchauffé *or* réjoui le cœur.
(b) (*wrinkle*) *[paper]* froissure *f*, pliure *f*; *[cloth]* faux pli.
2 *cpd*: **cockle shell** (*Zool*) (coquille *f* de) coque *f*; (*boat*) petit canot, coquille de noix.
3 *vt* (*wrinkle*) *paper* froisser; *cloth* chiffonner.
4 *vi* *[paper]* se froisser; *[cloth]* se chiffonner.

cockney [ˈkɒknɪ] **1** *n* **(a)** (*person*) Cockney *mf* (*personne née dans l'‘East End’ de Londres*). **(b)** (*Ling*) cockney *m*. **2** *adj* cockney, londonien.

cocktail [ˈkɒkteɪl] **1** *n* (*lit, fig*) cocktail *m* (*boisson*). **fruit** ~ salade *f* de fruits; **prawn** ~ coupe *f or* cocktail de crevettes.
2 *cpd*: **cocktail bar** bar *m* (*dans un hôtel*); **cocktail cabinet** bar *m* (*meuble*); **cocktail dress** robe *f* de cocktail; **cocktail lounge** bar *m* (*de luxe, dans un hôtel*); **cocktail onion** petit oignon (à apéritif); **cocktail party** cocktail *m* (*réunion*); **cocktail sausage** petite saucisse (à apéritif); **cocktail shaker** shaker *m*.

cocky [ˈkɒkɪ] *adj* (*pej*) suffisant, trop sûr de soi.

cocoa [ˈkəʊkəʊ] *n* (*drink, powder*) cacao *m*. ~ **butter** beurre *m* de cacao.

coconut [ˈkəʊkənʌt] **1** *n* noix *f* de coco. **2** *cpd*: **coconut matting** tapis *m* de fibre (*de noix de coco*); **coconut oil** huile *f* de coco; **coconut palm** cocotier *m*; **coconut shy** jeu *m* de massacre; **coconut tree** cocotier *m*.

cocoon [kəˈkuːn] **1** *n* cocon *m*; (*Mil*) *vernis or enveloppe de protection à base de vinyl*. **2** *vt* (*fig*) envelopper avec soin.

cod [kɒd] **1** *n, pl inv* (*Zool*) morue *f*; (*Culin*) (*also* **fresh** ~) morue fraîche, cabillaud *m*. **dried** ~ morue séchée, merluche *f*. **2** *cpd*: **codfish** *inv* morue *f*; **cod-liver oil** huile *f* de foie de morue; (*Brit*) **the C**~ **War** la guerre de la morue.

coda [ˈkəʊdə] *n* coda *f*.

coddle [ˈkɒdl] *vt* **(a)** *child, invalid* dorloter, choyer. **(b)** (*Culin*) *eggs* (faire) cuire à feu doux.

code [kəʊd] **1** *n* **(a)** (*Admin, Jur, fig*) code *m*. ~ **of behaviour/of honour** code de conduite/de l'honneur; *V* **highway, penal**.
(b) (*cipher*) code *m*, chiffre *m*; (*Bio, Computers, Post etc*) code. **in** ~ en code, chiffré; *V* **Morse, zip**.
2 *vt letter, despatch* chiffrer, coder.
3 *cpd*: **code letter** chiffre *m*; **code name** nom codé; (*Fin*) **code number** ≃ indice *m* des déductions fiscales.

codeine [ˈkəʊdiːn] *n* codéine *f*.

codex [ˈkəʊdeks] *n*, *pl* **codices** [ˈkɒdɪsiːz] manuscrit *m* (ancien).

codger‡ [ˈkɒdʒəʳ] *n* drôle de vieux bonhomme *m*.

codicil [ˈkɒdɪsɪl] *n* codicille *m*.

codify [ˈkəʊdɪfaɪ] *vt* codifier.

coding [ˈkəʊdɪŋ] *n* (*U*) *[telegram, message]* mise *f* en code, chiffrage *m*, codification *f*; (*Computers*) codage *m*; *V* **tax**.

co-driver [ˈkəʊdraɪvəʳ] *n* (*in race*) co-pilote *m*; *[lorry]* deuxième chauffeur *m*.

codswallop‡ [ˈkɒdzwɒləp] *n* (*U: Brit*) bobards* *mpl*, foutaises‡ *fpl*.

coed* [ˈkəʊˈed] **1** *adj abbr of* **coeducational**. **2** *n* (*US*) étudiante *f* (*dans un établissement mixte*).

coeducation [ˈkəʊˌedjʊˈkeɪʃən] *n* éducation *f* mixte.

coeducational [ˈkəʊˌedjʊˈkeɪʃənl] *adj school, teaching* mixte.

coefficient [ˌkəʊɪˈfɪʃənt] *n* coefficient *m*.

coequal [ˌkəʊˈiːkwəl] *adj, n* égal(e) *m(f)*.

coerce [kəʊˈɜːs] *vt* contraindre. **to** ~ **sb into obedience/into obeying** contraindre qn à l'obéissance/à obéir.

coercion [kəʊˈɜːʃən] *n* contrainte *f*, coercition *f*.

coercive [kəʊˈɜːsɪv] *adj* coercitif.

coeval [kəʊˈiːvəl] **1** *adj* contemporain (*with* de), du même âge (*with* que). **2** *n* contemporain(e) *m(f)*.

coexist [ˈkəʊɪgˈzɪst] *vi* coexister (*with* avec).

coexistence [ˈkəʊɪgˈzɪstəns] *n* coexistence *f*; *V* **peaceful**.

coexistent [ˈkəʊɪgˈzɪstənt] *adj* coexistant (*with* avec).

coextensive [ˈkəʊɪkˈstensɪv] *adv*: ~ **with** (*in space*) de même étendue que; (*in time*) de même durée que.

coffee [ˈkɒfɪ] **1** *n* café *m* (*grain, boisson*). **a (cup of)** ~ une tasse de café, un café; **black** ~ café noir *or* nature; (*Brit*) **white** ~ café au lait; **one white** ~, **please!** un (café-)crème s'il vous plaît!
2 *cpd*: **coffee bar** café *m*, cafétéria *f*; **coffee bean** grain *m* de café; **coffee break** pause(-)café *f*; **coffee-coloured** (couleur) café au lait *inv*; **coffee cup** tasse *f* à café, (*smaller*) tasse à moka; **coffee grounds** marc *m* de café; (*Hist*) **coffee house** café *m* (*au 18e siècle*); **coffee mill** moulin *m* à café; **coffee per-**

colator (*domestic*) cafetière *f* (*à pression or à l'italienne*); (*commercial*) percolateur *m*; **coffeepot** cafetière *f*; **coffee service, coffee set** service *m* à café; **coffee spoon** cuiller *f* à café *or* à moka; **coffee table** (petite) table basse; **a coffee table book** un beau livre grand format (*pour faire de l'effet*); **coffee tree** caféier *m*.

coffer ['kɒfəʳ] *n* **(a)** coffre *m*, caisse *f*. (*fig*) (*funds*) ~s coffres; **the ~s (of State)** les coffres de l'État, le trésor public. **(b)** (*Hydraulics*) caisson *m*. **(c)** (*also* **~dam**) batardeau *m*.

coffin ['kɒfɪn] *n* cercueil *m*, bière *f*. (*cigarette*) **~ nails**† sèches *f*.

cog [kɒg] *n* (*Tech*) dent *f* (*d'engrenage*). (*fig*) **he's only a ~ in the wheel** il n'est qu'un simple rouage (de *or* dans la machine); **~ wheel** roue dentée.

cogency ['kəʊdʒənsɪ] *n* [*argument etc*] puissance *f*, force *f*.

cogent ['kəʊdʒənt] *adj* (*compelling*) irrésistible; (*convincing*) puissant, convaincant; (*relevant*) pertinent, (fait) à-propos.

cogently ['kəʊdʒəntlɪ] *adv* (*V* **cogent**) irrésistiblement; puissamment; (avec) à-propos.

cogitate ['kɒdʒɪteɪt] **1** *vi* méditer, réfléchir ((*up*)*on* sur). **2** *vt scheme* méditer.

cogitation [ˌkɒdʒɪ'teɪʃən] *n* (*U*) réflexion *f*; (*liter, iro*) cogitations *fpl* (*liter, iro*).

cognac ['kɒnjæk] *n* cognac *m*.

cognate ['kɒgneɪt] **1** *adj* apparenté, analogue (*with* à), de même origine *or* source (*with* que); (*Ling*) *word, language* apparenté; (*Jur*) parent. **2** *n* (*Ling*) mot apparenté; (*Jur*) cognat *m*, parent *m* proche.

cognition [kɒg'nɪʃən] *n* (*U*) connaissance *f*; (*Philos*) cognition *f*.

cognizance ['kɒgnɪzəns] *n* **(a)** (*Jur, gen: frm*) connaissance *f*. **to take/have ~ of** prendre/avoir connaissance de; **this is outside his ~** ceci n'est pas de sa compétence; (*Jur*) **this case falls within the ~ of the court** cette affaire est de la compétence du tribunal.

(b) (*Her*) emblème *m*.

cognizant ['kɒgnɪzənt] *adj* (*frm*) instruit, ayant connaissance (*of* de); (*Jur*) compétent (*of* pour).

cognomen [kɒg'nəʊmen] *n* (*surname*) nom *m* de famille; (*nickname*) surnom *m*.

cohabit [kəʊ'hæbɪt] *vi* cohabiter (*with* avec).

cohabitation [ˌkəʊhæbɪ'teɪʃən] *n* cohabitation *f*.

coheir ['kəʊ'ɛəʳ] *n* cohéritier *m*.

coheiress ['kəʊ'ɛərɪs] *n* cohéritière *f*.

cohere [kəʊ'hɪəʳ] *vi* (*fig*) [*argument*] (se) tenir; [*reasoning*] se suivre logiquement; [*style*] être cohérent; (*lit: stick*) adhérer.

coherence [kəʊ'hɪərəns] *n* (*fig*) cohérence *f*; (*lit*) adhérence *f*.

coherent [kəʊ'hɪərənt] *adj* (*fig*) *person, words* cohérent, logique; *account, story, speech* facile à comprendre *or* à suivre; (*lit*) adhérent.

coherently [kəʊ'hɪərəntlɪ] *adv* (*fig*) avec cohérence, d'une façon cohérente.

cohesion [kəʊ'hiːʒən] *n* cohésion *f*.

cohesive [kəʊ'hiːsɪv] *adj* cohésif.

cohort ['kəʊhɔːt] *n* (*Mil*) cohorte *f*.

coif [kɔɪf] *n* (*headdress*) coiffe *f*; (*skullcap*) calotte *f*.

coiffure [kwɒ'fjʊəʳ] *n* coiffure *f* (*arrangement des cheveux*).

coil [kɔɪl] **1** *vt rope* enrouler; *hair* enrouler, torsader; (*Elec*) *wire* bobiner; (*Naut*) gléner. **the snake ~ed itself (up)** le serpent s'est lové.

2 *vi* [*river*] onduler, serpenter; [*rope*] s'enrouler (*round, about* autour de); [*snake*] se lover.

3 *n* **(a)** (*loops, roll*) [*rope, wire etc*] rouleau *m*; (*Naut*) glène *f*; [*hair*] rouleau; (*at back of head*) chignon *m*; (*over ears*) macaron *m*.

(b) (*one loop*) spire *f*; [*cable*] tour *m*, plet *m* (*rare*); [*hair*] boucle *f*; [*snake, smoke*] anneau *m*.

(c) (*Elec*) bobine *f*; (*one loop*) spire *f*.

(d) (*Med**: *contraceptive*) **the ~** le stérilet.

coin [kɔɪn] **1** *n* **(a)** pièce *f* de monnaie. **a 10p ~** une pièce de 10 pence; *V* **toss** *etc*.

(b) (*U*) monnaie *f*. **current ~** monnaie courante; **in (the) ~ of the realm** en espèces (sonnantes et trébuchantes); (*fig*) **to pay sb back in his own ~** rendre à qn la monnaie de sa pièce.

2 *cpd*: **coin-operated** automatique; **coin-operated laundry**, (*abbr*) **coin-op*** laverie *f* automatique (*à libre-service*).

3 *vt* **(a)** *money, medal* frapper. (*fig*) **he is ~ing money** il fait des affaires d'or.

(b) (*fig*) *word, phrase* inventer, fabriquer. (*hum, iro*) **to ~ a phrase** si je peux m'exprimer ainsi.

coinage ['kɔɪnɪdʒ] *n* (*U*) **(a)** (*coins*) monnaie *f*; (*system*) système *m* monétaire. **(b)** (*act*) [*money*] frappe *f*; (*fig*) [*word etc*] création *f*, invention *f*.

coincide [ˌkəʊɪn'saɪd] *vi* coïncider (*with* avec).

coincidence [kəʊ'ɪnsɪdəns] *n* coïncidence *f*.

coincidental [kəʊˌɪnsɪ'dentl] *adj* de coïncidence. **it's entirely ~** c'est une pure coïncidence.

coitus ['kɔɪtəs] *n* coït *m*.

coke [kəʊk] *n* coke *m*. **~ oven** four *m* à coke.

Coke [kəʊk] *n* ® coca *m* ®.

colander ['kʌləndəʳ] *n* passoire *f*.

cold [kəʊld] **1** *adj* **(a)** *day, drink, meal, meat, metal, water* froid. **as ~ as ice** *or* **as charity** *person, thing* glacé; **it's as ~ as charity** il fait un froid de canard* *or* un froid sibérien; **it's a ~ morning/day** il fait froid ce matin/aujourd'hui; **I am ~** j'ai froid; **my feet are ~** j'ai froid aux pieds; (*fig*) **to have** *or* **get ~ feet** avoir la frousse* *or* la trouille*; **to get ~** [*weather, room*] se refroidir; [*food*] refroidir; [*person*] commencer à avoir froid, (*catch a chill*) attraper froid; (*Met*) **~ front** front froid; (*Met*) **~ snap** courte offensive du froid; **a ~ colour** une couleur froide; **~ steel** arme blanche; **the scent is ~** la voie est froide, la piste a disparu (*also fig*); **that's ~ comfort** ce n'est pas tellement réconfortant *or* rassurant, c'est une maigre consolation; **to be in a ~ sweat (about)*** avoir des sueurs froides (au sujet de); **that brought him out in a ~ sweat** cela lui a donné des sueurs froides; *V also* **2** *and* **blow**[1], **icy** *etc*.

(b) (*fig*) (*unfriendly*) froid, manquant de *or* sans cordialité; (*indifferent*) froid, indifférent; (*dispassionate*) froid, calme, objectif. **a ~ reception** un accueil froid; **to be ~ to sb** se montrer froid envers qn; **that leaves me ~*** ça ne me fait ni chaud ni froid, cela me laisse froid; **in ~ blood** de sang-froid.

(c) (*: *unconscious*) sans connaissance. **he was out ~** il était sans connaissance *or* dans les pommes*.

2 *cpd*: **cold-blooded** (*Zool*) à sang froid; (*fig*) *person* insensible, sans pitié; (*fig*) **to be cold-blooded about sth** faire qch sans aucune pitié; **cold cream** crème *f* de beauté, cold-cream *m*; (*Culin*) **cold cuts** assiette anglaise; (*Agr*) **cold frame** châssis *m* de couches; **cold-hearted** impitoyable, sans pitié, au cœur dur; **cold room** chambre froide *or* frigorifique; (*fig*) **to give sb the cold shoulder*, to cold-shoulder sb*** battre froid à qn, se montrer froid envers qn; (*Med*) **cold sore** herpès *m*; **cold storage** conservation *f* par le froid; **to put into cold storage** *food* mettre en chambre froide *or* frigorifique; *fur coat* mettre en garde; (*fig*) *idea, book, scheme* mettre de côté *or* en attente; **cold store** entrepôt *m* frigorifique; (*Pol*) **the cold war** la guerre froide.

3 *n* **(a)** (*Met etc*) froid *m*. **I am beginning to feel the ~** je commence à avoir froid, je n'ai plus très chaud; **I never feel the ~** je ne crains pas le froid, je ne suis pas frileux; **don't go out in this ~!** ne sors pas par ce froid!; (*fig*) **to be left out in the ~** rester en plan*.

(b) (*Med*) rhume *m*. **~ in the head/on the chest** rhume de cerveau/de poitrine; **a heavy** *or* **bad ~** un gros *or* sale* rhume; **to have a ~** être enrhumé; **to get a ~** s'enrhumer, attraper un rhume; *V* **catch, head**.

coldly ['kəʊldlɪ] *adv look, say, behave* froidement, avec froideur.

coldness ['kəʊldnɪs] *n* (*lit, fig*) froideur *f*.

coleslaw ['kəʊlslɔː] *n* salade *f* de chou cru.

colic ['kɒlɪk] *n* colique(s) *f(pl)*.

Coliseum [ˌkɒlɪ'siːəm] *n* Colisée *m*.

colitis [kɒ'laɪtɪs] *n* colite *f*.

collaborate [kə'læbəreɪt] *vi* (*also pej*) collaborer. **to ~ with sb on** *or* **in sth** collaborer avec qn à qch.

collaboration [kəˌlæbə'reɪʃən] *n* (*also pej*) collaboration *f* (*in* à).

collaborator [kə'læbəreɪtəʳ] *n* (*gen*) collaborateur *m*, -trice *f*; (*pej: World War II*) collaborateur, -trice, collaborationniste *mf*, collabo* *mf*.

collage [kɒ'lɑːʒ] *n* (*Art*) collage *m*.

collapse [kə'læps] **1** *vi* **(a)** [*person, building, roof, floor*] s'écrouler, s'effondrer, s'affaisser; [*balloon*] se dégonfler; [*beam*] fléchir; (*fig*) [*one's health*] se délabrer, flancher*; [*government*] tomber, faire la culbute*; [*prices, defences*] s'effondrer; [*civilization, society, institution*] s'effondrer, s'écrouler; [*plan, scheme*] s'écrouler, tomber à l'eau; (*: *with laughter*) être plié (en deux) *or* se tordre (*de rire*). **he ~d at work and was taken to hospital** il a eu un grave malaise à son travail et on l'a emmené à l'hôpital.

(b) (*lit: fold for storage etc*) [*table, chairs*] se plier.

2 *vt table, chair* plier; (*fig*) *paragraphs, items* réduire, comprimer.

3 *n* [*person, building, roof*] écroulement *m*, effondrement *m*; [*lung etc*] collapsus *m*; [*beam*] fléchissement *m*; [*health*] délabrement *m*; [*government*] chute *f*; [*prices, defences*] effondrement; [*civilization, plan, scheme*] effondrement, écroulement.

collapsible [kə'læpsəbl] *adj table, chair, umbrella* pliant.

collar ['kɒləʳ] **1** *n* (*attached: on garment*) col *m*; (*separate*) (*for men*) faux-col *m*; (*for women*) col, collerette *f*; (*for dogs, horses etc*) collier *m*; (*part of animal's neck*) collier; (*Culin*) [*beef*] collier; [*mutton etc*] collet *m*; (*Tech: on pipe etc*) bague *f*. **to get hold of sb by the ~** saisir qn au collet; *V* **white** *etc*.

2 *vt* **(a)** (*) *person* (*lit*) prendre *or* saisir au collet, colleter; (*fig*) accrocher, intercepter*; *book, object* faire main basse sur.

(b) (*Tech*) baguer.

3 *cpd*: **collarbone** clavicule *f*; (*US*) **collar button**, (*Brit*) **collarstud** bouton *m* de col.

collate [kɒ'leɪt] *vt* **(a)** collationner (*with* avec). **(b)** (*Rel*) nommer (*to* à).

collateral [kɒ'lætərəl] **1** *adj* **(a)** (*parallel*) parallèle; *fact, phenomenon* concomitant; (*Jur*) *relationship*, (*Med*) *artery* collatéral.

(b) (*subordinate*) secondaire, accessoire; (*Fin*) subsidiaire. (*Fin*) **~ security** nantissement *m*.

2 *n* **(a)** (*Fin*) nantissement *m*. **securities lodged as ~** titres remis en nantissement.

(b) (*Jur*) collatéral(e) *m(f)*.

collation [kə'leɪʃən] *n* collation *f*.

colleague ['kɒliːg] *n* collègue *mf*, confrère *m*, consœur *f* (*rare*).

collect[1] ['kɒlekt] *n* (*Rel*) collecte *f* (*prière*).

collect[2] [kə'lekt] **1** *vt* **(a)** (*gather together, assemble*) *valuables, wealth* accumuler, amasser; *facts, information* rassembler, recueillir; *documents* recueillir, rassembler, grouper; *evidence, proof* rassembler. **the ~ed works of Shakespeare** les œuvres complètes de Shakespeare; **she ~ed (together) a group of volunteers** elle a rassemblé *or* réuni un groupe de volontaires; **the dam ~s the water from the mountains** le barrage accumule *or* retient l'eau des montagnes; (*fig*) **to ~ one's wits** rassembler ses esprits; (*fig*) **to ~ o.s.** (*regain control of o.s.*) se reprendre; (*reflect quietly*) se recueillir; (*fig*) **to ~ one's thoughts** se recueillir, se concentrer.

(b) (*pick up*) *seashells etc* ramasser; *eggs* lever, ramasser. **the children ~ed (up) the books for the teacher** les enfants ont ramassé les livres pour l'instituteur; **these vases ~ the dust*** ces vases prennent *or* ramassent* la poussière.

(c) (*obtain*) *money, subscriptions* recueillir; *taxes, dues, fines* percevoir; *rents* encaisser, toucher. (*US*) **~ on delivery** paiement *m* à la livraison, livraison contre remboursement.

(d) (*take official possession of*) *[bus or railway company] luggage etc* prendre à domicile; *[ticket collector] tickets* ramasser. (*Post*) **to ~ letters** faire la levée du courrier; **the rubbish is ~ed twice a week** les ordures sont enlevées *or* ramassées deux fois par semaine; **the firm ~s the empty bottles** la compagnie récupère les bouteilles vides.

(e) (*as hobby*) *stamps, antiques, coins* collectionner, faire collection de. (*pej*) **she ~s* poets/lame ducks** *etc* elle collectionne* les poètes/canards boiteux *etc.*

(f) (*call for*) *person* aller chercher, (passer) prendre. **I'll ~ you in the car/at 8 o'clock** j'irai vous chercher *or* je passerai vous prendre en voiture/à 8 heures; **to ~ one's mail/one's keys** *etc* (passer) prendre son courrier/ses clefs *etc*; **I'll come and ~ the book this evening** je passerai prendre le livre ce soir; **the bus ~s the children each morning** l'autobus ramasse les enfants tous les matins.

2 *vi* **(a)** *[people]* se rassembler, se réunir, se grouper; *[things]* s'amasser, s'entasser; *[dust, water]* s'amasser, s'accumuler.

(b) to ~ for the injured faire la quête *or* quêter pour les blessés.

3 *adv*: (*US Telec*) **to call ~** téléphoner en P.C.V.

collection [kəˈlekʃən] *n* **(a)** (*U: V* **collect**[2]) accumulation *f*; rassemblement *m*; ramassage *m*; fait *m* de recueillir; perception *f*; encaissement *m*.

(b) (*Rel etc*) *[money]* collecte *f*, quête *f*; (*Post*) *[mail]* levée *f*. **a ~ was made for the blind** on a fait une quête *or* collecte pour les aveugles; **there were several ~s for charity in the course of the evening** on a fait plusieurs quêtes *or* on a quêté pour plusieurs œuvres au cours de la soirée; (*Post*) **there are 5 ~s daily** il y a 5 levées par jour.

(c) (*group, also Fashion*) collection *f*. **the spring ~** la collection de printemps; **his ~ of foreign stamps** sa collection de timbres étrangers.

collective [kəˈlektɪv] *adj* (*gen, Jur*) *responsibility, farm, ownership, ticket, security* collectif. **~ bargaining** (négociations *fpl* pour une) convention collective de travail; (*Ling*) **~ noun** collectif *m*.

collectively [kəˈlektɪvlɪ] *adv* collectivement.

collectivism [kəˈlektɪvɪzəm] *n* collectivisme *m*.

collectivist [kəˈlektɪvɪst] *adj, n* collectiviste (*mf*).

collectivize [kəˈlektɪvaɪz] *vt* collectiviser.

collector [kəˈlektə^r] *n [taxes]* percepteur *m*; *[dues]* receveur *m*; *[rent, cash]* encaisseur *m*; *[stamps, coins etc]* collectionneur *m*, -euse *f*; (*also* **ticket ~**) contrôleur *m*, -euse *f*.

colleen [ˈkɒliːn] *n* jeune Irlandaise; (*in Ireland*) jeune fille *f*.

college [ˈkɒlɪdʒ] *n* **(a)** (*institution for higher education*) collège *m*, établissement *m* d'enseignement supérieur; (*for professional training*) école professionnelle, collège technique. **~ of agriculture** institut *m* agronomique; **~ of art** école des beaux-arts; **~ of domestic science** école *or* centre *m* d'enseignement ménager; **~ of music** conservatoire *m* de musique; **to go to ~*** faire des études supérieures; *V* **naval, teacher** *etc.*

(b) (*within a university*) collège *m*.

(c) (*association*) collège *m*, société *f*, académie *f*. **C~ of Physicians/Surgeons** Académie de médecine/de chirurgie; **the C~ of Cardinals** le Sacré Collège; *V* **electoral.**

collegiate [kəˈliːdʒɪɪt] *adj life* de collège; (*Can*) *studies* secondaire. **~ church** collégiale *f*.

collide [kəˈlaɪd] *vi* **(a)** (*lit*) entrer en collision, se heurter, se tamponner. **to ~ with** entrer en collision avec, heurter, tamponner; (*Naut*) aborder. **(b)** (*fig*) se heurter (*with* à), entrer en conflit (*with* avec).

collie [ˈkɒlɪ] *n* colley *m*.

collier [ˈkɒlɪə^r] *n* (*miner*) mineur *m*; (*ship*) charbonnier *m*.

colliery [ˈkɒlɪərɪ] *n* houillère *f*, mine *f* (de charbon).

collision [kəˈlɪʒən] **1** *n* **(a)** (*lit*) collision *f*, heurt *m*, choc *m*; (*Rail*) collision, tamponnement *m*; (*Naut*) abordage *m*. **to come into ~ with** *[car]* entrer en collision avec; *[train]* entrer en collision avec, tamponner; *[boat]* aborder.

(b) (*fig*) conflit *m*, opposition *f*.

2 *cpd*: **to be on a collision course** (*Naut etc*) être sur une route de collision; (*fig*) aller au-devant de l'affrontement (*with* avec).

colloquial [kəˈləʊkwɪəl] *adj* familier, parlé, de la conversation.

colloquialism [kəˈləʊkwɪəlɪzəm] *n* (*Ling*) expression familière.

colloquially [kəˈləʊkwɪəlɪ] *adv* familièrement, dans le langage de la conversation, dans la langue parlée.

colloquium [kəˈləʊkwɪəm] *n* colloque *m*.

colloquy [ˈkɒləkwɪ] *n* colloque *m*, conversation *f*.

collusion [kəˈluːʒən] *n* collusion *f*. **in ~ with** de complicité avec, de connivence avec.

collywobbles‡ [ˈkɒlɪˌwɒblz] *npl*: **to have the ~** (*be scared*) avoir la frousse* *or* la trouille*; (*have stomach trouble*) avoir des coliques.

colon[1] [ˈkəʊlən] *n* (*Anat*) côlon *m*.

colon[2] [ˈkəʊlən] *n* (*Gram*) deux-points *m inv*.

colonel [ˈkɜːnl] *n* colonel *m*. **C~ Smith** le colonel Smith.

colonial [kəˈləʊnɪəl] **1** *adj* colonial. **C~ Office** ministère *m* des Colonies; (*Mil*) **~ forces** (armée *f*) coloniale *f*. **2** *n* colonial(e) *m(f)*.

colonialism [kəˈləʊnɪəlɪzəm] *n* colonialisme *m*.

colonialist [kəˈləʊnɪəlɪst] *adj, n* colonialiste (*mf*).

colonic [kəʊˈlɒnɪk] *adj* du côlon. **~ irrigation** lavement *m*.

colonist [ˈkɒlənɪst] *n* colon *m* (*habitant etc d'une colonie*).

colonization [ˌkɒlənaɪˈzeɪʃən] *n* colonisation *f*.

colonize [ˈkɒlənaɪz] *vt* coloniser.

colonnade [ˌkɒləˈneɪd] *n* colonnade *f*.

colony [ˈkɒlənɪ] *n* (*all senses*) colonie *f*; *V* **leper.**

colophon [ˈkɒləfən] *n* colophon *m*, explicit *m*.

color [ˈkʌlə^r] *etc* (*US*) = **colour** *etc.*

Colorado [ˌkɒləˈrɑːdəʊ] *n* Colorado *m*. **~ beetle** doryphore *m*.

coloration [ˌkʌləˈreɪʃən] *n* coloration *f*, coloris *m*; *V* **protective.**

colorcast [ˈkʌləkɑːst] **1** *n* programme *m* (télévisé) en couleur. **2** *vt* téléviser en couleur.

colossal [kəˈlɒsl] *adj* (*lit, also fig*) colossal.

colossus [kəˈlɒsəs] *n* colosse *m*.

colour, (*US*) **color** [ˈkʌlə^r] **1** *n* **(a)** (*hue*) couleur *f*, teinte *f*. **what ~ is it?** de quelle couleur est-ce?; **there is not enough ~ in it** cela manque de couleur; **to take the ~ out of sth** décolorer qch; (*fig*) **the ~ of a newspaper** la couleur *or* les opinions *fpl* d'un journal; (*fig*) **let's see the ~ of your money*** fais voir la couleur de ton fric*; (*fig*) **a symphony/a poem full of ~** une symphonie pleine/un poème plein de couleur; (*fig*) **to give** *or* **lend ~ to a tale** colorer un récit; (*fig*) **to give a false ~ to sth** présenter qch sous un faux jour, dénaturer qch; (*fig*) **under (the) ~ of** sous prétexte *or* couleur de; *V* **primary.**

(b) (*complexion*) teint *m*, couleur *f* (*du visage*). **to change ~** changer de couleur; **to lose (one's) ~** pâlir, perdre ses couleurs; **to get one's ~ back** reprendre des couleurs; **he looks an unhealthy ~** il a très mauvaise mine; **to have a high ~** être haut en couleur; *V* **off.**

(c) (*Art*) (*pigment*) matière colorante, couleur *f*; (*paint*) peinture *f*; (*dye*) teinture *f*; (*shades, tones*) coloris *m*, couleur, ton *m*. (*lit, fig*) **to paint sth in bright/dark ~s** peindre qch de couleurs vives/sombres; (*fig*) **to see sth in its true ~s** voir qch sous son vrai jour (*V also* **d**); *V* **local, water** *etc.*

(d) (*symbol of allegiance*) **~s** couleurs *fpl* (*d'un club, d'un parti etc*); (*Mil*) couleurs, drapeau *m*; (*Naut*) couleurs, pavillon *m*; (*Sport*) **to get** *or* **win one's ~s** être sélectionné pour (faire partie de) l'équipe; **to salute the ~s** saluer le drapeau; **to fight with the ~s** combattre sous les drapeaux; (*fig*) **to stick to one's ~s** rester fidèle à ses principes *or* à ce qu'on a dit; (*fig*) **he showed his true ~s when he said ...** il s'est révélé tel qu'il est vraiment quand il a dit ...; *V* **flying, nail, troop.**

(e) (*Pol*) *[race]* couleur *f*. **his ~ counted against him** sa couleur jouait contre lui; **it is not a question of ~** ce n'est pas une question de race.

2 *cpd*: **colour bar** discrimination raciale; **colour-blind** daltonien; **colour blindness** daltonisme *m*, achromatopsie *f*; (*TV*) **colour camera** caméra *f* couleur *inv*; **colour film** (*for camera*) pellicule *f* (en) couleur; (*for movie camera; in cinema*) film *m* en couleur; (*Phot*) **colour filter** filtre coloré; **colour photograph** photographie *f* en couleur; **colour photography** photographie *f* en couleur; **colour problem** problème racial *or* du racisme; **colour scheme** combinaison *f* de(s) couleurs; **to choose a colour scheme** assortir les couleurs *or* les tons; (*Mil*) **colour sergeant** (sergent *m*) porte-drapeau *m*; **colour slide** diapositive *f* en couleur; (*Brit Press*) **colour supplement** supplément illustré; **colour television** télévision *f* (en) couleur; **colour television (set)** téléviseur *m* couleur *inv*.

3 *vt* **(a)** (*lit*) (*give ~ to*) colorer, donner de la couleur à; (*with paint*) peindre; (*with crayons etc*) colorier; (*dye*) teindre; (*tint*) teinter. **to ~ sth red** colorer (*or* colorier *etc*) qch en rouge; **to ~ (in) a picture** colorier une image; *[children]* **a ~ing book** un album à colorier.

(b) (*fig*) *story, description* colorer; *facts* (*misrepresent*) fausser; (*exaggerate*) exagérer.

4 *vi [things]* se colorer; *[persons]* (*also* **~ up**) rougir.

coloured, (*US*) **colored** [ˈkʌləd] **1** *adj* **(a)** *liquid, complexion* coloré; *drawing* colorié; *pencil* de couleur; *picture, photograph, slide, television* en couleur. (*fig*) **a highly ~ tale** un récit très coloré.

(b) (*adj ending in cpds*) **-coloured** (de) couleur. **a straw-coloured hat** un chapeau couleur paille; **muddy-coloured** couleur de boue.

(c) *person, race* de couleur.

2 *n*: **~s** (*US, Brit*) personnes *fpl* de couleur; (*in South Africa*) métis *mpl*; *V* **cape**[2].

colourful, (*US*) **colorful** [ˈkʌləfʊl] *adj* (*lit*) coloré, vif, éclatant; (*fig*) *personality* pittoresque, original; *account* coloré.

colouring, (*US*) **coloring** [ˈkʌlərɪŋ] **1** *n* **(a)** (*complexion*) teint *m*. **high ~** teint coloré.

(b) (*U*) coloration *f*; *[drawings etc]* coloriage *m*; (*fig*) *[news, facts etc]* travestissement *m*, dénaturation *f*. **~ book** album *m* à colorier.

(c) (*hue*) coloris *m*, coloration *f*.

colourless, (*US*) **colorless** [ˈkʌləlɪs] *adj* (*lit*) sans couleur, incolore; (*fig*) incolore, terne, fade.

colt [kəʊlt] **1** *n* **(a)** (*Zool*) poulain *m*; (*fig: a youth*) petit jeune (*pej*), novice *m*. **(b)** ® (*pistol*) colt *m*, pistolet *m* (automatique). **2** *cpd*: (*Bot*) **coltsfoot** pas-d'âne *m inv*, tussilage *m*.

coltish [ˈkɒltɪʃ] *adj* (*frisky*) guilleret, folâtre; (*inexperienced*) jeunet, inexpérimenté.

Columbia [kəˈlʌmbɪə] *n* Colombie *f*.

Columbian [kəˈlʌmbɪən] **1** *adj* colombien. **2** *n* Colombien(ne) *m(f)*.

columbine [ˈkɒləmbaɪn] *n* ancolie *f*.

Columbine [ˈkɒləmbaɪn] *n* (*Theat*) Colombine *f*.

Columbus [kəˈlʌmbəs] *n* Christophe Colomb *m*.

column [ˈkɒləm] *n* (*all senses*) colonne *f*; *V* **fifth** *etc.*

columnist [ˈkɒləmnɪst] *n* journaliste *mf*, collaborateur *m*, -trice *f* d'un journal (*chargé(e) d'une rubrique régulière*).

coma ['kəʊmə] *n* coma *m*. **in a ~** dans le coma.
comatose ['kəʊmətəʊs] *adj* comateux.
comb [kəʊm] **1** *n* **(a)** peigne *m*; (*large-toothed*) démêloir *m*. **to run a ~ through one's hair, to give one's hair a ~** se donner un coup de peigne, se peigner; *V* **tooth.**
(b) (*for horse*) étrille *f*; (*Tech: for wool etc*) peigne *m*, carde *f*; (*Elec*) balai *m*.
(c) *[fowl]* crête *f*; *[helmet]* cimier *m*.
(d) (*honeycomb*) rayon *m* de miel.
2 *vt* **(a)** peigner; (*Tech*) peigner, carder; *horse* étriller. **to ~ one's hair** se peigner; **to ~ sb's hair** peigner qn.
(b) (*fig: search*) *area, hills, town* fouiller, ratisser. **he ~ed (through) the papers looking for evidence** il a dépouillé le dossier à la recherche d'une preuve.
comb out *vt sep hair* peigner, démêler. **they combed out the useless members of the staff** on a passé le personnel au peigne fin et éliminé les incapables.
combat ['kɒmbæt] **1** *n* combat *m*; *V* **close[1], unarmed** *etc*. **2** *cpd*: **on combat duty** en service commandé; **combat zone** zone *f* de combat. **3** *vt* (*lit, fig*) combattre, lutter contre. **4** *vi* combattre, lutter (*for* pour, *with, against* contre).
combatant ['kɒmbətənt] *adj, n* combattant(e) *m(f)*.
combative ['kɒmbətɪv] *adj* combatif.
combe [ku:m] *n* = **coomb.**
combination [ˌkɒmbɪ'neɪʃən] **1** *n* (*gen, Chem, Math: also of lock*) combinaison *f*; *[people]* association *f*, coalition *f*; *[events]* concours *m*; *[interests]* coalition. (*undergarment*) **~s** combinaison-culotte *f* (de femme); (*Brit Aut*) **(motorcycle) ~** side-car *m*.
2 *cpd*: **combination lock** serrure *f* à combinaison.
combine [kəm'baɪn] **1** *vt* combiner (*with* avec), joindre (*with* à); (*Chem*) combiner. **he ~d generosity with discretion** il alliait la générosité à la discrétion; **they ~d forces/efforts** ils ont uni *or* joint leurs forces/efforts; **to ~ business with pleasure** joindre l'utile à l'agréable; **~d clock and radio** combiné *m* radio-réveil; **their ~d wealth was not enough** leurs richesses réunies n'ont pas suffi; **a ~d effort** un effort conjugué; (*Mil*) **~d forces** forces alliées; (*Mil*) **~d operation** (*by several nations*) opération alliée; (*by the different forces of the same nation*) opération interarmes *inv*.
2 *vi* s'unir, s'associer; *[parties]* fusionner; *[workers]* se syndiquer; (*Chem*) se combiner; (*fig*) se liguer (*against* contre).
3 ['kɒmbaɪn] *n* **(a)** association *f*; (*Comm, Fin*) trust *m*, cartel *m*; (*Jur*) corporation *f*.
(b) (*also* **~ harvester**) moissonneuse-batteuse *f*.
combustible [kəm'bʌstɪbl] *adj* combustible.
combustion [kəm'bʌstʃən] *n* combustion *f*; *V* **internal, spontaneous.**
come [kʌm] *pret* **came**, *ptp* **come 1** *vi* **(a)** (*move*) venir; (*arrive*) venir, arriver; (*reach*) gagner, atteindre. **~ with me** venez avec moi; **~ and see me soon** venez me voir bientôt; **he has ~ to mend the television** il est venu réparer la télévision; **he has ~ from Edinburgh** il est venu d'Édimbourg; **he has just ~ from Edinburgh** il arrive d'Édimbourg; (*fig: originate from*) **to ~ from** *[person]* venir de, être originaire *or* natif de; *[object, commodity]* provenir *or* venir de; **he ~s of a very poor family** il vient *or* est d'une famille très pauvre; **he has ~ a long way** (*lit*) il est venu de loin; (*fig: made much progress*) il a fait du chemin; **to ~ and go** aller et venir; **they were coming and going all day** ils n'ont fait qu'aller et venir toute la journée; (*TV*) **the picture ~s and goes** l'image saute; **the pain ~s and goes** la douleur est intermittente; **to ~ running/shouting** *etc* arriver en courant/en criant *etc*; **to ~ hurrying** arriver en toute hâte; **to ~ home** rentrer (chez soi *or* à la maison); **to ~ for sb/sth** venir chercher *or* venir prendre qn/qch; **you go on, I'll ~ after (you)** allez-y, je vous suis; **coming!** j'arrive!; (*excl*) **~, ~!, ~ now!** allons!, voyons!; **when did he ~?** quand est-il arrivé?; **no one has ~** personne n'est venu; **they came to a town** ils sont arrivés à une ville, ils ont atteint une ville; **the rain came closely after the thunderclap** la pluie a suivi de près le coup de tonnerre; **help came in time** les secours sont arrivés à temps; **it came into my head that** il m'est venu à l'esprit que; **it came as a shock to him** cela lui a fait un choc; **it came as a surprise to him** cela l'a (beaucoup) surpris; **when your turn ~s, when it ~s your turn** quand ce sera (à) votre tour, quand votre tour viendra; **when it ~s to mathematics, no one can beat him** pour ce qui est des mathématiques, personne ne peut le battre; **when it ~s to choosing** quand il faut choisir; (*fig*) **he will never ~ to much** il ne sera *or* fera jamais grand-chose; **the time will ~ when ...** il viendra un temps où ...; (*Jur*) **to ~ before a judge** *[accused]* comparaître devant un juge; *[case]* être entendu par un juge.
(b) (*have its place*) venir, se trouver, être placé. **May ~s before June** mai vient avant *or* précède juin; **July ~s after June** juillet vient après *or* suit juin; **this passage ~s on page 10** ce passage se trouve à la page 10; **the adjective must ~ before the noun** l'adjectif doit être placé devant *or* précéder le substantif; **a princess ~s before a duchess** une princesse prend le pas *or* a la préséance sur une duchesse.
(c) (*happen*) arriver, advenir (*to* à), se produire. **no harm will ~ to him** il ne lui arrivera rien de mal; **~ what may** quoi qu'il arrive (*subj*) *or* advienne, advienne que pourra; **recovery came slowly** la guérison a été lente; **nothing came of it** il n'en est rien résulté; **that's what ~s of disobeying!** voilà ce que c'est que de désobéir!, voilà ce qui arrive quand on désobéit; **no good will ~ of it** ça ne mènera à rien de bon, il n'en sortira rien de bon; **how do you ~ to be so late?** comment se fait-il que vous soyez si en retard?
(d) (+ *to* + *n*) **to ~ to a decision** parvenir à *or* prendre une décision; **to ~ to an end** toucher à sa fin; **to ~ to the throne** accéder au trône; *V* **agreement, blow[2], grief** *etc*.
(e) (+ *into* + *n*) **to ~ into sight** apparaître, devenir visible; *V* **bloom, blossom, effect** *etc*.
(f) (+ *adj, adv etc* = *be, become*) devenir, se trouver. **his dreams came true** ses rêves se sont réalisés; **the handle has ~ loose** le manche s'est desserré; **it ~s less expensive to shop in town** cela revient moins cher de faire ses achats en ville; **swimming/reading ~s naturally *or* natural* to him** il est doué pour la natation/la lecture; **everything came right in the end** tout s'est arrangé à la fin; **this dress ~s in 3 sizes** cette robe existe *or* se fait en 3 tailles; **to ~ undone** se défaire, se dénouer; **to ~ apart** (*come off*) se détacher; (*come unstuck*) se décoller; (*fall to pieces*) tomber en morceaux.
(g) (+ *infin* = *be finally in a position to*) en venir à, finir par. **I have ~ to believe him** j'en suis venu à le croire; **he came to admit he was wrong** il a fini par reconnaître qu'il avait tort; **now I ~ to think of it** réflexion faite, quand j'y songe; (*frm, liter*) **it came to pass that** il advint que (*liter*).
(h) (*phrases*) **the life to ~** la vie future; **the years to ~** les années à venir; **in time to ~** à l'avenir; **if it ~s to that, you shouldn't have done it either** à ce compte-là *or* à ce moment-là* tu n'aurais pas dû le faire non plus; **I've known him for 3 years ~ January** cela fera 3 ans en janvier que je le connais; **she will be 6 ~ August** elle aura 6 ans au mois d'août *or* en août; **she is coming* 6** elle va sur ses 6 ans, elle va avoir 6 ans; **a week ~ Monday** il y aura huit jours lundi; **she had it coming to her*** elle l'a *or* l'avait (bien) cherché; (*fig: cause trouble*) **to ~ between two people** (venir) se mettre entre deux personnes; **she's as clever as they ~*** elle est futée comme pas une*; **you could see that coming*** on voyait venir ça de loin, c'était gros comme le nez au milieu de sa figure; **~ again!‡** comment?, pardon?; **how ~?*** comment ça se fait?*; **how ~ you can't find it?*** comment se fait-il que tu n'arrives (*subj*) pas à le trouver?; **he tried to ~ the innocent with me‡** il a essayé de jouer aux innocents avec moi; **that's coming it a bit strong!‡** tu y vas un peu fort!*, tu pousses!*, tu charries!‡; (*Brit*) **don't ~ that game with me** ne jouez pas ce petit jeu-là avec moi; *V* **clean.**
2 *cpd*: **come-at-able*** accessible; **comeback** (*Theat etc*) retour *m*, rentrée *f*; (*US: response*) réplique *f*; **to make *or* stage a comeback** faire une rentrée; **comedown*** dégringolade* *f*, déchéance *f*; **it was rather a comedown for him to have to work*** c'était assez humiliant pour lui d'avoir à travailler; **she gave him a come-hither look*** elle lui a lancé un regard aguichant; **comeuppance*** *V* **comeuppance*.**
come about *vi* **(a)** (*impers: happen*) se faire (*impers*) + *que* + *subj*, arriver, se produire. **how does it come about that you are here?** comment se fait-il que vous soyez ici?; **this is why it came about** voilà pourquoi c'est arrivé *or* cela s'est produit.
(b) (*Naut*) *[wind]* tourner, changer de direction.
come across 1 *vi* **(a)** (*cross*) traverser.
(b) (*be received*) faire de l'effet. **his speech came across very well** son discours a fait beaucoup d'effet; **his speech came across very badly** son discours n'a pas fait d'effet *or* n'a pas passé la rampe; **despite his attempts to hide them, his true feelings came across quite clearly** malgré ses efforts pour les cacher, ses vrais sentiments se faisaient sentir clairement.
2 *vt fus* (*find or meet by chance*) *thing* trouver par hasard, tomber sur; *person* rencontrer par hasard, tomber sur. **if you come across my watch** si vous tombez sur ma montre.
come across with* *vt fus money* se fendre de*, y aller de; *information* donner, vendre. **he came across with £10** il s'est fendu* de 10 livres; **the criminal came across with the names of his accomplices** le criminel a donné* ses complices.
come along *vi* **(a)** (*imper only*) **come along!** (*impatiently*) (allons *or* voyons), dépêchez-vous!; (*in friendly tone*) (allez,) venez!
(b) (*accompany*) venir, suivre. **may my sister come along as well?** est-ce que ma sœur peut venir aussi?; **why don't you come along?** pourquoi ne viendrais-tu pas?; **come along with me** suivez-moi, accompagnez-moi, venez avec moi.
(c) (*develop*) avancer, faire des progrès. **how is your broken arm? — it's coming along quite well** comment va votre bras cassé? — il *or* ça se remet bien; **my book isn't coming along at all well** mon livre n'avance pas bien.
come at *vt fus* **(a)** (*reach, get hold of*) (*lit*) saisir, mettre la main sur; (*fig*) découvrir, déterminer. **we could not come at the documents** nous n'avons pas pu mettre la main sur les documents; **it was difficult to come at the exact facts/what exactly had happened** il était difficile de déterminer les faits exacts/ce qui s'était passé exactement.
(b) (*attack*) attaquer. **he came at me with an axe** il s'est jeté sur moi en brandissant une hache.
come away *vi* **(a)** (*leave*) partir, s'en aller. **she had to come away before the end** elle a dû partir avant la fin; **come away from there!** sors de là!, écarte-toi de là!
(b) (*become detached*) *[button etc]* se détacher, partir.
come back 1 *vi [person etc]* revenir; *[fashion etc]* revenir en vogue *or* à la mode. **he came back 2 hours later** il est revenu 2 heures plus tard; (*Sport*) **he came back strongly into the game** il est revenu en force dans le jeu; **I asked her to come back with me** je lui ai demandé de me raccompagner; **to come back to what I was saying** pour en revenir à ce que je disais; **I'll come back to you on that one*** nous en reparlerons (plus tard); (*fig*) **his face/name is coming back to me** son visage/son nom me revient (à la mémoire *or* à l'esprit).
2 comeback *n V* **come 2.**
come back with *vt fus* répondre par. **when accused, he came back with a counter-accusation** quand on l'a accusé il a répondu par une contre-accusation.
come by *vt fus* (*obtain*) *object* obtenir, se procurer; *idea, opinion* se faire. **how did you come by that book?** comment vous

êtes-vous procuré ce livre?, comment avez-vous déniché ce livre?

come down 1 *vi* **(a)** (*from ladder, stairs*) descendre (*from* de); (*from mountain*) descendre, faire la descente (*from* de); *[aircraft]* descendre. **come down from there at once!** descends de là tout de suite!; (*fig*) **to come down in the world** descendre dans l'échelle sociale, déchoir; (*fig*) **she had come down to begging** elle en était réduite à mendier *or* à la mendicité; **her hair comes down to her shoulders** ses cheveux lui descendent jusqu'aux épaules *or* lui tombent sur les épaules.

(b) *[buildings etc]* (*be demolished*) être démoli, être abattu; (*fall down*) s'écrouler.

(c) (*drop*) *[prices]* baisser.

(d) (*be transmitted*) *[traditions etc]* être transmis (de père en fils).

2 comedown* *n V* **come 2.**

come down (up)on *vt fus* **(a)** (*punish*) punir; (*rebuke*) s'en prendre à. **he came down on me like a ton of bricks*** il m'est tombé dessus à bras raccourcis.

(b) they came down on me* for a subscription ils m'ont mis le grappin dessus* pour que je souscrive.

come down with *vt fus* **(a)** (*become ill from*) attraper. **to come down with flu** attraper une grippe.

(b) (*: *pay out*) allonger‡.

come forward *vi* se présenter (*as* comme). **who will come forward as a candidate?** qui va se présenter comme candidat? *or* se porter candidat?; **after the burglary, her neighbours came forward with help/money** après le cambriolage, ses voisins ont offert de l'aider/lui ont offert de l'argent; **to come forward with a suggestion** offrir une suggestion; **to come forward with an answer** suggérer une réponse.

come in *vi* **(a)** *[person]* entrer; *[trains etc]* arriver; *[tide]* monter. (*fig*) **when do I come in?** quand est-ce que j'entre en jeu, moi?; (*fig*) **where does your brother come in?** (*how is he involved?*) qu'est-ce que ton frère a à voir là-dedans?; (*what's to be done with him?*) qu'est-ce qu'on fait de ton frère là-dedans?, qu'est-ce que ton frère devient là-dedans?

(b) *[fashion]* faire son entrée *or* apparition dans la mode. **when do strawberries come in?** quand commence la saison des fraises?

(c) (*in a race*) arriver. **he came in fourth** il est arrivé quatrième; (*Scol*) **he came in first in geography** il a eu la meilleure note en géographie, il a été premier en géographie.

(d) (*Pol: be elected to power*) être élu, arriver au pouvoir. **the socialists came in at the last election** les socialistes sont arrivés au pouvoir aux dernières élections.

(e) he has £5,000 coming in every year il touche *or* encaisse 5.000 livres chaque année; **there is at least £100 coming in each week to that household** c'est au moins 100 livres par semaine qui entrent dans ce ménage; **if I'm not working my pay won't be coming in** si je ne travaille pas ma paye ne tombera pas.

(f) to come in handy *or* **useful** avoir son utilité, venir à propos; **to come in handy** *or* **useful for sth** servir à qch, être commode pour qch.

come in for *vt fus* (*receive*) *criticism* être l'objet de, subir, être en butte à; *reproach* subir; *praise* recevoir.

come into *vt fus* (*inherit*) hériter de, entrer en possession de. (*fig*) **to come into one's own** se réaliser, trouver sa voie.

come near to *vt fus*: **to come near to doing** faillir faire, être près de faire, être à deux doigts de faire; **I came near to telling her everything** pour un peu je lui aurais tout dit, j'étais à deux doigts de tout lui dire; **he came near to (committing) suicide** il a failli se suicider.

come off 1 *vi* **(a)** *[button]* se détacher, se découdre; *[stains, marks]* s'enlever, partir.

(b) (*take place*) avoir lieu, se produire. **her wedding did not come off after all** son mariage n'a finalement pas eu lieu.

(c) (*succeed*) *[plans etc]* se réaliser; *[attempts, experiments]* réussir.

(d) (*acquit o.s.*) se tirer d'affaire, s'en tirer, s'en sortir. **he came off well by comparison with his brother** il s'en est très bien tiré en comparaison de son frère; **to come off best** gagner.

2 *vt fus* **(a) a button came off his coat** un bouton s'est détaché *or* décousu de son manteau; **he came off his bike** il est tombé de son vélo; (*Fin*) **to come off the gold standard** abandonner l'étalon-or.

(b) come off it!* et puis quoi encore?, à d'autres!, (et) mon œil!‡

come on 1 *vi* **(a)** (*follow*) suivre; (*continue to advance*) continuer de venir *or* d'avancer.

(b) (*imper only*) **come on, try again!** allons *or* voyons *or* allez, encore un effort!

(c) (*progress, develop*) faire des progrès, avancer, venir bien. **how are your lettuces/plans/children coming on?** où en sont vos laitues/vos projets/vos enfants?; **how are the children? — they're coming on** comment vont les enfants? — ils poussent bien *or* ça pousse!*

(d) (*start*) *[night]* tomber; *[illness]* se déclarer; *[storm]* survenir, éclater; *[seasons]* arriver. **it came on to rain, the rain came on** il s'est mis à pleuvoir; **I feel a cold coming on** je sens que je m'enrhume.

(e) (*arise for discussion or judgment*) *[subjects]* être soulevé, être mis *or* venir sur le tapis; *[questions]* être posé. (*Jur*) **his case comes on this afternoon** son affaire viendra devant le juge cet après-midi.

(f) (*Theat*) *[actor]* entrer en scène; *[play]* être joué *or* représenté *or* donné. **'Hamlet' is coming on next week** on donne 'Hamlet' la semaine prochaine.

2 *vt fus* = **come upon.**

come out *vi [person, object, car, drawer]* sortir (*of* de); *[sun, stars]* paraître, se montrer; *[flowers]* pousser, sortir, venir; *[spots, rash]* sortir; *[secret, news]* être divulgué *or* révélé; *[truth]* se faire jour; *[books, magazines]* paraître, sortir, être publié; *[films]* paraître, sortir; (*Brit Ind: also* **to come out on strike**) se mettre en grève, faire grève; (*go into society*) faire ses débuts dans le monde; (*Scol etc: in exams*) se classer; *[qualities]* se manifester, se révéler, se faire remarquer; *[stains]* s'enlever, s'en aller, partir; *[dyes, colours]* (*run*) déteindre; (*fade*) passer, se faner; (*Math*) *[problems]* se résoudre; *[division etc]* tomber juste. **this photo didn't come out well** cette photo n'a rien donné *or* est très mal venue; **the photo came out well** la photo a réussi *or* est très bonne; **you always come out well in photos** tu es toujours très bien sur les photos, tu es très photogénique; **the total comes out at** *or* **to 500** le total s'élève à 500; **he came out third in French** il s'est classé *or* il est troisième en français; (*Med*) **to come out in a rash** avoir une poussée de boutons, avoir une éruption; (*fig*) **to come out for/against sth** se déclarer ouvertement pour/contre qch.

come out with* *vt fus* (*say*) dire, sortir*, accoucher de‡. **you never know what she's going to come out with next** on ne sait jamais ce qu'elle va sortir*; **come out with it!** dis ce que tu as à dire!, accouche!‡

come over 1 *vi* **(a)** (*lit*) venir (de loin). **he came over to England for a few months** il est venu passer quelques mois en Angleterre; **his family came over with the Normans** sa famille s'est installée ici du temps des Normands.

(b) (*change one's opinions*) passer d'un camp dans l'autre *or* d'un parti à l'autre, changer de bord. **he came over to our side** il est passé de notre côté; **he came over to our way of thinking** il s'est rangé à notre avis.

(c) (*: *feel suddenly*) **to come over queer** *or* **giddy** *or* **funny** se sentir mal tout d'un coup, se sentir tout chose*; **she came over faint** elle a failli s'évanouir *or* tourner de l'œil‡.

(d) he came over well in his speech son discours l'a bien mis en valeur; **his speech came over well** son discours a fait bonne impression.

2 *vt fus [influences, feelings] person* affecter, saisir, s'emparer de. **a feeling of shyness came over her** la timidité la saisit, elle fut saisie de timidité; **I don't know what came over her to speak like that!** je ne sais pas ce qui lui a pris de parler comme cela!; **what's come over you?** qu'est-ce qui vous prend?

come round *vi* **(a)** faire le tour *or* un détour. **the road was blocked and we had to come round by the farm** la route était bloquée et nous avons dû faire un détour par la ferme.

(b) venir, passer. **do come round and see me one evening** passez me voir un de ces soirs.

(c) (*recur regularly*) revenir périodiquement. **your birthday will soon come round again** ce sera bientôt à nouveau ton anniversaire.

(d) (*change one's mind*) changer d'avis. **perhaps in time she will come round** peut-être qu'elle changera d'avis avec le temps.

(e) (*regain consciousness*) revenir à soi, reprendre connaissance; (*get better*) se rétablir, se remettre (*after* de).

(f) (*throw off bad mood etc*) se radoucir, redevenir aimable. **leave her alone, she'll soon come round** laissez-la tranquille, elle reviendra bientôt à d'autres sentiments.

(g) *[boat]* venir au vent.

come through 1 *vi* **(a)** (*survive*) s'en tirer.

(b) (*Telec*) **the call came through** on a reçu *or* eu la communication.

2 *vt fus* (*survive*) *illness, danger, war* se tirer indemne de.

come to 1 *vi* **(a)** (*regain consciousness*) revenir à soi, reprendre connaissance.

(b) (*Naut: stop*) s'arrêter.

2 *vt fus* (*Comm etc*) revenir à, se monter à. **how much does it come to?** cela fait combien?, cela se monte à combien?; **it comes to much less per metre if you buy a lot** cela revient beaucoup moins cher le mètre si vous en achetez beaucoup.

come together *vi* (*assemble*) se rassembler; (*meet*) se rencontrer. (*fig*) **to come together again** se réconcilier.

come under *vt fus* **(a)** (*be subjected to*) *sb's influence, domination* tomber sous, subir, être soumis à.

(b) (*be classified under*) être classé sous. **that comes under 'towns'** c'est classé *or* cela se trouve sous la rubrique 'villes'; (*Admin etc*) **this comes under another department** c'est du ressort *or* de la compétence d'un autre service.

come up *vi* **(a)** (*lit*) monter. (*fig*) **do you come up to town often?** est-ce que vous êtes souvent en ville?; **he came up to me with a smile** il m'a abordé en souriant; (*Brit*) **he came up to Oxford last year** il est entré à (l'université d')Oxford l'année dernière.

(b) (*Jur*) *[accused]* comparaître (*before* devant); *[case]* être entendu (*before* par).

(c) *[plants]* sortir, germer, pointer. **the tulips haven't come up yet** les tulipes ne sont pas encore sorties.

(d) (*fig*) *[matters for discussion]* être soulevé, être mis *or* venir sur le tapis; *[questions]* se poser, être soulevé. **the question of a subsidy came up** la question d'une subvention s'est posée *or* a été soulevée.

come up against *vt fus* se heurter (*fig*) à *or* contre. **he came up against total opposition to his plans** il s'est heurté à une opposition radicale à ses projets; **to come up against sb** entrer en conflit avec qn.

come up to *vt fus* **(a)** (*reach up to*) s'élever jusqu'à, arriver à. **the water came up to his knees** l'eau lui montait *or* venait *or* arrivait jusqu'aux genoux; **my son comes up to my shoulder** mon fils m'arrive à l'épaule.

(b) (*equal*) répondre à. **to come up to sb's hopes** réaliser les *or*

répondre aux espoirs de qn; **his work has not come up to our expectation** son travail n'a pas répondu à notre attente.
come up with *vt fus idea, plan* proposer, suggérer, sortir*. **he comes up with some good ideas** il sort* de bonnes idées.
come upon *vt fus* **(a)** (*attack by surprise*) tomber sur, fondre sur, surprendre.
(b) (*find or meet by chance*) *object* trouver par hasard, tomber sur; *person* rencontrer par hasard, tomber sur.
comedian [kəˈmiːdɪən] *n* **(a)** (*Theat*) *[variety]* comique *m*; *[plays]* comédien *m*; (*fig*) comique, pitre *m*, clown *m*. **(b)** (††: *author*) auteur *m* de comédies.
comedienne [kəˌmiːdɪˈen] *n* (*Theat*) *[variety]* actrice *f* comique; *[plays]* comédienne *f*.
comedy [ˈkɒmɪdɪ] *n* (*play: also fig*) comédie *f*; (*U: style of play*) la comédie, le genre comique. **C~ of Errors** Comédie des Méprises; **~ of manners** comédie de mœurs; **high ~** haute comédie; **low ~** farce *f*; (*fig*) **cut (out) the ~!*** pas de comédie!; *V* **musical.**
comeliness [ˈkʌmlɪnɪs] *n* (*V* **comely**) (*liter*) beauté *f*, charme *m*, grâce *f*; (††) bienséance *f*.
comely [ˈkʌmlɪ] *adj* (*liter: beautiful*) beau (*f* belle), charmant, gracieux; (††: *proper*) bienséant.
comer [ˈkʌməʳ] *n* (*gen in cpds*) arrivant(e) *m(f)*. **open to all ~s** ouvert à tout venant *or* à tous; **the first ~** le premier venu, le premier arrivant; *V* **late, new** *etc.*
comestible† [kəˈmestɪbl] **1** *adj* comestible. **2** *n* (*gen pl*) **~s** denrées *fpl* comestibles, comestibles *mpl*.
comet [ˈkɒmɪt] *n* comète *f*.
comeuppance* [ˌkʌmˈʌpəns] *n*: **to get one's ~*** recevoir ce qu'on mérite; **he got his ~*** il a échoué (*or* perdu *etc*) et il ne l'a pas volé* *or* et il l'a bien cherché.
comfort [ˈkʌmfət] **1** *n* **(a)** (*well-being: U*) confort *m*, bien-être *m*. (*material goods*) **~s** aises *fpl*, commodités *fpl* (de la vie); **he has always been used to ~** il a toujours eu tout le *or* son confort; **to live in ~** vivre dans l'aisance *or* à l'aise; **every (modern) ~** tout le confort moderne; **he likes his ~s** il aime ses aises; **he has never lacked ~s** il n'a jamais manqué des choses matérielles.
(b) (*consolation*) consolation *f*, réconfort *m*, soulagement *m*. **to take ~ from sth** trouver du réconfort *or* une consolation à *or* dans qch; **your presence is/you are a great ~ to me** votre présence est/vous êtes pour moi d'un grand réconfort; **if it's any ~ to you** si ça peut te consoler; **it is a ~ to know that ...** c'est un soulagement *or* c'est consolant de savoir que ...; **to take ~ from the fact that/from the knowledge that** trouver rassurant le fait que/de savoir que; *V* **cold.**
(c) (*peace of mind*) **the fighting was too close for (my) ~** les combats étaient trop près pour ma tranquillité (d'esprit) *or* mon goût.
2 *cpd*: (*US euph*) **comfort station** toilette(s) *f(pl)*.
3 *vt* (*console*) consoler; (*bring relief to*) soulager; (††: *hearten*) réconforter, encourager.
comfortable [ˈkʌmfətəbl] *adj armchair, bed* confortable; *temperature* agréable; *person* à l'aise; *thought, idea, news* rassurant, réconfortant; *win, majority* confortable. **I am quite ~ here** je me trouve très bien ici; **to make o.s. ~** se mettre à son aise, faire comme chez soi; **a very ~ hotel** un hôtel de grand confort; **to have a ~ income** avoir un revenu très suffisant; **he is in ~ circumstances** il mène une vie aisée *or* large; (*Sport etc*) **we've got a ~ lead** nous avons une bonne avance; (*fig*) **I am not very ~ about it** cela m'inquiète un peu.
comfortably [ˈkʌmfətəblɪ] *adv* (*V* **comfortable**) confortablement; agréablement; à son aise, à l'aise; *live* à l'aise, dans l'aisance. **they are ~ off** ils sont à l'aise.
comforter [ˈkʌmfətəʳ] *n* (*person*) consolateur *m*, -trice *f* (*liter*); (*scarf*) cache-nez *m inv*; (*dummy-teat*) tétine *f*, sucette *f*; (*US: quilt*) édredon *m*.
comforting [ˈkʌmfətɪŋ] *adj* (*V* **comfort** 3) consolant; soulageant; réconfortant, encourageant. **it is ~ to think that ...** il est réconfortant de penser que ... .
comfortless [ˈkʌmfətlɪs] *adj room* sans confort; *person* désolé, triste; *thought, prospect* désolant, peu rassurant, triste.
comfy* [ˈkʌmfɪ] *adj chair, room etc* confortable, agréable. **are you ~?** êtes-vous bien?
comic [ˈkɒmɪk] **1** *adj* comique, amusant; (*Theat*) comique, de la comédie. **~ opera** opéra *m* comique; **~ relief** (*Theat*) intervalle *m* comique; (*fig*) moment *m* de détente (comique); **~ verse** poésie *f* humoristique.
2 *n* **(a)** (*person*) (acteur *m*) comique *m*, actrice *f* comique.
(b) (*magazine*) comic *m*. **~s, ~ strip** bande dessinée.
comical [ˈkɒmɪkəl] *adj* drôle, amusant, comique.
comically [ˈkɒmɪkəlɪ] *adv* drôlement, comiquement.
coming [ˈkʌmɪŋ] **1** *n* **(a)** arrivée *f*, venue *f*. **~ and going** va-et-vient *m*; **~s and goings** allées *fpl* et venues; **~ away/back/down/in/out** *etc* départ *m*/retour *m*/descente *f*/entrée *f*/sortie *f etc.*
(b) (*Rel*) avènement *m*; *V* **second¹**.
2 *adj* **(a)** (*future*) à venir, futur; (*in the near future*) prochain. **the ~ year** l'année à venir, l'année prochaine; **~ generations** les générations à venir *or* futures.
(b) (*promising*) qui promet, d'avenir. **a ~ politician** un homme politique d'avenir; **it's the ~ thing*** c'est le truc* à la mode; *V* **up.**
comma [ˈkɒmə] *n* **(a)** (*Gram*) virgule *f*; *V* **invert. (b)** (*Mus*) comma *m*.
command [kəˈmɑːnd] **1** *vt* **(a)** (*order*) ordonner, commander, donner l'ordre (*sb to do* à qn de faire). **to ~ that ...** ordonner *or* commander que ... + *subj*; **to ~ sth to be done** donner l'ordre de (faire) faire qch.
(b) (*be in control of*) *army, ship* commander; *passions, instincts* maîtriser, dominer.
(c) (*be in position to use*) *money, services, resources* disposer de, avoir à sa disposition.
(d) (*deserve and get*) *respect etc* imposer, exiger. **that ~s a high price** cela se vend très cher.
(e) *[places, building]* (*overlook*) avoir vue sur, donner sur; (*overlook and control*) commander, dominer.
2 *vi* (*be in ~*) (*Mil, Naut*) commander, avoir le commandement; (*gen*) commander; (*order*) commander, donner un ordre.
3 *n* **(a)** (*order*) ordre *m*; (*Mil*) commandement *m*. **at** *or* **by the ~ of** sur l'ordre de; **at the word of ~** au commandement.
(b) (*U: Mil: power, authority*) commandement *m*. **to be in ~ of** être à la tête de, avoir sous ses ordres; **to have/take ~ of** avoir/prendre le commandement de; **under the ~ of** sous le commandement *or* les ordres de; (*gen*) **who's in ~ here?** qui est-ce qui commande ici?; *V* **second¹**.
(c) (*Mil*) (*troops*) troupes *fpl*; (*district*) région *f* militaire; (*military authority*) commandement *m*; *V* **high** *etc.*
(d) (*fig: possession, mastery*) maîtrise *f*, possession *f*. **~ of the seas** maîtrise des mers; **he has a ~ of 3 foreign languages** il possède 3 langues étrangères; **his ~ of English** sa maîtrise de l'anglais; **to have at one's ~** avoir à sa disposition; **all the money at my ~** tout l'argent à ma disposition *or* dont je peux disposer; **to be at sb's ~** être à la disposition de qn, être prêt à obéir à qn.
4 *cpd*: (*Space*) **command module** module *m* de commande; (*Brit Theat*) **command performance** ≃ représentation *f* de gala (*à la requête du souverain*); (*Mil*) **command post** poste *m* de commandement.
commandant [ˌkɒmənˈdænt] *n* (*Mil*) commandant *m* (*d'un camp militaire, d'une place forte etc*).
commandeer [ˌkɒmənˈdɪəʳ] *vt* réquisitionner.
commander [kəˈmɑːndəʳ] *n* **(a)** (*gen*) chef *m*; (*Mil*) commandant *m*; (*Naut*) capitaine *m* de frégate. **~-in-chief** commandant *m* en chef, généralissime *m*; *V* **lieutenant, wing. (b)** *[order of chivalry]* commandeur *m*.
commanding [kəˈmɑːndɪŋ] *adj* **(a)** (*person*) qui commande, en chef. (*Mil*) **~ officer** commandant *m*.
(b) *look* impérieux; *air* imposant; *voice, tone* impérieux, de commandement.
(c) *place* (*overlooking*) élevé; (*overlooking and controlling*) dominant. (*lit, fig*) **to be in a ~ position** avoir une position dominante.
commandment [kəˈmɑːndmənt] *n* commandement *m* (*de Dieu ou de l'Église*). **the Ten C~s** les dix commandements, le décalogue (*frm*).
commando [kəˈmɑːndəʊ] *n* (*all senses*) commando *m*.
commemorate [kəˈmeməreɪt] *vt* commémorer.
commemoration [kəˌmeməˈreɪʃən] *n* commémoration *f*; (*Rel*) commémoraison *f*.
commemorative [kəˈmemərətɪv] *adj* commémoratif.
commence [kəˈmens] *vti* commencer (*sth* qch, *to do, doing* à faire).
commencement [kəˈmensmənt] *n* **(a)** commencement *m*, début *m*; *[law]* date *f* d'entrée en vigueur. **(b)** (*Univ: Cambridge, Dublin, US*) remise *f* des diplômes.
commend [kəˈmend] *vt* (*praise*) louer, faire l'éloge de; (*recommend*) recommander, conseiller; (*entrust*) confier (*to* à), remettre (*to* aux soins de). **to ~ o.s. to** *[person]* se recommander à; *[idea, project]* être du goût de; **his scheme did not ~ itself to the public** son projet n'a pas été du goût du public; **his scheme has little to ~ it** son projet n'a pas grand-chose qui le fasse recommander; (†, *frm*) **~ me to Mr X** présentez mes devoirs à M X (*frm*), rappelez-moi au bon souvenir de M X; **to ~ one's soul to God** recommander son âme à Dieu.
commendable [kəˈmendəbl] *adj* (*V* **commend**) louable; recommandable.
commendably [kəˈmendəblɪ] *adv* d'une façon louable. **that was ~ short** cela avait le mérite de la brièveté.
commendation [ˌkɒmenˈdeɪʃən] *n* **(a)** (*V* **commend**) louange *f*, éloge *m*; recommandation *f*. **(b)** (*U*) remise *f* (*to* à, aux soins de).
commensurable [kəˈmenʃərəbl] *adj* commensurable (*with, to* avec).
commensurate [kəˈmenʃərɪt] *adj* (*of equal extent*) (*fig*) de même mesure (*with* que); (*Math*) coétendu (*with* à), de même mesure (*with* que); (*proportionate*) proportionné (*with, to* à).
comment [ˈkɒment] **1** *n* (*spoken, written*) commentaire *m* (*bref*), observation *f*, remarque *f*; (*written*) annotation *f*; (*critical*) critique *f*. **his action went** *or* **passed without ~** son action n'a donné lieu à aucun commentaire; (*Press*) **'no ~'** 'je n'ai rien à dire'; **he passed a sarcastic ~** il a fait une observation *or* une remarque sarcastique.
2 *vt text* commenter. **he ~ed that ...** il a remarqué que ..., il a fait la remarque que ... .
3 *vi* faire des remarques *or* des observations *or* des commentaires. **to ~ on sth** commenter qch, faire des remarques *or* des observations sur qch.
commentary [ˈkɒməntərɪ] *n* (*remark*) commentaire *m*, observation *f*; (*Rad, TV: on news, events*) commentaire; (*Sport*) reportage *m*; *V* **running.**
commentate [ˈkɒmenteɪt] **1** *vi* (*Rad, TV*) faire un reportage (*on* sur). **2** *vt* (*Rad, TV*) *match* commenter.
commentator [ˈkɒmenteɪtəʳ] *n* **(a)** (*Rad, TV*) reporter *m*; *V* **sport. (b)** (*on texts etc*) commentateur *m*, -trice *f*.
commerce [ˈkɒmɜːs] *n* **(a)** (*Comm*) commerce *m* (*généralement en gros ou international*), affaires *fpl*. **he is in ~** il est dans le commerce *or* dans les affaires; (*US*) **Secretary/Department of C~** ≃ ministre *m*/ministère *m* du Commerce; *V* **chamber.**
(b) (*fig: intercourse, dealings*) relations *fpl*, rapports *mpl*.
commercial [kəˈmɜːʃəl] **1** *adj* (*Admin, Comm, Fin, Jur*) *dealings, art, attaché* commercial; *world* du commerce; *value* mar-

chand, commercial; *district* commerçant. ~ **bank** banque commerciale *or* de commerce; ~ **college** école *f* de commerce; ~ **law** droit *m* commercial; ~ **traveller** voyageur *m or* représentant *m* de commerce, commis-voyageur† *m*; ~ **vehicle** véhicule *m* utilitaire; *V* **establishment.** 2 *n* (*Rad, TV*) annonce *f* publicitaire, publicité *f*, spot *m*.

commercialism [kəˈmɜːʃəlɪzəm] *n* (*U*) (*attitude*) mercantilisme *m* (*pej*), esprit commerçant; (*on large scale*) affairisme *m* (*pej*); (*business practice*) (pratique *f* du) commerce *m*, (pratique des) affaires *fpl*.

commercialization [kə,mɜːʃəlaɪˈzeɪʃən] *n* commercialisation *f*.

commercialize [kəˈmɜːʃəlaɪz] *vt* commercialiser.

commercially [kəˈmɜːʃəlɪ] *adv* commercialement.

commie* [ˈkɒmɪ] *adj, n* (*pej abbr of* **communist**) coco: (*mf*) (*pej*).

commiserate [kəˈmɪzəreɪt] *vi* **(a)** (*on bereavement, illness etc*) (*show commiseration for*) témoigner de la sympathie (*with* à); (*feel commiseration for*) éprouver de la commisération (*with* pour). **(b)** (*on bad luck etc*) s'apitoyer sur le sort (*with* de). **I ~ with you!** je compatis à votre sort!

commiseration [kə,mɪzəˈreɪʃən] *n* commisération *f*.

commissar [ˈkɒmɪsɑːʳ] *n* commissaire *m* du peuple (*en URSS etc*).

commissariat [,kɒmɪˈsɛərɪət] *n* (*Mil*) intendance *f*; (*Admin, Pol*) commissariat *m*; (*food supply*) ravitaillement *m*.

commissary [ˈkɒmɪsərɪ] *n* **(a)** (*Mil*) officier *m* d'intendance. ~ **general** intendant général. **(b)** (*delegate*) délégué *m*, commissaire *m*. **(c)** (*US Comm*) coopérative *f*. **(d)** (*Rel*) vicaire général.

commission [kəˈmɪʃən] **1** *n* **(a)** (*gen*) ordres *mpl*, instructions *fpl*; (*to artist etc*) commande *f*. **he gave the artist a ~** il a passé une commande à l'artiste.

(b) (*Comm*) commission *f*, courtage *m*. **on a ~ basis** à la commission; **he gets 10% ~** il reçoit une commission de 10%.

(c) (*errand*) commission *f*.

(d) (*U*) [*crime etc*] perpétration *f* (*Jur, liter*).

(e) (*official warrant*) pouvoir *m*, mandat *m*; (*Mil*) brevet *m*. **to get one's ~** être nommé officier; **to give up one's ~** démissionner.

(f) (*U: delegation of authority etc*) délégation *f* de pouvoir *or* d'autorité, mandat *m*.

(g) (*body of people*) commission *f*, comité *m*. **~ of inquiry** commission d'enquête; *V* **royal.**

(h) (*U: Naut*) armement *m* (*d'un navire*). **to put in ~** armer; **to take out of ~** désarmer; **in ~** en armement, en service; **out of ~** (*Naut*) hors de service; (*Naut: in reserve*) en réserve; (**gen: not in working order*) en panne, hors service, détraqué.

2 *cpd*: **commission agent** (*bookmaker*) bookmaker *m*; (*Comm*) courtier *m*.

3 *vt* **(a)** donner pouvoir *or* mission à, déléguer. **he was ~ed to inquire into ...** il reçut mission de faire une enquête sur ...; **I have been ~ed to say** j'ai été chargé de dire.

(b) *artist* passer une commande à; *book, painting* commander. **this work was ~ed by the town council** ce travail a été commandé par le conseil municipal.

(c) (*Mil etc*) *officer* nommer à un commandement. **~ed officer** officier *m*; **he was ~ed in 1970** il a été nommé officier en 1970; **he was ~ed sub-lieutenant** il a été nommé *or* promu au grade de sous-lieutenant.

(d) (*Naut*) *ship* mettre en service, armer.

commissionaire [kə,mɪʃəˈnɛəʳ] *n* (*Brit, Can*) commissionnaire *m* (*d'un hôtel etc*), chasseur *m*, coursier *m*.

commissioner [kəˈmɪʃənəʳ] *n* membre *m* d'une commission, commissaire *m*; (*Police*) préfet *m* (de police). (*Jur*) **~ for oaths** *officier m ayant qualité pour recevoir les déclarations sous serment*; (*Can*) **C~ of Official Languages** Commissaire *m* aux langues officielles; *V* **high, lord.**

commit [kəˈmɪt] *vt* **(a)** *crime, sacrilege* commettre; *mistake* commettre, faire. **to ~ hara-kiri** faire hara-kiri; **to ~ a perjury** se parjurer, (*Jur*) faire un faux serment; **to ~ suicide** se suicider.

(b) (*consign*) confier (*to* à), remettre (*to* à la garde de, aux soins de). (*Jur*) **to ~ sb (to prison)** faire incarcérer qn; **to ~ sb to a mental hospital** interner qn; (*Jur*) **to ~ sb for trial** mettre qn en accusation; **to ~ to writing** *or* **to paper** consigner *or* coucher par écrit; (*liter*) **to ~ to the flames** livrer aux flammes; **to ~ to memory** apprendre par cœur.

(c) (*Parl*) *bill* renvoyer à une commission.

(d) to ~ o.s. s'engager (*to* à); (*compromise o.s.*) se compromettre; **a ~ted writer** un écrivain engagé; **to be ~ted to a policy** s'être engagé à poursuivre une politique; **don't ~ yourself to giving her regular help** ne vous engagez pas à l'aider régulièrement.

commitment [kəˈmɪtmənt] *n* **(a)** (*responsibility, obligation*) charges *fpl*, responsabilité(s) *f(pl)*; (*Comm, Fin*) engagement financier. (*Comm*) **'without ~'** 'sans obligation'; **teaching ~s** (heures *fpl* d')enseignement *m*; **he has heavy teaching ~s** il a un enseignement chargé. **(b)** (*Jur: also* **~ order**) mandat *m* de dépôt. **(c)** (*Parl*) [*bill*] renvoi *m* à une commission.

committal [kəˈmɪtl] *n* **(a)** (*U*) remise *f* (*to* à, aux soins de); (*to prison*) incarcération *f*, emprisonnement *m*; (*to mental hospital*) internement *m*; (*burial*) mise *f* en terre. **~ for trial** mise en accusation; (*Jur*) **~ order** mandat *m* de dépôt.

(b) (*U*) [*crime etc*] perpétration *f* (*Jur, liter*).

(c) (*Parl*) = **commitment c.**

committee [kəˈmɪtɪ] **1** *n* commission *f*, comité *m*; (*Parl*) commission. **to be** *or* **sit on a ~** faire partie d'une commission *or* d'un comité; (*Parl*) **~ of inquiry** commission d'enquête; *V* **management, organize.**

2 *cpd*: **committee meeting** réunion *f* de commission *or* de comité; **committee member** membre *m* d'une commission *or* d'un comité.

commode [kəˈməʊd] *n* **(a)** (*chest of drawers*) commode *f*. **(b)** (*also* **night-~**) chaise percée.

commodious [kəˈməʊdɪəs] *adj* spacieux, vaste.

commodity [kəˈmɒdɪtɪ] *n* (*consumer goods*) produit *m*, article *m*, marchandise *f* (*U*); (*food*) denrée *f*. **staple commodities** produits de base; **household commodities** articles de ménage.

commodore [ˈkɒmədɔːʳ] *n* (*Naut*) commodore *m*; [*yacht club*] président *m*; [*shipping line*] doyen *m* (*des capitaines*).

common [ˈkɒmən] **1** *adj* **(a)** (*used by or affecting many*) *interest, cause, language* commun. **to make ~ cause with sb** faire cause commune avec qn; **by ~ consent** d'un commun accord; (*fig*) **~ ground** point commun, terrain *m* d'entente; **there is no ~ ground for negotiations** il n'y a aucun terrain d'entente pour (entreprendre) des négociations; **it's ~ knowledge** *or* **property that ...** chacun sait que ..., il est de notoriété publique que ...; **~ land** terrain communal *or* banal; **~ lodging house** hospice *m*, asile *m* de nuit; **the C~ Market** le Marché commun; **~ prostitute** fille publique; **~ wall** mur mitoyen; *V* **talk.**

(b) (*usual, ordinary*) commun, ordinaire; (*universal*) général, universel; (*not outstanding*) moyen, ordinaire. **it's quite ~** c'est très courant, ça n'a rien d'extraordinaire, c'est tout à fait banal (*pej*); **~ belief** croyance universelle; **it's a ~ experience** cela arrive à tout le monde, c'est une chose qui arrive à tout le monde; **it is only ~ courtesy to apologise** la politesse la plus élémentaire veut qu'on s'excuse (*subj*); (*pej*) **the ~ herd** la plèbe, la populace (*pej*); **~ honesty** la simple honnêteté; **the ~ man** l'homme du commun *or* du peuple; **the ~ people** le commun, le peuple, les gens du commun (*pej*); **a ~ occurrence** une chose fréquente *or* répandue; **in ~ parlance** dans le langage courant; (*Rel*) **the Book of C~ Prayer** *le livre du rituel anglican*; **the ~ run of mankind** le commun des hommes *or* des mortels; **out of the ~ run** hors du commun, exceptionnel; **~ salt** sel *m* (ordinaire); **a ~ sight** un spectacle familier; **a ~ soldier** un simple soldat; **~ or garden** vulgaire; (*Brit*) **I've a ~ or garden cold*** je n'ai qu'un vulgaire rhume.

(c) (*vulgar*) *accent, clothes, person* commun, vulgaire.

(d) (*Math*) commun. **~ denominator/factor** dénominateur/facteur commun; **~ multiple** commun multiple.

(e) (*Gram*) *noun* commun.

(f) (*Mus*) **~ time** *or* **measure** (*duple*) mesure *f* à deux temps; (*quadruple*) mesure à quatre temps.

2 *n* **(a)** (*land*) terrain communal. (*Jur*) **right of ~** [*land*] communauté *f* de jouissance; [*property*] droit *m* de servitude.

(b) in ~ en commun; **to hold in ~** partager; (*fig*) **they have nothing in ~** ils n'ont rien de commun; **in ~ with** en commun avec; (*by agreement with*) en accord avec.

3 *cpd*: (*US*) **common carrier** entreprise *f* de transport public, transporteur public; **common law** droit coutumier; **common-law wife** épouse *f* de droit coutumier; **commonplace** (*adj*) banal, commun, ordinaire; (*n*) lieu commun, platitude *f*, banalité *f*; **commonroom** salle commune; (*staffroom*) salle des professeurs; **commonsense** sens commun, bon sens; **commonsense attitude** attitude sensée *or* pleine de bon sens; **commonsense plan** projet sensé *or* plein de bon sens; (*US Fin*) **common stock** actions *fpl* ordinaires; **the commonweal** (*general good*) le bien public; (*the people*) l'État *m*.

commoner [ˈkɒmənəʳ] *n* (*not noble*) roturier *m*, -ière *f*; (*Parl*) député *m* (de la Chambre des Communes); (*Univ Oxford*) étudiant(e) *m(f)* non boursier (-ière); (*Jur*) personne *f* qui a droit de vaine pâture.

commonly [ˈkɒmənlɪ] *adv* **(a)** (*usually*) communément, ordinairement, généralement. **(b)** (*vulgarly*) vulgairement, d'une façon vulgaire *or* commune.

commonness [ˈkɒmənnɪs] *n* (*U*) (*frequency*) fréquence *f*; (*ordinariness*) caractère commun *or* ordinaire, banalité *f* (*pej*); (*universality*) généralité *f*, universalité *f*, caractère général *or* universel; (*vulgarity*) vulgarité *f*.

commons [ˈkɒmənz] *npl* **(a) the ~** le peuple, le tiers état; (*Parl*) **the C~** les Communes *fpl*; *V* **house. (b)** (*food*) nourriture *f* (*partagée en commun*). **to be on short ~** faire maigre chère, être réduit à la portion congrue.

commonwealth [ˈkɒmənwelθ] *n* **(a)** (*republican state*) état *m* démocratique, république *f*; (*federation*) confédération *f*. **the (British) C~** le Commonwealth; (*Brit*) **Minister of** *or* **Secretary of State for Commonwealth Affairs** ministre *m* du Commonwealth.

(b) (*Brit Hist*) **the C~** la république de Cromwell.

(c) (††) = **commonweal**; *V* **common 3.**

commotion [kəˈməʊʃən] *n* **(a)** (*U*) trouble *m*, agitation *f*, commotion *f*. **in a state of ~** *person* bouleversé, vivement ému; *town* en émoi.

(b) (*U: noise and movement*) agitation *f*, perturbation *f*, tumulte *m*. **to make** *or* **cause a ~** semer la perturbation.

(c) (*uprising*) insurrection *f*, révolte *f*, troubles *mpl*; *V* **civil.**

communal [ˈkɒmjuːnl] *adj* **(a)** (*of the community*) *benefit, profit, good* communautaire, de la communauté. **(b)** (*owned etc in common*) commun, public (*f* -ique). **a ~ bathroom** une salle de bains commune; **~ life** la vie collective.

communally [ˈkɒmjuːnəlɪ] *adv* en commun, collectivement.

commune [kəˈmjuːn] **1** *vi* **(a)** converser intimement, avoir un entretien à cœur ouvert (*with* avec). **to ~ with nature** communier avec la nature.

(b) (*US Rel*) communier.

2 [ˈkɒmjuːn] *n* (*administrative division*) commune *f*; (*community*) communauté *f*. **to live in a ~** vivre en communauté.

communicable [kəˈmjuːnɪkəbl] *adj* communicable; (*Med*) transmissible.

communicant [kəˈmjuːnɪkənt] **1** *n* **(a)** (*Rel*) communiant(e) *m(f)*. **(b)** (*informant*) informateur *m*, -trice *f*. **2** *adj* **(a)** qui communique (avec), communicant. **(b)** (*Rel*) ~ **member** fidèle *mf*, pratiquant(e) *m(f)*.

communicate [kəˈmjuːnɪkeɪt] **1** *vt* **(a)** *news etc* communiquer, transmettre, faire parvenir *or* connaître; *illness* transmettre (*to* à); *feelings, enthusiasm etc* communiquer, faire partager.
(b) (*Rel*) donner la communion à.
2 *vi* **(a)** communiquer, se mettre en rapport, entrer en contact *or* relations (*with* avec). **to ~ with sb by letter/by telephone** communiquer avec qn par lettre/par téléphone; **I no longer ~ with him** je n'ai plus aucun contact avec lui.
(b) *[rooms]* communiquer. **communicating rooms** des chambres qui communiquent *or* communicantes.
(c) (*Rel*) communier, recevoir la communion.

communication [kəˌmjuːnɪˈkeɪʃən] **1** *n* **(a)** (*U*) communication *f*. **to be in ~ with sb** être en contact *or* rapport *or* relations avec qn, avoir des communications avec qn; **to be in radio ~ with sb** communiquer avec qn par radio; **to get into ~ with sb** se mettre *or* entrer en contact *or* rapport *or* relations avec qn; **there is/has been no ~ between them** il n'y a/n'y a eu aucun contact entre eux.
(b) (*message transmitted*) communication *f*, message *m*, information *f*, renseignement *m*.
(c) (*roads, railways, telegraph lines etc*) **~s** communications *fpl*; (*Mil*) liaison *f*, communications.
2 *cpd*: (*Rail*) **communication cord** sonnette *f* d'alarme; (*Mil etc*) **communication line** ligne *f* de communication; **communication satellites** satellites *mpl* de transmission; **communications zone** (zone *f* des) arrières *mpl*.

communicative [kəˈmjuːnɪkətɪv] *adj* **(a)** (*talkative*) communicatif, expansif, bavard. **(b)** *difficulties etc* de communication.

communion [kəˈmjuːnɪən] **1** *n* (*gen*) communion *f*; (*Rel*) (*religious group*) communion; (*denomination*) confession *f*; (*also* **Holy C~**) communion. **a ~ of interests** des intérêts *mpl* en commun; **to make one's ~** communier; **to make one's Easter ~** faire ses pâques; **to take ~** recevoir la communion.
2 *cpd*: (*Rel*) **communion rail** table *f* de communion, balustre *m* du chœur; **communion service** office *m* de communion (*protestant*); **communion table** sainte table.

communiqué [kəˈmjuːnɪkeɪ] *n* communiqué *m*; *V* **joint.**

communism [ˈkɒmjʊnɪzəm] *n* communisme *m*.

communist [ˈkɒmjʊnɪst] *adj, n* communiste *(mf)*. **the C~ Manifesto** le Manifeste Communiste.

communistic [ˌkɒmjʊˈnɪstɪk] *adj* communisant.

community [kəˈmjuːnɪtɪ] **1** *n* **(a)** (*group of people*) communauté *f*, groupement *m*; *[monks, nuns]* communauté. **the French ~ in Edinburgh** la colonie française d'Édimbourg; **the student ~** les étudiants *mpl*, le monde étudiant; **to belong to the same ~** appartenir à la même communauté; **the ~** le public, la communauté; **for the good of the ~** pour le bien de la communauté.
(b) (*common ownership*) propriété collective; (*Jur*) communauté *f*. **~ of goods/interests** communauté de biens/d'intérêts.
2 *cpd*: (*US*) **community antenna distribution** câblodistribution *f*; **community centre** foyer socio-éducatif; (*US*) **community chest** fonds commun; **community health centre** centre médico-social; **community singing** chants *mpl* en chœur (*improvisés*); **community spirit** sens *m or* esprit *m* communautaire, sens de la solidarité; **community worker** animateur *m*, -trice *f* socio-culturel(le).

communize [ˈkɒmjuːnaɪz] *vt* **(a)** *people, countries* (*convert to communism*) convertir au communisme; (*impose communism on*) imposer le régime communiste à. **(b)** *land, factories* collectiviser.

commutable [kəˈmjuːtəbl] *adj* interchangeable, permutable; (*Jur*) commuable (*to* en).

commutability [kəˌmjuːtəˈbɪlɪtɪ] *n* interchangeabilité *f*, permutabilité *f*; (*Jur*) commuabilité *f*.

commutation [ˌkɒmjʊˈteɪʃən] *n* **(a)** échange *m*, substitution *f*; (*Fin*) échange; (*Elec, Jur*) commutation *f*. (*Jur*) **~ of punishment** commutation de peine. **(b)** (*US*) trajet journalier. **~ ticket** carte *f* d'abonnement.

commutative [kəˈmjuːtətɪv] *adj* (*Math*) **~ laws** lois commutatives.

commute [kəˈmjuːt] **1** *vt* substituer (*for, into* à); interchanger, échanger (*for, into* pour, contre, avec); (*Elec*) commuer; (*Jur*) commuer (*into* en). (*Jur*) **~d sentence** sentence commuée.
2 *vi* faire un *or* le trajet journalier, faire la navette (*between* entre, *from* de).

commuter [kəˈmjuːtəʳ] *n* banlieusard(e) *m(f)* (*qui fait un trajet quotidien pour se rendre à son travail*). (*Brit*) **I work in London but I'm a ~** je travaille à Londres mais je fais la navette; (*Brit*) **the ~ belt** la grande banlieue.

commuting [kəˈmjuːtɪŋ] *n* (*U*) migrations quotidiennes, trajets journaliers.

compact [kəmˈpækt] **1** *adj* (*lit*) compact, dense, serré; (*fig*) *style* concis, condensé. **a ~ mass** une masse compacte; **the house is very ~** la maison n'a pas de place perdue.
2 *vt* (*gen pass*) (*lit*) rendre compact, resserrer; (*fig*) condenser. (††) **~ed of** composé de.
3 [ˈkɒmpækt] *n* **(a)** (*agreement*) contrat *m*, convention *f*; entente *f*.
(b) (*also* **powder ~**) poudrier *m*.
(c) (*US Aut*) (voiture *f*) compact *f*.

compactly [kəmˈpæktlɪ] *adv* (*V* **compact 1**) d'une manière *or* de façon compacte; (*fig*) dans un style concis, d'une manière concise. **~ built/designed** construit/conçu sans perte de place *or* sans espace perdu.

compactness [kəmˈpæktnɪs] *n* (*V* **compact 1**) compacité *f*, densité *f*; (*fig*) concision *f*. **the ~ of the kitchen** l'économie *f* d'espace dans la cuisine.

companion [kəmˈpænjən] **1** *n* **(a)** compagnon *m*, compagne *f*; (*also* **lady ~**) dame *f* de compagnie; (*in order of knighthood*) compagnon. **travelling ~s** compagnons de voyage; **~s in arms/in misfortune** compagnons d'armes/d'infortune.
(b) (*one of pair of objects*) pendant *m*.
(c) (*handbook*) manuel *m*.
2 *cpd*: (*Naut*) **companion ladder** (*Navy*) échelle *f*; (*Merchant Navy*) escalier *m*; **companion volume** volume *m* qui va de pair (*to* avec); **companionway** (*Naut*) escalier *m* des cabines; *[small vessel]* montée *f*, descente *f*; (*in yacht: also* **companion hatch**) capot *m* (d'escalier).

companionable [kəmˈpænjənəbl] *adj person* sociable, d'une société agréable; *presence* sympathique.

companionship [kəmˈpænjənʃɪp] *n* (*U*) camaraderie *f*.

company [ˈkʌmpənɪ] **1** *n* **(a)** compagnie *f*. **to keep sb ~** tenir compagnie à qn; **to keep ~ with** fréquenter; **to part ~ with** se séparer de; **in ~ with** en compagnie de; **he is good ~** on ne s'ennuie pas avec lui; **he's bad ~** il n'est pas d'une compagnie très agréable; **she keeps a cat, it's ~ for her** elle a un chat, ça lui fait une compagnie *or* ça lui tient compagnie.
(b) (*guests*) assemblée *f*, compagnie *f*, société *f*. **we are expecting ~** nous attendons des visites *or* des invités; **we've got ~** nous avons de la visite*; **to be in good ~** être en bonne compagnie; *V* **present.**
(c) (*companions*) compagnie *f*, fréquentation *f*. **to keep *or* get into good/bad ~** avoir de bonnes/mauvaises fréquentations; **she is no(t) fit ~ for your sister** ce n'est pas une compagnie *or* une fréquentation pour votre sœur; (*Prov*) **a man is known by the ~ he keeps** dis-moi qui tu hantes, je te dirai qui tu es (*Prov*).
(d) (*Comm, Fin*) société *f*, compagnie *f*, firme *f*. **Smith & C~** Smith et Compagnie; **shipping ~** compagnie de navigation; *V* **affiliate, holding** *etc.*
(e) (*group*) compagnie *f*; *[actors]* troupe *f*, compagnie. **National Theatre C~** la troupe du Théâtre National; (*Naut*) **ship's ~** équipage *m*.
(f) (*Mil*) compagnie *f*.
2 *cpd*: (*Mil*) **company commander** capitaine *m* (de compagnie); **company manners*** belles manières; (*Comm*) **company secretary** secrétaire général (*d'une société*); (*Mil*) **company sergeant-major** adjudant *m*.

comparable [ˈkɒmpərəbl] *adj* comparable (*with, to* à). **the two things are not ~** il n'y a pas de comparaison possible entre les *or* ces deux choses.

comparative [kəmˈpærətɪv] **1** *adj* **(a)** comparatif, comparé; (*Gram*) comparatif. **~ linguistics/literature** linguistique/littérature comparée.
(b) (*relative*) relatif. **to live in ~ luxury** vivre dans un luxe relatif.
2 *n* (*Gram*) comparatif *m*. **in the ~** au comparatif.

comparatively [kəmˈpærətɪvlɪ] *adv* comparativement; (*relatively*) relativement.

compare [kəmˈpɛəʳ] **1** *vt* **(a)** comparer, mettre en comparaison *or* dans la balance (*with* à, avec). **~ the first letter with the second** comparez la première lettre à *or* avec la seconde; **~d with** en comparaison de, par comparaison avec; (*fig*) **to ~ notes** échanger ses impressions *or* ses vues.
(b) comparer, assimiler (*to* à). **the poet ~d her eyes to stars** le poète compara ses yeux à des étoiles.
(c) (*Gram*) *adjective, adverb* former les degrés de comparaison de.
2 *vi* se comparer; être comparable (*with* à). **how do the cars ~ for speed?** quelles sont les vitesses respectives des voitures?; **how do the prices ~?** est-ce que les prix sont comparables?; **he can't ~ with you** il n'y a pas de comparaison (possible) entre vous et lui; **it ~s very favourably** cela soutient la comparaison.
3 *n*: **beyond *or* without *or* past ~** (*adv*) incomparablement; (*adj*) sans pareil, sans comparaison possible.

comparison [kəmˈpærɪsn] *n* **(a)** comparaison *f*. **in ~ with** en comparaison de; **by ~ (with)** par comparaison (avec); **to stand ~ (with)** soutenir la comparaison (avec); **there's no ~** il n'y a pas de comparaison (possible).
(b) (*Gram*) comparaison *f*. **degrees of ~** degrés *mpl* de comparaison.

compartment [kəmˈpɑːtmənt] *n* compartiment *m*, subdivision *f*; (*Naut, Rail*) compartiment; *V* **water.**

compartmentalize [ˌkɒmpɑːtˈmentəlaɪz] *vt* compartimenter.

compass [ˈkʌmpəs] **1** *n* **(a)** boussole *f*; (*Naut*) compas *m*; *V* **box[1], point** *etc.*
(b) (*Math*) **~es** (*also* **a pair of ~es**) compas *m*.
(c) (*fig*) (*extent*) étendue *f*; (*reach*) portée *f*; (*scope*) rayon *m*, champ *m*; (*Mus*) *[voice]* étendue, portée; *V* **narrow.**
2 *cpd*: (*Naut*) **compass card** rose *f* des vents; **compass course** route *f* magnétique; **compass rose = compass card.**
3 *vt* (*go round*) faire le tour de; (*surround*) encercler, entourer.

compassion [kəmˈpæʃən] *n* compassion *f*.

compassionate [kəmˈpæʃənɪt] *adj* compatissant. **on ~ grounds** pour raisons de convenance personnelle *or* de famille; (*Mil*) **~ leave** permission exceptionnelle (*pour raisons de famille*).

compatibility [kəmˌpætəˈbɪlɪtɪ] *n* compatibilité *f* (*with* avec).

compatible [kəmˈpætɪbl] *adj* compatible (*with* avec).

compatibly [kəmˈpætɪblɪ] *adv* d'une manière compatible.

compatriot [kəmˈpætrɪət] *n* compatriote *mf*.

compel [kəmˈpel] *vt* **(a)** contraindre, obliger, forcer (*sb to do* qn à faire). **to be ~led to do** être contraint *or* obligé *or* forcé de faire.

(b) *admiration etc* imposer, forcer. **to ~ obedience/respect from sb** forcer *or* contraindre qn à obéir/à manifester du respect.

compelling [kəmˈpelɪŋ] *adj* irrésistible.

compellingly [kəmˈpelɪŋlɪ] *adv* irrésistiblement, d'une façon irrésistible.

compendious [kəmˈpendɪəs] *adj* compendieux, concis.

compendium [kəmˈpendɪəm] *n* **(a)** (*summary*) abrégé *m*, condensé *m*, compendium *m*. **(b)** (*Brit*) **~ of games** boîte *f* de jeux.

compensate [ˈkɒmpənseɪt] **1** *vt* (*indemnify*) dédommager, indemniser (*for* de); (*pay*) rémunérer (*for* pour); (*in weight, strength*) compenser, contrebalancer; (*Tech*) compenser, neutraliser.

2 *vi* être *or* constituer une compensation (*for* de), compenser; (*in money*) indemniser, dédommager (*for* pour).

compensation [ˌkɒmpənˈseɪʃən] *n* (*indemnity*) compensation *f*, dédommagement *m*, indemnité *f*; (*payment*) rémunération *f*; (*in weight etc*) contrepoids *m*; (*Tech*) compensation, neutralisation *f*. **in ~** en compensation.

compensatory [kəmˈpensətərɪ] *adj* compensateur (*f* -trice).

compère [ˈkɒmpɛəʳ] **1** *n* (*Brit: Rad, Theat, TV*) animateur *m*, -trice *f*, meneur *m*, -euse *f* de jeu. **2** *vt* (*Brit: Rad, Theat, TV*) *show, broadcast* animer, présenter.

compete [kəmˈpiːt] *vi* (*take part*) concourir, se mettre sur les rangs (*for* pour); (*vie*) rivaliser (*with* avec, *in* de), (*Comm*) faire concurrence (*with* à, *for* pour). **to ~ with one another** être rivaux (*f* rivales), se faire concurrence.

competence [ˈkɒmpɪtəns] *n* **(a)** compétence *f* (*for* pour, *in* en), capacité *f* (*for* pour, *in* en), aptitude *f* (*for* à, *in* en). **(b)** (*Jur*) compétence *f*. **within the ~ of the court** de la compétence du tribunal.

competency [ˈkɒmpɪtənsɪ] *n* **(a)** = **competence. (b)** (*money, means*) aisance *f*, moyens *mpl*.

competent [ˈkɒmpɪtənt] *adj* **(a)** (*capable*) compétent, capable; (*qualified*) qualifié (*for* pour), compétent (*for* pour). **he is a very ~ teacher** c'est un professeur très compétent *or* capable; **he is not ~ to teach English** il n'est pas compétent *or* qualifié pour enseigner l'anglais.

(b) (*adequate*) *qualities* suffisant, satisfaisant, honorable. **a ~ knowledge of the language** une connaissance suffisante de la langue.

(c) (*Jur*) *court* compétent; *evidence* admissible, recevable; *person* habile.

competently [ˈkɒmpɪtəntlɪ] *adv* (*V* **competent**) avec compétence, d'une façon compétente; suffisamment.

competition [ˌkɒmpɪˈtɪʃən] *n* **(a)** (*U*) compétition *f*, concurrence *f*, rivalité *f* (*for* pour); (*Comm*) concurrence. **unfair ~** concurrence *or* compétition déloyale; **there was keen ~ for it** on se l'est âprement disputé, il y a eu beaucoup de concurrence pour l'avoir; **in ~ with** en concurrence avec.

(b) concours *m* (*for* pour); (*Sport*) compétition *f*; (*Aut*) course *f*. **to choose by ~** choisir au concours; **to go in for a ~** se présenter à un concours; **beauty/swimming ~** concours de beauté/de natation; **I won it in a newspaper ~** je l'ai gagné en faisant un concours dans le journal.

competitive [kəmˈpetɪtɪv] *adj* **(a)** *entry, selection* par concours, déterminé par un concours. **~ examination** concours *m*. **(b)** *person* qui a l'esprit de compétition; *price* concurrentiel, compétitif; *goods* à prix concurrentiel *or* compétitif.

competitor [kəmˈpetɪtəʳ] *n* (*also Comm*) concurrent(e) *m(f)*.

compilation [ˌkɒmpɪˈleɪʃən] *n* compilation *f*.

compile [kəmˈpaɪl] *vt material* compiler; *dictionary* composer (par compilation); *list, catalogue, inventory* dresser.

compiler [kəmˈpaɪləʳ] *n* compilateur *m*, -trice *f*, rédacteur *m*, -trice *f*; (*Computers*) compilateur *m*.

complacence [kəmˈpleɪsəns] *n*, **complacency** [kəmˈpleɪsnsɪ] *n* contentement *m* de soi, suffisance *f*.

complacent [kəmˈpleɪsənt] *adj* content *or* satisfait de soi, suffisant.

complacently [kəmˈpleɪsəntlɪ] *adv* d'un air *or* ton suffisant, avec suffisance.

complain [kəmˈpleɪn] *vi* **(a)** se plaindre (*of, about* de). **to ~ that** se plaindre que + *subj or indic or* de ce que + *indic*. **how are you? — I can't ~*** comment vas-tu? — je ne peux pas me plaindre.

(b) (*make a complaint*) formuler une plainte *or* une réclamation (*against* contre), se plaindre. **you should ~ to the manager** vous devriez vous plaindre au directeur.

complaint [kəmˈpleɪnt] *n* **(a)** (*expression of discontent*) plainte *f*, récrimination *f*, doléances *fpl*; (*reason for ~*) grief *m*, sujet *m* de plainte; (*Comm*) réclamation *f*; (*Jur*) plainte. **don't listen to his ~s** n'écoutez pas ses doléances *or* ses récriminations; **I have no ~(s), I have no cause for ~** je n'ai aucun sujet *or* motif de plainte, je n'ai pas lieu de me plaindre; (*Comm*) **to make a ~** se plaindre (*about* de), faire une réclamation; (*Jur*) **to lodge *or* lay a ~ against** porter plainte contre.

(b) (*Med*) maladie *f*, affection *f*. **what is his ~?** de quoi souffre-t-il?, de quoi se plaint-il?; **a heart ~** une maladie de cœur; **bowel ~** affection intestinale.

complaisance [kəmˈpleɪzəns] *n* complaisance *f*, obligeance *f*.

complaisant [kəmˈpleɪzənt] *adj* complaisant, obligeant, aimable.

complement [ˈkɒmplɪmənt] **1** *n* (*gen, Gram, Math*) complément *m*; *[staff etc]* personnel tout entier, effectif complet. **with full ~** au grand complet. **2** [ˈkɒmplɪment] *vt* compléter, être le complément de.

complementary [ˌkɒmplɪˈmentərɪ] *adj* (*gen, Math*) complémentaire.

complete [kəmˈpliːt] **1** *adj* **(a)** *surprise, victory, failure* complet (*f* -ète), total; *satisfaction, approval* complet, entier, total. (*Literat*) **the ~ works** les œuvres complètes; **he's a ~ idiot*** il est complètement idiot; **it was a ~ disaster*** ça a été un désastre sur toute la ligne* *or* un désastre complet.

(b) (*finished*) achevé, terminé, fini. **his work is not yet ~** son travail n'est pas encore achevé.

2 *vt collection* compléter; *misfortune, happiness* mettre le comble à; *piece of work* achever, finir, terminer; *form, questionnaire* remplir. **and to ~ his happiness** et pour comble de bonheur; **and just to ~ things** et pour couronner le tout.

completely [kəmˈpliːtlɪ] *adv* complètement.

completeness [kəmˈpliːtnɪs] *n* état complet.

completion [kəmˈpliːʃən] **1** *n [work]* achèvement *m*; *[happiness, misfortune]* comble *m*; (*Jur*) *[contract, sale]* exécution *f*. **near ~** près d'être achevé; **payment on ~ of contract** paiement *m* à la signature du contrat.

2 *cpd*: (*Jur*) **completion date** date *f* d'achèvement (des travaux).

complex [ˈkɒmpleks] **1** *adj* (*all senses*) complexe.

2 *n* **(a)** complexe *m*, ensemble *m*, tout *m*. **industrial/mining ~** complexe industriel/minier; **housing ~** (ensemble de) résidences *fpl*, (*high rise*) grand ensemble.

(b) (*Psych*) complexe *m*. **he's got a ~ about it** ça lui a donné un complexe, il en fait (tout) un complexe; *V* **inferiority** *etc*.

complexion [kəmˈplekʃən] *n [face]* teint *m*; (*fig*) caractère *m*, aspect *m*. **that puts a new ~ on the whole affair** l'affaire se présente maintenant sous un tout autre aspect *or* jour.

complexity [kəmˈpleksɪtɪ] *n* complexité *f*.

compliance [kəmˈplaɪəns] *n* (*U*) **(a)** (*acceptance*) acquiescement *m* (*with* à); (*conformity*) conformité *f* (*with* avec). **in ~ with** conformément à, en accord avec. **(b)** (*submission*) basse complaisance, servilité *f*.

compliant [kəmˈplaɪənt] *adj* accommodant, docile.

complicate [ˈkɒmplɪkeɪt] *vt* compliquer (*with* de); (*muddle*) embrouiller. **that ~s matters** cela complique les choses; **she always ~s things** elle complique toujours tout, elle se crée des problèmes.

complicated [ˈkɒmplɪkeɪtɪd] *adj* (*involved*) compliqué, complexe; (*muddled*) embrouillé.

complication [ˌkɒmplɪˈkeɪʃən] *n* (*gen, Med*) complication *f*.

complicity [kəmˈplɪsɪtɪ] *n* complicité *f* (*in* dans).

compliment [ˈkɒmplɪmənt] **1** *n* **(a)** compliment *m*. **to pay sb a ~** faire *or* adresser un compliment à qn.

(b) (*frm*) **~s** compliments *mpl*, respects *mpl*, hommages *mpl* (*frm*); **give him my ~s** faites-lui mes compliments; **(I wish you) the ~s of the season** (je vous présente) tous les vœux d'usage *or* tous mes vœux; **'with the ~s of Mr X'** 'avec les hommages *or* les bons compliments de Monsieur X'; (*Comm*) **~s slip** ≃ papillon *m* (avec les bons compliments de l'expéditeur).

2 [ˈkɒmplɪment] *vt* complimenter, féliciter (*on* de), faire des compliments à (*on* de, sur).

complimentary [ˌkɒmplɪˈmentərɪ] *adj* **(a)** (*praising*) flatteur. **(b)** (*gratis*) gracieux, à titre gracieux. **~ copy** exemplaire offert en hommage; **~ ticket** billet *m* de faveur.

complin(e) [ˈkɒmplɪn] *n* (*Rel*) complies *fpl*.

comply [kəmˈplaɪ] *vi* obéir, céder, se soumettre (*with* à). **to ~ with sb's wishes** se conformer aux désirs de qn; **to ~ with a request** faire droit à une requête, accéder à une demande; (*Admin, Jur*) **to ~ with a clause** observer *or* respecter une disposition.

component [kəmˈpəʊnənt] **1** *adj* composant, constituant. **the ~ parts** les parties constituantes. **2** *n* (*Chem*) composant *m*; (*Aut, Tech*) pièce *f*. **~s factory** usine *f* de pièces détachées.

comport [kəmˈpɔːt] **1** *vt*: **to ~ o.s.** se comporter, se conduire. **2** *vi* convenir (*with* à), s'accorder (*with* avec).

comportment [kəmˈpɔːtmənt] *n* comportement *m*, conduite *f*.

compose [kəmˈpəʊz] *vt* (*Literat, Mus, Typ*) composer; (*gen, Chem, Tech*) composer, constituer. **to be ~d of** se composer de; **to ~ o.s.** se calmer; **to ~ one's features** composer son visage; **to ~ one's thoughts** mettre de l'ordre dans ses pensées.

composed [kəmˈpəʊzd] *adj* calme, tranquille, posé.

composedly [kəmˈpəʊzɪdlɪ] *adv* avec calme, posément, tranquillement.

composer [kəmˈpəʊzəʳ] *n* (*Mus*) compositeur *m*, -trice *f*.

composite [ˈkɒmpəzɪt] **1** *adj* (*gen, Archit, Phot*) composite; (*Bot, Math*) composé. (*Can*) **~ school** école polyvalente. **2** *n* (*Archit*) (ordre *m*) composite *m*; (*Bot*) composée *f*, composacée *f*.

composition [ˌkɒmpəˈzɪʃən] **1** *n* **(a)** (*U: gen, Art, Mus, Typ*) composition *f*. **music/verse of his own ~** de la musique/des vers de sa composition.

(b) (*thing composed*) composition *f*, œuvre *f*; (*Scol: essay*) rédaction *f*. **one of his most famous ~s** une de ses œuvres les plus célèbres.

(c) (*gen, Chem, Tech: parts composing whole*) composition *f*, constitution *f*; (*mixture of substances*) mélange *m*, composition, composé *m* (*of* de); (*Archit*) stuc *m*. **to study the ~ of a substance** étudier la constitution d'une substance.

(d) (*Gram*) *[sentence]* construction *f*; *[word]* composition *f*.

(e) (*temperament, make-up*) nature *f*, constitution intellectuelle *or* morale.

(f) (*Jur*) accommodement *m*, compromis *m*, arrangement *m* (*avec un créancier*). (*frm*) **to come to a ~** venir à composition (*frm*), arriver à une entente *or* un accord.

2 *cpd substance* synthétique. **composition rubber** caoutchouc *m* synthétique.

compositor [kəmˈpɒzɪtəʳ] *n* (*Typ*) compositeur *m*, -trice *f*.

compos mentis ['kɒmpɒs'mentɪs] *adj* sain d'esprit.
compost ['kɒmpɒst] **1** *n* compost *m*. **~ heap** tas *m* de compost. **2** *vt* composter.
composure [kəm'pəʊʒəʳ] *n* calme *m*, sang-froid *m*, maîtrise *f* de soi.
compote ['kɒmpəʊt] *n* compote *f*; (*US: dish*) compotier *m*.
compound ['kɒmpaʊnd] **1** *n* **(a)** (*Chem*) composé *m* (*of* de); (*Gram*) (mot *m*) composé; (*Tech*) compound *f*.
(b) (*enclosed area*) enclos *m*, enceinte *f*.
2 *adj* (*Chem*) composé, combiné; (*Math*) *number* complexe; *interest* composé; (*Med*) *fracture* compliqué; (*Tech*) *engine* compound *inv*; (*Gram*) *tense, word* composé; *sentence* complexe.
3 [kəm'paʊnd] *vt* **(a)** (*Chem, Pharm*) *mixture* composer (*of* de); *ingredients* combiner, mêler, mélanger; (*fig*) *problem, difficulties* aggraver.
(b) (*Jur etc*) *debt, quarrel* régler à l'amiable, arranger par des concessions mutuelles. **to ~ a felony** composer *or* pactiser (avec un criminel).
4 *vi* (*Jur etc*) composer, transiger (*with* avec, *for* au sujet de, pour), s'arranger à l'amiable (*with* avec, *for* au sujet de). **to ~ with one's creditors** s'arranger à l'amiable *or* composer avec ses créanciers.
comprehend [,kɒmprɪ'hend] *vt* **(a)** (*understand*) comprendre, saisir. **(b)** (*include*) comprendre, englober, embrasser.
comprehensible [,kɒmprɪ'hensəbl] *adj* compréhensible, intelligible.
comprehension [,kɒmprɪ'henʃən] *n* **(a)** (*understanding*) compréhension *f*, entendement *m*, intelligence *f*. **that is beyond my ~** cela dépasse ma compréhension *or* mon entendement.
(b) (*Scol*) exercice *m* de compréhension.
(c) (*inclusion*) inclusion *f*.
comprehensive [,kɒmprɪ'hensɪv] **1** *adj description, report, review, survey* détaillé, complet (*f* -ète); *knowledge* vaste, étendu; *label, rule* compréhensif. **~ measures** mesures *fpl* d'ensemble; (*Insurance*) **~ policy** assurance *f* tous-risques; (*Brit*) **~ school** ≈ collège *m* d'enseignement général, lycée polyvalent, école polyvalente (*Can*); **he is in favour of ~ schools** il est pour l'école unique. **2** *n* = **~ school**; *V* **1**.
compress [kəm'pres] **1** *vt substance* comprimer; *essay, facts* condenser, concentrer, réduire. **~ed air** air comprimé. **2** *vi* se comprimer; se condenser, se réduire. **3** ['kɒmpres] *n* compresse *f*.
compression [kəm'preʃən] *n* compression *f*; (*fig*) condensation *f*, concentration *f*, réduction *f*. (*Aut*) **~ ratio** taux *m* de compression.
compressor [kəm'presəʳ] *n* compresseur *m*. **~ unit** groupe *m* compresseur.
comprise [kəm'praɪz] *vt* comprendre, englober, embrasser.
compromise ['kɒmprəmaɪz] **1** *n* compromis *m*, transaction *f*. **to come to** *or* **reach a ~** aboutir à un compromis, transiger.
2 *vi* transiger (*over* sur), aboutir à *or* accepter un compromis.
3 *vt* **(a)** *reputation etc* compromettre. **to ~ o.s.** se compromettre.
(b) (*imperil*) mettre en péril, risquer.
4 *cpd*: **compromise decision** décision *f* de compromis; **compromise solution** solution *f* de compromis.
compromising ['kɒmprəmaɪzɪŋ] *adj* compromettant.
comptometer [kɒmp'tɒmɪtəʳ] *n* ® machine *f* comptable. **~ operator** (opérateur *m*, -trice *f*) mécanographe *mf*.
comptroller [kən'trəʊləʳ] *n* (*Admin*) économe *mf*, intendant(e) *m(f)*, administrateur *m*, -trice *f*; (*Fin*) contrôleur *m*, -euse *f*.
compulsion [kəm'pʌlʃən] *n* contrainte *f*, force *f*, coercition *f*. **under ~** de force, sous la contrainte; **you are under no ~** vous n'êtes nullement obligé, rien ne vous force.
compulsive [kəm'pʌlsɪv] *adj reason, demand* coercitif; (*Psych*) *desire, behaviour* compulsif. **he's a ~ smoker** c'est un fumeur invétéré, il ne peut pas s'empêcher de fumer; **she's a ~ talker** parler est un besoin chez elle.
compulsively [kəm'pʌlsɪvlɪ] *adv* (*Psych*) *drink, smoke, talk* d'une façon compulsive, sans pouvoir s'en empêcher. **she doodled ~** elle griffonnait machinalement *or* sans pouvoir s'en empêcher.
compulsorily [kəm'pʌlsərɪlɪ] *adv* obligatoirement, de force, par contrainte.
compulsory [kəm'pʌlsərɪ] *adj* **(a)** *action, education, military service* obligatoire; *loan* forcé. (*Brit*) **~ purchase (order)** (ordre *m* d')expropriation *f* pour cause d'utilité publique; (*Fin*) **~ liquidation** liquidation forcée; **~ retirement** mise *f* à la retraite d'office.
(b) (*compelling*) *powers* coercitif, contraignant; *regulations* obligatoire.
compunction [kəm'pʌŋkʃən] *n* remords *m*, scrupule *m*; (*Rel*) componction *f*. **without the slightest ~** sans le moindre scrupule *or* remords; **he had no ~ about doing it** il n'a eu aucun scrupule à le faire.
computation [,kɒmpjʊ'teɪʃən] *n* **(a)** calcul *m*. **(b)** (*U*) estimation *f*, évaluation *f*.
computational [,kɒmpjʊ'teɪʃənl] *adj*: **~ linguistics** application *f* des méthodes mathématiques de l'analyse à la linguistique.
compute [kəm'pjuːt] *vt* calculer, évaluer, estimer (*at* à).
computer [kəm'pjuːtəʳ] **1** *n* **(a)** (*electronic*) ordinateur *m*; (*mechanical*) calculatrice *f*. **he is in ~s** il est dans l'informatique; *V* **analog, digital**.
(b) (*person*) calculateur *m*, -trice *f*.
2 *cpd*: **the computer age** l'ère *f* de l'ordinateur *or* de l'informatique; **computer language** langage *m* de programmation, langage(-)machine *m*; **computer programmer** programmeur *m*, -euse *f*; **computer programming** programmation *f*; **computer science** informatique *f*; **computer scientist** informaticien(ne) *m(f)*; **the computer society** la société à l'heure de l'informatique.
computerization [kəm,pjuːtəraɪ'zeɪʃən] *n* **(a)** *[information etc]* traitement *m* (électronique). **(b)** *[system, process]* automatisation *f or* automation *f* électronique.
computerize [kəm'pjuːtəraɪz] *vt* traiter *or* gérer par ordinateur, informatiser.
comrade ['kɒmrɪd] *n* camarade *mf*. **~-in-arms** compagnon *m* d'armes.
comradeship ['kɒmrɪdʃɪp] *n* camaraderie *f*.
con¹ [kɒn] *vt* **(a)** (*study*) étudier soigneusement, apprendre par cœur. **(b)** (*Naut*) gouverner; (*US Naut*) piloter. **~ning tower** *[submarine]* kiosque *m*; *[warship]* centre opérationnel.
con² [kɒn] *prep, n* contre (*m*); *V* **pro**¹.
con³* [kɒn] **1** *adj*: **~ man** escroc *m*; **~ game** escroquerie *f*.
2 *vt* escroquer, duper. **to ~ sb into doing** amener qn à faire en l'abusant *or* en le dupant.
3 *n*: **it was all a big ~** (*empty boasting etc*) tout ça c'était de la frime*; (*swindle*) c'était une vaste escroquerie.
concatenation [kɒn,kætɪ'neɪʃən] *n [circumstances]* enchaînement *m*; (*series*) série *f*, chaîne *f*.
concave ['kɒn'keɪv] *adj* concave.
concavity [kɒn'kævɪtɪ] *n* concavité *f*.
conceal [kən'siːl] *vt* (*hide*) *object* cacher, dissimuler; (*keep secret*) *news, event* garder *or* tenir secret; *emotions, thoughts* dissimuler. **to ~ sth from sb** cacher qch à qn; **to ~ the fact that** dissimuler le fait que; **~ed lighting** éclairage indirect; (*Aut*) **~ed turning** *or* **road** intersection cachée.
concealment [kən'siːlmənt] *n* (*U*) dissimulation *f*; (*Jur*) *[criminal]* recel *m*; *[facts]* non-divulgation *f*; (*place of ~*) cachette *f*.
concede [kən'siːd] **1** *vt privilege* concéder, accorder; *point* concéder; (*Sport*) *match* concéder. **to ~ that** concéder *or* admettre *or* reconnaître que; **to ~ victory** s'avouer vaincu. **2** *vi* céder.
conceit [kən'siːt] *n* (*pride: U*) vanité *f*, suffisance *f*, prétention *f*; (*witty expression*) trait *m* d'esprit, expression brillante. (*liter*) **he is wise in his own ~** il se croit très sage; (*Literat*) **~s** concetti *mpl*.
conceited [kən'siːtɪd] *adj* vaniteux, suffisant, prétentieux.
conceitedly [kən'siːtɪdlɪ] *adv* avec vanité, avec suffisance, prétentieusement.
conceivable [kən'siːvəbl] *adj* concevable, imaginable. **it is hardly ~ that** il est à peine concevable que + *subj*.
conceivably [kən'siːvəblɪ] *adv* de façon concevable. **she may ~ be right** il est concevable *or* il se peut bien qu'elle ait raison.
conceive [kən'siːv] **1** *vt child, idea, plan* concevoir. **to ~ a hatred/love for sb/sth** concevoir de la haine/de l'amour pour qn/qch; **I cannot ~ why he wants to do it** je ne comprends vraiment pas pourquoi il veut le faire.
2 *vi*: **to ~ of** concevoir, avoir le concept de; **I cannot ~ of anything better** je ne conçois rien de mieux; **I cannot ~ of a better way to do it** je ne conçois pas de meilleur moyen de le faire.
concentrate ['kɒnsəntreɪt] **1** *vt attention* concentrer (*on* sur); *hopes* reporter (*on* sur); *supplies* concentrer, rassembler; (*Chem, Mil*) concentrer.
2 *vi* **(a)** (*converge*) *[troops, people]* se concentrer, converger. **the crowds began to ~ round the palace** la foule a commencé à se concentrer *or* à se rassembler autour du palais; **they ~d in the square** ils ont convergé vers la place.
(b) (*direct thoughts, efforts etc*) se concentrer, concentrer *or* fixer son attention (*on* sur). **to ~ on doing** s'appliquer à faire; **I just can't ~!** je n'arrive pas à me concentrer!; **try to ~ a little more** essaie de te concentrer un peu plus *or* de faire un peu plus attention; **~ on getting yourself a job** essaie avant tout de *or* occupe-toi d'abord de te trouver du travail; **the terrorists ~d on the outlying farms** les terroristes ont concentré leurs attaques sur les fermes isolées; **~ on getting well** occupe-toi d'abord de ta santé; *[speaker]* **today I shall ~ on the 16th century** aujourd'hui je traiterai en particulier le 16e siècle *or* m'occuperai en particulier du 16e siècle.
3 *adj, n* (*Chem*) concentré (*m*).
concentration [,kɒnsən'treɪʃən] *n* concentration *f*. **~ camp** camp *m* de concentration.
concentric [kən'sentrɪk] *adj* concentrique.
concept ['kɒnsept] *n* concept *m*.
conception [kən'sepʃən] *n* (*gen, Med*) conception *f*; *V* **immaculate**.
conceptual [kən'septjʊəl] *adj* conceptuel.
concern [kən'sɜːn] **1** *vt* **(a)** (*affect*) concerner, toucher, affecter; (*be of importance to*) concerner, intéresser, importer à; (*be the business of*) regarder, être l'affaire de. **as ~s** en ce qui concerne, à propos de; **that doesn't ~ you** cela ne vous regarde pas, ce n'est pas votre affaire; (*frm*) **to whom it may ~** à qui de droit; **as far as** *or* **so far as he is ~ed** en ce qui le concerne, quant à lui; **where we are ~ed** en ce qui nous concerne; **the persons ~ed** les intéressés; **the department ~ed** (*under discussion*) le service en question *or* dont il s'agit; (*relevant*) le service compétent; **my brother is the most closely ~ed** le premier intéressé c'est mon frère; **to be ~ed in** avoir un intérêt dans; **to ~ o.s. in** *or* **with** se mêler de, s'occuper de, s'intéresser à; **we are ~ed only with facts** nous ne nous occupons que des faits.
(b) (*trouble: gen pass*) inquiéter. **to be ~ed by** *or* **for** *or* **about** *or* **at** s'inquiéter de, être inquiet (*f* -ète) de; **I am ~ed about him** je m'inquiète à son sujet, je me fais du souci à son sujet; **I am ~ed to hear that ...** j'apprends avec peine *or* inquiétude que ... .
2 *n* **(a)** (*relation, connexion*) rapport *m* (*with* avec), relation *f* (*with* avec). **to have no ~ with** n'avoir rien à voir avec, être sans rapport avec.

(b) (*interest, business*) affaire *f*; (*responsibility*) responsabilité *f*. **it's no ~ of his, it's none of his ~** ce n'est pas son affaire, cela ne le regarde pas; **what ~ is it of yours?** en quoi est-ce que cela vous regarde?

(c) (*Comm: also* **business ~**) entreprise *f*, affaire *f*, firme *f*, maison *f* (de commerce); *V* **going.**

(d) (*interest, share*) intérêt(s) *m(pl)* (*in* dans). **he has a ~ in the business** il a des intérêts dans l'affaire.

(e) (*anxiety*) inquiétude *f*, souci *m*; (*stronger*) anxiété *f*. **he was filled with ~** il était très soucieux *or* inquiet; **a look of ~** un regard inquiet.

(f) (*: *object, contrivance*) truc* *m*, bidule: *m*.

concerned [kən'sɜːnd] *adj* (*worried*) inquiet (*f* -ète), soucieux; (*affected*) affecté (*about, at, for* de, par).

concerning [kən'sɜːnɪŋ] *prep* en ce qui concerne, au sujet de, à propos de, concernant.

concert ['kɒnsət] **1** *n* **(a)** (*Mus*) concert *m*.

(b) *[voices etc]* unisson *m*, chœur *m*. **in ~** à l'unisson, en chœur.

(c) (*fig*) accord *m*, harmonie *f*, entente *f*. **in ~ with** de concert avec.

2 *cpd ticket, hall* de concert. **concertgoer** habitué(e) *m(f)* des concerts, amateur *m* de concerts; **concert grand** piano *m* de concert; (*US*) **concertmaster** premier violon (soliste); **concert performer** concertiste *mf*; **concert pianist** pianiste *mf* de concert; (*Mus*) **concert pitch** diapason *m* (de concert); (*fig: on top form*) **at concert pitch** au maximum *or* à l'apogée de la forme; **when the enthusiasm reached concert pitch** quand l'enthousiasme a atteint son maximum *or* son point culminant; **concert tour** tournée *f* de concerts.

3 [kən'sɜːt] *vt* concerter, arranger (ensemble). **a ~ed effort** un effort concerté.

concertina [ˌkɒnsə'tiːnə] **1** *n* concertina *m*. (*Aut*) **~ crash** carambolage *m*. **2** *vi*: **the vehicles ~ed into each other** les véhicules se sont emboutis *or* télescopés (les uns les autres).

concerto [kən'tʃɛətəʊ] *n, pl* **~s** *or* **concerti** [kən'tʃɛətiː] concerto *m*.

concession [kən'seʃən] *n* (*gen, Jur*) concession *f*; (*Comm*) réduction *f*.

concessionaire [kənˌseʃə'nɛəʳ] *n* concessionnaire *mf*.

concessionary [kən'seʃənərɪ] **1** *adj* (*Fin, Jur etc*) concessionnaire; (*Comm*) *ticket, fare* à prix réduit. **2** *n* concessionnaire *mf*.

conch [kɒntʃ] *n* (*shell, Anat*) conque *f*; (*Archit*) voûte *f* semi-circulaire, (voûte d')abside *f*.

conciliate [kən'sɪlɪeɪt] *vt* **(a)** (*placate*) apaiser; (*win over*) se concilier, gagner. **(b)** (*reconcile*) *opposing views, extremes* concilier.

conciliation [kənˌsɪlɪ'eɪʃən] *n* (*V* **conciliate**) apaisement *m*; conciliation *f*. (*Ind*) **~ board** conseil *m* d'arbitrage.

conciliatory [kən'sɪlɪətərɪ] *adj person* conciliateur (*f* -trice), conciliant; *speech, words, manner* conciliant; *spirit* de conciliation; (*Jur, Pol*) *procedure* conciliatoire.

concise [kən'saɪs] *adj* concis.

concisely [kən'saɪslɪ] *adv* avec concision.

conciseness [kən'saɪsnɪs] *n*, **concision** [kən'sɪʒən] *n* concision *f*.

conclave ['kɒnkleɪv] *n* (*Rel*) conclave *m*; (*fig*) assemblée *f* (secrète), réunion *f* (privée). (*fig*) **in ~** en réunion privée.

conclude [kən'kluːd] **1** *vt* **(a)** (*end*) *business, agenda* conclure, achever, finir, terminer. **'to be ~d'** 'suite et fin au prochain numéro'.

(b) (*arrange*) *treaty* conclure, aboutir à.

(c) (*infer*) conclure, déduire, inférer (*from* de, *that* que).

(d) (*US: decide*) décider (*to do* de faire).

2 *vi* (*end*) *[things, events]* se terminer, s'achever (*with* par, sur); *[persons]* conclure. **to ~ I must say ...** pour conclure *or* en conclusion je dois dire ... .

concluding [kən'kluːdɪŋ] *adj* final.

conclusion [kən'kluːʒən] *n* **(a)** (*end*) conclusion *f*, fin *f*, terme *m*. **in ~** pour conclure, finalement, en conclusion; **to bring to a ~** mener à sa conclusion *or* à terme.

(b) (*settling*) *[treaty etc]* conclusion *f*.

(c) (*opinion, decision*) conclusion *f*, déduction *f*. **to come to the ~ that** conclure que; **to draw a ~ from** tirer une conclusion de; **this leads (one) to the ~ that ...** ceci amène à conclure que ...; *V* **foregone, jump.**

(d) (*Philos*) conclusion *f*.

(e) to try ~s with sb se mesurer avec *or* contre qn.

conclusive [kən'kluːsɪv] *adj* concluant, définitif.

conclusively [kən'kluːsɪvlɪ] *adv* de façon concluante, définitivement.

concoct [kən'kɒkt] *vt* (*Culin etc*) confectionner, composer; (*fig*) *scheme, excuse* fabriquer, inventer, combiner.

concoction [kən'kɒkʃən] *n* **(a)** (*Culin etc*) (*action*) confection *f*, préparation *f*; (*product*) mélange *m*, mixture *f* (*pej*). **(b)** (*U: fig*) *[scheme, excuse]* combinaison *f*, élaboration *f*.

concomitant [kən'kɒmɪtənt] **1** *adj* concomitant. **2** *n* événement concomitant.

concord ['kɒŋkɔːd] *n* **(a)** concorde *f*, harmonie *f*, entente *f*. **in complete ~** en parfaite harmonie. **(b)** (*Gram*) accord *m*. **to be in ~ with** s'accorder avec. **(c)** (*Mus*) accord *m*.

concordance [kən'kɔːdəns] *n* **(a)** (*agreement*) accord *m*. **(b)** (*index*) index *m*; *[Bible etc]* concordance *f*.

concordant [kən'kɔːdənt] *adj* concordant, s'accordant (*with* avec).

concordat [kɒn'kɔːdæt] *n* concordat *m*.

concourse ['kɒŋkɔːs] *n [circumstances]* concours *m*; *[people, vehicles]* multitude *f*, affluence *f*, concours; (*crowd*) foule *f*; (*place*) lieu *m* de rassemblement; (*US: in a park*) carrefour *m*; (*US: hall*) hall *m*; (*Rail*) hall; (*US: street*) cours *m*, boulevard *m*.

concrete ['kɒnkriːt] **1** *adj* **(a)** (*Philos*) concret (*f* -ète), réel, matériel; (*Gram, Math, Mus*) concret; *proof, advantage* concret, matériel.

(b) (*Constr*) en béton. **~ mixer** bétonnière *f*.

2 *n* **(a)** (*U: Constr*) béton *m*; *V* **prestressed, reinforce.**

(b) (*Philos*) **the ~** le concret.

3 *vt* (*Constr*) bétonner.

concretion [kən'kriːʃən] *n* concrétion *f*.

concubine ['kɒŋkjubaɪn] *n* concubine *f*; (*second wife*) seconde femme.

concupiscence [kən'kjuːpɪsəns] *n* concupiscence *f*.

concupiscent [kən'kjuːpɪsənt] *adj* concupiscent.

concur [kən'kɜːʳ] *vi* **(a)** (*agree*) être d'accord, s'entendre (*with sb* avec qn, *in sth* sur *or* au sujet de qch).

(b) (*happen together*) coïncider, arriver en même temps; (*contribute*) concourir (*to* à). **everything ~red to bring about this result** tout a concouru à produire ce résultat.

concurrent [kən'kʌrənt] *adj* **(a)** (*occurring at same time*) concomitant, coïncident, simultané. **(b)** (*acting together*) concerté. **(c)** (*in agreement*) concordant, d'accord. **(d)** (*Math, Tech*) concourant.

concurrently [kən'kʌrəntlɪ] *adv* simultanément.

concuss [kən'kʌs] *vt* **(a)** (*Med: gen pass*) commotionner. **to be ~ed** être commotionné, être sous l'effet d'un choc. **(b)** (*shake*) secouer violemment, ébranler.

concussion [kən'kʌʃən] *n* **(a)** (*Med*) commotion *f* (cérébrale). **(b)** (*shaking*) ébranlement *m*, secousse *f*.

condemn [kən'dem] *vt* **(a)** (*gen, Jur, Med, fig*) condamner (*to* à). (*Jur*) **to ~ to death** condamner à mort; **the ~ed man** le condamné; **the ~ed cell** la cellule des condamnés.

(b) (*Tech*) *building* déclarer inhabitable, condamner; (*Mil, Tech*) *materials* réformer, déclarer inutilisable.

condemnation [ˌkɒndem'neɪʃən] *n* (*gen, Jur, fig*) condamnation *f*; (*US Jur: of property*) expropriation *f* pour cause d'utilité publique.

condensation [ˌkɒnden'seɪʃən] *n* condensation *f*.

condense [kən'dens] **1** *vt* condenser, concentrer; (*Phys*) *gas* condenser; *rays* concentrer; (*fig*) condenser, résumer. **~d milk** lait condensé; **~d book** livre condensé. **2** *vi* se condenser, se concentrer.

condenser [kən'densəʳ] *n* (*Elec, Tech*) condensateur *m*; (*Phys*) *[gas]* condenseur *m*; *[light]* condensateur.

condescend [ˌkɒndɪ'send] *vi* **(a)** condescendre (*to do* à faire), daigner (*to do* faire). **to ~ to sb** se montrer condescendant envers *or* à l'égard de qn. **(b)** (†: *stoop to*) s'abaisser (*to* à), descendre (*to* à, jusqu'à).

condescending [ˌkɒndɪ'sendɪŋ] *adj* condescendant.

condescendingly [ˌkɒndɪ'sendɪŋlɪ] *adv* avec condescendance.

condescension [ˌkɒndɪ'senʃən] *n* condescendance *f*.

condign [kən'daɪn] *adj* (*fitting*) adéquat, proportionné; (*deserved*) mérité.

condiment ['kɒndɪmənt] *n* condiment *m*.

condition [kən'dɪʃən] **1** *n* **(a)** (*determining factor*) condition *f*. **on ~ that** à condition que + *fut indic or subj*, à condition de + *infin*; **on this ~** à cette condition; (*Comm*) **~ of sale** condition de vente; (*Jur*) **~ of a contract** condition d'un contrat; **he made the ~ that no one should accompany him** il a stipulé que personne ne devait l'accompagner; *V* **term.**

(b) (*circumstances*) **~s** conditions *fpl*, circonstances *fpl*; **under** *or* **in the present ~s** dans les conditions actuelles; **working/living ~s** conditions de travail/de vie; **weather ~s** conditions météorologiques.

(c) (*U: state, nature*) état *m*, condition *f*. **physical/mental ~** état physique/mental; **in ~** *thing* en bon état; *person* en forme, en bonne condition physique; **it's out of ~** c'est en mauvais état; **he's out of ~** il n'est pas en forme; **she was not in a ~** *or* **in any ~ to go out** elle n'était pas en état de sortir; (*euph*) **she is in an interesting ~*** elle est dans un état *or* une position intéressant(e) (*euph hum*).

(d) (*U: social position*) condition *f*, position *f*, situation *f*.

2 *vt* **(a)** (*determine*) déterminer, conditionner, être la condition de. **his standard of living is ~ed by his income** son niveau de vie dépend de ses revenus.

(b) (*bring into good ~*) *animals* mettre en forme; *things* remettre en bon état; *V* **air.**

(c) (*Psych, fig*) *person, animal* provoquer un réflexe conditionné chez, conditionner; (*by propaganda*) *person* conditionner (*into believing* à croire), mettre en condition. **~ed reflex** réflexe conditionné; **~ed response** réaction conditionnée; **the nation has been ~ed into believing that the government is right** on a conditionné la nation à croire que le gouvernement a raison.

conditional [kən'dɪʃənl] **1** *adj* **(a)** *promise, agreement* conditionnel. (*Jur*) **~ clause** clause conditionnelle.

(b) to be ~ (up)on dépendre de; **his appointment is ~ (up)on his passing his exams** sa nomination dépend de son succès aux examens, pour être nommé il faut qu'il soit reçu à ses examens.

(c) (*Gram*) *mood, clause* conditionnel.

2 *n* (*Gram*) conditionnel *m*. **in the ~** au conditionnel.

conditionally [kən'dɪʃnəlɪ] *adv* conditionnellement.

condole [kən'dəʊl] *vi* exprimer *or* offrir ses condoléances, exprimer sa sympathie (*with sb* à qn).

condolences [kən'dəʊlənsɪz] *npl* condoléances *fpl*.

condom ['kɒndəm] *n* préservatif *m*.

condominium [ˌkɒndə'mɪnɪəm] *n* **(a)** condominium *m*. **(b)** (*US*) (*ownership*) copropriété *f*; (*building*) immeuble *m* (en copropriété).

condone [kən'dəʊn] *vt* (*overlook*) fermer les yeux sur; (*forgive*) pardonner. (*Jur*) **to ~ adultery** ≃ pardonner un adultère.

condor [ˈkɒndɔːʳ] *n* condor *m*.
conduce [kənˈdjuːs] *vi*: to ~ to conduire à, provoquer.
conducive [kənˈdjuːsɪv] *adj* contribuant (*to* à). **to be ~ to** conduire à, provoquer, mener à.
conduct [ˈkɒndʌkt] **1** *n* **(a)** (*behaviour*) conduite *f*, tenue *f*, comportement *m*. **good/bad ~** bonne/mauvaise conduite *or* tenue; **his ~ towards me** sa conduite *or* son comportement à mon égard *or* envers moi; *V* **disorderly.**
(b) (*leading*) conduite *f*; *V* **safe.**
2 *cpd*: (*Scol*) **conduct report** rapport *m* (*sur la conduite d'un élève*); (*Mil*) **conduct sheet** feuille *f or* certificat *m* de conduite; (*Naut*) cahier *m* des punis.
3 [kənˈdʌkt] *vt* **(a)** (*lead*) conduire, mener. **he ~ed me round the gardens** il m'a fait faire le tour des jardins; **~ed visit** visite guidée; **~ed tour** excursion accompagnée, voyage organisé; *[building]* visite guidée.
(b) (*direct, manage*) diriger. **to ~ one's business** diriger ses affaires; **to ~ an orchestra** diriger un orchestre; (*Jur*) **to ~ an inquiry** conduire *or* mener une enquête; (*Jur*) **to ~ sb's case** assurer la défense de qn.
(c) to ~ o.s. se conduire, se comporter.
(d) (*Elec, Phys*) *heat etc* conduire, être conducteur *m*, -trice *f* de.
conduction [kənˈdʌkʃən] *n* (*Elec, Phys*) conduction *f*.
conductivity [ˌkɒndʌkˈtɪvɪtɪ] *n* (*Elec, Phys*) conductivité *f*.
conductor [kənˈdʌktəʳ] *n* **(a)** (*leader*) conducteur *m*, chef *m*; (*Mus*) chef d'orchestre. **(b)** *[bus]* receveur *m*; (*US Rail*) chef *m* de train. **(c)** (*Phys*) (corps *m*) conducteur *m*; *V* **lightning.**
conductress [kənˈdʌktrɪs] *n* receveuse *f*.
conduit [ˈkɒndɪt] *n* conduit *m*, tuyau *m*, canalisation *f*; (*Elec*) tube *m*.
cone [kəʊn] *n* (*Astron, Geol, Math, Mil, Naut, Opt, Rad, Tech*) cône *m*; (*Bot*) *[pine etc]* cône, pomme *f*; (*Culin*) *[ice cream]* cornet *m*.
coney [ˈkəʊnɪ] *n* = **cony.**
confab* [ˈkɒnfæb] *n* (brin *m* de) causette* *f*.
confabulate [kənˈfæbjʊleɪt] *vi* converser, bavarder, causer (*with* avec).
confabulation [kənˌfæbjʊˈleɪʃən] *n* conciliabule *m*, conversation *f*.
confection [kənˈfekʃən] *n* **(a)** (*Culin*) (*sweet*) sucrerie *f*, friandise *f*; (*cake*) gâteau *m*, pâtisserie *f*; (*dessert*) dessert *m* (sucré); (*Dress*) vêtement *m* de confection. **(b)** (*U*) confection *f*.
confectioner [kənˈfekʃənəʳ] *n* (*sweet maker*) confiseur *m*, -euse *f*; (*cakemaker*) pâtissier *m*, -ière *f*. **~'s (shop)** confiserie *f* (-pâtisserie *f*); (*US*) **~'s sugar** sucre *m* glace.
confectionery [kənˈfekʃənərɪ] *n* confiserie *f*; (*Brit: cakes etc*) pâtisserie *f*.
confederacy [kənˈfedərəsɪ] *n* **(a)** (*Pol: group of states*) confédération *f*. (*US Hist*) **the C~** les États Confédérés. **(b)** (*conspiracy*) conspiration *f*.
confederate [kənˈfedərɪt] **1** *adj* confédéré. **2** *n* confédéré(e) *m(f)*; (*in criminal act*) complice *mf*. **3** [kənˈfedəreɪt] *vt* confédérer. **4** *vi* se confédérer.
confederation [kənˌfedəˈreɪʃən] *n* confédération *f*.
confer [kənˈfɜːʳ] **1** *vt* conférer, accorder (*on* à). **to ~ a title** conférer un titre; (*at ceremony*) **to ~ a degree** remettre un diplôme. **2** *vi* conférer, s'entretenir (*with sb* avec qn, *on, about sth* de qch).
conference [ˈkɒnfərəns] **1** *n* (*meeting*) conférence *f*, réunion *f*, assemblée *f*, (*especially academic*) congrès *m*; (*discussion*) conférence, consultation *f*. **to be in ~** être en conférence; **the ~ decided ...** les participants à la conférence ont décidé ...; (*lit, fig*) **~ table** table *f* de conférence; *V* **press.**
2 *cpd*: **conference member** congressiste *mf*.
conferment [kənˈfɜːmənt] *n* action *f* de conférer; (*Univ*) *[degree]* remise *f* (de diplômes); *[title, favour]* octroi *m*.
confess [kənˈfes] **1** *vt* **(a)** (*also ~ to*) *crime* avouer, confesser; *mistake* reconnaître, avouer. **he ~ed that he had stolen the money/to having stolen the money** il a avoué *or* reconnu *or* confessé qu'il avait volé l'argent/avoir volé l'argent; **to ~ (to) a liking for sth** reconnaître qu'on aime qch.
(b) (*Rel*) *faith* confesser, proclamer; *sins* confesser, se confesser de; *penitent* confesser.
2 *vi* **(a)** avouer, passer aux aveux. **to ~ to having done** avouer *or* reconnaître *or* confesser avoir fait.
(b) (*Rel*) se confesser.
confessedly [kənˈfesɪdlɪ] *adv* (*generally admitted*) de l'aveu de tous; (*on one's own admission*) de son propre aveu.
confession [kənˈfeʃən] *n* (*V* **confess**) **(a)** aveu *m*, confession *f* (*of* de). (*Jur*) **to make a full ~** faire des aveux complets.
(b) (*Rel*) confession *f*. **to hear sb's ~** confesser qn; **to go to ~** aller se confesser; **to make one's ~** se confesser; **~ of faith** confession de foi; **general ~** confession générale; (*sects*) **~s** confessions.
confessional [kənˈfeʃənl] (*Rel*) **1** *n* confessionnal *m*. **under the seal of the ~** sous le secret de la confession. **2** *adj* confessionnel.
confessor [kənˈfesəʳ] *n* confesseur *m*.
confetti [kənˈfetiː] *n* confettis *mpl*.
confidant [ˌkɒnfɪˈdænt] *n* confident *m*.
confidante [ˌkɒnfɪˈdænt] *n* confidente *f*.
confide [kənˈfaɪd] *vt* **(a)** *object, person, job, secret* confier (*to sb* à qn). **to ~ sth to sb's care** confier qch à la garde *or* aux soins de qn; **to ~ secrets to sb** confier des secrets à qn.
(b) avouer en confidence. **she ~d to me that ...** elle m'a avoué en confidence que ..., elle m'a confié que ... .
confide in *vt fus* **(a)** (*have confidence in*) *sb's ability* se fier à, avoir confiance en. **you can confide in me** vous pouvez me faire confiance.
(b) (*tell secrets to*) s'ouvrir à, se confier à. **to confide in sb about sth** confier qch à qn; **to confide in sb about what one is going to do** révéler à qn ce qu'on va faire.
confidence [ˈkɒnfɪdəns] **1** *n* **(a)** (*trust, hope*) confiance *f*. **to have ~ in sb/sth** avoir confiance en qn/qch; **to put one's ~ in sb/sth** mettre sa confiance en qn/qch; **to have every ~ in sb** faire totalement confiance à qn, avoir pleine confiance en qn; **to have ~ in the future** faire confiance à l'avenir; **I have every ~ that he will come back** je suis sûr *or* certain qu'il reviendra; (*Pol etc*) **motion of no ~** motion *f* de censure; *V* **vote.**
(b) (*self-~*) confiance *f* en soi, assurance *f*. **he lacks ~** il manque d'assurance.
(c) (*U*) confidence *f*. **to take sb into one's ~** faire des confidences à qn, se confier à qn; **he told me that in ~** il me l'a dit en confidence *or* confidentiellement; **this is in strict ~** c'est strictement confidentiel; **'write in strict ~ to X'** 'écrire à X: discrétion garantie'.
(d) (*private communication*) confidence *f*. **they exchanged ~s** ils ont échangé des confidences.
2 *cpd*: **confidence game** abus *m* de confiance, escroquerie *f*; **confidence man** escroc *m*; **confidence trick** = **confidence game; confidence trickster** = **confidence man.**
confident [ˈkɒnfɪdənt] *adj* **(a)** (*sure*) assuré, sûr, persuadé (*of* de). **to be ~ of success** *or* **of succeeding** être sûr de réussir; **I am ~ that he will succeed** je suis sûr *or* persuadé qu'il réussira.
(b) (*assured*) sûr de soi, assuré.
confidential [ˌkɒnfɪˈdenʃəl] *adj letter, remark, information* confidentiel; *servant* de confiance. **~ clerk** homme *m* de confiance; **~ secretary** secrétaire *mf* particulier (-ière); **in a ~ tone of voice** sur le ton de la confidence.
confidentially [ˌkɒnfɪˈdənʃəlɪ] *adv* confidentiellement, en confidence.
confidently [ˈkɒnfɪdəntlɪ] *adv* avec confiance.
confiding [kənˈfaɪdɪŋ] *adj* confiant, sans méfiance.
configuration [kənˌfɪgjʊˈreɪʃən] *n* configuration *f*.
confine [kənˈfaɪn] **1** *vt* **(a)** (*imprison*) emprisonner, enfermer; (*shut up*) confiner, enfermer (*in* dans). **to ~ a bird in a cage** enfermer un oiseau dans une cage; **to be ~d to the house/to one's room/to bed** être obligé de rester chez soi/de garder la chambre/de garder le lit; (*Mil*) **to ~ sb to barracks** consigner qn.
(b) (*limit*) *remarks, opinions* limiter, borner, restreindre. **to ~ o.s. to doing** se borner à faire; **to ~ o.s. to generalities** s'en tenir à des généralités; **the damage is ~d to the back of the car** seul l'arrière de la voiture est endommagé.
(c) (*in childbirth*) **to be ~d** accoucher, être en couches.
2 ~s [ˈkɒnfaɪnz] *npl* (*lit, fig*) confins *mpl*, bornes *fpl*, limites *fpl*; **within the ~s of** dans les limites de.
confined [kənˈfaɪnd] *adj atmosphere, air* confiné. **in a ~ space** dans un espace restreint *or* réduit.
confinement [kənˈfaɪnmənt] *n* (*Med*) couches *fpl*; (*imprisonment*) emprisonnement *m*, détention *f*, réclusion *f* (*Jur, liter*); (*Mil: also* **~ to barracks**) consigne *f* (au quartier). (*Mil*) **to get 10 days' ~ to barracks** attraper 10 jours de consigne; **~ to bed** alitement *m*; **~ to one's room/the house** obligation *f* de garder la chambre/de rester chez soi; *V* **close**[1].
confirm [kənˈfɜːm] *vt statement, report, news, suspicions* confirmer, corroborer; *authority* (r)affermir, consolider; *one's resolve* fortifier, raffermir; *treaty, appointment* ratifier; (*Rel*) confirmer; (*Jur*) *decision* entériner, homologuer; *election* valider. **to ~ sb in an opinion** confirmer *or* fortifier qn dans une opinion; **to be ~ed in one's opinion** voir son opinion confirmée.
confirmation [ˌkɒnfəˈmeɪʃən] *n* (*V* **confirm**) confirmation *f*; corroboration *f*; raffermissement *m*, consolidation *f*; ratification *f*; (*Rel*) confirmation; (*Jur*) entérinement *m*.
confirmed [kənˈfɜːmd] *adj smoker, drunkard, liar* invétéré; *bachelor, sinner* endurci; *habit* incorrigible, invétéré. **I am a ~ admirer of ...** je suis un fervent admirateur de ... .
confiscate [ˈkɒnfɪskeɪt] *vt* confisquer (*sth from sb* qch à qn).
confiscation [ˌkɒnfɪsˈkeɪʃən] *n* confiscation *f*.
conflagration [ˌkɒnfləˈgreɪʃən] *n* incendie *m*, sinistre *m*; (*fig*) conflagration *f*.
conflict [ˈkɒnflɪkt] **1** *n* conflit *m*, lutte *f*; (*quarrel*) dispute *f*; (*Mil*) conflit, combat *m*; (*Jur*) conflit; (*fig*) *[interests, ideas, opinions]* conflit. (*Mil*) **armed ~** conflit armé; **to come into ~ with** entrer en conflit *or* en lutte avec.
2 [kənˈflɪkt] *vi* **(a)** être *or* entrer en conflit *or* en lutte (*with* avec).
(b) *[opinions, ideas]* s'opposer, se heurter. **~ing views** des opinions incompatibles *or* discordantes; **~ing evidence** des témoignages *mpl or* des preuves *fpl* contradictoires; **there have been ~ing reports** on a reçu des rapports contradictoires; **that ~s with what he told me** ceci est en contradiction avec *or* contredit ce qu'il m'a raconté.
confluence [ˈkɒnflʊəns] *n* *[rivers]* (*place*) confluent *m*; (*act*) confluence *f*; (*fig: crowd*) foule *f*, assemblée *f*.
conform [kənˈfɔːm] **1** *vt one's life, actions, methods* conformer, adapter, rendre conforme (*to* à). **2** *vi* **(a)** se conformer, s'adapter (*to, with* à); *[actions, sayings]* être en conformité (*to* avec). **(b)** (*gen, Rel*) être conformiste *mf*.
conformable [kənˈfɔːməbl] *adj* **(a)** conforme (*to* à). **(b)** (*in agreement with*) adapté (*to* à), compatible, en accord (*to* avec). **(c)** (*submissive*) docile, accommodant.
conformation [ˌkɒnfəˈmeɪʃən] *n* conformation *f*, structure *f*.
conformist [kənˈfɔːmɪst] *adj, n* (*gen, Rel*) conformiste (*mf*).
conformity [kənˈfɔːmɪtɪ] *n* (*likeness*) conformité *f*, ressemblance *f*; (*agreement*) conformité, accord *m*; (*submission*)

conformité, soumission *f*; (*Rel*) *adhésion f à la religion conformiste*. **in ~ with your wishes** en accord avec vos désirs, conformément à vos désirs.

confound [kən'faʊnd] *vt* (*perplex*) confondre, remplir de confusion; (*frm: defeat*) *enemy, plans* confondre (*frm*); (*mix up*) confondre (*sth with sth* qch avec qch), prendre (*sth with sth* qch pour qch). **~ it!*** diantre!*†; **~ him!*** qu'il aille au diable!, (que) le diable l'emporte!†; **it's a ~ed nuisance!*** c'est la barbe!*, quelle barbe!*

confront [kən'frʌnt] *vt* **(a)** (*bring face to face*) confronter (*with* avec), mettre en présence (*with* de). **the police ~ed the accused with the witnesses** la police a confronté l'accusé avec les témoins; **the police ~ed the accused with the evidence** la police a mis l'accusé en présence des témoignages; **to ~ two witnesses** confronter deux témoins (entre eux).

(b) *enemy, danger* affronter, faire face à; (*defy*) affronter, défier. **the problems which ~ us** les problèmes auxquels nous devons faire face.

confrontation [ˌkɒnfrən'teɪʃən] *n* confrontation *f*.

Confucius [kən'fju:ʃəs] *n* Confucius *m*.

confuse [kən'fju:z] *vt* **(a)** (*throw into disorder*) *opponents* confondre; *plans* semer le désordre dans, bouleverser; (*perplex*) jeter dans la perplexité; (*embarrass*) confondre, embarrasser; (*disconcert*) troubler, confondre; (*mix up*) *persons* embrouiller; *ideas* embrouiller, brouiller; *memory* brouiller. **you are just confusing me** tu ne fais que m'embrouiller (les idées).

(b) to ~ sth with sth confondre qch avec qch, prendre qch pour qch; **to ~ two problems** confondre deux problèmes.

confused [kən'fju:zd] *adj person* (*muddled*) confus; (*perplexed*) déconcerté; (*embarrassed*) embarrassé; *opponent* confondu; *mind* embrouillé, confus; *sounds, voices* confus, indistinct; *memories* confus, brouillé, vague; *ideas, situation* confus, embrouillé. **to have a ~ idea** avoir une vague idée; **to get ~** (*muddled up*) ne plus savoir où on en est, s'y perdre; (*embarrassed*) se troubler.

confusedly [kən'fju:zɪdlɪ] *adv* confusément.

confusing [kən'fju:zɪŋ] *adj* déroutant. **it's all very ~** on ne s'y retrouve plus, on s'y perd.

confusion [kən'fju:ʒən] *n* (*disorder, muddle*) confusion *f*, désordre *m*; (*embarrassment*) confusion, trouble *m*; (*mixing up*) confusion (*of sth with sth else* de qch avec qch d'autre). **he was in a state of ~** la confusion régnait dans son esprit, il avait l'esprit troublé; **the books lay about in ~** les livres étaient en désordre *or* pêle-mêle; *V* **throw**.

confute [kən'fju:t] *vt person* prouver *or* démontrer l'erreur de, réfuter les arguments de; *argument* réfuter.

congeal [kən'dʒi:l] **1** *vi* (*clot*) *[oil]* (se) figer; *[milk]* (se) cailler; *[blood]* se coaguler; (*freeze*) se congeler, geler. **2** *vt* (*clot*) *oil* faire figer; *milk* faire cailler; *blood* coaguler; (*freeze*) congeler, geler.

congenial [kən'dʒi:nɪəl] *adj person, atmosphere, surroundings* sympathique, agréable. **he found few people ~ to him** il y avait peu de gens qu'il trouvait sympathiques *or* avec lesquels il se trouvait en sympathie.

congenital [kən'dʒenɪtl] *adj* congénital.

conger ['kɒŋgəʳ] *n*: **~ eel** congre *m*.

congested [kən'dʒestɪd] *adj town, countryside* surpeuplé; *street* encombré, embouteillé; *corridors, pavement* encombré; *telephone lines* embouteillé; (*Med*) congestionné. **~ traffic** embouteillage(s) *m(pl)*, encombrement(s) *m(pl)*.

congestion [kən'dʒestʃən] *n [town, countryside]* surpeuplement *m*; *[street, traffic]* encombrement *m*, embouteillage *m*; (*Med*) congestion *f*.

conglomerate [kən'glɒmərеɪt] **1** *vt* conglomérer (*frm*), agglomérer. **2** *vi* s'agglomérer. **3** [kən'glɒmərɪt] *adj* congloméré (*also Geol*), aggloméré. **4** *n* conglomérat *m* (*also Geol*).

conglomeration [kənˌglɒmə'reɪʃən] *n* **(a)** (*U: act, state*) conglomération *f* (*frm*), agglomération *f*. **(b)** (*group*) *[objects]* groupement *m*, rassemblement *m*; *[houses]* agglomération *f*.

Congo ['kɒŋgəʊ] *n* (*river, state*) Congo *m*.

Congolese [ˌkɒŋgəʊ'li:z] **1** *adj* congolais. **2** *n, pl inv* Congolais(e) *m(f)*.

congratulate [kən'grætjʊleɪt] *vt* féliciter, complimenter (*sb on sth* qn de qch, *sb on doing* qn d'avoir fait). **to ~ o.s. on sth/on doing sth** se féliciter de qch/d'avoir fait qch.

congratulations [kənˌgrætjʊ'leɪʃənz] *npl* félicitations *fpl*, compliments *mpl*. **~!** toutes mes félicitations!; **~ on your success** je vous félicite de votre succès, (toutes mes) félicitations pour votre succès.

congratulatory [kən'grætjʊlətərɪ] *adj* de félicitations.

congregate ['kɒŋgrɪgeɪt] **1** *vi* se rassembler, s'assembler, se réunir (*round* autour de, *at* à). **2** *vt* rassembler, réunir, assembler.

congregation [ˌkɒŋgrɪ'geɪʃən] *n* rassemblement *m*, assemblée *f*; (*Rel*) *[worshippers]* assemblée (des fidèles), assistance *f*; *[cardinals, monks etc]* congrégation *f*; (*Univ*) *[professors]* assemblée générale.

congregational [ˌkɒŋgrɪ'geɪʃnl] *adj* (*V* **congregation**) de l'assemblée des fidèles, en assemblée; de congrégation, d'une congrégation. **the C~ Church** l'Église *f* congrégationaliste.

congress ['kɒŋgres] **1** *n* **(a)** congrès *m*. **education ~** congrès de l'enseignement; *V* **trade**.

(b) (*US Pol*) **C~** Congrès *m*; (*session*) session *f* du Congrès.

2 *cpd*: (*US Pol*) **congressman** membre *m* du Congrès, ≃ député *m*; **Congressman J. Smith said that ...** monsieur le Député J. Smith a dit que ...; **congress member** congressiste *mf*; **congresswoman** membre *m* du Congrès, ≃ député *m*.

congressional [kɒŋ'greʃənl] *adj* **(a)** d'un congrès. **(b)** (*US Pol*) **C~** du Congrès; **C~ Record** Journal Officiel du Congrès.

congruent ['kɒŋgrʊənt] *adj* d'accord, en harmonie (*with* avec), conforme (*with* à); (*suitable*) convenable (*with* à); (*Math*) *number* congru (*with* à); *triangle* congruent.

congruity [kɒŋ'gru:ɪtɪ] *n* convenance *f*, congruité *f*.

congruous ['kɒŋgrʊəs] *adj* qui convient, convenable (*to, with* à); approprié (*to, with* à), qui s'accorde (*to, with* avec); (*Rel*) congru.

conic(al) ['kɒnɪk(əl)] *adj* (de forme) conique.

conifer ['kɒnɪfəʳ] *n* conifère *m*.

coniferous [kə'nɪfərəs] *adj tree* conifère; *forest* de conifères.

conjectural [kən'dʒektʃərəl] *adj* conjectural.

conjecture [kən'dʒektʃəʳ] **1** *vt* conjecturer, supposer. **2** *vi* conjecturer, faire des conjectures. **3** *n* conjecture *f*.

conjoin [kən'dʒɔɪn] **1** *vt* adjoindre, unir. **2** *vi* s'unir.

conjoint ['kɒn'dʒɔɪnt] *adj* joint, uni, associé.

conjointly ['kɒn'dʒɔɪntlɪ] *adv* conjointement.

conjugal ['kɒndʒʊgəl] *adj state, rights, happiness* conjugal.

conjugate ['kɒndʒʊgeɪt] (*Bio, Gram*) **1** *vt* conjuguer. **2** *vi* se conjuguer.

conjugation [ˌkɒndʒʊ'geɪʃən] *n* conjugaison *f*.

conjunct [kən'dʒʌŋkt] *adj* conjoint.

conjunction [kən'dʒʌŋkʃən] *n* (*Astron, Gram*) conjonction *f*; (*U*) conjonction, connexion *f*, jonction *f*, union *f*. **in ~ with** conjointement avec.

conjunctive [kən'dʒʌŋktɪv] *adj* (*Anat, Gram*) conjonctif.

conjunctivitis [kənˌdʒʌŋktɪ'vaɪtɪs] *n* conjonctivite *f*.

conjuncture [kən'dʒʌŋktʃəʳ] *n* (*combination of circumstances*) conjoncture *f*, circonstance(s) *f(pl)*; (*crisis*) moment *m* critique.

conjure [kən'dʒʊəʳ] **1** *vt* **(a)** (*appeal to*) conjurer, prier, supplier (*sb to do* qn de faire).

(b) ['kʌndʒəʳ] faire apparaître (*par la prestidigitation*). **he ~d a rabbit from his hat** il a fait sortir un lapin de son chapeau.

2 *vi* (*lit, fig*) jongler (*with* avec). (*fig*) **a name to ~ with** un nom prestigieux.

conjure away *vt sep* faire disparaître (comme par magie).

conjure up *vt sep ghosts, spirits* faire apparaître; *memories* évoquer, rappeler. **to conjure up visions of ...** évoquer ... .

conjurer ['kʌndʒərəʳ] *n* prestidigitateur *m*, -trice *f*, illusionniste *mf*.

conjuring ['kʌndʒərɪŋ] *n* prestidigitation *f*, illusionnisme *m*. **~ trick** tour *m* de passe-passe *or* de prestidigitation.

conjuror ['kʌndʒərəʳ] *n* = **conjurer.**

conk‡ [kɒŋk] **1** *n* (*Brit: nose*) pif‡ *m*, blair‡ *m*.

2 *vi [engine, machine]* tomber *or* rester en panne.

conk out‡ *vi [person]* crever‡, clamecer‡; *[engine, machine]* tomber *or* rester en panne. **her car conked out** sa voiture est restée en carafe*.

conker ['kɒŋkəʳ] *n* (*Brit*) marron *m*.

connect [kə'nekt] **1** *vt [person]* joindre, réunir, relier, rattacher (*with, to* à); *[roads]* relier (*with, to* à); *[rail link, airline, rope]* relier, rattacher (*with, to* à); (*Elec*) *two objects* mettre en contact, connecter; (*Tech*) *pinions* embrayer; *wheels* engrener; *pipes* raccorder; *shafts etc* articuler, conjuguer; (*Telec*) mettre en communication (*with* avec); (*fig: associate*) associer, relier (*with, to* à). (*Telec*) **we are trying to ~ you** nous essayons d'obtenir votre communication; **~ed by telephone** relié par téléphone; (*Elec*) **to ~ to earth** remettre à la masse; **to ~ to the mains** brancher sur le secteur; **I always ~ Paris with springtime** j'associe toujours Paris au printemps, Paris me fait toujours penser au printemps; **to be ~ed with** (*be related to*) être allié à, être parent de; (*have dealings with*) avoir des rapports *or* des contacts *or* des relations avec; (*have a bearing on*) se rattacher à, avoir rapport à; **he is ~ed with many big firms** il a des rapports *or* des contacts *or* des relations avec beaucoup de firmes importantes, il est en relations avec beaucoup de firmes importantes; **his departure is not ~ed with the murder** son départ n'a aucun rapport *or* n'a rien à voir avec le meurtre; **he's very well ~ed** (*of good family*) il est de très bonne famille, il est très bien apparenté; (*of influential family*) sa famille a des relations; *V also* **connected.**

2 *vi* se relier, se réunir, se joindre, se raccorder; *[trains]* assurer la correspondance (*with* avec). (*Aut*) **~ing rod** bielle *f*; (*fig*) **my fist ~ed with his jaw*** je l'ai touché à la mâchoire, mon poing l'a cueilli à la mâchoire.

connected [kə'nektɪd] *adj languages* affin (*frm*), connexe; (*Bot, Jur*) connexe; (*fig*) *argument* logique; *speech* suivi. **(closely) ~ professions** des professions *fpl* connexes; *V also* **connect.**

connection, connexion [kə'nekʃən] *n* **(a)** (*V* **connect**) jonction *f*, liaison *f*; (*Elec*) prise *f*, contact *m*, connexion *f*; (*Tech*) embrayage *m*, engrenage *m*; raccord *m*, raccordement *m*; articulation *f*; (*Telec*) communication *f* (téléphonique); (*act of connecting*) connexion, (*fig*) association *f*, liaison. **wrong ~** faux numéro, fausse communication.

(b) rapport *m* (*with* avec), lien *m* (*between* entre), relation *f*, liaison *f*; (*relationship*) rapports, relations. **this has no ~ with what he did** ceci n'a aucun rapport avec ce qu'il a fait; **in this** *or* **that ~** à ce sujet, à ce propos, dans cet ordre d'idées; **in ~ with** à propos de, relativement à; **in another ~** dans un autre ordre d'idées; **to form a ~ with sb** établir des relations *or* des rapports avec qn; **to break off a ~ (with sb)** rompre les relations (avec qn); **to build up a ~ with a firm** établir des relations d'affaires avec une firme; **to have no further ~ with** rompre tout contact avec; (*Comm*) **we have no ~ with any other firm** toute ressemblance avec une autre compagnie est purement fortuite; **to have important ~s** avoir des relations (importantes).

(c) (*clientele, business contacts*) clientèle *f*, relations fpl d'affaires. **this grocer has a very good ~** cet épicier a une très bonne clientèle.

(d) *[family]* (*kinship*) parenté *f*; (*relative*) parent(e) *m(f)*. **~s**

famille *f*; **there is some family ~ between them** ils ont un lien de parenté; **he is a distant ~** c'est un parent éloigné; **she is a ~ of mine** c'est une de mes parentes.

(e) (*Jur*) **criminal ~** liaison criminelle *or* adultérine; **sexual ~** rapports sexuels.

(f) (*Rail*) correspondance *f* (*with* avec). **to miss one's ~** manquer la correspondance.

(g) (*Rel*) secte *f* (religieuse).

conniption* [kə'nɪpʃən] *n* (*US: also* **~s**) crise *f* de colère *or* de rage.

connivance [kə'naɪvəns] *n* connivence *f*. **this was done with her ~/in ~ with her** cela s'est fait avec sa connivence/de connivence avec elle.

connive [kə'naɪv] *vi*: **to ~ at** (*pretend not to notice*) fermer les yeux sur; (*aid and abet*) être de connivence dans, être complice de.

connoisseur [ˌkɒnə'sɜːʳ] *n* connaisseur *m*, -euse *f* (*of* de, en).

connotation [ˌkɒnəʊ'teɪʃən] *n* (*Ling*) connotation *f*, signification totale, sens total; (*Philos*) connotation, compréhension *f*; (*Logic*) implication *f*.

connote [kɒ'nəʊt] *vt* impliquer, suggérer, comporter l'idée de; (*Ling, Philos*) connoter; (*: *signify*) signifier.

connubial [kə'njuːbɪəl] *adj* conjugal.

conquer ['kɒŋkəʳ] *vt* (*lit*) *person, enemy* vaincre, battre; *nation, country* conquérir, subjuguer; *castle* conquérir; (*fig*) *feelings, habits* surmonter, vaincre; *sb's heart, one's freedom* conquérir; *one's audience* subjuguer.

conquering ['kɒŋkərɪŋ] *adj* victorieux.

conqueror ['kɒŋkərəʳ] *n* conquérant *m*, vainqueur *m*; *V* **William.**

conquest ['kɒŋkwest] *n* conquête *f*. **to make a ~*** faire une conquête; **she's his latest ~*** c'est sa dernière conquête*.

consanguinity [ˌkɒnsæŋ'gwɪnɪtɪ] *n* consanguinité *f*.

conscience ['kɒnʃəns] **1** *n* conscience *f*. **to have a clear *or* an easy ~** avoir bonne conscience, avoir la conscience tranquille; **he left with a clean ~** il est parti la conscience tranquille; **he has a bad *or* guilty ~** il a mauvaise conscience, il n'a pas la conscience tranquille; **to have sth on one's ~** avoir qch sur la conscience; **in (all) ~** en conscience; **for ~' sake** par acquit de conscience; **upon my ~, I swear ...** en mon âme et conscience, je jure ...; **to make sth a matter of ~** faire de qch un cas de conscience.

2 *cpd*: (*Jur*) **conscience clause** clause *f or* article *m* qui sauvegarde la liberté de conscience; **conscience money** argent restitué (*généralement au Trésor par scrupule de conscience*); **conscience-stricken** pris de remords.

conscientious [ˌkɒnʃɪ'enʃəs] *adj* **(a)** *person, worker, piece of work* consciencieux. **(b)** *scruple, objection* de conscience. **~ objector** objecteur *m* de conscience.

conscientiously [ˌkɒnʃɪ'enʃəslɪ] *adv* consciencieusement, avec conscience.

conscientiousness [ˌkɒnʃɪ'enʃəsnɪs] *n* conscience *f*.

conscious ['kɒnʃəs] *adj* **(a)** conscient, ayant conscience (*of* de). **to be ~ of one's responsibilities** être conscient de ses responsabilités; **to be ~ of doing** avoir conscience de faire; **to become ~ of sth** prendre conscience de qch, s'apercevoir de qch.

(b) (*Med*) conscient. **to become ~** revenir à soi, reprendre connaissance.

(c) (*clearly felt*) *guilt* conscient, dont on a conscience; ressenti clairement. **with ~ superiority** avec une supériorité consciente de soi, avec la nette conscience de sa (*or* leur *etc*) supériorité.

(d) (*deliberate*) *insult* conscient, intentionnel, délibéré. **~ humour** humour voulu.

(e) (*Philos*) conscient.

consciously ['kɒnʃəslɪ] *adv* consciemment; (*deliberately*) sciemment.

consciousness ['kɒnʃəsnɪs] *n* **(a)** (*Med*) connaissance *f*. **to lose ~** perdre connaissance; **to regain ~** revenir à soi, reprendre connaissance.

(b) (*Philos*) conscience *f*.

(c) (*awareness*) conscience *f* (*of* de), sentiment *m* (*of* de). **the ~ that he was being watched prevented him from ...** le sentiment qu'on le regardait l'empêchait de ... .

conscript [kən'skrɪpt] **1** *vt troops* enrôler, recruter (par conscription), appeler sous les drapeaux. **2** ['kɒnskrɪpt] *n* conscrit *m*. **3** *adj* conscrit.

conscription [kən'skrɪpʃən] *n* conscription *f*.

consecrate ['kɒnsɪkreɪt] *vt church etc* consacrer; *bishop* consacrer, sacrer; (*fig*) *custom, one's life* consacrer (*to* à). **he was ~d bishop** il a été sacré *or* consacré évêque.

consecration [ˌkɒnsɪ'kreɪʃən] *n* (*V* **consecrate**) consécration *f*; sacre *m*.

consecutive [kən'sekjʊtɪv] *adj* **(a)** consécutif. **on 4 ~ days** pendant 4 jours consécutifs *or* de suite. **(b)** (*Gram*) *clause* consécutif.

consecutively [kən'sekjʊtɪvlɪ] *adv* consécutivement. **he won 2 prizes ~** il a gagné consécutivement *or* coup sur coup 2 prix; (*Jur*) ... **the sentences to be served ~** ...avec cumul *m* de peines.

consensus [kən'sensəs] *n* consensus *m*, accord général. **~ of opinion** consensus d'opinion.

consent [kən'sent] **1** *vi* consentir (*to sth* à qch, *to do* à faire); (*to request*) accéder (*to sth* à qch). (*Jur*) **between ~ing adults** entre adultes consentants.

2 *n* consentement *m*, assentiment *m*. **to refuse one's ~ to** refuser son consentement *or* assentiment à; **by common ~** de l'aveu de tous *or* de tout le monde, de l'opinion de tous; **by mutual ~** (*general agreement*) d'un commun accord; (*private arrangement*) de gré à gré, à l'amiable; **divorce by (mutual) ~** divorce *m* par consentement mutuel; **age of ~** âge *m* nubile (légal); *V* **silence.**

consentient [kən'senʃɪənt] *adj* d'accord, en accord (*with* avec).

consequence ['kɒnsɪkwəns] *n* **(a)** (*result, effect*) conséquence *f*, suites *fpl*. **in ~** par conséquent; **in ~ of which** par suite de quoi; **to take *or* face the ~s** accepter *or* supporter les conséquences (*of* de).

(b) (*U: importance*) importance *f*, conséquence *f*. **it's of no ~** cela ne tire pas à conséquence, cela n'a aucune importance; **he's (a man) of no ~** c'est un homme de peu d'importance *or* de peu de poids.

consequent ['kɒnsɪkwənt] *adj* (*following*) consécutif (*on* à); (*resulting*) résultant (*on* de). **the loss of harvest ~ upon the flooding** la perte de la moisson résultant des *or* causée par les inondations.

consequential [ˌkɒnsɪ'kwenʃəl] *adj* **(a)** consécutif, conséquent (*to* à). **(b)** (*pej*) *person* suffisant, arrogant.

consequently ['kɒnsɪkwəntlɪ] *adv* par conséquent, donc, en conséquence.

conservancy [kən'sɜːvənsɪ] *n* **(a)** (*Brit: commission controlling forests, ports etc*) administration *f*. **(b)** = **conservation.**

conservation [ˌkɒnsə'veɪʃən] *n* préservation *f*; *[nature]* défense *f* de l'environnement; (*Phys*) conservation *f*.

conservationist [ˌkɒnsə'veɪʃənɪst] *n partisan(e) m(f) de la défense de l'environnement.*

conservatism [kən'sɜːvətɪzəm] *n* conservatisme *m*.

conservative [kən'sɜːvətɪv] **1** *adj* **(a)** conservateur (*f* -trice). (*Brit Pol*) **the C~ Party** le parti conservateur; **C~ and Unionist Party** parti conservateur et unioniste.

(b) *assessment* modeste; *style, behaviour* traditionnel. **at a ~ estimate** au bas mot.

2 *n* (*Pol*) conservateur *m*, -trice *f*.

conservatoire [kən'sɜːvətwɑːʳ] *n* (*Mus*) conservatoire *m*.

conservatory [kən'sɜːvətrɪ] *n* **(a)** (*greenhouse*) serre *f*. **(b)** (*Art, Mus, Theat*) conservatoire *m*.

conserve [kən'sɜːv] **1** *vt* conserver, préserver; *one's resources, one's strength* ménager. **2** *n* (*Culin*) **~s** confitures *fpl*, conserves *fpl* (de fruits).

consider [kən'sɪdəʳ] *vt* **(a)** (*think about*) *problem, possibility* considérer, examiner; *question, matter, subject* réfléchir à. **I had not ~ed taking it with me** je n'avais pas envisagé de l'emporter; **everything *or* all things ~ed** tout bien considéré, toute réflexion faite, tout compte fait; **it is my ~ed opinion that ...** après avoir mûrement réfléchi je pense que ...; **he is being ~ed for the post** on songe à lui pour le poste.

(b) (*take into account*) *facts* prendre en considération; *person's feelings* avoir égard à, ménager; *cost, difficulties, dangers* tenir compte de, considérer, regarder à. **when one ~s that ...** quand on considère *or* pense que ... .

(c) (*be of the opinion*) considérer, tenir. **she ~s him very mean** elle le considère comme très avare, elle le tient pour très avare; **to ~ o.s. happy** s'estimer heureux; **~ yourself lucky*** estimez-vous heureux; **~ yourself dismissed** considérez-vous comme renvoyé; **I ~ that we should have done it** je considère que *or* à mon avis nous aurions dû le faire; **to ~ sth as done** tenir qch pour fait; **I ~ it an honour to help you** je m'estime honoré de (pouvoir) vous aider.

considerable [kən'sɪdərəbl] *adj number, size* considérable; *sum of money* considérable, important. **there was a ~ number of ...** il y avait un nombre considérable de ...; **to a ~ extent** dans une large mesure; **we had ~ difficulty in finding you** nous avons eu beaucoup de mal à vous trouver.

considerably [kən'sɪdərəblɪ] *adv* considérablement.

considerate [kən'sɪdərɪt] *adj* prévenant (*towards* envers), plein d'égards (*towards* pour, envers).

considerately [kən'sɪdərɪtlɪ] *adv act* avec prévenance, avec égards.

consideration [kənˌsɪdə'reɪʃən] *n* **(a)** (*U: thoughtfulness*) considération *f*, estime *f*, égard *m*. **out of ~ for** par égard pour; **to show ~ for sb's feelings** ménager les susceptibilités de qn.

(b) (*U: careful thought*) considération *f*. **to take sth into ~** prendre qch en considération, tenir compte de qch; **taking everything into ~** tout bien considéré *or* pesé; **he left it out of ~** il n'en a pas tenu compte, il n'a pas pris cela en considération; **the matter is under ~** l'affaire est à l'examen *or* à l'étude; **in ~ of** en considération de, eu égard à; **after due ~** après mûre réflexion; **please give my suggestion your careful ~** je vous prie d'apporter toute votre attention à ma suggestion.

(c) (*fact etc to be taken into account*) préoccupation *f*, considération *f*; (*motive*) motif *m*. **money is the first ~** il faut considérer d'abord *or* en premier lieu la question d'argent; **many ~s have made me act thus** plusieurs considérations *or* motifs m'ont amené à agir ainsi; **on no ~** à aucun prix, en aucun cas; **it's of no ~** cela n'a aucune importance; **money is no ~** l'argent n'entre pas en ligne de compte; **his age was an important ~** son âge constituait un facteur important.

(d) (*reward, payment*) rétribution *f*, rémunération *f*. **to do sth for a ~** faire qch moyennant finance *or* contre espèces.

considering [kən'sɪdərɪŋ] *prep* étant donné, vu, eu égard à. **~ she has no money** étant donné (le fait) qu'elle n'a pas d'argent, vu qu'elle n'a pas d'argent; **~ the circumstances** vu *or* étant donné les circonstances; **he played very well ~** tout compte fait il a très bien joué, finalement il a quand même très bien joué.

consign [kən'saɪn] *vt* **(a)** (*send*) *goods* expédier (*to sb* à qn, à l'adresse de qn). **(b)** (*hand over*) *person, thing* confier, remettre. **to ~ a child to the care of** confier *or* remettre un enfant aux soins de.

consignee [ˌkɒnsaɪ'niː] *n* consignataire *mf*.

consigner [kən'saɪnəʳ] *n* = **consignor.**

consignment [kən'saɪnmənt] *n* **(a)** (*U*) envoi *m*, expédition *f*. **goods for ~ abroad** marchandises *fpl* à destination de l'étranger; (*Brit*) **~ note** bulletin *m* de chargement. **(b)** (*goods consigned*) arrivage *m*, envoi *m*.
consignor [kən'saɪnə(r)] *n* expéditeur *m*, -trice *f* (*de marchandises*), consignateur *m*, -trice *f*.
consist [kən'sɪst] *vi* **(a)** (*be composed*) consister (*of* en). **what does the house ~ of?** en quoi consiste la maison?, de quoi la maison est-elle composée?
(b) (*have as its essence*) consister (*in doing* à faire, *in sth* dans qch). **his happiness ~s in helping others** son bonheur consiste à aider autrui.
consistency [kən'sɪstənsɪ] *n* *[liquids etc]* consistance *f*; (*fig*) *[actions, argument, behaviour]* cohérence *f*, uniformité *f*. (*fig*) **to lack ~** manquer de logique.
consistent [kən'sɪstənt] *adj person, behaviour* conséquent, logique. **his arguments are not ~** ses arguments ne se tiennent pas; **~ with** compatible avec, d'accord avec.
consistently [kən'sɪstəntlɪ] *adv* **(a)** (*logically*) avec esprit de suite, avec logique. **(b)** (*unfailingly*) régulièrement, sans exception, immanquablement. **(c)** (*in agreement*) conformément (*with* à).
consolation [,kɒnsə'leɪʃən] **1** *n* consolation *f*, réconfort *m*. **2** *cpd prize* de consolation.
consolatory [kən'sɒlətərɪ] *adj* consolant, consolateur (*f* -trice), réconfortant.
console[1] [kən'səʊl] *vt* consoler (*sb for sth* qn de qch).
console[2] ['kɒnsəʊl] *n* **(a)** *[organ]* console *f*. **(b)** (*radio cabinet*) meuble *m* de radio. **(c)** (*Archit*) console *f*.
consolidate [kən'sɒlɪdeɪt] **1** *vt* **(a)** (*make strong*) *one's position* consolider, raffermir. **(b)** (*Comm, Fin: unite*) *businesses* réunir; *loan, funds, annuities* consolider. **~d fund** ≈ fonds consolidés. **2** *vi* se consolider, s'affermir.
consolidation [kən,sɒlɪ'deɪʃən] *n* (*V* **consolidate**) **(a)** consolidation *f*, affermissement *m*. **(b)** (*Comm, Fin*) unification *f*, consolidation *f*.
consoling [kən'səʊlɪŋ] *adj* consolant, consolateur (*f* -trice).
consols ['kɒnsɒlz] *npl* (*Brit Fin*) fonds consolidés.
consonance ['kɒnsənəns] *n* *[sounds]* consonance *f*, accord *m*; *[ideas]* accord, communion *f*.
consonant ['kɒnsənənt] **1** *n* (*Ling*) consonne *f*. **~ shift** mutation *f* consonantique. **2** *adj* en accord (*with* avec). **behaviour ~ with one's beliefs** comportement qui s'accorde avec ses croyances.
consonantal [,kɒnsə'næntl] *adj* consonantique.
consort ['kɒnsɔːt] **1** *n* **(a)** (*spouse*) époux *m*, épouse *f*; (*also* **prince ~**) (prince *m*) consort *m*.
(b) (*Naut*) conserve *f*. **in ~** de conserve.
2 [kən'sɔːt] *vi* **(a)** (*associate*) **to ~ with sb** fréquenter qn, frayer avec qn.
(b) (*be consistent*) *[behaviour]* s'accorder (*with* avec).
consortium [kən'sɔːtɪəm] *n* consortium *m*, comptoir *m*.
conspectus [kən'spektəs] *n* vue générale.
conspicuous [kən'spɪkjʊəs] *adj person, behaviour, clothes* voyant, qui attire la vue; *bravery* insigne; *difference, fact* notable, remarquable, manifeste. **the poster was ~** l'affiche attirait les regards, on ne pouvait pas manquer de voir l'affiche; **there was a ~ lack of ...** il y avait un manque manifeste de *or* une absence manifeste de ...; **he was in a ~ position** (*lit*) il était bien en évidence; (*fig*) il occupait une situation très en vue; **to make o.s. ~** se faire remarquer, se singulariser; **to be ~ by one's absence** briller par son absence.
conspicuously [kən'spɪkjʊəslɪ] *adv behave* d'une manière à se faire remarquer; *opposed, angry* visiblement, manifestement. **he was ~ absent** son absence se remarquait, il brillait par son absence.
conspiracy [kən'spɪrəsɪ] *n* conspiration *f*, complot *m*, conjuration *f*.
conspirator [kən'spɪrətə(r)] *n* conspirateur *m*, -trice *f*, conjuré(e) *m(f)*.
conspire [kən'spaɪə(r)] **1** *vi* **(a)** *[people]* conspirer (*against* contre). **to ~ to do** comploter de *or* se mettre d'accord pour faire. **(b)** *[events]* conspirer, concourir (*to do* à faire). **2** *vt* (†) comploter, méditer.
constable ['kʌnstəbl] *n* (*Brit: also* **police ~**) (*in town*) agent *m* de police, gardien *m* de la paix; (*in country*) gendarme *m*. **'yes, C~'** 'oui, monsieur l'agent (*or* monsieur le gendarme)'; *V* **chief, special.**
constabulary [kən'stæbjʊlərɪ] *collective n* (*Brit*) (*in town*) (la) police; (*in country*) (la) gendarmerie.
constancy ['kɒnstənsɪ] *n* (*firmness*) constance *f*, fermeté *f*; *[feelings, affection]* fidélité *f*, constance; *[temperature etc]* invariabilité *f*, constance.
constant ['kɒnstənt] **1** *adj* **(a)** (*occurring often*) *quarrels, interruptions* incessant, continuel, perpétuel. **(b)** (*unchanging*) *affection* inaltérable, constant; *friend* fidèle, loyal. **2** *n* (*Math, Phys*) constante *f*.
Constantinople [,kɒnstæntɪ'nəʊpl] *n* Constantinople.
constantly ['kɒnstəntlɪ] *adv* constamment, continuellement, sans cesse.
constellation [,kɒnstə'leɪʃən] *n* constellation *f*.
consternation [,kɒnstə'neɪʃən] *n* consternation *f*, accablement *m*. **filled with ~** frappé de consternation, consterné, accablé; **there was general ~** la consternation était générale.
constipate ['kɒnstɪpeɪt] *vt* constiper.
constipated ['kɒnstɪpeɪtɪd] *adj* (*lit, fig*) constipé.
constipation [,kɒnstɪ'peɪʃən] *n* constipation *f*.
constituency [kən'stɪtjʊənsɪ] *n* (*Pol*) (*place*) circonscription électorale; (*people*) électeurs *mpl* (d'une circonscription). **~ party** section locale (du parti).
constituent [kən'stɪtjʊənt] **1** *adj part, element* constituant, composant, constitutif. (*Pol*) **~ assembly** assemblée constituante.
2 *n* **(a)** (*Pol*) électeur *m*, -trice *f* (*de la circonscription d'un député*). **one of my ~s wrote to me ...** quelqu'un dans ma circonscription m'a écrit ...; **he was talking to one of his ~s** il parlait à un habitant *or* un électeur de sa circonscription.
(b) (*part, element*) élément constitutif.
constitute ['kɒnstɪtjuːt] *vt* **(a)** (*appoint*) constituer, instituer, désigner. **to ~ sb leader of the group** désigner qn (comme) chef du groupe.
(b) (*establish*) *organization* monter, établir; *committee* constituer.
(c) (*amount to, make up*) faire, constituer. **these parts ~ a whole** toutes ces parties font *or* constituent un tout; **paste ~d of flour and water** pâte faite *or* composée de farine et d'eau; **that ~s a lie** cela constitue un mensonge; **it ~s a threat to our sales** ceci représente une menace pour nos ventes; **so ~d that ...** fait de telle façon que ..., ainsi fait que ....
constitution [,kɒnstɪ'tjuːʃən] *n* **(a)** (*Pol*) constitution *f*. **under the French ~** selon *or* d'après la constitution française.
(b) *[person]* constitution *f*. **to have a strong/weak *or* poor ~** avoir une robuste/chétive constitution; **iron ~** santé *f* de fer.
(c) (*structure*) composition *f*, constitution *f*.
constitutional [,kɒnstɪ'tjuːʃənl] **1** *adj* **(a)** (*also Pol*) *government, reform, vote* constitutionnel, de constitution. **(b)** (*Med*) *weakness, tendency* diathésique. **2** *n* (**hum*) **to go for a ~** faire sa petite promenade *or* son petit tour.
constitutionally [,kɒnstɪ'tjuːʃənəlɪ] *adv* **(a)** (*Pol etc*) constitutionnellement, conformément à la constitution. **(b)** par nature, par tempérament.
constitutive ['kɒnstɪtjuːtɪv] *adj* constitutif.
constrain [kən'streɪn] *vt* **(a)** (*force*) contraindre, forcer, obliger (*sb to do* qn à faire). **I find myself ~ed to write to you** je me vois dans la nécessité de vous écrire; **to be/feel ~ed to do** être/se sentir contraint *or* forcé *or* obligé de faire.
(b) (*restrict*) *liberty, person* contraindre. **to feel ~ed by one's clothes** se sentir à l'étroit dans ses vêtements.
constrained [kən'streɪnd] *adj atmosphere* de gêne; *voice, manner* contraint.
constraint [kən'streɪnt] *n* **(a)** (*compulsion*) contrainte *f*. **to act under ~** agir sous la contrainte. **(b)** (*restriction*) contrainte *f*, retenue *f*, gêne *f*. **to speak freely and without ~** parler librement et sans contrainte.
constrict [kən'strɪkt] *vt* (*make smaller*) rétrécir, resserrer; (*tighten*) *muscle etc* serrer; (*hamper*) *movements* gêner. **a ~ed view of events** une vue bornée des événements.
constriction [kən'strɪkʃən] *n* (*esp Med*) constriction *f*, resserrement *m*, étranglement *m*.
construct [kən'strʌkt] *vt building* construire, bâtir; *novel, play* construire, composer; *theory, one's defence* bâtir.
construction [kən'strʌkʃən] *n* **(a)** *[roads, buildings]* construction *f*, édification *f*. **in course of ~, under ~** en construction.
(b) *[building, structure]* construction *f*, édifice *m*, bâtiment *m*.
(c) (*interpretation*) interprétation *f*. **to put a wrong ~ on sb's words** mal interpréter *or* interpréter à contresens les paroles de qn.
(d) (*Gram*) construction *f*.
constructional [kən'strʌkʃənl] *adj* de construction. **~ engineering** construction *f* mécanique.
constructive [kən'strʌktɪv] *adj* constructif.
constructively [kən'strʌktɪvlɪ] *adv* d'une manière constructive.
constructor [kən'strʌktə(r)] *n* constructeur *m*, -trice *f*; (*Naut*) ingénieur *m* des constructions navales.
construe [kən'struː] **1** *vt* (*translate, interpret*) *sentence* analyser, décomposer; *passage, Latin poem* expliquer. **his words were wrongly ~d** ses paroles ont été mal comprises, on a interprété ses paroles à contresens.
2 *vi* (*Gram*) s'analyser grammaticalement. **the sentence will not ~** la phrase n'a pas de construction.
consul ['kɒnsəl] *n* consul *m*. **~ general** consul général.
consular ['kɒnsjʊlə(r)] *adj* consulaire. **~ section** service *m* consulaire.
consulate ['kɒnsjʊlɪt] *n* consulat *m*. **~ general** consulat général.
consulship ['kɒnsəlʃɪp] *n* poste *m* *or* charge *f* de consul.
consult [kən'sʌlt] **1** *vt* **(a)** *book, person, doctor* consulter (*about* sur, au sujet de).
(b) (*show consideration for*) *person's feelings* avoir égard à, prendre en considération; *one's own interests* consulter.
2 *vi* consulter, être en consultation (*with* avec). **to ~ together over sth** se consulter sur *or* au sujet de qch.
3 *cpd*: **consulting engineer** ingénieur-conseil *m*, ingénieur consultant; (*Brit Med*) **consulting hours** heures *fpl* de consultation; (*Brit esp Med*) **consulting room** cabinet *m* de consultation.
consultant [kən'sʌltənt] **1** *n* (*gen*) consultant *m*, expert-conseil *m*, conseiller *m*; (*Brit Med*) médecin consultant, spécialiste *m*. **he acts as ~ to the firm** il est expert-conseil auprès de la compagnie; *V* **management** *etc.*
2 *cpd*: **consultant engineer** ingénieur-conseil *m*, ingénieur consultant; **consultant physician/psychiatrist** médecin/psychiatre consultant.
consultation [,kɒnsəl'teɪʃən] *n* **(a)** (*U*) consultation *f*. **in ~ with** en consultation avec. **(b)** consultation *f*. **to hold a ~** conférer (*about* de), délibérer (*about* sur), tenir une délibération.
consultative [kən'sʌltətɪv] *adj* consultatif.
consume [kən'sjuːm] *vt food, drink* consommer; *supplies, resources* consommer, dissiper; *[fire] buildings* consumer,

dévorer; *[engine] fuel* brûler, consommer. (*fig*) **to be ~d with grief** se consumer de chagrin; **to be ~d with desire** brûler de désir; **to be ~d with jealousy** être rongé par la jalousie.

consumer [kən'sjuːməʳ] **1** *n* consommateur *m*, -trice *f*.

2 *cpd*: **consumer credit** crédit *m* au consommateur; **consumer durables** biens *mpl* de consommation durable, articles *mpl* d'équipement; **consumer goods** biens *mpl* de consommation; **consumer protection** protection *f* du consommateur; (*Brit*) **Secretary of State for** *or* **Minister of Consumer Protection** ministre *m* pour la protection des consommateurs, ≃ secrétaire *m* d'État à la Consommation; **Department** *or* **Ministry of Consumer Protection** ministère *m* pour la protection des consommateurs, ≃ Secrétariat *m* d'État à la Consommation; **consumer research** études *fpl* de marchés; **consumer resistance** résistance *f* du consommateur; **consumer society** société *f* de consommation.

consuming [kən'sjuːmɪŋ] *adj desire, passion* dévorant, brûlant.

consummate [kən'sʌmɪt] **1** *adj* consommé, accompli, achevé.

2 ['kɒnsʌmeɪt] *vt* consommer.

consummation [ˌkɒnsʌ'meɪʃən] *n [union esp marriage]* consommation *f*; *[art form]* perfection *f*; *[one's desires, ambitions]* couronnement *m*, apogée *m*.

consumption [kən'sʌmpʃən] *n* (*U*) **(a)** *[food, fuel]* consommation *f*. **not fit for human ~** (*lit*) non-comestible; (**pej*) pas mangeable, immangeable.

(b) (*Med*†: *tuberculosis*) consomption *f* (pulmonaire)†, phtisie† *f*.

consumptive† [kən'sʌmptɪv] *adj, n* phtisique† (*mf*), tuberculeux *m*, -euse *f*.

contact ['kɒntækt] **1** *n* **(a)** contact *m*. **point of ~** point *m* de contact *or* de tangence; **to be in/come into/get into ~ with sb** être/entrer/se mettre en contact *or* rapport avec qn; **we have had no ~ with him for 6 months** nous sommes sans contact avec lui depuis 6 mois; **I seem to make no ~ with him** je n'arrive pas à communiquer avec lui.

(b) (*Elec*) contact *m*. **to make/break the ~** établir/couper le contact; (*Aviat*) **~!** contact!

(c) (*acquaintance*) connaissance *f*, relation *f*. **he has some ~s in Paris** il a des relations à Paris.

(d) (*Med*) contamineur *m* possible, contact *m*.

2 *vt person* se mettre en contact *or* en rapport avec, entrer en relations avec. **we'll ~ you soon** nous nous mettrons en rapport avec vous sous peu.

3 *cpd*: (*Elec*) **contact breaker** interrupteur *m*; **contact lenses** verres *mpl* de contact, lentilles cornéennes; (*Comm*) **contact man** agent *m* de liaison; (*Phot*) **contact print** négatif *m* contact *inv*.

contagion [kən'teɪdʒən] *n* contagion *f*.

contagious [kən'teɪdʒəs] *adj* (*Med*) *illness, person* contagieux; (*fig*) *laughter, emotion* contagieux, communicatif.

contain [kən'teɪn] *vt* **(a)** (*hold*) *[box, bottle, envelope etc]* contenir; *[book, letter, newspaper]* contenir, renfermer. **sea water ~s a lot of salt** l'eau de mer contient beaucoup de sel *or* a une forte teneur en sel; **the room will ~ 70 people** la salle peut contenir 70 personnes; *V* **self**.

(b) (*hold back, control*) *one's emotions, anger* contenir, refréner, maîtriser. **he couldn't ~ himself for joy** il ne se sentait pas de joie; (*Mil*) **to ~ the enemy forces** contenir les troupes ennemies.

(c) (*Math*) être divisible par.

container [kən'teɪnəʳ] **1** *n* **(a)** (*goods transport*) conteneur *m*. **(b)** (*jug, box etc*) récipient *m*.

2 *cpd train, ship* porte-conteneurs *inv*. **container dock** dock *m* pour la manutention de conteneurs; (*Naut*) **container line** ligne *f* transconteneurs *inv*; **container terminal** terminal *m* (à conteneurs); **container transport** transport *m* par conteneurs.

containerization [kənˌteɪnəraɪ'zeɪʃən] *n* conteneurisation *f*.

containerize [kən'teɪnəraɪz] *vt* mettre en conteneurs, conteneuriser.

contaminate [kən'tæmɪneɪt] *vt* (*lit, fig*) contaminer, souiller; *[radioactivity]* contaminer. **~d air** air vicié *or* contaminé.

contamination [kənˌtæmɪ'neɪʃən] *n* contamination *f*, souillure *f*.

contemplate ['kɒntəmpleɪt] *vt* **(a)** (*look at*) contempler, considérer avec attention. **(b)** (*plan, consider*) *action, purchase* envisager. **to ~ doing** envisager de *or* songer à *or* se proposer de faire; **I don't ~ a refusal from him** je ne m'attends pas à *or* je n'envisage pas un refus de sa part.

contemplation [ˌkɒntem'pleɪʃən] *n* (*U*) **(a)** (*act of looking*) contemplation *f*. **(b)** (*deep thought*) contemplation *f*, méditation *f*. **deep in ~** plongé dans de profondes méditations. **(c)** (*expectation*) prévision *f*. **in ~ of their arrival** en prévision de leur arrivée.

contemplative [kən'templətɪv] **1** *adj mood* contemplatif, méditatif; *attitude* recueilli; (*Rel*) *prayer, order* contemplatif. **2** *n* (*Rel*) contemplatif *m*, -ive *f*.

contemporaneous [kənˌtempə'reɪnɪəs] *adj* contemporain (*with* de).

contemporaneously [kənˌtempə'reɪnɪəslɪ] *adv* à la même époque (*with* que).

contemporary [kən'tempərərɪ] **1** *adj* (*of the same period*) contemporain (*with* de), de la même époque (*with* que); (*modern*) contemporain, moderne. **Dickens and ~ writers** Dickens et les écrivains contemporains *or* de son époque; **he's bought an 18th century house and is looking for ~ furniture** il a acheté une maison du 18e siècle et il cherche des meubles d'époque; **a ~ narrative** un récit de l'époque; **I like ~ art** j'aime l'art contemporain *or* moderne; **it's all very ~** c'est tout ce qu'il y a de plus moderne.

2 *n* contemporain(e) *m(f)*.

contempt [kən'tempt] *n* mépris *m*. **to hold in ~** mépriser, avoir du mépris pour; **this will bring you into ~** ceci vous fera mépriser; **in ~ of danger** au mépris *or* en dépit du danger; **it's beneath ~** c'est tout ce qu'il y a de plus méprisable, c'est audessous de tout; (*Jur*) **~ of court** outrage *m* à la Cour.

contemptible [kən'temptəbl] *adj* méprisable, indigne, vil.

contemptuous [kən'temptjuəs] *adj person* dédaigneux (*of* de); *manner etc* méprisant, altier, dédaigneux; *gesture* de mépris.

contemptuously [kən'temptjuəslɪ] *adv* avec mépris, dédaigneusement.

contend [kən'tend] **1** *vi* combattre, lutter (*with* contre). **to ~ with sb for sth** disputer qch à qn; **to ~ with sb over sth** se disputer *or* se battre avec qn au sujet de qch; **they had to ~ with very bad weather conditions** ils ont dû faire face à des conditions météorologiques déplorables; **we have many problems to ~ with** nous sommes aux prises avec de nombreux problèmes; **I should not like to have to ~ with him** je ne voudrais pas avoir affaire à lui; **you'll have me to ~ with** vous aurez affaire à moi.

2 *vt* soutenir, prétendre (*that* que).

contender [kən'tendəʳ] *n* prétendant(e) *m(f)* (*for* à); (*rival*) adversaire *mf*, rival(e) *m(f)*.

contending [kən'tendɪŋ] *adj* opposé, ennemi.

content[1] [kən'tent] **1** *adj* content, satisfait. **to be ~ with sth** se contenter *or* s'accommoder de qch; **she is quite ~ to stay there** elle ne demande pas mieux que de rester là.

2 *n* contentement *m*, satisfaction *f*; *V* **heart**.

3 *vt person* contenter, satisfaire. **to ~ o.s. with doing** se contenter de *or* se borner à faire.

content[2] ['kɒntent] *n* **(a)** **~s** (*thing contained*) contenu *m*; (*amount contained*) contenu, contenance *f*; *[book]* **(table of) ~s** table *f* des matières.

(b) (*U*) *[book, play, film]* contenu *m*; *[official document]* teneur *f*; *[metal]* teneur, titre *m*. **what do you think of the ~ of the article?** que pensez-vous du contenu *or* du fond de l'article?; **oranges have a high vitamin C ~** les oranges sont riches en vitamine C; **gold ~** teneur en or; **the play lacks ~** la pièce est mince *or* manque de profondeur.

contented [kən'tentɪd] *adj* content, satisfait (*with* de).

contentedly [kən'tentɪdlɪ] *adv* sans se plaindre, avec contentement. **to smile ~** avoir un sourire de contentement.

contentedness [kən'tentɪdnɪs] *n* contentement *m*, satisfaction *f*.

contention [kən'tenʃən] *n* **(a)** (*dispute*) démêlé *m*, dispute *f*, contestation *f*; *V* **bone**. **(b)** (*argument, point argued*) assertion *f*, affirmation *f*. **it is my ~ that** je soutiens que.

contentious [kən'tenʃəs] *adj person* querelleur, chamailleur; *subject, issue* contesté, litigieux.

contentment [kən'tentmənt] *n* contentement *m*, satisfaction *f*.

conterminous [ˌkɒn'tɜːmɪnəs] *adj* **(a)** (*contiguous*) *county, country* limitrophe (*with, to* de); *estate, house, garden* adjacent, attenant (*with, to* à). **(b)** (*end to end*) bout à bout. **(c)** (*coextensive*) de même étendue (*with* que).

contest [kən'test] **1** *vt* **(a)** (*argue, debate*) *question, matter, result* contester, discuter. **to ~ sb's right to do** contester à qn le droit de faire; (*Jur*) **to ~ a will** attaquer *or* contester un testament.

(b) (*compete for*) disputer. (*Parl*) **to ~ a seat** disputer un siège; (*Pol*) **to ~ an election** disputer une élection.

2 *vi* se disputer (*with, against* avec), contester.

3 ['kɒntest] *n* (*struggle: lit, fig*) combat *m*, lutte *f* (*with* avec, contre, *between* entre); (*Sport*) lutte; (*Boxing, Wrestling*) combat, rencontre *f*; (*competition*) concours *m*. **beauty ~** concours de beauté; **~ of skill** lutte d'adresse.

contestant [kən'testənt] *n* **(a)** (*for prize, reward*) concurrent(e) *m(f)*. **(b)** (*in fight*) adversaire *mf*.

contestation [ˌkɒntes'teɪʃən] *n* contestation *f*.

context ['kɒntekst] *n* contexte *m*.

contextual [kɒn'tekstjuəl] *adj* contextuel, d'après le contexte.

contiguous [kən'tɪgjuəs] *adj* contigu (*f* -guë). **~ to** contigu à *or* avec, attenant à; **the two fields are ~** les deux champs se touchent *or* sont contigus.

continence ['kɒntɪnəns] *n* (*V* **continent**[1]) continence *f*; chasteté *f*.

continent[1] ['kɒntɪnənt] *adj* (*chaste*) chaste; (*self-controlled*) continent†; (*Med*) qui n'est pas incontinent.

continent[2] ['kɒntɪnənt] *n* (*Geog*) continent *m*. (*Brit*) **the C~** l'Europe continentale; (*Brit*) **on the C~** en Europe (*continentale*).

continental [ˌkɒntɪ'nentl] **1** *adj* continental. **~ breakfast** petit déjeuner à la française; **~ drift** dérive *f* des continents; **~ quilt** couette *f*; **~ shelf** plateforme continentale, plateau continental.

2 *n* (*Brit*) Européen(ne) *m(f)* (*continental*).

contingency [kən'tɪndʒənsɪ] **1** *n* **(a)** éventualité *f*, événement imprévu *or* inattendu. **in a ~, should a ~ arise** en cas d'imprévu; **to provide for all contingencies** parer à toute éventualité.

(b) (*Statistics*) contingence *f*.

2 *cpd*: **contingency fund** caisse *f* de prévoyance; **contingency planning** mise *f* sur pied de plans d'urgence; **contingency plans** plans *mpl* d'urgence; (*Space*) **contingency sample** échantillon *m* lunaire (*prélevé dès l'alunissage*).

contingent [kən'tɪndʒənt] **1** *adj* contingent. **to be ~ upon sth** dépendre de qch. **2** *n* (*Mil etc*) contingent *m*.

continual [kən'tɪnjuəl] *adj* continuel.

continually [kən'tɪnjuəlɪ] *adv* continuellement, sans cesse.

continuance [kən'tɪnjuəns] *n* (*duration*) durée *f*; (*continuation*) continuation *f*; *[human race etc]* perpétuation *f*, continuité *f*.

continuation [kənˌtɪnjʊ'eɪʃən] *n* **(a)** (*no interruption*) continuation *f*. **(b)** (*after interruption*) reprise *f*. **the ~ of work after the**

holidays la reprise du travail après les vacances. **(c)** *[serial story]* suite *f.*

continue [kən'tɪnjuː] **1** *vt* continuer (*to do* à *or* de faire); *piece of work* continuer, poursuivre; *tradition* perpétuer, maintenir; *policy* maintenir; (*after interruption*) *conversation, work* reprendre. *[serial story etc]* **to be ~d** à suivre; **~d on page 10** suite page 10; **to ~ (on) one's way** continuer *or* poursuivre son chemin; (*after pause*) se remettre en marche; **'and so,' he ~d** 'et ainsi,' reprit-il *or* poursuivit-il; **to ~ sb in a job** maintenir qn dans un poste.

2 *vi* **(a)** (*go on*) *[road, weather, celebrations]* continuer; (*after interruption*) reprendre. **the forest ~s to the sea** la forêt s'étend jusqu'à la mer; **his speech ~d until 3 a.m.** son discours s'est prolongé jusqu'à 3 heures du matin.

(b) (*remain*) rester. **to ~ in one's job** garder *or* conserver son poste; **he ~d with his voluntary work** il a poursuivi son travail bénévole; **she ~d as his secretary** elle est restée sa secrétaire.

continuity [ˌkɒntɪnjuːɪtɪ] *n* (*gen, Cine, Rad*) continuité *f.* (*Cine, TV*) **~ girl** script-girl *f*, script *f.*

continuous [kən'tɪnjʊəs] *adj* continu. (*Cine*) **~ performance** spectacle permanent.

continuously [kən'tɪnjʊəslɪ] *adv* (*uninterruptedly*) sans interruption; (*repeatedly*) continuellement, sans arrêt.

continuum [kən'tɪnjʊəm] *n* continuum *m.*

contort [kən'tɔːt] *vt* **(a)** *one's features* tordre, crisper, contracter. **a face ~ed by pain** un visage tordu *or* crispé *or* contracté par la douleur. **(b)** (*fig*) *sb's words, story* déformer, fausser.

contortion [kən'tɔːʃən] *n [esp acrobat]* contorsion *f*; *[features]* torsion *f*, crispation *f*, convulsion *f.*

contortionist [kən'tɔːʃənɪst] *n* contorsionniste *mf.*

contour ['kɒntʊəʳ] **1** *n* contour *m*, profil *m* (*d'un terrain*). **2** *vt*: **to ~ a map** tracer les courbes de niveau sur une carte. **3** *cpd*: **contour line** courbe *f* de niveau; **contour map** carte *f* avec courbes de niveau.

contra... ['kɒntrə] *pref* contre-, contra... . **~flow (bus) lane** couloir *m* (d'autobus) à contre-courant.

contraband ['kɒntrəbænd] **1** *n* contrebande *f.* **2** *cpd goods* de contrebande.

contraception [ˌkɒntrə'sepʃən] *n* contraception *f.*

contraceptive [ˌkɒntrə'septɪv] **1** *n* contraceptif *m.* **2** *adj device, measures* contraceptif, anticonceptionnel.

contract[1] ['kɒntrækt] **1** *n* **(a)** contrat *m.* **marriage ~** contrat de mariage; **to enter into a ~ with sb for sth** passer un contrat avec qn pour qch; **to put work out to ~** mettre *or* donner du travail en adjudication *or* à l'entreprise; **by ~** par *or* sur contrat; (*fig: by killer*) **there's a ~ out for him**: sa tête a été mise à prix (*par un rival*); *V* **breach.**

(b) (*also* **~ bridge**) (bridge *m*) contrat *m.*

2 *cpd*: **~ party** partie contractante; **~ parties** contractants *mpl*; **contract work** travail *m* à forfait *or* à l'entreprise.

3 [kən'trækt] *vt* **(a)** *debts, illness* contracter; *habits, vices* prendre, contracter.

(b) *alliance* contracter. **to ~ to do** s'engager (par contrat) à faire; **to ~ with sb to do** passer un contrat avec qn pour faire.

4 [ˌkən'trækt] *vi* (*Comm*) s'engager (par contrat). **he has ~ed for the building of the motorway** il a un contrat pour la construction de l'autoroute.

contract in *vi* s'engager (par contrat).

contract out *vi* se libérer, se dégager (*of* de), se soustraire (*of* à). **to contract out of a pension scheme** cesser de cotiser à une caisse de retraite.

contract[2] [kən'trækt] **1** *vt* **(a)** *muscles* contracter, raidir; *one's brow, face* crisper. **(b)** (*Ling*) *word, phrase* contracter (*to* en). **2** *vi* se contracter, se resserrer.

contraction [kən'trækʃən] *n* **(a)** (*U*) *[metal, words etc]* contraction *f.* **(b) can't is a ~ of cannot** can't est une forme contractée de cannot. **(c)** *[a habit]* acquisition *f.* **~ of debts** endettement *m.*

contractor [kən'træktəʳ] *n* entrepreneur *m.* **army ~** fournisseur *m* de l'armée; *V* **building.**

contractual [kən'træktʃʊəl] *adj* contractuel.

contradict [ˌkɒntrə'dɪkt] *vt* **(a)** (*deny truth of*) *person, statement* contredire. **don't ~!** ne (me) contredites pas! **(b)** (*be contrary to*) *statement, event* contredire, démentir. **his actions ~ed his words** ses actions démentaient ses paroles.

contradiction [ˌkɒntrə'dɪkʃən] *n* contradiction *f*, démenti *m.* **to be in ~ with** être en contradiction avec, donner le démenti à; **a ~ in terms** une contradiction (dans les termes).

contradictory [ˌkɒntrə'dɪktərɪ] *adj* contradictoire, opposé (*to* à).

contradistinction [ˌkɒntrədɪs'tɪŋkʃən] *n* contraste *m*, opposition *f.* **in ~ to** en contraste avec, par opposition à.

contralto [kən'træltəʊ] **1** *n* (*voice, person*) contralto *m.* **2** *adj voice, part* de contralto.

contraption* [kən'træpʃən] *n* machin* *m*, bidule: *m*, truc* *m.*

contrapuntal [ˌkɒntrə'pʌntl] *adj* en contrepoint, contrapuntique.

contrarily [kən'treərɪlɪ] *adv* contrairement.

contrariness [kən'treərɪnɪs] *n* esprit *m* de contradiction, esprit contrariant.

contrariwise [kən'treərɪwaɪz] *adv* **(a)** (*on the contrary*) au contraire, par contre. **(b)** (*in opposite direction*) en sens opposé.

contrary ['kɒntrərɪ] **1** *adj* **(a)** (*opposite*) contraire, opposé (*to* à), en opposition (*to* avec); *statements, winds* contraire. **in a ~ direction** en sens inverse *or* opposé; **~ to nature** contre nature.

(b) [kən'treərɪ] (*self-willed*) *person, attitude* contrariant, entêté.

2 *adv* contrairement (*to* à), à l'encontre (*to* de). **~ to accepted ideas** à l'encontre des idées reçues; **~ to what I had thought** contrairement à ce que j'avais pensé.

3 *n* contraire *m.* **on the ~** au contraire; **quite the ~!** bien au contraire!; **come tomorrow unless you hear to the ~** venez demain sauf avis contraire *or* sauf contrordre; **I have nothing to say to the ~** je n'ai rien à dire contre *or* à redire, je n'ai pas d'objections (à faire); *[events]* **to go by contraries** se passer contrairement à ce à quoi on s'attendait.

contrast [kən'trɑːst] **1** *vt* mettre en contraste, contraster (*one thing with another* une chose avec une autre).

2 *vi* contraster, faire contraste (*with* avec). *[colour]* **to ~ strongly** contraster (*with* avec), trancher (*with* sur).

3 ['kɒntrɑːst] *n* (*gen, TV*) contraste *m* (*between* entre). **in ~** par contraste; **in ~ to** par opposition à, par contraste avec; **to stand out in ~** (*in landscapes, photographs*) se détacher (*to* de, sur); ressortir (*to* sur, contre); *[colours]* contraster (*to* avec), trancher (*to* sur).

contrasting [kən'trɑːstɪŋ] *adj colours, opinions* opposé, contrasté.

contravene [ˌkɒntrə'viːn] *vt* **(a)** *law* enfreindre, violer, contrevenir à (*frm*). **(b)** *statement* nier, opposer un démenti à.

contravention [ˌkɒntrə'venʃən] *n* infraction *f* (*of the law* à la loi). **in ~ of the rules** en violation des règles, en dérogation aux règles.

contribute [kən'trɪbjuːt] **1** *vt money* contribuer, cotiser. **he has ~d £5** il a offert *or* donné 5 livres; **to ~ an article to a newspaper** donner *or* envoyer un article à un journal; **his presence didn't ~ much to the success of the evening** sa présence n'a pas beaucoup contribué à faire de la soirée un succès.

2 *vi*: **to ~ to a charity** contribuer à une (bonne) œuvre; **he ~d to the success of the venture** il a contribué à assurer le succès de l'affaire; **to ~ to a discussion** prendre part *or* participer à une discussion; **to ~ to a newspaper** collaborer à un journal; **it all ~d to the muddle** tout cela a contribué au désordre.

contribution [ˌkɒntrɪ'bjuːʃən] *n [money, goods etc]* contribution *f*; (*Admin*) cotisation *f*; (*to publication*) article *m.*

contributor [kən'trɪbjʊtəʳ] *n* (*to publication*) collaborateur *m*, -trice *f*; *[money, goods]* donateur *m*, -trice *f.*

contributory [kən'trɪbjʊtərɪ] *adj* **(a)** *cause* accessoire. **it was a ~ factor in his downfall** cela a contribué à sa ruine *or* a été un des facteurs de sa ruine; **~ negligence** faute *f* de la victime; (*Jur*)compensation *f* des fautes.

(b) ~ pension scheme caisse *f* de retraite (à laquelle cotisent les employés).

contrite ['kɒntraɪt] *adj* contrit, pénitent.

contrition [kən'trɪʃən] *n* contrition *f*, pénitence *f.*

contrivance [kən'traɪvəns] *n* (*tool, machine etc*) dispositif *m*, mécanisme *m*; (*scheme*) invention *f*, combinaison *f.*

contrive [kən'traɪv] *vt* **(a)** (*invent, design*) *plan, scheme* combiner, inventer. **to ~ a means of doing** trouver moyen de faire *or* un moyen pour faire.

(b) (*manage*) s'arranger (*to do* pour faire), trouver (le) moyen (*to do* de faire). **can you ~ to be here at 3 o'clock?** est-ce que vous pouvez vous arranger pour être ici à 3 heures?; **he ~d to make matters worse** il a trouvé moyen d'aggraver les choses.

contrived [kən'traɪvd] *adj* artificiel, forcé, qui manque de naturel.

control [kən'trəʊl] **1** *n* **(a)** (*U*) (*authority, power to restrain*) autorité *f*; (*regulating*) *[traffic]* réglementation *f*; *[aircraft]* contrôle *m*; *[pests]* élimination *f*, suppression *f.* **the ~ of disease/forest fire** la lutte contre la maladie/les incendies de forêt; (*Pol*) **~ of the seas** maîtrise *f* des mers; **he has no ~ over his children** il n'a aucune autorité sur ses enfants; **to keep a dog under ~** tenir un chien, se faire obéir d'un chien; **to have a horse under ~** (savoir) maîtriser un cheval; **to lose ~ (of o.s.)** perdre tout contrôle de soi; **to lose ~ of a vehicle/situation** perdre le contrôle d'un véhicule/d'une situation, ne plus être maître d'un véhicule/d'une situation; **to be in ~ of a vehicle/situation, to have a vehicle/situation under ~** être maître d'un véhicule/d'une situation; **to get a fire under ~** maîtriser un incendie; **the situation is under ~** on a *or* on tient la situation bien en main; **everything's under ~*** tout est en ordre; **his car got out of ~** il a perdu le contrôle de sa voiture; **the children are quite out of ~** les enfants sont déchaînés; **under French ~** sous contrôle français; **under government ~** sous contrôle gouvernemental; **circumstances beyond our ~** circonstances indépendantes de notre volonté; **who is in ~ here?** qui *or* quel est le responsable ici?; (*Sport*) **his ~ of the ball is not very good** il ne contrôle pas très bien la balle; *V* **birth, self** *etc.*

(b) ~s *[train, car, ship, aircraft]* commandes *fpl*; *[radio, TV]* boutons *mpl* de commande; *[train etc]* **to be at the ~s** être aux commandes; (*Rad, TV*) **volume/tone ~** (bouton *m* de) réglage *m* de volume/de sonorité.

(c) price ~s le contrôle des prix.

(d) (*Phys, Psych etc: standard of comparison*) cas *m* témoin.

2 *vt* (*regulate, restrain*) *emotions* maîtriser, dominer, réprimer; *animal* se faire obéir de; *car* avoir la maîtrise de; *organization, business* diriger, être à la tête de; *expenditure* régler; *prices, wages* contrôler. **to ~ o.s.** se contrôler, se maîtriser, rester maître de soi; **~ yourself!** calmez-vous!; **she can't ~ the children** elle n'a aucune autorité sur les enfants; **to ~ traffic** régler la circulation; **to ~ a disease** enrayer une maladie; **to ~ immigration** restreindre et contrôler l'immigration; *V also* **controlled.**

3 *cpd*: (*Med, Psych etc*) **control case** cas *m* témoin; (*Aviat*) **control column** manche *m* à balai; (*Med, Psych etc*) **control group** groupe *m* témoin; **control knob** bouton *m* de commande *or* de réglage; **control panel** *[aircraft, ship]* tableau *m* de bord;

[TV, computer] pupitre *m* de commande; **control point** contrôle *m*; **control room** (*Naut*) poste *m* de commande; (*Mil*) salle *f* de commande, poste de contrôle; (*Rad, TV*) régie *f*; (*Aviat*) **control tower** tour *f* de contrôle.

controllable [kənˈtrəʊləbl] *adj child, animal* discipliné; *expenditure, inflation, imports, immigration* qui peut être freiné *or* restreint; *disease* qui peut être enrayé.

controlled [kənˈtrəʊld] *adj emotion* contenu. **he was very ~** il se dominait très bien; **... he said in a ~ voice** ... dit-il en se contrôlant *or* en se dominant; (*Econ*) **~ economy** économie dirigée.

controller [kənˈtrəʊləʳ] *n* **(a)** *[accounts etc]* contrôleur *m*, vérificateur *m*. **(b)** (*Admin, Ind etc: manager*) contrôleur *m*. **(c)** (*Tech: device*) appareil *m* de contrôle.

controlling [kənˈtrəʊlɪŋ] *adj factor* déterminant. (*Fin*) **~ interest** participation *f* majoritaire.

controversial [ˌkɒntrəˈvɜːʃəl] *adj speech, action, decision* discutable, sujet à controverse; *book, suggestion* contesté, discuté. **one of the most ~ figures of his time** l'un des personnages les plus discutés de son époque.

controversy [kənˈtrɒvəsɪ] *n* controverse *f*, polémique *f*. **there was a lot of ~ about it** ça a provoqué *or* soulevé beaucoup de controverses, ça a été très contesté *or* discuté; **to cause ~** provoquer *or* soulever une controverse; **they were having a great ~** ils étaient au milieu d'une grande polémique.

controvert [ˈkɒntrəvɜːt] *vt* (*rare*) disputer, controverser.

contumacious [ˌkɒntjʊˈmeɪʃəs] *adj* rebelle, insoumis, récalcitrant.

contumacy [ˈkɒntjʊməsɪ] *n* (*resistance*) résistance *f*, opposition *f*; (*rebelliousness*) désobéissance *f*, insoumission *f*; (*Jur*) contumace *f*.

contumelious [ˌkɒntjʊˈmiːlɪəs] *adj* (*liter*) insolent, méprisant.

contumely [ˈkɒntju(ː)mlɪ] *n* (*liter*) mépris *m*.

contusion [kənˈtjuːʒən] *n* contusion *f*.

conundrum [kəˈnʌndrəm] *n* devinette *f*, énigme *f*; (*fig*) énigme.

conurbation [ˌkɒnɜːˈbeɪʃən] *n* conurbation *f*.

convalesce [ˌkɒnvəˈles] *vi* relever de maladie, se remettre (d'une maladie). **to be convalescing** être en convalescence.

convalescence [ˌkɒnvəˈlesəns] *n* convalescence *f*.

convalescent [ˌkɒnvəˈlesənt] **1** *n* convalescent(e) *m(f)*. **2** *adj* convalescent. **~ home** maison *f* de convalescence *or* de repos.

convection [kənˈvekʃən] **1** *n* convection *f*. **2** *cpd heating* à convection.

convector [kənˈvektəʳ] *n* radiateur *m* (à convection).

convene [kənˈviːn] **1** *vt* convoquer. **2** *vi* se réunir, s'assembler; *V also* **convening.**

convener [kənˈviːnəʳ] *n* président(e) *m(f)* (*de commission etc*).

convenience [kənˈviːnɪəns] *n* **1 (a)** (*U*) (*suitability, comfort*) commodité *f*. **the ~ of a modern flat** la commodité *or* le confort d'un appartement moderne; **I doubt the ~ of an office in the suburbs** je ne suis pas sûr qu'un bureau en banlieue soit pratique; **for ~'(s) sake** par souci de commodité; (*Comm*) **at your earliest ~** dans les meilleurs délais; **to find sth to one's ~** trouver qch à sa convenance; **do it at your own ~** faites-le quand cela vous conviendra; *V* **marriage.**

(b) ~s commodités *fpl*; **the house has all modern ~s** la maison a tout le confort moderne.

(c) (*Brit euph*) toilettes *fpl*, W.-C. *mpl*; *V* **public.**

2 *cpd*: **convenience foods** aliments à préparation rapide *or* vite cuisinés.

convenient [kənˈviːnɪənt] *adj tool, place* commode. **if it is ~ to you** si vous n'y voyez pas d'inconvénient, si cela ne vous dérange pas; **will it be ~ for you to come tomorrow?** est-ce que cela vous arrange *or* vous convient de venir demain?; **what would be a ~ time for you?** quelle heure vous conviendrait?; **is it ~ to see Mr X now?** peut-on voir M X tout de suite sans le déranger?; **it is not a very ~ time** le moment n'est pas très *or* trop bien choisi; **we were looking for a ~ place to stop** nous cherchions un endroit convenable *or* un bon endroit où nous arrêter; **his cousin's death was very ~ for him** la mort de sa cousine est tombée au bon moment pour lui; **the house is ~ for shops and buses** la maison est bien située pour les magasins et les autobus; **he put it down on a ~ chair** il l'a posé sur une chaise qui se trouvait (là) à portée.

conveniently [kənˈviːnɪəntlɪ] *adv* d'une manière commode, sans inconvénient. **~ situated for the shops** bien situé pour les magasins; **her aunt ~ lent her a house** sa tante lui a prêté une maison fort à propos.

convening [kənˈviːnɪŋ] **1** *adj*: **~ authority** autorité habilitée à *or* chargée de convoquer; **~ country** pays *m* hôte. **2** *n* convocation *f*.

convenor [kənˈviːnəʳ] *n* = **convener.**

convent [ˈkɒnvənt] *n* couvent *m*. **to go into a ~** entrer au couvent.

conventicle [kənˈventɪkl] *n* conventicule *m*.

convention [kənˈvenʃən] *n* (*meeting, agreement*) convention *f*; (*accepted behaviour*) usage *m*, convenances *fpl*. **according to ~** selon l'usage, selon les convenances; **there is a ~ that ladies do not dine here** l'usage veut que les dames ne puissent pas dîner ici.

conventional [kənˈvenʃənl] *adj* **(a)** *method* conventionnel, classique. **~ weapons** armes classiques. **(b)** (*slightly pej*) *person* conventionnel, conformiste; *behaviour, remarks* conventionnel, de convention, banal.

converge [kənˈvɜːdʒ] *vi* converger (*on* sur).

convergence [kənˈvɜːdʒəns] *n* convergence *f*.

convergent [kənˈvɜːdʒənt] *adj*, **converging** [kənˈvɜːdʒɪŋ] *adj* convergent. **~ thinking** raisonnement convergent.

conversant [kənˈvɜːsənt] *adj*: **to be ~ with** *car, machinery* s'y connaître en; *language, science, laws, customs* connaître; *facts* être au courant de; **I am ~ with what he said** je suis au courant de ce qu'il a dit; **I am not ~ with mathematics** je ne comprends rien aux mathématiques; **I am not ~ with sports cars** je ne m'y connais pas en voitures de sport.

conversation [ˌkɒnvəˈseɪʃən] **1** *n* conversation *f*, entretien *m*. **to have a ~ with sb** avoir une conversation *or* un entretien avec qn, s'entretenir avec qn; **I have had several ~s with him** j'ai eu plusieurs entretiens *or* conversations avec lui; **to be in ~ with** s'entretenir avec, être en conversation avec; **what was your ~ about?** de quoi parliez-vous?; **she has no ~** elle n'a aucune conversation.

2 *cpd*: (*Art*) **conversation piece** tableau *m* de genre, scène *f* d'intérieur; **her hat was a real conversation piece*** son chapeau a fait beaucoup jaser; **that was a conversation stopper*** cela a arrêté net la conversation, cela a jeté un froid sur la conversation.

conversational [ˌkɒnvəˈseɪʃənl] *adj voice, words* de la conversation; *person* qui a la conversation facile, causeur. **to speak in a ~ tone** parler sur le ton de la conversation.

conversationalist [ˌkɒnvəˈseɪʃnəlɪst] *n* causeur *m*, -euse *f*. **she's a great ~** elle a de la conversation, elle brille dans la conversation.

conversationally [ˌkɒnvəˈseɪʃnəlɪ] *adv speak* sur le ton de la conversation. **'nice day' she said ~** 'il fait beau' dit-elle du ton de quelqu'un qui cherche à entamer une conversation.

converse[1] [kənˈvɜːs] *vi* converser, causer. **to ~ with sb about sth** s'entretenir avec qn de qch, causer avec qn de qch.

converse[2] [ˈkɒnvɜːs] **1** *adj* (*opposite, contrary*) *statement* contraire, inverse; (*Math, Philos*) inverse; *proposition* inverse, réciproque. **2** *n [statement]* contraire *m*, inverse *m*; (*Math, Philos*) inverse.

conversely [kɒnˈvɜːslɪ] *adv* inversement, réciproquement. **... and ~** ... et vice versa.

conversion [kənˈvɜːʃən] **1** *n* (*U: gen, Fin, Math, Philos, Rel*) conversion *f*; (*Rugby*) transformation *f*. **the ~ of salt water into drinking water** la conversion *or* la transformation d'eau salée en eau potable; **the ~ of an old house into flats** l'aménagement *m or* l'agencement *m* d'une vieille maison en appartements; **improper ~ of funds** détournement *m* de fonds, malversations *fpl*; **his ~ to Catholicism** sa conversion au catholicisme.

2 *cpd*: **conversion table** table *f* de conversion.

convert [ˈkɒnvɜːt] **1** *n* converti(e) *m(f)*. **to become a ~ to** se convertir à.

2 [kənˈvɜːt] *vt* **(a)** convertir, transformer, changer (*into* en); (*Rel etc*) convertir (*to* à). **to ~ pounds into francs** (*on paper*) convertir des livres en francs; (*by exchanging them*) changer *or* convertir des livres en francs; (*Rugby*) **to ~ a try** transformer un essai; **he has ~ed me to his way of thinking** il m'a converti *or* amené à sa façon de penser.

(b) (*alter*) *house* arranger, aménager, agencer (*into* en). **they have ~ed one of the rooms into a bathroom** ils ont aménagé une des pièces en salle de bains.

converter [kənˈvɜːtəʳ] *n* (*Elec, Metal*) convertisseur *m*; (*Rad*) changeur *m* de fréquence.

convertibility [kənˌvɜːtəˈbɪlɪtɪ] *n* convertibilité *f*.

convertible [kənˈvɜːtəbl] **1** *adj* convertible. **2** *n* (*Aut*) (voiture *f*) décapotable *f*.

convex [ˈkɒnˈveks] *adj* convexe.

convexity [kɒnˈveksɪtɪ] *n* convexité *f*.

convey [kənˈveɪ] *vt goods, passengers* transporter; *[pipeline etc]* amener; *sound* transmettre; (*Jur*) *property* transférer, transmettre, céder (*to* à); *opinion, idea* communiquer (*to* à); *order, thanks* transmettre (*to* à). **to ~ to sb that ...** faire comprendre à qn que ...; **I couldn't ~ my meaning to him** je n'ai pas pu lui communiquer ma pensée *or* me faire comprendre de lui; **would you ~ my congratulations to him?** voudriez-vous lui transmettre mes félicitations?; **words cannot ~ how I feel** les paroles ne peuvent traduire ce que je ressens; **the name ~s nothing to me** le nom ne me dit rien; **what does this music ~ to you?** qu'est-ce que cette musique évoque pour vous?

conveyance [kənˈveɪəns] *n* **(a)** (*U*) transport *m*. **~ of goods** transport de marchandises; **means of ~** moyens *mpl* de transport. **(b)** (*vehicle*) voiture *f*, véhicule *m*. **(c)** (*Jur*) *[property]* transmission *f*, transfert *m*, cession *f*; (*document*) acte translatif (*de propriété*), acte de cession.

conveyancing [kənˈveɪənsɪŋ] *n* (*Jur*) (*procedure*) procédure translative (de propriété); (*operation*) rédaction *f* d'actes translatifs.

conveyor [kənˈveɪəʳ] *n* transporteur *m*, convoyeur *m*. (*Tech*) **~ belt** convoyeur, tapis roulant.

convict [ˈkɒnvɪkt] **1** *n* forçat *m*, bagnard *m*.

2 [kənˈvɪkt] *vt* (*Jur*) *person* déclarer *or* reconnaître coupable (*sb of a crime* qn d'un crime). **he was ~ed** il a été déclaré *or* reconnu coupable; **a ~ed murderer** un homme reconnu coupable de meurtre; **the jury will not ~** le jury ne rendra pas un verdict de culpabilité.

conviction [kənˈvɪkʃən] *n* **(a)** (*Jur*) condamnation *f*. **there were 12 ~s for drunkenness** 12 personnes ont été condamnées pour ivresse; *V* **previous, record.**

(b) (*U*) persuasion *f*, conviction *f*. **to be open to ~** être ouvert à la persuasion; **to carry ~** être convaincant; **his explanation lacked ~** son explication manquait de conviction *or* n'était pas très convaincante.

(c) (*beliefs*) **~s** convictions *fpl*; *V* **courage.**

convince [kənˈvɪns] *vt* convaincre, persuader (*sb of sth* qn de qch). **he ~d her that she should leave** il l'a persuadée de partir, il l'a convaincue qu'elle devait partir; **I am ~d he won't do it** je suis persuadé qu'il ne le fera pas.

convincing [kənˈvɪnsɪŋ] *adj speaker, argument, manner, words* persuasif, convaincant; *win, victory* décisif, éclatant.

convincingly [kən'vɪnsɪŋlɪ] *adv speak* d'un ton *or* d'une façon convaincant(e), avec conviction; *win* de façon décisive *or* éclatante.
convivial [kən'vɪvɪəl] *adj person* amateur de bonnes choses, bon vivant; *atmosphere, evening* joyeux, plein d'entrain.
conviviality [kən,vɪvɪ'ælɪtɪ] *n* jovialité *f*, gaieté *f*.
convocation [,kɒnvə'keɪʃən] *n* (*act*) convocation *f*; (*assembly*) assemblée *f*, réunion *f*; (*Rel*) assemblée, synode *m*.
convoke [kən'vəʊk] *vt* convoquer.
convoluted ['kɒnvəlu:tɪd] *adj* (*Bot*) convoluté; (*fig*) compliqué, contourné, embarrassé.
convolution [,kɒnvə'lu:ʃən] *n* circonvolution *f*.
convolvulus [kən'vɒlvjʊləs] *n* volubilis *m*, liseron *m*.
convoy ['kɒnvɔɪ] **1** *n* **(a)** (*U: Mil, Naut*) convoi *m*. (*Naut*) **to sail under** *or* **in ~** naviguer en convoi *or* de conserve; (*Mil*) **to drive in ~** rouler en convoi.
(b) (*Naut: escort*) convoyeur(s) *m(pl)*, navire(s) *m(pl)* d'escorte, escorteur(s) *m(pl)*; (*Mil, Naut: ships or vehicles under escort*) convoi *m*.
2 *vt* convoyer, escorter.
convulse [kən'vʌls] *vt* ébranler, bouleverser. **a land ~d by war** un pays bouleversé par la guerre; **a land ~d by earthquakes** un pays ébranlé par des tremblements de terre; (*fig*) **to be ~d with laughter** se tordre de rire; **a face ~d with pain** un visage décomposé *or* contracté par la douleur.
convulsion [kən'vʌlʃən] *n* **(a)** (*Med*) convulsion *f*. **to have ~s** avoir des convulsions; (*fig*) **to go into ~s of laughter** se tordre de rire. **(b)** (*violent disturbance*) *[land]* convulsion *f*, bouleversement *m*, ébranlement *m*; *[sea]* violente agitation.
convulsive [kən'vʌlsɪv] *adj movement, laughter* convulsif.
cony ['kəʊnɪ] *n* (*US*) lapin *m*; (*also* **~ skin**) peau *f* de lapin.
coo[1] [ku:] **1** *vti [doves etc]* roucouler; *[baby]* gazouiller; *V* **bill**[2]. **2** *n* roucoulement *m*, roucoulade *f*.
coo[2]** [ku:] *excl* (*Brit*) ça alors!*
cooing ['ku:ɪŋ] *n* roucoulement *m*, roucoulade *f*.
cook [kʊk] **1** *n* cuisinier *m*, -ière *f*. **she is a good ~** elle est bonne cuisinière, elle fait bien la cuisine; **to be head** *or* **chief ~ and bottle-washer*** (*in a household*) servir de bonne à tout faire; (*elsewhere*) être le factotum.
2 *cpd*: **cookbook** livre *m* de cuisine; (*Mil, Naut*) **cookhouse** cuisine *f*; (*US*) **cookout** repas *m* (cuit) en plein air.
3 *vt* **(a)** *food* (faire) cuire. (*fig*) **to ~ sb's goose*** faire son affaire à qn, régler son compte à qn.
(b) (*Brit*: falsify*) *accounts, books* truquer, maquiller.
4 *vi [food]* cuire; *[person]* faire la cuisine, cuisiner. **she ~s well** elle fait bien la cuisine, elle cuisine bien; **what's ~ing?‡** qu'est-ce qui (se) mijote?*
cook up* *vt sep story, excuse* inventer, fabriquer.
cooker ['kʊkə'] *n* **(a)** (*Brit*) cuisinière *f* (*fourneau*); *V* **gas**. **(b)** (*apple*) pomme *f* à cuire.
cookery ['kʊkərɪ] *n* cuisine *f* (*activité*). **~ book** livre *m* de cuisine.
cookie ['kʊkɪ] *n* (*US*) **(a)** (*biscuit*) petit gâteau (sec). **(b)** (‡: *person*) type* *m*.
cooking ['kʊkɪŋ] **1** *n* cuisine *f* (*activité*). **plain/French ~** cuisine bourgeoise/française.
2 *cpd utensils* de cuisine; *apples, chocolate* à cuire. **cooking foil** papier *m* d'aluminium; **cooking salt** gros sel, sel de cuisine.
cool [ku:l] **1** *adj* **(a)** *water, weather* frais (*f* fraîche); *drink* rafraîchissant. (*Met*) **it is ~** il fait frais; (*Met*) **it's turning** *or* **getting ~er** le temps se rafraîchit; **to keep in a ~ place** tenir au frais; **I feel quite ~ now** j'ai bien moins chaud maintenant; **his brow is much ~er now** il a le front bien moins chaud maintenant.
(b) (*calm, unperturbed*) *person, manner, voice* calme. **to keep ~** garder son sang-froid; **keep ~!** du calme!; **play it ~!*** pas de panique!*, ne nous emballons pas!; **to be as ~ as a cucumber** garder son calme *or* son sang-froid *or* son flegme; **'I've lost it' he said as ~ as a cucumber** 'je l'ai perdu' dit-il sans sourciller *or* sans s'émouvoir *or* en gardant tout son flegme; **she looked as ~ as a cucumber** elle affichait un calme imperturbable.
(c) (*unenthusiastic, unfriendly*) *greeting, reception* froid. **to be ~ towards sb** battre froid à qn, traiter qn avec froideur.
(d) (*: *impertinent*) *behaviour* effronté. **he's a ~ customer** il a du culot*, il n'a pas froid aux yeux; **he spoke to her as ~ as you please** il lui a parlé sans la moindre gêne; **that was very ~ of him** quel toupet (il a eu)!*
(e) (*: *emphatic*) **he earns a ~ £10,000 a year** il se fait la coquette somme de 10.000 livres par an.
2 *cpd*: **cool-headed** calme, imperturbable; **cooling-off period** période *f* de détente.
3 *n* **(a)** fraîcheur *f*, frais *m*. **in the ~ of the evening** dans la fraîcheur du soir; **to keep sth in the ~** tenir qch au frais.
(b) (‡) **keep your ~!** t'énerve pas!*; **he lost his ~** (*panicked*) il a paniqué*; (*got angry*) il s'est fichu en rogne*.
4 *vt* **(a)** *air* rafraîchir, refroidir. (*fig*) **to ~ one's heels** faire le pied de grue; **to leave sb to ~ his heels** faire attendre qn, faire poireauter* qn.
(b) ~ it!‡ t'énerve pas!*, panique pas!*
5 *vi [air, liquid]* (se) rafraîchir, refroidir.
cool down 1 *vi* (*lit*) refroidir; (*fig*) *[anger]* se calmer, s'apaiser; *[critical situation]* se détendre; (*) *[person]* se calmer. **let the situation cool down!** attendez que la situation se détende! *or* que les choses se calment! (*subj*).
2 *vt sep* (*lit*) faire refroidir; (*fig*) calmer.
cool off *vi* (*lose enthusiasm*) perdre son enthousiasme, se calmer; (*change one's affections*) se refroidir (*towards sb* à l'égard de qn, envers qn); (*become less angry*) se calmer, s'apaiser.

cooler ['ku:lə'] *n* **(a)** (*for food*) glacière *f*. **in the ~** dans la glacière. **(b)** (*Prison sl*) taule‡ *f*. **in the ~** en taule‡; **to get put in the ~** se faire mettre au frais* *or* à l'ombre*.
coolie ['ku:lɪ] *n* coolie *m*.
cooling ['ku:lɪŋ] *adj* rafraîchissant. (*Tech*) **~ tower** refroidisseur *m*.
coolly ['ku:lɪ] *adv* (*calmly*) de sang-froid, calmement; (*unenthusiastically*) froidement, avec froideur; (*impertinently*) avec impertinence, sans la moindre gêne, avec (le plus grand) culot*.
coolness ['ku:lnɪs] *n [water, air, weather]* fraîcheur *f*; *[welcome]* froideur *f*; (*calmness*) sang-froid *m*, impassibilité *f*, flegme *m*; (*impudence*) toupet* *m*, culot* *m*.
coomb [ku:m] *n* petite vallée, combe *f*.
coon [ku:n] *n* **(a)** (*Zool: abbr of* **raccoon**) raton-laveur *m*. **(b)** (*‡pej: Negro*) nègre *m*.
coop [ku:p] **1** *n* (*also* **hen ~**) poulailler *m*, cage *f* à poules. **2** *vt hens* enfermer dans un poulailler.
coop up *vt sep person* claquemurer, cloîtrer, enfermer; *feelings* refouler.
co-op ['kəʊ'ɒp] *n* (*abbr of* **cooperative**) coopérative *f*, coop* *f*.
cooper ['ku:pə'] *n* tonnelier *m*.
cooperage ['ku:pərɪdʒ] *n* tonnellerie *f*.
cooperate [kəʊ'ɒpəreɪt] *vi* coopérer, collaborer (*with sb in sth* avec qn à qch). **I hope he'll ~** j'espère qu'il va se montrer coopératif; **everything ~d to make the visit successful** tout a contribué *or* concouru à faire de la visite un succès.
cooperation [kəʊ,ɒpə'reɪʃən] *n* coopération *f*, concours *m*. **in ~ with, with the ~ of** avec la coopération *or* le concours de.
cooperative [kəʊ'ɒpərətɪv] **1** *adj person, firm, attitude* coopératif. (*Comm etc*) **~ society** coopérative *f*, société coopérative *or* mutuelle; (*Can Pol*) **C~ Commonwealth Federation** parti *m* social démocratique (*Can*). **2** *n* coopérative *f*.
coopt [kəʊ'ɒpt] *vt* coopter (*onto* à).
coordinate [kəʊ'ɔ:dnɪt] **1** *adj* (*gen, Gram, Math*) coordonné. **~ geometry** géométrie *f* analytique. **2** *n* **(a)** (*gen, Math*) coordonnée *f*. **(b)** (*Dress*) **~s** ensemble *m* (coordonné), coordonnés *mpl*. **3** [kəʊ'ɔ:dɪneɪt] *vt* coordonner (*one thing with another* une chose avec une autre).
coordination [kəʊ,ɔ:dɪ'neɪʃən] *n* coordination *f*.
coordinator [kəʊ'ɔ:dɪneɪtə'] *n* coordinateur *m*, -trice *f*.
coot [ku:t] *n* **(a)** (*Orn*) foulque *f*; *V* **bald**. **(b)** (‡: *fool*) tourte* *f*.
cop‡ [kɒp] **1** *n* **(a)** (*policeman*) flic‡ *m*. **to play at ~s and robbers** jouer aux gendarmes et aux voleurs.
(b) (*Brit*) **it's no great ~*, it's not much ~*** ça ne vaut pas grand-chose *or* tripette.
2 *vt* pincer*, piquer‡. **to get ~ped** se faire piquer‡; (*Brit*) **to ~ it** écoper*, trinquer‡.
cop out‡ *vi* se défiler*.
copartner ['kəʊ'pɑ:tnə'] *n* coassocié(e) *m(f)*, coparticipant(e) *m(f)*.
copartnership ['kəʊ'pɑ:tnəʃɪp] *n* (*Fin*) société *f* en nom collectif; (*gen*) coassociation *f*, coparticipation *f*.
cope[1] [kəʊp] *n* (*Dress Rel*) chape *f*.
cope[2] [kəʊp] *vi* se débrouiller, s'en tirer. **to ~ with** *task, difficult person* se charger de, s'occuper de; *situation* faire face à; *difficulties, problems* (*tackle*) affronter; (*solve*) venir à bout de; **they ~ with 500 applications a day** 500 formulaires leur passent entre les mains chaque jour; **you get the tickets, I'll ~ with the luggage** va chercher les billets, moi je m'occupe *or* je me charge des bagages; **I'll ~ with him** je m'occupe *or* me charge de lui; **can you ~?** ça ira?, vous y arriverez?, vous vous débrouillerez?; **leave it to me, I'll ~** laissez cela, je m'en charge *or* je m'en occupe; **how are you coping without a secretary?** vous arrivez à vous débrouiller sans secrétaire?; **he's coping pretty well** il s'en tire *or* se débrouille très bien; **I can ~ in Spanish** je me débrouille en espagnol; **she just can't ~ any more** (*she's overworked etc*) elle ne s'en sort plus; (*work is too difficult for her*) elle n'est plus du tout dans la course*, elle est complètement dépassée.
Copenhagen [,kəʊpn'heɪgən] *n* Copenhague.
Copernicus [kə'pɜ:nɪkəs] *n* Copernic *m*.
copestone ['kəʊpstəʊn] *n* (*Archit*) couronnement *m*; *[wall]* chaperon *m*; (*fig*) *[career etc]* couronnement, point culminant.
copier ['kɒpɪə'] *n* machine *f* à photocopier.
co-pilot ['kəʊ'paɪlət] *n* (*Aviat*) copilote *m*, pilote *m* auxiliaire.
coping ['kəʊpɪŋ] *n* chaperon *m*. **~ stone = copestone**.
copious ['kəʊpɪəs] *adj food* copieux; *amount* ample, abondant; *harvest* abondant; *writer* fécond; *letter* prolixe.
copiously ['kəʊpɪəslɪ] *adv* copieusement.
copper ['kɒpə'] **1** *n* **(a)** (*U*) cuivre *m*.
(b) (*money*) **~s** la petite monnaie; **I gave the beggar a ~** j'ai donné une petite pièce au mendiant.
(c) (*washtub*) lessiveuse *f*.
(d) (*: *policeman*) flic‡ *m*. **~'s nark** indic‡ *m*, mouchard* *m*.
2 *cpd mine* de cuivre; *wire, bracelet* de *or* en cuivre. **copper beech** hêtre *m* pourpre; **copper-coloured** cuivré; (*in engraving*) **copperplate** (*n*) planche *f* (de cuivre) gravée; (*adj*) sur cuivre, en taille-douce; **copperplate handwriting** écriture moulée, belle ronde; **coppersmith** chaudronnier *m* (en cuivre).
coppery ['kɒpərɪ] *adj* cuivré.
coppice ['kɒpɪs] *n* taillis *m*, hallier *m*.
copra ['kɒprə] *n* copra *m*.
copse [kɒps] *n* = **coppice**.
copula ['kɒpjʊlə] *n* (*Gram*) copule *f*.
copulate ['kɒpjʊleɪt] *vi* copuler.
copulation [,kɒpjʊ'leɪʃən] *n* copulation *f*.
copulative ['kɒpjʊlətɪv] *adj* (*Gram*) copulatif.
copy ['kɒpɪ] **1** *n* **(a)** *[painting etc]* copie *f*, reproduction *f*; *[letter, document, memo]* copie; (*Phot: print*) épreuve *f*. **to take** *or*

make a ~ of sth faire une copie de qch; *V* **carbon, fair¹, rough** *etc.*

(b) *[book]* exemplaire *m*; *[magazine, newspaper]* exemplaire, numéro *m*; *V* **author, presentation.**

(c) (*U*) *[newspaper etc]* copie *f*, sujet *m* d'article, matière *f* à reportage; *[advertisement]* message *m*, texte *m*. **it gave him ~ for several articles** cela lui a fourni la matière de *or* un sujet pour *or* de la copie pour plusieurs articles; **that's always good ~** c'est un sujet qui rend toujours bien; **the murder will make good ~** le meurtre fera de l'excellente copie; **the journalist handed in his ~** le journaliste a remis son article *or* papier*; **they are short of ~** ils sont à court de copie.

2 *cpd*: **copybook** (*n*) cahier *m* (*V* **blot**); (*adj*) (*trite*) banal; (*ideal, excellent*) modèle; **copycat‡** copieur *m*, -ieuse *f*; (*Press*) **copy editor** secrétaire *mf* de rédaction; **copying ink** encre *f* à copier; **copy machine** machine *f* à photocopier; **copy press** presse *f* à copier; (*US Press*) **copyreader** secrétaire *mf* de rédaction; **copyright** *V* **copyright**; **copywriter** rédacteur *m*, -trice *f* publicitaire.

3 *vt* **(a)** (*also* **~ out**) *letter, passage from book* copier.

(b) (*imitate*) *person, gestures* copier, imiter.

(c) (*Scol etc*) *sb else's work* copier. **he copied in the exam** il a copié à l'examen.

copyist ['kɒpɪɪst] *n* copiste *mf*, scribe *m*.

copyright ['kɒpɪraɪt] **1** *n* droit *m* d'auteur, copyright *m*. **~ reserved** tous droits (de reproduction) réservés; **out of ~** dans le domaine public. **2** *vt book* obtenir les droits exclusifs sur *or* le copyright de.

coquetry ['kɒkɪtrɪ] *n* coquetterie *f*.

coquette [kə'ket] *n* coquette *f*.

coquettish [kə'ketɪʃ] *adj person* coquet, provocant; *look* aguichant, provocant.

cor‡ [kɔːʳ] *excl* (*Brit: also* **~ blimey**) mince alors!*

coracle ['kɒrəkl] *n* coracle *m*, canot *m* (d'osier).

coral ['kɒrəl] **1** *n* corail *m*. **2** *cpd necklace* de corail; *island* coralien; (*also* **coral-coloured**) (couleur) corail *inv*. (*liter*) **her coral lips** ses lèvres de corail; **coral reef** récif *m* de corail.

cord [kɔːd] **1** *n* **(a)** *[curtains, pyjamas etc]* cordon *m*; *[windows]* corde *f*; *[parcel etc]* ficelle *f*; (*US Elec*) cordon *or* fil *m* électrique; (*Anat: also* **umbilical ~**) cordon ombilical; *V* **spinal, vocal.**

(b) (*U: Tex*) = **corduroy.**

2 *cpd trousers* en velours côtelé. **cord carpet** tapis *m* de corde.

3 *vt* (*tie*) corder.

cordage ['kɔːdɪdʒ] *n* (*U*) cordages *mpl*.

corded ['kɔːdɪd] *adj fabric* côtelé.

cordial ['kɔːdɪəl] **1** *adj person, atmosphere* cordial; *welcome* chaleureux. **2** *n* cordial *m*.

cordiality [ˌkɔːdɪ'ælɪtɪ] *n* cordialité *f*.

cordially ['kɔːdɪəlɪ] *adv* cordialement. **I ~ detest him** je le déteste cordialement.

cordon ['kɔːdn] **1** *n* (*all senses*) cordon *m*. **~ bleu** cordon bleu. **2** *vt* (*also* **~ off**) *crowd* tenir à l'écart (*au moyen d'un cordon de police etc*); *area* interdire l'accès à (*au moyen d'un cordon de police etc*).

corduroy ['kɔːdərɔɪ] **1** *n* (*Tex*) velours côtelé. **~s** pantalon *m* en velours côtelé. **2** *cpd trousers, jacket* en velours côtelé; (*US*) *road* de rondins.

core [kɔːʳ] **1** *n* *[fruit]* trognon *m*, cœur *m*; *[magnet]* noyau *m*; *[cable]* âme *f*, noyau; (*Chem: of atom*) noyau enveloppé de son *or* ses électron(s); *[nuclear reactor]* cœur *m*; (*fig: of problem etc*)essentiel *m*. **apple ~** trognon de pomme; **the earth's ~** le noyau terrestre; (*fig*) **he is rotten to the ~** il est pourri jusqu'à l'os; **English to the ~** anglais jusqu'à la moelle (des os); *V* **hard.**

2 *vt fruit* enlever le trognon *or* le cœur de.

co-religionist ['kəʊrɪ'lɪdʒənɪst] *n* coreligionnaire *mf*.

corer [kɔːrəʳ] *n* (*Culin*) vide-pomme *m*.

co-respondent ['kəʊrɪs'pɒndənt] *n* (*Jur*) co-défendeur *m*, -deresse *f* (*d'un adultère*).

coriander [ˌkɒrɪ'ændəʳ] *n* coriandre *f*.

Corinthian [kə'rɪnθɪən] **1** *adj* corinthien. **2** *n* Corinthien(ne) *m(f)*.

Coriolanus ['kɒrɪə'leɪnəs] *n* Coriolan *m*.

cork [kɔːk] **1** *n* **(a)** (*U*) liège *m*.

(b) (*in bottle etc*) bouchon *m*. **to pull the ~ out of a bottle** déboucher une bouteille; (*Fishing: also* **~ float**) flotteur *m*, bouchon.

2 *vt* (*also* **~ up**) *bottle* boucher.

3 *cpd mat, tiles, flooring* de liège. **cork oak** = **cork tree**; **corkscrew** tire-bouchon *m*; **corkscrew curls** frisettes *fpl*; **cork-tipped** à bout de liège; **cork tree** chêne-liège *m*.

corkage ['kɔːkɪdʒ] *n* **(a)** (*U*) (*corking*) bouchage *m*; (*uncorking*) débouchage *m*. **(b)** (*charge*) droit *m* de bouchon (*payé par le client qui apporte dans un restaurant une bouteille achetée ailleurs*).

corked [kɔːkt] *adj wine* qui sent le bouchon.

corker‡ ['kɔːkəʳ] *n* (*lie*) mensonge *m* de taille, gros mensonge; (*story*) histoire fumante*; (*Sport: shot, stroke*) coup fumant*; (*player*) crack* *m*; (*girl*) beau morceau (de fille). **that's a ~!** ça vous en bouche un coin!*

corking*† ['kɔːkɪŋ] *adj* (*Brit*) épatant*†, fameux*, fumant*.

corm [kɔːm] *n* bulbe *m* (*de crocus etc*).

cormorant ['kɔːmərənt] *n* cormoran *m*.

corn¹ [kɔːn] **1** *n* **(a)** (*seed*) grain *m* (*de céréale*).

(b) (*Brit*) blé *m*; (*US*) maïs *m*. **~ on the cob** épi *m* de maïs.

(c) (*‡ pej*) salade* *f*, baratin* *m*.

2 *cpd*: (*US*) **corncob** épi *m* de maïs; (*Orn*) **corncrake** râle *m* des genêts; **corn crops** céréales *fpl*; **corn exchange** halle *f* au blé; **cornfield** (*Brit*) champ *m* de blé; (*US*) champ de maïs; **cornflakes** céréales *fpl*, cornflakes *fpl*; **cornflour** farine *f* de maïs, maïzena *f* ®; **cornflower** (*n*) bleuet *m*, barbeau *m*; (*adj*) (*also* **cornflower blue**) bleu vif *inv*, bleu barbeau *inv*; **corn oil** huile *f* de maïs; (*US*) **cornstarch** = **cornflour**; (*US*) **corn whiskey** whisky *m* (de maïs), bourbon *m*.

corn² [kɔːn] *n* (*Med*) cor *m*. (*Brit fig*) **to tread on sb's ~s** toucher qn à l'endroit sensible, blesser qn dans son amour-propre; (*Med*) **~ plaster** pansement *m* (*pour cors*).

cornea ['kɔːnɪə] *n* cornée *f*.

corneal ['kɔːnɪəl] *adj* cornéen.

corned ['kɔːnd] *adj*: **~ beef** corned-beef *m*.

cornelian [kɔː'niːlɪən] *n* cornaline *f*.

corner ['kɔːnəʳ] **1** *n* *[page, field, eye, mouth]* coin *m*; *[street, box, table]* coin, angle *m*; *[room]* coin, encoignure *f*, angle; (*Aut*) tournant *m*, virage *m*. **to put a child in the ~** mettre un enfant au coin; (*fig*) **to drive sb into a ~** mettre qn au pied du mur, coincer* qn; (*fig*) **to be in a (tight) ~** être dans le pétrin, être dans une situation difficile, être coincé*; **to look at sb out of the ~ of one's eye** regarder qn du coin de l'œil; **it's just round the ~** c'est à deux pas d'ici; **you'll find the church round the ~** vous trouverez l'église juste après le coin; **the little shop around the ~** la petite boutique du coin; **to take a ~** (*Aut*) prendre un tournant; (*Ftbl*) faire un corner; **in every ~ of the garden** dans tout le jardin; **treasures hidden in odd ~s** des trésors cachés dans des recoins; **in every ~ of the house** dans tous les coins et recoins de la maison; (*fig*) **in every ~ of Europe** dans toute l'Europe; **in (all) the four ~s of the earth** aux quatre coins du monde *or* de la planète; (*Fin*) **to make a ~ in wheat** accaparer le marché du blé; *V* **cut, turn** *etc.*

2 *vt* acculer; (*fig*) coincer*. (*Fin*) **to ~ the market** accaparer le marché; **she ~ed me in the hall** elle m'a coincé* dans l'entrée; (*fig*) **he's got you ~ed** il t'a coincé*, il t'a mis au pied du mur.

3 *vi* (*Aut*) prendre un virage.

4 *cpd*: **corner cupboard** placard *m* de coin; **corner flag** (*Ftbl*) piquet *m* de coin; (*flagstone in roadway*) dalle *f* de coin; **the corner house** la maison du coin, la maison qui fait l'angle (de la rue); (*Ftbl*) **corner kick** corner *m*; (*Rail*) **corner seat** (place *f* de) coin *m*; **corner shop** boutique *f* du coin; **the house has a corner situation** la maison fait l'angle; **cornerstone** (*lit, fig*) pierre *f* angulaire; (*foundation stone*) première pierre; **cornerways fold** pli *m* en triangle.

cornering ['kɔːnərɪŋ] *n* (*Aut*) façon *f* de prendre les virages.

cornet ['kɔːnɪt] *n* **(a)** (*Mus*) cornet *m* (à pistons). **~ player** cornettiste *mf*. **(b)** (*Brit*) *[sweets etc]* cornet *m*; *[ice cream]* cornet (de glace).

cornice ['kɔːnɪs] *n* corniche *f*.

Cornish ['kɔːnɪʃ] *adj* de Cornouailles, cornouaillais.

cornucopia [kɔːnjʊ'kəʊpɪə] *n* corne *f* d'abondance.

Cornwall ['kɔːnwəl] *n* (comté *m* de) Cornouailles *f*.

corny‡ ['kɔːnɪ] *adj joke, story* rebattu, galvaudé, banal.

corolla [kə'rɒlə] *n* corolle *f*.

corollary [kə'rɒlərɪ] *n* corollaire *m*.

corona [kə'rəʊnə] *n* (*Anat, Astron*) couronne *f*; (*Elec*) couronne électrique; (*Archit*) larmier *m*.

coronary ['kɒrənərɪ] **1** *adj* (*Anat*) coronaire. **~ thrombosis** infarctus *m* du myocarde, thrombose *f* coronarienne. **2** *n* (*Med*, *) infarctus *m*.

coronation [ˌkɒrə'neɪʃən] **1** *n* (*ceremony*) couronnement *m*; (*actual crowning*) sacre *m*. **2** *cpd ceremony, oath, robe* du sacre; *day* du couronnement.

coroner ['kɒrənəʳ] *n* coroner *m* (*officiel chargé de déterminer les causes d'un décès*). **~'s inquest** enquête *f* judiciaire (*menée par le coroner*); **~'s jury** jury *m* (*siégeant avec le coroner*).

coronet ['kɒrənɪt] *n* *[duke etc]* couronne *f*; *[lady]* diadème *m*.

corporal¹ ['kɔːpərəl] *n* *[infantry]* caporal-chef *m*; *[cavalry etc]* brigadier-chef *m*.

corporal² ['kɔːpərəl] *adj* corporel. **~ punishment** châtiment corporel.

corporate ['kɔːpərɪt] *adj* **(a)** (*of a corporation*) *property* appartenant à une corporation. **~ name** raison sociale.

(b) (*of members of a group*) *action, ownership* en commun. **~ responsibility** personnalité morale (*d'un groupement*).

(c) (*united in one group*) constitué (en corporation). **~ body** corps constitué.

corporation [ˌkɔːpə'reɪʃən] **1** *n* **(a)** *[town]* conseil municipal. **the Mayor and C~** le corps municipal, la municipalité.

(b) (*Comm, Fin*) société commerciale; (*US*) société à responsabilité limitée, compagnie commerciale.

(c) (*Brit**) bedaine* *f*, brioche* *f*. **to develop a ~** prendre de la bedaine* *or* de la brioche*.

2 *cpd* (*Brit*) *school, property* de la ville, municipal. (*Brit, US*) **corporation tax** impôt *m* sur les bénéfices.

corporeal [kɔː'pɔːrɪəl] *adj need* corporel, physique; *property* matériel.

corps [kɔːʳ] *n*, *pl* **corps** [kɔːz] corps *m*. **~ de ballet** corps de ballet; *V* **army, diplomatic** *etc.*

corpse [kɔːps] *n* cadavre *m*, corps *m*.

corpulence ['kɔːpjʊləns] *n* corpulence *f*, embonpoint *m*.

corpulent ['kɔːpjʊlənt] *adj* corpulent.

corpus ['kɔːpəs] *n* (*Literat*) corpus *m*, recueil *m*; (*Ling*) corpus; (*Fin*) capital *m*. (*Rel*) **C~ Christi** la Fête-Dieu.

corpuscle ['kɔːpʌsl] *n* **(a)** (*Anat, Bio*) corpuscule *m*. **(blood) ~** globule sanguin; **red/white ~s** globules rouges/blancs. **(b)** (*Phys*) électron *m*.

corral [kə'rɑːl] (*US*) **1** *n* corral *m*. **2** *vt cattle* enfermer dans un corral; (**fig*) pousser (en troupeau).

correct [kə'rekt] **1** *adj* **(a)** (*right, exact*) *answer, amount* correct, exact, juste; *temperature* exact; *forecast, estimate* correct. **have you the ~ time?** avez-vous l'heure exacte?; **the**

predictions proved ~ les prédictions se sont avérées justes; **am I ~ in thinking ...?** ai-je raison de penser ...?; **you are quite ~** vous avez parfaitement raison; **he was quite ~ to do it** il a eu tout à fait raison de le faire.

(b) (*seemly, suitable*) *person, behaviour, manners, language* correct, convenable; *dress* correct, bienséant. **~ dress must be worn** une tenue correcte est exigée; **it's the ~ thing** c'est l'usage, c'est ce qui se fait; **the ~ procedure** la procédure d'usage.

2 *vt* **(a)** *piece of work, text, manuscript* corriger; *error* rectifier, corriger; (*Typ*) *proofs* corriger. **to ~ sb's punctuation/spelling** corriger la ponctuation/l'orthographe de qn.

(b) (*put right*) *person* reprendre, corriger. **he ~ed me several times during the course of my speech** il m'a repris plusieurs fois pendant mon discours; **I stand ~ed** je reconnais mon erreur; **~ me if I'm wrong** corrigez-moi si je me trompe.

(c) (††: punish) réprimander, reprendre.

correction [kəˈrekʃən] *n* **(a)** (*U*) *[proofs, essay]* correction *f*; *[error]* correction, rectification *f*. **I am open to ~, but ...** corrigez-moi si je me trompe, mais ... .

(b) *[school work, proof]* correction *f*; *[text, manuscript]* correction, rectification *f*. **a page covered with ~s** une page couverte de corrections.

(c) (††: punishment) correction *f*, châtiment *m*. **house of ~**†† maison *f* de correction†.

corrective [kəˈrektɪv] *adj action* rectificatif; (*Jur, Med*) *measures, training* de rééducation, correctif.

correctly [kəˈrektlɪ] *adv* (*V* **correct**) correctement, d'une manière exacte, avec justesse; convenablement.

correctness [kəˈrektnɪs] *n* (*V* **correct**) correction *f*, exactitude *f*, justesse *f*; bienséance *f*.

correlate [ˈkɒrɪleɪt] **1** *vi* correspondre (*with* à), être en corrélation (*with* avec). **2** *vt* mettre en corrélation (*with* avec).

correlation [ˌkɒrɪˈleɪʃən] *n* corrélation *f*.

correlative [kɒˈrelətɪv] **1** *n* corrélatif *m*. **2** *adj* corrélatif.

correspond [ˌkɒrɪsˈpɒnd] *vi* **(a)** (*agree*) correspondre (*with* à), s'accorder (*with* avec). **that does not ~ with what he said** cela ne correspond pas à ce qu'il a dit.

(b) (*be similar, equivalent*) correspondre (*to* à), être l'équivalent (*to* de). **this ~s to what she was doing last year** ceci est semblable *or* correspond à ce qu'elle faisait l'année dernière; **his job ~s roughly to mine** son poste équivaut à peu près au mien *or* est à peu près l'équivalent du mien.

(c) (*exchange letters*) correspondre (*with* avec). **they ~** ils s'écrivent, ils correspondent.

correspondence [ˌkɒrɪsˈpɒndəns] **1** *n* (*V* **correspond**) **(a)** correspondance *f* (*between* entre, *with* avec).

(b) (*letter-writing*) correspondance *f*. **to be in ~ with sb** entretenir une *or* être en correspondance avec qn; **to read one's ~** lire son courrier *or* sa correspondance.

2 *cpd*: **correspondence card** carte-lettre *f*; **correspondence college** établissement *m* d'enseignement par correspondance; (*Press*) **correspondence column** courrier *m* (des lecteurs); **correspondence course** cours *m* par correspondance.

correspondent [ˌkɒrɪsˈpɒndənt] *n* (*gen, Comm, Press*) correspondant(e) *m(f)*. **foreign/sports ~** correspondant étranger/sportif; *V* **special.**

corresponding [ˌkɒrɪsˈpɒndɪŋ] *adj* correspondant. **~ to the original** conforme à l'original; **for a ~ period** pendant une période analogue *or* semblable.

correspondingly [ˌkɒrɪsˈpɒndɪŋlɪ] *adv* (*as a result*) en conséquence; (*proportionately*) proportionnellement.

corridor [ˈkɒrɪdɔːʳ] *n* couloir *m*, corridor *m*. (*Brit*) **~ train** train *m* à couloir.

corroborate [kəˈrɒbəreɪt] *vt* corroborer, confirmer.

corroboration [kəˌrɒbəˈreɪʃən] *n* confirmation *f*, corroboration *f*. **in ~ of** à l'appui de, en confirmation de.

corroborative [kəˈrɒbərətɪv] *adj* qui confirme *or* corrobore.

corrode [kəˈrəʊd] **1** *vt metal* corroder, attaquer, ronger; (*fig*) attaquer, corroder. **2** *vi [metals]* se corroder.

corrosion [kəˈrəʊʒən] *n* corrosion *f*.

corrosive [kəˈrəʊzɪv] **1** *adj* corrosif. **2** *n* corrosif *m*.

corrugated [ˈkɒrəgeɪtɪd] *adj* ridé, plissé; *road, surface* ondulé. **~ cardboard/paper** carton/papier ondulé; **~ iron** tôle ondulée.

corrupt [kəˈrʌpt] **1** *adj* **(a)** *person, action, behaviour* (*evil, immoral*) corrompu, dépravé; (*dishonest*) vénal. **~ practices** (*dishonesty*) tractations *fpl* malhonnêtes; (*Jur: bribery etc*) trafic *m* d'influence, malversations *fpl*; **a ~ society** une société corrompue *or* pourrie; **~ tastes** des goûts pervers.

(b) (*decaying, putrid*) vicié, corrompu.

(c) (*incorrect*) *text* altéré.

2 *vt person, morals* corrompre, dépraver, pervertir; (*bribe*) corrompre, soudoyer; *text* altérer.

corruption [kəˈrʌpʃən] *n* (*V* **corrupt**) corruption *f*; dépravation *f*; altération *f*.

corsage [kɔːˈsɑːʒ] *n* (*bodice*) corsage *m*; (*flowers*) petit bouquet (*de fleurs porté au corsage*).

corsair [ˈkɔːsɛəʳ] *n* (*ship, pirate*) corsaire *m*, pirate *m*.

corset [ˈkɔːsɪt] *n* (*Dress: also* **~s**) corset *m*; (*lightweight*) gaine *f*; (*Surgery*) corset.

Corsica [ˈkɔːsɪkə] *n* Corse *f*.

Corsican [ˈkɔːsɪkən] **1** *adj* corse. **2** *n* Corse *mf*.

cortège [kɔːˈtɛːʒ] *n* cortège *m*.

cortex [ˈkɔːteks] *n, pl* **cortices** [ˈkɔːtɪsiːz] (*Bot*) cortex *m*, écorce *f*; (*Anat*) cortex.

cortisone [ˈkɔːtɪzəʊn] *n* cortisone *f*.

corundum [kəˈrʌndəm] *n* corindon *m*.

coruscate [ˈkɒrəskeɪt] *vi* briller, scintiller.

coruscating [ˈkɒrəskeɪtɪŋ] *adj* (*fig*) *wit, humour* brillant, scintillant.

corvette [kɔːˈvet] *n* (*Naut*) corvette *f*.

cos[1] [kɒs] *n* (*Brit: lettuce*) (laitue *f*) romaine *f*.

cos[2] [kɒs] *n abbr of* **cosine.**

cosh [kɒʃ] (*Brit*) **1** *vt*(*) taper sur, cogner* sur (*gén avec un gourdin*). **2** *n* gourdin *m*, matraque *f*.

cosignatory [ˈkəʊˈsɪgnətərɪ] *n* cosignataire *mf*.

cosine [ˈkəʊsaɪn] *n* cosinus *m*.

cosiness [ˈkəʊzɪnɪs] *n* (*V* **cosy**) atmosphère douillette, confort *m*.

cosmetic [kɒzˈmetɪk] **1** *adj surgery* plastique, esthétique; *preparation* cosmétique. **2** *n* cosmétique *m*, produit *m* de beauté.

cosmic [ˈkɒzmɪk] *adj* (*lit*) cosmique; (*fig*) immense, incommensurable. **~ dust/rays** poussière *f*/rayons *mpl* cosmique(s).

cosmogony [kɒzˈmɒgənɪ] *n* cosmogonie *f*.

cosmographer [kɒzˈmɒgrəfəʳ] *n* cosmographe *mf*.

cosmography [kɒzˈmɒgrəfɪ] *n* cosmographie *f*.

cosmology [kɒzˈmɒlədʒɪ] *n* cosmologie *f*.

cosmonaut [ˈkɒzmənɔːt] *n* cosmonaute *mf*.

cosmopolitan [ˌkɒzməˈpɒlɪtən] *adj, n* cosmopolite (*mf*).

cosmos [ˈkɒzmɒs] *n* cosmos *m*.

Cossack [ˈkɒsæk] *n* cosaque *m*.

cosset [ˈkɒsɪt] *vt* dorloter, choyer.

cost [kɒst] **1** *vt* **(a)** (*pret, ptp* **cost**) (*lit, fig*) coûter. **how much** *or* **what does the dress ~?** combien coûte *or* vaut la robe?; **how much** *or* **what will it ~ to have it repaired?** combien est-ce que cela coûtera de le faire réparer?; **what does it ~ to get in?** quel est le prix d'entrée?; **it ~ him a lot of money** cela lui a coûté cher; **it ~s him £6 a week** cela lui revient à *or* lui coûte 6 livres par semaine, il en a pour 6 livres par semaine; **it ~s too much** cela coûte trop cher, c'est trop cher; **it ~s the earth*** cela coûte les yeux de la tête; **it ~ him a great effort** cela lui a coûté *or* demandé un gros effort; **it ~ him a lot of trouble** cela lui a causé beaucoup d'ennuis; **it will ~ you your life** il vous en coûtera la vie; **it will ~ you a present!** vous en serez quitte pour lui (*or* me *etc*) faire un cadeau!; **politeness ~s very little** il ne coûte rien d'être poli; (*fig*) **~ what it may, whatever it ~s** coûte que coûte.

(b) (*pret, ptp* **~ed**) (*Comm*) *articles for sale* établir le prix de revient de; *piece of work* évaluer le coût de. **the job was ~ed at £200** le devis pour (l'exécution de) ces travaux s'est monté à 200 livres.

2 *n* coût *m*. **the ~ of these apples** le coût *or* le prix de ces pommes; **to bear the ~ of** (*lit*) faire face aux frais *mpl or* aux dépenses *fpl* de; (*fig*) faire les frais de; (*lit, fig*) **at great ~** à grands frais; **at little ~** à peu de frais; (*fig*) **at little ~ to himself** sans que cela lui coûte (*subj*) beaucoup; **at ~ (price)** au prix coûtant; (*Jur*) **~s** dépens *mpl*, frais *mpl* judiciaires; (*Jur*) **to be ordered to pay ~s** être condamné aux dépens; (*fig*) **at all ~s, at any ~** coûte que coûte, à tout prix; **at the ~ of his life/health** au prix de sa vie/santé; (*fig*) **to my ~** à mes dépens; *V* **count**[1].

3 *cpd*: **cost-effective** rentable; **cost of living** coût *m* de la vie; **cost-of-living allowance** indemnité *f* de vie chère; **cost-of-living index** index *m* du coût de la vie; **cost plus** prix *m* de revient majoré du pourcentage contractuel; **cost price** prix coûtant *or* de revient.

co-star [ˈkəʊstɑːʳ] (*Cine, Theat*) **1** *n* partenaire *mf*. **2** *vi* partager l'affiche (*with* avec). '**~ring X**' 'avec X'.

Costa Rica [ˈkɒstəˈriːkə] *n* Costa Rica *m*.

Costa Rican [ˈkɒstəˈriːkən] **1** *adj* costaricain. **2** *n* Costaricain(e) *m(f)*.

coster [ˈkɒstəʳ] *n*, **costermonger** [ˈkɒstəˌmʌŋgəʳ] *n* (*Brit*) marchand(e) *m(f)* des quatre saisons.

costing [ˈkɒstɪŋ] *n* estimation *f* du prix de revient.

costive [ˈkɒstɪv] *adj* constipé.

costliness [ˈkɒstlɪnɪs] *n* (*value*) (grande) valeur; (*high price*) cherté *f*.

costly [ˈkɒstlɪ] *adj furs, jewels* de grande valeur, précieux; *undertaking, trip* coûteux; *tastes, habits* dispendieux, de luxe (*hum*).

costume [ˈkɒstjuːm] **1** *n* **(a)** (*U: style of dress, clothes*) costume *m*. **national ~** costume national; (*fancy dress*) **in ~** déguisé. **(b)** (*lady's suit*) tailleur *m*; (*fancy dress*) déguisement *m*, costume *m*. **2** *cpd*: **costume ball** bal masqué; **costume jewellery** bijoux *mpl* (de) fantaisie; (*Theat*) **costume play** pièce *f* historique (*en costume d'époque*).

costumier [kɒsˈtjuːmɪəʳ] *n*, (*esp US*) **costumer** [kɒsˈtjuːməʳ] *n* costumier *m*, -ière *f*.

cosy, (*US*) **cozy** [ˈkəʊzɪ] **1** *adj room* douillet, confortable; *atmosphere* douillet. **we are very ~ here** nous sommes très bien ici; **it is ~ in here** il fait bon ici; **a ~ little corner** un petit coin intime.

2 *adv* (*fig*) **to play it ~**‡ y aller mollo‡.

3 *n* (*tea* ~) couvre-théière *m*; (*egg* ~) couvre-œuf *m*.

4 *vi* (*esp US*) **to ~ up to sb**‡ faire de la lèche à qn‡.

cot [kɒt] *n* (*esp Brit*) lit *m* d'enfant, petit lit; (*US*) lit *m* de camp.

coterie [ˈkəʊtərɪ] *n* coterie *f*, cénacle *m*, cercle *m*.

cotillion [kəˈtɪljən] *n* cotillon *m*, quadrille *f*.

cottage [ˈkɒtɪdʒ] **1** *n* petite maison (à la campagne), cottage *m*; (*thatched*) chaumière *f*; (*in holiday village etc*) villa *f*.

2 *cpd*: **cottage cheese** fromage blanc (*maigre*); (*Brit*) **cottage hospital** petit hôpital; **cottage industry** industrie *f* à domicile; (*Brit*) **cottage loaf** miche *f*, pain *m* de ménage.

cottager [ˈkɒtɪdʒəʳ] *n* (*Brit*) paysan(ne) *m(f)*; (*US*) propriétaire *mf* de maison de vacances.

cottar, cotter [ˈkɒtəʳ] *n* (*Scot*) paysan(ne) *m(f)*.

cotton [ˈkɒtn] **1** *n* (*U*) (*Bot, Tex*) coton *m*; (*sewing thread*) fil *m* (de coton); *V* **absorbent.**

2 *cpd shirt, dress* de coton. (*US*) **cotton batting** = **cotton wool**; (*Agr*) **the cotton belt** la région de culture du coton; **cotton cake** tourteau *m* de coton; (*US*) **cotton candy** barbe à papa *f*; **cotton goods** cotonnades *fpl*; **cotton grass** linaigrette *f*, lin *m* des marais; **cotton industry** industrie cotonnière *or* du coton; **cotton lace** dentelle *f* de coton; **cotton mill** filature *f* de coton; **cottonseed oil** huile *f* de coton; (*US*) **cottontail** lapin *m*; **cotton waste** déchets *mpl* de coton, coton *m* d'essuyage; (*Brit*) **cotton wool** ouate *f*; **absorbent cotton wool** ouate *f or* coton *m* hydrophile; (*fig*) **to bring up a child in cotton wool** élever un enfant dans du coton; **my legs felt like cotton wool*** j'avais les jambes en coton; **cotton yarn** fil *m* de coton.

cotton on* *vi* piger*. **to cotton on to sth** piger qch, saisir qch.

cotton to‡ *vt fus person* avoir à la bonne‡; *plan, suggestion* apprécier, approuver. **I don't cotton to it much** je ne suis pas tellement pour*, ça ne me botte pas tellement!‡

cotyledon [ˌkɒtɪ'li:dən] *n* cotylédon *m*.

couch [kaʊtʃ] **1** *n* **(a)** (*settee*) canapé *m*, divan *m*, sofa *m*; (*bed*) lit *m*, couche *f* (*Literat, Poetry*).

(b) (*Bot: also* ~ **grass**) chiendent *m*.

2 *vt* formuler, exprimer. **request ~ed in insolent language** requête formulée *or* exprimée en des termes insolents; **request ~ed in the following terms** demande ainsi rédigée.

3 *vi [animal]* (*lie asleep*) être allongé *or* couché; (*ready to spring*) s'embusquer.

cougar ['ku:gər] *n* couguar *m or* cougouar *m*.

cough [kɒf] **1** *n* toux *f*. **to give sb a warning** ~ tousser pour avertir qn; **he has a (bad)** ~ il a une mauvaise toux, il tousse beaucoup.

2 *cpd*: **cough drop, cough lozenge** pastille *f* pour la toux; **cough mixture** sirop *m* pour la toux.

3 *vi* tousser.

cough out *vt sep* expectorer, cracher en toussant.

cough up* *vt sep* (*fig*) *money* cracher*.

could [kʊd] *pret, cond of* **can**[1].

couldn't ['kʊdnt] = **could not**; *V* **can**[1].

council ['kaʊnsl] **1** *n* conseil *m*, assemblée *f*. ~ **of war** conseil de guerre; **city** *or* **town** ~ conseil municipal; **they decided in** ~ **that ...** l'assemblée a décidé que ...; **the Security C~ of the U.N.** le conseil de Sécurité des Nations Unies; *V* **lord, parish, privy.**

2 *cpd*: **council flat** appartement loué à la municipalité, ≃ habitation *f* à loyer modéré, H.L.M. *m or f*; **council house** maison louée à la municipalité; **council housing** logements sociaux; **council housing estate** *or* **scheme** quartier *m* de logements sociaux, (*high rise*) ≃ grand ensemble; **councilman** membre *m* d'un conseil, conseiller *m*.

councillor ['kaʊnsɪlər] *n* conseiller *m*, -ère *f*, membre *m* d'un conseil. (*form of address*) **C~ X** Monsieur le conseiller municipal X, Madame la conseillère municipale X; *V* **privy, town.**

counsel ['kaʊnsəl] **1** *n* **(a)** (*U*) consultation *f*, conseil *m*, délibération *f*. **to take** ~ **with sb** prendre conseil de qn, consulter qn; **to keep one's own** ~ garder ses intentions *or* projets *or* ses opinions pour soi.

(b) (*pl inv: Jur*) avocat(e) *m(f)*. ~ **for the defence** (avocat de la) défense *f*; (*Brit*) ~ **for the prosecution** avocat du ministère public; **King's** *or* **Queen's C~** avocat de la couronne (*qui peut néanmoins plaider pour des particuliers*); *V* **defending, prosecute.**

2 *vt* (*frm, liter*) recommander, conseiller (*sb to do* à qn de faire). **to** ~ **caution** recommander la prudence.

counsellor, (*US also*) **counselor** ['kaʊnslər] *n* **(a)** conseiller *m*, -ère *f*; (*in social work, career guidance*) orienteur *m*; *V* **student. (b)** (*Ir, US: also* **~-at-law**) avocat *m*.

count[1] [kaʊnt] **1** *n* **(a)** compte *m*, dénombrement *m*, calcul *m*; *[votes at election]* dépouillement *m*. **to make a** ~ faire un compte; **at the last** ~ (*gen*) la dernière fois qu'on a compté; (*Admin*) au dernier recensement; (*Boxing*) **to be out for the ~, to take the** ~ être (mis) knock-out, aller au tapis pour le compte; **to be out for the ~*** être K.-O.*; **to keep (a)** ~ **of** tenir le compte de; (*fig*) **to take no** ~ **of** ne pas tenir compte de; **every time you interrupt you make me lose** ~ chaque fois que tu m'interromps je perds le fil; **I've lost** ~ je ne sais plus où j'en suis; **I've lost** ~ **of the number of times I've told you** je ne sais plus combien de fois je te l'ai dit; **he lost** ~ **of the tickets he had sold** il ne savait plus combien de billets il avait vendus.

(b) (*Jur*) chef *m* d'accusation. **guilty on 3 ~s** coupable à 3 chefs.

2 *cpd*: **countdown** compte *m* à rebours; **counting house** comptabilité *f* (*bureau*).

3 *vt* **(a)** (*add up*) compter; *inhabitants, injured, causes* dénombrer; *one's change etc* compter, vérifier. **to** ~ **the eggs in the basket** compter les œufs dans le panier; (*Admin, Pol*) **to** ~ **the votes** dépouiller le scrutin; (*Prov*) **don't** ~ **your chickens (before they're hatched)** il ne faut pas vendre la peau de l'ours (avant de l'avoir tué) (*Prov*); (*fig*) **to** ~ **sheep** compter les moutons; **to** ~ **the cost** (*lit*) compter *or* calculer la dépense; (*fig*) faire le bilan; (*lit, fig*) **without ~ing the cost** sans compter; **(you must)** ~ **your blessings** estimez-vous heureux; *V* **stand.**

(b) (*include*) compter. **10 people not ~ing the children** 10 personnes sans compter les enfants; **three more ~ing him** trois de plus lui inclus *or* compris; **to** ~ **sb among one's friends** compter qn parmi ses amis; **do not** ~ **his youth against him** ne lui faites pas grief de sa jeunesse; **will you** ~ **it against me if I refuse?** m'en tiendrez-vous rigueur *or* m'en voudrez-vous si je refuse?

(c) (*consider*) tenir, estimer. **to** ~ **sb as dead** tenir qn pour mort; **we must** ~ **ourselves fortunate** nous devons nous estimer heureux; **I** ~ **it an honour to help you** je m'estime honoré de pouvoir vous aider.

4 *vi* **(a)** compter. **can he ~?** est-ce qu'il sait compter?; **~ing from tonight** à compter de ce soir; **~ing from the left** à partir de la gauche.

(b) (*be considered*) compter. **you** ~ **among my best friends** vous comptez parmi *or* au nombre de mes meilleurs amis; **two children** ~ **as one adult** deux enfants comptent pour un adulte; **that doesn't** ~ cela ne compte pas.

(c) (*have importance*) compter. **every minute ~s** chaque minute compte, il n'y a pas une minute à perdre; **his lack of experience ~s against him** son inexpérience est un désavantage *or* un handicap; **that ~s for nothing** cela ne compte pas, cela compte pour du beurre*; **he ~s for a lot in that firm** il joue un rôle important dans cette compagnie; **a university degree ~s for very little nowadays** de nos jours un diplôme universitaire n'a pas beaucoup de valeur *or* ne pèse pas lourd*.

count down 1 *vi* faire le compte à rebours.

2 countdown *n V* **count**[1] **2.**

count in* *vt sep* compter. **to count sb in on a plan** inclure qn dans un projet; **you can count me in!** je suis de la partie!

count out *vt sep* **(a)** (*Boxing*) **to be counted out** être mis knock-out, être envoyé *or* aller au tapis pour le compte.

(b) *money* compter pièce par pièce; *small objects* compter, dénombrer.

(c) you can count me out of* this business ne comptez pas sur moi dans cette affaire.

(d) (*Parl etc*) **to count out a meeting** ajourner une séance (*le quorum n'étant pas atteint*); (*Brit*) **to count out the House** ajourner la séance (*du Parlement*).

count up *vt sep* faire le compte de, compter, additionner.

count (up)on *vt fus* compter (sur). **I'm counting (up)on you** je compte sur vous; **to count (up)on doing** compter faire.

count[2] [kaʊnt] *n* (*nobleman*) comte *m*.

countable ['kaʊntəbl] *adj* qui peut être compté, nombrable. (*Gram*) ~ **noun** substantif distributif.

countenance ['kaʊntɪnəns] **1** *n* **(a)** (*frm, liter: face, expression*) mine *f*, figure *f*, expression *f* (du visage). **out of** ~ décontenancé; **to keep one's** ~ ne pas se laisser décontenancer.

(b) (*approval*) **to give** ~ **to** *person* encourager; *plan* favoriser; *rumour, piece of news* accréditer.

2 *vt* approuver, admettre.

counter[1] ['kaʊntər] *n* **1 (a)** (*in shop, canteen*) comptoir *m*; (*position: in bank, post office etc*) guichet *m*; (*in pub*) comptoir *m*, zinc* *m*. **the girl behind the** ~ (*in shop*) la vendeuse; (*in pub*) la serveuse; (*fig*) **to buy/sell under the** ~ acheter/vendre clandestinement; **it was all very under the ~*** tout ceci se faisait sous le manteau *or* très en-dessous *or* très en sous-main.

(b) (*disc*) jeton *m*, fiche *f*.

(c) (*Tech*) compteur *m*; *V* **Geiger counter** *etc*.

2 *cpd*: **counter hand** (*in shop*) vendeur *m*, -euse *f*; (*in snack bar*) serveur *m*, -euse *f*.

counter[2] ['kaʊntər] **1** *adv*: ~ **to** à l'encontre de, à l'opposé de, contrairement à; **to go or run** ~ **to** aller à l'encontre de.

2 *vt decision, order* aller à l'encontre de, s'opposer à; *plans* contrecarrer, contrarier; *blow* parer.

3 *vi* (*fig*) contre-attaquer, riposter; (*Boxing, Fencing etc*) (parer un coup et) riposter. **he ~ed with a right** il a riposté par un droit.

counter ... ['kaʊntər] *pref* contre .... (*Mil, fig*) **~-attack** (*n*) contre-attaque *f*; (*vti*) contre-attaquer; **~-attraction** attraction rivale, spectacle rival; **~check** (*n*) deuxième contrôle *m or* vérification *f*; (*vt*) revérifier; (*Jur*) **~claim** demande reconventionnelle; **~-clockwise** en sens inverse des aiguilles d'une montre; **~-espionage** contre-espionnage *m*; **~-gambit** contre-gambit *m*; **~intelligence** contre-espionnage *m*; (*Med*) **~irritant** révulsif *m*; **~-measure** mesure défensive, contre-mesure *f*; (*Mil*) **~-move** mouvement *m* en contre-attaque, retour offensif; (*Mil*) **~-offensive** contre-offensive *f*; **~-order** contrordre *m*; (*Comm, Ind*) **~-productive** qui entrave la productivité; (*fig*) **that is ~-productive** c'est inefficace *or* improductif, ça ne donne rien; (*Hist*) **C~-Reformation** Contre-Réforme *f*; **~-revolution** contre-révolution *f*; **~-revolutionary** (*adj, n*) contre-révolutionnaire (*mf*); (*lit, fig*) **~-stroke** retour offensif; (*Mus*) **~tenor** (*singer*) haute-contre *m*; (*voice*) haute-contre *f*; **~weight** contrepoids *m*.

counteract [ˌkaʊntə'rækt] *vt influence, effect* neutraliser, contrebalancer.

counterbalance ['kaʊntəˌbæləns] **1** *n* contrepoids *m*. **2** *vt* contrebalancer, faire contrepoids à.

counterblast ['kaʊntəblɑ:st] *n* réfutation *f or* démenti *m* énergique.

countercharge ['kaʊntətʃɑ:dʒ] *n* (*Jur*) contre-accusation *f*.

counterfeit ['kaʊntəfi:t] **1** *adj* faux (*f* fausse). ~ **coin/money** fausse pièce/monnaie. **2** *n* faux *m*, contrefaçon *f*. **3** *vt banknote, signature* contrefaire. **to** ~ **money** fabriquer de la fausse monnaie.

counterfoil ['kaʊntəfɔɪl] *n [cheque etc]* talon *m*, souche *f*.

countermand ['kaʊntəmɑ:nd] *vt order* annuler. **unless ~ed** sauf contrordre.

counterpane ['kaʊntəpeɪn] *n* (*quilt*) courtepointe *f*, couvre-pieds *m inv*; (*bedspread*) dessus-de-lit *m inv*.

counterpart ['kaʊntəpɑ:t] *n [document etc]* (*duplicate*) double *m*, contrepartie *f*; (*equivalent*) équivalent *m*; *[person]* homologue *mf*.

counterpoint ['kaʊntəpɔɪnt] *n* (*Mus*) contrepoint *m*.

counterpoise ['kaʊntəpɔɪz] **1** *n* (*weight, force*) contrepoids *m*; (*equilibrium*) équilibre *m*. **in** ~ en équilibre. **2** *vt* contrebalancer, faire contrepoids à.

countersign ['kaʊntəsaɪn] **1** *vt* contresigner. **2** *n* mot *m* de passe *or* d'ordre.

countersink ['kaʊntəsɪŋk] *vt hole* fraiser; *screw* noyer.

countess ['kaʊntɪs] *n* comtesse *f*.

countless ['kaʊntlɪs] *adj* innombrable, sans nombre. **on ~ occasions** je ne sais combien de fois.

countrified ['kʌntrɪfaɪd] *adj* rustique, campagnard.

country ['kʌntrɪ] **1** *n* **(a)** pays *m*. **the different countries of the world** les divers pays du monde; **the ~ wants peace** le pays désire la paix; (*Brit Pol*) **to go to the ~** appeler le pays aux urnes.

(b) (*native land*) patrie *f*. **to die for one's ~** mourir pour la patrie; *V* **old.**

(c) (*U: as opposed to town*) campagne *f*. **in the ~** à la campagne; **the ~ round the town** les environs *mpl* de la ville; **the surrounding ~** la campagne environnante; **to live off the ~** vivre des produits de la terre.

(d) (*U: region*) pays *m*, région *f*. **there is some lovely ~ to the north** il y a de beaux paysages dans le nord; **mountainous ~** région montagneuse; **this is good fishing ~** c'est une bonne région pour la pêche; **this is unknown ~ to me** (*lit*) je ne connais pas la région; (*fig*) je suis en terrain inconnu; *V* **open.**

2 *cpd* de (la) campagne. (*US Mus*) **country and western** musique *f* américaine du Middle West; **country born** né à la campagne; **country bred** élevé à la campagne; (*pej*) **country bumpkin** péquenaud(e)*: *m(f)* (*pej*), cul-terreux* *m* (*pej*); **country club** club *m* de loisirs (*à la campagne*); **country cottage** petite maison (à la campagne); *[weekenders]* maison de campagne; (*fig*) **country cousin** cousin *m* de province; **country dancing** danse *f* folklorique; **to go country dancing** danser (des danses folkloriques); **country dweller** campagnard(e) *m(f)*; **country folk** gens *mpl* de la campagne, campagnards *mpl*, ruraux *mpl*; **country gentleman** gentilhomme campagnard; **country house** manoir *m*, (petit) château *m*; **country life** vie *f* de la *or* à la campagne, vie campagnarde; **countryman** (*also* **fellow countryman**) compatriote *m*, concitoyen *m*; (*opposed to town dweller*) habitant *m* de la campagne, campagnard *m*; **country people** campagnards *mpl*, gens *mpl* de la campagne; **country road** petite route (de campagne); **country seat** château *m*; **the countryside** la campagne; **country-wide** qui englobe tout le pays, qui couvre toute l'étendue du pays; **countrywoman** (*also* **fellow countrywoman**) compatriote *f*, concitoyenne *f*; (*opposed to town dweller*) habitante *f* de la campagne, campagnarde *f*.

county ['kaʊntɪ] **1** *n* **(a)** comté *m* (*division administrative*); *V* **home.**

(b) (*people*) habitants *mpl* d'un comté. (*Brit: nobility etc*) **the ~** l'aristocratie terrienne (*du comté*).

2 *adj* (*Brit: often pej*) *voice, accent* aristocratique. **he's very ~** il est *or* fait très hobereau; **she's very ~** elle est *or* fait très aristocratie terrienne.

3 *cpd:* (*US*) **county agent** ingénieur-agronome *m*; (*US*) **county seat,** (*esp Brit*) **county town** chef-lieu *m*.

coup [ku:] *n* (beau) coup *m* (*fig*); (*Pol*) coup d'État.

couple ['kʌpl] **1** *n [animals, people]* couple *m*. **to hunt in ~s** aller par deux; **the young (married) ~** les jeunes mariés *or* époux, le jeune ménage, le jeune couple; **a ~ of** deux; **I've seen him a ~ of times** je l'ai vu deux ou trois fois; **I did it in a ~ of hours** je l'ai fait en deux heures environ; **we had a ~* in the bar** nous avons pris un verre ou deux au bar; **when he's had a ~* he begins to sing** quand il a un verre dans le nez* il se met à chanter.

2 *vt* (*also* **~ up**) *railway carriages* atteler, (ac)coupler; *ideas, names* associer, accoupler.

3 *vi* (*mate*) s'accoupler.

coupler ['kʌplə^r] *n* (*US Rail*) attelage *m*.

couplet ['kʌplɪt] *n* distique *m*.

coupling ['kʌplɪŋ] *n* **(a)** (*U*) accouplement *m*, association *f*. **(b)** (*device*) (*Rail*) attelage *m*; (*Elec*) couplage *m*.

coupon ['ku:pɒn] *n [newspaper advertisements etc]* coupon *m* (*détachable*); *[cigarette packets etc]* bon *m*, prime *f*, vignette *f*; (*Comm: offering temporary price reductions*) bon de réduction; (*rationing*) ticket *m*, bon; (*Fin*) coupon, bon; *V* **football, international.**

courage ['kʌrɪdʒ] *n* courage *m*. **I haven't the ~ to refuse** je n'ai pas le courage de refuser, je n'ose pas refuser; **to take/lose ~** prendre/perdre courage; **to take ~ from sth** être encouragé par qch; **to have the ~ of one's convictions** avoir le courage de ses opinions; **to take one's ~ in both hands** prendre son courage à deux mains; *V* **Dutch, pluck up.**

courageous [kə'reɪdʒəs] *adj* courageux.

courageously [kə'reɪdʒəslɪ] *adv* courageusement.

courier ['kʊrɪə^r] *n* (*messenger*) courrier *m*, messager *m*; (*tourist guide*) guide *m*, cicérone *m*.

course [kɔ:s] **1** *n* **(a)** (*duration, process*) *[life, events, time, disease]* cours *m*. **in (the) ~ of time** à la longue, avec le temps; **in the ordinary ~ of things** *or* **events** normalement, en temps normal *or* ordinaire; **in the ~ of conversation** au cours *or* dans le courant de la conversation; **a house in (the) ~ of construction** une maison en cours de construction; **it is in (the) ~ of being investigated** c'est en cours d'investigation; **in the ~ of centuries** au cours des siècles; **in the ~ of the next few months** pendant les *or* au cours des prochains mois; **in the ~ of time** finalement, un beau jour; **in the ~ of the week** dans le courant de la semaine; **did he do it? — of ~!/of ~ not!** est-ce qu'il l'a fait? — bien entendu! *or* naturellement!/bien sûr que non!; **may I take it? — of ~!/of ~ not!** est-ce que je peux le prendre? — bien sûr! *or* mais oui!/certainement pas!; **of ~ I won't do it!** je ne vais évidemment pas faire ça!; **you'll come on Saturday of ~** il va sans dire que *or* bien entendu vous venez samedi; *V* **due, matter.**

(b) (*direction, way, route*) *[river]* cours *m*, lit *m*; *[ship]* route *f*; *[planet]* cours. **to keep** *or* **hold one's ~** poursuivre sa route; (*Naut*) **to hold (one's) ~** suivre son chemin; (*Naut*) **to set ~ for** mettre le cap sur; (*Naut*) **to change ~** changer de cap; (*Naut, fig*) **to go off ~** faire fausse route; **to take a certain ~ of action** adopter une certaine ligne de conduite; **we have no other ~ but to ...** nous n'avons d'autre moyen *or* ressource que de ..., aucune autre voie ne s'offre à nous que de ...; **there are several ~s open to us** plusieurs partis s'offrent à nous; **what ~ do you suggest?** quel parti (nous) conseillez-vous de prendre?; **let him take his own ~** laissez-le agir à sa guise *or* faire comme il veut; **the best ~ would be to leave at once** la meilleure chose *or* le mieux à faire serait de partir immédiatement; **to let sth take its ~** laisser qch suivre son cours, laisser qch prendre son cours naturel; **the affair/the illness has run its ~** l'affaire/la maladie a suivi son cours; *V* **middle.**

(c) (*Scol, Univ*) cours *m*. **to go to a French ~** suivre un cours *or* des cours de français; **he gave a ~ of lectures on Proust** il a donné une série de conférences sur Proust; **I have bought part two of the German ~** j'ai acheté la deuxième partie de la méthode *or* du cours d'allemand; (*Med*) **~ of treatment** traitement *m*; *V* **correspondence.**

(d) (*Sport*) terrain *m*, piste *f*; *V* **golf, race[1], stay[1]** *etc.*

(e) (*Culin*) plat *m*. **first ~** entrée *f*; *V* **main.**

(f) (*Constr*) assise *f* (*de briques etc*); *V* **damp.**

(g) (*Naut*) **~s** basses voiles.

2 *vi* **(a)** *[water etc]* couler à flots. **tears ~d down her cheeks** les larmes ruisselaient sur ses joues; **it sent the blood coursing through his veins** cela lui fouetta le sang.

(b) (*Sport*) chasser (le lièvre).

3 *vt* (*Sport*) *hare* courir, chasser.

courser ['kɔ:sə^r] *n* (*person*) chasseur *m* (*gén de lièvres*); (*dog*) chien courant; (*liter: horse*) coursier *m* (*liter*).

coursing ['kɔ:sɪŋ] *n* (*Sport*) chasse *f* au lièvre.

court [kɔ:t] **1** *n* **(a)** (*Jur*) cour *f*, tribunal *m*. (*Brit*) **~ of appeal,** (*US*) **~ of appeals** cour d'appel; **~ of enquiry** commission *f* d'enquête; **~ of justice** palais *m* de justice; (*Scot*) **C~ of Session** cour de cassation; **to settle a case out of ~** arranger une affaire à l'amiable; **to rule sth out of ~** déclarer qch inadmissible; **to take sb to ~ over** *or* **about sth** poursuivre *or* actionner qn en justice à propos de qch; **he was brought before the ~s several times** il est passé plusieurs fois en jugement; **to clear the ~** faire évacuer la salle; *V* **high, law.**

(b) *[monarch]* cour *f* (royale). **the C~ of St James** la cour de Saint-James; **to be at ~** (*for short time*) être à la cour; (*for long time*) faire partie de la cour.

(c) to pay ~ to a woman faire sa *or* la cour à une femme.

(d) (*Tennis*) court *m*. **they've been on ~ for 2 hours** cela fait 2 heures qu'ils jouent.

(e) (*also* **~yard**) cour *f*; (*passage between houses*) ruelle *f*, venelle *f*.

2 *cpd:* (*esp Brit*) **court card** figure *f* (*de jeu de cartes*); **court circular** bulletin quotidien de la cour; (*Jur*) **courthouse** palais *m* de justice, tribunal *m*; **a courting couple** un couple d'amoureux; (*Jur*) **court room** salle *f* de tribunal; (*Brit*) **court shoe** escarpin *m*; **courtyard** cour *f* (*de maison, de château*).

3 *vt woman* faire la *or* sa cour à, courtiser; *sb's favour* solliciter, rechercher; *danger, defeat* aller au-devant de, s'exposer à.

4 *vi:* **they are ~ing*** ils sortent ensemble; **are you ~ing?*** tu as un petit copain* (*or* une petite amie*)?

Courtelle [kɔ:'tel] *n* ® Courtelle *m* ®.

courteous ['kɜ:tɪəs] *adj* courtois, poli (*towards* envers).

courteously ['kɜ:tɪəslɪ] *adv* d'une manière courtoise, courtoisement, poliment.

courtesan [ˌkɔ: ɪ'zæn] *n* courtisane *f* (*liter*).

courtesy ['kɜ:tɪsɪ] **1** *n* courtoisie *f*, politesse *f*. **you might have had the ~ to explain yourself** vous auriez pu avoir la politesse de vous expliquer; **will you do me the ~ of reading it?** auriez-vous l'obligeance de le lire?; **exchange of courtesies** échange *m* de politesses; **by ~ of** avec la permission de.

2 *cpd:* **courtesy call** visite *f* de politesse; (*US*) **courtesy card** carte *f* de priorité (*utilisable dans les hôtels, banques etc*); (*Aut*) **courtesy light** plafonnier *m*; **courtesy title** titre *m* de courtoisie; **courtesy visit = courtesy call.**

courtier ['kɔ:tɪə^r] *n* courtisan *m*, dame *f* de la cour.

courtly ['kɔ:tlɪ] *adj* élégant, raffiné. (*Hist Literat*) **~ love** amour courtois.

court-martial ['kɔ:t'mɑ:ʃəl] **1** *n, pl* **courts-martial** (*Mil*) conseil *m* de guerre. **to be tried by ~** passer en conseil de guerre. **2** *vt* traduire *or* faire passer en conseil de guerre.

courtship ['kɔ:tʃɪp] *n:* **his ~ of her** la cour qu'il lui fait (*or* faisait *etc*); **during their ~** au temps où ils sortaient ensemble.

cousin ['kʌzn] *n* cousin(e) *m(f)*; *V* **country, first** *etc.*

cove[1] [kəʊv] *n* (*Geog*) crique *f*, anse *f*.

cove[2]‡ [kəʊv] *n* (*Brit: fellow*) mec‡ *m*.

covenant ['kʌvɪnənt] **1** *n* (*gen*) convention *f*, engagement formel; (*Fin*) obligation contractuelle; (*Jewish Hist*) alliance *f*; (*Scot Hist*) covenant *m* (*de 1638*); *V* **deed.**

2 *vt* s'engager (*to do* à faire), convenir (*to do* de faire). (*Fin*) **to ~ (to pay) £10 per annum to a charity** s'engager par obligation contractuelle à verser 10 livres par an à une œuvre.

3 *vi* convenir (*with sb for sth* de qch avec qn).

covenanter ['kʌvɪnəntə^r] *n* (*Scot Hist*) covenantaire *mf* (*adhérent au covenant de 1638*).

Coventry ['kɒvəntrɪ] *n* Coventry. (*Brit fig*) **to send sb to ~** mettre qn en quarantaine, boycotter qn.

cover ['kʌvə^r] **1** *n* **(a)** *[saucepan, bowl]* couvercle *m*; *[dish]* couvercle, dessus-de-plat *m inv*; *[table]* nappe *f*; *[umbrella]* (*fabric*) étoffe *f*; (*case*) fourreau *m*; (*for folding type*) étui *m*; (*over furniture, typewriter*) housse *f*; (*over merchandise, vehicle etc*) bâche *f*; (*bed~*) dessus-de-lit *m inv*; *[book]* couverture *f*; (*envelope*) enveloppe *f*; *[parcel]* emballage *m*. (*bedclothes*) **the ~s** les couvertures *fpl*; **to read a book from ~ to ~** lire un livre de la première à la dernière page; (*Comm*) **under separate ~** sous pli séparé; *V* **first, loose, plain.**

(b) (*shelter*) abri *m*; (*Hunting: for game*) fourré *m*, couvert *m*, abri; (*Mil etc: covering fire*) feu *m* de couverture *or* de protection. (*Mil, gen*) **there was no ~ for miles around** il n'y avait pas d'abri à des kilomètres à la ronde; **he was looking for some ~** il cherchait un abri; **the trees gave him ~** (*lit*) les arbres le cachaient; (*sheltered*) les arbres l'abritaient; (*to soldier etc*) **give me ~!** couvrez-moi!; **to take ~** (*hide*) se cacher; (*Mil*) s'embusquer; (*shelter*) s'abriter, se mettre à l'abri; **to take ~ from the rain/the bombing** se mettre à l'abri *or* s'abriter de la pluie/des bombes; (*Mil*) **to take ~ from enemy fire** se mettre à l'abri du feu ennemi; **under ~** à l'abri, à couvert; **to get under ~** se mettre à l'abri *or* à couvert; **under ~ of darkness** à la faveur de la nuit; **under ~ of friendship** sous le masque de l'amitié; *V* **break.**

(c) (*Fin*) couverture *f*, provision *f*; (*Brit: Insurance*) couverture. (*Fin*) **to operate without ~** opérer à découvert; (*Brit: Insurance*) **full ~** garantie totale *or* tous risques; **fire ~** assurance-incendie *f*.

(d) (*in espionage etc*) fausse identité. **what's your ~?** quelle est votre identité d'emprunt?

(e) (*at table*) couvert *m*. **~s laid for 6** une table de 6 couverts.

2 *cpd*: (*Dress*) **coveralls** bleu(s) *m(pl)* de travail, combinaison *f* (*d'ouvrier etc*); *[restaurant]* **cover charge** couvert *m*; **covergirl** cover-girl *f*; (*Brit: Insurance*) **cover note** = récépissé *m* (d'assurance); **cover story** (*Press*) article principal (*illustré en couverture*); (*in espionage etc*) couverture *f*; **cover-up** les tentatives faites pour étouffer l'affaire.

3 *vt* **(a)** (*gen*) *object, person* couvrir (*with* de); *book, chair* recouvrir, couvrir (*with* de). **snow ~s the ground** la neige recouvre le sol; **ground ~ed with leaves** sol couvert de feuilles; **he ~ed the paper with writing** il a couvert la page d'écriture; **the car ~ed us in mud** la voiture nous a couverts de boue; **to ~ one's eyes** se protéger les yeux; **to ~ one's face with one's hands** se couvrir le visage des mains; **~ed with confusion/ridicule** couvert de confusion/de ridicule; **to ~ o.s. with glory** se couvrir de gloire.

(b) (*hide*) *feelings, facts* dissimuler, cacher; *noise* couvrir.

(c) (*protect*) *person* couvrir, protéger. **the soldiers ~ed our retreat** les soldats ont couvert notre retraite; (*Insurance*) **to be ~ed against fire** être assuré contre l'incendie; **he only said that to ~ himself** il n'a dit cela que pour se couvrir.

(d) (*point gun at*) *person* braquer un revolver sur. **to keep sb ~ed** tenir qn sous la menace du revolver; **I've got you ~ed!** ne bougez pas ou je tire!

(e) (*Sport*) *opponent* marquer.

(f) *distance* parcourir, couvrir. **we ~ed 8 km in 2 hours** nous avons parcouru *or* couvert 8 km en 2 heures; **to ~ a lot of ground** (*lit*) faire beaucoup de chemin; (*fig*) (*in breadth*) traiter un large éventail de questions; (*in quantity*) faire du bon travail.

(g) (*be sufficient for*) couvrir; (*take in, include*) englober, traiter, comprendre. **his work ~s many different fields** son travail englobe *or* embrasse plusieurs domaines différents; **the book ~s the subject thoroughly** le livre traite le sujet à fond; **the article ~s the 18th century** l'article traite tout le 18e siècle; **his speech ~ed most of the points raised** dans son discours il a traité la plupart des points en question; **in order to ~ all possibilities** pour parer à toute éventualité; **to ~ one's costs** *or* **expenses** rentrer dans ses frais; **£5 will ~ everything** 5 livres payeront tout *or* suffiront à couvrir toutes les dépenses; **to ~ a deficit/a loss** combler un déficit/une perte.

(h) (*Press*) *news, story, scandal* assurer la couverture de; *lawsuit* faire le compte rendu de. **he was sent to ~ the riots** on l'a envoyé assurer le reportage des émeutes.

(i) *[animal]* couvrir.

4 *vi* (*US*) = **cover up 1b.**

cover in *vt sep trench, grave* remplir.

cover over *vt sep* recouvrir.

cover up 1 *vi* **(a)** se couvrir. **it's cold, cover up warmly** il fait froid, couvre-toi chaudement.

(b) to cover up for sb couvrir qn, protéger qn.

2 *vt sep* **(a)** *child, object* recouvrir, envelopper (*with* de).

(b) (*hide*) *truth, facts* dissimuler, cacher, étouffer. **to cover up one's tracks** (*lit*) couvrir sa marche; (*fig*) couvrir sa marche, brouiller les pistes.

3 cover-up *n V* **cover 2.**

coverage ['kʌvərɪdʒ] *n* **(a)** (*Press, Rad, TV*) reportage *m*. (*Press, Rad, TV*) **to give full ~ to an event** assurer la couverture complète d'un événement, traiter à fond un événement; **the match got nationwide ~** (*Rad*) le reportage du match a été diffusé sur l'ensemble du pays; (*TV*) le match a été retransmis *or* diffusé sur l'ensemble du pays; (*Press*) **it got full-page ~ in the main dailies** les principaux quotidiens y ont consacré une page entière.

(b) (*Insurance*) couverture *f*.

covering ['kʌvərɪŋ] **1** *n* (*wrapping etc*) couverture *f*, enveloppe *f*; (*of snow, dust etc*) couche *f*. **2** *adj*: **~ letter** lettre explicative; (*Mil*) **~ fire** feu *m* de protection *or* de couverture.

coverlet ['kʌvəlɪt] *n* dessus-de-lit *m inv*, couvre-lit *m*.

covert ['kʌvət] **1** *adj threat* voilé, caché; *attack* indirect; *glance* furtif, dérobé. **2** *n* (*Hunting*) fourré *m*, couvert *m*; (*animal's hiding place*) gîte *m*, terrier *m*.

covet ['kʌvɪt] *vt* convoiter.

covetous ['kʌvɪtəs] *adj person, attitude, nature* avide; *look* de convoitise. **to cast ~ eyes on sth** regarder qch avec convoitise.

covetously ['kʌvɪtəslɪ] *adv* avec convoitise, avidement.

covetousness ['kʌvɪtəsnɪs] *n* convoitise *f*, avidité *f*.

covey ['kʌvɪ] *n* compagnie *f* (*de perdrix*).

cow¹ [kaʊ] **1** *n* **(a)** vache *f*; (*female of elephant etc*) femelle *f*. (*fig*) **till the ~s come home*** jusqu'à la Trinité (*fig*), jusqu'au jour où les poules auront des dents*; (*fig*) **to wait till the ~s come home*** attendre la semaine des quatre jeudis*.

(b) (*‡pej: woman*) rosse* *f*, vache* *f*, chameau* *m*.

2 *cpd*: **cow elephant/buffalo** *etc* éléphant *m*/buffle *m etc* femelle; **cowbell** sonnaille *f*, clochette *f* (à bestiaux); **cowboy** cow-boy *m*; **to play cowboys and Indians** jouer aux cow-boys; **cowboy hat** chapeau *m* de cow-boy, feutre *m* à larges bords; (*Rail*) **cowcatcher** chasse-pierres *m inv*; (*US Scol*) **cow college*** boîte *f* dans le bled*; **cowherd** vacher *m*, bouvier *m*; **cowhide** (*n*) (*skin*) peau *f* de vache; (*US: whip*) fouet *m* (à lanière de cuir); (*vt: US*) fouetter (avec une lanière de cuir); **cowlick** mèche *f* (sur le front); (*Brit*) **cowman** = **cowherd**; (*Bot*) **cow parsley** cerfeuil *m* sauvage; **cowpox** variole *f* de la vache; **cowpox vaccine** vaccin *m* antivariolique; (*US*) **cowpuncher*** = **cowboy**; **cowshed** étable *f*; (*Bot*) **cowslip** coucou *m*, primevère *f*.

cow² [kaʊ] *vt person* effrayer, intimider. **a ~ed look** un air de chien battu.

coward ['kaʊəd] *n* lâche *mf*, poltron(ne) *m(f)*.

cowardice ['kaʊədɪs] *n*, **cowardliness** ['kaʊədlɪnɪs] *n* lâcheté *f*.

cowardly ['kaʊədlɪ] *adj person* lâche, poltron; *action, words* lâche.

cower ['kaʊə^r] *vi* (*also* **~ down**) se tapir, se recroqueviller. (*fig*) **to ~ before sb** trembler devant qn.

cowl [kaʊl] *n* **(a)** (*Dress*) *[monk etc]* capuchon *m* (*de moine*); *[penitent]* cagoule *f*. **(b)** *[chimney]* capuchon *m*.

co-worker ['kəʊ'wɜːkə^r] *n* collègue *mf*, camarade *mf* (de travail).

cowrie, cowry ['kaʊrɪ] *n* porcelaine *f* (*mollusque*).

cox [kɒks] **1** *n* barreur *m*. **2** *vt boat* barrer, gouverner. **3** *vi* barrer.

coxcomb† ['kɒkskəʊm] *n* fat *m*, poseur *m*, muscadin† *m*.

coxswain ['kɒksn] *n* (*Rowing*) barreur *m*; (*Naut*) patron *m*.

coy [kɔɪ] *adj* (*affectedly shy*) *person* qui joue à *or* fait l'effarouché(e), qui fait le *or* la timide; *smile* de sainte nitouche (*pej*); (*coquettish*) *woman* qui fait la coquette.

coyly ['kɔɪlɪ] *adv* (*V* **coy**) avec une timidité feinte; avec coquetterie.

coyness ['kɔɪnɪs] *n* (*V* **coy**) airs effarouchés, timidité affectée *or* feinte; coquetterie *f*.

coyote [kɔɪ'əʊtɪ] *n* coyote *m*.

cozy ['kəʊzɪ] (*US*) = **cosy.**

crab¹ [kræb] *n* **(a)** (*Zool*) crabe *m*; *V* **catch.** **(b)** (*Tech*) *[crane]* chariot *m*.

crab² [kræb] *n* (*also* **~apple**) pomme *f* sauvage; (*also* **~(apple) tree**) pommier *m* sauvage.

crabbed ['kræbd] *adj person* revêche, hargneux, grincheux. **in a ~ hand, in ~ writing** en pattes de mouche.

crabby ['kræbɪ] *adj person* revêche, grincheux, grognon.

crack [kræk] **1** *n* **(a)** (*split, slit*) fente *f*, fissure *f*; (*in glass, mirror, pottery, bone etc*) fêlure *f*; (*in wall*) fente, lézarde *f*, crevasse *f*; (*in ground*) crevasse; (*in skin*) (petite) crevasse; (*in paint, varnish*) craquelure *f*. **through the ~ in the door** (*slight opening*) par l'entrebâillement de la porte; **leave the window open a ~** laissez la fenêtre entrouverte; **at the ~ of dawn** au point du jour, dès potron-minet*.

(b) (*noise*) *[twigs]* craquement *m*; *[whip]* claquement *m*; *[rifle]* coup *m* (sec), détonation *f*. **~ of thunder** coup de tonnerre; **the ~ of doom** la trompette du Jugement dernier.

(c) (*sharp blow*) **to give sb a ~ on the head** assener à qn un grand coup sur la tête; (*fig*) **that was a ~* at your brother** ça, c'était pour votre frère; **that was a dirty ~* he made** c'est une vacherie‡ ce qu'il a dit là, c'était vache* *or* rosse* de dire ça; (*fig: try*) **to have a ~ at doing*** essayer (un coup*) de faire; (*fig*) **to have a ~ at sth*** se lancer dans qch, tenter le coup sur qch; (*fig*) **I'll have a ~ at it*** je vais essayer (un coup*).

2 *cpd sportsman, sportswoman* de première classe, fameux*. **a crack tennis player/skier** un as *or* un crack du tennis/du ski; **crack shot** bon *or* excellent fusil; (*Mil, Police etc*) tireur *m* d'élite; (*pej*) **crack-brained** détraqué, cinglé*; (*pej*) **crack-brained idea** une idée saugrenue *or* loufoque*; **crack-jaw*** impossible à prononcer, imprononçable; **crack-jaw* name** nom *m* à coucher dehors*; (*pej*) **crackpot*** (*n: person*) tordu(e)* *m(f)*, cinglé(e)* *m(f)*; (*adj*) *idea* tordu; (*Prison sl: burglar*) **cracksman** cambrioleur *m*, casseur *m* (*sl*); **crack-up*** *[plan, organization]* effondrement *m*, écroulement *m*; *[person]* (*physical*) effondrement; (*mental*) dépression nerveuse; (*US: accident*) *[vehicle]* collision *f*, accident *m*; *[plane]* accident (d'avion).

3 *vt* **(a)** *pottery, glass, bone* fêler; *wall* lézarder, crevasser; *ground* crevasser; *nut etc* casser. **to ~ one's skull** se fendre le crâne; **to ~ sb over the head** assommer qn; (*fig*) **to ~ a crib‡** faire un casse‡, faire un fric-frac‡; **to ~ a safe*** faire‡ *or* cambrioler un coffre-fort; **to ~ a bottle*** ouvrir *or* déboucher une bouteille; (*US*) **to ~ a book*** ouvrir un livre (pour l'étudier).

(b) *petroleum etc* craquer, traiter par craquage.

(c) *whip* faire claquer. **to ~ one's finger joints** faire craquer ses doigts; (*fig*) **to ~ jokes*** sortir des blagues* *or* des astuces.

(d) *code etc* déchiffrer. *[detective, police]* **to ~ a case (wide open)** (être sur le point de) résoudre une affaire.

4 *vi* **(a)** *[pottery, glass]* se fêler; *[ground]* se crevasser, se craqueler; *[wall]* se craqueler, se lézarder; *[skin]* se crevasser, (*from cold*) se gercer; *[ice]* se craqueler.

(b) *[whip]* claquer; *[dry wood]* craquer. **we heard the pistol ~** nous avons entendu partir le coup de pistolet.

(c) *[voice]* se casser; *[boy's voice]* muer.

(d) (*) **to get ~ing** s'y mettre, se mettre au boulot*; **let's get ~ing** allons-y!, au boulot!*; **get ~ing!** magne-toi!‡, grouille-toi!‡

crack down on *vt fus person* tomber à bras raccourcis sur; *expenditure, sb's actions* mettre le frein à.
crack up* 1 *vi* **(a)** (*physically*) ne pas tenir le coup; (*mentally*) être au bout de son rouleau, flancher*. (*hum*) **I must be cracking up!** ça ne tourne plus rond chez moi!*
(b) (*US*) *[vehicle]* s'écraser; *[plane]* s'écraser (au sol); *[person]* (*with laughter*) se tordre *or* éclater de rire.
2 *vt sep* **(a)** (*praise etc*) *person, quality, action, thing* vanter, louer; *method* prôner. **he's not all he's cracked up to be*** il n'est pas aussi sensationnel qu'on le dit *or* prétend.
(b) (*US*) *vehicle* emboutir; *plane* faire s'écraser.
3 crack-up *n V* **crack 2.**
cracked [krækt] *adj* **(a)** *plate* fêlé, fendu; *wall* lézardé. **(b)** (‡: *mad*) toqué*, timbré*, cinglé*.
cracker ['krækəʳ] *n* **(a)** (*esp US: biscuit*) craquelin *m*, cracker *m*, biscuit *m* (salé). **(b)** (*firework*) pétard *m*. **(c)** (*Brit: at parties etc*) diablotin *m*. **(d) (nut)**~**s** casse-noisettes *m inv*, casse-noix *m inv*.
crackers‡ ['krækəz] *adj* (*Brit*) cinglé*, dingue‡.
cracking ['krækɪŋ] *n* (*U*) **(a)** *[petroleum]* craquage *m*, cracking *m*. **(b)** (*cracks: in paint, varnish etc*) craquelure *f*.
crackle ['krækl] **1** *vi [twigs burning]* pétiller, crépiter; *[sth frying]* grésiller.
2 *n* **(a)** (*noise*) *[wood]* crépitement *m*, craquement *m*; *[food]* grésillement *m*; (*on telephone etc*) crépitement(s), friture* *f*.
(b) *[china, porcelain etc]* craquelure *f*. ~ **china** porcelaine craquelée.
crackling ['kræklɪŋ] *n* **(a)** (*sound*) crépitement *m*; (*Rad*) friture* *f* (*U*). **(b)** (*Culin*) couenne rissolée (*de rôti de porc*).
cracknel ['kræknl] *n* (*biscuit*) craquelin *m*; (*toffee*) nougatine *f*.
cradle ['kreɪdl] **1** *n* **(a)** (*lit, fig*) berceau *m*. **from the** ~ **to the grave** du berceau à la tombe; **the** ~ **of civilization** le berceau de la civilisation.
(b) (*Naut: framework*) ber *m*; (*Constr*) échafaudage *m*, pont volant; (*Telec*) support *m*; (*Med*) arceau *m*.
2 *vt*: **to** ~ **a child (in one's arms)** bercer un enfant (dans ses bras); **she** ~**d the vase in her hands** elle tenait délicatement le vase entre ses mains; **he** ~**d the telephone under his chin** il maintenait le téléphone sous son menton.
3 *cpd*: (*pej*) **she's a cradle snatcher*** elle les prend au berceau*; **cradlesong** berceuse *f*.
craft [krɑːft] **1** *n* **(a)** (*skill*) art *m*, métier *m*; (*job, occupation*) métier, profession *f* (*généralement de type artisanal*); *V* **art**[1], **needle** *etc*.
(b) (*tradesmen's guild*) corps *m* de métier, corporation *f*.
(c) (*pl inv: boat*) embarcation *f*, barque *f*, petit bateau; *V* **air, space** *etc*.
(d) (*U: cunning*) astuce *f*, ruse *f* (*pej*). **by** ~ par ruse; **his** ~ **in doing that** l'astuce dont il a fait preuve en le faisant.
2 *cpd*: **craftsman** artisan *m*, ouvrier *m*, homme *m* de métier; (*U*) **craftsmanship** connaissance *f* d'un métier; **a superb piece of craftsmanship** un *or* du travail superbe.
craftily ['krɑːftɪlɪ] *adv* astucieusement, avec ruse (*pej*).
craftiness ['krɑːftɪnɪs] *n* astuce *f*, finesse *f*, ruse *f* (*pej*).
crafty ['krɑːftɪ] *adj* malin (*f* -igne) astucieux, rusé (*pej*). **he's a** ~ **one*** c'est un malin; **a** ~ **little gadget*** un petit truc astucieux*; **that was a** ~ **move*** *or* **a** ~ **thing to do** c'était un coup très astucieux.
crag [kræg] *n* rocher escarpé *or* à pic.
craggy ['krægɪ] *adj rock* escarpé, à pic; *area* plein d'escarpements. ~ **features/ face** traits/visage taillé(s) à la serpe *or* à coups de hache.
cram [kræm] **1** *vt* **(a)** fourrer (*into* dans). **to** ~ **books into a case** fourrer des livres dans une valise, bourrer une valise de livres; **we can** ~ **in another book** nous pouvons encore faire place pour un autre livre *or* y faire tenir un autre livre; **to** ~ **food into one's mouth** enfourner* de la nourriture; **we can't** ~ **any more (people) into the hall/the bus** on n'a plus la place de faire entrer qui que ce soit dans la salle/l'autobus; **we were all** ~**med into one room** nous étions tous entassés *or* empilés dans une seule pièce; **he** ~**med his hat (down) over his eyes** il a enfoncé son chapeau sur ses yeux.
(b) bourrer (*with* de). **shop** ~**med with good things** magasin *m* qui regorge de bonnes choses; **drawer** ~**med with letters** tiroir bourré de lettres; **to** ~ **sb with food** bourrer *or* gaver qn de nourriture; **to** ~ **o.s. with food** se bourrer *or* se gaver de nourriture; (*fig*) **he has his head** ~**med with odd ideas** il a la tête bourrée *or* farcie d'idées bizarres.
(c) (*Scol**) *pupil* chauffer*, faire bachoter.
2 *vi* **(a)** *[people]* s'entasser, s'empiler. **they all** ~**med into the kitchen** tout le monde s'est entassé dans la cuisine.
(b) to ~ **for an exam** bachoter, préparer un examen.
3 *cpd*: **cram-full** *room, bus* bondé; *case* bourré (*of* de).
crammer ['kræməʳ] *n* (*slightly pej*) (*tutor*) répétiteur *m*, -trice *f* (*qui fait faire du bachotage*); (*student*) bachoteur *m*, -euse *f*; (*book*) précis *m*, aide-mémoire *m inv*; (*also* ~**'s**: *school*) boîte *f* à bachot*.
cramp[1] [kræmp] **1** *n* (*Med*) crampe *f*. **to have** ~ **in one's leg** avoir une crampe à la jambe; *V* **writer.**
2 *vt* **(a)** (*hinder*) *person* gêner, entraver. **to** ~ **sb's progress** gêner *or* entraver les progrès de qn; (*fig*) **to** ~ **sb's style** priver qn de ses moyens, enlever ses moyens à qn; (*fig*) **your presence is** ~**ing my style*** tu me fais perdre (tous) mes moyens.
(b) (*Med*) donner des crampes à.
cramp[2] [kræmp] **1** *n* (*Constr, Tech*) agrafe *f*, crampon *m*, happe *f*. **2** *vt stones* cramponner.
cramped [kræmpt] *adj* **(a)** *handwriting* en pattes de mouche. **(b)** *space* resserré, à l'étroit. **we were very** ~ **(for space)** on était à l'étroit, on n'avait pas la place de se retourner; **in a** ~ **position** dans une position inconfortable.

crampon ['kræmpən] *n* (*Alpinism, Constr*) crampon *m*.
cranberry ['krænbərɪ] *n* (*Bot*) canneberge *f*. **turkey with** ~ **sauce** dinde *f* aux canneberges.
crane [kreɪn] **1** *n* (*Orn, Tech*) grue *f*.
2 *cpd*: **crane driver** grutier *m*; **cranefly** tipule *f*; **crane operator** = **crane driver**; (*Bot*) **crane's-bill** géranium *m*.
3 *vt*: **to** ~ **one's neck** tendre le cou.
crane forward *vi* tendre le cou (*pour voir etc*).
crania ['kreɪnɪə] *npl of* **cranium.**
cranial ['kreɪnɪəl] *adj* crânien.
cranium ['kreɪnɪəm] *n, pl* **crania** crâne *m*, boîte crânienne.
crank[1] [kræŋk] *n* (*Brit**: *person*) excentrique *mf*, loufoque* *mf*. **a religious** ~ un fanatique religieux.
crank[2] [kræŋk] **1** *n* (*Tech*) manivelle *f*.
2 *vt* (*also* ~ **up**) *car* faire partir à la manivelle; *cine-camera, gramophone etc* remonter (à la manivelle); *barrel organ* tourner la manivelle de.
3 *cpd*: (*Aut*) **crankcase** carter *m*; (*Aut*) **crankshaft** vilebrequin *m*.
cranky* ['kræŋkɪ] *adj* (*eccentric*) excentrique, loufoque*; (*bad-tempered*) revêche, grincheux.
cranny ['krænɪ] *n* (petite) faille *f*, fissure *f*, fente *f*; *V* **nook.**
crap** [kræp] *n* (*excrement*) merde** *f*; (*nonsense*) conneries** *fpl*, couillonnades‡ *fpl*; (*junk*) merde**, saloperie‡ *f*.
crape [kreɪp] *n* **(a)** = **crêpe. (b)** (*for mourning*) crêpe *m* (*de deuil*). ~ **band** brassard *m* (de deuil).
crappy** ['kræpɪ] *adj* merdique**.
craps [kræps] *n* (*US*) jeu *m* de dés. **to shoot** ~ jouer aux dés.
crapulous ['kræpjʊləs] *adj* crapuleux.
crash[1] [kræʃ] **1** *n* **(a)** (*noise*) fracas *m*. **a** ~ **of thunder** un coup de tonnerre; **a sudden** ~ **of dishes** un soudain fracas d'assiettes cassées; ~**, bang, wallop!*** badaboum!, patatras!
(b) (*accident*) *[car]* collision *f*, accident *m*; *[aeroplane]* accident (d'avion). **in a car/plane** ~ dans un accident de voiture/d'avion; **we had a** ~ **on the way here** nous avons eu un accident en venant ici.
(c) (*Fin*) *[company, firm]* faillite *f*; (*St Ex*) krach *m*.
2 *adv*: **he went** ~ **into the tree** il est allé se jeter *or* se fracasser contre l'arbre.
3 *vt* **(a)** *car* avoir une collision *or* un accident avec. **he** ~**ed the car through the barrier** il a enfoncé la barrière (avec la voiture); **he** ~**ed the plane** il s'est écrasé (au sol).
(b) (*Brit**: *also* **gate**~) **to** ~ **a party** s'introduire dans une réception sans invitation, resquiller.
4 *vi* **(a)** *[aeroplane]* s'écraser au sol; *[vehicle]* s'écraser; *[two vehicles]* se percuter, se rentrer dedans*. **the cars** ~**ed at the junction** les voitures se sont percutées au croisement; **to** ~ **into sth** rentrer dans qch*, percuter qch, emboutir qch; **the plate** ~**ed to the ground** l'assiette s'est fracassée par terre; **the car** ~**ed through the gate** la voiture a enfoncé la barrière *or* s'est jetée à travers la barrière.
(b) (*Comm, Fin*) *[bank, firm]* faire faillite. **the stock market** ~**ed** les cours de la Bourse se sont effondrés.
5 *cpd*: **crash course** cours intensif; **crash helmet** casque *m* (protecteur); (*Aviat*) **crash-land** atterrir *or* se poser en catastrophe; **crash landing** atterrissage forcé *or* en catastrophe; **crash programme** programme intensif.
crash in, crash down *vi [roof etc]* s'effondrer (avec fracas).
crash[2] [kræʃ] *n* (*Tex*) grosse toile.
crass [kræs] *adj* grossier, crasse. ~ **ignorance/stupidity** ignorance *f*/bêtise *f* crasse.
crate [kreɪt] **1** *n* **(a)** cageot *m*, caisse *f* (à claire-voie); (*esp Naut*) caisse. **(b)** (‡: *aeroplane*) zinc* *m*; (‡: *car*) bagnole* *f*. **2** *vt goods* mettre en cageot(s) *or* en caisse(s).
crater ['kreɪtəʳ] *n [volcano, moon]* cratère *m*. **bomb** ~ entonnoir *m*; **shell** ~ trou *m* d'obus, entonnoir.
cravat(e) [krə'væt] *n* cravate *f*, foulard *m* (*noué autour du cou*).
crave [kreɪv] *vti* **(a)** (*also* ~ **for**) *drink, tobacco etc* avoir un besoin maladif *or* physiologique de; **to** ~ **(for) affection** avoir soif *or* avoir grand besoin d'affection.
(b) (*frm*) *attention* solliciter. **to** ~ **permission** avoir l'honneur de solliciter l'autorisation; **he** ~**d permission to leave** il supplia qu'on lui accordât la permission de partir; **may I** ~ **leave to ...?** j'ai l'honneur de solliciter l'autorisation de ...; **to** ~ **sb's pardon** implorer le pardon de qn.
craven ['kreɪvən] *adj, n* (*liter*) lâche (*mf*), poltron(ne) *m(f)*.
craving ['kreɪvɪŋ] *n [drink, drugs, tobacco]* besoin *m* (maladif *or* physiologique) (*for* de); *[affection]* grand besoin, soif *f* (*for* de); *[freedom]* désir *m* insatiable (*for* de).
crawfish ['krɔːfɪʃ] *n* = **crayfish.**
crawl [krɔːl] **1** *n* **(a)** *[vehicles]* allure très ralentie, poussette* *f*. **we had to go at a** ~ **through the main streets** nous avons dû avancer au pas *or* faire la poussette* dans les rues principales.
(b) (*Swimming*) crawl *m*. **to do the** ~ nager *or* faire le crawl, crawler.
2 *vi* **(a)** *[animals]* ramper, se glisser; *[person]* se traîner, ramper. **to** ~ **in/out** *etc* entrer/sortir *etc* en rampant *or* à quatre pattes; **to** ~ **on one's hands and knees** aller à quatre pattes; **the child has begun to** ~ **(around)** l'enfant commence à se traîner à quatre pattes; (*fig*) **to** ~ **to sb** s'aplatir devant qn, lécher les bottes de *or* à qn; **the fly** ~**ed up the wall/along the table** la mouche a grimpé le long du mur/a avancé le long de la table; **to make sb's skin** ~ rendre qn malade de dégoût, donner la chair de poule à qn; **to** ~ **with vermin** grouiller de vermine; (*pej*) **this street is** ~**ing* with policemen** la rue grouille d'agents de police.
(b) *[vehicles]* avancer au pas, faire la poussette*.
crawler* ['krɔːləʳ] *n* (*person*) lécheur* *m*, -euse* *f*, lèche-bottes* *mf inv*; (*vehicle*) véhicule lent. (*Brit Aut*) ~ **lane** file *f* or voie *f* pour véhicules lents.

crayfish ['kreɪfɪʃ] *n* (*freshwater*) écrevisse *f*; (*saltwater*) (*large*) langouste *f*; (*small*) langoustine *f*.
crayon ['kreɪən] **1** *n* (*coloured pencil*) crayon *m* (*de couleur*); (*Art: pencil, chalk etc*) pastel *m*; (*Art: drawing*) crayon, pastel. **2** *vt* crayonner, dessiner au crayon; (*Art*) colorier au crayon *or* au pastel.
craze [kreɪz] **1** *n* engouement *m* (*for* pour), manie *f* (*for* de). **it's all the ~*** cela fait fureur. **2** *vt* **(a)** rendre fou (*f* folle). **(b)** *glaze, pottery* craqueler.
crazed [kreɪzd] *adj* **(a)** affolé, rendu fou (*f* folle) (*with* par). **(b)** *glaze, pottery* craquelé.
crazily ['kreɪzɪlɪ] *adv* follement, d'une manière insensée.
crazy ['kreɪzɪ] *adj* **(a)** (*mad*) fou (*f* folle). **to go ~** devenir fou *or* cinglé* *or* dingue‡; **to be ~ with anxiety** être fou d'inquiétude; **it's enough to drive you ~** c'est à vous rendre fou *or* dingue‡; **it was a ~ idea** c'était une idée idiote; **you were ~ to want to go there** tu étais fou *or* dingue‡ de vouloir y aller, c'était de la folie de vouloir y aller.
(b) (*: *enthusiastic*) fou (*f* folle), fana* (*f inv*) (*about sb/sth* de qn/qch). **I am not ~ about it** ça ne m'emballe* pas; **he's ~ about her** il en est fou, il l'aime à la folie.
(c) *building* délabré, qui menace de s'écrouler. **~ paving** dallage irrégulier (*en pierres plates*); **the tower leant at a ~ angle** la tour penchait d'une façon menaçante *or* inquiétante.
(d) (*US*) **~ bone** petit juif* (*partie du coude*).
creak [kri:k] **1** *vi [door hinge]* grincer, crier; *[shoes, floorboard]* craquer, crisser. **2** *n* (*V* **1**) grincement *m*; craquement *m*.
creaky ['kri:kɪ] *adj stair, floorboard, joints, shoes* qui craque *or* crisse; *hinge* grinçant.
cream [kri:m] **1** *n* **(a)** crème *f*. **single/double ~** crème fraîche liquide/épaisse; **to take the ~ off the milk** écrémer le lait; (*fig*) **the ~ of society** la crème *or* la fine fleur de la société; (*Confectionery*) **chocolate ~** chocolat fourré (à la crème); **vanilla ~** (*dessert*) crème à la vanille; (*biscuit*) biscuit fourré à la vanille; *V* **clot**.
(b) (*face ~, shoe ~*) crème *f*; *V* **cold, foundation** *etc*.
2 *adj* (*~-coloured*) crème *inv*; (*made with ~*) *cake* à la crème.
3 *cpd*: **cream cheese** fromage *m* à la crème, fromage blanc *or* frais; (*Brit*) **cream jug** pot *m* à crème; **cream of tartar** crème *f* de tartre; **cream of tomato soup** crème *f* de tomates; **cream puff** chou *m* à la crème.
4 *vt* **(a)** *milk* écrémer.
(b) (*Culin*) *butter* battre. **to ~ (together) sugar and butter** travailler le beurre en crème avec le sucre; **~ed potatoes** purée *f* de pommes de terre.
cream off *vt sep* (*fig*) *best talents, part of profits* prélever, écrémer.
creamer ['kri:məʳ] *n* (*to separate cream*) écrémeuse *f*; (*US: pitcher*) pot *m* à crème.
creamery ['kri:mərɪ] *n* **(a)** (*on farm*) laiterie *f*; (*butter factory*) laiterie, coopérative laitière. **(b)** (*small shop*) crémerie *f*.
creamy ['kri:mɪ] *adj* crémeux; *complexion* crème *inv*, crémeux.
crease [kri:s] **1** *n [material, paper]* pli *m*, pliure *f*; *[trouser legs, skirt etc]* pli; (*unwanted fold*) faux pli; (*on face*) ride *f*. **~-resistant** infroissable.
2 *vt* (*crumple*) froisser, chiffonner, plisser; (*press ~ in*) plisser. (*fig*) **his face ~d with laughter** le rire a plissé son visage.
3 *vi* se froisser, se chiffonner, prendre un (faux) pli.
create [kri:'eɪt] **1** *vt* (*gen*) créer; *new fashion* lancer, créer; *work of art, character, role* créer; *impression* produire, faire; *problem, difficulty* créer, susciter, provoquer; *noise, din* faire. **to ~ a sensation** faire sensation; **he was ~d baron** il a été fait baron.
2 *vi* (*Brit*‡: *fuss*) faire une scène, faire un foin‡.
creation [kri:'eɪʃən] *n* **(a)** (*U*) création *f*. **since the ~** depuis la création du monde. **(b)** (*Art, Dress*) création *f*. **the latest ~s from Paris** les toutes dernières créations de Paris.
creative [kri:'eɪtɪv] *adj mind, power* créateur (*f* -trice); *person, atmosphere, activity* créatif.
creativity [,kri:eɪ'tɪvɪtɪ] *n* imagination créatrice, esprit créateur, créativité *f*.
creator [krɪ'eɪtəʳ] *n* créateur *m*, -trice *f*.
creature ['kri:tʃəʳ] **1** *n* (*animal*) bête *f*, animal *m*; (*human*) être *m*, créature *f*; (*fig: servile dependant, fool*) créature. **dumb ~s** les bêtes; **the ~s of the deep** les animaux marins; **she's a poor/lovely ~** c'est une pauvre/ravissante créature.
2 *cpd*: **creature comforts** confort matériel; **he likes his creature comforts** il aime son petit confort *or* ses aises.
crèche [kreɪʃ] *n* (*esp Brit*) pouponnière *f*; crèche *f*; (*daytime*) crèche, garderie *f*.
credence ['kri:dəns] *n* croyance *f*, foi *f*. **to give ~ to** ajouter foi à.
credentials [krɪ'denʃəlz] *npl* (*identifying papers*) pièce *f* d'identité; *[diplomat]* lettres *fpl* de créance; (*references*) références *fpl*, certificat *m*. **to have good ~** avoir de bonnes références.
credibility [,kredə'bɪlɪtɪ] **1** *n* crédibilité *f*. **2** *cpd*: **credibility gap** marge *f* de crédibilité; **his credibility rating is not very high** sa (marge de) crédibilité est très entamée.
credible ['kredɪbl] *adj witness* digne de foi; *person* crédible; *statement* plausible.
credit ['kredɪt] **1** *n* **(a)** (*Banking, Comm, Fin*) crédit *m*; (*Book-keeping*) crédit, avoir *m*. **to give sb ~** faire crédit à qn; **to sell on ~** vendre à crédit; **you have £10 to your ~** vous avez un crédit de 10 livres.
(b) (*belief, acceptance*) **to give ~ to** *[person]* ajouter foi à; *[event]* donner foi à, accréditer; **to gain ~ with** s'accréditer auprès de; **his ~ with the electorate** son crédit auprès des électeurs.
(c) honneur *m*. **to his ~ we must point out that ...** il faut faire remarquer à son honneur *or* à son crédit que ...; **he is a ~ to his family** il fait honneur à sa famille, il est l'honneur de sa famille; **I gave him ~ for more sense** je lui supposais *or* croyais plus de bon sens; **the only people to emerge with any ~** les seuls à s'en sortir à leur honneur; **to take (the) ~ for sth** s'attribuer le mérite de qch; **it does you (great) ~** cela est tout à votre honneur, cela vous fait grand honneur; (*Cine*) **~s** générique *m*.
(d) (*Scol*) unité *f* de valeur, U.V.*f*.
2 *vt* **(a)** (*believe*) *rumour, news* croire, ajouter foi à. **I could hardly ~ it** je n'arrivais pas à le croire; **you wouldn't ~ it** vous ne le croiriez pas.
(b) (*attribute*) *qualities* attribuer, prêter (*to* à). **to be ~ed with having done** passer pour avoir fait; **I ~ed him with more sense** je lui croyais *or* supposais plus de bon sens; **it is ~ed with (having) magic powers** on lui attribue des pouvoirs magiques.
(c) (*Banking*) **to ~ £5 to sb, to ~ sb with £5** créditer (le compte de) qn de 5 livres, porter 5 livres au crédit de qn.
3 *cpd*: (*US*) **credit agency** établissement *m or* agence *f* de crédit; (*Banking*) **credit balance** solde créditeur; **credit card** carte *f* de crédit; (*Fin*) **credit entry** inscription *f or* écriture *f* au crédit; **credit facilities** facilités *fpl* de paiement; **credit rating** limite *f or* plafond *m* de crédit; (*Book-keeping, also fig*) **on the credit side** à l'actif; (*Econ*) **credit squeeze** restrictions *fpl* de crédit; **credit terms** conditions *fpl* de crédit; (*Cine*) **credit titles** générique *m*; **creditworthiness** solvabilité *f*.
creditable ['kredɪtəbl] *adj* honorable, estimable.
creditably ['kredɪtəblɪ] *adv* honorablement, avec honneur.
creditor ['kredɪtəʳ] *n* créancier *m*, -ière *f*.
credo ['kreɪdəʊ] *n* credo *m*.
credulity [krɪ'dju:lɪtɪ] *n* crédulité *f*.
credulous ['kredjʊləs] *adj* crédule, naïf (*f* naïve).
credulously ['kredjʊləslɪ] *adv* avec crédulité, naïvement.
creed [kri:d] *n* credo *m*, principes *mpl*. (*Rel*) **the C~** le Credo, le symbole des Apôtres.
creek [kri:k] *n* **(a)** (*esp Brit: inlet*) crique *f*, anse *f*. **to be up the ~**‡ (*be wrong*) se fourrer le doigt dans l'œil (jusqu'au coude)*; (*be in trouble*) être dans le pétrin. **(b)** (*stream*) ruisseau *m*, petit cours d'eau.
creel [kri:l] *n* panier *m* de pêche (*en osier*).
creep [kri:p] *pret, ptp* **crept** **1** *vi [animal, person]* ramper; *[plants]* ramper, grimper; (*move silently*) se glisser. **to ~ between** se faufiler entre; **to ~ in/out/away** *etc* *[person]* entrer/sortir/s'éloigner *etc* à pas de loup; *[animal]* entrer/sortir/s'éloigner *etc* sans un bruit; **to ~ about on tiptoe** avancer sur la pointe des pieds; **to ~ up on sb** *[person]* surprendre qn, s'approcher de qn à pas de loup; *[old age etc]* prendre qn par surprise; **old age is ~ing on** on se fait vieux*; **the traffic crept along** les voitures avançaient au pas; (*fig*) **an error crept into it** une erreur s'y est glissée; **a feeling of peace crept over me** un sentiment de paix me gagnait peu à peu *or* commençait à me gagner; **it makes my flesh ~** cela me donne la chair de poule.
2 *n*: **it gives me the ~s**‡ cela me donne la chair de poule, cela me fait froid dans le dos; (*pej*) **he's a ~**‡ il vous dégoûte, c'est un saligaud‡.
creeper ['kri:pəʳ] *n* **(a)** (*Bot*) plante grimpante *or* rampante; *V* **Virginia**. **(b)** (*US*) **~s** barboteuse *f*. **(c)** (*: *person*) lécheur* *m*, -euse* *f*, lèche-bottes* *mf inv*.
creeping ['kri:pɪŋ] *adj plant* grimpant, rampant; (*fig*) *person* lécheur. (*Mil*) **~ barrage** barrage rampant; (*Med*) **~ paralysis** paralysie progressive.
creepy ['kri:pɪ] **1** *adj story, place* qui donne la chair de poule, qui fait frissonner, terrifiant. **2** *cpd*: (*Brit*) **creepy-crawly**‡ (*adj*) qui fait frissonner, qui donne la chair de poule, horrifiant; (*n*) petite bestiole; **I hate creepy-crawlies**‡ je déteste toutes les petites bestioles qui rampent.
cremate [krɪ'meɪt] *vt* incinérer (*un cadavre*).
cremation [krɪ'meɪʃən] *n* crémation *f*, incinération *f*.
crematorium [,kremə'tɔ:rɪəm] *n, pl* **crematoria** [,kremə'tɔ:rɪə] (*Brit*), **crematory** ['kremə,tɔ:rɪ] (*US*) *n* (*place*) crématorium *m*, crématoire *m*; (*furnace*) four *m* crématoire.
crenellated ['krenɪleɪtɪd] *adj* crénelé, à créneaux.
crenellations [,krenɪ'leɪʃənz] *npl* créneaux *mpl*.
Creole ['kri:əʊl] *adj, n* créole (*mf*).
creosote ['krɪəsəʊt] **1** *n* créosote *f*. **2** *vt* créosoter.
crêpe [kreɪp] **1** *n* (*Tex*) crêpe *m*. **2** *cpd*: **crêpe bandage** bande *f* Velpeau ®; **crêpe paper** papier *m* crêpon; **crêpe(-soled) shoes** chaussures *fpl* à semelles de crêpe.
crept [krept] *pret, ptp of* **creep**.
crepuscular [krɪ'pʌskjʊləʳ] *adj* crépusculaire.
crescendo [krɪ'ʃendəʊ] *n, pl* **~s** (*Mus, fig*) crescendo *m inv*.
crescent ['kresnt] **1** *n* **(a)** croissant *m*. (*Islamic faith etc*) **the C~** le Croissant. **(b)** (*street*) rue *f* (*en arc de cercle*). **2** *cpd*: **crescent moon** croissant *m* de (la) lune; (*Culin*) **crescent roll** croissant *m*; **crescent-shaped** en (forme de) croissant.
cress [kres] *n* cresson *m*; *V* **mustard, water**.
crest [krest] **1** *n [bird, wave]* crête *f*; *[helmet]* cimier *m*; *[mountain]* crête, (*long ridge*) arête *f*; *[road]* haut *m or* sommet *m* de côte; (*above coat of arms shield*) timbre *m*; (*on seal etc*) armoiries *fpl*. **the family ~** les armoiries familiales; (*fig*) **he is on the ~ of the wave** tout lui réussit en ce moment.
2 *vt wave, hill* franchir la crête de. **~ed notepaper** papier à lettres armorié.
crestfallen ['krest,fɔ:lən] *adj person* déçu, découragé, déconfit. **to look ~** avoir l'air penaud, avoir l'oreille basse.
cretaceous [krɪ'teɪʃəs] *adj* crétacé. (*Geol*) **the C~ (age)** le crétacé.

Cretan [ˈkriːtən] **1** *adj* crétois. **2** *n* Crétois(e) *m(f)*.
Crete [kriːt] *n* Crète *f*.
cretin [ˈkretɪn] *n* (*Med*) crétin(e) *m(f)*; (**pej*) crétin(e), imbécile *mf*, idiot(e) *m(f)*.
cretinism [ˈkretɪnɪzəm] *n* (*Med*) crétinisme *m*.
cretinous [ˈkretɪnəs] *adj* (*Med, also *pej*) crétin.
cretonne [kreˈtɒn] *n* cretonne *f*.
crevasse [krɪˈvæs] *n* (*Geol*) crevasse *f*.
crevice [ˈkrevɪs] *n* fissure *f*, fente *f*, lézarde *f*.
crew[1] [kruː] **1** *n* (*Aviat, Naut*) équipage *m*; (*Cine, Rowing etc*) équipe *f*; (*group, gang*) bande *f*, équipe. (*pej*) **what a ~!*** tu parles d'une équipe!*, quelle engeance!
2 *vi* (*Sailing*) être équipier, faire partie de l'équipage. **would you like me to ~ for you?** voulez-vous de moi comme équipier?
3 *vt yacht* armer.
4 *cpd*: **to have a crew-cut** avoir les cheveux en brosse; **crew-neck sweater** pull(-over) *m* à col ras.
crew[2] [kruː] *pret of* **crow**[2] **2a.**
crib [krɪb] **1** *n* **(a)** (*cot*) lit *m* d'enfant, berceau *m*; (*Rel*) crèche *f*.
(b) (*manger*) mangeoire *f*, râtelier *m*, crèche *f*.
(c) (*plagiarism*) plagiat *m*, copiage *m*; (*Brit Scol*) traduction *f*, traduc: *f* (*utilisée illicitement*).
2 *vt* (*Brit Scol*) copier. **to ~ sb's work** copier le travail de qn, copier sur qn.
3 *vi* copier. **to ~ from a friend** copier sur un camarade; **he had ~bed from Shakespeare** il avait plagié Shakespeare.
cribbage [ˈkrɪbɪdʒ] *n* (sorte *f* de) jeu *m* de cartes.
crick [krɪk] **1** *n* crampe *f*. **~ in the neck** torticolis *m*; **~ in the back** tour *m* de reins. **2** *vt*: **to ~ one's neck** attraper un torticolis; **to ~ one's back** se faire un tour de reins.
cricket[1] [ˈkrɪkɪt] *n* (*insect*) grillon *m*, cri-cri* *m inv*.
cricket[2] [ˈkrɪkɪt] **1** *n* (*Sport*) cricket *m*. (*fig*) **that's not ~** cela ne se fait pas, ce n'est pas fair-play. **2** *cpd*: **cricket ball/bat/match/pitch** balle *f*/batte *f*/match *m*/terrain *m* de cricket.
cricketer [ˈkrɪkɪtəʳ] *n* joueur *m* de cricket.
crier [ˈkraɪəʳ] *n* crieur *m*; *[law courts]* huissier *m*; *V* **town.**
crikey: [ˈkraɪkɪ] *excl* (*Brit*) mince (alors)!*
crime [kraɪm] *n* crime *m*; (*less serious*) délit *m*; (*U*) crime; (*Mil*) manquement *m* à la discipline, infraction *f*. **~ and punishment** le crime et le châtiment; **a life of ~** une vie de criminel *or* de crime; **~ wave** vague *f* de crimes; **~ is on the increase/decrease** il y a un accroissement/une régression de la criminalité; **~ doesn't pay** le crime ne paye pas; **it's a ~ to make him do it*** c'est un crime de le forcer à le faire.
Crimea [kraɪˈmɪə] *n*: **the ~** la Crimée.
Crimean [kraɪˈmɪən] *adj, n*: **the ~ (War)** la guerre de Crimée.
criminal [ˈkrɪmɪnl] **1** *n* criminel *m*, -elle *f*.
2 *adj action, motive, law* criminel. (*fig*) **it's ~* to stay indoors today** c'est un crime de rester enfermé aujourd'hui; (*Jur*) **~ assault** agression criminelle, voie *f* de fait; (*US Jur*) **~ conversation** adultère *m* (*de la femme*); **~ investigation** enquête criminelle; (*Brit*) **the C~ Investigation Department** la police judiciaire, la P.J.; **~ lawyer** pénaliste *m*, avocat *m* au criminel; (*Jur*) **to take ~ proceedings against sb** poursuivre qn au pénal; (*Brit*) **the C~ Records Office** l'identité *f* judiciaire.
criminologist [ˌkrɪmɪˈnɒlədʒɪst] *n* criminologiste *mf*.
criminology [ˌkrɪmɪˈnɒlədʒɪ] *n* criminologie *f*.
crimp [krɪmp] **1** *vt* **(a)** *hair* crêper, friser, frisotter; *pastry* pincer. **(b)** (*US: hinder*) gêner, entraver. **2** *n* (*US*) **to put a ~ in** mettre obstacle à, mettre des bâtons dans les roues de.
Crimplene [ˈkrɪmpliːn] *n* ® ≈ crêpe *m* acrylique.
crimson [ˈkrɪmzn] *adj, n* cramoisi (*m*).
cringe [krɪndʒ] *vi* (*shrink back*) avoir un mouvement de recul, reculer (*from* devant); (*fig: humble o.s.*) ramper, s'humilier (*before* devant). (*fig*) **the very thought of it makes me ~*** rien qu'à y penser j'ai envie de rentrer sous terre.
cringing [ˈkrɪndʒɪŋ] *adj movement* craintif, timide; *attitude, behaviour* servile, bas (*f* basse).
crinkle [ˈkrɪŋkl] **1** *vt paper* froisser, chiffonner. **2** *vi* se froisser. **3** *n* fronce *f*, pli *m*.
crinkly [ˈkrɪŋklɪ] *adj paper* gaufré; *hair* crépu, crêpelé.
crinoline [ˈkrɪnəliːn] *n* crinoline *f*.
cripple [ˈkrɪpl] **1** *n* (*lame*) estropié(e) *m(f)*, boiteux *m*, -euse *f*; (*disabled*) infirme *mf*, invalide *mf*; (*from accident, war*) invalide; (*maimed*) mutilé(e) *m(f)*.
2 *vt* **(a)** estropier. **~d with rheumatism** perclus de rhumatismes.
(b) (*fig*) *ship, plane* désemparer; (*Ind*) *[strikes etc] production, exports etc* paralyser. **crippling taxes** impôts écrasants; **activities ~d by lack of funds** activités paralysées par le manque de fonds.
crisis [ˈkraɪsɪs] *n, pl* **crises** [ˈkraɪsiːz] crise *f*. **to come to a ~, to reach a ~** entrer en crise; **to solve a ~** dénouer *or* résoudre une crise; **we've got a ~ on our hands** nous avons un problème urgent, nous sommes dans une situation critique.
crisp [krɪsp] **1** *adj biscuit* croquant, croustillant; *vegetables* croquant; *bread* croustillant; *snow* craquant; *paper* raide, craquant; *linen* apprêté; *weather* vif (*f* vive), piquant; *hair* crépu, crêpelé; *reply, style* vif, précis, tranchant (*pej*), brusque (*pej*); *tone, voice* acerbe, cassant (*pej*).
2 *n* (*Brit*) **(potato) ~s** (pommes) chips *fpl*; **packet of ~s** sachet *m or* paquet *m* de chips.
3 *cpd*: **crispbread** pain *m* scandinave.
4 *vt* (*Culin: also* **~ up**) faire réchauffer (*pour rendre croustillant*).
crisply [ˈkrɪsplɪ] *adv say etc* d'un ton acerbe *or* cassant (*pej*).
criss-cross [ˈkrɪskrɒs] **1** *adj lines* entrecroisés; (*in muddle*) enchevêtré. **in a ~ pattern** en croisillons. **2** *n* entrecroisement *m*; enchevêtrement *m*. **3** *vt* entrecroiser (*by* de). **4** *adv* formant (un) réseau.
criterion [kraɪˈtɪərɪən] *n, pl* **criteria** [kraɪˈtɪərɪə] *or* **~s** critère *m*.
critic [ˈkrɪtɪk] *n [books, painting, music, films etc]* critique *m*; (*faultfinder*) critique, censeur *m* (*frm*), détracteur *m*, -trice *f*. (*Press*) **film ~** critique de cinéma; **he is a constant ~ of the government** il ne cesse de critiquer le gouvernement; **his wife is his most severe ~** sa femme est son plus sévère critique.
critical [ˈkrɪtɪkəl] *adj* **(a)** (*Pol etc*) critique, crucial; *situation* critique; (*Med*) *condition, stage of illness* critique. **at a ~ moment** à un moment critique *or* crucial; (*Aviat, Opt*) **~ angle** angle *m* critique.
(b) (*Art, Literat*) *writings, essay* critique, de critique; *analysis, edition* critique. **~ work on Chaucer** travail *m or* travaux *mpl* critique(s) sur Chaucer.
(c) (*faultfinding*) *person, attitude, approach* sévère, critique. **to be ~ of** critiquer, trouver à redire à.
critically [ˈkrɪtɪkəlɪ] *adv* **(a)** (*discriminatingly*) *judge, consider, discuss* en critique, d'un œil critique. **(b)** (*adversely*) *review, report* sévèrement. **(c) ~ ill** dangereusement *or* gravement malade.
criticism [ˈkrɪtɪsɪzəm] *n* critique *f*.
criticize [ˈkrɪtɪsaɪz] *vt* **(a)** (*assess*) *book etc* critiquer, faire la critique de. **(b)** (*find fault with*) *behaviour, person* critiquer, réprouver, censurer (*frm*). **I don't want to ~, but ...** je ne veux pas avoir l'air de critiquer, mais ... .
critique [krɪˈtiːk] *n* critique *f*.
croak [krəʊk] **1** *vi* **(a)** *[frog]* coasser; *[raven]* croasser; *[person]* parler d'une voix rauque; (**: grumble*) maugréer, ronchonner.
(b) (*:: die*) claquer*, crever*.
2 *vt* dire avec une *or* d'une voix rauque *or* sourde. **'help' he ~ed feebly** 'au secours' appela-t-il d'une voix rauque *or* sourde.
3 *n [frog]* coassement *m*; *[raven]* croassement *m*. **his voice was a mere ~** il ne proférait que des sons rauques.
Croat [ˈkrəʊæt] *n* Croate *mf*.
Croatia [krəʊˈeɪʃɪə] *n* Croatie *f*.
Croatian [krəʊˈeɪʃɪən] *adj* croate.
crochet [ˈkrəʊʃeɪ] **1** *n* (*U: also* **~ work**) travail *m* au crochet. **~ hook** crochet *m*. **2** *vt garment* faire au crochet. **3** *vi* faire du crochet.
crock [krɒk] *n* **(a)** (*pot*) cruche *f*, pot *m* de terre. (*broken pieces*) **~s** débris *mpl* de faïence. **(b)** (*) (*horse*) vieille rosse, cheval fourbu; (*esp Brit: car etc*) guimbarde *f*, vieille bagnole*, vieux clou*. **he's an old ~** c'est un croulant*.
crockery [ˈkrɒkərɪ] *n* (*U*) (*earthenware*) poterie *f*, faïence *f*; (*cups, saucers, plates*) vaisselle *f*.
crocodile [ˈkrɒkədaɪl] **1** *n* **(a)** crocodile *m*. **~ tears** larmes *fpl* de crocodile. **(b)** (*Brit Scol*) cortège *m* en rangs (par deux). **to walk in a ~** aller deux par deux. **2** *cpd shoes, handbag* en crocodile, en croco*.
crocus [ˈkrəʊkəs] *n* crocus *m*.
croft [krɒft] *n* (*Brit*) petite ferme.
crofter [ˈkrɒftəʳ] *n* (*Brit*) petit fermier.
crone [krəʊn] *n* vieille ratatinée*, vieille bique.
crony* [ˈkrəʊnɪ] *n* copain* *m*, copine* *f*.
crook [krʊk] **1** *n* **(a)** *[shepherd]* houlette *f*; *[bishop]* crosse *f*. **(b)** *[road]* angle *m*; *[river]* angle, coude *m*, détour *m*. **(c)** (**: thief*) escroc *m*, filou *m*. **2** *vt one's finger* courber, recourber; *one's arm* plier.
crooked [ˈkrʊkɪd] **1** *adj* **(a)** *stick* courbé, crochu, tordu. **a ~ old man** un vieillard tout courbé; **a ~ path** un sentier tortueux; **she gave a ~ smile** elle a fait un pauvre sourire *or* un sourire contraint; **the picture is ~** le tableau est de travers.
(b) (*fig*) *person, action, method* malhonnête.
2 *adv* (*) de travers, de traviole:.
crookedness [ˈkrʊkɪdnɪs] *n* (*lit*) courbure *f*; (*fig*) malhonnêteté *f*, fausseté *f*.
croon [kruːn] *vti* (*sing softly*) chantonner, fredonner; (*in show business*) chanter (*en crooner*).
crooner [ˈkruːnəʳ] *n* chanteur *m*, -euse *f* de charme.
crop [krɒp] **1** *n* **(a)** (*produce*) produit *m* agricole, culture *f*; (*amount produced*) récolte *f*, (*of fruit etc*) récolte, cueillette *f*, (*of cereals*) moisson *f*; (*fig: of problems, questions*) série *f*, quantité *f*, tas* *m*. **one of the basic ~s** l'une des cultures de base; **we had a good ~ of strawberries** la récolte *or* la cueillette des fraises a été bonne; **to get the ~s in** faire la récolte *or* la cueillette *or* la moisson, rentrer les récoltes *or* la moisson.
(b) *[bird]* jabot *m*.
(c) *[whip]* manche *m*; (*also* **riding ~**) cravache *f*.
(d) (*Hairdressing*) **to give sb a (close) ~** couper ras les cheveux de qn; **Eton ~** cheveux *mpl* à la garçonne.
2 *cpd*: **crop dusting, crop spraying** pulvérisation *f* des cultures; **crop sprayer** (*device*) pulvérisateur *m*; (*plane*) avion-pulvérisateur *m*.
3 *vt* **(a)** *[animals] grass* brouter, paître.
(b) *tail* écourter; *hair* tondre. **~ped hair** cheveux coupés ras.
4 *vi [land]* donner *or* fournir une récolte.
crop out *vi* (*Geol*) affleurer.
crop up *vi* **(a)** *[questions, problems]* surgir, survenir, se présenter. **the subject cropped up during the conversation** le sujet a été amené *or* mis sur le tapis au cours de la conversation; **something's cropped up and I can't come** il s'est passé *or* il est survenu quelque chose qui m'empêche de venir; **he was ready for anything that might crop up** il était prêt à toute éventualité.
(b) (*Geol*) affleurer.
cropper: [ˈkrɒpəʳ] *n* (*lit, fig*) **to come a ~** se casser la figure*; **to come a ~ in an exam** être collé* à un examen.
croquet [ˈkrəʊkeɪ] **1** *n* croquet *m*. **2** *cpd*: **croquet hoop/mallet** arceau *m*/maillet *m* de croquet.
croquette [krəʊˈket] *n* croquette *f*. **potato ~** croquette de pommes de terre.

crosier ['krəʊʒəʳ] *n* crosse *f* (*d'évêque*).

cross [krɒs] **1** *n* **(a)** (*mark, emblem*) croix *f*. **to mark/sign with a ~** marquer/signer d'une croix; **the iron ~** la croix de fer; (*Rel*) **the C~** la Croix; (*fig*) **it is a ~ he has to bear** c'est sa croix, c'est la croix qu'il lui faut porter; **we each have our ~ to bear** chacun a *or* porte sa croix; *V* **market, red, sign** *etc*.

(b) (*Bio, Zool*) hybride *m*. **~ between two different breeds** mélange *m or* croisement *m* de deux races différentes, hybride; (*fig*) **it's a ~ between a novel and a poem** cela tient du roman et du poème.

(c) (*U*) *[material]* biais *m*. (*Sewing*) **to cut material on the ~** couper du tissu dans le biais; **a skirt cut on the ~** une jupe en biais; **line drawn on the ~** ligne tracée en biais *or* en diagonale.

2 *adj* **(a)** (*angry*) *person* de mauvaise humeur, en colère. **to be ~ with sb** être fâché *or* en colère contre qn; **it makes me ~ when ...** cela m'agace quand ...; **to get ~ with sb** se mettre en colère *or* se fâcher contre qn; **don't be ~ with me** ne m'en veuillez *or* voulez* pas; **to be as ~ as a bear with a sore head*** être d'une humeur massacrante *or* de chien*; **they haven't had a ~ word in 10 years** ils ne se sont pas disputés une seule fois en 10 ans.

(b) (*traverse, diagonal*) transversal, diagonal.

3 *cpd*: **crossbar** (*Rugby etc*) barre transversale; *[bicycle]* barre; **crossbeam** traverse *f*, sommier *m*; (*Parl*) **crossbencher** député non inscrit; (*Orn*) **crossbill** bec-croisé *m*; **crossbones** *V* **skull**; **crossbow** arbalète *f*; **crossbred** métis (*f* -isse); **crossbreed** (*n*) (*animal*) hybride *m*, métis(se) *m(f)*; (**pej*: *person*) sang-mêlé *mf inv*; (*vt: pret, ptp* **crossbred**) croiser, métisser; **cross-Channel** *ferry* qui traverse la Manche; **cross-check** (*n*) contre-épreuve *f*, recoupement *m*; (*vt*) *facts* vérifier par contre-épreuve, faire se recouper; **cross-country** à travers champs; **cross-country (race)** cross(-country) *m*; **cross-country skiing** ski *m* de randonnée; **cross-current** contre-courant *m*; **cross-cut chisel** bédane *m*; (*esp Jur*) **cross-examination** contre-interrogatoire *m*; **cross-examine** (*Jur*) faire subir un contre-interrogatoire à; (*gen*) interroger *or* questionner (de façon serrée); **cross-eyed** qui louche, bigleux*; (*Bot*) **cross-fertilize** *species* croiser avec une autre; *plants* faire un croisement de; (*Mil*) **crossfire** feux croisés; (*Mil*) **exposed to crossfire** pris entre deux feux; (*fig*) **caught in a crossfire of questions** pris dans un feu roulant de questions; **cross-grained** *wood* à fibre, irrégulier; *person* aigre, acariâtre, atrabilaire; **crosshatch** hachurer en croisillons; **crosshatching** hachures croisées; **cross-legged** les jambes croisées; **cross-over** *[roads]* (croisement *m* par) pont routier; (*Rail*) voie *f* de croisement; (*Dress*) **crossover bodice** corsage croisé; **cross-patch*** grincheux *m*, -euse *f*, grognon(ne) *m(f)*; **crosspiece** traverse *f*; **cross-pollination** pollinisation croisée; **to be at cross-purposes with sb** (*misunderstand*) comprendre qn de travers; (*disagree*) être en désaccord avec qn; **I think we are at cross-purposes** je crois qu'il y a malentendu, nous nous sommes mal compris; **we were talking at cross-purposes** notre conversation tournait autour d'un quiproquo; **cross-question** faire subir un interrogatoire à; **cross-refer** renvoyer (*to* à); **cross-reference** renvoi *m*, référence *f* (*to* à); (*Brit*) **crossroads** (*lit*) croisement *m*, carrefour *m*; (*fig*) carrefour; **cross section** (*Bio etc*) coupe transversale; *[population etc]* échantillon *m*; **cross-stitch** (*n*) point *m* de croix; (*vt*) coudre *or* broder au point de croix; **cross swell** houle traversière; **crosstalk** conversation *f*, échange *m* de propos; (*esp US*) **crosstie** traverse *f* (de voie ferrée); (*US*) **crosswalk** passage clouté; (*US*) **crossway** croisement *m*; **crosswind** vent *m* de travers; **crosswise** en travers, en croix; **crossword (puzzle)** mots croisés.

4 *vt* **(a)** *room, street, sea, continent* traverser; *river, bridge* traverser, passer; *threshold, fence, ditch* franchir. **the bridge ~es the river here** c'est ici que le pont franchit *or* enjambe la rivière; **it ~ed my mind that ...** il m'est venu à l'esprit que ..., l'idée m'est venue (à l'esprit) que ...; (*Prov*) **don't ~ your bridges before you come to them** chaque chose en son temps (*Prov*); (*fig*) **let's ~ that bridge when we come to it** on s'occupera de ce problème-là en temps et lieu; (*Ind*) **to ~ the picket lines** traverser un piquet de grève; (*fig*) **to ~ sb's path** se trouver sur le chemin de qn; (*Parl*) **to ~ the floor (of the House)** ≃ s'inscrire à un parti opposé.

(b) to ~ a t barrer un t; (*Brit*) **to ~ a cheque** barrer un chèque; **to ~ sb's palm with silver** donner la pièce à qn.

(c) to ~ one's arms/legs croiser les bras/les jambes; (*lit, fig*) **to ~ swords with sb** croiser le fer avec qn; (*Rel*) **to ~ o.s.** se signer, faire le signe de (la) croix; (*fig*) **~ my heart (and swear to die)!*** croix de bois croix de fer (si je mens je vais en enfer)!*; (*fig*) **to ~ one's fingers*** faire une petite prière (*fig*); (*fig*) **keep your fingers ~ed for me*** fais une petite prière pour moi (, ça me portera bonheur); (*Telec*) **the lines are ~ed** les lignes sont embrouillées; (*fig*) **they've got their lines ~ed*** il y a un malentendu quelque part.

(d) (*thwart*) *person* contrarier, contrecarrer; *plans* contrecarrer. **~ed in love** malheureux en amour.

(e) *animals, plants* croiser (*with* avec). **to ~ two animals/plants** croiser *or* métisser deux animaux/plantes.

5 *vi* **(a)** (*also* **~ over**) **he ~ed from one side of the room to the other to speak to me** il a traversé la pièce pour venir me parler; **to ~ from one place to another** passer d'un endroit à un autre; **to ~ from Newhaven to Dieppe** faire la traversée de Newhaven à Dieppe.

(b) *[roads, paths]* se croiser, se rencontrer; *[letters, people]* se croiser.

cross off *vt sep item on list* barrer, rayer, biffer.

cross out *vt sep word* barrer, rayer, biffer.

cross over **1** *vi* traverser; *V also* **cross 5a**.

2 crossover *n, adj V* **cross 3.**

crosse [krɒs] *n* crosse *f* (*au jeu de lacrosse*).

crossing ['krɒsɪŋ] *n* **(a)** (*esp by sea*) traversée *f*. **the ~ of the line** le passage de l'équateur *or* de la ligne.

(b) (*road junction*) croisement *m*, carrefour *m*; (*also* **pedestrian ~**) passage clouté; (*Rail: also* **level ~**) passage à niveau. **(school) ~ patrol** contractuel *m*, -elle *f* (*chargé(e) de faire traverser la rue aux enfants*); (*Aut*) **cross at the ~** traversez sur le passage clouté *or* dans les clous*; *V* **zebra.**

crossly ['krɒslɪ] *adv* avec (mauvaise) humeur.

crotch [krɒtʃ] *n [body, tree]* fourche *f*; *[garment]* entre-jambes *m inv*.

crotchet ['krɒtʃɪt] *n* (*Brit Mus*) noire *f*.

crotchety ['krɒtʃɪtɪ] *adj* grognon, grincheux.

crouch [kraʊtʃ] **1** *vi* (*also* **~ down**) *[person, animal]* s'accroupir, se tapir; (*before springing*) se ramasser. **2** *n* accroupissement *m*; action *f* de se ramasser.

croup[1] [kru:p] *n* (*Med*) croup *m*.

croup[2] [kru:p] *n [horse]* croupe *f*.

croupier ['kru:pɪeɪ] *n* croupier *m*.

crow[1] [krəʊ] **1** *n* (*Orn*) corneille *f*. **as the ~ flies** à vol d'oiseau, en ligne droite; (*US*) **to make sb eat ~*** faire rentrer les paroles dans la gorge à qn; **to eat ~*** faire des excuses humiliantes; *V* **carrion** *etc*.

2 *cpd*: **crowbar** (pince *f* à) levier *m*; **crowfoot** (*Bot*) renoncule *f*; (*Naut*) araignée *f*; (*Mil*) chausse-trape *f*; **crow's feet** pattes *fpl* d'oie (*rides*); (*Naut*) **crow's-nest** nid *m* de pie.

crow[2] [krəʊ] **1** *n [cock]* chant *m* du coq, cocorico *m*; *[baby]* gazouillis *m*; (*fig*) cri *m* de triomphe.

2 *vi* **(a)** *pret* **crowed** *or* **crew**, *ptp* **crowed** *[cock]* chanter.

(b) *pret, ptp* **crowed** *[baby]* gazouiller; (*fig*) chanter victoire. **he ~ed with delight** il poussait des cris de joie; **it's nothing to ~ about** il n'y a pas de quoi pavoiser.

crow over *vt fus person* se vanter d'avoir triomphé de, chanter sa victoire sur.

crowd [kraʊd] **1** *n* **(a)** foule *f*, multitude *f*, masse *f*; (*disorderly*) cohue *f*. **in ~s** en foule, en masse; **to get lost in the ~** se perdre dans la foule; **a large ~** *or* **large ~s had gathered** une foule immense s'était assemblée; **there was quite a ~** il y avait beaucoup de monde, il y avait foule; **how big was the ~?** est-ce qu'il y avait beaucoup de monde?; **there was quite a ~ at the concert** il y avait une bonne salle au concert; (*Cine, Theat*) **the ~** les figurants *mpl*; (*fig*) **that would pass in a ~*** ça peut passer si on n'y regarde pas de trop près, en courant vite on n'y verrait que du feu*; **there were ~s of books/people*** il y avait des masses* de livres/de gens.

(b) (*U: people in general*) **the ~** la foule, la masse du peuple; **to follow** *or* **go with the ~** suivre la foule *or* le mouvement.

(c) (**: group, circle*) bande *f*, clique *f*. **I don't like that ~ at all** je n'aime pas du tout cette bande.

2 *cpd*: (*Cine, Theat*) **crowd scene** scène *f* de foule.

3 *vi* s'assembler, se presser, s'attrouper. **they ~ed into the small room** ils se sont entassés dans la petite pièce; **don't all ~ together** ne vous serrez donc pas comme ça; **to ~ through the gates** passer en foule par le portail; **they ~ed round to see ...** ils ont fait cercle *or* se sont attroupés pour voir ...; **they ~ed round him** ils se pressaient autour de lui; **to ~ down/in/up** *etc* descendre/entrer/monter *etc* en foule.

4 *vt objects* entasser (*into* dans). **pedestrians ~ed the streets** les piétons se pressaient dans les rues; **he was ~ed off the pavement** la cohue l'a forcé à descendre du trottoir; **don't ~ me** ne poussez pas, écartez-vous; **the houses are ~ed together** les maisons sont les unes sur les autres; **a room ~ed with children** une pièce pleine d'enfants; **house ~ed with furniture** maison encombrée de meubles; **a house ~ed with guests** une maison pleine d'invités; **a week ~ed with incidents** une semaine riche en incidents; **memory ~ed with facts** mémoire bourrée de faits; (*Naut*) **to ~ on sail** mettre toutes voiles dehors; *V also* **crowded.**

crowd out *vt sep*: **we shall be crowded out** la cohue nous empêchera d'entrer; **this article was crowded out of yesterday's edition** cet article n'a pas pu être inséré dans l'édition d'hier faute de place.

crowded ['kraʊdɪd] *adj room, hall, train, café* bondé, plein; *bus* bondé, plein à craquer; *town* encombré (de monde); *streets* plein (de monde). **the streets are ~** il y a foule dans les rues; **the shops are too ~ for my liking** il y a trop d'affluence *or* de monde pour mon goût dans les magasins; (*Theat*) **~ house** salle *f* comble; **a ~ day** une journée chargée; **it is a very ~ profession** c'est une profession très encombrée *or* bouchée.

crown [kraʊn] **1** *n* **(a)** couronne *f*; (*fig*) couronne, pouvoir royal, monarchie *f*. **~ of roses/thorns** couronne de roses/d'épines; (*fig*) **to wear the ~** régner, porter la couronne; **to succeed to the ~** monter sur le trône; (*Jur*) **the C~** la Couronne, ≃ le ministère public; **the law officers of the C~** les conseillers *mpl* juridiques de la Couronne.

(b) (*money*) couronne *f* (*ancienne pièce de la valeur de cinq shillings*).

(c) *[head]* sommet *m* de la tête; *[hat]* fond *m*; *[road]* milieu *m*; *[roof]* faîte *m*; *[arch]* clef *f* (*d'une voûte*); *[tooth]* couronne *f*; *[anchor]* diamant *m*; *[hill]* sommet, faîte; *[tree]* cime *f*; (*size of paper*) couronne (*format 0,37 sur 0,47 cm*); (*fig: climax, completion*) couronnement *m*.

2 *vt* couronner (*with* de); *[draughts]* damer; *tooth* couronner; (**: hit*) flanquer* un coup sur la tête à. **he was ~ed king** il fut couronné roi; (*fig*) **all the ~ed heads of Europe** toutes les têtes couronnées d'Europe; **work ~ed with success** travail couronné de succès; **the hill is ~ed with trees** la colline est couronnée d'arbres; (*fig*) **to ~ it all* it began to snow** pour comble (de malheur) *or* pour couronner le tout il s'est mis à neiger; **that ~s it all!*** il ne manquait plus que ça!

3 *cpd*: (*Brit*) **crown colony** colonie *f* de la couronne; (*Jur*) **Crown court** ≃ Cour *f* d'assises (*en Angleterre et au Pays de Galles*); **crown estate** domaine *m* de la couronne; **crown jewels** joyaux *mpl* de la couronne; **crown lands** terres domaniales; **crown law** droit pénal; **crown prince** prince héritier; (*Aut*) **crown wheel** grande couronne; **crown wheel and pinion** couple *m* conique.

crowning ['kraʊnɪŋ] **1** *n* (*ceremony*) couronnement *m*. **2** *adj achievement, moment* suprême. **his ~ glory** son plus grand triomphe.

crucial ['kruːʃəl] *adj* critique, crucial, décisif; (*Med*) crucial.

crucible ['kruːsɪbl] *n* creuset *m*; (*fig: test*) (dure) épreuve *f*.

crucifix ['kruːsɪfɪks] *n* crucifix *m*, christ *m*; *[roadside]* calvaire *m*.

crucifixion [ˌkruːsɪ'fɪkʃən] *n* crucifiement *m*. (*Rel*) **the C~** la crucifixion, la mise en croix.

cruciform ['kruːsɪfɔːm] *adj* cruciforme.

crucify ['kruːsɪfaɪ] *vt* (*lit*) crucifier, mettre en croix; (*fig*) crucifier, mettre au pilori. (*Rel*) **to ~ the flesh** mortifier la chair.

crude [kruːd] *adj materials* brut; *sugar* non raffiné; *drawing* rudimentaire, qui manque de fini; *piece of work* à peine ébauché, mal fini, sommaire; *object* grossier, rudimentaire; *light, colour* cru, vif; *person, behaviour* grossier; *manners* fruste, de rustre. **~ oil** (pétrole *m*) brut *m*; **he managed to make a ~ hammer** il a réussi à fabriquer un marteau rudimentaire; **he made a ~ attempt at building a shelter** il a essayé tant bien que mal de construire un abri; **a ~ expression** *or* **word** une grossièreté.

crudely ['kruːdlɪ] *adv* (*make, fashion*) imparfaitement, sommairement; (*say, order, explain*) crûment, grossièrement, brutalement, sans ménagements. **to put it ~ I think he's mad** pour dire les choses crûment je pense qu'il est fou.

crudeness ['kruːdnɪs] *n*, **crudity** ['kruːdɪtɪ] *n* (*V* **crude**) état brut; grossièreté *f*; manque *m* de fini, caractère *m* rudimentaire.

cruel ['krʊəl] *adj* cruel (*to* envers).

cruelly ['krʊəlɪ] *adv* cruellement.

cruelty ['krʊəltɪ] *n* **(a)** cruauté *f* (*to* envers); *V* **prevention. (b)** (*Jur*) sévices *mpl*. **prosecuted for ~ to his wife** poursuivi pour sévices sur sa femme; **divorce on the grounds of ~** divorce *m* pour sévices; **mental ~** cruauté mentale.

cruet ['kruːɪt] *n* petit flacon; (*Rel*) burette *f*; (*oil bottle*) huilier *m*; (*vinegar bottle*) vinaigrier *m*; (*mustard jar*) moutardier *m*; (*all three*: *also* **~ stand**) ≃ huilier; (*Brit*: *also* **~ set**) salière *f* et poivrier *m*.

cruise [kruːz] **1** *vi* **(a)** *[fleet, ship]* croiser. **they are cruising in the Pacific** (*Naut*) ils croisent dans le Pacifique; *[tourists]* ils sont en croisière dans le Pacifique.

(b) *[cars]* rouler; *[aircraft]* voler. **the car was cruising (along) at 80 km/h** la voiture faisait 80 km/h sans effort; **we were cruising along the road when suddenly ...** nous roulions tranquillement quand tout à coup ...; (*Aut, Aviat*) **cruising speed** vitesse *f* or régime *m* de croisière; (*Aviat*) **cruising range** autonomie *f* de vol; **cruising yacht** yacht *m* de croisière.

(c) *[taxi, patrol car]* marauder, faire la maraude. **a cruising taxi** un taxi en maraude.

2 *n* (*Naut*) croisière *f*. **to go on** *or* **for a ~** partir en croisière, faire une croisière.

cruiser ['kruːzəʳ] *n* (*Naut*) croiseur *m*. (*Boxing*) **~ weight** poids *m* mi-lourd; *V* **battle** *etc*.

cruller ['krʌləʳ] *n* (*US*) beignet *m*.

crumb [krʌm] *n* miette *f*; (*U: inside of loaf*) mie *f*; (*fig*) miette, brin *m*; *[information]* miettes, fragments *mpl*. **a ~ of comfort** un brin de réconfort; **~s!*** ça alors!, zut!*; **he's a ~*** c'est un pauvre type*; *V* **bread.**

crumble ['krʌmbl] **1** *vt bread* émietter; *plaster* effriter; *earth* (faire s')ébouler.

2 *vi [bread]* s'émietter; *[buildings etc]* tomber en ruines, se désagréger; *[plaster]* s'effriter; *[earth]* s'ébouler; (*fig*) *[hopes etc]* s'effondrer, s'écrouler.

3 *n dessert à la compote (pommes, rhubarbe etc)*.

crumbly ['krʌmblɪ] *adj* friable.

crumby‡, **crummy**‡ ['krʌmɪ] *adj* minable*. **what a ~ thing to do!** c'est un coup minable!*, c'est vraiment mesquin de faire ça!

crump [krʌmp] *n* éclatement *m* (*d'un obus*); (*Mil sl: shell*) obus *m*.

crumpet ['krʌmpɪt] *n* (*Culin*) petite crêpe épaisse (*servie chaude et beurrée*). (*fig: girl*) **a bit of ~**‡ une belle poule*.

crumple ['krʌmpl] **1** *vt* froisser, friper; (*also* **~ up**) chiffonner. **he ~d the paper (up) into a ball** il a fait une boule de sa feuille (de papier).

2 *vi* se froisser, se chiffonner, se friper. (*fig*) **her features ~d when she heard the bad news** son visage s'est décomposé quand elle a appris la mauvaise nouvelle.

crunch [krʌntʃ] **1** *vt* **(a)** (*with teeth*) croquer. **to ~ an apple/a biscuit** croquer une pomme/un biscuit.

(b) (*underfoot*) écraser, faire craquer.

2 *vi*: **he ~ed across the gravel** il a traversé en faisant craquer le gravier sous ses pas.

3 *n* (*sound of teeth*) coup *m* de dents; (*of broken glass, gravel etc*) craquement *m*, crissement *m*. (*fig: moment of reckoning*) **the ~*** l'instant *m* critique; **here's the ~*** c'est le moment crucial; **when it comes to the ~* he ...** dans une situation critique, il ... .

crunch up *vt sep* broyer.

crunchy ['krʌntʃɪ] *adj apple, celery* croquant; *biscuit* croustillant, croquant; *bread* croustillant.

crupper ['krʌpəʳ] *n [harness]* croupière *f*; (*hindquarters*) croupe *f* (*de cheval*).

crusade [kruː'seɪd] **1** *n* (*Hist: also fig*) croisade *f*. **2** *vi* (*fig*) faire une croisade (*against* contre, *for* pour); (*Hist*) partir en croisade, être à la croisade.

crusader [kruː'seɪdəʳ] *n* (*Hist*) croisé *m*; (*fig*) champion *m* (*for* de).

crush [krʌʃ] **1** *n* **(a)** (*crowd*) foule *f*, cohue *f*. **there was a great ~ to get in** c'était la bousculade pour entrer; **there was a terrible ~ at the concert** il y avait une vraie cohue au concert; **he was lost in the ~** il était perdu dans la foule *or* la cohue.

(b) to have a ~ on sb* avoir le béguin* pour qn.

(c) (*Brit: drink*) jus *m* de fruit. **orange ~** orange pressée.

2 *cpd*: (*Brit*) **crush barrier** barrière *f* or rampe *f* de sécurité; **crush-resistant** infroissable.

3 *vt* **(a)** (*compress*) *stones, old cars* écraser, broyer; *grapes* écraser, presser; *ore* bocarder. **to ~ to a pulp** réduire en pulpe; **to ~ objects into a suitcase** tasser *or* entasser des objets dans une valise.

(b) (*crumple*) *clothes* froisser. **to ~ clothes into a bag** fourrer *or* bourrer des vêtements dans une valise; **we were very ~ed in the car** nous étions très tassés dans la voiture.

(c) (*overwhelm*) *enemy* écraser, accabler; *country* écraser; *revolution* écraser, réprimer; *hope* détruire; *opponent in argument* écraser; (*snub*) remettre à sa place, rabrouer.

4 *vi* **(a)** s'écraser, se presser, se serrer. **they ~ed round him** ils se pressaient autour de lui; **they ~ed into the car** ils se sont entassés *or* tassés dans la voiture; **to ~ (one's way) into/through** *etc* se frayer un chemin dans/à travers *etc*.

(b) *[clothes]* se froisser.

crush out *vt sep juice etc* presser, exprimer; *cigarette end* écraser, éteindre; (*fig*) *revolt* écraser, réprimer.

crushing ['krʌʃɪŋ] *adj defeat* écrasant; *reply* percutant.

crust [krʌst] **1** *n* (*on bread, pie, snow*) croûte *f*; (*piece of ~*) croûton *m*, croûte *f*; (*Med: on wound, sore*) croûte, escarre *f*; *[wine]* dépôt *m* (*de tanin*). **there were only a few ~s to eat** pour toute nourriture il n'y avait que quelques croûtes de pain; **a thin ~ of ice** une fine couche de glace; (*Geol*) **the earth's ~** la croûte terrestre; *V* **upper. 2** *vt*: **~ed snow** neige tôlée.

crustacean [krʌs'teɪʃən] *adj, n* crustacé (*m*).

crusty ['krʌstɪ] *adj loaf* croustillant; (**fig: irritable*) hargneux, bourru.

crutch [krʌtʃ] *n* **(a)** (*support*) soutien *m*, support *m*; (*Med*) béquille *f*; (*Archit*) étançon *m*; (*Naut*) support (de gui). **he gets about on ~es** il marche avec des béquilles; (*fig*) **alcohol is a ~ for him** l'alcool lui sert de soutien.

(b) (*Anat: crotch*) fourche *f*; *[trousers etc]* entre-jambes *m inv*.

crux [krʌks] *n* point crucial; *[problem]* cœur *m*, centre *m*. **the ~ of the matter** le nœud de l'affaire, le point capital dans l'affaire.

cry [kraɪ] **1** *n* **(a)** (*loud shout: also of sellers, paperboys etc*) cri *m*; *[hounds]* aboiements *mpl*, voix *f*. **to give a ~** pousser un cri; **he gave a ~ for help** il a crié *or* appelé au secours; **he heard a ~ for help** il a entendu crier au secours; **the cries of the victims** les cris des victimes; (*fig*) **there was a great ~ against the rise in prices** la hausse des prix a soulevé un tollé; *V* **far, full.**

(b) (*watchword*) slogan *m*. **'votes for women' was their ~** leur slogan était 'le vote pour les femmes'; *V* **battle, war.**

(c) (*weep*) **she had a good ~*** elle a pleuré un bon coup*.

2 *cpd*: **crybaby** pleurnicheur *m*, -euse *f*.

3 *vt* **(a)** (*shout out*) crier; (*announce*) crier, proclamer. **to ~ mercy** crier grâce; **to ~ shame** crier au scandale; **to ~ shame on sb/sth** crier haro sur qn/qch; (*fig*) **to ~ wolf** crier au loup; *V* **quits.**

(b) to ~ o.s. to sleep s'endormir à force de pleurer; **to ~ one's eyes** *or* **one's heart out** pleurer toutes les larmes de son corps.

4 *vi* **(a)** (*weep*) pleurer (*about, for, over* sur). **to ~ with rage** pleurer de rage; **to laugh till one cries** pleurer de rire, rire aux larmes; **to ~ for sth** pleurer pour avoir qch; (*fig*) **I'll give him sth to ~ for!*** je vais lui apprendre à pleurnicher!; (*Prov*) **it's no use ~ing over spilt milk** ce qui est fait est fait; *V* **shoulder.**

(b) (*call out*) *[person, animal, bird]* pousser un cri *or* des cris. **the baby cried at birth** l'enfant a poussé un cri *or* a crié en naissant; **he cried (out) with pain** il a poussé un cri de douleur; **to ~ for help** appeler à l'aide, crier au secours; **to ~ for mercy** demander miséricorde, implorer la pitié; **the starving crowd cried for bread** la foule affamée réclama du pain; *V* **moon.**

(c) (*shout*) s'écrier, crier. **'here I am' he cried** 'me voici' s'écria-t-il; **'go away' he cried to me** 'allez-vous-en' me cria-t-il.

(d) *[hunting dogs]* donner de la voix, aboyer.

cry down *vt sep* (*: *decry*) décrier.

cry off 1 *vi* (*from meeting*) se décommander; (*from promise*) se dédire, se rétracter. **I'm crying off!** je ne veux plus rien savoir!

2 *vt fus* (*cancel*) *arrangement, deal* annuler; (*withdraw from*) *project* ne plus se mêler à, se retirer de, se désintéresser de; *meeting* décommander.

cry out *vi* (*inadvertently*) pousser un cri; (*deliberately*) s'écrier. **he cried out with joy** il a poussé un cri de joie; **to cry out to sb** appeler qn à haute voix, crier pour appeler qn; **to cry out for sth** demander *or* réclamer qch à grands cris; (*fig*) **that floor is just crying out to be washed*** ce plancher a grandement besoin d'être lavé; (*fig*) **the door is crying out for a coat of paint*** la porte a bien besoin d'une couche de peinture.

cry up* *vt sep* (*praise*) vanter, exalter. **he's not all he's cried up to be** il n'est pas à la hauteur de sa réputation, il n'est pas aussi formidable* qu'on le dit.

crying ['kraɪɪŋ] **1** *adj* (*lit*) pleurant, qui pleure; (*fig*) criant, flagrant. **~ injustice** injustice criante *or* flagrante; **~ need for sth** besoin pressant *or* urgent de qch; **it's a ~ shame** c'est une honte, c'est honteux; (*excl*) **for ~ out loud!**‡ il ne manquait plus que ça!, c'est le bouquet!*

2 *n* (*shouts*) cris *mpl*; (*weeping*) larmes *fpl*, pleurs *mpl*.

crypt [krɪpt] *n* crypte *f*.

cryptic(al) ['krɪptɪk(əl)] *adj* (*secret*) secret; (*mysterious*) sibyllin, énigmatique; (*occult*) occulte; (*terse*)laconique.

cryptically ['krɪptɪkəlɪ] *adv* (*mysteriously*) énigmatiquement; (*tersely*) laconiquement.

cryptogram ['krɪptəʊgræm] *n* cryptogramme *m*.

cryptographer [krɪp'tɒgrəfəʳ] *n* cryptographe *mf*.

cryptographic(al) [,krɪptəʊ'græfɪk(əl)] *adj* cryptographique.

cryptography [krɪp'tɒgrəfɪ] *n* cryptographie *f*.

crystal ['krɪstl] **1** *n* **(a)** (*U*) cristal *m*; *V* **rock**[2].
(b) (*Chem, Min*) cristal *m*. **salt ~s** cristaux de sel.
(c) (*US: watch glass*) verre *m* de montre.
(d) (*Rad*) galène *f*.
2 *cpd* (*lit*) *vase* de cristal; (*fig*) *waters, lake* de cristal (*fig, liter*). **crystal ball** boule *f* de cristal; **crystal-clear** clair comme le jour *or* comme de l'eau de roche; **crystal-gazer** voyante *f* (*qui lit dans la boule de cristal*); **crystal-gazing** l'art *m* de la voyante; (*fig*) les prédictions *fpl*, les prophéties *fpl*; (*Rad*) **crystal set** poste *m* à galène.

crystalline ['krɪstəlaɪn] *adj* cristallin, clair *or* pur comme le cristal. (*Opt*) **~ lens** cristallin *m*.

crystallize ['krɪstəlaɪz] **1** *vi* (*lit, fig*) se cristalliser. **2** *vt* cristalliser; *sugar* (faire) cuire au cassé. **~d fruits** fruits confits *or* candis.

crystallography [,krɪstə'lɒgrəfɪ] *n* cristallographie *f*.

cub [kʌb] **1** *n* [*animal*] petit(e) *m(f)*; (*: *youth*) gosse *m*, petit morveux (*pej*); *V* **bear**[2], **fox, wolf** *etc*. **2** *cpd*: (*Scouting*) **cub master** chef *m*; **cub mistress** cheftaine *f*; (*Press*) **cub reporter** jeune reporter *m*; **cub scout** louveteau *m* (*scout*).

Cuba ['kju:bə] *n* Cuba *m* (*no art*). **in ~** à Cuba.

Cuban ['kju:bən] **1** *adj* cubain. **2** *n* Cubain(e) *m(f)*.

cubbyhole ['kʌbɪhəʊl] *n* (*room*) petit coin confortable; (*cupboard*) débarras *m*, cagibi *m*; (*Brit Aut*) vide-poches *m inv*.

cube [kju:b] **1** *n* (*gen, Culin, Math*) cube *m*. (*Math*) **~ root** racine *f* cubique; *V* **soup, stock**. **2** *vt* (*Math*) cuber; (*Culin*) couper en cubes *or* en dés.

cubic ['kju:bɪk] *adj* (*of shape, volume*) cubique; (*of measures*) cube. **~ capacity** volume *m*; **~ content** contenance *f* cubique; **~ measure** mesure *f* de volume; **~ metre** mètre *m* cube; (*Math*) **~ equation** équation *f* du troisième degré.

cubicle ['kju:bɪkəl] *n* [*hospital, dormitory*] box *m*, alcôve *f*; [*swimming baths*] cabine *f*.

cubism ['kju:bɪzəm] *n* cubisme *m*.

cubist ['kju:bɪst] *adj, n* cubiste (*mf*).

cuckold† ['kʌkəld] **1** *n* (mari *m*) cocu‡ *m*. **2** *vt* cocufier‡, faire cocu‡.

cuckoo ['kʊku:] **1** *n* (*Orn*) coucou *m*. **2** *adj*(‡) piqué*, toqué*. **to go ~**‡ perdre la boule*. **3** *cpd*: **cuckoo clock** coucou *m* (*pendule*); (*Bot*) **cuckoo spit** crachat *m* de coucou.

cucumber ['kju:kʌmbəʳ] *n* concombre *m*; *V* **cool**.

cud [kʌd] *n V* **chew 1**.

cuddle ['kʌdl] **1** *n* étreinte *f*, caresse(s) *f(pl)*. [*child*] **to have a ~** faire (un) câlin*.
2 *vt* embrasser, caresser; *child* bercer, câliner.
3 *vi* s'enlacer, se serrer, se blottir l'un contre l'autre.
cuddle down *vi* [*child in bed*] se pelotonner. **cuddle down now!** maintenant allonge-toi (et dors)!
cuddle up *vi* se pelotonner (*to, against* contre).

cuddly ['kʌdlɪ] *adj child* caressant, câlin; *animal* qui donne envie de le caresser; *toy* doux (*f* douce), qu'on a envie de câliner.

cudgel ['kʌdʒəl] **1** *n* gourdin *m*, trique *f*. (*fig*) **to take up the ~s for** *or* **on behalf of** prendre fait et cause pour. **2** *vt* frapper à coups de trique. (*fig*) **to ~ one's brains** se creuser la cervelle *or* la tête (*for* pour).

cue [kju:] **1** *n* **(a)** (*Theat*) (*verbal*) réplique *f* (*indiquant à un acteur qu'il doit parler*); (*action*) signal *m*; (*Mus*) signal d'entrée; (*Rad, TV*) signal. (*Theat*) **to give sb his ~** donner la réplique à qn; (*Theat*) **to take one's ~** entamer sa réplique; (*Theat*) **X's exit was the ~ for Y's entrance** la sortie d'X donnait à Y le signal de son entrée; (*fig*) **to take one's ~ from sb** emboîter le pas à qn (*fig*).
(b) (*Billiards*) queue *f* de billard.
(c) [*wig*] queue *f* (*de perruque*).
2 *vt* (*Theat*) donner la réplique à.
cue in *vt sep* (*Rad, TV*) donner le signal à; (*Theat*) donner la réplique à.

cuff [kʌf] **1** *n* **(a)** [*garment*] poignet *m*, manchette *f*; [*shirt*] manchette; [*coat*] parement *m*; (*US*) [*trousers*] revers *m inv* de pantalon. **~link** bouton *m* de manchette; (*fig*) **off the ~** impromptu, à l'improviste; (*US*) **to buy on the ~**‡ acheter à crédit. **(b)** (*blow*) gifle *f*, calotte* *f*. **2** *vt* (*strike*) gifler, calotter*.

cul-de-sac ['kʌldə'sæk] *n* (*esp Brit*) cul-de-sac *m*, impasse *f*. (*road sign*) '~' 'voie sans issue'.

culinary ['kʌlɪnərɪ] *adj* culinaire.

cull [kʌl] *vt* (*liter*) *flowers* cueillir; (*fig*) choisir, sélectionner.

culminate ['kʌlmɪneɪt] *vi* (*lit, fig*) culminer. **to ~ in sth** finir *or* se terminer par qch; **it ~ed in his throwing her out** pour finir il l'a mise à la porte.

culminating ['kʌlmɪneɪtɪŋ] *adj* culminant. **~ point** point culminant, sommet *m*.

culmination [,kʌlmɪ'neɪʃən] *n* (*Astron*) culmination *f*; (*fig*) [*success, career*] apogée *m*; [*disturbance, quarrel*] point culminant.

culotte(s) [kju(:)'lɒt(s)] *n(pl)* jupe-culotte *f*.

culpability [,kʌlpə'bɪlɪtɪ] *n* culpabilité *f*.

culpable ['kʌlpəbl] *adj* coupable (*of* de), blâmable. (*Jur*) **~ homicide** homicide *m* volontaire; (*Scot*) homicide sans préméditation; (*Jur*) **~ negligence** négligence *f* coupable.

culprit ['kʌlprɪt] *n* coupable *mf*; (*Jur*) accusé(e) *m(f)*, prévenu(e) *m(f)*.

cult [kʌlt] **1** *n* (*Rel, fig*) culte *m* (*of* de). **he made a ~ of cleanliness** il avait le culte de la propreté. **2** *cpd*: **cult figure** objet *m* d'un culte, idole *f*.

cultivable ['kʌltɪvəbl] *adj* cultivable.

cultivate ['kʌltɪveɪt] *vt* (*lit, fig*) cultiver. **to ~ the mind** se cultiver (l'esprit).

cultivated ['kʌltɪveɪtɪd] *adj land, person* cultivé; *voice* distingué. **~ pearls** perles *fpl* de culture.

cultivation [,kʌltɪ'veɪʃən] *n* culture *f*. **fields under ~** cultures *fpl*; **out of ~** en friche, inculte.

cultivator ['kʌltɪveɪtəʳ] *n* (*person*) cultivateur *m*, -trice *f*; (*machine*) cultivateur; (*power-driven*) motoculteur *m*.

cultural ['kʌltʃərəl] *adj* **(a)** (*fig*) culturel. **~ environment** environnement *or* milieu culturel. **(b)** (*Agr*) de culture, cultural.

culture ['kʌltʃəʳ] **1** *n* **(a)** (*physical, intellectual development*) culture *f*. **physical ~** culture physique; **a woman of no ~** une femme sans aucune culture *or* complètement inculte; **French ~** la culture française.
(b) (*Agr*) culture *f*; [*bees*] apiculture *f*; [*fish*] pisciculture *f*; [*farm animals*] élevage *m*.
(c) (*Med*) culture *f*.
2 *cpd tube* à culture. **culture fluid** bouillon *m* de culture; **culture medium** milieu *m* de culture; (*hum*) **culture vulture*** lèche-culture *m inv* (*hum*), intellectuel(le) *m(f)* de choc (*pej*).

cultured ['kʌltʃəd] *adj* (*gen, Agr, Med*) cultivé. **~ pearl** perle *f* de culture.

culvert ['kʌlvət] *n* caniveau *m*.

cumbersome ['kʌmbəsəm] *adj*, **cumbrous** ['kʌmbrəs] *adj* (*bulky*) encombrant, embarrassant; (*heavy*) lourd, pesant.

cumin ['kʌmɪn] *n* cumin *m*.

cummerbund ['kʌməbʌnd] *n* ceinture *f* (*de smoking; aussi portée par les Hindous*).

cumulative ['kju:mjʊlətɪv] *adj* cumulatif. (*Jur*) **~ evidence** preuve *f* par accumulation de témoignages; (*Fin*) **~ interest** intérêt cumulatif; **~ voting** vote plural.

cumulonimbus ['kju:mjələʊ'nɪmbəs] *n* cumulo-nimbus *m inv*.

cumulus ['kju:mjələs] *n* cumulus *m*.

cuneiform ['kju:nɪfɔ:m] **1** *adj* cunéiforme. **2** *n* écriture *f* cunéiforme.

cunning ['kʌnɪŋ] **1** *n* finesse *f*, astuce *f*; (*pej*) ruse *f*, fourberie *f*, duplicité *f*; (††: *skill*) habileté *f*, adresse *f*. **2** *adj* **(a)** astucieux, malin; (*pej*) rusé, fourbe. **a ~ little gadget*** un petit truc astucieux*. **(b)** (*US*‡) charmant, mignon.

cunningly ['kʌnɪŋlɪ] *adv* avec astuce, finement; (*pej*) avec ruse, avec fourberie; (*: *cleverly*) astucieusement.

cunt** [kʌnt] *n* con** *m*, chatte** *f*; (*woman*) nana‡ *f*; (*despicable person*) salaud‡ *m*, salope‡ *f*.

cup [kʌp] **1** *n* **(a)** tasse *f*; (*goblet*) coupe *f*; (*metal mug*) timbale *f*, gobelet *m*; (*cupful*) tasse, coupe. **~ of tea** tasse de thé; **he drank four ~s** *or* **~fuls** il (en) a bu quatre tasses; (*Culin*) **one ~** *or* **~ful of sugar/flour** *etc* une tasse de sucre/farine *etc*; **cider/champagne** *etc* **~** cup *m* au cidre/au champagne *etc*; (*fig*) **he was in his ~s** il était dans les vignes du Seigneur, il avait un verre dans le nez*; (*fig*) **that's just his ~ of tea*** c'est tout à fait à son goût, c'est exactement ce qui lui convient; (*fig*) **that's not my ~ of tea*** ce n'est pas du tout à mon goût, ça n'est vraiment pas mon genre*; (*fig*) **it isn't everyone's ~ of tea*** ça ne plaît pas à tout le monde; (*liter*) **his ~ of happiness was full** son bonheur était complet *or* parfait; (*liter*) **to drain the ~ of sorrow** vider *or* boire le calice (jusqu'à la lie); *V* **coffee, slip** *etc*.
(b) (*Tech*) godet *m*; [*flower*] corolle *f*; (*Rel: also* **communion ~**) calice *m*; (*Brit Sport etc: prize*) coupe *f*; (*Geog*) cuvette *f*; (*Anat*) [*bone*] cavité *f* articulaire, glène *f*; (*Med: cupping glass*) ventouse *f*; [*brassière*] bonnet *m* (*de soutien-gorge*); *V* **world**.
2 *vt* **(a) to ~ one's hands** mettre ses mains en coupe; **to ~ one's hands round sth** mettre ses mains autour de qch; **to ~ one's hands round one's ear/one's mouth** mettre ses mains en cornet/en porte-voix.
(b) (*Med* ††) appliquer des ventouses sur.
(c) (*Golf*) **to ~ the ball** faire un divot.
3 *cpd*: **cup bearer** échanson *m*; (*Culin*) **cupcake** petit gâteau; (*Brit Ftbl*) **cup final** finale *f* de la coupe; (*Brit Ftbl*) **cup-tie** match *m* de coupe *or* comptant pour la coupe.

cupboard ['kʌbəd] *n* (*esp Brit*) placard *m*. (*Brit*) **~ love** amour intéressé; *V* **skeleton**.

cupful ['kʌpfʊl] *n* (*contenu d'une*) tasse *f*; *V* **cup**.

Cupid ['kju:pɪd] *n* (*Myth*) Cupidon *m*; (*Art: cherub*) amour *m*. **C~'s darts** les flèches *fpl* de Cupidon.

cupidity [kju:'pɪdɪtɪ] *n* cupidité *f*.

cupola ['kju:pələ] *n* **(a)** (*Archit*) (*dome*) coupole *f*, dôme *m*; (*US: lantern, belfry*) belvédère *m*. **(b)** (*Naut*) coupole *f*. **(c)** (*Metal*) cubilot *m*.

cuppa‡ ['kʌpə] *n* (*Brit*) tasse *f* de thé.

cupric ['kju:prɪk] *adj* cuprique. **~ oxide** oxyde *m* de cuivre.

cur [kɜ:ʳ] *n* **(a)** (*pej: dog*) (*mongrel*) bâtard *m*, corniaud *m*; (*ill-tempered*) sale cabot* *m*. **(b)** (* *pej: man*) malotru *m*, mufle* *m*, rustre *m*.

curable ['kjʊərəbl] *adj* guérissable, curable.

curare [kjʊə'rɑ:rɪ] *n* curare *m*.

curate ['kjʊərɪt] *n* vicaire *m*. (*Brit*) **it's like the ~'s egg** il y a du bon et du mauvais.

curative ['kjʊərətɪv] *adj* curatif.

curator [kjʊə'reɪtəʳ] *n* **(a)** [*museum etc*] conservateur *m*. **(b)** (*Scot Jur*) curateur *m* (*d'un aliéné or d'un mineur*).

curb [kɜ:b] **1** *n* **(a)** [*harness*] gourmette *f*; (*fig*) frein *m*. (*fig*) **to put a ~ on** on mettre un frein à.
(b) (*US*) bord *m* du trottoir; *V* **kerb**.

2 *vt* (*US*) *horse* mettre un mors à; (*fig*) *impatience, passion* refréner, maîtriser, contenir; *expenditure* réduire, restreindre.

3 *cpd*: **curb bit** mors *m*; **curb chain** gourmette *f*; **curb reins** rênes *fpl* de filet; (*Archit*) **curb roof** comble brisé; **curbstone** pavé *m* (*pour bordure de trottoir*); (*US*) **curb(stone) market** marché *m* après bourse.

curd [kɜːd] *n* (*gen pl*) ~(s) lait caillé; *V* **lemon.**

curdle [ˈkɜːdl] **1** *vt milk* cailler; *blood* figer, cailler, coaguler; *oil* figer. **it was enough to ~ the blood** c'était à vous (faire) figer *or* glacer le sang dans les veines.

2 *vi milk* se cailler; *blood* se figer, se cailler, se coaguler. **his blood ~d** son sang s'est figé dans ses veines; (*fig*) **it made my blood ~** cela m'a glacé *or* figé le sang dans les veines.

cure [kjʊəʳ] **1** *vt* **(a)** (*Med*) *disease, patient* guérir (*of* de); (*fig*) *poverty* éliminer; *unfairness* éliminer, remédier à. **to ~ an injustice** réparer une injustice; **to ~ an evil** remédier à un mal; **to be ~d (of)** guérir (de); **to ~ a child of a bad habit** faire perdre une mauvaise habitude à un enfant; **to ~ o.s. of smoking** se déshabituer du tabac, se guérir de l'habitude de fumer; (*Prov*) **what can't be ~d must be endured** il faut savoir accepter l'inévitable.

(b) *meat, fish* (*salt*) saler; (*smoke*) fumer; (*dry*) sécher; *skins* traiter.

2 *n* **(a)** (*Med*) (*remedy*) remède *m*, cure *f*; (*recovery*) guérison *f*. **to take** *or* **follow a ~** faire une cure; **past** *or* **beyond ~** *person* inguérissable, incurable; *state, injustice, evil* irrémédiable, irréparable; *V* **rest.**

(b) (*Rel*) cure *f*. **~ of souls** charge *f* d'âmes.

3 *cpd*: **cure-all** panacée *f*.

curfew [ˈkɜːfjuː] *n* couvre-feu *m*. **to impose a/lift the ~** décréter/lever le couvre-feu.

curing [ˈkjʊərɪŋ] *n* (*V* **cure 1 b**) salaison *f*; fumaison *f*; séchage *m*.

curio [ˈkjʊərɪəʊ] *n* bibelot *m*, curiosité *f*.

curiosity [ˌkjʊərɪˈɒsɪtɪ] *n* **(a)** (*U: inquisitiveness*) curiosité *f* (*about* de). **out of ~** par curiosité; (*Prov*) **~ killed the cat** la curiosité est toujours punie. **(b)** (*rare object*) curiosité *f*, rareté *f*. **~ shop** magasin *m* de brocante *or* de curiosités.

curious [ˈkjʊərɪəs] *adj* **(a)** (*inquisitive*) curieux (*about* de). **I'm ~ to know what he did** je suis curieux de savoir ce qu'il a fait. **(b)** (*odd*) curieux, bizarre, singulier.

curiously [ˈkjʊərɪəslɪ] *adv* (*inquisitively*) avec curiosité; (*oddly*) curieusement, singulièrement. **~ enough, he didn't come** chose bizarre, il n'est pas venu.

curl [kɜːl] **1** *n* **(a)** *[hair]* boucle *f* (de cheveux).

(b) (*gen*) courbe *f*; *[smoke]* spirale *f*, volute *f*; *[waves]* ondulation *f*; *[wood grain]* ronce *f*. (*fig*) **with a ~ of the lip** avec une moue méprisante.

2 *cpd*: **curling irons, curling tongs** fer *m* à friser; **curl paper** papillote *f*.

3 *vt hair* (*loosely*) (faire) boucler; (*tightly*) friser. **she ~s her hair** elle frise *or* boucle ses cheveux; **he ~ed his lip in disdain** il a fait une moue méprisante.

4 *vi [hair]* (*tightly*) friser; (*loosely*) boucler. (*fig*) **it's enough to make your hair ~*** c'est à vous faire dresser les cheveux sur la tête; **his lip ~ed** sa lèvre s'est retroussée.

curl up 1 *vi* s'enrouler; *[person]* se pelotonner; (*: *from shame etc*) rentrer sous terre; *[cat]* se mettre en boule, se pelotonner; *[dog]* se coucher en rond; *[leaves, stale bread]* se racornir. **he lay curled up on the floor** il était couché en boule par terre; **to curl up with laughter** se tordre de rire; **the smoke curled up** la fumée montait en volutes *or* en spirales.

2 *vt sep* enrouler. **to curl o.s. up** *[person]* se pelotonner; *[cat]* se mettre en boule, se pelotonner; *[dog]* se coucher en rond.

curler [ˈkɜːləʳ] *n* **(a)** *[hair]* rouleau *m*, bigoudi *m*. **(b)** (*Scot Sport*) joueur *m*, -euse *f* de curling.

curlew [ˈkɜːluː] *n* courlis *m*.

curlicue [ˈkɜːlɪkjuː] *n [handwriting]* fioriture *f*; *[skating]* figure *f* (*de patinage*).

curling [ˈkɜːlɪŋ] *n* (*Sport*) curling *m*.

curly [ˈkɜːlɪ] *adj hair* (*loosely*) bouclé; (*tightly*) frisé. **~ eyelashes** cils recourbés; **~-haired, ~-headed** aux cheveux bouclés *or* frisés; **~ lettuce** laitue frisée.

currant [ˈkʌrənt] *n* **(a)** (*Bot*) (*fruit*) groseille *f*; (*also* **~ bush**) groseillier *m*; *V* **black, red. (b)** (*dried fruit*) raisin *m* de Corinthe, raisin sec. **~ bun** petit pain *m* aux raisins.

currency [ˈkʌrənsɪ] **1** *n* (*U*) **(a)** (*Fin: money*) monnaie *f*, argent *m*. **the ~ is threatened** la monnaie est en danger; **this coin is no longer legal ~** cette pièce n'a plus cours (légal); **foreign ~** devise *or* monnaie étrangère; *V* **hard, paper** *etc*.

(b) (*Fin*) circulation *f*. **this coin is no longer in ~** cette pièce n'est plus en circulation.

(c) (*acceptance, prevalence*) cours *m*, circulation *f*. **to gain ~** se répandre, s'accréditer; **to give ~ to** accréditer; **such words have short ~** de tels mots n'ont pas cours longtemps.

2 *cpd*: **currency note** billet *m*.

current [ˈkʌrənt] **1** *adj opinion* courant, commun, admis; *word, phrase* commun, courant; *price* courant, en cours; *fashion, tendency, popularity* actuel. **to be ~** *[report, rumour]* avoir cours; *[phrase, expression]* être accepté *or* courant; **to be in ~ use** être d'usage courant; (*Brit Banking*) **~ account** compte courant; **~ affairs** questions *fpl or* problèmes *mpl* d'actualité; (*Fin*) **~ assets** actif *m* réalisable et disponible, actifs de roulement; **~ events** événements actuels, actualité *f* (*U*); (*Press*) **~ issue** dernier numéro; **~ month** mois courant *or* en cours; **~ week** semaine *f* en cours; **his ~ job** le travail qu'il fait *or* le poste qu'il occupe en ce moment; **her ~ boyfriend*** le copain *or* petit ami du moment.

2 *n [air, water]* courant *m* (*also Elec*); (*fig: of events etc*) cours *m*, tendance *f*; (*of opinions*) tendance. (*lit, fig*) **to go with the ~** suivre le courant; **to drift with the ~** (*lit*) se laisser aller au fil de l'eau; (*fig*) aller selon le vent; **to go against the ~** (*lit*) remonter le courant; (*fig*) aller à contre-courant; *V* **alternating, direct.**

currently [ˈkʌrəntlɪ] *adv* actuellement, en ce moment. **it is ~ thought that ...** on pense maintenant *or* à présent que ... .

curriculum [kəˈrɪkjʊləm] *n* programme *m* scolaire *or* d'études. **~ vitae** curriculum vitae *m*, C.V.*m*.

curry[1] [ˈkʌrɪ] (*Culin*) **1** *n* curry *m or* cari *m*. **beef ~** curry de bœuf. **2** *cpd*: **curry powder** poudre *f* de curry. **3** *vt* accommoder au curry.

curry[2] [ˈkʌrɪ] **1** *vt horse* étriller; *leather* corroyer. (*fig*) **to ~ favour with sb** chercher à gagner la faveur de qn. **2** *cpd*: **curry-comb** (*n*) étrille *f*; (*vt*) étriller.

curse [kɜːs] **1** *n* **(a)** malédiction *f*. **a ~ on him!**† maudit soit-il!†; **to call down a ~ on sb** maudire qn.

(b) (*swearword*) juron *m*, imprécation *f*. **~s!*** zut!*

(c) (*fig: bane*) fléau *m*, malheur *m*, calamité *f*. **the ~ of drunkenness** le fléau de l'ivrognerie; **it has been the ~ of my life** c'est un sort qui m'a poursuivi toute ma vie; (*menstruation*) **she has the ~*** elle a ses règles; **this essay is a dreadful ~*** quelle corvée cette dissertation!; **the ~* of it is that ...** l'embêtant* c'est que ... .

2 *vt* maudire. **~ the child!*** maudit enfant!; (*fig*) **to be ~d with** être affligé de.

3 *vi* jurer, sacrer.

cursed* [ˈkɜːsɪd] *adj* sacré*, maudit, satané (*all before n*).

cursive [ˈkɜːsɪv] **1** *adj* cursif. **2** *n* (écriture *f*) cursive *f*.

cursorily [ˈkɜːsərɪlɪ] *adv* (*V* **cursory**) superficiellement; hâtivement, à la hâte.

cursory [ˈkɜːsərɪ] *adj* (*superficial*) superficiel; (*hasty*) hâtif. **to give a ~ glance at** *person, object* jeter un coup d'œil à; *book, essay, letter* lire en diagonale*.

curt [kɜːt] *adj person, manner* brusque, sec (*f* sèche), cassant; *explanation, question* brusque, sec. **in a ~ voice** d'un ton cassant; **with a ~ nod** avec un bref signe de tête.

curtail [kɜːˈteɪl] *vt account* écourter, raccourcir, tronquer; *proceedings, visit* écourter; *period of time* écourter, raccourcir; *wages* rogner, réduire; *expenses* restreindre, réduire.

curtailment [kɜːˈteɪlmənt] *n* (*V* **curtail**) raccourcissement *m*; réduction *f*.

curtain [ˈkɜːtn] **1** *n* **(a)** (*gen, Theat*) rideau *m*; (*fig*) rideau, voile *m*. **to draw** *or* **pull the ~s** tirer les rideaux; (*Mil*) **~ of fire** rideau de feu; (*fig*) **it was ~s for him‡** il était fichu* *or* foutu‡; *V* **iron, safety.**

(b) (*Theat: also* **~ call**) rappel *m*. **she took 3 ~s** elle a été rappelée 3 fois.

2 *cpd*: **curtain hook** crochet *m* de rideau; (*Theat*) **curtain raiser** lever *m* de rideau; **curtain ring** anneau *m* de rideau; **curtain rod** tringle *f* à rideau(x).

3 *vt window* garnir de rideaux.

curtain off *vt sep room* diviser par un *or* des rideau(x); *bed, kitchen area* cacher derrière un *or* des rideau(x).

curtly [ˈkɜːtlɪ] *adv* avec brusquerie, sèchement, d'un ton cassant.

curtness [ˈkɜːtnɪs] *n* brusquerie *f*, sécheresse *f*.

curtsey, curtsy [ˈkɜːtsɪ] **1** *n* révérence *f*. **to make** *or* **drop a ~** faire une révérence. **2** *vi* faire une révérence (*to* à).

curvaceous* [kɜːˈveɪʃəs] *adj woman* bien balancée*, bien roulée*.

curvature [ˈkɜːvətʃəʳ] *n* courbure *f*; (*Med*) déviation *f*. **~ of the spine** déviation de la colonne vertébrale, scoliose *f*; **the ~ of space** la courbure de l'espace.

curve [kɜːv] **1** *n* (*gen*) courbe *f*; *[arch]* voussure *f*; *[beam]* cambrure *f*; *[graph]* courbe. **~ in the road** courbe, tournant *m*, virage *m*; **a woman's ~s*** les rondeurs *fpl* d'une femme.

2 *vt* courber; (*Archit*) *arch, roof* cintrer. **space is ~d** l'espace est courbe.

3 *vi [surface, beam]* se courber, s'infléchir; *[road etc]* faire une courbe, être en courbe. **the road ~s down into the valley** la route descend en courbe dans la vallée; **the river ~s round the town** la rivière fait un méandre autour de la ville.

curvet [ˈkʌrvɪt] (*Equitation*) **1** *n* courbette *f*.**2** *vi* faire une courbette.

curvilinear [ˈkɜːvɪˈlɪnɪəʳ] *adj* curviligne.

cushion [ˈkʊʃən] **1** *n* **(a)** coussin *m*. **on a ~ of air** sur un coussin d'air; *V* **pin** *etc*.

(b) (*Billiards*) bande *f*. **stroke off the ~** doublé *m*.

2 *vt sofa* mettre des coussins à; *seat* rembourrer; (*Tech*) matelasser; (*fig*) *shock* amortir. **to ~ sb's fall** amortir la chute de qn; (*fig*) **to ~ sb against sth** protéger qn contre qch.

cushy‡ [ˈkʊʃɪ] *adj* (*Brit*) pépère‡, tranquille. **a ~ job** une bonne planque‡, un boulot pépère‡; **to have a ~ time** se la couler douce*; *V* **billet**[1].

cusp [kʌsp] *n* (*Bot*), *[tooth]* cuspide *f*; *[moon]* corne *f*.

cuspidor [ˈkʌspɪdɔːʳ] *n* (*US*) crachoir *m*.

cuss* [kʌs] (*US* = **curse**) **1** *n* **(a)** (*oath*) juron *m*. **he's not worth a tinker's ~** il ne vaut pas un pet de lapin*. **(b)** (*gen pej: person*) individu *m* (*pej*), type* *m*, bonne femme (*gen pej*). **he's a queer ~** c'est un drôle de type*. **2** *vi* jurer.

cussed* [ˈkʌsɪd] *adj* entêté, têtu comme une mule*.

cussedness* [ˈkʌsɪdnɪs] *n* esprit contrariant *or* de contradiction. **out of sheer ~** histoire d'embêter le monde*.

custard [ˈkʌstəd] **1** *n* (*pouring*) crème anglaise; (*set*) crème renversée. **2** *cpd*: (*Bot*) **custard apple** anone *f*; **custard cream (biscuit)** biscuit fourré; **custard powder** crème instantanée (en poudre); **custard tart** flan *m*.

custodian [kʌsˈtəʊdɪən] *n [building]* concierge *mf*, gardien(ne) *m(f)*; *[museum]* conservateur *m*, -trice *f*; *[tradition etc]* gardien(ne), protecteur *m*, -trice *f*.

custody ['kʌstədɪ] *n* **(a)** (*Jur etc*) garde *f*. **in safe ~** sous bonne garde; **the child is in the ~ of his aunt** l'enfant est sous la garde de sa tante; (*Jur*) **after the divorce she was given ~ of the children** après le divorce elle a reçu la garde des enfants.

(b) (*imprisonment*) emprisonnement *m*, captivité *f*. **in ~** en détention préventive; **to take sb into ~** mettre qn en état d'arrestation; **to give sb into ~** remettre qn aux mains de la police; *V* **protective.**

custom ['kʌstəm] **1** *n* **(a)** (*established behaviour*) coutume *f*, usage *m*, pratique courante; (*habit*) coutume, habitude *f*. **as ~ has it** selon la coutume, selon les us et coutumes; **it was his ~ to rest each morning** il avait l'habitude de se reposer chaque matin.

(b) (*Brit Comm*) clientèle *f*, pratique†† *f*. **the grocer wanted to get her ~** l'épicier voulait obtenir sa clientèle; **he has lost a lot of ~** il a perdu beaucoup de clients; **he took his ~ elsewhere** il est allé se fournir ailleurs.

(c) (*Jur*) coutume *f*, droit coutumier.

(d) (*duties payable*) **~s** droits *mpl* de douane; **the ~s** la douane; **to go through the ~s** passer la douane.

2 *cpd*: (*Comm*) **custom-built** (fait) sur commande; (*Comm*) **custom-made** *clothes* (fait) sur mesure; *other goods* (fait) sur commande; **customs duty** droit(s) *m(pl)* de douane; **customs house** (poste *m* *or* bureaux *mpl* de) douane *f*; **customs inspection** visite douanière *or* de douane; **customs officer** douanier *m*; **customs post** = **customs house**; **customs service** service *m* des douanes; **customs union** union douanière.

customary ['kʌstəmərɪ] *adj* habituel, coutumier, ordinaire; (*Jur*) coutumier. (*Jur*) **~ tenant** tenancier *m* censitaire; **it is ~ to do it** c'est ce qui se fait d'habitude, c'est la coutume.

customer ['kʌstəməʳ] *n* **(a)** (*Comm*) client(e) *m(f)*. **(b)** (*) type* *m*, individu *m* (*pej*). **he's an awkward ~** il n'est pas commode; **queer ~** drôle de type* *or* d'individu*; **ugly ~** sale type* *or* individu.

customize ['kʌstəmaɪz] *vt* fabriquer (*or* construire *or* arranger *etc*) sur commande.

cut [kʌt] (*vb*: *pret, ptp* **cut**) **1** *n* **(a)** (*stroke*) coup *m*; *[cards]* coupe *f*; (*mark, slit*) coupure *f*; (*notch*) entaille *f*; (*slash*) estafilade *f*; (*gash*) balafre *f*; (*Med*) incision *f*. **sabre ~** coup de sabre; **saw ~** trait *m* de scie; **a deep ~ in the leg** une profonde coupure à la jambe; **he had a shaving ~ on his chin** il s'était coupé au menton en se rasant; **there is a ~ in his jacket** il y a un accroc à sa veste; (*fig*) **the ~ and thrust of modern politics** les estocades *fpl* de la politique contemporaine; (*fig*) **that remark was a ~ at me** cette remarque était une pierre dans mon jardin; (*fig*) **the unkindest ~ of all** le coup le plus perfide; (*fig*) **he is a ~ above the others*** il vaut mieux que les autres, il est supérieur aux autres; (*fig*) **that's a ~ above him*** ça le dépasse; *V* **short.**

(b) (*reduction*) réduction *f*, diminution *f* (*in* de). **power** *or* **electricity ~** coupure *f* de courant; **to take a ~ in salary** subir une diminution *or* réduction de salaire; **to make ~s in a book/play** *etc* faire des coupures dans un livre/une pièce *etc*.

(c) *[meat]* (*piece*) morceau *m*; (*slice*) tranche *f*; (*: *share*) part *f*. **a nice ~ of beef** un beau morceau de bœuf; **a ~ off** *or* **from the joint** un morceau de rôti; **they all want a ~ in the profits*** ils veulent tous leur part du gâteau* (*fig*).

(d) *[clothes]* coupe *f*; *[jewel]* taille *f*. **I like the ~ of this coat** j'aime la coupe de ce manteau; *V* **jib.**

(e) (*also* **wood~**) planche *f*, gravure *f* (sur bois).

2 *adj* (*U*) **~ glass** cristal taillé; **~ flowers** fleurs coupées; **~ tobacco** tabac découpé; **~ prices** prix réduits; **well-~ coat** manteau bien coupé *or* de bonne coupe; (*fig*) **it was all ~ and dried** (*fixed beforehand*) c'était déjà décidé, tout était déjà arrangé; (*impossible to adapt*) il n'y avait pas moyen de changer quoi que ce soit; **~ and dried opinions** opinions toutes faites.

3 *cpd*: **cutaway (drawing** *or* **sketch)** (dessin *m*) écorché *m*; **cutback** (*reduction*) *[expenditure, production, staff]* réduction *f*, diminution *f* (*in* de); (*Cine*: *flashback*) flashback *m*; **cutoff** (*short cut*) raccourci *m*; (*Tech*: *stopping*) arrêt *m*; **cutoff switch** interrupteur *m*; **cutout** (*Elec*) disjoncteur *m*, coupe-circuit *m inv*; (*Aut*) échappement *m* libre; (*figure of wood or paper*) découpage *m*; **cutout book** livre *m* de découpages; (*Space*) **cutout point** point *m* de largage; **cut-price** au rabais, à prix réduit(s); **cut-price shop** *or* **store** magasin *m* à prix réduits; **cut-throat** assassin *m*; **cut-throat competition** compétition acharnée; (*Cards*) **cut-throat game** partie *f* à trois; (*Brit*) **cut-throat razor** rasoir *m* de coiffeur.

4 *vt* **(a)** couper; *joint of meat* découper; (*slice*) découper en tranches; (*Med*) *abscess* inciser; *tobacco* découper; (*notch*) encocher; (*castrate*) châtrer. **to ~ one's finger** se couper le doigt *or* au doigt; **to ~ sb's throat** couper la gorge à qn, égorger qn; (*fig*) **he is ~ting his own throat** il prépare sa propre ruine (*fig*); **to ~ in half/in three** *etc* couper en deux/en trois *etc*; **to ~ in pieces** (*lit*) couper en morceaux; (*fig*) *army* tailler en pièces; *reputation* démolir; **to ~ open** (*with knife*) ouvrir au *or* avec un couteau; (*with scissors etc*) ouvrir avec des ciseaux *etc*; **he ~ his arm open on a nail** il s'est ouvert le bras sur un clou; **he ~ his head open** il s'est fendu le crâne; **to ~ sb free** délivrer qn en coupant ses liens; (*fig*) **to ~ short** abréger, couper court à; **to ~ a visit short** écourter une visite; **to ~ sb short** couper la parole à qn; **to ~ a long story short, he came** bref *or* pour en finir, il est venu.

(b) (*shape*) couper, tailler; *steps* tailler; *channel* creuser, percer; *figure, statue* sculpter (*out of* dans); (*engrave*) graver; *jewel, key, glass, crystal* tailler; *screw* fileter; *dress* couper. **to ~ a (gramophone) record** graver un disque; **to ~ one's way through** se frayer *or* s'ouvrir un chemin à travers; (*fig*) **to ~ one's coat according to one's cloth** vivre selon ses moyens.

(c) (*mow, clip, trim*) *hedge, trees* tailler; *corn, hay* faucher; *lawn* tondre. **to ~ one's nails/hair** se couper les ongles/les cheveux; **to have** *or* **get one's hair ~** se faire couper les cheveux.

(d) (*: *ignore, avoid*) **to ~ sb (dead)** faire semblant de ne pas voir *or* reconnaître qn; **she ~ me dead** elle a fait comme si elle ne me voyait pas; **to ~ a lecture/class** sécher* un cours/une classe.

(e) (*cross, intersect*) couper, croiser, traverser; (*Math*) couper. **the path ~s the road here** le sentier coupe la route à cet endroit.

(f) (*reduce*) *profits, wages* réduire, diminuer; *text, book, play* réduire, faire des coupures dans. **to ~ prices** réduire les prix, vendre à prix réduit *or* au rabais; **we ~ the journey time by half** nous avons réduit de moitié la durée du trajet; (*Sport*) **he ~ 30 seconds off the record, he ~ the record by 30 seconds** il a amélioré le record de 30 secondes.

(g) (*fig*: *wound, hurt*) *person* blesser (profondément), affecter. **it ~ me to the heart** cela m'a profondément blessé; **the wind ~ his face** le vent lui coupait le visage; *V* **quick.**

(h) *[child]* **to ~ a tooth** percer une dent; **he is ~ting teeth** il fait ses dents; (*fig*) **to ~ one's teeth on sth** se faire les dents sur qch.

(i) *cards* couper.

(j) (*Sport*) **to ~ the ball** couper la balle.

(k) (*phrases*) **he ~ a sorry figure** il faisait piètre figure; **she ~s a fine figure in that dress** elle a grand air (*frm*) *or* elle a beaucoup d'allure dans cette robe; **to ~ a dash** faire de l'effet; **to ~ it fine** compter un peu juste, ne pas (se) laisser de marge; **you're ~ting it too fine** vous comptez trop juste; **that ~s no ice** *or* **that doesn't ~ much ice with me** ça ne me fait aucun effet, ça ne m'impressionne guère, ça me laisse froid; **to ~ the ground from under sb's feet** couper l'herbe sous le pied de qn; **to ~ one's losses** faire la part du feu, sauver les meubles*; (*Aut*) **to ~ a corner** prendre un virage à la corde; (*fig*) **to ~ corners** prendre des raccourcis (*fig*); **to ~ the Gordian knot** trancher le nœud gordien; **~ the cackle!‡** assez bavardé comme ça!*

5 *vi* **(a)** *[person, knife etc]* couper, tailler, trancher. **he ~ into the cake** il a fait une entaille dans le gâteau, il a entamé le gâteau; **~ along the dotted line** découper suivant le pointillé; **his sword ~ through the air** son épée fendit l'air; **this knife ~s well** ce couteau coupe bien; (*fig*) **this ~s across all I have learnt** ceci va à l'encontre de tout ce que j'ai appris; (*fig*) **what you say ~s both ways** ce que vous dites est à double tranchant; (*fig*) **that argument ~s both ways** c'est un argument à double tranchant; (*fig*) **to ~ and run*** mettre les bouts‡, filer*; (*Naut*) **to ~ loose** couper les amarres; (*fig*) **he ~ loose (from his family)** il a coupé les amarres (avec sa famille).

(b) *[material]* se couper. **paper ~s easily** le papier se coupe facilement; **this piece will ~ into 4** ce morceau peut se couper en 4.

(c) (*Math*) se couper. **lines A and B ~ at point C** les lignes A et B se coupent au point C.

(d) (*run, hurry*) **~ across the fields and you'll soon be there** coupez à travers champs et vous serez bientôt arrivé; **to ~ across country** couper à travers champs; **if you ~ through the lane you'll save time** si vous coupez *or* passez par la ruelle vous gagnerez du temps.

(e) (*Cine, TV*) **they ~ from the street to the shop scene** ils passent de la rue à la scène du magasin; **~!** coupez!

(f) (*Cards*) couper. **to ~ for deal** tirer pour la donne.

cut along *vi* s'en aller, filer*.

cut away 1 *vt sep branch* élaguer; *unwanted part* dégager, enlever (en coupant).

2 cutaway *n, adj V* **cut 3.**

cut back 1 *vt sep plants, shrubs* élaguer, tailler; (*fig*: *also* **cut back on**) *production, expenditure* réduire, diminuer.

2 *vi* revenir (sur ses pas). **he cut back to the village and gave his pursuers the slip** il est revenu au village par un raccourci et a semé ses poursuivants.

3 cutback *n V* **cut 3.**

cut down *vt sep* **(a)** *tree* couper, abattre; *corn* faucher; *person* (*by sword etc*) abattre (*d'un coup d'épée etc*); (*fig*: *through illness etc*) terrasser. **cut down by pneumonia** terrassé par la *or* une pneumonie.

(b) (*reduce*) réduire; *expenses* réduire, rogner; *article, essay* couper, tronquer; *clothes* rapetisser, diminuer. (*fig*) **to cut sb down to size*** remettre qn à sa place.

cut down on *vt fus food, drink, cigarettes* économiser sur; *expenditure* réduire.

cut in 1 *vi* (*into conversation*) se mêler à la conversation; (*Aut*) se rabattre. (*Aut*) **to cut in on sb** faire une queue de poisson à qn; (*Comm, Fin*) **to cut in on the market** s'infiltrer sur le marché.

2 *vt sep* **to cut sb in on a deal*** faire entrer qn dans une transaction.

cut off 1 *vi* (*†: *leave*) filer*, se trotter‡.

2 *vt sep* **(a)** *piece of cloth, cheese, meat, bread* couper (*from* dans); *limbs* amputer, couper. **to cut off sb's head** trancher la tête de *or* à qn, décapiter qn; (*loc*) **to cut off one's nose to spite one's face** agir contre son propre intérêt par dépit.

(b) (*disconnect*) *telephone caller, telephone, car engine, gas, electricity* couper. **our water supply has been cut off** on nous a coupé l'eau; (*Telec*) **we were cut off** nous avons été coupés; **to cut off sb's supplies** (*of food, money etc*) couper les vivres à qn.

(c) (*isolate*) isoler (*sb from sth* qn de qch). **to cut o.s. off from** rompre ses liens avec; **he feels very cut off in that town** il se sent très isolé dans cette ville; **town cut off by floods** ville isolée par des inondations; (*Mil*) **to cut off the enemy's retreat**

couper la retraite à l'ennemi; (*fig*) **to cut sb off with a shilling** déshériter qn.

3 cutoff *n, adj V* **cut 3.**

cut out 1 *vi* (*Aut, Aviat*) *[engine]* caler.

2 *vt sep* **(a)** *picture, article* découper (*of, from* de); *statue, figure* sculpter, tailler (*of* dans); *coat* couper, tailler (*of, from* dans). **to cut out a path through the jungle** se frayer un chemin à travers la jungle; (*fig*) **to be cut out for sth** avoir des dispositions pour qch; (*fig*) **he's not cut out for** *or* **to be a doctor** il n'est pas fait pour être médecin, il n'a pas l'étoffe d'un médecin; (*fig*) **he had his work cut out for him** il avait du pain sur la planche; (*fig*) **you'll have your work cut out to get there on time** vous n'avez pas de temps à perdre si vous voulez y arriver à l'heure; **you'll have your work cut out to persuade him to come** vous aurez du mal à le persuader de venir.

(b) (*fig*) *rival* supplanter.

(c) (*remove*) enlever, ôter; *unnecessary detail* élaguer. (*fig*) **cut it out!*** ça suffit!*, ça va comme ça!*; (*fig*) **cut out the talking!** assez bavardé!, vous avez fini de bavarder?; (*fig*) **you can cut out the tears for a start!*** et pour commencer arrête de pleurnicher!

(d) (*give up*) *tobacco* supprimer. **to cut out smoking/drinking** arrêter de fumer/boire.

3 cutout *n, adj V* **cut 3.**

cut up 1 *vi*: **to cut up rough*** se mettre en rogne* *or* en boule*; *V* **ugly.**

2 *vt sep* **(a)** *wood, food* couper; *meat* (*carve*) découper; (*chop up*) hacher; (*fig*) *enemy, army* tailler en pièces, anéantir.

(b) (*Brit*: pass only*) **to be cut up about sth** (*hurt*) être affecté *or* démoralisé par qch; (*annoyed*) être très embêté par qch*; **he's very cut up** il n'a plus le moral*; **he was very cut up by the death of his son** la mort de son fils l'a beaucoup affecté.

cutaneous [kjuːˈteɪnɪəs] *adj* cutané.

cute* [kjuːt] *adj* **(a)** (*bright, clever*) futé, rusé, astucieux. **(b)** (*esp US: sweet, attractive*) mignon, chouette.

cuticle [ˈkjuːtɪkl] *n* (*skin*) épiderme *m*; *[fingernails]* petites peaux, envie *f*; (*Bot*) cuticule *f*. ~ **remover** repousse-peaux *m*.

cutie‡ [ˈkjuːtɪ] *n* (*US*) (*girl*) jolie fille; (*shrewd person*) malin *m*, -igne *f*; (*shrewd action*) beau coup.

cutlass [ˈkʌtləs] *n* (*Naut*) coutelas *m*, sabre *m* d'abordage.

cutler [ˈkʌtlə^r] *n* coutelier *m*.

cutlery [ˈkʌtlərɪ] *n* **(a)** (*knives, forks, spoons etc*) couverts *mpl*; *V* **canteen. (b)** (*knives, daggers etc; also trade*) coutellerie *f*.

cutlet [ˈkʌtlɪt] *n* **(a)** *[mutton, veal]* côtelette *f*; *[veal]* escalope *f*. **(b)** (*US: croquette of meat, chicken etc*) croquette *f*.

cutter [ˈkʌtə^r] *n* **(a)** (*person*) *[clothes]* coupeur *m*, -euse *f*; *[stones, jewels]* tailleur *m*; *[films]* monteur *m*, -euse *f*. **(b)** (*tool*) coupoir *m*, couteau *m*. **(c)** (*Naut*) cotre *m*, cutter *m*; *[coastguards]* garde-côte *m*; *[warship]* canot *m*. **(d)** (*US: sleigh*) traîneau *m*.

cutting [ˈkʌtɪŋ] **1** *n* **(a)** (*U*) coupe *f*; *[diamond]* taille *f*; *[film]* montage *m*; *[trees]* coupe, abattage *m*.

(b) (*for road, railway*) tranchée *f*.

(c) (*piece cut off*) *[newspaper]* coupure *f*; *[cloth]* coupon *m*; (*Agr*) bouture *f*; *[vine]* marcotte *f*.

(d) (*reduction*) *[prices, expenditure]* réduction *f*, diminution *f*.

2 *adj* **(a)** *knife* coupant, tranchant. **the** ~ **edge** le tranchant; ~ **pliers** pinces coupantes; (*Sewing*) ~**-out scissors** ciseaux *mpl* à couture *or* de couturière; (*Cine*) ~ **room** salle *f* de montage.

(b) (*fig*) *wind* glacial, cinglant; *rain* cinglant; *cold* piquant, glacial; *words* blessant, cinglant, incisif; *remark* mordant, caustique, blessant. ~ **tongue** langue acérée.

cuttlebone [ˈkʌtlbəʊn] *n* os *m* de seiche.

cuttlefish [ˈkʌtlfɪʃ] *n* seiche *f*.

cyanide [ˈsaɪənaɪd] *n* cyanure *m*. ~ **of potassium** cyanure de potassium.

cybernetics [ˌsaɪbəˈnetɪks] *n* (*U*) cybernétique *f*.

cyclamen [ˈsɪkləmən] *n* cyclamen *m*.

cycle [ˈsaɪkl] **1** *n* **(a)** = **bicycle 1. (b)** *[poems, seasons etc]* cycle *m*. **2** *vi* faire de la bicyclette, faire du vélo. **he** ~**s to school** il va à l'école à bicyclette *or* à vélo *or* en vélo. **3** *cpd path* cyclable; *race* cycliste.

cyclic(al) [ˈsaɪklɪk(əl)] *adj* cyclique.

cycling [ˈsaɪklɪŋ] **1** *n* cyclisme *m*. **2** *cpd* de bicyclette. **cycling clothes** tenue *f* cycliste; **cycling holiday** randonnée *f* (de vacances) à bicyclette; **cycling tour** circuit *m* à bicyclette; **cycling track** vélodrome *m*.

cyclist [ˈsaɪklɪst] *n* cycliste *mf*; *V* **racing.**

cyclone [ˈsaɪkləʊn] *n* cyclone *m*. (*US*) ~ **cellar** abri *m* anticyclone.

cyclorama [ˌsaɪkləˈrɑːmə] *n* (*also Cine*) cyclorama *m*.

cyclostyle [ˈsaɪkləstaɪl] **1** *n* machine *f* à polycopier (*à stencils*). **2** *vt* polycopier.

cyclotron [ˈsaɪklətrɒn] *n* cyclotron *m*.

cygnet [ˈsɪgnɪt] *n* jeune cygne *m*.

cylinder [ˈsɪlɪndə^r] **1** *n* **(a)** (*Aut, Math, Tech*) cylindre *m*. **a 6-**~ **car** une 6-cylindres; **to fire on all 4** ~**s** (*lit*) avoir les 4 cylindres qui donnent; (*fig*) marcher *or* fonctionner à pleins gaz* *or* tubes*.

(b) *[typewriter]* rouleau *m*.

2 *cpd*: **cylinder block** bloc-cylindres *m*; **cylinder capacity** cylindrée *f*; **cylinder head** culasse *f*; **to take off the cylinder head** déculasser.

cylindrical [sɪˈlɪndrɪkəl] *adj* cylindrique.

cymbal [ˈsɪmbəl] *n* cymbale *f*.

cynic [ˈsɪnɪk] **1** *n* (*gen, Philos*) cynique *mf*. **2** *adj* = **cynical.**

cynical [ˈsɪnɪkəl] *adj* (*gen, Philos*) cynique.

cynically [ˈsɪnɪklɪ] *adv* cyniquement, avec cynisme.

cynicism [ˈsɪnɪsɪzəm] *n* (*gen, Philos*) cynisme *m*. ~**s** remarques *fpl* cyniques, sarcasmes *mpl*.

cynosure [ˈsaɪnəʃʊə^r] *n* (*also* ~ **of every eye**) point *m* de mire, centre *m* d'attraction.

cypher [ˈsaɪfə^r] = **cipher.**

cypress [ˈsaɪprɪs] *n* cyprès *m*.

Cypriot [ˈsɪprɪət] **1** *adj* cypriote, chypriote. **2** *n* Cypriote *mf*, Chypriote *mf*.

Cyprus [ˈsaɪprəs] *n* Chypre *f* (*no art*). **in** ~ à Chypre.

cyst [sɪst] *n* (*Med*) kyste *m*; (*Bio*) sac *m* (membraneux).

cystitis [sɪsˈtaɪtɪs] *n* cystite *f*.

cytology [saɪˈtɒlədʒɪ] *n* cytologie *f*.

czar [zɑː^r] *n* tsar *m* *or* czar *m*.

czarina [zɑːˈriːnə] *n* tsarine *f* *or* czarine *f*.

Czech [tʃek] **1** *adj* tchèque. **2** *n* **(a)** Tchèque *mf*. **(b)** (*Ling*) tchèque *m*.

Czechoslovak [ˈtʃekəʊˈsləʊvæk] **1** *adj* tchécoslovaque. **2** *n* Tchécoslovaque *mf*.

Czechoslovakia [ˈtʃekəʊsləˈvækɪə] *n* Tchécoslovaquie *f*.

Czechoslovakian [ˈtʃekəʊsləˈvækɪən] = **Czechoslovak.**

D

D, d [diː] **1** *n* **(a)** (*letter*) D, d *m*. (*Cine etc*) **(in) 3-D** en relief. **(b)** (*Mus*) ré *m*. **2** *cpd*: (*Med*) **D and C*** dilatation *f* et curetage *m*; (*Mil*) **D-day** le jour J.

dab[1] [dæb] **1** *n* **(a) a** ~ **of** un petit peu de; **a** ~ **of glue** une goutte de colle; **to give sth a** ~ **of paint** donner un petit coup *or* une petite touche de peinture à qch.

(b) (*esp Brit: fingerprints*) ~**s‡** empreintes digitales.

2 *vt* tamponner. **to** ~ **one's eyes** se tamponner les yeux; **to** ~ **paint on sth** donner un petit coup de peinture à qch, mettre un peu de peinture sur qch; **to** ~ **iodine on a wound** appliquer un peu de teinture d'iode sur une blessure.

dab on *vt sep* appliquer *or* mettre *or* étaler à petits coups.

dab[2] [dæb] *n* (*fish*) limande *f*.

dab[3] [dæb] *adj* (*Brit*) **to be a** ~ **hand* at sth/at doing sth** être doué en qch/pour faire qch.

dabble [ˈdæbl] **1** *vt*: **to** ~ **one's hands/feet in the water** barboter dans l'eau avec les mains/les pieds. **2** *vi* se mêler un peu (*in* de). **to** ~ **in politics** donner dans la politique; **to** ~ **in stocks and shares** boursicoter.

dabbler [ˈdæblə^r] *n* (*often pej*) amateur *m*.

dabchick [ˈdæbtʃɪk] *n* petit grèbe.

dace [deɪs] *n* vandoise *f*.

dachshund [ˈdækshʊnd] *n* teckel *m*.

Dacron [ˈdækrɒn] *n* ® dacron *m* ®.

dactyl [ˈdæktɪl] *n* dactyle *m*.

dactylic [dækˈtɪlɪk] *adj* dactylique.

dad [dæd] *n* **(a)** (*) papa *m*. **(b)** (‡: *to old man*) **come on,** ~**!** allez viens pépé!*; (*hum*) **D**~**'s army** l'armée *f* de (grand-)papa (*hum*).

Dada [ˈdɑːdɑː] **1** *n* Dada *m*. **2** *cpd school, movement* dada *inv*, dadaïste.

daddy [ˈdædɪ] **1** *n* (*) papa *m*. **2** *cpd*: **daddy-long-legs** (*harvestman*) faucheur *m* *or* faucheux *m*; (*Brit: cranefly*) tipule *f*.

dado [ˈdeɪdəʊ] *n* plinthe *f*; *[pedestal]* dé *m*; *[wall]* lambris *m* d'appui.

daffodil [ˈdæfədɪl] *n* jonquille *f*. ~ **yellow** (jaune) jonquille *inv*.

daffy‡ [ˈdæfɪ] *adj* toqué*, timbré*.

daft [dɑːft] *adj person* idiot, dingue*:*; *idea* stupide, idiot. **to be ~ about*** être fou (*f* folle) de.

dagger [ˈdægəʳ] *n* **(a)** poignard *m*, (*shorter*) dague *f*. (*fig*) **to be at ~s drawn with sb** être à couteaux tirés avec qn; **to look ~s at sb** lancer des regards furieux *or* meurtriers à qn, foudroyer qn du regard. **(b)** (*Typ*) croix *f*.

dago [ˈdeɪgəʊ] *n* (*pej*) métèque *m* (*pej*) (*gén d'origine italienne ou espagnole etc*).

daguerreotype [dəˈgerəʊtaɪp] *n* daguerréotype *m*.

dahlia [ˈdeɪlɪə] *n* dahlia *m*.

Dail Eireann [daɪlˈɛərən] *n* Chambre *f* des Députés (de la république d'Irlande).

daily [ˈdeɪlɪ] **1** *adj task* quotidien, journalier, de tous les jours. (*Rel*) **our ~ bread** notre pain quotidien *or* de chaque jour; **~ consumption** consommation journalière; **~ dozen*** gymnastique *f* (quotidienne); (*pej*) **the ~ grind*** le train-train (quotidien); **~ paper** quotidien *m* (*V also* **3a**).

2 *adv* quotidiennement, tous les jours, journellement.

3 *n* **(a)** (*newspaper*) quotidien *m*.

(b) (*Brit**: *also* **~ help, ~ woman**) femme *f* de ménage.

daintily [ˈdeɪntɪlɪ] *adv eat, hold* délicatement; *dress* coquettement; *walk* à petits pas élégants.

daintiness [ˈdeɪntɪnɪs] *n [form, shape, manners, taste]* délicatesse *f*; *[dress]* coquetterie *f*.

dainty [ˈdeɪntɪ] **1** *adj* **(a)** *food* de choix, délicat. **a ~ morsel** un morceau de choix.

(b) *figure* menu; *handkerchief, blouse* délicat. **she is a ~ little thing** elle est mignonne à croquer.

(c) (*difficult to please*) difficile. **he is a ~ eater** il est difficile (pour *or* sur la nourriture).

2 *n* mets délicat.

daiquiri [ˈdaɪkərɪ] *n* daiquiri *m*.

dairy [ˈdɛərɪ] **1** *n* (*on farm*) laiterie *f*; (*shop*) crémerie *f*, laiterie.

2 *cpd cow, farm* laitier. **dairy butter** beurre fermier; **dairy farming** industrie laitière; **dairy herd** troupeau *m* de vaches laitières; **dairy ice cream** glace *f* (faite à la crème); **dairymaid** fille *f* de laiterie; **dairyman** (*on farm etc*) employé *m* de laiterie; (*in shop*) crémier *m*; **dairy produce** produits laitiers.

dais [ˈdeɪɪs] *n* estrade *f*.

daisied [ˈdeɪzɪd] *adj* (*liter*) émaillé (*liter*) de pâquerettes.

daisy [ˈdeɪzɪ] *n* pâquerette *f*; (*cultivated*) marguerite *f*. **~ chain** guirlande *f* *or* collier *m* de pâquerettes; *V* **fresh, push up.**

Dalai Lama [ˈdælaɪˈlɑːmə] *n* dalaï-lama *m*.

dale [deɪl] *n* (*N Engl, also liter*) vallée *f*, vallon *m*.

dalliance [ˈdælɪəns] *n* (*liter*) badinage *m* (amoureux).

dally [ˈdælɪ] *vi* (*dawdle*) lambiner*, lanterner (*over sth* dans *or* sur qch). **to ~ with an idea** caresser une idée; **to ~ with sb**† badiner (amoureusement) avec qn.

Dalmatian [dælˈmeɪʃən] *n* (*dog*) dalmatien *m*.

dalmatic [dælˈmætɪk] *n* dalmatique *f*.

dam[1] [dæm] **1** *n* **(a)** (*wall*) *[river]* barrage *m* (de retenue), digue *f*; *[lake]* barrage (de retenue).

(b) (*water*) réservoir *m*, lac *m* de retenue.

2 *vt* **(a)** (*also* **~ up**) *river* endiguer; *lake* construire un barrage sur. **to ~ the waters of the Nile** faire *or* construire un barrage pour contenir les eaux du Nil.

(b) *flow of words, oaths* endiguer.

3 *cpd*: **dambuster** (*bomb*) bombe *f* à ricochets; (*person*) (aviateur *m*) briseur *m* de barrages (*se réfère à un épisode de la seconde guerre mondiale*).

dam[2] [dæm] *n* (*animal*) mère *f*.

dam' [dæm] = **damn 4, 5.**

damage [ˈdæmɪdʒ] **1** *n* **(a)** (*U*) dommage(s) *m(pl)*; (*visible, eg to car*) dégâts *mpl*, dommages; (*to ship, cargo*) avarie(s) *f(pl)*; (*fig*) préjudice *m*, tort *m*. **~ to property** dégâts matériels; **to make good the ~** réparer les dégâts; **the bomb did a lot of ~** la bombe a causé des dommages importants, la bombe a fait de gros dégâts; **there was a lot of ~ (done) to the house** la maison a beaucoup souffert; **there's no ~ done** il n'y a pas de mal; **that has done ~ to our cause** cela a fait du tort *or* porté préjudice à notre cause; (*fig: how much is it?*) **what's the ~?*** cela se monte à combien?

(b) (*Jur*) **~s** dommages *mpl* et intérêts *mpl*, dommages-intérêts *mpl*; **liable for ~s** tenu des dommages et intérêts; **war ~** dommages *or* indemnités *fpl* de guerre; *V* **sue.**

2 *vt furniture, goods, crops, machine, vehicle* endommager, causer des dégâts à, abîmer; *food* abîmer, gâter; *eyesight, health* abîmer; *good relations, reputation* nuire à, porter atteinte à.

damageable [ˈdæmɪdʒəbl] *adj* dommageable.

damaging [ˈdæmɪdʒɪŋ] *adj* préjudiciable, nuisible (*to* à); (*Jur*) préjudiciable.

Damascus [dəˈmɑːskəs] *n* Damas.

damask [ˈdæməsk] **1** *n* **(a)** (*cloth*) *[silk]* damas *m*, soie damassée; *[linen]* (linge *m*) damassé *m*. **(b) ~ (steel)** (acier *m*) damasquiné *m*. **2** *adj cloth* damassé. (*liter*) **her ~ cheeks** ses joues vermeilles (*liter*). **3** *cpd*: **damask rose** rose *f* de Damas.

dame [deɪm] *n* **(a)** (*esp Brit*) (†, *liter, also hum*) dame *f*; (*Theat*) la vieille dame (*rôle féminin de farce bouffonne joué par un homme*). (*Hist*) **~ school** école enfantine, petit cours privé; (†, *liter*) **D~ Fortune** Dame Fortune.

(b) (*Brit: in titles*) **D~** *titre porté par une femme décorée d'un ordre de chevalerie* (*eg Dame Margot Fonteyn, Dame Margot*).

(c) (*US*:) fille *f*, nana*:* *f*.

damfool: [ˈdæmˈfuːl] *adj* idiot, crétin, fichu*. **that ~ waiter** ce crétin de garçon, ce fichu* garçon.

dammit: [ˈdæmɪt] *excl* nom de nom!*, zut!*, nom d'une pipe!* **it weighs 2 kilos as near as ~** cela pèse 2 kilos à un cheveu près *or* à un poil* près.

damn [dæm] **1** *excl* (*: *also* **~ it!**) bon sang!*, merde!*:*; *V* **2c.**

2 *vt* **(a)** (*Rel*) damner; *book* condamner, éreinter. **to ~ with faint praise** éreinter sous couleur d'éloge; **his long hair ~ed him from the start** ses cheveux longs le condamnaient dès le départ *or* d'avance.

(b) (*swear at*) pester contre, maudire.

(c) (*:*) **~ him!** qu'il aille au diable!, qu'il aille se faire fiche!*; **the boy pinched my book, ~ him!** il a fauché mon livre, le petit salaud!*:*; **well I'll be ~ed!** ça c'est trop fort!; **I'll be ~ed if ...** je veux bien être pendu si..., que le diable m'emporte si ...; **~ this machine!** au diable cette machine!, il y en a marre de cette machine!*:*

3 *n* (*:*) **I don't care a ~, I don't give a ~** je m'en fiche pas mal *or* comme de l'an quarante*; **it's not worth a ~** cela ne vaut pas un clou*, ça ne vaut strictement rien, c'est de la foutaise*:*.

4 *adj* (*: *also* **dam', ~ed**) fichu*, sacré*:*. **it is one ~ thing after another** quand ce n'est pas une chose c'est l'autre; **it's a ~ nuisance!** quelle barbe!*, c'est la barbe!*

5 *adv* (*: *also* **dam', ~ed**) vachement*:*, sacrément*, rudement*. **I know ~ all about it** je n'en sais fichtre* rien; **can you see anything? — ~ all!** tu vois quelque chose? — zéro!* *or* rien de rien!*; **there's ~ all to drink in the house** il n'y a pas une goutte à boire dans la maison; **that's ~ all good *or* use** tu parles d'un truc utile!*, comme utilité c'est zéro!*; **he's done ~ all today** il n'a rien fichu* *or* foutu*:* aujourd'hui.

damnable* [ˈdæmnəbl] *adj* détestable, odieux.

damnably* [ˈdæmnəblɪ] *adv* vachement*:*, rudement*.

damnation [dæmˈneɪʃən] **1** *n* (*Rel*) damnation *f*. **2** *excl* (*:*) enfer et damnation! (*hum*), malheur!, misère!; merde!*:*

damned [dæmd] **1** *adj* **(a)** *soul* damné, maudit. **(b)** (*:*) *V* **damn 4.**

2 *adv* (*:*) *V* **damn 5. 3** *n* (*Rel, liter*) **the ~** les damnés.

damnedest: [ˈdæmdɪst] *n*: **to do one's ~ to help/to get away** faire l'impossible *or* tout (son possible) pour aider/pour s'évader.

damning [ˈdæmɪŋ] *adj words, facts, evidence* accablant. **the criticism was ~** c'était un éreintement.

damp [dæmp] **1** *adj air, room, clothes, heat* humide; *skin* moite. (*Brit*) **that was a ~ squib*** c'était un coup pour rien* *or* un coup d'épée dans l'eau.

2 *n* **(a)** *[atmosphere, walls]* humidité *f*.

(b) (*Min*) (*choke* **~**) mofette *f*; (*fire* **~**) grisou *m*.

3 *vt* **(a)** *a cloth, ironing* humecter.

(b) *sounds* amortir, étouffer; (*Mus*) étouffer; (*also* **~ down**) *fire* couvrir.

(c) *enthusiasm, courage* refroidir. **to ~ sb's spirits** décourager *or* déprimer qn.

4 *cpd*: (*Brit Constr*) **damp-course** couche isolante; **damp-proof** imperméable, étanche, hydrofuge.

dampen [ˈdæmpən] *vt* = **damp 3a, 3c.**

damper [ˈdæmpəʳ] *n*, (*US*) **dampener** [ˈdæmpənəʳ] *n* **(a)** *[chimney]* registre *m*. **(b)** (*: *depressing event*) douche *f* (froide)*. **to put a ~ on** jeter un froid sur. **(c)** (*Mus*) étouffoir *m*. **(d)** (*Aut, Elec, Tech*) amortisseur *m*. **(e)** (*for stamps, envelopes, clothes*) mouilleur *m*.

dampish [ˈdæmpɪʃ] *adj* un peu humide.

dampness [ˈdæmpnɪs] *n* (*V* **damp**) humidité *f*; moiteur *f*.

damsel [ˈdæmzəl] **1** *n* (††, *liter, also hum*) damoiselle *f*. **~ in distress** damoiselle en détresse. **2** *cpd*: (*Zool*) **damsel-fly** demoiselle *f*, libellule *f*.

damson [ˈdæmzən] *n* (*fruit*) prune *f* de Damas; (*tree*) prunier *m* de Damas.

dance [dɑːns] **1** *n* **(a)** (*movement*) danse *f*. **the D~ of Death** la danse macabre; (*Brit fig*) **to lead sb a (pretty) ~** donner à qn du fil à retordre; **may I have the next ~?** voudriez-vous m'accorder la prochaine danse?; *V* **folk, sequence** *etc*.

(b) (*social gathering*) bal *m*, soirée dansante, sauterie *f* (*more informal*). **to give *or* hold a ~** donner un bal; **to go to a ~** aller à un bal *or* à une soirée dansante.

2 *vt waltz etc* danser. (*fig*) **to ~ attendance on sb** être aux petits soins pour qn.

3 *vi [person, leaves in wind, boat on waves, eyes]* danser. **he ~d with her** il l'a fait danser; **she ~d with him** elle a dansé avec lui; (*fig*) **to ~ in/out *etc*** entrer/sortir *etc* joyeusement; **to ~ about, to ~ up and down** gambader, sautiller; **the child ~d away *or* off** l'enfant s'est éloigné en gambadant *or* en sautillant; **to ~ for joy** sauter de joie; **to ~ with rage** trépigner de colère.

4 *cpd*: **dance band** orchestre *m* (de danse); **dance floor** piste *f* (de danse); **dance hall** dancing *m*, salle *f* de danse *or* de bal; **dance hostess** entraîneuse *f*; **dance music** musique *f* de danse; **dance programme** carnet *m* de bal.

dancer [ˈdɑːnsəʳ] *n* danseur *m*, -euse *f*.

dancing [ˈdɑːnsɪŋ] **1** *n* (*U*) danse *f*.

2 *cpd master, school* de danse. **dancing-girl** danseuse *f*; **dancing-partner** cavalier *m*, -ière *f*, partenaire *mf*; **dancing shoes** *[men]* escarpins *mpl*; *[women]* souliers *mpl* de bal; (*for ballet*) chaussons *mpl* de danse.

dandelion [ˈdændɪlaɪən] *n* pissenlit *m*, dent-de-lion *f*.

dander* [ˈdændəʳ] *n*: **to get sb's ~ up** mettre qn hors de lui *or* en rogne*; **to have one's ~ up** être hors de soi *or* en rogne*.

dandified [ˈdændɪfaɪd] *adj* vêtu en dandy, qui a une allure de dandy.

dandle [ˈdændl] *vt child* (*on knees*) faire sauter sur ses genoux; (*in arms*) bercer dans ses bras, câliner.

dandruff [ˈdændrəf] *n* (*U*) pellicules *fpl* (*du cuir chevelu*).

dandy [ˈdændɪ] **1** *n* dandy *m*, élégant *m*. **2** *adj* (*: *esp US*) épatant*.

Dane [deɪn] *n* **(a)** Danois(e) *m(f)*. **(b)** *V* **great 3.**

danger [ˈdeɪndʒəʳ] **1** *n* danger *m*, péril *m*. **to be a ~ to** être un danger pour; **to put in ~** mettre en danger *or* en péril; **in ~** en danger; **he was in little ~** il ne courait pas grand risque; (*gen,*

Med) **out of ~** hors de danger; **in ~ of invasion** menacé d'invasion; **he was in ~ of losing his job** il risquait de *or* il était menacé de perdre sa place; **he was in ~ of falling** il risquait de tomber; **there was no ~ that she would be recognized** *or* **of her being recognized** elle ne courait aucun risque d'être reconnue; **there is a ~ of fire** il y a un risque d'incendie; (*Rail*) **signal at ~** signal à l'arrêt; **'~ road up'** 'attention (aux) travaux'; **'~ keep out'** 'danger: défense d'entrer'.

2 *cpd*: **danger area = danger zone**; (*Med*) **to be on the danger list** être dans un état critique *or* très grave; **danger money** prime *f* de risque; **danger point** point *m* critique, cote *f* d'alerte; **danger signal** signal *m* d'alarme; (*Rail*) arrêt *m*; **danger zone** zone dangereuse.

dangerous ['deɪndʒrəs] *adj person, animal, behaviour, example, maxim, topic, river, event, tool* dangereux; *expedition* dangereux, périlleux; *illness* grave. **it is ~ to do that** il est dangereux de faire cela; **in a ~ situation** dans une situation périlleuse, dans un mauvais pas; (*fig*) **to be on ~ ground** être sur un terrain glissant.

dangerously ['deɪndʒrəslɪ] *adv* dangereusement. **~ wounded** grièvement blessé; **he came ~ close to admitting it** il a été à deux doigts de l'avouer; **to live ~** risquer sa vie à tout instant, vivre dangereusement.

dangle ['dæŋgl] 1 *vt object on string* balancer, suspendre; *arm, leg* laisser pendre, balancer; (*fig*) *prospect, offer* faire miroiter (*before sb* aux yeux de qn).

2 *vi [object on string]* pendre, pendiller; *[arms, legs]* pendre, (se) balancer. **with arms dangling** les bras ballants; **with legs dangling** les jambes pendantes.

Danish ['deɪnɪʃ] 1 *adj* danois. **~ blue (cheese)** bleu *m* (du Danemark); **~ pastry** feuilleté *m* (fourré aux fruits *etc*). 2 *n* (*Ling*) danois *m*.

dank [dæŋk] *adj air, weather* humide et froid; *dungeon* humide et froid, aux murs suintants.

Dante ['dæntɪ] *n* Dante *m*.

Danube ['dænju:b] *n* Danube *m*.

daphnia ['dæfnɪə] *n* daphnie *f*.

dapper ['dæpəʳ] *adj* (*neat*) pimpant, soigné de sa personne; (*active*) vif, sémillant.

dapple ['dæpl] 1 *vt* tacheter. 2 *cpd*: **dapple grey** (cheval *m*) gris pommelé *inv*.

dappled ['dæpld] *adj surface* tacheté, moucheté; *sky* pommelé; *horse* miroité, (*grey*) pommelé.

Darby ['dɑ:bɪ] *n*: **~ and Joan** = Philémon et Baucis; (*Brit*) **~ and Joan club** cercle *m* (pour couples du troisième âge).

dare [dɛəʳ] *pret* **dared** *or* **durst**††, *ptp* **dared** 1 *modal aux vb* **(a)** oser. **he dare not** *or* **daren't climb that tree** il n'ose pas grimper à cet arbre; **he dared not do it** il n'a pas osé le faire; **dare you do it?** oserez-vous le faire?; **how dare you say such things?** comment osez-vous dire des choses pareilles?; **how dare you!** vous osez!, vous (en) avez du culot!*; **don't dare say that!** je vous défends d'oser dire cela!

(b) I dare say he'll come il viendra sans doute, il est probable qu'il viendra; **I dare say you're tired after your journey** vous êtes sans doute fatigué *or* j'imagine que vous êtes fatigué après votre voyage; **I dare say she's 40** elle pourrait bien avoir 40 ans, je lui donne dans les 40 ans; **he is very sorry** — (*iro*) **I dare say!** il le regrette beaucoup — c'est bien possible! (*iro*).

2 *vt* **(a)** (*face the risk of*) *danger, death* affronter, braver.

(b) (*challenge*) **to dare sb to do** défier qn de faire, mettre qn au défi de faire; **(I) dare you!** chiche!*

3 *n* défi *m*. **to do sth for a dare** faire qch pour relever un défi.

4 *cpd*: **daredevil** (*n*) casse-cou *m inv*, cerveau brûlé, risque-tout *m inv*; (*adj*) *behaviour* de casse-cou *inv*; *adventure* fou (*f* folle), audacieux.

daring ['dɛərɪŋ] 1 *adj person, attempt* audacieux, téméraire, hardi; *dress, opinion, proposal* osé, audacieux, hardi. 2 *n* audace *f*, hardiesse *f*.

daringly ['dɛərɪŋlɪ] *adv* audacieusement, témérairement.

dark [dɑ:k] 1 *adj* **(a)** (*lacking light*) obscur, noir; *room* sombre, obscur; *dungeon* noir, ténébreux. **it is ~** il fait nuit *or* noir; **it is getting ~** il commence à faire nuit; **it is as ~ as pitch** *or* **night** il fait nuit noire; **the sky is getting ~** le ciel s'assombrit; **the ~ side of the moon** la face cachée de la lune.

(b) *colour* foncé, sombre. **~ blue/green** bleu/vert foncé *inv*; **~ brown hair** cheveux châtain foncé *inv*; **a ~ blue** un bleu sombre; **~ glasses** lunettes noires; **~ chocolate** chocolat *m* à croquer; *V also* **blue**.

(c) *complexion, skin, hair* brun. **she is very ~** elle est très brune; **she has a ~ complexion** elle a le teint foncé *or* brun *or* basané; **she has ~ hair** elle est brune, elle a les cheveux bruns.

(d) mystérieux, obscur, secret (*f* -ète); (*sinister*) noir. **to keep sth ~** tenir qch secret; **keep it ~!** pas un mot!, pas un mot à la Reine Mère!*; **~ designs** noirs desseins; **~ hint** allusion sibylline *or* énigmatique; **~ threats** sourdes menaces.

(e) (*gloomy, sad*) *thoughts* sombre, triste. **to look on the ~ side of things** voir tout en noir.

2 *n* **(a)** (*absence of light*) nuit *f*, obscurité *f*, noir *m*. **after ~** la nuit venue, après la tombée de la nuit; **until ~** jusqu'à (la tombée de) la nuit; **to be afraid of the ~** avoir peur du noir.

(b) (*fig: ignorance*) noir *m*. **I am quite in the ~ about it** je suis tout à fait dans le noir là-dessus, j'ignore tout de cette histoire; **he has kept** *or* **left me in the ~ as to** *or* **about what he wants to do** il m'a laissé dans l'ignorance *or* il ne m'a donné aucun renseignement sur ce qu'il veut faire; **to work in the ~** travailler à l'aveuglette; *V* **shot**.

3 *cpd*: **the Dark Ages** l'âge des ténèbres *or* de l'ignorance, le Haut Moyen Âge; **dark-complexioned** brun (de teint), basané; **the Dark Continent** le continent noir; **dark-eyed** aux yeux noirs; (*fig*) **he is a dark horse** c'est une quantité inconnue, il cache son jeu; (*Phot*) **dark room** chambre noire; **dark-skinned** *person* brun (de peau), à peau brune; *race* de couleur.

darken ['dɑ:kən] 1 *vt room, landscape* obscurcir, assombrir; *sky* assombrir; *sun* obscurcir, voiler; *complexion* brunir, basaner; *colour* foncer; *brilliance* ternir; (*fig*) *reason* obscurcir; *future* assombrir; (*sadden*) assombrir, attrister. (††, *hum*) **never ~ my door again!** ne mettez plus les pieds chez moi!

2 *vi [sky, evening]* s'assombrir; *[room]* s'obscurcir, s'assombrir; *[colours]* foncer. **the night ~ed gradually** la nuit s'assombrit peu à peu *or* se fit peu à peu plus épaisse; (*fig*) **his brow ~ed** sa mine s'est rembrunie.

darkey‡, darkie‡ ['dɑ:kɪ] *n* (*pej*) moricaud(e) *m(f)* (*pej*), nègre *m* (*pej*), négresse *f* (*pej*).

darkish ['dɑ:kɪʃ] *adj sky* (un peu) sombre; *hair, person* plutôt brun.

darkly ['dɑ:klɪ] *adv* **(a)** *outlined* obscurément. **hills rose ~** des collines dressaient leurs silhouettes sombres. **(b)** *hint* mystérieusement, énigmatiquement. **(c)** (*gloomily*) tristement; (*sinisterly*) sinistrement, lugubrement.

darkness ['dɑ:knɪs] *n* (*U*) **(a)** *[night, room]* (*also fig*) obscurité *f*, ténèbres *fpl*. **in total** *or* **utter ~** dans une complète *or* totale obscurité; **the house was in ~** la maison était plongée dans l'obscurité; *V* **prince**.

(b) *[colour]* teinte foncée; *[face, skin]* teint brun *or* bronzé *or* basané.

darky‡ ['dɑ:kɪ] *n* = **darkey‡**.

darling ['dɑ:lɪŋ] 1 *n* favori(te) *m(f)*, idole *f*, bien-aimé(e) *m(f)*. **the ~ of the people** l'idole du peuple; **a mother's ~** un chouchou*, une chouchoute*, un(e) enfant gâté(e); **she's a little ~** c'est un petit amour, elle est adorable; **come here, ~** viens (mon) chéri *or* mon amour; (*to child*) viens (mon) chéri *or* mon petit chou; **be a ~* and bring me my glasses** sois un chou *or* un ange et apporte-moi mes lunettes; **she was a perfect ~ about it*** elle a été un ange (dans cette histoire).

2 *adj child* chéri, bien-aimé; (*liter*) *wish* le plus cher. **a ~ little place*** un petit coin ravissant *or* adorable.

darn[1] [dɑ:n] 1 *vt socks* repriser; *clothes etc* raccommoder. 2 *n* reprise *f*.

darn[2]* [dɑ:n], **darned*** [dɑ:nd] *euph for* **damn, damned**; *V* **damn 1, 2c, 3, 4, 5.**

darnel ['dɑ:nl] *n* ivraie *f*, ray-grass *m*.

darning ['dɑ:nɪŋ] 1 *n* **(a)** (*U*) raccommodage *m*, reprise *f*. **(b)** (*things to be darned*) raccommodage *m*, linge *m or* vêtements *mpl* à raccommoder. 2 *cpd*: **darning needle** aiguille *f* à repriser; **darning stitch** point *m* de reprise; **darning wool** laine *f* à repriser.

dart [dɑ:t] 1 *n* **(a) to make a sudden ~ at** foncer* sur, se précipiter sur.

(b) (*Sport*) fléchette *f*. **(game of) ~s** (jeu *m* de) fléchettes.

(c) (*weapon*) trait *m*, javelot *m*; (*liter*) *[serpent, bee]* dard *m*; (*fig*) trait, flèche *f*; *V* **Cupid**.

(d) (*Sewing*) pince *f*.

2 *vi* se précipiter, s'élancer, foncer* (*at* sur). **to ~ in/out** *etc* arriver/partir *etc* comme une flèche.

3 *vt rays* darder; *look* darder, décocher.

4 *cpd*: **dartboard** cible *f* (*de jeu de fléchettes*).

Darwinism ['dɑ:wɪnɪzəm] *n* darwinisme *m*.

dash [dæʃ] 1 *n* **(a)** (*sudden rush*) mouvement *m* brusque (*en avant*), ruée *f*, élan *m*; (*Sport*) sprint *m*. **to make a ~** se précipiter, se ruer, foncer* (*at* sur); **to make a ~ for freedom** saisir l'occasion de s'enfuir; **he made a ~ for it*** il a pris ses jambes à son cou; *V* **cut**.

(b) (*small amount*) petite quantité; *[spirits, flavouring]* goutte *f*, larme *f*, doigt *m*; *[seasonings etc]* pointe *f*; *[vinegar, lemon]* filet *m*; *[colour]* touche *f*, tache *f*. **a ~ of soda** un peu d'eau de Seltz.

(c) (*punctuation mark*) tiret *m*; (*in handwriting*) trait *m* de plume.

(d) (*Morse*) trait *m*.

2 *vt* **(a)** (*throw violently*) jeter *or* lancer violemment. **to ~ sth to pieces** casser qch en mille morceaux; **to ~ sth down** *or* **to the ground** jeter *or* flanquer* qch par terre; **to ~ one's head against** se cogner la tête contre; **the ship was ~ed against a rock** le navire a été jeté contre un écueil.

(b) (*fig*) *spirits* abattre; *person* démoraliser. **to ~ sb's hopes** anéantir les espoirs de qn.

3 *vi* **(a)** (*rush*) se précipiter, filer*. **to ~ away/back/up** *etc* s'en aller/revenir/monter *etc* à toute allure *or* en coup de vent; **to ~ into a room** se précipiter dans une pièce; **I must ~*** il faut que je file* (*subj*).

(b) (*crash*) *[waves]* se briser (*against* contre); *[car, bird, object]* se heurter (*against* à), se jeter (*against* contre).

4 *excl* (**euph for* **damn**) **~ (it)!**, **~ it all!** zut alors!*, flûte!*; **but ~ it all*, you can't do that!** mais quand même, tu ne peux faire ça!

dash off 1 *vi* partir précipitamment.

2 *vt sep letter etc* faire en vitesse; *drawing* dessiner en un tour de main.

dashboard ['dæʃbɔ:d] *n* (*Aut*) tableau *m* de bord.

dashed* [dæʃt] *adj, adv euph for* **damned**; *V* **damn 4, 5.**

dashing ['dæʃɪŋ] *adj person, behaviour* impétueux, plein d'allant; *person, appearance* fringant, qui a grande allure, plein de panache.

dashingly ['dæʃɪŋlɪ] *adv behave* avec brio, avec fougue, avec panache; *dress* avec une élégance fringante.

dastardly† ['dæstədlɪ] *adj person, action* lâche, ignoble.

data ['deɪtə] 1 *npl of* **datum** (*sometimes with sg vb*) données *fpl*, information *f* (brute), informations (brutes).

2 *cpd*: **data bank** banque *f* de *or* des données; **data file** fichier

m de données; **data processing** informatique *f*, traitement *m* de l'information.

date[1] [deɪt] **1** *n* **(a)** (*time of some event*) date *f*; (*Jur*) quantième *m* (du mois). ~ **of birth** date de naissance; **what is today's ~?** quelle est la date aujourd'hui?, nous sommes le combien aujourd'hui?; **what ~ is he coming (on)?** à quelle date vient-il?, quel jour arrive-t-il?; **what is the ~ of this letter?** de quand est cette lettre?; **to fix a ~ for a meeting** prendre date *or* convenir d'une date pour un rendez-vous.

(b) *[coins, medals etc]* millésime *m*.

(c) (*phrases*) **the announcement of recent ~ that ...** l'annonce récente *or* de fraîche date que ...; **to ~ we have accomplished nothing** jusqu'ici *or* à ce jour nous n'avons rien accompli; **to be out of ~** *[document]* ne plus être applicable; *[building]* être démodé, ne plus être au goût du jour, être de conception dépassée; *[person]* retarder, ne pas être de son temps *or* à la page; **he's very out of ~** il retarde vraiment; **to be out of ~ in one's opinions** avoir des opinions complètement dépassées; **to be up to ~** *[document]* être à jour; *[building]* être moderne, être au goût du jour; *[person]* être moderne *or* à la page *or* dans le vent; **to be up to ~ in one's work** *etc* être à jour dans son travail *etc*; **to bring up to ~** *accounts, correspondence etc* mettre à jour; *method etc* moderniser; **to bring sb up to ~** mettre qn au courant (*about sth* de qch); *V also* **out, up.**

(d) (*: *appointment*) rendez-vous *m*, rancard‡ *m*; (‡: *person*) petit(e) ami(e) *m(f)*. **to have a ~ with sb** avoir (pris) rendez-vous avec qn; **they made a ~ for 8 o'clock** ils ont pris rendez-vous *or* fixé un rendez-vous pour 8 heures; **have you got a ~ for tonight?** as-tu (un) rendez-vous ce soir?; *V* **blind.**

2 *cpd*: **date-line** (*Geog*) ligne *f* de changement de date *or* de changement de jour; (*Press*) date *f* (d'une dépêche); **date stamp** *[library etc]* tampon *m* (encreur) (*pour dater un document*), dateur *m*; (*Post*) tampon *or* cachet *m* (de la poste); ((*for cancelling*) oblitérateur *m*; (*postmark*) cachet de la poste; **date-stamp** *library book* tamponner; (*Post*) *envelope* apposer le cachet de la date sur; (*cancel*) *stamp* oblitérer.

3 *vt* **(a)** *letter* dater; *ticket, voucher* dater; (*with machine*) composter. **letter ~d August 7th** lettre datée du 7 août; **a coin ~d 1390** une pièce au millésime de 1390.

(b) *manuscript, ruins etc* donner *or* assigner une date à, fixer la date de. **his taste in ties certainly ~s him** son goût en matière de cravates trahit son âge; *V* **carbon.**

(c) (*) (*go out regularly with*) sortir avec; (*arrange meeting with*) prendre rendez-vous avec.

4 *vi* **(a)** **to ~ from, to ~ back to** dater de, remonter à.

(b) (*become old-fashioned*) *[clothes, expressions etc]* dater.

date[2] [deɪt] *n* (*fruit*) datte *f*; (*tree: also* ~ **palm**) dattier *m*.

dated ['deɪtɪd] *adj* démodé, qui date (*or* datait *etc*), suranné.

dateless ['deɪtlɪs] *adj book, picture, fashion* qui ne date jamais; *custom* immémorial.

dative ['deɪtɪv] **1** *n* datif *m*. **in the ~** au datif. **2** *adj*: ~ **case** (cas *m*) datif *m*; ~ **ending** flexion *f* du datif.

datum ['deɪtəm] *n, pl* **data** donnée *f*.

daub [dɔːb] **1** *vt* (*pej*) (*with paint, make-up*) barbouiller, peinturlurer* (*with* de); (*with clay, grease*) enduire, barbouiller (*with* de). **2** *n* **(a)** (*Constr*) enduit *m*. **(b)** (*pej: bad picture*) croûte* *f*, barbouillage *m*.

daughter ['dɔːtə^r] *n* (*lit, fig*) fille *f*. **~-in-law** belle-fille *f*, bru *f*.

daunt [dɔːnt] *vt* intimider, décourager, démonter. **nothing ~ed he continued** sans se (laisser) démonter il a continué.

daunting ['dɔːntɪŋ] *adj* décourageant, intimidant.

dauntless ['dɔːntlɪs] *adj person* intrépide; *courage* indomptable.

dauntlessly ['dɔːntlɪslɪ] *adv* intrépidement, avec intrépidité.

davenport ['dævnpɔːt] *n* **(a)** (*esp US: sofa*) canapé *m*. **(b)** (*Brit: desk*) secrétaire *m*.

David ['deɪvɪd] *n* David *m*.

davit ['dævɪt] *n* (*Naut*) bossoir *m*.

Davy ['deɪvɪ] *n* (*dim of* **David**). (*Naut*) **to go to ~ Jones' locker*** boire à la grande tasse‡; (*Min*) ~ **lamp** lampe *f* de sécurité (*de mineur*).

dawdle ['dɔːdl] *vi* (*also* ~ **about,** ~ **around**) flâner, traîner, lambiner*. **to ~ on the way** s'amuser en chemin; **to ~ over one's work** traînasser sur son travail.

dawdle away *vt sep*: **to dawdle away one's time** passer *or* perdre son temps à flâner.

dawdler ['dɔːdlə^r] *n* traînard(e) *m(f)*, lambin(e)* *m(f)*, flâneur *m*, -euse *f*.

dawdling ['dɔːdlɪŋ] **1** *adj* lambin*, traînard. **2** *n* flânerie *f*.

dawn [dɔːn] **1** *n* **(a)** aube *f*, point *m* du jour, aurore *f*. **at ~** à l'aube, au point du jour; **from ~ to dusk** du matin au soir; **it was the ~ of another day** c'était l'aube d'un nouveau jour.

(b) (*U*) *[civilization]* aube *f*; *[an idea, hope]* naissance *f*.

2 *vi* **(a)** *[day]* poindre, se lever. **the day ~ed bright and clear** l'aube parut, lumineuse et claire; **the day ~ed rainy** le jour a commencé dans la pluie, il pleuvait au lever du jour; **the day will ~ when ...** un jour viendra où ... .

(b) (*fig*) naître, se faire jour; *[hope]* luire. **an idea ~ed upon him** une idée lui vint à l'esprit; **the truth ~ed upon him** il a commencé à entrevoir la vérité; **it suddenly ~ed on him that no one would know** il lui vint tout d'un coup à l'esprit que personne ne saurait.

3 *cpd*: **dawn chorus** concert *m* (matinal) des oiseaux.

dawning ['dɔːnɪŋ] **1** *adj day, hope* naissant, croissant. **2** *n* = **dawn 1b.**

day [deɪ] **1** *n* **(a)** (*unit of time: 24 hours*) jour *m*. **3 ~s ago** il y a 3 jours; **to do sth in 3 ~s** faire qch en 3 jours, mettre 3 jours à faire qch; **he's coming in 3 ~s** *or* **3 ~s' time** il vient dans 3 jours; **what ~ is it today?** quel jour sommes-nous aujourd'hui?; **what ~ of the month is it?** nous sommes le combien?; **she arrived (on) the ~ they left** elle est arrivée le jour de leur départ; **on that ~** ce jour-là; **on a ~ like this** un jour comme aujourd'hui; **on the following ~** le lendemain; **from that ~ on** à partir *or* à dater de ce jour; **twice a ~** deux fois par jour; **the ~ before yesterday** avant-hier; **the ~ before/two ~s before her birthday** la veille/l'avant-veille de son anniversaire; **the ~ after, the following ~** le lendemain; **two ~s after her birthday** le surlendemain de son anniversaire, deux jours après son anniversaire; **the ~ after tomorrow** après-demain; **this ~ week** d'aujourd'hui en huit; **from that ~ onwards** dès lors, à partir de ce jour (-là); (*frm*) **from this ~ forth** désormais, dorénavant; **2 years ago to the ~** il y a 2 ans jour pour jour *or* exactement; **he will come any ~ now** il va venir d'un jour à l'autre; **every ~** tous les jours; **every other ~** tous les deux jours; **one ~ we saw the king** un (beau) jour nous vîmes le roi; **one ~ she will come** un jour (ou l'autre) elle viendra; **one of these ~s** un de ces jours, un jour ou l'autre; ~ **by ~** jour après jour; ~ **in ~ out** tous les jours que (le bon) Dieu fait; ~ **after ~** jour après jour; **for ~s on end** pendant des jours et des jours; **for ~s at a time** pendant des jours entiers; **to live from ~ to ~** vivre au jour le jour; **the other ~** l'autre jour, il y a quelques jours; **this ~ of all ~s** ce jour entre tous; **I remember it to this ~** je m'en souviens encore aujourd'hui; **he's fifty if he's a ~*** il a cinquante ans bien sonnés*; (*Rel*) **D~ of Atonement** jour *m* des propitiations *or* de l'expiation; (*Rel*) **the ~ of judgment, the ~ of reckoning** le jour du jugement dernier; (*fig*) **the ~ of reckoning will come** un jour il faudra rendre des comptes; *V* **Christmas, Easter** *etc.*

(b) (*daylight hours*) jour *m*, journée *f*. **during the ~** pendant la journée; **to work all ~** travailler toute la journée; **to travel by ~** voyager de jour; **to work ~ and night** travailler jour et nuit; (*liter*) **the ~ is done** le jour baisse, le jour tire à sa fin; **it's a fine ~** il fait beau aujourd'hui; **one summer's ~** un jour d'été; **on a wet ~** par une journée pluvieuse; (*Mil, fig*) **to carry the ~** remporter la victoire; (*Mil, fig*) **to lose the ~** perdre la bataille; *V* **break, good, time.**

(c) (*working hours*) journée *f*. **paid by the ~** payé à la journée; **it's all in the ~'s work!** ça fait partie de la routine!; **to take a ~ off** prendre un jour de congé; **it's my ~ off** c'est mon jour de congé *or* mon jour libre; ~ **of rest** jour de repos; **to work an 8-hour ~** travailler 8 heures par jour, faire une journée de 8 heures; *V* **call, working.**

(d) (*period of time: often pl*) époque *f*, temps *m*. **these ~s, in the present ~** à l'heure actuelle, de nos jours, actuellement; **in this ~ and age** par les temps qui courent; **in ~s to come** dans l'avenir, dans les jours à venir; **in his working ~s** au temps *or* à l'époque où il travaillait; **in his younger ~s** quand il était plus jeune; **in the ~s of Queen Victoria, in Queen Victoria's ~** du temps de *or* sous le règne de la reine Victoria; **in Napoleon's ~** à l'époque *or* du temps de Napoléon; **famous in her ~** célèbre à son époque; **in the good old ~s** au bon vieux temps; **they were sad ~s then** c'était une époque sombre; **the happiest ~s of my life** les jours les plus heureux *or* la période la plus heureuse de ma vie; **during the early ~s of the war** tout au début *or* pendant les premiers temps de la guerre; **to end one's ~s in misery** finir ses jours dans la misère; **he has known** *or* **seen better ~s** il a connu des jours meilleurs; **this dress has seen better ~s** cette robe a fait son temps; **that has had its ~** cela est passé de mode; **his ~ will come** son jour viendra; *V* **dog, olden** *etc.*

2 *cpd*: **day bed** banquette-lit *f*; (*Scol*) **day boarder** demi-pensionnaire *mf*; (*Comm*) **daybook** main courante *f*, brouillard *m*; (*Brit Scol*) **day boy** externe *m*; **daybreak** point *m* du jour, lever *m* du jour, aube *f*; **at daybreak** au point du jour, à l'aube; **daydream** (*n*) rêverie *f*, rêvasserie *f*; (*vi*) rêvasser, rêver (tout éveillé); (*Scol*) **day girl** externe *f*; **day labourer** journalier *m*, ouvrier *m* à la journée; (*US*) **day letter** ≃ télégramme-lettre *m*; **daylight** *V* **daylight**; (*liter*) **daylong** continuel, qui dure toute la journée; **day nurse** infirmière *f* (de jour); **day nursery** (*public*) pouponnière *f*, crèche *f*; (*in private house*) pièce *f* des enfants; **day-old chick** poussin *m* d'un jour; (*Brit: Comm, Ind*) **day release course** ≃ cours professionnel (de l'industrie *etc*) à temps partiel; (*Brit Rail*) **day return (ticket)** (billet *m* d')aller et retour *m* (*valable pour la journée*); **to go to day school** être externe *mf* (*Scol*); **day shift** (*workers*) équipe *f* or poste *m* de jour; **to be on day shift, to work day shift** travailler de jour, être de jour; **daytime** (*n*) jour *m*, journée *f*; (*adj*) de jour; **in the daytime** le jour, de jour, dans *or* pendant la journée; **day-to-day** *occurrence* qui se produit tous les jours, journalier; *routine* journalier, ordinaire; **on a day-to-day basis** au jour le jour; **day trip** excursion *f* (d'une journée); **to go on a day trip to Calais** faire une excursion (d'une journée) à Calais; **day-tripper** excursionniste *mf*.

daylight ['deɪlaɪt] **1** *n* **(a)** = **daybreak**; *V* **day 2.**

(b) (lumière *f* du) jour *m*. **it is still ~** il fait encore jour; **I begin to see ~*** (*understand*) je commence à voir clair; (*see the end appear*) j'en aperçois la fin; *V* **broad, living.**

2 *cpd attack* de jour. (*Brit*) **it's daylight robbery*** c'est du vol caractérisé; **daylight-saving (time)** l'heure *f* d'été.

daze [deɪz] **1** *n* (*after blow*) étourdissement *m*; (*at news*) stupéfaction *f*, ahurissement *m*, confusion *f*; (*from drug*) hébétement *m*. **in a ~** étourdi, stupéfait, ahuri, hébété, médusé.

2 *vt* *[drug]* stupéfier, hébéter; *[blow]* étourdir; *[news etc]* abasourdir, méduser, sidérer.

dazed [deɪzd] *adj* (*V* **daze**) hébété; tout étourdi; abasourdi, sidéré.

dazzle ['dæzl] **1** *vt* (*lit*) éblouir, aveugler; (*fig*) éblouir. **to ~ sb's eyes** éblouir qn. **2** *n* lumière aveuglante, éclat *m*. **blinded by the ~ of the car's headlights** ébloui par les phares de la voiture.

dazzling ['dæzlɪŋ] *adj* (*lit*) éblouissant; aveuglant; (*fig*) éblouissant.

de... [diː] *pref* de..., dé..., des..., dés... .

deacon ['di:kən] *n* diacre *m.*
deaconess ['di:kənes] *n* diaconesse *f.*
dead [ded] **1** *adj* **(a)** *person* mort, décédé; *animal, plant* mort. ~ **or alive** mort ou vif; **more ~ than alive** plus mort que vif; (*lit, fig*) ~ **and buried** mort et enterré; **to drop down ~, to fall (stone) ~** tomber (raide) mort; **as ~ as a doornail** *or* **as mutton** *or* **as the dodo** tout ce qu'il y a de plus mort; **to wait for a ~ man's shoes*** attendre que quelqu'un veuille bien mourir (pour prendre sa place); **will he do it? — over my ~ body!*** il le fera? — pas question!* *or* il faudra d'abord qu'il me passe (*subj*) sur le corps!; (*Prov*) ~ **men tell no tales** les morts ne parlent pas; **he's a ~ duck*** c'est un homme fini, il est cuit*; *V* **drop, strike.**
(b) *limbs* engourdi. **my fingers are** ~ j'ai les doigts gourds; **he's ~ from the neck up‡** il n'a rien dans la tête, il a la cervelle vide; **he was ~ to the world*** il dormait comme une souche.
(c) (*fig*) *custom* tombé en désuétude; *fire* mort, éteint; *cigarette* éteint; *town* mort, triste; *colour* éteint, terne; *sound* sourd, feutré. ~ **language** langue morte; (*Telec*) **the line has gone ~** *or* **is ~** on n'entend plus rien (sur la ligne).
(d) (*absolute, exact*) ~ **calm** calme plat; **to hit sth in the ~ centre** frapper qch au beau milieu *or* en plein milieu; **it's a ~ cert‡ that he'll come** il viendra à coup sûr, sûr qu'il viendra*; **this horse is a ~ cert‡** ce cheval est le gagnant sûr; **he's in ~ earnest** il ne plaisante pas; **on a ~ level with** exactement au même niveau que; **a ~ loss** (*Comm etc*) une perte sèche; (*: *person*) un bon à rien; **that idea was a ~ loss*** cette idée n'a absolument rien donné; **this book/knife is a ~ loss*** ce livre/couteau ne vaut rien; **to be a ~ shot** être un tireur d'élite; ~ **silence** silence *m* de mort; **he's the ~ spit of his father*** c'est son père tout craché; **to come to a ~ stop** s'arrêter net *or* pile.
2 *adv* (*completely*) absolument, complètement. ~ **ahead** tout droit; ~ **broke‡** fauché (comme les blés)*; **to be ~ certain about sth*** être absolument certain *or* convaincu de qch, être sûr et certain de qch*; ~ **drunk*** ivre mort; **to be ~ on time** être juste à l'heure *or* à l'heure pile; **it was ~ lucky‡** c'était le coup de pot monstre‡; (*order*) ~ **slow** (*Aut*) allez au pas; (*Naut*) en avant lentement; **to go ~ slow** aller aussi lentement que possible; **to stop ~** s'arrêter net *or* pile; ~ **tired** claqué*, éreinté, crevé*; **he went ~ white** il est devenu pâle comme un mort.
3 *n* **(a) the ~** les morts *mpl.*
(b) at ~ of night, in the ~ of night au cœur de *or* au plus profond de la nuit; **in the ~ of winter** au plus fort de l'hiver, au cœur de l'hiver.
4 *cpd*: **dead-and-alive** *town* triste, mort; **a dead-and-alive little place** un trou perdu; (*Ftbl*) **dead ball** ballon sorti; (*Rugby*) **dead-ball line** ligne *f* de ballon mort; **dead-beat*** (*n*) chiffe molle; (*US*) parasite *m*, pique-assiette *mf inv*; (*adj*) éreinté, crevé*, claqué*; **I'm dead-beat*** je suis claqué* *or* mort* *or* sur les rotules*; (*Tech*) **dead centre** point mort; (*lit, fig*) **dead end** impasse *f*; (*fig*) **to come to a dead end** être dans une impasse; **a dead-end job** un travail sans débouché; (*US*) **deadhead*** *V* **deadhead***; **the race was a dead heat** ils sont arrivés ex-aequo; (*Horse-racing*) la course s'est terminée par un dead-heat; (*Post*) **dead letter** lettre tombée au rebut; (*Jur*) **to become a dead letter** tomber en désuétude, devenir lettre morte; (*Post*) **dead-letter office** bureau *m* des rebuts; **deadline** (*Press etc*) date *f or* heure *f* limite, dernière limite; (*US: boundary*) limite *f* (qu'il est interdit de franchir); **to work to a deadline** travailler en vue d'une date *or* d'une heure limite; **he was working to a 6 o'clock deadline** son travail devait être terminé à 6 heures dernière limite; **deadlock** impasse *f*; **to reach (a) deadlock** aboutir à une impasse, être au point mort; **to be at (a) deadlock** être dans une impasse, être au point mort; **dead march** marche *f* funèbre; **dead matter** matière inanimée; (*Typ*) composition *f* à distribuer; **deadmen*** (*empty bottles*) bouteilles *fpl* vides, cadavres‡ *mpl*; **deadnettle** ortie blanche; **deadpan** (*adj*) *face* sans expression, figé, de marbre; *humour* pince-sans-rire *inv*; (*adv*) sans expression; (*Naut*) **dead reckoning** estime *f*; **by dead reckoning** à l'estime; **Dead Sea** mer Morte; **Dead Sea Scrolls** manuscrits *mpl or* parchemins *mpl* de la mer Morte; (*Comm, Press*) **dead season** morte-saison *f*; **to make a dead set at sth*** s'acharner comme un beau diable pour avoir qch; **to make a dead set at sb*** mettre le grappin sur qn*; **to be dead set on doing sth*** vouloir faire qch à tout prix; **to be dead set against sth*** s'opposer absolument à qch; **dead stock** invendu(s) *m(pl)*, rossignols* *mpl*; **dead weight** poids mort *or* inerte; (*Naut*) charge *f or* port *m* en lourd; (*Elec*) **dead wire** fil *m* sans courant; (*lit, fig*) **deadwood** bois mort; (*fig*) **to get rid of the deadwood in the office*** se débarrasser du personnel improductif *or* inutile.
deaden ['dedn] *vt shock, blow* amortir; *feeling* émousser; *sound* assourdir, feutrer; *passions* étouffer; *pain* calmer; *nerve* endormir.
deadening ['dednıŋ] *n* (*V* **deaden**) amortissement *m*; assourdissement *m.*
deadhead* ['dedhed] *n* (*US*) **(a)** (*person using free ticket*) (*Rail*) personne *f* possédant un titre de transport gratuit; (*Theat*) personne possédant un billet de faveur. **(b)** (*stupid person*) nullité *f.* **(c)** (*empty truck/train etc*) camion *m*/train *m etc* roulant à vide.
deadliness ['dedlınıs] *n* [*poison*] caractère mortel; [*aim*] précision *f* infaillible; (*boredom*) ennui mortel.
deadly ['dedlı] **1** *adj* **(a)** *blow, poison, sin, enemy* mortel; *hatred* mortel, implacable; *aim* qui ne rate jamais; *weapon* meurtrier; *pallor* de mort. (*Bot*) ~ **nightshade** belladone *f*; **the seven ~ sins** les sept péchés capitaux.
(b) (*: *boring*) casse-pieds* *inv*, rasoir* *inv.*
2 *adv dull* mortellement, terriblement. ~ **pale** d'une pâleur mortelle, pâle comme un(e) mort(e) *or* la mort.
deadness ['dednıs] *n* (*fig*) [*place*] absence *f* de vie *or* de vitalité; [*limbs*] engourdissement *m*; [*colour*] fadeur *f.*

deaf [def] **1** *adj* **(a)** sourd. ~ **in one ear** sourd d'une oreille; ~ **as a (door)post** *or* **a stone** sourd comme un pot; (*Prov*) **there are none so ~ as those who will not hear** il n'y a pire sourd que celui qui ne veut pas entendre (*Prov*).
(b) (*unwilling to listen*) sourd, insensible (*to* à). **to turn a ~ ear to sth** faire la sourde oreille à qch.
2 *n*: **the ~** les sourds *mpl.*
3 *cpd*: **deaf-aid** appareil *m* acoustique; **deaf-and-dumb** sourd-muet; **deaf-and-dumb alphabet** alphabet *m* des sourds et muets; **deaf-mute** sourd(e)-muet(te) *m(f).*
deafen ['defn] *vt* (*lit*) rendre sourd; (*fig*) assourdir, rendre sourd, casser les oreilles à*.
deafening ['defnıŋ] *adj* (*lit, fig*) assourdissant.
deafness ['defnıs] *n* surdité *f.*
deal[1] [di:l] (*vb: pret, ptp* **dealt**) **1** *n* **(a)** (*U: amount*) quantité *f*, tas *m.* **a good ~ of, a great ~ of, a ~ of** une grande quantité de, beaucoup de, pas mal de*, énormément de; **to have a great ~ to do** avoir beaucoup à faire, avoir bien des choses à faire; **a good ~ of the work is done** une bonne partie du travail est terminée; **that's saying a good ~** ce n'est pas peu dire; **there's a good ~ of truth in what he says** il y a beaucoup de vrai dans ce qu'il dit; **to think a great ~ of sb** avoir beaucoup d'estime pour qn; **to mean a great ~ to sb** compter beaucoup pour qn; (*adv phrase*) **a good ~** nettement, beaucoup; **she's a good ~ cleverer than her brother** elle est nettement plus intelligente que son frère; **she's a good ~ better today** elle va beaucoup mieux aujourd'hui; **they've travelled a good ~** ils ont beaucoup voyagé.
(b) (*Comm, Fin: also* **business ~**) affaire *f*, marché *m*; (*St Ex*) opération *f*, transaction *f.* **to do a ~ with sb** faire *or* passer un marché avec qn, faire (une) affaire avec qn; **it's a ~!*** d'accord!, marché conclu!; *V* **big, clinch.**
(c) (*fig*) (*agreement, bargain*) marché *m*, affaire *f*; (*pej*) coup *m.* **to do a ~ with sb** conclure un marché avec qn; (*pej*) monter un coup avec qn; **we might do a ~?** on pourrait (peut-être) s'arranger?
(d) (*treatment*) **he got a very bad ~ from them** ils se sont très mal conduits envers lui, ils ont agi très malhonnêtement avec lui; *V* **fair[1], raw, square** *etc.*
(e) (*Cards*) donne *f*, distribution *f.* **it's your ~** à vous la donne, à vous de distribuer *or* donner; (*Pol etc*) **a new ~** un programme de réformes.
2 *vt* **(a)** (*also* **~ out**) *cards* donner, distribuer.
(b) to ~ sb a blow porter *or* assener un coup à qn.
3 *vi* **(a) to have to ~ with sb** avoir affaire à qn; **to ~ well/badly by sb** agir bien/mal avec qn, se comporter bien/mal envers qn.
(b) (*Comm*) traiter, négocier (*with sb* avec qn); commercer (*with another firm* avec une autre maison). **I always ~ with that butcher** je vais *or* me fournis toujours chez ce boucher-là; **to ~ in wood** être dans le commerce du bois.
deal out *vt sep gifts, money* distribuer, répartir, partager (*between* entre). **to deal out justice** rendre (la) justice.
deal with *vt fus* **(a)** (*Comm, Fin*) négocier avec, avoir affaire à.
(b) (*have to do with*) *person* traiter. **to know how to deal with sb** savoir s'y prendre avec qn; **he's not very easy to deal with** il n'est pas commode.
(c) (*manage, handle*) *person, task* s'occuper de, se charger de; *problem* venir à bout de; (*Comm*) *order* régler. **I'll deal with him** je me charge de lui; **you bad boy, I'll deal with you later!*** vilain garçon, tu vas avoir affaire à moi *or* tu vas avoir de mes nouvelles tout à l'heure!
(d) (*be concerned with*) [*book, film etc*] traiter de, avoir pour sujet.
deal[2] [di:l] **1** *n* (*U*) (bois *m* de) sapin *m*, bois blanc. **2** *cpd* en bois blanc.
dealer ['di:ləʳ] *n* **(a)** (*Comm*) marchand *m* (*in* de), négociant *m* (*in* en); (*wholesaler*) stockiste *m*, fournisseur *m* (en gros) (*in* de); *V* **double, secondhand. (b)** (*Cards*) donneur *m.*
dealing ['di:lıŋ] *n* **(a)** (*U*) (*also* **~ out**) distribution *f*; [*cards*] donne *f*; *V* **wheel.**
(b) (*St Ex: gen pl*) opérations *fpl*, transactions *fpl.*
(c) ~s (*relationship with people*) relations *fpl*, rapports *mpl*; (*trafficking*) trafic *m.*
dealt [delt] *pret, ptp of* **deal[1]**.
dean [di:n] *n* (*Rel, Univ, US fig*) doyen *m.*
deanery ['di:nərı] *n* (*Univ*) demeure *f or* résidence *f* du doyen; (*Rel*) doyenné *m*, demeure du doyen.
dear [dıəʳ] **1** *adj* **(a)** (*loved*) *person, animal* cher; (*precious*) *object* cher, précieux; (*lovable*) adorable; *child* mignon, adorable. **she is very ~ to me** elle m'est très chère; **a ~ friend of mine** un de mes meilleurs amis, un de mes amis les plus chers; **to hold sb/sth ~** chérir qn/qch; **his ~est wish** son plus cher désir, son souhait le plus cher; **what a ~ child!** quel amour d'enfant!; **what a ~ little dress!*** quelle ravissante *or* mignonne petite robe!
(b) (*in letter-writing etc*) cher. ~ **Daddy** (mon) cher papa; ~ **Sir** Monsieur; ~ **Sirs** Messieurs; ~ **Mr Smith** cher Monsieur.
(c) (*expensive*) *prices, goods* cher, coûteux; *price* élevé; *shop* cher. **to get ~er** [*goods*] renchérir; [*prices*] augmenter.
2 *excl*: ~ **~!, ~ me!** mon Dieu!, vraiment!, pas possible!; **oh ~!** oh là là!, oh mon Dieu!
3 *n* cher *m*, chère *f*, chéri(e) *m(f).* **my ~** mon ami(e), mon cher ami, ma chère amie; (*to child*) mon petit; **my ~est** mon chéri, mon amour; **poor ~** (*to child*) pauvre petit, pauvre chou*; (*to woman*) ma pauvre; **your mother is a ~*** votre mère est un amour; **give it to me, there's a ~‡** sois gentil donne-le-moi, donne-le-moi tu seras (bien) gentil.
4 *adv* (*lit, fig*) *buy, pay, sell* cher.
dearie* ['dıərı] *n* mon petit chéri, ma petite chérie.
dearly ['dıəlı] *adv* **(a)** (*tenderly*) tendrement, avec tendresse.

he loves this country ~ il est très attaché à ce pays; **I should ~ like to live here** j'aimerais infiniment habiter ici.

(b) (*lit, fig*) **to pay ~ for sth** payer qch cher; (*fig*) **~ bought** chèrement payé.

dearness ['dɪənɪs] *n* **(a)** (*expensiveness*) cherté *f*. **(b)** (*lovableness*) **your ~ to me** la tendresse que j'ai pour vous.

dearth [dɜːθ] *n* *[food]* disette *f*; *[money, resources, water]* pénurie *f*; *[ideas etc]* stérilité *f*, pauvreté *f*. **there is no ~ of young men** les jeunes gens ne manquent pas.

deary* ['dɪərɪ] *n* = **dearie***.

death [deθ] **1** *n* mort *f*, décès *m* (*Jur, frm*); *[plans, hopes]* effondrement *m*, anéantissement *m*. **to be burnt to ~** mourir carbonisé; **he drank himself to ~** c'est la boisson qui l'a tué; **to be at ~'s door** être à (l'article de) la mort; (*Jur*) **to sentence sb to ~** condamner qn à mort; (*Jur*) **to put sb to ~** mettre qn à mort, exécuter qn; **a fight to the ~** une lutte à mort; (*fig*) **to be in at the ~** assister au dénouement (d'une affaire); (*lit*) **it will be the ~ of him** il le paiera de sa vie, cela va l'achever; (*fig*) **he will be the ~ of me** il me fera mourir, il sera ma mort; (*fig*) **he died the ~‡** il s'est fait massacrer; **to be bored to ~*** s'ennuyer à mourir *or* à crever*; **you look tired to ~*** tu as l'air crevé*; **I'm sick to ~*** *or* **tired to ~* of all this** j'en ai par-dessus la tête *or* j'en ai marre* de tout ceci; *V* **catch, dance, do**[1].

2 *cpd*: **deathbed** (*n*) lit *m* de mort; (*adj*) *repentance* de la dernière heure; (*Theat*) **this is a deathbed scene** la scène se passe au chevet du mourant; (*lit, fig*) **death-blow** coup mortel *or* fatal; **death cell** cellule *f* de condamné à mort; **death certificate** acte *m* de décès; (*Brit Jur*) **death duty** *or* **duties** droits *mpl* de succession; **deathlike** semblable à la mort, de mort; **death march** marche *f* funèbre; **death mask** masque *m* mortuaire; (*Jur*) **death penalty** peine *f* de mort; **death rate** (taux *m* de) mortalité *f*; **death rattle** râle *m* (d'agonie); **death ray** rayon *m* de la mort, rayon qui tue; **death roll** liste *f* des morts; (*US*) **death row** cellules *fpl* des condamnés à mort; **death sentence** arrêt *m* *or* sentence *f* de mort; **death's-head** tête *f* de mort; **death's-head moth** (sphinx *m*) tête *f* de mort; **death throes** affres *fpl* de la mort, agonie *f*; **death toll** chiffre *m* des morts; **deathtrap** endroit (*or* véhicule *etc*) dangereux; **that corner is a real death-trap** ce tournant est mortel; (*Jur*) **death warrant** ordre *m* d'exécution; (*fig*) **to sign the death warrant of a project** condamner un projet, signer la condamnation d'un projet; **deathwatch beetle** vrillette *f*, horloge *f* de la mort; (*Psych, also fig*) **death wish** désir *m* de mort.

deathless ['deθlɪs] *adj* immortel, impérissable, éternel.

deathly ['deθlɪ] **1** *adj appearance* semblable à la mort, de mort, cadavérique. **~ hush, ~ silence** silence mortel *or* de mort. **2** *adv* comme la mort. **~ pale** au teint blafard *or* cadavérique, d'une pâleur mortelle.

deb* [deb] *n abbr of* **débutante.**

debag‡ [diː'bæg] *vt* (*Brit*) déculotter.

debar [dɪ'bɑːʳ] *vt* (*from club, competition*) exclure (*from* de). **to ~ sb from doing** interdire *or* défendre à qn de faire.

debark [dɪ'bɑːk] *vti* débarquer.

debarkation [ˌdiːbɑː'keɪʃən] *n* débarquement *m*.

debarment [dɪ'bɑːmənt] *n* exclusion *f* (*from* de).

debase [dɪ'beɪs] *vt* **(a)** *person* avilir, ravaler. **to ~ o.s. (by doing)** s'avilir *or* se ravaler (en faisant). **(b)** (*reduce in value or quality*) rabaisser; *metal* altérer; (*Fin*) *coinage* déprécier, dévaloriser.

debasement [dɪ'beɪsmənt] *n* (*V* **debase**) avilissement *m*; baisse *f*, altération *f*; dépréciation *f*.

debatable [dɪ'beɪtəbl] *adj point* discutable, contestable, litigieux; *frontier* en litige.

debate [dɪ'beɪt] **1** *vt question* discuter, débattre.

2 *vi* discuter (*with* avec, *about* sur). **he was debating with himself whether to refuse or not** il se demandait bien s'il refuserait ou non, il s'interrogeait pour savoir s'il refuserait ou non.

3 *n* discussion *f*, débat *m*, délibération *f*; (*Parl*) débat(s); (*esp in debating society*) conférence *f* contradictoire, débat. **to hold long ~s** discuter longuement; **after much ~** après de longues discussions; **the ~ was on** *or* **about** la discussion portait sur; **the death penalty was under ~** on délibérait sur la peine de mort.

debater [dɪ'beɪtəʳ] *n* maître *m* dans l'art de la discussion. **he is a good ~** c'est un bon argumentateur *or* dialecticien.

debating [dɪ'beɪtɪŋ] *n* art *m* de la discussion. **~ society** société *f* de conférences *or* débats contradictoires.

debauch [dɪ'bɔːtʃ] **1** *vt person* débaucher, corrompre; *morals* corrompre; *woman* séduire; *taste* corrompre, vicier. **2** *n* débauche *f*.

debauchee [ˌdebɔː'tʃiː] *n* débauché(e) *m(f)*.

debaucher [dɪ'bɔːtʃəʳ] *n [person, taste, morals]* corrupteur *m*, -trice *f*; *[woman]* séducteur *m*.

debauchery [dɪ'bɔːtʃərɪ] *n* (*U*) débauche *f*, dérèglement *m* de(s) mœurs.

debenture [dɪ'bentʃəʳ] **1** *n* (*Customs*) certificat *m* de drawback; (*Fin*) obligation *f*, bon *m*. **2** *cpd*: **debenture bond** titre *m* d'obligation; **debenture holder** obligataire *mf*; **debenture stock** obligations *fpl* sans garantie.

debilitate [dɪ'bɪlɪteɪt] *vt* débiliter.

debility [dɪ'bɪlɪtɪ] *n* (*Med*) débilité *f*, faiblesse *f*.

debit ['debɪt] **1** *n* (*Comm*) débit *m*.

2 *cpd account* débiteur. **debit balance** solde débiteur; **debit entry** inscription *f* *or* écriture *f* au débit; **on the debit side** au débit; (*fig*) **on the debit side there is the bad weather** au passif il y a le mauvais temps.

3 *vt*: **to ~ sb's account with a sum, to ~ a sum against sb's account** porter une somme au débit du compte de qn; **to ~ sb with a sum, to ~ a sum to sb** porter une somme au débit de qn, débiter qn d'une somme.

debonair [ˌdebə'nɛəʳ] *adj* jovial, joyeux.

debouch [dɪ'baʊtʃ] (*Geog, Mil*) **1** *vi* déboucher. **2** *n* débouché *m*.

debrief [ˌdiː'briːf] *vt* faire faire un compte rendu (de fin de mission) à; (*Mil*) faire faire (un) rapport à. (*Mil*) **to be ~ed** faire rapport, aller au rapport.

debriefing [ˌdiː'briːfɪŋ] *n* compte rendu *m* (de fin de mission); (*Mil*) rapport *m*.

debris ['debriː] *n* débris *mpl*; (*Geol*) roches *fpl* détritiques.

debt [det] **1** *n* (*payment owed*) dette *f*, créance *f*. **bad ~s** créances irrécouvrables; **~ of honour** dette d'honneur; **outstanding ~** créance à recouvrer; **to be in ~** avoir des dettes, être endetté; **he is in ~ to everyone** il doit à tout le monde; **I am £5 in ~** je dois 5 livres; **to be out of sb's ~** être quitte envers qn; **to get** *or* **run into ~** faire des dettes, s'endetter; **to get out of ~** s'acquitter de ses dettes; **to be out of ~** n'avoir plus de dettes; (*fig*) **to repay a ~** acquitter une dette; (*fig*) **I am greatly in your ~ for sth/for having done** je vous suis très redevable de qch/d'avoir fait; *V* **eye, head, national** *etc*.

2 *cpd*: **debt collector** agent *m* de recouvrements; **debt-ridden** criblé de dettes.

debtor ['detəʳ] *n* débiteur *m*, -trice *f*.

debunk* [ˌdiː'bʌŋk] *vt person* déboulonner*; *claim* démentir; *institution* discréditer. **that ~s his claims!** autant pour ses prétentions!

début ['deɪbjuː] *n* (*Theat*) début *m*; (*in society*) entrée *f* dans le monde. **he made his ~ as a pianist** il a débuté comme pianiste.

débutante ['debjuːtɑ̃ːnt] *n* débutante *f* (*jeune fille qui fait son entrée dans le monde*).

decade ['dekeɪd] *n* **(a)** décennie *f*, décade *f*. **(b)** *[rosary]* dizaine *f*.

decadence ['dekədəns] *n* décadence *f*.

decadent ['dekədənt] **1** *adj person, civilization* en décadence, décadent; *book, attitude* décadent. **2** *n* (*Literat*) décadent *m*.

decaffeinate [ˌdiː'kæfɪneɪt] *vt* décaféiner.

decagramme, (*US*) **decagram** ['dekəgræm] *n* décagramme *m*.

decal [dɪ'kæl] *n* (*US*) décalcomanie *f*.

decalcification ['diːˌkælsɪfɪ'keɪʃən] *n* décalcification *f*.

decalcify [ˌdiː'kælsɪfaɪ] *vt* décalcifier.

decalitre, (*US*) **decaliter** ['dekəˌliːtəʳ] *n* décalitre *m*.

decalogue ['dekəlɒg] *n* décalogue *m*.

decametre, (*US*) **decameter** ['dekəˌmiːtəʳ] *n* décamètre *m*.

decamp [dɪ'kæmp] *vi* **(a)** (*) décamper, ficher le camp*. **(b)** (*Mil*) lever le camp.

decant [dɪ'kænt] *vt wine* décanter. **he ~ed the solution into another container** il a transvasé la solution.

decanter [dɪ'kæntəʳ] *n* carafe *f* (à liqueur *or* à vin); (*small*) carafon *m*.

decapitate [dɪ'kæpɪteɪt] *vt* décapiter.

decapitation [dɪˌkæpɪ'teɪʃən] *n* décapitation *f*, décollation *f* (*liter etc*).

decapod ['dekəpɒd] *n* décapode *m*.

decarbonization ['diːˌkɑːbənaɪ'zeɪʃən] *n* (*Aut*) décalaminage *m*; *[steel]* décarburation *f*.

decarbonize [ˌdiː'kɑːbənaɪz] *vt* (*Aut*) décalaminer; *steel* décarburer.

decathlon [dɪ'kæθlən] *n* décathlon *m*.

decay [dɪ'keɪ] **1** *vi* **(a)** (*go bad*) s'altérer, se détériorer; *[food]* pourrir, se gâter; *[flowers, vegetation, wood]* pourrir; *[tooth]* se carier, se gâter.

(b) (*crumble*) *[building]* se délabrer, tomber en ruines.

(c) (*Phys*) *[radioactive nucleus]* se désintégrer.

(d) (*fig*) *[hopes]* s'enfuir; *[beauty]* se faner; *[civilization]* décliner; *[race, one's faculties]* s'affaiblir.

2 *vt food, wood* faire pourrir; *tooth* carier.

3 *n* **(a)** (*Culin*) pourrissement *m*; (*Bot*) pourrissement, dépérissement *m*; (*Med*) carie *f*.

(b) (*Archit*) délabrement *m*, décrépitude *f*. **to fall into ~** tomber en ruines, se délabrer.

(c) (*Phys*) désintégration *f*.

(d) (*fig*) *[hopes, friendship, beauty]* ruine *f*; *[civilization]* décadence *f*, déclin *m*; *[race]* affaiblissement *m*, déchéance *f*; *[faculties]* affaiblissement, déclin.

decayed [dɪ'keɪd] *adj tooth* carié, gâté; *wood* pourri; *food* gâté, pourri; *building* délabré; (*Phys*) partiellement désintégré; *faculty, health, civilization* en déclin; *hopes, friendship* en ruines.

decaying [dɪ'keɪɪŋ] *adj nation* en décadence; *flesh* en pourriture; *food* en train de s'avarier; *tooth* qui se carie *or* se gâte.

decease [dɪ'siːs] (*Admin, frm*) **1** *n* décès *m*. **2** *vi* décéder.

deceased [dɪ'siːst] **1** *adj* (*Admin, frm*) décédé, défunt. **John Brown ~** feu John Brown. **2** *n*: **the ~** le défunt, la défunte.

deceit [dɪ'siːt] *n* **(a)** supercherie *f*, tromperie *f*, duperie *f*. **(b)** (*U*) = **deceitfulness.**

deceitful [dɪ'siːtfʊl] *adj person* trompeur, faux (*f* fausse), fourbe; *words, conduct* trompeur, mensonger.

deceitfully [dɪ'siːtfəlɪ] *adv* avec duplicité, faussement, par supercherie.

deceitfulness [dɪ'siːtfʊlnɪs] *n* fausseté *f*, duplicité *f*.

deceive [dɪ'siːv] **1** *vt* tromper, abuser, duper; *spouse* tromper; *hopes* tromper, décevoir. **to ~ sb into doing** amener qn à faire (en le trompant); **he ~d me into thinking that he had bought it** il m'a (faussement) fait croire qu'il l'avait acheté; **I thought my eyes were deceiving me** je n'en croyais pas mes yeux; **to be ~d by appearances** être trompé par *or* se tromper sur les apparences; **to ~ o.s.** s'abuser, se faire illusion.

2 *vi* tromper, être trompeur. **appearances ~** les apparences sont trompeuses.

deceiver [dɪ'siːvəʳ] *n* trompeur *m*, -euse *f*, imposteur *m*, fourbe *m*.

decelerate [diː'seləreɪt] *vti* ralentir.
deceleration ['diːˌselə'reɪʃən] *n [engine, programme]* ralentissement *m*; *[car]* décélération *f*, freinage *m*.
December [dɪ'sembəʳ] *n* décembre *m*; *for phrases V* **September.**
decency ['diːsənsɪ] *n* **(a)** (*U*) *[dress, conversation]* décence *f*, bienséance *f*; *[person]* pudeur *f*. **to have a sense of ~** avoir de la pudeur.
(b) (*good manners*) convenances *fpl*. **to observe the decencies** observer *or* respecter les convenances; **common ~** la simple politesse, le simple savoir-vivre; **for the sake of ~** par convenance, pour garder les convenances; **to have the ~ to do sth** avoir la décence de faire qch.
(c) (*: *niceness*) gentillesse *f*.
decent ['diːsənt] *adj* **(a)** (*respectable*) *person* convenable, honnête, bien* *inv*; *house, shoes* convenable; (*seemly*) *language, behaviour, dress* décent, bienséant. **no ~ person would do it** jamais une personne convenable ne ferait cela, quelqu'un de bien* ne ferait jamais cela.
(b) (*: *good, pleasant*) *person* bon, brave, chic* *inv*. **a ~ sort of fellow** un bon *or* brave garçon, un type bien*; **it was ~ of him** c'était chic* de sa part; **I've got quite a ~ flat** j'ai un appartement qui n'est pas mal; **I could do with a ~ meal** un bon repas ne me ferait pas de mal.
decently ['diːsəntlɪ] *adv dress, behave* décemment, convenablement, avec bienséance. **you can't ~ ask him that** décemment vous ne pouvez pas lui demander cela.
decentralization [diːˌsentrəlaɪ'zeɪʃən] *n* décentralisation *f*.
decentralize [diː'sentrəlaɪz] *vt* décentraliser.
deception [dɪ'sepʃən] *n* **(a)** (*U*) (*deceiving*) tromperie *f*, duperie *f*; (*being deceived*) illusion *f*, erreur *f*. **he is incapable of ~** il est incapable de tromperie. **(b)** (*deceitful act*) supercherie *f*.
deceptive [dɪ'septɪv] *adj* (*liable to deceive*) trompeur, illusoire; (*meant to deceive*) trompeur, mensonger, fallacieux.
deceptively [dɪ'septɪvlɪ] *adv* mensongèrement, faussement. **the village looks ~ near** le village donne l'illusion d'être proche.
deceptiveness [dɪ'septɪvnɪs] *n* caractère mensonger *or* trompeur.
decibel ['desɪbel] *n* décibel *m*.
decide [dɪ'saɪd] **1** *vt* **(a)** (*make up one's mind*) se décider (*to do* à faire), décider (*to do* de faire), se résoudre (*to do* à faire). **I ~d to go** *or* **that I would go** je me suis décidé à y aller, j'ai décidé d'y aller; **it has been ~d that** on a décidé *or* il a été décidé que.
(b) (*settle*) *question* décider, trancher; *quarrel* décider, arbitrer; *piece of business* régler; *difference of opinion* juger; *sb's fate, future* décider de.
(c) (*cause to make up one's mind*) décider, déterminer (*sb to do* qn à faire).
2 *vi* se décider. **you must ~** il vous faut prendre une décision, il faut vous décider; **to ~ for sth** se décider pour qch *or* en faveur de qch; **to ~ against sth** se décider contre qch; (*Jur*) **to ~ for/against sb** donner raison/tort à qn; (*Jur*) **to ~ in favour of sb** décider en faveur de qn, donner gain de cause à qn.
decide on *vt fus thing, course of action* se décider pour, choisir (finalement). **to decide on doing** se décider à faire.
decided [dɪ'saɪdɪd] *adj improvement, progress* incontestable; *difference* net, marqué; *refusal* catégorique; *character, person* résolu, décidé, déterminé; *manner, tone, look* résolu, décidé; *opinion* arrêté.
decidedly [dɪ'saɪdɪdlɪ] *adv act, reply* résolument, avec décision, d'une façon marquée. **~ lazy** incontestablement paresseux.
decider [dɪ'saɪdəʳ] *n* (*goal*) but décisif; (*point*) point décisif; (*factor*) facteur décisif. (*game*) **the ~** la belle.
deciding [dɪ'saɪdɪŋ] *adj factor, game, point* décisif.
deciduous [dɪ'sɪdjʊəs] *adj tree* à feuilles caduques; *leaves, antlers* caduc (*f* -uque).
decilitre, (*US*) **deciliter** ['desɪˌliːtəʳ] *n* décilitre *m*.
decimal ['desɪməl] **1** *adj number, system, coinage* décimal. **~ fraction** fraction décimale; **to three ~ places** (jusqu')à la troisième décimale; **~ point** virgule *f* (*de fraction décimale*).
2 *n* décimale *f*. **~s** le calcul décimal, la notation décimale; *V* **recurring.**
decimalization [ˌdesɪməlaɪ'zeɪʃən] *n* décimalisation *f*.
decimalize ['desɪməlaɪz] *vt* décimaliser.
decimate ['desɪmeɪt] *vt* (*lit, fig*) décimer.
decimetre, (*US*) **decimeter** ['desɪˌmiːtəʳ] *n* décimètre *m*.
decipher [dɪ'saɪfəʳ] *vt* (*lit, fig*) déchiffrer.
decipherable [dɪ'saɪfərəbl] *adj* déchiffrable.
decision [dɪ'sɪʒən] *n* **(a)** (*act of deciding*) décision *f*; (*Jur*) jugement *m*, arrêt *m*. **to come to a ~** arriver à *or* prendre une décision, prendre (un) parti, se décider; **his ~ is final** sa décision est irrévocable *or* sans appel; (*Jur*) **to give a ~ on a case** statuer sur un cas. **(b)** (*U*) décision *f*, résolution *f*, fermeté *f*. **a look of ~** un air décidé *or* résolu.
decisive [dɪ'saɪsɪv] *adj* **(a)** *battle, experiment, victory* décisif, concluant; *factor* décisif. **(b)** *manner, answer* décidé, catégorique. **he is very ~** il a de la décision.
decisively [dɪ'saɪsɪvlɪ] *adv speak* d'un ton décidé *or* catégorique; *act* d'une façon catégorique *or* décidée.
decisiveness [dɪ'saɪsɪvnɪs] *n* (*U*) *[experiment]* caractère décisif *or* concluant; *[person]* ton *or* air décidé *or* catégorique.
deck [dek] **1** *n* **(a)** (*Naut*) pont *m*. **to go up on ~** monter sur le pont; **below ~** dans l'entrepont; *V* **after, clear, flight[1], hand.**
(b) *[vehicle]* plate-forme *f*. **top ~, upper ~** *[bus]* impériale *f*; *[jumbo jet]* étage *m*.
(c) (*US*) **~ of cards** jeu *m* de cartes.
(d) *[record player etc]* table *f* de lecture; (*for recording*) platine *f* magnétophone; *V also* **cassette.**
2 *vt* (*also* **~ out**) orner, parer, agrémenter (*with* de). **to ~ o.s. (out) in one's Sunday best** se mettre sur son trente et un, s'endimancher (*pej*).
3 *cpd*: **deck cabin** cabine *f* (de pont); **deck cargo** pontée *f*; **deckchair** chaise longue, transat* *m*, transatlantique *m*; **deck hand** matelot *m*; **deckhouse** rouf *m*.
-decker ['dekəʳ] *n ending in cpds*: (*Naut*) **a three-decker** un vaisseau à trois ponts, un trois-ponts; (*bus*) **a single-decker** un autobus sans impériale; *V* **double** *etc*.
deckle ['dekl] *n* (*also* **~ edge**) barbes *fpl*.
declaim [dɪ'kleɪm] *vti* (*lit, fig*) déclamer (*against* contre).
declamation [ˌdeklə'meɪʃən] *n* déclamation *f*.
declamatory [dɪ'klæmətərɪ] *adj* déclamatoire.
declaration [ˌdeklə'reɪʃən] *n [love, war, intentions, taxes, goods at Customs]* déclaration *f*; (*Cards*) annonce *f*; (*public announcement*) proclamation *f*, déclaration (publique).
declare [dɪ'klɛəʳ] *vt* **(a)** *intentions, (Fin etc) income* déclarer; *results* proclamer. (*Customs*) **have you anything to ~?** avez-vous quelque chose à déclarer?; *[suitor]* **to ~ o.s.** faire sa déclaration, se déclarer; **to ~ war (on)** déclarer la guerre (à); **to ~ a state of emergency** déclarer l'état d'urgence.
(b) (*assert*) déclarer (*that* que). **to ~ o.s. for/against** se déclarer *or* se prononcer *or* prendre parti en faveur de/contre; **to ~ sb president/bankrupt** déclarer qn président/en faillite; **well I (do) ~!*** (ça) par exemple!
declared [dɪ'klɛəd] *adj* déclaré, avoué, ouvert.
declaredly [dɪ'klɛərɪdlɪ] *adv* ouvertement, formellement, de son propre aveu.
declarer [dɪ'klɛərəʳ] *n* (*Cards*) déclarant(e) *m(f)*.
declassify [diː'klæsɪfaɪ] *vt information, document* rendre accessible à tous.
declension [dɪ'klenʃən] *n* (*Gram*) déclinaison *f*.
declinable [dɪ'klaɪnəbl] *adj* (*Gram*) déclinable.
declination [ˌdeklɪ'neɪʃən] *n* (*Astron*) déclinaison *f*.
decline [dɪ'klaɪn] **1** *n [day, life]* déclin *m*; *[empire]* déclin, décadence *f*. **~ in price** baisse *f* de prix; **to be on the ~** *[prices]* être en baisse, baisser; *[fame, health]* décliner; **cases of real poverty are on the ~** les cas d'indigence réelle sont de moins en moins fréquents *or* sont en diminution; (*Med*) **to go into a ~** dépérir.
2 *vt* **(a)** *invitation, honour* refuser, décliner; *responsibility* décliner, rejeter. **he ~d to do it** il a refusé (poliment) de le faire.
(b) (*Gram*) décliner.
3 *vi* **(a)** *[health, influence]* décliner, baisser; *[empire]* tomber en décadence; *[prices]* baisser, être en baisse; *[business]* être en baisse, péricliter, décliner. **to ~ in importance** perdre de l'importance.
(b) (*slope*) s'incliner, descendre.
(c) *[sun]* décliner, se coucher; *[day]* tirer à sa fin, décliner.
(d) (*Gram*) se décliner.
declining [dɪ'klaɪnɪŋ] **1** *adj* sur son déclin. **in his ~ years** au déclin de sa vie; **in ~ health** d'une santé devenue chancelante *or* qui décline. **2** *n [invitation]* refus *m*; *[empire]* décadence *f*; (*Gram*) déclinaison *f*.
declivity [dɪ'klɪvɪtɪ] *n* déclivité *f*, pente *f*.
declutch ['diː'klʌtʃ] *vi* débrayer; *V* **double.**
decoction [dɪ'kɒkʃən] *n* décoction *f*.
decode ['diː'kəʊd] *vt* déchiffrer, traduire (en clair), décoder.
decoke [diː'kəʊk] (*Brit Aut*) **1** *vt* décalaminer. **2** ['diːkəʊk] *n* décalaminage *m*.
décolletage [deɪ'kɒltɑːʒ] *n*, **décolleté** [deɪ'kɒlteɪ] *n* décolletage *m*, décolleté *m*.
décolleté(e) [deɪ'kɒlteɪ] *adj* décolleté.
decompose [ˌdiːkəm'pəʊz] **1** *vt* décomposer. **2** *vi* se décomposer.
decomposition [ˌdiːkɒmpə'zɪʃən] *n* décomposition *f*.
decompression [ˌdiːkəm'preʃən] **1** *n* (*Med, Phys, Tech*) décompression *f*. **2** *cpd*: **decompression chamber** caisson *m* de décompression; **decompression sickness** maladie *f* des caissons.
decontaminate [ˌdiːkən'tæmɪneɪt] *vt* décontaminer, désinfecter.
decontamination ['diːkənˌtæmɪ'neɪʃən] *n* décontamination *f*, désinfection *f*.
decontrol [ˌdiːkən'trəʊl] *vt* (*Admin, Comm*) libérer des contrôles gouvernementaux. **to ~ (the price of) butter** lever *or* supprimer le contrôle du prix du beurre; **~led road** route non soumise à la limitation de vitesse.
décor ['deɪkɔːʳ] *n* décor *m*.
decorate ['dekəreɪt] *vt* **(a)** *cake* décorer; *hat* orner (*with* de); (*paint etc*) *room* peindre (et tapisser). **to ~ with flags** pavoiser.
(b) *soldier* décorer, médailler. **he was ~d for gallantry** il a été décoré pour son acte de bravoure.
decorating ['dekəreɪtɪŋ] *n* **(a) (painting and) ~** décoration intérieure; **they are doing some ~** ils sont en train de refaire les peintures. **(b)** *[cake etc]* décoration *f*.
decoration [ˌdekə'reɪʃən] *n* **(a)** (*U*) *[cake]* décoration *f*; *[hat]* ornementation *f*; *[room]* (*act*) décoration (intérieure); (*state*) décor *m*; *[town]* décoration; (*with flags*) pavoisement *m*.
(b) (*ornament*) *[hat]* ornement *m*; *[town]* décoration *f*. **Christmas ~s** décorations de Noël.
(c) (*Mil*) décoration *f*, médaille *f*.
decorative ['dekərətɪv] *adj* décoratif.
decorator ['dekəreɪtəʳ] *n* (*esp Brit*) décorateur *m*; *V* **painter[1].**
decorous ['dekərəs] *adj action* convenable, bienséant, comme il faut; *behaviour, person* digne.
decorously ['dekərəslɪ] *adv* (*V* **decorous**) convenablement, avec bienséance, comme il faut; avec dignité, d'un air digne.
decorum [dɪ'kɔːrəm] *n* décorum *m*, étiquette *f*, bienséance *f*. **with ~** avec bienséance, comme il faut; **a breach of ~** une

inconvenance; **to have a sense of** ~ avoir le sens des convenances.

decoy ['di:kɔɪ] **1** *n* (*bird*) (*live*) appeau *m*, chanterelle *f*; (*artificial*) leurre *m*; (*animal*) proie *f* (servant d'appât); (*person*) compère *m*. **police** ~ policier *m* en civil (*servant à attirer un criminel dans une souricière*).

2 *cpd*: **decoy duck** (*lit*) appeau *m*, chanterelle *f*; (*fig*) compère *m*.

3 [*also* dɪ'kɔɪ] *vt* (*V* 1) attirer avec un appeau *or* une chanterelle; leurrer; attirer dans un piège. **to ~ sb into doing sth** faire faire qch à qn en le leurrant.

decrease [di:'kri:s] **1** *vi [amount, numbers, supplies]* diminuer, décroître, s'amoindrir; *[birth rate, population]* décroître, diminuer; *[power]* s'affaiblir; *[strength, intensity]* s'affaiblir, décroître, aller en diminuant; *[price, value]* baisser; *[enthusiasm]* se calmer, se refroidir; (*Knitting*) diminuer.

2 *vt* diminuer, réduire.

3 ['di:kri:s] *n [amount, supplies]* diminution *f*, amoindrissement *m* (*in* de); *[numbers]* diminution, décroissance *f* (*in* de); *[birth rate, population]* diminution (*in* de); *[power]* affaiblissement *m* (*in* de); *[strength, intensity]* diminution, décroissance (*in* de); *[price, value]* baisse *f* (*in* de); *[enthusiasm]* baisse, refroidissement *m* (*in* de). **~ in speed** ralentissement *m*; **~ in strength** affaiblissement.

decreasing [di:'kri:sɪŋ] *adj amount, numbers, population* décroissant; *power* qui s'affaiblit; *enthusiasm, strength, intensity* décroissant, diminué; *price, value* en baisse.

decreasingly [di:'kri:sɪŋlɪ] *adv* de moins en moins.

decree [dɪ'kri:] **1** *n* (*Jur, Rel*) décret *m*; *[tribunal]* arrêt *m*, jugement *m*; (*municipal*) arrêté *m*. **by royal/government** ~ par décret du roi/du gouvernement; *[divorce]* **~ absolute** jugement définitif; **~ nisi** jugement provisoire de divorce.

2 *vt* décréter (*that* que + *indic*), ordonner (*that* que + *subj*), arrêter (*that* que + *indic*).

decrepit [dɪ'krepɪt] *adj wooden structure* vermoulu; *building* délabré; (*) *person* décrépit, décati*.

decrepitude [dɪ'krepɪtju:d] *n [person, object]* (état *m* de) décrépitude *f*, délabrement *m*.

decretal [dɪ'kri:tl] *n* décrétale *f*.

decry [dɪ'kraɪ] *vt* décrier, dénigrer, déprécier.

dedicate ['dedɪkeɪt] *vt church, shrine, book, one's life* dédier (*to* à); (*consecrate*) *church* consacrer. **to ~ o.s.** *or* **one's life to sth/to doing** se vouer *or* se consacrer à qch/à faire.

dedication [ˌdedɪ'keɪʃən] *n* **(a)** *[church]* dédicace *f*, consécration *f*. **(b)** (*in book*) dédicace *f*. **to write a ~ in a book** dédicacer un livre. **(c)** (*quality: devotion*) dévouement *m*.

deduce [dɪ'dju:s] *vt* déduire, inférer, conclure (*from* de, *that* que).

deducible [dɪ'dju:sɪbl] *adj* qu'on peut déduire *or* inférer.

deduct [dɪ'dʌkt] *vt amount* déduire, retrancher, défalquer (*from* de); *numbers* retrancher, soustraire (*from* de). **to ~ something from the price** faire une réduction sur le prix; **to ~ sth for expenses** retenir qch pour les frais; **to ~ 5% from the wages** faire une retenue de *or* prélever 5% sur les salaires; **after ~ing 5%** déduction faite de 5%.

deductible [dɪ'dʌktəbl] *adj* à déduire, à retrancher, à défalquer (*from* de); *expenses* déductible.

deduction [dɪ'dʌkʃən] *n* **(a)** (*sth deducted*) déduction *f*, défalcation *f* (*from* de); (*from wage*) retenue *f*, prélèvement *m* (*from* sur). **(b)** (*sth deduced*) déduction *f*, raisonnement déductif.

deductive [dɪ'dʌktɪv] *adj* déductif.

deed [di:d] **1** *n* **(a)** (*action*) action *f*, acte *m*; (*feat*) haut fait, exploit *m*. **good ~(s)** bonne(s) action(s); *V* **word**.

(b) in ~ de fait, en fait; **master in ~ if not in name** maître de *or* en fait sinon de *or* en titre.

(c) (*Jur*) acte notarié, contrat *m*. **~ of covenant** *or* **gift** (acte de) donation *f*; **~ of partnership** contrat de société.

2 *cpd*: (*Brit*) **(by) deed poll** (par) acte unilatéral.

deem [di:m] *vt* juger, estimer, considérer (*as* comme). **to ~ it prudent to do** juger prudent de faire; **to be ~ed worthy of (doing) sth** être jugé digne de (faire) qch.

deep [di:p] **1** *adj* **(a)** (*extending far down*) *water, hole, wound* profond; *snow* épais (*f* -aisse). **the water/pond was 4 metres ~** l'eau/l'étang avait 4 mètres de profondeur; (*fig*) **to be in ~ water(s)** avoir de gros ennuis, être dans de vilains draps; *[swimming pool]* **the ~ end** le grand bain; **to go off (at) the ~ end*** (*excited*) se mettre dans tous ses états; (*angry*) se flanquer* *or* se ficher* en colère; (*fig*) **he went in** *or* **plunged in** *or* **was thrown in at the ~ end** cela a été le baptême du feu (pour lui); **the snow lay ~** il y avait une épaisse couche de neige; **the streets were 2 feet ~ in snow** les rues étaient sous 60 cm *or* étaient recouvertes de 60 cm de neige.

(b) (*extending far back*) *shelf, cupboard* large, profond. **a plot of ground 15 metres ~** un terrain de 15 mètres de profondeur; **the spectators stood 10 ~** il y avait 10 rangs de spectateurs debout; **~ space** espace *m* interstellaire; (*US Geog*) **the ~ South** les États *mpl* du Sud les plus conservateurs (*aux Etats-Unis*).

(c) (*broad*) *edge, border* large, haut.

(d) (*fig*) *sound* grave; *voice, tones* grave, profond; (*Mus*) *note, voice* bas (*f* basse), grave; *sorrow, relief* profond, intense; *concern, interest* vif; *colour* intense, profond; *mystery, darkness* profond, total; *sleep* profond; *writer, thinker* profond; (*: *crafty*) *person* malin (*f* -igne), rusé. **~ in thought/in a book** plongé *or* absorbé dans ses pensées/dans un livre; **~ in debt** criblé de dettes, dans les dettes jusqu'au cou; **~ breathing** (*action, sound*) respiration profonde; (*exercises*) exercices *mpl* respiratoires; **he's a ~ one*** il est plus malin qu'il n'en a l'air, il cache bien son jeu; *V* **mourning**.

2 *adv* profondément. **don't go in too ~ if you can't swim** ne va pas trop loin si tu ne sais pas nager; **to go ~ into the forest** pénétrer profondément *or* très avant dans la forêt; **to read ~ into the night** lire tard dans la nuit; **to drink ~** boire à longs traits; **to breathe ~** respirer profondément *or* à pleins poumons; **to thrust one's hands ~ in one's pockets** enfoncer ses mains dans ses poches; **he's in it pretty ~*, he's pretty ~ in*** il s'est engagé très loin *or* à fond là-dedans, (*pej*) il est dedans jusqu'au cou; *V* **knee, skin, still**[2] *etc.*

3 *n* **(a)** (*liter*) **the ~** (les grands fonds de) l'océan *m*, les grandes profondeurs.

(b) (*rare: also* **depth**) **in the ~ of winter** au plus fort *or* au cœur de l'hiver.

4 *cpd*: **deep-breathing (exercises)** exercices *mpl* respiratoires; **deep-chested** *person* large de poitrine; *animal* à large poitrail; **deep-freeze** (*n: also* **Deepfreeze** ® *in US*) congélateur *m*; (*vt*) surgeler; (*US*) **deep freezer** congélateur *m*; **deep-freezing** surgélation *f*, quick-freezing *m*; **deep-frozen foods** aliments surgelés; **deep-fry** faire frire (en friteuse); **deep (ray) therapy** radiothérapie destructrice *or* à rayons X durs; **deep-rooted** *affection, prejudice* profond, profondément enraciné, vivace; *habit* invétéré, ancré; *tree* aux racines profondes; **deep-sea** *animal, plant* pélagique, abyssal; *current* pélagique; **deep-sea diver** plongeur sous-marin; **deep-sea diving** plongée sous-marine; **deep-sea fisherman** pêcheur hauturier *or* de haute mer; **deep-sea fishing** pêche hauturière, grande pêche; **deep-seated** *prejudice, dislike* profond, profondément enraciné; *conviction* fermement ancré; **deep-seated cough** toux bronchiale *or* caverneuse; **deep-set** *eyes* très enfoncé, creux, cave; *window* profond; (*Ling*) **deep structure** structure profonde.

deepen ['di:pən] **1** *vt hole* approfondir; *sorrow, interest* rendre plus intense *or* vif, augmenter; *darkness* épaissir, approfondir; *sound* rendre plus grave; *colour* foncer.

2 *vi* (*V* 1) devenir *or* se faire plus profond (*or* plus foncé *etc*), s'approfondir; *[night, mystery]* s'épaissir; *[voice]* se faire plus profond *or* plus grave.

deepening ['di:pənɪŋ] (*V* **deepen**) **1** *adj* qui s'approfondit; qui se fonce, qui se fait plus intense *etc.* **2** *n [meaning, mystery etc]* intensification *f*; *[colour, sound]* augmentation *f* d'intensité.

deeply ['di:plɪ] *adv* **(a)** *dig, cut* profondément, à une grande profondeur; (*fig*) *drink* abondamment, à longs traits; *think, consider* profondément. (*fig*) **to go ~ into sth** approfondir qch.

(b) (*very much*) *grateful, concerned* infiniment, extrêmement. **~ offended** profondément offensé; **to regret ~** regretter vivement.

deer [dɪəʳ] **1** *n, pl inv* cerf *m*, biche *f*; (*red* ~) cerf; (*fallow* ~) daim *m*; (*roe* ~) chevreuil *m*. **certain types of ~** certains types de cervidés *mpl*; **look at those ~!** regardez ces cerfs! *or* ces biches!

2 *cpd*: **deerhound** limier *m*; **deerskin** peau *f* de daim; **deerstalker** (*hat*) casquette *f* à la Sherlock Holmes; (*hunter*) chasseur *m* de cerf; **deer-stalking** chasse *f* au cerf à pied.

deface [dɪ'feɪs] *vt monument, door* dégrader; *work of art* mutiler; *poster* barbouiller; *inscription* barbouiller, rendre illisible.

de facto [deɪ'fæktəʊ] *adj, adv* de facto.

defamation [ˌdefə'meɪʃən] *n* diffamation *f*.

defamatory [dɪ'fæmətərɪ] *adj* diffamatoire, diffamant.

defame [dɪ'feɪm] *vt* diffamer.

default [dɪ'fɔ:lt] **1** *n* **(a)** (*Jur*) (*in civil cases*) défaut *m*, non-comparution *f*; (*in criminal cases*) contumace *f*. **judgment by ~** jugement *m or* arrêt *m* par contumace *or* par défaut.

(b) we must not let it go by ~ ne laissons pas échapper l'occasion (faute d'avoir agi); (*Sport*) **match won by ~** match gagné par forfait *or* par walk-over.

(c) (*lack, absence*) manque *m*, carence *f*. **in ~ of** à défaut de, faute de.

(d) (*Fin*) cessation *f* de paiements.

2 *vt* (*Jur*) condamner par défaut *or* par contumace, rendre un jugement par défaut contre.

3 *vi* **(a)** (*Jur*) faire défaut, être en état de contumace.

(b) (*gen*) manquer à ses engagements, être en défaut.

(c) (*Fin*) manquer à ses engagements.

defaulter [dɪ'fɔ:ltəʳ] *n* (*gen*) coupable *mf*; (*offender*) délinquant(e) *m(f)*; (*Mil, Naut*) soldat *m* (*or* marin *m*) en infraction; (*Mil, Naut: undergoing punishment*) consigné *m*; (*Jur*) contumace *mf*; (*Fin, St Ex*) défaillant(e) *m(f)*, débiteur *m*, -trice *f* (qui n'acquitte pas une dette); (*defaulting tenant*) locataire *mf* qui ne paie pas son loyer.

defaulting [dɪ'fɔ:ltɪŋ] *adj* **(a)** (*St Ex etc*) défaillant, en défaut. **(b)** (*Jur*) défaillant, qui n'a pas comparu.

defeat [dɪ'fi:t] **1** *n* (*act, state*) *[army, team]* défaite *f*; *[project, ambition]* échec *m*, insuccès *m*; *[legal case, appeal]* rejet *m*.

2 *vt opponent* vaincre, battre; *army* battre, défaire, mettre en déroute; *team* battre; *hopes* frustrer, ruiner; *ambitions, plans* faire échouer; (*Parl*) *government, opposition* mettre en minorité; *bill, amendment* rejeter. **to ~ one's own ends** *or* **object** aller à l'encontre du but que l'on s'est (*or* s'était *etc*) proposé; **that plan will ~ its own ends** ce plan sera auto-destructeur.

defeatism [dɪ'fi:tɪzəm] *n* défaitisme *m*.

defeatist [dɪ'fi:tɪst] *adj, n* défaitiste (*mf*).

defecate ['defəkeɪt] *vti* déféquer.

defecation [ˌdefə'keɪʃən] *n* défécation *f*.

defect ['di:fekt] **1** *n* défaut *m*, imperfection *f*, faute *f*. **physical ~** vice *m or* défaut de conformation; **mental ~** anomalie *or* déficience mentale; **moral ~** défaut.

2 [dɪ'fekt] *vi* (*Pol*) faire défection. **to ~ from one country to another** s'enfuir d'un pays pour aller dans un autre; **to ~ to the**

West/to another party/to the enemy passer à l'Ouest/à un autre parti/à l'ennemi.

defection [dɪˈfekʃən] *n* (*Pol*) défection *f*; (*Rel*) apostasie *f*.

defective [dɪˈfektɪv] **1** *adj machine* défectueux; *reasoning* mauvais; (*Med*) déficient; (*Gram*) défectif. **to be ~ in sth** manquer de qch; *V* **mental, mentally. 2** *n* (*Med*) déficient(e) *m(f)*; (*Gram*) mot défectif.

defector [dɪˈfektəʳ] *n* transfuge *mf*.

defence, (*US*) **defense** [dɪˈfens] **1** *n* **(a)** (*U*) défense *f*, protection *f*; *[action, belief]* justification *f*; (*Chess, Jur, Physiol, Sport*) défense. **in ~ of** à la défense de, pour défendre; (*Brit*) **Secretary (of State) for** *or* **Minister of D~,** (*US*) **Secretary of Defense** ministre *m* de la Défense nationale; (*Brit*) **Department** *or* **Ministry of D~,** (*US*) **Department of Defense** ministère *m* de la Défense nationale; *V* **civil.**

(b) défense *f*. **~s** défense(s), ouvrages défensifs; **the body's ~s against disease** la défense de l'organisme contre la maladie; **as a ~ against** pour se défendre contre; **to put up a stubborn ~** se défendre obstinément; **his conduct needs no ~** sa conduite n'a pas à être justifiée; **in his ~** (*Jur*) à sa décharge; (*gen*) à sa décharge, pour sa défense; (*Jur*) **witness for the ~** témoin *m* à décharge; (*Jur*) **the case for the ~** la défense.

2 *cpd* de défense. (*Mil*) **the defence forces** les forces défensives, la défense; **defence mechanism** (*Physiol*) système *m* de défense; (*Psych*) défenses *fpl*.

defenceless [dɪˈfenslɪs] *adj* sans défense. **he is quite ~** il est incapable de se défendre, il est sans défense.

defend [dɪˈfend] *vt country, town, person* défendre, protéger (*against* contre); (*Chess, Jur, Sport*) défendre; (*fig*) *friend* défendre, prendre le parti de; *action, decision, opinion* défendre, justifier. **to ~ o.s.** se défendre (*against* contre); **he is well able to ~ himself** il est très capable de *or* il sait se défendre; **he can't ~ himself** il est incapable de se défendre.

defendant [dɪˈfendənt] *n* (*Jur*) défendeur *m*, -deresse *f*; (*on appeal*) intimé(e) *m(f)*; (*in criminal case*) prévenu(e) *m(f)*; (*in assizes court*) accusé(e) *m(f)*.

defender [dɪˈfendəʳ] *n* (*lit, fig*) défenseur *m*, soutien *m*; (*Sport*) détenteur *m*, -trice *f*. (*Brit Hist*) **~ of the faith** défenseur de la foi.

defending [dɪˈfendɪŋ] *adj* (*Sport*) **~ champion** champion(ne) *m(f)* en titre; (*Jur*) **~ counsel** avocat *m* de la défense.

defense [dɪˈfens] (*US*) = **defence.**

defensible [dɪˈfensɪbl] *adj* (*lit*) défendable; (*fig*) justifiable, soutenable, défendable.

defensive [dɪˈfensɪv] **1** *adj* (*Mil, fig*) défensif. **2** *n* (*Mil, fig*) défensive *f*. (*lit, fig*) **to be on the ~** être sur la défensive.

defer¹ [dɪˈfɜːʳ] *vt* **(a)** *journey* différer, reporter, remettre; *meeting* ajourner, reporter; *business* renvoyer; *payment* différer, reculer, retarder; *decision, judgment* suspendre, différer. **to ~ doing** différer de *or* à faire; (*Fin*) **~red annuity** rente *f* à paiement différé; (*Comm etc*) **~red payment** paiement *m* par versements échelonnés.

(b) (*Mil*) mettre en sursis (d'incorporation). **to ~ sb on medical grounds** réformer qn (pour raisons médicales).

defer² [dɪˈfɜːʳ] *vi* (*submit*) **to ~ to sb** déférer (*frm*) à qn, s'incliner devant *or* s'en remettre à la volonté de qn; **to ~ to sb's knowledge** s'en remettre aux connaissances de qn.

deference [ˈdefərəns] *n* déférence *f*, égards *mpl* (*to* pour). **in ~ to, out of ~ for** par déférence *or* égards pour; **with all due ~ to you** avec tout le respect que je vous dois, sauf votre respect.

deferential [ˌdefəˈrenʃəl] *adj person, attitude* respectueux, plein de déférence *or* d'égards; *tone* de déférence. **to be ~ to sb** se montrer plein de déférence pour *or* envers qn.

deferentially [ˌdefəˈrenʃəlɪ] *adv* avec déférence.

deferment [dɪˈfɜːmənt] *n* (*V* **defer¹**) report *m*; ajournement *m*; renvoi *m*; retard *m* (*of* dans); suspension *f*. (*Mil*) **to apply for ~** faire une demande de sursis (d'incorporation).

defiance [dɪˈfaɪəns] *n* défi *m* (*of* à). **to act in ~ of** défier, braver, narguer; **in ~ of** *the law, instructions* au mépris de; *person* en dépit de, au mépris de.

defiant [dɪˈfaɪənt] *adj attitude, tone* de défi, provocant; *reply* provocant; *person* rebelle, intraitable. **to be ~ of sth** défier qch.

defiantly [dɪˈfaɪəntlɪ] *adv* d'un air *or* d'un ton provocant *or* de défi.

deficiency [dɪˈfɪʃənsɪ] **1** *n* **(a)** *[goods]* manque *m*, insuffisance *f*, défaut *m* (*of* de); (*Med*) carence *f*, déficience *f* (*of* de). (*Med*) **iron ~** carence de fer; *V* **mental, vitamin** *etc*.

(b) (*in character, system*) imperfection *f*, faille *f*, faiblesse *f* (*in* dans). **his ~ as an administrator** son incompétence en tant qu'administrateur.

(c) (*Fin*) déficit *m*, découvert *m*.

2 *cpd*: (*Med*) **deficiency disease** maladie *f* de carence.

deficient [dɪˈfɪʃənt] *adj* insuffisant, défectueux, faible (*in* en). **to be ~ in sth** manquer de qch.

deficit [ˈdefɪsɪt] *n* (*Fin etc*) déficit *m*.

defile¹ [ˈdiːfaɪl] *n* (*procession; place*) défilé *m*.

defile² [dɪˈfaɪl] *vi* (*march in file*) défiler.

defile³ [dɪˈfaɪl] *vt* (*pollute: lit, fig*) souiller (*liter*), salir; (*desecrate*) profaner.

defilement [dɪˈfaɪlmənt] *n* (*pollution: lit, fig*) souillure *f* (*liter*); (*desecration*) profanation *f*.

definable [dɪˈfaɪnəbl] *adj* définissable.

define [dɪˈfaɪn] *vt* **(a)** *word, feeling* définir; *attitude* préciser; *conditions* définir, déterminer; *boundaries, powers, duties* délimiter, définir.

(b) (*outline*) dessiner *or* dégager (les formes de). **the tower was clearly ~d against the sky** la tour se détachait nettement sur le ciel.

definite [ˈdefɪnɪt] *adj* **(a)** (*exact, clear*) *decision, agreement* bien déterminé, précis, net; *stain, mark* très visible; *improvement* net, manifeste; *intention, order, sale* ferme; *plan* déterminé, précis. **to come to a ~ understanding** parvenir à un accord précis *or* à une entente précise (*on sth* sur qch).

(b) (*certain*) certain, sûr; *manner, tone* assuré, positif. **it is ~ that** il est certain que + *indic*; **is it ~ that ...?** est-il certain que ...? + *subj*; **she was very ~ about it** elle a été très nette sur la question.

(c) (*Gram*) **~ article** article défini; **past ~ (tense)** prétérit *m*.

(d) (*Math*) **~ integral** intégrale définie.

definitely [ˈdefɪnɪtlɪ] *adv* **(a)** (*without doubt*) sans aucun doute, certainement. **he is ~ leaving** il part, c'est certain; **oh ~!** absolument!, bien sûr!

(b) (*appreciably*) nettement, manifestement. **she is ~ more intelligent than ...** elle est nettement *or* manifestement plus intelligente que ....

(c) (*emphatically*) catégoriquement, d'une manière précise *or* bien déterminée. **she said very ~ that she was not going out** elle a déclaré catégoriquement qu'elle ne sortirait pas.

definition [ˌdefɪˈnɪʃən] *n* **(a)** *[word, concept]* définition *f*. **by ~** par définition. **(b)** *[powers, boundaries, duties]* délimitation *f*. **(c)** (*Phot*) netteté *f*; (*TV*) définition *f*; (*Rad etc*) *[sound]* netteté; (*Opt*) *[lens]* (pouvoir *m* de) résolution *f*.

definitive [dɪˈfɪnɪtɪv] *adj biography* définitif; *result* décisif.

definitively [dɪˈfɪnɪtɪvlɪ] *adv* définitivement.

deflate [diːˈfleɪt] *vt* **(a)** *tyre* dégonfler. **~d tyre** pneu dégonflé *or* à plat.

(b) (*Fin*) **to ~ the currency** provoquer la déflation monétaire; **to ~ prices** faire tomber *or* faire baisser les prix.

(c) (*) *person* démonter, rabattre le caquet à.

deflation [diːˈfleɪʃən] *n* **(a)** (*Fin*) déflation *f*. **(b)** *[tyre, ball]* dégonflement *m*.

deflationary [diːˈfleɪʃənərɪ] *adj* (*Pol*) *measures, policy* de déflation, déflationniste.

deflect [dɪˈflekt] **1** *vt ball, projectile* faire dévier; *stream* dériver, détourner; *person* détourner (*from* de). **2** *vi* dévier, défléchir; *[magnetic needle]* décliner.

deflection [dɪˈflekʃən] *n* *[projectile]* déviation *f*; *[light]* déflexion *f*, déviation; *[magnetic needle]* déclinaison *f* (magnétique), déviation.

deflector [dɪˈflektəʳ] *n* déflecteur *m*.

defloration [ˌdiːflɔːˈreɪʃən] *n* (*lit, fig*) défloration *f*.

deflower [diːˈflaʊəʳ] *vt* **(a)** *girl* déflorer. **(b)** (*Bot*) défleurir.

defoliant [diːˈfəʊlɪənt] *n* défoliant *m*.

defoliate [diːˈfəʊlɪeɪt] *vt* défeuiller.

defoliation [ˌdiːfəʊlɪˈeɪʃən] *n* (*esp Mil*) défoliation *f*.

deforest [diːˈfɒrɪst] *vt* déboiser.

deform [dɪˈfɔːm] *vt outline, structure* déformer; (*Tech*) fausser; (*Phys*) déformer; *mind, tastes* déformer; *town* défigurer, enlaidir.

deformation [ˌdiːfɔːˈmeɪʃən] *n* déformation *f*.

deformed [dɪˈfɔːmd] *adj limb, body* difforme; *person* difforme, contrefait; *mind* déformé, tordu.

deformity [dɪˈfɔːmɪtɪ] *n* *[body]* difformité *f*; *[mind]* déformation *f*.

defraud [dɪˈfrɔːd] *vt Customs, state* frauder; *person* escroquer. **to ~ sb of sth** escroquer qch à qn, frustrer qn de qch (*Jur*).

defrauder [dɪˈfrɔːdəʳ] *n* fraudeur *m*, -euse *f*.

defray [dɪˈfreɪ] *vt* (*reimburse*) *expenses* payer, rembourser; (*cover*) *cost* couvrir. **to ~ sb's expenses** défrayer qn, rembourser ses frais à qn.

defrayal [dɪˈfreɪəl] *n*, **defrayment** [dɪˈfreɪmənt] *n* paiement *m* *or* remboursement *m* des frais.

defrock [diːˈfrɒk] *vt* défroquer.

defrost [diːˈfrɒst] *vt refrigerator, windscreen* dégivrer; *meat, vegetables* décongeler.

deft [deft] *adj hand, movement* habile, preste, adroit. **to be ~** avoir la main preste.

deftly [ˈdeftlɪ] *adv* adroitement, prestement.

deftness [ˈdeftnɪs] *n* adresse *f*, habileté *f*, dextérité *f*.

defunct [dɪˈfʌŋkt] **1** *adj* (*lit*) défunt, décédé; (*fig*) défunt. **2** *n*: **the ~** le défunt, la défunte.

defuse [diːˈfjuːz] *vt bomb* désamorcer. (*fig*) **to ~ the situation** désamorcer la situation.

defy [dɪˈfaɪ] *vt* **(a)** *person, law, danger, death* braver, défier.

(b) *attack* défier. **it defies description** cela défie toute description; **the window defied all efforts to open it** la fenêtre a résisté à tous nos efforts pour l'ouvrir.

(c) (*challenge*) **to ~ sb to do** défier qn de faire, mettre qn au défi de faire.

degeneracy [dɪˈdʒenərəsɪ] *n* dégénérescence *f*.

degenerate [dɪˈdʒenəreɪt] **1** *vi* *[race, people]* dégénérer (*into* en), s'abâtardir. (*fig*) **the expedition ~d into a farce** l'expédition a dégénéré en farce. **2** [dɪˈdʒenərɪt] *adj* dégénéré. **3** [dɪˈdʒenərɪt] *n* dégénéré(e) *m(f)*.

degeneration [dɪˌdʒenəˈreɪʃən] *n* *[mind, body, morals, race, people]* dégénérescence *f*.

degradation [ˌdegrəˈdeɪʃən] *n* *[person, character]* avilissement *m*, déchéance *f*; (*Chem, Geol, Mil, Phys*) dégradation *f*.

degrade [dɪˈgreɪd] *vt* **(a)** *official* dégrader; (*Mil*) dégrader, casser.

(b) (*debase*) dégrader. **he felt ~d** il se sentait avili *or* dégradé; **he ~d himself by accepting it** il s'est dégradé en l'acceptant; **I wouldn't ~ myself to do that** je n'irais pas m'abaisser *or* m'avilir à faire cela.

(c) (*Chem, Geol, Phys*) dégrader.

degrading [dɪˈgreɪdɪŋ] *adj* dégradant, avilissant, humiliant.

degree [dɪˈgriː] *n* **(a)** (*Geog, Math*) degré *m*. **angle of 90 ~s** angle *m* de 90 degrés; **40 ~s east of Greenwich** à 40 degrés de longitude est de Greenwich; **20 ~s of latitude** 20 degrés de latitude.

(b) *[temperature]* degré *m*. **it was 35 ~s in the shade** il faisait *or* il y avait 35 (degrés) à l'ombre.

(c) (*step in scale*) degré *m*, rang *m*, échelon *m*. **to do sth by ~s** faire qch par degrés *or* petit à petit; (*esp Brit*) **to a ~** énormément, extrêmement, au plus haut point *or* degré; **to some ~, to a certain ~** à un certain degré, jusqu'à un certain point, dans une certaine mesure; **to a high ~** au plus haut degré, au suprême degré; **not in the least ~ angry** pas le moins du monde fâché; **to such a ~ that** à (un) tel point que; (*Med*) **first-/second-/third- ~ burns** brûlures *fpl* au premier/deuxième/troisième degré; (*US Jur*) **first- ~ murder** assassinat *m*; (*US Jur*) **second- ~ murder** meurtre *m*; *V* **third.**

(d) (*Univ*) grade *m* (universitaire). **first ~** ≈ licence *f*; **higher ~** ≈ doctorat *m*; **I am taking a science ~ *or* a ~ in science** je prépare *or* fais une licence de sciences; **to have a ~ in** avoir une licence de *or* en, être licencié en; **to get one's ~** avoir sa licence; *V* **honorary.**

(e) (*Gram*) degré *m*. **three ~s of comparison** trois degrés de comparaison.

(f) (*liter: position in society*) rang *m*. **of high ~** de haut rang.

dehumanize [diːˈhjuːmənaɪz] *vt* déshumaniser.

dehydrate [ˌdiːˈhaɪdreɪt] *vt* déshydrater. **~d** *person, skin, vegetables* déshydraté; *milk, eggs* en poudre.

dehydration [ˌdiːhaɪˈdreɪʃən] *n* déshydratation *f*.

de-ice [ˈdiːˈaɪs] *vt* (*Aut, Aviat*) dégivrer.

de-icer [ˈdiːˈaɪsəʳ] *n* (*Aut, Aviat*) dégivreur *m*.

de-icing [ˈdiːˈaɪsɪŋ] *n* (*Aut, Aviat*) dégivrage *m*.

deification [ˌdiːɪfɪˈkeɪʃən] *n* déification *f*.

deify [ˈdiːɪfaɪ] *vt* déifier, diviniser.

deign [deɪn] *vt* daigner (*to do* faire), condescendre (*to do* à faire).

deism [ˈdiːɪzəm] *n* déisme *m*.

deist [ˈdiːɪst] *n* déiste *mf*.

deity [ˈdiːɪtɪ] *n* **(a)** (*Myth, Rel*) dieu *m*, déesse *f*, divinité *f*, déité *f*. **the D~** Dieu *m*. **(b)** (*U*) divinité *f*.

dejected [dɪˈdʒektɪd] *adj* abattu, découragé, déprimé. **to become *or* get ~** se décourager, se laisser abattre.

dejection [dɪˈdʒekʃən] *n* abattement *m*, découragement *m*.

dekko* [ˈdekəʊ] *n* (*Brit*) petit coup d'œil. **let's have a ~** fais voir ça, on va (y) jeter un œil*.

delay [dɪˈleɪ] **1** *vt* **(a)** (*postpone*) *action, event* retarder, différer; *payment* différer. **~ed - action bomb/mine** bombe *f*/mine *f* à retardement; **~ed effect** effet *m* à retardement; **to ~ doing sth** tarder *or* différer à faire qch.

(b) (*keep waiting, hold up*) *person* retarder, retenir; *train, plane* retarder; *traffic* retarder, ralentir, entraver. **I don't want to ~ you** je ne veux pas vous retenir *or* retarder.

2 *vi* s'attarder (*in doing* à faire). **don't ~!** dépêchez-vous!

3 *n* **(a)** (*waiting period*) délai *m*, retard *m*. **with as little ~ as possible** dans les plus brefs délais; **without ~** sans délai; **without further ~** sans plus tarder; **an hour's ~** une heure de retard.

(b) (*postponement*) retardement *m*, arrêt *m*. **after 2 or 3 ~s** après 2 ou 3 arrêts; **there will be ~s to trains on the London-Brighton line** on prévoit des retards pour les trains de la ligne Londres-Brighton; **there will be ~s to traffic** la circulation sera ralentie.

delaying [dɪˈleɪɪŋ] *adj action* dilatoire, qui retarde. **~ tactics** moyens *mpl* dilatoires.

delectable [dɪˈlektəbl] *adj* délectable, délicieux.

delectation [ˌdiːlekˈteɪʃən] *n* délectation *f*.

delegate [ˈdelɪgeɪt] **1** *vt authority, power* déléguer (*to* à). **to ~ sb to do sth** déléguer qn *or* se faire représenter par qn pour faire qch. **2** [ˈdelɪgɪt] *n* délégué(e) *m(f)* (*to* à). **~ to a congress** congressiste *mf*.

delegation [ˌdelɪˈgeɪʃən] *n* **(a)** (*U*) *[power]* délégation *f*; *[person]* nomination *f*, désignation *f* (*as* comme). **(b)** (*group of delegates*) délégation *f*.

delete [dɪˈliːt] *vt* barrer, rayer (*from* de), biffer. (*on forms etc*) **'~ where inapplicable'** 'rayer les mentions inutiles'.

deleterious [ˌdelɪˈtɪərɪəs] *adj effect, influence* nuisible, délétère (*to* à); *gas* délétère.

deletion [dɪˈliːʃən] *n* **(a)** (*U*) suppression *f*. **(b)** (*thing deleted*) rature *f*.

delft [delft] *n* faïence *f* de Delft. **D~ blue** (*colour*) bleu *m* (de) faïence.

deliberate [dɪˈlɪbərɪt] **1** *adj* **(a)** (*intentional*) *action, insult, lie* délibéré, voulu, intentionnel.

(b) (*cautious, thoughtful*) *action, decision* bien pesé, mûrement réfléchi; *character, judgment* réfléchi, circonspect, avisé; (*slow, purposeful*) *air, voice* décidé; *manner, walk* mesuré, posé.

2 [dɪˈlɪbəreɪt] *vi* **(a)** (*think*) délibérer, réfléchir (*upon* sur). **(b)** (*discuss*) délibérer, tenir conseil.

3 [dɪˈlɪbəreɪt] *vt* **(a)** (*study*) réfléchir sur, considérer, examiner.

(b) (*discuss*) délibérer sur, débattre.

deliberately [dɪˈlɪbərɪtlɪ] *adv* **(a)** (*intentionally*) *do, say* exprès, à dessein, délibérément, de propos délibéré. **(b)** (*slowly, purposefully*) *move, talk* avec mesure, posément.

deliberation [dɪˌlɪbəˈreɪʃən] *n* **(a)** (*consideration*) délibération *f*, réflexion *f*. **after due *or* careful ~** après mûre réflexion.

(b) (*discussion: gen pl*) **~s** débats *mpl*, délibérations *fpl*.

(c) (*slowness*) mesure *f*, manière posée.

deliberative [dɪˈlɪbərətɪv] *adj* **(a)** *speech* mûrement réfléchi. **(b) ~ assembly** assemblée délibérante.

delicacy [ˈdelɪkəsɪ] *n* **(a)** (*U: V* **delicate**) délicatesse *f*, finesse *f*; fragilité *f*; sensibilité *f*; tact *m*. **(b)** (*tasty food*) mets délicat, friandise *f*.

delicate [ˈdelɪkɪt] *adj* **(a)** (*fine, exquisite*) *silk, work* délicat, fin; *china, flower* délicat, fragile; *colour* délicat. **of ~ workmanship** d'un travail délicat.

(b) (*Med*) *health, person, liver* fragile. (*hum*) **in a ~ condition** dans une position intéressante (*hum*).

(c) (*sensitive*) *instrument* délicat; *compass* sensible; *touch* léger, délicat; *person* délicat, sensible; (*tactful*) plein de tact, délicat, discret (*f* -ète).

(d) (*requiring skilful handling*) *operation, subject, question, situation* délicat.

(e) *food, flavour* fin, délicat.

delicately [ˈdelɪkɪtlɪ] *adv* (*V* **delicate**) délicatement, avec délicatesse *or* finesse *or* tact *etc*.

delicatessen [ˌdelɪkəˈtesn] *n* **(a)** (*shop*) épicerie fine. **(b)** (*food*) plats cuisinés, charcuterie *f*.

delicious [dɪˈlɪʃəs] *adj dish, smell, person* délicieux, exquis.

delight [dɪˈlaɪt] **1** *n* **(a)** (*intense pleasure*) grand plaisir, joie *f*, délectation *f*. **to my ~** à *or* pour ma plus grande joie *or* mon plus grand plaisir; **to take ~ in sth/in doing** prendre grand plaisir à qch/à faire; **to watch/taste with ~** regarder/goûter avec délices; **to give ~** charmer.

(b) (*source of pleasure: often pl*) délice *m* (*f in pl*), joie *f*, charme *m*. **she is the ~ of her mother** elle fait les délices *or* la joie de sa mère; **this book is a great ~** ce livre est vraiment merveilleux; **a ~ to the eyes** un régal *or* un plaisir pour les yeux; **he's a ~ to watch** il fait plaisir à voir; **the ~s of life in the open** les charmes *or* les délices de la vie en plein air.

2 *vt person* réjouir, enchanter, faire les délices de; *V* **delighted.**

3 *vi* se délecter, prendre plaisir, se complaire (*in doing* à faire), adorer (*in doing* faire).

delighted [dɪˈlaɪtɪd] *adj* ravi, enchanté (*with, at, by* de, par, *to do* de faire, *that* que + *subj*). **absolutely ~!** tout à fait ravi!; **~ to meet you!** enchanté (de faire votre connaissance)!; **will you go? — (I shall be) ~** voulez-vous y aller? — avec grand plaisir *or* je ne demande pas mieux *or* très volontiers.

delightful [dɪˈlaɪtfʊl] *adj person, character, smile* délicieux, charmant; *evening, landscape, city, appearance, dress* ravissant. **it's ~ to live like this** c'est merveilleux de vivre ainsi.

delightfully [dɪˈlaɪtfəlɪ] *adv* délicieusement, d'une façon ravissante.

delimit [diːˈlɪmɪt] *vt* délimiter.

delimitation [ˌdiːlɪmɪˈteɪʃən] *n* délimitation *f*.

delineate [dɪˈlɪnɪeɪt] *vt* (*lit*) *outline* délinéer, esquisser, tracer; (*fig*) *character* représenter, dépeindre, décrire. **mountains clearly ~d** montagnes qui se détachent nettement à l'horizon.

delineation [dɪˌlɪnɪˈeɪʃən] *n* *[outline]* dessin *m*, tracé *m*; *[character]* description *f*, peinture *f*, esquisse *f*.

delinquency [dɪˈlɪŋkwənsɪ] *n* **(a)** (*U*) délinquance *f*; *V* **juvenile.** **(b)** (*act of ~*) faute *f*, délit *m*.

delinquent [dɪˈlɪŋkwənt] **1** *adj* délinquant; *V* **juvenile.** **2** *n* délinquant(e) *m(f)*; (*fig*) coupable *mf*, fautif *m*, -ive *f*.

deliquescence [ˌdelɪˈkwesəns] *n* déliquescence *f*.

delirious [dɪˈlɪrɪəs] *adj* (*Med*) qui a le délire, délirant. (*Med*) **to become ~** être pris de délire; (*Med*) **to be ~** avoir le délire, délirer; (*fig*) **~ with joy** délirant *or* fou (*f* folle) de joie; (*fig*) **the crowd was ~** la foule était en délire.

deliriously [dɪˈlɪrɪəslɪ] *adv* (*Med*) en délire; (*fig*) frénétiquement. **~ happy** débordant *or* transporté de joie.

delirium [dɪˈlɪrɪəm] *n* (*Med, fig*) délire *m*. **fit of ~** accès *m* de délire; **~ tremens** delirium *m* tremens.

deliver [dɪˈlɪvəʳ] *vt* **(a)** (*take*) remettre (*to* à); *letters etc* distribuer (*à domicile*); *goods* livrer. **to ~ a message to sb** remettre un message à qn; **milk is ~ed each day** le lait est livré tous les jours; (*Comm*) **'we ~ daily'** 'livraisons quotidiennes'; **'~ed free'** 'livraison gratuite'; **I will ~ the children to school tomorrow** j'emmènerai les enfants à l'école demain; **to ~ a child (over) into sb's care** confier un enfant aux soins de qn; **to ~ the goods*** tenir parole.

(b) (*rescue*) délivrer, sauver, retirer (*sb from sth* qn de qch). **~ us from evil** délivrez-nous du mal.

(c) (*utter*) *speech, sermon* prononcer. **to ~ an ultimatum** lancer un ultimatum.

(d) (*Med*) *woman* (faire) accoucher. (*frm*) **to be ~ed of a son** accoucher d'un fils.

(e) (*hand over: also* **~ over, ~ up**) céder, remettre, transmettre. **to ~ a town (up *or* over) into the hands of the enemy** livrer une ville à l'ennemi; *V* **stand.**

(f) *blow* porter, assener.

deliver over *vt sep V* **deliver a, e.**

deliver up *vt sep V* **deliver e.**

deliverance [dɪˈlɪvərəns] *n* **(a)** (*U*) délivrance *f*, libération *f* (*from* de). **(b)** (*statement of opinion*) déclaration *f* (formelle); (*Jur*) prononcé *m* (du jugement).

deliverer [dɪˈlɪvərəʳ] *n* **(a)** (*saviour*) sauveur *m*, libérateur *m*, -trice *f*. **(b)** (*Comm*) livreur *m*.

delivery [dɪˈlɪvərɪ] **1** *n* **(a)** *[goods]* livraison *f*; *[parcels]* remise *f*, livraison; *[letters]* distribution *f*. **to take ~ of** prendre livraison de; **to pay on ~** payer à la *or* sur livraison; **payable on ~** payable à la livraison; *V* **charge, free** *etc*.

(b) (*Med*) accouchement *m*.

(c) (*U*) *[speaker]* débit *m*, élocution *f*; *[speech]* débit. **his speech was interesting but his ~ dreary** son discours était intéressant mais son débit monotone.

2 *cpd*: **delivery man** livreur *m*; **delivery note** bulletin *m* de livraison; (*Med*) **delivery room** salle *f* de travail *or* d'accouchement; **delivery service** service *m* de livraison; **delivery truck,** (*Brit*) **delivery van** voiture *f* de livraison.

dell [del] *n* vallon *m*.

delouse [ˈdiːˈlaʊs] *vt person, animal* épouiller; *object* ôter les poux de.

Delphi ['delfaɪ] *n* Delphes.

Delphic ['delfɪk] *adj oracle* de Delphes; (*fig liter*) obscur.

delphinium [del'fɪnɪəm] *n* pied-d'alouette *m*, delphinium *m*.

delta ['deltə] **1** *n* delta *m*. **2** *cpd*: (*Aviat*) **delta-winged** à ailes (en) delta.

deltoid ['deltɔɪd] *adj, n* deltoïde (*m*).

delude [dɪ'lu:d] *vt* tromper, duper (*with* de); induire en erreur (*with* par). **to ~ sb into thinking that** amener qn à penser (par des mensonges) que, faire croire à qn (par des mensonges) que; **to ~ o.s.** se faire des illusions, se leurrer, se bercer d'illusions.

deluded [dɪ'lu:dɪd] *adj* induit en erreur, victime d'illusions.

deluding [dɪ'lu:dɪŋ] *adj* trompeur, illusoire.

deluge ['delju:dʒ] **1** *n* (*lit*) déluge *m*, inondation *f*; (*fig*) déluge. **the D~** le déluge; **a ~ of rain** une pluie diluvienne; **a ~ of protests** un déluge de protestations; **a ~ of letters** une avalanche de lettres. **2** *vt* (*lit, fig*) inonder, submerger (*with* de).

delusion [dɪ'lu:ʒən] *n* (*false belief*) illusion *f*; (*Psych*) fantasme *m*, hallucination *f*, psychose *f* paranoïaque. **to suffer from ~s** être en proie à des fantasmes; **to be under a ~** se faire illusion, s'abuser; **~s of grandeur** illusions de grandeur; **happiness is a ~** le bonheur est une illusion.

delusive [dɪ'lu:sɪv] *adj* = **deluding.**

delusiveness [dɪ'lu:sɪvnɪs] *n* caractère trompeur *or* illusoire.

de luxe [dɪ'lʌks] *adj* de luxe, somptueux. **a ~ flat** un appartement (de) grand standing.

delve [delv] *vi* (*lit, fig: also* **~ down**) creuser, fouiller. **to ~ (down) deep into a subject** creuser *or* approfondir un sujet, étudier un sujet à fond; **to ~ into books** fouiller dans des livres; **to ~ (down) into the past** fouiller le passé.

demagnetize [ˌdi:'mægnɪtaɪz] *vt* démagnétiser.

demagogic [ˌdemə'gɒgɪk] *adj* démagogique.

demagogue ['deməgɒg] *n* démagogue *m*.

demagoguery [ˌdemə'gɒgərɪ] *n* (*US*) agissements *mpl or* méthodes *fpl* de démagogue, démagogie *f*.

demagogy ['deməgɒgɪ] *n* démagogie *f*.

demand [dɪ'mɑ:nd] **1** *vt money, explanation, help* exiger, réclamer (*from, of* de); *higher pay etc* revendiquer, réclamer. **to ~ to do** exiger de faire, demander expressément à faire; **he ~s to be obeyed** il exige qu'on lui obéisse; **he ~s that you leave at once** il exige que vous partiez (*subj*) tout de suite; **a question/situation that ~s our attention** une question/une situation qui réclame *or* exige notre attention.

2 *n* **(a)** *[person]* exigence(s) *f(pl)*, demande *f*; *[duty, problem, situation etc]* exigence(s); (*claim*) (*for better pay etc*) revendication *f*, réclamation *f*; (*for help, money*) demande. **payable on ~** payable sur demande *or* sur présentation; **final ~ for payment** dernier avertissement d'avoir à payer; **to make ~s on sb** exiger beaucoup de qn *or* de la part de qn; **the ~s that the child made on her were heavy** l'enfant l'accaparait vraiment; **you make too great ~s on my patience** vous abusez de ma patience; **the ~s of the case** les nécessités *fpl* du cas; **I have many ~s on my time** je suis très pris, mon temps est très pris.

(b) (*U: Comm, Econ*) demande *f*. **to be in great ~** être très demandé *or* recherché; **the ~ for this product increases** ce produit est de plus en plus demandé; **to create a ~ for a product** créer la demande pour un produit; **do you stock suede hats? — no, there's no ~ for them** avez-vous des chapeaux en daim? — non, ils ne sont pas demandés; *V* **supply**[1].

3 *cpd*: (*Med*) **demand feeding** alimentation *f* libre; (*Econ*) **demand management** contrôle *m* (gouvernemental) de la demande; **demand note** feuille *f* de contributions, avertissement *m*.

demanding [dɪ'mɑ:ndɪŋ] *adj person* exigeant, difficile; *work* exigeant, astreignant. **physically ~** qui demande beaucoup de résistance (physique).

demarcate ['di:mɑ:keɪt] *vt* tracer la *or* une ligne de démarcation entre *or* de, délimiter.

demarcation [ˌdi:mɑ:'keɪʃən] *n* démarcation *f*, délimitation *f*. **~ line** ligne *f* de démarcation; **~ dispute** conflit *m* d'attributions.

démarche ['deɪmɑ:ʃ] *n* démarche *f*, mesure *f*.

demean [dɪ'mi:n] *vt*: **to ~ o.s.** s'abaisser (*to do* à faire), s'avilir, se ravaler.

demeanour, (*US*) **demeanor** [dɪ'mi:nəʳ] *n* (*behaviour*) comportement *m*, attitude *f*, conduite *f*; (*bearing*) maintien *m*.

demented [dɪ'mentɪd] *adj* (*Med*) dément, en démence; (*) fou (*f* folle), insensé. (*Med*) **to become ~** tomber en démence; **to drive sb ~** rendre qn fou, faire perdre la tête à qn.

dementedly [dɪ'mentɪdlɪ] *adv* comme un fou (*f* une folle).

dementia [dɪ'menʃɪə] *n* démence *f*. **~ praecox** démence précoce; *V* **senile.**

demerara [ˌdemə'reərə] *n* (*Brit: also* **~ sugar**) sucre roux (cristallisé), cassonade *f*.

demerit [di:'merɪt] *n* démérite *m*, tort *m*, faute *f*.

demesne [dɪ'meɪn] *n* domaine *m*, terre *f*; (*Jur*) possession *f*. (*Jur*) **to hold sth in ~** posséder qch en toute propriété.

demi... ['demɪ] *pref* demi-. **~god** demi-dieu *m*.

demijohn ['demɪdʒɒn] *n* dame-jeanne *f*, bonbonne *f*.

demilitarization ['di:ˌmɪlɪtəraɪ'zeɪʃən] *n* démilitarisation *f*.

demilitarize ['di:'mɪlɪtəraɪz] *vt* démilitariser.

demise [dɪ'maɪz] **1** *n* **(a)** (*death: frm, hum*) décès *m*, mort *f*. **(b)** (*Jur*) (*by legacy*) cession *f or* transfert *m* par legs, transfert par testament; (*by lease*) transfert par bail. **~ of the Crown** transmission *f* de la Couronne (*par décès ou abdication*).

2 *vt* (*Jur*) *estate* léguer; *the Crown, sovereignty* transmettre.

demisemiquaver ['demɪsemɪˌkweɪvəʳ] *n* (*Brit*) triple croche *f*.

demitasse ['demɪtæs] *n* (*US*) (*cup*) tasse *f* (à moka); (*contents*) (tasse de) café noir.

demo‡ ['deməʊ] *n* (*Brit abbr of* **demonstration**) manif* *f*; *V* **demonstration.**

demob* ['di:'mɒb] *vt, n* (*Brit*) *abbr of* **demobilize, demobilization.**

demobilization ['di:ˌməʊbɪlaɪ'zeɪʃən] *n* démobilisation *f*.

demobilize [di:'məʊbɪlaɪz] *vt* démobiliser.

democracy [dɪ'mɒkrəsɪ] *n* démocratie *f*. **they are working towards ~** ils sont en train de se démocratiser.

democrat ['deməkræt] *n* démocrate *mf*. (*US Pol*) **D~** démocrate.

democratic [ˌdemə'krætɪk] *adj institution, spirit* démocratique; (*believing in democracy*) démocrate. (*US Pol*) **the D~ Party** le parti démocrate.

democratically [ˌdemə'krætɪkəlɪ] *adv* démocratiquement. **to be ~ minded** avoir l'esprit démocrate.

democratize [dɪ'mɒkrətaɪz] **1** *vt* démocratiser. **2** *vi* se démocratiser.

demographer [dɪ'mɒgrəfəʳ] *n* démographe *mf*.

demographic [ˌdemə'græfɪk] *adj* démographique.

demography [dɪ'mɒgrəfɪ] *n* démographie *f*.

demolish [dɪ'mɒlɪʃ] *vt building* démolir, abattre; *fortifications* démanteler; (*fig*) *theory* démolir, détruire; (*) *cake* liquider*, dire deux mots à*.

demolisher [dɪ'mɒlɪʃəʳ] *n* (*lit, fig*) démolisseur *m*.

demolition [ˌdemə'lɪʃən] **1** *n* démolition *f*. **2** *cpd*: **demolition area** = **demolition zone; demolition squad** équipe *f* de démolition; **demolition zone** zone *f* de démolition.

demon ['di:mən] *n* (*all senses*) démon *m*. **the D~** le Démon; **the D~ drink** le démon de la boisson; **that child's a ~!*** cet enfant est un petit démon!; **to be a ~ for work** être un bourreau de travail.

demonetize [di:'mʌnɪtaɪz] *vt* démonétiser.

demoniac [dɪ'məʊnɪæk] *adj, n* démoniaque (*mf*).

demoniacal [ˌdi:məʊ'naɪəkəl] *adj* démoniaque, diabolique. **~ possession** possession *f* diabolique.

demonology [ˌdi:mə'nɒlədʒɪ] *n* démonologie *f*.

demonstrable ['demənstrəbl] *adj* démontrable.

demonstrably ['demənstrəblɪ] *adv* de façon évidente. **a ~ false statement** une affirmation dont la fausseté est facilement démontrable.

demonstrate ['demənstreɪt] **1** *vt* **(a)** *truth, need* démontrer, prouver; *system* expliquer, décrire.

(b) *appliance* faire une démonstration de. **to ~ how sth works** montrer le fonctionnement de qch, faire une démonstration de qch.

2 *vi* (*Pol etc*) manifester, faire une manifestation (*for* pour, *in favour of* en faveur de, *against* contre); (*Mil*) faire une démonstration.

demonstration [ˌdemən'streɪʃən] **1** *n* **(a)** (*U*) *[truth etc]* démonstration *f*.

(b) (*Comm*) démonstration *f*. **to give a ~ (of)** faire une démonstration (de).

(c) (*Pol etc*) manifestation *f*. **to hold a ~** faire une manifestation, manifester.

(d) *[love, affection]* manifestations *fpl*, témoignage(s) *m(pl)*.

2 *cpd car, lecture* de démonstration. (*Brit*) *[car, washing machine etc]* **demonstration model** modèle *m* de démonstration.

demonstrative [dɪ'mɒnstrətɪv] *adj behaviour, person* démonstratif, expansif; (*Gram, Math, Philos*) démonstratif.

demonstrator ['demənstreɪtəʳ] *n* (*Comm*) démonstrateur *m*, -trice *f*; (*Scol*) préparateur *m*, -trice *f*; (*Univ*) chargé(e) *m(f)* de travaux pratiques; (*Pol*) manifestant(e) *m(f)*.

demoralization [dɪˌmɒrəlaɪ'zeɪʃən] *n* démoralisation *f*, découragement *m*.

demoralize [dɪ'mɒrəlaɪz] *vt* démoraliser, décourager. **to become ~d** perdre courage *or* le moral*.

demoralizing [dɪ'mɒrəlaɪzɪŋ] *adj* démoralisant.

demote [dɪ'məʊt] *vt* (*also Mil*) rétrograder.

demotic [dɪ'mɒtɪk] **1** *adj* **(a)** (*of the people*) populaire. **(b)** (*Ling*) démotique. **2** *n* démotique *m*.

demotion [dɪ'məʊʃən] *n* rétrogradation *f*.

demulcent [dɪ'mʌlsənt] *adj, n* (*Med*) émollient (*m*), adoucissant (*m*).

demur [dɪ'mɜ:ʳ] **1** *vi* hésiter (*at sth* devant qch, *at doing* à faire), faire *or* soulever des difficultés (*at doing* pour faire); élever des objections (*at sth* contre qch); (*Jur*) opposer une exception.

2 *n* hésitation *f*, objection *f*. **without ~** sans hésiter, sans faire de difficultés.

demure [dɪ'mjʊəʳ] *adj smile, look* modeste, sage, réservé; *girl* modeste, sage, aux airs de sainte nitouche (*pej*); *child* très sage. **a ~ hat** un petit chapeau bien sage.

demurely [dɪ'mjʊəlɪ] *adv* modestement, sagement, avec réserve; (*coyly*) avec une modestie affectée.

demureness [dɪ'mjʊənɪs] *n* (*V* **demure**) air *m* modeste; sagesse *f*; air de sainte nitouche (*pej*).

den [den] *n* **(a)** *[lion, tiger]* tanière *f*, antre *m*; *[thieves]* repaire *m*, antre. (*lit, fig*) **the lion's ~** l'antre du lion; **~ of iniquity** *or* **vice** lieu *m* de perdition *or* de débauche; *V* **gambling, opium.**

(b) (*: *room, study*) antre *m*, turne‡ *f*, piaule‡ *f*.

denationalization ['di:ˌnæʃnəlaɪ'zeɪʃən] *n* dénationalisation *f*.

denationalize [di:'næʃnəlaɪz] *vt person, industry* dénationaliser.

denature [ˌdi:'neɪtʃəʳ] *vt* dénaturer.

dengue ['deŋgɪ] *n* dengue *f*.

denial [dɪ'naɪəl] *n* **(a)** *[rights, truth]* dénégation *f*; *[report, accusation]* démenti *m*; *[guilt]* dénégation; *[authority]* répudiation *f*, rejet *m*, reniement *m*. **~ of justice** déni *m* (de justice); **~ of self** abnégation *f*; **he met the accusation with a flat ~** il a nié catégoriquement l'accusation; **to issue a ~** publier un démenti.

(b) **Peter's ~ of Christ** le reniement du Christ par Pierre.

denier ['denɪəʳ] *n* **(a)** (*weight*) denier *m*. **25 ~ stockings** bas *mpl* de 25 deniers. **(b)** (*coin*) denier *m*.

denigrate ['denɪgreɪt] *vt* dénigrer, discréditer.

denim ['denɪm] *n* (*for jeans, skirts etc*) (toile *f* de) coton *m*, toile *f* de jean; (*heavier: for uniforms, overalls etc*) treillis *m*. (*Dress*) **~s** (*trousers*) blue-jean *m*, jean *m*; (*workman's overalls*) bleus *mpl* de travail.

denizen ['denɪzn] *n* **(a)** (*inhabitant*) habitant(e) *m(f)*. **~s of the forest** habitants *or* hôtes *mpl* (*liter*) des forêts. **(b)** (*Brit Jur*) étranger *m*, -ère *f* (ayant droit de cité). **(c)** (*naturalized plant/animal*) plante *f*/animal *m* acclimaté(e).

Denmark ['denmɑːk] *n* Danemark *m*.

denominate [dɪ'nɒmɪneɪt] *vt* dénommer.

denomination [dɪˌnɒmɪ'neɪʃən] *n* **(a)** (*group*) groupe *m*, catégorie *f*; (*Rel*) secte *f*, confession *f*; *[money]* valeur *f*; *[weight, measure]* unité *f*. **(b)** (*U*) dénomination *f*, appellation *f*.

denominational [dɪˌnɒmɪ'neɪʃənl] *adj* (*Rel*) confessionnel, appartenant à une secte *or* à une confession.

denominative [dɪ'nɒmɪnətɪv] *adj, n* dénominatif (*m*).

denominator [dɪ'nɒmɪneɪtəʳ] *n* dénominateur *m*; *V* **common**.

denotation [ˌdiːnəʊ'teɪʃən] *n* **(a)** (*U*) *[word, expression]* signification *f*; *[object]* dénotation *f*, désignation *f*; (*Philos*) dénotation. **(b)** (*symbol*) indices *mpl*, signes *mpl*.

denote [dɪ'nəʊt] *vt* dénoter, marquer, indiquer.

denounce [dɪ'naʊns] *vt* **(a)** (*speak against*) *person* dénoncer (*to* à); *action* dénoncer. **to ~ sb as an impostor** accuser publiquement qn d'imposture. **(b)** (*repudiate*) *treaty* dénoncer.

denouncement [dɪ'naʊnsmənt] *n* = **denunciation.**

denouncer [dɪ'naʊnsəʳ] *n* dénonciateur *m*, -trice *f*.

dense [dens] *adj* **(a)** *fog, forest* dense, épais (*f* -aisse); *crowd* dense, compact; *population* nombreux, dense. **(b)** (*Opt, Phot*) opaque. **(c)** (*: *stupid*) *person* bête, obtus, bouché*.

densely ['denslɪ] *adv*: **~ wooded** couvert de forêts épaisses; **~ populated** très peuplé, à forte densité de population.

denseness ['densnɪs] *n* **(a)** = **density. (b)** (*) stupidité *f*.

densitometer [ˌdensɪ'tɒmɪtəʳ] *n* densitomètre *m*.

density ['densɪtɪ] *n* (*Phys*) densité *f*; *[fog]* densité, épaisseur *f*; *[population]* densité.

dent [dent] **1** *n* (*in wood*) entaille *f*; (*in metal*) bosselure *f*. (*Aut*) **to have a ~ in the bumper** avoir le pare-choc bosselé *or* cabossé; **his holiday in Rome made a ~ in his savings*** ses vacances à Rome ont fait un trou dans *or* ont écorné *or* ont ébréché* ses économies.

2 *vt hat* cabosser; *car* bosseler, cabosser.

dental ['dentl] **1** *adj* **(a)** *treatment, school* dentaire. **~ surgeon** chirurgien *m* dentiste; **~ technician** mécanicien *m* dentiste. **(b)** (*Ling*) dental. **2** *n* (*Ling*) dentale *f*.

dentifrice ['dentɪfrɪs] *n* dentifrice *m*.

dentist ['dentɪst] *n* dentiste *mf*. **~'s chair** fauteuil *m* de dentiste; **~'s surgery** cabinet *m* de dentiste.

dentistry ['dentɪstrɪ] *n* art *m* dentaire.

dentition [den'tɪʃən] *n* dentition *f*.

denture ['dentʃəʳ] *n* dentier *m*, râtelier *m* (†, *hum*).

denude [dɪ'njuːd] *vt* (*lit, fig*) dénuder, dépouiller.

denunciation [dɪˌnʌnsɪ'eɪʃən] *n* **(a)** *[person]* dénonciation *f*; (*in public*) accusation publique, condamnation *f*; *[action]* dénonciation. **(b)** *[treaty]* dénonciation *f*.

denunciator [dɪ'nʌnsɪeɪtəʳ] *n* dénonciateur *m*, -trice *f*.

deny [dɪ'naɪ] *vt* **(a)** (*repudiate*) nier (*having done* avoir fait, *that* que + *indic or subj*); *fact, accusation* nier, refuser d'admettre; *sb's authority* rejeter. **there is no ~ing it** c'est indéniable; **I'm not ~ing the truth of it** je ne nie pas que ce soit vrai.

(b) (*refuse*) **to ~ sb sth** refuser qch à qn, priver qn de qch; **he was denied admittance** on lui a refusé l'entrée; **to ~ o.s. cigarettes** se priver de cigarettes; **to ~ sb the right to do** refuser *or* dénier à qn le droit de faire.

(c) (*disown*) *leader, religion* renier.

deodorant [diː'əʊdərənt] *adj, n* déodorant (*m*), désodorisant (*m*).

deodorize [diː'əʊdəraɪz] *vt* désodoriser.

deontology [ˌdiːɒn'tɒlədʒɪ] *n* déontologie *f*.

deoxidize [diː'ɒksɪdaɪz] *vt* désoxyder.

deoxyribonucleic [diːˌɒksɪ'raɪbəʊnjuːˌkliːɪk] *adj*: **~ acid** acide *m* désoxyribonucléique.

depart [dɪ'pɑːt] **1** *vi* **(a)** (*go away*) *[person]* partir, s'en aller; *[bus, plane, train etc]* partir. **to ~ from a city** quitter une ville, partir *or* s'en aller d'une ville; **to be about to ~** être sur le *or* son départ.

(b) (*deviate*) s'écarter. **he ~ed from his custom** il a fait une entorse à ses habitudes.

2 *vt* (*liter*) **to ~ this world *or* this life** quitter ce monde, trépasser (*liter*).

departed [dɪ'pɑːtɪd] **1** *adj* **(a)** (*liter: dead*) défunt. **the ~ leader** le chef défunt, le défunt chef. **(b)** (*bygone*) *glory, happiness* passé; *friends* disparu. **2** *n* (*liter*) **the ~** le défunt, la défunte, les défunts *mpl*.

department [dɪ'pɑːtmənt] **1** *n* (*Admin, Pol*) département *m*, ministère *m*; (*Ind*) bureau *m*, service *m*; *[shop, store]* rayon *m*; *[smaller shop]* comptoir *m*; (*Scol, Univ*) section *f*; (*French Admin, Geog*) département; (*fig: field of activity*) domaine *m*, rayon. (*Brit*) **D~ of Employment and Productivity** ≃ ministère du Travail; (*US*) **D~ of State** Département d'État; (*Ind*) **he works in the sales ~** il travaille au service des ventes; **which government ~ is involved?** de quel ministère cela relève-t-il?; **in all the ~s of public service** dans tous les services publics; (*Comm*) **the shoe ~** le rayon des chaussures; (*Scol, Univ*) **the French D~** la section de français; **gardening is my wife's ~*** le jardinage c'est le rayon de ma femme; *V* **head, state, trade** *etc*.

2 *cpd*: **department store** grand magasin.

departmental [ˌdiːpɑːt'mentl] *adj* (*V* **department**) d'un *or* du département *or* ministère *or* service; d'une *or* de la section; *[France]* départemental. *[shop]* **~ manager** chef *m* de rayon.

departure [dɪ'pɑːtʃəʳ] **1** *n* **(a)** (*from place*) *[person, vehicle]* départ *m*; (*from job*) départ, démission *f*. **on the point of ~** sur le point de partir, sur le départ; *V* **arrival** *etc*.

(b) (*from custom, principle*) dérogation *f*, entorse *f* (*from* à); (*from law*) manquement *m* (*from* à). **a ~ from the norm** une exception à la règle, un écart par rapport à la norme; **a ~ from the truth** une entorse à la vérité.

(c) (*change of course, action*) nouvelle voie *or* orientation *or* direction; (*Comm: new type of goods*) nouveauté *f*, innovation *f*. **it's a new ~ in biochemistry** c'est une nouvelle voie qui s'ouvre en *or* pour la biochimie.

(d) (*liter: death*) trépas *m* (*liter*).

2 *cpd preparations etc* de départ. (*Aviat*) **departure gate** porte *f* (de départ); (*Rail*) **departure indicator** horaire *m* des départs; (*Aviat*) **departure lounge** salle *f* de départ; (*Rail*) **departure platform** quai *m* de départ; (*Rail*) **departure signal** signal *m* de départ; **departure time** heure *f* de départ.

depend [dɪ'pend] *impers vi* dépendre (*on sb/sth* de qn/qch). **it all ~s, that ~s** cela dépend, c'est selon; **it ~s on you whether he comes or not** cela dépend de vous *or* il ne tient qu'à vous qu'il vienne ou non; **it ~s (on) whether he will do it or not** cela dépend s'il veut le faire ou non; **it ~s (on) what you mean** cela dépend de ce que vous voulez dire (*by* par); **~ing on what happens tomorrow ...** selon ce qui se passera demain ...

depend (up)on *vt fus* **(a)** (*rely on*) compter sur, se fier à, se reposer sur. **you can always depend (up)on him** on peut toujours compter sur lui *or* se fier à lui; **you may depend (up)on his coming** vous pouvez compter qu'il viendra *or* compter sur sa venue; **I'm depending (up)on you to tell me what he wants** je me fie à vous *or* je compte sur vous pour savoir ce qu'il veut; **you can depend (up)on it** soyez-en sûr, je vous le promets *or* garantis; **you can depend (up)on it that he'll do it wrong again** tu peux être sûr (et certain*) qu'il le fera de nouveau de travers.

(b) (*need support or help from*) dépendre de. **he depends (up)on his father for pocket money** il dépend de son père pour son argent de poche; **I'm depending (up)on you for moral support** votre appui moral m'est indispensable; **your success depends (up)on your efforts** votre succès dépendra de vos efforts.

dependability [dɪˌpendə'bɪlɪtɪ] *n* *[machine]* sécurité *f* de fonctionnement. **his ~ is well-known** tout le monde sait qu'on peut compter sur lui.

dependable [dɪ'pendəbl] *adj person* digne de confiance, sûr, sur qui on peut compter; *mechanism* fiable; *information* sûr. **this is a really ~ car** on peut vraiment avoir confiance en cette voiture, c'est vraiment une voiture solide; **he is not ~** on ne peut pas compter sur lui *or* se fier à lui *or* lui faire confiance.

dependant [dɪ'pendənt] *n* charge *f* de famille, personne *f* à charge. **he had many ~s** il avait de nombreuses personnes à (sa) charge.

dependence [dɪ'pendəns] *n* **(a)** (*state of depending: also* **dependency**) dépendance *f* (*on* à, à l'égard de, envers), sujétion *f* (*on* à). **~ on one's parents** dépendance à l'égard de *or* envers ses parents; **~ on drugs** (situation *f or* état *m* de) dépendance à l'égard de la drogue; **to place ~ on sb** faire confiance à *or* se fier à qn.

(b) ~ of success upon effort rapport *m or* dépendance *f* entre le succès et l'effort.

dependency [dɪ'pendənsɪ] *n* **(a)** = **dependence a. (b)** (*country*) dépendance *f*, colonie *f*.

dependent [dɪ'pendənt] **1** *adj* **(a)** *person* dépendant (*on* de); *condition, decision* dépendant (*on* de), subordonné (*on* à). **to be ~ on charity** dépendre de la charité, subsister de charité; **to be (financially) ~ on sb** vivre aux frais de qn, être à la charge de qn, dépendre de qn financièrement; **to be ~ on one another** dépendre l'un de l'autre; **to be ~ on drugs** avoir une dépendance psychologique à l'égard de la drogue.

(b) (*contingent*) **~ on** tributaire de; **tourism is ~ on the climate** le tourisme est tributaire du climat; **the time of his arrival will be ~ on the weather** son heure d'arrivée dépendra du temps.

(c) (*Gram*) subordonné.

(d) (*Math*) dépendant. **~ variable** variable dépendante, fonction *f*.

2 *n* = **dependant.**

depersonalize [diː'pɜːsənəlaɪz] *vt* dépersonnaliser.

depict [dɪ'pɪkt] *vt* (*in words*) peindre, dépeindre, décrire; (*in picture*) représenter. **surprise was ~ed on his face** la surprise se lisait sur son visage, son visage exprimait la surprise.

depiction [dɪ'pɪkʃən] *n* (*V* **depict**) peinture *f*; représentation *f*.

depilate ['depɪleɪt] *vt* épiler.

depilatory [dɪ'pɪlətərɪ] *adj, n* dépilatoire (*m*).

deplane [ˌdiː'pleɪn] *vi* descendre d'avion.

deplenish [dɪ'plenɪʃ] *vt* vider, dégarnir, démunir.

deplete [dɪ'pliːt] *vt* **(a)** (*reduce*) *supplies* réduire; *strength* diminuer, réduire; (*exhaust*) *supplies, strength* épuiser. (*Comm*) **our stock is very ~d** nos stocks sont très bas; (*Mil*) **the regiment was greatly ~d** (*by cuts etc*) l'effectif du régiment était très réduit; (*by war, sickness*) le régiment a été décimé; **numbers were greatly ~d** les effectifs étaient très réduits.

(b) (*Med*) décongestionner.

depletion [dɪ'pliːʃən] *n* (*V* **deplete**) réduction *f*; diminution *f*; épuisement *m*.

deplorable [dɪ'plɔːrəbl] *adj* déplorable, lamentable.

deplorably [dɪ'plɔːrəblɪ] *adv* déplorablement, lamentablement.

deplore [dɪ'plɔːʳ] *vt* déplorer, regretter vivement. **to ~ the fact that** déplorer le fait que + *indic*, regretter vivement que + *subj*.

deploy [dɪˈplɔɪ] (*Mil, fig*) **1** *vt* déployer. **2** *vi* se déployer.
deployment [dɪˈplɔɪmənt] *n* (*Mil, fig*) déploiement *m*.
depolarization [ˈdiːˌpəʊləraɪˈzeɪʃən] *n* dépolarisation *f*.
depolarize [diːˈpəʊləraɪz] *vt* dépolariser.
deponent [dɪˈpəʊnənt] **1** *n* **(a)** (*Gram*) déponent *m*. **(b)** (*Jur*) déposant(e) *m(f)*. **2** *adj* (*Gram*) déponent.
depopulate [ˌdiːˈpɒpjʊleɪt] *vt* dépeupler.
depopulation [ˈdiːˌpɒpjʊˈleɪʃən] *n* dépopulation *f*, dépeuplement *m*. **rural ~** exode rural.
deport [dɪˈpɔːt] *vt* **(a)** (*expel*) *alien* expulser; (*Hist*) *prisoner* déporter. **(b)** (*behave*) **to ~ o.s.** se comporter, se conduire.
deportation [ˌdiːpɔːˈteɪʃən] *n* expulsion *f*; (*Hist*) déportation *f*. (*Jur*) **~ order** arrêté *m* d'expulsion.
deportment [dɪˈpɔːtmənt] *n* maintien *m*, tenue *f*. **~ lessons** leçons *fpl* de maintien.
depose [dɪˈpəʊz] **1** *vt* *king* déposer, détrôner; *official* destituer. **2** *vti* (*Jur*) déposer, attester par déposition.
deposit [dɪˈpɒzɪt] **1** *vt* **(a)** (*put down*) *parcel etc* déposer, poser.
(b) *money, valuables* déposer, laisser *or* mettre en dépôt (*in or with the bank* à la banque), déposer (*sth with sb* qch chez qn), confier (*sth with sb* qch à qn).
(c) (*Geol*) déposer, former un dépôt de.
2 *n* **(a)** (*in bank*) dépôt *m*. **to make a ~ of £50** déposer 50 livres; **loan on ~** prêt *m* en nantissement.
(b) (*part payment*) arrhes *fpl*, acompte *m*, provision *f*; (*in hire purchase: down payment*) premier versement comptant; (*in hiring goods, renting accommodation: against damage etc*) caution *f*, cautionnement *m*; (*on bottle etc*) consigne *f*; (*Brit Pol*) cautionnement (*à verser pour faire acte de candidature*). (*Comm*) **to leave a ~ of £2** *or* **a £2 ~ on a dress** verser 2 livres d'arrhes *or* d'acompte sur une robe; (*Comm*) **'a small ~ will secure any goods'** 'on peut faire mettre tout article de côté moyennant (le versement d')un petit acompte'; (*Brit Pol*) **to lose one's ~** perdre son cautionnement.
(c) (*Chem*) dépôt *m*, précipité *m*, sédiment *m*; (*in wine*) dépôt; (*Geol*) (*alluvial*) dépôt; *[mineral, oil]* gisement *m*. **to form a ~** se déposer.
3 *cpd*: (*Banking*) **deposit account** compte *m* de dépôt; **deposit slip** bulletin *m* de versement.
depositary [dɪˈpɒzɪtərɪ] *n* **(a)** (*person*) dépositaire *mf*. **(b)** = **depository**.
deposition [ˌdiːpəˈzɪʃən] *n* **(a)** (*U*) *[king, official]* déposition *f*. **(b)** (*Jur*) déposition *f* sous serment, témoignage *m*.
depositor [dɪˈpɒzɪtəʳ] *n* déposant(e) *m(f)*.
depository [dɪˈpɒzɪtərɪ] *n* dépôt *m*, entrepôt *m*.
depot [ˈdepəʊ] **1** *n* **(a)** (*Mil*) dépôt *m*.
(b) (*Brit: garage*) garage *m*, dépôt *m*.
(c) [(*Brit*) ˈdepəʊ, (*US*) ˈdiːpəʊ] (*warehouse*) dépôt *m*, entrepôt *m*. **coal ~** dépôt *or* entrepôt de charbon.
(d) (*only* (*US*) [ˈdiːpəʊ]) (*railway station*) gare *f*; (*bus station*) dépôt *m*.
2 *cpd*: **depot ship** (navire *m*) ravitailleur *m*.
depravation [ˌdeprəˈveɪʃən] *n* dépravation *f*, corruption *f*, avilissement *m*.
deprave [dɪˈpreɪv] *vt* dépraver, corrompre.
depraved [dɪˈpreɪvd] *adj* dépravé, perverti, vicié. **to become ~** se dépraver.
depravity [dɪˈprævɪtɪ] *n* dépravation *f*, perversion *f*.
deprecate [ˈdeprɪkeɪt] *vt* *action, behaviour* désapprouver, s'élever contre. **I ~ his having spoken to you** j'estime qu'il n'aurait pas dû vous parler.
deprecating [ˈdeprɪkeɪtɪŋ] *adj* **(a)** (*disapproving*) *air, voice* désapprobateur (*f* -trice), de reproche. **(b)** (*apologetic*) *smile* d'excuse, humble.
deprecatingly [ˈdeprɪkeɪtɪŋlɪ] *adv* (*V* **deprecating**) d'un ton désapprobateur; avec l'air de s'excuser, humblement.
deprecatory [ˈdeprɪkətərɪ] *adj* = **deprecating**.
depreciate [dɪˈpriːʃɪeɪt] **1** *vt* (*Fin*) *property, currency* déprécier, dévaloriser; (*fig*) *help, talent* déprécier, dénigrer. **2** *vi* (*Fin, fig*) se déprécier, se dévaloriser.
depreciation [dɪˌpriːʃɪˈeɪʃən] *n* *[property, car]* dépréciation *f*, perte *f* de valeur; *[currency]* dépréciation, dévalorisation *f*; (*Comm, Econ*) *[goods]* moins-value *f*; (*fig*) *[talent etc]* dépréciation, dénigrement *m*.
depredation [ˌdeprɪˈdeɪʃən] *n* (*gen pl*) déprédation(s) *f(pl)*, ravage(s) *m(pl)*.
depress [dɪˈpres] *vt* **(a)** *person* déprimer, attrister, donner le cafard à; (*Med*) déprimer. **(b)** (*press down*) *lever* appuyer sur, abaisser. **(c)** *status* réduire; *trade* réduire, (faire) diminuer; *the market, prices* faire baisser.
depressant [dɪˈpresnt] *adj, n* (*Med*) dépresseur (*m*).
depressed [dɪˈprest] *adj* **(a)** *person* déprimé, abattu, découragé; (*Med*) déprimé. **to feel ~** se sentir déprimé *or* démoralisé, avoir le cafard; **to get ~** se décourager, se laisser abattre. **(b)** *industry, area* en déclin, touché par la crise; (*Fin*) *market, trade* en crise, languissant; *business* dans le marasme, languissant; (*Soc*) *class, group* économiquement faible.
depressing [dɪˈpresɪŋ] *adj* déprimant, attristant, décourageant. **I find it/him ~** cela/il me donne le cafard.
depressingly [dɪˈpresɪŋlɪ] *adv* d'une manière déprimante *or* décourageante.
depression [dɪˈpreʃən] *n* **(a)** (*U*) *[person]* découragement *m*; (*Med*) dépression *f*, état dépressif.
(b) (*in ground*) creux *m*; (*Geog*) dépression *f*; (*Met*) dépression (atmosphérique); (*Econ*) crise *f*, dépression, récession *f*. (*Met*) **a deep/shallow ~** une forte/faible dépression; (*Hist*) **the D~** la Crise (de 1929); **the country's economy was in a state of ~** l'économie du pays était dans le marasme *or* en crise.
(c) *[lever, key etc]* abaissement *m*.
depressive [dɪˈpresɪv] *adj, n* (*Med*) dépressif (*m*), -ive (*f*).
deprivation [ˌdeprɪˈveɪʃən] *n* (*act, state*) privation *f*; (*loss*) perte *f*; (*Psych*) carence(s) affective(s). (*Jur*) **~ of office** destitution *f* de fonction; *V* **maternal**.
deprive [dɪˈpraɪv] *vt* (*of sleep, food, company*) priver (*of* de); (*of right*) priver, déposséder (*of* de); (*of asset*) ôter, enlever (*sb of sth* qch à qn). **to ~ o.s. of** se priver de; (*Soc*) **~d child/family** enfant/famille déshérité(e).
depth [depθ] **1** *n* **(a)** *[water, hole]* profondeur *f*; *[shelf, cupboard]* profondeur, largeur *f*; *[snow]* épaisseur *f*; *[edge, border]* largeur, hauteur *f*, épaisseur; *[voice, tone]* registre *m* grave; *[knowledge, feeling]* profondeur; *[sorrow, relief]* profondeur, intensité *f*, acuité *f*; *[concern, interest]* acuité, intensité; *[colour]* intensité. **at a ~ of 3 metres** à 3 mètres de profondeur, par 3 mètres de fond; **the water is 3 metres in ~** l'eau a 3 mètres de profondeur, il y a 3 mètres de fond; (*lit, fig*) **to get out of one's ~** perdre pied; (*in swimming pool etc*) **don't go out of your ~** ne va pas là où tu n'as pas pied; (*fig*) **I am quite out of my ~** je nage complètement*; **the ~s of the ocean** les profondeurs océaniques; **from the ~s of the earth** des profondeurs *or* des entrailles *fpl* de la terre; **a great ~ of feeling** une grande profondeur de sentiment; **to study in ~** étudier en profondeur; (*Phot*) **~ of field/of focus** profondeur de champ/de foyer.
(b) (*fig*) **~s** fond *m*; **to be in the ~s of despair** toucher le fond du désespoir; **I would never sink to such ~s as to do that** je ne tomberais jamais assez bas pour faire cela; **in the ~ of winter** au plus fort *or* au cœur de l'hiver; **in the ~ of night** au milieu *or* au plus profond de la nuit; **in the ~s of the forest** au plus profond *or* au cœur de la forêt.
2 *cpd*: **depth charge** grenade sous-marine; **in-depth interview** interview *f* en profondeur; **depth psychology** psychologie *f* des profondeurs.
deputation [ˌdepjʊˈteɪʃən] *n* délégation *f*, députation *f*.
depute [dɪˈpjuːt] *vt* *power, authority* déléguer; *person* députer, déléguer (*sb to do* qn pour faire).
deputize [ˈdepjʊtaɪz] **1** *vi* assurer l'intérim (*for sb* de qn). **2** *vt* députer (*sb to do* qn pour faire).
deputy [ˈdepjʊtɪ] **1** *n* (*second in command*) adjoint(e) *m(f)*; (*replacement*) suppléant(e) *m(f)*, remplaçant(e) *m(f)*; (*in business*) fondé *m* de pouvoir; (*member of deputation*) délégué(e) *m(f)*; (*French Pol*) député *m*; (*US: also* **~ sheriff**) shérif adjoint.
2 *cpd* adjoint. **deputy chairman** vice-président *m*; **deputy head** directeur adjoint, sous-directeur *m*; **deputy judge** juge suppléant; **deputy mayor** maire adjoint.
derail [dɪˈreɪl] **1** *vt* faire dérailler. **2** *vi* dérailler.
derailment [dɪˈreɪlmənt] *n* déraillement *m*.
derange [dɪˈreɪndʒ] *vt* **(a)** *plan* déranger, troubler; *machine* dérégler. **(b)** (*Med*) déranger, aliéner. **~d person/mind** personne *f*/esprit *m* dérangé(e); **to be (mentally) ~d** avoir le cerveau dérangé.
derangement [dɪˈreɪndʒmənt] *n* **(a)** (*Med*) aliénation mentale. **(b)** *[machine]* dérèglement *m*.
Derby [ˈdɑːbɪ, (*US*) ˈdɜːbɪ] *n* **(a)** (*Brit*) (*Horse-racing*) **the ~** le Derby (d'Epsom); (*Sport*) **local ~** match *m* entre équipes voisines. **(b)** (*US*) **d~ (hat)** (chapeau *m*) melon *m*.
derelict [ˈderɪlɪkt] **1** *adj* **(a)** (*abandoned*) abandonné, délaissé; (*ruined*) (tombé) en ruines. **(b)** (*frm: neglectful of duty*) négligent. **2** *n* **(a)** (*Naut*) navire abandonné (*en mer*). **(b)** (*person*) épave *f* (humaine).
dereliction [ˌderɪˈlɪkʃən] *n* *[property]* état *m* d'abandon; *[person]* délaissement *m*. **~ of duty** négligence *f* (dans le service), manquement *m* au devoir.
derestricted [ˌdiːrɪˈstrɪktɪd] *adj* (*Brit*) *road, area* sans limitation de vitesse.
deride [dɪˈraɪd] *vt* rire de, railler, tourner en ridicule.
derision [dɪˈrɪʒən] *n* dérision *f*. **object of ~** objet *m* de dérision *or* de risée.
derisive [dɪˈraɪsɪv] *adj* **(a)** *smile, person* moqueur, railleur. **(b)** *amount, offer* dérisoire.
derisively [dɪˈraɪsɪvlɪ] *adv* d'un ton railleur *or* moqueur, d'un air *or* d'un ton de dérision.
derisory [dɪˈraɪsərɪ] *adj* **(a)** *amount, offer* dérisoire. **(b)** *smile, person* moqueur, railleur.
derivation [ˌderɪˈveɪʃən] *n* dérivation *f*.
derivative [dɪˈrɪvətɪv] **1** *adj* (*Chem, Ling, Math*) dérivé; (*fig*) *literary work etc* peu original. **2** *n* (*Chem, Ling*) dérivé *m*; (*Math*) dérivée *f*.
derive [dɪˈraɪv] **1** *vt* *profit, satisfaction* tirer (*from* de), trouver (*from* dans); *comfort, ideas* puiser (*from* dans); *name, origins* tenir (*from* de). **to ~ one's happiness from** devoir son bonheur à, trouver son bonheur dans; **to be ~d from** *V* **2**.
2 *vi*: **to ~ from** (*also* **be ~d from**) dériver de, provenir de, venir de; *[power, fortune]* provenir de; *[idea]* avoir sa source *or* ses origines dans; **it all ~s from the fact that** tout cela tient au fait que *or* provient du fait que.
dermatitis [ˌdɜːməˈtaɪtɪs] *n* dermatite *f*, dermite *f*.
dermatologist [ˌdɜːməˈtɒlədʒɪst] *n* dermatologue *mf*, dermatologiste *mf*.
dermatology [ˌdɜːməˈtɒlədʒɪ] *n* dermatologie *f*.
derogate [ˈderəgeɪt] *vi*: **to ~ from** porter atteinte à; **without derogating from his authority/his merits** sans rien enlever à *or* sans vouloir diminuer son autorité/ses mérites; (*liter*) **to ~ from one's position** déroger (à son rang) (*liter*).
derogation [ˌderəˈgeɪʃən] *n* (*V* **derogate**) atteinte *f* (*from* à), diminution *f* (*from* de); (*liter*) dérogation *f* (*liter*) (*from* à).
derogatory [dɪˈrɒgətərɪ] *adj* *remark* désobligeant (*of, to* à), peu flatteur, dénigrant; *attitude* de dénigrement.
derrick [ˈderɪk] *n* (*Naut: lifting device, crane*) mât *m* de charge; (*above oil well*) derrick *m*.
derring-do†† [ˈderɪŋˈduː] *n* bravoure *f*. **deeds of ~** hauts faits, prouesses *fpl*.

derringer ['derɪndʒəʳ] *n* (*US*) pistolet *m* (court et à gros calibre), derringer *m*.
derv [dɜːv] *n* (*Brit Aut*) gas-oil *m*.
dervish ['dɜːvɪʃ] *n* derviche *m*.
desalinate [diː'sælɪneɪt] *vt* dessaler.
desalination [diːˌsælɪ'neɪʃən] *n*, **desalinization** [diːˌsælɪnaɪ'zeɪʃən] *n* dessalage *m*, dessalaison *f*.
desalinize [diː'sælɪnaɪz] *vt* dessaler.
descale [diː'skeɪl] *vt* détartrer.
descant ['deskænt] *n* déchant *m*. **to sing ~** chanter une partie du déchant.
descend [dɪ'send] **1** *vi* **(a)** (*go down*) *[person, vehicle, road, hill etc]* descendre (*from* de); *[rain, snow]* tomber. **to ~ into oblivion** tomber dans l'oubli; **sadness ~ed upon him** la tristesse l'a envahi; **in ~ing order of importance** par ordre d'importance décroissante.
(b) (*by ancestry*) descendre, être issu (*from* de); *[plan, event etc]* tirer son origine (*from* de).
(c) (*pass by inheritance*) *[property, customs, rights]* passer (par héritage) (*from* de, *to* à).
(d) (*attack suddenly*) s'abattre, se jeter, tomber (*on, upon* sur); (*Mil, fig*) faire une descente. (*fig*) **visitors ~ed upon us** des gens sont arrivés (chez nous) sans crier gare.
(e) (*lower o.s. to*) s'abaisser (*to* à). **to ~ to lies** *or* **to lying** s'abaisser à mentir.
2 *vt* **(a)** *stairs* descendre.
(b) to be ~ed from sb descendre de qn, être issu de qn.
descendant [dɪ'sendənt] *n* descendant(e) *m(f)*.
descendible [dɪ'sendəbl] *adj* (*Jur*) transmissible.
descent [dɪ'sent] *n* **(a)** (*going down*) *[person]* descente *f* (*into* dans); (*fig: into crime etc*) chute *f*; (*Aviat, Sport*) descente; *[hill]* descente, pente *f*. **the street made a sharp ~** la rue était très en pente *or* descendait en pente très raide; **~ by parachute** descente en parachute.
(b) (*ancestry*) origine *f*, famille *f*. **of noble ~** de noble extraction; **to trace one's ~ back to** faire remonter sa famille à; **to trace back the ~ of** établir la généalogie de.
(c) *[property, customs etc]* transmission *f* (par héritage) (*to* à).
(d) (*Mil etc: attack*) descente *f*, irruption *f*. (*Mil*) **to make a ~ on the enemy camp** faire une descente sur *or* faire irruption dans le camp ennemi; (*Mil*) **to make a ~ on the enemy** faire une descente sur l'ennemi.
describe [dɪs'kraɪb] *vt* **(a)** *scene, person* décrire, faire la description de, dépeindre. **~ what it is like** racontez *or* dites comment c'est; **~ him for us** décrivez-le-nous; **which cannot be ~d** indescriptible, qu'on ne saurait décrire.
(b) (*represent*) décrire, représenter (*as* comme), qualifier (*as* de). **he ~s himself as a doctor** il se dit *or* se prétend docteur.
(c) (*Math*) décrire.
description [dɪs'krɪpʃən] *n* **(a)** *[person]* description *f*, portrait *m*; (*Police*) signalement *m*; *[scene, object]* description; *[event, situation]* description, exposé *m*. **to give an accurate/lively ~** faire *or* donner une description exacte/vivante; **beyond ~** indescriptible, qu'on ne saurait décrire; **it beggars** *or* **defies ~** cela défie toute description; *V* **answer**.
(b) (*sort*) sorte *f*, espèce *f*, genre *m*. **vehicles of every ~** véhicules de toutes sortes.
descriptive [dɪs'krɪptɪv] *adj* descriptif. **~ geometry/linguistics** géométrie/linguistique descriptive.
descry [dɪs'kraɪ] *vt* discerner, distinguer.
desecrate ['desɪkreɪt] *vt shrine, memory* profaner, souiller (*liter*).
desecration [ˌdesɪ'kreɪʃən] *n* profanation *f*.
desegregate [ˌdiː'segrɪgeɪt] *vt* abolir *or* supprimer la ségrégation raciale dans. **~d schools** écoles *fpl* où la ségrégation raciale n'est plus pratiquée.
desegregation ['diːˌsegrɪ'geɪʃən] *n* déségrégation *f*.
desensitize [ˌdiː'sensɪtaɪz] *vt* désensibiliser.
desert[1] ['dezət] **1** *n* (*lit, fig*) désert *m*.
2 *cpd region, climate* désertique. **desert boot** chaussure montante (en daim à lacets); **desert island** île déserte; (*Zool*) **desert rat** gerboise *f*; (*Brit Mil*) **Desert Rats*** *forces britanniques combattant en Libye (2e guerre mondiale)*.
desert[2] [dɪ'zɜːt] **1** *vt post, people, land* déserter, abandonner; *cause, party* déserter; *friend* délaisser. **his courage ~ed him** son courage l'a abandonné; **the place was ~ed** l'endroit était désert.
2 *vi* (*Mil*) déserter; (*from one's party*) faire défection. **to ~ to the rebels** passer du côté des rebelles.
desert[3] [dɪ'zɜːt] *n* (*gen pl*) dû *m*, ce qu'on mérite; (*reward*) récompense méritée; (*punishment*) châtiment mérité. **according to his ~s** selon ses mérites; **to get one's (just) ~s** avoir *or* recevoir ce que l'on mérite.
deserter [dɪ'zɜːtəʳ] *n* (*Mil*) déserteur *m*; (*to the enemy*) transfuge *m*.
desertion [dɪ'zɜːʃən] *n* (*V* **desert**[2]) désertion *f*, abandon *m*, défection *f*, délaissement *m*; (*Mil*) désertion; (*Jur*) *[spouse]* abandon du conjoint *or* du domicile conjugal. **~ to the enemy** désertion *or* défection à l'ennemi; **~ of one's family** abandon de sa famille.
deserve [dɪ'zɜːv] **1** *vt [person]* mériter, être digne de; *[object, suggestion]* mériter. **he ~s to win** il mérite de gagner; **he ~s to be pitied** il mérite qu'on le plaigne, il est digne de pitié; **he ~s more money** il mérite d'être mieux payé; **he got what he ~d** il n'a eu que ce qu'il méritait, il ne l'a pas volé*; **the idea ~s consideration** l'idée mérite réflexion; *V* **well**[2] *etc.*
2 *vi*: **to ~ well of one's country** bien mériter de la patrie; **man deserving of more respect** homme digne d'un plus grand respect.
deservedly [dɪ'zɜːvɪdlɪ] *adv* à bon droit, à juste titre (*also pej*).
deserving [dɪ'zɜːvɪŋ] *adj person* méritant; *action, cause* méritoire, louable. **she's a ~ case** c'est une personne méritante; **the ~ poor** les pauvres méritants; *V* **deserve**.
deshabille [ˌdezə'biːl] *n* = **dishabille.**
desiccant ['desɪkənt] *n* dessiccatif *m*.
desiccate ['desɪkeɪt] *vt* dessécher, sécher. **~d coconut** noix de coco séchée.
desiccation [ˌdesɪ'keɪʃən] *n* dessiccation *f*.
desiderata [dɪˌzɪdə'rɑːtə] *npl* desiderata *mpl*.
design [dɪ'zaɪn] **1** *n* **(a)** (*intention*) dessein *m*, intention *f*, projet *m*. **by ~** à dessein, exprès, de propos délibéré; **his ~s became obvious when ...** ses intentions *or* ses projets sont devenu(e)s manifestes quand ...; **to form a ~ to do** former le projet *or* concevoir le dessein de faire; **to have ~s on sb/sth** avoir des desseins *or* des visées sur qn/qch; **imperialist ~s against** *or* **on Ruritania** les visées *fpl* impérialistes sur la Ruritanie.
(b) (*U: planning*) *[building, book, machine, dress etc]* conception *f*, élaboration *f*, création *f*; (*Comm, Ind*) design *m*, esthétique industrielle. **a machine of good/bad ~** une machine bien/mal conçue; **of faulty ~** de conception défectueuse; **they worked for 2 years on the ~ of the new car** la nouvelle voiture a été à l'étude pendant 2 ans, la conception *or* la mise au point de la nouvelle voiture a pris 2 ans; **the ~ of this machine allows the customer to ...** la façon dont cette machine est conçue permet au client de ...; **improvements in ~ have transformed working conditions** les progrès du design *or* de l'esthétique industrielle ont transformé les conditions de travail; **industrial ~** dessin industriel.
(c) (*instance of this*) *[building, book etc]* plan *m*; *[car, industrial product, dress etc]* modèle *m*; (*Cine, Theat, TV*) décors *mpl*; (*pattern: on pottery, material etc*) dessin *m*, motif(s) *m(pl)*. **the general ~ of 'Paradise Lost'** le plan général *or* l'architecture *f* du 'Paradis Perdu'; **grand ~** plan d'ensemble; (*Mil*) stratégie *f* d'ensemble; **a new** *or* **fresh ~** un modèle inédit; *[dress etc]* **our latest ~s** nos derniers modèles, nos dernières créations; **this is a very practical ~** c'est un plan *or* un modèle très pratique, cela a été conçu de façon très pratique; **the ~ on this dress** les motifs sur cette robe.
2 *vt* **(a)** (*plan, think out*) *garden* dessiner, tracer le plan de; *machine* dresser le plan de, dessiner; *car, dress* créer, dessiner; *scheme* projeter, préparer. **a well-~ed house/machine** une maison/une machine bien conçue.
(b) (+ *for* = *intend for*) *machine, building etc* construire (*for* pour), concevoir (*for* pour); (*rare*) *person* destiner (*for* à). **this machine was ~ed for a special purpose** cette machine a été conçue pour un usage spécifique; **this room was ~ed as a study** cette pièce a été conçue pour être un cabinet de travail; **the jar was ~ed to hold wine** l'amphore était faite pour contenir du vin.
3 *vi* dessiner.
designate ['dezɪgneɪt] **1** *vt region, substance* désigner (*as* sous le nom de), qualifier (*as* de); *boundary* désigner; *officer* désigner, nommer. **to ~ sb to a post/as one's successor** désigner qn à une fonction/pour *or* comme son successeur.
2 ['dezɪgnɪt] *adj* désigné. **the chairman ~** le président désigné.
designation [ˌdezɪg'neɪʃən] *n* (*all senses*) désignation *f*.
designedly [dɪ'zaɪnɪdlɪ] *adv* à dessein, exprès.
designer [dɪ'zaɪnəʳ] *n* (*Archit, Art*) dessinateur *m*, -trice *f*, créateur *m*, -trice *f*; (*Comm, Ind*) concepteur-projeteur *m*, designer *m*; (*Cine, Theat*) décorateur *m*, -trice *f*; *V* **dress, industrial** *etc.*
designing [dɪ'zaɪnɪŋ] *adj* (*scheming*) intrigant; (*crafty*) rusé.
desirability [dɪˌzaɪərə'bɪlɪtɪ] *n [plan]* avantage *m*; *[woman]* charmes *mpl*, sex-appeal *m*.
desirable [dɪ'zaɪərəbl] *adj position, offer* désirable, enviable, tentant; *woman* désirable, séduisant; *action, progress* désirable, à désirer, souhaitable. **it is ~ that** il est désirable *or* souhaitable que + *subj*; **~ residence for sale** belle propriété à vendre.
desire [dɪ'zaɪəʳ] **1** *n* désir *m*, envie *f* (*for* de, *to do* de faire); (*sexual*) désir. **a ~ for peace** un désir (ardent) de paix; **it is my ~ that** c'est mon désir que + *subj*; **I have no ~** *or* **I haven't the least ~ to do it** je n'ai nullement envie de le faire.
2 *vt* **(a)** (*want*) désirer, vouloir (*to do* faire, *that* que + *subj*), avoir envie (*to do* de faire); *object* avoir envie de, désirer; *woman, peace* désirer. **his work leaves much to be ~d** son travail laisse beaucoup à désirer.
(b) (*request*) prier (*sb to do* qn de faire).
desirous [dɪ'zaɪərəs] *adj* désireux (*of* de). **to be ~ of sth/of doing** désirer qch/faire.
desist [dɪ'zɪst] *vi* cesser, s'arrêter (*from doing* de faire). **to ~ from sth** cesser qch; (*Jur*) se désister de qch; **to ~ from criticism** renoncer à *or* cesser de critiquer; **to ~ from one's efforts** abandonner ses efforts.
desk [desk] **1** *n* (*for pupil*) pupitre *m*; (*for teacher*) bureau *m*, chaire *f*; (*in office, home*) bureau; (*in shop, restaurant*) caisse *f*; (*in hotel, at airport*) réception *f*. (*Press*) **the ~** le secrétariat de rédaction; (*Press*) **the news/city ~** le service des informations/financier; *V* **cash, roll** *etc.*
2 *cpd*: **desk blotter** sous-main *m inv*; **desk-bound** sédentaire; (*US*) **desk clerk** réceptionniste *mf*; **desk diary** agenda *m* (de bureau); **he's got a desk job** il fait un travail de bureau; **desk lamp** lampe *f* de bureau; **desk pad** bloc *m* (de bureau), bloc-notes *m*.
desolate ['desəlɪt] **1** *adj* **(a)** *place* (*empty*) désolé, désert; (*in ruins*) ravagé, dévasté; (*fig*) *outlook, future* sombre, morne. **(b)** (*grief-stricken*) affligé, au désespoir; (*friendless*) délaissé, solitaire. **a ~ cry** un cri de désespoir. **2** ['desəleɪt] *vt country* désoler, ravager; *person* désoler, affliger.

desolately [ˈdesəlɪtlɪ] *adv* (*very sadly*) d'un air désolé *or* affligé, avec désolation; (*fig: friendlessly*) dans la solitude.
desolation [ˌdesəˈleɪʃən] *n* **(a)** (*grief*) désolation *f*, affliction *f*; (*friendlessness*) solitude *f*; *[landscape]* aspect désert, solitude. **(b)** (*of country, by war*) désolation *f* (*liter*), dévastation *f*.
despair [dɪsˈpɛəʳ] **1** *n* **(a)** (*U*) désespoir *m* (*about, at, over* au sujet de, *at having done* d'avoir fait). **to be in ~** être au désespoir, être désespéré; **in ~ she killed him** de désespoir elle l'a tué; **to drive sb to ~** désespérer qn, réduire qn au désespoir.
(b) (*cause of ~*) désespoir *m*. **this child is the ~ of his parents** cet enfant fait *or* est le désespoir de ses parents.
2 *vi* (se) désespérer, perdre l'espoir. **don't ~!** ne te désespère pas!; **to ~ of (doing) sth** désespérer de (faire) qch; **his life was ~ed of** on désespérait de le sauver.
despairing [dɪsˈpɛərɪŋ] *adj person* désespéré; *look, gesture* de désespoir, désespéré; (*) *situation* catastrophique*.
despairingly [dɪsˈpɛərɪŋlɪ] *adv say* d'un ton désespéré; *look* d'un air désespéré; *agree, answer* avec désespoir; *look for* désespérément.
despatch [dɪsˈpætʃ] = **dispatch.**
desperado [ˌdespəˈrɑːdəʊ] *n* hors-la-loi *m inv*, desperado *m*.
desperate [ˈdespərɪt] *adj* **(a)** *person, animal, measure, attempt, situation* désespéré; *fight, effort* désespéré, acharné; *criminal* capable de tout, prêt à tout. **to feel ~** être désespéré; **to do something ~** commettre un acte de désespoir; **he's a ~ man** c'est un désespéré; **I am ~ for money/for a rest** il me faut absolument de l'argent/du repos, j'ai désespérément besoin d'argent/de repos.
(b) (*: *very bad*) atroce*, abominable.
desperately [ˈdespərɪtlɪ] *adv* **(a)** *struggle* désespérément, avec acharnement, en désespéré; *regret* désespérément; *say, look* avec désespoir.
(b) *cold, needy* terriblement, désespérément. **~ in love** éperdument amoureux; **~ ill** très gravement malade.
desperation [ˌdespəˈreɪʃən] *n* (*U*) **(a)** (*state*) désespoir *m*. **to be in ~** être au désespoir; **to drive sb to ~** pousser qn à bout; **in ~ she killed him** poussée à bout elle l'a tué; **in sheer ~** en désespoir de cause.
(b) (*recklessness*) désespoir *m*, rage *f or* fureur *f* du désespoir. **to fight with ~** combattre avec la rage du désespoir.
despicable [dɪsˈpɪkəbl] *adj action, person* ignoble, abject, méprisable.
despicably [dɪsˈpɪkəblɪ] *adv* d'une façon méprisable *or* ignoble, bassement.
despise [dɪsˈpaɪz] *vt danger, person* mépriser. **to ~ sb for sth/for doing sth** mépriser qn pour qch/pour avoir fait qch.
despisingly [dɪsˈpaɪzɪŋlɪ] *adv* avec mépris, dédaigneusement.
despite [dɪsˈpaɪt] **1** *prep* malgré, en dépit de. **2** *n* (*liter*) dépit *m*.
despoil [dɪsˈpɔɪl] *vt* (*liter*) *person* dépouiller, spolier (*of* de); *country* piller.
despoiler [dɪsˈpɔɪləʳ] *n* (*liter*) spoliateur *m*, -trice *f*.
despoiling [dɪsˈpɔɪlɪŋ] *n* spoliation *f*.
despondence [dɪsˈpɒndəns] *n*, **despondency** [dɪsˈpɒndənsɪ] *n* découragement *m*, abattement *m*.
despondent [dɪsˈpɒndənt] *adj* découragé, abattu, déprimé (*about* par).
despondently [dɪsˈpɒndəntlɪ] *adv* avec découragement, d'un air *or* d'un ton découragé *or* abattu.
despot [ˈdespɒt] *n* (*lit, fig*) despote *m*, tyran *m*.
despotic [desˈpɒtɪk] *adj* (*lit*) despotique; (*fig*) despote.
despotically [desˈpɒtɪkəlɪ] *adv behave* d'une manière despotique, despotiquement; *govern* despotiquement, en despote.
despotism [ˈdespətɪzəm] *n* despotisme *m*.
dessert [dɪˈzɜːt] **1** *n* dessert *m*. **2** *cpd*: **dessert apple** pomme *f* à couteau; **dessert chocolate** chocolat *m* à croquer; **dessert plate** assiette *f* à dessert; **dessertspoon** cuiller *f* à dessert.
destination [ˌdestɪˈneɪʃən] *n* destination *f*.
destine [ˈdestɪn] *vt person, object* destiner (*for* à). **they were ~d to meet again later** ils étaient destinés à se rencontrer plus tard; **I was ~d never to see them again** je devais ne plus jamais les revoir; (*liter*) **at the ~d hour** à l'heure fixée par le destin.
destiny [ˈdestɪnɪ] *n* destin *m*, destinée *f*, sort *m*. **D~** le destin, le sort, la destinée; **the destinies of France during this period** le destin de la France pendant cette période; **it was his ~ to die in battle** il était écrit qu'il devait mourir au combat.
destitute [ˈdestɪtjuːt] **1** *adj* **(a)** (*poverty-stricken*) indigent, sans ressources. **to be utterly ~** être dans le dénuement le plus complet. **(b)** (*lacking*) dépourvu, dénué (*of* de). **2** *npl*: **the ~** les pauvres *mpl*, les indigents *mpl*.
destitution [ˌdestɪˈtjuːʃən] *n* dénuement *m*, indigence *f*, misère *f*.
destroy [dɪsˈtrɔɪ] *vt* **(a)** (*spoil completely*) *town, forest* détruire, ravager; *building* démolir; *toy, gadget* démolir; *document* détruire. **~ed by bombing** détruit par bombardement; **the village was ~ed by a fire** un incendie a ravagé le village.
(b) (*kill*) *enemy* détruire, anéantir; *population* détruire, exterminer, décimer; *dangerous animal, injured horse* abattre; *cat, dog* supprimer, faire piquer. **to ~ o.s.** se suicider, se tuer.
(c) (*put an end to*) *reputation, mood, beauty, influence, faith* détruire; *hope, love* anéantir, détruire.
destroyer [dɪsˈtrɔɪəʳ] *n* **(a)** (*Naut*) contre-torpilleur *m*, destroyer *m*. **(b)** (*person*) destructeur *m*, -trice *f*; (*murderer*) meurtrier *m*, -ière *f*.
destruct [dɪsˈtrʌkt] **1** *vt missile* détruire volontairement. **2** *vi* être détruit volontairement. **3** *n* destruction *f* volontaire. **4** *cpd*: **destruct button/mechanism** télécommande *f*/mécanisme *m* de destruction.
destructible [dɪsˈtrʌktəbl] *adj* destructible.
destruction [dɪsˈtrʌkʃən] *n* **(a)** (*U: act*) *[town, building]* destruction *f*; *[enemy]* destruction, anéantissement *m*; *[people, insects]* destruction, extermination *f*; *[documents]* destruction; *[reputation, hope]* destruction, ruine *f*; *[character, soul]* ruine, perte *f*. **~ by fire** destruction par un incendie *or* par le feu.
(b) (*U: damage: from war, fire*) destruction *f*, dégâts *mpl*, dommages *mpl*.
destructive [dɪsˈtrʌktɪv] *adj* **(a)** *wind, fire* destructeur (*f* -trice), qui cause des dégâts; *war* exterminateur (*f* -trice); *effect, person* destructeur; *power, instinct* destructif. **a ~ boy** un brise-fer. **(b)** (*not constructive*) *criticism, idea* destructif, destructeur (*f* -trice).
destructively [dɪsˈtrʌktɪvlɪ] *adv* de façon destructrice.
destructiveness [dɪˈstrʌktɪvnɪs] *n [fire, war, criticism etc]* caractère *or* effet destructeur; *[child etc]* penchant destructeur.
destructor [dɪsˈtrʌktəʳ] *n* (*Brit: also* **refuse ~**) incinérateur *m* (à ordures).
desuetude [dɪˈsjʊɪtjuːd] *n* (*liter*) désuétude *f*.
desultory [ˈdesəltərɪ] *adj reading* décousu, sans suite, sans méthode; *attempt* peu suivi, peu soutenu; *firing, contact* irrégulier, interrompu, intermittent. **to have a ~ conversation** échanger des propos décousus.
detach [dɪˈtætʃ] *vt hook, rope, cart* détacher, séparer (*from* de). **to ~ o.s. from a group** se détacher d'un groupe; **a section became ~ed from ...** une section s'est détachée de ...; **troops were ~ed to protect the town** on a envoyé un détachement de troupes pour protéger la ville.
detachable [dɪˈtætʃəbl] *adj part of machine, section of document* détachable (*from* de); *collar, lining* amovible. (*Phot*) **~ lens** objectif *m* mobile.
detached [dɪˈtætʃt] *adj* **(a)** (*separate*) *part, section* détaché, séparé. (*Brit*) **~ house** maison individuelle (entourée d'un jardin), ≃ pavillon *m*, petite villa.
(b) (*unbiased*) *opinion* désintéressé, objectif, sans préjugés; (*unemotional*) *manner* détaché, indifférent, dégagé. **he seemed very ~ about it** il semblait ne pas du tout se sentir concerné.
detachment [dɪˈtætʃmənt] *n* **(a)** (*U*) *[part, section etc]* séparation *f* (*from* de). (*Med*) **~ of the retina** décollement *m* de la rétine.
(b) (*U: fig: in manner*) détachement *m*, indifférence *f*; (*towards pleasure, friends*) indifférence (*towards* à, à l'égard de).
(c) (*Mil*) détachement *m*.
detail [ˈdiːteɪl] **1** *n* **(a)** (*also Archit, Art*) détail *m*. **in ~** en détail; **in great ~** dans les moindres détails; **his attention to ~** l'attention qu'il apporte au détail; **to go into ~s** entrer dans les détails; **in every ~ it resembles ...** de point en point *or* dans le moindre détail cela ressemble à ...; **but that's a tiny ~!** mais ce n'est qu'un (petit) détail!
(b) (*Mil*) détachement *m*.
2 *cpd*: (*Archit, Tech*) **detail drawing** épure *f*.
3 *vt* **(a)** *reason, fact* exposer en détail; *story, event* raconter en détail; *items, objects* énumérer, détailler.
(b) (*Mil*) *troops* affecter (*for* à, *to do* à *or* pour faire), détacher, désigner (*for* pour, *to do* pour faire).
detailed [ˈdiːteɪld] *adj work, account* détaillé, minutieux, circonstancié. (*Surv*) **a ~ survey** un levé de détail.
detain [dɪˈteɪn] *vt* **(a)** (*keep back*) retenir, garder. **Mr X has been ~ed at the office** M X a été retenu au bureau; **I don't want to ~ you any longer** je ne veux pas vous retarder *or* retenir plus longtemps.
(b) (*in captivity*) détenir; (*Scol*) mettre en retenue, consigner.
detect [dɪˈtekt] *vt culprit, secret, sadness* découvrir, surprendre, déceler; *object* apercevoir, discerner, distinguer; *movement* apercevoir, percevoir, distinguer; *noise* percevoir, distinguer; *mine, gas* détecter.
detectable [dɪˈtektəbl] *adj* qu'on peut découvrir *or* discerner, discernable, perceptible.
detection [dɪˈtekʃən] *n [criminal, secret]* découverte *f*; *[gas, mines]* détection *f*. **policemen engaged in the ~ of crime** les policiers qui s'emploient à démasquer les criminels; **the bloodstains led to the ~ of the criminal** les taches de sang ont mené à la découverte du criminel; **to escape ~** *[criminal]* échapper aux recherches; *[mistake]* passer inaperçu.
detective [dɪˈtektɪv] **1** *n* agent *m* de la sûreté, policier *m* en civil; (*also* **private ~**) détective *m* (privé).
2 *cpd*: (*Brit*) **detective constable** ≃ inspecteur *m or* officier *m* de police; **detective device** dispositif *m* de détection *or* de dépistage; **detective sergeant** ≃ brigadier *m* de police; **detective story** roman policier.
detector [dɪˈtektəʳ] **1** *n* (*device, person*) détecteur *m*; *V* **lie²**, **mine²** *etc*. **2** *cpd*: (*Brit TV*) **detector van** voiture *f* gonio.
detention [dɪˈtenʃən] **1** *n* (*captivity*) *[criminal, spy]* détention *f*; (*Mil*) arrêts *mpl*; (*Scol*) retenue *f*, consigne *f*. **to give a pupil 2 hours' ~** donner à un élève 2 heures de retenue *or* de consigne; **preventive ~** *prolongation de détention pour récidiviste.*
2 *cpd*: (*Brit Jur*) **detention centre**, (*US*) **detention home** centre *m* de redressement.
deter [dɪˈtɜːʳ] *vt* (*prevent*) détourner (*from sth* de qch); dissuader, empêcher (*from doing* de faire); (*discourage*) décourager (*from doing* de faire). **I was ~red by the cost** le coût m'a fait reculer; **don't let the weather ~ you** ne vous laissez pas arrêter par le temps; **a weapon which ~s no one** une arme qui ne dissuade personne.
detergent [dɪˈtɜːdʒənt] *adj, n* détersif (*m*), détergent (*m*).
deteriorate [dɪˈtɪərɪəreɪt] **1** *vt material, machine* détériorer, abîmer.
2 *vi [material]* se détériorer, s'altérer, s'abîmer; *[species,*

morals] dégénérer; *[one's health, relationships, weather]* se détériorer; *[situation]* se dégrader. **his schoolwork is deteriorating** il y a un fléchissement dans son travail scolaire.
deterioration [dɪˌtɪərɪəˈreɪʃən] *n [goods, weather, friendship]* détérioration *f*; *[situation, relations]* dégradation *f*; *[species]* dégénération *f*; (*in morality*) dégénérescence *f*; (*in taste, art*) déchéance *f*, décadence *f*.
determinable [dɪˈtɜːmɪnəbl] *adj* **(a)** *quantity* déterminable. **(b)** (*Jur*) résoluble.
determinant [dɪˈtɜːmɪnənt] *adj, n* déterminant (*m*).
determination [dɪˌtɜːmɪˈneɪʃən] *n* (*U*) **(a)** (*firmness of purpose*) détermination *f*, résolution *f* (*to do* de faire). **an air of ~** un air résolu. **(b)** (*gen, Math etc*) détermination *f*; *[frontiers]* délimitation *f*.
determinative [dɪˈtɜːmɪnətɪv] **1** *adj* déterminant; (*Gram*) déterminatif. **2** *n* facteur déterminant; (*Gram*) déterminant *m*.
determine [dɪˈtɜːmɪn] *vt* **(a)** (*settle, fix*) *conditions, policy, date* fixer, déterminer; *price* fixer, régler; *frontier* délimiter; *cause, nature, meaning* déterminer, établir; *sb's character, future* décider de, déterminer; (*Jur*) *contract* résoudre.
(b) (*resolve*) décider (*to do* de faire), se déterminer, se résoudre (*to do* à faire); (*cause to decide*) *person* décider, amener (*to do* à faire).
determine (up)on *vt fus* décider de, résoudre de (*doing* faire); *course of action* se résoudre à; *alternative* choisir.
determined [dɪˈtɜːmɪnd] *adj* **(a)** *person, appearance* décidé, déterminé, résolu. **to be ~ to do** être déterminé *or* bien décidé à faire; **to be ~ that** être déterminé *or* décidé à ce que + *subj*; **he's a very ~ person** il est très décidé *or* volontaire *or* résolu, il a de la suite dans les idées.
(b) *quantity* déterminé, établi.
determiner [dɪˈtɜːmɪnəʳ] *n* (*Gram*) déterminant *m*.
determining [dɪˈtɜːmɪnɪŋ] *adj* déterminant.
determinism [dɪˈtɜːmɪnɪzəm] *n* déterminisme *m*.
determinist [dɪˈtɜːmɪnɪst] *adj, n* déterministe (*mf*).
deterrent [dɪˈterənt] **1** *n* (*also Mil*) force *f* de dissuasion. **to act as a ~** exercer un effet de dissuasion; *V* **nuclear, ultimate. 2** *adj* de dissuasion, préventif.
detest [dɪˈtest] *vt* détester, avoir horreur de, haïr. **to ~ doing** détester (de) *or* avoir horreur de faire; **I ~ that sort of thing!** j'ai horreur de ce genre de chose!
detestable [dɪˈtestəbl] *adj* détestable, odieux.
detestably [dɪˈtestəblɪ] *adv* détestablement, d'une manière détestable *or* odieuse.
detestation [ˌdiːtesˈteɪʃən] *n* **(a)** (*U*) haine *f*. **(b)** (*object of hatred*) abomination *f*, chose *f* détestable.
dethrone [diːˈθrəʊn] *vt* détrôner.
dethronement [diːˈθrəʊnmənt] *n* déposition *f* (*d'un souverain*).
detonate [ˈdetəneɪt] **1** *vi* détoner. **2** *vt* faire détoner *or* exploser.
detonation [ˌdetəˈneɪʃən] *n* détonation *f*, explosion *f*.
detonator [ˈdetəneɪtəʳ] *n* détonateur *m*, amorce *f*, capsule fulminante; (*Rail*) pétard *m*.
detour [ˈdiːˌtʊəʳ] **1** *n* (*in river, road; also fig*) détour *m*; (*for traffic*) déviation *f*. **2** *vi* faire un détour.
detract [dɪˈtrækt] *vi*: **to ~ from** *quality, merit* diminuer; *reputation* porter atteinte à; **it ~s from the pleasure of walking** cela diminue le plaisir de se promener.
detraction [dɪˈtrækʃən] *n* détraction *f*.
detractor [dɪˈtræktəʳ] *n* détracteur *m*, -trice *f*, critique *m*.
detrain [diːˈtreɪn] **1** *vt* débarquer (*d'un train*). **2** *vi [troops]* débarquer (*d'un train*); (*US*) *[passengers]* descendre (*d'un train*).
detriment [ˈdetrɪmənt] *n* détriment *m*, préjudice *m*, tort *m*. **to the ~ of** au détriment de, au préjudice de; **without ~ to** sans porter atteinte *or* préjudice à; **that is no ~ to ...** cela ne nuit en rien à ... .
detrimental [ˌdetrɪˈmentl] *adj* (*to health, reputation*) nuisible, préjudiciable, qui nuit (*to* à); (*to a case, a cause, one's interests*) qui nuit, qui fait tort, qui cause un préjudice (*to* à).
detritus [dɪˈtraɪtəs] *n* (*Geol*) roches *fpl* détritiques, pierraille *f*; (*fig*) détritus *m*.
deuce[1] [djuːs] *n* (*Cards*) deux *m*; (*Tennis*) égalité *f*. **to be at ~** être à égalité.
deuce[2]†* [djuːs] *n* diantre*† *m*; *for phrases V* **devil.**
deuced†* [ˈdjuːsɪd] **1** *adj* satané (*before n*), sacré* (*before n*). **2** *adv* diablement†. **what ~ bad weather!** quel sale temps!
deuterium [djuːˈtɪərɪəm] *n* deutérium *m*. **~ oxide** eau lourde.
devaluate [diːˈvæljʊeɪt] *vt* = **devalue.**
devaluation [ˌdɪvæljʊˈeɪʃən] *n* dévaluation *f*.
devalue [ˈdiːˈvæljuː] *vt* (*Fin, fig*) dévaluer.
devastate [ˈdevəsteɪt] *vt town, land* dévaster, ravager; *opponent, opposition* anéantir; (*fig*) *person* terrasser, foudroyer.
devastating [ˈdevəsteɪtɪŋ] *adj wind, storm, power, passion* dévastateur (*f* -trice), ravageur; *news, grief* accablant; *argument, reply, effect* accablant, écrasant; *wit, humour, charm, woman* irrésistible.
devastatingly [ˈdevəsteɪtɪŋlɪ] *adv beautiful, funny* irrésistiblement.
devastation [ˌdevəˈsteɪʃən] *n* dévastation *f*.
develop [dɪˈveləp] **1** *vt* **(a)** *mind, body* développer, former; (*Math, Phot*) développer; *argument, thesis* développer, exposer (en détail), expliquer (en détail); *business* développer; *region* exploiter, mettre en valeur; (*change and improve*) aménager (*as* en). **this ground is to be ~ed** on va construire *or* bâtir sur ce terrain.
(b) *habit, taste, cold* contracter. **to ~ a tendency to/a talent for** manifester une tendance à/du *or* un talent pour.
2 *vi [person, region]* se développer; *[illness, tendency, talent]* se manifester, se déclarer; *[feeling]* se former; (*Phot*) se développer; *[plot, story]* se développer; *[event, situation]* se produire. **to ~ into** devenir; **it later ~ed that he had never seen her** plus tard il est devenu évident qu'il ne l'avait jamais vue.
developer [dɪˈveləpəʳ] *n* (*Phot*) révélateur *m*; *V* **property.**
developing [dɪˈveləpɪŋ] **1** *adj crisis, storm* qui se prépare; *country* en voie de développement; *industry* en expansion.
2 *n* **(a)** = **development 1a.**
(b) (*Phot*) développement *m*. **'~ and printing'** 'développement et tirage', 'travaux photographiques'.
3 *cpd*: (*Phot*) **developing bath** (bain *m*) révélateur *m*; **developing tank** cuve *f* à développement.
development [dɪˈveləpmənt] **1** *n* **(a)** (*U*) *[person, mind, body]* développement *m*, formation *f*; (*Math, Mus, Phot*) développement; *[subject, theme]* développement, exposé *m*; *[ideas]* développement, évolution *f*, progrès *m*; *[plot, story]* déroulement *m*, développement; *[region]* exploitation *f*, aménagement *m* (*as* en), mise *f* en valeur; *[site]* mise en exploitation; *[industry]* développement, expansion *f*.
(b) (*change in situation*) fait nouveau. **to await ~s** attendre la suite des événements.
2 *cpd*: (*Brit*) **development area** zone *f* à urbaniser en priorité, Z.U.P. *f*; **development company** société *f* d'exploitation.
deviant [ˈdiːvɪənt] **1** *adj behaviour* qui s'écarte de la norme; *development* anormal; (*sexually*) perverti. **2** *n* déviant(e) *m(f)*.
deviate [ˈdiːvɪeɪt] *vi* **(a)** (*from truth, former statement etc*) dévier, s'écarter (*from* de). **to ~ from the norm** s'écarter de la norme. **(b)** *[ship, plane]* dévier, dériver; *[projectile]* dévier.
deviation [ˌdiːvɪˈeɪʃən] *n* **(a)** (*Math, Med, Philos: also from principle, custom*) déviation *f* (*from* de); (*from law, instructions*) dérogation *f* (*from* à); (*from social norm*) déviance *f* (*from* de). **there have been many ~s from the general rule** on s'est fréquemment écarté de la règle générale; **mean ~** écart *m* type; **standard ~** déviation standard.
(b) *[ship, plane]* déviation *f*, dérive *f*; *[projectile]* déviation, dérivation *f*.
deviationism [ˌdiːvɪˈeɪʃənɪzəm] *n* déviationnisme *m*.
deviationist [ˌdiːvɪˈeɪʃənɪst] *adj, n* déviationniste (*mf*).
device [dɪˈvaɪs] *n* **(a)** (*mechanical*) appareil *m*, engin *m*, mécanisme *m* (*for* pour). **a clever ~** une invention astucieuse; **nuclear ~** engin nucléaire; *V* **safety.**
(b) (*scheme, plan*) formule *f*, truc* *m* (*to do* pour faire), moyen *m* (*to do* de faire). **to leave sb to his own ~s** livrer qn à lui-même, laisser qn se débrouiller.
(c) (*Her*) devise *f*, emblème *m*.
devil [ˈdevl] **1** *n* **(a)** (*evil spirit*) diable *m*, démon *m*. **the D~** le Diable, Satan *m*.
(b) (*) **poor ~!** pauvre diable!; **he's a nice little ~** c'est un bon petit diable; **you little ~!** petit monstre, va!; (*hum*) **go on, be a ~!** fais donc une folie!, laisse-toi tenter!
(c) (*: *as intensifier: also* **deuce, dickens**) **it's the ~ of a job to do ...** c'est un travail épouvantable à faire ...; **he had the ~ of a job to find it** il a eu toutes les peines du monde *or* un mal fou à le trouver; **the ~ of a wind** un vent du diable *or* de tous les diables; **he lives the ~ of a long way away** il habite au diable*; **it's the very ~** *or* **it's the ~ of a job to get him to come** c'est toute une affaire *or* c'est le diable pour le faire venir; **why the ~ didn't you say so?** pourquoi diable ne l'as-tu pas dit?; **how the ~ would I know?** comment voulez-vous que je (le) sache?; **where the ~ is he?** où diable peut-il bien être?; **oh well what the ~!** oh tant pis!, oh qu'est-ce que ça peut bien faire!; **what the ~ are you doing?** mais enfin que diable fais-tu? *or* qu'est-ce que tu fabriques?* *or* qu'est-ce que tu fiches?*; **to work/run/shout** *etc* **like the ~** travailler/courir/crier *etc* comme un fou; **to be in a ~ of a mess** être dans de beaux draps, être dans un sacré pétrin*; (*fig*) **there will be the ~ to pay** cela va faire du grabuge*, ça va barder‡; **they were making the ~ of a noise** ils faisaient un chahut de tous les diables.
(d) (*phrases*) **between the ~ and the deep blue sea** entre Charybde et Scylla; (*Prov*) **the ~ finds work for idle hands** l'oisiveté est la mère de tous les vices (*Prov*); **it will play the ~ with all your plans*** cela va bousiller* *or* foutre en l'air‡ tous vos projets; **go to the ~!‡** va te faire voir!*, va te faire foutre!‡; **he is going to the ~*** il court à sa perte; **his work has gone to the ~** son travail ne vaut plus rien; **he has the ~ in him today** il a le diable au corps aujourd'hui; **speak** *or* **talk of the ~!** quand on parle du loup (on en voit la queue)!; **to be the ~'s advocate** se faire l'avocat du diable; **to give the ~ his due ...** pour être honnête il faut reconnaître que ...; **he has the luck of the ~*** *or* **the ~'s own luck*** il a une veine insolente *or* une veine de pendu* *or* une veine de cocu‡; (*Prov*) **better the ~ you know (than the ~ you don't)** il vaut mieux un danger qu'on connaît qu'un danger qu'on ne connaît pas.
(e) (*printer's ~*) apprenti imprimeur; (*hack writer*) nègre *m* (*d'un écrivain etc*); (*Jur*) ≃ avocat *m* stagiaire.
2 *vi*: **to ~ for sb** (*Literat etc*) servir de nègre à qn; (*Jur*) ≃ faire office d'avocat stagiaire auprès de qn.
3 *vt* (*Culin*) *kidneys* (faire) griller au poivre et à la moutarde.
4 *cpd*: **devilfish** (*ray*) raie géante; (*octopus*) pieuvre *f*; **devil-may-care** insouciant, je-m'en-foutiste‡.
devilish [ˈdevlɪʃ] **1** *adj* **(a)** *invention* diabolique, infernal. **(b)** (‡) satané (*before n*), maudit (*before n*), sacré* (*before n*), du diable. **2** *adv difficult, beautiful* rudement*, diablement. **it's ~ cold** il fait un froid du diable *or* de canard*.
devilishly [ˈdevlɪʃlɪ] *adv* **(a)** *behave* diaboliquement. **(b)** = **devilish.**
devilishness [ˈdevlɪʃnɪs] *n [invention]* caractère *m* diabolique; *[behaviour]* méchanceté *f* diabolique.
devilment [ˈdevlmənt] *n* (*U*) (*mischief*) diablerie *f*, espièglerie *f*; (*spite*) méchanceté *f*, malice *f*. **a piece of ~** une espièglerie; **out of sheer ~** par pure malice *or* méchanceté.
devilry [ˈdevlrɪ], (*US*) **deviltry** [ˈdevltrɪ] *n* (*daring*) (folle) té-

mérité *f*; (*mischief*) diablerie *f*, espièglerie *f*; (*black magic*) magie noire, maléfices *mpl*; (*wickedness*) malignité *f*, méchanceté *f* (diabolique).

devious [ˈdiːvɪəs] *adj route* détourné; *path, mind* tortueux; *means, method* détourné, tortueux; *character* dissimulé, sournois (*pej*). **he's very ~** il a l'esprit tortueux, il n'est pas franc.

deviously [ˈdiːvɪəslɪ] *adv act, behave* d'une façon détournée.

deviousness [ˈdiːvɪəsnɪs] *n [person]* sournoiserie *f*; *[scheme, method]* complexité(s) *f(pl)*.

devise [dɪˈvaɪz] **1** *vt scheme, style* imaginer, inventer, concevoir; *plot* tramer, ourdir; *escape* combiner, machiner; (*Jur*) léguer. **of his own devising** de son invention. **2** *n* (*Jur*) legs *m*, clause *f* (constituant un legs).

deviser [dɪˈvaɪzəʳ] *n [scheme, plan]* inventeur *m*, -trice *f*, auteur *m*.

devitalization [diːˌvaɪtəlaɪˈzeɪʃən] *n* affaiblissement *m*.

devitalize [diːˈvaɪtəlaɪz] *vt* affaiblir.

devoid [dɪˈvɔɪd] *adj*: **~ of ornament/imagination** *etc* dépourvu *or* dénué d'ornement/d'imagination *etc*, sans ornement/imagination *etc*; **~ of sense** dénué de (bon) sens; **~ of error/guilt** *etc* exempt d'erreur/de culpabilité *etc*.

devolution [ˌdiːvəˈluːʃən] *n [power, authority]* délégation *f*; (*Jur*) *[property]* transmission *f*, dévolution *f*; (*Pol etc*) décentralisation *f*; (*Bio*) dégénérescence *f*.

devolve [dɪˈvɒlv] **1** *vi* **(a)** *[duty]* incomber (*on, upon* à); (*by chance*) échoir (*on, upon* à), retomber (*on, upon* sur). **it ~s on you to take this step** c'est à vous qu'il incombe de faire cette démarche; **all the work ~s on me** tout le travail retombe sur moi.

(b) (*Jur*) *[property]* passer (*on, upon* à), être transmis (*on, upon* à).

2 *vt* déléguer, transmettre, remettre (*on, upon* à).

devote [dɪˈvəʊt] *vt time, life, book, magazine* consacrer (*to* à); *resources* affecter (*to* à), consacrer (*to* à), réserver (*to* pour). **to ~ o.s. to** *a cause* se vouer à, se consacrer à; *pleasure* se livrer à; *study, hobby* s'adonner à, se consacrer à, se livrer à; **the money ~d to education** l'argent consacré à *or* (*Admin*) les crédits affectés à l'éducation; **2 chapters ~d to his childhood** 2 chapitres consacrés à son enfance; (*Rad, TV*) **they ~d the whole programme to ...** ils ont consacré toute l'émission à ... .

devoted [dɪˈvəʊtɪd] *adj husband, friend* dévoué; *admirer* fervent; *service, friendship* loyal, fidèle, dévoué. **to be ~ to** être dévoué *or* très attaché à.

devotedly [dɪˈvəʊtɪdlɪ] *adv* avec dévouement.

devotee [ˌdevəʊˈtiː] *n [doctrine, theory]* partisan(e) *m(f)*; *[religion]* adepte *mf*; *[sport, music, poetry]* passionné(e) *m(f)*, fervent(e) *m(f)*.

devotion [dɪˈvəʊʃən] *n* **(a)** (*U*) (*to duty*) dévouement *m* (*to* à); (*to friend*) dévouement (*to* à, envers), (profond) attachement *m* (*to* pour); (*to work*) dévouement (*to* à), ardeur *f* (*to* pour, à); (*Rel*) dévotion *f*, piété *f*. **with great ~** avec un grand dévouement. **(b)** (*Rel*) **~s** dévotions *fpl*, prières *fpl*.

devotional [dɪˈvəʊʃənl] *adj book* de dévotion, de piété; *attitude* de prière, pieux.

devour [dɪˈvaʊəʳ] *vt* **(a)** *food* dévorer, engloutir; (*fig*) *money* engloutir, dévorer; *book* dévorer. **to ~ sb with one's eyes** dévorer qn des yeux. **(b)** *[fire]* dévorer, consumer. (*fig*) **~ed by jealousy** dévoré de jalousie.

devouring [dɪˈvaʊərɪŋ] *adj hunger, passion* dévorant; *zeal, enthusiasm* ardent.

devout [dɪˈvaʊt] *adj person* pieux, dévot; *prayer, attention, hope* fervent.

devoutly [dɪˈvaʊtlɪ] *adv pray* dévotement, avec dévotion; *hope* sincèrement, bien vivement.

dew [djuː] **1** *n* rosée *f*; *V* **mountain**. **2** *cpd*: **dew claw** ergot *m*; **dewdrop** goutte *f* de rosée; *[cow, person]* **dewlap** fanon *m*; **dewpoint** point *m* de saturation; **dewpond** mare artificielle (*alimentée par les eaux de condensation*).

dewy [ˈdjuːɪ] **1** *adj grass* couvert de *or* humide de rosée. (*liter*) **~ lips** lèvres fraîches. **2** *cpd*: **dewy-eyed** (*tearful*) le regard brillant de larmes; (*innocent*) aux grands yeux ingénus; **to be (all) dewy-eyed** faire l'ingénu(e).

dexterity [deksˈterɪtɪ] *n* **(a)** (*skill: physical, mental*) dextérité *f*, adresse *f*, habileté *f*. **~ in doing** habileté à faire, adresse avec laquelle on fait; **a feat of ~** un tour d'adresse. **(b)** (*right-handedness*) **his ~** le fait qu'il est droitier.

dexterous [ˈdekstrəs] *adj* **(a)** (*skilful*) *person* adroit, habile; *movement* adroit, agile. **by the ~ use of** par l'habile emploi de. **(b)** (*right-handed*) droitier.

dexterously [ˈdekstrəslɪ] *adv* adroitement, habilement, avec dextérité.

dextrin [ˈdekstrɪn] *n* dextrine *f*.

dextrose [ˈdekstrəʊs] *n* dextrose *m*.

dextrous(ly) [ˈdekstrəs(lɪ)] = **dexterous(ly)**.

di... [daɪ] *pref* di... .

diabetes [ˌdaɪəˈbiːtiːz] *n* diabète *m*.

diabetic [ˌdaɪəˈbetɪk] *adj, n* diabétique (*mf*).

diabolic(al) [ˌdaɪəˈbɒlɪk(əl)] *adj action, invention, plan, power* diabolique, infernal, satanique; *laugh, smile* satanique, diabolique; (*) *child* infernal*; (*) *weather* atroce*, épouvantable.

diabolically [ˌdaɪəˈbɒlɪkəlɪ] *adv* diaboliquement, d'une manière diabolique.

diachronic [ˌdaɪəˈkrɒnɪk] *adj* diachronique.

diacid [daɪˈæsɪd] *n* biacide *m*, diacide *m*.

diacritic [ˌdaɪəˈkrɪtɪk] *adj, n* diacritique (*m*).

diacritical [ˌdaɪəˈkrɪtɪkəl] *adj* diacritique.

diadem [ˈdaɪədem] *n* (*lit, fig*) diadème *m*.

diaeresis, (*US*) **dieresis** [daɪˈerɪsɪs] *n* (*Ling*) diérèse *f*; (*sign for this*) tréma *m*.

diagnose [ˈdaɪəgnəʊz] *vt* (*Med, fig*) diagnostiquer. **his illness was ~d as bronchitis** on a diagnostiqué une bronchite, on a diagnostiqué que c'était d'une bronchite qu'il souffrait.

diagnosis [ˌdaɪəgˈnəʊsɪs] *n, pl* **diagnoses** [ˌdaɪəgˈnəʊsiːz] (*Med, fig*) diagnostic *m*; (*Bio, Bot*) diagnose *f*.

diagnostic [ˌdaɪəgˈnɒstɪk] *adj* diagnostique.

diagonal [daɪˈægənl] **1** *adj* diagonal. **2** *n* diagonale *f*.

diagonally [daɪˈægənəlɪ] *adv cut, fold* en diagonale, obliquement, diagonalement. **the bank is ~ opposite the church** la banque est diagonalement opposée à l'église; **to cut ~ across a street** traverser une rue en diagonale; **the car was struck ~ by a lorry** la voiture a été prise en écharpe par un camion; **ribbon worn ~ across the chest** ruban porté en écharpe sur la poitrine.

diagram [ˈdaɪəgræm] *n* (*Math*) figure *f*; *[book, leaflet]* schéma *m*, diagramme *m*. **as shown in the ~** comme le montre le diagramme *or* le schéma.

diagrammatic [ˌdaɪəgrəˈmætɪk] *adj* schématique.

dial [ˈdaɪəl] **1** *n* cadran *m*; (*‡: face*) tronche‡ *f*; *V* **sun**.

2 *vt* (*Telec*) *number* faire, composer. **you must ~ 336-1295** il faut faire le 336-12-95; **to ~ 999** ≈ appeler Police Secours; **to ~ a wrong number** faire un faux *or* mauvais numéro; **to ~ direct** appeler par l'automatique; **can I ~ London from here?** est-ce que d'ici je peux avoir Londres par l'automatique?

3 *cpd*: (*US Telec*) **dial tone** tonalité *f*.

dialect [ˈdaɪəlekt] **1** *n* (*regional*) dialecte *m*, parler *m*; (*local, rural*) patois *m*. **the Norman ~** le dialecte normand, les parlers normands; **in ~** en dialecte, en patois.

2 *cpd word* dialectal. **dialect atlas** atlas *m* linguistique; **dialect survey** étude *f* de géographie linguistique *or* de dialectologie.

dialectal [ˌdaɪəˈlektl] *adj* dialectal, de dialecte.

dialectical [ˌdaɪəˈlektɪkəl] *adj* dialectique. **~ materialism** matérialisme *m* dialectique.

dialectician [ˌdaɪəlekˈtɪʃən] *n* dialecticien(ne) *m(f)*.

dialectic(s) [ˌdaɪəˈlektɪk(s)] *n* (*U*) dialectique *f*.

dialectology [ˌdaɪəlekˈtɒlədʒɪ] *n* (*U*) dialectologie *f*.

dialling [ˈdaɪəlɪŋ] (*Telec*) **1** *n* composition *f* d'un numéro (de téléphone). **2** *cpd*: **dialling code** indicatif *m*; (*Brit*) **dialling tone** tonalité *f*.

dialogue [ˈdaɪəlɒg] *n* dialogue *m*.

dialysis [daɪˈæləsɪs] *n* dialyse *f*.

diamagnetism [ˌdaɪəˈmægnɪtɪzəm] *n* diamagnétisme *m*.

diamanté [ˌdaɪəˈmæntɪ] *n* tissu diamanté.

diameter [daɪˈæmɪtəʳ] *n* diamètre *m*. **the circle is one metre in ~** le cercle a un mètre de diamètre.

diametrical [ˌdaɪəˈmetrɪkəl] *adj* (*Math, fig*) diamétral.

diametrically [ˌdaɪəˈmetrɪkəlɪ] *adv* (*Math, fig*) diamétralement.

diamond [ˈdaɪəmənd] **1** *n* (*stone*) diamant *m*; (*Cards*) carreau *m*; (*Baseball*) terrain *m* (de baseball); (*Math*) losange *m*; *V* **rough**; *for other phrases V* **club**.

2 *cpd clip, ring* de diamant(s). **diamond-cutting** taille *f* du diamant; **diamond drill** foreuse *f* à pointe de diamant; **diamond jubilee** (célébration *f* du) soixantième anniversaire *m* (*d'un événement*); **diamond merchant** diamantaire *m*; **diamond necklace** rivière *f* de diamants; **diamond-shaped** en losange(s), (taillé) en losange; **diamond wedding** noces *fpl* de diamant.

diapason [ˌdaɪəˈpeɪzən] *n* diapason *m*. *[organ]* **open/stopped ~** diapason large/étroit.

diaper [ˈdaɪəpəʳ] *n* (*US*) couche *f* (*de bébé*).

diaphanous [daɪˈæfənəs] *adj* (*lit, fig*) diaphane.

diaphoretic [ˌdaɪəfəˈretɪk] *adj, n* diaphorétique (*m*).

diaphragm [ˈdaɪəfræm] *n* (*all senses*) diaphragme *m*.

diarist [ˈdaɪərɪst] *n [personal events]* auteur *m* d'un journal intime; *[contemporary events]* mémorialiste *mf*, chroniqueur *m*.

diarrhoea, (*US*) **diarrhea** [ˌdaɪəˈriːə] *n* diarrhée *f*. **to have ~** avoir la diarrhée *or* la colique.

diary [ˈdaɪərɪ] *n* (*record of events*) journal *m* (intime); (*for engagements*) agenda *m*. **to keep a ~** tenir un journal; **I've got it in my ~** je l'ai noté sur mon agenda.

Diaspora [daɪˈæspərə] *n* Diaspora *f*.

diastole [daɪˈæstəlɪ] *n* diastole *f*.

diatonic [ˌdaɪəˈtɒnɪk] *adj* diatonique.

diatribe [ˈdaɪətraɪb] *n* diatribe *f* (*against* contre).

dibasic [ˌdaɪˈbeɪsɪk] *adj* dibasique.

dibber [ˈdɪbəʳ] *n* = **dibble 1.**

dibble [ˈdɪbl] **1** *n* plantoir *m*. **2** *vt* repiquer au plantoir.

dibs [dɪbz] *npl* (*game, knucklebones*) osselets *mpl*; (*Cards: counters*) jetons *mpl*; (*‡†: money*) fric‡ *m*.

dice [daɪs] **1** *n, pl inv* dé *m* (à jouer). **to play ~** jouer aux dés; *V* **load**. **2** *vi* jouer aux dés. (*fig*) **he was dicing with death** il jouait avec la mort. **3** *vt vegetables* couper en dés *or* en cubes.

dicey* [ˈdaɪsɪ] *adj* (*Brit*) risqué. **it's ~, it's a ~ business** c'est bien risqué.

dichotomy [dɪˈkɒtəmɪ] *n* dichotomie *f*.

dick‡ [dɪk] *n* (*detective*) flic* *m*; *V* **clever**.

Dick [dɪk] *n* (*dim of* **Richard**) Richard *m*.

dickens* [ˈdɪkɪnz] *n* (*euph for* **devil**) diantre *m*; *for phrases V* **devil**.

dicker [ˈdɪkəʳ] *vi* (*US*) marchander.

dickey, dicky[1] [ˈdɪkɪ] *n* **(a)** (*also* **~ bird**: *baby talk*) petit zoziau (*baby talk*). **(b)** (*also* **~ seat**) strapontin *m*; (*Brit Aut*) spider *m*. **(c)** (*) *[shirt]* faux plastron (*de chemise*).

dicky[2] [ˈdɪkɪ] *adj* (*Brit*) *person* patraque*, pas solide*; *health, heart* qui flanche*, pas solide*; *situation* pas sûr*, pas solide*.

dicta [ˈdɪktə] *npl of* **dictum**.

Dictaphone [ˈdɪktəfəʊn] *n* ® Dictaphone *m* ®. **~ typist** dactylo *f* (qui travaille au dictaphone).

dictate [dɪkˈteɪt] **1** *vt letter, passage* dicter (*to* à); *terms, condi-*

tions dicter, prescrire, imposer. **his action was ~d by circumstances** il a agi comme le lui dictaient les circonstances.

2 *vi* **(a)** dicter.

(b) to ~ to sb imposer sa volonté à qn, régenter qn; **I won't be ~d to** je n'ai pas d'ordres à recevoir; **I don't like to be ~d to** je n'aime pas qu'on me commande (*subj*).

3 [ˈdɪkteɪt] *n* (*gen pl*) **~s** ordre(s) *m(pl)*, précepte(s) *m(pl)* (*de la raison etc*); **the ~s of conscience** la voix de la conscience.

dictation [dɪkˈteɪʃən] *n* (*in school, office etc*) dictée *f*. **to write to sb's ~** écrire sous la dictée de qn; **at ~ speed** à une vitesse de dictée.

dictator [dɪkˈteɪtəʳ] *n* **(a)** (*fig, Pol*) dictateur *m*. **(b)** *[letter etc]* personne *f* qui dicte.

dictatorial [ˌdɪktəˈtɔːrɪəl] *adj* (*fig, Pol*) dictatorial.

dictatorially [ˌdɪktəˈtɔːrɪəlɪ] *adv* (*fig, Pol*) autoritairement, dictatorialement, en dictateur.

dictatorship [dɪkˈteɪtəʃɪp] *n* (*fig, Pol*) dictature *f*.

diction [ˈdɪkʃən] *n* **(a)** (*Literat*) style *m*, langage *m*. **poetic ~** langage poétique. **(b)** diction *f*, élocution *f*. **his ~ is very good** il a une très bonne diction *or* une élocution très nette.

dictionary [ˈdɪkʃənrɪ] *n* dictionnaire *m*; (*short, specialized*) lexique *m*. **to look up a word in a ~** chercher un mot dans un dictionnaire.

dictum [ˈdɪktəm] *n, pl* **dicta** (*maxim*) dicton *m*, maxime *f*; (*pronouncement*) proposition *f*, affirmation *f*; (*Jur*) remarque *f* superfétatoire.

did [dɪd] *pret of* **do**[1].

didactic [dɪˈdæktɪk] *adj* didactique.

didactically [dɪˈdæktɪkəlɪ] *adv* didactiquement.

diddle* [ˈdɪdl] *vt* rouler*, escroquer. **you've been ~d** tu t'es fait rouler* *or* avoir*; **to ~ sb out of sth, to ~ sth out of sb** soutirer *or* carotter* qch à qn.

diddler‡ [ˈdɪdləʳ] *n* carotteur* *m*, -euse* *f*, escroc *m*.

didn't [ˈdɪdənt] = **did not**; *V* **do**[1].

die[1] [daɪ] *vi* **(a)** *[person]* mourir (*of* de), décéder (*frm*), s'éteindre (*euph*); *[animal, plant]* mourir, crever; *[engine, motor]* caler, s'arrêter. **to be dying** être à l'agonie *or* à la mort, se mourir; **to ~ a natural/violent death** mourir de sa belle mort/de mort violente; **to ~ by one's own hand** se suicider, mettre fin à ses jours; (*fig*) **to ~ with one's boots on*** mourir debout *or* en pleine activité; **he ~d a hero** il est mort en héros; **they were dying like flies** ils mouraient *or* tombaient comme des mouches; **never say ~!** il ne faut jamais désespérer; **you only ~ once** on ne meurt qu'une fois; (*fig*) **I nearly ~d** (*from laughing*) j'ai failli mourir de rire; (*from fear*) j'ai failli mourir de peur; (*from embarrassment*) je voulais rentrer sous terre; **to ~ a thousand deaths** être au supplice, souffrir mille morts (*liter*); (*fig*) **to be dying to do*** mourir d'envie de faire; **I'm dying* for a cigarette** j'ai une envie folle d'une cigarette.

(b) *[fire, love, memory, daylight]* s'éteindre, mourir; *[custom]* mourir, disparaître. **the secret ~d with him** il a emporté le secret dans la tombe; **rumours/bad habits ~ hard** les bruits qui courent/les mauvaises habitudes ont la vie dure.

die away *vi [sound, voice]* s'éteindre, mourir, s'affaiblir.

die down *vi [plant]* se flétrir, perdre ses feuilles et sa tige; *[emotion, protest]* se calmer, s'apaiser; *[wind]* tomber, se calmer; *[fire]* (*in blazing building*) diminuer, s'apaiser; (*in grate etc*) baisser, tomber; *[noise]* diminuer.

die off *vi* mourir *or* être emportés les uns après les autres.

die out *vi [custom, race]* disparaître, s'éteindre; *[showers etc]* disparaître.

die[2] [daɪ] **1** *n* **(a)** (*pl* **dice** [daɪs]) dé *m* (à jouer). **the ~ is cast** le sort en est jeté, les dés sont jetés; *V* **dice.**

(b) (*pl* **~s**) (*in minting*) coin *m*; (*Tech*) matrice *f*. **stamping ~** étampe *f*.

2 *cpd*: **die-casting** moulage *m* en coquille; **die-sinker** graveur *m* de matrices; **die-stamp** graver; **die-stock** (*frame*) cage *f* (de filière à peignes); (*tool*) filière *f* à main.

diehard [ˈdaɪhɑːd] **1** *n* (*one who resists to the last*) jusqu'au-boutiste *mf*; (*opponent of change*) conservateur *m*, -trice *f* (à tout crin); (*obstinate politician etc*) dur(e) à cuire* *m(f)*. **2** *adj* intransigeant, inébranlable.

dielectric [ˌdaɪəˈlektrɪk] *adj, n* diélectrique (*m*).

dieresis [daɪˈerɪsɪs] *n* (*US*) = **diaeresis.**

diesel [ˈdiːzəl] **1** *n* diesel *m*. **2** *cpd*: **diesel-electric** diesel-électrique; **diesel engine** (*Aut*) moteur *m* diesel; (*Rail*) motrice *f*; **diesel fuel, diesel oil** gas-oil *m*; **diesel train** autorail *m*.

diet[1] [ˈdaɪət] **1** *n* **(a)** (*restricted food*) régime *m*; (*light*) diète *f*. **milk ~** régime lacté; **to be/go on a ~** être/se mettre au régime *or* à la diète.

(b) (*customary food*) alimentation *f*, nourriture *f*. **to live on a (constant) ~ of** vivre *or* se nourrir de.

2 *vi* suivre un régime *or* une diète.

3 *vt* mettre au régime *or* à la diète.

diet[2] [ˈdaɪət] *n* (*esp Pol*) diète *f*.

dietary [ˈdaɪətərɪ] **1** *adj* de régime, diététique. **2** *n* régime *m* alimentaire (*d'un hôpital, d'une prison etc*).

dietetic [ˌdaɪəˈtetɪk] *adj* diététique.

dietetics [ˌdaɪəˈtetɪks] *n* (*U*) diététique *f*.

dietician [ˌdaɪəˈtɪʃən] *n* spécialiste *mf* de diététique, diététicien(ne) *m(f)*.

differ [ˈdɪfəʳ] *vi* (*be different*) différer, être différent, se distinguer (*from* de); (*disagree*) ne pas être d'accord, ne pas s'entendre (*from sb* avec qn, *on or about sth* sur qch). **the two points of view do not ~ much** les deux points de vue ne se distinguent guère l'un de l'autre *or* ne sont pas très différents l'un de l'autre; **I beg to ~** permettez-moi de ne pas partager cette opinion *or* de ne pas être de votre avis; **the texts ~** les textes ne s'accordent pas.

difference [ˈdɪfrəns] *n* différence *f*; (*in ideas, character, nature*) différence, divergence *f* (*in* de, *between* entre); (*in age, height, value, weight etc*) écart *m*, différence (*in* de, *between* entre); (*between numbers, amounts*) différence. **that makes a big ~ to me** c'est très important pour moi, ça ne m'est pas du tout égal, cela compte beaucoup pour moi; **to make a ~ in sb/sth** changer qn/qch; **that makes all the ~** voilà qui change tout; **what ~ does it make if ...?** qu'est-ce que cela peut faire que ...? + *subj*, quelle importance cela a-t-il si ...? + *indic*; **it makes no ~** peu importe, cela ne change rien (à l'affaire); **it makes no ~ to me** cela m'est égal, ça ne (me) fait rien; **for all the ~ it makes** pour ce que cela change *or* peut changer; **with this ~ that** à la différence que, à ceci près que; **a car with a ~** une voiture pas comme les autres*; **~ of opinion** différence *or* divergence d'opinions; (*quarrel*) différend *m*; **to pay the ~** payer la différence; *V* **know, split.**

different [ˈdɪfrənt] *adj* **(a)** *book* différent, autre; *belief, opinion* différent, divergent (*from, to* de). **completely ~ (from)** totalement différent (de), tout autre (que); **he wore a ~ tie each day** il portait chaque jour une cravate différente; **go and put on a ~ tie** va mettre une autre cravate; **I feel a ~ person** je me sens tout autre; (*rested etc*) j'ai l'impression de faire peau neuve; **let's do something ~** faisons quelque chose de nouveau; **quite a ~ way of doing** une tout autre manière de faire; **that's quite a ~ matter** ça c'est une autre affaire, c'est tout autre chose; **she's quite ~ from what you think** elle n'est pas du tout ce que vous croyez; **he wants to be ~** il veut se singulariser.

(b) (*various*) différent, divers, plusieurs.

differential [ˌdɪfəˈrenʃəl] **1** *adj* différentiel. (*Math*) **~ calculus/operator** calcul/opérateur différentiel; **~ equation** équation différentielle; **~ gear** (engrenage *m*) différentiel *m*.

2 *n* (*Math*) différentielle *f*; (*Econ*) écarts salariaux; (*Aut*) différentiel *m*.

differentially [ˌdɪfəˈrenʃəlɪ] *adv* (*Tech*) par action différentielle.

differentiate [ˌdɪfəˈrenʃɪeɪt] **1** *vt* **(a)** (*be the difference between*) *two things* distinguer, faire la différence entre.

(b) (*make different, perceive as different*) différencier, distinguer (*one thing from another* une chose d'une autre).

(c) (*Math*) différentier, calculer la différentielle de.

2 *vi* se différencier, se distinguer (*from* de); différencier, distinguer (*between* entre); (*Bio*) se différencier. **to ~ between people** faire la différence entre les gens.

differentiation [ˌdɪfərenʃɪˈeɪʃən] *n* différenciation *f*.

differently [ˈdɪfrəntlɪ] *adv* différemment, d'une manière différente (*from* de), autrement (*from* que). **he thinks ~ from you** il n'est pas de votre avis.

difficult [ˈdɪfɪkəlt] *adj problem, undertaking* difficile, dur, ardu; *writer, music, book* difficile; *person, character* difficile, peu commode; *child* difficile. **~ to live with, ~ to get on with** difficile à vivre; **this work is ~ to do** ce travail est difficile à faire *or* est ardu; **it is ~ to know** il est difficile de savoir; **it's ~ to deny that ...** on ne peut guère *or* on ne saurait (*frm*) nier que ... + *indic or subj*; **it is ~ for me** *or* **I find it ~ to believe** il m'est difficile de croire, j'ai de la peine *or* du mal à croire; **there's nothing ~ about it** cela ne présente aucune difficulté; **the ~ thing is to begin** le (plus) difficile *or* dur c'est de commencer.

difficulty [ˈdɪfɪkəltɪ] *n* **(a)** (*U*) *[problem, undertaking, writing]* difficulté *f*. **with/without ~** avec/sans difficulté *or* peine; **she has ~ in walking** elle marche difficilement *or* avec difficulté, elle a de la difficulté *or* elle éprouve de la difficulté *or* elle a du mal à marcher; **a slight ~ in breathing** un peu de gêne dans la respiration; **there was some ~ in finding him** on a eu du mal à le rouver; **the ~ is in choosing** *or* **to choose** le difficile *or* la difficulté c'est de choisir.

(b) difficulté *f*, obstacle *m*. **to make difficulties for sb** créer des difficultés à qn; **without meeting any difficulties** sans rencontrer d'obstacles *or* la moindre difficulté, sans accrocs; **to get into ~** *or* **difficulties** se trouver en difficulté; **to get into all sorts of difficulties** se trouver plongé dans toutes sortes d'ennuis; **to get o.s. into ~** se créer des ennuis; **to get out of a ~** se tirer d'affaire *or* d'embarras; **I am in ~** j'ai des difficultés, j'ai des problèmes; **to be in (financial) difficulties** être dans l'embarras, avoir des ennuis d'argent; **he was in ~** *or* **difficulties over the rent** il était en difficulté pour son loyer; **he was working under great difficulties** il travaillait dans des conditions très difficiles; **I can see no ~ in what you suggest** je ne vois aucun obstacle à ce que vous suggérez; **he's having ~** *or* **difficulties with his wife/his car** il a des ennuis *or* des problèmes avec sa femme/sa voiture.

diffidence [ˈdɪfɪdəns] *n* manque *m* de confiance en soi, manque d'assurance, défiance *f* de soi.

diffident [ˈdɪfɪdənt] *adj person* qui se défie de soi, qui manque de confiance *or* d'assurance; *smile* embarrassé. **to be ~ about doing** hésiter à faire (par modestie *or* timidité).

diffidently [ˈdɪfɪdəntlɪ] *adv* avec (une certaine) timidité, de façon embarrassée.

diffract [dɪˈfrækt] *vt* diffracter.

diffraction [dɪˈfrækʃən] *n* diffraction *f*. **~ grating** réseau *m* de diffraction.

diffuse [dɪˈfjuːz] **1** *vt light, heat, perfume, news* diffuser, répandre. **~d lighting** éclairage diffus *or* indirect. **2** *vi* se diffuser, se répandre. **3** [dɪˈfjuːs] *adj light, thought* diffus; *style, writer* prolixe, diffus.

diffuseness [dɪˈfjuːsnɪs] *n* prolixité *f*, verbiage *m* (*pej*).

diffuser [dɪˈfjuːzəʳ] *n* (*for light*) diffuseur *m*.

diffusion [dɪˈfjuːʒən] *n* diffusion *f*.

dig [dɪg] (*vb: pret, ptp* **dug**) **1** *n* **(a)** (*with hand/elbow*) coup *m* de poing/de coude. **to give sb a ~ in the ribs** donner un coup de coude dans les côtes de qn, pousser qn du coude.

(b) (*: *sly remark*) coup *m* de patte. **to have a ~ at sb** donner un coup de patte *or* de griffe à qn; **that's a ~ at John** c'est une pierre dans le jardin de Jean.
(c) (*with spade*) coup *m* de bêche.
(d) (*Archeol*) fouille *f*. **to go on a ~** aller faire des fouilles.
2 *vt* **(a)** *ground* bêcher, creuser, retourner; *grave, trench, hole* creuser; *tunnel* creuser, percer, ouvrir. **to ~ potatoes** arracher des pommes de terre; **they dug their way out of prison** ils se sont évadés de prison en creusant un tunnel.
(b) (*thrust*) enfoncer (*sth into sth* qch dans qch). (*fig*) **to ~ sb in the ribs** donner un coup de coude dans les côtes de qn, pousser qn du coude.
(c) (‡) (*understand*) piger‡; (*take notice of*) viser‡. **~ that guy!** vise un peu le mec!‡; **I ~ that!** ça me botte!‡; **he really ~s jazz** il est vraiment fou de jazz; **I don't ~ football** le football ne me dit rien *or* me laisse froid.
3 *vi* **(a)** *[dog, pig]* fouiller, fouir; *[person]* creuser (*into* dans); (*Tech*) fouiller; (*Archeol*) faire des fouilles. **to ~ for minerals** (creuser pour) extraire du minerai; (*fig*) **to ~ in one's pockets for sth** fouiller dans ses poches pour trouver qch.
(b) (*Brit*‡: *lodge*) loger (en garni) (*with* chez).

dig in 1 *vi* **(a)** (*Mil*) se retrancher; (*fig*) tenir bon, se braquer, se buter (*pej*).
(b) (*: *eat*) attaquer* un repas (*or* un plat *etc*). **dig in!** allez-y, mangez!
2 *vt sep compost etc* enterrer; *blade, knife* enfoncer. **to dig in one's spurs** éperonner son cheval, enfoncer ses éperons; (*fig*) **to dig one's heels in** se braquer, se buter (*pej*).

dig into *vt fus sb's past* fouiller dans; (*) *cake, pie* dire deux mots à*, entamer sérieusement*.

dig out *vt sep tree, plant* déterrer; *animal* déterrer, déloger; (*fig*) *facts, information* déterrer, dénicher. **to dig sb out of the snow** sortir qn de la neige (à coup de pelles et de pioches); **where did he dig out that old hat?*** où a-t-il été pêcher *or* dénicher ce vieux chapeau?

dig up *vt sep weeds* arracher; *vegetables, treasure, body* déterrer; *earth* retourner; *garden* piocher; (*fig*) *fact, solution, idea* déterrer, dénicher.

digest [daɪˈdʒest] **1** *vt food, idea* digérer, assimiler; *insult* digérer*. **this kind of food is not easily ~ed** ce genre de nourriture se digère mal *or* est un peu lourd.
2 *vi* digérer.
3 [ˈdaɪdʒest] *n [book, facts]* sommaire *m*, abrégé *m*, résumé *m*; (*magazine*) digest *m*. **in ~ form** en abrégé; (*Jur*) **the D~** le Digeste (*de Justinien*).

digestible [dɪˈdʒestəbl] *adj* (*lit, fig*) facile à digérer *or* à assimiler, digeste.

digestion [dɪˈdʒestʃən] *n* (*Anat, Chem, fig*) digestion *f*.

digestive [dɪˈdʒestɪv] *adj* digestif. **~ system** système digestif; **~ tract** appareil digestif; (*Brit*) **~ (biscuit)** (sorte *f* de) sablé *m*; *V* **juice**.

digger [ˈdɪgəʳ] *n* (*machine*) excavateur *m*, -trice *f*, pelleteuse *f*; (*miner*) ouvrier mineur *m*; (*navvy*) terrassier *m*; (‡) Australien *m or* Néo-Zélandais *m*; *V* **gold**.

digging [ˈdɪgɪŋ] *n* **(a)** (*U*) (*with spade*) bêchage *m*; *[hole etc]* forage *m*; (*Min*) terrassement *m*, creusement *m*, excavation *f*.
(b) ~s (*Miner*) placer *m*; (*Archeol*) fouilles *fpl*.

digit [ˈdɪdʒɪt] *n* (*Math*) chiffre *m*; (*finger*) doigt *m*; (*toe*) orteil *m*; (*Astron*) doigt.

digital [ˈdɪdʒɪtəl] *adj* (*Anat etc*) digital; *clock, watch* à affichage numérique. **~ computer** calculateur *m* numérique.

digitalin [ˌdɪdʒɪˈteɪlɪn] *n* digitaline *f*.

digitalis [ˌdɪdʒɪˈteɪlɪs] *n* (*Bot*) digitale *f*; (*Pharm*) digitaline *f*.

dignified [ˈdɪgnɪfaɪd] *adj person, manner* plein de dignité, digne, grave; *pause, silence* digne. **a ~ old lady** une vieille dame très digne; **he is very ~** il a beaucoup de dignité; **it is not very ~ to do that** cela manque de dignité (de faire cela).

dignify [ˈdɪgnɪfaɪ] *vt* donner de la dignité à. **to ~ with the name of** honorer du nom de.

dignitary [ˈdɪgnɪtərɪ] *n* dignitaire *m*.

dignity [ˈdɪgnɪtɪ] *n* **(a)** (*U*) *[person, occasion, character, manner]* dignité *f*. **it would be beneath his ~ to do such a thing** faire une chose pareille serait au-dessous de lui *or* de sa dignité; *V* **stand**.
(b) (*high rank*) dignité *f*, haut rang, haute fonction; (*title*) titre *m*, dignité.

digress [daɪˈgres] *vi* s'écarter, s'éloigner (*from* de); faire une digression.

digression [daɪˈgreʃən] *n* digression *f*. **this by way of ~** ceci (soit) dit en passant.

digs* [dɪgz] *npl* (*esp Brit*) chambre meublée, logement *m* (*avec ou sans pension*), piaule‡ *f*. **I'm looking for ~** je cherche une chambre *or* une piaule‡ à louer; **to be in ~** avoir une chambre (chez un particulier).

dihedral [daɪˈhiːdrəl] *adj, n* dièdre (*m*).

dike [daɪk] *n* = **dyke.**

dilapidated [dɪˈlæpɪdeɪtɪd] *adj house* délabré; *clothes* dépenaillé*; *book* déchiré. **in a ~ state** dans un état de délabrement.

dilapidation [dɪˌlæpɪˈdeɪʃən] *n [buildings]* délabrement *m*, dégradation *f*; *[clothes]* état dépenaillé*; (*Jur: gen pl*) détérioration *f* (*causée par un locataire*); (*Geol*) dégradation.

dilate [daɪˈleɪt] **1** *vt* dilater. **2** *vi* **(a)** se dilater. **(b)** (*talk at length*) **to ~ (up)on sth** s'étendre sur qch, raconter qch en détail.

dilation [daɪˈleɪʃən] *n* dilatation *f*. (*Med*) **~ and curettage** dilatation et curetage.

dilatoriness [ˈdɪlətərɪnɪs] *n* lenteur *f* (*in doing* à faire), caractère *m* dilatoire.

dilatory [ˈdɪlətərɪ] *adj person* traînard, lent; *action, policy* dilatoire. **to be ~** faire traîner les choses (en longueur).

dilemma [daɪˈlemə] *n* dilemme *m*. **to be in a ~** *or* **on the horns of a ~** être pris dans un dilemme.

dilettante [ˌdɪlɪˈtæntɪ] *pl* **dilettanti** [ˌdɪlɪˈtæntɪ] **1** *n* dilettante *mf*. **2** *cpd* de dilettante.

dilettantism [ˌdɪlɪˈtæntɪzəm] *n* dilettantisme *m*.

diligence [ˈdɪlɪdʒəns] *n* soins assidus *or* attentifs, zèle *m*, assiduité *f*. **his ~ in trying to save the child** les efforts assidus qu'il a déployés *or* le zèle dont il a fait preuve en essayant de sauver l'enfant; **his ~ in his work** le zèle *or* l'assiduité qu'il apporte à son travail.

diligent [ˈdɪlɪdʒənt] *adj student, work* appliqué, assidu; *person, search* laborieux. **to be ~ in doing sth** mettre du zèle à faire qch, faire qch avec assiduité *or* zèle.

diligently [ˈdɪlɪdʒəntlɪ] *adv* avec soin *or* application *or* assiduité, assidûment.

dill [dɪl] *n* aneth *m*, fenouil bâtard.

dillydally [ˈdɪlɪdælɪ] *vi* (*dawdle*) lanterner, lambiner*; (*fritter time away*) musarder; (*vacillate*) tergiverser, atermoyer. **no ~ing!** ne traînez pas!

dillydallying [ˈdɪlɪdælɪɪŋ] *n* (*hesitating*) tergiversation(s) *f(pl)*.

dilute [daɪˈluːt] **1** *vt liquid* diluer, couper d'eau; *sauce* délayer, allonger; *colour* délayer; (*Pharm*) diluer; (*fig*) diluer, édulcorer. **'~ to taste'** 'à diluer selon votre goût'; (*Ind*) **to ~ the work force** adjoindre de la main-d'œuvre non qualifiée aux ouvriers spécialisés.
2 *adj liquid* coupé *or* étendu d'eau, dilué; (*fig*) dilué, édulcoré.

dilutee [ˌdaɪluːˈtiː] *n* (*Ind*) manœuvre affecté à un travail spécialisé.

diluter [daɪˈluːtəʳ] *n* diluant *m*.

dilution [daɪˈluːʃən] *n* dilution *f*; *[wine, milk]* coupage *m*, mouillage *m*; (*fig*) édulcoration *f*. (*Ind*) **~ of labour** adjonction *f* de main-d'œuvre non qualifiée.

dim [dɪm] **1** *adj light* faible, pâle; *lamp* faible; *room, forest etc* sombre; *sight* faible, trouble; *colour, metal* terne, mat (*f* mate), sans éclat; *sound* vague, indistinct; *memory, outline* vague, incertain, imprécis; (*Brit**: *stupid*) bouché*, borné. **~ shapes** formes indécises; **to have a ~ remembrance of** avoir un vague souvenir de; **to take a ~ view of sth*** voir qch d'un mauvais œil; **to take a ~ view of sb*** avoir une piètre opinion de qn; **she took a ~ view of his selling the car*** elle n'a pas du tout apprécié qu'il ait vendu la voiture; *V also* **4**.
2 *cpd*: (*US*) **dim-out** black-out partiel; **dim-sighted** à la vue basse; **dimwit‡** imbécile *mf*, crétin(e)* *m(f)*; **dim-witted** gourde*, idiot; **a dim-witted mechanic** un crétin* de mécanicien.
3 *vt light* réduire, baisser; *lamp* mettre en veilleuse; *sight* brouiller, troubler; *colours, metals, beauty* ternir, obscurcir; *sound* affaiblir; *memory, outline* effacer, estomper; *mind, senses* affaiblir, troubler; *glory* ternir. (*Theat*) **to ~ the lights** baisser les lumières; (*Aut*) **to ~ the headlights** se mettre en code.
4 *vi* (*also* **grow ~**) *[light]* baisser, décliner; *[sight]* baisser, se troubler; *[metal, beauty, glory]* se ternir; *[colours]* devenir terne; *[outlines, memory]* s'effacer, s'estomper.

dim out (*US*) **1** *vt sep city* plonger dans un black-out partiel.
2 dim-out *n V* **dim 2.**

dime [daɪm] (*Can, US*) **1** *n* (pièce *f* de) dix cents. **it's not worth a ~*** cela ne vaut pas un clou* *or* un radis*; (*fig*) **they're a ~ a dozen*** il y en a *or* on en trouve à la pelle. **2** *cpd*: **dime store** ≃ prisunic *m*.

dimension [daɪˈmenʃən] *n* (*size, extension in space: also Math*) dimension *f*; (*fig: scope, extent*) étendue *f*.

dimensional [daɪˈmenʃənl] *adj ending in cpds*: **two-dimensional** à deux dimensions; *V* **three** *etc.*

diminish [dɪˈmɪnɪʃ] **1** *vt cost, speed* réduire, diminuer; *effect, enthusiasm, strength* diminuer, amoindrir; *staff* réduire; (*Mus*) diminuer.
2 *vi* diminuer, se réduire, s'amoindrir. **to ~ in numbers** diminuer en nombre, devenir moins nombreux.

diminished [dɪˈmɪnɪʃt] *adj numbers, speed, strength* diminué, amoindri, réduit; *character, reputation* diminué, rabaissé; (*Mus*) diminué. **a ~ staff** un personnel réduit; (*Jur*) **~ responsibility** responsabilité atténuée.

diminishing [dɪˈmɪnɪʃɪŋ] **1** *adj amount, importance, speed* qui diminue, qui va en diminuant; *value, price* qui baisse, en baisse. (*Art*) **~ scale** échelle fuyante *or* de perspective; (*Econ*) **law of ~ returns** loi *f* du rendement non-proportionnel *or* des rendements décroissants.
2 *n* diminution *f*, affaiblissement *m*, atténuation *f*.

diminuendo [dɪˌmɪnjʊˈendəʊ] *adv, n* diminuendo (*m*).

diminution [ˌdɪmɪˈnjuːʃən] *n [value]* baisse *f*, diminution *f*; *[speed]* réduction *f*; *[strength, enthusiasm]* diminution, affaiblissement *m* (*in* de); *[temperature]* baisse, abaissement *m* (*in* de); *[authority]* baisse (*in* de); (*Mus*) diminution.

diminutive [dɪˈmɪnjʊtɪv] **1** *adj* **(a)** *person, object* tout petit, minuscule; *house, garden* tout petit, exigu (*f* -guë), minuscule. **(b)** (*Gram*) diminutif. **2** *n* diminutif *m*.

dimity [ˈdɪmɪtɪ] *n* basin *m*.

dimly [ˈdɪmlɪ] *adv shine* faiblement, sans éclat; *see* indistinctement, vaguement; *recollect* vaguement, imparfaitement. **~ lit room** pièce mal *or* faiblement éclairée.

dimmer [ˈdɪməʳ] *n* (*Elec*) interrupteur *m* à gradation de lumière, rhéostat *m*. (*US Aut*) **~s** phares *mpl* code *inv*; (*parking lights*) feux *mpl* de position.

dimming [ˈdɪmɪŋ] *n [light]* affaiblissement *m*, atténuation *f*; *[mirror, reputation]* ternissement *m*; *[headlights]* mise *f* en code.

dimness [ˈdɪmnɪs] *n [light, sight]* faiblesse *f*; *[room, forest]* obscurité *f*; *[outline, memory]* imprécision *f*, vague *m*; *[colour,* *metal]* aspect *m* terne; *[intelligence]* faiblesse *f*, manque *m* de clarté; (*: *stupidity*) intelligence bornée.

dimorphism [ˌdaɪˈmɔːfɪzəm] *n* dimorphisme *m*.

dimple [ˈdɪmpl] **1** *n [chin, cheek]* fossette *f* (*on* à); *[water]* ride *f*. **2** *vi [cheeks]* former des fossettes; *[water]* se rider. **she ~d** un petit sourire creusa deux fossettes dans ses joues. **3** *vt*: **the wind ~d the water** le vent ridait la surface de l'eau.

dimpled [ˈdɪmpld] *adj cheek, chin* à fossettes; *hand, arm* potelé; *water* (doucement) ridé.

din [dɪn] **1** *n* (*from people*) vacarme *m*, tapage *m*; (*from factory, traffic*) vacarme; (*esp in classroom*) chahut *m*. **the ~ of battle** le fracas de la bataille; **to make** *or* **kick up* a ~** faire un boucan monstre*; (*esp Scol*) chahuter, faire un chahut monstre.

2 *vt*: **to ~ cleanliness into sb** dresser qn à être propre; **she ~ned into the child that he mustn't speak to strangers** elle ne cessait de dire et de répéter à l'enfant de ne pas parler à des inconnus; **try to ~ it into her that ...** essayez de lui faire entrer dans la tête le fait que ... .

dine [daɪn] **1** *vi* dîner (*off, on* de). **to ~ out** dîner en ville *or* dehors. **2** *vt* offrir à dîner à; *V* **wine.**

diner [ˈdaɪnəʳ] *n* **(a)** (*person*) dîneur *m*, -euse *f*. **(b)** (*Rail*) wagon-restaurant *m*. **(c)** (*US*) petit restaurant.

dinette [daɪˈnet] *n* coin-repas *m*; *V* **kitchen.**

ding-a-ling [ˈdɪŋəˈlɪŋ] = **ting-a-ling** *V* **ting.**

ding-dong [ˈdɪŋˈdɒŋ] **1** *n* ding dong *m*. **2** *adj* (*) *fight* acharné, dans les règles (*fig*). **3** *adv* ding dong.

dinghy [ˈdɪŋgɪ] *n* youyou *m*, petit canot; (*collapsible*) canot pneumatique; (*also* **sailing ~**) dériveur *m*.

dinginess [ˈdɪndʒɪnɪs] *n* aspect minable* *or* miteux.

dingo [ˈdɪŋgəʊ] *n* dingo *m*.

dingy [ˈdɪndʒɪ] *adj* minable*, miteux.

dining car [ˈdaɪnɪŋkɑːʳ] *n* (*Rail*) wagon-restaurant *m*.

dining hall [ˈdaɪnɪŋhɔːl] *n* réfectoire *m*, salle *f* à manger.

dining room [ˈdaɪnɪŋrʊm] **1** *n* salle *f* à manger. **2** *cpd table, chairs* de salle à manger. **dining room suite** salle *f* à manger (*meubles*).

dinky* [ˈdɪŋkɪ] *adj* (*Brit*) mignon, gentil.

dinner [ˈdɪnəʳ] **1** *n* (*meal; occasion*) dîner *m*; (*regional use: lunch*) déjeuner *m*; (*for dog, cat*) pâtée *f*. **have you given the dog his ~?** tu as donné à manger au chien?; **he was at ~, he was having his ~** il était en train de dîner; **we're having people to ~** nous avons du monde à dîner; **~'s ready!** le dîner est prêt!, à table!; **we had a good ~** nous avons bien dîné *or* mangé; **to go out to ~** (*in restaurant*) dîner dehors *or* en ville; (*at friends*) dîner chez des amis; **to give a (public) ~ in sb's honour** donner un banquet en l'honneur de qn; **a formal ~** un dîner officiel, un grand dîner.

2 *cpd*: **the dinner bell has gone** on a sonné (pour) le dîner; **dinner dance** dîner-dansant *m*; (*Scol*) **dinner duty** service *m* de réfectoire; (*Scol*) **to do dinner duty, to be on dinner duty** être de service *or* de surveillance au réfectoire; (*Brit*) **dinner jacket** smoking *m*; **dinner knife** grand couteau; **dinner party** dîner *m* (*par invitation*); **to give a dinner party** avoir du monde à dîner, donner un dîner; **dinner plate** (grande) assiette *f*; **dinner roll** petit pain; **dinner service** service *m* de table; **at the dinner table** pendant le dîner, au dîner, à table; **at dinner time** à l'heure du dîner; **it's dinner time** c'est l'heure du *or* de dîner; **dinner trolley, dinner wagon** table roulante; (*US*) **dinnerware** vaisselle *f*.

dinosaur [ˈdaɪnəsɔːʳ] *n* dinosaure *m*.

dint [dɪnt] **1** *n* **(a)** = **dent 1.** **(b)** **by ~ of (doing) sth** à force de (faire) qch. **2** *vt* = **dent 2.**

diocesan [daɪˈɒsɪsən] **1** *adj* diocésain. **2** *n* (évêque *m*) diocésain *m*.

diocese [ˈdaɪəsɪs] *n* diocèse *m*.

diode [ˈdaɪəʊd] *n* diode *f*.

diopter [daɪˈɒptəʳ] *n* dioptrie *f*.

diorama [daɪəˈrɑːmə] *n* diorama *m*.

dioxide [daɪˈɒksaɪd] *n* bioxyde *m*, déoxyde *m*.

dip [dɪp] **1** *vt* **(a)** (*into liquid*) *pen, hand, clothes* tremper, plonger (*into* dans); (*Tech*) tremper, décaper; *sheep* laver. **she ~ped her hand into the bag** elle a plongé la main dans le sac; **to ~ a spoon into a bowl** plonger une cuiller dans un bol; **to ~ water from a lake** puiser de l'eau dans un lac.

(b) (*Brit Aut*) **to ~ the headlights** se mettre en code; (*Naut*) **to ~ one's flag** saluer avec le pavillon.

2 *vi* **(a)** *[ground]* descendre, s'incliner; *[temperature, pointer on scale etc]* baisser; *[prices]* fléchir, baisser; *[sun]* baisser, descendre à l'horizon; *[boat, raft]* tanguer, piquer du nez*.

(b) puiser. **she ~ped into her handbag for money** elle a cherché de l'argent dans son sac à main; (*lit, fig*) **to ~ into one's pockets** puiser dans ses poches; **to ~ into one's savings** puiser dans ses économies; **to ~ into a book** feuilleter un livre.

3 *n* **(a)** (*: *in sea etc*) baignade *f*, bain *m* (*de mer etc*). **to have a (quick) ~** prendre un bain rapide (*en mer etc*), faire trempette (*hum*).

(b) (*for cleaning animals*) bain *m* parasiticide.

(c) (*in ground*) déclivité *f*; (*Geol*) pendage *m*; (*Phys: also* **angle of ~**) inclinaison *f* magnétique.

(d) (*Culin*) (*cheese: hot*) fondue savoyarde *or* au fromage; (*cheese: cold*) hors d'œuvre *m* au fromage (*que l'on mange sur des biscuits salés, des chips etc*); (*anchovy/shrimp etc*) mousse *f* aux anchois/aux crevettes *etc*.

(e) *V* **lucky.**

4 *cpd*: **dip needle, dipping needle** aiguille aimantée (de boussole); (*Aut*) **dipstick,** (*US*) **diprod** jauge *f* (*de niveau d'huile*).

diphtheria [dɪfˈθɪərɪə] *n* diphtérie *f*.

diphthong [ˈdɪfθɒŋ] *n* diphtongue *f*.

diphthongize [ˈdɪfθɒŋaɪz] **1** *vt* diphtonguer. **2** *vi* se diphtonguer.

diploid [ˈdɪplɔɪd] *adj* diploïde.

diploma [dɪˈpləʊmə] *n* diplôme *m*. **teacher's/nurse's ~** diplôme d'enseignement/d'infirmière; **to hold** *or* **have a ~ in** être diplômé de *or* en.

diplomacy [dɪˈpləʊməsɪ] *n* (*Pol, fig*) diplomatie *f*. (*fig*) **to use ~** user de diplomatie.

diplomat [ˈdɪpləmæt] *n* (*Pol*) diplomate *m*, femme *f* diplomate; (*fig*) diplomate *mf*.

diplomatic [ˌdɪpləˈmætɪk] *adj* **(a)** *mission, relations* diplomatique. **~ bag,** (*US*) **~ pouch** valise *f* diplomatique; **~ corps** corps *m* diplomatique; **~ immunity** immunité *f* diplomatique; **~ service** diplomatie *f*, service *m* diplomatique.

(b) (*fig: tactful*) *person* diplomate; *action, behaviour* diplomatique, plein de tact; *answer* diplomatique, habile. **to be ~ in dealing with sth** s'occuper de qch avec tact *or* en usant de diplomatie.

diplomatically [ˌdɪpləˈmætɪkəlɪ] *adv* (*Pol*) diplomatiquement; (*fig*) diplomatiquement, avec diplomatie.

diplomatist [dɪˈpləʊmətɪst] *n* = **diplomat.**

dipole [ˈdaɪˌpəʊl] *n* dipôle *m*.

dipper [ˈdɪpəʳ] *n* (*ladle*) louche *f*; *[mechanical shovel]* godet *m* (de pelleteuse); (*for river, sea*) benne *f* (de drague), hotte *f* à draguer; (*at fairground*) montagnes *fpl* russes; (*Aut: for headlamps*) basculeur *m* (de phares); (*Orn*) merle *m* d'eau, cincle *m* (plongeur). (*US Astron*) **the Big** *or* **Great D~** la Grande Ourse; **the Little D~** la Petite Ourse.

dippy‡ [ˈdɪpɪ] *adj* toqué*.

dipso‡ [ˈdɪpsəʊ] *n* (*abbr of* **dipsomaniac**) soûlard(e)‡ *m(f)*.

dipsomania [ˌdɪpsəʊˈmeɪnɪə] *n* (*Med*) dipsomanie *f*, alcoolisme *m*.

dipsomaniac [ˌdɪpsəʊˈmeɪnɪæk] *n* (*Med*) dipsomane *mf*, alcoolique *mf*.

diptera [ˈdɪptərə] *npl* diptères *mpl*.

dipterous [ˈdɪptərəs] *adj* diptère.

dire [daɪəʳ] *adj event* terrible, affreux; *poverty* extrême, noir; *prediction* sinistre. **~ necessity** dure nécessité; **they are in ~ need of food** ils ont un besoin urgent *or* extrême de nourriture; **in ~ straits** dans une situation désespérée.

direct [daɪˈrekt] **1** *adj link, road, responsibility, attack, reference, train* direct; *cause, result* direct, immédiat; *refusal, denial* direct, catégorique, absolu; *danger* immédiat, imminent; *person, character, question, answer* franc (*f* franche), direct. (*Computers*) **~ access** accès direct; (*Ind etc*) **~ action** action directe; **to be a ~ descendant of sb** descendre de qn en ligne directe; (*Elec*) **~ current** courant continu; (*Comm*) **~ debit** prélèvement *m*; (*Brit*) **~ grant school** lycée *m* privé (subventionné); **keep away from ~ heat** éviter l'exposition directe à la chaleur; **~ heating** chauffage direct; (*Mil*) **~ hit** coup *m* au but; **to make a ~ hit** porter un coup au but, frapper de plein fouet; *[bomb, projectile]* toucher *or* atteindre son objectif; **~-mail advertising** publicité *f* par courrier individuel; **~ method of teaching a language** méthode directe pour l'enseignement d'une langue; (*Astron*) **~ motion** mouvement direct; (*Gram*) **~ object** complément (d'objet) direct; (*Gram*) **~ speech,** (*US*) **~ discourse** discours *or* style direct; **~ tax** impôt direct.

2 *vt* **(a)** (*address, aim, turn*) *remark, letter* adresser (*to* à); *torch* diriger (*on* sur); *efforts* orienter (*towards* vers). **to ~ one's steps to(wards)** diriger ses pas *or* se diriger vers; **to ~ sb's attention to** attirer *or* appeler l'attention de qn sur; **can you ~ me to the town hall?** pourriez-vous m'indiquer le chemin de la mairie?

(b) (*control*) *sb's work* diriger; *conduct* diriger, gouverner; *business* diriger, gérer, administrer; *movements* guider; (*Theat*) *play* mettre en scène; (*Cine, Rad, TV*) *film, programme* réaliser; *group of actors* diriger.

(c) (*instruct*) charger (*sb to do* qn de faire); ordonner (*sb to do* à qn de faire). (*Jur*) **the judge ~ed the jury to find the accused not guilty** le juge imposa au jury un verdict de non-coupable; **he did it as ~ed** il l'a fait comme on le lui avait dit *or* comme on l'en avait chargé; (*Med*) **'as ~ed'** 'suivre les indications du médecin'.

3 *adv go, write* directement.

direction [dɪˈrekʃən] **1** *n* **(a)** (*way*) direction *f*, sens *m*; (*fig*) direction, voie *f*. **in every ~** dans toutes les directions, en tous sens; **in the wrong/right ~** (*lit*) dans le mauvais/bon sens, dans la mauvaise/bonne direction; (*fig*) sur la mauvaise/bonne voie; (*fig*) **it's a step in the right ~** voilà un pas dans la bonne direction; **in the opposite ~** en sens inverse; **in the ~ of** dans la direction de, en direction de; **what ~ did he go in?** quelle direction a-t-il prise?; **a sense of ~** le sens de l'orientation.

(b) (*management*) direction *f*, administration *f*. **under the ~ of** sous la direction de, sous la conduite de.

(c) (*Theat*) mise *f* en scène; (*Cine, Rad, TV*) réalisation *f*. **'under the ~ of'** (*Theat*) 'mise en scène de'; (*Cine, Rad, TV*) 'réalisation de'.

(d) (*instruction*) ordre *m*, indication *f*, instruction *f*. (*Comm*) **~s for use** mode *m* d'emploi; (*Theat*) **stage ~s** indications scéniques.

2 *cpd*: **direction finder** radiogoniomètre *m*; (*Aut*) **direction indicator** clignotant *m*.

directional [dɪˈrekʃənl] *adj* directionel. **~ antenna** antenne directionnelle.

directive [dɪˈrektɪv] *n* directive *f*, instruction *f*.

directly [dɪˈrektlɪ] **1** *adv* **(a)** (*without deviating*) directement, tout droit. **to be ~ descended from** descendre en droite ligne *or* en ligne directe de; **he's not ~ involved** cela ne le concerne pas directement, il n'est pas directement en cause.

(b) (*frankly*) *speak* sans détours, sans ambages, franchement. **to come ~ to the point** aller droit au fait.

(c) (*completely*) *opposite* exactement; *opposed* diamétralement, directement. ~ **contrary to** diamétralement opposé à, exactement contraire à.

(d) (*immediately*) tout de suite, sur-le-champ, immédiatement.

2 *conj* (*esp Brit*) aussitôt que, dès que. **he'll come ~ he's ready** il viendra dès qu'il sera prêt.

directness [daɪˈrektnɪs] *n* [*character, reply*] franchise *f*; [*remarks*] absence *f* d'ambiguïté; [*person*] franchise, francparler *m*; [*attack*] caractère direct. **to speak with great** ~ parler en toute franchise.

director [dɪˈrektəʳ] *n* **(a)** (*person*) [*company*] directeur *m*, -trice *f*, administrateur *m*, -trice *f*; [*institution*] directeur, -trice; (*Theat*) metteur *m* en scène; (*Cine, Rad, TV*) réalisateur *m*, -trice *f*; (*Rel*) directeur de conscience. ~ **general** directeur général; (*Mil*) ~ **of music** chef *m* de musique; (*Brit Jur*) **D~ of Public Prosecutions** ≃ procureur général; (*Univ*) ~ **of studies** (*for course*) directeur, -trice d'études *or* de travaux; (*for thesis*) directeur, -trice *or* patron(ne) *m(f)* de thèse; *V* **board, managing, stage** *etc*.

(b) (*device*) guide *m*.

directorate [daɪˈrektərɪt] *n* (*board of directors*) conseil *m* d'administration.

directorship [dɪˈrektəʃɪp] *n* poste *m or* fonctions *fpl* de directeur *or* d'administrateur, direction *f*.

directory [dɪˈrektərɪ] **1** *n* **(a)** [*addresses*] répertoire *m* (d'adresses); (*also* **street** ~) guide *m* des rues; (*Telec*) annuaire *m* (des téléphones); (*Comm*) annuaire du commerce.

(b) (*Hist*) **D~** Directoire *m*.

2 *adj* (*Brit Telec*) ~ **inquiries** (service *m* des) renseignements *mpl*.

directrix [daɪˈrektrɪks] *n* (*Math*) (ligne *f*) directrice *f*.

dirge [dɜːdʒ] *n* (*lit*) hymne *m or* chant *m* funèbre; (*fig*) chant lugubre.

dirigible [ˈdɪrɪdʒəbl] *adj, n* dirigeable (*m*).

dirk [dɜːk] *n* (*Scot*) dague *f*, poignard *m*.

dirt [dɜːt] **1** *n* **(a)** (*on skin, clothes, objects*) saleté *f*, crasse *f*; (*earth*) terre *f*; (*mud*) boue *f*; (*excrement*) crotte *f*, ordure *f*. **covered with** ~ (*gen*) couvert de crasse; *clothes, shoes, mudguards* couvert de boue, tout crotté; *cog, stylus* encrassé; **a layer of** ~ une couche de saleté *or* de crasse; **dog** ~ crotte de chien; **horse** ~ crottin *m* de cheval; **cow** ~ bouse *f* de vache; (*fig*) **to eat** ~* faire ses excuses les plus plates, ramper; **to treat sb like** ~* traiter qn comme un chien.

(b) (*fig*) (*obscenity*) obscénité *f*; (*: *scandal*) cancans *mpl*, ragots *mpl*, calomnies *fpl*. (*fig*) **to spread the** ~* **about sb** cancaner sur qn, calomnier qn; **what's the** ~ **on ...?*** qu'est-ce qu'on raconte sur ...?

(c) (*Ind*) impuretés *fpl*, corps étrangers; (*on machine, in engine*) encrassement *m*.

2 *cpd*: **dirt-cheap*** (*adv*) pour rien, pour une bouchée de pain; (*adj*) très bon marché *inv*; **it was dirt-cheap*** c'était donné, c'était pour (presque) rien; **dirt road** chemin non macadamisé; **dirt track** (*gen*) piste *f*; (*Sport*) cendrée *f*; **dirt track racing** courses *fpl* motocyclistes *or* de motos sur cendrée.

dirtily [ˈdɜːtɪlɪ] *adv eat, live* salement, malproprement; (*fig*) *act, behave* bassement.

dirty [ˈdɜːtɪ] **1** *adj* **(a)** *hands, clothes, house, person, animal* sale, malpropre, crasseux; *shoes* sale, (*mucky*) couvert de boue, crotté; *job* salissant; *machine, plug* encrassé; *cut, wound* infecté; *bomb* sale; *colour* sale, terne. **to get** ~ se salir; **to get sth** ~ salir qch; **that coat gets** ~ **very easily** ce manteau est très salissant.

(b) (*fig: lewd*) grossier, sale, cochon*. **to have a** ~ **mind** avoir l'esprit mal tourné; ~ **old man** vieux cochon*; ~ **remarks** propos orduriers; ~ **story** histoire sale *or* cochonne* *or* graveleuse; ~ **word** mot grossier, terme offensant; **'communist' is a** ~ **word* there** le mot 'communiste' est une insulte là-bas; **'smoking' is a** ~ **word* these days** c'est très mal vu de fumer de nos jours; **'work' is a** ~ **word*** ils ne veulent pas entendre de parler de travail.

(c) (*unpleasant*) sale (*before n*). **that was a** ~ **business** c'était une sale affaire *or* histoire; **politics is a** ~ **business** la politique est un sale métier; ~ **crack!*** vacherie!‡; **he's a** ~ **fighter** il se bat en traître; **to give sb a** ~ **look** regarder qn d'un sale œil; ~ **money** argent mal acquis; **he's a** ~ **rat*** c'est un sale type* *or* un salaud‡; **to play a** ~ **trick on sb** jouer un sale tour *or* un tour de cochon* à qn; ~ **weather** sale *or* vilain temps; **he left the** ~ **work for me to do** il m'a laissé le plus embêtant du boulot* à faire.

2 *adv* (*) *play, fight* déloyalement.

3 *vt hands, clothes* salir; *reputation* salir, souiller (*liter*); *machine* encrasser.

4 *n* (*Brit*) **to do the** ~ **on sb‡** faire une vacherie‡ *or* une saloperie‡ à qn, jouer un tour de cochon* à qn.

5 *cpd*: **dirty-faced** à *or* qui a la figure sale; **dirty-minded** à *or* qui a l'esprit mal tourné.

disability [ˌdɪsəˈbɪlɪtɪ] **1** *n* **(a)** (*U*) (*physical*) invalidité *f*, incapacité *f*; (*mental*) incapacité. ~ **for work** incapacité de travail; **complete/partial** ~ incapacité totale/partielle.

(b) (*infirmity*) infirmité *f*; (*handicap*) désavantage *m*, handicap *m*. **the disabilities of old age** les infirmités de la vieillesse; **this** ~ **made him eligible for a pension** cette infirmité lui donnait droit à une pension, étant infirme *or* invalide il avait droit à une pension; **to be under a** ~ être dans une position désavantageuse, avoir un handicap.

2 *cpd*: **disability pension** pension *f* d'invalidité.

disable [dɪsˈeɪbl] *vt* [*illness, accident, injury*] rendre infirme, (*stronger*) rendre impotent; (*maim*) estropier, mutiler; *tank, gun* mettre hors d'action; *ship* (*gen*) avarier, mettre hors d'état; (*by enemy action*) mettre hors de combat, désemparer; (*Jur: disqualify*) rendre (*or* prononcer) inhabile (*from doing* à faire).

disabled [dɪsˈeɪbld] **1** *adj* **(a)** (*permanently*) infirme, handicapé; (*esp Admin: unable to work*) invalide; (*maimed*) estropié, mutilé; (*through illness, old age*) impotent; (*Mil*) mis hors de combat. ~ **ex-servicemen** mutilés *mpl or* invalides *mpl* de guerre.

(b) (*Naut*) [*ship*] **to be** ~ avoir des avaries, être avarié *or* désemparé; [*propeller*] être immobilisé.

(c) (*Jur*) incapable (*from* de), inhabile (*from* à).

2 *n*: **the** ~ les infirmes *mpl*, les handicapés *mpl*, les invalides *mpl*; **the war** ~ les mutilés *mpl or* les invalides de guerre.

disablement [dɪsˈeɪblmənt] *n* infirmité *f*. ~ **insurance** assurance *f* invalidité; ~ **pension** pension *f* d'invalidité.

disabuse [ˌdɪsəˈbjuːz] *vt* détromper, désenchanter (*of* de).

disadvantage [ˌdɪsədˈvɑːntɪdʒ] **1** *n* **(a)** (*U*) désavantage *m*, inconvénient *m*. **to be at a** ~ être dans une position désavantageuse; **you've got me at a** ~ vous avez l'avantage sur moi; **to catch sb at a** ~ prendre qn en position de faiblesse.

(b) (*prejudice, injury*) préjudice *m*, désavantage *m*; (*Comm*) perte *f*. **it would be to your** ~ **to be seen with him** cela vous porterait préjudice *or* vous ferait du tort qu'on vous voie avec lui; **to sell at a** ~ vendre à perte.

2 *vt* désavantager, défavoriser.

disadvantageous [ˌdɪsædvɑːnˈteɪdʒəs] *adj* désavantageux, défavorable (*to* à).

disadvantageously [ˌdɪsædvɑːnˈteɪdʒəslɪ] *adv* d'une manière désavantageuse, désavantageusement.

disaffected [ˌdɪsəˈfektɪd] *adj* (*discontented*) mécontent, mal disposé; (*disloyal*) rebelle.

disaffection [ˌdɪsəˈfekʃən] *n* désaffection *f* (*from* pour), mécontentement *m* (*from* envers).

disagree [ˌdɪsəˈgriː] *vi* **(a)** se trouver *or* être en désaccord (*with* avec), ne pas être d'accord (*with* avec), ne pas être du même avis (*with* que). **I** ~ je ne suis pas de cet avis, je ne suis pas d'accord; **I** ~ **completely with you** je ne suis pas du tout d'accord avec vous *or* pas du tout de votre avis; **they always** ~ **(with each other)** ils ne sont jamais du même avis *or* d'accord; (*always quarrelling*) ils sont incapables de s'entendre; **to** ~ **with the suggestion that** être contre la suggestion que; **she** ~**s with everything he has done** elle se trouve en désaccord avec tout ce qu'il a fait.

(b) (*be different*) [*explanations, reports, sets of figures*] ne pas concorder.

(c) [*climate, food*] **to** ~ **with sb** ne pas convenir à qn, être nuisible à qn; **mutton** ~**s with him** il ne digère pas le mouton, le mouton ne lui réussit pas; **the mutton** ~**d with him** il a mal digéré le mouton, le mouton n'est pas bien passé*.

disagreeable [ˌdɪsəˈgriːəbl] *adj smell, work* désagréable, déplaisant; *experience* désagréable, fâcheux; *person, answer* désagréable, désobligeant, maussade (*towards* envers).

disagreeableness [ˌdɪsəˈgriːəblnɪs] *n* [*work, experience*] nature désagréable *or* fâcheuse; [*person*] mauvaise humeur, maussaderie *f*, attitude *f or* manière(s) *f(pl)* désagréable(s).

disagreeably [ˌdɪsəˈgriːəblɪ] *adv* désagréablement, d'un air *or* d'une manière désagréable *or* désobligeant(e).

disagreement [ˌdɪsəˈgriːmənt] *n* **(a)** (*of opinion, also between accounts etc*) désaccord *m*, différence *f*. **(b)** (*quarrel*) désaccord *m*, différend *m*, différence *f* d'opinion. **to have a** ~ **with sb** avoir un différend avec qn (*about* à propos de).

disallow [ˈdɪsəˈlaʊ] *vt* rejeter; (*Jur*) débouter, rejeter.

disappear [ˌdɪsəˈpɪəʳ] *vi* [*person, vehicle*] disparaître; [*lost object*] disparaître, s'égarer; [*snow, objection*] disparaître; [*memory*] disparaître, s'effacer; [*difficulties*] disparaître, s'aplanir; [*custom*] disparaître, tomber en désuétude; (*Ling*) s'amuïr. **he** ~**ed from sight** on l'a perdu de vue; **the ship** ~**ed over the horizon** le navire a disparu à l'horizon; (*fig*) **to do a** ~**ing trick*** s'éclipser*, s'esquiver; **to make sth** ~ faire disparaître qch; [*conjurer*] escamoter qch.

disappearance [ˌdɪsəˈpɪərəns] *n* disparition *f*; (*Ling*) [*sound*] amuïssement *m*.

disappoint [ˌdɪsəˈpɔɪnt] *vt person* décevoir, désappointer, tromper dans ses espoirs *or* son attente; (*after promising*) manquer de parole à; *hope* décevoir. **he promised to meet me but** ~**ed me several times** il m'a promis de me rencontrer mais il m'a fait faux bond plusieurs fois; **his schemes were** ~**ed** on a contrecarré ses plans.

disappointed [ˌdɪsəˈpɔɪntɪd] *adj person* déçu, désappointé; *hope, ambition* déçu; *plan* contrecarré. **I'm very** ~ **in you** vous m'avez beaucoup déçu *or* désappointé; **he was** ~ **with her reply** sa réponse l'a déçu; **I was** ~ **to learn that ...** *or* **when I learned that ...** j'ai été déçu *or* désappointé d'apprendre que ...; **we were** ~ **at not seeing her** *or* ~ **not to see her** cela a été une déception pour nous *or* nous avons été déçus de ne pas la voir; **to be** ~ **in one's hopes/in love** être déçu dans ses espoirs/en amour.

disappointing [ˌdɪsəˈpɔɪntɪŋ] *adj* décevant. **how** ~**!** quelle déception!, comme c'est décevant!

disappointment [ˌdɪsəˈpɔɪntmənt] *n* **(a)** (*U*) déception *f*, contrariété *f*, déconvenue *f*. **to my great** ~ à ma grande déception *or* contrariété *or* déconvenue.

(b) déception *f*, déboires *mpl*, désillusion *f*. **after a series of** ~**s** après une succession de déboires; ~**s in love** chagrins *mpl* d'amour; **he/that was a great** ~ **to me** il/cela a été une grosse déception pour moi, il/cela m'a beaucoup déçu.

disapprobation [ˌdɪsæprəˈbeɪʃən] *n* (*liter*), **disapproval** [ˌdɪsəˈpruːvəl] *n* désapprobation *f*; (*stronger*) réprobation *f*. **murmur** *etc* **of** ~ murmure *etc* désapprobateur *or* de désapprobation; **to show one's** ~ **of sb/sth** marquer sa désapprobation *or* sa réprobation à l'égard de qn/qch.

disapprove [ˌdɪsəˈpruːv] **1** *vi*: **to** ~ **of sb/sth** désapprouver qn/qch, trouver à redire à qn/qch; **to ~ of sb's doing sth** désapprouver *or* trouver mauvais que qn fasse qch; **your mother would ~** ta mère serait contre*, ta mère ne trouverait pas ça bien; **he entirely ~s of drink** il est tout à fait contre la boisson.

2 *vt action, event* désapprouver.

disapproving [ˌdɪsəˈpruːvɪŋ] *adj* désapprobateur (*f* -trice), de désapprobation.

disapprovingly [ˌdɪsəˈpruːvɪŋlɪ] *adv* avec désapprobation, d'un air *or* d'un ton désapprobateur.

disarm [dɪsˈɑːm] *vti* (*also fig*) désarmer.

disarmament [dɪsˈɑːməmənt] *n* désarmement *m*. **~ talks** conférence *f* sur le désarmement.

disarming [dɪsˈɑːmɪŋ] **1** *n* (*Mil*) désarmement *m*. **2** *adj smile* désarmant.

disarmingly [dɪsˈɑːmɪŋlɪ] *adv* d'une manière désarmante.

disarrange [ˈdɪsəˈreɪndʒ] *vt* déranger, mettre en désordre.

disarranged [ˈdɪsəˈreɪndʒd] *adj bed* défait; *hair, clothes* en désordre.

disarray [ˌdɪsəˈreɪ] *n* désordre *m*, confusion *f*. **the troops were in (complete) ~** le désordre *or* la confusion régnait parmi les troupes, les troupes étaient en déroute; **a political party in ~** un parti politique en plein désarroi *or* en proie au désarroi; **thoughts in complete ~** pensées très confuses; **she was *or* her clothes were in ~** ses vêtements étaient en désordre.

disassemble [ˈdɪsəˈsembl] *vt* désassembler, démonter.

disassociate [ˈdɪsəˈsəʊʃɪeɪt] *vt* = **dissociate.**

disassociation [ˌdɪsəsəʊsɪˈeɪʃən] *n* = **dissociation.**

disaster [dɪˈzɑːstəʳ] **1** *n* (*gen, also fig*) désastre *m*, catastrophe *f*; (*from natural causes*) catastrophe, sinistre *m*. **financial ~** désastre financier; **a record of ~s** une série de désastres *or* de calamités *or* de malheurs; **attempt doomed to ~** tentative vouée à l'échec (total) *or* à la catastrophe; **on the scene of the ~** sur les lieux du désastre *or* de la catastrophe *or* du sinistre; **their marriage/her hair style was a ~** leur mariage/sa coiffure était une catastrophe* *or* un (vrai) désastre.

2 *cpd*: **disaster area** région sinistrée; **earthquake disaster fund** collecte *f* au profit des victimes du tremblement de terre *or* des sinistrés.

disastrous [dɪˈzɑːstrəs] *adj* désastreux, funeste; (*) catastrophique*.

disastrously [dɪˈzɑːstrəslɪ] *adv* désastreusement.

disavow [ˈdɪsəˈvaʊ] *vt one's words, opinions* désavouer, renier; *faith, duties* renier.

disavowal [ˌdɪsəˈvaʊəl] *n* désaveu *m*, reniement *m*.

disband [dɪsˈbænd] **1** *vt army, corporation, club* disperser. **2** *vi* [*army*] se débander, se disperser; [*organization*] se disperser.

disbar [dɪsˈbɑːʳ] *vt barrister* rayer du tableau de l'ordre (des avocats). **to be ~red** se faire rayer du tableau de l'ordre (des avocats).

disbarment [dɪsˈbɑːmənt] *n* radiation *f* (du barreau *or* du tableau de l'ordre).

disbelief [ˈdɪsbəˈliːf] *n* incrédulité *f*. **in ~** avec incrédulité.

disbelieve [ˈdɪsbəˈliːv] **1** *vt person* ne pas croire; *news etc* ne pas croire à. **2** *vi* (*also Rel*) ne pas croire (*in* à).

disbeliever [ˈdɪsbəˈliːvəʳ] *n* (*also Rel*) incrédule *mf*.

disbelieving [ˈdɪsbəˈliːvɪŋ] *adj* incrédule.

disbud [dɪsˈbʌd] *vt* ébourgeonner.

disburden [dɪsˈbɜːdn] *vt* (*lit, fig*) décharger, débarrasser (*of* de); (*relieve*) soulager. **to ~ one's conscience** se décharger la conscience.

disburse [dɪsˈbɜːs] *vti* débourser.

disbursement [dɪsˈbɜːsmənt] *n* (*paying out*) déboursement *m*; (*money paid*) débours *mpl*.

disc [dɪsk] **1** *n* **(a)** (*also of moon etc*) disque *m*.

(b) (*Anat*) disque *m* (intervertébral); *V* **slip.**

(c) (*Mil: also* **identity ~**) plaque *f* d'identité.

(d) (*gramophone record*) disque *m*.

2 *cpd*: **disc brakes** freins *mpl* à disque(s); **disc harrow** pulvériseur *m*; (*Rad*) **disc jockey** animateur *m*, -trice *f* (de variétés), disc-jockey *m*.

discard [dɪsˈkɑːd] **1** *vt* **(a)** *clothes* se débarrasser de; *idea, plan* renoncer à, abandonner; *rocket, part of spacecraft* larguer.

(b) (*Bridge*) se défausser de, défausser; (*Cribbage*) écarter. **he was ~ing clubs** il se défaussait à trèfle; **he ~ed the three of hearts** il s'est défaussé du trois de cœur.

2 *vi* (*Bridge*) se défausser; (*Cribbage*) écarter.

3 [ˈdɪskɑːd] *n* **(a)** (*Bridge*) défausse *f*; (*Cribbage*) écart *m*.

(b) (*Comm, Ind*) pièce *f* de rebut, déchet *m*.

discern [dɪˈsɜːn] *vt person, object, difference* discerner, distinguer, percevoir; *feelings* discerner.

discernible [dɪˈsɜːnəbl] *adj object* visible; *likeness, fault* perceptible, sensible.

discernibly [dɪˈsɜːnəblɪ] *adv* visiblement, perceptiblement, sensiblement.

discerning [dɪˈsɜːnɪŋ] *adj person* judicieux, sagace, doué de discernement; *taste* délicat; *look* clairvoyant, perspicace.

discernment [dɪˈsɜːnmənt] *n* (*fig*) discernement *m*, pénétration *f*.

discharge [dɪsˈtʃɑːdʒ] **1** *vt* **(a)** *ship, cargo* décharger; *liquid* déverser; (*Elec*) décharger. (*Med*) **to ~ pus** suppurer.

(b) *employee* renvoyer, congédier; (*Mil*) *soldier* rendre à la vie civile; (*for health reasons*) réformer; (*Jur*) *prisoner* libérer, mettre en liberté, élargir; (*Jur*) *jury* congédier; (*Jur*) *accused* relaxer; *bankrupt* réhabiliter; (*Med*) *patient* renvoyer (guéri) de l'hôpital.

(c) *gun* tirer, faire partir; *arrow* décocher.

(d) (*Fin*) *debt, bill* acquitter, régler; *obligation, duty* remplir, s'acquitter de; *function* remplir.

2 *vi* [*wound*] suinter.

3 [ˈdɪstʃɑːdʒ] *n* **(a)** (*U*) [*cargo*] déchargement *m*; (*Elec*) décharge *f*; [*weapon*] décharge; [*liquid*] écoulement *m*; [*duty*] accomplissement *m*, exécution *f*, exercice *m*; [*debt*] acquittement *m*; [*employee*] renvoi *m*; [*prisoner*] libération *f*, élargissement *m*, mise *f* en liberté; [*patient*] renvoi. **the soldier got his ~ yesterday** le soldat a été libéré hier.

(b) (*Med*) pertes *fpl* (blanches); [*pus*] suppuration *f*.

disciple [dɪˈsaɪpl] *n* disciple *m*.

disciplinarian [ˌdɪsɪplɪˈnɛərɪən] *n* personne stricte en matière de discipline.

disciplinary [ˈdɪsɪplɪnərɪ] *adj* disciplinaire.

discipline [ˈdɪsɪplɪn] **1** *n* **(a)** (*U*) discipline *f*. **to keep ~** maintenir la discipline. **(b)** (*branch of knowledge*) discipline *f*, matière *f*. **2** *vt* (*control*) *person* discipliner; *mind* former, discipliner; (*punish*) punir.

disclaim [dɪsˈkleɪm] *vt* **(a)** désavouer, dénier. **to ~ all knowledge of** désavouer *or* nier toute connaissance de. **(b)** (*Jur*) se désister de, renoncer à.

disclaimer [dɪsˈkleɪməʳ] *n* désaveu *m*, dénégation *f*, démenti *m*; (*Jur*) désistement *m* (*of* de), renonciation *f* (*of* à). **to issue a ~** démentir officiellement, publier un démenti.

disclose [dɪsˈkləʊz] *vt secret* divulguer, dévoiler, mettre au jour; *news* divulguer; *intentions* révéler; *contents of envelope, box etc* exposer, montrer, laisser voir.

disclosure [dɪsˈkləʊʒəʳ] *n* **(a)** (*U*) divulgation *f*, révélation *f*. **(b)** (*fact etc revealed*) révélation *f*.

disco* [ˈdɪskəʊ] *n abbr of* **discotheque.**

discography [dɪsˈkɒgrəfɪ] *n* discographie *f*.

discolour, (*US*) **discolor** [dɪsˈkʌləʳ] **1** *vt* (*change, spoil colour of, fade*) décolorer; *white material, teeth* jaunir. **2** *vi* se décolorer, passer, s'altérer; [*white material, teeth*] jaunir; [*mirror*] se ternir.

discolouration, (*US*) **discoloration** [dɪsˌkʌləˈreɪʃən] *n* (*V* **discolour**) décoloration *f*; jaunissement *m*; ternissure *f*.

discomfit [dɪsˈkʌmfɪt] *vt* (*disappoint*) décevoir, tromper les espoirs de; (*confuse*) déconcerter, décontenancer, confondre.

discomfiture [dɪsˈkʌmfɪtʃəʳ] *n* (*disappointment*) déconvenue *f*; (*confusion*) embarras *m*, déconfiture* *f*.

discomfort [dɪsˈkʌmfət] *n* **(a)** (*U: physical, mental*) malaise *m*, gêne *f*, manque *m* de bien-être *or* de confort. (*Med*) **he is in some ~** il a assez mal; **I feel some ~ from it but not real pain** ça me gêne mais ça ne me fait pas vraiment mal; **this ~ will pass** cette gêne va passer.

(b) (*cause of ~*) inconvénient *m*, inconfort *m*, incommodité *f*.

discomposure [ˌdɪskəmˈpəʊʒəʳ] *n* trouble *m*, confusion *f*.

disconcert [ˌdɪskənˈsɜːt] *vt* déconcerter, décontenancer.

disconcerting [ˌdɪskənˈsɜːtɪŋ] *adj* déconcertant, troublant, déroutant.

disconcertingly [ˌdɪskənˈsɜːtɪŋlɪ] *adv* d'une manière déconcertante *or* déroutante.

disconnect [ˈdɪskəˈnekt] *vt* détacher, séparer, disjoindre; *pipe, radio, television* débrancher; *gas, electricity, water supply, telephone* couper. (*Telec*) **to ~ a call** couper *or* interrompre une communication; (*Telec*) **we've been ~ed** (*for non-payment etc*) on nous a coupé le téléphone; (*in mid-conversation*) nous avons été coupés.

disconnected [ˈdɪskəˈnektɪd] *adj speech, thought* décousu, sans suite.

disconsolate [dɪsˈkɒnsəlɪt] *adj* inconsolable.

disconsolately [dɪsˈkɒnsəlɪtlɪ] *adv* inconsolablement.

discontent [ˈdɪskənˈtent] *n* mécontentement *m*; (*Pol*) malaise *m* (social). **cause of ~** grief *m*.

discontented [ˈdɪskənˈtentɪd] *adj* mécontent (*with, about* de).

discontentment [ˈdɪskənˈtentmənt] *n* mécontentement *m*.

discontinue [ˈdɪskənˈtɪnjuː] *vt* cesser, interrompre; *series* interrompre; *story* interrompre la publication de; (*Jur*) *case* abandonner. **to ~ one's subscription to a newspaper** (*permanently*) cesser de s'abonner à un journal; (*temporarily*) suspendre *or* interrompre son abonnement à un journal; (*Comm*) **a ~d line** une série *or* un article qui ne se fait plus; (*on sale article*) '**~d**' 'fin de série'.

discontinuity [ˌdɪskɒntɪˈnjuːɪtɪ] *n* (*gen, Math*) discontinuité *f*; (*Geol*) zone *f* de discontinuité.

discontinuous [ˈdɪskənˈtɪnjʊəs] *adj* discontinu.

discord [ˈdɪskɔːd] *n* discorde *f*, dissension *f*, désaccord *m*; (*Mus*) dissonance *f*. **civil ~** dissensions civiles.

discordant [dɪsˈkɔːdənt] *adj opinions* incompatible; *sounds, colours* discordant; (*Mus*) dissonant.

discotheque [ˈdɪskəʊtek] *n* discothèque *f* (*dancing*).

discount [ˈdɪskaʊnt] **1** *n* escompte *m*; (*on article*) remise *f*, rabais *m*. **to give a ~** faire une remise (*on* sur); **to buy at a ~** acheter au rabais; **~ for cash** escompte au comptant; **at a ~** (*Fin*) en perte, au-dessous du pair; (*fig*) mal coté.

2 [dɪsˈkaʊnt] *vt sum of money* faire une remise de, escompter; *bill, note* prendre à l'escompte, escompter; (*fig*) ne pas tenir compte de. **I ~ half of what he says** je divise par deux tout ce qu'il dit.

3 *cpd*: **discount house, discount store** magasin *m* de demi-gros.

discourage [dɪsˈkʌrɪdʒ] *vt* **(a)** (*dishearten*) décourager, abattre. **to become ~d** se laisser décourager *or* rebuter, se laisser aller au découragement; **he isn't easily ~d** il ne se décourage pas facilement.

(b) (*advise against*) décourager, détourner, (essayer de) dissuader (*sb from sth/from doing* qn de qch/de faire).

(c) *suggestion* déconseiller; *offer of friendship* repousser. **she ~d his advances** elle a repoussé *or* découragé ses avances.

discouragement [dɪsˈkʌrɪdʒmənt] *n* (*act*) désapprobation *f* (*of* de); (*depression*) découragement *m*, abattement *m*.

discouraging [dɪsˈkʌrɪdʒɪŋ] *adj* décourageant, démoralisant.

discourse [ˈdɪskɔːs] **1** *n* **(a)** discours *m*; (*written*) dissertation *f*, traité *m*. **(b)** (††) conversation *f*. **2** [dɪsˈkɔːs] *vi* **(a)** discourir (*on* sur); traiter (*on* de). **(b)** (††) s'entretenir (*with* avec).

discourteous [dɪsˈkɜːtɪəs] *adj* impoli, peu courtois, discourtois (*towards* envers, avec).

discourteously [dɪsˈkɜːtɪəslɪ] *adv* d'une manière peu courtoise, de façon discourtoise. **to behave ~ towards** manquer de politesse envers, se montrer impoli *or* discourtois avec.

discourtesy [dɪsˈkɜːtɪsɪ] *n* incivilité *f*, manque *m* de courtoisie, impolitesse *f*.

discover [dɪsˈkʌvəʳ] *vt country, planet* découvrir; *treasure* découvrir, trouver; *secret, person hiding* découvrir, surprendre; *reason, cause* découvrir, comprendre, pénétrer; *mistake, loss* s'apercevoir de, se rendre compte de; (*after search*) *house, book* dénicher. **to ~ that** s'apercevoir que; **I can't ~ why he did it** je n'arrive pas à comprendre pourquoi il a fait cela.

discoverer [dɪsˈkʌvərəʳ] *n*: **the ~ of America/penicillin** celui qui le premier a découvert l'Amérique/la pénicilline.

discovery [dɪsˈkʌvərɪ] *n* **(a)** (*U*) *[fact, place, person]* découverte *f*. **it led to the ~ of penicillin** cela a conduit à la découverte de la pénicilline, cela a fait découvrir la pénicilline; *V* **voyage**. **(b)** (*happy find*) trouvaille *f*.

discredit [dɪsˈkredɪt] **1** *vt* (*cast slur on*) discréditer, déconsidérer; (*disbelieve*) ne pas croire, mettre en doute.

2 *n* discrédit *m*, déconsidération *f*. **to bring ~ upon sb** jeter le discrédit sur qn; **without any ~ to you** sans que cela nuise à votre réputation; **to be a ~ to** être une honte pour, faire honte à.

discreditable [dɪsˈkredɪtəbl] *adj* peu honorable, indigne, déshonorant.

discreet [dɪsˈkriːt] *adj person, silence, inquiry etc* discret (*f* -ète); *decor, colour* discret, sobre.

discreetly [dɪsˈkriːtlɪ] *adv speak, behave* discrètement; *dress* sobrement.

discrepancy [dɪsˈkrepənsɪ] *n* contradiction *f*, désaccord *m*, divergence *f* (*between* entre). **there is a slight ~ between the two explanations** les deux explications divergent légèrement *or* ne cadrent pas tout à fait.

discrete [dɪsˈkriːt] *adj* (*gen, Math, Med*) discret (*f* -ète).

discretion [dɪsˈkreʃən] *n* **(a)** (*tact*) discrétion *f*, réserve *f*, retenue *f*; (*prudence*) discrétion, sagesse *f*. (*Prov*) **~ is the better part of valour** prudence est mère de sûreté (*Prov*).

(b) (*freedom of decision*) discrétion *f*, arbitraire *m*, liberté *f* d'agir. **to leave sth to sb's ~** laisser qch à la discrétion de qn; **use your own ~** faites comme bon vous semblera, c'est à vous de juger; **at the ~ of the judge/the chairman** *etc* **it is possible to** ... c'est au juge/au président *etc* de décider s'il est possible de ...; **the age of ~** l'âge de raison.

discretionary [dɪsˈkreʃənərɪ] *adj powers* discrétionnaire.

discriminant [dɪsˈkrɪmɪnənt] *n* (*Math*) discriminant *m*.

discriminate [dɪsˈkrɪmɪneɪt] **1** *vi* **(a)** (*distinguish*) distinguer, établir une distinction, faire un choix (*between* entre). **the public should ~** le public ne devrait pas accepter n'importe quoi *or* devrait exercer son sens critique.

(b) (*make unfair distinction*) établir une discrimination (*against* contre, *in favour of* en faveur de).

2 *vt* distinguer (*from* de), discriminer (*liter*).

discriminating [dɪsˈkrɪmɪneɪtɪŋ] *adj judgment, mind* judicieux, sagace; *taste* fin, délicat; *tariff, tax* différentiel. **he's not very ~, he watches every television programme** il n'a aucun discernement, il regarde tous les programmes de la télévision.

discrimination [dɪsˌkrɪmɪˈneɪʃən] *n* **(a)** (*distinction*) distinction *f* (*between* entre), séparation *f* (*of one thing from another* d'une chose d'avec une autre); (*judgment*) discernement *m*, jugement *m*.

(b) discrimination *f* (*against* contre, *in favour of* en faveur de). **racial ~** discrimination raciale, racisme *m*; **sexual ~** discrimination sexuelle, sexisme *m*.

discriminatory [dɪsˈkrɪmɪnətərɪ] *adj* discriminatoire.

discursive [dɪsˈkɜːsɪv] *adj*, **discursory** [dɪsˈkɜːsərɪ] *adj* discursif, décousu (*pej*).

discus [ˈdɪskəs] *n* disque *m*. **~ thrower** lanceur *m* de disque, discobole *m* (*Hist*).

discuss [dɪsˈkʌs] *vt* (*examine in detail*) discuter, examiner; (*talk about*) *topic* discuter de *or* sur, débattre de. **we were ~ing him** nous parlions *or* discutions de lui; **I ~ed it with him** j'en ai discuté avec lui; **I won't ~ it any further** je ne veux plus (avoir à) revenir là-dessus.

discussant [dɪsˈkʌsənt] *n* (*US*) participant(e) *m(f)* (*à une discussion etc*).

discussion [dɪsˈkʌʃən] *n* discussion *f*, échange *m* de points de vue, débat *m* (*of, about* sur, au sujet de). **under ~** en discussion; **a subject for ~** un sujet de discussion.

disdain [dɪsˈdeɪn] **1** *vt* dédaigner (*to do* de faire). **2** *n* dédain *m*, mépris *m*. **in ~** avec dédain.

disdainful [dɪsˈdeɪnfʊl] *adj person* dédaigneux; *tone, look* dédaigneux, de dédain.

disdainfully [dɪsˈdeɪnfəlɪ] *adv* dédaigneusement, avec dédain.

disease [dɪˈziːz] *n* (*Med: mental, physical*) maladie *f*, affection *f*; (*Bot, Vet*) maladie; (*fig*) maladie, mal *m*; *V* **occupational, venereal, virus** *etc*.

diseased [dɪˈziːzd] *adj* malade.

disembark [ˌdɪsɪmˈbɑːk] *vti* débarquer.

disembarkation [ˌdɪsembɑːˈkeɪʃən] *n* débarquement *m*.

disembodied [ˈdɪsɪmˈbɒdɪd] *adj* désincarné.

disembowel [ˌdɪsɪmˈbaʊəl] *vt* éventrer, éviscérer, étriper*.

disenchant [ˈdɪsɪnˈtʃɑːnt] *vt* désabuser, désenchanter, désillusionner.

disenchantment [ˌdɪsɪnˈtʃɑːntmənt] *n* désenchantement *m*, désillusion *f*.

disenfranchise [ˈdɪsɪnˈfræntʃaɪz] *vt* = **disfranchise.**

disengage [ˌdɪsɪnˈgeɪdʒ] **1** *vt object, hand* dégager, libérer (*from* de); (*Tech*) *machine* déclencher, débrayer. **to ~ o.s. from** se dégager de; (*Aut*) **to ~ the clutch** débrayer. **2** *vi* (*Fencing*) dégager (le fer); (*Tech*) se déclencher.

disengaged [ˌdɪsɪnˈgeɪdʒd] *adj* libre, inoccupé; (*Tech*) débrayé.

disengagement [ˌdɪsɪnˈgeɪdʒmənt] *n* (*Pol*) désengagement *m*.

disentangle [ˈdɪsɪnˈtæŋgl] **1** *vt wool, problem, mystery* débrouiller, démêler; *plot* dénouer. (*lit, fig*) **to ~ o.s. from** se dépêtrer de, se sortir de. **2** *vi* se démêler.

disestablish [ˈdɪsɪsˈtæblɪʃ] *vt the Church* séparer de l'État.

disestablishment [ˌdɪsɪsˈtæblɪʃmənt] *n* séparation *f* (de l'Église et de l'État).

disfavour, (*US*) **disfavor** [dɪsˈfeɪvəʳ] **1** *n* défaveur *f*, désapprobation *f*, mécontentement *m*. **to fall into ~** tomber en défaveur *or* en disgrâce; **to fall into ~ with sb** mécontenter qn; **to be in ~ with sb** être mal vu de qn; **to incur sb's ~** s'attirer la défaveur de qn, encourir la désapprobation de qn; **to look with ~ on sth** regarder qch avec mécontentement *or* désapprobation.

2 *vt* (*dislike*) désapprouver, voir avec mécontentement; (*disadvantage*) être défavorable à, défavoriser.

disfigure [dɪsˈfɪgəʳ] *vt face* défigurer; *scenery* défigurer, déparer.

disfigured [dɪsˈfɪgəd] *adj* défiguré (*by* par).

disfigurement [dɪsˈfɪgəmənt] *n* défigurement *m*, enlaidissement *m*.

disfranchise [ˈdɪsˈfræntʃaɪz] *vt person* priver du droit électoral; *town* priver de ses droits de représentation.

disgorge [dɪsˈgɔːdʒ] **1** *vt food* dégorger, rendre; (*fig*) déverser. **2** *vi [river]* se dégorger, se décharger.

disgrace [dɪsˈgreɪs] **1** *n* **(a)** (*U*) (*dishonour*) honte *f*, déshonneur *m*; (*disfavour*) disgrâce *f*, défaveur *f*. **there is no ~ in doing** il n'y a aucune honte à faire; **to be in ~** *[politician etc]* être en disgrâce *or* en défaveur; *[child, dog]* être en pénitence; **to bring ~ on sb** déshonorer qn.

(b) (*cause of shame*) honte *f*. **it is a ~ to the country** cela est une honte pour *or* cela déshonore le pays; **the price of butter is a ~** le prix du beurre est une honte *or* un scandale; **she's a ~ to her family** elle est la honte de sa famille.

2 *vt family etc* faire honte à; *name, country* déshonorer, couvrir de honte *or* d'opprobre (*liter*). **don't ~ us** ne nous fais pas honte; **he ~d himself by drinking too much** il s'est très mal tenu *or* conduit en buvant trop; *[officer, politician]* **to be ~d** être disgracié.

disgraceful [dɪsˈgreɪsfʊl] *adj* honteux, scandaleux, déshonorant; (*) honteux, scandaleux. **it was ~ of him** c'était scandaleux de sa part.

disgracefully [dɪsˈgreɪsfəlɪ] *adv act* honteusement, scandaleusement. **~ badly paid** scandaleusement mal payé.

disgruntled [dɪsˈgrʌntld] *adj person* (*discontented*) mécontent (*about, with* de); (*in bad temper*) de mauvaise humeur, mécontent (*about, with* à cause de); *expression* maussade, renfrogné.

disguise [dɪsˈgaɪz] **1** *vt person* déguiser (*as* en); *mistake, voice* déguiser, camoufler; *building, vehicle, ship* camoufler (*as* en); *facts, feelings* masquer, dissimuler, déguiser. **to ~ o.s. as a woman** se déguiser en femme; **there is no disguising the fact that** ... on ne peut pas se dissimuler que ..., il faut avouer que ... .

2 *n* déguisement *m*; (*fig*) masque *m*, voile *m*, fausse apparence. **in ~** déguisé; **in the ~ of** déguisé en.

disgust [dɪsˈgʌst] **1** *n* dégoût *m*, aversion *f*, répugnance *f* (*for, at* pour). (*lit, fig*) **he left in ~** il est parti dégoûté *or* écœuré; **to his ~ they left** écœuré, il les a vus partir; **to my ~ he refused to do it** j'ai trouvé dégoûtant qu'il refuse (*subj*) de le faire.

2 *vt* inspirer du dégoût à, dégoûter, écœurer; (*infuriate*) dégoûter, révolter.

disgusted [dɪsˈgʌstɪd] *adj* dégoûté, écœuré (*at* de, par).

disgustedly [dɪsˈgʌstɪdlɪ] *adv* avec écœurement, avec dégoût. **... he said ~** ... dit-il, écœuré.

disgusting [dɪsˈgʌstɪŋ] *adj food, behaviour* dégoûtant, écœurant; *behaviour* révoltant, choquant; *smell* nauséabond. **what a ~ mess!** (*of room etc*) quelle pagaïe!*, quel bazar!*; (*of situation*) c'est dégoûtant!, c'est du propre! (*iro*); **it is quite ~ to have to pay** ... c'est tout de même écœurant d'avoir à payer ... .

disgustingly [dɪsˈgʌstɪŋlɪ] *adv* d'une manière dégoûtante. **~ dirty** d'une saleté dégoûtante *or* répugnante.

dish [dɪʃ] **1** *n* **(a)** plat *m*; (*in laboratory etc*) récipient *m*; (*Phot*) cuvette *f*. **vegetable ~** plat à légumes, légumier *m*; **the ~es** la vaisselle; **to do the ~es** faire la vaisselle.

(b) (*food*) plat *m*, mets *m*. (*fig*) **she's quite a ~*** c'est vraiment une belle fille, elle est rudement bien roulée*.

2 *cpd*: **dish aerial,** (*US*) **dish antenna** antenne *f* parabolique; **dish cloth** (*for washing*) lavette *f*; (*for drying*) torchon *m* (à vaisselle); **dish mop** lavette *f*; (*US*) **dishpan** bassine *f* (à vaisselle); **dishrack** égouttoir *m* (à vaisselle); **dishtowel** torchon *m* (à vaisselle); **dishwasher** (*machine*) machine *f* à laver la vaisselle, lave-vaisselle *m inv*; (*person*) laveur *m*, -euse *f* de vaisselle; (*in restaurant*) plongeur *m*, -euse *f*; **to work as (a) dishwasher** travailler à la plonge; **dishwater** eau *f* de vaisselle; **this coffee's like dishwater*** ce café est de la lavasse* *or* de l'eau de vaisselle*; *V* **dull.**

3 *vt* **(a)** *food, meal* verser dans un plat.

(b) (‡) *opponent* enfoncer*; *sb's chances, hopes* foutre en l'air‡, flanquer par terre*.

dish out *vt sep* (*lit, also fig**) distribuer. **to dish out a hiding to sb*** flanquer* une correction à qn.

dish up *vt sep* **(a)** *food, meal* servir, verser dans un plat. **the meal was ready to dish up** le repas était prêt à servir; **I'm dishing it up!** je sers!

(b) (*) *facts, statistics* sortir tout un tas de*.

dishabille [ˌdɪsəˈbiːl] *n* peignoir *m*, négligé *m*. **in ~** en déshabillé, en négligé.

disharmony [ˈdɪsˈhɑːmənɪ] *n* désaccord *m*, manque *m* d'harmonie; *[sound]* dissonance *f*.

dishearten [dɪsˈhɑːtn] *vt* décourager, abattre, démoraliser. **don't be ~ed** ne vous laissez pas décourager *or* abattre.

disheartening [dɪsˈhɑːtnɪŋ] *adj* décourageant, démoralisant.

dished [dɪʃt] *adj* (*Aut*) **~ wheel** roue désaxée *or* gauchie.

dishevelled [dɪˈʃevəld] *adj person, hair* échevelé, ébouriffé; *clothes* en désordre; (*scruffy*) *person, clothes* débraillé.

dishonest [dɪsˈɒnɪst] *adj* malhonnête, (*insincere*) déloyal, de mauvaise foi. **to be ~ with sb** être de mauvaise foi avec qn, être déloyal envers qn.

dishonestly [dɪsˈɒnɪstlɪ] *adv* (*V* **dishonest**) malhonnêtement, déloyalement, avec mauvaise foi.

dishonesty [dɪsˈɒnɪstɪ] *adv* (*V* **dishonest**) malhonnêteté *f*, déloyauté *f*, mauvaise foi. **an act of ~** une malhonnêteté.

dishonour [dɪsˈɒnəʳ] **1** *n* déshonneur *m*, infamie *f*, opprobre *m* (*liter*). **2** *vt* **(a)** *family* déshonorer, porter atteinte à l'honneur de; *woman* déshonorer, séduire. **(b)** *bill, cheque* refuser d'honorer. **a ~ed cheque** un chèque impayé *or* refusé *or* non honoré.

dishonourable [dɪsˈɒnərəbl] *adj* déshonorant, honteux.

dishonourably [dɪsˈɒnərəblɪ] *adv* avec déshonneur, de façon déshonorante.

dishy* [ˈdɪʃɪ] *adj* (*Brit*) *person* excitant, sexy, appétissant.

disillusion [ˌdɪsɪˈluːʒən] **1** *vt* désillusionner, désabuser. **to be ~ed** être désillusionné *or* désenchanté; **to grow ~ed** perdre ses illusions. **2** *n* désillusion *f*, désenchantement *m*, désabusement *m* (*liter*).

disillusionment [ˌdɪsɪˈluːʒənmənt] *n* = **disillusion 2**.

disincentive [ˌdɪsɪnˈsentɪv] **1** *n* effet décourageant, mesure décourageante. **to be a ~ to sth** décourager qch. **2** *adj* décourageant.

disinclination [ˌdɪsɪnklɪˈneɪʃən] *n* répugnance *f* (*for, to* pour).

disinclined [ˈdɪsɪnˈklaɪnd] *adj* peu disposé, peu porté, peu enclin (*for* à, *to do* à faire).

disinfect [ˌdɪsɪnˈfekt] *vt* désinfecter.

disinfectant [ˌdɪsɪnˈfektənt] *adj, n* désinfectant (*m*).

disinfection [ˌdɪsɪnˈfekʃən] *n* désinfection *f*.

disinflation [ˌdɪsɪnˈfleɪʃən] *n* déflation *f*.

disinflationary [ˌdɪsɪnˈfleɪʃənərɪ] *adj* de déflation, déflationniste.

disingenuous [ˌdɪsɪnˈdʒenjʊəs] *adj* déloyal, insincère, (*stronger*) fourbe.

disingenuousness [ˌdɪsɪnˈdʒenjʊəsnɪs] *n* déloyauté *f*, manque *m* de sincérité, fourberie *f*.

disinherit [ˈdɪsɪnˈherɪt] *vt* déshériter.

disintegrate [dɪsˈɪntɪgreɪt] **1** *vi* se désintégrer, se désagréger; (*Phys*) se désintégrer. **2** *vt* désintégrer, désagréger; (*Phys*) désintégrer.

disintegration [dɪsˌɪntɪˈgreɪʃən] *n* désintégration *f*, désagrégation *f*; (*Phys*) désintégration.

disinter [ˈdɪsɪnˈtɜːʳ] *vt* déterrer, exhumer.

disinterested [dɪsˈɪntrɪstɪd] *adj* (*impartial*) désintéressé; (*: *bored*) indifférent.

disinterestedness [dɪsˈɪntrɪstɪdnɪs] *n* désintéressement *m*, altruisme *m*.

disinterment [ˌdɪsɪnˈtɜːmənt] *n* déterrement *m*, exhumation *f*.

disjoint [dɪsˈdʒɔɪnt] *adj* (*Math*) disjoint.

disjointed [dɪsˈdʒɔɪntɪd] *adj lecture, account, conversation* sans suite, décousu, incohérent; *style* haché, décousu.

disjunction [dɪsˈdʒʌŋkʃən] *n* disjonction *f*.

disjunctive [dɪsˈdʒʌŋktɪv] *adj* disjonctif.

disk [dɪsk] = **disc**.

dislike [dɪsˈlaɪk] **1** *vt person, thing* ne pas aimer, avoir de l'aversion pour. **to ~ doing** ne pas aimer faire; **I don't ~ it** cela ne me déplaît pas, je ne le déteste pas; **I ~ her** je la trouve antipathique *or* désagréable, elle ne me plaît pas, je ne l'aime pas; **I ~ this intensely** j'ai cela en horreur. **2** *n* aversion *f*, antipathie *f*. **one's likes and ~s** ce que l'on aime et ce que l'on n'aime pas; **to take a ~ to sb/sth** prendre qn/qch en grippe.

dislocate [ˈdɪsləʊkeɪt] *vt limb etc* disloquer, démettre, luxer; (*fig*) *traffic, business* désorganiser; *plans, timetable* bouleverser. **he ~d his shoulder** il s'est déboîté *or* démis *or* luxé l'épaule.

dislocation [ˌdɪsləʊˈkeɪʃən] *n* (*V* **dislocate**) dislocation *f*, luxation *f*, déboîtement *m*, bouleversement *m*.

dislodge [dɪsˈlɒdʒ] *vt stone* déplacer, faire bouger; *cap, screw, nut* débloquer; *enemy* déloger; *person* faire bouger (*from* de).

disloyal [ˈdɪsˈlɔɪəl] *adj person, behaviour* déloyal, infidèle (*to* à, envers).

disloyalty [ˈdɪsˈlɔɪəltɪ] *n* déloyauté *f*, infidélité *f*.

dismal [ˈdɪzməl] *adj prospects, person, mood* lugubre, sombre, morne; *weather* maussade, morne.

dismally [ˈdɪzməlɪ] *adv* lugubrement, d'un air sombre *or* maussade. **to fail ~** échouer lamentablement.

dismantle [dɪsˈmæntl] *vt machine, furniture* démonter; (*Mil etc*) *fort, warship* démanteler.

dismast [dɪsˈmɑːst] *vt* démâter.

dismay [dɪsˈmeɪ] **1** *n* consternation *f*, désarroi *m*. **to my great ~** à ma grande consternation; **in ~** d'un air consterné. **2** *vt* consterner.

dismember [dɪsˈmembəʳ] *vt* démembrer (*also fig*).

dismemberment [dɪsˈmembəmənt] *n* démembrement *m*.

dismiss [dɪsˈmɪs] *vt* **(a)** *employee* renvoyer, congédier; *official, officer* destituer, casser; *class, visitors* laisser partir, congédier; *assembly* dissoudre; *troops* faire rompre les rangs à. (*Mil*) **to be ~ed (from) the service** être renvoyé de l'armée *or* rayé des cadres; (*Mil*) **~!** rompez (les rangs)!; (*Scol*) **class ~!** partez!

(b) *subject of conversation* écarter, abandonner; *thought, possibility* écarter; *request* rejeter; *suggestion* écarter, exclure.

(c) (*Jur*) *accused* relaxer; *appeal* rejeter; *jury* congédier. **to ~ sb's appeal** débouter qn de son appel; **to ~ a case** rendre une fin de non-recevoir; **to ~ a charge** rendre un (arrêt de *or* une ordonnance de) non-lieu.

dismissal [dɪsˈmɪsəl] *n* (*V* **dismiss**) **(a)** renvoi *m*, congédiement *m*; destitution *f*; départ *m*, congédiement; dissolution *f*. **he made a gesture of ~** d'un geste il les (*or* nous *etc*) a congédiés.

(b) rejet *m*, abandon *m*, exclusion *f*.

(c) (*Jur*) relaxe *f*, rejet *m*; *[jury]* congédiement *m*. **~ of case** fin *f* de non-recevoir; **~ of charge** non-lieu *m*.

dismount [dɪsˈmaʊnt] **1** *vi* descendre (*from* de); mettre pied à terre. **2** *vt rider* démonter, désarçonner; *troops, gun, machine* démonter (*from* de).

disobedience [ˌdɪsəˈbiːdɪəns] *n* (*U*) désobéissance *f*, insoumission *f* (*to* à). **an act of ~** une désobéissance.

disobedient [ˌdɪsəˈbiːdɪənt] *adj child* désobéissant (*to* à); *soldier* indiscipliné, insubordonné. **he has been ~** il a été désobéissant, il a désobéi.

disobey [ˈdɪsəˈbeɪ] *vt parents, officer* désobéir à, s'opposer à; *law* enfreindre, violer.

disobliging [ˈdɪsəˈblaɪdʒɪŋ] *adj* désobligeant, peu agréable.

disorder [dɪsˈɔːdəʳ] **1** *n* **(a)** (*U*) *[room, plans etc]* désordre *m*, confusion *f*. **to throw sth into ~** semer *or* jeter le désordre dans qch; **in ~** en désordre; (*Mil*) **to retreat in ~** être en déroute *or* en débâcle.

(b) (*Pol etc: rioting*) désordres *mpl*, émeute *f*.

(c) (*Med*) trouble(s) *m(pl)*. **kidney/stomach/mental ~** troubles rénaux/gastriques/psychiques.

2 *vt room* mettre en désordre; (*Med*) troubler, déranger.

disordered [dɪsˈɔːdəd] *adj room* en désordre; *imagination, existence* désordonné; (*Med*) *stomach* dérangé, malade; *mind* malade, déséquilibré.

disorderly [dɪsˈɔːdəlɪ] *adj* en désordre, sans ordre; *flight, mind* désordonné; *behaviour, life* désordonné, déréglé; *crowd, meeting* désordonné, tumultueux. **~ house** (*brothel*) maison *f* de débauche; (*gambling den*) maison de jeu, tripot *m*; (*Jur*) **~ conduct** conduite *f* contraire aux bonnes mœurs; *V* **drunk**.

disorganization [dɪsˌɔːgənaɪˈzeɪʃən] *n* désorganisation *f*.

disorganize [dɪsˈɔːgənaɪz] *vt* désorganiser, déranger. **she's very ~d*** elle est très désorganisée *or* brouillonne.

disorientate [dɪsˈɔːrɪənteɪt] *vt* désorienter.

disown [dɪsˈəʊn] *vt child, country, opinion* désavouer, renier; *debt, signature* nier, renier.

disparage [dɪsˈpærɪdʒ] *vt* dénigrer, décrier, déprécier.

disparagement [dɪsˈpærɪdʒmənt] *n* dénigrement *m*, dépréciation *f*.

disparaging [dɪsˈpærɪdʒɪŋ] *adj* peu flatteur, désobligeant, (un peu) méprisant (*to* pour). **to be ~ about** faire des remarques désobligeantes *or* peu flatteuses sur.

disparagingly [dɪsˈpærɪdʒɪŋlɪ] *adv look, speak* de façon désobligeante *or* peu flatteuse.

disparate [ˈdɪspərɪt] *adj* disparate.

disparity [dɪsˈpærɪtɪ] *n* disparité *f*, inégalité *f*, écart *m*.

dispassionate [dɪsˈpæʃənɪt] *adj* (*unemotional*) calme, froid; (*unbiased*) impartial, objectif.

dispassionately [dɪsˈpæʃənɪtlɪ] (*unemotionally*) sans émotion, avec calme; (*unbiasedly*) impartialement, sans parti pris.

dispatch [dɪsˈpætʃ] **1** *vt* **(a)** (*send*) *letter, goods* expédier, envoyer; *messenger* dépêcher; (*Mil*) *troops* envoyer, faire partir; *convoy* mettre en route; (*fig*) *food, drink* expédier.

(b) (*finish off*) *job* expédier, en finir avec; *animal* tuer, abattre.

2 *n* **(a)** *[letter, messenger, telegram etc]* envoi *m*, expédition *f*. **date of ~** date *f* d'expédition; **office of ~** bureau *m* d'origine.

(b) (*official report: also Mil*) dépêche *f*; (*Press*) dépêche (de presse). (*Mil*) **mentioned** *or* **cited in ~es** cité à l'ordre du jour.

(c) (*promptness*) promptitude *f*.

3 *cpd*: (*Brit Parl*) **dispatch box** ≃ tribune *f* (*d'où parlent les membres du gouvernement*); (*case*) valise officielle; **dispatch case** serviette *f*, porte-documents *m inv*; **dispatch rider** estafette *f*.

dispatcher [dɪsˈpætʃəʳ] *n* expéditeur *m*, -trice *f*.

dispel [dɪsˈpel] *vt* dissiper, chasser.

dispensable [dɪsˈpensəbl] *adj* dont on peut se passer; (*Rel*) dispensable.

dispensary [dɪsˈpensərɪ] *n* (*in hospital*) pharmacie *f*; (*in chemist's*) officine *f*; (*clinic*) dispensaire *m*.

dispensation [ˌdɪspenˈseɪʃən] *n* (*handing out*) *[food]* distribution *f*; *[justice, charity]* exercice *m*, pratique *f*; (*decreeing*) décret *m*, arrêt *m*; (*Jur, Rel*) dispense *f* (*from* de).

dispense [dɪsˈpens] *vt* **(a)** *food* distribuer; *charity* pratiquer; *justice, sacrament* administrer; *hospitality* accorder, offrir.

(b) (*Pharm*) *medicine, prescription* préparer. **dispensing chemist** (*person*) pharmacien(ne) *m(f)*; (*shop*) pharmacie *f*.

(c) (*also Rel: exempt*) dispenser, exempter (*sb from sth/from doing* qn de qch/de faire).

dispense with *vt fus* (*do without*) se passer de; (*make unnecessary*) rendre superflu.

dispenser [dɪsˈpensəʳ] *n* (*Brit*) (*person*) pharmacien(ne) *m(f)*; (*device*) distributeur *m*.

dispersal [dɪsˈpɜːsəl] *n* dispersion *f*.

disperse [dɪsˈpɜːs] **1** *vt crowd, mist* disperser; *sorrow* dissiper, chasser; *paper, seeds* disperser, éparpiller; *knowledge* disséminer, répandre, propager; (*Chem, Opt*) décomposer.

2 *vi* se disperser; se dissiper; se disséminer, se propager; se décomposer.

dispersion [dɪsˈpɜːʃən] *n* (*also Phys*) dispersion *f*.
dispirit [dɪsˈpɪrɪt] *vt* décourager, déprimer, abattre.
dispirited [dɪsˈpɪrɪtɪd] *adj* découragé, déprimé, abattu.
dispiritedly [dɪsˈpɪrɪtɪdlɪ] *adv* d'un air *or* d'un ton découragé, avec découragement.
displace [dɪsˈpleɪs] *vt* **(a)** (*move out of place*) *refugees* déplacer; *furniture* déplacer, changer de place. **~d person** personne déplacée.
(b) (*deprive of office*) *officer* destituer; *official* déplacer; (*replace*) supplanter, remplacer.
(c) (*Naut, Phys*) *water* déplacer.
displacement [dɪsˈpleɪsmənt] **1** *n* (*V* **displace**) déplacement *m*; destitution *f*; remplacement *m* (*by* par); (*Geol*) faille *f*.
2 *cpd*: **displacement activity** (*Zool*) activité *f* de substitution; (*Psych*) déplacement *m*; (*Naut*) **displacement tonnage** déplacement *m*.
display [dɪsˈpleɪ] **1** *vt* montrer; (*ostentatiously*) exhiber, faire parade de; *[peacock]* étaler; *notice, results* afficher; (*Press, Typ*) mettre en vedette; (*Comm*) *goods* étaler, mettre à l'étalage, exposer; (*Computers, Electronics*) visualiser; *courage, interest, ignorance* faire preuve de.
2 *vi* (*Zool*) parader.
3 *n* **(a)** (*U*) exposition *f*, déploiement *m*; (*ostentatious*) étalage *m*, parade *f*; *[paintings]* exposition; (*Comm*) étalage; (*Computers, Electronics*) visuel *m*; *[courage, emotion, ignorance]* manifestation *f*; *[force etc]* déploiement. **on ~** exposé; **to make a great ~ of learning** faire parade (*pej*) de son érudition, faire montre d'un grand savoir.
(b) military ~ parade *f* militaire; *V* **air.**
(c) (*Zool*) parade *f*.
4 *cpd* (*Comm*) *goods* d'étalage. (*Press*) **display advertising** placards *mpl* (publicitaires); **display cabinet, display case** vitrine *f* (*meuble*); **display window** étalage *m*, vitrine *f* (*de magasin*).
displease [dɪsˈpliːz] *vt* déplaire à, mécontenter, contrarier. **~d at** *or* **with** mécontent de.
displeasing [dɪsˈpliːzɪŋ] *adj* désagréable (*to* à), déplaisant (*to* pour). **to be ~ to sb** déplaire à qn.
displeasure [dɪsˈpleʒəʳ] *n* mécontentement *m*, déplaisir *m*. **to incur sb's ~** provoquer le mécontentement de qn; **to my great ~** à mon grand mécontentement *or* déplaisir.
disport [dɪsˈpɔːt] *vt*: **to ~ o.s.** s'amuser, s'ébattre, folâtrer.
disposable [dɪsˈpəʊzəbl] *adj* **(a)** (*not reusable*) à jeter; *nappy* à jeter, de cellulose. (*Comm*) **~ wrapping** emballage perdu. **(b)** (*available*) *objects, money* disponible.
disposal [dɪsˈpəʊzəl] **1** *n* **(a)** *[rubbish]* enlèvement *m*, destruction *f*; *[goods for sale]* vente *f*; *[bomb]* désamorçage *m*; (*Jur*) *[property]* disposition *f*, cession *f*; *[problem, question]* résolution *f*; *[matters under discussion, current business]* expédition *f*, exécution *f*; *V* **bomb, refuse²**.
(b) (*arrangement*) *[ornaments, furniture]* disposition *f*, arrangement *m*; *[troops]* disposition.
(c) (*control*) *[resources, funds, personnel]* disposition *f*. **the means at one's ~** les moyens à sa disposition *or* dont on dispose; **to put o.s./be at sb's ~** se mettre/être à la disposition de qn.
2 *cpd*: **(waste) disposal unit** broyeur *m* (*d'ordures*).
dispose [dɪsˈpəʊz] *vt* **(a)** (*arrange*) *papers, ornaments* disposer, arranger; *troops* disposer; *forces* déployer. (*Prov*) **man proposes, God ~s** l'homme propose, Dieu dispose (*Prov*).
(b) disposer, porter (*sb to do* qn à faire). **this does not ~ me to like him** ceci ne me rend pas bien disposé à son égard.
dispose of *vt fus* **(a)** *rubbish, unwanted goods* se débarrasser de, se défaire de; (*by selling*) écouler, vendre; *opponent* se débarasser de; *meal* liquider*, expédier; *question, problem, business* régler, expédier; (*kill*) liquider*.
(b) (*control*) *time, money* disposer de, avoir à sa disposition; (*settle*) *sb's fate* décider de.
disposed [dɪsˈpəʊzd] *adj* disposé, enclin (*to do* à faire). **well/ill-~ towards sb** bien/mal disposé *or* intentionné envers qn *or* à l'égard de qn.
disposer [dɪsˈpəʊzəʳ] *n* (*also* **waste ~**) broyeur *m* (*d'ordures*).
disposition [ˌdɪspəˈzɪʃən] *n* **(a)** (*temperament*) naturel *m*, caractère *m*, tempérament *m*. **(b)** (*readiness*) inclination *f* (*to do* à faire). **(c)** (*arrangement*) *[ornaments etc]* disposition *f*, arrangement *m*; *[troops]* disposition.
dispossess [ˈdɪspəˈzes] *vt* déposséder, priver (*of* de); (*Jur*) exproprier.
dispossession [ˌdɪspəˈzeʃən] *n* dépossession *f*; (*Jur*) expropriation *f*.
disproportion [ˌdɪsprəˈpɔːʃən] *n* disproportion *f*.
disproportionate [ˌdɪsprəˈpɔːʃnɪt] *adj* disproportionné (*to* à, avec).
disproportionately [ˌdɪsprəˈpɔːʃnɪtlɪ] *adv* d'une façon disproportionnée.
disprove [dɪsˈpruːv] *vt* établir *or* démontrer la fausseté de, réfuter.
disputable [dɪsˈpjuːtəbl] *adj* discutable, contestable, douteux.
disputably [dɪsˈpjuːtəblɪ] *adv* de manière contestable.
disputation [ˌdɪspjuːˈteɪʃən] *n* (*argument*) débat *m*, controverse *f*, discussion *f*; (††: *formal debate*) dispute†† *f*.
disputatious [ˌdɪspjuːˈteɪʃəs] *adj* raisonneur.
dispute [dɪsˈpjuːt] **1** *n* **(a)** (*U*) discussion *f*. **beyond ~** incontestable; **without ~** sans contredit; **there is some ~ about why he did it/what he's earning** on n'est pas d'accord sur ses motifs/le montant de son salaire; **there is some ~ about which horse won** il y a contestation sur le gagnant; **in** *or* **under ~** *matter* en discussion; *territory, facts, figures* contesté; (*Jur*) en litige; **statement open to ~** affirmation sujette à contradiction, affirmation contestable; **it is open to ~ whether he knew** on peut se demander s'il savait.
(b) (*quarrel*) dispute *f*; (*argument*) discussion *f*, débat *m*; (*Jur*) litige *m*; (*Ind, Pol*) conflit *m*. **to have a ~ with sb about sth** se disputer avec qn à propos de qch; (*Ind*) **industrial ~** conflit social; **wages ~** conflit salarial *or* sur les salaires.
2 *vt* **(a)** (*cast doubt on*) *statement, claim* contester, mettre en doute; (*Jur*) *will* attaquer, contester. **I do not ~ the fact that ...** je ne conteste pas (le fait) que ... + *subj*.
(b) (*debate*) *question, subject* discuter, débattre.
(c) (*try to win*) *victory, possession* disputer (*with sb* à qn).
disputed [dɪsˈpjuːtɪd] *adj decision* contesté, en discussion; *territory, fact* contesté; (*Jur*) en litige.
disqualification [dɪsˌkwɒlɪfɪˈkeɪʃən] *n* disqualification *f* (*also Sport*), exclusion *f* (*from* de); (*Jur*) incapacité *f*. **his ~ (from driving)** le retrait de son permis (de conduire).
disqualify [dɪsˈkwɒlɪfaɪ] *vt* **(a)** (*debar*) rendre inapte (*from sth* à qch, *from doing* à faire); (*Jur*) rendre inhabile (*from sth* à qch, *from doing* à faire); (*Sport*) disqualifier. (*Jur*) **to ~ sb from driving** retirer à qn son *or* le permis de conduire; (*Jur*) **he was disqualified for speeding** on lui a retiré son permis pour excès de vitesse; (*Jur*) **he was accused of driving while disqualified** il a été accusé d'avoir conduit alors qu'on lui avait retiré son permis.
(b) (*incapacitate*) rendre incapable, mettre hors d'état (*from doing* de faire).
disquiet [dɪsˈkwaɪət] **1** *vt* inquiéter, troubler, tourmenter. **to be ~ed about** s'inquiéter de. **2** *n* (*U*) inquiétude *f*, trouble *m*; (*unrest*) agitation *f*.
disquieting [dɪsˈkwaɪətɪŋ] *adj* inquiétant, alarmant, troublant.
disquietude [dɪsˈkwaɪɪtjuːd] *n* (*U*) inquiétude *f*, trouble *m*.
disquisition [ˌdɪskwɪˈzɪʃən] *n* (*treatise*) traité *m*, dissertation *f*, étude *f* (*on* sur); (*discourse*) communication *f* (*on* sur); (*investigation*) étude approfondie (*on* de).
disregard [ˈdɪsrɪˈgɑːd] **1** *vt fact, difficulty, remark* ne tenir aucun compte de, ne pas s'occuper de; *danger* mépriser, ne pas faire attention à; *feelings* négliger, faire peu de cas de; *authority, rules, duty* méconnaître, passer outre à.
2 *n* *[difficulty, comments, feelings]* indifférence *f* (*for* à); *[danger]* mépris *m* (*for* de); *[money]* mépris, dédain *m* (*for* de); *[safety]* négligence *f* (*for* en ce qui concerne); *[rule, law]* désobéissance *f* (*for* à), non-observation *f* (*for* de).
disrepair [ˈdɪsrɪˈpeəʳ] *n* (*U*) mauvais état, délabrement *m*, dégradation *f*. **in a state of ~** *building* délabré; *road* en mauvais état; **to fall into ~** *[building]* tomber en ruines, se délabrer; *[road]* se dégrader.
disreputable [dɪsˈrepjʊtəbl] *adj person* de mauvaise réputation, louche, peu recommandable; *behaviour* honteux, déshonorant; *clothes* minable*, miteux; *area* louche, mal famé. **a ~ crowd** une bande d'individus louches *or* peu reluisants.
disreputably [dɪsˈrepjʊtəblɪ] *adv behave* d'une manière honteuse *or* peu honorable; *dress* minablement*.
disrepute [ˈdɪsrɪˈpjuːt] *n* discrédit *m*, déconsidération *f*, déshonneur *m*. **to bring into ~** faire tomber dans le discrédit; **to fall into ~** tomber en discrédit.
disrespect [ˈdɪsrɪsˈpekt] *n* manque *m* d'égards *or* de respect, irrespect *m*, irrévérence *f*. **to show ~ to** manquer de respect envers.
disrespectful [ˌdɪsrɪsˈpektfʊl] *adj* irrespectueux, irrévérencieux (*towards, to* envers). **to be ~ to** manquer de respect envers, se montrer irrespectueux envers.
disrobe [ˈdɪsˈrəʊb] **1** *vi* se dévêtir, enlever ses vêtements; (*undress*) se déshabiller. **2** *vt* enlever les vêtements (de cérémonie) à, dévê ir, déshabiller.
disrupt [dɪsˈrʌpt] *vt peace, relations, train service* perturber; *conversation* interrompre; *plans* déranger, (*stronger*) mettre *or* semer la confusion dans; *communications* couper, interrompre.
disruption [dɪsˈrʌpʃən] *n* (*V* **disrupt**) perturbation *f*; interruption *f*; dérangement *m*.
disruptive [dɪsˈrʌptɪv] *adj element, factor* perturbateur (*f* -trice); (*Elec*) disruptif.
dissatisfaction [ˈdɪsˌsætɪsˈfækʃən] *n* mécontentement *m*, insatisfaction *f*. **growing/widespread ~** mécontentement croissant/général (*at, with* devant, provoqué par).
dissatisfied [ˈdɪsˈsætɪsfaɪd] *adj* mécontent, peu satisfait (*with* de).
dissect [dɪˈsekt] *vt animal, plant, truth* disséquer; *book, article* éplucher.
dissected [dɪˈsektɪd] *adj* (*Bot*) découpé.
dissection [dɪˈsekʃən] *n* (*Anat, Bot, fig*) dissection *f*.
dissemble [dɪˈsembl] **1** *vt* (*conceal*) dissimuler; (*feign*) feindre, simuler. **2** *vi* (*in speech*) dissimuler *or* déguiser *or* masquer sa pensée; (*in behaviour*) agir avec dissimulation.
disseminate [dɪˈsemɪneɪt] *vt* disséminer, semer. (*Med*) **~d sclerosis** sclérose *f* en plaques.
dissemination [dɪˌsemɪˈneɪʃən] *n* *[seeds]* dissémination *f*; *[ideas]* dissémination, propagation *f*.
dissension [dɪˈsenʃən] *n* dissension *f*, discorde *f*.
dissent [dɪˈsent] **1** *vi* différer (d'opinion *or* de sentiment); (*Rel*) être en dissidence, être dissident. **2** *n* dissentiment *m*, différence *f* d'opinion; (*Rel*) dissidence *f*.
dissenter [dɪˈsentəʳ] *n* (*esp Rel*) dissident(e) *m(f)*.
dissentient [dɪˈsenʃɪənt] **1** *adj* dissident, opposé. **2** *n* dissident(e) *m(f)*, opposant(e) *m(f)*.
dissertation [ˌdɪsəˈteɪʃən] *n* (*written*) mémoire *m* (*on* sur); (*spoken*) exposé *m* (*on* sur).
disservice [ˈdɪsˈsɜːvɪs] *n* mauvais service. **to do sb a ~** *[person]* ne pas rendre service à qn, rendre un mauvais service à qn; *[appearance etc]* constituer un handicap pour qn.
dissidence [ˈdɪsɪdəns] *n* dissidence *f* (*also Pol*), désaccord *m*, divergence *f* d'opinion.

dissident ['dɪsɪdənt] *adj, n* dissident(e) *m(f)*.
dissimilar ['dɪ'sɪmɪlər] *adj* dissemblable (*to* à), différent (*to* de).
dissimilarity [ˌdɪsɪmɪ'lærɪtɪ] *n* différence *f*, dissemblance *f* (*between* entre).
dissimulate [dɪ'sɪmjʊleɪt] = **dissemble.**
dissimulation [dɪˌsɪmjʊ'leɪʃən] *n* dissimulation *f*.
dissipate ['dɪsɪpeɪt] **1** *vt fog, clouds, fears, suspicions* dissiper; *hopes* anéantir; *energy, efforts* disperser, gaspiller; *fortune* dissiper, dilapider. **2** *vi* se dissiper.
dissipated ['dɪsɪpeɪtɪd] *adj life, behaviour* déréglé, de dissipation; *person* débauché. **to lead** *or* **live a ~ life** mener une vie déréglée *or* une vie de bâton de chaise.
dissipation [ˌdɪsɪ'peɪʃən] *n [clouds, fears]* dissipation *f*; *[energy, efforts]* gaspillage *m*; *[fortune]* dilapidation *f*; (*debauchery*) dissipation, débauche *f*.
dissociate [dɪ'səʊʃɪeɪt] *vt* dissocier, séparer (*from* de); (*Chem*) dissocier. **to ~ o.s. from** se dissocier de, se désolidariser de.
dissociation [dɪˌsəʊsɪ'eɪʃən] *n* (*all senses*) dissociation *f*.
dissoluble [dɪ'sɒljʊbl] *adj* soluble.
dissolute ['dɪsəlu:t] *adj person* débauché, dissolu (*liter*); *way of life* dissolu, déréglé, de débauche.
dissolution [ˌdɪsə'lu:ʃən] *n* (*all senses*) dissolution *f*.
dissolvable [dɪ'zɒlvəbl] *adj* soluble (*in* dans).
dissolve [dɪ'zɒlv] **1** *vt* (*Chem etc*) *substance* dissoudre, (faire) fondre (*in* dans); (*gen, Pol*) *alliance, marriage, assembly* dissoudre.
2 *vi* (*Chem*) se dissoudre, fondre; (*fig*) *[hopes, fears]* disparaître, s'évanouir; (*Jur, Pol*) se dissoudre. **to ~ into thin air** s'en aller en fumée; (*fig*) **to ~ into tears** fondre en larmes.
3 *n* (*Cine, TV*) fondu *m* (enchaîné). **~ in/out** ouverture *f*/fermeture *f* en fondu.
dissolvent [dɪ'zɒlvənt] **1** *adj* dissolvant, dissolutif. **2** *n* dissolvant *m*, solvant *m*.
dissonance ['dɪsənəns] *n* dissonance *f*, discordance *f*.
dissonant ['dɪsənənt] *adj* dissonant, discordant.
dissuade [dɪ'sweɪd] *vt* dissuader (*sb from doing* qn de faire), détourner (*sb from sth* qn de qch). **to try to ~ sb from doing** déconseiller à qn de faire.
dissuasion [dɪ'sweɪʒən] *n* dissuasion *f*.
dissuasive [dɪ'sweɪsɪv] *adj voice, person* qui cherche à dissuader; *powers* de dissuasion.
distaff ['dɪstɑ:f] *n* quenouille *f*. (*fig*) **on the ~ side** du côté maternel *or* des femmes.
distance ['dɪstəns] **1** *n* **(a)** (*in space*) distance *f* (*between* entre). **the ~ between the boys/the houses/the towns** la distance qui sépare les garçons/les maisons/les villes; **the ~ between the eyes/rails/posts** *etc* l'écartement *m* des yeux/des rails/des poteaux *etc*; **at a ~** assez loin, à quelque distance; **at a ~ of 2 metres** à une distance de 2 mètres; **what ~ is it from London?** c'est à quelle distance de *or* c'est à combien de Londres?; **what ~ is it from here to London?** nous sommes *or* on est à combien de Londres?; **it's a good ~** c'est assez loin; **in the ~** au loin, dans le lointain; **from a ~** de loin; **seen from a ~** vu de loin; **it's within walking ~** on peut y aller à pied; **5 minutes' walking ~ away** à 5 minutes de marche; **a short ~ away** à une faible distance; **within hailing ~** à portée de voix; **it's no ~*** c'est à deux pas, c'est tout près; **to cover the ~ in 2 hours** franchir *or* parcourir la distance en 2 heures; **to go part of the ~ alone** faire une partie du trajet seul; **at an equal ~ from each other** à égale distance l'un de l'autre; *V* **long**[1], **middle** *etc.*
(b) (*in time*) distance *f*, intervalle *m*, écart *m*. **at a ~ of 400 years** à 400 ans d'écart; **at this ~ in time** après un tel intervalle de temps, après tant d'années.
(c) (*in rank etc*) distance *f*. **to keep sb at a ~** tenir qn à distance *or* à l'écart; **to keep one's ~** garder ses distances.
2 *vt* (*Sport etc*) distancer.
3 *cpd*: (*Sport*) **(long-)distance race** épreuve *f* de fond.
distant ['dɪstənt] *adj* **(a)** *country, town* lointain, éloigné. **we had a ~ view of the church** nous avons vu l'église de loin; **the school is 2 km ~ from the church** l'école est à (une distance de) 2 km de l'église.
(b) (*in time, age*) éloigné, reculé; *recollection* lointain. **in the ~ future/past** dans un avenir/un passé lointain.
(c) (*fig*) *cousin, relationship* éloigné; *likeness* vague, lointain.
(d) (*reserved*) *person, manner* distant, froid.
distantly ['dɪstəntlɪ] *adv* **(a)** *resemble* vaguement, un peu. **~ related** d'une parenté éloignée. **(b)** (*haughtily*) froidement, avec hauteur, d'une manière distante.
distaste ['dɪs'teɪst] *n* dégoût *m*, répugnance *f* (*for* pour).
distasteful [dɪs'teɪstfʊl] *adj* déplaisant, désagréable. **to be ~ to** déplaire à, être désagréable à.
distemper[1] [dɪs'tempər] **1** *n* (*paint*) détrempe *f*, badigeon *m*. **2** *vt* peindre en détrempe *or* à la détrempe, badigeonner.
distemper[2] [dɪs'tempər] *n* (*Vet*) maladie *f* des jeunes chiens *or* de Carré.
distend [dɪs'tend] **1** *vt* distendre. (*Med*) **~ed stomach** ventre dilaté. **2** *vi* se distendre, se ballonner.
distension [dɪs'tenʃən] *n* distension *f*, dilatation *f*.
distich ['dɪstɪk] *n* distique *m*.
distil, (*US*) **distill** [dɪs'tɪl] **1** *vt* **(a)** *water, alcohol, knowledge* distiller. **(b)** (*drip slowly*) laisser couler goutte à goutte. **2** *vi* se distiller; couler goutte à goutte.
distillation [ˌdɪstɪ'leɪʃən] *n* (*Chem etc, fig*) distillation *f*.
distiller [dɪs'tɪlər] *n* distillateur *m*.
distillery [dɪs'tɪlərɪ] *n* distillerie *f*.
distinct [dɪs'tɪŋkt] *adj* **(a)** (*clear*) *landmark, voice, memory* distinct, clair, net; *promise, offer* précis, formel; *preference, likeness* marqué, net; *increase, progress* sensible, net.
(b) (*different*) distinct, différent, séparé (*from* de). **as ~ from** par opposition à.
distinction [dɪs'tɪŋkʃən] *n* **(a)** (*difference*) distinction *f*, différence *f*; (*act of keeping apart*) distinction (*of ... from* de ... et de, *between* entre). **to make a ~ between two things** faire la *or* une distinction entre deux choses.
(b) (*U*) (*pre-eminence*) distinction *f*, mérite *m*; (*refinement*) distinction. **to win ~** se distinguer, acquérir une *or* de la réputation; **a pianist of ~** un pianiste réputé *or* de marque; **she has great ~** elle est d'une grande distinction.
(c) (*Univ etc*) **he got a ~ in French** il a été reçu en français avec mention très bien.
distinctive [dɪs'tɪŋktɪv] *adj* distinctif, caractéristique. **to be ~ of sth** caractériser qch.
distinctly [dɪs'tɪŋktlɪ] *adv speak, hear, see* distinctement, clairement; *promise* sans équivoque; *stipulate* expressément, formellement. **~ better** incontestablement *or* sensiblement mieux; **he was told ~ that** on lui a bien précisé que, on lui a stipulé formellement que.
distinguish [dɪs'tɪŋgwɪʃ] **1** *vt* **(a)** (*discern*) *landmark* distinguer, apercevoir; *change* discerner, percevoir.
(b) *object, series, person* (*make different*) distinguer (*from* de); (*characterize*) caractériser. **to ~ o.s.** se distinguer (*as* en tant que); (*iro*) **you've really ~ed yourself!** tu t'es vraiment distingué! (*iro*).
2 *vi*: **to ~ between A and B** distinguer *or* faire la distinction entre A et B, distinguer A de B.
distinguishable [dɪs'tɪŋgwɪʃəbl] *adj* **(a)** (*which can be differentiated*) *problems, people* qui peut être distingué, qu'on peut distinguer (*from* de). **easily ~ from each other** faciles à distinguer l'un de l'autre.
(b) (*discernible*) *landmark, change* visible, perceptible.
distinguished [dɪs'tɪŋgwɪʃt] *adj* (*refined etc*) distingué, qui a de la distinction; (*eminent*) *pianist, scholar* distingué. **~ for his bravery** remarquable par *or* remarqué pour son courage.
distinguishing [dɪs'tɪŋgwɪʃɪŋ] *adj* distinctif, caractéristique. **~ mark** caractéristique *f*; (*on passport*) signe particulier.
distort [dɪs'tɔ:t] *vt* (*physically*) déformer, altérer; (*fig*) *truth* défigurer, déformer; *text* déformer; *judgment* fausser; *words, facts* dénaturer, déformer. **she has a ~ed impression of what is happening** elle se fait une idée fausse de ce qui se passe; **he gave us a ~ed version of the events** il a dénaturé les événements en les racontant.
distortion [dɪs'tɔ:ʃən] *n* (*gen, Electronics, Med, Opt*) distorsion *f*; *[tree etc]* déformation *f*; *[features]* distorsion, altération *f*, décomposition *f*; *[shape, facts, text]* déformation, altération. **by ~ of the facts** en dénaturant les faits.
distract [dɪs'trækt] *vt* (*all senses*) distraire. **the noise ~ed him from working** le bruit le distrayait de son travail; **the noise ~ed him** le bruit l'empêchait de se concentrer *or* le distrayait; **you mustn't ~ him** il ne faut pas le déranger dans son travail; **to ~ sb's attention** détourner *or* distraire l'attention de qn (*from sth* de qch).
distracted [dɪs'træktɪd] *adj* éperdu, fou (*f* folle) (*with worry etc* d'anxiété *etc*), égaré; *look* égaré, affolé. **to drive sb ~** faire perdre la tête à qn, rendre qn fou; **she was quite ~** elle était dans tous ses états.
distractedly [dɪs'træktɪdlɪ] *adv behave, run* comme un fou (*or* une folle), d'un air affolé; *love, weep* éperdument.
distracting [dɪs'træktɪŋ] *adj* gênant, qui empêche de se concentrer.
distraction [dɪs'trækʃən] *n* **(a)** (*U: lack of attention*) distraction *f*, inattention *f*. **(b)** (*interruption: to work etc*) interruption *f*; (*entertainment*) divertissement *m*, distraction *f*. **(c)** (*U: perplexity*) confusion *f*, trouble *m* d'esprit; (*madness*) affolement *m*. **to love to ~** aimer à la folie; **to drive sb to ~** faire perdre la tête à qn, rendre qn fou (*f* folle).
distrain [dɪs'treɪn] *vi* (*Jur*) **to ~ upon sb's goods** saisir les biens de qn, opérer la saisie des biens de qn.
distraint [dɪs'treɪnt] *n* (*Jur*) saisie *f*, saisie-exécution *f* (*sur les meubles d'un débiteur*).
distraught [dɪs'trɔ:t] *adj* éperdu (*with, from* de), égaré, affolé.
distress [dɪs'tres] **1** *n* **(a)** (*physical*) douleur *f*; (*mental*) douleur, chagrin *m*, affliction *f*. **to be in great ~** (*physical*) souffrir beaucoup; (*mental*) être (plongé) dans l'affliction; **to be in great ~ over sth** être profondément affligé de qch; **to cause ~ to** causer une grande peine *or* douleur à.
(b) (*great poverty*) détresse *f*, misère *f*. **in ~** dans la détresse.
(c) (*danger*) péril *m*, détresse *f*. **a ship in ~** un navire en perdition; **a plane in ~** un avion en détresse; **comrades in ~** compagnons *mpl* d'infortune.
2 *vt* affliger, peiner.
3 *cpd*: **distress rocket, distress signal** signal *m* de détresse.
distressed [dɪs'trest] *adj* affligé, peiné (*by* par, de). **she was very ~** elle était bouleversée; (*Brit*) **~ area** zone sinistrée; **in ~ circumstances** dans la détresse *or* la misère; **~ gentlewomen** dames *fpl* de bonne famille dans le besoin.
distressing [dɪs'tresɪŋ] *adj* pénible, affligeant.
distributary [dɪs'trɪbjʊtərɪ] **1** *n* (*Geog*) défluent *m*. **2** *adj* de distribution.
distribute [dɪs'trɪbju:t] *vt leaflets, prizes, type* distribuer; *dividends, load, weight* répartir; *money* distribuer, partager, répartir; (*Comm*) *goods* être concessionnaire de; *films* être distributeur de. **to ~ into categories** répartir en catégories.
distribution [dɪstrɪ'bju:ʃən] *n* (*V* **distribute**) distribution *f* (*also Comm*); répartition *f*. (*Econ*) **the ~ of wealth** la répartition *or* distribution des richesses.
distributive [dɪs'trɪbjʊtɪv] **1** *adj* (*Comm, Gram, Philos etc*) distributif. (*Econ*) **the ~ trades** le secteur de la distribution. **2** *n* (*Gram*) pronom *or* adjectif distributif.

distributor [dɪsˈtrɪbjʊtəʳ] *n* **(a)** (*Comm*) *[goods over an area]* concessionnaire *mf*; *[films]* distributeur *m*. **(b)** (*machine*) distributeur *m*; (*Aut*) delco *m* ®, distributeur.

district [ˈdɪstrɪkt] **1** *n* (*of a country*) région *f*; (*in town*) quartier *m*; (*administrative area*) district *m*, arrondissement *m*; *V* **electoral, postal.**

2 *cpd*: (*US Jur*) **district attorney** magistrat-fédéral *m*, ≃ Procureur *m* de la République; (*Brit*) **district commissioner** commissaire *m*; (*US Jur*) **district court** cour fédérale; (*Comm*) **district manager** directeur régional; **district nurse** infirmière visiteuse.

distrust [dɪsˈtrʌst] **1** *vt* se méfier de, se défier de. **2** *n* méfiance *f*. **to feel some ~ of sb/sth** éprouver de la méfiance à l'égard de qn/qch.

distrustful [dɪsˈtrʌstfʊl] *adj* méfiant, qui se méfie (*of* de).

disturb [dɪsˈtɜːb] *vt* **(a)** (*inconvenience*) *person* déranger. **don't ~ yourself!** ne vous dérangez pas!; **sorry to ~ you** excusez-moi de vous déranger; (*on notice*) **'please do not ~'** 'prière de ne pas déranger'.

(b) (*alarm*) *person* troubler, inquiéter. **the news ~ed him greatly** la nouvelle l'a beaucoup troublé *or* ébranlé.

(c) (*interrupt*) *silence, balance* troubler, rompre; *sleep, rest* troubler.

(d) (*disarrange*) *waters, sediment* troubler, remuer. **don't ~ those papers** ne dérangez pas ces papiers, laissez ces papiers comme ils sont.

disturbance [dɪsˈtɜːbəns] *n* **(a)** (*political, social*) troubles *mpl*, émeute *f*; (*in house, street*) bruit *m*, tapage *m*. **to cause a ~** faire du bruit *or* du tapage; (*Jur*) **~ of the peace** tapage injurieux *or* nocturne.

(b) (*U*) *[routine, papers]* dérangement *m*; *[liquid]* agitation *f*; *[atmosphere]* perturbation *f*.

(c) (*U: alarm, uneasiness*) trouble *m* (d'esprit), perturbation *f* (de l'esprit).

disturbed [dɪsˈtɜːbd] *adj* **(a)** *person* agité, troublé; (*Psych*) perturbé, troublé. **to be greatly ~** être très troublé (*at, by* par). **(b)** *waters* troublé; *night, sleep* agité, troublé.

disturbing [dɪsˈtɜːbɪŋ] *adj* (*alarming*) inquiétant, alarmant; (*distracting*) gênant, ennuyeux.

disunite [ˈdɪsjuːˈnaɪt] *vt* désunir.

disunity [ˌdɪsˈjuːnɪtɪ] *n* désunion *f*.

disuse [ˈdɪsˈjuːs] *n* désuétude *f*. **to fall into ~** tomber en désuétude.

disused [ˈdɪsˈjuːzd] *adj building* désaffecté, abandonné.

disyllabic [ˌdɪsɪˈlæbɪk] *adj* dissyllabe, dissyllabique.

ditch [dɪtʃ] **1** *n* (*by roadside, between fields etc*) fossé *m*; (*for irrigation*) rigole *f*; (*around castle*) douve *f*. (*Aviat sl*) **the ~** la patouille‡, la baille (*sl*); *V* **last**[1].

2 *vt* (‡: *get rid of*) *person* plaquer‡, laisser tomber*; *car etc* abandonner. **to ~ a plane** faire un amerrissage forcé.

ditcher [ˈdɪtʃəʳ] *n* terrassier *m*.

ditching [ˈdɪtʃɪŋ] *n* **(a)** creusement *m* de fossés. **hedging and ~** entretien *m* des haies et fossés. **(b)** (*Aviat*) amerrissage forcé (*d'un avion*).

dither* [ˈdɪðəʳ] (*esp Brit*) **1** *n* panique *f*. **to be in a ~, to be all of a ~** être dans tous ses états, paniquer*.

2 *vi* se tâter. **to ~ over a decision** se tâter pour prendre une décision; **stop ~ing and get on with it!** il n'y a pas à tortiller*, il faut que tu t'y mettes!

dither about*, dither around* *vi* tourner en rond (*fig*).

ditto [ˈdɪtəʊ] **1** *adv* idem. **you made a mistake and Robert ~*** tu t'es trompé et Robert idem* *or* aussi. **2** *cpd*: **ditto mark, ditto sign** guillemets *mpl* de répétition.

ditty [ˈdɪtɪ] *n* chansonnette *f*.

diuretic [ˌdaɪjʊəˈretɪk] *adj, n* diurétique (*m*).

diurnal [daɪˈɜːnl] **1** *adj* (*Astron, Bot*) diurne. **2** *n* (*Rel*) diurnal *m*.

divan [dɪˈvæn] **1** *n* divan *m*. **2** *cpd*: **divan bed** divan-lit *m*.

dive [daɪv] **1** *n* **(a)** *[swimmer, goalkeeper]* plongeon *m*; *[submarine, deep-sea diver etc]* plongée *f*; *[aircraft]* piqué *m*. **to make a ~*** foncer (tête baissée).

(b) (‡*pej: club, café etc*) bouge *m*.

2 *cpd*: **dive-bomb** bombarder en piqué; **dive bomber** bombardier *m* (*qui bombarde en piqué*); **dive bombing** bombardement *m* en piqué.

3 *vi* **(a)** *[swimmer etc]* plonger, faire un plongeon; *[submarine]* plonger, s'immerger; *[aircraft]* piquer du nez, plonger, descendre en piqué. **he ~d in head first** il a piqué une tête dans l'eau; **to ~ for pearls** pêcher des perles; (*fig*) **he ~d under the table** il s'est jeté sous la table.

(b) (*: *rush*) **to ~ in/out** *etc* entrer/sortir *etc* tête baissée; **he ~d for the exit** il a foncé (tête baissée) vers la sortie; **he ~d into the crowd** il s'est engouffré dans la foule; **to ~ for cover** se précipiter pour se mettre à l'abri; (*Ftbl*) **the goalie ~d for the ball** le gardien de but a plongé pour bloquer le ballon; (*fig*) **to ~ into one's pocket** plonger la main dans sa poche; **the child ~d into the meal** l'enfant s'est jeté sur la nourriture.

dive in *vi* **(a)** *[swimmer]* plonger.

(b) (‡: *start to eat*) **dive in!** attaquez!*

diver [ˈdaɪvəʳ] *n* **(a)** (*person*) plongeur *m*; (*in suit*) scaphandrier *m*; (*in diving bell*) plongeur (sous-marin); *V* **skin.** **(b)** (*Orn*) plongeon *m*, plongeur *m*.

diverge [daɪˈvɜːdʒ] *vi [lines, paths]* diverger, s'écarter; *[opinions, stories, explanations]* diverger.

divergence [daɪˈvɜːdʒəns] *n* divergence *f*.

divergent [daɪˈvɜːdʒənt] *adj* divergent. **~ thinking** raisonnement divergent.

divers [ˈdaɪvɜːz] *adj* (*liter*) divers, plusieurs.

diverse [daɪˈvɜːs] *adj* divers, différent.

diversification [daɪˌvɜːsɪfɪˈkeɪʃən] *n* diversification *f*.

diversify [daɪˈvɜːsɪfaɪ] *vt* diversifier, varier.

diversion [daɪˈvɜːʃən] *n* **(a)** (*Brit: redirecting*) *[traffic]* déviation *f*; *[stream]* dérivation *f*, détournement *m*.

(b) (*relaxation*) divertissement *m*, distraction *f*, diversion *f*. **it's a ~ from work** cela change *or* distrait du travail.

(c) (*Mil etc*) diversion *f*. **to create a ~** (*Mil*) opérer une diversion; (*in class, during argument etc*) faire diversion.

diversionary [daɪˈvɜːʃnərɪ] *adj remark, behaviour* destiné à faire diversion; (*Mil*) *landing, manoeuvre* de diversion.

diversity [daɪˈvɜːsɪtɪ] *n* diversité *f*, variété *f*.

divert [daɪˈvɜːt] *vt* **(a)** (*turn away*) *stream* détourner, dériver; *train, plane, ship* dérouter, détourner; *traffic* dévier; *attention, eyes* détourner; *conversation* détourner, faire dévier; *blow* écarter.

(b) (*amuse*) divertir, distraire, amuser.

diverting [daɪˈvɜːtɪŋ] *adj* divertissant, amusant.

divest [daɪˈvest] *vt* (*of clothes, weapons*) dévêtir, dépouiller (*of* de); (*of rights, property*) dépouiller, priver (*of* de); *room* dégarnir.

divide [dɪˈvaɪd] **1** *vt* **(a)** (*separate*) séparer (*from* de). **the Pyrenees ~ France from Spain** les Pyrénées séparent la France de l'Espagne.

(b) (*split: also* **~ up**) *money, work* diviser, partager, répartir (*into parts* en morceaux, en parties, *between, among* entre); *property, kingdom* diviser, démembrer, morceler; *apple, room* diviser, couper (*into* en). **she ~s her time between home and the office** elle partage son temps entre la maison et le bureau; **to ~ a large house into several flats** diviser *or* partager une grande maison en plusieurs appartements; **to ~ a class into several groups** diviser une classe en plusieurs groupes.

(c) (*Math*) diviser. **to ~ 6 into 36, to ~ 36 by 6** diviser **36** par **6**.

(d) (*cause disagreement among*) *friends, political parties etc* diviser. **they were ~d on (the question of) the death penalty** ils étaient divisés sur la question de la peine de mort; **opinions are ~d on that** les avis sont partagés là-dessus; (*Pol etc*) **policy of ~ and rule** politique *f* consistant à diviser pour régner.

(e) (*Brit Parl*) **to ~ the House** faire voter la Chambre.

2 *vi* **(a)** *[river]* se diviser; *[road]* bifurquer.

(b) (*also* **~ up**) *[people]* se diviser, se séparer (*into groups* en groupes); (*Bio*) *[cells etc]* se diviser.

(c) (*Math*) être divisible (*by* par).

(d) (*Brit Parl*) **the House ~d** la Chambre a procédé au vote *or* a voté.

3 *n* (*Geog*) ligne *f* de partage des eaux. **the Great D~** ligne de partage des montagnes Rocheuses.

divide off **1** *vi* se séparer (*from* de).

2 *vt sep* séparer (*from* de).

divide out *vt sep* répartir, distribuer (*among* entre).

divide up **1** *vi* = **divide 2b.**

2 *vt sep* = **divide 1b.**

divided [dɪˈvaɪdɪd] *adj* **(a)** (*lit*) divisé; (*Bot*) découpé. (*US*) **~ highway** route *f* à chaussées séparées *or* à quatre voies; **~ skirt** jupe-culotte *f*.

(b) (*fig: in disagreement*) *opinion* partagé; *couple, country* désuni; (*vacillating*) indécis. **I feel ~ (in my own mind) about this** je me sens partagé *or* indécis à cet égard.

dividend [ˈdɪvɪdend] *n* (*Fin, Math*) dividende *m*; *V* **pay.**

divider [dɪˈvaɪdəʳ] *n* **(a)** **~s** compas *m* à pointes sèches. **(b)** *V* **room 3.**

dividing [dɪˈvaɪdɪŋ] *adj wall, fence* mitoyen. **~ line** ligne *f* de démarcation.

divination [ˌdɪvɪˈneɪʃən] *n* (*lit, fig*) divination *f*.

divine[1] [dɪˈvaɪn] **1** *adj* (*Rel,* **fig*) divin. (*Rel*) **~ office** l'office divin; **D~ Providence** la divine Providence; (*Hist*) **~ right of kings** le droit divin des rois; **by ~ right** de droit divin; (*Rel*) **~ service** service *or* office divin; **my wife/that music *etc* is ~*** ma femme/cette musique *etc* est divine.

2 *n* ecclésiastique *m*, théologien *m*.

divine[2] [dɪˈvaɪn] **1** *vt* **(a)** (*foretell*) *the future* présager, prédire. **(b)** (*make out*) *sb's intentions* deviner, pressentir. **(c)** (*find*) *water, metal* découvrir par la radiesthésie. **2** *cpd*: **divining rod** baguette *f* divinatoire *or* de sourcier.

divinely [dɪˈvaɪnlɪ] *adv* (*Rel,* **fig*) divinement.

diviner [dɪˈvaɪnəʳ] *n [future etc]* devin *m*, devineresse *f*; *V* **water.**

diving [ˈdaɪvɪŋ] **1** *n* **(a)** (*underwater*) plongée sous-marine; (*skill*) art *m or* (*trade*) métier *m* du plongeur *or* du scaphandrier; *V* **skin.**

(b) (*from diving board*) plongeon(s) *m(pl)*.

2 *cpd*: **diving bell** cloche *f* à plongeur; **diving board** plongeoir *m*; (*springboard*) tremplin *m*; **diving suit** scaphandre *m*.

divinity [dɪˈvɪnɪtɪ] *n* **(a)** (*quality; god*) divinité *f*. **the D~** la Divinité. **(b)** (*theology*) théologie *f*.

divisible [dɪˈvɪzəbl] *adj* divisible (*by* par).

division [dɪˈvɪʒən] **1** *n* **(a)** (*act, state*) division *f*, séparation *f* (*into* en); partage *m*, répartition *f*, distribution *f* (*between, among* entre); (*Bot, Math*) division. **~ of labour** division du travail; *V* **long**[1], **simple.**

(b) (*Admin, Comm, Mil, Naut*) division *f*; (*category*) classe *f*, catégorie *f*, section *f*; (*in box, case*) division, compartiment *m*.

(c) (*that which divides*) séparation *f*; (*in room*) cloison *f*; (*fig: between social classes etc*) barrière *f*; (*dividing line: lit, fig*) division *f*.

(d) (*discord*) division *f*, désaccord *m*, brouille *f*.

(e) (*Brit Parl*) **to call a ~** passer au vote; **to call for a ~** demander la mise aux voix; **the ~ took place at midnight** la Chambre a procédé au vote à minuit; **without a ~** sans procéder au vote; **to carry a ~** avoir la majorité des voix.

2 *cpd*: (*Brit Parl*) **division bell** sonnerie *f* qui annonce la mise aux voix; (*Math*) **division sign** symbole *m* de division.

divisive [dɪˈvaɪsɪv] *adj* qui entraîne la division, qui sème le désaccord.
divisor [dɪˈvaɪzəʳ] *n* (*Math*) diviseur *m*.
divorce [dɪˈvɔːs] **1** *n* (*Jur, fig*) divorce *m* (*from* d'avec). **to get a ~ from** obtenir le divorce d'avec.
2 *vt* (*Jur*) divorcer avec *or* d'avec; (*fig*) séparer (*from* de).
3 *cpd*: **divorce court** ≃ tribunal *m* de grande instance; **divorce proceedings** procédure *f* de divorce; **to start divorce proceedings** former une requête de divorce, demander le divorce.
divorced [dɪˈvɔːst] *adj* (*Jur*) divorcé (*from* d'avec); (*fig*) divorcé (*from* de).
divorcee [dɪˌvɔːˈsiː] *n* divorcé(e) *m(f)*.
divot [ˈdɪvɪt] *n* (*esp Golf*) motte *f* de gazon.
divulge [daɪˈvʌldʒ] *vt* divulguer, révéler.
dixie [ˈdɪksɪ] *n* (*Brit Mil sl*) gamelle *f*.
Dixie [ˈdɪksɪ], **Dixieland** [ˈdɪksɪlænd] **1** *n* (*US*) États *mpl* du Sud. **2** *cpd*: **Dixieland jazz** le jazz (genre) Dixieland.
dizzily [ˈdɪzɪlɪ] *adv* **(a)** (*giddily*) *walk* avec un sentiment de vertige; *rise, fall, spin* d'une façon vertigineuse, vertigineusement. **(b)** (*fig: foolishly*) bêtement, de façon étourdie, étourdiment.
dizziness [ˈdɪzɪnɪs] *n* (*state*) vertige(s) *m(pl)*; (*also* **attack of ~**) vertige, étourdissement *m*, éblouissement *m*.
dizzy [ˈdɪzɪ] *adj* **(a)** (*Med*) *person* pris de vertige *or* d'étourdissement; (*fig*) pris de vertige. **it makes me ~** cela me donne le vertige, j'en ai la tête qui tourne; **it makes one ~ to think of it** c'est à donner le vertige (rien que d'y penser).
(b) *height, speed, rise in price* vertigineux.
(c) (*fig*) (*heedless*) tête de linotte, étourdi; (*foolish*) sot (*f* sotte).
djinn [dʒɪn] *n* djinn *m*.
do[1] [duː] *3rd person sg present* **does**, *pret* **did**, *ptp* **done** **1** *aux vb* **(a)** (*used to form interrog and neg in present and pret verbs*). **~ you understand?** comprenez-vous?, (est-ce que) vous comprenez?; **I ~ not** *or* **don't understand** je ne comprends pas; **didn't you** *or* **did you not speak?** n'avez-vous pas parlé?; **never did I see so many** jamais je n'en ai vu autant.
(b) (*for emphasis: with stress on 'do'*) **DO come!** venez donc, je vous en prie!; **DO tell him that ...** dites-lui bien que ...; **but I DO like it!** mais si je l'aime!, mais bien sûr que je l'aime!; **he DID say it** bien sûr qu'il l'a dit, il l'a bien dit; **so you DO know them!** alors c'est vrai que vous les connaissez!; **I DO wish I could come with you** je voudrais tant pouvoir vous accompagner; **do you like Paris? — DO I like Paris!**; Paris te plaît? — ah si Paris me plaît!*
(c) (*vb substitute: used to avoid repeating verb*) **you speak better than I ~** vous parlez mieux que moi *or* que je ne le fais; **she always says she will go but she never does** elle dit toujours qu'elle ira mais elle n'y va jamais; **so ~ I** moi aussi; **she used to like him and so did I** elle l'aimait bien et moi aussi (je l'aimais); **neither ~ I** ni moi, moi non plus; **he doesn't like butter and neither ~ I** il n'aime pas le beurre et moi non plus; **he said he would write to me and I believe he will ~ (so)** il a dit qu'il m'écrirait et je crois qu'il le fera; **they said he would go and so he did** on a dit qu'il s'en irait et c'est ce qui est arrivé *or* et c'est bien ce qu'il a fait; **you know him, don't you?** vous le connaissez, n'est-ce pas?; **(so) you know him, ~ you?** alors vous le connaissez?; **you DO agree, don't you?** vous êtes bien d'accord, n'est-ce pas?; **he didn't go, did he?** il n'y est pas allé, tout de même?; **she said that, did she?** elle a vraiment dit ça?, elle a osé dire ça?; **she said that, didn't she?** elle a bien dit ça, n'est-ce pas?; **I like them, don't you?** je les aime, pas vous?; **~ you see them often? — yes, I ~** vous les voyez souvent? — oui bien sûr *or* oui (je les vois souvent); **they speak French — oh, ~ they?** ils parlent français — ah oui? *or* vraiment? *or* c'est vrai?; **they speak French — ~ they really?** ils parlent français — non, c'est vrai? *or* vraiment?; **may I come in? — ~!** puis-je entrer? — bien sûr! *or* je vous en prie! (*frm*); **shall I open the window? — no, don't!** si j'ouvrais la fenêtre? — ah non!; **I'll tell him — don't!** je vais le lui dire — surtout pas!; **who broke the mirror? — I did** qui est-ce qui a cassé le miroir? — (c'est) moi.
2 *vt* **(a)** (*be busy with, involved in, carry out*) faire. **what are you ~ing (now)?** qu'est-ce que tu fais? *or* tu es en train de faire?; **what are you ~ing (these days** *or* **with yourself)?** qu'est-ce que tu deviens?; **what do you ~ (for a living)?** que faites-vous dans la vie?; **what shall I ~ next?** qu'est-ce que je dois faire ensuite?; **I've got plenty to ~** j'ai beaucoup à faire, j'ai largement de quoi m'occuper; **there's nothing to ~ here** il n'y a rien à faire ici; **I don't know what to ~** je ne sais que faire, je ne sais pas quoi faire; **are you ~ing anything this evening?** êtes-vous pris ce soir?, vous faites quelque chose ce soir?; **I shall ~ nothing of the sort** je n'en ferai rien; **don't ~ too much!** n'en faites pas trop!; (*don't overwork*) ne vous surmenez pas!; **he does nothing but complain** il ne fait que se plaindre, il ne cesse (pas) de se plaindre; **what must I ~ to get better?** que dois-je faire pour guérir?; **what shall we ~ for money?** comment allons-nous faire pour trouver de l'argent?; **what have you done with my gloves?** qu'avez-vous fait de mes gants?
(b) (*perform, accomplish*) faire, accomplir, rendre. **I'll ~ all I can** je ferai tout mon possible; **to ~ one's best** faire (tout) son possible, faire de son mieux; **I'll ~ my best to come** je ferai (tout) mon possible *or* je ferai de mon mieux pour venir; **how do you ~ it?** comment faites-vous?, comment vous y prenez-vous?; **what's to be done?** que faire?; **what can I ~ for you?** en quoi puis-je vous aider? *or* vous être utile?; **what do you want me to ~ (about it)?** qu'est-ce que vous voulez que je fasse? *or* que j'y fasse?; **to ~ sth again** refaire qch; **it's all got to be done again** tout est à refaire *or* à recommencer; **~ something for me, will you?** rends-moi (un) service, veux-tu?; **what's done cannot be undone** ce qui est fait est fait; **that's just not done!** cela ne se fait pas!; **well done!** bravo!, très bien!; **that's done it!*** (*dismay*) il ne manquait plus que ça!; (*satisfaction*) (voilà) ça y est!; **it's as good as done** c'est comme si c'était fait; **no sooner said than done** aussitôt dit aussitôt fait; **it's easier said than done** c'est plus facile à dire qu'à faire; **I've done a stupid thing** j'ai fait une bêtise; (*Theat*) **to ~ a play** monter une pièce; (*Cine*) **to ~ a film** tourner un film; **to ~ one's military service** faire son service militaire; **to ~ 6 years (in jail)** faire 6 ans de prison; *V* **bit**[2], **credit, good** *etc*.
(c) (*make, produce*) faire. **~ this letter and 6 copies** faites cette lettre et 6 copies; **I'll ~ a translation for you** je vais vous (en) faire *or* donner la traduction, je vais vous le traduire; *V* **wonder** *etc*.
(d) (*Scol etc: study*) faire, étudier. **we've done Milton** nous avons étudié *or* fait Milton; **I've never done any German** je n'ai jamais fait d'allemand.
(e) (*solve*) faire. **to ~ a crossword/a problem** faire des mots croisés/un problème; (*Math*) **to ~ a sum** faire un calcul *or* une opération.
(f) (*translate*) traduire, mettre (*into* en).
(g) (*arrange*) **to ~ the flowers** arranger les fleurs (dans les vases); **to ~ one's hair** se coiffer; **I can't ~ my tie** je n'arrive pas à faire mon nœud de cravate.
(h) (*clean, tidy*) faire, laver, nettoyer. **to ~ one's nails** se faire les ongles; **to ~ one's teeth** se laver *or* se brosser les dents; **to ~ the shoes** cirer les chaussures; **this room needs ~ing today** cette pièce est à faire aujourd'hui; **to ~ the dishes/housework** faire la vaisselle/le ménage; *V* **washing** *etc*.
(i) (*deal with*) faire, s'occuper de. **the barber said he'd ~ me next** le coiffeur a dit qu'il me prendrait après *or* qu'il s'occuperait de moi après; **he does the film criticism for the 'Gazette'** il fait la critique du cinéma dans la 'Gazette'; (*Comm*) **we only ~ one make of gloves** nous n'avons *or* ne faisons qu'une marque de gants; **I'll ~ you; if I get hold of you!** tu vas le payer cher *or* tu auras affaire à moi si je t'attrape!; **he's hard done by** on le traite durement; **he's been badly done by** on s'est très mal conduit à son égard.
(j) (*in pret, ptp only*) (*complete, accomplish*) faire; (*use up*) finir. **the work's done now** le travail est fait maintenant; **I've only done 3 pages** je n'ai fait que 3 pages; **a woman's work is never done** une femme n'est jamais au bout de sa tâche; **the soap is (all) done** il ne reste plus de savon; **I haven't done telling you what I think of you*** je n'ai pas fini de vous dire ce que je pense de vous; (*Comm*) **done!** marché conclu!, entendu!; (*frm*) **have done!** finissez donc!; **when all's said and done** tout compte fait, en fin de compte; **it's all over and done (with)** tout ça c'est fini *or* classé; **to ~ sb to death** tuer qn, frapper qn à mort; **this theme has been done to death** ce thème est rebattu; **to get done with sth** en finir avec qch.
(k) (*visit, see sights of*) *city, country, museum* visiter, faire*.
(l) (*Aut etc*) faire; rouler; parcourir. **the car was ~ing 100** la voiture roulait à 100 à l'heure *or* faisait du 100 (à l'heure); **this car does** *or* **can ~** *or* **will ~ 100** cette voiture fait *or* peut faire du 100; **we did London to Edinburgh in 8 hours** nous avons fait (le trajet) Londres-Édimbourg en 8 heures; **we've done 200 km since 2 o'clock** nous avons fait *or* parcouru 200 km depuis 2 heures.
(m) (*suit*) aller à; (*be sufficient for*) suffire à. **that will ~ me nicely** (*that's what I want*) cela fera très bien mon affaire, ça m'ira bien; (*that's enough*) cela me suffit.
(n) (*Theat, fig*) (*play part of*) faire, jouer le rôle de; (*pretend to be*) faire; (*mimic*) faire. **she does the worried mother very convincingly** elle joue à la mère inquiète avec beaucoup de conviction; **he does his maths master to perfection** il fait *or* imite son professeur de math à la perfection.
(o) (*Brit: cheat*) avoir*, refaire*. **you've been done!** on vous a eu!* *or* refait!*; **to ~ sb out of £10** carotter* 10 livres à qn, refaire* qn de 10 livres; **to ~ sb out of a job** prendre à qn son travail.
(p) (*: *provide food, lodgings for*) **they ~ you very well at that restaurant** on mange rudement* bien à ce restaurant; **Mrs X does her lodgers proud** Mme X mitonne *or* dorlote ses pensionnaires; **to ~ o.s. well** *or* **proud** ne se priver de rien.
(q) (*Culin*) (*cook*) faire (cuire); (*prepare*) *vegetables* éplucher, préparer; *salad* faire, préparer. **to ~ the cooking** faire la cuisine; **to ~ an omelette** faire une omelette; **how do you like your steak done?** comment aimez-vous votre bifteck?; **steak well done** bifteck bien cuit; **steak done to a turn** bifteck à point.
(r) (*: *tire out*) éreinter*. **I'm absolutely done!** je n'en peux plus!, je suis crevé!*
(s) (*phrases*) **what am I to ~ with you?** qu'est-ce que je vais bien pouvoir faire de toi?; **he didn't know what to ~ with himself all day** il ne savait pas quoi faire de lui-même *or* de sa peau* toute la journée; **tell me what you did with yourself last week** raconte-moi ce que tu as fait *or* fabriqué* la semaine dernière; **what have you been ~ing with yourself?** (*greeting*) qu'est-ce que vous devenez?; (*mother to child*) qu'est-ce que tu as bien pu fabriquer?*; **I shan't know what to ~ with all my free time** je ne saurai pas quoi faire de *or* comment occuper mon temps libre.
3 *vi* **(a)** (*act: be occupied*) faire, agir. **~ as your friends ~** faites comme vos amis; (*Prov*) **~ as you would be done by** ne faites pas aux autres ce que vous ne voudriez pas qu'on vous fasse; **he did well by his mother** il a bien agi envers sa mère; **he did well to take advice** il a bien fait de demander des conseils; **you would ~ well to rest more** vous feriez bien de vous reposer davantage; **he did right** il a bien fait; **he did right to go** il a bien fait d'y aller; **she was up and ~ing at 6 o'clock** elle était (debout et) à l'ouvrage dès 6 heures du matin.

(b) (*get on, fare*) aller, marcher, se porter; être. **how do you ~?** (*greeting*) bonjour, comment allez-vous?; (*on being introduced*) très heureux *or* enchanté (de faire votre connaissance); **how are you ~ing?*** comment ça va?, comment ça marche?*; **the patient is ~ing very well** le malade est en très bonne voie; **the patient is ~ing better now** le malade va mieux; **he's ~ing well at school** il marche bien* en classe; **he *or* his business is ~ing well** ses affaires vont *or* marchent bien; **the roses are ~ing well this year** les roses viennent bien cette année.

(c) (*finish*) finir, terminer. **have you done?** (vous avez) terminé?, ça y est?; **I've done with all that nonsense** je ne veux plus rien avoir à faire avec toutes ces bêtises; **have you done with that book?** vous n'avez plus besoin de ce livre?; **I've done with smoking** je ne fume plus.

(d) (*suit, be convenient*) faire l'affaire, convenir. **that will never ~!** (ah non!) ça ne peut pas aller!; **this room will ~** cette chambre ira bien *or* fera l'affaire; **will it ~ if I come back at 8?** ça (vous) va si je reviens à 8 heures?; **it doesn't ~ to tell him what you think of him** ce n'est pas (la chose) à faire (que) de lui dire ce que vous pensez de lui; **these shoes won't ~ for walking** ces chaussures ne conviennent pas *or* ne vont pas pour la marche; **this coat will ~ for *or* as a cover** ce manteau servira de couverture; **nothing would ~ but that he should come** il a fallu absolument qu'il vienne; **to make ~** s'arranger, faire aller* (*with* avec); (*fig*) **to make ~ and mend** faire des économies de bouts de chandelle; **you'll have to (make) ~ with £10** il faudra vous contenter de *or* vous débrouiller* avec 10 livres; **she hadn't much money but she made ~ with what she had** elle n'avait pas beaucoup d'argent mais elle s'en est tirée *or* elle s'est débrouillée* avec ce qu'elle avait.

(e) (*be sufficient*) suffire. **half a kilo of flour will ~ (for the cake/for the weekend)** un demi-kilo de farine suffira (pour le gâteau/pour le week-end); **can you lend me some money? — will £1 ~?** pouvez-vous me prêter de l'argent? — une livre, ça suffit? *or* ça (vous) va?; **that will ~!** ça suffit!, assez!

(f) (*do housework*) faire le ménage (et la cuisine) (*for* chez). **the woman who does for me** ma femme de ménage.

(g) (*phrases*) **what's ~ing?*** qu'est-ce qu'on fait?, qu'est-ce qui se passe?; **there's nothing ~ing in this town*** il n'y a rien d'intéressant *or* il ne se passe rien dans cette ville; **could you lend me £5? — nothing ~ing!‡** tu pourrais me prêter 5 livres? — rien à faire!* *or* pas question! *or* tu peux toujours courir!*; **this debate has to ~ with the cost of living** ce débat a à voir avec *or* concerne le coût de la vie; **a doctor has to ~ with all kinds of people** un médecin a affaire à toutes sortes de gens; **his business activities have nothing to ~ with how much I earn** ses affaires n'ont aucune influence sur ce que je touche; **money has a lot to ~ with it** l'argent y est pour beaucoup, c'est surtout une question d'argent; **he has something to ~ with the government** il a quelque chose à voir dans *or* avec le gouvernement; **he has to ~ with the steel industry** il est dans la sidérurgie; **what has that got to ~ with it?** et alors, qu'est-ce que cela a à voir?; **that has nothing to ~ with it!** cela n'a rien à voir!, cela n'y est pour rien!, cela n'a aucun rapport!; **that's got a lot to ~ with it!** cela y est pour beaucoup!; **that has nothing to ~ with the problem** cela n'a rien à voir avec le problème; **that has nothing to ~ with you!** cela ne vous regarde pas!; **I won't have anything to ~ with it** je ne veux pas m'en mêler; **to have to ~ with sb** avoir affaire à qn.

4 *n* (*) **(a)** (*party*) soirée *f*, (*ceremony*) fête *f*, grand tralala*. **there's a big ~ at the Ritz tonight** il y a (un) grand tralala* ce soir au Ritz; **there's a big Air Force ~ tomorrow at noon** l'armée de l'air organise une grande fête demain à midi.

(b) (*Brit: swindle*) escroquerie *f*. **the whole business was a real ~ from start to finish** tout ça, c'était une escroquerie du début jusqu'à la fin.

(c) (*phrases*) **it's a poor ~!** c'est plutôt minable!*; **the ~s and don'ts** ce qu'il faut faire ou ne pas faire; **fair ~s all round** à chacun son dû; *V* **hair** *etc*.

do away with *vt fus* **(a)** (*get rid of*) *custom, law, document* supprimer; *building* démolir.

(b) (*kill*) *person* liquider*, supprimer. **to do away with o.s.** se suicider, se supprimer, mettre fin à ses jours.

do down* *vt sep* (*Brit*) *person* rouler*, refaire*.

do for‡ *vt fus person* (*finish off*) démolir*, (*ruin*) ruiner; *project* flanquer en l'air*, bousiller*; *ambition* mettre fin à. **he/it is done for** il/cela est fichu* *or* foutu‡; *V also* **do¹ 3f.**

do in‡ *vt sep* **(a)** (*kill*) supprimer, liquider*.

(b) (*gen pass: exhaust*) éreinter. **to be *or* feel (quite) done in** être claqué* *or* éreinté.

do out *vt sep room* faire *or* nettoyer (à fond).

do over *vt sep* **(a)** (*redecorate*) refaire.

(b) (‡: *beat up*) passer à tabac, tabasser‡.

do up 1 *vi [dress etc]* s'attacher, se fermer.

2 *vt sep* **(a)** (*fasten*) *buttons* boutonner; *zip* fermer, remonter; *dress* attacher; *shoes* attacher (les lacets de).

(b) (*parcel together*) *goods* emballer, empaqueter. **to do sth up in a parcel** emballer *or* empaqueter qch; **to do up a parcel** faire un paquet; **books done up in brown paper** des livres emballés *or* empaquetés dans du papier d'emballage.

(c) (*renovate*) *house, room* remettre à neuf, refaire; *old dress etc* rafraîchir. **to do o.s. up** se faire beau (*f* belle).

do with *vt fus* **(a)** (*with 'can' or 'could': need*) avoir besoin de, avoir envie de. **I could do with a cup of tea** je prendrais bien une tasse de thé.

(b) (*in neg, with 'can' or 'could': tolerate*) supporter, tolérer. **I can't do with whining children** je ne peux pas supporter les enfants qui pleurnichent.

(c) = **make do**; *V* **do¹ 3d.**

do without *vt fus* se passer de, se priver de. **I can do without your advice!** je vous dispense de vos conseils!; **I could well have done without that!** je m'en serais très bien passé!; **you'll have to do without then!** alors il faudra bien que tu t'en passes (*subj*)! *or* que tu en fasses ton deuil!*

do² [dəʊ] *n* (*Mus*) do *m*, ut *m*.

doc* [dɒk] *n* (*US abbr of* **doctor**) toubib* *m*. **yes ~*** oui docteur.

docile [ˈdəʊsaɪl] *adj* docile, maniable.

docility [dəʊˈsɪlɪtɪ] *n* docilité *f*, soumission *f*.

dock¹ [dɒk] **1** *n* (*for berthing*) bassin *m*, dock *m*; (*for loading, unloading, repair: often pl*) dock(s). (*Brit fig*) **my car is in ~*** ma voiture est en réparation; *V* **dry, graving** *etc*.

2 *cpd*: **dock house** bureaux *mpl* des docks; **dock labourer** docker *m*; **dockyard** chantier naval *or* de constructions navales (*V* **naval**).

3 *vt* mettre à quai.

4 *vi* **(a)** (*Naut*) entrer au bassin *or* aux docks, arriver *or* se mettre à quai. **the ship has ~ed** le bateau est à quai.

(b) (*Space*) *[two spacecraft]* s'arrimer, s'amarrer.

dock² [dɒk] *n* (*Jur*) banc *m* des accusés *or* des prévenus. **'prisoner in the ~ ...'** 'accusé ...'.

dock³ [dɒk] *vt animal's tail* écourter, couper; (*fig*) *wages* rogner. **to ~ 50p off sb's wages** retenir *or* rogner 50 pence sur le salaire de qn; **he had his wages ~ed for being late** on lui a fait une retenue sur son salaire pour retard; **to ~ a soldier of 2 days' pay/leave** supprimer 2 jours de solde/de permission à un soldat.

dock⁴ [dɒk] *n*, **docken** [ˈdɒkn] *n* (*Bot*) patience *f*.

docker [ˈdɒkəʳ] *n* docker *m*, débardeur *m*.

docket [ˈdɒkɪt] **1** *n* **(a)** (*paper: on document, parcel etc*) étiquette *f*, fiche *f* (*indiquant le contenu d'un paquet etc*).

(b) (*Jur*) (*register*) registre *m* des jugements rendus; (*list of cases*) rôle *m* des causes; (*abstract of letters patent*) table *f* des matières, index *m*.

(c) (*Brit: Customs certificate*) récépissé *m* de douane, certificat *m* de paiement des droits de douane.

2 *vt* **(a)** *contents* résumer; (*Jur*) *judgment* enregistrer *or* consigner sommairement; (*fig*) *information etc* consigner, prendre note de.

(b) *packet, document* faire une fiche pour, étiqueter.

docking [ˈdɒkɪŋ] *n* (*Space*) arrimage *m*, amarrage *m*.

doctor [ˈdɒktəʳ] **1** *n* **(a)** (*Med*) docteur *m*, médecin *m*. **who is your ~?** qui est votre docteur?, qui est votre médecin traitant?; **D~ Smith** le docteur Smith; (*more formally*) Monsieur *or* Madame le docteur Smith; yes ~ oui docteur; **to send for the ~** appeler *or* faire venir le médecin *or* le docteur; **he/she is a ~** il/elle est médecin *or* docteur; **a woman ~** une femme docteur, une femme médecin; **he's under the ~*** il est suivi par le docteur, il est entre les mains du docteur; (*fig*) **it's just what the ~ ordered*** c'est exactement ce qu'il me (*or* te *etc*) fallait.

(b) (*Univ etc*) docteur *m*. **D~ of Law/of Science** *etc* docteur en droit/ès sciences *etc*; *V* **medicine.**

2 *vt* **(a)** *sick person* soigner.

(b) (*: *castrate*) châtrer (*un animal*).

(c) (**pej: mend*) rafistoler* (*pej*).

(d) (*tamper with*) *wine* frelater; *food* altérer; *text, document* arranger, tripatouiller*.

doctorate [ˈdɒktərɪt] *n* doctorat *m*. **~ in science/in philosophy** doctorat ès sciences/en philosophie.

doctrinaire [ˌdɒktrɪˈnɛəʳ] *adj, n* doctrinaire (*mf*).

doctrinal [dɒkˈtraɪnl] *adj* doctrinal.

doctrine [ˈdɒktrɪn] *n* (*Philos, Rel*) doctrine *f*.

document [ˈdɒkjʊmənt] **1** *n* document *m*. **~s relating to a case** dossier *m* d'une affaire; **official ~** document officiel; (*Jur*) acte authentique public.

2 [ˈdɒkjʊment] *vt* **(a)** *case* documenter.

(b) *ship* munir des papiers nécessaires.

3 *cpd*: **document case** porte-documents *m inv*.

documentary [ˌdɒkjʊˈmentərɪ] **1** *adj* documentaire. (*Jur*) **~ evidence** documents *mpl*, preuve *f* documentaire *or* par écrit. **2** *n* (*Cine*) (film *m*) documentaire *m*.

documentation [ˌdɒkjʊmenˈteɪʃən] *n* documentation *f*.

dodder [ˈdɒdəʳ] *vi* ne pas tenir sur ses jambes, marcher d'un pas branlant; (*fig*) tergiverser, atermoyer.

dodderer [ˈdɒdərəʳ] *n* vieux (*or* vieille) gaga*, croulant(e)* *m(f)*, gâteux *m*, -euse *f*.

doddering [ˈdɒdərɪŋ] *adj*, **doddery** [ˈdɒdərɪ] *adj* (*trembling*) branlant; (*senile*) gâteux.

dodge [dɒdʒ] **1** *n* **(a)** (*movement*) mouvement *m* de côté, détour *m*; (*Boxing, Ftbl*) esquive *f*.

(b) (*) (*trick*) tour *m*, truc* *m*; (*ingenious scheme*) combine* *f*, truc*. **he's up to all the ~s** il connaît (toutes) les ficelles; **that's an old ~** c'est le coup classique*; **I've got a good ~ for making money** j'ai une bonne combine* pour gagner de l'argent.

2 *vt blow, ball* esquiver; *pursuer* échapper à; (*fig: avoid ingeniously*) *question* esquiver, éluder; *difficulty* esquiver; *tax* éviter de payer; (*shirk*) *work, duty* esquiver, se dérober à. **he ~d the issue** il est volontairement passé à côté de la question; **I managed to ~ him before he saw me** j'ai réussi à l'éviter avant qu'il ne me voie.

3 *vi* faire un saut de côté *or* un brusque détour; (*Boxing, Ftbl*) faire une esquive. **to ~ out of sight *or* out of the way** s'esquiver; **to ~ behind a tree** disparaître derrière un arbre; **to ~ through the traffic/the trees** se faufiler entre les voitures/les arbres; **he saw the police and ~d round the back (of the house)** il a vu les agents et s'est esquivé (en faisant le tour de la maison) par derrière.

dodge about *vi* aller et venir, remuer.

dodgems [ˈdɒdʒəmz] *npl* autos tamponneuses.

dodger [ˈdɒdʒəʳ] *n* **(a)** (*: *trickster*) roublard(e)* *m(f)*, finaud(e) *m(f)*; (*shirker*) tire-au-flanc *m inv*; *V* **artful. (b)**

(*Naut*) toile *f* de passerelle de commandement. **(c)** (*US: handbill*) prospectus *m*.
dodgy* ['dɒdʒɪ] *adj* **(a)** (*Brit: tricky*) *situation* délicat, épineux, pas commode*. **the whole business seemed a bit ~** toute cette affaire était un peu épineuse *or* douteuse; **he's very ~** *or* **in a very ~ situation financially** il est dans une mauvaise passe financièrement.
(b) (*artful*) malin (*f* -igne), rusé.
dodo ['dəʊdəʊ] *n* dronte *m*, dodo *m*; *V* **dead.**
doe [dəʊ] *n* **(a)** (*deer*) biche *f*. **(b)** (*rabbit*) lapine *f*; (*hare*) hase *f*. **(c)** *V* **John.**
doer ['du(:)ə^r] *n* **(a)** (*author of deed*) auteur *m* d'une action, personne *f* qui commet une action. **he's a great ~ of crosswords*** c'est un cruciverbiste fervent; **he's a great ~ of jigsaw puzzles*** il adore faire *or* il se passionne pour les puzzles; *V* **evil.**
(b) (*active person*) personne *f* efficace *or* dynamique.
does [dʌz] *V* **do**[1].
doeskin ['dəʊskɪn] *n* peau *f* de daim.
doesn't ['dʌznt] = **does not;** *V* **do**[1].
doff [dɒf] *vt* (†, *hum*) *garment, hat* ôter, enlever.
dog [dɒg] **1** *n* **(a)** chien(ne) *m(f)*. (*Brit Sport*) **the ~s*** les courses *fpl* de lévriers; **to lead a ~'s life** mener une vie de chien; **she led him a ~'s life** elle lui a fait une vie de chien; (*fig*) **to go to the ~s*** *[person]* gâcher sa vie, mal tourner; *[institution, business]* aller à vau-l'eau; **he is being a ~ in the manger** il fait l'empêcheur de tourner en rond; (*Prov*) **every ~ has his day** à chacun vient sa chance, à chacun son heure de gloire; **he hasn't a ~'s chance*** il n'a pas la moindre chance (de réussir); **it's (a case of) ~ eat ~** c'est un cas où les loups se mangent entre eux; (*Prov*) **give a ~ a bad name (and hang him)** qui veut noyer son chien l'accuse de la rage (*Prov*); (*US*) **to put on the ~‡** faire de l'épate*; *V* **cat, hair** *etc.*
(b) (*male*) *[fox etc]* mâle *m*.
(c) (‡: *person*) **lucky ~** veinard(e)* *m(f)*; **gay ~** joyeux luron; **dirty ~** sale type* *m*; **sly ~** (petit) malin *m*, (petite) maligne *f*.
(d) (*Tech*) (*clamp*) crampon *m*; (*pawl*) cliquet *m*.
(e) (*feet*) **~s‡** panards‡ *mpl*.
2 *cpd* canin, de chien. **dog biscuit** biscuit *m* pour chien; **dog-cart** charrette anglaise, dog-cart *m*; **dog collar** (*lit*) collier *m* de chien; (*hum*) col *m* de pasteur, (faux-)col *m* d'ecclésiastique; **dog days** canicule *f*; **dog-eared** écorné; **dog fancier** (*connoisseur*) connaisseur *m*, -euse *f* en chiens; (*breeder*) éleveur *m*, -euse *f* de chiens; **dogfight** (*lit*) bataille *f* de chiens; (*Aviat*) combat *m* entre avions de chasse; (*between people*) bagarre *f*; **dogfish** chien *m* de mer; **dogfood** (*gen*) nourriture *f* pour chiens; (*mushy*) pâtée *f*; **dog fox** renard *m* (mâle); **to lie doggo*** rester peinard‡ dans son coin, se tenir *or* rester coi, se terrer; **doghouse** chenil *m*, niche *f* à chien; **he is in the doghouse‡** il n'est pas en odeur de sainteté; **dog Latin** latin *m* de cuisine; **dog leg** (*n*) (*in road etc*) coude *m*, angle abrupt; (*adj*) qui fait un coude; **dog licence** permis *m* de posséder un chien; **dog paddle** (*n*) nage *f* en chien; (*vi*) nager en chien; **dog rose** (*flower*) églantine *f*; (*bush*) églantier *m*; **she's the general dogsbody** elle fait le factotum, elle est la bonne à tout faire; **dogshow** exposition canine; **Dog Star** Sirius *m*; **dog-tired*** claqué*, crevé*; **dog track** piste *f* (pour les courses de lévriers); **dogtrot** petit trot; (*US: passageway*) passage couvert; (*Naut*) **dog-watch** petit quart, quart de deux heures; **dog wolf** loup *m*; **dogwood** cornouiller *m*.
3 *vt* **(a)** (*follow closely*) *person* suivre (de près). **he ~s my footsteps** il marche sur mes talons, il ne me lâche pas d'une semelle.
(b) (*harass*) harceler. **~ged by ill fortune** poursuivi par la malchance.
doge [dəʊdʒ] *n* doge *m*.
dogged ['dɒgɪd] *adj person, character* déterminé, tenace, persévérant; *courage* opiniâtre, obstiné.
doggedly ['dɒgɪdlɪ] *adv* obstinément, avec ténacité *or* obstination.
doggedness ['dɒgɪdnɪs] *n* obstination *f*, entêtement *m*, ténacité *f*.
Dogger Bank ['dɒgəbæŋk] *n* Dogger Bank *m*.
doggerel ['dɒgərəl] *n* vers *mpl* de mirliton.
doggie ['dɒgɪ] *n* = **doggy.**
doggone(d)* [ˌdɒg'gɒn(d)] *adj* (*US*) *euph for* **damn, damned;** *V* **damn 1, 2c, 3, 4, 5.**
doggy ['dɒgɪ] **1** *n* (*baby talk*) chienchien* *m*, toutou* *m* (*langage enfantin*). **2** *adj smell* de chien. **she is a very ~ woman** elle a la folie des chiens.
doglike ['dɒglaɪk] *adj* de chien.
dogma ['dɒgmə] *n* dogme *m*.
dogmatic [dɒg'mætɪk] *adj* (*Rel, fig*) dogmatique. **to be very ~ about sth** être très dogmatique sur qch.
dogmatically [dɒg'mætɪkəlɪ] *adv* dogmatiquement.
dogmatism ['dɒgmətɪzəm] *n* (*Philos, Rel*) dogmatisme *m*; (*fig*) caractère *m* *or* esprit *m* dogmatique.
dogmatize ['dɒgmətaɪz] *vi* (*Rel, fig*) dogmatiser.
do-gooder ['du:'gʊdə^r] *n* (*slightly pej*) faiseur *m*, -euse *f* *or* pilier *m* de bonnes œuvres.
doh [dəʊ] *n* (*Mus*) = **do**[2].
doily ['dɔɪlɪ] *n* (*under plate*) napperon *m*; (*on plate*) dessus *m* d'assiette.
doing ['du:ɪŋ] *n* **(a)** action *f* de faire. **this is your ~** c'est vous qui avez fait cela; **it was none of my ~** je n'y suis pour rien, ce n'est pas moi qui l'ai fait; **that takes some ~** ce n'est pas facile *or* commode, (il) faut le faire!*
(b) **~s** faits *mpl* et gestes *mpl*.
(c) (*Brit‡: thingummy*) **~s** machin* *m*, truc* *m*; **that ~s over there** ce machin* là-bas.
do-it-yourself ['du:ɪtjə'self] *adj shop* de bricolage. **~ enthusiast** bricoleur *m*, -euse *f*; **the ~ craze** la passion du bricolage, l'engouement *m* pour le bricolage; **~ kit** kit *m*, ensemble *m* de pièces détachées (à assembler soi-même).
doldrums ['dɒldrəmz] *npl* (*area*) zone *f* des calmes; (*weather*) calme équatorial. (*fig*) **to be in the ~** *[person]* avoir le cafard*, broyer du noir; *[business]* être dans le marasme.
dole [dəʊl] *n* allocation *f* *or* indemnité *f* de chômage. (*Brit*) **to go/be on the ~** s'inscrire/être au chômage.
dole out *vt sep* distribuer *or* accorder au compte-gouttes *or* avec parcimonie.
doleful ['dəʊlfʊl] *adj face, tone* dolent, plaintif, morne; *prospect, song* lugubre, morne.
dolefully ['dəʊlfəlɪ] *adv* d'un ton *or* d'une manière lugubre *or* morne, plaintivement.
dolichocephalic ['dɒlɪkəʊse'fælɪk] *adj* dolichocéphale.
doll [dɒl] *n* **(a)** poupée *f*. **to play with a ~** *or* **~s** jouer à la poupée; **~'s house/pram** maison *f*/voiture *f* de poupée.
(b) (‡: *esp US: girl*) nana‡ *f*, pépée‡ *f*; (*pretty girl*) poupée *f*.
doll up‡ *vt sep person, thing* bichonner. **to doll o.s. up, to get dolled up** se faire (tout) beau* (*or* (toute) belle*), se bichonner.
dollar ['dɒlə^r] **1** *n* dollar *m*; *V* **half, sixty. 2** *cpd*: **dollar area** zone *f* dollar; (*US*) **dollar bill** billet *m* d'un dollar; **dollar gap** déficit *m* de la balance dollar.
dollop* ['dɒləp] *n* *[butter]* gros *or* bon morceau; *[cream]* bonne cuillerée.
dolly ['dɒlɪ] **1** *n* **(a)** (*: *doll*) poupée *f*.
(b) (*for washing clothes*) agitateur *m*. **~ tub** (*for washing*) baquet *m* à lessive; (*Min*) cuve *f* à rincer.
(c) (*wheeled frame*) chariot *m*; (*Cine, TV*) chariot, travelling *m* (*dispositif*); (*Rail: truck*) plate-forme *f*.
2 *adj* (*Sport**) facile.
3 *vt* (*Cine, TV*) **to ~ the camera in/out** avancer/reculer la caméra.
dolman ['dɒlmən] *n* dolman *m*. **~ sleeve** (sorte *f* de) manche *f* kimono *inv*.
dolmen ['dɒlmen] *n* dolmen *m*.
dolomite ['dɒləmaɪt] *n* dolomite *f*, dolomie *f*. (*Geog*) **the D~s** les Dolomites.
dolphin ['dɒlfɪn] *n* (*Zool*) dauphin *m*.
dolt [dəʊlt] *n* gourde* *f*, cruche* *f* (*personne*).
doltish ['dəʊltɪʃ] *adj* gourde*, cruche*.
domain [dəʊ'meɪn] *n* (*liter*) domaine *m* (*also fig, Math etc*), propriété *f*, terres *fpl*. **in the ~ of science** dans le domaine des sciences.
dome [dəʊm] *n* (*Archit: on building*) dôme *m*, coupole *f*; (*liter: stately building*) (noble) édifice *m*; *[hill]* sommet arrondi, dôme; *[skull]* calotte *f*; *[heaven, branches]* dôme.
domed [dəʊmd] *adj forehead* bombé; *building* à dôme, à coupole.
Domesday Book ['du:mzdeɪ,bʊk] *n* Domesday Book *m* (*recueil cadastral établi par Guillaume le Conquérant*).
domestic [də'mestɪk] **1** *adj* **(a)** *duty, happiness* familial, de famille, domestique. **his public and his ~ life** sa vie publique et sa vie privée; **everything of a ~ nature** tout ce qui se rapporte au ménage; (*esp Brit*) **~ science** arts ménagers; **~ science college** école ménagère *or* d'art ménager; **~ science teaching** enseignement ménager; **~ servants, ~ staff** domestiques *mfpl*, employé(e)s *m(f)pl* de maison; **she was in ~ service** elle était employée de maison *or* domestique.
(b) (*Econ, Pol*) *policy, affairs, flights* intérieur. **~ quarrels** querelles intestines; **~ rates** tarifs *mpl* en régime intérieur.
(c) *animal* domestique.
2 *n* domestique *mf*.
domesticate [də'mestɪkeɪt] *vt person* habituer à la vie du foyer; *animal* apprivoiser.
domesticated [də'mestɪkeɪtɪd] *adj person* qui aime son intérieur, pantouflard* (*pej*), pot-au-feu *inv* (*slightly pej*); *animal* domestiqué. **she's very ~** elle est très femme d'intérieur *or* femme au foyer.
domesticity [ˌdəʊmes'tɪsɪtɪ] *n* (*home life*) vie *f* de famille, vie casanière (*slightly pej*); (*love of household duties*) attachement *m* aux tâches domestiques.
domicile ['dɒmɪsaɪl] (*Brit Admin, Fin, Jur*) **1** *n* domicile *m*. **2** *vt* domicilier. **~d at** domicilié à, demeurant à.
domiciliary [ˌdɒmɪ'sɪlɪərɪ] *adj* domiciliaire.
dominance ['dɒmɪnəns] *n* *[person, country etc]* prédominance *f*; (*Ecol, Genetics, Psych*) dominance *f*.
dominant ['dɒmɪnənt] **1** *adj* **(a)** *nations, species* dominant; (*Genetics*) dominant; *feature* dominant, principal; *position* dominant, élevé; *personality, tone* dominateur (*f* -trice).
(b) (*Mus*) de dominante.
2 *n* (*Mus*) dominante *f*; (*Ecol, Genetics*) dominance *f*.
dominate ['dɒmɪneɪt] *vti* dominer.
domination [ˌdɒmɪ'neɪʃən] *n* domination *f*.
domineer [ˌdɒmɪ'nɪə^r] *vi* agir en maître (autoritaire), se montrer autoritaire (*over* avec).
domineering [ˌdɒmɪ'nɪərɪŋ] *adj* dominateur (*f* -trice), impérieux, autoritaire.
Dominica [ˌdɒmɪ'ni:kə] *n* (*Geog*) Dominique *f*.
Dominican[1] [də'mɪnɪkən] *adj* (*Geog*) dominicain. **~ Republic** République dominicaine.
Dominican[2] [də'mɪnɪkən] *adj, n* (*Rel*) dominicain(e) *m(f)*.
dominion [də'mɪnɪən] *n* **(a)** (*U*) domination *f*, empire *m* (*over* sur). **to hold ~ over sb** maintenir qn sous sa domination *or* sous sa dépendance. **(b)** (*territory*) territoire *m*, possessions *fpl*; (*Brit Pol*) dominion *m*.
domino ['dɒmɪnəʊ] *n, pl* **~es (a)** domino *m*. **to play ~es** jouer aux dominos. **(b)** (*costume, mask, person*) domino *m*.
don[1] [dɒn] *n* **(a)** (*Brit Univ*) professeur *m* d'université (*surtout à*

Oxford et à Cambridge). **(b)** (*Spanish title*) don *m.* **a D~ Juan** un don Juan.
don[2] [dɒn] *vt garment* revêtir, endosser.
donate [dəʊ'neɪt] *vt* faire don de. **to ~ blood** donner son sang.
donation [dəʊ'neɪʃən] *n* (*act of giving*) donation *f*; (*gift*) don *m.* **to make a ~ to a fund** faire un don *or* une contribution à une caisse.
done [dʌn] **1** *ptp of* **do**[1]. **2** *adj* (*V* **do**[1]) **(a) the ~ thing** ce qui se fait. **(b)** (*: *tired out*) claqué*, crevé*. **(c)** (*used up*) fini. **the butter is ~** le beurre est terminé, il n'y a plus de beurre.
donjon ['dʌndʒən] *n* donjon *m.*
donkey ['dɒŋkɪ] **1** *n* **(a)** âne(sse) *m(f)*, baudet* *m.* (*Brit*) **she hasn't been here for ~'s years*** il y a une éternité qu'elle n'est pas venue ici.
(b) (*: *fool*) âne *m*, imbécile *mf.*
2 *cpd*: (*Tech*) **donkey engine** auxiliaire *m*, petit cheval, cheval alimentaire; **donkey jacket** grosse veste; **donkey ride** promenade *f* à dos d'âne; **the donkey work** le gros du travail.
donnish ['dɒnɪʃ] *adj look, tone* d'érudit, de savant; *person* érudit.
donor ['dəʊnəʳ] *n* (*to charity etc*) donateur *m*, -trice *f*; (*Med*) *[blood, organ for transplant]* donneur *m*, -euse *f.*
don't [dəʊnt] **1** *vb* = **do not**; *V* **do**[1]. **2** *n*: **~s** choses *fpl* à ne pas faire; *V* **do**[1] **4c.**
donut ['dəʊnʌt] *n* (*US*) = **doughnut**; *V* **dough 2.**
doodah‡ ['du:dɑ:] *n* (*gadget*) petit bidule*.
doodle ['du:dl] **1** *vi* griffonner (distraitement). **2** *n* griffonnage *m.* **3** *cpd*: (*Brit*) **doodlebug*** bombe volante.
doom [du:m] **1** *n* (*ruin*) ruine *f*, perte *f*; (*fate*) destin *m*, sort *m.* **2** *vt* condamner (*to* à), destiner (*to* à). **~ed to failure** voué à l'échec; **the project was ~ed from the start** le projet était voué à l'échec dès le début.
doomsday ['du:mzdeɪ] *n* jour *m* du Jugement dernier. (*fig*) **till ~** jusqu'à la fin des siècles *or* des temps; **D~ Book** = **Domesday Book.**
door [dɔ:ʳ] **1** *n* **(a)** *[house, room, cupboard]* porte *f*; *[railway carriage, car]* portière *f.* **he shut** *or* **closed the ~ in my face** il m'a fermé la porte au nez; **in the ~(way)** dans (l'embrasure de) la porte; (*outside door*) sous le porche; (*Theat etc*) **'pay at the ~'** 'billets à l'entrée'; *[salesman etc]* **to go from ~ to ~** faire du porte à porte (*V also* **2**); **he lives 2 ~s down the street** il habite 2 portes plus loin; **out of ~s** (au-)dehors; *V* **answer, front, next door** *etc.*
(b) (*phrases*) **to lay sth at sb's ~** imputer qch à qn, charger qn de qch; **to open the ~ to further negotiations** ouvrir la voie à des négociations ultérieures; **to leave** *or* **keep the ~ open for further negotiations** laisser la porte ouverte à des négociations ultérieures; **to close** *or* **shut the ~ to sth** barrer la route à qch, rendre qch irréalisable; *V* **death, show** *etc.*
2 *cpd*: **doorbell** sonnette *f*; **there's the doorbell!** on sonne (à la porte)!; **door curtain** portière *f* (*tenture*); **doorframe** chambranle *m*, châssis *m* de porte; **door handle** poignée *f or* bouton *m* de porte; (*Aut*) poignée de portière; **doorjamb** montant *m* de porte, jambage *m*; **doorkeeper** = **doorman**; **door knob** poignée *f or* bouton *m* de porte; **door-knocker** marteau *m* (de porte), heurtoir *m*; **doorman** *[hotel]* portier *m*; *[block of flats]* concierge *m*; **doormat** (*lit*) paillasson *m* (d'entrée), essuie-pieds *m inv*; (*: *downtrodden person*) chiffe molle; **doornail** clou *m* de porte (*V* **dead**); **doorpost** montant *m* de porte, jambage *m* (*V* **deaf**); **door scraper** grattoir *m*; **doorstep** (*lit*) pas *m* de porte, seuil *m* de porte; (**hum: hunk of bread*) grosse tartine; **the bus-stop is just at my doorstep** l'arrêt du bus est (juste) à ma porte; **door-to-door salesman** démarcheur *m*, vendeur *m* à domicile; **door-to-door selling** démarchage *m*, vente *f* à domicile, porte à porte *m inv*; **door stopper** butoir *m* de porte; **doorway** (embrasure *f* de) porte *f*, (*outside*) porche *m.*
dope [dəʊp] **1** *n* **(a)** (‡: *drugs*) drogue *f*; (*for athlete, horse*) dopant *m*, doping *m*; (*US*‡: *drug addict*) drogué(e) *m(f)*, toxico* *mf.* **to take ~, to be on ~** se droguer, se doper*.
(b) (‡*U: information*) tuyaux* *mpl.* **to give sb the ~** tuyauter* qn, affranchir‡ qn; **what's the ~ on ...?** qu'est-ce qu'on a comme tuyaux* sur ... ?
(c) (‡: *stupid person*) andouille‡ *f*, nouille* *f.*
(d) (*varnish*) enduit *m*; (*Aut, Chem*) dopant *m.*
(e) (*for explosives*) absorbant *m.*
2 *vt horse, person* doper; *food, drink* verser une drogue *or* un dopant dans.
3 *cpd*: **dope fiend** toxicomane *mf*, drogué(e) *m(f)*; **dope peddler, dope pusher** revendeur *m*, -euse *f* de stupéfiants *or* de drogue; **dope test*** (*n*) contrôle *m* anti-doping *inv*; (*vt*) faire subir le contrôle anti-doping à.
dopey ['dəʊpɪ] *adj* (*drugged*) drogué, dopé; (*very sleepy*) (à moitié) endormi; (‡: *stupid*) abruti*.
Doppler effect ['dɒplərˌɪfekt] *n* effet *m* Doppler-Fizeau.
dopy ['dəʊpɪ] *adj* = **dopey.**
Doric ['dɒrɪk] *adj* (*Archit*) dorique.
dorm [dɔ:m] *n* (*Scol sl*) = **dormitory.**
dormant ['dɔ:mənt] *adj energy, passion* en veilleuse, qui sommeille; (*Bio, Bot*) dormant; *volcano* en repos, en sommeil; *rule, law* inappliqué; *title* tombé en désuétude; (*Her*) dormant. **to let a matter lie ~** laisser une affaire en sommeil.
dormer window ['dɔ:mə'wɪndəʊ] *n* lucarne *f.*
dormie ['dɔ:mɪ] *adj* (*Golf*) dormie.
dormice ['dɔ:maɪs] *npl of* **dormouse.**
dormitory ['dɔ:mɪtrɪ] **1** *n* dortoir *m.* **2** *cpd*: (*esp Brit*) **dormitory suburb** banlieue *f* dortoir; **dormitory town** ville *f* dortoir.
Dormobile ['dɔ:məbi:l] *n* ® (*Brit*) auto-camping *f*, voiture-camping *f.*
dormouse ['dɔ:maʊs] *n, pl* **dormice** loir *m.*
dorsal ['dɔ:sl] *adj* dorsal.
dory[1] ['dɔ:rɪ] *n* (*fish*) dorée *f*, saint-pierre *m inv.*
dory[2] ['dɔ:rɪ] *n* (*boat*) doris *m.*
dosage ['dəʊsɪdʒ] *n* dosage *m*; (*amount*) dose *f*; (*on medicine bottle*) posologie *f.*
dose [dəʊs] **1** *n* **(a)** (*Pharm*) dose *f.* **give him a ~ of medicine** donne-lui son médicament; **in small/large ~s** à faible/haute dose; **she's all right in small ~s*** elle est supportable à petites doses; (*fig*) **to give sb a ~ of his own medicine** rendre à qn la monnaie de sa pièce.
(b) (*bout of illness*) attaque *f* (*of* de). **to have a ~ of flu** avoir une bonne grippe*.
(c) (*‡: *venereal disease*) vérole‡ *f.*
2 *vt person* administrer un médicament à. **she's always dosing herself** elle se bourre de médicaments.
doss‡ [dɒs] (*Brit*) **1** *n* (*cheap bed for night*) pieu‡ *m*; (*sleep*) roupillon* *m*, somme *m.* **2** *cpd*: **doss house** asile *m* (de nuit). **3** *vi* coucher à l'asile (de nuit).
doss down‡ *vi* crécher‡ (quelque part). **to doss down for the night** (trouver à) crécher quelque part pour la nuit.
dossier ['dɒsɪeɪ] *n* dossier *m*, documents *mpl.*
dot [dɒt] **1** *n* (*over i, on horizon, Math, Mus*) point *m*; (*on material*) pois *m.* (*Morse*) **~s and dashes** points et traits *mpl*; (*in punctuation*) '**~, ~, ~**' 'points de suspension'; (*fig*) **on the ~*** à l'heure pile* *or* tapante; (*Brit*) **in the year ~‡** il y a des siècles, dans la nuit des temps.
2 *vt* **(a)** *paper, wall* marquer avec des points, pointiller. **to ~ an i** mettre un point sur un i; (*fig*) **to ~ one's i's (and cross one's t's)** mettre les points sur les i; **to ~ and carry one** (*Math*) reporter un chiffre; (*: *limp*) boiter, clopiner; **field ~ted with flowers** champ parsemé de fleurs; **cars ~ted along the route** des voitures échelonnées sur le parcours; **~ted line** ligne pointillée *or* en pointillé; (*Aut*) ligne discontinue; **to tear along the ~ted line** détacher suivant le pointillé; **to sign on the ~ted line** (*lit*) signer à l'endroit indiqué *or* sur la ligne pointillée *or* sur les pointillés; (*fig*) (*agree officially*) donner son consentement (en bonne et due forme); (*accept uncritically*) s'incliner (*fig*); (*Mus*) **~ted note** note pointée.
(b) to ~ sb one‡ flanquer un gnon à qn‡.
dotage ['dəʊtɪdʒ] *n* **(a)** (*senility*) gâtisme *m*, seconde enfance. **to be in one's ~** être gâteux. **(b)** (*blind love*) adoration folle (*on* pour).
dote [dəʊt] *vi* (*be senile*) être gâteux, être gaga*.
dote on *vt fus person, thing* aimer à la folie, être fou (*f* folle) de, raffoler de.
doting ['dəʊtɪŋ] *adj* **(a)** (*adoring*) qui aime follement, qui adore. **her ~ father** son père qui l'adore. **(b)** (*senile*) gâteux.
dotterel ['dɒtrəl] *n* pluvier *m* (guignard).
dotty‡ ['dɒtɪ] *adj* (*Brit*) toqué*, piqué*. **to be ~ about sb/sth** être toqué* de qn/qch.
double ['dʌbl] **1** *adj* **(a)** (*twice as much: also Bot*) double. **a ~ amount of work** une double quantité de travail; (*Ind*) **to earn ~ time (on Sundays etc)** être payé (au tarif) double (le dimanche *etc*); *V also* **4.**
(b) (*twofold; having two similar parts; in pairs*) deux fois, double. (*in numerals*) **~ seven five four** (*7754*) deux fois sept cinq quatre, (*as telephone number*) soixante-dix-sept cinquante-quatre; **spelt with a ~ 'p'** écrit avec deux 'p'; (*Dominoes*) **the ~ 6** le double 6; **box with a ~ bottom** boîte à double fond; *V also* **4.**
(c) (*made for two users*) pour *or* de deux personnes; *V also* **4.**
(d) (*for two purposes*) double. **with a ~ meaning** à double sens; **~ advantage** double avantage *m*; **that table serves a ~ purpose** cette table a une double fonction; *V also* **4.**
(e) (*underhand, deceptive*) double, à double face, faux (*f* fausse), trompeur. **to lead a ~ life** mener une double vie; **to play a ~ game** jouer un double jeu; *V also* **4.**
2 *adv* **(a)** (*twice*) deux fois. **that costs ~ what it did last year** cela coûte deux fois plus que l'année dernière, cela a doublé de prix depuis l'année dernière; **I've got ~ what you've got** j'en ai deux fois plus que toi, j'ai le double de ce que tu as; **her salary is ~ what it was 10 years ago** son salaire est le double de ce qu'il était il y a 10 ans; **he did it in ~ the time it took me** il a mis deux fois plus de temps que moi à le faire; **he's ~ your age** il est deux fois plus âgé que vous, il a le double de votre âge; **~ 6 is 12** deux fois 6 font 12, le double de 6 est 12.
(b) (*in two; twofold*) en deux, double. **to see ~** voir double; **bent ~ with pain** plié en deux de douleur; **fold the paper ~** pliez le papier en deux.
3 *n* **(a)** (*twice a quantity, number, size etc*) double *m.* **12 is the ~ of 6** 12 est le double de 6; (*Sport, fig*) **~ or quits** quitte ou double; **he earns the ~ of what I do** il gagne le double de ce que je gagne *or* deux fois plus que moi; **he arrived at the ~** il est arrivé au pas de course.
(b) (*exactly similar thing*) réplique *f*; (*exactly similar person*) double *m*, sosie *m.*
(c) (*Cine: stand-in*) doublure *f*; (*Theat: actor taking two parts*) acteur *m*, -trice *f* qui tient deux rôles (*dans la même pièce*); (*Cards*) contre *m*; (*Betting*) pari doublé (*sur deux chevaux de deux courses différentes*); (*Dominoes*) double *m.* (*Tennis*) **~s** double; **mixed ~s** double mixte; **ladies'/men's ~s** double dames/messieurs.
4 *cpd*: **double-acting** à double effet; (*Mus*) **double bar** double barre *f*, signe *m* de reprise; **double-barrelled** *gun* à deux coups; (*Brit fig*) *surname* à rallonges*, à tiroir*; **double bass** (*instrument, player*) contrebasse *f*; **double bassoon** contrebasson *m*; **double bed** grand lit, lit de deux personnes; (*Brit Aut*) **double bend** virage *m* en S; **double boiler** casserole *f* à double fond; (*Dress*) **double-breasted** croisé; **double chin** double menton *m*; **double consonant** consonne *f* double *or* redoublée *or* géminée;

(*Brit*) **double cream** crème fraîche *or* à fouetter; **double-cross*** (*vt*) trahir, doubler*; (*n*) traîtrise *f*, duplicité *f*; **double-dealer** fourbe *m*; **double-dealing** (*n*) double jeu *m*, duplicité *f*; (*adj*) hypocrite, faux (*f* fausse) comme un jeton*; **double-decker** (*bus*) autobus *m* à impériale; (*aircraft*) deux-ponts *m inv*; (*sandwich*) sandwich *m* à deux garnitures (superposées); (*Aut*) **double declutch** faire un double débrayage; **double door** porte *f* à deux battants; (*Brit*) **double dutch*** baragouin *m*, charabia *m*; **to talk double dutch*** baragouiner; **it was double dutch to me*** pour moi c'était de l'hébreu; (*lit, fig*) **double-edged** à double tranchant, à deux tranchants; **double entendre** ambiguïté *f*, double entente *f*; (*Book-keeping*) **double entry** comptabilité *f* en partie double; (*Phot*) **double exposure** surimpression *f*, double exposition *f*; **double-faced** *material* réversible; (*pej*) *person* hypocrite; (*Tennis*) **double fault** (*n*) double faute *f*; (*vi*) faire *or* servir une double faute; (*Cine*) **double feature** programme *m* à deux longs métrages; (*Mus*) **double flat** double bémol *m*; (*Brit*) **to double-glaze a window** poser une double fenêtre; (*Brit*) **to put in double glazing** faire installer des doubles fenêtres; **double helix** double hélice *f*; (*US Insurance*) **double indemnity** indemnité *f* double; **double-jointed** désarticulé; **double knitting wool** laine *f* sport; **double knot** double nœud *m*; **double-lock** fermer à double tour; **double lock** serrure *f* de sécurité; **double negative** double négation *f*; (*Aut*) **double-park** stationner en double file; (*Aut*) **double-parking** stationnement *m* en double file; (*Med*) **double pneumonia** pneumonie *f* double; **double-quick, in double-quick time** *run etc* au pas de course *or* de gymnastique; *do, finish* en vitesse, en deux temps trois mouvements*; **double room** chambre *f* pour deux personnes; **double saucepan** = **double boiler**; (*Mus*) **double sharp** double dièse *m*; (*Typ*) **in double spacing, double-spaced** à double interligne; **double star** étoile *f* double; (*Mus*) **double stopping** doubles cordes *fpl*; **to do a double take*** y regarder à deux fois; **double talk** paroles ambiguës *or* trompeuses; **to do a double think*** *tenir un raisonnement ou suivre une démarche où l'on s'accommode (sans vergogne) de contradictions flagrantes*; (*Mil*) **in double time** au pas redoublé (*V also* **time**); **double track** (*Cine*) double bande *f*; (*tape*) double piste *f*; (*Rail*) **double track line** ligne *f* à deux voies; **a double whisky** un double whisky; **double windows** doubles fenêtres *fpl*; **egg with a double yolk** œuf *m* à deux jaunes.

5 *vt* **(a)** (*multiply by two*) *number* doubler; *salary, price* doubler, augmenter du double.

(b) (*fold in two: also* ~ **over**) plier en deux, replier, doubler.

(c) (*Theat*) **he ~s the parts of courtier and hangman** il joue les rôles *or* il a le double rôle du courtisan et du bourreau; **he's doubling the hero's part for X** il est la doublure de X dans le rôle du héros.

(d) (*Cards*) *one's opponent, his call* contrer; *one's stake* doubler. (*Bridge*) ~! contre!

6 *vi* **(a)** *[prices, incomes, quantity etc]* doubler.

(b) (*run*) courir, aller au pas de course.

(c) (*Cine*) **to ~ for sb** doubler qn.

double back 1 *vi [animal, person]* revenir sur ses pas; *[road]* faire un brusque crochet.

2 *vt sep blanket* rabattre, replier; *page* replier.

double over 1 *vi* = **double up a.**

2 *vt sep* = **double 5b.**

double up *vi* **(a)** (*bend over sharply*) se plier, se courber. **to double up with laughter/pain** se tordre *or* être plié en deux de rire/de douleur.

(b) (*share room*) partager une chambre (*with* avec).

(c) (*Brit Betting*) parier sur deux chevaux.

doublet ['dʌblɪt] *n* **(a)** (*Dress*) pourpoint *m*, justaucorps *m*. **(b)** (*Ling*) doublet *m*.

doubleton ['dʌbltən] *n* (*Cards*) deux cartes *fpl* d'une (même) couleur, doubleton *m*.

doubling ['dʌblɪŋ] *n [number, letter]* redoublement *m*, doublement *m*.

doubly ['dʌblɪ] *adv difficult, grateful* doublement, deux fois plus. **to be ~ careful** redoubler de prudence.

doubt [daʊt] **1** *n* (*U*) doute *m*, incertitude *f*. **his honesty is in ~** (*in this instance*) son honnêteté est en doute; (*in general*) son honnêteté est sujette à caution; **I am in (some) ~(s) about his honesty** j'ai des doutes sur son honnêteté; **the outcome is in ~** l'issue est indécise *or* dans la balance; **I am in no ~ as to** *or* **about what he means** je n'ai aucun doute sur ce qu'il veut dire; **to be in great ~ about sth** être dans une grande incertitude au sujet de qch; **there is room for ~** il est permis de douter; **there is some ~ about whether he'll come or not** on ne sait pas très bien s'il viendra ou non; **to have one's ~s about sth** avoir des doutes sur *or* au sujet de qch; **I have my ~s (about) whether he will come** je doute qu'il vienne; **to cast** *or* **throw ~(s) on sth** mettre qch en doute, jeter le doute sur qch; **I have no ~(s) about it** je n'en doute pas; **no ~** sans doute; **there is no ~ that ...** il n'y a pas de doute que ... + *indic*; **he'll come without any ~, there's no ~ that he'll come** il viendra sûrement, nul doute qu'il vienne; **no ~ he will come tomorrow** sans doute qu'il viendra demain; **without (a) ~** sans aucun doute, sans le moindre doute; **beyond ~** indubitablement, à n'en pas douter; **if** *or* **when in ~** s'il y a (un) doute, en cas de doute; *V* **benefit.**

2 *vt* **(a)** *person, sb's honesty, truth of statement* douter de. **I ~ it (very much)** j'en doute (fort); **I ~ed my own eyes** je n'en croyais pas mes yeux.

(b) douter. **I ~ whether he will come** je doute qu'il vienne; **I don't ~ that he will come** je ne doute pas qu'il vienne; **she didn't ~ that he would come** elle ne doutait pas qu'il viendrait; **I ~ he won't come now** je doute (beaucoup) qu'il vienne maintenant; **I ~ if that is what she wanted** je doute que ce soit ce qu'elle voulait.

3 *vi* douter (*of* de), avoir des doutes (*of* sur), ne pas être sûr (*of* de). **~ing Thomas** Thomas l'incrédule; **don't be a ~ing Thomas** ne fais pas ton (petit) saint Thomas.

doubter ['daʊtəʳ] *n* incrédule *mf*, sceptique *mf*.

doubtful ['daʊtfʊl] *adj* **(a)** (*undecided*) *person* incertain, indécis, peu convaincu; *question* douteux, discutable; *result* indécis. **to be ~ about sb/sth** douter de qn/qch, avoir des doutes sur qn/qch; **to be ~ about doing** hésiter à faire; **to look ~** avoir l'air peu convaincu; **it is ~ whether ...** il est douteux que ... + *subj*, on ne sait pas si ... + *indic*, on se demande si ... + *indic*; **it is ~ that ...** il est douteux que ... + *subj*.

(b) (*questionable*) *person* suspect, louche; *affair* douteux, louche. **in ~ taste** d'un goût douteux.

doubtfully ['daʊtfəlɪ] *adv* (*unconvincedly*) d'un air *or* d'un ton de doute, avec doute; (*hesitatingly*) en hésitant, d'une façon indécise.

doubtfulness ['daʊtfʊlnɪs] *n* (*hesitation*) indécision *f*, irrésolution *f*; (*uncertainty*) incertitude *f*; (*suspicious quality*) caractère *m* équivoque *or* suspect *or* louche.

doubtless ['daʊtlɪs] *adv* (*probably*) très probablement; (*indubitably*) sans aucun doute, sûrement, indubitablement.

douche [du:ʃ] **1** *n* (*shower bath*) douche *f*; (*Med*) *[nose, ear]* lavage *m* interne; (*as contraceptive etc*) lavage *or* injection *f* vaginal(e); (*instrument*) poire *f* à lavage vaginal. (*fig*) **it was (like) a cold ~** cela a été une douche froide*.

2 *vt* doucher.

dough [dəʊ] **1** *n* **(a)** pâte *f*. **bread ~** pâte à pain; (*fig*) **to be ~ in sb's hands** être comme une cire molle entre les mains de qn.

(b) (*‡: money*) fric‡ *m*, pognon‡ *m*.

2 *cpd*: **doughboy** (*Culin*) boulette *f* (de pâte); (*US*‡) soldat américain; **doughnut** beignet *m*.

doughty ['daʊtɪ] *adj* (*liter*) preux (*liter*), vaillant. **~ deeds** hauts faits (*liter*).

doughy ['dəʊɪ] *adj consistency* pâteux; *bread* mal cuit; (*pej*) *complexion* terreux.

dour ['dʊəʳ] *adj* austère, dur; (*stubborn*) buté. **a ~ Scot** un austère Écossais.

douse [daʊs] *vt* **(a)** (*drench*) plonger dans l'eau, tremper, inonder; *head* tremper. **(b)** *flames, light* éteindre.

dove [dʌv] *n* colombe *f*. **~-grey** gris perle *inv*; **~cote** colombier *m*, pigeonnier *m*; *V* **hawk**[1], **turtle** *etc*.

Dover ['dəʊvəʳ] *n* Douvres; *V* **strait.**

dovetail ['dʌvteɪl] **1** *n* (*Carpentry*) queue *f* d'aronde. **~ joint** assemblage *m* à queue d'aronde.

2 *vt* (*Carpentry*) assembler à queue d'aronde; (*fig*) *plans etc* faire concorder, raccorder.

3 *vi* (*Carpentry*) se raccorder (*into* à); (*fig*) concorder, coïncider.

dowager ['daʊədʒəʳ] *n* douairière *f*. **~ duchess** duchesse *f* douairière.

dowdiness ['daʊdɪnɪs] *n* manque *m* de chic.

dowdy ['daʊdɪ] *adj person* mal fagoté*, mal ficelé*; *clothes* démodé.

dowel ['daʊəl] **1** *n* cheville *f* en bois, goujon *m*. **2** *vt* assembler avec des goujons, goujonner.

dower house ['daʊəhaʊs] *n* (*Brit*) petit manoir (de douairière).

down[1] [daʊn] (*phr vb elem*) **1** *adv* **(a)** (*indicating movement to lower level*) en bas, vers le bas; (*~ to the ground*) à terre, par terre. (*said to a dog*) **~!** couché!; **~ with traitors!** à bas les traîtres!; **to come** *or* **go ~** descendre; **to fall ~** tomber; **to go/fall ~ and ~** descendre/tomber de plus en plus bas; **to run ~** descendre en courant; *V* **bend down, knock down, slide down** *etc*.

(b) (*indicating position at lower level*) en bas. **~ there** en bas (là-bas); **I shall stay ~ here** je vais rester ici *or* en bas; **don't hit a man when he is ~** ne frappez pas un homme à terre; **head ~** (*upside down*) la tête en bas; (*looking down*) la tête baissée; **face ~** *[object]* face en dessous; *[person]* face contre terre; **the sun is ~** le soleil est couché; **the blinds were ~** les stores étaient baissés; **John isn't ~ yet** Jean n'est pas encore descendu; (*Boxing*) **to be ~ for the count** être mis knock-out; **I've been ~ with flu** j'ai été au lit avec une grippe; **I'm feeling rather ~ today*** j'ai un peu le cafard aujourd'hui*; *V* **stay down** *etc*.

(c) (*to less important place; to the coast; from university*) **he came ~ from London yesterday** il est arrivé de Londres hier; **we're going ~ to the sea tomorrow** demain nous allons à la mer; **we're going ~ to Dover tomorrow** demain nous descendons à Douvres; **he came ~ from Oxford in 1973** il a terminé ses études à Oxford *or* il est sorti d'Oxford en 1973; *V* **come down, go down, send down** *etc*.

(d) (*indicating diminution in volume, degree, activity*) **his shoes were quite worn ~** ses chaussures étaient tout éculées; **the tyres are ~** les pneus sont à plat; **his temperature has gone ~** sa température a baissé; **I'm £2 ~ on what I expected** j'ai 2 livres de moins que je ne pensais; **she's very run ~** elle est en mauvaise forme, elle est très à plat*; *V* **close down, put down** *etc*.

(e) (*in writing*) inscrit. **I've got it ~ in my diary** je l'ai (mis) *or* c'est inscrit sur mon agenda; **let's get it ~ on paper** mettons-le par écrit; **to be ~ for the next race** être inscrit dans *or* pour la course suivante; *V* **note, take down, write down** *etc*.

(f) (*indicating a series or succession*) **~ to** jusqu'à; **from 1700 ~ to the present** de *or* depuis 1700 jusqu'à nos jours; **from the biggest ~ to the smallest** du plus grand (jusqu')au plus petit; **from the king ~ to the poorest beggar** depuis le roi jusqu'au plus pauvre des mendiants.

(g) (*phrases*) **to be ~ on sb*** avoir une dent contre qn; **I know the subject ~ to the ground** je connais le sujet à fond; **I am ~ on my luck** je n'ai pas de chance *or* de veine; **to be ~ in the mouth**

être abattu, avoir le moral à zéro*; **to look ~ in the mouth** avoir l'air abattu, faire une sale tête*; *V also* **5** *and* **cash, come down, up** *etc.*

2 *prep* **(a)** (*indicating movement to lower level*) en descendant, du haut en bas de. (*lit*) **he went ~ the hill** il a descendu la colline (*V also* **5**); **to slide ~ a wall** se laisser tomber d'un mur; **her hair hung ~ her back** ses cheveux lui tombaient dans le dos; **he ran his finger ~ the list** il a parcouru la liste du doigt.

(b) (*at a lower part of*) **he's ~ the hill** il est au pied *or* en bas de la côte; **she lives ~ the street (from us)** elle habite plus bas *or* plus loin (que nous) dans la rue; (*fig*) **~ the ages** au cours des siècles.

(c) (*along*) le long de. **he was walking ~ the street** il descendait la rue; **he has gone ~town** il est allé *or* descendu *or* parti en ville; **looking ~ this street, you can see ...** si vous regardez le long de cette rue, vous verrez ... .

3 *n* (*Brit*) **to have a ~ on sb*** avoir une dent contre qn, en vouloir à qn; *V* **up.**

4 *vt* (*: *replacing vb + down*) **to ~ an opponent** terrasser *or* abattre un adversaire; **he ~ed 3 enemy planes** il a descendu* 3 avions ennemis; **to ~ tools** (*stop work*) cesser le travail; (*strike*) se mettre en grève, débrayer; **he ~ed a glass of beer** il a vidé *or* s'est envoyé* un verre de bière.

5 *cpd*: **to be down-and-out** (*Boxing*) aller au tapis pour le compte, être hors de combat; (*destitute*) être sur le pavé; **he's a down-and-out** (*tramp*) c'est un clochard; (*penniless*) c'est un sans-le-sou *or* un fauché*; **down-at-heel** *person, appearance* miteux; *shoes* éculé; **downbeat** (*n: Mus*) (temps *m*) frappé *m*; (*adj: fig*) *ending etc* pessimiste; **downcast** (*adj*) (*discouraged*) abattu, démoralisé, découragé; *look, eyes* baissé; (*n: Min*) puits *m* d'aérage; **downfall** *[person, empire]* chute *f*, ruine *f*, effondrement *m*; *[hopes]* ruine; *[rain]* chute de pluie; **downgrade** (*vt*) *person* rétrograder; *hotel* déclasser; *work, job* dévaloriser, déclasser; (*n*) (*Rail etc*) rampe descendante, descente *f*; (*fig*) **on the downgrade** sur le déclin, sur le retour; **downhearted** abattu, découragé, déprimé; **don't be downhearted** ne te laisse pas décourager!; **downhill** (*adj*) en pente, incliné; **to go downhill** *[road]* aller en descendant, descendre; *[car]* descendre la côte *or* la pente; (*fig*) *[person]* être sur le déclin; *[company, business etc]* péricliter; (*Rail*) **downline** voie descendante; (*Fin*) **down payment** acompte *m*, premier versement; **to make a down payment of £10** payer un acompte de 10 livres, payer 10 livres d'acompte; (*Brit*) **downpipe** (tuyau *m* de) descente *f*; (*Brit Rail*) **down platform** quai *m* (du train) en provenance de Londres; **downpour** averse *f*, (chute *f* de) pluie torrentielle, déluge *m*; **downright** *V* **downright**; **down-river** = **downstream**; (*US*) **downspout** = **downpipe**; (*Theat*) **downstage** sur *or* vers le devant de la scène (*from* par rapport à); **downstairs** (*adj*) (*on the ground floor*) du rez-de-chaussée; (*on the floor underneath*) de l'étage au-dessous; (*below*) d'en bas; (*adv*) au rez-de-chaussée; à l'étage inférieur, en bas; **to come** *or* **go downstairs** descendre (l'escalier); **downstream** en aval; **to go downstream** descendre le courant; **downstroke** (*in writing*) plein *m*; *[piston etc]* course descendante, mouvement *m* de descente; (*Aviat*) **downswept wings** ailes surbaissées; **down-to-earth** terre à terre *inv or* terre-à-terre *inv*, réaliste; **it was a very down-to-earth plan** c'était un projet très terre à terre; **he's a very down-to-earth person** il a les pieds sur terre, il est très terre à terre; **downtown** en ville; **downtown Chicago** le centre *or* le quartier commerçant de Chicago; (*Brit Rail*) **downtrain** train *m* en provenance de Londres; (*fig*) **downtrodden** opprimé, tyrannisé; **down under** aux Antipodes (*Australie etc*); (*Naut*) **downwind** sous le vent (*from* par rapport à); (*Hunting etc*) **to be downwind of sth** avoir le vent *or* être sous le vent de qch.

down[2] [daʊn] *n [bird, person, plant]* duvet *m*; *[fruit]* peau *f* (veloutée); *V* **eider, thistle** *etc.*

down[3] [daʊn] *n* **(a)** (*hill*) colline dénudée. (*Brit*) **the D~s** les Downs *fpl* (*collines crayeuses dans le sud de l'Angleterre*). **(b)** (*Brit Geog: Straits of Dover*) **the D~s** les Dunes *fpl*.

downright ['daʊnraɪt] **1** *adj person* franc (*f* franche), direct; *refusal* catégorique; *lie* effronté. **it's ~ cheek on his part*** il a un sacré culot* *or* un fier toupet*; **it's a ~ lie to say ...** c'est mentir effrontément *or* c'est purement et simplement mentir que de dire ...; **it's a ~ lie for him to say ...** il ment carrément quand il dit ...; **it is ~ rudeness** c'est d'une impolitesse flagrante.

2 *adv rude* carrément, franchement; *refuse* catégoriquement. **it's ~ impossible** c'est purement et simplement impossible.

downward ['daʊnwəd] **1** *adj movement, pull* vers le bas; *road* qui descend en pente; *glance* baissé. (*fig*) **the ~ path** la pente fatale, le chemin qui mène à la ruine; (*St Ex*) **~ trend** tendance *f* à la baisse. **2** *adv* = **downwards.**

downwards ['daʊnwədz] (*phr vb elem*) *adv go* vers le bas, de haut en bas, en bas. **to slope (gently) ~** descendre (en pente douce); **to look ~** regarder en bas *or* vers le bas; **looking ~** les yeux baissés, la tête baissée; **place the book face ~** posez le livre face en dessous; (*fig*) **from the 10th century ~** à partir du 10e siècle; (*fig*) **from the king ~** depuis le roi (jusqu'au plus humble), du haut en bas de l'échelle sociale.

downy ['daʊnɪ] *adj* **(a)** *skin, leaf* couvert de duvet, duveté; *softness* duveteux; *peach* duveté, velouté; *cushion* de duvet. **(b)** (*Brit*: *sly, sharp*) malin (*f* -igne), roublard*.

dowry ['daʊrɪ] *n* dot *f*.

dowse [daʊz] **1** *vi* (*search for water*) faire de l'hydroscopie *or* de la radiesthésie; (*search for ore*) faire de la radiesthésie. **dowsing rod** baguette *f* (de sourcier). **2** *vt* = **douse.**

dowser ['daʊzəʳ] *n* (*for water*) sourcier *m*, radiesthésiste *mf*; (*for ore*) radiesthésiste.

doxology [dɒk'sɒlədʒɪ] *n* doxologie *f*.

doxy ['dɒksɪ] *n* (‡, ††) catin†† *f*.

doyen ['dɔɪən] *n* doyen *m* (d'âge).

doyenne ['dɔɪen] *n* doyenne *f*.

doze [dəʊz] **1** *n* somme *m*. **to have a ~** faire un petit somme. **2** *vi* sommeiller.

doze off *vi* s'assoupir, s'endormir.

dozen ['dʌzn] *n* douzaine *f*. **3 ~** 3 douzaines; **a ~ shirts** une douzaine de chemises; **a round ~** une bonne douzaine; **half-a-~, a half-~** une demi-douzaine; **20p a ~** 20 pence la douzaine; **~s of times** des douzaines de fois; **there are ~s like that** des choses (*or* des gens) comme cela, on en trouve à la douzaine; (*fig*) **~s of people came** il est venu des dizaines de gens; *V* **baker, nineteen.**

dozy ['dəʊzɪ] *adj* **(a)** (*sleepy*) assoupi, somnolent. **(b)** (*: *stupid*) gourde*, pas très dégourdi.

drab [dræb] **1** *adj colour* terne, fade; *surroundings, existence* terne, morne, gris. **2** *n* **(a)** (*U: Tex*) grosse toile bise. **(b)** (††) (*slattern*) souillon *f*; (*prostitute*) grue‡ *f*.

drabness ['dræbnɪs] *n* (*V* **drab**) caractère *m or* aspect *m* terne *or* morne; fadeur *f*.

drachm [dræm] *n* **(a)** (*Measure, Pharm*) drachme *f*. **(b)** = **drachma.**

drachma ['drækmə] *n, pl* **~s** *or* **~e** ['drækmiː] (*coin*) drachme *f*.

draconian [drə'kəʊnɪən] *adj* draconien.

Dracula ['drækjʊlə] *n* Dracula *m*.

draft [drɑːft] **1** *n* **(a)** (*outline*) *[letter]* brouillon *m*; *[novel]* premier jet, ébauche *f*.

(b) (*Comm, Fin*) *[money]* retrait *m*; (*bill*) traite *f*. **to make a ~ on** tirer sur.

(c) (*Mil: group of men*) détachement *m*; (*US Mil: conscript intake*) contingent *m*.

(d) (*US*) = **draught.**

2 *cpd*: (*US Mil*) **draft board** conseil *m* de révision; (*US Mil*) **draft card** ordre *m* d'incorporation; (*US Mil*) **draft dodger** insoumis *m*; **a draft letter** une lettre au brouillon, un brouillon de lettre; **a draft version** une version préliminaire.

3 *vt* **(a)** (*also* **~ out**) *letter* faire le brouillon de; *speech* (*gen*) écrire, préparer; (*first* ~) faire le brouillon de; (*final version*) rédiger; (*Parl*) *bill*, (*Comm, Fin*) *contract* rédiger, dresser; *plan* esquisser, dresser; *diagram* esquisser.

(b) (*US Mil*) *conscript* appeler (sous les drapeaux), incorporer. (*esp Mil*) **to ~ sb to a post/to do sth** détacher *or* désigner qn à un poste/pour faire qch.

draftiness ['drɑːftɪnɪs] *n* (*US*) = **draughtiness.**

draftsman ['drɑːftsmən] *n* (*US*) = **draughtsman a.**

draftsmanship ['drɑːftsmənʃɪp] *n* (*US*) = **draughtsmanship.**

drafty ['drɑːftɪ] *adj* (*US*) = **draughty.**

drag [dræg] **1** *n* **(a)** (*for dredging etc*) drague *f*; (*Naut: cluster of hooks*) araignée *f*; (*also* **~net**) drège *f*; (*heavy sledge*) traîneau *m*; (*Agr: harrow*) herse *f*.

(b) (*Aviat, Naut: resistance*) résistance *f*, traînée *f*.

(c) (*Aut, Rail etc: brake*) sabot *m or* patin *m* de frein.

(d) (*Hunting*) drag *m*.

(e) (*hindrance*) boulet *m*, entrave *f*, frein *m* (*on* à); (*: *person*) raseur* *m*, -euse* *f*, casse-pieds* *mf inv*; (*tedium*) corvée *f*. **he's an awful ~ on them** ils le traînent comme un boulet; **what a ~ to have to go there!*** quelle corvée *or* quelle barbe* d'avoir à y aller!; **this thing is a ~!*** quelle barbe* *or* ce que c'est embêtant ce truc-là!

(f) (‡: *pull on cigarette, pipe*) bouffée *f*. **here, have a ~** tiens, tire une bouffée.

(g) (‡: *women's clothing worn by men*) travesti *m*. **in ~** en travesti.

(h) (*US*‡: *influence*) piston *m*. **to use one's ~** travailler dans la coulisse, user de son influence.

2 *cpd*: (*Aut, Rail etc*) **drag shoe** sabot *m or* patin *m* (de frein); (*Theat*) **drag show**‡ spectacle *m* de travestis.

3 *vi* **(a)** (*trail along*) *[object]* traîner (à terre); *[anchor]* chasser.

(b) (*lag behind*) rester en arrière, traîner.

(c) (*Aut*) *[brakes]* frotter, (se) gripper.

(d) (*fig*) *[time, work, an entertainment]* traîner; *[conversation]* traîner, languir.

4 *vt* **(a)** *person, object* traîner, tirer; *person* entraîner. **to ~ one's feet** (*lit*) traîner les pieds; (*fig*) traîner (exprès); (*Naut*) **to ~ anchor** chasser sur ses ancres; (*fig*) **to ~ the truth from sb** arracher la vérité à qn.

(b) *river* draguer (*for* à la recherche de).

drag about 1 *vi* traîner.

2 *vt sep* traîner, trimbaler*. **to drag o.s. about (in pain** *etc***)** se traîner péniblement (sous l'effet de la douleur *etc*).

drag along *vt sep person* entraîner (à contrecœur); *toy etc* tirer. **to drag o.s. along** se traîner, avancer péniblement.

drag apart *vt sep* séparer de force.

drag away *vt sep* tirer, arracher, emmener de force (*from* de). **she dragged him away from the television*** elle l'a arraché à la télévision.

drag down *vt sep* tirer du haut, entraîner (en bas). (*fig*) **to drag sb down to one's own level** rabaisser qn à son niveau; **his illness is dragging him down** sa maladie l'affaiblit.

drag in *vt sep* (*fig*) *subject, remark* tenir à placer, amener à tout prix.

drag on *vi [meeting, conversation]* se prolonger, s'éterniser.

drag out 1 *vi* = **drag on.**

2 *vt sep discussion* faire traîner.

drag up *vt sep* **(a)** (‡ *pej*) *child* élever à la diable *or* tant bien que mal.

(b) *scandal, story* remettre sur le tapis, déterrer.

dragnet ['drægnet] *n* (*for fish*) seine *f*, drège *f*; (*for birds*) tirasse *f*.

dragoman ['drægəʊmən] *n* drogman *m*.

dragon ['drægən] **1** *n* **(a)** (*Myth, Zool, also fig: fierce person*) dragon *m*. **(b)** (*Mil: armoured tractor*) tracteur blindé. **2** *cpd*: **dragonfly** libellule *f*, demoiselle *f*.

dragoon [drə'gu:n] **1** *n* (*Mil*) dragon *m*. **2** *vt* tyranniser, opprimer. **to ~ sb into doing** contraindre *or* forcer qn à faire.

drain [dreɪn] **1** *n* **(a)** (*pipe, channel*) canal *m* (de décharge *or* d'écoulement), égout *m*, tuyau *m* d'écoulement; (*Agr, Med*) drain *m*; (*grid etc*) (*in street*) bouche *f* d'égout; (*beside house*) puisard *m*. **~s** (*in town*) égouts; (*in house*) canalisations *fpl* sanitaires; (*Agr*) drains; **open ~** canal *or* fossé *m or* égout à ciel ouvert; (*fig*) **to throw one's money down the ~** jeter son argent par les fenêtres; **all his hopes have gone down the ~*** voilà tous ses espoirs fichus* *or* à l'eau*.

(b) (*fig*) (*on resources, manpower*) saignée *f* (*on* de), perte *f* (*on* en); (*on strength*) épuisement *m* (*on* de). **looking after her father has been a great ~ on her** s'occuper de son père l'a complètement épuisée; *V* **brain.**

(c) (*small amount of liquid*) goutte *f*.

2 *cpd*: **draining board,** (*US*) **drainboard** égouttoir *m*, paillasse *f*; **drainpipe** tuyau *m* d'écoulement *or* de drainage; (*Brit*) **drainpipe trousers** pantalon-cigarette *m*.

3 *vt land, marshes* drainer, assécher; *vegetables* égoutter; *mine* vider, drainer; *reservoir* mettre à sec, vider; *boiler* vider, vidanger; (*Med*) *wound* drainer; *glass* vider complètement; *wine in glass* boire jusqu'à la dernière goutte. (*fig*) **to ~ sb of strength** épuiser qn; (*fig*) **to ~ a country of resources** saigner un pays.

4 *vi [liquid]* s'écouler; *[stream]* s'écouler (*into* dans); *[vegetables]* (s')égoutter.

drain away, drain off 1 *vi [liquid]* s'écouler; *[strength]* s'épuiser.

2 *vt sep liquid* faire couler (*pour vider un récipient*).

drainage ['dreɪnɪdʒ] **1** *n* (*act of draining*) drainage *m*, assèchement *m*; (*system of drains*) (*on land*) système *m* de fossés *or* de tuyaux de drainage; *[town]* système d'égouts; *[house]* système d'écoulement des eaux; (*sewage*) eaux usées; (*Geol*) système hydrographique fluvial.

2 *cpd*: (*Geol*) **drainage area, drainage basin** bassin *m* hydrographique; (*Constr*) **drainage channel** barbacane *f*; (*Med*) **drainage tube** drain *m*.

drainer ['dreɪnəʳ] *n* égouttoir *m*, paillasse *f*.

drake [dreɪk] *n* canard *m* (mâle); *V* **duck¹**.

dram [dræm] *n* **(a)** (*Measure, Pharm*) drachme *f*. **(b)** (*: *small drink*) goutte *f*, petit verre.

drama ['drɑ:mə] **1** *n* **(a)** (*U: dramatic art*) théâtre *m*, art *m* dramatique. **English ~** le théâtre anglais.

(b) (*play*) drame *m*, pièce *f* de théâtre; (*fig*) drame.

(c) (*U: quality of being dramatic*) drame *m*.

2 *cpd*: **drama critic** critique *m* dramatique.

dramatic [drə'mætɪk] *adj* **(a)** (*Literat, Theat*) *art, criticism, artist* dramatique. (*Literat*) **~ irony** ironie *f* dramatique; *V* **amateur. (b)** (*fig*) *effect, entry* théâtral; *situation, event, change* dramatique, spectaculaire.

dramatically [drə'mætɪkəlɪ] *adv* (*V* **dramatic**) dramatiquement, d'une manière dramatique *or* théâtrale *or* spectaculaire.

dramatics [drə'mætɪks] *npl* (*Theat*) art *m* dramatique; (*) comédie *f* (*fig*); *V* **amateur.**

dramatis personae ['dræmətɪspɜ:'səʊnaɪ] *npl* personnages *mpl* (*d'une pièce etc*).

dramatist ['dræmətɪst] *n* auteur *m* dramatique, dramaturge *m*.

dramatization [,dræmətaɪ'zeɪʃən] *n* (*V* **dramatize**) adaptation *f* pour la scène *etc*; dramatisation *f*.

dramatize ['dræmətaɪz] *vt* **(a)** *novel* adapter pour la scène *or* (*Cine*) pour l'écran *or* (*TV*) pour la télévision. **they ~d several episodes from his life** ils ont présenté plusieurs épisodes de sa vie sous forme de sketch.

(b) (*make vivid*) *event* dramatiser, rendre dramatique *or* émouvant; (*exaggerate*) dramatiser, faire un drame de.

Drambuie [dræm'bju:ɪ] *n* ® Drambuie *f* ®.

drank [dræŋk] *pret of* **drink.**

drape [dreɪp] **1** *vt window, statue, person* draper (*with* de); *room, altar* tendre (*with* de); *curtain, length of cloth* draper. **she ~d herself over the settee*** elle s'est étalée sur le canapé. **2** *n* **(a) ~s** tentures *fpl*. **(b)** (*US*) **~s** rideaux *mpl*.

draper ['dreɪpəʳ] *n* marchand(e) *m(f)* de nouveautés.

drapery ['dreɪpərɪ] *n* **(a)** (*material*) draperie *f*, étoffes *fpl*; (*hangings*) tentures *fpl*, draperies. **(b)** (*also* **draper's shop**) magasin *m* de nouveautés.

drastic ['dræstɪk] *adj remedy* énergique; *effect, change* radical; *measures* énergique, sévère, draconien; *price reduction* massif.

drastically ['dræstɪkəlɪ] *adv* (*V* **drastic**) énergiquement, radicalement, sévèrement, de façon massive.

drat* [dræt] *excl* (*euph for* **damn**) sapristi!*, diable! **~ the child!** au diable cet enfant!, quelle barbe* que cet enfant!

dratted* ['drætɪd] *adj* sacré* (*before n*), maudit (*before n*). **this ~ weather** ce sacré* temps, ce maudit temps.

draught, (*US*) **draft** [drɑ:ft] **1** *n* **(a)** courant *m* d'air; (*for fire*) tirage *m*; (*Naut*) tirant *m* d'eau. **beer on ~** bière *f* à la pression; (*fig*) **to feel the ~** devoir se serrer la ceinture*.

(b) (*drink*) coup *m*; (*Med*) potion *f*, breuvage *m*. **a ~ of cider** un coup de cidre; **to drink in long ~s** boire à longs traits.

(c) **(game of) ~s** (jeu *m* de) dames *fpl*.

(d) (*rough sketch*) = **draft 1a.**

2 *cpd animal* de trait; *cider, beer* à la pression. **draughtboard** damier *m*; **draught excluder** bourrelet *m* (*de porte, de fenêtre*); **draughtproof** (*adj*) calfeutré; (*vt*) calfeutrer; **draughtproofing** calfeutrage *m*, calfeutrement *m*.

draughtiness, (*US*) **draftiness** ['drɑ:ftɪnɪs] *n* (*U*) courants *mpl* d'air.

draughtsman ['drɑ:ftsmən] *n* **(a)** ((*US*) **draftsman**) (*Art*) dessinateur *m*, -trice *f*; (*in drawing office*) dessinateur, -trice industriel(le). **(b)** (*in game*) pion *m*.

draughtsmanship, (*US*) **draftsmanship** ['drɑ:ftsmənʃɪp] *n [artist]* talent *m* de dessinateur, coup *m* de crayon; (*in industry*) art *m* du dessein industriel.

draughty, (*US*) **drafty** ['drɑ:ftɪ] *adj room* plein de courants d'air; *street corner* exposé à tous les vents *or* aux quatre vents.

draw [drɔ:] *pret* **drew,** *ptp* **drawn 1** *vt* **(a)** (*move by pulling*) *object, cord, string, bolt* tirer. **to ~ a bow** tirer à l'arc; **to ~ the curtains** (*open*) tirer *or* ouvrir les rideaux; (*shut*) tirer *or* fermer les rideaux; **to ~ one's hand over one's eyes** se passer la main sur les yeux; **I drew her arm through mine** j'ai passé *or* glissé son bras sous le mien; **to ~ a book towards one** tirer un livre vers soi; **to ~ one's finger along a surface** passer le doigt sur une surface; **to ~ one's hat over one's eyes** baisser son chapeau sur ses yeux; **to ~ one's belt tighter** serrer sa ceinture; (*Med*) **to ~ an abscess** faire mûrir un abcès; (*aim*) **to ~ a bead on sth** viser qch.

(b) (*pull*) *coach, cart* tirer, traîner; *train* tirer; *caravan, trailer* remorquer.

(c) (*extract, remove*) *teeth* extraire, arracher; *cork* retirer, enlever. (*fig*) **to ~ sb's teeth** mettre qn hors d'état de nuire; (*Sewing*) **to ~ threads** tirer des fils; **to ~ a ticket out of a hat** tirer un billet d'un chapeau; **to ~ one's gun** tirer son revolver; **he drew a gun on me** il a tiré un revolver et l'a braqué sur moi; (*fig*) **to ~ the sword** passer à l'attaque; **with ~n sword** l'épée dégainée; **to ~ the bolt of a door** ouvrir *or* tirer le verrou d'une porte.

(d) (*obtain from source*) *wine* tirer (*from* de); *water* (*from tap, pump*) tirer (*from* de); (*from well*) puiser (*from* dans). **to ~ a bath** faire couler un bain, préparer un bain; **the stone hit him and drew blood** la pierre l'a frappé et l'a fait saigner; (*Med*) **to ~ blood from sb's arm** faire une prise de sang à qn; (*fig*) **that remark drew blood** cette remarque a porté; **to ~ (a) breath** aspirer, respirer; (*fig*) souffler; **to ~ lots (for sth)** tirer (qch) au sort; **to ~ straws** tirer à la courte paille; **they drew lots as to who should do it** ils ont tiré au sort (pour décider) qui le ferait; **to ~ the first prize** gagner *or* décrocher le gros lot; **to ~ a card from the pack** tirer une carte du jeu; (*Cards*) **to ~ trumps** tirer *or* faire tomber les atouts; **to ~ a blank** (*lit*) tirer un billet (de loterie) blanc; (*fig*) revenir bredouille, faire chou blanc*; **to ~ inspiration from** puiser *or* tirer son inspiration de; **to ~ comfort from** puiser une *or* sa consolation dans; **her singing drew tears from the audience** sa façon de chanter a fait pleurer les auditeurs; **her singing drew applause from the audience** sa façon de chanter a provoqué les applaudissements des auditeurs; **to ~ a smile/a laugh from sb** faire sourire/rire qn; **to ~ money from the bank** retirer de l'argent à la banque *or* de la banque; **to ~ a cheque on a bank** tirer un chèque sur une banque; **to ~ one's salary/pay** toucher son traitement/son salaire.

(e) (*attract*) *attention, customer, crowd* attirer. **the play has ~n a lot of criticism** la pièce a donné lieu à *or* s'est attiré de nombreuses critiques; **to feel ~n towards sb** se sentir attiré par *or* porté vers qn.

(f) (*cause to move, do, speak etc*) **her shouts drew me to the scene** ses cris m'ont attiré sur les lieux; **to ~ sb into a plan** entraîner qn dans un projet; **I could ~ no reply from him** je n'ai pu tirer de lui aucune réponse; **he refuses to be ~n** (*will not speak*) il refuse de parler; (*will not be provoked*) il refuse de se laisser provoquer; **to ~ sth to a close or an end** mettre fin à qch.

(g) *picture* dessiner; *plan, line, circle* tracer; (*fig*) *situation* faire un tableau de; *character* peindre, dépeindre. **to ~ sb's portrait** faire le portrait de qn; **to ~ a map** (*Geog*) dresser une carte; (*Scol*) faire *or* dessiner une carte; (*fig*) **I ~ the line at scrubbing floors** je n'irai pas jusqu'à *or* je me refuse à frotter les parquets; **I ~ the line at murder** (*personally*) je n'irai pas jusqu'au *or* je me refuse au meurtre; (*as far as others are concerned*) je n'admets pas *or* je ne tolère pas le meurtre; **we must ~ the line somewhere** il faut se fixer une limite, il y a des limites *or* une limite à tout; **it's hard to know where to ~ the line** il n'est pas facile de savoir où fixer les limites.

(h) (*establish, formulate*) *conclusion* tirer (*from* de); *comparison, parallel* établir, faire (*between* entre); *distinction* faire, établir (*between* entre).

(i) (*Naut*) **the boat ~s 4 metres** le bateau a un tirant d'eau de 4 mètres, le bateau cale 4 mètres.

(j) **to ~ (a match)** (*Sport*) faire match nul; (*Chess*) faire partie nulle.

(k) (*infuse*) *tea* faire infuser.

(l) (*Culin*) *fowl* vider; *V* **hang.**

(m) (*Hunting*) **to ~ a fox** débusquer *or* lancer un renard.

(n) *metal* étirer; *wire* tréfiler.

2 *vi* **(a)** (*move, come*) *[person]* s'approcher (de), se rapprocher (de); *[time, event]* approcher (de). **he drew towards the door** il s'est dirigé vers la porte; **to ~ to one side** s'écarter; **to ~ round the table** se rassembler *or* s'assembler autour de la table; **the train drew into the station** le train est entré en gare; **the car drew over towards the centre of the road** la voiture a dévié vers le milieu de la chaussée; **he drew ahead of the other runners** il s'est détaché des autres coureurs; **the 2 horses drew level** les 2 chevaux sont arrivés à la hauteur l'un de l'autre; **to ~ near (to)** s'approcher (de); **to ~ nearer (to)** s'approcher un peu plus (de); **to ~ to an end** *or* **a close** tirer à *or* toucher à sa fin.

(b) *[chimney, pipe]* tirer.

(c) (*be equal*) *[two teams]* faire match nul; (*in exams, competitions*) être ex æquo *inv.* **the competitors/the teams drew for second place** les concurrents *mpl*/les équipes *fpl* sont arrivé(e)s deuxièmes ex æquo *or* ont remporté la deuxième place ex æquo.
(d) (*Cards*) **to ~ for partners** tirer pour les partenaires.
(e) (*Art*) dessiner. **he ~s well** il dessine bien, il sait bien dessiner.
(f) *[tea]* infuser.
3 *n* **(a)** (*lottery*) loterie *f*, tombola *f*; (*act of ~ing a lottery*) tirage *m* au sort; *V* **luck.**
(b) (*Sport*) match nul, partie nulle. **the match ended in a ~** ils ont fini par faire match nul; **5 wins and 2 ~s** 5 matches gagnés et 2 matches nuls.
(c) (*attraction*) attraction *f*, succès *m*; (*Comm*) réclame *f*. **Laurence Olivier was the big ~** Laurence Olivier était la grande attraction.
(d) to be quick on the ~ (*lit*) avoir la détente rapide; (*fig*) avoir la repartie facile.
4 *cpd*: **drawback** (*disadvantage*) inconvénient *m*; désavantage *m* (*to* à); (*refund*) drawback *m*; **drawbridge** pont-levis *m*, pont basculant *or* à bascule; **draw-sheet** alaise *f*; **drawstring** cordon *m*; **draw(-top) table** table *f* à rallonge.
draw along *vt sep cart* tirer, traîner; (*fig*) *person* entraîner.
draw apart *vi* s'éloigner *or* s'écarter l'un de l'autre, se séparer.
draw aside 1 *vi [people]* s'écarter.
2 *vt sep person* tirer *or* prendre à l'écart; *object* écarter.
draw away 1 *vi* **(a)** *[person]* s'éloigner, s'écarter (*from* de); *[car etc]* démarrer. **to draw away from the kerb** s'éloigner du trottoir.
(b) (*move ahead*) *[runner, racehorse etc]* se détacher (*from* de), prendre de l'avance (*from* sur).
2 *vt sep person* éloigner, emmener; *object* retirer, ôter.
draw back 1 *vi* (*move backwards*) (se) reculer (*from* de), faire un mouvement en arrière; (*fig*) se retirer, reculer (*at, before, from* devant).
2 *vt sep person* faire reculer; *object, one's hand* retirer.
3 drawback *n V* **draw 4.**
draw down *vt sep blind* baisser, descendre; (*fig*) *blame, ridicule* attirer (*on* sur).
draw in 1 *vi* **(a)** (*Aut*) **to draw in by the kerb** (*pull over*) se rapprocher du trottoir; (*stop*) s'arrêter le long du trottoir.
(b) (*get shorter*) **the days are drawing in** les jours diminuent *or* raccourcissent.
2 *vt sep* **(a)** *air* aspirer, respirer.
(b) (*attract*) *crowds* attirer. **the play is drawing in huge returns** la pièce fait des recettes énormes; (*fig*) **to draw sb in on a project** recruter qn pour un projet.
(c) rentrer; *reins* tirer sur. (*lit, fig*) **to draw in one's claws** rentrer ses griffes; *V* **horn.**
draw off 1 *vi [army, troops]* se retirer.
2 *vt sep gloves* retirer, ôter; *garment* ôter, enlever; *pint of beer* tirer; (*Med*) *blood* prendre.
draw on 1 *vi [time]* s'avancer.
2 *vt sep* **(a)** *stockings, gloves, garment* enfiler; *shoes* mettre.
(b) (*fig: encourage*) *person* entraîner, encourager.
draw out 1 *vi* (*become longer*) **the days are drawing out** les jours rallongent.
2 *vt sep* **(a)** (*bring out, remove*) *handkerchief, purse* sortir, tirer (*from* de); *money* retirer (*from* de); *secret, plan* soutirer (*from* à); (*fig*) *person* faire parler. **he's shy, try and draw him out (of his shell)** il est timide, essayez de le faire parler *or* de le faire sortir de sa coquille.
(b) *wire* étirer, tréfiler; (*fig*) *speech, meeting* faire traîner, (faire) tirer en longueur; *meal* prolonger.
draw up 1 *vi* (*stop*) *[car etc]* s'arrêter, stopper.
2 *vt sep* **(a)** *chair* approcher; *troops* aligner, ranger; *boat* tirer à sec. **to draw o.s. up (to one's full height)** se redresser (fièrement).
(b) (*formulate, set out*) *contract, agreement* dresser, rédiger; *plan, scheme* formuler, établir; (*Fin*) *bill* établir, dresser.
draw (up)on *vt fus*: **to draw (up)on one's savings** prendre *or* tirer sur ses économies; **to draw (up)on one's imagination** faire appel à son imagination.
drawee [drɔːˈiː] *n* (*Fin*) tiré *m*.
drawer [drɔːʳ] *n* **(a)** *[furniture]* tiroir *m*; *V* **bottom, chest**[1] *etc.*
(b) [ˈdrɔːəʳ] (*person*) *[cheque etc]* tireur *m*; (*Art*) *[pictures]* dessinateur *m*, -trice *f*. **(c) ~s**† *[men]* caleçon *m*; *[women]* culotte *f*, pantalon(s)† *m(pl)*.
drawing [ˈdrɔːɪŋ] **1** *n* **(a)** (*Art*) dessin *m*. **pencil ~** dessin au crayon; **chalk ~** pastel *m*; **rough ~** ébauche *f*, esquisse *f*, croquis *m*.
(b) (*U: extending, tapering*) *[metals]* étirage *m*.
2 *cpd*: **drawing board** planche *f* à dessin; (*fig*) **the scheme is still on the drawing board** le projet est encore à l'étude; (*Brit*) **drawing office** bureau *m* de dessin industriel; (*Art*) **drawing paper** papier *m* à dessin; (*Art*) **drawing pen** tire-ligne *m*; (*Brit*) **drawing pin** punaise *f* (*à papier*); **drawing room** salon *m*; (*larger*) salle *f or* salon de réception.
drawl [drɔːl] **1** *vi* parler d'une voix traînante. **2** *vt* dire *or* prononcer d'une voix traînante. **3** *n* débit traînant, voix traînante. **a slight American ~** un léger accent américain; **... he said with a ~** ... dit-il d'une voix traînante.
drawn [drɔːn] **1** *ptp of* **draw.**
2 *adj* **(a)** (*haggard*) *features* tiré, crispé. **to look ~** avoir les traits tirés; **face ~ with pain** visage crispé par la douleur.
(b) (*equal*) *game, match* nul. **~ battle** bataille indécise.
(c) long-~-out qui tire en longueur, qui traîne.
3 *cpd*: (*Sewing*) **drawn work** ouvrage *m* à fils tirés *or* à jour(s).
dray [dreɪ] *n [brewer]* haquet *m*; *[wood, stones]* fardier *m*; *[quarry work]* binard *m*.
dread [dred] **1** *vt* redouter, appréhender. **to ~ doing** redouter de faire; **to ~ that ...** redouter que ... ne + *subj.* **2** *n* terreur *f*, effroi *m*, épouvante *f*. **in ~ of doing** dans la crainte de faire; **to be** *or* **stand in ~ of** redouter, vivre dans la crainte de. **3** *adj* (*liter*) redoutable, terrible.
dreadful [ˈdredfʊl] *adj crime, sight, suffering* épouvantable, affreux, atroce; *weapon, foe* redoutable; (*) *weather* affreux, atroce; (*) *child* insupportable, terrible. **what a ~ nuisance!*** quelle barbe!*, c'est rudement embêtant!*; **it's a ~ thing but ...** c'est terrible mais ...; **what a ~ thing to happen!** quelle horreur!; **I feel ~!** (*ill*) je ne me sens pas bien (du tout)!; (*ashamed*) j'ai vraiment honte!; *V* **penny.**
dreadfully [ˈdredfəlɪ] *adv frightened, late* terriblement, affreusement, horriblement. **I'm ~ sorry but ...** je regrette infiniment mais ...; **I'm ~ sorry** je suis absolument désolé.
dreadnought [ˈdrednɔːt] *n* (*Naut*) cuirassé *m* (d'escadre).
dream [driːm] (*vb: pret, ptp* **dreamed** *or* **dreamt**) **1** *n* **(a)** (*during sleep*) rêve *m*. **to have a ~ about sth** faire un rêve sur qch, rêver de qch; **I've had a bad ~** j'ai fait un mauvais rêve *or* un cauchemar; **the whole business was (like) a bad ~** toute cette affaire a été comme un mauvais rêve; **it was like a ~ come true** c'était comme dans un rêve; **sweet ~s!** fais de beaux rêves!; **to see sth in a ~** voir qch en rêve; **life is but a ~** la vie n'est qu'un songe.
(b) (*when awake*) rêverie *f*, rêve *m*, songerie *f*. **half the time she goes around in a ~*** la moitié du temps elle est dans un rêve *or* elle est dans les nuages *or* elle rêvasse.
(c) (*fantasy*) rêve *m*, vision *f*. **the house of his ~s** la maison de ses rêves; **his fondest ~ was to see her again** son vœu le plus cher était de la revoir; **to have ~s of doing** rêver de faire; **all his ~s came true** tous ses rêves se sont réalisés; **idle ~s** rêvasseries *fpl*; **rich beyond his wildest ~s** plus riche qu'il n'aurait jamais pu rêver de l'être.
(d) (*) merveille *f*, amour* *m*. **a ~ of a hat** un amour de chapeau*, une merveille de petit chapeau; **isn't he a ~?** n'est-ce pas qu'il est adorable?
2 *cpd car, holiday* de rêve. **his dream house** la maison de ses rêves; **dreamland** pays *m* des rêves *or* des songes; **dream world** monde *m* imaginaire; **he lives in a dream world** il plane complètement.
3 *vi* **(a)** (*in sleep*) rêver. **to ~ about** *or* **of sb/sth** rêver de qn/qch; **to ~ about** *or* **of doing** rêver qu'on a fait.
(b) (*when awake*) rêvasser, se perdre en rêveries. **I'm sorry, I was ~ing** excusez-moi, j'étais dans la lune *or* je rêvais.
(c) (*imagine, envisage*) songer, penser (*of* à), avoir l'idée (*of* de). **I should never have dreamt of doing such a thing** l'idée ne me serait jamais passée par la tête de faire une chose pareille, je n'aurais jamais songé *or* pensé à faire une chose pareille; **I shouldn't ~ of telling her!** jamais il ne me viendrait à l'idée de lui dire cela!; **will you come? — I shouldn't ~ of it!** vous allez venir? — jamais de la vie! *or* pas question!
4 *vt* **(a)** (*in sleep*) rêver, voir en rêve. **to ~ a dream** faire un rêve; **I dreamt that she came** j'ai rêvé qu'elle venait; **you must have dreamt it!** vous avez dû le rêver!
(b) (*imagine*) **if I had dreamt you would do that ...** si j'avais pu imaginer un instant que tu ferais cela ...; **I didn't ~ he would come!** je n'ai jamais songé *or* imaginé un instant qu'il viendrait!
dream away *vt sep time, one's life* perdre en rêveries.
dream up* *vt sep idea* imaginer, concevoir. **where did you dream that up?** où est-ce que vous êtes allés pêcher cela?*
dreamer [ˈdriːməʳ] *n* (*lit*) rêveur *m*, -euse *f*; (*fig*) rêveur, songe-creux *m inv*; (*politically*) utopiste *mf*.
dreamily [ˈdriːmɪlɪ] *adv* (*V* **dreamy**) d'un air *or* d'un ton rêveur *or* songeur, rêveusement, d'une manière distraite.
dreamless [ˈdriːmlɪs] *adj* sans rêves.
dreamt [dremt] *pret, ptp of* **dream.**
dreamy [ˈdriːmɪ] *adj* **(a)** *nature* rêveur, romanesque, songeur. **(b)** (*absent-minded*) rêveur, distrait, dans la lune *or* les nuages; *expression* rêveur. **(c)** *music* langoureux. **(d)** (*) ravissant.
dreariness [ˈdrɪərɪnɪs] *n* (*V* **dreary**) aspect *m* morne *etc*; monotonie *f*.
dreary [ˈdrɪərɪ] *adj weather* morne, lugubre; *landscape* morne, désolé, monotone; *life* morne, monotone; *work* monotone, ennuyeux; *speech, person* ennuyeux (comme la pluie).
dredge[1] [dredʒ] **1** *n* (*net, vessel*) drague *f*. **2** *vt river, canal* draguer. **3** *vi* draguer.
dredge up *vt sep* (*lit*) draguer; (*fig*) *unpleasant facts* déterrer, ressortir.
dredge[2] [dredʒ] *vt* (*Culin*) saupoudrer (*with* de, *on to, over* sur).
dredger[1] [ˈdredʒəʳ] *n* (*Naut*) (*ship*) dragueur *m*; (*machine*) drague *f*.
dredger[2] [ˈdredʒəʳ] *n* (*Culin*) saupoudreuse *f*, saupoudroir *m*.
dredging[1] [ˈdredʒɪŋ] *n* (*Naut*) dragage *m*.
dredging[2] [ˈdredʒɪŋ] *n* (*Culin*) saupoudrage *m*.
dregs [dregz] *npl* lie *f* (*also fig*). **to drink sth to the ~** boire qch jusqu'à la lie; **the ~ of society** la lie de la société; **he is the ~*** c'est la dernière des crapules.
drench [drentʃ] **1** *vt* **(a)** tremper, mouiller. **to get ~ed to the skin** se faire tremper jusqu'aux os, se faire saucer*; *V* **sun. (b)** (*Vet*) administrer *or* faire avaler un médicament à. **2** *n* (*Vet*) (dose *f* de) médicament *m* (*pour un animal*).
drenching [ˈdrentʃɪŋ] **1** *n*: **to get a ~** se faire tremper *or* saucer*. **2** *adj*: **~ rain** pluie battante *or* diluvienne.
Dresden [ˈdrezdən] *n* (*also* **~ china**) porcelaine *f* de Saxe, saxe *m*. **a piece of ~** un saxe.

dress [dres] **1** *n* **(a)** robe *f*. **a long/silk/summer ~** une robe longue/de soie/d'été; *V* **cocktail, wedding** *etc*.
(b) (*U: clothing*) habillement *m*, tenue *f*, vêtements *mpl*; (*way of dressing*) tenue, mise *f*. **articles of ~** vêtements; **in eastern ~** en tenue orientale; **careless in one's ~** d'une tenue *or* mise négligée; *V* **evening, full, national** *etc*.
2 *cpd*: **dress circle** premier balcon, corbeille *f*; **dress coat** habit *m*, queue-de-pie *f*; **dress designer** couturier *m*, dessinateur *m*, -trice *f* de mode, modéliste *mf*; **dress length** (*of material*) hauteur *f* (de robe); **dressmaker** couturière *f*; **dressmaking** couture *f*; travaux *mpl* de couture, confection *f* de robes; **dress rehearsal** (*Theat*) (répétition *f*) générale *f*; (*fig*) répétition générale; **dress shield** dessous-de-bras *m*; **dress shirt** chemise *f* de soirée; **dress suit** habit *m or* tenue *f* de soirée *or* de cérémonie; (*Mil*) **dress uniform** tenue *f* de cérémonie.
3 *vt* **(a)** (*clothe*) *child, family, recruits, customer* habiller. **to ~ o.s.** s'habiller; **to be ~ed for the country/for town/for tennis** être en tenue de sport/de ville/de tennis; **~ed in black** habillé de *or* en noir; **to be ~ed to kill*** être sur son trente et un, *[woman only]* être parée comme une mariée (*hum*).
(b) (*Theat*) *play* costumer.
(c) (*arrange, decorate*) *gown* parer, orner; (*Naut*) *ship* pavoiser. **to ~ a shop window** faire l'étalage, faire la vitrine; **to ~ sb's hair** coiffer qn.
(d) (*Culin*) *salad* assaisonner, garnir (*d'une vinaigrette, d'une sauce*); *food for table* apprêter, accommoder; *chicken* préparer. **~ed crab** du crabe tout préparé (*pour la table*).
(e) *skins* préparer, apprêter; *material* apprêter; *leather* corroyer; *timber* dégrossir; *stone* tailler, dresser.
(f) (*Agr*) *field* façonner.
(g) *troops* aligner.
(h) *wound* panser. **to ~ sb's wound** faire le pansement de qn.
4 *vi* **(a)** s'habiller, se vêtir. **to ~ in black** s'habiller de noir; **she ~es very well** elle s'habille avec goût; **to ~ for dinner** se mettre en tenue de soirée; *[man]* se mettre en smoking; *[woman]* se mettre en robe du soir; **we don't ~ (for dinner)** nous ne nous habillons pas pour le dîner.
(b) *[soldiers]* s'aligner. **right ~!** à droite, alignement!

dress down **1** *vt sep* **(a)** (*: *scold*) passer un savon à*.
(b) *horse* panser.
2 dressing-down* *n V* **dressing 2.**

dress up **1** *vi* **(a)** (*put on smart clothes*) s'habiller, se mettre en grande toilette, s'endimancher (*pej*). (*Brit*) **to be dressed up to the nines*** être sur son trente et un; **there's no need to dress up*** il n'y a pas besoin de vous habiller.
(b) (*put on fancy dress*) se déguiser, se costumer (*as* en). **the children love dressing up** les enfants adorent se déguiser.
2 *vt sep* **(a)** déguiser (*as* en). **(b) it dresses up the skirt** cela rend la jupe plus habillée.

dresser^1 ['dresə^r] *n* **(a)** (*Theat*) habilleur *m*, -euse *f*; (*Comm: window ~*) étalagiste *mf*. **she's a stylish ~** elle s'habille avec chic; *V* **hair. (b)** (*tool*) (*for wood*) raboteuse *f*; (*for stone*) rabotin *m*.

dresser^2 ['dresə^r] *n* **(a)** (*furniture*) buffet *m*, vaisselier *m*. **(b)** (*US*) = **dressing table**; *V* **dressing 2.**

dressing ['dresɪŋ] **1** *n* **(a)** (*providing with clothes*) habillement *m*. **~ always takes me a long time** je mets beaucoup de temps à m'habiller; *V* **hair** *etc*.
(b) (*Med*) pansement *m*.
(c) (*Culin*) (*presentation*) présentation *f*; (*seasoning*) assaisonnement *m*, sauce *f*; (*stuffing*) farce *f*. **oil and vinegar ~** vinaigrette *f*; *V* **salad.**
(d) (*manure*) engrais *m*, fumages *mpl*.
(e) (*for material, leather*) apprêt *m*.
(f) (*Constr*) parement *m*.
2 *cpd*: **dressing case** nécessaire *m* de toilette, trousse *f* de toilette *or* de voyage; **to give sb a dressing-down*** passer un savon à qn*; **to get a dressing-down*** recevoir *or* se faire passer un savon*, se faire enguirlander*; **dressing gown** robe *f* de chambre; *[bather, boxer etc]* peignoir *m*; (*negligée*) déshabillé *m*; **dressing room** (*in house*) dressing-room *m*, vestiaire *m*; (*Theat*) loge *f* (d'acteur); **dressing table** coiffeuse *f*, (table *f* de) toilette *f*; **dressing table set** accessoires *mpl* pour coiffeuse.

dressy ['dresɪ] *adj person* chic *inv*, élégant; *party* (très) habillé; *clothes, material* (qui fait) habillé.

drew [druː] *pret of* **draw.**

dribble ['drɪbl] **1** *vi [liquids]* tomber goutte à goutte, couler lentement; *[baby]* baver; (*Sport*) dribbler. *[people]* **to ~ back/in** *etc* revenir/entrer *etc* par petits groupes *or* un par un.
2 *vt* **(a)** (*Sport*) *ball* dribbler.
(b) he ~d his milk all down his chin son lait lui dégoulinait le long du menton.
3 *n* **(a)** *[water]* petite goutte.
(b) (*Sport*) dribble *m*.

driblet ['drɪblɪt] *n [liquid]* gouttelette *f*. **in ~s** (*lit*) goutte à goutte, (*fig*) au compte-gouttes.

dribs and drabs ['drɪbzən'dræbz] *npl* petites quantités. **in ~** (*gen*) petit à petit, peu à peu; *arrive* en *or* par petits groupes; *pay, give* au compte-gouttes.

dried [draɪd] **1** *pret, ptp of* **dry. 2** *adj fruit, beans* sec (*f* sèche); *vegetables* séché, déshydraté; *eggs, milk* en poudre; *flowers* séché. **~ fruit** fruits secs.

drier ['draɪə^r] *n* = **dryer.**

drift [drɪft] **1** *vi* **(a)** (*on sea, river etc*) aller à la dérive, dériver; (*in wind/current*) être poussé *or* emporté (par le vent/le courant); (*Aviat*) dériver; *[snow, sand etc]* s'amonceler, s'entasser. **to ~ downstream** descendre le courant à la dérive; *[person]* **to ~ away/out/back** *etc* s'en aller/sortir/revenir *etc* d'une allure nonchalante; **he was ~ing aimlessly about** il flânait (sans but), il déambulait.
(b) (*fig*) *[person]* se laisser aller, aller à la dérive; *[events]* tendre (*towards* vers). **to let things ~** laisser les choses aller à la dérive *or* à vau-l'eau; **he ~ed into marriage** il s'est retrouvé marié; **the nation was ~ing towards a crisis** le pays glissait vers une crise.
(c) (*Rad*) se décaler.
2 *n* **(a)** (*U: driving movement or force*) mouvement *m*, force *f*; *[air, water current]* poussée *f*. **the ~ of the current** (*speed*) la vitesse du courant; (*direction*) le sens *or* la direction du courant; **carried north by the ~ of the current** emporté vers le nord par le courant; (*fig*) **the ~ of events** le cours *or* la tournure des événements.
(b) (*mass*) *[clouds]* traînée *f*; *[dust]* nuage *m*; *[falling snow]* rafale *f*; *[fallen snow]* congère *f*, amoncellement *m*; *[sand, leaves]* amoncellement, entassement *m*; (*Geol: deposits*) apports *mpl*.
(c) (*U*) (*act of drifting*) *[ships, aircraft]* dérivation *f*; *[projectile]* déviation *f*; (*deviation from course*) dérive *f*; (*Ling*) évolution *f* (de la langue). **continental ~** dérive des continents.
(d) (*general meaning*) *[question etc]* but *m*, portée *f*, sens *m* (général). **I caught the ~ of what he said, I caught his general ~** j'ai compris le sens général de ses paroles, j'ai compris où il voulait en venir.
(e) (*Min*) galerie chassante.
3 *cpd*: **drift anchor** ancre flottante; **drift ice** glaces *fpl* en dérive; **drift-net** filet dérivant, traîne *f*; **driftwood** bois flotté.

drifter ['drɪftə^r] *n* (*boat*) chalutier *m*, drifter *m*; (*person*) personne *f* qui se laisse aller *or* qui est sans but dans la vie. **he's a bit of a ~** il manque un peu de stabilité.

drill^1 [drɪl] **1** *n* (*for metal, wood*) foret *m*, mèche *f*; (*for oil well*) trépan *m*; (*complete tool*) porte-foret *m*, perceuse *f*; (*Min*) perforatrice *f*, foreuse *f*; *[dentist]* roulette *f*, fraise *f* (de dentiste). **electric (hand) ~** perceuse électrique; *V* **pneumatic.**
2 *vt wood, metal* forer, driller, percer; *tooth* fraiser. **to ~ an oil well** forer un puits de pétrole.
3 *vi* forer.

drill^2 [drɪl] **1** *n* (*U*) (*esp Mil: exercises etc*) exercice(s) *m(pl)*, manœuvre(s) *f(pl)*; (*in grammar etc*) exercices. (*fig*) **what's the ~?*** quelle est la marche à suivre?; **he doesn't know the ~*** il ne connaît pas la marche à suivre *or* la marche des opérations.
2 *vt soldiers* faire faire l'exercice à. **these troops are well-~ed** ces troupes sont bien entraînées; **to ~ pupils in grammar** faire faire des exercices de grammaire à des élèves; **to ~ good manners into a child** dresser un enfant à bien se tenir; **I ~ed it into him that he must not ...** je lui ai bien fait entrer dans la tête qu'il ne doit pas ... .
3 *vi* (*Mil*) faire l'exercice, être à l'exercice.
4 *cpd*: (*Mil*) **drill sergeant** sergent instructeur.

drill^3 [drɪl] (*Agr*) **1** *n* (*furrow*) sillon *m*; (*machine*) drill *m*, semoir *m*. **2** *vt seeds* semer en sillons; *field* tracer des sillons dans.

drill^4 [drɪl] *n* (*Tex*) coutil *m*, treillis *m*.

drilling^1 ['drɪlɪŋ] **1** *n* (*U*) *[metal, wood]* forage *m*, perçage *m*, perforation *f*; (*by dentist*) fraisage *m*. **~ for oil** forage (pétrolier). **2** *cpd*: **drilling rig** derrick *m*; (*at sea*) plate-forme *f*; **drilling ship** navire *m* de forage.

drilling^2 ['drɪlɪŋ] *n* (*Mil*) exercices *mpl*, manœuvres *fpl*.

drily ['draɪlɪ] *adv* (*coldly*) sèchement, d'un ton sec; (*with dry humour*) d'un ton *or* d'un air pince-sans-rire.

drink [drɪŋk] (*vb: pret* **drank**, *ptp* **drunk**) **1** *n* **(a)** (*liquid to ~*) boisson *f*. **have you got ~s for the children?** est-ce que tu as des boissons pour les enfants?; **there's food and ~ in the kitchen** il y a de quoi boire et manger à la cuisine; **there's plenty of food and ~ in the house** il y a tout ce qu'il faut à boire et à manger dans la maison; **may I have a ~?** est-ce que je pourrais boire quelque chose?; **to give sb a ~** donner à boire à qn.
(b) (*glass of alcoholic ~*) verre *m*, coup* *m*, pot* *m*; (*before meal*) apéritif *m*; (*after meal*) digestif *m*. **have a ~!** tu prendras bien un verre?; **let's have a ~** on va prendre *or* boire quelque chose, on va prendre un verre *or* un pot*; **let's have a ~ on it** on va boire un coup* pour fêter ça; **I need a ~!** il me faut quelque chose à boire!, vite à boire!; **he likes a ~** il aime bien boire un verre *or* un coup*; **to ask friends in for ~s** inviter des amis à venir prendre un verre *or* boire un pot*; **to stand sb a ~** offrir un verre *or* un pot* à qn, offrir à boire à qn; **to stand a round of ~s** *or* **~s all round** payer une tournée; **he had a ~ in him*** il avait un verre dans le nez*; *V* **short, soft, strong** *etc*.
(c) (*U: alcoholic liquor*) la boisson, l'alcool *m*. **to be under the influence of ~, to be the worse for ~** être en état d'ébriété, être plutôt éméché* *or* parti*; **to take to ~** s'adonner à la boisson; **to smell of ~** sentir l'alcool; **his worries drove him to ~** ses soucis l'ont poussé à boire *or* à la boisson; **it's enough to drive you to ~!** ça vous pousserait un honnête homme à la boisson!*; *V* **demon.**
(d) (*: *sea*) flotte* *f*. **to be in the ~** être à la baille* *or* à la patouille*.
2 *cpd*: **the drink problem** le problème de l'alcoolisme; **to have a drink problem** être alcoolique.
3 *vt wine, coffee* boire, prendre; *soup* manger. **would you like something to ~?** voulez-vous boire quelque chose?; **give me something to ~** donnez-moi (quelque chose) à boire; **is the water fit to ~?** est-ce que l'eau est potable?; **this coffee isn't fit to ~** ce café n'est pas buvable; **to ~ sb's health** boire à (la santé de) qn; **this wine should be drunk at room temperature** ce vin se boit chambré; (*fig*) **he ~s all his wages** il boit tout ce qu'il gagne; **to ~ o.s. to death** se tuer à force de boire; **to ~ sb under the table** faire rouler qn sous la table; *V* **toast** *etc*.
4 *vi* boire. **he doesn't ~** il ne boit pas; **his father drank** son père buvait; **to ~ from the bottle** boire à (même) la bouteille; **to ~ out of a glass** boire dans un verre; (*notice*) **'don't ~ and drive'** 'attention, au volant l'alcool tue'; **to ~ like a fish*** boire comme

un trou*; **to ~ to sb/to sb's success** boire à *or* porter un toast à qn/au succès de qn.
drink away *vt sep fortune* boire; *sorrows* noyer (dans l'alcool).
drink down *vt sep* avaler, boire d'un trait.
drink in *vt sep [plants, soil]* absorber, boire; *(fig) story* avaler*. **he drank in the fresh air** il a respiré *or* humé l'air frais; *(fig)* **the children were drinking it all in** les enfants n'en perdaient pas une goutte* *(fig)*.
drink up 1 *vi* boire, vider son verre. **drink up!** finis *or* bois ton vin! (*or* ton café! *etc*).
2 *vt sep* boire (jusqu'au bout), finir.
drinkable ['drɪŋkəbl] *adj (not poisonous) water* potable; *(palatable) wine* buvable.
drinker ['drɪŋkəʳ] *n* buveur *m*, -euse *f*. **whisky ~** buveur de whisky; **he's a hard** *or* **heavy ~** il boit beaucoup, il boit sec.
drinking ['drɪŋkɪŋ] **1** *n (U) (act)* boire *m*, acte *m* de boire; *(drunkenness)* boisson *f*, alcoolisme *m*, ivrognerie *f*.
2 *cpd*: **drinking bout** (séance *f* de) beuverie *f*; **drinking fountain** (*in street*) fontaine publique; (*in toilets etc*) jet *m* d'eau potable; **drinking song** chanson *f* à boire; **drinking trough** abreuvoir *m*, auge *f* à boire; **drinking water** eau *f* potable.
drip [drɪp] **1** *vi [water, sweat, rain]* tomber goutte à goutte, dégoutter, dégouliner; *[tap]* couler, goutter; *[cheese, washing]* s'égoutter; *[hair, trees etc]* dégoutter, ruisseler (*with* de). **the rain was ~ping down the wall** la pluie dégouttait *or* dégoulinait le long du mur; **sweat was ~ping from his brow** il avait le front ruisselant de sueur; **to be ~ping with sweat** ruisseler de sueur, être en nage; **his hands were ~ping with blood** il avait les mains dégoulinantes de sang; **the walls were ~ping (with water)** les murs suintaient; **he's ~ping wet*** il est trempé jusqu'aux os; **my coat is ~ping wet*** mon manteau est trempé *or* est à tordre.
2 *vt liquid* faire tomber *or* laisser tomber goutte à goutte; *washing, cheese* égoutter. **you're ~ping paint all over the floor** tu mets de la peinture partout.
3 *n* **(a)** *(sound) [water, rain]* bruit *m* de l'eau qui tombe goutte à goutte; *[tap]* bruit d'un robinet qui goutte; *(drop)* goutte *f*; (**fig: spineless person*) nouille* *f*, lavette* *f*.
(b) *(Med) (liquid)* perfusion *f*; *(device)* goutte-à-goutte *m inv*. **to put up a ~** mettre un goutte-à-goutte; **to be on a ~** être sous perfusion, avoir le goutte-à-goutte.
(c) *(Archit: also* **~stone**) larmier *m*.
4 *cpd*: **drip-dry** *shirt* qui ne nécessite aucun repassage; *(Comm: on label)* 'ne pas repasser'; *(Med)* **drip-feed** alimenter par perfusion; **drip mat** dessous-de-verre *m inv*.
dripping ['drɪpɪŋ] **1** *n* **(a)** *(Culin)* graisse *f* (de rôti). **bread and ~** tartine *f* à la graisse.
(b) *(action) [water etc]* égouttement *m*, égouttage *m*.
2 *adj* **(a)** *tap* qui goutte *or* fuit; *rooftop, tree* ruisselant, qui dégoutte; *washing* qui dégoutte, trempé; (*) *coat, hat* trempé, dégoulinant*, saucé*.
(b) *(Culin)* **~ pan** lèchefrite *f*.
drive [draɪv] (*vb: pret* **drove**, *ptp* **driven**) **1** *n* **(a)** *(Aut: journey)* promenade *f or* trajet *m* en voiture. **to go for a ~** faire une promenade en voiture; **it's about one hour's ~ from London** c'est à environ une heure de voiture de Londres.
(b) *(private road) (into castle)* allée *f*, avenue *f*; *(into house)* allée.
(c) *(Golf)* drive *m*; *(Tennis)* coup droit, drive.
(d) *(energy)* dynamisme *m*, énergie *f*; *(Psych etc)* besoin *m*, instinct *m*. **the sex ~** les pulsions sexuelles; **to have plenty of ~** avoir de l'énergie *or* du dynamisme *or* de l'allant, être dynamique *or* entreprenant; **to lack ~** manquer d'allant *or* de dynamisme.
(e) *(Pol etc)* campagne *f*, propagande *f*; *(Mil)* poussée *f*. **a ~ to boost sales** une promotion systématique de vente; **output ~** effort *m* de production; *V* **export, whist** *etc*.
(f) *(Tech: power transmission)* commande *f*, transmission *f*, actionnement *m*. *(Aut)* **front-wheel ~** traction *f* avant; **rear-wheel ~** propulsion *f* arrière; **left-hand ~** conduite *f* à gauche.
2 *cpd*: **drive-in** (*adj, n*) drive-in (*m*); *(Aut etc)* **driveshaft** arbre *m* de transmission; **driveway = drive 1b.**
3 *vt* **(a)** *people, animals* chasser *or* pousser devant soi; *(Hunting) game* rabattre; *clouds* charrier, chasser, pousser; *leaves* chasser. **to ~ sb out of the country** chasser qn du pays; *(fig)* **to ~ sb into a corner** mettre qn au pied du mur *(fig)*; **the dog drove the sheep into the farm** le chien a fait rentrer les moutons à la ferme; **the gale drove the ship off course** la tempête a fait dériver le navire; **the wind drove the rain against the windows** le vent rabattait la pluie contre les vitres.
(b) *cart, car, train* conduire; *racing car* piloter; *passenger* conduire. **he ~s a lorry/taxi** *(for a living)* il est camionneur/chauffeur de taxi; **he ~s a Peugeot** il a une Peugeot; **he ~s racing cars** il est pilote de course; *(Aut)* **to ~ sb back/off** *etc* ramener/emmener *etc* qn en voiture; **I'll ~ you home** je vais vous ramener en voiture, je vais vous reconduire chez vous; **he drove me down to the coast** il m'a conduit (en voiture) jusqu'à la côte.
(c) *(operate) motor* actionner, commander, entraîner. **steam-driven train** locomotive *f* à vapeur; **machine driven by electricity** machine fonctionnant à l'électricité.
(d) *nail* enfoncer; *stake* enfoncer, ficher; *rivet* poser; *(Golf, Tennis)* driver; *tunnel* percer, creuser; *well* forer, percer. **to ~ a nail home** enfoncer un clou à fond; *(fig)* **to ~ a point home** réussir à faire comprendre un argument; *(fig)* **to ~ sth into sb's head** enfoncer qch dans la tête de qn; **to ~ sth out of sb's head** faire complètement oublier qch à qn; **to ~ a bargain** conclure un marché; **to ~ a hard bargain with sb** soutirer le maximum à qn.
(e) *(fig)* **to ~ sb hard** surcharger qn de travail, surmener qn; **to ~ sb mad** rendre qn fou (*f* folle); **to ~ sb to despair** réduire qn au désespoir; **to ~ sb to rebellion** pousser *or* inciter qn à la révolte; **to ~ sb to do** *or* **into doing sth** pousser qn à faire qch; **I was driven to it** j'y ai été poussé malgré moi, j'y ai été contraint.
4 *vi* **(a)** *(Aut)* conduire (une voiture), aller en voiture. **to ~ away/back/down** *etc* partir/revenir/aller *etc* en voiture; **can you ~?** savez-vous conduire?; **to ~ at 50 km/h** rouler à 50 km/h; **to ~ on the right** rouler à droite, tenir la droite; **did you come by train? — no, we drove** êtes-vous venus par le train? — non, (nous sommes venus) en voiture; **we have been driving all day** nous avons fait de la route *or* nous avons roulé toute la journée.
(b) the rain was driving in our faces la pluie nous fouettait le visage.
drive along 1 *vi [vehicle]* rouler, circuler; *[person]* rouler.
2 *vt sep [wind, current]* chasser, pousser.
drive at *vt fus (fig: intend, mean)* en venir à, vouloir dire. **what are you driving at?** où voulez-vous en venir?, que voulez-vous dire?
drive away 1 *vi [car]* démarrer; *[person]* s'en aller *or* partir en voiture.
2 *vt sep (lit, fig) person, suspicions, cares* chasser.
drive back 1 *vi [car]* revenir; *[person]* rentrer en voiture.
2 *vt sep* **(a)** *(cause to retreat) (Mil etc)* repousser, refouler, faire reculer. **the storm drove him back** la tempête lui a fait rebrousser chemin.
(b) *(convey back)* ramener *or* reconduire en voiture.
drive in 1 *vi [car]* entrer; *[person]* entrer (en voiture).
2 *vt sep nail* enfoncer; *screw* visser. *(fig)* **to drive an idea into sb's head** enfoncer *or* faire entrer une idée dans la tête de qn.
3 drive-in *adj, n V* **drive 2.**
drive off 1 *vi* **(a) = drive away 1.**
(b) *(Golf)* driver.
2 *vt sep* **= drive away 2.**
drive on 1 *vi [person, car]* poursuivre sa route; *(after stopping)* reprendre sa route, repartir.
2 *vt sep (incite, encourage)* pousser, inciter, entraîner (*to* à).
drive out 1 *vi [car]* sortir; *[person]* sortir (en voiture).
2 *vt sep person* faire sortir, chasser; *thoughts, desires* chasser.
drive over 1 *vi* venir *or* aller en voiture. **we drove over in 2 hours** nous avons fait le trajet en 2 heures.
2 *vt sep (convey)* conduire en voiture.
3 *vt fus (crush)* écraser.
drive up *vi [car]* arriver; *[person]* arriver (en voiture).
drivel ['drɪvl] **1** *n (U)* radotage *m*, sornettes *fpl*, imbécillités *fpl*. **what utter ~!** quelles imbécillités! *or* sornettes! **2** *vi* radoter. **what's he ~ling about?** qu'est-ce qu'il radote?*
driven ['drɪvn] *ptp of* **drive.**
driver ['draɪvəʳ] *n* **(a)** *[car]* conducteur *m*, -trice *f*; *[taxi, truck, bus]* chauffeur *m*, conducteur, -trice; *[racing car]* pilote *m*; *(Brit) [locomotive]* mécanicien *m*, conducteur; *[cart]* charretier *m*. **car ~s** automobilistes *mpl*; **to be a good ~** conduire bien; **he's a very careful ~** il conduit très prudemment; *(US)* **~'s license** permis *m* de conduire; *(Aut)* **the ~'s** *or* **driving seat** la place du conducteur; **to be in the ~'s** *or* **driving seat** *(lit)* être au volant; *(fig)* tenir les rênes, être aux commandes; *V* **back, lorry, racing** *etc*.
(b) *[animals]* conducteur *m*; *V* **slave.**
(c) *(golf club)* driver *m*.
driving ['draɪvɪŋ] **1** *n (Aut)* conduite *f*. **his ~ is awful** il conduit très mal; **bad ~** conduite imprudente *or* maladroite; **dangerous ~** conduite dangereuse; **~ is his hobby** conduire est sa distraction favorite.
2 *adj* **(a)** *necessity* impérieux, pressant. **he is the ~ force** c'est lui qui est la force agissante, il est la locomotive*.
(b) ~ rain pluie battante.
3 *cpd*: **driving belt** courroie *f* de transmission; **driving instructor** moniteur *m*, -trice *f* de conduite *or* d'auto-école; **driving lesson** leçon *f* de conduite; *(Brit)* **driving licence** permis *m* de conduire; **driving mirror** rétroviseur *m*; **driving school** auto-école *f*; **driving seat** *V* **driver a**; **driving test** examen *m* du permis de conduire; **to pass one's driving test** avoir son permis; **to fail the driving test** être refusé *or* recalé* à son permis; *(Tech)* **driving wheel** roue motrice.
drizzle ['drɪzl] **1** *n* bruine *f*, crachin *m*. **2** *vi* bruiner.
drizzly ['drɪzlɪ] *adj* de bruine, de crachin.
droll [drəʊl] *adj (comic)* comique, drôle; *(odd)* bizarre, drôle, curieux.
dromedary ['drɒmɪdərɪ] *n* dromadaire *m*.
drone [drəʊn] **1** *n* **(a)** *(bee)* abeille *f* mâle, faux-bourdon *m*; *(pej: idler)* fainéant(e) *m(f)*.
(b) *(sound) [bees]* bourdonnement *m*; *[engine, aircraft]* ronronnement *m*, *(louder)* vrombissement *m*; *(fig: monotonous speech)* débit *m* soporifique *or* monotone, ronronnement.
(c) *(Mus)* bourdon *m*.
(d) *(robot plane)* avion téléguidé, drone *m*.
2 *vi [bee]* bourdonner; *[engine, aircraft]* ronronner, *(louder)* vrombir; *(speak monotonously: also* **~ away, ~ on**) parler d'une voix monotone *or* endormante. **he ~d on and on for hours** il n'a pas cessé pendant des heures de parler de sa voix monotone.
3 *vt*: **to ~ (out) a speech** débiter un discours d'un ton monotone.
drool [dru:l] *vi (lit)* baver; (**fig*) radoter. *(fig)* **to ~ over sth*** baver d'admiration *or* s'extasier devant qch.
droop [dru:p] **1** *vi [body]* s'affaisser; *[shoulders]* tomber; *[head]* pencher; *[eyelids]* s'abaisser; *[flowers]* commencer à se faner *or* à baisser la tête; *[feathers, one's hand]* retomber. **his spirits ~ed** il fut pris de découragement; **the heat made him ~** il était accablé par la chaleur.
2 *vt head* baisser, pencher.

3 *n [body]* attitude penchée *or* affaissée; *[eyelids]* abaissement *m*; *[spirits]* langueur *f*, abattement *m*.

drop [drɒp] **1** *n* **(a)** *[water, rain etc]* goutte *f*; *[alcohol]* goutte, larme *f*. **~ by ~** goutte à goutte; (*Med*) **~s** gouttes; **just a ~!** (juste) une goutte! *or* une larme!, une (petite) goutte!; **there's only a ~ left** il n'en reste qu'une goutte; **to fall in ~s** tomber en gouttes; **we haven't had a ~ of rain** nous n'avons pas eu une goutte de pluie; (*fig*) **it's a ~ in the ocean** c'est une goutte d'eau dans la mer; **he's had a ~ too much*** il a un verre dans le nez; *V* **nose, tear²** *etc*.

(b) (*pendant*) *[chandelier]* pendeloque *f*; *[earring]* pendant *m*, pendeloque; *[necklace]* pendentif *m*. (*sweet*) **acid ~** bonbon acidulé.

(c) (*fall*) *[temperature]* baisse *f* (*in* de); *[prices]* baisse, chute *f* (*in* de). (*Elec*) **~ in voltage** chute de tension; (*fig*) **at the ~ of a hat** sans hésitation.

(d) (*difference in level*) dénivellation *f*, descente *f* brusque; (*abyss*) précipice *m*; (*fall*) chute *f*; (*distance of fall*) hauteur *f* de chute; (*parachute jump*) saut *m* (en parachute); *[supplies, arms]* parachutage *m*, droppage *m*; *[gallows]* trappe *f*. **there's a ~ of 10 metres between the roof and the ground** il y a (une hauteur de) 10 mètres entre le toit et le sol; **sheer ~** descente à pic.

(e) (*Theat: also* **~ curtain**) rideau *m* d'entracte; *V* **back**.

2 *cpd*: **drop-forge** marteau-pilon *m*; (*Rugby*) **drop goal** drop(-goal) *m*; **drop-hammer = drop-forge**; (*Rugby*) **drop kick** drop *m* (*coup de pied*); **drop-leaf table** table *f* à volets, table anglaise; **drop-off** (*in sales, interest etc*) diminution *f*; **dropout** (*from society*) drop-out* *mf*; (*from college etc*) étudiant(e) *m(f)* qui abandonne ses études; (*Comm*) **drop shipment** drop shipment *m*; (*Tennis*) **drop shot** amorti *m*.

3 *vt* **(a)** *rope, ball, cup* (*let fall*) laisser tomber; (*release, let go*) lâcher; *bomb* lancer, larguer; *liquid* laisser tomber goutte à goutte; *price* baisser; (*from car*) *person, thing* déposer; (*from boat*) *cargo, passengers* débarquer. (*Aut*) **I'll ~ you here** je vous dépose *or* laisse ici; **to ~ one's eyes/voice** baisser les yeux/la voix; **to ~ a letter in the postbox** mettre *or* jeter une lettre à la boîte; **to ~ soldiers/supplies by parachute** parachuter des soldats/du ravitaillement; (*Tennis*) **he ~ped the ball over the net** son amorti a juste passé le filet; (*Naut*) **to ~ anchor** mouiller *or* jeter l'ancre; (*fig*) **to ~ a brick*** faire une gaffe* *or* une bourde*; (*Theat*) **to ~ the curtain** baisser le rideau; **to ~ a curtsy** faire une révérence; (*Rugby*) **to ~ a goal** marquer un drop; (*Knitting*) **to ~ a stitch** sauter *or* laisser échapper *or* laisser tomber une maille; **to ~ a hem** ressortir un ourlet.

(b) (*kill*) *bird* abattre; (**:**) *person* descendre**:**.

(c) (*utter casually*) *remark, clue* laisser échapper. **to ~ a hint about sth** (laisser) suggérer qch; **are you ~ping hints?** c'est une allusion?, ce sont des allusions?; **to ~ a word in sb's ear** glisser un mot à l'oreille de qn; **he let ~ that he had seen her** (*accidentally*) il a laissé échapper qu'il l'avait vue; (*deliberately*) il a fait comprendre qu'il l'avait vue.

(d) *letter, card* envoyer, écrire (*to* à). **to ~ sb a line** faire *or* écrire un (petit) mot à qn; **~ me a note** écrivez-moi *or* envoyez-moi un petit mot.

(e) (*omit*) *word, syllable* (*spoken*) avaler, (*written*) omettre; (*intentionally*) *programme, word, scene from play* supprimer; (*unintentionally*) *word, letter in type* laisser tomber, omettre. **to ~ one's h's** *or* **aitches** ne pas aspirer les h, avoir un accent vulgaire.

(f) (*abandon*) *habit, idea* renoncer à; *work* lâcher*, abandonner; *plan* renoncer à, ne pas donner suite à; *discussion, conversation* abandonner; *friend* laisser tomber, lâcher, cesser de voir; *girlfriend, boyfriend* rompre avec, lâcher, laisser tomber. (*Sport*) **to ~ sb from a team** écarter qn d'une équipe; **let's ~ the subject** parlons d'autre chose, laissons ce sujet, ne parlons plus de cela; **~ it!*** laisse tomber!*, finis!, assez!

(g) (*lose*) *money* perdre, laisser; (*Cards, Tennis etc*) *game* perdre.

(h) *[animal]* (*give birth to*) mettre bas.

4 *vi* **(a)** *[object]* tomber, retomber; *[liquids]* tomber goutte à goutte; *[person]* descendre, se laisser tomber; (*sink to ground*) se laisser tomber, tomber; (*collapse*) s'écrouler, s'affaisser. (*Theat*) **the curtain ~s** le rideau tombe; **you could have heard a pin ~** on aurait entendu voler une mouche; **to ~ into sb's arms** tomber dans les bras de qn; **to ~ on one's knees** se jeter *or* tomber à genoux; **I'm ready to ~*** je tombe de fatigue, je ne tiens plus debout, je suis claqué*; **she ~ped into an armchair** elle s'écroula dans un fauteuil; **~ dead!:** va te faire voir!*, va te faire foutre!**:**; (*select*) **to ~ on sth*** choisir qch; **to ~ on sb (like a ton of bricks)*** passer un fameux savon à qn*, secouer les puces à qn*; *V* **penny**.

(b) (*decrease*) *[wind]* se calmer, tomber; *[temperature, voice]* baisser; *[price]* baisser, diminuer.

(c) (*end*) *[conversation, correspondence]* en rester là, être interrompu, cesser. **there the matter ~ped** l'affaire en est restée là; **let it ~!*** laisse tomber!*, finis!, assez!

drop across* *vi*: **we dropped across to see him** nous sommes passés *or* allés le voir; **he dropped across to see us** il est passé *or* venu nous voir.

drop away *vi [numbers, attendance]* diminuer, tomber.

drop back, drop behind *vi* rester en arrière, se laisser devancer *or* distancer; (*in work etc*) prendre du retard.

drop down *vi* tomber.

drop in *vi*: **to drop in on sb** passer voir qn, débarquer* chez qn; **to drop in at the grocer's** passer chez l'épicier; **do drop in if you're in town** passez à la maison si vous êtes en ville.

drop off 1 *vi* **(a)** (*fall asleep*) s'endormir; (*for brief while*) faire un (petit) somme.

(b) *[leaves]* tomber; *[sales, interest]* diminuer.

(c) (*: *alight*) descendre.

2 *vt sep* (*set down from car etc*) *person, parcel* déposer, laisser.

3 drop-off *n V* **drop 2**.

drop out 1 *vi [contents etc]* tomber; (*fig*) se retirer, renoncer. **to drop out of a competition** se retirer d'une compétition, abandonner une compétition *or* un concours; **to drop out** (*from society*) être un *or* une drop-out*, s'évader de la société (de consommation); (*from college etc*) abandonner.

2 dropout *n V* **drop 2**.

droplet ['drɒplɪt] *n* gouttelette *f*.

dropper ['drɒpəʳ] *n* (*Med*) compte-gouttes *m inv*.

droppings ['drɒpɪŋz] *npl [birds]* fiente *f*; *[animals]* crottes *fpl*; *[flies]* chiures *fpl*, crottes.

dropsical ['drɒpsɪkəl] *adj* hydropique.

dropsy ['drɒpsɪ] *n* hydropisie *f*.

drosophila [drəʊ'sɒfɪlə] *n* drosophile *f*.

dross [drɒs] *n* (*U*) (*Metal*) scories *fpl*, crasse *f*, laitier *m*; (*Brit: coal*) menu *m* (de houille *or* de coke), poussier *m*; (*refuse*) impuretés *fpl*, déchets *mpl*; (*fig: sth worthless*) rebut *m*.

drought [draʊt] *n* sécheresse *f*.

drove [drəʊv] **1** *pret of* **drive**. **2** *n* **(a)** *[animals]* troupeau *m* en marche. **~s of people** des foules *fpl* de gens; **they came in ~s** ils arrivèrent en foule. **(b)** (*channel*) canal *m or* rigole *f* d'irrigation.

drover ['drəʊvəʳ] *n* toucheur *m or* conducteur *m* de bestiaux.

drown [draʊn] **1** *vt person, animal* noyer; *land* inonder, submerger; (*fig*) *sorrows* noyer; *noise, voice* couvrir, noyer, étouffer. **because he couldn't swim he was ~ed** il s'est noyé parce qu'il ne savait pas nager; **he ~ed himself in despair** il s'est noyé de désespoir; **he's like a ~ed rat*** il est trempé jusqu'aux os *or* comme une soupe*; (*fig*) **to ~ one's sorrows** noyer ses chagrins; (*of whisky etc*) **don't ~ it!*** n'y mets pas trop d'eau!, ne le noie pas!; (*fig*) **they were ~ed with offers of help*** ils ont été inondés *or* submergés d'offres d'assistance.

2 *vi* se noyer, être noyé.

drowning ['draʊnɪŋ] **1** *adj* qui se noie. (*Prov*) **a ~ man will clutch at a straw** un homme qui se noie se raccroche à un fétu de paille.

2 *n* (*death*) (mort *f or* asphyxie *f* par) noyade *f*; *[noise, voice]* étouffement *m*. **there were 3 ~s here last year** 3 personnes se sont noyées ici *or* il y a eu 3 noyades ici l'année dernière.

drowse [draʊz] *vi* être à moitié endormi *or* assoupi, somnoler. **to ~ off** s'assoupir.

drowsily ['draʊzɪlɪ] *adv* d'un air endormi, d'un air *or* d'un ton somnolent, à demi endormi.

drowsiness ['draʊzɪnɪs] *n* somnolence *f*, assoupissement *m*, engourdissement *m*.

drowsy ['draʊzɪ] *adj person* somnolent, assoupi, qui a envie de dormir; *smile, look* somnolent; *afternoon, atmosphere* assoupissant, soporifique. **to grow ~** s'assoupir; **to feel ~** avoir envie de dormir.

drub [drʌb] *vt* (*thrash*) rosser*, rouer de coups; (*abuse*) injurier, traiter de tous les noms; (*defeat*) battre à plate(s) couture(s). (*fig*) **to ~ an idea into sb** enfoncer une idée dans la tête de qn; (*fig*) **to ~ an idea out of sb** arracher une idée de la tête de qn.

drubbing ['drʌbɪŋ] *n* (*thrashing*) volée *f* de coups, raclée* *f*; (*defeat*) raclée*. **to give sb a ~** donner *or* administrer une belle raclée* à qn.

drudge [drʌdʒ] **1** *n* bête *f* de somme (*fig*). **the household ~** la bonne à tout faire, la Cendrillon de la famille. **2** *vi* trimer**:**, peiner.

drudgery ['drʌdʒərɪ] *n* (*U*) grosse besogne, corvée *f*, travail pénible et ingrat *or* fastidieux. **it's sheer ~** c'est (une corvée) d'un fastidieux!

drug [drʌg] **1** *n* drogue *f*, stupéfiant *m*, narcotique *m*; (*Med, Pharm*) drogue, médicament *m*. **he's on ~s, he's taking ~s** (*gen*) il se drogue; (*Med*) il est sous médication, on lui fait prendre des médicaments; (*fig*) **a ~ on the market** un article *or* une marchandise invendable; **television is a ~** la télévision est comme une drogue; *V* **hard, soft** etc.

2 *cpd*: **drug addict** drogué(e) *m(f)*, intoxiqué(e) *m(f)*, toxicomane *mf*; (*on morphine*) morphinomane *mf*; (*on cocaine*) cocaïnomane *mf*; (*on heroin*) héroïnomane *mf*; **drug addiction** toxicomanie *f*; (*to morphine*) morphinomanie *f*; (*to cocaine*) cocaïnomanie *f*; (*to heroin*) héroïnomanie *f*; **the drug habit** l'accoutumance *f* à la drogue; **drug peddler, drug pusher** revendeur *m*, -euse *f* de drogue, ravitailleur *m*, -euse *f* en drogue; **drug runner** trafiquant(e) *m(f)* (de la drogue); **drug-running = drug traffic**; (*US*) **drugstore** drugstore *m*; **drug-taker** consommateur *m*, -trice *f* de drogue *or* de stupéfiants; **drug-taking** usage *m* de la drogue *or* de stupéfiants; **drug traffic** trafic *m* de la drogue *or* des stupéfiants.

3 *vt person* droguer (*also Med*); *food, wine etc* mêler un narcotique à. **to be in a ~ged sleep** dormir sous l'effet d'un narcotique; (*fig*) **to be ~ged with sleep/from lack of sleep** être abruti de sommeil/par manque de sommeil.

druggist ['drʌgɪst] *n* **(a)** (*Brit*) pharmacien(ne) *m(f)*. **~'s** pharmacie *f*, droguerie médicinale. **(b)** (*US*) droguiste-épicier *m*, -ière *f*.

druid ['druːɪd] *n* druide *m*.

drum [drʌm] **1** *n* **(a)** (*Mus: instrument, player*) tambour *m*. **the big ~** la grosse caisse; (*Mil Mus*) **the ~s** la batterie; **to beat the ~** battre le *or* du tambour; *V* **kettle, tight** *etc*.

(b) (*for oil*) tonnelet *m*, bidon *m*; (*for tar*) gonne *f*; (*cylinder for wire etc*) tambour *m*; (*machine part*) tambour; (*Aut: brake ~*) tambour (de frein); (*Computers*) tambour magnétique; (*of figs, sweets*) caisse *f*.

(c) (*sound*) = **drumming.**
2 *cpd*: (*Aut*) **drum brake** frein *m* à tambour; (*Mil*) **drumfire** tir *m* de barrage, feu roulant; (*Mus*) **drumhead** peau *f* de tambour; (*Mil*) **drumhead court-martial** conseil *m* de guerre prévôtal; (*Mil*) **drumhead service** office religieux en plein air; **drum major** (*Brit Mil*) tambour-major *m*; (*US*) chef *m* des tambours; (*US*) **drum majorette** majorette *f*; **drumstick** (*Mus*) baguette *f* de tambour; *[chicken]* pilon *m*.
3 *vi* (*Mus*) battre le *or* du tambour; *[person, fingers]* tambouriner, pianoter (*with* de, avec, *on* sur); *[insect etc]* bourdonner. **the noise was ~ming in my ears** le bruit me tambourinait aux oreilles.
4 *vt tune* tambouriner. **to ~ one's fingers on the table** tambouriner *or* pianoter des doigts *or* avec les doigts sur la table; **to ~ one's feet on the floor** tambouriner des pieds sur le plancher; (*fig*) **to ~ sth into sb** enfoncer *or* fourrer* qch dans le crâne *or* la tête de qn, seriner* qch à qn; **I don't want to ~ it in but ...** je ne veux pas trop insister mais ... .
drum out *vt sep* (*Mil, also fig*) expulser (à grand bruit) (*of* de).
drum up *vt sep* (*fig*) *enthusiasm, support* susciter; *supporters* rassembler, racoler, battre le rappel de; *customers* racoler, raccrocher.
drumlin ['drʌmlɪn] *n* drumlin *m*.
drummer ['drʌməʳ] *n* **(a)** (joueur *m* de) tambour *m*. **~ boy** petit tambour. **(b)** (*US Comm**) commis voyageur.
drumming ['drʌmɪŋ] *n [drum]* bruit *m* du tambour; *[insect]* bourdonnement *m*; (*in the ears*) bourdonnement; *[fingers]* tambourinage *m*, tambourinement *m*.
drunk [drʌŋk] **1** *ptp of* **drink.**
2 *adj* ivre, soûl*; (*fig*) ivre, enivré, grisé (*with* de, par). **to get ~** s'enivrer, se griser, se soûler* (*on* de); (*Jur*) **~ and disorderly, ~ and incapable** ≃ en état d'ivresse publique *or* manifeste; **as ~ as a lord** soûl comme une grive* *or* un Polonais*; **~ with success** enivré *or* grisé par le succès; *V* **blind, dead.**
3 *n* (*) ivrogne(sse) *m(f)*, homme *or* femme soûl(e)*, soûlard(e)‡ *m(f)*.
drunkard ['drʌŋkəd] *n* ivrogne(sse) *m(f)*, alcoolique *mf*, buveur *m*, -euse *f*, soûlard(e)‡ *m(f)*.
drunken ['drʌŋkən] *adj person* (*habitually drunk*) ivrogne; (*intoxicated*) ivre, soûl*; *orgy, quarrel* d'ivrogne(s); *fury* causé par la boisson, d'ivrogne; *voice* aviné. **a ~ old man** un vieil ivrogne, un vieux soûlard‡; **accused of ~ driving** accusé d'avoir conduit en état d'ivresse.
drunkenly ['drʌŋkənlɪ] *adv quarrel* comme un ivrogne; *sing* d'une voix avinée; *walk* en titubant, en zigzag.
drunkenness ['drʌŋkənnɪs] *n* (*state*) ivresse *f*, ébriété *f*; (*problem, habit*) ivrognerie *f*.
drunkometer [drʌŋ'kɒmɪtəʳ] *n* (*US*) alcooltest *m or* alcootest *m*.
dry [draɪ] **1** *adj* **(a)** *ground, climate, weather, skin, clothes* sec (*f* sèche); *day* sans pluie; *country* sec, aride; *riverbed, well* tari, à sec; (*Geol*) *valley* sec; (*Elec*) *cell* sec; *battery* à piles sèches. **on ~ land** sur la terre ferme; **as ~ as a bone** tout sec, sec comme de l'amadou; **to keep sth ~** tenir qch au sec; (*on label*) **'to be kept ~'** 'craint l'humidité'; **to wipe sth ~** essuyer *or* sécher qch; **the river ran ~** la rivière s'est asséchée *or* s'est tarie *or* a tari; **his mouth was ~ with fear** la peur lui desséchait la bouche; **~ bread** pain sec; **piece of ~ toast** tartine *f* de pain grillé sans beurre; (*Met*) **a ~ spell** une période sèche *or* de sécheresse; *V also* **2.**
(b) *wine, vermouth etc* sec (*f* sèche); *champagne* brut, dry *inv*.
(c) *country, state* (qui a le régime) sec. (*fig*: *thirsty*) **to feel** *or* **to be ~*** avoir le gosier sec*; **it's ~ work*** c'est un boulot* qui donne soif.
(d) *humour* pince-sans-rire *inv*; *sarcasm, wit* caustique, mordant. **he has a ~ sense of humour** il est pince-sans-rire, c'est un pince-sans-rire, il a l'esprit caustique.
(e) (*dull*) *lecture, book, subject* aride. **as ~ as dust** mortel*, ennuyeux comme la pluie.
2 *cpd*: **dry-as-dust** aride, dépourvu d'intérêt, sec (*f* sèche); **dry-clean** (*vt*) nettoyer à sec, dégraisser; (*on label*) **'dry-clean only'** 'nettoyage à sec'; **to have a dress dry-cleaned** donner une robe à nettoyer *or* à la teinturerie, porter une robe chez le teinturier; **dry cleaner** teinturier *m*; **to take a coat to the dry cleaner's** porter un manteau à la teinturerie *or* chez le teinturier *or* au pressing; **dry cleaning** nettoyage *m* à sec, pressing *m*, dégraissage *m*; (*Naut*) **dry dock** cale sèche, bassin *m or* cale de radoub; **dry-eyed** les yeux secs, d'un œil sec, sans larmes; (*Agr*) **dry farming** culture sèche, dry-farming *m*; (*Fishing*) **dry fly** mouche sèche; (*Comm*) **dry goods** tissus *mpl*, mercerie *f*; (*US Comm*) **dry goods store** magasin *m* de nouveautés; **dry ice** neige *f* carbonique; **dry measure** mesure *f* de capacité pour matières sèches; **dry rot** pourriture sèche (*du bois*); (*fig*) **dry run** (coup *m* d')essai *m*; (*Brit*) **drysalter** marchand *m* de couleurs; **dry shampoo** shampooing sec; **dry-shod** à pied sec; **dry ski slope** piste (de ski) artificielle; (*Constr*) **dry(stone) wall** mur *m* de pierres sèches.
3 *vt clothes, paper, fruit, skin* sécher; (*with cloth*) essuyer, sécher; *clothes* faire sécher. (*on label*) **'~ away from direct heat'** 'ne pas sécher près d'une source de chaleur'; **to ~ one's eyes** *or* **one's tears** sécher ses larmes *or* ses pleurs; **to ~ the dishes** essuyer la vaisselle; **to ~ o.s.** s'essuyer, se sécher, s'éponger.
4 *vi* sécher; (*) *[actor, speaker]* sécher, rester sec.
dry off *vi [clothes etc]* sécher.
dry out 1 *vi* **(a)** = **dry off.**
(b) *[alcoholic]* se désintoxiquer.
2 *vt sep alcoholic* désintoxiquer.
dry up *vi* **(a)** *[stream, well]* se dessécher, (se) tarir; *[moisture]* s'évaporer; *[clay]* sécher; *[cow]* tarir; *[source of supply, inspiration]* se tarir.
(b) (*dry the dishes*) essuyer la vaisselle.
(c) (*) se taire; *[actor, speaker]* sécher, rester sec. **dry up!*** tais-toi!, laisse tomber!*, boucle-la!‡
dryer ['draɪəʳ] *n* **(a)** (*apparatus*) *[clothes]* séchoir *m* (à linge); *[hair]* (*gen*) séchoir (à cheveux), (*helmet type*) casque *m* (sèche-cheveux); *V* **spin, tumble** *etc.* **(b)** (*for paint*) siccatif *m*.
drying ['draɪɪŋ] **1** *n [river, clothes]* séchage *m*; (*with a cloth*) essuyage *m*. **2** *cpd*: **drying cupboard, drying room** séchoir *m*; **to do the drying-up** essuyer la vaisselle; **drying-up cloth** torchon *m* (à vaisselle).
dryly ['draɪlɪ] *adv* = **drily.**
dryness ['draɪnɪs] *n [soil, weather]* sécheresse *f*, aridité *f*; *[clothes, skin]* sécheresse; *[wit, humour]* causticité *f*; *[humorist]* ton *m or* air *m* pince-sans-rire.
dual ['djʊəl] **1** *adj* double, à deux. (*Brit*) **~ carriageway** route *f* à chaussées séparées *or* à quatre voies; (*Aut, Aviat*) **~ controls** double commande *f*; **~-control** (*adj*) à double commande; **~ national** personne *f* ayant la double nationalité, binational(e) *m(f)*; **~ nationality** double nationalité *f*; **~ ownership** copropriété *f* (*à deux*); (*Psych*) **~ personality** dédoublement *m* de la personnalité; **~-purpose** (*adj*) à double usage, à double emploi.
2 *n* (*Gram*) duel *m*.
dualism ['djʊəlɪzəm] *n* (*Philos, Pol, Rel*) dualisme *m*.
duality [djʊ'ælɪtɪ] *n* dualité *f*, dualisme *m*.
dub [dʌb] *vt* **(a) to ~ sb a knight** donner l'accolade à qn; (*Hist*) adouber *or* armer qn chevalier; (*nickname*) **to ~ sb 'Ginger'** qualifier qn de *or* surnommer qn 'Poil de Carotte'. **(b)** (*Cine*) doubler (*dialogue*).
dubbin ['dʌbɪn] *n* dégras *m*, graisse *f* pour les chaussures.
dubbing ['dʌbɪŋ] *n* (*Cine*) doublage *m*.
dubiety [djuː'baɪətɪ] *n* doute *m*, incertitude *f*.
dubious ['djuːbɪəs] *adj company, offer, privilege* douteux, suspect; *reputation* douteux, équivoque; *person* qui doute (*of* de), hésitant, incertain (*of* de). **he was ~ (about) whether he should come or not** il se demandait s'il devait venir ou non; **~ of success** incertain du succès; **I'm very ~ about it** j'en doute fort, je n'en suis pas du tout sûr; **with a ~ air** d'un air de doute.
dubiously ['djuːbɪəslɪ] *adv* avec doute, d'un ton *or* d'un air incertain *or* de doute.
Dublin ['dʌblɪn] *n* Dublin. **~ Bay prawn** langoustine *f*.
ducal ['djuːkəl] *adj* ducal, de duc.
ducat ['dʌkɪt] *n* ducat *m*.
duchess ['dʌtʃɪs] *n* duchesse *f*.
duchy ['dʌtʃɪ] *n* duché *m*.
duck[1] [dʌk] **1** *n, pl* **~s**, (*collectively*) **~** canard *m*; (*female*) cane *f*; (*Mil*: *vehicle*) véhicule *m* amphibie. **wild ~** canard sauvage; (*Culin*) **roast ~** canard rôti; **to play (at) ~s and drakes** faire des ricochets (sur l'eau); **to play (at) ~s and drakes with one's money** jeter son argent par les fenêtres*, gaspiller son argent; **he took to it like a ~ to water** il était comme un poisson dans l'eau, c'était comme s'il l'avait fait toute sa vie; **yes ~s‡, yes duckie‡** (*to child, friend*) oui mon chou*; (*to unknown adult*) oui mon petit monsieur *or* ma petite dame *or* ma petite demoiselle; **he is a ~** c'est un chou* *or* un amour; *V* **Bombay, dying, lame** *etc.*
2 *cpd*: **duckbill, duck-billed platypus** ornithorynque *m*; **duckboard** caillebotis *m*; **duck-egg blue** bleu-vert (pâle) *inv*; **duck pond** mare *f* aux canards, canardière *f*; **duck shooting** chasse *f* au canard (sauvage); **duckweed** lentille *f* d'eau, lenticule *f*.
3 *vi* (*also* **~ down**) se baisser vivement *or* subitement; (*in fight etc*) esquiver un coup. **to ~ (down) under the water** plonger subitement sous l'eau.
4 *vt* **(a) to ~ sb** (*push under water*) plonger qn dans l'eau; (*as a joke*) faire faire le plongeon à qn; (*head only*) faire boire la tasse à qn*.
(b) to ~ one's head baisser vivement *or* subitement la tête.
duck[2] [dʌk] *n* (*Tex*) coutil *m*, toile fine. **~s** pantalon *m* de coutil.
duckie‡ ['dʌkɪ] *n* (*Brit*) *V* **duck**[1] **1.**
ducking ['dʌkɪŋ] *n* plongeon *m*, bain forcé. **to give sb a ~** faire faire le plongeon à qn; (*head only*) faire boire la tasse à qn*.
duckling ['dʌklɪŋ] *n* (*also Culin*) caneton *m*; (*female*) canette *f*; (*older*) canardeau *m*.
duct [dʌkt] *n [liquid, gas, electricity]* conduite *f*, canalisation *f*; (*Bot*) trachée *f*; (*Anat*) canal *m*, conduit *m*. **respiratory ~** conduit respiratoire.
ductile ['dʌktaɪl] *adj metal* ductile; *person* maniable, malléable, docile.
ductless ['dʌktlɪs] *adj*: **~ gland** glande *f* endocrine.
dud* [dʌd] **1** *adj shell, bomb* non éclaté, qui a raté; *object, tool* à la noix*; *note, coin* faux (*f* fausse); *cheque* sans provision, en bois*; *person* à la manque, (très) mauvais, nul. (*Press*) **~ (story)** canard *m*.
2 *n* **(a)** (*shell*) obus non éclaté; (*bomb*) bombe non éclatée; (*: *person*) type nul*, raté(e) *m(f)*. **this coin is a ~** cette pièce est fausse; **this watch is a ~** cette montre ne marche pas; **to be a ~* at geography** être nul en géographie; **to be a ~* at tennis** être un zéro *or* une nullité au tennis.
(b) (‡†: *clothes*) **~s** nippes* *fpl*.
dude* [djuːd] *n* (*US*) dandy *m*, (*young*) gommeux* *m*. **~ ranch** (hôtel *m*) ranch *m*.
dudgeon ['dʌdʒən] *n*: **in (high) ~** offensé dans sa dignité, furieux.
due [djuː] **1** *adj* **(a)** (*owing*) *sum, money* dû (*f* due). **the sum which is ~ to him** la somme qui lui est due *or* qui lui revient; **our thanks are ~ to X** nous aimerions remercier X, notre gratitude va à X (*frm*); **to fall ~** échoir, venir à (l')échéance; **~ on the 8th** payable le 8; **when is the rent ~?** quand faut-il payer le loyer?; I

am ~ 6 days' leave on me doit 6 jours de permission; **he is ~ for a rise** (*will get it*) il doit recevoir une augmentation; (*should get it*) il devrait recevoir une augmentation; **I am ~ for a holiday in September** en principe j'aurai des vacances en septembre.

(b) (*proper, suitable*) *respect, regard* qu'on doit, qui convient. (*Jur*) **driving without ~ care and attention** conduite imprudente; **after ~ consideration** après mûre réflexion; **it will come about in ~ course** cela arrivera en temps utile *or* voulu; **in ~ course it transpired that ...** à la longue il s'est révélé que ...; **in ~ time** à la longue, finalement; **in ~ form** en bonne et due forme; **with all ~ respect, I believe ...** sauf votre respect *or* sans vouloir vous contredire, je crois ... .

(c) when is the plane ~ (in)? à quelle heure l'avion doit-il atterrir?; **the train is ~ (in *or* to arrive) at midday** le train doit arriver à midi; **they are ~ to start at 6** l'heure du départ est fixée pour 6 heures, ils doivent partir à 6 heures; **I am ~ there tomorrow** je dois être là-bas demain, on m'attend là-bas demain.

(d) ~ to dû (*f* due) à, attribuable à; **it is ~ to his ineptitude that ...** c'est à cause de son incompétence que ...; **the accident was ~ to a drunken driver** l'accident a été provoqué par un conducteur en état d'ivresse; **the accident was ~ to the icy road** l'accident était dû au verglas; **it is ~ to you that he is alive today** c'est grâce à vous qu'il est en vie aujourd'hui; **what's it ~ to?** comment cela se fait-il?, quelle en est la cause?

2 *adv* (tout) droit. **to go ~ west** aller droit vers l'ouest, faire route plein ouest; **to sail ~ north** avoir le cap au nord; **to face ~ north** être (en) plein nord *or* au nord; **~ east of the village** plein est par rapport au village.

3 *n* **(a) to give sb his ~** être juste envers qn, faire *or* rendre justice à qn; **(to) give him his ~, he did try hard** il faut (être juste et) reconnaître qu'il a quand même fait tout son possible; *V* **devil.**

(b) (*fees*) **~s** *[club etc]* cotisation *f*; *[harbour]* droits *mpl* (de port).

duel ['djʊəl] **1** *n* duel *m*, rencontre *f*; (*fig*) duel, lutte *f*. **~ to the death** duel à mort; *V* **challenge, fight. 2** *vi* se battre en duel (*with* contre, avec). **3** *cpd*: **duelling pistols** pistolets *mpl* de duel.

duellist ['djʊəlɪst] *n* duelliste *m*.

duet [djuː'et] *n* duo *m*. **to sing/play a ~** chanter/jouer en duo; **violin ~** duo de violon; **piano ~** morceau *m* à quatre mains.

duff[1] [dʌf] *n* (*Culin*) pudding *m*; *V* **plum.**

duff[2] [dʌf] **1** *vt*(‡) (*bungle*) saboter*, bousiller‡; (*alter, fake*) *stolen goods etc* maquiller, truquer. **2** *adj* (*Brit**) *shot* raté, loupé*; *suggestion, idea* stupide, inepte.

duffel ['dʌfəl] *adj*: **~ bag** sac *m* de paquetage, sac marin; **~ coat** duffel-coat *m*.

duffer* ['dʌfəʳ] *n* cruche* *f*, gourde* *f*; (*Scol*) cancre* *m*, âne *m*. **he is a ~ at French** il est nul *or* c'est un cancre* en français; **to be a ~ at games** n'être bon à rien en sport.

duffle ['dʌfəl] *adj* = **duffel.**

dug[1] [dʌg] *n* mamelle *f*, tétine *f*; *[cow]* pis *m*.

dug[2] [dʌg] **1** *pret, ptp of* **dig. 2** *cpd*: **dugout** (*Mil*) tranchée-abri *f*; (*canoe*) pirogue *f*.

duke [djuːk] *n* duc *m*.

dukedom ['djuːkdəm] *n* (*territory*) duché *m*; (*title*) titre *m* de duc.

dulcet ['dʌlsɪt] *adj* (*liter*) suave, doux (*f* douce), harmonieux.

dulcimer ['dʌlsɪməʳ] *n* tympanon *m*.

dull [dʌl] **1** *adj* **(a)** *sight, hearing* faible; (*slow-witted*) *person, mind* borné, obtus. (*Scol*) **the ~ ones** les moins doués; **his senses/his intellectual powers are growing ~** ses sens/ses capacités intellectuelles s'émoussent *or* s'amoindrissent; **to be ~ of hearing** être dur d'oreille.

(b) (*boring*) *book, evening, lecture* ennuyeux, dépourvu d'intérêt; *style* terne; *person* terne, insignifiant. **deadly ~*** assommant*, mortel*; **as ~ as ditchwater *or* dishwater** ennuyeux comme la pluie; **a ~ old stick*** un vieux raseur*.

(c) *colour, light, eyes, mirror* sans éclat, terne; *metal* terne; *sound* sourd, étouffé; *weather, sky* couvert, gris, sombre, maussade; *blade* émoussé; *pain* sourd, vague; (*St Ex*) *market* calme, terne, lourd; (*Comm*) *trade, business* lent, languissant, stagnant; *person* déprimé, las (*f* lasse) (d'esprit), triste; *mood, humour* déprimé, triste, las; *look* terne, atone. **it's ~ today** il fait un temps maussade *or* il fait gris aujourd'hui; **a ~ day** un jour maussade; **a ~ thud** un bruit sourd *or* mat.

2 *vt senses* émousser, engourdir; *mind* alourdir, engourdir; *pain, grief, impression* amortir, atténuer; *thing remembered* atténuer; *pleasure* émousser; *sound* assourdir, amortir; *edge, blade* émousser; *colour, mirror, metal* ternir.

3 *vi* s'émousser; s'engourdir; s'alourdir; s'atténuer; s'amortir; s'assourdir; se ternir.

dullard ['dʌləd] *n* lourdaud(e) *m(f)*, balourd(e) *m(f)*; (*Scol*) cancre* *m*, âne *m*.

dullness ['dʌlnɪs] *n* **(a)** (*slow-wittedness*) lourdeur *f* d'esprit; *[senses]* affaiblissement *m*. **~ of hearing** dureté *f* d'oreille.

(b) (*tedium*) *[book, evening, lecture, person]* caractère ennuyeux, manque *m* d'intérêt.

(c) *[colour, metal, mirror etc]* manque *m or* peu *m* d'éclat, aspect *m* terne; *[sound]* caractère sourd *or* étouffé; *[person]* ennui *m*, lassitude *f*, tristesse *f*; *[landscape, room]* tristesse. **the ~ of the weather** le temps couvert.

dully ['dʌllɪ] *adv* (*depressedly*) *behave, walk* lourdement; *answer, listen* avec lassitude, avec découragement; (*boringly*) *talk, write* d'une manière ennuyeuse *or* insipide, avec monotonie.

duly ['djuːlɪ] *adv* (*properly*) comme il faut, ainsi qu'il convient; (*Jur etc*) dûment; (*on time*) en temps voulu, en temps utile. **he ~ protested** il a protesté comme on s'y attendait; **he said he would come and he ~ came at 6 o'clock** il avait promis de venir et est en effet venu à 6 heures; **everybody was ~ shocked** tout le monde a bien entendu été choqué.

dumb [dʌm] **1** *adj* **(a)** muet; (*fig: with surprise, shock*) muet (*with, from* de), sidéré*, abasourdi (*with, from* de, par). **a ~ person** un(e) muet(te); **~ animals** les animaux *mpl*; **~ creatures** les bêtes *fpl*; **our ~ friends** nos amis les bêtes; **to be struck ~** rester muet, être sidéré*; *V* **deaf.**

(b) (‡: *stupid*) *person* bête, nigaud, bêta* (*f* -asse), gourde*; *action* bête. **a ~ blonde** une blonde évaporée; **to act ~** faire l'innocent.

2 *cpd*: **dumbbell** (*Sport*) haltère *m*; (‡: *fool: also* **dumb cluck**‡) imbécile *mf*; **in dumb show** en pantomime, par (des) signes; **dumbwaiter** (*US: lift*) monte-plats *m inv*; (*Brit: trolley*) table roulante; (*revolving stand*) plateau tournant.

dumbfound [dʌm'faʊnd] *vt* confondre, abasourdir, ahurir, sidérer*. **I'm ~ed** j'en suis ahuri *or* sidéré*, je n'en reviens pas.

dumbness ['dʌmnɪs] *n* (*Med*) mutisme *m*; (‡: *stupidity*) bêtise *f*, niaiserie *f*.

dum-dum ['dʌmdʌm] *n* balle *f* dumdum *inv*.

dummy ['dʌmɪ] **1** *n* (*Comm: sham object*) factice *m*; *[book]* maquette *f*; (*Comm, Sewing: model*) mannequin *m*; *[ventriloquist]* pantin *m*; (*Theat*) personnage muet, figurant *m*; (*Fin etc: person replacing another*) prête-nom *m*, homme *m* de paille; (*Bridge*) mort *m*; (*baby's teat*) sucette *f*, tétine *f*; (*Sport*) feinte *f*. (*Sport*) **to sell (sb) the ~** feinter (qn); (*Bridge*) **to be ~** faire *or* être le mort; (*Bridge*) **to play from ~** jouer du mort.

2 *adj* faux (*f* fausse), factice. (*Cards*) **~ bridge** bridge *m* à trois; (*Sport*) **~ pass** passe feinte; **~ run** (*Aviat*) attaque *f or* bombardement *m* simulé(e); (*Comm, Ind*) (coup *m* d')essai *m*.

3 *vti* (*Sport*) feinter.

dump [dʌmp] **1** *n* **(a)** (*pile of rubbish*) tas *m or* amas *m* d'ordures; (*place*) décharge *f* (publique), dépotoir *m*, terrain *m* de décharge; (*Mil*) dépôt *m*. (*fig*) **to be (down) in the ~s*** avoir le cafard*, broyer du noir; *V* **ammunition.**

(b) (‡*pej*) (*place*) trou* *m*, bled‡ *m*; (*house, hotel*) baraque‡ *f*, boîte‡ *f*.

2 *vt* **(a)** (*get rid of*) *rubbish* déposer, jeter; (*Comm*) *goods* vendre *or* écouler à bas prix (*sur les marchés extérieurs*), pratiquer le dumping pour; (‡) *person* plaquer‡; (‡) *thing* se débarrasser de, bazarder*.

(b) (*put down*) *package* déposer; *sand, bricks* décharger, déverser; (*) *passenger* déposer. **~ your bag on the table** plante *or* fiche* ton sac sur la table.

3 *cpd*: **dump truck** = **dumper.**

dumper ['dʌmpəʳ] *n* tombereau *m* automoteur, dumper *m*.

dumping ['dʌmpɪŋ] **1** *n [load, rubbish]* décharge *f*; (*Ecol: in sea etc*) versement *m* (de produits nocifs); (*Comm*) dumping *m*. **2** *cpd*: **dumping ground** dépotoir *m* (*also fig*).

dumpling ['dʌmplɪŋ] *n* (*Culin: savoury*) boulette *f* (de pâte); (*: *person*) boulot(te) *m(f)*; *V* **apple.**

dumpy ['dʌmpɪ] *adj* courtaud, boulot (*f* -otte).

dun[1] [dʌn] **1** *adj* (*colour*) brun foncé *inv*, brun grisâtre *inv*. **2** *n* cheval louvet, jument louvette.

dun[2] [dʌn] *vt*: **to ~ sb (for money owed)** harceler *or* relancer qn (pour lui faire payer ses dettes).

dunce [dʌns] *n* (*Scol*) âne *m*, cancre* *m*. **to be a ~ at maths** être nul *or* un cancre* en math; **~'s cap** bonnet *m* d'âne.

dunderhead ['dʌndəhed] *n* imbécile *mf*, souche* *f*.

dune [djuːn] *n* dune *f*. **~ buggy** buggy *m*.

dung [dʌŋ] **1** *n* (*U*) (*excrement*) excrément(s) *m(pl)*, crotte *f*; *[horse]* crottin *m*; *[cattle]* bouse *f*; *[bird]* fiente *f*; *[wild animal]* fumées *fpl*; (*manure*) fumier *m*, engrais *m*. **2** *cpd*: **dung beetle** bousier *m*; **dunghill** (tas *m* de) fumier *m*.

dungarees [ˌdʌŋgə'riːz] *npl [workman]* bleu(s) *m(pl)* (de travail); (*Brit*) *[child etc]* salopette *f*.

dungeon ['dʌndʒən] *n* (*underground*) cachot *m* (souterrain); (*Hist: castle tower*) donjon *m*.

dunk [dʌŋk] *vt* tremper. **to ~ one's bread in one's coffee** *etc* faire trempette.

Dunkirk [dʌn'kɜːk] *n* Dunkerque.

dunlin ['dʌnlɪn] *n* bécasseau *m* variable.

dunnock ['dʌnək] *n* (*Brit*) accenteur *m* mouchet.

duo ['djuːəʊ] *n* (*Mus, Theat*) duo *m*.

duodecimal [ˌdjuːəʊ'desɪməl] *adj* duodécimal.

duodenal [ˌdjuːəʊ'diːnl] *adj* duodénal. **~ ulcer** ulcère *m* du duodénum.

duodenum [ˌdjuːəʊ'diːnəm] *n* duodénum *m*.

dupe [djuːp] **1** *vt* duper, tromper. **2** *n* dupe *f*.

duple ['djuːpl] *adj* (*gen*) double; (*Mus*) binaire. (*Mus*) **~ time** rythme *m or* mesure *f* binaire.

duplex ['djuːpleks] *adj, n* duplex (*m*).

duplicate ['djuːplɪkeɪt] **1** *vt document, map, key* faire un double de; (*on machine*) *document* polycopier; *action etc* répéter exactement. **duplicating machine** machine *f* à polycopier; **that is merely duplicating work already done** cela fait double emploi avec ce qu'on a déjà fait.

2 ['djuːplɪkɪt] *n [document, map]* double *m*, copie exacte; (*Jur etc*) duplicata *m inv*, ampliation *f*; *[key, ornament, chair]* double. **in ~** en deux exemplaires, (*Jur etc*) en *or* par duplicata.

3 ['djuːplɪkɪt] *adj copy* en double; *bus, coach* supplémentaire. **a ~ receipt** un reçu en duplicata; **a ~ cheque** un duplicata; **I've got a ~ key** j'ai un double de la clef; **~ bridge** bridge *m* de compétition *or* de tournoi.

duplication [ˌdjuːplɪ'keɪʃən] *n* (*U*) *[document]* action *f* de copier, (*on machine*) polycopie *f*; *[efforts, work]* répétition *f*, reproduction *f*.

duplicator ['djuːplɪkeɪtəʳ] *n* duplicateur *m*.

duplicity [djuː'plɪsɪtɪ] *n* duplicité *f*, fausseté *f*, double jeu *m*.

durability [ˌdjʊərəˈbɪlɪtɪ] (*V* **durable**) solidité *f*, résistance *f*; durabilité *f*.
durable [ˈdjʊərəbl] *adj material, metal* solide, résistant; *friendship* durable, de longue durée. (*Comm*) ~ **goods,** ~**s** biens *mpl* de consommation durable, articles *mpl* d'équipement.
Duralumin [djʊəˈræljʊmɪn] *n* ® duralumin *m*.
duration [djʊəˈreɪʃən] *n* durée *f*. **of long** ~ de longue durée; **for the** ~ **of the war** jusqu'à la fin de la guerre.
duress [djʊəˈres] *n* contrainte *f*, coercition *f*. **under** ~ sous la contrainte, contraint et forcé (*Jur*).
during [ˈdjʊərɪŋ] *prep* pendant, durant, au cours de.
durst†† [dɜːst] *pret of* **dare.**
dusk [dʌsk] *n* (*twilight*) crépuscule *m*; (*gloom*) (semi-) obscurité *f*. **at** ~ au crépuscule, entre chien et loup, à la brune (*liter*); **in the** ~ dans la semi-obscurité, dans l'obscurité.
duskiness [ˈdʌskɪnɪs] *n [complexion]* teint brun *or* bistré, teint olivâtre.
dusky [ˈdʌskɪ] *adj complexion* foncé, bistré; *person* au teint foncé *or* mat; *colour* sombre, brunâtre; *room* sombre, obscur. ~ **pink** vieux rose *inv*.
dust [dʌst] **1** *n* (*U*) (*on furniture, ground*) poussière *f*; *[coal, gold]* poussière, poudre *f*; *[dead body]* poudre. **there was thick** ~, **the** ~ **lay thick** il y avait une épaisse couche de poussière; **I've got a speck of** ~ **in my eye** j'ai une poussière dans l'œil; **to raise a lot of** ~ (*lit*) faire de la poussière; (*fig*) faire tout un scandale, faire beaucoup de bruit; **to lay the** ~ (*lit*) mouiller la poussière; (*fig*) ramener le calme, dissiper la fumée; (*fig*) **to throw** ~ **in sb's eyes** jeter de la poudre aux yeux de qn; **to kick up** *or* **raise a** ~* faire un *or* du foin*; *V* **ash², bite, shake off** *etc*.
2 *cpd*: **dust bag** sac *m* à poussière (*d'aspirateur*); *[bird]* **to take a dust bath** s'ébrouer dans la poussière, prendre un bain de poussière; (*Brit*) **dustbin** poubelle *f*, boîte *f* à ordures; (*Geog*) **dust bowl** désert *m* de poussière, cratère(s) *m(pl)* de poussière; (*Brit*) **dustcart** tombereau *m* aux ordures, camion *m* des boueux; **dustcloud** nuage *m* de poussière; **dust cover** *[book]* jaquette *f*, couvre-livre *m*; *[furniture]* housse *f* (de protection); **dustheap** (*lit*) tas *m* d'ordures; (*fig*) poubelle *f* (*fig*), rebut *m*; **dust jacket** jaquette *f*, couvre-livre *m*; (*Brit*) **dustman** boueux *m*, éboueur *m*; (*Brit*) **dustmen's strike** grève *f* des éboueurs; **dustpan** pelle *f* à poussière; **dustproof** anti-poussière; **dust sheet** housse *f* (de protection); **dust storm** tourbillon *m* de poussière; **dust-up*** accrochage* *m*, bagarre* *f*; **to have a dust-up with sb*** avoir un accrochage* *or* se bagarrer* avec qn.
3 *vt* **(a)** *furniture, room* enlever la poussière de, épousseter, essuyer.
(b) (*with talc, sugar etc*) saupoudrer (*with* de).
dust down *vt sep* (*with brush*) brosser, épousseter; (*with hand*) épousseter.
dust off *vt sep* enlever (*en époussetant*).
dust out *vt sep box, cupboard* épousseter.
duster [ˈdʌstəʳ] *n* chiffon *m* (à poussière); (*blackboard* ~) chiffon (à effacer); *V* **feather.**
dusting [ˈdʌstɪŋ] **1** *n* **(a)** *[furniture]* époussetage *m*. **to do the** ~ épousseter, essuyer (la poussière); **to give sth a** ~ donner un coup de chiffon à qch.
(b) (*Culin etc: sprinkling*) saupoudrage *m*.
2 *cpd*: **dusting powder** (poudre *f* de) talc *m*.
dusty [ˈdʌstɪ] *adj* **(a)** *table, path* poussiéreux, couvert de *or* plein de poussière. **to get** ~ se couvrir de poussière; **not so** ~* pas mal; **to get a** ~ **answer*** en être pour ses frais; **to give sb a** ~ **answer*** envoyer promener qn.
(b) ~ **pink** vieux rose *inv*, rose fané *inv*; ~ **blue** bleu cendré *inv*.
Dutch [dʌtʃ] **1** *adj* hollandais, de Hollande, néerlandais. **the** ~ **government** le gouvernement néerlandais *or* hollandais; **the** ~ **embassy** l'ambassade néerlandaise *or* des Pays-Bas; **the** ~ **East Indies** les Indes néerlandaises; (*Art*) **the** ~ **School** l'école hollandaise; ~ **cheese** fromage *m* de Hollande, hollande *m*.
2 *cpd*: (*fig*) **Dutch auction** enchères *fpl* au rabais; **Dutch barn** hangar *m* à récoltes; (*fig*) **Dutch courage** courage puisé dans la bouteille; **the drink gave him Dutch courage** il a trouvé du courage dans la bouteille; (*US*) **Dutch door** porte *f* à double vantail, porte d'étable; **Dutch elm disease** champignon *m* parasite de l'orme; **to go Dutch*, to go on a Dutch treat** partager les frais; (*casserole*) **Dutch oven** grosse cocotte (*en métal*); **to talk to sb like a Dutch uncle*** dire à qn ses quatre vérités.
3 *n* **(a) the** ~ les Hollandais *mpl*, les Néerlandais *mpl*.
(b) (*Ling*) hollandais *m*, néerlandais *m*. (*fig*) **it's (all)** ~ **to me*** c'est du chinois *or* du javanais pour moi; *V* **double.**
Dutchman [ˈdʌtʃmən] *n* Hollandais *m*. **he did say that or I'm a** ~* il a bien dit ça, j'en mettrais ma tête à couper; *V* **flying.**
Dutchwoman [ˈdʌtʃˌwʊmən] *n* Hollandaise *f*.
dutiable [ˈdjuːtɪəbl] *adj* taxable; (*Customs*) soumis à des droits de douane.
dutiful [ˈdjuːtɪfʊl] *adj child* obéissant, respectueux, soumis; *husband* plein d'égards; *employee* consciencieux.
dutifully [ˈdjuːtɪfəlɪ] *adv obey, act* avec soumission, respectueusement; *work* consciencieusement.
duty [ˈdjuːtɪ] **1** *n* **(a)** (*U: moral, legal*) devoir *m*, obligation *f*. **to do one's** ~ s'acquitter de *or* faire son devoir (*by sb* envers qn); **it is my** ~ **to say that ..., I feel (in)** ~ **bound to say that ...** il est de mon devoir de faire remarquer que ...; ~ **calls** le devoir m'appelle; **one's** ~ **to one's parents** le respect dû à *or* son devoir envers ses parents; **to make it one's** ~ **to do** se faire un devoir *or* prendre à tâche de faire.
(b) (*gen pl: responsibility*) fonction *f*, responsabilité *f*. **to take up one's duties** assumer ses fonctions, commencer *or* prendre son service; **to neglect one's duties** négliger ses fonctions; **my duties consist of ...** mes fonctions comprennent ... .
(c) (*U*) **on** ~ (*Mil*) de service; (*Med*) de garde; (*Admin, Scol*) de jour, de permanence; **to be on** ~ être de service *or* de garde *or* de jour *or* de permanence; **to be off** ~ être libre, n'être pas de service *or* de garde *or* de jour *or* de permanence; (*Mil*) avoir quartier libre; **to go on/off** ~ prendre/quitter le service *or* la garde *or* la permanence; **in the course of** ~ (*Mil, Police etc*) en service commandé; (*civilian*) dans l'accomplissement de mes (*or ses etc*) fonctions; **to do** ~ **for sb, to do sb's** ~ remplacer qn; (*fig*) **the box does** ~ **for a table** la boîte fait fonction *or* office de table, la boîte sert de table; *V* **spell², tour.**
(d) (*Fin: tax*) droit *m*, impôt *m* (indirect), taxe *f* (indirecte). **to pay** ~ **on** payer un droit *or* une taxe sur; *V* **death, estate** *etc*.
2 *cpd*: **a duty call** une visite de politesse; **duty-free** exempté de douane, (admis) en franchise de douane; **duty-free shop** magasin *m* hors-taxe; **duty officer** (*Mil etc*) officier *m* de permanence; (*Admin*) officiel *m or* préposé *m* de service; **duty roster, duty rota** liste *f* de service, (*esp Mil*) tableau *m* de service.
duvet [ˈduːveɪ] *n* couette *f* (*édredon*). ~ **cover** housse *f* de couette.
dwarf [dwɔːf] **1** *n* (*person, animal*) nain(e) *m(f)*; (*tree*) arbre nain.
2 *adj person, tree, star* nain.
3 *vt* **(a)** *[skyscraper, person]* rapetisser, écraser (*fig*); *[achievement]* écraser, éclipser.
(b) *plant* rabougrir, empêcher de croître.
dwell [dwel] *pret, ptp* **dwelt** *vi* (*liter*) habiter (*in* dans), demeurer, résider (*frm*) (*in* à); (*fig*) *[interest, difficulty]* résider (*in* dans). **the thought dwelt in his mind** la pensée lui resta dans l'esprit, la pensée demeura dans son esprit.
dwell (up)on *vt fus* (*think about*) s'arrêter sur, arrêter sa pensée sur; (*talk at length on*) s'étendre sur; (*Mus*) *note* appuyer sur. **to dwell (up)on the past** s'appesantir sur le passé, revenir sans cesse sur le passé; **to dwell (up)on the fact that ...** insister *or* appuyer *or* s'appesantir sur le fait que ...; **don't let's dwell (up)on it** passons là-dessus, glissons.
dweller [ˈdweləʳ] *n* habitant(e) *m(f)*; *V* **country** *etc*.
dwelling [ˈdwelɪŋ] **1** *n* (*liter: also* ~ **place**) habitation *f*, résidence *f*. **to take up one's** ~ s'installer, élire domicile (*Admin*). **2** *cpd*: **dwelling house** maison *f* d'habitation.
dwelt [dwelt] *pret, ptp of* **dwell.**
dwindle [ˈdwɪndl] *vi [strength]* diminuer, décroître, s'affaiblir; *[numbers, resources]* diminuer, tomber (peu à peu); *[supplies, interest]* diminuer, baisser.
dwindle away *vi* diminuer; *[person]* dépérir.
dwindling [ˈdwɪndlɪŋ] **1** *n* diminution *f* (graduelle). **2** *adj interest* décroissant, en baisse; *strength* décroissant; *resources* en diminution.
dye [daɪ] **1** *n* (*substance*) teinture *f*, colorant *m*; (*colour*) teinte *f*, couleur *f*, ton *m*. **hair** ~ teinture pour les cheveux; **the** ~ **will come out in the wash** la teinture ne résistera pas au lavage, cela déteindra au lavage; (*fig liter*) **a villain of the deepest** ~ une canaille *or* crapule de la pire espèce.
2 *vt* teindre. **to** ~ **sth red** teindre qch en rouge; **to** ~ **one's hair** se teindre (les cheveux); *V* **also 4** *and* **tie.**
3 *vi [cloth etc]* prendre la teinture, se teindre.
4 *cpd*: (*fig*) **dyed-in-the-wool** bon teint, invétéré; **dyestuffs** matières colorantes, colorants *mpl*; **dyeworks** teinturerie *f*.
dyeing [ˈdaɪɪŋ] *n* (*U*) teinture *f*.
dyer [ˈdaɪəʳ] *n* teinturier *m*. ~**'s and cleaner's** teinturier (dégraisseur).
dying [ˈdaɪɪŋ] **1** *adj person* mourant, agonisant, moribond; *animal, plant* mourant; (*fig*) *custom* en train de disparaître. **to my** ~ **day** jusqu'à ma dernière heure *or* mon dernier jour; (*hum*) **he looked like a** ~ **duck (in a thunderstorm)*** il avait un air lamentable *or* pitoyable.
2 *n* **(a)** (*death*) mort *f*; (*just before death*) agonie *f*.
(b) the ~ les mourants *mpl*, les agonisants *mpl*, les moribonds *mpl*; **prayer for the** ~ prière *f* des agonisants.
dyke [daɪk] *n* (*channel*) fossé *m*; (*wall barrier*) digue *f*; (*causeway*) levée *f*, chaussée *f*; (*Geol*) filon *m* stérile, dyke *m*; (*‡: lesbian*) gouine‡ *f*.
dynamic [daɪˈnæmɪk] *adj* (*Phys etc*) dynamique; *person etc* dynamique, énergique, plein d'entrain.
dynamics [daɪˈnæmɪks] *n* (*U or pl*) dynamique *f*.
dynamism [ˈdaɪnəmɪzəm] *n* dynamisme *m*.
dynamite [ˈdaɪnəmaɪt] **1** *n* dynamite *f*. (*fig*) **he's** ~! c'est de la dynamite!*, il pète le feu!*, il est d'un dynamisme!; **that business is** ~ ça pourrait t'exploser dans les mains; **it's political** ~ sur le plan politique c'est un sujet explosif *or* une affaire explosive; *V* **stick.**
2 *vt* faire sauter à la dynamite, dynamiter.
dynamo [ˈdaɪnəməʊ] *n* (*esp Brit*) dynamo *f*. **he is a human** ~ il déborde d'énergie.
dynastic [daɪˈnæstɪk] *adj* dynastique.
dynasty [ˈdɪnəstɪ] *n* dynastie *f*.
dyne [daɪn] *n* dyne *f*.
dysentery [ˈdɪsɪntrɪ] *n* dysenterie *f*.
dyslexia [dɪsˈleksɪə] *n* dyslexie *f*.
dyslexic [dɪsˈleksɪk] *adj, n* dyslexique (*mf*).
dysmenorrhaea, (*US*) **dysmenorrhea** [ˌdɪsmenəˈrɪə] *n* dysménorrhée *f*.
dyspepsia [dɪsˈpepsɪə] *n* dyspepsie *f*.
dyspeptic [dɪsˈpeptɪk] *adj, n* dyspepsique (*mf*), dyspeptique (*mf*).
dysphasia [dɪsˈfeɪzɪə] *n* dysphasie *f*.
dystrophy [ˈdɪstrəfɪ] *n* dystrophie *f*; *V* **muscular.**

E

E, e [i:] *n* **(a)** (*letter*) E, e *m*. **(b)** (*Mus*) mi *m*.

each [i:tʃ] **1** *adj* chaque. **~ passport** chaque passeport, tout passeport; **~ day** chaque jour, tous les jours; **~ one of us** chacun(e) de *or* d'entre nous; **~ (and every) one of us, ~ and all of us** chacun(e) de nous sans exception.

2 *pron* **(a)** (*thing, person, group*) chacun(e) *m(f)*. **~ of the boys** chacun des garçons; **~ of us** chacun(e) de *or* d'entre nous; **~ of them gave their*** *or* **his opinion** chacun a donné son avis, ils ont donné chacun leur avis; **we ~ had our own idea about it** nous avions chacun notre idée là-dessus; **~ of them was given a present** on leur a offert à chacun un cadeau, chacun d'entre eux a reçu un cadeau; **a little of ~ please** un peu de chaque s'il vous plaît.

(b) (*apiece*) chacun(e). **we gave them one apple ~** nous leur avons donné une pomme chacun; **2 classes of 20 pupils ~** 2 classes de chacune 20 élèves *or* de 20 élèves chacune; **the records are £2 ~** les disques coûtent 2 livres chacun *or* chaque; **carnations at one franc ~** des œillets à un franc (la) pièce.

(c) ~ other l'un(e) l'autre *m(f)*, *mpl* les uns les autres, *fpl* les unes les autres; **they love ~ other** ils s'aiment (l'un l'autre); **they write to ~ other often** ils s'écrivent souvent; **they were sorry for ~ other** ils avaient pitié l'un de l'autre; **they respected ~ other** ils avaient du respect l'un pour l'autre, ils se respectaient mutuellement; **you must help ~ other** il faut vous entraider; **separated from ~ other** séparés l'un de l'autre; **they used to carry ~ other's books** ils s'aidaient à porter leurs livres.

eager ['i:gə^{r}] *adj* (*keen*) désireux, avide (*for* de, *to do* de faire); (*impatient*) impatient, pressé (*to do* de faire); *scholar, supporter* passionné; *lover* ardent, passionné; *desire* ardent, passionné, violent; *search, glance* avide; *pursuit, discussion* âpre. **to be ~ for** *happiness* rechercher avidement; *knowledge, affection* être avide de; *power, vengeance, pleasure* être assoiffé de; *praise, fame, knowledge* avoir soif de; *nomination, honour* désirer vivement, ambitionner; **~ for profit** âpre au gain; **to be ~ to do** (*keen*) être extrêmement désireux *or* avoir très envie de faire, désirer vivement faire; (*impatient*) brûler *or* être impatient *or* être pressé de faire; **to be ~ to help** être empressé à *or* très désireux d'aider; **to be an ~ student of** se passionner pour l'étude de; **~ beaver*** bourreau *m* de travail, travailleur *m*, -euse *f* acharné(e).

eagerly ['i:gəlɪ] *adv* (*V* **eager**) avidement; avec impatience, avec empressement; passionnément, ardemment, âprement.

eagerness ['i:gənɪs] *n* (*V* **eager**) (vif) désir *m*, avidité *f* (*for* de) (*liter*), désir ardent (*to do* de faire, *for* de); impatience *f* (*to do* de faire), empressement *m* (*to do* à faire); ardeur *f* (*for* à); âpreté *f* (*for* à).

eagle ['i:gl] **1** *n* (*Orn*) aigle *mf* (*gen m*); (*Rel: lectern*) aigle *m*; (*Her, Hist, Mil*) aigle *f*; (*Golf*) eagle *m*; *V* **golden. 2** *cpd*: **eagle-eyed** qui a des yeux d'aigle.

ear[1] [ɪə^{r}] **1** *n* oreille *f*. (*fig*) **to keep one's ~s open** ouvrir l'oreille; (*fig*) **to close** *or* **shut one's ~s to sth** faire la sourde oreille à qch; **to keep one's ~ to the ground** être aux écoutes; **to be all ~s*** être tout oreilles *or* tout ouïe; (*fig*) **that set them by the ~s!** ça a semé la zizanie (entre eux)!, cela les a mis aux prises!; **your ~s must have been burning** les oreilles ont dû vous tinter; **if that came to his ~s** si cela venait à ses oreilles; **it goes in one ~ and out of the other** cela lui (*or* vous *etc*) entre par une oreille et lui (*or* vous *etc*) sort par l'autre; **he has the ~ of the President** il a l'oreille du Président; **to be up to the ~s in work** avoir du travail par-dessus la tête; **to be up to the ~s in debt** être endetté jusqu'au cou; **to have an ~ for music** avoir l'oreille musicale; (*Mus*) **to have a good ~** avoir de l'oreille, avoir l'oreille juste; (*Mus*) **to play by ~** jouer d'instinct *or* à l'oreille; (*fig*) **I'll play it by ~** je déciderai quoi faire *or* j'improviserai le moment venu; *V* **box**[2]**, deaf, half.**

2 *cpd operation* à l'oreille. **earache** mal *m* d'oreille(s); **to have earache** avoir mal à l'oreille *or* aux oreilles; **eardrum** tympan *m* (*de l'oreille*); **earmark** (*n*) (*fig*) marque *f*, signe distinctif, caractéristique *f*; (*vt*) *cattle* marquer (au fer rouge); (*fig*) *object, seat* réserver (*for* à); *funds, person* assigner, affecter, destiner (*for* à); **earmuff** serre-tête *m inv*; (*Med*) **ear nose and throat department** service *m* d'oto-rhino-laryngologie; **ear nose and throat specialist** oto-rhino-laryngologiste *mf*, oto-rhino* *mf*; (*Rad, Telec etc*) **earphone** écouteur *m*; **to listen on earphones** écouter au casque; (*Rad, Telec etc*) **earpiece** écouteur *m*; **earplugs** (*for sleeping*) boules *fpl* Quiès ®; (*for underwater*) protège-tympan *m inv*; **earring** boucle *f* d'oreille; **out of earshot** hors de portée de voix; **within earshot** à portée de voix; **ear-splitting** *sound, scream* strident; *din* fracassant; **ear trumpet** cornet *m* acoustique; **ear wax** cérumen *m*, cire *f*; **earwig** perce-oreille *m*.

ear[2] [ɪə^{r}] *n [grain, plant]* épi *m*.

earl [3:l] *n* comte *m*.

earldom ['3:ldəm] *n* (*title*) titre *m* de comte; (*land*) comté *m*.

early ['3:lɪ] **1** *adj man, Church* primitif; *apple, plant* précoce, hâtif; *death* prématuré. **don't go, it's still ~** ne t'en va pas, il est encore tôt *or* il n'est pas tard; **you're ~ today!** vous arrivez de bonne heure *or* tôt aujourd'hui!; **his ~ arrival** son arrivée de bonne heure, le fait qu'il arrive (*or* est arrivé *etc*) de bonne heure; **an ~ text** un texte très ancien, un des premiers textes; **to be an ~ riser** *or* **an ~ bird*** être matinal, se lever tôt *or* de bon matin; (*Prov*) **it's the ~ bird that catches the worm** l'avenir appartient à qui se lève matin (*Prov*); (*Prov*) **~ to bed, ~ to rise** tôt couché, tôt levé; (*Mil*) **~ warning system** dispositif *m* de première alerte; (*Brit Comm*) **it's ~ closing day today** aujourd'hui les magasins ferment l'après-midi; **it is too ~** *or* (*Brit*) **it is ~ days*** *or* **it's ~ in the day yet to say** il est trop tôt pour dire; **~ fruit** *or* **vegetables** primeurs *fpl*; **at an ~ hour** de bonne heure, très tôt; **at an ~ hour (of the morning)** à une heure matinale; **it was ~ in the morning** c'était tôt le matin, c'était le début de la matinée; **in the ~ morning** de bon *or* grand matin; **in the ~ afternoon/spring** au commencement *or* au début de l'après-midi/du printemps; **she's in her ~ forties** elle a juste dépassé la quarantaine; **from an ~ age** dès l'enfance, de bonne heure; **in his ~ youth** dans sa première *or* prime jeunesse; **his ~ life** sa jeunesse; **in ~ life** tôt dans la vie, de bonne heure; **in the ~ part of the century** au début *or* au commencement du siècle; (*Archit*) **E~ English** premier gothique anglais; (*Brit Hist*) **the ~ Victorians** les Victoriens *mpl* du début du règne; **an ~ Victorian table** une table du début de l'époque victorienne; **at an ~ date** bientôt, prochainement; **at an earlier date** à une date plus rapprochée; **at the earliest possible moment** le plus tôt possible, au plus tôt, dès que possible; (*Comm*) **at your earliest convenience** dans les meilleurs délais; (*Comm*) **to promise ~ delivery** promettre une livraison rapide; *V* **hour.**

2 *adv* de bonne heure, tôt. **too ~** trop tôt, de trop bonne heure; **as ~ as possible** le plus tôt possible, dès que possible; **she left 10 minutes ~** elle est partie 10 minutes plus tôt; **she had left 10 minutes earlier** elle était partie 10 minutes plus tôt *or* 10 minutes auparavant; **I get up earlier in summer** je me lève plus tôt en été; **not earlier than Thursday** pas avant jeudi; **earlier on** précédemment, plus tôt; **the earliest he can come is ...** le plus tôt qu'il puisse venir c'est ...; **post ~** expédiez votre courrier à l'avance; **book ~** réservez longtemps à l'avance; **~ in the morning** de bon *or* de grand matin; **~ in the year/in the book** au commencement *or* au début de l'année/du livre; **he took his summer holiday ~ this year** il a pris ses vacances tôt cette année; **~ in (my) life** dans *or* dès ma jeunesse.

earn [3:n] *vt money* gagner; *salary* toucher; (*Fin*) *interest* rapporter; *praise, rest* mériter, gagner. **to ~ one's living** gagner sa vie; **his success ~ed him praise** sa réussite lui a valu des éloges; **~ed income** revenus salariaux, traitement(s) *m(pl)*, salaire(s) *m(pl)*.

earnest ['3:nɪst] **1** *adj* (*conscientious*) sérieux, consciencieux; (*eager*) ardent; (*sincere*) sincère; *prayer* fervent; *desire, request* pressant.

2 *n* **(a) in ~** (*with determination*) sérieusement; (*without joking*) sans rire. **this time I am in ~** cette fois je ne plaisante pas; **it is snowing in ~** il neige pour de bon.

(b) (*also* **~ money**) arrhes *fpl*; (*fig: guarantee*) garantie *f*, gage *m*. **as an ~ of his good intentions** en gage de ses bonnes intentions.

earnestly ['3:nɪstlɪ] *adv speak* avec conviction, avec (grand) sérieux; *work* consciencieusement, avec ardeur; *beseech* instamment; *pray* avec ferveur.

earnestness ['3:nɪstnɪs] *n [person, tone]* gravité *f*, sérieux *m*; *[effort]* ardeur *f*; *[demand]* véhémence *f*.

earnings ['3:nɪŋz] *npl [person]* salaire *m*, gain(s) *m(pl)*; *[business]* profits *mpl*, bénéfices *mpl*.

earth [3:θ] **1** *n* **(a)** (*the world*) terre *f*, monde *m*. **(the) E~** la Terre; **on ~** sur terre; **here on ~** ici-bas, en ce bas monde; (*fig*) **it's heaven on ~** c'est le paradis sur terre; **to the ends of the ~** au bout du monde; **where/why/how on ~ ...?** où/pourquoi/comment ...?; **nowhere on ~ will you find ...** nulle part au monde vous ne trouverez ...; **nothing on ~** rien au monde; (*fig*) **to promise sb the ~** promettre la lune à qn; **it must have cost the ~!*** ça a dû coûter les yeux de la tête!*

(b) (*U*) (*ground*) terre *f*, sol *m*; (*soil*) terre; (*Elec*) masse *f*, terre; (*Art: also* **~ colour**) terre, couleur minérale. **to fall to ~** tomber à terre *or* par terre *or* au sol; (*lit, fig*) **to come back to ~** redescendre sur terre; **my boots are full of ~** j'ai les bottes pleines de terre; *V* **down**[1]**.**

(c) *[fox, badger etc]* terrier *m*, tanière *f*. (*lit, fig*) **to run** *or* **go to ~** se terrer; **to run sth/sb to ~** découvrir *or* dépister *or* dénicher qch/qn.

2 *cpd*: (*liter*) **earthborn** humain; **earthbound** (*moving towards* **~**) qui se dirige vers la terre; (*stuck on* **~**) attaché à la terre; (*fig: unimaginative*) terre à terre *inv or* terre-à-terre *inv*; **earthmover** bulldozer *m*; **earthquake** tremblement *m* de terre, séisme *m*; **earth sciences** sciences *fpl* de la terre; **earth tremor** secousse *f* sismique; **earthwork** (*Constr*) terrassement *m*; (*Mil*) ouvrage *m* de terre; **earthworm** ver *m* de terre.

3 *vt* (*Elec*) *apparatus* mettre à la masse *or* à la terre.

earth up *vt sep plant* butter.

earthen ['3:θən] **1** *adj* de terre, en terre. **2** *cpd*: **earthenware**

poterie *f*; (*glazed*) faïence *f*; **earthenware jug** *etc* cruche *f etc* en faïence *or* en terre (cuite).
earthly ['ɜːθlɪ] **1** *adj being, paradise, possessions* terrestre. (*fig*) **there is no ~ reason to think** il n'y a pas la moindre raison de croire; **for no ~ reason** sans aucune raison; **he hasn't an ~ chance of succeeding** il n'a pas la moindre chance de réussir; **of no ~ use** d'aucune utilité, sans aucun intérêt; **it's no ~ use telling him that** ça ne sert absolument à rien de lui dire ça.
2 *n* (*Brit*) **not an ~**: pas la moindre chance, pas l'ombre d'une chance.
earthward(s) ['ɜːθwəd(z)] *adv* dans la direction de la terre, vers la terre.
earthy ['ɜːθɪ] *adj taste, smell* terreux, de terre; (*fig*) *person* matériel, terre à terre *inv or* terre-à-terre *inv*; *humour* truculent.
ease [iːz] **1** *n* (*U*) **(a)** (*mental*) tranquillité *f*; (*physical*) bien-être *m*. **at (one's) ~** à l'aise; **to put sb at (his) ~** mettre qn à l'aise; **not at ~, ill-at-~** mal à son aise, mal à l'aise; **my mind is at ~** j'ai l'esprit tranquille; **to put sb's mind at ~** tranquilliser qn; **the feeling of ~ after a good meal** la sensation de bien-être qui suit un bon repas; **to take one's ~** prendre ses aises; **he lives a life of ~** il a une vie facile; (*Mil*) **(stand) at ~!** repos!
(b) (*lack of difficulty*) aisance *f*, facilité *f*. **with ~** facilement, aisément, sans difficulté.
2 *vt* **(a)** *pain* atténuer, soulager; *mind* calmer, rassurer, tranquilliser; (*liter*) *person* délivrer, soulager (*of a burden* d'un fardeau); *cord* détendre, desserrer; *strap* relâcher; *dress, coat* donner plus d'ampleur à; *pressure, tension* diminuer, modérer; *speed* ralentir. (*Naut*) **to ~ a rope** donner du mou à *or* mollir un cordage.
(b) to ~ a key into a lock introduire doucement *or* lentement une clef dans une serrure; (*Aviat*) **to ~ back the stick** redresser doucement le manche (à balai); (*Aut*) **to ~ in the clutch** embrayer en douceur; (*Aut*) **he ~d the car into gear** il a passé la première en douceur; **he ~d out the screw** il a desserré délicatement la vis; **he ~d himself into the chair** il s'est laissé glisser dans le fauteuil; **he ~d himself through the gap in the fence** il s'est glissé par le trou de la barrière; **he ~d himself into his jacket** il a passé *or* enfilé doucement sa veste.
3 *vi* se détendre. **the situation has ~d** une détente s'est produite; **prices have ~d** les prix ont baissé, il y a eu une baisse des prix.
ease off 1 *vi* (*slow down*) ralentir; (*work less hard*) se relâcher; *[situation]* se détendre; *[pressure]* diminuer; *[work, business]* devenir plus calme; *[traffic]* diminuer; *[pain]* se calmer; *[demand]* baisser.
2 *vt sep bandage, stamp etc* enlever délicatement; *lid* enlever doucement.
ease up *vi [person]* se détendre, se reposer, dételer; *[situation]* se détendre. **ease up a bit!** vas-y plus doucement!
easel ['iːzl] *n* chevalet *m*.
easily ['iːzɪlɪ] *adv* **(a)** (*without difficulty*) facilement, sans difficulté, aisément. **the engine was running ~** le moteur tournait régulièrement.
(b) (*unquestionably*) sans aucun doute, de loin; (*with amounts, measurements etc*) facilement. **he is ~ the best** il est de loin *or* sans aucun doute le meilleur; **that's ~ 4 km** cela fait facilement 4 km.
(c) (*possibly*) bien. **he may ~ change his mind** il pourrait bien changer d'avis; **he could ~ be right** il pourrait bien avoir raison.
(d) (*calmly*) *smile etc* avec calme, tranquillement. **'yes' he said ~** 'oui' dit-il tranquillement.
easiness ['iːzɪnɪs] *n* facilité *f*, aisance *f*.
east [iːst] **1** *n* est *m*, orient *m* (*frm*), levant† *m*. **the E~** (*Pol*) les pays *mpl* de l'Est; (*US Geog*) (les états *mpl* de) l'Est; **the mysterious E~** l'Orient mystérieux; **(to the) ~ of** à l'est de; **in the ~ of Scotland** dans l'est de l'Écosse; **house facing the ~** maison exposée à l'est; *[wind]* **to veer to the ~, to go into the ~** tourner à l'est; **the wind is in the ~** le vent est à l'est; **the wind is from the ~** le vent vient *or* souffle de l'est; **to live in the ~** habiter dans l'Est; (*in London*) **the E~ End** les quartiers *mpl* est de Londres (*quartiers pauvres*); (*in New York*) **the E~ Side** les quartiers est de New York; *V* **far, middle** *etc.*
2 *adj* est *inv*, de *or* à l'est, oriental. **~ wind** vent *m* d'est; **~ coast** côte est *or* orientale; **on the ~ side** du côté est; **room with an ~ aspect** pièce exposée à l'est; (*Archit*) **~ transept/door** transept/portail est *or* oriental; *V also* **4**.
3 *adv* à l'est, vers l'est. **the town lies ~ of the border** la ville est située à l'est de la frontière; **we drove ~ for 100 km** nous avons roulé pendant 100 km en direction de l'est; **go ~ till you get to Crewe** aller en direction de l'est jusqu'à Crewe; **to sail due ~** aller droit vers l'est; (*Naut*) avoir le cap à l'est; **~ by north-~** est quart nord-est.
4 *cpd*: **East Africa** l'Afrique orientale, l'Est *m* de l'Afrique; **East African** (*adj*) d'Afrique orientale; (*n*) Africain(e) *m(f)* de l'Est; **eastbound** *traffic, vehicles* (se déplaçant) en direction de l'est; *carriageway* est *inv*; **east-facing** exposé à l'est; **East Indies** Indes orientales.
Easter ['iːstəʳ] **1** *n* Pâques *fpl or msg*. **at ~** à Pâques; **Happy ~!** joyeuses Pâques!; **~ is celebrated between ...** Pâques est célébré entre ... .
2 *cpd egg* de Pâques; *holidays* pascal, de Pâques. **Easter bonnet** chapeau *m* de printemps; **Easter Day** le jour de Pâques; **Easter Monday** le lundi de Pâques; **Easter parade** défilé pascal; **Easter Sunday** le dimanche de Pâques; **Eastertide** le temps pascal, la saison de Pâques; **Easter week** la semaine pascale.
easterly ['iːstəlɪ] **1** *adj wind* d'est; *situation* à l'est, à l'orient (*frm*). **in an ~ direction** en direction de l'est, vers l'est; **~ aspect** exposition *f* à l'est. **2** *adv* vers l'est.
eastern ['iːstən] **1** *adj* est *inv*, de l'est. **the ~ coast** la côte est *or* orientale; **house with an ~ outlook** maison exposée à l'est; **~ wall** mur exposé à l'est; **E~ Africa** Afrique orientale; **E~ France** l'Est *m* de la France; (*Pol*) **the E~ bloc** les pays *mpl* de l'Est; (*US*) **E~ Standard Time** l'heure normale de l'Est.
2 *cpd*: **easternmost** le plus à l'est.
easterner ['iːstənəʳ] *n* (*esp US*) homme *m or* femme *f* de l'Est. **he is an ~** il vient de l'Est; **the ~s** les gens *mpl* de l'Est.
eastward ['iːstwəd] **1** *adj* à l'est. **2** *adv* (*also* **~s**) vers l'est.
easy ['iːzɪ] **1** *adj* **(a)** (*not difficult*) *problem, sum, decision* facile; *person* facile, accommodant. **as ~ as anything*, as ~ as pie*** facile comme tout *or* comme bonjour; **it is ~ to see that ...** on voit bien que ..., cela se voit que ...; **it is ~ for him to do that** il lui est facile de faire cela; **it's ~ to see why** il est facile de comprendre pourquoi; **it was ~ to get them to be quiet** on a eu vite fait de les faire taire; **it's easier said than done!** c'est vite dit!; **you've got an ~ life** tu as une vie sans problèmes, tu n'as pas de problèmes; **it's an ~ house to run** c'est une maison facile à tenir; **it's ~ money** c'est comme si on était payé à ne rien faire; **within ~ reach of** à distance commode de; **in ~ stages** *travel* par petites étapes; *learn* par degrés; **he is ~ to work with** il est agréable *or* accommodant dans le travail; **~ to get on with** facile à vivre; **to be ~ on the eye*** être bien balancé*; (*Brit*) **I'm ~*** ça m'est égal; **he came in an ~ first** il est arrivé bon premier *or* dans un fauteuil*.
(b) (*relaxed, comfortable*) aisé, facile, tranquille; *manners* aisé, naturel; *life* tranquille, sans souci; *style* facile, aisé, coulant; *conditions* favorable. **to feel ~ in one's mind** être tout à fait tranquille, ne pas se faire de souci; **in ~ circumstances** dans l'aisance; **to be on ~ street*** se la couler douce*; **at an ~ pace** à une allure modérée; **woman of ~ virtue** femme *f* facile *or* de petite vertu; **to be on ~ terms with** avoir des relations cordiales avec; (*Comm*) **on ~ terms, by ~ payments** avec facilités *fpl* de paiement; (*St Ex*) **~ market** marché tranquille *or* mou; **prices are ~ today** les prix sont un peu moins hauts aujourd'hui; **~ there!** tout doucement!; *V* **mark**^{2}.
2 *adv* (*) doucement, tranquillement. **to take things** *or* **it ~** ne pas se fatiguer, en prendre à son aise (*pej*), se la couler douce*; **take it ~!** (*don't worry*) ne vous en faites pas!; (*calm down*) ne vous emballez pas!; (*relax*) ne vous fatiguez pas!; (*go slow*) ne vous pressez pas!; **go ~ on** *or* **with the sugar** ne mets pas trop de sucre, vas-y doucement avec le sucre; **go ~ on** *or* **with the whisky** ne verse pas trop de whisky, vas-y doucement *or* mollo: avec le whisky; **to go ~ on** *or* **with sb** ne pas être trop dur envers qn, ménager qn, traiter qn avec ménagement; (*Prov*) **~ come, ~ go** ce n'est que de l'argent!, c'est fait pour être dépensé! (*V also* **3**); **~ does it!** allez-y doucement! *or* mollo!:; (*Mil*) **stand ~!** repos!
3 *cpd*: **easy chair** fauteuil *m* (rembourré); **easy-going** accommodant, facile à vivre, qui ne s'en fait pas; *attitude* complaisant; **easy come-easy go*** *person* qui gagne et dépense sans compter.
eat [iːt] *pret* **ate**, *ptp* **eaten 1** *vt food* manger. **to ~ (one's) breakfast** déjeuner, prendre son petit déjeuner; **to ~ (one's) lunch** déjeuner; **to ~ (one's) dinner** dîner; **to ~ a meal** prendre un repas; **to have nothing to ~** n'avoir rien à manger *or* à se mettre sous la dent; **to ~ one's fill** manger à sa faim; (*lit*) **fit to ~** mangeable, bon à manger; (*fig*) **she looks good enough to ~** elle est belle à croquer; (*fig*) **to ~ one's words** se rétracter, ravaler ses paroles; (*fig*) **to make sb ~ his words** faire rentrer ses mots dans la gorge à qn; **I'll ~ my hat if ...*** je veux bien être pendu si ...; **he won't ~ you*** il ne va pas te manger; **what's ~ing you?**: qu'est-ce qui ne va pas?, qu'est-ce qui te tracasse?
2 *vi* manger. **we ~ at 8** nous dînons à 20 heures; **to ~ like a horse** manger comme quatre *or* comme un ogre; **he is ~ing us out of house and home**: son appétit va nous mettre à la rue; (*fig*) **to ~ out of sb's hand** faire les quatre volontés de qn; **I've got him ~ing out of my hand** il fait tout ce que je lui dis *or* tout ce que je veux.
3 *n* (*Brit*) **~s**: bouffe: *f*, boustifaille: *f*.
eat away *vt sep [sea]* saper, éroder; *[acid, mice]* ronger.
eat into *vt fus [acid, insects]* ronger; *[moths]* manger; *[expenditure]* entamer, écorner*.
eat out 1 *vi* aller au restaurant, déjeuner *or* dîner en ville.
2 *vt sep* (*fig*) **to eat one's heart out** se ronger d'inquiétude.
eat up *vt sep* **(a)** finir. **eat up your meat** finis ta viande; **eat up your meal** finis ton repas, finis de manger; (*fig*) **to be eaten up with envy** être dévoré d'envie *or* rongé par l'envie.
(b) (*fig*) manger, dévorer. **this car eats up the miles** cette voiture dévore la route; **this car eats up petrol** cette voiture bouffe: l'essence *or* consomme beaucoup; **it eats up the electricity/coal** cela consomme beaucoup d'électricité/de charbon.
eatable ['iːtəbl] **1** *adj* (*fit to eat*) mangeable, bon à manger; (*edible*) comestible. **2** *n*: **~s*** comestibles *mpl*, victuailles *fpl* (*hum*).
eaten ['iːtn] *ptp of* **eat**.
eater ['iːtəʳ] *n* **(a)** (*person*) mangeur *m*, -euse *f*. **to be a big ~** être un grand *or* gros mangeur; **to be a big meat ~** être un gros mangeur de viande. **(b)** (*eating apple/pear*) pomme *f*/poire *f* à couteau *or* de dessert.
eatery ['iːtərɪ] *n* (*US*) crémerie *f*, café-restaurant *m*.
eating ['iːtɪŋ] **1** *n*: **these apples make good ~** ces pommes sont bonnes à manger. **2** *cpd apple* à couteau, de dessert. **eating chocolate** chocolat *m* à croquer; (*US*) **eating hall** réfectoire *m*; **eating house, eating place** restaurant *m*.
eau de Cologne ['əʊdəkə'ləʊn] *n* eau *f* de Cologne.
eaves ['iːvz] **1** *npl* avant-toit(s) *m(pl)*. **2** *cpd*: **eavesdrop** écouter de façon indiscrète; **to eavesdrop on a conversation** écouter une conversation privée; **eavesdropper** oreille indiscrète.
ebb [eb] **1** *n [tide]* reflux *m*, (*Naut*) jusant *m*. **~ and flow** le flux

et le reflux; **the tide is on the ~** la marée descend; (*fig*) **to be at a low ~** *[person, spirits]* être bien bas; *[business]* aller mal.

2 *cpd*: **ebb tide** marée descendante, reflux *m*; (*Naut*) jusant *m*.

3 *vi* **(a)** *[tide]* refluer, descendre. **to ~ and flow** monter et baisser.

(b) (*fig: also* **~ away**) *[enthusiasm etc]* décliner, baisser, être sur le déclin.

ebonite ['ebənaɪt] *n* ébonite *f*.

ebony ['ebənɪ] **1** *n* ébène *f*. **2** *cpd* (*~-coloured*) noir d'ébène; (*made of ~*) en ébène, d'ébène.

ebullience [ɪ'bʌlɪəns] *n* (*fig, lit*) effervescence *f*.

ebullient [ɪ'bʌlɪənt] *adj person* plein de vie, exubérant; *spirits, mood* exubérant.

eccentric [ɪk'sentrɪk] **1** *adj* (*fig*) *person, behaviour, clothes, ideas* excentrique, original, bizarre; (*Math, Tech*) *orbit, curve, circles* excentrique. **2** *n* (*person*) original(e) *m(f)*, excentrique *mf*; (*Tech*) excentrique *m*.

eccentrically [ɪk'sentrɪkəlɪ] *adv* (*V* **eccentric**) excentriquement, avec excentricité, d'une manière originale, bizarrement.

eccentricity [ˌeksən'trɪsɪtɪ] *n* **(a)** (*V* **eccentric**) excentricité *f*, originalité *f*, bizarrerie *f*. **(b)** *[action, whim]* excentricité *f*.

ecclesiastic [ɪˌkliːzɪ'æstɪk] *adj, n* ecclésiastique (*m*).

ecclesiastical [ɪˌkliːzɪ'æstɪkəl] *adj* ecclésiastique.

ecdysis ['ekdɪsɪs] *n* ecdysis *f*.

echelon ['eʃəlɒn] *n* (*Mil*) échelon *m*.

echinoderm [ɪkiːnədɜːm] *n* échinoderme *m*.

echo ['ekəʊ] **1** *n* écho *m*; (*fig*) écho, rappel *m*. **to cheer to the ~** applaudir à tout rompre.

2 *vt* (*lit*) répercuter, renvoyer. (*fig*) **he ~ed my words incredulously** il a répété ce que j'avais dit d'un ton incrédule; **'go home?' he ~ed** 'rentrer?' répéta-t-il; **to ~ sb's ideas** se faire l'écho de la pensée de qn.

3 *vi* *[sound]* retentir, résonner, se répercuter; *[room]* faire écho. (*liter*) **to ~ with music** retentir de musique; (*liter*) **the valley ~ed with their laughter** la vallée résonnait *or* retentissait de leurs rires.

4 *cpd*: (*Rad, TV*) **echo chamber** chambre *f* sonore; (*Naut*) **echo-sounder** sondeur *m* (à ultra-sons).

éclair ['eɪkleəʳ] *n* (*Culin*) éclair *m* (à la crème).

eclampsia [ɪ'klæmpsɪə] *n* éclampsie *f*.

eclectic [ɪ'klektɪk] *adj, n* éclectique (*mf*).

eclecticism [ɪ'klektɪsɪzəm] *n* éclectisme *m*.

eclipse [ɪ'klɪps] **1** *n* (*Astron, fig*) éclipse *f*. (*Astron, fig*) **to be in** *or* **go into ~** être éclipsé; **partial/total ~** éclipse partielle/totale. **2** *vt* (*Astron*) éclipser; (*fig*) éclipser, faire pâlir, surpasser. **eclipsing binary** étoile *f* double.

ecliptic [ɪ'klɪptɪk] *adj* écliptique.

eclogue ['eklɒg] *n* églogue *f*.

eclosion [ɪ'kləʊʒən] *n* éclosion *f*.

eco... ['ɪːkəʊ] *pref* éco... . **~system** écosystème *m*; **~type** écotype *m*; *V* **ecology** *etc*.

ecological [ˌiːkəʊ'lɒdʒɪkəl] *adj* écologique.

ecologist [ɪ'kɒlədʒɪst] *n* écologiste *mf*.

ecology [ɪ'kɒlədʒɪ] *n* écologie *f*.

economic [ˌiːkə'nɒmɪk] *adj* **(a)** *development, geography, factor* économique. **the ~ system of a country** l'économie *f* d'un pays.

(b) (*profitable*) rentable, qui rapporte. **an ~ rent** un loyer rentable; **this business is no longer ~** *or* **an ~ proposition** cette affaire n'est plus rentable; **it isn't ~** *or* **it isn't an ~ proposition** *or* **it doesn't make ~ sense to own a car in town** si l'on habite en ville il n'est pas intéressant d'avoir une voiture.

economical [ˌiːkə'nɒmɪkəl] *adj person* économe; *method, appliance, speed* économique. **to be ~ with** économiser, ménager.

economically [ˌiːkə'nɒmɪkəlɪ] *adv* économiquement. **to use sth ~** économiser qch, ménager qch.

economics [ˌiːkə'nɒmɪks] *n* (*U*) (*science*) (science *f*) économique *f*, économie *f* politique; (*financial aspect*) côté *m* économique. **the ~ of the situation/the project** le côté économique de la situation/du projet; *V* **home**.

economist [ɪ'kɒnəmɪst] *n* économiste *mf*, spécialiste *mf* d'économie politique.

economize [ɪ'kɒnəmaɪz] **1** *vi* économiser (*on* sur), faire des économies. **2** *vt time, money* économiser, épargner. **to ~ 20% on the costs** faire une économie de 20% sur la dépense.

economy [ɪ'kɒnəmɪ] **1** *n* **(a)** (*saving: in time, money etc*) économie *f* (*in* de). **to make economies in** faire des économies de.

(b) (*U: system*) économie *f*, système *m* économique. **the country's ~ depends on ...** l'économie du pays dépend de ... .

2 *cpd*: (*esp Aviat*) **economy class** classe *f* touriste; **economy drive** (campagne *f* *or* mesures *fpl* de) restrictions *fpl* budgétaires; (*Comm*) **economy pack/size** paquet *m*/taille *f* économique.

ecstasy ['ekstəsɪ] *n* extase *f* (*also Rel*), ravissement *m*, transport *m* (de joie) (*liter*). **with ~** avec ravissement, avec extase; **to be in ecstasies over** *object* s'extasier sur; *person* être en extase devant.

ecstatic [eks'tætɪk] *adj* extasié. **to be ~ over** *or* **about** *object* s'extasier sur; *person*, être en extase devant.

ecstatically [eks'tætɪkəlɪ] *adv* avec extase, avec ravissement, d'un air extasié.

ectoplasm ['ektəʊplæzəm] *n* ectoplasme *m*.

Ecuador ['ekwədɔːʳ] *n* Équateur *m*, Ecuador *m*.

Ecuador(i)an [ˌekwə'dɔːr(ɪ)ən] **1** *adj* équatorien. **2** *n* Équatorien(ne) *m(f)*.

ecumenical [ˌiːkjʊ'menɪkəl] *adj* œcuménique.

eczema ['eksɪmə] *n* eczéma *m*.

eddy ['edɪ] **1** *n* *[water, air]* remous *m*, tourbillon *m*; *[snow, dust, smoke]* tourbillon; *[leaves]* tournoiement *m*, tourbillon. **2** *vi* *[air, smoke, leaves]* tourbillonner; *[people]* tournoyer; *[water]* faire des remous *or* des tourbillons.

edelweiss ['eɪdlvaɪs] *n* edelweiss *m inv*.

edema [ɪ'diːmə] *n* (*esp US*) œdème *m*.

Eden ['iːdn] *n* Éden *m*, paradis *m* terrestre. **the garden of ~** le jardin d'Éden.

edentate [ɪ'denteɪt] *adj, n* édenté (*m*).

edge [edʒ] **1** *n* **(a)** *[knife, razor]* tranchant *m*, fil *m*. **a blade with a sharp ~** une lame bien affilée; **to put an ~ on** aiguiser, affiler, affûter; **to take the ~ off** *knife, sensation* émousser; *appetite* calmer; **it sets my teeth on ~** cela m'agace les dents; **he is on ~** il est énervé *or* à cran*; **my nerves are all on ~*** j'ai les nerfs à vif *or* en pelote* *or* en boule*; (*fig*) **to have the ~ on sb/sth** être légèrement supérieur à qn/qch, l'emporter de justesse *or* d'un poil* sur qn/qch.

(b) *[table, plate]* bord *m*; *[river, lake]* bord, rive *f*; *[sea]* rivage *m*, bord; *[cliff]* bord; *[forest]* lisière *f*, orée *f*; *[road]* bord, côté *m*; *[town]* abords *mpl*; *[cloth]* (*uncut*) lisière, bord; (*cut*) bord; *[coin]* tranche *f*; *[page]* marge *f*; *[cube, brick]* arête *f*; (*distance round the ~ of an object*) pourtour *m*. **a book with gilt ~s** un livre doré sur tranches; **to stand sth on its ~** poser qch de chant; **the trees at the ~ of the road** les arbres en bordure de la route; (*fig*) **to be on the ~ of disaster** être au bord du désastre, courir au désastre.

2 *cpd*: **edgeways, edgewise** de côté; **I couldn't get a word in edgeways*** je n'ai pas réussi à placer un mot.

3 *vt* **(a)** (*put a border on*) border (*with* de). **to ~ a collar with lace** border un col de dentelle.

(b) (*sharpen*) *tool, blade* aiguiser, affiler, affûter.

(c) to ~ one's chair nearer the door rapprocher sa chaise tout doucement de la porte; **to ~ one's way through** *etc* = **to edge through** *etc*; *V* **4**.

4 *vi* se glisser, se faufiler. **to ~ through/into** *etc* se glisser *or* se faufiler à travers/dans *etc*; **to ~ forward** avancer petit à petit; **to ~ away** s'éloigner tout doucement *or* furtivement; **to ~ up to sb** s'approcher tout doucement *or* furtivement de qn; **to ~ out of a room** se glisser hors d'une pièce, sortir furtivement d'une pièce.

edginess ['edʒɪnɪs] *n* (*U*) nervosité *f*, énervement *m*, irritation *f*.

edging ['edʒɪŋ] **1** *n* bordure *f*; *[ribbon, silk]* liseré *m* *or* liséré *m*. **2** *cpd*: **edging shears** cisaille *f* de jardinier *or* d'horticulteur.

edgy ['edʒɪ] *adj* énervé, à cran*, crispé*.

edible ['edɪbl] *adj mushroom, berry* comestible, bon à manger; *meal* mangeable. **~ snail** escargot *m* comestible.

edict ['iːdɪkt] *n* (*Hist*) édit *m*; (*Jur, Pol*) décret *m*.

edification [ˌedɪfɪ'keɪʃən] *n* édification *f*, instruction *f*.

edifice ['edɪfɪs] *n* édifice *m*.

edify ['edɪfaɪ] *vt* édifier (*moralement*).

Edinburgh ['edɪnbərə] *n* Édimbourg.

edit ['edɪt] *vt magazine, review* diriger; *daily newspaper* être le rédacteur *or* la rédactrice en chef de; *article* mettre au point, préparer; *series of texts* diriger la publication de; *text, author* éditer, donner une édition de; *film* monter; *tape* mettre au point, couper et recoller.

edition [ɪ'dɪʃən] *n* *[newspaper, book]* édition *f*; *[print, etching]* tirage *m*. **limited ~** édition à tirage restreint *or* limité; **revised ~** édition revue et corrigée; **to bring out an ~ of a text** publier *or* faire paraître l'édition d'un texte; **a one volume ~ of Corneille** une édition de Corneille en un volume.

editor ['edɪtəʳ] *n* *[daily newspaper]* rédacteur *m*, -trice *f* en chef; *[magazine, review]* directeur *m*, -trice *f*; *[text]* éditeur *m*, -trice *f*; *[series]* directeur, -trice de la publication; *[dictionary, encyclopaedia]* rédacteur, -trice; (*Rad, TV*) *[programme]* réalisateur *m*, -trice *f*. (*Press*) **political ~** rédacteur, -trice politique; **sports ~** rédacteur sportif, rédactrice sportive; *V* **news** *etc*.

editorial [ˌedɪ'tɔːrɪəl] **1** *adj office* de (la) rédaction; *comment, decision* de la rédaction, du rédacteur. **~ staff** rédaction *f*. **2** *n* *[newspaper etc]* éditorial *m*, article *m* de tête.

editorialist [ˌedɪ'tɔːrɪəlɪst] *n* (*US*) éditorialiste *mf*.

editorship ['edɪtəʃɪp] *n* (*V* **editor**) rédaction *f*; direction *f*. **under the ~ of** sous la direction de.

educable ['edjʊkəbl] *adj* éducable.

educate ['edjʊkeɪt] *vt pupil* instruire, donner de l'instruction à; *the mind, one's tastes* former; (*bring up*) *family, children* élever, éduquer. **he is being ~d in Paris** il fait ses études à Paris; **to ~ the public** éduquer le public.

educated ['edjʊkeɪtɪd] **1** *ptp of* **educate**. **2** *adj person* instruit, cultivé; *handwriting* distingué; *voice* cultivé. **well-~** qui a reçu une bonne éducation; **hardly ~ at all** qui n'a guère d'instruction.

education [ˌedjʊ'keɪʃən] *n* éducation *f*; (*teaching*) instruction *f*, enseignement *m*; (*studies*) études *fpl*; (*training*) formation *f*; (*knowledge*) culture *f*; (*Univ etc: subject*) pédagogie *f*. **Department** *or* **Ministry of E~** ministère *m* de l'Éducation nationale; (*Brit*) **Secretary of State for** *or* **Minister of E~**, (*US*) **Secretary for E~** ministre *m* de l'Éducation (nationale); **primary/secondary ~** enseignement primaire/secondaire; **he had a good ~** il a reçu une bonne éducation; **physical/political ~** éducation physique/politique; **~ is free** l'instruction est gratuite; **the ~ he received at school** l'instruction qu'il a reçue à l'école (*or* au lycée *etc*); **his ~ was neglected** on a negligé son éducation; **his ~ was interrupted** ses études ont été interrompues; **literary/professional ~** formation littéraire/professionnelle; **man with a sound ~** homme *m* qui a une solide culture; (*Univ etc*) **diploma in ~** diplôme *m* de pédagogie; *V* **adult, further** *etc*.

educational [ˌedjʊ'keɪʃənl] *adj methods* pédagogique; *establishment, institution* d'enseignement; *system* d'éducation; *supplies* scolaire; *film, games* éducatif; *role, function* éducateur (*f* -trice). ~ **psychology** psychopédagogie *f*; (*US*) ~ **park** complexe *m* d'écoles primaires et secondaires; **we found the visit very** ~ cette visite a été très instructive.

education(al)ist [ˌedjʊˈkeɪʃn(əl)ɪst] *n* pédagogue *mf*, éducateur *m*, -trice *f*.

educationally [ˌedjʊˈkeɪʃnəlɪ] *adv* (*as regards teaching methods*) du point de vue pédagogique, pédagogiquement; (*as regards education, schooling*) sous l'angle scolaire *or* de l'éducation. **it is** ~ **wrong to do so** il est faux d'un point de vue pédagogique *or* il est pédagogiquement faux de procéder ainsi; ~ **subnormal** dont la performance est inférieure à la normale; sous-performant (du point de vue scolaire); ~ **deprived children** enfants déshérités sous l'angle scolaire *or* de l'éducation, enfants sous-scolarisés.

educative [ˈedjʊkətɪv] *adj* éducatif, éducateur (*f* -trice).

educator [ˈedjʊkeɪtəʳ] *n* éducateur *m*, -trice *f*.

educe [ɪˈdjuːs] *vt* dégager, faire sortir.

Edward [ˈedwəd] *n* Édouard *m*.

Edwardian [edˈwɔːdɪən] (*Brit*) **1** *adj lady, architect, society* de l'époque du roi Édouard VII; *clothes, manners, design* dans le style 1900. **in** ~ **days** à l'époque d'Édouard VII, juste après 1900; **the** ~ **era** ≃ la Belle Époque.

2 *n personne f qui vivait sous le règne d'Édouard VII ou qui a les caractéristiques de cette époque.*

eel [iːl] *n* anguille *f*. ~**worm** anguillule *f*; *V* **electric, slippery.**

e'en [iːn] *adv* (*liter*) = **even**[2] **2.**

e'er [ɛəʳ] *adv* (*liter*) = **ever.**

eerie, eery [ˈɪərɪ] *adj* inquiétant, sinistre, qui donne le frisson.

efface [ɪˈfeɪs] *vt* (*lit, fig*) effacer, oblitérer (*liter*).

effect [ɪˈfekt] **1** *n* **(a)** (*result*) effet *m* (*also Phys*), action *f*, conséquence *f*. ~ **of an acid on** action d'un acide sur; **to have an** ~ **on** produire un effet sur, influer sur; **to have no** ~ ne produire aucun effet, rester sans effet *or* sans suite; **it won't have any** ~ **on him** ça ne lui fera aucun effet, ça n'aura aucun effet sur lui; **this rule will have the** ~ **of preventing ..., the** ~ **of this rule will be to prevent ...** cette règle aura pour conséquence *or* effet d'empêcher ...; **the** ~ **of all this is that ...** il résulte de tout ceci que ...; **to feel the** ~**s of an accident** ressentir les effets d'un accident, se ressentir d'un accident; **the** ~**s of the new law are already being felt** les effets de la nouvelle loi se font déjà sentir; (*Phys*) **the Doppler** ~ l'effet Doppler-Fizeau; **to no** ~ en vain; **to such good** ~ **that** si bien que; **to put into** ~ mettre à exécution *or* en application; **to take** ~ *[drug]* produire *or* faire son effet, agir; *[law]* prendre effet, entrer en vigueur; **to be of no** ~ être inefficace *or* inopérant; **to come into** ~ entrer en vigueur; **in** ~ en fait, en réalité.

(b) (*impression*) effet *m*. (*Theat*) **stage** ~**s** effets scéniques; **sound** ~**s** bruitage *m*; **to make an** ~ faire effet *or* de l'effet; **to give a good** ~ faire (un) bon effet; **literary** ~ effet littéraire; (*Art*) ~**s of light** effets de lumière; **he said it just for** ~ il ne l'a dit que pour faire de l'effet *or* pour impressionner.

(c) (*meaning*) sens *m*. **his letter is to the** ~ **that ...** sa lettre nous apprend que ...; **an announcement to the** ~ **that ...** un communiqué déclarant que *or* dont la teneur est que ...; **orders to the** ~ **that ...** ordres suivant lesquels ...; **he used words to that** ~ il s'est exprimé dans ce sens; **... or words to that** ~ ... ou quelque chose d'analogue *or* de ce genre; **we got a letter to the same** ~ nous avons reçu une lettre dans le même sens.

(d) (*property*) ~**s** biens *mpl*; (*Banking*) **'no** ~**s'** 'sans provision'; *V* **personal.**

2 *vt cure* obtenir; *improvement* apporter; *transformation* opérer, effectuer; *reform, reduction, payment* effectuer; *reconciliation, reunion* amener; *sale, purchase* réaliser, effectuer. **to** ~ **a saving (in** *or* **of)** faire une économie (de); **to** ~ **a settlement** arriver à un accord; **to** ~ **an entry** entrer de force.

effective [ɪˈfektɪv] **1** *adj* **(a)** (*efficient*) *cure* efficace; *word, remark* qui porte, qui a de l'effet. **the measures were** ~ les mesures ont été efficaces *or* ont fait leur effet; **the system is** ~ le système fonctionne bien; **an** ~ **argument** un argument décisif; **to become** ~ *[law, regulation]* prendre effet, entrer en vigueur (*from* à partir de); *[ticket]* être valide (*from* à partir de); **it was an** ~ **way of stopping him** c'était une bonne façon *or* une façon efficace de l'arrêter.

(b) (*striking, impressive*) frappant, saisissant, qui fait *or* qui produit de l'effet.

(c) (*actual*) *aid, contribution* effectif. **the** ~ **head of the family** le chef réel *or* véritable de la famille; (*Mil*) ~ **troops** hommes *mpl* valides.

2 *npl* (*Mil*) ~**s** effectifs *mpl*.

effectively [ɪˈfektɪvlɪ] *adv* (*efficiently*) efficacement, d'une manière effective; (*usefully*) utilement; (*strikingly*) d'une manière frappante, avec beaucoup d'effet; (*in reality*) effectivement, réellement.

effectiveness [ɪˈfektɪvnɪs] *n* (*efficiency*) efficacité *f*; (*striking quality*) effet frappant *or* saisissant.

effector [ɪˈfektəʳ] **1** *adj* effecteur (*f* -trice). **2** *n* effecteur *m*.

effectual [ɪˈfektjʊəl] *adj remedy, punishment* efficace, qui produit l'effet voulu; *document, agreement* valide.

effectually [ɪˈfektjʊəlɪ] *adv* efficacement.

effectuate [ɪˈfektjʊeɪt] *vt* effectuer, opérer, réaliser.

effeminacy [ɪˈfemɪnəsɪ] *n* caractère efféminé.

effeminate [ɪˈfemɪnɪt] *adj* efféminé.

efferent [ˈefərənt] *adj* efférent.

effervesce [ˌefəˈves] *vi [liquids]* être *or* entrer en effervescence; *[drinks]* pétiller, mousser; *[gas]* se dégager (en effervescence); (*fig*) *[person]* déborder (*with* de), être excité.

effervescence [ˌefəˈvesns] *n* effervescence *f*, pétillement *m*; (*fig*) excitation *f*.

effervescent [ˌefəˈvesnt] *adj liquid, tablet* effervescent; *drink* gazeux; (*fig*) plein d'entrain.

effete [ɪˈfiːt] *adj person* mou (*f* molle), veule; *empire, civilization* décadent; *government* affaibli; *method* (devenu) inefficace, stérile.

effeteness [ɪˈfiːtnɪs] *n* (*V* **effete**) veulerie *f*; décadence *f*; inefficacité *f*.

efficacious [ˌefɪˈkeɪʃəs] *adj cure, means* efficace; *measure, method* efficace, opérant.

efficacy [ˈefɪkəsɪ] *n*, **efficaciousness** [ˌefɪˈkeɪʃəsnɪs] *n* efficacité *f*.

efficiency [ɪˈfɪʃənsɪ] **1** *n [person]* capacité *f*, compétence *f*; *[method]* efficacité *f*; *[organization, system]* efficacité, bon fonctionnement; *[machine]* bon rendement, bon fonctionnement. **2** *cpd*: (*US*) **efficiency apartment** studio *m*.

efficient [ɪˈfɪʃənt] *adj person* capable, compétent, efficace; *method, system* efficace, opérant; *plan, organization* efficace; *machine* d'un bon rendement, qui fonctionne bien. **the** ~ **working of a machine** le bon fonctionnement d'une machine.

efficiently [ɪˈfɪʃəntlɪ] *adv* (*V* **efficient**) avec compétence, efficacement. *[machine]* **to work** ~ bien fonctionner, avoir un bon rendement.

effigy [ˈefɪdʒɪ] *n* effigie *f*. **in** ~ en effigie.

effloresce [ˌeflɒˈres] *vi* (*Chem*) effleurir.

efflorescence [ˌefləˈresns] *n* (*Chem, Med: also liter*) efflorescence *f*; (*Bot*) floraison *f*.

efflorescent [ˌeflɔːˈresnt] *adj* (*Chem*) efflorescent; (*Bot*) en fleur(s).

effluence [ˈeflʊəns] *n* émanation *f*, effluence *f* (*liter, rare*).

effluent [ˈeflʊənt] *adj, n* effluent (*m*).

effluvium [eˈfluːvɪəm] *n* effluve(s) *m(pl)*, émanation *f*, exhalaison *f*; (*pej*) exhalaison *or* émanation fétide.

effort [ˈefət] *n* effort *m*. **to make an** ~ **to do** faire un effort pour faire, s'efforcer de faire; **to make every** ~ *or* **a great** ~ **to do** (*try hard*) faire tous ses efforts *or* (tout) son possible pour faire, s'évertuer à faire; (*take great pains*) se donner beaucoup de mal *or* de peine pour faire; **to make an** ~ **to concentrate/to adapt** faire un effort de concentration/d'adaptation; **do make some** ~ **to help!** fais un petit effort pour aider!, essaie d'aider un peu!; **he made no** ~ **to be polite** il ne s'est pas donné la peine d'être poli; (*Scol*) **he makes no** ~ il ne fait aucun effort, il ne s'applique pas; **it's not worth the** ~ cela ne vaut pas la peine; **without** ~ sans peine, sans effort; **the government's** ~ **to avoid ...** les efforts *or* les tentatives *fpl* du gouvernement pour éviter ...; **it's an awful** ~ **to get up!** il en faut du courage pour se lever!*; **what do you think of his latest** ~**?*** qu'est-ce que tu penses de ce qu'il vient de faire?; **it's not bad for a first** ~ ça n'est pas (si) mal pour un coup d'essai; **that's a good** ~***** ça n'est pas mal (réussi); **it's a pretty poor** ~***** ça n'est pas une réussite *or* un chef d'œuvre.

effortless [ˈefətlɪs] *adj success, victory* facile; *style, movement* aisé.

effortlessly [ˈefətlɪslɪ] *adv* sans effort, sans peine, aisément, facilement.

effrontery [ɪˈfrʌntərɪ] *n* effronterie *f*.

effusion [ɪˈfjuːʒən] *n [liquid]* écoulement *m*; *[blood, gas]* effusion *f*; (*fig*) effusion, épanchement *m*.

effusive [ɪˈfjuːsɪv] *adj person, character* expansif, démonstratif; *welcome* chaleureux; *style* expansif; *thanks, apologies* sans fin.

effusively [ɪˈfjuːsɪvlɪ] *adv greet, praise* avec effusion. **to thank sb** ~ se confondre *or* se répandre en remerciements auprès de qn.

eft [eft] *n* (*Zool*) triton *m* (crêté), salamandre *f* d'eau.

egalitarian [ɪˌgælɪˈtɛərɪən] **1** *n* égalitariste *mf*. **2** *adj person* égalitariste; *principle* égalitaire.

egalitarianism [ɪˌgælɪˈtɛərɪənɪzəm] *n* égalitarisme *m*.

egest [ɪˈdʒest] *vt* évacuer.

egg [eg] **1** *n* (*Culin, Zool*) œuf *m*. **in the** ~ dans l'œuf; ~**s and bacon** œufs au bacon; (*fig*) **to put all one's** ~**s in one basket** mettre tous ses œufs dans le même panier; **as sure as** ~**s is** ~**s‡** c'est sûr et certain*; (*fig*) **to have** ~ **on one's face** avoir l'air plutôt ridicule; **he's a good/bad** ~**‡** c'est un brave/sale type*; *V* **boil**[1], **Scotch** *etc.*

2 *cpd*: **eggbeater** (*rotary*) batteur *m* (à œufs); (*whisk*) fouet *m* (à œufs); **eggcup** coquetier *m*; **egg custard** ≃ crème renversée; **egg flip** (*with milk*) lait *m* de poule; (*with spirits*) flip *m*; **egghead‡** intellectuel(le) *m(f)*, cérébral(e) *m(f)*; **eggnog** flip *m*; **eggplant** aubergine *f*; **egg roll** pâté *or* rouleau impérial; **egg-shaped** ovoïde; **eggshell** coquille *f* (d'œuf); **eggshell china** coquille *f* d'œuf (*porcelaine*); **paint with an eggshell finish** peinture presque mate; **egg timer** (*sand*) sablier *m*; (*automatic*) minuteur *m*; **egg whisk** fouet *m* (à œufs); **egg white** blanc *m* d'œuf; **egg yolk** jaune *m* d'œuf.

3 *vt* (*) pousser, inciter (*to do* à faire).

egg on* *vt sep* pousser, inciter (*to do* à faire).

eglantine [ˈegləntaɪn] *n* (*flower*) églantine *f*; (*bush*) églantier *m*.

ego [ˈiːgəʊ] *n* (*Psych*) **the** ~ le moi, l'ego *m*. ~ **trip** fête *f* pour soi.

egocentric(al) [ˌegəʊˈsentrɪk(əl)] *adj* égocentrique.

egoism [ˈegəʊɪzəm] *n* égoïsme *m*.

egoist [ˈegəʊɪst] *n* égoïste *mf*.

egoistical [ˌegəʊˈɪstɪkəl] *adj* égoïste.

egomania [ˌegəʊˈmeɪnɪə] *n* manie *f* égocentrique.

egotism [ˈegəʊtɪzəm] *n* égotisme *m*.

egotist [ˈegəʊtɪst] *n* égotiste *mf*.

egotistic(al) [ˌegəʊˈtɪstɪk(əl)] *adj* égotiste.

egregious [ɪˈgriːdʒəs] *adj* (*pej*) énorme (*iro*), fameux* (*iro: before n*); *folly, blunder* insigne. **he's an** ~ **ass** c'est un fameux* imbécile.

egress ['iːgres] *n (gen: frm)* sortie *f*, issue *f*; *(Astron)* émersion *f*.
egret ['iːgrɪt] *n* aigrette *f*.
Egypt ['iːdʒɪpt] *n* Égypte *f*.
Egyptian [ɪ'dʒɪpʃən] **1** *adj* égyptien, d'Égypte. **2** *n* Égyptien(ne) *m(f)*.
eh [eɪ] *excl* **(a)** *(what did you say?)* comment?, quoi?, hein?* **(b) you'll do it for me, ~?** tu le feras pour moi, n'est-ce pas? *or* hein?*
eider ['aɪdə^r] *n* eider *m*. **~down** *(quilt)* édredon *m*; *(U: down)* duvet *m* (d'eider).
eidetic [aɪ'detɪk] *adj* eidétique.
eight [eɪt] **1** *adj* huit *inv*; *for phrases V* **six**. **2** *n* huit *m inv* *(also Rowing)*. *(fig)* **he's had one over the ~*** il a du vent dans les voiles*, il a un verre dans le nez*; *V* **figure**.
eighteen ['eɪ'tiːn] **1** *adj* dix-huit *inv*. **2** *n* dix-huit *m inv*; *for phrases V* **six**.
eighteenth ['eɪ'tiːnθ] **1** *adj* dix-huitième. **2** *n* dix-huitième *mf*; *(fraction)* dix-huitième *m*; *for phrases V* **sixth**.
eighth [eɪtθ] **1** *adj* huitième. *(US: Mus)* **~ note** croche *f*. **2** *n* huitième *mf*; *(fraction)* huitième *m*; *for phrases V* **sixth**.
eightieth ['eɪtɪəθ] **1** *adj* quatre-vingtième. **2** *n* quatre-vingtième *mf*; *(fraction)* quatre-vingtième *m*.
eighty ['eɪtɪ] **1** *adj* quatre-vingts *inv*. **about ~ books** environ *or* à peu près quatre-vingts livres; *for other phrases V* **sixty**.
2 *n* quatre-vingts *m*. **about ~** environ *or* à peu près quatre-vingts; **~-one** quatre-vingt-un; **~-two** quatre-vingt-deux; **~-first** quatre-vingt-unième; **page ~** page quatre-vingt; *for other phrases V* **sixty**.
Eire ['ɛərə] *n* République *f* d'Irlande, Irlande *f* du Sud.
Eisteddfod [aɪs'teðvɒd] *n* concours *m* de musique et de poésie *(en gallois)*.
either ['aɪðə^r] **1** *adj* **(a)** *(one or other)* l'un(e) ou l'autre, n'importe lequel *(f* laquelle) (des deux). **~ day would suit me** l'un ou l'autre jour *or* l'un de ces deux jours me conviendrait; **do it ~ way** faites-le de l'une ou l'autre façon; **~ way* I can't do anything about it** de toute façon *or* quoi qu'il arrive *(subj)* je n'y peux rien; **I don't like ~ book** je n'aime ni l'un ni l'autre de ces livres.
(b) *(each)* chaque. **in ~ hand** dans chaque main; **on ~ side of the street** des deux côtés *or* de chaque côté de la rue; **on ~ side lay fields** de part et d'autre s'étendaient des champs.
2 *pron* l'un(e) *m(f)* ou l'autre, n'importe lequel *m* (*or* laquelle *f*) (des deux). **which bus will you take? — ~** quel bus prendrez-vous? — l'un ou l'autre *or* n'importe lequel (des deux); **there are 2 boxes on the table, take ~** il y a 2 boîtes sur la table, prenez celle que vous voulez *or* n'importe laquelle *or* l'une ou l'autre; **I don't admire ~** je n'admire ni l'un ni l'autre; **I don't believe ~ of them** je ne les crois ni l'un ni l'autre; **give it to ~ of them** donnez-le soit à l'un soit à l'autre; **if ~ is attacked the other helps him** si l'un des deux est attaqué l'autre l'aide.
3 *adv* *(after neg statement)* non plus. **he sings badly and he can't act ~** il chante mal et il ne sait pas jouer non plus *or* et il ne joue pas mieux; **I have never heard of him — no I haven't ~** je n'ai jamais entendu parler de lui — moi non plus.
4 *conj* **(a) ~ ... or** ou (bien) ... ou (bien), soit ... soit; *(after neg)* ni ... ni. **he must be ~ lazy or stupid** il doit être ou paresseux ou stupide; **he must ~ change his policy or resign** il faut soit qu'il change *(subj)* de politique soit qu'il démissionne *(subj)*; **~ be quiet or go out!** tais-toi ou sors d'ici!, ou (bien) tu te tais ou (bien) tu sors d'ici!; **I have never been ~ to Paris or to Rome** je ne suis jamais allé ni à Paris ni à Rome; **it was ~ he or his sister** c'était soit lui soit sa sœur, c'était ou (bien) lui ou(bien) sa sœur.
(b) *(moreover)* **she got a sum of money and not such a small one ~** elle a reçu une certaine somme pas si petite que ça d'ailleurs.
ejaculate [ɪ'dʒækjʊleɪt] *vti* *(cry out)* s'exclamer, s'écrier; *(Physiol)* éjaculer.
ejaculation [ɪˌdʒækjʊ'leɪʃən] *n* *(cry)* exclamation *f*, cri *m*; *(Physiol)* éjaculation *f*.
eject [ɪ'dʒekt] *vt* *(Aviat, Tech etc)* éjecter; *tenant, troublemaker* expulser; *trespasser* chasser, reconduire; *customer* expulser, vider*.
ejection [ɪ'dʒekʃən] *n* *(U)* *[person]* expulsion *f*; *(Aviat, Tech)* éjection *f*.
ejector [ɪ'dʒektə^r] *n* *(Tech)* éjecteur *m*. *(Aviat)* **~ seat** siège *m* éjectable.
eke [iːk] *vt*: **to ~ out** *(by adding)* accroître, augmenter; *(by saving)* économiser, faire durer; **to ~ out one's pension by doing ...** augmenter un peu sa retraite en faisant ... .
elaborate [ɪ'læbərɪt] **1** *adj* *scheme, programme* complexe; *ornamentation, design, sewing* détaillé, compliqué; *preparations* minutieux; *pattern, joke, excuse* compliqué, recherché; *meal* soigné, raffiné; *style* recherché, travaillé; *clothes* recherché, raffiné; *sculpture* ouvragé, travaillé; *drawing* minutieux, travaillé. **with ~ care** très soigneusement, minutieusement; **he made an ~ plan for avoiding ...** il a établi un projet détaillé *or* minutieux pour éviter ...; **his plan was so ~ that I couldn't follow it** son projet était si complexe *or* compliqué que je n'arrivais pas à le comprendre; **the work was so ~ that it took her years to finish it** le travail était si complexe *or* minutieux qu'elle a mis des années à le finir.
2 [ɪ'læbəreɪt] *vt* élaborer.
3 [ɪ'læbəreɪt] *vi* donner des détails (*on* sur), entrer dans *or* expliquer les détails (*on* de).
elaborately [ɪ'læbərɪtlɪ] *adv* *(V* **elaborate**) en détail; minutieusement; soigneusement, avec soin; avec recherche.
elaboration [ɪˌlæbə'reɪʃən] *n* élaboration *f*.
elapse [ɪ'læps] *vi* s'écouler, (se) passer.
elastic [ɪ'læstɪk] **1** *adj* élastique *(also fig)*. *(Brit)* **~ band** élastique *m*, caoutchouc *m*; **~ stockings** bas *mpl* à varices. **2** *n* *(U)* élastique *m*.
elasticity [ˌiːlæs'tɪsɪtɪ] *n* élasticité *f*.
elate [ɪ'leɪt] *vt* transporter, ravir, enthousiasmer.
elated [ɪ'leɪtɪd] *adj* transporté (de joie), rempli d'allégresse. **to be ~** exulter.
elation [ɪ'leɪʃən] *n* allégresse *f*, exultation *f*.
elbow ['elbəʊ] **1** *n* *[person, road, river, pipe]* coude *m*. **to lean one's ~s on** s'accouder à *or* sur, être accoudé à; **to lean on one's ~** s'appuyer sur le coude; **at his ~** à ses côtés; **out at the ~s** *garment* percé *or* troué aux coudes; *person* déguenillé, loqueteux; *(euph)* **he lifts his ~* a bit** il lève le coude*, il picole*.
2 *cpd*: **to use a bit of elbow grease** mettre de l'huile de coude*; **elbow-rest** accoudoir *m*; *[armchair]* bras *m*; **to have enough elbow room** *(lit)* avoir de la place pour se retourner; *(fig)* avoir les coudées franches; **to have no elbow room** *(lit)* être à l'étroit; *(fig)* ne pas avoir de liberté d'action.
3 *vi*: **to ~ through** se frayer un passage à travers (en jouant des coudes); **to ~ forward** avancer en jouant des coudes.
4 *vt*: **to ~ sb aside** écarter qn du coude *or* d'un coup de coude; **to ~ one's way through** *etc* = **to elbow through** *etc*; *V* 3.
elder[1] ['eldə^r] **1** *adj* aîné (de deux). **my ~ sister** ma sœur aînée; **Pliny the ~** Pline l'Ancien; **Alexandre Dumas the ~** Alexandre Dumas père; **~ statesman** vétéran *m* de la politique, homme politique chevronné.
2 *n* aîné(e) *m(f)*; *[Presbyterian Church]* membre *m* du conseil d'une église presbytérienne. *[tribe, Church]* **~s** Anciens *mpl*; **one's ~s and betters** ses aînés.
elder[2] ['eldə^r] **1** *n* *(Bot)* sureau *m*. **2** *cpd*: **elderberry** baie *f* de sureau; **elderberry wine** vin *m* de sureau.
elderly ['eldəlɪ] *adj* assez âgé. **he's getting ~** il prend de l'âge, il se fait vieux.
eldest ['eldɪst] *adj* aîné *(de plusieurs)*. **their ~ (child)** leur aîné(e), l'aîné(e) de leurs enfants; **my ~ brother** l'aîné de mes frères.
Eleanor ['elɪnə^r] *n* Éléonore *f*.
elect [ɪ'lekt] **1** *vt* **(a)** *(by vote)* élire; *(more informally)* nommer. **he was ~ed chairman/M.P.** il a été élu président/député; **to ~ sb to the senate** élire qn au sénat.
(b) *(choose)* choisir, opter *(to do* de faire). **to ~ French nationality** opter pour *or* choisir la nationalité française.
2 *adj* futur. **the president ~** le président désigné, le futur président.
3 *npl* *(esp Rel)* **the ~** les élus *mpl*.
election [ɪ'lekʃən] **1** *n* élection *f*. **to hold an ~** procéder à une élection; **to stand for ~ to Parliament** se porter candidat *or* se présenter aux élections législatives; *V* **general**. **2** *cpd* *campaign, speech, agent* électoral; *day, results* du scrutin.
electioneer [ɪˌlekʃə'nɪə^r] *vi* mener une campagne électorale, faire de la propagande électorale.
electioneering [ɪˌlekʃə'nɪərɪŋ] **1** *n* *(campaign)* campagne électorale; *(propaganda)* propagande électorale. **2** *adj* *speech* de propagande électorale.
elective [ɪ'lektɪv] *adj* *(with power to elect)* *body, assembly, power* électoral; *(elected)* *official, body* électif, élu; *(Chem, fig)* électif; *(US: optional)* *class, course* facultatif, à option.
elector [ɪ'lektə^r] *n* *(gen, Parl)* électeur *m*, -trice *f*; *(US Parl)* membre *m* du collège électoral. *(Hist)* **E~** Électeur *m*, prince électeur.
electoral [ɪ'lektərəl] *adj* électoral. *(US)* **~ college** collège électoral *(présidentiel)*; **~ district *or* division** circonscription électorale; **~ roll** liste électorale.
electorate [ɪ'lektərɪt] *n* électorat *m*, électeurs *mpl*.
electric [ɪ'lektrɪk] **1** *adj* *appliance, current, wire* électrique; *meter, account, generator* d'électricité, électrique. *(fig)* **the atmosphere was ~** il y avait de l'électricité dans l'air*.
2 *cpd*: **electric (arc) welding** soudure *f* électrique (à l'arc); **electric blanket** couverture chauffante; **electric chair** chaise *f* électrique; **electric charge/current** charge *f*/courant *m* électrique; *(Zool)* **electric eel** anguille *f* électrique, gymnote *m*; **electric field** champ *m* électrique; *(Brit)* **electric fire** radiateur *m* électrique; **electric furnace** four *m* électrique; **electric guitar** guitare *f* électrique; **electric heater** = **electric fire**; **electric light** lumière *f* électrique; *(U: lighting)* éclairage *m* électrique *or* à l'électricité; **electric potential** potentiel *m* électrique; *(Zool)* **electric ray** torpille *f*; **electric shock** choc *m* électrique; **to get an electric shock** recevoir une décharge électrique, recevoir le courant, prendre le jus*; **to give sb an electric shock** donner une décharge électrique à qn; *(Med)* **electric shock treatment*** électrochoc *m*; **to give sb electric shock treatment*** traiter qn par électrochocs; **electric storm** orage *m* magnétique.
electrical [ɪ'lektrɪkəl] *adj* électrique. **~ engineer** ingénieur *m* électricien; **~ engineering** électrotechnique *f*; **~ failure** panne *f* d'électricité; **~ fitter** monteur *m* électricien.
electrician [ɪlek'trɪʃən] *n* électricien *m*.
electricity [ɪlek'trɪsɪtɪ] *n* *(also fig)* électricité *f*. **to switch off/on the ~** couper/rétablir le courant; *(Brit)* **~ board** office régional de l'électricité; *V* **supply**[1].
electrification [ɪˌlektrɪfɪ'keɪʃən] *n* électrification *f*.
electrify [ɪ'lektrɪfaɪ] *vt* **(a)** *(Rail)* électrifier; *(charge with electricity)* électriser. **(b)** *(fig)* *audience* électriser, galvaniser.
electrifying [ɪ'lektrɪfaɪɪŋ] *adj* *(fig)* électrisant, galvanisant.
electro ... [ɪ'lektrəʊ] *pref* électro ... .
electrocardiogram [ɪ'lektrəʊ'kɑːdɪəgræm] *n* électrocardiogramme *m*.
electrocardiograph [ɪ'lektrəʊ'kɑːdɪəgræf] *n* électrocardiographe *m*.
electrochemical [ɪˌlektrəʊ'kemɪkəl] *adj* électrochimique.

electrochemistry [ɪˌlektrəʊ'kemɪstrɪ] *n* électrochimie *f.*

electroconvulsive [ɪ'lektrəkən'vʌlsɪv] *adj*: ~ **therapy** électrochoc(s) *m(pl)*; **to give sb ~ therapy** traiter qn par électrochocs.

electrocute [ɪ'lektrəkjuːt] *vt* électrocuter.

electrocution [ɪˌlektrə'kjuːʃən] *n* électrocution *f.*

electrode [ɪ'lektrəʊd] *n* électrode *f.*

electrodynamics [ɪ'lektrəʊdaɪ'næmɪks] *n* (*U*) électrodynamique *f.*

electroencephalogram [ɪˌlektrəʊen'sefələˌgræm] *n* électroencéphalogramme *m.*

electroencephalograph [ɪˌlektrəʊen'sefələˌgræf] *n* électroencéphalographe *m.*

electroforming [ɪ'lektrəʊˌfɔːmɪŋ] *n* électroformage *m.*

electrolysis [ɪlek'trɒlɪsɪs] *n* électrolyse *f.*

electrolytic [ɪˌlektrəʊ'lɪtɪk] *adj* électrolytique.

electromagnet [ɪ'lektrəʊ'mægnɪt] *n* électro-aimant *m.*

electromagnetic [ɪ'lektrəʊmæg'netɪk] *adj* électromagnétique.

electromotive [ɪˌlektrəʊ'məʊtɪv] *adj* électromoteur (*f* -trice).

electron [ɪ'lektrɒn] **1** *n* électron *m.* **2** *cpd microscope, telescope* électronique. **electron beam** faisceau *m* électronique; **electron camera** caméra *f* électronique; **electron gun** canon *m* à électrons.

electronic [ɪlek'trɒnɪk] *adj* électronique. ~ **computer** ordinateur *m* électronique; ~ **data processing** traitement *m* électronique de données; ~ **flash** flash *m* électronique; ~ **music/organ** musique *f*/orgue *m* électronique; ~ **surveillance** utilisation *f* d'appareils d'écoute.

electronics [ɪlek'trɒnɪks] *n* (*U*) électronique *f.*

electroplate [ɪ'lektrəʊpleɪt] **1** *vt* plaquer par galvanoplastie; (*with gold*) dorer *or* (*with silver*) argenter par galvanoplastie. **~d silver** ruolz *m.* **2** *n* (*U*) articles plaqués *etc* par galvanoplastie; (*silver*) articles de ruolz.

electroshock [ɪ'lektrəʊʃɒk] **1** *n* électrochoc *m.* **to give sb ~ treatment** traiter qn par électrochocs. **2** *cpd*: **electroshock therapy, electroshock treatment** (traitement *m* par) électrochocs *mpl.*

electrostatic [ɪ'lektrəʊ'stætɪk] *adj* électrostatique.

electrostatics [ɪ'lektrəʊ'stætɪks] *n* (*U*) électrostatique *f.*

electrotype [ɪ'lektrəʊˌtaɪp] **1** *n* galvanotype *m*, galvano* *m.* **2** *vt* clicher par galvanotypie.

electrovalency [ɪˌlektrəʊ'veɪlənsɪ] *n* électrovalence *f.*

electrovalent [ɪˌlektrəʊ'veɪlənt] *adj*: ~ **bond** liaison *f* électrostatique.

elegance ['elɪgəns] *n* (*V* **elegant**) élégance *f*; chic *m*; distinction *f*; grâce *f.*

elegant ['elɪgənt] *adj person, clothes* élégant, chic *inv*, distingué; *style, design* élégant, chic; *proportions, building* élégant, harmonieux; *manners, movement* élégant, gracieux.

elegantly ['elɪgəntlɪ] *adv* (*V* **elegant**) élégamment, avec élégance; avec chic *or* distinction; avec grâce.

elegiac [ˌelɪ'dʒaɪək] **1** *adj* élégiaque. **2** *n*: **~s** poèmes *mpl* élégiaques.

elegy ['elɪdʒɪ] *n* élégie *f.*

element ['elɪmənt] *n* (*Chem, Gram, Med, Phys, fig*) élément *m*; *[heater, kettle]* résistance *f.* (*Met*) **the ~s** les éléments; **the ~s of mathematics** les éléments *or* les rudiments *mpl* des mathématiques; **an ~ of danger/truth** une part de danger/de vérité; **the ~ of chance** le facteur chance; **it's the personal ~ that matters** c'est le rapport personnel qui compte; **the comic/tragic ~ in X's poetry** le comique/le tragique dans la poésie de X; **the communist ~ in the trade unions** l'élément communiste dans les syndicats; **to be in/out of one's ~** être/ne pas être dans son élément; (*Rel*) **the E~s** les Espèces *fpl.*

elemental [ˌelɪ'mentl] **1** *adj forces* des éléments, élémentaire; (*Chem, Phys*) élémentaire; (*basic*) essentiel. ~ **truth** vérité première. **2** *n* (*Occult*) esprit *m* (élémental).

elementary [ˌelɪ'mentərɪ] *adj* élémentaire. (*Math*) ~ **particle** particule *f* élémentaire; ~ **geometry course** cours élémentaire *or* fondamental de géométrie; ~ **science** les rudiments *mpl* de la science; ~ **school/education** école *f*/enseignement *m* primaire; ~ **politeness requires that ...** la plus élémentaire politesse exige que ... + *subj.*

elephant ['elɪfənt] *n* (*bull* ~) éléphant *m* (mâle); (*cow* ~) éléphant *m* (femelle); (*young* ~) éléphanteau *m.* ~ **seal** éléphant de mer; *V* **white.**

elephantiasis [ˌelɪfən'taɪəsɪs] *n* éléphantiasis *f.*

elephantine [ˌelɪ'fæntaɪn] *adj* (*heavy, clumsy*) gauche, lourd; (*large*) éléphantesque; (*iro*) *wit* lourd. **with ~ grace** avec la grâce d'un éléphant.

elevate ['elɪveɪt] *vt* hausser, élever (*also fig, Rel*); *voice* hausser; *mind* élever; *soul* élever, exalter. **to ~ to the peerage** élever à la pairie, anoblir; **elevating reading** lectures exaltantes *or* qui élèvent l'esprit.

elevated ['elɪveɪtɪd] *adj position* élevé; *railway* aérien; *rank* éminent; *style* soutenu; *thoughts* noble, sublime.

elevation [ˌelɪ'veɪʃən] *n* **(a)** (*U*: *V* **elevate**; *also Archit, Gunnery, Surv*) élévation *f.* **angle of ~** angle *m* d'élévation; (*Archit*) **front ~** façade *f*; **sectional ~** coupe verticale.

(b) (*altitude*) altitude *f*, hauteur *f*; (*hill*) hauteur, éminence *f.* **at an ~ of 1000 metres** à 1000 mètres d'altitude.

elevator ['elɪveɪtə^r] *n* élévateur *m*; (*esp US: lift*) ascenseur *m*; (*hoist*) monte-charge *m inv*; (*grain storehouse*) silo *m* (à élévateur pneumatique), élévator *m*; (*Aviat*) gouvernail *m* de profondeur.

eleven [ɪ'levn] **1** *adj* onze *inv*; *for phrases V* **six. 2** *n* **(a)** (*number*) onze *m inv.* **number ~** le numéro onze, le onze; (*Brit Scol*) **the ~ plus** l'examen *m* d'entrée en sixième. **(b)** (*Sport*) **the French ~** le onze de France; **the first ~** le onze, la première équipe; **the second ~** la deuxième équipe.

elevenses* [ɪ'levnzɪz] *npl* (*Brit*) ≈ pause-café *f* (*dans la matinée*).

eleventh [ɪ'levnθ] **1** *adj* onzième. (*fig*) **at the ~ hour*** à la onzième heure, à la dernière minute. **2** *n* onzième *mf*; (*fraction*) onzième *m*; *for phrases V* **sixth.**

elf [elf] *n, pl* **elves** (*lit*) elfe *m*, lutin *m*, farfadet *m*; (*fig*) lutin.

elfin ['elfɪn] *adj* d'elfe, de lutin; *light, music* féerique.

elicit [ɪ'lɪsɪt] *vt truth* arracher (*from* à), mettre à jour; *admission* arracher (*from* à), provoquer; *reply, explanation, information* tirer, obtenir (*from* de); *smile* faire naître; *secret* tirer (*from* de), arracher (*from* à). **to ~ the facts of a case** tirer au clair les faits dans une affaire, tirer une affaire au clair; **to ~ the truth about a case** faire le jour *or* la clarté sur une affaire.

elide [ɪ'laɪd] *vt* élider. **to be ~d** s'élider.

eligibility [ˌelɪdʒə'bɪlɪtɪ] *n* (*for election*) éligibilité *f*; (*for employment*) admissibilité *f.*

eligible ['elɪdʒəbl] *adj* (*for membership, office*) éligible (*for* à); (*for job*) admissible (*for* à). **to be ~ for a pension** avoir droit à la retraite; **to be ~ for promotion** avoir les conditions requises pour obtenir de l'avancement; **an ~ young man** un beau *or* bon parti; **he's very ~*** c'est un parti très acceptable.

eliminate [ɪ'lɪmɪneɪt] *vt alternative, suspicion, competitor, candidate* éliminer, écarter; *possibility* écarter, exclure; *competition, opposition, suspect* éliminer; *mark, stain* enlever, faire disparaître; *bad language, expenditure, detail* éliminer, supprimer; (*Math, Physiol*) éliminer; (*kill*) supprimer.

elimination [ɪˌlɪmɪ'neɪʃən] *n* élimination *f.* **by (the process of) ~** par élimination.

elision [ɪ'lɪʒən] *n* élision *f.*

élite [eɪ'liːt] *n* élite *f.*

élitism [eɪ'liːtɪzəm] *n* élitisme *m.*

elixir [ɪ'lɪksə^r] *n* élixir *m.* ~ **of life** élixir de longue vie.

Elizabeth [ɪ'lɪzəbəθ] *n* Élisabeth *f.*

Elizabethan [ɪˌlɪzə'biːθən] *adj* élisabéthain.

elk [elk] *n* (*Zool*) élan *m.* **Canadian ~** orignac *m or* orignal *m.*

ellipse [ɪ'lɪps] *n* (*Math*) ellipse *f.*

ellipsis [ɪ'lɪpsɪs] *n, pl* **ellipses** [ɪ'lɪpsiːz] (*Gram*) ellipse *f.*

ellipsoid [ɪ'lɪpsɔɪd] *adj, n* ellipsoïde (*m*).

elliptic(al) [ɪ'lɪptɪk(əl)] *adj* (*Gram, Math, fig*) elliptique.

elm [elm] *n* (*tree, wood*) orme *m.* **young ~** ormeau *m*; *V* **Dutch.**

elocution [ˌelə'kjuːʃən] *n* élocution *f*, diction *f.*

elocutionist [ˌelə'kjuːʃənɪst] *n* (*teacher*) professeur *m* d'élocution *or* de diction; (*entertainer*) diseur *m*, -euse *f.*

elongate ['iːlɒŋgeɪt] **1** *vt* allonger, étirer. **2** *vi* s'allonger, s'étirer.

elongation [ˌiːlɒŋ'geɪʃən] *n [shape]* allongement *m*; *[line etc]* prolongement *m*; (*Astron, Med*) élongation *f.*

elope [ɪ'ləʊp] *vi*: **to ~ with sb** *[woman]* se faire *or* se laisser enlever par qn; *[man]* enlever qn; **they ~d** ils se sont enfuis (ensemble).

elopement [ɪ'ləʊpmənt] *n* fugue *f* (amoureuse).

eloquence ['eləkwəns] *n* éloquence *f.*

eloquent ['eləkwənt] *adj person* éloquent, qui a le don de la parole; *speech* éloquent; *words* entraînant; (*fig*) *look, gesture* éloquent, expressif, parlant. **his silence was ~** son silence en disait long; *V* **wax².**

eloquently ['eləkwəntlɪ] *adv* éloquemment, avec éloquence.

else [els] **1** *adv* **(a)** (*other, besides, instead*) autre, d'autre, de plus. **anybody ~ would have done it** tout autre *or* n'importe qui d'autre l'aurait fait; **is there anybody ~ there?** y a-t-il quelqu'un d'autre?, y a-t-il encore quelqu'un?; **I'd prefer anything ~** je préférerais n'importe quoi d'autre; **have you anything ~ to say?** avez-vous encore quelque chose à dire?, avez-vous quelque chose à ajouter?; **will there be anything ~ sir?** *[shop assistant]* désirez-vous quelque chose d'autre monsieur?, et avec ça* monsieur?; *[servant]* monsieur ne désire rien d'autre?; **nothing ~, thank you** plus rien, merci; **I couldn't do anything ~ but leave** il ne me restait plus qu'à partir; **anywhere ~ nobody would have noticed, but ...** n'importe où ailleurs personne ne s'en serait aperçu mais ...; **can you do it anywhere ~?** pouvez-vous le faire ailleurs?; **you won't find this flower anywhere ~** vous ne trouverez cette fleur nulle part ailleurs; **how ~ can I do it?** de quelle autre façon est-ce que je peux le faire?, comment est-ce que je peux le faire autrement?; **nobody ~, no one ~** personne d'autre; **nothing ~** rien d'autre; **nowhere ~** nulle part ailleurs; **someone *or* somebody ~** quelqu'un d'autre; **may I speak to someone ~?** puis-je parler à quelqu'un d'autre?; **this is someone ~'s umbrella** c'est le parapluie de quelqu'un d'autre; **something ~** autre chose, quelque chose d'autre; **somewhere ~, (*US*) someplace ~** ailleurs, autre part; **where ~?** à quel autre endroit?, où encore?; **who ~?** qui encore?, qui d'autre?; **what ~?** quoi encore, quoi d'autre?; **what ~ could I do?** que pouvais-je faire d'autre *or* de plus?; **they sell books and toys and much ~** ils vendent des livres, des jouets et bien d'autres choses (encore) *or* et toutes sortes d'autres choses; **there is little ~ to be done** il n'y a *or* il ne reste pas grand-chose d'autre à faire.

(b) or ~ ou bien, sinon, autrement; **do it or ~ go away** faites-le, ou bien allez-vous en; **do it now or ~ you'll be punished** faisle tout de suite, sans ça *or* sinon tu seras puni; **do it or ~!*** faites-le sinon ...!

2 *cpd*: **elsewhere** ailleurs, autre part; **from elsewhere** (venu) d'ailleurs *or* d'un autre endroit (*or* pays *etc*).

elucidate [ɪ'luːsɪdeɪt] *vt text* élucider, expliquer, dégager le sens de; *mystery* élucider, tirer au clair, éclaircir.

elucidation [ɪˌluːsɪ'deɪʃən] *n* explication *f*, éclaircissement *m*, élucidation *f.*

elude [ɪ'luːd] *vt enemy, pursuit, arrest* échapper à; *the law, question* éluder; *sb's gaze, police, justice* se dérober à; *obligation, responsibility* se soustraire à, se dérober à; *blow* esquiver, éviter. **to ~ sb's grasp** échapper aux mains de qn; **the name ~s me** le nom m'échappe; **success ~d him** le succès restait hors de sa portée.

elusive [ɪ'luːsɪv] *adj enemy, prey, thoughts* insaisissable; *word, happiness, success* qui échappe; *glance, personality* fuyant; *answer* évasif.

elusively [ɪ'luːsɪvlɪ] *adv* de façon insaisissable *or* évasive.

elusiveness [ɪ'luːsɪvnɪs] *n* nature *f* insaisissable, caractère évasif.

elusory [ɪ'luːsərɪ] *adj* = **elusive.**

elver ['elvəʳ] *n* civelle *f.*

elves [elvz] *npl of* **elf.**

Elysian [ɪ'lɪzɪən] *adj* élyséen.

elytron ['elɪtrɒn] *n, pl* **elytra** ['elɪtrə] élytre *m.*

emaciated [ɪ'meɪsɪeɪtɪd] *adj person, face* émacié, amaigri; *limb* décharné. **to become ~** s'émacier, s'amaigrir, se décharner.

emaciation [ɪ,meɪsɪ'eɪʃən] *n* émaciation *f,* amaigrissement *m.*

emanate ['eməneɪt] *vi [light, odour]* émaner (*from* de); *[rumour, document, instruction]* émaner, provenir (*from* de).

emanation [,emə'neɪʃən] *n* émanation *f.*

emancipate [ɪ'mænsɪpeɪt] *vt women* émanciper; *slaves* affranchir; (*fig*) émanciper, affranchir, libérer (*from* de). **to be ~d from** s'affranchir de, s'émanciper de.

emancipation [ɪ,mænsɪ'peɪʃən] *n* (*V* **emancipate**) émancipation *f*; affranchissement *m*; libération *f.*

emasculate [ɪ'mæskjʊleɪt] **1** *vt* émasculer (*also fig*). **2** *adj* émasculé (*also fig*).

embalm [ɪm'bɑːm] *vt* (*all senses*) embaumer.

embankment [ɪm'bæŋkmənt] *n [path, railway line]* talus *m,* remblai *m; [road]* banquette *f* (de sûreté); *[canal, dam]* digue *f,* chaussée *f* (de retenue); *[river]* berge *f,* levée *f,* quai *m. [London]* **the E~** *l'un des quais le long de la Tamise;* (*fig*) **to sleep on the E~** ≈ coucher sous les ponts.

embargo [ɪm'bɑːgəʊ] **1** *n* **(a)** (*Comm, Naut*) (*prohibition*) embargo *m*; (*sequestration*) confiscation *f.* **to lay** *or* **put an ~ on** mettre l'embargo sur; **arms ~** embargo sur les armes; **to lift an ~** lever l'embargo; **under (an) ~** confisqué, mis sous séquestre.

(b) (*fig*) interdiction *f,* restriction *f.* **to put an ~ on sth** interdire qch.

2 *vt* (*prohibit*) mettre l'embargo sur; (*sequester*) séquestrer, confisquer.

embark [ɪm'bɑːk] **1** *vt passengers* embarquer, prendre à bord; *goods* embarquer, charger.

2 *vi* (*Aviat, Naut*) (s')embarquer (*on* à bord de, sur). (*fig*) **to ~ on** *journey* commencer; *business undertaking, deal* s'engager dans, se lancer dans; *doubtful or risky affair, explanation, story* se lancer dans, s'embarquer dans*; *discussion* entamer.

embarkation [,embɑː'keɪʃən] *n [passengers]* embarquement *m; [cargo]* chargement *m.* (*Aviat, Naut*) **~ card** carte *f* d'embarquement.

embarrass [ɪm'bærəs] *vt* (*disconcert*) embarrasser, gêner, déconcerter; (*hamper*) *[clothes, parcels]* embarrasser, gêner, encombrer. **I feel ~ed about it** j'en suis gêné, cela m'embarrasse; **to be (financially) ~ed** avoir des embarras *or* des ennuis d'argent, être gêné *or* à court.

embarrassing [ɪm'bærəsɪŋ] *adj* embarrassant, gênant. **to get out of an ~ situation** se tirer d'embarras.

embarrassment [ɪm'bærəsmənt] *n* embarras *m,* gêne *f,* confusion *f* (*at* devant). **to cause sb ~** mettre qn dans l'embarras; **financial ~** des embarras d'argent *or* financiers.

embassy ['embəsɪ] *n* ambassade *f.* **the French E~** l'ambassade de France.

embattled [ɪm'bætld] *adj army* rangé *or* formé en bataille; *town, camp* fortifié; *castle etc* garni de remparts, crénelé.

embed [ɪm'bed] *vt* (*in wood*) enfoncer; (*in cement*) noyer; (*in stone*) sceller; *jewel* enchâsser; (*encrust*) incruster; (*Ling*) enchâsser. (*fig*) **~ded in the memory/mind** fixé *or* gravé dans la mémoire/l'esprit.

embedding [ɪm'bedɪŋ] *n* action *f* de sceller; fixation *f;* (*Ling*) enchâssement *m.*

embellish [ɪm'belɪʃ] *vt* (*adorn*) embellir, orner, décorer (*with* de); *manuscript* relever, rehausser, enjoliver (*with* de); (*fig*) *tale, account* enjoliver; *truth* broder sur, orner.

embellishment [ɪm'belɪʃmənt] *n* (*V* **embellish**) embellissement *m,* ornement *m,* décoration *f,* enjolivement *m; [style, handwriting]* fioritures *fpl* (*gen pej*).

ember ['embəʳ] *n* charbon ardent. **~s** braise *f,* charbons ardents; **the dying ~s** les tisons *mpl*; *V* **fan¹.**

Ember ['embəʳ] *adj* (*Rel*) **~ days** Quatre-Temps *mpl.*

embezzle [ɪm'bezl] *vt* détourner, escroquer (*des fonds*).

embezzlement [ɪm'bezlmənt] *n* détournement *m* de fonds.

embezzler [ɪm'bezləʳ] *n* escroc *m.*

embitter [ɪm'bɪtəʳ] *vt person* aigrir, remplir d'amertume; *relations, disputes* envenimer.

embitterment [ɪm'bɪtəmənt] *n* amertume *f,* aigreur *f.*

emblazon [ɪm'bleɪzən] *vt* (*extol*) chanter les louanges de; (*Her*) blasonner.

emblem ['embləm] *n* (*all senses*) emblème *m.*

emblematic [,emblə'mætɪk] *adj* emblématique.

embodiment [ɪm'bɒdɪmənt] *n* **(a)** incarnation *f,* personnification *f.* **to be the ~ of progress** incarner le progrès; **he is the ~ of kindness** c'est la bonté incarnée *or* personnifiée. **(b)** (*inclusion*) incorporation *f.*

embody [ɪm'bɒdɪ] *vt* **(a)** (*give form to*) *thoughts, theories [person]* exprimer, concrétiser, formuler (*in* dans, en); *[work]* exprimer, donner forme à, mettre en application (*in* dans). **embodied spirit** esprit incarné.

(b) (*include*) *[person] ideas* résumer (*in* dans); *[work] ideas* renfermer; *[machine] features* réunir.

embolden [ɪm'bəʊldən] *vt* enhardir. **to ~ sb to do** donner à qn le courage de faire, enhardir qn à faire.

embolism ['embəlɪzəm] *n* embolie *f.*

emboss [ɪm'bɒs] *vt metal* travailler en relief, repousser, estamper; *leather, cloth* frapper, gaufrer. **~ed wallpaper** papier gaufré; **~ed writing paper** papier à lettres à en-tête en relief.

embrace [ɪm'breɪs] **1** *vt* **(a)** *person* embrasser, étreindre, enlacer; (*fig*) *religion* embrasser; *opportunity* saisir; *cause* épouser, embrasser; *offer* profiter de.

(b) (*include*) *[person] theme, experience* embrasser; *topics, hypotheses* inclure; *[work] theme, period* embrasser, englober; *ideas, topics* renfermer, comprendre. **his charity ~s all mankind** sa charité s'étend à l'humanité tout entière; **an all-embracing review** une revue d'ensemble.

2 *vi* s'étreindre, s'embrasser.

3 *n* (*hug*) étreinte *f,* enlacement *m.* **they were standing in a tender ~** ils étaient tendrement enlacés; **he held her in a tender ~** il l'a enlacée tendrement.

embrasure [ɪm'breɪʒəʳ] *n* embrasure *f.*

embrocation [,embrəʊ'keɪʃən] *n* embrocation *f.*

embroider [ɪm'brɔɪdəʳ] *vt* broder; (*fig*) *facts, truth* broder sur; *story* enjoliver.

embroidery [ɪm'brɔɪdərɪ] **1** *n* broderie *f.* **2** *cpd:* **embroidery frame** métier *m or* tambour *m* à broder; **embroidery silk/thread** soie *f*/coton *m* à broder.

embroil [ɪm'brɔɪl] *vt* entraîner (*in* dans), mêler (*in* à). **to get (o.s.) ~ed in** être entraîné dans, se trouver mêlé à.

embroilment [ɪm'brɔɪlmənt] *n* implication *f* (*in* dans), participation *f* (*in* à).

embryo ['embrɪəʊ] *n* (*lit, fig*) embryon *m.* **in ~** (*lit*) à l'état *or* au stade embryonnaire; (*fig*) en germe.

embryology [,embrɪ'ɒlədʒɪ] *n* embryologie *f.*

embryonic [,embrɪ'ɒnɪk] *adj* embryonnaire; (*fig*) en germe.

embus [ɪm'bʌs] **1** *vt* (faire) embarquer dans un car. **2** *vi* s'embarquer dans un car.

emcee ['em'siː] (*esp US*) **1** *n* animateur *m,*-trice *f,* maître *m* de cérémonie, présentateur *m,* -trice *f.* **2** *vt* animer, présenter.

emend [ɪ'mend] *vt text* corriger.

emendation [,iːmen'deɪʃən] *n* correction *f.*

emerald ['emərəld] **1** *n* (*stone*) émeraude *f;* (*colour*) (vert *m*) émeraude *m.* **2** *cpd* (*set with ~s*) (serti) d'émeraudes; (*also* **emerald green**) émeraude *inv.* **the Emerald Isle** l'île *f* d'Émeraude (*Irlande*); **emerald necklace** collier *m* d'émeraudes.

emerge [ɪ'mɜːdʒ] *vi* (*gen*) apparaître, surgir (*from* de, *from behind* de derrière); (*from water*) émerger, surgir, s'élever (*from* de); (*from hole, room*) sortir, surgir (*from* de); (*from confined space*) déboucher, sortir (*from* de); (*fig*) *[truth]* émerger (*from* de), apparaître, se faire jour; *[facts]* émerger (*from* de), apparaître; *[difficulties]* surgir, s'élever, apparaître; *[new nation]* naître; *[theory, school of thought]* apparaître, naître. **it ~s that** il ressort que, il apparaît que.

emergence [ɪ'mɜːdʒəns] *n [truth, facts]* apparition *f; [theory, school of thought]* naissance *f.*

emergency [ɪ'mɜːdʒənsɪ] **1** *n* cas urgent, imprévu *m* (*U*). **in case of ~, in an ~** en cas d'urgence *or* d'imprévu *or* de nécessité; **to be prepared for any ~** être prêt à *or* parer à toute éventualité; **in this ~** dans cette situation critique, dans ces circonstances critiques; *V* **state.**

2 *cpd measures, treatment, operation, repair* d'urgence; *brake, airstrip* de secours; (*improvised*) *mast* de fortune. (*Med*) **an emergency case** une urgence; **emergency centre** poste *m* de secours; **emergency exit** issue *f or* sortie *f* de secours; (*Mil*) **emergency force** force *f* d'urgence *or* d'intervention; (*Aviat*) **emergency landing** atterrissage forcé; **emergency powers** pouvoirs *mpl* extraordinaires; **emergency rations** vivres *mpl* de réserve; (*Med*) **emergency service** service *m* des urgences; (*Med*) **emergency ward** salle *f* des urgences.

emergent [ɪ'mɜːdʒənt] *adj* qui émerge; (*Opt, Philos*) émergent. **~ nations** pays *mpl* en voie de développement.

emeritus [ɪ'merɪtəs] *adj* (*Univ*) **professor ~** professeur *m* émérite† *or* honoraire.

emery ['emərɪ] *n* émeri *m.* **~ cloth** toile *f* (d')émeri; **~ paper** papier *m* (d')émeri, papier de verre.

emetic [ɪ'metɪk] *adj, n* émétique (*m*).

emigrant ['emɪgrənt] *n* émigrant(e) *m(f).* **~ ship** bateau *m* d'émigrants.

emigrate ['emɪgreɪt] *vi* émigrer.

emigration [,emɪ'greɪʃən] *n* émigration *f.*

émigré ['emɪgreɪ] *n* émigré(e) *m(f).*

eminence ['emɪnəns] *n* **(a)** (*U: distinction*) distinction *f.* **to achieve ~ in one's profession** parvenir à un rang éminent dans sa profession; **to win ~ as a surgeon** acquérir un grand renom comme chirurgien; **the ~ of his position** sa position éminente; (*Rel*) **His/Your E~** Son/Votre Éminence.

(b) (*high ground*) éminence *f,* élévation *f,* butte *f.*

eminent ['emɪnənt] *adj person* éminent, très distingué; *quality, services* éminent, insigne. (*Rel*) **Most E~** éminentissime.

eminently ['emɪnəntlɪ] *adv* éminemment, parfaitement, admirablement. **~ suitable** qui convient admirablement *or* parfaitement; **an ~ respectable gentleman** un monsieur des plus respectables *or* éminemment respectable.

emir [e'mɪəʳ] *n* émir *m.*

emirate [e'mɪərɪt] *n* émirat *m.*

emissary ['emɪsərɪ] *n* émissaire *m.*

emission [ɪ'mɪʃən] **1** *n* (*V* **emit**) émission *f,* dégagement *m.* **2** *cpd:* **emission spectrum** spectre *m* d'émission.

emit [ɪ'mɪt] *vt gas, heat, smoke* dégager, émettre; *sparks* lancer, jeter; *light, electromagnetic waves, banknotes* émettre; *vapour, smell* dégager, répandre, exhaler; *lava* émettre, cracher, vomir; *cry* laisser échapper; *sound* rendre, émettre.

emitter [ɪ'mɪtəʳ] *n* (*Electronics*) émetteur *m*.

emollient [ɪ'mɒlɪənt] *adj, n* émollient (*m*).

emolument [ɪ'mɒljʊmənt] *n* émoluments *mpl*, rémunération *f*; (*fee*) honoraires *mpl*; (*salary*) traitement *m*.

emote* [ɪ'məʊt] *vi* donner dans le sentiment* *or* dans le genre exalté*.

emotion [ɪ'məʊʃən] *n* **(a)** (*U*) émotion *f*. **voice full of ~** voix émue. **(b)** (*jealousy, love etc*) sentiment *m*.

emotional [ɪ'məʊʃənl] *adj shock, disturbance* émotif; *reaction* émotionnel, affectif; *moment* d'émotion profonde *or* intense; *story, writing* qui fait appel aux sentiments *or* à l'émotion. **he's very ~, he's a very ~ person** il est facilement ému *or* très sensible; **he was being very ~ *or* he was in a very ~ state about it** il prenait cela très à cœur, il laissait paraître son émotion *or* ses sentiments à ce sujet; **his ~ state** son état émotionnel.

emotionalism [ɪ'məʊʃnəlɪzəm] *n* émotivité *f*, sensiblerie *f* (*pej*). **the article was sheer ~** l'article *m* n'était qu'un étalage de sensiblerie.

emotionally [ɪ'məʊʃnəlɪ] *adv speak* avec émotion. **~ worded article** article qui fait appel aux sentiments; **~ deprived** privé d'affection; **to be ~ disturbed** avoir des troubles émotifs *or* de l'affectivité; **he is ~ involved** ses sentiments sont en cause.

emotionless [ɪ'məʊʃənlɪs] *adj face etc* impassible, qui ne montre aucune émotion; *person* indifférent.

emotive [ɪ'məʊtɪv] *adj* émotif.

empanel [ɪm'pænl] *vt*: **to ~ a juror** inscrire quelqu'un sur la liste du jury; **to ~ a jury** dresser la liste du jury.

empathy ['empəθɪ] *n* communauté *f* d'âme, communion *f* d'idées (*or* de sentiments *etc*).

emperor ['empərəʳ] **1** *n* empereur *m*. **2** *cpd*: **emperor butterfly** paon *m* de nuit; **emperor penguin** manchot *m* empereur.

emphasis ['emfəsɪs] *n* (*in word, phrase*) accentuation *f*, accent *m* d'intensité; (*fig*) accent. **to speak with ~** parler sur un ton d'insistance; **the ~ is on the first syllable** l'accent d'intensité *or* l'accentuation tombe sur la première syllabe; **to lay ~ on a word** souligner un mot, insister sur *or* appuyer sur un mot; (*fig*) **to lay ~ on one aspect of...** mettre l'accent sur *or* insister sur *or* attacher de l'importance à un aspect de ...; **the ~ is on sport** on accorde une importance particulière au sport; **this year the ~ is on femininity** cette année l'accent est sur la féminité.

emphasize ['emfəsaɪz] *vt* (*stress*) *word, fact, point* appuyer sur, insister sur, souligner; *syllable* insister sur, appuyer sur; (*draw attention to*) mettre en valeur, faire valoir, accentuer. **this point cannot be too strongly ~d** on ne saurait trop insister sur ce point; **I must ~ that ...** je dois souligner le fait que ...; **the long coat ~d his height** le long manteau faisait ressortir sa haute taille; **to ~ the eyes with mascara** mettre les yeux en valeur *or* souligner les yeux avec du mascara.

emphatic [ɪm'fætɪk] *adj tone, manner* énergique; *denial, speech, condemnation* catégorique, énergique; *person* vigoureux, énergique. **I am ~ about this point** j'insiste sur ce point, sur ce point je suis formel.

emphatically [ɪm'fætɪkəlɪ] *adv speak* énergiquement; *deny, refuse* catégoriquement, énergiquement. **yes, ~!** oui, absolument!; **~ no!** non, en aucun cas!, non, absolument pas!; **I must say this ~** je ne saurais trop insister sur ceci, sur ce point je suis formel.

emphysema [emfɪ'si:mə] *n* emphysème *m*.

empire ['empaɪəʳ] **1** *n* (*all senses*) empire *m*. **2** *cpd*: **Empire** *costume, furniture* Empire *inv*; (*fig*) **empire builder** bâtisseur *m* d'empires; **he is empire-building, it is empire building on his part** il joue les bâtisseurs d'empire.

empiric [em'pɪrɪk] **1** *adj* empirique. **2** *n* empiriste *mf*; (*Med*) empirique *m*.

empirical [em'pɪrɪkəl] *adj* empirique.

empiricism [em'pɪrɪsɪzəm] *n* empirisme *m*.

empiricist [em'pɪrɪsɪst] *adj, n* empiriste (*mf*).

emplacement [ɪm'pleɪsmənt] *n* (*Mil*) emplacement *m* (*d'un canon*).

employ [ɪm'plɔɪ] **1** *vt person* employer (*as* comme); *means, method, process* employer, utiliser; *time* employer (*in or by doing* à faire); *force, cunning* recourir à, employer; *skill* faire usage de, employer. **to be ~ed in doing** être occupé à faire.

2 *n*: **to be in the ~ of** être employé par, travailler chez *or* pour; [*domestic staff*] être au service de.

employee [ˌɪmplɔɪ'i:] *n* employé(e) *m(f)*.

employer [ɪm'plɔɪəʳ] *n* (*Comm, Ind; also domestic*) patron(ne) *m(f)*; (*Jur*) employeur *m*, -euse *f*. (*Ind: collectively*) **~s** le patronat *m*; **~s' federation** syndicat patronal, fédération patronale; (*Insurance*) **~'s contribution** cotisation patronale.

employment [ɪm'plɔɪmənt] **1** *n* (*U: jobs collectively*) emploi *m* (*U*); (*a job*) emploi, travail *m*; (*modest*) place *f*; (*important*) situation *f*. **full ~** le plein emploi; **to take up ~** prendre un emploi; **without ~** sans emploi, au *or* en chômage; **to seek/find ~** chercher/trouver un emploi *or* du travail; **in sb's ~** employé par qn; [*domestic staff*] au service de qn; **conditions/place of ~** conditions *fpl*/lieu *m* de travail; (*Brit*) **Secretary (of State) for *or* Minister of E~,** (*US*) **Secretary for E~** ministre *m* de l'Emploi; **Department *or* Ministry of E~** ministère *m* de l'Emploi.

2 *cpd*: **employment agency** agence *f* de placement; (*Brit*) **employment exchange** bourse *f* du travail.

emporium [em'pɔ:rɪəm] *n* (*shop*) grand magasin, bazar *m*; (*market*) centre commercial, marché *m*.

empower [ɪm'paʊəʳ] *vt*: **to ~ sb to do** autoriser qn à faire; (*Jur*) habiliter qn à faire; **to be ~ed to do** avoir pleins pouvoirs pour faire.

empress ['emprɪs] *n* impératrice *f*.

emptiness ['emptɪnɪs] *n* vide *m*; [*pleasures etc*] vanité *f*. **the ~ of life** le vide de l'existence.

empty ['emptɪ] **1** *adj jar, box, car* vide; *house, room* inoccupé, vide; *lorry, truck* vide, sans chargement; *ship* lège; *post, job* vacant; *town, theatre* vide, désert. **~ of** vide de, dénué de, sans; **on an ~ stomach** à jeun; **my stomach is ~** j'ai le ventre *or* l'estomac creux; (*Prov*) **~ vessels make most noise** les grands diseurs ne sont pas les grands faiseurs; **~ words** paroles creuses, discours *mpl* creux; **~ talk** verbiage *m*; **~ promises** promesses *fpl* en l'air; **~ threats** menaces vaines; **to look into ~ space** regarder dans le vide.

2 *n*: **empties** (*bottles*) bouteilles *fpl* vides; (*boxes etc*) boîtes *fpl or* emballages *mpl* vides.

3 *cpd*: **empty-handed** les mains vides; **to return empty-handed** revenir bredouille *or* les mains vides; **empty-headed** sot (*f* sotte), sans cervelle; **an empty-headed girl** une écervelée, une évaporée.

4 *vt* **(a)** *box, glass* vider; *pond, tank* vider, vidanger; *vehicle* décharger. **the burglars emptied the shop** les voleurs ont dévalisé *or* nettoyé* le magasin; **television has emptied the cinemas** la télévision a vidé les cinémas.

(b) (*also* **~ out**) *box, tank, pocket* vider; *bricks, books* sortir (*of, from* de, *into* dans); *liquid* vider (*of, from* de), verser (*of, from* de, *into* dans), transvaser (*into* dans).

5 *vi* [*water*] se déverser, s'écouler; [*river*] se jeter (*into* dans); [*building, container*] se vider.

empyema [ˌempaɪ'i:mə] *n* empyème *m*.

emu ['i:mju:] *n* émeu *m or* émou *m*.

emulate ['emjʊleɪt] *vt person* (*imitate*) imiter, essayer d'égaler; (*successfully*) être l'émule de.

emulation [ˌemjʊ'leɪʃən] *n* émulation *f*.

emulsify [ɪ'mʌlsɪfaɪ] *vt* émulsionner.

emulsion [ɪ'mʌlʃən] *n* émulsion *f*. **~ paint** peinture *f* mate *or* à émulsion.

enable [ɪ'neɪbl] *vt*: **to ~ sb to do** (*give opportunity*) permettre à qn de faire, donner à qn la possibilité de faire; (*give means*) permettre à qn de faire, donner à qn le moyen de faire, mettre qn à même de faire; (*Jur etc: authorize*) habiliter qn à faire, donner pouvoir à qn de faire.

enact [ɪ'nækt] *vt* **(a)** (*Jur*) (*make into law*) promulguer, donner force de loi à; (*decree*) décréter, ordonner, arrêter. **as by law ~ed** aux termes de la loi, selon la loi. **(b)** (*perform*) *play* représenter, jouer; *part* jouer. (*fig*) **the drama which was ~ed yesterday** le drame qui s'est déroulé hier.

enactment [ɪ'næktmənt] *n* promulgation *f*.

enamel [ɪ'næməl] **1** *n* **(a)** (*U: most senses*) émail *m*. **nail ~** vernis *m* à ongles (laqué).

(b) (*Art*) **an ~** un émail.

2 *vt* émailler.

3 *cpd saucepan, ornament, brooch* en émail. **enamel paint** peinture laquée, ripolin *m* ®; (*Art*) **enamel painting** peinture *f* sur émail; **enamelware** articles *mpl* en métal émaillé.

enamelled [ɪ'næməld] *adj brooch* en émail; *metal* émaillé; *saucepan* en émail, émaillé.

enamelling [ɪ'næməlɪŋ] *n* émaillage *m*.

enamour, (*US*) **enamor** [ɪ'næməʳ] *vt*: **to be ~ed of *person*** être amoureux *or* épris de, s'être amouraché de (*pej*); *thing* être enchanté de, être séduit par; **she was not ~ed of the idea** l'idée ne l'enchantait pas.

encamp [ɪn'kæmp] **1** *vi* camper. **2** *vt* faire camper.

encampment [ɪn'kæmpmənt] *n* campement *m*.

encapsulate [ɪn'kæpsjʊleɪt] *vt* (*Pharm, Space*) mettre en capsule; (*fig*) renfermer, résumer.

encase [ɪn'keɪs] *vt* (*contain*) enfermer, enchâsser (*in* dans); (*cover*) entourer, recouvrir (*in* de).

encaustic [en'kɔ:stɪk] **1** *adj painting* encaustique; *tile, brick* céramique. **2** *n* (*painting*) encaustique *f*.

encephalitis [ˌensefə'laɪtɪs] *n* encéphalite *f*.

enchain [ɪn'tʃeɪn] *vt* enchaîner; (*fig*) enchaîner, retenir.

enchant [ɪn'tʃɑ:nt] *vt* (*put under spell*) enchanter, ensorceler, charmer; (*delight*) enchanter, ravir, charmer. **the ~ed wood** le bois enchanté.

enchanter [ɪn'tʃɑ:ntəʳ] *n* enchanteur *m*.

enchanting [ɪn'tʃɑ:ntɪŋ] *adj* enchanteur (*f* -eresse), charmant, ravissant.

enchantingly [ɪn'tʃɑ:ntɪŋlɪ] *adv smile, dance* d'une façon ravissante. **she is ~ beautiful** elle est belle à ravir.

enchantment [ɪn'tʃɑ:ntmənt] *n* (*V* **enchant**) enchantement *m*; ensorcellement *m*; ravissement *m*.

enchantress [ɪn'tʃɑ:ntrɪs] *n* enchanteresse *f*.

encircle [ɪn'sɜ:kl] *vt* (*gen*) entourer; [*troops, men, police*] encercler, cerner, entourer; [*walls, belt, bracelet*] entourer, ceindre.

encirclement [ɪn'sɜ:klmənt] *n* encerclement *m*.

encircling [ɪn'sɜ:klɪŋ] **1** *n* encerclement *m*. **2** *adj* qui encercle. **~ movement** manœuvre *f* d'encerclement.

enclave ['enkleɪv] *n* enclave *f*.

enclitic [ɪn'klɪtɪk] *n* enclitique *m*.

enclose [ɪn'kləʊz] *vt* **(a)** (*fence in*) enclore, clôturer; (*surround*) entourer, ceindre (*with* de); (*Rel*) cloîtrer. **to ~ within** enfermer dans; **an ~d space** un espace clos; (*Rel*) **~d order** ordre cloîtré.

(b) (*with letter etc*) joindre (*in* à). **to ~ sth in a letter** joindre qch à une lettre, inclure qch dans une lettre; **letter enclosing a receipt** lettre contenant un reçu; **please find ~d** veuillez trouver ci-joint *or* sous ce pli; **the ~d cheque** le chèque ci-joint *or* ci-inclus.

enclosure [ɪn'kləʊʒəʳ] **1** *n* **(a)** (*U*) [*land*] fait *m* de clôturer; (*Brit Hist*) enclosure *f*, clôture *f* des terres.

(b) (*document etc enclosed*) pièce jointe, document ci-joint *or* ci-inclus; (*ground enclosed*) enclos *m*, enceinte *f*; *[monastery]* clôture *f*; (*fence etc*) enceinte *f*, clôture *f*. *[racecourse]* the ~ le pesage; **the public** ~ la pelouse; **royal** ~ enceinte réservée à la famille royale.

2 *cpd*: **enclosure wall** mur *m* d'enceinte.

encomium [ɪnˈkəʊmɪəm] *n* panégyrique *m*, éloge *m*.

encompass [ɪnˈkʌmpəs] *vt* (*lit*) entourer, ceindre, environner (*with* de); (*fig*) (*include*) contenir, inclure; (*beset*) assaillir.

encore [ɒŋˈkɔːʳ] **1** *excl* bis! **2** [ˈɒŋkɔːʳ] *n* bis *m*. **to call for an** ~ bisser, crier 'bis'; **the pianist gave an** ~ le pianiste a joué un (morceau en) bis. **3** *vt song, act* bisser.

encounter [ɪnˈkaʊntəʳ] **1** *vt person* rencontrer (à l'improviste), tomber sur; *enemy* affronter, rencontrer; *opposition* se heurter à; *difficulties* affronter, rencontrer, éprouver; *danger* affronter. **to** ~ **enemy fire** essuyer le feu de l'ennemi.

2 *n* rencontre *f* (inattendue); (*Mil*) rencontre, engagement *m*, combat *m*.

encourage [ɪnˈkʌrɪdʒ] *vt person* encourager; *arts, industry, projects, development, growth* encourager, favoriser; *bad habits* encourager, flatter. **to** ~ **sb to do** encourager *or* inciter *or* pousser qn à faire; **to** ~ **sb in his belief that ...** confirmer qn dans sa croyance que ..., encourager qn à croire que ...; **to** ~ **sb in his desire to do** encourager le désir de qn de faire.

encouragement [ɪnˈkʌrɪdʒmənt] *n* encouragement *m*; (*to a deed*) incitation *f* (*to* à); (*support*) encouragement, appui *m*, soutien *m*.

encouraging [ɪnˈkʌrɪdʒɪŋ] *adj* encourageant.

encouragingly [ɪnˈkʌrɪdʒɪŋlɪ] *adv speak etc* d'une manière encourageante. **we had** ~ **little difficulty** le peu de difficulté rencontré a été encourageant *or* nous a encouragés.

encroach [ɪnˈkrəʊtʃ] *vi* (*on sb's land, time, rights*) empiéter (*on* sur). **the sea is** ~**ing on the land** la mer gagne (du terrain).

encroachment [ɪnˈkrəʊtʃmənt] *n* empiètement *m* (*on* sur).

encrust [ɪnˈkrʌst] *vt* (*with earth, cement*) encroûter, couvrir (d'une croûte) (*with* de); (*with jewels etc*) incruster (*with* de).

encumber [ɪnˈkʌmbəʳ] *vt person, room* encombrer (*with* de). **estate** ~**ed with debts** succession grevée de dettes.

encumbrance [ɪnˈkʌmbrəns] *n* (*burden*) embarras *m*, charge *f*; (*Jur: on estate*) charge. **to be an** ~ **to sb** gêner *or* embarrasser qn.

encyclical [ɪnˈsɪklɪkəl] *adj, n* encyclique (*f*).

encyclop(a)edia [ɪnˌsaɪkləʊˈpiːdɪə] *n* encyclopédie *f*; *V* **walking.**

encyclop(a)edic [ɪnˌsaɪkləʊˈpiːdɪk] *adj* encyclopédique.

end [end] **1** *n* **(a)** (*farthest part*) *[road, string, table, branch, finger]* bout *m*, extrémité *f*; *[procession, line of people]* bout, queue *f*; *[garden, estate]* bout, limite *f*. **the southern** ~ **of the town** l'extrémité sud de la ville; **the fourth from the** ~ le quatrième avant la fin; **from** ~ **to** ~ d'un bout à l'autre, de bout en bout; **on** ~ debout (*V also* **1b**); **to stand a box** *etc* **on** ~ mettre une caisse *etc* debout; **his hair stood on** ~ ses cheveux se dressèrent sur sa tête; **the ships collided** ~ **on** les bateaux se sont heurtés de front *or* nez à nez; ~ **to** ~ bout à bout; **to the** ~**s of the earth** jusqu'au bout du monde; (*Sport*) **to change** ~**s** changer de côté *or* de camp; (*fig*) **to make (both)** ~**s meet** (faire) joindre les deux bouts; (*fig*) **he can't see beyond the** ~ **of his nose** il ne voit pas plus loin que le bout de son nez; (*fig*) **to begin at the wrong** ~ s'y prendre mal *or* par le mauvais bout; **to keep one's** ~ **up*** se défendre (assez bien); *V* **hair, loose, stick** *etc.*

(b) (*conclusion*) *[story, chapter, month]* fin *f*; *[work]* achèvement *m*; *[efforts]* fin, aboutissement *m*; *[meeting]* fin, issue *f*. **to read a book to the very** ~ lire un livre de A à Z *or* jusqu'à la dernière page; **it succeeded in the** ~ cela a réussi à la fin *or* finalement *or* en fin de compte; **he got used to it in the** ~ il a fini par s'y habituer; **in the** ~ **they decided to use ...** ils ont décidé en définitive *or* ils ont fini par décider d'employer ...; **at the** ~ **of the day** à la fin de la journée; (*fig*) en fin de compte; **at the** ~ **of December** à la fin de décembre; (*Comm*) fin décembre; **at the** ~ **of the century** à *or* vers la fin du siècle; **at the** ~ **of the winter** à la fin *or* au sortir de l'hiver; **at the** ~ **of three weeks** au bout de trois semaines; **the** ~ **of a session** la clôture d'une séance; **that was the** ~ **of my watch** ma montre était fichue*; **that was the** ~ **of that!** on n'en a plus reparlé; **that was the** ~ **of him** on n'a plus reparlé de lui, on ne l'a plus revu; (*fig*) **there is no** ~ **to it all** cela n'en finit plus; **to be at an** ~ *[action]* être terminé *or* fini; *[time, period]* être écoulé; *[material, supplies]* être épuisé; **to be at the** ~ **of one's patience/strength** être à bout de patience/forces; **my patience is at an** ~ ma patience est à bout; (*fig*) **to be at the** ~ **of one's tether** être au bout de son rouleau; **to bring to an** ~ *speech, writing* achever, conclure; *work* terminer; *relations* mettre fin à; **to come to an** ~ prendre fin, se terminer, arriver à son terme (*liter, frm*); **to get to the** ~ **of** *supplies, food* finir; *work, essay* venir à bout de; *troubles* (se) sortir de; *holiday* arriver à la fin de; **to put an** ~ **to, to make an** ~ **of** mettre fin à, mettre un terme à; **to put an** ~ **to one's life** mettre fin à ses jours; (*euph, liter*) **to be nearing one's** ~ être à (l'article de) la mort, se mourir (*liter*); **to come to a bad** ~ mal finir; **we shall never hear the** ~ **of it** on n'a pas fini d'en entendre parler; **there was no** ~* **of ...** il y avait une masse* de *or* un tas de *or* énormément de ...; **it pleased her no** ~* cela lui a fait un plaisir fou *or* énorme; **that's the (bitter)** ~**!*** il ne manquait plus que cela!, c'est la fin de tout!, c'est le comble!; **he's (just) the** ~**!*** c'est une vraie plaie!*; **for two hours on** ~ deux heures de suite *or* d'affilée; **for days on** ~ jour après jour, pendant des jours et des jours; **for several days on** ~ pendant plusieurs jours de suite; *V* **bitter, meet[1], sticky, untimely.**

(c) (*remnant*) *[rope, candle]* bout *m*; *[loaf, meat]* reste *m*, restant *m*. *V* **cigarette** *etc.*

(d) (*purpose*) but *m*, fin *f*, dessein *m*. **with this** ~ **in view** dans ce dessein *or* but, à cette fin, avec cet objectif en vue; **an** ~ **in itself** une fin en soi; **to no** ~ en vain; (*Prov*) **the** ~ **justifies the means** la fin justifie les moyens (*Prov*).

2 *cpd*: **end-all** *V* **be 5**; (*Cards, Chess*) **end game** fin *f* de partie, phase finale du jeu; **the end house in the street** la dernière maison de la rue; (*Typ*) **endpapers** gardes *fpl*, pages *fpl* de garde; **end product** (*Comm, Ind*) produit fini; (*fig*) résultat *m*; **end result** résultat final *or* définitif; (*US*) **end table** table *f* basse; **endways** *V* **endways.**

3 *vt work* finir, achever, terminer; *period of service* accomplir; *speech, writing* conclure, achever (*with* avec, par); *broadcast, series* terminer (*with* par); *speculation, gossip, rumour* mettre fin à, mettre un terme à; *quarrel, war* mettre fin à, faire cesser. **to** ~ **one's days** finir *or* achever ses jours; **this is the dictionary to** ~ **all dictionaries*** c'est ce qu'il y a de mieux comme dictionnaire; **that was the lie to** ~ **all lies!*** comme mensonge on ne fait pas mieux!* (*iro*).

4 *vi [speech, programme, holiday, marriage, series]* finir, se terminer, s'achever; *[road]* se terminer. **the winter is** ~**ing** l'hiver tire à sa fin; **where's it all going to** ~**?, how will it all** ~**?** comment tout cela finira-t-il?; **word** ~**ing in an s/in -re** mot se terminant par un s/en -re; **stick which** ~**s in a point** bâton qui se termine en pointe; **it** ~**ed in a fight** cela s'est terminé par une bagarre*; **the plan** ~**ed in failure** le projet s'est soldé par un échec; **the film** ~**s with the heroine dying** le film se termine par la mort de l'héroïne.

end off *vt sep* finir, achever, terminer.

end up *vi* **(a)** finir, se terminer, s'achever (*in* en, par); *[road]* aboutir (*in* à). **it ended up in a fight** cela s'est terminé par une *or* en bagarre*.

(b) (*finally arrive at*) se retrouver, échouer (*in* à, en); (*finally become*) finir par devenir. **he ended up in Paris** il s'est retrouvé à Paris; **you'll end up in jail** tu vas finir *or* te retrouver *or* échouer en prison; **he ended up a rich man** il a fini (par devenir) riche; **the book she had planned ended up (being) an article** le livre qu'elle avait projeté a fini par n'être qu'un article.

endanger [ɪnˈdeɪndʒəʳ] *vt life, interests, reputation* mettre en danger, exposer; *future, chances, health* compromettre.

endear [ɪnˈdɪəʳ] *vt* faire aimer (*to* de). **this** ~**ed him to the whole country** cela l'a fait aimer de tout le pays; **what** ~**s him to me is ...** ce qui me plaît en lui c'est ...; **to** ~ **o.s. to everybody** se faire aimer de tout le monde; **that speech didn't** ~ **him to the public** ce discours ne l'a pas fait apprécier du public.

endearing [ɪnˈdɪərɪŋ] *adj smile* engageant; *personality* attachant, qui inspire l'affection; *characteristic* (qui rend) sympathique. **she's a very** ~ **person** elle est très attachante *or* sympathique.

endearingly [ɪnˈdɪərɪŋlɪ] *adv* de façon engageante *or* attachante *or* sympathique.

endearment [ɪnˈdɪəmənt] *n*: ~**s** (*words*) paroles affectueuses *or* tendres; (*acts*) marques *fpl* d'affection; **term of** ~ terme *m* d'affection, **words of** ~ paroles *fpl* tendres.

endeavour [ɪnˈdevəʳ] **1** *n* effort *m*, tentative *f* (*to do* pour faire). **to make an** ~ **to do** essayer *or* s'efforcer de faire, se donner la peine de faire; **he made every** ~ **to go** il a fait tout son possible pour y aller, il a tout fait pour y aller; **in an** ~ **to please** dans l'intention de plaire, dans un effort pour plaire.

2 *vi* essayer, s'efforcer, tenter (*to do* de faire), (*stronger*) s'évertuer, s'appliquer (*to do* à faire).

endemic [enˈdemɪk] **1** *adj* endémique. **2** *n* endémie *f*.

ending [ˈendɪŋ] *n* **(a)** *[story, book]* fin *f*, dénouement *m*; *[events]* fin, conclusion *f*; *[day]* fin; (*outcome*) issue *f*; *[speech etc]* conclusion. **story with a happy** ~ histoire qui finit bien.

(b) (*Ling*) terminaison *f*, désinence *f*. **feminine** ~ terminaison féminine; *V* **nerve.**

endive [ˈendaɪv] *n* (*curly*) chicorée *f*; (*smooth, flat*) endive *f*.

endless [ˈendlɪs] *adj road* interminable, sans fin; *plain* sans bornes, infini; *speech, vigil* interminable, qui n'en finit plus, sans fin; *times, attempts* innombrable, sans nombre; *discussion, argument* continuel, incessant; *chatter* intarissable; *patience* infini; *resources, supplies* inépuisable; *possibilities* illimité, sans limites. **this job is** ~ c'est à n'en plus finir, on n'en voit pas la fin; (*Tech*) ~ **belt** courroie *f* sans fin.

endlessly [ˈendlɪslɪ] *adv stretch out* interminablement, sans fin, à perte de vue; *chatter, argue* continuellement, interminablement; *speak* sans cesse, continuellement; *repeat* sans cesse, infatigablement. ~ **kind/willing** d'une bonté/d'une bonne volonté à toute épreuve.

endocarp [ˈendəkɑːp] *n* endocarpe *m*.

endocrine [ˈendəʊkraɪn] *adj* endocrine. ~ **gland** glande *f* endocrine.

endorse [ɪnˈdɔːs] *vt* (*sign*) *document, cheque* endosser; (*guarantee*) *bill* avaliser; (*approve*) *claim, candidature* appuyer; *opinion* souscrire à, adhérer à; *action, decision* approuver, sanctionner. (*Brit Jur*) **to** ~ **a driving licence** ≃ porter une contravention au permis de conduire; **he has had his licence** ~**d** une contravention a été portée à son permis de conduire.

endorsement [ɪnˈdɔːsmənt] *n* (*V* **endorse**) endossement *m*, endos *m*; aval *m*; appui *m* (*of* de); adhésion *f* (*of* à); approbation *f*, sanction *f* (*of* de). (*Brit Jur: on driving licence*) **she has had 2** ~**s** ≃ elle a eu 2 contraventions portées à son permis.

endoskeleton [ˌendəʊˈskelɪtən] *n* squelette *m* interne, endosquelette *m*.

endothermic [ˌendəʊˈθɜːmɪk] *adj* endothermique.

endow [ɪnˈdaʊ] *vt institution, church* doter (*with* de); *hospital bed, prize, chair* fonder. (*fig*) **to be** ~**ed with brains/beauty** *etc* être doté d'intelligence/de beauté *etc.*

endowment [ɪnˈdaʊmənt] **1** *n* (*V* **endow**) dotation *f*; fondation *f*.

2 *cpd*: **endowment assurance** *or* **policy** assurance *f* à capital différé.
endue [ɪn'djuː] *vt* revêtir, douer (*with* de).
endurable [ɪn'djʊərəbl] *adj* supportable, tolérable, endurable.
endurance [ɪn'djʊərəns] 1 *n* endurance *f*, résistance *f*. **to have great powers of ~ against pain** être dur au mal; **he has come to the end of his ~** il n'en peut plus, il est à bout; **beyond ~, past ~** intolérable, au-delà de ce que l'on peut supporter; **tried beyond ~** excédé.
2 *cpd*: (*Sport*) **endurance race** épreuve *f* de fond; **endurance test** (*Sport, Tech, fig*) épreuve *f* de résistance; (*Aut*) épreuve d'endurance.
endure [ɪn'djʊəʳ] 1 *vt pain, insults* supporter, endurer, tolérer; *domination* subir; (*put up with*) supporter, souffrir (*doing* de faire). **she can't ~ being teased** elle ne peut pas supporter *or* souffrir qu'on la taquine (*subj*); **I cannot ~ him** je ne peux pas le supporter *or* le voir *or* le sentir*.
2 *vi [building, peace, friendship]* durer; *[book, memory]* rester.
enduring [ɪn'djʊərɪŋ] *adj friendship, fame, peace* durable; *government, regime* stable; *illness, hardship* persistant, qui persiste.
endways ['endweɪz] *adv*, **endwise** ['endwaɪz] *adv* (~ *on*) en long, par le petit bout; (*end to end*) bout à bout.
enema ['enɪmə] *n* (*act*) lavement *m*; (*apparatus*) poire *f or* bock *m* à lavement.
enemy ['enəmɪ] 1 *n* (*person*) ennemi(e) *m(f)*, adversaire *mf*. (*Mil*) **the ~** l'ennemi; **to make enemies** se faire *or* s'attirer des ennemis; **to make an ~ of sb** (se) faire un ennemi de qn; **he is his own worst ~** il est son pire ennemi, il n'a de pire ennemi que lui-même; **they are deadly enemies** ils sont à couteaux tirés, ils sont ennemis jurés; (*fig*) **corruption is the ~ of the state** la corruption est l'ennemie de l'État; *V* **public.**
2 *cpd tanks, forces, tribes* ennemi; *morale, strategy* de l'ennemi. **enemy action** attaque ennemie; **killed by enemy action** tombé à l'ennemi; **enemy alien** ressortissant(e) *m(f)* d'un pays ennemi; **enemy-occupied territory** territoire occupé par l'ennemi.
energetic [,enə'dʒetɪk] 1 *adj* (a) *person* énergique, plein d'énergie, actif. **~ children** enfants pleins d'énergie *or* débordants d'activité; **I've had a very ~ day** je me suis beaucoup dépensé aujourd'hui; **do you feel ~ enough to come for a walk?** est-ce que tu te sens assez d'attaque* pour faire une promenade?
(b) *measure* énergique, rigoureux; *denial, refusal* énergique, vigoureux; *government* énergique, à poigne.
2 *n* (*U*) **~s** énergétique *f*.
energetically [,enə'dʒetɪkəlɪ] *adv move, behave* énergiquement, avec énergie, avec vigueur; *speak, reply* avec force, avec vigueur.
energize ['enədʒaɪz] *vt person* stimuler, donner de l'énergie à; (*Elec*) alimenter (en courant).
energizing ['enədʒaɪzɪŋ] *adj food* énergétique.
energy ['enədʒɪ] 1 *n* (*gen*) énergie *f*, vigueur *f*; (*Phys*) énergie. **potential/kinetic ~** énergie potentielle/cinétique; **he has a lot of ~** il a beaucoup d'énergie, il est très dynamique; (*Brit*) **Secretary (of State) for** *or* **Minister of E~** ministre *m* de l'Énergie; **Department** *or* **Ministry of E~** ministère *m* de l'Énergie; **in order to save ~** pour faire des économies d'énergie; **with all one's ~** de toutes ses forces; **to put all one's ~** *or* **energies into sth/into doing** se consacrer tout entier à qch/à faire, appliquer toute son énergie à qch/à faire; **I haven't the ~ to go back** je n'ai pas l'énergie *or* le courage de retourner; **he seems to have no ~ these days** il semble sans énergie *or* à plat* en ce moment; **don't waste your ~** ne te fatigue pas*, ne te donne pas du mal pour rien; **he used up all his ~** *or* **energies doing it** il a épuisé ses forces à le faire; *V* **atomic** *etc.*
2 *cpd*: **the energy crisis** la crise énergétique *or* de l'énergie; **energy level** niveau *m or* état *m* énergétique.
enervate ['enɜːveɪt] *vt* affaiblir.
enervating ['enɜːveɪtɪŋ] *adj* débilitant, amollissant.
enfeeble [ɪn'fiːbl] *vt* affaiblir.
enfeeblement [ɪn'fiːblmənt] *n* affaiblissement *m*.
enfilade [,enfɪ'leɪd] (*Mil*) 1 *vt* soumettre à un tir d'enfilade. 2 *n* tir *m* d'enfilade.
enfold [ɪn'fəʊld] *vt* envelopper (*in* de). **to ~ sb in one's arms** entourer qn de ses bras, étreindre qn.
enforce [ɪn'fɔːs] *vt decision, policy* mettre en application *or* en vigueur, appliquer; *ruling, law* faire obéir *or* respecter; *discipline* imposer; *demand* appuyer; *argument, rights* faire valoir. **to ~ obedience** se faire obéir.
enforced [ɪn'fɔːst] *adj* forcé, obligé, obligatoire.
enforcement [ɪn'fɔːsmənt] *n [decision, policy, law]* mise *f* en application *or* en vigueur; *[discipline]* imposition *f*.
enfranchise [ɪn'fræntʃaɪz] *vt* (*give vote to*) accorder le droit de vote à, admettre au suffrage; (*set free*) affranchir.
enfranchisement [ɪn'fræntʃɪzmənt] *n* (*V* **enfranchise**) admission *f* au suffrage; affranchissement *m*.
engage [ɪn'geɪdʒ] 1 *vt servant* engager; *workers* embaucher; *lawyer* prendre; (†) *room* retenir, réserver; (*fig*) *sb's attention, interest* éveiller, retenir; (*Mil*) *the enemy* engager le combat avec, attaquer; (*Tech*) engager; *gearwheels* mettre en prise. **to ~ sb in conversation** engager la *or* lier conversation avec qn; (*frm*) **to ~ o.s. to do** s'engager à faire; (*Aut*) **to ~ a gear** engager une vitesse; **to ~ gear** mettre en prise; **to ~ the clutch** embrayer.
2 *vi [person]* s'engager (*to do* à faire); (*Tech*) *[wheels]* s'engrener, s'engager, se mettre en prise; *[bolt]* s'enclencher; *[clutch]* s'embrayer. **to ~ in** *politics, transaction* se lancer dans; *controversy* s'engager dans, s'embarquer dans; **to ~ in a discussion/in a conversation/in competition** entrer en discussion/en conversation/en concurrence (*with* avec).
engaged [ɪn'geɪdʒd] *adj* (a) (*betrothed*) fiancé (*to* à, avec). **to get ~** se fiancer (*to* à, avec); **the ~ couple** les fiancés.
(b) *seat* occupé, pris, retenu; *taxi* pris, pas libre; *toilet* occupé; (*Brit Telec*) *number, line* occupé; *person* occupé, pris. **Mr X is ~ just now** M X est occupé *or* est pris *or* n'est pas libre en ce moment; **to be ~ in doing** être occupé à faire; **to be ~ on sth** s'occuper de qch; (*Brit Telec*) **the ~ signal** *or* **tone** la tonalité occupé *inv or* pas libre.
engagement [ɪn'geɪdʒmənt] 1 *n* (a) (*appointment*) rendez-vous *m inv*; *[actor etc]* engagement *m*. **public ~** obligation officielle; **previous ~** engagement antérieur; **I have an ~** j'ai un rendez-vous, je ne suis pas libre, je suis pris.
(b) (*betrothal*) fiançailles *fpl*. **to break off one's ~** rompre ses fiançailles.
(c) (*frm: undertaking*) engagement *m*, obligation *f*, promesse *f*. **to give an ~ to do sth** s'engager à faire qch.
(d) (*Mil*) action *f*, combat *m*, engagement *m*.
2 *cpd*: **engagement book** agenda *m*; **engagement ring** bague *f* de fiançailles.
engaging [ɪn'geɪdʒɪŋ] *adj smile, look, tone* engageant; *personality* attirant, at achant.
engender [ɪn'dʒendəʳ] *vt* engendrer (*fig*), produire (*fig*).
engine ['endʒɪn] 1 *n* (*Tech*) machine *f*, moteur *m*; *[ship]* machine; (*Rail*) locomotive *f*; (*Aut, Aviat*) moteur; *V* **back, jet**[1] *etc.*
2 *cpd*: (*Brit Rail*) **engine driver** mécanicien *m*; (*US Rail*) **engine house** = **engine shed**; (*Naut*) **engine room** salle *f or* chambre *f* des machines; (*Brit Rail*) **engine shed** rotonde *f*; **engine unit** bloc-moteur *m*.
-engined ['endʒɪnd] *adj ending in cpds*: **twin-engined** à deux machines, bimoteur; *V* **single** *etc.*
engineer [,endʒɪ'nɪəʳ] 1 *n* (a) (*professional*) ingénieur *m*; (*tradesman*) technicien *m*; (*repairer: for domestic appliances etc*) dépanneur *m*, réparateur *m*. **woman ~** (femme *f*) ingénieur; (*Mil*) **the E~s** le génie; **the TV ~ came** le dépanneur est venu pour la télé*; *V* **civil, highway** *etc.*
(b) (*Merchant Navy*) mécanicien *m*; (*Navy*) mécanicien de la marine; (*US Rail*) mécanicien, agent *m* de conduite; *V* **chief.**
2 *vt scheme, plan* machiner, manigancer.
engineering [,endʒɪ'nɪərɪŋ] 1 *n* (a) (*U*) engineering *m*, ingénierie *f*. **to study ~** faire des études d'ingénieur; *V* **civil, electrical, mechanical** *etc.*
(b) (*fig, gen pej*) machination(s) *f(pl)*, manœuvre(s) *f(pl)*.
2 *cpd*: **engineering factory** atelier *m* de construction mécanique; **engineering industries** industries *fpl* d'équipement; **engineering works** = **engineering factory.**
England ['ɪŋglənd] *n* Angleterre *f*.
English ['ɪŋglɪʃ] 1 *adj* anglais; *king, throne* d'Angleterre.
2 *n* (a) **the ~** les Anglais *mpl*.
(b) (*Ling*) anglais *m*. **the King's** *or* **Queen's ~** l'anglais correct; **in plain** *or* **simple ~** en termes très simples, ≃ en bon français.
3 *cpd*: **the English Channel** la Manche; **Englishman** Anglais *m*; (*Prov*) **an Englishman's home is his castle** charbonnier est maître chez soi (*Prov*); **English speaker** anglophone *mf*; **English-speaking** qui parle anglais; *nation etc* anglophone; **Englishwoman** Anglaise *f*.
engraft [ɪn'grɑːft] *vt* (*Agr, Surg, fig*) greffer (*into, on* sur).
engram ['engræm] *n* engramme *m*.
engrave [ɪn'greɪv] *vt wood, metal, stone* graver; (*Typ*) graver au burin; (*fig*) graver, empreindre. **~d on the heart/the memory** gravé dans le cœur/la mémoire.
engraver [ɪn'greɪvəʳ] *n* graveur *m*.
engraving [ɪn'greɪvɪŋ] *n* gravure *f*; *V* **wood** *etc.*
engross [ɪn'grəʊs] *vt* (a) *attention, person* absorber, captiver. **to be ~ed in** *work* être absorbé par, s'absorber dans; *reading, thoughts* être plongé dans, s'abîmer dans (*liter*). **(b)** (*Jur*) grossoyer.
engrossing [ɪn'grəʊsɪŋ] *adj book, game* absorbant, captivant; *work* absorbant.
engulf [ɪn'gʌlf] *vt* engouffrer, engloutir. **to be ~ed in** s'engouffrer dans, sombrer dans.
enhance [ɪn'hɑːns] *vt attraction, beauty* mettre en valeur, rehausser; *powers* accroître, étendre; *numbers, price, value* augmenter; *position, chances* améliorer; *prestige, reputation* accroître, rehausser.
enharmonic [,enhɑː'mɒnɪk] *adj* enharmonique.
enigma [ɪ'nɪgmə] *n* énigme *f*. (*fig*) **he is an ~** cet homme est une énigme.
enigmatic [,enɪg'mætɪk] *adj* énigmatique.
enigmatically [,enɪg'mætɪkəlɪ] *adv* d'une manière énigmatique.
enjambement [ɪn'dʒæmmənt] *n* enjambement *m*.
enjoin [ɪn'dʒɔɪn] *vt silence, obedience* imposer (*on* à); *discretion, caution* recommander (*on* à). **to ~ sb to do** ordonner *or* prescrire à qn de faire; (*Jur*) **to ~ sb from doing** enjoindre à qn de ne pas faire.
enjoy [ɪn'dʒɔɪ] *vt* (a) (*take pleasure in*) *theatre, cinema, football, music* aimer; *game, pastime* aimer, trouver agréable; *evening, walk, holiday, company, conversation* aimer, prendre plaisir à; *book, meal* apprécier, trouver bon, goûter (*frm*). **to ~ doing** trouver du plaisir *or* prendre plaisir à faire, aimer faire, trouver agréable de faire; **I ~ed doing it** cela m'a fait (grand) plaisir de le faire; **to ~ greatly** se délecter (*sth* de qch, *doing* à faire); **to ~ life** jouir de *or* profiter de la vie; **to ~ a weekend/an evening/holidays** passer un bon weekend/une soirée très agréable/de bonnes vacances; **did you ~ the concert?** le concert vous a-t-il plu?; **to ~ one's dinner** bien manger *or* dîner;

the children ~ed their meal les enfants ont bien mangé *or* ont mangé de bon appétit.

(b) **to ~ o.s.** s'amuser, prendre *or* se donner du bon temps; **did you ~ yourself in Paris?** est-ce que tu t'es bien amusé à Paris?; **~ yourself!** amusez-vous bien!; (*tonight/at weekend*) passez une bonne soirée/ un bon week-end!; **she always ~s herself in the country** elle se plaît toujours à la campagne, elle est toujours contente d'être à la campagne.

(c) (*benefit from*) *income, rights, health, advantage* jouir de.

enjoyable [ɪn'dʒɔɪəbl] *adj visit, evening* agréable; *meal* excellent.

enjoyment [ɪn'dʒɔɪmənt] *n* (*U*) **(a)** plaisir *m.* **to get ~ from (doing) sth** trouver du plaisir à (faire) qch. **(b)** *[rights etc]* jouissance *f*, possession *f* (*of* de).

enlarge [ɪn'lɑːdʒ] **1** *vt house, territory* agrandir; *empire, influence, field of knowledge, circle of friends* étendre; (*Med*) *organ* hypertrophier; *pore* dilater; (*Phot*) agrandir; *business* développer, agrandir; *hole* élargir, agrandir; *numbers* augmenter; *majority* accroître. **~ed edition** édition augmentée.

2 *vi* **(a)** (*grow bigger*) s'agrandir, s'étendre, s'hypertrophier, se dilater, se développer, s'élargir, s'accroître.

(b) to ~ (up)on *subject, difficulties etc* s'étendre sur; *idea* développer.

enlargement [ɪn'lɑːdʒmənt] *n* **(a)** (*V* **enlarge**) agrandissement *m*; dilatation *f*; élargissement *m*; accroissement *m*; hypertrophie *f*. **(b)** (*Phot*) agrandissement *m.*

enlarger [ɪn'lɑːdʒəʳ] *n* (*Phot*) agrandisseur *m.*

enlighten [ɪn'laɪtn] *vt* éclairer (*sb on sth* qn sur qch).

enlightened [ɪn'laɪtnd] *adj person, views, mind* éclairé. (*gen iro*) **in this ~ age** dans notre siècle de lumières, à notre époque éclairée.

enlightening [ɪn'laɪtnɪŋ] *adj* révélateur (*f* -trice) (*about* au sujet de).

enlightenment [ɪn'laɪtnmənt] *n* (*explanations*) éclaircissements *mpl*; (*knowledge*) instruction *f*, édification *f*. **we need some ~ on this point** nous avons besoin de quelques éclaircissements *or* lumières *fpl* sur ce point; **the Age of E~** le Siècle des lumières.

enlist [ɪn'lɪst] **1** *vi* (*Mil etc*) s'engager, s'enrôler (*in* dans). (*US Mil*) **~ed man** simple soldat *m*. **2** *vt recruits* enrôler, engager; *soldiers, supporters* recruter. **to ~ sb's support/sympathy** s'assurer le concours/la sympathie de qn.

enlistment [ɪn'lɪstmənt] *n* (*V* **enlist**) engagement *m*, enrôlement *m*; recrutement *m.*

enliven [ɪn'laɪvn] *vt conversation, visit, evening* animer; *decor, design* mettre une note vive dans, égayer.

enmesh [ɪn'meʃ] *vt* (*lit, fig*) prendre dans un filet. **to get ~ed in** s'empêtrer dans.

enmity ['enmɪtɪ] *n* inimitié *f*, hostilité *f*.

ennoble [ɪ'nəʊbl] *vt* (*lit*) anoblir; (*fig*) *person, mind* ennoblir, élever.

enologist [iː'nɒlədʒɪst] (*US*) = **oenologist.**

enology [iː'nɒlədʒɪ] (*US*) = **oenology.**

enormity [ɪ'nɔːmɪtɪ] *n* **(a)** (*U*) *[action, offence]* énormité *f*. **(b)** (*crime*) crime *m* très grave, outrage *m*; (*blunder*) énormité *f*.

enormous [ɪ'nɔːməs] *adj object, animal, influence, difference* énorme; *patience* immense; *strength* prodigieux; *stature* colossal. **an ~ quantity of** énormément de; **an ~ number of** une masse *or* un tas de; **an ~ number of people** un monde fou, un tas de gens*.

enormously [ɪ'nɔːməslɪ] *adv* (+ *vb or ptp*) énormément; (+ *adj*) extrêmement. **the village has changed ~** le village a énormément changé; **he told an ~ funny story** il a raconté une histoire extrêmement drôle.

enosis ['enəʊsɪs] *n* Enosis *m.*

enough [ɪ'nʌf] **1** *adj, n* assez (de). **~ books** assez de livres; **~ money** assez *or* suffisamment d'argent; **~ to eat** assez à manger; **he earns ~ to live on** il gagne de quoi vivre; **I've had ~ of this novel/of obeying him** j'en ai assez de ce roman/de lui obéir; **you can never have ~ of this music** on ne se lasse jamais de cette musique; **one song was ~ to show he couldn't sing** une chanson a suffi à prouver qu'il ne savait pas chanter; **it is ~ for us to know that ...** il nous suffit de savoir que ...; **that's ~, thanks** cela suffit *or* c'est assez, merci; **that's ~!** ça suffit!; **~ of this!** ça suffit comme ça!*; **~** *or* **'nuff said!**‡ assez parlé! *or* causé!*; **this noise is ~ to drive you mad** ce bruit est à (vous) rendre fou; **I've had more than ~ wine** j'ai bu plus de vin que je n'aurais dû, j'ai bu un peu trop de vin; **there's more than ~ for all** il y en a largement (assez) *or* plus qu'assez pour tous; **~'s ~!*** n'en jetez plus!*; (*Prov*) **~ is as good as a feast** il ne faut pas abuser des meilleures choses.

2 *adv* **(a)** (*sufficiently*) assez, suffisamment. **are you warm ~?** avez-vous assez chaud?; **he has slept long ~** il a suffisamment dormi; **he is old ~ to go alone** il est suffisamment *or* assez grand pour y aller tout seul; **your work is good ~** votre travail est assez bon *or* est honorable; **that's a good ~ excuse** c'est une excuse satisfaisante; **he knows well ~ what I've said** il sait très bien ce que j'ai dit; **I was fool ~** *or* **~ of a fool to believe him** j'ai été assez bête pour le croire.

(b) (*disparaging*) assez. **she is pretty ~** elle est assez jolie, elle n'est pas mal; **he writes well ~** il écrit assez bien, il n'écrit pas mal; **it's good ~ in its way** ce n'est pas (si) mal dans son genre*.

(c) (*intensifying*) **oddly ~, I saw him too** chose curieuse *or* c'est curieux, je l'ai vu aussi; **sure ~ he didn't come** comme je l'avais (*or* on l'avait *etc*) bien prévu il n'est pas venu; **sure ~ I'll be there*** je serai là sans faute.

enquire [ɪn'kwaɪəʳ] *etc* = **inquire** *etc.*

enrage [ɪn'reɪdʒ] *vt* mettre en rage *or* en fureur, rendre furieux. **it ~s me to think that ...** j'enrage *or* je rage* de penser que ... .

enrapture [ɪn'ræptʃəʳ] *vt* ravir, enchanter. **~d by** ravi de, enchanté par.

enrich [ɪn'rɪtʃ] *vt person, language, collection, mind* enrichir; *soil* fertiliser, amender.

enrichment [ɪn'rɪtʃmənt] *n* enrichissement *m*; *[soil]* fertilisation *f*, amendement *m.*

enrol, (*gen US*) enroll [ɪn'rəʊl] **1** *vt workers* embaucher; *students* immatriculer, inscrire; *members* inscrire; *soldiers* enrôler.

2 *vi [labourer etc]* se faire embaucher (*as* comme); (*Univ etc*) se faire immatriculer *or* inscrire, s'inscrire (*in* à, *for* pour); (*Mil*) s'enrôler, s'engager (*in* dans). **to ~ as a member of a club/party** s'inscrire à un club/un parti.

enrolment [ɪn'rəʊlmənt] *n* (*U: V* **enrol**) embauchage *m*; immatriculation *f*; inscription *f*; enrôlement *m*. **school with an ~ of 600** une école avec un effectif de 600 élèves.

ensconce [ɪn'skɒns] *vt*: **to ~ o.s.** bien se caler, bien s'installer; **to be ~d** être bien installé *or* calé.

ensemble [ɑ̃ːnsɑ̃ːmbl] *n* (*Dress, Mus*) ensemble *m.*

enshrine [ɪn'ʃraɪn] *vt* (*Rel*) enchâsser; (*fig*) *memory* conserver pieusement *or* religieusement.

ensign ['ensaɪn] *n* **(a)** ['ensən] (*flag*) drapeau *m*; (*Naut*) pavillon *m*; (*Brit*) **red/white ~** pavillon de la marine marchande/de la marine de guerre; **~-bearer** porte-étendard *m.*

(b) (*emblem*) insigne *m*, emblème *m.*

(c) (*Mil Hist*) (officier *m*) porte-étendard *m.*

(d) (*US Naut*) enseigne *m* de vaisseau.

enslave [ɪn'sleɪv] *vt* (*lit*) réduire en esclavage, asservir; (*fig*) asservir. **to be ~d by tradition** être l'esclave de la tradition.

enslavement [ɪn'sleɪvmənt] *n* asservissement *m.*

ensnare [ɪn'sneəʳ] *vt* (*lit, fig*) prendre au piège; *[woman, charms]* séduire.

ensue [ɪn'sjuː] *vi* s'ensuivre, résulter (*from, on* de).

ensuing [ɪn'sjuːɪŋ] *adj events* qui s'ensuit; *year, day* suivant.

ensure [ɪn'ʃʊəʳ] *vt* **(a)** assurer, garantir. **he did everything to ~ that she came** il a tout fait pour qu'elle vienne *or* pour s'assurer qu'elle viendrait. **(b)** = **insure b.**

entail [ɪn'teɪl] *vt* **(a)** *expense, work, delay* occasionner; *inconvenience, risk, difficulty* comporter; *suffering, hardship* imposer, entraîner. **it ~ed buying a car** cela nécessitait l'achat d'une voiture. **(b)** (*Jur*) **to ~ an estate** substituer un héritage; **~ed estate** biens *mpl* inaliénables.

entangle [ɪn'tæŋgl] *vt* (*catch up*) empêtrer, enchevêtrer; (*twist together*) *hair* emmêler; *wool, thread* emmêler, embrouiller; (*fig*) *person* entraîner, impliquer (*in* dans), mêler (*in* à). **to become ~d in an affair** s'empêtrer *or* se laisser entraîner dans une affaire; **to become ~d in ropes/lies/explanations** s'empêtrer dans des cordages/des mensonges/des explications.

entanglement [ɪn'tæŋglmənt] *n* (*V* **entangle**) (*lit*) enchevêtrement *m*, emmêlement *m*; (*fig*) implication *f*. **his ~ with the police** son affaire *f* avec la police.

enter ['entəʳ] **1** *vt* **(a)** (*come or go into*) *house etc* entrer dans, pénétrer dans; *vehicle* monter dans, entrer dans; *path, road etc* s'engager dans. **he ~ed the grocer's** il est entré chez l'épicier *or* dans l'épicerie; (*Naut*) **to ~ harbour** entrer au port *or* dans le port; **the thought never ~ed my head** cette pensée ne m'est jamais venue à l'esprit; **he is ~ing his sixtieth year** il entre dans sa soixantième année.

(b) (*become member of*) *a profession, the army etc* entrer dans; *university, college etc* s'inscrire à, se faire inscrire à *or* dans. **to ~ the Church** se faire prêtre, recevoir la prêtrise; **to ~ society** faire ses débuts dans le monde.

(c) (*submit, write down*) *amount, name, fact, order* (*on list etc*) inscrire; (*in notebook*) noter. **to ~ an item in the ledger** porter un article sur le livre de comptes; (*Comm*) **~ these purchases to me** mettez *or* portez ces achats à *or* sur mon compte; **to ~ a horse for a race** engager *or* inscrire un cheval dans une course; **to ~ a dog for a show** présenter un chien dans un concours; **to ~ a pupil for an exam/a competition** présenter un élève à un examen/à un concours; **he has ~ed his son for Eton** il a inscrit son fils (à l'avance) à Eton; **to ~ a protest** rédiger *or* élever *or* présenter une protestation; (*Jur*) **to ~ an appeal** interjeter appel.

2 *vi* **(a)** entrer. (*Theat*) **~ Macbeth** entre Macbeth.

(b) to ~ for a race s'inscrire pour une course; **to ~ for an examination** se présenter à un examen.

enter into *vt fus* **(a)** *explanation, apology* se lancer dans; *correspondence, conversation* entrer en; *plot* prendre part à; *negotiations* entamer; *contract* passer; *alliance* conclure.

(b) *sb's plans, calculations* entrer dans. (*lit, fig*) **to enter into the spirit of the game** entrer dans le jeu; **her money doesn't enter into it at all** son argent n'y est pour rien *or* n'a rien à voir là-dedans.

enter up *vt sep sum of money, amount* inscrire; *diary, ledger* tenir à jour.

enter (up)on *vt fus career* débuter dans, entrer dans; *negotiations* entamer; *alliance* conclure; *subject* aborder; *inheritance* prendre possession de.

enteric [en'terɪk] *adj* entérique. **~ fever** (fièvre *f*) typhoïde *f*.

enteritis [ˌentə'raɪtɪs] *n* entérite *f*.

enterprise ['entəpraɪz] *n* **(a)** (*undertaking, company*) entreprise *f*. **(b)** (*U: spirit*) (esprit *m* d')initiative *f*, esprit entreprenant, hardiesse *f*; *V* **free** *etc.*

enterprising ['entəpraɪzɪŋ] *adj person* plein d'initiative, entreprenant; *venture* audacieux, hardi. **that was ~ of you!** vous avez fait preuve d'initiative!, vous avez eu de l'idée!*

enterprisingly ['entəpraɪzɪŋlɪ] *adv* hardiment, audacieusement, avec audace.

entertain [ˌentə'teɪn] *vt* **(a)** (*amuse*) amuser, divertir; distraire.

(b) *guests* recevoir. **to ~ sb to dinner** offrir un dîner à qn; (*at home*) recevoir qn à dîner; **they ~ a lot** ils reçoivent beaucoup.
(c) (*bear in mind*) *thought* considérer, méditer; *intention, suspicion, doubt, hope* nourrir; *proposal* accueillir favorablement. **I wouldn't ~ it for a moment** je repousserais tout de suite une telle idée.
entertainer [ˌentəˈteɪnəʳ] *n* artiste *mf* (de music-hall *etc*), fantaisiste *mf*. **a well-known radio ~** un(e) artiste bien connu(e) à la radio; **he's a born ~** c'est un amuseur né.
entertaining [ˌentəˈteɪnɪŋ] **1** *adj* amusant, divertissant. **2** *n*: **she does a lot of ~** elle reçoit beaucoup; **their ~ is always sumptuous** ils reçoivent toujours avec faste, leurs réceptions sont toujours fastueuses.
entertainingly [ˌentəˈteɪnɪŋlɪ] *adv* d'une façon amusante *or* divertissante.
entertainment [ˌentəˈteɪnmənt] **1** *n* **(a)** (*U: amusement*) amusement *m*, divertissement *m*, distraction *f*. **much to the ~ of** au grand amusement de; **for your ~ we have invited ...** pour vous distraire *or* amuser nous avons invité ...; **for my own ~** pour mon divertissement personnel; **the cinema is my favourite ~** le cinéma est ma distraction préférée.
(b) (*performance*) spectacle *m*, attractions *fpl*. **musical ~** soirée musicale.
2 *cpd*: **entertainment allowance** frais *mpl* de représentation; **entertainment tax** taxe *f* sur les spectacles; **the entertainment world** le monde du spectacle.
enthral(l) [ɪnˈθrɔːl] *vt [book, film, talk etc]* captiver, passionner; *[beauty, charm]* séduire, ensorceler; (††: *enslave*) asservir. **enthralled by what one is reading** captivé par une lecture.
enthralling [ɪnˈθrɔːlɪŋ] *adj story, film* passionnant; *beauty* ensorcelant.
enthrone [ɪnˈθrəʊn] *vt king* placer sur le trône, introniser; *bishop* introniser. (*liter*) **to sit ~d** trôner; (*fig*) **~d in the hearts of his countrymen** vénéré par ses compatriotes.
enthuse* [ɪnˈθuːz] *vi*: **to ~ over sb/sth** porter qn/qch aux nues, parler avec (beaucoup d')enthousiasme de qn/qch, être emballé par qn/qch.
enthusiasm [ɪnˈθuːzɪæzəm] *n* (*U*) enthousiasme *m* (*for* pour). **to move *or* arouse to ~** enthousiasmer; **I haven't much ~ for going out** cela ne me dit pas grand-chose de sortir*.
enthusiast [ɪnˈθuːzɪæst] *n* enthousiaste *mf*. **he is a jazz/bridge/sport** *etc* **~** il se passionne pour le *or* il est passionné de jazz/bridge/sport *etc*; **all these football ~s** tous ces passionnés *or* enragés* de football; **a Vivaldi ~** un(e) fervent(e) de Vivaldi.
enthusiastic [ɪnˌθuːzɪˈæstɪk] *adj person, attitude, response* enthousiaste; *welcome* enthousiaste, chaleureux; *shout* enthousiaste, d'enthousiasme. **an ~ swimmer** un nageur passionné *or* enragé*; **an ~ supporter** un partisan enthousiaste *or* fervent *or* passionné (*of* de); **to grow *or* wax ~ over** s'enthousiasmer *or* se passionner pour; **to be ~ about** être passionné de; **he was very ~ about the plan** il a accueilli le projet avec enthousiasme.
enthusiastically [ɪnˌθuːzɪˈæstɪkəlɪ] *adv receive, speak, applaud* avec enthousiasme; *work* avec zèle, avec ferveur, avec élan; *support* avec enthousiasme, avec ferveur.
entice [ɪnˈtaɪs] *vt* (*attract*) attirer; (*lure*) entraîner; (*with blandishments*) séduire; (*with food, prospects*) allécher; (*with false promises*) leurrer; *animal* attirer; (*with food*) allécher; (*with bait*) appâter. **to ~ sb away from sb** éloigner qn de qn (par la ruse); **to ~ sb away from a place** entraîner qn (par la ruse) à l'écart d'un endroit; **to ~ sb into a room** attirer qn (par la ruse) dans une pièce; **to ~ sb to do** entraîner qn (par la ruse) à faire.
enticement [ɪnˈtaɪsmənt] *n* (*act*) séduction *f*; (*attraction*) attrait *m*.
enticing [ɪnˈtaɪsɪŋ] *adj person* séduisant; *prospects, offer* attrayant; *food* alléchant, appétissant.
entire [ɪnˈtaɪəʳ] *adj* **(a)** (*total*) entier, tout. **the ~ week** la semaine entière, toute la semaine; **the ~ world** le monde entier.
(b) (*complete*) entier, complet (*f* -ète); (*unreserved*) total, absolu. **the ~ house** la maison (tout) entière; **the ~ text** le texte tout entier; (*unexpurgated*) le texte intégral; **my ~ confidence** mon entière confiance, ma confiance totale *or* absolue.
(c) (*unbroken*) entier, intact.
entirely [ɪnˈtaɪəlɪ] *adv* entièrement, tout à fait, totalement, absolument, complètement; *change* du tout au tout.
entirety [ɪnˈtaɪərətɪ] *n* intégralité *f*, intégrité *f*, totalité *f*. **in its ~** en (son) entier, intégralement.
entitle [ɪnˈtaɪtl] *vt* **(a)** *book* intituler. **to be ~d** s'intituler.
(b) (*bestow right on*) autoriser, habiliter (*Jur*) (*to do* à faire). **to ~ sb to sth** donner droit à qch à qn; **to ~ sb to do** donner à qn le droit de faire; **this ticket ~s the bearer to do ...** ce billet donne au porteur le droit de faire ...; **to be ~d to sth** avoir droit à qch; **to be ~d to do** (*by position, qualifications*) avoir qualité pour faire, être habilité à faire (*Jur*); (*by conditions, rules*) avoir le droit *or* être en droit de faire; **these statements ~ us to believe that ...** ces déclarations nous autorisent à croire que ... .
entity [ˈentɪtɪ] *n* entité *f*.
entomb [ɪnˈtuːm] *vt* mettre au tombeau, ensevelir; (*fig*) ensevelir.
entombment [ɪnˈtuːmmənt] *n* mise *f* au tombeau, ensevelissement *m*.
entomological [ˌentəməˈlɒdʒɪkəl] *adj* entomologique.
entomologist [ˌentəˈmɒlədʒɪst] *n* entomologiste *mf*.
entomology [ˌentəˈmɒlədʒɪ] *n* entomologie *f*.
entourage [ˌɒntʊˈrɑːʒ] *n* entourage *m*.
entr'acte [ˈɒntrækt] *n* entracte *m*.
entrails [ˈentreɪlz] *npl* (*lit, fig*) entrailles *fpl*.
entrain [ɪnˈtreɪn] **1** *vt* (faire) embarquer dans un train. **2** *vi* s'embarquer dans un train.
entrance[1] [ˈentrəns] **1** *n* **(a)** (*way in*) entrée *f* (*to* de); (*hall*) entrée, vestibule *m*; *V* **trade**.
(b) (*act*) entrée *f*. **on his ~** à son entrée; (*esp Theat*) **to make an ~** faire son entrée; **to force an ~ into** forcer l'entrée de; **door giving ~ to a room** porte qui donne accès à une pièce.
(c) (*right to enter*) admission *f*. **~ to a school** admission à *or* dans une école; **to gain ~ to a university** être admis à *or* dans une université.
2 *cpd*: **entrance card** carte *f or* billet *m* d'entrée *or* d'admission; **entrance examination** examen *m* d'entrée; (*Brit*) **entrance fee** droit *m* d'inscription; **entrance ticket = entrance card**.
entrance[2] [ɪnˈtrɑːns] *vt* transporter, ravir, enivrer. **she stood there ~d** elle restait là extasiée *or* en extase.
entrancing [ɪnˈtrɑːnsɪŋ] *adj* enchanteur (*f* -teresse), ravissant, séduisant.
entrancingly [ɪnˈtrɑːnsɪŋlɪ] *adv dance, sing* à ravir; *smile* d'une façon ravissante *or* séduisante. **she is ~ beautiful** elle est belle à ravir.
entrant [ˈentrənt] *n* (*to profession*) débutant(e) *m(f)* (*to* dans, en); (*in race*) concurrent(e) *m(f)*, participant(e) *m(f)*; (*in competition*) candidat(e) *m(f)*, concurrent(e); (*in exam*) candidat(e).
entrap [ɪnˈtræp] *vt* prendre au piège. **to ~ sb into doing sth** amener qn à faire qch par la ruse *or* la feinte.
entreat [ɪnˈtriːt] *vt* supplier, implorer, prier instamment (*sb to do* qn de faire). **listen to him I ~ you** écoutez-le je vous en supplie *or* je vous en conjure; **to ~ sth of sb** demander instamment qch à qn; **to ~ sb for help** implorer le secours de qn.
entreatingly [ɪnˈtriːtɪŋlɪ] *adj look* d'un air suppliant; *ask* d'un ton suppliant, d'une voix suppliante.
entreaty [ɪnˈtriːtɪ] *n* prière *f*, supplication *f*. **at his (earnest) ~** sur ses (vives) instances *fpl*; **a look of ~** un regard suppliant.
entrée [ˈɒntreɪ] *n* entrée *f*.
entrench [ɪnˈtrentʃ] *vt* (*Mil*) retrancher. (*fig*) **customs ~ed by long tradition** coutumes implantées par une longue tradition; **to be ~ed in one's post** être bien ancré à son poste, être indélogeable.
entrenchment [ɪnˈtrentʃmənt] *n* (*Mil*) retranchement *m*.
entrepôt [ˈɒntrəpəʊ] *n* entrepôt *m*.
entrepreneur [ˌɒntrəprəˈnɜːʳ] *n* entrepreneur *m*.
entropy [ˈentrəpɪ] *n* entropie *f*.
entrust [ɪnˈtrʌst] *vt secrets, valuables, letters,* confier (*to* à); *child* confier (*to sb* à qn, à la garde de qn); *prisoner* confier (*to* à la garde de). **to ~ sb/sth to sb's care** confier *or* remettre qn/qch aux soins de qn; **to ~ sb with a task** charger qn d'une tâche, confier à qn une tâche; **to ~ sb with the job of doing** charger qn de faire qch, confier à qn le soin de faire qch.
entry [ˈentrɪ] **1** *n* **(a)** (*action*) entrée *f*. **to make an ~** faire son entrée; (*Theat*) **to make one's ~** entrer en scène; **'no ~'** (*on gate etc*) 'défense d'entrer', 'entrée interdite'; (*in one-way street*) 'sens interdit'.
(b) (*way in*) *[building, mine etc]* entrée *f*; *[cathedral]* portail *m*.
(c) (*item*) *[list]* inscription *f*; *[account book, ledger]* écriture *f*; *[dictionary]* (*term*) entrée *f*; (*headword*) adresse *f*, entrée; (*article*) article *m*. (*Book-keeping*) **single/double ~** comptabilité *f* en partie simple/double; (*Naut*) **~ in the log** entrée du journal de bord.
(d) (*Sport etc*) **there is a large ~ for the 200 metres** il y a une longue liste de concurrents pour le 200 mètres; **there are only 3 entries** (*for race, competition*) il n'y a que 3 concurrents; (*for exam*) il n'y a que 3 candidats.
2 *cpd*: **entry form** feuille *f* d'inscription; **entry permit** visa *m* d'entrée; (*US Lexicography*) **entry word** entrée *f*, adresse *f*.
entwine [ɪnˈtwaɪn] **1** *vt stems, ribbons* entrelacer; *garland* tresser; (*twist around*) enlacer (*with* de). **2** *vi* s'entrelacer, s'enlacer, s'entortiller (*around* autour de).
enumerate [ɪˈnjuːməreɪt] *vt* énumérer, dénombrer.
enumeration [ɪˌnjuːməˈreɪʃən] *n* énumération *f*, dénombrement *m*.
enunciate [ɪˈnʌnsɪeɪt] *vt sound, word* prononcer, articuler; *principle, theory* énoncer, exposer. **to ~ clearly** bien articuler.
enunciation [ɪˌnʌnsɪˈeɪʃən] *n [sound, word]* articulation *f*; *[theory]* énonciation *f*, exposition *f*; *[problem]* énoncé *m*.
enuresis [ˌenjʊˈriːsɪs] *n* énurésie *f*.
enuretic [ˌenjəˈretɪk] *adj* énurétique.
envelop [ɪnˈveləp] *vt* envelopper (*also fig*). **~ed in a blanket** enveloppé dans une couverture; **~ed in clouds/snow** enveloppé de nuages/neige; **~ed in mystery** enveloppé *or* entouré de mystère.
envelope [ˈenvələʊp] *n [letter, balloon, airship]* enveloppe *f*; (*Bio, Bot*) enveloppe, tunique *f*; (*Math*) enveloppe. **to put a letter in an ~** mettre une lettre sous enveloppe; **in a sealed ~** sous pli cacheté; **in the same ~** sous le même pli.
envelopment [ɪnˈveləpmənt] *n* enveloppement *m*.
envenom [ɪnˈvenəm] *vt* (*lit, fig*) envenimer.
enviable [ˈenvɪəbl] *adj position, wealth, beauty* enviable; *fate* enviable, digne d'envie.
envious [ˈenvɪəs] *adj person* envieux; *look, tone* envieux, d'envie. **to be ~ of sth** être envieux de qch; **to be ~ of sb** être jaloux de qn, envier qn; **to make sb ~** exciter *or* attirer l'envie de qn; **people were ~ of his success** son succès a fait des envieux *or* des jaloux.
enviously [ˈenvɪəslɪ] *adv* avec envie.
environment [ɪnˈvaɪərənmənt] *n* (*Bio, Bot, Geog*) milieu *m*; (*Admin, Pol*) environnement *m*; (*physical*) cadre *m*, milieu, environnement; (*social*) milieu, environnement; (*moral*) milieu, climat *m*, ambiance *f*. **cultural ~** climat *or* milieu culturel; (*fig*) **hostile ~** climat d'hostilité, ambiance hostile;

natural ~ milieu naturel; **his normal ~** son cadre *or* son milieu normal; **working-class ~** milieu ouvrier; **heredity or ~** l'hérédité ou l'environnement; **pollution/protection of the ~** la pollution/la protection de l'environnement; (*Brit*) **Secretary (of State) for** *or* **Minister of the E~** ministre *m* de l'Environnement; **Department** *or* **Ministry of the E~** ministère *m* de l'Environnement.

environmental [ɪnˌvaɪərənˈmentl] *adj conditions, changes* écologique, du milieu; *influence* exercé par le milieu *or* l'environnement. **~ studies** l'écologie *f*.

environmentalist [ɪnˌvaɪərənˈmentəlɪst] *n* environnementaliste *mf*.

environs [ɪnˈvaɪərənz] *npl* environs *mpl*, alentours *mpl*, abords *mpl*.

envisage [ɪnˈvɪzɪdʒ] *vt* (*foresee*) prévoir; (*imagine*) envisager. **it is ~d that ...** on prévoit que ...; **an increase is ~d next year** on prévoit une augmentation pour l'année prochaine; **it is hard to ~ such a situation** il est difficile d'envisager une telle situation.

envoy[1] [ˈenvɔɪ] *n* (*gen*) envoyé(e) *m(f)*, représentant(e) *m(f)*; (*diplomat, also* **~ extraordinary**) ministre *m* plénipotentiaire.

envoy[2] [ˈenvɔɪ] *n* (*Poetry*) envoi *m*.

envy [ˈenvɪ] **1** *n* envie *f*, jalousie *f*. **out of ~** par envie, par jalousie; **filled with ~** dévoré de jalousie; **it was the ~ of everyone** cela faisait *or* excitait l'envie de tout le monde; *V* **green**. **2** *vt person, thing* envier. **to ~ sb sth** envier qch à qn.

enzyme [ˈenzaɪm] *n* enzyme *f*.

eolithic [ˌiːəʊˈlɪθɪk] *adj* éolithique.

eon [ˈiːɒn] *n* = **aeon**.

epaulette [ˈepɔːlet] *n* (*Mil*) épaulette *f*.

ephedrine [ˈefɪdrɪn] *n* éphédrine *f*.

ephemeral [ɪˈfemərəl] *adj* (*Bot, Zool*) éphémère; (*fig*) éphémère, fugitif.

ephemerid [ɪˈfemərɪd] *n* éphémère *m*.

ephemeris [ɪˈfemərɪs] *n* éphéméride *f*.

epic [ˈepɪk] **1** *adj* (*Literat*) épique; (*fig*) héroïque, épique; (*hum*) épique, homérique. **2** *n* épopée *f*, poème *m or* récit *m* épique. (*Cine*) **an ~ of the screen** un film à grand spectacle.

epicarp [ˈepɪkɑːp] *n* épicarpe *m*.

epicene [ˈepɪsiːn] *adj manners, literature* efféminé; (*Gram*) épicène.

epicentre [ˈepɪsentəʳ] *n* épicentre *m*.

epicure [ˈepɪkjʊəʳ] *n* (fin) gourmet *m*, gastronome *mf*.

epicurean [ˌepɪkjʊəˈriːən] *adj, n* épicurien(ne) *m(f)*.

epicureanism [ˌepɪkjʊəˈrɪənɪzəm] *n* épicurisme *m*.

epicyclic [epɪˈsaɪklɪk] *adj*: **~ gear** *or* **train** train épicycloïdal.

epidemic [ˌepɪˈdemɪk] **1** *n* épidémie *f*. **2** *adj* épidémique.

epidermis [ˌepɪˈdɜːmɪs] *n* (*Anat, Bot, Zool*) épiderme *m*.

epigenesis [ˌepɪˈdʒenɪsɪs] *n* (*Biol*) épigénèse *f*; (*Geol*) épigénie *f*.

epiglottis [ˌepɪˈglɒtɪs] *n* épiglotte *f*.

epigram [ˈepɪgræm] *n* épigramme *f*.

epigrammatic(al) [ˌepɪgrəˈmætɪk(əl)] *adj* épigrammatique.

epigraph [ˈepɪgrɑːf] *n* épigraphe *f*.

epilepsy [ˈepɪlepsɪ] *n* épilepsie *f*.

epileptic [ˌepɪˈleptɪk] **1** *adj* épileptique. **~ fit** crise *f* d'épilepsie. **2** *n* épileptique *mf*.

epilogue [ˈepɪlɒg] *n* (*Literat*) épilogue *m*.

epinephrine [ˌepəˈnefrɪn] *n* (*US*) adrénaline *f*.

Epiphany [ɪˈpɪfənɪ] *n* Épiphanie *f*, jour *m or* fête *f* des Rois.

epiphytic [ˌepɪˈfɪtɪk] *adj* épiphyte.

episcopal [ɪˈpɪskəpəl] *adj* épiscopal. **~ ring** anneau pastoral *or* épiscopal; **the E~ Church** l'Église épiscopale.

episcopalian [ɪˌpɪskəˈpeɪlɪən] **1** *adj* épiscopal (*de l'Église épiscopale*). **2** *n* membre *m* de l'Église épiscopale. **the ~s** les épiscopaux *mpl*.

episode [ˈepɪsəʊd] *n* épisode *m*.

episodic [ˌepɪˈsɒdɪk] *adj* épisodique.

epistemology [ɪˌpɪstəˈmɒlədʒɪ] *n* épistémologie *f*.

epistle [ɪˈpɪsl] *n* épître *f*.

epistolary [ɪˈpɪstələrɪ] *adj* épistolaire.

epitaph [ˈepɪtɑːf] *n* épitaphe *f*.

epithelium [ˌepɪˈθiːlɪəm] *n* épithélium *m*.

epithet [ˈepɪθet] *n* épithète *f*.

epitome [ɪˈpɪtəmɪ] *n* [*book*] abrégé *m*, résumé *m*; (*fig*) [*virtue, goodness*] modèle *m*, type *m or* exemple *m* même; [*idea, subject*] quintessence *f*.

epitomize [ɪˈpɪtəmaɪz] *vt book* abréger, résumer; *quality, virtue* incarner, personnifier.

epoch [ˈiːpɒk] **1** *n* époque *f*, période *f*. (*fig*) **to mark an ~** faire époque, faire date. **2** *cpd*: **epoch-making** qui fait époque, qui fait date.

epoxy [ɪˈpɒksɪ] *n*: **~ resin** résine *f* époxyde.

Epsom salts [ˈepsəmˈsɔːltz] *npl* sel *m* d'Epsom, sulfate *m* de magnésium.

equable [ˈekwəbl] *adj temperament, climate* égal. **he is very ~** il a un tempérament très égal.

equably [ˈekwəblɪ] *adv* tranquillement.

equal [ˈiːkwəl] **1** *adj* (*Math, gen*) égal (*to* à); *temperament* égal. **~ in number** égal en nombre; **to be ~ to sth** égaler qch; **~ pay for ~ work** à travail égal salaire égal; **~ pay for women** salaire égal pour les femmes; **other** *or* **all things (being) ~** toutes choses égales d'ailleurs; **an ~ sum of money** une même somme d'argent; **with ~ indifference** avec la même indifférence; (*in value etc*) **they are about ~** ils se valent à peu près; **to talk to sb on ~ terms** parler à qn d'égal à égal; **to be on an ~ footing (with sb)** être sur un pied d'égalité (avec qn); **to be ~ to the task/the emergency** être à la hauteur de la tâche/des circonstances critiques; **to be ~ to doing** être de force à *or* de taille à faire; **she did not feel ~ to going out** elle ne se sentait pas le courage *or* la force de sortir, elle ne se sentait pas capable de sortir.

2 *n* égal(e) *m(f)*, pair *m*, pareil(le) *m(f)*. **our ~s** nos égaux; **to treat sb as an ~** traiter qn d'égal à égal; **she has no ~** elle n'a pas sa pareille, elle est hors pair; (*in rank, standing*) **she is his ~** elle est son égale.

3 *vt* (*Math, gen*) égaler (*in* en). **not to be ~led** sans égal, qui n'a pas son égal; **there is nothing to ~ it** il n'y a rien de tel *or* de comparable; (*Math*) **let x ~ y** si x égale y.

4 *cpd*: (*Math*) **equal(s) sign** signe *m* d'égalité *or* d'équivalence.

equality [ɪˈkwɒlɪtɪ] *n* égalité *f*. **~ in the eyes of the law** égalité devant la loi.

equalize [ˈiːkwəlaɪz] **1** *vt chances, opportunities* égaliser; *wealth, possessions* niveler. **2** *vi* (*Sport*) égaliser.

equalizer [ˈiːkwəlaɪzəʳ] *n* (*Sport*) but *or* point égalisateur.

equally [ˈiːkwəlɪ] *adv* également. **to divide sth ~** diviser qch en parts *or* parties égales; **her mother was ~ disappointed** sa mère a été tout aussi déçue; **she did ~ well in history** elle a eu de tout aussi bons résultats en histoire; **it would be ~ wrong to suggest** il serait tout aussi faux de suggérer; **~ gifted brothers** frères également *or* pareillement doués; **they were ~ guilty** ils étaient également coupables *or* coupables au même degré.

equanimity [ˌekwəˈnɪmɪtɪ] *n* égalité *f* d'humeur, sérénité *f*, équanimité *f* (*frm*). **with ~** avec sérénité, d'une âme égale.

equate [ɪˈkweɪt] *vt* (*identify*) assimiler (*with* à); (*compare*) mettre sur le même pied (*with* que); (*Math*) mettre en équation (*to* avec); (*make equal*) égaler, égaliser. **to ~ Eliot with Shakespeare** mettre Eliot sur le même pied que Shakespeare; **to ~ black with mourning** assimiler le noir au deuil; **to ~ supply and demand** égaler *or* égaliser l'offre à la demande.

equation [ɪˈkweɪʒən] *n* (*V* **equate**) assimilation *f*; égalisation *f*; (*Chem, Math*) équation *f*. (*Astron*) **~ of time** équation du temps; *V* **quadratic, simple**.

equator [ɪˈkweɪtəʳ] *n* équateur *m* (terrestre), ligne équinoxiale. **at the ~** sous l'équateur.

equatorial [ˌekwəˈtɔːrɪəl] *adj* équatorial.

equerry [ɪˈkwerɪ] *n* écuyer *m* (*au service d'un membre de la famille royale*).

equestrian [ɪˈkwestrɪən] **1** *adj* équestre. **2** *n* (*gen*) cavalier *m*, -ière *f*; (*in circus*) écuyer *m*, -ère *f*.

equi ... [ˈiːkwɪ] *pref* équi ... .

equidistant [ˈiːkwɪˈdɪstənt] *adj* équidistant.

equilateral [ˈiːkwɪˈlætərəl] *adj* équilatéral.

equilibrium [ˌiːkwɪˈlɪbrɪəm] *n* (*physical, mental*) équilibre *m*. **to lose one's ~** (*physically*) perdre l'équilibre; (*mentally*) devenir déséquilibré; **in ~** en équilibre.

equine [ˈekwaɪn] *adj species, profile* chevalin.

equinoctial [ˌiːkwɪˈnɒkʃəl] *adj* équinoxial; *gales, tides* d'équinoxe.

equinox [ˈiːkwɪnɒks] *n* équinoxe *m*. **vernal** *or* **spring ~** équinoxe de printemps, point vernal; **autumnal ~** équinoxe d'automne.

equip [ɪˈkwɪp] *vt* **(a)** (*fit out*) *factory* équiper, outiller; *kitchen, laboratory* aménager (*as* en), installer, équiper; *ship, soldier, worker, astronaut* équiper. **to ~ a household** monter un ménage; (*fig*) **he is well ~ped for the job** il a les compétences *or* les qualités nécessaires pour ce travail.

(b) (*provide*) *person* équiper, pourvoir, munir (*with* de); *ship, car, factory, army etc* équiper, munir, doter (*with* de). **to ~ o.s. with** s'équiper de, se munir de, se pourvoir de; **she is well ~ped with cookery books** elle est bien montée *or* pourvue en livres de cuisine; **to ~ a ship with radar** installer le radar sur un bateau.

equipage [ˈekwɪpɪdʒ] *n* équipage *m* (*chevaux et personnel*).

equipment [ɪˈkwɪpmənt] *n* (*U*) équipement *m*. **factory ~** outillage *m*; **laboratory/office/lifesaving/camping ~** matériel *m* de laboratoire/de bureau/de sauvetage/de camping; **electrical ~** appareillage *m* électrique; **domestic ~** appareils ménagers.

equisetum [ˌekwɪˈsiːtəm] *n* equisetum *m*, prêle *f*.

equitable [ˈekwɪtəbl] *adj* équitable, juste.

equitably [ˈekwɪtəblɪ] *adv* équitablement, avec justice.

equitation [ˌekwɪˈteɪʃən] *n* (*frm*) équitation *f*.

equity [ˈekwɪtɪ] *n* **(a)** (*U*) équité *f*. **(b)** (*Brit St Ex*) **equities** actions *fpl* (cotées en bourse).

equivalence [ɪˈkwɪvələns] *n* équivalence *f*.

equivalent [ɪˈkwɪvələnt] **1** *adj* équivalent. **to be ~ to** être équivalent à, équivaloir à. **2** *n* équivalent *m* (*in* en). **the French ~ of the English word** l'équivalent en français du mot anglais.

equivocal [ɪˈkwɪvəkəl] *adj* (*ambiguous*) *attitude* équivoque, peu net; *words* équivoque, ambigu (*f* -guë); (*suspicious*) *behaviour* louche, douteux; (*unclear*) *outcome* incertain, douteux.

equivocally [ɪˈkwɪvəkəlɪ] *adv* d'une manière équivoque, avec ambiguïté.

equivocate [ɪˈkwɪvəkeɪt] *vi* user de faux-fuyants *or* d'équivoques, équivoquer (*liter*).

equivocation [ɪˈkwɪvəˈkeɪʃən] *n* (*often pl*) paroles *fpl* équivoques, emploi *m* d'équivoques.

era [ˈɪərə] *n* (*Geol, Hist*) ère *f*; (*gen*) époque *f*, temps *m*. **the Christian ~** l'ère chrétienne; **the end of an ~** la fin d'une époque; **the ~ of crinolines** le temps des crinolines; **to mark an ~** marquer une époque, faire époque.

eradicate [ɪˈrædɪkeɪt] *vt vice, malpractices* extirper, supprimer; *disease* faire disparaître, supprimer; *superstition* bannir, mettre fin à; *weeds* détruire.

eradication [ɪˌrædɪˈkeɪʃən] *n* (*V* **eradicate**) suppression *f*, fin *f*; destruction *f*.

erase [ɪˈreɪz] **1** *vt writing, marks* effacer, gratter; (*with rubber*) gommer; (*Computers, Sound Recording; also from the mind*) effacer. **2** *cpd*: **erase head** tête *f* d'effacement.

eraser [ɪˈreɪzəʳ] *n (rubber)* gomme *f*; *(liquid: for typing)* liquide correcteur.

Erasmus [ɪˈræzməs] *n* Érasme *m*.

erasure [ɪˈreɪʒəʳ] *n* rature *f*, grattage *m*; *(act of erasing)* grattage, effacement *m*.

ere [ɛəʳ] *(liter, ††)* **1** *prep* avant. ~ **now** déjà; ~ **then** d'ici là; ~ **long** sous peu. **2** *conj* avant que + *subj*.

erect [ɪˈrekt] **1** *adj (straight)* (bien) droit; *(standing)* debout. **to hold o.s.** ~ se tenir droit; **with head** ~ la tête haute; **with tail** ~ la queue levée *or* dressée en l'air.

2 *vt temple, statue* ériger, élever; *wall, flats, factory* bâtir, construire; *machinery, traffic signs* installer; *scaffolding, furniture* monter; *altar, tent, mast, barricade* dresser; *(fig) theory* bâtir; *obstacles* élever.

erection [ɪˈrekʃən] *n* **(a)** *(U: V* **erect***)* érection *f*, construction *f*; installation *f*; montage *m*; dressage *m*; *[theory, obstacle]* édification *f*. **(b)** *(building, structure)* construction *f*, bâtiment *m*. **(c)** *(Physiol)* érection *f*.

erg [ɜːg] *n* erg *m*.

ergonomics [ˌɜːgəʊˈnɒmɪks] *n (U)* ergonomie *f*.

ergot [ˈɜːgət] *n (Agr)* ergot *m*; *(Pharm)* ergot de seigle.

ergotism [ˈɜːgətɪzəm] *n* ergotisme *m*.

Erin [ˈɪərɪn] *n (liter, ††)* Irlande *f*.

ermine [ˈɜːmɪn] *n (animal, fur, robes)* hermine *f*.

erode [ɪˈrəʊd] *vt [water, wind, sea]* éroder, ronger; *[acid, rust]* ronger, corroder; *(fig)* ronger, miner, corroder.

erogenous [ɪˈrɒdʒənəs] *adj* érogène.

Eros [ˈiːrɒs] *n* Éros *m*.

erosion [ɪˈrəʊʒən] *n (V* **erode***)* érosion *f*; corrosion *f*.

erosive [ɪˈrəʊzɪv] *adj (V* **erode***)* érosif; corrosif.

erotic [ɪˈrɒtɪk] *adj* érotique.

erotica [ɪˈrɒtɪkə] *npl (Art)* art *m* érotique; *(Literat)* littérature *f* érotique.

eroticism [ɪˈrɒtɪsɪzəm] *n* érotisme *m*.

err [ɜːʳ] *vi (be mistaken)* se tromper; *(sin)* pécher, commettre une faute. **to** ~ **in one's judgment** faire une erreur de jugement; **to** ~ **on the side of caution** pécher par excès de prudence; **to** ~ **is human** l'erreur est humaine.

errand [ˈerənd] *n* commission *f*, course *f*. **to go on** *or* **run** ~**s** faire des commissions *or* des courses; **to be on an** ~ être en course; ~ **of mercy** mission *f* de charité; ~ **boy** garçon *m* de courses; *V* **fool**[1].

errant [ˈerənt] *adj (sinful)* dévoyé; *(wandering)* errant; *V* **knight**.

errata [eˈrɑːtə] *npl of* **erratum**.

erratic [ɪˈrætɪk] *adj person* fantasque, capricieux; *record, results* irrégulier; *performance* irrégulier, inégal; *mood* changeant; *(Geol, Med)* erratique. **his driving is** ~ il conduit de façon déconcertante.

erratically [ɪˈrætɪkəlɪ] *adv act* capricieusement; *work* irrégulièrement, par à-coups. **to drive** ~ conduire de façon déconcertante.

erratum [eˈrɑːtəm] *n, pl* **errata** erratum *m*.

erroneous [ɪˈrəʊnɪəs] *adj* erroné, faux (*f* fausse).

erroneously [ɪˈrəʊnɪəslɪ] *adv* erronément, faussement, à tort.

error [ˈerəʳ] *n* **(a)** *(mistake)* erreur *f (also Math)*, faute *f*. **to make** *or* **commit an** ~ faire (une) erreur, commettre une erreur, se tromper; **it would be an** ~ **to underestimate him** on aurait tort de le sous-estimer; ~ **of judgment** erreur de jugement; ~ **in calculation** erreur de calcul; *(Naut)* **compass** ~ variation *f* du compas; *(Comm)* ~**s and omissions excepted** sauf erreur ou omission; *V* **margin, spelling** *etc*.

(b) *(U)* erreur *f*. **in** ~ par erreur, par méprise; *(Rel)* **to be in/fall into** ~ être/tomber dans l'erreur; **to see the** ~ **of one's ways** revenir de ses erreurs.

ersatz [ˈɛəzæts] **1** *n* ersatz *m*, succédané *m*. **2** *adj*: **this is** ~ **coffee** c'est de l'ersatz *or* du succédané de café; **this coffee is** ~ ce café est un ersatz *or* de l'ersatz *or* un succédané.

erstwhile [ˈɜːstwaɪl] *(liter, †)* **1** *adj* d'autrefois, d'antan *(liter)*. **2** *adv* autrefois, jadis.

eructate [ɪˈrʌkteɪt] *vi* éructer.

erudite [ˈerʊdaɪt] *adj person, work* érudit, savant; *word* savant.

eruditely [ˈerʊdaɪtlɪ] *adv* d'une manière savante, avec érudition.

erudition [ˌerʊˈdɪʃən] *n* érudition *f*.

erupt [ɪˈrʌpt] *vi [volcano]* entrer en éruption; *[spots]* sortir, apparaître; *[teeth]* percer; *[anger]* exploser; *[war, fighting, quarrel]* éclater. **he** ~**ed into the room** il a fait irruption dans la pièce.

eruption [ɪˈrʌpʃən] *n [volcano]* éruption *f*; *[spots, rash]* éruption, poussée *f*; *[teeth]* percée *f*; *[anger]* explosion *f*, accès *m*; *[violence]* accès. **a volcano in a state of** ~ un volcan en éruption.

erysipelas [ˌerɪˈsɪpɪləs] *n* érysipèle *m or* érésipèle *m*.

escalate [ˈeskəleɪt] **1** *vi [fighting, bombing, violence]* s'intensifier; *[costs]* monter en flèche. **the war is escalating** c'est l'escalade militaire; **prices are escalating** c'est l'escalade des prix.

2 *vt fighting etc* intensifier; *prices, wage claims* faire monter en flèche.

escalation [ˌeskəˈleɪʃən] *n (V* **escalate***)* escalade *f*, intensification *f*; montée *f* en flèche.

escalator [ˈeskəleɪtəʳ] **1** *n* escalier roulant *or* mécanique, escalator *m*. **2** *cpd*: *(Comm, Pol)* **escalator clause** clause *f* d'échelle mobile.

escapade [ˌeskəˈpeɪd] *n (misdeed)* fredaine *f*; *(prank)* frasque *f*; *(adventure)* équipée *f*.

escape [ɪsˈkeɪp] **1** *vi [person, animal]* échapper *(from sb* à qn), s'échapper *(from somewhere* de quelque part); *[prisoner]* s'évader *(from* de); *[water]* s'échapper, fuir; *[gas]* s'échapper. **to** ~ **from sb/from sb's hands** échapper à qn/des mains de qn; **an** ~**d prisoner** un évadé; **to** ~ **to a neutral country** s'enfuir dans *or* gagner un pays neutre; **he** ~**d with a few scratches** il s'en est tiré avec quelques égratignures; **to** ~ **with a fright/a warning** en être quitte pour la peur/un avertissement; **to seek to** ~ **from the world/the crowd** fuir le monde/la foule; **to** ~ **from o.s.** se fuir; *V* **skin**.

2 *vt* **(a)** *(avoid) pursuit* échapper à; *consequences* éviter; *punishment* se soustraire à. **he narrowly** ~**d danger/death** il a échappé de justesse au danger/à la mort; **he narrowly** ~**d being run over** il a failli *or* manqué être écrasé.

(b) *(be unnoticed, forgotten by)* échapper à. **his name** ~**s me** son nom m'échappe; **nothing** ~**s him** rien ne lui échappe; **to** ~ **observation** *or* **notice** passer inaperçu; **it had not** ~**d her notice that ...** elle n'avait pas été sans s'apercevoir que ..., il ne lui avait pas échappé que ...; **the thoughtless words which** ~**d me** les paroles irréfléchies qui m'ont échappé.

3 *n [person]* fuite *f*, évasion *f*; *[animal]* fuite; *[water, gas]* fuite; *[steam, gas in machine]* échappement *m*. **to plan an** ~ combiner un plan d'évasion; **to make an** *or* **one's** ~ s'échapper, s'évader; **to have a lucky** *or* **narrow** ~ l'échapper belle, s'en tirer de justesse; *(fig)* ~ **from reality** évasion hors de la réalité.

4 *cpd*: *(Jur)* **escape clause** échappatoire *f*; **escape device** dispositif *m* de sortie; *(Naut)* **escape hatch** sas *m* de secours; **escape mechanism** *(lit)* mécanisme *m* de défense *or* de protection; *(Psych)* fuite *f (devant la réalité)*; **escape pipe** tuyau *m* d'échappement *or* de refoulement, tuyère *f*; **escape plan** plan *m* d'évasion; **escape route** chemin *m* d'évasion; **escape valve** soupape *f* d'échappement; *(Space)* **escape velocity** vitesse *f* de libération.

escapee [ɪskeɪˈpiː] *n [prison]* évadé(e) *m(f)*.

escapement [ɪsˈkeɪpmənt] *n [clock, piano]* échappement *m*.

escapism [ɪsˈkeɪpɪzəm] *n* (désir *m* d')évasion *f*. **it's sheer** ~! c'est simplement s'évader du réel!

escapist [ɪsˈkeɪpɪst] **1** *n* personne *f* qui se complaît dans l'évasion. **2** *adj film, reading etc* d'évasion.

escapologist [ˌeskəˈpɒlədʒɪst] *n (conjurer)* virtuose *m* de l'évasion; *(fig)* champion *m* de l'esquive.

escarpment [ɪsˈkɑːpmənt] *n* escarpement *m*.

eschatology [ˌeskəˈtɒlədʒɪ] *n* eschatologie *f*.

eschew [ɪsˈtʃuː] *vt (†, frm)* éviter; *wine etc* s'abstenir de; *temptation* fuir.

escort [ˈeskɔːt] **1** *n* **(a)** *(Mil, Naut)* escorte *f*; *(guard of honour)* escorte, cortège *m*, suite *f*. **under the** ~ **of** sous l'escorte de; **under** ~ sous escorte.

(b) *(male companion)* cavalier *m*.

2 *cpd*: **escort agency** bureau *m* d'hôtesses; **to be on escort duty** *[soldiers]* être assigné au service d'escorte; *[ship]* être en service d'escorte; *(Naut)* **escort vessel** vaisseau *m or* bâtiment *m* d'escorte, (vaisseau *m*) escorteur *m*.

3 [ɪsˈkɔːt] *vt (Mil, Naut, gen)* escorter; *(accompany)* accompagner, escorter. **to** ~ **sb in** *(Mil, Police)* faire entrer qn sous escorte; *(gen: accompany)* faire entrer qn; **to** ~ **sb out** *(Mil, Police)* faire sortir qn sous escorte; *(gen)* raccompagner qn jusqu'à la sortie.

escutcheon [ɪsˈkʌtʃən] *n (Her)* écu *m*, écusson *m*; *V* **blot**.

esker [ˈeskəʳ] *n (Geol)* os *m*.

Eskimo [ˈeskɪməʊ] **1** *n* **(a)** Esquimau(de) *m(f)*. **(b)** *(Ling)* esquimau *m*. **2** *adj* esquimau (*f* -aude *or inv*), eskimo *inv*. ~ **dogs** chiens esquimaux.

esophagus [ɪˈsɒfəgəs] *n* œsophage *m*.

esoteric [ˌesəʊˈterɪk] *adj* ésotérique, secret (*f* -ète).

espalier [ɪˈspæljəʳ] **1** *n (trellis)* treillage *m* d'un espalier; *(tree)* arbre *m* en espalier; *(method)* culture *f* en espalier. **2** *vt* cultiver en espalier.

esparto [eˈspɑːtəʊ] *n (also* ~ **grass***)* alfa *m*.

especial [ɪsˈpeʃəl] *adj* particulier, exceptionnel, spécial.

especially [ɪsˈpeʃəlɪ] *adv (to a marked degree)* particulièrement, spécialement; *(principally)* particulièrement, spécialement, en particulier, surtout; *(expressly)* exprès. **more** ~ **as** d'autant plus que; **it is** ~ **awkward** c'est particulièrement fâcheux; ~ **as it's so late** d'autant plus qu'il est si tard; **you** ~ **ought to know** tu devrais le savoir mieux que personne; **why me** ~? pourquoi moi en particulier *or* tout particulièrement?; **I came** ~ **to see you** je suis venu exprès pour vous voir.

Esperantist [ˌespəˈræntɪst] *n* espérantiste *mf*.

Esperanto [ˌespəˈræntəʊ] **1** *n* espéranto *m*. **2** *adj* en espéranto.

espionage [ˌespɪəˈnɑːʒ] *n* espionnage *m*.

esplanade [ˌespləˈneɪd] *n* esplanade *f*.

espouse [ɪsˈpaʊz] *vt cause* épouser, embrasser; *(††) person* épouser.

espresso [esˈpresəʊ] *n* (café *m*) express *m*. ~ **bar** café *m (où l'on sert du café express)*.

espy [ɪsˈpaɪ] *vt (†, frm)* apercevoir, aviser *(frm)*.

esquire [ɪsˈkwaɪəʳ] *n*: **Brian Smith E**~ Monsieur Brian Smith *(sur une enveloppe etc)*.

essay [ˈeseɪ] **1** *n (Literat)* essai *m (on* sur); *(Scol)* rédaction *f*, composition *f (on* sur); *(Univ)* dissertation *f (on* sur); *(attempt)* essai. **2** [eˈseɪ] *vt (try)* essayer, tenter *(to do* de faire); *(test)* mettre à l'épreuve.

essayist [ˈeseɪɪst] *n* essayiste *mf*.

essence [ˈesəns] *n (gen)* essence *f*, fond *m*, essentiel *m*; *(Chem)* essence; *(Culin)* extrait *m*; *(Philos)* essence, nature *f*. **in** ~ par essence, essentiellement; **the** ~ **of what was said** l'essentiel de ce qui a été dit; **speed/precision is of the** ~ la vitesse/la précision est essentielle *or* s'impose; **the** ~ **of stupidity*** le comble de la stupidité; ~ **of violets** essence de violette; **meat** ~ extrait de viande; **the divine** ~ l'essence divine.

essential [ɪˈsenʃəl] **1** *adj equipment, action* essentiel, indispensable *(to* à); *fact* essentiel; *role, point* capital, essentiel; *question* essentiel, fondamental; *commodities* essentiel, de première nécessité; *(Chem)* essentiel. **it is** ~ **to act quickly** il est indispensable *or* essentiel d'agir vite; **it is ~ that ...** il est indispensable que ... + *subj*; **it's not ~** ce n'est pas indispensable; **the ~ thing is to act** l'essentiel est d'agir; **man's ~ goodness** la bonté essentielle de l'homme; (*Chem*) **~ oil** essence *f*, huile essentielle.

2 *n* qualité *f* (*or* objet *m etc*) indispensable. **the ~s** l'essentiel *m*; **to see to the ~s** s'occuper de l'essentiel; **accuracy is an ~** *or* **one of the ~s** la précision est une des qualités indispensables; (*rudiments*) **the ~s of German grammar** les éléments *mpl or* les rudiments *mpl* de la grammaire allemande.

essentially [ɪ'senʃəlɪ] *adv* (*in essence*) essentiellement, fondamentalement, par essence; (*principally*) essentiellement, avant tout, principalement.

establish [ɪs'tæblɪʃ] *vt* **(a)** (*set up*) *government* constituer, établir; *state, business* fonder, créer; *factory* établir, monter; *society, tribunal* constituer; *laws, custom* instaurer; *relations* établir, nouer; *post* créer; *power, authority* affermir; *peace, order* faire régner; *list, sb's reputation* établir. **to ~ one's reputation as a scholar/as a writer** se faire une réputation de savant/comme écrivain; **to ~ o.s. as a grocer** s'établir épicier.

(b) (*prove*) *fact, identity, one's rights* établir; *necessity, guilt* prouver, démontrer; *innocence* établir, démontrer.

established [ɪs'tæblɪʃt] *adj reputation* établi, bien assis; *fact* acquis, reconnu; *truth* établi, démontré; *custom, belief* établi, enraciné; *government* établi, au pouvoir; *laws* établi, en vigueur; *order* établi. **well-~ business** maison solide; **the ~ Church** l'Église établie, la religion d'État *or* officielle.

establishment [ɪs'tæblɪʃmənt] *n* **(a)** (*U*) (*V* **establish**) établissement *m*; fondation *f*, création *f*; constitution *f*; instauration *f*.

(b) (*institution etc*) établissement *m*. **commercial ~** établissement commercial, maison *f* de commerce, firme *f*; **teaching ~** établissement d'enseignement.

(c) (*Mil, Naut etc: personnel*) effectif *m*. **war/peace ~** effectifs de guerre/de paix; (*household*) **to keep up a large ~** avoir un grand train de maison.

(d) (*Brit*) **the E~** (*the authorities*) les pouvoirs établis, les milieux dirigeants, l'establishment *m* (*esp Brit or US*); (*their power*) le pouvoir effectif; (*the values they represent*) l'ordre établi, les valeurs reconnues; (*Rel*) l'Église établie; **these are the values of the E~** ce sont là les valeurs traditionnelles *or* conformistes *or* bien reconnues; **he has always been against the E~** il a toujours été anticonformiste; **he has joined the E~** il s'est rangé, il n'est plus rebelle; **the literary/political E~** ceux qui font la loi dans le monde littéraire/politique.

estate [ɪs'teɪt] **1** *n* **(a)** (*land*) propriété *f*, domaine *m*. **country ~** terre(s) *f(pl)*; (*esp Brit*) **housing ~** lotissement *m*; *V* **real** *etc*.

(b) (*Jur: possessions*) bien(s) *m(pl)*, fortune *f*; *[deceased]* succession *f*. **he left a large ~** il a laissé une grosse fortune (en héritage); **to liquidate the ~** liquider la succession.

(c) (*order, rank, condition*) état *m*, rang *m*, condition *f*. **the three ~s** les trois états; **the Third ~** le Tiers État, la bourgeoisie; **the fourth ~** la presse, le quatrième pouvoir; (*liter*) **a man of high/low ~** un homme de haut rang/d'humble condition; (*liter*) **to reach man's ~** parvenir à l'âge d'homme.

2 *cpd*: (*esp Brit*) **estate agency** agence immobilière; (*esp Brit*) **estate agent** agent immobilier; (*Brit*) **estate car** break *m*; (*Brit*) **estate duty** droits *mpl* de succession.

esteem [ɪs'ti:m] **1** *vt* **(a)** (*think highly of*) *person* avoir de l'estime pour, estimer; *quality* estimer, apprécier. **our (highly) ~d colleague** notre (très) estimé collègue *or* confrère.

(b) (*consider*) estimer, considérer. **I ~ it an honour (that)** je m'estime très honoré (que + *subj*); **I ~ it an honour to do** je considère comme un honneur de faire.

2 *n* estime *f*, considération *f*. **to hold in high ~** tenir en haute estime; **he went up/down in my ~** il a monté/baissé dans mon estime.

esthete ['i:sθi:t] *etc* = **aesthete** *etc*.

Esthonia [es'təʊnɪə] *n* Estonie *f*.

Esthonian [es'təʊnɪən] **1** *adj* estonien. **2** *n* **(a)** Estonien(ne) *m(f)*. **(b)** (*Ling*) estonien *m*.

estimable ['estɪməbl] *adj* estimable, digne d'estime.

estimate ['estɪmɪt] **1** *n* (*judgement*) jugement *m*, évaluation *f*; (*calculation*) évaluation, estimation *f*, calcul approximatif; (*Comm*) devis *m*. (*Comm*) **give me an ~ for (building) a greenhouse** donnez-moi *or* établissez-moi un devis pour la construction d'une serre; **give me an ~ of what your trip will cost** donnez-moi un état estimatif du coût de votre voyage; **this price is only a rough ~** ce prix n'est que très approximatif; **at a rough ~** approximativement, à vue de nez*; **at the lowest ~ it will cost 100 francs** cela coûtera 100 F au bas mot; (*Admin, Pol*) **the ~s** le budget, les crédits *mpl* budgétaires; **the Army ~s** le budget de l'armée; **to form an ~ of sb's capabilities** évaluer les capacités de qn; **his ~ of 400 people was very far out** il s'était trompé de beaucoup en évaluant le nombre de gens à 400.

2 ['estɪmeɪt] *vt* estimer, juger (*that* que); *cost, number, price, quantity* estimer, évaluer; *distance, speed* estimer, apprécier. **his fortune is ~d at ...** on évalue sa fortune à ...; **I ~ that there must be 40 of them** j'estime *or* je juge qu'il doit y en avoir 40, à mon avis il doit y en avoir 40.

estimation [,estɪ'meɪʃən] *n* **(a)** jugement *m*, opinion *f*. **in my ~** à mon avis, selon moi. **(b)** (*esteem*) estime *f*, considération *f*. **he went up/down in my ~** il a monté/baissé dans mon estime.

estrange [ɪs'treɪndʒ] *vt* brouiller (*from* avec), éloigner (*from* de). **to become ~d (from)** se brouiller (avec), se détacher (de); **the ~d couple** les époux désunis *or* séparés.

estrangement [ɪs'treɪndʒmənt] *n* (*V* **estrange**) brouille *f* (*from* avec), éloignement *m* (*from* de); désunion *f*, séparation *f*.

estrogen ['i:strəʊdʒən] *n* (*US*) = **oestrogen.**

estrus ['i:strəs] *n* (*US*) = **oestrus.**

estuary ['estjʊərɪ] *n* estuaire *m*.

et cetera [ɪt'setərə] **1** *adv* et caetera. **2** *n*: **the ~s** les extras *mpl*, les et caetera *mpl*.

etch [etʃ] *vti* graver à l'eau forte.

etching ['etʃɪŋ] *n* **(a)** (*U*) gravure *f* à l'eau forte. **~ needle** pointe *f* (sèche). **(b)** (*picture*) (gravure *f* à l')eau-forte *f*.

eternal [ɪ'tɜ:nl] **1** *adj* (*Philos, Rel, gen*) éternel; (*pej*) *complaints, gossip etc* continuel, perpétuel, sempiternel (*pej*). **the ~ triangle** l'éternelle situation de trio, le ménage à trois. **2** *n*: **the E~** l'Éternel *m*.

eternally [ɪ'tɜ:nəlɪ] *adv* (*V* **eternal**) éternellement; continuellement, perpétuellement, sempiternellement (*pej*).

eternity [ɪ'tɜ:nɪtɪ] **1** *n* éternité *f*. **it seemed like an ~** on aurait dit une éternité; **we waited an ~*** nous avons attendu (toute) une éternité *or* des éternités*. **2** *cpd*: **eternity ring** bague *f* de fidélité (*offerte par un mari à sa femme*).

ethane ['i:θeɪn] *n* éthane *m*.

ethanol ['eθənɒl] *n* alcool *m* éthylique, éthanol *m*.

ether ['i:θər] *n* (*Chem, Phys*) éther *m*. (*liter*) **the ~** l'éther, les espaces *mpl* célestes; (*Rad*) **over the ~** sur les ondes.

ethereal [ɪ'θɪərɪəl] *adj* (*delicate*) éthéré, aérien; (*spiritual*) éthéré, sublime.

ethic ['eθɪk] **1** *n* morale *f*, éthique *f*. **2** *adj* = **ethical.**

ethical ['eθɪkəl] *adj* éthique (*frm*), moral. **not ~** contraire à la morale; (*Med*) **~ code** code *m* déontologique.

ethics ['eθɪks] *n* (*U*) (*study*) éthique *f*, morale *f*; (*system, principles*) morale; (*morality*) moralité *f*. **medical ~** code *m* déontologique *or* de déontologie.

Ethiopia [,i:θɪ'əʊpɪə] *n* Éthiopie *f*.

Ethiopian [,i:θɪ'əʊpɪən] **1** *adj* éthiopien. **2** *n* Éthiopien(ne) *m(f)*.

ethnic ['eθnɪk] *adj* ethnique.

ethnographer [eθ'nɒgrəfər] *n* ethnographe *mf*.

ethnography [eθ'nɒgrəfɪ] *n* ethnographie *f*.

ethnologist [eθ'nɒlədʒɪst] *n* ethnologue *mf*.

ethnology [eθ'nɒlədʒɪ] *n* ethnologie *f*.

ethology [ɪ'θɒlədʒɪ] *n* éthologie *f*, éthographie *f*.

ethos ['i:θɒs] *n* génie *m* (*d'un peuple, d'une culture*).

ethyl ['i:θaɪl] *n* éthyle *m*. **~ acetate** acétate *m* d'éthyle.

ethylene ['eθɪli:n] *n* éthylène *m*.

etiology [,i:tɪ'ɒlədʒɪ] *n* (*Med, gen*) étiologie *f*.

etiquette ['etɪket] *n* étiquette *f*, convenances *fpl*, bon usage. **diplomatic ~** protocole *m*; **court ~** cérémonial *m* de cour; **that isn't ~** c'est contraire aux convenances *or* au bon usage, cela ne se fait pas; **it's against medical ~** c'est contraire à la déontologie médicale; **it's not professional ~** c'est contraire aux usages de la profession.

Etruscan [ɪ'trʌskən] **1** *adj* étrusque. **2** *n* **(a)** Étrusque *mf*. **(b)** (*Ling*) étrusque *m*.

etymological [,etɪmə'lɒdʒɪkəl] *adj* étymologique.

etymologically [,etɪmə'lɒdʒɪkəlɪ] *adv* étymologiquement.

etymology [,etɪ'mɒlədʒɪ] *n* étymologie *f*.

eucalyptus [,ju:kə'lɪptəs] *n* (*Bot, Pharm*) eucalyptus *m*. **~ oil** essence *f* d'eucalyptus.

Eucharist ['ju:kərɪst] *n* Eucharistie *f*.

eugenics [ju:'dʒenɪks] *n* (*U*) eugénique *f*, eugénisme *m*.

eulogize ['ju:lədʒaɪz] *vt* faire l'éloge *or* le panégyrique de.

eulogy ['ju:lədʒɪ] *n* panégyrique *m*.

eunuch ['ju:nək] *n* eunuque *m*.

euphemism ['ju:fəmɪzəm] *n* euphémisme *m*.

euphemistic [,ju:fə'mɪstɪk] *adj* euphémique.

euphemistically [,ju:fə'mɪstɪkəlɪ] *adv* par euphémisme, euphémiquement.

euphonic [ju:'fɒnɪk] *adj*, **euphonious** [ju:'fəʊnɪəs] *adj* euphonique.

euphonium [ju:fəʊnɪəm] *n* saxhorn *m*.

euphony ['ju:fənɪ] *n* euphonie *f*.

euphorbia [ju:'fɔ:rbɪə] *n* euphorbe *f*.

euphoria [ju:'fɔ:rɪə] *n* euphorie *f*.

euphoric [ju:'fɒrɪk] *adj* euphorique.

Euphrates [ju:'freɪti:z] *n* Euphrate *m*.

euphuism ['ju:fju:ɪzəm] *n* préciosité *f*, euphuisme *m*.

Eurasia [jʊə'reɪʃə] *n* Eurasie *f*.

Eurasian [jʊə'reɪʃn] **1** *adj population* eurasien; *continent* eurasiatique. **2** *n* Eurasien(ne) *m(f)*.

eureka [jʊə'ri:kə] *excl* eurêka!

eurhythmics [ju:'rɪðmɪks] *n* (*U*) gymnastique *f* rythmique.

Euripides [jʊ'rɪpɪdi:z] *n* Euripide *m*.

euro... ['jʊərəʊ] *pref* euro... . **~crat** eurocrate *mf*; **~dollar** eurodollar *m*; **~market, ~mart** Communauté Économique Européenne; (*Comm*) **~size 1** modèle *m* E1; (*TV*) **E~vision** Eurovision *f*.

Europe ['jʊərəp] *n* Europe *f*. (*Pol*) **to go into ~, to join ~** entrer dans le marché commun.

European [,jʊərə'pi:ən] **1** *adj* européen. **the ~ Economic Community** (*abbr* **EEC**) la Communauté Économique Européenne (*abbr* CEE *f*); (*US: in hotel*) **~ plan** chambre *f* sans petit déjeuner. **2** *n* Européen(ne) *m(f)*.

Eustachian [ju:'steɪʃən] *adj*: **~ tube** trompe *f* d'Eustache.

eustatic [ju:'stætɪk] *adj* eustatique.

euthanasia [,ju:θə'neɪzɪə] *n* euthanasie *f*.

evacuate [ɪ'vækjʊeɪt] *vt* (*all senses*) évacuer.

evacuation [ɪ,vækjʊ'eɪʃən] *n* évacuation *f*.

evacuee [ɪ,vækjʊ'i:] *n* évacué(e) *m(f)*.

evade [ɪ'veɪd] *vt blow, difficulty* esquiver, éviter; *pursuers* échapper à, tromper; *obligation* éviter, esquiver, se dérober à; *punishment* échapper à, se soustraire à; *sb's gaze* éviter; *question* éluder; *law* tourner, contourner. **to ~ military service** se dérober à ses obligations militaires; **to ~ taxation/customs duty** frauder le fisc/la douane.

evaluate [ɪ'væljʊeɪt] *vt damages, property, worth* évaluer (*at* à),

déterminer le montant or la valeur or le prix de; effectiveness, usefulness mesurer; evidence, reasons, argument peser, évaluer; achievement porter un jugement sur la valeur de. to ~ sth at £100 évaluer qch à 100 livres.
evaluation [ɪˌvæljuˈeɪʃən] n évaluation f.
evanescent [ˌiːvəˈnesnt] adj évanescent, fugitif, éphémère.
evangelic(al) [ˌiːvænˈdʒelɪk(əl)] adj, n évangélique (mf).
evangelist [ɪˈvændʒəlɪst] n (Bible) évangéliste m; (preacher) évangélisateur m, -trice f; (itinerant) évangéliste.
evangelize [ɪˈvændʒəlaɪz] 1 vt évangéliser, prêcher l'Évangile à. 2 vi prêcher l'Évangile.
evaporate [ɪˈvæpəreɪt] 1 vt (liquid) faire évaporer. ~d milk lait concentré. 2 vi [liquid] s'évaporer; [hopes, fear] se volatiliser, s'évanouir, s'envoler.
evaporation [ɪˌvæpəˈreɪʃən] n évaporation f.
evasion [ɪˈveɪʒən] n (a) (U) fuite f, dérobade f (of devant); V tax. (b) (excuse) détour m, faux-fuyant m, échappatoire f.
evasive [ɪˈveɪzɪv] adj évasif. ~ answer réponse évasive or de Normand; to take ~ action (Mil) se replier; (gen) prendre la tangente.
evasively [ɪˈveɪzɪvlɪ] adv évasivement; reply en termes évasifs, en Normand.
Eve [iːv] n Ève f.
eve[1] [iːv] n veille f; (Rel) vigile f. (lit, fig) on the ~ of sth/of doing à la veille de qch/de faire; V Christmas.
eve[2] [iːv] n (liter: evening) soir m.
even[1] [ˈiːvən] n = eve[2].
even[2] [ˈiːvən] 1 adj (a) (smooth, flat) surface, ground uni, plat, plan. to make ~ égaliser, aplanir, niveler; V keel.
(b) (regular) progress régulier; temperature, breathing, step, temper, distribution égal. his work is not ~ son travail est inégal or variable.
(c) (equal) quantities, distances, values égal. our score is ~ nous sommes à égalité (de points); they are an ~ match (Sport) la partie est égale; (fig) ils sont (bien) assortis; to get ~ with sb se venger de qn; I will get ~ with you for that je vous revaudrai ça*; (fig) the odds or chances are about ~ les chances sont à peu près égales; I'll give you ~ money or ~s that ... (Betting) je vous parie le même enjeu que ...; (gen) il y a cinquante pour cent de chances or une chance sur deux que ... + subj.
(d) ~ number/date nombre/jour pair.
2 adv (a) même, jusqu'à. ~ in the holidays même pendant les vacances; ~ the most optimistic même les plus optimistes; ~ the guards were asleep les gardes mêmes dormaient, même les gardes dormaient; I have ~ forgotten his name j'ai oublié jusqu'à son nom, j'ai même oublié son nom; they ~ denied its existence ils ont nié jusqu'à son existence, ils ont été jusqu'à nier or ils ont même nié son existence.
(b) (+ comp adj or adv) encore. ~ better encore mieux; ~ more easily encore plus facilement; ~ less money encore moins d'argent.
(c) (+ neg) même, seulement. without ~ saying goodbye sans même or sans seulement dire au revoir; he can't ~ swim il ne sait même pas nager.
(d) (phrases) ~ if même si + indic; ~ though quand (bien) même + cond, alors même que + cond; ~ though or ~ if he came himself I would not do it il viendrait lui-même que je ne le ferais pas; if he ~ made an effort si encore or si au moins il faisait un effort; ~ then même alors; ~ so quand même, pourtant, cependant; ~ so he was disappointed il a quand même or malgré tout été déçu, cependant or pourtant il a été déçu; yes but ~ so ... oui mais quand même ...; ~ as he spoke, the door opened au moment même où il or alors même qu'il disait cela, la porte s'ouvrit; (liter, frm) ~ as he had wished it précisément comme il l'avait souhaité; (liter, frm) ~ as ... so ... de même que ... de même ...
3 cpd: even-handed impartial, équitable; even-tempered d'humeur égale, placide.
4 vt surface égaliser, aplanir, niveler.
even out 1 vi [prices] s'égaliser; [ground] s'aplanir, s'égaliser, se niveler.
2 vt sep prices égaliser; burden, taxation répartir or distribuer plus également (among entre).
even up vt sep égaliser. that will even things up cela rétablira l'équilibre; (financially) cela compensera.
evening [ˈiːvnɪŋ] 1 n soir m; (length of time) soirée f. in the ~ le soir; to go out in the ~ sortir le soir; let's have an ~ out (tonight) si on sortait ce soir?; (some time) nous devrions sortir un soir; 6 o'clock in the ~ 6 heures du soir; this ~ ce soir; that ~ ce soir-là; tomorrow ~ demain soir; the previous ~ la veille au soir; on the ~ of the next day le lendemain soir; on the ~ of the twenty-ninth le vingt-neuf au soir; on the ~ of his birthday le soir de son anniversaire; every ~ tous les soirs, chaque soir; every Monday ~ tous les lundis soir(s); one fine summer ~ (par) un beau soir d'été; the warm summer ~s les chaudes soirées d'été; a long winter ~ une longue soirée or veillée d'hiver; all ~ toute la soirée; to spend one's ~ reading passer sa soirée à lire; where shall we finish off the ~? où allons-nous terminer la soirée?; (liter) in the ~ of life au soir or au déclin de la vie; V good etc.
2 cpd: evening class cours m du soir; evening dress [man] tenue f de soirée, habit m; [woman] robe f du soir; in evening dress man en tenue de soirée; woman en toilette de soirée, en robe du soir; evening paper journal m du soir; evening performance (représentation f en) soirée f; evening prayer(s) office m du soir; (Rel) evening service service m (religieux) du soir; evening star étoile f du berger.
evenly [ˈiːvənlɪ] adv spread, paint etc de façon égale, uniment; breathe, space régulièrement; distribute, divide également.
evenness [ˈiːvənnɪs] n [movements, performance] régularité f; [ground] caractère uni, égalité f. ~ of temper égalité d'humeur, sérénité f, calme m.
evensong [ˈiːvənsɒŋ] n (Rel) vêpres fpl, office m du soir (de l'Église anglicane).
event [ɪˈvent] n (a) (happening) événement m. course of ~s suite f des événements, succession f or déroulement m des faits; in the course of ~s par la suite; in the normal or ordinary course of ~s normalement; after the ~ après coup; it's quite an ~ c'est un (véritable) événement; V happy.
(b) cas m. in the ~ of death en cas de décès; in the ~ of his failing au cas or dans le cas or pour le cas où il échouerait; in the unlikely ~ that ... s'il arrivait par hasard que ... + subj; in the ~ en fait, en réalité; in that ~ dans ce cas; in any ~, at all ~s en tout cas, de toute façon; in either ~ dans l'un ou l'autre cas.
(c) (Sport) épreuve f; (Racing) course f. field ~s concours mpl; track ~s courses.
eventful [ɪˈventfʊl] adj life, day, period mouvementé, fertile en événements; journey mouvementé, plein d'incidents; (momentous) mémorable, de grande importance.
eventide [ˈiːvəntaɪd] n (liter) tombée f du jour, soir m. ~ home maison f de retraite.
eventual [ɪˈventʃʊəl] adj (resulting) qui s'ensuit; (probably resulting) éventuel, possible. his many mistakes and his ~ failure ses nombreuses erreurs et l'échec qui s'en est ensuivi or qui en a résulté or auquel elles ont mené; it resulted in the ~ disappearance of ... cela a abouti finalement à la disparition de ...; any ~ profits les profits éventuels.
eventuality [ɪˌventʃʊˈælɪtɪ] n éventualité f.
eventually [ɪˈventʃʊəlɪ] adv (finally) finalement, en fin de compte, en définitive; (after interval) à la longue, à la fin. to do sth ~ finir par faire qch, faire qch finalement or à la longue.
ever [ˈevəʳ] 1 adv (a) (with negation, doubt) jamais; (with interrogation) jamais, déjà. nothing ~ happens il ne se passe jamais rien; if you ~ see her si jamais vous la voyez; do you ~ see her? est-ce qu'il vous arrive de la voir?; have you ~ seen her? l'avez-vous jamais or déjà vue?; I haven't ~ seen her je ne l'ai jamais vue; we seldom if ~ go nous n'y allons jamais ou rarement, nous n'y allons pour ainsi dire jamais; now if ~ is the moment to ... c'est le moment ou jamais de ...; he's a liar if ~ there was one c'est un menteur ou je ne m'y connais pas.
(b) (after comp or superl) jamais. more beautiful than ~ plus beau que jamais; faster than ~ plus vite que jamais; the best meal I have ~ eaten le meilleur repas que j'aie jamais fait; the best grandmother ~ la meilleure grand-mère du monde; the coldest night ~ la nuit la plus froide qu'on ait jamais connue.
(c) (at all times) toujours, sans cesse. ~ ready toujours prêt; ~ after à partir de ce jour; they lived happily ~ after ils vécurent (toujours) heureux; ~ since I was a boy depuis mon enfance; ~ since I have lived here depuis que j'habite ici; ~ since (then) they have been very careful depuis (lors) or depuis ce moment-là ils sont très prudents; for ~ (and ~) à jamais, pour toujours, éternellement; for ~ (and ~), amen dans tous les siècles (des siècles), amen; he has gone for ~ il est parti pour toujours or sans retour; (liter) for ~ and a day jusqu'à la fin des temps; (†, liter) ~ and anon de temps à autre, parfois; he is for ~ changing his mind il change d'avis sans cesse or continuellement or à tout bout de champ; they are for ~ quarrelling ils ne font que se disputer, ils ne cessent de se disputer; (in letters) yours ~ bien amicalement or cordialement (à vous); ~ increasing anxiety inquiétude qui va (or allait) croissant; ~ present constant; (†, frm) he was ~ courteous il était toujours poli.
(d) (intensive) although he is or (frm) be he ~ so charming quelque or si or pour charmant qu'il soit; as quickly as ~ you can aussi vite que vous le pourrez; as soon as ~ he arrives aussitôt or dès qu'il arrivera; the first ~ le tout premier; before ~ she came in avant même qu'elle (ne) soit entrée; ~ so slightly drunk tant soit peu ivre; ~ so pretty joli comme tout*; he is ~ so nice il est tout ce qu'il y a de plus gentil*; I am ~ so sorry je regrette infiniment, je suis (vraiment) désolé; it's ~ such a pity c'est vraiment dommage; thank you ~ so much, thanks ~ so; merci mille fois, merci bien; she is ~ so much prettier than her sister elle est autrement jolie que sa sœur; as if I ~ would! comme si je ferais ça moi!, moi faire ça!; what ~ shall we do? qu'est-ce que nous allons bien faire?; where ~ can he have got to? où a-t-il bien pu passer?; when ~ will they come? quand donc viendront-ils?; why ~ not? pourquoi pas donc?, pourquoi pas Grand Dieu?; did you ~!* a-t-on jamais vu cela!, (ça) par exemple!
2 cpd: (US) everglade terres marécageuses; evergreen V evergreen; everlasting V everlasting; evermore toujours; for evermore à tout jamais.
evergreen [ˈevəgriːn] 1 adj trees, shrubs vert, à feuilles persistantes; song qui ne vieillit pas; subject of conversation éternel, qui revient toujours. ~ oak yeuse f, chêne vert. 2 n (tree) arbre vert or à feuilles persistantes; (plant) plante f à feuilles persistantes.
everlasting [ˌevəˈlɑːstɪŋ] adj (a) God éternel; gratitude, mercy infini, éternel; fame, glory éternel, immortel; materials inusable, qui ne s'use pas. ~ flower immortelle f. (b) (*: repeated) perpétuel, éternel, sempiternel (pej).
everlastingly [ˌevəˈlɑːstɪŋlɪ] adv éternellement; sans cesse, sempiternellement (pej).
every [ˈevrɪ] adj (a) (each) tout, chaque; tous (or toutes) les. ~ shop in the town tous les magasins de la ville; not ~ child has the same advantages les enfants n'ont pas tous les mêmes avantages; not ~ child has the advantages you have tous les enfants n'ont pas les avantages que tu as; he spends ~ penny he earns il dépense tout ce qu'il gagne (jusqu'au dernier sou); I have ~ confidence in him j'ai entièrement or pleine confiance en lui;

there is ~ chance that he will come il y a toutes les chances *or* de fortes chances (pour) qu'il vienne; **you have ~ reason to complain** vous avez tout lieu de vous plaindre; **I have ~ reason to think that ...** j'ai de bonnes raisons *or* de fortes raisons *or* toutes les raisons de penser que ..., j'ai tout lieu de penser que ...; **we wish you ~ success** nous vous souhaitons très bonne chance, tous nos souhaits pour l'avenir; **there was ~ prospect of success** tout faisait croire au succès; **~ (single) one of them** chacun d'eux; **~ child had brought something** chaque enfant avait apporté quelque chose; **~ movement is painful to him** chaque *or* tout mouvement lui fait mal; **from ~ country** de tous (les) pays; **at ~ moment** à tout moment, à chaque instant; **of ~ sort** de toute sorte; **from ~ side** de toutes parts; **of ~ age** de tout âge; **he became weaker ~ day** il devenait plus faible chaque jour *or* de jour en jour.

(b) (*showing recurrence*) tout. **~ fifth day, ~ five days** tous les cinq jours, un jour sur cinq; **~ second child** un enfant sur deux; **~ quarter of an hour** tous les quarts d'heure; **~ other day, ~ second day** tous les deux jours; **~ other Wednesday** un mercredi sur deux; **to write on ~ other line** écrire en sautant une ligne sur deux; **~ few days** tous les deux ou trois jours; **once ~ week** une fois par semaine; **~ 15 metres** tous les 15 mètres.

(c) (*after poss*) tout, chacun, moindre. **his ~ action** chacune de ses actions, tout ce qu'il faisait; **his ~ wish** son moindre désir, tous ses désirs.

(d) (*phrases*) **he is ~ bit as clever as his brother** il est tout aussi doué que son frère; **he is ~ bit as much of a liar as his brother** il est tout aussi menteur que son frère; **~ now and then, ~ now and again, ~ so often** de temps en temps, de temps à autre; **~ time (that) I see him** chaque fois *or* toutes les fois que je le vois; **~ single time** chaque fois sans exception; **you must examine ~ one** il faut les examiner tous; **~ single one of these peaches is bad** toutes ces pêches sans exception sont pourries; **~ one of us is afraid of something** tous tant que nous sommes nous craignons quelque chose; **~ one of them was there** ils étaient tous là (au grand complet); **~ man for himself** chacun pour soi; (*excl: save yourself*) sauve qui peut!; **~ man to his trade** à chacun son métier; **~ man Jack of them** tous tant qu'ils sont (*or* étaient *etc*), tous sans exception; **in ~ way** (*from every point of view*) à tous (les) égards, en tous points, sous tous les rapports; (*by ~ means*) par tous les moyens; *V* **bit**[1].

everybody ['evrɪbɒdɪ] *pron* tout le monde, chacun. **~ has finished** tout le monde a fini; **~ has his *or* their* own ideas about it** chacun a ses (propres) idées là-dessus; **~ else** tous les autres; **~ knows ~ else here** tout le monde se connaît ici; **~ knows that** tout le monde *or* n'importe qui sait cela.

everyday ['evrɪdeɪ] *adj* de tous les jours, banal, ordinaire, commun. **my ~ coat** mon manteau de tous les jours; **words in ~ use** mots d'usage courant; **it was an ~ occurrence** c'était un événement banal, cela se produisait tous les jours; **it was not an ~ event** c'était un événement hors du commun.

everyone ['evrɪwʌn] *pron* = **everybody.**

everyplace ['evrɪpleɪs] *adv* (*US*) = **everywhere.**

everything ['evrɪθɪŋ] *n* tout. **~ is ready** tout est prêt; **~ you have** tout ce que vous avez; **stamina is ~** c'est la résistance qui compte, l'essentiel c'est d'avoir de la résistance; **money isn't ~** l'argent ne fait pas le bonheur.

everywhere ['evrɪwɛə^r] *adv* partout, en tous lieux, de tous côtés. **~ in the world** partout dans le monde, dans le monde entier; **~ you go you meet the British** où qu'on aille *or* partout où on va on rencontre des Britanniques.

evict [ɪ'vɪkt] *vt* (*from house, lodgings*) expulser, chasser (*from* de); (*from meeting*) expulser (*from* de).

eviction [ɪ'vɪkʃən] *n* expulsion *f.*

evidence ['evɪdəns] **1** *n* (*U*) **(a)** (*ground for belief*) évidence *f*; (*testimony*) témoignage *m.* **the clearest possible ~** l'évidence même; **the ~ of the senses** le témoignage des sens.

(b) (*Jur*) (*data*) preuve *f*; (*testimony*) témoignage *m*, déposition *f.* **to give ~** témoigner, déposer (en justice); **to give ~ for/against sb** témoigner *or* déposer en faveur de/contre qn; **to take sb's ~** recueillir la déposition de qn; (*Brit*) **to turn King's *or* Queen's ~**, (*US*) **to turn state's ~** témoigner contre ses complices.

(c) signe *m*, marque *f.* **to bear ~ of** porter la marque *or* les marques de; **to show ~ of** témoigner de, offrir des signes de, attester.

(d) his father was nowhere in ~ son père n'était nulle part dans les parages, il n'y avait pas trace de son père; **a man very much in ~ at the moment** un homme très en vue à l'heure actuelle.

2 *vt* manifester, témoigner de.

evident ['evɪdənt] *adj* évident, manifeste, patent. **that is very ~** c'est l'évidence même; **we must help her, that's ~** il faut l'aider, c'est évident *or* cela va de soi; **he's guilty, that's ~** il est coupable, c'est évident *or* cela saute aux yeux; **it was ~ from the way he walked** cela se voyait à sa démarche; **it is ~ from his speech that ...** il ressort de son discours que ... .

evidently ['evɪdəntlɪ] *adv* **(a)** (*obviously*) évidemment, manifestement, de toute évidence. **he was ~ frightened** il était évident qu'il avait peur.

(b) (*apparently*) à ce qu'il paraît. **they are ~ going to change the rule** il paraît qu'ils vont changer le règlement; **are they going too? — ~** ils y vont aussi? — à ce qu'il paraît *or* on dirait.

evil ['i:vl] **1** *adj deed* mauvais; *person* mauvais, malveillant; *example, advice, reputation* mauvais; *influence* néfaste; *doctrine, spell, spirit* malfaisant; *course of action, consequence* funeste. **the E~ One** le Malin; **the ~ eye** le mauvais œil; **in an ~ hour** dans un moment funeste.

2 *n* mal *m.* **to wish sb ~** vouloir du mal à qn; **to speak ~ of sb** dire du mal de qn; **of two ~s one must choose the lesser** de deux maux il faut choisir le moindre; **it's the lesser ~** c'est le moindre mal; **social ~s** maux sociaux, plaies sociales; **the ~s of drink** les conséquences *fpl* funestes de la boisson; **one of the great ~s of our time** un des grands fléaux de notre temps.

3 *cpd*: **evildoer** scélérat *m*, méchant(e) *m(f)*, gredin(e) *m(f)*; **evil-minded** malveillant, mal intentionné; **evil-smelling** malodorant, nauséabond.

evilly ['i:vɪlɪ] *adv* avec malveillance.

evince [ɪ'vɪns] *vt surprise, desire* montrer, manifester; *qualities, talents* faire preuve de, manifester.

eviscerate [ɪ'vɪsəreɪt] *vt* éventrer, étriper.

evocation [ˌevə'keɪʃən] *n* évocation *f.*

evocative [ɪ'vɒkətɪv] *adj style, scent, picture, words* évocateur (*f* -trice); *incantation, magic* évocatoire.

evoke [ɪ'vəʊk] *vt spirit, memories* évoquer; *admiration* susciter.

evolution [ˌi:və'lu:ʃən] *n* **(a)** (*Bio, Zool etc*) évolution *f*; *[language, events]* évolution; *[culture, technology, machine]* évolution, développement *m.* **(b)** *[troops, skaters etc]* évolutions *fpl.*

evolutionary [ˌi:və'lu:ʃnərɪ] *adj* évolutionniste.

evolve [ɪ'vɒlv] **1** *vt system, theory, plan* élaborer, développer. **2** *vi [system, plan]* se développer; *[idea, science]* évoluer.

ewe [ju:] *n* brebis *f.* **~ lamb** (*lit*) agnelle *f*; (*fig*) trésor *m.*

ewer ['ju:ə^r] *n* aiguière *f.*

ex [eks] *n* (*former girlfriend or boyfriend*) **his ~*** son ex* *f inv*; **her ~*** son ex* *m inv.*

ex- [eks] *pref* **(a)** (*former*) ex-. **~president** ancien président, ex-président; **~serviceman** ancien combattant; **~husband** ex-mari *m*; **~wife** ex-femme *f.*

(b) (*out of*) ex-. (*Telec*) **his number is ~directory, he has an ~directory number** son numéro ne figure pas au Bottin *or* à l'annuaire; (*St Ex*) **~dividend** ex-dividende; (*Comm, Ind*) **price ~works** prix *m* départ usine; *V* **ex officio.**

exacerbate [eks'æsəbeɪt] *vt person* irriter, exaspérer; *pain, disease, hate* exacerber.

exact [ɪg'zækt] **1** *adj* **(a)** (*accurate*) *description, time, measurements* exact, juste, précis; *forecast* juste, exact; *copy [picture]* exact, fidèle à l'original; *[document]* textuel; *transcript* littéral; *likeness* parfait. **that is ~** c'est exact *or* juste; **these were his ~ words** voilà textuellement ce qu'il a dit.

(b) (*precise*) *number, amount, value* exact, précis; *notions, meaning, time, moment, place, instructions* précis. **to give ~ details** donner des précisions; **he's 44 to be ~** il a très exactement 44 ans; **to be ~ it was 4 o'clock** il était 4 heures, plus précisément *or* plus exactement; **or, to be more ~ ...** ou pour mieux dire ...; **can you be more ~?** pouvez-vous préciser un peu?; **can you be more ~ about how many came?** pouvez-vous préciser le nombre des gens qui sont venus?

(c) (*rigorous*) *observation of rule etc* strict, exact; *analysis* exact; *study, work* rigoureux, précis; *instrument* de précision. **the ~ sciences** les sciences exactes.

2 *vt money, ransom* extorquer (*from* à); *payment, obedience* exiger (*from* de). **work that ~s great care** travail qui exige beaucoup de soin.

exacting [ɪg'zæktɪŋ] *adj person* exigeant; *profession* exigeant, astreignant; *task, activity, work* astreignant, qui exige beaucoup d'attention *or* d'efforts.

exaction [ɪg'zækʃən] *n* (*act*) exaction *f* (*pej*); (*money exacted*) impôt *m*, contribution *f*; (*excessive demand*) extorsion *f.*

exactitude [ɪg'zæktɪtju:d] *n* exactitude *f.*

exactly [ɪg'zæktlɪ] *adv* **(a)** (*accurately*) avec précision, précisément, exactement.

(b) (*precisely, quite*) exactement, précisément, justement, (tout) juste. **~ the same thing** exactement *or* précisément la même chose; **we don't ~ know** nous ne savons pas au juste; **that's ~ what I thought** c'est exactement ce que je pensais; **I had ~ £3** j'avais 3 livres tout juste; **it is 3 o'clock ~** il est 3 heures juste(s); **~!** précisément!, parfaitement!; **~ so!** c'est précisément cela!, c'est cela même!

exactness [ɪg'zæktnɪs] *n* (*V* **exact**) exactitude *f*, justesse *f*; précision *f*; rigueur *f.*

exaggerate [ɪg'zædʒəreɪt] **1** *vt* (*overstate*) *dangers, fears, size, beauty* exagérer; *story* amplifier; (*give undue importance to*) s'exagérer; (*intensify*) accentuer; *effect* outrer, forcer. **the dress ~d her paleness** la robe accentuait sa pâleur; **he ~s the importance of the task** il s'exagère l'importance de la tâche, il prête *or* attribue une importance excessive à la tâche.

2 *vi* exagérer, forcer la note. **he always ~s a little** il exagère *or* il en rajoute* toujours un peu.

exaggerated [ɪg'zædʒəreɪtɪd] *adj* exagéré; *praise, fashion* outré. **to have an ~ opinion of o.s.** avoir (une) trop bonne opinion de soi-même.

exaggeration [ɪgˌzædʒə'reɪʃən] *n* exagération *f.*

exalt [ɪg'zɔ:lt] *vt* (*in rank, power*) élever (*à un rang plus important*); (*extol*) porter aux nues, exalter.

exaltation [ˌegzɔ:l'teɪʃən] *n* (*U*) exaltation *f.*

exalted [ɪg'zɔ:ltɪd] *adj* (*high*) *rank, position, style* élevé; *person* haut placé, de haut rang; (*elated*) *mood, person* exalté, surexcité.

exam [ɪg'zæm] *n* (*abbr of* **examination a**) exam*** *m.*

examination [ɪgˌzæmɪ'neɪʃən] *n* **(a)** (*Scol, Univ*) (*test*) examen *m*; (*each paper*) épreuve *f.* (*Scol*) **class ~** composition *f.*

(b) (*study, inspection*) examen *m*; *[machine]* inspection *f*, examen; *[premises]* visite *f*, inspection; *[question]* étude *f*, considération *f*; *[accounts]* vérification *f*; *[passports]* contrôle *m.* **Custom's ~** fouille douanière; **close ~** examen rigoureux *or* minutieux; **expert's ~** expertise *f*; **on ~** après examen; *V* **medical** *etc.*

(c) (*Jur*) *[suspect, accused]* interrogatoire *m*; *[witness]* audition *f*; *[case, documents]* examen *m*. **legal ~** examen légal; *V* **cross.**

examine [ɪg'zæmɪn] *vt* **(a)** (*gen, Med*) examiner; *machine* inspecter; *proposition* examiner, étudier; *accounts* vérifier; *passport* contrôler; *dossier, documents* compulser, étudier, examiner; (*Customs*) *luggage* visiter, fouiller; *question, problem* examiner. **to ~ a question thoroughly** approfondir une question, examiner une question à fond.

(b) *pupil, candidate* examiner (*in* en); (*orally*) interroger (*on* sur).

(c) (*Jur*) *witness* interroger; *suspect, accused* interroger, faire subir un interrogatoire à; *case, document, evidence* examiner.

examinee [ɪg,zæmɪ'niː] *n* candidat(e) *m(f)*.

examiner [ɪg'zæmɪnəʳ] *n* examinateur *m*, -trice *f* (*in* de); *V* **board.**

example [ɪg'zɑːmpl] *n* (*model*) exemple *m*, modèle *m*; (*illustration*) exemple, cas *m*; (*sample*) spécimen *m*, exemple. **for ~** par exemple; **to set a good ~** donner l'exemple; **to be an ~** *[sb's conduct, deeds]* être un modèle; *[person]* être un exemple (*to* pour); **to take sb as an ~** prendre exemple sur qn; **to follow sb's ~** suivre l'exemple de qn; **following the ~ of** à l'exemple de; **to hold sb up as an ~** proposer qn en exemple; **to make an ~ of sb** faire un exemple en punissant qn; **to punish sb as an ~ to others** punir qn pour l'exemple; **to quote the ~ of ...** citer l'exemple de *or* le cas de ...; **to quote sth as an ~** citer qch en exemple; **here is an ~ of the work** voici un spécimen du travail.

exasperate [ɪg'zɑːspəreɪt] *vt person* exaspérer, mettre hors de soi, pousser à bout; *feeling* exaspérer, exacerber. **to become ~d** s'exaspérer; **~d at his lack of attention** exaspéré de *or* poussé à bout par son inattention; **~d with the boy** exaspéré par *or* furieux contre le garçon.

exasperating [ɪg'zɑːspəreɪtɪŋ] *adj* exaspérant, énervant (au possible).

exasperatingly [ɪg'zɑːspəreɪtɪŋlɪ] *adv* d'une manière exaspérante. **~ slow/stupid** d'une lenteur/d'une stupidité exaspérante.

exasperation [ɪg,zɑːspə'reɪʃən] *n* exaspération *f*, irritation *f*. **'hurry!' he cried in ~** 'dépêchez-vous!' cria-t-il, exaspéré.

excavate ['ekskəveɪt] **1** *vt ground* excaver; (*Archeol*) fouiller; *trench* creuser; *remains* dégager, déterrer. **2** *vi* (*Archeol*) faire des fouilles.

excavation [,ekskə'veɪʃən] *n* **(a)** (*U*) *[tunnel etc]* creusage *m*, creusement *m*, percement *m*. **(b)** (*Archeol: activity, site*) fouille *f*.

excavator ['ekskəveɪtəʳ] *n* (*machine*) excavateur *m*, excavatrice *f*; (*Archeol: person*) fouilleur *m*, -euse *f*.

exceed [ɪk'siːd] *vt* (*in value, amount, length of time etc*) dépasser, excéder (*in* en, *by* de); *powers* outrepasser, excéder; *instructions* outrepasser, dépasser; *expectations, limits, capabilities* dépasser; *desires* aller au-delà de, dépasser. (*Aut*) **to ~ the speed limit** dépasser la vitesse permise, commettre un excès de vitesse; (*Jur*) **a fine not ~ing £50** une amende ne dépassant pas 50 livres.

exceedingly [ɪk'siːdɪŋlɪ] *adv* extrêmement, infiniment, excessivement.

excel [ɪk'sel] **1** *vi* briller (*at, in* en), exceller (*at or in doing* à faire). **he doesn't exactly ~ in Latin** on ne saurait dire qu'il brille en latin, on ne peut pas dire qu'il fasse des étincelles* en latin. **2** *vt person* surpasser, l'emporter sur (*in* en). (*often iro*) **to ~ o.s.** se surpasser, se distinguer.

excellence ['eksələns] *n* **(a)** (*U*) excellence *f*, supériorité *f*. **(b)** (*outstanding feature*) qualité *f* (supérieure).

Excellency ['eksələnsɪ] *n* Excellence *f*. **Your/His ~** Votre/Son Excellence.

excellent ['eksələnt] *adj* excellent, admirable, parfait. **what an ~ idea!** (quelle) excellente idée!; **~!** parfait!; **that's ~!** c'est parfait!, c'est on ne peut mieux!

excellently ['eksələntlɪ] *adv* admirablement, parfaitement, excellemment (*liter*). **to do sth ~** faire qch à la perfection *or* on ne peut mieux.

except [ɪk'sept] **1** *prep* (*also* **excepting**) **(a)** sauf, excepté, à l'exception de, hormis. **all ~ the eldest daughter** tous excepté la fille aînée *or* la fille aînée exceptée; **~ for** à part, à l'exception de, si ce n'est; **~ that** sauf que, excepté que, sinon que, si ce n'est que, à cela près que; **~ if** sauf si; **~ when** sauf quand, excepté quand.

(b) (*after neg and certain interrogs*) sinon, si ce n'est. **what can they do ~ wait?** que peuvent-ils faire sinon *or* si ce n'est attendre?

2 *conj* (*also* **excepting**) (†, *liter*) à moins que + ne + *subj*. **~ he be a traitor** à moins qu'il ne soit un traître.

3 *vt* excepter, exclure (*from* de), faire exception de. **present company ~ed** exception faite des personnes présentes.

excepting [ɪk'septɪŋ] *prep, conj* (*V* **except 1, 2**) **not** *or* **without ~** sans exclure, sans oublier; **always ~** à l'exception (bien entendu) de, exception faite (bien entendu) de.

exception [ɪk'sepʃən] *n* **(a)** (*U*) exception *f*. **without ~** sans (aucune) exception; **with the ~ of** à l'exception de, exception faite de; **to take ~ to** (*demur*) trouver à redire à, désapprouver; (*be offended*) s'offenser de, s'offusquer de; **I take ~ to that remark** je suis indigné par cette remarque.

(b) (*singularity*) exception *f*. **to make an ~** faire une exception (*to sth* à qch, *for sb/sth* pour qn/qch, en faveur de qn/qch); **these strokes of luck are the ~** ces coups de chance sont l'exception; **this case is an ~ to the rule** ce cas est *or* constitue une exception à la règle; **the ~ proves the rule** l'exception confirme la règle; **with this ~** à cette exception près, à ceci près; **apart from a few ~s** à part quelques exceptions, à de rares exceptions près.

exceptional [ɪk'sepʃənl] *adj* (*unusual*) *weather, temperature* exceptionnel; (*outstanding*) *quality, talent* exceptionnel, peu commun, hors ligne.

exceptionally [ɪk'sepʃənəlɪ] *adv* (*unusually*) exceptionnellement, par exception; (*outstandingly*) exceptionnellement, extraordinairement.

excerpt ['eksɜːpt] *n* (*Literat, Mus etc*) extrait *m*, passage *m*, morceau *m*.

excess [ɪk'ses] **1** *n* **(a)** (*U*) *[precautions, enthusiasm]* excès *m*; *[details, adjectives]* luxe *m*, surabondance *f*. **to ~** (jusqu')à l'excès; **to carry to ~** pousser à l'excès, pousser trop loin; **carried to ~** outré; **in ~ of** qui dépasse, dépassant; **to drink to ~** boire à l'excès *or* avec excès, faire des excès de boisson; **the ~ of imports over exports** l'excédent *m* des importations sur les exportations.

(b) (*Insurance*) franchise *f*.

(c) ~es (*debauchery*) excès *mpl*, débauche *f*; (*cruelty, violence*) excès, abus *m*, cruauté *f*; (*overindulgence*) excès, écart *m*; **the ~es of the regime** les abus du régime.

2 *cpd profit, weight, production* excédentaire. (*Econ*) **excess demand** excès *m* de la demande; **excess fare** supplément *m*; **excess luggage** excédent *m* de bagages; **excess profits tax** impôt *m* sur les bénéfices exceptionnels; (*Econ*) **excess supply** excès *m* de l'offre.

excessive [ɪk'sesɪv] *adj demands, price, use* excessif; *ambition* démesuré, sans mesure; *expenditure* immodéré; *praise* outré. **~ drinking** abus *m* de la boisson.

excessively [ɪk'sesɪvlɪ] *adv* **(a)** (*to excess*) *eat, drink, spend* avec excès, plus que de raison; *optimistic* par trop; *proud* démesurément. **I was not ~ worried** je ne m'inquiétais pas outre mesure.

(b) (*extremely*) extrêmement, infiniment, excessivement; *pretty* extrêmement, infiniment; *boring, ugly* atrocement.

exchange [ɪks'tʃeɪndʒ] **1** *vt glances, gifts, letters, blows* échanger; *photographs, records, books* échanger, faire un *or* des échange(s) de; *houses, cars, jobs* faire un échange de. **to ~ one thing for another** échanger une chose contre une autre; **they ~d a few words** ils échangèrent quelques mots; (*euph: quarrel*) **they ~d words** ils se sont disputés, ils ont eu des mots ensemble*.

2 *n* **(a)** *[objects, prisoners, ideas, secrets, notes, greetings]* échange *m*. **in ~** en échange (*for* de), en retour (*for* de); **to gain/lose on the ~** gagner/perdre au change; *V* **fair[1], part** *etc.*

(b) (*Fin*) change *m*. **the dollar ~** le change du dollar; **on the (stock) ~** à la Bourse, au change; *V* **bill[1], foreign** *etc.*

(c) (*telephone ~*) central *m*; (*labour ~*) bourse *f* du travail.

3 *cpd*: (*Fin*) **exchange control** contrôle *m* des changes; **exchange rate** taux *m* de change.

exchangeable [ɪks'tʃeɪndʒəbl] *adj* échangeable (*for* contre).

exchequer [ɪks'tʃekəʳ] *n* (*Parl*) ministère *m* des Finances, (*in Britain*) Échiquier *m*; (*one's own funds*) fonds *mpl*, finances* *fpl*; *V* **chancellor.**

excisable [ek'saɪzəbl] *adj* imposable, soumis aux droits de régie.

excise[1] ['eksaɪz] **1** *n* taxe *f* (*on* sur). (*Brit*) **the E~** la Régie. **2** *cpd*: **excise duties** impôts prélevés par la régie, ≃ contributions indirectes; (*Brit*) **exciseman** employé *m* de la régie.

excise[2] [ek'saɪz] *vt* (*Med*) exciser; (*gen*) retrancher, supprimer.

excision [ek'sɪʒən] *n* (*V* **excise[2]**) excision *f*; retranchement *m*, suppression *f*.

excitable [ɪk'saɪtəbl] *adj person* excitable, prompt à l'excitation, nerveux; *animal, temperament* nerveux; (*Med*) excitable.

excite [ɪk'saɪt] *vt* **(a)** (*agitate*) exciter, agiter; (*rouse enthusiasm in*) passionner; (*move*) mettre en émoi, impressionner; *animal* exciter. **to ~ sb to sth** provoquer *or* pousser *or* inciter qn à qch.

(b) *sentiments, envy, attention, pity* exciter; *imagination, passion* exciter, enflammer; *desire, anger* exciter, aviver; *admiration* exciter, susciter; *curiosity* exciter, piquer. **to ~ enthusiasm/interest in sb** enthousiasmer/intéresser qn.

(c) (*Med*) *nerve* exciter, stimuler.

excited [ɪk'saɪtɪd] *adj person, animal* excité, agité, énervé; *laughter* énervé; *crowd* excité, agité, en émoi; *voice* animé; *imagination* surexcité, enflammé; (*Phys*) *atom, molecule* excité. **to get ~** *[person]* s'exciter, s'énerver, se monter la tête (*about* au sujet de, à propos de); *[crowd]* s'agiter, devenir houleux; **don't get ~!** du calme!, ne t'énerve pas!; **to make ~ gestures** faire de grands gestes, gesticuler.

excitedly [ɪk'saɪtɪdlɪ] *adv behave* avec agitation, d'une manière agitée; *speak* sur un ton animé, avec agitation; *laugh* d'excitation. **to wave ~** faire de grands gestes, gesticuler.

excitement [ɪk'saɪtmənt] *n* (*agitation*) excitation *f*, agitation *f*, fièvre *f*; (*exhilaration*) vive émotion, exaltation *f*. **the ~ of the departure/elections** la fièvre du départ/des élections; **the ~ of victory** l'ivresse *f* *or* l'exaltation de la victoire; **to be in a state of great ~** être très agité, être en proie à une vive émotion; **the book caused great ~ in literary circles** le livre a fait sensation dans les milieux littéraires; **he likes ~** il aime les émotions fortes *or* l'aventure.

exciting [ɪk'saɪtɪŋ] *adj events, story, film* passionnant; *account* saisissant; *holiday, experience* excitant. **we had an ~ time** ça a été très excitant.

exclaim [ɪks'kleɪm] *vi* s'exclamer, s'écrier. **he ~ed in surprise when he saw it** il s'est exclamé de surprise en le voyant; **'at last!' she ~ed** 'enfin!' s'écria-t-elle; **to ~ at sth** (*indignantly*) se récrier (d'indignation) devant *or* contre qch; (*admiringly*) se récrier d'admiration devant qch.

exclamation [,ekskləˈmeɪʃən] **1** *n* exclamation *f*. **2** *cpd*: **exclamation mark,** (*US*) **exclamation point** point *m* d'exclamation.

exclamatory [ɪksˈklæmətərɪ] *adj* exclamatif.

exclude [ɪksˈklu:d] *vt* (*from team, society*) exclure (*from* de), rejeter; (*from list*) écarter (*from* de), ne pas retenir; *doubt, possibility* exclure, écarter, éliminer. **he was ~d from the senior posts** il n'a jamais eu droit aux postes supérieurs; **he was ~d from taking part** il n'a pas eu le droit de participer.

exclusion [ɪksˈklu:ʒən] *n* exclusion *f* (*from* de). **to the ~ of** à l'exclusion de.

exclusive [ɪksˈklu:sɪv] *adj* **(a)** (*excluding others*) *group, gathering* select *inv or* sélect; *club, society* fermé; *person, friendship, interest, occupation* exclusif. **~ gatherings** réunions select *or* sélectes.
(b) (*owned by one person, one firm*) *rights, information, dress, design* exclusif. **to have/buy ~ rights for** avoir/acheter l'exclusivité de; (*Press*) **an interview ~ to X** une interview accordée exclusivement à X; (*Press*) **~ story** reportage exclusif.
(c) (*not including*) **from 15th to 20th June ~** du 15 (jusqu')au 20 juin exclusivement; **~ of** non compris, sans compter; **the price is ~ of transport charges** le prix ne comprend pas les frais de transport; (*Comm*) **~ of post and packing** frais d'emballage et d'envoi en sus *or* non compris.

exclusively [ɪksˈklu:sɪvlɪ] *adv* exclusivement.

excommunicate [ˌekskəˈmju:nɪkeɪt] *vt* excommunier.

excommunication [ˈekskəˌmju:nɪˈkeɪʃən] *n* excommunication *f*.

excrement [ˈekskrɪmənt] *n* excrément *m*.

excrescence [ɪksˈkresns] *n* (*lit, fig*) excroissance *f*.

excreta [ɪksˈkri:tə] *npl* excrétions *fpl*.

excrete [ɪksˈkri:t] *vt* excréter; *[plant]* sécréter.

excretion [ɪksˈkri:ʃən] *n* excrétion *f*, sécrétion *f*.

excruciating [ɪksˈkru:ʃɪeɪtɪŋ] *adj pain* atroce; *suffering* déchirant; *noise* infernal, insupportable; (*: *unpleasant*) épouvantable, atroce.

excruciatingly [ɪksˈkru:ʃɪeɪtɪŋlɪ] *adv* atrocement, affreusement. **it's ~ funny*** c'est désopilant, c'est à mourir de rire.

exculpate [ˈekskʌlpeɪt] *vt person* disculper, innocenter (*from* de).

excursion [ɪksˈkɜ:ʃən] **1** *n* excursion *f*, balade* *f*; (*in car, on cycle*) randonnée *f*; (*fig: digression*) digression *f*. **2** *cpd*: **excursion ticket** billet *m* d'excursion; **excursion train** train spécial (*pour excursions*).

excusable [ɪksˈkju:zəbl] *adj* excusable, pardonnable. **your hesitation is ~** votre hésitation s'excuse *or* est excusable.

excuse [ɪksˈkju:z] **1** *vt* **(a)** (*justify*) *action, person* excuser, défendre. **such rudeness cannot be ~d** une telle impolitesse est sans excuse *or* inexcusable; **to ~ o.s.** s'excuser (*for* de, *for doing* de faire, d'avoir fait), présenter ses excuses.
(b) (*pardon*) excuser (*sb for having done* qn d'avoir fait). **to ~ sb's insolence** excuser l'insolence de qn, pardonner à qn son insolence; **one can be ~d for not understanding what he says** on est excusable de ne pas comprendre ce qu'il dit; **if you will ~ the expression** passez-moi l'expression; **and now if you will ~ me I have work to do** maintenant, si vous (le) permettez, j'ai à travailler; **~ me for wondering if ...** permettez-moi de me demander si ...; **~ me!** excusez-moi!, (je vous demande) pardon!; **~ me, but I don't think this is true** excusez-moi *or* permettez, mais je ne crois pas que ce soit vrai; **~ me for not seeing you out** excusez-moi si je ne vous raccompagne pas *or* de ne pas vous raccompagner.
(c) (*exempt*) exempter (*sb from sth* qn de qch), dispenser (*sb from sth* qn de qch, *sb from doing* qn de faire), excuser. (*to children*) **you are ~d** vous pouvez vous en aller; **he ~d himself after 10 minutes** au bout de 10 minutes, il s'est excusé et est parti; **to ask to be ~d** se faire excuser; **he was ~d from the afternoon session** on l'a dispensé d'assister à la séance de l'après-midi; **to ~ sb from an obligation** faire grâce à qn *or* exempter qn d'une obligation.
2 [ɪksˈkju:s] *n* **(a)** (*reason, justification*) excuse *f*. **there is no ~ for it**, (*frm*) **it admits of no ~** cela est inexcusable *or* sans excuse; **his only ~ was that ...** il avait comme seule excuse le fait que ...; **that is no ~ for his leaving so abruptly** cela ne l'excuse pas d'être parti si brusquement; **in ~ for** pour excuser; **without ~** sans excuse, sans raison, sans motif valable; *V* **ignorance** *etc*.
(b) (*pretext*) excuse *f*, prétexte *m*. **lame ~** faible excuse, excuse boiteuse; **to find an ~ for sth** trouver une excuse à qch; **I have a good ~ for not going** j'ai une bonne excuse pour ne pas y aller; **he is only making ~s** il cherche tout simplement des prétextes *or* de bonnes raisons; **he is always making ~s to get away** il trouve *or* invente toujours des excuses pour s'absenter; **what's your ~ this time?** qu'avez-vous comme excuse cette fois-ci?; **he gave the bad weather as his ~ for not coming** il a prétexté *or* allégué le mauvais temps pour ne pas venir; **it's only an ~** ce n'est qu'un prétexte; **his success was a good ~ for a family party** sa réussite a servi de prétexte à une fête de famille.

execrable [ˈeksɪkrəbl] *adj* exécrable, affreux, détestable; *manners, temper* exécrable, épouvantable.

execrably [ˈeksɪkrəblɪ] *adv* exécrablement, détestablement.

execrate [ˈeksɪkreɪt] *vt* **(a)** (*hate*) exécrer, détester. **(b)** (*curse*) maudire.

execration [ˌeksɪˈkreɪʃən] *n* **(a)** (*U*) exécration *f*, horreur *f*. **to hold in ~** avoir en horreur *or* en exécration, exécrer. **(b)** (*curse*) malédiction *f*, imprécation *f*.

executant [ɪgˈzekjʊtənt] *n* (*Mus*) interprète *mf*, exécutant(e) *m(f)*.

execute [ˈeksɪkju:t] *vt* **(a)** (*put to death*) exécuter.
(b) (*carry out*) *order, piece of work, dance, movement* exécuter; *work of art* réaliser; *project, plan* exécuter, mettre à exécution, réaliser; *purpose, sb's wishes* accomplir; *duties* exercer, remplir, accomplir; *task* accomplir, s'acquitter de, mener à bien; (*Mus*) exécuter, interpréter; (*Jur*) *will* exécuter; (*Jur*) *document* valider; *contract* valider, exécuter.

execution [ˌeksɪˈkju:ʃən] *n* **(a)** (*killing*) exécution *f*.
(b) (*V* **execute b**) exécution *f*; réalisation *f*; accomplissement *m*; validation *f*; (*Mus: of musical work*) exécution, interprétation *f*; (*Mus: performer's skill*) jeu *m*, technique *f*. **to put into ~** mettre à exécution; **in the ~ of his duties** dans l'exercice de ses fonctions; *V* **stay**.

executioner [ˌeksɪˈkju:ʃnə^r] *n* (*also* **public ~**) bourreau *m*, exécuteur *m* des hautes œuvres.

executive [ɪgˈzekjʊtɪv] **1** *adj powers, committee* exécutif; *talent, quality* d'exécution; *job, position* administratif, de cadre. **senior ~ post** poste *m* de direction; **~ capability** capacité *f* d'exécution; (*Can, US*) **~ director** directeur *m* (général), directrice *f*; (*US*) **~ order** décret-loi *m*; **~ secretary** secrétaire *m* général; (*Can, US: Parl*) **~ session** séance *f* parlementaire (*à huis clos*).
2 *n* **(a)** (*power*) (pouvoir *m*) exécutif *m*.
(b) (*Admin, Ind etc*) (*person*) cadre *m*, administrateur *m*; (*group of managers*) bureau *m*. **to be on the ~** faire partie du bureau; **the trades union ~** le bureau du syndicat.
3 *cpd*: (*Ind etc*) **executive car** voiture *f* de directeur; (*US*) **the Executive Mansion** (*White House*) la Maison Blanche; (*Governor's House*) la résidence officielle du gouverneur (*d'un État*); (*Ind etc*) **executive plane** avion *m* de directeur; **the executive suite (of offices)** les bureaux *mpl* de la direction; **executive unemployment** chômage *m* des cadres.

executor [ɪgˈzekjʊtə^r] *n* (*Jur*) exécuteur *m* testamentaire.

executrix [ɪgˈzekjʊtrɪks] *n* (*Jur*) exécutrice *f* testamentaire.

exegesis [ˌeksɪˈdʒi:sɪs] *n* exégèse *f*.

exemplary [ɪgˈzemplərɪ] *adj conduct, virtue* exemplaire; *pupil etc* modèle; *punishment* exemplaire. (*Brit Jur*) **~ damages** dommages-intérêts très élevés (à titre de réparation exemplaire).

exemplify [ɪgˈzemplɪfaɪ] *vt* (*illustrate*) exemplifier, illustrer, démontrer; (*be example of*) servir d'exemple de, être un exemple de.

exempt [ɪgˈzempt] **1** *adj* exempt (*from* de). **2** *vt* exempter (*from sth* de qch), dispenser (*from doing* de faire).

exemption [ɪgˈzempʃən] *n* exemption *f* (*from* de).

exercise [ˈeksəsaɪz] **1** *n* **(a)** (*U*) *[right, caution, power]* exercice *m*; *[religion]* pratique *f*, exercice. **in the ~ of his duties** dans l'exercice de ses fonctions; **physical ~** exercice physique; **to take ~** prendre de l'exercice.
(b) (*in gymnastics, school subjects*) exercice *m*. **a grammar ~** un exercice de grammaire; **to do (physical) ~s every morning** faire de la gymnastique tous les matins.
(c) (*Mil etc: gen pl*) exercice *m*, manœuvre *f*. **to go on (an) ~** (*Mil*) aller à la manœuvre, partir à l'exercice; (*Naut*) partir en exercice *or* en manœuvre; **NATO ~s** manœuvres de l'OTAN.
(d) (*US: gen pl: ceremony*) cérémonies *fpl*.
2 *cpd*: **exercise book** cahier *m* (de devoirs).
3 *vt* **(a)** *body, mind* exercer; *troops* faire faire l'exercice à; *horse* exercer. **to ~ a dog** exercer *or* promener un chien.
(b) *one's authority, control, power* exercer; *a right* exercer, faire valoir, user de; *one's talents* employer, exercer; *patience, tact, restraint* faire preuve de. **to ~ care in doing** apporter du soin à faire, s'appliquer à bien faire.
(c) (*frm: disquiet*) inquiéter. **the problem which is exercising my mind** le problème qui me préoccupe.
4 *vi* se donner de l'exercice. **you don't ~ enough** vous ne prenez pas assez d'exercice.

exert [ɪgˈzɜ:t] *vt* **(a)** *pressure* exercer; *force* employer; *talent, influence* exercer, déployer; *authority* exercer, faire sentir.
(b) to ~ o.s. (*physically*) se dépenser; (*take trouble*) se donner du mal, s'appliquer; **to ~ o.s. to do** s'appliquer à *or* s'efforcer de faire; **he didn't ~ himself unduly** il ne s'est pas donné trop de mal, il ne s'est pas trop fatigué; (*iro*) **don't ~ yourself!** ne vous fatiguez pas!

exertion [ɪgˈzɜ:ʃən] *n* **(a)** effort *m*. **by his own ~s** par ses propres moyens; **after the day's ~s** après les fatigues *fpl* de la journée; **it doesn't require much ~** cela n'exige pas un grand effort. **(b)** (*U*) *[force, strength]* emploi *m*; *[authority, influence]* exercice *m*. **by the ~ of a little pressure** en exerçant une légère pression.

exeunt [ˈeksɪʌnt] *vi* (*Theat*) ils sortent. **~ Macbeth and Lady Macbeth** Macbeth et Lady Macbeth sortent.

exfoliate [eksˈfəʊlɪeɪt] *vt* exfolier.

exfoliation [eksˌfəʊlɪˈeɪʃən] *n* exfoliation *f*.

exhalation [ˌekshəˈleɪʃən] *n* (*act*) exhalation *f*; (*odour, fumes etc*) exhalaison *f*.

exhale [eksˈheɪl] **1** *vt* **(a)** (*breathe out*) expirer (*Physiol*). **(b)** (*give off*) *smoke, gas, perfume* exhaler. **2** *vi* expirer. **~ please** expirez s'il vous plaît; **he ~d slowly in relief** il a laissé échapper un long soupir de soulagement.

exhaust [ɪgˈzɔ:st] **1** *vt* **(a)** (*use up*) *supplies, energy, mine, subject* épuiser. **to ~ sb's patience** épuiser la patience de qn, mettre qn à bout de patience; **my patience is ~ed** ma patience est à bout; **until funds are ~ed** jusqu'à épuisement des fonds.
(b) (*tire*) épuiser, exténuer.
2 *n* (*Aut etc*) (*also* **~ system**) échappement *m*; (*also* **~ pipe**) tuyau *m or* pot *m* d'échappement; (*also* **~ fumes**) gaz *m* d'échappement.

exhausted [ɪgˈzɔ:stɪd] *adj person* épuisé, exténué, brisé de fatigue; *supplies* épuisé. **I'm ~** je n'en peux plus, je suis à bout, je tombe de fatigue.

exhausting [ɪgˈzɔ:stɪŋ] *adj climate, activity* épuisant; *work* exténuant, épuisant.

exhaustion [ɪgˈzɔːstʃən] *n* (*U: tiredness*) épuisement *m*, fatigue *f* extrême.
exhaustive [ɪgˈzɔːstɪv] *adj account, report* complet (*f* -ète); *study, description, list* complet, exhaustif; *inquiry, inspection* minutieux; *research* approfondi. **to make an ~ study of** étudier à fond.
exhaustively [ɪgˈzɔːstɪvlɪ] *adv* à fond, complètement, exhaustivement.
exhibit [ɪgˈzɪbɪt] **1** *vt painting, handicrafts* exposer; *merchandise* exposer, étaler; *document, identity card* montrer, présenter, produire; *courage, skill, ingenuity* faire preuve de, déployer.
2 *n* (*in exhibition*) objet exposé; (*Jur*) pièce *f* à conviction. **~ A** première pièce à conviction.
exhibition [ˌeksɪˈbɪʃən] *n* **(a)** (*show*) *[paintings, furniture etc]* exposition *f*; *[articles for sale]* étalage *m*. **the Van Gogh ~** l'exposition Van Gogh; (*fig*) **to make an ~ of o.s.** se donner en spectacle.
(b) (*act of exhibiting*) *[technique etc]* démonstration *f*; *[film]* présentation *f*. **what an ~ of bad manners!** quelle belle démonstration d'impolitesse!, quel étalage de mauvaise éducation!
(c) (*Brit Univ*) bourse *f* (d'études).
exhibitioner [ˌeksɪˈbɪʃənəʳ] *n* (*Brit Univ*) boursier *m*, -ière *f*.
exhibitionism [ˌeksɪˈbɪʃənɪzəm] *n* exhibitionnisme *m*.
exhibitionist [ˌeksɪˈbɪʃənɪst] *adj, n* exhibitionniste (*mf*).
exhibitor [ɪgˈzɪbɪtəʳ] *n* exposant(e) *m(f)* (*dans une exposition*).
exhilarate [ɪgˈzɪləreɪt] *vt [sea air etc]* vivifier; *[music etc]* transporter (de joie), mettre la joie au cœur à; *[wine, good company]* stimuler.
exhilarating [ɪgˈzɪləreɪtɪŋ] *adj air, wind etc* vivifiant; *music* enivrant, grisant; *conversation, work* stimulant, passionnant. **she found his presence very ~** elle trouvait sa présence très stimulante.
exhilaration [ɪgˌzɪləˈreɪʃən] *n* joie *f*, allégresse *f*, ivresse *f*.
exhort [ɪgˈzɔːt] *vt* (*urge*) exhorter, inciter, appeler (*sb to sth* qn à qch, *sb to do* qn à faire); (*advise*) conseiller *or* recommander vivement (*sb to do* à qn de faire).
exhortation [ˌegzɔːˈteɪʃən] *n* (*V* **exhort**) exhortation *f* (*to* à), incitation *f* (*to* à); conseil *m*, recommandation *f*.
exhumation [ˌekshjuːˈmeɪʃən] *n* exhumation *f*. (*Jur*) **~ order** autorisation *f* d'exhumer.
exhume [eksˈhjuːm] *vt* exhumer.
exigence [ˈeksɪdʒəns] *n*, **exigency** [ɪgˈzɪdʒənsɪ] *n* (*urgency*) urgence *f*; (*emergency*) circonstance *f or* situation *f* critique; (*gen pl: demand*) exigence *f*. **according to the exigencies of the situation** selon les exigences de la situation.
exigent [ˈeksɪdʒənt] *adj* (*urgent*) urgent, pressant; (*exacting*) exigeant.
exiguity [ˌegzɪˈgjuːɪtɪ] *n* exiguïté *f*.
exiguous [ɪgˈzɪgjʊəs] *adj space* exigu (*f* -guë), minuscule, fort petit; *income, revenue* modique.
exile [ˈeksaɪl] **1** *n* **(a)** (*person*) (*voluntarily*) exilé(e) *m(f)*, expatrié(e) *m(f)*; (*expelled*) exilé(e), expulsé(e) *m(f)*, banni(e) *m(f)*.
(b) (*U: condition: lit, fig*) exil *m*. **in ~** en exil; **to send into ~** envoyer en exil, exiler, bannir; **to go into ~** partir *or* s'en aller en exil, s'exiler, s'expatrier.
2 *vt* exiler, bannir (*from* de).
exist [ɪgˈzɪst] *vi* **(a)** *[person, animal, plant, belief, custom]* exister; (*Philos etc*) exister, être. **everything that ~s** tout ce qui existe *or* est; **it only ~s in her imagination** cela n'existe que dans son imagination; **to continue to ~** exister encore, subsister; **doubt still ~s** le doute subsiste; **the understanding which ~s between the two countries** l'entente qui règne *or* existe entre les deux pays; **the tradition ~s that ...** il existe une tradition selon laquelle ...; **can life ~ on Mars?** la vie existe-t-elle sur Mars?, y a-t-il de la vie sur Mars?
(b) (*live*) vivre, subsister. **we cannot ~ without water** nous ne pouvons pas vivre *or* subsister sans eau; **she ~s on very little** elle vit de très peu; **we manage to ~** nous subsistons tant bien que mal, nous vivotons; **can one ~ on such a small salary?** est-il possible de subsister avec un salaire aussi modique?
existence [ɪgˈzɪstəns] *n* **(a)** (*U*) *[God, person, object, institution]* existence *f*. **to be in ~** exister; **to come into ~** naître, être créé; **to call into ~** faire naître, créer; **it came into ~ 30 years ago** cela a été créé il y a 30 ans, cela existe depuis 30 ans; **it went out of ~ 10 years ago** cela n'existe plus depuis 10 ans; **the only one in ~** le seul *or* la seule qui existe (*subj*) *or* qui soit.
(b) (*life*) existence *f*, vie *f*.
existent [ɪgˈzɪstənt] *adj* existant.
existential [ˌegzɪsˈtenʃəl] *adj* existentiel.
existentialism [ˌegzɪsˈtenʃəlɪzəm] *n* existentialisme *m*.
existentialist [ˌegzɪsˈtenʃəlɪst] *adj, n* existentialiste (*mf*).
existing [ɪgˈzɪstɪŋ] *adj law* existant; *state of affairs, regime* actuel; *circumstances* présent, actuel.
exit [ˈeksɪt] **1** *n* **(a)** (*from stage*) sortie *f*. **to make one's ~** (*Theat*) quitter la scène; (*gen*) sortir, faire sa sortie.
(b) (*way out, door*) sortie *f*, issue *f*; *V* **emergency**.
2 *vi* **(a)** (*Theat*) **~ the King** le roi sort.
(b) (*: *leave*) sortir, faire sa sortie.
3 *cpd*: **exit permit/visa** permis *m*/visa *m* de sortie.
exocrine [ˈeksəʊˌkraɪn] *adj* exocrine.
exodus [ˈeksədəs] *n* exode *m*; (*Bible*) **E~** l'Exode.
ex officio [ˌeksəˈfɪʃɪəʊ] **1** *adv act* ex officio, d'office. **2** *adj member* ex officio, nommé d'office.
exonerate [ɪgˈzɒnəreɪt] *vt* (*prove innocent*) disculper, justifier (*from* de), innocenter; (*release from obligation*) exempter, dispenser, décharger (*from* de).
exoneration [ɪgˌzɒnəˈreɪʃən] *n* (*V* **exonerate**) disculpation *f*, justification *f*; exemption *f*, dispense *f*, décharge *f* (*from* de).
exorbitance [ɪgˈzɔːbɪtəns] *n [demands]* outrance *f*; *[price]* énormité *f*.
exorbitant [ɪgˈzɔːbɪtənt] *adj price* exorbitant, excessif, exagéré; *demands, pretensions* exorbitant, démesuré, extravagant.
exorbitantly [ɪgˈzɔːbɪtəntlɪ] *adv* démesurément.
exorcise [ˈeksɔːsaɪz] *vt* exorciser.
exorcism [ˈeksɔːsɪzəm] *n* exorcisme *m*.
exorcist [ˈeksɔːsɪst] *n* exorciste *m*.
exoskeleton [ˌeksəʊˈskelɪtən] *n* exosquelette *m*.
exoteric [ˌeksəʊˈterɪk] *adj doctrine* exotérique; *opinions* populaire.
exothermic [ˌeksəʊˈθɜːmɪk] *adj* exothermique.
exotic [ɪgˈzɒtɪk] **1** *adj* exotique. **an ~-sounding name** un nom aux consonances exotiques. **2** *n* (*Bot*) plante *f* exotique.
exoticism [ɪgˈzɒtɪsɪzəm] *n* exotisme *m*.
expand [ɪksˈpænd] **1** *vt gas, liquid, metal* dilater; *one's business, trade, ideas* développer; *production* accroître, augmenter; *horizons, study* élargir; *influence, empire, property, knowledge, experience* étendre; (*Math*) *formula* développer. **to ~ one's lungs** se dilater les poumons; **exercises to ~ one's chest** exercices physiques pour développer le torse; **to ~ a few notes into a complete article** développer quelques notes pour en faire un article complet; **~ed polystyrene** polystyrène *m* expansé.
2 *vi* (*V* 1) se dilater; se développer; s'accroître, augmenter; s'élargir; s'étendre. **the market is ~ing** les débouchés se multiplient; **a rapidly ~ing industry** une industrie en pleine expansion *or* en plein essor; **the ~ing universe theory** la théorie de l'expansion de l'univers.
expanse [ɪksˈpæns] *n* étendue *f*.
expansion [ɪksˈpænʃən] **1** *n [gas]* expansion *f*, dilatation *f*; *[business]* extension *f*, agrandissement *m*; *[trade]* développement *m*, essor *m*; *[production]* accroissement *m*, augmentation *f*; (*territorial, economic, colonial*) expansion; *[subject, idea]* développement; (*Math*) développement.
2 *cpd*: **expansion bolt** écrou *m* de serrage *or* de scellement.
expansionism [ɪksˈpænʃənɪzəm] *n* expansionnisme *m*.
expansionist [ɪksˈpænʃənɪst] *adj, n* expansionniste (*mf*).
expansive [ɪksˈpænsɪv] *adj* **(a)** *person* expansif, démonstratif, communicatif. **to be in an ~ mood** être en veine d'épanchements *or* d'effusion(s). **(b)** (*Phys*) (*causing expansion*) expansif; (*capable of expanding*) expansible, dilatable.
expansively [ɪksˈpænsɪvlɪ] *adv* avec abondance. **he was smiling ~** il arborait un large sourire.
expatiate [ɪksˈpeɪʃɪeɪt] *vi* discourir, disserter, s'étendre (*upon* sur).
expatriate [eksˈpætrɪeɪt] **1** *vt* expatrier. **2** *adj* expatrié. **3** *n* expatrié(e) *m(f)*.
expect [ɪksˈpekt] *vt* **(a)** (*anticipate*) s'attendre à, attendre, prévoir; (*with confidence*) escompter; (*count on*) compter sur; (*hope for*) espérer. **to ~ to do** penser *or* compter *or* espérer faire, s'attendre à faire; **we were ~ing rain** nous nous attendions à de la pluie; **to ~ the worst** s'attendre au pire, prévoir le pire; **that was to be ~ed** c'était à prévoir, il fallait s'y attendre; **I ~ed as much** je m'y attendais; **I know what to ~** je sais à quoi m'attendre *or* m'en tenir; **I did not ~ that from him** je n'attendais pas cela de lui; **he did not have the success he ~ed** il n'a pas eu le succès qu'il escomptait; **we were ~ing war** on attendait la guerre; **to ~ that** s'attendre à ce que + *subj*, escompter que + *indic*; **it is ~ed that** il est vraisemblable que + *indic*, il y a des chances pour que + *subj*, il faut s'attendre à ce que + *subj*; **it is hardly to be ~ed that** il ne faut pas *or* guère s'attendre à ce que + *subj*, il y a peu de chances pour que + *subj*; **I ~ him to come, I ~ that he'll come** je m'attends à ce qu'il vienne; **this suitcase is not as heavy as I ~ed** cette valise n'est pas aussi lourde que je le croyais; **he failed, as we had ~ed** il a échoué, comme nous l'avions prévu; **as might have been ~ed, as was to be ~ed** comme il fallait *or* comme on pouvait s'y attendre; **as ~ed** comme on s'y attendait, comme prévu.
(b) (*suppose*) penser, croire, supposer, se douter de. **I ~ so** je (le) crois, je crois que oui; **this work is very tiring — yes, I ~ it is** ce travail est très fatigant — oui, je m'en doute *or* je veux bien le croire; **I ~ he'll soon have finished** je pense *or* suppose qu'il aura bientôt fini; **I ~ it was your father** je suppose que c'était ton père.
(c) (*demand*) exiger, attendre (*sth from sb* qch de qn), demander (*sth from sb* qch à qn). **to ~ sb to do sth** exiger *or* vouloir *or* demander que qn fasse qch; **you can't ~ too much from him** il ne faut pas trop lui en demander, on ne peut pas trop exiger de lui; **I ~ you to tidy your own room** tu es censé ranger ta chambre toi-même, je compte que tu rangeras ta chambre toi-même; **what do you ~ me to do about it?** que voulez-vous que j'y fasse?; **what do you ~ of me?** qu'attendez-vous *or* qu'exigez-vous de moi?; **England ~s that every man will do his duty** l'Angleterre compte que chacun fera son devoir; **are we ~ed to leave now?** est-ce que nous sommes censés *or* est-ce qu'on doit partir tout de suite?
(d) (*await*) *person, baby, thing, action* attendre. **I am ~ing her tomorrow** je l'attends demain; **I am ~ing them for dinner** je les attends à dîner; **~ me when you see me!*** vous (me) verrez bien quand je serai là!*; **we'll ~ you when we see you*** on ne t'attend pas à une heure précise; **she is ~ing*** elle est enceinte, elle attend un bébé *or* un heureux événement.
expectancy [ɪksˈpektənsɪ] *n* attente *f*; *[money, inheritance]* espérances *fpl*. **air of ~** air *m* d'attente; **awaited with eager ~** attendu avec une vive impatience; *V* **life**.
expectant [ɪksˈpektənt] *adj* qui attend. **an ~ attitude** une attitude d'expectative *or* expectante (*liter*); **with an ~ look** d'un air de quelqu'un qui attend quelque chose; **~ mother** femme enceinte, future maman.

expectantly [ɪks'pektəntlɪ] *adv look, listen* avec l'air d'attendre quelque chose. **to wait ~** être dans l'expectative, attendre avec espoir.

expectation [ˌekspek'teɪʃən] *n* **(a)** (*U*) prévision *f*, attente *f*, espoir *m*. **in ~ of** dans l'attente *or* l'espoir de, en prévision de; **to live in ~** vivre dans l'expectative; **happiness in ~** bonheur en perspective; **his ~ of life** son espérance *f* de vie, la durée de sa vie.

(b) (*sth expected*) attente *f*, espérance *f*. **contrary to all ~** contre toute attente *or* espérance; **to come up to sb's ~s** répondre à l'attente *or* aux espérances de qn, remplir les espérances de qn; **beyond ~** au-delà de mes (*or* de nos *etc*) espérances; **his (financial) ~s are good** ses espérances sont considérables.

expectorate [ɪks'pektəreɪt] *vti* expectorer, cracher.

expedience [ɪks'piːdɪəns] *n*, **expediency** [ɪks'piːdɪənsɪ] *n* (*convenience*) convenance *f*; (*self-interest*) recherche *f* de l'intérêt personnel, opportunisme *m*; (*advisability*) *[project, course of action]* opportunité *f*.

expedient [ɪks'piːdɪənt] **1** *adj* **(a)** (*suitable, convenient*) indiqué, opportun, expédient (*frm*).

(b) (*politic*) politique, opportun. **this solution is more ~ than just** cette solution est plus politique que juste; **it would be ~ to change the rule** il serait opportun de changer le règlement.

2 *n* expédient *m*.

expedite ['ekspɪdaɪt] *vt preparations, process* accélérer; *operations, legal or official matters* activer, hâter; *business, deal* pousser; *task* expédier; († *or frm: dispatch*) expédier.

expedition [ˌekspɪ'dɪʃən] *n* **(a)** (*journey*) expédition *f*; (*group of people*) (membres *mpl* d'une) expédition. **(b)** (*U:* † *or frm: speed*) promptitude *f*.

expeditionary [ˌekspɪ'dɪʃənrɪ] *adj* expéditionnaire. (*Mil*) **~ force** corps *m* expéditionnaire.

expeditious [ˌekspɪ'dɪʃəs] *adj* expéditif.

expeditiously [ˌekspɪ'dɪʃəslɪ] *adv* promptement, d'une façon expéditive.

expel [ɪks'pel] *vt* (*from country, meeting*) expulser; (*from society, party*) exclure, expulser; (*from school*) renvoyer; *the enemy* chasser, refouler; *gas, liquid* évacuer, expulser; (*from the body*) éliminer, évacuer.

expend [ɪks'pend] *vt* **(a)** *time, energy, care* consacrer, employer (*on sth* à qch, *on doing* à faire); *money* dépenser (*on sth* pour qch, *on doing* à faire). **(b)** (*use up*) *ammunition, resources* épuiser.

expendable [ɪks'pendəbl] *adj* (*not reusable*) *equipment* non-réutilisable; (*Mil*) *troops* sacrifiable; (*of little value*) *person, object* remplaçable. (*Mil*) **~ stores** matériel *m* de consommation; **this watch is ~** cette montre est facile à remplacer; **he is really ~** il n'est vraiment pas irremplaçable, on peut se passer de lui.

expenditure [ɪks'pendɪtʃəʳ] *n* (*U*) **(a)** (*money spent*) dépense(s) *f(pl)*. **public ~** dépenses publiques; **to limit one's ~** limiter ses dépenses; **project which involves heavy ~** projet qui entraîne une grosse dépense *or* de gros frais.

(b) (*U*) *[money, time, energy]* dépense *f*; *[ammunition, resources]* consommation *f*. **the ~ of public funds on this project** l'utilisation *f* des fonds publics pour ce projet.

expense [ɪks'pens] **1** *n* **(a)** (*U*) dépense *f*, frais *mpl*. **at my ~** à mes frais; **at the public ~** aux frais de l'État; **at little ~** à peu de frais; **at great ~** à grands frais; **to go to the ~ of buying a car** faire la dépense d'une voiture; **to go to great ~ on sb's account** s'engager *or* se lancer dans de grosses dépenses pour qn; **to go to great ~ to repair the house** faire beaucoup de frais pour réparer la maison; **to go to some ~** faire des frais; **don't go to any ~ over our visit** ne faites pas de frais pour notre visite; **regardless of ~** sans regarder à la dépense; **we have spared no ~** nous n'avons pas reculé devant la dépense *or* pas cherché à faire des économies; **to put sb to ~** faire faire *or* causer des dépenses à qn; **that will involve him in some ~** cela lui occasionnera des frais; **to meet the ~ of sth** faire face aux frais de qch *or* à la dépense occasionnée par qch, supporter les frais de qch.

(b) (*gen pl*) **~s** (*Fin*) frais *mpl*, débours *mpl*, dépenses *fpl*; (*Comm*) sortie *f*; **your ~s will be entirely covered** vous serez défrayé entièrement *or* en totalité; **after all ~s have been paid** tous frais payés.

(c) (*fig*) **to have a good laugh at sb's ~** bien rire aux dépens de qn; **to get rich at other people's ~** s'enrichir aux dépens d'autrui *or* au détriment des autres; **to live at other people's ~** vivre aux dépens *or* à la charge *or* aux crochets des autres; **at the ~ of great sacrifices** au prix de grands sacrifices.

2 *cpd*: (*Comm*) **expense account** frais *mpl* de représentation; **this will go on his expense account** cela passera aux frais de représentation *or* sur sa note de frais; **expense account lunch** déjeuner *m* qui passe aux frais de représentation *or* sur la note de frais.

expensive [ɪks'pensɪv] *adj goods, seats, shop, restaurant* cher (*f* chère); *holidays, medicine, undertaking* coûteux; *tastes* dispendieux, de luxe; *journey* onéreux. **to be ~** coûter cher *inv*, valoir cher *inv*; **that vase must be ~** ce vase doit valoir cher, ce doit être un vase de prix; **this car comes ~** cette voiture revient cher; **to be extremely ~** être hors de prix, coûter les yeux de la tête*.

expensively [ɪks'pensɪvlɪ] *adv* (*sparing no expense*) *entertain* à grands frais; (*in costly way*) *dress* de façon coûteuse.

expensiveness [ɪks'pensɪvnɪs] *n* cherté *f*.

experience [ɪks'pɪərɪəns] **1** *n* **(a)** (*U: knowledge, wisdom*) expérience *f*. **~ of life/of men** expérience du monde/des hommes; **~ shows that ...** l'expérience démontre que ...; **I know by ~** je (le) sais par expérience *or* pour en avoir fait l'expérience; **from my own** *or* **personal ~** d'après mon expérience personnelle; **I know from bitter ~ that ...** j'ai appris à mes dépens que ...; **he has no ~ of real grief** il n'a jamais éprouvé *or* ressenti un vrai chagrin; **he has no ~ of living in the country** il ne sait pas ce que c'est que de vivre à la campagne; **the greatest disaster in the ~ of this nation** le plus grand désastre que cette nation ait connu.

(b) (*U: practice, skill*) pratique *f*, expérience *f*. **practical ~** pratique; **business ~** expérience des affaires; **he has a lot of teaching ~** il a une longue pratique *or* expérience *or* habitude de l'enseignement; **he has considerable driving ~** il a l'expérience de la route *or* du volant, c'est un conducteur expérimenté; **he lacks ~** il manque d'expérience *or* de pratique; **have you any previous ~ (in this kind of work)?** avez-vous déjà fait ce genre de travail?; **I've (had) no ~ of driving this type of car** je n'ai jamais conduit une voiture de ce type.

(c) (*event experienced*) expérience *f*, aventure *f*, sensation *f*. **I had a pleasant/frightening ~** il m'est arrivé une chose *or* une aventure agréable/effrayante; **she's had** *or* **gone through some terrible ~s** elle est passée par de rudes épreuves *fpl*, elle en a vu de dures*; **it was a new ~ for me** cela a été une nouveauté *or* une nouvelle expérience pour moi; **we had many unforgettable ~s there** nous y avons vécu *or* passé bien des moments inoubliables; **she swam in the nude and it was an agreeable ~** elle a nagé toute nue et a trouvé cela agréable; **it wasn't an ~ I would care to repeat** ça n'est pas une aventure que je tiens à recommencer; **unfortunate ~** mésaventure *f*.

2 *vt* **(a)** (*undergo*) *misfortune, hardship* connaître; *setbacks, losses* essuyer; *privations* souffrir de; *conditions* vivre sous *or* dans; *ill treatment* subir; *difficulties* rencontrer. **he doesn't know what it is like to be poor for he has never ~d it** il ne sait pas ce que c'est que d'être pauvre car il n'en a jamais fait l'expérience *or* cela ne lui est jamais arrivé; **he ~s some difficulty in speaking** il a *or* éprouve de la difficulté *or* du mal à parler.

(b) (*feel*) *sensation, terror, remorse* éprouver; *emotion, joy, elation* ressentir.

experienced [ɪks'pɪərɪənst] *adj teacher, secretary* expérimenté, qui a de l'expérience, qui a du métier; *technician etc* confirmé, expérimenté; *driver, politician* expérimenté, chevronné; *eye, ear* exercé. **wanted, ~ secretary/journalist** on cherche secrétaire/journaliste expérimenté(e); **she is not ~ enough** elle n'a pas assez d'expérience, elle est trop inexpérimentée; **someone ~ in the trade** quelqu'un qui a l'habitude du métier; **he is ~ in business/driving/teaching** il a de l'expérience en affaires/en matière de conduite/en matière d'enseignement, il est rompu aux affaires/à la conduite/à l'enseignement.

experiment [ɪks'perɪmənt] **1** *n* (*Chem, Phys*) expérience *f*; (*fig*) expérience, essai *m*. **to carry out an ~** faire une expérience; **by way of ~, as an ~** à titre d'essai *or* d'expérience.

2 [ɪks'perɪment] *vi* (*Chem, Phys*) faire une expérience, expérimenter; (*fig*) faire une *or* des expérience(s). **to ~ with a new vaccine** expérimenter un nouveau vaccin; **to ~ on guinea pigs** faire des expériences sur des cobayes; **they are ~ing with communal living** ils font une expérience de vie communautaire.

experimental [ɪksˌperɪ'mentl] *adj laboratory, research, method, science* expérimental; *evidence* établi *or* confirmé par l'expérience; *engine, novel* expérimental; *cinema, period* d'essai. **at the ~ stage** au stade expérimental; **this system is merely ~** ce système est encore à l'essai; **~ chemist** chimiste *mf* de laboratoire.

experimentally [ɪksˌperɪ'mentəlɪ] *adv test, establish, discover* expérimentalement; *organise* à titre expérimental *or* d'expérience.

experimentation [ɪksˌperɪmen'teɪʃən] *n* expérimentation *f*.

expert ['ekspɜːt] **1** *n* expert *m*, spécialiste *mf*, connaisseur *m*. **he is an ~ on wines** il est grand *or* fin connaisseur en vins; **he is an ~ on the subject** c'est un expert en la matière; **~ at pigeon shooting** spécialiste du tir aux pigeons; **nineteenth century ~** spécialiste du dix-neuvième siècle; **he's an ~ at repairing watches** il est expert à réparer les montres; **he's an ~ at that sort of negotiation** il est spécialiste de ce genre de négociations; **with the eye of an ~** d'un œil *or* regard connaisseur.

2 *adj knowledge*, (*Jur*) *evidence* d'expert. (*Jur*) **~ witness** (témoin *m*) expert *m*; **to be ~ in an art/a science** être expert dans un art/une science; **he is ~ in this field** il est expert en la matière, il s'y connaît; **he is ~ in handling a boat** il est expert à manœuvrer un bateau; **to judge sth with an ~ eye** juger qch en connaisseur *or* en expert; **to cast an ~ eye on sth** jeter un coup d'œil connaisseur sur qch; **with an ~ touch** avec beaucoup d'habileté, avec une grande adresse; **~ opinion believes that ...** d'après les avis autorisés ...; **~ advice** l'avis *m* d'un expert; **~ valuation** expertise *f*.

expertise [ˌekspə'tiːz] *n* compétence *f* (*in* en), adresse *f* (*in* à).

expertly ['ekspɜːtlɪ] *adv* de façon experte, habilement, adroitement.

expertness ['ekspɜːtnɪs] *n* = **expertise.**

expiate ['ekspɪeɪt] *vt* expier.

expiation [ˌekspɪ'eɪʃən] *n* expiation *f*. **in ~ of** en expiation de.

expiatory ['ekspɪətərɪ] *adj* expiatoire.

expiration [ˌekspaɪə'reɪʃən] *n* **(a)** = **expiry. (b)** (*breathing out*) expiration *f*. **(c)** (††: *death*) trépas *m* (*liter*), décès *m*.

expire [ɪks'paɪəʳ] *vi* **(a)** *[lease, passport, licence]* expirer; *[period, time limit]* arriver à terme. **(b)** (*liter: die*) expirer, rendre l'âme *or* le dernier soupir. **(c)** (*breathe out*) expirer.

expiry [ɪks'paɪərɪ] *n [time limit, period, term of office]* expiration *f*, fin *f*; *[passport, lease]* expiration. **date of ~ of the lease** expiration *or* terme *m* du bail.

explain [ɪks'pleɪn] *vt* **(a)** (*make clear*) *how sth works, rule, meaning of a word, situation* expliquer; *mystery* élucider, éclaircir; *motives, thoughts* expliquer, éclairer; *reasons, points of view* exposer. **~ what you intend to do** expliquez ce que vous voulez faire; **'it's raining' she ~ed** 'il pleut' expliqua-t-elle; **that is easy to ~, that is easily ~ed** cela s'explique facilement; **this may seem confused, I will ~ myself** ceci peut paraître confus, je m'explique donc (*V also* **b**); **to ~ why/how** *etc* expliquer pourquoi/comment *etc*; **he ~ed to us why he had been absent** il nous a expliqué pourquoi il avait été absent; **to ~ to sb how to do sth** expliquer à qn comment (il faut) faire qch.

(b) (*account for*) *phenomenon* expliquer, donner l'explication de; *behaviour* expliquer, justifier. **the bad weather ~s why he is absent** le mauvais temps explique son absence *or* qu'il soit absent; **come now, ~ yourself!** allez, expliquez-vous!

explain away *vt sep* justifier, trouver une explication convaincante de.

explainable [ɪks'pleɪnəbl] *adj* explicable. **that is easily ~** cela s'explique facilement.

explanation [,eksplə'neɪʃən] *n* **(a)** (*act, statement*) explication *f*, éclaircissement *m*. **a long ~ of what he meant by democracy** une longue explication de ce qu'il entendait par la démocratie; **these instructions need some ~** ces instructions demandent quelques éclaircissements.

(b) (*cause, motive*) explication *f*. **to find an ~ for sth** trouver l'explication de qch, s'expliquer qch.

(c) (*U: justification*) explication *f*, justification *f*. **has he something to say in ~ of his conduct?** est-ce qu'il peut fournir une explication de sa conduite?; **what have you to say in ~?** qu'avez-vous à dire pour votre justification?

explanatory [ɪks'plænətərɪ] *adj* explicatif.

expletive [ɪks'pliːtɪv] **1** *n* (*exclamation*) exclamation *f*, interjection *f*; (*oath*) juron *m*; (*Gram*) explétif *m*. **2** *adj* (*Gram*) explétif.

explicable [ɪks'plɪkəbl] *adj* explicable.

explicably [ɪks'plɪkəblɪ] *adv* d'une manière explicable.

explicit [ɪks'plɪsɪt] *adj* (*plainly stated*) explicite (*also Math*); (*definite*) catégorique, formel. **the intention is ~ in the text** l'intention est explicite dans le texte; **in ~ terms** en termes explicites; **he was ~ on this point** il a été explicite sur ce point, il a été catégorique là-dessus; **~ denial/order** démenti/ordre formel.

explicitly [ɪks'plɪsɪtlɪ] *adv* (*V* **explicit**) explicitement; catégoriquement, formellement.

explode [ɪks'pləʊd] **1** *vi [bomb, boiler, plane]* exploser, éclater; *[gas]* exploser, détoner; *[building, ship, ammunition]* exploser, sauter; *[joy, anger]* éclater; *[person]* (*: *from rage, impatience*) exploser. **to ~ with laughter** éclater de rire; (*Art etc*) **~d drawing** *or* **view** éclaté *m*.

2 *vt* (*V* 1) faire exploser *or* éclater *or* détoner *or* sauter; (*fig*) *theory, argument* discréditer, démontrer la fausseté de; *rumour* montrer la fausseté de.

exploit ['eksplɔɪt] **1** *n* (*heroic*) exploit *m*, haut fait; (*feat*) prouesse *f*. (*adventures*) **~s** aventures *fpl*.

2 [ɪks'plɔɪt] *vt* **(a)** (*use unfairly*) *workers, sb's credulity* exploiter.

(b) (*make use of*) *minerals, land, talent* exploiter; *situation* exploiter, profiter de, tirer parti *or* profit de.

exploitation [,eksplɔɪ'teɪʃən] *n* exploitation *f*.

exploration [,eksplɔː'reɪʃən] *n* (*lit, fig, Med*) exploration *f*. **voyage of ~** voyage *m* d'exploration *or* de découverte; *[ground, site]* **preliminary ~** reconnaissance *f*.

exploratory [ɪks'plɒrətərɪ] *adj expedition* d'exploration, de découverte; *step, discussion* préliminaire, préparatoire. (*Med*) **~ operation** sondage *m*; **~ drilling of a piece of land** sondage d'un terrain; (*Pol etc*) **~ talks** entretiens *mpl* préliminaires *or* préparatoires.

explore [ɪks'plɔːʳ] *vt territory, house, question, matter* explorer; (*Med*) sonder. **to go exploring** partir en exploration *or* à la découverte; **to ~ every corner of** fouiller partout dans; (*lit, fig*) **to ~ the ground** tâter *or* sonder le terrain; (*fig*) **to ~ every avenue** examiner toutes les possibilités; **to ~ the possibilities** étudier les possibilités.

explorer [ɪks'plɔːrəʳ] *n* explorateur *m*, -trice *f*.

explosion [ɪks'pləʊʒən] *n* (*V* **explode**) explosion *f*; éclatement *m*; *[joy, mirth]* explosion, débordement *m*. **noise of ~** détonation *f*; *V* **population**.

explosive [ɪks'pləʊzɪv] **1** *adj gas, matter* explosible; *weapons, force* explosif; *mixture* détonant; *situation, temper* explosif; (*Ling*) explosif. **2** *n* **(a)** (*gen, Chem*) explosif *m*; *V* **high**. **(b)** (*Ling*) consonne explosive.

exponent [ɪks'pəʊnənt] *n [theory etc]* interprète *m*; (*Math*) exposant *m*. **the principal ~ of this movement/this school of thought** le chef de file *or* le principal représentant de ce mouvement/de cette école de pensée.

exponential [,ekspəʊ'nenʃəl] *adj* exponentiel. (*Statistics*) **~ distribution** distribution exponentielle.

export [ɪks'pɔːt] **1** *vt* exporter (*to* vers). **countries which ~ coal** pays exportateurs de charbon.

2 ['ekspɔːt] *n* **(a)** (*U*) exportation *f*, sortie *f*. **for ~ only** réservé à l'exportation.

(b) (*object, commodity*) (article *m* d')exportation *f*. **invisible ~s** exportations invisibles; **ban on ~s** prohibition sur les sorties.

3 ['ekspɔːt] *cpd goods, permit* d'exportation. **export drive** campagne *f* pour (encourager) l'exportation; **export duty** droit *m* de sortie; **export reject** article *m* impropre à l'exportation; **export trade** commerce *m* d'exportation.

exportable [ɪks'pɔːtəbl] *adj* exportable.

exportation [,ekspɔː'teɪʃən] *n* (*U*) exportation *f*, sortie *f*.

exporter [ɪks'pɔːtəʳ] *n* (*person*) exportateur *m*, -trice *f*; (*country*) pays *m* exportateur.

expose [ɪks'pəʊz] *vt* **(a)** (*uncover; leave unprotected*) découvrir, exposer, mettre au jour; *wire, nerve* mettre à nu, dénuder; (*Phot*) exposer. **a dress which leaves the back ~d** une robe qui découvre *or* dénude le dos; **to ~ to radiation/rain/sunlight/danger** exposer à la radiation/à la pluie/au soleil/au danger; **not to be ~d to air** ne pas laisser *or* exposer à l'air; **to be ~d to view** s'offrir à la vue; **~d to the general view** exposé aux regards de tous; (*Mil*) **~d position** lieu découvert; **~d ground** terrain découvert; **an ~d hillside** un flanc de coteau battu par les vents *or* mal abrité; **digging has ~d the remains of a temple** les fouilles ont mis au jour les restes d'un temple; (*Tech*) **~d parts** parties apparentes; (*Hist*) **to ~ a child (to die)** exposer un enfant; **to ~ o.s. to criticism/censure** *etc* s'exposer à la critique/aux reproches *etc*; **he ~d himself to the risk of losing his job** il s'est exposé à perdre sa place; (*fig*) **he is in a very ~d position** il est très exposé; (*Jur*: *indecently*) **to ~ o.s.** commettre un outrage à la pudeur.

(b) (*display*) *goods* étaler, exposer; *pictures* exposer; *one's ignorance* afficher, étaler.

(c) (*unmask, reveal*) *vice* mettre à nu; *scandal, plot* révéler, dévoiler, exposer au grand jour; *secret* éventer; *person* démasquer, dénoncer.

exposition [,ekspə'zɪʃən] *n* **(a)** (*U*) *[facts, theory, plan]* exposition *f*; *[text]* exposé *m*, commentaire *m*, interprétation *f*. **(b)** (*exhibition*) exposition *f*.

expostulate [ɪks'pɒstjʊleɪt] **1** *vt* protester. **2** *vi*: **to ~ with sb about sth** faire des remontrances à qn au sujet de qch.

expostulation [ɪks,pɒstjʊ'leɪʃən] *n* (*V* **expostulate**) protestation *f*; remontrances *fpl*.

exposure [ɪks'pəʊʒəʳ] **1** *n* **(a)** (*V* **expose**) découverte *f*; mise *f* à nu; exposition *f* (*to* à), étalage *m*; révélation *f*, dénonciation *f*. **to threaten sb with ~** menacer qn d'un scandale; **to die of ~** mourir de froid; *V* **indecent**.

(b) (*position of building*) exposition *f*. **southern/eastern ~** exposition *f* au midi/à l'est; **house with a northern ~** maison exposée *or* orientée au nord.

(c) (*Phot*) (temps *m* de) pose *f*. **to make an ~** prendre un cliché; **film with 36 ~s** film de 36 poses; *V* **double**.

2 *cpd*: (*Phot*) **exposure meter** posemètre *m*, photomètre *m*.

expound [ɪks'paʊnd] *vt theory* expliquer; *one's views* exposer; *the Bible* expliquer, interpréter.

express [ɪks'pres] **1** *vt* **(a)** (*make known*) *appreciation, feelings, sympathy* exprimer; *opinions* émettre, exprimer; *surprise, displeasure* exprimer, manifester; *thanks* présenter, exprimer; *a truth, proposition* énoncer; *wish* formuler. **to ~ o.s.** s'exprimer; **I haven't the words to ~ my thoughts** les mots me manquent pour traduire ma pensée.

(b) (*in another language or medium*) rendre, exprimer; *[face, actions]* exprimer; (*Math*) exprimer. **this ~es exactly the meaning of the word** ceci rend exactement le sens du mot; **you cannot ~ that so succinctly in French** on ne peut pas exprimer cela aussi succinctement en français.

(c) *juice* exprimer, extraire.

(d) (*send*) *letter, parcel* expédier par exprès.

2 *adj* **(a)** (*clearly stated*) *instructions* exprès (*f* -esse), formel; *intention* explicite. **with the ~ purpose of** dans le seul but de, dans le but même de.

(b) (*fast*) extrêmement rapide; *letter* exprès *inv*.

3 *cpd*: **express coach** (auto)car *m* express; **express company** compagnie *f* de messageries; (*Brit Post*) **express delivery** distribution *f* exprès; (*US*) **expressman** employé *m* de messageries; **express rifle** fusil *m* de chasse express; **express train** rapide *m*; (*esp US*) **expressway** voie *f* express.

4 *adv* très rapidement. **to send a parcel ~** envoyer un colis exprès; (*Rail*) **to travel ~** prendre le rapide.

5 *n* **(a)** (*train*) rapide *m*.

(b) to send goods by ~ envoyer des marchandises par transport rapide *or* par messagerie.

expressage [ɪks'presɪdʒ] *n* (*US*) service *m* transport-express, colis-express *m*.

expression [ɪks'preʃən] *n* **(a)** (*U*) *[opinions]* expression *f*; *[friendship, affection]* témoignage *m*; *[joy]* manifestation *f*. **to give ~ to one's fears** formuler ses craintes.

(b) (*U: feeling*) expression *f*. **to play with ~** jouer avec expression.

(c) (*phrase etc*) expression *f*, tournure *f*, tour *m*, locution *f* (*esp Gram*); (*Math*) expression. **it's an ~ he's fond of** c'est une expression *or* une tournure qu'il affectionne; **a figurative ~** une expression figurée; **an original/common ~** une tournure originale/fréquente; **that is a set ~ in English** c'est une expression consacrée *or* une locution figée (*Ling*) en anglais.

(d) (*facial ~*) expression *f*.

expressionism [ɪks'preʃənɪzəm] *n* expressionnisme *m*.

expressionist [ɪks'preʃənɪst] *adj, n* expressionniste (*mf*).

expressionless [ɪks'preʃənlɪs] *adj voice* sans expression, plat; *face* inexpressif, éteint; *style* dénué d'expression. **he remained ~** il est resté sans expression.

expressive [ɪks'presɪv] *adj language, face, hands* expressif; *gestures, silence* éloquent; *look, smile* significatif. **poems ~ of despair** poèmes qui expriment le désespoir.

expressively [ɪks'presɪvlɪ] *adv* avec expression, d'une manière expressive.

expressiveness [ɪks'presɪvnɪs] *n [face]* caractère expressif, expressivité *f*; *[words]* force expressive. **picture remarkable for its ~** tableau remarquable par (la force de) l'expression.

expressly [ɪks'preslɪ] *adv* expressément.

expropriate [eks'prəʊprɪeɪt] *vt person, land* exproprier.
expropriation [eks,prəʊprɪ'eɪʃən] *n* expropriation *f.*
expulsion [ɪks'pʌlʃən] *n* expulsion *f*, bannissement *m*; (*Scol etc*) renvoi *m.* ~ **order** arrêté *m* d'expulsion.
expunge [ɪks'pʌndʒ] *vt* (*from book*) supprimer. **to ~ sth from the record** supprimer *or* effacer qch.
expurgate ['ekspɜːgeɪt] *vt* expurger. **~d edition** édition expurgée.
exquisite [ɪks'kwɪzɪt] *adj sewing, painting, sweetness, politeness* exquis; *sensibility* raffiné, délicat; *sense of humour* exquis, subtil; *satisfaction, pleasure* vif (*f* vive); *pain* aigu (*f* -guë), vif. **woman of ~ beauty** femme d'une beauté exquise *or* exquise de beauté; **chair of ~ workmanship** chaise d'une facture exquise.
exquisitely [ɪks'kwɪzɪtlɪ] *adv* **(a)** *paint, embroider, decorate, dress* d'une façon exquise, exquisément; *describe* avec beaucoup de finesse. **(b)** (*extremely*) extrêmement, excessivement. ~ **beautiful/polite** d'une beauté/d'une politesse exquise.
extant [eks'tænt] *adj* qui existe encore, existant. **the only ~ manuscript** le seul manuscrit conservé; **a few examples are still ~** quelques exemples subsistent (encore).
extemporaneous [ɪks,tempə'reɪnɪəs] *adj*, **extemporary** [ɪks'tempərərɪ] *adj* improvisé, impromptu.
extempore [ɪks'tempərɪ] **1** *adv* impromptu, sans préparation. **2** *adj* improvisé, impromptu. **to give an ~ speech** improviser un discours, faire un discours au pied levé.
extemporize [ɪks'tempəraɪz] *vti* improviser.
extend [ɪks'tend] **1** *vt* **(a)** (*stretch out*) *arm* étendre. **to ~ one's hand (to sb)** tendre la main (à qn).
(b) (*prolong*) *street, line* prolonger (*by* de); *visit, leave* prolonger (*for 2 weeks* de 2 semaines).
(c) (*enlarge*) *house, property* agrandir; *research* porter *or* pousser plus loin; *powers* étendre, augmenter; *business* étendre, accroître; *knowledge* élargir, accroître; *limits* étendre. **to ~ the frontiers of a country** reculer les frontières d'un pays; **to ~ the field of human knowledge/one's sphere of influence** agrandir le champ des connaissances humaines/sa sphère d'influence; **to ~ one's vocabulary** enrichir *or* élargir son vocabulaire; **to ~ a time limit (for payment)** proroger l'échéance (d'un paiement), accorder des délais (de paiement); **to grant ~ed credit** accorder un long crédit; **an ~ed play record** un disque double (durée).
(d) (*offer*) *help* apporter; *hospitality, friendship* offrir; *thanks, condolences, congratulations* présenter. **to ~ a welcome to sb** souhaiter la bienvenue à qn; **to ~ an invitation** faire *or* lancer une invitation.
(e) (*make demands on*) *person, pupil* pousser à la limite de ses capacités, faire donner son maximum à. **the staff are fully ~ed** le personnel travaille à la limite de ses possibilités *or* fournit un maximum d'effort; **the child is not being fully ~ed in this class** l'enfant ne donne pas son maximum dans cette classe.
2 *vi* [*wall, estate*] s'étendre (*to, as far as* jusqu'à); [*meeting, visit*] se prolonger, continuer (*over* pendant, *for* durant, *till* jusqu'à, *beyond* au-delà de). **holidays which ~ into September** des vacances qui durent *or* se prolongent jusqu'en septembre; **enthusiasm which ~s even to the children** enthousiasme qui gagne (*or* a gagné) les enfants eux-mêmes.
extensible [ɪks'tensɪbl] *adj* extensible.
extension [ɪks'tenʃən] **1** *n* **(a)** (*U*) (*V* **extend**) prolongation *f*; agrandissement *m*; extension *f*; augmentation *f*; prorogation *f*.
(b) (*addition*) (*to road, line*) prolongement *m*; (*for table, wire, electric flex*) rallonge *f*; (*to holidays, leave*) prolongation *f*. **to get an ~ (of time for payment)** obtenir un délai; **to have an ~ built on to the house** faire agrandir la maison; **there is an ~ at the back of the house** la maison a été agrandie par derrière; **come and see our ~** venez voir nos agrandissements *mpl*.
(c) (*telephone*) [*private house*] appareil *m* supplémentaire; [*office*] poste *m*. ~ **21** poste 21.
2 *cpd*: **(university) extension courses** cours publics du soir (organisés par l'Université); **extension ladder** échelle coulissante.
extensive [ɪks'tensɪv] *adj estate, forest* étendu, vaste; *grounds, gardens* vaste, très grand; *knowledge* vaste, étendu; *study, research* approfondi; *investments, operations, alterations* considérable, important; *plans, reforms, business* de grande envergure; *use* large, répandu, fréquent.
extensively [ɪks'tensɪvlɪ] *adv* (*in place*) sur un large espace; (*in quantity*) largement, considérablement. ~ **used method** méthode très répandue; **he has travelled ~ in Asia** il a beaucoup voyagé en Asie.
extensor [ɪks'tensəʳ] *n* (muscle *m*) extenseur *m*.
extent [ɪks'tent] *n* **(a)** (*length*) longueur *f*; (*size*) étendue *f*, superficie *f*. **avenue bordered with trees along its entire ~** allée bordée d'arbres sur toute sa longueur; **to open to its fullest ~** ouvrir entièrement *or* tout grand; **over the whole ~ of the ground** sur toute la superficie du terrain; **she could see the full ~ of the park** elle voyait le parc dans toute son étendue.
(b) (*range, scope*) [*damage*] importance *f*, ampleur *f*; [*commitments, losses*] importance; [*knowledge, activities, power, influence*] étendue *f*.
(c) (*degree*) mesure *f*, degré *m*. **to what ~** dans quelle mesure; **to a certain ~** jusqu'à un certain point *or* degré, dans une certaine mesure; **to a large ~** en grande partie; **to a small *or* slight ~** dans une faible mesure, quelque peu; **to such an ~ that** à tel point que; **to the ~ of doing** au point de faire.
extenuate [ɪks'tenjʊeɪt] *vt* atténuer. **extenuating circumstances** circonstances atténuantes.
extenuation [ɪks,tenjʊ'eɪʃən] *n* atténuation *f*.
exterior [ɪks'tɪərɪəʳ] **1** *adj surface, paintwork* extérieur; *decorating* du dehors. **~ to** extérieur à, en dehors de; **~ angle** angle *m* externe; **~ decoration** peintures *fpl* d'extérieur; **paint for ~ use** peinture *f* pour bâtiment.
2 *n* [*house, box*] extérieur *m*, dehors *m*; (*Art, Cine*) extérieur. **on the ~** à l'extérieur; **he has a rough ~** il a des dehors rudes, il a un extérieur rude.
exteriorize [ɪks'tɪərɪəraɪz] *vt* extérioriser.
exterminate [ɪks'tɜːmɪneɪt] *vt pests, group of people* exterminer; *race* anéantir; *disease* abolir; *beliefs, ideas* supprimer, détruire, abolir.
extermination [ɪks,tɜːmɪ'neɪʃən] *n* (*V* **exterminate**) extermination *f*; anéantissement *m*; abolition *f*, suppression *f*; destruction *f*.
external [eks'tɜːnl] **1** *adj surface* externe, extérieur; *wall* extérieur; *influences* du dehors; *factor* extérieur. (*Pharm*) **for ~ use only** pour (l')usage externe; (*Brit Univ*) **~ examiner** examinateur (venu) de l'extérieur (*d'une autre université*); (*US*) **~ trade** commerce extérieur.
2 *n* (*fig*) **the ~s** l'extérieur *m*, les apparences *fpl*.
externally [eks'tɜːnəlɪ] *adv* extérieurement, à l'extérieur. **he remained ~ calm** il gardait une apparence calme, il restait calme extérieurement; (*Pharm*) **to be used ~** pour (l')usage externe.
extinct [ɪks'tɪŋkt] *adj volcano* éteint; *feelings, passion* éteint, mort; *race, species* disparu.
extinction [ɪks'tɪŋkʃən] *n* (*U*) [*fire*] extinction *f*; [*race, family*] extinction, disparition *f*; [*hopes*] anéantissement *m*.
extinguish [ɪks'tɪŋgwɪʃ] *vt fire, light* éteindre; *candle* éteindre, souffler; *hopes* anéantir, mettre fin à.
extinguisher [ɪks'tɪŋgwɪʃəʳ] *n* extincteur *m*; *V* **fire**.
extirpate ['ekstɜːpeɪt] *vt* extirper.
extirpation [,ekstə'peɪʃən] *n* (*U*) extirpation *f*.
extirpator ['ekstəpeɪtəʳ] *n* (*Agr, Tech*) extirpateur *m*.
extol [ɪks'təʊl] *vt person* louer, chanter les louanges de; *act, quality* prôner, exalter.
extort [ɪks'tɔːt] *vt promise, money* extorquer, soutirer (*from* à); *consent, confession, secret* arracher (*from* à); *signature* extorquer.
extortion [ɪks'tɔːʃən] *n* (*also Jur*) extorsion *f*. (*fig*) **this is sheer ~!** c'est du vol (manifeste)!
extortionate [ɪks'tɔːʃənɪt] *adj price* exorbitant, inabordable; *demand, tax* excessif, exorbitant.
extortioner [ɪks'tɔːʃənəʳ] *n* extorqueur *m*, -euse *f*.
extra ['ekstrə] **1** *adj* **(a)** (*additional*) supplémentaire, de plus, en supplément; *homework, credit, bus* supplémentaire. **we need an ~ chair** il nous faut une chaise de plus; **to work ~ hours** faire des heures supplémentaires; (*Ftbl*) **after ~ time** après prolongation *f*; **to make an ~ effort** faire un surcroît d'efforts; **I have had ~ work this week** j'ai eu plus de travail que d'habitude *or* un surcroît de travail cette semaine; **to order an ~ dish** commander un plat en supplément; **there is an ~ charge for wine, the wine is ~** le vin est en supplément, le vin n'est pas compris; **there will be no ~ charge** on ne vous comptera pas de supplément; **to go to ~ expense** faire des frais supplémentaires; **take ~ care!** faites particulièrement attention!; **~ pay** supplément *m* de salaire, indemnité *f* (*for* de); (*Mil*) supplément de solde; **for ~ safety** pour plus de sécurité, pour être plus sûr; **for ~ whiteness** pour plus de blancheur; **I have set an ~ place at table** j'ai ajouté un couvert; **postage and packing ~** frais de port et d'emballage en plus *or* en sus.
(b) (*spare*) de trop, en trop, de réserve. **I bought a few ~ tins** j'ai acheté quelques boîtes de réserve *or* pour mettre en réserve; **these copies are ~** ces exemplaires sont en trop *or* en supplément.
2 *adv* plus que d'ordinaire *or* d'habitude, particulièrement. **she was ~ kind that day** elle fut plus gentille que d'habitude ce jour-là.
3 *n* **(a)** (*perk*) à-côté *m*; (*luxury*) agrément *m*. (*expenses*) **~s** frais *mpl or* dépenses *fpl* supplémentaires, faux frais *mpl*; **singing and piano are ~s** (*optional*) les leçons de chant et de piano sont en supplément; (*obligatory*) les leçons de chant et de piano ne sont pas comprises.
(b) (*in restaurant*: **~ dish**) supplément *m*.
(c) (*Cine, Theat*: *actor*) figurant(e) *m(f)*.
extra- ['ekstrə] *pref* **(a)** (*outside*) extra-; *V* **extramarital** *etc*.
(b) (*specially, ultra*) extra-. **~dry** *wine etc* très sec, extra-sec; *champagne, vermouth* extra-dry *inv*; **~fine** extra-fin; **~smart** ultra-chic* *inv*; **~strong** *person* extrêmement fort; *material* extra-solide; *V* **extraspecial**.
extract [ɪks'trækt] **1** *vt juice, minerals, oil, bullet, splinter* extraire (*from* de); *tooth* arracher (*from* à); *cork* tirer; (*fig*) *secrets* extraire (*from* de), arracher (*from* à); *confession, permission, promise* arracher (*from* à); *information* tirer (*from* de); *money* tirer (*from* de), soutirer (*from* à); *meaning, moral* tirer, dégager (*from* de); *quotation, passage* extraire, relever (*from* de). **to ~ pleasure from sth** tirer du plaisir de qch; (*Math*) **to ~ the square root** extraire la racine carrée.
2 ['ekstrækt] *n* **(a)** [*book etc*] extrait *m*. **~s from Voltaire** morceaux choisis de Voltaire.
(b) (*Pharm*) extrait *m*; (*Culin*) extrait, concentré *m*. **meat ~** extrait de viande.
extraction [ɪks'trækʃən] *n* **(a)** (*U*) (*V* **extract**) extraction *f*; arrachement *m*.
(b) (*Dentistry*) extraction *f*, arrachement *m*.
(c) (*U*: *descent*) origine *f*, extraction *f*. **of noble ~** d'origine noble; **of low/high ~** de basse/de haute extraction; **of Spanish ~** d'origine espagnole.
extractor [ɪks'træktəʳ] *n* extracteur *m*. (*Brit*) **~ fan** ventilateur *m*.
extracurricular ['ekstrəkə'rɪkjʊləʳ] *adj activities* en dehors du

programme, hors programme; *sports* en dehors des heures de classe.

extraditable ['ekstrədaɪtəbl] *adj offence* qui peut donner lieu à l'extradition; *person* passible *or* susceptible d'extradition.

extradite ['ekstrədaɪt] *vt* extrader.

extradition [ˌekstrə'dɪʃən] *n* extradition *f*.

extragalactic [ˌekstrəgə'læktɪk] *adj* extragalactique. ~ **nebula** nébuleuse *f* extragalactique.

extramarital ['ekstrə'mærɪtl] *adj* en dehors du mariage.

extramural ['ekstrə'mjʊərəl] *adj* **(a)** (*esp Brit*) *course* hors faculté (*donné par des professeurs accrédités par la faculté et ouvert au public*). ~ **lecture** conférence *f* publique. **(b)** *district* extra-muros *inv*.

extraneous [ɪks'treɪnɪəs] *adj detail, idea* accessoire. ~ **to** étranger à, qui n'a aucun rapport avec, qui n'a rien à voir avec.

extraordinarily [ɪks'trɔːdnrɪlɪ] *adv* extraordinairement, remarquablement.

extraordinary [ɪks'trɔːdnrɪ] *adj* **(a)** (*beyond the ordinary*) *measure* extraordinaire, d'exception; *success* remarquable, extraordinaire; *career, quality* remarquable, exceptionnel; *destiny* hors du commun; (*Admin etc*) extraordinaire. **envoy** ~ délégué *or* ambassadeur extraordinaire; (*Brit*) **an** ~ **meeting of the shareholders** une assemblée extraordinaire des actionnaires.

(b) (*unusual, surprising*) *appearance, dress* extraordinaire, insolite, singulier; *tale, adventure* bizarre, curieux, invraisemblable; *action, speech, behaviour* étonnant, surprenant; *courage, skill* incroyable, extraordinaire; *insults, violence* inouï. **I find it** ~ **that he hasn't replied** je trouve extraordinaire *or* inouï qu'il n'ait pas répondu; **there's nothing** ~ **about that** cela n'a rien d'étonnant; **it's** ~ **to think that ...** il semble incroyable que ... + *subj*; **the** ~ **fact is that he succeeded** ce qu'il y a d'étonnant c'est qu'il a *or* ait réussi; **it's** ~ **how much he resembles his brother** c'est inouï ce qu'il peut ressembler à son frère.

extrapolate [eks'træpəleɪt] *vt* extrapoler.

extrasensory ['ekstrə'sensərɪ] *adj* extra-sensoriel. ~ **perception** perception extra-sensorielle.

extraspecial ['ekstrə'speʃəl] *adj* exceptionnel. **to take** ~ **care over sth** apporter un soin tout particulier à qch; ~ **occasion** grande occasion; **to make something** ~ **to eat** préparer quelque chose de particulièrement bon.

extraterrestrial [ˌekstrətɪ'restrɪəl] *adj* extraterrestre.

extraterritorial ['ekstrəˌterɪ'tɔːrɪəl] *adj* d'exterritorialité, d'extra-territorialité.

extravagance [ɪks'trævəgəns] *n* (*excessive spending*) prodigalité *f*; (*wastefulness*) gaspillage *m*; (*thing bought*) dépense excessive, folie *f*; (*action, notion*) extravagance *f*, fantaisie *f*. **that hat was a great** ~ ce chapeau était une vraie folie.

extravagant [ɪks'trævəgənt] *adj* **(a)** (*wasteful*) *person* dépensier, prodigue, gaspilleur; *taste, habit* dispendieux. **he is very** ~ **with his money** il gaspille son argent, il jette l'argent par les fenêtres*; **it was very** ~ **of him to buy this ring** il a fait une folie en achetant cette bague.

(b) (*exaggerated*) *ideas, theories, behaviour* extravagant; *opinions, claims* exagéré; *praise* outré; *prices* exorbitant, inabordable; *dress* extravagant, excentrique. ~ **talk** paroles excessives, propos extravagants *or* outranciers.

extravagantly [ɪks'trævəgəntlɪ] *adv* **(a)** (*lavishly*) *spend* largement, avec prodigalité; *furnish* avec luxe. **to use sth** ~ gaspiller qch.

(b) (*flamboyantly*) d'une façon extravagante. **to praise sth** ~ louer qch à outrance; **to act** *or* **behave** ~ faire des extravagances; **to talk** ~ tenir des propos extravagants *or* outranciers.

extravaganza [ɪksˌtrævə'gænzə] *n* (*Liter, Mus*) fantaisie *f*; (*story*) histoire extravagante *or* invraisemblable; (*fig*) fantaisie, folie *f*, caprice *m*.

extravehicular [ˌekstrəvɪ'hɪkjʊlə'] *adj* (*Space*) extravéhiculaire.

extreme [ɪks'triːm] **1** *adj* **(a)** (*exceptional*) *courage, pleasure, concern, urgency* extrême; *joy* extrême, suprême, intense; (*exaggerated*) *praise, flattery* outré, excessif; *measures* extrême, rigoureux, très sévère; *views, person* extrême. **in** ~ **danger** en très grand danger; **of** ~ **importance** de (la) toute première importance; **the most** ~ **poverty** la plus grande misère, l'extrême misère; **an** ~ **case** un cas exceptionnel *or* extrême; ~ **in one's opinions** d'opinions extrêmes, extrémiste; (*Pol*) **the** ~ **right** l'extrême droite *f*.

(b) (*furthest off*) extrême; *limit* dernier, extrême. **to the** ~ **right** à l'extrême droite; **in the** ~ **distance** dans l'extrême lointain; **at the** ~ **end of the path** tout au bout du chemin, à l'extrémité du chemin; **at the** ~ **edge of the wood** tout à fait à la lisière du bois; **the** ~ **opposite** l'extrême opposé; **to carry sth to the** ~ **limits** pousser qch à son point extrême *or* à l'extrême.

(c) (*last, final*) dernier, extrême. **the** ~ **penalty** le dernier supplice; ~ **old age** l'extrême vieillesse *f*; (*Rel*) ~ **unction** extrême-onction *f*.

(d) (*ostentatious*) *hat, design* m'as-tu-vu* *inv*; *idea, suggestion* exagéré. **how** ~**!** c'est un peu fort!* *or* poussé!

2 *n* extrême *m*. **in the** ~ à l'extrême, au plus haut degré, au dernier degré; **irritating in the** ~ agaçant au possible; **to go from one** ~ **to the other** passer d'un extrême à l'autre; ~**s of temperature** températures *fpl* extrêmes; ~**s meet** les extrêmes se touchent; **to go to** ~**s** pousser les choses à l'extrême; **I won't go to that** ~ je ne veux pas aller jusqu'à ces extrémités.

extremely [ɪks'triːmlɪ] *adv* extrêmement, à l'extrême, au plus haut degré *or* point. **to be** ~ **talented** avoir un grand talent *or* énormément de talent; **he is** ~ **helpful** il est on ne peut plus serviable.

extremism [ɪks'triːmɪzəm] *n* extrémisme *m*.

extremist [ɪks'triːmɪst] **1** *adj opinion* extrême; *person* extrémiste. **an** ~ **party** un parti d'extrémistes. **2** *n* extrémiste *mf*.

extremity [ɪks'tremɪtɪ] *n* **(a)** (*furthest point*) extrémité *f*, bout *or* point le plus éloigné. (*hands and feet*) **extremities** extrémités.

(b) *[despair, happiness]* extrême *or* dernier degré; (*extreme act*) extrémité *f*. **to drive sb to extremities** pousser qn à une extrémité.

(c) (*danger, distress*) extrémité *f*. **to help sb in his** ~ venir en aide à qn qui est aux abois.

extricate ['ekstrɪkeɪt] *vt object* dégager (*from* de). **to** ~ **o.s.** s'extirper (*from* de); (*fig*) se tirer (*from* de); **to** ~ **sb from a nasty situation** tirer qn d'un mauvais pas.

extrinsic [eks'trɪnsɪk] *adj* extrinsèque.

extrovert ['ekstrəʊvɜːt] **1** *adj* extraverti *or* extroverti. **2** *n* extraverti(e) *m(f)* *or* extroverti(e) *m(f)*. **he's an** ~ il s'extériorise (beaucoup).

extrude [ɪks'truːd] *vt* rejeter (*from* hors de), expulser (*from* de); *metal, plastics* extruder.

extrusion [ɪks'truːʒən] *n* (*Tech*) extrusion *f*.

extrusive [ɪks'truːsɪv] *adj* extrusif.

exuberance [ɪg'zuːbərəns] *n [person]* exubérance *f*, trop-plein *m* de vie; *[vegetation]* exubérance, luxuriance *f*; *[words, images]* richesse *f*, exubérance.

exuberant [ɪg'zuːbərənt] *adj person* exubérant, débordant de vie; *mood* exubérant, expansif; *joy, imagination* exubérant, débordant; *style* abondant, exubérant; *vegetation* exubérant, luxuriant; *foliage* abondant.

exude [ɪg'zjuːd] **1** *vi* suinter, exsuder (*from* de). **2** *vt resin, blood* exsuder. **to** ~ **water** *or* **moisture** suinter; **he** ~**d charm** le charme lui sortait par tous les pores*.

exult [ɪg'zʌlt] *vi* (*rejoice*) se réjouir (*in* de, *over* (à propos) de), exulter; (*triumph*) jubiler, chanter victoire. **to** ~ **at finding** *or* **to find** se réjouir grandement *or* exulter de trouver.

exultant [ɪg'zʌltənt] *adj joy* triomphant; *expression, shout* de triomphe. **to be** ~, **to be in an** ~ **mood** jubiler, triompher, être transporté de joie.

exultantly [ɪg'zʌltəntlɪ] *adv* triomphalement.

exultation [ˌegzʌl'teɪʃən] *n* exultation *f*, jubilation *f*.

eye [aɪ] **1** *n* **(a)** *[person, animal]* œil *m* (*pl* yeux). **girl with blue** ~**s** fille aux yeux bleus; **to have brown** ~**s** avoir les yeux bruns; **with tears in her** ~**s** les larmes aux yeux; **with** ~**s half-closed** *or* **half-shut** les yeux à demi fermés, les paupières mi-closes (*liter*); **with one's** ~**s closed** *or* **shut** les yeux fermés; (*lit*) **to keep one's** ~**s wide open** garder les yeux grand(s) ouverts; **he couldn't keep his** ~**s open*** il dormait debout (*fig*), il sentait ses yeux se fermer (*V also* 1b); **to have the sun in one's** ~**s** avoir le soleil dans les yeux; *V* **black**.

(b) (*phrases*) **before my very** ~**s** sous mes yeux; **it's there in front of your very** ~**s** tu l'as sous les yeux, c'est sous ton nez*; **as far as the** ~ **can see** à perte de vue; **in the** ~**s of** aux yeux de; **in his** ~**s** à ses yeux; **in the** ~**s of the law** aux yeux *or* au regard de la loi; **through someone else's** ~**s** par les yeux d'un autre; **to look at a question through the** ~**s of an economist** envisager une question du point de vue de l'économiste; **under the** ~ **of** sous la surveillance de, sous l'œil de; **with my own** ~**s** de mes propres yeux; **I saw him with my own** ~**s** je l'ai vu de mes yeux vu; **with a critical/jealous/uneasy** ~ d'un œil critique/jaloux/inquiet; **with an** ~ **to the future** en prévision de l'avenir; **with an** ~ **to buying** en vue d'acheter; **that's one in the** ~ **for him*** c'est bien fait pour lui *or* pour sa poire‡; **to be all** ~**s** être tout yeux; **to be up to the** *or* **one's** ~**s in work/debts** être dans le travail/dans les dettes jusqu'au cou; **he's in it up to the** ~**s*** il est (compromis) dans l'affaire jusqu'au cou, il est dedans jusqu'au cou; **to close** *or* **shut one's** ~**s to sb's shortcomings** fermer les yeux *or* s'aveugler sur les faiblesses de qn; **to close** *or* **shut one's** ~**s to the evidence** se refuser à l'évidence; **to close** *or* **shut one's** ~**s to the dangers of sth/the truth** se dissimuler les périls de qch/la vérité; **one can't close** *or* **shut one's** ~**s to the fact that ...** on ne peut pas se dissimuler que ..., on est bien obligé d'admettre que ...; **his** ~ **fell on a small door** son regard rencontra une petite porte; **to get one's** ~ **in** ajuster son coup d'œil; **he's got his** ~ **on the championship** il guigne le championnat; **I've already got my** ~ **on a house** j'ai déjà une maison en vue; **to have an** ~ **on sb for a job** avoir qn en vue pour une place; **he had his** ~ **on a job in the Foreign Office** il visait un poste *or* il lorgnait une place au ministère des Affaires étrangères; **to have an** ~ **to the main chance** ne jamais perdre de vue ses propres intérêts, ne négliger aucune occasion de soigner ses intérêts; **she has an** ~ **for a bargain** elle flaire *or* elle reconnaît tout de suite une bonne affaire; **she has got an** ~ **for antique furniture** elle a du coup d'œil pour les meubles anciens; **he had** ~**s for no one but her** il n'avait d'yeux que pour elle; **to keep one's** ~ **on the ball** fixer la balle, regarder sa balle; **keeping his** ~ **on the beast, he seized his gun** sans quitter l'animal des yeux, il a empoigné son fusil; **keep your** ~ **on the main objective** ne perdez pas de vue le but principal; **to keep a watchful** ~ **on the situation** suivre de près la situation, avoir l'œil sur la situation; **to keep an** ~ **on things*** *or* **on everything** avoir l'œil (à tout); **to keep a strict** ~ **on sb** surveiller qn de près, avoir *or* tenir qn à l'œil*; **will you keep an** ~ **on the child/shop?** voudriez-vous surveiller l'enfant/le magasin?; **to keep an** ~ **on expenditure** surveiller la dépense; **to keep one's** ~**s open** *or* **peeled‡** *or* **skinned‡** être attentif (*for a danger* à un danger), être vigilant, ouvrir l'œil; **keep your** ~**s open for** *or* **keep an** ~ **out for* a hotel** essayez de repérer* un hôtel; **to go into sth with one's** ~**s wide open** *or* **with open** ~**s** se lancer dans qch en connaissance de cause; **his will open his** ~**s to the truth** ça va lui ouvrir *or* dessiller (*liter*) les yeux (*about* au sujet de); **to let one's ~ rest on sth** poser *or* arrêter son regard sur qch; **to look sb straight in the ~** regarder qn dans les yeux *or* dans le blanc des yeux *or* bien en face; **to make ~s at*** faire de l'œil à*, lancer des œillades à; **to run** *or* **cast one's ~s over** jeter un coup d'œil sur; **he ran his ~ over the letter** il a parcouru la lettre (en diagonale); **to see ~ to ~ with sb** voir les choses exactement comme qn *or* du même œil que qn, partager les opinions *or* le point de vue de qn; **I've never set** *or* **clapped*** *or* **laid ~s on him** je ne l'ai jamais vu de ma vie; **he didn't take his ~s off her, he kept his ~s fixed on her** il ne l'a pas quittée des yeux; **she couldn't take her ~s off the cakes** elle ne pouvait pas s'empêcher de reluquer *or* lorgner les gâteaux, elle dévorait les gâteaux des yeux; **he never uses his ~s** il ne sait pas voir; **why don't you use your ~s?** tu es aveugle?*, tu n'as donc pas les yeux en face des trous?‡; (*loc*) **an ~ for an ~ and a tooth for a tooth** œil pour œil, dent pour dent; (*Mil*) **~s right!** tête (à) droite!; (*Mil*) **~s front!** fixe!; **it's all my ~‡** tout ça, c'est des histoires*; **my ~!‡** mon œil!‡; *V* **catch, half, mind, open, private** *etc.*

(c) *[needle]* chas *m*, œil *m*, trou *m*; *[potato, peacock's tail]* œil; *[hurricane]* œil, centre *m*; (*photoelectric cell*) œil électrique.

2 *vt person* regarder, mesurer du regard; *thing* regarder, observer. **to ~ sb from head to toe** toiser qn de haut en bas; **he was ey(e)ing the girls** il reluquait *or* lorgnait les filles.

3 *cpd*: **eyeball** globe *m* oculaire; (*Med*) **eye bank** banque *f* des yeux; (*esp Brit*) **eyebath** œillère *f* (*pour bains d'œil*); **eyebrow** sourcil *m*; **eyebrow pencil** crayon *m* (à sourcils); **eyebrow tweezers** pince *f* à épiler; **eye-catcher** personne *f* *or* chose *f* qui tire l'œil *or* qui tape dans l'œil*; **eye-catching** *dress, colour* qui tire l'œil, qui tape dans l'œil*, tape-à-l'œil* *inv* (*pej*); *publicity, poster* accrocheur; (*US*) **eyecup** = **eyebath**; **eyedrops** gouttes *fpl* pour les yeux; **eyeglass** monocle *m*; **eyeglasses** lorgnon *m*, binocle *m*, pince-nez *m inv*; **eyelash** cil *m*; **at eye level** au niveau de l'œil; **eye-level grill** gril surélevé; **eyelid** paupière *f*; **eyeliner** eye-liner *m*; **eye-opener*** révélation *f*, surprise *f*; **that was an eye-opener for him*** cela lui a ouvert les yeux; **his speech was an eye-opener*** son discours a été très révélateur; **eyepiece** oculaire *m*; **eyeshade** visière *f*; **eyeshadow** fard *m* à paupières; **eyesight** vue *f*; **to have good eyesight** avoir une bonne vue *or* de bons yeux; **to lose one's eyesight** perdre la vue; **his eyesight is failing** sa vue baisse; **eyesore** horreur *f*; **these ruins are an eyesore** ces ruines sont une horreur *or* sont hideuses, ces ruines choquent la vue; **her hat was an eyesore** son chapeau était une horreur; **to have eyestrain** avoir la vue fatiguée; **eye test** examen *m* de la vue; **eye tooth** canine supérieure; (*Med*) **eyewash** collyre *m*; (*fig*) **that's a lot of eyewash‡** (*nonsense*) ce sont des fadaises, c'est du vent; (*to impress*) c'est de la frime*, c'est de la poudre aux yeux; **eyewitness** témoin oculaire *or* direct.

-eyed [aɪd] *adj ending in cpds*: **big-eyed** aux grands yeux; **one-eyed** (*lit*) borgne, qui n'a qu'un œil; (**fig*) miteux, minable; *V* **dry, hollow, wall** *etc.*

eyeful ['aɪfʊl] *n*: **he got an ~ of mud** il a reçu de la boue plein les yeux; **she's quite an ~‡** on se rince l'œil à la regarder‡; **get an ~ of this!‡** vise ça un peu!‡

eyelet ['aɪlɪt] *n* œillet *m* (*dans du tissu etc*).

eyrie ['ɪərɪ] *n* aire *f* (*d'aigle*).

F

F, f [ef] *n* **(a)** (*letter*) F, f *m or f*. **(b)** (*Mus*) fa *m*.

fa [fɑː] *n* (*Mus*) fa *m*.

fab‡ [fæb] *adj* (*Brit*: *abbr of* **fabulous**) sensass*, terrible‡.

fable ['feɪbl] *n* (*Literat*) fable *f*, légende *f*; (*fig*) fable; *V* **fact.**

fabled ['feɪbld] *adj* légendaire, fabuleux.

fabric ['fæbrɪk] *n* **(a)** (*cloth*) tissu *m*, étoffe *f*. **(b)** *[building, system, society]* structure *f*.

fabricate ['fæbrɪkeɪt] *vt goods etc* fabriquer; (*fig*) *document* fabriquer, forger; *story, account* inventer, fabriquer. **a ~d story** une histoire inventée *or* fabriquée *or* controuvée.

fabrication [ˌfæbrɪ'keɪʃən] *n* **(a)** (*U*: *V* **fabricate**) fabrication *f*; invention *f*. **(b)** (*false statement etc*) invention *f*. **it is (a) pure ~** c'est une pure invention, c'est de la fabrication pure (et simple).

fabulous ['fæbjʊləs] *adj* (*incredible*) extraordinaire, fabuleux; (*legendary*) légendaire, fabuleux; (*: *wonderful*) formidable*, sensationnel*. **a ~ price*** un prix fou *or* astronomique; (*excl*) **~!** chouette!*, sensass!*

façade [fə'sɑːd] *n* (*Archit, fig*) façade *f*.

face [feɪs] **1** *n* (*Anat*) visage *m*, figure *f*; (*expression*) mine *f*, physionomie *f*; *[building]* façade *f*, devant *m*, front *m*; *[clock]* cadran *m*; *[cliff]* paroi *f*; *[coin]* côté *m*; *[the earth]* surface *f*; *[document]* recto *m*; *[type]* œil *m*; *[playing card]* face *f*, dessous *m*; (*U*: *prestige*) face; (*: *U*: *impertinence*) toupet* *m*. **a pleasant ~** un visage *or* une figure agréable; **to fall (flat) on one's ~** tomber à plat ventre, tomber face contre terre; **he was lying ~ down(wards)** il était étendu (la) face contre terre *or* à plat ventre; **he was lying ~ up(wards)** il était étendu sur le dos *or* le visage tourné vers le ciel; **the card fell ~ up** la carte est tombée retournée; **the card fell ~ down** la carte est tombée sens dessous dessus; **to turn sth ~ up** retourner *or* mettre qch à l'endroit; (*Med*) **injuries to the ~** blessures *fpl* à la face *or* au visage; **to have one's ~ lifted** se faire faire un lifting; **you can shout till you're black** *or* **blue in the ~, nobody will come** tu auras beau t'exténuer à crier, personne ne viendra; **to change the ~ of a town** changer le visage d'une ville; **he vanished off the ~ of the earth** il a complètement disparu de la circulation; **I know that ~** je connais ce visage *or* cette tête-là; **I've got a good memory for ~s** j'ai la mémoire des visages, je suis physionomiste; **he's a good judge of ~s** il sait lire sur les visages; **the rain was blowing in our ~s** la pluie nous fouettait le visage *or* la figure; **he laughed in my ~** il m'a ri au nez; **he won't show his ~ here again** il ne se montrera plus ici, il ne remettra plus le nez ici; **he told him the truth to his ~** il lui a dit la vérité sans ambages; **he told him so to his ~** il le lui a dit tout cru; **to come ~ to ~ with sb** se trouver face à face *or* nez à nez avec qn (*V also* 2); **to bring two people ~ to ~** confronter deux personnes; **courage in the ~ of the enemy** courage *m* face à l'ennemi; **in the ~ of this threat** devant cette menace; **he succeeded in the ~ of great difficulties** il a réussi en dépit de grandes difficultés; **to set one's ~ against sth** s'élever contre qch; **to set one's ~ against doing** se refuser à faire; **to put a bold** *or* **brave ~ on things** faire bonne contenance *or* bon visage; **you'll just have to put a good ~ on it** tu n'auras qu'à faire contre mauvaise fortune bon cœur; **to save (one's) ~** sauver la face; **to lose ~** perdre la face; **to make** *or* **pull ~s (at)** faire des grimaces (à); **to make** *or* **pull a (disapproving) ~** faire une moue de désapprobation; **on the ~ of it his evidence is false** à première vue son témoignage est faux; **to have the ~ to do*** avoir le toupet* de faire; *V* **coal, fly[3], straight** *etc.*

2 *cpd*: **face card** figure *f*; **face cream** crème *f* pour le visage; (*Brit*) **face flannel** gant *m* de toilette; **face lift** lifting *m*, déridage *m*; **to have a face lift** se faire faire un lifting; (*fig*) **to give the house a face lift** retaper la maison; **face pack** masque *m* de beauté; **face powder** poudre *f* de riz; **it was clearly a face-saver** *or* **a piece of face-saving on their part** ils l'ont visiblement fait pour sauver la face; **face-saving** (*adj*) qui sauve la face; **face-to-face** face à face, en tête à tête *or* en tête-à-tête; (*TV etc*) **face-to-face discussion** face à face *m inv* *or* face-à-face *m inv*; **face value** *[coin]* valeur nominale; *[stamp, card]* valeur; (*fig*) **to take a statement at its face value** prendre une déclaration pour argent comptant *or* au pied de la lettre; **to take sb at his face value** juger qn sur les apparences; **you can't take it at its face value** il ne faut pas vous laisser tromper par les apparences.

3 *vt* **(a)** *[window]* donner sur; *[building]* donner sur, faire face à; *[person]* faire face à. **he was facing me at the dinner** il était assis en face de moi *or* je l'avais comme vis-à-vis au dîner; **he stood facing the wall** il se tenait face au mur; **the man facing us** l'homme en face de nous; **the problem facing us** le problème devant lequel nous nous trouvons *or* qui se pose à nous; **facing one another** en face l'un de l'autre, l'un vis-à-vis de l'autre, en vis-à-vis; **the picture facing page 16** l'illustration en regard de la page 16; (*Rail*) **facing the engine** dans le sens de la marche; **to be ~d with defeat** être menacé par la défaite; **he was ~d with having to pay £10** il se voyait contraint à payer 10 livres; **he was ~d with a bill for £10** il se voyait contraint à payer une note de 10 livres; **he was ~d with the prospect of doing it himself** il risquait d'avoir à le faire lui-même; **~d with the prospect of having to refuse, he ...** face à *or* devant la perspective d'avoir à refuser, il ... .

(b) (*meet confidently*) *danger* faire face à. (*fig*) **to ~ the music** braver l'orage *or* la tempête, ne pas reculer, ne pas se dérober; **we'll have to ~ the music** allons-y gaiement (*iro*), il ne faut pas reculer; **to ~ it out*** faire face, ne pas reculer, ne pas se dérober; **to ~ (the) facts** regarder les choses en face, se rendre à l'évidence; **she won't ~ the fact that he will not come back** elle ne veut pas se rendre à l'évidence et comprendre *or* admettre qu'il ne reviendra pas; **let's ~ it*** regardons les choses en face, admettons-le; **I can't ~ doing it** je ne trouve pas *or* je n'ai pas le courage de le faire.

(c) (*line*) *wall* revêtir (*with* de). **coat ~d with silk** habit à revers de soie.

4 *vi* *[person]* se tourner; *[house]* être exposé *or* orienté. **~ this**

way! tournez-vous de ce côté!; (*fig*) to ~ **both ways** ménager la chèvre et le chou; **which way does the house ~?** comment la maison est-elle orientée?; **house facing north** maison exposée *or* orientée au nord; **room facing towards the sea** chambre donnant sur la mer, chambre face à la mer; (*US Mil*) **right ~!** à droite, droite!; (*US Mil*) **about ~!** demi-tour!

face about *vi* (*Mil*) faire demi-tour.

face up to *vt fus danger, difficulty* faire face à, affronter. **to face up to the fact that** admettre *or* accepter (le fait) que.

faceless ['feɪslɪs] *adj* anonyme.

facer: ['feɪsəʳ] *n* (*Brit*) tuile* *f*, os* *m*. **well there's a ~ for us** nous voilà tombés sur un os*, voilà une belle tuile* qui nous tombe dessus.

facet ['fæsɪt] *n* (*lit, fig*) facette *f*.

faceted ['fæsɪtɪd] *adj* à facettes.

facetious [fə'siːʃəs] *adj person* facétieux, plaisant; *remark* plaisant, bouffon.

facetiously [fə'siːʃəslɪ] *adv* facétieusement.

facetiousness [fə'siːʃəsnɪs] *n* (*V* **facetious**) caractère facétieux *or* plaisant.

facial ['feɪʃəl] **1** *adj nerve, massage* facial. **2** *n* (*) soin *m* (complet) du visage. **to have a ~** se faire faire un soin du visage; **to give o.s. a ~** se faire un nettoyage de peau.

facies ['feɪʃɪiːz] *n* faciès *m*.

facile ['fæsaɪl] *adj* (*gen pej*) *victory, style* facile; *talk, idea* superficiel, creux; *person* complaisant; *style, manner* aisé, coulant.

facilely ['fæsaɪllɪ] *adv* complaisamment.

facilitate [fə'sɪlɪteɪt] *vt* faciliter.

facility [fə'sɪlɪtɪ] *n* **(a)** (*U*) facilité *f*. **to write with ~** écrire avec facilité; **~ in learning** facilité pour apprendre.

(b) **you will have all facilities** *or* **every ~ for study** vous aurez toutes facilités pour étudier; **sports/educational facilities** équipements sportifs/scolaires; **transport/production facilities** moyens *mpl* de transports/de production; **harbour facilities** installations *fpl* portuaires; **the flat has no cooking facilities** l'appartement n'est pas équipé pour qu'on y fasse la cuisine; *V* **credit**.

facing ['feɪsɪŋ] *n* (*Constr*) revêtement *m*; (*Sewing*) revers *m*.

-facing ['feɪsɪŋ] *adj ending in cpds*: **south-facing** exposé au sud.

facsimile [fæk'sɪmɪlɪ] *n* fac-similé *m*. **in ~** en fac-similé.

fact [fækt] **1** *n* **(a)** (*sth known, accepted as true*) fait *m*. **the ~ that he is here** le fait qu'il est là; **it is a ~ that** il est de fait que + *indic*; **is it a ~ that** est-il vrai que + *subj* (*often indic in conversation*); **I know it for a ~** c'est un fait certain, je le sais de source sûre; **to know (it) for a ~ that** savoir de science *or* source sûre que, savoir pertinemment que; **to stick to ~s** s'en tenir aux faits; **it's time he knew the ~s of life** il est temps de lui apprendre les choses de la vie; (*fig*) il est temps qu'on le mette devant les réalités de la vie; *V* **face**.

(b) (*U: reality*) faits *mpl*, réalité *f*. **~ and fiction** le réel et l'imaginaire; (*fig*) **he can't tell ~ from fiction** *or* **from fable** il ne sait pas séparer le vrai du faux; **story founded on ~** histoire basée sur des faits *or* sur la réalité; **in point of ~** en fait, par le fait; **in ~, as a matter of ~** en fait, en réalité, à vrai dire; **the ~ of the matter is that** ... le fait est que ..., la réalité c'est que ...; **I accept what he says as ~** je crois à la réalité de ce qu'il dit.

(c) (*Jur*) fait *m*, action *f*; *V* **accessary**.

2 *cpd*: **fact-finding committee** commission *f* d'enquête; **they were on a fact-finding mission to the war front** ils étaient partis enquêter au front.

faction ['fækʃən] *n* (*group*) faction *f*; (*U: strife*) discorde *f*, dissension *f*.

factious ['fækʃəs] *adj* factieux.

factitious [fæk'tɪʃəs] *adj* artificiel.

factitive ['fæktɪtɪv] *adj* (*Gram*) factitif.

factor ['fæktəʳ] **1** *n* **(a)** facteur *m* (*also Bio, Math etc*), élément *m*. **determining ~** facteur décisif *or* déterminant; (*Tech*) **~ of safety, safety ~** facteur de sécurité; **human ~** élément humain; *V* **common, prime**.

(b) (*agent*) agent *m*; (*Scot: estate manager*) régisseur *m*, intendant *m*.

2 *cpd*: (*Statistics*) **factor analysis** analyse factorielle.

factorial [fæk'tɔːrɪəl] **1** *adj* factoriel. **2** *n* factorielle *f*.

factory ['fæktərɪ] **1** *n* usine *f*, (*gen smaller*) fabrique *f*; (*fig*) usine. **shoe/soap** *etc* **~** usine *or* fabrique de chaussures/de savon *etc*; **car/textile** *etc* **~** usine d'automobiles/de textile *etc*; **arms/china/tobacco ~** manufacture *f* d'armes/de porcelaine/de tabac.

2 *cpd*: **Factory Acts** législation industrielle; **factory chimney** cheminée *f* d'usine; **factory farming** élevage industriel; **factory hand = factory worker**; **factory inspector** inspecteur *m* du travail; **factory ship** navire-usine *m*; **factory work** travail *m* en *or* d'usine; **factory worker** ouvrier *m*, -ière *f* (d'usine).

factotum [fæk'təʊtəm] *n* factotum *m*, intendant *m*; (*hum: man or woman*) bonne *f* à tout faire (*fig hum*).

factual ['fæktjʊəl] *adj report, description* basé sur les *or* des faits; *happening* réel; (*Philos*) factuel. **~ error** erreur *f* de fait *or* sur les faits.

factually ['fæktjʊəlɪ] *adv* en se tenant aux faits. **~ speaking** pour s'en tenir aux faits.

faculty ['fækəltɪ] **1** *n* **(a)** faculté *f*. **the mental faculties** les facultés mentales; **to have all one's faculties** avoir toutes ses facultés.

(b) (*U: aptitude*) aptitude *f*, facilité *f* (*for doing* à faire).

(c) (*Univ*) faculté *f*. **the F~ of Arts** la faculté des lettres; **the medical ~** la Faculté de Médecine; (*US*) **the F~** le corps enseignant; *V* **law, science** *etc*.

2 *cpd*: **Faculty board** Conseil *m* de faculté; **Faculty meeting** réunion *f* du Conseil de faculté.

fad [fæd] *n* (*personal*) marotte *f*, manie *f*; (*general*) folie *f*. **she has her ~s** elle a ses (petites) marottes *or* manies; **a passing ~** une lubie; **this ~ for long skirts** cette folie des *or* cet engouement pour les jupes longues.

faddy ['fædɪ] *adj* (*Brit*) *person* maniaque, capricieux, à marottes; *distaste, desire* capricieux.

fade [feɪd] **1** *vi* **(a)** *[flower]* se faner, se flétrir; *[light]* baisser, diminuer, s'affaiblir; *[colour]* passer, perdre son éclat; *[material]* passer, se décolorer. **guaranteed not to ~** garanti bon teint; **the daylight was fast fading** le jour baissait rapidement.

(b) (*also* **~ away**) *[one's sight, memory, hearing etc]* baisser; *[thing remembered, vision]* s'effacer; *[hopes, smile]* s'éteindre, s'évanouir; *[sound]* s'affaiblir; *[person]* dépérir. **the castle ~d from sight** le château disparut aux regards; (*Rad*) **the sound is fading** il y a du fading, le son s'en va.

2 *cpd*: **fade-in** (*Cine*) ouverture *f* en fondu; (*TV*) apparition graduelle; (*Rad*) fondu *m* sonore; **fade-out** (*Cine*) fermeture *f* en fondu; (*TV*) disparition graduelle; (*Rad*) fondu *m* sonore.

3 *vt* **(a)** *curtains etc* décolorer; *colours, flowers* faner.

(b) (*Rad*) *conversation* couper par un fondu sonore. (*Cine, TV*) **to ~ one scene into another** faire un fondu enchaîné.

fade away *vi* = **fade 1b**.

fade in **1** *vi* (*Cine, TV*) apparaître en fondu.

2 *vt sep* (*Cine, TV*) faire apparaître en fondu; (*Rad*) monter.

3 fade-in *n V* **fade 2**.

fade out **1** *vi [sound]* s'affaiblir, disparaître; (*Cine, TV*) *[picture]* disparaître en fondu; (*Rad*) *[music, dialogue]* être coupé par fondu sonore.

2 *vt sep* (*Cine, TV*) faire disparaître en fondu; (*Rad*) couper par un fondu sonore.

3 fade-out *n V* **fade 2**.

faded ['feɪdɪd] *adj material* décoloré, passé; *flowers* fané, flétri; *beauty* défraîchi, fané.

faeces, (*US*) **feces** ['fiːsiːz] *npl* fèces *fpl*.

faerie, faery ['fɛərɪ] († *or liter*) **1** *n* féerie *f*. **2** *adj* imaginaire, féerique.

fag [fæg] **1** *n* **(a)** (*U: Brit*:) corvée *f*. **what a ~!** quelle barbe!*; **it's too much of a ~** c'est trop la barbe*.

(b) (*Brit*: *cigarette*) sèche: *f*.

(c) (*Brit Scol*) petit *m* (*élève au service d'un grand*).

(d) (*: homosexual*) pédé: *m*.

2 *cpd*: **fag end** (*remainder*) restes *mpl*; *[material]* bout *m*; *[conversation]* dernières bribes; (:) *[cigarette]* mégot* *m*, clope: *m*.

3 *vt* (*also* **~ out**) *person, animal* éreinter, épuiser, fatiguer. **to ~ o.s. (out)** s'éreinter; **to be ~ged (out)*** être éreinté *or* claqué* *or* crevé*; **I can't be ~ged**: j'ai la flemme*.

4 *vi* **(a)** (*also* **~ away**) s'échiner, s'éreinter (*at* à).

(b) (*Brit Scol*) **to ~ for sb** faire les menues corvées de qn.

faggot, (*US*) **fagot** ['fægət] *n* (*wood*) fagot *m*; (*Culin*) (*sorte de*) crépinette *f*; (:*: homosexual*) pédé: *m*, tante: *f*.

fah [fɑː] *n* (*Mus*) = **fa**.

Fahrenheit ['færənhaɪt] *adj* Fahrenheit *inv*. **~ thermometer/scale** thermomètre *m*/échelle *f* Fahrenheit; **degrees ~** degrés *mpl* Fahrenheit.

fail [feɪl] **1** *vi* **(a)** (*be unsuccessful*) *[candidate]* échouer, être collé* *or* recalé* (*in an exam* à un examen, *in Latin* en latin); *[plans, attempts, treatment]* échouer, ne pas réussir; *[negotiations]* ne pas aboutir, échouer; *[play, show]* faire *or* être un four; *[bank, business]* faire faillite. **I ~ed (in my attempts) to see him** je n'ai pas réussi *or* je ne suis pas arrivé à le voir; **to ~ by 5 votes** échouer à 5 voix près.

(b) (*grow feeble*) *[hearing, eyesight, health]* faiblir, baisser; *[person, invalid, voice]* s'affaiblir; *[light]* baisser; (*run short*) *[power, gas, electricity, water supply]* faire défaut, manquer; (*break down*) *[engine]* tomber en panne, flancher*. **his eyes are ~ing** sa vue faiblit *or* baisse; **crops ~ed because of the drought** la sécheresse a causé la perte des récoltes; **to ~ in one's duty** faillir à *or* manquer à son devoir.

2 *vt* **(a)** *examination* échouer à, être collé* *or* recalé* à; *candidate* refuser, coller*, recaler* (*in an exam* à un examen). **to ~ one's driving test** échouer à *or* être recalé* à son permis (de conduire); **he's a ~ed writer** il n'a pas réussi comme écrivain; **he ~ed Latin** il a échoué en latin.

(b) (*let down*) *person* manquer à ses engagements envers, laisser tomber*. **don't ~ me!** ne me laissez pas tomber!*, je compte sur vous!; **his heart ~ed him** le cœur lui a manqué; **words ~ me!** les mots me manquent!; **his memory often ~s him** sa mémoire lui fait souvent défaut, sa mémoire le trahit souvent.

(c) (*omit*) manquer, négliger, omettre (*to do* de faire). **he never ~s to write** il ne manque jamais d'écrire; **he ~ed to visit her** il a négligé *or* omis de lui rendre visite; **he ~ed to keep his word** il a manqué à sa parole; (*Jur*) **to ~ to appear** faire défaut; **he ~ed to appear at the dinner** il ne s'est pas montré au dîner; **I ~ to see why** je ne vois pas pourquoi; **I ~ to understand** je n'arrive pas à comprendre.

3 *n* **(a)** **without ~** *come, do* à coup sûr, sans faute; *happen, befall* immanquablement, inévitablement.

(b) (*Scol, Univ*) échec *m*. **she got a ~ in history** elle a échoué *or* a été recalée* en histoire.

4 *cpd*: (*Tech*) **failsafe** à sûreté intégrée.

failing ['feɪlɪŋ] **1** *n* défaut *m*. **2** *prep* à défaut de. **~ this** à défaut.

failure ['feɪljəʳ] *n* **(a)** (*lack of success*) échec *m* (*in an exam* à un examen); *[plan]* échec, insuccès *m*, avortement *m*; *[play, show etc]* échec; *[bank, business]* faillite *f*; *[discussions, negotiations]* échec, fiasco *m*. **after two ~s he gave up** il a abandonné après deux échecs; **the play was a ~** la pièce a été un four *or* a fait un four *or* a été un fiasco *or* a fait fiasco; **this new machine/this plan is a total ~** cette nouvelle machine/ce projet est un fiasco complet; **his ~ to convince them** son incapacité *f* *or* son impuissance *f* à les convaincre.

(b) (*unsuccessful person*) raté(e) *m(f)*. **to be a ~ at maths** être nul en math; **to be a ~ at gardening** n'être pas doué pour le jardinage; **he's a ~ as a writer** il ne vaut rien comme écrivain.

(c) (*breakdown, insufficiency*) *[electricity, engine]* panne *f*. **~ of oil/water supply** manque *m* de pétrole/d'eau; **~ of the crops** perte *f* des récoltes; *V* **heart**.

(d) (*omission*) manquement *m*, défaut *m*. **his ~ to answer** le fait qu'il n'a pas répondu; **because of his ~ to help us** du fait qu'il ne nous a pas aidés; (*Jur*) **~ to appear** défaut *m* de comparution; **~ to observe a by-law** inobservation *f* d'un règlement (de police).

fain†† [feɪn] *adv* (*only after 'would'*) volontiers.

faint [feɪnt] **1** *adj* **(a)** *breeze, smell, sound, hope, trace* léger, faible; *colour* pâle, délavé; *voice* faible, éteint; *breathing* faible; *idea* vague, peu précis, flou. **I haven't the ~est idea (about it)** je n'en ai pas la moindre idée; **a ~ smile** (*indifferent*) un vague sourire; (*sad*) un pauvre sourire; **to make a ~ attempt at doing** essayer sans conviction de faire; **to grow ~(er)** s'affaiblir, diminuer; (*Prov*) **~ heart never won fair lady** la pusillanimité n'est point la clef des cœurs féminins.

(b) (*Med*) défaillant, prêt à s'évanouir. **to feel ~** se trouver mal, être pris d'un malaise; **~ with hunger/weariness** défaillant de faim/de fatigue.

2 *n* évanouissement *m*, défaillance *f*. **to fall in a ~** s'évanouir, avoir une défaillance.

3 *cpd*: **fainthearted** craintif, timide, timoré; **fainting fit** évanouissement *m*; **faint-ruled paper** papier réglé (en impression légère).

4 *vi* (*also* **~ away**) s'évanouir, tomber dans les pommes*; (*from hunger etc*) défaillir (*from* de).

faintly ['feɪntlɪ] *adv call, say* d'une voix éteinte, faiblement; *breathe, shine* faiblement; *write, mark, scratch* légèrement; (*slightly*) légèrement, vaguement. **~ reminiscent of** qui rappelle vaguement; **in a ~ disappointed tone** d'un ton un peu déçu, avec une nuance de déception dans la voix.

faintness ['feɪntnɪs] *n [sound, voice etc]* faiblesse *f*; *[breeze etc]* légèreté *f*.

fair[1] [fɛəʳ] **1** *adj* **(a)** *person, decision* juste, équitable; *deal* équitable, honnête; *fight, competition* loyal; *profit, warning, comment* justifié, mérité. **he is strict but ~** il est sévère mais juste *or* équitable *or* impartial; **it's not ~** ce n'est pas juste; **to be ~ (to him)** *or* **let's be ~ (to him), he thought he had paid for it** rendons-lui cette justice, il croyait l'avoir payé; **it wouldn't be ~ to his brother** ce ne serait pas juste *or* honnête *or* équitable vis-à-vis de son frère; **as is (only) ~** et ce n'est que justice; **~ enough!** d'accord!, très bien!; c'est bien normal!; **it's (a) ~ comment** la remarque est juste; **to give sb ~ warning of sth** prévenir qn honnêtement de qch; **to give sb a ~ deal** agir équitablement envers qn; **it's a ~ exchange** c'est équitable, c'est un échange honnête; (*loc*) **~ exchange is no robbery** échange n'est pas vol; **he was ~ game for the critics** c'était une proie rêvée *or* idéale pour les critiques; **by ~ means or foul** par tous les moyens, par n'importe quel moyen; **~ play** fair-play *m*; **~ sample** échantillon représentatif; **he got his ~ share of the money** il a eu tout l'argent qui lui revenait (de droit); **he's had his ~ share of trouble*** il a eu sa part de soucis; **~ shares for all** (à) chacun son dû; **he's ~ and square** il est honnête *or* franc *or* loyal; **through ~ and foul** à travers toutes les épreuves.

(b) (*average*) *work, achievements* passable, assez bon. **it's ~ to middling** c'est passable, ce n'est pas mal, c'est assez bien; **he has a ~ chance of success** il a des chances de réussir; **in ~ condition** en assez bon état.

(c) (*quite large*) *sum* considérable; *number* respectable. **to go at a ~ pace** aller bon train, aller à (une) bonne allure; **he is in a ~ way to doing** il y a de bonnes chances pour qu'il fasse; **he's travelled a ~ amount** il a pas mal voyagé; **there's a ~ amount of money left** il reste pas mal d'argent.

(d) (*light-coloured*) *hair etc* blond; *complexion, skin* clair, de blond(e). **she's ~** elle est blonde, c'est une blonde.

(e) (*fine*) *wind* propice, favorable; *weather* beau (*f* belle); (†: *beautiful*) beau. **it's set ~** le temps est au beau fixe; **the ~ sex** le beau sexe; **~ promises** belles promesses; **~ words** belles phrases.

(f) (*clean, neat*) propre, net. **to make a ~ copy of sth** recopier qch au propre *or* au net; **~ copy** (*rewritten*) copie *f* au propre *or* au net; (*model answer etc*) corrigé *m*.

2 *adv* **(a) to play ~** jouer franc jeu; **to act ~ and square** agir loyalement, faire preuve de loyauté, jouer cartes sur table; **the branch struck him ~ and square in the face** la branche l'a frappé au beau milieu du visage *or* en plein (milieu du) visage; **the car ran ~ and square into the tree** la voiture est entrée de plein fouet *or* en plein dans l'arbre.

(b) (*: or dial*) = **fairly c.**

(c) (††) *speak* courtoisement. **~ spoken** qui parle avec courtoisie.

3 *cpd*: **fair-haired** blond, aux cheveux blonds; (*US fig*) **the fair-haired boy*** le chouchou*, le chéri; **fair-haired girl** blonde *f*; **fair-minded** impartial, équitable; **fair-sized** assez grand, d'une bonne taille; **fair-skinned** à la peau claire; (*US*) **fair-trade price** prix imposé; **fairway** (*Naut*) chenal *m*, passe *f*; (*Golf*) fairway *m*; (*fig*) **fair-weather friends** les amis *mpl* des bons *or* beaux jours.

fair[2] [fɛəʳ] **1** *n* foire *f*; (*Comm*) foire; (*for charity*) fête *f*, kermesse *f*. (*Comm*) **the Book F~** la Foire du livre; *V* **world** *etc.* **2** *cpd*: **fairground** champ *m* de foire.

fairing ['fɛərɪŋ] *n* (*Aut, Aviat*) carénage *m*.

fairly ['fɛəlɪ] *adv* **(a)** (*justly*) *treat* équitablement, avec justice, impartialement; *obtain* honnêtement, loyalement.

(b) (*reasonably*) assez, moyennement. **it's ~ straightforward** c'est assez facile; **he plays ~ well** il joue passablement; **he's ~ good** il n'est pas mauvais; **they lead a ~ quiet life** ils mènent une vie plutôt tranquille; **I'm ~ sure that ...** je suis presque sûr que ... .

(c) (*utterly*) absolument, vraiment. **he was ~ beside himself with rage** il était absolument hors de lui.

(d) ~ and squarely = fair and square; *V* **fair**[1] **2a.**

fairness ['fɛənɪs] *n* **(a)** (*lightness*) *[hair]* couleur blonde, blond *m*, blondeur *f*; *[skin]* blancheur *f*.

(b) (*honesty, justice*) justice *f*, honnêteté *f*; *[decision, judgment]* équité *f*, impartialité *f*. **in all ~** en toute justice; **in ~ to him** pour être juste envers lui.

fairy ['fɛərɪ] **1** *n* **(a)** fée *f*. **the wicked ~** la fée Carabosse; **she is his good/wicked ~** elle est son bon/mauvais ange.

(b) (*‡pej: homosexual*) pédé‡ *m*, tapette‡ *f*.

2 *adj helper, gift* magique; *child, dance, music* des fées.

3 *cpd*: **fairy cycle** bicyclette *f* d'enfant; (*iro*) **fairy footsteps** pas *mpl* (légers) de danseuse (*iro*); **fairy godmother** (*lit*) bonne fée; (*fig*) marraine *f* gâteau *inv*; **fairyland** royaume *m* des fées; (*fig*) féerie *f*; **fairy lights** guirlande *f* électrique; **fairy-like** féerique, de fée; **fairy queen** reine *f* des fées; **fairy story, fairy tale** conte *m* de fées; (*untruth*) mensonge *m*, conte à dormir debout.

faith [feɪθ] **1** *n* **(a)** (*U: trust, belief*) foi *f*, confiance *f*. **F~, Hope and Charity** la foi, l'espérance et la charité; **~ in God** foi en Dieu; **to have ~ in sb** avoir confiance en qn; **I've lost ~ in him** je ne lui fais plus confiance; **to put one's ~ in, to pin one's ~ on*** mettre tous ses espoirs en.

(b) (*religion*) foi *f*, religion *f*.

(c) (*U*) **to keep ~ with sb** tenir ses promesses envers qn; **to break ~ with sb** manquer à sa parole envers qn.

(d) (*U*) **good ~** bonne foi; **to do sth in all good ~** faire qch en toute bonne foi; **bad ~** déloyauté *f*, perfidie *f*; **to act in bad ~** agir de mauvaise foi *or* déloyalement.

2 *cpd*: **faith healer** guérisseur *m*, -euse *f* (mystique); **faith healing** guérison *f* par la foi.

faithful ['feɪθfʊl] **1** *adj* **(a)** *person* fidèle (*to* à). **(b)** (*accurate*) *account, translation* fidèle, exact; *copy* conforme. **2** *n* (*Rel*) **the ~** (*Christians*) les fidèles *mpl*; (*Muslims*) les croyants *mpl*.

faithfully ['feɪθfəlɪ] *adv follow* fidèlement; *behave* loyalement; *translate* exactement, fidèlement. **to promise ~ that** donner sa parole que; (*in correspondence*) **yours ~** veuillez agréer mes *or* nos salutations distinguées.

faithfulness ['feɪθfʊlnɪs] *n* fidélité *f* (*to* à), loyauté *f* (*to* envers); *[account, translation]* fidélité, exactitude *f*; *[copy]* conformité *f*.

faithless ['feɪθlɪs] *adj* déloyal, perfide.

faithlessness ['feɪθlɪsnɪs] *n* (*U*) déloyauté *f*, perfidie *f*.

fake [feɪk] **1** *n* (*object*) article *or* objet truqué; (*picture*) faux *m*. **he's a ~** c'est un imposteur, il n'est pas ce qu'il prétend être.

2 *adj document* maquillé, falsifié, faux (*f* fausse); *picture, beam, furniture* faux; *elections* truqué; (*Rad, TV*) *interview* truqué, monté d'avance.

3 *vt document* faire un faux de, (*alter*) maquiller, falsifier; (*Art*) *picture* faire un faux de, contrefaire; *beam, furniture* imiter; *photograph, sound tape, elections, trial* truquer; (*Rad, TV*) *interview* truquer, monter d'avance. **to ~ illness/death** *etc* faire semblant d'être malade/mort *etc.*

4 *vi* faire semblant.

fakir ['fɑːkɪəʳ] *n* fakir *m*.

falcon ['fɔːlkən] *n* faucon *m*.

falconer ['fɔːlkənəʳ] *n* fauconnier *m*.

falconry ['fɔːlkənrɪ] *n* fauconnerie *f*.

Falkland Islands ['fɔːlklənd,aɪləndz] *npl* îles *fpl* Falkland.

fall [fɔːl] (*vb: pret* **fell**, *ptp* **fallen**) **1** *n* **(a)** (*lit, fig*) chute *f*; (*Mil*) chute, prise *f*. **to have a ~** tomber, faire une chute; **without a ~** sans tomber; (*fig*) **to be heading** *or* **riding for a ~** courir à l'échec, aller au-devant de la défaite; (*Rel*) **the F~ (of Man)** la chute (de l'homme); **the ~ of Saigon** la chute *or* la prise de Saigon; **the ~ of the Bastille** la prise de la Bastille; **~ of earth** éboulement *m* de terre, éboulis *m*; **~ of rock** chute de pierres; **there has been a heavy ~ of snow** il y a eu de fortes chutes de neige, il est tombé beaucoup de neige; *V* **free.**

(b) (*lowering: in price, demand, temperature*) baisse *f* (*in* de); (*more drastic*) chute *f*; (*Fin*) dépréciation *f*, baisse.

(c) (*slope: of ground, roof*) pente *f*, inclinaison *f*.

(d) (*waterfall*) **~s** chute *f* d'eau, cascade *f*; **the Niagara F~s** les chutes du Niagara.

(e) (*US: autumn*) automne *m*. **in the ~** en automne.

2 *vi* **(a)** *[person, object]* tomber; (*Rel etc: sin*) tomber, pécher; *[building]* s'écrouler, s'effondrer; *[rain, leaves, bombs, night, darkness, hair, garment, curtains]* tomber; *[temperature, price, level, voice, wind]* baisser, tomber; *[ground]* descendre, aller en pente; (*Mil*) *[soldier etc]* tomber (au champ d'honneur); *[country, city, fortress]* tomber; *[government]* tomber, être renversé. **he let ~ the cup, he let the cup ~** il a laissé tomber la tasse (*V also* 2b); **he fell into the river** il est tombé dans la rivière; **to ~ out of a car/off a bike** tomber d'une voiture/d'un vélo; **to ~ over a chair** tomber en butant contre une chaise (*V also* 2b); **to ~ (flat) on one's face** tomber face contre terre *or* à plat ventre; **he fell full length** il est tombé de tout son long; **to ~ to** *or* **on one's knees** tomber à genoux; (*lit, fig*) **to ~ on one's feet** retomber sur ses pieds; **he fell into bed exhausted** il s'est jeté au lit épuisé; **they fell into each other's arms** ils sont tombés dans les bras l'un de l'autre; **her hair fell to her shoulders** les cheveux lui tombaient sur les épaules; *V* **neck** *etc.*

(b) (*fig phrases*) **to ~ into a trap/an ambush** tomber *or* donner dans un piège/une embuscade; **he was ~ing over himself to be polite*** il se mettait en quatre pour être poli; **they were ~ing**

over each other to get it* ils se battaient pour l'avoir; **to let ~ a hint that** laisser entendre que, donner à entendre que; **the accent ~s on the second syllable** l'accent tombe sur la deuxième syllabe; **strange sounds fell on our ears** des bruits étranges parvinrent à nos oreilles; **his face fell** son visage s'est assombri *or* s'est allongé; **her eyes fell on a strange object** son regard est tombé sur un objet étrange; **the students ~ into 3 categories** les étudiants se divisent en 3 catégories; **the responsibility ~s on you** la responsabilité retombe sur vous; **to ~ on bad times** tomber dans la misère, avoir des revers de fortune; **Christmas Day ~s on a Sunday** Noël tombe un dimanche; **he fell to wondering if ...** il s'est mis à se demander si ...; **it ~s to me to say** il m'appartient de dire, c'est à moi de dire; **not a word fell from his lips** il n'a pas laissé échapper un mot; **to ~ by the way** abandonner en cours de route; **he fell among thieves** il est tombé aux mains de voleurs; **his work fell short of what we had expected** son travail n'a pas répondu à notre attente; **the copy fell far short of the original** la copie était loin de valoir l'original; **to ~ short of perfection** ne pas atteindre la perfection; *V* **foul, stool** *etc.*

(c) (*become, find o.s. etc*) **to ~ asleep** s'endormir; **to ~ into a deep sleep** tomber dans un profond sommeil; **to ~ into bad habits** prendre *or* contracter de mauvaises habitudes; **to ~ into conversation with sb** entrer en conversation avec qn; **to ~ into despair** sombrer dans le désespoir; **to ~ into disgrace** tomber en disgrâce; **to ~ from grace** (*Rel*) perdre la grâce; (*fig*) tomber en disgrâce, ne plus avoir la cote; (*hum*) faire une gaffe*; *[rent, bill]* **to ~ due** venir à échéance; **to ~ flat** *[joke]* tomber à plat; *[scheme]* échouer, rater; **to ~ into the hands of** tomber aux *or* entre les mains de; **to ~ heir to sth** hériter de qch; **to ~ ill** *or* **sick** tomber malade; **to ~ lame** se mettre à boiter; (*lit, fig*) **to ~ into line** s'aligner; (*fig*) **to ~ into line with sb** se ranger *or* se conformer à l'avis de qn; **to ~ in love** tomber amoureux (*with* de); **to ~ for sb*** tomber amoureux de qn; **to ~ for an idea*** *etc* s'enthousiasmer pour une idée *etc*; (*pej: be taken in by*) **to ~ for a suggestion** se laisser prendre à une suggestion; **he really fell for it!*** il s'est vraiment laissé prendre!, il s'est vraiment fait avoir!*; **to ~ silent** se taire; **to ~ under suspicion** devenir suspect; **to ~ vacant** *[job, position]* se trouver vacant; *[room, flat]* se trouver libre; **to ~ (a) victim to** devenir (la) victime de.

3 *cpd*: (*US*) **fall guy‡** (*scapegoat*) bouc *m* émissaire; (*easy victim*) pigeon* *m*, dindon *m* (de la farce), dupe *f*; **falling-off** réduction *f*, diminution *f*, décroissance *f* (*in* de); **falling star** étoile filante; **fall-off** = **falling-off**; (*U*) **fallout** retombées *fpl* (radioactives); (*fig*) retombées; **fallout shelter** abri *m* antiatomique.

fall about* *vi* (*fig: laugh*) se tordre (de rire).

fall apart *vi [object]* tomber en morceaux; *[scheme, plan, one's life, marriage]* se désagréger.

fall away *vi [ground]* descendre en pente; *[plaster]* s'écailler; *[supporters]* déserter; *[numbers, attendances]* diminuer; *[anxiety, fears]* se dissiper, s'évanouir.

fall back *vi* (*also Mil*) reculer, se retirer. (*fig*) **to fall back on sth** avoir recours à qch; **a sum to fall back on** une somme en réserve, un matelas*.

fall behind *vi* rester en arrière, être à la traîne; *[racehorse, runner]* se laisser distancer. **to fall behind with one's work** prendre du retard dans son travail; **she fell behind with the rent** elle était en retard pour son loyer.

fall down *vi* **(a)** *[person, book]* tomber (par terre); *[building]* s'effondrer, s'écrouler; *[tree]* tomber; *[plans]* s'effondrer, s'écrouler; *[hopes]* s'évanouir.

(b) (*fig: fail*) échouer. **to fall down on the job** se montrer incapable de faire le travail, ne pas être à la hauteur; **he fell down badly that time** il a fait un vrai fiasco *or* il a vraiment raté son coup cette fois; **that was where we fell down** c'est là que nous avons achoppé *or* que nous nous sommes fichus dedans*; **she fell down on the last essay** elle a raté la dernière dissertation.

fall in 1 *vi* **(a)** *[building]* s'effondrer, s'écrouler, s'affaisser. **she leaned over the pool and fell in** elle s'est penchée au-dessus de la mare et est tombée dedans.

(b) (*Mil*) *[troops]* former les rangs; *[one soldier]* rentrer dans les rangs. **fall in!** à vos rangs!

2 *vt sep troops* (faire) mettre en rangs.

fall in with *vt fus* **(a)** (*meet*) *person* rencontrer. **he fell in with bad company** il a fait de mauvaises rencontres *or* connaissances.

(b) (*agree to*) *proposal, suggestion* accepter, agréer. **to fall in with sb's views** entrer dans les vues de qn.

(c) this decision fell in very well with our plans cette décision a cadré avec nos projets.

fall off 1 *vi* **(a)** (*lit*) tomber.

(b) *[supporters]* déserter; *[sales, numbers, attendances]* diminuer; *[curve on graph]* décroître; *[interest]* se relâcher, tomber; *[enthusiasm]* baisser, tomber.

2 fall(ing)-off *n V* **fall 3**.

fall out 1 *vi* **(a)** (*quarrel*) se brouiller, se fâcher (*with* avec).

(b) (*Mil*) rompre les rangs. **fall out!** rompez!

(c) (*come to pass*) advenir, arriver. **everything fell out as we had hoped** tout s'est passé comme nous l'avions espéré.

2 *vt sep troops* faire rompre les rangs à.

3 fallout *n, adj V* **fall 3**.

fall over *vi* tomber (par terre).

fall through *vi [plans]* échouer. **all their plans have fallen through** tous leurs projets ont échoué *or* sont (tombés) à l'eau.

fall to *vi* (*start eating*) se mettre à l'œuvre, attaquer (un repas).

fall (up)on *vt fus* **(a)** se jeter sur, se lancer sur. (*Mil*) **to fall (up)on the enemy** fondre *or* s'abattre sur l'ennemi.

(b) (*find*) trouver, découvrir. **to fall (up)on a way of doing sth** trouver *or* découvrir un moyen de faire qch.

fallacious [fəˈleɪʃəs] *adj* fallacieux, faux (*f* fausse), trompeur.

fallaciousness [fəˈleɪʃəsnɪs] *n* caractère fallacieux, fausseté *f*.

fallacy [ˈfæləsɪ] *n* (*false belief*) erreur *f*, illusion *f*; (*false reasoning*) faux raisonnement, sophisme *m*.

fallen [ˈfɔːlən] **1** *ptp of* **fall**.

2 *adj* tombé; (*morally*) perdu; *angel, woman* déchu. **~ leaf** feuille morte; (*Med*) **~ arches** affaissement *m* de la voûte plantaire.

3 *n* (*Mil*) **the ~** ceux qui sont morts à la guerre, ceux qui sont tombés (au champ d'honneur).

fallibility [ˌfælɪˈbɪlɪtɪ] *n* faillibilité *f*.

fallible [ˈfæləbl] *adj* faillible.

fallopian [fəˈləʊpɪən] *adj*: **~ tube** trompe utérine *or* de Fallope.

fallow[1] [ˈfæləʊ] **1** *n* (*Agr*) jachère *f*. **2** *adj land* en jachère. **the land lay ~** la terre était en jachère; **his mind lay ~ for years** il a laissé son esprit en friche pendant des années.

fallow[2] [ˈfæləʊ] *adj*: **~ deer** daim *m*.

false [fɔːls] **1** *adj* **(a)** (*mistaken, wrong*) *idea, information* faux (*f* fausse). (*lit, fig*) **~ alarm** fausse alerte; **~ dawn** lueurs annonciatrices de l'aube; (*fig*) lueur d'espoir trompeuse; **to take a ~ step** faire un faux pas; **to put a ~ interpretation on sth** interpréter qch à faux; **in a ~ position** dans une position fausse; **~ ribs** fausses côtes; (*Sport, also fig*) **~ start** faux départ.

(b) (*deceitful*) perfide, faux (*f* fausse), mensonger. **to be ~ to one's wife†** tromper sa femme; (*Jur*) **~ pretences** moyens *mpl* frauduleux; (*Jur etc*) **on** *or* **under ~ pretences** par des moyens frauduleux; (*by lying*) sous des prétextes fallacieux; **~ promises** promesses mensongères, fausses promesses; **~ witness** faux témoin; († *or frm*) **to bear ~ witness** porter un faux témoignage.

(c) (*counterfeit*) *coin* faux (*f* fausse); (*artificial*) artificiel; *ceiling* faux. **~ eyelashes** faux cils *mpl*; **a box with a ~ bottom** une boîte à double fond; **~ hem** faux ourlet; **~ teeth** fausses dents, dentier *m*, râtelier *m*.

2 *adv* (*liter*) **to play sb ~** trahir qn.

3 *cpd*: **false-hearted** fourbe.

falsehood [ˈfɔːlshʊd] *n* **(a)** (*lie*) mensonge *m*. **to tell a ~** mentir, dire un mensonge. **(b)** (*U*) faux *m*. **truth and ~** le vrai et le faux. **(c)** (*U*) = **falseness**.

falsely [ˈfɔːlslɪ] *adv claim, declare* faussement; *interpret* à faux; *accuse* à tort; *act* déloyalement.

falseness [ˈfɔːlsnɪs] *n* fausseté *f*; († *or liter: of lover etc*) infidélité *f*.

falsetto [fɔːlˈsetəʊ] **1** *n* (*Mus*) fausset *m*. **2** *cpd voice, tone* de fausset, de tête.

falsies‡ [ˈfɔːlsɪz] *npl* soutien-gorge rembourré.

falsification [ˌfɔːlsɪfɪˈkeɪʃən] *n* falsification *f*.

falsify [ˈfɔːlsɪfaɪ] *vt* **(a)** (*forge*) *document* falsifier; *evidence* maquiller; (*misrepresent*) *story, facts* dénaturer. **(b)** (*disprove*) *theory* réfuter.

falsity [ˈfɔːlsɪtɪ] *n* = **falseness**.

falter [ˈfɔːltə^r] **1** *vi [voice, speaker]* hésiter, s'entrecouper; (*waver*) vaciller, chanceler; *[sb's steps]* chanceler; *[courage, memory]* faiblir. **2** *vt* (*also* **~ out**) *words, phrases* bredouiller, prononcer d'une voix hésitante *or* entrecoupée.

faltering [ˈfɔːltərɪŋ] *adj voice* hésitant, entrecoupé; *steps* chancelant.

falteringly [ˈfɔːltərɪŋlɪ] *adv speak* d'une voix hésitante *or* entrecoupée; *walk* d'un pas chancelant *or* mal assuré.

fame [feɪm] *n* renommée *f*, renom *m*. **his ~ as a writer** sa renommée d'écrivain; **he wanted ~** il était avide de gloire, il voulait se faire une renommée *or* un grand nom; **to win ~ for o.s.** bâtir sa renommée; **Margaret Mitchell of 'Gone with the Wind' ~** Margaret Mitchell connue pour son livre 'Autant en emporte le vent' *or* l'auteur célèbre de 'Autant en emporte le vent'; **Bader of 1940 ~** Bader célèbre pour ses prouesses *or* exploits en 1940; († *or liter*) **of ill ~** mal famé.

famed [feɪmd] *adj* célèbre, renommé (*for* pour).

familiar [fəˈmɪljə^r] **1** *adj* **(a)** (*usual, well-known*) *sight, scene, street* familier; *complaint, event, protest* habituel. **he's a ~ figure in the town** c'est un personnage bien connu *or* tout le monde le connaît de vue dans la ville; **it's a ~ feeling** c'est une sensation bien connue; **his face is ~** je l'ai déjà vu (quelque part), sa tête me dit quelque chose*; **among ~ faces** parmi des visages familiers *or* connus; **his voice seems ~ (to me)** il me semble connaître sa voix.

(b) (*conversant*) **to be ~ with sth** bien connaître qch, être au fait de qch; **to make o.s. ~ with** se familiariser avec; **he is ~ with our customs** il connaît bien nos coutumes.

(c) (*intimate*) familier, intime. **~ language** langue familière; **to be on ~ terms with sb** être intime avec qn, avoir des rapports d'intimité avec qn; **~ spirit** démon familier; (*pej*) **he got much too ~, he was very ~** il s'est permis des familiarités (*with* avec).

2 *n* **(a)** (**~ spirit**) démon familier.

(b) (*friend*) familier *m*.

familiarity [fəˌmɪlɪˈærɪtɪ] *n* **(a)** (*U*) *[sight, event etc]* caractère familier *or* habituel. (*Prov*) **~ breeds contempt** la familiarité engendre le mépris.

(b) (*U: with book, poem, customs etc*) familiarité *f* (*with* avec), (parfaite) connaissance *f* (*with* de).

(c) (*pej: gen pl*) **familiarities** familiarités *fpl*, privautés *fpl*.

familiarize [fəˈmɪlɪəraɪz] *vt* **(a) to ~ sb with sth** familiariser qn avec qch, habituer qn à qch; **to ~ o.s. with** se familiariser avec. **(b)** *theory* répandre, vulgariser.

familiarly [fəˈmɪljəlɪ] *adv* familièrement.

family [ˈfæmɪlɪ] **1** *n* (*all senses*) famille *f*. **has he any ~?** (*relatives*) a-t-il de la famille?; (*children*) a-t-il des enfants?; **it runs**

in the ~ cela tient de famille; **of good** ~ de bonne famille; **he's one of the** ~ il fait partie *or* il est de la famille.

2 *cpd dinner, jewels, likeness, name* de famille; *Bible, life* familial, de famille. (*Brit Admin*) **family allowance** allocations familiales; **family business** affaire *f* de famille; **family butcher** boucher *m* de quartier; **family doctor** médecin *m* de famille; **a family friend** un(e) ami(e) de la famille; **family hotel** pension *f* de famille; **he's a family man** c'est un bon père de famille, il aime la vie de famille; **family planning** planning *or* planisme familial; **family planning clinic** centre *m* de planning *or* planisme familial; (*Comm*) **family-size(d) packet** paquet familial; **family tree** arbre *m* généalogique; **she's in the family way*** elle est enceinte, elle attend un bébé *or* un enfant.

famine ['fæmɪn] *n* famine *f*, disette *f*.

famished ['fæmɪʃt] *adj* affamé. **I'm absolutely ~*** je meurs de faim, j'ai une faim de loup; ~ **looking** d'aspect famélique.

famishing ['fæmɪʃɪŋ] *adj*: **I'm ~*** je crève* de faim, j'ai une faim de loup.

famous ['feɪməs] *adj* célèbre, (bien) connu, renommé (*for* pour); (*†: *excellent*) fameux, formidable*. (*iro*) ~ **last words!*** on verra bien!, c'est ce que tu crois!; (*iro*) **so much for his ~ motorbike!** maintenant on sait ce que vaut sa fameuse moto!

famously* ['feɪməslɪ] *adv* fameusement*, rudement bien*, à merveille. **they get on** ~ ils s'entendent rudement bien* *or* comme larrons en foire.

fan[1] [fæn] **1** *n* éventail *m*; (*mechanical*) ventilateur *m*; (*Agr*) tarare *m*. **electric** ~ ventilateur électrique.

2 *cpd*: (*Aut*) **fan belt** courroie *f* de ventilateur; (*Brit*) **fan heater** radiateur soufflant; **fan light** imposte *f* (*semi-circulaire*); **fan-shaped** en éventail; **fantail (pigeon)** pigeon-paon *m*; (*Archit*) **fan vaulting** voûte(s) *f(pl)* en éventail.

3 *vt person, object* éventer. **to ~ the fire** attiser le feu; **to ~ the embers** souffler sur la braise; **to ~ o.s.** s'éventer; (*fig*) **to ~ the flames** jeter de l'huile sur le feu (*fig*); **to ~ a quarrel** attiser une querelle.

fan out **1** *vi [troops, searchers]* se déployer (en éventail).

2 *vt sep cards etc* étaler (en éventail).

fan[2] [fæn] **1** *n* (*) enthousiaste *mf*; (*Sport*) supporter *m*; *[pop star etc]* fan *mf*, admirateur *m*, -trice *f*. **he is a jazz/bridge/sports/football** *etc* ~ il se passionne pour le *or* c'est un passionné du *or* c'est un mordu* du jazz/bridge/sport/football *etc*; **all these football** ~**s** tous ces enragés *or* mordus* *or* fanas* de football; **a Vivaldi** ~ un(e) fervent(e) de Vivaldi; **I'm definitely not one of his** ~**s** je suis loin d'être un de ses admirateurs.

2 *cpd*: **fan club** (*Cine etc*) cercle *m or* club *m* de fans; (*fig*) cercle d'adorateurs *or* de fervents (admirateurs); **the Colin Smith fan club** le club des fans de Colin Smith; **his fan mail** le courrier *or* les lettres *fpl* de ses admirateurs.

fanatic [fə'nætɪk] *n* fanatique *mf*.

fanatic(al) [fə'nætɪk(əl)] *adj* fanatique.

fanaticism [fə'nætɪsɪzəm] *n* fanatisme *m*.

fancied ['fænsɪd] *adj* imaginaire.

-fancier ['fænsɪəʳ] *n ending in cpds*: **dog-fancier** amateur *m* de chiens.

fanciful ['fænsɪfʊl] *adj* (*whimsical*) *person* capricieux, fantasque; *ideas* fantasque; (*quaint*) *ideas etc* bizarre; *hat* extravagant; (*imaginative*) *design, drawing* plein d'imagination, imaginatif; (*imaginary*) *story, account* imaginaire.

fancy ['fænsɪ] **1** *n* **(a)** (*whim*) caprice *m*, fantaisie *f*. **it was just a (passing)** ~ ce n'était qu'un caprice (passager) *or* qu'une fantaisie (passagère) *or* qu'une lubie; **as the ~ takes her** comme l'idée la prend; **he only works when the ~ takes him** il ne travaille que quand cela lui plaît *or* lui chante*; **he took a ~ to go swimming** il a eu tout à coup envie *or* il lui a pris l'envie d'aller se baigner.

(b) (*taste, liking*) goût *m*, envie *f*. **to take a ~ to sb** se prendre d'affection pour qn; **to take a ~ to sth** se mettre à aimer qch; **it took** *or* **caught** *or* **tickled his** ~ d'un seul coup il en a eu envie; **the hat took** *or* **caught my** ~ le chapeau m'a fait envie *or* m'a tapé dans l'œil‡; **it caught the public's** ~ le public l'a tout de suite aimé; **he had a ~ for her** il a eu un petit béguin* *or* une toquade* pour elle; **he had a ~ for sports cars** il a eu une toquade* *or* un engouement pour les voitures de sport.

(c) (*U*) imagination *f*, fantaisie *f*. **that is in the realm of** ~ cela appartient au domaine de l'imaginaire, c'est chimérique.

(d) (*delusion*) chimère *f*, fantasme *m*; (*whimsical notion*) idée *f* fantasque. **I have a ~ that ...** j'ai idée que ... .

2 *vt* **(a)** (*imagine*) se figurer, s'imaginer; (*rather think*) croire, penser. **he fancies he can succeed** il se figure pouvoir réussir, il s'imagine qu'il peut réussir; **I rather ~ he's gone out** je crois (bien) qu'il est sorti; **he fancied he heard the car arrive** il a cru entendre arriver la voiture; ~ **that!*** tiens!, voyez-vous cela!, vous m'en direz tant!*; ~ **seeing you here!*** si je m'imaginais vous voir ici!*, je ne m'imaginais pas vous voir ici!; ~ **him winning!*** qui aurait cru qu'il allait gagner!

(b) (*want*) avoir envie de; (*like*) aimer. **do you ~ going for a walk?** as-tu envie *or* ça te dit* d'aller faire une promenade?; **I don't ~ the idea** cette idée ne me dit rien*; **I don't ~ his books** je n'aime pas tellement ce qu'il écrit, ses livres ne m'emballent pas*; (*Brit*) **he fancies himself*** il ne se prend pas pour rien* (*iro*); **he fancies himself as an actor*** il ne se prend pas pour une moitié d'acteur* (*iro*); (*Brit*) **he fancies her*** il la trouve pas mal du tout*, il la trouve attirante.

3 *adj* **(a)** *hat, buttons, pattern* (de) fantaisie *inv*. ~ **cakes** pâtisseries *fpl*; ~ **dog** chien *m* de luxe.

(b) (*pej: overrated*) *ideal, cure* fantaisiste. **a ~ price** un prix exorbitant; **it was all very** ~ c'était très recherché, ça faisait très chic; **with his ~ house and his ~ car how can he know how the ordinary man lives?** avec sa belle maison et sa voiture grand luxe, comment peut-il se mettre à la place de l'homme de la rue?

(c) (*US: extra good*) *goods, foodstuffs* de qualité supérieure, de luxe.

4 *cpd*: **fancy dress** travesti *m*, déguisement *m*; **in fancy dress** déguisé, travesti; **fancy-dress ball** bal masqué *or* costumé; **he is fancy-free** c'est un cœur à prendre (*V* **foot**); (*Comm*) **fancy goods** nouveautés *fpl*, articles *mpl* de fantaisie; († *or pej*) **fancy woman** maîtresse *f*, bonne amie (*pej*); **fancy work** ouvrages *mpl* d'agrément.

fanfare ['fænfɛəʳ] *n* fanfare *f* (*morceau de musique*).

fang [fæŋ] *n [dog, vampire]* croc *m*, canine *f*; *[snake]* crochet *m*.

fanny‡ ['fænɪ] *n* cul‡ *m*, fesses* *fpl*.

fantasia [fæn'teɪzjə] *n* (*Literat, Mus*) fantaisie *f*.

fantasize ['fæntəsaɪz] *vi* (*Psych etc*) faire des fantasmes, fantasmer*.

fantastic [fæn'tæstɪk] *adj story, adventure* fantastique, bizarre; *idea* impossible, invraisemblable; *success* inouï, fabuleux, fantastique; (*fig: excellent*) *dress, plan, news, holiday* sensationnel, fantastique.

fantastically [fæn'tæstɪkəlɪ] *adv* fantastiquement, extraordinairement, terriblement. **he's ~ rich** il est extraordinairement *or* fabuleusement riche.

fantasy ['fæntəzɪ] *n* **(a)** (*U*) imagination *f*, fantaisie *f*. **(b)** idée *f* fantasque; (*Psych etc*) fantasme *m*. **(c)** (*Literat, Mus*) fantaisie *f*.

far [fɑːʳ] *comp* **farther** *or* **further**, *superl* **farthest** *or* **furthest** **1** *adv* **(a)** (*lit*) loin. **how ~ is it to ...?** combien y a-t-il jusqu'à ...?; **is it ~?** est-ce loin?; **is it ~ to London?** c'est loin pour aller à Londres?; **we live not ~ from here** nous habitons pas loin d'ici; **we live quite** ~ nous habitons assez loin; **have you come from ~?** vous venez de loin?; **how ~ are you going?** jusqu'où allez-vous?; *V also* **1c**.

(b) (*fig*) **how ~ have you got with your plans?** où en êtes-vous de vos projets?; **he is very gifted and will go** ~ il est très doué et il ira loin *or* il fera son chemin; **to make one's money go** ~ faire durer son argent; **£10 doesn't go ~ these days** 10 livres ne vont pas loin de nos jours; **that will go ~ towards placating him** cela contribuera beaucoup à le calmer; **this scheme does not go ~ enough** ce projet ne va pas assez loin; **I would even go so ~ as to say that ...** j'irais même jusqu'à dire que ..., je dirais même que ...; **that's going too** ~ cela passe *or* dépasse les bornes *or* la mesure; **now you're going a bit too** ~ alors là vous exagérez un peu; **he's gone too ~ this time!** il a vraiment exagéré cette fois!; **he has gone too ~ to back out now** il est trop engagé pour reculer maintenant; **he was ~ gone*** (*ill*) il était bien bas; (*drunk*) il était bien parti*; **he carried the joke too** ~ il a poussé trop loin la plaisanterie; **just so ~, so ~ and no further** jusque-là mais pas plus loin; **so ~ so good** jusqu'ici ça va; **so ~ this year** jusqu'ici cette année; **we have 10 volunteers so** ~ nous avons 10 volontaires jusqu'ici *or* jusqu'à présent; ~ **be it from me to try to dissuade you** loin de moi l'idée de vous dissuader.

(c) (*phrases*) **as ~ as** jusqu'à, autant que; **we went as ~ as the town** nous sommes allés jusqu'à la ville; **we didn't go as** *or* **so ~ as the others** nous ne sommes pas allés aussi loin que les autres; **as** *or* **so ~ as I know** (pour) autant que je (le) sache; **as ~ as I can** dans la mesure du possible; **as** *or* **so ~ as I can foresee** autant que je puisse (le) prévoir; **as ~ as the eye can see** à perte de vue; **as** *or* **so ~ as that goes** pour ce qui est de cela; **as** *or* **so ~ as I'm concerned** en ce qui me concerne, pour ma part; **as ~ back as I can remember** d'aussi loin que je m'en souvienne; **as ~ back as 1945** dès 1945, déjà en 1945; ~ **and away** *V* **1d**; ~ **and wide**, ~ **and near** de tous côtés, partout; **they came from ~ and wide** *or* ~ **and near** ils sont venus de partout; ~ **above** loin au-dessus; ~ **above the hill** loin au-dessus de la colline; **he is ~ above the rest of the class** il est de loin supérieur au *or* il domine nettement le reste de la classe; ~ **away** au loin, au lointain; **he could see them ~ away in the distance** il les voyait là-bas au loin *or* dans le lointain; ~ **beyond** bien au-delà; ~ **beyond the forest** très loin au-delà de la forêt; **it's ~ beyond what I can afford** c'est bien au-dessus de mes moyens; ~ **from** loin de; **your work is ~ from satisfactory** votre travail est loin d'être satisfaisant, il s'en faut de beaucoup que votre travail soit satisfaisant (*frm*); ~ **from it!** loin de là!, tant s'en faut!; ~ **from liking him I find him rather objectionable** bien loin de l'aimer je le trouve (au contraire) tout à fait désagréable; **I am ~ from believing him** je suis très loin de le croire; ~ **into** très avant dans; ~ **into the night** tard dans la nuit, très avant dans la nuit; **I won't look so ~ into the future** je ne regarderai pas si avant dans l'avenir; **they went ~ into the jungle** ils ont pénétré très avant dans la jungle; ~ **off** au loin, dans le lointain (*V also* **3**); **he wasn't ~ off when I caught sight of him** il n'était pas loin quand je l'ai aperçu; **his birthday is not ~ off** c'est bientôt son anniversaire, son anniversaire approche; **she's not ~ off fifty** elle n'est pas loin de la cinquantaine; ~ **out at sea** au (grand) large; ~ **out on the branch** tout au bout de la branche; **our calculations are ~ out** nous avons fait une énorme erreur de calcul, nous sommes très loin du compte.

(d) (*with comp and superl adv or adj: also* ~ **and away**) beaucoup, bien. **this is ~ better** ceci est beaucoup *or* bien mieux; **this is ~ (and away) the best, this is by ~ the best** *or* **the best by** ~ ceci est de très loin ce qu'il y a de mieux; **it is ~ more serious** c'est (bien) autrement sérieux; **she is ~ prettier than her sister** elle est bien plus jolie que sa sœur; **by** ~ de loin, beaucoup.

2 *adj* **(a)** (*liter*) *country, land* lointain, éloigné. **it's a ~ cry from what he promised** on est loin de ce qu'il a promis.

(b) autre, plus éloigné. **on the ~ side of** de l'autre côté de; **at the ~ end of** à l'autre bout de, à l'extrémité de.

3 *cpd*: **faraway** *place* lointain, éloigné; *look* distrait, absent, perdu dans le vague; *voice* lointain; *memory* flou, vague; **far-distant** lointain; **the Far East** l'Extrême-Orient *m*; **far-fetched** forcé, tiré par les cheveux; **far-flung** vaste, très étendu; **the Far North** le Grand Nord; **far-off** lointain, éloigné; *(fig)* **far-reaching** d'une portée considérable, d'une grande portée; **far-seeing, far-sighted** *person* prévoyant, clairvoyant, qui voit loin; *decision, measure* fait (*or* pris *etc*) avec clairvoyance; *(lit)* **far-sighted** hypermétrope; *(in old age)* presbyte; **far-sightedness** *(fig)* prévoyance *f*, clairvoyance *f*; *(lit)* hypermétropie *f*; *(in old age)* presbytie *f*; *(US)* **the Far West** le far west, l'Ouest américain.

farad ['færəd] *n* farad *m*.

farce [fɑːs] *n* *(Theat, fig)* farce *f*. **the whole thing's a~!, what a ~ it all is!** tout ça c'est une vaste rigolade* *or* ce n'est pas sérieux *or* c'est grotesque.

farcical ['fɑːsɪkəl] *adj* risible, grotesque, ridicule. **it's ~** cela tient de la farce, c'est vraiment grotesque.

fare [fɛəʳ] **1** *n* **(a)** *(charge)* *(on train, bus etc)* prix *m* du ticket *or* du billet; *(on boat, plane)* prix du billet. *(in bus)* **~s, please!** les places, s'il vous plaît!; **~s are going up** les (tarifs *mpl* des) transports *mpl* vont augmenter; **let me pay your ~** laissez-moi payer pour vous; **I haven't got the ~** je n'ai pas assez d'argent pour le billet; *V* **half, return** *etc*.

(b) *(passenger)* voyageur *m*, -euse *f*; *[taxi]* client(e) *m(f)*.

(c) *(food)* chère *f*. **hospital ~** régime *m* d'hôpital; *V* **bill[1]**.

2 *cpd*: *[bus]* **fare stage** section *f*; **farewell** *V* **farewell**.

3 *vi* aller, se porter. **he ~d well at his first attempt** il a réussi à sa première tentative; **we all ~d alike** nous avons tous partagé le même sort, nous étions tous au même régime*; **how did you ~?** comment cela s'est-il passé (pour vous)?, comment ça a marché?*; († *or hum*) **how ~s it with you?** les choses vont-elles comme vous voulez?

farewell [fɛə'wel] **1** *n, excl* adieu *m*. **to make one's ~s** faire ses adieux; **to take one's ~ of** faire ses adieux à; **to bid ~ to** dire adieu à; *(fig)* **you can say ~ to your wallet!** tu peux dire au revoir à ton portefeuille!*, ton portefeuille tu peux en faire ton deuil!*

2 *cpd dinner etc* d'adieu.

farinaceous [ˌfærɪ'neɪʃəs] *adj* farinacé, farineux.

farm [fɑːm] **1** *n* *(Agr)* ferme *f*; *(fish ~ etc)* centre *m* d'élevage. **to work on a ~** travailler dans une ferme; *V* **sheep** *etc*.

2 *cpd*: **farmhand** valet *m or* fille *f* de ferme; **farmhouse** (maison *f* de) ferme *f*; **farm labourer = farm worker; farmland** terres cultivées *or* arables; **farm produce** produits *mpl* agricoles *or* de ferme; **farmstead** ferme *f*; **farm worker** ouvrier *m*, -ière *f* agricole; **farmyard** cour *f* de ferme.

3 *vt* cultiver.

4 *vi* être fermier, être cultivateur.

farm out *vt sep shop* mettre en gérance. **to farm out work** céder un travail à un sous-traitant *or* en sous-traitance; **the firm farmed out the plumbing to a local tradesman** l'entreprise a confié la plomberie à un sous-traitant local; **to farm out children on sb*** donner des enfants à garder à qn, parquer* des enfants chez qn.

farmer ['fɑːməʳ] *n* fermier *m*, cultivateur *m*, agriculteur *m*. **~'s wife** fermière *f*, femme *f* du cultivateur.

farming ['fɑːmɪŋ] **1** *n* agriculture *f*, exploitation *f* agricole. **fish/mink** *etc* **~** élevage *m* de poissons/du vison *etc*; *V* **dairy, factory, mixed** *etc*.

2 *cpd*: *(Agr)* **farming communities** collectivités rurales; **farming methods** méthodes *fpl* d'agriculture.

Faroes ['fɛərəuz] *npl* *(also* **Faroe Islands***)* îles *fpl* Féroé *or* Faeroe.

farrago [fə'rɑːgəu] *n* méli-mélo* *m*, mélange *m*.

farrier ['færɪəʳ] *n* maréchal-ferrant *m*.

farrow ['færəu] **1** *vti* mettre bas. **2** *n* portée *f* (de cochons).

fart∵ [fɑːt] **1** *n* pet∵ *m*. **2** *vi* péter∵.

farther ['fɑːðəʳ] *comp of* **far 1** *adv* plus loin. **how much ~ is it?** c'est encore à combien?; **it is ~ than I thought** c'est plus loin que je ne pensais; **have you got much ~ to go?** est-ce que vous avez encore loin à aller?; **we will go no ~** *(lit)* nous n'irons pas plus loin; *(fig)* nous en resterons là; **I got no ~ with him** je ne suis arrivé à rien de plus avec lui; **nothing could be ~ from the truth** rien n'est plus éloigné de la vérité; **nothing is ~ from my thoughts** rien n'est plus éloigné de ma pensée; **to get ~ and ~ away** s'éloigner de plus en plus; **~ back** plus (loin) en arrière; **push it ~ back** repousse-le plus loin; **move ~ back** reculez-vous; **~ back than 1940** avant 1940; **~ off** plus éloigné, plus loin; **he went ~ off than I thought** il est allé plus loin que je ne pensais; **~ on, ~ forward** plus en avant, plus loin; *(fig)* **he is ~ on *or* ~ forward than his brother** il est plus avancé que son frère, il est en avance sur son frère; *(fig)* **we're no ~ forward after all that** on n'est pas plus avancé, tout ça n'a rien donné.

2 *adj* plus éloigné, plus lointain. **at the ~ end of the room** à l'autre bout de la salle, au fond de la salle; **at the ~ end of the branch** à l'autre bout *or* à l'extrémité de la branche.

farthest ['fɑːðɪst] *superl of* **far 1** *adj* le plus lointain, le plus éloigné. **in the ~ depths of the forest** au fin fond de la forêt; **the ~ way** la route la plus longue; **it's 5 km at the ~** il y a 5 km au plus *or* au maximum. **2** *adv* le plus loin.

farthing ['fɑːðɪŋ] *n quart m d'un ancien penny*. **I haven't a ~** je n'ai pas le sou; *V* **brass** *etc*.

fascia ['feɪʃə] *n* *(Brit Aut)* tableau *m* de bord.

fascicle ['fæsɪkl] *n*, **fascicule** ['fæsɪkjuːl] *n* *(Bot)* rameau fasciculé; *[book]* fascicule *m*.

fascinate ['fæsɪneɪt] *vt [speaker, tale]* fasciner, captiver; *[sight]* fasciner; *[snake etc]* fasciner.

fascinating ['fæsɪneɪtɪŋ] *adj person* fascinant, séduisant; *speaker, tale* fascinant, captivant; *sight* fascinant.

fascination [ˌfæsɪ'neɪʃən] *n* fascination *f*, attrait *m* (irrésistible), charme *m*. **his ~ with the cinema** la fascination qu'exerce sur lui le cinéma.

fascism ['fæʃɪzəm] *n* fascisme *m*.

fascist ['fæʃɪst] *adj, n* fasciste *(mf)*.

fashion ['fæʃən] **1** *n* **(a)** *(U: manner)* façon *f*, manière *f*. **in a queer ~** d'une manière *or* façon bizarre; **after a ~** tant bien que mal, si l'on peut dire; **after the ~ of** à la manière de; **in the French ~** à la française; **in his own ~** à sa manière *or* façon; **it's not my ~ to lie** ce n'est pas mon genre de mentir.

(b) *(latest style)* mode *f*, vogue *f*. **in ~** à la mode, en vogue; **it's the latest ~** c'est la dernière mode *or* le dernier cri; **to dress in the latest ~** s'habiller à la dernière mode; **the Paris ~s** les collections (de mode) parisiennes; **out of ~** démodé, passé de mode; **to set the ~** donner le ton, lancer la mode; **to set the ~ for** lancer la mode de; **to bring sth into ~** mettre qch à la mode; **to come into ~** devenir à la mode; **to go out of ~** se démoder; **it is the ~ to say** il est bien porté *or* de bon ton de dire; **a man of ~** un homme élégant.

(c) *(habit)* coutume *f*, habitude *f*. **as was his ~** selon sa coutume *or* son habitude.

2 *vt carving* façonner; *model* fabriquer; *dress* confectionner.

3 *cpd*: **fashion designer** (grand) couturier *m*; **fashion editor** rédacteur *m*, -trice *f* de mode; **fashion house** maison *f* de couture; **fashion magazine** journal *m* de mode; **fashion model** mannequin *m* *(personne)*; **fashion parade = fashion show; fashion plate** gravure *f* de mode; **she's a real fashion plate*** à la voir on dirait une gravure de mode, on dirait qu'elle sort des pages d'un magazine; **fashion show** présentation *f* de modèles *or* de collections, défilé *m* de mannequins; **to go to the Paris fashion shows** faire les collections parisiennes.

fashionable ['fæʃnəbl] *adj dress* à la mode; *district, shop, hotel* chic *inv*; *dressmaker, subject* à la mode, en vogue. **the ~ world** les gens à la mode; **it is ~ to say** il est bien porté *or* de bon ton de dire.

fashionably ['fæʃnəblɪ] *adv* à la mode, élégamment.

fast[1] [fɑːst] **1** *adj* **(a)** *(speedy)* rapide. *(Aut)* **the ~ lane** ≃ la voie la plus à gauche; **~ train** rapide *m*; *(Phys)* **~ breeder reactor** breeder *m*, pile couveuse *or* surrégénératrice; **he's a ~ thinker** il a l'esprit très rapide, il sait réfléchir vite; **he's a ~ worker** *(lit)* il va vite en besogne; (*: *with the girls*) c'est un tombeur* *or* un don Juan; **to pull a ~ one on sb*** rouler qn*, avoir qn*; *(Tennis)* **a grass court is ~er** le jeu est plus rapide sur gazon; *(Phot)* **~ film** pellicule *f* rapide.

(b) *[clock etc]* **to be ~** avancer; **my watch is 5 minutes ~** ma montre avance de 5 minutes.

(c) *(dissipated)* de mœurs légères, dissolu. **~ life *or* living** vie dissolue *or* de dissipation; **~ woman** femme légère *or* de mœurs légères; **one of the ~ set** un viveur.

(d) *(firm) rope, knot* solide; *grip* tenace; *colour* bon teint *inv*, grand teint *inv*; *friend* sûr. **to make a boat ~** amarrer un bateau; **is the dye ~?** est-ce que ça déteindra?, est-ce que la teinture s'en ira?

2 *adv* **(a)** *(quickly)* vite, rapidement. **he ran off as ~ as his legs could carry him** il s'est sauvé à toutes jambes; **don't speak so ~** ne parlez pas si vite; **how ~ can you type?** à quelle vitesse pouvez-vous taper (à la machine)?; *(interrupting)* **not so ~!** doucement!, minute!*; **as ~ as I advanced he drew back** à mesure que j'avançais il reculait.

(b) *(firmly, securely)* ferme, solidement. **to be ~ asleep** être profondément endormi, dormir à poings fermés; **a door shut ~** une porte bien close; **~ by† the church** qui jouxte l'église; *V* **hard, hold, play** *etc*.

fast[2] [fɑːst] **1** *vi* jeûner, rester à jeun; *(Rel)* jeûner, faire maigre. **2** *n* jeûne *m*. **to break one's ~** rompre le jeûne; *(Rel)* **~ day** jour *m* maigre *or* de jeûne.

fasten ['fɑːsn] **1** *vt* **(a)** *(lit)* attacher (*to* à); *(with rope, string etc)* lier (*to* à); *(with nail)* clouer (*to* à); *(with paste)* coller (*to* à); *box, door, window* fermer (solidement); *dress* fermer, attacher. **to ~ two things together** attacher deux choses ensemble *or* l'une à l'autre; **to ~ one's seat belt** attacher *or* mettre sa ceinture de sécurité; *(fig)* **to ~ one's eyes on sth** fixer son regard *or* les yeux sur qch.

(b) *(fig) responsibility* attribuer (*on sb* à qn); *a crime* imputer (*on sb* à qn). **to ~ the blame on sb** rejeter la faute sur (le dos de) qn; **you can't ~ it on me!** tu ne peux pas me mettre ça sur le dos!

2 *vi [box, door, lock, window]* se fermer; *[dress]* s'attacher.

fasten down *vt sep blind, flap* fixer en place; *envelope* coller.

fasten on *vt sep* fixer (en place).

fasten on to *vt fus* **(a) = fasten (up)on.**

(b) se cramponner à, s'accrocher à. **he fastened on to my arm** il s'est cramponné *or* accroché à mon bras.

fasten up *vt sep dress, coat* fermer, attacher.

fasten (up)on *vt fus* saisir. **to fasten (up)on an excuse** saisir un prétexte; **to fasten (up)on the idea of doing** se mettre en tête l'idée de faire.

fastener ['fɑːsnəʳ] *n*, **fastening** ['fɑːsnɪŋ] *n* attache *f*; *[box, door, window]* fermeture *f*; *[bag, necklace, book]* fermoir *m*; *[garment]* fermeture, *(button)* bouton *m*, *(hook)* agrafe *f*, *(press stud)* pression *f*, *(zip)* fermeture *f* éclair *inv*. **what kind of ~ has this dress got?** comment se ferme *or* s'attache cette robe?

fastidious [fæs'tɪdɪəs] *adj person* difficile (à contenter), tatillon *(pej)*; *(about cleanliness etc)* exigeant (*about* pour, en ce qui concerne), méticuleux; *taste* délicat; *mind* méticuleux, minutieux.

fastigiate [fæ'stɪdʒɪɪt] *adj* fastigié.

fastness ['fɑːstnɪs] *n* **(a)** *(stronghold)* place forte. **mountain ~** repaire *m* de montagne. **(b)** *(U: speed)* rapidité *f*, vitesse *f*. **(c)** *[colours]* solidité *f*.

fat [fæt] **1** *n* *(Anat)* graisse *f*; *(on meat)* gras *m*; *(for cooking)* graisse, matière grasse. **to fry in deep ~** (faire) frire *or* cuire à la grande friture; **beef/mutton ~** graisse de bœuf/de mouton; **pork ~** saindoux *m*; **he's got rolls of ~ round his waist** il a des bourrelets de graisse autour de la taille; (*fig*) **the ~'s in the fire** le feu est aux poudres, ça va barder‡ *or* chauffer*; (*fig*) **to live off the ~ of the land** vivre grassement.

2 *adj* **(a)** *person* gras (*f* grasse), corpulent; *limb* gros (*f* grosse), gras; *face* joufflu; *cheeks* gros; *meat, bacon* gras. **to get ~** grossir, engraisser, prendre de l'embonpoint; **she has got a lot ~ter** elle a beaucoup grossi; (*fig*) **he grew ~ on the profits** il s'est engraissé avec les bénéfices.

(b) (*thick, big*) *volume, cheque, salary* gros (*f* grosse). **he paid a ~ price for it*** il l'a payé un gros prix.

(c) *land* riche, fertile, gras (*f* grasse). **he's got a nice ~ job in an office*** il a un bon fromage dans un bureau.

(d) (*: *phrases*) **a ~ lot you did to help!** tu as vraiment été d'un précieux secours! (*iro*), comme aide c'était réussi!*; **a ~ lot of good that did!*** ça a bien avancé les choses! (*iro*); **and a ~ lot of good it did you!, that did you a ~ lot of good anyway!*** ça t'a *or* te voilà bien avancé! (*iro*); **a ~ lot that's worth!*** c'est fou ce que ça a comme valeur! (*iro*), ça ne vaut pas tripette!*; **a ~ lot he knows about it!*** comme s'il en savait quelque chose!; **a ~ lot he cares!*** comme si ça lui faisait quelque chose!; **a ~ chance he's got of getting rich!*** tu parles comme il a une chance de s'enrichir!*; **you've got a ~ chance of seeing her!*** comme si tu avais une chance *or* la moindre chance de la voir!

3 *vt* = **fatten 1. to kill the ~ted calf** tuer le veau gras.

4 *cpd*: **fathead*** idiot(e) *m(f)*, imbécile *mf*, cruche* *f*; **fatheaded*** idiot, imbécile; (*Agr*) **fatstock** animaux *mpl* de boucherie.

fatal [ˈfeɪtl] *adj* **(a)** *injury, disease, shot, accident* mortel; *blow* mortel, fatal; *consequences, result* fatal; (*fig*) *mistake* fatal; *influence* néfaste, pernicieux; *consequences, result* désastreux, catastrophique. **his illness was ~ to their plans** sa maladie a porté un coup fatal *or* le coup de grâce à leurs projets; **it was absolutely ~ to mention that** c'était une grave erreur *or* c'était la mort que de parler de cela.

(b) = fateful.

fatalism [ˈfeɪtəlɪzəm] *n* fatalisme *m*.

fatalist [ˈfeɪtəlɪst] *n* fataliste *mf*.

fatalistic [ˌfeɪtəˈlɪstɪk] *adj* fataliste.

fatality [fəˈtælɪtɪ] *n* (*at sea, on road*) accident mortel; (*in natural disaster*) mort *m*. **bathing fatalities** noyades *fpl*; **road fatalities** accidents mortels de la route; **luckily there were no fatalities** heureusement il n'y a pas eu de morts.

fatally [ˈfeɪtəlɪ] *adv wounded* mortellement. **~ ill** condamné, perdu.

fate [feɪt] *n* **(a)** (*force*) destin *m*, sort *m*. (*Myth*) **the F~s** les Parques *fpl*; **what ~ has in store for us** ce que le destin *or* le sort nous réserve.

(b) (*one's lot*) sort *m*. **to leave sb to his ~** abandonner qn à son sort; **to meet one's ~** trouver la mort; **that sealed his ~** ceci a décidé de son sort.

fated [ˈfeɪtɪd] *adj friendship, person* voué au malheur. **to be ~ to do** être destiné *or* condamné à faire.

fateful [ˈfeɪtfʊl] *adj words* fatidique; *day, event, moment* fatal, décisif.

father [ˈfɑːðəʳ] 1 *n* **(a)** père *m*. (*Rel*) **Our F~** Notre Père; **from ~ to son** de père en fils; (*Prov*) **like ~ like son** tel père tel fils (*Prov*); **to act like a ~** agir en père *or* comme un père; **he was like a ~ to me** il était comme un père pour moi; (*ancestors*) **~s** ancêtres *mpl*, pères; **there was the ~ and mother of a row!*** il y a eu une dispute à tout casser!* *or* une dispute maison!‡; *V also* **3.**

(b) (*founder, leader*) père *m*, créateur *m*. **the F~s of the Church** les Pères de l'Église; *V* **city.**

(c) (*Rel*) père *m*. **F~ X** le (révérend) père X, l'abbé X; **yes, F~** oui, mon père; **the Capuchin F~s** les pères capucins; *V* **holy.**

2 *vt* **(a)** *child* engendrer; *idea, plan* concevoir, inventer.

(b) (*saddle with responsibility*) **to ~ sth on sb** attribuer la responsabilité de qch à qn; **to ~ the blame on sb** imputer la faute à qn, faire porter le blâme à qn.

3 *cpd*: (*Brit*) **Father Christmas** le père Noël; **Father's Day** la Fête des Pères; (*Rel*) **father confessor** directeur *m* de conscience, père spirituel; **father-figure** personne *f* qui tient *or* joue le rôle du père; **he is the father-figure** il joue le rôle du père; **father-in-law** beau-père *m*; **fatherland** patrie *f*, mère *f* patrie; **(Old) Father Time** le Temps.

fatherhood [ˈfɑːðəhʊd] *n* paternité *f*.

fatherless [ˈfɑːðəlɪs] *adj* orphelin de père, sans père.

fatherly [ˈfɑːðəlɪ] *adj* paternel.

fathom [ˈfæðəm] 1 *n* (*Naut*) brasse *f* (= *1,83m*). **a channel with 5 ~s of water** un chenal de 9m de fond; **to lie 25 ~s deep** *or* **down** reposer par 45m de fond.

2 *vt* (*Naut*) sonder; (*fig: also* **~ out**) *mystery, person* sonder, pénétrer. **I just can't ~ it (out)** je n'y comprends absolument rien.

fathomless [ˈfæðəmlɪs] *adj* (*lit*) insondable; (*fig*) insondable, impénétrable.

fatigue [fəˈtiːg] 1 *n* **(a)** fatigue *f*, épuisement *m*. **metal ~** fatigue du métal.

(b) (*Mil*) corvée *f*. **to be on ~** être de corvée.

2 *vt* fatiguer, lasser; (*Tech*) *metals etc* fatiguer.

3 *cpd*: (*Mil*) **fatigue dress** tenue *f* de corvée, treillis *m*; (*Mil*) **fatigue duty** corvée *f*; (*Tech*) **fatigue limit** limite *f* de fatigue; (*Mil*) **fatigue party** corvée *f*.

fatiguing [fəˈtiːgɪŋ] *adj* fatigant, épuisant.

fatness [ˈfætnɪs] *n* [*person*] embonpoint *m*, corpulence *f*.

fatten [ˈfætn] 1 *vt* (*also* **~ up**) *cattle, chickens etc* engraisser; *geese* gaver. 2 *vi* (*also* **~ out**) engraisser, grossir.

fattening [ˈfætnɪŋ] 1 *adj food* qui fait grossir. 2 *n* (*also* **~-up**) [*cattle, chickens etc*] engraissement *m*; [*geese*] gavage *m*.

fatty [ˈfætɪ] 1 *adj* **(a)** (*greasy*) *chips etc* gras (*f* grasse), graisseux. **~ food** nourriture grasse, aliments gras; (*Chem*) **~ acid** acide gras.

(b) *tissue* adipeux. (*Med*) **~ degeneration** dégénérescence graisseuse.

2 *n* (*) gros *m* (bonhomme), grosse *f* (bonne femme). **hey ~!** eh toi le gros! (*or* la grosse!).

fatuity [fəˈtjuːɪtɪ] *n* imbécillité *f*, stupidité *f*, sottise *f*.

fatuous [ˈfætjʊəs] *adj person, remark* imbécile, sot (*f* sotte), stupide; *smile* stupide, niais.

fatuousness [ˈfætjʊəsnɪs] *n* = **fatuity.**

faucet [ˈfɔːsɪt] *n* (*US*) robinet *m*.

faugh [fɔː] *excl* pouah!

fault [fɔːlt] 1 *n* **(a)** [*person, scheme*] défaut *m*; (*Tech*) défaut, anomalie *f*; (*mistake*) erreur *f*; (*Tennis*) faute *f*; (*Geol*) faille *f*. **in spite of all her ~s** malgré tous ses défauts; **her big ~ is ...** son gros défaut est ...; **there is a mechanical ~ in this hair-dryer** ce séchoir a un défaut mécanique; **a ~ has been found in the engine** une anomalie a été constatée dans le moteur; **there is a ~ in the gas supply** il y a un défaut dans l'arrivée du gaz; **to find ~ with sth** trouver à redire à qch; **to find ~ with sb** critiquer qn; **I have no ~ to find with him** je n'ai rien à lui reprocher; **he is always finding ~** il trouve toujours à redire; **he's always finding ~ with my work** il trouve toujours à redire dans mon travail, il critique toujours mon travail; **she is generous to a ~** elle est généreuse à l'excès; **to be at ~** être fautif, être coupable; **you were at ~ in not telling me** vous avez eu tort de ne pas me le dire; **he's at ~ in this matter** il est fautif *or* c'est lui le fautif en cette affaire; **my memory was at ~** ma mémoire m'a trompé *or* m'a fait défaut.

(b) (*U: blame, responsibility*) faute *f*. **whose ~ is it?** qui est fautif?; (*iro*) **whose ~ is it if we're late?** et à qui la faute si nous sommes en retard?; **it's not my ~** ce n'est pas (de) ma faute; **it's all your ~** c'est entièrement (de) ta faute; **it's your own ~** vous n'avez à vous en prendre qu'à vous-même.

2 *vt*: **to ~ sth/sb** trouver des défauts à qch/chez qn; **you can't ~ him** on ne peut pas le prendre en défaut; **I can't ~ his reasoning** je ne trouve aucune faille dans son raisonnement.

3 *cpd*: **faultfinder** mécontent(e) *m(f)*, grincheux *m*, -euse *f*; **faultfinding** (*adj*) chicanier, grincheux; (*n*) critiques *fpl*; **she's always faultfinding** elle est toujours à critiquer; (*Geol*) **fault plane** plan *m* de faille.

faultless [ˈfɔːltlɪs] *adj person, behaviour* irréprochable; *work, manners, dress* impeccable, irréprochable. **he spoke ~ English** il parlait un anglais impeccable.

faulty [ˈfɔːltɪ] *adj work* défectueux, mal fait; *machine* défectueux; *style* incorrect, mauvais; *reasoning* défectueux, erroné.

faun [fɔːn] *n* faune *m*.

fauna [ˈfɔːnə] *n* faune *f*.

favour, (US) favor [ˈfeɪvəʳ] 1 *n* **(a)** (*act of kindness*) service *m*, faveur *f*, grâce *f*. **to do sb a ~, to do a ~ for sb** rendre (un) service à qn, obliger qn; **to ask a ~ of sb** demander un service à qn, solliciter une faveur *or* une grâce de qn (*frm*); **I ask you as a ~ to wait a moment** je vous demande d'avoir la gentillesse d'attendre un instant; **he did it as a ~ to his brother** il l'a fait pour rendre service à son frère; (*frm*) **do me the ~ of closing the door** soyez assez gentil pour fermer la porte; **do me a ~!*** je t'en prie!; **do me a ~ and ...** sois gentil et ...; **a woman's ~s** les faveurs d'une femme; (*Comm*) **your ~ of the 7th inst** votre honorée du 7 courant.

(b) (*U: approval, regard*) faveur *f*, approbation *f*. **to be in ~** [*person*] être bien en cour, avoir la cote; [*style, fashion*] être à la mode *or* en vogue; **to be out of ~** [*person*] être mal en cour, ne pas avoir la cote; [*style, fashion*] être démodé *or* passé de mode; **to be in ~ with sb** être bien vu de qn, jouir des bonnes grâces de qn; **to win sb's ~, to find ~ with sb** [*person*] s'attirer les bonnes grâces de qn; [*suggestion*] gagner l'approbation de qn; **to get back into sb's ~** rentrer dans les bonnes grâces de qn; **to look with ~ on sth** approuver qch; **to look with ~ on sb** bien considérer qn.

(c) (*U: support, advantage*) faveur *f*, avantage *m*. **the court decided in her ~** le tribunal lui a donné gain de cause; **will in ~ of sb** testament en faveur de qn; **cheque in ~ of sb** chèque payable à qn; (*Banking*) **'balance in your ~'** 'à votre crédit'; **it's in our ~ to act now** c'est (à) notre avantage d'agir maintenant; **the exchange rate is in our ~** le taux de change joue en notre faveur *or* pour nous; **the traffic lights are in our ~** les feux sont pour nous; **that's a point in his ~** c'est quelque chose à mettre à son actif, c'est un bon point pour lui; **to be in ~ of capital punishment** être partisan de la peine de mort; **I'm not in ~ of letting him decide** je ne suis pas d'avis de lui laisser prendre la décision.

(d) (*U: partiality*) faveur *f*, indulgence *f*. **to show ~ to sb** montrer un *or* des préjugé(s) en faveur de qn; *V* **curry², fear.**

(e) (*ribbon, token*) faveur *f*.

2 *vt* (*approve*) *political party, scheme, suggestion* être partisan de; *undertaking* favoriser, appuyer; (*prefer*) *person* préférer; *candidate, pupil* montrer une préférence pour; *team, horse* être pour; († *or dial: resemble*) ressembler à. **I don't ~ the idea** je ne suis pas partisan de cette idée; **he ~ed us with a visit** il a eu l'amabilité *or* la bonté de nous rendre visite; **the weather ~ed the journey** le temps a favorisé *or* facilité le voyage.

favourable, (US) favorable [ˈfeɪvərəbl] *adj reception, impression, report* favorable (*to* à); *weather, wind* propice (*for, to* à). **is he ~ to the proposal?** est-ce qu'il approuve la proposition?

favourably, (US) favorably [ˈfeɪvərəblɪ] *adv receive, impress* favorablement; *consider* d'un œil favorable. ~ **disposed** bien disposé (*towards sb* envers qn, à l'égard de qn, *towards sth* en ce qui concerne qch).

favoured, (*US*) **favored** ['feɪvəd] *adj* favorisé. **the ~ few** les élus; **ill-~** disgracieux.

favourite, (*US*) **favorite** ['feɪvərɪt] **1** *n* (*gen*) favori(te) *m(f)*, préféré(e) *m(f)*; (*at court, Racing*) favori. **he's his mother's ~** c'est le préféré *or* le favori *or* le chouchou* de sa mère; (*US fig*) **the ~ son** l'enfant chéri, le chouchou*; **he is a universal ~** tout le monde l'adore; **that song is a great ~ of mine** cette chanson est une de mes préférées; **he sang a lot of old ~s** il a chanté beaucoup de vieux succès; *V* **hot.**

2 *adj* favori, préféré.

favouritism, (*US*) **favoritism** ['feɪvərɪtɪzəm] *n* favoritisme *m.*

fawn¹ [fɔːn] **1** *n* faon *m.* **2** *adj* (*colour*) fauve.

fawn² [fɔːn] *vi*: **to ~ (up)on sb** [*dog*] faire fête à qn; (*fig*) flatter qn (servilement), lécher les bottes de qn.

fawning ['fɔːnɪŋ] *adj person, manner* servile, flagorneur; *dog* trop démonstratif, trop affectueux.

fay [feɪ] *n* (†† *or liter*) fée *f.*

fealty ['fiːəltɪ] *n* (*Hist*) fidélité *f*, allégeance *f.*

fear [fɪəʳ] **1** *n* **(a)** (*fright*) crainte *f*, peur *f.* **he obeyed out of ~** il a obéi sous l'effet de la peur; **a sudden ~ came over him** la peur s'est soudain emparée de lui; **grave ~s have arisen for the safety of the hostages** on est dans l'anxiété *or* la plus vive inquiétude en ce qui concerne le sort des otages; **there are ~s that ...** on craint fort que ... + ne + *subj*; **he has ~s for his sister's life** il craint pour la vie de sa sœur; **have no ~(s)** ne craignez rien, soyez sans crainte; **without ~ nor favour** impartialement, sans distinction de personnes; **to live** *or* **go in ~** vivre dans la peur; **to go in ~ of one's life** craindre pour sa vie; **he went in ~ of being discovered** il craignait toujours d'être découvert; **in ~ and trembling** en tremblant de peur, transi de peur; **for ~ of waking him** de peur de le réveiller; **for ~ (that)** de peur que + ne + *subj*; **~ of heights** vertige *m.*

(b) (*U: awe*) crainte *f*, respect *m.* **the ~ of God** le respect *or* la crainte de Dieu; **to put the ~ of God into sb*** (*frighten*) faire une peur bleue à qn; (*scold*) passer à qn une semonce *or* un savon* qu'il n'oubliera pas de si tôt.

(c) (*risk, likelihood*) risque *m*, danger *m.* **there's not much ~ of his coming** il est peu probable qu'il vienne, il ne risque guère de venir; **there's no ~ of that!** ça ne risque pas d'arriver!; **no ~!*** jamais de la vie!, pas de danger!*

2 *vt* **(a)** craindre, avoir peur de, redouter. **to ~ the worst** redouter *or* craindre le pire; **to ~ that** avoir peur que *or* craindre que + ne + *subj*; **I ~ he may come all the same** j'ai (bien) peur *or* je crains (bien) qu'il ne vienne quand même; **I ~ he won't come** j'ai (bien) peur *or* je crains (bien) qu'il ne vienne pas; **I ~ so** je crains que oui; **I ~ not** je crains que non; **he's a man to be ~ed** c'est un homme redoutable; **never ~!** ne craignez rien!, n'ayez crainte!, soyez tranquille!; **they did not ~ to die** ils ne craignaient pas la mort *or* de mourir, ils n'avaient pas peur de la mort *or* de mourir.

(b) (*feel awe for*) *God, gods* craindre, avoir le respect de.

3 *vi*: **to ~ for one's life** craindre pour sa vie; **I ~ for him** j'ai peur *or* je tremble pour lui; **he ~s for the future of the country** l'avenir du pays lui inspire des craintes *or* des inquiétudes.

fearful ['fɪəfʊl] *adj* **(a)** (*frightening*) *spectacle, noise* effrayant, affreux; *accident* épouvantable.

(b) (*fig*) affreux. **it really is a ~ nuisance** c'est vraiment empoisonnant* *or* embêtant*; **she's a ~ bore** Dieu qu'elle est *or* peut être ennuyeuse!

(c) (*timid*) *person* peureux, craintif. **I was ~ of waking her** je craignais de la réveiller.

fearfully ['fɪəfəlɪ] *adv* **(a)** (*timidly*) peureusement, craintivement. **(b)** (*fig*) affreusement, terriblement. **she's ~ ugly** elle est laide à faire peur.

fearfulness ['fɪəfʊlnɪs] *n* (*fear*) crainte *f*, appréhension *f*; (*shyness*) extrême timidité *f.*

fearless ['fɪəlɪs] *adj* intrépide, courageux. (*liter*) **~ of** sans peur *or* appréhension de.

fearlessly ['fɪəlɪslɪ] *adv* intrépidement, avec intrépidité, courageusement.

fearlessness ['fɪəlɪsnɪs] *n* intrépidité *f.*

fearsome ['fɪəsəm] *adj opponent* redoutable; *apparition* terrible, effroyable.

fearsomely ['fɪəsəmlɪ] *adv* effroyablement, affreusement.

feasibility [ˌfiːzə'bɪlɪtɪ] **1** *n* **(a)** (*practicability: of plan, suggestion*) possibilité *f* (de réalisation). **~ of doing** possibilité de faire; **to doubt the ~ of a scheme** douter qu'un plan soit réalisable.

(b) (*plausibility: of story, report*) vraisemblance *f*, plausibilité *f.*

2 *cpd*: **feasibility study** (*of scheme etc*) étude *f* des possibilités; (*of machine etc*) étude des faisabilités.

feasible ['fiːzəbl] *adj* **(a)** (*practicable*) *plan, suggestion* faisable, possible, réalisable. **can we do it? — yes, it's quite ~** pouvons-nous le faire? — oui, c'est très faisable. **(b)** (*likely, probable*) *story, theory* plausible, vraisemblable.

feast [fiːst] **1** *n* **(a)** (*lit, fig*) festin *m*, banquet *m.*

(b) (*Rel*) fête *f.* **~ day** (jour *m* de) fête; **the ~ of St John** la Saint-Jean; **the ~ of the Assumption** la fête de l'Assomption; *V* **movable.**

2 *vi* banqueter, festoyer. **to ~ on sth** se régaler de qch; (*fig*) se délecter de qch.

3 *vt* († *or liter*) *guest* fêter, régaler. **to ~ o.s.** se régaler; (*fig*) **to ~ one's eyes on** repaître ses yeux de, se délecter à regarder.

feat [fiːt] *n* exploit *m*, prouesse *f.* **~ of architecture** *etc* chef d'œuvre *m or* réussite *f* de l'architecture *etc*; **~ of arms** fait *m* d'armes; **~ of skill** tour *m* d'adresse; **getting him to speak was quite a ~** cela a été un exploit de (réussir à) le faire parler.

feather ['feðəʳ] **1** *n* plume *f*; [*wing, tail*] penne *f.* (*fig*) **to make the ~s fly** mettre le feu aux poudres (*fig*); **that smoothed her ruffled** *or* **rumpled ~s** cela lui a rendu le sourire; **in fine** *or* **high ~** en pleine forme; **that's a ~ in his cap** c'est une réussite dont il peut être fier *or* se féliciter, c'est un fleuron à sa couronne; **you could have knocked me over with a ~** les bras m'en sont tombés, j'en suis resté baba* *inv*; *V* **bird, light², white.**

2 *vt* **(a)** *arrow etc* empenner. (*fig*) **to ~ one's nest** faire sa pelote; **to ~ one's nest at sb's expense** s'engraisser sur le dos de qn.

(b) (*Aviat*) *propeller* mettre en drapeau. (*Rowing*) **to ~ an oar** plumer.

3 *cpd mattress etc* de plumes; *headdress* à plumes. **feather bed** (*n*) lit *m* de plume(s); (*: *sinecure*) sinécure *f*, bonne planque; (*fig*) **feather-bed** (*vt*) *person, project* protéger; *child* élever dans du coton; (*Ind*) protéger (*afin de lutter contre les licenciements pour raisons économiques*); **featherbrain** hurluberlu *m*, écervelé(e) *m(f)*; **featherbrained** étourdi, écervelé; **feather duster** plumeau *m*; (*Carpentry*) **featheredge** biseau *m*; **feather-edged** en biseau; (*Boxing*) **featherweight** (*n*) poids *m* plume *inv*; (*adj*) *championship etc* poids plume *inv.*

feathery ['feðərɪ] *adj* duveteux, doux (*f* douce) comme la plume.

feature ['fiːtʃəʳ] **1** *n* **(a)** (*part of the face*) trait *m* (du visage). **the ~s** la physionomie; **delicate ~s** traits fins.

(b) [*countryside, person, building*] particularité *f*, caractéristique *f*, trait *m.* **her most striking ~ is her hair** son trait le plus frappant ce sont ses cheveux; **one of his most outstanding ~s is his patience** une de ses caractéristiques les plus remarquables est sa patience; **one of the main ~s in the kidnapping story was ...** un des traits les plus frappants dans l'affaire du kidnapping a été ...; **scepticism is a ~ of our age** le scepticisme est caractéristique *or* un trait de notre temps.

(c) (*Comm etc*) spécialité *f.* **this store makes a ~ of its ready-to-wear department** ce magasin se spécialise dans le prêt-à-porter.

(d) (*Cine*) grand film, long métrage; (*Press: column*) chronique *f.* **this cartoon is a regular ~ in 'The Observer'** cette bande dessinée paraît régulièrement dans 'The Observer'.

2 *cpd*: (*Press*) **feature article** article *m*; (*Cine*) **feature (-length) film** grand film, long métrage; **feature story** = **feature article**; (*Press*) **feature writer** journaliste *mf.*

3 *vt* **(a)** (*give prominence to*) *person, event, story* mettre en vedette; *name, news* faire figurer. **this film ~s an English actress** ce film a pour vedette une actrice anglaise; **the murder was ~d on the front page** le meurtre tenait la vedette (en première page) *or* était à la une.

(b) (*depict*) représenter.

4 *vi* **(a)** (*Cine*) figurer, jouer (*in* dans).

(b) a lack of public concern ~d prominently in the car-bomb story l'indifférence du public a été un trait frappant dans l'affaire des voitures piégées.

featureless ['fiːtʃəlɪs] *adj* anonyme, sans traits distinctifs.

febrifuge ['febrɪfjuːdʒ] *adj, n* fébrifuge (*m*).

febrile ['fiːbraɪl] *adj* fébrile, fiévreux.

February ['febrʊərɪ] *n* février *m*; *for phrases V* **September.**

feces ['fiːsiːz] *npl* (*US*) = **faeces.**

feckless ['feklɪs] *adj person* inepte, incapable; *attempt* maladroit. **a ~ girl** une tête sans cervelle, une évaporée.

fecund ['fiːkənd] *adj* fécond.

fecundity [fɪ'kʌndɪtɪ] *n* fécondité *f.*

fed [fed] **1** *pret, ptp of* **feed.**

2 *cpd*: **to be fed up*** en avoir assez, en avoir marre*; **I'm fed up waiting for him*** j'en ai assez *or* j'en ai marre* de l'attendre; **he got fed up with it*** il en a eu assez, il en a eu marre*; **to be fed (up) to the back teeth‡** en avoir ras le bol‡ (*with doing* de faire).

federal ['fedərəl] **1** *adj* fédéral. **F~ Republic of Germany** Allemagne fédérale, République fédérale d'Allemagne. **2** *n* (*US Hist*) fédéral *m*, nordiste *m.*

federalism ['fedərəlɪzəm] *n* fédéralisme *m.*

federalist ['fedərəlɪst] *adj, n* fédéraliste (*mf*).

federate ['fedəreɪt] **1** *vt* fédérer. **2** *vi* se fédérer. **3** ['fedərɪt] *adj* fédéré.

federation [ˌfedə'reɪʃən] *n* fédération *f.*

fee [fiː] **1** *n* [*doctor, lawyer etc*] honoraires *mpl*; [*artist, footballer etc*] cachet *m*; [*director, administrator etc*] honoraires, jeton *m*; [*private tutor*] appointements *mpl*; (*Scol, Univ etc*) (*for tuition*) frais *mpl* de scolarité; (*for examination*) droits *mpl*; (*for board*) prix *m* de la pension. **entrance ~** prix *or* droit d'entrée; **membership ~** montant *m* de la cotisation; **registration ~** droits d'inscription; **retaining ~** provision *f*; **one had to pay a ~ in order to speak at the meetings** il fallait payer une cotisation *or* participer aux frais pour prendre la parole aux réunions; **you can borrow more books on payment of a small ~** contre une somme modique vous pouvez emprunter d'autres livres.

2 *cpd*: **fee-paying school** établissement (d'enseignement) privé.

feeble ['fiːbl] **1** *adj person* faible, débile, frêle; *light, pulse, sound* faible; *attempt, excuse* pauvre, piètre; *joke* piteux, faiblard*. **a ~ old man** un frêle vieillard; **she's such a ~ sort of person** c'est une fille si molle.

2 *cpd*: **feeble-minded** imbécile; **feeble-mindedness** imbécillité *f.*

feebleness ['fiːblnɪs] *n* [*person, pulse etc*] faiblesse *f.*

feebly ['fiːblɪ] *adv stagger, smile* faiblement; *say, explain* piteusement.

feed [fiːd] (*vb: pret, ptp* **fed**) **1** *n* **(a)** (*U: gen*) alimentation *f*, nourriture *f*; (*pasture*) pâture *f*; (*hay etc*) fourrage *m*. **he's off his ~‡** (*not hungry*) il n'a pas d'appétit; (*dejected*) il a un peu le cafard; (*unwell*) il est un peu patraque*.

(b) (*portion of food*) ration *f*. **the baby has 5 ~s a day** (*breastfeeds*) le bébé a 5 tétées par jour; (*bottles*) le bébé a 5 biberons par jour; **~ of oats** picotin *m* d'avoine; **we had a good ~*** on a bien mangé *or* bien boulotté* *or* bien bouffé‡.

(c) (*Theat**) (*comedian's cue line*) réplique *f* (*donnée par un faire-valoir*); (*straight man*) faire-valoir *m inv*.

2 *cpd*: **feedback** (*Elec*) réaction *f*, (*unwanted*) réaction parasite; (*Cybernetics*) rétroaction *f*, feed-back *m*; (*gen*) feed-back, réactions *fpl*; **feedbag** musette *f* mangeoire; **feedpipe** tuyau *m* d'amenée; **feedstuffs** nourriture *f or* aliments *mpl* (pour animaux).

3 *vt* **(a)** *person, animal* donner à manger à, nourrir; *family* nourrir; *army etc* ravitailler; *baby* (*breastfed*) allaiter; (*bottle-fed*) donner le biberon à; *birds [mother bird]* donner la becquée à; *[person]* donner à manger à. **there are 6 people to ~ in this house** il y a 6 personnes *or* bouches à nourrir dans cette maison; **what do you ~ your cat on?** que donnez-vous à manger à votre chat?; **have you fed the horses?** avez-vous donné à manger aux chevaux?; *[child]* **he can ~ himself now** il sait manger tout seul maintenant; **to ~ sth to sb** donner qch à manger à qn, nourrir qn de qch; **you shouldn't ~ him that** vous ne devriez pas lui faire manger cela *or* lui donner cela à manger; **we've fed him all the facts*** nous lui avons fourni toutes les données.

(b) *fire* entretenir, alimenter; *furnace, machine* alimenter. **to ~ the flames** (*lit*) attiser le feu; (*fig*) jeter de l'huile sur le feu (*fig*); **2 rivers ~ this reservoir** 2 rivières alimentent ce réservoir; **to ~ the parking meter** rajouter une pièce dans le parcmètre; **to ~ sth into a machine** mettre *or* introduire qch dans une machine; **to ~ data into a computer** alimenter un ordinateur en données.

(c) (*Theat**) *comedian* donner la réplique à (*pour obtenir de lui la réponse comique*); (*prompt*) souffler à.

4 *vi [animal]* manger, se nourrir; (*on pasture*) paître, brouter; *[baby]* manger, (*at breast*) téter. (*lit, fig*) **to ~ on** se nourrir de.

feed back 1 *vt sep facts, information, results* donner (en retour).

2 feedback *n V* **feed 2**.

feed in *vt sep tape, wire* introduire (*to* dans); *facts, information* fournir (*to* à).

feed up 1 *vt sep animal* engraisser; *geese* gaver; *person* faire manger plus *or* davantage.

2 fed up* *adj V* **fed 2**.

feeder ['fi:dər] **1** *n* **(a)** (*one who gives food*) nourrisseur *m*; (*eater: person, animal*) mangeur *m*, -euse *f*. **a heavy ~** un gros mangeur.

(b) (*device*) (*for chickens*) mangeoire *f* automatique; (*for cattle*) nourrisseur *m* automatique; (*for machine*) chargeur *m*.

(c) (*Elec*) conducteur *m* alimentaire.

(d) (*Brit: bib*) bavette *f*, bavoir *m*.

2 *cpd canal* d'amenée; *railway, road etc* secondaire; *stream* affluent.

feeding ['fi:dɪŋ] **1** *n* alimentation *f*. **2** *cpd*: (*esp Brit*) **feeding bottle** biberon *m*; **feeding stuffs** nourriture *f or* aliments *mpl* (pour animaux).

feel [fi:l] (*vb: pret, ptp* **felt**) **1** *n* (*U*) (*sense of touch*) toucher *m*; (*sensation*) sensation *f*. **cold to the ~** froid au toucher; **at the ~ of** au contact de; **to know sth by the ~ (of it)** reconnaître qch au toucher; **I don't like the ~ of wool against my skin** je n'aime pas la sensation de la laine contre la peau; (*fig*) **I don't like the ~ of it** ça ne me dit rien de bon *or* rien qui vaille; **let me have a ~!*** laisse-moi toucher!; (*fig*) **he wants to get the ~ of the factory*** il veut se faire une impression générale de l'usine; **you have to get the ~ of a new car** il faut se faire à une nouvelle voiture.

2 *vt* **(a)** (*touch, explore*) palper, tâter. **the blind man felt the object to find out what it was** l'aveugle a palpé *or* tâté l'objet pour découvrir ce que c'était; **to ~ sb's pulse** tâter le pouls à qn; **~ the envelope and see if there's anything in it** palpez l'enveloppe pour voir s'il y a quelque chose dedans; (*lit*) **to ~ one's way** avancer *or* marcher à tâtons; (*fig*) **you'll have to ~ your way** il faut y aller à tâtons; **we are ~ing our way towards an agreement** nous tâtons le terrain pour parvenir à un accord; (*fig*) **I'm still ~ing my way around** j'essaie de m'y retrouver.

(b) (*experience, be aware of*) *blow, caress* sentir; *pain* sentir, ressentir; *sympathy, grief* éprouver, ressentir. **I can ~ something pricking me** je sens quelque chose qui me pique; **I'm so cold I can't ~ anything** j'ai si froid que je ne sens plus rien; **I felt it getting hot** je l'ai senti se réchauffer; **she could ~ the heat from the radiator** elle sentait la chaleur du radiateur; **to ~ the heat/cold** être sensible à *or* incommodé par la chaleur/le froid; **I don't ~ the heat much** la chaleur ne me gêne pas beaucoup; **she ~s the cold terribly** elle est terriblement frileuse; **I felt a few drops of rain** j'ai senti quelques gouttes de pluie; **he felt it move** il l'a senti bouger; **I ~ no interest in it** cela ne m'intéresse pas du tout; **he felt a great sense of relief** il a éprouvé *or* ressenti un grand soulagement; **they couldn't help ~ing the justice of his remarks** ils ne pouvaient qu'apprécier la justesse de ses paroles, ils étaient pleinement conscients de la justesse de ses paroles; **I do ~ the importance of this** j'ai pleinement conscience de l'importance de ceci; **you must ~ the beauty of this music before you can play it** il faut que vous sentiez (*subj*) la beauté de la musique avant de pouvoir la jouer vous-même; **the effects will be felt later** les effets se feront sentir plus tard; **he ~s his position very much** il est très conscient de la difficulté de sa situation; **she felt the loss of her father greatly** elle a été très affectée par la mort de son père, elle a vivement ressenti la perte de son père.

(c) (*think*) avoir l'impression, considérer, estimer. **I ~ he has spoilt everything** j'ai l'impression *or* il me semble qu'il a tout gâché; **I ~ that he ought to go** je considère *or* j'estime qu'il devrait y aller; **I ~ it in my bones that I am right** quelque chose (en moi) me dit que j'ai raison; **he felt it necessary to point out ...** il a jugé *or* estimé nécessaire de faire remarquer ...; **I ~ strongly that** je suis convaincu que; **if you ~ strongly about it** si cela vous tient à cœur, si cela vous semble important; **what do you ~ about this idea?** que pensez-vous de cette idée?, quel est votre sentiment sur cette idée?

3 *vi* **(a)** (*of physical state*) se sentir. **to ~ cold/hot/hungry/thirsty/sleepy** avoir froid/chaud/faim/soif/sommeil; **to ~ old/ill** se sentir vieux/malade; **he felt like a young man again** il se sentait redevenu jeune homme; **I ~ (like) a new man** (*or* **woman**) je me sens renaître *or* revivre; **how do you ~ today?** comment vous sentez-vous aujourd'hui?; **I ~ much better** je me sens beaucoup mieux; **you'll ~ all the better for a rest** vous vous sentirez mieux après vous être reposé; **he doesn't ~ quite himself today** il ne se sent pas tout à fait dans son assiette aujourd'hui; **I felt as if I was going to faint** j'avais l'impression que j'allais m'évanouir; **to ~ up to doing** se sentir capable de faire; **I'm afraid I don't ~ up to it** je crois malheureusement que je ne m'en sens pas capable; *V* **equal**.

(b) (*of mental or moral state*) être. **I ~ sure that ...** je suis sûr que ...; **they don't ~ able to recommend him** ils estiment qu'ils ne peuvent pas le recommander; **he ~s confident of success** il s'estime capable de réussir; **we felt very touched by his remarks** nous avons été très touchés par ses remarques; **I don't ~ ready to see her again yet** je ne me sens pas encore prêt à la revoir; **I ~ very bad about leaving you here** cela m'ennuie beaucoup de vous laisser ici; **how do you ~ about him?** que pensez-vous de lui?; **how do you ~ about (going for) a walk** est-ce que cela vous dit d'aller vous promener?; **I ~ as if there's nothing we can do** j'ai le sentiment que nous ne pouvons rien faire; **she felt as if she could do whatever she liked** elle avait l'impression qu'elle pouvait faire tout ce qu'elle voulait; **what does it ~ like** *or* **how does it ~ to know that you are a success?** quel effet cela vous fait-il de savoir que vous avez réussi?; **to ~ like doing** avoir envie de faire; **he felt like an ice cream** il avait envie d'une glace; **if you ~ like it** si le cœur vous en dit; **I don't ~ like it** je n'en ai pas envie, cela ne me dit rien; **to ~ for sb** compatir aux malheurs de qn; **we ~ for you in your sorrow** nous partageons votre douleur; **I ~ for you!** comme je vous comprends!; *V* **sorry** *etc*.

(c) *[objects]* **to ~ hard/soft** être dur/doux (*f* douce) au toucher; **the house ~s damp** la maison donne l'impression d'être humide; **the box ~s as if** *or* **as though it has been mended** au toucher on dirait que la boîte a été réparée; **this material is so soft it ~s like silk** ce tissu est si doux qu'on dirait de la soie; **the car travelled so fast it felt like flying** la voiture filait si rapidement qu'on se serait cru en avion; **it ~s like rain** on dirait qu'il va pleuvoir; **it ~s like thunder** il y a de l'orage dans l'air.

(d) (*grope: also* **~ about, ~ around**) tâtonner, fouiller. **she felt (about** *or* **around) in her pocket for some change** elle a fouillé dans sa poche pour trouver de la monnaie; **he was ~ing (about** *or* **around) in the dark for the door** il tâtonnait dans le noir pour trouver la porte.

feeler ['fi:lər] **1** *n [insect]* antenne *f*; *[octopus etc]* tentacule *m*. (*fig*) **to throw out** *or* **put out a ~** *or* **~s** tâter le terrain (*to discover* pour découvrir), tâter l'opinion, lancer un ballon d'essai.

2 *cpd*: (*Tech*) **feeler gauge** calibre *m* (d'épaisseur).

feeling ['fi:lɪŋ] *n* **(a)** (*U: physical*) sensation *f*. **I've lost all ~ in my right arm** j'ai perdu toute sensation dans le bras droit, mon bras droit ne sent plus rien; **a ~ of cold, a cold ~** une sensation de froid.

(b) (*awareness, impression*) sentiment *m*. **a ~ of isolation** un sentiment d'isolement; **he had the ~ (that) something dreadful would happen to him** il avait le sentiment *or* le pressentiment que quelque chose de terrible lui arriverait; **I've a funny ~ she will succeed** j'ai comme l'impression *or* comme le sentiment qu'elle va réussir; **the ~ of the meeting was against the idea** le sentiment *or* l'opinion *f* de l'assemblée était contre l'idée; **there was a general ~ that ...** on avait l'impression que ..., le sentiment général a été que ... ; *V* **strong**.

(c) (*emotions*) **~s** sentiments *mpl*, sensibilité *f*; **he appealed to their ~s rather than their reason** il faisait appel à leurs sentiments plutôt qu'à leur raison; **a ~ of joy came over her** la joie l'a envahie; **you can imagine my ~s** tu t'imagines ce que je ressens (*or* j'ai ressenti *etc*); **~s ran high about the new motorway** la nouvelle autoroute a déchaîné les passions; **his ~s were hurt** on l'avait blessé *or* froissé (dans ses sentiments); *V* **hard**.

(d) (*U*) (*sensitivity*) sentiment *m*, émotion *f*, sensibilité *f*; (*compassion*) sympathie *f*. **a woman of great ~** une femme très sensible; **she sang with ~** elle a chanté avec sentiment; **he spoke with great ~** il a parlé avec chaleur *or* avec émotion; **he doesn't show much ~ for his sister** il ne fait pas preuve de beaucoup de sympathie pour sa sœur; **he has no ~ for the suffering of others** les souffrances d'autrui le laissent insensible *or* froid; **he has no ~ for music** il n'apprécie pas du tout la musique; **he has a certain ~ for music** il est assez sensible à la musique; **ill** *or* **bad ~** animosité *f*, hostilité *f*.

feelingly ['fi:lɪŋlɪ] *adv speak, write* avec émotion, avec chaleur.

feet [fi:t] *npl of* **foot 1**.

feign [feɪn] *vt surprise* feindre; *madness* simuler. **to ~ illness/sleep** faire semblant d'être malade/de dormir; **~ed modesty** fausse modestie, modestie feinte.

feint [feɪnt] (*Boxing, Fencing, Mil*) **1** *n* feinte *f*. **to make a ~** faire une feinte (*at* à). **2** *vi* feinter. **3** *cpd*: **feint-ruled paper** papier réglé (en impression légère).

feldspar ['feldspɑ:r] *n* = **felspar**.

felicitate [fɪˈlɪsɪteɪt] *vt* féliciter, congratuler.
felicitous [fɪˈlɪsɪtəs] *adj* (*happy*) heureux; (*well-chosen*) bien trouvé, à propos, heureux.
felicity [fɪˈlɪsɪtɪ] *n* (*happiness*) félicité *f*, bonheur *m*; (*aptness*) bonheur, justesse *f*, à-propos *m*.
feline [ˈfiːlaɪn] *adj, n* félin(e) *m(f)*.
fell[1] [fel] *pret of* **fall**.
fell[2] [fel] *vt tree, enemy* abattre; *ox* assommer, abattre.
fell[3] [fel] *n* (*Brit*) (*mountain*) montagne *f*, mont *m*. (*moorland*) **the ~s** la lande.
fell[4] [fel] *adj* (*liter*) *blow* féroce, cruel; *disease* cruel; *V* **swoop.**
fell[5] [fel] *n* (*hide, pelt*) fourrure *f*, peau *f* (d'animal).
fellow [ˈfeləʊ] **1** *n* **(a)** garçon *m*, homme *m*, type* *m*, individu *m* (*pej*). **a nice ~** un brave garçon, un brave type*; **an old ~** un vieux (bonhomme); **a poor old ~** un pauvre vieux; **some poor ~ will have to rewrite this** il y aura un pauvre malheureux qui devra récrire ceci; **poor little ~** pauvre petit (bonhomme *or* gars); **a young ~** un jeune homme, un garçon; **a ~ must have a bit of a rest!*** il faut bien qu'on se repose (*subj*) un peu!; **my dear ~** mon cher; **look here, old ~** écoute, mon vieux; **this journalist ~** ce journaliste, le journaliste en question.
(b) (*comrade*) camarade *m*, compagnon *m*; (*equal, peer*) pair *m*, semblable *m*. **~s in misfortune** frères *mpl* dans le malheur, compagnons d'infortune; **I can't find the ~ to this glove** je ne trouve pas le deuxième gant de cette paire *or* le frère de ce gant; **the ~ to this sock** la deuxième chaussette de cette paire, la sœur de cette chaussette; *V* **school**[1] *etc.*
(c) *[association, society etc]* membre *m*, associé *m* (*d'une société savante, d'une académie*).
(d) (*Univ*) chargé *m* de cours (*qui est aussi membre du conseil d'administration d'un collège*); *V* **research.**
2 *cpd*: **fellow being** semblable *mf*, pareil(le) *m(f)*; **fellow citizen** concitoyen(ne) *m(f)*; **fellow countryman** compatriote *m*; **fellow creature** semblable *mf*, pareil(le) *m(f)*; **fellow feeling** sympathie *f*; **fellow member** confrère *m*, consœur *f*, collègue *mf*; **fellow men** semblables *mpl*; **fellow passenger** compagnon *m* de voyage, compagne *f* de voyage; **fellow traveller** (*lit*) compagnon *m* de voyage, compagne *f* de voyage; (*Pol: with communists*) communisant(e) *m(f)*, cryptocommuniste *mf*; (*gen*) sympathisant(e) *m(f)*; **fellow worker** (*in office*) collègue *mf*; (*in factory*) camarade *mf* (de travail).
fellowship [ˈfeləʊʃɪp] *n* **(a)** (*U: comradeship*) amitié *f*, camaraderie *f*; (*Rel etc*) communion *f*. **(b)** (*society etc*) association *f*, corporation *f*; (*Rel*) confrérie *f*. **(c)** (*membership of learned society*) titre *m* de membre *or* d'associé (*d'une société savante*). **(d)** (*Univ*) (*scholarship*) bourse *f* universitaire; (*post*) poste *m* de 'fellow' (*V* **fellow 1d**).
felon [ˈfelən] *n* (*Jur*) criminel(le) *m(f)*.
felonious [fɪˈləʊnɪəs] *adj* (*Jur*) criminel.
felony [ˈfelənɪ] *n* (*Jur*) crime *m*, forfait *m*.
felspar [ˈfelspɑːʳ] *n* feldspath *m*.
felt[1] [felt] *pret, ptp of* **feel.**
felt[2] [felt] **1** *n* feutre *m*; *V* **roofing. 2** *cpd* de feutre. **a felt hat** un feutre; **a felt-tip (pen)** un (crayon) feutre.
female [ˈfiːmeɪl] **1** *adj animal, plant* (*also Tech*) femelle; *subject, slave* du sexe féminin; *company, vote* des femmes; *sex, character, quality* féminin. **a ~ child** une enfant, une fille, un enfant du sexe féminin; **~ students** les étudiantes *fpl*; **~ labour** main-d'œuvre féminine; (*Theat*) **~ impersonator** travesti *m*.
2 *n* (*person*) femme *f*, fille *f*; (*animal, plant*) femelle *f*. (*pej*) **there was a ~ there who ...*** il y avait là une espèce de bonne femme qui ...* (*pej*).
feminine [ˈfemɪnɪn] **1** *adj* (*also Gram*) féminin. **2** *n* (*Gram*) féminin *m*. **in the ~** au féminin.
femininity [ˌfemɪˈnɪnɪtɪ] *n* féminité *f*.
feminism [ˈfemɪnɪzəm] *n* féminisme *m*.
feminist [ˈfemɪnɪst] *n* féministe *mf*.
femlib* [ˈfemˈlɪb] *n* (*abbr of* **female liberation**) M.L.F. *m*.
femur [ˈfiːməʳ] *n* fémur *m*.
fen [fen] *n* marais *m*, marécage *m*. **the F~s** les plaines marécageuses du Norfolk.
fence [fens] **1** *n* **(a)** barrière *f*, palissade *f*, clôture *f*; (*Racing*) obstacle *m*. (*fig*) **to sit on the ~** ménager la chèvre et le chou, s'abstenir de prendre position; *V* **barbed.**
(b) (*machine guard*) barrière protectrice.
(c) (‡: *of stolen goods*) fourgue *m*, fourgat *m*, receleur *m*.
2 *vt* **(a)** (*also* **~ in**) *land* clôturer, entourer d'une clôture.
(b) (*fig*) *question* éluder.
3 *vi* (*Sport*) faire de l'escrime; (*fig*) éluder la question, se dérober. (*Sport*) **to ~ with sword/sabre** *etc* tirer à l'épée/au sabre *etc.*
fence in *vt sep* **(a)** (*lit*) = **fence 2a.**
(b) (*fig*) **to feel fenced in by restrictions** se sentir gêné *or* entravé par des restrictions.
fence off *vt sep* **(a)** *piece of land* séparer par une clôture.
(b) *attack* détourner; *blow* parer; (*fig*) *question* parer, éluder.
fencer [ˈfensəʳ] *n* escrimeur *m*, -euse *f*.
fencing [ˈfensɪŋ] **1** *n* **(a)** (*Sport*) escrime *f*. **(b)** (*for making fences*) matériaux *mpl* pour clôture. **2** *cpd*: **fencing master** maître *m* d'armes; **fencing match** assaut *m* d'escrime; **fencing school** salle *f* d'armes.
fend [fend] *vi*: **to ~ for o.s.** se débrouiller (tout seul).
fend off *vt sep blow* parer; *attack* détourner; *attacker* repousser; *awkward question* écarter, éluder.
fender [ˈfendəʳ] *n* (*in front of fire*) garde-feu *m inv*; (*US Aut*) pare-chocs *m inv*; (*US Rail*) chasse-pierres *m inv*; (*Naut*) défense *f*, pare-battage *m inv*.
fenestration [ˌfenɪsˈtreɪʃən] *n* (*Archit*) fenêtrage *m*; (*Med*) fenestration *f*; (*Bot, Zool*) aspect fenêtré.
fennel [ˈfenl] *n* fenouil *m*.
ferment [fəˈment] **1** *vi* (*lit, fig*) fermenter. **2** *vt* (*lit, fig*) faire fermenter. **3** [ˈfɜːment] *n* (*lit*) ferment *m*; (*fig*) agitation *f*, effervescence *f*. **city in a state of ~** ville en effervescence.
fermentation [ˌfɜːmenˈteɪʃən] *n* (*lit, fig*) fermentation *f*.
fern [fɜːn] *n* fougère *f*.
ferocious [fəˈrəʊʃəs] *adj* féroce.
ferociously [fəˈrəʊʃəslɪ] *adv* férocement, avec férocité.
ferociousness [fəˈrəʊʃəsnɪs] *n*, **ferocity** [fəˈrɒsɪtɪ] *n* férocité *f*.
ferret [ˈferɪt] **1** *n* (*Zool*) furet *m*.
2 *vi* **(a)** (*also* **~ about, ~ around**) fouiller, fureter. **she was ~ing (about *or* around) among my books** elle furetait dans mes livres.
(b) to go ~ing chasser au furet.
ferret out *vt sep secret, person* dénicher, découvrir.
Ferris wheel [ˈferɪswiːl] *n* grande roue (*dans une foire*).
ferroconcrete [ˈferəʊˈkɒŋkriːt] *n* béton armé.
ferrous [ˈferəs] *adj* ferreux.
ferrule [ˈferuːl] *n* virole *f*.
ferry [ˈferɪ] **1** *n* **(a)** (*also* **~boat**) (*small: for people, cars*) bac *m*; (*larger: for people, cars, trains*) ferry(-boat) *m*; (*between ship and quayside*) va-et-vient *m inv*. **~man** passeur *m*; *V* **air, car.**
(b) (*place*) passage *m*.
2 *vt* **(a)** (*also* **~ across, ~ over**) *person, car, train* faire passer (en bac *or* par bateau *or* par avion *etc*).
(b) (*fig*) *people* transporter, emmener, conduire; (*) *things* porter, apporter. **he ferried voters to and from the polls** il a fait la navette avec sa voiture pour emmener les électeurs au bureau de vote.
fertile [ˈfɜːtaɪl] *adj land* fertile; *person, animal, mind, egg* fécond; *imagination* fécond, fertile.
fertility [fəˈtɪlɪtɪ] **1** *n* (*V* **fertile**) fertilité *f*; fécondité *f*. **2** *cpd cult, symbol* de fertilité. (*Med*) **fertility drug** médicament *m* contre la stérilité.
fertilization [ˌfɜːtɪlaɪˈzeɪʃən] *n* fertilisation *f*.
fertilize [ˈfɜːtɪlaɪz] *vt land, soil* fertiliser, amender; *animal, plant, egg* féconder, fertiliser.
fertilizer [ˈfɜːtɪlaɪzəʳ] *n* engrais *m*. **artificial ~** engrais chimique.
fervent [ˈfɜːvənt] *adj*, **fervid** [ˈfɜːvɪd] *adj* fervent, ardent.
fervour, (*US*) **fervor** [ˈfɜːvəʳ] *n* ferveur *f*.
fester [ˈfestəʳ] *vi [cut, wound]* suppurer; *[anger, resentment]* couver. **the insult ~ed** l'injure lui est restée sur le cœur.
festival [ˈfestɪvəl] *n* (*Rel etc*) fête *f*; (*Mus etc*) festival *m*. **the Edinburgh F~** le festival d'Édimbourg.
festive [ˈfestɪv] *adj* de fête. **the ~ season** la période des fêtes; **to be in a ~ mood** être en veine de réjouissances.
festivity [fesˈtɪvɪtɪ] *n* **(a)** (*U: also* **festivities**) fête *f*, réjouissances *fpl*. **(b)** (*festival*) fête *f*.
festoon [fesˈtuːn] **1** *n* feston *m*, guirlande *f*. **2** *vt* festonner, orner de festons; *building, town* pavoiser. **a room ~ed with posters** une pièce tapissée d'affiches.
fetch [fetʃ] **1** *vt* **(a)** (*go and get*) *person, thing* aller chercher; (*bring*) *person* amener; *thing* apporter. (*fig*) **to ~ and carry for sb** faire la bonne pour qn; (*to dog*) **~ it!** rapporte!, va chercher!; **he ~ed out a handkerchief from his pocket** il a sorti *or* tiré un mouchoir de sa poche; **~ in the dustbin** rentre la poubelle.
(b) *sigh, groan* pousser.
(c) (*sell for*) *money* rapporter. **they won't ~ much** ils ne rapporteront pas grand-chose; **it ~ed a good price** ça a atteint *or* fait* une jolie somme *or* un joli prix, c'est parti pour une jolie somme.
(d) *blow* flanquer*.
2 *vi* (*Naut*) manœuvrer.
3 *n* (*Naut*) fetch *m*.
fetch up 1 *vi* finir par arriver, se retrouver (*at* à, *in* dans).
2 *vt sep* **(a)** *object* apporter, monter; *person* faire monter.
(b) (*Brit fig: vomit*) rendre, vomir.
fetching [ˈfetʃɪŋ] *adj smile* attrayant; *person* charmant, séduisant; *dress, hat* ravissant, très seyant.
fête [feɪt] **1** *n* fête *f*; (*for charity*) fête, kermesse *f*. **village ~** fête de village. **2** *vt person, success* faire fête à, fêter.
fetid [ˈfetɪd] *adj* fétide, puant.
fetish [ˈfiːtɪʃ] *n* fétiche *m* (*objet de culte*); (*Psych*) objet *m* de la fétichisation. (*fig*) **she makes a real ~ of cleanliness** elle est obsédée par la propreté, c'est une maniaque de la propreté.
fetishism [ˈfiːtɪʃɪzəm] *n* fétichisme *m*.
fetishist [ˈfiːtɪʃɪst] *n* fétichiste *mf*.
fetlock [ˈfetlɒk] *n* (*joint*) boulet *m*; (*hair*) fanon *m*.
fetter [ˈfetəʳ] **1** *vt person* enchaîner, lier; *horse, slave* entraver; (*fig*) entraver. **2** *npl*: **~s** *[prisoner]* fers *mpl*, chaînes *fpl*; *[horse, slave]* (*also fig*) entraves *fpl*; **to put a prisoner in ~s** mettre un prisonnier aux fers; **in ~s** dans les fers *or* les chaînes.
fettle [ˈfetl] *n*: **in fine *or* good ~** en pleine forme, en bonne condition.
fetus [ˈfiːtəs] *n* (*US*) = **foetus.**
feu [fjuː] *n* (*Scot Jur*) bail perpétuel (*à redevance fixe*). **~ duty** loyer *m* (de la terre).
feud[1] [fjuːd] **1** *n* (*between families, tribes*) querelle *f*, dissension *f*. **family ~s** querelles de famille, dissensions domestiques. **2** *vi* se quereller, se disputer. **to ~ with sb** être l'ennemi juré de qn, être à couteaux tirés avec qn.
feud[2] [fjuːd] *n* (*Hist*) fief *m*.
feudal [ˈfjuːdl] *adj* féodal. **the ~ system** le système féodal.
feudalism [ˈfjuːdəlɪzəm] *n* (*Hist*) féodalité *f*; (*fig*) *[society, institution etc]* féodalisme *m*.
fever [ˈfiːvəʳ] *n* (*Med, fig*) fièvre *f*. **a bout of ~** un accès de fièvre; **high ~** forte fièvre, fièvre de cheval; **he has no ~** il n'a pas de fièvre *or* de température; (*fig*) **the gambling ~** le démon

E-I

du jeu; a ~ **of impatience** une impatience fébrile; **enthusiasm reached** ~ **pitch** l'enthousiasme était à son comble; *V* **glandular, scarlet** *etc.*

feverish ['fiːvərɪʃ] *adj (Med) person* fiévreux; *condition* fiévreux, fébrile; *swamp, climate* malsain; *(fig) state, activity, excitement* fiévreux, fébrile.

feverishly ['fiːvərɪʃlɪ] *adv* fiévreusement, fébrilement.

few [fjuː] *adj, pron* **(a)** *(not many)* peu (de). ~ **books** peu de livres; **very** ~ **books** très peu de livres; ~ **of them came** peu d'entre eux sont venus, quelques-uns d'entre eux seulement sont venus; ~ **(people) come to see him** peu de gens viennent le voir; **he is one of the** ~ **people who** ... c'est l'une des rares personnes qui ... + *indic or subj*; **we have travelled a lot in the past** ~ **days** nous avons beaucoup voyagé ces jours-ci; **the next** ~ **days** les (quelques) jours qui viennent; **with** ~ **exceptions** à de rares exceptions près; **the exceptions are** ~ les exceptions sont rares *or* peu nombreuses; **she goes to town every** ~ **days** elle va à la ville tous les deux ou trois jours; ~ **and far between** rares; **such occasions are** ~ de telles occasions sont rares; **we are very** ~ **(in number)** nous sommes peu nombreux; *(liter)* **our days are** ~ nos jours sont comptés; **I'll spend the remaining** ~ **minutes alone** je passerai seul le peu de *or* les quelques minutes qui me restent; **there are always the** ~ **who think that** ... il y a toujours la minorité qui croit que ...; **the** ~ **who know him** les rares personnes qui le connaissent; *(Brit Aviat Hist)* **the F**~ *les héros de la Bataille d'Angleterre*; *V* **happy, word** *etc.*

(b) *(after adv)* **I have as** ~ **books as you** j'ai aussi peu de livres que vous; **I have as** ~ **as you** j'en ai aussi peu que vous; **there were as** ~ **as 6 objections** il n'y a eu en tout et pour tout que 6 objections; **how** ~ **there are!** qu'il y en a peu!; **how** ~ **they are!** qu'ils sont peu nombreux!; **however** ~ **books you (may) buy** si peu de livres que l'on achète (*subj*), même si l'on achète peu de livres; **however** ~ **there may be** si peu qu'il y en ait; **I've got so** ~ **already (that ...)** j'en ai déjà si peu (que ...); **so** ~ **have been sold** si peu se sont vendus; **so** ~ **books** tellement peu *or* si peu de livres; **there were too** ~ il y en avait trop peu; **too** ~ **cakes** trop peu de gâteaux; **there were 3 too** ~ il en manquait 3; **10 would not be too** ~ 10 suffiraient, il (en) suffirait de 10; **I've got too** ~ **already** j'en ai déjà (bien) trop peu; **he has too** ~ **books** il a trop peu de livres; **there are too** ~ **of you** vous êtes trop peu nombreux, vous n'êtes pas assez nombreux; **too** ~ **of them realize that** ... trop peu d'entre eux sont conscients que ... .

(c) *(some, several)* **a** ~ quelques(-uns), quelques(-unes); **a** ~ **books** quelques livres; **I know a** ~ **of these people** je connais quelques-uns de ces gens; **a** ~ *or (liter)* **some** ~ **thought otherwise** quelques-uns pensaient autrement; **I'll take just a** ~ j'en prendrai quelques-uns (*or* quelques-unes) seulement; **I'd like a** ~ **more** j'en voudrais quelques-un(e)s de plus; **quite a** ~ **books** pas mal* de livres; **quite a** ~ **did not believe him** pas mal* de gens ne l'ont pas cru; **I saw a good** ~ *or* **quite a** ~ **people there** j'y ai vu pas mal* de gens; **he has had a good** ~ **drinks** il a pas mal* bu; **we'll go in a** ~ **minutes** nous partirons dans quelques minutes; **a** ~ **of us** quelques-un(e)s d'entre nous; **there were only a** ~ **of us** nous n'étions qu'une poignée; **a good** ~ **of the books are** bon nombre de ces livres sont; **we must wait a** ~ **more days** il nous faut attendre encore quelques jours.

fewer ['fjuːə^r] *adj, pron, comp of* **few** moins (de). **we have sold** ~ **this year** nous en avons moins vendu cette année; **he has** ~ **books than you** il a moins de livres que vous; **we are** ~ **(in number) than last time** nous sommes moins nombreux que la dernière fois; ~ **people than we expected** moins de gens que nous (ne) l'escomptions; **there are** ~ **opportunities for doing it** les occasions de le faire sont plus rares, il y a moins d'occasions de le faire; **no** ~ **than 37 pupils were ill** il y a eu pas moins de 37 élèves malades; **the** ~ **the better** moins il y en a mieux c'est *or* mieux ça vaut; **few came and** ~ **stayed** peu sont venus et encore moins sont restés.

fewest ['fjuːɪst] *adj, pron, superl of* **few** le moins (de). **he met her on the** ~ **occasions possible** il l'a rencontrée le moins souvent possible; **we were** ~ **in number then** c'est à ce moment-là que nous étions le moins nombreux; **we sold** ~ **last year** c'est l'année dernière que nous en avons le moins vendu; **I've got (the)** ~ c'est moi qui en ai le moins.

fey [feɪ] *adj* extra-lucide, visionnaire.

fiancé [fɪ'ɑ̃ːŋseɪ] *n* fiancé *m.*

fiancée [fɪ'ɑ̃ːŋseɪ] *n* fiancée *f.*

fiasco [fɪ'æskəʊ] *n* fiasco *m.* **the play was a** ~ la pièce a fait un four *or* a été un four *or* a été un fiasco; **the whole undertaking was a** ~ l'entreprise tout entière a tourné au désastre *or* a fait fiasco.

fiat ['faɪæt] *n* décret *m,* ordonnance *f.*

fib* [fɪb] **1** *n* bobard* *m,* blague* *f,* mensonge *m.* **2** *vi* raconter des bobards* *or* des blagues*. **you're** ~**bing!** ce que tu racontes c'est des blagues!*

fibber ['fɪbə^r] *n* blagueur* *m,* -euse *f,* menteur *m,* -euse *f.*

fibre, *(US)* **fiber** ['faɪbə^r] **1** *n [wood, cotton, muscle etc]* fibre *f.* **cotton** ~ fibre de coton; **synthetic** ~**s** fibres synthétiques, synthétiques *mpl*; *(fig)* **a man of** ~ un homme qui a de la trempe; **a man of great moral** ~ un homme d'une grande force morale.

2 *cpd*: **fibreboard** panneau fibreux; **fibre-glass,** *(US)* **fiberglass, Fiberglas** ® fibre *f* de verre.

fibrillation [ˌfaɪbrɪ'leɪʃən] *n* fibrillation *f.*

fibroid ['faɪbrɔɪd] *n,* **fibroma** [faɪ'brəʊmə] *n (Med)* fibrome *m.*

fibrositis [ˌfaɪbrə'saɪtɪs] *n* cellulite *f.*

fibrous ['faɪbrəs] *adj* fibreux.

fibula ['fɪbjʊlə] *n* péroné *m.*

fickle ['fɪkl] *adj* inconstant, volage.

fickleness ['fɪklnɪs] *n* inconstance *f.*

fiction ['fɪkʃən] *n* **(a)** *(U: Literat)* **(works of)** ~ romans *mpl*; **light** ~ romans faciles à lire; **romantic** ~ romans à l'eau-de-rose *(pej)*; *V* **science. (b)** fiction *f,* création *f* de l'imagination. **legal** ~ une fiction légale. **(c)** *(U: the unreal)* le faux; *V* **fact.**

fictional ['fɪkʃənl] *adj* fictif. **a** ~ **character** un personnage imaginaire *or* fictif.

fictitious [fɪk'tɪʃəs] *adj (false, not genuine)* fictif; *(imaginary)* fictif, imaginaire.

fiddle ['fɪdl] **1** *n* **(a)** *(violin)* violon *m,* crincrin* *m (pej)*; *V* **fit[1], long[1], second[1].**

(b) *(esp Brit*: cheating)* truc* *m,* combine‡ *f.* **it was all a** ~ tout ça c'était une combine‡; **tax** ~ fraude fiscale; **he's on the** ~ il traficote*.

2 *cpd*: *(excl)* **fiddle-faddle!*, fiddlesticks!*** quelle blague!*

3 *vi* **(a)** *(Mus)* jouer du violon, violoner*.

(b) do stop fiddling (about *or* **around)!** tiens-toi donc tranquille!; **to** ~ **(about** *or* **around) with a pencil** tripoter un crayon; **he's fiddling (about** *or* **around) with the car** il tripote *or* bricole la voiture; **stop fiddling (about** *or* **around) over that job** arrête de perdre ton temps à faire ça.

(c) (*: *cheat*) faire de la fraude, traficoter*.

4 *vt* **(a)** (*) *accounts, expenses claim* truquer. **to** ~ **one's tax return** truquer sa déclaration d'impôts; **he's** ~**d himself (into) a job** il s'est débrouillé* pour se faire nommer à un poste.

(b) *(Mus)* violoner*.

fiddle about, fiddle around *vi*: **he's fiddling about in the garage** il est en train de s'occuper vaguement *or* de bricoler dans le garage; **we just fiddled about yesterday** on n'a rien fait de spécial hier, on a seulement traînassé hier; *V also* **fiddle 3b.**

fiddler ['fɪdlə^r] *n* **(a)** joueur *m,* -euse *f* de violon, violoneux* *m (often pej).* **(b)** (*: *cheat*) combinard‡ *m.*

fiddling ['fɪdlɪŋ] **1** *adj* futile, insignifiant. ~ **little jobs** menus travaux sans importance. **2** *n* (*: *dishonesty*) combine(s)‡ *f(pl).*

fiddly ['fɪdlɪ] *adj task* minutieux, délicat *(et agaçant)*; *object* délicat à utiliser, embêtant* à manier.

fidelity [fɪ'delɪtɪ] *n* **(a)** fidélité *f,* loyauté *f (to* à); *(in marriage)* fidélité. **(b)** *[translation etc]* exactitude *f,* fidélité *f*; *V* **high.**

fidget ['fɪdʒɪt] **1** *vi (also* ~ **about,** ~ **around)** se trémousser, remuer, gigoter*. **stop** ~**ing!** reste donc tranquille!, arrête de bouger!; **to** ~ **(about** *or* **around) with sth** tripoter qch.

2 *n*: **to be a** ~ *[child]* être très remuant, ne jamais se tenir tranquille; *[adult]* être très nerveux, ne jamais tenir en place; **to have the** ~**s** avoir la bougeotte*.

fidgety ['fɪdʒɪtɪ] *adj child etc* remuant, agité.

fiduciary [fɪ'djuːʃɪərɪ] *adj, n* fiduciaire *(mf).*

fief [fiːf] *n* fief *m.*

field [fiːld] **1** *n* **(a)** *(Agr etc)* champ *m*; *(Miner)* gisement *m.* **in the** ~**s** dans les champs, aux champs; **this machine had a year's trial in the** ~ cette machine a eu un an d'essais sur le terrain; *(Comm)* **to be first in the** ~ **with sth** être le premier à lancer qch; **work in the** ~ enquête *f* sur place *or* sur le terrain; *(Mil)* ~ **of battle** champ de bataille; *(Mil)* **to take the** ~ entrer en campagne (*V also* **1b**); **to hold the** ~ *(Mil)* se maintenir sur ses positions; *(fig)* tenir tête à l'adversaire; *(Mil)* **to die in the** ~ tomber *or* mourir au champ d'honneur; *V* **coal, gold, oil** *etc.*

(b) *(Sport)* terrain *m*; *(Racing)* concurrents *mpl (sauf le favori)*; *(Hunting)* chasseurs *mpl.* **football** ~ terrain de football; **to take the** ~ entrer en jeu; *V* **play.**

(c) *(sphere of activity etc)* domaine *m,* sphère *f.* **in the** ~ **of painting** dans le domaine de la peinture; **it's outside my** ~ ce n'est pas de mon domaine *or* de ma compétence *or* dans mes cordes; **his particular** ~ **is Renaissance painting** la peinture de la Renaissance est sa spécialité.

(d) *(Phys: also* ~ **of force)** champ *m.* ~ **of vision** champ visuel *or* de vision; **gravitational** ~ champ de gravitation.

(e) *(expanse)* étendue *f*; *(Her)* champ *m.*

2 *vt (Sport) ball* attraper; *team* faire jouer.

3 *cpd*: **field day** *(Mil)* jour *m* de grandes manœuvres; *(fig)* grande occasion, grand jour; *(fig)* **the ice-cream sellers had a field day*** cela a été une bonne journée pour les marchands de glaces; *(Sport)* **field event** concours *m*; *(Orn)* **fieldfare** litorne *f*; **field glasses** jumelles *fpl*; **field gun** canon *m* (de campagne); *(US)* **field hockey** hockey *m*; **field hospital** *(Mil)* antenne chirurgicale; *(Hist)* hôpital *m* de campagne; *(US)* **field house** *(for changing)* vestiaire *m*; *(sports hall)* complexe sportif couvert; *(Mil)* **field kitchen** cuisine roulante; *(Brit Mil)* **field marshal** maréchal *m*; *(Zool)* **field mouse** mulot *m,* rat *m* des champs; *(Mil)* **field officer** officier supérieur; **field sports** activités *fpl* de plein air *(surtout la chasse et la pêche)*; *(US Tech etc)* **field-test** soumettre aux essais sur le terrain, tester *(Tech)*; *(Tech etc)* **field tests** essais *mpl* sur le terrain; **field trials** *[gundogs etc]* field trials *mpl*; *[machine etc]* essais *mpl* sur le terrain; **fieldwork** *(Archeol, Geol etc)* recherches *fpl or* enquête *f* sur le terrain; *(Soc)* travail *m* avec des cas sociaux; **fieldworker** *(Archeol/Geol etc)* archéologue *mf*/géologue *mf etc* qui fait des recherches *or* une enquête sur le terrain; *(Soc)* ≃ assistant(e) *m(f)* de service social, assistant social.

fiend [fiːnd] *n* **(a)** démon *m*; *(cruel person)* monstre *m,* démon. **that child's a real** ~* cet enfant est un petit monstre *or* est infernal*. **(b)** (*: *fanatic*) enragé(e) *m(f),* mordu(e)* *m(f).* **tennis** ~ enragé *or* mordu* du tennis; **drug** ~† toxicomane *mf.*

fiendish ['fiːndɪʃ] *adj* diabolique, satanique. **to take a** ~ **delight in doing** prendre un plaisir diabolique à faire; **I had a** ~ **time* getting him to agree** j'ai eu un mal fou *or* un mal de chien* à obtenir son accord.

fiendishly ['fiːndɪʃlɪ] *adv* diaboliquement; (*) *expensive, difficult* abominablement.

fierce [fɪəs] *adj animal, person, look, tone, gesture* féroce; *wind* furieux; *desire* ardent; *attack (lit)* violent; *(fig)* virulent, violent; *hatred* implacable; *heat* intense, torride; *competition, fighting* serré, acharné; *opponent, partisan, advocate* acharné.

fiercely ['fɪəslɪ] *adv behave* férocement; *attack* violemment; *fight, pursue, advocate, oppose* avec acharnement; *speak* d'un ton féroce; *look* d'un air féroce *or* farouche.

fierceness ['fɪəsnɪs] *n* (*V* **fierce**) férocité *f*; fureur *f*; ardeur *f*; violence *f*; virulence *f*; implacabilité *f*; intensité *f*; acharnement *m*. **his ~ of manner** la violence de son comportement.

fiery ['faɪərɪ] *adj coals, sun* ardent; *heat, sands* brûlant; *sky* rougeoyant, embrasé (*liter*); *person* fougueux, ardent; *speech* fougueux; *temper* violent. **~ eyes** des yeux qui étincellent *or* brillent de colère (*or* d'enthousiasme *etc*); **~-tempered** irascible, coléreux.

fiesta [fɪ'estə] *n* fiesta *f*.

fife [faɪf] *n* fifre *m* (*instrument*).

fifteen [fɪf'ti:n] 1 *adj* quinze *inv*. **about ~ books** une quinzaine de livres. 2 *n* (a) quinze *m inv*. **about ~** une quinzaine. (b) (*Rugby*) quinze *m*. **the French ~** le quinze de France; *for other phrases V* **six**.

fifteenth [fɪf'ti:nθ] 1 *adj* quinzième. 2 *n* quinzième *mf*; (*fraction*) quinzième *m*; *for phrases V* **sixth**.

fifth [fɪfθ] 1 *adj* cinquième. (*fig: Pol etc*) **~ column** cinquième colonne *f*; (*fig*) **~-rate** de dernier ordre, de dernière catégorie; *for other phrases V* **sixth**. 2 *n* (*gen*) cinquième *mf*; (*fraction*) cinquième *m*; (*Mus*) quinte *f*; *for phrases V* **sixth**.

fiftieth ['fɪftɪɪθ] 1 *adj* cinquantième. 2 *n* cinquantième *mf*; (*fraction*) cinquantième *m*.

fifty ['fɪftɪ] 1 *adj* cinquante *inv*. **about ~ books** une cinquantaine de livres.

2 *n* cinquante *m inv*. **about ~** une cinquantaine; (*fig*) **to go ~-~ with sb** se mettre de moitié avec qn, partager moitié-moitié avec qn; **we have a ~-~ chance of success** nous avons cinquante pour cent de chances *or* une chance sur deux de réussir; *for other phrases V* **sixty**.

fig [fɪg] 1 *n* (*fruit*) figue *f*; (*also* **~ tree**) figuier *m*. (*fig*) **I don't care a ~*** je m'en fiche*; **I don't give a ~ for that*** je m'en moque comme de ma première chemise; **a ~ for all your principles!**† zut à tous vos principes!*

2 *cpd*: **fig leaf** (*Bot*) feuille *f* de figuier; (*on statue etc*) feuille de vigne.

fight [faɪt] (*vb: pret, ptp* **fought**) 1 *n* (a) (*between persons*) bagarre* *f*; (*brawl*) rixe *f*; (*Mil*) combat *m*, bataille *f*; (*Boxing*) combat; (*against disease, poverty etc*) lutte *f*; (*argument*) dispute *f*. (*lit, fig*) **he put up a good ~** il s'est bien défendu; **to have a ~ with sb** se battre avec qn, se bagarrer* avec qn; (*argue*) se disputer avec qn; **we're going to make a ~ of it** nous n'allons pas nous laisser battre comme ça, nous allons contre-attaquer; *V* **pick**.

(b) (*U: spirit*) **there was no ~ left in him** il n'avait plus envie de lutter, il n'avait plus de ressort; **he certainly shows ~** il faut reconnaître qu'il sait montrer les dents *or* qu'il ne se laisse pas faire.

2 *cpd*: (*Sport*) **fightback** reprise *f*.

3 *vi [person, animal]* se battre (*with* avec, *against* contre); *[troops, countries]* se battre, combattre (*against* contre); (*fig*) lutter (*for* pour, *against* contre); (*quarrel*) se disputer (*with* avec). **the boys were ~ing in the street** les garçons se battaient dans la rue; **the dogs were ~ing over a bone** les chiens se disputaient un os; (*fig*) **to ~ shy of sth/sb** fuir devant qch/qn, tout faire pour éviter qch/qn; **to ~ shy of doing** éviter à tout prix de *or* répugner à faire; **to ~ against sleep** lutter contre le sommeil; **to ~ against disease** lutter contre *or* combattre la maladie; (*lit, fig*) **to ~ for sb** se battre pour qn; (*lit, fig*) **to ~ for one's life** lutter pour la *or* sa vie; **he went down ~ing** il s'est battu jusqu'au bout.

4 *vt person, army* se battre avec *or* contre; *fire, disease* lutter contre, combattre. **to ~ a battle** livrer bataille; (*fig*) **to ~ a losing battle against sth** combattre qch en pure perte, se battre en pure perte contre qch; **we're ~ing a losing battle** nous livrons une bataille perdue d'avance; **to ~ a duel** se battre en duel; (*Jur*) **to ~ a case** défendre une cause; **we shall ~ this decision all the way** nous combattrons cette décision jusqu'au bout; **to ~ one's way out through the crowd** sortir en se frayant un passage à travers la foule.

fight back 1 *vi* (*in fight*) rendre les coups, répondre; (*Mil*) se défendre, résister; (*in argument*) répondre, se défendre; (*after illness*) se remettre, réagir; (*Sport*) se reprendre, effectuer une reprise.

2 *vt sep tears* refouler; *despair* lutter contre; *doubts* vaincre.

3 **fightback** *n V* **fight 2**.

fight down *vt sep anxiety, doubts* vaincre; *desire* réprimer.

fight off *vt sep* (*Mil*) *attack* repousser; (*fig*) *disease, sleep* lutter contre, résister à; *criticisms* répondre à.

fight on *vi* continuer le combat *or* la lutte.

fight out *vt sep*: **they fought it out** ils se sont bagarrés* pour régler la question; **leave them to fight it out** laissez-les se bagarrer* entre eux.

fighter ['faɪtə^r] 1 *n* (a) combattant *m*; (*Boxing*) boxeur *m*, pugiliste *m*. (*fig*) **he's a ~** c'est un lutteur; *V* **prize**[1] *etc*.

(b) (*plane*) avion *m* de chasse, chasseur *m*.

2 *cpd*: (*Aviat*) **fighter-bomber** chasseur bombardier *m*, avion *m* de combat polyvalent; **fighter pilot** pilote *m* de chasse.

fighting ['faɪtɪŋ] 1 *n* (*Mil*) combat *m*. **there was some ~ in the town** il y a eu des échauffourées dans la ville; *V* **bull**[1], **street** *etc*.

2 *adj person* combatif; (*Mil*) *troops* de combat. (*Mil*) **~ soldier, ~ man** combattant *m*; **he's got a lot of ~ spirit** c'est un lutteur, il a du cran*; **there's a ~ chance for her recovery** elle a une assez bonne chance de s'en tirer; **~ cock** coq *m* de combat; **to live like a ~ cock** vivre comme un coq en pâte; (*Mil*) **~ forces** forces armées; **~ line** front *m*; **~ strength** effectif *m* mobilisable.

figment ['fɪgmənt] *n*: **a ~ of the imagination** une invention *or* création de l'imagination; **it's all a ~ of his imagination** il l'a purement et simplement inventé, il a inventé ça de toutes pièces.

figurative ['fɪgjʊrətɪv] *adj* (a) *language* figuré, métaphorique. **in the literal and in the ~ meaning** au (sens) propre et au (sens) figuré. (b) (*Art*) figuratif.

figure ['fɪgə^r] 1 *n* (a) chiffre *m*. **in round ~s** en chiffres ronds; **I can't give you the exact ~s** je ne peux pas vous donner les chiffres exacts; **he's good at ~s** il est doué pour le calcul; **there's a mistake in the ~s** il y a une erreur de calcul; **to get into double ~s** atteindre la dizaine; **to reach three ~s** atteindre la centaine; **a 3-~ number** un nombre *or* un numéro de 3 chiffres; **to sell sth for a high ~** vendre qch cher *or* à un prix élevé; **I got it for a low ~** je l'ai eu pour pas cher *or* pour peu de chose; **he earns well into** *or* **over five ~s** il gagne bien plus de dix mille livres.

(b) (*diagram, drawing*) (*Math*) figure *f*; *[animal, person etc]* figure, image *f*. **to draw a ~ on the blackboard** tracer une figure au tableau; **he drew the ~ of a bird** il a dessiné (l'image d')un oiseau; **draw a ~ of eight** dessinez un huit (*V also* **f**).

(c) (*of human form*) forme *f*, silhouette *f*. **I saw a ~ approach** j'ai vu une forme *or* une silhouette s'approcher de moi; **she has a good ~** elle est bien faite *or* bien tournée; **to keep one's ~** garder la ligne; **remember your ~!** pense à ta ligne!; **she's a fine ~ of a woman** c'est une belle femme; **he cut a poor ~** il faisait piètre figure.

(d) (*important person*) figure *f*, personnage *m*. **the great ~s of history** les grandes figures *or* les grands personnages de l'histoire; **a ~ of fun** un guignol; *V* **public**.

(e) (*Literat*) figure *f*. **~ of speech** figure de rhétorique; (*fig*) **it's just a ~ of speech** ce n'est qu'une façon de parler.

(f) (*Dancing, Skating*) figure *f*. **~ of eight** huit *m*.

2 *cpd*: **to be figure-conscious*** penser à sa ligne; **figurehead** (*lit, fig*) figure *f* de proue; (*pej: person*) prête-nom *m* (*pej*), homme *m* de paille (*pej*); **figure-skate** (*in competition*) faire les figures imposées (*en patinage*); (*in display etc*) faire du patinage artistique; **figure skating** figures imposées; patinage *m* artistique.

3 *vt* (a) (*represent*) représenter; (*illustrate by diagrams*) illustrer par un *or* des schéma(s), mettre sous forme de schéma.

(b) (*decorate*) orner; *silk etc* brocher, gaufrer. **~d velvet** velours façonné.

(c) (*Mus*) **~d bass** basse chiffrée.

(d) (*imagine*) penser, s'imaginer.

(e) (*US: guess*) penser, supposer. **I ~ it like this** je vois la chose comme ceci; **I ~ he'll come** je pense *or* suppose qu'il va venir.

4 *vi* (a) (*appear*) figurer. **he ~d in a play of mine** il a joué *or* tenu un rôle dans une de mes pièces; **his name doesn't ~ on this list** son nom ne figure pas sur cette liste.

(b) (*US**: *make sense*) **it doesn't ~** ça n'a pas de sens, ça ne s'explique pas; **that ~s** ça cadre, ça se tient, ça s'explique.

figure on *vt fus* (*US*) compter sur. **I figured on his coming** je comptais qu'il viendrait.

figure out *vt sep* arriver à comprendre, résoudre. **I can't figure that fellow out at all** je n'arrive pas du tout à comprendre ce type*; **I can't figure out how much money we need** je n'arrive pas à (bien) calculer la somme qu'il nous faut; **I can't figure it out** ça me dépasse*.

Fiji ['fi:dʒi:] *n* (*also* **~ Islands**) (îles *fpl*) Fi(d)ji *fpl*.

filament ['fɪləmənt] *n* filament *m*.

filariasis [,fɪlə'raɪəsɪs] *n* filariose *f*.

filbert ['fɪlbɜ:t] *n* aveline *f*.

filch [fɪltʃ] *vt* voler, chiper*.

file[1] [faɪl] 1 *n* (*for wood, fingernails etc*) lime *f*. **triangular ~** tiers-point *m*; *V* **nail**.

2 *vt* limer. **to ~ one's nails** se limer les ongles.

file away *vt sep* limer (*pour enlever*).

file down *vt sep* limer (*pour raccourcir*).

file[2] [faɪl] 1 *n* (*folder*) dossier *m*, chemise *f*; (*with hinges*) classeur *m*; (*for drawings: also in filing drawers*) carton *m*; (*for card index*) fichier *m*; (*cabinet*) classeur; (*papers*) dossier; (*Computers*) fichier *m*. **have we a ~ on her?** est-ce que nous avons un dossier sur elle?; **there's something in** *or* **on the file about him** le dossier contient des renseignements sur lui; **to put a document on the ~** joindre une pièce au dossier; (*fig*) **to close the ~ on a question** classer une affaire; (*Computers*) **data on ~** données fichées.

2 *cpd*: (*US*) **file clerk** documentaliste *mf*.

3 *vt* (a) (*also* **~ away**) *notes* classer; *letters* ranger, classer; (*into file*) joindre au dossier; (*on spike*) enfiler.

(b) (*Jur*) **to ~ a claim** déposer *or* faire enregistrer une requête *or* demande; **to ~ a claim for damages** intenter un procès en dommages-intérêts; **to ~ a petition** déposer *or* faire enregistrer une requête *or* demande; **to ~ a petition (in bankruptcy)** déposer son bilan; **to ~ a suit against sb** intenter un procès à qn.

file[3] [faɪl] 1 *n* file *f*. **in Indian ~** à la *or* en file indienne; **in single ~** en *or* à la file; *V* **rank**[1].

2 *vi* marcher en file. **to ~ in/out** *etc* entrer/sortir *etc* en file; **to ~ past** défiler; **the soldiers ~d past the general** les soldats ont défilé devant le général; **they ~d slowly past the ticket collector** ils sont passés lentement un à un devant le poinçonneur.

filial ['fɪlɪəl] *adj* filial.

filiation [,fɪlɪ'eɪʃən] *n* filiation *f*.

filibuster ['fɪlɪbʌstə^r] 1 *n* (*US Pol*) obstructionniste *mf*; (*pirate*) flibustier *m*. 2 *vi* (*US Pol*) faire de l'obstructionnisme.

filigree ['fɪlɪgri:] 1 *n* filigrane *m* (*en métal*). 2 *cpd* en filigrane.

filing ['faɪlɪŋ] 1 *n [documents]* classement *m*; *[claim etc]* enregistrement *m*. 2 *cpd*: **filing cabinet** classeur *m*; (*Brit*) **filing clerk** documentaliste *mf*.

filings [ˈfaɪlɪŋz] *npl* limaille *f*. **iron ~** limaille de fer.

fill [fɪl] 1 *vt* (a) *bottle, bucket* remplir (*with* de); *hole* remplir (*with* de), boucher (*with* avec); *teeth* plomber. **smoke ~ed the room** la pièce s'est remplie de fumée; **the wind ~ed the sails** le vent a gonflé les voiles; **they ~ed the air with their cries** l'air s'emplissait de leurs cris; **~ed with admiration** rempli *or* plein d'admiration; **~ed with anger** très en colère; **~ed with despair** en proie au désespoir, plongé dans le désespoir.

(b) *post, job* remplir. **to ~ a vacancy** *[employer]* pourvoir à un emploi; *[employee]* prendre un poste vacant; **the position is already ~ed** le poste est déjà pris; **he ~s the job well** il remplit bien ses fonctions; **he ~s all our requirements** il répond à tous nos besoins; **to ~ a need** répondre à un besoin; **to ~ a void** remplir *or* combler un vide; **that ~s the bill** cela fait l'affaire; (*Comm*) **to ~ an order** livrer une commande.

2 *vi* (*also* **~ up**) *[bath etc]* se remplir, s'emplir; *[hole]* se boucher. **her eyes ~ed with tears** ses yeux se sont remplis de larmes.

3 *n*: **to eat one's ~** manger à sa faim, se rassasier; **he had eaten his ~** il était rassasié; **to drink/have one's ~** boire/avoir tout son content; **I've had my ~ of listening to her!** j'en ai assez de l'écouter, j'en ai jusque-là* de l'écouter; **a ~ of tobacco** une pipe, de quoi bourrer sa pipe.

fill in 1 *vi*: **to fill in for sb** remplacer qn (temporairement).

2 *vt sep* (a) *form, questionnaire* remplir; *account, report* mettre au point, compléter. **would you fill in the details for us?** voudriez-vous nous donner les détails?; **to fill sb in on sth*** mettre qn au courant de qch.

(b) *hole* boucher. **we had that door filled in** nous avons fait murer *or* condamner cette porte; **to fill in gaps in one's knowledge** combler des lacunes dans ses connaissances; **draw the outline in black and fill it in in red** dessinez le contour en noir et remplissez-le en rouge.

fill out 1 *vi* (a) *[sails etc]* gonfler, s'enfler.

(b) (*become fatter*) *[person]* forcir, grossir. **her cheeks *or* her face had filled out** elle avait pris de bonnes joues.

2 *vt sep form, questionnaire* remplir.

fill up 1 *vi* (a) = **fill 2**.

(b) (*Aut*) faire le plein d'essence.

2 *vt sep* (a) *tank, cup* remplir. **to fill up to the brim** remplir jusqu'au bord *or* à ras bord; (*Aut*) **fill her up!*** (faites) le plein!

(b) *hole* boucher.

(c) *form, questionnaire* remplir.

filler [ˈfɪləʳ] *n* (a) (*utensil*) récipient *m* (de remplissage); *[bottle]* remplisseuse *f*; (*funnel*) entonnoir *m*. (b) (*U: for cracks in wood etc*) mastic *m*; (*Press*) article *m* bouche-trou.

fillet [ˈfɪlɪt] 1 *n* (a) (*Culin*) *[beef, pork, fish]* filet *m*. **veal ~** (*U*) longe *f* de veau; (*one piece*) escalope *f* de veau; **~ steak** (*U*) filet de bœuf, tournedos *m*; (*one piece*) bifteck *m* dans le filet, tournedos.

(b) (*for the hair*) serre-tête *m inv*.

2 *vt meat* désosser; *fish* découper en filets. **~ed sole** filets *mpl* de sole.

filling [ˈfɪlɪŋ] 1 *n* (a) (*in tooth*) plombage *m*. **my ~'s come out** mon plombage est parti *or* a sauté.

(b) (*in pie, tart, sandwich*) garniture *f*; (*for vegetables*) farce *f*. **chocolates with a coffee ~** chocolats fourrés au café.

2 *adj food* substantiel, bourratif*.

3 *cpd*: **filling station** poste *m* d'essence, station-service *f*.

fillip [ˈfɪlɪp] *n* (*with finger*) chiquenaude *f*, pichenette *f*; (*fig*) coup *m* de fouet (*fig*). **our advertisements gave a ~ to our business** notre publicité a donné un coup de fouet à nos affaires.

filly [ˈfɪlɪ] *n* pouliche *f*; (*†: *girl*) jeune fille *f*.

film [fɪlm] 1 *n* (a) (*Cine: motion picture*) film *m*. (*esp Brit*) **to go to the ~s** aller au cinéma; **the ~ is on at the Odeon just now** le film passe actuellement à l'Odéon; **he's in ~s** il travaille dans le cinéma; **he's been in many ~s** il a joué dans beaucoup de films; *V* **feature** *etc*.

(b) (*Phot*) (*U*) pellicule *f* (photographique); (*spool*) pellicule, film *m*; (*Cine*) (*U*) film *or* pellicule (cinématographique); (*spool*) film.

(c) (*thin layer*) (*of dust, mud*) couche *f*, pellicule *f*; (*of mist*) voile *m*.

2 *vt play* filmer; *scene* filmer, tourner.

3 *vi* (a) *[windscreen, glass]* (*also* **~ over**) se voiler, s'embuer.

(b) (*Cine*) **the story ~ed very well** l'histoire a bien rendu au cinéma *or* en film; **she ~s well** elle est photogénique.

4 *cpd*: (*Cine*) **film camera** caméra *f*; **film fan** cinéphile *mf*, amateur *mf* de cinéma; **film library** cinémathèque *f*; **film première** première *f*; **film rights** droits *mpl* d'adaptation (cinématographique); **film script** scénario *m*; **film sequence** séquence *f*; **film star** vedette *f* (de cinéma), star *f*; **filmstrip** film *m* (pour projection) fixe; **film studio** studio *m* (de cinéma); **film test** bout *m* d'essai; **to give sb a film test** faire tourner un bout d'essai à qn.

filmy [ˈfɪlmɪ] *adj clouds, material* léger, transparent, vaporeux; *glass* embué.

filter [ˈfɪltəʳ] 1 *n* (a) (*gen, also Phot*) filtre *m*; *V* **colour, oil** *etc*.

(b) (*Brit: in traffic lights*) flèche *f* (*permettant à une file de voitures de passer*).

2 *cpd*: **filter bed** bassin *m* de filtration; (*Aut*) **filter lane** ≈ file *f or* voie *f* de droite; (*Aut*) **filter light** flèche *f*; **filter paper** papier *m* filtre; (*cigarette, tip*) **filter tip** bout *m* filtre; **filter-tipped** à bout filtre.

3 *vt liquids* filtrer; *air* purifier, épurer.

4 *vi [light, liquid, sound]* filtrer. **the light ~ed through the shutters** la lumière filtrait à travers les volets; (*Aut*) **to ~ to the left** tourner à la flèche; *[people]* **to ~ back/in/out** revenir/entrer/sortir par petits groupes (espacés).

filter in *vi*: **the news of the massacre began to filter in** on a commencé petit à petit à avoir des renseignements sur le massacre.

filter out *vt sep impurities* éliminer par filtrage; (*fig*) éliminer.

filter through *vi [light]* filtrer. **the news filtered through at last** les nouvelles ont fini par se savoir.

filth [fɪlθ] *n* (*lit*) saleté *f*, crasse *f*; (*excrement*) ordure *f*; (*fig*) saleté, ordure (*liter*). (*fig*) **this book is sheer ~** ce livre est une vraie saleté; **the ~ shown on television** les saletés *or* les grossièretés *fpl* que l'on montre à la télévision.

filthy [ˈfɪlθɪ] *adj room, clothes, face, object* sale, crasseux, dégoûtant; *language* ordurier, obscène; (*) *weather etc* affreux, abominable. **~ talk** propos grossiers *or* orduriers; **it's a ~ habit** c'est une habitude dégoûtante *or* répugnante; **she's got a ~ mind** elle a l'esprit mal tourné; **he's ~ rich‡** il est pourri de fric*.

filtrate [ˈfɪltreɪt] *n* filtrat *m*.

filtration [fɪlˈtreɪʃən] *n* filtration *f*.

fin [fɪn] *n [fish, whale, seal]* nageoire *f*; *[shark]* aileron *m*; *[aircraft, spacecraft]* empennage *m*; *[ship]* dérive *f*; *[radiator etc]* ailette *f*. (*for swimmer's feet*) **~s** palmes *fpl*.

final [ˈfaɪnl] 1 *adj* (a) (*last*) dernier. **to put the ~ touches to a book** *etc* mettre la dernière main à un livre *etc*; (*in speech, lecture*) **one ~ point ...** enfin ..., un dernier point ...; (*Univ etc*) **~ examinations** examens *mpl* de dernière année; (*Fin*) **~ instalment** versement *m* libératoire; (*Comm*) **~ demand *or* notice** dernière demande (de règlement), dernier avertissement.

(b) (*conclusive*) *decision* définitif; *answer* définitif, décisif; *judgment* sans appel. **the umpire's decision is ~** la décision de l'arbitre est sans appel; **and that's ~!** un point c'est tout!

(c) (*Philos*) *cause* final.

2 *n* (a) (*Univ*) **the ~s** les examens *mpl* de dernière année.

(b) (*Sport*) finale *f*.

(c) (*Press*) **late night ~** dernière édition (du soir).

finale [fɪˈnɑːlɪ] *n* (*Mus, fig*) finale *m*. (*fig*) **the grand ~** l'apothéose *f*.

finalist [ˈfaɪnəlɪst] *n* (*Sport*) finaliste *mf*.

finality [faɪˈnælɪtɪ] *n [decision etc]* caractère définitif, irrévocabilité *f*. **with an air of ~** avec fermeté, avec décision.

finalization [ˌfaɪnəlaɪˈzeɪʃən] *n* (*V* **finalize**) rédaction définitive; dernière mise au point; confirmation définitive.

finalize [ˈfaɪnəlaɪz] *vt text, report* rédiger la version définitive de; *arrangements, plans* mettre au point les derniers détails de, parachever, mettre la dernière main à; *preparations* mettre la dernière main à; *decision* rendre définitif, confirmer de façon définitive; *date* fixer de façon définitive.

finally [ˈfaɪnəlɪ] *adv* (a) (*lastly*) enfin, en dernier lieu, pour terminer. **~ I would like to say ...** pour terminer je voudrais dire ... .

(b) (*eventually*) enfin, finalement. **they ~ decided to leave** ils se sont finalement décidés à partir, ils ont fini par décider de partir.

(c) (*once and for all*) définitivement.

finance [faɪˈnæns] 1 *n* (a) (*U*) finance *f*. **high ~** la haute finance; **Minister/Ministry of F~** ministre *m*/ministère *m* des Finances.

(b) **~s** finances *fpl*; **his ~s aren't sound** ses finances ne sont pas solides; **the country's ~s** la situation financière du pays; **he hasn't the ~s to do that** il n'a pas les finances *or* les fonds *mpl* pour cela.

2 *vt scheme etc* (*supply money for*) financer, commanditer; (*obtain money for*) trouver des fonds pour.

3 *cpd* (*Press*) *news, page* financier. **finance company, finance house** compagnie financière.

financial [faɪˈnænʃəl] *adj* financier. (*Brit*) **the ~ year** l'année *f* budgétaire.

financier [faɪˈnænsɪəʳ] *n* financier *m*.

finch [fɪntʃ] *n* fringillidé *m* (*pinson, bouvreuil, gros-bec etc*).

find [faɪnd] *pret, ptp* **found** 1 *vt* (a) (*gen sense*) trouver; *lost person or object* retrouver. **I never found my book** je n'ai jamais retrouvé mon livre; **your book is not to be found** on ne parvient pas à retrouver votre livre, votre livre reste introuvable; **to ~ one's place in a book** retrouver sa page dans un livre; **they soon found him again** ils l'ont vite retrouvé; **he found himself in Paris** il s'est retrouvé à Paris; (*fig*) **he found himself at last** il a enfin trouvé sa voie; **they couldn't ~ the way back** ils n'ont pas pu trouver le chemin du retour; **I'll ~ my way about all right by myself** je trouverai très bien mon chemin tout seul; **can you ~ your own way out?** pouvez-vous trouver la sortie tout seul?; **to ~ one's way into a building** trouver l'entrée d'un bâtiment; **it found its way into my handbag** ça s'est retrouvé *or* ça a atterri* dans mon sac; **it found its way into his essay** ça s'est glissé dans sa dissertation; **we left everything as we found it** nous avons tout laissé tel quel; **he was found dead in bed** on l'a trouvé mort dans son lit; **the castle is to be found near Tours** le château se trouve près de Tours; **this flower is found all over England** on trouve cette fleur *or* cette fleur se trouve partout en Angleterre.

(b) (*fig*) trouver (*that* que); *cure* découvrir; *solution* trouver, découvrir; *answer* trouver. **I can never ~ anything to say to him** je ne trouve jamais rien à lui dire; (*in health*) **how did you ~ him?** comment l'avez-vous trouvé?; **how did you ~ the steak?** comment avez-vous trouvé le bifteck?; **to ~ that** trouver que, s'apercevoir que, découvrir que, constater que; **you will ~ that I am right** vous trouverez *or* vous verrez *or* vous constaterez *or* vous vous apercevrez que j'ai raison; **it has been found that one person in ten does so** on a constaté qu'une personne sur dix le fait; to ~ **a house damp** trouver une maison humide; **I ~ her very pleasant** je la trouve très agréable; **I went there yesterday, only to ~ her out** j'y suis allé hier, pour constater qu'elle était sortie; **I found myself quite at sea among all those scientists** je me suis trouvé *or* senti complètement dépaysé *or* perdu au milieu de tous ces scientifiques; **he ~s it impossible to leave** il ne peut se résoudre à partir; **he ~s it impossible to walk** il lui est impossible de marcher; **to ~ the courage to do** trouver le courage de faire; **you won't ~ it easy** vous ne le trouverez pas facile; **to ~ some difficulty in doing** éprouver une certaine difficulté à faire; (*fig*) **to ~ one's feet** s'adapter, s'acclimater; **I couldn't ~ it in my heart to refuse** je n'ai pas eu le cœur de refuser; **I can't ~ time to read** je n'arrive pas à trouver le temps de lire; **to ~ fault with sth** trouver à redire à qch; **to ~ fault with sb** critiquer qn; **to ~ favour with sb** *[person]* s'attirer les bonnes grâces de qn; *[idea, suggestion, action]* recevoir l'approbation de qn.

(c) (*Jur*) **to ~ sb guilty** prononcer qn coupable; **how do you ~ the accused?** quel est votre verdict?; **to ~ a verdict of guilty** retourner un verdict de culpabilité; **the court found that ...** le tribunal a conclu que ... .

(d) (*supply*) fournir; (*obtain*) obtenir, trouver. **wages £50 all found** salaire 50 livres logé et nourri; (*US*) **wages 100 dollars and found** salaire 100 dollars logé et nourri; **you'll have to ~ yourself in clothes** vous aurez à fournir vos propres vêtements; **who will ~ the money for the journey?** qui va fournir l'argent pour le voyage?; **where will they ~ the money for the journey?** où est-ce qu'ils trouveront *or* obtiendront l'argent pour le voyage?; **I can't ~ the money to do it** je ne peux pas trouver l'argent nécessaire; **go and ~ me a needle** va me chercher une aiguille; **can you ~ me a pen?** peux-tu me trouver un stylo?; **there are no more to be found** il n'en reste plus.

2 *vi* (*Jur*) **to ~ for/against the accused** se prononcer en faveur de/contre l'accusé.

3 *n* trouvaille *f*, découverte *f*. **that was a lucky ~** nous avons (*or* vous avez *etc*) eu de la chance de trouver *or* de découvrir cela.

find out 1 *vi* **(a)** (*make enquiries*) se renseigner (*about* sur).

(b) (*discover*) **we didn't find out about it in time** nous ne l'avons pas su *or* appris à temps.

2 *vt sep* **(a)** (*discover*) *answer* découvrir (*that* que); trouver; *sb's secret, character* découvrir. **I found out what he was really like** j'ai découvert son vrai caractère; **your mother will find out if you ...** ta mère le saura si tu ... .

(b) (*discover the misdeeds etc of*) *person* démasquer. **he thought we wouldn't know, but we found him out** il pensait que nous ne saurions rien, mais nous l'avons démasqué *or* nous avons découvert le pot aux roses; **this affair has really found him out** il s'est bel et bien révélé tel qu'il est *or* sous son vrai jour dans cette affaire.

finder ['faɪndəʳ] *n* **(a)** (*of lost object*) celui *or* celle qui a trouvé (*or* qui trouvera *etc*); (*Jur*) inventeur *m*, -trice *f*. **~s keepers!** (celui) qui le trouve le garde! **(b)** *[telescope etc]* chercheur *m*; *V* **view**.

finding ['faɪndɪŋ] *n*: **~s** *[person, committee]* conclusions *fpl*, constatations *fpl*; *[scientist etc]* conclusions, résultats *mpl* (des recherches); (*Jur*) conclusions *fpl*, verdict *m*.

fine[1] [faɪn] **1** *n* amende *f*, contravention *f* (*esp Aut*). **I got a ~ for going through a red light** j'ai attrapé une contravention pour avoir brûlé un feu rouge.

2 *vt* (*V* 1) condamner à une amende, donner une contravention à. **he was ~d £10** il a eu une amende de 10 livres, il a eu 10 livres d'amende.

fine[2] [faɪn] **1** *adj* **(a)** (*not coarse*) *cloth, dust, needle, rain, rope* fin; *metal* pur; *workmanship, feelings* délicat; *distinction* subtil (*f* subtile); *taste* raffiné, délicat. **~ handwriting** écriture fine *or* délicate; **he has no ~r feelings** il n'a aucune noblesse de sentiments; (*fig*) **not to put too ~ a point on it ...** bref ...; **he's got it down to a ~ art** il le fait à la perfection; **~ art, the ~ arts** les beaux arts; *V* **print**.

(b) *weather* beau (*f* belle). **it's going to be ~ this afternoon** il va faire beau cet après-midi; **one ~ day** (*lit*) par une belle journée; (*fig*) un beau jour; (*fig*) **one of these ~ days** un de ces quatre matins, un de ces jours; **the weather is set ~** le temps est au beau (fixe); **I hope it keeps ~ for you!** je vous souhaite du beau temps!

(c) (*excellent*) beau (*f* belle). **~ clothes** de beaux vêtements; **meat of the finest quality** viande de première qualité; **you have a ~ future ahead of you** un bel avenir vous attend; **it's a ~ thing to help others** c'est beau d'aider autrui; (*iro*) **a ~ thing!*** c'est du beau! *or* du propre!*; (*iro*) **you're a ~ one!** tu en as de bonnes!*; (*iro*) **you're a ~ one to talk!** c'est bien à toi de le dire!; (*iro*) **that's a ~ excuse** en voilà une belle excuse; (*iro*) **a ~ friend you are!** c'est beau l'amitié!; **that's all very ~ but ...** tout cela (c')est bien beau *or* bien joli mais ...; **she likes to play at being the ~ lady** elle aime jouer les grandes dames; *V* **figure**.

2 *adv* **(a)** (très) bien. **you're doing ~!** ce que tu fais est très bien!, tu te débrouilles bien!*, ça va!; **I'm feeling ~ now** je me sens très bien maintenant; **that suits me ~** ça me convient très bien.

(b) finement, fin. **to cut/chop sth up ~** couper/hacher qch menu; (*fig*) **you've cut it a bit ~** vous avez calculé un peu juste; **he writes so ~ I can hardly read it** il écrit si fin *or* si petit que je peux à peine le lire.

3 *cpd*: **fine-drawn** *wire, thread* finement étiré; *features* délicat, fin; **fine-grained** au grain fin *or* menu; (*Phot*) à grain fin; **fine-spun** *yarn etc* très fin, ténu; (*fig*) *hair* très fin; **fine toothcomb** peigne fin; (*fig*) **he went through the document with a fine toothcomb** il a passé les documents au peigne fin *or* au crible.

fine down 1 *vi* (*get thinner*) s'affiner.

2 *vt sep* (*reduce*) réduire; (*simplify*) simplifier; (*refine*) raffiner.

finely ['faɪnlɪ] *adv* **(a)** (*splendidly*) admirablement, magnifiquement. **~ dressed** magnifiquement habillé.

(b) to chop up ~ hacher menu *or* fin; **the meat was ~ cut up** la viande était coupée en menus morceaux.

(c) (*subtly*) **the distinction was ~ drawn** la distinction était très subtile.

fineness ['faɪnnɪs] *n* **(a)** (*V* **fine**[2]) finesse *f*; pureté *f*; délicatesse *f*; subtilité *f*; raffinement *m*. **(b)** (*Metal*) titre *m*.

finery ['faɪnərɪ] *n* parure *f*. **she wore all her ~** elle s'était parée de ses plus beaux atours.

finesse [fɪ'nes] **1** *n* finesse *f*; (*Cards*) impasse *f*. **2** *vi* (*Cards*) **to ~ against the King** faire l'impasse au roi. **3** *vt* (*Cards*) **to ~ the Queen** faire l'impasse en jouant la dame.

finger ['fɪŋgəʳ] **1** *n* (*Anat*) doigt *m*; (*of cake etc*) petite part, petit rectangle. **first** *or* **index ~** index *m*; **little ~** auriculaire *m*, petit doigt; **middle ~** médius *m*, majeur *m*; **ring ~** annulaire *m*; **between ~ and thumb** entre le pouce et l'index; **to point one's ~ at sb** (*lit*) montrer qn du doigt; (*fig*) (*identify*) identifier qn; (*accuse*) accuser qn; (*fig*) **to point the ~ of scorn at sb** pointer un doigt accusateur vers qn; **to put one's ~ on the difficulty** mettre le doigt sur la difficulté; **there's something wrong, but I can't put my ~ on it** il y a quelque chose qui cloche* mais je ne peux pas mettre le doigt dessus; **to keep one's ~s crossed** dire une petite prière (*fig*) (*for sb* pour qn); **keep your ~s crossed!** dis une petite prière!, touchons du bois!; **his ~s are all thumbs** il est très maladroit de ses mains, il est adroit de ses mains comme un cochon de sa queue*; **she can twist** *or* **wind him round her little ~** elle fait de lui ce qu'elle veut, elle le mène par le bout du nez; **Robert has a ~ in the pie** (*gen*) il y a du Robert là-dessous, Robert y est pour quelque chose; (*financially*) Robert a des intérêts là-dedans *or* dans cette affaire; **he's got a ~ in every pie** il se mêle de tout, il est mêlé à tout; **he wouldn't lift a ~ to help me** il ne lèverait pas le petit doigt pour m'aider; **to pull one's ~ out‡** se décarcasser*, faire un effort; *V* **fish, green, lay**[1], **snap** *etc*.

2 *vt* **(a)** toucher *or* manier (des doigts), (*pej*) tripoter; *money* palper; *keyboard, keys* toucher.

(b) (*Mus: mark fingering on*) doigter, indiquer le doigté sur.

3 *cpd*: **finger alphabet** alphabet *m* des sourds-muets; (*Mus*) **finger board** touche *f* (*de guitare ou de violon etc*); **finger bowl** rince-doigts *m inv*; (*for piano etc*) **finger exercises** exercices *mpl* de doigté; **finger mark** trace *f* de doigt; **fingernail** ongle *m* (*de la main*); **finger painting** peinture *f* avec les doigts; (*on door*) **finger plate** plaque *f* de propreté; **fingerprint** (*n*) empreinte digitale; (*vt*) *car, weapon* relever les empreintes digitales sur; *person* prendre les empreintes digitales de; **fingerprint expert** expert *m* en dactyloscopie; **fingerstall** doigtier *m*; **fingertip** *V* **fingertip**.

fingering ['fɪŋgərɪŋ] *n* **(a)** (*Mus*) doigté *m*. **(b)** (*fine wool*) laine *f* (fine) à tricoter. **(c)** (*of goods in shop etc*) maniement *m*.

fingertip ['fɪŋgətɪp] *n* bout *m* du doigt. **he has the whole matter at his ~s** il connaît l'affaire sur le bout du doigt; **he's a Scot right to his ~s** il est écossais jusqu'au bout des ongles; (*fig*) **a machine with ~ control** une machine d'un maniement (très) léger.

finial ['faɪnɪəl] *n* fleuron *m*, épi *m* (de faîtage).

finicky ['fɪnɪkɪ] *adj person* pointilleux, tatillon; *work, job* minutieux, qui demande de la patience. **she is ~ about her food** elle est difficile pour *or* sur la nourriture.

finish ['fɪnɪʃ] **1** *n* **(a)** (*end*) fin *f*; (*Sport*) arrivée *f*; (*Hunting*) mise *f* à mort. (*fig*) **to be in at the ~** assister au dénouement (d'une affaire); **to fight to the ~** se battre jusqu'au bout; **from start to ~** du début jusqu'à la fin; *V* **photo**.

(b) *[woodwork, manufactured articles etc]* finition *f*. **it's a solid car but the ~ is not good** la voiture est solide mais les finitions sont mal faites; **a car with a two-tone ~** une voiture (peinte) en deux tons; **paint with a matt ~** peinture mate; **paint with a gloss ~** laque *f*; **table with an oak ~** (*stained*) table teintée chêne; (*veneered*) table plaquée *or* à placage chêne; **a table with rather a rough ~** une table à la surface plutôt rugueuse.

2 *vt* (*end*) *activity, work, letter, meal, game* finir, terminer, achever; (*use up*) *supplies, cake* finir, terminer. **~ your soup** finis *or* mange ta soupe; **to ~ doing sth** finir de faire qch; **I'm in a hurry to get this job ~ed** je suis pressé de finir *or* de terminer *or* d'achever ce travail; **to ~ a book** *[reader]* finir (de lire) un livre; *[author]* finir *or* terminer *or* achever un livre; **~ing school** institution *f* pour jeunes filles (de bonne famille); **to put the ~ing touch to sth** mettre la dernière main *or* la touche finale à qch; (*fig*) **that last mile nearly ~ed me*** ces derniers quinze cents mètres ont failli être ma mort *or* m'ont mis à plat*; *V also* **finished**.

3 *vi* **(a)** *[book, film, game, meeting]* finir, s'achever, se terminer; *[holiday, contract]* prendre fin. **the meeting was ~ing** la réunion tirait à sa fin; **he ~ed by saying that ...** il a terminé en disant que ...; (*Sport*) **to ~ first** arriver *or* terminer premier; (*Sport*) **~ing line** ligne *f* d'arrivée.

(b) I've ~ed with the paper je n'ai plus besoin du journal; **I've ~ed with politics once and for all** j'en ai fini avec la politique, j'ai dit une fois pour toutes adieu à la politique; **she's ~ed with him** elle a rompu avec lui; **you wait till I've ~ed with you!*** attends un peu que je t'aie réglé ton compte!*

finish off 1 *vi* terminer, finir. **let's finish off now** maintenant finissons-en; **to finish off with a glass of brandy** terminer (le repas) par *or* sur un verre de cognac; **the meeting finished off with a prayer** la réunion a pris fin sur une prière, à la fin de la réunion on a récité une prière.

2 *vt sep* **(a)** *work* terminer, mettre la dernière main à.
(b) *food, meal* terminer, finir. **finish off your potatoes!** finis *or* mange tes pommes de terre!
(c) (*fig: kill*) *person, wounded animal* achever. **his illness last year almost finished him off** sa maladie de l'année dernière a failli l'achever.
finish up 1 *vi* **(a)** = **finish off 1.**
(b) se retrouver. **he finished up in Rome** il s'est retrouvé à Rome, il a fini par arriver à Rome.
2 *vt sep* = **finish off 2b.**
finished ['fɪnɪʃt] *adj* **(a)** *woodwork* poli; *performance* accompli; *appearance* soigné. **the ~ product** le produit fini.
(b) (*done for*) fichu*. **as a politician he's ~** sa carrière politique est finie; **if that gets around you're ~** si ça se sait tu es fichu* *or* fini.
(c) (*: *tired*) à plat*, crevé*.
finite ['faɪnaɪt] *adj* **(a)** fini, limité. **a ~ number** un nombre fini.
(b) (*Gram*) *mood, verb* fini.
Finland ['fɪnlənd] *n* Finlande *f*.
Finn [fɪn] *n* (*Finnish speaker*) Finnois(e) *m(f)*; (*inhabitant or native of Finland*) Finlandais(e) *m(f)*.
Finnish ['fɪnɪʃ] 1 *adj* (*of Finnish speakers*) finnois; (*of Finland*) finlandais. 2 *n* (*Ling*) finnois *m*.
fiord [fjɔːd] *n* fjord *m or* fiord *m*.
fir [fɜːʳ] *n* (*also* **~ tree**) sapin *m*. **~ cone** pomme *f* de pin.
fire [faɪəʳ] 1 *n* **(a)** (*gen*) feu *m*; (*house-~ etc*) incendie *m*. **the house was on ~** la maison était en feu *or* en flammes; **the chimney was on ~** il y avait un feu de cheminée; (*fig*) **he's playing with ~** il joue avec le feu; **forest ~** incendie de forêt; **to insure o.s. against ~** s'assurer contre l'incendie; (*fig*) **~ and brimstone** les tourments *mpl* de l'enfer; **by ~ and sword** par le fer et par le feu; (*fig*) **he would go through ~ and water for her** il se jetterait au feu pour elle; **to set ~ to sth, set sth on ~** mettre le feu à qch; **to lay/light/make up the ~** préparer/allumer/faire le feu; **come and sit by the ~** venez vous installer près du feu *or* au coin du feu; **they were sitting in front of a roaring ~** ils étaient assis devant une belle flambée; *V* **catch, electric, Thames** *etc*.
(b) (*Mil*) feu *m*. **to open ~** ouvrir le feu, faire feu; **~!** feu!; (*also fig*) **between two ~s** entre deux feux; (*also fig*) **running ~** feu roulant; **to come under ~** (*Mil*) essuyer le feu (de l'ennemi); (*fig: be criticized*) être (vivement) critiqué; *V* **cease, hang, line**[1].
(c) (*U: passion*) ardeur *f*, fougue *f*, feu *m*. **to speak with ~** parler avec feu *or* avec ardeur *or* avec fougue.
2 *cpd*: **fire alarm** avertisseur *m* d'incendie; **firearm** arme *f* à feu; **fireball** (*meteor*) bolide *m*; (*lightning, nuclear*) boule *f* de feu; (*Mil*) bombe explosive; (*fig*) **he's a real fireball** *or* **firebrand** il a un dynamisme à tout casser*; **firebrand** brandon *m*, tison *m*; (*mischief-maker*) fauteur *m*, -trice *f* de troubles; **firebreak** pare-feu *m inv*, coupe-feu *m inv*; **firebrick** brique *f* réfractaire; **fire brigade** (régiment *m* de sapeurs-)pompiers *mpl*; (*US*) **firebug** incendiaire *mf*, pyromane *mf*; (*US*) **fire chief** capitaine *m* de pompiers; (*Brit*) **fire clay** argile *f* réfractaire; (*US*) **firecracker** pétard *m*; (*Theat*) **fire curtain** rideau *m* de fer; (*Min*) **firedamp** grisou *m*; (*US*) **fire department** = **fire brigade**; **firedogs** chenets *mpl*; **fire door** porte *f* anti-incendie *or* coupe-feu; **fire drill** exercice *m* anti-incendie; répétition *f* des consignes d'incendie; **fire-eater** (*lit*) avaleur *m* de feu; (*fig*) belliqueux *m*, -euse *f*; **fire engine** pompe *f* à incendie; **fire escape** (*staircase*) escalier *m* de secours; (*ladder*) échelle *f* d'incendie; **fire exit** sortie *f* de secours; **fire extinguisher** extincteur *m* (d'incendie); **fire fighter** (*fireman*) pompier *m*; (*volunteer*) volontaire *mf* dans la lutte contre l'incendie; **firefly** luciole *f*; **fireguard** garde-feu *m inv*, pare-étincelles *m inv*; **it's a fire hazard** ça constitue un danger d'incendie; (*US*) **firehouse** = **fire station**; **fire hydrant** bouche *f* d'incendie; **fire insurance** assurance-incendie *f*; **fire irons** garniture *f* de foyer; **firelight** lueur *f* du feu; **by firelight** à la lueur du feu; **firelighter** allume-feu *m inv*; **fireman** (*in fire brigade*) pompier *m*, sapeur-pompier *m*; (*Rail*) chauffeur *m*; **fireplace** cheminée *f*, foyer *m*; (*US*) **fireplug** = **fire hydrant**; (*Mil*) **fire power** puissance *f* de feu; **fire prevention** mesures *fpl* de sécurité contre l'incendie; **fireproof** (*vt*) ignifuger; (*adj*) ignifuge; **fireproof door** porte ignifugée *or* à revêtement ignifuge; (*Culin*) **fireproof dish** plat *m* à feu *or* allant au feu; (*Brit*) **fire-raiser** incendiaire *mf*, pyromane *mf*; (*Brit*) **fire-raising** pyromanie *f*; **fire regulations** consignes *fpl* en cas d'incendie; **fire risk** = **fire hazard**; **fire screen** = **fireguard**; **fireside** foyer *m*, coin *m* du feu; **fireside chair** fauteuil *m* club; (*without arms*) chauffeuse *f*; **fire station** caserne *f* de pompiers; (*US*) **fire warden** responsable *mf* de la lutte anti-incendie; **firewood** bois *m* de chauffage, bois à brûler; **firework** feu *m* d'artifice; **fireworks (display)** feu *m* d'artifice (*U*).
3 *vt* **(a)** (*set ~ to*) incendier, mettre le feu à; (*fig*) *imagination, passions, enthusiasm* enflammer, échauffer, exciter; *pottery* cuire; *furnace* chauffer; *V* **gas, oil** *etc*.
(b) *gun* décharger, tirer; *rocket* tirer; (*: *throw*) balancer*. **to ~ a gun at sb** tirer (un coup de fusil) sur qn; **to ~ a shot** tirer un coup de feu (*at* sur); **without firing a shot** sans tirer un coup (de feu); **to ~ a salute** *or* **a salvo** lancer *or* tirer une salve; **to ~ a salute of 21 guns** saluer de 21 coups de canon; (*fig*) **to ~ (off) questions at sb** bombarder qn de questions; **'your name?' he suddenly ~d at me** 'votre nom?' me demanda-t-il à brûle-pourpoint; **~ me over that book*** balance-moi ce bouquin*.
(c) (*: *dismiss*) renvoyer, flanquer à la porte*, vider*, licencier (*Ind*). **you're ~d!** vous êtes renvoyé! *or* vidé!*
4 *vi* (*shoot*) tirer, faire feu (*at* sur). **~ ahead!, ~ away!*** vas-y, raconte!, tu peux y aller!
fire off *vt sep V* **fire 3b.**
firing ['faɪrɪŋ] 1 *n* **(a)** [*pottery*] cuite *f*, cuisson *f*. **(b)** (*Mil*) feu *m*, tir *m*. 2 *cpd*: **firing line** ligne *f* de tir; **firing squad** peloton *m* d'exécution.
firm[1] [fɜːm] *n* (*Comm*) compagnie *f*, firme *f*, maison *f* (de commerce). (*Brit Med*) **there are 4 doctors in the ~*** 4 médecins se partagent le cabinet.
firm[2] [fɜːm] *adj* **(a)** *table, rock, tomato* ferme; **on ~ ground** (*lit*) sur le sol ferme, sur la terre ferme, (*fig*) sur une base solide; (*fig*) **I'm on ~ ground** je suis sur mon terrain; **he's as ~ as a rock** il est ferme comme le *or* un roc.
(b) (*unshakeable, stable*) *faith, friendship* constant, solide; *character* résolu, déterminé; *intention, purpose* ferme, résolu; *step, voice* ferme, assuré; *look* résolu; (*Comm, Fin*) *market* ferme. **you must be ~ with your children** il vous faut être ferme avec vos enfants; **I have a ~ belief in telling the truth** je crois fermement qu'il faut dire la vérité; (*fig*) **to stand ~** tenir bon, tenir ferme.
(c) (*definite*) *date* ferme, sûr; *sale, offer* ferme.
firmament ['fɜːməmənt] *n* firmament *m*.
firmly ['fɜːmlɪ] *adv close, screw* fermement; *speak* d'une voix ferme, d'un ton ferme, avec fermeté. **I ~ believe he's right** je crois fermement *or* je suis convaincu qu'il a raison.
firmness ['fɜːmnɪs] *n* (*V* **firm**[2]) fermeté *f*; solidité *f*; résolution *f*; détermination *f*; assurance *f*.
first [fɜːst] 1 *adj* premier. **the ~ of May** le premier mai; **the twenty-~ time** la vingt et unième fois; **Charles the F~** Charles Premier, Charles Ier; **in the ~ place** en premier lieu, d'abord; **~ principles** principes premiers; **he did it the very ~ time** il l'a fait du premier coup; **it's not the ~ time and it won't be the last** ce n'est pas la première fois et ce ne sera pas la dernière; **they won for the ~ and last time in 1932** ils ont gagné une seule et unique fois en 1932 *or* pour la première et dernière fois en 1932; **he goes out ~ thing in the morning** il sort dès le matin; **I'll do it ~ thing in the morning** *or* **~ thing tomorrow** je le ferai dès demain matin, je le ferai demain à la première heure; **take the pills ~ thing in the morning** prenez les pilules dès le réveil; **~ things first!** les choses importantes d'abord! (*hum*); **she's past her ~ youth** elle n'est plus de la première *or* prime jeunesse; (*fig*) **of the ~ water** de tout premier ordre; *V also* **4** *and* **lord, love, sight** *etc*.
2 *adv* **(a)** (*in time*) d'abord, premièrement. **~ you take off the string, then you ...** d'abord on enlève la ficelle, ensuite on ..., premièrement on enlève la ficelle, deuxièmement on ...; **~ of all** tout d'abord, pour commencer; **~ and foremost** tout d'abord, en tout premier lieu; **~ come ~ served** les premiers arrivés seront les premiers servis; **you go ~!** vas-y d'abord!; **ladies ~!** les dames d'abord!, place aux dames!; **women and children ~** les femmes et les enfants d'abord; **he came ~ in the exam** il a été reçu premier à l'examen *or* au concours; **he says ~ one thing and then another** il se contredit sans cesse, il dit tantôt ceci, tantôt cela; **she looked at ~ one thing then another** elle regardait tantôt ceci tantôt cela, elle a regardé plusieurs choses l'une après l'autre; **~ you agree, then you change your mind!** d'abord *or* pour commencer tu acceptes, et ensuite tu changes d'avis!; **~ and last** avant tout; **I must finish this ~** il faut que je termine (*subj*) ceci d'abord.
(b) (*for the first time*) pour la première fois. **when did you ~ meet him?** quand est-ce que vous l'avez rencontré pour la première fois?
(c) (*in preference*) plutôt. **I'd die ~!** plutôt mourir!; **I'd give up my job ~, rather than do that** j'aimerais mieux renoncer à mon travail que de faire cela.
3 *n* **(a)** premier *m*, -ière *f*. **he was among the very ~ to arrive** il est arrivé parmi les tout premiers; **they were the ~ to come** ils sont arrivés les premiers; **he was among the ~ to meet her** il a été l'un des premiers à la rencontrer, il a été l'un des premiers qui l'ont *or* l'aient rencontrée.
(b) (*U*) commencement *m*, début *m*. **at ~** d'abord, au commencement, au début; **from ~ to last** du début *or* depuis le début (jusqu')à la fin; **they liked him from the ~** ils l'ont aimé dès le début *or* dès le premier jour *or* d'emblée.
(c) (*Aut: also* **~ gear**) première *f* (vitesse). **in ~** en première.
(d) (*Brit Univ*) **he got a ~** ≈ il a eu sa licence avec mention très bien.
4 *cpd*: **first aid** *V* **first aid**; (*Baseball*) **first base** première base; (*US fig*) **he didn't even get to first base*** il n'a même pas franchi le premier obstacle (*fig*); **these ideas didn't even get to first base** ces idées n'ont jamais rien donné; **first-born** (*adj, n*) premier-né (*m*), première-née (*f*); **first-class** *V* **first-class**; **first cousin** cousin(e) *m(f)* germain(e) *or* au premier degré; (*Post*) **first-day cover** émission *f* du premier jour; **first edition** première édition, (*valuable*) édition originale *or* princeps; **on the first floor** (*Brit*) au premier (étage); (*US*) au rez-de-chaussée; (*Scol*) **first form** ≈ sixième *f*; **he's a first-generation American** il n'est américain que depuis une génération; **first-hand** *article, news, information* de première main; **I got it at first-hand** je l'ai appris de première main; **first lady** première dame; (*Naut*) **first lieutenant** lieutenant *m* de vaisseau; (*Naut*) **first mate** second *m*; **first name** prénom *m*, nom *m* de baptême; **my first name is Ellis** je m'appelle Ellis de mon prénom *or* de mon petit nom, mon prénom est Ellis; **to be on first-name terms with sb** appeler qn par son prénom; (*frm*) **the first-named** le premier, la première; (*Theat etc*) **first night** première *f*; (*Theat etc*) **first-nighter** habitué(e) *m(f)* des premières; (*Jur*) **first offender** délinquant *m* primaire; (*Naut*) **first officer** = **first mate**; **first performance** (*Cine, Theat*) première *f*; (*Mus*) première audition; (*Gram*) **first person** première personne; **first-rate** *V* **first-rate**; **first violin** premier violon.
first aid ['fɜːst'eɪd] 1 *n* premiers secours *or* soins, secours d'urgence. **to give ~** donner les soins *or* secours d'urgence.
2 *cpd*: **first-aid box** = **first-aid kit**; **first-aid classes** cours *mpl*

de secourisme *m*; **first-aid kit** trousse *f* de premiers secours *or* à pharmacie; **first-aid post, first-aid station** poste *m* de secours.

first-class [ˌfɜːstˈklɑːs] *adj* **(a)** (*Aviat, Naut, Rail etc*) *seat, ticket* de première (classe); *hotel* de première catégorie. ~ **mail** *or* **post** courrier (tarif) normal (*rapide*); ~ **ticket** billet *m* de première (classe); **to travel** ~ voyager en première (classe).
(b) = **first-rate.**
(c) (*Univ*) ~ **honours (degree)** ≈ (licence *f* avec) mention *f* très bien.

firstly [ˈfɜːstlɪ] *adv* premièrement, en premier lieu, primo.

first-rate [ˈfɜːstˈreɪt] *adj* excellent, de première classe, de premier ordre, extra*. ~ **vegetables** légumes *mpl* de première qualité; ~ **wine** vin *m* de haute qualité; ~ **idea** excellente idée; **there is some** ~ **photography in that film** il y a des prises de vues excellentes *or* exceptionnelles dans ce film; **he is** ~ il est de première force, il est formidable*; **he is a** ~ **engineer** c'est un ingénieur de premier ordre; **he's** ~ **at his job/at tennis** il est de premier ordre *or* de première force *or* de première* dans son travail/au tennis; (*iro*) **that's** ~**!** c'est absolument parfait! (*iro*); ~! de première!*

firth [fɜːθ] *n* (*gen Scot*) estuaire *m*, bras *m* de mer.

fiscal [ˈfɪskəl] **1** *adj* fiscal. ~ **year** année *f* budgétaire; *V* **procurator. 2** *n* (*Scot Jur*) ≈ procureur *m* de la République.

fish [fɪʃ] **1** *n, pl* ~ *or* ~**es (a)** poisson *m*. **I caught 2** ~ j'ai pris 2 poissons; (*fig*) **I've got other** ~ **to fry** j'ai d'autres chats à fouetter; (*loc*) **there's as good** ~ **in the sea as ever came out of it** un(e) de perdu(e) dix de retrouvé(e)s; (*fig*) **it's neither** ~ **nor fowl** (*or* **nor flesh**) **nor good red herring** ce n'est ni chair ni poisson; **he's like a** ~ **out of water** il est complètement dépaysé, il est comme un poisson hors de l'eau; **he's a queer** ~**!*** c'est un drôle de numéro* *or* de lascar* (celui-là)!; **poor** ~**!*** pauvre type!*; (*Astron*) **the F**~**es** les Poissons; *V* **drink, gold, kettle.**
(b) (*U: Culin*) poisson *m*. (*esp Brit*) ~ **and chips** du poisson frit avec des frites.
2 *cpd*: **fish-and-chip shop** débit *m* de fritures; **fishbone** arête *f* (de poisson); **fishbowl** bocal *m* (à poissons); (*Culin*) **fish cake** croquette *f* de poisson; (*Phot*) **fish-eye lens** objectif *m* à (champ de) 180°; **fish farm** centre *m* de pisciculture, centre d'élevage de poissons; **fish farming** alevinage *m*, pisciculture *f*, élevage *m* de poissons; (*Brit*) **fish fingers** bâtonnets *mpl* de poisson; **fish glue** colle *f* de poisson; **fish hook** hameçon *m*; (*Culin*) **fish kettle** poissonnière *f*; **fish knife** couteau *m* à poisson; **fish knife and fork** couvert *m* à poisson; **fish ladder** barrages *mpl* à saumons; **fish manure** engrais *m* de poisson; **fish market** marché *m* au poisson; **fish meal** guano *m* de poisson; **fishmonger** marchand(e) *m(f)* de poisson, poissonnier *m*, -ière *f*; **fish net** (*on fishing boat*) filet *m* (de pêche); *[angler]* épuisette *f*; **fishnet tights** collant *m* en résille; (*Culin*) **fish paste** pâte *f* d'anchois (*or* de homard *or* d'écrevisse *etc*); (*Rail*) **fishplate** éclisse *f*; (*US*) **fish-pole** canne *f* à pêche; **fishpond** étang *m* à poissons, vivier *m*; **fish shop** poissonnerie *f*; (*Brit Culin*) **fish slice** pelle *f* à poisson; (*US*) **fish sticks** = **fish fingers**; (*US*) **fish store** = **fish shop**; **fish tank** aquarium *m*; **fishwife** marchande *f* de poisson, poissonnière *f*; (*pej*) harengère *f*, poissarde *f*; (*pej*) **she gossips like a fishwife** elle est bavarde comme une pipelette* *or* une concierge; (*pej*) **she talks like a fishwife** elle a un langage de poissarde *or* de charretier.
3 *vi* pêcher. **to go** ~**ing** aller à la pêche; **to go salmon** ~**ing** aller à la pêche au saumon; **to** ~ **for trout** pêcher la truite; (*fig*) **to** ~ **in troubled waters** pêcher en eau trouble (*fig*); **to** ~ **(for compliments)** chercher les compliments; **to** ~ **for information from sb** tâcher de tirer des renseignements de qn.
4 *vt trout, salmon* pêcher; *river, pool* pêcher dans; (*fig: find*) pêcher*. **they** ~**ed a cat out of the well** ils ont repêché un chat du puits; **he** ~**ed a handkerchief out of his pocket** il a extirpé un mouchoir de sa poche; **where on earth did you** ~ **that (up) from?*** où diable as-tu été pêcher ça?*

fish out *vt sep* (*from water*) sortir, repêcher; (*from box, drawer etc*) sortir, extirper (*from* de). **he fished out a piece of string from his pocket** il a extirpé un bout de ficelle de sa poche; **to fish sb out of a river** repêcher qn d'une rivière; *V also* **fish 4.**

fish up *vt sep* (*from water*) pêcher, repêcher; (*from bag etc*) sortir; *V also* **fish 4.**

fisherman [ˈfɪʃəmən] *n* pêcheur *m*. **he's a keen** ~ il aime beaucoup la pêche.

fishery [ˈfɪʃərɪ] *n* pêcherie *f*, pêche *f*.

fishing [ˈfɪʃɪŋ] **1** *n* pêche *f*. **'~ prohibited'** 'pêche interdite', 'défense de pêcher'; **'~ private'** 'pêche réservée'.
2 *cpd*: **fishing boat** barque *f* de pêche; **fishing fleet** flottille *f* de pêche; **fishing grounds** pêches *fpl*, lieux *mpl* de pêche; **fishing harbour** port *m* de pêche; **fishing line** ligne *f* de pêche; **fishing net** (*on fishing boat*) filet *m* (de pêche); *[angler]* épuisette *f*; **fishing port** port *m* de pêche; **fishing rod** canne *f* à pêche; **fishing tackle** attirail *m* de pêche.

fishy [ˈfɪʃɪ] *adj* **(a)** *smell* de poisson. **it smells** ~ **in here** ça sent le poisson ici. **(b)** (*) suspect, douteux, louche. **the whole business seems very** ~ **to me** toute cette histoire m'a l'air bien louche; **it seems rather** ~ ça ne me paraît pas très catholique*.

fissile [ˈfɪsaɪl] *adj* fissile.

fission [ˈfɪʃən] *n* fission *f*; *V* **nuclear.**

fissionable [ˈfɪʃnəbl] *adj* fissible.

fissure [ˈfɪʃəʳ] *n* fissure *f*, fente *f*, crevasse *f*.

fissured [ˈfɪʃəd] *adj* fissuré.

fist [fɪst] *n* **(a)** poing *m*. **he hit me with his** ~ il m'a donné un coup de poing; **he shook his** ~ **at me** il m'a menacé du poing. **(b)** (*: *handwriting*) écriture *f*.

-fisted [ˈfɪstɪd] *adj ending in cpds* aux poings ...; *V* **ham, tight** *etc*.

fistful [ˈfɪstfʊl] *n* poignée *f*.

fisticuffs [ˈfɪstɪkʌfs] *npl* coups *mpl* de poing.

fistula [ˈfɪstjʊlə] *n* fistule *f*.

fit[1] [fɪt] **1** *adj* **(a)** (*suitable, suited*) *person* capable (*for* de); *time, occasion* propice; (*worthy*) digne (*for* de); (*right and proper*) convenable, correct. ~ **to eat** (*palatable*) mangeable; (*not poisonous*) comestible, bon à manger; **a meal** ~ **for a king** un repas digne d'un roi, un festin de roi; (*qualified etc*) **to be** ~ **for a job** avoir la compétence nécessaire pour faire un travail; **he isn't** ~ **to rule the country** il n'est pas capable *or* digne de gouverner; (*after illness*) ~ **for duty** en état de reprendre le travail; (*Mil*) en état de reprendre le service; **he's not** ~ **to drive** il n'est pas capable de *or* pas en état de conduire; **I'm not** ~ **to be seen** je ne suis pas présentable; **that shirt isn't** ~ **to wear** cette chemise n'est pas mettable; **the house is** ~ **for habitation** cette maison est habitable; (*frm*) **it is not** ~ **that you should be here** il est inconvenant que vous soyez ici (*frm*); **it is not a** ~ **moment to ask that question** ce n'est pas le moment de poser cette question; **to see** *or* **think** ~ **to do** trouver convenable *or* bon de faire; **I'll do as I think** ~ je ferai comme bon me semblera; **he's not** ~ **company for my son** ce n'est pas une compagnie pour mon fils.
(b) (*in health*) en bonne santé, en pleine forme. **he is not a** ~ **man** il n'est pas en bonne santé; **she is not yet** ~ **to travel** elle n'est pas encore en état de voyager; **to be as** ~ **as a fiddle** être en pleine forme, se porter comme un charme*; *V* **keep.**
(c) (*: *ready*) **to laugh** ~ **to burst** rigoler* comme un fou (*f* une folle) *or* un(e) bossu(e)*, se tenir les côtes; **she was crying** ~ **to break one's heart** elle sanglotait à (vous) fendre le cœur; **she goes on until she's** ~ **to drop** elle continue jusqu'à tomber *or* jusqu'à ce qu'elle tombe (*subj*) de fatigue.
2 *n*: **your dress is a very good** ~ votre robe est tout à fait à votre taille; **it's rather a tight** ~ c'est un peu juste.
3 *vt* **(a)** *[clothes etc]* aller à. **this coat** ~**s you (well)** ce manteau vous va bien *or* est bien à votre taille; **the key doesn't** ~ **the lock** la clef ne va pas pour *or* ne correspond pas à la serrure; **these shoes** ~ **very badly** ces souliers chaussent très mal; **it** ~**s like a glove** cela me (*or* vous *etc*) va comme un gant; *V* **cap.**
(b) (*correspond to, match*) *description* répondre à. **his account doesn't** ~ **the facts** son explication ne colle pas *or* ne concorde pas avec les faits; **the punishment should** ~ **the crime** la punition doit être proportionnée à l'offense; **the curtains won't** ~ **the colour scheme** les rideaux n'iront pas avec les couleurs de la pièce, la couleur des rideaux va jurer avec le reste.
(c) adapter, ajuster. **her sister** ~**ted the dress on her** sa sœur a ajusté la robe sur elle; **to** ~ **a key in the lock** engager une clef dans la serrure; **to** ~ **a handle on a broom** emmancher un balai; **to** ~ **2 things together** ajuster 2 objets; **I'm having a new window** ~**ted** je suis en train de faire poser une nouvelle fenêtre; **car** ~**ted with a radio** voiture équipée d'une radio; **he has been** ~**ted with a new hearing aid** on lui a mis *or* posé un nouvel appareil auditif.
(d) to ~ **sb for sth/to do** préparer qn *or* rendre qn apte à qch/à faire; **to** ~ **o.s. for a job** se préparer à un travail.
4 *vi* **(a)** *[clothes]* aller. **the dress doesn't** ~ **very well** la robe n'est pas très bien ajustée.
(b) *[key, machine, part]* entrer, aller. **this key doesn't** ~ cette clef n'entre pas, ce n'est pas la bonne clef; **the saucepan lid doesn't** ~ **any more** le couvercle ne va plus sur la casserole; **that lid won't** ~ **on this saucepan** ce couvercle ne va pas avec cette casserole.
(c) *[facts etc]* s'accorder, cadrer. **if the description** ~**s, he must be the thief** si la description est la bonne, ce doit être lui le voleur; **it all** ~**s now!** tout s'éclaire!; **it doesn't** ~ **with what he said to me** ceci ne correspond pas à *or* ne s'accorde pas avec *or* ne cadre pas avec ce qu'il m'a dit.

fit in 1 *vi* **(a)** *[fact]* s'accorder (*with* avec). **this doesn't fit in with what I myself learnt** ceci ne correspond pas à *or* ne s'accorde pas avec *or* ne cadre pas avec ce que j'ai appris de mon côté.
(b) *[remark]* être en harmonie (*with* avec). **he left the firm because he didn't fit in** il a quitté la compagnie parce qu'il n'arrivait pas à s'intégrer; **he doesn't fit in with our group** il n'est pas au diapason de notre groupe.
(c) entrer. **this dictionary won't fit in on the shelf** ce dictionnaire n'entre pas sur le rayon.
2 *vt sep* **(a)** faire entrer. **can you fit another book in?** pouvez-vous faire entrer encore un livre?
(b) adapter, faire concorder. **I'll try to fit my plans in with yours** je tâcherai de faire concorder mes projets avec les tiens.
(c) prendre, caser*. **the doctor can fit you in tomorrow at 3** le docteur peut vous prendre *or* vous caser* demain à 15 heures.

fit on 1 *vi*: **this bottle top won't fit on any more** cette capsule ne ferme plus.
2 *vt sep* attacher, fixer, poser.

fit out *vt sep expedition, person* équiper; *ship* armer.

fit up *vt sep* pourvoir (*with* de). **they have fitted their house up with all modern conveniences** ils ont pourvu leur maison de tout le confort moderne.

fit[2] [fɪt] *n* **(a)** (*Med*) accès *m*, attaque *f*. ~ **of coughing** quinte *f* de toux; **to have** *or* **throw*** **a** ~ avoir *or* piquer* une crise; **to fall down in a** ~ tomber en convulsions; (*fig*) **she'll have a** ~ **when we tell her*** elle aura une attaque *or* elle piquera une crise quand on lui dira ça*; *V* **blue, epileptic, faint.**
(b) (*outburst*) mouvement *m*, accès *m*. **in a** ~ **of anger** dans un mouvement *or* accès de colère; ~ **of crying** crise *f* de larmes; **to be in** ~**s (of laughter), to get a** ~ **of the giggles** avoir le fou rire; **he has** ~**s of enthusiasm** il a des accès d'enthousiasme; **in** ~**s and starts** par à-coups.

fitful [ˈfɪtfʊl] *adj showers* intermittent; *wind* capricieux,

changeant; *sleep* troublé, agité. ~ **enthusiasm/anger** des accès *mpl* d'enthousiasme/de colère.
fitfully [ˈfɪtfəlɪ] *adv move, work* par à-coups; *sleep* de façon intermittente.
fitment [ˈfɪtmənt] *n* **(a)** (*Brit: built-in furniture*) meuble encastré; (*cupboard*) placard encastré; (*in kitchen*) élément *m* (de cuisine). **you can't move the table, it's a** ~ on ne peut pas déplacer la table, elle est encastrée.
(b) (*for vacuum cleaner, mixer etc*) accessoire *m*. **it's part of the light** ~ cela fait partie de l'appareil d'éclairage.
fitness [ˈfɪtnɪs] *n* **(a)** (*health*) santé *f or* forme *f* (physique). **(b)** (*suitability*) *[remark]* à-propos *m*, justesse *f*; *[person]* aptitudes *fpl* (*for* pour).
fitted [ˈfɪtɪd] *adj garment* ajusté. **to be** ~ **for sth/to do** être apte à qch/à faire, être fait pour qch/pour faire; (*Brit*) ~ **carpet** moquette *f*; ~ **sheet** drap-housse *m*.
fitter [ˈfɪtəʳ] *n* **(a)** (*Dress*) essayeur *m*, -euse *f*. **(b)** (*Tech*) monteur *m*; (*Naut*) arrimeur *m*; *[carpet etc]* poseur *m*.
fitting [ˈfɪtɪŋ] **1** *adj remark* approprié (*to* à), juste.
2 *n* **(a)** (*Dress*) essayage *m*. ~ **room** salon *m* d'essayage.
(b) (*Brit: gen pl: in house etc*) ~**s** installations *fpl*; **bathroom** ~**s** installations sanitaires; **electrical** ~**s** installations électriques, appareillage *m* électrique; **furniture and** ~**s** mobilier *m* et installations; **office** ~**s** équipement *m* de bureau; *V* **light**[1].
fittingly [ˈfɪtɪŋlɪ] *adv dress* convenablement (pour l'occasion); *speak* à propos; *say* avec justesse, avec à-propos.
five [faɪv] **1** *adj* cinq; *for phrases V* **six**.
2 *n* **(a)** cinq *m*; *for phrases V* **six**.
(b) (*Sport*) ~**s** *sorte de jeu de pelote* (*à la main*).
3 *cpd*: (*US*) **five-and-ten-cent store** bazar *m*; **fivefold** (*adj*) quintuple; (*adv*) au quintuple; **five-star restaurant** ≈ restaurant *m* (à) trois étoiles; **five-star hotel** palace *m*; **five-year** quinquennal; **five-year plan** plan quinquennal.
fiver* [ˈfaɪvəʳ] *n* (*Brit*) billet *m* de cinq livres; (*US*) billet de cinq dollars.
fix [fɪks] **1** *vt* **(a)** (*make firm*) (*with nails etc*) fixer; (*with ropes etc*) attacher. **to** ~ **a stake in the ground** enfoncer un pieu en terre; (*Mil*) **to** ~ **bayonets** mettre (la) baïonnette au canon; *V also* **fixed**.
(b) *attention* fixer. **to** ~ **one's eyes on sth** fixer qch du regard; **he** ~**ed his eye on me** son regard s'est fixé sur moi; **all eyes were** ~**ed on her** tous les regards *or* tous les yeux étaient fixés sur elle; **he** ~**ed him with an angry glare** il l'a fixé d'un regard furieux, il a dardé sur lui un regard furieux; **to** ~ **sth in one's mind** graver *or* imprimer qch dans son esprit; **to** ~ **one's hopes on sth** mettre tous ses espoirs en qch; **to** ~ **the blame on sb** attribuer la responsabilité à qn, mettre la responsabilité sur le dos de qn.
(c) (*arrange, decide*) décider, arrêter; *time, price* fixer, arrêter; *limit* fixer, établir. **on the date** ~**ed** à la date convenue; **nothing has been** ~**ed yet** rien n'a encore été décidé, il n'y a encore rien d'arrêté.
(d) (*Phot*) fixer. ~**ing bath** (*liquid*) bain *m* de fixage; (*container*) cuvette *f* de fixage.
(e) (*US**) arranger, préparer. **to** ~ **one's hair** se passer un coup de peigne; **can I** ~ **you a drink?** qu'est-ce que je vous donne à boire?; **I'll go and** ~ **us something to eat** je vais vite nous faire quelque chose à manger; **to** ~ **a flat tyre** réparer un pneu.
(f) (*deal with*) arranger; (*mend*) réparer. **don't worry, I'll** ~ **it all** ne vous en faites pas, je vais tout arranger; **he** ~**ed it with the police before he called the meeting** il a attendu d'avoir le feu vert* de la police *or* il s'est arrangé avec la police avant d'organiser la réunion; **I'll soon** ~ **him*** je vais lui régler son compte.
(g) (*: *bribe etc*) *jury* acheter, soudoyer; *match, fight, election, trial* truquer.
2 *n* **(a)** (*) ennui *m*, embêtement* *m*. **to be in/get into a** ~ être/se mettre dans le pétrin *or* dans de beaux draps; **what a** ~! nous voilà dans de beaux draps! *or* dans le pétrin!
(b) (*Drugs sl: injection*) piqûre *f*, piquouse *f* (*sl*). **to get** *or* **give o.s. a** ~ se shooter (*sl*), se piquer.
(c) (*Aviat, Naut*) position *f*. **I've got a** ~ **on him now** j'ai sa position maintenant; (*Naut*) **to take a** ~ **on** faire un relèvement par rapport à.
fix on 1 *vt fus* choisir. **they finally fixed on that house** leur choix s'est finalement arrêté sur cette maison-là.
2 *vt sep lid* fixer, attacher.
fix up 1 *vi* s'arranger (*to do* pour faire).
2 *vt sep* combiner, arranger. **I'll try to fix something up** je tâcherai d'arranger quelque chose; **let's fix it all up now** décidons tout de suite des détails; **to fix sb up with sth** faire avoir qch à qn, obtenir qch pour qn; **I fixed him up with a job** je lui ai trouvé un travail; **we fixed them up for one night** nous leur avons trouvé à coucher pour une nuit.
fixation [fɪkˈseɪʃən] *n* (*Chem, Phot, Psych*) fixation *f*. **to have a** ~ **about** (*Psych*) avoir une fixation à; (*fig*) être obsédé par.
fixative [ˈfɪksətɪv] *n* fixatif *m*.
fixed [fɪkst] *adj* **(a)** *idea, star, stare* fixe; *smile* figé; *determination* inébranlable. (*Jur*) **of no** ~ **abode** sans domicile fixe; (*Mil*) **with** ~ **bayonets** baïonnette *f* au canon; ~ **menu** (menu *m* à) prix *m* fixe; ~ **price** prix *m* fixe *or* imposé; (*Fin*) ~ **assets** immobilisations *fpl*; (*Fin*) ~ **costs** frais *mpl* fixes; (*Computers*) ~**-point notation** *or* **representation** notation *f* en virgule fixe.
(b) (*) **how are we** ~ **for time?** on a combien de temps?; **how are you** ~ **for cigarettes?** vous avez des cigarettes?; **how are you** ~ **for tonight?** qu'est-ce que vous faites ce soir?, vous êtes libre ce soir?
fixedly [ˈfɪksɪdlɪ] *adv* fixement.
fixer [ˈfɪksəʳ] *n* **(a)** (*Phot*) fixateur *m*. **(b)** (*: *person*) combinard(e)*: *m(f)*.
fixings [ˈfɪksɪŋz] *npl* (*US Culin*) garniture *f*, accompagnement *m*.
fixture [ˈfɪkstʃəʳ] *n* **(a)** (*gen pl: in building etc*) installation *f*; (*Jur*) immeuble *m* par destination. **the house was sold with** ~**s and fittings** on a vendu la maison avec toutes les installations; **she's a** ~* elle fait partie du mobilier*; **lighting** ~**s** appareillage *m* électrique.
(b) (*Brit Sport*) match *m* (prévu), épreuve *f* (prévue). ~ **list** calendrier *m*.
fizz [fɪz] **1** *vi [champagne etc]* pétiller, mousser; *[steam etc]* siffler.
2 *n* **(a)** pétillement *m*, sifflement *m*.
(b) (*) champagne *m*, champ* *m*; (*US*) eau *or* boisson gazeuse.
fizz up *vi* monter (en pétillant).
fizzle [ˈfɪzl] *vi* pétiller.
fizzle out *vi [firework]* rater (*une fois en l'air*); *[party, event]* finir en eau de boudin; *[book, film, plot]* se terminer en queue de poisson; *[business started]* s'en aller en eau de boudin; *[plans]* aller à vau-l'eau; *[enthusiasm, interest]* tomber.
fizzy [ˈfɪzɪ] *adj soft drink* pétillant, gazeux; *wine* mousseux, pétillant.
fjord [fjɔːd] *n* = **fiord**.
flabbergast* [ˈflæbəgɑːst] *vt* sidérer*, époustoufler*, ahurir. **I was** ~**ed at this** j'ai été sidéré* *or* époustouflé* d'apprendre ça.
flabby [ˈflæbɪ] *adj handshake, muscle, flesh* mou (*f* molle), flasque; *person* flasque; (*fig*) *character* mou, mollasse, indolent.
flaccid [ˈflæksɪd] *adj muscle, flesh* flasque, mou (*f* molle).
flag[1] [flæg] **1** *n* **(a)** drapeau *m*; (*Naut*) pavillon *m*. ~ **of truce, white** ~ drapeau blanc; *[pirates]* **black** ~ pavillon noir; **red** ~ drapeau rouge; **'The Red F~'** 'l'Internationale' *f*; ~ **of convenience** pavillon de complaisance; **to go down with** ~**s flying** (*Naut*) couler pavillon haut; (*fig*) mener la lutte jusqu'au bout; (*fig*) **to keep the** ~ **flying** tenir bon, assurer la permanence *or* la continuité; *V* **show**.
(b) *[taxi]* **the** ~ **was down** le taxi était pris.
(c) (*for charity*) insigne *m* (*d'une œuvre charitable*).
2 *vt* **(a)** orner *or* garnir de drapeaux; *street, building, ship* pavoiser.
(b) (*also* ~ **down**) *taxi, bus, car* héler, faire signe à.
3 *cpd*: (*Brit*) **flag day** journée *f* de vente d'insignes (*pour une œuvre charitable*); (*Brit*) **flag day in aid of the war-blinded** journée *f* des *or* pour les aveugles de guerre; (*US*) **Flag Day** le 14 juin (*anniversaire du drapeau américain*); (*Naut*) **flag officer** officier supérieur; **flagpole** mât *m* (*pour drapeau*); **flagship** vaisseau *m* amiral; **flagstaff** mât *m* (*pour drapeau*); (*Naut*) mât de pavillon; (*US*) **flag stop** arrêt facultatif.
flag[2] [flæg] *vi [plants etc]* languir, dépérir; *[athlete, walker, health]* s'affaiblir, s'alanguir; *[worker, zeal, courage etc]* fléchir, se relâcher; *[conversation]* traîner, languir; *[interest]* faiblir; *[enthusiasm]* tomber. **his steps were** ~**ging** il commençait à traîner la jambe.
flag[3] [flæg] *n* (*Bot*) iris *m* (des marais).
flag[4] [flæg] *n* (*also* ~**stone**) dalle *f*.
flagellate [ˈflædʒəleɪt] **1** *adj, n* (*Bio*) flagellé (*m*). **2** *vt* flageller, fouetter.
flagellation [ˌflædʒəˈleɪʃən] *n* flagellation *f*.
flagon [ˈflægən] *n* (*of glass*) (grande) bouteille *f*, (*larger*) bonbonne *f*; (*jug*) (grosse) cruche *f*.
flagrant [ˈfleɪgrənt] *adj* flagrant.
flail [fleɪl] **1** *n* (*Agr*) fléau *m*. **2** *vt* (*Agr*) *corn* battre au fléau. **3** *vi [arms etc]* (*also* ~ **about**) battre l'air.
flair [fleəʳ] *n* flair *m*, perspicacité *f*. **to have a** ~ **for** avoir du flair *or* du nez pour.
flak [flæk] *n* (*Mil*) (*firing*) tir antiaérien *or* de D.C.A.; (*guns*) canons antiaériens *or* de D.C.A.; (*flashes*) éclairs *mpl*. ~ **ship** bâtiment *m* de D.C.A.
flake [fleɪk] **1** *n [snow, cereal etc]* flocon *m*; *[metal etc]* paillette *f*, écaille *f*; *V* **corn**[1].
2 *cpd*: **flake-white** blanc *m* de plomb.
3 *vi [stone, plaster etc]* (*also* ~ **off**) s'effriter, s'écailler; *[paint]* s'écailler; *[skin]* peler, se desquamer (*Med*).
4 *vt* (*also* ~ **off**) effriter, écailler.
flake out* *vi* (*faint*) tomber dans les pommes*, tourner de l'œil*; (*fall asleep*) s'endormir *or* tomber (tout d'une masse).
flaky [ˈfleɪkɪ] *adj* floconneux; *pastry, biscuit* feuilleté.
flamboyant [flæmˈbɔɪənt] *adj colour* flamboyant, éclatant; *person, character* haut en couleur; *rudeness* ostentatoire; *speech* retentissant; *dress* voyant; *manners* extravagant; (*Archit*) flamboyant.
flame [fleɪm] **1** *n* **(a)** flamme *f*; (*fig*) *[passion, enthusiasm]* flamme, ardeur *f*, feu *m*. **in** ~**s** en flammes, en feu; **to burst into** ~**s, to go up in** ~**s** (*lit*) s'enflammer (brusquement), prendre feu (tout à coup); (*fig*) éclater; *V* **fan**[1], **fuel**.
(b) she's one of his old ~**s*** c'est un de ses anciens béguins*.
2 *cpd*: **flame-coloured** (rouge) feu *inv*; **flame-proof dish** plat *m* à feu *or* allant au feu; **flamethrower** lance-flammes *m inv*.
3 *vi [fire]* flamber; *[passion]* brûler. **her cheeks** ~**d** ses joues se sont empourprées.
flame up *vi [fire]* flamber; *[anger]* exploser; (*fig*) *[person]* exploser*, se mettre en colère.
flamenco [fləˈmeŋkəʊ] *adj, n* flamenco (*m*).
flaming [ˈfleɪmɪŋ] *adj* **(a)** *sun, fire etc* ardent, flamboyant. **(b)** (*Brit**: *furious*) furibard*, furax*. **(c)** (*) fichu*, foutu*. **you and your** ~ **radio!** toi et ta fichue* *or* foutue* radio!; **it's a** ~ **nuisance!** c'est empoisonnant!*, ce que c'est enquiquinant!*
flamingo [fləˈmɪŋgəʊ] *n, pl* ~**s** *or* ~**es** flamant *m* (rose).

flammable ['flæməbl] *adj* inflammable (*lit*).
flan [flæn] *n* (*Brit Culin*) tarte *f*.
Flanders ['flɑːndəz] *n* Flandre(s) *f(pl)*.
flange [flændʒ] *n* (*on wheel*) boudin *m*; (*on pipe*) collerette *f*, bride *f*; (*on I-beam*) aile *f*; (*on railway rail*) patin *m*.
flanged [flændʒd] *adj wheel etc* à boudin, à rebord; *tube etc* à brides.
flank [flæŋk] 1 *n* (*Anat, Geog, Mil*) flanc *m*; (*Culin*) flanchet *m*.
2 *vt* (a) flanquer. **~ed by 2 policemen** flanqué de *or* encadré par 2 gendarmes. (b) (*Mil*) flanquer; (*turn the ~ of*) contourner le flanc de.
flannel ['flænl] 1 *n* (*Tex: U*) flanelle *f*; (*Brit: face ~*) gant *m* de toilette. (*Brit: trousers*) **~s** pantalon *m* de flanelle; (*Brit‡ fig: waffle*) baratin‡ *m*. 2 *cpd* de flanelle. 3 *vi* (*Brit‡: waffle*) baratiner‡.
flannelette [,flænə'let] 1 *n* finette *f*, pilou *m*. 2 *cpd sheet* de finette, de pilou.
flap [flæp] 1 *n* (a) *[wings]* battement *m*, coup *m*; *[sails]* claquement *m*.
(b) *[pocket, envelope]* rabat *m*; *[counter, table]* abattant *m*; *[door]* battant *m*; (*Aviat*) volet *m*.
(c) (*Brit**: *panic*) panique* *f*. **to be in a ~** être affolé *or* dans tous ses états; **to get into a ~** s'affoler, se mettre dans tous ses états, paniquer*.
2 *cpd*: (*Culin*) **flapjack** (*pancake*) crêpe épaisse; (*biscuit*) galette *f*.
3 *vi* (a) *[wings]* battre; *[shutters]* battre, claquer; *[sails]* claquer. **his cloak ~ped about his legs** sa cape lui battait les jambes.
(b) (*Brit**: *be panicky*) paniquer*. **don't ~!** pas de panique!, pas d'affolement!
4 *vt [bird]* **to ~ its wings** battre des ailes.
flapper*† ['flæpəʳ] *n* mignonne *f* (des années 1920).
flare [flɛəʳ] 1 *n* (a) (*light*) *[torch, fire]* flamme *f*, éclat *m*, flamboiement *m*; *[sun]* éclat, flamboiement.
(b) (*signal*) feu *m*, signal *m* (lumineux); (*Mil*) fusée éclairante, fusée-parachute *f*; (*Aviat: for target*) bombe éclairante *or* de jalonnement; (*for runway*) balise *f*.
(c) (*Dress*) évasement *m*.
2 *cpd*: (*Aviat*) **flare path** rampe *f* de balisage; **flare-up** *[fire]* flambée *f* (soudaine); *[war]* intensification soudaine; *[quarrel, fighting]* recrudescence *f*; (*outburst of rage*) crise *f* de colère; (*sudden dispute*) altercation *f*, prise *f* de bec*.
3 *vi* (a) *[match]* s'enflammer; *[candle]* briller; *[sunspot]* brûler.
(b) *[sleeves, skirt]* s'évaser, s'élargir.
4 *vt skirt, trouser legs* évaser. **~d skirt** jupe évasée; **~d trousers** pantalon *m* à pattes d'éléphant.
flare up 1 *vi [fire]* s'embraser, prendre (brusquement); *[person]* se mettre en colère, s'emporter; *[political situation]* exploser; *[anger, fighting, revolt]* éclater; *[epidemic]* éclater, se déclarer (soudain).
2 **flare-up** *n V* **flare 2**.
flash [flæʃ] 1 *n* (a) *[flame, jewels]* éclat *m*. **~ of lightning** éclair *m*; **~ of wit** saillie *f*, boutade *f*; **it happened in a ~** c'est arrivé en un clin d'œil; **it came to him in a ~ that ...** l'idée lui est venue tout d'un coup que ...; (*fig*) **a ~ in the pan** un feu de paille (*fig*); **~ of inspiration** éclair de génie.
(b) (*also* **news ~**) flash *m* (d'information). **we've just had a ~ that ...** nous venons de recevoir une dépêche indiquant que ... .
(c) (*Mil*) parement *m*.
(d) (*Phot*) flash *m*.
2 *vi* (a) *[jewels]* étinceler, briller; *[light, traffic lights etc]* clignoter; *[eyes]* lancer des éclairs. **lightning was ~ing** il y avait des éclairs.
(b) *[person, vehicle]* **to ~ in/out/past** *etc* entrer/sortir/passer *etc* comme un éclair; **the news ~ed round** la nouvelle s'est répandue comme un éclair; **the thought ~ed through his mind that ...** un instant, il a pensé que ...; **it ~ed upon me** *or* **into my mind that ...** l'idée m'est venue tout d'un coup que ... .
(c) (‡: *expose o.s. indecently*) s'exhiber.
3 *vt* (a) *light* projeter. **to ~ a torch on** diriger une lampe (de poche) sur; **she ~ed him a look of contempt** elle lui a jeté un regard de mépris; (*Aut*) **to ~ one's headlights** faire un appel de phares (*at sb* à qn).
(b) (*show, wave*) *diamond ring* étaler (aux yeux de tous), mettre (bien) en vue. **don't ~ all that money around** n'étale pas tout cet argent de cette façon.
4 *cpd*: (*Cine*) **flashback** flashback *m inv*, retour *m* en arrière; (*Phot*) **flash bulb** ampoule *f* de flash; (*Med*) **flash burn** brûlure *f* de la peau (*causée par un flux thermique*); (*Phot*) **flash cube** cube-flash *m*; **flash flood** crue subite; (*Phot*) **flash gun** flash *m*; **flashlight** (*Phot*) flash *m*; (*torch*) lampe *f* électrique *or* de poche; (*on lighthouse etc*) fanal *m*; (*Chem*) **flash point** point *m* d'ignition; (*fig*) **the situation had nearly reached flash point** la situation était sur le point d'exploser.
flasher ['flæʃəʳ] *n* (*light, device*) clignotant *m*; (‡: *in indecent exposure case*) exhibitionniste *m*.
flashy ['flæʃɪ] *adj* (*pej*) *person* tapageur; *jewellery, car* tape-à-l'œil *inv*, clinquant; *dress* tapageur, tape-à-l'œil *inv*, voyant; *colour, taste* criard, tapageur.
flask [flɑːsk] *n* (*Pharm*) fiole *f*; (*Chem*) ballon *m*; (*bottle*) bouteille *f*; (*for pocket*) flacon *m* (plat); (*also* **vacuum ~**) (bouteille) Thermos *f* ®.
flat¹ [flæt] 1 *adj* (a) *countryside, surface, the earth* plat; *tyre* dégonflé, à plat. **as ~ as a pancake*** *tyre* plat comme une galette; *surface, countryside* tout plat; (*after bombing*) complètement rasé; **a ~ dish** un plat creux; **~ roof** toit plat *or* en terrasse; **~ nose** nez épaté *or* camus; **a ~ stomach** un ventre plat; **to have ~ feet** avoir les pieds plats; **he was lying ~ on the floor** il était (étendu) à plat par terre; **to fall ~ on one's face** tomber à plat ventre *or* sur le nez; **lay the book ~ on the table** pose le livre à plat sur la table; **the earthquake laid the whole city ~** le tremblement de terre a rasé la ville entière; **a ~ race** une course de plat; (**fig*) **to be in a ~ spin** être dans tous ses états.
(b) (*listless*) *taste, style* monotone, plat; *battery* à plat; *beer etc* éventé. **I was feeling rather ~** je me sentais sans ressort, je me sentais plutôt vidé* *or* à plat*; **the beer tastes ~** la bière a un goût fade *or* d'éventé.
(c) (*Mus*) *instrument, voice* faux (*f* fausse). **B ~** si *m* bémol.
(d) *refusal, denial* net (*f* nette), catégorique. **and that's ~!*** un point c'est tout!*
(e) (*Comm*) **~ rate of pay** salaire *m* fixe; *[price, charge]* **~ rate** taux *m* fixe.
(f) (*not shiny*) *colour* mat.
(g) (*US: penniless*) **to be ~‡** être fauché (comme les blés)*, n'avoir plus un rond*.
2 *adv* (a) carrément, nettement, sans ambages. **he told me ~ that ...** il m'a dit carrément *or* sans ambages que ...; **he turned it down ~** il l'a carrément refusé, il l'a refusé tout net; (*Brit*) **to be ~ broke‡** être fauché (comme les blés)*, n'avoir plus un rond*; **in 10 seconds ~** en 10 secondes pile.
(b) **to go ~ out** (*Sport*) *[runner]* donner son maximum; *[person running in street]* courir comme un dératé; *[car]* être à sa vitesse de pointe; **to go ~ out for sth** faire tout son possible pour avoir qch; **to be working ~ out** travailler d'arrache-pied; **to be lying ~ out** être étendu *or* couché de tout son long; **to be ~ out** (*exhausted*) être à plat* *or* vidé*; (*asleep*) dormir, ronfler* (*fig*); (*drunk*) être complètement rétamé, être K.-O.*
(c) (*Mus*) *sing* faux.
3 *n* (a) *[hand, blade]* plat *m*.
(b) (*Geog*) (*dry land*) plaine *f*; (*marsh*) marécage *m*; *V* **salt**.
(c) (*Mus*) bémol *m*.
(d) (*US Aut*) crevaison *f*, pneu crevé.
(e) (*Racing*) **the ~** = **flat racing, the flat season**; *V* **4**.
4 *cpd*: **flat-bottomed boat** bateau *m* à fond plat; **she is flat-chested** elle est plate (comme une limande*), elle n'a pas de poitrine; **flat fish** poisson plat; **flatfooted** (*lit*) aux pieds plats; (*Brit‡ pej*) *person* balourd, maladroit; *attitude* maladroit; **flatiron** fer *m* à repasser; (*Racing*) **flat racing** plat *m*; (*Racing*) **flat season** (saison *f* du) plat *m*; (*US*) **flat silver** couverts *mpl* en argent; **flatworm** plathelminthe *m*.
flat² [flæt] *n* (*Brit*) appartement *m*. **to go ~-hunting** chercher un appartement; **my ~mate** la fille (*or* le garçon *or* la personne) avec qui je partage mon appartement.
flatlet ['flætlɪt] *n* (*Brit*) studio *m*.
flatly ['flætlɪ] *adv deny, oppose, refuse* catégoriquement, absolument. **'I'm not going' he said ~** 'je n'y vais pas' dit-il tout net.
flatness ['flætnɪs] *n [countryside, surface]* égalité *f*, aspect plat; *[curve]* aplatissement *m*; *[refusal]* netteté *f*; (*dullness*) monotonie *f*.
flatten ['flætn] *vt* (a) *path, road* aplanir; *metal* aplatir.
(b) *[wind, storm etc] crops* coucher, écraser; *tree* abattre; *town, building* raser. **to ~ o.s. against** s'aplatir *or* se plaquer contre.
(c) (*: *snub*) *person* clouer le bec à*, river son clou à. **that'll ~ him!** ça lui clouera le bec!*
flatten out 1 *vi [countryside, road]* s'aplanir; *[aircraft]* se redresser.
2 *vt sep path* aplanir; *metal* aplatir; *map etc* ouvrir à plat.
flatter ['flætəʳ] *vt* (*all senses*) flatter. **he ~s himself he's a good musician** il se flatte d'être bon musicien; **you ~ yourself!** tu te flattes!
flatterer ['flætərəʳ] *n* flatteur *m*, -euse *f*, flagorneur *m*, -euse *f* (*pej*).
flattering ['flætərɪŋ] *adj* flatteur. **that's not very ~** ce n'est pas très flatteur; **she wears very ~ clothes** elle porte des vêtements très seyants *or* qui l'avantagent.
flatteringly ['flætərɪŋlɪ] *adv* flatteusement.
flattery ['flætərɪ] *n* flatterie *f*.
flatulence ['flætjʊləns] *n* flatulence *f*.
flatulent ['flætjʊlənt] *adj* flatulent.
flaunt [flɔːnt] *vt wealth* étaler; *knowledge* faire étalage de; (*US*) *rules, regulations* faire fi de, passer outre à. **she ~ed her femininity at him** elle lui jetait sa féminité à la tête; **to ~ o.s.** poser (pour la galerie).
flautist ['flɔːtɪst] *n*, (*US*) **flutist** ['fluːtɪst] *n* flûtiste *mf*.
flavour, (*US*) **flavor** ['fleɪvəʳ] 1 *n* goût *m*, saveur *f*; *[ice cream]* parfum *m*. **with a rum ~** (parfumé) au rhum; (*fig*) **a slight ~ of irony** une légère pointe d'ironie; **the film gives the ~ of Paris in the twenties** le film rend bien l'atmosphère du Paris des années vingt.
2 *vt* (*give ~ to*) donner du goût à; (*with fruit, spirits*) parfumer; (*with herbs, salt etc*) assaisonner. **to ~ a sauce with garlic** relever une sauce avec de l'ail; **pineapple-~ed** (parfumé) à l'ananas.
flavouring, (*US*) **flavoring** ['fleɪvərɪŋ] *n* (*Culin*) (*in sauce etc*) assaisonnement *m*; (*in cake etc*) parfum *m*. **vanilla ~** essence de vanille.
flavourless, (*US*) **flavorless** ['fleɪvəlɪs] *adj* insipide, sans saveur, sans goût.
flaw [flɔː] *n* (*in jewel, character, argument etc*) défaut *m*, imperfection *f*; (*Jur: in contract, procedure etc*) vice *m* de forme; (*obstacle*) inconvénient *m*. **everything seems to be working out, but there is just one ~** tout semble s'arranger, il n'y a qu'un seul inconvénient *or* qu'un hic*.
flawed [flɔːd] *adj* imparfait.

flawless ['flɔ:lɪs] *adj* parfait, sans défaut. **he spoke ~ English** il parlait un anglais impeccable, il parlait parfaitement l'anglais.
flax [flæks] *n* lin *m*.
flaxen ['flæksən] *adj hair* blond, de lin, filasse *inv* (*pej*); (*Tex*) de lin. **~-haired** aux cheveux de lin *or* filasse.
flay [fleɪ] *vt animal* (*skin*) écorcher; (*beat*) fouetter, rosser; *person* (*beat*) fouetter, rosser, battre (comme plâtre); (*criticize*) éreinter.
flea [fli:] **1** *n* puce *f*. **to send sb off with a ~ in his ear*** envoyer promener qn; *V* **sand**. **2** *cpd*: **fleabite** (*lit*) piqûre *f* de puce; (*fig*) vétille *f*, broutille *f*; **flea market** marché *m* aux puces; (*Brit*) **flea-pit**: ciné* miteux, ciné* de quartier.
fleck [flek] **1** *n [colour]* moucheture *f*; *[sunlight]* petite tache; *[dust]* particule *f*.
2 *vt* tacheter, moucheter. **dress ~ed with mud** robe éclaboussée de boue; **blue ~ed with white** bleu moucheté de blanc; **sky ~ed with little clouds** ciel pommelé.
fled [fled] *pret, ptp of* **flee**.
fledged [fledʒd] *adj*: **fully-~ bird** oiseau *m* qui a toutes ses plumes; **he's now a fully-~ doctor/architect** il est maintenant médecin/architecte diplômé; **a fully-~ British citizen** un citoyen britannique à part entière.
fledg(e)ling ['fledʒlɪŋ] *n* (*Orn*) oiselet *m*, oisillon *m*; (*fig: novice*) blanc-bec *m*.
flee [fli:] *pret, ptp* **fled** **1** *vi* fuir (*before, in face of* devant), s'enfuir (*from* de), se réfugier (*to* auprès de). **they fled** ils ont fui, ils se sont enfuis, ils se sont sauvés; **I fled when I heard she was expected** je me suis sauvé *or* j'ai pris la fuite lorsque j'ai appris qu'elle devait venir; **to ~ from temptation** fuir la tentation.
2 *vt town, country* s'enfuir de; *temptation, danger* fuir. **to ~ the country** quitter le pays, s'enfuir du pays.
fleece [fli:s] **1** *n* toison *f*; *V* **golden**. **2** *vt* **(a)** (*rob*) voler; (*swindle*) escroquer, filouter; (*overcharge*) estamper*, tondre*. **(b)** *sheep* tondre.
fleecy ['fli:sɪ] *adj clouds, snow* floconneux; *blanket* laineux.
fleet[1] [fli:t] **1** *n* (*Naut*) flotte *f*. (*fig*) **a ~ of vehicles** un parc automobile; **the company has a ~ of cars** la compagnie possède un certain nombre de voitures; *V* **admiral, fishing** *etc*.
2 *cpd*: (*US Naut*) **fleet admiral** amiral *m* (à cinq étoiles); (*Brit*) **Fleet Air Arm** aéronavale *f*.
fleet[2] [fli:t] *adj* (*also* **~-footed, ~ of foot**) rapide, au pied léger.
fleeting ['fli:tɪŋ] *adj time, memory* fugace, fugitif; *beauty, pleasure* éphémère, passager. **for a ~ moment** pendant un bref instant *or* moment; **a ~ visit** une visite éclair *or* en coup de vent*; (*liter*) **the ~ years** les années qui s'enfuient.
Fleming ['flemɪŋ] *n* Flamand(e) *m(f)*.
Flemish ['flemɪʃ] **1** *adj* flamand. **2** *n* **(a) the ~** les Flamands *mpl*. **(b)** (*Ling*) flamand *m*.
flesh [fleʃ] **1** *n [person, animal]* chair *f*; *[fruit, vegetable]* chair, pulpe *f*. **to put on ~** *[animal]* engraisser; *[person]* grossir, engraisser, prendre de l'embonpoint; (*fig*) **to make sb's ~ creep** donner la chair de poule à qn; **creatures of ~ and blood** êtres *mpl* de chair et de sang; **I'm only ~ and blood** je ne suis qu'un homme (*or* une femme) comme les autres; **my own ~ and blood** la chair de ma chair; **it is more than ~ and blood can stand** c'est plus que la nature humaine ne peut endurer; **in the ~** en chair et en os, en personne; **to exact one's pound of ~** exiger son dû; **he's gone the way of all ~** il a payé le tribut de la nature; (*Rel*) **the sins of the ~** les péchés *mpl* de la chair; (*Rel*) **the ~ is weak** la chair est faible; *V* **fish**.
2 *cpd*: **flesh colour** couleur *f* (de) chair; (*Art*) carnation *f*; **flesh-coloured** (couleur *f*) chair *inv*; **fleshpots** lieux *mpl* de plaisir; (*Art*) **flesh tints** carnations *fpl*; **flesh wound** blessure *f* superficielle.
fleshy ['fleʃɪ] *adj* charnu.
flew [flu:] *pret of* **fly**[3].
flex [fleks] **1** *vt body, knees* fléchir, ployer; *muscle* tendre, bander (*liter*). **2** *n* (*Brit*) *[lamp, iron]* fil *m* (souple); *[telephone]* cordon *m*; (*heavy duty*) câble *m*. **3** *cpd*: **flextime** les horaires *mpl* libres.
flexibility [ˌfleksɪ'bɪlɪtɪ] *n* (*V* **flexible**) flexibilité *f*, élasticité *f*, souplesse *f*.
flexible ['fleksəbl] *adj wire, branch* flexible, souple; *shoes, sole etc* flexible, souple, élastique; (*fig*) *person* maniable, flexible, souple; *plans, attitude* flexible, souple. **~ working hours** heures de travail souples *or* élastiques.
flexion ['flekʃən] *n* flexion *f*, courbure *f*.
flexor ['fleksər] *adj, n* fléchisseur (*m*).
flibbertigibbet ['flɪbətɪ'dʒɪbɪt] *n* tête *f* de linotte, étourdi(e) *m(f)*.
flick [flɪk] **1** *n* **(a)** *[tail, duster]* petit coup; (*with finger*) chiquenaude *f*, pichenette *f*; (*with wrist*) petit mouvement (rapide).
(b) (*Brit*) **~s**: ciné* *m*.
2 *cpd*: (*Brit*) **flick knife** couteau *m* à cran d'arrêt.
3 *vt* donner un petit coup à. **he ~ed the horse lightly with the reins** il a donné au cheval un (tout) petit coup avec les rênes; **I'll just ~ a duster round the sitting room** je vais donner *or* passer un petit coup de chiffon au salon*.
flick off *vt sep dust, ash* enlever d'une chiquenaude.
flick over *vt sep pages of book* feuilleter, tourner rapidement.
flick through *vt fus pages of book, document* feuilleter, lire en diagonale*.
flicker ['flɪkər] **1** *vi [flames, light]* danser; (*before going out*) trembloter, vaciller; *[needle on dial]* osciller. **the snake's tongue ~ed in and out** le serpent a dardé sa langue.
2 *n [flames, light]* danse *f*; (*before going out*) vacillement *m*. **in the ~ of an eyelid** en un clin d'œil; **without a ~** sans sourciller *or* broncher; **a ~ of hope** une lueur d'espoir.
flier ['flaɪər] *n* **(a)** (*Aviat: person*) aviateur *m*, -trice *f*. *[passenger]* **to be a good ~** supporter (bien) l'avion; **to be a bad ~** ne pas supporter *or* mal supporter l'avion; *V* **high**.
(b) (*esp US: fast train*) rapide *m*; (*fast coach*) car *m* express.
(c) (*leap*) **to take a ~** sauter avec élan; (* *fig*) foncer tête baissée, risquer le tout pour le tout.
(d) (*St Ex*) (folle) aventure *f*.
(e) (*US: handbill*) prospectus *m*.
flight[1] [flaɪt] **1** *n* **(a)** (*U: action, course*) *[bird, insect, plane etc]* vol *m*; *[ball, bullet]* trajectoire *f*. **the principles of ~** les rudiments *mpl* du vol *or* de la navigation aérienne; **in ~** en plein vol.
(b) (*Aviat*) vol *m*. **~ number 776 from/to Madrid** le vol numéro 776 en provenance/à destination de Madrid; *V* **reconnaissance, test** *etc*.
(c) (*group*) *[birds]* vol *m*, volée *f*; *[planes]* escadrille *f*. (*fig*) **in the first** *or* **top ~ of scientists/novelists** parmi les scientifiques/les romanciers les plus marquants; **a firm in the top ~** une compagnie de pointe.
(d) *[fancy, imagination]* élan *m*, envolée *f*.
(e) ~ of stairs escalier *m*, volée *f* d'escalier. **we had to climb 3 ~s to get to his room** nous avons dû monter 3 étages pour arriver à sa chambre; **he lives three ~s up** il habite au troisième; **~ of hurdles** série *f* de haies; **~ of terraces** escalier *m* de terrasses.
2 *cpd*: **flight deck** (*Aviat*) poste *m or* cabine *f* de pilotage; (*Naut*) pont *m* d'envol; (*Brit Aviat*) **flight lieutenant** capitaine *m* (de l'armée de l'air); (*Aviat*) **flight log** suivi *m* de vol; **flight path** trajectoire *f* (de vol); **flight plan** plan *m* de vol; (*Aviat*) **flight recorder** enregistreur *m* de vol; (*Brit Aviat*) **flight sergeant** sergent(-chef) *m* (de l'armée de l'air); **flight simulator** simulateur *m* de vol; **flight-test** essayer en vol.
flight[2] [flaɪt] *n* (*U: act of fleeing*) fuite *f*. **to put to ~** mettre en fuite; **to take (to) ~** prendre la fuite, s'enfuir; (*Fin*) **the ~ of capital abroad** la fuite des capitaux à l'étranger.
flightless ['flaɪtlɪs] *adj* (*Orn*) coureur.
flighty ['flaɪtɪ] *adj person* (*fickle*) volage, inconstant; (*light-headed*) étourdi, écervelé; *remark* frivole, superficiel.
flimsily ['flɪmzɪlɪ] *adv*: **~ built** *or* **constructed** (d'une construction) peu solide.
flimsiness ['flɪmzɪnɪs] *n [dress]* fragilité *f*; *[house]* construction *f* peu solide; *[paper]* minceur *f*; *[excuse, reasoning]* faiblesse *f*, futilité *f*.
flimsy ['flɪmzɪ] **1** *adj dress* trop léger; *cloth, paper* mince; *house* peu solide; *excuse, reasoning* piètre, pauvre. **2** *n* papier *m* pelure *inv*.
flinch [flɪntʃ] *vi* broncher, tressaillir. **to ~ from a task** reculer devant une tâche; **he didn't ~ from warning her** il ne s'est pas dérobé au devoir de la prévenir; **without ~ing** sans sourciller *or* broncher.
flinders ['flɪndəz] *npl*: **to break** *or* **fly into ~** voler en éclats.
fling [flɪŋ] (*vb: pret, ptp* **flung**) **1** *n* (*throw*) lancer *m*. (*fig*) **to have one's ~** s'en payer, se payer du bon temps; **youth must have its ~** il faut que jeunesse se passe (*Prov*); **to go on a ~** aller faire la noce *or* la foire*, (*in shops*) faire des folies; (*attempt*) **to have a ~** tenter sa chance; **to have a ~ at sth** s'essayer la main à qch; **to have a ~ at doing** essayer de faire; *V* **highland**.
2 *vt stone etc* jeter, lancer (*at sb* à qn, *at sth* sur qch); (*fig*) *remark, insult, accusation* lancer (*at sb* à qn). **he flung his opponent to the ground** il a jeté son adversaire à terre; **to ~ sb into jail** jeter *or* flanquer* qn en prison; **to ~ the window open** ouvrir toute grande la fenêtre; **the door was flung open** la porte s'est ouverte à la volée; **to ~ one's arms round sb's neck** sauter *or* se jeter au cou de qn; **to ~ a coat over one's shoulders** jeter un manteau sur ses épaules; **to ~ on/off one's coat** enfiler/enlever son manteau d'un geste brusque; **to ~ sb a look of contempt** lancer un regard de mépris à qn; **to ~ an accusation at sb** lancer une accusation à la tête de qn; **to ~ o.s. into a job/a hobby** se jeter *or* se lancer à corps perdu dans un travail/une activité; (*fig*) **she flung herself* at him** *or* **at his head** elle s'est jetée à sa tête.
3 *vi*: **to ~ off/out** *etc* partir/sortir *etc* brusquement; **he was ~ing about like a madman** il gesticulait *or* se démenait comme un possédé.
fling away *vt sep unwanted object* jeter, ficher en l'air*; (*fig*) *money* gaspiller, jeter par les fenêtres.
fling off *vt sep* (*fig liter*) se débarrasser de.
fling out *vt sep person* flanquer* *or* mettre à la porte; *unwanted object* jeter, ficher en l'air*.
fling up *vt sep* jeter en l'air. **to fling one's arms up in exasperation** lever les bras en l'air *or* au ciel d'exaspération; **he flung up his head** il a brusquement relevé la tête.
flint [flɪnt] **1** *n* (*gen: also tool, weapon*) silex *m*; (*for cigarette lighter*) pierre *f* (à briquet). **2** *cpd axe* de silex. **flint glass** flint(-glass) *m*.
flinty ['flɪntɪ] *adj soil* à silex; *rocks* siliceux; *heart* dur, insensible, de pierre.
flip [flɪp] **1** *n* **(a)** chiquenaude *f*, pichenette *f*, petit coup.
(b) (*Aviat**) petit tour en zinc:.
2 *cpd*: (*Computers*) **flip-flop** bascule *f*; (*sandals*) **flip-flops** tongs *fpl* ®; **the flip side of a record** l'autre face *f* d'un disque (*celle qui a le moins de succès*).
3 *vt* donner un petit coup à, donner une chiquenaude *or* une pichenette à. **to ~ a book open** ouvrir un livre d'une chiquenaude *or* d'une pichenette; **he ~ped the letter over to me** il m'a passé la lettre d'une pichenette *or* d'une chiquenaude.
flip off *vt sep cigarette ash* secouer, faire tomber.
flip over *vt sep stone* retourner d'un coup léger; *pages* feuilleter.
flip through *vt fus book* feuilleter.

flippancy ['flɪpənsɪ] n *[attitude]* désinvolture *f*; *[speech, remark]* irrévérence *f*, légèreté *f*.
flippant ['flɪpənt] *adj remark* désinvolte, irrévérencieux; *person, tone, attitude* cavalier, (trop) désinvolte, irrévérencieux.
flippantly ['flɪpəntlɪ] *adv* avec désinvolture; irrévérencieusement; cavalièrement.
flipper ['flɪpəʳ] *n [seal etc]* nageoire *f*. *[swimmer]* ~s palmes *fpl*.
flipping* ['flɪpɪŋ] *adj* (*Brit*) fichu* (*before n*), maudit (*before n*).
flirt [flɜːt] **1** *vi* flirter (*with* avec). **to ~ with an idea** caresser une idée. **2** *n*: **he's a great ~** il adore flirter, il est très flirteur.
flirtation [flɜː'teɪʃən] *n* flirt *m*, amourette *f*.
flirtatious [flɜː'teɪʃəs] *adj* flirteur.
flit [flɪt] **1** *vi* **(a)** *[bats, butterflies etc]* voleter, voltiger. **the idea ~ted through his head** l'idée lui a traversé l'esprit; *[person]* **she ~ted in and out** elle n'a fait qu'entrer et sortir.
(b) (*Brit: move house stealthily*) déménager à la cloche de bois; (*N Engl, Scot: move house*) déménager.
2 *n* (*N Engl, Scot*) déménagement *m*. (*Brit*) **to do a moonlight ~** déménager à la cloche de bois.
flitch [flɪtʃ] *n* flèche *f* (de lard).
flitting ['flɪtɪŋ] *n* (*N Engl, Scot*) déménagement *m*.
float [fləʊt] **1** *n* (*Fishing, Plumbing*) flotteur *m*, flotte *f*; (*of cork*) bouchon *m*; *[seaplane etc]* flotteur *m*; (*vehicle in a parade*) char *m*; *V* **milk**.
2 *vi* (*on water, in air*) flotter; *[ship]* être à flot; *[bather]* faire la planche; *[vision etc]* planer; (*Fin*) *[currency]* flotter. **the raft ~ed down the river** le radeau a descendu la rivière; **to ~ back up to the surface** remonter à la surface (de l'eau).
3 *vt* **(a)** *boat* faire flotter, mettre à flot *or* sur l'eau; (*refloat*) remettre à flot *or* sur l'eau.
(b) (*Fin*) *currency* laisser flotter; *company* fonder, créer, constituer. **to ~ a share issue** émettre des actions; **to ~ a loan** lancer un emprunt.
float (a)round* *vi [rumour, news]* circuler, courir.
float away *vi* dériver, partir à la dérive.
float off **1** *vi [wreck etc]* se renflouer, se déséchouer.
2 *vt sep* renflouer, déséchouer, remettre à flot *or* sur l'eau.
floating ['fləʊtɪŋ] **1** *adj population* instable. (*Fin*) **~ assets** capitaux circulants; **~ currency** devise flottante; **~ debt** dette *f* à court terme *or* flottante; (*Naut*) **~ dock** dock flottant; **~ exchange** change flottant; (*Computers*) **~ point representation** notation *f* en virgule flottante; (*Anat*) **~ rib** côte flottante; (*Pol*) **~ vote** vote flottant; **~ voter** électeur *m*, -trice *f* indécis(e) *or* non-engagé(e).
2 *n [boat]* mise *f* en flottement; *[loan]* lancement *m*; *[currency]* flottement *m*, flottaison *f*.
flocculent ['flɒkjʊlənt] *adj* floconneux.
flock[1] [flɒk] **1** *n [animals, geese]* troupeau *m*; *[birds]* vol *m*, volée *f*; *[people]* foule *f*, troupeau; (*Rel*) ouailles *fpl*. **they came in ~s** ils sont venus en masse.
2 *vi* aller *or* venir en masse *or* en foule, affluer. **to ~ in/out** *etc* entrer/sortir *etc* en foule; **to ~ together** s'assembler; **to ~ round sb** s'attrouper *or* s'assembler *or* se grouper autour de qn.
flock[2] [flɒk] *n* (*U*) (*wool*) bourre *f* de laine; (*cotton*) bourre de coton.
floe [fləʊ] *n* banquise *f*, glaces flottantes.
flog [flɒg] *vt* **(a)** flageller, fustiger. (*fig*) **to ~ an idea to death*** rabâcher une idée; (*fig*) **to ~ a dead horse** perdre sa peine et son temps. **(b)** (*Brit*‡) vendre. **how much did you ~ it for?** tu en as tiré combien?
flogging ['flɒgɪŋ] *n* flagellation *f*, fustigation *f*; (*Jur*) fouet *m* (*sanction*).
flood [flʌd] **1** *n* inondation *f*; (*fig*) flot *m*, torrent *m*, déluge *m*; (*also* **~tide**) flux *m*, marée montante. (*Sport*) **~s*** = **floodlights** (*V* **floodlight**); **the F~** le déluge; **river in ~** rivière en crue; **~s of tears** un torrent *or* déluge de larmes; **a ~ of light** un flot de lumière; **a ~ of letters** un déluge de lettres *or* de courrier.
2 *cpd*: **flood control** prévention *f* des inondations; **floodgate** vanne *f*, porte *f* d'écluse; (*fig*) **to open the floodgates** ouvrir les vannes (*to* à); **floodlight** *V* **floodlight**; **floodlighting** *V* **floodlighting**; **flood plain** lit majeur, plaine *f* inondable.
3 *vt* **(a)** *fields, town* inonder, submerger; (*Aut*) *carburettor* noyer; (*fig*) inonder. **he was ~ed with letters/with applications** il a été inondé de lettres/de demandes; **room ~ed with light** pièce inondée de lumière.
(b) *[storm, rain] river, stream* faire déborder. (*Comm*) *[suppliers, goods]* **to ~ the market** inonder le marché (*with* de).
4 *vi [river]* déborder, être en crue; *[people]* affluer, aller *or* venir en foule. **the crowd ~ed into the streets** la foule a envahi les rues *or* s'est répandue dans les rues.
flood in *vi [sunshine]* entrer à flots; *[people]* entrer en foule, affluer.
flood out *vt sep house* inonder. **the villagers were flooded out** les inondations ont forcé les villageois à évacuer leurs maisons.
flooding ['flʌdɪŋ] *n* inondation *f*.
floodlight ['flʌdlaɪt] *pret, ptp* **floodlit** ['flʌdlɪt] **1** *vt buildings* illuminer; (*Sport*) *match* éclairer (aux projecteurs); (*fig*) mettre en lumière, éclairer.
2 *n* (*device*) projecteur *m*; (*light*) lumière *f* (des projecteurs). **to play a match under ~s** jouer un match en nocturne.
floodlighting ['flʌdlaɪtɪŋ] *n [building]* illumination *f*; *[match]* éclairage *m* (aux projecteurs). **let's go and see the ~** allons voir les illuminations.
floor [flɔːʳ] **1** *n* **(a)** (*gen*) sol *m*; (*~boards*) plancher *m*, parquet *m*; (*for dance*) piste *f* (de danse); (*fig*) *[prices etc]* plancher. **stone/tiled ~** sol dallé/carrelé; **put it on the ~** pose-le par terre *or* sur le sol; **she was sitting on the ~** elle était assise par terre *or* sur le sol; (*fig*) **a question from the ~ of the house** une question de l'auditoire *m or* de l'assemblée *f*; **to take the ~** (*speak*) prendre la parole; (*dance*) (aller) faire un tour de piste; **sea ~** fond *m* de la mer; *V* **cross, wipe** *etc*.
(b) (*storey*) étage *m*. **first ~** (*Brit*) premier étage, (*US*) rez-de-chaussée *m*; **he lives on the second ~** il habite au deuxième étage *or* au second; **we live on the same ~** nous habitons au même étage *or* sur le même palier; *V* **ground**[1] *etc*.
2 *vt* **(a)** faire le sol de; (*with boards*) planchéier, parqueter.
(b) (*knock down*) *opponent* terrasser; (*Boxing*) envoyer au tapis.
(c) (*silence*) réduire au silence, couper le sifflet à*; (*puzzle*) stupéfier, souffler*. **he was completely ~ed by this** il n'a rien trouvé à répondre.
3 *cpd*: **floorboard** planche *f* (*de plancher*), latte *f* (de plancher); **floorcloth** serpillière *f*; **floor covering** revêtement *m* de sol; (*US Pol*) **floor leader** serre-file *m*; **floor polish** encaustique *f*, cire *f*; (*tool*) **floor polisher** cireuse *f*; **floor show** attractions *fpl*, spectacle *m* de variétés (*dans un restaurant, cabaret etc*); (*Comm*) **floorwalker** chef *m* de rayon.
floozy‡ ['fluːzɪ] *n* poule* *f*, pouffiasse‡ *f*.
flop [flɒp] **1** *vi* **(a)** (*drop etc*) s'effondrer, s'affaler. **he ~ped down on the bed** il s'est affalé *or* s'est effondré sur le lit; **I'm ready to ~*** je suis claqué* *or* crevé* *or* sur les rotules*; **the fish ~ped feebly in the basket** le poisson s'agitait faiblement dans le panier.
(b) (*fail*) *[play]* faire un four; *[scheme etc]* faire fiasco, être un fiasco. **he ~ped as Hamlet** il a complètement raté son interprétation d'Hamlet.
2 *n* (*: *failure*) *[business venture, scheme]* fiasco *m*. **the play was a ~** la pièce a été un four *or* a fait fiasco; **he was a terrible ~** il s'est payé un échec monumental*, il a échoué dans les grandes largeurs*.
3 *adv*: **the whole business went ~** toute l'affaire s'est effondrée.
4 *cpd*: (*US*) **flophouse** asile *m* de nuit.
floppy ['flɒpɪ] *adj hat* à bords flottants; *clothes* lâche, flottant, flou.
flora ['flɔːrə] *n* flore *f*.
floral ['flɔːrəl] *adj* floral. **material with a ~ pattern** étoffe *f* à ramages *or* à motifs floraux; **~ tribute** fleurs *fpl* et couronnes *fpl*.
Florence ['flɒrəns] *n* Florence.
Florentine ['flɒrəntaɪn] *adj* florentin.
floribunda [flɔrə'bʌndə] *n* polyanta floribunda *m*.
florid ['flɒrɪd] *adj person, complexion* rubicond, rougeaud; *literary style* fleuri, plein de fioritures; *architecture* tarabiscoté, très chargé *or* orné.
Florida ['flɒrɪdə] *n* Floride *f*.
florin ['flɒrɪn] *n* florin *m* (*ancienne pièce de deux shillings*).
florist ['flɒrɪst] *n* fleuriste *mf*. **~'s shop** magasin *m or* boutique *f* de fleuriste.
floss [flɒs] *n* bourre *f* de soie; *V* **candy**.
flotation [fləʊ'teɪʃən] *n [boat etc]* action *f* de flotter; *[log]* flottage *m*; (*Fin*) lancement *m*. (*Space*) **~ collar** flotteur *m* (*de module lunaire*).
flotilla [flə'tɪlə] *n* flotille *f*.
flotsam ['flɒtsəm] *n* épave *f* (flottante). (*fig*) **the ~ and jetsam of our society** les épaves de notre société.
flounce [flaʊns] **1** *vi* avoir des mouvements brusques. **to ~ in/out** *etc* entrer/sortir *etc* dans un mouvement d'humeur (*or* d'indignation *etc*). **2** *n* **(a)** (*gesture*) geste impatient, mouvement vif. **(b)** (*Dress*) volant *m*.
flounced [flaʊnst] *adj skirt, dress* à volants.
flounder[1] ['flaʊndəʳ] *n* (*fish*) flet *m*, carrelet *m*.
flounder[2] ['flaʊndəʳ] *vi* (*in mud etc*) patauger (péniblement), patouiller*, barboter. **we ~ed along in the mud** nous avons poursuivi notre chemin en pataugeant dans la boue; **I watched him ~ing about in the water** je le regardais se débattre dans l'eau; (*fig*) **he was ~ing about upstairs** il allait et venait bruyamment en haut; **he ~ed through the rest of the speech** il a fini le discours en bredouillant; **he ~ed on in bad French** il continuait de patauger* *or* baragouiner en mauvais français.
flour ['flaʊəʳ] **1** *n* farine *f*. **2** *vt* fariner; *one's hands, face* enfariner. **3** *cpd*: **flour-bin** boîte *f* à farine; **flour mill** minoterie *f*; **flour shaker** saupoudreuse *f* (à farine); **flour sifter** tamis *m* à farine.
flourish ['flʌrɪʃ] **1** *vi [plants etc]* bien venir, se plaire; *[business etc]* prospérer; *[writer, artist etc]* avoir du succès; *[literature, the arts, painting]* fleurir, être en plein essor. **the children were all ~ing** les enfants étaient tous en pleine forme *or* d'une santé florissante.
2 *vt stick, book etc* brandir.
3 *n* (*curve, decoration*) fioriture *f*, ornement *m*; (*in handwriting*) fioriture; (*under signature*) parafe *m or* paraphe *m*; (*Mus*) fioriture. **with a ~ of his stick** en faisant un moulinet avec sa canne; **he took the lid off with a ~** il a enlevé le couvercle avec un grand moulinet *or* geste du bras; **a ~ of trumpets** une fanfare, un air de trompettes.
flourishing ['flʌrɪʃɪŋ] *adj business* prospère, florissant; *plant* florissant, en très bon état; *person* resplendissant de santé, d'une santé florissante.
floury ['flaʊərɪ] *adj hands* enfariné; *potatoes* farineux; *loaf, dish* saupoudré de farine, fariné.
flout [flaʊt] *vt orders, advice* faire fi de, se moquer de, passer outre à; *conventions, society* mépriser, se moquer de.
flow [fləʊ] **1** *vi [river, blood from wound]* couler; *[electric current, blood in veins]* circuler; *[tide]* monter, remonter; *[dress, hair etc]* flotter, ondoyer; (*fig: result*) découler, résulter, provenir (*from* de). *[people]* **to ~ in** affluer, entrer à flots; **to ~ out of** s'écouler de, sortir de; **the money keeps ~ing in** l'argent

rentre bien; to ~ past sth passer devant qch; to ~ back refluer; the water ~ed over the fields l'eau s'est répandue dans les champs; let the music ~ over you laisse la musique t'envahir; the river ~s into the sea le fleuve se jette dans la mer; tears were ~ing down her cheeks les larmes coulaient *or* ruisselaient sur ses joues; land ~ing with milk and honey une terre d'abondance.

2 *n* [*tide*] flux *m*; [*river*] courant *m*; [*electric current, blood in veins*] circulation *f*; [*donations, orders, replies, words*] flot *m*; [*music*] déroulement *m*. he always has a ready ~ of conversation il a toujours la conversation facile; he stopped the ~ of blood il a arrêté l'écoulement *m or* l'épanchement *m* du sang, il a étanché le sang; *V* ebb.

3 *cpd*: flow chart, flow sheet (*Admin, Ind*) planning *m*, plan *m* de travail, organigramme *m*; (*Computers*) organigramme.

flower ['flaʊəʳ] 1 *n* fleur *f*. in ~ en fleur; to say sth with ~s dire qch avec des fleurs; no ~s by request ni fleurs ni couronnes; the ~ of the army la (fine) fleur *or* l'élite *f* de l'armée; ~s of rhetoric fleurs de rhétorique; *V* bunch.

2 *vi* (*lit, fig*) fleurir.

3 *cpd*: flower arrangement (*art*) art *m* de faire des bouquets; (*exhibit*) composition florale; flower bed plate-bande *f*, parterre *m*; flower garden jardin *m* d'agrément; flower head capitule *m*; (*fig*) flower people* hippies *mpl*; flowerpot pot *m* (à fleurs); flower-seller bouquetière *f*; flower shop (boutique *f* de) fleuriste *m*; at the flower shop chez le marchand (*or* la marchande) de fleurs, chez le fleuriste; flower show floralies *fpl*; (*smaller*) exposition *f* de fleurs.

flowered ['flaʊəd] *adj cloth, shirt etc* à fleurs.

flowering ['flaʊərɪŋ] 1 *n* (*lit*) floraison *f*; (*fig*) floraison, épanouissement *m*. 2 *adj* (*in flower*) en fleurs. ~ shrub arbuste *m* à fleurs.

flowery ['flaʊərɪ] *adj meadow* fleuri, couvert *or* émaillé (*liter*) de fleurs; *material* à fleurs; *style, essay, speech* fleuri, orné.

flowing ['fləʊɪŋ] *adj movement* gracieux; *beard, dress, hair* flottant; *style* coulant; *tide* montant.

flown [fləʊn] *ptp of* fly³; *V* high 4.

flu [fluː] *n* (*abbr of* influenza) grippe *f*; *V* Asian.

fluctuate ['flʌktjʊeɪt] *vi* [*prices, temperature etc*] varier, fluctuer; [*person, attitude*] varier (*between* entre).

fluctuation [ˌflʌktjʊ'eɪʃən] *n* fluctuation *f*, variation *f*.

flue [fluː] *n* [*chimney*] conduit *m* (de cheminée); [*stove*] tuyau *m* (de poêle). ~ brush hérisson *m* (*de ramoneur*).

fluency ['fluːənsɪ] *n* (*in speech*) facilité *f or* aisance *f* (d'élocution); (*in writing*) facilité, aisance. his ~ in English son aisance à s'exprimer en anglais.

fluent ['fluːənt] *adj style* coulant, aisé. to be a ~ speaker avoir la parole facile; he is ~ in Italian, he speaks ~ Italian, his Italian is ~ il parle couramment l'italien.

fluently ['fluːəntlɪ] *adv speak a language* couramment; *speak, write, express o.s.* avec facilité, avec aisance.

fluff [flʌf] 1 *n* (*U*) (*on birds, young animals*) duvet *m*; (*from material*) peluche *f*; (*dust on floors*) mouton(s) *m(pl)* (*de poussière*). (*fig*) a bit of ~‡ une nénette‡.

2 *vt* (a) (*also* ~ out) *feathers* ébouriffer; *pillows, hair* faire bouffer.

(b) (*) *audition, lines in play, exam* rater, louper*.

fluffy ['flʌfɪ] *adj bird* duveteux; *hair* bouffant; *toy* en peluche; *material* pelucheux.

fluid ['fluːɪd] 1 *adj substance* fluide, liquide; *situation* fluide, indécis; *drawing, outline, style* fluide, coulant. ~ ounce *mesure de capacité* (= 0,028L); my plans are still fairly ~ je n'ai pas encore de plans très fixes; (*US Fin*) ~ assets liquidités *fpl*, disponibilités *fpl*.

2 *n* fluide *m* (*also Chem*), liquide *m*. (*as diet*) he's on ~s only il ne peut prendre que des liquides.

fluidity [fluː'ɪdɪtɪ] *n* [*gas, liquid, situation etc*] fluidité *f*; [*style, speech*] aisance *f*, coulant *m*.

fluke¹ [fluːk] *n* coup *m* de chance *or* de veine* extraordinaire, hasard *m* extraordinaire. by a (sheer) ~ par raccroc, par un hasard extraordinaire.

fluke² [fluːk] *n* (*Naut*) patte *f* (*d'ancre*).

fluke³ [fluːk] *n* (*Zool*) douve *f* (du foie *etc*).

fluky ['fluːkɪ] *adj wind* capricieux. ~ shot raccroc *m*.

flummery ['flʌmərɪ] *n* (*Culin*) bouillie *f*; (*fig*) flagornerie *f*.

flummox* ['flʌməks] *vt person* démonter, couper le sifflet à*. he was ~ed ça lui avait coupé le sifflet*, il était complètement démonté.

flung [flʌŋ] *pret, ptp of* fling; *V* far 3.

flunk‡ [flʌŋk] 1 *vi* (*fail*) être recalé* *or* collé*; (*shirk*) se dégonfler*, caner‡.

2 *vt* (a) (*fail*) to ~ French/an exam être recalé* *or* être collé* *or* se faire étendre* en français/à un examen; they ~ed 10 candidates ils ont recalé* *or* collé* 10 candidats.

(b) (*give up*) laisser tomber.

flunk(e)y ['flʌŋkɪ] *n* (*lit*) laquais *m*; (*fig*) larbin* *m*.

fluorescence [flʊə'resns] *n* fluorescence *f*.

fluorescent [flʊə'resnt] *adj lighting* fluorescent. ~ strip tube fluorescent *or* au néon.

fluoridation [ˌflʊərɪ'deɪʃən] *n* traitement *m* au fluor.

fluoride ['flʊəraɪd] *n* fluor *m*. ~ toothpaste dentifrice fluoré *or* au fluor.

fluorine ['flʊəriːn] *n* fluor *m*.

fluorspar ['flʊəspaːʳ] *n* spath *m* fluor.

flurry ['flʌrɪ] 1 *n* [*snow*] rafale *f*; [*wind*] rafale, risée *f*; (*fig*) agitation *f*, émoi *m*. a ~ of activity une soudaine poussée *or* un soudain accès d'activité; in a ~ of excitement dans un accès d'agitation.

2 *vt* agiter, effarer. to get flurried perdre la tête, s'affoler (*at* pour).

flush¹ [flʌʃ] 1 *n* (a) (*in sky*) lueur *f* rouge, rougeoiement *m*; [*blood*] flux *m*; (*blush*) rougeur *f*. (*Med*) (hot) ~es bouffées *fpl* de chaleur.

(b) [*beauty, health, youth*] éclat *m*; [*joy*] élan *m*; [*excitement*] accès *m*. in the (first) ~ of victory dans l'ivresse de la victoire; she's not in the first ~ of youth elle n'est pas de la première jeunesse.

(c) [*lavatory*] chasse *f* (d'eau).

2 *vi* [*face, person*] rougir. to ~ crimson s'empourprer, piquer un fard*; to ~ with shame/anger rougir de honte/de colère.

3 *vt* (a) nettoyer à grande eau; *drain, pipe* curer à grande eau. to ~ the lavatory tirer la chasse (d'eau).

(b) to ~ a door rendre une porte plane.

flush away *vt sep* (*down sink/drain*) faire partir par l'évier/par l'égout; (*down lavatory*) faire partir (en tirant la chasse d'eau).

flush out *vt sep* nettoyer à grande eau.

flush² [flʌʃ] *adj* (a) au même niveau (*with* que), au *or* à ras (*with* de). ~ with the ground à ras de terre, au ras de terre; rocks ~ with the water des rochers à *or* au ras de l'eau, des rochers à fleur d'eau *or* qui affleurent; a door ~ with the wall une porte dans l'alignement du mur; a cupboard ~ with the wall un placard encastré dans le mur; ~ against tout contre.

(b) to be ~ (with money)‡ être plein de fric‡, être plein aux as‡.

flush³ [flʌʃ] *vt* (*also* ~ out) *game, birds* lever; *thieves, spies* forcer à se montrer.

flush⁴ [flʌʃ] *n* (*Cards*) flush *m*; *V* royal *etc*.

flushed ['flʌʃt] *adj person, face* (tout) rouge. ~ with fever rouge de fièvre; they were ~ with success le succès leur tournait la tête.

fluster ['flʌstəʳ] 1 *vt* énerver, agiter, troubler. don't ~ me! ne me trouble pas!, ne m'énerve pas!; to get ~ed s'énerver, se troubler. 2 *n* agitation *f*, trouble *m*. in a ~ énervé, troublé, agité.

flute [fluːt] *n* (*Mus*) flûte *f*.

fluted ['fluːtɪd] *adj pillar* cannelé, strié; (*Mus*) *tone, note* flûté.

flutist ['fluːtɪst] *n* (*US*) = flautist.

flutter ['flʌtəʳ] 1 *vi* (a) [*flag, ribbon*] flotter, voleter, s'agiter; [*bird, moth, butterfly*] voltiger, voleter; [*wings*] battre. the bird ~ed about the room l'oiseau voletait çà et là dans la pièce; the butterfly ~ed away le papillon a disparu en voltigeant; a leaf came ~ing down une feuille est tombée en tourbillonnant.

(b) [*person*] papillonner, virevolter, aller et venir dans une grande agitation. she ~ed into the room elle a fait une entrée très agitée dans la pièce.

(c) [*heart*] palpiter; [*pulse*] battre (faiblement).

2 *vt fan, paper* jouer de. the bird ~ed its wings l'oiseau a battu des ailes; to ~ one's eyelashes battre des cils (*at sb* dans la direction de qn).

3 *n* (a) [*eyelashes, wings*] battement *m*; [*heart*] palpitation *f*; [*pulse*] (faible) battement; (*nervousness*) agitation *f*, émoi *m*, trouble *m*. (all) in a ~ tout troublé, dans un grand émoi.

(b) (*Brit: gamble*) to have a ~* parier *or* risquer (de petites sommes) (*on* sur); (*St Ex*) boursicoter.

fluvial ['fluːvɪəl] *adj* fluvial.

flux [flʌks] *n* (*U*) (a) changement continuel, fluctuation *f*. to be in a state of ~ changer sans arrêt, fluctuer continuellement. (b) (*Med*) flux *m*, évacuation *f* (*de sang etc*); (*Phys*) flux; (*Metal*) fondant *m*.

fly¹ [flaɪ] 1 *n* (*insect: also Fishing*) mouche *f*. the epidemic killed them off like flies ils mouraient *or* tombaient comme des mouches, frappés par l'épidémie; (*fig*) there's a ~ in the ointment il y a un ennui *or* un hic* *or* un os*; he's the ~ in the ointment le gros obstacle c'est lui, c'est lui l'empêcheur de tourner en rond; there are no flies on him‡ il n'est pas né d'hier, il n'est pas tombé de la dernière averse *or* pluie; *V* die¹, house.

2 *cpd*: fly-blown couvert *or* plein de chiures de mouches; (*tainted*) gâté; flycatcher (*bird*) gobe-mouches *m inv*; (*plant*) plante *f* carnivore; (*trap*) attrape-mouches *m inv*; fly fishing pêche *f* à la mouche; fly paper papier *m* tue-mouches; (*Fishing*) fly rod canne *f* à mouche; fly swat(ter) tapette *f*; fly trap *V* Venus; (*Boxing*) fly weight poids *m* mouche.

fly² [flaɪ] *adj* (*esp Brit: astute*) malin (*f* -igne), rusé, astucieux.

fly³ [flaɪ] *pret* flew, *ptp* flown 1 *vi* (a) [*bird, insect, plane*] voler; [*air passenger*] aller *or* voyager en avion. to ~ over London survoler Londres, voler au-dessus de Londres; the planes flew past *or* over at 3 p.m. les avions sont passés (au-dessus de nos têtes) à 15 heures; to ~ across *or* over the Channel [*bird, plane, person*] survoler la Manche; [*passenger*] traverser la Manche en avion; [*bird*] to ~ away s'envoler; (*fig*) all her worries flew away tous ses soucis se sont envolés; we flew in from Rome this morning nous sommes venus de Rome en *or* par avion ce matin; to ~ off [*bird, plane*] s'envoler; [*plane*] (*take off*) s'envoler, décoller; (*disappear*) s'évanouir; [*passenger*] partir en avion, s'envoler (*to* pour); (*fig*) he is ~ing high il voit grand, il vise haut; (*fig*) to find that the bird has flown trouver l'oiseau envolé; I don't like ~ing je n'aime pas l'avion; *V* fury.

(b) (*fig*) [*time*] passer vite, filer*; [*sparks*] jaillir, voler; [*car, people*] filer*. [*person*] to ~ in/out/back *etc* entrer/sortir/retourner *etc* à toute vitesse *or* à toute allure *or* comme un bolide; it's late, I must ~! il est tard, il faut que je me sauve! (*subj*) *or* que je file*! (*subj*); to ~ to sb's assistance voler au secours de qn; to ~ in the face of danger lancer un défi au danger; to ~ in the face of authority battre en brèche l'ordre établi; to ~ into a rage *or* a passion s'emporter, se mettre dans une violente colère; (*fig*) to ~ off the handle s'emporter, sortir de ses gonds; to let ~ at sb (*in angry words*) s'en prendre violemment à qn, prendre qn violemment à parti, traiter qn de tous les noms; (*by shooting*) tirer sur qn; to let ~ **a stone** jeter une pierre; to ~ **at sb** sauter *or* se ruer sur qn; to ~ **at sb's throat** sauter à la gorge de qn; **the door flew open** la porte s'est ouverte brusquement *or* soudain *or* en coup de vent; **the handle flew off** la poignée s'est détachée brusquement *or* soudain; **the lid and the box flew apart** le couvercle et la boîte se sont brusquement *or* soudain séparés; **the cup flew to bits** *or* **into pieces** la tasse a volé en éclats; *V* **feather, send, spark.**

(c) (*flee*) fuir (*before* devant), s'enfuir (*from* de), se réfugier (*to* auprès de). to ~ **from temptation** fuir la tentation; ~ **for your life!** fuyez!

(d) *[flag]* se déployer; *V* **flag**[1].

2 *vt* **(a)** *aircraft* piloter; *person* emmener par avion; *goods* transporter par avion; *standard, admiral's flag etc* arborer. to ~ **the French flag** battre pavillon français; to ~ **a kite** (*lit*) faire voler un cerf-volant; (*fig*) lancer un ballon d'essai (*fig*); **we will ~ you to Italy and back for £80** nous vous offrons le voyage d'Italie aller et retour par avion pour 80 livres.

(b) to ~ **the country** quitter le pays, s'enfuir du pays.

3 *n* **(a)** (*on trousers: also* **flies**) braguette *f*; (*on tent*) auvent *m*.

(b) (*vehicle*) fiacre *m*.

(c) *[flag]* battant *m*.

(d) (*Theat*) **flies** cintres *mpl*, dessus *mpl*.

4 *cpd*: **flyaway** *hair* difficile, intraitable*; (*frivolous*) frivole, futile; **fly-button** bouton *m* de braguette; **fly-by-night** (*n*) (*irresponsible person*) tout-fou* *m*, écervelé(e) *m(f)*; (*decamping debtor*) débiteur *m*, -trice *f* qui déménage à la cloche de bois *or* qui décampe en douce*; (*adj*) *person* tout-fou* (*m only*), écervelé; (*Comm, Fin*) *firm, operation* véreux; **flyleaf** page *f* de garde; **flyover** (*Brit Aut*) autopont *m*; (*temporary*) toboggan *m*; (*US Aviat*) défilé aérien; (*Brit*) **flypast** défilé aérien; (*Brit*) **fly sheet** feuille volante; **flywheel** volant *m* (*Tech*).

flying ['flaɪɪŋ] **1** *n* (*action*) vol *m*; (*activity*) aviation *f*. **he likes ~** il aime l'avion; *V* **formation, stunt.**

2 *adj* volant. (*fig*) **to come through with ~ colours** remporter une victoire magnifique *or* complète; **~ insect** insecte volant; **~ jump** saut *m* avec élan; **to take a ~ jump** sauter avec élan; (*Sport*) **~ start** départ lancé; (*fig*) **to get off to a ~ start** *[racing car, runner]* prendre un départ très rapide *or* en flèche; *[scheme, plan]* prendre un bon *or* un excellent départ; **~ visit** visite *f* éclair *inv*.

3 *cpd*: **flying ambulance** (*plane*) avion *m* sanitaire; (*helicopter*) hélicoptère *m* sanitaire; **flying boat** hydravion *m*; **flying bomb** bombe volante, V1 *m*; **flying buttress** arc-boutant *m*; **flying doctor** médecin volant; **the Flying Dutchman** (*legend*) le Hollandais volant; (*opera*) le Vaisseau fantôme; **flying fish** poisson volant; **flying fortress** forteresse volante; **flying fox** roussette *f*; **flying machine** machine volante, appareil volant; **flying saucer** soucoupe volante; (*Police*) **Flying Squad** brigade volante de la police judiciaire; **flying time** heures *fpl* de vol; **flying trapeze** trapèze volant.

foal [fəʊl] **1** *n* (*horse*) poulain *m*; (*donkey*) ânon *m*. **the mare is in ~** la jument est pleine. **2** *vi* mettre bas (*un poulain etc*), pouliner.

foam [fəʊm] **1** *n [sea, animal]* écume *f*; *[beer etc]* mousse *f*; (*in fire fighting*) mousse (*carbonique*). (*liter*) **the ~** les flots *mpl* (*liter*).

2 *cpd*: **foam-backed** *carpet* à sous-couche de mousse; **foam plastic** mousse *f* de plastique; **foam rubber** caoutchouc *m* mousse; **foam sprayer** extincteur *m* à mousse.

3 *vi [sea]* écumer, moutonner; *[soapy water]* mousser, faire de la mousse. **to ~ at the mouth** *[animal]* baver, écumer; *[person]* (*lit*) avoir de l'écume aux lèvres; (*fig*) écumer de rage; **he was absolutely ~ing**‡ il écumait (de rage).

foam up *vi [liquid in container]* mousser.

foamy ['fəʊmɪ] *adj sea* écumeux; *beer* mousseux.

fob [fɒb] **1** *vt*: **to ~ sth off on sb, to ~ sb off with sth** refiler* *or* fourguer‡ qch à qn; **to ~ sb off with promises** payer qn de promesses. **2** *n* (†) (*pocket*) gousset *m* (de pantalon); (*ornament*) breloque *f*. **~ watch** montre *f* de gousset.

focal ['fəʊkəl] *adj* focal. **~ length** distance focale, focale *f*; **~ plane** plan focal; **~ plane shutter** obturateur focal; **~ point** foyer *m*; (*fig*) point central, point de mire.

foci ['fəʊkaɪ] *npl of* **focus.**

fo'c'sle ['fəʊksl] *n* = **forecastle.**

focus ['fəʊkəs] **1** *n, pl* **~es** *or* **foci** (*Math, Phys*) foyer *m*; *[interest]* centre *m*; *[illness, unrest]* foyer, siège *m*. (*Phot*) **the picture is in/out of ~** l'image est/n'est pas au point; (*Phot*) **to bring a picture into ~** mettre une image au point; **he was the ~ of attention** il était le point de mire *or* le centre d'attention *or* le centre d'intérêt.

2 *vt instrument, camera* mettre au point; *light, heat rays* faire converger; *one's efforts, attention* concentrer (*on* sur). **to ~ one's eyes on sth** fixer ses yeux sur qch; **all eyes were ~ed on him** il était le point de mire de tous.

3 *vi [light, heat rays]* converger (*on* sur); *[eyes, person]* accommoder. **to ~ on sth** fixer son regard sur; **his eyes ~ed on the book** ses yeux se sont fixés sur le livre; **I can't ~ properly** je n'arrive pas à accommoder.

fodder ['fɒdə^r] *n* fourrage *m*; *V* **cannon.**

foe [fəʊ] *n* (*liter: lit, fig*) ennemi(e) *m(f)*, adversaire *mf*.

foetal ['fiːtl] *adj* fœtal.

foetid ['fiːtɪd] *adj* = **fetid.**

foetus ['fiːtəs] *n* fœtus *m*.

fog [fɒg] **1** *n* **(a)** (*Met*) brouillard *m*; (*Naut*) brume *f*, brouillard (de mer); (*fig*) brouillard, confusion *f*. (*fig*) **to be in a ~** être dans le brouillard, ne plus savoir où l'on en est.

(b) (*Phot*) voile *m*.

2 *vt mirror, glasses* embuer; *person* embrouiller, brouiller les idées à; *photo* voiler. **to ~ the issue** (*accidentally*) embrouiller *or* obscurcir la question; (*purposely*) brouiller les cartes.

3 *vi [mirror, glasses]* (*also* **~ over**) s'embuer; *[landscape]* s'embrumer; (*Phot*) *[negative]* se voiler.

4 *cpd*: **fog bank** banc *m* de brume; **fogbound** pris dans la brume, bloqué par le brouillard; (*Naut*) **foghorn** corne *f or* sirène *f* de brume; **she has a voice like a foghorn** elle a une voix tonitruante *or* de stentor; (*Aut*) **foglamp, foglight** phare *m* antibrouillard; **fog signal** (*Naut*) signal *m* de brume; (*Rail*) pétard *m*.

fogey* ['fəʊgɪ] *n*: **old ~** vieille baderne*, vieux bonze*.

foggy ['fɒgɪ] *adj landscape, weather* brumeux; *ideas, reasoning* confus. **it was ~ yesterday** hier il a fait du brouillard; **on a ~ day** par un jour de brouillard; **I haven't the foggiest (idea** *or* **notion)!*** aucune idée!, pas la moindre idée!

foible ['fɔɪbl] *n* marotte *f*, petite manie.

foil[1] [fɔɪl] *n* **(a)** (*U: metal sheet*) feuille *f or* lame *f* de métal; (*also* **cooking** *or* **kitchen ~**) papier *m* d'aluminium, (papier) alu* *m*. (*Culin*) **fish cooked in ~** poisson cuit (au four) dans du papier d'aluminium; *V* **tin** *etc*.

(b) (*fig*) repoussoir *m*. **to act as a ~ to sb/sth** servir de repoussoir à qn/qch, mettre qn/qch en valeur.

foil[2] [fɔɪl] *n* (*Fencing*) fleuret *m*.

foil[3] [fɔɪl] *vt plans, attempts* déjouer, contrecarrer.

foist [fɔɪst] *vt*: **to ~ sth (off) on sb** refiler* *or* repasser* qch à qn; **this job was ~ed (off) on to me** c'est moi qui ai hérité de ce boulot*; **to ~ o.s. on (to) sb** s'imposer à qn; (*as uninvited guest*) s'imposer *or* s'installer chez qn.

fold[1] [fəʊld] **1** *n* (*in paper, cloth, skin, earth's surface*) pli *m*. (*Geol*) **~s** plissement *m*.

2 *cpd*: **foldaway** *bed etc* pliant.

3 *vt* **(a)** *paper, blanket, bed, chair* plier. **to ~ a sheet in two** plier un drap en deux; **to ~ one's arms** (se) croiser les bras.

(b) (*wrap up*) envelopper (*in* dans), entourer (*in* de). **to ~ sb/sth in one's arms** serrer qn/qch dans ses bras, étreindre qn/qch; **to ~ sb to one's heart** serrer qn sur son cœur; (*liter*) **hills ~ed in mist** des collines enveloppées dans la brume *or* de brume.

4 *vi* **(a)** *[chair, table]* se (re)plier.

(b) (*: *fail*) *[newspaper]* disparaître, cesser de paraître; *[business]* fermer (ses portes).

fold away 1 *vi [table, bed]* (être capable de) se (re)plier.

2 *vt sep clothes, one's book, newspaper* plier (*pour ranger*).

3 foldaway *adj V* **fold**[1] **2.**

fold back *vt sep shutters* ouvrir, rabattre; *bedclothes, collar* replier, rabattre, retourner.

fold down *vt sep chair* plier; *corner of page* corner.

fold over *vt sep paper* plier, replier; *blanket* replier, rabattre, retourner.

fold up 1 *vi* (**fig*) *[plan, business venture]* faire fiasco, s'écrouler; *[play etc]* échouer, faire un four. **to fold up with laughter*** se tordre (de rire), être plié (en deux)*.

2 *vt sep paper etc* plier, replier.

fold[2] [fəʊld] *n* (*enclosure*) parc *m* à moutons; (*Rel*) sein *m* de l'Église. (*fig*) **to come back to the ~** rentrer au bercail.

...fold [fəʊld] *suf*: **twenty~** (*adj*) par vingt; (*adv*) vingt fois; *V* **two** *etc*.

folder ['fəʊldə^r] *n* **(a)** (*file*) chemise *f*; (*with hinges*) classeur *m*; (*for drawings*) carton *m*; (*papers*) dossier *m*. **(b)** (*circular*) dépliant *m*, brochure *f*.

folding ['fəʊldɪŋ] *adj bed etc* pliant. **~ chair** (*with back*) chaise pliante; (*with back and arms*) fauteuil pliant; **~ door** porte *f* (en) accordéon; **~ seat** (*gen: also* **~ stool**) pliant *m*; (*Aut, Theat*) strapontin *m*; **~ table** table pliante.

foliage ['fəʊlɪɪdʒ] *n* feuillage *m*.

foliation [ˌfəʊlɪ'eɪʃən] *n* (*Bot*) foliation *f*, feuillaison *f*; *[book]* foliotage *m*; (*Geol*) foliation; (*Archit*) rinceaux *mpl*.

folio ['fəʊlɪəʊ] *n* (*sheet*) folio *m*, feuillet *m*; (*volume*) (volume *m*) in-folio *m*.

folk [fəʊk] **1** *n* **(a)** (*pl: people: also* **~s**) gens *fpl*. **they are good ~(s)** ce sont de braves gens, ce sont de bonnes gens, ce sont des gens gentils; **a lot of ~(s) believe ...** beaucoup de gens croient ...; **there were a lot of ~ at the concert** il y avait beaucoup de gens *or* de monde au concert; **old ~(s)** les vieux, les vieilles gens; **young ~(s)** les jeunes *mpl*, les jeunes gens; **the old ~s stayed at home** les vieux* sont restés à la maison; **hullo ~s!*** bonjour tout le monde!*; *V* **country, old** *etc*.

(b) (*pl: people in general: also* **~s**) les gens, on. **what will ~(s) think?** qu'est-ce que les gens vont penser?, qu'est-ce qu'on va penser?; **~ get worried when they see that** les gens s'inquiètent quand ils voient ça.

(c) (*pl: relatives*) **~s*** famille *f*, parents *mpl*; **my ~s** ma famille, mes parents, les miens.

(d) (*U*) = **~ music**; *V* **2.**

2 *cpd*: **folk dance, folk dancing** danse *f* folklorique; **folklore** folklore *m*; **folk music** (*gen*) musique *f* folklorique; (*contemporary*) musique folk *inv*, folk *m*; **folk singer** (*gen*) chanteur *m*, -euse *f* de chansons folkloriques; (*contemporary*) chanteur, -euse de (chansons) folk *m inv*; **folksong** (*gen*) chanson *f or* chant *m* folklorique; (*contemporary*) chanson folk *inv*; **folk tale** conte *m* populaire *or* folklorique.

folksy* ['fəʊksɪ] *adj manner, story, humour* populaire; *person* bon enfant *inv*, sans façon.

follicle ['fɒlɪkl] *n* follicule *m*.

follow ['fɒləʊ] **1** *vt* **(a)** *person, road, vehicle* suivre; (*in procession*) aller *or* venir à la suite de, suivre; *suspect* filer. **we're being ~ed** on nous suit; **~ that car!** suivez cette voiture!; **~ me** suivez-moi; **the child ~s him everywhere** l'enfant le suit partout, l'enfant est toujours sur ses talons; **they ~ed the guide**

ils ont suivi le guide; **to have sb ~ed** faire filer qn; **the detectives ~ed the suspect for a week** les détectives ont filé le suspect pendant une semaine; **a bodyguard ~ed the president everywhere** un garde du corps accompagnait le président partout; **he was ~ed by one of our staff** il a été suivi par l'un de nos employés; **he arrived first, ~ed by the ambassador** il est arrivé le premier, suivi de l'ambassadeur *or* et après lui est venu l'ambassadeur; **this was ~ed by a request for ...** ceci a été suivi d'une demande de ...; **the boat ~ed the coast** le bateau suivait *or* longeait la côte; **~ your nose** continue tout droit; **he ~ed his father into the business** il est entré dans l'affaire sur les traces de son père; **as ~s** comme suit; **his argument was as ~s** son raisonnement était le suivant; **the earthquake was ~ed by an epidemic** une épidémie a suivi le tremblement de terre; **the dinner will be ~ed by a concert** le dîner sera suivi d'un concert; **the years ~ed one another** les années se suivirent *or* se succédèrent.

(b) *fashion* suivre, se conformer à; *instructions, course of study* suivre; *serial, strip cartoon* lire (régulièrement); *speech, lecture* suivre, écouter (attentivement). **to ~ sb's advice/example** suivre les conseils/l'exemple de qn; **to ~ suit** (*Cards*) fournir (*in clubs etc* à trèfle *etc*); (*fig*) en faire autant, faire de même; **do you ~ football?** vous suivez le football?; **which team do you ~?** tu es supporter de quelle équipe?

(c) *profession* exercer, suivre; *career* poursuivre. (*liter*) **to ~ the sea** être *or* devenir *or* se faire marin.

(d) (*understand*) suivre, comprendre. **do you ~ me?** vous me suivez?; **I don't quite ~ (you)** je ne vous suis pas bien *or* pas tout à fait.

2 *vi* **(a)** (*come after*) suivre. **to ~ right behind sb, to ~ hard on sb's heels** être sur les talons de qn; (*fig*) **to ~ in sb's footsteps** *or* **tracks** suivre les traces *or* marcher sur les traces de qn; (*at meals*) **what is there to ~?** qu'est-ce qu'il y a après?, qu'est-ce qui suit?

(b) (*result*) s'ensuivre, résulter (*from* de). **it ~s that** il s'ensuit que + *indic*; **it doesn't ~ that** il ne s'ensuit pas nécessairement que + *subj or indic*, cela ne veut pas forcément dire que + *subj or indic*; **that doesn't ~** pas forcément, les deux choses n'ont rien à voir (l'une avec l'autre); **that ~s from what he said** cela découle de ce qu'il a dit.

(c) (*understand*) suivre, comprendre.

3 *cpd*: **follow-my-leader** *jeu où les enfants doivent imiter tous les mouvements d'un joueur désigné*; **follow-through** (*Billiards*) coulé *m*; (*Golf, Tennis*) accompagnement *m* (du coup); (*to a project, survey*) suite *f*, continuation *f*; **follow-up** (*event, programme etc coming after another*) suite *f* (*to* de); (*letter, circular*) rappel *m*; (*Med*) **follow-up care** soins post-hospitaliers; **follow-up survey** étude *f* complémentaire; (*Med, Soc etc*) **follow-up visit** visite *f* de contrôle.

follow about, follow around *vt sep* suivre (partout), être toujours sur les talons de.

follow on *vi* **(a)** (*come after*) suivre. **you go ahead and I'll follow on when I can** allez-y, je vous suivrai quand je pourrai.

(b) (*result*) résulter (*from* de). **it follows on from what I said** cela découle de ce que j'ai dit, c'est la conséquence logique de ce que j'ai dit.

follow out *vt sep idea, plan* poursuivre jusqu'au bout *or* jusqu'à sa conclusion.

follow through 1 *vi* (*Billiards*) faire *or* jouer un coulé; (*Golf, Tennis*) accompagner son coup *or* sa balle.

2 *vt sep* = **follow out.**

3 follow-through *n V* **follow 3.**

follow up 1 *vi* **(a)** (*pursue an advantage*) exploiter un *or* tirer parti d'un avantage.

(b) (*Ftbl etc*) suivre l'action.

2 *vt sep* **(a)** (*benefit from*) *advantage, success, victory* exploiter, tirer parti de; *offer* donner suite à.

(b) (*not lose track of*) suivre; *[social worker]* maintenir une liaison avec, suivre, surveiller. **we must follow this business up** il faudra suivre cette affaire; **this is a case to follow up** c'est un cas à suivre; **'to be followed up'** 'cas à suivre'.

(c) (*reinforce*) *victory* asseoir; *remark* faire suivre (*with* de), compléter (*with* par). **they followed up the programme with another equally good** ils ont donné à cette émission une suite qui a été tout aussi excellente; **they followed up the insults with threats** ils ont fait suivre leurs insultes de menaces.

3 follow-up *n, adj V* **follow 3.**

follower ['fɒləʊə^r] *n* **(a)** partisan(e) *m(f)*, disciple *m*. **the ~s of fashion** ceux qui suivent la mode; **as all football ~s know** comme le savent tous ceux qui s'intéressent au football. **(b)** (†: *admirer*) amoureux *m* -euse *f*, admirateur *m* -trice *f*.

following ['fɒləʊɪŋ] **1** *adj* suivant. **the ~ day** le jour suivant, le lendemain; **he made the ~ remarks** il a fait les remarques suivantes *or* les remarques que voici; **he said the ~** il a dit ceci; (*in documents etc*) **see the ~ for an explanation** voir ce qui suit pour toute explication; **~ wind** vent *m* arrière.

2 *n [idea, doctrine]* partisans *mpl*, disciples *mpl*, adeptes *mpl*. **he has a large ~** il a de nombreux partisans *or* disciples *or* fidèles.

folly ['fɒlɪ] *n* **(a)** (*U: foolishness*) folie *f*, sottise *f*. **it's sheer ~ to do that** c'est de la pure folie *or* de la démence de faire cela. **(b)** (*foolish thing, action*) sottise *f*, folie *f*. **(c)** (*Archit*) folie *f*.

foment [fəʊ'ment] *vt* (*lit, fig*) fomenter.

fomentation [ˌfəʊmen'teɪʃən] *n* (*lit, fig*) fomentation *f*.

fond [fɒnd] *adj* **(a) to be ~ of sb** aimer qn, avoir de l'affection pour qn; **to be very ~ of music** aimer beaucoup la musique, être très amateur de musique; **to be ~ of sweet things** être friand de sucreries, aimer les sucreries.

(b) (*loving*) *husband, friend* affectueux, tendre; *parent* (trop) bon, (trop) indulgent; *look* tendre; *hope* fervent; *ambition, wish* cher. **it is my ~est hope that ...** mon espoir le plus cher est que ...

(c) (*foolish*) *hope, ambition, wish* naïf (*f* naïve).

fondle ['fɒndl] *vt* caresser.

fondly ['fɒndlɪ] *adv* **(a)** (*lovingly*) tendrement, affectueusement.

(b) (*foolishly, credulously*) *believe, think* naïvement. **he ~ expected to learn it quickly** il avait la naïveté de croire qu'il l'apprendrait vite; **after that, he ~ imagined that** après cela, il était allé s'imaginer que *or* il s'imaginait naïvement que.

fondness ['fɒndnɪs] *n* (*for things*) prédilection *f*, penchant *m* (*for* pour); (*for people*) affection *f*, tendresse *f* (*for* pour).

font [fɒnt] *n* **(a)** (*Rel*) fonts baptismaux. **(b)** (*US Typ*) = **fount b.**

food [fu:d] **1** *n* **(a)** (*U*) nourriture *f*; *[grazing animals]* pâture *f*; *[poultry, pigs, dogs, cats]* pâtée *f*; *[plants]* engrais *m*. **there was no ~ in the house** il n'y avait rien à manger *or* il n'y avait pas de nourriture dans la maison; **there's not enough ~** il n'y a pas assez à manger, il n'y a pas assez de nourriture; **most of the ~ had gone bad** la plus grande partie de la nourriture *or* des vivres *mpl* s'était avariée; **to give sb ~** donner à manger à qn; **to buy ~** acheter à manger, acheter de la nourriture, faire des provisions; **the cost of ~** le prix des denrées *fpl* alimentaires *or* de la nourriture; **~ and clothing** la nourriture et les vêtements; **to be off one's ~*** avoir perdu l'appétit, n'avoir plus d'appétit; **the ~ is very good here** la cuisine est excellente ici, on mange très bien ici; **he likes plain ~** il aime la cuisine simple, il aime se nourrir simplement; (*fig*) **it gave me ~ for thought** cela m'a donné à penser *or* à réfléchir.

(b) ~s aliments *mpl*; **all these ~s must be kept in a cool place** tous ces aliments doivent être conservés au froid; **such ~s must be avoided** il faut s'abstenir de tels aliments; *V* **frozen, health** *etc*.

2 *cpd*: (*Ecol*) **food chain** chaîne *f* alimentaire; **food parcel** colis *m* (de vivres); **food poisoning** intoxication *f* alimentaire; **food prices** prix *mpl* des denrées *fpl* alimentaires *or* de la nourriture; **food rationing** rationnement *m* alimentaire; **foodstuffs** denrées *fpl* alimentaires, aliments *mpl*, comestibles *mpl*; **food subsidy** subvention *f* sur les denrées alimentaires; **food supplies** vivres *mpl*; **food value** valeur nutritive.

fool[1] [fu:l] **1** *n* **(a)** imbécile *mf*, idiot(e) *m(f)*, sot(te) *m(f)*. **stupid ~!** espèce d'imbécile!* *or* d'idiot(e)! *or* d'abruti(e)!*; **don't be a ~!** ne sois pas stupide!, ne fais pas l'idiot(e)!; **some ~ of a doctor, some ~ doctor**‡ un imbécile *or* un abruti* de médecin; **he was a ~ not to accept** il a été idiot *or* stupide de ne pas accepter; **he's more of a ~ than I thought** il est (encore) plus idiot que je ne pensais; **he was ~ enough to accept** il a été assez stupide pour accepter, il a eu la bêtise d'accepter; **to play** *or* **act the ~** faire l'imbécile* *or* le pitre; **he's nobody's ~** il n'est pas né d'hier *or* tombé de la dernière pluie; **more ~ you!*** tu n'avais qu'à ne pas faire l'idiot! *or* être idiot!; **he made himself look a ~** *or* **he made a ~ of himself in front of everybody** il s'est rendu ridicule devant tout le monde; **to make a ~ of sb** (*ridicule*) ridiculiser qn, se payer la tête de qn*; (*trick*) avoir* *or* duper qn; **I went on a ~'s errand** j'y suis allé pour rien, je me suis dépensé en pure perte; **to live in a ~'s paradise** se bercer d'un bonheur illusoire, poursuivre son rêve, planer.

(b) (*jester*) bouffon *m*, fou *m*.

2 *cpd*: **foolproof** *method* infaillible, à toute épreuve; *piece of machinery* indétraquable, indéréglable.

3 *vi* faire l'imbécile *or* l'idiot(e). **stop ~ing!** arrête de faire l'idiot(e)! *or* l'imbécile!; **no ~ing*, he really said it** sans blague*, il a vraiment dit ça; **I was only ~ing** je ne faisais que plaisanter, c'était pour rire.

4 *vt* avoir*, berner, duper. **you won't ~ me so easily!** vous ne m'aurez pas comme ça!* *or* si facilement!*; **it ~ed nobody** personne n'a été dupe.

fool about, fool around *vi* **(a)** (*waste time*) perdre son temps. **stop fooling about and get on with your work** cesse de perdre ton temps et fais ton travail.

(b) (*play the fool*) faire l'idiot(e) *or* l'imbécile *or* le pitre. **stop fooling about!** arrête de faire l'idiot! *or* l'imbécile! *or* le pitre!, cesse tes idioties!; **to fool about with sth** faire l'imbécile avec qch.

fool away *vt sep time, money* perdre *or* gaspiller (en futilités).

fool[2] [fu:l] *n* (*Brit Culin: also* **fruit ~**) mousse *f* de fruits.

foolery ['fu:lərɪ] *n* (*U*) (*foolish acts*) sottises *fpl*, bêtises *fpl*; (*behaviour*) bouffonnerie *f*, pitrerie(s) *f(pl)*.

foolhardiness ['fu:lˌhɑ:dɪnɪs] *n* témérité *f*, imprudence *f*.

foolhardy ['fu:lˌhɑ:dɪ] *adj* téméraire, imprudent.

foolish ['fu:lɪʃ] *adj* idiot, bête, insensé. **it would be ~ to believe her** ce ne serait pas (très) malin de la croire; **don't be so ~** ne fais pas l'idiot(e), ne sois pas bête; **that was very ~ of you** ça n'a pas été très malin de votre part, (*more formally*) vous avez vraiment été imprudent; **to look ~** avoir l'air idiot *or* tout bête*; **to make sb look ~** rendre qn ridicule; **I felt very ~** je me suis senti plutôt idiot *or* bête.

foolishly ['fu:lɪʃlɪ] *adv* sottement, bêtement. **and ~ I believed him** et je l'ai cru comme un(e) imbécile *or* un(e) idiot(e) (que j'étais).

foolishness ['fu:lɪʃnɪs] *n* (*U*) bêtise *f*, sottise *f*.

foolscap ['fu:lskæp] **1** *n* (*also* **~ paper**) = papier *m* pot *or* écolier. **2** *cpd*: **foolscap sheet** feuille *f* de papier pot *or* écolier; **foolscap size** format *m* pot *or* écolier.

foot [fʊt] **1** *n, pl* **feet (a)** *[person]* pied *m*; *[horse, cow etc]* pied; *[dog, cat, bird]* patte *f*. **to be on one's feet** (*lit*) être *or* se tenir debout; (*fig: after illness*) être sur pied, être rétabli *or* remis; **a little rest will set** *or* **put her on her feet again** un peu de repos la remettra sur pied *or* d'aplomb; **I'm on my feet all day long** je suis debout toute la journée; **to go on ~** aller à pied; **to get** *or* **to**

rise to one's feet se lever, se mettre debout; (*fig*) **to put** *or* **set sb on his feet again** (*healthwise*) remettre qn d'aplomb *or* d'attaque*; (*financially*) remettre qn en selle; **to keep one's feet** garder l'équilibre; **it's very wet under ~** c'est très mouillé par terre; **he was trampled under ~ by the horses** les chevaux l'ont piétiné; **the children have been under my** (*or* **our** *etc*) **feet the whole day** les enfants ont été dans mes (*or* nos *etc*) jambes toute la journée; **to get under sb's feet** venir dans les jambes de qn; (*fig*) **you've got to put your ~ down** il faut faire acte d'autorité, il faut être catégorique; **he let it go on for several weeks before finally putting his ~ down** il l'a supporté pendant plusieurs semaines avant d'y mettre le holà; (*Aut*: accelerate*) **to put one's ~ down** appuyer sur le champignon*; (*fig*) **to put one's ~ in it*** mettre les pieds dans le plat*; (*fig*) **to put one's best ~ forward** (*hurry*) se dépêcher, allonger *or* presser le pas; (*do one's best*) faire de son mieux; (*fig*) **he didn't put a ~ wrong** il n'a pas commis la moindre erreur *or* maladresse; *[people, relationship]* **to get off on the right/wrong ~** être bien/mal parti; **I got off on the wrong ~ with him** j'ai mal commencé avec lui; (*fig*) **to get one's** *or* **a ~ in the door** faire le premier pas, établir un premier contact; **to put one's feet up*** (s'étendre *or* s'asseoir pour) se reposer un peu; (*fig*) **he's got one ~ in the grave*** il a un pied dans la tombe; **to set ~ on land** poser le pied sur la terre ferme; **I've never set ~ there** je n'y ai jamais mis le(s) pied(s); **never set ~ here again!** ne remettez pas les pieds ici!; *V* **cold, drag, fall, find** *etc.*

(b) *[hill, bed, stocking]* pied *m*; *[table]* (bas) bout *m*; *[page, stairs]* bas *m*. **at the ~ of the page** au *or* en bas de la page.

(c) (*measure*) pied *m* (anglais); (*Poetry*) pied.

(d) (*U: Mil*) infanterie *f*. **ten thousand ~** dix mille fantassins *mpl or* soldats *mpl* d'infanterie; **the 91st of ~** le 91e (régiment) d'infanterie.

2 *vt*: **to ~ the bill*** payer (la note *or* la douloureuse*), casquer‡; **to ~ it*** (*walk*) (y) aller à pied *or* à pattes*; (*dance*) danser.

3 *cpd*: **foot-and-mouth (disease)** fièvre aphteuse; **football** *V* **football**; **footbath** bain *m* de pieds; **footboard** marchepied *m*; **footbrake** frein *m* à pied; **footbridge** passerelle *f*; **footfall** (bruit *m* de) pas *m*; **footgear*** chaussures *fpl*; **foothills** contreforts *mpl*; **foothold** prise *f* (de pied); **to gain a foothold** (*lit*) prendre pied; (*fig*) mettre le pied à l'étrier (*fig*); (*Theat*) **footlights** rampe *f*; (*fig*) **the lure of the footlights** l'attrait du théâtre *or* des planches*; **footloose** libre de toute attache; (*fig*) **footloose and fancy-free** libre comme l'air; **footman** valet *m* de pied; **footmark** empreinte *f* (de pied); **footnote** (*lit*) note *f* en bas de la page; (*fig*) post-scriptum *m*; **footpath** (*path*) sentier *m* (*V also* **public**); (*Brit: pavement*) trottoir *m*; (*by highway*) chemin *m*; (*esp Brit Rail*) **footplate** plate-forme *f* (*d'une locomotive*); **footplatemen, footplate workers** agents *mpl* de conduite; **footprint** = **footmark**; **footpump** pompe *f* à pied; **footrest** tabouret *m* (*pour les pieds*), marchepied† *m*; **footslog‡** s'envoyer* de la marche à pied; **footslogger‡** (*walker*) marcheur *m*, -euse *f*; (*soldier*) pousse-cailloux‡† *m inv*; **foot soldier** fantassin *m*; **footsore** aux pieds endoloris; **to be footsore** avoir mal aux pieds; **footstep** pas *m* (*V* **follow**); **footstool** = **footrest**; (*U*) **footwear** chaussure *f* (*U*), chaussures *fpl*; (*U: Boxing, Dancing*) **footwork** jeu *m* de jambes.

football ['fʊtbɔːl] **1** *n* (*sport*) football *m*; (*ball*) ballon *m* (de football), balle *f*.

2 *cpd ground, match, team* de football. **football coupon** fiche *f* de pari (sur les matchs de football); **football hooligan** vandale *m* (*qui assiste à un match de football*); **football hooliganism** vandalisme *m* (*lors d'un match de football*); **football league** championnat *m* de football; **Football League** ≈ Fédération française de football; **football pools** pronostics *mpl* (sur les matchs de football); **to do the football pools** parier *or* faire des paris (sur les matchs de football); **he won £20 on the football pools** il a gagné 20 livres en pariant sur les matchs de football; **football season** saison *f* du football; (*Brit Rail*) **football special** train *m* de supporters (*d'une équipe de football*).

footballer ['fʊtbɔːləʳ] *n* joueur *m* de football, footballeur *m*.

-footed ['fʊtɪd] *adj ending in cpds*: **light-footed** au pied léger; *V* **four** *etc.*

-footer ['fʊtəʳ] *n ending in cpds*: (*boat*) **a 15-footer** ≈ un bateau de 5 mètres de long; *V* **six** *etc.*

footing ['fʊtɪŋ] *n* (*lit*) prise *f* (de pied); (*fig*) position *f*, relations *fpl*. **to lose** *or* **miss one's ~** perdre pied *or* son équilibre *or* l'équilibre; **to get a ~ in society** se faire une position dans le monde; **to be on a friendly ~ with sb** être traité en ami par qn, avoir des relations d'amitié avec qn; **on an equal ~** sur un pied d'égalité; **on a war ~** sur le pied de guerre; **we should put this on a regular ~** (*do it regularly*) nous devrions faire ceci régulièrement; (*make it official*) nous devrions régulariser ceci; **to put sth on an official ~** officialiser qch, rendre qch officiel.

footle* ['fuːtl] *vi*: **to ~ about** faire l'âne‡, perdre son temps à des futilités.

footling ['fuːtlɪŋ] *adj* insignifiant, futile.

footsie‡ ['fʊtsɪ] *n*: **to play ~ with sb‡** faire du pied à qn.

fop [fɒp] *n* dandy *m*.

foppish ['fɒpɪʃ] *adj man* dandy; *manners, behaviour, clothes* de dandy.

for [fɔːʳ] (*phr vb elem*) **1** *prep* **(a)** (*indicating intention*) pour, à l'intention de; (*destination*) pour, à destination de, dans la direction de. **a letter ~ you** une lettre pour toi; **is this ~ me?** c'est pour moi?; **I sent a present ~ the child** j'ai envoyé un cadeau pour l'enfant; **he put it aside ~ me** il l'a mis de côté pour moi *or* à mon intention; **votes ~ women!** le droit de vote pour les femmes!; **clothes ~ children** vêtements pour enfants; **~ sale** à vendre; **~ example** par exemple; **it's time ~ dinner** c'est l'heure du dîner; **I've got news ~ you** j'ai une nouvelle pour toi, j'ai quelque chose à t'apprendre; **a job ~ next week** un travail à faire la semaine prochaine; **to write ~ the papers** faire des articles pour les journaux; **6 children to provide ~** 6 enfants à élever; **she's the wife ~ me** voilà *or* c'est la femme qu'il me faut; **he's the man ~ the job** il est l'homme idéal *or* c'est l'homme qu'il (nous) faut pour ce travail; **a weakness ~ sweet things** un faible pour les sucreries; **a liking ~ work** le goût du travail; **a gift ~ languages** un don pour les langues; **he's got a genius ~ saying the wrong thing*** il a le don de *or* un don pour dire ce qu'il ne faut pas; **he left ~ Italy** il est parti pour l'Italie; **trains ~ Paris** trains en direction de *or* à destination de Paris; **the train ~ Paris** le train pour *or* de Paris; **the ship left ~ Australia** le navire est parti pour l'Australie; **ship bound ~ Australia** (*before sailing*) navire en partance pour l'Australie; (*en route*) navire à destination de *or* en route pour l'Australie; **he swam ~ the shore** il a nagé dans la direction du rivage *or* vers le rivage; **to make ~ home** prendre la direction de la maison; **to make ~ the open sea** mettre le cap sur le (grand) large; **where are you ~?** où allez-vous?; **destined ~ greatness** promis à la célébrité; *V* **head** *etc.*

(b) (*indicating purpose*) pour, par. **what ~?** pourquoi?; **what did you do that ~?** pourquoi avez-vous fait cela?; **what's this knife ~?** à quoi sert ce couteau?; **it's not ~ cutting wood** ça n'est pas fait pour couper du bois; **it's been used ~ a hammer** on s'en est servi comme d'un marteau, ça a servi de marteau; **this will do ~ a hammer** ça ira comme marteau, ça servira de *or* comme marteau; **a room ~ studying in** une pièce réservée à l'étude *or* comme salle d'étude; **a bag ~ carrying books in** un sac pour porter des livres; **we went there ~ our holidays** nous y sommes allés pour les vacances; **he went there ~ a holiday/a rest** il y est allé pour des vacances/pour se reposer; **he does it ~ pleasure** il le fait par plaisir *or* pour son plaisir; **to work ~ exams** travailler pour des examens; **to work ~ one's living** travailler pour gagner sa vie; **to get ready ~ a journey** se préparer pour un voyage; **do you feel ready ~ bed now?** vous voulez aller vous coucher tout de suite?; **fit ~ nothing** bon à rien; **eager ~ praise** avide d'éloges; **a collection ~ the blind** une quête pour les *or* en faveur des aveugles; **a campaign ~ free education** une campagne pour la gratuité de l'enseignement; **to pray ~ peace** prier pour la paix; **to hope ~ news** espérer des nouvelles; **to look ~ sth** chercher qch; *V* **ask, good** *etc.*

(c) (*as representing*) **D ~ Daniel** D comme Daniel; (*Parl*) **member ~ Brighton** député *m* de Brighton; **agent ~ Ford cars** concessionnaire *mf* Ford; **I'll see her ~ you if you like** je la verrai à ta place si tu veux; **will you go ~ me?** voulez-vous y aller à ma place?; **the government will do it ~ them** le gouvernement le fera à leur place; **to act ~ sb** agir pour qn *or* au nom de qn *or* pour le compte de qn; **what does G.B. stand ~?** qu'est-ce que G.B. veut dire?; **I took you ~ a burglar** je vous ai pris pour un cambrioleur.

(d) (*in exchange for*) **I'll give you this book ~ that one** je vous échange ce livre-ci contre celui-là; **to exchange one thing ~ another** échanger une chose contre une autre; **to pay 5 francs ~ a ticket** payer 5 F le billet; **I sold it ~ £2** je l'ai vendu 2 livres; **he'll do it ~ £5** il le fera pour 5 livres; **word ~ word** mot à mot; **there is one French passenger ~ every 10 English** sur 11 passagers il y a un Français et 10 Anglais, il y a un passager français pour 10 Anglais; **~ one man like that there are 10 his opposite** pour un homme comme lui il y en a 10 qui sont (tout à fait) l'opposé; **what's (the) German ~ 'dog'?** comment est-ce qu'on dit 'chien' en allemand?

(e) (*in favour of*) pour. **~ or against** pour ou contre; **I'm ~ the government** je suis pour le *or* partisan du gouvernement; **I'm (all) ~ helping him if we can** je suis (tout à fait) partisan de l'aider si cela peut se faire; **I'm all ~ it*** je suis tout à fait pour*; **they voted ~ the bill** ils ont voté en faveur de la loi.

(f) (*because of*) pour, en raison de. **~ this reason** pour cette raison; **~ fear of being left behind** de peur d'être oublié; **noted ~ his jokes** connu pour ses plaisanteries; **famous ~ its church** célèbre pour son église; **to shout ~ joy** hurler de joie; **to weep ~ rage** pleurer de rage; **to go to prison ~ theft/~ stealing** aller en prison pour vol/pour avoir volé; **~ old times' sake** en souvenir du passé; **~ my sake** pour moi; **to choose sb ~ his ability** choisir qn en raison de sa compétence; **if it weren't ~ him, but ~ him** sans lui.

(g) (*considering; with regard to*) pour. **anxious ~ sb** inquiet (*f* -ète) pour qn; **~ my part** pour ma part, quant à moi; **as ~ him** quant à lui; **as ~ that** pour ce qui est de cela, quant à cela; **~ sure** à coup sûr; **it is warm ~ January** il fait bon pour (un mois de) janvier; **he's tall ~ his age** il est grand pour son âge; **he's small ~ a policeman** il est petit pour un agent de police; **he's young ~ a prime minister** il est jeune pour un *or* pour être premier ministre.

(h) (*in spite of*) **~ all his wealth** malgré toute sa richesse, tout riche qu'il soit; **~ all that, you should have warned me** malgré tout vous auriez dû me prévenir, vous auriez néanmoins dû me prévenir; **~ all he promised to come, he didn't** en dépit de *or* malgré ses (belles) promesses il n'est pas venu.

(i) (*in time*) (*future*) pour, pendant; (*past*) pendant; (*present and past continuous*) depuis. **I am going away ~ a few days** je pars pour quelques jours; **I shall be away ~ a month** je serai absent (pendant) un mois; **he won't be back ~ a week** il ne sera pas de retour avant huit jours; **that's enough ~ the moment** cela suffit pour le moment; **he's gone ~ good** il est parti pour de bon; **he went away ~ two weeks** il est parti (pendant) quinze jours; **I have not seen her ~ 2 years** voilà 2 ans *or* il y a 2 ans que je ne l'ai vue; **he's been here ~ 10 days** il est ici depuis 10 jours; **I had known her ~ years** je la connaissais depuis des années.

(j) (*distance*) pendant. **a road lined with trees ~ 3 km** une route bordée d'arbres pendant *or* sur 3 km; **we walked ~ 2 km** nous avons marché (pendant) 2 km; **we drove ~ 50 km** nous avons conduit pendant 50 km; **there was nothing to be seen ~ miles** il n'y avait rien à voir pendant des kilomètres; **there were small drab houses ~ mile upon mile** de petites maisons monotones se succédaient kilomètre après kilomètre, c'était pendant des kilomètres un défilé de petites maisons monotones.

(k) (*with infin phrases*) pour que + *subj*. **~ this to be possible** pour que cela se puisse, pour que cela puisse être; **it's easy ~ him to do it** il lui est facile de le faire; **I brought it ~ you to see** je l'ai apporté pour que vous le voyiez (*subj*); **it's not ~ you to blame him** ce n'est pas à vous de le critiquer, il ne vous appartient pas de le critiquer (*frm*); **it's not ~ me to say** ce n'est pas à moi de le dire; **the best would be** *or* **it would be best ~ you to go away** le mieux serait que vous vous en alliez (*subj*); **there is still time ~ him to come** il a encore le temps d'arriver; **their one hope is ~ him to return** leur seul espoir est qu'il revienne; *V* **arrange, wait** *etc.*

(l) (*phrases*) **now ~ it!** (bon alors) allons-y!; **you're ~ it!*** qu'est-ce que tu vas prendre!*, ça va être ta fête!‡; **I'll be ~ it if he catches me here!*** qu'est-ce que je vais prendre* *or* dérouiller‡ s'il me trouve ici!; **oh ~ a cup of tea!** je donnerais n'importe quoi pour une tasse de thé!; **oh ~ a horse!** si seulement j'avais un cheval!

2 *conj* car.

forage ['fɒrɪdʒ] **1** *n* fourrage *m*. (*Mil*) **~ cap** calot *m*. **2** *vi* fourrager, fouiller (*for* pour trouver).

foray ['fɒreɪ] **1** *n* incursion *f*, raid *m*, razzia *f* (*into* en). **to go on** *or* **make a ~** faire une incursion *or* un raid. **2** *vi* faire une incursion *or* un raid.

forbad(e) [fə'bæd] *pret of* **forbid.**

forbear [fɔː'bɛər] *pret* **forbore,** *ptp* **forborne** *vi* s'abstenir. **to ~ from doing, to ~ to do** s'abstenir *or* se garder de faire; **he forbore to make any comment** il s'abstint de tout commentaire.

forbearance [fɔː'bɛərəns] *n* patience *f*, tolérance *f*.

forbears ['fɔːbɛəz] *npl* = **forebears.**

forbid [fə'bɪd] *pret* **forbad(e),** *ptp* **forbidden** *vt* **(a)** (*not allow*) défendre, interdire (*sb to do* à qn de faire). **to ~ sb alcohol** interdire l'alcool à qn; **employees are ~den to do this** il est interdit aux employés de faire cela, les employés n'ont pas le droit de faire cela; **it is ~den to talk** il est défendu de parler; (*on signs*) 'défense de parler'; **smoking is strictly ~den** il est formellement interdit de fumer, défense absolue de fumer; **that's ~den** c'est défendu; **~den fruit** fruit défendu.

(b) (*prevent*) empêcher. **my health ~s my attending the meeting** ma santé m'empêche d'assister à la réunion; (*liter*) **God ~ that this might be true!** à Dieu ne plaise que ceci soit vrai! (*liter*); **God ~!*** pourvu que non!, j'espère bien que non!

forbidden [fə'bɪdn] *ptp of* **forbid.**

forbidding [fə'bɪdɪŋ] *adj building, cliff, cloud* menaçant; *person* sévère. **a ~ look** un air *or* un aspect rébarbatif.

forbore [fɔː'bɔːr] *pret of* **forbear.**

forborne [fɔː'bɔːn] *ptp of* **forbear.**

force [fɔːs] **1** *n* **(a)** (*U: strength*) force *f*, violence *f*; (*Phys*) force; *[phrase, word etc]* importance *f*, force, poids *m*. (*Phys*) **~ of gravity** pesanteur *f*; **centrifugal/centripetal ~** force centrifuge/centripète; **by sheer ~** de vive force; **by ~ of** à force de; **~ of circumstances** contrainte *f or* force des circonstances; **by ~ of habit** par la force de l'habitude; **through sheer ~ of will** purement à force de volonté; **~ of a blow** violence d'un coup; **to resort to ~** avoir recours à la force *or* à la violence; **to settle a dispute by ~** régler une querelle par la force *or* par la violence; **his argument lacked ~** son argument manquait de conviction; **I don't quite see the ~ of his argument** je ne vois pas bien la force de son argument; **I can see the ~ of that** je comprends la force que cela peut avoir; *[law, prices etc]* **to come into ~** entrer en vigueur *or* en application; **the rule is now in ~** le règlement est actuellement en vigueur; **the police were there in ~** la police était là en force *or* en grand nombre; **they came in ~ to support him** ils sont arrivés en force pour lui prêter leur appui; *V* **brute.**

(b) (*power*) force *f*. **~s of Nature** forces de la nature; **he is a powerful ~ in the Trade Union movement** il exerce une influence puissante dans le mouvement syndical; **there are several ~s at work** plusieurs influences se font sentir; *V* **life.**

(c) (*body of men*) force *f*. (*Mil*) **the ~s** les forces armées; (*Mil*) **allied ~s** armées alliées; **police ~** forces de police; (*Police*) **the ~*** la police; (*Comm*) **our sales ~** (l'effectif *m* de) nos représentants *mpl* de commerce; *V* **join, land.**

2 *cpd*: **force-feed** nourrir de force; **he was force-fed** on l'a nourri de force; (*Bridge*) **forcing bid** annonce forcée *or* de forcing.

3 *vt* **(a)** (*constrain*) contraindre, forcer, obliger (*sb to do* qn à faire). **to be ~d to do** être contraint *or* forcé *or* obligé de faire; **to ~ o.s. to do** se forcer *or* se contraindre à faire; **I find myself ~d to say that** force m'est de dire que, je me vois contraint de dire que; **he was ~d to conclude that** il a été forcé de conclure que, force lui a été de conclure que.

(b) (*impose*) *conditions, obedience* imposer (*on sb* à qn). **the decision was ~d on me by events** la décision m'a été imposée par les événements, les événements ont dicté ma décision; **they ~d action on the enemy** ils ont contraint l'ennemi à la bataille; **I don't want to ~ myself on you, but ...** je ne veux pas m'imposer (à vous), mais ...

(c) (*push, thrust*) pousser. **to ~ books into a box** fourrer des livres dans une caisse; **he ~d himself through the gap in the hedge** il s'est frayé un passage par un trou dans la haie; **to ~ one's way into** entrer *or* pénétrer de force dans; **to ~ one's way through** se frayer un passage à travers; **to ~ a bill through Parliament** forcer la Chambre à voter une loi; **to ~ sb into a corner** (*lit*) pousser qn dans un coin; (*fig*) acculer qn; **the lorry ~d the car off the road** le camion a forcé la voiture à quitter la route.

(d) (*break open*) *lock etc* forcer. **to ~ open a drawer/a door** forcer un tiroir/une porte; (*fig*) **to ~ sb's hand** forcer la main à qn.

(e) (*extort*) arracher; (*stronger*) extorquer (*from* à). **he ~d a confession from me** il m'a arraché *or* extorqué une confession; **we ~d the secret out of him** nous lui avons arraché le secret.

(f) *plants etc* forcer, hâter. **to ~ the pace** forcer l'allure *or* le pas.

(g) *smile, answer* forcer. **he ~d a reply** il s'est forcé à répondre.

4 *vi* (*Bridge*) faire un forcing.

force back *vt sep* **(a)** (*Mil*) *enemy* obliger à reculer, faire reculer; *crowd* repousser, refouler, faire reculer.

(b) to force back one's desire to laugh réprimer son envie de rire; **to force back one's tears** refouler ses larmes.

force down *vt sep* **(a)** *aircraft* forcer à atterrir.

(b) to force food down se forcer à manger.

(c) if you force the clothes down you will get more into the suitcase si tu tasses les vêtements tu en feras entrer plus dans la valise.

force out *vt sep* **(a)** faire sortir (de force). **he forced the cork out** il a sorti le bouchon en forçant; **they forced the rebels out into the open** ils ont forcé *or* obligé les insurgés à se montrer.

(b) he forced out a reply/an apology il s'est forcé à répondre/à s'excuser.

forced [fɔːst] *adj smile* forcé, contraint, artificiel; *plant* forcé. (*Aviat*) **~ landing** atterrissage forcé; (*Mil*) **~ march** marche forcée.

forceful ['fɔːsfʊl] *adj person, character* énergique; *argument, reasoning* vigoureux, puissant; *influence* puissant.

forcefully ['fɔːsfʊlɪ] *adv* avec force, avec vigueur.

forcemeat ['fɔːsmiːt] *n* (*Culin*) farce *f*, hachis *m* (*de viande et de fines herbes*).

forceps ['fɔːseps] *npl* (*also* **pair of ~**) forceps *m*.

forcible ['fɔːsəbl] *adj* **(a)** (*done by force*) de *or* par force. (*Jur*) **~ entry** effraction *f*; **~ feeding** alimentation forcée. **(b)** (*powerful*) *language, style* vigoureux, énergique; *personality* puissant.

forcibly ['fɔːsəblɪ] *adv* **(a)** (*by force*) de force, par la force. **the prisoner was ~ fed** le prisonnier a été nourri de force. **(b)** (*vigorously*) *speak, object* énergiquement, avec véhémence, avec vigueur.

ford [fɔːd] **1** *n* gué *m*. **2** *vt* passer à gué.

fordable ['fɔːdəbl] *adj* guéable.

fore [fɔːr] **1** *adj* à l'avant, antérieur. (*Naut*) **~ and aft rig** gréement *m* aurique; (*Naut*) **~ and aft sail** voile *f* aurique; *V* **foreleg** *etc.*

2 *n* (*Naut*) avant *m*. (*fig*) **to come to the ~** se mettre en évidence, se faire remarquer; **he was well to the ~ during the discussion** il a été très en évidence pendant la discussion; (*at hand*) **to the ~** à portée de main.

3 *adv* (*Naut*) à l'avant. **~ and aft** de l'avant à l'arrière.

4 *excl* (*Golf*) gare!, attention!

forearm ['fɔːrɑːm] *n* avant-bras *m inv*.

forebears ['fɔːbɛəz] *npl* aïeux *mpl* (*liter*), ancêtres *mpl*.

forebode [fɔː'bəʊd] *vt* présager, annoncer.

foreboding [fɔː'bəʊdɪŋ] *n* pressentiment *m*, prémonition *f* (*néfaste*). **to have a ~ that** avoir le pressentiment que, pressentir que; **to have ~s** avoir des pressentiments *or* des prémonitions; **with many ~s he agreed to do it** il a consenti à le faire en dépit de *or* malgré toutes ses appréhensions.

forecast ['fɔːkɑːst] *pret, ptp* **forecast 1** *vt* (*also Met*) prévoir.

2 *n* prévision *f*; (*Betting*) pronostic *m*. **according to all the ~s** selon toutes les prévisions; (*Comm*) **sales ~** prévisions de vente; **the racing ~** les pronostics hippiques *or* des courses; **weather ~** bulletin *m* météorologique, météo* *f*; (*Met*) **the ~ is good** les prévisions sont bonnes, la météo* est bonne.

forecastle ['fəʊksl] *n* (*Naut*) gaillard *m* d'avant; (*Merchant Navy*) poste *m* d'équipage.

foreclose [fɔː'kləʊz] **1** *vt* (*Jur*) saisir. **to ~ (on) a mortgage** saisir un bien hypothéqué. **2** *vi [bank etc]* saisir le bien hypothéqué. **to ~ on** = **to ~;** *V* **1.**

foreclosure [fɔː'kləʊʒər] *n* forclusion *f*.

forecourt ['fɔːkɔːt] *n* avant-cour *f*, cour *f* de devant; *[filling station]* devant *m*.

foredoomed [fɔː'duːmd] *adj* condamné d'avance, voué à l'échec.

forefathers ['fɔːˌfɑːðəz] *npl* aïeux *mpl* (*liter*), ancêtres *mpl*.

forefinger ['fɔːˌfɪŋgər] *n* index *m*.

forefoot ['fɔːfʊt] *n [horse, cow etc]* pied antérieur *or* de devant; *[cat, dog]* patte antérieure *or* de devant.

forefront ['fɔːfrʌnt] *n*: **in the ~ of** au premier rang *or* premier plan de.

foregather [fɔː'gæðər] *vi* se réunir, s'assembler.

forego [fɔː'gəʊ] *pret* **forewent,** *ptp* **foregone** *vt* renoncer à, se priver de, s'abstenir de.

foregoing ['fɔːgəʊɪŋ] *adj* précédent, déjà cité, susdit. **according to the ~** d'après ce qui précède.

foregone ['fɔːgɒn] *adj*: **it was a ~ conclusion** c'était à prévoir, c'était réglé *or* prévu d'avance.

foreground ['fɔːgraʊnd] *n* (*Art, Phot*) premier plan. **in the ~** au premier plan.

forehand ['fɔːhænd] *n* (*Tennis: also* **~ stroke**) coup droit.

forehead ['fɒrɪd] *n* front *m*.

foreign ['fɒrən] **1** *adj* **(a)** *language, visitor* étranger; *politics, trade* extérieur. **he comes from a ~ country** il vient de l'étranger; **our relations with ~ countries** nos rapports avec l'étranger *or* l'extérieur; **~ affairs** affaires étrangères; **Minister of F~ Affairs, F~ Minister,** (*Brit*) **Secretary (of State) for F~ Affairs, F~ Secretary** ministre *m* des Affaires étrangères; **Ministry of F~ Affairs, F~ Ministry,** (*Brit*) **F~ Office** ministère *m* des Affaires étrangères; **~ agent** (*spy*) agent étranger; (*Comm*) représentant *m* à l'étranger; (*Press, Rad, TV*) **~ correspondent** correspondant(e) *m(f) or* envoyé(e) *m(f)* permanent(e) à l'étranger; **~ currency** devises étrangères; **the ~ exchange market** le marché des changes; **F~ Legion** Légion *f* (étrangère); **~ national** ressortissant étranger, ressortissante étrangère; **~ policy** politique étrangère *or* extérieure; **~ relations** relations *fpl* avec l'étranger *or* l'extérieur.

(b) (*not natural*) étranger (*to* à). **lying is quite ~ to him** *or* **to his nature** le mensonge lui est (complètement) étranger; (*Med*) **~ body** corps étranger.

2 *cpd*: **foreign-born** né à l'étranger.

foreigner ['fɒrənəʳ] *n* étranger *m*, -ère *f*.

foreknowledge ['fɔːˈnɒlɪdʒ] *n* fait *m* de savoir à l'avance, connaissance anticipée. **I had no ~ of his intentions** je ne savais pas à l'avance ce qu'il voulait faire; **it presupposes a certain ~ of ...** ceci présuppose une certaine connaissance anticipée de ... .

foreland ['fɔːlənd] *n* cap *m*, promontoire *m*, pointe *f* (de terre).

foreleg ['fɔːleg] *n [horse, cow etc]* jambe antérieure; *[dog, cat etc]* patte *f* de devant.

forelock ['fɔːlɒk] *n* mèche *f*, toupet *m*. **to touch one's ~ to sb** saluer qn en portant la main à son front; (*fig*) **to take time by the ~** saisir l'occasion par les cheveux*, sauter sur l'occasion*.

foreman ['fɔːmən] *n, pl* **foremen (a)** (*Ind*) contremaître *m*, chef *m* d'équipe. **(b)** *[jury]* président *m*.

foremast ['fɔːmɑːst] *n* (*Naut*) mât *m* de misaine.

foremen ['fɔːmən] *npl of* **foreman.**

foremost ['fɔːməʊst] **1** *adj* (*fig*) *writer, politician* principal, le plus en vue; (*lit*) le plus en avant. **2** *adv*: **first and ~** tout d'abord, en tout premier lieu.

forename ['fɔːneɪm] *n* prénom *m*.

forenoon ['fɔːnuːn] *n* matinée *f*.

forensic [fə'rensɪk] *adj eloquence* du barreau; *chemistry, medicine* légal. **~ evidence** expertise médico-légale; **~ expert** expert *m* en médecine légale; **~ laboratory** laboratoire médico-légal.

foreplay ['fɔːpleɪ] *n* travaux *mpl* d'approche* (*stimulation érotique*).

forequarters ['fɔːˌkwɔːtəz] *npl* quartiers *mpl* de devant.

forerunner ['fɔːˌrʌnəʳ] *n* avant-coureur *m*, précurseur *m*.

foresail ['fɔːseɪl] *n* (*Naut*) (voile *f* de) misaine *f*.

foresee [fɔː'siː] *vt* prévoir, présager.

foreseeable [fɔː'siːəbl] *adj* prévisible. **in the ~ future** dans un avenir prévisible.

foreshadow [fɔː'ʃædəʊ] *vt [event etc]* présager, annoncer, laisser prévoir.

foreshore ['fɔːʃɔːʳ] *n* (*Geog, Jur*) laisse *f* de mer; (*beach*) plage *f*.

foreshorten [fɔː'ʃɔːtn] *vt* (*Art, Phot*) faire un raccourci de.

foreshortening [fɔː'ʃɔːtnɪŋ] *n* (*Art, Phot*) raccourci *m*.

foresight ['fɔːsaɪt] *n* prévoyance *f*. **lack of ~** imprévoyance *f*.

foreskin ['fɔːskɪn] *n* prépuce *m*.

forest ['fɒrɪst] *n* forêt *f*. (*US*) **~ ranger** garde *m* forestier.

forestall [fɔː'stɔːl] *vt competitor* devancer; *desire, eventuality, objection* anticiper, prévenir, devancer.

forester ['fɒrɪstəʳ] *n* (garde *m or* agent *m*) forestier *m*.

forestry ['fɒrɪstrɪ] *n* sylviculture *f*. (*Brit*) **the F~ Commission** les Eaux et Forêts *fpl*.

foretaste ['fɔːteɪst] *n* avant-goût *m*.

foretell [fɔː'tel] *pret, ptp* **foretold** *vt* prédire.

forethought ['fɔːθɔːt] *n* prévoyance *f*.

forever [fər'evəʳ] *adv* **(a)** (*incessantly*) toujours, sans cesse. **she's ~ complaining** elle se plaint sans cesse, elle est toujours à se plaindre. **(b)** (*US: eternally*) pour toujours, à jamais (*liter*). **it won't go on ~** cela ne durera pas toujours.

forewarn [fɔː'wɔːn] *vt* prévenir, avertir. (*Prov*) **~ed is forearmed** un homme averti en vaut deux (*Prov*).

foreword ['fɔːwɜːd] *n* avant-propos *m inv*, avis *m* au lecteur, avertissement *m* (au lecteur).

forfeit ['fɔːfɪt] **1** *vt* (*Jur*) *property* perdre (par confiscation); *one's rights* perdre; (*fig*) *one's life, health* payer de; *sb's respect* perdre. **2** *n* prix *m*, peine *f*. (*game*) **~s** gages *mpl* (*jeu de société*); (*in game*) **to pay a ~** avoir un gage.

forfeiture ['fɔːfɪtʃəʳ] *n [property]* perte *f* (par confiscation) (*of* de); *[right etc]* renoncement *m* (*of* à).

forgather [fɔː'gæðəʳ] *vi* = **foregather.**

forgave [fə'geɪv] *pret of* **forgive.**

forge [fɔːdʒ] **1** *vt* **(a)** (*counterfeit*) *signature, banknote* contrefaire; *document* faire un faux de; (*alter*) maquiller, falsifier; (*Art*) *picture* faire un faux de, contrefaire; (*invent*) *story* inventer, fabriquer. **(b)** *metal, friendship, plan* forger. **2** *vi*: **to ~ ahead** prendre de l'avance, pousser de l'avant; (*Racing*) foncer. **3** *n* forge *f*.

forger ['fɔːdʒəʳ] *n* faussaire *mf*; (*Jur*) contrefacteur *m*.

forgery ['fɔːdʒərɪ] *n* **(a)** (*U*) *[banknote, signature]* contrefaçon *f*; *[document, will]* falsification *f*; *[story]* invention *f*; (*Jur*) contrefaçon (frauduleuse). **to prosecute sb for ~** poursuivre qn pour faux (et usage de faux). **(b)** (*thing forged*) faux *m*.

forget [fə'get] *pret* **forgot,** *ptp* **forgotten 1** *vt* **(a)** *name, fact, experience* oublier. **I shall never ~ what he said** je n'oublierai jamais ce qu'il a dit; **on that never-to-be-forgotten day** ce jour (à jamais) inoubliable; **I've forgotten all my Spanish** j'ai oublié tout l'espagnol que je savais *or* tout mon espagnol; **she never ~s a face** elle a la mémoire des visages; **he quite forgot himself** *or* **his manners and behaved abominably** il s'est tout à fait oublié *or* il a oublié toutes ses bonnes manières et s'est comporté abominablement; **he works so hard for others that he ~s himself** il travaille tant pour autrui qu'il en oublie son propre intérêt; **don't ~ the guide!** n'oubliez pas le guide!; **we quite forgot the time** nous avons complètement oublié l'heure; **and don't you ~ it!*** et tâche de ne pas l'oublier!, et tâche de te le rappeler!; **let's ~ it!** passons *or* on passe l'éponge!; **~ it*** (*when thanked*) de rien*; (*let's drop the subject*) ça n'a aucune importance; (*when irritated*) rien, tant pis; **to ~ to do** oublier *or* omettre de faire; **I forgot I'd seen her** j'ai oublié que je l'avais vue.

(b) (*leave behind*) oublier, laisser. **she forgot her umbrella in the train** elle a oublié *or* laissé son parapluie dans le train.

2 *vi* oublier. **I quite forgot** j'ai complètement oublié, ça m'est complètement sorti de l'esprit*.

3 *cpd*: (*Bot*) **forget-me-not** myosotis *m*; **forget-me-not blue** (bleu *m*) myosotis *m inv*.

forget about *vt fus* oublier. **I forgot all about it** je l'ai complètement oublié; **I've forgotten all about it (already)** je n'y pense (déjà) plus; **forget about it!*** n'y pensez plus!; **he seemed willing to forget about the whole business** il semblait prêt à passer l'éponge sur l'affaire.

forgetful [fə'getfʊl] *adj* (*absent-minded*) distrait; (*careless*) négligent, étourdi. **he is very ~** il a très mauvaise mémoire, il oublie tout; **how ~ of me!** que je suis étourdi!; **~ of the danger** oublieux du danger.

forgetfulness [fə'getfʊlnɪs] *n* (*absent-mindedness*) manque *m* de mémoire; (*carelessness*) négligence *f*, étourderie *f*. **in a moment of ~** dans un moment d'oubli *or* d'étourderie.

forgivable [fə'gɪvəbl] *adj* pardonnable.

forgive [fə'gɪv] *pret* **forgave,** *ptp* **forgiven** [fə'gɪvn] *vt* **(a)** *person, sin, mistake* pardonner. **to ~ sb (for) sth** pardonner qch à qn; **to ~ sb for doing** pardonner à qn de faire *or* d'avoir fait; **you must ~ him his rudeness** pardonnez-lui son impolitesse; **~ me, but ...** pardonnez-moi *or* excusez-moi, mais ... .

(b) to ~ (sb) a debt faire grâce (à qn) d'une dette.

forgiveness [fə'gɪvnɪs] *n* (*U*) (*pardon*) pardon *m*; (*compassion*) clémence *f*, miséricorde *f*.

forgiving [fə'gɪvɪŋ] *adj* indulgent, clément.

forgo [fɔː'gəʊ] *pret* **forwent,** *ptp* **forgone** *vt* = **forego.**

forgot [fə'gɒt] *pret of* **forget.**

forgotten [fə'gɒtn] *ptp of* **forget.**

fork [fɔːk] **1** *n* **(a)** (*at table*) fourchette *f*; (*Agr*) fourche *f*.

(b) *[branches]* fourche *f*; *[roads, railways]* embranchement *m*.

2 *cpd*: **fork-lift truck** chariot *m* de levage, chariot élévateur; (*Brit*) **fork luncheon** buffet *m* (*repas*).

3 *vt* **(a)** (*also* **~ over**) *hay, ground* fourcher.

(b) he ~ed the food into his mouth il enfournait* la nourriture (à coups de fourchette).

4 *vi [roads]* bifurquer. **we ~ed right on leaving the village** nous avons pris *or* bifurqué à droite à la sortie du village; **~ left for Oxford** prenez *or* bifurquez à gauche pour Oxford.

fork out‡ 1 *vi* casquer‡.

2 *vt sep money* allonger‡, abouler‡.

fork over *vt sep* = **fork 3a.**

fork up *vt sep* **(a)** *soil* fourcher.

(b) (‡) = **fork out 2.**

forked [fɔːkt] *adj* fourchu. **~ lightning** éclair *m* en zigzags.

forlorn [fə'lɔːn] *adj* (*miserable*) *person, sb's appearance* triste, malheureux; (*deserted*) *person* abandonné, délaissé; (*despairing*) *attempt* désespéré. **he looked very ~** il avait l'air très triste *or* malheureux; *[house etc]* **~ look, ~ appearance** air abandonné *or* négligé; **it is a ~ hope** c'est un mince espoir.

form [fɔːm] **1** *n* **(a)** (*type, particular kind*) forme *f*, genre *m*, espèce *f*. **a new ~ of government** une nouvelle forme *or* un nouveau système de gouvernement; **a different ~ of life** une autre forme *or* un autre genre de vie; **the various ~s of energy** les différentes formes *or* espèces d'énergie; **you could say it was a ~ of apology** on pourrait appeler cela une sorte d'excuse.

(b) (*style, condition*) forme *f*. **in the ~ of** sous forme de; **medicine in the ~ of tablets** *or* **in tablet ~** médicament sous forme de comprimés; **the first prize will take the ~ of a trip to Rome** le premier prix consistera en un voyage à Rome; **what ~ should my application take?** comment dois-je faire *or* formuler ma demande?; **the same thing in a new ~** la même chose sous un aspect nouveau; **their discontent took various ~s** leur mécontentement s'est manifesté de différentes façons; (*Gram*) **the plural ~** la forme du pluriel.

(c) (*U: Art, Literat, Mus etc*) forme *f*. **~ and content** la forme et le fond.

(d) (*U: shape*) forme *f*. **to take ~** prendre forme; **his thoughts lack ~** il n'y a aucun ordre dans ses pensées.

(e) (*figure*) forme *f*. **the human ~** la forme humaine; **I saw a ~ in the fog** j'ai vu une forme dans le brouillard.

(f) (*Philos*) (*structure, organization*) forme *f*; (*essence*) essence *f*.

(g) (*U: etiquette*) forme *f*, formalité *f*. **for ~'s sake, as a matter of ~** pour la forme; **it's good/bad ~ to do that** cela se fait/ne se fait pas.

(h) (*formula, established practice*) forme *f*, formule *f*. **he pays attention to the ~s** il respecte les formes; **choose another ~ of words** choisissez une autre expression *or* tournure; **the correct ~ of address for a bishop** *etc* le titre à utiliser en s'adressant *or* la manière correcte de s'adresser à un évêque *etc*; **~s of politeness** formules de politesse; **~ of worship** liturgie *f*; **what's the ~?*** quelle est la marche à suivre?

(i) (*document*) (*sheet*) formulaire *m*, formule *f*, feuille *f*; (*card*) fiche *f*. **telegraph ~** formule de télégramme; **printed ~** imprimé *m*; **to fill up** *or* **in** *or* (*US*) **out a ~** remplir un formulaire; *V* **application, tax** *etc*.
(j) (*U: fitness*) forme *f*, condition *f*. **on ~** en forme; **he is not on ~, he is off ~, he is out of ~** il n'est pas en forme; **in fine ~** en pleine forme, en excellente condition; **he was in great ~** *or* **on top ~** il était en pleine forme; **in good ~** en bonne forme.
(k) to study (the) ~ (*Racing*) ≈ préparer son tiercé; (*fig*) établir un pronostic.
(l) (*Brit: bench*) banc *m*, banquette *f*.
(m) (*Brit Scol: class*) classe *f*. **he's in the sixth ~** ≈ il est en première.
(n) (*U: Prison etc sl: criminal record*) **he's got ~** il a fait de la taule*.
2 *cpd*: (*Brit Scol*) **form master, form mistress** professeur principal *or* de classe.
3 *vt* **(a)** (*shape*) former, construire. (*Gram*) **~ the plural** formez le pluriel; **he ~s his sentences well** il construit bien ses phrases; **he ~s his style on that of Dickens** il forme *or* modèle son style sur celui de Dickens; **he ~ed it out of a piece of wood** il l'a façonné *or* fabriqué *or* sculpté dans un morceau de bois; **he ~ed the clay into a ball** il a roulé *or* pétri l'argile en boule.
(b) (*train, mould*) *child* former, éduquer; *sb's character* former, façonner.
(c) (*develop*) *habit* contracter; *plan* arrêter. **to ~ an opinion** se faire *or* se former une opinion; **to ~ an impression** avoir une impression; **you mustn't ~ the idea that ...** il ne faut pas que vous ayez l'idée que ... .
(d) (*organize*) *government* former; *classes, courses* organiser, instituer; (*Comm*) *company* former, fonder, créer. **to ~ a committee** former un comité.
(e) (*constitute*) composer, former. **to ~ part of** faire partie de; **the ministers who ~ the government** les ministres qui composent *or* constituent le gouvernement; **those who ~ the group** les gens qui font partie du groupe; **to ~ a** *or* **the basis for** former *or* constituer la base de, servir de base à.
(f) (*take the shape or order of*) former, faire, dessiner. (*Mil*) **to ~ fours** se mettre par quatre; **to ~ a line** se mettre en ligne, s'aligner; **~ a circle please** mettez-vous en cercle s'il vous plaît; **to ~ a queue** se mettre en file, former la queue; **the road ~s a series of curves** la route fait *or* dessine une série de courbes.
4 *vi* **(a)** (*take shape*) prendre forme, se former. **an idea ~ed in his mind** une idée a pris forme dans son esprit.
(b) (*also* **~ up**) se former. **to ~ (up) into a square** se former en carré.
form up *vi* **(a)** se mettre *or* se ranger en ligne, s'aligner. **form up behind your teacher** mettez-vous *or* rangez-vous en ligne derrière votre professeur.
(b) *V* **form 4b.**

formal [ˈfɔːməl] *adj* **(a)** (*austere: not familiar or relaxed*) *person* compassé, guindé, formaliste; *manner, style* raide, compassé. **he is very ~** il est très à cheval sur les convenances; **don't be so ~** soyez donc un peu plus naturel; **in ~ language** dans la (*or* une) langue soignée; **~ gardens** jardins *mpl* à la française.
(b) (*ceremonious*) *bow, greeting, welcome* cérémonieux; *function* officiel, protocolaire. **a ~ dance** un grand bal; **a ~ dinner** un grand dîner, un dîner officiel; **~ dress** tenue *f* de cérémonie; (*evening dress*) tenue de soirée.
(c) (*in the accepted form*) *announcement* officiel; *acceptance* dans les règles, en bonne et due forme; (*specific*) formel, explicite, clair. **~ agreement** accord *m* en bonne et due forme (*V also* **d**); **~ denial** démenti formel; **~ surrender** reddition *f* dans les règles; **~ instructions** instructions formelles *or* explicites; **he had little ~ education** il a reçu une éducation scolaire très réduite; **she has no ~ training in teaching** elle n'a reçu aucune formation pédagogique.
(d) (*superficial, in form only*) de forme. **a ~ agreement** un accord de forme; **a certain ~ resemblance** une certaine ressemblance dans la forme; **a lot of ~ handshaking** beaucoup de poignées de mains échangées pour la forme; **he is the ~ head of state** c'est lui qui est théoriquement chef d'État *or* qui est le chef d'État officiel.
(e) (*Philos etc*) formel. **~ grammar** grammaire formelle.
formaldehyde [fɔːˈmældɪhaɪd] *n* formaldéhyde *m*.
formalin(e) [ˈfɔːməlɪn] *n* formol *m*.
formalism [ˈfɔːməlɪzəm] *n* formalisme *m*.
formalist [ˈfɔːməlɪst] *adj, n* formaliste (*mf*).
formalistic [ˌfɔːməˈlɪstɪk] *adj* formaliste.
formality [fɔːˈmælɪtɪ] *n* **(a)** (*U*) (*convention*) formalité *f*; (*stiffness*) raideur *f*, froideur *f*; (*ceremoniousness*) cérémonie *f* (*U*).
(b) formalité *f*. **it's a mere ~** ce n'est qu'une simple formalité; **the formalities** les formalités; **let's do without the formalities!** trêve de formalités!, dispensons-nous des formalités!
formalize [ˈfɔːməlaɪz] *vt* formaliser.
formally [ˈfɔːməlɪ] *adv* **(a)** (*ceremoniously*) cérémonieusement. **to be ~ dressed** être en tenue de cérémonie (*or* de soirée).
(b) (*officially*) officiellement, en bonne et due forme, dans les règles. **to be ~ invited** recevoir une invitation officielle.
format [ˈfɔːmæt] *n* format *m*.
formation [fɔːˈmeɪʃən] **1** *n* **(a)** (*U*) *[child, character]* formation *f*; *[plan]* élaboration *f*, mise *f* en place; *[government]* formation; *[classes, courses]* création *f*, organisation *f*, mise en place; *[club]* création; *[committee]* formation, création, mise en place.
(b) (*U: Mil etc*) formation *f*, disposition *f*. **battle ~** formation de combat; **in close ~** en ordre serré.
(c) (*Geol*) formation *f*.
2 *cpd*: (*Aviat*) **formation flying** vol *m* en formation.
formative [ˈfɔːmətɪv] **1** *adj* formateur (*f* -trice). **~ years** années formatrices. **2** *n* (*Gram*) formant *m*, élément formateur.
former[1] [ˈfɔːməʳ] *n* (*Tech*) gabarit *m*.
former[2] [ˈfɔːməʳ] **1** *adj* **(a)** (*earlier, previous*) ancien, précédent. **the ~ mayor** l'ancien maire, le maire précédent; **he is a ~ mayor of Brighton** c'est un ancien maire de Brighton; **my ~ husband** mon ex-mari; **in a ~ life** au cours d'une vie antérieure; **in ~ times, in ~ days** autrefois, dans le passé; **he was very unlike his ~ self** il ne se ressemblait plus du tout.
(b) (*first of two mentioned*) premier. **the ~ method seems better** la première méthode semble préférable; **your ~ suggestion** votre première suggestion.
2 *pron* celui-là, celle-là. **the ~ ... the latter** celui-là ... celui-ci; **of the two ideas I prefer the ~** des deux idées je préfère celle-là *or* la première.
-former [ˈfɔːməʳ] *n ending in cpds* (*Scol*) élève *mf* de ... . **fourth-former** ≈ élève de troisième.
formerly [ˈfɔːməlɪ] *adv* autrefois, anciennement, jadis.
formic [ˈfɔːmɪk] *adj* formique.
Formica [fɔːˈmaɪkə] *n* ® Formica *m* ®.
formidable [ˈfɔːmɪdəbl] *adj person, enemy, opposition* redoutable, effrayant, terrible; *obstacles, debts* terrible, énorme.
formless [ˈfɔːmlɪs] *adj* informe.
Formosa [fɔːˈməʊsə] *n* Formose *f*, Tai-wan *f*.
formula [ˈfɔːmjʊlə] *n, pl* **~s** *or* **~e** [ˈfɔːmjʊliː] (*also Chem, Math etc*) formule *f*; (*US: for baby's feed*) mélange *m* (lacté pour biberon).
formulate [ˈfɔːmjʊleɪt] *vt* formuler.
formulation [ˌfɔːmjʊˈleɪʃən] *n* formulation *f*, expression *f*.
fornicate [ˈfɔːnɪkeɪt] *vi* forniquer.
fornication [ˌfɔːnɪˈkeɪʃən] *n* fornication *f*.
forsake [fəˈseɪk] *pret* **forsook**, *ptp* **forsaken** *vt person* abandonner, délaisser; *place* quitter; *habit* renoncer à. **my willpower ~s me on these occasions** la volonté me fait défaut dans ces cas-là.
forsaken [fəˈseɪkən] **1** *ptp of* **forsake**. **2** *adj*: **an old ~ farmhouse** une vieille ferme abandonnée; *V* **god.**
forsook [fəˈsʊk] *pret of* **forsake.**
forsooth [fəˈsuːθ] *adv* (†† *or hum*) en vérité, à vrai dire. (*excl*) **~!** par exemple!
forswear [fɔːˈswɛəʳ] *pret* **forswore**, *ptp* **forsworn** *vt* (*frm*) (*renounce*) renoncer à, abjurer; (*deny*) désavouer. (*perjure*) **to ~ o.s.** se parjurer.
forsythia [fɔːˈsaɪθɪə] *n* forsythia *m*.
fort [fɔːt] *n* (*Mil*) fort *m*; (*small*) fortin *m*; *V* **hold.**
forte[1] [ˈfɔːtɪ, (*US*) fɔːt] *n* fort *m*. **generosity is not his ~** la générosité n'est pas son fort*.
forte[2] [ˈfɔːtɪ] *adj, adv* (*Mus*) forte.
forth [fɔːθ] (*phr vb elem*) *adv* **(a)** en avant. (*frm*) **to set ~** se mettre en route; (*frm*) **to stretch ~ one's hand** tendre la main; **to go back and ~ between** aller et venir entre, faire la navette entre; *V* **bring forth, sally forth** *etc*. **(b) and so ~** et ainsi de suite; (*frm*) **from this day ~** dorénavant, désormais.
forthcoming [fɔːθˈkʌmɪŋ] *adj* **(a)** *book* qui va paraître, à paraître; *film* qui va sortir; *play* qui va débuter; *event* à venir, futur. **his ~ film** son prochain film; **in a ~ film he studies ...** dans un film qui va bientôt sortir *or* dans son prochain film il examine ...; (*Theat etc*) '**~ attractions**' 'prochains spectacles', 'prochainement'.
(b) (*available etc*) **if help is ~** si on nous (*or* les *etc*) aide; **if funds are ~** si on nous (*or* leur *etc*) donne de l'argent, si on met de l'argent à notre (*or* leur *etc*) disposition; **no answer was ~** il n'y a pas eu de réponse; **this was not ~** ceci ne nous (*or* leur *etc*) a pas été accordé.
(c) (*friendly, sociable*) *person* ouvert, communicatif; *manners* accueillant, cordial. **I asked him what his plans were but he wasn't ~ about them** je lui ai demandé quels étaient ses projets mais il s'est montré peu disposé à en parler.
forthright [ˈfɔːθraɪt] *adj answer, remark* franc (*f* franche), direct; *person* direct, carré; *look* franc. **he is very ~** il ne mâche pas ses mots.
forthwith [ˈfɔːθˈwɪθ] *adv* sur-le-champ, aussitôt, tout de suite.
fortieth [ˈfɔːtɪɪθ] **1** *adj* quarantième. **2** *n* quarantième *mf*; (*fraction*) quarantième *m*.
fortification [ˌfɔːtɪfɪˈkeɪʃən] *n* fortification *f*.
fortify [ˈfɔːtɪfaɪ] *vt* **(a)** *place* fortifier, armer (*against* contre); *person* réconforter. **fortified place** place forte; **have a drink to ~ you*** prenez un verre pour vous remonter. **(b)** *wine* accroître la teneur en alcool de; *food* renforcer en vitamines.
fortitude [ˈfɔːtɪtjuːd] *n* courage *m*, fermeté *f* d'âme, force *f* d'âme.
fortnight [ˈfɔːtnaɪt] *n* (*esp Brit*) quinzaine *f*, quinze jours *mpl*. **a ~'s holiday** quinze jours de vacances; **a ~ tomorrow** demain en quinze; **adjourned for a ~** remis à quinzaine; **for a ~** pour une quinzaine, pour quinze jours; **in a ~, in a ~'s time** dans quinze jours; **a ~ ago** il y a quinze jours.
fortnightly [ˈfɔːtnaɪtlɪ] (*esp Brit*) **1** *adj* bimensuel. **2** *adv* tous les quinze jours.
fortran [ˈfɔːtræn] *n* fortran *m*.
fortress [ˈfɔːtrɪs] *n* (*prison*) forteresse *f*; (*mediaeval castle*) château fort; *V* **flying.**
fortuitous [fɔːˈtjuːɪtəs] *adj* fortuit, imprévu, accidentel.
fortuitously [fɔːˈtjuːɪtəslɪ] *adv* fortuitement, par hasard.
fortunate [ˈfɔːtʃənɪt] *adj person* heureux, chanceux; *circumstances, meeting, event* heureux, favorable, propice. **to be ~** avoir de la chance; **we were ~ enough to meet him** nous avons eu la chance *or* le bonheur de le rencontrer; **how ~!** quelle chance!

fortunately ['fɔːtʃənɪtlɪ] *adv* heureusement, par bonheur.

fortune ['fɔːtʃən] **1** *n* **(a)** (*chance*) fortune *f*, chance *f*, hasard *m*. **the ~s of war** la fortune des armes; **by good ~** par chance, par bonheur; **I had the good ~ to meet him** j'ai eu la chance *or* le bonheur de le rencontrer; **to try one's ~** tenter sa chance; **~ favoured him** la chance *or* la fortune lui a souri; **to tell sb's ~** dire la bonne aventure à qn; **whatever my ~ may be** quel que soit le sort qui m'est réservé.

(b) (*riches*) fortune *f*, richesse *f*, prospérité *f*. **to make a ~** faire fortune; **to come into a ~** hériter d'une fortune, faire un gros héritage; **to seek one's ~** (aller) chercher fortune; **a man of ~** un homme d'une fortune *or* d'une richesse considérable; **to marry a ~** épouser une grosse fortune *or* un sac‡; **to spend/cost/lose** *etc* **a (small) ~** dépenser/coûter/perdre *etc* une (petite) fortune *or* un argent fou*.

2 *cpd*: **fortune hunter** coureur *m* de dot; **fortuneteller** diseur *m*, -euse *f* de bonne aventure; (*with cards*) tireuse *f* de cartes; **fortunetelling** pratique *f* de dire la bonne aventure; (*with cards*) cartomancie *f*.

forty ['fɔːtɪ] **1** *adj* quarante *inv*. **about ~ books** une quarantaine de livres; **to have ~ winks*** faire un petit somme, piquer un roupillon‡. **2** *n* quarante *m inv*. **about ~** une quarantaine; *for other phrases V* **sixty**.

forum ['fɔːrəm] *n* (*Hist*) forum *m*; (*fig*) tribune *f* (*sur un sujet d'actualité*).

forward ['fɔːwəd] (*phr vb elem*) **1** *adv* (*also* **~s**) en avant. **to rush ~** se précipiter *or* s'élancer (en avant); **to go ~** avancer; **to go straight ~** aller droit devant soi; **~!**, (*Mil*) **~ march!** en avant, marche!; **from this time ~** à partir de maintenant, désormais, à l'avenir, dorénavant (*frm*); (*lit, fig*) **to push o.s. ~** se mettre en avant; (*fig*) **to come ~** s'offrir, se présenter, se proposer; **he went backward(s) and ~(s) between the station and the house** il allait et venait entre *or* il faisait la navette entre la gare et la maison; *V* **bring forward, look forward** *etc*.

2 *adj* **(a)** (*in front, ahead*) *movement* en avant. **the ~ ranks of the army** les premiers rangs de l'armée; **I am ~ with my work** je suis en avance dans mon travail; **this seat is too far ~** cette banquette est trop en avant; **~ gears** vitesses *fpl* avant; **~ line** (*Mil*) première ligne; (*Sport*) ligne des avants; (*Rugby*) **~ pass** (passe *f*) en-avant *m inv*; (*Admin*) **~ planning** planning *m* à long terme; (*Mil*) **~ post** avant-poste *m*, poste avancé.

(b) (*well-advanced*) *season, plant* précoce; *child* précoce, en avance.

(c) (*pert*) effronté, insolent.

(d) (*Comm etc*) *prices* à terme. **~ buying** vente *f* à terme; **~ delivery** livraison *f* à terme.

3 *n* (*Sport*) avant *m*.

4 *vt* **(a)** (*advance*) *plans etc* favoriser, avancer.

(b) (*dispatch*) *goods* expédier, envoyer; (*send on*) *letter, parcel* faire suivre. **please ~** faire suivre S.V.P., prière de faire suivre.

5 *cpd*: **forwarding address** (*gen*) adresse *f* (pour faire suivre le courrier); (*Comm*) adresse pour l'expédition; **he left no forwarding address** il est parti sans laisser d'adresse; (*Comm*) **forwarding agent** transitaire *m*; **forward-looking** *person* ouvert sur *or* tourné vers les possibilités de l'avenir; *plan* tourné vers l'avenir *or* le progrès.

forwardness ['fɔːwədnɪs] *n [seasons, children etc]* précocité *f*; (*pertness*) effronterie *f*, audace *f*.

forwards ['fɔːwədz] *adv* = **forward 1**.

fossil ['fɒsl] **1** *n* fossile *m*. (*fig*) **he's an old ~!*** c'est un vieux fossile!* *or* une vieille croûte!* **2** *adj insect* fossilisé. **~ fuel** combustible *m* fossile.

fossilized ['fɒsɪlaɪzd] *adj* fossilisé; (*fig*) *person, customs* fossilisé, figé.

foster ['fɒstə^{r}] **1** *vt* **(a)** (*Jur: care for*) *child* élever (*sans obligation d'adoption*). **the authorities ~ed the child with Mr and Mrs X** les autorités ont placé l'enfant chez M et Mme X.

(b) (*encourage*) *friendship, development* favoriser, encourager, stimuler.

(c) (*entertain*) *idea, thought* entretenir, nourrir.

2 *cpd child* (*gen, Admin, Soc: officially arranged*) adoptif; (*where wet-nursed*) nourricier, de lait; *father, parents, family* adoptif, nourricier; *brother, sister* adoptif, de lait. **foster home** famille adoptive; famille nourricière; **foster mother** mère adoptive; (*wet-nurse*) nourrice *f*.

fought [fɔːt] *pret, ptp of* **fight**.

foul [faʊl] **1** *adj weather, food, meal, taste* infect; *place* immonde, crasseux; *smell* infect, nauséabond, fétide; *breath* fétide; *water* croupi; *air* vicié, pollué; *calumny, behaviour* vil (*f* vile), infâme; *language* ordurier, grossier; (*unfair*) déloyal. **a ~ blow** un coup en traître; (*liter*) **~ deed** scélératesse *f* (*liter*), acte crapuleux; **~ play** (*Sport*) jeu irrégulier *or* déloyal; (*Cards*) tricherie *f*; (*fig*) **he suspected ~ play** il soupçonnait qu'il y avait quelque chose de louche; (*fig*) **the explosion was put down to ~ play** l'explosion a été attribuée à la malveillance *or* à un acte criminel *or* à un geste criminel; **the police found a body but do not suspect ~ play** la police a découvert un cadavre mais écarte l'hypothèse d'un meurtre; **~ weather** sale temps, temps de chien; **to fall ~ of sb** se mettre qn à dos, s'attirer le mécontentement de qn; **to fall ~ of a ship** entrer en collision avec un bateau; *V* **fair**[1].

2 *n* (*Sport*) coup défendu *or* interdit *or* irrégulier; (*Boxing*) coup bas; (*Ftbl*) faute *f*; *V* **fair**[1].

3 *cpd*: **foulmouthed** au langage ordurier *or* grossier, qui parle comme un charretier; **foul-smelling** puant, nauséabond, fétide.

4 *vt* (*pollute*) *air* polluer, infecter; (*clog*) *pipe, chimney, gun barrel* encrasser, obstruer; (*collide with*) *ship* entrer en collision avec; (*entangle*) *fishing line* embrouiller, emmêler, entortiller; *propeller* s'emmêler dans; (*tarnish*) *reputation* salir.

5 *vi [rope, line]* s'emmêler, s'entortiller, s'embrouiller.

foul up *vt sep river* polluer; (‡) *relationship* ficher en l'air*. **that has fouled things up‡** ça a tout mis *or* flanqué par terre*, ça a tout fichu en l'air*.

found[1] [faʊnd] *pret, ptp of* **find**.

found[2] [faʊnd] *vt town, school etc* fonder, créer; *hospital* fonder; *business enterprise* fonder, constituer, établir; *colony* établir; (*fig*) *belief, opinion* fonder, baser, appuyer (*on* sur). **my suspicions were ~ed on the fact that ...** mes soupçons étaient basés sur le fait que ...; **our society is ~ed on this** notre société est fondée là-dessus; **the novel is ~ed on fact** le roman est basé sur des faits réels.

found[3] [faʊnd] *vt* (*Metal*) fondre.

foundation [faʊn'deɪʃən] **1** *n* **(a)** (*U: act of founding*) *[town, school]* fondation *f*, création *f*, établissement *m*; *[hospital, business enterprise]* fondation, création.

(b) (*establishment*) fondation *f*, institution dotée. **Carnegie F~** fondation Carnegie.

(c) (*Constr*) **~s** fondations *fpl*; **to lay the ~s** (*lit*) poser les fondations (*of* de); (*fig*) *V* **1d**.

(d) (*fig: basis*) *[career, social structure]* assises *fpl*, base *f*; *[idea, religious belief, theory]* base, fondement *m*. **his work laid the ~(s) of our legal system** son travail a posé les bases de notre système judiciaire; **the rumour is entirely without ~** la rumeur est dénuée de tout fondement.

(e) (*also* **~ cream**) fond *m* de teint.

2 *cpd*: **foundation garment** gaine *f*, combiné *m*; (*Brit*) **foundation stone** pierre commémorative; (*lit, fig*) **to lay the foundation stone** poser la première pierre.

founder[1] ['faʊndə^{r}] *n* fondateur *m*, -trice *f*.

founder[2] ['faʊndə^{r}] *vi [ship]* sombrer, chavirer, couler; *[horse]* (*in mud etc*) s'embourber, s'empêtrer; (*from fatigue*) (se mettre à) boiter; *[plans etc]* s'effondrer, s'écrouler; *[hopes]* s'en aller en fumée.

founding ['faʊndɪŋ] **1** *n* = **foundation 1a**. **2** *adj* (*US*) **~ fathers** pères fondateurs (*qui élaborèrent la Constitution Fédérale des États-Unis*).

foundling ['faʊndlɪŋ] *n* enfant trouvé(e) *m(f)*. **~ hospital** hospice *m* pour enfants trouvés.

foundry ['faʊndrɪ] *n* fonderie *f*.

fount [faʊnt] *n* **(a)** (*liter*) source *f*. **the ~ of knowledge/wisdom** la source du savoir/de la sagesse. **(b)** ((*US*) **font**) (*Brit Typ*) fonte *f*.

fountain ['faʊntɪn] **1** *n* (*natural*) fontaine *f*, source *f*; (*artificial*) fontaine, jet *m* d'eau; (*also* **drinking ~**) jet *m* d'eau potable; (*fig*) source; *V* **soda**.

2 *cpd*: **fountainhead** source *f*, origine *f*; **to go to the fountainhead** aller (directement) à la source, retourner aux sources; **fountain pen** stylo *m* (à encre).

four [fɔː^{r}] **1** *adj* quatre *inv*. **to the ~ corners of the earth** aux quatre coins du monde; **it's in ~ figures** c'est dans les milliers (*V also* 3); **open to the ~ winds** ouvert à tous les vents *or* aux quatre vents; *V* **stroke**.

2 *n* quatre *m inv*. **on all ~s** à quatre pattes; (*Rowing*) **a ~** un quatre; **will you make up a ~ for bridge?** voulez-vous faire le quatrième au bridge?; *V* **form**; for other phrases *V* **six**.

3 *cpd*: (*Golf*) **four-ball** (*adj, n*) fourball (*m*); (*Aut*) **four-door** à quatre portes; (*Aviat*) **four-engined** à quatre moteurs; **four-engined plane** quadrimoteur *m*; **four-figure salary** traitement annuel de plus de mille; (*US*) **fourflusher‡** bluffeur* *m*, -euse* *f*; **fourfold** (*adj*) quadruple; (*adv*) au quadruple; **fourfooted** quadrupède, à quatre pattes; (*Mus*) **in four-four time** à quatre/quatre; (*Mus*) **four-handed** à quatre mains; **four-leaf clover, four-leaved clover** trèfle *m* à quatre feuilles; (*fig*) **four-letter word** obscénité *f*, gros mot, mot grossier; **he let out a four-letter word** il a sorti le mot de cinq lettres (*euph*); (*Sport*) **four-minute mile** course d'un mille courue en quatre minutes; **four-part** *song* à quatre voix; *serial* en quatre épisodes; **fourposter** lit *m* à baldaquin *or* à colonnes; (*liter*) **fourscore** (*adj, n*) quatre-vingt(s); (*Aut*) **four-seater** (voiture *f* à) quatre places *f inv*; **foursome** (*game*) partie *f* à quatre; (*two women, two men*) deux couples; **we went in a foursome** nous y sommes allés à quatre; **foursquare** (*square*) carré; (*firm*) *attitude, decision* ferme, inébranlable; (*forthright*) *account, assessment* franc (*f* franche); (*Aut*) **four-stroke** (*adj, n*) (moteur *m*) à quatre temps; (*Aut*) **four-wheel drive** propulsion *f* à quatre roues motrices; **with four-wheel drive** à quatre roues motrices.

fourteen ['fɔː'tiːn] *adj, n* quatorze (*m inv*); *for phrases V* **six**.

fourteenth ['fɔː'tiːnθ] **1** *adj* quatorzième. **Louis the F~** Louis Quatorze. **2** *n* quatorzième *mf*; (*fraction*) quatorzième *m*. **the ~ of July** le quatorze juillet, la fête du quatorze juillet; *for other phrases V* **sixth**.

fourth [fɔːθ] **1** *adj* quatrième. **the ~ dimension** la quatrième dimension; **he lives on the ~ floor** il habite au quatrième *or* (*US*) au cinquième (étage); (*Aut*) **to change into ~ gear** passer en quatrième; **the ~ estate** la presse (toute puissante); **~ finger** annulaire *m*.

2 *n* quatrième *mf*; (*fraction*) quart *m*; (*Mus*) quarte *f*. **we need a ~ for our game of bridge** il nous faut un quatrième pour notre bridge; (*US*) **the F~ (of July)** le quatre juillet (*Fête de l'Indépendance américaine*); *for other phrases V* **sixth**.

3 *cpd*: **fourth-floor flat** (appartement *m* au) quatrième *m* (*or* (*US*) cinquième); **fourth-rate** de dernier ordre, de dernière catégorie.

fourthly ['fɔːθlɪ] *adv* quatrièmement, en quatrième lieu.

fowl [faʊl] **1** *n* **(a)** (*hens etc*) (*collective n*) volaille *f*, oiseaux *mpl* de basse-cour; (*one bird*) volatile *m*, volaille *f*. (*Culin*) **roast ~** volaille rôtie, poulet rôti.

(b) (††) oiseau *m*. (*liter*) **the ~s of the air** les oiseaux; *V* **fish, water, wild** *etc*.

2 *vi*: **to go ~ing** chasser le gibier à plumes.
3 *cpd*: **fowling piece** fusil *m* de chasse léger, carabine *f*; **fowl pest** peste *f* aviaire.

fox [fɒks] **1** *n* renard *m*. (*fig*) **a (sly) ~** un rusé, un malin, un fin renard.
2 *vt* (*) (*puzzle*) rendre perplexe, mystifier; (*deceive*) tromper, berner.
3 *cpd*: **fox cub** renardeau *m*; (*Bot*) **foxglove** digitale *f* (pourprée); **foxhole** terrier *m* de renard, renardière *f*; (*Mil*) gourbi *m*; **foxhound** chien courant, fox-hound *m*; **foxhunt(ing)** chasse *f* au renard; **to go foxhunting** aller à la chasse au renard; **fox terrier** fox *m*, fox-terrier *m*; **foxtrot** slow *m*, slow-fox *m*.

foxed [fɒkst] *adj book, paper* marqué de rousseurs.

foxy ['fɒksɪ] *adj* (*crafty*) rusé, malin (*f* -igne), finaud.

foyer ['fɔɪeɪ] *n [theatre]* foyer *m*; *[hotel]* vestibule *m*, foyer, hall *m*; (*US*) *[house]* vestibule, entrée *f*.

fracas ['frækɑː] *n* (*scuffle*) rixe *f*, échauffourée *f*, bagarre *f*; (*noise*) fracas *m*.

fraction ['frækʃən] *n* (*Math*) fraction *f*; (*fig*) fraction, partie *f*. **for a ~ of a second** pendant une fraction de seconde; *V* **decimal, vulgar**.

fractional ['frækʃənl] *adj* (*Math*) fractionnaire; (*fig*) infime, tout petit. **~ part** fraction *f*; (*Chem*) **~ distillation** distillation fractionnée.

fractionally ['frækʃnəlɪ] *adv* un tout petit peu.

fractious ['frækʃəs] *adj child* grincheux, pleurnicheur; *old person* grincheux, hargneux.

fracture ['fræktʃəʳ] **1** *n* fracture *f*. **2** *vt* fracturer. **3** *vi* se casser, se fracturer.

fragile ['frædʒaɪl] *adj china* fragile; *complexion, health* fragile, délicat; *person* fragile, (*from age, ill-health*) frêle; *happiness* fragile, précaire. (*hum*) **I feel ~ this morning** je me sens déliquescent* ce matin.

fragility [frə'dʒɪlɪtɪ] *n* fragilité *f*.

fragment ['frægmənt] **1** *n [china, paper]* fragment *m*, morceau *m*; *[shell]* éclat *m*. **he smashed it to ~s** il l'a réduit en miettes *or* en mille morceaux; **~s of conversation** bribes *fpl* de conversation.
2 [fræg'ment] *vt* fragmenter.
3 [fræg'ment] *vi* se fragmenter.

fragmental [fræg'mentl] *adj* fragmentaire; (*Geol*) clastique.

fragmentary ['frægməntərɪ] *adj* fragmentaire.

fragmentation ['frægmen'teɪʃən] *n* fragmentation *f*.

fragmented [fræg'mentɪd] *adj story, version* morcelé, fragmentaire.

fragrance ['freɪgrəns] *n* parfum *m*, senteur *f*, fragrance *f* (*liter*). (*Comm*) **a new ~ by X** un nouveau parfum de X.

fragrant ['freɪgrənt] *adj* parfumé, odorant. (*fig liter*) **~ memories** doux souvenirs.

frail [freɪl] *adj person* frêle, fragile; *health* délicat, fragile; *happiness* fragile, éphémère. **it's a ~ hope** c'est un espoir fragile.

frailty ['freɪltɪ] *n [person, health, happiness]* fragilité *f*; (*morally*) faiblesse *f*.

frame [freɪm] **1** *n [building]* charpente *f*; *[ship]* carcasse *f*; *[car]* châssis *m*; *[bicycle]* cadre *m*; *[window]* châssis, chambranle *m*; *[door]* encadrement *m*, chambranle; *[picture]* cadre, encadrement; *[embroidery, tapestry]* cadre; (*Tech*) métier *m*; *[spectacles]* (*also* **~s**) monture *f*; (*Cine*) image *f*, photogramme *m*; (*in garden*) châssis, cloche *f*; *[racket]* armature *f*, cadre; *[human, animal]* charpente *f*, ossature *f*, corps *m*. **her ~ was shaken by sobs** toute sa personne était secouée par les sanglots; **his large ~** son grand corps; **~ of mind** humeur *f*, disposition *f* d'esprit; **I'm not in a ~ of mind for singing** je ne suis pas d'humeur à chanter; (*Math, fig*) **~ of reference** système *m* de référence.
2 *cpd*: **frame house** maison *f* à charpente de bois; **frame rucksack** sac *m* à dos à armature; **frame-up**‡ coup monté, machination *f*; **framework** (*lit*: *V* **frame 1**) charpente *f*, carcasse *f*, ossature *f*, encadrement *m*, châssis *m*, chambranle *m*; (*fig*) *[society, government etc]* structure *f*, cadre *m*, ossature; *[play, novel]* structure, ossature; **in the framework of a totalitarian society** dans le cadre d'une société totalitaire.
3 *vt* **(a)** *picture* encadrer. **he appeared ~d in the door** il apparut dans l'encadrement de la porte; **a face ~d in a mass of curls** un visage encadré par une profusion de boucles.
(b) (*construct*) *house* bâtir *or* construire la charpente de; *idea, plan* concevoir, formuler; *plot* combiner, ourdir (*liter*); *sentence* construire.
(c) (‡: *also* **~ up**) **to ~ sb (up), to have sb ~d** monter un coup contre qn (*pour faire porter l'accusation contre lui*); **he claimed he had been ~d** il a prétendu être victime d'un coup monté.
4 *vi* (*develop*) **the child is framing well** l'enfant montre des dispositions *or* fait des progrès; **his plans are framing well/badly** ses projets se présentent bien/mal, ses projets prennent une bonne/une mauvaise tournure.

franc [fræŋk] *n* franc *m*.

France [frɑːns] *n* France *f*. **in ~** en France.

Frances ['frɑːnsɪs] *n* Françoise *f*.

franchise ['fræntʃaɪz] *n* **(a)** (*Pol*) droit *m* de suffrage *or* de vote. **(b)** (*US Comm*) autorisation *f*, permis *m*.

Francis ['frɑːnsɪs] *n* François *m*, Francis *m*.

Franciscan [fræn'sɪskən] *adj, n* franciscain (*m*).

francophile ['fræŋkəʊfaɪl] *adj, n* francophile (*mf*).

francophobe ['fræŋkəʊfəʊb] *adj, n* francophobe (*mf*).

frangipane ['frændʒɪpeɪn] *n*, **frangipani** [ˌfrændʒɪ'pænɪ] *n* (*perfume, pastry*) frangipane *f*; (*shrub*) frangipanier *m*.

Frank [fræŋk] *n* **(a)** (*Hist*) Franc *m*, Franque *f*. **(b)** (*dim of* **Francis**) François *m*.

frank[1] [fræŋk] *adj* franc (*f* franche), ouvert, sincère. **to be ~ with sb** être franc *or* sincère avec qn, parler avec qn à cœur ouvert; **I'll be quite ~ with you** je vais être très franc avec vous, je vais vous parler franchement *or* en toute franchise.

frank[2] [fræŋk] *vt letter* affranchir. **~ing machine** machine *f* à affranchir.

Frankenstein ['fræŋkənstaɪn] *n* Frankenstein *m*.

frankfurter ['fræŋkˌfɜːtəʳ] *n* (*Culin*) saucisse *f* de Francfort.

frankincense ['fræŋkɪnsens] *n* encens *m*.

Frankish ['fræŋkɪʃ] **1** *adj* (*Hist*) franc (*f* franque). **2** *n* (*Ling*) francique *m*, langue franque.

frankly ['fræŋklɪ] *adv* franchement, sincèrement. **~, I don't think that ...** franchement, je ne pense pas que ... .

frankness ['fræŋknɪs] *n* franchise *f*, droiture *f*, sincérité *f*.

frantic ['fræntɪk] *adj agitation, activity, cry, effort* frénétique; *need, desire, effort* effréné; *person* hors de soi, fou (*f* folle). **she's ~** elle est hors d'elle, elle est dans tous ses états; **~ with joy/rage** fou de joie/de rage; **she was ~ with pain** la douleur la rendait folle; **he was driven ~ by anxiety** il était fou d'inquiétude, il était dans tous ses états, il commençait à paniquer*; **the noise was driving him ~** le bruit l'exaspérait *or* le rendait fou; **he drives me ~*** il me rend dingue*.

frantically ['fræntɪkəlɪ] *adv* frénétiquement, comme un fou (*or* une folle), avec frénésie.

fraternal [frə'tɜːnl] *adj* fraternel.

fraternity [frə'tɜːnɪtɪ] *n* **(a)** (*U*) fraternité *f*. **(b)** (*community*) confrérie *f*, communauté *f*; (*US Univ*) confrérie (d'étudiants).

fraternization [ˌfrætənaɪ'zeɪʃən] *n* fraternisation *f*.

fraternize ['frætənaɪz] *vi* fraterniser (*with* avec).

fratricide ['frætrɪsaɪd] *n* fratricide *m*.

fraud [frɔːd] *n* **(a)** (*criminal deception*) supercherie *f*, imposture *f*, tromperie *f*; (*financial*) escroquerie *f*; (*Jur*) fraude *f*.
(b) (*person*) imposteur *m*, fraudeur *m*, -euse *f*; (*object*) attrape-nigaud *m*. **he isn't a doctor, he's a ~** ce n'est pas un médecin, c'est un imposteur; **he's not ill, he's a ~** il n'est pas malade, il joue la comédie* *or* c'est un simulateur; **this whole thing is a ~!** c'est de la frime!* *or* de la fumisterie!*

fraudulence ['frɔːdjʊləns] *n*, **fraudulency** ['frɔːdjʊlənsɪ] *n* caractère frauduleux.

fraudulent ['frɔːdjʊlənt] *adj* frauduleux. (*Jur*) **~ conversion** malversation *f*, détournement *m* de fonds.

fraught [frɔːt] *adj* plein, chargé, gros (*f* grosse), lourd (*with* de); (*tense*) tendu. **situation ~ with danger** situation pleine de danger *or* dangereuse; **atmosphere ~ with hatred** atmosphère chargée de haine; **silence ~ with menace** silence chargé de *or* gros de *or* lourd de menaces; **the situation/discussion was very ~** la situation/discussion était très tendue; **the whole business is a bit ~*** tout ça c'est un peu risqué*.

fray[1] [freɪ] *n* rixe *f*, échauffourée *f*, bagarre *f*; (*Mil*) combat *m*. (*lit, fig*) **ready for the ~** prêt à se battre; (*fig*) **to enter the ~** descendre dans l'arène, entrer en lice.

fray[2] [freɪ] **1** *vt cloth, garment* effilocher, effiler; *cuff* user le bord de, effranger; *trousers* user le bas de, effranger; *rope* user; raguer (*Naut*). **tempers were getting ~ed** tout le monde commençait à perdre patience *or* s'énerver; **my nerves are quite ~ed** je suis à bout de nerfs.
2 *vi [cloth, garment]* s'effilocher, s'effiler; *[rope]* s'user; se raguer (*Naut*). **his sleeve was ~ing at the cuff** sa manche était usée *or* s'effrangeait *or* s'effilochait au poignet.

frazzle* ['fræzl] **1** *n*: **worn to a ~** éreinté, claqué*, crevé*; **to beat sb to a ~** battre qn à plate(s) couture(s). **2** *vt* (*US*) éreinter, crever*.

freak [friːk] **1** *n* **(a)** (*abnormal person or animal*) monstre *m*, phénomène *m*; (*eccentric*) phénomène; (*absurd idea*) lubie *f*, idée saugrenue *or* farfelue*; (*anomalous idea*) anomalie *f*. **~ of nature** accident *m* de la nature; **~ of fortune** caprice *m* de la fortune; **he won by a ~** il a gagné grâce à un hasard extraordinaire.
(b) (‡) hippie *mf*.
(c) (‡) **he's an acid ~** il se drogue au LSD, c'est un habitué du LSD; **a jazz ~** un(e) dingue* *or* un(e) fana* du jazz; **a health food ~** un(e) fana* des aliments naturels.
2 *cpd storm, weather* anormal, insolite; *error* bizarre; *victory* inattendu; (‡) *culture, clothes* hippie. **freak-out**‡ partie *f* de came‡.

freak out‡ **1** *vi* (*abandon convention*) se défouler*; (*get high on drugs*) se défoncer‡; (*drop out of society*) devenir marginal, se mettre en marge de la société; (*become a hippie*) devenir hippie.
2 freak-out‡ *n V* **freak 2**.

freakish ['friːkɪʃ] *adj weather* anormal, insolite; *error* bizarre; *idea* saugrenu, insolite.

freckle ['frekl] **1** *n* tache *f* de rousseur *or* de son. **2** *vi* se couvrir de taches de rousseur.

freckled ['frekld] *adj* plein de taches de rousseur, taché de son.

Fred [fred] *n* (*dim of* **Frederick** *or* **Alfred**) Freddy *m*.

Frederick ['fredrɪk] *n* Frédéric *m*.

free [friː] **1** *adj* **(a)** (*at liberty, unrestricted*) *person, animal, object, activity, translation, choice* libre; *government* autonome, libre; *gas* libre, non combiné. **they tied him up but he managed to get ~** ils l'ont attaché mais il a réussi à se libérer; **to set a prisoner ~** libérer *or* mettre en liberté *or* élargir (*frm*) un prisonnier; **her aunt's death set her ~ to follow her own career** la mort de sa tante lui a donné toute liberté pour poursuivre sa carrière; **the ~ world** le monde libre; **the land of the ~** le pays de la liberté; (*Hist*) **the F~ French** les Français libres; **to go ~** être relâché, être mis en liberté; **you're ~ to choose** vous êtes libre de choisir, libre à vous de choisir; **I'm not ~ to do it** je ne suis pas libre de le faire, j'ai les mains liées et je ne peux pas le faire; **the fishing is ~** la pêche est autorisée; **he left one end of the string ~** il a laissé un bout de la ficelle flotter libre; **a dress**

which leaves my arms ~ une robe qui me laisse les bras libres; **I am leaving you ~ to do as you please** je vous laisse libre de faire comme bon vous semble; **to be ~ from care/responsibility** être dégagé de tout souci/de toute responsabilité; **~ from the usual ruling** non soumis au règlement habituel; **a surface ~ from dust** une surface dépoussiérée; **to get ~ of sb** se débarrasser de qn; **to be ~ of sb** être débarrassé de qn; **area ~ of malaria** zone non touchée par la malaria; **we chose a spot ~ of tourists** nous avons choisi un endroit sans touristes; **~ of charge** (*adj*) gratuit; (*adv*) gratuitement, gratis; **~ of tax** *or* **duty** exonéré, hors taxe; **to be a ~ agent** avoir toute liberté d'action; **~ and easy** décontracté, désinvolte, à l'aise; (*Psych*) **~ association** association *f* libre; **~ church** église *f* non-conformiste; (*Pol etc*) **~ elections** élections *fpl* libres; **~ enterprise** libre entreprise *f*; (*Space*) **~ fall** chute *f* libre; **in ~ fall** en chute libre; **to have a ~ hand to do sth** avoir carte blanche pour faire qch; **to give sb a ~ hand** donner carte blanche à qn (*V also* 1c, 3); (*Brit*) **~ house** pub *m* en gérance libre; (*Ind*) **~ labour** main d'œuvre non syndiquée; **~ love** amour *m* libre, union *f* libre; **~ port** port franc; (*newspapers etc*) **~ press** presse *f* libre; **to give ~ rein to** donner libre cours à; **~ speech** liberté *f* de parole; (*Econ*) **~ trade** libre-échange *m* (*V also* 3); **~ verse** vers *m* libre; (*Philos*) **~ will** libre arbitre *m* (*V also* 3); **he did it of his own ~ will** il l'a fait de son propre gré; *V also* 3 *and* **break** *etc*.

(b) (*costing nothing*) *object, ticket* gratuit. **admission ~** entrée gratuite *or* libre; **we got in ~** *or* **for ~*** nous sommes entrés gratuitement *or* gratis *or* à l'œil*; **they'll send it ~ on request** ils l'enverront gratuitement *or* franco sur demande; (*Comm*) **~ on board** franco à bord; (*Comm*) **~ delivery, delivery ~** livraison gratuite, franco de port; (*Comm*) **~ sample** échantillon gratuit; (*Comm: on packets etc*) **~ mug with each towel** une chope gratuite pour tout achat d'une serviette; **he got a ~ ticket** il a eu un billet gratuit *or* gratuitement *or* sans payer; *V* **post**[3].

(c) (*not occupied*) *room, seat, hour, person* libre. **there are 2 ~ rooms left** il reste 2 chambres de libre; **is this table ~?** cette table est-elle libre?; **I wasn't able to get ~ earlier** je n'ai pas pu me libérer plus tôt; **I will be ~ at 2 o'clock** je serai libre à 2 heures; (*lit, fig*) **to have one's hands ~** avoir les mains libres.

(d) (*lavish, profuse*) généreux, prodigue, large. **to be ~ with one's money** dépenser son argent sans compter; (*iro*) **you're very ~ with your advice** pour donner des conseils vous êtes un peu là (*iro*); **he makes ~ with all my things** il ne se gêne pas pour se servir de mes affaires; **feel ~!*** je t'en prie!, sers-toi!; *V also* 1e.

(e) (*improper*) *language* grivois, licencieux, libre. **to make ~ with a woman**† prendre des libertés *or* se permettre des familiarités *or* se permettre des privautés (*hum*) avec une femme.

2 *vt nation, slave* affranchir, libérer; *caged animal* libérer; *prisoner* libérer, élargir (*frm*), mettre en liberté; (*untie*) *person, animal* détacher, dégager; *knot* défaire, dénouer; *tangle* débrouiller; (*unblock*) *pipe* débloquer, déboucher; (*rescue*) sauver (*from* de); (*from burden*) soulager, débarrasser (*from* de); (*from tax*) exempter, exonérer (*from* de). **to ~ sb from anxiety** libérer *or* délivrer qn de l'angoisse; (*lit, fig*) **to ~ o.s. from** se débarrasser de, se libérer de.

3 *cpd*: **freeboard** (hauteur *f* de) franc-bord *m*; **freebooter** (*buccaneer*) pirate *m*; (*Hist*) flibustier *m*; **free fight, free-for-all** mêlée générale; **freehand** (*adj, adv*) à main levée; (*Sport*) **free hit** coup franc; (*Brit*) **freehold** (*n*) propriété foncière libre (*de toute obligation*); (*adv*) en propriété libre; (*Brit*) **freeholder** propriétaire foncier (*sans obligation*); (*Sport*) **free kick** coup franc; (*Comm, Press etc*) **freelance** (*n*) collaborateur *m*, -trice *f* indépendant(e); (*adj*) *journalist, designer, player etc* indépendant; (*vi*) *[journalist/designer etc]* être journaliste/dessinateur *m*, -trice *f etc* indépendant(e), faire du journalisme/du dessin *etc* indépendant; (*Hist*) **freeman** homme *m* libre; **freeman of a city** citoyen(ne) *m(f)* d'honneur d'une ville; **freemason** franc-maçon *m*; **freemasonry** franc-maçonnerie *f*; **free-range eggs/poultry** œufs *mpl*/poulets *mpl* de ferme; **free-standing** *furniture* sur pied, non encastré; (*U*) **freestone** pierre *f* de taille; **freestyle swimming** nage *f* libre; **200 metres freestyle** 200 mètres nage libre; **freethinker** libre-penseur *m*, -euse *f*; **freethinking** (*adj*) libre-penseur; (*n*) libre pensée *f*; (*Econ*) **free trader** libre-échangiste *m*; (*US*) **freeway** autoroute *f* (*sans péage*); **freewheel** (*vi*) *[cyclist]* se mettre en roue libre, être en roue libre; *[motorist]* rouler au point mort; (*n*) *[bicycle]* roue *f* libre; **free-will gift/offering** don *m*/offrande *f* volontaire.

freedom ['fri:dəm] **1** *n* liberté *f*. **~ of action** liberté d'action *or* d'agir; **~ of the press** liberté de la presse; **~ of speech** liberté de parole; **~ of worship** liberté religieuse *or* du culte; **~ of the seas** franchise *f* des mers; **to give sb ~ to do as he wishes** laisser les mains libres à qn, donner carte blanche à qn; **to speak with ~** parler en toute liberté; **~ from care/responsibility** le fait d'être dégagé de tout souci/de toute responsabilité; **to give sb the ~ of a city** nommer qn citoyen d'honneur d'une ville; **he gave me the ~ of his house** il m'a permis de me servir comme je voulais de sa maison, il m'a dit de faire comme chez moi.

2 *cpd*: **freedom fighter** guérillero *m*, partisan *m*.

freely ['fri:lɪ] *adv* **(a)** (*lavishly*) *give* libéralement, à profusion. **he spends his money ~** il dépense son argent sans compter, il est dépensier.

(b) (*unrestrictedly*) *speak* franchement, sans contrainte, à cœur ouvert; *act* sans contrainte, librement, en toute liberté; *grow* avec luxuriance.

freesia ['fri:zɪə] *n* freesia *m*.

freeze [fri:z] *pret* **froze**, *ptp* **frozen 1** *vi* (*Met*) geler; *[liquids, pipes, lakes, rivers etc]* geler; (*fig*) se figer. **it will ~ hard tonight** il gèlera dur cette nuit; **I'm freezing** je suis gelé *or* glacé; **my hands are freezing** j'ai les mains gelées *or* glacées; **to ~ to death** mourir de froid; **the lake has frozen** le lac est pris *or* gelé; (*Aut*) **the windscreen was frozen** le pare-brise était givré; (*fig*) **his smile froze on his lips** son sourire s'est figé sur ses lèvres; **he froze (in his tracks)** il est resté figé sur place; **~!** pas un geste!; **to ~ on to sb*** se cramponner à qn; (*Culin*) **meat ~s well but lettuce won't ~** la viande se congèle bien mais la laitue se congèle mal.

2 *vt food* congeler; (*industrially*) surgeler; (*Econ*) *assets, credits* geler; *prices, wages* bloquer, stabiliser. (*fig*) **she froze him with a look** elle lui a lancé un regard qui l'a glacé sur place; *V also* **frozen**.

3 *n* **(a)** (*Met*) temps *m* de gelée, gel *m*. **the big ~ of 1948** le gel rigoureux *or* le grand gel de 1948; *V* **deep**.

(b) (*Econ*) *[prices, wages]* blocage *m*; *[credits]* gel *m*.

4 *cpd*: **freeze-dry** (*vt*) lyophiliser; (*Met*) **freeze-up** gel *m*.

freeze over *vi [lakes, rivers]* geler, se prendre en glace; (*Aut*) *[windscreen etc]* givrer. **the river has frozen over** *or* **up** la rivière est gelée *or* est prise (en glace).

freeze up 1 *vi* **(a)** = **freeze over.**

(b) *[pipes]* geler.

2 *vt sep*: **the pipes** *or* **we* were frozen up last winter** les conduits ont gelé l'hiver dernier.

3 freeze-up *n V* **freeze 4.**

freezer ['fri:zə^r] *n* **(a)** (*deep-freeze*) (*domestic*) congélateur *m*; (*industrial*) surgélateur *m*. **(b)** (*in fridge*) freezer *m*.

freezing ['fri:zɪŋ] **1** *adj weather, look* glacial. **2** *n* congélation *f*, gel *m*. **~ point** point *m* de congélation; **below ~ point** au-dessous de zéro (centigrade).

freight [freɪt] **1** *n* **(a)** (*goods*) fret *m*, cargaison *f*; (*transport*) transport *m*; (*charge*) fret. **to send sth by ~** faire transporter qch par petite vitesse *or* en régime ordinaire; **air ~** transport *or* fret par avion.

(b) (*Brit: by water*) (*inland*) transport fluvial; (*at sea*) transport maritime *or* par voie de mer; (*cargo*) cargaison *f*; (*goods*) marchandises *fpl*.

2 *vt boat, ship* affréter, charger; *goods* transporter.

3 *cpd*: (*US*) (*Rail*) **freight car** wagon *m* de marchandises, fourgon *m*; **freight plane** avion-cargo *m*, avion *m* de fret; **freight train** train *m* de marchandises; **freight yard** dépôt *m or* cour *f* des marchandises.

freightage ['freɪtɪdʒ] *n* (*charge*) fret *m*; (*goods*) fret, cargaison *f*.

freighter ['freɪtə^r] *n* (*Naut*) cargo *m*, navire *m* de charge; (*Aviat*) avion-cargo *m*, avion *m* de fret.

French [frentʃ] **1** *adj* français. **the ~ Academy** l'Académie française; **~ teacher** professeur de français; **the ~ king/embassy** le roi/l'ambassade de France; **the ~ way of life** la vie française; **~ cooking** cuisine française; **the ~ people** les Français; **the ~ Riviera** la côte d'Azur.

2 *n* **(a) the ~** les Français *mpl*; *V* **free**.

(b) (*Ling*) français *m*.

3 *cpd*: **French bean** haricot vert; **French Canadian** (*adj*) canadien français; (*n*) (*person*) Canadien(ne) français(e) *m(f)*; (*Ling*) français canadien; **French chalk** craie *f* de tailleur; (*US*) **French door** porte-fenêtre *f*; (*Culin*) **French dressing** vinaigrette *f*; **French fried (potatoes)**, (*esp US*) **French fries** (pommes *fpl* de terre) frites *fpl*; (*Mus*) **French horn** cor *m* d'harmonie; (*fig*) **to take French leave** filer à l'anglaise*; (*fig: contraceptive*) **French letter*** capote anglaise*; **French loaf** baguette *f* (*de pain*); **Frenchman** Français *m*; **French marigold** œillet *m* d'Inde; **French pastry** pâtisserie *f*; **French polish** vernis *m* (à l'alcool); **French-polish** vernir (à l'alcool); (*Sewing*) **French seam** couture anglaise; **French-speaking** qui parle français; *nation etc* francophone (*V* **Switzerland**); **French window** porte-fenêtre *f*; **Frenchwoman** Française *f*.

Frenchify ['frentʃɪfaɪ] *vt* franciser. (*pej*) **his Frenchified ways** ses maniérismes copiés sur les Français.

frenetic [frə'netɪk] *adj* frénétique, effréné, forcené.

frenzied ['frenzɪd] *adj person* effréné, forcené; *joy, despair* frénétique, délirant.

frenzy ['frenzɪ] *n* frénésie *f*. **~ of delight** transport *m* de joie.

frequency ['fri:kwənsɪ] **1** *n* fréquence *f*. **~ band** bande *f* de fréquence; *V* **high, ultrahigh, very. 2** *cpd*: (*Statistics*) **frequency distribution** distribution *f* des fréquences; (*Electronics*) **frequency modulation** modulation *f* de fréquence.

frequent ['fri:kwənt] **1** *adj* (*numerous, happening often*) *visits, rests, changes* fréquent, nombreux; (*common*) *objection, criticism* fréquent, habituel, courant. **it's quite ~** c'est très courant, cela arrive souvent; **he is a ~ visitor (to our house)** c'est un habitué (de la maison).

2 [frɪ'kwent] *vt* fréquenter, hanter, courir.

frequentative [frɪ'kwentətɪv] *adj, n* (*Gram*) fréquentatif (*m*).

frequenter [frɪ'kwentə^r] *n [house etc]* familier *m*, habitué(e) *m(f)*; *[pub etc]* habitué(e). **he was a great ~ of night clubs** il courait les boîtes de nuit, c'était un pilier de boîtes de nuit.

frequently ['fri:kwəntlɪ] *adv* fréquemment, souvent.

fresco ['freskəʊ] *n* (*pigment, picture*) fresque *f*. **to paint in ~** peindre à fresque.

fresh [freʃ] **1** *adj* **(a)** (*recent, new*) *news, report, paint, make-up, flowers* frais (*f* fraîche); (*not stale*) *air, milk, eggs, butter, food* frais; *food* (*not frozen*) frais, non congelé, non surgelé; (*not tinned*) frais; (*additional*) *supplies* nouveau (*f* nouvelle), supplémentaire; (*new, different*) *clothes, horse* nouveau. **milk ~ from the cow** lait fraîchement trait; **~ butter** (*not stale*) beurre frais; (*unsalted*) beurre sans sel; **the bread is ~ from the oven** le pain est tout frais, le pain sort (à l'instant) du four; **is there any ~ news?** y a-t-il du nouveau? *or* des nouvelles fraîches?; **a ~ sheet of paper** une nouvelle feuille de papier; **he**

put ~ courage into me il m'a redonné courage, il m'a insufflé un courage nouveau; (*fig*) **to break ~ ground** faire œuvre de pionnier, faire quelque chose d'entièrement nouveau; **he has had a ~ heart attack** il a eu une nouvelle crise cardiaque; **it's nice to see some ~ faces here** c'est agréable de voir des visages nouveaux ici; **to make a ~ start** prendre un nouveau départ; **~ water** (*not salt*) eau douce (*V also* **3**); **it is still ~ in my memory** j'en ai encore le souvenir tout frais *or* tout récent; **I'm going out for some ~ air** *or* **for a breath of ~ air** je sors prendre l'air *or* le frais; **in the ~ air** au grand air, en plein air; **let's have some ~ air!** un peu d'air!

(b) (*Met: cool*) *wind* frais (*f* fraîche). **it is getting ~** il commence à faire frais; (*Naut*) **~ breeze** vent frais.

(c) *colours* frais (*f* fraîche), gai; *complexion* frais. **she was as ~ as a daisy** elle était fraîche comme une rose; *V also* **1d.**

(d) (*lively*) *person* plein d'entrain, fringant, sémillant; *horse* fougueux, fringant. **as ~ as a daisy** tout fringant *or* sémillant.

(e) (*: *cheeky*) familier, trop libre, culotté* (*with* envers). **don't get ~ with me!** pas d'impertinences!; **he's very ~!** il a du toupet!*, il est culotté!*

2 *adv*: **boy ~ from school** garçon frais émoulu du lycée; **~ from Scotland** nouvellement *or* fraîchement arrivé d'Écosse; **he's just come ~ from a holiday by the sea** il revient de vacances au bord de la mer; **we're ~ out of cream*** nous venons de vendre le dernier pot de crème.

3 *cpd*: (*Univ*) **freshman** bizut(h) *m*, nouveau *m*, nouvelle *f* (*étudiant(e) de première année*); **freshwater fish** poisson *m* d'eau douce.

freshen [ˈfreʃn] *vi* (*Met*) *[wind, air]* fraîchir.

freshen up 1 *vi* (*fig*) faire un brin de toilette *or* une petite toilette; *[woman]* se refaire une beauté*, faire un raccord (à son maquillage)*.

2 *vt sep child, invalid etc* faire un brin de toilette à, faire une petite toilette à; *child* débarbouiller. **that will freshen you up** cela vous ravigotera* *or* vous requinquera*.

fresher [ˈfreʃəʳ] *n* (*Brit Univ sl*) = **freshman**; *V* **fresh 3.**

freshly [ˈfreʃlɪ] *adv* nouvellement, récemment. **~-cut flowers** des fleurs fraîches cueillies *or* nouvellement cueillies.

freshness [ˈfreʃnɪs] *n [air, food, fruit, milk, wind etc]* fraîcheur *f*; *[manner]* franchise *f*, spontanéité *f*, naturel *m*; *[outlook, approach]* fraîcheur, jeunesse *f*; *[colour]* fraîcheur, gaieté *f or* gaîté *f*.

fret[1] [fret] **1** *vi* **(a)** (*become anxious*) s'agiter, se tourmenter, se tracasser; *[baby]* pleurer, geindre. **don't ~!** ne t'en fais pas!, ne te tracasse pas!; **she ~s over trifles** elle se fait du mauvais sang pour des vétilles; **the child is ~ting for its mother** le petit pleure parce qu'il veut sa mère.

(b) *[horse]* **to ~ (at the bit)** ronger le mors.

2 *vt*: **to ~ o.s.*** se tracasser, se faire de la bile, se biler*.

3 *n*: **to be in a ~*** se faire du mauvais sang *or* de la bile, se biler*.

fret[2] [fret] **1** *vt wood etc* découper, chantourner. **the stream has ~ted its way through the rock** le ruisseau s'est creusé un chenal dans le rocher. **2** *cpd*: **fretsaw** scie *f* à découper; **fretwork** (*piece*) pièce chantournée; (*work*) découpage *m*.

fret[3] [fret] **1** *n [guitar]* touchette *f*. **2** *vt*: **~ted** à touchettes.

fretful [ˈfretfʊl] *adj person* agité, énervé; *baby, child* grognon, pleurnicheur; *sleep* agité.

fretfully [ˈfretfəlɪ] *adv do* avec agitation *or* énervement, d'un air énervé; *say* d'un ton agité. *[baby]* **to cry ~** pleurnicher, être grognon.

fretfulness [ˈfretfʊlnɪs] *n* irritabilité *f*.

Freudian [ˈfrɔɪdɪən] *adj* (*Psych, fig*) freudien. **~ slip** lapsus *m*.

friable [ˈfraɪəbl] *adj* friable.

friar [ˈfraɪəʳ] *n* moine *m*, frère *m*, religieux *m*. **F~ John** Frère Jean.

fricassee [ˈfrɪkəsiː] *n* fricassée *f*.

fricative [ˈfrɪkətɪv] *adj, n*: **~ (consonant)** (consonne *f*) fricative (*f*).

friction [ˈfrɪkʃən] *n* (*Phys etc*) friction *f*, frottement *m*; (*fig*) désaccord *m*, frottement, friction. (*fig*) **there is a certain amount of ~ between them** il y a des frottements *or* des désaccords *or* de la friction entre eux; (*US*) **~ tape** chatterton *m*.

Friday [ˈfraɪdɪ] *n* vendredi *m*. **~ the thirteenth** vendredi treize; *V* **good**; *for other phrases V* **Saturday.**

fridge [frɪdʒ] *n* (*Brit abbr of* **refrigerator**) frigo* *m*, frigidaire *m* ®.

fried [fraɪd] *pret, ptp of* **fry**[2].

friend [frend] *n* ami(e) *m(f)*; (*schoolmate, workmate etc*) camarade *mf*, copain* *m*, copine* *f*; (*helper, supporter*) ami(e), bienfaiteur *m*, -trice *f*. **a ~ of mine** un de mes amis; **~s of ours** des amis (à nous); **he's one of my son's ~s** c'est un ami *or* un camarade *or* un copain* de mon fils; **her best ~** sa meilleure amie; **he's no ~ of mine** je ne le compte pas au nombre de mes amis; **to make ~s with sb** devenir ami avec qn, se lier d'amitié avec qn; **he made a ~ of him** il en a fait son ami; **he makes ~s easily** il se fait facilement des amis, il se lie facilement; **to be ~s with sb** être ami *or* lié avec qn; **let's be ~s again** on fait la paix?; **we're just good ~s** nous sommes simplement bons amis; **we're all ~s here** nous sommes entre amis; **a ~ of the family** un ami de la famille *or* de la maison; (*Prov*) **a ~ in need is a ~ indeed** c'est dans le besoin que l'on connaît ses vrais amis; (*loc*) **the best of ~s must part** il n'est si bonne compagnie qui ne se sépare (*Prov*); **he's been a true ~ to us** il a fait preuve d'une véritable amitié envers nous; (*fig*) **a ~ at court** un ami influent; (*fig*) **to have ~s at court** avoir des amis influents *or* des protections; (*Parl*) **my honourable ~**, (*Jur*) **my learned ~** mon cher *or* distingué confrère, ma distinguée collègue; **~ of the poor** bienfaiteur *or* ami des pauvres; **F~s of the National Theatre** (Société *f* des) Amis du Théâtre National; (*Rel*) **Society of F~s** Société *f* des Amis, Quakers *mpl*.

friendless [ˈfrendlɪs] *adj* seul, isolé, sans amis.

friendliness [ˈfrendlɪnɪs] *n* attitude amicale, bienveillance *f*.

friendly [ˈfrendlɪ] *adj person, attitude, feelings* amical; *child, dog* gentil, affectueux; *advice* d'ami; *smile, welcome* amical; (*from superiors*) bienveillant, aimable. **people here are so ~** les gens sont si gentils ici; **I am quite ~ with her** je suis (assez) ami avec elle; **to be on ~ terms with sb** être en termes amicaux *or* avoir des rapports d'amitié avec qn; **that wasn't a very ~ thing to do** ce n'était pas très gentil de faire cela; (*Sport*) **~ match** match amical; (*Brit*) **F~ Society** Société *f* de prévoyance, (société *f*) mutuelle *f*; (*Geog*) **the F~ Islands** les îles *fpl* des Amis, Tonga *m*.

friendship [ˈfrendʃɪp] *n* amitié *f*. **out of ~** par amitié.

frieze[1] [friːz] *n* (*Archit*) frise *f*, bordure *f*.

frieze[2] [friːz] *n* (*Tex*) ratine *f*.

frigate [ˈfrɪgɪt] *n* frégate *f*.

fright [fraɪt] *n* **(a)** effroi *m*, peur *f*. **to take ~** prendre peur, s'effrayer (*de* at); **to get** *or* **have a ~** avoir peur; **it gave me such a ~** ça m'a fait une de ces peurs* *or* une belle peur; *V* **stage.**

(b) (*: *person*) horreur* *f*, épouvantail *m*. **she's** *or* **she looks a ~** elle est à faire peur.

frighten [ˈfraɪtn] *vt* effrayer, faire peur à. **did he ~ you?** est-ce qu'il vous a fait peur?; **it nearly ~ed him out of his wits** *or* **his skin** cela lui a fait une peur bleue; **to ~ sb into doing sth** effrayer qn pour lui faire faire qch, faire faire qch à qn par (l')intimidation; **he was ~ed into doing it** il l'a fait sous le coup de la peur; **to be ~ed of (doing) sth** avoir peur de (faire) qch; **to be ~ed to death** mourir de peur; **she is easily ~ed** elle prend peur facilement, elle est peureuse; *V* **living.**

frighten away, frighten off *vt sep birds* effaroucher; *children etc* chasser (en leur faisant peur).

frightened [ˈfraɪtnd] *adj* effrayé. **don't be ~** n'ayez pas peur, ne vous effrayez pas.

frightening [ˈfraɪtnɪŋ] *adj* effrayant.

frightful [ˈfraɪtfʊl] *adj* épouvantable, affreux, effroyable. **she looks ~ in that hat*** elle est affreuse avec ce chapeau.

frightfully [ˈfraɪtfəlɪ] *adv* affreusement, effroyablement. **I am ~ late** je suis terriblement *or* affreusement en retard; **I am ~ sorry** je regrette énormément, je suis (absolument) désolé; **it's ~ good of you** c'est vraiment trop gentil à vous *or* de votre part, vous êtes vraiment trop bon; **~ ugly** affreusement *or* effroyablement laid; **he's ~ sweet** il est terriblement mignon.

frightfulness [ˈfraɪtfʊlnɪs] *n [crime etc]* atrocité *f*, horreur *f*.

frigid [ˈfrɪdʒɪd] *adj* (*Geog, Met*) glacial; *manner, reaction, welcome* froid, glacé; (*Psych*) *woman* frigide.

frigidity [frɪˈdʒɪdɪtɪ] *n* (*V* **frigid**) froideur *f*, frigidité *f*.

frill [frɪl] *n [dress]* ruche *f*, volant *m*; *[shirt]* jabot *m*; (*Culin*) papillote *f*; (*Orn*) collerette *f*. (*fig*) **~s** manières *fpl*, façons *fpl*, chichis* *mpl*; (*fig*) **without any ~s** simple, sans manières, sans façons; *V* **furbelow.**

frilly [ˈfrɪlɪ] *adj dress* à fanfreluches; (*fig*) *speech* à fioritures, fleuri.

fringe [frɪndʒ] **1** *n [rug, shawl, hair]* frange *f*; *[wood]* bord *m*, bordure *f*, lisière *f*; *[crowd]* derniers rangs. **on the ~ of the forest** en bord *or* bordure de forêt, à la lisière *or* à l'orée de la forêt; **to live on the ~ of society** vivre en marge de la société; **the outer ~s** *[large town]* la grande banlieue; *[town]* la périphérie; *V* **lunatic.**

2 *vt shawl etc* franger (*with* de). (*fig*) **road ~d with trees** route bordée d'arbres; (*Geog*) **fringing reef** récif frangeant.

3 *cpd*: (*TV*) **fringe area** zone *f* limitrophe (de réception); **fringe benefits** avantages *mpl* supplémentaires, indemnités *fpl*, avantages divers; **fringe group** groupe marginal.

frippery [ˈfrɪpərɪ] *n* (*pej*) (*cheap ornament*) colifichets *mpl*; (*on dress*) fanfreluches *fpl*; (*ostentation*) préciosité *f*, maniérisme *m*.

frisbee [ˈfrɪzbɪ] *n* ® frisbee *m* ®.

frisk [frɪsk] **1** *vi* gambader, batifoler*, folâtrer. **2** *vt criminal, suspect* fouiller.

friskiness [ˈfrɪskɪnɪs] *n* vivacité *f*.

frisky [ˈfrɪskɪ] *adj* vif (*f* vive), sémillant, fringant.

fritillary [frɪˈtɪlərɪ] *n* fritillaire *f*.

fritter[1] [ˈfrɪtəʳ] *vt* (*also* **~ away**) *money, time* gaspiller, perdre; *energy* gaspiller.

fritter[2] [ˈfrɪtəʳ] *n* (*Culin*) beignet *m*. **apple ~** beignet aux pommes.

frivolity [frɪˈvɒlɪtɪ] *n* frivolité *f*.

frivolous [ˈfrɪvələs] *adj person, behaviour* frivole, léger; *remark* frivole, superficiel.

frizz [frɪz] *vt hair* faire friser *or* frisotter.

frizzle [ˈfrɪzl] **1** *vi* grésiller. **2** *vt* (*also* **~ up**) *food* faire trop griller, laisser brûler *or* calciner. **the joint was all ~d (up)** le rôti était complètement calciné.

frizzly [ˈfrɪzlɪ] *adj*, **frizzy** [ˈfrɪzɪ] *adj hair* crépu, crêpelé.

fro [frəʊ] *adv*: **to and ~** de long en large; **to go to and ~ between** aller et venir entre, faire la navette entre; **journeys to and ~ between London and Edinburgh** allers *mpl* et retours *mpl* entre Londres et Édimbourg; *V also* **to.**

frock [frɒk] *n [woman, baby]* robe *f*; *[monk]* froc *m*. **~ coat** redingote *f*.

frog[1] [frɒg] **1** *n* **(a)** (*Zool*) grenouille *f*. (*fig*) **to have a ~ in one's throat** avoir un chat dans la gorge.

(b) (*pej*) **F~**: Français(e) *m(f)*.

2 *cpd*: **frogman** homme-grenouille *m*; **to frog-march sb in/out** *etc* (*hustle*) amener/sortir *etc* qn de force; (*carry*) amener/sortir *etc* qn en le prenant par les quatre membres; **frogspit** crachat *m* de coucou.

frog[2] [frɒg] *n* (*Dress*) brandebourg *m*, soutache *f*.

frolic ['frɒlɪk] 1 *vi* (*also* ~ **about**, ~ **around**) folâtrer, batifoler*, gambader. 2 *n* ébats *mpl*, gambades *fpl*; (*prank*) espièglerie *f*, gaminerie *f*; (*merry-making*) ébats.

frolicsome ['frɒlɪksəm] *adj* folâtre, gai, espiègle.

from [frɒm] *prep* **(a)** (*place: starting point*) de. ~ **house to house** de maison en maison; **to jump** ~ **a wall** sauter d'un mur; **to travel** ~ **London to Paris** voyager de Londres à Paris; **train** ~ **Manchester** train (en provenance) de Manchester; **programme transmitted** ~ **Lyons** programme retransmis de *or* depuis Lyon; **he comes** ~ **London** il vient de Londres, il est (originaire) de Londres; **where are you** ~? d'où êtes-vous *or* venez-vous?

(b) (*time: starting point*) de, dès, à partir de. **(as)** ~ **the 14th July** à partir du 14 juillet; ~ **that day onwards** à partir de ce jour-là; ~ **beginning to end** du début jusqu'à la fin; ~ **his childhood** dès son enfance; **he comes** ~ **time to time** il vient de temps en temps; **counting** ~ **last Monday** à dater de lundi dernier.

(c) (*distance: lit, fig*) de. **the house is 10 km** ~ **the coast** la maison est à 10 km de la côte; **to go away** ~ **home** quitter la maison; **not far** ~ **here** pas loin d'ici; **far** ~ **blaming you** loin de vous le reprocher.

(d) (*origin*) de, de la part de, d'après. **a letter** ~ **my mother** une lettre de ma mère; **tell him** ~ **me** dites-lui de ma part; **an invitation** ~ **the Smiths** une invitation (de la part) des Smith; **painted** ~ **life** peint d'après nature; ~ **a picture by Picasso** d'après un tableau de Picasso.

(e) (*used with prices, numbers*) à partir de, depuis. **wine** ~ **6 francs a bottle** vins à partir de 6 F la bouteille; **dresses** ~ **150 francs** robes à partir de 150 F; **there were** ~ **10 to 15 people there** il y avait là de 10 à 15 personnes.

(f) (*source*) **to drink** ~ **a brook** boire à un ruisseau; **to drink** ~ **a glass** boire dans un verre; **to drink straight** ~ **the bottle** boire à (même) la bouteille; **he took it** ~ **the cupboard** il l'a pris dans le placard, il l'a sorti du placard; **to pick sb** ~ **the crowd** choisir qn dans la foule; **a quotation** ~ **Racine** une citation (tirée) de Racine; **to speak** ~ **notes** parler avec des notes; **to judge** ~ **appearances** juger d'après les apparences; ~ **your point of view** à *or* de votre point de vue; **to draw a conclusion** ~ **the information** tirer une conclusion des renseignements.

(g) (*prevention, escape, deprivation etc*) à, de. **take the knife** ~ **this child!** ôtez *or* enlevez *or* prenez le couteau à cet enfant!; **he prevented me** ~ **coming** il m'a empêché de venir; **he took/stole it** ~ **them** il le leur a pris/volé; **the news was kept** ~ **her** on lui a caché la nouvelle; **to shelter** ~ **the rain** s'abriter de la pluie.

(h) (*change*) de. ~ **bad to worse** de mal en pis; **price increase** ~ **one franc to one franc fifty** augmentation de prix d'un franc à un franc cinquante; **he went** ~ **office boy to director in 5 years** de garçon de bureau il est passé directeur en 5 ans.

(i) (*cause, motive*) **to act** ~ **conviction** agir par conviction; **to die** ~ **fatigue** mourir de fatigue; ~ **what I heard ...** d'après ce que j'ai entendu ...; ~ **what I can see ...** à ce que je vois ...; ~ **the look of things ...** à en juger par les apparences ...; ~ **the way he talks you would think that ...** à l'entendre on penserait que ... .

(j) (*difference*) de. **he is quite different** ~ **the others** il est complètement différent des autres; **to distinguish the good** ~ **the bad** distinguer le bon du mauvais.

(k) (*with other preps and advs*) **seen** ~ **above** vu d'en haut; ~ **above the clouds** d'au-dessus des nuages; ~ **henceforth** à partir d'aujourd'hui, désormais, dorénavant (*frm*); **I saw him** ~ **afar** je l'ai vu de loin; **she was looking at him** ~ **over the wall** elle le regardait depuis l'autre côté du mur; ~ **under the table** de dessous la table.

frond [frɒnd] *n* [*fern*] fronde *f*; [*palm*] feuille *f*.

front [frʌnt] 1 *n* **(a)** (*forepart*) devant *m*, avant *m*; [*class, crowd, audience*] premier rang; [*building*] façade *f*, devant, front *m*; [*boat, coach, train*] avant; [*shirt, dress*] devant; [*book*] début *m*. **in** ~ devant, en avant; **in** ~ **of the table** devant la table; **to send sb on in** ~ envoyer qn en avant; **he was walking in** ~ il marchait devant; (*Sport*) **to be in** ~ mener; (*fig*) **to come to the** ~ se faire connaître *or* remarquer, percer; **to sit in the** ~ **of the train/bus** s'asseoir en tête de *or* du train/à l'avant de l'autobus; **in the** ~ **of the class** au premier rang de la classe; **in the** ~ **of the book** au début du livre; **she spilt it down the** ~ **of her dress** elle l'a renversé sur le devant de sa robe; **he pushed his way to the** ~ **of the crowd** il s'est frayé un chemin jusqu'au premier rang de la foule; (*fig*) **to put on a bold** ~ faire bonne contenance; (*fig*) **it's all just a** ~ **with him** tout ça n'est que façade chez lui.

(b) (*Met, Mil, Pol*) front *m*. **to fall at the** ~ mourir au front; **there was fighting on several** ~**s** on se battait sur plusieurs fronts; (*gen, Mil, Pol etc*) **on all** ~**s** partout, de tous côtés; **cold/warm** ~ front froid/chaud; **popular** ~ front populaire; (*Pol, fig*) **we must present a common** ~ nous devons offrir un front commun, il faut faire front commun; *V* **home** *etc.*

(c) (*Brit: also* **sea** ~) (*beach*) bord *m* de mer, plage *f*; (*prom*) front *m* de mer. **along the** ~ (*on the beach*) en bord de mer; (*on the prom*) sur le front de mer; **a house on the** ~ une maison sur le front de mer.

(d) (*liter: forehead*) front *m*.

2 *adj* **(a)** de devant, (en) avant, premier. ~ **door** [*house*] porte d'entrée *or* principale; [*car*] portière *f* avant; **in the** ~ **end of the train** en tête de *or* du train, à l'avant du train; ~ **garden** jardin *m* de devant; (*Mil*) ~ **line(s)** front *m*; (*Press*) **on the** ~ **page** en première page, à la une* (*V also* 6); **the** ~ **page** la première page, la une*; (*fig*) **in the** ~ **rank** parmi les premiers; ~ **room** pièce *f* donnant sur la rue, pièce de devant; (*lounge*) salon *m*; **in the** ~ **row** au premier rang; **to have a** ~ **seat** (*lit*) avoir une place (assise) au premier rang; (*fig*) être aux premières loges (*fig*); ~ **tooth** dent *f* de devant; ~ **wheel** roue *f* avant.

(b) de face. ~ **view** vue *f* de face; (*Archit*) ~ **elevation** élévation frontale.

(c) (*Ling*) ~ **vowel** voyelle frontale *or* antérieure.

3 *adv* par devant. **to attack** ~ **and rear** attaquer par devant et par derrière; (*Mil*) **eyes** ~! fixe!

4 *vi*: **to** ~ **on to** donner sur; **the house** ~**s north** la maison fait face *or* est exposée au nord; **the windows** ~ **on to the street** les fenêtres donnent sur la rue.

5 *vt building* donner une façade à. **house** ~**ed with stone** maison avec façade en pierre.

6 *cpd*: (*Parl*) **front bench** banc *m* des ministres et celui des membres du cabinet fantôme; (*Brit Parl*) **frontbencher** *député siégeant au banc des ministres ou à celui des membres du cabinet fantôme*; **it's merely a front organization** cette organisation n'est qu'une façade *or* une couverture; **front-page news** gros titres, manchettes *fpl*; **it was front-page news for a month** cela a été à la une* (des journaux) pendant un mois; **front-rank** de premier plan; (*Athletics*) **front runner** coureur *m* de tête; (*fig*) **he is a front runner for the party leadership** il est un des favoris pour être leader du parti; (*Aut*) **front-wheel drive** traction *f* avant; **front-wheel drive car** traction *f* avant.

frontage ['frʌntɪdʒ] *n* [*shop*] devanture *f*, façade *f*; [*house*] façade.

frontal ['frʌntl] 1 *adj* (*Mil*) *attack* de front; (*Anat, Med etc*) frontal. **full** ~ **nude** nu(e) *m(f)* de face. 2 *n* (*Rel*) parement *m*.

frontier ['frʌntɪəʳ] 1 *n* frontière *f*. 2 *cpd town, zone* frontière *inv*. **frontier dispute** incident *m* de frontière; **frontier post** = **frontier station**; **frontiersman** frontalier *m*; **frontier station** poste *m* frontière.

frontispiece ['frʌntɪspiːs] *n* frontispice *m*.

frontwards ['frʌntwədz] *adv* en avant, vers l'avant.

frost [frɒst] 1 *n* gel *m*, gelée *f*; (*also* **hoar**~) givre *m*, gelée blanche. **late** ~**s** gelées tardives *or* printanières *or* de printemps; (*Brit*) **10 degrees of** ~ 10 degrés au-dessous de zéro; *V* **ground**[1], **hoarfrost**, **jack** *etc.*

2 *vt* (*freeze*) *plants, vegetables* geler; (*US: ice*) *cake* glacer. ~**ed glass** (*for window*) verre dépoli; (*for drink*) verre givré.

3 *cpd*: **frostbite** gelure *f*; **to get frostbite in one's hands** avoir les mains qui gèlent; **frostbitten** *hands, feet* gelé; *rosebushes, vegetables* gelé, grillé par la gelée *or* le gel; **frostbound** *ground* gelé.

frosting ['frɒstɪŋ] *n* (*US Culin: icing*) glace *f*, glaçage *m*.

frosty ['frɒstɪ] *adj morning, weather etc* de gelée, glacial; *window* couvert de givre; (*fig*) *welcome, look* glacial, froid. **it is going to be** ~ **tonight** il va geler cette nuit.

froth [frɒθ] 1 *n* [*liquids in general*] écume *f*, mousse *f*; [*beer*] mousse; (*fig: frivolities*) futilités *fpl*, vent *m* (*fig*), paroles creuses.

2 *vi* écumer, mousser. **this detergent does not** ~ **(up)** ce détergent ne mousse pas; **the beer** ~**ed over the edge of the glass** la mousse débordait du verre (de bière); **the dog was** ~**ing at the mouth** le chien avait de l'écume à la gueule.

frothy ['frɒθɪ] *adj water* mousseux, écumeux; *sea* écumeux; *beer* mousseux; (*fig*) *lace, nightdress* léger, vaporeux; *play, entertainment* léger, vide (*pej*), creux (*pej*).

frown [fraʊn] 1 *n* froncement *m* (de sourcils). **to give a** ~ froncer les sourcils; **he looked at her with a disapproving** ~ il l'a fixée avec un froncement de sourcils désapprobateur.

2 *vi* froncer les sourcils, se renfrogner. **to** ~ **at sb** regarder qn en fronçant les sourcils, regarder qn de travers; **to** ~ **at a child** faire les gros yeux à un enfant; **he** ~**ed at the news/the interruption** l'information/l'interruption lui a fait froncer les sourcils.

frown (up)on *vt fus* (*fig*) *person, suggestion, idea* désapprouver.

frowning ['fraʊnɪŋ] *adj face, look* renfrogné, sombre; *forehead* plissé, orageux.

frowsty* ['fraʊstɪ] *adj* (*Brit*) = **frowsy a.**

frowsy, frowzy ['fraʊzɪ] *adj* **(a)** *room* qui sent le renfermé. **(b)** *person, clothes* sale, négligé, peu soigné.

froze [frəʊz] *pret of* **freeze.**

frozen ['frəʊzn] 1 *ptp of* **freeze.** 2 *adj pipes, river* gelé;(*) *person* gelé, glacé. **I am** ~ je suis gelé *or* glacé; **my hands are** ~ j'ai les mains gelées *or* glacées; **to be** ~ **stiff** être gelé jusqu'aux os; ~ **food** aliments congelés; (*industrially* ~) aliments surgelés; *V* **marrow.**

fructification [ˌfrʌktɪfɪ'keɪʃən] *n* fructification *f*.

fructify ['frʌktɪfaɪ] *vi* fructifier.

frugal ['fruːgəl] *adj person* économe (*with* de); *meal* frugal, simple.

frugality [fruː'gælɪtɪ] *n* [*meal*] frugalité *f*; [*person*] frugalité; (*fig*) parcimonie *f*.

frugally ['fruːgəlɪ] *adv give out* parcimonieusement; *live* simplement, avec simplicité.

fruit [fruːt] 1 *n*, *pl* ~ *or* (*rare*) ~**s** fruit *m*. **may I have some** ~? puis-je avoir un fruit?; **more** ~ **is eaten nowadays** on mange actuellement plus de fruits; ~ **is good for you** les fruits sont bons pour la santé; **the** ~**s of the earth** les fruits de la terre; (*lit, fig*) **to bear** ~ porter fruit; **it is the** ~ **of much hard work** c'est le fruit d'un long travail; **hullo, old** ~!‡ salut, mon pote!‡; *V* **dried**, **forbid** *etc.*

2 *vi* [*tree*] donner.

3 *cpd*: **fruit basket** corbeille *f* à fruits; **fruit cake** cake *m*; **fruit cup** (*drink*) boisson *f* aux fruits (*parfois faiblement alcoolisée*); (*US*) (coupe *f* de) fruits rafraîchis; **fruit dish** (*for dessert*) (*small*) petite coupe *or* coupelle *f* à fruits; (*large*) coupe à fruits, compotier *m*; (*basket etc*) corbeille *f* à fruits; **fruit drop** bonbon *m* au fruit; **fruit farm** exploitation *or* entreprise fruitière; **fruit farmer** arboriculteur *m* (fruitier); **fruit farming** arboriculture *f* (fruitière); **fruit fly** mouche *f* du vinaigre, drosophile *f*; (*Brit*) **fruit gum** boule *f* de gomme (*bonbon*); **fruit knife** couteau *m* à fruits; (*Brit*) **fruit machine** machine *f* à sous; **fruit salad** salade *f* de fruits; (*Med*) **fruit salts** sels purgatifs; **fruit tree** arbre fruitier.

fruiterer ['fruːtərəʳ] *n* (*Brit*) marchand(e) *m(f)* de fruits, fruitier *m*, -ière *f*. **at the ∼'s (shop)** chez le fruitier, à la fruiterie.

fruitful ['fruːtfʊl] *adj plant* fécond; *soil* fertile, fécond; *career, attempt* fructueux; *discussion, investigation* fructueux, utile.

fruitfully ['fruːtfəlɪ] *adv* (*fig*) fructueusement, avec profit.

fruitfulness ['fruːtfʊlnɪs] *n [soil]* fertilité *f*, fécondité *f*; *[plant]* fécondité; *[discussion etc]* caractère fructueux *or* profitable, profit *m*.

fruition [fruː'ɪʃən] *n [aims, plans, ideas]* réalisation *f*. **to bring to ∼** réaliser, concrétiser; **to come to ∼** se réaliser.

fruitless ['fruːtlɪs] *adj plant* stérile, inféconď; *attempt, discussion, investigation* stérile, vain, sans résultat.

fruity ['fruːtɪ] *adj* **(a)** *flavour* fruité, de fruit. **it has a ∼ taste** cela a un goût de fruit; **it has a ∼ smell** cela sent le fruit. **(b)** *voice* bien timbré, posé. **(c)** (:) *joke* corsé, raide*.

frump [frʌmp] *n* bonne femme fagotée *or* ficelée*. **old ∼** vieux tableau, vieille sorcière *or* rombière*.

frumpish ['frʌmpɪʃ] *adj* fagoté, mal ficelé*.

frustrate [frʌs'treɪt] *vt hopes* frustrer, tromper; *attempts, plans* contrecarrer, faire échouer; *plot* déjouer, faire échouer, faire avorter; *person* décevoir, frustrer. **he was ∼d in his efforts to win** il a été frustré dans les tentatives qu'il a faites pour gagner; **his hopes were ∼d** ses espoirs ont été frustrés.

frustrated [frʌs'treɪtɪd] *adj person* frustré, déçu; (*sexually*) frustré. **he feels very ∼ in his present job** il se sent très insatisfait dans son poste actuel; **in a ∼ effort to speak to him** dans un vain effort pour lui parler.

frustrating [frʌs'treɪtɪŋ] *adj* déprimant, désespérant. **it's very ∼ having *or* to have no money** c'est vraiment pénible de ne pas avoir d'argent.

frustration [frʌs'treɪʃən] *n* **(a)** (*U*) frustration *f* (*also Psych*), déception *f*. **(b)** déception *f*. **many ∼s** de nombreux déboires, de nombreuses déceptions.

fry[1] [fraɪ] *collective n [fish]* fretin *m*; *[frogs]* têtards *mpl*. **small ∼** (*unimportant people*) le menu fretin; (*children*) les gosses* *mfpl*, les mioches* *mfpl*, la marmaille*.

fry[2] [fraɪ] *pret, ptp* **fried 1** *vt meat, fish etc* faire frire, frire. **to ∼ eggs** faire des œufs sur le plat; **fried eggs** œufs sur le plat; **fried fish** poisson frit; **fried potatoes** (*chips*) pommes (de terre) frites, frites *fpl*; (*sauté*) pommes (de terre) sautées; *V* **fish, French.**

2 *vi* frire.

3 *n* friture *f*. (*US*) **∼-pan = frying pan** (*V* **frying**); *V* **French.**

frying ['fraɪɪŋ] *n*: **there was a smell of ∼** il y avait une odeur de friture; **∼ pan** poêle *f* (à frire); (*fig*) **to jump out of the ∼ pan into the fire** tomber de Charybde en Scylla.

fuchsia ['fjuːʃə] *n* fuchsia *m*.

fuck∵ [fʌk] **1** *n* (*act*) baisage∵ *m*. **she's a good ∼** elle baise bien∵.

2 *cpd*: **fuck-all** rien de rien; **I know fuck-all about it** je n'en sais foutre rien:; **there's fuck-all to drink in the house** il n'y a pas une goutte à boire dans cette putain de baraque:; **that's fuck-all good *or* use** comme utilité, mon cul:; **he's done fuck-all today** il n'a rien branlé aujourd'hui:.

3 *vt* baiser∵. **∼!, ∼ it!** putain de bordel!∵, putain de merde!∵; **∼ me!** putain!:, merde alors!:; **∼ you!** va te faire foutre!:; **to feel ∼ed (out)** se sentir vidé: *or* vanné:.

4 *vi* baiser∵.

fuck about∵, fuck around∵ *vi* déconner:. **to fuck about *or* around with sth** tripatouiller* qch.

fuck off∵ *vi* foutre le camp:.

fuck up∵ *vt sep plans* foutre la merde dans:; *people* foutre dans la merde:.

fucking∵ ['fʌkɪŋ] **1** *adj*: **∼ hell!** putain de bordel!∵, putain de merde!∵; **this ∼ machine** cette putain de machine:; **this ∼ phone** ce putain *or* ce bordel de téléphone:.

2 *adv* vachement:. **it's ∼ cold** il fait un putain de froid:; **it's ∼ good** c'est chié; **a ∼ awful film** un film complètement con:.

fuddled ['fʌdld] *adj ideas* embrouillé, brouillé, confus; *person* (*muddled*) désorienté, déconcerté; (*tipsy*) éméché, gris. **he was slightly ∼** il était un peu éméché *or* gris *or* pompette*.

fuddy-duddy* ['fʌdɪ,dʌdɪ] **1** *adj* (*old-fashioned*) vieux jeu *inv*; (*fussy*) tatillon, maniaque. **2** *n* vieux machin:, vieux schnock: *or* schnoque:.

fudge [fʌdʒ] **1** *n* **(a)** (*Culin*) fondant *m*.

(b) (*Press*) (*space for stop press*) emplacement *m* de la dernière heure; (*stop press news*) (insertion *f* de) dernière heure, dernières nouvelles.

2 *excl* (*) balivernes!

3 *vt* **(a)** (*fake up*) *story, excuse* monter.

(b) (*US: dodge*) *question, issue* esquiver, tourner.

fuel [fjʊəl] **1** *n* (*U: also Aviat, Space*) combustible *m*; (*Aut*) carburant *m*; (*specifically coal*) charbon *m*; (*wood*) bois *m*. **what kind of ∼ do you use in your central heating?** quel combustible utilisez-vous dans votre chauffage central?; (*fig*) **to add ∼ to the flames *or* fire** jeter de l'huile sur le feu; **the statistics gave him ∼ for further attacks on the government** les statistiques sont venues alimenter ses attaques *or* lui ont fourni des munitions pour continuer ses attaques contre le gouvernement; *V* **aviation, diesel, solid** *etc.*

2 *vt stove, furnace etc* alimenter (en combustible); *ships, aircraft etc* ravitailler en combustible *or* carburant.

3 *vi [ship, engine, aircraft]* s'approvisionner *or* se ravitailler en combustible *or* en carburant. (*Aviat etc*) **a ∼ling stop** une escale technique.

4 *cpd*: **fuel injection** injection *f* (de carburant); **fuel injection engine** moteur *m* à injection; **fuel oil** mazout *m*, fuel *m*; **fuel pump** pompe *f* d'alimentation; **fuel tank** réservoir *m* à carburant; *[ship]* soute *f* à mazout.

fug* [fʌg] *n* (*esp Brit*) forte odeur de renfermé. **what a ∼!** (ce que) ça pue le renfermé!

fuggy* ['fʌgɪ] *adj* (*esp Brit*) *room* qui sent le renfermé, mal aéré; *atmosphere* confiné.

fugitive ['fjuːdʒɪtɪv] **1** *n* fugitif *m*, -ive *f*, fuyard(e) *m(f)*; (*refugee*) réfugié(e) *m(f)*. **he was a ∼ from justice** il fuyait la justice. **2** *adj thought, impression* fugitif; (*liter*) *happiness* fugace, éphémère; (*running away*) fugitif.

fugue [fjuːg] *n* (*Mus, Psych*) fugue *f*.

fulcrum ['fʌlkrəm] *n* pivot *m*, point *m* d'appui (*de levier*).

fulfil, (*US*) **fulfill** [fʊl'fɪl] *vt task, prophecy* accomplir, réaliser; *order* exécuter; *condition* remplir; *plan* réaliser; *norm* obéir à, répondre à; *desire* satisfaire, répondre à; *one's duties* s'acquitter de, remplir. **all my prayers have been ∼led** toutes mes prières ont été exaucées; **he ∼s all my hopes** il répond à *or* satisfait toutes mes espérances, il comble tous mes espoirs; **to feel *or* be ∼led** se sentir profondément satisfait, se réaliser (dans la vie).

fulfilling [fʊl'fɪlɪŋ] *adj work etc* profondément satisfaisant.

fulfilment, (*US*) **fulfillment** [fʊl'fɪlmənt] *n [duty, desire]* accomplissement *m*; *[prayer, wish]* exaucement *m*; *[conditions, plans]* réalisation *f*, exécution *f*; (*satisfied feeling*) (sentiment *m* de) contentement *m*.

full [fʊl] **1** *adj* **(a)** (*filled*) *container, stomach* plein, rempli (*of* de); *room, hall, theatre* comble, plein; *hotel, bus, train* complet (*f* -ète). **pockets ∼ of money** des poches pleines d'argent; **the house was ∼ of people** la maison était pleine de monde; **∼ to overflowing** plein à déborder; **he's had a ∼ life** il a eu une vie (bien) remplie; **I have a ∼ day ahead of me** j'ai une journée chargée devant moi; **look ∼ of hate** regard plein *or* chargé de haine; **he's ∼ of good ideas** il est plein de *or* il déborde de bonnes idées; **he's ∼ of hope** il est rempli *or* plein d'espoir; (*liter*) **to die ∼ of years** mourir chargé d'ans (*liter*); **his heart was ∼** il avait le cœur gros; (*Theat*) '**∼ house**' 'complet'; (*Theat*) **to play to a ∼ house** jouer à bureaux fermés; **we are ∼ (up) for July** nous sommes complets pour juillet; **you'll work better on a ∼ stomach** tu travailleras mieux après avoir mangé *or* le ventre plein; (*not hungry*) **I am ∼ (up)!*** je n'en peux plus!, j'ai trop mangé!; **∼ of life** qui déborde d'entrain; **∼ of oneself** imbu de soi-même, plein de soi; **∼ of one's own importance** imbu or pénétré de sa propre importance; **she was/the papers were ∼ of the murder** elle ne parlait/les journaux ne parlaient que du meurtre; *V* **house** *etc.*

(b) (*maximum, complete*) **the ∼ particulars** tous les détails; **ask for ∼ information** demandez des renseignements complets; **we must have ∼er information** il nous faut des informations plus complètes *or* un complément d'information, il nous faut un plus ample informé (*Jur*); **I waited 2 ∼ hours** j'ai attendu 2 bonnes heures *or* 2 grandes heures *or* pas moins de 2 heures; **a ∼ 10 kilometres** 10 bons kilomètres, pas moins de 10 kilomètres; (*Mil*) **a ∼ colonel** un colonel; **a ∼ general** un général d'armée, ≃ un général à cinq étoiles; **to go (at) ∼ blast*** *[car etc]* aller à toute pompe* *or* à toute bitture*; *[radio, television]* marcher à pleins tubes*; **a radio on at ∼ blast** une radio (marchant) à pleins tubes*; **roses in ∼ bloom** roses épanouies; (*fig*) **the wheel has come ∼ circle** la boucle est bouclée; (*Hunting*) **the pack was in ∼ cry** toute la meute donnait de la voix; **the crowd was in ∼ cry after the thief** la foule poursuivait le voleur en criant; **∼ dress** (*Mil etc*) grande tenue; (*evening dress*) tenue *f* de soirée (*V also* 4); **∼ employment** plein emploi; **to pay ∼ fare** payer place entière *or* plein tarif; **in ∼ flight** en plein vol; **to fall ∼ length** tomber de tout son long; **∼ member** membre *m* à part entière; **∼ moon** pleine lune; **∼ name** nom et prénom(s); **at ∼ speed** à toute vitesse; (*Naut*) **∼ steam ahead!** en avant toute!; (*Gram*) **∼ stop** point *m*; (*fig*) **I'm not going, ∼ stop!*** je n'y vais pas, un point c'est tout!; **working at the factory came to a ∼ stop** ça a été l'arrêt complet du travail à l'usine; **battalion at ∼ strength** bataillon *m* au (grand) complet; **party in ∼ swing** soirée qui bat son plein; *V* **coverage, tilt** *etc.*

(c) (*rounded; ample*) *lips* charnu; *face* plein, rond, joufflu; *figure* replet (*f* -ète), rondelet; *skirt etc* large, ample; (*Naut*) *sails* plein, gonflé.

2 *adv*: **∼ well** fort bien, parfaitement; **to hit sb ∼ in the face** frapper qn en plein visage; **to look sb ∼ in the face** regarder qn droit dans les yeux; **to go ∼ out** aller à toute vitesse, filer à toute allure.

3 *n*: **to write one's name in ∼** écrire son nom en toutes lettres; **to publish a letter in ∼** publier une lettre intégralement; **text in ∼** texte intégral; **he paid in ∼** il a tout payé; **to the ∼** complètement, tout à fait.

4 *cpd*: (*Sport*) **fullback** arrière *m*; **full-blooded** (*vigorous*) *person* vigoureux, robuste; (*of unmixed race*) de race pure; **full-blown** *flower* épanoui; (*fig*) *dentist, doctor, architect etc* qui a (obtenu) tous ses diplômes, à part entière; **full-bodied** *wine* qui a du corps; **full-dress** *clothes* de cérémonie; (*Parl*) **full-dress debate** débat *m* dans les règles; **they had a full-dress discussion on what to do** ils ont eu un débat en règle pour décider de ce qu'il fallait faire; (*US*) **full-fledged = fully-fledged** (*V* **fully 2**); **full-grown** *child* grand, qui est parvenu au terme de sa croissance; *animal, man, woman* adulte; (*Cards*) **full house** full *m*; **full-length** *portrait* en pied; *film* (de) long métrage; **full-scale** *V* **full-scale**; **full-sized** *model, drawing* grandeur nature *inv*; **full-time** (*adv*) *work* à temps plein, à plein temps; (*n*) (*Sport*) fin *f* de match; (*adj*) *employment* à plein temps; **she's a full-time secretary** elle est secrétaire à plein temps; **it's a full-time job looking after those children*** il faut s'occuper de ces enfants 24 heures sur 24; (*Sport*) **full-time score** score final.

fuller ['fʊlə^r] *n*: **~'s earth** terre savonneuse.
ful(l)ness ['fʊlnɪs] *n [details etc]* abondance *f*; *[voice, sound, garment]* ampleur *f*. **out of the ~ of his heart** le cœur débordant de joie (*or* de chagrin *etc*); **out of the ~ of his sorrow** le cœur débordant de chagrin; **in the ~ of time** (*eventually*) avec le temps; (*at predestined time*) en temps et lieu.
full-scale ['fʊl'skeɪl] *adj* **(a)** *drawing, replica* grandeur nature *inv*. **(b)** (*fig*) *operation, retreat* de grande envergure. **to mount a ~ search for** mettre sur pied des recherches de grande envergure pour trouver; **~ fighting** une *or* la bataille rangée; **the factory starts ~ operations next month** l'usine va commencer à marcher à plein régime le mois prochain.
fully ['fʊlɪ] **1** *adv* **(a)** (*completely*) entièrement, complètement. **I am ~ satisfied** je suis entièrement *or* pleinement satisfait; *V* **laden.**
(b) (*at least*) au moins, bien, largement. **it is ~ 2 hours since he went out** il y a au moins *or* bien *or* largement 2 heures qu'il est sorti.
2 *cpd*: **fully-fashioned** (entièrement) diminué; (*Brit*) **fully-fledged bird** oiseau *m* qui a toutes ses plumes; (*Brit*) **he's now a fully-fledged doctor/architect** il est maintenant médecin/architecte diplômé; (*Brit*) **a fully-fledged British citizen** un citoyen britannique à part entière.
fulmar ['fʊlmə^r] *n* (pétrel *m*) fulmar *m*.
fulminate ['fʌlmɪneɪt] **1** *vi* fulminer, pester (*against* contre). **2** *n*: **~ of mercury** fulminate *m* de mercure.
fulsome ['fʊlsəm] *adj* (*pej*) *praise* excessif, exagéré; *manner, tone, welcome* plein d'effusions. **~ compliments** *or* **thanks** *or* **praises** *etc* effusions *fpl*.
fumarole ['fju:mə,rəʊl] *n* fumerolle *f*.
fumble ['fʌmbl] **1** *vi* (*also* **~ about, ~ around**) (*in the dark*) tâtonner; (*in one's pockets*) fouiller. **to ~ (about) for sth in the dark** chercher qch à tâtons dans l'obscurité; **to ~ (about) for sth in a pocket/a drawer** fouiller dans une poche/un tiroir pour trouver qch; **to ~ with sth** manier *or* tripoter qch (maladroitement); **to ~ for words** chercher ses mots.
2 *vt* manier gauchement *or* maladroitement. (*Sport*) **to ~ the ball** mal attraper la balle.
fume [fju:m] **1** *vi* **(a)** *[liquids, gases]* exhaler des vapeurs, fumer. **(b)** (*: *be furious*) rager. **he is fuming** il est furibard* *or* furax* *inv*. **2** *n*: **~s** exhalaisons *fpl*, vapeurs *fpl*, fumées *fpl*; **petrol ~s** vapeurs d'essence.
fumigate ['fju:mɪgeɪt] *vt* désinfecter par fumigation, fumiger (*frm*).
fun [fʌn] **1** *n* (*U*) (*amusement*) amusement *m*; (*joke*) plaisanterie *f*. **he had great** *or* **good ~** il s'est bien *or* beaucoup amusé; **have ~!*** amuse-toi bien!; **he's great** *or* **good ~** il est très drôle, on s'amuse bien avec lui; **the book is great** *or* **good ~** le livre est très amusant; **the visit is great** *or* **good ~** la visite est très amusante; **sailing is good ~** on s'amuse bien en faisant de la voile; **what ~!** ce que c'est drôle! *or* amusant!; **for ~, in ~** pour rire, par plaisanterie, en plaisantant; **I don't see the ~ of it** je ne trouve pas cela drôle; **I only did it for the ~ of it** je ne l'ai fait que pour m'amuser; **I'm not doing this for the ~ of it** je ne fais pas cela pour m'amuser *or* pour mon plaisir; **it's not much ~ for us** ce n'est pas très amusant, cela ne nous amuse pas beaucoup; **it's only his ~** il fait cela pour rire, c'est tout; **to spoil sb's ~** empêcher qn de s'amuser; **to spoil the ~** jouer les trouble-fête *or* les rabat-joie; **the children had ~ and games at the picnic** les enfants se sont follement amusés pendant le pique-nique; (*iro*) **there'll be ~ and games over this decision*** cette décision va faire du potin* *or* du boucan*; (*euph*) **he's having ~ and games with the au-pair girl*** il ne s'ennuie pas avec la jeune fille au pair (*euph*); (*difficulty*) **she's been having ~ and games with the washing machine*** la machine à laver lui en a fait voir de toutes les couleurs*; (*difficulty*) **we had a bit of ~ getting the car started*** pour faire partir la voiture ça n'a pas été de la rigolade* *or* ça n'a pas été une partie de plaisir *or* on a rigolé* cinq minutes; **to make ~ of** *or* **poke ~ at sb/sth** rire *or* se moquer de qn/qch; **did he go?—like ~ he did!‡** y est-il allé?—je t'en fiche!* *or* tu rigoles!* *or* tu parles!*
2 *adj* (‡) marrant*, rigolo*, amusant. **it's a ~ thing to do** c'est marrant à faire*; **she's a really ~ person** elle est vraiment marrante* *or* rigolote*.
3 *cpd*: **fun fair** fête *f* (foraine); **fun-loving** aimant s'amuser, aimant les plaisirs.
function ['fʌŋkʃən] **1** *n* **(a)** *[heart, tool etc]* fonction *f*; *[person]* fonction, charge *f*. **in his ~ as judge** en sa qualité de juge; **it is not part of my ~ to do that** cela n'entre pas dans mes fonctions, il ne m'appartient pas de faire cela.
(b) (*meeting*) réunion *f*; (*reception*) réception *f*; (*official ceremony*) cérémonie publique.
(c) (*Math*) fonction *f*.
2 *cpd*: (*Ling*) **function word** mot grammatical.
3 *vi* fonctionner, marcher. *[person, thing]* **to ~ as** faire fonction de, servir de, jouer le rôle de.
functional ['fʌŋkʃnəl] *adj* fonctionnel.
functionary ['fʌŋkʃənərɪ] *n* employé(e) *m(f)* (*d'une administration*); (*in civil service, local government*) fonctionnaire *mf*.
fund [fʌnd] **1** *n* **(a)** (*Fin*) caisse *f*, fonds *m*. **to start a ~** lancer une souscription; **~s** fonds *mpl*; **to be in ~s** être en fonds; **the public ~s** les fonds publics, la dette publique; (*Banking*) **no ~s** défaut *m* de provision; **he hasn't the ~s to buy a house** il n'a pas assez de capitaux pour acheter une maison.
(b) (*supply*) *[humour, good sense etc]* fond *m*. **a ~ of knowledge** un trésor de connaissances; **he has a ~ of stories** il connaît des quantités d'histoires.
2 *vt debt* consolider.
fundamental [,fʌndə'mentl] **1** *adj rule, question* fondamental, de base; *quality* fondamental, essentiel; (*Mus*) fondamental. **it is ~ to our understanding of the problem** c'est fondamental *or* essentiel si nous voulons comprendre le problème.
2 *n* (*often pl*) les principes essentiels *or* de base; (*Mus*) fondamental *m*. **when you get down to (the) ~s** quand on en vient à l'essentiel.
fundamentalism [,fʌndə'mentəlɪzəm] *n* (*Rel*) fondamentalisme *m*.
fundamentalist [,fʌndə'mentəlɪst] *n* (*Rel*) fondamentaliste *mf*.
fundamentally [,fʌndə'mentəlɪ] *adv* fondamentalement, essentiellement. **there is something ~ wrong in what he says** il y a quelque chose de radicalement *or* fondamentalement faux dans ce qu'il dit; **he is ~ good** il a un bon fond.
funeral ['fju:nərəl] **1** *n* enterrement *m*, obsèques *fpl* (*frm*); (*also* **state ~**) funérailles *fpl* (nationales). **my uncle's ~** l'enterrement de mon oncle; **Churchill's ~** les funérailles de Churchill; **that's his ~ if he wants to do it*** s'il veut le faire c'est tant pis pour lui; **that's your ~!*** tant pis pour toi!, tu te débrouilles!*
2 *cpd*: **funeral director** entrepreneur *m* des pompes funèbres; (*US*) **funeral home** = **funeral parlour**; **funeral march** marche *f* funèbre; **funeral oration** oraison *f* funèbre; **funeral parlour** dépôt *m* mortuaire; **funeral procession** (*on foot*) cortège *m* funèbre; (*in car*) convoi *m* mortuaire; **funeral pyre** bûcher *m* (funéraire); **funeral service** service *m or* cérémonie *f* funèbre.
funereal [fju:'nɪərɪəl] *adj expression* funèbre, lugubre; *voice* sépulcral, lugubre.
fungi ['fʌŋgaɪ] *npl of* **fungus.**
fungoid ['fʌŋgɔɪd] *adj*, **fungous** ['fʌŋgəs] *adj* (*Med*) fongueux; (*Bot*) cryptogamique.
fungus ['fʌŋgəs] *n*, *pl* **fungi** (*Bot*) (*generic term*) champignon *m*; (*mould*) moisissure *f*; (*Med*) fongus *m*; (‡ *hum: whiskers etc*) excroissance *f* (*hum*).
funicular [fju:'nɪkjʊlə^r] **1** *adj* funiculaire. **2** *n* (*also* **~ railway**) funiculaire *m*.
funk* [fʌŋk] **1** *n* (*coward*) froussard(e)* *m(f)*, trouillard(e)‡ *m(f)*. **to be in a blue ~** avoir la frousse* *or* la trouille‡.
2 *vt*: **he ~ed it** il s'est dégonflé*, il a cané*; **he ~ed his exams** il s'est dégonflé* *or* il a cané* et il n'a pas passé ses examens; **he ~ed doing it** il s'est dégonflé*, il a cané*.
funky‡ ['fʌŋkɪ] *adj* froussard*, trouillard‡.
funnel ['fʌnl] **1** *n* **(a)** (*for pouring through*) entonnoir *m*. **(b)** *[ship, engine etc]* cheminée *f*. **a two-~led liner** un paquebot à deux cheminées. **2** *vt* (faire) passer dans un entonnoir; (*fig*) canaliser.
funnily ['fʌnɪlɪ] *adv* **(a)** (*amusingly*) drôlement, comiquement. **(b)** (*strangely*) curieusement, bizarrement. **~ enough ...** chose curieuse ..., c'est drôle ... .
funny ['fʌnɪ] **1** *adj* **(a)** (*comic*) drôle, amusant, comique. **~ story** histoire *f* drôle; **he was always trying to be ~** il cherchait toujours à faire de l'esprit; **don't (try to) be ~!*** ce n'est pas le moment de plaisanter *or* de faire de l'esprit!; **its not ~** ça n'a rien de drôle.
(b) (*strange*) curieux, bizarre, drôle. **a ~ idea** une drôle d'idée; **the ~ thing about it is ...** ce qu'il y a de drôle *or* de bizarre *or* de curieux c'est ...; **he is ~ that way*** il est comme ça*; **the meat tastes ~** la viande a un drôle de goût; **I find it ~ that he should want to see her** je trouve (cela) bizarre qu'il veuille la voir; **there's something ~ about this affair** il y a quelque chose de bizarre *or* qui cloche* dans cette affaire; **there's something ~** *or* **some ~ business* going on** il se passe quelque chose de louche; **I felt ~*** je me suis senti tout chose*; **it gave me a ~ feeling** cela m'a fait tout drôle; **~! I thought he'd left** c'est drôle *or* c'est curieux, je pensais qu'il était parti.
(c) ~ bone* petit juif*.
2 *n* (*US Press: gen pl*) **the funnies‡** les bandes dessinées.
fur [fɜ:^r] **1** *n* **(a)** *[animal]* poil *m*, pelage *m*, fourrure *f*. (*fig*) **it will make the ~ fly** cela va faire du grabuge*; **the ~ was flying** ça bardait‡, il y avait du grabuge*, les plumes volaient.
(b) (*animal skins: often pl*) fourrure(s) *f(pl)*. **she was dressed in ~s** elle portait des fourrures *or* de la fourrure.
(c) (*in kettle etc*) incrustation *f*, (dépôt *m* de) tartre *m*. (*Med*) **to have ~ on one's tongue** avoir la langue pâteuse *or* empâtée *or* chargée.
2 *vi*: **to ~ (up)** *[kettle, boiler]* s'entartrer, s'incruster; *[tongue]* se charger; **his tongue is ~red** sa langue est chargée *or* empâtée.
furbelow† ['fɜ:bɪləʊ] *n* falbala *m*. **(frills and) ~s** fanfreluches *fpl*, falbalas.
furbish ['fɜ:bɪʃ] *vt* (*polish*) fourbir, astiquer, briquer; (*smarten*) remettre à neuf, retaper*; (*revise*) revoir, repasser*.
furious ['fjʊərɪəs] *adj person* furieux (*with sb* contre qn, *at having done* d'avoir fait); *storm, sea* déchaîné; *struggle* acharné; *speed* fou (*f* folle). **to get ~** se mettre en rage (*with sb* contre qn); **the fun was fast and ~** la fête battait son plein.
furiously ['fjʊərɪəslɪ] *adv* (*violently, angrily*) furieusement; *fight* avec acharnement; *drive* à une allure folle; *ride a horse* à bride abattue.
furl [fɜ:l] *vt* (*Naut*) *sail* ferler, serrer; *umbrella, flag* rouler. **the flags are ~ed** les drapeaux sont en berne.
furlong ['fɜ:lɒŋ] *n* furlong *m* (*201,17 mètres*).
furlough ['fɜ:ləʊ] *n* (*esp Admin, Mil*) permission *f*, congé *m*. **on ~** en permission.
furnace ['fɜ:nɪs] *n* (*Metal*) fourneau *m*, four *m*; (*for central heating etc*) chaudière *f*. **this room is like a ~** cette pièce est une vraie fournaise.
furnish ['fɜ:nɪʃ] *vt* **(a)** *house* meubler (*with* de). (*Brit*) **~ed flat**, (*US*) **~ed apartment** appartement meublé; **in ~ed rooms** en meublé.

(b) (*supply*) *information, excuse, reason* fournir, donner. **to ~ sb with sth** pourvoir *or* munir qn de qch; **to ~ an army with provisions** ravitailler une armée.

furnishing ['fɜːnɪʃɪŋ] *n*: **~s** mobilier *m*, ameublement *m*; **house sold with ~s and fittings** maison vendue avec objets mobiliers divers; **~ fabrics** tissus *mpl* d'ameublement.

furniture ['fɜːnɪtʃəʳ] **1** *n* (*U*) meubles *mpl*, mobilier *m*, ameublement *m*. **a piece of ~** un meuble; **I must buy some ~** il faut que j'achète (*subj*) des meubles; **the ~ was very old** les meubles étaient très vieux, le mobilier était très vieux; **the ~ was scanty** l'ameublement était insuffisant, c'était à peine meublé; **one settee and three chairs were all the ~** un sofa et trois chaises constituaient tout l'ameublement *or* le mobilier; **he treats her as part of the ~** il la traite comme si elle faisait partie du décor; **dining-room ~** des meubles *or* du mobilier de salle à manger; **Empire ~** mobilier *or* meubles Empire.

2 *cpd*: **furniture depot** garde-meubles *m inv*; **furniture polish** encaustique *f*; **furniture remover** déménageur *m*; **furniture shop** magasin *m* d'ameublement *or* de meubles; **furniture store** = **furniture depot** *or* **furniture shop**; **furniture van** camion *m* de déménagement.

furore [fjʊə'rɔːrɪ] *n*, (*US*) **furor** [fjʊ'rɔːʳ] *n* (*protests*) scandale *m*; (*enthusiasm*) débordement *m* d'enthousiasme.

furrier ['fʌrɪəʳ] *n* fourreur *m*.

furrow ['fʌrəʊ] **1** *n* (*Agr*) sillon *m*; (*for flowers etc*) rayon *m*; (*on brow*) ride *f*, ligne *f*, sillon; (*liter: on sea*) sillage *m*. **2** *vt earth* sillonner, labourer; *face, brow* rider.

furry ['fɜːrɪ] *adj animal* à poil; *toy* en peluche.

further ['fɜːðəʳ] *comp of* **far** **1** *adv* **(a)** = **farther 1**.

(b) (*more*) davantage, plus. **he questioned us no ~** il ne nous a pas interrogés davantage, il ne nous a pas posé d'autres questions; **without troubling any ~** sans se tracasser davantage, sans plus se tracasser; **I got no ~ with him** je ne suis arrivé à rien de plus avec lui; **unless I hear any ~** à moins qu'on ne me prévienne du contraire, sauf avis contraire; **until you hear ~** jusqu'à nouvel avis; **we heard nothing ~ from him** nous n'avons plus rien reçu de lui, nous n'avons pas eu d'autres nouvelles de lui; **and ~ I believe ...** et de plus je crois ...; **he said that he would do it and ~ that he WANTED to** il a dit qu'il le ferait et en outre *or* et en plus *or* ajoutant qu'il avait envie de le faire; (*Comm*) **~ to your letter** par suite à votre lettre (*Comm*).

2 *adj* **(a)** = **farther 2**.

(b) (*additional*) nouveau (*f* nouvelle), additionnel, supplémentaire. **~ education** enseignement *m* post-scolaire *or* de promotion sociale; **college of ~ education** centre *m* d'enseignement post-scolaire *or* de promotion sociale; **until ~ notice** jusqu'à nouvel ordre; (*Jur*) **to remand a case for ~ inquiry** renvoyer une cause à plus ample informé; **without ~ delay** sans autre délai, sans plus attendre; **without ~ ado** sans plus de cérémonie; **upon ~ consideration** après plus ample réflexion, à la réflexion; **awaiting ~ details** en attendant de plus amples détails; **one or two ~ details** un ou deux autres points; **there are one or two ~ things I must say** il y a encore un ou deux remarques à faire.

3 *vt one's interests, a cause* servir, avancer, favoriser.

4 *cpd*: **furthermore** en outre, de plus, qui plus est, par ailleurs; **furthermost** le plus éloigné, le plus reculé, le plus lointain.

furtherance ['fɜːðərəns] *n* avancement *m*. **in ~ of sth** pour avancer *or* servir qch.

furthest ['fɜːðɪst] = **farthest**.

furtive ['fɜːtɪv] *adj action, behaviour, look* furtif; *person* sournois.

furtively ['fɜːtɪvlɪ] *adv* furtivement, à la dérobée.

fury ['fjʊərɪ] *n* [*person*] fureur *f*, furie *f*; [*storm, wind*] fureur, violence *f*; [*struggle*] acharnement *m*. **to be in a ~** être en furie, être dans une rage *or* colère folle; **to put sb into a ~** mettre qn dans une colère folle; **to fly into a ~** entrer en fureur *or* en furie, se mettre dans une rage folle, faire une colère terrible; **she's a little ~** c'est une petite furie *or* harpie; (*Myth*) **the Furies** les Furies *fpl*, les Euménides *fpl*; **to work like ~*** travailler d'arrache-pied *or* comme un nègre; **to run like ~** courir comme un dératé.

furze [fɜːz] *n* (*U*) ajoncs *mpl*.

fuse, (*US*) **fuze** [fjuːz] **1** *vt* **(a)** (*unite*) *metal* fondre, mettre en fusion; (*fig*) fusionner, unifier, amalgamer.

(b) (*Brit Elec*) faire sauter. **to ~ the television *or* the iron *or* the lights *etc*** faire sauter les plombs.

(c) *bomb* amorcer.

2 *vi* **(a)** [*metals*] fondre; (*fig: also* **~ together**) s'unifier, fusionner.

(b) (*Brit Elec*) [*apparatus, lights*] faire sauter les plombs.

3 *n* **(a)** (*Elec: wire*) plomb *m*, fusible *m*. **to blow a ~** faire sauter un plomb *or* un fusible; **there's been a ~ somewhere** il y a un plomb de sauté quelque part.

(b) [*bomb etc*] amorce *f*, détonateur *m*, fusée(-détonateur) *f*, (*Min*) cordeau *m*.

4 *cpd*: **fuse box** boîte *f* à fusibles, coupe-circuit *m inv*; **fuse wire** fusible *m*.

fused [fjuːzd] *adj* (*Elec*) avec fusible incorporé. **~ plug** prise *f* avec fusible incorporé.

fusel ['fjuːzl] *n*: **~ oil** fusel *m*, huile *f* de fusel.

fuselage ['fjuːzəlɑːʒ] *n* fuselage *m*.

fusible ['fjuːzɪbl] *n*: **~ metal *or* alloy** alliage *m* fusible.

fusilier [ˌfjuːzɪ'lɪəʳ] *n* (*Brit*) fusilier *m*.

fusillade [ˌfjuːzɪ'leɪd] *n* fusillade *f*.

fusion ['fjuːʒən] *n* (*Metal*) fonte *f*, fusion *f*; (*Phys*) fusion; [*parties, races*] fusion, fusionnement *m*.

fuss [fʌs] **1** *n* (*U*) (*excitement*) tapage *m*, agitation *f*; (*activity*) façons *fpl*, embarras *m*, cérémonie *f*. **a lot of ~ about very little** beaucoup d'agitation *or* de bruit pour pas grand-chose; **to make a ~, to kick up a ~*** faire un tas d'histoires*; **to make a ~ about *or* over sth** faire des histoires pour qch, faire tout un plat de qch*; **you were quite right to make a ~** vous avez eu tout à fait raison de protester *or* de ne pas laisser passer ça; **what a ~ just to get a passport!** que d'histoires rien que pour obtenir un passeport!; **don't make such a ~ about accepting** ne faites pas tant d'embarras *or* de manières pour accepter; **to make a ~ of sb** être aux petits soins pour qn.

2 *cpd*: **fusspot***, (*US*) **fussbudget*** (*nuisance*) enquiquineur* *m*, -euse* *f*; (*finicky person*) coupeur *m*, -euse *f* de cheveux en quatre; **don't be such a fusspot!*** ne fais pas tant d'histoires!, arrête d'enquiquiner le monde!*

3 *vi* (*become excited*) s'agiter; (*rush around busily*) s'affairer, faire la mouche du coche; (*worry*) se tracasser, s'en faire*. **to ~ over sb** être aux petits soins pour qn; (*pej*) embêter* qn (par des attentions excessives).

4 *vt person* ennuyer, embêter*.

fuss about, fuss around *vi* faire l'affairé, s'affairer, faire la mouche du coche.

fussily ['fʌsɪlɪ] *adv* (*V* **fussy**) de façon tatillonne *or* méticuleuse *or* tarabiscotée.

fussy ['fʌsɪ] *adj person* tatillon, méticuleux, pointilleux; *dress* surchargé de fanfreluches, tarabiscoté; *style* trop orné, tarabiscoté. **she's very ~ about what she eats/what she wears** elle fait très attention à *or* elle est très tatillonne sur ce qu'elle mange/ce qu'elle porte; **what do you want to do? — I'm not ~*** que veux-tu faire? — ça m'est égal.

fustian ['fʌstɪən] *n* futaine *f*.

fusty ['fʌstɪ] *adj smell* de renfermé, de moisi; *room* qui sent le renfermé; (*fig*) *idea, outlook* suranné, vieillot.

futile ['fjuːtaɪl] *adj remark* futile, vain; *attempt* vain.

futility [fjuː'tɪlɪtɪ] *n* futilité *f*.

future ['fjuːtʃəʳ] **1** *n* **(a)** avenir *m*. **in (the) ~** à l'avenir; **in the near ~** dans le *or* un proche avenir; **what the ~ holds for us** ce que l'avenir nous réserve; **his ~ is assured** son avenir est assuré; **there is a real ~ for bright boys in this firm** cette firme offre de réelles possibilités d'avenir pour des jeunes gens doués; **there's no ~ in this type of research** ce type de recherche n'a aucun avenir; **there's no ~ in it*** ça n'aboutira à rien, ça ne servira à rien.

(b) (*Gram*) futur *m*. **in the ~** au futur; **~ perfect** futur antérieur.

(c) (*St Ex*) **~s** marchandises (achetées) à terme; **~s market** marché *m* à terme; **coffee ~s** café *m* (acheté) à terme.

2 *adj life, events* futur, à venir; (*Comm*) *delivery* à terme. **her ~ husband** son futur (époux); **at some ~ date** à une date ultérieure (non encore précisée); (*Gram*) **the ~ tense** le futur.

futurism ['fjuːtʃərɪzəm] *n* futurisme *m*.

futuristic [ˌfjuːtʃə'rɪstɪk] *adj* futuriste.

futurologist [ˌfjuːtʃər'ɒlədʒɪst] futurologue *mf*.

futurology [ˌfjuːtʃər'ɒlədʒɪ] futurologie *f*.

fuze [fjuːz] (*US*) = **fuse**.

fuzz [fʌz] *n* **(a)** (*U*) (*frizzy hair*) cheveux crépus *or* crêpelés (et bouffants); (*whiskers etc*) excroissance *f* (*hum*).

(b) (*light growth*) (*on body*) duvet *m*, poils fins; (*on head*) duvet, cheveux fins.

(c) (*‡: policeman*) flic‡ *m*. (*collective*) **the ~** la flicaille‡, les flics‡.

fuzzy ['fʌzɪ] *adj* **(a)** *hair* crépu, crêpelé. **(b)** (*Phot*) flou. **(c)** (*muddled: also* **~-headed**) désorienté, déconcerté; (**: tipsy*) pompette*, un peu parti*. **I feel ~** j'ai la tête qui tourne.

G

G, g [dʒiː] **1** *n* **(a)** (*letter*) G, g *m*. **(b)** (*Mus*) sol *m*. **(c)** (*Phys: gravity, acceleration*) g *m*. **2** *cpd*: (*US*) **G.I.** *V* **G.I.**; (*US*) **G-man‡** agent *m* du FBI; (*Med*) **G.P.** = **general practitioner** (*V* **general 1b**); **G-string** (*Mus*) (corde *f* de) sol *m*; (*garment*) cache-sexe *m inv*; (*Space*) **G-suit** combinaison spatiale (*anti-gravité*).

gab‡ [gæb] **1** *n* bagou(t)‡ *m*. **shut your ~!** la ferme!‡; *V* **gift**. **2** *vi* jacasser, bavasser‡.

gabardine [ˌgæbəˈdiːn] *n* gabardine *f*.

gabble [ˈgæbl] **1** *vi* (*talk indistinctly*) bredouiller, bafouiller. (*talk quickly*) **he ~d on about the accident** il nous a fait une description volubile de l'accident.

2 *vt* bredouiller, bafouiller. **he ~d (out) an excuse** il a bredouillé *or* bafouillé une excuse.

3 *n* baragouin *m*, charabia* *m*, flot *m* de paroles (inintelligibles).

gabble away *vi* jacasser sans arrêt. **they were gabbling away in French** ils baragouinaient *or* jacassaient en français.

gabbro [ˈgæbrəʊ] *n* gabbro *m*.

gabby‡ [ˈgæbɪ] *adj* jacasseur, bavard comme une pie, bavasson‡.

gable [ˈgeɪbl] **1** *n* pignon *m*. **2** *cpd*: **gable end** pignon *m*; **gable roof** comble *m* sur pignon(s).

gad[1] [gæd] *n* (*Agr*) aiguillon *m*. **~fly** taon *m*.

gad[2] [gæd] **1** *vi*: **to ~ about** vadrouiller*, (se) baguenauder; **she's been ~ding about town all day** elle a couru la ville *or* elle a vadrouillé* en ville toute la journée. **2** *cpd*: **gadabout** vadrouilleur* *m*, -euse* *f*.

gad[3]* [gæd] *excl* (*also* **by ~**) sapristi!†, bon sang!

gadget [ˈgædʒɪt] *n* (*device*) gadget *m*, (petit) instrument *m or* dispositif *m*; (*: *thingummy*) (petit) truc* *m or* machin* *m or* bidule* *m*, gadget.

gadgetry [ˈgædʒɪtrɪ] *n [car etc]* tous les gadgets *mpl*.

Gael [geɪl] *n* Gaël *mf*.

Gaelic [ˈgeɪlɪk] **1** *adj* gaélique. **2** *n* (*Ling*) gaélique *m*.

gaff[1] [gæf] **1** *n* (*Fishing*) gaffe *f*; (*Naut*) corne *f*. **2** *vt* gaffer, harponner.

gaff[2]‡ [gæf] *n* (*Brit: music hall etc*) (sorte *f* de) beuglant‡ *m*.

gaff[3]‡ [gæf] *n* (*nonsense*) foutaises‡ *fpl*; *V* **blow[1]**.

gaffe [gæf] *n* gaffe *f*, bévue *f*.

gaffer‡ [ˈgæfə^r] *n* **(a)** (*old man*) vieux *m*. **this old ~** ce vieux (bonhomme). **(b)** (*Brit*) (*foreman*) contremaître *m*; (*boss*) patron *m*, chef *m*.

gag [gæg] **1** *n* **(a)** (*in mouth*) bâillon *m*; (*Med*) ouvre-bouche *m inv*. (*fig*) **it put an effective ~ on press reports of the incident** ceci a eu pour effet de bâillonner très efficacement la presse dans sa façon de rapporter l'incident.

(b) (*Theat**) (*joke*) plaisanterie *f*, blague *f*; (*unscripted*) improvisation *f* comique; (*visual*) gag *m*.

(c) (**gen*) (*joke*) blague *f*, plaisanterie *f*; (*hoax*) canular *m*. **is this a ~?** c'est une plaisanterie?; **it's a ~ to raise funds** c'est un truc* comique pour ramasser de l'argent.

2 *vt* (*silence*) bâillonner; (*fig*) *press etc* bâillonner, museler.

3 *vi* **(a)** (*Theat*) faire une *or* des improvisation(s) comique(s).

(b) (*: *joke*) plaisanter, blaguer.

(c) (*: *retch*) avoir des haut-le-cœur.

gaga‡ [ˈgɑːˈgɑː] *adj* (*senile*) gaga‡, gâteux; (*crazy*) cinglé‡.

gage [geɪdʒ] **1** *n* **(a)** (*challenge*) défi *m*; (*glove*) gant *m*. **(b)** (*pledge*) gage *m*, garantie *f*; (*article pledged*) gage. **(c)** (*US Tech*) = **gauge 1**. **2** *vt* (*US Tech*) = **gauge 2**.

gaggle [ˈgægl] **1** *n [geese etc]* troupeau *m*; (*hum*) *[girls etc]* (petite) troupe *f*, troupeau (*hum*). **2** *vi [geese]* cacarder.

gaiety [ˈgeɪɪtɪ] *n* **(a)** (*U*) gaieté *f or* gaîté *f*; (*in dress etc*) gaieté, couleur *f*. **(b)** (*gen pl*) **gaieties** réjouissances *fpl*.

gaily [ˈgeɪlɪ] *adv behave, speak* gaiement, avec bonne humeur; *decorate* de façon gaie. **to dress ~** porter des couleurs gaies; **~ coloured** aux couleurs vives.

gain [geɪn] **1** *n* (*Comm, Fin*) gain *m*, profit *m*, bénéfice *m*; (*fig*) avantage *m*; (*increase*) augmentation *f*; (*in wealth*) accroissement *m* (*in* de); (*in knowledge etc*) acquisition *f* (*in* de). **to do sth for ~** faire qch pour le profit; **his loss is our ~** là où il perd nous gagnons; **~s** (*profits*) bénéfices *mpl*; (*winnings*) gains *mpl*; **~ in weight** augmentation de poids; (*St Ex*) **there have been ~s of up to 3 points** des hausses allant jusqu'à 3 points ont été enregistrées.

2 *vt* **(a)** (*earn, obtain*) *money* gagner; *approval, respect* conquérir, gagner; *liberty* conquérir. **to ~ a hearing** (*make people listen*) se faire écouter; (*with king etc*) obtenir une audience; **to ~ sb's goodwill** se concilier qn, gagner les bonnes grâces de qn; (*fig*) **to ~ ground** gagner du terrain, progresser; **to ~ one's objective** atteindre son objectif; **the idea slowly ~ed popularity** l'idée gagna petit à petit en popularité; **to ~ time** gagner du temps (*by doing* en faisant); **what have you ~ed by doing it?** qu'est-ce que tu as gagné à faire ça?; **he'll ~ nothing by being rude** il ne gagnera rien à être impoli.

(b) (*increase*) **to ~ experience** acquérir de l'expérience; (*St Ex*) **these shares have ~ed 3 points** ces valeurs ont enregistré une hausse de 3 points; **to ~ speed** prendre de la vitesse; **to ~ weight** prendre du poids; **she's ~ed 3 kg (in weight)** elle a pris 3 kg; **my watch has ~ed 5 minutes** ma montre a pris 5 minutes d'avance.

(c) (*win*) *battle* gagner; *friends* se faire. **to ~ the day** (*Mil*) remporter la victoire; (*fig*) l'emporter; **to ~ the upper hand** prendre le dessus.

(d) (*reach*) *place* atteindre, parvenir à.

3 *vi [watch]* avancer; *[runners]* prendre de l'avance. **to ~ in prestige** gagner en prestige; **to ~ in weight** prendre du poids; **he hasn't ~ed by the exchange** il n'a rien gagné au change.

gain (up)on *vt fus* **(a)** (*Sport, fig*) (*catch up with*) rattraper; (*outstrip*) prendre de l'avance sur.

(b) *[sea]* gagner sur.

gainer [ˈgeɪnə^r] *n* gagnant(e) *m(f)*. **he is the ~ by it** c'est lui qui y gagne.

gainful [ˈgeɪnfʊl] *adj occupation etc* profitable, lucratif, rémunérateur (*f* -trice); *business* rentable. (*Admin etc*) **in ~ employment** dans un emploi rémunéré.

gainsay [ˌgeɪnˈseɪ] *pret, ptp* **gainsaid** [ˌgeɪnˈsed] *vt person, thing* contredire, démentir; *fact* nier. **facts that cannot be gainsaid** faits *mpl* indéniables; **evidence that cannot be gainsaid** preuve *f* irrécusable; **argument that cannot be gainsaid** argument *m* irréfutable; **it cannot be gainsaid, there's no ~ing it** c'est indéniable, il n'y a pas de contradiction possible; **I don't ~ it** je ne dis pas le contraire.

gait [geɪt] *n* démarche *f*. **with an awkward ~** d'une démarche *or* d'un pas gauche; **to know sb by his ~** reconnaître qn à sa démarche.

gaiter [ˈgeɪtə^r] **1** *n* guêtre *f*. **2** *vt* guêtrer.

gal* [gæl] *n* († *or hum*) = **girl 1**.

gala [ˈgɑːlə] **1** *n* fête *f*, gala *m*. **swimming/sports ~** grand concours de natation/d'athlétisme. **2** *cpd*: **gala day** jour *m* de gala *or* de fête; **gala dress** tenue *f* de gala; **gala occasion** grande occasion.

galactic [gəˈlæktɪk] *adj* galactique.

galantine [ˈgæləntiːn] *n* galantine *f*.

galaxy [ˈgæləksɪ] *n* (*Astron*) galaxie *f*; (*fig*) *[beauty, talent]* constellation *f*, brillante assemblée.

gale [geɪl] **1** *n* coup *m* de vent, grand vent. (*Met*) **a force 8 ~** un vent de force 8; **it was blowing a ~** le vent soufflait très fort; **there's a ~ blowing in through that window** c'est une véritable bourrasque qui entre par cette fenêtre; (*fig*) **~s of laughter** grands éclats de rire.

2 *cpd*: **gale force winds** vent *m* soufflant en tempête, coups *mpl* de vent; (*Met*) **gale warning** avis *m* de coup de vent.

galena [gəˈliːnə] *n* galène *f*.

Galilean [ˌgæləˈliːən] **1** *adj* (*Bible, Geog*) galiléen; (*Astron*) de Galilée. **2** *n* Galiléen(ne) *m(f)*. (*Bible*) **the ~** le Galiléen.

Galilee [ˈgælɪliː] *n* Galilée *f*. **the Sea of ~** le lac de Tibériade, la mer de Galilée.

gall[1] [gɔːl] **1** *n* (*Med*) bile *f*; (*Zool*) bile, fiel *m*; (*fig: bitterness*) fiel, amertume *f*; (*: *impertinence*) effronterie *f*, culot* *m*. **she had the ~ to say that*...** elle a eu l'effronterie *or* le culot* de dire que ...

2 *cpd*: **gall-bladder** vésicule *f* biliaire; **gallstone** calcul *m* biliaire.

gall[2] [gɔːl] **1** *n* (*on animal*) écorchure *f*, excoriation *f*; (*Bot*) galle *f*. **2** *vt* (*fig*) irriter, ulcérer, exaspérer. **it ~s me to have to admit it** je suis ulcéré d'avoir à le reconnaître.

gallant [ˈgælənt] **1** *adj* **(a)** (*noble, brave*) *person* courageux, brave, vaillant (*liter*); *horse* noble, vaillant (*liter*); *appearance, dress* élégant, magnifique, superbe. **~ deed** action *f* d'éclat.

(b) [gəˈlænt] (*attentive to women*) galant, empressé auprès des dames.

2 [gəˈlænt] *n* galant *m*.

gallantly [ˈgæləntlɪ] *adv* (*V* **gallant**) **(a)** courageusement, bravement, vaillamment. **(b)** [gəˈlæntlɪ] galamment.

gallantry [ˈgæləntrɪ] *n* (*V* **gallant**) **(a)** courage *m*, bravoure *f*, vaillance *f* (*liter*). **(b)** galanterie *f*.

galleon [ˈgælɪən] *n* galion *m*.

gallery [ˈgælərɪ] *n* (*Archit, Art, Min*) galerie *f*; (*for spectators*) tribune *f*. (*Theat*) **in the ~** au dernier balcon; (*fig*) **to play to the ~** poser *or* parler pour la galerie; *V* **minstrel, press, shooting** *etc*.

galley [ˈgælɪ] *n* **(a)** (*ship*) galère *f*; (*ship's kitchen*) cuisine *f*. **~ slave** galérien *m*. **(b)** (*Typ*) galée *f*. **~ (proof)** (épreuve *f* en) placard *m*.

Gallic [ˈgælɪk] *adj* (*of Gaul*) gaulois; (*French*) français. **~ charm** charme latin.

gallic [ˈgælɪk] *adj* (*Chem*) gallique.

gallicism [ˈgælɪsɪzəm] *n* gallicisme *m*.

galling [ˈgɔːlɪŋ] *adj* (*irritating*) irritant, exaspérant; (*humiliating*) blessant, humiliant.

gallinule [ˈgælɪnjuːl] *n* (*US*) **common ~** poule *f* d'eau.

gallivant [ˌgælɪˈvænt] *vi* (*also* **~ about, ~ around**) (*on pleasure*) courir le guilledou*; (*: *busily*) courir. **I've been ~ing about the shops all day*** j'ai couru les magasins toute la journée.

gallon [ˈgælən] *n* gallon *m* (*Brit* = *4,546 litres, US* = *3,785 litres*).

gallop ['gæləp] 1 *n* galop *m*. **to go for a ~** faire un temps de galop; **to break into a ~** prendre le galop; **at a** *or* **the ~** au galop; **at full ~** *[horse]* au grand galop, ventre à terre; *[rider]* à bride abattue.

2 *vi [horse, rider]* galoper. **to ~ away/back** *etc* partir/revenir *etc* au galop; *(fig)* **to go ~ing down the street** descendre la rue au galop; **to ~ through a book*** lire un livre à toute allure *or* à la va-vite*, lire un livre en diagonale.

3 *vt horse* faire galoper.

galloping ['gæləpɪŋ] *adj horse* au galop; *(fig) inflation* galopant; *pneumonia, pleurisy* galopant. **~ consumption** phtisie galopante.

gallows ['gæləʊz] 1 *n* (*U: also* **~ tree**) gibet *m*, potence *f*. **he'll end up on the ~** il finira à la potence *or* par la corde; **to send sb to the ~** envoyer qn à la potence *or* au gibet. 2 *cpd*: **gallows bird*** gibier *m* de potence.

Gallup poll ['gæləp,pəʊl] *n* sondage *m* (d'opinion), gallup *m*.

galore [gə'lɔːʳ] *adv* en abondance, à gogo*, à la pelle*.

galosh [gə'lɒʃ] *n* (*gen pl*) **~es** caoutchoucs *mpl* (*enfilés par-dessus les souliers*).

galumph* [gə'lʌmf] *vi* cabrioler *or* caracoler lourdement *or* avec la légèreté d'un éléphant. **to go ~ing in/out** *etc* entrer/sortir *etc* en cabriolant *or* caracolant comme un (gros) balourd.

galvanic [gæl'vænɪk] *adj* (*Elec*) galvanique; *jerk* crispé; *(fig) effect* galvanisant, électrisant.

galvanism ['gælvənɪzəm] *n* galvanisme *m*.

galvanization [,gælvənaɪ'zeɪʃən] *n* galvanisation *f*.

galvanize ['gælvənaɪz] *vt* (*Elec, Med*) galvaniser. **~d iron** fer galvanisé; *(fig)* **to ~ sb into action** donner un coup de fouet à qn.

Gambia ['gæmbɪə] *n* Gambie *f*.

gambit ['gæmbɪt] *n* (*Chess*) gambit *m*. *(fig)* **(opening) ~** manœuvre *f or* ruse *f* (stratégique).

gamble ['gæmbl] 1 *n* entreprise risquée. **life's a ~** la vie est un jeu de hasard; **it's a pure ~** c'est affaire de chance; **the ~ came off** *or* **paid off** le jeu en a valu la chandelle, ça a payé de prendre ce risque*; (*Racing, St Ex*) **to have a ~ on** jouer.

2 *vi* **(a)** (*lit*) jouer (*on* sur, *with* avec). **to ~ on the stock exchange** jouer à la Bourse.

(b) *(fig)* **to ~ on** compter sur; (*less sure*) miser sur. **we had been gambling on fine weather** nous avions compté sur le beau temps; (*less sure*) nous avions misé sur le beau temps; **he was gambling on her being late** il comptait qu'elle allait être en retard, il escomptait son retard.

gamble away *vt sep money etc* perdre *or* dilapider au jeu.

gambler ['gæmbləʳ] *n* joueur *m*, -euse *f*; *V* **big**.

gambling ['gæmblɪŋ] 1 *n* jeu *m*, jeux d'argent. **his ~ ruined his family** sa passion du jeu a *or* ses pertes de jeu ont entraîné la ruine de sa famille.

2 *cpd*: **gambling debts** dettes *fpl* de jeu; (*pej*) **gambling den,** (*pej*) **gambling hell*, gambling house,** (*US*) **gambling joint‡** maison *f* de jeu, tripot *m* (*pej*); **gambling losses** pertes *fpl* au jeu.

gamboge [gæm'buːʒ] *n* gomme-gutte *f*.

gambol ['gæmbəl] 1 *n* gambade *f*, cabriole *f*. 2 *vi* gambader, cabrioler, faire des cabrioles. **to ~ away/back** *etc* partir/revenir *etc* en gambadant *or* cabriolant.

game¹ [geɪm] 1 *n* **(a)** (*gen*) jeu *m*; *[football, rugby, cricket etc]* match *m*; *[tennis]* partie *f*; *[billiards, chess]* partie. **~ of cards** partie de cartes; **card ~** jeu de cartes (*belotte, bridge etc*); **~ of skill/of chance** jeu d'adresse/de hasard; **he plays a good ~ of football** il est bon au football; **to have** *or* **play a ~ of** faire une partie de, jouer un match de (*V also* **play**); (*Scol*) **~s** sport *m*, (activités *fpl* de) plein air; **to be good at ~s** être sportif; (*Scol*) **we get ~s on Thursdays** nous avons plein air le jeudi; **that's ~** (*Tennis*) ça fait jeu; (*Bridge*) ça fait la manche; **they were ~ all** (*Tennis*) on était à un jeu partout; (*Bridge*) on était manche A, on était à une manche partout; (*Tennis*) **~, set and match** jeu, set, et match; **he's off his ~** il n'est pas en forme; **to put sb off his ~** troubler qn; **this isn't a ~!** on n'est pas en train de jouer!, c'est sérieux!; *V* **highland, indoor** *etc*.

(b) *(fig)* (*scheme, plan*) plan *m*, projet *m*; (*dodge, trick*) (petit) jeu *m*, manège *m*, combinaison *f*; (**: occupation*) travail *m*, boulot* *m*. **it's a profitable ~** c'est une entreprise rentable; **the ~ is up** tout est fichu* *or* à l'eau; **they saw the ~ was up** ils ont vu que la partie était perdue; **I'll play his ~ for a while** je ferai son jeu pendant un certain temps; **don't play his ~** n'entre pas dans son jeu; **we soon saw through his ~** nous avons vite vu clair dans son (petit) jeu; **two can play at that ~** à bon chat bon rat (*Prov*); **what's the ~?*** qu'est-ce qui se passe? *or* se manigance? (*pej*); **I wonder what his ~ is** je me demande ce qu'il manigance (*pej*) *or* mijote*; **what's your little ~?** à quoi est-ce que tu joues?; **to beat sb at his own ~** battre qn sur son propre terrain; **to spoil sb's ~** déjouer les combinaisons *or* manigances (*pej*) *or* machinations de qn; **how long have you been in this ~?*** cela fait combien de temps que vous faites ça?; *[prostitute]* **to be on the ~‡** faire le trottoir*; **the ~ isn't worth the candle** le jeu n'en vaut pas la chandelle; **to make a ~ of sb/sth** se moquer de qn/qch, tourner qn/qch en dérision; *V* **fun, waiting** *etc*.

(c) (*Culin, Hunting*) gibier *m*. **big/small ~** gros/petit *or* menu gibier; *V also* **big, fair¹**.

2 *cpd*: **gamebag** gibecière *f*, carnier *m*, carnassière *f*; **game birds** gibier *m* (*U*) à plume; **gamecock** coq *m* de combat; **gamekeeper** garde-chasse *m*; **game laws** réglementation *f* de la chasse; (*Culin*) **game pie** pâté *m* de gibier en croûte; (*Hunting*) **game reserve** réserve *f* de grands fauves; (*Scol*) **games master, games mistress** professeur *m* d'éducation physique; **games theory** théorie *f* des jeux; **game warden** agent chargé de la police de la chasse; (*on reserve*) gardien chargé de la protection des animaux.

3 *vi* jouer.

4 *adj* courageux, brave. **to be ~** avoir du cran, avoir du cœur au ventre; **are you ~?** tu t'en sens capable?, tu te sens de taille?; **are you ~ to do it again?** tu te sens le courage de recommencer?; **to be ~ for sth** se sentir de force *or* de taille à faire qch; **he's ~ for anything** il est prêt à tout, il ne recule devant rien.

game² [geɪm] *adj* (*lame*) *arm, leg* estropié. **to have a ~ leg** être boiteux, boiter.

gamesmanship ['geɪmzmənʃɪp] *n* art *m* de gagner par des astuces. **to be good at ~** être rusé; **it's a piece of ~ on his part** c'est un truc pour gagner.

gamester ['geɪmstəʳ] *n* joueur *m*, -euse *f*.

gamete ['gæmiːt] *n* gamète *m*.

gamin ['gæmɛ̃] *n* gamin *m*.

gamine [gæ'miːn] 1 *n* (*cheeky girl*) gamine *f* (espiègle); (*tomboy*) garçon manqué. 2 *cpd appearance, hat* gamin. **she had a gamine haircut** elle avait les cheveux coupés très court; **the gamine look** le style gavroche.

gaming ['geɪmɪŋ] 1 *n* = **gambling.** 2 *cpd*: **gaming laws** réglementation *f* des jeux de hasard.

gamma ['gæmə] *n* gamma *m*. **~ rays** rayons *mpl* gamma.

gammon ['gæmən] *n* (*bacon*) quartier *m* de lard fumé; (*ham*) jambon fumé. **~ steak** (épaisse) tranche *f* de jambon fumé *or* salé.

gammy* ['gæmɪ] *adj* (*Brit*) = **game²**.

gamp‡ [gæmp] *n* (*Brit hum*) pépin* *m*, parapluie *m*.

gamut ['gæmət] *n* (*Mus, fig*) gamme *f*. *(fig)* **to run the ~ of** passer par toute la gamme de.

gamy ['geɪmɪ] *adj meat etc* faisandé.

gander ['gændəʳ] *n* (*Orn*) jars *m*. *(fig)* **to take a ~‡** filer* un coup d'œil (*at* vers); *V* **sauce**.

gang [gæŋ] 1 *n [workmen]* équipe *f*; *[criminals]* bande *f*, gang *m*; *[youths, friends etc]* bande, clique *f*; *[prisoners]* convoi *m*; (*Tech*) série *f* (d'outils multiples). **the little boy wanted to be like the rest of his ~** le petit garçon voulait être comme le reste de sa bande; **he's one of the ~ now*** il est maintenant un des nôtres; *V* **chain** *etc*.

2 *cpd*: **gang bang‡** viol collectif; **gangland*** le milieu; **gangplank** passerelle *f* (de débarquement); (*Navy*) échelle *f* de coupée; **gangway** (*gen*) passage *m* (planchéié); (*Naut*) = **gangplank**; (*in bus etc*) couloir *m*; (*in theatre*) allée *f*; (*excl*) **gangway!** dégagez!

gang together* *vi* se mettre à plusieurs.

gang up* *vi* se mettre à plusieurs. **to gang up on** *or* **against sb‡** se liguer contre qn, se mettre à plusieurs contre qn.

ganger ['gæŋəʳ] *n* (*Brit*) chef *m* d'équipe (*de travailleurs*).

Ganges ['gændʒiːz] *n* Gange *m*.

ganglia ['gæŋglɪə] *npl of* **ganglion**.

gangling ['gæŋglɪŋ] *adj person* dégingandé. **a ~ boy** un échalas, une perche (*hum*).

ganglion ['gæŋglɪən] *n, pl* **ganglia** ganglion *m*; *(fig) [activity]* centre *m*; *[energy]* foyer *m*.

gangrene ['gæŋgriːn] *n* gangrène *f*.

gangrenous ['gæŋgrɪnəs] *adj* gangreneux. **to go ~** se gangrener.

gangster ['gæŋstəʳ] 1 *n* gangster *m*, bandit *m*. 2 *cpd story, film* de gangsters.

gangsterism ['gæŋstərɪzəm] *n* gangstérisme *m*.

gannet ['gænɪt] *n* (*Orn*) fou *m* (de Bassan).

gantry ['gæntrɪ] *n* (*for crane*) portique *m*; (*Space*) tour *f* de lancement; (*Rail*) portique à signaux; (*for barrels*) chantier *m*.

gaol [dʒeɪl] (*Brit*) = **jail.**

gaoler ['dʒeɪləʳ] *n* (*Brit*) = **jailer.**

gap [gæp] 1 *n* **(a)** trou *m*, vide *m*; (*in wall*) trou, brèche *f*, ouverture *f*; (*in hedge*) trou, ouverture; (*in print, text*) vide, intervalle *m*, blanc *m*; (*between floorboards*) interstice *m*, jour *m*; (*in pavement*) brèche; (*between curtains*) intervalle, jour; (*between teeth*) vide, interstice; (*mountain pass*) trouée *f*. **to stop up** *or* **fill in a ~** boucher un trou *or* une brèche, combler un vide; **leave a ~ for the name** laissez un blanc pour (mettre) le nom.

(b) *(fig)* vide *m*; (*in education*) lacune *f*, manque *m*; (*in time*) intervalle *m*; (*in conversation, narrative*) interruption *f*, vide. **a ~ in his memory** un trou de mémoire; **he left a ~ which will be hard to fill** il a laissé un vide qu'il sera difficile de combler; **to close the ~ between two points of view** supprimer l'écart entre *or* rapprocher deux points de vue; **to close the ~ in the balance of payments** supprimer le déficit dans la balance des paiements; *V* **bridge¹, credibility, generation.**

2 *cpd*: **gap-toothed** (*teeth wide apart*) aux dents écartées; (*teeth missing*) brèche-dent *inv*.

gape [geɪp] 1 *vi* **(a)** (*open mouth*) *[person]* bâiller, ouvrir la bouche toute grande; *[bird]* ouvrir le bec tout grand; *[seam etc]* bâiller; *[chasm etc]* être ouvert *or* béant.

(b) (*stare*) rester bouche bée (*at* devant), bayer aux corneilles. **to ~ at sb/sth** regarder qn/qch bouche bée.

2 *n* **(a)** *[chasm etc]* trou béant.

(b) (*stare*) regard ébahi.

gaping ['geɪpɪŋ] *adj hole, chasm, wound* béant; *seam* qui bâille; *person* bouche bée *inv*.

garage ['gærɑːʒ] 1 *n* garage *m*. 2 *vt* garer, mettre au garage. 3 *cpd*: **garageman, garage mechanic** mécanicien *m*; **garageman, garage proprietor** garagiste *m*.

garb [gɑːb] 1 *n* (*U: often hum*) costume *m*, mise *f*, atours *mpl* (*hum*). **in medieval ~** en costume médiéval. 2 *vt* (*gen pass*) vêtir (*in* de). **to ~ o.s. in** se revêtir de, s'affubler de (*hum*).

garbage ['gɑːbɪdʒ] 1 *n* (*U*) ordures *fpl*, détritus *mpl*; (*Culin*) déchets *mpl*; *(fig)* rebut *m*.

2 *cpd*: (*US*) **garbage can** boîte *f* à ordures, poubelle *f*; (*US*) **garbage collector** boueur *m or* boueux *m*, éboueur *m*; **garbage disposal unit** broyeur *m* d'ordures; (*US*) **garbage man** = **gar-**

bage collector; (*US*) **garbage truck** camion *m* des boueurs.

garble ['gɑːbl] *vt story* raconter de travers; *quotation* déformer; *facts* dénaturer; *instructions* embrouiller.

garbled ['gɑːbld] *adj account* parfaitement embrouillé; *text* altéré; *question* erroné; *instructions* confus; *words, speech* incompréhensible.

garden ['gɑːdn] 1 *n* jardin *m*. **the G~ of Eden** le jardin d'Éden; **~s** parc *m*, jardin public; (*fig*) **to lead sb up the ~ (path)*** mener qn en bateau*; (*fig*) **everything in the ~'s lovely** tout va pour le mieux; *V* **back, flower, kitchen** *etc.*

2 *vi* jardiner, faire du jardinage. **I like ~ing** j'aime le jardinage, j'aime jardiner.

3 *cpd*: **garden centre** garden-centre *m*, pépinière *f*; (*Brit*) **garden city** cité-jardin *f*; **garden hose** tuyau *m* d'arrosage; **garden(ing) tools** outils *mpl* de jardinage; **garden party** garden-party *f*, réception *f* en plein air; **garden path** *V* 1; **garden produce** produits maraîchers; **garden seat** banc *m* de jardin; **garden shears** cisaille *f* de jardinier; **garden snail** escargot *m*; **he lives just over the garden wall from us** il habite juste à côté de chez nous.

gardener ['gɑːdnəʳ] *n* jardinier *m*, -ière *f*. **I'm no ~** je ne connais rien au jardinage; **he's a good ~** il est très bon jardinier; *V* **landscape.**

gardenia [gɑː'diːnɪə] *n* gardénia *f*.

gardening ['gɑːdnɪŋ] *n* jardinage *m*; *V also* **garden** *and* **landscape.**

gargantuan [gɑː'gæntjʊən] *adj* gargantuesque.

gargle ['gɑːgl] 1 *vi* se gargariser, se faire un gargarisme. 2 *vt*: **to ~ one's throat** se gargariser, se faire un gargarisme. 3 *n* gargarisme *m*.

gargoyle ['gɑːgɔɪl] *n* gargouille *f*.

garish ['gɛərɪʃ] *adj clothes, colour, decorations* voyant, criard, tapageur; *light* cru, éblouissant.

garishness ['gɛərɪʃnɪs] *n [clothes]* aspect criard *or* tapageur; *[colours, light]* crudité *f*, violence *f*.

garland ['gɑːlənd] 1 *n* guirlande *f*, couronne *f* de fleurs. (*fig*) **a ~ of verse** un florilège (de poèmes). 2 *vt* orner de guirlandes, enguirlander.

garlic ['gɑːlɪk] 1 *n* (*U*) ail *m*; *V* **clove**[1]. 2 *cpd*: **garlic salt** sel *m* d'ail; **garlic sausage** saucisson *m* à l'ail.

garlicky ['gɑːlɪkɪ] *adj flavour, smell* d'ail; *sauce* à l'ail; *food* aillé; *breath* qui sent l'ail.

garment ['gɑːmənt] *n* vêtement *m*.

garner ['gɑːnəʳ] 1 *vt* (*also* **~ in, ~ up**) *grain etc* engranger, mettre en grenier; (*fig*) *memories etc* recueillir. 2 *n* (*liter*) (*granary*) grenier *m*; (*anthology*) recueil *m*.

garnet ['gɑːnɪt] 1 *n* (*gem, colour*) grenat *m*. 2 *adj*: **~ (-coloured)** grenat *inv*.

garnish ['gɑːnɪʃ] 1 *vt* garnir, orner, parer (*with* de); (*Culin*) garnir (*with* de). 2 *n* garniture *f*.

garnishing ['gɑːnɪʃɪŋ] *n* garnissage *m*, embellissement *m*; (*Culin*) garniture *f*; *[style]* ornement *m*, fioriture *f*.

garret ['gærət] *n* (*room*) mansarde *f*; (*attic*) grenier *m*.

garrison ['gærɪsən] 1 *n* garnison *f*. 2 *vt fort etc* placer une garnison dans; *troops* mettre en garnison. 3 *cpd*: **garrison duty** service *m* de garnison *or* de place; **garrison life** vie *f* de garnison; **garrison town** ville *f* de garnison; **garrison troops** troupes *fpl* de garnison.

garrotte [gə'rɒt] 1 *vt* (*strangle*) étrangler (*au cours d'un vol*); (*Spanish Hist*) faire périr par le garrot. 2 *n* (*gen*) cordelette *f* (*pour étrangler*); (*Spanish Hist*) garrot *m*.

garrulity [gə'ruːlɪtɪ] *n* (*U*) *[person]* loquacité *f*; *[style]* verbosité *f*.

garrulous ['gærʊləs] *adj person* loquace, volubile, bavard; *style* verbeux; (*liter*) *stream* babillard (*liter*), jaseur (*liter*).

garrulously ['gærʊləslɪ] *adv* avec volubilité.

garter ['gɑːtəʳ] 1 *n* (*gen*) jarretière *f*; (*for men's socks*) fixe-chaussette *m*; (*US: from belt*) jarretelle *f*. (*Brit*) **Order of the G~** Ordre *m* de la Jarretière; (*Brit*) **Knight of the G~** chevalier *m* de l'Ordre de la Jarretière. 2 *cpd*: (*US*) **garter belt** porte-jarretelles *m inv*.

gas [gæs] 1 *n* **(a)** (*Chem, Culin, Phys etc*) gaz *m*; (*Min*) méthane *m*; (*Mil*) gaz (asphyxiant *or* vésicant *etc*); (*anaesthetic*) (gaz) anesthésique *m*. **to cook by** *or* **with ~** faire la cuisine au gaz; **to turn on/off the ~** allumer/fermer *or* éteindre le gaz; (*Med etc*) **I had ~** j'ai eu une anesthésie au masque; *V* **laughing, natural, supply** *etc.*

(b) (*US: gasoline*) essence *f*. (*Aut*) **to step on the ~*** appuyer sur le champignon*; (*fig*) se magner‡, se presser; **to take one's foot off the ~*** ralentir.

(c) (‡: *idle words*) bla-bla-bla* *m*. (*chat*) **to have a ~** avoir une bonne parlotte (*about* à propos de).

(d) (‡: *fun*) rigolade* *f*. **to do sth for a ~** faire qch pour rigoler* *or* pour se marrer‡; **what a ~ it was!** quelle rigolade!*, ce qu'on s'est marrés!‡

2 *cpd industry* du gaz, gazier; *engine* à gaz. **gasbag** (enveloppe *f* de) ballon *m* à gaz; (‡*pej: talkative person*) moulin *m* à paroles* (*pej*); (*boastful*) baratineur‡ *m*, -euse‡ *f*; **gas bracket** applique *f* à gaz; **gas burner = gas jet**; **gas chamber** chambre *f* à gaz; **gas cooker** cuisinière *f* à gaz; (*portable*) réchaud *m* à gaz; **gas fire** appareil *m* de chauffage à gaz; **to light the gas fire** allumer le gaz; **gas-fired** chauffé au gaz; **gas-fired central heating** chauffage central au gaz; **gas fitter** ajusteur-gazier *m*; **gas fittings** appareillage *m* du gaz; (*US*) **gas fixture = gas bracket**; **gas heater** appareil *m* de chauffage à gaz; (*for heating water*) chauffe-eau *m inv* (à gaz); **gasholder** gazomètre *m*; **gas jet** brûleur *m* à gaz; **gaslight** lumière *f* du gaz; **by gaslight** au gaz, à la lumière du gaz; **gas lighter** (*for cooker etc*) allume-gaz *m inv*; (*for cigarettes*) briquet *m* à gaz; **gas lighting** éclairage *m* au gaz; **gaslit** éclairé au gaz; **gas main** canalisation *f* de gaz; **the gasman*** l'homme *m* du gaz; **gas mantle** manchon *m* à incandescence; **gasmask** masque *m* à gaz; **gas meter** compteur *m* à gaz; **gas oil** gas-oil *m*; **gas oven** four *m* à gaz; **he put his head in the gas oven** il s'est suicidé en se mettant la tête dans le four à gaz; **she felt like putting her head in the gas oven** elle avait envie de se jeter par la fenêtre; **gas pipe** tuyau *m* à gaz; **gas pipeline** gazoduc *m*; **gas range** fourneau *m* à gaz; **gas ring** (*part of cooker*) brûleur *m*; (*small stove*) réchaud *m* à gaz; (*US*) **gas station** poste *m* d'essence, station-service *f*; **gas stove** (*portable*) réchaud *m* à gaz; (*larger*) cuisinière *f or* fourneau *m* à gaz; (*US*) **gas tank** réservoir *m* à essence; **gas tap** (*on pipe*) robinet *m* à gaz; (*on cooker*) bouton *m* (de cuisinière à gaz); **gas turbine** turbine *f* à gaz; **gas worker** gazier *m*; **gasworks** usine *f* à gaz.

3 *vt* asphyxier, intoxiquer; (*Mil*) gazer. **to ~ o.s.** s'asphyxier.

4 *vi* **(a)** (*Chem*) dégager des gaz.

(b) (‡: *talk*) parler; (*chat*) bavarder.

gas up* *vi* (*US Aut*) faire le plein (de carburant).

Gascony ['gæskənɪ] *n* Gascogne *f*.

gaseous ['gæsɪəs] *adj* gazeux.

gash [gæʃ] 1 *n* (*in flesh*) entaille *f*, estafilade *f*; (*on face*) balafre *f*; (*in cloth, leather*) (grande) déchirure *f*, (grand) accroc *m*.

2 *vt flesh* entailler, entamer; *face* balafrer; *cloth, leather* déchirer, faire un (grand) accroc à.

3 *adj* (‡) de trop, en surplus. **if that box is ~ I'll take it** si vous n'avez plus besoin de cette boîte, je la prends.

gasket ['gæskɪt] *n* **(a)** *[piston]* garniture *f* de piston; *[joint]* joint *m* d'étanchéité; *[cylinder head]* joint de culasse; *V* **blow**[1]. **(b)** (*Naut*) raban *m* de ferlage.

gasoline ['gæsəʊliːn] *n* (*US*) essence *f*.

gasometer [gæ'sɒmɪtəʳ] *n* gazomètre *m*.

gasp [gɑːsp] 1 *n* halètement *m*. **to give a ~ of surprise/fear** *etc* avoir le souffle coupé par la surprise/la peur *etc*; **to be at one's last ~** (*lit*) être à l'agonie, agoniser, être à la dernière extrémité; (**fig*) n'en pouvoir plus; (*lit, fig*) **to the last ~** jusqu'au dernier souffle.

2 *vi* (*choke*) haleter, suffoquer; (*from astonishment*) avoir le souffle coupé. (*lit, fig*) **to make sb ~** couper le souffle à qn; **to ~ for breath** *or* **air** haleter, suffoquer, chercher sa respiration.

3 *vt*: **'no!' she ~ed** 'pas possible!' souffla-t-elle.

gasp out *vt sep plea* dire dans un souffle *or* d'une voix entrecoupée; *word* souffler.

gasper‡ ['gɑːspəʳ] *n* (*Brit*) sèche‡ *f*, clope‡ *f*.

gassy ['gæsɪ] *adj* (*Chem etc*) gazeux; *drink* gazeux; (‡*pej*) *person* bavard, jacasseur.

gastric ['gæstrɪk] *adj* gastrique. **~ flu** grippe gastro-intestinale; **~ juices** sucs *mpl* gastriques; **~ ulcer** ulcère *m* de l'estomac.

gastritis [gæs'traɪtɪs] *n* gastrite *f*.

gastro... ['gæstrəʊ] *pref* gastro...

gastroenteritis [ˌgæstrəʊˌentə'raɪtɪs] *n* gastro-entérite *f*.

gastronome ['gæstrənəʊm] *n* gastronome *mf*.

gastronomic [ˌgæstrə'nɒmɪk] *adj* gastronomique.

gastronomist [gæs'trɒnəmɪst] *n* gastronome *mf*.

gastronomy [gæs'trɒnəmɪ] *n* gastronomie *f*.

gastropod ['gæstrəpɒd] *n* gastéropode *m*.

gat[1]†† [gæt] *pret of* **get.**

gat[2]‡ [gæt] *n* (*US: gun*) flingue‡ *m*, pétard‡ *m*.

gate [geɪt] 1 *n* **(a)** *[castle, town]* porte *f*; *[field, level crossing]* barrière *f*; *[garden]* porte, portail *m*; (*of wrought iron*) grille *f*; (*low*) portillon *m*; (*tall, into courtyard etc*) porte cochère; (*Rail: in Underground*) portillon; *[lock, sluice]* vanne *f*, porte (d'écluse); *[sports ground]* entrée *f*. (*at airport*) **~ 5** sortie *f* 5, porte 5; **five-bar ~ = barrière**; (*US*) **to give sb the ~‡** (*employee*) sacquer‡ qn, virer‡ qn; (*boyfriend etc*) plaquer* qn.

(b) (*Sport*) (*attendance*) spectateurs *mpl*; (*money*) recette *f*, entrées *fpl*. **there was a ~ of 5,000** il y a eu 5.000 spectateurs; **the match got a good ~** le match a fait de grosses entrées*.

(c) (*Ski*) porte *f*.

2 *vt* (*Brit**: *Scol, Univ*) consigner, coller*. **to be ~d** se faire consigner *or* coller*.

3 *cpd*: **gatecrash*** (*vi*) (*without invitation*) s'introduire sans invitation; (*without paying*) resquiller; **to gatecrash a party*** s'introduire dans une réception sans invitation; **to gatecrash a match*** assister à un match sans payer; **gatecrasher*** (*without invitation*) intrus(e) *m(f)*; (*without paying*) resquilleur* *m*, -euse* *f*; **gatehouse** *[castle]* corps *m* de garde; *[park etc]* loge *f*; **gatekeeper** portier *m*, -ière *f*; (*Rail*) garde-barrière *mf*; **gateleg(ged) table** table *f* à abattants sur pieds mobiles; (*Sport*) **gate money** recette *f*, (montant *m* des) entrées *fpl*; **gatepost** montant *m* (de porte); (*fig*) **between you, me and the gatepost*** soit dit entre nous, entre quat'z'yeux‡; **gateway** porte *f*, entrée *f*, portail *m*; **New York, the gateway to America** New York, porte de l'Amérique; (*fig*) **it proved the gateway to success/fame/fortune** cela s'avéra être la porte ouverte au succès/à la gloire/à la fortune.

gather ['gæðəʳ] 1 *vt* **(a)** (*also* **~ together**) *people* rassembler, grouper, réunir; *objects* rassembler, ramasser; (*Typ*) *pages* assembler; *troops* amasser. **the accident ~ed quite a crowd** l'accident a provoqué *or* causé un grand rassemblement.

(b) (*collect*) *flowers* cueillir; *wood, sticks, mushrooms* ramasser; *taxes etc* percevoir; *information* recueillir. **to ~ dirt** s'encrasser; **to ~ dust** ramasser la poussière; **to ~ one's energies** rassembler *or* ramasser ses forces; **to ~ one's senses** *or* **one's thoughts** méditer, s'absorber, se concentrer; **to ~ speed**, (*Naut*) **to ~ way** prendre de la vitesse; **to ~ strength** *[person]* reprendre des forces; *[feeling, movement]* se renforcer; **to ~ volume** croître en volume.

(c) she ~ed him in her arms/to her elle l'a serré dans ses bras/contre elle; **he ~ed his cloak around him** il a resserré sa cape contre lui; she ~ed (up) her skirts elle a ramassé ses jupes; her hair was ~ed (up) into a bun ses cheveux étaient ramassés en chignon; (*liter: euph*) he was ~ed to his fathers il alla rejoindre ses ancêtres *or* aïeux.

(d) (*Sewing*) froncer. ~ed skirt jupe froncée; to ~ one's brows froncer le(s) sourcil(s).

(e) (*infer*) déduire, conclure (*from* de). I ~ from the papers ... d'après ce que disent les journaux, je déduis *or* je crois comprendre ...; I ~ from him that ... je comprends d'après ce qu'il me dit que ...; what are we to ~ from that? que devons-nous en déduire?; as far as I can ~ à ce que je comprends; I ~ she won't be coming je crois comprendre qu'elle ne viendra pas; as you will have ~ed comme vous avez dû le deviner; as will be ~ed from my report comme il ressort de mon rapport.

2 *vi* (a) (*collect*) *[people]* s'assembler, se rassembler, se réunir, se grouper; *[crowd]* se former, se masser; *[troops etc]* s'amasser; *[objects]* s'accumuler, s'amonceler, s'amasser; *[clouds]* se former, s'amonceler; *[dust]* s'accumuler, s'amasser. they ~ed round him ils se sont groupés *or* se sont rassemblés autour de lui.

(b) (*increase*) (*in volume, intensity etc*) croître, grandir; (*in size, content etc*) grossir. the ~ing darkness l'obscurité croissante; with ~ing force avec une force croissante; with ~ing speed avec une vitesse croissante; the ~ing storm l'orage qui se prépare (*or* se préparait).

(c) *[abscess etc]* mûrir; *[pus]* se former. tears ~ed in her eyes ses yeux se remplirent de larmes.

3 *n* (*Sewing*) fronce *f*.

gather in *vt sep crops* rentrer, récolter; *money, contributions, taxes* faire rentrer, percevoir; *papers, essays* ramasser.

gather round *vi* faire cercle, s'approcher. gather round! approchez-vous!

gather together 1 *vi* s'amasser, se rassembler.

2 *vt sep* = gather 1a. to gather o.s. together (*collect one's thoughts*) se ressaisir; (*for jump etc*) se ramasser.

gather up *vt sep papers, essays, toys* ramasser. to gather up the threads of a discussion rassembler les principaux points d'une discussion; to gather up one's strength rassembler ses forces; (*for jump etc*) to gather o.s. up se ramasser; he gathered himself up to his full height il s'est redressé de toute sa stature; *V also* gather 1c.

gathering ['gæðərɪŋ] *n* (a) (*U: act*) *[people]* rassemblement *m*; *[objects]* accumulation *f*, amoncellement *m*; *[fruits etc]* cueillette *f*; *[crops]* récolte *f*; (*Typ*) assemblage *m*. ~ of speed accélération *f*.

(b) (*group*) *[people]* assemblée *f*, réunion *f*, rassemblement *m*; *[objects]* accumulation *f*, amoncellement *m*. family ~ réunion de famille.

(c) (*U: Sewing*) fronces *fpl*, froncis *m*.

gauche [gəʊʃ] *adj* gauche, maladroit, inhabile.

gaucho ['gaʊtʃəʊ] *n* gaucho *m*.

gaudy ['gɔːdɪ] 1 *adj colour* éclatant, voyant (*pej*), criard (*pej*); (*pej*) *display etc* tapageur, de mauvais goût. 2 *n* (*Brit Univ*) fête annuelle (*de collège*).

gauge [geɪdʒ] 1 *n* (*standard measure: also of gun*) calibre *m*; (*Rail*) écartement *m*; (*Tex*) jauge *f*; (*instrument*) jauge, indicateur *m*. (*Aut, Aviat*) fuel ~ jauge de carburant; (*Aviat etc*) height ~ altimètre *m*; oil ~ indicateur *or* jauge du niveau d'huile; (*Aut*) petrol ~, (*US*) gasoline ~ jauge d'essence; pressure ~ manomètre *m*; temperature ~ indicateur de température; tyre ~ indicateur de pression des pneus; (*Aut*) wheel ~ écartement des essieux; rain ~ pluviomètre *m*; wind ~ anémomètre *m*; (*fig*) it is a ~ of his experience c'est un test qui permettra de juger *or* de jauger *or* d'évaluer son expérience; the incident was a ~ of public feeling on the subject l'incident a permis de jauger *or* d'évaluer le sentiment du public sur le sujet.

2 *vt* (a) (*measure*) *nut, temperature* mesurer; *oil* jauger; *wind* mesurer la vitesse de; *gun* calibrer; *sb's capacities* jauger, mesurer; *course of events* prévoir. to ~ the distance with one's eye jauger *or* mesurer la distance de l'œil; he was trying to ~ how far he should move it il essayait d'évaluer de combien il devait le déplacer; to ~ the right moment calculer le bon moment; we must try to ~ how strong public opinion is nous devons essayer de jauger *or* de mesurer la force de l'opinion publique.

(b) *tools* standardiser.

3 *cpd*: narrow-/standard-/broad-gauge railway voie étroite/à écartement normal/à grand écartement.

Gaul [gɔːl] *n* (*country*) Gaule *f*; (*person*) Gaulois(e) *m(f)*.

gaunt [gɔːnt] *adj* (*very thin*) *person* émacié, décharné; *face* creux; (*grim*) *appearance* lugubre; *landscape* désolé.

gauntlet ['gɔːntlɪt] *n* (*glove*) gant *m* (à crispin); (*part of glove*) crispin *m*; *[armour]* gantelet *m*. (*Hist, also fig*) to throw down/ take up the ~ jeter/ relever le gant; to run the ~ (*Mil Hist*) passer par les baguettes; (*Naut Hist*) courir la bouline; (*fig*) he had to run the ~ through the crowd il a dû foncer à travers une foule hostile; (*fig*) he ran the ~ of public criticism il essuya le feu des critiques du public.

gauss [gaʊs] *n* gauss *m*.

gauze [gɔːz] *n* (*all senses*) gaze *f*.

gave [geɪv] *pret of* give.

gavel ['gævl] *n* marteau *m* (*de président de réunion, de commissaire-priseur*).

gavotte [gə'vɒt] *n* gavotte *f*.

gawk [gɔːk] 1 *n* godiche* *mf*, grand dadais*. 2 *vi* rester bouche bée (*at* devant).

gawky ['gɔːkɪ] *adj* godiche*, gauche.

gawp* [gɔːp] *vi* = gape 1.

gay [geɪ] 1 *adj* (a) (*cheerful*) *person, music* gai, joyeux; *appearance* gai; *company, occasion* joyeux; *laughter* enjoué; *colour* éclatant, vif; (*pleasure-loving*) adonné aux plaisirs. ~ with lights resplendissant de lumières; ~ with flowers égayé de fleurs; to become ~(er) s'égayer; with ~ abandon avec une belle désinvolture; they danced with ~ abandon ils se sont abandonnés joyeusement au plaisir de la danse; ~ dog* joyeux drille, gai luron; to lead a *or* the ~ life mener une vie de plaisirs, mener joyeuse vie; to have a ~ time prendre du bon temps.

(b) (*: *homosexual*) homosexuel, homo* (*f inv*).

2 *n* homosexuel(le) *m(f)*. G~ Liberation Movement mouvement *m* pour la libération des homosexuels.

gaze [geɪz] 1 *n* regard *m* (fixe). his ~ met mine son regard a croisé le mien. 2 *vi* regarder. to ~ into space regarder dans *or* fixer le vide; to ~ at *or* (*liter*) upon sth regarder *or* contempler qch.

gaze about, gaze around *vi* regarder autour de soi.

gazebo [gə'ziːbəʊ] *n* belvédère *m*.

gazelle [gə'zel] *n* gazelle *f*.

gazette [gə'zet] 1 *n* (*official publication*) (journal *m*) officiel *m*; (*newspaper*) gazette *f*. 2 *vt* publier à l'Officiel. (*Mil etc*) to be ~d avoir sa nomination publiée à l'Officiel.

gazetteer [ˌgæzɪ'tɪə^r] *n* index *m* (géographique).

gazpacho [gəz'pætʃəʊ] *n* gazpacho *m*.

gazump [gə'zʌmp] *vi* (*Brit*) *revenir sur une promesse de vente pour accepter un prix plus élevé.*

gear [gɪə^r] 1 *n* (a) (*U*) (*equipment*) équipement *m*, matériel *m*, attirail *m*; (*harness*) harnachement *m*; *[camping, skiing, climbing, photography]* matériel, équipement; *[sewing, painting]* matériel; *[gardening]* matériel, outils *mpl*. fishing *etc* ~ matériel *or* équipement de pêche *etc*; the kitchen ~ is in this cupboard les ustensiles *mpl* de cuisine sont dans ce placard.

(b) (*U: belongings*) effets *mpl* (personnels), affaires* *fpl*. he leaves his ~ all over the house* il laisse traîner ses affaires* dans toute la maison.

(c) (*U: clothing*) vêtements *mpl*. he had his tennis ~ on il était en tenue de tennis; put on your tennis ~ mets tes affaires de tennis.

(d) (‡*U: modern clothes*) fringues‡ *fpl* à la mode.

(e) (*U: apparatus*) mécanisme *m*, dispositif *m*; *V* landing, steering *etc*.

(f) (*Tech*) engrenage *m*. in ~ engrené, en prise; it's out of ~ c'est désengrené, ce n'est pas *or* plus en prise.

(g) (*Aut*) (*mechanism*) embrayage *m*; (*speed*) vitesse *f*. in ~ en prise; not in ~ au point mort; he put the car into ~ il a mis (la voiture) en prise; the car slipped *or* jumped out of ~ la vitesse a sauté; neutral ~ point mort; to change *or* (*US*) to shift ~ changer de vitesse; first *or* bottom *or* low ~ première vitesse; second/third/fourth ~ deuxième/troisième/quatrième vitesse; top ~ (*fourth*) quatrième vitesse; (*fifth*) cinquième vitesse; in second ~ en seconde; to change *or* (*US*) to shift into third ~ passer en troisième (vitesse); you're in too high a ~ tu devrais rétrograder; (*fig*) production has moved into high *or* top ~ la production a atteint sa vitesse maxima; *V* engage, reverse *etc*.

2 *cpd*: (*Aut*) gearbox boîte *f* de vitesses; gear change changement *m* de vitesse; (*Brit*) gear-lever, (*US*) gearshift levier *m* de (changement de) vitesse; *[bicycle]* gearwheel pignon *m*.

3 *vt* (a) adapter. they ~ed their output to seasonal demands ils ont adapté leur production à la demande saisonnière; he ~ed his timetable to collecting his children from school il a adapté *or* combiné son emploi du temps de façon à pouvoir aller chercher les enfants à l'école; they were not ~ed to cope with the influx of immigrants ils n'étaient pas préparés pour cet afflux d'immigrants; the factory was not ~ed to cope with an increase of production la capacité de l'usine n'était pas calculée pour une production supérieure.

(b) *wheel* engrener.

4 *vi* s'engrener.

gear down *vi* (*Tech*) démultiplier.

gear up 1 *vi* (*Tech*) produire une multiplication.

2 *vt sep* (*: *make ready*) he geared himself up for the interview il s'est préparé pour l'entrevue; we're geared up (and ready) to do it nous sommes tout prêts à le faire; they were all geared up for the new sales campaign ils étaient parés* *or* fin prêts pour la nouvelle promotion de vente.

gecko ['gekəʊ] *n* gecko *m*.

gee[1]* [dʒiː] *excl* (**esp US*) eh bien!

gee[2] [dʒiː] 1 *n* (‡: *also* ~-~: *baby talk*) dada *m*. 2 *excl* (*to horse*) ~ up! hue!

geese [giːs] *npl of* goose.

geezer‡ ['giːzə^r] *n* type* *m*. (silly) old ~ vieux schnock‡.

Geiger counter ['gaɪgəˌkaʊntə^r] *n* compteur *m* Geiger.

geisha ['geɪʃə] *n* geisha *f or* ghesha *f*.

gel [dʒel] 1 *n* (*Chem*) colloïde *m*; (*gen*) gelée *f*. 2 *vi* se coaguler.

gelatin(e) ['dʒelətiːn] *n* gélatine *f*.

gelatinous [dʒɪ'lætɪnəs] *adj* gélatineux.

geld [geld] *vt horse* hongrer; *pig etc* châtrer.

gelding ['geldɪŋ] *n* (a) (*horse*) (cheval *m*) hongre *m*. (b) (*U*) castration *f*.

gelignite ['dʒelɪgnaɪt] *n* gélignite *f*.

gem [dʒem] 1 *n* gemme *f*, pierre précieuse; (*fig: work of art*) (vrai) bijou *m*, chef-d'œuvre *m*, merveille *f*. his painting was the ~ of the collection son tableau était le joyau de la collection; it's a little ~ of a house la maison est un vrai petit bijou; this miniature is a perfect ~ cette miniature est une vraie merveille; your char's a ~* votre femme de ménage est une perle; her aunt's a real ~* sa tante est un chou*; I must read you this ~* from the newspaper il faut que je te lise cette perle dans le journal.

2 *cpd*: gemstone pierre *f* gemme *inv*.

Gemini ['dʒemɪniː] *npl* (*Astron*) les Gémeaux *mpl*.

gemology [dʒeˈmɒlədʒɪ] *n* gemmologie *f.*
gen* [dʒen] *(Brit)* **1** *n* coordonnées* *fpl.* **to give sb the ~ on sth** donner à qn les coordonnées* *or* tous les tuyaux* de qch, rencarder: qn sur qch; **what's the ~ on this?** qu'est-ce qu'on doit savoir *or* qu'on sait là-dessus?; **I want all the ~ on him** je voudrais avoir toutes ses coordonnées*; **have you got the ~ on the new house?** avez-vous une documentation sur la nouvelle maison?
2 *adj* vrai, vrai de vrai:, véritable.
gen up: **1** *vi*: **to gen up on sth** se rencarder sur qch:.
2 *vt sep*: **to gen sb up on sth** mettre qn au parfum: de qch, rencarder: qn sur qch, donner à qn les coordonnées* de qch.
gender [ˈdʒendəʳ] *n (Gram)* genre *m*; (*: *sex*) sexe *m.* **common ~** genre commun; **of common ~** épicène.
gene [dʒiːn] *n* gène *m.* **~ pool** bagage *m or* patrimoine *m* héréditaire (de l'espèce).
genealogical [ˌdʒiːnɪəˈlɒdʒɪkəl] *adj* généalogique.
genealogist [ˌdʒiːnɪˈælədʒɪst] *n* généalogiste *mf.*
genealogy [ˌdʒiːnɪˈælədʒɪ] *n* généalogie *f.*
genera [ˈdʒenərə] *npl of* **genus.**
general [ˈdʒenərəl] **1** *adj* **(a)** (*common, not limited or specialized*) général; (*not in detail*) *view, plan, inquiry* d'ensemble. **in a ~ way** d'une manière générale; **as a ~ rule** en règle générale; **in ~ use** d'usage courant, généralement répandu; **for ~ use** à l'usage du public; **if you go in the ~ direction of the church** si vous allez grosso modo dans la direction de l'église; **he was a ~ favourite** il était universellement aimé *or* aimé par tout le monde; **the book was a ~ favourite** le livre a été très apprécié du (grand) public; **~ meeting** assemblée générale (*V* **annual**); **the ~ public** le grand public; **the ~ reader** le lecteur moyen; **~ servant** bonne *f* à tout faire; **there has been ~ opposition to the scheme** l'opposition à ce plan a été générale; **this type of behaviour is fairly ~ amongst young people** ce genre de comportement est assez répandu parmi les jeunes; **the rain has been fairly ~** il a plu un peu partout; **to give sb a ~ idea** *or* **outline of a subject** donner à qn un aperçu (d'ensemble) sur un sujet; **I've got the ~ idea** j'ai une idée d'ensemble sur la question.
(b) (*specific terms*) (*Med*) **~ anaesthetic** anesthésie générale; **~ assembly** assemblée générale; (*Rel*) **~ confession** (*Church of England*) confession collective (*lors de la prière en commun*); (*Roman Catholic Church*) confession générale; (*US*) **~ dealer = ~ shop**; (*US, Can: Post*) **~ delivery** poste restante; **~ election** élections législatives *or* générales; (*Mil*) **~ headquarters** quartier général; **~ holiday** fête publique, jour férié; **~ hospital** centre hospitalier; **~ knowledge** connaissances générales; **~ linguistics** linguistique générale; **~ manager** directeur général; (*Mil*) **G~ Officer Commanding** (*abbr* **G.O.C.**) général *m* commandant en chef; **there was ~ post within the department** (*changing desks*) tout le monde dans le service a changé de bureau; (*changing jobs*) il y a eu une réorganisation complète du personnel dans le service; **G~ Post Office** (*abbr* **G.P.O.**) (*Admin*) Postes et Télécommunications; (*building*) poste centrale; (*Med*) **to be in ~ practice** faire de la médecine générale; **~ practitioner** (*abbr* **G.P.**) (médecin *m*) généraliste *m*; **he's a G.P.** il fait de la médecine générale, il est (médecin) généraliste; **go to your G.P.** allez voir votre médecin habituel *or* de famille; **who is your G.P.?** qui est votre médecin traitant?; **~ shop** magasin *m* qui vend de tout; (*Mil etc*) **~ staff** état-major *m*; **~ store** grand magasin; **~ strike** grève générale; *V* **paralysis** *etc.*
(c) (*after official title*) général, en chef; *V* **secretary** *etc.*
2 *cpd*: **general-purpose** *tool, dictionary* universel.
3 *n* **(a)** général *m.* **in ~** en général; **the particular and the ~** le particulier et le général.
(b) (*Mil*) général *m*; *V* **brigadier** *etc.*
(c) (*: *servant*) bonne *f* à tout faire.
generality [ˌdʒenəˈrælɪtɪ] *n* **(a)** (*gen pl*) généralité *f*, considération générale. **we talked only of generalities** nous n'avons parlé que de généralités *or* qu'en termes généraux *or* que de questions *fpl* d'ordre général.
(b) (*most of*) **the ~ of** la plupart de.
(c) (*U*) caractère général. **a rule of great ~** une règle très générale.
generalization [ˌdʒenərəlaɪˈzeɪʃən] *n* généralisation *f.*
generalize [ˈdʒenərəlaɪz] *vti* généraliser.
generally [ˈdʒenərəlɪ] *adv* (*usually*) généralement, en général; (*for the most part*) dans l'ensemble. **~ speaking** en général, d'une manière générale.
generalship [ˈdʒenərəlʃɪp] *n* (*Mil*) tactique *f.*
generate [ˈdʒenəreɪt] **1** *vt children* engendrer; *electricity, heat* produire; (*Ling*) générer; (*fig*) *hope, fear* engendrer, donner naissance à.
2 *cpd*: **generating set** groupe *m* électrogène; **generating station** centrale *f* électrique; **generating unit** groupe *m* électrogène.
generation [ˌdʒenəˈreɪʃən] **1** *n* **(a)** génération *f.* **the younger ~** la jeune génération; **the postwar ~** la génération d'après-guerre; **a ~ ago** il y a une génération; (*fig*) **it's ~s since ...*** ça fait des siècles que ...; *V* **rising.**
(b) (*U*) *[electricity, heat]* production *f*; (*Ling*) génération *f*; *[hatred etc]* engendrement *m.*
2 *cpd*: **the generation gap** le conflit *or* l'opposition *f* des générations.
generative [ˈdʒenərətɪv] *adj* (*Ling*) génératif. **~ grammar** grammaire générative.
generator [ˈdʒenəreɪtəʳ] *n* **(a)** (*apparatus*) (*Elec*) génératrice *f*, *[steam]* générateur *m*, chaudière *f*; *[gas]* gazogène *m*; *[lighting]* dynamo *f* (d'éclairage). **(b)** (*person*) générateur *m*, -trice *f.*
generatrix [ˈdʒenəreɪtrɪks] *n* (*Math*) génératrice *f.*
generic [dʒɪˈnerɪk] *adj* générique.
generically [dʒɪˈnerɪkəlɪ] *adv* génériquement.
generosity [ˌdʒenəˈrɒsɪtɪ] *n* (*U*) générosité *f*, libéralité *f.*
generous [ˈdʒenərəs] *adj person, character, action, wine* généreux; *gift, donation, quantity* généreux; *supply, harvest* abondant; *meal* copieux, abondant; *size* ample. **he is very ~ with his time** il est très généreux de son temps; **he took a ~ helping of carrots** il s'est servi abondamment de carottes; **a ~ spoonful of sugar** une bonne cuillerée de sucre; **the seams in this dress are very ~** les coutures de cette robe ont une bonne largeur.
generously [ˈdʒenərəslɪ] *adv give etc* généreusement; *say, offer* avec générosité; *pardon, reprieve* avec magnanimité. **a dress cut ~ around the waist** une robe ample à la taille; **you've salted this meat rather ~** tu as eu la main un peu lourde en salant cette viande.
genesis [ˈdʒenɪsɪs] *n, pl* **geneses** [ˈdʒenɪsiːz] genèse *f*, origine *f.* (*Bible*) **G~** la Genèse.
genetic [dʒɪˈnetɪk] *adj* (*Bio: of the genes*) génétique, génique; (*hereditary*) génétique; (*Philos*) génétique. (*Bio*) **~ code** code *m* génétique; **~ engineering** sélection *f* eugénique.
geneticist [dʒɪˈnetɪsɪst] *n* généticien(ne) *m(f).*
genetics [dʒɪˈnetɪks] *n* (*U*) génétique *f.*
Geneva [dʒɪˈniːvə] *n* Genève. **Lake ~** le lac Léman; **~ Convention** convention *f* de Genève.
genial [ˈdʒiːnɪəl] *adj* **(a)** (*kindly, pleasant*) *person* cordial, affable, aimable; *climate* doux (*f* douce), clément, agréable; *smile, look, voice* chaleureux, cordial; *warmth* réconfortant, vivifiant. **(b)** (*having genius*) génial.
geniality [ˌdʒiːnɪˈælɪtɪ] *n [person, smile]* cordialité *f*, chaleur *f*; *[climate]* douceur *f*, clémence *f.*
genially [ˈdʒiːnɪəlɪ] *adv* **(a)** (*pleasantly*) cordialement. **(b)** (*as a genius*) génialement.
genie [ˈdʒiːnɪ] *n, pl* **genii** génie *m*, djinn *m.*
genii [ˈdʒiːnɪaɪ] *npl of* **genie** *and* **genius d.**
genital [ˈdʒenɪtl] **1** *adj* génital. **2** *npl*: **~s** organes génitaux.
genitive [ˈdʒenɪtɪv] *adj, n* (*Gram*) génitif (*m*). **in the ~** au génitif.
genius [ˈdʒiːnɪəs] *n* **(a)** (*U*) (*cleverness*) génie *m*; (*ability, aptitude*) génie (*for* de), don *m* extraordinaire (*for* pour). **man of ~** (homme *m* de) génie; **his ~ lay in his ability to assess ...** il était supérieurement doué pour juger ...; **he has a ~ for publicity** il a le génie de la publicité; **he's got a ~ for saying the wrong thing** il a le génie de *or* un certain génie pour dire ce qu'il ne faut pas.
(b) *pl* **~es** génie *m.* **he's a ~** c'est un génie, il est génial.
(c) (*U: distinctive character*) *[period, country etc]* génie *m* (particulier).
(d) *pl* **genii** (*spirit*) génie *m.* **evil ~** mauvais génie.
Genoa [ˈdʒenəʊə] *n* Gênes.
genocidal [ˌdʒenəʊˈsaɪdl] *adj* génocide.
genocide [ˈdʒenəʊsaɪd] *n* génocide *m.*
Genoese [ˌdʒenəʊˈiːz] **1** *adj* génois. **2** *n* Génois(e) *m(f).*
genotype [ˈdʒenəʊtaɪp] *n* génotype *m.*
genre [ˈʒɑːŋrə] *n* genre *m.* **~ (painting)** tableau *m* de genre.
gent [dʒent] *n* (*abbr of* **gentleman**) **(a)** (*Comm*) **~s' outfitters** magasin *m* d'habillement *or* de confection pour hommes; (*Comm*) **~s' shoes/suitings** *etc* chaussures/tissus *etc* (pour) hommes; **the ~s*** les toilettes *fpl* (pour hommes); (*sign*) '**~s**' 'messieurs'.
(b) (:) monsieur *m*, type* *m.* **he's a (real) ~:** c'est un monsieur (tout ce qu'il y a de) bien.
genteel [dʒenˈtiːl] *adj* (†*or iro*) *person, behaviour, family* distingué, élégant; *school* de bon ton. **~ poverty** une décente misère; **she has a very ~ way of holding her glass** elle a une façon qu'elle croit distinguée de tenir son verre; *V* **shabby.**
gentian [ˈdʒenʃɪən] *n* gentiane *f.* **~ blue** bleu *m* gentiane; **~ violet** bleu de méthylène.
Gentile [ˈdʒentaɪl] **1** *n* Gentil(e) *m(f).* **2** *adj* des Gentils.
gentility [dʒenˈtɪlɪtɪ] *n* (*iro*) prétention *f* à la distinction *or* au bon ton; (†: *good birth*) bonne famille, bonne naissance. (†: *gentry*) **the ~** la haute bourgeoisie, la petite noblesse.
gentle [ˈdʒentl] **1** *adj* **(a)** (*kind, not rough*) *person, disposition* doux (*f* douce), aimable; *voice, animal* doux. (*liter*) **the ~ sex** le beau sexe; **to be ~ with one's hands** avoir la main douce; **to use ~ methods** employer la douceur; **~ as a lamb** doux comme un agneau.
(b) (*not violent or strong*) *rebuke* gentil, peu sévère; *exercise, heat* modéré; *slope* doux (*f* douce); *tap, breeze, push, sound, touch* léger; *progress* mesuré; *transition* sans heurts; *hint, reminder* discret (*f* -ète). **in a ~ voice** d'une voix douce; **the car came to a ~ stop** la voiture s'est arrêtée doucement; **try a little ~ persuasion and he ...** essaie de le persuader en douceur et il ... .
(c) (†: *wellborn*) noble, bien né, de bonne famille. **of ~ birth** bien né; († *or hum*) **~ reader** aimable lecteur; (*Hist*) **~ knight** noble chevalier *m.*
2 *cpd*: **gentlewoman** (*by birth*) dame *f or* demoiselle *f* de bonne famille; (*in manner*) dame *or* demoiselle très bien *or* comme il faut*; (*at court*) dame d'honneur *or* de compagnie.
gentleman [ˈdʒentlmən] *pl* **gentlemen** **1** *n* **(a)** (*man*) monsieur *m.* **there's a ~ to see you** il y a un monsieur qui voudrait vous voir; **the ~ I was speaking to** le monsieur à qui je parlais; (*sign*) **'gentlemen'** 'messieurs'.
(b) (*man of breeding*) homme bien élevé, gentleman *m.* **he is a perfect ~** c'est un vrai gentleman; **a ~ never uses such language** un monsieur bien élevé ne se sert jamais de mots pareils; **one of nature's gentlemen** un gentleman né; **~'s agreement** accord *m* reposant sur l'honneur; (*hum*) **~'s ~** valet *m* de

chambre; **be a ~ and give her your seat** montre-toi bien élevé et donne-lui ta place; **he's no ~!** ce n'est pas un monsieur!
(c) (*man of substance*) rentier *m*. **to lead the life of a ~** vivre de ses rentes.
(d) (*at court etc*) gentilhomme *m*.
2 *cpd*: **Gentleman-at-Arms** gentilhomme *m* de la garde; **gentleman farmer** gentleman-farmer *m*; **gentleman-in-waiting** gentilhomme *m* (*attaché à la personne du roi etc*).
gentlemanly [ˈdʒentlmənlɪ] *adj person, manner* bien élevé, courtois; *voice, appearance* distingué; *behaviour* courtois.
gentlemen [ˈdʒentlmən] *npl of* **gentleman.**
gentleness [ˈdʒentlnɪs] *n [person, animal, character]* douceur *f*, bonté *f*; *[action, touch]* douceur.
gently [ˈdʒentlɪ] *adv push, touch, stroke* doucement, avec douceur; *say, smile, rebuke* avec douceur, gentiment; *remind, suggest* gentiment; *walk, move* (tout) doucement; *exercise* doucement, sans forcer. **the road slopes ~ down to the river** la route descend doucement *or* va en pente douce vers la rivière; **~ does it!** (allons-y) doucement!; **to go ~ with** *or* **on sth*** y aller doucement *or* mollo* avec qch; **to treat sb ~, to deal ~ with sb** ménager qn; **~ born**† bien né, de bonne naissance†.
gentry [ˈdʒentrɪ] *n* (*lit*) petite noblesse; (*fig pej: people*) gens *mpl*.
genuflect [ˈdʒenjʊflekt] *vi* faire une génuflexion.
genuflexion, (*US*) **genuflection** [ˌdʒenjʊˈflekʃən] *n* génuflexion *f*.
genuine [ˈdʒenjʊɪn] *adj* **(a)** (*authentic*) *wool, silver, jewel etc* véritable; *manuscript, antique* authentique; *coin* de bon aloi; (*Comm*) *goods* garanti d'origine. **a ~ Persian rug** un authentique tapis persan; **I'll only buy the ~ article** (*of furniture etc*) je n'achète que de l'authentique; (*of jewellery, cheeses etc*) je n'achète que du vrai; **that's the ~ article!*** ça c'est du vrai!
(b) (*sincere*) *laughter* franc (*f* franche); *tears* vrai, sincère; *emotion, belief* sincère; *simplicity* vrai, franc; *person* franc, sincère. **he is a very ~ person** il est très (simple et) direct; (*Comm*) **~ buyer** acheteur sérieux.
genuinely [ˈdʒenjʊɪnlɪ] *adv* (*V* **genuine**) authentiquement, véritablement; *feel, think* sincèrement.
genus [ˈdʒenəs] *n, pl* **genera** (*Bio*) genre *m*.
ge(o)... [ˈdʒiː(əʊ)] *pref* géo....
geodesic [ˌdʒiːəʊˈdesɪk] *adj* géodésique. **~ dome** dôme *m* géodésique.
geodesy [dʒiːˈɒdɪsɪ] *n* géodésie *f*.
geographer [dʒɪˈɒgrəfəʳ] *n* géographe *mf*.
geographic(al) [dʒɪəˈgræfɪk(əl)] *adj* géographique.
geography [dʒɪˈɒgrəfɪ] *n* (*science*) géographie *f*. **I don't know the ~ of the district** je ne connais pas la topographie de la région.
geological [dʒɪəʊˈlɒdʒɪkəl] *adj* géologique.
geologist [dʒɪˈɒlədʒɪst] *n* géologue *mf*.
geology [dʒɪˈɒlədʒɪ] *n* géologie *f*.
geometric(al) [dʒɪəʊˈmetrɪk(əl)] *adj* géométrique. (*Math*) **~ mean** moyenne *f* géométrique; **by ~ progression** par progression géométrique.
geometry [dʒɪˈɒmɪtrɪ] *n* géométrie *f*; *V* **analytical** *etc*.
geomorphology [ˌdʒiːəʊmɔːˈfɒlədʒɪ] *n* géomorphologie *f*.
geophysics [ˌdʒiːəʊˈfɪzɪks] *n* (*U*) géophysique *f*.
geopolitics [ˌdʒiːəʊˈpɒlɪtɪks] *n* (*U*) géopolitique *f*.
Geordie* [ˈdʒɔːdɪ] *n* (*Brit*) *natif m, -ive f de Tyneside*.
George [dʒɔːdʒ] *n* Georges *m*. **by ~!*** mon Dieu!
georgette [dʒɔːˈdʒet] *n* (*also* **~ crêpe**) crêpe *m* georgette.
Georgia [ˈdʒɔːdʒɪə] *n* Géorgie *f*.
Georgian [ˈdʒɔːdʒɪən] *adj* (*Brit Hist*) du temps des rois George I-IV (*1714-1830*). (*Brit Archit*) **~ style** *style anglais (environ 1720-1830) d'inspiration classique*.
geosyncline [ˌdʒiːəʊˈsɪnklaɪn] *n* géosynclinal *m*.
geotropism [dʒɪˈɒtrəpɪzəm] *n* géotropisme *m*.
geranium [dʒɪˈreɪnɪəm] **1** *n* géranium *m*. **2** *adj* (*colour: also* **~ red**) rouge vif *inv*, rouge géranium *inv*.
geriatric [ˌdʒerɪˈætrɪk] *adj* gériatrique, des vieillards. **~ medicine** gériatrie *f*; **~ nursing** soins *mpl* aux vieillards; **~ social work** aide sociale aux vieillards.
geriatrics [ˌdʒerɪˈætrɪks] *n* (*U*) (*Med*) gériatrie *f*; (*research*) gérontologie *f*.
germ [dʒɜːm] **1** *n* **(a)** (*Bio, also fig*) germe *m*. **the ~ of an idea** un embryon d'idée, le germe d'une idée.
(b) (*Med*) microbe *m*, germe *m*.
2 *cpd*: (*Med*) **germ carrier** porteur *m* de microbes; (*Bio*) **germ cell** cellule germinale *or* reproductrice, gamète *m*; (*Med*) **germ-free** stérilisé; **germ-killer** antiseptique *m*, germicide *m*, microbicide *m*; **germproof** résistant aux microbes; **germ warfare** guerre *f* bactériologique.
German [ˈdʒɜːmən] **1** *adj* allemand. (*Med*) **~ measles** rubéole *f*; (*US*) **~ sheep dog** chien *m* loup, berger allemand; **~-speaking** qui parle allemand; *V* **Switzerland. 2** *n* **(a)** Allemand(e) *m(f)*.
(b) (*Ling*) allemand *m*.
germane [dʒɜːˈmeɪn] *adj* allié, apparenté, se rapportant (*to* à).
Germanic [dʒɜːˈmænɪk] *adj* germanique.
germanium [dʒɜːˈmeɪnɪəm] *n* germanium *m*.
germanophile [dʒɜːˈmænəʊfaɪl] *n* germanophile *mf*.
germanophobe [dʒɜːˈmænəʊfəʊb] *n* germanophobe *mf*.
Germany [ˈdʒɜːmənɪ] *n* Allemagne *f*. **East/West ~** Allemagne de l'Est/de l'Ouest.
germicidal [ˌdʒɜːmɪˈsaɪdl] *adj* microbicide, germicide.
germicide [ˈdʒɜːmɪsaɪd] *n* microbicide *m*, germicide *m*.
germinate [ˈdʒɜːmɪneɪt] **1** *vi* germer. **2** *vt* faire germer; (*fig*) donner naissance à, engendrer.
germination [ˌdʒɜːmɪˈneɪʃən] *n* germination *f*.
gerontologist [ˌdʒerɒnˈtɒlədʒɪst] *n* gérontologue *mf*.
gerontology [ˌdʒerɒnˈtɒlədʒɪ] *n* gérontologie *f*.
gerrymander [ˈdʒerɪmændəʳ] **1** *vt election* truquer; *business* truquer, tripatouiller*. **2** *n* = **gerrymandering.**
gerrymandering [ˈdʒerɪmændərɪŋ] *n* tripotage(s) *m(pl)*.
gerund [ˈdʒerənd] *n* (*in English*) gérondif *m*, substantif verbal; (*in Latin*) gérondif.
gerundive [dʒɪˈrʌndɪv] **1** *adj* du gérondif. **2** *n* adjectif verbal.
gesso [ˈdʒesəʊ] *n [moulding etc]* plâtre *m* (de Paris); (*Art*) enduit *m* au plâtre.
gestalt [gəˈʃtɑːlt] *n* gestalt *f*. **~ psychology** gestaltisme *m*.
Gestapo [gesˈtɑːpəʊ] *n* Gestapo *f*.
gestate [dʒesˈteɪt] **1** *vi* être en gestation. **2** *vt* (*Bio*) garder en gestation; (*fig*) mûrir.
gestation [dʒesˈteɪʃən] *n* gestation *f*.
gesticulate [dʒesˈtɪkjʊleɪt] **1** *vi* gesticuler. **2** *vt* mimer, exprimer par gestes.
gesticulation [dʒesˌtɪkjʊˈleɪʃən] *n* gesticulation *f*.
gesture [ˈdʒestʃəʳ] **1** *n* (*lit, fig*) geste *m*. **a ~ of refusal** un geste de refus; (*fig*) **friendly ~** geste *or* témoignage *m* d'amitié; **they did it as a ~ of support** ils l'ont fait pour manifester leur soutien; **an empty ~** un geste qui ne signifie rien; **what a nice ~!** c'est un très joli geste!
2 *vi*: **to ~ to sb to do sth** faire signe à qn de faire qch; **he ~d towards the door** il désigna la porte d'un geste.
3 *vt* mimer, exprimer par gestes.
get [get] *pret, ptp* **got,** (*US*) *ptp* **gotten 1** *vt* **(a)** (*obtain*) *hat, book* obtenir, avoir, trouver; *permission, result* obtenir (*from* de); *commodity* (se) procurer, trouver, avoir; (*Rad*) *station* avoir, capter; (*Telec*) *person, number* avoir, obtenir; (*Scol*) *marks* obtenir, avoir. **to ~ sth cheap** avoir qch (à) bon marché; **I ~ my meat from the local butcher** je me fournis chez le boucher du quartier; **I must go and ~ some bread** il faut que j'aille acheter du pain; **I'll ~ some milk as well** je prendrai aussi du lait; **to ~ something to eat** (*find food*) trouver de quoi manger; (*eat*) manger quelque chose; **I'm going to ~ a new hat** je vais acheter un nouveau chapeau; **where did you ~ that hat?** où as-tu trouvé ce chapeau?; **I don't ~ much from his lectures** je ne tire pas grand-chose de ses cours; **to ~ sth for sb** trouver qch pour qn, procurer qch à qn; **he got the book for me** il m'a trouvé le livre; **he got me a job** il m'a trouvé un emploi; (*fig*) **we'll never ~ anything out of him** nous ne tirerons jamais rien de lui; *V* **answer, right, sleep** *etc*.
(b) (*acquire, win*) *power, wealth* acquérir, accéder à; *ideas, reputation* se faire; *wages, salary* recevoir, gagner, toucher; *prize* gagner. **if I'm not working I ~ no pay** si je ne travaille pas ma paye ne tombe pas*; **to ~ sth for nothing** avoir *or* obtenir qch pour rien; *[collection, set]* **I've still 3 to ~** il m'en manque encore 3; **it got him fame/glory** *etc* cela lui a valu *or* rapporté la célébrité/la gloire *etc*; **he got fame/glory** *etc* il a connu la célébrité/la gloire *etc*; **he got support from the crowd** il s'est fait soutenir par la foule; **he got himself a wife** il a trouvé à se marier; *V* **best** *etc*.
(c) (*receive*) *letter, present* recevoir, avoir; *shock* recevoir, ressentir, avoir; *surprise* avoir; *wound, punishment* recevoir. **to ~ one in the eye‡** recevoir *or* prendre un coup dans l'œil; **you'll ~ it!*** tu te fais passer un (bon) savon!*, tu vas écoper!*; **to ~ 2 years (in prison)** écoper* de *or* attraper* 2 ans (de prison); **he ~s it from his mother** il le tient de sa mère; **this room ~s all the sun** cette pièce reçoit tout le soleil; *V* **neck, sack**[1]**, worst** *etc*.
(d) (*catch*) *ball, disease* attraper; *quarry* attraper, prendre; *person* prendre, attraper. *[pain]* **it ~s me here** cela me prend ici; **I've got him** *or* **it!** ça y est (je l'ai)!, je le tiens!; **got you at last!** enfin je te tiens!; **we'll ~ them yet!** on les aura!; **I'll ~ you!*** je t'aurai!, j'aurai ta peau!‡; **he'll ~ you for that!*** qu'est-ce que tu vas prendre!*; **to ~ religion*** devenir bigot *or* calotin‡; **he's got it bad (for her)*** il en pince sérieusement (pour elle)‡.
(e) (*hit*) *target etc* atteindre, avoir. **the bullet got him in the arm** il a pris la balle dans le bras.
(f) (*seize*) prendre, saisir. **to ~ sb round the neck/by the throat** saisir *or* prendre qn au cou/à la gorge; **to ~ sb by the arm** saisir le bras de qn, attraper *or* saisir qn par le bras; *V* **grip, hold.**
(g) (*fetch*) *person, doctor* aller chercher, faire venir; *object* chercher, apporter. **(go and) ~ my books** allez chercher mes livres; **can I ~ you a drink?** voulez-vous boire quelque chose?
(h) (*have, possess*) **to have got** avoir, posséder; **I've got toothache** j'ai mal aux dents; **I have got 3 sisters** j'ai 3 sœurs; **how many have you got?** (de choses) combien en avez-vous?; **she's got too much to do** elle a trop de choses à faire; *V also* **have.**
(i) (*causative etc*) **to ~ sb to do sth** persuader qn de faire qch, faire faire qch à qn, obtenir que qn fasse qch; **to ~ sth done** faire faire qch; **to ~ sth going** faire démarrer qch; **to ~ one's hair cut** se faire couper les cheveux; **I got him to cut my hair** je me suis fait couper les cheveux par lui; **~ him to clean the car** fais-lui laver la voiture; **he knows how to ~ things done!** il sait faire activer les choses!; **she got her arm broken** elle a eu le bras cassé.
(j) (*cause to be: gen + adj*) **to ~ sth ready** préparer qch; **to ~ o.s. ready** se préparer; **to ~ sb drunk** enivrer *or* soûler qn; **to ~ one's hands dirty** se salir les mains; **try to ~ him into a good humour** essaie de le mettre de bonne humeur; **to ~ sb into trouble** attirer des ennuis à qn; (*euph*) **he got her into trouble*** il l'a mise dans une situation intéressante (*euph*); **we got him on to the subject of the war** nous l'avons amené à parler de la guerre; *V* **straight** *etc*.
(k) (*put, take*) faire parvenir. **they got him home somehow** ils l'ont fait rentrer tant bien que mal; **I'll come if you can ~ me home** je veux bien venir si vous pouvez assurer mon retour; **how can we ~ it home?** comment faire pour le rapporter à la

maison?; to ~ sth to sb faire parvenir qch à qn; **to ~ a child to bed** (faire) coucher un enfant; **to ~ sb upstairs** faire monter l'escalier à qn, aider qn à monter l'escalier; **to ~ sth upstairs/downstairs** monter/descendre qch; **he managed to ~ the card into the envelope** il a réussi à faire entrer la carte dans l'enveloppe; **I'll never ~ the car through here** je n'arriverai jamais à faire passer la voiture par ici; **to ~ a horse/vehicle over a bridge** faire franchir un pont à un cheval/un véhicule; **to ~ sth past the customs** passer qch à la douane; (*fig*) **to ~ something off one's chest** dire ce que l'on a sur le cœur; **he got the blood off his hand** il a fait disparaître le sang de sa main; (*fig*) **to ~ sth off one's hands** se débarrasser de qch (*fig*); **where does that ~ us?*** où est-ce que ça nous mène?

(l) (†† *or liter: beget*) engendrer.

(m) (*understand*) *meaning* comprendre, saisir. **~ it?*, do you ~ me?‡** tu saisis?*; **(I've) got it!** j'y suis!, ça y est!; **I don't ~ it*** je ne comprends pas, je ne saisis pas*, je n'y suis pas (du tout).

(n) (*take note of*) observer, remarquer. **I didn't ~ your name** je n'ai pas saisi votre nom; (*to secretary etc*) **did you ~ that last sentence?** avez-vous pris la dernière phrase?; **~ (a load of) that!‡** regarde-moi ça!, vise-moi ça!‡; **~ her!‡** (*look*) regardez-la donc!; (*listen*) écoutez-la donc!

(o) (*: *annoy*) ennuyer, chiffonner, embêter*, (*stronger*) mettre en rogne* *or* en boule*. **that sort of behaviour really ~s me** ce genre de conduite me met hors de moi; **that's what ~s me in all this business** c'est ça qui me chiffonne *or* me met en rogne* dans cette histoire; *V* **goat** *etc.*

(p) (*: *impress, thrill*) **that tune ~s me!** cet air me fait quelque chose!; **that really ~s me!** ça m'emballe!*

2 *vi* **(a)** (*go, arrive*) aller, se rendre (*to, at* à, *from* de). **how do you ~ there?** comment fait-on pour y aller?; **can you ~ there from London by bus?** est-ce qu'on peut y aller de Londres en autobus?; **he should ~ here soon** il devrait être là *or* arriver bientôt; **how did that box ~ here?** comment se fait-il que cette boîte se trouve ici?; **to ~ to the top** (*lit*) arriver au *or* atteindre le sommet; (*fig: also* **to ~ there**) arriver, réussir; (*fig*) **now we're ~ting somewhere!*** enfin on avance!; (*fig*) **we're ~ting nowhere, we're ~ting nowhere fast‡** on fait du sur place*; (*fig*) **you won't ~ anywhere if you behave like that** tu n'arriveras à rien en te conduisant comme ça; (*fig*) **we'll ~ nowhere** *or* **we won't ~ anywhere with him** nous n'arriverons à rien *or* nous perdons notre temps avec lui; **where did you ~ to?** où êtes-vous allé?; (*in book, work etc*) **where have you got to?** où en êtes-vous?; **where has he got to?, where can he have got to?** qu'est-ce qu'il est devenu?, où est-il passé?; **I got as far as speaking to him** je suis allé jusqu'à lui parler; (*excl*) **~!‡** fous le camp!‡; *V* **above** *etc.*

(b) (+ *adj or ptp: become, be*) devenir, se faire. **to ~ old** devenir vieux, vieillir; **to ~ fat** devenir gros (*f* grosse), grossir; **to ~ paid** se faire payer; **to ~ killed** se faire tuer; **to ~ used to sth/to doing** s'habituer à qch/à faire; **to ~ married** se marier; **it's ~ting late** il se fait tard; **you're ~ting grey** vous commencez à grisonner; **how do people ~ like that?** comment peut-on en arriver là?; **to ~ with it‡** se mettre à la mode *or* dans le vent*; (*excl*) **~ with it!‡** mets-toi un peu à la mode!, sois un peu dans le vent!*; *V* **catch** *etc.*

(c) (+ *infin*) parvenir à. **to ~ to know sb** parvenir *or* apprendre à connaître qn; **we soon got to like them** nous nous sommes vite mis à les apprécier *or* aimer; **we got to like him in the end** nous avons fini par l'aimer, finalement nous nous sommes mis à l'aimer; **it got to be quite pleasant after a while*** après un certain temps c'est devenu assez agréable.

(d) (+ *prp: begin*) se mettre à. **to ~ going** commencer, s'y mettre; **I got talking to him in the train** je me suis mis à parler avec lui *or* je suis entré en conversation avec lui dans le train; **to ~ working** se mettre au travail; **I got to thinking*** je me suis dit comme ça‡; *V* **crack, weave** *etc.*

3 (*modal auxiliary usage: la forme* **have got to** *est moins littéraire que la forme* **have to** *et la remplace généralement au présent en anglais parlé*) **you've got to come** il vous faut absolument venir; **I haven't got to leave yet** je ne suis pas obligé de partir tout de suite; **have you got to go and see her?** est-ce que vous êtes obligé d'aller la voir?; *V also* **have 2.**

4 *cpd*: **get-at-able*** *place* accessible, d'accès facile; *person* accessible; **getaway** (*Aut*) démarrage *m*; (*Racing*) départ *m*; *[criminals]* fuite *f*; **to make a** *or* **one's getaway** filer, décamper; **they had a getaway car waiting** ils avaient une voiture pour filer; **the gangsters' getaway car was later found abandoned** on a retrouvé plus tard, abandonnée, la voiture qui avait permis aux gangsters de s'enfuir; **get-rich-quick scheme*** projet *m* pour faire fortune rapidement; **get-together** (petite) réunion *f*; **getup*** (*clothing*) mise *f*, tenue *f*, accoutrement *m* (*pej*); (*fancy dress*) déguisement *m*; (*presentation*) présentation *f*; **he's got lots of get-up-and-go*** il a un allant *or* un dynamisme fou*, il est très dynamique; **get-well card** carte *f* de vœux (de bon rétablissement).

get about *vi* **(a)** *[person]* se déplacer. **she gets about quite well despite her lameness** elle se déplace très bien malgré son infirmité; **he gets about with a stick/on crutches** il marche *or* se déplace avec une canne/avec des béquilles; (*after illness*) **he's getting about again now** il est de nouveau sur pied.

(b) *[news]* se répandre, circuler, s'ébruiter. **it has got about that ...** le bruit court que ... .

get above *vt fus*: **to get above o.s.** se prendre pour plus important qu'on n'est; **you're getting above yourself!** pour qui te prends-tu?

get across 1 *vi* (*lit*) traverser, passer d'un côté à l'autre; (*fig*) *[play]* passer la rampe; *[speaker]* se faire comprendre, se faire accepter; *[meaning, message]* passer*. **he didn't get across to the audience** il n'a pas réussi à établir la communication avec le public; **he managed to get across to her at last** il a enfin réussi à s'en faire entendre.

2 *vt sep* (*lit*) *load* traverser; *person* faire traverser, faire passer; (*fig*) *play, song* faire passer la rampe à; *ideas, intentions, desires* communiquer (*to sb* à qn). **to get sth across to sb** faire comprendre qch à qn.

3 *vt fus* (*annoy*) **to get across sb** se faire mal voir de qn.

get along 1 *vi* **(a)** (*go*) aller, s'en aller, se rendre (*to* à). **I must be getting along** il faut que je m'en aille; **get along with you!*** (*go away*) va-t-en!, file!; (*Brit: stop joking*) ça va, hein!, allons (allons)!

(b) (*manage*) se débrouiller*. **to get along without sth/sb** se passer de *or* se débrouiller* sans qch/qn.

(c) (*progress*) avancer, faire des progrès, faire du chemin. **he's getting along well in French** il fait de gros progrès en français; *[invalid etc]* **he's getting along nicely** il est en bonne voie, il fait des progrès.

(d) (*be on good terms*) s'entendre (bien). **they get along very well** ils s'entendent très bien; **I don't get along with him at all** je ne m'entends pas du tout avec lui.

2 *vt sep* faire avancer, faire venir, amener.

get around *vi* = **get about.**

get at 1 *vt fus* **(a)** (*reach*) *place* parvenir à, atteindre; *person* accéder jusqu'à. **house difficult to get at** maison difficile à atteindre *or* difficile d'accès, maison peu *or* difficilement accessible; **he's not easy to get at** il est d'un abord peu facile; **let me get at him!*** que je l'attrape! (*subj*), que je mette la main sur lui!

(b) (*find, ascertain*) *facts, truth* parvenir à, découvrir.

(c) (*suggest*) **what are you getting at?** où voulez-vous en venir?

(d) (*attack, jibe at*) s'en prendre à, en avoir à‡. **she's always getting at her brother** elle est toujours sur le dos de son frère *or* après son frère*; **who are you getting at?** à qui voulez-vous faire allusion?, qui est-ce que vous visez?

(e) (*: *bribe*) acheter, suborner.

(f) (*start work on*) se mettre à. **I must get at this essay tonight** il faut que je me mette à cette dissertation ce soir; **I want to get at the redecorating this weekend** je veux commencer à refaire les peintures ce week-end.

2 get-at-able *adj V* **get 4.**

get away 1 *vi* **(a)** (*leave*) s'en aller, partir; *[vehicle]* partir, démarrer. **to get away from a place** quitter un endroit; **to get away from work** quitter son travail; **I couldn't get away any sooner** je n'ai pas pu m'échapper *or* me libérer plus tôt; **can you get away for a holiday?** pouvez-vous vous libérer pour partir en vacances?; **get away!** allez-vous-en!; **get away (with you)!*** (*go away*) va-t-en!, file!*; (*stop joking*) ça va, hein!, allons (allons)!

(b) (*escape*) s'échapper, se sauver (*from* de). **to get away from one's environment** se soustraire à *or* échapper à son environnement; **to get away from sb** échapper à qn; **he went to the Bahamas to get away from it all** il est allé aux Bahamas pour laisser tous ses ennuis *or* problèmes derrière lui; **the doctor told her she must get away from it all** le médecin lui a ordonné de partir se reposer loin de tout; **the thief got away with the money** le voleur est parti avec l'argent; **he got away with a mere apology** il en a été quitte pour une simple excuse; **you'll never get away with that!** on ne te laissera pas passer ça!*; (*fig*) **he'd get away with murder*** il tuerait père et mère qu'on lui pardonnerait; (*fig*) **you can't get away from it!, there's no getting away from it!** il faut bien le reconnaître!, le fait est là, on ne peut rien y changer!

2 *vt sep* **(a)** *person* faire partir, emmener, entraîner, éloigner. **you must get her away to the country for a while** il faut que vous l'emmeniez (*subj*) un peu à la campagne; **I must get this letter away today** il faut que je mette cette lettre à la poste *or* que je fasse partir cette lettre aujourd'hui.

(b) (*remove*) **to get sth away from sb** arracher qch à qn.

3 getaway *n, adj V* **get 4.**

get back 1 *vi* **(a)** (*return*) revenir, retourner. **to get back (home)** rentrer chez soi; **to get back to bed** se recoucher, retourner au lit; **to get back upstairs** remonter *or* retourner en haut; **to get back to work** (*after pause*) se remettre au travail; (*after illness, holiday*) retourner au travail; **to get back to the point** revenir au sujet; **let's get back to why you didn't come yesterday** revenons à la question de savoir pourquoi vous n'êtes pas venu hier; *V also* **get on 3.**

(b) (*move backwards*) reculer. (*excl*) **get back!** reculez!

2 *vt sep* **(a)** (*recover*) *sth lent* se faire rendre, reprendre possession de; *sth lost* retrouver; *possessions* recouvrer; *good opinion* retrouver; *strength* reprendre; *person* faire revenir. **now that we've got you back** maintenant que tu nous es revenu; **to get one's money back** se faire rembourser, (*with difficulty*) récupérer son argent; *V* **own.**

(b) (*replace*) remettre, replacer.

(c) (*return*) *object* renvoyer; *person* raccompagner, reconduire, faire reconduire (chez lui).

get back at* *vt fus* (*retaliate against*) se venger de, rendre la monnaie de sa pièce à.

get by *vi* **(a)** (*pass*) passer. **let me get by** laissez-moi passer; **this work just gets by** ce travail est tout juste passable *or* acceptable.

(b) (*manage*) se débrouiller, s'en sortir*, s'en tirer*. **she gets by on very little money** elle s'en tire* *or* elle s'en sort* *or* elle se débrouille* avec très peu d'argent; **he'll get by!** il s'en sortira!*, il se débrouillera toujours!*

get down 1 *vi* descendre (*from, off* de). (*at table*) **may I get down?** est-ce que je peux sortir (de table)?; **to get down on one's knees** se mettre à genoux; **get down!** descends!

2 *vt sep* **(a)** *book, plate* descendre; *hat, picture* décrocher.

get that child down off the table! descends cet enfant de (sur) la table!
(b) *bird, game* abattre, descendre*.
(c) (*swallow*) *food, pill* avaler, faire descendre.
(d) (*make note of*) noter, prendre (en note).
(e) (*: *depress*) déprimer, démoraliser. **he gets me down** il me tape sur le système‡; **all that worry has got him down** tous ces soucis l'ont déprimé *or* lui ont mis le moral à zéro*; **don't let it get you down!** ne vous laissez pas abattre!, du cran!*
get down to *vt fus*: **to get down to doing sth** se mettre à faire qch; **to get down to work** se mettre au travail; **to get down to a task** s'attaquer *or* s'atteler à une besogne; **you'll have to get down to it** il faut vous y mettre; (*fig*) **when you get down to it there's not much difference between the two** à bien regarder les faits il n'y a pas beaucoup de différence entre les deux.
get in 1 *vi* **(a)** *[person]* (*enter*) entrer, réussir à entrer; (*be admitted*) se faire admettre; (*reach home*) rentrer; *[sunshine, air, water]* pénétrer, entrer, s'introduire. **to get in between two people** se glisser *or* s'introduire entre deux personnes.
(b) (*arrive*) *[train, bus, plane]* arriver.
(c) (*Parl: be elected*) *[member]* être élu; *[party]* accéder au pouvoir.
2 *vt sep* **(a)** (*lit*) *object* rentrer; *person* faire entrer; *crops, harvest* rentrer, engranger; *debts, taxes* percevoir, recouvrer.
(b) (*plant*) *seeds* planter, semer; *bulbs* planter.
(c) (*buy, obtain*) *groceries, coal* acheter, faire rentrer. **to get in supplies** s'approvisionner, faire des provisions.
(d) (*summon*) *doctor, police, tradesman* faire venir.
(e) (*insert etc*) **to get a word in edgeways** glisser *or* placer un mot; **he got in a reference to his new book** il a glissé une allusion à son dernier livre; (*fig*) **to get one's hand in** se faire la main; **he managed to get in a couple of blows on his opponent's head** il a réussi à frapper deux fois son adversaire à la tête; *V* **eye**.
get into *vt fus* **(a)** (*enter*) *house, park* entrer dans, pénétrer dans; *car, train* monter dans. (*fig*) **to get into a club** se faire accepter comme membre d'un club; **he got into a good school** il a été accepté dans une bonne école; (*fig*) **how did I get into all this?** comment me suis-je fourré dans un pareil pétrin?, que suis-je allé faire dans cette galère?; **to get into the way of doing sth** (*become used to*) s'habituer à faire qch; (*make a habit of*) prendre l'habitude de faire qch; *V* **company, habit, mischief** *etc.*
(b) *clothes* mettre, enfiler*; *coat, dressing gown* endosser, mettre.
get in with *vt fus* **(a)** (*gain favour of*) (réussir à) se faire bien voir de, s'insinuer dans les bonnes grâces de. **he tried to get in with the headmaster** il a essayé de se faire bien voir du directeur.
(b) (*become friendly with*) **he got in with a bad crowd** il s'est mis à avoir de mauvaises fréquentations.
get off 1 *vi* **(a)** (*from vehicle*) descendre. (*fig*) **to tell sb where to get off*** envoyer qn sur les roses*, envoyer promener qn; **he was told where he got off*** on lui a fait comprendre que la plaisanterie avait assez duré.
(b) (*depart*) *[person]* partir, filer, se sauver; *[car]* démarrer; *[plane]* décoller. (*fig*) **to get off to a good start** prendre un bon départ; **to get off (to sleep)** s'endormir.
(c) (*escape*) s'en tirer. **to get off lightly** s'en tirer à bon compte; **to get off with a reprimand/a fine** en être quitte pour une semonce/une amende.
(d) (*leave work*) sortir, s'en aller, se libérer. **I can't get off early today** je ne peux pas m'en aller de bonne heure aujourd'hui; **can you get off tomorrow?** est-ce que tu peux te libérer *or* être libre demain?; **we get off at 5 o'clock** nous sortons à 5 heures.
2 *vt sep* **(a)** (*remove*) *clothes, shoes* ôter, enlever; *jewellery* enlever; *stains* faire partir, faire disparaître, enlever.
(b) (*despatch*) *mail* expédier, envoyer, mettre à la poste. **to get the children off to school** expédier les enfants à l'école; **to get sb off to work** faire partir qn au travail; **to get a child off to sleep** endormir un enfant.
(c) (*save from punishment*) (*in court*) faire acquitter; (*gen*) tirer d'affaire *or* de là*. **a good lawyer will get him off** un bon avocat le tirera d'affaire *or* le fera acquitter.
(d) (*learn*) **to get sth off (by heart)** apprendre qch (par cœur).
(e) (*Naut*) *boat* renflouer; *crew, passengers* débarquer.
3 *vt fus* **(a) to get off a bus/a cycle** descendre d'un autobus/d'une bicyclette; **he got off his horse** il est descendu de cheval; **to get off a chair** se lever d'une chaise; **get (up) off the floor!** levez-vous!, debout!; (*fig*) **I wish you would get off my back!*** ne sois donc pas constamment sur mon dos!, vas-tu me laisser tranquille!; **let's get off this subject of conversation** parlons d'autre chose; **we've rather got off the subject** nous nous sommes plutôt éloignés du sujet.
(b) (*: *avoid etc*) **to get off doing the homework/washing up** se faire dispenser de (faire ses) devoirs/(faire la) vaisselle; **he got off visiting his aunt** il s'est fait dispenser d'aller rendre visite à sa tante; **to get off work** se libérer.
get off with* *vt fus*: **he got off with a blonde he met on a bus** il a eu la touche* avec une blonde qu'il a rencontrée dans un autobus.
get on 1 *vi* **(a)** (*advance, make progress*) avancer, progresser, faire des progrès. **how are you getting on?** comment ça marche?*; **how did you get on?** ça a bien marché?*, comment ça c'est passé?; **to be getting on (in years)** se faire vieux; **he's getting on for forty** il frise la quarantaine; **time is getting on** il se fait tard; **it's getting on for 3 o'clock** il est bientôt 3 heures, il n'est pas loin de 3 heures; **there were getting on for 100 people** il y avait pas loin de 100 personnes; **we have getting on for 500 books** nous avons près de *or* pas loin de 500 livres.
(b) (*succeed*) réussir, arriver, faire son chemin. **if you want to get on, you must ...** si tu veux réussir, tu dois ...; **to get on in life** *or* **in the world** faire son chemin *or* réussir dans la vie; **the art of getting on** le moyen de parvenir dans la vie *or* de réussir dans la vie *or* d'arriver.
(c) (*continue, proceed*) continuer, poursuivre. **we must be getting on** il faut aller de l'avant; **get on (with you)!*** (*go away*) va-t-en!, file!*; (*stop joking*) ça va, hein!, allons (allons)!; **get on with it!, get on with the job!** allez, au travail!; **he got on with the job** il s'est (re)mis au travail; **while he was getting on with the job** pendant qu'il travaillait; **this will do to be getting on with** ça ira pour le moment.
(d) (*agree*) s'accorder, s'entendre, faire bon ménage (*with* avec). **we don't get on** nous ne nous entendons pas; **I get on well with her** je m'entends bien avec elle.
2 *vt sep clothes, shoes* mettre, enfiler.
3 *vt fus*: **to get on a horse** monter (sur un cheval); **to get on a bicycle** monter sur *or* enfourcher une bicyclette; **to get on a bus/train** monter dans un autobus/un train; **to get on one's feet** se mettre debout, se lever; (*after illness, setback*) **to get back on one's feet** se remettre.
get on to *vt fus* **(a)** = **get on 3**.
(b) (*find, recognize*) *facts, truth* découvrir. **the police got on to him at once** la police l'a dépisté *or* a été sur sa trace immédiatement.
(c) (*nag*) **she's always getting on to me** elle est toujours après moi*.
(d) (*get in touch with*) se mettre en rapport avec; (*speak to*) parler à; (*Telec*) téléphoner à.
get out 1 *vi* **(a)** sortir (*of* de); (*from vehicle*) descendre (*of* de). **get out!** sortez!, fichez le camp!*
(b) (*escape*) s'échapper (*of* de). (*fig*) **to get out of** *obligation* se dérober à, échapper à; *duty* se soustraire à; *difficulty* se tirer de; **there's no getting out of it, he's just not good enough** il n'y a pas à dire, il n'est pas à la hauteur; **you'll have to do it, there's no getting out of it** il faut que tu le fasses, il n'y a pas moyen d'y échapper; *V* **clutch, depth, trouble** *etc.*
(c) *[news etc]* se répandre, s'ébruiter; *[secret]* s'éventer.
2 *vt sep* **(a)** (*remove*) *plug* enlever; *tooth* enlever, arracher; *stain* enlever, faire partir, faire disparaître. **to get a cork out of a bottle** déboucher une bouteille; **I can't get it out of my mind** je ne peux m'empêcher d'y penser, cela me trotte par la tête*.
(b) (*bring out*) *object* sortir (*of* de); *words, speech* prononcer, sortir*; *book [publisher]* publier, sortir; *[library-user]* emprunter, sortir. **get the cards out and we'll have a game** sors les cartes et on va faire une partie.
(c) (*prepare*) *plan, scheme* préparer, mettre sur pied; *list* établir, dresser.
(d) (*solve*) *problem, puzzle* venir à bout de.
get over 1 *vi* (*lit*) traverser; *[message, meaning]* passer.
2 *vt fus* **(a)** (*cross*) *river, road* franchir, traverser; *fence [horse]* franchir, passer par-dessus; *[person]* escalader, passer par-dessus.
(b) (*recover from*) **to get over an illness** guérir *or* se remettre d'une maladie; **to get over a loss** se consoler *or* se remettre d'une perte; **to get over a surprise** revenir d'une surprise; **I can't get over it** je n'en reviens pas; **I can't get over the fact that ...** je n'en reviens pas que ... + *subj*; **you'll get over it!** tu n'en mourras pas!, on n'en meurt pas!; **she never really got over him*** elle ne l'a jamais vraiment oublié.
(c) (*overcome*) *obstacle* surmonter; *objections, difficulties* triompher de, venir à bout de.
3 *vt sep* **(a)** (*lit*) *person, animal, vehicle* faire passer pardessus. **we couldn't get the car over** nous n'avons pas pu (faire) passer la voiture.
(b) (*swallow*) *food, pill* avaler.
(c) (*have done with*) en finir avec. **let's get it over (with)** finissons-en (avec*); **I was glad to get that over (with)** j'étais ravi d'en avoir fini (avec*).
(d) (*Theat*) *play* faire passer la rampe à; *song etc* faire accepter; (*gen: communicate*) faire comprendre. **he couldn't get his ideas over to his readers** il était incapable de faire comprendre *or* de communiquer ses idées à ses lecteurs; **I couldn't get it over to him that he must come** je n'ai pas pu lui faire comprendre qu'il devait venir.
get round 1 *vi* = **get about**.
2 *vt sep* **(a)** *unconscious person* ranimer.
(b) **to get sb round to one's way of thinking** amener qn à partager sa façon de voir.
3 *vt fus* **(a)** (*circumvent*) *obstacle* contourner; *difficulty, law, regulation* tourner.
(b) (*coax, persuade*) entortiller, embobiner*. **he knows how to get round her** il sait la prendre; **she got round him in the end** elle a fini par l'entortiller*.
get round to* *vt fus*: **to get round to doing sth** arriver à faire qch; **if I get round to it** si j'y arrive; **I never got round to going to see her** jamais je n'ai réussi à aller la voir; **I shan't get round to that before next week** je n'arriverai pas à trouver l'occasion *or* le temps de m'en occuper avant la semaine prochaine.
get through 1 *vi* **(a)** *[message, news]* parvenir (*to* à); *[signal]* être reçu.
(b) (*be accepted, pass*) *[candidate]* être reçu, passer; *[motion, bill]* passer, être voté. *[football team etc]* **to get through to the third round** se classer pour le troisième tour.
(c) (*Telec*) obtenir la communication (*to* avec). **I phoned you several times but couldn't get through** je t'ai téléphoné plusieurs fois mais je n'ai pas pu t'avoir; **could you get through to him straight away?** pouvez-vous le contacter immédiatement?
(d) (*communicate with*) **to get through to sb** se faire com-

prendre de qn; **he can't get through to his son at all** il n'arrive pas à se faire comprendre de son fils, il n'est pas sur la même longueur d'ondes que son fils; **she was so angry I couldn't get through to her** elle était tellement en colère que je ne pouvais rien lui faire entendre.

(e) (*finish*) terminer, finir. **I shan't get through before 6 o'clock** je n'aurai pas terminé *or* fini avant 6 heures; **to get through with sth*** en finir avec qch.

2 *vt fus* **(a)** *hole, window* passer par; *hedge* traverser, passer à travers; *crowd* se frayer un chemin dans *or* à travers; (*Mil*) *enemy lines* percer, franchir.

(b) (*finish*) *task* accomplir, achever, venir au bout de; *book* achever, finir; *supplies, sugar, fuel* venir au bout de. **he got through a lot of work** il a abattu de la besogne; **to get through all one's money** (*salary*) dépenser tout ce qu'on gagne; (*inheritance etc*) manger toute sa fortune; **I've got through the £20 you lent me** je suis venu à bout des 20 livres *or* j'ai dépensé les 20 livres *or* il ne reste plus rien des 20 livres que vous m'avez prêtées; **how can I get through the week without you?** comment vais-je pouvoir vivre une semaine sans toi?

(c) (*consume, use*) *food, drink, coal, supplies* consommer. **we get through 10 bottles a week** il nous faut 10 bouteilles par semaine; **we get through £50 per week** nous n'avons pas trop de 50 livres par semaine.

3 *vt sep* **(a)** (*lit*) *person, object* faire passer; (*fig*) *message* faire parvenir (*to* à). **can you get this message through to him?** pouvez-vous lui transmettre *or* faire passer ce message?; **I can't get it through to him that ...** je n'arrive pas à lui faire comprendre que ...; (*Telec*) **to get sb through** to passer qn à, donner à qn la communication avec; (*Telec*) **get me through to Paris at once** donnez-moi *or* passez-moi Paris tout de suite.

(b) (*fig*) **to get a law through** faire adopter une loi; **he got his pupils through** ses élèves ont été reçus grâce à lui; **it was his English that got him through** c'est à son anglais qu'il doit d'avoir été reçu.

get together 1 *vi* se rassembler, se réunir. **let's get together on Thursday and decide what to do** on se retrouve jeudi pour décider ce qu'il faut faire; **you'd better get together with him before you decide** vous feriez bien de le consulter *or* de vous entendre avec lui avant de décider.

2 *vt sep people* rassembler, réunir; *things* ramasser, rassembler; *thoughts, ideas* rassembler.

3 **get-together** *n V* **get 4.**

get under 1 *vi* (*pass underneath*) passer par-dessous; se mettre *or* se glisser dessous.

2 *vt fus*: **to get under a fence/a rope** *etc* passer sous une barrière/une corde *etc.*

3 *vt sep* (*lit*) mettre dessous, faire passer par-dessous; (*fig: control*) *fire, revolt* maîtriser.

get up 1 *vi* **(a)** (*rise*) *[person]* se lever (*from* de), se mettre debout; *[wind]* se lever. **the sea is getting up** la houle se lève; **get up out of bed!** sors du lit!

(b) (*on horse*) monter. (*on horse, cycle*) **to get up behind sb** monter en croupe derrière qn.

2 *vt fus tree, ladder* monter à; *hill* gravir.

3 *vt sep* **(a)** (*lit*) *person* (*on to ladder etc*) faire monter; (*from chair etc*) faire lever; *thing* monter; *sail* hisser. **to get sb's back up*** mettre qn en boule*, braquer qn; **to get sb's temper up** mettre qn en colère; **to get up speed** prendre de la vitesse; **to get up steam** (*Tech*) faire monter la pression; (*fig*) rassembler ses forces; **when she gets up steam she can ...** quand elle s'y met elle peut ... .

(b) (*from bed*) *person* faire lever; (*wake*) réveiller.

(c) (*organize*) *play* monter; *entertainment* monter, organiser; *plot* ourdir, monter; *story* fabriquer, forger. **to get up a petition** mettre sur pied *or* organiser une pétition.

(d) (*prepare, arrange*) *article for sale* apprêter, préparer; (*Comm*) *book* présenter. **to get o.s. up as** se déguiser en, se travestir en; **to get o.s. up beautifully** se faire beau (*f* belle), se mettre sur son trente et un; **she was very nicely got up** elle était très bien habillée.

(e) (*study*) *history, literature etc* travailler, bûcher*; *speech, lecture* préparer.

4 **getup** *n V* **get 4.**

get up to *vt fus* **(a)** (*catch up with*) rattraper.

(b) (*reach*) arriver à. **I've got up to page 17** j'en suis à la page 17; **where did we get up to last week?** où en sommes-nous arrivés la semaine dernière?

(c) (*be involved in, do*) **to get up to mischief** faire des bêtises *or* des sottises; **you never know what he'll get up to next** on ne sait jamais ce qu'il va encore inventer *or* fabriquer*, on ne sait jamais ce qu'il va encore trouver moyen de faire.

Gethsemane [geθ'seməni] *n* Gethsémani *m.*

geum ['dʒi:əm] *n* benoîte *f.*

gewgaw ['gju:gɔ:] *n* bibelot *m*, babiole *f.*

geyser ['gi:zəʳ] *n* (*Geol*) geyser *m*; (*Brit: in house*) chauffe-bain *m inv.*

Ghana ['gɑ:nə] *n* Ghana *m.*

Ghanaian [gɑ:'neɪən] **1** *adj* ghanéen. **2** *n* Ghanéen(ne) *m(f).*

ghastly ['gɑ:stlɪ] *adj* (*pale*) *appearance* blême, livide, mortellement pâle; *pallor* mortel; *light* blafard, spectral; (*horrible, frightening*) horrible, effrayant, affreux; (*unpleasant*) horrible, affreux, épouvantable. **he looked** ~ il avait une mine de déterré.

Ghent [gent] *n* Gand.

gherkin ['gɜ:kɪn] *n* (*Culin*) cornichon *m.*

ghetto ['getəʊ] *n* ghetto *m.*

ghost [gəʊst] **1** *n* (*apparition*) fantôme *m*, revenant *m*, spectre *m*; (*fig*) ombre *f*; (*TV*) image *f* secondaire; (††: *soul*) âme *f.* **I don't believe in ~s** je ne crois pas aux fantômes; **the ~ of a smile** une ombre de sourire, un pâle *or* vague sourire; **I haven't the ~ of a chance** je n'ai pas la moindre chance *or* pas l'ombre d'une chance; (*liter*) **to give up the ~** rendre l'âme; *V* **holy** *etc.*

2 *vt*: **to ~ sb's books/speeches** écrire les livres/les discours de qn; **his book was ~ed by a journalist** c'est un journaliste qui lui a servi de nègre.

3 *cpd film, story* de revenants, de fantômes; *ship, train* fantôme. **ghost town** ville morte; **ghost writer** rédacteur *m* anonyme, nègre *m* (*pej*).

ghostly ['gəʊstlɪ] *adj* **(a)** spectral, fantomatique. **(b)** (††: *Rel etc*) spirituel.

ghoul [gu:l] *n* goule *f*, vampire *m*; (*grave robber*) déterreur *m* de cadavres. (*fig*) **he's a ~** il est morbide, il a des goûts dépravés.

ghoulish ['gu:lɪʃ] *adj* (*lit*) de goule, vampirique; (*fig*) *humour, tastes* morbide, macabre.

G.I.* [,dʒi:'aɪ] (*US*) **1** *n* soldat *m* (américain), G.I. *m.* **2** *adj* militaire. ~ **bride** *épouse étrangère d'un G.I.*

giant ['dʒaɪənt] **1** *n* géant *m.* (*Ir Geog*) **the G~'s Causeway** la chaussée des Géants. **2** *adj tree, star etc* géant; *strides* de géant; *helping, amount* gigantesque.

gibber ['dʒɪbəʳ] *vi [person, ape etc]* baragouiner. **to ~ with rage** bégayer *or* bafouiller de colère; **~ing idiot*** crétin patenté*.

gibberish ['dʒɪbərɪʃ] *n* (*U*) charabia* *m*, baragouin *m.*

gibbet ['dʒɪbɪt] *n* potence *f*, gibet *m.*

gibbon ['gɪbən] *n* gibbon *m.*

gibbous ['gɪbəs] *adj* (*hump-backed*) gibbeux (*liter*), bossu. ~ **moon** lune *f* dans le deuxième *or* troisième quartier.

gibe [dʒaɪb] **1** *vi* **(a)** **to ~ at sb** railler qn, se moquer de qn. **(b)** (*Naut*) *[boat]* virer lof pour lof; *[sail]* passer d'un bord à l'autre du mât. **2** *n* raillerie *f*, moquerie *f*, sarcasme *m.*

giblets ['dʒɪblɪts] *npl* abattis *mpl* (*de volaille*).

Gibraltar [dʒɪ'brɔ:ltəʳ] *n* Gibraltar *m*; *V* **rock**², **strait.**

giddily ['gɪdɪlɪ] *adv* (*lit*) vertigineusement; (*light-heartedly*) à la légère; (*heedlessly*) avec insouciance, à l'étourdie.

giddiness ['gɪdɪnɪs] *n* (*U*) (*Med*) vertiges *mpl*, étourdissements *mpl*; (*lightheartedness*) légèreté *f*; (*heedlessness*) étourderie *f.* **a bout of ~** un vertige, un étourdissement.

giddy ['gɪdɪ] *adj person* (*dizzy*) pris de vertige *or* d'un étourdissement; (*heedless*) étourdi, écervelé; (*not serious*) léger; *height* vertigineux, qui donne le vertige. **I feel ~** la tête me tourne; **to turn** *or* **go ~** être pris de vertige; **to make sb ~** donner le vertige à qn; ~ **round of pleasure** tourbillon *m* de plaisirs; (*fig, iro*) **the ~ heights of senior management** les hautes sphères de la direction générale; **that's the ~ limit!**‡ ça c'est le bouquet!*; *V* **goat.**

gift [gɪft] **1** *n* **(a)** (*present*) cadeau *m*, présent *m*; (*Comm*) prime *f*, cadeau. **New Year ~** étrennes *fpl*; (*in shop*) **is it for a ~?** c'est pour offrir?; **it was a ~** (*lit*) on me l'a offert; (*: *fig: it was easy*) c'était du gâteau‡; **I wouldn't have it as a ~** on m'en ferait cadeau que je n'en voudrais pas; **he thinks he's God's ~* to the human race** il se prend pour le nombril du monde; **people like us are God's ~* to dentists** des gens comme nous c'est le rêve* pour les dentistes; (*Comm*) **'free ~ inside the packet'** 'ce paquet contient un cadeau'.

(b) (*Jur etc*) don *m*, donation *f.* **to make sb a ~ of sth** faire don *or* cadeau de qch à qn; **by free ~** à titre gratuit; **in the ~ of** à la discrétion de; *V* **deed.**

(c) (*talent*) don *m* (*for* de, pour), talent *m* (*for* pour). **he has a ~ for maths** il a un don pour les maths *or* le don des maths; **he has great artistic ~s** il a de grands dons artistiques; **to have the ~ of the gab*** avoir la langue bien pendue, avoir du bagou*.

2 *vt* (*esp Jur*) donner. (*fig*) **to be ~ed with patience** *etc* être doué de patience *etc.*

3 *cpd*: (*Comm*) **gift coupon** bon-prime *m*; (*Prov*) **don't look a gift horse in the mouth** à cheval donné on ne regarde pas la bride (*Prov*), on ne critique pas le cadeau qu'on reçoit; **gift token** chèque-cadeau *m*; **gift voucher** = **gift coupon**; **to giftwrap a package** faire un paquet-cadeau; **giftwrapping** emballage-cadeau *m.*

gifted ['gɪftɪd] *adj* (*fig*) doué (*for* pour). **the ~ child** l'enfant surdoué.

gig [gɪg] *n* **(a)** (*vehicle*) cabriolet *m*; (*boat*) petit canot, youyou *m.* **(b)** (‡) (*jazz etc session*) gig *f* (*engagement occasionnel de courte durée*).

gigantic [dʒaɪ'gæntɪk] *adj* géant, gigantesque.

gigantism [dʒaɪ'gæntɪzəm] *n* gigantisme *m.*

giggle ['gɪgl] **1** *vi* rire nerveusement, rire sottement, glousser. **stop giggling!** arrête de rigoler!*; **she was giggling helplessly** elle ne pouvait pas se retenir de pouffer.

2 *n* petit rire sot *or* nerveux, gloussement sot *or* nerveux. **to have/get the ~s** avoir/attraper le fou rire; (*Brit*) **it was a bit of a ~*** ça nous a bien fait rigoler*.

giggly ['gɪglɪ] *adj* qui glousse sans arrêt, qui glousse pour un rien.

gigolo ['ʒɪgələʊ] *n* (*sexually*) gigolo *m*; (*dancing partner*) danseur mondain.

gild [gɪld] *pret* **gilded**, *ptp* **gilded** *or* **gilt** *vt* dorer. (*fig*) **to ~ the lily** renchérir sur la perfection; **to ~ the pill** dorer la pilule; **~ed youth** la jeunesse dorée.

gilding ['gɪldɪŋ] *n* dorure *f.*

gill¹ [gɪl] *n [mushrooms]* lamelle *f.* *[fish]* **~s** ouïes *fpl*, branchies *fpl*; **he was looking rather green around the ~s*** il était vert (*de peur etc*).

gill² [dʒɪl] *n* (*measure*) quart *m* de pinte (= *0,142 litre*).

gillie ['gɪlɪ] *n* (*Scot*) gillie *m*, accompagnateur *m* (*d'un chasseur, d'un pêcheur etc*).

gillyflower ['dʒɪlɪ,flaʊəʳ] *n* giroflée *f.*

gilt [gɪlt] **1** *ptp of* **gild.**

2 *n* dorure *f.* (*fig*) **to take the ~ off the gingerbread** enlever tout le charme, gâter le plaisir.

3 *adj* doré.

4 *cpd*: **gilt-edged** *book* doré sur tranche; (*Fin*) **gilt-edged securities** *or* **stock** valeurs *fpl* de premier ordre *or* de tout repos *or* de père de famille.

gimbal(s) ['dʒɪmbəl(z)] *n* (*Aut, Naut*) cardan *m*.

gimcrack ['dʒɪmkræk] *adj furniture* de camelote, de pacotille; *jewellery* en toc; *house* de carton.

gimlet ['gɪmlɪt] *n* vrille *f*. **to have eyes like ~s, to be ~-eyed** avoir des yeux perçants, avoir un regard perçant comme une vrille.

gimmick ['gɪmɪk] *n* (*Comm, Pol, Theat etc*) truc* *m*, trouvaille *f*, gadget *m*; (*Theat: catchphrase*) réplique *f* à effet; (*gadget*) machin* *m*, truc*. **advertising ~** trouvaille *or* truc* *or* gadget publicitaire; **it's just a sales ~** c'est simplement un gadget promotionnel *or* une astuce promotionnelle; **the comedian put on a Scots accent as a ~** le comique a pris un accent écossais pour l'effet; **her glasses are just a ~ to make her look intellectual** ses lunettes sont simplement un truc* pour lui donner l'air intellectuel.

gimmickry ['gɪmɪkrɪ] *n* (recherche *f* d')astuces *fpl*, trucs *mpl*.

gimmicky ['gɪmɪkɪ] *adj* (*pej*) *photography* à trucs; *presentation* à astuces.

gin[1] [dʒɪn] *n* gin *m*. **~ and tonic** gin-tonic *m*; (*Brit*) **~ and it** gin-vermouth *m*; (*Cards*) **~ (rummy)** *variante f du rami*; *V* **pink**.

gin[2] [dʒɪn] *n* **(a)** (*also* **~ trap**) piège *m*. **(b)** (*Tech*) égreneuse *f* (de coton).

ginger ['dʒɪndʒəʳ] **1** *n* gingembre *m*; (*fig*) dynamisme *m*, énergie *f*, vitalité *f*. (*nickname*) **G~** Poil de Carotte.

2 *adj* **(a)** *hair* roux (*f* rousse), rouquin*.

(b) (*Culin*) *biscuit etc* au gingembre.

3 *cpd*: **ginger ale, ginger beer** boisson gazeuse au gingembre; **gingerbread** (*n*) pain *m* d'épice; (*adj*) (*Culin*) en pain d'épice; (*: *Archit*) *style* tarabiscoté; (*esp Brit Pol*) **ginger group** groupe *m* de pression; **gingernut** gâteau sec au gingembre; **ginger pop*** = **ginger ale**; **gingersnap** = **gingernut**.

ginger up *vt sep person* secouer, secouer les puces à‡; *action, event* mettre de la vie *or* de l'entrain dans. **he gingered up his talk with a few jokes** il a relevé *or* égayé sa causerie de quelques plaisanteries.

gingerly ['dʒɪndʒəlɪ] **1** *adj prod* léger, doux (*f* douce); *touch* délicat.

2 *adv touch, move* précautionneusement, avec précaution. **to walk** *or* **tread ~** (*lit*) marcher à pas précautionneux *or* avec précaution *or* comme sur des œufs; (*fig*) y aller avec des gants* *or* doucement.

gingham ['gɪŋəm] *n* (*Tex*) vichy *m*.

gink‡ [gɪŋk] *n* (*US pej*) (drôle de) type* *m*.

gipsy ['dʒɪpsɪ] **1** *n* (*gen*) bohémien(ne) *m(f)*; (*Spanish*) gitan(e) *m(f)*; (*Central European*) Tsigane *mf*; (*pej*) romanichel(le) *m(f)*. **she's so dark she looks like a ~** elle est si foncée de peau qu'elle a l'air d'une bohémienne *or* d'une gitane.

2 *cpd caravan, custom* de bohémien, de gitan, tsigane, de romanichel (*pej*); *music* des gitans, tsigane. **gipsy moth** zigzag *m* (*Zool*).

giraffe [dʒɪ'rɑːf] *n* girafe *f*. **baby ~** girafeau *m*.

gird [gɜːd] *pret, ptp* **girded** *or* **girt** *vt* (*liter*) (*encircle*) ceindre (*liter*); (*clothe*) revêtir (*with* de).

gird on *vt sep sword etc* ceindre (*liter*).

gird up *vt sep robe* ceindre. (*Bible*) **to gird up one's loins** se ceindre les reins.

girder ['gɜːdəʳ] *n* poutre *f*; (*smaller*) poutrelle *f*.

girdle[1] ['gɜːdl] **1** *n* (*belt: lit, fig*) ceinture *f*; (*corset*) gaine *f*. **2** *vt* (*fig liter*) ceindre (*with* de).

girdle[2] ['gɜːdl] *n* (*Culin*) = **griddle 1**.

girl [gɜːl] **1** *n* **(a)** (jeune *or* petite) fille *f*. **a little ~** une petite fille, une fillette; **a ~ of 17** une (jeune) fille de 17 ans; **an English ~** une jeune Anglaise; **a little English ~** une petite Anglaise; **poor little ~** pauvre petite; **the Smith ~s** les filles des Smith; **the little Smith ~s** les petites Smith.

(b) (*daughter*) fille *f*; (*pupil*) élève *f*; (*servant*) bonne *f*; (*factory-worker*) ouvrière *f*; (*shop assistant*) vendeuse *f*, jeune fille; (*: *sweetheart*) petite amie. (*Brit Scol*) **old ~** ancienne élève; **yes, old ~‡** oui, ma vieille*; **the old ~** (*wife*) la patronne‡, la bourgeoise*; (*mother*) ma mère, ma vieille‡; **the old ~ next door** la vieille (dame) d'à côté.

2 *cpd*: (*in office*) **girl Friday** aide *f* de bureau; **girlfriend** *[boy]* petite amie; *[girl]* amie *f*, camarade *f*, copine* *f*; (*Brit*) **girl guide**, (*US*) **girl scout** éclaireuse *f*; (*Roman Catholic*) guide *f*.

girlhood ['gɜːlhʊd] *n* enfance *f*, jeunesse *f*.

girlie ['gɜːlɪ] *adj*: **~ magazine*** magazine déshabillé.

girlish ['gɜːlɪʃ] *adj behaviour, appearance* (*woman's*) de petite fille, de jeune fille; (*man's, boy's*) de fille, efféminé.

giro ['dʒaɪrəʊ] *n* (*Brit*) **bank ~ system** système *m* de virement bancaire; **National G~** (service *m* des) Comptes Chèques Postaux.

girt [gɜːt] **1** *pret, ptp of* **gird**. **2** *n* = **girth b**.

girth [gɜːθ] *n* **(a)** (*circumference*) *[tree]* circonférence *f*; *[waist/hips etc]* tour *m* (de taille/de hanches *etc*). **in ~** de circonférence, de tour; **his (great) ~** sa corpulence. **(b)** *[saddle]* sangle *m*. **to loosen the ~s** dessangler.

gist [dʒɪst] *n* (*U*) *[report, conversation etc]* fond *m*, essentiel *m*; *[question]* point principal. **to get the ~ of sth** comprendre l'essentiel de qch; **give me the ~ of what he said** mettez-moi au courant de ce qu'il a dit, en deux mots.

give [gɪv] *pret* **gave**, *ptp* **given** **1** *vt* **(a)** (*bestow, confer*) donner (*to* à); (*as gift*) donner, faire don *or* cadeau de, offrir (*to* à); *honour, title* conférer (*to* à), donner; *help, support* prêter (*to* à); *food, hospitality* donner, offrir; *meal* offrir; (*dedicate*) *one's time, fortune, energies* donner, consacrer (*to* à). **to ~ alms** faire l'aumône; **to ~ sb one's hand** donner *or* tendre la main à qn; (†: *in marriage*) accorder sa main à qn†; **to ~ one's daughter in marriage**† donner sa fille en mariage†; **to ~ sb one's trust** donner sa confiance à qn, reposer sa confiance en qn; **to ~ sb good day**†† souhaiter le bonjour à qn; **one must ~ and take** il faut faire des concessions (*V also* **4**); (*fig*) **he gave as good as he got** il a rendu coup pour coup (*fig*); **to ~ sb something to eat/drink** donner à manger/boire à qn; **can you ~ him something to do?** pouvez-vous lui donner quelque chose à faire?; **what name will you ~ him?** quel nom lui donnerez-vous?; **can you ~ me a bed for the night?** pouvez-vous me loger pour la nuit?; **I wouldn't have it if you gave it to me*** tu m'en ferais cadeau que je n'en voudrais pas; **you've ~n me your cold** tu m'as donné *or* passé ton rhume; **he gave all his free time to golf** il consacrait tout son temps libre au golf; **he gave his life/himself to helping the needy** il a consacré sa vie/il s'est consacré aux nécessiteux; (*Telec*) **~ me Newtown 231** passez-moi le 231 à Newtown; **I'll ~ him something to cry about!*** je lui apprendrai à pleurer!; **to ~ sb what for‡, to ~ it to sb‡** passer un savon à qn‡, faire sa fête à qn‡; **I don't ~ a damn*** *or* **a hoot*** **for culture** la culture j'en ai rien à faire* *or* à foutre‡; **he just doesn't ~ a damn*** il se fiche* *or* se fout‡ de tout; (*US*) **O.K., now ~!‡** allez, crache!‡; *V* **thank, thought** *etc*.

(b) (*grant; cause to have*) donner; *pain, pleasure* occasionner (*to* à); *punishment* infliger (*to* à); *time* donner, laisser (*to* à); *damages* accorder (*to* à). **(God) ~ me strength to do it!** que Dieu me donne la force de le faire!; (*liter*) **it was not ~n to him to achieve happiness** il ne lui fut pas donné de trouver le bonheur; **the judge gave him 5 years** le juge l'a condamné à 5 ans de prison; **the doctors gave him 2 years (to live)** les médecins lui ont donné 2 ans (à vivre); **how long do you ~ that marriage?** combien de temps crois-tu que ce mariage tiendra?; **I can't ~ you any longer, you must pay me now** je ne peux plus vous accorder de délai, il faut que vous payiez (*subj*) maintenant; **I can ~ you half an hour tomorrow** je peux vous consacrer une demi-heure demain; (*in age*) **I can ~ him 10 years** il est de 10 ans mon cadet; (*fig: agreeing*) **I'll ~ you that** je vous accorde cela; **he wants £10? I'll ~ him £10 indeed!** il veut 10 livres? tu penses comme je vais lui donner 10 livres!*; **~ yourself time to think about it before you decide** accordez-vous le temps d'y réfléchir *or* de la réflexion avant de prendre une décision; **~ me time and I'll manage it** laissez-moi du temps et j'y arriverai; **~ me Mozart every time!*** pour moi, rien ne vaut Mozart; *V* **due, ground**[1] *etc*.

(c) (*state, deliver*) donner; *message* remettre (*to* à); *description, particulars* donner, fournir (*to* à). **to ~ sb to understand that ...** donner à qn à entendre que ...; **to ~ sb to believe sth** faire croire *or* faire supposer qch à qn; (*Jur etc*) **to ~ the case for/against sb** décider en faveur de/contre qn; (*Jur*) **~n under my hand and seal** signé et scellé par moi; **what name did he ~?** quel nom a-t-il donné?; (*lit, fig*) **he gave no sign of life** il n'a pas donné signe de vie; **to ~ a decision** donner *or* faire connaître sa décision; (*Jur*) prononcer *or* rendre un arrêt; **~ him my love** faites-lui mes amitiés; *V* **account, evidence, hint** *etc*.

(d) (*pay, exchange*) donner, payer, offrir. **what will you ~ me for it?** combien m'en offrez-vous *or* m'en donnez-vous?; **what did you ~ for it?** combien l'avez-vous payé?; **to ~ one thing in exchange for another** échanger une chose pour *or* contre une autre; **I'd ~ a lot/anything to know** je donnerais gros/n'importe quoi pour savoir.

(e) (*perform etc*) *jump, gesture* faire; *answer, lecture* faire, donner; *sigh, cry, laugh* pousser; (*Theat*) *play* donner, représenter. **to ~ a party/ball** *etc* donner une soirée/un bal *etc*; **to ~ sb a look** jeter *or* lancer un regard à qn; **to ~ sb a blow** porter un coup à qn; **to ~ sb a slap** donner *or* allonger* *or* flanquer* une gifle à qn; **to ~ sb's hand a squeeze** presser la main à qn; **to ~ one's hair a brush** donner un coup de brosse à ses cheveux; **to ~ sb a smile** adresser *or* faire un sourire à qn; **she gave a little smile** elle a eu un petit sourire; **to ~ a recitation** dire des vers; **~ us a song** chantez-nous quelque chose; **~ us a laugh*** faites-nous rire; (*frm*) **I ~ you the Queen!** je lève mon verre à la santé de la Reine!

(f) (*produce, provide, supply*) donner, rendre; *sound* rendre; (*Math etc*) *result, answer* donner. **it ~s 16% per annum** cela rapporte 16% par an; **this lamp ~s a poor light** cette lampe éclaire mal; **5 times 4 ~s 20** 5 fois 4 font *or* égalent 20; **it ~s a total of 100** cela fait 100 en tout; **~ the answer to the 4th decimal place/in pence** donnez la réponse à la 4e décimale/en pence.

(g) **to ~ way** (*break, collapse*) *[building, ceiling]* s'effondrer, s'affaisser; *[ground]* s'affaisser, se dérober; *[plaster]* s'effriter; *[cable, rope, ladder etc]* casser; se rompre; *[legs]* fléchir, mollir; *[health]* s'altérer; (*yield*) *[person]* lâcher pied, céder (*to* devant); (*make room for*) céder la place (*to* à); (*Aut*) céder (la priorité) (*to* à); (*Mil: retreat*) battre en retraite. **my legs are giving way*** mes jambes se dérobent sous moi; **his strength gave way** ses forces lui ont manqué.

2 *vi* (*collapse, yield*) *[road, ground, beam etc]* céder (*to* à, *under* sous); s'affaisser (*under* sous); (*lose firmness*) *[cloth, elastic etc]* prêter, se détendre, se relâcher. **the frost is giving** il commence à dégeler.

3 *n* (*) élasticité *f*, souplesse *f*. **there is not much ~ in this cloth** ce tissu ne prête pas.

4 *cpd*: **give-and-take** concessions mutuelles; **there must be a certain amount of give-and-take in any family** dans toute famille, il faut que chacun fasse des concessions *or* y mette un peu du sien; (*fig*) **giveaway** (*n*) révélation *f* involontaire; (*Comm: free gift*) prime *f*; (*US: Rad, TV*) jeu radiophonique *or* télévisé (*doté de prix*); (*adj*) *price* dérisoire; **it was a real giveaway when he said that ...** il s'est vraiment trahi en disant que ...; **the fact that she knew his name was a giveaway** le simple fait qu'elle sache son nom était révélateur.

give away 1 *vt sep* **(a)** (*bestow, distribute*) *prizes* distribuer; *bride* conduire à l'autel; *money, goods* donner, faire cadeau de. **I'm giving it away** j'en fais cadeau.
(b) (*tell, betray*) *names, details* révéler; *person* dénoncer, trahir, donner*. **to give o.s. away** se trahir, se révéler; **don't give anything away** ne dis rien; **his face gave nothing away** son visage ne trahissait rien; (*fig*) **to give the game** *or* **show away*** vendre la mèche*.
2 giveaway *n, adj V* **give 4.**
give back *vt sep object, health, freedom* rendre (*to* à); *property* restituer (*to* à); *echo* renvoyer; *image* refléter.
give forth *vt sep sound* émettre, faire entendre.
give in 1 *vi* (*yield*) se rendre, renoncer, abandonner, s'avouer vaincu. **to give in to sb** céder à qn; (*in games*) **I give in!** je donne ma langue au chat!*
2 *vt sep parcel, document* remettre; *one's name* donner; *accounts* rendre.
give off *vt sep heat* émettre, dégager; *smell* émettre, exhaler; (*Chem*) *gas* dégager; (*Bot*) *shoots* former.
give on to *vt fus [door, window]* donner sur.
give out 1 *vi [supplies]* s'épuiser, manquer; *[patience]* être à bout; (*) *[car, engine]* tomber en panne. **my strength is giving out** je suis à bout de forces, je n'en peux plus; **my patience gave out** j'ai perdu patience, la patience m'a manqué; **my watch is giving out*** ma montre est en train de rendre l'âme (*hum*).
2 *vt sep* **(a)** (*distribute*) *books, food etc* distribuer.
(b) (*announce*) *news* annoncer, proclamer; *list etc* faire connaître. **it was given out that ...** on annonça que ... .
(c) = **give off.**
give over 1 *vt sep* (*dedicate, devote*) donner, consacrer (*to* à); (*transfer*) affecter (*to* à). **this building is now given over to offices** ce bâtiment est maintenant affecté à des bureaux; **to give o.s. over to** s'adonner à, s'abandonner à; **to give over all one's time to doing** consacrer tout son temps à faire.
2 *vt fus* (*: *stop*) cesser, finir. **to give over doing** cesser de faire, arrêter de faire*; **give over!** arrête!, assez!, finis donc!
give up 1 *vi* abandonner, renoncer. **don't give up!** tenez bon!; **I give up** j'y renonce, je renonce; (*in guessing etc*) je donne ma langue au chat*.
2 *vt sep* **(a)** (*devote*) vouer, consacrer. **to give up one's life to music** vouer *or* consacrer sa vie à la musique; **to give o.s. up to sth** se livrer à qch, se plonger dans qch.
(b) (*renounce, part with*) *friends, interests* abandonner, délaisser; *seat, place* céder; *habit, idea* abandonner, renoncer à; *job* quitter; *appointment* démissionner de; *business* se retirer de; *subscription* cesser. **he'll never give her up** il n'acceptera jamais qu'elle le quitte (*subj*); **to give up doing** renoncer à *or* cesser de faire; **to give up smoking** renoncer au tabac, cesser de fumer; (*fig*) **to give up the game** *or* **the struggle** abandonner la partie; **I gave it up as a bad job** (comme ça ne menait à rien) j'ai laissé tomber*; **she gave him up as a bad job*** comme elle n'arrivait à rien avec lui elle l'a laissé tomber*.
(c) (*deliver, hand over*) *prisoner* livrer (*to* à); *authority* se démettre de; *keys of city etc* rendre. **to give o.s. up** se livrer (*to the police* à la police), se rendre, se constituer prisonnier.
(d) (*abandon hope for*) *patient* condamner; *expected visitor* ne plus attendre, ne plus espérer voir; *problem, riddle* renoncer à (résoudre). **to give sb up for lost** considérer qn comme perdu; **to give o.s. up for lost** se croire perdu.
given ['gɪvn] **1** *ptp of* **give.**
2 *adj* **(a)** donné, déterminé. **at a ~ time** à une heure déterminée, à un moment donné; **of a ~ size** d'une taille donnée *or* bien déterminée; **under the ~ conditions** dans les conditions données *or* requises; (*Scot, US*) **~ name** prénom *m*, nom *m* de baptême.
(b) ~ the triangle ABC soit *or* étant donné le triangle ABC; **~ that he is capable of learning** supposé qu'il soit capable d'apprendre.
(c) (*having inclination*) adonné, enclin (*to* à). **I am not ~ to doing** je n'ai pas l'habitude de faire, je ne suis pas enclin à faire.
giver ['gɪvəʳ] *n* donateur *m*, -trice *f*.
gizzard ['gɪzəd] *n* gésier *m*; *V* **stick.**
glacé ['glæseɪ] *adj* (*Culin*) *fruit* glacé, confit; *cake* recouvert de sucre glace. **~ icing** sucre *m* glace.
glacial ['gleɪsɪəl] *adj* (*Geol*) glaciaire; *wind, winter* glacial; (*Chem*) cristallisé, en cristaux.
glaciated ['gleɪsɪeɪtɪd] *adj* (*Geol*) **~ landscape** relief *m* glaciaire.
glaciation [ˌgleɪsɪ'eɪʃən] *n* glaciation *f*.
glacier ['glæsɪəʳ] *n* glacier *m*.
glad [glæd] *adj person* heureux, content (*of, about* de); *news, occasion* heureux, joyeux. **I am ~ about it** cela me fait plaisir, j'en suis bien content; **I'm ~ (that) you came** je suis ravi que tu sois venu; **I'm ~ to hear it** je suis ravi de l'apprendre; **I shall be ~ to come** je serai heureux de venir; **~ to know you!*** ravi!*, enchanté!, très heureux!; **~ tidings, ~ news** heureuses *or* bonnes nouvelles; (*esp US*) **to give sb the ~ hand:** accueillir qn les bras ouverts; **~ rags:** beaux atours, belles fringues:, belles frusques:; **she's in her ~ rags:** elle est en grand tralala:, elle est sur son trente et un; **to give sb the ~ eye:** faire de l'œil* à qn.
gladden ['glædn] *vt person* rendre heureux; *heart, occasion* réjouir, égayer.
glade [gleɪd] *n* clairière *f*.
gladiator ['glædɪeɪtəʳ] *n* gladiateur *m*.
gladiolus [ˌglædɪ'əʊləs] *n, pl* **gladioli** [ˌglædɪ'əʊlaɪ] glaïeul *m*.
gladly ['glædlɪ] *adv* (*joyfully*) avec joie; (*willingly*) avec plaisir, volontiers, de bon cœur. **will you help me? — ~** voulez-vous m'aider? — volontiers *or* avec plaisir.
gladness ['glædnɪs] *n* joie *f*, contentement *m*.
glamorize ['glæməraɪz] *vt place, event, act etc* montrer *or* présenter sous des couleurs séduisantes.
glamorous ['glæmərəs] *adj spectacle, life* brillant; *production* à grand spectacle; *dress, photo* splendide; *person* séduisant, fascinant; *job* prestigieux.
glamour ['glæməʳ] **1** *n [person]* séductions *fpl*, fascination *f*; *[occasion, situation etc]* prestige *m*, éclat *m*. **the ~ of life in Hollywood** la vie brillante d'Hollywood; **the ~ of being an M.P.** la gloire d'être membre du parlement; **to lend ~ to sth** prêter de l'éclat à qch.
2 *cpd*: **glamour boy*** beau gars*, beau mec:; **glamour girl*** pin-up: *f inv*, beauté *f*.
glance [glɑːns] **1** *n* **(a)** regard *m*, coup *m* d'œil. **at a ~** d'un coup d'œil; **at first ~** au premier coup d'œil, à première vue; **without a backward ~** (*lit*) sans se retourner; (*fig*) sans plus de cérémonies; **to have** *or* **take a ~ at** jeter un coup d'œil sur.
(b) (*gleam*) (*of light*) lueur *f*; (*of metal*) reflet *m*. **a ~ of sunlight** un rayon de soleil.
2 *vi* **(a)** (*look*) jeter un coup d'œil (*at* sur, à), lancer un regard (*at* à). **she ~d in my direction** elle a jeté un coup d'œil vers moi; **she ~d over her shoulder** elle a jeté un coup d'œil par-dessus son épaule; **he ~d over the paper** il a parcouru le journal du regard, il a lu le journal en diagonale*; **he ~d through the book** il a jeté un coup d'œil sur *or* feuilleté le livre.
(b) (*glint*) étinceler.
(c) to ~ off sth *[bullet]* ricocher sur qch; *[arrow, sword]* dévier sur qch.
glance away *vi* détourner le regard.
glance down *vi* jeter un coup d'œil en bas, regarder en bas.
glance off *vi [bullet etc]* ricocher, dévier; *[arrow, sword]* dévier.
glance round *vi* jeter un coup d'œil autour de soi.
glance up *vi* (*raise eyes*) lever les yeux; (*look upwards*) regarder en l'air.
glancing ['glɑːnsɪŋ] *adj* **(a)** *blow* oblique. **(b)** (*glinting*) *metal etc* étincelant.
gland [glænd] *n* glande *f*.
glanders ['glændəz] *n* (*Vet*) morve *f*.
glandular ['glændjʊləʳ] *adj* glandulaire. **~ fever** mononucléose infectieuse.
glare [glɛəʳ] **1** *vi* **(a)** *[person]* lancer un regard furieux *or* de colère (*at* à).
(b) *[sun, lights]* éblouir, briller d'un éclat éblouissant *or* aveuglant.
2 *vt*: **to ~ defiance** *etc* **at sb** lancer un regard plein de défi *etc* à qn.
3 *n* **(a)** *[person]* regard furieux. **'no' he said with a ~** 'non' jeta-t-il avec un regard furieux; **he gave me an angry ~** il m'a jeté un regard furieux.
(b) *[light]* éclat aveuglant, lumière éblouissante; (*Aut*) éblouissement *m*; *[publicity]* feux *mpl*.
glaring ['glɛərɪŋ] *adj light* éblouissant, éclatant; *sun* aveuglant; *colour* hurlant, criard; *eyes* furieux, flamboyant (de colère); *fact, mistake* (plus qu')évident, qui saute aux yeux, qui crève les yeux; *injustice, lie* flagrant.
glass [glɑːs] **1** *n* **(a)** (*U*) verre *m*. **pane of ~** carreau *m*, vitre *f*; **window ~** verre à vitre; *V* **cut, plate** *etc.*
(b) (*tumbler*) verre *m*; (*glassful*) (plein) verre. **a ~ of wine** un verre de vin; **a wine ~** un verre à vin; *V* **balloon, beer, champagne.**
(c) (*U: also* **~ware**) (*gen*) verrerie *f*; (*glasses*) gobeleterie *f*.
(d) (*mirror*) miroir *m*, glace *f*; (*Opt*) lentille *f*; (*magnifying ~*) verre grossissant, loupe *f*; (*telescope*) longue-vue *f*; (*barometer*) baromètre *m*; (*for plants*) cloche *f*, châssis *m*; (*Comm etc*) vitrine *f*. (*Met*) **the ~ is falling** le baromètre baisse; **grown under ~** cultivé sous verre; **object displayed under ~** objet exposé en vitrine; **~es** (*spectacles*) lunettes *fpl*; (*binoculars*) jumelles *fpl*; *V* **sun** *etc.*
2 *vt* (*also* **~ in**) *door, shelves* vitrer; *picture* mettre sous verre.
3 *cpd bottle, ornament* de verre, en verre. **glassblower** verrier *m*, souffleur *m* (de verre); **glassblowing** soufflage *m* (du verre); **glass case** (*Comm*) vitrine *f*; *[clock etc]* globe *m*; **to keep sth in a glass case** garder qch sous verre *or* sous globe; **glasscloth** essuie-verres *m inv*, torchon *m* à verres; **glasscutter** (*tool*) diamant *m*, coupe-verre *m inv*; (*person*) vitrier *m*; **glass door** porte vitrée; **glass eye** œil *m* de verre; **glass factory** = **glassworks**; **glass fibre** (*n*) fibre *f* de verre; (*cpd*) en fibre de verre; **glasshouse** (*Brit: for plants*) serre *f*; (*US: glassworks*) verrerie *f* (*fabrique*); (*Brit Mil sl*) **in the glasshouse** au trou:; (*Prov*) **people in glass houses shouldn't throw stones** critiquer les autres, c'est s'exposer à la critique; **glass industry** industrie *f* du verre, verrerie *f*; (*Brit*) **glasspaper** papier *m* de verre; **glass slipper** pantoufle *f* de verre; **glass wool** laine *f* de verre; **glassworks** verrerie *f* (*fabrique*).
glassful ['glɑːsfʊl] *n* (plein) verre *m*.
glassy ['glɑːsɪ] *adj* semblable au verre, qui ressemble au verre; *substance* vitreux; *surface* uni, lisse; *water, sea* transparent, uni comme un miroir; *eye, look* vitreux, terne. **~-eyed** au regard terne *or* vitreux.
Glaswegian [glæs'wiːdʒjən] **1** *n*: **he's a ~** (*living there*) c'est un habitant de Glasgow, il habite Glasgow; (*born there*) il est originaire de Glasgow. **2** *adj* de Glasgow.
glaucoma [glɔː'kəʊmə] *n* glaucome *m*.
glaucous ['glɔːkəs] *adj* glauque.
glaze [gleɪz] **1** *vt* **(a)** *door, window* vitrer; *picture* mettre sous verre; *V* **double.**
(b) *pottery* vernisser; *tiles* vitrifier, vernisser; *leather* vernir; *cotton etc* satiner, lustrer; *paper, photograph, cake, meat* glacer.

2 *vi* (*also* ~ over) *[eyes]* devenir vitreux *or* terne.
3 *n* **(a)** (*U*) (*on pottery, leather, tiles etc*) vernis *m*; (*on cotton etc*) lustre *m*; (*on paper, photograph*) glacé *m*; (*Culin*) glaçage *m*.
(b) (*substance*) (*for tiles etc*) enduit vitrifié; (*for pottery*) vernis *m*.
(c) (*US: ice*) verglas *m*.

glazed [gleɪzd] *adj door, window etc* vitré; *picture* sous verre; *pottery* émaillé, vernissé; *tiles* vernissé, vitrifié; *leather* glacé, verni; *material* lustré, satiné; *paper, photograph* brillant; *cake, meat* glacé. **his eyes** *or* **he had a ~ look** il avait les yeux ternes *or* vitreux.

glazier [ˈgleɪzɪəʳ] *n* vitrier *m*.

gleam [gliːm] **1** *n* lueur *f*, rayon *m* (de lumière); *[metal]* reflet *m*; *[water]* miroitement *m*. ~ **of hope** lueur d'espoir, rayon d'espérance; ~ **of humour/of intelligence** lueur d'humour/d'intelligence; **she had a dangerous ~ in her eye** il y avait une lueur dangereuse dans ses yeux *or* dans son regard.
2 *vi [lamp, star etc]* luire; *[polished metal, shoes etc]* reluire; *[knife, blade etc]* luire, briller; *[water]* miroiter. **his eyes ~ed with delight/mischief** la joie/la malice luisait dans ses yeux.

gleaming [ˈgliːmɪŋ] *adj lamp, star* brillant; *polished metal, shoes etc* reluisant, brillant; *kitchen* étincelant; *water* miroitant.

glean [gliːn] *vti* (*lit, fig*) glaner.

gleaner [ˈgliːnəʳ] *n* glaneur *m*, -euse *f*.

gleanings [ˈgliːnɪŋz] *npl* glanure(s) *f(pl)*.

glebe [gliːb] *n* (*Rel*) terre attachée à un bénéfice ecclésiastique; (†† *or liter*) terre, glèbe *f* (*liter*).

glee [gliː] *n* **(a)** (*U*) joie *f*, allégresse *f*. **in high ~** jubilant, débordant *or* plein d'allégresse. **(b)** (*Mus*) chant choral à plusieurs voix. ~ **club** chorale *f*.

gleeful [ˈgliːfʊl] *adj* joyeux, allègre, plein d'allégresse.

gleefully [ˈgliːfəlɪ] *adv* joyeusement, allègrement, avec allégresse.

glen [glen] *n* vallée encaissée, vallon *m*; (*steep-sided*) gorge *f*.

glib [glɪb] *adj person* qui a la parole facile, qui a du bagou*; *tongue* délié, affilé; *speech, style* facile, désinvolte; *excuse* désinvolte, spécieux; *lie* désinvolte. **he's very ~** il est beau parleur.

glibly [ˈglɪblɪ] *adv speak* avec aisance, facilement; *reply* sans hésiter; *make excuses, lie* avec désinvolture.

glibness [ˈglɪbnɪs] *n [person]* facilité *f* de parole, bagou* *m*; *[excuses, lies, style etc]* désinvolture *f*.

glide [glaɪd] **1** *vi* **(a)** *[door, drawer]* glisser (en douceur); *[vehicle]* s'avancer en douceur *or* silencieusement; *[person]* circuler à pas feutrés *or* comme en flottant. **to ~ in/out** *etc [waiter etc]* entrer/sortir *etc* silencieusement; *[woman etc]* entrer/sortir *etc* avec grâce; *[car]* entrer/sortir *etc* comme en glissant; **to ~ along** *or* **past** *[person]* passer sans bruit; *[car]* passer en douceur; *[water]* couler; *[time]* s'écouler.
(b) *[birds]* planer; (*Aviat*) planer, faire du vol plané. (*Aviat*) **he ~d down to land** il a atterri en vol plané.
2 *vt* faire glisser, faire avancer sans heurts *or* en douceur.
3 *n* **(a)** glissement *m*; (*Dancing*) glissé *m*, glissade *f*.
(b) (*Mus*) port *m* de voix; (*Gram*) son *m* de transition.
(c) (*Aviat*) vol plané.

glider [ˈglaɪdəʳ] *n* **(a)** (*Aviat*) planeur *m*. ~ **pilot** pilote *m* de planeur. **(b)** (*US: swing*) balançoire *f*.

gliding [ˈglaɪdɪŋ] *n* (*Aviat*) vol plané; (*gen: movement*) glissement *m*.

glimmer [ˈglɪməʳ] **1** *vi [lamp, light, fire]* luire faiblement; *[water]* miroiter; *[sea]* miroiter, brasiller (*liter*). **2** *n [light, candle etc]* faible *or* petite lueur; *[water]* miroitement *m*; (*fig: of hope, intelligence etc*) (faible) lueur.

glimpse [glɪmps] **1** *n* vision rapide *or* momentanée *or* fugitive. **to catch a ~ of** entrevoir *or* entr'apercevoir (un bref instant). **2** *vt* entrevoir *or* entr'apercevoir (un bref instant).

glint [glɪnt] **1** *n [light]* trait *m* de lumière, éclair *m*; *[metal]* reflet *m*. **he had a ~ in his eye** il avait une étincelle *or* une lueur dans le regard. **2** *vi [metal object, glass, wet road]* luire, briller; *[dewdrop]* briller.

glissade [glɪˈseɪd] (*Alpinism*) **1** *n* ramasse *f*. **2** *vi* descendre en ramasse.

glisten [ˈglɪsn] **1** *vi [water]* miroiter, scintiller, chatoyer; *[wet surface]* luire, briller; *[light]* scintiller; *[metal object]* briller, miroiter. **her eyes ~ed (with tears)** ses yeux brillaient (de larmes). **2** *n* miroitement *m*; chatoiement *m*; scintillement *m*.

glister†† [ˈglɪstəʳ] = **glitter.**

glitter [ˈglɪtəʳ] **1** *vi [snow, ice, lights]* scintiller, briller; *[jewel]* chatoyer, rutiler, scintiller; *[water]* miroiter, scintiller. **her eyes ~ed** ses yeux brillaient *or* flambaient de haine (*or* de convoitise *etc*); (*Prov*) **all that ~s is not gold** tout ce qui brille n'est pas or (*Prov*).
2 *n* scintillement *m*; (*fig*) éclat *m*.

glittering [ˈglɪtərɪŋ] *adj* brillant, étincelant, scintillant; (*fig*) éclatant, resplendissant.

gloaming [ˈgləʊmɪŋ] *n* (*liter*) crépuscule *m*. **in the ~** au crépuscule, entre chien et loup.

gloat [gləʊt] *vi* exulter, jubiler*; (*maliciously*) se réjouir avec malveillance (*over, upon* de). **to ~ over** *money, possessions* jubiler à la vue *or* à l'idée de; *beaten enemy* triompher de; **he was ~ing over his success** son succès l'avait fait jubiler; **it's nothing to ~ over** il n'y a pas de quoi se frotter les mains.

glob [glɒb] *n [liquid]* globule *m*; *[clay etc]* petite boule.

global [ˈgləʊbl] *adj* **(a)** (*world-wide*) *peace* universel, mondial. **(b)** (*comprehensive*) *sum, view, method* global, entier. **(c)** (*globe-shaped*) globulaire, en forme de globe.

globe [gləʊb] **1** *n* (*sphere*) globe *m*, sphère *f*; (*with map on it*) globe; (*lampshade etc*) globe; (*fishbowl*) bocal *m*; (*Anat*) globe. **terrestrial/celestial ~** globe terrestre/céleste; (*Geog*) **the ~** le globe, la terre; **all over the ~** sur toute la surface du globe.
2 *cpd*: **globe artichoke** artichaut *m*; **globe lightning** éclair *m* en boule; **globe-trotter** globe-trotter *m*; **globe-trotting** voyages *mpl* à travers le monde.

globular [ˈglɒbjʊləʳ] *adj* **(a)** (*composed of globules*) globuleux. **(b)** (*globe-shaped*) globulaire, en forme de globe, sphérique.

globule [ˈglɒbjuːl] *n* (*Anat*) globule *m*; (*of water etc*) gouttelette *f*.

gloom [gluːm] *n* (*darkness*) obscurité *f*, ténèbres *fpl*; (*melancholy*) mélancolie *f*, tristesse *f*. **to cast a ~ over sth** assombrir qch, jeter une ombre sur qch; **to cast a ~ over sb** rendre qn triste *or* sombre *or* mélancolique, attrister qn; **it was all ~ and doom*** tout était sombre, l'avenir se présentait sous les plus sombres couleurs.

gloomily [ˈgluːmɪlɪ] *adv* tristement, mélancoliquement, d'un air sombre *or* morne *or* lugubre.

gloomy [ˈgluːmɪ] *adj* **(a)** *person, character* sombre, triste, mélancolique, (*stronger*) lugubre; *tone, voice, look* morne, triste, mélancolique, (*stronger*) lugubre; *atmosphere, place* morne, (*stronger*) lugubre; *forecast, future, prospects* sombre; *thoughts* sombre, noir; *weather* sombre, morne. **he took a ~ view of everything** il voyait tout en noir; **to feel ~** avoir des idées noires.
(b) (*dark*) obscur, sombre, ténébreux (*liter*).

glorification [ˌglɔːrɪfɪˈkeɪʃən] *n* glorification *f*.

glorify [ˈglɔːrɪfaɪ] *vt God* glorifier, rendre gloire à; *person* exalter, célébrer, chanter les louanges de; (*fig*) *event, place etc* embellir. **the 'luxury hotel' was nothing but a glorified boarding house** c'était une pension de famille, qualifiée pompeusement d'hôtel de luxe, c'était en fait une pension de famille qui n'avait d'hôtel de luxe que le nom.

glorious [ˈglɔːrɪəs] *adj saint, martyr* glorieux; *person* illustre; *mansion, clothes, view, countryside* magnifique, splendide; *victory* éclatant; *holiday etc* merveilleux, sensationnel*. ~ **deed** action *f* d'éclat; **we had a ~ evening*** nous avons passé une soirée sensationnelle*; (*iro*) **a ~ mess** un joli *or* beau gâchis.

glory [ˈglɔːrɪ] **1** *n* **(a)** (*U*) gloire *f* (*also Rel*); (*magnificence*) splendeur *f*, magnificence *f*, éclat *m*. **to give ~ to God** rendre gloire à Dieu; **Christ in ~** le Christ en majesté *or* en gloire; **the saints in ~** les glorieux *mpl*; **Solomon in all his ~** Salomon dans toute sa gloire; **covered with ~** couvert de gloire; **Rome at the height of its ~** Rome à l'apogée *or* au sommet de sa gloire; **there she was in all her ~*, dressed in gold from head to foot** elle était là dans toute sa splendeur, vêtue d'or de la tête aux pieds; **she was in her ~* as president of the club** elle était tout à fait à son affaire en tant que présidente du club; (*die*) **to go to ~*†** aller ad patres*; ~ **be!*** Seigneur!, grand Dieu!; (*US*) **Old G~*** le drapeau américain.
(b) (*object etc*) gloire *f*. **the church was the village's greatest ~** l'église était le principal titre de gloire du village; **her hair was her greatest** *or* **crowning ~** sa chevelure était sa gloire; **this sonnet is one of the glories of English poetry** ce sonnet est un des fleurons de la poésie anglaise; **the glories of Nature** les splendeurs *fpl* de la nature.
2 *vi*: **to ~ in sth** être très fier de qch. (*iro*) **the café glories in the name of 'The Savoy'** le café porte le nom ronflant de 'Savoy'.
3 *cpd*: **glory hole*** capharnaüm* *m*; (*Naut*) cambuse *f*.

gloss[1] [glɒs] **1** *n* (*shine*) lustre *m*, vernis *m*, brillant *m*, éclat *m*; (*on cloth*) cati *m*. **to take the ~ off** *metal etc* dépolir, délustrer; *cloth* décatir; (*fig*) *event, success* retirer *or* enlever tout son charme *or* attrait à; *victory, compliment* gâcher; **to lose its ~** *[metal etc]* se dépolir, se délustrer; *[cloth]* se décatir; (*fig*) *[event, success]* perdre tout son charme *or* son attrait; *[victory, compliment]* être gâché.
2 *cpd paint* brillant, laqué; *paper* glacé, brillant. **gloss finish** brillant *m*; (*Phot*) glaçage *m*.
3 *vt metal etc* faire briller, polir; *material* catir, lustrer.

gloss[2] [glɒs] **1** *n* (*insertion*) glose *f*; (*note*) commentaire *m*; (*translation*) traduction *f* (interlinéaire); (*interpretation*) paraphrase *f*, interprétation *f*.
2 *vt* commenter, gloser.

gloss over *vt fus* (*play down*) atténuer, glisser sur, passer sur; (*cover up*) dissimuler.

glossary [ˈglɒsərɪ] *n* glossaire *m*, lexique *m*.

glossy [ˈglɒsɪ] **1** *adj fur, material* luisant, lustré; *photograph* glacé; *paint* brillant, laqué; *hair* brillant; *leaves etc* vernissé; *metal* brillant, poli. ~ **magazine** magazine *m* de luxe (*sur papier couché*); ~ **paper** (*Typ*) papier couché; (*esp Phot*) papier brillant *or* glacé.
2 *n*: **the glossies*** les magazines *mpl* de luxe.

glottal [ˈglɒtl] *adj* (*Anat*) glottique; (*Ling*) glottal. (*Ling*) ~ **stop** coup *m* de glotte.

glottis [ˈglɒtɪs] *n* glotte *f*.

glove [glʌv] **1** *n* (*also Baseball, Boxing*) gant *m*. **to put on one's ~s** mettre *or* enfiler ses gants; **to take off one's ~s** enlever *or* retirer ses gants; **he had ~s on** il portait des gants, il avait mis des gants; (*fig*) **the ~s are off!** j'y vais (*or* il y va *etc*) sans gants! *or* sans prendre de gants!; *V* **fit, hand, kid.**
2 *vt* ganter. **~d hand** main gantée; **white-~d hand** main gantée de blanc.
3 *cpd*: (*Aut*) **glove compartment** vide-poches *m inv*, boîte *f* à gants; **glove factory** ganterie *f* (*fabrique*); **glove maker** gantier *m*, -ière *f*; **glove puppet** marionnette *f* (à gaine); **glove shop** ganterie *f* (*magasin*).

glover [ˈglʌvəʳ] *n* gantier *m*, -ière *f*.

glow [gləʊ] **1** *vi [coal, fire]* rougeoyer; *[sky]* rougeoyer, s'embraser; *[metal]* luire rouge, être incandescent; *[cigarette end, lamp]* luire; *[colour, jewel]* rutiler; *[complexion, face]* rayonner; *[eyes]* rayonner, flamboyer. **her cheeks ~ed** elle avait les joues en feu; **he was ~ing with health** il était florissant (de santé); (*fig*) **to ~ with enthusiasm/love** *etc* brûler d'enthousiasme/d'amour *etc*; **~ing with admiration** transporté d'admiration; **a walk in the cold makes your body ~** une marche par temps froid vous fouette le sang; **the compliment made her ~ (with pleasure)** le compliment la rendit radieuse.

2 *n [coal, fire]* rougeoiement *m*; *[metal]* rougeoiement, incandescence *f*; *[sun]* feux *mpl*, embrasement *m*; *[complexion, skin]* éclat *m*; *[colour, jewel]* éclat; *[lamp]* lueur *f*; *[passion]* feu *m*; *[youth]* ardeur *f*. **a ~ of enthusiasm** un élan d'enthousiasme.

3 *cpd*: **glow-worm** ver luisant.

glower ['glaʊər] 1 *vi*: **to ~ at sb/sth** lancer à qn/qch des regards mauvais *or* noirs, regarder qn/qch de travers; **he sat there ~ing silently** il était assis là en silence, jetant à la ronde des regards mauvais *or* noirs. 2 *n* regard noir.

glowering ['glaʊərɪŋ] *adj look* hostile, mauvais, noir; *person* à l'air mauvais *or* hostile.

glowing ['gləʊɪŋ] *adj coals, fire* rougeoyant; *sky* rougeoyant, embrasé; *colour, jewel* rutilant; *lamp, cigarette end* luisant; *eyes* brillant, flamboyant, de braise; *complexion, skin* rayonnant, éclatant; *person* florissant (de santé); *style, words etc* chaleureux. **to give a ~ account/description of sth** raconter/décrire qch en termes chaleureux *or* avec enthousiasme; (*fig*) **to paint sth in ~ colours** présenter qch en rose.

gloxinia [glɒk'sɪnɪə] *n* gloxinia *m*.

glucose ['glu:kəʊs] *n* glucose *m*.

glue [glu:] 1 *n* colle *f*, glu *f*; *V* **sniff**.

2 *vt* coller (*to, on* à). **to ~ sth together** recoller qch; **you must ~ down the envelope** il faut que tu colles (*subj*) l'enveloppe; **it's broken off! — ~ it back on then!** c'est cassé! — eh bien! recolle-le!; (*fig*) **her face was ~ed to the window** son visage était collé au carreau (de la fenêtre); **to keep one's eyes ~d to sb/sth*** avoir les yeux fixés sur qn/qch, ne pas détacher les yeux de qn/qch; **he stood there ~d to the spot*** il était là comme s'il avait pris racine; **he was ~d to the television all evening*** il est resté cloué devant la télévision toute la soirée.

gluey ['glu:ɪ] *adj* gluant, collant, poisseux.

glum [glʌm] *adj person, face* mélancolique, triste, (*stronger*) lugubre; *appearance* triste, morne, sombre; *thoughts* noir. **to feel ~** avoir des idées noires, avoir le cafard.

glumly ['glʌmlɪ] *adv walk, shake one's head* d'un air triste; *answer* d'un ton *or* d'une voix triste; *look, inspect* d'un œil *or* d'un regard morne.

glut [glʌt] 1 *vt* rassasier, gaver, gorger; (*Comm*) *the market* surcharger, embouteiller (*with* de). **~ted with food** repu, gavé (de nourriture); **~ted with pleasure** rassasié *or* gavé de plaisirs.

2 *n [appetite etc]* rassasiement *m*; *[foodstuffs, goods]* surplus *m*, excès *m*, surabondance *f*. **a ~ on the market** un surplus *or* un excès *or* une surabondance sur le marché; **there is a ~ of ...** il y a surplus *or* excès *or* surabondance de ... .

glutamic [glu:'tæmɪk] *adj*: **~ acid** acide *m* glutamique.

gluten ['glu:tən] 1 *n* gluten *m*. 2 *cpd*: **gluten-free** sans gluten.

glutenous ['glu:tənəs] *adj* glutineux.

glutinous ['glu:tɪnəs] *adj* visqueux, gluant.

glutton ['glʌtn] *n* glouton(ne) *m(f)*, gourmand(e) *m(f)*. (*fig*) **to be a ~ for work** être un bourreau de travail; **he's a ~ for punishment** c'est un masochiste (*fig*).

gluttonous ['glʌtənəs] *adj* glouton, gourmand, goulu.

gluttony ['glʌtənɪ] *n* gloutonnerie *f*, gourmandise *f*.

glycerin(e) [,glɪsə'ri:n] *n* glycérine *f*.

glycerol ['glɪsərɒl] *n* glycérine *f*, glycérol *m*.

glycin(e) ['glaɪsi:n] *n* glycine *f*.

glycogen ['glaɪkəʊdʒen] *n* glycogène *m*.

glycol ['glaɪkɒl] *n* glycol *m*.

gnarled [nɑ:ld] *adj wood, hand* noueux.

gnash [næʃ] *vt*: **to ~ one's teeth** grincer des dents.

gnat [næt] *n* moucheron *m*.

gnaw [nɔ:] 1 *vi* ronger. **to ~ at** *or* **on a bone** ronger un os; **the rat had ~ed through the chair-leg** le rat avait coupé le pied de la chaise à force de ronger.

2 *vt bone etc* ronger. (*fig*) **~ed by hunger** tenaillé par la faim; **~ed by remorse** rongé par le remords.

gnaw away, gnaw off *vt sep* ronger.

gnawing ['nɔ:ɪŋ] *adj sound* comme une bête qui ronge; (*fig*) *remorse, anxiety etc* torturant, tenaillant; *hunger* dévorant, tenaillant; *pain* harcelant. **I had a ~ feeling that something had been forgotten** j'étais tenaillé par le sentiment qu'on avait oublié quelque chose.

gneiss [naɪs] *n* gneiss *m*.

gnome [nəʊm] *n* gnome *m*, lutin *m*. (*Fin: fig*) **the G~s of Zurich** les gnomes de Zurich.

gnomic ['nəʊmɪk] *adj* gnomique.

gnostic ['nɒstɪk] *adj, n* gnostique (*m*).

gnu [nu:] *n* gnou *m*.

go [gəʊ] *3rd person sg* **goes**, *pret* **went**, *ptp* **gone** 1 *vi* (a) (*proceed, travel, move*) aller, se rendre (*to* à, en, *from* de); *[vehicle]* aller, rouler. **to ~ to France/to Canada/to London** aller en France/au Canada/à Londres; **to ~ for a walk** (aller) se promener, (aller) faire une promenade; **to ~ on a journey** faire un voyage; **to ~ up/down the hill** monter/descendre la colline; **to ~ fishing/shooting** aller à la pêche/à la chasse; **to ~ riding** faire du cheval *or* de l'équitation, monter (à cheval); **to ~ swimming** faire de la natation, (aller) nager; **to ~ looking for sth** aller *or* partir à la recherche de qch; **we can talk as we ~** nous pouvons parler chemin faisant *or* en chemin; **what shall I ~ in?** qu'est-ce que je mets *or* vais mettre pour y aller?; **~ after him!** suivez-le!, poursuivez-le!; **there he ~es!** le voilà (qui passe)!; **there he ~es again!** (*there he is*) le voilà qui repasse!; (*fig: he's at it again*) le voilà qui recommence!; **here ~es!*** allez, on y va!; (*Mil*) **who ~es there?** qui va là?, qui vive?; **you ~ first** passe devant, vas-y le premier; **you ~ next** à toi après; (*in games etc*) **whose turn is it to ~?** à qui le tour?; **~ and shut the door** va fermer la porte; **~ and get me it** va me le chercher; **don't ~ doing that!, don't ~ and do that!** ne va pas faire ça!, ne fais pas ça!; **don't ~ and say ...** ne va pas dire ...; **you've gone and torn my dress!** il a fallu que tu déchires (*subj*) ma robe!; **she went and broke a cup** elle a trouvé le moyen de casser une tasse; **to ~ to do sth** aller faire qch; **the child went to his mother** l'enfant est allé vers sa mère; **she went to the headmaster** elle est allée voir *or* trouver le directeur; **to ~ to the doctor** aller voir le médecin; **to ~ to sb for sth** aller demander qch à qn; aller trouver qn pour avoir qch; **the train ~es at 90 km/h** le train fait (du) *or* roule à 90 km/h; **the train ~es from London to Glasgow** le train va de Londres à Glasgow; **we had gone only 3 km** nous n'avions fait que 3 km; **I wouldn't ~ as far as to say that** je n'irais pas jusqu'à dire cela; **that's ~ing too far!** c'est un peu poussé!, il y a de l'exagération!, il y a de l'abus!; **you've gone too far!** tu exagères!, tu as été trop loin!; (*at auction*) **I went up to £100 but didn't get it** je suis monté jusqu'à 100 livres mais je ne l'ai pas eu; (*in buying*) **I'll ~ as high as £100** j'irai *or* je mettrai jusqu'à 100 livres; *V* **far, place, school**[1] *etc.*

(b) (*depart*) partir, s'en aller; (*disappear*) disparaître; (*euph: die*) s'éteindre (*euph*), disparaître (*euph*); *[time]* passer, s'écouler; (*be dismissed*) s'en aller; (*be abolished*) être aboli *or* supprimé, disparaître; (*be sold*) se vendre; (*be finished*) *[money]* disparaître, filer; *[strength]* manquer; *[hearing, sight etc]* baisser. **his health is ~ing** il n'a plus la santé*, sa santé se détériore; **his mind is ~ing** (*losing ability*) il commence à baisser, il n'a plus toute sa tête *or* toutes ses facultés; (*losing reason*) il perd l'esprit *or* la raison; **my hat has gone** mon chapeau n'est plus là; **the coffee has all gone** il n'y a plus de café; **the trees have been gone for years** cela fait des années qu'il n'y a plus d'arbres; **he is gone** (*lit*) il est parti; (*euph: dead*) il n'est plus; **after I ~ or have gone** (*lit*) après mon départ; (*euph: death*) après ma mort, quand je ne serai plus là (*euph*); **gone are the days when** le temps n'est plus où; **we (or I etc) must ~ or must be ~ing** il faut partir; (*Sport*) **~!** partez!; (*fig*) **from the word ~** dès le départ, dès le commencement; (*hum*) **how ~es the time?** quelle heure est-il?; (*US*) **it's ~ing on 3** il va être 3 heures; **to let sb ~** (*allow to leave*) laisser partir qn; (*stop gripping*) lâcher qn; **to let ~ or leave ~** lâcher prise; **let ~!, leave ~!** lâchez!; **to let ~ or leave ~ of sth/sb** lâcher qch/qn; **to let o.s. ~** (*lose control of o.s.*) se laisser aller; (*burst into tears*) se laisser aller à pleurer; (*lose interest in one's appearance etc*) se laisser aller, se négliger; **they have let their garden ~** ils ont laissé leur jardin à l'abandon; **I've let my music ~ as I've been so busy** j'ai eu trop à faire et je n'ai pas travaillé (à) ma musique; **to ~ to the bad** mal tourner; **to ~ to ruin** tomber en ruine(s); **we'll let it ~ at that** ça ira comme ça; **you're wrong, but let it ~** vous avez tort, mais passons; (†† *or hum*) **be gone!** partez!, allez-vous-en!; **he'll have to ~** il va falloir se débarrasser de lui; **'X must ~!' 'à bas X!'**; **luxuries will have to ~** il va falloir se priver *or* se passer de tout ce qui est luxe; **it was ~ing cheap** cela se vendait à bas prix; **~ing, ~ing, gone!** une fois, deux fois, adjugé!; (*fig*) **7 down and 3 to ~** 7 de faits il n'en reste plus que 3; *V* **here, ready, song, west** *etc.*

(c) (*start up*) *[car]* partir; *[machine]* démarrer; (*function*) *[machine, watch, car etc]* marcher, fonctionner. **to ~ by steam** marcher à la vapeur; **it ~es on petrol** ça marche *or* fonctionne à l'essence; *[machine, engine]* **to be ~ing** marcher, être en marche; **to set or get ~ing** *machine* mettre en marche, faire démarrer; *work, business* mettre en train; **to keep ~ing** *[person]* se maintenir en activité, continuer ses activités; *[business]* se maintenir à flot; *[machine]* continuer à marcher, marcher toujours; **he's not well but he manages to keep ~ing** il n'est pas en bonne santé mais il se maintient *or* se défend*; **to keep a factory ~ing** maintenir une usine en activité; **to keep the fire ~ing** entretenir le feu; **she needs these pills/his friendship to keep her ~ing** elle a besoin de ces pilules/de son amitié pour tenir le coup; **this medicine/prospect etc kept her ~ing** elle a tenu le coup grâce à ce médicament/à cette perspective *etc*; **to keep sb ~ing in food/money etc** donner à qn ce qu'il lui faut de nourriture/d'argent *etc*; **to make the party ~** animer la soirée; **to get things ~ing** faire démarrer les choses; **to make things ~** faire marcher les choses, mener les choses rondement; **to get ~ing on or with sth** commencer à *or* se mettre à faire qch, s'attaquer à qch; **once he gets ~ing ...** une fois lancé ... .

(d) (*progress*) aller, marcher*; (*turn out*) *[events]* se passer, se développer, se dérouler, se présenter; *[contest]* aboutir; *[judgment]* être rendu *or* prononcé. **how did your holiday ~?** comment se sont passées tes vacances?; **the evening went very well** la soirée s'est très bien passée; **the project was ~ing well** le projet marchait bien *or* était en bonne voie; **how's it ~ing?**, (*hum*) **how ~es it?** (comment) ça va?*; **the decision went in his favour** la décision lui a été favorable; **how does the story ~?** comment c'est* cette histoire?; **the tune ~es like this** voici *or* écoutez l'air; **let's wait and see how things ~** attendons de voir ce qui va se passer *or* comment cjp6a va tourner*; **as things ~** dans l'état actuel des choses; **I don't know how things will ~** je ne sais pas comment les choses vont tourner*; **I hope that all will ~ well** j'espère que tout ira bien; **all went well for him until ...** tout a bien marché *or* s'est bien passé pour lui jusqu'à ce que ...; *V* **bomb, clockwork, strong** *etc.*

(e) (*be, become*) devenir, se faire. **the children went in rags** les enfants étaient en haillons; **he must not ~ unpunished** il ne faut pas qu'il s'en tire (*subj*) sans châtiment; **to ~ armed** porter une arme; **to ~ red** rougir; **the constituency went Labour at the last election** aux dernières élections la circonscription est passée aux travaillistes; we never went short nous n'avons jamais manqué du nécessaire; to ~ short of manquer de; *V* free, piece, sick *etc.*

(f) (*be about to, intend to*) to be ~ing to do aller faire, être sur le point de faire, avoir l'intention de faire; I'm ~ing to do it tomorrow je vais le faire demain; it's ~ing to rain il va pleuvoir; I was just ~ing to do it j'allais le faire, j'étais sur le point de le faire; I was ~ing to do it yesterday but he stopped me j'allais le faire *or* j'étais sur le point de le faire *or* j'avais l'intention de le faire hier mais il m'en a empêché; I was ~ing to do it yesterday but I forgot j'allais le faire hier *or* j'avais l'intention de le faire hier mais j'ai oublié; I'm ~ing to do as I please je ferai *or* je vais faire ce qu'il me plaira.

(g) (*be current, be accepted*) *[story, rumour]* circuler, passer; *[money]* avoir cours. the story *or* rumour ~es that ... le bruit court que ...; anything ~es these days* tout est permis de nos jours; that ~es without saying cela va sans dire; what he says ~es c'est lui qui fait la loi, tout le monde fait ce qu'il dit; what I say ~es! faites ce que je dis!; that ~es for me too (*that applies to me*) cela s'applique à moi aussi; (*I agree with that*) je suis (aussi) de cet avis.

(h) (*break, yield*) *[rope, cable]* céder; *[fuse]* sauter; *[lamp, bulb]* sauter, griller*; *[material]* s'user. the skirt went at the seams la jupe a craqué aux coutures; this jacket has gone at the elbows cette veste est percée aux coudes; there ~es another button! voilà encore un bouton de sauté!

(i) (*extend or cover a certain distance*) aller, s'étendre. the garden ~es as far as the river le jardin va *or* s'étend jusqu'à la rivière; (*fig*) as far as that ~es pour ce qui est de cela; this book is good, as far as it ~es c'est un bon livre, compte tenu de ses limites; he's not bad, as boys ~ il n'est pas trop mal, pour un garçon; it's a fairly good garage as garages ~ comme garage cela peut aller *or* ce n'est pas trop mal; money does not ~ very far nowadays l'argent ne va pas loin aujourd'hui; a pound note does not ~ very far on ne va pas loin avec un billet d'une livre; the difference between them ~es deep il y a une profonde différence entre eux; *V* expense, length, trouble *etc.*

(j) (*have recourse*) avoir recours (*to* à); *V* country, law, war.

(k) (*be placed, contained, arranged*) aller, se mettre, se ranger. 4 into 12 ~es 3 times 12 divisé par 4 égale 3; 2 won't ~ exactly into 11 11 n'est pas exactement divisible par 2; 4 into 3 won't ~ 3 divisé par 4 (il) n'y va pas; the books ~ in that cupboard les livres se rangent *or* se mettent *or* vont dans ce placard-là; where does this box ~? où est-ce que l'on met cette boîte?; this screw ~es here cette vis va là.

(l) *[prize, reward etc]* aller, être donné (*to* à); *[inheritance]* passer (*to* à).

(m) (*be available*) are there any houses ~ing? y-a-t-il des maisons à vendre?, trouve-t-on des maisons (à acheter)?; are there any jobs ~ing? trouve-t-on du travail, y a-t-il des postes vacants?, peut-on trouver du travail?; is there any coffee ~ing? est-ce qu'il y a du café?; I'll have what's ~ing donnez-moi *or* je prendrai de ce qu'il y a.

(n) (*contribute*) contribuer, servir (*to* à). that will ~ to make him happy cela contribuera à son bonheur *or* à le rendre heureux; it only ~es to show that ... cela sert à vous montrer que ..., cela montre bien que ...; it only ~es to show! ça fait la preuve!; the qualities that ~ to make a great man les qualités qui font un grand homme; the money will ~ towards a new car on mettra l'argent de côté pour une nouvelle auto.

(o) (*make specific sound or movement*) faire; *[bell, clock]* sonner. ~ like that with your left foot faites comme ça du pied gauche; to ~ bang faire 'pan'; he went 'psst' 'psst' fit-il.

2 *vt*: the car was fairly ~ing it* la voiture roulait *or* filait à une bonne vitesse; he was fairly ~ing it* (*driving fast*) il allait bon train, il filait à toute allure; (*working hard*) il travaillait d'arrache-pied; (*having fun*) il faisait la noce*; to ~ it alone (*gen*) se débrouiller tout seul; (*Pol etc*) faire cavalier seul; to ~ one better faire (*or* dire) mieux (*than sb* que qn); (*Cards*) he went 3 spades il a annoncé *or* demandé *or* dit 3 piques; (*Gambling*) he went £10 on the red il a misé 10 livres sur le rouge; I can only ~ £5 je ne peux mettre que 5 livres; I could ~ a beer‡ je m'enverrais‡ bien une bière; *V* bail[1], half, share *etc.*

3 *n, pl* ~es (a) (*U: energy*) dynamisme *m*, entrain *m*, allant *m*. to be full of ~ être plein d'énergie, avoir beaucoup de dynamisme; there's no ~ about him il n'a aucun ressort, il est mou comme une chiffe*.

(b) to be always on the ~ être toujours sur la brèche *or* en mouvement; to keep sb on the ~ ne pas laisser souffler qn; he has 2 books on the ~ at the moment il a 2 livres en train en ce moment; it's all ~!* ça n'arrête pas!

(c) (*attempt*) coup *m*, essai *m*, tentative *f*. to have a ~ essayer, tenter le coup; to have a ~ at sth essayer de faire qch; to have another ~ faire une nouvelle tentative, ressayer; have another ~! encore un coup!*; at one *or* a ~ d'un seul coup, d'un seul trait; (*in games*) it's your ~ c'est à toi (de jouer).

(d) (*Med**: *attack*) accès *m*, attaque *f*.

(e) (*: *event, situation*) that was a queer ~ c'était une drôle d'histoire; that was a near ~ on l'a échappé belle, il s'en est fallu de peu; what a ~! quelle affaire!, quelle histoire!

(f) (*success*) to make a ~ of sth réussir qch; no ~!* rien à faire!; it's all the ~* ça fait fureur, c'est le dernier cri.

4 *adj* (*: *esp Space*) paré (à démarrer), en bon état de marche *or* de fonctionnement. all systems are ~ tout est O.K.; you are ~ for (moon-) landing vous êtes 'bon' *or* vous êtes 'go' *or* vous avez le feu vert pour l'alunissage.

5 *cpd*: go-ahead (*adj*) *person, government* dynamique, entreprenant, plein d'allant, qui va de l'avant; *business, attitude* dynamique; (*n*) to give sb the go-ahead (for sth/to do)* donner à qn le feu vert (pour qch/pour faire); go-between intermédiaire *mf*; to give sth/sb the go-by* laisser tomber qch/qn; go-cart (*vehicle: also* go-kart) kart *m*; (*toy*) chariot *m* (*que se construisent les enfants*); (*handcart*) charrette *f*; (*pushchair*) poussette *f*; (*baby-walker*) trotteur *m*, trotte-bébé *m inv*; (*esp US*) go-getter* arriviste *mf*, ambitieux *m*, -euse *f*; (*Brit*) go-slow (strike) grève perlée.

go about 1 *vi* (a) circuler, aller (çà et là). *[sick person]* to be going about again être de nouveau sur pied; he goes about in a Rolls il roule *or* circule en Rolls; they go about in gangs ils vont *or* circulent en *or* par bandes; he's going about with an unpleasant set of people il fréquente des gens peu recommandables; she's going about with Paul now elle sort avec Paul en ce moment.

(b) *[rumour]* courir, se répandre.

(c) (*Naut: change direction*) virer de bord.

2 *vt fus* (a) (*set to work at*) *task, duties* se mettre à, vaquer à. he knows how to go about it il sait s'y prendre; we must go about it carefully nous devons y aller *or* nous y prendre avec précaution; how does one go about getting seats? comment doit-on s'y prendre *or* comment fait-on pour avoir des places?

(b) (*be occupied with*) *affairs, business* s'occuper de. to go about one's normal work vaquer à ses occupations habituelles.

go across *vt fus river, road* traverser, passer de l'autre côté de.

go after *vt fus*: to go after a girl faire la cour à *or* courir après* une fille; to go after a job essayer d'obtenir un emploi, viser un poste; he went after first prize il a essayé d'avoir *or* il a visé le premier prix.

go against *vt fus* (a) (*prove hostile to*) *[luck, events etc]* tourner contre, être hostile *or* contraire à; *[appearance, evidence]* militer contre, nuire à, être préjudiciable à. the decision went against him la décision lui a été défavorable, la décision a été prise contre lui; if fate goes against us si la fortune nous est contraire; this behaviour will go against his chances of promotion cette conduite nuira à ses chances de promotion.

(b) (*oppose*) (*fig*) to go against the tide aller contre le courant; to go against public opinion aller à l'encontre de *or* heurter l'opinion publique; to go against sb's wishes aller contre *or* contrarier les désirs de qn; it goes against my conscience ma conscience s'y oppose; *V* grain.

go along *vi* aller, avancer. I'll tell you as we go along je vous le dirai chemin faisant *or* en cours de route *or* en chemin; (*lit*) to go along with sb aller avec qn, accompagner qn; (*fig*) I don't go along with you on that là, je ne vous suis pas; I can't go along with that at all je ne suis pas du tout d'accord là-dessus, je suis tout à fait contre*; no one will mind if you go along too personne n'y verra d'objection si vous y allez aussi; (*fig*) I check as I go along je vérifie au fur et à mesure.

go around *vi* = go about 1a, 1b.

go at *vt fus* (*attack*) *person* attaquer, se jeter sur; (*undertake*) *task* s'attaquer à. he went at it with a will il s'y est mis *or* attaqué avec acharnement; he was still going at it 3 hours later il était toujours à la tâche 3 heures plus tard.

go away *vi* partir, s'en aller. he's gone away with my keys il est parti avec mes clefs; don't go away with the idea that* ... n'allez pas penser que ... .

go back *vi* (a) (*return*) revenir, retourner, s'en retourner. to go back on one's steps revenir sur ses pas, rebrousser chemin; to go back to a subject revenir sur un sujet; to go back to the beginning recommencer.

(b) (*retreat*) reculer.

(c) (*in time*) remonter. my memory doesn't go so far back ma mémoire ne remonte pas si loin; the family goes back to the Norman Conquest la famille remonte à la conquête normande.

(d) (*revert*) revenir (*to* à). I don't want to go back to coal fires je ne veux pas en revenir aux feux de charbon; to go back to one's former habits retomber dans ses anciennes habitudes; he's gone back to childhood il est retombé en enfance.

(e) (*extend*) s'étendre. the garden goes back to the river le jardin s'étend jusqu'à la rivière; the cave goes back 300 metres la grotte a 300 mètres de profondeur.

go back on *vt fus decision* revenir sur; *promise* revenir sur, se dédire de, manquer à; *friend* trahir, faire faux bond à.

go before *vi* (a) aller au devant. all that has gone before tout ce qui s'est passé avant.

(b) (*euph: die*) to be gone before être mort *or* disparu.

go below *vi* (*Naut*) descendre dans l'entrepont.

go by 1 *vi [person]* passer; *[period of time]* (se) passer, s'écouler. we've let the opportunity go by nous avons manqué *or* raté *or* laissé échapper l'occasion; as time goes by à mesure que le temps passe, avec le temps.

2 *vt fus* (*base judgment or decision on*) juger d'après, (se) fonder sur; (*be guided by*) suivre, se régler sur. that's nothing to go by ce n'est pas une preuve*, on ne peut rien fonder là-dessus; I'll go by what he does je ferai comme lui; I go by what I'm told je me fonde sur ce qu'on me dit; you can never go by what he says on ne peut jamais se fonder sur *or* se fier à ce qu'il dit; to go by appearances juger d'après *or* selon les apparences; to go by the instructions suivre les instructions; the only thing to go by la seule chose qui puisse nous guider *or* sur laquelle nous puissions nous baser, le seul indice sérieux que nous ayons.

3 go-by *n V* go 5.

go down *vi* (a) (*descend*) descendre.

(b) (*fall*) *[person]* tomber; *[building]* s'écrouler; *V* knee, nine.

(c) (*sink*) *[ship]* couler, sombrer; *[person]* couler, disparaître (*sous les flots*). (*Naut*) to go down by the bows sombrer par l'avant.

(d) (*Brit Univ*) *[student]* (*go on holiday*) terminer (le trimestre), partir en vacances; (*finish studies*) terminer (ses études), quitter l'université. **the university goes down on June 20th** les vacances universitaires commencent le 20 juin.

(e) (*set*) *[sun, moon]* se coucher.

(f) (*be swallowed*) **to go down the wrong way** passer de travers; **it went down the wrong way** j'ai (*or* il a *etc*) avalé de travers; **the cake just won't go down** le gâteau n'arrive pas à descendre.

(g) (*be accepted, approved*) être accepté, plaire. **that won't go down with me** ça ne prend pas avec moi, je n'avalerai pas ça*; **to go down well/badly** être bien/mal reçu; **his speech didn't go down at all in Exeter** son discours a été très mal reçu à Exeter; **he didn't go down at all well in Exeter** il n' a pas été du tout apprécié à Exeter.

(h) (*become calmer*) *[wind, storm]* baisser, tomber; (*become lower*) *[tide]* descendre; *[floods, temperature]* baisser, s'abaisser; (*diminish*) diminuer; *[value, price]* baisser. **the picture has gone down in value** le tableau a perdu de sa valeur; **this neighbourhood has gone down** ce quartier n'est plus ce qu'il était.

(i) (*be defeated, fail*) s'incliner (*to* devant), être battu (*to* par); (*Bridge*) chuter; (*fail examination*) échouer, être refusé, se faire coller* (*in* en). (*Ftbl*) **Spain went down to Scotland 2-1** l'Espagne s'est inclinée devant l'Écosse par 2 à 1.

(j) (*Theat*) *[curtain]* tomber. **when the curtain goes down** au tomber du rideau, quand le rideau tombe.

(k) (*go as far as*) aller, continuer. **go down to the bottom of the page** continuez jusqu'au bas de la page; **this history book goes down to the present day** ce livre d'histoire va jusqu'à nos jours.

(l) *[balloon, tyre]* se dégonfler; *[swelling]* désenfler, (se) dégonfler.

(m) (*be noted, remembered*) être noté, être pris par écrit. **to go down to posterity** passer à la postérité; *[event, day, decision]* **it will go down in history** ce sera historique; **he will go down in history for what he did then** il entrera dans l'histoire pour ce qu'il a fait là.

(n) (*become ill*) **to go down with flu** attraper la grippe.

(o) (*Mus: lower pitch*) **can you go down a bit?** vous ne pouvez pas chanter (*or* jouer) un peu plus bas?

go for *vt fus* **(a)** (*attack*) *person* tomber sur, fondre sur, s'élancer sur; (*verbally*) s'en prendre à; (*in newspaper*) attaquer. **they went for each other** (*physically*) ils en sont venus aux coups, ils se sont empoignés; (*verbally*) ils ont eu une prise de bec*; (*to dog*) **go for him!** mors-le!

(b) (*: *admire*) *person, object* s'enticher de, se toquer de:. **he rather goes for that** il adore ça*; **I don't go much for television** la télévision ne me dit pas grand-chose.

(c) (*strive for*) essayer d'avoir; (*choose*) choisir.

go forth *vi* (*liter, frm*) **(a)** *[person]* sortir.

(b) *[order]* paraître, être promulgué. **the order went forth that ...** il fut décrété que ... .

go forward *vi [person, vehicle]* avancer. (*fig*) **they let the suggestion go forward that ...** ils ont transmis la proposition que ... .

go in *vi* **(a)** (*enter*) entrer, rentrer. **I must go in now** il faut que je rentre (*subj*) maintenant; **go in and win!** (allez,) bonne chance!; **what time does the theatre go in?** à quelle heure commence la pièce?; **the troops are going in tomorrow** les troupes attaquent demain.

(b) *[sun, moon]* (*behind clouds*) se cacher (*behind* derrière).

go in for *vt fus* (*fig*) **(a)** *examination* se présenter à; *appointment* poser sa candidature à, être candidat à; *competition, race* prendre part à.

(b) *sport, hobby* pratiquer, s'adonner à, faire; *style, idea, principle, cause* adopter; *lectures* s'inscrire à, suivre; *profession* entrer dans, se consacrer à; *politics* s'occuper de, se mêler de, faire. **she goes in for tennis/painting** *etc* elle fait du tennis/de la peinture *etc*; **I don't go in for bright colours** je ne suis pas (très) porté sur les couleurs vives, je n'aime pas beaucoup les couleurs vives; **we don't go in for that sort of thing here** nous n'aimons pas beaucoup ce genre de chose ici; **he doesn't go in much for reading** il ne s'intéresse pas beaucoup à la lecture; **he's going in for science** il va se spécialiser dans les sciences, il va faire des sciences; **he's going in for vegetables** *[grower]* il va cultiver *or* il va faire* des légumes; *[merchant]* il va vendre des légumes, il va faire* les légumes.

go into *vt fus* **(a)** (*join, take up*) entrer à *or* dans; *V* **church, parliament** *etc.*

(b) (*embark on*) (se mettre à) donner, se lancer dans. **he went into a long explanation** il s'est lancé *or* embarqué dans une longue explication; **let's not go into that now** laissons cela pour le moment; **to go into fits of laughter** être pris de fou rire; *V* **action, decline, detail, hysterics** *etc.*

(c) (*investigate*) examiner, étudier. **to go into a question closely** approfondir une question; **this matter is being gone into** on s'occupe de *or* on étudie cette affaire, cette affaire est à l'étude.

(d) (*begin to wear*) (se mettre à) porter. **she goes into woollen stockings in September** elle se met à porter des bas en laine en septembre; *V* **mourning.**

go in with *vt fus* se joindre à (*in* dans, *to do* pour faire). **she went in with her sister to buy the present** elle s'est mise* *or* cotisée avec sa sœur pour acheter le cadeau.

go off 1 *vi* **(a)** (*leave*) partir, s'en aller; (*Theat*) quitter la scène. **to go off with sth** enlever *or* emporter qch; **to go off with sb** partir avec qn; **they went off together** ils sont partis ensemble; *V* **deep.**

(b) *[gun]* partir. **it didn't go off** le coup n'est pas parti; **the pistol went off in his hand** le pistolet lui est parti dans la main.

(c) (*Brit: lose excellence*) *[meat]* s'avarier, se gâter; *[milk]* tourner; *[butter]* rancir; *[sportsman, athlete]* perdre de sa forme, baisser; *[woman]* perdre de sa beauté, se défraîchir.

(d) (*lose intensity*) *[feeling, effect]* passer.

(e) (*go to sleep*) s'endormir.

(f) *[event]* se passer. **the evening went off very well** la soirée s'est très bien passée; **how did it go off?** comment cela s'est-il passé?

2 *vt fus* (*Brit: lose liking for*) perdre le goût de. **I've gone off skiing** je n'ai plus envie de faire du ski, j'ai perdu le goût (de faire) du ski; **I've gone off my boyfriend/Dickens** *etc* je n'ai plus envie de sortir avec mon petit ami/de lire Dickens *etc.*

go on 1 *vi* **(a)** (*be placed*) **the lid won't go on** le couvercle ne va pas (dessus); **these shoes won't go on** je n'entre pas dans ces chaussures.

(b) (*proceed on one's way*) (*without stopping*) poursuivre son chemin; (*after stopping*) repartir, se remettre en route, poursuivre sa course.

(c) (*continue*) continuer (*doing* de *or* à faire). **go on with your work** continuez votre travail; **to go on speaking** continuer de parler; (*after pause*) reprendre (la parole); **go on trying!** essaie encore!; **go on!** continuez!; **go on (with you)!*** allons donc!, à d'autres!*; **the war went on until 1945** la guerre a continué *or* s'est prolongée jusqu'en 1945; **if you go on doing that, you'll be punished** si tu continues *or* persistes à faire cela, tu seras puni; **you have enough to go on with** *or* **be going on with** tu as de quoi faire* pour le moment; **she just goes on and on*** elle ne cesse pas de parler, c'est un moulin à paroles*; **he goes on and on about it*** il ne finit pas d'en parler, il est intarissable sur le sujet.

(d) (*proceed*) passer. **to go on to another matter** passer à une autre question; **he went on to say that ...** puis il a dit que ..., il a dit ensuite que ... .

(e) (*happen*) se passer, se dérouler. **while this was going on** pendant que cela se passait, au même moment, pendant ce temps; **this has been going on for a long time** cela dure depuis longtemps; **how long will this go on for?** combien de temps cela va-t-il durer?; **several arguments were going on at the same time** plusieurs disputes étaient en train à la fois; **what's going on here?** qu'est-ce qui se passe ici?

(f) (*pass*) *[time]* passer; *[years]* s'écouler, passer. **as the years went on he ...** avec le passage des années, il ... .

(g) (*gen pej: behave*) se conduire. **what a way to go on!** en voilà des manières!; **she went on in a dreadful way** elle nous a fait une scène épouvantable*.

(h) (*Theat: enter*) entrer en scène; (*Sport*) *[substitute]* prendre sa place, entrer en jeu.

(i) (*progress*) *[person, esp patient]* se porter, aller; *[life, affairs]* marcher, continuer, aller son train.

2 *vt fus* **(a)** (*be guided by*) se fonder sur, se laisser guider par, s'appuyer sur. **what have you to go on?** sur quoi vous fondez-vous?; **the police had no clue to go on** la police n'avait aucun indice sur lequel s'appuyer; **we don't have much to go on yet** nous ne pouvons pas encore nous fonder sur grand-chose.

(b) (*: *appreciate, be impressed by*) s'intéresser à. **I don't go much on that** ça ne me dit pas grand-chose*.

3 goings-on *npl V* **going 3.**

go on at *vt fus* (*nag*) s'en prendre à, être (toujours) sur le dos de*. **she goes on at him** elle ne cesse pas de s'en prendre à lui, elle est toujours sur son dos* *or* après lui:.

go on for *vt fus*: **to be going on for** approcher de, être près de; **he's going on for fifty** il frise la cinquantaine, il va sur la cinquantaine; **it's going on for 5 o'clock** il est presque 5 heures *or* près de 5 heures.

go out *vi* **(a)** (*leave*) sortir. **to go out of a room** quitter une pièce, sortir d'une pièce; **to go out riding** faire une sortie *or* sortir à cheval; **to go out for a meal** manger en ville (*or* chez des amis); **he goes out a lot** il sort beaucoup; **she doesn't go out with him any more** elle ne sort plus avec lui; **to go out to work** travailler au dehors; **to go out charring** aller faire des ménages; **she doesn't want to go out to work** elle ne veut pas travailler hors de chez elle *or* au dehors; **since she's gone out of his life** depuis qu'elle est sortie de sa vie; *V* **mind, way.**

(b) *[fashion]* passer de mode, se démoder; *[custom]* disparaître; *[fire, light]* s'éteindre. **he was so tired he went out like a light*** il était si fatigué qu'il s'est endormi d'un seul coup; **the happiness went out of his face** le bonheur disparut de son visage.

(c) (*depart*) partir (*to* pour, à); (*emigrate, travel*) émigrer (*to* à, en). **he's gone out to the Middle East with his regiment** il est parti (servir) au Moyen-Orient avec son régiment.

(d) *[sea, tide]* descendre, se retirer. **the tide is going out** la marée descend, la mer se retire; **the tide** *or* **the sea goes out 2 km** la mer se retire à 2 km.

(e) **my heart went out to him in his sorrow** j'ai été de tout cœur avec lui dans son chagrin; **all our sympathy goes out to you** toute notre sympathie va vers vous.

(f) (*Cards etc*) terminer.

(g) (*be issued*) *[pamphlet, circular]* être distribué (*to* à).

(h) (*end*) *[year, month]* finir, se terminer.

go over 1 *vi* **(a)** (*cross*) **to go over to America** aller aux États-Unis; **how long does it take to go over?** combien de temps faut-il pour faire la traversée?; (*fig*) **his speech went over well** son discours a été très bien reçu.

(b) (*change allegiance*) passer, se joindre (*to* à). **to go over to the other side** changer de parti (*or* de religion), passer de l'autre côté (de la barrière); **to go over to the enemy** passer à l'ennemi.

(c) (*be overturned*) *[vehicle etc]* verser, se retourner; *[boat]* chavirer, se retourner.

2 *vt fus* **(a)** (*examine*) *accounts, report* examiner, vérifier;

[doctor] patient examiner. **to go over a house** *[visitor]* parcourir *or* visiter une maison; *[purchaser]* examiner une maison; (*lit, fig*) **to go over the ground** reconnaître le terrain.

(b) (*rehearse, review*) *lesson, rôle* repasser, revoir; *speech* revoir; *facts etc* revoir, récapituler. **to go over sb's faults** passer au crible *or* éplucher les défauts de qn; **to go over sth in one's mind** repasser qch dans son esprit; **to go over the events of the day** retracer les événements de la journée; **let's go over the facts again** reprenons les faits; **let's go over what happened again** récapitulons les faits *or* les événements.

(c) (*touch up*) retoucher, faire des retouches à. **to go over a drawing in ink** repasser un dessin à l'encre.

3 going-over *n V* **going 3.**

go round *vi* **(a)** (*turn*) tourner. **the wheels go round** les roues tournent; **my head is going round** j'ai la tête qui tourne.

(b) (*make a detour*) faire un détour, faire le tour. **to go a long way round** faire un grand détour; **to go the long way round** prendre le chemin le plus long *or* le chemin des écoliers; **there's no bridge, we'll have to go round** il n'y a pas de pont, il faut faire le tour; **we went round by Manchester** nous avons fait le détour par Manchester.

(c) to go round to sb's house/to see sb passer chez qn/voir qn.

(d) (*be sufficient*) suffire (pour tout le monde). **there's enough food to go round** il y a assez de nourriture pour tout le monde; **to make the money go round** ménager son argent, s'arranger pour joindre les deux bouts*.

(e) (*circulate*) *[bottle, document, story]* circuler; *[rumour]* courir, circuler.

go through 1 *vi* (*be agreed, voted etc*) *[law, bill]* passer, être voté; *[business deal]* être conclu, être fait, se faire. **the deal did not go through** l'affaire n'a pas été conclue *or* ne s'est pas faite.

2 *vt fus* **(a)** (*suffer, endure*) subir, souffrir, endurer. **we've all gone through it** nous avons tous passé par là; **the experiences I have gone through** les épreuves que j'ai subies; **after all he's gone through** après tout ce qu'il a subi *or* enduré.

(b) (*examine carefully*) *list, book* éplucher; *mail* dépouiller; *subject* discuter *or* examiner à fond; *clothes, wardrobe* trier; *one's pockets* fouiller dans, explorer; (*Customs*) *suitcases, trunks* fouiller. **to go through sb's pockets** faire les poches à qn*.

(c) (*use up*) *money* dépenser; (*wear out*) user. **to go through a fortune** engloutir une fortune; **he goes through a pair of shoes a month** il use une paire de chaussures par mois; **he has gone through the seat of his trousers** il a usé *or* troué le fond de son pantalon; **this book has already gone through 13 editions** il y a déjà eu 13 éditions de ce livre.

(d) (*perform, accomplish, take part in*) *lesson* réciter; *formalities* remplir, accomplir; *programme, entertainment* exécuter; *course of study* suivre; *apprenticeship* faire; *V* **motion** *etc.*

go through with *vt fus* (*complete*) *plan, crime, undertaking* aller jusqu'au bout de, réaliser, exécuter. **in the end she couldn't go through with it** en fin de compte elle n'a pas pu aller jusqu'au bout; **they nevertheless went through with their marriage** ils se sont mariés malgré tout.

go to 1 *vi* (*excl*) go to!†† allons donc!, laissez donc!

2 *vt fus*: **go to it!** allez-y!, au travail!

go together *vi [people]* aller ensemble; *[colours, ideas]* s'accorder, s'harmoniser, aller bien ensemble; *[events, conditions]* marcher ensemble, aller de pair. **they go well together** ils vont bien ensemble.

go under *vi* **(a)** (*sink*) *[ship]* sombrer, couler; *[person]* couler, disparaître (*sous les flots*).

(b) (*fail*) *[person]* succomber, être vaincu; *[business etc]* couler.

go up *vi* **(a)** (*rise*) *[price, value, temperature]* monter, être en hausse, s'élever; (*Theat*) *[curtain]* se lever. **when the curtain goes up** au lever du rideau; **to go up in price** renchérir; (*Scol*) **to go up a class** monter d'une classe; *V* **estimation** *etc.*

(b) (*ascend, climb*) monter, aller en haut; (*go upstairs to bed*) monter se coucher.

(c) (*explode, be destroyed*) sauter, exploser; *V* **flame, smoke.**

(d) (*Brit Univ*) entrer à l'université. **he went up to Oxford** il est entré à Oxford.

go with *vt fus* **(a)** *[circumstances, event, conditions]* marcher *or* aller (de pair) avec. **poverty goes with laziness** la pauvreté va de pair avec la paresse; **the house goes with the job** le logement va avec le poste; (*fig*) **to go with the times** marcher avec son temps; **to go with the crowd** suivre la foule.

(b) (*harmonize with, suit*) *[colours]* s'assortir avec, se marier avec; *[furnishings]* aller avec, être assorti à, s'accorder avec; *[behaviour, opinions]* cadrer avec, s'accorder avec. **I want a hat to go with my new coat** je cherche un chapeau assorti à mon *or* qui aille avec mon nouveau manteau; **his accent doesn't go with his appearance** son accent ne va pas *or* ne s'accorde pas avec son allure.

(c) (*agree with*) avoir les mêmes idées que, être du même avis que. **I'll go with you there** là, je suis de votre avis.

(d) (*: *also* **go steady with**) sortir avec.

go without *vt fus* se passer de, se priver de.

goad [gəʊd] **1** *n* aiguillon *m*, pique-bœuf *m*.

2 *vt cattle* aiguillonner, piquer; (*fig*) aiguillonner, stimuler. **to goad sb into doing** talonner *or* harceler qn jusqu'à ce qu'il fasse; **fright goaded him into action** l'aiguillon de la peur le fit passer à l'action.

goad on *vt sep* aiguillonner, stimuler. **to goad sb on to doing** inciter qn à faire.

goal [gəʊl] **1** *n* **(a)** but *m*, objectif *m*. **his ~ was to become president** son ambition *or* son but était de devenir président, il avait pour ambition *or* pour but de devenir président; **his ~ was in sight** il approchait du but.

(b) (*Sport*) but *m*. **to keep ~, to play in ~** être gardien de but; **to win by 3 ~s to 2** gagner par 3 buts à 2; **the ball went into the ~** le ballon est entré dans le but *or* est allé au fond du filet.

2 *cpd*: (*Sport*) **goal-area** surface *f* de but; **goalkeeper** gardien *m* de but, goal* *m*; (*Ftbl*) **goal-kick** coup *m* de pied de but; **goal-line** ligne *f* de but; **in the goalmouth** juste devant les poteaux; **goal-post** montant *m or* poteau *m* de but; **the main goal scorer was Jones** c'est Jones qui a marqué le plus de buts.

goalie* ['gəʊlɪ] *n* (*abbr of* **goalkeeper**) goal* *m*.

goat [gəʊt] **1** *n* **(a)** chèvre *f*, bouc *m*. **young ~** chevreau *m*, chevrette *f*; *V* **sheep.**

(b) (*: *silly person*) imbécile *mf*, andouille* *f*. (*Brit*) **to act the (giddy) ~*** faire l'imbécile *or* l'andouille*.

(c) (*fig: irritate*) **to get sb's ~*** énerver qn*, taper sur le système‡ *or* les nerfs* de qn; **it gets my ~*** ça me tape sur les nerfs*.

2 *cpd*: (*Myth*) **the goat God** le divin chèvre-pied, le dieu Pan; **goatherd** chevrier *m*, -ière *f*; **goatskin** (*clothing*) peau *f* de chèvre *or* de bouc; (*container*) outre *f* en peau de bouc.

goatee [gəʊ'tiː] *n* barbiche *f*, bouc *m*.

gob [gɒb] **1** *n* **(a)** (∵: *spit*) crachat *m*, mollard∵ *m*. **(b)** (‡: *esp Brit: mouth*) gueule∵ *f*. **shut your ~!** ferme-la!‡, ta gueule!∵ **2** *cpd*: (*Brit*) **gob-stopper*** (gros) bonbon *m*.

gobble ['gɒbl] **1** *n [turkey]* glouglou *m*. **2** *vi [turkey]* glousser, glouglouter. **3** *vt* (*also* **~ down, ~ up**) *food* engloutir, engouffrer, avaler gloutonnement.

gobbledygook* ['gɒbldɪguːk] *n* charabia *m*.

gobbler ['gɒbləʳ] *n* (*turkey*) dindon *m*.

goblet ['gɒblɪt] *n* verre *m* à pied; (†*liter*) coupe *f*.

goblin ['gɒblɪn] *n* lutin *m*, farfadet *m*.

goby ['gəʊbɪ] *n* gobie *m*.

god [gɒd] **1** *n* **(a) G~** Dieu *m*, le bon Dieu*; **G~ the Father, the Son, the Holy Spirit** Dieu le Père, le Fils, le Saint-Esprit; **for G~'s sake!‡** pour l'amour du ciel!, nom d'un chien!*; **(my) G~!‡** mon Dieu!, bon Dieu!‡; **G~ (only) knows‡** Dieu seul le sait; **G~ forbid!*** à Dieu ne plaise!, Dieu m'en garde!; **G~ forbid that she should come!** prions le ciel *or* Dieu veuille qu'elle ne vienne pas!; **G~ willing** s'il plaît à Dieu; **would to G~ that** plût à Dieu que + *subj*; (*fig*) **G~'s acre** cimetière *m*; (*US*) **G~'s own country‡** les États-Unis; *V* **gift, love, thank.**

(b) dieu *m*, divinité *f*; (*fig*) dieu, idole *f*. **ye ~s!*** grands dieux!; (*fig*) **money is his ~** l'argent est son dieu *or* son idole; (*fig*) **to make a little tin ~ of sb** dresser des autels à qn, mettre qn sur un piédestal; (*Brit Theat*) **the ~s*** le poulailler*.

2 *cpd*: **godchild** filleul(e) *m(f)*; **goddam(n)‡, goddamned‡** sacré, fichu*, foutu‡; **it's no goddam use!‡** ça ne sert à rien de rien!*; **goddaughter** filleule *f*; **godfather** parrain *m*; **to stand godfather to a child** être parrain d'un enfant; (*at ceremony*) tenir un enfant sur les fonts baptismaux; **god-fearing** (très) religieux, (très) croyant; **any god-fearing man** tout croyant digne de ce nom; **godforsaken** *town, place* perdu, paumé‡; *person* malheureux, misérable; **godforsaken existence** chienne *f* de vie*; **godforsaken spot** trou perdu *or* paumé‡, bled* *m*; **godhead** divinité *f*; **godlike** divin; *stature etc* de dieu; **godmother** marraine *f* (*V* **fairy 3**); **to stand godmother to a child** être marraine d'un enfant; (*at ceremony*) tenir un enfant sur les fonts baptismaux; **his godparents** son parrain et sa marraine; **godsend** aubaine *f*, bénédiction *f*, don *m* (du ciel); **to be a** *or* **come as a godsend** être une bénédiction *or* aubaine (*to* pour); **godson** filleul *m*; **godspeed!**† bonne chance!, bon voyage!

goddess ['gɒdɪs] *n* déesse *f*; (*fig*) idole *f*.

godless ['gɒdlɪs] *adj person, action, life* impie.

godly ['gɒdlɪ] *adj person* dévot, pieux, religieux; *actions, life* pieux.

...goer ['gəʊəʳ] *n ending in cpds*: **cinemagoer** cinéphile *mf*; *V* **opera, theatre** *etc.*

goes [gəʊz] *V* **go.**

goggle ['gɒgl] **1** *vi [person]* rouler de gros yeux ronds; *[eyes]* être saillants *or* exorbités, sortir de la tête. **to ~ at sb/sth** regarder qn/qch en roulant de gros yeux ronds, regarder qn/qch des yeux en billes de loto*.

2 *n*: **~s** *[motorcyclist]* (grosses) lunettes protectrices *or* de motocycliste; *[skindiver]* lunettes de plongée; (*industrial*) lunettes protectrices *or* de protection; (*: *glasses*) lunettes, besicles *fpl* (*hum*).

3 *cpd*: (*Brit*) **goggle-box‡** télé* *f*; **goggle-eyed** aux yeux saillants *or* exorbités *or* en billes de loto*.

go-go ['gəʊgəʊ] *adj dancer, dancing* go-go *inv.*

going ['gəʊɪŋ] **1** *n* **(a)** (*departure*) départ *m*; *V* **coming.**

(b) (*pace*) allure *f*, marche *f*, train *m*. (*lit, fig*) **that was good ~** ça a été rapide; **it was slow ~** on n'avançait pas, les progrès étaient lents.

(c) (*conditions*) état *m* du sol *or* du terrain (*pour la marche etc*). **it's rough ~** (*walking*) on marche mal; (*Aut etc*) la route est mauvaise; **let's cross while the ~ is good** traversons pendant que nous le pouvons *or* que la circulation le permet; (*lit, fig*) **he got out while the ~ was good** il est parti au bon moment *or* au moment où les circonstances le permettaient; *V* **heavy.**

2 *adj price* existant, actuel. **a ~ concern** une affaire prospère *or* qui marche *or* florissante; **the shop was sold as a ~ concern** le magasin a été vendu comme une affaire qui marche.

3 *cpd*: **going-over** *[accounts]* vérification *f*, révision *f*; (*medical*) examen *m*; *[rooms, house etc]* nettoyage *m*; (*fig: beating*) brutalités *fpl*, passage *m* à tabac*; **goings-on** (**pej: behaviour*) activités *fpl*, conduite *f*, manigances *fpl*; (*happenings*) événements *mpl*; **fine goings-on!*** en voilà du joli!; **your letters keep me in touch with goings-on at home** tes lettres me tiennent au courant de ce qui se passe à la maison.

goitre, (*US*) **goiter** [ˈgɔɪtəʳ] *n* goitre *m*.

gold [gəʊld] **1** *n* (*U*) or *m*. **£500 in** ~ 500 livres en or; (*Prov*) **all is not** ~ **that glisters** tout ce qui brille n'est pas or (*Prov*); (*fig*) **heart of** ~ cœur *m* d'or; *V* **good, heart, rolled.**

2 *cpd watch, tooth* en or; *coin, cloth, ingot* d'or; (*also* **gold-coloured**) or *inv*, couleur d'or. **gold braid** galon *m* d'or; (*lit*) **goldbrick** barre *f* d'or; (*US fig*) **to sell sb a goldbrick*** escroquer *or* filouter qn; (*fig pej*) **she's a gold-digger*** c'est une aventurière; **gold dust** poudre *f* d'or; **gold fever** la fièvre de l'or; **goldfield** région *f or* terrain *m* aurifère; **gold-filled** *watch etc* en doublé (or); *tooth* aurifié; (*Dentistry*) **gold filling** obturation *f* en or; (*Orn*) **goldfinch** chardonneret *m*; **goldfish** poisson *m* rouge, cyprin *m* (doré); **goldfish bowl** bocal *m* (à poissons); (*fig*) **to live in a goldfish bowl** vivre comme dans un bocal en verre; **gold-headed cane** canne *f* à pommeau d'or; (*on uniform*) **gold lace** = **gold braid; gold leaf** feuille *f* d'or, or *m* en feuille; (*lit, fig*) **gold mine** mine *f* d'or; **gold plate** vaisselle *f* d'or; (*fig*) **to eat off gold plates** rouler sur l'or, nager dans l'opulence; **gold-plated** plaqué or; (*Fin*) **the gold pool** le pool de l'or; (*Econ*) **gold reserves** réserves *fpl* d'or; **gold-rimmed spectacles** lunettes *fpl* à montures en or; **gold rush** ruée *f* vers l'or; **goldsmith** orfèvre *m*; **goldsmith's shop** magasin *m or* atelier *m* d'orfèvre; **goldsmith's trade** orfèvrerie *f*; **gold standard** étalon-or *m*; **to come off** *or* **leave the gold standard** abandonner l'étalon-or.

golden [ˈgəʊldən] *adj* (*of a* ~ *colour*) d'or, doré, (couleur d')or; (*made of gold*) en or, d'or; (*fig*) *voice etc* d'or, en or; (*happy, prosperous etc*) *era* idéal. ~ **age** âge *m* d'or; (*fig*) ~ **boy** enfant chéri, chouchou* *m*; **the** ~ **calf** le veau d'or; ~ **deed** action *f* d'éclat; *[pop star etc]* ~ **disc** disque *m* d'or; ~ **eagle** aigle royal; **the G**~ **Fleece** la Toison d'or; ~ **hair** cheveux d'or *or* dorés; (*Brit fig*) ~ **handshake** gratification *f* de fin de service; ~ **hours** heures précieuses *or* merveilleuses; ~ **jubilee** fête *f* du cinquantième anniversaire; ~ **legend** légende dorée; **the** ~ **mean** le juste milieu; ~ **opportunity** occasion magnifique *or* sensationnelle*; **it's your** ~ **opportunity to do it** c'est pour vous le moment ou jamais de le faire; ~ **oriole** loriot *m* jaune *or* d'Europe; ~ **pheasant** faisan doré; ~ **remedy** remède souverain *or* infaillible; ~ **retriever** golden retriever *m*; (*Bot*) ~ **rod** solidage *f*, gerbe *f* d'or; ~ **rule** règle *f* d'or; (*Brit*) ~ **syrup** mélasse raffinée; ~ **wedding** noces *fpl* d'or; ~ **yellow** jaune d'or.

Goldilocks [ˈgəʊldɪlɒks] *n* Boucles d'Or *f*.

golf [gɒlf] **1** *n* golf *m*; *V* **clock.**

2 *vi* faire du golf, jouer au golf.

3 *cpd*: **golf ball** balle *f* de golf; **golf club** (*stick*) club *m or* crosse *f or* canne *f* (de golf); (*place*) club de golf; **golf course, golf links** (terrain *m* de) golf *m*; **she's a golf widow** son mari la délaisse pour aller jouer au golf *or* lui préfère le golf.

golfer [ˈgɒlfəʳ] *n* joueur *m*, -euse *f* de golf, golfeur *m*, -euse *f*.

Goliath [gəʊˈlaɪəθ] *n* (*lit, fig*) Goliath *m*.

golliwog [ˈgɒlɪwɒg] *n* poupée *f* nègre de chiffon (*aux cheveux hérissés*).

golly* [ˈgɒlɪ] **1** *excl* mince (alors)!*, flûte!* **2** *n* (*Brit*) = **golliwog.**

golosh [gəˈlɒʃ] *n* = **galosh.**

gonad [ˈgəʊnæd] *n* gonade *f*.

gondola [ˈgɒndələ] *n* **(a)** gondole *f*. **(b)** *[balloon, airship]* nacelle *f*.

gondolier [ˌgɒndəˈlɪəʳ] *n* gondolier *m*.

Gondwanaland [gɒndˈwɑːnəlænd] *n* continent *m* de Gondwana.

gone [gɒn] **1** *ptp of* **go.**

2 *adj* **(a) to be** ~ *[person]* être parti *or* absent; (*euph: dead*) être disparu *or* mort; **to be far** ~ (*ill*) être très bas (*f* basse) *or* mal; (*: *drunk*) être parti* *or* beurré‡; (*Med*) **she was 6 months** ~* elle était enceinte de 6 mois; (*liter*) **she was far** ~ **with child** elle approchait de son terme; **to be** ~ **on sb‡** en pincer pour qn‡; (†† *or hum*) **be**~! allez-vous-en!; ~ **with the wind** autant en emporte le vent.

(b) (*Brit*) **it's just** ~ **3** il vient de sonner 3 heures, 3 heures viennent de sonner; **it was** ~ **4 before he came** il était plus de 4 heures *or* passé 4 heures quand il est arrivé.

goner‡ [ˈgɒnəʳ] *n*: **to be a** ~ être fichu* *or* foutu‡.

gong [gɒŋ] *n* **(a)** (*also Boxing*) gong *m*. **(b)** (*Brit Mil sl*) médaille *f*.

gonorrhoea [ˌgɒnəˈrɪə] *n* blennorragie *f*, blennorrhée *f*.

goo [guː] *n* (‡*pej*) matière visqueuse *or* gluante; (*sentimentality*) sentimentalité *f* mièvre *or* à l'eau de rose.

good [gʊd] **1** *adj, comp* **better,** *superl* **best (a)** (*excellent, satisfactory*) *artist, book, meal, quality* bon (*f* bonne); (*virtuous, honourable*) bon, brave (*before n*), vertueux; (*well-behaved*) *child, animal* sage; (*kind*) bon, gentil, bienveillant. **a** ~ **man** un homme bien, un brave homme; **all** ~ **people** toutes les braves gens; (*liter*) ~ **men and true** hommes vaillants; **a** ~ **and holy man** un saint homme; **to live** *or* **lead a** ~ **life** mener une vie vertueuse; **the child was as** ~ **as gold** l'enfant était sage comme une image; **be** ~! sois sage!; **be** ~ **to him** soyez gentil avec lui; **that's very** ~ **of you** c'est bien aimable *or* très gentil de votre part, vous êtes bien aimable *or* gentil; **would you be** ~ **enough to tell me** seriez-vous assez aimable pour *or* auriez-vous la bonté de me dire, voudriez-vous avoir l'obligeance (*frm*) de me dire; **he asked us to be** ~ **enough to sit** il nous a priés de bien vouloir nous asseoir; **she is a** ~ **mother** c'est une bonne mère; **she was a** ~ **wife to him** elle a été pour lui une épouse dévouée; **he's a** ~ **chap** *or* **sort*** c'est un brave *or* chic type*; **she's a** ~ **sort** c'est une brave *or* chic* fille; ~ **old Charles!*** ce (bon) vieux Charles!; **my** ~ **friend** (mon) cher ami; **your** ~ **lady**† votre épouse; **your** ~ **man**† votre époux; **yes, my** ~ **man** oui, mon brave; **the** ~ **ship Domino** le Domino; **very** ~, **sir!** (très) bien monsieur!; **to do** ~ **works** faire de bonnes œuvres; **the G**~ **Book** la Bible; **she was wearing a** ~ **dress** elle portait une robe de (belle) qualité; **she was wearing her** ~ **dress** elle portait sa robe bien; **nothing was too** ~ **for his wife** rien n'était trop beau pour sa femme; **he sat on the only** ~ **chair** il s'est assis sur la seule bonne chaise; (*in shop*) **I want something** ~ je veux quelque chose de bien; **that's not** ~ **enough** ça ne va pas; **that's** ~ **enough for me** cela me suffit; ~ **for you! bravo!**, très bien!; **(that's)** ~! bon!, très bien!; (*joke, story*) **that's a** ~ **one!** elle est (bien) bonne celle-là!; (*iro*) à d'autres!*; ~ **heavens!***, ~ **Lord!*** mon Dieu!, Seigneur!; **he's as** ~ **as you** il vous vaut, il vaut autant que vous; **he's as** ~ **a writer as his brother** il est aussi bon écrivain que son frère; **it's as** ~ **a way as any other** c'est une façon comme une autre *or* qui en vaut une autre; **he was as** ~ **as his word** il a tenu sa promesse; **his hearing/eyesight is** ~ il a l'ouïe fine/une bonne vue; *V* **form, part** *etc*.

(b) (*beneficial, wholesome*) bon (*for* pour), salutaire (*for* à). **milk is** ~ **for children** le lait est bon pour les enfants; **drink up your milk, it's** ~ **for you** bois ton lait, c'est bon pour toi *or* c'est bon pour ta santé *or* ça te fait du bien; **oil of cloves is** ~ **for toothache** l'essence de girofle est bonne pour les maux de dents; **exercise is** ~ **for you** l'exercice vous fait du bien, il est sain de prendre de l'exercice; **you don't know what's** ~ **for you** (*of food etc*) tu ne sais pas apprécier les bonnes choses; (*fig*) tu ne sais pas profiter des bonnes occasions; **if you know what's** ~ **for you you'll say yes** si tu as le moindre bon sens tu accepteras; **the shock was** ~ **for him** le choc lui a été salutaire; **this climate is not** ~ **for one's health** ce climat est mauvais pour la santé *or* est insalubre; **all this running isn't** ~ **for me!** ce n'est pas bon pour moi de courir comme ça!; **to drink more than is** ~ **for one** boire plus qu'on ne le devrait *or* plus que de raison; **he's had more (to drink) than is** ~ **for him*** il a largement son compte*, il a trop bu; *[food]* **to keep** *or* **stay** ~ (bien) se conserver.

(c) (*efficient, competent*) bon, compétent, expert. **I've got a** ~ **teacher/doctor/lawyer** j'ai un bon professeur/médecin/avocat; **a** ~ **businessman** un excellent homme d'affaires; ~ **at French** bon *or* fort *or* calé* en français, doué pour le français; **he's** ~ **at everything** il est bon *or* il brille en tout; **she's** ~ **with children/dogs** elle sait s'y prendre avec les enfants/les chiens; **he's** ~ **at telling stories, he tells a** ~ **story** il sait bien raconter les histoires; **he's not** ~ **enough to do it alone** il n'est pas assez expert *or* il ne s'y connaît pas assez pour le faire tout seul; **he's too** ~ **for that** il mérite mieux que cela; ~ **for nothing** bon *or* propre à rien (*V also* **4**).

(d) (*pleasing, agreeable*) *visit, holiday* bon, agréable, plaisant; *weather, day* beau (*f* belle); *news* bon, heureux; *humour* bon, joyeux. **he has a** ~ **temper** il a bon caractère; **he's in a** ~ **temper** *or* **humour** il est de bonne humeur; **his** ~ **nature** son bon naturel *or* caractère; **we had a** ~ **time** nous nous sommes bien amusés; **I've had a** ~ **life** j'ai eu une belle vie; **it's too** ~ **to be true** c'est trop beau pour être vrai; **it's** ~ **to be alive** il fait bon vivre; **it's** ~ **to be here** cela fait plaisir d'être ici; **I feel** ~ je me sens bien; **I don't feel too** ~ **about that*** (*worried*) cela m'inquiète *or* m'ennuie un peu; (*ashamed*) j'en ai un peu honte; **Robert sends (his)** ~ **wishes** Robert envoie ses amitiés; **with every** ~ **wish, with all** ~ **wishes** tous mes meilleurs vœux; *V* **cheer** *etc*.

(e) (*in greetings*) ~ **afternoon** (*early*) bonjour, (*later*) bonsoir, (*on leaving*) bonsoir; ~**bye** au revoir, adieu†; **to bid sb** ~**bye** faire ses adieux à qn, prendre congé de qn; ~**bye to all that!** fini tout cela!; **you can say** ~**bye to all your hopes** tu peux dire adieu à toutes tes espérances; ~ **day**† = ~**bye** *or* ~ **morning**; ~ **evening** bonsoir; ~ **morning** bonjour; ~**night** bonsoir, bonne nuit; **to bid sb** ~**night** souhaiter le *or* dire bonsoir à qn; **to give sb a** ~**night kiss** embrasser qn avant qu'il s'endorme *or* qu'il aille se coucher, donner à qn le baiser du soir (*frm*).

(f) (*handsome, well-made*) *appearance etc* bon, beau (*f* belle), joli; *features* beau, joli. ~ **looks** beauté *f*; **you look** ~ **in that, that looks** ~ **on you** ça vous va bien; **you look** ~! tu es très bien!; **she's got a** ~ **figure** elle a une jolie ligne, elle est bien faite; **she's got** ~ **legs** elle a les jambes bien faites *or* dessinées.

(g) (*advantageous, favourable*) *terms, contract, deal* avantageux, favorable; *offer* favorable, bon; *omen, chance* bon; *opportunity* bon, favorable. **to make a** ~ **marriage** faire un beau mariage; **to live at a** ~ **address** avoir une adresse chic; **people of** ~ **position** *or* **standing** des gens bien; (*Betting etc*) **I've had a** ~ **day** la chance était avec moi aujourd'hui; **you've never had it so** ~!* vous n'avez jamais eu la vie si belle!; **he thought it** ~ **to say** il crut bon *or* il jugea à propos de dire; **he's on to a** ~ **thing*** il a trouvé un filon*; **to make a** ~ **thing out of sth*** tirer bon parti de qch, faire de gros bénéfices sur qch; **it would be a** ~ **thing to ask him** il serait bon de lui demander; **it's a** ~ **thing I was there** heureusement que j'étais là, c'est une chance que j'aie été là; **that's a** ~ **thing!** tant mieux!, très bien!; **to put in a** ~ **word for sb** glisser un mot en faveur de qn; **this is as** ~ **a time as any to do it** autant le faire maintenant; *V* **fortune, job, time** *etc*.

(h) (*reliable, valid*) *car, tools, machinery* bon, sûr; *cheque* bon; *reason, excuse* bon, valable. (*Insurance*) **he is a** ~ **risk** il est un bon risque; (*Fin*) **is his credit** ~? peut-on lui faire crédit?; **he is** *or* **his credit is** ~ **for £3,000** on peut lui faire crédit jusqu'à 3.000 livres; **what** *or* **how much is he** ~ **for?** de combien (d'argent) dispose-t-il?; **how much will you be** ~ **for?** combien (d'argent) pouvez-vous mettre?; (*lending money*) **he's** ~ **for £500** il nous (*or* vous *etc*) prêtera bien 500 livres; **this ticket is** ~ **for 3 months** ce billet est bon *or* valable 3 mois; **this note is** ~ **for £5** ce bon vaut 5 livres; **he's** ~ **for another 20 years yet** il en a encore bien pour 20 ans; **my car is** ~ **for another few years** ma voiture fera *or* tiendra encore bien quelques années; **are you** ~ **for a long walk?** te sens-tu en état de *or* de taille à *or* de force à faire une longue promenade?; **I'm ~ for another mile or two** je me sens de force à faire encore un ou deux kilomètres; *V* **reason.**

(i) (*thorough*) bon, grand, complet (*f* -ète). **a ~ thrashing** une bonne correction; **to give sb a ~ scolding** passer un bon savon* à qn, tancer qn vertement; **to give sth a ~ clean*** nettoyer qch à fond, faire le nettoyage complet de qch; **to have a ~ cry** avoir une bonne crise de larmes, pleurer un bon coup *or* tout son soûl; **I've a ~ mind to tell him everything!** j'ai bien envie de tout lui dire!; *V* **care, grounding.**

(j) (*considerable, not less than*) bon, grand. **a ~ deal (of)** beaucoup (de); **a ~ many** beaucoup de, bon nombre de; **a ~ distance** une bonne distance; **a ~ way** un bon bout de chemin; **a ~ while** pas mal de temps, assez longtemps; **it will take you a ~ hour** vous n'aurez pas trop d'une heure, il vous faudra une bonne heure; **a ~ 8 kilometres** 8 bons kilomètres, 8 kilomètres pour le moins; **that was a ~ 10 years ago** il y a bien 10 ans de cela; **a ~ round sum** une somme rondelette; **he came in a ~ third** il s'est honorablement classé troisième; *V* **bit²**.

(k) (*adv phrases*) **as ~ as** pour ainsi dire, à peu de choses près, pratiquement; **as ~ as new** comme neuf (*f* neuve); **to make sth as ~ as new** remettre qch à neuf; **the matter is as ~ as settled** c'est comme si l'affaire était réglée, l'affaire est pour ainsi dire *or* pratiquement réglée; **he's as ~ as lost it** c'est comme s'il l'avait perdu; **she as ~ as told me that ...** elle m'a dit à peu de chose près que ..., elle m'a pour ainsi dire déclaré que ...; **he as ~ as called me a liar** il n'a pas dit que je mentais mais c'était tout comme*; **it's as ~ as saying that ...** autant dire que ...; **it was as ~ as a play!** c'était une vraie comédie!; **it was as ~ as a holiday** c'étaient presque des vacances.

(l) to make ~ (*succeed*) faire son chemin, réussir; *[ex-criminal etc]* se refaire une vie, racheter son passé; **to make ~** *deficit* combler; *deficiency, losses* compenser; *expenses* rembourser; *injustice, damage* réparer; **to make ~ a loss to sb** dédommager qn d'une perte; **to make ~ a promise** tenir *or* remplir une promesse; **to make ~ one's escape** réussir son évasion; **to make ~ an assertion** justifier une affirmation.

2 *adv* **(a)** bien. **a ~ strong stick** un bâton bien solide; **a ~ long walk** une bonne *or* une grande promenade; **we had a ~ long talk** nous avons discuté bien longuement; **in ~ plain English** en termes simples.

(b) ~ and* bien, tout à fait; **the soup was served ~ and hot** la soupe a été servie bien chaude; **the house is ~ and clean** la maison est scrupuleusement propre; **I told him off ~ and proper‡** je lui ai passé un bon savon*, je l'ai bien engueulé‡.

(c) (*US*) **to be in ~ with sb‡** être dans les petits papiers de qn.

3 *n* **(a)** (*virtue, righteousness*) bien *m*. **to do ~** faire du bien *or* le bien; **to return ~ for evil** rendre le bien pour le mal; **he is a power for ~** il exerce une influence salutaire; **she's up to no ~*** elle prépare quelque mauvais coup; **there's some ~ in him** il a du bon; **for ~ or ill, for ~ or evil, for ~ or bad** que ce soit un bien ou un mal; **he'll come to no ~** il finira *or* tournera mal.

(b) (*collective n: people*) **the ~** les bons *mpl*, les gens *mpl* de bien, les gens vertueux; **the ~ and the bad** les bons et les méchants; (*loc*) **only the ~ die young** seuls les bons meurent jeunes.

(c) (*advantage, profit*) bien *m*, avantage *m*, profit *m*. **the common ~** l'intérêt commun; **I did it for your ~** je l'ai fait pour votre bien; **it's for his own ~** c'est pour son bien; **he went for the ~ of his health** il est parti pour des raisons de santé; **that will do you ~** cela vous fera du bien; **it does my heart ~ to see him** cela me réjouit *or* me réchauffe le cœur de le voir; **what ~ will that do you?** ça t'avancera à quoi?; **what's the ~?** à quoi bon?; **what's the ~ of hurrying?** à quoi bon se presser?; **a (fat) lot of ~ that will do (you)!*** tu seras bien avancé!, ça te fera une belle jambe!*; **much ~ may it do you!** grand bien vous fasse!; **a lot of ~ that's done!** nous voilà bien avancés!; **a lot of ~ that's done him!** le voilà bien avancé!; **so much to the ~** autant de gagné; **we were £5 to the ~** nous avons fait 5 livres de bénéfice, cela nous a fait 5 livres de gagnées; **that's all to the ~!** tant mieux!, c'est autant de gagné!; **it's no ~** ça ne sert à rien, c'est en pure perte; **that's no ~** cela ne vaut rien, cela ne va pas, cela ne peut pas aller; **that won't be much ~** cela ne servira pas à grand-chose; **if that is any ~ to you** si ça peut vous être utile *or* vous rendre service; **it's no ~ saying that** ce n'est pas la peine de dire cela, inutile de dire cela.

(d) (*adv phrase*) **for ~** pour de bon, à jamais; **to settle down for ~** se fixer définitivement; **he's gone for ~** il est parti pour toujours *or* pour de bon *or* pour ne plus revenir; **for ~ and all** à tout jamais, une (bonne) fois pour toutes, pour tout de bon.

(e) *V* **goods.**

4 *cpd*: **goodbye** *V* **1e**; **good-for-nothing** (*adj*) bon *or* propre à rien; (*n*) propre *mf* à rien, vaurien(ne) *m(f)*; **Good Friday** Vendredi saint; **good-hearted** qui a bon cœur, bon, généreux; **good-heartedness** bonté *f*; **good-humoured** *person* de bonne humeur, jovial, bon enfant *inv*; *appearance, smile etc* plein de bonhomie, bonhomme *inv*, bon enfant *inv*; *joke* sans malice; **good-humouredly** avec bonne humeur, avec bonhomie; **good-looker*** (*man*) beau garçon, bel homme; (*woman*) belle *or* jolie femme; (*horse etc*) beau cheval *etc*; **good-looking** beau (*f* belle), bien *inv*, joli; **good-natured** *person* qui a un bon naturel, accommodant, facile à vivre; *smile, laughter* bon enfant *inv*; **goodnight** *V* **1e**; **good-tempered** *person* qui a bon caractère, de caractère égal; *smile, look* aimable, gentil; (*pej*) **good-time girl*** fille *f* qui ne pense qu'à s'amuser *or* qu'à se donner du bon temps; **goodwill** *V* **goodwill.**

goodly ['gʊdlɪ] *adj* († *or liter*) **(a)** *appearance* beau (*f* belle), gracieux. **(b)** *size* grand, large, ample. **a ~ number** un nombre considérable; **a ~ heritage** un bel héritage.

goodness ['gʊdnɪs] *n [person]* bonté *f*; *[thing]* (bonne) qualité *f*. **(my) ~!*, ~ gracious!*** Seigneur!, bonté divine!; **~ (only) knows*** Dieu (seul) sait; **for ~ 'sake*** pour l'amour de Dieu, par pitié; **I wish to ~ I had gone there!*** si seulement j'y étais allé!; *V* **thank.**

goods [gʊdz] **1** *npl* **(a)** (*Comm*) marchandises *fpl*, articles *mpl*. **leather ~** articles *mpl* de cuir, maroquinerie *f*; **knitted ~** articles en tricot; **that's/he's just the ~!‡** c'est/il est exactement ce qu'il (nous *or* vous *etc*) faut!; (*US*) **to have the ~ on sb‡** en savoir long sur qn; *V* **consumer, deliver** *etc*.

(b) (*Jur*) biens *mpl*, meubles *mpl*. **all his ~ and chattels** tous ses biens et effets.

2 *cpd*: (*Brit Rail*) **to send by fast/slow goods service** envoyer en grande/petite vitesse; **goods siding** voie *f* de garage pour wagons de marchandises; **goods station** gare *f* de marchandises; **goods train** train *m* de marchandises; **goods yard** dépôt *m or* cour *f* des marchandises.

goodwill [ˌgʊd'wɪl] *n* **(a)** bonne volonté, bon vouloir, bienveillance *f*. **to gain sb's ~** se faire bien voir de qn; (*Pol*) **~ mission** mission *f* de conciliation *or* de médiation.

(b) (*willingness*) zèle *m*. **to work with ~** travailler de bon cœur *or* avec zèle.

(c) (*Comm*) (biens *mpl*) incorporels *mpl*, clientèle *f*. **the ~ goes with the business** les incorporels sont vendus *or* la clientèle est vendue avec le fonds de commerce.

goody* ['gʊdɪ] **1** *excl* (*also* **~ ~**) chic!*, chouette!‡ **2** *n* **(a)** (*Cine*) **the goodies and the baddies*** les bons *mpl* et les méchants *mpl*. **(b)** (*Culin*) **goodies*** friandises *fpl*, bonnes choses.

goody-goody* ['gʊdɪˌgʊdɪ] **1** *adj* (*pej*) *[person]* **to be ~** être l'image du petit garçon (*or* de la petite fille) modèle. **2** *n* modèle *m* de vertu (*iro*), petit saint, sainte nitouche *f*.

gooey‡ ['gu:ɪ] *adj* (*pej*) *substance* gluant; *cake* qui colle aux dents; (*fig*) *film, story* sentimental, à l'eau de rose.

goof‡ [gu:f] **1** *n* (*idiot*) toqué(e)‡ *m(f)*. (*Drugs sl*) **~ball** barbiturique *m*.

2 *vi* faire une gaffe, mettre les pieds dans le plat*.

goof off‡ *vi* (*US*) tirer au flanc.

goof up‡ **1** *vi* (*US*) faire une gaffe, gaffer‡.

2 *vt sep* foutre en l'air‡, bousiller‡.

goofy‡ ['gu:fɪ] *adj* maboul‡, toqué‡.

goon [gu:n] *n* (‡: *fool*) idiot(e)* *m(f)*, imbécile* *mf*; (*US*‡: *hired thug*) gangster *m*.

goosander [gu:'sændəʳ] *n* harle *m*.

goose [gu:s] *pl* **geese** **1** *n* oie *f*. (*fig*) **all his geese are swans** d'après lui tout ce qu'il fait tient du prodige; (*fig*) **to kill the ~ that lays the golden eggs** tuer la poule aux œufs d'or; **don't be such a ~!*** ne sois pas si bébête!* *or* si dinde!*; **silly little ~!*** petite dinde!*, petite niaise!*; *V* **boo, cook, mother** *etc*.

2 *cpd*: **gooseberry** *V* **gooseberry**; **to come out in gooseflesh** *or* **goosepimples** *or* (*US*) **goosebumps** avoir la chair de poule; **that gives me gooseflesh** *or* **goosepimples** *or* (*US*) **goosebumps** cela me donne la chair de poule; (*Mil*) **goose-step** (*n*) pas *m* de l'oie; (*vi*) faire le pas de l'oie.

gooseberry ['gʊzbərɪ] *n* (*fruit*) groseille *f* à maquereau; (*also* **~ bush**) groseiller *m*. (*Brit*) **to play ~** tenir la chandelle.

gopher ['gəʊfəʳ] *n* (*squirrel*) spermophile *m*; (*rodent*) geomys *m*, saccophore *m*, thomomys *m*.

Gordian ['gɔ:dɪən] *n*: **to cut the ~ knot** trancher le nœud gordien.

gore¹ [gɔ:ʳ] *n* (*blood*) sang *m*.

gore² [gɔ:ʳ] *vt* (*injure*) encorner, blesser *or* éventrer d'un coup de corne. **~d to death** tué d'un coup de corne.

gore³ [gɔ:ʳ] **1** *n* (*Sewing*) godet *m*; *[sail]* pointe *f*. **2** *vt sail* mettre une pointe à. **~d skirt** jupe *f* à godets.

gorge [gɔ:dʒ] **1** *n* **(a)** (*Geog*) gorge *f*, défilé *m*. **(b)** (*Anat*) gorge *f*, gosier *m*. (*fig*) **it makes my ~ rise** cela me soulève le cœur. **2** *vt meal, food* engloutir, engouffrer*. **to ~ o.s.** se gorger, se rassasier. **3** *vi* se bourrer, se gorger, se rassasier (*on* de).

gorgeous ['gɔ:dʒəs] *adj sunset, colours* somptueux, splendide, magnifique, fastueux; *woman* magnifique, splendide; *weather* splendide, magnifique; (*) *holiday* sensationnel*, formidable*. **we had a ~ time*** on a passé un moment sensationnel*; **hullo there, ~!‡** bonjour, ma beauté! *or* ma belle! *or* ma mignonne!; **it was a ~ feeling** c'était une sensation merveilleuse.

gorilla [gə'rɪlə] *n* (*Zool*) gorille *m*; (‡*pej: man*) brute *f*; (‡: *thug*) gangster *m*; (‡: *bodyguard*) gorille* *m*.

gormandize ['gɔ:məndaɪz] *vi* bâfrer‡, se goinfrer‡, s'empiffrer‡.

gormless* ['gɔ:mlɪs] *adj* (*Brit*) lourdaud, bêta (*f* -asse)*.

gorse [gɔ:s] *n* (*U*) ajoncs *mpl*. **~ bush** ajonc *m*.

gory ['gɔ:rɪ] *adj wound, battle etc* sanglant; *person* ensanglanté. (*fig*) **all the ~ details** tous les détails les plus horribles.

gosh* [gɒʃ] *excl* ça alors!*, mince (alors)!*, nom d'un chien!*

goshawk ['gɒshɔ:k] *n* autour *m*.

gosling ['gɒzlɪŋ] *n* oison *m*.

gospel ['gɒspəl] **1** *n* évangile *m*. **the G~ according to St John** l'Évangile selon St Jean; (*fig*) **that's ~*** c'est parole d'évangile, c'est la vérité pure; (*fig*) **to take sth for ~*** accepter qch comme *or* prendre qch pour parole d'évangile.

2 *cpd*: **Gospel oath** serment prêté sur l'Évangile; (*fig*) **it's the gospel truth*** c'est parole d'évangile, c'est la vérité pure.

gossamer ['gɒsəməʳ] **1** *n* (*U*) (*cobweb*) fils *mpl* de la Vierge; (*gauze*) gaze *f*; (*light fabric*) étoffe translucide *or* très légère; (*US: waterproof*) imperméable léger. **2** *adj* arachnéen (*liter*), léger. **~ thin** très fin, fin comme de la gaze.

gossip ['gɒsɪp] **1** *n* **(a)** (*U*) (*chatter*) bavardage *m*, commérage *m* (*pej*), cancans *mpl* (*pej*), potins *mpl* (*pej*); (*in newspaper*) propos familiers, échos *mpl*. **I never listen to ~** je n'écoute jamais les cancans *or* les racontars *mpl*; **what's the latest ~?** quels sont les derniers potins?; **a piece of ~** un cancan, un ragot; **we had a good old ~** nous nous sommes raconté tous les potins, nous avons taillé une bonne bavette.

(b) (*person*) bavard(e) *m(f)*, commère *f* (*pej*). **he's a real ~** c'est une vraie commère *or* un vrai pipelet*.

2 *vi* bavarder, papoter; (*maliciously*) potiner, cancaner, faire des commérages (*about* sur).

3 *cpd*: (*Press*) **gossip column** échos *mpl*; **gossip columnist, gossip writer** échotier *m*, -ière *f*.

gossiping ['gɒsɪpɪŋ] **1** *adj* bavard, cancanier (*pej*). **2** *n* bavardage *m*, papotage *m*, commérage *m* (*pej*).

gossipy ['gɒsɪpɪ] *adj person* bavard, cancanier (*pej*); *style* anecdotique; *conversation* cancanier, de commère.

got [gɒt] *pret, ptp of* **get**; *for* **have ~** *V* **have.**

Goth [gɒθ] *n* Goth *m.*

Gothic ['gɒθɪk] **1** *adj* (*Archit etc*) gothique; (*Hist*) des Goths. **~ type** caractère *m* gothique. **2** *n* (*Archit, Ling etc*) gothique *m.*

gotten ['gɒtn] (*US*) *ptp of* **get.**

gouge [gaʊdʒ] **1** *n* gouge *f.*

2 *vt* gouger.

gouge out *vt sep* (*with gouge*) gouger; (*with thumb, pencil etc*) évider. **to gouge sb's eyes out** crever les yeux à qn.

goulash ['guːlæʃ] *n* goulache *f.*

gourd [gʊəd] *n* (*fruit*) gourde *f*; (*container*) gourde, calebasse *f.*

gourmand ['gʊəmənd] *n* gourmand(e) *m(f)*, glouton(ne) *m(f).*

gourmet ['gʊəmeɪ] *n* gourmet *m*, gastronome *mf.*

gout [gaʊt] *n* (*Med*) goutte *f.*

gouty ['gaʊtɪ] *adj person, joint* goutteux.

gov* [gʌv] *n abbr of* **governor b.**

govern ['gʌvən] **1** *vt* **(a)** (*rule*) *country* gouverner; *province, city etc* administrer; *household* diriger, gérer; *affairs* administrer, gérer; *business, company* gérer, administrer, diriger.

(b) (*Tech*) régler; (*fig: control*) *passions, emotions etc* maîtriser, contenir, gouverner, dominer. **to ~ one's tongue** tenir sa langue, contrôler ses paroles; **to ~ one's temper** se maîtriser.

(c) (*influence*) *events* déterminer, régir; *opinions* guider; *speed* déterminer.

(d) (*Gram*) *case, mood* gouverner, régir.

2 *vi* (*Pol*) gouverner.

governess ['gʌvənɪs] *n* gouvernante *f*, institutrice *f* (*à domicile*).

governing ['gʌvənɪŋ] *adj* (*Pol etc*) gouvernant; (*fig*) *belief etc* dominant. **~ body** conseil *m* d'administration, directeurs *mpl*; **~ principle** idée directrice *or* dominante.

government ['gʌvənmənt] **1** *n* **(a)** (*U: act: V* **govern 1**) gouvernement *m*; gestion *f*, direction *f*, administration *f.*

(b) (*Pol*) (*governing body*) gouvernement *m*, cabinet *m*, ministère *m*; (*system*) régime *m*, gouvernement; (*the State*) l'État *m*. **to form a ~** former un gouvernement *or* un cabinet *or* un ministère; **democratic ~** gouvernement *or* régime démocratique; **local ~** administration locale; **minority ~** gouvernement minoritaire; **~ by the people and for the people** gouvernement du peuple pour le peuple; **that country needs a strong ~** ce pays a besoin d'un gouvernement fort; **the ~ is taking measures to stop pollution** le gouvernement prend des mesures pour empêcher la pollution; **a dam built by the ~** un barrage construit par l'État; **the G~ and the Opposition** le gouvernement et l'opposition; **the ~ has fallen** le cabinet *or* le ministère *or* le gouvernement est tombé; **a socialist ~** un gouvernement *or* un ministère socialiste; **he was invited to join the ~** il a été invité à entrer dans le gouvernement.

2 *cpd policy, decision* gouvernemental, du gouvernement; *responsibility, loan* de l'État, public (*f* -ique). (*Fin*) **government bonds** bons *mpl* du Trésor; **government department** département *or* service gouvernemental; **government expenditure** dépenses publiques; (*Brit*) **Government House** palais *m* du gouverneur, résidence *f*; **government issue** (*adj*) *equipment* fourni par le gouvernement; *bonds etc* émis par le gouvernement; (*Fin*) **government securities** effets publics; (*Fin*) **government stock** fonds publics *or* d'État.

governmental [ˌgʌvən'mentl] *adj* gouvernemental, du gouvernement.

governor ['gʌvənəʳ] *n* **(a)** *[state, bank]* gouverneur *m*; (*esp Brit*) *[prison]* directeur *m*, -trice *f*; *[school, institution etc]* administrateur *m*, -trice *f*. **G~ General** gouverneur général.

(b) (*Brit**) (*employer*) patron *m*; (*father*) paternel* *m*. **thanks ~!** merci chef! *or* patron!

(c) (*Tech*) régulateur *m.*

governorship ['gʌvənəʃɪp] *n* fonctions *fpl* de gouverneur. **during my ~** pendant la durée de mes fonctions (de gouverneur).

gown [gaʊn] **1** *n* robe *f*; (*Jur, Univ*) toge *f*; *V* **town. 2** *vt* (*liter*) revêtir (*in* de), habiller (*in* de).

goy [gɔɪ] *n, pl* **goyim** ['gɔɪɪm] goy *m or* goï *m* (*pl* goym *or* goyim).

grab [græb] **1** *n* **(a) to make a ~ for** *or* **at sth** faire un geste vif *or* un mouvement vif pour saisir qch.

(b) (*esp Brit: Tech*) benne preneuse.

2 *cpd*: (*US*) **grab bag*** sac *m* (pour jouer à la pêche miraculeuse).

3 *vt object* saisir, agripper, empoigner; (*fig*) *land* se saisir de, prendre, mettre la main sur; *power* se saisir de, prendre. **he ~bed the pen from me** il m'a arraché le stylo; (*fig*) **how does that ~ you?*** qu'est-ce que ça te dit?*

4 *vi*: **to ~ at a rope** essayer d'agripper une corde; (*to child*) **don't ~!** doucement!, ne te précipite pas dessus!, ne te jette pas dessus!

grab away *vt sep*: **to grab sth away from sb** arracher qch à qn, enlever qch à qn d'un geste brusque.

grace [greɪs] **1** *n* **(a)** (*U*) *[person]* grâce *f*, charme *m*, distinction *f*, élégance *f*; *[animal, movement]* grâce.

(b) (*Rel*) grâce *f*. **by the ~ of God** par la grâce de Dieu; **in a state of ~** en état de grâce; **to fall from ~** (*Rel*) perdre la grâce; (*fig hum*) tomber en disgrâce; **to say ~** (*before meals*) dire le bénédicité; (*after meals*) dire les grâces; *V* **year.**

(c) (*phrases*) **to be in sb's good/bad ~s** être bien/mal vu de qn, être en faveur/défaveur auprès de qn; **to get into sb's good/bad ~s** se faire bien/mal voir de qn; **to do sth with good/bad ~** faire qch de bonne/mauvaise grâce; **he had the ~ to apologize** il a eu la bonne grâce de s'excuser; **his saving ~** ce qui le rachète (*or* rachetait *etc*); (*Myth*) **the three G~s** les trois Grâces; *V* **air.**

(d) (*U: respite*) grâce *f*, répit *m*. **a day's ~** un jour de grâce *or* de répit; (*Comm*) **days of ~** jours de grâce; (*Jur*) **as an act of ~, he ...** en exerçant son droit de grâce, il ... .

(e) (*title*) **His G~ (the Archbishop)** Monseigneur l'Archevêque, Son Excellence l'Archevêque; **His G~ (the Duke)** Monsieur le duc; **Her G~ (the Duchess)** Madame la duchesse; **yes, your G~** oui, Monseigneur (*or* Monsieur le duc *or* Madame la duchesse).

2 *cpd*: (*Brit*) **grace and favour residence** *résidence attribuée à une personne pour la durée de sa vie par un roi ou un noble*; (*Mus*) **grace note** note *f* d'agrément, fioriture *f*, ornement *m.*

3 *vt* **(a)** (*adorn*) orner, embellir (*with* de).

(b) honorer (*with* de). **the queen ~d the performance with her presence** la reine honora la représentation de sa présence.

graceful ['greɪsfʊl] *adv movement, animal, person* gracieux; *style, appearance etc* gracieux, élégant; *apology, retraction* élégant, plein d'élégance.

gracefully ['greɪsfəlɪ] *adv move, dance* gracieusement, élégamment, avec élégance, avec grâce; *apologize, withdraw* avec élégance, élégamment. **we cannot ~ refuse** nous ne pouvons pas trouver une excuse élégante pour refuser.

gracefulness ['greɪsfʊlnɪs] *n* = **grace 1a.**

graceless ['greɪslɪs] *adj person, conduct* peu élégant, inélégant; *gesture* gauche.

gracious ['greɪʃəs] *adj person, smile, gesture* gracieux, bienveillant (*to* envers); *action* courtois, plein de bonne grâce; *God* miséricordieux (*to* envers); *house, room, gardens* d'une élégance raffinée. **our ~ Queen** notre gracieuse souveraine; (*frm*) **by the ~ consent of** par la grâce de; **he was very ~ to me** il s'est montré très affable *or* bienveillant envers moi; **Lord be ~ unto him** Seigneur soyez-lui miséricordieux; **~ living** vie élégante *or* raffinée; **(good) ~!*** juste ciel!, bonté divine!

graciously ['greɪʃəslɪ] *adv wave, smile* gracieusement, avec grâce; *agree, accept* avec bonne grâce; *live* élégamment, avec élégance; (*frm*) *consent, allow* gracieusement; (*Rel*) miséricordieusement. **the king was ~ pleased to accept** le roi eut la bonté d'accepter, le roi accepta gracieusement.

graciousness ['greɪʃəsnɪs] *n* (*U*) *[person]* bienveillance *f*, condescendance *f* (*towards* envers); *[action, style]* grâce *f*, aménité *f*; *[house, room, gardens]* élégance raffinée; *[wave, smile]* grâce; *[God]* miséricorde *f*, clémence *f.*

grad* [græd] *n* (*US*) *abbr of* **graduate 3a.**

gradate [grə'deɪt] **1** *vt* graduer. **2** *vi* être gradué.

gradation [grə'deɪʃən] *n* gradation *f*, progression *f*, échelonnement *m.*

grade [greɪd] **1** *n* **(a)** (*in hierarchy*) catégorie *f*; (*on scale*) échelon *m*, grade *m*; (*Mil: rank*) rang *m*; (*Comm: of steel, butter, goods etc*) qualité *f*; (*Comm: size: of eggs, apples, anthracite nuts etc*) calibre *m*; (*US: level*) niveau *m*. **the lowest ~ of skilled worker** la catégorie la plus basse des ouvriers qualifiés; **the highest ~ of clerical post** la catégorie supérieure *or* la plus élevée des employés de bureau; **~ C eggs** œufs *mpl* de calibre C; **~ B milk** lait *m* de qualité B; **high-~ meat/fruit** viande *f*/fruits *mpl* de premier choix *or* de première qualité; **high-~ steel/coal** acier *m*/charbon *m* de haute qualité; **he was classed as ~ 3 for physical fitness** on le mit en catégorie 3 en ce qui concerne la forme physique; (*fig*) **to make the ~** se montrer à la hauteur, y arriver*; **he'll never make the ~** il n'y arrivera jamais*, il ne sera jamais assez bon *or* jamais à la hauteur.

(b) (*US Scol*) (*class*) classe *f*; (*mark*) note *f.*

(c) (*slope*) rampe *f*, pente *f.*

2 *cpd*: (*US Rail*) **grade crossing** passage *m* à niveau; (*US*) **grade school** école *f* primaire; (*US Aut*) **grade separation** séparation *f* des niveaux de circulation.

3 *vt* **(a)** (*sort out*) *butter, milk, fruit, old clothes, accommodation, colours, questions* classer; (*by size*) *apples, eggs etc* calibrer. **the exercises are ~d according to difficulty** les exercices sont classés selon leur degré de difficulté.

(b) (*make progressively easier, more difficult, darker, lighter etc*) *work, exercises, colours etc* graduer.

(c) (*US Scol: mark*) *pupil, work* noter.

(d) (*Animal Husbandry: also* **~ up**) améliorer par sélection.

(e) (*US: level*) *ground* niveler.

grade down *vt sep* classer *or* mettre *or* placer dans une catégorie inférieure.

grade up *vt sep* classer *or* mettre *or* placer dans une catégorie supérieure; *V also* **grade 3d.**

gradient ['greɪdɪənt] *n* (*esp Brit*) rampe *f*, pente *f*, inclinaison *f*; (*Math, Phys*) gradient *m*. **a ~ of one in ten** une inclinaison de dix pour cent.

gradual ['grædjʊəl] **1** *adj change, improvement* graduel, progressif; *slope* doux (*f* douce). **2** *n* (*Rel*) graduel *m.*

gradually ['grædjʊəlɪ] *adv* graduellement, petit à petit, peu à peu.

graduate ['grædjʊeɪt] **1** *vt* **(a)** (*mark out*) *thermometer, container* graduer (*in* en).

(b) (*make progressively easier, more difficult, darker etc*) *work, exercises, colours etc* graduer. *[buyer]* **to ~ payments** payer par fractionnements progressifs (*or* dégressifs).

(c) (*US Scol, Univ*) conférer un diplôme à.

2 *vi* **(a)** (*Univ*) ≃ obtenir sa licence (*or* son diplôme *etc*); (*US*

Scol) ≃ obtenir son baccalauréat. **he ~d as an architect/a teacher** *etc* il a eu son diplôme d'architecte/de professeur *etc*.
(b) *[colours etc]* se changer graduellement (*into* en), passer graduellement (*into* à).
3 [ˈgrædjʊɪt] *n* **(a)** (*Univ*) ≃ licencié(e) *m(f)*, diplômé(e) *m(f)*. **(b)** (*Pharm*) verre (*or* bocal *etc*) gradué.
4 [ˈgrædjʊɪt] *adj* (*Univ*) *student, teacher, staff* ≃ diplômé, licencié. **~ course** études *fpl* de troisième cycle.
graduated [ˈgrædjʊeɪtɪd] *adj tube, flask* gradué; *tax etc* progressif. **in ~ stages** par paliers, graduellement, progressivement.
graduation [ˌgrædjʊˈeɪʃən] *n* **(a)** (*V* **graduate 1a, 1b**) graduation *f*. **(b)** (*Univ, also US Scol*) (*ceremony*) remise *f* des diplômes *etc*; (*by student*) réception *f* d'un diplôme *etc*. **~ day/ceremony** jour *m*/cérémonie *f* de la remise des diplômes.
graffiti [grəˈfiːtɪ] *npl* graffiti *mpl*.
graft [grɑːft] **1** *n* **(a)** (*Agr*) greffe *f*, greffon *m*, ente *f*; (*Med*) greffe. **they did a skin ~** ils ont fait une greffe de la peau; **they did a kidney ~ on him** on lui a greffé un rein.
(b) (*U: bribery etc*) corruption *f*. (*Brit*) **hard ~:** boulot* acharné.
2 *vt* **(a)** (*Agr, Med*) greffer (*on, in* sur).
(b) (*get by bribery etc*) obtenir par la corruption; (*get by swindling*) obtenir par (l')escroquerie.
3 *vi* (*engage in bribery*) donner (*or* recevoir) des pots-de-vin *mpl or* enveloppes* *fpl*; (*swindle*) faire de l'escroquerie.
grail [greɪl] *n*: **the Holy G~** le Saint Graal.
grain [greɪn] **1** *n* **(a)** (*U*) grain(s) *m(pl)*, céréale(s) *f(pl)*; (*US*) blé *m*.
(b) *[cereal, salt, sand etc]* grain *m*; *[sense, malice]* grain, brin *m*; *[truth]* ombre *f*, miette *f*. **a few ~s of rice** quelques grains de riz; **that's a ~ of comfort** c'est une petite consolation; *V* **salt**.
(c) (*in leather; also Phot*) grain *m*; (*in wood, meat*) fibre *f*; (*in cloth*) fil *m*; (*in stone, marble*) veine *f*. **with the ~** dans le sens de la fibre (*or* de la veine *etc*); **against the ~** en travers de la fibre (*or* de la veine *etc*); (*fig*) **it goes against the ~ for him to apologize** cela va à l'encontre de sa nature de s'excuser; **I'll do it, but it goes against the ~** je le ferai, mais pas de bon cœur *or* mais cela va à l'encontre de mes idées.
(d) (*weight*) *mesure de poids* (= *0,065 gramme*).
2 *cpd*: **grain alcohol** alcool *m* de grain; (*US*) **grain elevator** silo *m* à céréales.
3 *vt* **(a)** *salt etc* grener, grainer, réduire en graine; *powder* granuler.
(b) *leather, paper* greneler; (*paint in imitation of wood*) veiner.
gram [græm] *n* gramme *m*.
grammar [ˈgræmə^{r}] **1** *n* **(a)** (*U*) grammaire *f*. **that is bad ~** cela n'est pas grammatical; *V* **generative** *etc*. **(b)** (*also* **~ book**) (livre *m* de) grammaire *f*. **2** *cpd*: **grammar school** (*Brit*) lycée *m*; (*US*) cours moyen.
grammarian [grəˈmɛərɪən] *n* grammairien(ne) *m(f)*.
grammatical [grəˈmætɪkəl] *adj* grammatical.
grammatically [grəˈmætɪkəlɪ] *adv* grammaticalement.
gramme [græm] *n* = **gram**.
gramophone [ˈgræməfəʊn] **1** *n* (*esp Brit*) phonographe *m*. **2** *cpd*: **gramophone needle** aiguille *f* de phonographe; **gramophone record** disque *m*.
grampus [ˈgræmpəs] *n* épaulard *m*, orque *m*; *V* **puff**.
granary [ˈgrænərɪ] *n* grenier *m* (*à blé etc*).
grand [grænd] **1** *adj* **(a)** grand, magnifique, splendide; *person* magnifique, splendide; (*in official titles*) grand; *character* grand, noble; *style* grandiose, noble; *scenery, house* grandiose, magnifique, impressionnant; *job, post* important, considérable; *chorus, concert* grand. **~ duke** grand duc; **in the ~ manner** dans un style de grand seigneur; **the ~ old man of music/French politics** *etc* le patriarche de la musique/de la politique française *etc*; **~ vizier** grand vizir; *V also* **3**.
(b) (*excellent*) magnifique, sensationnel*, formidable*. **we had a ~ time** nous nous sommes formidablement* amusés; **it was a ~ game** le match a été magnifique.
2 *n* **(a)** (*US*:) mille dollars *mpl*.
(b) piano *m* à queue *or* de concert; *V* **baby**.
3 *cpd*: **grandchild** petit(e)-enfant *m(f)*, petit-fils *m*, petite-fille *f*; **grand(d)ad*** grand-papa* *m*, pépé* *m*, bon-papa* *m*; **granddaughter** petite-fille *f*; **grandfather** grand-père *m*; **grandfather clock** ≃ horloge *f* de parquet; **grand jury** jury *m* d'accusation; (*US Jur*) **grand larceny** vol qualifié; **grand(ma)ma*** grand-maman* *f*, mémé* *f*, mamie* *f*, bonne-maman* *f*; **grandmother** grand-mère *f*; (*Racing*) **the Grand National** le Grand National; **grand opera** grand opéra; **grand(pa)pa*** = **grand(d)ad**; **grandparents** grands-parents *mpl*; **grand piano** piano *m* à queue *or* de concert; (*Bridge*) **grand slam** grand chelem; **grandson** petit-fils *m*; **grand staircase** escalier *m* d'honneur; (*Sport*) **grandstand** tribune *f*; (*fig*) **to have a grandstand view** être aux premières loges (*fig*) (*of sth* pour voir qch); **grand total** somme globale; (*Hist*) **the Grand Tour** le tour d'Europe; le tour complet; **we did a** *or* **the grand tour of the Louvre** nous avons fait le tour complet *or* une visite complète du Louvre.
grandee [grænˈdiː] *n* (*in Spain*) grand *m* d'Espagne; (*fig*) grand manitou*.
grandeur [ˈgrændjə^{r}] *n [person]* grandeur *f*; *[scenery, house etc]* splendeur *f*, magnificence *f*; *[character, style]* noblesse *f*; *[position]* éminence *f*.
grandiloquence [grænˈdɪləkwəns] *n* grandiloquence *f*.
grandiloquent [grænˈdɪləkwənt] *adj* grandiloquent.
grandiose [ˈgrændɪəʊz] *adj* grandiose; *style* grandiloquent, pompeux.
grand mal [ˈgrɑ̃ːnˈmæl] *n* épilepsie *f*, haut mal†.
grange [greɪndʒ] *n* **(a)** (*esp Brit: country house*) château *m*, manoir *m*. **(b)** (*US: farm*) ferme *f*. **the G~** la fédération agricole. **(c)** (††) = **granary**.
granger [ˈgreɪndʒə^{r}] **1** *n* (*US*) fermier *m*.
granite [ˈgrænɪt] **1** *n* granit *m*. **2** *cpd* de granit. (*Brit*) **the Granite City** la cité de granit (*Aberdeen*); (*US*) **the Granite State** l'État *m* du granit (*le New Hampshire*).
granny [ˈgrænɪ] *n* **(a)** (*) grand-maman* *f*, bonne-maman* *f*, mémé* *f*, mamie* *f*. **(b)** (*also* **~ knot**) nœud *m* de vache.
grant [grɑːnt] **1** *vt* **(a)** *favour, permission* accorder, octroyer; *prayer* exaucer; *wish* accorder; *request* accéder à, faire droit à; *pension etc* accorder, allouer. **to ~ sb permission to do** accorder à qn l'autorisation de faire; **to ~ sb his request** accorder à qn sa requête; **I beg your pardon! — ~ed!** je vous demande pardon! — je vous en prie!; **God ~ that** plaise à Dieu que + *subj*.
(b) (*admit*) admettre, accorder, concéder. **to ~ a proposition** admettre la vérité d'une proposition; **it must be ~ed that ...** il faut admettre *or* reconnaître que ...; **~ed that this is true** en admettant que ce soit vrai; **I ~ you that** je vous l'accorde; **I ~ that he is honest** je vous accorde qu'il est honnête; **~ed!** soit!, d'accord!; **he takes her for ~ed** il la considère comme faisant partie du décor; **stop taking me for ~ed!** j'existe moi aussi!, tu pourrais avoir quelques égards pour moi!; **to take details/sb's agreement** *etc* **for ~ed** considérer les détails/l'accord de qn *etc* comme convenu(s) *or* admis; **we may take it for ~ed that he will come** nous pouvons tenir pour certain *or* compter qu'il viendra; **you take too much for ~ed** (*take too many liberties*) vous prenez trop de libertés *or* de privautés; (*assume things are further forward than they are*) vous croyez que c'est arrivé*.
2 *n* **(a)** (*U*) *[favour, permission]* octroi *m*; *[land]* concession *f*; (*Jur*) *[property]* cession *f*; *[money, pension]* allocation *f*.
(b) (*sum given*) subvention *f*, allocation *f*; (*scholarship*) bourse *f*. **they have a government ~ to aid research** ils ont une subvention gouvernementale pour aider la recherche; **this student is on a ~ of £900** cet étudiant a une bourse de 900 livres.
3 *cpd*: **grant-aided** subventionné par l'État; **grant-in-aid** subvention *f* de l'État.
granular [ˈgrænjʊlə^{r}] *adj* granuleux, granulaire.
granulate [ˈgrænjʊleɪt] *vt metal, powder* granuler; *salt, sugar, soil* grener, grainer; *surface* rendre grenu. **~d paper** papier grenelé; **~d surface** surface grenue; **~d sugar** sucre *m* semoule.
granule [ˈgrænjuːl] *n* granule *m*.
grape [greɪp] **1** *n* (grain *m* de) raisin *m*, grume *f*. **~s** raisin (*U*), raisins; **to harvest the ~s** vendanger, faire la (*or* les) vendange(s); *V* **bunch, sour** *etc*. **2** *cpd*: **grapefruit** pamplemousse *m*; **grape harvest** vendange *f*; **grape hyacinth** muscari *m*; **grape juice** jus *m* de raisin; **grapeshot** mitraille *f*; (*lit*) **grapevine** vigne *f*; (*fig*) **I hear on** *or* **through the grapevine that ...** j'ai appris par le téléphone arabe *or* de mes sources personnelles que ..., mon petit doigt m'a dit que ... .
graph [grɑːf] *n* graphique *m*, courbe *f*. **~ paper** papier quadrillé; (*in millimetres*) papier millimétré.
graphic [ˈgræfɪk] **1** *adj* (*also Math*) graphique; (*fig*) *description* pittoresque, vivant, animé. **~ arts** arts *mpl* graphiques.
2 *n*: **~s** (*U: art of drawing*) art *m* graphique; (*U: Math etc: use of graphs*) (utilisation *f* des) graphiques *mpl*; (*npl: process*) procédés *mpl* graphiques; (*npl: sketches*) représentations *fpl* graphiques; (*TV etc*) **~s by ...** art graphique (de) ... .
graphite [ˈgræfaɪt] *n* graphite *m*, mine *f* de plomb, plombagine *f*.
graphologist [græˈfɒlədʒɪst] *n* graphologue *mf*.
graphology [græˈfɒlədʒɪ] *n* graphologie *f*.
grapnel [ˈgræpnəl] *n* grappin *m*.
grapple [ˈgræpl] **1** *n* (*Tech: also* **grappling iron**) grappin *m*. **2** *vt* (*Tech*) saisir avec un grappin *or* au grappin. **3** *vi [people]* se bagarrer*, se battre (*with sb* avec qn, *for sth* pour qch). (*fig*) **to ~ with difficulties** affronter résolument les difficultés.
grasp [grɑːsp] **1** *vt* **(a)** (*seize*) *object* saisir, empoigner; (*fig*) *power, opportunity, territory* saisir, se saisir de, s'emparer de. **to ~ sb's hand** saisir *or* empoigner la main de qn; (*fig*) **to ~ the nettle** aborder de front la difficulté, prendre le taureau par les cornes.
(b) (*understand*) saisir, comprendre.
2 *n* **(a)** poigne *f*. **a strong ~** une forte poigne.
(b) prise *f*, étreinte *f*. (*lit*) **to lose one's ~** lâcher prise; (*lit*) **to lose one's ~ on** *or* **of sth** lâcher qch; (*lit, fig*) **to have sth within one's ~** avoir qch à portée de la main; **to have sb in one's ~** avoir *or* tenir qn en son pouvoir; **prosperity is within everyone's ~** la prospérité est à la portée de chacun.
(c) (*understanding*) compréhension *f*. **he has a good ~ of mathematics** il a une solide connaissance des mathématiques; **he has no ~ of our difficulties** il ne se rend pas compte de nos difficultés, il ne saisit pas la nature de nos difficultés; **it is beyond my ~** je n'y comprends rien, cela me dépasse; **this subject is within everyone's ~** ce sujet est à la portée de tout le monde.
grasping [ˈgrɑːspɪŋ] *adj* (*fig*) avare, cupide, avide.
grass [grɑːs] **1** *n* **(a)** (*U*) herbe *f*; (*lawn*) gazon *m*, pelouse *f*; (*grazing*) herbage *m*, pâturage *m*. **'keep off the ~'** 'défense de marcher sur le gazon'; (*fig*) **to let the ~ grow under one's feet** laisser traîner les choses, perdre son temps; **he can hear the ~ growing*** rien ne lui échappe; (*fig*) **the ~ is greener on the other side of the fence** on jalouse le sort du voisin; **at ~** au vert; **to put out to ~** *horse* mettre au vert; (*fig*) *person* mettre au repos; (*Agr*) **to put under ~** enherber, mettre en pré; *V* **blade, green, sparrow** *etc*.
(b) (*Bot*) **~es** graminées *fpl*.
(c) (*Drugs sl: marijuana*) herbe *f* (*sl*).

(d) (*Brit Prison sl: informer*) indic *m* (*sl*), mouchard: *m*.
2 *vt* (*also* ~ **over**) *garden* gazonner; *field* couvrir d'herbe, enherber.
3 *vi* (*Brit Prison sl*) moucharder:. **to ~ on sb** donner *or* vendre qn.
4 *cpd*: (*Tennis*) **grass court** court *m* (en gazon); (*Tennis*) **to play on grass** *or* **on a grass court** jouer sur herbe *or* sur gazon; **grass cutter** (grosse) tondeuse *f* à gazon; **grass green** vert pré *inv*; **grasshopper** sauterelle *f*; (*U*) **grassland** prairie *f*, herbages *mpl*; (*fig, esp Pol: of movement, party*) **the grass roots** la base; (*Pol*) **grass-roots candidate/movement** *etc* candidat *m*/mouvement *m etc* populaire *or* du peuple *or* de la masse; **grass snake** couleuvre *f*; (*esp US*) **grass widow** divorcée *f*, femme séparée (de son mari); (*Brit fig*) **I'm a grass widow this week*** cette semaine je suis veuve (*hum*) *or* sans mari; (*esp US*) **grass widower** divorcé *m*, homme séparé de sa femme.

grassy [ˈgrɑːsɪ] *adj* herbeux, herbu.

grate[1] [greɪt] *n* (*metal framework*) grille *f* de foyer; (*fireplace*) foyer *m*, âtre *m*, cheminée *f*.

grate[2] [greɪt] **1** *vt* **(a)** (*Culin*) *cheese, carrot etc* râper.
(b) *metallic object* faire grincer; *chalk* faire grincer *or* crisser. **to ~ one's teeth** grincer des dents.
2 *vi* [*metal*] grincer; [*chalk*] grincer, crisser (*on* sur). (*fig*) **to ~ on the ears** écorcher les oreilles; **it ~d on his nerves** cela lui tapait sur les nerfs* *or* le système*; **his constant chatter ~d on me** son bavardage incessant me tapait sur les nerfs* *or* m'agaçait.

grateful [ˈgreɪtfʊl] *adj* reconnaissant (*to, towards* à, envers, *for* de). **I am most ~ to you** je vous suis très reconnaissant; **I am ~ for your support** je vous suis reconnaissant de votre soutien; **he sent me a very ~ letter** il m'a envoyé une lettre exprimant sa vive reconnaissance; **I should be ~ if you would come** je vous serais reconnaissant de venir; **the ~ warmth of the fire** la chaleur réconfortante *or* l'agréable chaleur du feu; **with ~ thanks** avec mes (*or* nos *etc*) plus sincères remerciements.

gratefully [ˈgreɪtfəlɪ] *adv* avec reconnaissance.

grater [ˈgreɪtəʳ] *n* râpe *f*. **cheese ~** râpe à fromage.

gratification [ˌgrætɪfɪˈkeɪʃən] *n* satisfaction *f*, plaisir *m*, contentement *m*; [*desires etc*] assouvissement *m*. **to his ~ he learnt that ...** à sa grande satisfaction il apprit que ... .

gratify [ˈgrætɪfaɪ] *vt person* faire plaisir à, être agréable à; *desire etc* satisfaire, assouvir; *whim* satisfaire. **I was gratified to hear that** j'ai appris avec grand plaisir que, cela m'a fait plaisir d'apprendre que; **he was very gratified** il a été très content *or* très satisfait.

gratifying [ˈgrætɪfaɪɪŋ] *adj* agréable, plaisant; *attentions etc* flatteur. **it is ~ to learn that** il est très agréable d'apprendre que, j'ai (*or* nous avons) appris avec plaisir que.

grating[1] [ˈgreɪtɪŋ] *n* grille *f*, grillage *m*.

grating[2] [ˈgreɪtɪŋ] **1** *adj sound* grinçant; *voice* discordant, de crécelle; (*annoying*) irritant, énervant, agaçant. **2** *n* (*U: sound*) grincement *m*.

gratis [ˈgrætɪs] **1** *adv* gratis, gratuitement. **2** *adj* gratis *inv*, gratuit.

gratitude [ˈgrætɪtjuːd] *n* reconnaissance *f*, gratitude *f* (*towards* envers, *for* de).

gratuitous [grəˈtjuːɪtəs] *adj* **(a)** (*uncalled for*) gratuit, injustifié, sans motif. **(b)** (*freely given*) gratuit.

gratuitously [grəˈtjuːɪtəslɪ] *adv* **(a)** (*for no reason*) gratuitement, sans motif. **(b)** (*without payment*) gratuitement, gratis.

gratuity [grəˈtjuːɪtɪ] *n* **(a)** (*Brit Mil etc*) prime *f* de démobilisation. **(b)** (*tip*) pourboire *m*, gratification *f*.

grave[1] [greɪv] **1** *n* tombe *f*; (*more elaborate*) tombeau *m*. **from beyond the ~** d'outre-tombe; **he'll come to an early ~** il aura une fin prématurée; **someone is walking over my ~*** j'ai eu un frisson; *V* **foot, silent** *etc*.
2 *cpd*: **gravedigger** fossoyeur *m*; **graverobber** déterreur *m* de cadavres; **gravestone** pierre tombale; **graveyard** cimetière *m*; (*fig*) **the graveyard of his hopes** l'enterrement *m* de ses espoirs; (*fig*) **a graveyard cough** une toux qui sent le sapin.

grave[2] [greɪv] *adj* **(a)** *error, illness, misfortune, news* grave, sérieux; *matter* grave, important, de poids; *manner* grave, sérieux, solennel; *look* sérieux; *symptoms* grave, inquiétant. **(b)** [grɑːv] (*Ling*) *accent* grave.

gravel [ˈgrævəl] **1** *n* **(a)** (*U*) gravier *m*; (*finer*) gravillon *m*. **(b)** (*Med*) gravelle *f*. **2** *vt* couvrir de gravier. **3** *cpd*: **gravel path** chemin *m* de gravier; **gravel pit** carrière *f* de cailloux.

gravelly [ˈgrævəlɪ] *adj road* caillouteux, de gravier; *riverbed* pierreux, caillouteux; (*fig*) *voice* râpeux. **~ soil** gravier *m*.

gravely [ˈgreɪvlɪ] *adv move, nod, beckon* gravement, sérieusement, solennellement; *speak* gravement, sérieusement, d'un ton grave *or* sérieux. **~ ill** gravement malade; **~ wounded** grièvement *or* gravement blessé; **~ displeased** extrêmement mécontent.

graven [ˈgreɪvən] *adj* (††) taillé, sculpté. (*Rel etc*) **~ image** image *f*; (*fig*) **~ on his memory** gravé dans sa mémoire.

graveness [ˈgreɪvnɪs] *n* (*U: all senses*) gravité *f*.

graving [ˈgreɪvɪŋ] *n* (*Naut*) **~ dock** bassin *m* de radoub.

gravitate [ˈgrævɪteɪt] *vi* (*Phys etc*) graviter (*round* autour de); (*fig*) être attiré (*towards* vers). **to ~ to the bottom** se déposer *or* descendre au fond (*par gravitation*).

gravitation [ˌgrævɪˈteɪʃən] *n* (*Phys, fig*) gravitation *f* (*round* autour de, *towards* vers).

gravitational [ˌgrævɪˈteɪʃənl] *adj* de gravitation, attractif. **~ constant/field/force** constante *f*/champ *m*/force *f* de gravitation; **~ pull** gravitation *f*.

gravity [ˈgrævɪtɪ] *n* (*U*) **(a)** (*Phys*) pesanteur *f*. **the law of ~** la loi de la pesanteur; **~ feed** alimentation *f* par gravité; *V* **centre, specific**. **(b)** (*seriousness*) gravité *f*, sérieux *m*. **to lose one's ~** perdre son sérieux.

gravy [ˈgreɪvɪ] **1** *n* **(a)** (*Culin*) jus *m* de viande, sauce *f* (au jus). **(b)** (*US*:) (*easy money*) profit *m* facile, bénef: *m*; (*dishonest money*) argent mal acquis. **2** *cpd*: **gravy boat** saucière *f*; (*US*) **to get on the gravy train:** trouver un fromage (*fig*).

gray [greɪ] (*esp US*) = **grey**.

grayling [ˈgreɪlɪŋ] *n* ombre *m* (de rivière).

graze[1] [greɪz] **1** *vi* brouter, paître. **2** *vt* **(a)** [*cattle*] *grass* brouter, paître; *field* pâturer (dans). **(b)** [*farmer*] *cattle* paître, faire paître.

graze[2] [greɪz] **1** *vt* **(a)** (*touch lightly*) frôler, raser, effleurer. (*Naut*) **to ~ bottom** labourer le fond; **it only ~d him** cela n'a fait que l'effleurer.
(b) (*scrape*) *skin, hand etc* érafler, écorcher. **to ~ one's knees** s'écorcher les genoux; **the bullet ~d his arm** la balle lui a éraflé le bras.
2 *n* écorchure *f*, éraflure *f*.

grazing [ˈgreɪzɪŋ] *n* (*U*) (*land*) pâturage *m*; (*act*) pâture *f*.

grease [griːs] **1** *n* (*gen, also Culin*) graisse *f*; (*Aut, Tech*) lubrifiant *m*, graisse; (*dirt*) crasse *f*, saleté *f*. **to remove the ~ from sth** dégraisser qch; **his collar was thick with ~** son col était couvert d'une épaisse couche de crasse; *V* **axle, elbow** *etc*.
2 *vt* graisser; (*Aut etc*) lubrifier, graisser. **like ~d lightning*** à toute allure, en quatrième vitesse*, à toute pompe:, tel l'éclair (*hum*); *V* **palm**[1], **wheel** *etc*.
3 *cpd*: **grease gun** (pistolet *m*) graisseur *m*; (*Aut*) **grease nipple** graisseur *m*; **greasepaint** fard gras; **stick of greasepaint** crayon gras; (*Brit*) **greaseproof** imperméable à la graisse; **greaseproof paper** papier parcheminé *or* sulfurisé; **grease-stained** graisseux.

greasiness [ˈgriːsɪnɪs] *n* graisse *f*, nature graisseuse, état graisseux; [*ointment etc*] onctuosité *f*; (*slipperiness*) [*road etc*] surface grasse *or* glissante.

greasy [ˈgriːsɪ] *adj substance, hair, food* graisseux, gras (*f* grasse), huileux; *tools* graisseux; *ointment* gras, huileux; (*slippery*) *surface, road etc* gras, glissant; *clothes, collar* (*oily*) plein de graisse; (*grubby*) sale, crasseux. **~ hands** mains pleines de graisse, mains graisseuses; (*fig*) **a ~ character** un personnage fuyant; **~ pole** mât *m* de cocagne; (*US*) **~ spoon:** gargote *f* (*pej*).

great [greɪt] **1** *adj* **(a)** *building, tree, fire, height, depth* grand; *cliff* grand, haut, élevé; *parcel* grand, gros (*f* grosse); *crowd, swarm* grand, gros, nombreux; *number, amount* grand, élevé; *heat* grand, gros, fort, intense; *pain* fort, intense; *pleasure, satisfaction, annoyance* grand, intense; *power* grand, énorme; *determination, will-power* fort; *person* (*in achievement*) grand, éminent, insigne; (*in character*) grand, supérieur, noble; (*in appearance*) magnifique, splendide; (*in importance*) grand, important, notable; (*chief*) grand, principal. **Alexander the G~** Alexandre le Grand; **a ~ man** un grand homme; **she's a ~ lady** c'est une grande dame; **the ~ masters** les grands maîtres; **a ~ painter** un grand peintre; **Dickens is a ~ storyteller** Dickens est un grand conteur; **the ~est names in football/poetry** *etc* les plus grands noms du football/de la poésie *etc*; **a ~ deal (of)** beaucoup (de); **a ~ many** beaucoup (de); **to a ~ extent** en grande partie; **to reach a ~ age** parvenir à un âge avancé; **~ big** énorme, immense; **with ~ care** avec grand soin, avec beaucoup de soin; **they are ~ friends** ce sont de grands amis; **Robert is my ~ friend** Robert est mon grand ami; **he has a ~ future** il a un bel avenir devant lui *or* beaucoup d'avenir; **to take a ~ interest in** prendre grand intérêt à; **I have a ~ liking for/hatred of** j'éprouve une grande affection pour/une violente haine pour; **I have a ~ mind to do it** j'ai bien *or* très envie de le faire; **I have no ~ opinion of ...** je n'ai pas une haute opinion de ...; **at a ~ pace** à vive allure; **with ~ pleasure** avec grand plaisir, avec beaucoup de plaisir; **with the ~est pleasure** avec le plus grand plaisir; **a ~ while ago** il y a bien longtemps; *V* **also 3**.
(b) (*: *excellent*) *holiday, results etc* merveilleux, magnifique, sensationnel*, génial*, terrible:. **it was a ~ joke** c'était une bonne blague; **it's ~!** magnifique!, sensass!:, terrible!:, génial!*; **you were ~!** tu as été magnifique! *or* merveilleux! *or* sensationnel!* *or* terrible!:; **we had a ~ time** nous nous sommes follement amusés; **wouldn't it be ~ to do that** ce serait merveilleux de faire cela; **he's a ~ angler** (*keen*) il est passionné de pêche; (*expert*) c'est un pêcheur émérite; **he's ~ at football/maths** *etc* il est doué pour le football/les maths *etc*; **he's a ~ one for cathedrals*** il adore visiter les cathédrales; **he's a ~ one for criticizing others*** il ne rate pas une occasion de critiquer les autres; **he's a ~ arguer** il est toujours prêt à discuter; **he's ~ on jazz*** il connaît à fond le jazz; **~ Scott!*** grands dieux!; **he's a ~ guy*** c'est un type sensass: *or* génial* *or* terrible:; **he's the ~est!:** c'est lui le roi!:, il est champion!:; *V* **gun**.
2 *n* **(a)** **the ~** les grands *mpl*.
(b) (*Oxford Univ*) **G~s** = licence *f* de lettres classiques.
3 *cpd*: **great-aunt** grand-tante *f*; **the Great Barrier Reef** la Grande Barrière; (*Astron*) **Great Bear** Grande Ourse; **Great Britain** Grande-Bretagne *f*; **greatcoat** pardessus *m*; (*Mil*) manteau *m*, capote *f*; (*dog*) **Great Dane** danois *m*; **Greater London** le grand Londres; **great-grandchild** arrière-petit(e)-enfant *m(f)*; **great-granddaughter** arrière-petite-fille *f*; **great-grandfather** arrière-grand-père *m*, bisaïeul *m* (*liter*); **great-grandmother** arrière-grand-mère *f*, bisaïeule *f* (*liter*); **great-grandson** arrière-petit-fils *m*; **great-great-grandfather** arrière-arrière-grand-père *m*, trisaïeul *m*; **great-great-grandson** arrière-arrière-petit-fils *m*; **great-hearted** au grand cœur, magnanime; **the Great Lakes** les Grands Lacs; **great-nephew** petit-neveu *m*; **great-niece** petite-nièce *f*; (*Pol*) **the Great Powers** les grandes puissances; (*Orn*) **great tit** mésange *f* charbonnière; **great-uncle** grand-oncle *m*; **the Great War** la Grande Guerre, la guerre de 1914-18.

greatly [ˈgreɪtlɪ] *adv* grandement, fort, bien, très, (de) beaucoup. **it is ~ to be feared/regretted** *etc* il est fort *or* bien à craindre/à regretter *etc*, il y a tout lieu de craindre/de regretter *etc*; **~ admired/amused/surprised** très admiré/amusé/surpris; **~ superior** bien *or* de très loin *or* de beaucoup supérieur; **~ annoyed** vivement *or* fort *or* très contrarié; **it was ~ improved/increased** *etc* c'était bien amélioré/augmenté *etc*.

greatness ['greɪtnɪs] *n* **(a)** (*in size*) grandeur *f*; (*hugeness*) énormité *f*, immensité *f*; (*in degree*) intensité *f*. **(b)** (*of person: V* **great 1a**) grandeur *f*, éminence *f*; noblesse *f*; splendeur *f*, importance *f*.

grebe [gri:b] *n* grèbe *m*.

Grecian ['gri:ʃən] (*liter*) **1** *adj* grec (*f* grecque). **hair in a ~ knot** coiffure *f* à la grecque. **2** *n* (*Greek*) Grec(que) *m(f)*; (*scholar*) helléniste *mf*.

Greece [gri:s] *n* Grèce *f*.

greed [gri:d] *n* (*U*) (*for money, power etc*) avidité *f*, cupidité *f*; (*for food*) gourmandise *f*, gloutonnerie *f*.

greedily ['gri:dɪlɪ] *adv* avidement, cupidement; *eat* voracement, gloutonnement; *drink* avidement, avec avidité. **he eyed the food ~** il a regardé la nourriture d'un air vorace; **he licked his lips ~** il s'est léché les babines *or* les lèvres d'un air vorace.

greediness ['gri:dɪnɪs] *n* = **greed**.

greedy ['gri:dɪ] *adj* (*for money, power etc*) avide (*for* de), rapace, cupide; (*for food*) vorace, glouton, goulu. **~ for gain** âpre au gain; **don't be ~!** (*at table*) ne sois pas si gourmand!; (*gen*) n'en demande pas tant!; (*pej*) **~ guts‡** goinfre *m*, empiffreur‡ *m*, -euse‡ *f*; *V* **hog**.

Greek [gri:k] **1** *adj* grec (*f* grecque). (*on china etc*) **~ key pattern, ~ fret** grecque *f*; **the ~ Orthodox Church** l'Église orthodoxe grecque.

2 *n* **(a)** Grec(que) *m(f)*.

(b) (*Ling*) grec *m*. **ancient/modern ~** grec classique/moderne; (*fig*) **that's (all) ~ to me*** tout ça c'est de l'hébreu *or* du chinois pour moi*.

green [gri:n] **1** *adj* **(a)** (*colour*) vert; *complexion* vert, verdâtre. **light/dark ~** vert clair *inv*/vert foncé *inv*; **to turn ~** verdir; **he looked quite ~** il était vert; **she went ~** elle *or* son visage verdit; (*fig*) **to be ~ with envy** être vert de jalousie; **to make sb ~ with envy** faire pâlir *or* loucher qn de jalousie; *V also* **3** *and* **baize** *etc*.

(b) (*unripe*) *fruit etc* vert, pas mûr; *bacon* non fumé; *wood* vert. **~ corn** blé *m* en herbe; **~ meat** viande trop fraîche.

(c) (*inexperienced*) jeune, inexpérimenté; (*naïve*) naïf (*f* naïve). **I'm not as ~ as I look!*** je ne suis pas si naïf que j'en ai l'air!; **he's as ~ as grass*** il ne connaît rien de la vie, c'est un niais.

(d) (*flourishing*) vert, vigoureux. **~ old age** verte vieillesse; **to keep sb's memory ~** chérir la mémoire de qn; **memories still ~** souvenirs encore vivaces *or* vivants.

2 *n* **(a)** (*colour*) vert *m*. **dressed in ~** habillé de *or* en vert.

(b) pelouse *f*, gazon *m*; (*also* **village ~**) place *f* (du village) (*gazonnée*); *V* **bowling** *etc*.

(c) (*Culin*) **~s** légumes verts.

3 *cpd*: (*US*) **greenback** billet *m* (de banque); **green bean** haricot vert; (*Town Planning*) **green belt** ceinture verte, zone *f* de verdure; **green-eyed** aux yeux verts; (*fig*) jaloux, envieux; (*fig*) **the green-eyed monster** la jalousie; **greenfinch** verdier *m*; (*Brit*) **he's got green fingers** il a le pouce vert, il a un don pour faire pousser les plantes; **greenfly** puceron *m* (des plantes); **greengage** reine-claude *f*; (*esp Brit*) **greengrocer** marchand(e) *m(f)* de légumes, fruitier *m*, -ière *f*; **greengrocer's (shop)** fruiterie *f*; **greenhorn** blanc-bec *m*, béjaune† *m*; **greenhouse** serre *f*; (*Aut*) **green light** feu vert; (*fig*) **to give sb the green light** donner le feu vert à qn; **to get the green light from sb** obtenir *or* recevoir le feu vert de qn; **green peas** petits pois; **green pepper** poivron vert; (*Econ*) **the green pound** la livre verte; (*Theat*) **green room** foyer *m* des acteurs *or* des artistes; (*Med*) **greenstick fracture** fracture incomplète; **greenstuff** verdure *f*; (*Culin*) légumes verts, verdure; **greensward††** pelouse *f*, gazon *m*, tapis *m* de verdure; (*US*) **he's got a green thumb** = **he's got green fingers**; **green vegetables** légumes verts; **greenwood††** forêt verdoyante.

greenery ['gri:nərɪ] *n* verdure *f*.

greenish ['gri:nɪʃ] *adj* tirant sur le vert, verdâtre (*pej*).

Greenland ['gri:nlənd] *n* Groenland *m*.

Greenlander ['gri:nləndəʳ] *n* Groenlandais(e) *m(f)*.

greenness ['gri:nnɪs] *n* couleur verte, vert *m*; *[countryside etc]* verdure *f*; *[wood, fruit etc]* verdeur *f*; *[person]* (*inexperience*) inexpérience *f*, manque *m* d'expérience; (*naïvety*) naïveté *f*.

Greenwich ['grɪnɪdʒ] *n*: **~ (mean) time** heure *f* de Greenwich.

greet[1] [gri:t] *vt person* saluer, accueillir. **they ~ed him with cries of delight** ils l'ont salué *or* accueilli avec des cris de joie; **he ~ed me with the news that ...** il m'a accueilli en m'apprenant que ...; **the statement was ~ed with laughter** la déclaration fut accueillie *or* saluée par des rires; **this was ~ed with relief by everyone** ceci a été accueilli avec soulagement par tous; **to ~ the ear** parvenir à l'oreille; **an awful sight ~ed me** *or* **my eyes** un spectacle affreux s'offrit à mes regards.

greet[2] [gri:t] *vi* (*Scot: weep*) pleurer.

greeting ['gri:tɪŋ] *n* salut *m*, salutation *f*; (*welcome*) accueil *m*. **~s** compliments *mpl*, salutations; **Xmas ~s** souhaits *mpl* *or* vœux *mpl* de Noël; **~(s) card** carte *f* de vœux; **he sent ~s to my brother** il s'est rappelé au bon souvenir de mon frère; **my mother sends you her ~s** ma mère vous envoie son bon souvenir.

gregarious [grɪ'gɛərɪəs] *adj animal, instinct, tendency* grégaire; *person* sociable. **men are ~** l'homme est un animal grégaire.

Gregorian [grɪ'gɔ:rɪən] *adj* grégorien. **~ calendar/chant** calendrier/chant grégorien.

gremlin* ['gremlɪn] *n* (*hum*) diablotin *m* (malfaisant).

grenade [grɪ'neɪd] *n* (*Mil*) grenade *f*; *V* **hand**.

grenadier [ˌgrenə'dɪəʳ] *n* grenadier *m* (*soldat*).

grenadine ['grenədi:n] *n* grenadine *f*.

grew [gru:] *pret of* **grow**.

grey [greɪ] **1** *adj* gris; *hair* gris, grisonnant; *complexion* blême; (*fig*) *outlook, prospect* sombre, morne. **he is going ~** il grisonne; **he nearly went ~ over it** il s'en est fait des cheveux blancs; **he turned quite ~ when he heard the news** il a blêmi en apprenant la nouvelle; **~ skies** ciel gris *or* morne; **it was a ~ day** (*lit*) c'était un jour gris; (*fig*) c'était un jour triste; (*fig*) **~ matter*** matière grise, cervelle* *f*; (*fig*) **there is a ~ area between what is clearly acceptable and what is clearly unacceptable** il existe une zone sombre *or* zone d'incertitude entre ce qui est évidemment acceptable et ce qui est évidemment inacceptable; *V also* **4**.

2 *n* **(a)** gris *m*. **dressed in ~** habillé de *or* en gris; **hair touched with ~** cheveux grisonnants.

(b) (*horse*) cheval gris.

3 *vi [hair]* grisonner. **he was ~ing at the temples** il avait les tempes grisonnantes.

4 *cpd*: **greybeard** vieil homme; **Grey Friar** franciscain *m*; **grey-haired** aux cheveux gris, grisonnant; **greyhound** (*dog*) lévrier *m*; (*bitch*) levrette *f*; **grey lag goose** oie cendrée; **grey squirrel** écureuil gris, petit-gris *m*; **grey wolf** loup *m* (gris).

greyish ['greɪɪʃ] *adj* tirant sur le gris, grisâtre (*pej*); *hair, beard* grisonnant.

grid [grɪd] **1** *n* (*grating*) grille *f*, grillage *m*; (*network of lines on chart, map etc; also Rad*) grille; (*Culin: utensil*) gril *m*; (*Theat*) gril (*pour manœuvrer les décors*); (*Aut: on roof*) galerie *f*, porte-bagages *m inv*; (*electrode*) grille; (*Brit Elec: system*) réseau *m*; (*Surv*) treillis *m*. (*Brit Elec*) **the (national) ~** le réseau électrique (national).

2 *cpd*: **grid(iron)** (*utensil*) gril *m*; (*US Sport*) terrain *m* de football.

griddle ['grɪdl] **1** *n* (*Culin*) plaque *f* en fonte (*pour cuire*); (*part of stove*) plaque chauffante. **~ cake** (sorte *f* de) crêpe épaisse. **2** *vt* (*Culin*) cuire à la poêle (plate).

grief [gri:f] **1** *n* **(a)** (*U*) chagrin *m*, douleur *f*, peine *f*, (*stronger*) affliction *f*, désolation *f*. **to come to ~** *[person]* avoir un malheur *or* des ennuis; *[vehicle]* avoir un accident; *[plan, marriage etc]* tourner mal, échouer; **we came to ~** il nous est arrivé malheur; **good ~!*** ciel!, grands dieux!

(b) (*cause of grief*) (cause *f* de) chagrin *m*.

2 *cpd*: **grief-stricken** accablé de douleur, affligé.

grievance ['gri:vəns] *n* (*ground for complaint*) grief *m*, sujet *m* de plainte; (*complaint*) doléance *f*; (*injustice*) injustice *f*, tort *m*; (*Ind*) différend *m*, conflit *m*. **to have a ~ against sb** avoir un grief *or* un sujet de plainte contre qn, en vouloir à qn; **he was filled with a sense of ~** il avait le sentiment profond d'être victime d'une injustice; *V* **redress**.

grieve [gri:v] **1** *vt* peiner, chagriner; (*stronger*) affliger, désoler. **it ~s us to see** nous sommes peinés de voir.

2 *vi* avoir de la peine *or* du chagrin (*at, about, over* à cause de); (*stronger*) s'affliger, se désoler (*at, about, over* de). **to ~ for sb/sth** pleurer qn/qch.

grievous ['gri:vəs] *adj pain* affreux, cruel; *loss, blow* cruel; *wounds, injury* grave, sérieux; *fault* grave, lourd, sérieux; *wrongs* grave; *crime, offence* atroce, odieux; *news* pénible, cruel; *cry* douloureux. (*Jur*) **~ bodily harm** coups *mpl* et blessures *fpl*.

grievously ['gri:vəslɪ] *adv* (*V* **grievous**) affreusement; cruellement; gravement; sérieusement; odieusement; douloureusement. **~ wounded** grièvement blessé.

griffin ['grɪfɪn] *n* (*Myth*) griffon *m*.

griffon ['grɪfən] *n* (*Myth, Zool*) griffon *m*.

grift‡ [grɪft] (*US*) **1** *n* filouterie* *f*, escroquerie *f*. **2** *vi* filouter*, vivre d'escroquerie.

grifter‡ ['grɪftəʳ] *n* (*US*) estampeur* *m*, filou *m*.

grill [grɪl] **1** *n* **(a)** (*Culin*) (*cooking utensil*) gril *m*; (*dish*) grillade *f*; (*restaurant: also* **~room**) rôtisserie *f*, grill *m*. (*Culin*) **brown it under the ~** faites-le dorer au gril; *V* **mixed**.

(b) = **grille**.

2 *vt* **(a)** (*Culin*) (faire) griller.

(b) (*: *interrogate*) faire subir un interrogatoire serré à, cuisiner‡.

3 *vi* (*Culin*) griller. **~ed fish** poisson grillé; **it's ~ing (hot) in here*** on grille ici*.

grille [grɪl] *n* (*grating*) grille *f*, grillage *m*; *[convent etc]* grille; *[door]* judas *m* (grillé); (*Aut: also* **radiator ~**) calandre *m*.

grilse [grɪls] *n* grilse *m*.

grim [grɪm] *adj* **(a)** *aspect* menaçant, sinistre; *outlook, prospects* sinistre; *landscape* lugubre; *joke* macabre; *smile* sardonique; *face* sévère, rébarbatif; *silence* sinistre. **to look ~** avoir une mine sinistre *or* sévère; **~ reality** la dure réalité; **~ necessity** la dure *or* cruelle nécessité; **the ~ truth** la vérité brutale; **with ~ determination** avec une volonté inflexible; **to hold on to sth like ~ death** rester cramponné à qch de toutes ses forces *or* comme quelqu'un qui se noie.

(b) (*: *unpleasant*) désagréable. **life is rather ~ at present** les choses vont plutôt mal à présent, la vie n'est pas drôle actuellement*; **she's feeling pretty ~*** (*ill*) elle ne se sent pas bien du tout; (*depressed*) elle se sent très déprimée, elle n'a pas le moral*.

grimace [grɪ'meɪs] **1** *n* grimace *f*. **2** *vi* (*from disgust, pain etc*) grimacer, faire la grimace; (*for fun*) faire des grimaces. **he ~d at the taste/the sight of ...** il a fait une grimace en goûtant/voyant ...

grime [graɪm] *n* (*U*) crasse *f*, saleté *f*.

grimly ['grɪmlɪ] *adv frown, look* d'un air mécontent; *continue,* *hold on* inexorablement, inflexiblement; *fight, struggle* avec acharnement. **'no surrender' they said** ~ 'nous ne nous rendrons pas' dirent-ils d'un air résolu; **'this is not good enough' he said** ~ 'ceci est insuffisant' dit-il d'un air mécontent.

grimness ['grɪmnɪs] *n [situation]* réalité accablante; *[landscape]* aspect *m* lugubre *or* sinistre; *[sb's appearance, expression]* sévérité *f*, aspect lugubre *or* sinistre.

grimy ['graɪmɪ] *adj* sale, encrassé, noirci; (*with soot*) noir; *face, hands* crasseux, sale, noir.

grin [grɪn] **1** *vi* **(a)** (*smile*) sourire; (*broadly*) avoir un large *or* grand sourire. **to ~ broadly at sb** adresser un large sourire à qn; **to ~ like a Cheshire cat** avoir un sourire fendu jusqu'aux oreilles; **we must just ~ and bear it** il faut le prendre avec le sourire, il faut faire contre mauvaise fortune bon cœur.

(b) (*in pain*) avoir un rictus, grimacer; *[snarling dog]* montrer les dents.

2 *vt*: **he ~ned his approval** il a manifesté son approbation d'un large sourire.

3 *n* (*smile*) (large) sourire *m*; (*in pain*) rictus *m*, grimace *f* de douleur.

grind [graɪnd] (*vb: pret, ptp* **ground**) **1** *n* **(a)** (*sound*) grincement *m*, crissement *m*.

(b) (*: *dull hard work*) boulot* *m* pénible, (lourde) corvée *f*. **the daily ~** le boulot*, (*stronger*) le labeur quotidien; **I find maths a dreadful ~** pour moi les maths sont un cauchemar; **that essay was a terrible ~** cette dissertation a été un vrai cauchemar à écrire; **it was an awful ~ for the exam** il a fallu bûcher ferme pour l'exam*.

(c) (*US**: *swot*) bûcheur *m*, -euse *f*.

2 *cpd*: **grindstone** meule *f* (à aiguiser); *V* **nose**.

3 *vt* **(a)** *corn, coffee, pepper etc* moudre; (*crush*) écraser, broyer; (*in mortar*) piler, concasser; (*rub together*) écraser l'un contre l'autre; (*fig: oppress*) écraser, opprimer. **to ~ sth to pieces** réduire qch en pièces par broyage *or* en le broyant *or* en l'écrasant; **to ~ sth to a powder** pulvériser qch, réduire qch en poudre; **to ~ one's teeth** grincer des dents; **he ground his heel into the soil** il a enfoncé son talon dans la terre; (*fig*) **they were ground (down) by taxation** ils étaient accablés *or* écrasés d'impôts; **ground down by poverty** accablé par la misère; (*loc*) **to ~ the faces of the poor** opprimer les pauvres.

(b) *gems* égriser, polir; *knife, blade* aiguiser *or* affûter (à la meule), meuler; *lens* polir; *V* **axe**.

(c) *handle* tourner; *barrel organ* faire jouer, jouer de. **to ~ a pepper mill** tourner un moulin à poivre.

4 *vi* **(a)** grincer. **the ship ground against the rocks** le navire a heurté les rochers en grinçant; **to ~ to a halt** *or* **to a standstill** *[vehicle]* s'arrêter *or* s'immobiliser dans un grincement de freins; *[process, production, business]* s'arrêter progressivement, s'immobiliser peu à peu.

(b) (*: *work hard*) bûcher‡ *or* boulonner‡ (dur *or* ferme).

grind away* *vi* bûcher‡ *or* boulonner‡ (dur *or* ferme). **to grind away at grammar** bûcher‡ *or* potasser‡ la grammaire.

grind down *vt sep* (*lit*) pulvériser; (*fig: oppress*) opprimer, écraser. **he gradually ground down all opposition to his plans** il a écrasé petit à petit toute tentative d'opposition à ses plans; *V also* **grind 3a**.

grind out *vt sep*: **to grind out a tune on a barrel organ** jouer un air sur un orgue de Barbarie; (*fig*) **he ground out an oath** il a proféré un juron entre ses dents; **he managed to grind out 2 pages of his essay** il est laborieusement arrivé à pondre‡ *or* à écrire 2 pages de sa dissertation.

grind up *vt sep* pulvériser.

grinder ['graɪndəʳ] *n* **(a)** (*apparatus*) broyeur *m*, machine *f or* moulin *m* à broyer; (*in kitchen*) broyeur, moulin; (*Tech*) affûteuse *f*, appareil *m* à aiguiser *or* à meuler.

(b) (*person*) broyeur *m*, -euse *f*; (*for knives*) rémouleur *m*, -euse *f*; *V* **organ**.

(c) (*tooth*) molaire *f*.

grinding ['graɪndɪŋ] *n* (*U: sound*) grincement *m*.

gringo ['grɪŋgəʊ] *n* (*US pej*) gringo *m*, ≃ Amerloque‡ *mf*.

grip [grɪp] **1** *n* **(a)** (*handclasp*) poigne *f*; (*hold*) prise *f*, étreinte *f*. **he has a strong ~** il a la poigne forte; **he held my arm in a vice-like ~** il me tenait le bras d'une poigne d'acier, il me serrait le bras comme un étau; **to get a ~ on** *or* **of sth** empoigner qch; (*fig*) **to get a ~ on** *or* **of o.s.*** se secouer*, se ressaisir; **get a ~ on yourself!*** secoue-toi un peu!*, ressaisis-toi!; (*lit*) **to lose one's ~** lâcher prise; **he lost his ~ on the rope** il a lâché la corde; **the tyres lost their ~ on the icy road** les pneus perdirent leur adhérence sur la chaussée gelée; (*fig*) **he's losing his ~*** il baisse*; (*hum*) **I must be losing my ~!*** je ne fais que des bêtises!; (*fig*) **he had a good ~ on his audience** il tenait (parfaitement) son auditoire; **he had lost his ~ on his audience** il ne tenait plus son auditoire; **he has a good ~ on** *or* **of his subject** il possède bien son sujet, il connaît à fond son sujet; **he came to ~s with the intruder** il en est venu aux prises avec l'intrus; **to come** *or* **get to ~s with a problem** s'attaquer à un problème, s'efforcer de résoudre un problème; **we have never had to come to ~s with such a situation** nous n'avons jamais été confrontés à pareille situation; **in the ~ of winter** paralysé par l'hiver; **country in the ~ of a general strike** pays en proie à *or* pays paralysé par une grève générale.

(b) (*device*) serrage *m*.

(c) (*handle*) poignée *f*.

(d) (*suitcase*) valise *f*; (*bag: also US* **~sack**) trousse *f*.

2 *vt* **(a)** (*grasp*) *rope, handrail, sb's arm* saisir; *pistol, sword etc* saisir, empoigner; (*hold*) serrer, tenir serré. **to ~ sb's hand** (*grasp*) saisir *or* prendre la main de qn; (*hold*) tenir la main de qn serrée; *[tyres]* **to ~ the road** adhérer à la chaussée; **the car ~s the road well** la voiture colle à la route.

(b) *[fear etc]* saisir, étreindre. **~ped by terror** saisi de terreur.

(c) (*interest strongly*) *[film, story etc]* empoigner. **a film that really ~s you** un film vraiment palpitant, un film qui vous empoigne vraiment.

3 *vi [wheels]* adhérer, mordre; *[screw, vice, brakes]* mordre; *[anchor]* crocher (sur le fond).

gripe [graɪp] **1** *vt* (*Med*) donner des coliques à. (‡: *anger*) **this ~d him** cela lui a mis l'estomac en boule*.

2 *vi* (‡: *grumble*) ronchonner*, rouspéter* (*at* contre).

3 *n* (*Med: also* **~s**) coliques *fpl*.

4 *cpd*: (*Brit*) **gripe water** calmant *m* (*pour coliques infantiles*).

griping‡ ['graɪpɪŋ] *n* (*U: grumbling*) rouspétance* *f*, ronchonnements* *mpl*.

gripping ['grɪpɪŋ] *adj story, play* passionnant, palpitant.

grisly ['grɪzlɪ] *adj* (*gruesome*) macabre, sinistre; (*terrifying*) horrible, effroyable.

grist [grɪst] *n* blé *m* (à moudre). (*fig*) **that's all ~ to his mill** tout cela apporte de l'eau à son moulin.

gristle ['grɪsl] *n* (*U*) cartilage *m*, tendons *mpl* (*surtout dans la viande cuite*).

gristly ['grɪslɪ] *adj* cartilagineux, croquant (*pej*) (*se dit surtout de la viande cuite*).

grit [grɪt] **1** *n* **(a)** (*U*) (*sand*) sable *m*; (*gravel*) gravillon *m*; (*rock: also* **~stone**) grès *m*; (*for fowl*) gravier *m*; (*: *courage*) cran* *m*. **I've got (a piece of) ~ in my eye** j'ai une poussière dans l'œil; **he's got ~*** il a du cran*.

(b) (*US*) **~s** gruau *m* de maïs.

2 *vi* craquer, crisser.

3 *vt* **(a) to ~ one's teeth** serrer les dents.

(b) to ~ a road répandre du gravillon sur une route.

gritty ['grɪtɪ] *adj path etc* (couvert) de gravier *or* de cailloutis; *fruit* graveleux, grumeleux; (*: *plucky*) *person* qui a du cran*.

grizzle ['grɪzl] *vi* (*Brit*) (*whine*) pleurnicher, geindre; (*complain*) ronchonner*.

grizzled ['grɪzld] *adj hair, person* grisonnant.

grizzly ['grɪzlɪ] **1** *adj* **(a)** (*grey*) grisâtre; *hair, person* grisonnant. **(b)** (*whining*) pleurnicheur, geignard. **2** *n* (*also* **~ bear**) ours gris.

groan [grəʊn] **1** *n* (*of pain etc*) gémissement *m*, plainte *f*; (*of disapproval, dismay*) grognement *m*. **this was greeted with ~s** ceci fut accueilli par des murmures (désapprobateurs).

2 *vi* **(a)** (*in pain*) gémir, pousser un *or* des gémissement(s) (*with* de); (*in disapproval, dismay*) grogner. **he ~ed inwardly at the thought** il a étouffé un grognement à l'idée.

(b) (*creak*) *[planks etc]* gémir; *[door]* crier. **the table ~ed under the weight of the food** la table ployait sous le poids de la nourriture; (*hum*) **the ~ing board** la table ployant sous l'amoncellement de victuailles.

groat [grəʊt] *n* (*Brit*) *ancienne petite pièce de monnaie*.

groats [grəʊts] *npl* gruau *m* d'avoine *or* de froment.

grocer ['grəʊsəʳ] *n* épicier *m*. **at the ~'s (shop)** à l'épicerie, chez l'épicier; **the ~'s wife** l'épicière *f*.

grocery ['grəʊsərɪ] *n* **(a)** (*shop*) épicerie *f*. **he's in the ~ business** il est dans l'épicerie. **(b) I spent £7 on groceries** j'ai dépensé 7 livres en épicerie (*U*) *or* en provisions; **all the groceries are in this basket** toute l'épicerie est dans ce panier.

grog [grɒg] *n* grog *m*.

groggy* ['grɒgɪ] *adj person* (*weak*) faible; (*unsteady*) vacillant, chancelant, groggy*; (*from blow etc*) groggy*, sonné*. **I still feel a bit ~** j'ai toujours un peu les jambes comme du coton, je me sens toujours un peu sonné* *or* groggy*; **that chair looks rather ~** cette chaise a l'air un peu bancale.

grogram ['grɒgrəm] *n* gros-grain *m*.

groin [grɔɪn] *n* **(a)** (*Anat*) aine *f*. **(b)** (*Archit*) arête *f*. **(c)** = **groyne**.

grommet ['grɒmɪt] *n* (*ring of rope, metal*) erse *f*, erseau *m*; (*metal eyelet*) œillet *m*.

groom [gru:m] **1** *n* (*for horses*) valet *m* d'écurie, palefrenier *m*; (*bridegroom*) (*just married*) (jeune) marié *m*; (*about to be married*) (futur) marié; (*in royal household*) chambellan *m*.

2 *vt horse* panser. **the animal was ~ing itself** l'animal faisait sa toilette; **she is always well-~ed** elle est toujours très soignée; (*fig*) **to ~ sb for a post** préparer *or* former qn pour un poste; (*Cine*) **she is being ~ed for stardom** on la façonne pour en faire une star; (*fig: in business etc*) **to ~ sb for stardom** préparer qn pour une promotion; **he is ~ing him as his successor** il en a fait son poulain.

groove [gru:v] **1** *n* (*for sliding door etc*) rainure *f*; (*for pulley etc*) cannelure *f*, gorge *f*; (*in column, screw*) cannelure; (*in record*) sillon *m*; (*in penknife blade*) onglet *m*. **it's in the ~‡** (*up-to-date*) c'est dans le vent‡; (*functioning perfectly*) ça baigne dans l'huile*, ça marche comme sur des roulettes*; **to get into a ~*** s'encroûter, devenir routinier; **he's in a ~*** il est pris dans la routine, il s'est encroûté.

2 *vt* canneler, rainer, rainurer.

groovy‡ ['gru:vɪ] *adj* (*marvellous*) sensass‡, vachement bien‡; (*up-to-date*) dans le vent‡.

grope [grəʊp] *vi* tâtonner, aller à l'aveuglette. **to ~ for sth** chercher qch à tâtons *or* à l'aveuglette; **to ~ for words** chercher ses mots; **to ~ (one's way) towards** avancer à tâtons *or* à l'aveuglette vers; **to ~ (one's way) in/out** *etc* entrer/sortir *etc* à tâtons *or* à l'aveuglette.

grope about, grope around *vi* tâtonner, aller à l'aveuglette. **to grope about for sth** chercher qch à tâtons *or* à l'aveuglette.

groping ['grəʊpɪŋ] *adj* tâtonnant.

gropingly ['grəʊpɪŋlɪ] *adv* à tâtons, en tâtonnant, à l'aveuglette.

grosgrain ['grəʊgreɪn] *n* gros-grain *m*.

gross [grəʊs] **1** *adj* **(a)** (*coarse*) *person* grossier, fruste, sans délicatesse; *food* grossier; *joke etc* cru, grossier. ~ **eater** goulu(e) *m(f)*, glouton(ne) *m(f)*.

(b) (*flagrant*) *injustice* flagrant; *abuse* choquant; *error* gros (*f* grosse), lourd. ~ **ignorance** ignorance crasse.

(c) (*fat*) *person* obèse, bouffi, adipeux.

(d) (*Comm, Econ, Fin*) *weight, income, product, tonnage* brut. ~ **national product** (*abbr* **GNP**) revenu national brut (*abbr* R.N.B.).

2 *n* **(a)** **in (the)** ~ (*wholesale*) en gros, en bloc; (*fig*) en général, à tout prendre.

(b) (*pl inv: twelve dozen*) grosse *f*, douze douzaines *fpl*.

3 *vt* (*Comm*) faire *or* obtenir une recette brute de. **the company ~ed £100,000 last year** la compagnie a fait *or* obtenu une recette brute de 100.000 livres l'an dernier.

grossly ['grəʊslɪ] *adv* **(a)** (*very much*) *exaggerate, overrate etc* énormément, extrêmement. **(b)** (*coarsely*) *behave, talk* grossièrement.

grossness ['grəʊsnɪs] *n [person]* (*coarseness*) grossièreté *f*; (*fatness*) obésité *f*, adiposité *f*; *[joke, language]* grossièreté, crudité *f*; *[crime, abuse etc]* énormité *f*.

grotesque [grəʊ'tesk] **1** *adj* grotesque, saugrenu. **2** *n* grotesque *m*.

grotto ['grɒtəʊ] *n, pl* ~**s** *or* ~**es** grotte *f*.

grotty* ['grɒtɪ] *adj* (*Brit*) *room, surroundings, food, evening* minable*, affreux. **he was feeling** ~ il ne se sentait pas bien, il se sentait tout chose*.

grouch* [graʊtʃ] **1** *vi* rouspéter, ronchonner*. **2** *n* rouspéteur* *m*, -euse* *f*.

grouchy* ['graʊtʃɪ] *adj* ronchon*, grognon, maussade.

ground[1] [graʊnd] **1** *n* **(a)** (*U*) terre *f*, sol *m*. **to lie/sit (down) on the** ~ se coucher/s'asseoir par terre *or* sur le sol; **above** ~ en surface (*du sol*); (*fig*) **to have one's feet firmly on the** ~ avoir (bien) les pieds sur terre; **to fall to the** ~ (*lit*) tomber à *or* par terre; (*fig*) *[plans etc]* tomber à l'eau, s'écrouler; **to dash sb's hopes to the** ~ anéantir *or* ruiner les espérances de qn; **to get off the** ~ (*Aviat*) décoller; (*fig*) *[scheme etc]* démarrer*; (*fig*) **to run a car into the** ~ user une voiture jusqu'à ce qu'elle soit bonne pour la casse; (*fig*) **to run a business into the** ~ laisser péricliter une entreprise; (*fig*) **that suits me down to the** ~* ça me va tout à fait *or* comme un gant, ça me botte‡; (*Naut*) **to touch** ~ toucher le fond; *V* **thick, thin** *etc*.

(b) (*U: soil*) sol *m*, terre *f*, terrain *m*. **to till the** ~ labourer la terre; **stony** ~ terre(s) caillouteuse(s), sol *or* terrain caillouteux; *V* **break**.

(c) (*U*) (*area, position*) terrain *m*; (*larger*) domaine *m*, terres *fpl*; (*territory*) territoire *m*, sol *m*. **hilly** ~ contrée vallonnée, pa' s vallonné; **all this** ~ **is owned by X** c'est X qui possède toutes ces terres *or* tout ce domaine; **to hold** *or* **stand one's** ~ tenir bon *or* ferme, ne pas lâcher pied; (*fig*) **to change** *or* **shift one's** ~ changer son fusil d'épaule; **to gain** ~ (*Mil*) gagner du terrain; *[idea etc]* faire son chemin; (*Mil, also fig*) **to give** ~ céder du terrain; (*Mil, also fig*) **to lose** ~ perdre du terrain; (*fig*) **to be on dangerous** ~ être sur un terrain glissant; (*fig*) **forbidden** ~ domaine interdit; (*fig*) **to be on sure** *or* **firm** ~ partir de *or* reposer sur des bases solides; **to be sure of one's** ~ être sur son terrain, être sûr de son fait, parler en connaissance de cause; (*fig*) **to meet sb on his own** ~ se battre avec qn sur son propre terrain; *V* **common, cover, cut** *etc*.

(d) (*area for special purpose*) terrain *m*. **football** ~ terrain de football; *V* **landing, parade, recreation** *etc*.

(e) (*gardens etc*) ~**s** parc *m*.

(f) (*US Elec*) masse *f*, terre *f*.

(g) (*reason: gen* ~**s**) motif *m*, raison *f*. **on personal/medical** ~**s** pour (des) raisons personnelles/médicales; ~**s for divorce** motifs de divorce; **on what** ~**s?** à quel titre?; **on the** ~**(s) of** pour raison de, à cause de; ~ **for complaint** grief *m*; **there are** ~**s for believing that ...** il y a des raisons de penser que ...; **the situation gives** ~**s for anxiety** la situation est (nettement) préoccupante.

(h) **(coffee)** ~**s** marc *m* (de café).

(i) (*background*) fond *m*. **on a blue** ~ sur fond bleu.

2 *vt* **(a)** *plane, pilot* empêcher de voler, interdire de voler à; (*keep on ground*) retenir au sol. **all aircraft have been** ~**ed** tous les avions ont reçu l'ordre de ne pas décoller.

(b) *ship* échouer.

(c) (*US Elec*) mettre une prise de terre à.

(d) (*fig*) *hopes etc* fonder (*on* sur). **well-~ed belief/rumour** croyance/rumeur bien fondée; (*Scol*) **well** ~**ed in Latin** ayant de solides connaissances *or* bases en latin, possédant bien *or* à fond le latin.

3 *vi [ship]* s'échouer.

4 *cpd*: (*Mil*) **ground attack** offensive *f* au sol; (*Fishing*) **ground bait** amorce *f* de fond; (*Mus*) **ground bass** basse contrainte, basso *m* ostinato; (*US*) **ground cloth** = **groundsheet**; **ground colour** (*base coat*) première couche; (*background colour*) teinte *f* de fond; (*Aviat*) **ground control** contrôle *m* au sol; (*Aviat*) **ground crew** équipe *f* au sol; **ground floor** rez-de-chaussée *m*; **ground-floor** *adj flat* au rez-de-chaussée; (*fig*) **he got in on the ground floor** il est là depuis le début; (*Mil*) **ground forces** armée *f* de terre; **ground frost** gelée blanche; (*US*) **ground hog** marmotte *f* d'Amérique; **ground ice** glaces *fpl* de fond; **groundkeeper** gardien *m* de parc (*or* de cimetière, stade *etc*); **at ground level** au ras du sol, à fleur de terre; **groundnut** arachide *f*; **groundnut oil** huile *f* d'arachide; **ground plan** (*Archit*) plan *m*, projection horizontale; (*fig*) plan de base; (*esp Brit*) **ground rent** redevance foncière; **groundsheet** tapis *m* de sol; (*Brit*) **groundsman** gardien *m* de stade; (*Aviat*) **groundspeed** vitesse-sol *f*; (*Aviat*) **ground staff** personnel *m* au sol; **groundswell** lame *f* de fond; (*Mil*) **ground-to-air missile** engin *m* sol-air; (*Mil*) **ground-to-ground missile** engin *m* sol-sol; (*US Elec*) **ground wire** fil *m* neutre; **groundwork** *[undertaking]* base *f*, préparation *f*; *[novel, play etc]* plan *m*, canevas *m*.

ground[2] [graʊnd] **1** *pret, ptp of* **grind**. **2** *adj coffee etc* moulu. ~ **glass** verre pilé; ~ **rice** semoule *f or* farine *f* de riz.

grounding ['graʊndɪŋ] *n* **(a)** *[ship]* échouage *m*.

(b) *[plane]* interdiction *f* de vol.

(c) (*in education*) connaissances fondamentales *or* de fond, base *f* (*in* en). **she had a good** ~ **in French** elle avait une base solide *or* de solides connaissances en français.

groundless ['graʊndlɪs] *adj* sans fond, mal fondé, sans motif.

groundsel ['graʊnsl] *n* séneçon *m*.

group [gru:p] **1** *n [people, statues, houses, languages, figures]* groupe *m*; *[mountains]* massif *m*. **to form a** ~ se grouper; **literary** ~ cercle *m* littéraire; *V* **blood, in, pressure** *etc*.

2 *cpd*: (*Brit Aviat*) **Group Captain** colonel *m* de l'armée de l'air; (*Med*) **group practice is expanding in this country** la médecine de groupe est en expansion dans notre pays; (*Med*) **he belongs to a group practice** il fait partie d'un cabinet collectif; (*Psych*) **group therapy** psychothérapie *f* de groupe; (*Soc*) **group work** travail *m* en groupe *or* en équipe.

3 *vi* (*also* ~ **together**) *[people]* se grouper, former un groupe. **to** ~ **round sth/sb** se grouper *or* se rassembler autour de qch/de qn.

4 *vt* (*also* ~ **together**) *objects, people* grouper, rassembler, réunir; *ideas, theories, numbers* grouper.

groupie‡ ['gru:pɪ] *n* groupie‡ *f*, minette *f* sexivore (dans le sillage d'un groupe pop).

grouse[1] [graʊs] (*Orn*) **1** *n, pl inv* grouse *f*; *V* **black, red. 2** *cpd*: **to go grouse-beating** faire le rabatteur; **grouse moor** chasse réservée (*où l'on chasse la grouse*); **to go grouse-shooting** chasser la grouse, aller à la chasse à la grouse.

grouse[2]* [graʊs] **1** *vi* (*grumble*) rouspéter*, râler*, récriminer (*at, about* contre). **stop grousing!** pas de rouspétance!‡ **2** *n* motif *m* de râler*, motif à rouspétance*, grief *m*.

grout [graʊt] **1** *n* enduit *m* de jointoiement. **2** *vt* mastiquer.

grove [grəʊv] *n* bocage *m*, bosquet *m*. **olive** ~ oliveraie *f*; **chestnut** ~ châtaigneraie *f*; **pine** ~ pinède *f*.

grovel ['grɒvl] *vi* se vautrer (*in* dans); (*fig*) ramper, s'aplatir (*to, before* devant, aux pieds de).

grovelling ['grɒvlɪŋ] *adj* (*lit*) rampant; (*fig*) rampant, servile.

grow [grəʊ] *pret* **grew**, *ptp* **grown 1** *vi* **(a)** *[plant]* pousser, croître; *[hair]* pousser; *[person]* grandir, se développer; *[animal]* grandir, grossir. **that plant does not** ~ **in England** cette plante ne pousse pas en Angleterre; **how you've** ~**n!** comme tu as grandi!; **to** ~ **into a man** devenir un homme; **he's** ~**n into quite a handsome boy** il est devenu très beau garçon en grandissant (*V also* **grow into**); (*liter*) **to** ~ **in wisdom/beauty** croître en sagesse/beauté; **she has** ~**n in my esteem** elle est montée dans mon estime; **we have** ~**n away from each other** nous nous sommes éloignés l'un de l'autre avec les années.

(b) *[numbers, amount]* augmenter, grandir; *[club, group]* s'agrandir; *[rage, fear, love, influence, knowledge]* augmenter, croître, s'accroître. **their friendship grew as time went on** leur amitié grandit avec le temps; **our friendship grew from a common love of gardening** notre amitié s'est développée à partir d'un amour partagé pour le jardinage.

(c) **to** ~ **to like/dislike/fear sth** finir par aimer/détester/redouter qch.

(d) (+ *adj* = *become: often translated by vi or vpr*) devenir. **to** ~ **big(ger)** grandir; **to** ~ **red(der)** rougir; **to** ~ **fat(ter)** grossir; **to** ~ **old(er)** vieillir; **to** ~ **angry** se fâcher, se mettre en colère; **to** ~ **rare(r)** se faire (plus) rare; **to** ~ **better** s'améliorer; **to** ~ **worse** empirer; **to** ~ **dark(er)** s'assombrir, s'obscurcir; **to** ~ **tired** se fatiguer, se lasser; **to** ~ **used to sth** s'habituer *or* s'accoutumer à qch.

2 *vt plants, crops* cultiver, faire pousser *or* venir; *one's hair, beard, nails etc* laisser pousser.

grow in *vi [nail]* s'incarner; *[hair]* repousser.

grow into *vt fus clothes* devenir assez grand pour mettre. **he grew into the job** c'est en forgeant qu'il devint forgeron; **to grow into the habit of doing** acquérir (avec le temps) l'habitude de faire, prendre le pli de faire.

grow on *vt fus [habit etc]* s'imposer petit à petit à; *[book, music etc]* plaire de plus en plus à. **his paintings grow on one** on finit par se faire à ses tableaux, plus on voit ses tableaux plus on les apprécie.

grow out of *vt fus clothes* devenir trop grand pour. **he's grown out of this jacket** cette veste est trop petite pour lui; **to grow out of the habit of doing** perdre (avec le temps) l'habitude de faire.

grow up *vi* **1 (a)** *[person, animal]* devenir adulte. **when I grow up I'm going to be a doctor** quand je serai grand je serai médecin; **grow up!*** ne sois pas si enfant! *or* si gamin!

(b) *[friendship, hatred etc]* naître, se développer; *[custom]* naître, se répandre.

2 grown-up *adj, n V* **grown 3**.

grower ['grəʊə^r] *n* **(a)** (*person*) producteur *m*, -trice *f*, cultivateur *m*, -trice *f*. **vegetable** ~ maraîcher *m*, -ère *f*; *V* **rose**[2] *etc*. **(b)** **this plant is a slow** ~ cette plante pousse lentement.

growing ['grəʊɪŋ] **1** *adj* **(a)** *plant* qui pousse. ~ **crops** récoltes *fpl* sur pied; **fast-/slow-** ~ à croissance rapide/lente.

(b) *child* en pleine croissance, qui grandit. **he's a** ~ **boy** c'est un enfant qui grandit.

(c) (*increasing*) *number, amount* grandissant, qui augmente; *club, group* qui s'agrandit; *friendship, hatred* grandissant, croissant. **a** ~ **opinion** opinion de plus en plus répandue; **a** ~ **feeling of frustration** un sentiment croissant *or* grandissant de frustration; **to have a** ~ **desire to do sth** avoir de plus en plus envie de faire qch.

2 *n* (*act*) croissance *f*; (*Agr*) culture *f*. ~ **pains*** (*Med*) douleurs *fpl* de croissance; (*fig*) *[business, project]* difficultés *fpl* de croissance.

growl [graʊl] **1** *vi [animal]* grogner, gronder (*at* contre); *[person]* grogner, ronchonner*; *[thunder]* tonner, gronder. **2** *vt reply etc* grogner, grommeler. **3** *n* grognement *m*, grondement *m*. **to give a ~** grogner.

grown [grəʊn] **1** *ptp of* **grow**.
2 *adj* **(a)** (*also* **fully ~**) *person, animal* adulte, qui a fini sa croissance. **he's a ~ man** il est adulte.
(b) wall ~ over with ivy mur (tout) couvert de lierre.
3 *cpd*: **grown-up** (*adj*) *behaviour* de grande personne, adulte; (*n*) grande personne, adulte *mf*; **when he is grown-up** quand il sera grand; **the grown-ups** les grandes personnes.

growth [grəʊθ] **1** *n* **(a)** (*U: development*) *[plant]* croissance *f*, développement *m*; *[person]* croissance. **to reach full ~** *[plant]* arriver à maturité; *[person]* avoir fini sa croissance.
(b) (*U: increase*) *[numbers, amount]* augmentation *f*; *[club, group]* croissance *f*; *[fear, love]* croissance, poussée *f*; *[influence, economy, knowledge, friendship]* croissance, développement *m*. **the ~ of public interest in ...** l'intérêt croissant du public pour ... .
(c) (*what has grown*) pousse *f*, poussée *f*. **a thick ~ of weeds** des mauvaises herbes qui ont poussé dru; **a 5 days' ~ of beard** une barbe de 5 jours; **a new ~ of hair** une nouvelle pousse *or* poussée de cheveux.
(d) (*Med*) grosseur *f*, excroissance *f*, tumeur *f*. **benign/malignant ~** tumeur bénigne/maligne.
2 *cpd market, point, town, industry* en voie de développement *or* de croissance, en (pleine) expansion. (*Fin*) **growth shares**, (*US*) **growth stock** actions *fpl* susceptibles d'une hausse rapide.

groyne [grɔɪn] *n* (*esp Brit*) brise-lames *m inv*.

grub [grʌb] **1** *n* **(a)** (*larva*) larve *f*.
(b) (*ː food*) boustifailleː *f*, bouffeː *f*. **~ up!*** à la soupe!*
2 *vt [animal] ground, soil* fouir.
3 *vi* (*also* **~ about, ~ around**) fouiller, fouiner (*in, among* dans). **he was ~bing (about *or* around) in the earth for a pebble** il fouinait dans la terre *or* fouillait le sol pour trouver un caillou.

grub up *vt sep soil* fouir; *object* déterrer.

grubbiness ['grʌbɪnɪs] *n* saleté *f*.

grubby ['grʌbɪ] *adj* sale, (*stronger*) crasseux.

grudge [grʌdʒ] **1** *vt* donner *or* accorder à contrecœur *or* en rechignant. **he ~s her even the food she eats** il lui mesure jusqu'à sa nourriture, il lésine même sur sa nourriture; **do you ~ me these pleasures?** me reprochez-vous ces (petits) plaisirs?; **they ~d him his success** ils lui en voulaient de sa réussite; **she ~s paying £2 a ticket** cela lui fait mal au cœur de *or* elle la trouve mauvaise de payer 2 livres un billet; **it's not the money I ~ but the time** ce n'est pas sur la dépense mais sur le temps que je rechigne.
2 *n* rancune *f*. **to bear *or* have a ~ against sb** en vouloir à qn, garder rancune à qn, avoir une dent contre qn; **to pay off a ~** satisfaire une rancune.

grudging ['grʌdʒɪŋ] *adj person, attitude* radin, mesquin, peu généreux; *contribution* parcimonieux; *gift, praise etc* accordé *or* donné à regret *or* à contrecœur. **with ~ admiration** avec une admiration réticente.

grudgingly ['grʌdʒɪŋlɪ] *adv give, help* à contrecœur, de mauvaise grâce; *say, agree* de mauvaise grâce.

gruel [grʊəl] *n* gruau *m*.

gruelling ['grʊəlɪŋ] *adj march, match, race etc* exténuant, épuisant, éreintant*.

gruesome ['gruːsəm] *adj* horrible, épouvantable, infâme, révoltant. **in ~ detail** jusque dans les plus horribles détails.

gruff [grʌf] *adj person* brusque, bourru; *voice* gros (*f* grosse), bourru.

gruffly ['grʌflɪ] *adv* d'un ton bourru *or* rude, avec brusquerie.

grumble ['grʌmbl] **1** *vi [person]* grogner, grommeler, bougonner*, ronchonner*, rouspéter* (*at, about* contre), se plaindre (*about, at* de); *[thunder]* gronder. **he's always grumbling** il est toujours à grommeler.
2 *n* grognement *m*, ronchonnement* *m*. **to do sth without a ~** faire qch sans se plaindre; **after a long ~ about ...** après une longue lamentation à propos de ... .

grummet ['grʌmɪt] *n* = **grommet.**

grumpily ['grʌmpɪlɪ] *adv* d'un ton *or* d'une façon maussade, en bougonnant* *or* ronchonnant*.

grumpy ['grʌmpɪ] *adj* maussade, renfrogné, grincheux, grognon.

grunt [grʌnt] **1** *vi [pig, person]* grogner.
2 *vt* grogner. **to ~ a reply** grommeler *or* grogner une réponse; **'no' he ~ed** 'non' grommela-t-il.
3 *n* grognement *m*. **to give a ~** pousser *or* faire entendre un grognement; (*in reply*) répondre par un grognement; **with a ~ of distaste** avec un grognement dégoûté *or* de dégoût.

gryphon ['grɪfən] *n* = **griffin.**

guano ['gwɑːnəʊ] *n* (*U*) guano *m*.

guarantee [ˌgærən'tiː] **1** *n* **(a)** (*Comm etc: promise, assurance*) garantie *f*. **there is a year's ~ on this watch** cette montre est garantie un an, cette montre a une garantie d'un an; **a ~ against defective workmanship** une garantie contre les malfaçons; **'money-back ~ with all items'** 'remboursement garanti sur tous articles'; **you must read the ~ carefully** il faut lire attentivement la garantie; **you have/I give you my ~ that ...** vous avez/je vous donne ma garantie que ...; **there's no ~ that it will happen** il n'est pas garanti *or* dit que cela arrivera; **there's no ~ that it actually happened** il n'est pas certain que cela soit arrivé; **health is not a ~ of happiness** la santé n'est pas une garantie de bonheur.
(b) (*Jur etc: pledge, security*) garantie *f*, caution *f*. **to give sth as (a) ~** donner qch en caution; **he left his watch as a ~ of payment** il a laissé sa montre en garantie de paiement *or* en gage; **what ~ can you offer?** quelle caution pouvez-vous donner?
(c) = **guarantor.**
2 *cpd*: **guarantee form** garantie *f* (*fiche*).
3 *vt goods etc* garantir, assurer (*against* contre, *for 2 years* pendant 2 ans). **~d waterproof** garanti imperméable; **~d not to rust** garanti inoxydable; **~d price** prix garanti; **I will ~ his good behaviour** je me porte garant de sa bonne conduite; **to ~ a loan** se porter garant *or* caution d'un emprunt; **I will ~ him for a £500 loan** je lui servirai de garant *or* de caution pour un emprunt de 500 livres; **I ~ that it won't happen again** je garantis *or* certifie que cela ne se reproduira pas; **I can't ~ that he will come** je ne peux pas garantir sa venue, je ne peux pas certifier qu'il viendra; **I can't ~ that he did it** je ne peux pas certifier qu'il l'ait fait; **we can't ~ good weather** nous ne pouvons pas garantir le beau temps *or* certifier qu'il fera beau.

guarantor [ˌgærən'tɔːʳ] *n* garant(e) *m(f)*, caution *f*. **to stand ~ for sb** se porter garant *or* caution de qn; **will you be my ~ for the loan?** me servirez-vous de garant *or* de caution pour l'emprunt?

guaranty ['gærəntɪ] *n* (*Fin*) garantie *f*, caution *f*; (*agreement*) garantie; (*sth held as security*) garantie, caution.

guard [gɑːd] **1** *n* **(a)** (*U*) garde *f*, surveillance *f*; (*Boxing, Fencing, Mil etc*) garde. **to go on/come off ~** prendre/finir son tour de garde; **to be on ~** être de garde *or* de faction; **to keep *or* stand ~** être de garde, monter la garde; **to keep *or* stand ~ on sb/sth** garder *or* surveiller qn/qch; **he was taken under ~ to ...** il fut emmené sous escorte à ...; **to keep sb under ~** garder qn sous surveillance; **to put a ~ on sb/sth** faire surveiller qn/qch; (*Sport*) **on ~!** en garde!; **to be on one's ~** se méfier (*against* de), être *or* se tenir sur ses gardes (*against* contre); **to put sb on his ~** mettre qn en garde (*against* contre); **to put sb off (his) ~** tromper la vigilance de qn; **to catch sb off his ~** prendre qn au dépourvu; **he wears goggles as a ~ against accidents** il porte des lunettes protectrices par précaution contre les accidents; *V* **mount** *etc*.
(b) (*Mil etc*) (*squad of men*) garde *f*; (*one man*) garde *m*. (*lit, fig*) **~ of honour** garde d'honneur; (*on either side*) haie *f* d'honneur; **one of the old ~** un vieux de la vieille*; (*Brit Mil*) **the G~s** les régiments *mpl* de la garde royale; *V* **change, life, security** *etc*.
(c) (*Brit Rail*) chef *m* de train.
(d) (*on machine*) dispositif *m* de sûreté; (*on sword*) garde *f*; *V* **fire** *etc*.
2 *cpd*: **guard dog** chien *m* de garde; (*Mil*) **to be on guard duty** être de garde *or* de faction; (*Mil*) **guardhouse** (*for guards*) corps *m* de garde; (*for prisoners*) salle *f* de police; **guardrail** barrière *f* de sécurité; (*Mil*) **guardroom** corps *m* de garde; **guardsman** (*Brit Mil*) garde *m* (*soldat m de la garde royale*); (*US*) soldat de la garde nationale; (*Brit Rail*) **guard's van** fourgon *m* du chef de train.
3 *vt person, place* défendre, protéger (*from, against* contre); *prisoner* garder; (*Cards, Chess*) garder; (*fig*) *one's tongue, passions etc* surveiller. **the frontier is heavily ~ed** la frontière est solidement gardée.

guard against *vt fus* se protéger contre, se défendre contre, se prémunir contre. **to guard against doing** (bien) se garder de faire; **in order to guard against this** pour éviter cela; **we must try to guard against this happening** nous devons essayer d'empêcher que cela ne se produise.

guarded ['gɑːdɪd] *adj machinery* protégé; *prisoner* sous surveillance, gardé à vue; *remark, smile* prudent, circonspect, réservé.

guardedly ['gɑːdɪdlɪ] *adv* avec réserve, avec circonspection, prudemment.

guardian ['gɑːdɪən] **1** *n* **(a)** gardien(ne) *m(f)*, protecteur *m*, -trice *f*. **(b)** *[minor]* tuteur *m*, -trice *f*. **2** *adj* gardien. **~ angel** ange gardien.

Guatemala [ˌgwɑːtɪ'mɑːlə] *n* Guatemala *m*.

Guatemalan [ˌgwɑːtɪ'mɑːlən] **1** *adj* guatémaltèque. **2** *n* Guatémaltèque *mf*.

guava ['gwɑːvə] *n* (*fruit*) goyave *f*; (*tree*) goyavier *m*.

gubernatorial [ˌguːbənə'tɔːrɪəl] *adj* (*frm*) de *or* du gouverneur.

gudgeon¹ ['gʌdʒən] *n* (*fish*) goujon *m*.

gudgeon² ['gʌdʒən] *n* (*Tech*) tourillon *m*; (*Naut*) goujon *m*. (*Brit Aut*) **~ pin** goupille *f*.

guelder rose [ˌgeldə'rəʊz] *n* (*Bot*) boule-de-neige *f*.

Guernsey ['gɜːnzɪ] *n* **(a)** (*Geog*) Guernesey *m*. **(b)** (*cow*) vache *f* de Guernesey. **(c)** (*garment*) **g~** jersey *m*.

guerrilla [gə'rɪlə] **1** *n* guérillero *m*. **2** *cpd tactics etc* de guérilla. **guerrilla band, guerrilla group** guérilla *f* (*troupe*); (*Ind*) **guerrilla strike** grève *f* sauvage; **guerrilla war(fare)** guérilla *f* (*guerre*).

guess [ges] **1** *n* supposition *f*, conjecture *f*. **to have *or* make a ~** tâcher de *or* essayer de deviner, hasarder une conjecture; **to have *or* make a ~ at sth** essayer de deviner qch; **I give you three ~es!, have a ~!** essaie de deviner!, devine un peu!; **that was a good ~** tu as deviné juste, ton intuition ne t'a pas trompé; **that was a good ~ but ...** c'était une bonne intuition *or* idée mais ...; **it was just a lucky ~** j'ai (*or* il a *etc*) deviné juste, c'est tout; **at a ~ I would say there were 200** au jugé je dirais qu'il y en avait 200; **at a rough ~** à vue de nez, approximativement, grosso modo; **my ~ is that he refused** d'après moi il aura refusé; **your ~ is as good as mine!*** tu en sais autant que moi!, je n'en sais pas plus que toi!; **it's anyone's ~ who will win*** impossible de prévoir qui va gagner; **will he come tomorrow? — it's anyone's ~*** viendra-t-il demain? — qui sait? *or* Dieu seul le sait; **by ~ and by God*** Dieu sait comment.
2 *cpd*: **guesswork** conjecture *f*, hypothèse *f*; **it was sheer**

guesswork ce n'étaient que des conjectures, on n'a fait que deviner; **by guesswork** en devinant, par flair.

3 *vt* **(a)** deviner; (*surmise*) supposer, conjecturer; (*estimate*) estimer, évaluer. **to ~ sb's age** deviner l'âge de qn; (*make a rough guess*) évaluer l'âge de qn; **I ~ed him to be about 20** j'estimais *or* je jugeais qu'il avait à peu près 20 ans; **~ how heavy he is** devine combien il pèse; **I'd already ~ed who had done it** j'avais déjà deviné qui l'avait fait; **you've ~ed (it)!** tu as deviné!, c'est ça!; **to ~ the answer** deviner la réponse; **I haven't a recipe, I just ~ the quantities** je n'ai pas de recette, je mesure à vue de nez; **can you ~ what it means?** peux-tu arriver à deviner ce que cela veut dire?; **I ~ed as much** je m'en doutais; **~ who!*** devine qui c'est!; **you'll never ~ who's coming to see us!** tu ne devineras jamais qui va venir nous voir!

(b) (*US: believe, think*) croire, penser. **he'll be about 40 I ~** il doit avoir dans les 40 ans je pense *or* j'imagine, moi je lui donne *or* donnerais la quarantaine; **I ~ it's going to rain** j'ai l'impression *or* je crois qu'il va pleuvoir; **I ~ so** je crois, je suppose, j'ai l'impression que oui; **I ~ not** j'ai l'impression que non, je ne crois pas.

4 *vi* deviner. **try to ~!** essaie de deviner!, devine un peu!; **you'll never ~!** tu ne devineras jamais!; **to ~ right** deviner juste; **to ~ wrong** tomber à côté*; **to keep sb ~ing** laisser qn dans le doute; **to ~ at the height of a building/the number of people present** *etc* évaluer *or* estimer (au jugé) la hauteur d'un bâtiment/le nombre de personnes présentes *etc*.

guesstimate* ['gestɪmɪt] *n* calcul *m* au pifomètre*.

guest [gest] 1 *n* (*at home*) invité(e) *m(f)*, hôte *mf*; (*at table*) convive *mf*; (*in hotel*) client(e) *m(f)*; (*in boarding house*) pensionnaire *mf*. **~ of honour** invité(e) d'honneur; **we were their ~s last summer** nous avons été leurs invités l'été dernier; **be my ~!*** à toi!, (fais) comme chez toi!*; *V* **house, paying.**

2 *cpd*: (*Theat*) **guest artist** (artiste *mf*) invité(e) *m(f)*; **guest-house** pension *f* de famille; **guest list** liste *f* des invités; **guest night** *soirée f où les membres d'un club peuvent inviter des non-membres*; **guest room** chambre *f* d'amis; **guest speaker** orateur invité (*par un club, une organisation*).

guff‡ [gʌf] *n* (*U*) bêtises *fpl*, idioties *fpl*.

guffaw [gʌ'fɔː] 1 *vi* rire bruyamment, pouffer (de rire), partir d'un gros rire. 2 *vt* pouffer. 3 *n* gros (éclat de) rire.

Guiana [gaɪ'ænə] *n* les Guyanes *fpl*.

guidance ['gaɪdəns] *n* **(a)** conseils *mpl*. **for your ~** pour votre gouverne, à titre d'indication *or* d'information; **he needs some ~ about** *or* **as to how to go about it** il a besoin de conseils quant à la façon de procéder; **your ~ was very helpful** vos conseils ont été très utiles; *V* **child, vocational.**

(b) *[rocket etc]* guidage *m*. **~ system** système *m* de guidage.

guide [gaɪd] 1 *n* **(a)** (*gen, also for climbers, tourists etc*) guide *m*; (*spiritualism*) esprit *m*; (*fig*) guide, indication *f*. **you must let reason be your ~** il faut vous laisser guider par la raison; **this figure is only a ~** ce chiffre n'est qu'une indication; **last year's figures will be a good ~** les statistiques de l'année dernière serviront de guide; **these results are not a very good ~ as to his ability** ces résultats ne donnent pas d'indication sûre touchant ses compétences; **as a rough ~, count 4 apples to the pound** comptez en gros *or* à peu près 4 pommes par livre.

(b) (*also* **~book**) guide *m*. **~ to Italy** guide d'Italie.

(c) (*book of instructions*) guide *m*, manuel *m*. **beginner's ~ to sailing** manuel d'initiation à la voile.

(d) (*for curtains etc*) glissière *f*; (*on sewing machine*) pied-de-biche *m*.

(e) (*also* **girl ~**) éclaireuse *f*; (*Roman Catholic*) guide *f*.

2 *vt* **(a)** *blind man* conduire, guider; *stranger, visitor* guider, piloter. **he ~d us through the town** il nous a pilotés *or* guidés à travers la ville; **he ~d us to the main door** il nous a montré le chemin jusqu'à la porte d'entrée; (*lit, fig*) **to be ~d by sb/sth** se laisser guider par qn/qch.

(b) *rocket, missile* guider.

3 *cpd*: **guidebook** *V* 1b; **guide dog** chien *m* d'aveugle; **guide line** (*for writing*) ligne *f* (*permettant une écriture horizontale régulière*); (*fig: hints, suggestions*) ligne directrice; (*rope*) main courante; **guidepost** poteau indicateur.

guided ['gaɪdɪd] *adj* **(a)** *rocket etc* téléguidé. **~ missile** engin téléguidé. **(b) ~ tour** visite guidée.

guiding ['gaɪdɪŋ] *adj*: **~ principle** principe directeur; (*fig*) **~ star** guide *m*; **he needs a ~ hand from time to time** il a besoin qu'on l'aide (*subj*) de temps en temps.

guild [gɪld] 1 *n* **(a)** (*Hist*) guilde *f*, corporation *f*. **goldsmiths' ~** guilde des orfèvres.

(b) association *f*, confrérie *f*. **the church ~** le cercle paroissial; **women's ~** association féminine.

2 *cpd*: **guildhall** (*Hist*) palais *m* des corporations; (*town hall*) hôtel *m* de ville.

guile [gaɪl] *n* (*U*) (*deceit*) fourberie *f*, tromperie *f*; (*cunning*) ruse *f*, astuce *f*.

guileful ['gaɪlfʊl] *adj* (*deceitful*) fourbe, trompeur; (*cunning*) rusé, astucieux.

guileless ['gaɪllɪs] *adj* (*straightforward*) sans astuce, candide; (*open*) franc (*f* franche), loyal, sincère.

guillemot ['gɪlɪmɒt] *n* guillemot *m*.

guillotine [ˌgɪlə'tiːn] 1 *n* (*for beheading*) guillotine *f*; (*for paper-cutting*) massicot *m*. **a ~ was imposed on the bill** une limite de temps a été imposée au débat sur le projet de loi.

2 *vt person* guillotiner; *paper* massicoter. (*Brit Parl*) **to ~ a bill** ≃ poser la question de confiance.

guilt [gɪlt] *n* (*U*) culpabilité *f*. **he was tormented by ~** il était torturé par un sentiment de culpabilité; (*Psych*) **to have ~ feelings about sb/sth** se sentir coupable *or* avoir des sentiments de culpabilité vis-à-vis de qn/qch.

guiltless ['gɪltlɪs] *adj* innocent (*of* de).

guilty ['gɪltɪ] *adj* **(a)** (*Jur etc*) *person* coupable (*of* de). **~ person** *or* **party** coupable *mf*; **to plead ~/not ~** plaider coupable/non coupable; **to find sb ~/not ~** déclarer qn coupable/non coupable; **verdict of ~/not ~** verdict *m* de culpabilité/d'acquittement; **'not ~' he replied** 'non coupable' répondit-il; **he was ~ of taking the book without permission** il s'est rendu coupable de prendre le livre sans permission; **I have been ~ of that myself** j'ai moi-même commis la même erreur; **I feel very ~ about not writing to her** j'ai des *or* je suis plein de remords de ne pas lui avoir écrit.

(b) *look* coupable, confus; *thought, act* coupable. **~ conscience** conscience lourde *or* chargée *or* coupable.

guinea ['gɪnɪ] *n* (*Brit: money*) guinée *f* (= *21 shillings*).

Guinea ['gɪnɪ] 1 *n* (*Geog*) Guinée *f*. 2 *cpd*: **guinea-fowl** pintade *f*; **guinea-pig** (*Zool*) cochon *m* d'Inde, cobaye *m*; (*fig*) cobaye; (*fig*) **to be a guinea-pig** servir de cobaye.

guise [gaɪz] *n*: **in the ~ of a soldier** sous l'aspect d'un soldat; **in** *or* **under the ~ of friendship** sous l'apparence *or* les traits de l'amitié.

guitar [gɪ'tɑːʳ] *n* guitare *f*.

guitarist [gɪ'tɑːrɪst] *n* guitariste *mf*.

gulch [gʌlʃ] *n* (*US*) ravin *m*.

gulf [gʌlf] *n* **(a)** (*in ocean*) golfe *m*. **the (Persian) G~** le golfe Persique; **G~ of Mexico** golfe du Mexique; **G~ Stream** Gulf Stream *m*. **(b)** (*abyss: lit, fig*) gouffre *m*, abîme *m*.

gull[1] [gʌl] *n* (*bird*) mouette *f*, goéland *m*.

gull[2] [gʌl] (*dupe*) 1 *vt* duper, rouler‡. 2 *n* jobard‡ *m*, dindon‡ *m*.

gullet ['gʌlɪt] *n* (*Anat*) œsophage *m*; (*throat*) gosier *m*.

gullibility [ˌgʌlɪ'bɪlɪtɪ] *n* crédulité *f*.

gullible ['gʌlɪbl] *adj* crédule, facile à duper.

gully ['gʌlɪ] *n* **(a)** (*ravine*) ravine *f*, couloir *m*. **(b)** (*drain*) caniveau *m*, rigole *f*.

gulp [gʌlp] 1 *n* **(a)** (*action*) coup *m* de gosier; (*from emotion*) serrement *m* de gorge. **to swallow sth at one ~** avaler qch d'un seul coup; **he emptied the glass at one ~** il a vidé le verre d'un (seul) trait; **'yes' he replied with a ~** 'oui' répondit-il la gorge serrée *or* avec une boule dans la gorge.

(b) (*mouthful*) *[food]* bouchée *f*, goulée* *f*; *[drink]* gorgée *f*, lampée *f*. **he took a ~ of milk** il a avalé une gorgée de lait.

2 *vt* (*also* **~ down**) *food* avaler à grosses bouchées, engloutir, enfourner*; *drink* avaler à pleine gorge, lamper. **don't ~ your food** mâche ce que tu manges.

3 *vi* essayer d'avaler; (*from emotion etc*) avoir un serrement *or* une contraction de la gorge. **he ~ed** sa gorge s'est serrée *or* s'est contractée.

gulp back *vt sep*: **to gulp back one's tears/sobs** ravaler *or* refouler ses larmes/sanglots.

gum[1] [gʌm] *n* (*Anat*) gencive *f*. **~boil** fluxion *f* dentaire.

gum[2] [gʌm] 1 *n* **(a)** (*U*) (*Bot*) gomme *f*; (*glue*) gomme, colle *f*; (*rubber*) caoutchouc *m*.

(b) (*U*) chewing-gum *m*.

(c) (*sweet: also* **~drop**) boule *f* de gomme.

2 *cpd*: **gum arabic** gomme *f* arabique; (*esp Brit*) **gumboots** bottes *fpl* de caoutchouc; (‡: *detective*) **gumshoe** privé‡ *m*; (*US*) **gumshoes** (*overshoes*) caoutchoucs *mpl*; (*sneakers*) (chaussures *fpl* de) tennis *mpl*; **gum tree** gommier *m*; (*Brit fig*) **to be up a gum tree‡** être dans le lac (*fig*), être dans la merde‡.

3 *vt* gommer, coller. **~med envelope/label** enveloppe/étiquette collante *or* gommée; **to ~ sth back on** recoller qch; **to ~ down an envelope** coller *or* cacheter une enveloppe.

gum up‡ *vt sep machinery, plans* abîmer, bousiller‡. (*fig*) **it's gummed up the works** ça a tout bousillé‡.

gum[3]* [gʌm] (*euph of God*) **by ~!** nom d'un chien!*, mince alors!*

gumbo ['gʌmbəʊ] *n* (*Bot*) gombo *m*; (*Culin*) soupe *f* au gombo.

gummy ['gʌmɪ] *adj* gommeux; (*sticky*) collant, gluant.

gumption* ['gʌmpʃən] *n* (*U: Brit*) jugeote* *f*, bon sens. **use your ~!** aie un peu de jugeote!*; **he's got a lot of ~** il sait se débrouiller; **he's got no ~** il n'a pas deux sous de jugeote* *or* de bon sens.

gun [gʌn] 1 *n* **(a)** (*small*) pistolet *m*, revolver *m*, (*rifle*) fusil *m*; (*cannon*) canon *m*. **he's got a ~!** il est armé!, il a un pistolet!; **the thief was carrying a ~** le voleur avait une arme (à feu); **to draw a ~ on sb** braquer une arme sur qn; **a 21-~ salute** une salve de 21 coups de canon; (*Mil*) **the ~s** les canons, l'artillerie *f*; **the big ~s** (*Mil*) les gros canons, l'artillerie lourde‡; (*fig: people*) les grosses légumes‡, les huiles‡ *fpl*; **to be going great ~s‡** *[business]* marcher à pleins gaz‡; *[person]* être en pleine forme (*V also* **blow**[1]); (*fig*) **he's the fastest ~ in the West** de tous les cowboys il est le plus rapide sur la détente; *V* **jump, son, stick** *etc*.

(b) (*Brit: member of shooting party*) fusil *m*.

(c) (*US‡: gunman*) bandit armé.

(d) (*Tech*) pistolet *m*. **paint ~** pistolet *m* à peinture; *V* **grease.**

2 *cpd*: (*Naut*) **gunboat** canonnière *f*; **gunboat diplomacy** diplomatie appuyée par la force armée; **gun carriage** affût *m* de canon; (*at funeral*) prolonge *f* d'artillerie; **gun cotton** fulmicoton *m*, coton-poudre *m*; (*Mil*) **gun crew** peloton *m or* servants *mpl* de pièce; **gun dog** chien *m* de chasse; **gunfight** échange *m* de coups de feu; **gunfire** *[rifles etc]* coups *mpl* de feu, fusillade *f*; *[cannons]* feu *m or* tir *m* d'artillerie; **gun licence** permis *m* de port d'armes; **gunman** bandit armé; (*Pol etc*) terroriste *m*; **gunmetal** (*n*) bronze *m* à canon; (*adj: colour*) vert-de-gris *inv*; (*US*) **gunplay** échange *m* de coups de feu; **to have** *or* **hold sb at gunpoint** tenir qn sous son pistolet *or* au bout de son fusil; **he did it at gunpoint** il l'a fait sous la menace du pistolet; **gunpowder** poudre *f* à canon; (*Brit Hist*) **the Gunpowder Plot** la conspiration des Poudres; **gun room** (*in house*) armurerie *f*; (*Brit Naut*) poste *m* des aspirants; **gunrunner** trafiquant *m* d'armes; **gunrunning** contrebande *f or* trafic *m* d'armes; **gunshot** *V* **gunshot**; **gun-shy** qui a peur des coups de

feu *or* des détonations; (*US*) **gunslinger**: bandit armé; **gunsmith** armurier *m*; (*Mil etc*) **gun turret** tourelle *f*.

3 *vt* **(a)** (*also* ~ **down**) abattre, tuer (à coups de pistolet *etc*).

(b) (*Aut*) **to ~ the engine** faire ronfler le moteur; **to ~ it**: appuyer sur le champignon:.

4 *vi*: (*fig*) **to be ~ning for sb*** chercher qn; **watch out, he's ~ning for you!** fais gaffe, il te cherche!

gunner ['gʌnəʳ] *n* (*Mil, Naut*) artilleur *m*.

gunnery ['gʌnərɪ] **1** *n* **(a)** (*science, art, skill*) tir *m* au canon, canonnage *m*. **(b)** (*Mil: collective n: guns*) artillerie *f*. **2** *cpd*: (*Mil*) **gunnery officer** officier *m* de tir.

gunny ['gʌnɪ] *n* (*U*) toile *f* de jute grossière; (*also* ~ **bag**, ~ **sack**) sac *m* de jute.

gunshot ['gʌnʃɒt] **1** *n* (*sound*) coup *m* de feu. **within ~** à portée de fusil. **2** *cpd*: **gunshot wound** blessure *f* de *or* par balle; **to get a gunshot wound** être blessé par une balle, recevoir un coup de feu.

gunwale ['gʌnl] *n* (*Naut*) plat-bord *m*.

guppy ['gʌpɪ] *n* guppy *m*.

gurgle ['gɜ:gl] **1** *n* [*water*] glouglou *m*, gargouillis *m*, gargouillement *m*; [*rain*] gargouillis, gargouillement; [*stream*] murmure *m*; (*of laughter*) gloussement *m*; [*baby*] gazouillis *m*. **to give a ~ of delight** gazouiller de joie.

2 *vi* [*water*] glouglouter, gargouiller; [*rain*] gargouiller; [*stream*] murmurer; [*person*] (*with delight*) gazouiller; (*with laughter*) glousser.

gurnard ['gɜ:nəd] *n* grondin *m*.

guru ['gʊru:] *n* (*lit, fig*) gourou *m*.

gush [gʌʃ] **1** *n* [*oil, water, blood*] jaillissement *m*, bouillonnement *m*; [*tears, words*] flot *m*; (**pej*) effusion(s) *f(pl)*, épanchement(s) *m(pl)*.

2 *vi* **(a)** [*spring, water, blood*] jaillir; [*tears, words*] jaillir. [*water etc*] **to ~ in/out/through** *etc* entrer/sortir/traverser *etc* en bouillonnant.

(b) (**pej*) [*person*] se répandre en compliments (*over* sur, *about* à propos de, au sujet de).

gushing ['gʌʃɪŋ] *adj water etc* jaillissant, bouillonnant; (*pej*) *person* trop exubérant, trop démonstratif, trop expansif.

gusset ['gʌsɪt] *n* (*Sewing*) soufflet *m*.

gust [gʌst] **1** *n* [*wind*] coup *m* de vent, rafale *f*, bourrasque *f*; [*smoke*] bouffée *f*; [*flame*] jet *m*; (*fig*) [*rage etc*] accès *m*, crise *f*, bouffée. **~ of rain** averse *f*; **there was a ~ of laughter from the audience** un grand éclat de rire s'est élevé du public.

2 *vi* [*wind*] souffler en bourrasque. (*Met*) **wind ~ing to force 7** vent (soufflant en bourrasque) atteignant force 7.

gusto ['gʌstəʊ] *n* (*U*) enthousiasme *m*, plaisir *m*. **... he said with ~** ... dit-il vivement; **he ate his meal with great ~** il a dévoré son repas.

gusty ['gʌstɪ] *adj weather* venteux. **a ~ day** un jour de grand vent *or* à bourrasques; **~ wind** des rafales *fpl* de vent.

gut [gʌt] **1** *n* (*Anat*) boyau *m*, intestin *m*; (*Med: for stitching*) catgut *m*; (*Mus etc*) (corde *f* de) boyau. **~s** (*Anat*) boyaux; (**fig: courage*) cran* *m*; **he stuck his bayonet into my ~s** il m'a enfoncé sa baïonnette dans le ventre; (*fig*) **I hate his ~s**: je ne peux pas le blairer:, je ne peux pas le voir en peinture*; **his speech had no ~s to it** son discours manquait de nerf; **the real ~s of his speech came when he described ...** le point fondamental de son discours a été sa description de ...; **he's got ~s*** il a du cran*, il a du cœur au ventre*; **he's got no ~s*** il n'a rien dans le ventre*, il manque de cran*; **it takes a lot of ~s to do that*** il faut beaucoup de cran* *or* d'estomac pour faire ça.

2 *vt* (*Culin*) *animal* vider, étriper; *fish* vider; (*) *book etc* piller*. **fire ~ted the house** le feu n'a laissé que les quatre murs de la maison; **the vandals ~ted the hall** les vandales n'ont laissé de la salle que les murs.

gutless* ['gʌtlɪs] *adj* (*cowardly*) qui a les foies blancs:.

gutsy: ['gʌtsɪ] *adj person, advertising, style* qui a du punch.

gutta-percha [ˌgʌtə'pɜ:tʃə] *n* (*U*) gutta-percha *f*.

gutter ['gʌtəʳ] **1** *n* [*roof*] gouttière *f*; [*road*] caniveau *m*; (*ditch*) rigole *f*. (*fig*) **language of the ~** langage *m* de corps de garde; **to rise from the ~** sortir de la boue *or* du ruisseau.

2 *vi* [*candle*] couler; [*flame*] vaciller, crachoter.

3 *cpd*: **gutter-press** presse *f* de bas étage *or* à scandales, bas-fonds *mpl* du journalisme; **guttersnipe** gamin(e) *m(f)* des rues.

guttural ['gʌtərəl] **1** *adj* guttural. **2** *n* (*Ling*) gutturale *f*.

guv: [gʌv] *n* = **gov**.

Guy [gaɪ] *n* Guy *m*. (*Brit*) **~ Fawkes Day** le cinq novembre (*anniversaire de la conspiration des Poudres*).

guy[1] [gaɪ] **1** *n* **(a)** (*: *esp US*) type* *m*, individu *m*. **nice ~** chic type*, type bien*; **smart** *or* **wise ~** malin *m*, type qui fait le malin*; **tough ~** dur* *m*; *V* **fall, great**. **(b)** (*Brit**) effigie *f* (*de Guy Fawkes, brûlée en plein air le 5 novembre*); (*oddly dressed person*) épouvantail *m* (*fig*). **2** *vt person* tourner en ridicule. (*Theat*) **to ~ a part** travestir un rôle.

guy[2] [gaɪ] *n* (*also* **~-rope**) corde *f* de tente.

Guyana [gaɪ'ænə] *n* Guyane *f*.

guzzle ['gʌzl] **1** *vi* (*eat*) s'empiffrer*; (*drink*) siffler* du vin *etc*. **2** *vt food* bâfrer, bouffer:; *drink* siffler*. **3** *n* glouton(ne) *m(f)*, goinfre *m*.

guzzler ['gʌzləʳ] *n* glouton(ne) *m(f)*.

gybe [dʒaɪb] *vi* = **gibe 1b**.

gym [dʒɪm] **1** *n* **(a)** (*abbr of* **gymnastics**) gymnastique *f*, gym* *f*. **(b)** (*abbr of* **gymnasium**) gymnase *m*; (*Scol*) gymnase, salle *f* de gym*. **2** *cpd*: **gym shoes** (chaussures *fpl* de) tennis *mpl*, chaussures de gym*; (*Brit*) **gym slip**, (*US*) **gym suit** tunique *f* (*d'écolière*).

gymkhana [dʒɪm'kɑ:nə] *n* (*esp Brit*) gymkhana *m*.

gymnasium [dʒɪm'neɪzɪəm] *n*, *pl* **~s** *or* **gymnasia** [dʒɪm'neɪzɪə] gymnase *m*; (*Scol*) gymnase, salle *f* de gymnastique.

gymnast ['dʒɪmnæst] *n* gymnaste *mf*.

gymnastic [dʒɪm'næstɪk] *adj* gymnastique.

gymnastics [dʒɪm'næstɪks] *n* **(a)** (*pl: exercises*) gymnastique *f*. **to do ~** faire de la gymnastique; **mental ~** gymnastique intellectuelle. **(b)** (*U: art, skill*) gymnastique *f*.

gynaecological, (*US*) **gynecological** [ˌgaɪnɪkə'lɒdʒɪkəl] *adj* gynécologique.

gynaecologist, (*US*) **gynecologist** [ˌgaɪnɪ'kɒlədʒɪst] *n* gynécologue *mf*.

gynaecology, (*US*) **gynecology** [ˌgaɪnɪ'kɒlədʒɪ] *n* gynécologie *f*.

gyp [dʒɪp] *n* **(a)** (*US*:) (*swindler*) carotteur *m*, escroc *m*; (*swindle*) escroquerie *f*.

(b) (*Brit*:) **he gave me ~** il m'a passé une engueulade:; **my leg is giving me ~** j'ai atrocement *or* sacrément* mal à la jambe.

(c) (*Brit Univ**) domestique *m* (de collège).

gypsophila [dʒɪp'sɒfɪlə] *n* gypsophile *f*.

gypsum ['dʒɪpsəm] *n* (*U*) gypse *m*.

gypsy ['dʒɪpsɪ] = **gipsy**.

gyrate [ˌdʒaɪə'reɪt] *vi* tournoyer, décrire des girations.

gyration [ˌdʒaɪə'reɪʃən] *n* giration *f*.

gyratory [ˌdʒaɪə'reɪtərɪ] *adj* giratoire.

gyro ['dʒaɪərəʊ] *n abbr of* **gyrocompass, gyroscope**.

gyro... ['dʒaɪərəʊ] *pref* gyro... .

gyrocompass ['dʒaɪərəʊ'kʌmpəs] *n* gyrocompas *m*.

gyroscope ['dʒaɪərəskəʊp] *n* gyroscope *m*.

gyrostabilizer [ˌdʒaɪərəʊ'steɪbɪlaɪzəʳ] *n* gyrostabilisateur *m*.

H

H, h [eɪtʃ] *n* (*letter*) H, h *m or f*. **aspirate/silent h** h aspiré/muet; **H-bomb** bombe *f* H; *V* **drop**.

ha [hɑ:] *excl* ha!, ah! **~, ~!** (*surprise, humour*) ha! ha!; (*laughter*) hi! hi! hi!

habeas corpus ['heɪbɪəs'kɔ:pəs] *n* (*Jur*) habeas corpus *m*; *V* **writ**[1].

haberdasher ['hæbədæʃəʳ] *n* (*Brit*) mercier *m*, -ière *f*; (*US*) chemisier *m*, -ière *f*.

haberdashery [ˌhæbə'dæʃərɪ] *n* (*Brit*) mercerie *f*; (*US*) chemiserie *f*.

habit ['hæbɪt] **1** *n* **(a)** (*custom*) habitude *f*, coutume *f*. **to be in the ~** *or* **to make a ~ of doing** avoir l'habitude *or* avoir pour habitude de faire; **I don't make a ~ of it** je le fais rarement, je ne le fais pas souvent; **don't make a ~ of it!** et ne recommence pas!; **let's hope he doesn't make a ~ of it** espérons qu'il n'en prendra pas l'habitude; **to get** *or* **fall into bad ~s** prendre *or* contracter de mauvaises habitudes; **to get into/out of the ~ of doing** prendre/perdre l'habitude de faire; **to get sb into the ~ of doing** habituer qn à faire, faire prendre à qn l'habitude de faire; **to get out of a ~** perdre une habitude, se débarrasser *or* se défaire d'une habitude; **to have a ~ of doing** avoir l'habitude *or* la manie (*slightly pej*) de faire; **to grow out of the ~ of doing** perdre en grandissant *or* avec l'âge l'habitude de faire; **by** *or* **out of** *or* **from (sheer) ~** par (pure) habitude; **their ~ of shaking hands surprised him** cette habitude qu'ils avaient de donner des poignées de main l'a surpris; (*drug-taking*) **they couldn't cure him of the ~*** ils n'ont pas réussi à le désaccoutumer *or* faire décrocher*; **~ of mind**† tournure *f* d'esprit; *V* **force**.

(b) (*costume*) habit *m*, tenue *f*. **(nun's) ~** habit (de religieuse); **(riding) ~** tenue de cheval *or* d'équitation.

2 *cpd*: **habit-forming** qui crée une accoutumance.

habitable ['hæbɪtəbl] *adj* habitable.

habitat [ˈhæbɪtæt] *n* habitat *m*.
habitation [ˌhæbɪˈteɪʃən] *n* **(a)** (*U*) habitation *f*. **the house showed signs of ~** la maison avait l'air habitée; **fit for ~** habitable. **(b)** (*house etc*) habitation *f*, demeure *f*, domicile *m*; (*settlement*) établissement *m*, colonie *f*.
habitual [həˈbɪtjʊəl] *adj smile, action, courtesy* habituel, accoutumé; *smoker, liar, drinker* invétéré. **this had become ~** ceci était devenu une habitude.
habitually [həˈbɪtjʊəlɪ] *adv* habituellement, d'habitude, ordinairement.
habituate [həˈbɪtjʊeɪt] *vt* habituer, accoutumer (*sb to sth* qn à qch).
hack[1] [hæk] **1** *n* (*cut*) entaille *f*, taillade *f*, coupure *f*; (*blow*) (grand) coup *m*; (*kick*) coup *m* de pied; (*cough*) toux sèche.
2 *cpd*: **hacksaw** scie *f* à métaux.
3 *vt* **(a)** (*cut*) hacher, tailler, taillader. **to ~ sth to pieces** tailler qch en pièces; **the regiment was ~ed to pieces** le régiment fut mis *or* taillé en pièces; (*fig*) **the editor ~ed his story to pieces** le rédacteur a fait des coupes sombres dans son reportage; **to ~ one's way in/out** entrer/sortir en se taillant un chemin à coups de couteau (*or* de hache *or* d'épée *etc*).
(b) (*strike*) frapper; (*kick*) donner des coups de pied à.
hack down *vt sep* abattre à coups de couteau (*or* de hache *or* d'épée *etc*).
hack out *vt sep* enlever grossièrement à coups de couteau (*or* de hache *or* d'épée *etc*).
hack up *vt sep* hacher, tailler en pièces.
hack[2] [hæk] **1** *n* **(a)** (*Brit: horse*) cheval *m* de selle; (*hired*) cheval de louage; (*worn-out*) haridelle *f*, rosse *f*; (*ride*) promenade *f* à cheval. **to go for a ~** (aller) se promener à cheval.
(b) (*pej*) **~ writer, (literary) ~** nègre *m* (*pej*); **as a writer/painter he was just a ~** il ne faisait que de la littérature/qu'une peinture alimentaire.
(c) (*US:*) taxi *m*.
2 *vi* (*Brit*) monter (à cheval). **to go ~ing** (aller) se promener à cheval.
3 *cpd*: (*U: pej*) **hackwork** travail *m* de nègre; (*pej*) **hack writer** *V* 1.
hacking[1] [ˈhækɪŋ] *adj*: **~ cough** toux sèche (et opiniâtre).
hacking[2] [ˈhækɪŋ] *adj* (*Brit*) **~ jacket** veste *f* de cheval *or* d'équitation.
hackle [ˈhækl] *n* plume *f* du cou (*des gallinacés*). **~s** camail *m* (*U*); (*fig*) **his ~s rose at the very idea** il se hérissait rien que d'y penser; **with his ~s up** en colère, en fureur; **to get sb's ~s up** mettre qn en colère *or* en fureur.
hackney [ˈhæknɪ] *adj*: **~ cab** fiacre *m*; **~ carriage** voiture *f* de place *or* de louage.
hackneyed [ˈhæknɪd] *adj subject* rebattu; *phrase, metaphor* usé, galvaudé. **~ expression** cliché *m*.
had [hæd] *pret, ptp of* **have.**
haddock [ˈhædək] *n, pl* **~** *or* **~s** églefin *m*. **smoked ~** haddock *m*.
Hades [ˈheɪdiːz] *n* (*Myth*) les Enfers *mpl*.
hadn't [ˈhædnt] = **had not**; *V* **have.**
Hadrian [ˈheɪdrɪən] *n* Hadrien *m*, Adrien *m*.
haematology, (*US*) **hematology** [ˌhiːməˈtɒlədʒɪ] *n* hématologie *f*.
haemoglobin, (*US*) **hemoglobin** [ˌhiːməʊˈgləʊbɪn] *n* hémoglobine *f*.
haemophilia, (*US*) **hemophilia** [ˌhiːməʊˈfɪlɪə] *n* hémophilie *f*.
haemophiliac, (*US*) **hemophiliac** [ˌhiːməʊˈfɪlɪæk] *adj, n* hémophile (*mf*).
haemorrhage, (*US*) **hemorrhage** [ˈhemərɪdʒ] *n* hémorragie *f*.
haemorrhoids, (*US*) **hemorrhoids** [ˈhemərɔɪdz] *npl* hémorroïdes *fpl*.
haft [hɑːft] **1** *n* [*knife*] manche *m*; [*sword*] poignée *f*. **2** *vt* emmancher, mettre un manche à.
hag [hæg] **1** *n* (*ugly old woman*) vieille sorcière, vieille harpie; (*witch*) sorcière; (*: *unpleasant woman*) chameau* *m*. **she's a real ~*** elle est un vrai chameau*. **2** *cpd*: **hag-ridden** tourmenté, obsédé.
haggard [ˈhægəd] *adj face* hâve, émacié, décharné; *expression* hagard, égaré. **he looked ~** il avait la mine hagarde, il avait le visage défait *or* décomposé; **he had a ~ expression** il avait l'œil hagard *or* l'air égaré.
haggis [ˈhægɪs] *n* (*Culin*) haggis *m* (*plat national écossais*).
haggish [ˈhægɪʃ] *adj* (*V* **hag**) de (vieille) sorcière; (*: *nasty*) vache*.
haggle [ˈhægl] *vi* marchander. **to ~ about** *or* **over the price** chicaner sur le prix, débattre le prix; **I'm not going to ~ over a penny here or there** je ne vais pas chicaner sur un centime par-ci par-là.
haggling [ˈhæglɪŋ] *n* marchandage *m*.
hagiographer [ˌhægɪˈɒgrəfə^r] *n* hagiographe *mf*.
hagiography [ˌhægɪˈɒgrəfɪ] *n* hagiographie *f*.
Hague [heɪg] *n*: **The ~** La Haye.
ha-ha [ˈhɑːˈhɑː] *n* (*fence*) clôture *f* en contrebas; (*ditch*) saut-de-loup *m*.
hail[1] [heɪl] **1** *n* (*Met*) grêle *f*; (*fig*) grêle, pluie *f*. (*fig*) **a ~ of bullets** une pluie *or* grêle de balles.
2 *cpd*: **hailstone** grêlon *m*; **hailstorm** averse *f* de grêle.
3 *vi* grêler. **it is ~ing** il grêle.
hail down 1 *vi*: **stones hailed down on him** il reçut une pluie de cailloux.
2 *vt sep* (*liter*) **to hail down curses on sb** faire pleuvoir des malédictions sur qn.
hail[2] [heɪl] **1** *vt* **(a)** saluer, acclamer. **he was ~ed (as) emperor** (*saluted*) ils le saluèrent aux cris de 'vive l'empereur'; (*fig: acknowledged*) on l'acclama *or* il fut acclamé comme empereur; (*excl*) **~!** salut à vous!, je vous salue!
(b) (*call loudly*) *ship, taxi, person* héler. **within ~ing distance** à portée de (la) voix.
2 *vi* (*Naut*) être en provenance (*from* de); [*person*] être originaire (*from* de). **a ship ~ing from London** un navire en provenance de Londres; **they ~ from Leeds** ils viennent de Leeds; **where do you ~ from?** d'où êtes-vous?
3 *n* appel *m*. **within ~** à portée de (la) voix.
4 *cpd*: **to be hail-fellow-well-met** être liant *or* exubérant, tutoyer tout le monde (*fig*); (*Rel*) **the Hail Mary** le 'Je vous Salue Marie', l'Avé Maria *m*.
hair [hɛə^r] **1** *n* **(a)** (*U*) [*head*] cheveux *mpl*. **he has black ~** il a les cheveux noirs; **a man with long ~** un homme aux cheveux longs; **a fine head of ~** une belle chevelure; **to wash one's ~** se laver les cheveux *or* la tête; **to do one's ~** se coiffer; **she always does my ~ very well** elle me coiffe toujours très bien; **her ~ is always very well done** *or* **very neat** *or* **very nice** elle est toujours très bien coiffée; **to have one's ~ done** se faire coiffer; **to have one's ~ set** se faire faire une mise en plis; **to get one's ~ cut** se faire couper les cheveux; **to make sb's ~ stand on end** faire dresser les cheveux sur la tête à qn; **it was enough to make your ~ stand on end** il y avait de quoi vous faire dresser les cheveux sur la tête; **his ~ stood on end at the sight** le spectacle lui fit dresser les cheveux sur la tête; **to put up one's ~** mettre ses cheveux en chignon, se faire un chignon; (*fig*) **to let one's ~ down*** se laisser aller, se défouler*; **his ~ is getting thin, he's losing his ~** il perd ses cheveux; (*Brit*) **keep your ~ on!*** du calme!, pas de panique!*; **he gets in my ~*** il me tape sur les nerfs* *or* sur le système*; *V* **part, tear**[1] *etc.*
(b) (*single hair*) [*head*] cheveu *m*; [*body*] poil *m*. **not a ~ of his head was harmed** on ne lui a pas touché un cheveu; **it was hanging by a ~** cela ne tenait qu'à un cheveu; (*fig*) **he won the race by a ~** il a gagné la course à un millimètre près *or* à un quart de poil*; **to remove sb's unwanted ~** épiler qn; **to get rid of unwanted ~** s'épiler; (*fig*) **he's got him by the short ~s** il lui tient le couteau sur la gorge; *V* **hairbreadth, split, turn** *etc.*
(c) (*of animal: single ~*) poil *m*; (*U*) [*any animal*] pelage *m*; [*horse*] pelage, robe *f*; (*bristles*) soies *fpl*. **to stroke an animal against the ~** caresser un animal à rebrousse-poil *or* à rebours; (*fig*) **try a ~ of the dog (that bit you)*** reprends un petit verre (pour faire passer ta gueule de bois*).
2 *cpd sofa, mattress etc* de crin. **I've a hair appointment tomorrow** j'ai un rendez-vous chez le coiffeur demain; **hairband** bandeau *m*; **hairbreadth** *V* **hairbreadth**; **hairbrush** brosse *f* à cheveux; **hair clippers** (*npl*) tondeuse *f*; **hair cream** brillantine *f*, crème *f* capillaire; **hair-curler** bigoudi *m*; **to have** *or* **get a haircut** se faire couper les cheveux; **I'd like a haircut** je voudrais une coupe; **I like your haircut** j'aime ta coupe de cheveux; **he's got a dreadful haircut** on lui a très mal coupé les cheveux; **hairdo*** coiffure *f*; **I'm going to have a hairdo*** je vais me faire coiffer; **do you like my hairdo?*** tu aimes ma coiffure *or* mes cheveux comme ça?*; **hairdresser** coiffeur *m*, -euse *f*; **hairdresser's (shop** *or* **salon)** salon *m* de coiffure; **I'm going to the hairdresser's** je vais chez le coiffeur; (*skill, job*) **hairdressing** coiffure *f* (*métier*); **hairdressing salon** salon *m* de coiffure; **I've a hairdressing appointment** j'ai un rendez-vous chez le coiffeur; **hair-drier** séchoir *m* à cheveux, sèche-cheveux *m*; (*Brit*) **hair grip** pince *f* à cheveux; **hair lacquer** laque *f* (*capillaire*); **hairline** (*on head*) naissance *f* des cheveux; (*in handwriting*) délié *m*; **he has a receding hairline** son front se dégarnit; (*Med*) **hairline fracture** fêlure *f*; **hairline crack** mince *or* légère fêlure; **hairnet** résille *f*, filet *m* à cheveux; **hair oil** huile *f* capillaire; **hairpiece** postiche *m*; **hairpin** épingle *f* à cheveux; **hairpin bend** virage *m* en épingle à cheveux; **hair-raising** horrifique, à (vous) faire dresser les cheveux sur la tête; **prices are hair-raising* these days** le coût de la vie est affolant* en ce moment; **driving in Paris is a hair-raising business** conduire dans Paris c'est à vous faire dresser les cheveux sur la tête; **hair remover** crème *f* épilatoire *or* à épiler; **hair restorer** régénérateur *m* des cheveux; **hair roller** rouleau *m*; **hair's breadth** *V* **hairbreadth**; **hair set** mise *f* en plis; (*Rel*) **hair shirt** haire *f*, cilice *m*; **hair specialist** capilliculteur *m*, -trice *f*; **hair-splitter** coupeur *m*, -euse *f* de cheveux en quatre; **hair-splitting** (*n*) ergotage *m*, chicane *f*, chicanerie *f*; (*adj*) ergoteur, chicanier; **hair spray** laque *f* (en aérosol *or* en bombe); **a can of hair spray** un aérosol *or* une bombe de laque; **hairspring** (ressort *m*) spiral *m* (*de montre*); **hair style** coiffure *f* (*arrangement des cheveux*); **hair stylist** coiffeur *m*, -euse *f*.
hairbreadth [ˈhɛəbretθ] *n* (*also* **hair's breadth, hairsbreadth**) **by a ~** d'un cheveu, tout juste, de justesse; **the bullet missed him by a ~** la balle l'a manqué d'un cheveu; **we missed death by a ~** nous avons frisé la mort, nous étions à deux doigts de la mort, il s'en est fallu d'un cheveu qu'on y reste (*subj*); **the car missed the taxi by a ~** la voiture a évité le taxi de justesse; **he was within a ~ of giving in** il a tenu à un cheveu qu'il ne cède (*subj*); **he was within a ~ of bankruptcy** il était à deux doigts de la faillite.
-haired [hɛəd] *adj ending in cpds*: **long-haired** *person* aux cheveux longs; *animal* à longs poils; **short-haired** *person* aux cheveux courts; *animal* à poils ras; *V* **curly, fair**[1] *etc.*
hairless [ˈhɛəlɪs] *adj head* chauve; *face, chin* glabre; *body, animal* sans poils.
hairy [ˈhɛərɪ] *adj* **(a)** *body, animal* velu, poilu; *scalp* chevelu; *person* hirsute; (*Bot*) velu.
(b) (**fig*) (*frightening*) horrifique, à (vous) faire dresser les cheveux sur la tête; (*difficult*) hérissé de difficultés, épouvantable. **they had a few ~ moments*** ils ont eu des sueurs froides*.
Haiti [ˈheɪtɪ] *n* Haïti *f*.
Haitian [ˈheɪʃɪən] **1** *adj* haïtien. **2** *n* Haïtien(ne) *m(f)*.

hake [heɪk] *n, pl* ~ *or* ~**s** colin *m*, merlu *m*.
halberd ['hælbəd] *n* hallebarde *f*.
halcyon ['hælsɪən] 1 *n* (*Myth, Orn*) alcyon *m*. 2 *adj* paisible, serein. ~ **weather** temps paradisiaque *or* enchanteur; ~ **days** jours de bonheur, jours heureux.
hale [heɪl] *adj* vigoureux, robuste. **to be** ~ **and hearty** être vigoureux, être en pleine santé, se porter comme un charme.
half [hɑːf] *pl* **halves** 1 *n* **(a)** moitié *f*; demi(e) *m(f)*. **to cut in** ~ couper en deux; **it broke in** ~ cela s'est cassé en deux; **will you have one** ~ **of my apple?** veux-tu une moitié de ma pomme?; **to take** ~ **of** prendre la moitié de; **two halves make a whole** deux demis font un tout; **he doesn't do things by halves** il ne fait pas les choses à moitié; **two and a** ~ deux et demi; **two and a** ~ **hours, two hours and a** ~ deux heures et demie; **two and a** ~ **kilos, two kilos and a** ~ deux kilos et demi; **will you go halves with me in buying the book?** est-ce que tu te mettras de moitié avec moi pour acheter le livre?; **they had always gone halves in everything** ils avaient toujours tout partagé (également); **bigger by** ~ moitié plus grand; **he is too clever by** ~ il est un peu trop malin; **and that's not the** ~ **of it!*, I haven't told you the** ~ **of it yet!*** et ce n'est pas le mieux!, que je te raconte (*subj*) le meilleur!*; (*hum*) **my better** *or* **other** ~* ma (douce) moitié* (*hum*); (*fig*) **to see how the other** ~ **lives*** aller voir comment vivent les autres; *[rail ticket]* **outward/return** ~ billet *m or* coupon *m* aller/retour.
(b) (*Sport*) (*player*) demi *m*; (*part of match*) mi-temps *f*. **the first/second** ~ la première/seconde mi-temps.
(c) (*Scol: term*) semestre *m*.
2 *adj* demi. **a** ~ **cup,** ~ **a cup** une demi-tasse; **two and a** ~ **cups** deux tasses et demie; (*fig*) **in** ~ **a second*** en moins de rien; ~ **one thing** ~ **another** ni chair ni poisson; ~ **man** ~ **beast** mi-homme mi-bête; ~ **French** ~ **English** mi-français mi-anglais, moitié français moitié anglais; **to listen with** ~ **an ear** n'écouter que d'une oreille; **you can see that with** ~ **an eye** cela saute aux yeux, cela crève les yeux; **to go at** ~ **speed** aller à une vitesse modérée; **she was working with** ~ **her usual energy** elle ne travaillait qu'avec la moitié de son énergie coutumière; **I don't like** ~ **measures** je n'aime pas faire les choses à moitié; **the dress had** ~**-sleeves** la robe avait des manches mi-longues; *V* **tick**[1].
3 *adv* **(a)** (à) moitié; à demi. ~ **asleep** à moitié endormi; **the work is only** ~ **done** le travail n'est qu'à moitié fait; ~ **laughing** ~ **crying** moitié riant moitié pleurant; ~ **dressed** à demi vêtu; **I've only** ~ **read it** je ne l'ai qu'à moitié lu; **he** ~ **rose to his feet** il s'est levé à demi; **I** ~ **think** je serais tenté de penser; **he only** ~ **understands** il ne comprend qu'à moitié; **I** ~ **suspect that ...** je soupçonne presque que ...; **I'm** ~ **afraid that** j'ai un peu peur *or* quelque crainte que+ne+*subj*; **she has only** ~ **recovered from her illness** elle n'est qu'à moitié remise de sa maladie, elle est loin d'avoir entièrement récupéré depuis sa maladie.
(b) (*: intensive*) **he's not** ~ **rich!** il est rudement* *or* drôlement* riche!, il n'est pas à plaindre!; **she didn't** ~ **swear!** elle a juré comme un charretier!; **she didn't** ~ **cry!** elle a pleuré comme une madeleine; **not** ~**!** tu parles!*, et comment!*
(c) it is ~ **past three** il est trois heures et demie.
(d) he is ~ **as big as his sister** il est moitié moins grand que sa sœur; ~ **as big again** moitié plus grand; **he earns** ~ **as much as you** il gagne moitié moins que vous; ~ **as much again** moitié plus.
4 *cpd*: **half-and-half** moitié-moitié; (*Sport*) **half-back** demi *m*; **half-baked** (*Culin*) à moitié cuit; (*fig pej*) *person* mal dégrossi*; *plan, idea* qui ne tient pas debout, à la noix; **a half-baked philosopher/politician** un philosophe/politicien à la manque; *[book]* **half-binding** demi-reliure *f*; (*US*) **half-blood, half-breed** (*person*) métis(se) *m(f)*; (*horse*) demi-sang *m inv*; (*dog*) hybride *m*; **half-brother** demi-frère *m*; **half-caste** (*adj, n*) métis(se) *m(f)*; **half-circle** demi-cercle *m*; (*fig*) **to go off at half-cock** rater; **half-cocked** *gun* à moitié armé, au cran de sûreté; *plan, scheme* mal préparé, bâclé; **a half-crown** (*coin*), **half-a-crown** (*value*) une demi-couronne; **half-cup brassière** soutien-gorge *m* à balconnet; (*lit, fig*) **half-dead** à moitié mort, à demi mort (*with* de), plus mort que vif; (*Naut*) **half-deck** demi-pont *m*; **a half-dollar** (*coin*), **half-a-dollar** (*value*) (*US*) un demi-dollar; (*Brit*:†) une demi-couronne; **a half-dozen, half-a-dozen** une demi-douzaine; **half-empty** (*adj*) à moitié vide; (*vt*) vider à moitié; **half-fare** (*n*) demi-place *f*, demi-tarif *m*; (*adv*) à demi-tarif; **half fill** remplir à moitié; **half-full** à moitié plein; **half-hearted** *manner, person* tiède, sans enthousiasme; *attempt* timide, sans conviction; *welcome* peu enthousiaste; **half-heartedly** avec tiédeur, sans enthousiasme, sans conviction; **half-heartedness** tiédeur *f*, manque *m* d'enthousiasme *or* de conviction; **half-hitch** demi-clef *f*; **half-holiday** demi-journée *f* de congé; **a half-hour, half-an-hour** une demi-heure; **half-hourly** (*adv*) toutes les demi-heures, de demi-heure en demi-heure; (*adj*) (de) toutes les demi-heures; **half-length** (*n*) (*Swimming etc*) demi-longueur *f*; (*adj*) *portrait* en buste; (*Phys*) **half-life** période *f*; **half-light** demi-jour *m*; **at half-mast** en berne, à mi-mât; **half-moon** demi-lune *f*; (*on fingernail*) lunule *f*; **half-naked** à demi nu, à moitié nu; (*Wrestling*) **half-nelson** clef *f* du cou; (*Mus*) **half note** blanche *f*; **half-open** *eye, mouth* entrouvert; *window* entrebâillé; *door* entrouvert, entrebâillé; **half open** entrouvrir, entrebâiller; **on half-pay** (*gen*) à demi-salaire, à *or* en demi-traitement; (*Mil*) en demi-solde; **half-penny** (*n*) (*coin: pl* **halfpennies**; *value: pl* **halfpence**) demi-penny *m*; (*adj*) d'un demi-penny; **he hasn't got a halfpenny** il n'a pas le sou, il n'a pas un sou; **half-pint** ≈ quart *m* de litre; **a half-pint (of beer)** ≈ un bock; **at half-price** à moitié prix; **the goods were reduced to half-price** le prix des articles était réduit de moitié; **children admitted (at) half-price** les enfants paient demi-tarif *or* demi-place; **a half-price hat** un chapeau à moitié prix; (*Mus*) **half-rest** demi-pause *f*; **to be half-seas over**: être parti*, être dans les vignes du Seigneur; **half-sister** demi-sœur *f*; *[shoes]* **half-size** demi-pointure *f*; **half-size(d) model** modèle réduit de moitié; (*US*) **at half-staff** en berne, à mi-mât; (*Brit Scol etc*) **half-term** congé *m* de demi-trimestre; **half-timbered** à colombage; (*Sport*) **half-time** mi-temps *f*; **at half-time** à la mi-temps; (*Ind*) **on half-time** à mi-temps; **they are working half-time** ils travaillent à mi-temps *or* à la demi-journée; **a half-time job** un poste à mi-temps; **half-time score** score *m* à mi-temps; **they are on half-time (work)** = **they are working half-time**; **half-tone** (*Art*) demi-teinte *f*; (*Phot*) similigravure *f*; **half-track** (*tread*) chenille *f*; (*vehicle*) half-track *m*; **half-truth** demi-vérité *f*; (*Tennis etc*) **half-volley** demi-volée *f*; **half-way** *V* **halfway**; **half-wit** idiot(e) *m(f)*, imbécile *mf*; **half-witted** idiot, imbécile, faible d'esprit; (*esp Brit*) **half-yearly** (*adj*) semestriel; (*adv*) tous les six mois, par semestre.
halfway ['hɑːf'weɪ] 1 *adv* à mi-chemin. ~ **to Paris** à mi-chemin de Paris; (*lit, fig*) **to be** ~ **between** être à mi-chemin entre; (*lit*) **to go** ~ faire la moitié du chemin; (*fig*) **the decision goes** ~ **to giving the strikers what they want** avec cette décision on est à mi-chemin de donner satisfaction aux grévistes; ~ **up** *or* ~ **down (the hill)** à mi-côte, à mi-pente; (*lit, fig*) **we're** ~ **there** nous n'avons plus que la moitié du chemin à faire; (*lit*) **to meet sb** ~ (faire la moitié du chemin pour) aller à la rencontre de qn; (*fig*) **let's meet** ~**, I'll meet you** ~ coupons la poire en deux, je vous propose un compromis, faisons un compromis; (*fig*) **he agreed to meet them** (*or* **us** *etc*) ~ il a accepté de couper la poire en deux, il a accepté un compromis; ~ **through the book/film** à la moitié du livre/du film.
2 *adj*: **halfway house** maison *f or* bâtiment *m etc* à mi-chemin; (*Hist: inn*) hôtellerie *f* à mi-chemin entre deux relais; (*fig*) juste milieu *m*; (*also* **halfway hostel**: *for prisoners, mental patients etc*) centre *m* (ouvert) de réadaptation (*pour prisonniers, malades mentaux etc*).
halibut ['hælɪbət] *n, pl* ~ *or* ~**s** flétan *m* (holibut).
halitosis [ˌhælɪ'təʊsɪs] *n* mauvaise haleine.
hall [hɔːl] 1 *n* **(a)** (*large public room*) salle *f*; *[castle, public building]* (grande) salle; (*village* ~, *church* ~) salle paroissiale; (*Brit Univ: refectory*) réfectoire *m*.
(b) (*mansion*) château *m*, manoir *m*; (*Brit Univ: also* ~ **of residence**) pavillon *m* universitaire, foyer *m* d'étudiants. **the** ~**s of residence** la cité universitaire; (*Theat*) **to play the** ~**s** faire du music-hall; *V* **concert, music, town** *etc*.
(c) (*entrance way*) *[house]* vestibule *m*, entrée *f*, hall *m*; *[hotel]* hall; (*corridor*) couloir *m*, corridor *m*.
2 *cpd*: **hallmark** *[gold, silver]* poinçon *m*; (*fig*) sceau *m*, marque *f*; **the hallmark of genius** le sceau *or* la marque *or* l'empreinte *f* du génie; **hall porter** concierge *mf*, portier *m*; **hall-stand,** (*US*) **hall tree** portemanteau *m*; **hallway** vestibule *m*; (*corridor*) couloir *m*.
hallelujah [ˌhælɪ'luːjə] *excl, n* alléluia (*m*).
hallo [hə'ləʊ] *excl* (*in greeting*) bonjour!, salut!*; (*Telec*) allô!; (*to attract attention*) hé!, ohé!; (*in surprise*) tiens!
halloo [hə'luː] 1 *excl* (*Hunting*) taïaut!; (*gen*) ohé! 2 *vi* (*Hunting*) crier taïaut; (*gen*) appeler (à grands cris).
hallow ['hæləʊ] *vt* sanctifier, consacrer. ~**ed be Thy name** que ton nom soit sanctifié; ~**ed ground** terre sainte *or* bénie.
Hallowe'en ['hæləʊ'iːn] *n* veille *f* de la Toussaint.
hallucination [həˌluːsɪ'neɪʃən] *n* hallucination *f*.
hallucinatory [hə'luːsɪnətərɪ] *adj* hallucinatoire.
halo ['heɪləʊ] *n, pl* ~**(e)s** *[saint etc]* auréole *f*, nimbe *m*; (*Astron*) halo *m*.
halogen ['heɪləʊdʒɪn] *n* halogène *m*.
halt[1] [hɔːlt] 1 *n* **(a)** halte *f*, arrêt *m*. **5 minutes'** ~ 5 minutes d'arrêt; **to come to a** ~ faire halte, s'arrêter; **to call a** ~ (*order a stop*) commander halte; (*stop*) faire halte; (*fig*) **to call a** ~ **to sth** mettre fin à qch.
(b) (*Brit Rail*) halte *f*.
2 *vi* faire halte, s'arrêter. ~! halte!
3 *vt vehicle* faire arrêter; *process* interrompre.
halt[2] [hɔːlt] *adj* (††: *lame*) boiteux. **the** ~ les estropiés *mpl*.
halter ['hɔːltəʳ] *n [horse]* licou *m*, collier *m*; (*hangman's noose*) corde *f* (*de pendaison*). **a dress with a** ~ **top** *or* ~ **neckline** une robe dos nu *inv*.
halting ['hɔːltɪŋ] *adj speech, voice* hésitant, haché, entrecoupé; *progress* hésitant; *verse* boiteux; *style* heurté.
haltingly ['hɔːltɪŋlɪ] *adv* de façon hésitante, de façon heurtée.
halve [hɑːv] *vt apple etc* partager *or* diviser en deux (moitiés égales); *expense, time* réduire *or* diminuer de moitié.
halves [hɑːvz] *npl of* **half.**
halyard ['hæljəd] *n* (*Naut*) drisse *f*.
ham [hæm] 1 *n* **(a)** (*Culin*) jambon *m*. ~ **and eggs** œufs *mpl* au jambon.
(b) (*Anat*) (*thigh*) cuisse *f*; (*buttock*) fesse *f*.
(c) (*Theat**) cabotin(e)* *m(f)* (*pej*).
(d) (*Rad**) radio-amateur *m*.
2 *cpd sandwich* au jambon. **ham-fisted, ham-handed** maladroit, gauche; **hamstring** (*n*) tendon *m* du jarret; (*vt*) couper les jarrets à; (*fig*) couper ses moyens à, paralyser.
3 *vi* (*Theat**) forcer son rôle.
Hamburg ['hæmbɜːg] *n* Hambourg.
hamburger ['hæmˌbɜːgəʳ] *n* hamburger *m*.
Hamitic [hæ'mɪtɪk] *adj* chamitique.
hamlet ['hæmlɪt] *n* hameau *m*. **H**~ Hamlet *m*.
hammer ['hæməʳ] 1 *n* (*gen; auctioneer's; Mus, Sport, Tech etc*) marteau *m*; *[gun]* chien *m*. **the** ~ **and sickle** la faucille et le marteau; **they were going at it** ~ **and tongs** (*working*) ils y allaient de tout leur cœur *or* à bras raccourcis; (*arguing*) ils discutaient passionnément *or* avec feu; (*quarrelling*) ils se disputaient

avec violence; (*at auction*) **to come under the ~** être mis aux enchères.

2 *cpd*: **hammertoe** orteil *m* en marteau; **hammertoed** aux orteils en marteau.

3 *vt* **(a)** battre au marteau, marteler. **to ~ a nail into a plank** enfoncer un clou dans une planche (à coups de marteau); **to ~ a nail home** enfoncer un clou (à fond); (*fig*) **to ~ a point home** revenir sur un point avec une insistance tenace *or* acharnée; **to ~ into shape** *metal* façonner au marteau; (*fig*) *plan, agreement* mettre au point; **I tried to ~ some sense into him** je me suis efforcé de lui faire entendre raison; **to ~ an idea into sb's head** enfoncer de force *or* faire entrer de force une idée dans la tête de qn.

(b) (**fig*) (*defeat*) battre à plate(s) couture(s); (*criticize severely*) éreinter, démolir. **the critics ~ed the film** les critiques ont éreinté *or* ont démoli le film.

(c) (*St Ex*) *stockbroker* déclarer en faillite *or* failli.

4 *vi* (*also* **~ away**) frapper au marteau. (*fig*) **he was ~ing (away) at the door** il frappait à la porte à coups redoublés; **he was ~ing (away) on the piano** il tapait sur le piano (à bras raccourcis); **to ~ (away) at a problem** s'acharner sur *or* travailler d'arrache-pied à un problème.

hammer down *vt sep metal* aplatir au marteau; *loose plank* fixer.

hammer in *vt sep* enfoncer (au marteau). **he hammered the nail in with his shoe** il a enfoncé le clou avec son soulier.

hammer out *vt sep metal* étendre au marteau; (*fig*) *plan, agreement* élaborer (avec difficulté); *difficulties* démêler, aplanir; *verse, music* marteler.

hammer together *pieces of wood etc* assembler au marteau.

hammering ['hæmərɪŋ] *n* (*action*) martelage *m*; (*sound*) martèlement *m*; (*fig*) (*defeat*) punition* *f*, dérouillée: *f*; (*criticism*) esquintement *m*. **to take a ~** *[team, boxer, player]* prendre une punition* *or* une dérouillée:; *[book, play, film]* se faire esquinter.

hammock ['hæmək] *n* hamac *m*.

hamper[1] ['hæmpər] *n* panier *m* d'osier, manne *f*; (*for oysters, fish, game*) bourriche *f*. **a ~ of food** un panier garni (*de nourriture*); *V* **picnic**.

hamper[2] ['hæmpər] *vt person* gêner; *movement* gêner, entraver.

hamster ['hæmstər] *n* hamster *m*.

hand [hænd] **1** *n* **(a)** (*Anat*) main *f*. **on (one's) ~s and knees** à quatre pattes; **to have** *or* **hold in one's ~** *book* tenir à la main; *money* avoir dans la main; (*fig*) *victory* tenir entre ses mains; **give me your ~** donne-moi la main; **to take sb's ~** prendre la main de qn; **he took her by the ~** il l'a prise par la main; **to lead sb by the ~** conduire *or* mener qn par la main; **to take sth with** *or* **in both ~s** prendre qch à deux mains; (*fig*) **he clutched at my offer with both ~s** il s'est jeté sur ma proposition; (*Mus*) **for four ~s** pour *or* à quatre mains; **~s up!** (*at gunpoint*) haut les mains!; (*in school etc*) levez la main!; **~s off!*** pas touche!*, bas les pattes!:; **~s off the sweets!*** touche pas aux bonbons!*; (*fig*) **~s off our village*** laissez notre village tranquille; (*lit*) **~ over ~, ~ over fist** main sur main; (*fig*) **he's making money ~ over fist** il fait des affaires d'or; **he's very good** *or* **clever with his ~s** il est très adroit de ses mains; **I'm no good with my ~s at all** je ne sais (strictement) rien faire de mes mains *or* de mes dix doigts; (*fig*) **I'm always putting my ~ in my pocket** je n'arrête pas de débourser *or* de mettre la main à la poche; (*fig*) **you could see his ~ in everything the committee did** on reconnaissait son empreinte *or* influence dans tout ce que faisait le comité.

(b) (*phrases*) **at ~** à portée de la main, sous la main; **to keep sth at ~** garder qch à portée de la main; **he has enough money at ~** il a assez d'argent disponible; **summer is (close) at ~** l'été est (tout) proche; **at first ~** de première main; **the information at** *or* **to ~** les renseignements *mpl* disponibles; **by ~** à la main; **made by ~** fait à la main; **the letter was written by ~** c'était une lettre manuscrite, la lettre était manuscrite *or* écrite à la main; **to send a letter by ~** faire porter une lettre (*à la main*); **from ~ to ~** de main en main (*V also* **2**); **to live from ~ to mouth** vivre au jour le jour (*V also* **2**); **pistol in ~** pistolet *m* au poing; **in one's own ~s** entre ses mains; (*lit, fig*) **to put sth into sb's ~s** remettre qch entre les mains de qn; **to put o.s. in sb's ~s** s'en remettre à qn, se mettre entre les mains de qn; **my life is in your ~s** ma vie est entre vos mains; **to fall into the ~s of** tomber aux mains *or* entre les mains de; **to be in good ~s** être en bonnes mains; **I have this matter in ~ at the moment** je suis en train de m'occuper de cette affaire; **he had £6,000 in ~** il avait 6.000 livres de disponibles; (*Comm*) **stock in ~** existence *f or* marchandises *fpl* en magasin; **cash in ~** encaisse *f*; **the matter in ~** l'affaire en question; **he had the situation well in ~** il avait la situation bien en main; **she took the child in ~** elle a pris l'enfant en main; **to keep o.s. well in ~** se contrôler; **work in ~** travail *m* en cours *or* en chantier; **the matter in** *or* **on ~** le sujet en discussion *or* en délibération *or* sur le tapis; **to have sth on one's ~s** avoir qch sur les bras (*V also* **time**); (*Comm*) **goods left on our ~s** marchandises invendues; **on the right/left ~** du côté droit/gauche; **on my right ~** à ma droite; **on every ~, on all ~s** partout, de tous (les) côtés; **on the one ~ ... on the other ~** d'une part ... d'autre part; **yes, but on the other ~ he is very rich** oui, mais par contre il est très riche; **to get sth off one's ~s** se décharger de qch; **I'll take it off your ~s** je m'en chargerai, je vous en déchargerai *or* débarrasserai; **his daughter was off his ~s** sa fille n'était plus à sa charge; **to condemn sb out of ~** condamner qn sans jugement; **to execute sb out of ~** exécuter qn sommairement; *[child, dog, situation]* **to get out of ~** devenir impossible; **this child/dog is quite out of ~** il n'y a plus moyen de tenir cet enfant/ce chien; **to ~** sous la main, à portée de la main; **I have not got the letter to ~** je n'ai pas la lettre sous la main; (*Comm*) **your letter has come to ~** votre lettre m'est parvenue; (*Comm*) **your letter of 6th inst. to ~** en mains votre lettre du 6 courant (*Comm*); **he seized the first weapon to ~** il s'est emparé de la première arme venue; **to rule with a firm ~** gouverner d'une main ferme; **with a heavy ~** avec poigne, à la cravache; **they are ~ in glove** ils s'entendent comme larrons en foire; **he's ~ in glove with them** il est de mèche avec eux; **he never does a ~'s turn** il ne remue pas le petit doigt, il n'en fiche pas une rame:; **the hedgehog ate out of his ~** le hérisson lui mangeait dans la main; (*fig*) **he's got the boss eating out of his ~*** il fait marcher le patron au doigt et à l'œil; **to force sb's ~** forcer la main à qn; **to get one's ~ in** se faire la main; **to keep one's ~ in** garder *or* s'entretenir la main; **he can't keep his ~s off the money** il ne peut pas s'empêcher de toucher à l'argent; **I have my ~s full at the moment** je suis très occupé en ce moment; **to have one's ~s full with** avoir fort à faire avec, avoir du pain sur la planche avec; (*lit, fig*) **to have one's ~s tied** avoir les mains liées; **to have a ~ in** *piece of work, decision* être pour quelque chose dans, jouer un rôle dans; *crime* être mêlé à; *plot* tremper dans; **she had a ~ in it** elle y était pour quelque chose; **I have no ~ in it** je n'y suis pour rien; **I will have no ~ in it** je ne veux rien avoir à faire là-dedans; **to take a ~ in sth** se mêler de qch; **to take a ~ in doing sth** participer à qch, contribuer à qch; **to give sb a (helping) ~ (to do), to lend sb a ~ (to do)** donner un coup de main à qn (pour faire); **he got his brother to give him a ~** il s'est fait aider par son frère, il a obtenu de son frère qu'il lui donne (*subj*) un coup de main; **give me a ~, will you?** tu peux me donner un coup de main?; (*Theat: applause*) **they gave him a big ~*** ils l'ont applaudi bien fort; (*Theat*) **give him a (big) ~ now!*** (et maintenant) on l'applaudit bien fort!; **to get the upper ~ of sb** prendre l'avantage *or* le dessus sur qn; **to have the upper ~** avoir le dessus; **to put** *or* **set one's ~ to sth** entreprendre qch; **he can set his ~ to most things** il sait tout faire; (*fig liter*) **to put** *or* **set one's ~ to the plough** se mettre à l'ouvrage *or* à l'œuvre; **to hold** *or* (*liter*) **stay one's ~** se retenir; **to win sth ~s down** gagner qch haut la main; **to be waited on ~ and foot** se faire servir comme un prince; (*fig*) **he asked for her ~ (in marriage)** il a demandé sa main (en mariage); (*liter*) **she gave him her ~** elle lui a accordé sa main; *V* **free, high, lay**[1] *etc.*

(c) (*worker*) travailleur *m*, -euse *f* manuel(le), ouvrier *m*, -ière *f*. **~s** (*Ind etc*) main d'œuvre *f*; (*Naut*) équipage *m*, hommes *mpl*; **to take on ~s** embaucher (de la main d'œuvre); (*Naut*) **all ~s on deck** tout le monde sur le pont; (*Naut*) **lost with all ~s** perdu corps et biens; (*fig*) **he's a great ~ at (doing) that** il a le coup de main pour (faire) cela, il est vraiment doué pour (faire) cela; (*fig*) **old ~** vétéran *m*, vieux routier; **he's an old ~ (at it)** il n'en est pas à son coup d'essai, il connaît la musique*; *V* **dab**[3], **factory, farm** *etc.*

(d) *[clock etc]* aiguille *f*; (*Typ*) index *m*.

(e) (*Measure*) paume *f*. **a horse 13 ~s high** un cheval de 13 paumes.

(f) (*handwriting*) écriture *f*. **the letter was in his ~** la lettre était (écrite) de sa main; **he writes a good ~** il a une belle écriture *or* une belle main.

(g) (*Cards*) main *f*, jeu *m*; (*game etc*) partie *f*. **I've got a good ~** j'ai une belle main *or* un beau jeu; **we played a ~ of bridge** nous avons fait une partie de bridge.

(h) (*Culin*) **~ of pork** jambonneau *m*; **~ of bananas** régime *m* de bananes.

2 *cpd*: **handbag** sac *m* à main; (*Sport*) **handball** handball *m*; **handbasin** lavabo *m*; **handbell** sonnette *f*, clochette *f*; **handbill** prospectus *m*; **handbook** (*instructions*) manuel *m* (*V also* **teacher**); *[tourist]* guide *m*; *[museum]* livret *m*, catalogue *m*; (*Aut*) **handbrake** frein *m* à main; **handcart** charrette *f* à bras; **handclasp** poignée *f* de main; **hand cream** crème *f* pour les mains; **handcuff** mettre *or* passer les menottes à; **to be handcuffed** avoir les menottes aux poignets; **handcuffs** menottes *fpl*; (*Mil*) **hand grenade** grenade *f* (à main); **handgrip** (*on cycle, machine etc*) poignée *f*; (*handshake*) poignée de main; **handhold** prise *f* de main; **hand-in-hand** (*lit*) la main dans la main; (*fig*) ensemble, de concert; (*fig*) **to go hand-in-hand (with)** aller de pair (avec); **hand-knitted** tricoté à la main; **hand lotion** lotion *f* pour les mains; **hand-luggage** bagages *mpl* à main; **handmade** fait (à la) main; (*lit, fig*) **handmaid(en)** servante *f*; **it's a hand-me-down* from my sister** c'est un vieux vêtement que m'a refilé* ma sœur; **hand-me-downs*** (*npl*) vêtements *mpl* d'occasion; (*scruffier*) friperie *f*; **handout** (*leaflet*) prospectus *m*; (*at lecture, meeting*) dossier *m*, documentation *f*; (*press release*) communiqué *m*; (*money*) charité *f*, aumône *f*; **hand-picked** trié sur le volet; **hand-printed** imprimé à la main; **handrail** *[stairs etc]* rampe *f*, main courante, balustrade *f*; *[bridge, quay]* gardefou *m*; **handsaw** scie *f* à main; (*Telec*) **handset** combiné *m*; **handshake** poignée *f* de main (*V* **golden**); **hand-spray** douchette *f* (amovible); **handspring** saut *m* de mains; **to do a handstand** faire l'arbre droit; **hand-stitched** cousu main; **to fight hand-to-hand** combattre corps à corps; **a hand-to-hand fight** un corps à corps; **hand-to-hand fighting** du corps à corps *m*; **to lead a hand-to-mouth existence** vivre au jour le jour; **handwork** = **handiwork**; **hand-woven** tissé à la main; **handwriting** écriture *f*; **handwritten** manuscrit, écrit à la main.

3 *vt* **(a)** (*give*) passer, donner, tendre (*to* à). (*fig*) **you've got to ~ it to him*** c'est une justice à lui rendre; (*fig*) **it was ~ed to him (on a plate)*** ça lui a été apporté sur un plateau; (*fig*) **to ~ sb a line about sth:** raconter des bobards: à qn à propos de qch.

(b) he ~ed the lady into/out of the car il tendit sa main à la dame pour l'aider à monter dans/à descendre de la voiture.

hand back *vt sep* rendre (*to* à).

hand down *vt sep* **(a)** (*lit*) **hand me down the vase** descends-moi le vase; **he handed me down the book from the shelf** il a descendu le livre du rayon et me l'a tendu.

(b) (*fig*) transmettre. **the story/the sword was handed down from father to son** l'histoire/l'épée était transmise *or* se transmettait de père en fils.
(c) (*US Jur*) *decision* rendre.
hand in *vt sep* remettre (*to* à). **hand this in at the office** remettez cela à quelqu'un au bureau.
hand on *vt sep* transmettre (*to* à). (*fig*) **to hand on the torch** passer *or* transmettre le flambeau.
hand out 1 *vt sep* distribuer. **to hand out advice*** distribuer des conseils.
2 handout *n V* **hand 2.**
hand over *vt sep book, object* remettre (*to* à); *criminal, prisoner* livrer (*to* à); *authority, powers* (*transfer*) transmettre (*to* à); (*surrender*) céder (*to* à); *property, business* céder.
hand round *vt sep bottles, papers* faire circuler; *cakes* (faire) passer (à la ronde), *[hostess]* offrir.
hand up *vt sep* passer (*de bas en haut*).
-handed ['hændɪd] *adj ending in cpds* qui a la main ... . **empty-handed** les mains vides; **heavy-handed** qui a la main lourde; *V* **left², short** *etc.*
handful ['hændfʊl] *n [coins, objects etc]* poignée *f*. **by the ~, in ~s** à *or* par poignées; **there was only a ~ of people at the concert** il n'y avait qu'une poignée de gens au concert, il y avait quatre pelés et un tondu au concert*; (*fig*) **the children are a ~*** les enfants ne me (*or* lui *etc*) laissent pas une minute de répit.
handicap ['hændɪkæp] **1** *n* **(a)** (*Sport*) handicap *m*. *[racehorse]* **weight ~** surcharge *f*; **time ~** handicap (de temps).
(b) (*disadvantage*) désavantage *m*. **his appearance is a great ~** son aspect physique le handicape beaucoup; **to be under a great ~** avoir un désavantage *or* un handicap énorme; *V* **physical.**
2 *vt* (*Sport, gen*) handicaper. **he was greatly ~ped by his accent** il était très handicapé par son accent.
handicapped ['hændɪkæpt] **1** *adj* handicapé. **~ children** enfants handicapés; **mentally/physically ~** handicapé mentalement/physiquement. **2** *npl*: **the ~** les handicapés *mpl*; **the mentally/physically ~** les handicapés mentaux/physiques.
handicraft ['hændɪkrɑːft] *n* (*work*) (travail *m* d')artisanat *m*; (*skill*) habileté manuelle; (*trade*) métier *m* d'artisanat.
handiness ['hændɪnɪs] *n* (*V* **handy**) *[object, method]* commodité *f*, aspect *m* pratique; *[person]* adresse *f*, dextérité manuelle. **because of the ~ of the library** parce qu'il est si facile de se rendre à la bibliothèque.
handiwork ['hændɪwɜːk] *n* (*lit*) travail manuel, ouvrage *m*; (*fig*) œuvre *f*, ouvrage. (*fig*) **that is his ~** c'est son œuvre.
handkerchief ['hæŋkətʃɪf] *n* mouchoir *m*; (*fancy*) pochette *f*; (*for neck*) foulard *m*.
handle ['hændl] **1** *n [basket, bucket]* anse *f*; *[broom, spade, knife]* manche *m*; *[door, drawer, suitcase]* poignée *f*; *[handcart]* brancard *m*; *[saucepan]* queue *f*; *[pump, stretcher, wheelbarrow]* bras *m*; *[tap]* clef *f*, poignée *f*. *[car]* **(starting) ~** manivelle *f*; (*fig*) **to have a ~ to one's name*** avoir un titre; *V* **fly³.**
2 *vt* **(a)** (*touch*) manipuler, manier. **please do not ~ the goods** prière de ne pas toucher aux marchandises; (*label*) '**~ with care**' 'fragile'; (*Ftbl*) **to ~ the ball** toucher le ballon de la main.
(b) (*control, deal with*) *ship* manœuvrer, gouverner; *car* conduire, manœuvrer; *person, animal* manier, s'y prendre avec. **he knows how to ~ a gun** il sait se servir d'un pistolet; **he ~d the situation very well** il a très bien conduit l'affaire; **I'll ~ this** je m'en charge, je vais m'en occuper; **he knows how to ~ his son** il sait très bien s'y prendre avec son fils; **this child is very hard to ~** cet enfant est très difficile *or* dur*; **can you ~ dogs?** savez-vous (comment) vous y prendre avec les chiens?; **she can certainly ~ children** il n'y a pas de doute qu'elle sait s'y prendre avec les enfants; **the crowd ~d him roughly** (*lit*) la foule l'a malmené; (*fig*) la foule l'a hué.
(c) (*Comm*) *commodity, product* avoir, faire. **we don't ~ that type of product** nous ne faisons pas ce genre de produit; **we don't ~ that type of business** nous ne traitons pas ce type d'affaires; **do you ~ tax matters?** est-ce que vous vous occupez de fiscalité?; **Orly ~s 5 million passengers a year** 5 millions de passagers passent par Orly chaque année; **we ~ 200 passengers a day** 200 voyageurs par jour passent par nos services; **can the port ~ big ships?** le port peut-il recevoir les gros bateaux?
3 *vi*: **to ~ well/badly** *[ship]* être facile/difficile à manœuvrer; *[car, gun]* être facile/difficile à manier.
4 *cpd*: **handlebar** guidon *m*; (*hum*) **handlebar moustache** moustache *f* en crocs *or* en guidon de vélo* (*hum*).
-handled ['hændld] *adj ending in cpds* au manche de, à la poignée de. **a wooden-handled spade** une pelle au manche de bois *or* avec un manche de bois.
handler ['hændləʳ] *n* (*also* **dog ~**) dresseur *m*, -euse *f* (de chiens). **the dog looked at his ~** le chien a regardé son maître.
handling ['hændlɪŋ] *n [ship]* manœuvre *f*; *[car]* maniement *m*; *[goods, objects]* (*Ind*) manutention *f*; (*fingering*) maniement, manipulation *f*. **his ~ of the matter** la façon dont il a traité l'affaire; *[person, object]* **to get some rough ~** se faire malmener.
handsome ['hænsəm] *adj* **(a)** (*good-looking*) *person* beau (*f* belle); *furniture, building* beau, élégant; (*fig*) *conduct, compliment* généreux; *gift* riche, généreux. **~ apology** excuse *f* honorable.
(b) (*considerable*) **a ~ amount** une jolie somme; **~ fortune** belle fortune; **to make a ~ profit out of sth** réaliser de jolis bénéfices sur qch; **to sell sth for a ~ price** vendre qch un bon prix *or* pour une jolie somme.
handsomely ['hænsəmlɪ] *adv* (*elegantly*) élégamment, avec élégance; (*generously*) *contribute, donate* généreusement, avec générosité; *apologise, agree* avec bonne grâce, élégamment. **he behaved very ~** il s'est conduit très généreusement *or* élégamment.

handy ['hændɪ] **1** *adj* **(a)** *person* adroit. **he's a very ~ person** il est très adroit de ses mains, il sait se servir de ses mains; **he's ~ with his fists*** il sait se servir de ses poings; **he's ~ with a gun*** il sait se servir d'un pistolet; **she's ~ with a sewing machine*** elle sait très bien se servir d'une machine à coudre; **he's ~ in the kitchen*** il sait très bien se débrouiller dans la cuisine.
(b) (*close at hand*) *tool* accessible, sous la main, prêt. **in a ~ place** dans un endroit commode, à portée de la main; **I always have an aspirin ~** j'ai toujours une aspirine sous la main; **the shops are very ~** les magasins sont très accessibles; **the house is ~ for the shops** la maison est très bien placée *or* située pour les magasins.
(c) (*convenient*) *tool, method* commode, pratique. **a ~ little car** une petite voiture pratique; **that's ~!** ça tombe bien!; **that would come in very ~** cela tomberait bien.
(d) (*ship*) maniable.
2 *cpd*: **handyman** (*servant*) factotum *m*, homme *m* à tout faire; (*do-it-yourself*) bricoleur *m*.
hang [hæŋ] *pret, ptp* **hung 1** *vt* **(a)** (*suspend*) *lamp* suspendre, accrocher (*on* à); *curtains, hat, decorations* accrocher; *painting* accrocher, (*in gallery: exhibit*) exposer; *door* monter; *clothes* pendre (*on, from* à); *wallpaper* poser, tendre; (*Culin*) *game* faire faisander; *dangling object* laisser pendre. **he hung the rope over the side of the boat** il a laissé pendre le cordage par-dessus bord; **to ~ one's head** baisser la tête.
(b) (*decorate*) garnir, orner (*with* de). **trees hung with lights** arbres chargés de lumières; **balconies hung with flags** balcons pavoisés; **room hung with paintings** pièce ornée de tableaux *or* aux murs couverts de tableaux; **study/wall hung with hessian** bureau/mur tapissé *or* tendu de jute.
(c) **to ~ fire** *[guns]* faire long feu; *[plans etc]* traîner (en longueur).
(d) (*pret, ptp* **hanged**) *criminal* pendre. **he was ~ed for murder** il fut pendu pour meurtre; (*loc*) **(may) as well be ~ed for a sheep as a lamb** autant être pendu pour un mouton que pour un agneau; (*Hist*) **he was ~ed, drawn and quartered** il a été pendu, éviscéré et écartelé; **he ~ed himself from** *or* **out of despair** il s'est pendu de désespoir; **~ him!*** qu'il aille se faire voir!‡; **(I'll be) ~ed if I know!*** je veux bien être pendu si je le sais!*; **~ it!*, ~ it all!*** zut!*
2 *vi* **(a)** *[rope, dangling object]* pendre, être accroché *or* suspendu (*on, from* à); *[drapery]* pendre, tomber, retomber. **her hair hung down her back** ses cheveux tombaient sur ses épaules *or* lui tombaient dans le dos; **a picture ~ing on the wall** un tableau accroché au mur; **to ~ out of the window** *[person]* se pencher par la fenêtre; *[thing]* pendre à la fenêtre; (*fig*) **to ~ by a hair** ne tenir qu'à un cheveu.
(b) planer, peser. **a fog ~s over the town** un brouillard plane *or* pèse sur la ville; **the hawk hung motionless in the sky** le faucon était comme suspendu immobile dans le ciel; (*fig*) **the threat which ~s over us** la menace qui plane *or* pèse sur nous, la menace qui est suspendue au-dessus de nos têtes; *V* **time.**
(c) *[criminal etc]* être pendu. **he ought to ~** il devrait être pendu; **he'll ~ for it** cela lui vaudra d'être pendu, cela lui vaudra la corde.
3 *n* (*) **to get the ~ of doing sth** attraper le coup* pour faire qch; **you'll soon get the ~ of it** tu auras vite fait de t'y mettre; **I'll never get the ~ of it** je n'arriverai jamais à le comprendre, je ne comprendrai jamais ce truc-là*; **he can't get the ~ of this machine** il n'arrive pas à prendre le coup de main avec cette machine; **I don't give** *or* **care a ~*** je m'en fiche*, je n'en ai rien à fiche‡.
4 *cpd*: **to have a hangdog look** *or* **expression** avoir un air de chien battu; **hang-glider** aile *f* delta, deltaplane *m*, aile volante; **hang-gliding** vol *m* libre; **to go hang-gliding** faire du vol libre; **hangman** bourreau *m*; **hangnail** petite peau, envie *f*; (*house, flat etc*) **hang-out‡** crèche‡ *f*, perchoir‡ *m*; (*after drinking*) **to have a hangover** avoir mal aux cheveux*, avoir une *or* la gueule de bois‡; **this problem is a hangover from the previous administration** ce problème est un reliquat de l'administration précédente; **hang-up*** complexe *m* (*about* en ce qui concerne).
hang about, hang around 1 *vi* rôder, errer, traîner. **he's always hanging about here** il est toujours à rôder *or* à errer par ici; **to keep sb hanging about** faire attendre qn, faire poireauter* qn.
2 *vt fus*: **to hang about sb** coller à qn, être toujours sur le dos de qn; **he's always hanging about that café** il hante toujours ce café.
hang back *vi* (*in walking etc*) rester en arrière, hésiter à aller de l'avant. (*fig*) **she hung back from offering ...** elle ne voulait pas offrir ..., elle était réticente pour offrir ... .
hang down *vi, vt sep* pendre.
hang on 1 *vi* **(a)** (*: *wait*) attendre. **hang on!** attendez!; (*on phone*) ne quittez pas!; (*on phone*) **I had to hang on for ages** j'ai dû attendre des siècles.
(b) (*hold out*) tenir bon, résister. **he managed to hang on till help came** il réussit à tenir bon *or* à résister jusqu'à ce que des secours arrivent (*subj*).
(c) **to hang on to sth*** (*keep hold of*) ne pas lâcher qch, rester cramponné à qch; (*keep*) garder qch; **hang on to the branch** tiens bien la branche, ne lâche pas la branche.
2 *vt fus* **(a)** (*lit, fig*) se cramponner à, s'accrocher à. **to hang on sb's arm** se cramponner au *or* s'accrocher au bras de qn; **to hang on sb's words** *or* **lips** boire les paroles de qn, être suspendu aux lèvres de qn.
(b) (*depend on*) dépendre de, être suspendu à. **everything hangs on his decision** tout dépend de *or* est suspendu à sa décision; **everything hangs on whether he saw her or not** le tout est de savoir s'il l'a vue ou non.

hang out 1 *vi* (a) *[tongue]* pendre; *[shirt tails etc]* pendre (dehors), pendouiller*.
(b) (‡: *live*) percher*, crécher‡.
(c) (*: *resist, endure*) tenir bon, résister. **they managed to hang out till help came*** ils réussirent à tenir bon *or* à résister jusqu'à l'arrivée des secours; **they are hanging out for more pay*** ils tiennent bon pour avoir une augmentation.
2 *vt sep streamer* suspendre (dehors); *washing* étendre (dehors); *flag* arborer.
3 **hang-out‡** *n V* **hang 4**.
hang together *vi* (a) *[people]* se serrer les coudes.
(b) *[argument]* se tenir; *[story]* tenir debout; *[statements]* s'accorder, concorder. **it all hangs together** tout ça se tient, c'est logique.
hang up 1 *vi* (*Telec*) raccrocher.
2 *vt sep hat, picture* accrocher, pendre (*on* à, sur); (*Telec*) *receiver* raccrocher; *V* **hung 2**.
3 **hang-up*** *n V* **hang 4**.
hangar ['hæŋəʳ] *n* (*Aviat*) hangar *m*.
hanger ['hæŋəʳ] 1 *n* (*clothes* ~) cintre *m*, portemanteau *m*; (*hook*) crochet *m*. 2 *cpd*: (*fig*) **hanger-on** personne *f* de la suite, parasite *m* (*pej*); **there was a crowd of hangers-on** il y avait toute une suite.
hanging ['hæŋɪŋ] 1 *n* (a) (*execution*) pendaison *f*.
(b) (*U*) accrochage *m*, suspension *f*; *[bells, wallpaper]* pose *f*; *[door]* montage *m*; *[picture]* accrochage.
(c) (*curtains etc*) ~**s** tentures *fpl*, draperies *fpl*; **bed** ~**s** rideaux *mpl* de lit.
2 *adj* (a) *bridge, staircase* suspendu; *door* battant; *lamp, light* pendant; *sleeve* tombant. **the** ~ **gardens of Babylon** les jardins suspendus de Babylone; ~ **wardrobe** penderie *f*; (*Art*) ~ **committee** jury *m* d'exposition.
(b) (*Hist*) ~ **judge** *juge m qui envoyait régulièrement à la potence*; (*lit*) **it's a** ~ **offence** c'est un crime pendable; (*fig*) **it's not a** ~ **matter** ce n'est pas grave, ce n'est pas un cas pendable.
hank [hæŋk] *n [wool etc]* écheveau *m*.
hanker ['hæŋkəʳ] *vi*: **to** ~ **for** *or* **after** aspirer à, avoir envie de.
hankering ['hæŋkərɪŋ] *n*: **to have a** ~ **for sth/to do** avoir envie de qch/de faire.
hankie* ['hæŋkɪ] *n abbr of* **handkerchief**.
hanky-panky* ['hæŋkɪ'pæŋkɪ] *n* entourloupette* *f*. **there's some** ~ **going on** il se passe quelque chose de louche, il y a une entourloupette* là-dessous.
Hannibal ['hænɪbəl] *n* Annibal *m*.
Hanover ['hænəʊvəʳ] *n* Hanovre.
Hanoverian [ˌhænəʊ'vɪərɪən] *adj* hanovrien.
Hansard ['hænsɑːd] *n* (le) Hansard (*sténographie des débats du parlement britannique*).
Hanseatic [ˌhænzɪ'ætɪk] *adj*: **the** ~ **League** la Hanse, la ligue hanséatique.
hansom ['hænsəm] *n* cab *m*.
ha'pence ['heɪpəns] *npl of* **ha'penny**.
ha'penny ['heɪpnɪ] *n* = **halfpenny**; *V* **half 4**.
haphazard [ˌhæp'hæzəd] *adj* (fait) au hasard, (fait) au petit bonheur. **a** ~ **arrangement** une disposition fortuite; **the whole thing was very** ~ tout était fait au petit bonheur.
haphazardly [ˌhæp'hæzədlɪ] *adv arrange* au petit bonheur, au hasard; *select* à l'aveuglette, au petit bonheur, au hasard.
hapless ['hæplɪs] *adj* infortuné (*before n*), malchanceux (*after n*).
happen ['hæpən] *vi* (a) arriver, se passer, se produire. **something** ~**ed** il est arrivé *or* il s'est passé quelque chose; **what's** ~**ed?** qu'est-ce qui s'est passé? *or* est arrivé?, qu'est-ce qu'il y a eu?; **just as if nothing had** ~**ed** tout comme s'il n'était rien arrivé, comme si de rien n'était; **whatever** ~**s** quoi qu'il arrive (*subj*) *or* advienne; **don't let it** ~ **again!** et que ça ne se reproduise pas!; **these things** ~ ce sont des choses qui arrivent, ça peut arriver; **what has** ~**ed to him?** (*befallen*) qu'est-ce qui lui est arrivé?; (*become of*) qu'est-ce qu'il est devenu?; **if anything** ~**ed to me my wife would have enough money** s'il m'arrivait quelque chose *or* si je venais à disparaître ma femme aurait assez d'argent; **something has** ~**ed to him** il lui est arrivé quelque chose; **a funny thing** ~**ed to me this morning** il m'est arrivé quelque chose de bizarre ce matin; **let's pretend it never** ~**ed** c'est *or* faisons comme si ça n'était pas arrivé.
(b) (*come about, chance*) **how does it** ~ **that?** d'où vient que? + *indic*, comment se fait-il que? + *subj*; **it might** ~ **that** il pourrait se faire que + *subj*; **it so** ~**ed that** il s'est trouvé que + *indic*; **it so** ~**s that I'm going there today, as it** ~**s, I'm going there today** (il se trouve que) j'y vais justement aujourd'hui; **he** ~**ed to call on me** il s'est trouvé qu'il est venu me voir; **do you** ~ **to have a pen?** aurais-tu par hasard un stylo?; **how did you** ~ **to go?** comment se fait-il que tu y sois allé?; **I** ~ **to know he is not rich** il se trouve que je sais qu'il n'est pas riche; **if he does** ~ **to see her** s'il lui arrive de la voir.
happen (up)on† *vt fus object* trouver par hasard; *person* rencontrer par hasard.
happening ['hæpnɪŋ] *n* événement *m*; (*Theat*) happening *m*.
happenstance* ['hæpənstæns] *n* (*US*) événement fortuit, circonstance fortuite.
happily ['hæpɪlɪ] *adv* (a) (*contentedly*) *play, walk, talk* tranquillement; *say, smile* joyeusement. **to live** ~ vivre heureux (*V also* **live**); **she smiled** ~ elle eut un sourire épanoui *or* de contentement.
(b) (*fortunately*) heureusement, par bonheur.
(c) (*felicitously*) *word, choose* heureusement, avec bonheur.
happiness ['hæpɪnɪs] *n* bonheur *m*, félicité *f*.
happy ['hæpɪ] 1 *adj* (a) (*contented*) heureux. **as** ~ **as a king** heureux comme un roi; **as** ~ **as a lark** *or* **a sandboy** gai comme un pinson; **a** ~ **marriage** un mariage heureux *or* réussi; **I'm not** ~ **about the plan** je ne suis pas très heureux de ce projet; **I'm not** ~ **about leaving him alone** je ne suis pas tranquille de le laisser seul; **I'll be quite** ~ **to do it** je le ferai volontiers, ça ne me dérange pas de le faire; **she was** ~ **to be able to help** elle a été heureuse *or* contente de pouvoir aider; **she was quite** ~ **to stay there alone** cela ne l'ennuyait pas (du tout) de rester là toute seule; **I'm** ~ **here reading** je suis très bien ici à lire; **the child is** ~ **playing in the sand** l'enfant est heureux *or* content de jouer dans le sable; ~ **ending** fin heureuse; **the film has a** ~ **ending** le film se termine bien; **the** ~ **few** les rares privilégiés; ~ **birthday!** bon *or* joyeux anniversaire!; ~ **Christmas!** joyeux Noël!; ~ **New Year!** bonne année!
(b) (*felicitous*) *phrase, gesture, words* heureux, à propos. (*euph*) **a** ~ **event** un heureux événement (*euph*); **a** ~ **thought** une heureuse inspiration; **a** ~ **medium** un moyen terme; (*fig*) **a** ~ **hunting ground for collectors** une terre promise pour les collectionneurs, un paradis des collectionneurs.
(c) (*: *tipsy*) (un peu) gai, (un peu) pompette*.
2 *cpd*: **happy-go-lucky** *person* insouciant, sans souci; *attitude* insouciant; **the arrangements were very happy-go-lucky** c'était organisé au petit bonheur (la chance), l'organisation était à la va comme je te pousse*; **to do sth in a happy-go-lucky way** faire qch au petit bonheur (la chance) *or* à la va comme je te pousse*.
Hapsburg ['hæpsbɜːg] *n* Habsbourg.
hara-kiri ['hærə'kɪrɪ] *n* hara-kiri *m*. **to commit** ~ faire hara-kiri.
harangue [hə'ræŋ] 1 *vt* haranguer (*about* à propos de); *individuals* haranguer, sermonner (*about* à propos de). **he** ~**d her into getting her hair cut** il n'a eu de cesse qu'elle ne se fasse couper les cheveux. 2 *n* harangue *f*, sermon *m*.
harass ['hærəs] *vt* (a) (*harry*) *troops, the enemy, crowd etc* harceler. (b) (*worry*) tracasser; (*stronger*) harceler, tourmenter. ~**ed by doubts** harcelé de doutes.
harassed ['hærəst] *adj* tracassé, (*stronger*) harcelé.
harbinger ['hɑːbɪndʒəʳ] *n* (*liter*) avant-coureur *m* (*liter*), présage *m*. (*fig*) **a** ~ **of doom** un funeste présage.
harbour, (*US*) **harbor** ['hɑːbəʳ] 1 *n* (*for boats*) port *m*; (*fig*) port, havre *m* (*liter*), refuge *m*.
2 *cpd*: **harbour master** capitaine *m* de port.
3 *vt* (a) (*give shelter to*) héberger, abriter. **to** ~ **a criminal** receler un criminel.
(b) *suspicions* entretenir, nourrir; *fear, hope* entretenir. **to** ~ **a grudge against sb** garder rancune à qn.
(c) *dirt, dust* retenir, garder.
hard [hɑːd] 1 *adj* (a) *substance* dur; *mud, snow* durci; *muscle* ferme; (*Med*) *tissue* scléreux, sclérosé. **to get** *or* **become** *or* **grow** ~ durcir; (*fig*) **that's a** ~ **nut to crack** ce n'est pas un petit problème; (*fig*) **he's a** ~ **nut to crack** c'est un dur à cuire; **he is as** ~ **as nails** (*physically*) c'est un paquet de muscles; (*mentally*) il est dur.
(b) (*difficult*) *problem, examination* difficile, dur; *question* ardu, difficile; *task* pénible, dur. **it was** ~ **to understand** c'était difficile *or* dur à comprendre; **I find it** ~ **to explain** j'ai du mal à l'expliquer; **I find it** ~ **to believe that ...** j'ai du mal à croire que ... + *subj*, j'ai peine à croire que ... + *subj*; **he is** ~ **to please** il est exigeant *or* difficile; **he is** ~ **to get on with** il est difficile à vivre; **that is** ~ **to beat** on peut difficilement faire mieux; ~ **of hearing** dur d'oreille; *V also* **3**.
(c) (*severe*) dur, sévère, strict (*on, to* avec, *towards* envers); *master* sévère, exigeant; *voice, tone* dur, sec (*f* sèche); *face, expression* dur, sévère; *heart* dur, impitoyable. **he's a** ~ **man** il est dur, c'est un homme impitoyable; **he's a** ~ **(task)master** il mène ses subordonnés à la baguette; **duty is a** ~ **(task)master** le devoir est un maître exigeant; **to be** ~ **on sb** être dur *or* sévère avec qn, traiter qn avec sévérité; **to grow** ~ s'endurcir; *V also* **3**.
(d) (*harsh*) *life* dur, pénible, difficile; *fate* dur; *climate, winter* rude, rigoureux; *rule, decision* sévère; (*tough*) *battle, fight* acharné, âpre, rude; *match* âprement disputé; *work* dur; *worker* dur (à la tâche), endurant. **it's** ~ **work!** c'est dur!; **he drives a** ~ **bargain** il ne fait pas de cadeaux (*fig*); **it was a** ~ **blow** ce fut un coup dur *or* un rude coup; (*Brit*) ~ **cheese!‡**, (*Brit*) ~ **luck!***, ~ **lines!*** pas de veine!*, pas de pot!*; (*Brit*) **it was** ~ **luck** *or* **lines that he didn't win*** c'est manque de pot* qu'il ait perdu; **it's** ~ **lines** *or* **luck on him*** il n'a pas de veine* *or* de pot!*; ~ **drink**, ~ **liquor** boisson fortement alcoolisée; **he's a** ~ **drinker** c'est un gros buveur, il boit sec; **a** ~ **core of juvenile offenders** un noyau irréductible de jeunes délinquants; (*Pol*) **the** ~ **core of the party** les inconditionnels *mpl* parmi les membres du parti (*V also* **3**); **the** ~ **facts** la réalité brutale *or* non déguisée; **he had a** ~ **fall** il a fait une mauvaise chute; **there's still a lot of** ~ **feeling about it** il en reste beaucoup d'amertume; **no** ~ **feelings!** sans rancune!; ~ **frost** forte gelée; (*lit, fig*) **it was** ~ **going** on a eu du mal, ça a été dur*; (*Jur*) ~ **labour** travaux forcés; ~ **study** étude assidue; **she had a** ~ **time of it after her husband's death** elle a traversé des moments difficiles après la mort de son mari; **you'll have a** ~ **time of it trying to get him to help you** vous allez avoir du mal à lui persuader de vous aider; **these are** ~ **times** les temps sont durs; **they fell upon** ~ **times** ils connurent des temps difficiles; ~ **treatment** traitement *m* sévère; **those are** ~ **words to use** c'est s'exprimer en termes très durs; *V also* **3**.
(e) (*fig*) *light, line, colour, outline, consonant* dur. (*Fin*) **the market is** ~ le marché est ferme *or* soutenu; ~ **cash** espèces *fpl*; ~ **currency** devise forte; ~ **drug** drogue dure (*gén opiacée*); (*Press*) **what we want is** ~ **news** ce qu'il nous faut c'est de l'information (sérieuse); ~ **water** eau *f* calcaire *or* dure; *V also* **3**.
2 *adv* (a) (*strongly, energetically*) **as** ~ **as one can** de toutes

ses forces; **it's raining** ~ il pleut à verse, il tombe des cordes; **it's snowing** ~ il neige dru; **it's freezing** ~ il gèle fort *or* ferme *or* dur *or* à pierre fendre; **the lake was frozen** ~ le lac était profondément gelé; **the ground was frozen** ~ le sol était durci par le gel; **to beg** ~ prier instamment, supplier; **he's drinking fairly** ~ **these days** il boit beaucoup *or* sec en ce moment; **to fall down** ~ tomber durement; **to hit** ~ frapper dur *or* fort, cogner dur; **to hold on** ~ tenir bon *or* ferme; **to look** ~ **at** *person* regarder fixement, dévisager; *thing* regarder *or* examiner de près; **pull** ~! tirez fort!; **to run** ~ courir à toutes jambes *or* comme un dératé*; **to think** ~ réfléchir sérieusement *or* profondément; **to try** ~ faire *or* fournir un gros effort; **to study** ~ étudier assidûment *or* d'arrache-pied; **to work** ~ travailler dur *or* d'arrache-pied; **to be** ~ **at work** *or* ~ **at it*** être attelé à la tâche, travailler d'arrache-pied; (*Naut*) ~ **a-port** (à) bâbord toute; (*Navy*) à gauche toute; *V* **drive, hold.**

(b) (*closely*) ~ **by** tout près, tout contre, tout à côté; **to follow** ~ **upon sb's heels** suivre qn de très près, être sur les talons de qn; **the revolution followed** ~ **on (the heels of) the strike** la révolution suivit de très près la grève *or* suivit immédiatement la grève; **it was** ~ **on 10 o'clock** il était bientôt 10 heures.

(c) (*phrases*) **to be** ~ **put (to it)** *or* **pressed to do** avoir beaucoup de mal *or* de peine à faire, éprouver les plus grandes difficultés à faire; **to be** ~ **pressed for time/money** *etc* être très à court de temps/d'argent *etc*; **I'm rather** ~ **pressed** (*for time*) je suis débordé; (*for money*) je suis à court; **she took it pretty** ~ elle a été très affectée; **he took the news very** ~ il a très mal pris la nouvelle; (*Brit*) **to be** ~ **done by** être traité injustement, être mal traité; **he feels very** ~ **done by** il a l'impression d'avoir été brimé *or* très mal traité; **it will go** ~ **for him if ...** cela tournera *or* ira mal pour lui si ....

3 *cpd*: **hard-and-fast** strict, inflexible; *rule* absolu; **hardback** (*adj*) *book* relié, cartonné; (*n*) livre relié *or* cartonné; (*fig*) **hard-bitten** dur à cuire*; **hardboard** Isorel *m* ®; **hard-boiled** *egg* dur; (*fig*) *person* dur à cuire*; **hard-core support/opposition** soutien *m*/opposition *f etc* inconditionnel(le); **hard-core pornography** pornographie (dite) dure; **hard-earned** *money, salary* (si) durement gagné; *holiday* bien mérité; **hard-faced, hard-featured** au visage sévère, aux traits durs; **hard-fought** *battle* âprement mené; *election, competition* âprement disputé; **hard hat** casque *m*; (*riding hat*) bombe *f*; **hardhead** réaliste *mf*; **hard-headed** réaliste, à la tête froide; **hard-headed businessman** homme d'affaires réaliste; **hard-hearted** insensible, impitoyable, au cœur dur; **he was very hard-hearted towards them** il était très dur avec eux; **hard-packed snow** neige tassée; (*by wind*) congère *f*; (*Comm*) **hard sell** promotion (de vente) agressive; (*Comm*) **hardsell tactics** politique *f* de promotion (de vente) agressive; **hardtack** (*Mil*) biscuit *m*; (*Naut*) galette *f*; **hard-up*** fauché*; **I'm hard-up*** je suis fauché*, je suis à sec*; **I'm hard-up for books about it*** j'ai bien du mal à trouver des livres sur ce sujet; **the country is hard-up for dentists*** le pays manque de dentistes; (*U*) **hardware** (*Comm*) quincaillerie *f* (*marchandises*); (*Mil, Police etc*) matériel *m*; (*Computers, Space*) matériel, hardware *m*; **hardware dealer** quincaillier *m*, -ère *f*; **hardware shop** quincaillerie *f* (*magasin*); (*Computers*) **hardware specialist** technicien(ne) *m(f)* du hardware; **hardware store** = **hardware shop; hard-wearing** solide, résistant; **hard-won** (si) durement gagné, remporté de haute lutte; **hardwood** bois dur; **hard-working** (*gen*) travailleur; *student, pupil* travailleur, bûcheur*.

harden ['hɑːdn] **1** *vt* durcir; *steel* tremper; *muscle* affermir, durcir; (*Med*) indurer, scléroser. **his years in the Arctic** ~**ed him considerably** les années qu'il a passées dans l'Arctique l'ont considérablement endurci; **to** ~ **o.s. to sth** s'endurcir *or* s'aguerrir à qch; **to** ~ **one's heart** s'endurcir; **this** ~**ed his heart** cela lui a endurci le cœur; *V also* **hardened.**

2 *vi* **(a)** *[substances]* durcir, s'affermir; (*Med*) s'indurer, se scléroser; *[steel]* se tremper. **his voice** ~**ed** sa voix se fit dure.

(b) (*St Ex*) *[shares]* se raffermir; *[prices]* être en hausse. **the market** ~**ed** le marché s'affermit.

hardened ['hɑːdnd] *adj* durci; *steel* trempé; *criminal* endurci; *sinner* invétéré. **I'm** ~ **to it** j'y suis accoutumé *or* fait, j'ai l'habitude.

hardening ['hɑːdnɪŋ] *n* durcissement *m*, affermissement *m*; *[steel]* trempe *f*; (*Med*) induration *f*, sclérose *f*; (*fig*) durcissement *m*, endurcissement *m*. **I noticed a** ~ **of his attitude** je remarquais un durcissement de son attitude *or* que son attitude se durcissait; (*Med*) ~ **of the arteries** durcissement des artères.

hardihood ['hɑːdɪhʊd] *n* hardiesse *f*.

hardiness ['hɑːdɪnɪs] *n* force *f*, vigueur *f*.

hardly ['hɑːdlɪ] *adv* **(a)** (*scarcely*) à peine, ne ... guère. **he can** ~ **write** il sait à peine écrire, c'est à peine s'il sait écrire; **I can** ~ **hear you** je vous entends à peine, c'est à peine si je vous entends; **he had** ~ **spoken when ...** à peine eut-il parlé que ..., il n'eut pas plus tôt parlé que ...; **you'll** ~ **believe it** vous aurez de la peine *or* du mal à le croire; **it's** ~ **his business if ...** ce n'est guère son affaire si ...; **I need** ~ **point out that** je n'ai pas besoin de faire remarquer que; **I** ~ **know** je n'en sais trop rien; ~ **anyone** presque personne; ~ **anywhere** presque nulle part; ~ **ever** presque jamais; ~! (*not at all*) certainement pas!; (*not exactly*) pas précisément!; **he would** ~ **have said that** il n'aurait tout de même pas dit cela.

(b) (*harshly*) durement, rudement, sévèrement. **to treat sb** ~ être *or* se montrer sévère avec qn, traiter qn sévèrement.

hardness ['hɑːdnɪs] *n* (*V* **hard**) **(a)** dureté *f*; fermeté *f*; (*Med*) induration *f*.

(b) difficulté *f*.

(c) dureté *f*, sévérité *f*.

(d) dureté *f*, difficulté *f*; rigueur *f*; sévérité *f*. (*St Ex*) **the** ~ **of the market** le raffermissement du marché; (*Med*) ~ **of hearing** surdité *f* (partielle); (*fig*) **his** ~ **of heart** sa dureté de cœur, son insensibilité *f*.

hardship ['hɑːdʃɪp] *n* **(a)** (*U*) (*circumstances*) épreuves *fpl*; (*suffering*) souffrance *f*; (*deprivation*) privation *f*. **he has suffered great** ~ il a connu de dures épreuves; **there's a certain amount of** ~ **involved but it's worth it** ça n'ira pas tout seul *or* ça sera dur mais ça en vaut la peine; **a life of** ~ une vie pleine d'épreuves; **it is no** ~ **to him to stop smoking** pour lui cesser de fumer n'est pas une privation; **it's no great** ~ **to go and see her once a month** ce n'est tout de même pas une épreuve *or* la mer à boire* d'aller la voir une fois par mois.

(b) ~**s** épreuves *fpl*, privations *fpl*; **the** ~**s of war** les privations *or* les rigueurs *fpl* de la guerre.

hardy ['hɑːdɪ] *adj* **(a)** (*strong*) *person* vigoureux, robuste; *plant* résistant (au gel); *tree* de plein vent. ~ **perennial** plante *f* vivace; ~ **annual** (*Bot*) plante annuelle résistante au gel; (**fig*) (vieille) histoire *f* qui a la vie dure.

(b) (*bold*) hardi, audacieux, intrépide.

hare [hɛəʳ] **1** *n* lièvre *m*. (*game*) ~ **and hounds** (*sorte de*) jeu *m* de piste; *V* **jug, mad** *etc.*

2 *cpd*: **harebell** campanule *f*; **hare-brained** *person* écervelé; *plan* insensé; **to be hare-brained** avoir *or* être une tête de linotte, être écervelé; (*Med*) **harelip** bec-de-lièvre *m*.

3 *vi* (*Brit*) **to** ~ **in/out/through*** *etc* entrer/sortir/traverser *etc* en trombe *or* à fond de train*.

harem [hɑːˈriːm] *n* harem *m*.

haricot ['hærɪkəʊ] *n*: ~ **(bean)** haricot blanc; (*Culin*) ~ **mutton** haricot de mouton.

hark [hɑːk] *vi* (*liter*) **to** ~ **to** écouter, prêter une oreille attentive à; (*liter*, †) ~! écoutez!; ~ **at him!*** mais écoutez-le (donc)!*

hark back *vi* revenir (*to* sur). **he's always harking back to that** il y revient toujours, il en est toujours à cette histoire.

harken ['hɑːkən] *vi* = **hearken.**

Harlequin ['hɑːlɪkwɪn] *n* (*Theat*) Arlequin *m*. ~ **costume** costume bigarré *or* d'Arlequin.

harlot†† ['hɑːlət] *n* courtisane *f*.

harm [hɑːm] **1** *n* mal *m*, tort *m*, dommage *m*. **to do sb** ~ faire du mal *or* du tort à qn, nuire à qn; **what** ~ **has he done you?** quel mal vous a-t-il fait?, qu'est-ce qu'il vous a fait?*; **the** ~**'s done now** le mal est fait maintenant; **it can't do you any** ~ ça ne peut pas te faire de mal; **it will do more** ~ **than good** cela fera plus de mal que de bien; **he means no** ~ il n'a pas de mauvaises intentions, il a de bonnes intentions; **he meant no** ~ **by what he said** il ne l'a pas dit méchamment; **he doesn't mean us any** ~ il ne nous veut pas de mal; **you will come to no** ~ il ne t'arrivera rien; **I don't see any** ~ **in it, I see no** ~ **in it** je n'y vois aucun mal; **there's no** ~ **in an occasional drink** un petit verre de temps en temps ne peut pas faire de mal; **there's no** ~ **in doing that** il n'y a pas de mal à faire cela; **keep** *or* **stay out of** ~**'s way** (*out of danger*) mettez-vous en sûreté; (*out of the way*) ne restez pas dans les parages; **to keep a child out of** ~**'s way** mettre un enfant à l'abri du danger; **to put a vase out of** ~**'s way** mettre un vase en lieu sûr.

2 *vt person* faire du mal *or* du tort à, nuire à; *crops, harvest* endommager; *object* abîmer; *reputation* salir, souiller (*liter*); *sb's interests, a cause* causer du tort à *or* un dommage à. **this will** ~ **his case considerably** ceci sera très préjudiciable à sa cause.

harmful ['hɑːmfʊl] *adj person* malfaisant, nuisible; *influence, thing* nocif, nuisible (*to* à).

harmless ['hɑːmlɪs] *adj animal, joke* inoffensif, pas méchant; *person* sans méchanceté, sans malice, pas méchant; *action, game* innocent; *suggestion, conversation* anodin. **a** ~ **child** un enfant innocent; **it was all fairly** ~ tout ça était assez innocent.

harmonic [hɑːˈmɒnɪk] **1** *adj* (*Math, Mus, Phys*) harmonique. **2** *n* **(a)** (*Mus*) ~s (*U: science*) harmonie *f*; (*pl: overtones*) harmoniques *mpl or fpl*. **(b)** (*Phys*) ~s harmoniques *mpl or fpl*.

harmonica [hɑːˈmɒnɪkə] *n* harmonica *m*.

harmonious [hɑːˈməʊnɪəs] *adj* (*Mus*) harmonieux, mélodieux; (*fig*) harmonieux.

harmonium [hɑːˈməʊnɪəm] *n* harmonium *m*.

harmonize ['hɑːmənaɪz] **1** *vt* (*Mus*) harmoniser; (*fig*) *ideas, views* harmoniser, mettre en harmonie (*with* avec); *colours* assortir, harmoniser, marier; *texts, statements* faire accorder, concilier.

2 *vi* (*Mus*) chanter en harmonie; *[colours etc]* s'harmoniser (*with* avec), s'allier (*with* à), s'assortir (*with* à); *[person, facts]* s'accorder (*with* avec).

harmony ['hɑːmənɪ] *n* (*Mus*) harmonie *f*; (*fig*) harmonie, accord *m*. **in perfect** ~ en parfaite harmonie, en parfait accord; **in** ~ **with** en harmonie *or* en accord avec; **his ideas are in** ~ **with mine** ses idées s'accordent avec les miennes, nos idées s'accordent; *V* **close**¹.

harness ['hɑːnɪs] **1** *n [horse]* harnais *m*, harnachement *m*; *[loom, parachute]* harnais. (*fig*) **to get back in(to)** ~ reprendre le collier; (*fig*) **to die in** ~ mourir debout *or* à la tâche.

2 *vt* **(a)** *horse* harnacher. **to** ~ **a horse to a carriage** atteler un cheval à une voiture.

(b) (*fig*) *river, resources, energy etc* exploiter.

harp [hɑːp] **1** *n* harpe *f*.

2 *vi* **(a)** (*) **to** ~ **on (about) sth** rabâcher qch; **stop** ~**ing on (about) it!** cesse de répéter toujours la même chose!; **I don't want to** ~ **on about it** je ne veux pas revenir toujours là-dessus; **she's always** ~**ing on about her troubles** elle nous rebat les oreilles de ses malheurs.

(b) (*Mus*) jouer de la harpe.

harpist ['hɑːpɪst] *n* harpiste *mf*.

harpoon [hɑːˈpuːn] **1** *n* harpon *m*. **2** *vt* harponner.

harpsichord ['hɑːpsɪkɔːd] *n* clavecin *m*.

harpsichordist ['hɑːpsɪkɔːdɪst] *n* claveciniste *mf.*

harpy ['hɑːpɪ] *n* (*Myth*) harpie *f.* **old ~** vieille harpie *or* sorcière.

harridan ['hærɪdən] *n* vieille harpie *or* sorcière.

harrier ['hærɪəʳ] *n* **(a)** (*dog*) harrier *m.* **~s** meute *f.* **(b)** (*cross-country runners*) **~s** coureurs *mpl* de cross. **(c)** (*Orn*) busard *m.*

Harris ['hærɪs] *adj*: ® **~ tweed** (gros) tweed *m* (*des Hébrides*).

harrow ['hærəʊ] **1** *n* herse *f.* **2** *vt* (*Agr*) herser. (*fig*) **to ~ sb** *or* **sb's feelings** déchirer le cœur de qn, torturer qn.

harrowing ['hærəʊɪŋ] **1** *adj story* poignant, navrant; *cry* déchirant. **2** *n* (*Agr*) hersage *m.*

Harry ['hærɪ] *n* (*dim of* **Henry**) Riri *m.* (*fam*) **to play old ~ with*** *person* en faire voir des vertes et des pas mûres* à; *machine, sb's digestion* détraquer; *timetable, plans etc* chambouler*; *sb's chances* gâcher, bousiller‡.

harry ['hærɪ] *vt country* dévaster, ravager; *person* harceler, tourmenter; (*Mil*) harceler.

harsh [hɑːʃ] *adj* **(a)** (*cruel, severe*) *person, punishment* dur, sévère; *words* dur, âpre; *tone, voice, reply* cassant, dur; *fate* cruel, dur; *climate* dur, rude, rigoureux. **to be ~ with sb** être dur avec *or* envers qn; **that's a ~ thing to say** c'est méchant de dire cela, (*more formally*) c'est une déclaration très dure.

(b) (*to the touch*) *material* rêche; *surface* rugueux, râpeux, rude.

(c) (*to the ear*) *woman's voice* criard, aigre; *man's voice* discordant; *bird cry* criard; *sound* discordant. **a ~ squeal of brakes** un grincement de freins strident.

(d) (*to the eye*) *colours* criard; *contrast* dur, heurté.

(e) (*to the taste*) âpre, râpeux; *wine* âpre.

harshly ['hɑːʃlɪ] *adv reply* rudement, durement; *treat* sévèrement.

harshness ['hɑːʃnɪs] *n* **(a)** (*severity, cruelty*) *[manner]* rudesse *f*; *[words]* dureté *f*; *[fate, climate]* rigueur *f*; *[punishment]* sévérité *f.*

(b) (*to the eye*) aspect déplaisant *or* heurté; (*to the touch*) rudesse *f*, dureté *f*, rugosité *f*; (*to the taste*) âpreté *f*; (*to the ear*) discordance *f.*

hart [hɑːt] *n* cerf *m.*

harum-scarum ['heərəm'skeərəm] **1** *adj* écervelé, étourdi, tête de linotte *inv.* **2** *n* tête *f* en l'air, tête de linotte, écervelé(e) *m(f).*

harvest ['hɑːvɪst] **1** *n [corn]* moisson *f*; *[fruit]* récolte *f*, cueillette *f*; *[grapes]* vendange *f*; (*fig*) moisson. **to get in the ~** faire la moisson, moissonner.

2 *vt corn* moissonner; *fruit* récolter, cueillir; *grapes* vendanger, récolter; (*fig*) *reward* moissonner; *insults* récolter. **to ~ the fields** faire les moissons, moissonner (les champs).

3 *vi* faire la moisson, moissonner.

4 *cpd*: **harvest festival** fête *f* de la moisson; **harvest home** (*festival*) fête *f* de la moisson; (*season*) fin *f* de la moisson; **harvestman** (*insect*) faucheur *m*; **harvest moon** pleine lune (de l'équinoxe d'automne); **at harvest time** pendant *or* à la moisson.

harvester ['hɑːvɪstəʳ] *n* (*person*) moissonneur *m*, -euse *f*; (*machine*) moissonneuse *f*; *V* **combine.**

has [hæz] **1** *V* **have. 2** *cpd*: **has-been*** (*man*) type fini* *or* fichu*; (*hat, carpet etc*) vieillerie *f*, vieux truc*; **he's/she's a has-been*** il/elle a fait son temps.

hash [hæʃ] **1** *n* **(a)** (*Culin*) hachis *m*; (**fig*) gâchis *m.* **he made a ~ of it*** il a saboté ça, il en a fait un beau gâchis; **a ~-up* of old ideas** un réchauffé *or* une resucée‡ de vieilles idées; *V* **settle[2].**

(b) (*Drugs sl: hashish*) hasch *m* (*sl*).

2 *vt* (*Culin*) hacher.

hash over‡ *vt sep problem, plan, difficulty* discuter ferme de. **they were hashing it over when I came** ils discutaient le coup* quand je suis arrivé.

hash up 1 *vt sep* **(a)** (*Culin*) hacher menu.

(b) (‡: *spoil*) bousiller‡, faire un beau gâchis de.

2 hash-up* *n V* **hash 1a.**

hashish ['hæʃɪʃ] *n* haschisch *m or* hachisch *m.*

hasn't ['hæznt] = **has not;** *V* **have.**

hasp [hɑːsp] *n [book cover, necklace]* fermoir *m*; *[door, lid, window]* moraillon *m.*

hassle* ['hæsl] *n* (*squabble*) chamaillerie* *f*, bagarre* *f*; (*bustle, confusion*) pagaïe *f or* pagaille *f.* **it's a ~!** c'est toute une histoire!*

hassock ['hæsək] *n* coussin *m* (d'agenouilloir).

haste [heɪst] *n* hâte *f*, diligence *f*, célérité *f*; (*excessive*) précipitation *f.* **to do sth in ~** faire qch à la hâte *or* en hâte; **in great ~** en toute hâte; **to be in ~ to do** avoir hâte de faire; **to make ~ (to do)** se hâter *or* se dépêcher (de faire); (*Prov*) **more ~ less speed** hâtez-vous lentement (*loc*); **why all this ~?** pourquoi tant de précipitation?

hasten ['heɪsn] **1** *vi* se hâter, se dépêcher, se presser, s'empresser (*to do* de faire). **I ~ to add ...** je m'empresse d'ajouter ..., j'ajoute tout de suite ...; **to ~ down/away** *etc* se hâter de descendre/partir *etc*, descendre/partir *etc* à la hâte.

2 *vt* hâter, presser, accélérer; *reaction* activer. **to ~ one's steps** presser le pas, accélérer l'allure *or* le pas; **to ~ sb's departure** hâter le départ de qn.

hastily ['heɪstɪlɪ] *adv* **(a)** *leave, write, work* (*speedily*) en hâte, à la hâte; (*too speedily*) hâtivement, précipitamment. **he ~ suggested that** il s'est empressé de suggérer que. **(b)** (*without reflexion*) *speak, act* sans réfléchir, trop hâtivement.

hasty ['heɪstɪ] *adj departure, marriage* précipité, hâtif; *visit, glance, meal* rapide, hâtif; *sketch* fait à la hâte; *action, decision, move* hâtif, inconsidéré, irréfléchi. **don't be so ~!** ne va pas si vite (en besogne)!; **to have a ~ temper, to be ~-tempered** être (très) emporté, s'emporter facilement, être soupe au lait; **~ words** paroles irréfléchies, paroles lancées à la légère.

hat [hæt] **1** *n* chapeau *m.* **to put on one's ~** mettre son chapeau; *[man]* se couvrir; **to keep one's ~ on** garder son chapeau; *[man]* rester couvert; **to take off one's ~** enlever son chapeau; *[man]* se découvrir; **~ in hand** (*lit*) chapeau bas; (*fig*) obséquieusement; **~s off!** chapeau bas!; (*fig*) **to take off one's ~ to** tirer son chapeau à; **I take my ~ off to him!** chapeau!; **to keep sth under one's ~*** garder qch pour soi; **keep it under your ~!*** motus!; (*fig*) **to pass round the ~ for sb** faire la quête pour qn; **that's old ~!*** c'est vieux *or* c'est de l'histoire ancienne* tout ça!; *V* **bowler[2], eat, talk, top** *etc.*

2 *cpd*: **hatband** ruban *m* de chapeau; **hatbox** carton *m* à chapeau; (*US*) **hatcheck girl** dame *f* du vestiaire; **hatpin** épingle *f* à chapeau; **hatrack** porte-chapeaux *m inv*; (*US*) **hat tree** portemanteau *m*; (*Conjuring*) **the hat trick** le tour *or* le coup du chapeau; (*Sport etc*) **to do the hat trick, to get a hat trick** réussir trois coups (*or* gagner trois matchs *etc*) consécutifs.

hatch[1] [hætʃ] **1** *vt* **(a)** (*also* **~ out**) *chick, egg* faire éclore. (*loc*) **don't count your chickens before they are ~ed** il ne faut pas vendre la peau de l'ours avant de l'avoir tué.

(b) *plot* ourdir, tramer; *plan* couver. **I wonder what he's ~ing (up)** je me demande ce qu'il manigance.

2 *vi* (*also* **~ out**) *[chick, egg]* éclore.

3 *n* (*act*) éclosion *f*; (*brood*) couvée *f.*

hatch[2] [hætʃ] **1** *n* **(a)** (*Naut: also* **~way**) écoutille *f*; (*floodgates*) vanne *f* d'écluse. **under ~es** dans la cale; (*fig*) **down the ~!‡** à la tienne!

(b) (service) ~ passe-plats *m inv*, guichet *m.*

(c) (*Aut*) hayon *m* arrière.

2 *cpd*: (*Aut*) **hatchback** (*two-door*) coupé *m* avec hayon (à l')arrière; (*four-door*) berline *f* avec hayon (à l')arrière.

hatch[3] [hætʃ] *vt* (*Art*) hachurer.

hatchery ['hætʃərɪ] *n [chicks]* couvoir *m*, incubateur *m*; *[fish]* appareil *m* à éclosion.

hatchet ['hætʃɪt] **1** *n* hachette *f*; *V* **bury.**

2 *cpd*: **hatchet-faced** au visage en lame de couteau; (*killer*) **hatchet man*** tueur *m* (à gages); (*fig*) **he was the firm's hatchet man when they sacked 200 workers** c'est lui que la compagnie a chargé de faire tomber les têtes quand elle a licencié 200 travailleurs; (*fig*) **in his vicious speech he acted as hatchet man for the opposition** dans son violent discours il s'est fait l'homme de main de l'opposition.

hatching[1] ['hætʃɪŋ] *n [chicks etc]* (*act*) éclosion *f*; (*brood*) couvée *f.*

hatching[2] ['hætʃɪŋ] *n* (*Art*) hachures *fpl.*

hate [heɪt] **1** *vt* haïr, avoir en horreur, exécrer; (*weaker*) détester, avoir horreur de. **she ~s him like poison*** elle le hait à mort, (*weaker*) elle ne peut pas le voir en peinture; **she ~s me for not helping her** elle m'en veut à mort de ne pas l'avoir aidée; **to ~ to do** *or* **doing** détester faire, avoir horreur de faire; **he ~s to be** *or* **being ordered about** il a horreur *or* il ne peut pas souffrir qu'on lui donne (*subj*) des ordres; **what he ~s most of all is ...** ce qu'il déteste le plus au monde c'est ...; **I ~ being late** je déteste être en retard, j'ai horreur d'être en retard; **I ~ to say so, I ~ having to say it** cela m'ennuie beaucoup de *or* je suis désolé de devoir le dire; **I ~ seeing her in pain** je ne peux pas supporter de la voir souffrir; **I should ~ to keep you waiting** je ne voudrais surtout pas vous faire attendre; **I should ~ it if he thought ..., I should ~ him to think ...** je détesterais qu'il vienne à penser ...

2 *n* **(a)** (*U*) haine *f.*

(b) one of my pet ~s* une de mes bêtes noires.

hateful ['heɪtfʊl] *adj* haïssable, odieux, détestable.

hatless ['hætlɪs] *adj* sans chapeau, tête nue, nu-tête.

hatred ['heɪtrɪd] *n* (*U*) haine *f.* **out of ~ of** *or* **for sth/sb** en *or* par haine de qch/qn; **to feel ~ for sb/sth** haïr qn/qch.

hatter ['hætəʳ] *n* chapelier *m*; *V* **mad.**

haughtily ['hɔːtɪlɪ] *adv* avec hauteur, avec arrogance, hautainement.

haughtiness ['hɔːtɪnɪs] *n* hauteur *f*, morgue *f*, arrogance *f.*

haughty ['hɔːtɪ] *adj* hautain, plein de morgue, arrogant.

haul [hɔːl] **1** *n* **(a)** (*Aut etc*) **the long ~ between Paris and Grenoble** le long voyage entre Paris et Grenoble; (*lit, fig*) **it's a long ~** la route est longue.

(b) *[fishermen]* prise *f*; *[thieves]* butin *m.* (*Fishing*) **a good ~** une belle prise, un beau coup de filet; **the thieves made a good ~** les voleurs ont eu un beau butin; **a good ~ of jewels** un beau butin en joyaux; (*fig*) **a good ~ of presents*** une bonne récolte de cadeaux; (*fig*) **what a ~!*** quelle récolte!

2 *vt* **(a)** (*pull*) traîner, tirer; (*Naut*) haler. (*fig*) **to ~ sb over the coals** passer un savon* à qn, réprimander sévèrement qn.

(b) (*transport by truck*) camionner.

(c) (*Naut*) haler. **to ~ into the wind** faire lofer.

3 *vi* (*Naut*) *[boat]* lofer; *[wind]* refuser.

haul down *vt sep flag, sail* affaler, amener; (*gen*) *object* faire descendre (*en tirant*).

haul in *vt sep line, catch* amener; *drowning man* tirer (de l'eau).

haul up *vt sep flag, sail* hisser. (*Naut*) **to haul up a boat** (*aboard ship*) rentrer une embarcation (à bord); (*on to beach*) tirer un bateau au sec.

haulage ['hɔːlɪdʒ] *n* remorquage *m*, halage *m*; (*Brit: road transport*) transport routier, camionnage *m*, roulage *m*; (*Min*) herschage *m*, roulage. (*Brit*) **~ contractor = haulier.**

haulier ['hɔːlɪəʳ] *n* (*Brit*) entrepreneur *m* de transports (routiers), transporteur *m* (routier), camionneur *m.*

haunch [hɔːntʃ] *n* hanche *f.* *[animal]* **~es** derrière *m*, arrière-train *m*; **(squatting) on his ~es** *person* accroupi; *dog etc* assis (sur son derrière); (*Culin*) **~ of venison** cuissot *m* de chevreuil.

haunt [hɔːnt] **1** *vt* (*lit, fig*) hanter. (*fig*) **he ~ed the café in the hope of seeing her** il hantait le café dans l'espoir de la voir; **to be ~ed by memories** être hanté *or* obsédé par des souvenirs; **he is**

~ed by the fear of losing all his money il est hanté par la peur de *or* il a la hantise de perdre tout son argent; *V also* **haunted.**
2 *n [criminals]* repaire *m.* **one of the favourite ~s of this animal is ...** un des lieux où l'on trouve souvent cet animal est ...; **it is a favourite ~ of artists** c'est un lieu fréquenté des artistes; **that café is one of his favourite ~s** ce café est un de ses coins favoris.

haunted ['hɔːntɪd] *adj house* hanté; *look, expression* égaré; *face* hagard, à l'air égaré.

haunting ['hɔːntɪŋ] **1** *adj tune* obsédant, qui vous trotte par la tête *or* qui vous hante; *doubt* obsédant. **2** *n*: **there have been several ~s here** il y a eu plusieurs apparitions *fpl* ici.

Havana [hə'vænə] *n* **(a)** Havane *f.* **(b) a ~ (cigar)** un havane.

have [hæv] *3rd person sg pres* **has,** *pret, ptp* **had 1** *aux vb* **(a)** avoir; être. **to have been** avoir été; **to have eaten** avoir mangé; **to have gone** être allé; **to have got up** s'être levé; **I have been** j'ai été; **I have eaten** j'ai mangé; **I have gone** je suis allé; **I have got up** je me suis levé; **I have not** *or* **I've not** *or* **I haven't seen him** je ne l'ai pas vu; **I had been** j'avais été; **I had eaten** j'avais mangé; **I had gone** j'étais allé; **I had got up** je m'étais levé; **I had not** *or* **I hadn't** *or* **I'd not seen him** je ne l'avais pas vu; **had I seen him** *or* **if I had seen him I should have spoken to him** si je l'avais vu je lui aurais parlé; **having seen him** l'ayant vu; **after** *or* **when I had seen him I went out** après l'avoir vu je suis sorti; **when he had seen me I went out** une fois qu'il m'eut vu je sortis; **I have lived** *or* **have been living here for 10 years/since January** j'habite ici depuis 10 ans/depuis janvier; **I had lived** *or* **had been living there for 10 years** j'habitais là depuis 10 ans; **you HAVE grown!** ce que tu as grandi!; **have got** *V* **2, 3a, 3b, 3f, 3l.**
(b) *(in tag questions etc)* **you've seen her, haven't you?** vous l'avez vue, n'est-ce pas?; **you haven't seen her, have you?** vous ne l'avez pas vue, je suppose?; **you haven't seen her — yes I have!** vous ne l'avez pas vue — si!; **you've made a mistake — no I haven't!** vous vous êtes trompé — mais non!; **you've dropped your book — so I have!** vous avez laissé tomber votre livre — en effet! *or* c'est vrai!; **have you been there? if you have ...** y êtes-vous allé? si oui ...; **have you been there? if you haven't ...** y avez-vous été? si non ... .
(c) to have just done sth venir de faire qch; **I have just seen him** je viens de le voir; **I had just seen him** je venais de le voir; **I've just come from London** j'arrive à l'instant de Londres.
2 *modal aux usage (+ infin: be obliged) (au présent la forme* **have got to** *est plus usuelle en anglais parlé que la forme* **have to) to have (got) to do** devoir faire, être obligé *or* forcé de faire; **I have (got) to speak to you at once** je dois vous parler *or* il faut que je vous parle *(subj)* immédiatement; **I haven't got to do it, I don't have to do it** je ne suis pas obligé *or* forcé de le faire; **I've got** *or* **I have to hurry or I'll be late** il faut que je me dépêche *(subj)* sinon je serai en retard, si je ne me dépêche pas je serai en retard; **do you have to go now?, have you got to go now?** est-ce que vous êtes obligé de *or* est-ce que vous devez partir tout de suite?; **do you have to make such a noise?** tu ne pourrais pas faire un peu moins de bruit?; **you didn't have to tell her!** tu n'avais pas besoin de le lui dire! *or* d'aller le lui dire!; **haven't you got to** *or* **don't you have to write to your mother?** est-ce que tu ne dois pas écrire à ta mère?; **if you go through Dijon you haven't got to** *or* **you don't have to go to Lyons** si vous passez par Dijon vous n'avez pas besoin d'aller à Lyon; **you haven't (got) to say a word about it!*** tu ne dois pas en dire un mot!; **he doesn't have to work, he hasn't got to work** il n'est pas obligé de travailler, il n'a pas besoin de travailler; **she was having to get up at 6 each morning** elle devait se lever *or* il fallait qu'elle se lève *(subj)* à 6 heures tous les matins; **we've had to go and see her twice this week** nous avons dû aller *or* il nous a fallu aller la voir deux fois cette semaine; **we shall have to leave tomorrow** nous devrons *or* nous serons obligés de *or* il nous faudra partir demain; **the letter will have to be written tomorrow** il va falloir que la lettre soit écrite demain; **I had to send for the doctor** j'ai été obligé d'appeler *or* j'ai dû appeler le médecin; *(US)* **it's got to be** *or* **it has to be the biggest scandal this year** ça va sûrement être le plus grand scandale de l'année.
3 *vt* **(a)** *(also* **have got:** *possess)* avoir, posséder. **she has (got) blue eyes** elle a les yeux bleus; **he has (got) big feet** il a de grands pieds; **I have** *or* **I've got 3 books** j'ai 3 livres; **have you (got)** *or (esp US)* **do you have a suitcase?** avez-vous une valise?; **all I have (got)** tout ce que je possède; **I haven't (got) any more** je n'en ai plus; **she has (got) a shop** elle a *or* tient une boutique; **I must have more time** il me faut davantage de temps; **have you (got) any money? if you have ...** avez-vous de l'argent? si vous en avez ...; **have you got a cigarette?** (est-ce que) tu as une cigarette?; **have you got the time (on you)?** avez-vous *or* est-ce que vous avez l'heure?; **I have (got) no German** je ne parle pas un mot d'allemand; *(Cards)* **I had (got) no hearts** je n'avais pas de cœur; *(in shop)* **have you (got) any bananas?** avez-vous des bananes?
(b) *meals etc* avoir, prendre. **he has dinner at 8** il dîne à 8 heures; **he has had lunch** il a déjeuné; **to have tea with sb** prendre le thé avec qn; **will you have tea or coffee?** voulez-vous du thé ou du café?; **what will you have? — I'll have an egg** qu'est-ce que vous prendrez? — je prendrai *or* donnez-moi un œuf; **how will you have your eggs? — boiled** comment voulez-vous vos œufs? — à la coque; **he had eggs for breakfast** il a eu *or* mangé des œufs au petit déjeuner; **will you ~ some more?** en reprendrez-vous?; **I have had some more** j'en ai repris; **will you have a drink?** voulez-vous prendre *or* boire un verre?; **he had a cigarette** il a fumé une cigarette; **will you have a cigarette?** voulez-vous une cigarette?; **do you have coffee at breakfast?** est-ce que vous prenez du café au petit déjeuner?; **have you (got) coffee now or is that tea?** est-ce que c'est du café ou du thé que vous buvez là?
(c) *(receive, obtain, get)* avoir, recevoir, tenir. **to have news from sb** recevoir des nouvelles de qn; **I had a telegram from him** j'ai reçu un télégramme de lui; **I have it from my sister that ...** je tiens de ma sœur que ...; **I have it on good authority that ...** je tiens de bonne source que ...; **I shall let you have the books tomorrow** je vous donnerai les livres demain; **I must have them by this afternoon** il me les faut pour cet après-midi; **let me have your address** donnez-moi votre adresse; **let me have a reply soon** répondez-moi rapidement; **I shall let you have it for 10 francs** je vous le cède *or* laisse pour 10 F; **we had a lot of visitors** nous avons reçu beaucoup de visites; **I must have £5 at once** il me faut 5 livres immédiatement; **there are no newspapers to be had** on ne trouve pas de journaux; **it is to be had at the chemist's** cela se trouve en pharmacie.
(d) *(maintain, insist)* **he will have it that Paul is guilty** il soutient que Paul est coupable; **he won't have it that Paul is guilty** il n'admet pas que Paul soit coupable; **rumour has it that ...** le bruit court que ...; **as gossip has it** selon les racontars; **as the Bible has it** comme il est dit dans la Bible.
(e) *(neg: refuse to allow)* **I won't have this nonsense!** je ne tolérerai pas cette absurdité!; **I won't have this sort of behaviour!** je ne supporterai *or* tolérerai pas une pareille conduite!; **I won't have it!** je ne tolérerai pas ça!, cela ne va pas se passer comme ça!; **I won't have him hurt** je ne veux pas qu'on lui fasse du mal.
(f) *(hold)* tenir. **he had (got) me by the throat/the hair** il me tenait à la gorge/par les cheveux; **the dog had (got) him by the ankle** le chien le tenait par la cheville; *(fig)* **I have (got) him where I want him!*** je le tiens (à ma merci)!
(g) *(to give birth to)* **to have a child** avoir un enfant; **she is having a baby in April** elle va avoir un bébé en avril; **our cat has had kittens** notre chatte a eu des petits.
(h) *(+* **will** *or* **would:** *wish)* **which one will you have?** lequel voulez-vous?; **will you have this one?** voulez-vous (prendre) celui-ci?; **what more would you have?** que vous faut-il de plus?; **as fate would have it he did not get the letter** la fatalité a voulu qu'il ne reçoive pas la lettre; **what would you have me say?** que voulez-vous que je dise?; **I would have you know that ...** sachez que ... .
(i) *(causative)* **to have sth done** faire faire qch; **to have one's hair cut** se faire couper les cheveux; **I had my luggage brought up** j'ai fait monter mes bagages; **have it mended!** faites-le réparer!; **to have sb do sth** faire faire qch à qn; **I had him clean the car** je lui ai fait nettoyer la voiture.
(j) *(experience, suffer)* **he had his car stolen** il s'est fait voler sa voiture, on lui a volé sa voiture; **I've had 3 windows broken this week** on m'a cassé 3 fenêtres cette semaine.
(k) *(+n = vb identical with n)* **to have a walk** faire une promenade; *V* **dream, sleep, talk** *etc.*
(l) *(phrases)* **I had better go now** je devrais partir (maintenant); **you'd better not tell him that!** tu ferais mieux de *or* tu as intérêt à ne pas lui dire ça!; **I had as soon not see him** j'aimerais autant ne pas le voir; **I had rather do it myself** j'aimerais mieux le faire moi-même; **I'd rather not speak to him** j'aimerais mieux *or* je préférerais ne pas lui parler; **to have a good time** bien s'amuser; **to have a pleasant evening** passer une bonne soirée; **to have good holidays** passer de bonnes vacances; **he has (got) flu** il a la grippe; **I've (got) a headache** j'ai mal à la tête; **I've (got) an idea** j'ai une idée; **I've (got) £6 left** il me reste 6 livres; **I've (got) a half left** il m'en reste la moitié; **I had my camera ready** j'avais mon appareil tout prêt; **I shall have everything ready** je veillerai à ce que tout soit prêt; **I have (got) letters to write** j'ai des lettres à écrire; **to have (got) sth to do/to read** *etc* avoir qch à faire/à lire *etc*; **I have (got) nothing to do** je n'ai rien à faire; **I have (got) nothing to do with it** je n'y suis pour rien; **there you have me!** ça je n'en sais rien; **I have it!** j'y suis!, ça y est, j'ai trouvé!; **you've been had*** tu t'es fait avoir*, on t'a eu*; **he's had it!*** il est fichu!*; **I'm not having any‡** ça ne prend pas*; *V* **cheek, cold, lesson** *etc.*
4 *n*: **the haves and the have-nots** les riches *mpl* et les pauvres *mpl*, les nantis *mpl* et les démunis *mpl*; **the have-nots** les démunis, les déshérités *mpl.*

have at *vt fus (Fencing) person* attaquer. **have at thee!†** défends-toi!

have down *vt sep*: **we are having the Smiths down for a few days** nous avons invité les Smith à venir passer quelques jours chez nous, les Smith viennent passer quelques jours chez nous.

have in *vt sep* **(a)** faire entrer. **I had the children in to speak to them** j'ai fait entrer les enfants pour leur parler.
(b) *doctor* faire venir.
(c) to have it in for sb* garder *or* avoir une dent contre qn.

have off *vt sep (Brit‡)* **to have it off with sb** s'envoyer** qn.

have on *vt sep* **(a)** *clothes* porter. **he had (got) nothing on** il était nu.
(b) *(Brit: be occupied or busy)* **I've got so much on this week that ...** j'ai tant à faire cette semaine que ...; **I have got nothing on (for) this evening** je ne suis pas pris ce soir, je n'ai rien ce soir.
(c) *(Brit‡: deceive, tease) person* faire marcher*.

have out *vt sep* **(a) to have a tooth out** se faire arracher une dent.
(b) to have it out with sb s'expliquer avec qn.

have up *vt person* faire venir; *(from below)* faire monter. **I had him up to see me** je l'ai fait venir *(or* monter) me voir; **he was had up by the headmaster** il a été appelé chez le proviseur; *[magistrate etc]* **to have sb up** convoquer qn; **to be had up for dangerous driving** être convoqué devant les tribunaux pour conduite dangereuse.

haven ['heɪvn] *n (harbour)* port *m*; *(safe place)* havre *m*, abri *m*, refuge *m.*

haven't ['hævnt] = have not; *V* have.

haver ['heɪvəʳ] *vi* (*N Engl, Scot*) dire des âneries.

haversack ['hævəsæk] *n* (*over shoulder*) musette *f*; (*on back*) sac *m* à dos; (*Mil*) havresac *m*, musette.

havoc ['hævək] *n* (*U*) ravages *mpl*, dégâts *mpl*. to wreak ~ in, to make ~ of ravager, causer des ravages dans; (*fig*) to play ~ with désorganiser complètement.

haw[1] [hɔː] *n* (*Bot*) cenelle *f*.

haw[2] [hɔː] *vi*: to hem and ~, to hum and ~ bafouiller.

Hawaii [hə'waɪiː] *n* Hawaii *m*.

Hawaiian [hə'waɪjən] 1 *adj* hawaïen. 2 *n* (a) Hawaïen(ne) *m(f)*. (b) (*Ling*) hawaïen *m*.

hawk[1] [hɔːk] 1 *n* (*Orn*) faucon *m*. to have eyes like a ~ avoir un regard d'aigle *or* des yeux de lynx; (*Pol fig*) ~s and doves faucons et colombes *fpl*. 2 *vi* chasser au faucon. 3 *cpd*: hawk-eyed au regard d'aigle, aux yeux de lynx.

hawk[2] [hɔːk] *vi* (*clear one's throat*) se racler la gorge.
hawk up *vt sep* expectorer.

hawk[3] [hɔːk] *vt* (*peddle*) colporter; (*in street*) crier (*des marchandises*).

hawker ['hɔːkəʳ] *n* (*street*) colporteur *m*; (*door-to-door*) démarcheur *m*, -euse *f*.

hawser ['hɔːzəʳ] *n* haussière *f or* aussière *f*.

hawthorn ['hɔːθɔːn] *n* aubépine *f*.

hay [heɪ] 1 *n* foin *m*. (*Agr*) to make ~ faner, faire les foins; (*Prov*) to make ~ while the sun shines battre le fer pendant qu'il est chaud, profiter de l'occasion; to make ~ of* *argument* démolir*; *enemy, team* battre à plate(s) couture(s); *V* hit.
2 *cpd*: haycock meulon *m* (de foin); (*Med*) hay fever rhume *m* des foins; hayloft grenier *m* à foin, fenil *m*; haymaker faneur *m*, -euse *f*; haymaking fenaison *f*; hayrick, haystack meule *f* de foin; to go haywire* *[person]* perdre la tête *or* la boule*; *[plans etc]* mal tourner; *[equipment etc]* se détraquer.

hazard ['hæzəd] 1 *n* (a) (*chance*) hasard *m*, chance *f*. it was pure ~ that he ... ce fut pur hasard qu'il ... + *subj*.
(b) (*risk*) risque *m*, (*stronger*) danger *m*, péril *m*; (*Golf*) hazard *m*. natural ~s risques naturels; professional ~ risque du métier; this constitutes a ~ for pedestrians ceci constitue un danger pour les piétons; *V* health.
2 *vt* (a) (*risk*) *life, reputation* hasarder, risquer.
(b) (*venture to make*) *remark, forecast* hasarder. to ~ a suggestion hasarder une proposition; to ~ an attempt risquer une tentative; to ~ a guess faire une conjecture, hasarder *or* risquer une hypothèse; if I might ~ a guess si je peux me permettre de risquer une hypothèse; 'I could do it' she ~ed 'moi je pourrais bien le faire' se risqua-t-elle à dire *or* risqua-t-elle.

hazardous ['hæzədəs] *adj* (a) (*risky*) *enterprise, situation* hasardeux, risqué, périlleux. (b) (*problematical*) *outcome* aléatoire, incertain, hasardeux.

haze[1] [heɪz] *n* brume *f* (légère), vapeur *f*. a ~ of tobacco filled the room des vapeurs de tabac emplissaient la pièce; (*fig*) to be in a ~ être dans le brouillard; *V* heat.

haze[2] [heɪz] *vt* (*US: tease*) brimer.

hazel ['heɪzl] 1 *n* (*Bot*) noisetier *m*, coudrier *m*. 2 *adj* (*colour*) (couleur) noisette *inv*. ~ eyes yeux (couleur) noisette. 3 *cpd*: hazel grove coudraie *f*; hazelnut noisette *f*; hazelwood (bois *m* de) noisetier *m*.

haziness ['heɪzɪnɪs] *n* *[day, weather]* état brumeux; *[ideas etc]* vague *m*, flou *m*.

hazy ['heɪzɪ] *adj* *day, weather* brumeux; *sun, moon* voilé; *outline, photograph* flou; *idea* vague, nébuleux; *thinking* fumeux. he's ~ about dates il ne se rappelle pas bien les dates; I'm ~ about maths j'ai des notions mathématiques (très) vagues; I'm ~ about what really happened j'ai une idée assez vague de *or* je ne sais pas (très) bien ce qui s'est vraiment passé.

he [hiː] 1 *pers pron* (a) (*unstressed*) il. ~ has come il est venu; here ~ is le voici; ~ is a doctor il est médecin, c'est un médecin; ~ is a small man c'est un homme petit.
(b) (*stressed*) lui. (*frm*) it is ~ c'est lui; (*frm*) if I were ~ si j'étais lui, si j'étais à sa place; (*frm*) younger than ~ plus jeune que lui; HE didn't do it ce n'est pas lui qui l'a fait.
(c) (+*rel pron*) celui. ~ who *or* that can celui qui peut.
2 *cpd* mâle. he-bear ours *m* mâle; he-goat bouc *m*; a he-man* un (vrai) mâle.
3 *n* (a) (*) mâle *m*. it's a ~ (*animal*) c'est un mâle; (*baby*) c'est un garçon.
(b) (*Scol sl*) you're ~! (c'est toi le) chat!

head [hed] 1 *n* (a) (*Anat*) tête *f*. ~ of hair chevelure *f*; covered *etc* from ~ to foot couvert *etc* de la tête aux pieds; armed from ~ to foot armé de pied en cap; ~ down, ~ hanging la tête baissée; ~ downwards la tête en bas; ~ first, ~ foremost la tête la première; my ~ aches, I've got a bad ~ j'ai mal à la tête; *[person, stone etc]* to hit sb on the ~ frapper qn à la tête; to stand on one's ~ faire le poirier; he stands ~ and shoulders above everybody else (*lit*) il dépasse tout le monde d'une tête; (*fig*) il surpasse tout le monde; she is ~ and shoulders above her sister in maths elle est cent fois supérieure à sa sœur en maths; she is a ~ taller than her sister, she is taller than her sister by a ~ elle dépasse sa sœur d'une tête; *[horse]* to win by a (short) ~ gagner d'une (courte) tête; to be ~ over ears in debt être criblé *or* accablé de dettes, être dans les dettes jusqu'au cou; to turn *or* go ~ over heels (*accidentally*) faire la culbute; (*on purpose*) faire une galipette; to be ~ over heels in love with sb être follement *or* éperdument amoureux de qn; to keep one's ~ above water (*lit*) garder la tête au-dessus de l'eau; (*fig*) se maintenir à flot; he was talking his ~ off* il n'arrêtait pas de parler; to sing/shout one's ~ off* chanter/crier à tue-tête; he's talking off the top of his ~* il dit n'importe quoi; I'm saying that off the top of my ~* je dis ça sans savoir exactement; to give a horse its ~ lâcher la bride à un cheval; to give sb his ~ lâcher la bride à qn; on your ~ be it! à vos risques et périls!; *V* bang[1], crown, hold, lion *etc*.
(b) (*mind, intellect*) tête *f*. to get sth into one's ~ s'enfoncer *or* se mettre qch dans la tête; I wish he would get it into his ~ that ... j'aimerais qu'il se mette (bien) dans la tête que ...; I can't get that into his ~ je ne peux pas lui enfoncer *or* mettre ça dans la tête; he has taken it into his ~ that ... il s'est mis dans la tête que ...; to take it into one's ~ to do se mettre en tête de *or* s'aviser de faire; it didn't enter his ~ that .../to do il ne lui vint pas à l'idée *or* à l'esprit que .../de faire; you never know what's going on in his ~ on ne sait jamais ce qui lui passe par la tête; what put that (idea) into his ~? qu'est-ce qui lui a mis cette idée-là dans la tête?; don't put ideas into his ~ ne lui donnez pas des idées, ne lui mettez pas d'idées dans la tête; I can't get it out of my ~ je ne peux pas me sortir ça de la tête, ça me trotte par la tête; his name has gone out of my ~ son nom m'est sorti de la tête *or* de la mémoire; it's gone right out of my ~ ça m'est tout à fait sorti de la tête; that tune has been running through my ~ all day cet air m'a trotté par la tête toute la journée; he has a good ~ for mathematics il a des dispositions *fpl* pour les mathématiques, il a la bosse* des mathématiques; he has a good ~ for heights il n'a jamais le vertige; he has no ~ for heights il a le vertige; he has a good business ~ il a le sens des affaires; he has a good ~ (on his shoulders) il a de la tête; he's got his ~ screwed on (right)* il a la tête sur les épaules, il a la tête bien plantée entre les deux épaules; (*Prov*) two ~s are better than one deux avis valent mieux qu'un; we put our ~s together nous nous y sommes mis à deux, nous nous sommes consultés; don't bother *or* worry your ~ about it ne vous en faites pas pour cela; to count in one's ~ calculer mentalement *or* de tête; I can't do it in my ~ je ne peux pas faire *or* calculer ça de tête; he spoke above *or* over their ~s ce qu'il a dit les a complètement dépassés; he gave orders over my ~ il a donné des ordres sans me consulter; he went over my ~ to the director il m'a court-circuité pour parler au directeur; it's quite above my ~ cela me dépasse complètement; to keep one's ~ garder son sang-froid; to lose one's ~ perdre la tête; the wine/his success went to his ~ le vin/son succès lui est monté à la tête; he has gone *or* he is off his ~* il a perdu la boule* *or* le nord*; weak *or* soft* in the ~ un peu demeuré, faible *or* simple d'esprit.
(c) (*pl inv*) 20 ~ of cattle 20 têtes *or* pièces de bétail; 20 ~ of oxen 20 bœufs; they paid 10 francs a ~ *or* per ~ ils ont payé 10 F par tête.
(d) *[tree, flower, lettuce, cabbage, nail, pin, abscess]* tête *f*; *[asparagus, arrow]* pointe *f*; *[celery]* pied *m*; *[corn]* épi *m*; *[bed]* chevet *m*; *[hammer]* tête *f*; *[spear]* fer *m*; *[cane]* pommeau *m*; *[mountain]* faîte *m*, sommet *m*, haut *m*; *[violin]* crosse *f*; *[pillar]* chapiteau *m*; *[page, staircase]* haut; *[river]* source *f*; *[beer]* mousse *f*, faux col*; *[jetty, pier]* extrémité *f*; *[ship etc]* nez *m*, avant *m*, proue *f*; *[mast]* tête. to collide with a ship ~-on aborder un navire par l'avant; the cars collided ~-on les voitures se sont heurtées de plein fouet; the car ran ~-on into a tree la voiture heurta l'arbre de plein fouet; (*Naut*) ~ to wind vent debout; ~ of steam pression *f*; ~ of water hauteur *f* de chute, hauteur piézométrique; at the ~ of the lake à l'extrémité du lac, à l'amont du lac; at the ~ of the valley à la tête *or* en tête de la vallée; at the ~ of the table au haut bout de la table; to come to a ~ *[abscess etc]* mûrir; *[situation etc]* arriver à son point critique; the situation is coming to a ~ la situation devient critique; it all came to a ~ when he met her yesterday les choses sont arrivées au point critique quand il l'a rencontrée hier; to bring things to a ~ précipiter une crise.
(e) (*leader*) *[family, business etc]* chef *m*. (*Scol*) the ~ le directeur, la directrice; ~ of department *[business firm]* chef de service; *[shop]* chef de rayon; *[school, college etc]* chef de section; (*Pol*) ~ of state chef d'État; the ~ of the government le chef du gouvernement.
(f) (*front place*) tête *f*. at the ~ of (*in charge of*) à la tête de; (*in front row of, at top of*) en tête de; at the ~ of his army/the organization à la tête de son armée/de l'organisation; to be at the ~ of the list venir en tête de liste; at the ~ of the queue en tête de file, au début de la queue.
(g) (*title*) titre *m*; (*subject heading*) rubrique *f*. under this ~ sous ce titre *or* cette rubrique; this comes under the ~ of ceci se classe sous la rubrique de, ceci vient au chapitre de; the speech/essay was divided into several ~s le discours/la dissertation était divisé(e) en plusieurs têtes de chapitre *or* en plusieurs parties; *V* letter.
(h) *[coin]* face *f*. to toss ~s or tails jouer à pile ou face; ~s or tails? pile ou face?; ~s I win! face je gagne!; he called ~s il a annonçé 'face'; I can't make ~ nor tail of what he's saying je ne comprends rien à ce qu'il dit; I can't make ~ nor tail of it je n'y comprends rien, pour moi ça n'a ni queue ni tête.
2 *cpd typist, assistant etc* principal. headache *V* headache; headband bandeau *m*; (*Brit Scol*) head boy/girl *élève m/f de terminale chargé(e) d'un certain nombre de responsabilités*; (*US Culin*) headcheese fromage *m* de tête; head clerk (*Comm*) premier commis, chef *m* de bureau; (*Jur*) principal *m*; head cold rhume *m* de cerveau; headdress (*of feathers etc*) coiffure *f*; (*of lace*) coiffe *f*; head gardener jardinier *m* en chef; (*U*) headgear couvre-chef *m*; I haven't any headgear for this weather je n'ai rien à me mettre sur la tête par ce temps; headhunter chasseur *m* de têtes; headhunting chasse *f* aux têtes; headlamp (*Aut*) phare *m*; *[train]* fanal *m*, feu *m* avant; headland promontoire *m*, cap *m*; headlight = headlamp; headline *V* headline; headlong *V* headlong; headman chef *m* (*d'une tribu etc*); headmaster *[school]* directeur *m*; *[lycée]* proviseur *m*; headmistress directrice *f*; head office bureau *or* siège central *or* principal, agence centrale; head-on (*adj*) *collision* de plein fouet, de front; *meeting, confrontation* en face à face; (*adv*) *collide de plein*

fouet, de front; *meet* face à face; (*Rad, Telec*) **headphones** casque *m* (à écouteurs); **head post office** bureau central des postes, poste principale; **headquarters** *[bank, business company, political party]* bureau *or* siège principal *or* central; (*Mil*) quartier général; (*Mil*) **headquarters staff** état-major *m*; **headrest,** (*Aut*) **head restraint** appui-tête *m*; (*on roadsign*) **5 metres headroom** hauteur *f* limite de 5 mètres; **there is not enough headroom in this car** le toit de cette voiture n'est pas assez haut; **have you got enough headroom?** est-ce que vous avez assez de place (pour ne pas vous cogner la tête)?; **headscarf** foulard *m*, pointe *f*; **headset** = **headphones**; **headship** (*post*) poste *m* de directeur *or* de directrice (*school*) *or* de proviseur (*lycée*); **under the headship of X** sous la direction de X; **headshrinker**: psy: *m*, psychiatre *mf*; **headsman** bourreau *m*; **headsquare** = **headscarf**; **to do a headstand** faire le poirier; (*fig*) **to have a head start** avoir une grosse avance (*over or on sb* sur qn); **headstone** *[grave]* pierre tombale (de tête); (*Archit*) clef *f* de voûte, pierre angulaire; **headstrong** (*obstinate*) têtu, entêté, volontaire, obstiné; (*rash*) impétueux; **head waiter** maître *m* d'hôtel; **headwaters** sources *fpl*; **headway** progrès *m*; **to make headway** (*in journey, studies etc*) avancer, faire des progrès; *[ship]* faire route; **I didn't make much headway with him** je n'ai pas fait beaucoup de progrès avec lui; **headwind** vent *m* contraire, vent debout (*Naut*); **headword** entrée *f*, adresse *f*.

3 *vt* **(a)** *procession, list, poll* venir *or* être en tête de; *group of people* être à la tête de.

(b) (*direct*) **he ~ ed the car towards town** il a pris la direction de *or* il s'est dirigé vers la ville; (*Naut*) **to ~ a ship for port** mettre le cap sur le port.

(c) (*put at ~ of*) *chapter* intituler. **to ~ a chapter/a letter** *etc* **with sth** mettre qch en tête d'un chapitre/d'une lettre *etc*; (*Brit*) **~ed writing paper** papier *m* à lettres à en-tête.

(d) (*Ftbl*) **to ~ the ball** faire une tête.

4 *vi* se diriger. **to ~ for** *[person, car etc]* se diriger vers; *[ship]* mettre le cap sur; **he ~ed up the hill** il s'est mis à monter la colline; **he was ~ing home(wards)** il était sur le chemin du retour; **they were ~ing back to town** ils rentraient *or* retournaient à la ville; (*fig*) **he's ~ing for a disappointment** il va vers une déception; **he's ~ing for a fall** il court à un échec.

head off **1** *vi* partir (*for* pour, *towards* vers). (*fig*) **he headed off on to the subject of ...** il est passé à la question de ... .

2 *vt sep enemy* forcer à se rabattre; *person* (*lit*) détourner de son chemin; (*fig*) détourner (*from* de); *questions* parer, faire dévier.

headache ['hedeɪk] *n* mal *m* de tête, migraine *f*; (*fig*) problème *m*. **to have a ~** avoir mal à la tête, avoir la migraine; **terrible ~s** de terribles maux de tête, des migraines affreuses; (*fig*) **that's his ~** c'est son problème (à lui); **the whole business was a ~ from beginning to end** nous n'avons (*or* ils n'ont *etc*) connu que des ennuis avec cette affaire; **geography is a ~ to me** la géographie est une de mes bêtes noires.

-headed ['hedɪd] *adj ending in cpds*: **bare-headed** nu-tête *inv*; **curly-headed** frisé, aux cheveux frisés; *V* **hard** *etc*.

header ['hedəʳ] *n* **(a)** (*: *dive*) plongeon *m*; (*fall*) chute *f* *or* plongeon *or* dégringolade *f* (la tête la première). **to take a ~** (*fall*) piquer une tête, se flanquer* par terre la tête la première; **to take a ~ into the water** piquer une tête dans l'eau, se flanquer* à l'eau la tête la première.

(b) (*Ftbl**) (coup *m* de) tête *f*.

(c) (*Constr*) boutisse *f*.

headiness ['hedɪnɪs] *n* (*V* **heady**) **(a)** bouquet capiteux; qualité entêtante; griserie *f*, ivresse *f*. **(b)** impétuosité *f*.

heading ['hedɪŋ] *n* (*title: at top of page, chapter, article, column of figures etc*) titre *m*; (*subject title*) rubrique *f*; (*printed: on letter, document etc*) en-tête *m*. **under this ~** sous ce titre *or* cette rubrique; **this comes under the ~ of** ceci se classe sous la rubrique de, ceci vient au chapitre de; **under the ~ of 'Science' may be found ...** sous la rubrique des 'Sciences' on peut trouver ...; **the essay was divided into several ~s** la dissertation était divisée en plusieurs têtes de chapitre *or* en plusieurs parties.

headless ['hedlɪs] *adj body, nail* sans tête; (*Zool*) acéphale.

headline ['hedlaɪn] **1** *n [newspaper]* manchette *f*, titre *m*; (*Rad, TV*) grand titre. **it's in the ~s in the papers** c'est en gros titre *or* en manchette dans les journaux; **to hit the ~s*** faire les gros titres, être en manchette, défrayer la chronique; **have you seen the ~s?** as-tu vu les (gros) titres?; **I've only glanced at the ~s** je n'ai fait que jeter un coup d'œil aux gros titres *or* sur les titres; (*Rad, TV*) **here are the news ~s** voici les grands titres de l'actualité; **here are the ~s again** et maintenant le rappel des (grands) titres; **I only heard the ~s** je n'ai entendu que les (grands) titres.

2 *vt* mettre en manchette.

headlong ['hedlɒŋ] **1** *adv fall* la tête la première; *run, rush* (*head down*) tête baissée; (*at uncontrollable speed*) à toute allure *or* vitesse. **the car drove ~ into the wall** la voiture s'est littéralement jetée dans le mur.

2 *adj fall etc* la tête la première; (*reckless*) impétueux, fougueux. **~ flight** débandade *f*, sauve-qui-peut *m inv*; **there was a ~ dash for the gates** ce fut une ruée générale vers la sortie.

heady ['hedɪ] *adj* **(a)** (*intoxicating*) *wine* capiteux, qui monte à la tête; *perfume* capiteux, entêtant; *success* grisant, enivrant. **the ~ delights of ...** les plaisirs grisants de ... . **(b)** (*impetuous*) emporté, impétueux.

heal [hiːl] **1** *vi* (*also* **~ over, ~ up**) *[wound]* se cicatriser. **2** *vt* (*Med*) *person* guérir (*of* de); *wound* cicatriser; (*fig*) *differences* régler; *troubles* apaiser. **time will ~ the pain** le temps guérit les chagrins.

healer ['hiːləʳ] *n* guérisseur *m*, -euse *f*; *V* **faith**.

healing ['hiːlɪŋ] **1** *n [person]* guérison *f*; *[wound]* cicatrisation *f*.

2 *adj* (*Med*) *ointment* cicatrisant; *remedy* curatif; (*fig*) apaisant; *hands* de guérisseur.

health [helθ] **1** *n* **(a)** (*Med, fig*) santé *f*. **in good/bad ~** en bonne/mauvaise santé; **mental ~** *[person]* santé mentale; (*Admin etc*) prévention *f* en (matière de) médecine mentale; **to regain one's ~** recouvrer la santé, guérir, se remettre; **he enjoys good ~** il jouit d'une bonne santé; **from a ~ point of view** du point de vue de la santé; (*Brit*) **Secretary (of State) for** *or* **Minister of H~**, (*US*) **Secretary for H~** ministre *m* de la Santé publique; **Department** *or* **Ministry of H~** ministère *m* de la Santé publique; (*fig*) **the ~ of the economy** la santé de l'économie; *V* **national, restore**.

(b) to drink (to) sb's ~ boire à la santé de qn; **your ~!, good ~!** à votre santé!

2 *cpd*: **health centre** ≈ centre médico-social; **health foods** aliments naturels; **health food shop** magasin *m* diététique; **health-giving** *V* **healthful**; **health hazard** risque *m* pour la santé; **health insurance** assurance *f* maladie; **health officer** inspecteur *m*, -trice *f* de la santé (publique); **health resort** (*watering place*) station thermale, ville *f* d'eau; (*in mountains*) station climatique; **health risk** = **health hazard**; (*Brit*) **the Health Service** ≈ la Sécurité Sociale; **I got my specs on the Health Service*** la Sécurité Sociale m'a remboursé mes lunettes; **Health Service doctor** médecin conventionné; **Health Service nursing home** clinique conventionnée; **health visitor** ≈ infirmière visiteuse.

healthful ['helθfʊl] *adj*, **health-giving** ['helθ,gɪvɪŋ] *adj air* salubre; *exercise etc* salutaire, bon pour la santé.

healthily ['helθɪlɪ] *adv live etc* sainement. (*fig*) **~ sceptical about ...** manifestant un *or* des doute(s) salutaire(s) à propos de ... .

healthy ['helθɪ] *adj person* sain, bien portant, en bonne santé; *animal, plant* en bonne santé; *climate, air* salubre; *food, skin, surroundings* sain; *appetite* robuste, bon; (*fig*) *economy, finances, attitude* sain. **he is very ~** il se porte très bien, il est très bien portant; **to make sth ~** *or* **healthier** assainir qch; (*fig*) **his interest in this is not very ~** l'intérêt qu'il porte à cela n'est pas très sain; (*fig*) **to have a ~ respect for sb/sth** éprouver un respect salutaire pour qn/qch.

heap [hiːp] **1** *n* **(a)** tas *m*, monceau *m*, amas *m*. **in a ~** en tas; **I was struck all of a ~!**: cela m'a coupé bras et jambes!, cela m'a sidéré!*

(b) (**fig*) tas* *m*, masse* *f*. **~s of** *or* **a whole ~ of things to do** un tas* *or* des masses* de choses à faire; **~s of** des tas* de, des masses* de, des monceaux de; **she has ~s of money** elle a des tas* *or* des monceaux d'argent, elle a de l'argent à ne savoir qu'en faire; **we've got ~s of time** nous avons grandement *or* largement le temps, nous avons tout notre temps; **~s of times** des tas* de fois, mille fois; **a whole ~ of people** tout un tas* de gens; **a whole ~ of trouble** tout un tas* d'ennuis.

(c) (:: *car etc*) **an old ~** un vieux clou* (*pej*).

2 *vt* (*also* **~ up**) entasser, amonceler, empiler. **to ~ sth (up) on top of sth** empiler *or* entasser qch sur qch; **to ~ gifts on sb** couvrir qn de cadeaux; **to ~ praises/favours on sb** combler qn d'éloges/de faveurs; **to ~ insults on sb** accabler *or* couvrir qn d'injures; **to ~ work on sb** accabler qn de travail; (*fig*) **to ~ coals of fire (on sb)** rendre le bien pour le mal (à qn); **she ~ed (up) her plate with cakes** elle a empilé des gâteaux sur son assiette, elle a chargé son assiette de gâteaux; (*Culin*) **~ed spoonful**, (*US*) **~ing spoonful** grosse cuillerée.

hear [hɪəʳ] *pret, ptp* **heard** **1** *vt* **(a)** entendre. **did you ~ what he said?** avez-vous entendu ce qu'il a dit?; **can you ~ him?** l'entendez-vous?, vous l'entendez bien?; **I can't ~ you!** je ne vous entends pas!, je n'entends pas ce que vous dites!; **I ~ you speaking** je vous entends parler; **I heard him say that ...** je l'ai entendu dire que ...; **I heard someone come in** j'ai entendu entrer quelqu'un *or* quelqu'un entrer; **a noise was heard** un bruit se fit entendre; **he was heard to say that ...** on l'a entendu dire que ...; **to make o.s. heard** se faire entendre; **he likes to ~ himself talk** il aime s'écouter parler; **to ~ him (talk) you'd think he was an expert** à l'entendre vous le prendriez pour un expert; **I have heard it said that ..., I've heard tell that ...** j'ai entendu dire que ...; **I've heard tell of ...** j'ai ouï parler de ...; **have you heard the story about her going to Paris?** tu as su l'histoire de son voyage à Paris?; **have you heard the one about the Scotsman who ...** tu connais l'histoire de l'Écossais qui ...; **I've heard bad reports of him** j'ai eu sur lui des échos défavorables; **I've never heard such rubbish!** c'est d'une imbécillité inouïe!, jamais je n'ai entendu pareilles âneries!

(b) (*learn*) *piece of news, facts* apprendre. **have you heard the news?** connaissez-vous la nouvelle?; **have you heard the rumour that they're going to leave?** avez-vous entendu dire qu'ils partent?; **he had heard that they had left** il avait appris qu'ils étaient partis; **I ~ you've been ill** il paraît que vous avez été malade.

(c) (*listen to*) *lecture etc* assister à, écouter. **to ~ a child's lessons** faire répéter *or* réciter ses leçons à un enfant; (*Jur*) **to ~ a case** entendre une cause; (*Rel*) **to ~ mass** assister à *or* entendre la messe; **Lord, ~ our prayers** Seigneur, écoutez *or* exaucez nos prières; (*excl*) **~, ~!** bravo!

2 *vi* **(a)** entendre. **he does not** *or* **cannot ~ very well** il n'entend pas très bien.

(b) (*get news*) recevoir *or* avoir des nouvelles (*from* de). **I ~ from my daughter every week** je reçois *or* j'ai des nouvelles de ma fille chaque semaine; **you will ~ from me soon** vous aurez bientôt de mes nouvelles; (*threatening*) **you'll be ~ing from me!** tu vas avoir de mes nouvelles!, tu vas entendre parler de moi!; **to ~ about** *or* **of sb/sth** avoir des nouvelles de qn/qch, entendre parler de qn/qch; **I ~ about** *or* **of him from his mother**

j'ai de ses nouvelles par sa mère, sa mère me donne de ses nouvelles; **he wasn't heard of for a long time** on n'entendit plus parler de lui pendant longtemps; **I've never heard of him!** je ne le connais pas!, connais pas!*; **everyone has heard of him** tout le monde a entendu parler de lui; **he was never heard of again** on n'a jamais plus entendu parler de lui; **the ship was never heard of again** on n'a jamais retrouvé trace du navire; **I've never heard of such a thing!** je n'ai jamais entendu parler d'une chose pareille!; **the first I heard (tell) of it was when ...** la première fois que j'en ai entendu parler c'était lorsque ...; **that's the first I've heard of it!** c'est la première fois que j'entends parler de ça!; **I ~ of nothing but that!** j'en ai les oreilles rebattues!, je n'entends plus que cela!; **I won't ~ of you going there** je ne veux absolument pas que tu y ailles; **Mother won't ~ of it!** Maman ne veut pas en entendre parler!; **can I wash the dishes? — I wouldn't ~ of it!** puis-je faire la vaisselle? — (il n'en est) pas question!

hear out *vt sep person, story* écouter *or* entendre jusqu'au bout.

heard [hɜːd] *pret, ptp of* **hear.**

hearer ['hɪərəʳ] *n* auditeur *m*, -trice *f*. **~s** auditoire *m*, auditeurs *mpl*.

hearing ['hɪərɪŋ] **1** *n* **(a)** (*U: sense*) ouïe *f*. **to have good ~** avoir l'oreille fine; **within ~ (distance)** à portée de voix; **in my ~** en ma présence, devant moi; *V* **hard.**

(b) (*act*) audition *f*. (*Jur*) **~ of witnesses** audition des témoins; (*Jur*) **~ of the case** audience *f*; **give him a ~!** laissez-le parler!, écoutez ce qu'il a à dire!; **he was refused a ~** on refusa de l'entendre; **to condemn sb without a ~** condamner qn sans entendre sa défense *or* sans l'entendre.

(c) (*meeting: of commission, committee etc*) séance *f*.

2 *cpd*: **hearing aid** appareil *m* acoustique, audiophone *m*.

3 *adj person* qui entend (bien), (bien) entendant.

hearken ['hɑːkən] *vi* (*liter*, †) prêter l'oreille (*to* à).

hearsay ['hɪəseɪ] **1** *n* ouï-dire *m inv*. **from** *or* **by ~** par ouï-dire; **it's only ~** ce ne sont que des rumeurs. **2** *cpd report, account* fondé sur des ouï-dire. (*Jur*) **hearsay evidence** déposition *f* sur la foi d'un tiers *or* d'autrui.

hearse [hɜːs] *n* corbillard *m*, fourgon *m* mortuaire.

heart [hɑːt] **1** *n* **(a)** (*Anat*) cœur *m*. (*Med*) **to have a weak ~** avoir le cœur malade, être cardiaque; **to clasp sb to one's ~** serrer qn sur son cœur; *V* **beat, cross, hole** *etc.*

(b) (*fig phrases*) **at ~** au fond; **a man after my own ~** un homme selon mon cœur; **he knew in his ~** il savait instinctivement; **in his ~ (of ~s) he thought ...** en son for intérieur il pensait ...; **with all my ~** de tout mon cœur; **from the ~, from (the bottom of) one's ~** du fond du cœur; **to take sth to ~** prendre qch à cœur; **don't take it to ~** ne prenez pas cela trop à cœur; **I hadn't the ~ to tell him, I couldn't find it in my ~ to tell him** je n'ai pas eu le courage *or* le cœur de lui dire; **I have his future at ~** c'est son avenir qui me tient à cœur; **have a ~!*** pitié!*; **to sing to one's ~'s content** chanter tout son content *or* à cœur joie; **to eat/drink/sleep to one's ~'s content** manger/boire/dormir tout son soûl *or* tout son content; **it did my ~ good to see them** cela m'a réchauffé le cœur de les voir; **~ and soul** corps et âme; **he put his ~ and soul into his work** il s'est donné à son travail corps et âme, il a mis tout son cœur dans son travail; **his ~ isn't in his work** il n'a pas le cœur à l'ouvrage; **his ~ is not in it** le cœur n'y est pas; **to lose/take ~** perdre/prendre courage; **we may take ~ from the fact that ...** nous pouvons nous sentir encouragés du fait que ...; **to put new ~ into sb** donner du courage *or* du cœur à qn; **to be in good ~** avoir (un) bon moral; **to put** *or* **set sb's ~ at rest** calmer les inquiétudes de qn; **to have a ~ of gold** avoir un cœur d'or; **his ~ is in the right place** il a bon cœur; **to have a ~ of stone** avoir un cœur de pierre; **to lose one's ~ to sb** tomber amoureux de qn; **the cause is close to** *or* **near his ~** c'est une cause chère à son cœur *or* qui lui est chère *or* qui lui tient à cœur; **he has set his ~ on** *or* **his ~ is set on a new car** il veut à tout prix une nouvelle voiture, il a jeté son dévolu sur une nouvelle voiture; **he has set his ~ on going to Paris** il veut à tout prix *or* désire absolument aller à Paris; **to have** *or* **wear one's ~ on one's sleeve** laisser voir ses sentiments; **his ~ was in his boots** il avait la mort dans l'âme; **my ~ sank** j'ai eu un coup au cœur; **she had her ~ in her mouth** son cœur battait la chamade; **to learn sth by ~** apprendre qch par cœur; **to know** *or* **have sth by ~** savoir qch par cœur; *V* **bless, break** *etc.*

(c) (*centre*) *[town etc]* cœur *m*, centre *m*; *[cabbage, lettuce]* cœur; *[artichoke]* fond *m*, cœur; *[celery]* cœur. **in the ~ of winter** au cœur de l'hiver, en plein hiver; **the ~ of the matter** le fond du problème, le vif du sujet; **in the ~ of the country** en pleine campagne; **in the ~ of the forest** au cœur *or* au (beau) milieu de la forêt, en pleine forêt; **in the ~ of the desert** au cœur *or* au (fin) fond du désert.

(d) (*Cards*) **~s** cœur *m*; **queen of ~s** dame *f* de cœur; **have you any ~s?** avez-vous du cœur?; **he played a ~** il a joué (un) cœur; **the 6 of ~s** le 6 de cœur; **~ are trumps** atout cœur.

2 *cpd*: **heartache** chagrin *m*, douleur *f*; **heart attack** crise *f* cardiaque; **heartbeat** pulsation *f*, battement *m* de cœur; **heartbreak** immense chagrin *m or* douleur *f*; **heartbreaking** navrant, déchirant, qui fend le cœur; **it was heartbreaking to see him thus** c'était à fendre le cœur de le voir ainsi; **a heartbreaking sight** un spectacle navrant; **heartbroken** navré, au cœur brisé; **to be heartbroken** avoir un immense chagrin; (*stronger*) avoir le cœur brisé; *[child]* avoir un gros chagrin; **she was heartbroken about it** elle en a eu un immense chagrin; (*stronger*) elle en a eu le cœur brisé; (*Med*) **heartburn** brûlures *fpl* d'estomac; **heartburning** (*ill-feeling*) animosité *f*, rancœur *f*; (*regret*) regret(s) *m(pl)*; **there was much heartburning over the decision** la décision a causé beaucoup de rancœur; (*Med*) **heart case** cardiaque *mf*; (*Med*) **heart complaint** maladie *f* de cœur; (*Med*) **to have a heart condition** avoir une maladie de cœur, être cardiaque; **heart disease = heart complaint**; (*Med*) **heart failure** arrêt *m* du cœur; **heartfelt** sincère, senti, qui vient du fond du cœur; **to make a heartfelt appeal** faire un appel bien senti; **heartfelt sympathy** condoléances *fpl* sincères; **heart-lung machine** cœur-poumon *m* (artificiel) ; **heartrending** *cry, appeal* déchirant, qui fend le cœur; *sight* navrant; **it was heart-rending to see him** c'était à fendre le cœur de le voir; **after much heart-searching he ...** après s'être longuement interrogé, il ...; **heart-shaped** en (forme de) cœur; **to be heartsick** avoir la mort dans l'âme; **to touch** *or* **pull at** *or* **tug sb's heartstrings** toucher *or* faire vibrer les cordes sensibles de qn, prendre qn par les sentiments; (*Med*) **heart surgeon** chirurgien *m* cardiologue; (*Med*) **heart surgery** chirurgie *f* du cœur; **heart-throb** (*: *person*) idole *f*, coqueluche *f* (*du cinéma, de la jeunesse etc*); (*US: heartbeat*) battement *m* de cœur; **heart-to-heart** (*adj*) intime, à cœur ouvert; (*adv*) à cœur ouvert; **to have a heart-to-heart*** parler à cœur ouvert; (*Med*) **heart transplant** greffe *f* du cœur; (*Med*) **to have heart trouble** souffrir du cœur, être cardiaque; **~ trouble in the over-50's** les troubles *mpl* cardiaques dont on souffre après la cinquantaine; **heartwarming** réconfortant, qui réchauffe le cœur; **heart-whole** (qui a le cœur) libre.

-hearted ['hɑːtɪd] *adj ending in cpds*: **open-hearted** sincère; **warm-hearted** chaleureux, généreux; *V* **broken, hard** *etc.*

hearten ['hɑːtn] *vt* encourager, donner du courage à.

heartening ['hɑːtnɪŋ] *adj* encourageant, réconfortant. **I found it very ~** cela m'a donné du courage, j'ai trouvé cela très encourageant *or* réconfortant.

hearth [hɑːθ] *n* foyer *m*, cheminée *f*, âtre† *m*. **~ rug** devant *m* de foyer.

heartily ['hɑːtɪlɪ] *adv say, welcome* chaleureusement, de tout cœur; *laugh, work* de tout son cœur; *eat* avec appétit, de bon appétit. **I ~ agree** je suis on ne peut plus d'accord; **I'm ~ tired** *or* **sick* of ...** j'en ai par-dessus la tête* de ...; **to be ~ glad** être ravi.

heartless ['hɑːtlɪs] *adj person* sans cœur, sans pitié, insensible; *treatment* cruel.

heartlessly ['hɑːtlɪslɪ] *adv* sans pitié.

heartlessness ['hɑːtlɪsnɪs] *n* (*V* **heartless**) manque *m* de cœur, insensibilité *f*; cruauté *f*.

hearty ['hɑːtɪ] **1** *adj greeting, welcome* (très) cordial, chaleureux; *approval, support* chaleureux; *laugh* franc, gros; *meal* copieux; *appetite* gros, solide; *kick, slap* bien senti, vigoureux; *person* (*healthy*) vigoureux, robuste, solide; (*cheerful*) jovial. **he is a ~ eater** c'est un gros mangeur, il a un bon coup de fourchette; **to have a ~ dislike of sth** détester qch de tout son cœur; *V* **hale.**

2 *npl* (*: *esp Naut*) **... my hearties!** ... les gars!*

heat [hiːt] **1** *n* **(a)** (*U*) (*gen, Phys*) chaleur *f*; *[fire, flames, sun]* ardeur *f*; *[oven, kiln]* température *f*. **extremes of ~ and cold** extrêmes *mpl* de chaleur et de froid; **I can't stand ~** je ne supporte pas la chaleur; **in the ~ of the day** au (moment le) plus chaud de la journée; (*Culin*) **at low ~** à feu doux; (*Culin*) **lower the ~ and allow to simmer** réduire la chaleur et laisser frémir; **in the ~ of the moment** dans le feu de l'action; **in the ~ of the battle** dans le feu du combat; **in the ~ of his departure they forgot ...** dans l'agitation qui entoura son départ ils oublièrent ...; **in the ~ of the argument** dans le feu de la discussion; **to speak with (some) ~** parler avec feu *or* avec passion; **we had no ~ all day at the office** nous avons été sans chauffage toute la journée au bureau; **to turn on the ~** (*in house, office etc*) mettre le chauffage; (*fig*) **to put** *or* **turn the ~ on sb*** faire pression sur qn; *V* **red, specific, white** *etc.*

(b) (*Sport*) (épreuve *f*) éliminatoire *f*; *V* **dead.**

(c) (*U: Zool*) chaleur *f*, rut *m*. **in** *or* (*Brit*) **on ~** en chaleur, en rut.

2 *cpd*: (*Phys*) **heat constant** constante *f* calorifique; **heat efficiency** rendement *m* calorifique; (*Med*) **heat exhaustion** épuisement *m* dû à la chaleur; **heat haze** brume *f* de chaleur; **heat lightning** éclair(s) *m(pl)* de chaleur; **heat loss** perte *f* calorifique; **heatproof** *material* résistant à la chaleur; *dish* allant au four; (*Med*) **heat rash** irritation *f or* inflammation *f* (due à la chaleur); **heat-resistant, heat-resisting = heatproof**; (*Space*) **heat shield** bouclier *m* thermique; (*Med: U*) **heatstroke** coup *m* de chaleur; (*Med*) **heat treatment** traitement *m* par la chaleur, thermothérapie *f*; **heatwave** vague *f* de chaleur.

3 *vt* (*Culin, Phys, Tech etc*) chauffer; (*Med*) *blood etc* échauffer; (*fig*) enflammer.

4 *vi [liquids etc]* chauffer; *[room]* se réchauffer.

heat up 1 *vi [liquids etc]* chauffer; *[room]* se réchauffer.

2 *vt sep* réchauffer.

heated ['hiːtɪd] *adj* (*lit*) chauffé; (*fig*) *argument, discussion* passionné; *words* vif (*f* vive); *person* échauffé. **to get** *or* **grow ~** *[conversation etc]* s'échauffer, se passionner; *[person]* s'échauffer, s'enflammer, s'exciter.

heatedly ['hiːtɪdlɪ] *adv speak, argue, debate* avec passion.

heater ['hiːtəʳ] *n* appareil *m* de chauffage; *V* **electric, immersion** *etc.*

heath [hiːθ] *n* (*moorland*) lande *f*; (*plant*) bruyère *f*.

heathen ['hiːðən] **1** *adj* (*unbelieving*) païen; (*barbarous*) barbare, sauvage. **2** *n* païen(ne) *m(f)*. **the ~** les païens *mpl*; (*savages*) les barbares *mpl*, les sauvages *mpl*.

heathenish ['hiːðənɪʃ] *adj* (*pej*) de païen, barbare.

heathenism ['hiːðənɪzəm] *n* paganisme *m*.

heather ['heðəʳ] *n* bruyère *f*.

heating ['hiːtɪŋ] **1** *n* chauffage *m*; *V* **central. 2** *cpd*: **heating apparatus** (*heater*) appareil *m* de chauffage; (*equipment*) appareillage *m* de chauffage; **heating plant** système *m or* installation *f* de chauffage; **heating power** pouvoir *m* calorifique; **heating system** système *m* de chauffage.

heave [hi:v] (*vb: pret, ptp* **heaved,** (*Naut*) **hove**) **1** *n [sea]* houle *f*; *[bosom]* soulèvement *m*; *(retching)* haut-le-cœur *m inv*, nausée *f*; (*vomiting*) vomissement *m*. **to give a ~** (*lift/throw/tug*) faire un effort pour soulever/lancer/tirer; **to give sb the ~(-ho)**: *[employer]* sacquer* *or* virer* qn; *[girlfriend etc]* plaquer: qn.
2 *cpd*: (*Naut excl*) **heave-ho!** oh-hisse!
3 *vt* (*lift*) lever *or* soulever (avec effort); (*pull*) tirer (avec effort); (*drag*) traîner (avec effort); (*throw*) lancer. **to ~ a sigh** pousser un (gros) soupir; (*Naut*) **to ~ a boat astern/ahead** déhaler un bateau sur l'arrière/sur l'avant.
4 *vi* **(a)** *[sea, chest]* se soulever; *[person, horse]* (*pant*) haleter; (*retch*) avoir des haut-le-cœur *or* des nausées; (*vomit*) vomir. **his stomach was heaving** son estomac se soulevait.
(b) (*Naut*) *[ship]* **to ~ in(to) sight** poindre (à l'horizon), paraître.

heave to (*Naut*) **1** *vi* se mettre en panne.
2 *vt sep* mettre en panne.

heave up *vt sep* (*vomit*) vomir.

heaven ['hevn] **1** *n* **(a)** (*paradise*) ciel *m*, paradis *m*. **to go to ~** aller au ciel, aller au *or* en paradis; **in ~** au ciel, au *or* en paradis; **he was in ~** *or* **in the seventh ~ (of delight)** il était au septième ciel *or* aux anges, il nageait dans la félicité; **an injustice that cries out to ~** une injustice criante *or* flagrante; **~ forbid that I should accept** Dieu me garde d'accepter; **~ forbid that he should come here** Dieu fasse *or* veuille qu'il ne vienne pas ici; **~ forbid!*** mon Dieu non!, surtout pas!; **~ knows what/when** *etc* Dieu sait quoi/quand *etc*; **when will you come back? — ~ knows!*** quand reviendras-tu? — Dieu seul le sait!; **(good) ~s!*** mon Dieu!, Seigneur!, ciel! (*hum*); **for ~'s sake*** (*pleading*) pour l'amour de Dieu* *or* du ciel*; (*protesting*) zut alors!*; **I wish to ~* that he hadn't left!** comme je voudrais qu'il ne soit pas parti!; **it was ~*** c'était divin *or* merveilleux; **he found a ~ on earth** ce fut pour lui le paradis sur terre; **he's ~!**: il est divin! *or* merveilleux!; *V* **move, stink, thank** *etc.*
(b) (*gen liter: sky*) **the ~s** le ciel, le firmament (*liter*); **the ~s opened** le ciel se mit à déverser des trombes d'eau.
2 *cpd*: **heaven-sent** providentiel.

heavenly ['hevnlı] *adj* (*lit*) céleste, du ciel; (*fig: delightful*) divin, merveilleux. **~ body** corps *m* céleste; (*Rel*) **H~ Father** Père *m* céleste.

heavenward(s) ['hevnwəd(z)] *adv go* vers le ciel; *look* au ciel.

heavily ['hevılı] **1** *adv load, tax* lourdement; *underline* fortement; *sleep, sigh* profondément; *breathe* péniblement, bruyamment; *move* péniblement, avec difficulté; *walk* lourdement, d'un pas pesant; *drink, smoke* beaucoup. **to lean ~ on** s'appuyer de tout son poids sur; **to lose ~** *[team]* se faire écraser; *[gambler]* perdre gros; **it was raining ~** il pleuvait à verse; **it was snowing ~** il neigeait dru *or* très fort; **... he said ~** ... dit-il d'une voix accablée.
2 *cpd*: **heavily-built** solidement bâti, fortement charpenté; **heavily-laden** lourdement chargé.

heaviness ['hevınıs] *n* pesanteur *f*, lourdeur *f*, poids *m*. **~ of heart** tristesse *f*.

heavy ['hevı] **1** *adj* **(a)** *weight, parcel* lourd, pesant. **~ vehicle** (véhicule *m*) poids lourd *m*; **~ luggage** gros bagages *mpl*; (*Zool*) **~ with young** gravide, grosse; **to make heavier** alourdir; **how ~ are you?** combien pesez-vous?; (*Phys*) **~ bodies** corps *mpl* graves; **~ water** eau lourde; **heavier than air** plus lourd que l'air.
(b) (*fig*) *expenses, payments, movement, cloth* lourd; *step* pesant, lourd; *crop* abondant, gros (*f* grosse) (*before n*); *loss* gros (*before n*), lourd; *rain, shower* fort (*before n*), gros (*before n*); *fog* épais (*f* -aisse), à couper au couteau; *meal, food* lourd, indigeste; *defeat* grave; *odour* fort, lourd; *book, film* indigeste; *evening* ennuyeux; *humour, irony* lourd, peu subtil (*f* subtile); (*Theat*) *part* (*demanding*) lourd, difficile, (*tragic*) tragique; *population* dense; *sigh* gros (*before n*), profond; *silence, sleep* lourd, pesant, profond; *sky* chargé, couvert, lourd; *soil* lourd, gras (*f* grasse); *task* lourd, pénible; *work* gros (*before n*). **to be a ~ drinker/smoker** *etc* boire/fumer *etc* beaucoup, être un grand buveur/fumeur *etc*; **to be a ~ sleeper** avoir le sommeil profond *or* lourd; **air ~ with scents** air chargé *or* lourd de parfums; **atmosphere ~ with suspicion** atmosphère pleine de soupçon; **eyes ~ with sleep** yeux lourds de sommeil; **~ eyes** yeux battus; **the car is ~ on petrol** la voiture consomme beaucoup (d'essence); **I've had a ~ day** j'ai eu une journée chargée; (*Mil*) **~ artillery, ~ guns** artillerie lourde, grosse artillerie; **~ (gun) fire** feu nourri; **~ blow** (*lit*) coup violent; (*fig: from fate etc*) rude coup; **man of ~ build** homme fortement charpenté *or* solidement bâti; **there were ~ casualties** il y a eu de nombreuses victimes; (*Med*) **~ cold** gros rhume; **a ~ concentration of** une forte concentration de; (*Naut*) **~ cruiser** croiseur lourd; **~ dew** rosée abondante; (*fig*) **to play the ~ father** jouer les pères nobles, faire l'autoritaire; **~ features** gros traits, traits épais *or* lourds; **the going was ~ because of the rain** le terrain était lourd à cause de la pluie; **the conversation was ~ going** la conversation traînait; **this book is very ~ going** ce livre est d'une lecture difficile; **with a ~ heart** le cœur gros; **~ industry** industrie lourde; **~ line** gros trait, trait épais; (*Typ*) **~ type** caractères gras; **~ sea** grosse mer; **a ~ sea was running** la mer était grosse; **traffic was ~** la circulation était dense, il y avait une grosse circulation; (*Naut etc*) **~ weather** gros temps; **the weather's ~ today** il fait lourd aujourd'hui; (*fig*) **he made ~ weather of it** il s'est compliqué la tâche *or* l'existence*; **he made ~ weather of cleaning the car** il a fait toute une histoire pour laver la voiture; **~ wine** vin corsé *or* lourd; **he did all the ~ work** c'est lui qui a fait le gros travail; (*Ind etc*) **~ workers** travailleurs *mpl* de force.
2 *adv* (*rare*) lourd, lourdement. **to weigh** *or* **lie ~ on** peser lourd (sur); *V also* **lie**[1].
3 *cpd*: **heavy-duty** très résistant; **to be heavy-handed** (*clumsy*) être maladroit, avoir la main lourde; (*harsh*) être dur, avoir une main *or* une poigne de fer; **to be heavy-hearted** avoir le cœur gros; **heavy-laden** lourdement chargé; **heavyweight** *V* **heavyweight.**

heavyweight ['hevıweıt] **1** *n* (*Boxing*) poids lourd; (**fig: influential person*) huile: *f*, grosse légume:. **2** *adj* **(a)** (*Boxing*) *bout, champion* poids lourd. **in the ~ class** dans la catégorie (des) poids lourds. **(b)** *cloth* lourd.

Hebrew ['hi:bru:] **1** *adj* hébreu (*m only*), hébraïque. **2** *n* **(a)** (*Hist*) Hébreu *m*, Israélite *mf*. **(b)** (*Ling*) hébreu *m*.

Hebrides ['hebrıdi:z] *n*: **the ~** les Hébrides *fpl*.

heck* [hek] *excl* zut!*, flûte!*

heckle ['hekl] *vti* (*Pol etc*) (*shout*) chahuter; (*interrupt*) interrompre bruyamment.

heckler ['heklə^r] *n* (*Pol etc*) interrupteur *m*, -trice *f*.

heckling ['heklıŋ] *n* (*Pol etc*) interpellations *fpl*, chahut m (*pour troubler l'orateur*).

hectare ['hektɑ:^{r}] *n* hectare *m*.

hectic ['hektık] *adj* **(a)** *period* très bousculé, très agité, trépidant; *traffic* intense, fou (*f* folle), terrible. **~ life** (*busy*) vie trépidante; (*eventful*) vie très mouvementée; **we had 3 ~ days** nous avons été très bousculés pendant 3 jours, nous avons passé 3 jours mouvementés; **the journey was fairly ~** le voyage a été assez mouvementé; **I've had a ~ rush** ça a vraiment été une course folle.
(b) (*Med*) *person* fiévreux; *fever* hectique.

hectogramme, (*US*) **hectogram** ['hektəʊgræm] *n* hectogramme *m*.

hectolitre, (*US*) **hectoliter** ['hektəʊ,li:tə^r] *n* hectolitre *m*.

hector ['hektə^r] **1** *vt* malmener, rudoyer. **2** *vi* faire l'autoritaire, être tyrannique. **in a ~ing voice** d'un ton autoritaire *or* impérieux.

he'd [hi:d] = **he had, he would**; *V* **have, would.**

hedge [hedʒ] **1** *n* haie *f*. **beech ~** haie *f* de hêtres.
2 *cpd*: **hedge clippers** sécateur *m* à haie; **hedgehog** hérisson *m*; (*Aviat*) **hedgehop** voler en rase-mottes, faire du rase-mottes; **hedgerow(s)** haies *fpl*; **hedge sparrow** fauvette *f* des haies *or* d'hiver, traîne-buisson *m*.
3 *vi* (*in answering*) répondre à côté, éviter de répondre; (*in explaining/recounting etc*) expliquer/raconter avec des détours. **don't ~** dis-le franchement *or* directement.
4 *vt* **(a)** (*also* **~ about, ~ in**) entourer d'une haie, enclore. **~d (about** *or* **in) with difficulties** entouré de difficultés.
(b) (*bet, risk*) couvrir. (*fig*) **to ~ one's bet** se couvrir.

hedge off *vt sep garden* entourer d'une haie; *part of garden* séparer par une haie (*from* de).

hedonism ['hi:dənızəm] *n* hédonisme *m*.

hedonist ['hi:dənıst] *adj, n* hédoniste (*mf*).

heebie-jeebies: ['hi:bı'dʒi:bız] *npl* frousse* *f*, trouille: *f*. **it gives me the ~** (*revulsion*) ça me donne la chair de poule; (*fright, apprehension*) ça me donne la frousse* *or* la trouille: *or* les chocottes:.

heed [hi:d] **1** *vt* faire attention à, prendre garde à, tenir compte de.
2 *n* attention *f*. **to take ~ of sth, to pay** *or* **give ~ to sth** faire attention *or* prendre garde à qch, tenir compte de qch; **take no ~ of what they say** ne faites pas attention à ce qu'ils disent; **he paid no ~ to the warning** il n'a tenu aucun compte de l'avertissement; **to take ~ to do** prendre garde *or* soin de faire.

heedless ['hi:dlıs] *adj* étourdi, insouciant. **~ of what was going on** inattentif à ce qui se passait; **~ of danger** sans se soucier du danger; **~ of complaints** sans tenir compte des réclamations.

heedlessly ['hi:dlıslı] *adv* (*without reflection*) étourdiment, à la légère, sans (faire) attention; (*without caring*) avec insouciance.

heehaw ['hi:hɔ:] **1** *n* hi-han *m*. **2** *vi* faire hi-han, braire.

heel[1] [hi:l] **1** *n* **(a)** *[foot, sock, shoe, tool, golf club etc]* talon *m*. **to tread** *or* **be on sb's ~s** marcher sur les talons de qn; **they followed close on his ~s** ils étaient sur ses talons; **to take to one's ~s, to show a clean pair of ~s** tourner les talons, prendre ses jambes à son cou; **he turned on his ~ and departed** il tourna les talons et partit; **down-at-~** *person* miteux; *shoe* éculé; (*fig*) **under the ~ of** sous le joug *or* la botte de; (*to dog*) **~!** au pied!; **he brought the dog to ~** il a fait venir le chien à ses pieds; (*fig*) **to bring sb to ~** rappeler qn à l'ordre, faire rentrer qn dans le rang; *V* **cool, kick** *etc.*
(b) (**: unpleasant person*) (*man*) salaud: *m*; (*man or woman*) chameau* *m*.
2 *vt shoes, socks* remettre *or* refaire un talon à; (*Sport*) *ball* talonner. (*fig*) **to be well-~ed*** être plein de sous*.

heel[2] [hi:l] *vi* (*also* **~ over**) *[ship]* gîter, donner de la bande; *[truck, structure]* s'incliner *or* pencher (dangereusement).

heft* [heft] *vt* (*lift*) soulever; (*feel weight of*) soupeser.

hefty* ['heftı] *adj person* costaud*; *parcel* lourd; *part, piece, debt, price* gros (*f* grosse). **it's a ~ sum** c'est une grosse *or* une jolie somme.

hegemony [hı'gemənı] *n* hégémonie *f*.

hegira [he'dʒaıərə] *n* hégire *f*.

heifer ['hefə^r] *n* génisse *f*.

heigh [heı] *excl* hé!, eh!, oh!, hé là-bas! **~-ho!** eh bien!

height [haıt] *n* **(a)** *[building]* hauteur *f*; *[person]* taille *f*, grandeur *f*; *[mountain, plane]* altitude *f*; *[star, sun]* élévation *f*. **what ~ are you?** combien mesurez-vous?; **he is 1 metre 80 in ~** il a 1 mètre 80 de haut; **of average ~** de taille moyenne; **he drew himself up to his full ~** il se dressa de toute sa hauteur; **a building**

40 metres in ~ un bâtiment qui a *or* un bâtiment de 40 mètres de haut; **~ above sea level** altitude au-dessus du niveau de la mer.

(b) (*high ground*) éminence *f*, hauteur *f*. **the ~s** les sommets *mpl*; **fear of ~s** vertige *m*; (*fig*) **his performance never reached the ~s** il n'a jamais brillé; *V* **giddy, head.**

(c) (*fig: highest point etc*) *[fortune]* apogée *m*; *[success]* point culminant; *[glory]* sommet *m*; *[grandeur]* sommet, faîte *m*, point culminant; *[absurdity, folly, ill manners]* comble *m*. **at the ~ of his power** au summum de sa puissance; **at the ~ of summer/of the storm/of the battle** au cœur de l'été/de l'orage/de la bataille; **at the ~ of the season** en pleine saison; **the ~ of fashion** la toute dernière mode, le dernier cri; **the fair was at its ~** la fête battait son plein; **excitement was at its ~** l'animation était à son apogée *or* à son maximum.

heighten ['haɪtn] **1** *vt* (*lit: raise*) relever, rehausser; (*Med*) *fever* faire monter, aggraver; (*fig*) *effect, absurdity, interest, tension, fear* augmenter, intensifier; *flavour* relever. *[person]* **with ~ed colour** le teint animé. **2** *vi [fear, tension]* augmenter, monter.

heinous ['heɪnəs] *adj* odieux, atroce, abominable.

heir [ɛə^r] *n* héritier *m*, légataire *mf* (*to* de). **he is ~ to a fortune** il héritera d'une fortune; **~ apparent** héritier présomptif; **~ presumptive** héritier présomptif (*sauf naissance d'un héritier en ligne directe*); **~ to the throne** héritier du trône *or* de la couronne; (*Jur*) **~ at law, rightful ~** héritier légitime *or* naturel; *V* **fall.**

heiress ['ɛəres] *n* héritière *f*.

heirloom ['ɛəlu:m] *n* héritage *m*. **this picture is a family ~** c'est un tableau de famille.

heistᵡ [haɪst] (*US*) **1** *n* hold-up *m inv*; (*burglary*) casseᵡ *m*. **2** *vt* voler.

held [held] *pret, ptp of* **hold.**

Helen ['helɪn] *n* Hélène *f*.

helicopter ['helɪkɒptə^r] **1** *n* hélicoptère *m*. **2** *cpd patrol, rescue* en hélicoptère; *pilot* d'hélicoptère.

heliograph ['hi:lɪəʊgrɑ:f] *n* héliographe *m*.

heliostat ['hi:lɪəʊstæt] *n* héliostat *m*.

heliotrope ['hi:lɪətreʊp] **1** *n* (*Bot*) héliotrope *m*. **2** *adj* (couleur d')héliotrope *inv*.

heliport ['helɪpɔ:t] *n* héliport *m*.

helium ['hi:lɪəm] *n* hélium *m*.

hell [hel] **1** *n* **(a)** (*Rel etc*) enfer *m*; (*Myth*) les enfers. **in ~** (*Rel, gen*) en enfer; (*Myth*) aux enfers; **until ~ freezes (over)** jusqu'à la Saint-glinglin*; **all ~ was let loose** ça a été une pagaïe* monstre; **when he heard about it all ~ was let loose** quand il l'a appris il y a eu une scène infernale; **life became ~** la vie est devenue infernale *or* un enfer; **come ~ or high water** en dépit de tout, quoi qu'il arrive (*subj*); **to ride ~ for leather** aller au triple galop *or* à bride abattue, aller à un train d'enfer; **he went off home ~ for leather** il est rentré chez lui au triple galop; *V* **raise.**

(b) (*: *phrases*) **to make a ~ of a noise** faire un boucan *or* un raffut du diable*; **a ~ of a lot of cars** tout un tas de bagnoles*; **a ~ of a lot of people** des masses* de gens; **he's a ~ of a nice guy** c'est un type vachement bien*; **we had a ~ of a time** (*bad*) ça n'a pas été marrantᵡ, on en a bavéᵡ; (*good*) on s'est vachement marrésᵡ, ça a été terribleᵡ *or* du tonnerreᵡ; **to work like ~** travailler comme un nègre *or* comme une brute; **to run like ~** courir comme un dératé* *or* comme un fou; **to give sb ~** (*make his life a misery*) (faire) mener une vie infernale à qn*; (*scold*) faire sa fête à qn (*iro*), passer une engueuladeᵡ à qn; **oh ~!** flûte!*, merde!ᵡ; **to ~ with him!** qu'il aille se faire voir!*; **to ~ with it!** la barbe!ᵡ; **get the ~ out of here!** fous-moi le camp d'ici!ᵡ; **let's get the ~ out of here** foutons le camp d'iciᵡ; **he got the ~ out** il a foutu le campᵡ; **what the ~ does he want now?** qu'est-ce qu'il peut bien vouloir maintenant?; **what the ~ is he doing?** qu'est-ce qu'il peut bien fabriquer?* *or* foutre?ᵡ; **where the ~ have I put it?** où est-ce que j'ai bien pu le fourrer?* *or* foutre?ᵡ; **how the ~ did you get in?** mais enfin! comment as-tu fait pour entrer?; **why the ~ did you do it?** qu'est-ce qui t'a pris de faire ça?; **go to ~!** va te faire voir!* *or* foutre!ᵡ; **will you do it? — like ~ (I will)!** tu le feras? — tu parles!* *or* tu rigoles!ᵡ *or* pas si con!ᵡᵡ

2 *cpd*: **hellbent* (on doing)** acharné (à faire); **hellcat** harpie *f*, mégère *f*; **hellfire** feu *m* de l'enfer; **hellhole*** bouge *m*.

he'll [hi:l] = **he will**; *V* **will.**

Hellene ['heli:n] *n* Hellène *mf*.

Hellenic [he'li:nɪk] *adj* hellénique.

hellish ['helɪʃ] **1** *adj intentions, actions* diabolique; (*: *unpleasant*) infernal. **2** *adv* (ᵡ) vachementᵡ, atrocement*.

hellishly* ['helɪʃlɪ] *adv* atrocement*, vachementᵡ.

hello [hə'ləʊ] *excl* = **hallo.**

helm [helm] **1** *n* (*Naut*) barre *f*. **to be at the ~** (*Naut*) tenir la barre; (*fig*) diriger l'entreprise, tenir la barre *or* les rênes. **2** *cpd*: (*Naut*) **helmsman** timonier *m*, homme *m* de barre.

helmet ['helmɪt] *n* casque *m*; *V* **crash**[1] *etc.*

helminth ['helmɪnθ] *n* helminthe *m*.

help [help] **1** *n* **(a)** aide *f*, secours *m*, assistance *f*. (*excl*) **~!** au secours!, à l'aide!; **thank you for your ~** merci de votre aide; **with his brother's ~** avec l'aide de son frère; **with the ~ of a knife** à l'aide d'un couteau; **he did it without ~** il l'a fait tout seul; **to shout for ~** appeler *or* crier au secours, appeler à l'aide; **to go to sb's ~** aller au secours de qn, prêter secours *or* assistance à qn; **to come to sb's ~** venir à l'aide de qn *or* en aide à qn; **to be of ~ to sb** prêter assistance *or* secours à qn; **can I be of ~?** puis-je faire quelque chose pour vous?; **I was glad to be of ~** j'ai été content d'avoir pu rendre service; **he's a (great) ~ to me** il m'est d'un grand secours, il m'aide beaucoup; (*iro*) **you're a great ~!** tu es d'un précieux secours! (*iro*); **you can't get (domestic) ~ nowadays** on ne trouve plus à se faire aider de nos jours; **she has no ~ in the house** elle n'a pas de femme de ménage; **we need more ~ in the shop** il nous faut davantage de personnel au magasin; (*fig*) **he's beyond ~** on ne peut plus rien pour lui; **there's no ~ for it** il n'y a rien à faire, on n'y peut rien.

(b) (*person*) (*servant*) domestique *mf*; (*charwoman*) femme *f* de ménage; (*in shop etc*) employé(e) *m(f)*; *V* **daily, home, mother** *etc.*

2 *cpd*: **helpmate, helpmeet** (*spouse*) époux *m*, épouse *f*; (*companion*) compagnon *m*, compagne *f*, aide *mf*.

3 *vt* **(a)** aider (*sb to do* qn à faire), secourir, venir à l'aide de. **let me ~ you with that suitcase** laissez-moi vous aider à porter votre valise; **she ~s her son with his homework** elle aide son fils à faire ses devoirs; **he got his brother to ~ him** il s'est fait aider par son frère; **that doesn't ~ much** cela ne sert pas à *or* n'arrange pas grand-chose; **that won't ~ you** cela ne vous servira à rien; (*Prov*) **God ~s those who ~ themselves** aide-toi et le ciel t'aidera (*Prov*); **so ~ me God!** je le jure devant Dieu!; **so ~ me* I'll kill him!** je le tuerai, je le jure!; **this money will ~ to save the church** cet argent contribuera à sauver l'église; (*loc*) **every little ~s** les petits ruisseaux font les grandes rivières (*Prov*); (*in shops etc*) **can I ~ you?** vous désirez?; **he is ~ing the police with their inquiries** il est en train de répondre aux questions de la police; **to ~ sb across/down/in** *etc* aider qn à traverser/à descendre/à entrer *etc*; **to ~ sb up/down/out with a suitcase** aider qn à monter/à descendre/à sortir une valise; **to ~ sb on/off with his coat** aider qn à mettre/à enlever son manteau.

(b) servir. **she ~ed him to potatoes** elle l'a servi de pommes de terre; **he ~ed himself to vegetables** il s'est servi de légumes; **~ yourself!** servez-vous!; **~ yourself to wine/bread** prenez du vin/du pain, servez-vous de vin/de pain; (*euph*) **he's ~ed himself to my pencil*** il m'a piqué mon crayon*.

(c) (*with 'can' or 'cannot'*) **I couldn't ~ laughing** je ne pouvais pas m'empêcher de rire; **one cannot ~ wondering whether ...** on ne peut s'empêcher de se demander si ...; **it can't be ~ed** tant pis!, on n'y peut rien!; **I can't ~ it if he always comes late, I can't ~ him *or* his always coming late** je n'y peux rien *or* ce n'est pas de ma faute s'il arrive toujours en retard; **he can't ~ it** ce n'est pas de sa faute, il n'y peut rien; **why are you laughing? — I can't ~ it** pourquoi riez-vous? — c'est plus fort que moi; **not if I can ~ it!** sûrement pas!, il faudra d'abord me passer sur le corps! (*hum*); **he won't come if I can ~ it** je vais faire tout mon possible pour l'empêcher de venir; **can I ~ it if it rains?** est-ce que c'est de ma faute s'il pleut?; **it's rather late now — I can't ~ that, you should have come earlier** il est un peu tard maintenant — je n'y peux rien, tu aurais dû venir plus tôt; **he can't ~ his nature** il ne peut rien (changer) à sa nature; **he can't ~ his deafness** ce n'est pas de sa faute s'il est sourd; **he can't ~ being stupid** ce n'est pas de sa faute s'il est idiot; **don't say more than you can ~** n'en dites pas plus qu'il ne faut.

help along *vt sep person* aider à marcher; *scheme* (faire) avancer, faire progresser.

help out 1 *vi* aider, donner un coup de main.

2 *vt sep person* tirer d'embarras, aider à se sortir d'une difficulté. **would £5 help you out?** est-ce que 5 livres pourraient vous être utiles?

helper ['helpə^r] *n* aide *mf*, assistant(e) *m(f)*, auxiliaire *mf*.

helpful ['helpfʊl] *adj person* serviable, obligeant; *book, tool, gadget etc* utile; *medicine etc* efficace, salutaire; *advice* efficace, utile. *[person, thing]* **to be extremely ~** être d'un grand secours; **you have been most ~** votre aide m'a été très utile.

helpfully ['helpfəlɪ] *adv* gentiment, avec obligeance.

helpfulness ['helpfʊlnɪs] *n* obligeance *f*.

helping ['helpɪŋ] **1** *n* (*at table*) portion *f*. **to take a second ~ of sth** reprendre de qch; **I've had three ~s** j'en ai repris deux fois.

2 *adj* secourable. **to give *or* lend a ~ hand (to)** aider, donner un coup de main (à).

helpless ['helplɪs] *adj* (*powerless*) sans ressource, sans recours, sans appui; (*mentally, morally*) impuissant, incapable de s'en sortir; (*physically*) faible, impotent. **she looked at him with a ~ expression** elle lui jeta un regard où se lisait son impuissance; **~ as a child** aussi désarmé qu'un enfant; **he is quite ~ (in this matter)** il n'y peut rien, il est absolument impuissant; **we were ~ to do anything about it** nous avons été impuissants à y faire quoi que ce soit; **her illness has left her ~** sa maladie l'a laissée impotente; **she is a ~ invalid** elle est complètement impotente; (*fig*) **to feel ~** se sentir impuissant; **she was quite ~ (with laughter)** elle n'en pouvait plus de rire*, elle était malade de rire.

helplessly ['helplɪslɪ] *adv struggle* en vain; *try, agree* désespérément. **he was lying there ~** il était allongé là sans pouvoir bouger; **... he said ~** ... dit-il d'un ton où se sentait son impuissance; **to laugh ~** être pris d'un fou rire, ne pas pouvoir s'empêcher de rire.

helplessness ['helplɪsnɪs] *n* (*V* **helpless**) impuissance *f*, incapacité *f* à s'en sortir; impotence *f*.

helter-skelter ['heltə'skeltə^r] **1** *adv* à la débandade, à la six-quatre-deux*. **2** *adj* désordonné, à la débandade. **3** *n* (*rush*) débandade *f*, bousculade *f*; (*Brit: in fairground*) toboggan *m*.

hem[1] [hem] **1** *n* ourlet *m*; (*edge*) bord *m*. **I've let the ~ down on my skirt** j'ai défait l'ourlet de ma jupe pour la rallonger.

2 *cpd*: **hemline** (bas *m* de l')ourlet *m*; **hemlines are lower this year** les robes rallongent cette année; **hemstitch** (*vt*) ourler à jour; (*n*) ourlet *m* à jour.

3 *vt* (*sew*) ourler.

hem in *vt sep [houses, objects, people]* cerner; *[rules etc]* entraver. **I feel hemmed in** ça me donne la claustrophobie, ça m'écrase *or* m'oppresse.

hem[2] [hem] *vi V* **haw**[2].

hema(t)... ['hi:mə(t)] *pref* héma(t)... .

hemato... [ˈhiːmətəʊ] *pref* hémato... .

hematology [ˌhiːməˈtɒlədʒɪ] *n* (*US*) = **haematology.**

hemicycle [ˈhemɪsaɪkl] *n* hémicycle *m.*

hemiplegia [hemɪˈpliːdʒɪə] *n* hémiplégie *f.*

hemisphere [ˈhemɪsfɪəʳ] *n* hémisphère *m.* **the northern** ~ l'hémisphère nord *or* boréal; **the southern** ~ l'hémisphère sud *or* austral.

hemistich [ˈhemɪstɪk] *n* hémistiche *m.*

hemlock [ˈhemlɒk] *n* ciguë *f.*

hem(o)... [ˈhiːm(əʊ)] *pref* hémo... .

hemoglobin [ˌhiːməʊˈgləʊbɪn] *n* (*US*) = **haemoglobin.**

hemophilia [ˌhiːməʊˈfɪlɪə] *n* (*US*) = **haemophilia.**

hemophiliac [ˌhiːməʊˈfɪlɪæk] *n* (*US*) = **haemophiliac.**

hemorrhage [ˈhemərɪdʒ] *n* (*US*) = **haemorrhage.**

hemorrhoids [ˈhemərɔɪdz] *npl* (*US*) = **haemorrhoids.**

hemp [hemp] *n* (*plant, fibre*) chanvre *m*; (*drug*) haschisch *m or* hachisch *m*, chanvre indien.

hen [hen] **1** *n* poule *f*; (*female bird*) femelle *f.* ~ **bird** oiseau *m* femelle.

2 *cpd*: (*Bot*) **henbane** jusquiame *f* (noire), herbe *f* aux poules; **hen coop** cage *f* à poules, mue *f*; **henhouse** poulailler *m*; **hen party*** réunion *f* de femmes *or* filles *or* nanas‡; **he is henpecked** sa femme le mène par le bout du nez, c'est sa femme qui porte la culotte; **henpecked husband** mari dominé par sa femme.

hence [hens] **1** *adv* **(a)** (*therefore*) d'où, de là. **(b)** (*from now on*) d'ici. **2 years** ~ d'ici 2 ans, dans 2 ans (d'ici). **(c)** (††*liter*) (**get thee**) ~! hors d'ici! **2** *cpd*: **henceforth, henceforward** dorénavant, désormais, à l'avenir.

henchman [ˈhentʃmən] *n* (*pej*) acolyte *m* (*pej*), suppôt *m* (*pej*); (*supporter*) partisan *m*, adepte *m*; (*Hist*) écuyer *m.*

henna [ˈhenə] *n* henné *m.*

Henry [ˈhenrɪ] *n* Henri *m.*

hep‡ [hep] *adj* dans le vent*.

hepatitis [ˌhepəˈtaɪtɪs] *n* hépatite *f.*

her [hɜːʳ] **1** *pers pron* **(a)** (*direct*) (*unstressed*) la; (*before vowel*) l'; (*stressed*) elle. **I see** ~ je la vois; **I have seen** ~ je l'ai vue; **I know HIM but I have never seen HER** je le connais, lui, mais elle je ne l'ai jamais vue.

(b) (*indirect*) lui. **I give** ~ **the book** je lui donne le livre; **I'm speaking to** ~ je lui parle.

(c) (*after prep etc*) elle. **I am thinking of** ~ je pense à elle; **without** ~ sans elle; **if I were** ~ si j'étais elle; **it's** ~ c'est elle; **younger than** ~ plus jeune qu'elle.

(d) celle. **to** ~ **who objects I would explain it thus** à celle qui n'est pas d'accord je l'expliquerais ainsi.

2 *poss adj* son, sa, ses. ~ **book** son livre; ~ **table** sa table; ~ **friend** son ami(e); ~ **clothes** ses vêtements.

herald [ˈherəld] **1** *n* héraut *m.* (*fig liter*) **the** ~ **of spring** le messager du printemps (*liter*). **2** *vt* annoncer. **to** ~ **(in)** annoncer l'arrivée de.

heraldic [heˈrældɪk] *adj* héraldique. ~ **bearing** armoiries *fpl*, blason *m.*

heraldry [ˈherəldrɪ] *n* (*U*) (*science*) héraldique *f*; (*coat of arms*) blason *m*; (*ceremonial*) pompe *f* héraldique. **book of** ~ armorial *m.*

herb [hɜːb] **1** *n* herbe *f.* **(sweet)** ~**s** (fines) herbes; **pot** ~**s** herbes potagères; **medicinal** ~**s** herbes médicinales, simples *mpl.* **2** *cpd*: **herb garden** jardin *m* d'herbes aromatiques.

herbaceous [hɜːˈbeɪʃəs] *adj* herbacé. ~ **border** bordure *f* de plantes herbacées.

herbage [ˈhɜːbɪdʒ] *n* (*Agr*) herbages *mpl*; (*Jur*) droit *m* de pâturage *or* de pacage.

herbal [ˈhɜːbəl] **1** *adj* d'herbes. **2** *n* herbier *m* (*livre*).

herbalist [ˈhɜːbəlɪst] *n* herboriste *mf.*

herbarium [hɜːˈbɛərɪəm] *n* herbier *m* (*collection*).

herbivorous [hɜːˈbɪvərəs] *adj* herbivore.

Herculean [ˌhɜːkjuˈliːən] *adj* herculéen.

Hercules [ˈhɜːkjuliːz] *n* Hercule *m*; (*fig: strong man*) hercule *m.*

herd [hɜːd] **1** *n* **(a)** *[cattle etc]* troupeau *m*; *[stags]* harde *f*; *[horses]* troupe *f*, bande *f*; *[people]* troupeau, foule *f*; *V* **common.**

(b) (*person*) pâtre *m* (*liter*); *V* **cow¹, goat** *etc.*

2 *cpd*: **the herd instinct** l'instinct grégaire; **herdsman** gardien *m* de troupeau; (*shepherd*) berger *m*; (*cowman*) vacher *m*, bouvier *m.*

3 *vt animals, people* mener, conduire (*along* le long de).

herd together **1** *vi [animals, people]* s'attrouper, s'assembler en troupeau.

2 *vt sep animals, people* rassembler en troupeau.

here [hɪəʳ] **1** *adv* **(a)** (*place*) ici. **I live** ~ j'habite ici; **come** ~ venez ici; (*at roll call*) ~! présent!; ~ **I am** me voici; ~ **is my brother** voici mon frère; ~ **are the others** voici les autres; ~ **we are at last** nous voici enfin arrivés; (*bringing sth*) ~ **we are!** voici!; (*giving sth*) ~ **you are!** tenez!; ~ **come my friends** voici mes amis qui arrivent; **he's** ~ **at last** le voici enfin, il est enfin là *or* arrivé; **spring is** ~ c'est le printemps, le printemps est là; **my sister** ~ **says ...** ma sœur que voici dit ...; **this man** ~ **saw it** cet homme-ci l'a vu; ~**'s to you!** à la tienne! *or* vôtre!; ~**'s to your success!** à votre succès!; **about** *or* **around** ~ par ici; **far from** ~ loin d'ici; **put it in** ~ mettez-le ici; **come in** ~ venez (par) ici; **in** ~ **please** par ici s'il vous plaît; **near** ~ près d'ici; **over** ~ ici; **it's cold up** ~ il fait froid ici (en haut); **up to** *or* **down to** ~ jusqu'ici; **from** ~ **to there** d'ici (jusqu')à là-bas; **it's 10 km from** ~ **to Paris** il y a 10 km d'ici à Paris; **Mr X is not** ~ **just now** M X n'est pas là *or* ici en ce moment; **are you there? — yes I'm** ~ vous êtes là? — oui je suis là; **I shan't be** ~ **this afternoon** je ne serai pas là cet après-midi; ~ **and there** çà et là, par-ci par-là; ~, **there and everywhere** un peu partout; **I can't be** ~, **there and everywhere** je ne peux pas être partout (à la fois), je ne peux pas être à la fois au four et au moulin*; (*fig*) **it's neither** ~ **nor there** tout cela n'a aucun rapport; ~ **goes!*** allons-y!; ~ **and now** en ce moment précis, en ce moment même (*V also* **3**); ~ **below** ici-bas; ~ **lies** ci-gît; *V* **look** *etc.*

(b) (*time*) alors, à ce moment-là. **and** ~ **I stopped work to answer the telephone** et alors j'ai laissé mon travail pour répondre au téléphone.

2 *excl* tenez!, écoutez! ~, **I didn't promise that at all!** mais écoutez, *or* dites donc, je n'ai jamais promis cela!; ~, **you try to open it** tiens, essaie de l'ouvrir; ~, **hold this a minute** tiens, prends ça une minute.

3 *cpd*: **hereabouts** par ici, près d'ici, dans les environs, dans les parages; **hereafter** (*in the future*) après, plus tard; (*in books etc: following this*) ci-après; (*after death*) dans l'autre vie *or* monde; **the hereafter** l'au-delà *m*, la vie future; **the here and now** le présent, l'instant présent; (*frm: Comm, Jur etc*) **hereby** (*in letter*) par la présente; (*in document*) par le présent document; (*in act*) par le présent acte; (*in will*) par le présent testament; (*in declaration*) par la présente (déclaration); (*frm*) **herein** (*in this matter*) en ceci, en cela; (*in this writing*) ci-inclus; (*frm*) **hereof** de ceci, de cela; (*frm*) **heretofore** jusque-là, jusqu'ici, ci-devant; **hereupon** là-dessus, sur ce; **herewith** avec ceci; **I am sending you herewith** je vous envoie ci-joint *or* sous ce pli.

hereditary [hɪˈredɪtərɪ] *adj* héréditaire.

heredity [hɪˈredɪtɪ] *n* hérédité *f.*

heresy [ˈherəsɪ] *n* hérésie *f.* **an act of** ~ une hérésie.

heretic [ˈherətɪk] *n* hérétique *mf.*

heretical [hɪˈretɪkəl] *adj* hérétique.

heritable [ˈherɪtəbl] *adj objects, property etc* dont on peut hériter; *person* qui peut hériter.

heritage [ˈherɪtɪdʒ] *n* (*lit, fig*) héritage *m.*

hermaphrodite [hɜːˈmæfrədaɪt] *adj, n* hermaphrodite (*m*).

hermetic [hɜːˈmetɪk] *adj* hermétique.

hermetically [hɜːˈmetɪkəlɪ] *adv* hermétiquement. ~ **sealed** bouché *or* fermé hermétiquement.

hermit [ˈhɜːmɪt] *n* ermite *m*, solitaire *m.* ~ **crab** bernard-l'ermite *m inv.*

hermitage [ˈhɜːmɪtɪdʒ] *n* ermitage *m.*

hernia [ˈhɜːnɪə] *n* hernie *f.*

hero [ˈhɪərəʊ] *pl* ~**es** **1** *n* (*all senses*) héros *m.* **2** *cpd*: **hero-worship** (*n*) culte *m* (du héros); (*vt*) aduler, idolâtrer; *one's brother, a pop star etc* avoir un culte pour.

Herod [ˈherəd] *n* Hérode *m*; *V* **out.**

heroic [hɪˈrəʊɪk] *adj act, behaviour, person* héroïque. (*Poetry*) **in** ~ **verse** en décasyllabes *mpl*; ~ **couplet** distique *m* héroïque.

heroically [hɪˈrəʊɪkəlɪ] *adv* héroïquement.

heroics [hɪˈrəʊɪks] *npl* (*slightly pej*) grandiloquence *f.*

heroin [ˈherəʊɪn] *n* héroïne *f* (*drogue*). ~ **addict** héroïnomane *mf.*

heroine [ˈherəʊɪn] *n* héroïne *f* (*femme*).

heroism [ˈherəʊɪzəm] *n* héroïsme *m.*

heron [ˈherən] *n* héron *m.*

herpes [ˈhɜːpiːz] *n* herpès *m.*

herring [ˈherɪŋ] **1** *n* hareng *m*; *V* **fish, red** *etc.*

2 *cpd*: **herring boat** harenguier *m*; **herringbone** (*lit*) arête *f* de hareng; (*Archit*) appareil *m* en épi; (*Ski*) montée *f* en canard; **herringbone pattern** (dessin *m* à) chevrons *mpl*; **herringbone stitch** point *m* d'épine (en chevron); (*Atlantic*) **the herring-pond‡** la mare aux harengs (*hum*), l'Atlantique nord.

hers [hɜːz] *poss pron* le sien, la sienne, les siens, les siennes. **my hands are clean,** ~ **are dirty** mes mains sont propres, les siennes sont sales; ~ **is a specialized department** sa section est une section spécialisée; **this book is** ~ ce livre est à elle, ce livre est le sien; **the house became** ~ la maison est devenue la sienne; **it is not** ~ **to decide** ce n'est pas à elle de décider, il ne lui appartient pas de décider; **a friend of** ~ un de ses amis (à elle); **it's no fault of** ~ ce n'est pas de sa faute (à elle); **no advice of** ~ **could prevent him** aucun conseil de sa part ne pouvait l'empêcher; **is this poem** ~? ce poème est-il d'elle?; (*pej*) **that car of** ~ sa fichue* voiture; **that stupid son of** ~ son idiot de fils; **that temper of** ~ son sale caractère.

herself [hɜːˈself] *pers pron* (*reflexive: direct and indirect*) se; (*emphatic*) elle-même; (*after prep*) elle. **she has hurt** ~ elle s'est blessée; **she said to** ~ elle s'est dit; **she told me** ~ elle me l'a dit elle-même; **I saw the girl** ~ j'ai vu la jeune fille elle-même *or* en personne; **she kept 3 for** ~ elle s'en est réservé 3; **he asked her for a photo of** ~ il lui a demandé une de ses photos *or* une photo d'elle; **(all) by** ~ toute seule; **she is not** ~ **today** elle n'est pas dans son état normal *or* dans son assiette* aujourd'hui.

he's [hiːz] = **he is, he has**; *V* **be, have.**

hesitancy [ˈhezɪtənsɪ] *n* hésitation *f.*

hesitant [ˈhezɪtənt] *adj* hésitant, irrésolu, indécis. **I am** ~ **about offering him money** j'hésite à lui offrir de l'argent.

hesitantly [ˈhezɪtəntlɪ] *adv* avec hésitation; *speak, suggest* d'une voix hésitante.

hesitate [ˈhezɪteɪt] *vi* hésiter (*over, about, at* sur, devant, *to do* à faire). (*Prov*) **he who** ~**s is lost** une minute d'hésitation peut coûter cher, ≃ aux audacieux les mains pleines (*Prov*); **he** ~**s at nothing** il ne recule devant rien, rien ne l'arrête; **I** ~ **to condemn him** j'hésite à le condamner; **I am hesitating about what I should do** j'hésite sur ce que je dois faire; **don't** ~ **to ask me** n'ayez pas peur de *or* n'hésitez pas à me demander.

hesitation [ˌheziˈteɪʃən] *n* hésitation *f.* **without the slightest** ~ sans la moindre hésitation; **I have no** ~ **in saying that ...** je n'hésite pas à dire que ... .

hessian [ˈhesɪən] *n* (toile *f* de) jute *m.*

hetero... [ˈhetərəʊ] *pref* hétér(o)... .

heterodox [ˈhetərədɒks] *adj* hétérodoxe.

heterodoxy [ˈhetərədɒksɪ] *n* hétérodoxie *f.*

heterogeneous [ˈhetərəʊˈdʒiːnɪəs] *adj* hétérogène.
heterosexual [ˈhetərəʊˈseksjʊəl] *adj, n* hétérosexuel(le) *m(f)*.
het up* [ˈhetˈʌp] *adj* agité, excité, énervé. **he gets very ~ about it** cela le met dans tous ses états.
hew [hjuː] 1 *pret* **hewed**, *ptp* **hewn** [hjuːn] *or* **hewed** *vt stone* tailler, équarrir; *wood* couper; *coal* abattre. **to ~ sth out of wood** *etc* tailler qch dans du bois *etc*; **to ~ one's way through the jungle** se tailler un chemin à travers la jungle (à coups de hache *etc*).
 2 *pret, ptp* **hewed** *vi* (*US*) **to ~ to sth** se conformer à qch, suivre qch.
hex [heks] (*US*) 1 *n* sort *m*. 2 *vt* jeter un sort sur.
hexagon [ˈheksəgən] *n* hexagone *m*.
hexagonal [hekˈsægənəl] *adj* hexagonal.
hexameter [hekˈsæmɪtəʳ] *n* hexamètre *m*.
hey [heɪ] *excl* hé!, holà! **~ presto!** *[magician]* passez muscade!; (*fig*) ô miracle!
heyday [ˈheɪdeɪ] *n [person]* apogée *m*; *[thing]* âge *m* d'or, beaux jours. **in his ~** (*in his prime*) quand il était dans la force de l'âge; (*at his most famous*) à l'apogée de sa gloire; **the ~ of the crinoline/the theatre** l'âge d'or de la crinoline/du théâtre.
hi [haɪ] *excl* hé!, ohé!; (*: *greeting*) salut!*
hiatus [haɪˈeɪtəs] *n* (*in series, manuscript etc*) lacune *f*; (*Ling, Poetry*) hiatus *m*.
hibernate [ˈhaɪbəneɪt] *vi* hiberner.
hibernation [ˌhaɪbəˈneɪʃən] *n* hibernation *f*.
hibiscus [hɪˈbɪskəs] *n* hibiscus *m*.
hiccough, hiccup [ˈhɪkʌp] 1 *n* hoquet *m*. **to have ~s** avoir le hoquet; **to give a ~** hoqueter, avoir un hoquet. 2 *vi* hoqueter. 3 *vt* dire en hoquetant.
hick‡ [hɪk] (*US*) 1 *n* péquenaud(e)‡ *m(f)* (*pej*). 2 *adj ideas* de péquenaud‡ (*pej*). **~ town** bled‡ *m* (*pej*).
hickory [ˈhɪkərɪ] *n* hickory *m*.
hid [hɪd] *pret*, (††) *ptp of* **hide**[1].
hidden [ˈhɪdn] *ptp of* **hide**[1].
hide[1] [haɪd] *pret* **hid**, *ptp* **hidden** *or* **hid**†† 1 *vt* cacher (*from sb* à qn); *feelings* dissimuler (*from sb* à qn). **to ~ o.s.** se cacher; **I've got nothing to ~** je n'ai rien à cacher *or* à dissimuler; **he's hiding something** il nous cache quelque chose; **to ~ one's face** se cacher le visage; **to ~ sth from sight** dérober qch aux regards, cacher qch; **hidden from sight** dérobé aux regards, caché; (*fig*) **to ~ one's light under a bushel** cacher ses talents; (*fig*) **he doesn't ~ his light under a bushel** ce n'est pas la modestie qui l'étouffe; **clouds hid the sun** des nuages cachaient *or* voilaient le soleil; **a small village hidden in a valley** un petit village caché *or* niché dans une vallée; **a hidden meaning** un sens caché.
 2 *vi* se cacher (*from sb* de qn). (*fig*) **he's hiding behind his boss** il se réfugie derrière son patron (*fig*).
 3 *n* (*Brit*) cachette *f*.
 4 *cpd*: **hide-and-(go-)seek** cache-cache *m*; **hideaway, hideout** cachette *f*, planque‡ *f*.
hide away 1 *vi* se cacher (*from* de).
 2 *vt sep* cacher.
 3 **hideaway** *n V* **hide**[1] 4.
hide out, hide up 1 *vi* se cacher (*from* de), rester caché (*from* de).
 2 **hideout** *n V* **hide**[1] 4.
hide[2] [haɪd] 1 *n* (*skin*) peau *f*; (*leather*) cuir *m*. **to save one's ~*** sauver sa peau*; **they found neither ~ nor hair of him** ils n'ont pas trouvé la moindre trace de son passage; *V* **tan**.
 2 *cpd chair etc* de *or* en cuir. **hidebound** *person* borné, obtus, à l'esprit étroit *or* limité; *view* étroit, borné, rigide.
hideous [ˈhɪdɪəs] *adj appearance, sight, person* hideux, affreux; *crime* atroce, abominable, horrible; (*fig*) terrible*. **it was a ~ disappointment** ce fut une terrible déception.
hideously [ˈhɪdɪəslɪ] *adv* hideusement, atrocement, affreusement; (*fig: very*) terriblement*, horriblement*.
hiding[1] [ˈhaɪdɪŋ] 1 *n* acte *m* de cacher; *[feelings etc]* dissimulation *f*; *[criminals]* recel *m*. **to be in ~** se tenir caché; **to go into ~** se cacher. 2 *cpd*: **hiding place** cachette *f*.
hiding[2] [ˈhaɪdɪŋ] *n* (*beating*) correction *f*, volée *f* de coups. **to give sb a good ~** donner une bonne correction à qn; (*fig*) **the team got a ~*** l'équipe a pris une raclée *or* une déculottée‡.
hie [haɪ] *vi* (†† *or hum*) se hâter. **~ thee hence!** hors d'ici!
hierarchic(al) [ˌhaɪəˈrɑːkɪk(əl)] *adj* hiérarchique.
hierarchy [ˈhaɪərɑːkɪ] *n* hiérarchie *f*.
hieroglyph [ˈhaɪərəglɪf] *n* hiéroglyphe *m*.
hieroglyphic [ˌhaɪərəˈglɪfɪk] 1 *adj* hiéroglyphique. 2 *n* hiéroglyphe *m*.
hi-fi [ˈhaɪˈfaɪ] (*abbr of* **high fidelity**) 1 *n* **(a)** (*U*) hi-fi* *f inv*, haute fidélité *inv*. **(b)** (*gramophone*) chaîne *f* hi-fi* *inv*; (*radio*) radio *f* hi-fi* *inv*. 2 *cpd reproduction, record* hi-fi* *inv*, haute fidélité *inv*. **hi-fi equipment** *or* **system** chaîne *f* (hi-fi*).
higgledy-piggledy* [ˈhɪgldɪˈpɪgldɪ] *adj, adv* pêle-mêle *inv*, n'importe comment.
high [haɪ] 1 *adj* **(a)** *building, mountain, tide* haut; *altitude* haut, élevé. **building 40 metres ~** bâtiment haut de 40 mètres, bâtiment de 40 mètres de haut, bâtiment qui a *or* fait 40 mètres de haut; **how ~ is that tower?** quelle est la hauteur de cette tour?; **when he was so ~*** quand il était grand comme ça; **~ cheekbones** pommettes saillantes; (*Sport*) **~ jump** saut *m* en hauteur; (*Brit fig*) **he's for the ~ jump*** il est bon *or* mûr pour une engueulade*; **you're for the ~ jump!*** qu'est-ce que tu vas prendre!*; **at ~ tide** *or* **water** à marée haute.
 (b) (*fig*) *frequency, latitude, opinion* haut (*before n*); *speed, value* grand (*before n*); *fever* gros (*f* grosse) (*before n*), fort (*before n*), intense; *respect* grand (*before n*), profond; *complexion* rougeaud; *colour* vif (*f* vive); *polish* brillant; *pressure* élevé, haut (*before n*), fort (*before n*); *salary* haut, élevé, gros (*before n*); *rent, price* élevé; *tension* haut (*before n*); *number* grand (*before n*), élevé; *sound* aigu (*f* -guë); *note* haut; (*shrill*) aigu; *voice* aigu; *calling, character* noble; *ideal* noble, grand (*before n*), élevé; (*Culin*) *game, meat* avancé, faisandé; *butter* fort, rance; (‡: *intoxicated*) paf*, parti*. **to be ~‡ on drugs/hashish** *etc* être défoncé‡ par la drogue/au haschisch; **~ caste** caste supérieure; (*Math*) **the ~est common factor** le plus grand commun diviseur; **in the ~est degree** au plus haut degré, à l'extrême; **~ official** haut fonctionnaire; **to have a ~ opinion of sb/sth** avoir une haute opinion de qn/qch; **to buy sth at a ~ price** acheter qch cher; (*lit, fig*) **to pay a ~ price for sth** payer qch cher; **he has a ~ temperature** il a de la température *or* une forte température; **it boils at a ~ temperature** cela bout à une température élevée; **it's ~ time you went home** il est grand temps que tu rentres (*subj*); **to have a ~ old time*** s'amuser follement, faire une noce* fantastique; **to set a ~ value on sth** attacher une grande valeur à qch; **in a ~ voice** d'une voix aiguë; **a ~ wind was blowing** il soufflait un vent violent, il faisait grand vent; *V also* **4** *and* **lord, octane, stink, very** *etc*.
 2 *adv* **(a)** (*lit*) haut, en haut; *fly etc* à haute altitude, à une altitude élevée. **~ up** (en) haut; **~er up** plus haut; **~er and ~er** de plus en plus haut; **the balloon rose ~ in the air** le ballon s'est élevé *or* est monté haut dans le ciel *or* dans les airs; **the kite sailed ~ over the house** le cerf-volant est passé très haut au-dessus de la maison; **~ above our heads** bien au-dessus de nos têtes; (*lit, fig*) **to aim ~** viser haut.
 (b) (*fig*) **the numbers go as ~ as 200** les nombres montent jusqu'à 200; **I had to go as ~ as 200 francs for it** j'ai dû aller *or* monter jusqu'à 200 F pour l'avoir; **the bidding went as ~ as 400 francs** les enchères sont montées jusqu'à 400 F; **to hunt ~ and low for sb** chercher qn partout; **to hunt ~ and low for sth** chercher qch partout *or* dans tous les coins; **to hold one's head (up) ~** avoir la tête haute; *[gambler etc]* **to play ~** jouer gros (jeu); (*fig*) **to fly ~** voir grand, viser haut; **to live ~** mener grand train, mener la grande vie; **the sea is running ~** la mer est grosse *or* houleuse; **the river is running ~** la rivière est en crue; **feelings ran ~** les passions se donnaient libre cours.
 3 *n* **(a) on ~** en haut, au ciel; **from on ~** d'en haut.
 (b) (*Rel*) **the Most H~** le Très-Haut.
 (c) the cost of living reached a new ~ le coût de la vie a atteint une nouvelle pointe *or* un nouveau plafond; (*Met*) **a ~ over the North Sea** une zone de haute pression sur la mer du Nord.
 4 *cpd*: **high altar** maître-autel *m*; **high and dry** *boat* échoué; (*fig*) **to leave sb high and dry** laisser qn en plan*; **high and mighty** *monarch, dignitary* tout-puissant; **to be** *or* **act high and mighty*** se donner de grands airs, faire le grand seigneur; (*US*) **highball** whisky *m* à l'eau (avec de la glace); **highborn** de haute naissance, bien né; (*US*) **highboy** commode *f* (haute); (*slightly pej*) **highbrow** (*n*) intellectuel(le) *m(f)*; (*adj*) *tastes, interests* intellectuel; *music* pour intellectuels; **highchair** chaise haute (*pour enfants*); **High Church** Haute Église; **high-class** *hotel, food, service* de premier ordre; *house* de grand style; *neighbourhood, flat, publicity* (de) grand standing; *person* du grand monde; (*Mil*) **high command** haut commandement; (*Admin*) **high commissioner** haut commissaire; (*Jur*) **high court** cour *f* suprême; **high explosive** explosif *m* (puissant); **high-explosive shell** obus explosif; **highfalutin(g)*** affecté, prétentieux, ampoulé; **high-fidelity** haute fidélité *inv*; (*fig*) **high flier** ambitieux *m*, -euse *f*; (*gifted*) doué(e) *m(f)*; **high-flown** *style* ampoulé; *discourse* ampoulé, boursouflé; **high-flying** *aim, ambition* extravagant; *person* ambitieux; **high-frequency** de *or* à haute fréquence (*V also* **ultrahigh, very**); **High German** haut allemand; **high-grade** *goods* de haute qualité, de premier choix; **high-grade mineral** minerai *m* à haute teneur; **to rule sb with a high hand** imposer sa loi à qn; **high-handed** très autoritaire, tyrannique; **high-handedly** très autoritairement; **high-hat*** (*adj*) snob, poseur; (*vt*) faire le snob (*f* la snobinette); **high-heeled shoes** chaussures *fpl* à hauts talons; (*shoes*) **high heels*** hauts talons*; (*fig*) **to be/get up on one's high horse** être/monter sur ses grands chevaux; **highjack = hijack**; **highjacker = hijacker**; **highjacking = hijacking**; **to have high jinks*** se payer du bon temps*; **there were high jinks* last night** on s'amusait comme des fous hier soir; **highland** *V* **highland**; (*Admin, Ind, Pol etc*) **high-level** *talks, discussions* à très haut niveau; **high life** vie mondaine, grande vie; **highlight** *V* **highlight**; **he likes high living** il aime (mener) la grande vie; **High Mass** grand-messe *f*; **high-minded** *person* à l'âme noble, de caractère élevé; *ambition, wish* noble, élevé; **high-necked** à col haut; **high noon** plein midi; **high-pitched** (*Mus*) *song* (chanté) dans les aigus; *voice, sound, note* aigu (*f* -guë); (*Archit*) *roof* à forte pente; *ambitions etc* noble, haut (*before n*); **high-powered** *car* de haute puissance, très puissant; (*fig*) *person* très important; **high-powered businessman** important homme d'affaires, gros industriel; (*Tech*) **high-pressure** à haute pression; (*Met*) **high-pressure area** anticyclone *m*, zone *f* de hautes pressions (atmosphériques); (*fig*) **a high-pressure salesman** vendeur *m* de choc*; **high-priced** coûteux, cher (*f* chère); **high priest** grand prêtre; **high-principled** qui a des principes élevés; **high-ranking official** haut fonctionnaire, fonctionnaire de haut rang; **high-rise block, high-rise flats** tour *f* (d'habitation); (*esp Brit*) **highroad** grand-route *f*; **high school** (*Brit*) lycée *m*; (*US*) établissement *m* d'enseignement supérieur; **on the high seas** en haute mer; **high society** haute société; **high-sounding** sonore, grandiloquent (*pej*), ronflant (*pej*); **high-speed** ultra-rapide; **high-speed lens** objectif *m* à obturation (ultra-)rapide; **high-spirited** *person* plein d'entrain *or* de vivacité; *horse* fougueux, fringant, vif (*f* vive); **high spirits** entrain *m*, vivacité *f*, pétulance *f*; **in high spirits** plein d'entrain *or* de vivacité, tout joyeux; (*fig: climax*) **the high spot**

[evening, show] le clou, le point culminant;*[visit, holiday]* le grand moment; **to hit the high spots*** faire la foire‡ *or* la noce* (*dans un night-club, restaurant etc*); (*lit, fig*) **to play for high stakes** jouer gros (jeu); **high street** *[village]* grand-rue *f*; *[town]* rue principale; **the (little) high-street shops** le petit commerce; **high-strung** = **highly strung** (*V* **highly**); **high summer** le cœur *or* le plus chaud de l'été; **in high summer** en plein été, au cœur de l'été, au plus chaud de l'été; **high table** table *f* d'honneur; (*Scol, Univ*) table des professeurs (*au réfectoire*); (*US*) **high-tail*** se débiner‡, prendre la tangente*; (*US*) **they hightailed it* back to town** ils sont revenus à toute blinde‡ en ville; (*Brit*) **high tea** goûter *m* dînatoire; (*Elec*) **high-tension** à haute tension; **high treason** haute trahison; **high-up** (*adj*) *person, post* de haut rang, très haut placé; (*n*) grosse légume*, huile* *f*; **high-water mark** niveau *m* des hautes eaux; **highway** *V* **highway**.

higher ['haɪəʳ] *comp of* **high 1** *adj mathematics, animals, post* supérieur (*f* -eure). **any number ~ than 6** tout nombre supérieur à 6; **~ education** enseignement supérieur; (*Scol*) **the ~ forms** *or* **classes** les grandes classes. **2** *adv* plus haut; *V* **high**. **3** *cpd*: **higher-up*** supérieur(e) *m(f)*.

highland ['haɪlənd] **1** *npl*: **~s** région montagneuse, montagnes *fpl*; (*Brit Geog*) **the H~s** les Highlands *mpl*. **2** *adj* (*Brit*) **H~** *scenery, air* des Highlands; *holiday* dans les Highlands; **H~ fling** *danse écossaise*; **H~ games** jeux *mpl* écossais.

highlander ['haɪləndəʳ] *n* montagnard *m*. (*Brit*) **H~** natif *m*, -ive *f* des Highlands.

highlight ['haɪlaɪt] **1** *n* (*Art*) rehaut *m*. **to have ~s put in one's hair** se faire faire des reflets; (*fig*) **the ~ of the evening** le clou de la soirée; **the ~s of the match** les instants les plus marquants du match.

2 *vt* souligner, mettre en lumière. **his report ~ed the lack of new houses** son rapport a mis en lumière *or* a souligné le manque de maisons nouvelles.

highly ['haɪlɪ] *adv* très, fort, hautement, extrêmement; *recommend* chaudement. **~ interesting** fort *or* très intéressant; **~ coloured** (*lit*) haut en couleur; (*fig*) *description etc* exagéré, enjolivé; **~ paid** *person, job* très bien payé *or* rémunéré; *[person]* **to be ~ paid** être très bien payé *or* rémunéré, toucher un gros salaire *or* traitement; **he pays me very ~** il me paye très bien; **~ placed official** officiel *m* de haut rang, officiel haut placé, (*in administration, government circles*) haut fonctionnaire; **~ seasoned** fortement assaisonné; (*Brit*) **~ strung** nerveux, toujours tendu; **to praise sb ~** chanter (haut) les louanges de qn; **to speak/think ~ of sb/sth** dire/penser beaucoup de bien de qn/qch.

highness ['haɪnɪs] *n* **(a) His** *or* **Her/Your H~** Son/Votre Altesse *f*; *V* **royal**. **(b)** *[building etc]* hauteur *f*; *[wind]* violence *f*, force *f*; *[fever]* intensité *f*.

highway ['haɪweɪ] **1** *n* grande route, route nationale; (*also* **public ~**) voie publique. **the king's** *or* **queen's ~** la voie publique; **through the ~s and byways of Sussex** par tous les chemins du Sussex.

2 *cpd*: (*Brit*) **the highway code** le code de la route; **highwayman** voleur *m* *or* bandit *m* de grand chemin; **highway robbery** banditisme *m* de grand chemin; (*Admin*) **Highways Department** administration *f* des Ponts et Chaussées; **highways engineer** ingénieur *m* des Ponts et Chaussées.

hijack ['haɪdʒæk] **1** *vt* détourner (*par la force*). **2** *n* détournement *m*.

hijacker ['haɪdʒækəʳ] *n* *[plane]* pirate *m* (de l'air); *[coach, train]* terroriste *mf*, gangster *m*; *[truck]* gangster *m*.

hijacking ['haɪdʒækɪŋ] *n* détournement *m*.

hike [haɪk] **1** *n* **(a)** (*walk etc*) excursion *f* à pied; (*shorter*) promenade *f* (à pied); (*Mil, Sport*) marche *f* à pied. **to go on** *or* **for a ~** faire une excursion *or* une promenade *or* une randonnée à pied.

(b) (*US: increase: of prices etc*) hausse *f*, augmentation *f*.

2 *vi* **(a)** aller *or* marcher à pied. **we spent our holidays hiking in France** nous avons passé nos vacances à excursionner à pied à travers la France; **they go hiking a lot** ils font beaucoup d'excursions à pied.

(b) (*US: increase*) *[price etc]* augmenter, s'élever.

hiker ['haɪkəʳ] *n* excursionniste *mf* (à pied), marcheur *m*.

hiking ['haɪkɪŋ] *n* excursions *fpl* *or* randonnées *fpl* (à pied).

hilarious [hɪ'lɛərɪəs] *adj* (*merry*) hilare; (*funny*) désopilant, tordant*, marrant*.

hilariousness [hɪ'lɛərɪəsnɪs] *n*, **hilarity** [hɪ'lærɪtɪ] *n* hilarité *f*. **it caused a lot of ~** cela a provoqué *or* déchaîné l'hilarité.

hill [hɪl] **1** *n* colline *f*; (*gen lower*) coteau *m*; (*rounded*) mamelon *m*; (*slope*) côte *f*, pente *f*; (*up*) montée *f*; (*down*) descente *f*. **he was going up the ~** il montait la colline; **up ~ and down dale, over ~ and dale** par monts et par vaux; **as old as the ~s** immémorial, vieux (*f* vieille) comme Hérode; **this car is not good on ~s** cette voiture ne grimpe pas bien; *V* **ant, mole[1], up** *etc*.

2 *cpd*: (*US: often pej*) **hillbilly*** péquenaud* *m* (*pej*), rustaud *m* (*pej*) (*montagnard du sud des U.S.A.*); (*Mus*) **hillbilly music** musique *f* folk* *inv* (*originaire des montagnes du sud des U.S.A.*); **hillside** (flanc *m* de) coteau *m*; **on the hillside** à flanc de coteau; **on the hilltop** en haut de *or* au sommet de la colline.

hilliness ['hɪlɪnɪs] *n* caractère accidenté, vallonnement *m*.

hillock ['hɪlək] *n* petite colline, tertre *m*, butte *f*; (*rounded*) mamelon *m*.

hilly ['hɪlɪ] *adj country* vallonné, accidenté; *road* accidenté, à fortes côtes, montueux (*liter*).

hilt [hɪlt] *n* *[sword]* poignée *f*, garde *f*; *[dagger etc]* manche *m*; *[pistol]* crosse *f*. **he's in this business up to the ~** il est (plongé) dans cette affaire jusqu'au cou; **to back sb up to the ~** être derrière qn quoiqu'il arrive (*subj*), apporter son soutien inconditionnel à qn.

him [hɪm] *pers pron* **(a)** (*direct*) (*unstressed*) le; (*before vowel*) l'; (*stressed*) lui. **I see ~** je le vois; **I have seen ~** je l'ai vu; **I know** HER **but I've never seen** HIM je la connais, elle, mais lui je ne l'ai jamais vu.

(b) (*indirect*) lui. **I give ~ the book** je lui donne le livre; **I'm speaking to ~** je lui parle, c'est à lui que je parle.

(c) (*after prep etc*) lui. **I am thinking of ~** je pense à lui; **without ~** sans lui; **if I were ~** si j'étais lui; **it's ~** c'est lui; **younger than ~** plus jeune que lui.

(d) celui. **to ~ who objects I would explain it thus** à celui qui n'est pas d'accord je l'expliquerais ainsi.

Himalayas [ˌhɪmə'leɪəz] *npl* (montagnes *fpl* de l')Himalaya *m*.

himself [hɪm'self] *pers pron* (*reflexive: direct and indirect*) se; (*emphatic*) lui-même; (*after prep*) lui. **he has hurt ~** il s'est blessé; **he said to ~** il s'est dit; **he told me ~** il me l'a dit lui-même; **I saw the teacher ~** j'ai vu le professeur lui-même *or* en personne; **he kept 3 for ~** il s'en est réservé 3; **she asked him for a photo of ~** elle lui a demandé une de ses photos *or* une photo de lui; **(all) by ~** tout seul; **he is not ~ today** il n'est pas dans son état normal *or* dans son assiette* aujourd'hui.

hind[1] [haɪnd] *n* (*Zool*) biche *f*.

hind[2] [haɪnd] *adj* postérieur (*f* -eure), de derrière. **~ legs, ~ feet** pattes *fpl* de derrière; **to get up on one's ~ legs*** se lever (*pour parler*); **she could** *or* **would talk the ~ leg(s) off a donkey*** c'est un vrai moulin à paroles*.

hinder[1] ['haɪndəʳ] *adj comp of* **hind[2]**.

hinder[2] ['hɪndəʳ] *vt* (*obstruct, impede*) gêner, entraver (*sb* qn); (*oppose*) faire obstacle à (*sth* qch); (*delay*) retarder; (*prevent*) empêcher, arrêter, retenir (*sb from doing* qn de faire).

Hindi ['hɪndiː] *n* (*Ling*) hindi *m*.

hindmost ['haɪndməʊst] *adv* dernier, ultime, le plus en arrière. (*Prov*) **every man for himself and the devil take the ~** sauve qui peut.

hindquarters ['haɪndˌkwɔːtəz] *npl* arrière-train *m*, train *m* de derrière.

hindrance ['hɪndrəns] *n* gêne *f*, entrave *f*, obstacle *m*. **he is more of a ~ than a help** il gêne plus qu'il n'aide.

hindsight ['haɪndsaɪt] *n* sagesse rétrospective. **with the benefit of ~** rétrospectivement, en réfléchissant après coup.

Hindu ['hɪn'duː] **1** *adj people, customs, religion* hindou; *religion* hindouiste. **2** *n* (*all senses including Rel*) Hindou(e) *m(f)*; (*Rel only*) hindouiste *mf*.

Hinduism ['hɪnduːɪzəm] *n* hindouisme *m*.

Hindustan [ˌhɪndʊ'stɑːn] *n* Hindoustan *m*.

Hindustani [ˌhɪndʊ'stɑːnɪ] **1** *adj* hindou. **2** *n* **(a)** Hindoustani(e) *m(f)*. **(b)** (*Ling*) hindoustani *m*.

hinge [hɪndʒ] **1** *n* *[door]* gond *m*, charnière *f*; *[box]* charnière; (*fig*) pivot *m*, charnière; (*stamp ~*) charnière. **the door came off its ~s** la porte est sortie de ses gonds.

2 *vt door* mettre dans ses gonds; *box* mettre des charnières à. **~d lid** couvercle *m* à charnière(s); *[counter]* **~d flap** battant *m* relevable; (*Tech*) **~d girder** poutre articulée.

3 *vi* (*Tech*) pivoter (*on* sur); (*fig*) dépendre (*on* de). **everything ~s on his decision** tout dépend de sa décision.

hint [hɪnt] **1** *n* **(a)** allusion *f*, insinuation *f* (*pej*). **to drop** *or* **throw out** *or* **let fall a ~** faire une allusion; **to drop a ~ that ...** faire une allusion au fait que ...; **he dropped me a ~ that he would like an invitation** il m'a fait comprendre (par une allusion) qu'il aimerait être invité; **he dropped a gentle ~ about it** il y a fait une allusion discrète; **broad ~** allusion transparente *or* à peine voilée; **no need to drop ~s!** pas la peine* de faire des allusions! *or* des insinuations (*pej*)!; **he knows how to take a ~** il comprend à demi-mot, il comprend les allusions; **he took the ~ and left at once** il a compris sans qu'on ait besoin de lui expliquer et est parti sur-le-champ; **I can take a ~** (ça va) j'ai compris‡; (*in guessing etc*) **give me a ~** donne-moi une indication; **he gave no ~ of his feelings** il n'a donné aucune indication sur ce qu'il ressentait, il n'a rien laissé transparaître de ses sentiments; **~s for travellers** conseils *mpl* aux voyageurs; **~s on maintenance** conseils d'entretien.

(b) (*trace*) nuance *f*, trace *f*, soupçon *m*. **a ~ of garlic** un soupçon d'ail; **there was not the slightest ~ of a dispute** il n'y a pas eu l'ombre d'une dispute; **there was a ~ of sadness about him** il avait un je ne sais quoi de mélancolique.

2 *vt* insinuer, laisser entendre *or* comprendre. **he ~ed to me that he was unhappy** il m'a laissé entendre *or* comprendre qu'il était malheureux.

3 *vi*: **to ~ at sth** faire (une) allusion à qch; **what are you ~ing at?** qu'est-ce que vous voulez dire par là?; **are you ~ing at something?** c'est une allusion?

hinterland ['hɪntəlænd] *n* arrière-pays *m inv*.

hip[1] [hɪp] **1** *n* **(a)** (*Anat*) hanche *f*. **with one's hands on one's ~s** les mains sur les hanches.

(b) (*Archit*) arête *f* (*d'un toit*).

2 *cpd*: **hip bath** bain *m* de siège; **hipbone** os *m* iliaque *or* de la hanche; **hip flask** flacon plat (pour la poche); **hip joint** articulation *f* iliaque *or* de la hanche; **hip measurement** = **hip size**; **hip pocket** poche *f* revolver; **hip size** tour *m* de hanches; **what is her hip size?** quel est son tour de hanches?, combien fait-elle de tour de hanches?

hip[2] [hɪp] *n* (*Bot*) fruit *m* d'églantier *or* de rosier, gratte-cul *m*, cynorrhodon *m*.

hip[3] [hɪp] *excl*: **~ ~ hurrah!** hip hip hip hourra!

hip[4]‡ [hɪp] *adj* (*up-to-date*) dans le vent*, à la page; (*hippie*) hippie.

hipped‡ [hɪpt] *adj* (*US*) (*interested*) engoué, entiché (*on* de); (*annoyed*) vexé. (*Brit: depressed*) **to be ~** avoir le cafard*.

-hipped [hɪpt] *adj ending in cpds*: **broad-hipped** large de hanches.

hippie* ['hɪpɪ] *adj, n* hippie (*mf*).

hippo* [ˈhɪpəʊ] *n abbr of* **hippopotamus.**
Hippocratic [ˌhɪpəʊˈkrætɪk] *adj*: **the ~ oath** le serment d'Hippocrate.
hippodrome [ˈhɪpədrəʊm] *n* hippodrome *m.*
hippopotamus [ˌhɪpəˈpɒtəməs] *n, pl* **~es** *or* **hippopotami** [ˌhɪpəˈpɒtəmaɪ] hippopotame *m.*
hippy[1]* [ˈhɪpɪ] = **hippie*.**
hippy[2]* [ˈhɪpɪ] *adj* aux hanches larges, large de hanches.
hipster [ˈhɪpstəʳ] *n* (*Brit*) **~s** pantalon *m* taille basse; **~ skirt** jupe *f* taille basse.
hire [ˈhaɪəʳ] **1** *n* **(a)** (*U*) *[car, clothes, hall]* location *f*; *[boat, horse]* louage *m.* **for ~** à louer; (*on taxi*) 'libre'; **on ~** en location; **to let (out) sth on ~** louer qch.
(b) (*money*) *[person]* paye *f*; *[car, hall etc]* prix *m* de (la) location.
2 *cpd*: (*Brit*) **hire purchase** achat *m* à crédit; **on hire purchase** à crédit.
3 *vt thing* louer; *person* engager, embaucher (*esp Ind*). **~d man** ouvrier *m* à la saison *or* à la journée; **~d car** voiture louée *or* de louage.
hire out *vt sep car, tools* louer, donner en location. (*US*) **he hires himself out as a gardener** il fait des journées (*or* des heures) de jardinier.
hireling [ˈhaɪəlɪŋ] *n* (*pej*) larbin *m* (*pej*), laquais *m* (*pej*).
hirsute [ˈhɜːsjuːt] *adj* hirsute, velu, poilu.
his [hɪz] **1** *poss adj* son, sa, ses. **~ book** son livre; **~ table** sa table; **~ friend** son ami(e); **~ clothes** ses vêtements.
2 *poss pron* le sien, la sienne, les siens, les siennes. **my hands are clean, ~ are dirty** mes mains sont propres, les siennes sont sales; **~ is a specialized department** sa section est une section spécialisée; **this book is ~** ce livre est à lui, ce livre est le sien; **the house became ~** la maison est devenue la sienne; **it is not ~ to decide** ce n'est pas à lui de décider, il ne lui appartient pas de décider; **a friend of ~** un de ses amis (à lui); **it's no fault of ~** ce n'est pas de sa faute (à lui); **no advice of ~ could prevent her** aucun conseil de sa part ne pouvait l'empêcher; (*pej*) **that car of ~** sa fichue* voiture; **that stupid son of ~** son idiot de fils; **that temper of ~** son sale caractère.
Hispanic [hɪsˈpænɪk] *adj* hispanique.
hiss [hɪs] **1** *vi [person, snake]* siffler; *[gas, steam]* chuinter, siffler. **2** *vt actor, speaker* siffler. **'come here,' he ~ed** 'viens ici,' siffla-t-il. **3** *n* sifflement *m.* (*Theat etc*) **~es** sifflet(s) *m(pl).*
historian [hɪsˈtɔːrɪən] *n* historien(ne) *m(f).*
historic [hɪsˈtɒrɪk] *adj* (*gen*) historique; (*important*) historique, qui fait date.
historical [hɪsˈtɒrɪkəl] *adj novel, fact* historique. **~ linguistics** linguistique *f* diachronique.
historiography [ˌhɪstɒrɪˈɒgrəfɪ] *n* historiographie *f.*
history [ˈhɪstərɪ] *n* **(a)** (*U*) histoire *f.* **to make ~** être historique; **he will go down in ~ for what he did** il entrera dans l'histoire pour ce qu'il a fait; (*fig*) *[event, day, decision]* **it will go down in ~** ce sera historique; **that's ancient ~** c'est de l'histoire ancienne (*fig*); *V* **natural.**
(b) I don't know the ~ of this necklace je ne connais pas l'histoire de ce collier; **the patient has a ~ of psychiatric disorders** le patient a dans son passé (médical) des désordres psychiatriques; **what is his medical ~?** quel est son passé médical?; *V* **case**[1]**.**
histrionic [ˌhɪstrɪˈɒnɪk] *adj* théâtral; (*pej*) histrionique, de cabotin* (*pej*). **~ ability** talent *m* dramatique.
histrionics [ˌhɪstrɪˈɒnɪks] *npl* art *m* dramatique. (*pej*) **to indulge in ~** prendre des airs dramatiques, cabotiner* (*pej*); (*pej*) **I'm tired of his ~** j'en ai assez de ses airs dramatiques *or* de son cinéma* (*fig*).
hit [hɪt] (*vb: pret, ptp* **hit**) **1** *n* **(a)** (*stroke, blow*) coup *m*; (*Baseball, Cricket etc*) coup de batte *etc*; (*Tennis*) coup de raquette. (*fig*) **that's a ~ at me** ça c'est pour moi, c'est une pierre dans mon jardin; **he made a ~ at the government** il a attaqué le gouvernement; *V* **free.**
(b) (*successful stroke etc*) coup réussi, beau coup; (*Archery*) coup dans le mille; (*with bullet, shell etc*) tir réussi; (*Fencing*) touche *f*; (*good guess*) coup dans le mille (*fig*). (*gen*) **3 ~s and 3 misses** 3 succès et 3 échecs; **direct ~** coup (en plein) dans le mille; *V* **score.**
(c) (*success*) coup réussi, beau coup; (*Theat*) (gros) succès *m*; (*song*) chanson *f* à succès, tube**:** *m.* **to make a ~ of sth*** réussir (pleinement) qch; **to make a ~ with sb*** faire une grosse impression sur qn; **he made a great ~ with her*** il a eu un gros succès avec elle, il lui a tapé dans l'œil**:**; **the play/song was a big ~** la pièce/chanson a eu un énorme succès.
2 *cpd*: **hit-and-run driver** chauffard* *m* (coupable du délit de fuite); (*Mil*) **hit-and-run raid** raid *m* éclair *inv*; **hit or miss** (*adv*) au petit bonheur (la chance), un peu n'importe comment; **hit-or-miss** (*adj*) *work* fait au petit bonheur (la chance); *attitude* désinvolte; **the way she painted the room was rather hit-or-miss** elle a peint la pièce un peu n'importe comment; **it was all rather hit-or-miss** tout se passait plutôt au petit bonheur (la chance), tout était à la va-comme-je-te-pousse; **hit parade** hit parade *m*; (*Theat*) **hit show** revue *f* à succès; **hit song** chanson *f* à succès, tube**:** *m.*
3 *vt* **(a)** (*strike*) frapper, taper sur; (*knock against*) heurter, cogner; (*reach*) atteindre; (*Billiards, Fencing*) toucher; (*fig: hurt, annoy*) affecter, blesser, piquer. **he ~ his brother** il a frappé son frère; **he ~ me!** il m'a frappé!, il m'a tapé dessus!; **his father used to ~ him** son père le battait; **to ~ sb a blow** porter *or* donner *or* envoyer *or* flanquer* un coup à qn; (*fig*) **to ~ a man when he's down** frapper un homme à terre; **to ~ one's head/arm against sth** se cogner *or* se heurter la tête/le bras contre qch; **his head ~ the pavement, he ~ his head on the pavement** sa tête a donné contre *or* porté contre *or* heurté le trottoir; **the stone ~ the window** la pierre atteignit la fenêtre; **he was ~ by a stone** il fut atteint par une pierre, il reçut une pierre; (*fig*) **it ~s you in the eye** cela (vous) saute aux yeux; **he ~ the nail with a hammer** il a tapé sur le clou avec un marteau; (*fig*) **to ~ the nail on the head** mettre dans le mille, faire mouche; (*fig*) **to ~ the mark** atteindre le *or* son but; (*fig*) **that ~ home!** le coup a porté!; (*Shooting etc*) **you couldn't ~ an elephant!** tu raterais (même) un éléphant!; **the president was ~ by 3 bullets** le président reçut 3 balles; **the house was ~ by a bomb** la maison fut atteinte par *or* reçut une bombe; **my plane had been ~** mon avion avait été touché; (*fig*) **he was hard ~ by his losses** ses pertes l'ont durement touché *or* atteint; (*fig*) **the crops were ~ by the rain** la pluie a causé des dégâts aux récoltes; (*fig*) **production was ~ by the strike** la production a été atteinte *or* touchée par la grève; **the public was hardest ~ by the strike** c'est le public qui a été le plus atteint par la grève; **the rise in prices will ~ the poorest families first** la hausse des prix affectera *or* touchera d'abord les familles les plus pauvres.
(b) (*fig*) *[news, story]* **to ~ the papers** être à la une* des journaux, faire les gros titres des journaux; **what will happen when the story ~s the front page?** que se passera-t-il quand on lira cette histoire en première page des journaux?; (*realization*) **then it ~ me*** alors j'ai réalisé* d'un seul coup! *or* brusquement!; **you've ~ it!*** ça y est* tu as trouvé!; **~ it!**: fiche le camp!*; **to ~ the bottle**: (se mettre à) picoler*; (*fig*) **to ~ the ceiling*** sortir de ses gonds; (*fig*) **to ~ the hay**: se pieuter**:**; **to ~ the road*** *or* **the trail*** se mettre en route, mettre les voiles*; **this car can ~* 160 km/h** cette voiture fait du 160 (km) à l'heure; **the troops ~ the beach at dawn*** les troupes ont débarqué sur la plage à l'aube; **when will Jim ~ town?*** quand est-ce que Jim va débarquer en ville?; (*US fig*) **it ~s the spot** c'est justement ce qu'il me faut!, ça me redonne le moral!; *V* **headline, high.**
(c) (*collide with*) entrer en collision avec, heurter, rentrer dans*.
(d) (*find*) trouver, tomber sur; *problems, difficulties* rencontrer. **at last we ~ the right road** nous sommes tombés enfin sur la bonne route.
4 *vi* (*collide*) se heurter, se cogner (*against* à, contre).
hit back **1** *vi* (*fig*) riposter. **to hit back at sb** riposter, répondre à qn.
2 *vt sep*: **to hit sb back** rendre son coup à qn.
hit off *vt sep* **(a) to hit off a likeness** saisir une ressemblance; **he hit him off beautifully** il l'a imité à la perfection.
(b) (*) **to hit it off with sb** s'entendre bien avec qn; **they hit it off well together** ils s'entendent très bien *or* comme larrons en foire; **they just don't hit it off** ils n'arrivent pas à s'entendre, entre eux ça n'accroche pas*.
hit out at *vt fus* (*lit*) envoyer un coup à; (*fig*) attaquer, lancer une attaque contre.
hit (up)on *vt fus* tomber sur, trouver.
hitch [hɪtʃ] **1** *n* **(a) to give sth a ~ (up)** remonter qch (d'une saccade).
(b) (*any knot*) nœud *m*; (*specific knot*) deux demi-clefs *fpl.*
(c) (*fig: obstacle*) anicroche *f*, contretemps *m*, os* *m.* **without a ~** sans accroc *or* anicroche; **there's been a ~** il y a eu une anicroche *or* un os*; **there was some ~ in their plans** il y a eu une anicroche *or* un contretemps quelconque dans leurs projets; *V* **technical.**
2 *cpd*: **hitch-hike** faire du stop* *or* de l'auto-stop; **they hitch-hiked to Paris** ils sont allés à Paris en stop, ils ont fait du stop* *or* de l'auto-stop jusqu'à Paris; **hitch-hiker** auto-stoppeur *m*, -euse *f*, stoppeur* *m*, -euse* *f*; **hitch-hiking** auto-stop *m*, stop* *m.*
3 *vt* **(a)** (*also* **~ up**) remonter (d'une saccade).
(b) (*fasten*) accrocher, attacher, fixer; (*Naut*) amarrer. **to get ~ed**: se marier.
(c) (*) **to ~ a lift** *or* **a ride to Paris** faire du stop* jusqu'à Paris; **I ~ed a lift to Paris with my father** je me suis fait emmener en voiture jusqu'à Paris par mon père.
4 *vi* (*) = **~-hike**; *V* **2.**
hitch up *vt sep* **(a)** *horses, oxen* atteler (*to* à).
(b) *trousers* remonter (d'une saccade).
hither [ˈhɪðəʳ] **1** *adv* (††) ici. (*not* ††) **~ and thither** çà et là; (†† *or hum*) **come ~** venez çà (†† *or hum*); *V also* **come.** **2** *adj* (††) de ce côté-ci. **3** *cpd*: **hitherto** jusqu'ici.
hive [haɪv] **1** *n* (*place, also fig*) ruche *f*; (*bees in it*) essaim *m.* (*fig*) **a ~ of industry** une vraie ruche. **2** *vt* mettre dans une ruche. **3** *vi* entrer à la ruche.
hive off (*Brit*) **1** *vi* **(a)** (*: *separate*) se séparer (*from* de).
(b) (**:** *rush off*) filer*, se tirer**:**.
2 *vt sep* séparer (*from* de). **they hived off the infant school to a different building** ils ont décentralisé la maternelle pour l'installer dans un autre bâtiment.
hives [haɪvz] *npl* (*Med*) urticaire *f.*
hiya: [ˈhaɪjə] *excl* salut!*
hoard [hɔːd] **1** *n* réserve(s) *f(pl)*, provision *f*, stock *m* (*pej*); (*treasure*) trésor *m*; *[money]* trésor, magot *m.* **a ~ of food** des provisions, des réserves; **a squirrel's ~ of nuts** les réserves *or* provisions de noisettes d'un écureuil; **I've a ~ of** *or* **~s of things to tell you*** j'ai un tas* *or* une masse* de choses à te dire.
2 *vt* (*also* **~ up**) *food etc* amasser, mettre en réserve, stocker (*pej*); *money* accumuler, amasser.
hoarding[1] [ˈhɔːdɪŋ] *n* entassement *m*, accumulation *f*; *[capital]* thésaurisation *f.*
hoarding[2] [ˈhɔːdɪŋ] *n* (*Brit*) (*fence*) palissade *f*; (*for advertisements*) panneau *m* d'affichage *or* publicitaire.
hoarfrost [ˈhɔːˈfrɒst] *n* gelée blanche, givre *m.*
hoarse [hɔːs] *adj person* enroué; *voice* rauque, enroué. **to be ~** avoir la voix prise *or* enrouée *or* rauque, être enroué; **he**

shouted himself ~ il a tant crié qu'il a fini par s'enrouer.

hoarsely ['hɔːslɪ] *adv* d'une voix rauque *or* enrouée.

hoarseness ['hɔːsnɪs] *n* enrouement *m*.

hoary ['hɔːrɪ] *adj hair* blanchi, blanc neigeux *inv*; *person* (*lit: also* ~**-headed**) chenu; (*fig*) vénérable; (*Bot*) couvert de duvet blanc. **a** ~ **old joke** une blague éculée.

hoax [həʊks] **1** *n* canular *m*. **to play a** ~ **on sb** monter *or* faire un canular à qn. **2** *vt* faire *or* monter un canular à. **we were completely** ~**ed** on nous a eus*.

hob [hɒb] *n* (*by fireplace*) plaque *f* (de foyer) (*où la bouilloire etc est tenue au chaud*); (*on old-fashioned cooker*) rond *m*; (*on modern cooker*) plaque (chauffante).

hobble ['hɒbl] **1** *vi* clopiner, boitiller. **to** ~ **along** aller clopin-clopant; **to** ~ **in/out** *etc* entrer/sortir *etc* en clopinant. **2** *vt horse* entraver. **3** *n* (*for horses*) entrave *f*. **4** *cpd*: **hobble skirt** jupe entravée.

hobbledehoy ['hɒbldɪ'hɔɪ] *n* grand dadais *or* niais.

hobby ['hɒbɪ] **1** *n* passe-temps *inv* favori, hobby *m*. **his** ~ **is sailing** son passe-temps favori *or* son hobby (c')est la voile; **he began to paint as a** ~ il a commencé la peinture à titre de passe-temps; **he's got several hobbies** il a plusieurs passe-temps.

2 *cpd*: **hobby-horse** (*toy*) tête *f* de cheval (*sur un manche*); (*rocking horse*) cheval *m* à bascule; (*fig*) **he's off on his hobby-horse** le voilà reparti (sur son dada).

hobgoblin ['hɒbˌgɒblɪn] *n* (*elf*) lutin *m*; (*fig: bugbear*) croque-mitaine *m*.

hobnail ['hɒbneɪl] *n* caboche *f*, clou *m*. ~**(ed) boots** souliers à clous *or* cloutés *or* ferrés.

hobnob ['hɒbnɒb] *vi*: **to** ~ **with** frayer avec.

hobo ['həʊbəʊ] *n* (*US*) **(a)** (*tramp*) (*in town*) clochard *m*, vagabond *m*; (*in country*) chemineau *m*, vagabond. **(b)** (*migratory worker*) saisonnier *m*.

hock[1] [hɒk] *n* [*animal*] jarret *m*; [*human*] partie postérieure du genou; (*Culin*) jarret (de bœuf).

hock[2] [hɒk] *n* (*wine*) vin *m* du Rhin.

hock[3]**‡** [hɒk] **1** *vt* (*pawn*) mettre au clou‡. **2** *n*: **in** ~ au clou‡, au mont-de-piété.

hockey ['hɒkɪ] **1** *n* hockey *m*; *V* **ice**. **2** *cpd match, pitch* de hockey. **hockey player** hockeyeur *m*, -euse *f*; (*Can*) joueur *m*, -euse *f* de hockey; **hockey stick** crosse *f* de hockey; (*Can*) hockey *m*.

hocus-pocus ['həʊkəs'pəʊkəs] *n* (*trickery*) supercherie *f*, attrape *f*; (*conjuring trick*) tour *m* de passe-passe; (*talk*) charabia* *m*, galimatias *m*.

hod [hɒd] *n* (*for coal*) seau *m* à charbon; (*for bricks, mortar*) oiseau *m*, hotte *f*.

hodgepodge ['hɒdʒpɒdʒ] *n* = **hotchpotch.**

hoe [həʊ] **1** *n* houe *f*, binette *f*. **2** *vt* biner, sarcler. **3** *cpd*: (*US*) **hoedown** danse *f* (de village).

hog [hɒg] **1** *n* (*Zool*) sanglier *m* d'Europe; (*US*) porc *m*; (*castrated*) verrat châtré. **he's a greedy** ~ c'est un vrai goinfre, il se goinfre* comme un pourceau; *V* **road, whole.**

2 *vt* **(a)** (*) *food* se goinfrer* de; (*take selfishly*) accaparer, monopoliser. **don't** ~ **all the sweets** ne garde pas tous les bonbons pour toi; **he was** ~**ging the only armchair** il accaparait *or* monopolisait le seul fauteuil; **to** ~ **the credit** s'attribuer tout le mérite.

(b) they were ~**ging it‡ in a dirty little room** ils vivaient dans un petit galetas qui était comme une porcherie.

3 *cpd*: **hogshead** barrique *f*; (*US*) **hogtie** lier par les pieds et les poings; (*fig*) entraver; **hogwash** (*pigswill*) eaux grasses (*pour nourrir les porcs*); (‡: *nonsense*) foutaises‡ *fpl*.

Hogmanay ['hɒgməneɪ] *n* (*Scot*) la Saint-Sylvestre, le réveillon du jour de l'an.

hoi polloi [ˌhɔɪpə'lɔɪ] *n* (*pej*) **the** ~ les gens *mpl* du commun, le commun (*pej*), la plèbe (*pej*).

hoist [hɔɪst] **1** *vt* hisser, remonter; *sails, flag* hisser. (*fig*) ~ **with his own petard** pris à son propre piège.

2 *n* **(a)** (*equipment*) appareil *m* de levage, palan *m*; (*winch*) treuil *m*; (*crane*) grue *f*; (*for goods*) monte-charge *m inv*; (*made of rope*) corde *f*, palan.

(b) to give sth a ~ **(up)** hisser *or* remonter qch.

hoity-toity ['hɔɪtɪ'tɔɪtɪ] **1** *adj* (*arrogant*) prétentieux, qui se donne de grands airs, bêcheur* (*f* -euse); (*touchy*) susceptible. **2** *excl* (†) taratata!†.

hokum‡ ['həʊkəm] *n* (*US*) (*nonsense*) foutaises‡ *fpl*; (*sentimentality*) blablabla* sentimental, niaiseries *fpl*.

hold [həʊld] (*vb: pret, ptp* **held**) **1** *n* **(a)** (*U*) prise *f*, étreinte *f*; (*fig*) empire *m*, influence *f* (*over sb* sur qn). **to catch** *or* **lay** *or* **seize** ~ **of, to get** *or* **take (a)** ~ **of** saisir, se saisir de, s'emparer de; **catch** ~**!, take** ~**!** tiens!, attrape!; **he got** *or* **caught** ~ **of her arm** il lui a saisi le bras; (*fig*) **we're trying to get** ~ **of him** nous essayons de le contacter *or* joindre; **can you get** ~ **of a piece of wire?** est-ce que tu peux trouver *or* dénicher* un morceau de fil de fer?; **where did you get** ~ **of that hat?** où as-tu été trouver *or* dénicher* ce chapeau?; **where did you get** ~ **of that idea?** où as-tu été pêcher* cette idée?; (*fig*) **to get (a)** ~ **of o.s.** se maîtriser, se contrôler; **get (a)** ~ **of yourself!** ressaisis-toi!, ne te laisse pas aller!; **to have** ~ **of** tenir; **I've got a good** *or* **firm** ~ **on the rope** je tiens bien *or* bon la corde; **to keep** ~ **of** tenir fermement, ne pas lâcher; **keep** ~ **of the idea that ...** dites-vous bien que ...; (*fig*) **to have a** ~ **over sb** avoir barre *or* avoir prise sur qn; **I don't know what kind of a** ~ **he has over them but they all obey him** je ne sais pas quel pouvoir *or* quelle prise il a sur eux mais ils lui obéissent.

(b) prise *f*. **the rock offered him few** ~**s** le rocher lui offrait peu de prises; *V* **foot, hand** *etc*.

(c) (*Wrestling*) prise *f*. (*fig*) **no** ~**s barred*** tous les coups sont permis.

(d) (*Naut*) cale *f*.

2 *cpd*: (*esp Brit*) **holdall** fourre-tout *m inv*; **holdup** (*robbery*) hold-up *m inv*, attaque *f* à main armée; (*delay*) retard *m*; (*in traffic*) embouteillage *m*, bouchon *m*; **there's been a holdup in ...** il y a eu un retard dans ...; **a big holdup owing to roadworks** un gros bouchon dû aux travaux.

3 *vt* **(a)** (*grasp, carry*) tenir. **she was** ~**ing a book in her hand** elle tenait un livre à la main; **she was** ~**ing a coin in her hand** elle tenait une pièce de monnaie dans la main; ~ **this for a moment** tiens *or* prends ça un moment; (*lit, fig*) **she was** ~**ing her sister's hand** elle tenait la main de sa sœur; **they were** ~**ing hands** ils se tenaient par la main, ils s'étaient donné la main; **he held my arm** il me tenait le bras; **to** ~ **one's sides with laughter** se tenir les côtes de rire; **the dog held the stick in his mouth** le chien tenait le bâton dans sa gueule; **she held him tight for a moment** elle l'a serré très fort pendant un instant; ~ **him tight or he'll fall** tenez-le bien (pour) qu'il ne tombe (*subj*) pas; **to** ~ **fast** tenir bien *or* bon *or* solidement; **the ladder won't** ~ **you** *or* **your weight** l'échelle ne supportera pas ton poids; **the nails** ~ **the carpet in place** les clous maintiennent la moquette en place; **he** ~**s the key to the mystery** il détient la clef du mystère; **to** ~ **o.s. upright** se tenir droit; (*lit, fig*) **to** ~ **one's head high** porter la tête haute.

(b) (*fig*) **to** ~ **o.s. ready** se tenir prêt; **he held us all spellbound** il nous tenait tous sous son charme; **can he** ~ **an audience?** est-ce qu'il sait tenir un auditoire?; **to** ~ **sb's attention/interest** retenir l'attention/l'intérêt de qn; **he was left** ~**ing the baby** tout est retombé sur sa tête; **to** ~ **one's breath** retenir son souffle; **he can't** ~ **a candle to his brother** il n'arrive pas à la cheville de son frère; (*Naut*) **to** ~ **course** tenir le cap, continuer à faire route (*for* vers); **to** ~ **one's ground** *or* **one's own** tenir bon, tenir ferme; (*Telec*) ~ **the line!** ne quittez pas!; (*Telec*) **I've been** ~**ing the line for several minutes** cela fait plusieurs minutes que je suis en ligne *or* que j'attends; **to** ~ **in mind** garder en mémoire; (*Mus*) **to** ~ **a note** tenir une note; **to** ~ **an opinion** avoir une opinion; **the invalid is** ~**ing his own** le malade se maintient; **he can** ~ **his own with anybody** il ne s'en laisse pas remontrer; **he can** ~ **his own in German** il se débrouille très bien en allemand; **this car** ~**s the road well** cette voiture tient bien la route; **he held his tongue about it** il a tenu sa langue; ~ **your tongue!** taisez-vous!

(c) *meeting, election, session, debate, conversation etc* tenir; (*Scol*) *examination* organiser. **the exhibition is always held here** l'exposition se tient toujours *or* a toujours lieu ici; **to** ~ **a check** faire un contrôle; (*Rel*) **to** ~ **a service** célébrer un office; [*employer*] **to** ~ **an interview** recevoir des candidats.

(d) (*contain*) contenir. **this box will** ~ **all my books** cette boîte contiendra tous mes livres; **this bottle** ~**s one litre** cette bouteille contient un litre; **this room** ~**s 20 people** 20 personnes peuvent tenir dans cette salle; *V* **water** *etc*.

(e) (*believe, maintain*) tenir, maintenir, considérer, estimer, juger. **he** ~**s that matter does not exist** il maintient *or* considère que la matière n'existe pas; **to** ~ **sth to be true** considérer qch comme vrai; **this is held to be true** ceci passe pour vrai; **to** ~ **in high esteem** tenir en haute estime; (*Jur*) **it was held by the judge that** le juge a statué que; **to** ~ **sb responsible for sth** tenir qn pour *or* considérer qn responsable de qch; **to** ~ **sb guilty** considérer qn coupable; **to** ~ **sb dear** aimer beaucoup qn; **all that he** ~**s dear** tout ce qui lui est cher.

(f) (*keep back, restrain*) *person* tenir, retenir. **I will** ~ **the money until ...** je garderai l'argent jusqu'à ce que ... + *subj*; **to** ~ **a train** empêcher un train de partir; ~ **the letter until ...** n'envoyez pas la lettre avant que ... + *subj*; **the police held him for 2 days** la police l'a gardé (à vue) pendant 2 jours; **there's no** ~**ing him** il n'y a pas moyen de le (re)tenir; (*fig*) ~ **your horses!*** arrêtez!, minute!*; ~ **it!*** (*stay still*) restez là!, ne bougez plus!; (*stop: also* ~ **everything!***) arrêtez!, ne faites plus rien!

(g) (*possess*) avoir, posséder; (*Mil*) tenir; *post, position* avoir, occuper; (*Fin*) *shares* détenir; (*Sport*) *record* détenir; (*Rel*) *living* jouir de. (*Parl*) **to** ~ **office** avoir *or* tenir un portefeuille; **he** ~**s the post of headmaster** il occupe le poste de directeur; **he** ~**s the record for the long jump** il détient le record du saut en longueur; **Spain held vast territories in South America** l'Espagne possédait de vastes territoires en Amérique du Sud; **the army held the castle against the enemy** l'armée a tenu le château fort malgré les attaques de l'ennemi; (*fig*) **to** ~ **the fort** garder la maison, monter la garde (*hum*), assurer la continuité; (*fig*) **to** ~ **the stage** tenir le devant de la scène.

4 *vi* [*rope, nail etc*] tenir (bon), être solide; [*weather*] continuer, se maintenir; [*statement, argument*] (*also* ~ **good**) valoir. **that objection does not** ~ **(good)** cette objection n'est pas valable; **his promise still** ~**s (good)** sa promesse tient *or* vaut toujours; **to** ~ **firm** *or* **tight** *or* **fast** tenir bon *or* ferme; ~ **hard!** arrêtez!, minute!*

hold back 1 *vi* (*lit*) rester en arrière; (*fig*) se retenir (*from sth* de qch, *from doing* de faire).

2 *vt sep fears, emotions* retenir, maîtriser. **the police held back the crowd** la police a contenu la foule; **to hold sb back from doing** retenir qn de faire; **they held back the names of the victims** on n'a pas donné le nom des victimes; **he was holding something back from me** il me cachait quelque chose.

hold down *vt sep* **(a)** (*keep on ground*) *rug etc* maintenir à terre; *person* maintenir au sol, forcer à rester par terre; (*keep in place*) maintenir en place. **to hold one's head down** avoir *or* tenir la tête baissée; **we couldn't hold him down** nous ne pouvions arriver à le maintenir au sol.

(b) (*have*) *job* avoir, occuper; (*keep*) garder. **he's holding down a good job** il occupe *or* a une belle situation; **he can't hold down a job** il ne garde jamais longtemps une situation.

hold forth 1 *vi* pérorer, faire des discours (*on* sur).
2 *vt sep* (*frm*) tendre.
hold in *vt sep* retenir. **hold your stomach in!** rentre ton ventre!; **to hold in one's temper, to hold o.s. in** se contenir, se retenir; **he managed to hold in his horse** il réussit à maîtriser *or* retenir son cheval.
hold off 1 *vi* (*fig*) **the rain has held off so far** jusqu'ici il n'a pas plu.
2 *vt sep* tenir éloigné *or* à distance. **they held off the enemy** ils tenaient l'ennemi à distance; (*fig*) **I can't hold him off any longer, you'll have to see him** je ne peux pas le faire attendre plus longtemps, il faut que vous le voyiez (*subj*); **try to hold him off a little longer** essayez de le faire patienter encore un peu.
hold on 1 *vi* (*endure*) tenir bon, tenir le coup; (*wait*) attendre. **hold on!** attendez!; (*Telec*) ne quittez pas!; (*Telec*) **I've been holding on for several minutes** j'attends depuis plusieurs minutes.
2 *vt sep* maintenir (à sa place), tenir en place. **this screw holds the lid on** cette vis maintient le couvercle (en place).
hold on to *vt fus* **(a)** (*cling to*) *rope, raft, branch* tenir bien, tenir bon à, se cramponner à, s'accrocher à; (*fig*) *hope, idea* se raccrocher à.
(b) (*keep*) conserver. **hold on to this for me** tiens-moi ça.
hold out 1 *vi* **(a)** *[supplies etc]* durer. **how long will the food hold out?** combien de temps est-ce que les provisions vont durer?
(b) (*endure, resist*) tenir bon, tenir le coup. **to hold out against** *enemy, attacks* tenir bon devant; *change, improvements, progress, threats, fatigue* résister à; **they are holding out for more pay** ils tiennent bon pour avoir une augmentation.
2 *vt sep* **(a)** tendre, présenter, offrir (*sth to sb* qch à qn). **to hold out one's arms** ouvrir *or* étendre les bras.
(b) (*fig*) offrir. **his case holds out little hope of recovery** son cas offre peu d'espoir de guérison; **the doctor holds out little hope for him** le médecin laisse peu d'espoir pour lui.
hold out on* *vt fus* (*fig*) **you've been holding out on me!** tu m'as caché quelque chose!
hold over *vt sep* remettre. **the meeting was held over until Friday** la séance fut reportée *or* remise à vendredi.
hold to *vt fus* s'en tenir à, rester attaché à. **I hold to what I said** je m'en tiens à ce que j'ai dit; **he held to his religious beliefs** il restait attaché à ses croyances religieuses.
hold together 1 *vi [objects]* tenir (ensemble); *[groups, people]* rester unis. **this door hardly holds together any more** cette porte ne tient plus beaucoup; **we must hold together** il faut se serrer les coudes *or* rester unis.
2 *vt sep objects* maintenir (ensemble); (*fig*) *dissenting factions* assurer l'union de. (*Pol*) **this held the party together** ceci a maintenu l'union du parti.
hold up 1 *vi*: **that building won't hold up much longer** ce bâtiment ne tiendra plus longtemps debout.
2 *vt sep* **(a)** (*raise*) lever, élever. **hold up your hand** levez la main; (*fig*) **I shall never hold up my head again** je ne pourrai plus jamais regarder personne en face; **to hold sth up to the light** élever qch à la lumière; (*fig*) **to hold sb up to ridicule** tourner qn en ridicule.
(b) (*support*) soutenir. **this pillar holds the roof up** cette colonne soutient le toit.
(c) (*stop*) arrêter; (*delay*) retarder. **the traffic was held up by the accident** la circulation fut retardée par l'accident; **I'm sorry, I was held up** excusez-moi, j'ai été mis en retard *or* retenu.
(d) *[robber] bank, shop* faire un hold-up dans; *coach, person* attaquer (à main armée).
3 **holdup** *n V* **hold 2**.
hold with* *vt fus* approuver, être pour. **she doesn't hold with people smoking** elle est contre les gens qui fument, elle désapprouve que l'on fume (*subj*).
holder [ˈhəʊldəʳ] *n* **(a)** *[ticket, card]* détenteur *m*, -trice *f*; *[passport, office, post, title]* titulaire *mf*; *[stocks]* porteur *m*, -euse *f*, détenteur *m*, -trice *f*; *[farm]* exploitant *m*; (*Sport*) *[record]* détenteur, -trice; *[title]* détenteur, -trice, tenant(e) *m(f)*.
(b) (*object*) support *m*. **pen~** porte-plume *m inv*; *V* **cigarette** *etc*.
holding [ˈhəʊldɪŋ] 1 *n* **(a)** (*act*) tenue *f*; (*Tech*) fixation *f*.
(b) (*possession*) *[lands]* possession *f*, jouissance *f*; *[stocks]* possession. (*Fin*) ~s (*lands*) avoirs fonciers; (*stocks*) intérêts *mpl*.
(c) (*farm*) propriété *f*, ferme *f*.
2 *adj* (*Fin*) ~ **company** holding *m*.
hole [həʊl] 1 *n* **(a)** (*in ground, road, wall, belt, strap etc; for mouse; also Golf*) trou *m*; (*in defences, dam*) brèche *f*; *[rabbit, fox]* terrier *m*. **these socks are in ~s** *or* **full of ~s** ces chaussettes sont toutes trouées *or* pleines de trous; **these socks got ~s in them** *or* **went into ~s** *or* **wore into ~s very quickly** ces chaussettes se sont trouées très vite; **through a ~ in the clouds** par une trouée dans les nuages; (*fig*) **it made a ~ in his savings** cela a fait un trou dans ses économies; **there are ~s in his argument** il y a des failles *fpl* *or* des faiblesses *fpl* dans son argumentation; **he's talking through a ~ in his head‡** il dit des idioties, il débloque‡; **I need it like a ~ in the head!‡** il ne manquait plus que ça!; *V* **knock, pick** *etc*.
(b) (*: *trouble*) **to be in a (nasty)** ~ avoir des ennuis, être dans l'embarras; **he got me out of a ~** il m'a tiré d'embarras *or* d'un mauvais pas.
(c) (**pej*) (*town*) trou *m* (paumé)‡; (*room, house*) bouge *m*.
2 *cpd*: (*pej*) **hole-and-corner** (*secret*) clandestin, secret (*f* -ète); (*furtive*) furtif; (*underhand*) fait en douce*; (*Golf*) **to get a hole in one** faire un trou en un; (*Med*) **hole-in-the-heart** communication *f* interventriculaire.
3 *vt socks etc* faire un trou dans, trouer. (*Golf*) **to ~ one's ball in 3** faire un *or* le trou en 3; **he holed the 5th in 3** il a fait 3 sur le 5.
4 *vi* **(a)** *[socks etc]* se trouer.
(b) (*Golf: also ~ out*) terminer le trou; (*Billiards*) bloquer. (*Golf*) **to ~ in one** faire un trou en un.
hole up *vi [animal]* se terrer; *[wanted man etc]* se terrer, se cacher.
holey [ˈhəʊlɪ] *adj* plein de trous, (tout) troué.
holiday [ˈhɒlədɪ] 1 *n* (*vacation*) vacances *fpl*; (*day off*) (jour *m* de) congé *m*. **to take a ~** prendre des vacances *or* un congé; **on ~** en vacances, en congé; **to take a month's ~** prendre un mois de vacances; **~s with pay** congés payés; **school ~(s)** vacances scolaires; **Christmas ~(s)** vacances de Noël; *V* **bank**[2].
2 *vi* (*esp Brit*) passer les vacances. **they were ~ing at home** ils prenaient leurs vacances à la maison.
3 *cpd mood etc* gai, joyeux. (*Brit*) **holiday camp** *[families]* camp *m* de vacances; *[children only]* colonie *f or* camp de vacances; **holiday clothes** tenue *f* de vacances; **holiday feeling** atmosphère *f or* ambiance *f* de vacances; (*Brit*) **holiday-maker** vacancier *m*, -ière *f*; (*in summer*) estivant(e) *m(f)*; **holiday pay** salaire dû pendant les vacances; **holiday resort** villégiature *f*, lieu *m* de vacances; **holiday season** saison *f* des vacances; **holiday spirit** esprit *m* de vacances; **holiday traffic** circulation *f* des départs (*or* des rentrées) de vacances, rush *m* des vacances.
holiness [ˈhəʊlɪnɪs] *n* sainteté *f*. **His H~** Sa Sainteté.
holism [ˈhəʊlɪzəm] *n* holisme *m*.
holistic [həʊˈlɪstɪk] *adj* holistique.
Holland [ˈhɒlənd] *n* **(a)** Hollande *f*, Pays-Bas *mpl*. **(b)** (*Tex*) **h~** toile *f* de Hollande.
holler* [ˈhɒləʳ] 1 *n* braillement *m*. 2 *vti* (*also ~ out*) brailler.
hollow [ˈhɒləʊ] 1 *adj tooth, tree, cheeks* creux; *eyes* cave; *sound* creux, caverneux; *voice* caverneux; (*fig*) *sympathy, friendship, victory* faux (*f* fausse); *promise* vain, trompeur. (*hungry*) **to feel ~*** avoir le ventre *or* l'estomac creux; **to give a ~ laugh** rire jaune.
2 *cpd*: **hollow-cheeked** aux joues creuses *or* creusées; **hollow-eyed** aux yeux caves *or* creux.
3 *adv* (*lit, fig*) **to sound ~** sonner creux; (*Brit*) **they beat us ~*** ils nous ont battus à plate(s) couture(s).
4 *n [back, hand, tree]* creux *m*; *[tooth]* cavité *f*; (*in ground*) dépression *f*, dénivellation *f*; (*valley*) cuvette *f*. (*fig*) **to hold sb in the ~ of one's hand** mener qn par le bout du nez.
5 *vt* (*also ~ out*) creuser, évider.
holly [ˈhɒlɪ] 1 *n* houx *m*. 2 *cpd*: **holly berry** baie *f* de houx; **hollyhock** rose trémière.
holm oak [ˈhəʊmˈəʊk] *n* chêne vert, yeuse *f*.
holocaust [ˈhɒləkɔːst] *n* holocauste *m*.
holograph [ˈhɒləgrɑːf] 1 *n* document *m* (h)olographe. 2 *adj* (h)olographe.
holster [ˈhəʊlstəʳ] *n* étui *m* de revolver; (*on saddle*) fonte *f*.
holy [ˈhəʊlɪ] 1 *adj person, oil, poverty* saint; *bread, water* bénit; *ground* sacré. **H~ Bible** Sainte Bible; **H~ City** Ville sainte; **H~ Communion** Sainte communion; **the H~ Father** le Saint-Père; **the H~ Ghost** *or* **Spirit** le Saint-Esprit, l'Esprit Saint; **H~ Land** Terre Sainte; **~ orders** ordres *mpl* (majeurs) (*V also* **order**); **H~ Rood** Sainte Croix; **H~ Saturday** Samedi saint; **the H~ See** le Saint-Siège; **H~ Sepulchre** Saint Sépulcre; **H~ Trinity** Sainte Trinité; **H~ Week** Semaine Sainte; **H~ Writ** Saintes Écritures, Écriture sainte; **that child is a ~ terror*** cet enfant est un vrai démon; **~ cow!‡, ~ mackerel!*, ~ smoke!*** zut alors!*, ça alors!*, Seigneur!*
2 *n*: **the ~ of holies** le Saint des Saints.
3 *cpd*: (*Naut*) **holystone** (*n*) brique *f* à pont; (*vt*) briquer.
homage [ˈhɒmɪdʒ] *n* (*U*) hommage *m*. **to pay** *or* **do ~ to** rendre hommage à.
homburg [ˈhɒmbɜːg] *n* chapeau mou, feutre *m* (souple).
home [həʊm] 1 *n* **(a)** maison *f*, foyer *m*, chez-soi *m inv*. **he left ~ in 1978** il a quitté la maison en 1978; **he was glad to see his ~ again** il fut content de revoir sa maison; **it is quite near my ~** c'est tout près de chez moi; **his ~ is in Paris** il habite Paris; **we live in Paris but my ~ is in London** nous habitons Paris mais je suis de Londres; **~ for me is Edinburgh** c'est à Édimbourg que j'ai mes racines; **for some years he made his ~ in France** pendant quelques années il a habité en France *or* la France; **refugees who made their ~ in Britain** réfugiés qui se sont installés en Grande-Bretagne; **he is far from ~** il est loin de chez lui; **he has been away from ~ for some months** il est loin de chez lui depuis quelques mois; (*Prov*) **there's no place like ~** on n'est vraiment bien que chez soi; (*Prov*) **~ is where the heart lies** où le cœur aime, là est le foyer; **to have a ~ of one's own** avoir un foyer *or* un chez-soi; **he has no ~** il n'a pas de foyer *or* de chez-soi; **to give sb a ~** recueillir qn chez soi; **he needed a wife to make a ~ for him** il fallait qu'il se marie (*subj*) pour avoir un foyer; **she made a ~ for her brothers** elle a fait un (vrai) foyer pour ses frères; (*Brit*) **it's a ~ from ~** c'est un second chez-soi; **she has a lovely ~** elle a un joli intérieur; **he comes from a good ~** il a une famille comme il faut; **'good ~ wanted for kitten'** 'cherche foyer accueillant pour chaton'; **he comes from a broken ~** il vient d'un foyer désuni; **safety in the ~** prudence à la maison; **accidents in the ~** accidents qui se produisent au foyer; **at ~** chez soi, à la maison; (*Ftbl*) **Celtic are at ~ to Rangers, Celtic are playing Rangers at ~** le Celtic joue à domicile contre les Rangers, le Celtic reçoit les Rangers; (*fig*) **Mrs X is not at ~ to anyone** Mme X ne reçoit personne; (*fig*) **Mrs X is not at ~** Mme X ne reçoit pas; (*fig*) **Mrs X is at ~ on Fridays** Mme X reçoit le vendredi; **to be** *or* **feel at ~ with sb** se sentir à l'aise avec qn; **he doesn't feel at ~ in English** il n'est pas à l'aise en anglais; **to make o.s. at ~** se mettre à l'aise, faire comme chez soi.

(b) pays natal, patrie *f*. **at ~ and abroad** chez nous *or* dans notre pays et à l'étranger; (*fig*) **let us consider something nearer ~** considérons quelque chose qui nous intéresse plus directement.
(c) (*institution*) (*for aged, children, blind, handicapped etc*) maison *f*, institution *f*; (*for sailors*) foyer *m*. **children's ~** maison pour enfants; *V* **maternity, mental, nursing** *etc*.
(d) (*Bot, Zool*) habitat *m*. (*fig*) **Scotland is the ~ of the haggis** l'Écosse est le pays *or* la patrie du haggis.
(e) (*Racing*) arrivée *f*.
2 *adv* **(a)** chez soi, à la maison. **to go** *or* **get ~** rentrer (à la maison); **I'll be ~ at 5 o'clock** je serai à la maison à 5 heures, je rentrerai (à la maison) à 5 heures; **I met him on the journey ~** je l'ai rencontré sur le chemin du retour; **to see sb ~** accompagner qn jusque chez lui, raccompagner qn; **I must write ~** il faut que j'écrive à la maison; **it's nothing to write ~ about*** ça ne casse rien*, c'est pas merveilleux*; (*fig*) **~ and dry,** (*US*) **~ free*** sauvé; *V* **head, roost.**
(b) (*from abroad*) au pays natal. **he came ~ from abroad** il est rentré de l'étranger; **to send sb ~** rapatrier qn; **to go** *or* **return ~** rentrer dans son pays.
(c) (*right in etc*) à fond. **to drive a nail ~** enfoncer un clou à fond; **to bring sth ~ to sb** faire comprendre *or* faire voir qch à qn; **the horror of the situation was brought ~ to him when ...** l'horreur de la situation lui apparut pleinement quand ...; **his words went ~ to her** ses paroles la touchèrent au vif; *V* **hit** *etc*.
3 *cpd atmosphere* de famille, familial; *troubles* de famille, domestique; (*Econ, Pol etc*) du pays, national; *policy, market, sales etc* intérieur (*f* -eure). **home address** (*on forms etc*) domicile *m* (permanent); (*as opposed to business address*) adresse personnelle; **home-baked** (fait à la) maison *inv*; **home-baked bread** pain *m* fait à la maison; (*US*) **homebody*** = **home-lover; home brew (beer/wine** *etc*) bière *f*/vin *m etc* fait(e) à la maison; **home comforts** confort *m* du foyer; **homecoming** retour *m* au foyer *or* à la maison *or* au pays; **home cooking** cuisine familiale; (*Brit Geog*) **the Home Counties** *les comtés mpl qui entourent Londres*; **the home country** le vieux pays; **home economics** économie *f* domestique; (*Pol etc*) **on the home front** à l'intérieur; **home-grown** (*not foreign*) du pays; (*from own garden*) du jardin; (*Brit*) **Home Guard** *volontaires mpl pour la défense du territoire* (*en 1940-45*); **home help** aide ménagère; **homeland** patrie *f*; **home leave** congé *m* de longue durée; **home life** vie *f* de famille; **homelike** accueillant, confortable; **it's very homelike here** on se sent vraiment chez soi *or* comme en famille ici; **home-lover** casanier *m*, -ière *f*; (*woman*) femme *f* d'intérieur; **home-loving** casanier; **home-made** (fait à la) maison *inv*; (*Sport*) **home match** match *m* (joué) à domicile *or* sur son (*or* notre *etc*) terrain; **home news** (*gen*) nouvelles *fpl* de chez soi; (*Pol*) nouvelles de l'intérieur; (*Brit*) **Home Office** ministère *m* de l'Intérieur; (*Naut*) **home port** port *m* d'attache; **home rule** autonomie *f*; **the ship was on the home run** le navire effectuait son voyage de retour; (*Brit*) **Home Secretary** ministre *m* de l'Intérieur; **homesick** nostalgique; **to be homesick** avoir le mal du pays, s'ennuyer de sa famille *or* de son chez-soi; **to be homesick for sth** avoir la nostalgie de qch; **homesickness** nostalgie *f* (*for* de), mal *m* du pays; (*Ftbl etc*) **the home side** l'équipe *f* qui reçoit; **homespun** (*adj*) *cloth* filé à la maison; (*fig*) simple, sans recherche; (*n*) homespun *m*; **homestead** (*house etc*) propriété *f*; (*farm*) ferme *f*; **to be in the home straight** *or* **stretch** (*Sport*) être dans la (dernière) ligne droite; (*fig*) voir la lumière au bout du tunnel; (*Ftbl*) **the home team** = **the home side; my home town** (*place of birth*) ma ville natale; (*where I grew up*) la ville où j'ai grandi; **I'll tell him a few home truths** je vais lui dire ses quatre vérités, je vais lui dire quelques vérités bien senties; (*by doctor etc*) **home visit** visite *f* à domicile; (*Naut*) **home waters** (*territorial waters*) eaux territoriales; (*near home port*) eaux voisines du port d'attache; (*Scol*) **homework** devoirs *mpl* (à la maison); **homework exercise** devoir *m* (à la maison).
4 *vi* revenir *or* rentrer chez soi; *[pigeons]* revenir au colombier.
home in on, home on to *vt fus [missile]* se diriger (automatiquement) vers *or* sur.
homeless ['həʊmlɪs] 1 *adj* sans foyer, sans abri. 2 *npl*: **the ~** les sans-abri *mpl*; *V* **single.**
homely ['həʊmlɪ] *adj* **(a)** *food* simple, ordinaire; *person* tout à fait simple, sans prétentions; *atmosphere* accueillant, confortable; *style* simple, sans recherche. **(b)** (*US: plain*) *person* laid, sans charme; *appearance* peu attrayant.
homeopath ['həʊmɪəʊpæθ] *etc* (*US*) = **homoeopath** *etc*.
Homer ['həʊməʳ] *n* Homère *m*.
homeward ['həʊmwəd] 1 *adj* du retour. **~ voyage** (voyage *m* de) retour *m*; **to be ~ bound** être sur le chemin du retour. 2 *adv* (*also* **~s**) vers la maison *or* la patrie; *V* **head.**
homey ['həʊmɪ] *adj* (*US*) = **homelike;** *V* **home 3.**
homicidal [ˌhɒmɪ'saɪdl] *adj* homicide.
homicide ['hɒmɪsaɪd] *n* (*act*) homicide *m*; (*person*) homicide *mf*.
homily ['hɒmɪlɪ] *n* (*Rel*) homélie *f*; (*fig*) sermon *m*, homélie.
homing ['həʊmɪŋ] *adj missile* à tête chercheuse. **~ pigeon** pigeon voyageur.
homo‡ ['həʊməʊ] *adj,n* (*abbr of* **homosexual**) pédé‡ (*m*), homo* (*mf*).
homoeopath, (*US*) **homeopath** ['həʊmɪəʊpæθ] *n* homéopathe *mf*.
homoeopathic, (*US*) **homeopathic** [ˌhəʊmɪəʊ'pæθɪk] *adj medicine, methods* homéopathique; *doctor* homéopathe.
homoeopathy, (*US*) **homeopathy** [ˌhəʊmɪ'ɒpəθɪ] *n* homéopathie *f*.
homogeneity [ˌhɒməʊdʒə'niːɪtɪ] *n* homogénéité *f*.
homogeneous [ˌhɒmə'dʒiːnɪəs] *adj* homogène.
homogenize [hə'mɒdʒənaɪz] *vt* homogénéiser, homogénéifier.
homograph ['hɒməʊgrɑːf] *n* homographe *m*.
homonym ['hɒmənɪm] *n* homonyme *m*.
homophone ['hɒməfəʊn] *n* homophone *m*.
homosexual ['hɒməʊ'seksjʊəl] *adj, n* homosexuel(le) *m(f)*.
homosexuality ['hɒməʊseksjʊ'ælɪtɪ] *n* homosexualité *f*.
Honduran [hɒn'djʊərən] 1 *adj* hondurien. 2 *n* Hondurien(ne) *m(f)*.
Honduras [hɒn'djʊərəs] *n* Honduras *m*.
hone [həʊn] 1 *n* pierre *f* à aiguiser. 2 *vt* affûter, affiler, aiguiser.
honest ['ɒnɪst] *adj person* honnête, probe, intègre; *action* honnête, loyal; *opinion* sincère, franc (*f* franche); *face* franc, ouvert; *money, profit* honnêtement acquis *or* gagné; (*Jur*) *goods* loyal et marchand. **they are ~ people** ce sont de braves *or* d'honnêtes gens; **the ~ truth** la pure vérité; **tell me your ~ opinion of it** dites-moi sincèrement ce que vous en pensez; **to be ~ with you, I don't like it** à (vous) dire la vérité, je n'aime pas ça; **now, be ~!** (*say what you think*) allons, dis ce que tu penses!; (*tell the truth*) allons, sois franc!; (*be objective*) allons, sois objectif!; **you've not been ~ with me** tu n'as pas été franc avec moi; **to earn an ~ penny** gagner honnêtement son pain; **an ~ day's work** une bonne journée de travail; **by ~ means** par des moyens légitimes *or* honnêtes; **~ to goodness!*, ~ to God!‡** parole d'honneur!; **he made an ~ woman of her*** il a régularisé sa situation (*en l'épousant*).
honestly ['ɒnɪstlɪ] *adv act, behave* honnêtement. **~, I don't care** franchement, ça m'est égal; **I didn't do it, ~** je ne l'ai pas fait, je vous le jure; **~?** c'est vrai?
honesty ['ɒnɪstɪ] *n* **(a)** (*V* **honest**) honnêteté *f*, probité *f*, intégrité *f*; loyauté *f*; *[words, report]* exactitude *f*, véracité *f*. **in all ~** en toute sincérité; (*Prov*) **~ is the best policy** l'honnêteté paie.
(b) (*Bot*) monnaie-du-pape *f*.
honey ['hʌnɪ] 1 *n* **(a)** miel *m*. **clear/thick ~** miel liquide/solide; (*fig*) **he was all ~** il était (tout sucre) tout miel.
(b) yes, **~*** oui, chéri(e); **she's a ~*** elle est adorable*, c'est un chou*.
2 *cpd*: **honey-bee** abeille *f*; **honeycomb** *V* **honeycomb; honeydew** miellée *f*; **honeydew melon** melon *m* d'hiver *or* d'Antibes; **honeymoon** (*n*) (*time*) lune *f* de miel; (*journey*) voyage *m* de noces; (*vi*) passer sa lune de miel; **the honeymoon couple** les nouveaux mariés; **honeypot** pot *m* à miel (*V* **bee**); **honeysuckle** chèvrefeuille *m*.
honeycomb ['hʌnɪkəʊm] 1 *n* (*lit*) rayon *m* de miel; (*Tex*) nid *m* d'abeille; (*Metal*) soufflure *f*. 2 *cpd textile, pattern* en nid d'abeille. 3 *vt* (*fig*) cribler (*with* de). **the palace was ~ed with corridors** le palais était un dédale de couloirs.
honeyed ['hʌnɪd] *adj* (*fig*) *words* mielleux, doucereux.
honk [hɒŋk] 1 *vi [car]* klaxonner, corner; *[geese]* cacarder. 2 *n [car]* coup *m* de klaxon; *[geese]* cri *m*. **~, ~!** *[car]* tut-tut!; *[goose]* couin-couin!
honky-tonk* ['hɒŋkɪ'tɒŋk] *n* **(a)** (*US: club*) boîte* *f*, beuglant‡ *m*. **(b)** (*Mus*) musique *f* de bastringue.
Honolulu [ˌhɒnə'luːluː] *n* Honolulu.
honor ['ɒnəʳ] *n* (*US*) = **honour.**
honorable ['ɒnərəbl] *adj* (*US*) = **honourable.**
honorably ['ɒnərəblɪ] *adv* (*US*) = **honourably.**
honorarium [ˌɒnə'rɛərɪəm] *n, pl* **honoraria** [ˌɒnə'rɛərɪə] *n* honoraires *mpl* (*no sg*).
honorary ['ɒnərərɪ] *adj official, member* honoraire; *duties, titles* honorifique. (*Univ*) **~ degree** grade *m* honoris causa.
honour, (*US*) **honor** ['ɒnəʳ] 1 *n* **(a)** honneur *m*. **in ~ of** en l'honneur de; (*Prov*) **(there is) ~ among thieves** les loups ne se mangent pas entre eux; **to lose one's ~** être déshonoré; **for ~'s sake** pour l'honneur; **on my ~!, ~ bright!*†** parole d'honneur!; **to be on one's ~ to do** être engagé sur son honneur *or* sur l'honneur à faire; **to put sb on his ~ to do** engager qn sur son honneur *or* sur l'honneur à faire; **it is a great ~ for me** c'est un grand honneur pour moi; (*frm*) **I have the ~ to tell you** j'ai l'honneur de vous dire; **I had the ~ to do** *or* **of doing** j'ai eu l'honneur de faire; (*frm*) **may I have the ~?** me ferez-vous l'honneur?; (*title*) **Your/His H~** Votre/Son Honneur; **he is an ~ to his father/his regiment** il fait honneur à son père/son régiment; **to do the ~s of one's house** faire les honneurs de sa maison; (*introductions*) **to do the ~s** faire les présentations (*entre invités*); (*Mil etc*) **the last ~s** les derniers honneurs, le dernier hommage; *V* **debt, guard, word** *etc*.
(b) (*Univ*) **to take ~s in English** ≈ faire une licence d'anglais; **an ~s degree in English** ≈ une licence d'anglais; **he got first-/second-class ~s in English** ≈ il a eu sa licence d'anglais avec mention très bien/mention bien.
(c) (*Bridge*) honneur *m*.
2 *cpd*: **to be honour-bound to do** être tenu par l'honneur de faire; (*Brit*) **Honours List** *liste f de distinctions honorifiques conférées par le monarque à l'occasion de son anniversaire officiel* **(Birthday Honours List)** *ou le 1er janvier* **(New Year Honours List).**
3 *vt* **(a)** *person* honorer, faire honneur à. (*in dancing*) **to ~ one's partner** saluer son cavalier (*or* sa cavalière).
(b) *cheque* honorer.
honourable, (*US*) **honorable** ['ɒnərəbl] *adj person, action* honorable. (*title*) **the H~ ...** l'honorable ...; *V* **right.**
honourably, (*US*) **honorably** ['ɒnərəblɪ] *adv* honorablement.
hooch‡ [huːtʃ] *n* gnôle‡ *f*.
hood [hʊd] 1 *n* **(a)** (*gen*) capuchon *m*; (*Ku Klux Klan type*) cagoule *f*; (*Univ*) épitoge *f*. **rain-~** capuche *f*.
(b) (*Brit Aut*) capote *f*; (*US Aut*) capot *m*; *[pram]* capote; (*over fire, cooker etc*) hotte *f*; *[falcon]* chaperon *m*; *[cobra]* capuchon *m*.

(c) (*US*:) *abbr of* **hoodlum.**
2 *vt falcon* chaperonner enchaperonner.
3 *cpd*: **hoodwink** tromper, avoir*.
hooded ['hʊdɪd] *adj person, figure* encapuchonné; *cloak etc* à capuchon. ~ **crow** corneille mantelée; ~ **falcon** faucon chaperonné *or* enchaperonné.
hoodlum ['hu:dləm] *n* (*US*) voyou *m*.
hoodoo* ['hu:du:] 1 *n* (*bad luck*) guigne* *f*, poisse* *f*; (*object, person*) porte-guigne* *m*. 2 *vt* porter la guigne* *or* la poisse* à.
hooey: ['hu:ɪ] *n* (*US*) chiqué* *m*, blague* *f*, fumisterie* *f*; **to talk a lot of** ~ dire des bêtises.
hoof [hu:f] 1 *n, pl* ~s *or* **hooves** sabot *m* (*d'animal*); *V* **cloven.** 2 *cpd*: (*US*) **hoof and mouth disease** fièvre aphteuse. 3 *vt*: **to** ~ **it**: aller à pinces:, aller pedibus-cum-jambis*.
hoofed [hu:ft] *adj* à sabots.
hoo-ha* ['hu:ˌhɑ:] *n* (*noise*) brouhaha *m*, boucan* *m*; (*confusion*) pagaïe* *f or* pagaille* *f*; (*bustle*) tohu-bohu *m*; (*excitement*) animation *f*; (*pej: publicity*) baratin* *m*. **there was a great** ~ **about it** on en a fait tout un foin: *or* tout un plat*, il y a eu des tas d'histoires*.
hook [hʊk] 1 *n* (a) crochet *m*; (*for coats*) patère *f*; (*on dress*) agrafe *f*; (*Fishing*) hameçon *m*. (*Sewing*) ~**s and eyes** agrafes; (*fig*) **to take the** ~ avaler le morceau, mordre à *or* gober* l'hameçon; **he swallowed the story** ~**, line and sinker*** il a gobé* tout ce qu'on lui a raconté, il a tout avalé; **by** ~ **or by crook** coûte que coûte, par tous les moyens; (*fig*) **to get sb off the** ~* tirer qn d'affaire; **I'll let you off the** ~* je laisse passer*, je vous libère de vos obligations; **he's off the** ~* il est tiré d'affaire.
(b) (*Boxing*) crochet *m*; (*Golf*) coup hooké. (*Boxing*) **right** ~ crochet (du) droit.
(c) (*Agr*) faucille *f*.
2 *cpd*: **hook-nosed** au nez recourbé *or* crochu; (*Rad, TV etc*) **hookup*** relais *m* temporaire; **hookworm** ankylostome *m*.
3 *vt* (a) accrocher (*to* à); (*Naut*) gaffer; (*Boxing*) donner un crochet à; (*Fishing*) prendre; (*Golf*) hooker; *dress* agrafer. **she finally** ~**ed him*** elle a fini par lui passer la corde au cou; *V also* **hooked.**
(b) (*Rugby*) **to** ~ **the ball** talonner le ballon.
hook on 1 *vi* s'accrocher (*to* à).
2 *vt sep* accrocher (*to* à).
hook up 1 *vi* [*dress*] s'agrafer.
2 *vt sep* (a) *dress etc* agrafer.
(b) (*: *Rad, TV etc*) faire un duplex entre.
3 **hookup*** *n V* **hook 2.**
hookah ['hʊkɑ:] *n* narguilé *m*.
hooked [hʊkt] *adj* (a) (*hook-shaped*) *nose* recourbé, crochu. **the end of the wire was** ~ le bout du fil (de fer) était recourbé.
(b) (*having hooks*) muni de crochets *or* d'agrafes *or* d'hameçons (*V* **hook 1a**).
(c) (**fig*) dépendant (*on* de). **he's** ~ **on it** il ne peut plus s'en passer; **to get** ~ **on** *drugs* se camer à*; *jazz, television* devenir enragé* de; **he's really** ~ **on that girl** il est complètement dingue: de cette fille; **once I'd seen the first episode I was** ~ après avoir vu le premier épisode j'étais accroché*.
hooker ['hʊkə^r] *n* (*Rugby*) talonneur *m*; (:: *esp US: prostitute*) sauteuse: *f*, putain: *f*.
hooky: ['hʊkɪ] *n* (*esp US*) **to play** ~ sécher les cours, faire l'école buissonnière.
hooligan ['hu:lɪgən] *n* voyou *m*, vandale *m*.
hooliganism ['hu:lɪgənɪzəm] *n* vandalisme *m*.
hoop [hu:p] *n* [*barrel*] cercle *m*; (*toy; in circus; for skirt*) cerceau *m*; (*Croquet*) arceau *m*. (*fig*) **they put him through the** ~* ils l'ont mis sur la sellette.
hoopla ['hu:plɑ:] *n* (a) (*Brit*) jeu *m* d'anneaux (*dans les foires*). (b) (*US**) = **hoo-ha.**
hoopoe ['hu:pu:] *n* huppe *f*.
hoosegow: ['hu:sgaʊ] *n* (*US*) taule: *f or* tôle: *f*, bloc* *m*, trou* *m*.
hoot [hu:t] 1 *n* [*owl*] hululement *m*; (*Aut*) coup *m* de klaxon; [*siren*] mugissement *m*; [*train*] sifflement *m*; (*jeer*) huée *f*. **she gave a** ~ **of laughter** elle s'est esclaffée; **I don't care a** ~* *or* **two** ~**s*** je m'en fiche* comme de ma première chemise, je n'en ai rien à fiche*; **it was a** ~: c'était tordant* *or* marrant:.
2 *vi* [*owl*] hululer; (*Aut*) klaxonner, corner; [*siren*] mugir; [*train*] siffler; (*jeer*) huer, pousser des huées. **to** ~ **with laughter** s'esclaffer, rire aux éclats.
3 *vt actor, speaker* huer, conspuer.
hooter ['hu:tə^r] *n* [*factory*] sirène *f*; (*Aut*) klaxon *m*; [*train*] sifflet *m*.
Hoover ['hu:və^r] (*Brit*) ® 1 *n* aspirateur *m*. 2 *vt*: **to h**~ **a carpet/a room** passer l'aspirateur sur un tapis/dans une pièce, passer un tapis/une pièce à l'aspirateur.
hooves [hu:vz] *npl of* **hoof.**
hop[1] [hɒp] 1 *n* (a) [*person, animal*] saut *m*; [*person, bird*] sautillement *m*. (*fig*) **to catch sb on the** ~ prendre qn au dépourvu.
(b) (*: *dance*) sauterie *f*.
(c) (*Aviat*) étape *f*. **from London to Athens in 2** ~**s** de Londres à Athènes en 2 étapes; **it's a short** ~ **from Paris to Brussels** ce n'est qu'un saut de Paris à Bruxelles.
2 *cpd*: **hop-o'-my-thumb** le Petit Poucet; **hopscotch** marelle *f*.
3 *vi* [*person*] sauter à cloche-pied; (*jump*) sauter; [*animal*] sauter; [*bird*] sautiller. **he** ~**ped over to the window** il est allé à cloche-pied jusqu'à la fenêtre; (*in car etc*) ~ **in!** montez!; **he** ~**ped out of bed** il a sauté du lit; *V* **mad.**
4 *vt* sauter. **to** ~ **it*** décamper, mettre les bouts* *or* les voiles*; ~ **it!*** fiche le camp!*
hop off* *vi* (*leave*) décamper, ficher le camp*. **he hopped off with all the silver** il a fichu le camp* avec toute l'argenterie.
hop[2] [hɒp] 1 *n* (*Bot: also* ~s) houblon *m*. 2 *cpd*: **hopfield** houblonnière *f*; **hop picker** cueilleur *m*, -euse *f* de houblon.
hope [həʊp] 1 *n* espoir *m*, espérance *f*. **past** *or* **beyond (all)** ~ sans espoir, désespéré; **we must live in** ~ nous devons vivre d'espoir; **she lives in (the)** ~ **of seeing her son again** c'est l'espoir de revoir son fils qui la fait vivre; **in the** ~ **of sth/of doing** dans l'espoir de qch/de faire; **to have** ~**s of doing** avoir l'espoir de faire; **I haven't much** ~ **of succeeding** je n'ai pas beaucoup d'espoir de réussir; **there is no** ~ **of that** n'y comptez nullement; **he set out with high** ~**s** il s'est lancé avec l'espoir de faire de grandes choses; **to raise sb's** ~**s** susciter *or* faire naître l'espoir chez qn; **don't raise her** ~**s too much** ne lui laisse *or* donne pas trop d'espoir; **to lose (all)** ~ **of sth/of doing** perdre l'espoir *or* tout espoir de qch/de faire; **my** ~ **is that ...** ce que j'espère *or* mon espoir c'est que ...; **he's the** ~ **of his family** c'est l'espoir de sa famille; **you're my last** ~ tu es mon dernier espoir; **what a** ~**!*, some** ~**(s)!*** tu parles!:, tu crois au père Noël!*; *V* **faith.**
2 *vi* espérer. **to** ~ **in God** espérer en Dieu, mettre son espoir en Dieu; **to** ~ **for money/for success** espérer gagner de l'argent/avoir du succès; **if I were you I shouldn't** ~ **for too much from the meeting** à votre place je n'attendrais pas trop de la réunion; **don't** ~ **for too much** n'en attendez pas trop; **to** ~ **for better days** espérer (connaître) des jours meilleurs; **we must** ~ **for better things** il faut espérer que de meilleurs jours viendront *or* que ça ira mieux; **to** ~ **against hope** espérer en dépit de tout *or* contre tout espoir.
3 *vt* espérer. **I** ~ **to see you, I** ~ **I'll see you** j'espère te voir; **hoping to hear from you** dans l'espoir d'avoir de vos nouvelles; **what do you** ~ **to gain by that?** qu'espères-tu obtenir par là?; **I** ~ **so** j'espère que oui; **I** ~ **not** j'espère que non.
4 *cpd*: (*US*) **hope chest** (armoire *f* à) trousseau *m*.
hopeful ['həʊpfʊl] 1 *adj person* plein d'espoir; *situation, response* encourageant, prometteur, qui promet. **we are** ~ **about the results** nous attendons avec confiance les résultats; **I am** ~ **that ...** j'ai bon espoir que ...; **I'll ask her but I'm not too** ~ je lui demanderai mais je n'ai pas tellement d'espoir; **it's a** ~ **sign** c'est bon signe.
2 *n*: **he's a young** ~ c'est un jeune loup (*fig*).
hopefully ['həʊpfəlɪ] *adv* (a) *speak, assess, smile* avec (bon) espoir, avec optimisme; *develop, progress* d'une façon encourageante. ... **he said** ~ ... dit-il avec optimisme. (b) (*esp US*) ~ **it won't rain** on espère qu'il ne va pas pleuvoir.
hopeless ['həʊplɪs] *adj* (a) *person* sans espoir, désespéré; *task* impossible; *situation* désespéré, qui ne permet *or* ne laisse aucun espoir, irrémédiable; *outlook* désespéré. **he's a** ~ **teacher*** il est nul comme professeur*; **I'm** ~ **at maths*** je suis nul en maths; **it's** ~**!** c'est impossible *or* désespérant.
(b) *liar, drunkard etc* invétéré, incorrigible. **he's** ~***, he's a** ~ **case*** c'est un cas désespéré.
hopelessly ['həʊplɪslɪ] *adv act* sans espoir; *speak* avec désespoir. **they were** ~ **lost** ils étaient complètement perdus.
hopper ['hɒpə^r] *n* (*person, animal, insect*) sauteur *m*, -euse *f*; (*: *Australia*) kangourou *m*; (*bin*) trémie *f*. (*Rail*) ~ **car** wagon-trémie *m*.
Horace ['hɒrɪs] *n* Horace *m*.
horde [hɔ:d] *n* horde *f*.
horizon [hə'raɪzn] *n* (*lit*) horizon *m*; (*fig*) vue *f*, horizon. (*lit, fig*) **on the** ~ à l'horizon; (*fig*) **a man of narrow** ~**s** un homme de vues étroites; **to open new** ~**s for sb** ouvrir des horizons à qn.
horizontal [ˌhɒrɪ'zɒntl] 1 *adj* horizontal. ~ **bar** barre *f* fixe. 2 *n* horizontale *f*.
horizontally [ˌhɒrɪ'zɒntəlɪ] *adv* horizontalement.
hormone ['hɔ:məʊn] *n* hormone *f*.
horn [hɔ:n] 1 *n* (a) corne *f*. ~ **of plenty** corne d'abondance; (*fig*) **to draw in** *or* **pull in one's** ~**s** (*back down*) diminuer d'ardeur; (*spend less*) restreindre son train de vie; *V* **dilemma.**
(b) (*Mus*) cor *m*; *V* **French etc.**
(c) (*Aut, Naut*) klaxon *m*. **to sound** *or* **blow the** ~ corner, klaxonner; *V* **fog.**
2 *cpd handle, ornament* en corne. (*Bot*) **hornbeam** charme *m*; **hornbill** calao *m*; (*Naut*) **hornpipe** matelote *f* (*danse*); **horn-rimmed spectacles** lunettes *fpl* à monture d'écaille *or* à grosse monture.
horn in: *vi* (*esp US*) mettre son grain de sel.
horned [hɔ:nd] *adj* cornu. ~ **owl** (*variété de*) duc *m* (*Orn*); ~ **toad** crapaud cornu.
hornet ['hɔ:nɪt] *n* frelon *m*. (*fig*) **his inquiries stirred up a** ~**'s nest** ses investigations ont mis le feu aux poudres.
hornless ['hɔ:nlɪs] *adj* sans cornes.
horny ['hɔ:nɪ] *adj* (a) (*like horn*) corné; *hands etc* calleux.
(b) (:: *esp US: sexually aroused*) en rut*, excité* (*sexuellement*).
horology [hɒ'rɒlədʒɪ] *n* horlogerie *f*.
horoscope ['hɒrəskəʊp] *n* horoscope *m*.
horrendous [hɒ'rendəs] *adj* horrible, affreux.
horrible ['hɒrɪbl] *adj sight, murder* horrible, affreux; *holiday, weather, person* affreux*, atroce*.
horribly ['hɒrɪblɪ] *adv* horriblement, affreusement. **I'm going to be** ~ **late** je vais être affreusement* en retard.
horrid ['hɒrɪd] *adj* méchant, vilain; (†: *stronger*) horrible, affreux, hideux. **a** ~ **child** un méchant enfant, une horreur d'enfant*.
horrific [hɒ'rɪfɪk] *adj* horrible, terrifiant, horrifique.
horrify ['hɒrɪfaɪ] *vt* horrifier.
horrifying ['hɒrɪfaɪɪŋ] *adj* horrifiant.
horror ['hɒrə^r] 1 *n* (*feeling, object, person*) horreur *f*. **to have a** ~ **of sth/of doing** avoir horreur de qch/de faire; (*excl*) ~**s!*** quelle horreur!*, quelle chose affreuse!*; **that child is a** ~**!*** cet enfant est un petit monstre!*; **you** ~**!*** monstre!*; **that gives me the** ~**s*** cela me donne le frisson, cela me donne la chair de poule; *V* **chamber.** 2 *cpd book, film, comic* d'épouvante. **horror-stricken** glacé *or* frappé d'horreur.

horse [hɔːs] **1** *n* **(a)** cheval *m*. **he eats like a ~** il mange comme quatre; **to work like a ~** travailler comme un forcené; (*fig*) **(straight) from the ~'s mouth** de source sûre; (*lit, fig*) **to back the wrong ~** miser sur le mauvais cheval; *V* **dark, gift, white, willing** *etc*.
(b) (*Gymnastics*) cheval *m* d'arçons; *V* **clothes.**
(c) (*Mil: U*) cavalerie *f*. **light ~** cavalerie légère.
2 *cpd*: **horse-artillery** artillerie montée; **on horseback** à cheval; **horse-box** fourgon *m* à chevaux; (*in stable*) box *m*; **horse brass** médaillon *m* de cuivre (fixé à une martingale); **horse-breaker** dresseur *m*, -euse *f* de chevaux; **horse breeder** éleveur *m*, -euse *f* de chevaux; (*US*) **horsecar** fourgon *m* à chevaux; **horse chestnut** marron *m* (d'Inde); **horse chestnut tree** marronnier *m* (d'Inde); **horse-collar** collier *m* (*de harnais*); **horse-dealer** maquignon *m*; **horse-doctor*** vétérinaire *mf*; **horse-drawn** tiré par des chevaux, à chevaux; **horsefly** taon *m*; (*Brit Mil*) **the Horse Guards** (le régiment de) la Garde à cheval; **horsehair** (*n*) crin *m* (de cheval); (*cpd*) de *or* en crin (de cheval); **horsehide** cuir *m* de cheval; **horse latitudes** ceintures subtropicales; **horse-laugh** gros rire; **horseman** cavalier *m*; **he's a good horseman** il est bon cavalier, il monte bien (à cheval); **horsemanship** (*activity*) équitation *f*; (*skill*) talent *m* de cavalier; **horse manure** crottin *m* de cheval; (*US: Cine, TV*) **horse opera*** western *m*; **horseplay** chahut brutal, jeux brutaux; **horsepower** puissance *f* (en chevaux); (*unit*) cheval-vapeur *m*; **a ten-horsepower car** une dix-chevaux; **horse-race** course *f* de chevaux; **horse-racing** courses *fpl* (de chevaux), hippisme *m*; (*Bot*) **horseradish** raifort *m*; **horse-sense*** (gros) bon sens; **horseshoe** (*n*) fer *m* à cheval; (*cpd*) en fer à cheval; **horse show** concours *m* hippique; (*lit, fig*) **horse-trade** maquignonner; (*lit, fig*) **horse-trader** maquignon *m*; (*lit, fig*) **horse-trading** maquignonnage *m*; **horse trials** concours *m* hippique; **horsewhip** (*n*) cravache *f*; (*vt*) cravacher; **horsewoman** cavalière *f*, amazone *f*, écuyère *f*; **she's a good horsewoman** elle est bonne cavalière, elle monte bien (à cheval).

horse about‡, horse around‡ *vi* chahuter, jouer brutalement.

horsey* ['hɔːsɪ] *adj person* féru de cheval; *appearance, face* chevalin. **~ people** les passionnés *mpl* de chevaux.

horticultural [ˌhɔːtɪ'kʌltʃərəl] *adj* horticole. **~ show** exposition *f* horticole *or* d'horticulture.

horticulture ['hɔːtɪkʌltʃəʳ] *n* horticulture *f*.

horticulturist [ˌhɔːtɪ'kʌltʃərɪst] *n* horticulteur *m*, -trice *f*.

hose [həʊz] **1** *n* **(a)** (*also* **~pipe**) tuyau *m*; (*garden* **~**) tuyau d'arrosage; (*fire* **~**) tuyau d'incendie; (*Tech*) manche *f* (à eau *or* à air *etc*); (*Aut*) tuyau.
(b) (*Comm: stockings etc*) bas *mpl*; (*Hist*) (*tights*) chausses *fpl*; (*knee breeches*) culotte courte (*jusqu'aux genoux*).
2 *vt* (*in garden*) arroser au jet; *[firemen]* arroser à la lance.

hose down, hose out *vt sep* laver au jet.

hosier ['həʊʒəʳ] *n* bonnetier *m*, -ière *f*.

hosiery ['həʊʒərɪ] *n* (*business*) bonneterie *f*; (*Comm: stocking department*) (rayon *m* des) bas *mpl*; (*stockings*) bas *mpl*.

hospice ['hɒspɪs] *n* hospice *m*, asile *m*.

hospitable [hɒs'pɪtəbl] *adj* hospitalier.

hospitably [hɒs'pɪtəblɪ] *adv* avec hospitalité.

hospital ['hɒspɪtl] **1** *n* hôpital *m*. **in ~** à l'hôpital; *V* **maternity, mental** *etc*.
2 *cpd treatment, staff* hospitalier; *bed etc* d'hôpital. **90% of hospital cases are released within 3 weeks** 90% des patients hospitalisés peuvent sortir dans les 3 semaines; **this is a hospital case, I'll call an ambulance** le patient doit être hospitalisé, je vais appeler une ambulance; **the hospital doctors** les médecins *mpl* des hôpitaux; **the junior hospital doctors** les internes *mpl* des hôpitaux; **the hospital facilities were inadequate** le service hospitalier n'était pas à la hauteur; **hospital nurse** infirmier *m*, -ière *f* (*d'hôpital*); **the hospital service** le service hospitalier; **hospital ship** navire-hôpital *m*; **hospital train** train *m* sanitaire.

hospitality [ˌhɒspɪ'tælɪtɪ] *n* hospitalité *f*.

hospitalize ['hɒspɪtəlaɪz] *vt* hospitaliser.

host¹ [həʊst] **1** *n* hôte *m*; (*in hotel etc*) aubergiste *m*, hôtelier *m*; (*Bot, Zool*) hôte. (*hum*) **mine ~** notre hôte (*hum*). **2** *cpd plant, animal* hôte; *town etc* qui reçoit.

host² [həʊst] *n* (*crowd*) foule *f*; (††) armée *f*. **a ~ of friends** une foule d'amis; **a whole ~ of reasons** toute une série *or* tout un tas* de raisons.

host³ [həʊst] *n* (*Rel*) hostie *f*.

hostage ['hɒstɪdʒ] *n* otage *m*. **to take sb ~** prendre qn comme otage.

hostel ['hɒstəl] **1** *n* **(a)** *[students, workers etc]* foyer *m*. **(youth) ~** auberge *f* de jeunesse. **(b)** (††) auberge *f*. **2** *vi*: **to go (youth) ~ling** aller passer ses vacances en auberges de jeunesse; **they were ~ling in Sweden** ils étaient en Suède dans les auberges de jeunesse.

hosteller ['hɒstələʳ] *n* ≃ ajiste *mf*.

hostelling ['hɒstəlɪŋ] *n* mouvement *m* des auberges de jeunesse.

hostelry ['hɒstəlrɪ] *n* hostellerie *f*.

hostess ['həʊstes] *n* hôtesse *f*; (*in night club*) entraîneuse *f*; *V* **air.**

hostile ['hɒstaɪl] *adj* hostile (*to* à).

hostility [hɒs'tɪlɪtɪ] *n* hostilité *f*.

hostler ['ɒsləʳ] *n* = **ostler.**

hot [hɒt] **1** *adj* **(a)** (*lit*) chaud. **to be ~** *[person]* avoir (très *or* trop) chaud; *[thing]* être (très) chaud; (*Met*) faire (très) chaud; **this room is ~** il fait (très *or* trop) chaud dans cette pièce; **it's too ~ in here** il fait trop chaud ici, on étouffe ici; **to get ~** *[person]* s'échauffer; *[thing]* devenir chaud, chauffer; (*Met*) commencer à faire chaud; **~ spring** source chaude; **it was a very ~ day** c'était un jour très chaud, c'était un jour de grande *or* forte chaleur; **the ~ sun** le soleil brûlant; **in the ~ weather** pendant les chaleurs; **it was a ~ and tiring walk** ce fut une marche épuisante par la grande chaleur; **bread ~ from the oven** pain tout chaud sorti du four; (*on menu*) **~ dishes** plats chauds; **I can't drink ~ things** je ne supporte pas le chaud; **the food must be served ~** la nourriture doit être servie bien chaude; (*fig*) **he's had more trips to Paris than I've had ~ dinners‡** il va plus souvent à Paris que je ne change (*subj*) de chemise; (*fig*) **to be in the ~ seat** être sur la sellette; **~ and cold running water** eau courante chaude et froide; (*Med*) **~ flush** bouffée *f* de chaleur; (*fig*) **to get into ~ water** se mettre dans une mauvaise passe *or* dans le pétrin, s'attirer une sale histoire*; **to be (all) ~ and bothered** (*perspiring*) être en nage*; (*flustered*) être dans tous ses états, être tourneboulé* (*about sth* au sujet de qch); **to be/get ~ under the collar* (about sth)** être/se mettre dans tous ses états *or* en colère (au sujet de qch); *V* **cake, coal, iron** *etc*.
(b) (*fig*) *curry, spices etc* fort, épicé; *news, report* tout frais (*f* fraîche); *struggle, contest, dispute* acharné; *temperament* passionné, violent; *supporter* enthousiaste, passionné. **~ jazz** hot *m*; **he's got a ~ temper** il est de caractère violent, il est très colérique; (*Pol*) **a ~ war*** une guerre ouverte; (*Sport*) **~ favourite** grand favori; **~ tip** tuyau sûr *or* increvable*; **to be ~ on the trail** être sur la bonne piste; **to be ~ on sb's trail** être sur les talons de qn; (*in guessing games etc*) **you're getting ~!** tu brûles!; **news ~ from the press** informations de dernière minute; **he was ~ from Paris** il était tout frais arrivé de Paris; **he made the town too ~ for his enemies** il a rendu l'atmosphère de la ville irrespirable pour *or* à ses ennemis; **to make it *or* things ~ for sb*** mener la vie dure à qn, en faire baver à qn*; **not so ~‡** pas formidable*, pas merveilleux, pas fameux*; **how are things? — not so ~*** comment ça va? — ce n'est pas fameux*; **he's pretty ~* at maths** il a la bosse des maths; **he's pretty ~* at football** il est très calé en foot*; **he's a ~ player*** c'est un joueur sensationnel*; (*sexually*) **she's a ~ piece‡** elle est (très) sexy‡; (*fig: stolen*) **it's ~‡** ça a été volé; *V* **also 3** and **pursuit** *etc*.
2 *adv*: **he went at it ~ and strong** il n'y est pas allé de main morte*; **to give it to sb ~ and strong*** passer un savon à qn*, sonner les cloches à qn*; *V* **blow¹**.
3 *cpd*: (*fig*) **hot air*** blablabla* *m*, foutaises‡ *fpl*; **hot-air balloon** montgolfière *f*; **a hotbed of vice/social unrest** *etc* un foyer de vice/de troubles sociaux *etc*; (*fig*) **hot-blooded** ardent, passionné; (*Culin*) **hot dog** hot-dog *m*; **hotfoot** à toute vitesse, à toute allure; **to hotfoot it*** galoper; **hot gospeller** prêcheur enragé (du protestantisme); (*fig*) **hothead** (*n*) tête brûlée; (*adj*: *also* **hotheaded**) *person* exalté, impétueux; *attitude* impétueux; **hothouse** (*n*) serre *f* (chaude); (*adj*: *lit, fig*) de serre (chaude); (*Telec*) **hot line** téléphone *m* rouge (*to* avec); **hotplate** *[cooker]* plaque chauffante; (*plate-warmer*) chauffe-plats *m inv*; (*esp Brit Culin*) **hotpot** ragoût *m* (*cuit au four avec des pommes de terre*); (*fig*) **hot potato*** sujet brûlant; **he dropped the idea like a hot potato*** il a laissé tomber comme si ça lui brûlait les doigts; (*US*) **hotrod*** voiture gonflée*; (*US*) **hotshot‡** (*adj*) terrible*; (*n*) crack* *m*; (*US*) **hot spot*** (*trouble area*) point *m* *or* coin *m* névralgique; (*night club*) boîte *f* (de nuit); **to be hot stuff*** être terrible* *or* sensationnel* *or* sensass‡; **hot-tempered** emporté, colérique; **hot-water bag *or* bottle** bouillotte *f*.

hot up* **1** *vi* (*lit*) réchauffer; (*fig*) se chauffer, s'échauffer, se réchauffer. **things are hotting up in the Middle East** cela commence à chauffer* au Moyen-Orient; (*at a party*) **things are hotting up** l'atmosphère commence à chauffer* *or* balancer*.
2 *vt sep* **(a)** *food* faire chauffer, (faire) réchauffer.
(b) (*fig*) *music* faire balancer*; *car engine* gonfler*. **he was driving a hotted-up Mini ®** il conduisait une Mini ® au moteur gonflé*; (*fig*) **to hot up the pace** forcer l'allure.

hotchpotch ['hɒtʃpɒtʃ] *n* salmigondis *m*, fatras *m*.

hotel [həʊ'tel] **1** *n* hôtel *m*.
2 *cpd furniture, prices, porter* d'hôtel. **the hotel industry** l'industrie hôtelière; **hotelkeeper** hôtelier *m*, -ière *f*, patron(ne) *m(f)* (d'hôtel); **hotel manager** gérant *m* *or* directeur *m* d'hôtel; **hotel receptionist** réceptionniste *mf* d'hôtel; **a hotel room** une chambre d'hôtel; **the hotel staff** le personnel hôtelier *or* de l'hôtel; **he's looking for hotel work** il cherche un travail dans l'hôtellerie; **hotel workers** personnel hôtelier.

hotelier [həʊ'telɪəʳ] *n* hôtelier *m*, -ière *f*.

hotly ['hɒtlɪ] *adv* avec feu, passionnément, violemment. **it was ~ disputed** ce fut contredit violemment.

Hottentot ['hɒtəntɒt] **1** *adj* hottentot. **2** *n* **(a)** Hottentot *mf*. **(b)** (*Ling*) hottentot *m*.

hound [haʊnd] **1** *n* **(a)** chien courant, chien de meute; (*often hum: any dog*) chien. **the ~s** la meute *f*; **to ride to ~s** chasser à courre; *V* **fox, master** *etc*.
(b) (*pej: person*) canaille *f*, crapule *f*.
2 *vt debtor etc* poursuivre avec acharnement, s'acharner sur, traquer. **they ~ed the lepers out of town** ils chassèrent les lépreux hors de la ville; **they ~ed him for the money** ils l'ont harassé *or* se sont acharnés sur lui pour lui soutirer l'argent.

hound down *vt sep* (traquer et) capturer.

hound out *vt sep* chasser.

hour ['aʊəʳ] **1** *n* **(a)** (*period*) heure *f*. **a quarter of an ~** un quart d'heure; **half an ~, a half-~** une demi-heure; **an ~ and a half** une heure et demie; **~ by ~** heure par heure; **80 km an ~** 80 km à l'heure; **4 ~s' walk from here** (à) 4 heures de marche d'ici; **she is paid £2 an ~** elle est payée 2 livres (de) l'heure; **he took ~s to do it** il a mis des heures *or* un temps fou* à le faire; **she's been waiting for ~s** elle attend depuis des heures; **to be ~s late** (*lit*) être en retard de plusieurs heures; (*fig*) être terriblement en retard.
(b) (*time of day, point in time*) heure *f*; (*fig*) heure, moment

m. **this clock strikes the ~s** cette horloge sonne les heures; **on the ~** toutes les heures à l'heure juste; **at the ~ stated** à l'heure dite; **the ~ has come** l'heure est venue, c'est l'heure; **his ~ has come** son heure est venue; **he realized his last ~ had come** il comprit que sa dernière heure était venue *or* arrivée; **in the early** *or* **small ~s (of the morning)** au petit matin *or* jour, aux premières heures (du jour); **at all ~s (of the day and night)** à toute heure (du jour et de la nuit); **not at this ~ surely!** tout de même pas à cette heure-ci *or* à l'heure qu'il est!; (*fig*) **at this late ~** à ce stade avancé; **in the ~ of danger** à l'heure du danger; **the problems of the ~** les problèmes du jour *or* de l'heure; **Book of H~s** livre *m* d'Heures; *V* **eleventh.**

(c) to keep early ~s être un(e) couche-tôt *inv*, se coucher tôt; **to keep late ~s** être un(e) couche-tard *inv*, veiller tard; **to keep regular ~s** avoir une vie réglée; **to work long ~s** avoir une journée très longue; (*Brit*) **after ~s** *[shops, pubs]* après l'heure de fermeture; *[offices]* après les heures de bureau; **out of ~s** en dehors des heures d'ouverture; **out of visiting ~s** en dehors des heures de visite; *V* **office, school**[1] *etc.*

2 *cpd*: **hourglass** sablier *m*; *[watch etc]* **hour hand** petite aiguille.

hourly ['aʊəlɪ] **1** *adj* **(a)** (*every hour*) *bus service etc* toutes les heures. (*Ind*) **~ rate** taux *m* horaire.

(b) (*fig: incessant*) *dread, fear* constant.

2 *adv* (*lit*) une fois par heure, chaque heure, toutes les heures; (*fig*) continuellement. **they expected him ~** ils l'attendaient d'une heure à l'autre *or* incessamment *or* à tout moment; (*Ind*) **~ paid workers** ouvriers payés à l'heure.

house [haʊs] **1** *n, pl* **houses** ['haʊzɪz] **(a)** maison *f*. **at** *or* **to my ~** chez moi; **on the ~*** aux frais de la maison, aux frais de la princesse*; (*fig*) **they got on like a ~ on fire** ils s'entendaient à merveille *or* comme larrons en foire; **the children were playing at ~(s)** les enfants jouaient à papa et maman; **doll's ~** maison de poupée; **~ of cards** château *m* de cartes; **she looks after the ~ herself** elle tient son ménage, c'est elle qui s'occupe de son ménage; **she needs more help in the ~** il faudrait qu'elle soit plus aidée à la maison; **to keep ~ (for sb)** tenir la maison *or* le ménage (de qn); **to set up ~** s'installer, monter son ménage; **they set up ~ together** ils se sont mis en ménage; **to keep open ~** tenir table ouverte; (*fig*) **to put** *or* **set one's ~ in order** mettre de l'ordre dans ses affaires; *V* **move, public, safe** *etc.*

(b) (*Parl etc*) **the H~** la Chambre; (*Brit*) **H~ of Commons/of Lords** Chambre des communes/des lords; (*US*) **H~ of Representatives** Chambre des députés; **the H~s of Parliament** (*building*) le Palais de Westminster; (*members*) le Parlement, les Chambres; *V* **floor.**

(c) (*Theat etc*) salle *f*, auditoire *m*, spectateurs *mpl*. **is there a doctor in the ~?** y a-t-il un médecin dans l'auditoire?; **in the front of the ~** parmi les spectateurs; **a full** *or* **good ~** une salle pleine; **to have a full ~** faire salle pleine, jouer à guichets fermés; **'~ full'** 'complet'; **the second ~** la deuxième séance; (*fig*) **to bring the ~ down** faire crouler la salle sous les applaudissements.

(d) (*Comm*) maison *f* (de commerce), compagnie *f*; (*noble family*) maison; (*Rel*) maison religieuse; (*Brit Scol*) maison *f*. **the H~ of Windsor** la maison des Windsors; **banking ~** établissement *m* bancaire; **business ~** compagnie, maison (de commerce); **publishing ~** maison d'édition.

2 *cpd*: (*Brit*) **house agent** agent immobilier; **house arrest** assignation *f* à domicile *or* à résidence; **to put sb under house arrest** assigner qn à domicile *or* à résidence; **to be under house arrest** être assigné à domicile, être en résidence surveillée; **houseboat** péniche *f* (aménagée); **housebound** confiné chez soi; **the housebound** les personnes isolées; **housebreaker** (*burglar*) cambrioleur *m*; (*Brit: demolition worker*) démolisseur *m*; **housebreaking** (*burglary*) cambriolage *m*; (*Brit: demolition*) démolition *f*; **housebroken** *animal* propre; (*fig*) *person* docile, obéissant; (*US*) **house-clean** faire le ménage; **housecleaning** ménage *m*, nettoyage *m* (*d'une maison*); **housecoat** peignoir *m*; **housedress** robe *f* d'intérieur; **housefather** responsable *m* (de groupe) (*dans une institution*); **housefly** mouche *f* (commune *or* domestique); **houseguest** invité(e) *m(f)*; **I've got houseguests** j'ai des amis de passage; **household** *V* **household**; (*Brit*) **house-hunt** chercher un appartement *or* une maison, être à la recherche d'un appartement *or* d'une maison; **house journal** = **house magazine**; **housekeeper** (*in sb else's house*) gouvernante *f*; (*in institution*) économe *f*, intendante *f*; **his wife is a good housekeeper** sa femme est bonne ménagère *or* maîtresse de maison; **housekeeping** (*skill*) économie *f* domestique *or* ménagère; (*work*) ménage *m*; **housekeeping (money)** argent *m* du ménage; (*Theat*) **houselights** lumières *fpl or* éclairage *m* de la salle; *[company, organization]* **house magazine** bulletin *m* (*à usage interne dans une entreprise*); **housemaid** bonne *f*, femme *f* de chambre; (*Med*) **housemaid's knee** inflammation *f* du genou; (*Theat*) **house manager** directeur *m* de théâtre; (*Brit Scol*) **housemaster, housemistress** professeur *m* responsable d'une maison; **housemother** responsable *f* (de groupe) (*dans une institution*); **house organ** = **house magazine**; **house painter** peintre *m* en bâtiments; **she had a large house party last weekend** elle a organisé une grande partie de campagne le week-end dernier; **house physician** *[hospital]* ≃ interne *mf* en médecine; *[hotel etc]* médecin *m* (*attaché à un hôtel etc*); **house prices** prix immobiliers; **to be house-proud** être une femme d'intérieur méticuleuse, avoir la manie de l'astiquage (*pej*); **houseroom** place *f* (*pour loger qch ou qn*); (*fig*) **I wouldn't give it houseroom** je n'en voudrais pas chez moi; **house sale** vente immobilière; **house surgeon** ≃ interne *mf* en chirurgie; **house-to-house** porte à porte *inv*; **to make a house-to-house search for sb** aller de porte en porte à la recherche de qn; **housetop** toit *m*; **to proclaim sth from the housetops** crier qch sur les toits; (*Brit*) **house-trained** = **housebroken**; **housewares** articles *mpl* de ménage; **house warming (party)** pendaison *f* de crémaillère; **to give a house warming (party)** pendre la crémaillère; **housewife** *V* **housewife**; **housewifely** *V* **housewifely**; **housewifery** *V* **housewifery**; **housework** (travaux *mpl* de) ménage *m*; **to do the housework** faire le ménage.

3 [haʊz] *vt person* loger, héberger, recevoir. **she was housing refugees** elle logeait *or* hébergeait des réfugiés; **the town offered to ~ six refugee families** la ville a proposé de loger six familles de réfugiés; **this building ~s 5 families/3 offices** ce bâtiment abrite 5 familles/3 bureaux; **the school can't ~ more than 100** l'école ne peut recevoir plus de 100 élèves; **the papers were ~d in a box** les papiers étaient rangés dans une boîte; **the freezer is ~d in the basement** on garde le congélateur au sous-sol.

houseful ['haʊsfʊl] *n*: **a ~ of people** une pleine maisonnée de gens; **a ~ of dogs** une maison pleine de chiens.

household ['haʊshəʊld] **1** *n* (*persons*) (gens *mpl* de la) maison *f*, maisonnée *f*, ménage *m* (*also Admin, Econ etc*). **there were 7 people in his ~** sa maison était composée de 7 personnes; **the whole ~ was there to greet him** tous les gens de la maison étaient *or* toute la maisonnée était là pour l'accueillir; **give below details of your ~** indiquez ci-dessous le nom des personnes qui résident chez vous; **~s with more than 3 wage-earners** des ménages *or* des familles *fpl* à plus de 3 salariés; (*Brit*) **H~** maison royale.

2 *cpd accounts, expenses, equipment* de *or* du ménage. **household ammonia** ammoniaque *f* (d'usage domestique); **the household arts** l'économie *f* domestique; (*Brit*) **the Household Cavalry** la Cavalerie de la Garde Royale; **household chores** (travaux *mpl* du) ménage *m*; **household gods** pénates *mpl*; **household linen** linge *m* de maison; **household soap** savon *m* de Marseille; (*Brit*) **Household troops** Garde Royale; (*fig*) **it's a household word** c'est un mot que tout le monde connaît.

householder ['haʊsˌhəʊldəʳ] *n* occupant(e) *m(f)*; (*owner*) propriétaire *mf*; (*lessee*) locataire *mf*; (*head of house*) chef *m* de famille.

housewife ['haʊswaɪf] *n, pl* **housewives** ['haʊswaɪvz] **(a)** ménagère *f*; (*as opposed to career woman*) femme *f* au foyer. **a born ~** une ménagère née, une femme au foyer type; **housewives refused to pay these prices** les ménagères ont refusé de payer ces prix; **we wish to see housewives paid for their work** nous voulons qu'on rémunère (*subj*) les femmes au foyer; **I'd rather be a ~** j'aimerais mieux être femme au foyer.

(b) ['hʌzɪf] (*sewing box*) trousse *f* de couture.

housewifely ['haʊswaɪflɪ] *adj* de ménagère.

housewifery ['haʊswɪfərɪ] *n* économie *f* domestique, tenue *f* du ménage.

housewives ['haʊswaɪvz] *npl of* **housewife.**

housing ['haʊzɪŋ] **1** *n* **(a)** logement *m*. (*Brit*) **Minister/Ministry of H~**, (*US*) **Secretary/Department of H~** ministre *m*/ministère *m* du Logement; **there's a lot of new ~** il y a beaucoup de résidences *or* de constructions nouvelles; **the ~ of workers proved difficult** le logement des ouvriers a posé un problème; *V* **low**[1].

(b) (*Tech: for mechanism etc*) boîtier *m*; (*Archit, Constr*) encastrement *m*.

2 *cpd problem, shortage, crisis* du logement. **housing estate, housing scheme,** (*US*) **housing project** cité *f*, lotissement *m*.

hove [həʊv] *pret, ptp of* **heave.**

hovel ['hɒvəl] *n* taudis *m*, bouge *m*.

hover ['hɒvəʳ] **1** *vi* **(a)** *[bird]* voltiger (*about, over* autour de); *[bird of prey, helicopter, danger, threat]* planer (*above, over* au-dessus de); *[person]* (*also* **~ about, ~ around**) rôder; *[smile]* errer. **a waiter ~ed over** *or* **round us** un garçon (de café) rôdait *or* tournait autour de nous; **he was ~ing between life and death** il restait suspendu entre la vie et la mort.

(b) (*waver*) hésiter, vaciller (*between* entre).

2 *cpd*: **hovercraft** aéroglisseur *m*.

how [haʊ] **1** *adv* **(a)** (*in what way*) **~ did you come?** comment êtes-vous venu?; **tell me ~ you came** dites-moi comment vous êtes venu; **to learn ~ to do sth** apprendre à faire qch; **I know ~ to do it** je sais le faire; **~ do you like your steak?** comment aimez-vous votre bifteck?; **~ did you like the steak?** comment avez-vous trouvé le bifteck?; **~ was the play?** comment avez-vous trouvé la pièce?; **~ is it that ...?** comment se fait-il que ...? + *subj*; **~ so?, ~'s that?, ~ can that be?** comment cela (se fait-il)?; **~ come?*** comment ça se fait?*, comment cela?, pourquoi?; **~ come you aren't going out?*** comment ça se fait que tu ne sors pas?*; **~ about going for a walk?** si on allait se promener?; **and ~!*** et comment!*

(b) (*health*) **~ are you?** comment allez-vous?; **tell me ~ she is** dites-moi comment elle va; **~ do you do?** (*greeting*) bonjour; (*on being introduced*) (enchanté) Monsieur (*or* Madame *or* Mademoiselle).

(c) (*with adj, adv: degree, quantity etc*) que, comme. **~ big he is!** comme *or* qu'il est grand!; **~ splendid!** c'est merveilleux!; **~ kind of you!** c'est très aimable à vous; **~ glad I am to see you!*** que *or* comme je suis content de vous voir!; **~ he's grown!** comme il a grandi, ce qu'il a grandi!*, comme il est grand!; **~ long is the boat?** quelle est la longueur du bateau?, quelle longueur fait le bateau?; **~ long shall I make it?** je le fais de quelle longueur?, je le fais long comment?*; **~ tall is he?** quelle est sa taille?, combien mesure-t-il?; **~ old is he?** quel âge a-t-il?; **~ soon can you come?** quand pouvez-vous venir?, quel est le plus tôt que vous puissiez venir?; **~ much does this book cost?** combien coûte ce livre?; **~ many days in a week?** combien de jours dans une semaine?

(d) (*that*) que. **she told me ~ she had seen the child lying on**

the ground elle m'a raconté qu'elle avait vu l'enfant couché par terre.

2 *n*: **the ~ and the why of it** le comment et le pourquoi de cela.

3 *cpd*: **here's a (fine) how-d'ye-do!*** en voilà une affaire!, en voilà une histoire!*; **it was a real how-d'ye-do*** c'était un joli gâchis!*; **however** *V* **however.**

howdy* ['haʊdɪ] *excl* (*US*) salut!*

however [haʊ'evəʳ] **1** *adv* **(a)** de quelque manière *or* façon que + *subj.* **~ you may do it, it will never be right** de quelque manière que vous le fassiez, ce ne sera jamais bien fait; **~ that may be** quoi qu'il en soit.

(b) (+ *adj*) quelque *or* si ... que + *subj.* **~ tall he may be** *or* **is** quelque *or* si grand qu'il soit; **~ much money he has** quelque argent qu'il ait, pour riche qu'il soit; **~ little** si peu que ce soit; **~ few people come, we'll do the play** pour peu nombreux que soit le public, nous jouerons la pièce.

(c) (*: *in questions*) **~ did you do it?*** comment avez-vous bien pu faire ça?*

2 *conj* pourtant, cependant, toutefois, néanmoins.

howitzer ['haʊɪtsəʳ] *n* obusier *m.*

howl [haʊl] **1** *n* *[person, animal]* hurlement *m*; *[baby]* braillement *m*, hurlement; *[wind]* mugissement *m*. **there were ~s of laughter** on entendit d'énormes éclats de rire.

2 *vi* *[person, animal]* hurler; (*: *cry*) pleurer; *[baby]* brailler; *[wind]* mugir. **to ~ with laughter** rire aux éclats *or* à gorge déployée; **to ~ with pain/fury** hurler de douleur/de rage; **to ~ with derision** lancer des huées.

3 *vt* (*also* **~ out**) hurler, crier. **they ~ed their disapproval** ils hurlaient leur désapprobation.

howl down *vt sep*: **they howled the speaker down** ils ont réduit l'orateur au silence par leurs huées.

howler* ['haʊləʳ] *n* gaffe* *f*, bourde *f*. **(schoolboy) ~** perle *f* (d'écolier).

howling ['haʊlɪŋ] **1** *n* *[person, animal]* hurlement(s) *m(pl)*; *[baby]* braillement(s) *m(pl)*; *[wind]* mugissement(s) *m(pl)*. **2** *adj* **(a)** *person, animal* hurlant. **a ~ gale** une violente tempête. **(b)** (**fig*) *mistake* énorme. **~ success** succès fou*.

hoy [hɔɪ] *excl* ohé!

hoyden ['hɔɪdn] *n* garçon manqué.

hoydenish ['hɔɪdənɪʃ] *adj* garçonnier, de garçon manqué.

hub [hʌb] *n* *[wheel]* moyeu *m*; (*fig*) pivot *m*, centre *m*. (*Aut*) **~ cap** enjoliveur *m.*

hubbub ['hʌbʌb] *n* brouhaha *m*, vacarme *m.*

hubby‡ ['hʌbɪ] *n* (*abbr of* **husband**) petit mari*, bonhomme* *m*. **my ~** le patron*.

hubris ['hju:brɪs] *n* orgueil *m* (démesuré).

huckleberry ['hʌklbərɪ] *n* (*US*) myrtille *f*, airelle *f.*

huckster ['hʌkstəʳ] *n* (*US*) (*hawker*) colporteur *m*; (*fig pej*) mercanti *m*; (*: *salesman*) vendeur *m* de choc*.

huddle ['hʌdl] **1** *n* *[people]* petit groupe (compact); *[books etc]* tas *m*, amas *m*. **a ~ of houses in the valley** quelques maisons blotties dans la vallée; **to go into a ~*** se réunir en petit comité (*fig*).

2 *vi* se blottir (les uns contre les autres). **we ~d round the fire** nous nous sommes blottis près du feu; **the baby birds ~d in the nest** les oisillons se blottissaient les uns contre les autres dans le nid; *V also* **huddled.**

huddle down *vi* (*crouch*) se recroqueviller, se faire tout petit; (*snuggle*) se blottir, se pelotonner.

huddle together *vi* se serrer *or* se blottir les uns contre les autres, se réunir en (un) petit groupe. **they were huddling together for warmth** ils se serraient *or* se blottissaient les uns contre les autres pour se tenir chaud; **they huddled together to discuss the proposal** ils ont formé un petit groupe pour discuter de la proposition; *V also* **huddled.**

huddle up *vi* se blottir, se pelotonner.

huddled ['hʌdld] *adj*: **the chairs were ~ in a corner** les chaises étaient rassemblées *or* groupées dans un coin; **houses ~ (together) round the church** des maisons blotties autour de l'église; **he lay ~ under the blankets** il était blotti *or* pelotonné sous les couvertures; **the children lay ~ under the blankets** les enfants étaient blottis *or* pelotonnés les uns contre les autres sous les couvertures; **he was ~ over his books** il était penché sur ses livres.

Hudson Bay ['hʌdsən'beɪ] *n* baie *f* d'Hudson.

hue[1] [hju:] *n*: **~ and cry** clameur *f* (de haro); **with ~ and cry** à cor et à cri; **to raise a ~ and cry against** crier haro sur.

hue[2] [hju:] *n* (*colour*) teinte *f*, nuance *f.*

-hued [hju:d] *adj ending in cpds*: **many-hued** multicolore.

huff* [hʌf] *n*: **to be in a ~** être froissé *or* fâché; **to take (the) ~, to get into a ~** prendre la mouche, s'offusquer; **he left in a ~** il est parti froissé *or* fâché.

huffed* [hʌft] *adj* froissé, fâché.

huffily* ['hʌfɪlɪ] *adv* *leave* avec humeur; *say* d'un ton froissé *or* fâché.

huffiness* ['hʌfɪnɪs] *n* mauvaise humeur.

huffy* ['hʌfɪ] *adj* (*annoyed*) froissé, fâché; (*sulky*) boudeur; (*touchy*) susceptible.

hug [hʌg] **1** *vt* **(a)** (*hold close*) serrer dans ses bras, étreindre; *[bear, gorilla]* écraser entre ses bras; (*fig*) *opinion etc* tenir à, ne pas démordre de. (*fig*) **to ~ o.s. over** *or* **about sth** jubiler de qch.

(b) serrer. (*Naut*) **to ~ the shore/wind** serrer la côte/le vent; *[car]* **to ~ the kerb** serrer le trottoir.

2 *n* étreinte *f*. **to give sb a ~** serrer qn dans ses bras, étreindre qn; **he gave the child a big (bear) ~** il a serré l'enfant bien fort dans ses bras.

huge [hju:dʒ] *adj* énorme, immense, vaste.

hugely ['hju:dʒlɪ] *adv* énormément; (*very*) extrêmement.

hugeness ['hju:dʒnɪs] *n* immensité *f.*

hugger-mugger* ['hʌgə,mʌgəʳ] **1** *n* (*muddle*) fouillis *m*, pagaïe* *f or* pagaille* *f*, désordre *m*; (*secrecy*) secret *m*. **2** *adj* désordonné; secret (*f* -ète). **3** *adv* en désordre; en secret.

Hugh [hju:] *n* Hugues *m.*

Huguenot ['hju:gənəʊ] **1** *adj* huguenot. **2** *n* Huguenot(e) *m(f).*

huh [hʌ] *excl* (*dismay*) oh!; (*surprise, disbelief*) hein?; (*disgust*) berk!*, beuh!

hulk [hʌlk] *n* (*prison etc ship*) ponton *m*; (*wrecked ship*) épave *f*; (*ramshackle ship*) vieux rafiot‡; (*wrecked vehicle, building etc*) carcasse *f*. **(big) ~ of a man** mastodonte* *m*, malabar* *m.*

hulking ['hʌlkɪŋ] *adj* balourd, lourdaud, gros (*f* grosse). **he was a ~ great brute** c'était un gros malabar*.

hull [hʌl] **1** *n* **(a)** *[ship, plane]* coque *f*; *[tank]* caisse *f*. **a ship ~ down on the horizon** un navire coque noyée *or* dont la coque disparaissait sous l'horizon.

(b) *[nuts]* coque *f*; *[peas, beans]* cosse *f*, gousse *f.*

2 *vt* **(a)** *peas* écosser; *barley* émonder; *oats, rice* décortiquer; *nuts* écaler.

(b) *ship, plane* percer la coque de.

hullabaloo* [,hʌləbə'lu:] *n* (*noise*) chambard* *m*, boucan* *m*, raffut* *m*. (*fuss*) **there was quite a ~ about the missing money** on a fait toute une histoire* *or* tout un foin‡ à propos de l'argent disparu.

hullo [hʌ'ləʊ] *excl* = **hallo.**

hum [hʌm] **1** *vi* **(a)** *[insect]* bourdonner; *[person]* fredonner, chantonner; *[aeroplane, engine, machine]* vrombir; *[top, wireless etc]* ronfler; *[wire]* bourdonner. (*fig*) **to make things ~*** mener *or* faire marcher les choses rondement; **then things began to ~*** alors les choses ont commencé à chauffer* *or* à s'animer; *V* **haw**[2].

(b) (‡: *stink*) puer, sentir mauvais, taper‡.

2 *vt* *tune* fredonner, chantonner.

3 *n* **(a)** *[insect, voices]* bourdonnement *m*; *[aeroplane, machine, engine]* vrombissement *m*; *[top etc]* ronflement *m.*

(b) (‡: *stink*) puanteur *f.*

4 *excl* hem!, hum!

human ['hju:mən] **1** *adj* humain. **~ being** être humain; **the ~ race** la race humaine, le genre humain; **~ nature** nature humaine; **it's only ~ nature to want revenge** c'est normal *or* humain de chercher à se venger; **he's only ~ after all** il n'est pas un saint, personne n'est parfait; **to lack the ~ touch** manquer de chaleur humaine; **it needs the ~ touch to bring the situation home to the public** le public ne comprend la situation que lorsqu'il la voit sous l'angle humain.

2 *n* humain *m*, être humain.

3 *cpd*: (*U*) **humankind** humanité *f*, genre humain, race humaine.

humane [hju:'meɪn] *adj* **(a)** (*compassionate*) *person, attitude* humain, plein d'humanité; *method* humain. **(b) ~ studies** humanités *fpl*, sciences humaines.

humanism ['hju:mənɪzəm] *n* humanisme *m.*

humanist ['hju:mənɪst] *n* humaniste *mf.*

humanistic [,hju:mə'nɪstɪk] *adj* humaniste.

humanitarian [hju:,mænɪ'tɛərɪən] *adj, n* humanitaire (*mf*).

humanity [hju:'mænɪtɪ] *n* humanité *f*. **the humanities** les humanités.

humanize ['hju:mənaɪz] *vt* humaniser.

humanly ['hju:mənlɪ] *adv* humainement, avec humanité. **if it is ~ possible** si c'est humainement possible.

humanoid ['hju:mənɔɪd] *adj, n* humanoïde (*mf*).

humble ['hʌmbl] **1** *adj* humble, modeste. **of ~ birth** *or* **extraction** d'humble extraction; **of ~ origin** d'origine modeste; **in my ~ opinion** à mon humble avis; (*fig*) **to eat ~ pie** faire des excuses humiliantes; (*in letters: frm*) **I am, Sir, your ~ servant** veuillez agréer, Monsieur, l'assurance de ma considération très distinguée; (*hum: oneself*) **your ~ servant** votre serviteur (*hum*).

2 *vt* humilier, mortifier. **to ~ o.s.** s'humilier, s'abaisser.

3 *cpd*: **humble-bee** bourdon *m.*

humbleness ['hʌmblnɪs] *n* humilité *f.*

humbly ['hʌmblɪ] *adv* humblement, modestement.

humbug ['hʌmbʌg] *n* **(a)** (*person*) charlatan *m*, fumiste* *m*; (*behaviour, talk*) blague* *f*, fumisterie* *f*. **(b)** (*Brit: sweet*) bonbon *m* à la menthe.

humdinger‡ ['hʌmdɪŋəʳ] *n* quelqu'un *or* quelque chose de terrible* *or* de sensationnel*. **it's a ~!** c'est terrible* *or* sensass!‡; **she's a ~** elle est extra* *or* terrible* *or* sensass‡; **a ~ of a speech** un discours sensationnel*; (*Sport*) **that shot was a real ~** c'est un coup sans bavure*.

humdrum ['hʌmdrʌm] **1** *adj* monotone, banal, routinier. **2** *n* monotonie *f*, banalité *f.*

humerus ['hju:mərəs] *n* humérus *m.*

humid ['hju:mɪd] *adj* humide.

humidifier [hju:'mɪdɪfaɪəʳ] *n* humidificateur *m.*

humidity [hju:'mɪdɪtɪ] *n* humidité *f.*

humidor ['hju:mɪdɔ:ʳ] *n* humidificateur *m.*

humiliate [hju:'mɪlɪeɪt] *vt* humilier.

humiliating [hju:'mɪlɪeɪtɪŋ] *adj* humiliant.

humiliation [hju:,mɪlɪ'eɪʃən] *n* humiliation *f.*

humility [hju:'mɪlɪtɪ] *n* humilité *f.*

humming ['hʌmɪŋ] **1** *n* *[insect, voices]* bourdonnement *m*; *[aeroplane, engine, machine]* vrombissement *m*; *[person]* fredonnement *m*. **2** *cpd*: **hummingbird** oiseau-mouche *m*, colibri *m*; **humming-top** toupie ronflante.

hummock ['hʌmək] *n* (*hillock*) mamelon *m*, tertre *m*, monticule *m*; (*in ice field*) hummock *m.*

humor ['hju:məʳ] *n* (*US*) = **humour.**

-humored ['hju:məd] *adj ending in cpds* (*US*) = **-humoured.**

humorist ['hju:mərɪst] *n* humoriste *mf.*

humorless ['hju:məlɪs] *adj* (*US*) = **humourless.**

humorous ['hju:mərəs] *adj genre, book, story* humoristique; *person, writer, remark* plein d'humour, amusant.

humorously ['hju:mərəslı] *adv* avec humour.

humour, (*US*) **humor** ['hju:məʳ] **1** *n* **(a)** (*sense of fun*) humour *m.* **he has no sense of ~** il n'a pas le sens de l'humour; **I see no ~ in that** je ne vois pas où est l'humour; **this is no time for ~** ce n'est pas le moment de faire de l'humour.

(b) (*temper*) humeur *f*, disposition *f.* **to be in a good/bad ~** être de bonne/mauvaise humeur; **he is in no ~ for working** il n'est pas d'humeur à travailler; **to be out of ~** être de mauvaise humeur.

(c) (*Med††*) humeur *f.*

2 *vt person* faire plaisir à, ménager; *sb's wishes, whims* se prêter à, se plier à.

-humoured, (*US*) **-humored** ['hju:məd] *adj ending in cpds*: **good-humoured** de bonne humeur; **bad-humoured** de mauvaise humeur.

humourless, (*US*) **humorless** ['hju:məlıs] *adj person* qui manque d'humour *or* du sens de l'humour; *attitude, book, voice* sans humour.

hump [hʌmp] **1** *n* **(a)** (*Anat*) bosse *f*; *[camel]* bosse.

(b) (*hillock*) bosse *f*, mamelon *m.* (*fig*) **we're over the ~ now*** le plus difficile est passé *or* fait maintenant, on a doublé le cap maintenant.

(c) (*Brit:*) cafard* *m.* **he's got the ~** il a le cafard*, il a le moral à zéro*; **that gives me the ~** ça me donne le cafard*, ça me met le moral à zéro*.

2 *vt* **(a)** arrondir, voûter. **to ~ one's back** *[person]* arrondir *or* voûter le dos; *[cat]* faire le gros dos; **to ~ one's shoulders** voûter les épaules, rentrer la tête dans les épaules.

(b) (*: *carry*) porter.

3 *cpd*: **humpbacked** *person* bossu; *bridge* en dos d'âne.

humph [mm] *excl* hum!

humpy ['hʌmpı] *adj ground* inégal, accidenté.

humus ['hju:məs] *n* humus *m.*

Hun [hʌn] *n* (*Hist*) Hun *m*; (**pej*) Boche: *m* (*pej*).

hunch [hʌntʃ] **1** *vt* (*also* **~ up**) *back* arrondir; *shoulders* voûter. **to ~ one's back** arrondir le dos, se voûter; **~ed shoulders** épaules voûtées *or* remontées; **with ~ed shoulders** la tête rentrée dans les épaules; **he sat ~ed (up) over his books** il était assis courbé *or* penché sur ses livres.

2 *n* **(a)** (*hump*) bosse *f.*

(b) (*hunk*) morceau *m.* **~ of bread** (gros) morceau *or* quignon *m* de pain; **~ of cheese** gros morceau de fromage.

(c) (*: *premonition*) pressentiment *m*, intuition *f.* **to have a ~ that ...** avoir comme une (petite) idée *or* comme un pressentiment que* ...; **you should follow your ~** il faut suivre son intuition; **it's only a ~** ce n'est qu'une idée (comme ça*); **~es sometimes pay off** on fait quelquefois bien de suivre son intuition.

3 *cpd*: **hunchback** bossu(e) *m(f)*; **hunchbacked** bossu.

hundred ['hʌndrıd] **1** *adj* cent. **a ~ books/chairs** cent livres/chaises; **two ~ chairs** deux cents chaises; **about a ~ books** une centaine de livres.

2 *n* **(a)** cent *m.* **about a ~, a ~-odd*** une centaine; **I've got a ~** j'en ai cent; **a** *or* **one ~ and one** cent un; **two ~** deux cents; **two ~ and one** deux cent un; **the ~ and first** le *or* la cent unième; **a ~ per cent** cent pour cent; (*fig*) **it was a ~ per cent successful** cela a réussi à cent pour cent; **in seventeen ~** en dix-sept cents; **in seventeen ~ and ninety-six** en dix-sept cent quatre-vingt-seize; (*Comm*) **sold by the ~** vendus au cent; **to live to be a ~** devenir centenaire; **they came in (their) ~s** ils sont venus par centaines; (*Hist*) **the H~ Days** les Cent Jours; (*Hist*) **the H~ Years' War** la guerre de Cent Ans; *for other phrases V* **sixty.**

(b) (**fig*) **~s of** des centaines de, des tas* de; **I've told you ~s of times!** je te l'ai dit cent fois!

3 *cpd*: **hundredfold** (*adj*) centuple; (*adv*) au centuple; **hundredweight** (*Brit, Can*) poids *m* de cent douze livres (*50,7 kg*); (*US*) (poids de) cent livres (*45,3 kg*); **a hundred-year-old tree** un arbre centenaire *or* séculaire.

hundredth ['hʌndrıdθ] **1** *adj* centième. **2** *n* centième *mf*; (*fraction*) centième *m.*

hung [hʌŋ] **1** *pret, ptp of* **hang. 2** *adj*: **he's ~ up: about it** il en fait tout un complexe*.

Hungarian [hʌŋ'gɛərıən] **1** *adj* hongrois. **2** *n* **(a)** Hongrois(e) *m(f).* **(b)** (*Ling*) hongrois *m.*

Hungary ['hʌŋgərı] *n* Hongrie *f.*

hunger ['hʌŋgəʳ] **1** *n* faim *f*; (*fig*) faim, soif *f*, désir ardent (*for* de).

2 *cpd*: (*Brit Hist*) **the hunger marches** les marches *fpl* de la faim; **to go on a hunger strike** faire la grève de la faim.

3 *vi* (*liter*) avoir faim. (*fig*) **to ~ for** *or* **after** avoir faim *or* soif de, désirer ardemment.

hungrily ['hʌŋgrılı] *adv* (*lit*) voracement, avidement; (*fig*) avidement. **to look ~ at sth, to eye sth ~** convoiter qch du regard, jeter un regard de convoitise sur qch.

hungry ['hʌŋgrı] *adj*: **to be ~** avoir faim, avoir l'estomac creux; **to be very ~** avoir très faim, être affamé; **to feel ~** avoir faim, se sentir (le ventre) creux; **to make sb ~** donner faim à qn; **to go ~** (*starve*) souffrir de la faim; (*miss a meal*) se passer de manger; **if you don't eat your spinach you'll have to go ~** si tu ne manges pas tes épinards tu n'auras rien d'autre; **you look ~** tu as l'air d'avoir faim; (*fig*) **~ for** avide de.

hunk [hʌŋk] *n* = **hunch 2b.**

hunky-dory* ['hʌŋkı'dɔ:rı] *adj* (*esp US*) chouette*, au poil*. **it's all ~** tout marche comme sur des roulettes*.

hunt [hʌnt] **1** *n* **(a)** (*Sport*) chasse *f.* **elephant/tiger ~** chasse à l'éléphant/au tigre; **the ~ rode by** les chasseurs sont passés à cheval.

(b) (*gen*) chasse *f*, recherche *f.* **the ~ for the murderer** la chasse au meurtrier; **we all went on a ~ for the missing key/child** nous nous sommes tous mis à la recherche de la clef perdue/de l'enfant disparu; **I've had a ~ for my gloves** j'ai cherché mes gants partout, j'ai tout retourné pour trouver mes gants; **to be on the ~ for a cheap house** chercher une *or* être à la recherche d'une maison pas chère.

2 *vt* (*Sport*) chasser, faire la chasse à; (*pursue*) poursuivre, pourchasser; (*seek*) chercher. (*Sport*) **to ~ a horse** monter un cheval à la chasse; **we ~ed the town for a green vase** nous avons fait* toute la ville à la recherche d'un vase vert; **I've ~ed my desk for it** j'ai retourné tout mon bureau pour le trouver.

3 *vi* (*Sport*) chasser. **to go ~ing** aller à la chasse; **to ~ for** (*Sport*) faire la chasse à, chasser; (*gen*) *object, details, facts* rechercher (partout), être à la recherche de; **he ~ed in his pocket for his pen** il a fouillé dans sa poche pour trouver son stylo; **I've been ~ing (about** *or* **around) for that book everywhere** j'ai cherché ce livre partout, j'ai tout retourné pour trouver ce livre.

hunt down *vt sep animal* forcer; *person* traquer; *object, facts, details, quotation* dénicher.

hunt out *vt sep* dénicher, découvrir.

hunt up *vt sep* rechercher.

hunter ['hʌntəʳ] *n* (*person: Sport*) chasseur *m*; (*fig*) poursuivant *m*; (*horse*) cheval *m* de chasse; (*watch*) (montre *f* à) savonnette *f*; *V* **lion** *etc.*

hunting ['hʌntıŋ] **1** *n* (*Sport*) chasse *f* à courre; (*fox~*) chasse au renard; (*pursuit*) chasse *f* (*for* à), poursuite *f* (*for* de).

2 *cpd*: **hunting ground** (terrain *m* de) chasse *f* (*V* **happy**); **hunting horn** cor *m or* trompe *f* de chasse; **hunting lodge** pavillon *m* de chasse; **hunting pink** rouge chasseur *inv*; **the hunting season** la saison de la chasse.

huntress ['hʌntrıs] *n* (*liter*) chasseresse *f.*

huntsman ['hʌntsmən] *n, pl* **huntsmen** ['hʌntsmən] chasseur *m.*

hurdle ['hɜ:dl] **1** *n* (*for fences*) claie *f*; (*Sport*) haie *f*; (*fig*) obstacle *m.* (*Sport*) **the 100-metre ~s** le 100 mètres haies; **to take a ~** (*Sport*) franchir une haie; (*fig*) franchir un obstacle.

2 *cpd*: (*Sport*) **the hurdles champion** le champion de course de haies; (*Sport*) **hurdle race** course *f* de haies.

3 *vi* (*Sport*) faire de la course de haies.

hurdler ['hɜ:dləʳ] *n* (*Sport*) coureur *m*, -euse *f* (qui fait des courses de haies).

hurdy-gurdy ['hɜ:dı,gɜ:dı] *n* orgue *m* de Barbarie.

hurl [hɜ:l] *vt stone* jeter *or* lancer (avec violence) (*at* contre). **they were ~ed to the ground by the blast** ils ont été précipités à terre par le souffle de l'explosion; **to ~ o.s. at sb/sth** se ruer sur qn/qch; **they ~ed themselves into the fray** ils se sont jetés dans la mêlée; **he ~ed himself over a cliff** il s'est jeté *or* précipité (du haut) d'une falaise; (*fig*) **to be ~ed into** être précipité dans; **to ~ abuse at sb** lancer des injures à qn, accabler *or* agonir qn d'injures.

hurly-burly ['hɜ:lı'bɜ:lı] *n* (*commotion*) tohu-bohu *m*; (*uproar*) tintamarre *m*, tumulte *m*, brouhaha *m.* **the ~ of politics** le tourbillon de la politique.

hurrah [hʊ'rɑ:] *n,* **hurray** [hʊ'reı] *n* hourra *m.* **~ for Robert!** vive Robert!; *V* **hip**[3].

hurricane ['hʌrıkən] *n* ouragan *m.* **~ lamp** lampe-tempête *f.*

hurried ['hʌrıd] *adj steps* précipité, pressé; *remark* dit à la hâte; *departure* précipité; *reading* très rapide; *work* fait à la hâte, fait à la va-vite* (*pej*), bâclé (*pej*). **a ~ line to tell you ...** un mot bref *or* à la hâte pour te dire ...; **to have a ~ meal** manger à la hâte; **we had a ~ discussion about it** nous en avons discuté rapidement.

hurriedly ['hʌrıdlı] *adv do* précipitamment, à la hâte. **he explained ~** il s'est empressé d'expliquer; **... she said ~** ... dit-elle précipitamment.

hurry ['hʌrı] **1** *n* (*haste*) hâte *f*, précipitation *f*; (*eagerness*) empressement *m.* **to be in a ~** être pressé; **to be in a ~ to do** avoir hâte de faire; **it was done in a ~** cela a été fait à la hâte; **I won't do that again in a ~!*** je ne recommencerai pas de sitôt!, je ne suis pas près de recommencer!; **he won't come back here in a ~!*** il ne reviendra pas de sitôt!, il n'est pas près de revenir!; **are you in a ~ for this?** vous le voulez très vite?; **what's the** *or* **your ~?** qu'est-ce qui (vous) presse?; **there's no ~** rien ne presse, il n'y a pas le feu*; **there's no ~ for it** ça ne presse pas.

2 *vi* **(a)** se dépêcher, se presser, se hâter (*to do* de faire). **do ~** dépêchez-vous; **don't ~** ne vous pressez *or* dépêchez pas; **I must ~** il faut que je me dépêche (*subj*) *or* presse (*subj*); **don't ~ over that essay** ne faites pas cette dissertation à la va-vite, prenez votre temps pour faire cette dissertation; **if we ~ over the meal** si nous mangeons rapidement, si nous nous dépêchons de manger.

(b) to ~ in/out/through *etc* entrer/sortir/traverser *etc* à la hâte *or* en toute hâte *or* précipitamment; **she hurried (over) to her sister's** elle s'est précipitée chez sa sœur, elle s'est rendue chez sa sœur en toute hâte; **he hurried (over) towards me** il s'est précipité vers moi; **he hurried after her** il a couru pour la rattraper; **they hurried up the stairs** ils ont monté l'escalier précipitamment *or* en toute hâte *or* quatre à quatre; **she hurried home** elle s'est dépêchée de rentrer, elle est rentrée en hâte.

3 *vt* **(a)** *person* faire presser, bousculer, faire se dépêcher; *piece of work* presser. **don't ~ your meal** ne mangez pas trop vite; **you can't ~ him, he won't be hurried** vous ne le ferez pas se dépêcher; **this plan can't be hurried** ce projet exige d'être exécuté sans hâte; *V also* **hurried.**

(b) to ~ sb in/out/through *etc* faire entrer/sortir/traverser qn à la hâte *or* en (toute) hâte; **they hurried him to a doctor** ils l'ont emmené d'urgence chez un médecin; **troops were hurried to the spot** des troupes ont été envoyées d'urgence sur place.

hurry along 1 *vi* marcher d'un pas pressé. **hurry along please!** pressons un peu *or* activons*, s'il vous plaît!
2 *vt sep* = **hurry on 2.**
hurry back *vi* se presser de revenir. (*to guest*) **hurry back!** revenez-nous bientôt!; **don't hurry back, I shall be here till 6 o'clock** ne te presse pas de revenir, je serai ici jusqu'à 6 heures.
hurry on 1 *vi* se dépêcher, continuer à la hâte *or* en hâte. **she hurried on to the next stop** elle s'est pressée de gagner l'arrêt suivant; **they hurried on to the next question** ils sont vite passés à la question suivante.
2 *vt sep person* faire presser le pas à, faire se dépêcher, activer; *work etc* activer, accélérer. **we're trying to hurry things on a little** nous essayons d'accélérer *or* d'activer un peu les choses.
hurry up 1 *vi* se dépêcher, se presser. **hurry up!** dépêchez-vous!, activez!*
2 *vt sep person* faire se dépêcher, (faire) activer; *work* activer, pousser.
hurry-scurry ['hʌrɪ'skʌrɪ] 1 *vi* courir dans tous les sens. 2 *n* bousculade *f*, débandade *f*. 3 *adv* à la débandade.
hurt [hɜ:t] *pret, ptp* **hurt** 1 *vt* **(a)** (*physically*) faire du mal à, blesser. **to ~ o.s.** se faire (du) mal, se blesser; **to ~ one's arm** se blesser au bras; **my arm ~s me** mon bras me fait mal; **I hope I haven't ~ you** j'espère que je ne vous ai pas fait mal?; **where does it ~ you?** où avez-vous mal?, où cela vous fait-il mal?; **to get ~** se faire (du) mal; **someone is bound to get ~** quelqu'un va se faire mal, il va y avoir quelqu'un de blessé.
(b) (*mentally etc*) faire de la peine à. **in such cases someone is bound to get ~** en pareils cas il y a toujours quelqu'un qui pâtit *or* qui écope*; **wine never ~ anyone** un peu de vin n'a jamais fait de mal à personne; **a little rest won't ~ him** un peu de repos ne lui fera pas de mal; **what ~ most was ...** ce qui faisait le plus mal c'était ...; **to ~ sb's feelings** offenser *or* froisser *or* blesser qn; **his feelings were ~ by what you said** ce que vous avez dit l'a froissé; **that will ~ his reputation** cela nuira à sa réputation; **that rumour will ~ his business** cette rumeur fera du tort à *or* nuira à son commerce.
(c) *thing* abîmer, endommager. **moths can't ~ this material** les mites ne peuvent pas attaquer ce tissu; **it wouldn't ~ the grass to water it** ça ne ferait pas de mal au gazon d'être arrosé.
2 *vi* faire mal. **that ~s** ça fait mal; **my arm ~s** mon bras me fait mal; **it doesn't ~ much** ça ne fait pas très mal; **where does it ~?** où avez-vous mal?; (*loc*) **nothing ~s like the truth** il n'y a que la vérité qui blesse (*loc*); **it won't ~ for being left for a while** il n'y aura pas de mal à laisser cela de côté un instant.
3 *n* (*physical*) mal *m*, blessure *f*. (*fig*) **the real ~ lay in his attitude to her** ce qui la blessait réellement *or* lui faisait vraiment mal c'était l'attitude qu'il avait envers elle.
4 *adj* (*physically injured*) blessé; (*offended*) offensé, froissé, blessé. **with a ~ expression** avec un regard meurtri *or* blessé; **she's feeling ~ about it** elle en est *or* a été blessée.
hurtful ['hɜ:tfʊl] *adj* nocif, nuisible, préjudiciable (*to* à); *remark* blessant, offensant. **~ to his health** nuisible *or* préjudiciable à sa santé; **what a ~ thing to say!** comme c'est méchant *or* (*stronger*) cruel de dire cela!
hurtle ['hɜ:tl] 1 *vi [car, person]* **to ~ along** avancer à toute vitesse *or* allure; **to ~ past sb** passer en trombe à côté de qn; **the stone ~d through the air** la pierre a fendu l'air; **great masses of snow ~d down the mountain** d'énormes masses de neige dévalèrent de la montagne; **she went hurtling down the hill** elle a dégringolé *or* dévalé la pente.
2 *vt* lancer (de toutes ses forces *or* violemment).
husband ['hʌzbənd] 1 *n* mari *m*, époux *m*. **now they're ~ and wife** ils sont maintenant mari et femme; **they were living together as ~ and wife** ils vivaient maritalement *or* en ménage.
2 *vt strength* ménager, économiser; *supplies, resources* bien gérer.
husbandry ['hʌzbəndrɪ] *n* (*Agr*) agriculture *f*; (*fig*) économie *f*, gestion *f*. **good ~** bonne gestion; *V* **animal.**
hush [hʌʃ] 1 *n* calme *m*, silence *m*. **the ~ before the storm** le calme avant la tempête; **there was a sudden ~, a ~ fell** il y a eu un silence, tout à coup tout le monde s'est tu; **in the ~ of the night** dans le silence de la nuit; **~!** chut!, silence!; *V also* **hushed.**
2 *cpd*: **hush-hush*** (ultra-)secret (*f* -ète); **hush money*** pot-de-vin *m* (*pour acheter le silence*), prix *m* du silence; **to pay sb hush money*** acheter le silence de qn.
3 *vt* (*silence*) faire taire; (*soothe*) apaiser, calmer. **she ~ed the baby to sleep** elle endormit le bébé en le berçant.
hush up *vt sep scandal, news* étouffer; *person* faire taire, empêcher de parler.
hushed [hʌʃt] *adj voice, conversation* étouffé. **there was a ~ silence** il y eut un grand *or* profond silence.
husk [hʌsk] 1 *n [wheat]* balle *f*; *[maize, rice]* enveloppe *f*; *[chestnut]* bogue *f*; *[nut]* écale *f*; *[peas]* cosse *f*, gousse *f*. **rice in the ~** riz non décortiqué. 2 *vt maize, rice* décortiquer; *nut* écaler; *grain* vanner; *peas* écosser; *barley, oats* monder.
huskily ['hʌskɪlɪ] *adv speak, whisper* d'une voix rauque; *sing* d'une voix voilée.
huskiness ['hʌskɪnɪs] *n* enrouement *m*.
husky[1] ['hʌskɪ] *adj* **(a)** (*hoarse*) *person* enroué; *voice* rauque; *singer's voice* voilé. **(b)** (*burly*) costaud*.
husky[2] ['hʌskɪ] *n* (*dog*) chien esquimau *or* de traîneau.
hussar [hʊ'zɑ:ʳ] *n* hussard *m*.
hussy ['hʌsɪ] *n* **(a)** (*minx*) coquine* *f*, mâtine* *f*. **you little ~!** petite coquine!* **(b)** (*pej*) garce: *f*, traînée: *f*.
hustings ['hʌstɪŋz] *npl* (*esp Brit*) plate-forme électorale. **he said it on the ~** il l'a dit pendant *or* au cours de sa campagne électorale.
hustle ['hʌsl] 1 *vt person* pousser, bousculer, presser. **to ~ sb in/out** *etc* pousser *or* bousculer qn pour le faire entrer/sortir *etc*; **they ~d him into a car** ils l'ont poussé *or* enfourné* dans une voiture; **I won't be ~d into anything** je ne ferai rien si on me bouscule; **I don't want to ~ you but ...** je ne veux pas vous bousculer mais ...; **to ~ things (on *or* along)** faire activer les choses.
2 *vi* se bousculer. **to ~ in/out/away** entrer/sortir/partir en se bousculant.
3 *n* (*jostling*) bousculade *f*, presse *f*; (*activity*) grande activité. **~ and bustle** tourbillon *m* d'activité; **the ~ and bustle of city life** le tourbillon de la vie dans les grandes villes.
hustler* ['hʌsləʳ] *n* type* *m* dynamique, débrouillard(e)* *m(f)*.
hut [hʌt] *n* (*primitive dwelling*) hutte *f*; (*hovel*) masure *f*, baraque* *f*; (*shed*) cabane *f*; (*Mil*) baraquement *m*; (*in mountains*) (chalet-)refuge *m*; *V* **mud.**
hutch [hʌtʃ] *n [rabbit etc]* clapier *m*; (*US: dresser*) vaisselier *m*.
hyacinth ['haɪəsɪnθ] *n* (*Bot*) jacinthe *f*; (*stone*) hyacinthe *f*. (*Bot*) **wild ~** jacinthe des bois *or* sauvage, endymion *m*.
hyaena [haɪ'i:nə] *n* hyène *f*.
hybrid ['haɪbrɪd] *adj, n* hybride (*m*).
hybridism ['haɪbrɪdɪzəm] *n* hybridisme *m*.
hybridization [,haɪbrɪdaɪ'zeɪʃən] *n* hybridation *f*.
hybridize ['haɪbrɪdaɪz] *vt* hybrider, croiser.
hydra ['haɪdrə] *n* hydre *f*.
hydrangea [haɪ'dreɪndʒə] *n* hortensia *m*.
hydrant ['haɪdrənt] *n* prise *f* d'eau; (*also* **fire ~**) bouche *f* d'incendie.
hydrate ['haɪdreɪt] 1 *n* hydrate *m*. 2 *vt* hydrater.
hydraulic [haɪ'drɒlɪk] *adj* hydraulique.
hydraulics [haɪ'drɒlɪks] *n* (*U*) hydraulique *f*.
hydro ['haɪdrəʊ] 1 *n* **(a)** (*Brit: hotel etc*) établissement thermal (*hôtel*). **(b)** (*Can*) (*power*) énergie *f* hydro-électrique; (*plant*) centrale *f* d'énergie hydro-électrique. 2 *adj* (*Can*) hydro-électrique.
hydr(o)... ['haɪdr(əʊ)] *pref* hydr(o)... .
hydrocarbon ['haɪdrəʊ'kɑ:bən] *n* hydrocarbure *m*.
hydrochloric ['haɪdrə'klɒrɪk] *adj* chlorhydrique.
hydrocyanic ['haɪdrəsaɪ'ænɪk] *adj* cyanhydrique.
hydrodynamics ['haɪdrəʊdaɪ'næmɪks] *n* (*U*) hydrodynamique *f*.
hydroelectric ['haɪdrəʊɪ'lektrɪk] *adj* hydro-électrique. **~ power** énergie *f* hydro-électrique.
hydrofoil ['haɪdrəfɔɪl] *n* hydrofoil *m*.
hydrogen ['haɪdrɪdʒən] *n* hydrogène *m*. **~ bomb** bombe *f* à hydrogène; **~ peroxide** eau oxygénée.
hydrography [haɪ'drɒgrəfɪ] *n* hydrographie *f*.
hydrolysis [haɪ'drɒlɪsɪs] *n* hydrolyse *f*.
hydrometer [haɪ'drɒmɪtəʳ] *n* hydromètre *m*.
hydropathic [,haɪdrə'pæθɪk] *adj* hydrothérapique.
hydrophobia [,haɪdrə'fəʊbɪə] *n* hydrophobie *f*.
hydrophobic [,haɪdrə'fəʊbɪk] *adj* hydrophobe.
hydroplane ['haɪdrəʊpleɪn] *n* hydroglisseur *m*.
hydroponics [,haɪdrə'pɒnɪks] *n* (*U*) culture *f* hydroponique.
hydroxide [haɪ'drɒksaɪd] *n* hydroxyde *m*, hydrate *m*.
hyena [haɪ'i:nə] *n* = **hyaena.**
hygiene ['haɪdʒi:n] *n* hygiène *f*.
hygienic [haɪ'dʒi:nɪk] *adj* hygiénique.
hymen ['haɪmen] *n* (*Anat*) hymen *m*.
hymn [hɪm] 1 *n* hymne *m*, cantique *m*. **~ book** livre *m* de cantiques. 2 *vt* (*liter*) chanter un hymne à la gloire de.
hymnal ['hɪmnəl] *n* livre *m* de cantiques.
hyper... ['haɪpəʳ] *pref* hyper... .
hyperacidity ['haɪpərə'sɪdɪtɪ] *n* hyperacidité *f*.
hyperbola [haɪ'pɜ:bələ] *n* (*Math*) hyperbole *f*.
hyperbole [haɪ'pɜ:bəlɪ] *n* (*Literat*) hyperbole *f*.
hyperbolic(al) [,haɪpə'bɒlɪk(əl)] *adj* hyperbolique.
hypercritical ['haɪpə'krɪtɪkəl] *adj* hypercritique.
hypermarket ['haɪpəmɑ:kɪt] *n* (*Brit*) hypermarché *m*.
hypersensitive ['haɪpə'sensɪtɪv] *adj* hypersensible.
hypersonic [,haɪpə'sɒnɪk] *adj* hypersonique.
hypertension ['haɪpə'tenʃən] *n* hypertension *f*.
hyphen ['haɪfən] *n* trait *m* d'union.
hyphenate ['haɪfəneɪt] *vt* mettre un trait d'union à. **~d word** mot *m* à trait d'union.
hypnosis [hɪp'nəʊsɪs] *n* hypnose *f*. **under ~** en état d'hypnose, en état hypnotique.
hypnotic [hɪp'nɒtɪk] 1 *adj* hypnotique. 2 *n* (*drug*) hypnotique *m*; (*person*) hypnotique *mf*.
hypnotism ['hɪpnətɪzəm] *n* hypnotisme *m*.
hypnotist ['hɪpnətɪst] *n* hypnotiseur *m*, -euse *f*.
hypnotize ['hɪpnətaɪz] *vt* (*lit, fig*) hypnotiser. **to ~ sb into doing sth** faire faire qch à qn sous hypnose.
hypo... ['haɪpəʊ] *pref* hypo... .
hypochondria [,haɪpəʊ'kɒndrɪə] *n* hypocondrie *f*.
hypochondriac [,haɪpəʊ'kɒndrɪæk] 1 *adj* hypocondriaque. 2 *n* malade *mf* imaginaire, hypocondriaque *mf*. **he's a ~** il se croit toujours malade.
hypocrisy [hɪ'pɒkrɪsɪ] *n* hypocrisie *f*.
hypocrite ['hɪpəkrɪt] *n* hypocrite *mf*.
hypocritical [,hɪpə'krɪtɪkəl] *adj* hypocrite.
hypocritically [,hɪpə'krɪtɪkəlɪ] *adv* hypocritement.
hypodermic [,haɪpə'dɜ:mɪk] 1 *adj* hypodermique. 2 *n* (*syringe*) seringue *f* hypodermique; (*injection*) injection *f* hypodermique.
hypotenuse [haɪ'pɒtɪnju:z] *n* hypoténuse *f*.
hypothermia [,haɪpəʊ'θɜ:mɪə] *n* hypothermie *f*.
hypothesis [haɪ'pɒθɪsɪs] *n, pl* **hypotheses** [haɪ'pɒθɪsi:z] hypothèse *f*.
hypothetic(al) [,haɪpəʊ'θetɪk(əl)] *adj* hypothétique.
hypothetically [,haɪpəʊ'θetɪkəlɪ] *adv* hypothétiquement.

hysterectomy [ˌhɪstəˈrektəmɪ] *n* hystérectomie *f.*

hysteria [hɪsˈtɪərɪə] *n* (*Psych*) hystérie *f.* **she felt a wave of mounting ~** elle sentait monter la crise de nerfs; **there were signs of ~ among the crowd** la foule semblait être sur le point de perdre tout contrôle; *V* **mass**[1].

hysterical [hɪsˈterɪkəl] *adj* (*Psych*) hystérique; (*gen*) *person* très nerveux, surexcité; *laugh, sobs, weeping* convulsif. **to become ~** avoir une (violente) crise de nerfs.

hysterically [hɪsˈterɪkəlɪ] *adv* (*Med, Psych*) hystériquement. **to weep ~** avoir une violente crise de larmes; **to laugh ~** rire convulsivement, être saisi d'un rire convulsif; **'come here,' she shouted ~** 'viens ici,' hurla-t-elle comme une hystérique.

hysterics [hɪsˈterɪks] *npl* **(a)** (*tears, shouts etc*) (violente) crise *f* de nerfs. **to have ~, to go into ~** avoir une (violente) crise de nerfs; **she was nearly in ~** elle était au bord de la crise de nerfs.

(b) (*: *laughter*) crise *f* de rire. **to have ~, to go into ~** attraper un fou rire*; **we were in ~ about it** on en était malade (de rire)*, on en a ri jusqu'aux larmes.

I

I[1], **i** [aɪ] *n* (*letter*) I, i *m*; *V* **dot.**

I[2] [aɪ] *pers pron* (*unstressed*) je, (*before vowel*) j'; (*stressed*) moi. **he and ~ are going to sing** lui et moi (nous) allons chanter; **no, I'LL do it** non, c'est moi qui vais le faire; (*frm*) **it's ~** c'est moi.

iambic [aɪˈæmbɪk] **1** *adj* iambique. **~ pentameter** pentamètre *m* iambique. **2** *n* iambe *m*, vers *m* iambique.

Iberia [aɪˈbɪərɪə] *n* Ibérie *f.*

Iberian [aɪˈbɪərɪən] **1** *adj* ibérique, ibérien. **~ Peninsula** péninsule *f* ibérique. **2** *n* **(a)** Ibère *mf.* **(b)** (*Ling*) ibère *m.*

ibex [ˈaɪbeks] *n* bouquetin *m*, ibex *m.*

ibis [ˈaɪbɪs] *n* ibis *m.*

ice [aɪs] **1** *n* **(a)** (*U*) glace *f*; (*on road*) verglas *m.* **to be as cold as ~** *[object]* être froid comme de la glace; *[room]* être glacial; *[person]* être glacé jusqu'aux os; **my hands are like ~** *or* **as cold as ~** j'ai les mains glacées; (*fig*) **to be (skating** *or* **treading) on thin ~** se trouver *or* être sur la corde raide (*fig*); **to keep on ~** (*lit*) mettre à la glacière; (*fig*) mettre en attente *or* au frigidaire*; (*Theat*) **'Cinderella on ~'** 'Cendrillon, spectacle sur glace'; *V* **black, break, cut** *etc.*

(b) (*Brit:* **~** *cream*) glace *f.* **raspberry ~** glace à la framboise; *V* **water** *etc.*

2 *cpd*: **ice age** période *f* glaciaire; **ice-age** (qui date) de la période glaciaire; **ice axe** piolet *m*; **iceberg** iceberg *m*; (**fig*: *person*) glaçon* *m* (*V also* **tip**[1]); **ice blue** bleu glacier *inv*; **iceboat** (*Sport*) = **ice yacht**; (*Naut*) = **icebreaker**; **icebound** *harbour* fermé par les glaces; *ship* pris dans les glaces; **icebox** (*US: refrigerator*) frigidaire *m* ®, réfrigérateur *m*; (*Brit: part of refrigerator*) compartiment *m* à glace, freezer *m*; (*insulated box*) glacière *f*; **this room is like an icebox** cette pièce est une vraie glacière, on gèle dans cette pièce; (*Naut*) **icebreaker** brise-glace(s) *m inv*; **ice bucket** seau *m* à glace *or* à champagne; **icecap** calotte *f* glaciaire; **ice-cold** *drink, hands* glacé; *room* glacial; *manners, person* glacé, glacial; **ice cream** glace *f*; **strawberry ice cream** glace *f* à la fraise; (*US*) **ice-cream soda** ice-cream soda *m*; **ice cube** glaçon *m*, cube *m* de glace; (*Brit*) **ice(d) lolly** glace *f* (sur un bâtonnet); **ice field** champ *m* de glace; **ice floe** banquise *f*; **ice hockey** hockey *m* sur glace; **icehouse** glacière *f*; (*US*) **iceman** marchand *m or* livreur *m* de glace; **ice pick** pic *m* à glace; **ice rink** patinoire *f*; (*Theat*) **ice show** spectacle *m* sur glace; **iceskate** patin *m* (à glace); **ice-skate** patiner (sur glace), faire du patin (à glace) *or* du patinage (sur glace); **ice-skating** patinage *m* (sur glace); (*in refrigerator*) **ice-tray** bac *m* à glaçons; **ice yacht** yacht *m* à glace.

3 *vt* **(a)** *drink* (*chill*) (faire) rafraîchir, mettre à rafraîchir; (*put ~ cubes in*) mettre des glaçons dans, ajouter des glaçons à. **~d tea/coffee** thé/café glacé; **~d champagne** champagne frappé; **~(d) lolly** *V* 2; **~d melon** melon rafraîchi.

(b) *cake* glacer.

(c) (*cover with ~: also* **~ over, ~ up**) *windscreen, aircraft wings* givrer.

(d) (*freeze: also* **~ over**) *lake, river* geler.

4 *vi* (*also* **~ over, ~ up**) *[aircraft wings, windscreen]* givrer.

ice over 1 *vi* **(a)** *[river]* geler. **the lake has iced over** le lac a gelé *or* est pris (de glace).

(b) *V* **ice 4.**

2 *vt sep V* **ice 3c, 3d.**

ice up 1 *vi V* **ice 4.**

2 *vt sep V* **ice 3c.**

Iceland [ˈaɪslənd] *n* Islande *f.*

Icelander [ˈaɪsləndəʳ] *n* Islandais(e) *m(f).*

Icelandic [aɪsˈlændɪk] **1** *adj* islandais. **2** *n* (*Ling*) islandais *m.*

ichthyology [ˌɪkθɪˈɒlədʒɪ] *n* ichtyologie *f.*

ichthyosaurus [ˌɪkθɪəˈsɔːrəs] *n* ichtyosaure *m.*

icicle [ˈaɪsɪkl] *n* glaçon *m* (*naturel*).

icily [ˈaɪsɪlɪ] *adv look, bow* d'un air glacial; *speak* d'une voix *or* d'un ton glacial(e).

icing [ˈaɪsɪŋ] *n* (*U*) **(a)** (*Culin*) glace *f*, glaçage *m.* (*Brit*) **~ sugar** sucre *m* glace; **chocolate/coffee** *etc* **~** glaçage au chocolat/au café *etc*; *V* **butter. (b)** (*on aircraft etc*) givre *m.*

icon [ˈaɪkɒn] *n* icône *f.*

iconoclast [aɪˈkɒnəklæst] *n* iconoclaste *mf.*

iconoclastic [aɪˌkɒnəˈklæstɪk] *adj* iconoclaste.

icy [ˈaɪsɪ] *adj wind, weather, stare, reception* glacial, glacé; *ground, hands* glacé; *road* couvert de verglas, verglacé. **it will be ~ cold today** aujourd'hui le temps sera glacial; **it's ~ cold in here** on gèle ici, il fait glacial ici; **her hands were ~ cold** elle avait les mains glacées.

I'd [aɪd] = **I had, I should, I would**; *V* **have, should, would.**

id [ɪd] *n* (*Psych*) ça *m.*

idea [aɪˈdɪə] *n* **(a)** (*thought, purpose*) idée *f.* **man of ~s** homme *m* à idées; **he's the firm's ~s man*** c'est lui qui trouve les idées nouvelles dans cette compagnie; **he hasn't an ~ in his head** il n'a rien dans la tête; **brilliant** *or* **bright ~** idée géniale *or* de génie; **good ~!** bonne idée!; **what an ~!, the very ~ (of it)!** quelle idée!, en voilà une idée!; **I can't bear the ~ (of it)** je n'ose pas y penser; **I've got an ~ for a play** j'ai l'idée d'une pièce; **I hit (up)on** *or* **I suddenly had the ~ of going to see her** d'un seul coup l'idée m'est venue d'aller la voir; **I had an ~ of buying a car but didn't do so** j'avais l'idée d'acheter une voiture mais je ne l'ai pas fait; **it might not be a bad ~ to wait a few days** ce ne serait peut-être pas une mauvaise idée d'attendre quelques jours; **the ~ is to sell the car to him** il s'agit de lui vendre la voiture; **whose ~ was it to take this route?** qui a eu l'idée de prendre ce chemin?; **it wasn't my ~!** ce n'est pas moi qui en ai eu l'idée!; **the ~ never entered my head** l'idée ne m'en est jamais venue *or* ne m'a jamais effleuré; **he got the ~ (into his head) that she wouldn't help him** il s'est mis en tête l'idée qu'elle ne l'aiderait pas; **where did you get that ~?** où est-ce que tu as pris cette idée-là?; **what gave you the ~ that I couldn't come?** qu'est-ce qui t'a fait penser que je ne pourrais pas venir?; **don't get any ~s!*** ne te fais pas d'illusions!, ce n'est pas la peine de t'imaginer des choses!*; **once he gets an ~ into his head** une fois qu'il s'est mis une idée en tête; **to put ~s into sb's head, to give sb ~s** mettre *or* fourrer des idées dans la tête de qn; **that gave me the ~ of inviting her** cela m'a donné l'idée de l'inviter.

(b) (*opinion*) idée *f*, opinion *f*; (*way of thinking*) conception *f*, façon *f* de penser. **she has some odd ~s about how to bring up children** elle a de drôles d'idées sur la façon d'élever les enfants; **according to his ~** selon sa façon de penser; **if that's your ~ of fun** si c'est ça que tu appelles t'amuser; **it wasn't my ~ of a holiday** ce n'était pas ce que j'appelle des vacances.

(c) (*vague knowledge*) idée *f*, notion *f.* **I've got some ~ of physics** j'ai quelques notions de physique; **have you any ~ of what he meant to do?** avez-vous la moindre idée de ce qu'il voulait faire?; **I haven't the least** *or* **slightest** *or* **foggiest* ~** je n'en ai pas la moindre idée; **I have an ~ that he was going to Paris** j'ai idée *or* j'ai dans l'idée qu'il allait à Paris; **I had no ~ they knew each other** je n'avais aucune idée *or* j'ignorais absolument *or* j'étais loin de soupçonner qu'ils se connaissaient; **can you give me a rough ~ of how many you want?** pouvez-vous m'indiquer en gros *or* approximativement combien vous en voulez?; **he gave me a general ~ of what they would do** il m'a donné une indication générale sur ce qu'ils allaient faire; **you're getting the ~!*** tu y es!, tu as compris! *or* pigé!*; **I've got the general ~*** je vois à peu près (ce dont il s'agit); **that's the ~!*** c'est ça!; **what's the big ~?*** qu'est-ce que c'est que cette histoire?

ideal [aɪˈdɪəl] **1** *adj* idéal, parfait. **her ~ man** son homme idéal; **it would be ~ if she could come with us** ce serait idéal *or* parfait si elle pouvait venir avec nous; **it's ~!** c'est (l')idéal! **2** *n* idéal *m.* **the ~ of beauty** le beau idéal, la beauté idéale.

idealism [aɪˈdɪəlɪzəm] *n* idéalisme *m.*

idealist [aɪˈdɪəlɪst] *adj, n* idéaliste (*mf*).

idealistic [aɪˌdɪəˈlɪstɪk] *adj* idéaliste.

idealize [aɪˈdɪəlaɪz] *vt* idéaliser.

ideally [aɪˈdɪəlɪ] *adv* idéalement, d'une manière idéale. **the village is ~ situated** le village jouit d'une situation idéale; **he is ~ suited to the job** il est parfait pour ce poste; **~ the house should have 4 rooms** l'idéal serait que la maison ait 4 pièces.

identical [aɪˈdentɪkəl] *adj* identique (*to* à). **~ twins** vrais jumeaux, vraies jumelles.

identically [aɪˈdentɪkəlɪ] *adv* identiquement.

identification [aɪˌdentɪfɪˈkeɪʃən] **1** *n* **(a)** (*U*) identification *f*. **(b)** (*papers etc*) pièce *fpl* d'identité. **have you got any (means of) ~ to back up this cheque?** avez-vous une pièce d'identité pour garantir la validité de ce chèque?
2 *cpd*: **identification mark** signe *m* d'identification; **identification papers** pièces *fpl or* papiers *mpl* d'identité; (*Brit Police*) **identification parade** séance *f* d'identification (d'un suspect); (*US*) **identification tag** plaque *f* d'identité.

identify [aɪˈdentɪfaɪ] **1** *vt* **(a)** (*establish identity of*) identifier, établir l'identité de. **she identified him as the man who attacked her** elle l'a identifié comme étant l'homme qui l'a attaquée; **the police have identified the man they want to question** la police a identifié *or* établi l'identité de l'homme qu'elle veut interroger; **to ~ a body** identifier un cadavre.
(b) (*consider as the same*) identifier (*A with B* A avec *or* à *or* et B). **to ~ o.s. with** s'identifier à *or* avec, s'assimiler à; **he refused to ~ himself with the rebels** il a refusé de s'identifier avec les rebelles; **he refused to be identified with the rebels** il a refusé d'être identifié *or* assimilé aux rebelles.
2 *vi* s'identifier (*with* avec, à), s'assimiler (*with* à).

identikit [aɪˈdentɪkɪt] *n*: **~ (picture)** portrait-robot *m*, photo-robot *f*.

identity [aɪˈdentɪtɪ] **1** *n* identité *f*. **show me some proof of ~** montrez-moi une pièce d'identité; **this is not a proof of ~** ceci ne constitue pas une preuve d'identité; **a case of mistaken ~** une erreur d'identité.
2 *cpd*: **identity card** carte *f* d'identité; (*Psych*) **identity crisis** crise *f* d'identité; (*Mil etc*) **identity disc** plaque *f* d'identité; **identity papers** pièces *fpl or* papiers *mpl* d'identité; **identity parade** séance *f* d'identification (d'un suspect).

ideogram [ˈɪdɪəgræm] *n*, **ideograph** [ˈɪdɪəgrɑːf] *n* idéogramme *m*.

ideographic [ˌɪdɪəˈgræfɪk] *adj* idéographique.

ideological [ˌaɪdɪəˈlɒdʒɪkəl] *adj* idéologique.

ideologist [ˌaɪdɪˈɒlədʒɪst] *n* idéologue *mf*.

ideology [ˌaɪdɪˈɒlədʒɪ] *n* idéologie *f*.

ides [aɪdz] *npl* ides *fpl*.

idiocy [ˈɪdɪəsɪ] *n* (*U*) stupidité *f*, idiotie *f*, imbécillité *f*; (*Med* ††) idiotie. **a piece of ~** une stupidité, une idiotie.

idiolect [ˈɪdɪəʊlekt] *n* idiolecte *m*.

idiom [ˈɪdɪəm] *n* **(a)** (*phrase, expression*) idiotisme *m*, locution *f or* expression *f or* tournure *f* idiomatique. **(b)** (*language*) [*country*] idiome *m*, langue *f*; [*region*] idiome; [*person*] idiome, langue, parler *m*.

idiomatic [ˌɪdɪəˈmætɪk] *adj* idiomatique, de la langue courante *or* populaire. **he speaks ~ French** il parle un français idiomatique; **~ expression** idiotisme *m*, expression *f or* locution *f or* tournure *f* idiomatique.

idiomatically [ˌɪdɪəˈmætɪkəlɪ] *adv speak, explain* de façon idiomatique.

idiosyncrasy [ˌɪdɪəˈsɪŋkrəsɪ] *n* particularité *f*, caractéristique *f*. **one of his little idiosyncrasies** une de ses particularités *or* petites manies.

idiosyncratic [ˌɪdɪəsɪŋˈkrætɪk] *adj* particulier, caractéristique.

idiot [ˈɪdɪət] **1** *n* idiot(e) *m(f)*, imbécile *mf*, crétin(e)* *m(f)*; (*Med*††) idiot(e) (de naissance). **to act/speak like an ~** faire/dire des idioties *or* des imbécillités; **to behave like an ~** se conduire en idiot *or* en imbécile *or* en crétin*, faire l'idiot *or* l'imbécile; **you ~!** espèce d'idiot! *or* d'imbécile!; **what an ~ I am!** que je suis idiot! *or* bête!, quel imbécile je fais!; *V* **village.**
2 *cpd*: (*TV*) **idiot board** nègre *m*; **idiot card, idiot sheet** point *m* de repère.

idiotic [ˌɪdɪˈɒtɪk] *adj* idiot, bête, stupide. **that was ~ of you!** quel idiot tu as été!

idiotically [ˌɪdɪˈɒtɪkəlɪ] *adv* bêtement, stupidement, idiotement. **to behave ~** se conduire en idiot *or* en imbécile, faire l'imbécile *or* l'idiot.

idle [ˈaɪdl] **1** *adj* **(a)** *person* (*doing nothing*) sans occupation, inoccupé, désœuvré; (*unemployed*) en chômage; (*lazy*) paresseux, fainéant, oisif. **the ~ rich** les riches désœuvrés, l'élite oisive; **in my ~ moments** à mes moments de loisir, à mes moments perdus; **~ life** vie oisive *or* d'oisiveté; (*Ind*) **to make sb ~** réduire qn au chômage.
(b) (*not in use*) *machine* au repos. **this machine is never ~** cette machine n'est jamais au repos *or* ne s'arrête jamais; **the whole factory stood ~** l'usine entière était arrêtée *or* chômait *or* était en chômage; *V* **lie**[1].
(c) *speculation, question, wish, threat* oiseux, futile, vain. **out of ~ curiosity** par curiosité pure et simple; **~ promises** vaines promesses, promesses en l'air; **~ words** *or* **talk** paroles oiseuses *or* en l'air; **~ fears** craintes non justifiées *or* sans fondement; **~ pleasures** plaisirs *mpl* futiles; **it is ~ to hope that ...** il est inutile d'espérer que ... .
2 *vi* **(a)** (*also* **~ about, ~ around**) [*person*] paresser, fainéanter, se laisser aller à la paresse. **to ~ about the streets** traîner dans les rues.
(b) [*engine, machine*] tourner au ralenti.

idle away *vt sep*: **to idle away one's time** gaspiller *or* perdre son temps (à ne rien faire).

idleness [ˈaɪdlnɪs] *n* **(a)** (*state of not working*) oisiveté *f*, inaction *f*, inactivité *f*, désœuvrement *m*; (*unemployment*) chômage *m*; (*laziness*) paresse *f*, fainéantise *f*. **to live in ~** vivre oisif *or* dans l'oisiveté.
(b) [*threat, wish, question, speculation*] futilité *f*, inutilité *f*; [*promises, pleasures*] futilité; [*fears*] manque *m* de justification; [*words*] manque de sérieux; [*effort*] inutilité.

idler [ˈaɪdləʳ] *n* **(a)** (*person*) (*doing nothing*) oisif *m*, -ive *f*, désœuvré(e) *m(f)*; (*lazy*) paresseux *m*, -euse *f*, fainéant(e) *m(f)*.
(b) (*Tech*) (*wheel*) roue folle; (*pinion*) pignon *m* libre; (*pulley*) poulie-guide *f*, poulie folle.

idly [ˈaɪdlɪ] *adv* (*without working*) sans travailler; (*lazily*) paresseusement; (*without thought*) *reply, say, suggest* négligemment.

idol [ˈaɪdl] *n* (*lit, fig*) idole *f*. (*Cine, TV etc*) **the current ~** l'idole du jour *or* du moment.

idolater [aɪˈdɒlətəʳ] *n* idolâtre *mf*.

idolatrous [aɪˈdɒlətrəs] *adj* idolâtre.

idolatry [aɪˈdɒlətrɪ] *n* idolâtrie *f*.

idolize [ˈaɪdəlaɪz] *vt* idolâtrer, adorer. **to ~ sb** idolâtrer *or* adorer qn, faire de qn son idole.

idyll [ˈɪdɪl] *n* (*Literat, also fig*) idylle *f*.

idyllic [ɪˈdɪlɪk] *adj* idyllique.

if [ɪf] **1** *conj* **(a)** (*condition: supposing that*) si. **I'll go ~ you come with me** j'irai si tu m'accompagnes; **~ it is fine I shall be pleased** s'il fait beau je serai content; **~ it were fine I should be pleased** s'il faisait beau je serais content; **~ it is fine and (~ it is) not too cold I shall go with you** s'il fait beau et (s'il ne fait *or* qu'il ne fasse) pas trop froid je vous accompagnerai; **~ I had known, I would have visited them** si j'avais su, je leur aurais rendu visite; **~ you wait a minute, I'll come with you** si vous attendez *or* voulez attendre une minute, je vais vous accompagner; **~ you were a bird you could fly** si tu étais (un) oiseau tu pourrais voler; **~ I were you** si j'étais vous, (si j'étais) à votre place; **(even) ~ I knew I wouldn't tell you** quand même je le saurais *or* même si je le savais je ne te le dirais pas; **~ they are to be believed** à les en croire; **~ it is true that ...** s'il est vrai que ... + *indic*, si tant est que ... + *subj*; *V also* **1i.**
(b) (*whenever*) si. **~ I asked him he helped me** si je le lui demandais il m'aidait; **~ she wants any help she asks me** si elle a besoin d'aide elle s'adresse à moi.
(c) (*although*) si. **(even) ~ it takes me all day I'll do it** (même) si cela doit *or* quand bien même cela devrait me prendre toute la journée je le ferai; **(even) ~ they are poor at least they are happy** s'ils sont pauvres du moins ils sont *or* sont-ils heureux; **even ~ it is a good film it's rather long** c'est un bon film bien qu'(il soit) un peu long; **even ~ he tells me himself I won't believe it** même s'il me le dit lui-même je ne le croirai pas.
(d) (*granted that, admitting that*) si. **~ I am wrong, you are wrong too** si je me trompe *or* en admettant que je me trompe (*subj*), vous vous trompez aussi; **(even) ~ he DID say that, he didn't mean to hurt you** quand (bien) même il l'aurait dit, il n'avait aucune intention de vous faire de la peine.
(e) (*whether*) si. **do you know ~ they have gone?** savez-vous s'ils sont partis?; **I wonder ~ it's true** je me demande si c'est vrai.
(f) (*unless*) **~ ... not** si ... ne; **that's the house, ~ I'm not mistaken** voilà la maison, si je ne me trompe; **they're coming at Christmas ~ they don't change their minds** ils viennent à Noël à moins qu'ils ne changent (*subj*) d'avis.
(g) (*excl*) **~ only I had known!** si seulement j'avais su!
(h) **as ~** comme, comme si; **he acts as ~ he were rich** il se conduit comme s'il était riche; **as ~ by chance** comme par hasard; **he stood there as ~ he were dumb** il restait là comme (s'il était) muet; **it isn't as ~ we were rich** ce n'est pas comme si nous étions riches, nous ne sommes pourtant pas riches.
(i) (*phrases*) **~ necessary** s'il le faut, au besoin, s'il est nécessaire; **~ anything, this one is bigger** c'est plutôt celui-ci qui est le plus grand; **~ so,** (*liter*) **~ it be so** s'il en est ainsi, si c'est le cas; **~ not** sinon; **~ only for a moment** ne serait-ce *or* ne fût-ce que pour un instant; **well ~ he didn't try to steal my bag!*** (ne) voilà-t-il pas qu'il essaie de me voler mon sac!*; **~ it isn't our old friend Smith!** tiens! *or* par exemple! ce vieux Smith!; **~ I know HER, she'll refuse** telle que je la connais, elle refusera.
2 *n*: **~s and buts** les si *mpl* et les mais *mpl*; **it's a big ~** c'est un grand point d'interrogation.

iffy‡ [ˈɪfɪ] *adj* aléatoire, problématique; *problem* plein d'inconnues.

igloo [ˈɪgluː] *n* igloo *m or* iglou *m*.

igneous [ˈɪgnɪəs] *adj* igné.

ignite [ɪgˈnaɪt] **1** *vt* mettre le feu à, enflammer. **2** *vi* prendre feu, s'enflammer.

ignition [ɪgˈnɪʃən] **1** *n* **(a)** ignition *f*. **(b)** (*Aut*) allumage *m*. **to switch on the ~** mettre le contact. **2** *cpd*: (*Aut*) **ignition coil** bobine *f* d'allumage; **ignition key** clef *f* de contact; **ignition switch** contact *m*.

ignoble [ɪgˈnəʊbl] *adj* ignoble, infâme, indigne, vil.

ignominious [ˌɪgnəˈmɪnɪəs] *adj* ignominieux, honteux.

ignominiously [ˌɪgnəˈmɪnɪəslɪ] *adv* ignominieusement, honteusement.

ignominy [ˈɪgnəmɪnɪ] *n* ignominie *f*.

ignoramus [ˌɪgnəˈreɪməs] *n* ignare *mf*, ignorant(e) *m(f)*.

ignorance [ˈɪgnərəns] *n* **(a)** ignorance *f* (*of* de). **to be in ~ of sth** ignorer qch; **to keep sb in ~ of sth** tenir qn dans l'ignorance de qch, laisser ignorer qch à qn; **~ of the law is no excuse** nul n'est censé ignorer la loi; **his ~ of chemistry astonished me** son ignorance en matière de chimie m'a ahuri.
(b) (*lack of education*) ignorance *f*. **he was ashamed of his ~** il avait honte de son ignorance *or* de ne rien savoir; **don't show your ~!** ce n'est pas la peine d'étaler ton ignorance!

ignorant [ˈɪgnərənt] *adj* **(a)** (*unaware*) **~ of** ignorant de; **to be ~ of the facts** ignorer les faits, être ignorant des faits. **(b)** (*lacking education*) *person* ignorant; *words, behaviour* d'(un) ignorant, qui trahit l'ignorance.

ignorantly [ˈɪgnərəntlɪ] *adv* par ignorance.

ignore [ɪgˈnɔːʳ] *vt* **(a)** (*take no notice of*) *interruption, remark, objection* ne tenir aucun compte de, ne pas relever, passer sous silence; *sb's behaviour* ne pas prêter attention à, faire semblant de ne pas s'apercevoir de; *person* faire semblant de ne pas reconnaître; *invitation, letter* ne pas répondre à; *facts* méconnaître; *rule, prohibition* ne pas respecter; *awkward fact* faire semblant de ne pas connaître, ne tenir aucun compte de. **I shall ~ your impertinence** je ne relèverai pas votre impertinence; **we cannot ~ this behaviour any longer** nous ne pouvons plus fermer les yeux sur ces agissements.

(b) (*Jur*) **to ~ a bill** prononcer un verdict d'acquittement.

iguana [ɪˈgwɑːnə] *n* iguane *m*.

ikon [ˈaɪkɒn] *n* = **icon.**

ilex [ˈaɪleks] *n* **(a)** (*holm oak*) yeuse *f*, chêne vert. **(b)** (*genus: holly*) houx *m*.

ilk [ɪlk] *n*: **of that ~** (*fig*) de cet acabit; (*Scot: in names*) de ce nom.

ill [ɪl] **1** *adj, comp* **worse**, *superl* **worst** **(a)** (*sick*) malade, souffrant. **to be ~** être malade; **to fall** *or* **be taken ~** tomber malade; **to feel ~** se sentir malade *or* souffrant; **to look ~** avoir l'air malade; **~ with a fever** malade d'une fièvre; **~ with anxiety/jealousy** *etc* malade d'inquiétude/de jalousie *etc*.

(b) (*bad*) mauvais, méchant. **~ deed** mauvaise action, méfait *m*; **~ effects** conséquences désastreuses; **~ fame** mauvaise réputation; **house of ~ fame** *or* **repute** maison mal famée; **~ feeling** ressentiment *m*, rancune *f*; **no ~ feeling!** sans rancune!; **~ health** mauvaise santé; **~ humour, ~ temper** mauvaise humeur; **~ luck** malchance *f*; **by ~ luck** par malheur, par malchance; **as ~ luck would have it, he ...** le malheur a voulu qu'il ... + *subj*; **~ nature** méchanceté *f*; **~ omen** mauvais augure; **~ repute** = **~ fame**; **~ will** malveillance *f*; **I bear him no ~ will** je ne lui en veux pas; (*Prov*) **it's an ~ wind that blows nobody any good** à quelque chose malheur est bon (*Prov*).

2 *n* **(a)** (*U: evil, injury*) mal *m*. **to think/speak ~ of** penser/dire du mal de; *V* **good.**

(b) (*misfortunes*) **~s** maux *mpl*, malheurs *mpl*.

3 *adv* mal. **he can ~ afford the expense** il peut difficilement se permettre la dépense; **he can ~ afford to refuse** il ne peut guère se permettre de refuser; (*liter*) **to take sth ~** prendre mal qch, prendre qch en mauvaise part; (*liter*) **to go ~ with** tourner mal pour, aller mal pour; (*frm, liter*) **it ~ becomes you to do that** il vous sied mal (*frm*) de faire cela.

4 *cpd* mal. **ill-advised** *decision, remark* peu judicieux; **you would be ill-advised to do that** vous auriez tort de faire cela, vous seriez malavisé (*liter*) de faire cela; **ill-assorted** mal assorti; **ill-at-ease** mal à l'aise, gêné; **ill-bred** mal élevé; **ill-breeding** manque *m* de savoir-vivre *or* d'éducation, impolitesse *f*; **ill-considered** *action, words* irréfléchi; *measures* hâtif; **ill-disposed** malintentionné; **ill-disposed towards** mal disposé *or* malintentionné envers; **ill-fated** *person* infortuné, malheureux; *day* fatal, néfaste; *action, effort* malheureux; **ill-favoured** (*ugly*) laid; (*objectionable*) déplaisant, désagréable, (*stronger*) répugnant; **ill-founded** *belief, argument* mal fondé; *rumour* sans fondement; **ill-gotten gains** biens *mpl* mal acquis; **ill-humoured** de mauvaise humeur, maussade, grincheux; **ill-informed** *person* mal renseigné, mal informé; *essay, speech* plein d'inexactitudes; **ill-judged** peu judicieux, peu sage; **ill-mannered** *person* mal élevé; *behaviour* grossier, impoli; **ill-natured** *person, reply* désagréable; *child* méchant, désagréable; **ill-nourished** mal nourri; **ill-omened** de mauvais augure; **ill-prepared** mal préparé; (*liter*) **ill-starred** *person* né sous une mauvaise étoile, infortuné; *day, undertaking* malheureux, néfaste; **ill-suited** mal assorti; **ill-suited to** qui ne convient guère à, qui convient mal à; **ill-tempered** (*habitually*) grincheux, désagréable, qui a mauvais caractère; (*on one occasion*) de mauvaise humeur, maussade, grincheux; **ill-timed** inopportun, malencontreux, intempestif, mal à propos; **ill-treat** maltraiter, brutaliser, rudoyer; **ill treatment** mauvais traitements; **ill-use** = **ill-treat.**

I'll [aɪl] = **I shall, I will**; *V* **shall, will.**

illegal [ɪˈliːgəl] *adj* illégal.

illegality [ˌɪliːˈgælɪtɪ] *n* illégalité *f*.

illegally [ɪˈliːgəlɪ] *adv* illégalement, d'une manière illégale *or* contraire à la loi.

illegible [ɪˈledʒəbl] *adj* illisible.

illegibly [ɪˈledʒəblɪ] *adv* illisiblement.

illegitimacy [ˌɪlɪˈdʒɪtɪməsɪ] *n* illégitimité *f*.

illegitimate [ˌɪlɪˈdʒɪtɪmɪt] *adj action* illégitime; *child* illégitime, naturel; (*fig*) *argument* illogique; *conclusion* injustifié.

illegitimately [ˌɪlɪˈdʒɪtɪmɪtlɪ] *adv* illégitimement.

illiberal [ɪˈlɪbərəl] *adj* **(a)** (*narrow-minded*) intolérant, à l'esprit étroit. **(b)** (†: *niggardly*) ladre†.

illicit [ɪˈlɪsɪt] *adj* illicite.

illicitly [ɪˈlɪsɪtlɪ] *adv* illicitement.

illimitable [ɪˈlɪmɪtəbl] *adj* illimité, sans bornes, sans limites.

illiteracy [ɪˈlɪtərəsɪ] *n* analphabétisme *m*.

illiterate [ɪˈlɪtərɪt] **1** *adj person* illettré, analphabète; *letter, sentence* plein de fautes. **in an ~ hand** dans une écriture de primaire. **2** *n* illettré(e) *m(f)*, analphabète *mf*.

illness [ˈɪlnɪs] *n* maladie *f*. **to have a long ~** faire une longue maladie.

illogical [ɪˈlɒdʒɪkəl] *adj* illogique.

illogicality [ɪˈlɒdʒɪˈkælɪtɪ] *n* illogisme *m*.

illogically [ɪˈlɒdʒɪkəlɪ] *adv* illogiquement.

illuminate [ɪˈluːmɪneɪt] *vt* **(a)** *room, street* éclairer; *building* illuminer; *sky* embraser, illuminer; (*fig*) *question, subject* éclairer, faire la lumière sur. **~d sign** enseigne lumineuse. **(b)** (*Art*) *manuscript* enluminer.

illuminating [ɪˈluːmɪneɪtɪŋ] *adj* (*lit, fig*) éclairant. (*fig*) **his comments proved very ~** ses commentaires se sont avérés très éclairants *or* ont beaucoup éclairci la question.

illumination [ɪˌluːmɪˈneɪʃən] *n* **(a)** (*U*) *[street, room]* éclairage *m*; *[building]* illumination *f*; *[sky etc]* illumination, embrasement *m*; (*fig*) lumière *f*, inspiration *f*. **(b)** (*decorative lights*) **~s** illuminations *fpl*. **(c)** *[manuscript]* enluminure *f*.

illuminator [ɪˈluːmɪneɪtəʳ] *n* **(a)** (*lighting device*) dispositif *m* d'éclairage. **(b)** *[manuscript]* enlumineur *m*.

illumine [ɪˈluːmɪn] *vt* éclairer, éclaircir, faire la lumière sur.

illusion [ɪˈluːʒən] *n* illusion *f*. **it gives an ~ of space** cela donne une illusion d'espace; **to be under an ~** avoir *or* se faire une illusion; **to be under the ~ that** avoir *or* se faire l'illusion que + *indic*; **to have** *or* **to be under no ~(s)** ne se faire aucune illusion; **I have no ~s about what will happen to him** je ne me fais aucune illusion sur le sort qui l'attend; **he cherishes the ~ that ...** il caresse l'illusion que ...; *V* **optical.**

illusive [ɪˈluːsɪv] *adj*, **illusory** [ɪˈluːsərɪ] *adj* (*unreal*) illusoire, irréel; (*deceptive*) illusoire, trompeur, chimérique.

illustrate [ˈɪləstreɪt] *vt* **(a)** *book, story* illustrer. **~d paper** (journal *m or* magazine *m etc*) illustré *m*.

(b) (*fig: exemplify*) *idea, problem* illustrer, éclairer, mettre en lumière; *rule* donner un exemple de. **I can best ~ this as follows** la meilleure façon d'illustrer ceci est la suivante.

illustration [ˌɪləsˈtreɪʃən] *n* (*lit, fig*) illustration *f*. (*fig*) **by way of ~** à titre d'exemple.

illustrative [ˈɪləstrətɪv] *adj example* explicatif, servant d'explication, qui illustre *or* explique. **~ of this problem** qui sert à illustrer ce problème.

illustrator [ˈɪləstreɪtəʳ] *n* illustrateur *m*, -trice *f*.

illustrious [ɪˈlʌstrɪəs] *adj* illustre, célèbre.

illustriously [ɪˈlʌstrɪəslɪ] *adv* glorieusement.

I'm [aɪm] = **I am**; *V* **be.**

image [ˈɪmɪdʒ] *n* (*all senses*) image *f*. **God created man in his own ~** Dieu créa l'homme à son image; **real/virtual ~** image réelle/virtuelle; **~ in the glass/lake** *etc* réflexion *f* dans la vitre/à la surface du lac *etc*; (*fig*) **he is the (living** *or* **very** *or* **spitting*) ~ of his father** c'est le portrait (vivant) de son père, c'est son père tout craché; **I had a sudden (mental) ~ of her, alone and afraid** soudain je l'ai vue en imagination, qui était seule et qui avait peur; **they had quite the wrong ~ of him** ils se faisaient une idée tout à fait fausse de lui; *[politician, town etc]* **(public) ~** image de marque (*fig*); **he has to think of his ~** il faut qu'il prenne en considération son image de marque; (*Cine, Theat etc*) **he's got the wrong ~ for that part** le public ne le voit pas dans ce genre de rôle, son image de marque ne convient guère à ce rôle; *V* **brand, graven, mirror** *etc*.

imagery [ˈɪmɪdʒərɪ] *n* (*Literat*) images *fpl*. **style/language full of ~** style/langage imagé.

imaginable [ɪˈmædʒɪnəbl] *adj* imaginable. **she's the quietest person ~** c'est la personne la plus silencieuse qu'on puisse imaginer; **the best thing ~ would be for him to leave at once** le mieux qu'on puisse imaginer serait qu'il parte tout de suite.

imaginary [ɪˈmædʒɪnərɪ] *adj danger* imaginaire; *character, place* imaginaire, fictif.

imagination [ɪˌmædʒɪˈneɪʃən] *n* (*U*) imagination *f*. **to have a lively** *or* **vivid ~** avoir l'imagination fertile; **he's got ~** il a de l'imagination; **she lets her ~ run away with her** elle se laisse emporter *or* entraîner par son imagination; **it existed only in his ~** cela n'existait que dans son imagination; **in (his) ~ he saw ...** en imagination il a vu ...; **it is only** *or* **all (your) ~!** vous vous faites des idées!, vous rêvez!; **haven't you got any ~?** tu n'as donc aucune imagination?; **use your ~!** aie donc un peu d'imagination!

imaginative [ɪˈmædʒɪnətɪv] *adj person* imaginatif, plein d'imagination; *book, film, approach* plein d'imagination.

imaginativeness [ɪˈmædʒɪnətɪvnɪs] *n* imagination *f*, esprit imaginatif *or* inventif.

imagine [ɪˈmædʒɪn] *vt* **(a)** (*picture to o.s.*) (s')imaginer, se figurer, se représenter. **~ life 100 years ago** imaginez(-vous) *or* représentez-vous *or* figurez-vous la vie il y a 100 ans; **try to ~ a huge house far from anywhere** essayez d'imaginer *or* de vous imaginer *or* de vous figurer *or* de vous représenter une immense maison loin de tout; **~ that you were** *or* **~ yourself at school now** imagine que tu sois à l'école en ce moment; **I can't ~ myself at 60** je ne m'imagine *or* ne me vois pas du tout à 60 ans; **~ a situation in which ...** imaginez(-vous) une situation où ...; **(just) ~!** tu (t')imagines!; **(you can) ~ how I felt!** imaginez(-vous) *or* vous imaginez ce que j'ai pu ressentir!; **(you can) ~ my fury when ...** (vous) imaginez *or* vous vous représentez ma rage quand ...; **(you can) ~ how pleased I was!** vous pensez si j'étais content!; **you can't ~ how difficult it is** vous ne pouvez pas (vous) imaginer *or* vous figurer combien c'est difficile.

(b) (*suppose, believe*) supposer, imaginer, penser, croire (*that* que). **he's rich, I ~** il est riche, j'imagine *or* je suppose.

(c) (*believe wrongly*) croire, s'imaginer, se figurer. **don't ~ that I can help you** n'allez pas croire que *or* ne vous imaginez pas que *or* ne vous figurez pas que je puisse vous aider; **he fondly ~d she was still willing to obey him** il s'imaginait naïvement qu'elle était encore prête à lui obéir; **I ~d I heard someone speak** j'ai cru entendre parler; **he's (always) imagining things** il se fait des idées.

imbalance [ɪmˈbæləns] *n* (*lit, fig*) déséquilibre *m*.

imbecile [ˈɪmbəsiːl] **1** *n* imbécile *mf*, idiot(e) *m(f)*; (*Med*††) imbécile. **to behave like an ~** se conduire comme un imbécile *or* en imbécile, se conduire comme un idiot *or* en idiot, faire l'imbécile *or* l'idiot; **to act/speak like an ~** faire/dire des imbécillités *or* des bêtises; **you ~!** espèce d'imbécile! *or* d'idiot!; **this ~ said ...** cette espèce d'imbécile *or* d'idiot a dit ... .

2 *adj action, laugh, words* imbécile; *person* imbécile, idiot; (*Med*††) imbécile.

imbecility [ˌɪmbɪˈsɪlɪtɪ] *n* **(a)** (*U*) imbécillité *f*, stupidité *f*; (*Med*††) imbécillité. **(b)** (*act etc*) imbécillité *f*, stupidité *f*.

imbibe [ɪmˈbaɪb] **1** *vt* **(a)** (*drink*) boire, avaler, absorber; (*fig*) *ideas, information* absorber, assimiler. **(b)** (*absorb*) *water, light, heat* absorber. **2** *vi* (**hum: drink to excess*) picoler*.

imbroglio [ɪmˈbrəʊlɪəʊ] *n* imbroglio *m*.

imbue [ɪm'bjuː] *vt (fig)* imprégner (*with* de). ~**d with** imbu de, imprégné de.
imitable ['ɪmɪtəbl] *adj* imitable.
imitate ['ɪmɪteɪt] *vt (all senses)* imiter.
imitation [ˌɪmɪ'teɪʃən] **1** *n (all senses)* imitation *f*. **in ~ of** à l'imitation de, en imitant, sur le modèle de; (*Comm*) **'beware of ~s'** 'se méfier des contrefaçons'; **it's only ~** c'est de l'imitation.
2 *cpd*: **imitation fur coat** manteau *m* en fourrure synthétique *or* artificielle; **imitation gold** similor *m*; **imitation jewellery** faux bijoux; **imitation leather** imitation *f* cuir *inv*, similicuir *m*; **imitation marble** imitation *f* marbre, faux marbre, similimarbre *m*; **imitation mink coat** manteau *m* (en) imitation vison; **imitation pearl/stone** perle/pierre artificielle *or* d'imitation, fausse perle/pierre.
imitative ['ɪmɪtətɪv] *adj word, art* imitatif; *person* imitateur (*f* -trice).
imitator ['ɪmɪteɪtə^r] *n* imitateur *m*, -trice *f*.
immaculate [ɪ'mækjʊlɪt] *adj snow* immaculé; *dress, appearance* irréprochable, impeccable; *person* impeccable, tiré à quatre épingles; *room* impeccable, d'une propreté irréprochable; *behaviour, manners, courtesy* irréprochable, impeccable, parfait; (*Rel*) immaculé, sans tache. **the I~ Conception** l'Immaculée Conception.
immaculately [ɪ'mækjʊlɪtlɪ] *adv dress* avec un soin impeccable; *behave* de façon irréprochable, parfaitement.
immanent ['ɪmənənt] *adj* immanent.
immaterial [ˌɪmə'tɪərɪəl] *adj* **(a)** (*unimportant*) négligeable, insignifiant, peu important, sans importance. **it is ~ whether he did or not** il importe peu *or* il est indifférent qu'il l'ait fait ou non; **that's (quite) ~** la question n'est pas là; **that is quite ~ to me** cela m'est tout à fait indifférent.
(b) (*Philos etc*) immatériel.
immature [ˌɪmə'tjʊə^r] *adj fruit* (qui n'est) pas mûr, vert; *animal, tree* jeune. *[person, book etc]* **to be ~** manquer de maturité.
immaturity [ˌɪmə'tjʊərɪtɪ] *n* manque *m* de maturité, immaturité *f*.
immeasurable [ɪ'meʒərəbl] *adj amount, height, space* incommensurable; *joy* incommensurable, infini; *precautions, care* infini.
immeasurably [ɪ'meʒərəblɪ] *adv (lit)* incommensurablement; (*fig*) infiniment.
immediacy [ɪ'miːdɪəsɪ] *n* caractère immédiat *or* d'urgence.
immediate [ɪ'miːdɪət] *adj successor, reaction, result, neighbour, risk* immédiat; *information, knowledge* immédiat, direct; *reply* immédiat, instantané; *measures, need* immédiat, urgent, pressant; (*Philos*) *cause, effect* immédiat. **I shall take ~ steps** *or* **action to ensure that ...** je vais agir immédiatement *or* tout de suite *or* sans retard pour m'assurer que ..., je vais prendre des mesures immédiates pour m'assurer que ...; **the ~ future** le futur proche, l'avenir immédiat; **in the ~ future** dans l'immédiat, dans un avenir immédiat; **my ~ object** mon premier but; **for ~ delivery** à livrer d'urgence; **in the ~ neighbourhood** dans le voisinage immédiat, dans le proche voisinage; **the ~ area** les environs immédiats *or* les plus proches.
immediately [ɪ'miːdɪətlɪ] **1** *adv* **(a)** (*at once*) *reply, react, depart* immédiatement, tout de suite, aussitôt, instantanément. **~ after** aussitôt après.
(b) (*directly*) directement. **it does not ~ concern you** cela ne vous regarde pas directement.
2 *conj* (*Brit*) dès que. **~ he had finished he went home** dès qu'il eut fini il rentra chez lui; **~ I returned** dès mon retour.
immemorial [ˌɪmɪ'mɔːrɪəl] *adj* immémorial. **from time ~** de toute éternité, de temps immémorial.
immense [ɪ'mens] *adj space* immense, vaste; *size* immense; *possibilities, achievements, fortune, difficulty* immense, énorme.
immensely [ɪ'menslɪ] *adv* extrêmement, immensément. **~ rich** immensément *or* extrêmement riche; **to enjoy o.s. ~** s'amuser énormément.
immensity [ɪ'mensɪtɪ] *n* immensité *f*.
immerse [ɪ'mɜːs] *vt* immerger, plonger; (*Rel*) baptiser par immersion. **to ~ one's head in water** plonger la tête dans l'eau; (*fig*) **to ~ o.s. in** se plonger dans; **to be ~d in one's work/one's reading** être absorbé *or* plongé dans son travail/sa lecture.
immersion [ɪ'mɜːʃən] **1** *n* immersion *f*; (*fig*) absorption *f*; (*Rel*) baptême *m* par immersion. **2** *cpd*: (*Brit*) **immersion heater** chauffe-eau *m inv* électrique.
immigrant ['ɪmɪgrənt] *adj, n* (*newly arrived*) immigrant(e) *m(f)*; (*well-established*) immigré(e) *m(f)*. (*Ind*) **~ labour, ~ workers** main-d'œuvre immigrée.
immigrate ['ɪmɪgreɪt] *vi* immigrer.
immigration [ˌɪmɪ'greɪʃən] *n* immigration *f*. (*Admin*) **~ authorities** service *m* de l'immigration.
imminence ['ɪmɪnəns] *n* imminence *f*.
imminent ['ɪmɪnənt] *adj* imminent.
immobile [ɪ'məʊbaɪl] *adj* immobile.
immobility [ˌɪməʊ'bɪlɪtɪ] *n* immobilité *f*.
immobilize [ɪ'məʊbɪlaɪz] *vt* (*also Fin*) immobiliser.
immoderate [ɪ'mɒdərɪt] *adj desire, appetite* immodéré, démesuré; *conduct* déréglé.
immoderately [ɪ'mɒdərɪtlɪ] *adv* immodérément.
immodest [ɪ'mɒdɪst] *adj* **(a)** (*indecent*) immodeste, impudique, indécent. **(b)** (*presumptuous*) impudent, présomptueux.
immodestly [ɪ'mɒdɪstlɪ] *adv* **(a)** (*indecently*) immodestement, impudiquement, indécemment. **to behave ~** avoir une conduite indécente. **(b)** (*presumptuously*) impudemment, présomptueusement.
immodesty [ɪ'mɒdɪstɪ] *n* **(a)** (*indecency*) immodestie *f*, impudeur *f*, indécence *f*. **(b)** (*presumption*) impudence *f*, présomption *f*.
immolate ['ɪməʊleɪt] *vt* immoler.
immoral [ɪ'mɒrəl] *adj action, suggestion, person* immoral.
immorality [ˌɪmə'rælɪtɪ] *n* immoralité *f*.
immortal [ɪ'mɔːtl] **1** *adj person, God* immortel; *fame* immortel, impérissable. **2** *n* immortel(le) *m(f)*.
immortality [ˌɪmɔː'tælɪtɪ] *n* immortalité *f*.
immortalize [ɪ'mɔːtəlaɪz] *vt* immortaliser.
immovable [ɪ'muːvəbl] **1** *adj object* fixe; (*Jur*) *belongings* immobilier; (*fig*) *courage, decision* inflexible, inébranlable, immuable; *person* insensible, impassible. **2** *n* (*Jur*) **~s** immeubles *mpl*, biens immobiliers.
immune [ɪ'mjuːn] *adj* (*Med*) immunisé (*from* contre); (*gen*) à l'abri (*against* de), immunisé, protégé (*against* contre).
immunity [ɪ'mjuːnɪtɪ] *n* (*Med, gen*) immunité *f* (*from* contre). **diplomatic/parliamentary ~** immunité diplomatique/parlementaire.
immunization [ˌɪmjʊnaɪ'zeɪʃən] *n* immunisation *f* (*against* contre).
immunize ['ɪmjʊnaɪz] *vt* immuniser (*against* contre).
immure [ɪ'mjʊə^r] *vt* (*lit*) emmurer; (*fig*) enfermer.
immutability [ɪˌmjuːtə'bɪlɪtɪ] *n* immutabilité *f*, immuabilité *f* (*frm*).
immutable [ɪ'mjuːtəbl] *adj* immuable, inaltérable.
imp [ɪmp] *n* diablotin *m*, lutin *m*; (*child*) petit(e) espiègle *m(f)*, petit diable.
impact ['ɪmpækt] **1** *n* impact *m* (*on* sur), choc *m* (*on, against* contre); (*fig*) impact, effet *m* (*on* sur). (*fig*) **to make an ~ on sb** faire une forte impression sur qn. **2** [ɪm'pækt] *vt* enfoncer, presser (*into* dans). **~ed tooth** dent incluse.
impair [ɪm'pɛə^r] *vt abilities, faculties* détériorer, diminuer; *negotiations, relations* porter atteinte à; *health* abîmer, détériorer; *sight, hearing* affaiblir, abîmer; *mind, strength* diminuer.
impala [ɪm'pɑːlə] *n* impala *m*.
impale [ɪm'peɪl] *vt* empaler (*on* sur).
impalpable [ɪm'pælpəbl] *adj* impalpable.
impanel [ɪm'pænl] *vt* = **empanel.**
imparity [ɪm'pærɪtɪ] *n* inégalité *f*.
impart [ɪm'pɑːt] *vt* **(a)** (*make known*) *news* communiquer, faire connaître, faire part de; *knowledge* communiquer, transmettre. **(b)** (*bestow*) donner, transmettre.
impartial [ɪm'pɑːʃəl] *adj person, attitude* impartial, objectif, équitable; *verdict, decision, speech* impartial, objectif.
impartiality [ɪmˌpɑːʃɪ'ælɪtɪ] *n* impartialité *f*.
impartially [ɪm'pɑːʃəlɪ] *adv* impartialement, objectivement, sans parti pris.
impassable [ɪm'pɑːsəbl] *adj barrier, river* infranchissable; *road* impraticable.
impasse [æm'pɑːs] *n* (*lit, fig*) impasse *f*.
impassioned [ɪm'pæʃnd] *adj feeling* exalté; *plea, speech* passionné.
impassive [ɪm'pæsɪv] *adj person, attitude, face* impassible, imperturbable.
impassively [ɪm'pæsɪvlɪ] *adv* impassiblement, imperturbablement, sans s'émouvoir.
impatience [ɪm'peɪʃəns] *n* **(a)** impatience *f* (*to do* de faire). **(b)** (*intolerance*) intolérance *f*, impatience *f* (*with sb* vis-à-vis de qn, à l'égard de qn).
impatient [ɪm'peɪʃənt] *n* **(a)** *person, answer* impatient. **~ to leave** impatient de partir; **to become** *or* **get** *or* **grow ~** s'impatienter. **(b)** intolérant (*of sth* à l'égard de qch, *with sb* vis-à-vis de qn, à l'égard de qn).
impatiently [ɪm'peɪʃəntlɪ] *adv* avec impatience, impatiemment.
impeach [ɪm'piːtʃ] *vt* **(a)** (*Jur: accuse*) *public official* mettre en accusation (*en vue de destituer*), (*US*) entamer la procédure d'impeachment contre; *person* accuser (*for or of sth* de qch, *for doing* de faire).
(b) (*question, challenge*) *sb's character* attaquer; *sb's motives, honesty* mettre en doute. (*Jur*) **to ~ a witness** récuser un témoin.
impeachment [ɪm'piːtʃmənt] *n* **(a)** (*Jur*) *[public official]* mise *f* en accusation (*en vue d'une destitution*), (*US*) procédure *f* d'impeachment; *[person]* accusation *f* (*for sth* de qch, *for doing* de faire).
(b) *[sb's character etc]* dénigrement *m*; *[sb's honesty]* contestation *f*.
impeccable [ɪm'pekəbl] *adj* impeccable, irréprochable, parfait.
impecunious [ˌɪmpɪ'kjuːnɪəs] *adj* impécunieux, nécessiteux.
impede [ɪm'piːd] *vt* empêcher (*sb from doing* qn de faire); *action, success, movement* gêner, faire obstacle à, entraver; *traffic* gêner, entraver.
impediment [ɪm'pedɪmənt] *n* **(a)** obstacle *m*. **(b)** (*also* **speech ~**) défaut *m* d'élocution. **(c) ~s = impedimenta.**
impedimenta [ɪmˌpedɪ'mentə] *npl* (*also Mil*) impedimenta *mpl*.
impel [ɪm'pel] *vt* **(a)** (*drive forward*) pousser, faire avancer. **(b)** (*compel*) obliger, forcer (*to do* à faire); (*urge*) inciter, pousser (*to do* à faire). **to ~ sb to crime** pousser qn au crime.
impend [ɪm'pend] *vi* (*be about to happen*) être imminent; (*menace, hang over*) *[danger, storm]* menacer; *[threat]* planer.
impending [ɪm'pendɪŋ] *adj* (*about to happen*) *birth, arrival* imminent, prochain (*after n*); (*threateningly close*) *danger, storm* imminent, menaçant, qui menace. **his ~ fate** le sort qui le menace (*or* menaçait *etc*); **his ~ retirement** la retraite qu'il va (*or* allait *etc*) prendre sous peu, sa retraite prochaine; **we discussed our ~ removal** nous avons parlé de notre déménagement imminent.

impenetrability [ɪm,penɪtrəˈbɪlɪtɪ] *n* impénétrabilité *f*.
impenetrable [ɪmˈpenɪtrəbl] *adj substance* impénétrable (*to, by* à); *mystery, secret* insondable.
impenitence [ɪmˈpenɪtəns] *n* impénitence *f*.
impenitent [ɪmˈpenɪtənt] *adj* impénitent. **he was quite ~ about it** il ne s'en repentait nullement.
impenitently [ɪmˈpenɪtəntlɪ] *adv* sans repentir.
imperative [ɪmˈperətɪv] **1** *adj* **(a)** *need, desire* urgent, pressant, impérieux; *order* impératif; *voice, manner* impérieux, autoritaire. **silence is ~** le silence s'impose; **it is ~ that you leave, it is ~ for you to leave** il faut absolument que vous partiez (*subj*), votre départ s'impose.
(b) (*Gram*) impératif.
2 *n* (*Gram*) impératif *m*. **in the ~ (mood)** à l'impératif, au mode impératif.
imperceptible [,ɪmpəˈseptəbl] *adj sight, movement* imperceptible (*to* à); *sound* imperceptible, inaudible; *difference* imperceptible, insensible.
imperceptibly [,ɪmpəˈseptəblɪ] *adv* imperceptiblement.
imperceptive [,ɪmpəˈseptɪv] *adj* peu perspicace.
imperfect [ɪmˈpɜːfɪkt] **1** *adj* **(a)** (*faulty*) *reasoning* imparfait; *car, machine* défectueux; (*incomplete*) incomplet (*f* -ète), inachevé. **(b)** (*Gram*) imparfait. **2** *n* (*Gram*) imparfait *m*. **in the ~ (tense)** à l'imparfait.
imperfection [,ɪmpəˈfekʃən] *n* (*V* **imperfect**) imperfection *f*; défectuosité *f*; état imparfait *or* incomplet.
imperfectly [ɪmˈpɜːfɪktlɪ] *adv* imparfaitement.
imperial [ɪmˈpɪərɪəl] **1** *adj* **(a)** (*gen*) *territory, troops* impérial; (*of British Empire*) de l'Empire britannique. (*Brit Hist*) **~ preference** tarif préférentiel (*à l'intérieur de l'Empire britannique*).
(b) (*lordly*) *splendour, dignity* majestueux, grandiose; *look, gesture* impérieux, autoritaire, hautain.
(c) (*Brit*) *weight, measure* légal (*adopté dans tout le Royaume Uni*).
2 *n* (*beard*) (barbe *f* à l')impériale *f*.
imperialism [ɪmˈpɪərɪəlɪzəm] *n* impérialisme *m*.
imperialist [ɪmˈpɪərɪəlɪst] *adj, n* impérialiste (*mf*).
imperialistic [ɪm,pɪərɪəˈlɪstɪk] *adj* impérialiste.
imperially [ɪmˈpɪərɪəlɪ] *adv* majestueusement; *say, gesture* impérieusement.
imperil [ɪmˈperɪl] *vt* mettre en péril *or* danger; *fortune, life* exposer, risquer; *health, reputation* compromettre.
imperious [ɪmˈpɪərɪəs] *adj gesture, look, command* impérieux, autoritaire; *need, desire* urgent, pressant, impérieux.
imperiously [ɪmˈpɪərɪəslɪ] *adv gesture, look* impérieusement, d'un air *or* d'un ton impérieux; *need* impérativement, de façon urgente.
imperishable [ɪmˈperɪʃəbl] *adj* impérissable.
impermanent [ɪmˈpɜːmənənt] *adj* éphémère, fugitif, transitoire, passager.
impermeable [ɪmˈpɜːmɪəbl] *adj rock* imperméable; *wall, roof* étanche.
impersonal [ɪmˈpɜːsnl] *adj* **(a)** *manner, style* impersonnel, froid; *decision, discussion, remark* impersonnel, objectif. **(b)** (*Gram*) impersonnel.
impersonality [ɪm,pɜːsəˈnælɪtɪ] *n* impersonnalité *f*, froideur *f*; objectivité *f*.
impersonally [ɪmˈpɜːsnəlɪ] *adv* impersonnellement.
impersonate [ɪmˈpɜːsəneɪt] *vt* (*gen*) se faire passer pour; (*Jur*) usurper l'identité de; (*Theat*) imiter.
impersonation [ɪm,pɜːsəˈneɪʃən] *n* (*Theat*) imitation *f*; (*Jur*) usurpation *f* d'identité, supposition *f* de personne. (*Theat*) **he does ~s** il fait des imitations (de personnages); **his ~ of his uncle caused him a lot of trouble** s'être fait passer pour son oncle lui a attiré beaucoup d'ennuis.
impersonator [ɪmˈpɜːsəneɪtəʳ] *n* (*Theat*) imitateur *m*, -trice *f*; (*Jur*) usurpateur *m*, -trice *f* d'identité; *V* **female**.
impertinence [ɪmˈpɜːtɪnəns] *n* impertinence *f*, insolence *f*, impudence *f*. **it's the height of ~** c'est le comble de l'impertinence; **a piece of ~** une impertinence; **it would be an ~ to say** il serait impertinent de dire.
impertinent [ɪmˈpɜːtɪnənt] *adj* **(a)** (*impudent*) impertinent, insolent, impudent. **to be ~ to sb** être *or* se montrer insolent envers qn; **don't be ~!** ne soyez pas impertinent!
(b) (*irrelevant*) non pertinent, hors de propos, sans rapport avec la question.
impertinently [ɪmˈpɜːtɪnəntlɪ] *adv* **(a)** (*impudently*) avec impertinence, d'un air insolent, avec impudence. **(b)** (*irrelevantly*) sans pertinence, hors de propos; *reply* en dehors de la question.
imperturbable [,ɪmpəˈtɜːbəbl] *adj* imperturbable.
impervious [ɪmˈpɜːvɪəs] *adj substance, rock* imperméable (*to* à); *wall, roof* étanche (*to* à). (*fig*) **~ to the sufferings of others** imperméable *or* fermé aux souffrances d'autrui; **~ to reason/suggestions** inaccessible *or* sourd à la raison/aux suggestions; **he is ~ to criticism** la critique le laisse indifférent *or* ne le touche pas; (*pej*) il est fermé *or* sourd à la critique.
impetigo [,ɪmpɪˈtaɪgəʊ] *n* (*Med*) impétigo *m*; (*in children*) gourme *f*.
impetuosity [ɪm,petjʊˈɒsɪtɪ] *n* impétuosité *f*, fougue *f*.
impetuous [ɪmˈpetjʊəs] *adj* impétueux, fougueux.
impetuousness [ɪmˈpetjʊəsnɪs] *n* = **impetuosity.**
impetus [ˈɪmpɪtəs] *n [object]* force *f* d'impulsion; *[runner]* élan *m*; (*fig*) impulsion *f*, élan. (*fig*) **to give an ~ to** donner l'impulsion à, donner son élan à, mettre en branle.
impiety [ɪmˈpaɪətɪ] *n* impiété *f*.
impinge [ɪmˈpɪndʒ] *vi* **(a)** (*make impression: also* **make an impingement on**) **to ~ on** affecter, toucher; **her death did not ~ on him** sa mort ne l'a pas affecté *or* touché; **it didn't ~ on his daily life** cela n'affectait pas sa vie quotidienne, cela n'avait pas de répercussion sur sa vie quotidienne; **what was happening around him suddenly ~d on him** il a pris brusquement conscience de ce qui se passait autour de lui.
(b) to ~ on sb's rights empiéter sur les droits de qn.
(c) rays of light impinging on the eye des rais de lumière qui frappent l'œil.
impingement [ɪmˈpɪndʒmənt] *n* **(a)** *V* **impinge a. (b)** *[sb's rights etc]* empiétement *m* (*of, on* sur).
impious [ˈɪmpɪəs] *adj* impie.
impiously [ˈɪmpɪəslɪ] *adv* avec impiété.
impish [ˈɪmpɪʃ] *adj* espiègle, malicieux.
implacable [ɪmˈplækəbl] *adj* implacable.
implant [ɪmˈplɑːnt] *vt* **(a)** *idea* implanter (*in sb* dans la tête de qn); *principle* inculquer (*in sb* à qn); *desire, wish* inspirer (*in sb* à qn). **(b)** (*Med*) implanter (*in* dans).
implausible [ɪmˈplɔːzəbl] *adj* peu plausible, peu vraisemblable.
implement [ˈɪmplɪmənt] **1** *n* outil *m*, instrument *m*; (*fig*) instrument. **~s** équipement *m* (*U*), matériel *m* (*U*); (*for gardening, painting, carpentry*) matériel, outils; (*for cooking*) ustensiles *mpl*; **~s of war** matériel de guerre; **farm ~s** matériel *or* outillage *m* agricole.
2 [ˈɪmplɪment] *vt contract* exécuter; *decision* donner suite à, exécuter; *promise* accomplir; *engagement* remplir, exécuter; *plan* réaliser.
implementation [,ɪmplɪmenˈteɪʃən] *n* (*V* **implement 2**) exécution *f*; accomplissement *m*; réalisation *f*.
implicate [ˈɪmplɪkeɪt] *vt* impliquer, compromettre (*in* dans).
implication [,ɪmplɪˈkeɪʃən] *n* **(a)** insinuation *f*, implication *f*. **by ~** implicitement; **I know only from ~** je ne sais que d'après ce qui a été insinué; **there were ~s of dishonesty** on a insinué qu'il y avait eu de la malhonnêteté; **I don't like the ~s of that question** je n'aime pas ce que cette question insinue *or* sous-entend, je n'aime pas les implications contenues dans cette question; **he didn't realize the full ~s of his words** il n'avait pas pleinement mesuré la portée de ses paroles; **we shall have to study all the ~s** il nous faudra étudier toutes les conséquences (possibles); **this has serious ~s for the youth of the country** ceci pourrait avoir des répercussions sérieuses *or* un retentissement sérieux sur la jeunesse du pays.
(b) (*U*) implication *f* (*in* dans).
implicit [ɪmˈplɪsɪt] *adj* **(a)** (*implied*) implicite (*in* dans); *threat* implicite; *recognition* tacite. **(b)** (*unquestioning*) *belief, faith* absolu; *confidence* absolu, sans réserve, aveugle, parfait; *obedience* aveugle, parfait.
implicitly [ɪmˈplɪsɪtlɪ] *adv* (*V* **implicit**) **(a)** *make known* implicitement, tacitement. **(b)** *believe* absolument, sans réserves. **to obey sb ~** obéir à qn aveuglément *or* au doigt et à l'œil.
implied [ɪmˈplaɪd] *adj* implicite, tacite, sous-entendu.
implode [ɪmˈpləʊd] **1** *vi* imploser; (*Ling*) faire implosion. **2** *vt* causer l'implosion de.
implore [ɪmˈplɔːʳ] *vt* implorer, conjurer, supplier (*sb to do* qn de faire). **to ~ sb's help** implorer le secours de qn; **I ~ you!** je vous en supplie! *or* conjure!
imploring [ɪmˈplɔːrɪŋ] *adj look, voice* suppliant, implorant; *person* suppliant.
imploringly [ɪmˈplɔːrɪŋlɪ] *adv ask* d'un ton suppliant; *look* avec *or* d'un regard suppliant.
implosion [ɪmˈpləʊʒən] *n* implosion *f*.
implosive [ɪmˈpləʊzɪv] **1** *adj* implosif. **2** *n* (*Ling*) plosive *f*, implosive *f*.
imply [ɪmˈplaɪ] *vt* **(a)** *[person]* suggérer, laisser entendre, laisser supposer, (*insinuate*) insinuer (*pej*). **he implied that he would come** il a laissé entendre *or* laissé supposer qu'il viendrait; **he implied that I was lying** il a laissé entendre *or* insinué que je mentais; **are you ~ing that ...?** voulez-vous suggérer *or* insinuer que ...?; **it is implied that ...** il faut sous-entendre que ..., cela sous-entend que ...; *V also* **implied.**
(b) (*indicate*) suggérer, impliquer, (laisser) supposer. **that implies some intelligence** cela suppose *or* implique une certaine intelligence; **this fact implies that he was already aware of the incident** ce fait suggère *or* laisse supposer qu'il était déjà au courant de l'incident; *V also* **implied.**
impolite [,ɪmpəˈlaɪt] *adj* impoli (*to, towards* envers).
impolitely [,ɪmpəˈlaɪtlɪ] *adv* impoliment, d'une manière impolie, avec impolitesse.
impoliteness [,ɪmpəˈlaɪtnɪs] *n* impolitesse *f* (*to, towards* envers).
impolitic [ɪmˈpɒlɪtɪk] *adj* peu politique, impolitique.
imponderable [ɪmˈpɒndərəbl] *adj, n* impondérable (*m*).
import [ˈɪmpɔːt] **1** *n* **(a)** (*Comm*) importation *f*. **~ of goods** importation de marchandises; **~s** articles *mpl or* marchandises *fpl* d'importation, importations; **~s from England** importations en provenance d'Angleterre.
(b) (*meaning*) *[action, decision, speech, words]* sens *m*, signification *f*; *[document]* teneur *f*.
(c) importance *f*. **questions of great ~** questions de grande importance.
2 *cpd*: (*Comm*) **import duty** droits *mpl* d'importation, taxe *f* à l'importation; **import-export trade** import-export *m*; **import licence** licence *f* d'importation; **import surcharge** surcharge *f* d'importation; **import trade** (commerce *m* d')importation *f*.
3 [ɪmˈpɔːt] *vt* **(a)** (*Comm*) importer. **~ed goods** marchandises d'importation *or* importées.
(b) (*mean, imply*) signifier, vouloir dire.
importance [ɪmˈpɔːtəns] *n* importance *f*. **to be of ~** avoir de l'importance; **of some ~** assez important, d'une certaine importance; **of great ~** très important, de grande importance;

it is of the highest ~ that ... il est de la plus haute importance que ... + *subj*, il importe au premier chef que ... + *subj*; **it is of ~ to do** il est important de faire, il importe de faire (*frm*); **it is of no (great) ~** c'est sans (grande) importance; **we attach the greatest ~ to establishing the facts** nous attachons la plus haute importance à l'établissement des faits; **man of ~** homme important, personnage *m* (important); **person of no ~** personne *f* sans importance *or* de peu de conséquence; **his position gives him considerable ~** sa position lui donne une influence considérable; **he is full of his own ~** il est plein de lui-même, il est imbu *or* pénétré de sa propre importance.

important [ɪm'pɔːtənt] *adj* important. **it is ~ that you (should) know** il importe (*frm*) *or* il est important que vous sachiez; **that's not ~** ça n'a pas d'importance, cela n'est pas important; **his presence is ~ to** *or* **for the success of our plan** sa présence est importante pour la réussite de notre projet; **he played an ~ part in abolishing slavery** il a joué un rôle important dans l'abolition de l'esclavage; **he was trying to look ~** il essayait de se donner *or* de prendre des airs importants.

importantly [ɪm'pɔːtəntlɪ] *adv* (*pej*) d'un air important *or* d'importance.

importation [ˌɪmpɔː'teɪʃən] *n* (*Comm*) importation *f*.

importer [ɪm'pɔːtə^r] *n* (*person*) importateur *m*, -trice *f*; (*country*) (pays *m*) importateur *m*.

importunate [ɪm'pɔːtjʊnɪt] *adj visitor, demand* importun, gênant; *creditor* harcelant.

importune [ˌɪmpɔː'tjuːn] **1** *vt [questioner etc]* importuner, ennuyer; *[creditor]* harceler, presser; (*Jur*) *[prostitute etc]* racoler. **2** *vi* (*Jur*) racoler. **she was arrested for importuning** elle a été arrêtée pour racolage.

importunity [ˌɪmpɔː'tjuːnɪtɪ] *n* importunité *f*.

impose [ɪm'pəʊz] **1** *vt* **(a)** *task, conditions* imposer (*on* à); *sanctions* infliger (*on* à). **to ~ a penalty/a fine on sb** infliger une peine/une amende à qn, frapper qn d'une peine/d'une amende; **to ~ a tax on sth** imposer qch, taxer qch, mettre un impôt *or* une taxe sur qch; **to ~ o.s. on sb** s'imposer à qn; **to ~ one's presence on sb** imposer sa présence à qn.

(b) (*Typ*) imposer.

2 *vi*: **to ~ on sb** (*deceive*) tromper *or* duper qn, en faire accroire à qn; (*take advantage of*) abuser de la gentillesse *or* de la bonté *or* de l'amabilité de qn; **to ~ on sb's generosity** abuser de la générosité de qn.

imposing [ɪm'pəʊzɪŋ] *adj figure, amount, appearance* imposant, impressionnant. **~ height** *[person]* taille imposante; *[building etc]* hauteur impressionnante.

imposition [ˌɪmpə'zɪʃən] *n* **(a)** (*U*) *[tax, condition, sanction]* imposition *f*.

(b) (*tax imposed*) impôt *m*, taxe *f*.

(c) (*fig*) **it's rather an ~ on her** c'est abuser de sa gentillesse *or* de sa bonté *or* de son amabilité; **I'm afraid it's an ~ for you** je crains que cela ne vous dérange (*subj*).

(d) (*Typ*) imposition *f*.

(e) (*Scol*) punition *f*.

impossibility [ɪmˌpɒsə'bɪlɪtɪ] *n* impossibilité *f* (*of sth* de qch, *of doing* de faire). **the moral/physical ~ of** l'impossibilité morale/matérielle de; **it's a physical ~ for her to get there before 3 o'clock** elle est dans l'impossibilité matérielle *or* il lui est matériellement impossible d'y être avant 3 heures; **it's an ~** c'est une impossibilité, c'est une chose impossible, c'est quelque chose d'impossible.

impossible [ɪm'pɒsəbl] **1** *adj* **(a)** impossible. **it is ~ for him to leave** il lui est impossible *or* il est dans l'impossibilité de partir; **he made it ~ for me to accept** il m'a mis dans l'impossibilité d'accepter; **it is/is not ~ that ...** il est/n'est pas impossible que ... + *subj*; **I'm afraid it's quite ~!** c'est malheureusement absolument impossible!

(b) *person, child, condition, situation* impossible, insupportable; *excuse, account, adventure, story, reason* impossible, invraisemblable, extravagant. **he made her life ~** il lui a rendu la vie *or* l'existence impossible.

2 *n* impossible *m*. **to do/ask for the ~** faire/demander l'impossible.

impossibly [ɪm'pɒsəblɪ] *adv* **(a)** de façon impossible. **if, ~, he were to succeed** si, par impossible, il réussissait; **an ~ difficult problem** un problème d'une difficulté insurmontable.

(b) *dress* d'une façon invraisemblable; *behave* d'une façon impossible *or* insupportable. **we're ~ late** nous sommes incroyablement *or* épouvantablement en retard; **she is ~ eccentric** elle est incroyablement *or* follement excentrique.

impostor [ɪm'pɒstə^r] *n* (*impersonator*) imposteur *m*; (*fraud*) charlatan *m*.

imposture [ɪm'pɒstʃə^r] *n* imposture *f*.

impotence ['ɪmpətəns] *n* (*lit, fig*) impuissance *f*, faiblesse *f*; (*sexual*) impuissance; (*Med gen*) impotence *f*.

impotent ['ɪmpətənt] *adj* (*V* **impotence**) impuissant; faible; impotent.

impound [ɪm'paʊnd] *vt* (*Jur*) confisquer, saisir.

impoverish [ɪm'pɒvərɪʃ] *vt* appauvrir. **~ed** appauvri, pauvre.

impoverishment [ɪm'pɒvərɪʃmənt] *n* appauvrissement *m*.

impracticability [ɪmˌpræktɪkə'bɪlɪtɪ] *n* impraticabilité *f*.

impracticable [ɪm'præktɪkəbl] *adj idea, plan, scheme, suggestion* impraticable, irréalisable; *road etc* impraticable.

impractical [ɪm'præktɪkəl] *adj person* qui manque d'esprit pratique; *plan, idea* peu réaliste, pas pratique.

imprecation [ˌɪmprɪ'keɪʃən] *n* imprécation *f*, malédiction *f*.

imprecise [ˌɪmprɪ'saɪs] *adj* imprécis.

imprecision [ˌɪmprɪ'sɪʒən] *n* imprécision *f*, manque *m* de précision.

impregnable [ɪm'pregnəbl] *adj* (*Mil*) *fortress, defences* imprenable, inexpugnable; (*fig*) *position* inattaquable; *argument* irréfutable.

impregnate ['ɪmpregneɪt] *vt* **(a)** (*fertilize*) féconder. **(b)** (*saturate*) imprégner, imbiber (*with* de); (*fig*) imprégner, pénétrer (*with* de).

impregnation [ˌɪmpreg'neɪʃən] *n* (*V* **impregnate**) fécondation *f*; imprégnation *f*.

impresario [ˌɪmpre'sɑːrɪəʊ] *n* impresario *m*.

impress [ɪm'pres] **1** *vt* **(a)** *person* impressionner, faire impression sur. **how did he ~ you?** quelle impression vous a-t-il faite?; **he ~ed me favourably/unfavourably** il m'a fait une bonne/mauvaise impression; **his novel greatly ~ed me** son roman m'a beaucoup impressionné, son roman m'a fait une forte *or* grosse impression; **he is not easily ~ed** il ne se laisse pas facilement impressionner; **I am not ~ed** ça ne m'impressionne pas, ça me laisse froid, ça me laisse de marbre; **I am not in the least ~ed** ça ne m'impressionne absolument pas, ça ne me fait ni chaud ni froid; **he does it just to ~ people** il ne le fait que pour (impressionner) la galerie.

(b) imprimer, marquer (*on* sur). **to ~ a seal on wax** imprimer un sceau sur la cire; (*fig*) **to ~ sth on sb** faire (bien) comprendre qch à qn; **you must ~ on him that he should be on time** il faut que tu lui fasses (bien) comprendre qu'il doit arriver à l'heure; **his words are (forever) ~ed on my memory** ses paroles sont (à jamais) gravées dans ma mémoire.

2 ['ɪmpres] *n* marque *f*, empreinte *f*.

impression [ɪm'preʃən] *n* **(a)** (*effect*) impression *f*. **to make an ~** faire impression *or* de l'effet (*on sb* à qn); **to make a good/bad ~ on sb** faire une bonne/mauvaise impression à qn; **what ~ does he make on you?, what's your ~ of him?** quelle impression vous fait-il?; **the water made no ~ on the stains** l'eau n'a fait aucun effet sur *or* n'a pas agi sur les taches; **first ~s are most important** ce sont les premières impressions qui comptent (le plus); **he gave the ~ of power** il donnait une impression de puissance.

(b) (*vague idea*) impression *f*. **I am under the ~ that ..., my ~ is that ...** j'ai l'impression que ...; **that wasn't my ~!** ce n'est pas l'impression que j'ai eue!; **his ~s of Paris** les impressions qu'il a gardées de Paris; **he had the ~ of falling** il avait l'impression de tomber.

(c) *[seal, stamp, footprint]* empreinte *f*, impression *f*, trace *f*, marque *f*; (*on wax*) impression.

(d) *[engraving etc]* impression *f*; *[book etc]* tirage *m*.

impressionable [ɪm'preʃnəbl] *adj* impressionnable, sensible. **at an ~ age** à un âge où l'on est impressionnable.

impressionism [ɪm'preʃənɪzəm] *n* (*Art*) impressionnisme *m*.

impressionist [ɪm'preʃənɪst] *adj, n* (*Art*) impressionniste (*mf*).

impressionistic [ɪmˌpreʃə'nɪstɪk] *adj story, account* impressionniste, subjectif; (*Art*) impressionniste.

impressive [ɪm'presɪv] *adj appearance, building, ceremony, person, sight, sum* impressionnant, imposant; *amount, account, achievement, result* impressionnant; *speech* impressionnant, frappant. **~ height** *[person]* taille imposante; *[building]* hauteur impressionnante.

impressively [ɪm'presɪvlɪ] *adv* de façon impressionnante, d'une manière impressionnante.

impressment [ɪm'presmənt] *n [person]* enrôlement forcé; *[property, goods]* réquisition *f*.

imprint [ɪm'prɪnt] **1** *vt* imprimer, marquer (*on* sur); (*fig*) imprimer, graver, implanter (*on* dans). **2** ['ɪmprɪnt] *n* (*lit, fig*) marque *f*, empreinte *f*; (*Psych*) empreinte perceptive. **published under the Collins ~** édité chez Collins.

imprinting [ɪm'prɪntɪŋ] *n* (*Psych: U*) empreinte *f*.

imprison [ɪm'prɪzn] *vt* emprisonner, mettre en prison; (*fig*) emprisonner. **he had been ~ed for 3 months when ...** il avait été en prison 3 mois quand ..., il avait fait 3 mois de prison quand ...; **the judge ~ed him for 10 years** le juge l'a envoyé en prison pour 10 ans, le juge l'a condamné à 10 ans de prison.

imprisonment [ɪm'prɪznmənt] *n* (*action, state*) emprisonnement *m*. **to sentence sb to one month's ~/to life ~** condamner qn à un mois de prison/à la prison à vie; **sentence of life ~** condamnation *f* à la prison à perpétuité; **to serve a sentence of ~** faire de la prison.

improbability [ɪmˌprɒbə'bɪlɪtɪ] *n* (*V* **improbable**) **(a)** improbabilité *f*. **(b)** invraisemblance *f*.

improbable [ɪm'prɒbəbl] *adj* **(a)** (*unlikely to happen*) improbable. **it is ~ that ...** il est improbable *or* il est peu probable que ... + *subj*. **(b)** (*of doubtful truth*) *story, excuse* invraisemblable.

impromptu [ɪm'prɒmptjuː] **1** *adv* impromptu. **2** *adj* impromptu. **to make an ~ speech** faire un discours impromptu *or* au pied levé *or* à l'improviste. **3** *n* (*Mus*) impromptu *m*.

improper [ɪm'prɒpə^r] *adj* (*unsuitable*) déplacé, malséant, de mauvais goût; (*indecent*) indécent, inconvenant; *conduct, suggestion* indécent; *story* indécent, scabreux; (*dishonest*) malhonnête; (*wrong*) *diagnosis* incorrect, erroné; *term* inexact, impropre, incorrect; *use, interpretation* abusif, incorrect; (*Sport*) *play etc* incorrect.

improperly [ɪm'prɒpəlɪ] *adv* (*indecently*) d'une manière malséante *or* inconvenante, indécemment; (*wrongly*) incorrectement, à tort. **word ~ used** mot employé incorrectement *or* improprement *or* abusivement.

impropriety [ˌɪmprə'praɪətɪ] *n* **(a)** *[behaviour etc]* inconvenance *f*. **to commit an ~** commettre une inconvenance; **to behave with ~** se conduire avec inconvenance. **(b)** (*Ling*) *[expression, phrase]* impropriété *f*.

improve [ɪm'pruːv] **1** *vt* **(a)** (*make better*) améliorer; *situation, position, one's work, health, wording, property, building* améliorer; *knowledge* améliorer, augmenter, accroître; *physique* développer; *machine, invention* améliorer, perfectionner; *site* embellir; *soil, land* amender, fertiliser, bonifier. **to ~ sb's looks** *or* **appearance** embellir *or* avantager qn; **to ~ one's looks** s'embellir; **that should ~ his chances of success** ceci devrait lui donner de meilleures chances de réussir; **she's trying to ~ her mind** elle essaie de se cultiver (l'esprit); **he wants to ~ his French** il veut se perfectionner en français.

(b) (*make good use of*) tirer parti de, profiter de. **to ~ the occasion,** (*hum*) **to ~ the shining hour** tirer parti de l'occasion, mettre l'occasion à profit.

2 *vi* **(a)** (*V* **1a**) s'améliorer; s'augmenter, s'accroître; se développer; être amélioré, être perfectionné; s'embellir; s'amender, se bonifier. **this wine ~s with age** ce vin se bonifie *or* s'améliore en vieillissant; **to ~ with use** s'améliorer à l'usage; *[person, town etc]* **to ~ on acquaintance** gagner à être connu; **this book ~s on rereading** ce livre gagne à être relu; **his chances of success are improving** ses chances de réussir augmentent *or* s'améliorent; **she's improving in appearance, her appearance is improving** elle embellit; **the invalid is improving** l'état du malade s'améliore; **his work is improving** (la qualité de) son travail s'améliore; **he has ~d in maths, his maths have ~d** il a fait des progrès en maths; **his French is improving** son français s'améliore; **business is improving** les affaires reprennent; **things are improving** les choses vont mieux, la situation s'améliore; **this child is difficult but he's improving** c'est un enfant difficile mais il s'améliore *or* il fait des progrès; **the weather is improving** le temps s'améliore *or* s'arrange.

(b) to ~ on sth faire mieux que qch, apporter des améliorations à qch; **it can't be ~d on** on ne peut pas faire mieux; (*Comm, Fin*) **to ~ on sb's offer** enchérir sur qn.

improvement [ɪm'pruːvmənt] **1** *n* **(a)** (*U*) amélioration *f*; *[gifts, mind, physique]* développement *m*; *[studies]* progrès *m*; *[health, situation, land, soil]* amélioration; *[machine]* perfectionnement *m*. (*gen*) **there's been quite an ~** il y a un *or* du mieux; **the ~ in the appearance of the house** l'embellissement *m* de la maison; **there has been a great ~ in her looks since ...** elle a beaucoup embelli depuis ..., elle s'est beaucoup arrangée depuis ...; **there has been some ~ in the patient's condition** l'état du malade s'est un peu amélioré; **to be open to ~** être susceptible d'amélioration; **he has shown some ~ in French** il a fait quelques progrès en français; **this car is an ~ on the previous one** cette voiture marque un progrès sur la précédente; **there is room for ~** cela pourrait être mieux, on pourrait faire mieux.

(b) (*gen pl*) **~s** améliorations *fpl*; **to carry out ~s to a town/a house** apporter des améliorations à *or* faire des travaux *mpl* d'aménagement dans une ville/une maison.

2 *cpd*: **he got an improvement grant from the council for his kitchen** il a obtenu une aide financière de la ville pour la modernisation de sa cuisine.

improvidence [ɪm'prɒvɪdəns] *n* imprévoyance *f*, manque *m* de prévoyance.

improvident [ɪm'prɒvɪdənt] *adj* (*not providing for future*) imprévoyant; (*spendthrift*) prodigue, dépensier.

improvidently [ɪm'prɒvɪdəntlɪ] *adv* avec imprévoyance.

improving [ɪm'pruːvɪŋ] *adj book, conversation* édifiant, instructif.

improvisation [ˌɪmprəvaɪ'zeɪʃən] *n* improvisation *f*.

improvise ['ɪmprəvaɪz] *vti* improviser.

imprudence [ɪm'pruːdəns] *n* imprudence *f*.

imprudent [ɪm'pruːdənt] *adj* imprudent.

imprudently [ɪm'pruːdəntlɪ] *adv* imprudemment.

impudence ['ɪmpjʊdəns] *n* impudence *f*, effronterie *f*, insolence *f*.

impudent ['ɪmpjʊdənt] *adj* impudent, effronté, insolent.

impudently ['ɪmpjʊdəntlɪ] *adv* impudemment, effrontément, insolemment.

impugn [ɪm'pjuːn] *vt* contester, attaquer.

impulse ['ɪmpʌls] **1** *n* **(a)** (*spontaneous act etc*) impulsion *f*, élan *m*. **rash ~** coup *m* de tête; **on a sudden ~ he ...** pris d'une impulsion soudaine il ...; **man of ~** impulsif *m*; **to act on (an) ~** agir par impulsion; **my first ~ was to refuse** ma première impulsion *or* réaction a été de refuser.

(b) impulsion *f*, poussée *f*. **to give an ~ to business** donner une impulsion aux affaires.

2 *cpd*: **impulse buy** achat *m* sur un coup de tête; **impulse buying** (tendance *f* à faire des) achats *mpl* sur un coup de tête.

impulsion [ɪm'pʌlʃən] *n* impulsion *f*.

impulsive [ɪm'pʌlsɪv] *adj* **(a)** (*spontaneous, acting on impulse*) *movement* impulsif; *temperament* primesautier; *temper, passion* fougueux; *action* impulsif, spontané, irréfléchi; *remark* irréfléchi. **(b)** (*impelling*) *force* irrésistible.

impulsively [ɪm'pʌlsɪvlɪ] *adv act, speak* par *or* sur impulsion.

impulsiveness [ɪm'pʌlsɪvnɪs] *n* (*U*) caractère impulsif, impulsivité *f*.

impunity [ɪm'pjuːnɪtɪ] *n* impunité *f*. **with ~** impunément, avec impunité.

impure [ɪm'pjʊəʳ] *adj air, water, milk, motive* impur; *thought, action* impur, impudique; (*Archit etc*) *style* bâtard.

impurity [ɪm'pjʊərɪtɪ] *n* **(a)** (*U: V* **impure**) impureté *f*; impudicité *f*. **(b)** (*in water etc*) **impurities** impuretés *fpl*.

imputation [ˌɪmpjʊ'teɪʃən] *n* **(a)** (*accusation*) imputation *f*, accusation *f*. **(b)** (*U*) attribution *f*, imputation *f* (*of sth to sb/sth* de qch à qn/qch).

impute [ɪm'pjuːt] *vt* imputer, attribuer (*sth to sb/sth* qch à qn/qch).

in [ɪn] (*phr vb elem*) **1** *prep* **(a)** (*place*) en, à, dans. **~ the garden** dans le *or* au jardin; **~ the country** à la campagne; **~ town** en ville; **~ here** ici; **~ there** là-dedans; **~ the street** dans la rue; **~ the shop window** à la vitrine, en vitrine; **sitting ~ the doorway** assis dans l'embrasure de la porte; **sitting ~ the window** assis devant la fenêtre; **~ school** à l'école; **~ the school** dans l'école; **~ a friend's house** chez un ami; *V* **bed, hand, place** *etc*.

(b) (*towns*) à; (*countries*) en, au(x). **~ London** à Londres; **~ France** en France; **~ Yorkshire** dans le Yorkshire; **~ Denmark** au Danemark; **~ the United States** aux États-Unis.

(c) (*people, works*) chez, en, dans. **we find it ~ Dickens** nous le trouvons chez *or* dans Dickens; **rare ~ a child of that age** rare chez un enfant de cet âge; **he has/hasn't got it ~ him to succeed** il est capable/incapable de réussir; **you find this instinct ~ animals** on trouve cet instinct chez les animaux; **they will have a great leader ~ him** ils trouveront en lui un excellent dirigeant.

(d) (*time: during*) **~ 1969** en 1969; **~ the sixties** dans les années soixante; **~ the reign of** sous le règne de; **~ June** en juin, au mois de juin; **~ spring** au printemps; **~ summer/autumn/winter** en été/automne/hiver; **~ the morning** le matin, dans la matinée; **~ the afternoon** l'après-midi, dans l'après-midi; **~ the mornings** le(s) matin(s); **~ the daytime** pendant la journée; **~ the evening** le soir, pendant la soirée; **~ the night** la nuit, pendant la nuit, de nuit; **3 o'clock ~ the afternoon** 3 heures de l'après-midi; **at any time ~ the day** à n'importe quelle heure du jour *or* de la journée; **~ those days** à cette époque-là; **~ these days** de nos jours, à notre époque, actuellement; **I haven't seen him ~ years** cela fait des années que je ne l'ai (pas) vu; *V* **end, future, life** *etc*.

(e) (*time: in the space of*) en. **I did it/will do it ~ 2 hours** je l'ai fait/je le ferai en 2 heures, j'ai mis/je mettrai 2 heures à le faire.

(f) (*time: at the end of*) dans, au bout de. **~ a moment** *or* **a minute** dans un moment *or* une minute; **~ a short time** sous peu, dans peu de temps; **~ a week's time** dans (l'espace d')une semaine; **he will arrive ~ a fortnight** il arrivera dans quinze jours; **he returned ~ a week** il rentra au bout d'une semaine; *V* **time** *etc*.

(g) (*manner*) **~ a loud voice** d'une voix forte; **~ a soft voice** à voix basse; **to speak ~ a whisper** parler en chuchotant, chuchoter; **to dress ~ fashion** s'habiller à la mode; **~ self-defence** pour se défendre; (*Jur*) en légitime défense; **~ ink** à l'encre; **~ pencil** au crayon; **~ French** en français; **to reply ~ writing** répondre par écrit; **to paint ~ oils** peindre à l'huile; **to pay ~ cash/~ kind** payer (en argent) comptant/en nature; **it is written ~ black and white** c'est écrit noir sur blanc; **to stand ~ a row** être en ligne; **~ alphabetical order** par ordre alphabétique; **to walk ~ groups** se promener en *or* par groupes; **packed ~ hundreds** en *or* par paquets de cent; **~ rags** en haillons, en lambeaux; **dressed ~ white/black** habillé en *or* vêtu de blanc/noir; **~ his shirt** en chemise; **~ his slippers** en pantoufles; **you look nice ~ that dress** tu es jolie avec cette robe.

(h) (*substance, material*) en. **~ velvet** en velours; **~ marble** en marbre.

(i) (*physical surroundings, circumstances*) **~ the rain** sous la pluie; **~ the sun** au soleil; **~ the shade** à l'ombre; **~ darkness** dans l'obscurité; **~ the moonlight** au clair de (la) lune; **to go out ~ all weathers/~ a high wind** sortir par tous les temps/par grand vent; **~ public** en public; **~ itself** en soi.

(j) (*state, condition*) **~ good/bad health** en bonne/mauvaise santé; **~ tears** en larmes; **~ despair** au désespoir; **to be ~ a rage** être en rage, être furieux; **~ good repair** en bon état; **~ ruins** en ruines; **to live ~ luxury/poverty** vivre dans le luxe/la misère; **~ private** en privé; **~ secret** en secret; **~ fun** pour rire, par plaisanterie; **~ earnest** sérieusement, pour de bon.

(k) (*ratio*) **one man ~ ten** un homme sur dix; **once ~ a hundred years** une fois tous les cent ans; **a day ~ a thousand** un jour entre mille; **15 pence ~ the pound** 15 pence par livre sterling.

(l) (*degree, extent*) **~ large/small quantities** en grande/petite quantité; **~ some measure** dans une certaine mesure; **~ part** en partie; **~ hundreds** par centaines.

(m) (*in respect of*) **blind ~ the left eye** aveugle de l'œil gauche; **poor ~ maths** faible en maths; **10 metres ~ height by 30 ~ length** 10 mètres de haut sur 30 de long; **5 ~ number** au nombre de 5; **~ that, he resembles his father** en cela, il ressemble à son père; *V* **respect** *etc*.

(n) (*occupation, activity*) **he is ~ the army** il est dans l'armée; **he is ~ the motor trade** il travaille dans l'(industrie) automobile; **he spends his time ~ reading** il passe son temps à lire.

(o) (*after superlative*) de. **the best pupil ~ the class** le meilleur élève de la classe; **the highest mountain ~ Europe** la montagne la plus haute d'Europe, la plus haute montagne d'Europe.

(p) (+ *gerund*) **~ saying this, ~ so saying** en disant cela; **~ trying to save her he fell into the water himself** en essayant de la sauver il est tombé lui-même à l'eau.

(q) ~ that there are 5 of them étant donné qu'il y en a 5; **~ so** *or* **as far as** dans la mesure où; **~ all** en tout.

2 *adv* **(a)** dedans, à l'intérieur. **to be ~** (*at home*) être là, être à la maison, être chez soi; (*in room, office etc*) être là; **there is nobody ~** il n'y a personne (à la maison); **is Paul ~?** est-ce que Paul est là?; **they will be ~ at 6 o'clock** ils seront rentrés *or* là à 6 heures; **we were asked ~** on nous invita à entrer; **the train is ~** le train est en gare *or* est arrivé; **the harvest is ~** la moisson est rentrée; **oranges are now ~** c'est maintenant la saison des oranges, les oranges sont maintenant en saison; **straw hats are ~** les chapeaux de paille sont en vogue *or* à la mode; **the socialists are ~** les socialistes sont au pouvoir; (*Pol*) **to put sb ~** porter qn au pouvoir; **the Communist candidate is ~** le candidat communiste a été élu; **the fire is still ~** le feu brûle encore, il y a encore du feu; *V* **call in, move in** *etc*.

(b) (*phrases*) **~ between** (*space*) entre, au milieu; (*time*) dans l'intervalle, entre-temps (*V also* 5); **we are ~ for trouble** nous allons avoir des ennuis; **we are ~ for rain** nous allons avoir de la pluie; **he's ~ for it!*** il va écoper!*, il va en prendre pour son grade!*; **you don't know what you're ~ for!*** tu ne sais pas ce qui t'attend!; **are you ~ for the race?** est-ce que tu es inscrit pour la course?; **he's ~ for the job of ...** il est candidat au poste de ...; **to have it ~ for sb*** avoir une dent contre qn*, garder une dent à qn*; **to be ~ on a plan/secret** être au courant d'un plan/d'un secret; **are you ~ on it?** tu es au courant?, tu es dans le coup?*; **to be (well) ~ with sb** être en bons termes avec qn, être bien avec qn; **day ~ day out** jour après jour; *V* **all, eye, luck** *etc.*

3 *adj* **(a)** **'~' door** porte *f* d'entrée; **'~' tray** corbeille *f* du courrier du jour; *V also* **5.**

(b) (*) **it's the ~ thing to ...** c'est très dans le vent* de ... + *infin*; **it's the ~ place to eat** c'est le restaurant dans le vent* *or* à la mode; **an ~ joke** une plaisanterie qui n'est comprise que des initiés.

4 *n* **(a)** **to know the ~s and outs of a matter** connaître une affaire dans ses moindres détails, connaître les tenants et les aboutissants d'une affaire; **all the ~s and outs of the question** les tenants et les aboutissants de la question.

(b) (*US Pol**) **the ~s** le parti au pouvoir.

5 *cpd*: **inasmuch** *V* **inasmuch**; **the in-betweens** ceux qui sont entre les deux; **it's in-between** c'est entre les deux; **in-between times** dans les intervalles; **it was in-between* weather** il faisait un temps moyen; **a coat for in-between weather** un manteau de demi-saison; (*Naut*) **inboard** (*adv*) à l'intérieur, à bord; (*prep*) à bord de; (*adj*) intérieur (*f* -eure); (*Naut*) **inboard motor** (moteur *m*) inboard *m*; **inborn** *feeling, desire* inné; *weakness* congénital; **inbred** *quality* inné, naturel; **an inbred family/tribe** une famille/tribu qui a un fort degré de consanguinité; **an inbred animal** une bête issue de parents consanguins; **inbreeding** *[animals]* croisement *m* d'animaux de même souche; **there is a lot of inbreeding in the tribe** il y a beaucoup d'unions consanguines au sein de la tribu; **in-car entertainment** détente *f* en voiture, détente-voiture *f*; **incoming** *people, crowd* qui arrive, qui entre; *tenant, resident* nouveau (*f* nouvelle); *mayor, president* nouveau, entrant; **incoming mail** courrier *m* du jour; **incoming tide** marée montante; (*Book-keeping*) **incomings** rentrées *fpl*, recettes *fpl*; **indoor** *V* **indoor**; **in-fighting** (*Mil*) (*hand-to-hand*) corps à corps *m*; (*close-range*) combat rapproché; (*Boxing*) corps à corps; (*fig*) (*within group etc*) luttes *fpl or* querelles *fpl* internes; (*hard struggles etc*) bagarre* *f*; **infix** *V* **infix**; **inflight entertainment/film** *etc* distractions *fpl*/film *m etc* en vol; **ingoing** *people, crowd* qui entre; *tenant* nouveau (*f* nouvelle); **ingroup** noyau *m* (fermé); (*Med*) **ingrowing** *or* (*US*) **ingrown nail** ongle incarné; **inlaid** *V* **inlaid**; **inland** *V* **inland**; **my in-laws*** (*parents-in-law*) mes beaux-parents *mpl*; (*others*) ma belle-famille; **inlay** *V* **inlay**; **inlet** *V* **inlet**; **inmate** *V* **inmate**; **inmost** *V* **inmost**; (*Med*) **in-patient** malade *mf* hospitalisé(e); **input** *V* **input**; *[water, people etc]* **in-rush** irruption *f*; (*Ind etc*) **to have in-service training** faire un stage de formation professionnelle (continue) *or* de promotion sociale; **inset** *V* **inset**; **inshore** *V* **inshore**; **insight** *V* **insight**; **insole** (*removable sole*) semelle intérieure; (*part of shoe*) première *f*; **insomuch** *V* **insomuch**; **instep** *V* **instep**; **intake** *V* **intake.**

inability [ˌɪnəˈbɪlɪtɪ] *n* incapacité *f* (*to do* de faire), impuissance *f* (*to do* à faire).

inaccessibility [ˈɪnækˌsesəˈbɪlɪtɪ] *n* inaccessibilité *f.*

inaccessible [ˌɪnækˈsesəbl] *adj country, town* inaccessible (*to* à); *forest* impénétrable (*to* par); *person* inabordable, inaccessible.

inaccuracy [ɪnˈækjʊrəsɪ] *n* **(a)** (*U*) *[calculation, information, quotation, statement]* inexactitude *f*; *[person]* imprécision *f*, manque *m* de précision; *[expression, term, word]* inexactitude, impropriété *f.*

(b) **there are several inaccuracies in his account/calculations** il y a plusieurs inexactitudes dans son rapport/ses calculs.

inaccurate [ɪnˈækjʊrɪt] *adj calculation, information* inexact, erroné; *word, expression* incorrect, impropre; *mind, person* manquant de précision; *account, statement, report, quotation* inexact.

inaccurately [ɪnˈækjʊrɪtlɪ] *adv answer, quote, report* avec inexactitude, inexactement; *multiply* incorrectement.

inaction [ɪnˈækʃən] *n* inaction *f*, inactivité *f.* **policy of ~** politique *f* de l'inaction *or* de non-intervention.

inactive [ɪnˈæktɪv] *adj person* inactif, peu actif; *life* peu actif; *mind* inerte; *volcano* qui n'est pas en activité, en léthargie.

inactivity [ˌɪnækˈtɪvɪtɪ] *n* (*V* **inactive**) inactivité *f*, manque *m* d'activité; inertie *f.*

inadequacy [ɪnˈædɪkwəsɪ] *n [heating, punishment, resources]* insuffisance *f*; *[piece of work]* insuffisance, médiocrité *f*; (*Psych*) inadaptation *or* insuffisance socio-affective.

inadequate [ɪnˈædɪkwɪt] *adj amount, measures, precautions, punishment, resources, supply, strength* insuffisant, inadéquat; *piece of work* insuffisant, médiocre; *person* insuffisant, incapable, inadéquat; (*Psych*) mal adapté *or* inadapté (sur le plan socio-affectif). **the proposed legislation is quite ~ for this purpose** la législation en projet est tout à fait insuffisante pour atteindre ce but; **the amount offered is ~ to cover the expenses** la somme proposée ne suffit pas à couvrir les frais; **he felt totally ~** il ne se sentait absolument pas à la hauteur.

inadequately [ɪnˈædɪkwɪtlɪ] *adv* insuffisamment.

inadmissible [ˌɪnədˈmɪsəbl] *adj attitude, opinion, behaviour* inadmissible; *suggestion, offer* inacceptable. (*Jur*) **~ evidence** témoignage *m* irrecevable.

inadvertence [ˌɪnədˈvɜːtəns] *n* inattention *f*, manque *m* d'attention, étourderie *f.* **by ~** par mégarde, par inadvertance, par étourderie.

inadvertent [ˌɪnədˈvɜːtənt] *adj person* (*inattentive*) inattentif, étourdi; (*heedless*) insouciant (*to* de); *action* commis par inadvertance *or* par mégarde. **an ~ insult** une insulte lâchée par étourderie.

inadvertently [ˌɪnədˈvɜːtəntlɪ] *adv* par inadvertance, par mégarde, par étourderie.

inadvisability [ˈɪnədˌvaɪzəˈbɪlɪtɪ] *n* inopportunité *f* (*of doing* de faire).

inadvisable [ˌɪnədˈvaɪzəbl] *adj action, scheme* inopportun, à déconseiller. **it is ~ to ...** il est déconseillé de ... + *infin.*

inalienable [ɪnˈeɪlɪənəbl] *adj* (*Jur, fig*) *rights, affection* inaliénable.

inamorata [ɪnˌæməˈrɑːtə] *n* anoureuse *f.*

inane [ɪˈneɪn] *adj person, action* inepte, stupide; *hope* vain, insensé. **~ remark** observation *f* inepte, ineptie *f*; **what an ~ thing to do!** faut-il être inepe *or* stupide pour faire une chose pareille!

inanimate [ɪnˈænɪmɪt] *adj* inanimé.

inanition [ˌɪnəˈnɪʃən] *n* inanition *f.*

inanity [ɪˈnænɪtɪ] *n* ineptie *f.*

inapplicable [ɪnˈæplɪkəbl] *adj* inapplicable (*to* à).

inappropriate [ˌɪnəˈprəʊprɪɪt] *adj action, behaviour, remark* inopportun, mal à propos; *word, expression* impropre; *moment* inopportun, mauvais.

inappropriately [ˌɪnəˈprəʊprɪɪtlɪ] *adv behave, remark, reply* mal à propos, inopportunément; *use word* improprement.

inapt [ɪnˈæpt] *adj* **(a)** *remark, behaviour* peu approprié. **(b)** *person* inapte, incapable.

inaptitude [ɪnˈæptɪtjuːd] *n* **(a)** *[remark, behaviour]* manque *m* d'à-propos. **(b)** *[person]* inaptitude *f*, incapacité *f.*

inarticulate [ˌɪnɑːˈtɪkjʊlɪt] *adj* **(a)** *person* incapable de s'exprimer, qui parle *or* s'exprime avec difficulté; *speech* mal prononcé, indistinct; *sound* inarticulé. **~ with anger** bafouillant *or* bégayant de colère; **his ~ fury** la rage qui le faisait bégayer; **she is a very ~ person** c'est une personne qui a beaucoup de difficulté *or* de mal à s'exprimer.

(b) (*Zool*) *body, structure* inarticulé.

inartistic [ˌɪnɑːˈtɪstɪk] *adj work* peu artistique, sans valeur artistique; *person* dépourvu de sens artistique, peu artiste.

inartistically [ˌɪnɑːˈtɪstɪkəlɪ] *adv* sans talent (artistique), de façon peu artistique.

inasmuch [ɪnəzˈmʌtʃ] *adv*: **~ as** (*seeing that*) attendu que, vu que; (*insofar as*) en ce sens que.

inattention [ˌɪnəˈtenʃən] *n* manque *m* d'attention, inattention *f.* **~ to details** manque d'attention accordée aux détails; **his ~ to his mother** son manque d'égards *or* d'attentions envers sa mère, le manque d'égards *or* d'attentions qu'il témoigne à sa mère.

inattentive [ˌɪnəˈtentɪv] *adj* (*not paying attention*) inattentif, distrait; (*neglectful*) peu attentionné, négligent (*towards sb* envers qn). **~ to details** qui accorde peu d'attention aux détails.

inattentively [ˌɪnəˈtentɪvlɪ] *adv* distraitement, sans prêter attention.

inaudible [ɪnˈɔːdəbl] *adj sound* inaudible, imperceptible; *voice* inaudible, faible. **an ~ whisper** un murmure inaudible *or* imperceptible; **he was almost ~** on l'entendait à peine.

inaudibly [ɪnˈɔːdəblɪ] *adv* de manière inaudible.

inaugural [ɪˈnɔːgjʊrəl] *adj meeting* inaugural; *address, speech* d'inauguration, inaugural. (*Univ*) **~ lecture** leçon inaugurale *or* d'ouverture.

inaugurate [ɪˈnɔːgjʊreɪt] *vt* **(a)** *policy* inaugurer, instaurer, mettre en vigueur *or* en application; *new rail service etc* inaugurer; *era* inaugurer, commencer. **(b)** *president, official* investir de ses fonctions; *bishop, king* introniser.

inauguration [ɪˌnɔːgjʊˈreɪʃən] *n* (*V* **inaugurate**) **(a)** inauguration *f.* **(b)** investiture *f*; intronisation *f.*

inauspicious [ˌɪnɔːsˈpɪʃəs] *adj beginning, event* peu propice, de mauvais augure; *circumstances* malencontreux, fâcheux.

inauspiciously [ˌɪnɔːsˈpɪʃəslɪ] *adv* d'une façon peu propice; malencontreusement.

incalculable [ɪnˈkælkjʊləbl] *adj* (*Math*) incalculable; *amount* inévaluable; *consequences* incalculable, imprévisible; *person, character, mood* inégal, changeant.

incandescence [ˌɪnkænˈdesns] *n* incandescence *f.*

incandescent [ˌɪnkænˈdesnt] *adj* (*lit, fig*) incandescent.

incantation [ˌɪnkænˈteɪʃən] *n* incantation *f.*

incapability [ɪnˌkeɪpəˈbɪlɪtɪ] *n* (*Jur, fig*) incapacité *f* (*of doing* de faire).

incapable [ɪnˈkeɪpəbl] *adj person* incapable (*of doing* de faire); (*Jur*) incapable, incompétent. **he was ~ of movement** il était incapable de bouger; **~ of tenderness** incapable de montrer de la tendresse *or* de faire preuve de tendresse; **~ of proof** impossible à prouver; *V* **drunk.**

incapacitate [ˌɪnkəˈpæsɪteɪt] *vt* **(a)** rendre incapable. **to ~ sb for work** *or* **from working** mettre qn dans l'incapacité de travailler, rendre qn incapable de travailler. **(b)** (*Jur*) frapper d'incapacité.

incapacity [ˌɪnkəˈpæsɪtɪ] *n* **(a)** incapacité *f* (*to do* de faire), incompétence *f* (*to do* pour faire), impuissance *f* (*to do* à faire, *for sth* en matière de qch). **(b)** (*Jur*) incapacité *f* (légale).

incarcerate [ɪnˈkɑːsəreɪt] *vt* incarcérer.

incarnate [ɪnˈkɑːnɪt] (*Rel, fig*) **1** *adj* incarné. (*Rel*) **the I~ Word** le Verbe incarné; **he's the devil ~** c'est le diable incarné; **liberty ~** la liberté incarnée. **2** [ˈɪnkɑːneɪt] *vt* incarner.

incarnation [ˌɪnkɑːˈneɪʃən] *n* (*Rel, fig*) incarnation *f.* **she is the ~ of virtue** c'est la vertu incarnée.

incautious [ɪnˈkɔːʃəs] *adj person* imprudent; *remark, promise, action* irréfléchi, imprudent, inconsidéré.

incautiously [ɪnˈkɔːʃəslɪ] *adv* imprudemment, sans réfléchir.

incendiary [ɪnˈsendɪərɪ] **1** *adj* (*lit, fig*) incendiaire. **~ device** dispositif *m* incendiaire. **2** *n* (*bomb*) engin *m* or bombe *f* incendiaire; (*arsonist*) incendiaire *mf*; (*fig: agitator*) brandon *m* de discorde.

incense[1] [ɪn'sens] *vt* (*anger*) mettre en colère, courroucer; (*stronger*) exaspérer. **he was quite ~d** il était dans une violente colère, il était hors de lui; **~d by** *or* **at sth** outré de *or* par qch.

incense[2] ['ɪnsens] **1** *n* encens *m*. **2** *vt* encenser. **3** *cpd*: **incense bearer** thuriféraire *m*; **incense burner** encensoir *m*.

incentive [ɪn'sentɪv] **1** *n* objectif *m*, bonne raison (pour faire qch). **in this system there is no ~ to hard work** *or* **to working hard** ce système n'incite pas *or* ne pousse pas *or* n'encourage pas à travailler dur; **he has no ~ to do more than he does at present** il n'a rien qui l'incite (*subj*) à travailler plus qu'il ne le fait en ce moment.

2 *adj* encourageant, stimulant. (*Ind*) **~ bonus** prime *f* d'encouragement, (*for manual workers*) prime de rendement.

inception [ɪn'sepʃən] *n* commencement *m*, début *m*.

incertitude [ɪn'sɜːtɪtjuːd] *n* incertitude *f*.

incessant [ɪn'sesnt] *adj complaints* incessant, perpétuel; *rain, efforts* incessant.

incessantly [ɪn'sesntlɪ] *adv* sans cesse, incessamment, constamment.

incest ['ɪnsest] *n* inceste *m*.

incestuous [ɪn'sestjʊəs] *adj* incestueux.

inch [ɪntʃ] **1** *n* pouce *m* (= *2,54 cm*). **he has grown a few ~es since last year** il a grandi de quelques centimètres depuis l'année dernière; **not an ~ from my face** *or* **nose** en plein *or* juste devant mon nez; **he couldn't see an ~ in front of him** il n'y voyait pas à deux pas; **not an ~ of the cloth is wasted** on ne perd pas un centimètre de tissu; **not an ~ of French territory will be conceded** on ne cédera pas un pouce de territoire français; **he knows every ~ of the district** il connaît la région comme sa poche *or* (jusque) dans ses moindres recoins; **we searched every ~ of the room** nous avons cherché partout dans la pièce, nous avons passé la pièce au peigne fin; **he wouldn't budge an ~** (*lit*) il n'a pas voulu bouger d'un pouce; (*fig*) il n'a pas voulu faire la plus petite concession *or* céder d'un pouce; **he looked every ~ a king** son allure était en tous points celle d'un roi; **he's every ~ a soldier** il est soldat jusqu'à la moelle; **she's every ~ a lady** elle est raffinée jusqu'au bout des ongles; **within an ~ of succeeding/of death** *etc* à deux doigts *or* à un doigt *or* à un cheveu de réussir/de la mort *etc*; **he missed being run over by ~es** il a été à deux doigts de se faire écraser; **~ by ~** petit à petit; (*loc*) **give him an ~ and he'll take a yard** *or* **an ell** donnez-lui-en long comme le doigt et il en prendra long comme le bras.

2 *cpd*: **inchtape** centimètre *m* (de couturière).

3 *vi*: **to ~ (one's way) forward/out/in** *etc* avancer/sortir/entrer *etc* peu à peu *or* petit à petit; **prices are ~ing up** les prix augmentent petit à petit.

4 *vt*: **to ~ sth forward/in/out** *etc* faire avancer/entrer/sortir *etc* qch peu à peu *or* petit à petit.

inchoate ['ɪnkəʊeɪt] *adj* (*just begun*) naissant, débutant; (*half-formed*) rudimentaire, fruste; (*unfinished*) incomplet (*f* -ète), inachevé.

incidence ['ɪnsɪdəns] *n* **(a)** *[crime, disease]* fréquence *f*. **the high ~ of heart trouble in men over 40** le taux élevé des troubles cardiaques chez les hommes de plus de 40 ans; **the low ~ of TB** la faible fréquence des cas de tuberculose.

(b) (*Opt, Phys etc*) incidence *f*. **angle of ~** angle *m* d'incidence.

incident ['ɪnsɪdənt] **1** *n* incident *m*, événement *m*; (*in book, play etc*) épisode *m*, péripétie *f*. **a life full of ~** une vie mouvementée; **we arrived without ~** nous sommes arrivés sans incident *or* sans encombre *or* sans anicroche; **there were several ~s on the border last month** il y a eu plusieurs incidents *or* accrochages frontaliers le mois dernier; **this caused a diplomatic ~** cela provoqua un incident diplomatique; **the Birmingham ~** l'incident de Birmingham *or* qui a eu lieu à Birmingham.

2 *adj* **(a)** (*frm*) **~ to** qui s'attache à, attaché à.

(b) (*Opt*) incident.

3 *cpd*: (*Police etc*) **incident room** salle *f* d'opérations.

incidental [ˌɪnsɪ'dentl] **1** *adj* (*accompanying*) accessoire; (*secondary*) d'importance secondaire; (*unplanned*) accidentel, fortuit. **~ expenses** frais *mpl* accessoires; **~ music** musique *f* de fond *or* d'accompagnement; (*Theat*) musique de scène; (*Cine*) musique de film; **the ~ music to the play** la musique qui accompagne la pièce; **~ to sth** qui accompagne qch; **the dangers ~ to such exploration** les dangers que suppose *or* que comporte une telle exploration; **but that is ~ to my purpose** mais ceci est en marge de mon propos *or* n'a qu'un rapport secondaire avec mon propos.

2 *n* (*event etc*) chose fortuite. **that's just an ~** ça n'a pas de rapport avec la question; **~s** (*expenses*) frais *mpl* accessoires; (*objects*) accessoires *mpl*.

incidentally [ˌɪnsɪ'dentəlɪ] *adv* **(a)** *happen etc* incidemment, accidentellement. **it was interesting only ~** cela n'avait qu'un intérêt secondaire. **(b)** (*by the way*) à propos, entre parenthèses.

incinerate [ɪn'sɪnəreɪt] *vt* incinérer.

incineration [ɪnsɪnə'reɪʃən] *n* incinération *f*.

incinerator [ɪn'sɪnəreɪtəʳ] *n* (*also in garden*) incinérateur *m*; *[crematorium]* four *m* crématoire.

incipient [ɪn'sɪpɪənt] *adj quarrel, disease, revolt* naissant, qui commence. **the ~ uprising was suppressed** la révolte naissante a été étouffée, la révolte a été réprimée à ses débuts *or* écrasée dans l'œuf.

incise [ɪn'saɪz] *vt* **(a)** inciser, faire une incision dans. **(b)** (*Art*) graver.

incision [ɪn'sɪʒən] *n* incision *f*, coupure *f*, entaille *f*; (*Surg*) incision.

incisive [ɪn'saɪsɪv] *adj* (*trenchant*) *style, report, tone, person* incisif, acerbe, acéré, tranchant; (*biting*) *person, voice, tone, criticism* mordant, incisif; (*acute*) *criticism, mind, person* pénétrant, perspicace.

incisively [ɪn'saɪsɪvlɪ] *adv* (*V* **incisive**) d'une façon tranchante; d'un ton mordant *or* incisif; d'une façon pénétrante.

incisiveness [ɪn'saɪsɪvnɪs] *n* (*V* **incisive**) tranchant *m*; ton mordant *or* incisif; pénétration *f*, perspicacité *f*. **the ~ of his style** son style incisif *or* tranchant; **the ~ of his criticism** la pénétration *or* la perspicacité de sa critique.

incisor [ɪn'saɪzəʳ] *n* (*tooth*) incisive *f*.

incite [ɪn'saɪt] *vt* pousser, inciter, entraîner (*to* à). **to ~ sb to violence/revolt** *etc* pousser *or* inciter qn à la violence/la révolte *etc*; **to ~ sb to do** pousser *or* entraîner *or* inciter qn à faire.

incitement [ɪn'saɪtmənt] *n* (*U*) incitation *f*, provocation *f* (*to* à).

incivility [ˌɪnsɪ'vɪlɪtɪ] *n* (*U*) impolitesse *f*, incivilité *f*. **a piece of ~** une impolitesse, une incivilité.

inclemency [ɪn'klemənsɪ] *n* inclémence *f*, dureté *f*, rigueur *f*.

inclement [ɪn'klemənt] *adj* inclément, dur, rigoureux.

inclination [ˌɪnklɪ'neɪʃən] *n* **(a)** (*slope, leaning*) *[head, body]* inclination *f*; *[hill etc]* inclinaison *f*, pente *f*.

(b) (*liking, wish etc*) inclination *f*, penchant *m*, propension *f*. **my ~ is to leave** j'incline à partir; **I have no ~ to help him** je n'ai aucune envie *or* aucun désir de l'aider; **he has an ~ to(wards) meanness** il a tendance à être mesquin *or* à la mesquinerie; **to follow one's (own) ~** suivre son inclination *or* ses penchants (naturels).

incline [ɪn'klaɪn] **1** *vt* **(a)** (*bend, bow*) incliner, baisser, pencher. **~d plane** plan incliné; **~d at an angle of ...** incliné à un angle de ... .

(b) (*fig: gen pass*) **to ~ sb to do** incliner qn *or* porter qn *or* rendre qn enclin à faire; *[person]* **to be ~d to do** (*feel desire to*) incliner à *or* être enclin à *or* être porté à faire; (*have tendency to*) incliner à *or* avoir tendance à faire; **he is ~d to be lazy** il a tendance à être paresseux, il est enclin à la paresse; **it's ~d to break** cela se casse facilement, c'est fragile; **he's that way ~d** il a tendance à être comme ça; **if you feel (so) ~d** si le cœur vous en dit, si l'envie vous en prend; **to be well ~d towards sb** être bien disposé *or* être dans de bonnes dispositions à l'égard de qn.

2 *vi* **(a)** (*slope*) s'incliner; (*bend, bow*) s'incliner, pencher, se courber.

(b) (*tend towards*) **to ~ to an opinion/a point of view** *etc* pencher pour une opinion/un point de vue *etc*; **he ~s to laziness** il incline à la paresse, il a tendance à être paresseux; **the colour ~s towards blue** la couleur tend vers le bleu; **his politics ~ towards socialism** ses idées politiques tendent vers le socialisme.

3 ['ɪnklaɪn] *n* pente *f*, inclinaison *f*, déclivité *f*; (*Rail etc*) plan incliné.

inclose [ɪn'kləʊz] *vt* = **enclose.**

inclosure [ɪn'kləʊʒəʳ] *n* = **enclosure.**

include [ɪn'kluːd] *vt* comprendre, compter, englober, embrasser, inclure. **your name is not ~d on the list** votre nom n'est pas inclus dans la liste, votre nom ne paraît pas *or* ne figure pas sur la liste, la liste ne comporte pas votre nom; **the tip is not ~d in the bill** le service n'est pas compris *or* compté *or* inclus dans la note; **the wine was ~d in the overall price** le vin était compris *or* compté *or* inclus dans le prix total; **all** *or* **everything ~d** tout compris; **does that remark ~ me?** est-ce que cette remarque s'applique aussi à moi?; **he ~d my mother in the invitation** ma mère était comprise dans son invitation; **the invitation ~s everybody** tout le monde est compris dans l'invitation, l'invitation s'adresse à *or* englobe tout le monde; **they were all ~d in the accusation** ils étaient tous visés par l'accusation; **the children/tables** *etc* **~d** y compris les enfants/les tables *etc*; **the district ~s ...** la région comprend *or* englobe ... .

including [ɪn'kluːdɪŋ] *prep* y compris, compris, inclus. **that comes to 200 francs ~ packing** cela fait 200 F y compris l'emballage *or* l'emballage compris *or* l'emballage inclus; **there were 6 rooms ~ the kitchen** il y avait 6 pièces en comprenant la cuisine *or* si on comprend la cuisine *or* la cuisine (y) comprise *or* y compris la cuisine; **~ the service charge** service compris; **not ~ tax** taxe non comprise; **up to and ~ chapter 5** jusqu'au chapitre 5 inclus, jusques et y compris le chapitre 5; **up to and ~ 4th May** jusqu'au 4 mai inclus.

inclusion [ɪn'kluːʒən] *n* inclusion *f*.

inclusive [ɪn'kluːsɪv] *adj* inclus, compris. **from 1st to 6th May ~** du 1er au 6 mai inclus(ivement); **to the fifth page ~** (jusqu')à la cinquième page incluse; **to be ~ of** inclure, comprendre; **~ terms** (prix *m*) tout compris; **~ sum** somme globale.

inclusively [ɪn'kluːsɪvlɪ] *adv* inclusivement.

incognito [ɪn'kɒgnɪtəʊ] **1** *adv* incognito. **2** *adj traveller* dans l'incognito. **to remain ~** garder l'incognito. **3** *n* incognito *m*.

incoherence [ˌɪnkəʊ'hɪərəns] *n* incohérence *f*.

incoherent [ˌɪnkəʊ'hɪərənt] *adj conversation, speech, person* incohérent; *style* décousu.

incoherently [ˌɪnkəʊ'hɪərəntlɪ] *adv* sans cohérence, d'une façon incohérente; d'une façon décousue.

incohesive [ˌɪnkəʊ'hiːsɪv] *adj* sans cohésion.

incombustible [ˌɪnkəm'bʌstəbl] *adj* incombustible.

income ['ɪnkʌm] **1** *n* revenu *m*. **(private) ~** rente(s) *f(pl)*; **annual/taxable ~** revenu annuel/imposable; **to live beyond/within one's ~** dépasser/ne pas dépasser son revenu; *V* **price.**

2 *cpd*: (*Econ*) **the lowest income group** les économiquement faibles *mpl*; **the middle income group** la classe à revenus moyens; **the upper** *or* **highest income group** la classe à revenus élevés; **incomes policy** politique *f* des revenus; **income tax** impôt *m* sur le revenu; **income tax inspector** inspecteur *m* des contributions directes; **income tax return** déclaration *f* des revenus, feuille *f* d'impôts.

incomer [ˈɪnˌkʌməʳ] *n* (*new arrival*) arrivant(e) *m(f)*, nouveau venu, nouvelle venue; (*immigrant*) immigrant(e) *m(f)*.

incommensurable [ˌɪnkəˈmenʃərəbl] *adj* (*lit, fig*) incommensurable (*with* avec).

incommensurate [ˌɪnkəˈmenʃərɪt] *adj* **(a)** (*out of proportion*) sans rapport (*to* avec), disproportionné (*to* à); (*inadequate*) insuffisant (*to* pour). **(b)** = **incommensurable.**

incommode [ˌɪnkəˈməʊd] *vt* (†, *frm*) incommoder, gêner.

incommodious [ˌɪnkəˈməʊdɪəs] *adj* (*inconvenient*) incommode; (*not spacious*) *house, room* où l'on est à l'étroit.

incommunicado [ˌɪnkəmjʊnɪˈkɑːdəʊ] *adj* (tenu) au secret.

incomparable [ɪnˈkɒmpərəbl] *adj* incomparable (*to, with* à); *talent, beauty etc* incomparable, inégalable, sans pareil.

incomparably [ɪnˈkɒmpərəblɪ] *adv* incomparablement, infiniment.

incompatibility [ˈɪnkəmˌpætəˈbɪlɪtɪ] *n [people, aims, wishes]*, (*Med*) *[blood groups etc]* incompatibilité *f*. **divorce on the grounds of ~** divorce *m* pour incompatibilité d'humeur.

incompatible [ˌɪnkəmˈpætəbl] *adj* incompatible, inconciliable (*with* avec); (*Med*) incompatible.

incompetence [ɪnˈkɒmpɪtəns] *n*, **incompetency** [ɪnˈkɒmpɪtənsɪ] *n* **(a)** incompétence *f*, incapacité *f*, insuffisance *f*. **(b)** (*Jur*) incompétence *f*.

incompetent [ɪnˈkɒmpɪtənt] *adj* **(a)** incompétent, incapable. **to be ~ in business** être incompétent en *or* n'avoir aucune compétence en affaires; **he is ~ to teach** *or* **for teaching music** il n'a pas les compétences nécessaires pour enseigner la musique. **(b)** (*Jur*) incompétent.

incomplete [ˌɪnkəmˈpliːt] *adj* (*unfinished*) incomplet (*f* -ète), inachevé; (*with some parts missing*) *collection, series, kit, machine* incomplet.

incompletely [ˌɪnkəmˈpliːtlɪ] *adv* incomplètement.

incompleteness [ˌɪnkəmˈpliːtnɪs] *n* inachèvement *m*.

incomprehensible [ɪnˌkɒmprɪˈhensəbl] *adj person, speech, reasoning* incompréhensible, inintelligible; *writing* indéchiffrable.

incomprehensibly [ɪnˌkɒmprɪˈhensəblɪ] *adv* de manière incompréhensible, incompréhensiblement.

inconceivable [ˌɪnkənˈsiːvəbl] *adj* inconcevable.

inconceivably [ˌɪnkənˈsiːvəblɪ] *adv* à un degré inconcevable. **~ stupid** d'une stupidité inconcevable.

inconclusive [ˌɪnkənˈkluːsɪv] *adj result, discussion* peu concluant; *evidence, argument* peu convaincant; *action* sans résultat, qui n'aboutit pas.

inconclusively [ˌɪnkənˈkluːsɪvlɪ] *adv* (*V* **inconclusive**) d'une manière peu concluante *or* peu convaincante; sans résultat.

incongruity [ˌɪnkɒŋˈgruːɪtɪ] *n* manque *m* d'harmonie *or* d'appropriation (*with* avec); *[behaviour, dress, remark]* incongruité *f*, inconvenance *f*; *[age, condition]* disproportion *f*, incompatibilité *f*.

incongruous [ɪnˈkɒŋgrʊəs] *adj* (*not in harmony*) en désaccord (*with* avec), peu approprié (*with* à), sans rapport (*with* avec); (*incompatible*) disparate, incompatible; (*out of place*) *remark, act* incongru, déplacé; (*absurd*) absurde, grotesque. **it seems ~ that** il semble absurde que+*subj*.

inconsequent [ɪnˈkɒnsɪkwənt] *adj person, remark, behaviour, reasoning* illogique, inconséquent.

inconsequential [ɪnˌkɒnsɪˈkwenʃəl] *adj* **(a)** = **inconsequent. (b)** (*unimportant*) sans importance, sans conséquence.

inconsiderable [ˌɪnkənˈsɪdərəbl] *adj* insignifiant.

inconsiderate [ˌɪnkənˈsɪdərɪt] *adj* **(a)** (*thoughtless*) *person* qui manque d'égards *or* de considération; *action, reply* inconsidéré, irréfléchi. **to be ~ towards sb** manquer d'égards *or* de considération envers qn; **you were very ~, that was most ~ of you** tu as agi sans aucun égard *or* sans aucune considération; **it was a very ~ thing to do** c'était vraiment agir sans aucun égard *or* sans aucune considération.
(b) (*hasty*) *action, words* inconsidéré, irréfléchi.

inconsistency [ˌɪnkənˈsɪstənsɪ] *n [person]* inconsistance *f*, inconséquence *f*; *[facts, accusation]* inconsistance; *[behaviour, reasoning]* inconsistance, inconséquence, illogisme *m*.

inconsistent [ˌɪnkənˈsɪstənt] *adj action, speech, attitude, person* inconséquent, inconsistant. **his report was ~** son rapport était inconsistant *or* présentait des contradictions; **~ with** en contradiction avec, incompatible avec; **this is ~ with what you told me** ceci ne concorde pas avec *or* ceci est incompatible avec ce que vous m'avez dit.

inconsolable [ˌɪnkənˈsəʊləbl] *adj* inconsolable.

inconspicuous [ˌɪnkənˈspɪkjʊəs] *adj person, action, dress* qui passe inaperçu, qui ne se fait pas remarquer. **he tried to make himself ~** il a essayé de passer inaperçu, il s'est efforcé de ne pas se faire remarquer.

inconspicuously [ˌɪnkənˈspɪkjʊəslɪ] *adv behave, move* sans se faire remarquer, discrètement; *dress* de façon discrète.

inconstancy [ɪnˈkɒnstənsɪ] *n* (*V* **inconstant**) inconstance *f*; instabilité *f*.

inconstant [ɪnˈkɒnstənt] *adj person* (*in friendship*) changeant, instable; (*in love*) inconstant, volage; (*unstable*) *weather* instable, changeant; (*variable*) *quality etc* variable.

incontestable [ˌɪnkənˈtestəbl] *adj* incontestable, indiscutable.

incontinence [ɪnˈkɒntɪnəns] *n* (*Med, fig*) incontinence *f*.

incontinent [ɪnˈkɒntɪnənt] *adj* (*Med*) incontinent; (*fig*) intempérant.

incontrovertible [ɪnˌkɒntrəˈvɜːtəbl] *adj fact* indéniable; *argument, explanation* irréfutable; *sign, proof* irrécusable.

inconvenience [ˌɪnkənˈviːnɪəns] **1** *n* **(a)** inconvénient *m*, désagrément *m*, ennui *m*. **there are ~s in living in the country** il y a des inconvénients à habiter la campagne, habiter la campagne présente des inconvénients *or* des désagréments.
(b) (*U*) dérangement *m*, gêne *f*. **to put sb to great ~** causer beaucoup de dérangement à qn; **I don't want to put you to any ~** je ne veux surtout pas vous déranger; **he went to a great deal of ~ to help me** il s'est donné beaucoup de mal pour m'aider.
2 *vt* déranger, incommoder, (*stronger*) gêner.

inconvenient [ˌɪnkənˈviːnɪənt] *adj time, place* inopportun, mal choisi; *house, equipment* incommode, malcommode; *visitor* gênant, importun. **if it is not ~ (to you)** si cela ne vous dérange pas; **it is most ~** c'est très gênant; **it is very ~ for him to have to wait** cela le dérange *or* gêne beaucoup d'avoir à attendre.

inconveniently [ˌɪnkənˈviːnɪəntlɪ] *adv design* incommodément; *happen* d'une manière gênante; *arrive* inopportunément.

inconvertibility [ˈɪnkənˌvɜːtɪˈbɪlɪtɪ] *n* non-convertibilité *f*.

inconvertible [ˌɪnkənˈvɜːtəbl] *adj* (*Fin etc*) inconvertible.

incorporate[1] [ɪnˈkɔːpəreɪt] **1** *vt* **(a)** (*introduce as part*) *territory, suggestions, revisions* incorporer (*into* dans). **they ~d him into their group** ils l'ont incorporé dans *or* associé à leur groupe, ils l'ont pris dans leur groupe.
(b) (*include, contain*) contenir. **his book ~s his previous articles** son livre contient *or* englobe ses précédents articles; **this essay ~s all his thoughts on the subject** cette étude contient *or* rassemble toutes ses pensées sur la question.
(c) (*Comm, Jur*) se constituer en société (unique) avec. (*esp US*) **~d company** société *f* (*enregistrée*).
(d) (*mix, add*) incorporer (*into* à). **to ~ eggs into a sauce** incorporer des œufs à une sauce.
2 *vi [business firm]* fusionner (*with* avec); *[two firms]* se constituer en (une seule) société.

incorporate[2] [ɪnˈkɔːpərɪt] *adj* (*Philos*) incorporel.

incorporation [ɪnˌkɔːpəˈreɪʃən] *n* (*V* **incorporate**[1]) incorporation *f* (*into* dans, à); (*Comm, Jur*) constitution *f* en société (unique).

incorrect [ˌɪnkəˈrekt] *adj* **(a)** (*wrong*) *wording, calculation* incorrect; *statement, opinion, assessment* inexact, erroné; *text* fautif, inexact, erroné. (*Ling*) **~ expression** expression incorrecte, incorrection *f*, impropriété *f* (de langage); **you are ~** vous faites erreur, vous vous trompez; **he is ~ in stating that ...** il se trompe *or* il fait erreur quand il affirme que ...; **it would be ~ to say that ...** il serait inexact de dire que ...; **that's quite ~** c'est tout à fait inexact.
(b) (*out of place*) *behaviour* incorrect, déplacé; *dress* incorrect, indécent. **it would be ~ to mention it** il serait incorrect *or* déplacé d'en faire mention.

incorrectly [ˌɪnkəˈrektlɪ] *adv* **(a)** (*wrongly*) inexactement; *spell, address, translate* incorrectement, mal. **he was ~ reported as having said ...** on a raconté faussement *or* inexactement qu'il avait dit ... .
(b) *behave, act* incorrectement, de façon déplacée.

incorrigible [ɪnˈkɒrɪdʒəbl] *adj* incorrigible.

incorruptible [ˌɪnkəˈrʌptəbl] *adj* incorruptible.

increase [ɪnˈkriːs] **1** *vi [taxes]* augmenter; *[pain]* augmenter, s'intensifier; *[amount, numbers]* augmenter, croître; *[price, sales]* augmenter, monter; *[demand, strength, supply]* augmenter, croître, s'accroître; *[speed]* augmenter, s'accroître; *[joy, rage]* augmenter, croître, s'intensifier; *[sorrow, surprise]* augmenter, croître; *[possessions, riches, trade]* s'accroître, augmenter; *[darkness, noise]* s'intensifier, grandir; *[pride]* croître, grandir; *[business firm, institution, town]* s'agrandir, se développer, croître; *[crime]* s'intensifier, augmenter; *[rain, wind]* augmenter, redoubler; *[population]* augmenter, croître, s'accroître; *[friendship]* se renforcer, se consolider; *[effort]* s'intensifier. **to ~ in volume** augmenter de volume, prendre du volume; **to ~ in weight** prendre du poids, s'alourdir; **to ~ in width** s'élargir; **to ~ in height** *[person]* grandir; *[tree]* pousser; *[building]* gagner de la hauteur.
2 *vt numbers, strength, taxes* augmenter; *pain* augmenter, intensifier; *price, sales* augmenter, faire monter; *demand, supply, population* augmenter, accroître; *delight, joy, pride, rage* augmenter, ajouter à; *sorrow, surprise* augmenter, ajouter à, accroître; *possessions, riches, trade* accroître, augmenter; *darkness, noise* intensifier; *business firm, institution, town* agrandir, développer; *rain, wind* faire redoubler; *friendship* renforcer, consolider; *effort* redoubler de, intensifier. **he ~d his efforts** il redoubla ses efforts *or* d'effort; **to ~ speed** accélérer, augmenter *or* accroître la vitesse; (*Aut*) **he ~d his speed to 90 km/h** il a accéléré jusqu'à 90 km/h, il a atteint le 90*.
3 [ˈɪnkriːs] *n* (*gen*) augmentation *f* (*in, of* de); *[pain]* augmentation, intensification *f*; *[numbers]* augmentation, accroissement *m*, multiplication *f*; *[price, sales]* augmentation, montée *f*; *[demand, strength, supply]* augmentation, croissance *f*, accroissement; *[speed]* augmentation, accroissement; *[joy, rage]* intensification; *[possessions, riches, trade]* accroissement; *[darkness, noise]* intensification; *[pride]* accroissement; *[business firm, institution, town]* agrandissement *m*, développement *m*, croissance; *[crime]* intensification, augmentation; *[rain, wind]* redoublement *m*; *[population]* augmentation, croissance, accroissement; *[friendship]* renforcement *m*, consolidation *f*; *[effort]* redoublement *m*, intensification. (*Fin*) **~ in value** plus-value *f*; **he had a big ~ in his workload** il a vu une grosse augmentation *or* un gros accroissement de ses charges professionnelles; **there has been an ~ in police activity** la police a intensifié ses activités *or* redoublé d'activité; **an ~ in pay** une hausse de salaire, une augmentation (de salaire); **on the ~** en augmentation; **to be on the ~** augmenter, aller en augmentant, être en hausse; **the problem of crime is on the ~** le problème de la criminalité s'accentue.

increasing [ɪnˈkriːsɪŋ] *adj* croissant. **an ~ number/amount of ...** un nombre/une quantité croissant(e) de ... .

increasingly [ɪnˈkriːsɪŋlɪ] *adv* de plus en plus.

incredible [ɪnˈkredəbl] *adj number, amount, error, behaviour* incroyable; *story* incroyable, invraisemblable, inimaginable.

incredibly [ɪnˈkredəblɪ] *adv* incroyablement.
incredulity [ˌɪnkrɪˈdjuːlɪtɪ] *n* incrédulité *f.*
incredulous [ɪnˈkredjʊləs] *adj person* incrédule; *look* incrédule, d'incrédulité.
incredulously [ɪnˈkredjʊləslɪ] *adv* d'un air *or* d'un ton incrédule *or* d'incrédulité.
increment [ˈɪnkrɪmənt] *n (in salary)* augmentation *f*; *(Math)* différentielle *f*; *V* **unearned.**
incriminate [ɪnˈkrɪmɪneɪt] *vt* incriminer, compromettre, impliquer. **his evidence ~s his friends** son témoignage incrimine *or* implique *or* compromet ses amis; **don't say anything that could ~** you ne dites rien qui puisse vous incriminer *or* vous compromettre.
incriminating [ɪnˈkrɪmɪneɪtɪŋ] *adj* compromettant. **~ document** *or* **evidence** pièce *f* à conviction.
incrimination [ɪnˌkrɪmɪˈneɪʃən] *n* accusation *f*, incrimination *f.*
incriminatory [ɪnˈkrɪmɪnətərɪ] *adj* = **incriminating.**
incrust [ɪnˈkrʌst] *vt* = **encrust.**
incrustation [ˌɪnkrʌsˈteɪʃən] *n* incrustation *f.*
incubate [ˈɪnkjʊbeɪt] **1** *vt eggs* couver, incuber; *bacteria cultures, disease* incuber; *(fig) plan, scheme* couver. **2** *vi (also fig)* couver; *(Med)* être en incubation.
incubation [ˌɪnkjʊˈbeɪʃən] *n [eggs, disease, scheme etc]* incubation *f.* **~ period** période *f* d'incubation.
incubator [ˈɪnkjʊbeɪtə^r] *n [chicks, eggs, infants]* couveuse *f*, incubateur *m*; *[bacteria cultures]* incubateur. **(to put) an infant in an ~** (mettre) un nouveau-né en couveuse.
incubus [ˈɪŋkjʊbəs] *n (demon)* incube *m*; *(fig)* cauchemar *m.*
inculcate [ˈɪnkʌlkeɪt] *vt* inculquer *(sth in sb, sb with sth* qch à qn).
inculcation [ˌɪnkʌlˈkeɪʃən] *n* inculcation *f.*
incumbency [ɪnˈkʌmbənsɪ] *n (Rel)* charge *f.*
incumbent [ɪnˈkʌmbənt] **1** *adj*: **to be ~ upon sb to do sth** incomber *or* appartenir à qn de faire qch. **2** *n (Rel etc)* titulaire *m.*
incunabula [ˌɪnkjʊˈnæbjʊlə] *npl* incunables *mpl.*
incunabular [ˌɪnkjʊˈnæbjʊlə^r] *adj* incunable.
incur [ɪnˈkɜː^r] *vt anger, blame* s'attirer, encourir; *risk* courir; *obligation, debts* contracter; *loss* subir, éprouver; *expenses* encourir.
incurable [ɪnˈkjʊərəbl] **1** *adj (Med, fig)* incurable, inguérissable. **2** *n* incurable *mf.*
incurably [ɪnˈkjʊərəblɪ] *adv* incurablement. **~ inquisitive** d'une curiosité incurable.
incurious [ɪnˈkjʊərɪəs] *adj* sans curiosité, incurieux *(liter).*
incursion [ɪnˈkɜːʃən] *n* incursion *f.*
indebted [ɪnˈdetɪd] *adj (Fin)* redevable *(to sb for sth* à qn de qch), endetté; *(fig)* redevable *(to sb for sth* à qn pour qch). **he was ~ to his brother for a large sum** il était redevable d'une grosse somme à son frère; **I am greatly ~ to him for his generosity** je lui dois beaucoup pour sa générosité; **I am ~ to him for pointing out that ...** je lui suis redevable d'avoir fait remarquer que ... .
indebtedness [ɪnˈdetɪdnɪs] *n (Fin, fig)* dette(s) *f(pl).* **my ~ to my friend** ma dette envers mon ami, ce dont je suis redevable à mon ami.
indecency [ɪnˈdiːsnsɪ] *n (V* **indecent***)* indécence *f*; inconvenance *f*; *(Jur)* outrage public à la pudeur, outrage aux bonnes mœurs.
indecent [ɪnˈdiːsnt] *adj* **(a)** *(offensive)* indécent, peu décent. *(Jur)* **~ assault (on sb)** attentat *m* à la pudeur (sur *or* contre qn); *(Jur)* **~ exposure** outrage public à la pudeur.
(b) *(unseemly)* malséant, inconvenant. **with ~ haste** avec une précipitation malséante *or* inconvenante.
indecently [ɪnˈdiːsntlɪ] *adv (V* **indecent***)* indécemment; de façon inconvenante. **he arrived ~ early** il est arrivé si tôt que c'en était inconvenant.
indecipherable [ˌɪndɪˈsaɪfərəbl] *adj* indéchiffrable.
indecision [ˌɪndɪˈsɪʒən] *n* indécision *f*, irrésolution *f.*
indecisive [ˌɪndɪˈsaɪsɪv] *adj* **(a)** *(hesitating) person, manner* indécis, irrésolu. **(b)** *(inconclusive) discussion, argument* peu concluant; *battle* indécis. **(c)** *(vague) outline* indécis, flou.
indecisively [ˌɪndɪˈsaɪsɪvlɪ] *adv* avec indécision, de façon indécise.
indeclinable [ˌɪndɪˈklaɪnəbl] *adj* indéclinable.
indecorous [ɪnˈdekərəs] *adj* peu convenable, inconvenant, incorrect, peu digne *(hum).*
indecorously [ɪnˈdekərəslɪ] *adv* d'une manière incorrecte *or* inconvenante *or* peu convenable.
indecorum [ˌɪndɪˈkɔːrəm] *n* faute *f* contre le bon ton, manquement *m* aux usages.
indeed [ɪnˈdiːd] *adv* **(a)** *(really, in reality, in fact)* en effet, vraiment. **he promised to help and ~ he helped us a lot** il a promis de nous aider et en effet il nous a beaucoup aidés; **I feel, ~ I know he is right** je sens, et même je sais qu'il a raison; **I am ~ quite tired** je suis en effet assez fatigué; **he was ~ as tall as she had said** il était vraiment *or* en effet aussi grand qu'elle l'avait dit; **are you coming? — ~ I am!** *or* yes **~!** vous venez? — mais certainement! *or* (mais) bien sûr!; **I may ~ come** il se peut effectivement *or* en effet que je vienne; **if ~ he were wrong** s'il est vrai qu'il a tort, si tant est qu'il ait tort.
(b) *(as intensifier)* **I am very pleased ~** je suis extrêmement content *or* vraiment très content; **he was very grateful ~** il était infiniment reconnaissant; **thank you very much ~** merci mille fois.
(c) *(showing interest, irony, surprise etc)* **(oh) ~?** vraiment?, c'est vrai?; **is it ~!, did you** *(or* **he** *etc)* **~!** vraiment?; **who is that man? — who is he ~?** qui est cet homme? — ah, là est la question!
indefatigable [ˌɪndɪˈfætɪgəbl] *adj* infatigable, inlassable.
indefatigably [ˌɪndɪˈfætɪgəblɪ] *adv* infatigablement, inlassablement.
indefensible [ˌɪndɪˈfensəbl] *adj action, behaviour* indéfendable, injustifiable, inexcusable; *crime* injustifiable; *cause, theory, argument* indéfendable, insoutenable; *(Mil etc)* indéfendable.
indefinable [ˌɪndɪˈfaɪnəbl] *adj* indéfinissable, vague.
indefinite [ɪnˈdefɪnɪt] *adj* **(a)** *intentions, doubts, feelings* incertain, indéfini, vague; *answer* vague; *outline* indistinct, mal défini; *size* indéterminé; *number, duration, period* indéterminé, illimité. **our plans are still somewhat ~** nos plans ne sont encore que mal définis *or* que peu précis, nos plans sont encore assez nébuleux; **~ leave of absence** congé illimité *or* indéfini.
(b) *(Gram)* indéfini.
indefinitely [ɪnˈdefɪnɪtlɪ] *adv* **(a)** *wait etc* indéfiniment. **the meeting has been postponed ~** la réunion a été remise à une date indéterminée. **(b)** *speak etc* vaguement, avec imprécision.
indelible [ɪnˈdeləbl] *adj* **(a)** *stain, ink* indélébile. **~ pencil** crayon *m* à copier. **(b)** *impression* ineffaçable, indélébile; *memory* ineffaçable, inoubliable; *shame* ineffaçable.
indelibly [ɪnˈdelɪblɪ] *adv* de façon indélébile, ineffaçablement.
indelicacy [ɪnˈdelɪkəsɪ] *n (V* **indelicate***)* **(a)** *(U) [person, behaviour, comment]* indélicatesse *f*, manque *m* de délicatesse; manque de discrétion. **(b)** *[action, remark etc]* inconvenance *f*; grossièreté *f*; indiscrétion *f.*
indelicate [ɪnˈdelɪkɪt] *adj person* indélicat, peu délicat; *(tactless)* manquant de tact, indiscret *(f* -ète); *act, remark (out of place)* indélicat, inconvenant, déplacé; *(tactless)* indiscret, manquant de tact; *(coarse)* grossier.
indemnification [ɪnˌdemnɪfɪˈkeɪʃən] *n* **(a)** *(U)* indemnisation *f (for, against* de). **(b)** *(sum paid)* indemnité *f*, dédommagement *m.*
indemnify [ɪnˈdemnɪfaɪ] *vt* **(a)** *(compensate)* indemniser, dédommager *(sb for sth* qn de qch). **(b)** *(safeguard)* garantir, assurer *(sb against or for sth* qn contre qch).
indemnity [ɪnˈdemnɪtɪ] *n* **(a)** *(compensation)* indemnité *f*, dédommagement *m*, compensation *f.* **(b)** *(insurance)* assurance *f*, garantie *f.*
indent [ɪnˈdent] **1** *vt* **(a)** *border* denteler, découper *(en dentelant).* **~ed edge** bord dentelé; **~ed coastline** littoral échancré *or* découpé.
(b) *(Typ) word, line* renfoncer, mettre en retrait. **~ed line** ligne *f* en alinéa *or* en retrait.
(c) *(make dent in)* faire *or* laisser une marque *or* une empreinte sur; *sheet of metal, car door etc* bosseler, cabosser.
2 *vi (Brit Comm)* **to ~ on sb for sth** passer une commande de qch à qn, commander qch à qn.
3 [ˈɪndent] *n* **(a)** *(Brit Comm: V* 2) commande *f.*
(b) = **indentation.**
indentation [ˌɪndenˈteɪʃən] *n* **(a)** *(act)* découpage *m*; *(notched edge)* dentelure *f*, découpure *f*; *[coastline]* échancrures *fpl.*
(b) *(Typ)* renfoncement *m*, retrait *m*, alinéa *m.*
(c) *(hollow mark)* empreinte *f*, impression *f* (en creux); *(in metal, car)* bosse *f.* **the ~ of tyres on the soft ground** l'empreinte des pneus sur le sol mou.
indenture [ɪnˈdentʃə^r] **1** *n (Jur)* contrat *m* synallagmatique; *[apprentice]* contrat d'apprentissage. **2** *vt (Jur)* lier par contrat (synallagmatique); *apprentice* mettre en apprentissage *(to* chez).
independence [ˌɪndɪˈpendəns] **1** *n* indépendance *f (from* par rapport à); *(Pol)* indépendance, autonomie *f.* **to show ~** faire preuve d'indépendance, manifester son indépendance; **the country got its ~ in 1970** le pays est devenu indépendant *or* autonome en 1970, le pays a obtenu son indépendance *or* son autonome en 1970.
2 *cpd*: *(US)* **Independence Day** fête *f or* anniversaire *m* de l'Indépendance américaine *(le 4 juillet).*
independent [ˌɪndɪˈpendənt] **1** *adj* **(a)** *(free) person, attitude, thinker, artist* indépendant; *country, nation* indépendant, autonome. **to become ~** *[person]* devenir indépendant, s'affranchir; *[country, nation]* devenir indépendant *or* autonome, s'affranchir; **to be ~ of sb/sth** être indépendant de qn/qch, ne pas dépendre de qn/qch; **she is quite ~** elle est tout à fait indépendante; **he is an ~ thinker** c'est un penseur original; *(Pol)* **an I~ member** un député non inscrit *or* non affilié; **~ means** rentes *fpl*, revenus indépendants; **he has ~ means** il a une fortune personnelle, il vit de ses rentes.
(b) *(unrelated) proof, research* indépendant; *opinions, reports* émanant de sources différentes. **to ask for an ~ opinion** demander l'avis d'un tiers; *(Aut)* **~ suspension** suspension indépendante.
(c) *(Gram)* indépendant.
2 *n (Pol)* **I~** non-inscrit *m*, non-affilié *m.*
independently [ˌɪndɪˈpendəntlɪ] *adv* de façon indépendante. **~ of** indépendamment de; **he acted ~** il a agi de son côté *or* de façon indépendante; **quite ~ he had offered to help** de façon tout à fait indépendante il avait proposé son aide.
indescribable [ˌɪndɪsˈkraɪbəbl] *adj disorder, event* indescriptible; *emotion* indescriptible, inexprimable, indicible *(liter).*
indescribably [ˌɪndɪsˈkraɪbəblɪ] *adv (V* **indescribable***)* indescriptiblement; inexprimablement, indiciblement *(liter).* **it was ~ awful** c'était affreux au-delà de toute expression.
indestructible [ˌɪndɪsˈtrʌktəbl] *adj* indestructible.
indeterminate [ˌɪndɪˈtɜːmɪnɪt] *adj amount, sound* indéterminé; *shape* indéterminé, imprécis, vague; *(Math)* indéterminé.
indeterminately [ˌɪndɪˈtɜːmɪnɪtlɪ] *adv* de façon indéterminée, vaguement.
index [ˈɪndeks] **1** *n* **(a)** *(pl* **~es***: list) (in book etc)* index *m*, table *f* alphabétique; *(on cards, in files: in library etc)* catalogue *m or*

répertoire *m* (alphabétique). (*Rel*) **to put a book on the I~** mettre un livre à l'Index.

(b) (*pl* **~es**: *pointer*) *[instrument]* aiguille *f*, index *m*.

(c) (*pl* **indices**: *number expressing ratio*) indice *m*. **cost-of-living ~** indice du coût de la vie; **~ of growth** indice de croissance; **~ of intelligence** *etc* taux *m* d'intelligence *etc*; (*Opt*) **~ of refraction** indice de réfraction.

(d) (*pl* **indices**: *fig*) indice *m*, signe *m* (révélateur *or* indicateur), indication *f*, symptôme *m*. **it was a true ~ of his character** c'était un signe bien révélateur de son caractère; **it is an ~ of how much poorer people were then** c'est un signe *or* une indication qui permet de se rendre compte combien les gens étaient plus pauvres en ce temps-là, c'est un signe révélateur de la plus grande pauvreté qui régnait alors.

(e) (*pl* **~es**) **~ (finger)** index *m*.

(f) (*pl* **~es**: *Typ*) index *m*.

(g) (*pl* **indices**: *Math*) exposant *m*.

2 *vt* **(a)** *book* mettre un index *or* une table alphabétique à. **the book is badly ~ed** l'index *or* la table alphabétique du livre est mal fait(e).

(b) *word* mettre dans l'index *or* la table alphabétique; (*on cards, in files etc*) *information* répertorier *or* cataloguer (alphabétiquement). **it is ~ed under 'Europe'** c'est classé *or* ça se trouve sous *or* à 'Europe', l'entrée est à 'Europe'.

3 *cpd*: **index card** fiche *f*; (*Statistics*) **index figure** indice *m*; **index finger** index *m*; (*Econ*) **index-linked** indexé; **index number = index figure.**

indexation [ˌɪndekˈseɪʃən] *n* indexation *f*.

India [ˈɪndɪə] **1** *n* Inde *f*. **2** *cpd*: **India ink** encre *f* de Chine; (*Naut Hist*) **Indiaman** navire *m* faisant le voyage des Indes; **India paper** papier *m* bible; **indiarubber** (*n*) (*U: substance*) caoutchouc *m*; (*eraser*) gomme *f* (*à effacer*); (*cpd*) de *or* en caoutchouc.

Indian [ˈɪndɪən] **1** *n* **(a)** (*in India*) Indien(ne) *m(f)*.

(b) (*in America*) Indien(ne) *m(f)* (d'Amérique).

(c) (*Ling*) amérindien *m*.

2 *adj* **(a)** (*in India*) indien, de l'Inde; (*Brit Hist*) des Indes.

(b) **(American** *or* **Red) ~** indien, des Indiens (d'Amérique).

3 *cpd*: **Indian clubs** massues *fpl* de gymnastique; **Indian elephant** éléphant *m* d'Asie; **Indian Empire** empire *m* des Indes; **Indian ink** encre *f* de Chine; (*Hist*) **Indian Mutiny** révolte *f* des Cipayes; **Indian Ocean** océan Indien; (*fig*) **Indian summer** été *m* de la Saint-Martin; **Indian tea** thé indien *or* de l'Inde.

indicate [ˈɪndɪkeɪt] *vt* **(a)** (*point to*) indiquer, montrer (*with one's hand* de la main). **he ~d the spot on the map** il indiqua *or* montra l'endroit sur la carte.

(b) (*be a sign of*) indiquer, dénoter, révéler, être l'indice de. **it ~s the presence of acid** ceci révèle la présence d'acide; **that ~s a clear conscience** cela dénote *or* révèle une conscience nette, c'est l'indice d'une conscience nette; **it ~s that he is dissatisfied** ceci indique *or* révèle qu'il est mécontent, ceci témoigne de son mécontentement.

(c) (*make known*) signaler, indiquer, faire connaître; *feelings, intentions* manifester, montrer. **he ~d that I was to leave** il m'a fait comprendre que je devais partir; (*Aut*) **he was indicating left** il avait mis son clignotant gauche.

(d) (*Med etc*) indiquer. **the use of penicillin is clearly ~d** le recours à la pénicilline est nettement indiqué; **a new approach to the wages problem is ~d** une approche nouvelle du problème salarial est indiquée *or* semble nécessaire.

indication [ˌɪndɪˈkeɪʃən] *n* **(a)** (*sign, suggestion etc*) indice *m*, signe *m*, indication *f*. **there is every ~ that he is right** tout porte à croire qu'il a raison; **there is no ~ that he will come** rien ne porte à croire qu'il vienne; **we had no ~ that it was going to take place** aucun signe ne nous permettait de prévoir *or* nous n'avions aucun indice nous permettant de prévoir que cela allait arriver; **it is some ~ of how much remains to be done** cela permet de se rendre compte de ce qu'il reste à faire; **he gave us some ~ of what he meant** il nous a donné quelque idée de ce qu'il voulait dire; **to give sb an ~ of one's feelings/intentions** manifester ses sentiments/ses intentions à qn; **it was an ~ of his guilt** c'était une indication *or* un signe *or* un indice de sa culpabilité; **all the ~s lead one to believe that ...** tout porte à croire que ..., il y a toute raison de croire que ... .

(b) (*U*) indication *f*.

indicative [ɪnˈdɪkətɪv] **1** *adj* **(a)** indicatif (*of* de). **(b)** (*Gram*) indicatif. **2** *n* (*Gram*) **~ (mood)** (mode *m*) indicatif *m*; **in the ~** à l'indicatif.

indicator [ˈɪndɪkeɪtəʳ] *n* (*device*) indicateur *m*; (*needle on scale etc*) aiguille *f*, index *m*; (*Aut*) (*flashing*) clignotant *m*, (*projecting*) flèche *f*; (*Ling*) indicateur. **altitude/pressure ~** indicateur d'altitude/de pression; **speed ~** indicateur *or* compteur *m* de vitesse; (*plan*) **town ~** table *f* d'orientation; (*Rail*) **arrival/departure ~** tableau *m* *or* indicateur des arrivées/des départs.

indices [ˈɪndɪsiːz] *npl of* **index 1c, 1d, 1g.**

indict [ɪnˈdaɪt] *vt* **(a)** (*Jur*) accuser (*on a charge of* de), mettre en accusation. **(b)** (*fig*) accuser, porter une accusation contre.

indictable [ɪnˈdaɪtəbl] *adj* (*Jur*) *person, action* tombant sous le coup de la loi. **~ offence** délit pénal, délit punissable (par la loi).

indictment [ɪnˈdaɪtmənt] *n* (*Jur*) (*bill*) acte *m* d'accusation (*for* de); (*process*) mise *f* en accusation (*for* de); (*US*) mise en accusation (*par le grand jury*). (*Brit Hist*) **bill of ~** résumé *m* d'instruction (*présenté au grand jury*); **to bring an ~ against sb for sth** mettre qn en accusation pour qch; (*fig*) **such poverty is an ~ of the political system** une telle pauvreté constitue une mise en accusation *or* une condamnation du système politique.

Indies [ˈɪndɪz] *npl* Indes *fpl*; *V* east, west.

indifference [ɪnˈdɪfrəns] *n* **(a)** (*lack of interest, of feeling*) indifférence *f* (*to* à, *towards* envers), manque *m* d'intérêt (*to, towards* pour, à l'égard de). **he greeted the suggestion with ~** il accueillit la suggestion avec indifférence *or* sans manifester d'intérêt; **it is a matter of supreme ~ to me** cela m'est parfaitement indifférent *or* égal.

(b) (*poor quality*) médiocrité *f*.

indifferent [ɪnˈdɪfrənt] *adj* **(a)** (*lacking feeling, interest*) indifférent (*to* à); (*impartial*) impartial, neutre. **it is quite ~ to me** cela m'est tout à fait indifférent *or* égal. **(b)** (*pej*) *talent, performance, player* médiocre, quelconque.

indifferently [ɪnˈdɪfrəntlɪ] *adv* **(a)** indifféremment. **she went ~ to one shop or the other** elle fréquentait indifféremment une boutique ou l'autre. **(b)** (*pej*) *paint, perform* médiocrement, de façon quelconque.

indigence [ˈɪndɪdʒəns] *n* indigence *f*.

indigenous [ɪnˈdɪdʒɪnəs] *adj* (*lit, fig*) indigène (*to* de); *population, language, customs* indigène, autochtone.

indigent [ˈɪndɪdʒənt] *adj* (*frm*) indigent, nécessiteux.

indigestible [ˌɪndɪˈdʒestəbl] *adj* (*Med, fig*) indigeste.

indigestion [ˌɪndɪˈdʒestʃən] *n* (*U: Med*) dyspepsie *f*. **to have an attack of ~** avoir une indigestion; **she gets a lot of ~** elle a la digestion difficile, elle a une mauvaise digestion.

indignant [ɪnˈdɪgnənt] *adj* indigné, plein *or* rempli d'indignation (*at sth* de *or* devant qch, *with sb* contre qn); *look* indigné, d'indignation. **to get** *or* **grow ~** s'indigner (*at sth* de *or* devant qch, *with sb about sth* contre qn à propos de qch); **to make sb ~** indigner qn.

indignantly [ɪnˈdɪgnəntlɪ] *adv* avec indignation, d'un air *or* d'un ton indigné.

indignation [ˌɪndɪgˈneɪʃən] *n* indignation *f* (*at* devant, *with* contre). **~ meeting*** réunion *f* de protestation.

indignity [ɪnˈdɪgnɪtɪ] *n* **(a)** (*act etc*) indignité *f*, affront *m*, offense *f*, outrage *m*. **it was a gross ~** c'était un grave outrage; **he suffered the ~ of having to ...** il subit l'indignité d'avoir à ... .

(b) (*U*) indignité *f*.

indigo [ˈɪndɪgəʊ] **1** *n* indigo *m*. **2** *adj*: **~ (blue)** (bleu) indigo *inv*.

indirect [ˌɪndɪˈrekt] *adj* **(a)** *route, means etc* indirect, oblique, détourné; *consequence, reference* indirect. **~ lighting** éclairage indirect; **~ taxes** contributions indirectes; **~ taxation** imposition indirecte, impôts indirects.

(b) (*Gram*) *object* indirect. **~ speech** discours indirect.

indirectly [ˌɪndɪˈrektlɪ] *adv* indirectement.

indirectness [ˌɪndɪˈrektnɪs] *n* caractère indirect; *[route etc]* détours *mpl*.

indiscernible [ˌɪndɪˈsɜːnəbl] *adj* indiscernable, imperceptible.

indiscipline [ɪnˈdɪsɪplɪn] *n* indiscipline *f*.

indiscreet [ˌɪndɪsˈkriːt] *adj* (*tactless*) indiscret (*f* -ète); (*rash*) imprudent, peu judicieux.

indiscreetly [ˌɪndɪsˈkriːtlɪ] *adv* (*tactlessly*) indiscrètement; (*rashly*) imprudemment, avec imprudence.

indiscretion [ˌɪndɪsˈkreʃən] *n* **(a)** (*U: V* **indiscreet**) manque *m* de discrétion, indiscrétion *f*; imprudence *f*. **(b)** (*action, remark*) indiscrétion *f*. **youthful ~** bêtise *f* *or* péché *m* de jeunesse.

indiscriminate [ˌɪndɪsˈkrɪmɪnɪt] *adj* *punishment, blows* distribué au hasard *or* à tort et à travers; *killings* commis au hasard; *person* manquant de discernement; *faith, admiration, confidence* aveugle.

indiscriminately [ˌɪndɪsˈkrɪmɪnɪtlɪ] *adv* *choose, kill* au hasard; *make friends* sans discrimination; *read, watch TV* sans aucun sens critique; *accept, admire* aveuglément.

indispensable [ˌɪndɪsˈpensəbl] *adj* indispensable (*to* à). **you're not ~!** on peut se passer de toi!

indisposed [ˌɪndɪsˈpəʊzd] *adj* **(a)** (*unwell*) indisposé, souffrant.

(b) (*disinclined*) peu disposé, peu enclin (*to do* à faire).

indisposition [ˌɪndɪspəˈzɪʃən] *n* **(a)** (*illness*) indisposition *f*, malaise *m*. **(b)** (*disinclination*) manque *m* d'inclination (*to do* à faire).

indisputable [ˌɪndɪsˈpjuːtəbl] *adj* incontestable, indiscutable.

indisputably [ˌɪndɪsˈpjuːtəblɪ] *adv* sans conteste, incontestablement, indisputablement.

indissoluble [ˌɪndɪˈsɒljʊbl] *adj* *friendship etc* indissoluble; (*Chem*) insoluble.

indissolubly [ˌɪndɪˈsɒljʊblɪ] *adv* (*also Jur*) indissolublement.

indistinct [ˌɪndɪsˈtɪŋkt] *adj* *object, voice, words* indistinct; *memory* vague, confus; *noise* confus, sourd. (*on telephone*) **you're very ~** je ne vous entends pas bien, je vous entends mal.

indistinctly [ˌɪndɪsˈtɪŋktlɪ] *adv* *see, hear, speak* indistinctement; *feel* vaguement.

indistinguishable [ˌɪndɪsˈtɪŋgwɪʃəbl] *adj* **(a)** indifférenciable (*from* de). **(b)** (*very slight*) *noise, difference, change* insaisissable, imperceptible, indiscernable.

individual [ˌɪndɪˈvɪdjʊəl] **1** *adj* **(a)** (*separate*) *opinion, attention* individuel. **(b)** (*distinctive, characteristic*) original, particulier. **he has an ~ style** il a un style particulier *or* personnel *or* bien à lui. **2** *n* individu *m*.

individualism [ˌɪndɪˈvɪdjʊəlɪzəm] *n* individualisme *m*.

individualist [ˌɪndɪˈvɪdjʊəlɪst] *n* individualiste *mf*.

individualistic [ˌɪndɪˌvɪdjʊəˈlɪstɪk] *adj* individualiste.

individuality [ˌɪndɪˌvɪdjʊˈælɪtɪ] *n* individualité *f*.

individualize [ˌɪndɪˈvɪdjʊəlaɪz] *vt* individualiser.

individually [ˌɪndɪˈvɪdjʊəlɪ] *adv* **(a)** (*separately*) individuellement. **he spoke to them ~** il leur a parlé à chacun individuellement *or* séparément; **they're all right ~** (pris chacun) individuellement ils sont très bien.

(b) (*for o.s. alone*) pour soi-même. **he is speaking ~** il parle pour lui-même, il parle en son nom personnel.

indivisible [ˌɪndɪˈvɪzəbl] *adj* indivisible; (*Math, Philos*) insécable.

Indo- [ˈɪndəʊ] **1** *pref* indo-. **2** *cpd*: **Indo-China** Indochine *f*; **Indo-European** (*adj*) indo-européen; (*n: Ling*) indo-européen *m*.

indoctrinate [ɪn'dɒktrɪneɪt] *vt* endoctriner. **he's been well ~d** on l'a bien endoctriné; **to ~ sb with political ideas/with hatred of the enemy** inculquer des doctrines politiques/la haine de l'ennemi à qn.
indoctrination [ɪn,dɒktrɪ'neɪʃən] *n* endoctrinement *m*.
indolence ['ɪndələns] *n* indolence *f*, nonchalance *f*.
indolent ['ɪndələnt] *adj* indolent, nonchalant.
indolently ['ɪndələntlɪ] *adv* indolemment, nonchalamment.
indomitable [ɪn'dɒmɪtəbl] *adj* indomptable, invincible.
Indonesia [,ɪndəʊ'ni:zɪə] *n* Indonésie *f*.
Indonesian [,ɪndəʊ'ni:zɪən] **1** *adj* indonésien. **2** *n* **(a)** Indonésien(ne) *m(f)*. **(b)** (*Ling*) indonésien *m*.
indoor ['ɪndɔ:'] *adj shoes etc* d'intérieur; *plant* d'appartement; *swimming pool, tennis court* couvert; (*Cine, Theat*) *scene* d'intérieur. **it's an ~ hobby/occupation/job** c'est un passe-temps/une activité/un travail qui se pratique en intérieur *or* en appartement; (*TV*) **~ aerial** antenne intérieure; **~ athletics** athlétisme *m* en salle; **~ games** (*squash etc*) sports pratiqués en intérieur; (*table games*) jeux *mpl* de société; **~ photography** photographie *f* d'intérieur *or* en studio.
indoors [ɪn'dɔ:z] *adv* (*in building*) à l'intérieur; (*at home*) à la maison; (*under cover*) à l'abri. **to stay ~** rester à l'intérieur *or* à la maison; **to go ~** entrer, rentrer; **~ and outdoors** à l'intérieur et au-dehors, dedans et dehors.
indorse [ɪn'dɔ:s] *vt* = **endorse.**
indubitable [ɪn'dju:bɪtəbl] *adj* indubitable, incontestable.
indubitably [ɪn'dju:bɪtəblɪ] *adv* indubitablement, sans aucun doute, sans conteste, incontestablement.
induce [ɪn'dju:s] *vt* **(a)** (*persuade*) persuader (*sb to do* qn de faire), décider, inciter (*sb to do* qn à faire).
(b) (*bring about*) *reaction* produire, provoquer, amener; *sleep, illness, hypnosis* provoquer. (*Med*) **to ~ labour** déclencher l'accouchement (*artificiellement*); **~d labour** accouchement déclenché; **she was ~d** elle a été déclenchée.
(c) (*Philos: infer*) déduire, induire, conclure.
(d) (*Elec*) produire par induction.
inducement [ɪn'dju:smənt] *n* **(a)** (*U*) encouragement *m*, incitation *f* (*to do* à faire).
(b) (*incentive*) motif *m*, but *m*; (*pej: bribe*) pot-de-vin *m*. **he can't work without ~s** il est incapable de travailler sans motif *or* but précis; **and as an added ~ we are offering ...** et comme avantage supplémentaire nous offrons ...; **he received £100 as an ~** il a reçu 100 livres à titre de gratification, il a reçu un pot-de-vin de 100 livres (*pej*).
induct [ɪn'dʌkt] *vt* **(a)** *clergyman* instituer, installer; *president etc* établir dans ses fonctions, installer. **(b) to ~ sb into the mysteries of ...** initier qn aux mystères de .... **(c)** (*US Mil*) incorporer.
induction [ɪn'dʌkʃən] **1** *n* **(a)** (*U*) (*Elec, Philos*) induction *f*; *[sleep, hypnosis etc]* provocation *f*. **(b)** *[clergyman, president etc]* installation *f*. **(c)** (*US Mil*) incorporation *f*. **2** *cpd*: (*Elec*) **induction coil** bobine *f* d'induction.
inductive [ɪn'dʌktɪv] *adj* **(a)** *reasoning, process* inductif. **(b)** (*Elec*) *current, charge* inducteur (*f* -trice).
indue [ɪn'dju:] *vt* = **endue.**
indulge [ɪn'dʌldʒ] **1** *vt* **(a)** *person* (*spoil*) gâter; (*give way to*) céder à; (*gratify*) *sb's desires, wishes* se prêter à; *one's own desires* satisfaire; *one's own laziness* s'abandonner à, se laisser aller à, donner libre cours à. **to ~ sb's whim** passer une fantaisie à qn, céder à un caprice de qn; **to ~ o.s.** se passer tous ses caprices.
(b) (*Comm: extend time for payment*) *person, firm* accorder des délais de paiement à.
2 *vi*: **to ~ in doing sth** se livrer à qch, s'adonner à qch; **to ~ in a cigarette** se permettre une cigarette; **to ~ in sth to excess** abuser de qch; (*: *refusing cigarette etc*) **I'm afraid I don't ~** non merci, ce n'est pas un de mes vices; (*: *drink*) **he tends to ~** il est assez porté sur *or* il a un faible pour la bouteille*.
indulgence [ɪn'dʌldʒəns] *n* **(a)** (*U*) (*tolerance etc*) indulgence *f*, complaisance *f*; *[desires etc]* satisfaction *f*. **(b)** satisfaction *f*, gâterie *f*. **his little ~s** les petites douceurs qu'il se permet, les petites faiblesses qu'il s'autorise. **(c)** (*Rel*) indulgence *f*.
indulgent [ɪn'dʌldʒənt] *adj* (*not severe*) indulgent (*to* envers, pour), clément (*to* envers); (*permissive*) indulgent (*to* envers, pour), complaisant (*to* à l'égard de, pour), accommodant (*to* avec).
indulgently [ɪn'dʌldʒəntlɪ] *adv* (*V* **indulgent**) avec indulgence; complaisamment.
industrial [ɪn'dʌstrɪəl] *adj application, experience, psychology, research, training* industriel; *expansion* industriel, de l'industrie; *worker* de l'industrie; *disease* professionnel; *accident, injury, medicine* du travail; *dispute* ouvrier; *fabric, equipment* pour l'industrie, industriel. **~ action** action revendicative; **~ designer** concepteur-dessinateur industriel, designer *m*; **~ diamond** diamant naturel *or* industriel; (*Brit*) **~ estate** zone industrielle; **~ injury benefit** indemnité *f* d'accident du travail; **~ insurance** assurance *f* contre les accidents du travail, assurance des salariés de l'industrie; (*US*) **~ park** zone industrielle; **~ rehabilitation** réadaptation fonctionnelle; (*Hist*) **the ~ revolution** la révolution industrielle; (*US*) **~ school** école *f* technique; **~ unrest** troubles sociaux, agitation ouvrière.
industrialism [ɪn'dʌstrɪəlɪzəm] *n* industrialisme *m*.
industrialist [ɪn'dʌstrɪəlɪst] *n* industriel *m*.
industrialization [ɪn,dʌstrɪəlaɪ'zeɪʃən] *n* industrialisation *f*.
industrialize [ɪn'dʌstrɪəlaɪz] *vt* industrialiser.
industrious [ɪn'dʌstrɪəs] *adj* industrieux, travailleur.
industriously [ɪn'dʌstrɪəslɪ] *adv* industrieusement.
industriousness [ɪn'dʌstrɪəsnɪs] *n* = **industry b.**
industry ['ɪndəstrɪ] *n* **(a)** industrie *f*. **basic** *or* **heavy ~** industrie lourde; **the hotel ~** l'hôtellerie *f*, l'industrie hôtelière; **tourist ~** tourisme *m*, industrie touristique; (*Brit*) **Secretary of State for/Department of I~** ministre *m*/ministère *m* de l'Industrie; *V* **coal, textile** *etc*.
(b) (*U: industriousness*) zèle *m*, assiduité *f*, application *f*.
inebriate [ɪ'ni:brɪɪt] **1** *n* alcoolique *mf*. **2** *adj* ivre. **3** [ɪ'ni:brɪeɪt] *vt* (*lit, fig*) enivrer, griser. **~d** (*lit*) ivre; (*fig*) ivre, enivré, grisé (*by* de).
inebriation [ɪ,ni:brɪ'eɪʃən] *n*, **inebriety** [,ɪni:'braɪətɪ] *n* état *m* d'ébriété.
inedible [ɪn'edɪbl] *adj* (*not meant to be eaten*) non comestible; (*not fit to be eaten*) immangeable.
ineducable [ɪn'edjʊkəbl] *adj* inéducable.
ineffable [ɪn'efəbl] *adj* (*liter*) indicible (*liter*), ineffable, inexprimable.
ineffaceable [,ɪnɪ'feɪsəbl] *adj* ineffaçable, indélébile.
ineffective [,ɪnɪ'fektɪv] *adj remedy, measures, reasoning* inefficace, sans effet, sans résultat; *style* plat, fade, terne; *person* incapable, incompétent. **he made an ~ attempt to apologize** il a vainement *or* en vain essayé de s'excuser.
ineffectively [,ɪnɪ'fektɪvlɪ] *adv* inefficacement, vainement, en vain.
ineffectual [,ɪnɪ'fektjʊəl] *adj* = **ineffective.**
inefficacious [,ɪnefɪ'keɪʃəs] *adj* inefficace, sans effet, sans résultat.
inefficacy [ɪn'efɪkəsɪ] *n* inefficacité *f*.
inefficiency [,ɪnɪ'fɪʃənsɪ] *n [action, machine, measures]* inefficacité *f*, insuffisance *f*; *[person]* incompétence *f*, incapacité *f*, insuffisance.
inefficient [,ɪnɪ'fɪʃənt] *adj action, machine, measures* inefficace; *person* incapable, incompétent. **an ~ use of** une mauvaise utilisation de.
inefficiently [,ɪnɪ'fɪʃəntlɪ] *adv* (*V* **inefficient**) inefficacement; sans compétence. **work ~ done** travail mal exécuté.
inelastic [,ɪnɪ'læstɪk] *adj* inélastique; (*fig*) rigide, sans souplesse, sans élasticité. (*Econ*) **~ demand** demande *f* inélastique.
inelegant [ɪn'elɪgənt] *adj* inélégant, peu élégant, sans élégance.
inelegantly [ɪn'elɪgəntlɪ] *adv* inélégamment, sans élégance, peu élégamment.
ineligible [ɪn'elɪdʒəbl] *adj candidate* inéligible. **~ for military service** inapte au service militaire; **~ for social security benefits** n'ayant pas droit aux prestations de la Sécurité sociale; **he is ~ to vote** il n'a pas le (droit de) vote.
ineluctable [,ɪnɪ'lʌktəbl] *adj* (*frm*) inéluctable, inévitable.
inept [ɪ'nept] *adj behaviour* inapproprié, mal *or* peu à propos; *remark, refusal* inepte, stupide, absurde; *person* inepte, stupide.
ineptitude [ɪ'neptɪtju:d] *n*, **ineptness** [ɪ'neptnɪs] *n [behaviour]* manque *m* d'à-propos; *[remark, person]* ineptie *f*, sottise *f*, stupidité *f*.
inequality [,ɪnɪ'kwɒlɪtɪ] *n* inégalité *f*.
inequitable [ɪn'ekwɪtəbl] *adj* inéquitable, injuste.
inequity [ɪn'ekwɪtɪ] *n* injustice *f*, iniquité *f*.
ineradicable [,ɪnɪ'rædɪkəbl] *adj* indéracinable, tenace.
inert [ɪ'nɜ:t] *adj* (*Chem, Phys, fig*) inerte.
inertia [ɪ'nɜ:ʃə] **1** *n* **(a)** *[person]* inertie *f*, apathie *f*. **(b)** (*Chem, Phys*) inertie *f*. **2** *cpd*: (*Aut*) **inertia reel seat belts** ceintures *fpl* (de sécurité) à enrouleurs; (*Comm*) **inertia selling** vente(s) *f(pl)* par envoi forcé.
inescapable [,ɪnɪs'keɪpəbl] *adj* inéluctable, inévitable.
inessential [,ɪnɪ'senʃəl] *adj* superflu, non-essentiel.
inestimable [ɪn'estɪməbl] *adj gift, friendship* inestimable, inappréciable; *fortune, work* incalculable.
inevitability [ɪn,evɪtə'bɪlɪtɪ] *n* caractère *m* inévitable, inévitabilité *f*.
inevitable [ɪn'evɪtəbl] *adj consequence* inévitable, inéluctable, fatal; *day, event* fatal. **the ~ result of this war** le résultat inéluctable *or* inévitable de cette guerre; **it was ~ that she should discover ...** elle devait inévitablement *or* fatalement *or* forcément découvrir ...; **I'm afraid it's ~** j'ai bien peur que ce ne soit inévitable *or* inéluctable; **the tourist had the ~ camera** le touriste avait l'inévitable appareil-photo.
inevitably [ɪn'evɪtəblɪ] *adv* inévitablement, inéluctablement, fatalement.
inexact [,ɪnɪg'zækt] *adj information* inexact, erroné, incorrect; *description, measurement* inexact.
inexactly [,ɪnɪg'zæktlɪ] *adv* inexactement, incorrectement.
inexcusable [,ɪnɪks'kju:zəbl] *adj* inexcusable, impardonnable, injustifiable.
inexcusably [,ɪnɪks'kju:zəblɪ] *adv* inexcusablement. **~ lazy** d'une paresse inexcusable.
inexhaustible [,ɪnɪg'zɔ:stəbl] *adj* inépuisable.
inexorable [ɪn'eksərəbl] *adj* inexorable.
inexorably [ɪn'eksərəblɪ] *adv* inexorablement.
inexpedient [,ɪnɪks'pi:dɪənt] *adj action, decision, policy* inopportun, malavisé.
inexpensive [,ɪnɪks'pensɪv] *adj* bon marché *inv*, pas cher (*f* chère), peu coûteux.
inexpensively [,ɪnɪks'pensɪvlɪ] *adv buy* à bon marché, à bon compte; *live* à peu de frais.
inexperience [,ɪnɪks'pɪərɪəns] *n* inexpérience *f*, manque *m* d'expérience.
inexperienced [,ɪnɪks'pɪərɪənst] *adj* inexpérimenté, manquant d'expérience, novice. **I am very ~ in matters of this kind** j'ai très peu d'expérience en ces matières.
inexpert [ɪn'ekspɜ:t] *adj* inexpert, maladroit (*in* en).
inexpertly [ɪn'ekspɜ:tlɪ] *adv* maladroitement.
inexplicable [,ɪnɪks'plɪkəbl] *adj* inexplicable.
inexplicably [,ɪnɪks'plɪkəblɪ] *adv* inexplicablement.
inexpressible [,ɪnɪks'presəbl] *adj* inexprimable; indicible (*liter*).

inexpressive [ˌɪnɪksˈpresɪv] *adj* inexpressif, sans expression.
inextinguishable [ˌɪnɪksˈtɪŋgwɪʃəbl] *adj passion etc* inextinguible; *fire* impossible à éteindre *or* à maîtriser.
inextricable [ˌɪnɪksˈtrɪkəbl] *adj* inextricable.
inextricably [ˌɪnɪksˈtrɪkəblɪ] *adv* inextricablement.
infallibility [ɪnˌfæləˈbɪlɪtɪ] *n* (*also Rel*) infaillibilité *f.*
infallible [ɪnˈfæləbl] *adj* infaillible.
infallibly [ɪnˈfæləblɪ] *adv* infailliblement.
infamous [ˈɪnfəməs] *adj conduct, person, thing* infâme, abominable; *place* mal famé.
infamy [ˈɪnfəmɪ] *n* infamie *f.*
infancy [ˈɪnfənsɪ] *n* (toute) petite enfance, bas âge; (*Jur*) minorité *f;* (*fig*) enfance, débuts *mpl.* **from his** ~ depuis sa petite enfance; **child still in** ~ enfant encore en bas âge; **this process is still in its** ~ ce procédé en est encore à ses débuts, ce procédé est encore dans l'enfance.
infant [ˈɪnfənt] **1** *n* (*newborn*) nouveau-né(e) *m(f);* (*baby*) bébé *m,* nourrisson *m;* (*young child*) petit(e) enfant *m(f),* enfant en bas âge; (*Jur*) mineur(e) *m(f);* (*Brit Scol*) enfant, petit(e) *m(f)* (*de 5 à 7 ans*).
2 *cpd disease etc* infantile. (*Brit*) **infant class** ≃ cours *m* préparatoire; **the infant classes** les classes enfantines, les petites classes; **infant mortality** mortalité *f* infantile; (*Brit*) **infant school** ≃ classes *fpl* préparatoires (*entre 5 et 7 ans*).
infanta [ɪnˈfæntə] *n* infante *f.*
infante [ɪnˈfæntɪ] *n* infant *m.*
infanticide [ɪnˈfæntɪsaɪd] *n* (*act*) infanticide *m;* (*person*) infanticide *mf.*
infantile [ˈɪnfəntaɪl] *adj* **(a)** (*childish*) enfantin, infantile, puéril. **(b)** (*Med*) infantile. ~ **paralysis**† paralysie *f* infantile†, poliomyélite *f.*
infantry [ˈɪnfəntrɪ] *n* (*U: Mil*) infanterie *f* (*U*), fantassins *mpl.* ~**man** fantassin *m;* *V* **light²**.
infatuate [ɪnˈfætjʊeɪt] *vt* (*gen pass*) tourner la tête à. **to be** ~**d with** *person* être entiché de, avoir le béguin* pour; *idea etc* avoir la tête pleine de, être engoué de; **to become** ~**d with** *person* s'enticher de, se toquer de*; *idea etc* s'engouer pour; **after he met her he was clearly** ~**d** après sa rencontre avec elle il était évident qu'il avait la tête tournée.
infatuation [ɪnˌfætjʊˈeɪʃən] *n* **(a)** (*U: V* **infatuate**) engouement *m,* toquade* *f,* béguin* *m* (*with* pour). **(b)** (*object of* ~) folie *f.*
infect [ɪnˈfekt] *vt* **(a)** (*Med*) *air, well, wound etc* infecter, contaminer. **his wound became** ~**ed** sa blessure s'infecta; **to** ~ **sb with a disease** transmettre *or* communiquer une maladie à qn; ~**ed with leprosy** atteint de la lèpre, ayant contracté la lèpre; (*fig*) **to** ~ **sb with one's enthusiasm** communiquer son enthousiasme à qn.
(b) (*fig pej*) *person* corrompre; *morals* corrompre, infecter (*liter*), souiller (*liter*).
infection [ɪnˈfekʃən] *n* (*Med*) infection *f,* contagion *f,* contamination *f;* (*fig*) contagion. **she has a slight** ~ elle est légèrement souffrante; **a throat** ~ une angine; **an ear** ~ une infection de l'oreille, une otite.
infectious [ɪnˈfekʃəs] *adj* (*Med*) *disease* infectieux; *person* contagieux; (*fig*) *idea* contagieux; *enthusiasm, laughter* communicatif.
infectiousness [ɪnˈfekʃəsnɪs] *n* (*Med*) nature infectieuse; (*fig*) contagion *f.*
infelicitous [ˌɪnfɪˈlɪsɪtəs] *adj* malheureux, fâcheux.
infelicity [ˌɪnfɪˈlɪsɪtɪ] *n* **(a)** (*U: misfortune*) malheur *m.* **(b)** (*tactless act, remark*) maladresse *f.*
infer [ɪnˈfɜːʳ] *vt* déduire, conclure, inférer (*sth from sth* qch de qch, *that* que).
inference [ˈɪnfərəns] *n* déduction *f,* inférence *f,* conclusion *f.* **by** ~ par déduction; **the** ~ **is that he is unwilling to help us** on doit en conclure qu'il n'est pas disposé à nous aider; **to draw an** ~ **from sth** tirer une conclusion de qch.
inferential [ˌɪnfəˈrenʃəl] *adj method* déductif; *proof* obtenu par déduction.
inferentially [ˌɪnfəˈrenʃəlɪ] *adv* par déduction.
inferior [ɪnˈfɪərɪəʳ] **1** *adj* inférieur (*f* -eure) (*to* à); *products, goods* de qualité inférieure, de second choix; (*Bot*) infère. (*Typ*) ~ **letter** lettre inférieure; **he makes me feel** ~ il me donne un sentiment d'infériorité.
2 *n* (*in quality, social standing*) inférieur(e) *m(f);* (*in authority, rank: also Mil*) subalterne *mf,* subordonné(e) *m(f).*
inferiority [ɪnˌfɪərɪˈɒrɪtɪ] *n* infériorité *f* (*to* par rapport à). ~ **complex** complexe *m* d'infériorité.
infernal [ɪnˈfɜːnl] *adj* infernal, de l'enfer; (*fig*) *cruelty* diabolique, abominable; (*: *infuriating*) *noise, impudence* infernal*. **it's an** ~ **nuisance!** que c'est enquiquinant!*
infernally* [ɪnˈfɜːnəlɪ] *adv difficult, unpleasant* abominablement, épouvantablement, atrocement. **it is** ~ **hot** il fait une chaleur infernale *or* à crever*.
inferno [ɪnˈfɜːnəʊ] *n* (scène *f* d')enfer *m.*
infertile [ɪnˈfɜːtaɪl] *adj land* stérile, infertile, infécond (*liter*); *person* stérile, infécond (*liter*); *discussion* stérile.
infertility [ˌɪnfɜːˈtɪlɪtɪ] *n* (*V* **infertile**) infertilité *f;* stérilité *f.*
infest [ɪnˈfest] *vt* infester (*with* de).
infestation [ˌɪnfesˈteɪʃən] *n* infestation *f.*
infidel [ˈɪnfɪdəl] **1** *n* (*liter*) (*Hist, Rel*) infidèle *mf;* (*Rel*) incroyant(e) *m(f).* **2** *adj* infidèle; incroyant.
infidelity [ˌɪnfɪˈdelɪtɪ] *n* infidélité *f.* (*Jur*) **divorce on the grounds of** ~ divorce *m* pour cause d'adultère.
infiltrate [ˈɪnfɪltreɪt] **1** *vi* [*troops, person, light, liquid, ideas*] s'infiltrer (*into* dans).
2 *vt liquid* infiltrer (*into* dans, *through* à travers). (*Mil*) **to** ~ **troops into a territory** faire s'infiltrer des troupes dans un territoire; (*Mil*) **to** ~ **the enemy lines** s'infiltrer dans les lignes ennemies; (*Pol*) **disruptive elements have** ~**d the group** des éléments perturbateurs se sont infiltrés dans le groupe *or* ont noyauté le groupe.
infiltration [ˌɪnfɪlˈtreɪʃən] *n* (*V* **infiltrate**) infiltration *f;* (*Pol*) noyautage *m.*
infinite [ˈɪnfɪnɪt] **1** *adj* (*Math, Philos, Rel etc*) infini; (*fig*) infini, illimité, sans bornes. **it gave her** ~ **pleasure** cela lui a fait infiniment plaisir; **he took** ~ **pains to do it** il mit un soin infini à le faire. **2** *n* infini *m.*
infinitely [ˈɪnfɪnɪtlɪ] *adv* infiniment.
infiniteness [ˈɪnfɪnɪtnɪs] *n* = **infinity c.**
infinitesimal [ˌɪnfɪnɪˈtesɪməl] *adj* (*Math etc*) infinitésimal; (*gen*) *amount, majority etc* infinitésimal, infime.
infinitive [ɪnˈfɪnɪtɪv] (*Gram*) **1** *n* infinitif *m.* **in the** ~ à l'infinitif. **2** *adj* infinitif.
infinitude [ɪnˈfɪnɪtjuːd] *n:* **an** ~ **of** une infinité de.
infinity [ɪnˈfɪnɪtɪ] *n* **(a)** (*that which is infinite*) infinité *f,* infini *m.* **in time and space or in** ~ dans le temps et dans l'espace ou dans l'infinité *or* l'infini.
(b) (*infinite quantity, number etc*) infinité *f.* (*fig*) **an** ~ **of reasons** *etc* une infinité de raisons *etc.*
(c) (*infiniteness*) infinitude *f.* **the** ~ **of God** l'infinitude de Dieu.
(d) (*Math*) infini *m.* **to** ~ à l'infini.
infirm [ɪnˈfɜːm] *adj* **(a)** (*sick*) infirme. **the old and** ~ ceux qui sont âgés et infirmes *or* âgés et invalides. **(b)** (*liter*) ~ **of purpose** irrésolu, indécis.
infirmary [ɪnˈfɜːmərɪ] *n* (*hospital*) hôpital *m;* (*in school etc*) infirmerie *f.*
infirmity [ɪnˈfɜːmɪtɪ] *n* **(a)** (*U*) infirmité *f,* débilité *f,* faiblesse *f.* (*liter*) ~ **of purpose** irrésolution *f,* indécision *f.* **(b)** infirmité *f.* **the infirmities of old age** les infirmités de l'âge.
infix [ɪnˈfɪks] *vt habit, idea* inculquer (*in* à), implanter (*in* dans); (*Ling*) insérer (*in* dans).
inflame [ɪnˈfleɪm] **1** *vt* (*set alight*) enflammer, mettre le feu à; (*Med*) enflammer; (*fig*) *courage* enflammer; *anger, desire, hatred, discord* attiser, allumer. **2** *vi* s'enflammer, prendre feu; (*Med*) s'enflammer; (*fig*) s'allumer, s'échauffer.
inflammable [ɪnˈflæməbl] *adj* (*lit, fig*) inflammable.
inflammation [ˌɪnfləˈmeɪʃən] *n* (*also Med, fig*) inflammation *f.*
inflammatory [ɪnˈflæmətərɪ] *adj speech etc* incendiaire; (*Med*) inflammatoire.
inflate [ɪnˈfleɪt] *vt tyre, balloon* gonfler (*with* de); (*fig*) *prices* faire monter, hausser; *bill, account* grossir, charger. (*Econ*) **to** ~ **the currency** recourir *or* avoir recours à l'inflation.
inflated [ɪnˈfleɪtɪd] *adj tyre etc* gonflé; (*fig*) *style* enflé, boursouflé; *value* exagéré; *prices* exagéré, gonflé. ~ **with pride** bouffi *or* gonflé d'orgueil; **he has an** ~ **sense of his own importance** il a une idée exagérée de sa propre importance.
inflation [ɪnˈfleɪʃən] *n* (*U*) (*Econ*) inflation *f;* [*tyre etc*] gonflement *m;* [*prices*] hausse *f.*
inflationary [ɪnˈfleɪʃnərɪ] *adj* inflationniste.
inflect [ɪnˈflekt] **1** *vt* **(a)** (*Ling*) *word* mettre une désinence à, modifier la désinence de, fléchir; (*conjugate*) conjuguer; (*decline*) décliner. ~**ed vowel** voyelle infléchie.
(b) *voice* moduler; (*Mus*) *note* altérer.
(c) (*bend*) courber, fléchir, infléchir.
2 *vi* (*Ling*) prendre une désinence. **a verb which** ~**s** un verbe flexionnel *or* qui prend des désinences; **a noun** ~**s in the plural** un nom prend le signe du pluriel; **an** ~**ing language** une langue désinentielle *or* flexionnelle.
inflection [ɪnˈflekʃən] *n* = **inflexion.**
inflectional [ɪnˈflekʃənl] *adj* (*Ling*) **an** ~ **ending** une désinence; **an** ~ **language** une langue désinentielle *or* flexionnelle.
inflexibility [ɪnˌfleksɪˈbɪlɪtɪ] *n* (*lit*) rigidité *f;* (*fig*) inflexibilité *f,* rigidité.
inflexible [ɪnˈfleksəbl] *adj object* rigide; *person, attitude, opinion* inflexible, rigide.
inflexion [ɪnˈflekʃən] *n* **(a)** (*U: Ling: V* **inflect 1a**) [*word*] flexion *f,* adjonction *f* de désinence, modification *f* de désinence; conjugaison *f;* déclinaison *f;* [*vowel*] inflexion *f.* **the** ~ **of nouns/verbs** la flexion nominale/verbale.
(b) (*Ling: affix*) désinence *f.*
(c) (*U*) [*voice*] inflexion *f,* modulation *f;* [*note*] altération *f;* [*body*] inflexion, inclination *f;* (*Geom, Opt etc*) inflexion, déviation *f.*
(d) the ~**s of her voice** les inflexions *fpl* de sa voix.
inflict [ɪnˈflɪkt] *vt punishment, fine, torture* infliger (*on* à); *pain, suffering* faire subir, infliger, occasionner (*on* à). **to** ~ **a wound on sb** blesser qn; **to** ~ **o.s.** *or* **one's company on sb** infliger *or* imposer sa compagnie à qn.
infliction [ɪnˈflɪkʃən] *n* **(a)** (*U*) infliction *f.* **to avoid the unnecessary** ~ **of pain/punishment** éviter d'infliger inutilement la douleur/un châtiment. **(b)** (*misfortune*) affliction *f.*
inflow [ˈɪnfləʊ] **1** *n* **(a)** [*water*] afflux *m,* arrivée *f,* flot *m.* **(b)** = **influx a. 2** *cpd:* **inflow pipe** tuyau *m* d'arrivée; **water-inflow pipe** arrivée *f or* adduction *f* d'eau.
influence [ˈɪnflʊəns] **1** *n* (*effect, impression*) [*person, moon, climate etc*] influence *f* (*on* sur); (*power*) influence, autorité *f* (*on* sur). **under his** ~ sous son influence; **under the** ~ **of drugs/anger** sous l'effet *m or* l'empire *m* des drogues/de la colère; **under the** ~ **of drink** sous l'effet *or* l'empire de la boisson, en état d'ébriété (*Jur*); (*Jur*) **convicted of driving under the** ~ **of drink** condamné pour avoir conduit en état d'ébriété *or* d'ivresse; **he was a bit under the** ~* il avait bu un coup de trop*, il était paf*; **his book had** *or* **was a great** ~ **on her** son livre a eu beaucoup d'influence sur elle *or* l'a beaucoup influencée; **I've got a lot of** ~ **with her** j'ai beaucoup d'influence *or* d'ascendant auprès d'elle; **to use one's** ~ **with sb to get sth** user de son influence auprès de qn pour obtenir qch; **I shall bring all my** ~ *or* **every** ~ **to bear on him** j'essaierai d'exercer toute mon in-

fluence *or* toute l'influence dont je dispose sur lui; **he has got ~** il a de l'influence *or* de l'autorité *or* de l'importance *or* du crédit, il a le bras long; **a man of ~** un homme influent; **she is a good ~ in the school/on the pupils** elle a *or* exerce une bonne influence dans l'établissement/sur les élèves.

2 *vt attitude, behaviour, decision, person* influencer, influer sur, agir sur. **don't let him ~ you** ne le laissez pas vous influencer; **don't be ~d by him** ne vous laissez pas influencer par lui; **she's easily ~d** elle est très influençable, elle se laisse facilement influencer; **the artist has been ~d by Leonardo da Vinci** l'artiste a été influencé par *or* a subi l'influence de *or* a été sous l'influence de Léonard de Vinci.

influential [ˌɪnflʊˈenʃəl] *adj* influent. **to be ~** avoir de l'influence *or* du crédit *or* de l'autorité *or* de l'importance, avoir le bras long.

influenza [ˌɪnflʊˈenzə] *n* (*U*) grippe *f*. **he's got ~** il a la grippe.

influx [ˈɪnflʌks] *n* **(a)** *[people]* afflux *m*, flot *m*; *[new ideas, attitudes]* flot, flux *m*. **a great ~ of people into the neighbourhood** un gros afflux d'arrivants dans le voisinage; **the ~ of tourists/foreign workers** *etc* l'afflux *or* le flot de touristes/de travailleurs étrangers *etc*. **(b) = inflow 1a. (c)** (*meeting place of rivers etc*) confluent *m*.

info* [ˈɪnfəʊ] *n* (*U: abbr of* **information 1a**) tuyaux* *mpl*.

inform [ɪnˈfɔːm] **1** *vt* informer, avertir, aviser (*of* de); renseigner (*about* sur). **to ~ sb of sth** informer *or* avertir *or* aviser qn de qch, faire savoir qch à qn, faire part de qch à qn; **I should like to be ~ed as soon as he arrives** j'aimerais être informé *or* averti *or* avisé dès qu'il sera là, prévenez-moi s'il vous plaît dès qu'il arrivera; **keep me ~ed (of what is happening)** tenez-moi au courant (de ce qui se passe); **why was I not ~ed?** pourquoi ne m'a-t-on rien dit?, pourquoi n'ai-je pas été averti? *or* informé? *or* tenu au courant?; **we must ~ the police** il (nous) faut avertir la police; **can you ~ me about the recent developments?** pouvez-vous me mettre au courant des *or* me faire connaître les derniers faits?; **he was well ~ed about what had been happening** il était bien informé sur *or* bien au courant de ce qui s'était passé; **he was ill ~ed *or* not well ~ed about what had been happening** il était mal informé *or* il n'était pas bien au courant de ce qui s'était passé; *V also* **informed**.

2 *vi*: **to ~ against sb** dénoncer qn, informer contre qn.

informal [ɪnˈfɔːməl] *adj* **(a)** (*simple, relaxed*) *tone, manner, style* simple, familier, sans façon. **~ language** le langage de la conversation; **he is very ~** il est très simple, il ne fait pas de façons; **we had an ~ talk about it** nous en avons discuté entre nous.

(b) (*without ceremony*) *welcome, greeting, visit* dénué de cérémonie *or* de formalité; *discussion* dénué de formalité, informel. **~ dance** sauterie *f* entre amis; **~ dinner** repas *m* simple (entre amis); **'dress ~'** 'tenue de ville'; **~ meeting** réunion *f* sans caractère officiel; **it was a very ~ occasion** c'était une occasion dénuée de toute formalité *or* de toute cérémonie *or* de tout protocole; **it's just an ~ get-together*** ce ne sera qu'une réunion toute simple; **it will be quite ~** ce sera sans cérémonie *or* en toute simplicité *or* à la bonne franquette, on ne fera pas de cérémonies*.

(c) (*not official*) *announcement, acceptance, communication* officieux, non-officiel; *instructions, invitation* non-officiel, dénué de caractère officiel. **there was an ~ arrangement that ...** il y avait une entente officieuse selon laquelle ...; **we had an ~ agreement to do it thus** nous nous étions mis d'accord officieusement *or* entre nous pour le faire ainsi; **there is an ~ suggestion that ...** il est suggéré de façon officieuse que ... .

informality [ˌɪnfɔːˈmælɪtɪ] *n [person, manner, style]* simplicité *f*; *[visit, welcome etc]* simplicité, absence *f* de formalité *or* de cérémonie; *[arrangement, agreement etc]* caractère officieux. **we liked the ~ of the meeting** nous avons aimé l'absence de cérémonie qui a marqué la réunion.

informally [ɪnˈfɔːməlɪ] *adv invite* sans cérémonie; *arrange, agree, meet* officieusement, en privé; *behave, speak* de façon toute simple, sans cérémonie. **to dress ~** s'habiller simplement.

informant [ɪnˈfɔːmənt] *n* **(a)** informateur *m*, -trice *f*. **my ~ tells me ...** mon informateur me dit que ...; **who is your ~?** de qui tenez-vous cette information?, quelles sont vos sources?; **a reliable ~** un informateur bien renseigné.

(b) (*Ling: also* **native ~**) informant(e) *m(f)*.

information [ˌɪnfəˈmeɪʃən] **1** *n* (*U*) **(a)** (*facts*) renseignements *mpl*, information(s) *f(pl)*. **a piece of ~** un renseignement, une information; **to give sb ~ about *or* on sth/sb** renseigner qn sur qch/qn; **to get ~ about *or* on sth/sb** se renseigner sur qch/qn; **to ask for ~ about *or* on sth/sb** demander des renseignements *or* des informations sur qch/qn; **I need more ~ about it** il me faut des renseignements plus complets *or* des informations plus complètes *or* une information plus complète là-dessus; **we are collecting as much ~ as we can on that organization** nous sommes en train de réunir le plus possible d'informations *or* de renseignements sur cette organisation; **we have no ~ on that point** nous n'avons aucune information *or* aucun renseignement là-dessus; **until more ~ is available** jusqu'à plus ample informé; **have you any ~ about the accident?** avez-vous des renseignements *or* des détails sur l'accident?; **the police are seeking ~ about ...** la police recherche des renseignements sur ..., la police enquête sur ... .

(b) (*knowledge*) connaissances *fpl*, savoir *m*, science *f*. **his ~ on the subject is astonishing** ses connaissances en la matière sont stupéfiantes, son savoir en la matière est stupéfiant; **for your ~ ...** à titre de renseignement ..., pour vous tenir au courant ...; **I enclose for your ~ a copy of ...** à titre d'information je joins une copie de ... .

(c) (*Jur: not U*) (*denunciation*) dénonciation *f*; (*charge*) acte *m* d'accusation. **to lay an ~ against sb** (*bring charge against*) former *or* porter une accusation contre qn; (*denounce*) dénoncer qn à la police.

2 *cpd*: **information bureau** bureau *m* de renseignements; **information content** contenu informationnel; **information office = information bureau; information retrieval** recherche *f* documentaire, retrouve *f* de l'information; **information retrieval system** système *m* de recherche documentaire; **information theory** théorie *f* de l'information.

informative [ɪnˈfɔːmətɪv] *adj book, meeting* instructif. **he's not very ~ about his plans** il ne s'ouvre pas beaucoup de *or* il ne dit pas grand-chose de ses projets.

informatory [ɪnˈfɔːmətərɪ] *adj* (*Bridge*) d'information. **~ double** contre *m* d'appel.

informed [ɪnˈfɔːmd] *adj* informé, renseigné. **there is a body of ~ opinion which claims that ...** il y a une opinion (bien) informée selon laquelle ...; **~ observers believe that ...** des observateurs informés *or* bien renseignés croient que ...; **an ~ guess** une hypothèse fondée sur la connaissance des faits; *V also* **inform**.

informer [ɪnˈfɔːməʳ] *n* dénonciateur *m*, -trice *f*, délateur *m*, -trice *f*. **police ~** indicateur *m*, -trice *f* (de police); **to turn ~** dénoncer *or* vendre ses complices.

infraction [ɪnˈfrækʃən] *n [law, rule etc]* infraction *f* (*of* à).

infra dig* [ˈɪnfrəˈdɪg] *adj* au-dessous de sa (*or* ma *etc*) dignité, indigne *or* au-dessous de soi (*or* moi *etc*), déshonorant.

infrared [ˈɪnfrəˈred] *adj* infrarouge.

infrequency [ɪnˈfriːkwənsɪ] *n* rareté *f*.

infrequent [ɪnˈfriːkwənt] *adj* peu fréquent, rare.

infrequently [ɪnˈfriːkwəntlɪ] *adv* peu fréquemment, rarement.

infringe [ɪnˈfrɪndʒ] **1** *vt obligation* contrevenir à; *law, rule* enfreindre, transgresser, contrevenir à. **to ~ a patent** commettre une contrefaçon (en matière) de brevet. **2** *vi*: **to ~ (up)on sb's rights** empiéter sur les droits de qn.

infringement [ɪnˈfrɪndʒmənt] *n* (*V* **infringe**) infraction *f* (*of* à); contravention *f* (*of* à); transgression *f* (*of* de). **~ of patent** contrefaçon *f* d'une invention brevetée *or* d'une fabrication brevetée.

infuriate [ɪnˈfjʊərɪeɪt] *vt* rendre furieux, mettre en fureur. **it ~s me** cela me rend fou, cela m'exaspère, ça m'enquiquine*.

infuriating [ɪnˈfjʊərɪeɪtɪŋ] *adj* exaspérant, rageant, enquiquinant*.

infuriatingly [ɪnˈfjʊərɪeɪtɪŋlɪ] *adv* de façon exaspérante. **~ slow** d'une lenteur exaspérante.

infuse [ɪnˈfjuːz] *vt* infuser (*into* dans); (*Culin*) *tea, herbs* (faire) infuser; (*fig*) *ideas etc* infuser, insuffler (*into* à); *enthusiasm* inspirer, insuffler.

infusion [ɪnˈfjuːʒən] *n* infusion *f*.

ingenious [ɪnˈdʒiːnɪəs] *adj* ingénieux, astucieux.

ingeniously [ɪnˈdʒiːnɪəslɪ] *adv* ingénieusement, astucieusement.

ingenuity [ˌɪndʒɪˈnjuːɪtɪ] *n* ingéniosité *f*.

ingenuous [ɪnˈdʒenjʊəs] *adj* (*naïve*) ingénu, naïf (*f* naïve), simple; (*candid*) sincère, franc (*f* franche), ouvert.

ingenuousness [ɪnˈdʒenjʊəsnɪs] *n* (*V* **ingenuous**) ingénuité *f*, naïveté *f*, simplicité *f*; sincérité *f*, franchise *f*.

ingest [ɪnˈdʒest] *vt* (*Med*) ingérer.

ingestion [ɪnˈdʒestʃən] *n* (*Med*) ingestion *f*.

inglenook [ˈɪŋglnʊk] *n* coin *m* du feu. **~ fireplace** grande cheminée à l'ancienne.

inglorious [ɪnˈglɔːrɪəs] *adj* peu glorieux, (*stronger*) déshonorant, honteux.

ingot [ˈɪŋgət] *n* lingot *m*.

ingrained [ˈɪnˈgreɪnd] *adj habit* invétéré; *prejudice* enraciné. **an ~ hatred of** une haine tenace pour; **~ dirt** crasse *f*; **~ with dirt** encrassé.

ingratiate [ɪnˈgreɪʃɪeɪt] *vt*: **to ~ o.s. with sb** s'insinuer dans les bonnes grâces *or* dans la confiance de qn.

ingratiating [ɪnˈgreɪʃɪeɪtɪŋ] *adj* insinuant, patelin.

ingratitude [ɪnˈgrætɪtjuːd] *n* ingratitude *f*.

ingredient [ɪnˈgriːdɪənt] *n* (*Culin etc*) ingrédient *m*; *[character etc]* élément *m*.

ingress [ˈɪngres] *n* (*Jur*) entrée *f*. **to have free ~** avoir le droit d'entrée.

inhabit [ɪnˈhæbɪt] *vt town, country* habiter; *house* habiter (dans). **~ed** habité.

inhabitable [ɪnˈhæbɪtəbl] *adj* habitable.

inhabitant [ɪnˈhæbɪtənt] *n* habitant(e) *m(f)*.

inhalation [ˌɪnhəˈleɪʃən] *n* inhalation *f*, aspiration *f*.

inhalator [ˈɪnhəleɪtəʳ] *n* (appareil *m*) inhalateur *m*.

inhale [ɪnˈheɪl] **1** *vt vapour, gas etc* inhaler; *[smoker]* avaler; *perfume* aspirer, respirer, humer. **2** *vi* (*in smoking*) avaler la fumée.

inhaler [ɪnˈheɪləʳ] *n* = **inhalator**.

inharmonious [ˌɪnhɑːˈməʊnɪəs] *adj* inharmonieux, peu harmonieux.

inhere [ɪnˈhɪəʳ] *vi* être inhérent (*in* à); être intrinsèque (*to, in* à).

inherent [ɪnˈhɪərənt] *adj* inhérent, naturel (*in, to* à); (*Jur*) propre (*in, to* à). **with all the ~ difficulties** avec toutes les difficultés qui s'y rattachent.

inherently [ɪnˈhɪərəntlɪ] *adv* en soi; (*Philos*) par inhérence; (*Jur*) en propre. **it's not ~ difficult** ce n'est pas difficile en soi; **he is ~ curious** il est fondamentalement curieux, il est né curieux.

inherit [ɪnˈherɪt] *vt* hériter de, hériter. **to ~ a house/fortune** hériter (d')une maison/(d')une fortune; **to ~ a house/fortune from sb** hériter une maison/une fortune de qn; **he ~ed the estate from his father** il a succédé à son père à la tête du domaine, il a hérité le domaine de son père; **to ~ a title** succéder à un titre; **he is due to ~ on the death of his uncle** il doit hériter à la mort de son oncle; **she ~ed her mother's beauty** elle a hérité (de) la beauté de sa mère; **he ~s his patience/his red hair from his father** il tient sa patience/ses cheveux roux de son père; (*hum*) **I've ~ed my brother's coat** j'ai hérité du manteau de mon frère.

inheritance [ɪnˈherɪtəns] *n* **(a)** (*U*) succession *f*. (*Jur*) **law of ~** droit *m* de succession. **(b)** héritage *m*; patrimoine *m*. **to come into an ~** faire un héritage; **he wasted all his ~** il a dilapidé tout son héritage; **our national ~** notre patrimoine national.

inhibit [ɪnˈhɪbɪt] *vt* **(a)** (*restrain*) *impulse, desire* dominer, maîtriser; (*Psych*) inhiber. **to ~ sb from doing** (*restrain*) retenir qn de faire; (*prevent*) empêcher qn de faire; **his presence ~ed the discussion** sa présence gênait *or* entravait la discussion; **he found his principles very ~ing** ses principes lui apparaissaient comme une entrave; **he was greatly ~ed by his lack of education** son manque d'instruction le gênait beaucoup; (*Psych*) **he is very ~ed** il a beaucoup d'inhibitions.
(b) (*Jur: prohibit*) interdire, défendre (*sb from doing* à qn de faire).

inhibition [ˌɪnhɪˈbɪʃən] *n* **(a)** (*Physiol, Psych*) inhibition *f*. **(b)** (*Jur: prohibition*) interdiction *f*.

inhibitory [ɪnˈhɪbɪtərɪ] *adj* **(a)** (*Physiol, Psych*) inhibiteur (*f* -trice). **(b)** (*Jur*) prohibitif.

inhospitable [ˌɪnhɒsˈpɪtəbl] *adj person, country, climate* inhospitalier; *attitude, remark* inamical, désobligeant.

inhospitably [ˌɪnhɒsˈpɪtəblɪ] *adv* (*V* **inhospitable**) d'une manière inhospitalière *or* peu hospitalière; de façon inamicale *or* désobligeante.

inhospitality [ˈɪnˌhɒspɪˈtælɪtɪ] *n* inhospitalité *f*; inimitié *f*.

inhuman [ɪnˈhjuːmən] *adj* (*lit, fig*) inhumain.

inhumane [ˌɪnhju(ː)ˈmeɪn] *adj* inhumain, brutal, cruel.

inhumanity [ˌɪnhjuːˈmænɪtɪ] *n* inhumanité *f*, brutalité *f*, cruauté *f*.

inhumation [ˌɪnhjuːˈmeɪʃən] *n* inhumation *f*, enterrement *m*.

inimical [ɪˈnɪmɪkəl] *adj* (*hostile*) hostile, inamical, ennemi. **~ to** défavorable à, (l')ennemi de.

inimitable [ɪˈnɪmɪtəbl] *adj* inimitable.

inimitably [ɪˈnɪmɪtəblɪ] *adv* d'une façon inimitable.

iniquitous [ɪˈnɪkwɪtəs] *adj* inique, d'une injustice monstrueuse.

iniquitously [ɪˈnɪkwɪtəslɪ] *adv* iniquement, monstrueusement.

iniquity [ɪˈnɪkwɪtɪ] *n* iniquité *f*.

initial [ɪˈnɪʃəl] **1** *adj* initial, premier, du début. *[shop, firm etc]* **~ expenses** frais *mpl* d'installation; **in the ~ stages** dans les débuts, au début, dans un premier temps, au commencement; **my ~ reaction was to refuse** ma première réaction *or* ma réaction initiale a été de refuser; (*Typ*) **~ letter** initiale *f*.
2 *n* (lettre *f*) initiale *f*. **~s** initiales *fpl*; (*as signature*) parafe *m or* paraphe *m*.
3 *vt letter, document* parafer *or* parapher; (*approve*) viser.

initially [ɪˈnɪʃəlɪ] *adv* initialement, au commencement, au début, à l'origine.

initiate [ɪˈnɪʃɪeɪt] **1** *vt* **(a)** *reform* promouvoir; *negotiations* entreprendre, amorcer, engager; *enterprise* se lancer dans; *scheme, programme* inaugurer, instaurer, mettre en action; *fashion* lancer. (*Jur*) **to ~ proceedings against sb** intenter une action à qn.
(b) (*Rel etc*) *person* initier. **to ~ sb into a society** admettre qn au sein d'une société (secrète); **to ~ sb into a science/a secret** initier qn à une science/un secret.
2 [ɪˈnɪʃɪɪt] *adj, n* initié(e) *m(f)*.

initiation [ɪˌnɪʃɪˈeɪʃən] **1** *n* (*V* **initiate**) **(a)** *[negotiations, enterprise]* commencement *m*, début *m*, amorce *f*; *[scheme]* inauguration *f*.
(b) (*into society*) admission *f* (*into* dans), initiation *f*; (*into knowledge, secret*) initiation (*into* à).
2 *cpd*: **initiation rite** rite *m* d'initiation.

initiative [ɪˈnɪʃətɪv] *n* initiative *f*. **to take the ~** prendre l'initiative (*in doing sth* de faire qch); **on one's own ~** de sa propre initiative, par soi-même; **he's got ~** il a de l'initiative.

inject [ɪnˈdʒekt] *vt liquid, gas* injecter (*into* dans). (*Med*) **to ~ sb with sth** injecter qch à qn, faire une piqûre *or* une injection de qch à qn; **to ~ sb's arm with penicillin, to ~ penicillin into sb's arm** faire une piqûre *or* injection de pénicilline dans le bras de qn; (*fig*) **to ~ sb with enthusiasm** *etc* communiquer *or* insuffler de l'enthousiasme *etc* à qn; **to ~ new life into a club** insuffler une vie nouvelle à un club.

injection [ɪnˈdʒekʃən] *n* injection *f*; (*Med*) injection, piqûre *f*.

injudicious [ˌɪndʒʊˈdɪʃəs] *adj* peu judicieux, malavisé.

injudiciously [ˌɪndʒʊˈdɪʃəslɪ] *adv* peu judicieusement.

injunction [ɪnˈdʒʌŋkʃən] *n* (*gen*) ordre *m*, recommandation formelle; (*Jur*) injonction *f*; (*court order*) ordonnance *f* (*to do* de faire, *against doing* de ne pas faire). **to give sb strict ~s to do** enjoindre formellement *or* strictement à qn de faire.

injure [ˈɪndʒəʳ] *vt* **(a)** (*Med*) *person, limb* blesser. **to ~ o.s.** se blesser, se faire du mal; **to ~ one's leg** se blesser à la jambe; **fatally ~d** blessé mortellement *or* à mort; **no one was ~d** il n'y a pas eu de blessés, personne n'a été blessé; *V also* **injured**.
(b) (*wrong*) *person* faire du tort à, nuire à; (*Jur*) porter préjudice à, léser; (*offend*) blesser, offenser; (*damage*) *reputation, sb's interests, chances, trade* compromettre; (*Comm*) *cargo, goods* avarier. **to ~ sb's feelings** offenser *or* outrager *or* offusquer qn; **to ~ one's health** compromettre sa santé, se détériorer la santé; *V also* **injured**.

injured [ˈɪndʒəd] **1** *adj* (*Med*) blessé; (*maimed*) estropié; (*in accident etc*) accidenté; *limb* blessé; (*fig*) *person* offensé; *look, voice* blessé, offensé; (*Jur*) *wife, husband* outragé, trompé. (*Jur*) **the ~ party** la partie lésée.
2 *n*: **the ~** (*gen*) les blessés *mpl*; (*in road accident etc*) les accidentés *mpl*, les blessés.

injurious [ɪnˈdʒʊərɪəs] *adj* nuisible, préjudiciable (*to* à). **~ to the health** nuisible *or* préjudiciable à la santé, mauvais pour la santé.

injury [ˈɪndʒərɪ] **1** *n* **(a)** (*Med*) blessure *f*, lésion *f*. **to do sb an ~** blesser qn; **to do o.s. an ~** se blesser, se faire mal; (*Sport*) **3 players have injuries** il y a 3 joueurs (de) blessés; *V* **internal**.
(b) (*wrong*) (*to person*) tort *m*, préjudice *m*; (*to reputation etc*) atteinte *f*; (*Jur*) lésion *f*, préjudice. **to the ~ of sb** au détriment *or* au préjudice de qn.
(c) (*Comm, Naut*) avarie *f*.
2 *cpd*: (*Ftbl*) **injury time** arrêts *mpl* de jeu.

injustice [ɪnˈdʒʌstɪs] *n* injustice *f*. **to do sb an ~** être *or* se montrer injuste envers qn.

ink [ɪŋk] **1** *n* **(a)** encre *f*. **written in ~** (écrit) à l'encre; *V* **Indian, invisible** *etc*.
(b) *[cuttlefish etc]* encre *f*, sépia *f*.
2 *cpd*: (*Zool*) **ink bag** sac *m or* poche *f* d'encre; **ink blot** tache *f* d'encre, pâté *m*; **ink bottle** bouteille *f* d'encre; **ink eraser** gomme *f* à encre; **inkpad** tampon *m* (encreur); **inkpot** encrier *m*; **ink rubber = ink eraser**; **inkstain** tache *f* d'encre; **inkstand** (grand) encrier *m* (de bureau); **inkwell** encrier *m* (de pupitre *etc*).
3 *vt* (*Typ*) encrer.
ink in *vt sep* repasser à l'encre.
ink out *vt sep* raturer *or* barrer à l'encre.
ink over *vt sep* = **ink in**.

inkling [ˈɪŋklɪŋ] *n* soupçon *m*, vague *or* petite idée. **I had no ~ that ...** je n'avais pas la moindre idée que ..., je ne me doutais pas du tout que ..., j'étais à cent lieues de me douter que ...; **he had no ~ of it** il n'en avait pas la moindre idée, il ne s'en doutait pas le moins du monde; **we had some ~ of their plan** nous soupçonnions leur plan, nous avions une petite idée de leur plan; **there was no ~ of the disaster to come** rien ne laissait présager le désastre qui allait se produire.

inky [ˈɪŋkɪ] *adj* taché *or* couvert d'encre; *book, hand* barbouillé d'encre; *pad, rubber stamp* encré; (*fig*) *darkness etc* noir comme de l'encre, noir d'encre.

inlaid [ˈɪnˈleɪd] *adj brooch, sword etc* incrusté (*with* de); *box, table* marqueté; *metal* damasquiné. **ivory ~ with gold** ivoire incrusté d'or; **~ floor** parquet *m*; **~ work** incrustation *f*, marqueterie *f*.

inland [ˈɪnlænd] **1** *adj* **(a)** (*not coastal*) *sea, town* intérieur (*f* -eure). **~ navigation** navigation fluviale; **~ waterways** canaux *mpl* et rivières *fpl*.
(b) (*Brit: domestic*) *mail, trade* intérieur (*f* -eure). **~ revenue** (*organization, system*) fisc *m*; (*payments*) contributions directes; **~ revenue stamp** timbre fiscal.
2 [ɪnˈlænd] *adv* à l'intérieur. **to go ~** pénétrer à l'intérieur *or* dans les terres.

inlay [ˈɪnleɪ] (*vb: pret, ptp* **inlaid**) **1** *n* incrustation *f*; *[table, box]* marqueterie *f*; *[floor]* parquet *m*; *[metal]* damasquinage *m*.
2 [ˌɪnˈleɪ] *vt* incruster (*with* de); *table, box* marqueter; *floor* parqueter; *metal* damasquiner; *V also* **inlaid**.

inlet [ˈɪnlet] **1** *n* **(a)** *[sea]* crique *f*, anse *f*, bras *m* de mer; *[river]* bras de rivière. **(b)** (*Tech*) arrivée *f*, admission *f*; *[ventilator]* prise *f* (d'air). **2** *cpd*: **inlet pipe** tuyau *m* d'arrivée; *V* **valve**.

inmate [ˈɪnmeɪt] *n [house]* occupant(e) *m(f)*, résident(e) *m(f)*; *[prison]* détenu(e) *m(f)*; *[asylum]* interné(e) *m(f)*; *[hospital]* hospitalisé(e) *m(f)*, pensionnaire* *mf*.

inmost [ˈɪnməʊst] *adj part* le plus profond; *corner, thoughts, feelings* le plus secret (*f* -ète). **one's ~ being** le tréfonds de son être (*liter*); **in one's ~ heart** dans le fond de son cœur.

inn [ɪn] **1** *n* **(a)** (*small, wayside*) auberge *f*; (*larger, wayside*) hostellerie *f*; (*in town*) hôtel *m*; (†: *tavern*) cabaret† *m*.
(b) (*Brit Jur*) **the I~s of Court** les (quatre) écoles de droit (*londoniennes*).
2 *cpd*: **innkeeper** aubergiste *mf*; hôtelier *m*, -ière *f*; **inn sign** enseigne *f* d'auberge.

innards* [ˈɪnədz] *npl* entrailles *fpl*, intérieurs* *mpl*.

innate [ɪˈneɪt] *adj knowledge, gift* inné, infus; *sense, wisdom, qualities* inné, naturel, foncier.

inner [ˈɪnəʳ] **1** *adj* **(a)** *room, court* intérieur (*f* -eure), interne, de dedans. **on the ~ side** à l'intérieur, en dedans; **they formed an ~ circle within the society** ils formaient un petit noyau *or* un petit cercle (fermé) *or* une chapelle à l'intérieur de la société; **~ city** centre *m* d'une *or* de la zone urbaine; **~ city schools** les établissements scolaires situés dans le centre de la *or* des zone(s) urbaine(s); (*Naut*) **~ dock** arrière-bassin *m*; (*Anat*) **~ ear** oreille *f* interne; **~ harbour** arrière-port *m*; **the ~ man** (*spiritual self*) l'homme intérieur; (*hum: stomach*) l'estomac *m*; *[shoe]* **~ sole** semelle *f* (intérieure); *[tyre]* **~ tube** chambre *f* à air.
(b) (*fig*) *emotions, thoughts* intime, secret (*f* -ète), profond; *life* intérieur (*f* -eure). **~ meaning** sens *m* intime *or* profond.
2 *n* (*Archery etc*) zone *f* entourant le visuel.
3 *cpd*: **innermost = inmost**; (*US*) **inner spring mattress** matelas *m* à ressorts.

inning [ˈɪnɪŋ] *n* (*Baseball*) tour *m* de batte.

innings [ˈɪnɪŋz] *n* (*pl inv*) (*Cricket*) tour *m* de batte; (*fig*) tour. (*fig*) **I've had a good ~** j'ai bien profité de l'existence (*etc*).

innocence [ˈɪnəsns] *n* (*gen, Jur*) innocence *f*; (*simplicity*) innocence, naïveté *f*, candeur *f*. **to put on an air of ~** faire l'innocent; **in all ~** en toute innocence; **in his ~ he believed it all** naïf comme il (l')est *or* dans son innocence il a tout cru.

innocent [ˈɪnəsnt] **1** *adj* (*Jur etc*) innocent, non coupable (*of* de); (*Rel*) innocent, sans péché, pur; (*simple*) naïf (*f* naïve), candide, innocent; *question, remark* innocent, sans malice; *mistake* innocent; *amusement, pastime* innocent, inoffensif. **as ~ as a newborn babe** innocent comme l'enfant qui vient de naître; **to put on an ~ air** faire l'innocent; **he was ~ of any desire to harm her** il était dénué de tout désir de *or* il n'avait nulle intention de lui faire du mal; **she was dressed in black, ~ of all jewellery** elle était vêtue de noir et sans aucun bijou; **room ~ of all ornament** pièce dépourvue de tout ornement.

2 *n*: **he's one of Nature's ~s*, he's a bit of an ~*** c'est un grand innocent; (*Rel*) **Massacre of the Holy I~s** massacre *m* des saints Innocents.

innocently [ˈɪnəsntlɪ] *adv* innocemment.

innocuous [ɪˈnɒkjʊəs] *adj* inoffensif.

innovate [ˈɪnəʊveɪt] *vti* innover.

innovation [ˌɪnəʊˈveɪʃən] *n* innovation *f* (*in* en, en matière de); changement *m* (*in* dans, en matière de). **to make ~s in sth** apporter des innovations *or* des changements à qch; **scientific/technical ~s** innovations scientifiques/techniques.

innovator [ˈɪnəʊveɪtəʳ] *n* innovateur *m*, -trice *f*, novateur *m*, -trice *f*.

innuendo [ˌɪnjʊˈendəʊ] *n, pl* **~es** insinuation *f*, allusion *f* (malveillante). **to make ~es against sb** faire des insinuations (malveillantes) à l'égard de qn.

innumerable [ɪˈnjuːmərəbl] *adj* innombrable, sans nombre. **there are ~ reasons** il y a une infinité de raisons; **I've told you ~ times** je te l'ai dit cent fois *or* trente-six fois.

inoculate [ɪˈnɒkjʊleɪt] *vt* (*Med*) *person* inoculer, vacciner (*against* contre). (*lit, fig*) **to ~ sb with sth** inoculer qch à qn.

inoculation [ɪˌnɒkjʊˈleɪʃən] *n* (*Med*) inoculation *f*.

inoffensive [ˌɪnəˈfensɪv] *adj* inoffensif.

inoperable [ɪnˈɒpərəbl] *adj* inopérable.

inoperative [ɪnˈɒpərətɪv] *adj* inopérant.

inopportune [ɪnˈɒpətjuːn] *adj arrival, demand, request* inopportun, intempestif; *moment* inopportun, mal choisi; *behaviour* déplacé, hors de saison.

inopportunely [ɪnˈɒpətjuːnlɪ] *adv speak* inopportunément, mal à propos; *arrive, demand* inopportunément, intempestivement.

inordinate [ɪˈnɔːdɪnɪt] *adj size* démesuré; *quantity, demands* excessif; *passion* immodéré. **an ~ amount of time** un temps fou*; **an ~ amount of butter** énormément de beurre; **an ~ sum (of money)** une somme exorbitante *or* astronomique.

inordinately [ɪˈnɔːdɪnɪtlɪ] *adv* démesurément, immodérément, excessivement.

inorganic [ˌɪnɔːˈgænɪk] *adj* inorganique.

input [ˈɪnpʊt] *n* (*Elec*) énergie *f*, puissance *f*; (*Tech*) *[machine]* consommation *f*; *[computer]* données *fpl*, information fournie, input *m*.

inquest [ˈɪnkwest] *n* (*Jur*) enquête *f* (criminelle); *V* **coroner**.

inquietude [ɪnˈkwaɪətjuːd] *n* inquiétude *f*.

inquire [ɪnˈkwaɪəʳ] **1** *vi* demander; s'enquérir, s'informer (*about* de); se renseigner (*about* sur).

2 *vt* demander, s'informer de, s'enquérir de; *the time, a name* demander. **to ~ the way of** *or* **from sb** demander le (*or* son) chemin à qn; **to ~ the price of sth from sb** demander à qn le prix de qch, s'enquérir *or* s'informer du prix de qch auprès de qn; '**~ within**' 'renseignements ici', 's'adresser ici'; '**~ at the information desk**' 's'adresser aux renseignements *or* au bureau de renseignements'; **he ~d how to get to the theatre** il a demandé le chemin du théâtre; **he ~d what she wanted** il a demandé ce qu'elle voulait.

inquire after *vt fus person, sb's health* demander des nouvelles de, s'informer de, s'enquérir de.

inquire for *vt fus person* demander.

inquire into *vt fus subject* faire des recherches *or* des investigations sur; *possibilities* se renseigner sur, se documenter sur, examiner; (*Admin, Jur*) enquêter sur, faire une enquête sur. **to inquire into the truth of sth** vérifier la véracité de qch.

inquiring [ɪnˈkwaɪərɪŋ] *adj attitude, frame of mind* curieux, investigateur (*f* -trice); *look* interrogateur (*f* -trice).

inquiringly [ɪnˈkwaɪərɪŋlɪ] *adv* avec curiosité; d'un air interrogateur. **to look ~ at sb/sth** regarder qn/qch d'un air interrogateur, interroger qn/qch du regard.

inquiry [ɪnˈkwaɪərɪ] **1** *n* **(a)** (*from individual*) demande *f* de renseignements. **to make inquiries about sb/sth (of sb)** se renseigner sur qn/qch (auprès de qn), demander des renseignements sur qn/qch (à qn) (*V also* **1b**); **on ~ he found that ...** renseignements pris il a découvert que ...; **a look of ~** un regard interrogateur; **he gave me a look of ~** il m'a interrogé du regard; **'all inquiries to ...'** 'pour tous renseignements s'adresser à ...'; (*sign*) **'Inquiries'** 'Renseignements'; **ask at the Inquiries** demandez aux Renseignements.

(b) (*Admin, Jur*) enquête *f*, investigation *f*. **to set up** *or* **open an ~ into** ouvrir une enquête sur; **committee of ~** commission *f* d'enquête; **to hold an ~ into** enquêter *or* faire une enquête sur; **judicial ~** enquête judiciaire; (*Jur*) **remanded for further ~** renvoyé pour complément d'instruction *or* d'information; **this is a fruitful line of ~** c'est une bonne direction dans laquelle pousser cette enquête; **there will have to be an ~ into this** il va falloir enquêter *or* faire une enquête sur cette affaire; **the police are making inquiries** la police enquête; *V* **help**.

2 *cpd*: **inquiry desk, inquiry office** (bureau *m* de) renseignements *mpl*.

inquisition [ˌɪnkwɪˈzɪʃən] *n* investigation *f*, recherches *fpl*; (*Jur*) enquête *f* (judiciaire). (*Rel*) **the I~** l'Inquisition *f*.

inquisitive [ɪnˈkwɪzɪtɪv] *adj person, mind* curieux; (*pej*) inquisiteur (*f* -trice), indiscret (*f* -ète), (trop) curieux.

inquisitively [ɪnˈkwɪzɪtɪvlɪ] *adv* avec curiosité; (*pej*) indiscrètement, trop curieusement.

inquisitiveness [ɪnˈkwɪzɪtɪvnɪs] *n* curiosité *f*; (*pej*) curiosité indiscrète, indiscrétion *f*.

inquisitor [ɪnˈkwɪzɪtəʳ] *n* (*Jur*) enquêteur *m*, -euse *f*; (*Rel*) inquisiteur *m*.

inquisitorial [ɪnˌkwɪzɪˈtɔːrɪəl] *adj* inquisitorial.

inroad [ˈɪnrəʊd] *n* (*Mil*) incursion *f* (*into* en, dans). (*fig*) **to make ~s upon** *or* **into** *sb's rights* empiéter sur; *savings* entamer, ébrécher.

insalubrious [ˌɪnsəˈluːbrɪəs] *adj* insalubre, malsain.

insane [ɪnˈseɪn] **1** *adj* (*Med*) aliéné, dément; (*gen*) *person, desire* fou (*f* folle), insensé; *project* démentiel. **to become ~** perdre la raison; **to drive sb ~** rendre qn fou; **he must be ~ to think of going** il faut qu'il soit fou pour envisager d'y aller; **you must be ~!** tu es fou!; *V* **certify**.

2 *npl* (*Med*) **the ~** les aliénés *mpl*, les malades *mpl* psychiatriques.

insanely [ɪnˈseɪnlɪ] *adv laugh* comme un fou (*f* une folle); *behave* de façon insensée. **to act/talk ~** faire/dire des insanités; **~ jealous** follement jaloux.

insanitary [ɪnˈsænɪtərɪ] *adj* insalubre, malsain.

insanity [ɪnˈsænɪtɪ] *n* (*Med*) aliénation *f* (mentale), démence *f*; (*gen*) folie *f*, démence, insanité *f*.

insatiable [ɪnˈseɪʃəbl] *adj* insatiable (*of* de).

inscribe [ɪnˈskraɪb] *vt* **(a)** (*in book etc*) inscrire (*in* dans); (*on monument etc*) inscrire, graver (*on* sur); *surface etc* marquer, graver; (*fig*) *ideas* graver, inscrire, fixer (*on* sur). **to ~ a tomb with a name** *or* **a name on a tomb** graver un nom sur une tombe; **a watch ~d with his name** une montre gravée à son nom; (*Fin*) **~d stock** titres nominatifs *or* inscrits.

(b) (*dedicate*) *book* dédier, dédicacer (*to* à).

inscription [ɪnˈskrɪpʃən] *n* (*on coin, monument etc*) inscription *f*; (*on cartoon*) légende *f*; (*dedication*) dédicace *f*.

inscrutability [ɪnˌskruːtəˈbɪlɪtɪ] *n* impénétrabilité *f* (*fig*).

inscrutable [ɪnˈskruːtəbl] *adj* impénétrable, insondable. **~ face** visage impénétrable *or* fermé.

insect [ˈɪnsekt] **1** *n* insecte *m*.

2 *cpd*: **insect bite** piqûre *f*, morsure *f* d'insecte; **insect eater** insectivore *m*; **insect powder** poudre *f* insecticide; **insect repellent** (*adj*) anti-insecte *inv*; (*n*) (*cream, ointment etc*) crème *f* anti-insecte *inv*; **insect spray** aérosol *m or* bombe *f* insecticide.

insecticide [ɪnˈsektɪsaɪd] *adj, n* insecticide (*m*).

insectivorous [ˌɪnsekˈtɪvərəs] *adj* insectivore.

insecure [ˌɪnsɪˈkjʊəʳ] *adj* **(a)** (*not firm, badly fixed*) *bolt, nail, padlock* peu solide, qui tient mal; *rope* mal attaché, peu solide; *structure, ladder* branlant, mal affermi, qui tient mal; *lock* peu sûr; *door, window* qui ferme mal.

(b) (*uncertain*) *career, future* incertain.

(c) (*dangerous*) *place* peu sûr, exposé au danger.

(d) (*worried*) *person* anxieux, inquiet (*f* -ète); (*Psych etc*) insécurisé. **he is very ~** c'est un anxieux.

insecurity [ˌɪnsɪˈkjʊərɪtɪ] *n* (*also Psych*) insécurité *f*.

inseminate [ɪnˈsemɪneɪt] *vt* inséminer.

insemination [ɪnˌsemɪˈneɪʃən] *n* insémination *f*; *V* **artificial**.

insensate [ɪnˈsenseɪt] *adj* (*senseless*) insensé; (*inanimate*) inanimé, insensible; (*unfeeling*) insensible.

insensibility [ɪnˌsensəˈbɪlɪtɪ] *n* **(a)** (*Med: unconsciousness*) insensibilité *f*, inconscience *f*. **(b)** (*fig: unfeelingness*) insensibilité *f* (*to* à), indifférence *f* (*to* à, pour).

insensible [ɪnˈsensəbl] *adj* **(a)** (*Med: unconscious*) inconscient, sans connaissance. **the blow knocked him ~** le coup lui fit perdre connaissance; **he drank himself ~** il a bu à en tomber ivre mort.

(b) (*without sensation*) *limb etc* insensible. **~ to cold/heat** insensible au froid/à la chaleur.

(c) (*emotionless*) insensible, indifférent (*to* à).

(d) (*unaware*) **~ of danger** *etc* insensible *or* indifférent au danger *etc*.

(e) (*imperceptible*) *change, shift* insensible, imperceptible. **by ~ degrees** petit à petit, insensiblement, imperceptiblement.

insensitive [ɪnˈsensɪtɪv] *adj* (*all senses*) insensible (*to* à).

insensitivity [ɪnˌsensɪˈtɪvɪtɪ] *n* insensibilité *f*.

inseparable [ɪnˈsepərəbl] *adj* inséparable (*from* de).

inseparably [ɪnˈsepərəblɪ] *adv join* indissolublement.

insert [ɪnˈsɜːt] **1** *vt* insérer (*in, into* dans, *between* entre); *paragraph, word etc* insérer, introduire (*in* dans), ajouter (*in* à); *key, knife, finger* insérer, introduire, enfoncer (*in* dans); (*Typ*) *page, leaflet* encarter, insérer; *advertisement* insérer (*in* dans).

2 [ˈɪnsɜːt] *n* (*page*) encart *m*; (*advertisement, note, word*) insertion *f*; (*Tech*) pièce insérée, ajout *m*; (*Sewing*) entre-deux *m inv*, incrustation *f*.

insertion [ɪnˈsɜːʃən] *n* **(a)** (*U*) insertion *f*, introduction *f*. **(b)** = **insert 2**.

inset [ˈɪnset] *pret, ptp* **inset 1** *vt map, illustration* insérer en cartouche (*into* dans); *jewel, ornamentation* insérer (*into* dans), incruster (*into* sur); *lace* incruster (*into* sur); (*Typ*) *page, leaflet* encarter, insérer (*into* dans). (*Sewing*) **to ~ a panel into a skirt** rapporter un panneau sur une jupe; **to ~ a map into the corner of a larger one** insérer une carte en cartouche sur une plus grande.

2 *n* (*diagram/map/portrait etc*) schéma *m*/carte *f*/portrait *m etc* en cartouche; (*Typ: leaflet, pages*) encart *m*; (*Sewing*) entre-deux *m inv*, incrustation *f*.

inshore [ˈɪnˈʃɔːʳ] **1** *adj area, fisherman, navigation* côtier; *fishing boat* côtier, caboteur. **~ fishing, ~ fisheries** pêche côtière; **~ lifeboat** canot *m* de sauvetage côtier; **~ wind** vent *m* de mer.

2 *adv be, fish* près de la côte; *blow, flow, go* vers la côte.

inside [ˈɪnˈsaɪd] (*phr vb elem*) **1** *adv* **(a)** dedans, au dedans, à l'intérieur. **~ and outside** au dedans et au dehors; **come** *or* **step ~!** entrez (donc)!; **it is warmer ~** il fait plus chaud à l'intérieur *or* dedans; **wait for me ~** attendez-moi à l'intérieur.

(b) (*‡: in jail*) en taule‡, à l'ombre*, au frais‡.

2 *prep* **(a)** (*of place*) à l'intérieur de, dans. **he was waiting ~ the house** il attendait à l'intérieur (de la maison); **she was standing just ~ the gate** (*seen from inside*) elle était juste de ce côté-ci de la barrière; (*seen from outside*) elle était juste de l'autre côté de la barrière.

(b) (*of time*) en moins de. **he came back ~ 3 minutes** *or* (*US**) **~ of 3 minutes** il est revenu en moins de 3 minutes; (*Sport*) **he was well ~ the record time** il avait largement battu le record.

3 *n* (a) dedans *m*, intérieur *m*; *[house, box]* intérieur. **on the ~** en dedans, au dedans, à l'intérieur; **walk on the ~ of the pavement** *or* (*US*) **sidewalk** marchez sur le trottoir du côté maisons; **on the ~ of the road** (*Brit*) sur la gauche; (*US, Europe etc*) sur la droite; **the door is bolted on** *or* **from the ~** la porte est fermée au verrou du dedans; (*fig*) **to know the ~ of an affair** connaître les dessous *mpl* d'une affaire; **I see the firm from the ~** je vois la compagnie de l'intérieur.

(b) **your coat is ~ out** ton manteau est à l'envers; **the wind blew the umbrella ~ out** le vent a retourné le parapluie; **I turned the bag ~ out but there was no money in it** j'ai retourné le sac (entièrement) mais il n'y avait pas d'argent dedans; (*fig*) **the children turned everything ~ out** les enfants ont tout mis sens dessus dessous; **he knows his subject ~ out** il connaît son sujet à fond; **he knows the district ~ out** il connaît le quartier comme sa poche.

(c) (*: *stomach: also* ~s) ventre *m*. **he's got a pain in his ~(s)** il a mal au ventre *or* aux entrailles (*hum*); **my ~ is playing me up** j'ai les intestins détraqués, je suis tout détraqué.

4 *adj* (a) intérieur (*f* -eure), d'intérieur. **~ pocket** poche intérieure; **~ leg measurement** mesure *f or* hauteur *f* de l'entrejambes; *[plane]* **~ seat** place *f* de fenêtre; (*fig*) **to get ~ information** obtenir des renseignements *mpl* à la source; (*Press*) **'the ~ story of the plot'** 'le complot raconté par un des participants'; (*of theft etc*) **it must have been an ~ job*** c'est un coup qui a dû être monté de l'intérieur *or* par quelqu'un de la maison.

(b) (*Aut*) *wheel, headlight etc* (*Brit*) gauche; (*US, Europe etc*) droit. **the ~ lane** (*Brit*) la voie de gauche; (*US, Europe etc*) la voie de droite; **to be on the ~ track** (*Sport*) être à la corde, tenir la corde; (*fig*) être avantagé.

5 *cpd*: (*Sport*) **inside-forward** intérieur *m*, inter* *m*; **inside-left/-right** intérieur *m* gauche/droit.

insidious [ɪn'sɪdɪəs] *adj promises, flattery* insidieux, traître (*f* traîtresse), trompeur; *enemy, disease* insidieux; *argument* insidieux, captieux, spécieux.

insidiously [ɪn'sɪdɪəslɪ] *adv* insidieusement.

insight ['ɪnsaɪt] *n* (*discernment*) pénétration *f*, perspicacité *f*. **I got** *or* **gained an ~ into his way of thinking** cela m'a permis de comprendre *or* de pénétrer sa façon de penser; **that will give you an ~ into his reasons for doing it** cela vous éclairera sur les raisons qui l'ont poussé à le faire.

insignia [ɪn'sɪgnɪə] *npl* insignes *mpl*.

insignificance [ˌɪnsɪg'nɪfɪkəns] *n* insignifiance *f*; *V* **pale**[1].

insignificant [ˌɪnsɪg'nɪfɪkənt] *adj detail, fact, person* insignifiant, sans importance; *amount, quantity* insignifiant, négligeable.

insincere [ˌɪnsɪn'sɪəʳ] *adj person* de mauvaise foi, hypocrite, insincère (*liter*); *smile, remark* faux (*f* fausse), hypocrite.

insincerity [ˌɪnsɪn'serɪtɪ] *n* manque *m* de sincérité, fausseté *f*, hypocrisie *f*.

insinuate [ɪn'sɪnjʊeɪt] *vt* (a) insinuer (*into* dans). **to ~ o.s. into sb's favour** s'insinuer dans les bonnes grâces de qn.

(b) (*hint, suggest*) laisser entendre, insinuer (*sth to sb* qch à qn, *that* que); sous-entendre (*sth* qch, *that* que). **what are you insinuating?** que voulez-vous dire *or* insinuer par là?

insinuating [ɪn'sɪnjʊeɪtɪŋ] *adj* insinuant.

insinuation [ɪnˌsɪnjʊ'eɪʃən] *n* (a) (*U*) insinuation *f*. (b) (*suggestion*) insinuation *f*, allusion *f*, sous-entendu *m*.

insipid [ɪn'sɪpɪd] *adj* insipide, fade.

insipidity [ˌɪnsɪ'pɪdɪtɪ] *n* insipidité *f*, fadeur *f*.

insist [ɪn'sɪst] 1 *vi* (*demand, urge*) insister; (*stress*) insister, appuyer. **to ~ on doing** insister pour faire, vouloir absolument faire, tenir à faire; **I ~ on your coming** je veux absolument que tu viennes; **he ~ed on my waiting for him** il a tenu à ce que *or* insisté pour que je l'attende; **they ~ed on silence/our help** ils ont exigé le silence/notre aide; **if you ~** si vous insistez, si vous y tenez; **I shan't ~ if you object** si vous avez des objections je n'insisterai pas; **please don't ~, I should like to pay for it!** inutile d'insister, je tiens à le payer!; **if he refuses, I will ~** s'il refuse, j'insisterai; **he ~s on the justice of his claim** il affirme *or* soutient *or* maintient que sa revendication est juste; **to ~ on a point in a discussion** appuyer *or* insister sur un point dans une discussion.

2 *vt* (a) insister. **I must ~ that you let me help** j'insiste pour que tu me permettes d'aider; **she ~ed that I should come** elle a insisté pour que je vienne; **I ~ that you should come** je veux absolument que tu viennes.

(b) affirmer, soutenir, maintenir. **he ~s that he has seen her before** il affirme *or* soutient *or* maintient qu'il l'a déjà vue.

insistence [ɪn'sɪstəns] *n* insistance *f*. **his ~ on coming with me** l'insistance qu'il met (*or* a mis *etc*) à vouloir venir avec moi; **his ~ on his innocence** ses protestations *fpl* d'innocence; **with ~** avec insistance, avec instance; **I did it on** *or* **at his ~** je l'ai fait parce qu'il a insisté.

insistent [ɪn'sɪstənt] *adj person* insistant, pressant; *demands etc* instant, insistant, pressant. **he was most ~ about it** il a beaucoup insisté là-dessus, il a été très pressant; **... he said in ~ tones ...** dit-il d'une voix pressante.

insistently [ɪn'sɪstəntlɪ] *adv* avec insistance, avec instance, instamment; (*repeatedly*) avec insistance, à maintes reprises.

insolence ['ɪnsələns] *n* (*U*) insolence *f* (*to* envers).

insolent ['ɪnsələnt] *adj* insolent (*to* envers).

insolently ['ɪnsələntlɪ] *adv* insolemment.

insolubility [ɪnˌsɒljʊ'bɪlɪtɪ] *n* insolubilité *f*.

insoluble [ɪn'sɒljʊbl] *adj* insoluble.

insolvable [ɪn'sɒlvəbl] *adj* insoluble.

insolvency [ɪn'sɒlvənsɪ] *n* insolvabilité *f*; (*bankruptcy*) faillite *f*.

insolvent [ɪn'sɒlvənt] *adj* (a) (*Fin*) insolvable.

(b) (*Jur*) en faillite. **to become ~** *[trader etc]* tomber en *or* faire faillite; *[individual]* tomber en déconfiture; **to declare oneself ~** *[trader etc]* déposer son bilan; *[individual]* se déclarer insolvable.

insomnia [ɪn'sɒmnɪə] *n* insomnie *f*.

insomniac [ɪn'sɒmnɪæk] *adj, n* insomniaque (*mf*).

insomuch [ˌɪnsəʊ'mʌtʃ] *adv*: **~ that** à tel point *or* au point *or* tellement que; **~ as** d'autant que.

insouciance [ɪn'suːsɪəns] *n* insouciance *f*.

inspect [ɪn'spekt] *vt* (a) (*examine*) *document, object* examiner (avec attention *or* de près), inspecter; *ticket* contrôler; *machinery* inspecter, vérifier; *school, teacher* inspecter. (b) *troops etc* (*check*) inspecter; (*review*) passer en revue.

inspection [ɪn'spekʃən] 1 *n* (a) *[document, object]* examen *m* (attentif); *[ticket]* contrôle *m*; *[machinery]* vérification *f*, inspection *f*; *[school]* (visite *f* d')inspection. **close ~** (*gen*) examen minutieux; (*for checking purposes*) inspection; **customs ~** visite douanière *or* de douane; **factory ~** inspection d'usine; **on ~ everything proved normal** une vérification a permis de s'assurer que tout était normal.

(b) *[troops etc]* (*check*) inspection *f*; (*review*) revue *f*.

2 *cpd*: (*Aut*) **inspection pit** fosse *f* (à réparations).

inspector [ɪn'spektəʳ] *n* *[schools, police etc]* inspecteur *m*, -trice *f*; (*on bus, train*) contrôleur *m*, -euse *f*. **~ general** inspecteur général.

inspectorate [ɪn'spektərɪt] *n* (*body of inspectors*) corps *m* des inspecteurs, inspection *f*; (*office*) inspection *f*.

inspiration [ˌɪnspə'reɪʃən] *n* (a) (*U*) inspiration *f*. **to draw one's ~ from** s'inspirer de.

(b) *[person, thing]* **to be an ~ to sb** être une source d'inspiration pour qn; **you've been an ~ to us all** vous avez été notre source d'inspiration à tous.

(c) (*good idea*) inspiration *f*. **to have a sudden ~** avoir une inspiration subite.

inspire [ɪn'spaɪəʳ] *vt person, work of art, action, decision* inspirer. **to ~ confidence in sb, to ~ sb with confidence** inspirer confiance à qn; **to ~ courage in sb** insuffler du courage à qn; **to ~ sb with an idea** inspirer une idée à qn; **her beauty ~d him** *or* **he was ~d by her beauty to write the song** inspiré par sa beauté il a écrit la chanson; **what ~d you to offer to help?** qu'est-ce qui vous a donné l'idée de *or* où avez-vous pris l'idée de proposer votre aide?; **an ~d poet/book** un poète/livre inspiré; **in an ~d moment** dans un moment d'inspiration; **an ~d idea** une inspiration.

inspiring [ɪn'spaɪərɪŋ] *adj book, poem etc* qui suscite l'inspiration. **this subject isn't particularly ~** ce sujet n'a rien de particulièrement inspirant.

instability [ˌɪnstə'bɪlɪtɪ] *n* instabilité *f*.

install [ɪn'stɔːl] *vt* (*also Rel*) installer. **to ~ o.s. in** s'installer dans.

installation [ˌɪnstə'leɪʃən] *n* (*all senses*) installation *f*.

instalment, (*US*) **installment** [ɪn'stɔːlmənt] 1 *n* (a) (*Comm*) acompte *m*, versement partiel. **to pay an ~** faire un versement partiel, verser un acompte *or* des arrhes *fpl*; **to pay in ~s** *or* **by ~s** payer en plusieurs versements *or* par acomptes *or* par traites échelonnées; **~ on account** acompte provisionnel; **monthly ~** versement *or* acompte mensuel.

(b) *[story, serial]* épisode *m*; *[book]* fascicule *m*, livraison *f*. (*TV etc*) **this is the first ~ of a 6-part serial** voici le premier épisode d'un feuilleton qui en comportera 6; **this story will appear in ~s over the next 8 weeks** ce récit paraîtra par épisodes pendant les 8 semaines à venir; **to publish a work in ~s** publier un ouvrage par fascicules.

2 *cpd*: **instalment plan** système *m* de crédit, vente *f* à tempérament; **to buy on the instalment plan** acheter à tempérament.

instance ['ɪnstəns] 1 *n* (a) (*example*) exemple *m*, cas *m*; (*occasion*) circonstance *f*, occasion *f*. **for ~** par exemple; **in the present ~** dans le cas actuel *or* présent, dans cette circonstance; **in many ~s** dans bien des cas; **in the first ~** en premier lieu; **as an ~ of** comme exemple de; **let's take an actual ~** prenons un exemple *or* un cas concret; **this is an ~ of what I was talking about** c'est un exemple de ce dont je parlais.

(b) (*Jur*) **at the ~ of** sur *or* à la demande de, sur l'instance de.

2 *vt* (*cite*) donner en exemple, citer en exemple; (*exemplify*) illustrer.

instant ['ɪnstənt] 1 *adj* (a) *obedience, relief* immédiat, instantané; *need* urgent, pressant. **this calls for ~ action** ceci nécessite des mesures immédiates; (*US TV*) **~ replay** répétition immédiate (*d'une séquence*).

(b) (*Culin*) *coffee* soluble; *potatoes* déshydraté; *food* à préparation rapide. **~ soup** potage *m* (instantané) en poudre.

(c) (*Comm*) courant. **your letter of the 10th inst(ant)** votre lettre du 10 courant.

2 *n* instant *m*, moment *m*. **come here this ~** viens ici tout de suite *or* immédiatement *or* à l'instant; **on the ~** tout de suite, à l'instant, immédiatement, sur-le-champ; **I did it in an ~** je l'ai fait en un instant; **I'll be ready in an ~** je serai prêt dans un instant; **he left the ~ he heard the news** il est parti dès qu'il *or* aussitôt qu'il a appris la nouvelle.

instantaneous [ˌɪnstən'teɪnɪəs] *adj* instantané.

instantaneously [ˌɪnstən'teɪnɪəslɪ] *adv* instantanément.

instantly ['ɪnstəntlɪ] *adv* à l'instant, sur-le-champ, immédiatement, tout de suite.

instead [ɪn'sted] *adv* au lieu de cela, à la place, plutôt. **the water**

is not good, drink wine ~ l'eau n'est pas bonne, buvez plutôt du vin; **if he isn't going, I shall go** ~ s'il n'y va pas, j'irai à sa place; **I didn't go home, I went to the pictures** ~ je ne suis pas rentré, au lieu de cela je suis allé au cinéma; ~ **of** au lieu de; ~ **of going to school** au lieu d'aller à l'école; ~ **of sb** à la place de qn; **his brother came** ~ **of him** son frère est venu à sa place; **this is** ~ **of a birthday present** ceci tient lieu de cadeau d'anniversaire.

instep ['ɪnstep] *n* **(a)** (*Anat*) cou-de-pied *m*. **to have a high** ~ avoir le pied cambré. **(b)** *[shoe]* cambrure *f*.

instigate ['ɪnstɪgeɪt] *vt* inciter, pousser (*sb to do* qn à faire); *rebellion etc* fomenter, provoquer, susciter.

instigation [ˌɪnstɪ'geɪʃən] *n* instigation *f*, incitation *f*. **at sb's** ~ à l'instigation de qn.

instigator ['ɪnstɪgeɪtəʳ] *n* instigateur *m*, -trice *f*; *[riot, plot]* auteur *m*.

instil [ɪn'stɪl] *vt courage etc* insuffler (*into sb* à qn); *knowledge* inculquer (*into sb* à qn).

instinct ['ɪnstɪŋkt] **1** *n* instinct *m*. **by** *or* **from** ~ d'instinct; **to have an** ~ **for business** *or* **a good business** ~ avoir l'instinct des affaires. **2** [ɪn'stɪŋkt] *adj* (*liter*) ~ **with** qui exhale *or* respire (*liter*), plein de.

instinctive [ɪn'stɪŋktɪv] *adj* instinctif.

instinctively [ɪn'stɪŋktɪvlɪ] *adv* instinctivement, d'instinct.

institute ['ɪnstɪtjuːt] **1** *vt* **(a)** (*establish*) instituer, établir; (*found*) fonder, créer, constituer. **newly** ~**d** *post* récemment créé, de création récente; *organization* de fondation récente.

(b) (*Jur etc*) *inquiry* ouvrir; *action* entreprendre (*against sb* à qn); *proceedings* entamer (*against sb* contre qn).

(c) (*Rel*) investir.

2 *n* institut *m*.

institution [ˌɪnstɪ'tjuːʃən] *n* **(a)** (*U: V* **institute 1**) institution *f*, établissement *m*; fondation *f*, constitution *f*; (*Jur*) *[action, proceedings]* mise *f* en train; (*Rel*) investiture *f*.

(b) (*organization*) établissement *m*, organisme *m*; (*school, college*) établissement, (*private*) institution *f*; (*mental hospital*) hôpital *m* psychiatrique; (*hospital*) hôpital; (*workhouse etc*) asile *m*, hospice *m*. **he has been in** ~**s all his adult life** il a passé toute sa vie d'adulte dans des établissements hospitaliers (*etc*).

(c) (*long-established structure, custom etc*) institution *f*. **the family is an important** ~ la famille est une institution importante; **the morning coffee break is too much of an** ~ **to abolish** la pause café matinale est une telle institution qu'il serait impossible de la supprimer; **tea is a British** ~ le thé est une institution britannique; **he's been with the firm so long that he's now an** ~* il fait partie de la compagnie depuis si longtemps qu'il en est devenu une véritable institution.

institutional [ˌɪnstɪ'tjuːʃənl] *adj* **(a)** *reform etc* institutionnel; (*St Ex*) *buying, selling* de(s) grands organismes. **she needs** ~ **care** (*in hospital*) elle a besoin de soins hospitaliers; (*in old people's home*) elle a besoin d'être placée dans une maison de retraite; ~ **life** la vie (organisée) d'un établissement (*d'ordre social, médical ou pédagogique*); ~ **life in hospital/in prison** la vie réglementée de l'hôpital/de la prison.

(b) (*fig pej*) *food* d'internat; *furniture, aspect* d'hospice.

(c) (*US*) ~ **advertising** promotion *f* de l'image de marque.

institutionalize [ˌɪnstɪ'tjuːʃnəlaɪz] *vt* **(a)** *person* placer dans un établissement (*d'ordre médical ou social*). (*pej*) **to become** ~**d** être marqué par la vie en collectivité. **(b)** *procedure etc* institutionnaliser.

instruct [ɪn'strʌkt] *vt* **(a)** (*teach*) *person* instruire. **to** ~ **sb in sth** instruire qn en qch, enseigner *or* apprendre qch à qn; **to** ~ **sb in how to do sth** enseigner *or* apprendre à qn comment (il faut) faire qch.

(b) (*order, direct*) *person* donner des instructions *or* des ordres à. **to** ~ **sb to do** charger qn de faire, ordonner à qn de faire; (*frm*) **I am** ~**ed to inform you that ...** j'ai mission de vous informer que ... .

(c) (*Jur*) (*Brit*) **to** ~ **a solicitor** donner ses instructions à un notaire; **to** ~ **counsel** constituer avocat; *[judge]* **to** ~ **the jury** donner des instructions au jury (*to do* pour qu'il fasse).

instruction [ɪn'strʌkʃən] **1** *n* **(a)** (*U: teaching*) instruction *f*, enseignement *m*. **to give** ~ **to sb (in sth)** instruire qn (en qch); **driving** ~ leçons *fpl* de conduite.

(b) (*gen pl*) ~**s** directives *fpl*, instructions *fpl*; (*Mil*) consigne *f*; (*Comm, Pharm, Tech*) indications *fpl*; (*Comm, Tech: on packet etc*) **'**~**s for use'** 'mode d'emploi'; (*Comm, Tech*) **the** ~**s are on the back of the box** le mode d'emploi est (indiqué) au dos de la boîte; **he gave me careful** ~**s on what to do if ...** il m'a donné des directives *or* des instructions précises sur ce qu'il faut faire au cas où ...; **I gave** ~**s for him to be brought to me** j'ai donné des instructions *or* des directives pour qu'on me l'amène (*subj*); **he gave me** ~**s not to leave until ...** il m'a donné des instructions selon lesquelles je ne devais pas partir avant ...; **to act according to** ~**s** se conformer à la consigne.

2 *cpd*: (*Comm, Tech*) **instruction book** manuel *m* d'entretien.

instructive [ɪn'strʌktɪv] *adj speech, report* instructif; *book* éducatif.

instructor [ɪn'strʌktəʳ] *n* **(a)** maître *m*, professeur *m*; (*Mil*) instructeur *m*; (*Ski*) moniteur *m*. **the geography/tennis** ~ le professeur de géographie/de tennis; *V* **driving** *etc.* **(b)** (*US Univ*) ≃ maître assistant *m*.

instructress [ɪn'strʌktrɪs] *n* maîtresse *f*, professeur *m*; (*Ski*) monitrice *f*.

instrument ['ɪnstrʊmənt] **1** *n* (*Med, Mus, Tech etc*) instrument *m*; (*domestic*) ustensile *m*; (*fig*) instrument; (*Jur*) instrument, acte *m* juridique. **to fly by** *or* **on** ~**s** naviguer aux instruments; ~ **of government** instrument du gouvernement; *V* **blunt, wind**[1] *etc.*

2 *cpd* (*Aviat*) *flying, landing* aux instruments (de bord). (*Aut, Aviat*) **instrument board** tableau *m* de bord; (*Aviat, US Aut*) **instrument panel** = **instrument board.**

3 [ˌɪnstrʊ'ment] *vt* (*Mus*) orchestrer; (*Jur*) instrumenter.

instrumental [ˌɪnstrʊ'mentl] *adj* **(a)** **to be** ~ **in** contribuer à, être pour quelque chose dans; **he was** ~ **in founding the organization** il a contribué à la fondation de *or* à fonder l'organisation.

(b) (*Mus*) instrumental. ~ **music** musique instrumentale; ~ **performer** instrumentiste *mf*.

instrumentalist [ˌɪnstrʊ'mentəlɪst] *n* (*Mus*) instrumentiste *mf*.

instrumentation [ˌɪnstrʊmen'teɪʃən] *n* (*Mus*) orchestration *f*; (*Jur*) instrumentation *f*.

insubordinate [ˌɪnsə'bɔːdənɪt] *adj* insubordonné, indiscipliné.

insubordination ['ɪnsəˌbɔːdɪ'neɪʃən] *n* insubordination *f*, indiscipline *f*, désobéissance *f*.

insubstantial [ˌɪnsəb'stænʃəl] *adj meal, work* peu substantiel; *structure* peu solide, léger; *argument* peu solide, sans substance; *evidence* insuffisant; (*unreal*) *vision etc* imaginaire, chimérique, irréel.

insufferable [ɪn'sʌfərəbl] *adj* insupportable, intolérable.

insufferably [ɪn'sʌfərəblɪ] *adv* insupportablement, intolérablement. ~ **rude** d'une grossièreté intolérable.

insufficiency [ˌɪnsə'fɪʃənsɪ] *n* insuffisance *f*.

insufficient [ˌɪnsə'fɪʃənt] *adj* insuffisant.

insufficiently [ˌɪnsə'fɪʃəntlɪ] *adv* insuffisamment.

insular ['ɪnsjələʳ] *adj* (*lit*) *administration, climate* insulaire; *attitude* d'insulaire; (*fig pej*) *mind, outlook* borné, étriqué; *person* aux vues étroites.

insularity [ˌɪnsjʊ'lærɪtɪ] *n* insularité *f*; (*fig pej*) *[person]* étroitesse *f* d'esprit; *[outlook, views]* étroitesse.

insulate ['ɪnsjʊleɪt] *vt* (*Elec*) isoler; (*against cold, heat*) *room, roof* isoler; *water tank* calorifuger; (*against sound*) *room, wall* insonoriser; (*fig*) *person* (*separate*) séparer (*from* de); (*protect*) protéger (*against* de). ~**d handle** manche isolant; ~**d pliers** pince isolante; **insulating material** isolant *m*; (*Brit*) **insulating tape** (ruban *m*) isolant *m*, (*adhesive*) chatterton *m*.

insulation [ˌɪnsjʊ'leɪʃən] *n* **(a)** (*U*) *[house, room]* (*against cold*) calorifugeage *m*, isolation *f* (calorifuge); (*against sound*) insonorisation *f*. **the** ~ **in this house is bad** l'isolation de cette maison est défectueuse. **(b)** (*U: material*) isolant *m*.

insulator ['ɪnsjʊleɪtəʳ] *n* (*Elec*) (*device*) isolateur *m*; (*material*) isolant *m*.

insulin ['ɪnsjʊlɪn] **1** *n* insuline *f*. **2** *cpd treatment* à l'insuline; *injection* d'insuline. (*Med*) **insulin shock** choc *m* insulinique; **insulin treatment** insulinothérapie *f*.

insult [ɪn'sʌlt] **1** *vt* insulter, injurier; faire (un) affront à.

2 ['ɪnsʌlt] *n* insulte *f*, injure *f*, affront *m*. **the book is an** ~ **to the reader's intelligence** le livre est une insulte à *or* fait affront à l'intelligence du lecteur; **these demands are an** ~ **to the profession** ces revendications sont un affront à la profession; *V* **add.**

insulting [ɪn'sʌltɪŋ] *adj* insultant, injurieux, offensant. **to use** ~ **language to sb** adresser à qn des paroles offensantes *or* injurieuses *or* insultantes.

insultingly [ɪn'sʌltɪŋlɪ] *adv* d'un ton *or* d'une voix insultant(e); d'une manière insultante.

insuperable [ɪn'suːpərəbl] *adj* insurmontable.

insuperably [ɪn'suːpərəblɪ] *adv* d'une façon insurmontable.

insupportable [ˌɪnsə'pɔːtəbl] *adj* insupportable, intolérable.

insurable [ɪn'ʃʊərəbl] *adj* assurable.

insurance [ɪn'ʃʊərəns] **1** *n* (*on life, against fire etc*) assurance *f*. **he pays £30 a year in** ~ il paie 30 livres (de primes) d'assurance par an; **to take out (an)** ~ **against** s'assurer contre, se faire assurer contre; **he buys property as an** ~ **against inflation** il achète de l'immobilier pour se protéger de l'inflation; *V* **fire, life** *etc.*

2 *cpd*: **insurance agent** agent *m* d'assurances; **insurance broker** courtier *m* d'assurances; (*Aut*) **insurance certificate** carte *f* d'assurance (automobile); **insurance company** compagnie *f* *or* société *f* d'assurances; **to work in an insurance office** travailler pour une compagnie d'assurances; **insurance policy** police *f* d'assurance, assurances* *fpl*; **insurance premium** prime *f* (d'assurance); **insurance scheme** régime *m* d'assurances; (*Brit Admin*) **insurance stamp** vignette *f* *or* timbre *m* de contribution à la Sécurité sociale.

insure [ɪn'ʃʊəʳ] *vt* **(a)** *car, house* (faire) assurer. **to** ~ **o.s.** *or* **one's life** s'assurer *or* se faire assurer sur la vie, prendre une assurance-vie; **I am** ~**d against fire** je suis assuré contre l'incendie; **the** ~**d** l'assuré(e) *m(f)*; (*fig*) **we** ~**d (ourselves) against possible disappointment** nous avons paré aux déceptions possibles; **in order to** ~ **against any delay** ... pour nous (*or* les *etc*) garantir contre les délais ... .

(b) *power, success* assurer, garantir. **this will** ~ **that you will be notified when ...** grâce à ceci vous êtes assuré d'être averti quand ... .

insurer [ɪn'ʃʊərəʳ] *n* assureur *m*.

insurgent [ɪn'sɜːdʒənt] *adj, n* insurgé(e) *m(f)*, révolté(e) *m(f)*.

insurmountable [ˌɪnsə'maʊntəbl] *adj* insurmontable.

insurrection [ˌɪnsə'rekʃən] *n* **(a)** (*U*) insurrection *f*. **to rise in** ~ se soulever, s'insurger. **(b)** (*uprising*) insurrection *f*, émeute *f*, soulèvement *m*.

insurrectionary [ˌɪnsə'rekʃnərɪ] *adj* insurrectionnel.

insurrectionist [ˌɪnsə'rekʃənɪst] *n* insurgé(e) *m(f)*.

intact [ɪn'tækt] *adj* intact.

intake ['ɪnteɪk] **1** *n* **(a)** (*U: Tech*) *[water]* prise *f*, adduction *f*; *[gas, steam]* adduction, admission *f*. **air** ~ admission d'air.

(b) (*Scol, Univ*) admission(s) *f(pl)*; (*Mil*) contingent *m*, recrues *fpl*.

(c) *[protein, liquid etc]* consommation *f*. **food** ~ *[animals]* ration *f* alimentaire; *[person]* consommation de nourriture.

2 *cpd*: (*Scol*) intake class cours *m* préparatoire; (*Tech*) intake valve soupape *f* d'admission.

intangible [ɪn'tændʒəbl] 1 *adj* intangible, impalpable. (*Jur*) ~ property biens incorporels; (*Jur*) ~ assets valeurs immatérielles. 2 *n* impondérable *m*.

integer ['ɪntɪdʒəʳ] *n* nombre entier.

integral ['ɪntɪgrəl] 1 *adj* (a) *part* intégrant, constituant. to be an ~ part of sth faire partie intégrante de qch.
(b) (*whole*) intégral, complet (*f*-ète), entier. ~ payment paiement intégral.
(c) (*Math*) intégral. ~ calculus calcul intégral.
2 *n* (*Math, fig*) intégrale *f*.

integrate ['ɪntɪgreɪt] 1 *vt* (a) (*combine into a whole*) *people, objects, ideas* intégrer; incorporer (*in, into* dans).
(b) (*complete by adding parts*) compléter. (*Psych*) an ~d personality une personnalité bien intégrée.
(c) (*combine, desegregate*) *races, religions, ethnic groups etc* intégrer, unifier. to ~ Catholic and non-Catholic schools intégrer *or* unifier les établissements catholiques et non-catholiques; (*US*) to ~ a school *etc* imposer la déségrégation raciale dans un établissement scolaire *etc*; (*US*) ~d school établissement scolaire où se pratique la déségrégation raciale.
(d) (*Math*) intégrer.
2 *vi* (a) (*US: racially*) *[school, neighbourhood etc]* pratiquer la déségrégation raciale.
(b) *[person, religious or ethnic group etc]* s'intégrer (*into* dans).

integration [ˌɪntɪ'greɪʃən] *n* (*V* integrate) intégration *f* (*also Math, Psych*); incorporation *f*; unification *f*. racial ~, (*US*) ~ déségrégation raciale; the ~ of the country's various ethnic groups l'intégration des divers groupes ethniques du pays.

integrity [ɪn'tegrɪtɪ] *n* (a) (*honesty*) intégrité *f*, honnêteté *f*, probité *f*. man of ~ homme *m* intègre. (b) (*totality*) intégrité *f*, totalité *f*. in its ~ dans son intégrité, dans sa totalité, en entier; territorial ~ l'intégrité du territoire.

integument [ɪn'tegjʊmənt] *n* tégument *m*.

intellect ['ɪntɪlekt] *n* (a) (*U*) (*reasoning power*) intellect *m*, intelligence *f*; (*cleverness*) intelligence, esprit *m*. a man of (great) ~ un homme d'une grande intelligence. (b) (*person*) intelligence *f*, esprit *m*.

intellectual [ˌɪntɪ'lektjʊəl] *adj, n* intellectuel(le) *m(f)*.

intelligence [ɪn'telɪdʒəns] 1 *n* (*U*) (a) intelligence *f*. man of little ~ homme peu intelligent; he shows ~ il fait preuve d'intelligence; his book shows ~ son livre est intelligent.
(b) (*information*) renseignement(s) *m(pl)*, information(s) *f(pl)*. (*Press*) latest ~ informations de dernière minute.
(c) Military/Naval I~ service *m* de renseignements de l'armée de Terre/de la Marine; he was in I~ during the war il était dans les services de renseignements pendant la guerre.
2 *cpd*: intelligence agent agent *m* de renseignements, agent secret; (*Brit Mil*) Intelligence Corps *arme f du service de renseignements et de sécurité militaires*; Intelligence officer officier *m* du deuxième bureau *or* de renseignements; intelligence quotient quotient intellectuel; (*Pol*) Intelligence Service service secret *or* de renseignements; intelligence test test *m* d'aptitude intellectuelle; to do intelligence work être dans *or* travailler dans les services de renseignements, être agent secret.

intelligent [ɪn'telɪdʒənt] *adj* intelligent.

intelligently [ɪn'telɪdʒəntlɪ] *adv* intelligemment, avec intelligence.

intelligentsia [ɪnˌtelɪ'dʒentsɪə] *n* (*collective sg*) the ~ l'intelligentsia *f*, l'élite *f* intellectuelle.

intelligibility [ɪnˌtelɪdʒə'bɪlɪtɪ] *n* intelligibilité *f*.

intelligible [ɪn'telɪdʒəbl] *adj* intelligible.

intelligibly [ɪn'telɪdʒəblɪ] *adv* intelligiblement.

intemperance [ɪn'tempərəns] *n* (*lack of moderation*) manque *m* de modération; (*drunkenness*) ivrognerie *f*.

intemperate [ɪn'tempərɪt] *adj climate* sévère, peu clément, rigoureux; *wind* violent; *haste, zeal* excessif; *person* (*lacking moderation*) immodéré; (*drinking too much*) adonné à la boisson.

intend [ɪn'tend] *vt* avoir l'intention, se proposer, projeter (*to do, doing* de faire), penser (*to do* faire); *gift etc* destiner (*for* à). I ~ going to see him *or* to go and see him j'ai l'intention d'aller le voir, je pense aller le voir; I didn't ~ to let him know je n'avais pas l'intention de lui en parler; I ~ him to go with me, I ~ that he should go with me j'ai (bien) l'intention qu'il m'accompagne (*subj*); I fully ~ to punish him j'ai la ferme intention de le punir; he ~s to be a doctor il a l'intention de *or* il projette de faire médecine, il se destine à la médecine; we ~ him to be a doctor nous le destinons à la médecine; this scheme is ~ed to help the poor ce projet est destiné à venir en aide aux indigents; he ~ed that remark for you sa remarque était à votre intention, c'est à vous qu'il destinait *or* adressait cette observation; I ~ it as a present for Robert c'est un cadeau que je destine à Robert; I ~ed it as a compliment (dans mon esprit) cela voulait être un compliment; he ~ed no harm il l'a fait sans mauvaise intention; to ~ marriage avoir des intentions de mariage; what do you ~ by that? que voulez-vous dire par là?; did you ~ that? est-ce que vous avez fait cela exprès? *or* à dessein? *or* avec intention?; *V also* intended.

intended [ɪn'tendɪd] 1 *adj* (a) (*deliberate*) *insult etc* intentionnel, fait intentionnellement. (b) (*planned*) *journey, enterprise* projeté; *effect* voulu. 2 *n* (†) his ~ sa promise †, sa future (*hum*); her ~ son promis †, son futur (*hum*).

intense [ɪn'tens] *adj cold, heat, sunlight* intense; *hatred, love, rage* intense, violent, profond; *enthusiasm, interest* vif, énorme; *person, tone* véhément. ~ expression (*interested*) expression concentrée *or* d'intérêt profond; (*fervent*) expression exaltée *or* d'intense ferveur; I find her too ~ je la trouve trop véhémente.

intensely [ɪn'tenslɪ] *adv* (a) *live, look* intensément, avec intensité. (b) profondément, extrêmement. ~ moved profondément ému; it was ~ cold il faisait extrêmement froid.

intensification [ɪnˌtensɪfɪ'keɪʃən] *n [heat]* intensification *f*; *[production]* accélération *f*, intensification; (*Mil*) *[fighting]* intensification; (*Phot*) renforcement *m*.

intensify [ɪn'tensɪfaɪ] 1 *vt* intensifier, augmenter; (*Mil*) *fighting* intensifier; *colour* intensifier, renforcer; *sound* intensifier. 2 *vi* s'intensifier, augmenter.

intensity [ɪn'tensɪtɪ] *n [anger, hatred, love]* intensité *f*, force *f*, violence *f*; *[cold, heat]* intensité; *[current, light, sound]* intensité, puissance *f*; *[tone]* véhémence *f*. her ~ disturbs me sa véhémence me met mal à l'aise.

intensive [ɪn'tensɪv] *adj* (*also Ling*) intensif. ~ course in French cours accéléré *or* intensif de français; (*Med*) ~ care unit service *m* de réanimation.

intensively [ɪn'tensɪvlɪ] *adv* intensivement.

intent [ɪn'tent] 1 *n* intention *f*, dessein *m*, projet *m*. to all ~s and purposes en fait, pratiquement, virtuellement; with ~ to do dans l'intention *or* dans le dessein *or* dans le but de faire; with good ~ dans une bonne intention; to do sth with ~ faire qch de propos délibéré; (*Jur*) with criminal ~ dans un but délictueux; *V* loiter.
2 *adj* attentif, absorbé. ~ stare regard *m* fixe; he was ~ on his work il était absorbé par son travail; ~ on revenge résolu *or* (bien) décidé à se venger; I am ~ on leaving je suis résolu *or* (bien) décidé à partir, j'ai la ferme intention de partir; he was so ~ on catching the bus that he didn't see the car dans sa préoccupation d'attraper l'autobus il n'a pas vu la voiture.

intention [in'tenʃən] *n* intention *f*, but *m*, dessein *m*. to have the ~ of doing avoir l'intention de faire; to have no ~ of doing n'avoir aucune intention de faire; I haven't the least *or* slightest ~ of staying je n'ai pas la moindre intention de rester ici, il n'est nullement dans mes intentions de rester ici; with the ~ of doing dans l'intention de *or* dans le but de *or* dans le dessein de faire; with this ~ à cette intention, à cette fin; with good ~s avec de bonnes intentions; with the best of ~s avec les meilleures intentions (du monde); what are your ~s? quelles sont vos intentions?, que comptez-vous faire?; I don't know what his ~s were when he did it je ne sais pas quelles étaient ses intentions *or* quel était son dessein *or* quel était son but quand il l'a fait; she thinks his ~s are honourable elle pense qu'il a des intentions honorables.

intentional [ɪn'tenʃənl] *adj* intentionnel, voulu, délibéré. it wasn't ~ ce n'était pas fait exprès, je ne l'ai (*or* il ne l'a *etc*) pas fait exprès.

intentionally [ɪn'tenʃnəlɪ] *adv* intentionnellement. the wording was ~ vague l'imprécision de l'énoncé était voulue *or* intentionnelle; he did it ~ il l'a fait exprès *or* intentionnellement *or* de propos délibéré *or* à dessein.

intently [ɪn'tentlɪ] *adv listen, look* avec une vive attention.

inter [ɪn'tɜːʳ] *vt* enterrer, ensevelir.

inter... ['ɪntəʳ] *pref* inter... . ~-schools interscolaire.

interact [ˌɪntər'ækt] *vi* (ré)agir réciproquement, avoir une action réciproque.

interaction [ˌɪntər'ækʃən] *n* interaction *f*.

interbreed ['ɪntə'briːd] *pret, ptp* interbred 1 *vt animals* croiser. 2 *vi* se croiser (*with* avec).

intercalate [ɪn'tɜːkəleɪt] *vt* intercaler.

intercalation [ɪnˌtɜːkə'leɪʃən] *n* intercalation *f*.

intercede [ˌɪntə'siːd] *vi* intercéder (*with* auprès de, *for* pour, en faveur de).

intercept [ˌɪntə'sept] *vt message, light* intercepter, capter; *plane, suspect* intercepter; *person* arrêter au passage.

interception [ˌɪntə'sepʃən] *n* interception *f*.

interceptor [ˌɪntə'septəʳ] *n* (*Aviat*) intercepteur *m*.

intercession [ˌɪntə'seʃən] *n* intercession *f*.

interchange ['ɪntəˌtʃeɪndʒ] 1 *n* (a) (*U*) (*exchange*) échange *m*; (*alternation*) alternance *f*.
(b) (*on motorway*) échangeur *m*.
2 [ˌɪntə'tʃeɪndʒ] *vt* (*exchange*) *gifts, letters, ideas* échanger (*with sb* avec qn); (*alternate*) faire alterner (*with* avec); (*change positions of*) changer de place, mettre à la place l'un de l'autre.

interchangeable [ˌɪntə'tʃeɪndʒəbl] *adj* interchangeable.

intercollegiate ['ɪntəkə'liːdʒɪɪt] *adj* entre collèges.

intercom ['ɪntəkɒm] *n* interphone *m*.

intercommunicate [ˌɪntəkə'mjuːnɪkeɪt] *vi* communiquer (réciproquement).

intercommunication ['ɪntəkəˌmjuːnɪ'keɪʃən] *n* intercommunication *f*, communication *f* réciproque.

intercommunion [ˌɪntəkə'mjuːnɪən] *n* (*Rel*) intercommunion *f*; (*gen*) intercommunication *f*.

interconnect [ˌɪntəkə'nekt] 1 *vt* connecter (entre eux *or* elles). ~ed facts faits intimement *or* étroitement liés; ~ed rooms pièces communicantes. 2 *vi [rooms]* communiquer (entre eux *or* elles).

intercontinental ['ɪntəˌkɒntɪ'nentl] *adj* intercontinental.

intercourse ['ɪntəkɔːs] *n* (*U*) (a) relations *fpl*, rapports *mpl*, commerce *m*. business ~ relations commerciales; human ~ relations humaines. (b) (sexual) ~ rapports *mpl* (sexuels); to have ~ avoir des rapports (*with* avec).

interdenominational ['ɪntədɪˌnɒmɪ'neɪʃənl] *adj* entre confessions, interconfessionnel.

interdepartmental ['ɪntəˌdiːpɑːt'mentl] *adj* (*within firm*) entre services; (*within ministry*) entre départements.

interdependence [ˌɪntədɪ'pendəns] *n* interdépendance *f*.

interdependent [ˌɪntədɪ'pendənt] *adj* interdépendant.

interdict [ˈɪntədɪkt] **1** *vt* **(a)** (*Jur, frm*) interdire, prohiber. **(b)** (*Rel*) *priest, person* jeter l'interdit sur. **2** *n* **(a)** (*Jur*) prohibition *f*, interdiction *f*. **(b)** (*Rel*) interdit *m*.

interdiction [ˌɪntəˈdɪkʃən] *n* (*Jur, Rel*) interdiction *f*.

interest [ˈɪntrɪst] **1** *n* **(a)** (*U: understanding etc*) intérêt *m*. **to take** *or* **have** *or* **feel an ~ in sb** s'intéresser à qn; **to take** *or* **have** *or* **feel an ~ in sth** s'intéresser à qch, prendre de l'intérêt à qch; **he took no further ~ in it** il ne s'y est plus intéressé; **to show an ~ in sb/sth** manifester *or* montrer de l'intérêt pour qn/qch; **to take a great ~ in sb/sth** s'intéresser vivement à qn/qch; **to arouse sb's ~** éveiller l'intérêt de qn; **that's of great ~ to me** ceci m'intéresse beaucoup, ceci a beaucoup d'intérêt pour moi; **that's of no ~ to me** ceci ne m'intéresse pas, ceci a peu d'intérêt pour moi; **a subject of little ~** un sujet présentant peu d'intérêt; **questions of public ~** questions d'intérêt public *or* qui intéressent le public (*V also* **1c**); **I'm doing it just for ~** *or* **just for ~'s sake** je le fais seulement parce que cela m'intéresse; **it adds ~ to the story** ça ajoute un certain intérêt à l'histoire; **matters of vital ~** questions d'un intérêt *or* d'une importance capital(e).

(b) (*hobby etc*) **my main ~ is reading** ce qui m'intéresse le plus c'est la lecture; **what are your ~s?** quelles sont les choses qui vous intéressent?, à quoi vous intéressez-vous?

(c) (*advantage, well-being*) intérêt *m*, avantage *m*, profit *m*. **in one's (own) ~(s)** dans son (propre) intérêt; **it is in your own ~ to do so** il est de votre (propre) intérêt d'agir ainsi, vous avez intérêt à agir ainsi; **to act in sb's ~(s)** agir dans l'intérêt de qn *or* au profit de qn *or* pour le compte de qn; **in the ~ of hygiene** par souci d'hygiène; **in the ~ of peace** dans l'intérêt de la paix; **in the public ~** dans l'intérêt public, pour le bien public.

(d) (*Comm, Jur etc: share, stake*) intérêts *mpl*, participation *f*. **I have an ~ in a hairdressing business** j'ai des intérêts dans un salon de coiffure; **he has business ~s abroad** il a des intérêts commerciaux à l'étranger; **Switzerland is looking after British ~s** la Suisse défend les intérêts britanniques; **he has sold his ~ in the company** il a vendu la participation *or* les intérêts qu'il avait dans la compagnie; (*fig*) **we have an ~ in knowing what is to happen** il est de notre intérêt de *or* nous avons intérêt à savoir ce qui va se produire; *V* **vest**[2].

(e) (*people*) **the coal/oil ~(s)** les (gros) intérêts houillers/pétroliers; **shipping ~s** les intérêts maritimes; **the landed ~s** les propriétaires terriens.

(f) (*U: Fin*) intérêt(s) *m(pl)*. **simple/compound ~** intérêts simples/composés; **~ on an investment** intérêts d'un placement; **loan with ~** prêt à intérêt; **to lend at ~** prêter à intérêt; **at an ~ of 10%** à un taux d'intérêt de 10%; **to bear ~** rapporter un intérêt; **to bear ~ at 8%** donner un intérêt de 8%, porter intérêt à 8%.

2 *cpd*: (*Fin*) **interest rate** taux *m* d'intérêt.

3 *vt* **(a)** intéresser. **to be ~ed in sth/sb, to become** *or* **grow** *or* **get ~ed in sth/sb** s'intéresser à qch/qn; **I am not ~ed in football** le football ne m'intéresse pas, je ne m'intéresse pas au football; **the company is ~ed in buying land** cela intéresse la firme d'acheter des terrains; **I am ~ed in going** ça m'intéresse d'y aller; **she was ~ed to see what he would do** cela l'intéressait *or* elle était curieuse de voir ce qu'il ferait; **I am trying to ~ her in our sale of work** j'essaie de lui faire prendre un intérêt actif à notre vente de charité; **his teacher succeeded in ~ing him in geography** son professeur a réussi à l'intéresser *or* à le faire s'intéresser à la géographie; **can I ~ you in this problem?** puis-je attirer votre attention sur ce problème?; **can I ~ you in contributing to ...?** est-ce que cela vous intéresserait de contribuer à ...?

(b) (*concern*) intéresser, concerner, toucher. **the struggle against inflation ~s us all** la lutte contre l'inflation touche chacun d'entre nous *or* nous concerne tous, nous sommes tous intéressés par la lutte contre l'inflation.

interested [ˈɪntrɪstɪd] *adj* (*V also* **interest 3a**) **(a)** (*attentive*) *look, attitude* d'intérêt. **~ spectators** spectateurs intéressés.

(b) (*biased, involved*) *person, motive* intéressé. **~ party** partie intéressée; (*Jur*) ayant droit *m*; **the ~ parties** les intéressés *mpl*; (*Jur*) les ayants droit.

interesting [ˈɪntrɪstɪŋ] *adj story, offer, proposition* intéressant. (*euph*) **she's in an ~ condition*** elle est dans une position intéressante (*euph*).

interestingly [ˈɪntrɪstɪŋlɪ] *adv* de façon intéressante. **~ enough I saw him only yesterday** ce qui est très intéressant, c'est que je l'ai vu pas plus tard qu'hier.

interface [ˈɪntəfeɪs] *n* (*Computers, Tech*) interface *f*.

interfacing [ˈɪntəfeɪsɪŋ] *n* entoilage *m*.

interfere [ˌɪntəˈfɪəʳ] *vi [person]* s'immiscer, s'ingérer (*in* dans); (*Phys*) interférer. **to ~ in a quarrel** s'interposer dans une dispute; **stop interfering!** ne vous mêlez pas de mes (*or* leurs *etc*) affaires!; **he's always interfering** il se mêle toujours de tout, il met *or* fourre* son nez partout; *[weather, accident, circumstances etc]* **to ~ with sb's plans** contrecarrer les *or* entraver les *or* se mettre en travers des projets de qn; **he never allows his hobbies to ~ with his work** il ne laisse jamais ses distractions empiéter sur son travail; **don't ~ with my camera*** ne touche pas à *or* ne tripote pas mon appareil, laisse mon appareil tranquille*.

interference [ˌɪntəˈfɪərəns] *n* (*U*) ingérence *f*, intrusion *f* (*in* dans); (*Phys*) interférence *f*; (*Rad*) parasites *mpl*, interférence.

interfering [ˌɪntəˈfɪərɪŋ] *adj person* importun. **she's an ~ busybody** elle se mêle toujours de ce qui ne la regarde pas, elle fourre son nez partout*, il faut qu'elle mette partout son grain de sel*.

interim [ˈɪntərɪm] **1** *n* intérim *m*. **in the ~** dans l'intérim, entre-temps.

2 *adj administration, government* provisoire; *report, arrangements* provisoire, temporaire; *post, holder of post* par intérim, intérimaire. (*Fin*) **~ dividend** dividende *m* intérimaire; **the ~ period** l'intérim *m*.

interior [ɪnˈtɪərɪəʳ] **1** *adj* intérieur (*f* -eure). (*Math*) **~ angle** angle *m* interne.

2 *n* **(a)** *[building, country]* intérieur *m*. **Minister/Ministry of the I~**, (*US*) **Secretary/Department of the I~** ministre *m*/ministère *m* de l'Intérieur.

(b) (*Art*) (tableau *m* d')intérieur *m*.

3 *cpd*: **interior decoration/decorator** décoration *f*/décorateur *m*, -trice *f* (d'intérieurs *or* d'appartements); **interior sprung mattress** matelas *m* à ressorts.

interject [ˌɪntəˈdʒekt] *vt remark, question* lancer, placer. **'yes' he ~ed** 'oui' réussit-il à placer.

interjection [ˌɪntəˈdʒekʃən] *n* interjection *f*.

interlace [ˌɪntəˈleɪs] **1** *vt* entrelacer, entrecroiser. **2** *vi* s'entrelacer, s'entrecroiser.

interlard [ˌɪntəˈlɑːd] *vt* entrelarder, entremêler (*with* de).

interleave [ˌɪntəˈliːv] *vt* interfolier.

interline [ˌɪntəˈlaɪn] *vt* **(a)** (*Typ*) interligner. **(b)** (*Sewing*) mettre une doublure intermédiaire à.

interlinear [ˌɪntəˈlɪnɪəʳ] *adj* interlinéaire.

interlining [ˌɪntəˈlaɪnɪŋ] *n* (*Sewing*) doublure *f* intermédiaire.

interlock [ˌɪntəˈlɒk] **1** *vt* (*Tech*) enclencher. **2** *vi* (*Tech*) s'enclencher; (*fig*) s'entremêler, s'entrecroiser, s'imbriquer.

interlocutor [ˌɪntəˈlɒkjʊtəʳ] *n* interlocuteur *m*, -trice *f*.

interloper [ˈɪntələʊpəʳ] *n* intrus(e) *m(f)*; (*Comm*) commerçant marron.

interlude [ˈɪntəluːd] *n* intervalle *m*; (*Theat*) intermède *m*. **in the ~** (*gen*) dans l'intervalle, entre-temps; (*Theat*) pendant l'intermède; **musical ~** interlude *m*, intermède musical.

intermarriage [ˌɪntəˈmærɪdʒ] *n* (*U*) (*within family/tribe etc*) mariage *m* entre membres de la même famille/tribu *etc*; (*between families/tribes etc*) mariage *m* entre membres de familles/tribus *etc* différentes.

intermarry [ˈɪntəˈmærɪ] *vi* (*V* **intermarriage**) se marier. **these tribes do not ~** les membres de ces tribus ne se marient pas entre eux; **this tribe doesn't ~ with its neighbours** les membres de cette tribu ne se marient pas avec leurs voisins.

intermediary [ˌɪntəˈmiːdɪərɪ] *adj, n* intermédiaire (*mf*).

intermediate [ˌɪntəˈmiːdɪət] *adj* **(a)** intermédiaire. *[ship, plane]* **~ stop** escale *f*; **the ~ stages of the project** les phases *fpl* *or* étapes *fpl* intermédiaires du projet. **(b)** (*Scol etc*) moyen. **~ course/exam** cours *m*/examen *m* (de niveau) moyen.

interment [ɪnˈtɜːmənt] *n* enterrement *m*, inhumation *f*.

intermezzo [ˌɪntəˈmetsəʊ] *n* intermède *m*; (*Mus*) intermezzo *m*.

interminable [ɪnˈtɜːmɪnəbl] *adj* interminable, sans fin.

intermingle [ˌɪntəˈmɪŋgl] **1** *vt* entremêler (*with* de), mélanger. **2** *vi* s'entremêler (*with* de), se confondre, se mélanger (*with* avec).

intermission [ˌɪntəˈmɪʃən] *n* interruption *f*, pause *f*; (*in hostilities, quarrel, work, session*) trêve *f*; (*Cine, Theat*) entracte *m*; (*Med*) intermission *f*. **without ~** sans arrêt, sans relâche.

intermittent [ˌɪntəˈmɪtənt] *adj* intermittent.

intermittently [ˌɪntəˈmɪtəntlɪ] *adv* par intermittence, par intervalles.

intern [ɪnˈtɜːn] **1** *vt* (*Pol etc*) interner (*pour raisons de sécurité*). **2** [ˈɪntɜːn] *n* (*US Med*) interne *mf*.

internal [ɪnˈtɜːnl] *adj* **(a)** (*Math, Med, Tech*) interne. **~ combustion engine** moteur *m* à explosion, moteur à combustion interne; **~ injuries** lésions *fpl* internes.

(b) (*Ind, Pol*) *dispute, trouble, reorganization* intérieur (*f* -eure), interne. (*Pol*) **~ wars** guerres intestines *or* intérieures *or* civiles; (*Pol*) **~ quarrels** querelles intestines; (*US*) **~ revenue** recette *f* des finances, fisc *m*; (*US*) **I~ Revenue Service** (service *m* de la) recette des finances.

(c) (*intrinsic*) *proof, evidence* intrinsèque.

(d) *hope* secret (*f* -ète). **~ conviction** conviction *f* intime.

internally [ɪnˈtɜːnəlɪ] *adv* intérieurement. (*Pharm*) **'not to be taken ~'** 'pour usage externe'.

international [ˌɪntəˈnæʃnəl] **1** *adj* international. **~ law** droit international; **~ reply coupon** coupon-réponse international; *V* **road**. **2** *n* **(a)** (*Sport: match, player*) international *m*. **(b)** (*Pol*) **I~** Internationale *f* (*association*).

Internationale [ˌɪntəˌnæʃəˈnɑːl] *n* Internationale *f* (*hymne*).

internationalism [ˌɪntəˈnæʃnəlɪzəm] *n* internationalisme *m*.

internationalize [ˌɪntəˈnæʃnəlaɪz] *vt* internationaliser.

internecine [ˌɪntəˈniːsaɪn] *adj feud, war, struggle* de destruction réciproque.

internee [ˌɪntɜːˈniː] *n* interné(e) *m(f)* (politique).

internist [ɪnˈtɜːnɪst] *n* (*US Med*) ≈ spécialiste *mf* des maladies organiques.

internment [ɪnˈtɜːnmənt] *n* internement *m* (politique). **~ camp** camp *m* d'internement.

interplanetary [ˌɪntəˈplænɪtərɪ] *adj journey* interplanétaire. **~ vessel** vaisseau spatial.

interplay [ˈɪntəpleɪ] *n* (*U*) effet *m* réciproque *or* combiné, jeux combinés.

interpolate [ɪnˈtɜːpəleɪt] *vt* **(a)** *text, manuscript* altérer par interpolation. **(b)** *phrase etc* interpoler (*into* dans). **(c)** (*interpose*) intercaler.

interpolation [ɪnˌtɜːpəˈleɪʃən] *n* interpolation *f*.

interpose [ˌɪntəˈpəʊz] **1** *vt remark* intercaler; *objection, veto* opposer.

2 *vi* intervenir, s'interposer.

interpret [ɪnˈtɜːprɪt] **1** *vt* (*all senses*) interpréter. **2** *vi* interpréter, traduire, servir d'interprète, faire l'interprète.

interpretation [ɪnˌtɜːprɪˈteɪʃən] *n* (*all senses*) interprétation *f*. **what ~ am I to put** *or* **place on your conduct?** comment dois-je interpréter votre conduite?

interpretative [ɪnˈtɜːprɪtətɪv] *adj* interprétatif.

interpreter [ɪn'tɜːprɪtəʳ] *n* interprète *mf.*
interregnum [ˌɪntə'regnəm] *n, pl* **~s** *or* **interregna** [ˌɪntə'regnə] interrègne *m.*
interrelate [ˌɪntərɪ'leɪt] *vt* mettre en corrélation. **~d** en corrélation, en relation mutuelle *or* réciproque; **~d facts** faits *mpl* en corrélation *or* intimement liés.
interrelation [ˌɪntərɪ'leɪʃən] *n* corrélation *f,* relation mutuelle *or* réciproque.
interrogate [ɪn'terəgeɪt] *vt* interroger, soumettre à une interrogation *or* (*Police*) un interrogatoire.
interrogation [ɪnˌterə'geɪʃən] *n* interrogation *f;* (*Police*) interrogatoire *m.* **~ mark, ~ point** point *m* d'interrogation.
interrogative [ˌɪntə'rɒgətɪv] **1** *adj look, tone* interrogateur (*f* -trice); (*Ling*) interrogatif. **2** *n* (*Ling*) interrogatif *m.* **in the ~** à l'interrogatif.
interrogatively [ˌɪntə'rɒgətɪvlɪ] *adv* d'un air *or* d'un ton interrogateur; (*Ling*) interrogativement.
interrogator [ɪn'terəgeɪtəʳ] *n* interrogateur *m,* -trice *f.*
interrogatory [ˌɪntə'rɒgətərɪ] *adj* interrogateur (*f* -trice).
interrupt [ˌɪntə'rʌpt] *vt speech, traffic, circuit* interrompre; *communication* interrompre, couper; *person* interrompre, couper la parole à; *view* gêner, boucher, cacher. **to ~ a private conversation** rompre un tête à tête; **don't ~!** n'interrompez pas!, pas d'interruptions!; **I don't want to ~, but ...** je ne voudrais pas vous interrompre, mais ... .
interruption [ˌɪntə'rʌpʃən] *n* interruption *f.* **without ~** sans interruption, sans arrêt, d'affilée.
intersect [ˌɪntə'sekt] **1** *vt* couper, croiser; (*Math*) intersecter. **2** *vi [lines, wires, roads etc]* s'entrecouper, s'entrecroiser, se couper, se croiser; (*Math*) s'intersecter. (*Math*) **~ing arcs/lines** arcs *mpl*/lignes *fpl* intersecté(e)s.
intersection [ˌɪntə'sekʃən] *n* (*crossroads*) croisement *m,* carrefour *m;* (*Math*) intersection *f.*
intersperse [ˌɪntə'spɜːs] *vt* répandre, semer, parsemer (*among, between* dans, parmi). **book ~d with quotations** livre parsemé *or* émaillé de citations; **speech ~d with jokes** discours émaillé de plaisanteries; **lawns ~d with flowerbeds** pelouses agrémentées de parterres de fleurs.
interstate [ˌɪntə'steɪt] *adj* (*US*) *commerce etc* entre états.
interstice [ɪn'tɜːstɪs] *n* interstice *m.*
intertwine [ˌɪntə'twaɪn] **1** *vt* entrelacer. **2** *vi* s'entrelacer. **intertwining branches** branches entrelacées.
interurban [ˌɪntɜː'ɜːbən] *adj* interurbain.
interval ['ɪntəvəl] *n* **(a)** (*in time*) intervalle *m.* **at ~s** par intervalles; **at frequent ~s** à intervalles rapprochés; **at rare ~s** à intervalles espacés, de loin en loin; **at regular ~s** à intervalles réguliers (*V also* **c**); **there was an ~ for discussion** il y eut une pause pour la discussion; (*Med*) **he has lucid ~s** il a des moments de lucidité; (*Met*) **bright ~s** (belles) éclaircies *fpl;* (*Met*) **showery ~s** averses *fpl.*
(b) (*Scol*) récréation *f;* (*Sport*) mi-temps *f,* pause *f;* (*Theat*) entracte *m;* (*Mus*) intervalle *m.* (*Mus*) **second/third ~** intervalle de seconde/de tierce.
(c) (*space between objects*) intervalle *m,* écartement *m,* distance *f.* **the ~s between the trees grew longer** les arbres s'espaçaient, la distance *or* l'intervalle entre les arbres grandissait; **lampposts (placed) at regular ~s along the road** des réverbères placés à intervalles réguliers *or* échelonnés régulièrement le long de la route.
intervene [ˌɪntə'viːn] *vi* **(a)** *[person]* intervenir, s'interposer (*in* dans).
(b) *[event, circumstances etc]* survenir, intervenir, arriver. **war ~d** survint la guerre; **if nothing ~s** s'il n'arrive *or* ne se passe rien entre-temps.
(c) *[time]* s'écouler, s'étendre (*between* entre). **12 years ~ between the two events** 12 ans séparent les deux événements.
intervening [ˌɪntə'viːnɪŋ] *adj event* survenu; *period of time* intermédiaire. **the ~ years were happy** les années qui s'écoulèrent entre-temps furent heureuses.
intervention [ˌɪntə'venʃən] *n* intervention *f.*
interview ['ɪntəvjuː] **1** *n* **(a)** (*for job etc*) entrevue *f.* **to call** *or* **invite sb to an ~** convoquer qn; **I had an ~ with the manager** j'ai été convoqué par le directeur; **the ~s will be held next week** les entrevues auront lieu la semaine prochaine.
(b) (*Press, Rad, TV*) interview *f.*
2 *vt* **(a)** (*for job etc*) avoir une entrevue avec. **he is being ~ed on Monday** on le convoque (pour) lundi.
(b) (*Press, Rad, TV*) interviewer.
interviewer ['ɪntəvjuːəʳ] *n* (*Press, Rad, TV*) interviewer *m;* (*in market research, opinion poll*) enquêteur *m,* -euse *f.* (*for job etc*) **the ~ asked me ...** la personne qui me faisait passer mon entrevue me demanda ... .
interwar ['ɪntə'wɔːʳ] *adj:* **the ~ period** *or* **years** l'entre-deux-guerres *m.*
interweave [ˌɪntə'wiːv] **1** *vt threads* tisser ensemble; *lines etc* entrelacer; (*fig*) entremêler. **2** *vi* s'entrelacer, s'emmêler.
intestate [ɪn'testɪt] *adj* (*Jur*) intestat (*f inv*). **to die ~** mourir intestat; **~ estate** succession *f* ab intestat.
intestinal [ɪn'testɪnl] *adj* intestinal. (*US fig*) **to have ~ fortitude**‡ avoir quelque chose dans le ventre*.
intestine [ɪn'testɪn] *n* (*Anat*) intestin *m.* **small ~** intestin grêle; **large ~** gros intestin.
intimacy ['ɪntɪməsɪ] *n* **(a)** (*U*) intimité *f.* **(b)** (*U: euph: sexual*) rapports *mpl* (intimes *or* sexuels). **(c) intimacies** familiarités *fpl,* gestes familiers.
intimate[1] ['ɪntɪmɪt] **1** *adj* **(a)** (*close*) *friend* intime, proche; *friendship* profond. **to be on ~ terms with** être ami intime de, avoir des relations intimes avec; **to become ~ with sb** se lier (d'amitié) avec qn, devenir (ami) intime avec qn, devenir l'intime de qn; **they became ~** ils se sont liés d'amitié, ils sont devenus amis intimes.
(b) (*euph: sexually*) **he had been ~ with her** il avait eu des rapports (intimes) avec elle; **they were ~ several times** ils ont eu des rapports (intimes) plusieurs fois.
(c) (*private*) *feelings* intime, personnel, secret (*f* -ète); *beliefs, life* intime. **one's ~ affairs** ses affaires privées.
(d) (*cosy*) *restaurant etc* intime. **an ~ atmosphere** une atmosphère intime *or* d'intimité.
(e) (*detailed*) **to have an ~ knowledge of a subject** avoir une connaissance approfondie d'un sujet, connaître à fond un sujet; **a more ~ analysis** une analyse plus approfondie *or* plus détaillée.
2 *n* intime *mf,* familier *m,* -ière *f.*
intimate[2] ['ɪntɪmeɪt] *vt* **(a)** (*make known officially*) annoncer, faire savoir, faire connaître (*that* que). **he ~d his approval** il annonça *or* fit connaître son approbation. **(b)** (*make known indirectly*) suggérer, donner à entendre, laisser entendre.
intimately ['ɪntɪmɪtlɪ] *adv know, talk* intimement. **to be ~ acquainted with a subject** connaître à fond *or* intimement un sujet; **to be ~ connected with sth** avoir un rapport très étroit avec qch; **to be ~ involved in sth** être mêlé de près à qch.
intimation [ˌɪntɪ'meɪʃən] *n* (*announcement*) (*gen*) annonce *f;* *[death]* avis *m;* *[birth, wedding]* annonce; (*notice*) signification *f,* notification *f;* (*hint*) suggestion *f;* (*sign*) indice *m,* indication *f.* **this was the first ~ we had of their refusal/that they had refused** cela a été la première indication que nous avons eue de leur refus/du fait qu'ils avaient refusé; **we had had no previous ~ that** rien ne nous faisait pressentir que.
intimidate [ɪn'tɪmɪdeɪt] *vt* intimider.
intimidation [ɪnˌtɪmɪ'deɪʃən] *n* (*U*) intimidation *f;* (*Jur*) menaces *fpl.*
into ['ɪntʊ] (*phr vb elem*) *prep* dans, en. **to come** *or* **go ~ a room** entrer dans une pièce; **to go ~ town** aller en ville; **to get ~ a car** monter dans une voiture *or* en voiture; **he helped his mother ~ the car** il a aidé sa mère à monter en voiture; **she fell ~ the lake** elle est tombée dans le lac; **he went off ~ the desert** il est parti dans le désert; **to put sth ~ a box** mettre qch dans une boîte; **it broke ~ a thousand pieces** ça s'est cassé en mille morceaux; **to change traveller's cheques ~ francs** changer des chèques de voyage contre des francs; **to translate** *or* **put sth ~ French** traduire qch en français; **he went further ~ the forest** il a pénétré *or* s'est enfoncé plus avant dans la forêt; **far ~ the night** très avant dans la nuit; **let's not go ~ that again!** ne recommençons pas à discuter là-dessus!, ne revenons pas là-dessus!; **we must go ~ this very carefully** nous devons étudier la question de très près; **4 ~ 12 goes 3** 12 divisé par 4 donne 3; **the children are ~ everything*** les enfants touchent à tout; (*fig*) **she's ~‡ health foods/Marxism** *etc* elle donne à fond* dans les aliments naturels/le marxisme *etc;* *V* **burst, get into, grow** *etc.*
intolerable [ɪn'tɒlərəbl] *adj* intolérable, insupportable. **it is ~ that ...** il est intolérable *or* il n'est pas tolérable que ... + *subj.*
intolerably [ɪn'tɒlərəblɪ] *adv* de manière intolérable *or* insupportable, insupportablement.
intolerance [ɪn'tɒlərəns] *n* (*U: also Med*) intolérance *f.*
intolerant [ɪn'tɒlərənt] *adj* intolérant (*of* de; (*Med*) *of* à).
intolerantly ɪn'tɒlərəntlɪ] *adv* avec intolérance.
intonation [ˌɪntəʊ'neɪʃən] *n* (*Ling*) intonation *f.*
intone [ɪn'təʊn] *vt* entonner; (*Rel*) psalmodier.
intoxicant [ɪn'tɒksɪkənt] **1** *adj* enivrant, grisant. **2** *n* alcool *m,* boisson *f* alcoolique.
intoxicate [ɪn'tɒksɪkeɪt] *vt* (*lit, fig*) enivrer, griser.
intoxicated [ɪn'tɒksɪkeɪtɪd] *adj* (*lit*) ivre; (*Jur*) en état d'ivresse *or* d'ébriété; (*fig*) ivre, grisé. **~ with success** grisé par le succès, ivre de succès.
intoxication [ɪnˌtɒksɪ'keɪʃən] *n* ivresse *f;* (*Med*) intoxication *f* (par l'alcool); (*fig*) ivresse, griserie *f.* (*Jur*) **in a state of ~** en état d'ivresse *or* d'ébriété.
intra... ['ɪntrə] *pref* intra... .
intractability [ɪnˌtræktə'bɪlɪtɪ] *n* (*V* **intractable**) caractère *m* intraitable, manque *m* de docilité; insolubilité *f;* opiniâtreté *f.*
intractable [ɪn'træktəbl] *adj child, temper* intraitable, indocile; *problem* insoluble; *illness* opiniâtre; *machine* difficile à régler *or* à manipuler.
intramural [ˌɪntrə'mjʊərəl] *adj* intra-muros *inv.*
intramuscular [ˌɪntrə'mʌskjʊləʳ] *adj* intramusculaire.
intransigence [ɪn'trænsɪdʒəns] *n* intransigeance *f.*
intransigent [ɪn'trænsɪdʒənt] *adj, n* intransigeant(e) *m(f).*
intransitive [ɪn'trænsɪtɪv] *adj, n* (*Gram*) intransitif (*m*).
intravenous [ˌɪntrə'viːnəs] *adj* intraveineux.
intrepid [ɪn'trepɪd] *adj* intrépide.
intrepidity [ˌɪntrɪ'pɪdɪtɪ] *n* intrépidité *f.*
intrepidly [ɪn'trepɪdlɪ] *adv* avec intrépidité, intrépidement.
intricacy ['ɪntrɪkəsɪ] *n [problem, plot, pattern, mechanism]* complexité *f,* complication *f.* **the intricacies of the law** les complexités *or* les détours *mpl* de la loi.
intricate ['ɪntrɪkɪt] *adj mechanism, pattern, style* compliqué; *plot, problem, situation* complexe. **all the ~ details** tous les détails dans leur complexité.
intricately ['ɪntrɪkɪtlɪ] *adv* de façon complexe *or* compliquée.
intrigue [ɪn'triːg] **1** *vi* intriguer, comploter (*with sb* avec qn, *to do* pour faire).
2 *vt* intriguer, éveiller la curiosité de, intéresser. **she ~s me** elle m'intrigue; **go on, I'm ~d** continue, ça m'intrigue *or* m'intéresse; **I'm ~d to know whether he did arrive** je suis curieux de savoir s'il est vraiment arrivé; **your news ~s me** ce que vous m'annoncez m'intrigue; **we were ~d by a road sign** un panneau a éveillé notre curiosité *or* nous a intrigués.
3 *n* (*plot*) intrigue *f;* (*love affair*) intrigue, liaison *f.*
intriguer [ɪn'triːgəʳ] *n* intrigant(e) *m(f).*

intriguing [ɪn'tri:gɪŋ] **1** *adj* fascinant. **2** *n* (*U*) intrigues *fpl.*
intrinsic [ɪn'trɪnsɪk] *adj* intrinsèque.
intrinsically [ɪn'trɪnsɪklɪ] *adv* intrinsèquement.
intro... ['ɪntrəʊ] *pref* intro... .
introduce [ˌɪntrə'dju:s] *vt* **(a)** (*bring in*) *reform, new method, innovation* présenter, introduire; *subject, question* aborder, amener, présenter; *practice* faire adopter, établir, introduire. (*Rad, TV*) **to ~ a programme** présenter une émission; (*Parl*) **to ~ a bill** déposer un projet de loi; **it was I who ~d him into the firm** c'est moi qui l'ai introduit *or* fait entrer dans la compagnie; **potatoes were ~d into Europe from America** la pomme de terre a été introduite d'Amérique en Europe; **he ~d me to the delights of skiing** il m'a initié aux plaisirs du ski; **I was ~d to Shakespeare too young** on m'a fait connaître Shakespeare quand j'étais trop jeune; **this ~d a new note into the conversation** ceci a donné un ton nouveau à la conversation; **I don't know how to ~ the subject** je ne sais pas comment présenter *or* aborder la question; **he ~d the tape recorder surreptitiously into the meeting** il a introduit sans se faire remarquer le magnétophone dans la réunion; (*frm*) **we were ~d into a dark room** on nous introduisit dans une pièce sombre.
(b) (*make acquainted*) présenter. **he ~d me to his friend** il m'a présenté à son ami; **I ~d myself to my new neighbour** je me suis présenté à mon nouveau voisin; **who ~d them?** qui les a présentés l'un à l'autre?; **we haven't been ~d** on ne nous a pas présentés (l'un à l'autre); (*frm*) **may I ~ Mr X?** puis-je (me permettre de) vous présenter M X?
(c) (*insert*) *key etc* introduire, insérer (*into* dans).
introduction [ˌɪntrə'dʌkʃən] *n* **(a)** (*U*) introduction *f* (*into* dans). **my ~ to chemistry/to life in London** mon premier contact avec la chimie/la vie londonienne.
(b) présentation *f* (*of sb to sb* de qn à qn). **to give sb an ~** *or* **a letter of ~ to sb** donner à qn une lettre de recommandation auprès de qn; **will you make** *or* **do* the ~s?** voulez-vous faire les présentations?
(c) (*to book etc*) avant-propos *m*, introduction *f.*
(d) (*elementary course*) introduction *f* (*to* à), manuel *m* élémentaire. **'an ~ to German'** 'initiation *f* à l'allemand'.
introductory [ˌɪntrə'dʌktərɪ] *adj* préliminaire, préalable, d'introduction. **a few ~ words** quelques mots d'introduction; **~ remarks** remarques *fpl* préliminaires *or* préalables, préambule *m.*
introit ['ɪntrɔɪt] *n* introït *m.*
introspection [ˌɪntrəʊ'spekʃən] *n* (*U*) introspection *f.*
introspective [ˌɪntrəʊ'spektɪv] *adj* introspectif, replié sur soi-même.
introspectiveness [ˌɪntrəʊ'spektɪvnɪs] *n* tendance *f* à l'introspection.
introversion [ˌɪntrəʊ'vɜ:ʃən] *n* introversion *f.*
introvert ['ɪntrəʊvɜ:t] **1** *n* (*Psych*) introverti(e) *m(f).* **he's something of an ~** c'est un caractère plutôt fermé. **2** *adj* introverti. **3** *vt one's thoughts etc* tourner sur soi-même. (*Psych*) **to become ~ed** se replier sur soi-même.
intrude [ɪn'tru:d] **1** *vt* introduire de force (*into* dans), imposer (*into* à). **the thought that ~d itself into my mind** la pensée qui s'est imposée à mon esprit; **to ~ one's views (on sb)** imposer ses idées (à qn).
2 *vi* [*person*] être importun, s'imposer; [*feeling, emotion*] se manifester. **to ~ on sb's conversation** s'immiscer dans la conversation de qn; **to ~ on sb's privacy** s'ingérer dans la vie privée de qn; **to ~ on sb's time** empiéter sur le temps de qn; **to ~ into sb's affairs** s'immiscer *or* s'ingérer dans les affaires de qn; **sometimes a note of sentimentality ~s** quelquefois s'insinue une note sentimentale; **he lets no feelings of pity ~** il ne laisse intervenir aucun sentiment de pitié; **am I intruding?** est-ce que je (vous) dérange?, (*stronger*) est-ce que je (vous) gêne?
intruder [ɪn'tru:dəʳ] *n* (*person*) intrus(e) *m(f)*; (*Aviat/Naut*) avion/navire isolé (*qui pénètre chez l'ennemi*); (*animal*) intrus(e). **the ~ fled when he heard the car** l'intrus s'enfuit quand il entendit la voiture; **she treated us like ~s** elle nous a traités comme des intrus *or* des étrangers; **I felt like an ~** je me sentais étranger *or* de trop.
intrusion [ɪn'tru:ʒən] *n* (*V* **intrude**) intrusion *f* (*into* dans); imposition *f* (*on* à). **~s on sb's privacy** ingérences *fpl* dans la vie privée de qn; **~s on sb's time** empiètement *m* sur le temps de qn; **his ~ into our conversation/meeting** son intrusion dans notre conversation/réunion; **excuse my ~** excusez-moi de vous déranger.
intrusive [ɪn'tru:sɪv] *adj* importun, indiscret (*f* -ète), gênant. (*Ling*) **the ~ 'r'** *le 'r' rajouté en anglais en liaison abusive.*
intuit [ɪn'tjuɪt] *vt* (*esp US*) **to ~ that ...** savoir intuitivement *or* par intuition que ..., avoir l'intuition que ... .
intuition [ˌɪntju:'ɪʃən] *n* intuition *f.*
intuitive [ɪn'tju:ɪtɪv] *adj* intuitif.
intuitively [ɪn'tju:ɪtɪvlɪ] *adv* par intuition, intuitivement.
inundate ['ɪnʌndeɪt] *vt* (*lit, fig*) inonder (*with* de). **to be ~d with work** être débordé (de travail), être submergé de travail; **to be ~d with visits** être inondé de visiteurs, être débordé de visites.
inundation [ˌɪnʌn'deɪʃən] *n* inondation *f.*
inure [ɪn'jʊəʳ] *vt* endurcir, accoutumer, habituer, aguerrir (*to* à).
invade [ɪn'veɪd] *vt* **(a)** (*Mil, fig*) envahir. **city ~d by tourists** ville envahie par les touristes; **he was suddenly ~d by doubts** il fut soudain envahi de doutes. **(b)** *privacy* violer, s'ingérer dans. **to ~ sb's rights** empiéter sur les droits de qn.
invader [ɪn'veɪdəʳ] *n* envahisseur *m*, -euse *f.* **the ~s were generally detested** les envahisseurs étaient haïs de tous, l'envahisseur était haï de tous.
invading [ɪn'veɪdɪŋ] *adj army, troops* d'invasion. **the ~ Romans** l'envahisseur romain.
invalid¹ ['ɪnvəlɪd] **1** *n* (*sick person*) malade *mf*; (*with disability*) invalide *mf*, infirme *mf.* **chronic ~** malade chronique.
2 *adj* (*ill*) malade; (*with disability*) invalide, infirme.
3 *cpd*: (*Brit*) **invalid car, invalid carriage** voiture *f* d'infirme; **invalid chair** fauteuil *m* d'infirme *or* de malade; (*Brit*) **invalid tricycle** tricyclecar *m.*
4 [ˌɪnvə'li:d] *vt* (*esp Brit Mil*) **he was ~ed home from the front** il fut rapatrié du front pour blessures *or* pour raisons de santé.
invalid out *vt sep* (*Mil*) **to invalid sb out (of the army)** réformer qn (pour blessures *or* pour raisons de santé).
invalid² [ɪn'vælɪd] *adj* (*esp Jur*) non valide, non valable. [*ticket*] **to become ~** ne plus être valable, se périmer.
invalidate [ɪn'vælɪdeɪt] *vt* invalider, annuler; (*Jur*) *judgment* casser, infirmer; *will* rendre nul et sans effet; *contract etc* vicier; *statute* abroger.
invaluable [ɪn'væljʊəbl] *adj* (*lit, fig*) inestimable, inappréciable. **her help** *or* **she has been ~ to me** elle m'a été d'une aide inestimable *or* inappréciable.
invariable [ɪn'vɛərɪəbl] *adj* invariable.
invariably [ɪn'vɛərɪəblɪ] *adv* invariablement, immanquablement.
invasion [ɪn'veɪʒən] *n* **(a)** (*Mil, fig*) invasion *f*, envahissement *m.* **(b)** [*rights*] empiètement *m* (*of* sur). **it is an ~ of his privacy to ask him such questions** c'est une incursion dans sa vie privée que de lui poser de telles questions.
invective [ɪn'vektɪv] *n* invective *f.* **torrent** *or* **stream of ~** flot *m* d'invectives *or* d'injures.
inveigh [ɪn'veɪ] *vi*: **to ~ against sb/sth** invectiver qn/qch; (*more violently*) fulminer *or* tonner contre qn/qch.
inveigle [ɪn'vi:gl] *vt*: **to ~ sb into sth** entraîner *or* attirer qn dans qch (sous de faux prétextes *or* par la flatterie *or* par la ruse); **to ~ sb into doing** entraîner *or* amener qn à faire (sous de faux prétextes *or* par la flatterie *or* par la ruse).
invent [ɪn'vent] *vt* (*lit, fig*) inventer.
invention [ɪn'venʃən] *n* **(a)** invention *f.* **the ~ of the telephone** l'invention du téléphone; **one of his most practical ~s** une de ses inventions les plus pratiques.
(b) (*falsehood*) invention *f*, mensonge *m.* **it was sheer ~ on her part** c'était pure invention de sa part; **it was (an) ~ from start to finish** c'était (une) pure invention du début à la fin.
inventive [ɪn'ventɪv] *adj* inventif.
inventiveness [ɪn'ventɪvnɪs] *n* (*U*) esprit inventif *or* d'invention.
inventor [ɪn'ventəʳ] *n* inventeur *m*, -trice *f.*
inventory ['ɪnvəntrɪ] **1** *n* inventaire *m*; (*US: Comm*) stock *m.* **to draw up an ~ of sth** inventorier qch, faire *or* dresser un inventaire de qch; **~ of fixtures** état *m* des *or* de lieux. **2** *vt* inventorier.
inverse ['ɪn'vɜ:s] **1** *adj* inverse. **in ~ order** en sens inverse; **in ~ proportion to** inversement proportionnel à; **in ~ ratio (to)** en raison inverse (de). **2** *n* inverse *m*, contraire *m.*
inversely [ɪn'vɜ:slɪ] *adv* inversement.
inversion [ɪn'vɜ:ʃən] *n* (*Anat, Chem, Gram, Math, Psych etc*) inversion *f*; (*Mus*) renversement *m*; [*values, roles etc*] renversement.
invert [ɪn'vɜ:t] **1** *vt* **(a)** *elements, order, words* intervertir; *roles* renverser, intervertir. **to ~ a process** renverser une opération; (*Mus*) **~ed chord** accord renversé; (*Brit*) **~ed commas** guillemets *mpl*; **in ~ed commas** entre guillemets.
(b) *cup, object* retourner.
2 ['ɪnvɜ:t] *n* (*Psych*) inverti(e) *m(f).*
3 ['ɪnvɜ:t] *cpd*: **invert sugar** sucre inverti.
invertebrate [ɪn'vɜ:tɪbrɪt] *adj, n* invertébré (*m*).
invest [ɪn'vest] **1** *vt* **(a)** (*Fin*) *money* placer (*in* dans, en); *capital, funds* investir (*in* dans, en). **to ~ money** faire un *or* des placement(s), placer de l'argent; **they ~ed large sums in books** ils ont investi des sommes énormes dans l'achat de livres; **I have ~ed a lot of time in this project** j'ai consacré beaucoup de temps à ce projet.
(b) (*Mil: surround*) investir, cerner.
(c) (*endow*) revêtir, investir (*sb with sth* qn de qch). **the event was ~ed with an air of mystery** l'événement revêtait un caractère de mystère; **she seems to ~ it with some importance** elle semble lui attribuer une certaine importance.
2 *vi*: **to ~ in shares/property** placer son argent en valeurs/dans l'immobilier; (*hum*) **I've ~ed in a new car** je me suis payé* *or* offert une nouvelle voiture.
investigate [ɪn'vestɪgeɪt] *vt question, possibilities* examiner, étudier; *motive, reason* scruter, sonder; *crime* se livrer à des investigations sur, enquêter sur, faire une enquête sur.
investigation [ɪnˌvestɪ'geɪʃən] *n* **(a)** (*U*) [*facts, question*] examen *m*; [*crime*] enquête *f* (*of* sur). **the matter under ~** la question à l'étude.
(b) investigation *f*, enquête *f.* **his ~s led him to believe that ...** ses investigations l'ont amené à penser que ...; **criminal/scientific ~** enquête criminelle/scientifique; **to institute an ~** ouvrir une enquête; **preliminary ~** enquête *or* investigations préalable(s) *or* préparatoire(s); **it calls for (an) immediate ~** cela demande une étude immédiate *or* à être étudié immédiatement; **he called for (an) immediate ~ into** il a demandé qu'on fasse *or* ouvre (*subj*) immédiatement une enquête sur; **we have made ~s** nous avons fait une enquête *or* des recherches.
investigator [ɪn'vestɪgeɪtəʳ] *n* investigateur *m*, -trice *f*; *V* **private.**
investiture [ɪn'vestɪtʃəʳ] *n* investiture *f.*
investment [ɪn'vestmənt] **1** *n* **(a)** (*Fin*) investissement *m*, placement *m.* **by careful ~ of his capital/the money he inherited** en investissant *or* plaçant soigneusement son capital/l'argent dont il a hérité; **he regretted his ~ in the company** il regrettait d'avoir investi dans la firme; **~ in shares** placement

en valeurs; ~ **in property** placement *or* investissement immobilier; **I have a large ~ in the business** j'ai une grosse somme investie dans cette affaire *or* de gros intérêts dans cette affaire; (*money invested*) ~s placements, investissements; **he has large ~s in Africa** il a de grosses sommes investies en Afrique.

(b) (*Mil*) investissement *m*.

(c) = **investiture.**

2 *cpd*: (*Fin*) **investment bank** banque *f* d'investissement; **investment company** société *f* de placement; **investment trust** société *f* d'investissement.

investor [ɪnˈvestəʳ] *n* actionnaire *mf*. **(the) big ~s** les gros actionnaires; **(the) small ~s** les petits actionnaires, la petite épargne (*U*).

inveterate [ɪnˈvetərɪt] *adj habit* invétéré, (bien) enraciné; *thief, smoker* invétéré; *gambler* invétéré, acharné. **an ~ liar** un fieffé menteur.

invidious [ɪnˈvɪdɪəs] *adj decision, distinction, choice* injuste, propre à susciter la jalousie; *comparison* blessant, désobligeant; *task* ingrat, déplaisant.

invigilate [ɪnˈvɪdʒɪleɪt] **1** *vi* (*Brit*) être de surveillance (à un examen). **2** *vt examination* surveiller.

invigilator [ɪnˈvɪdʒɪleɪtəʳ] *n* (*Brit*) surveillant(e) *m(f)* (*à un examen*).

invigorate [ɪnˈvɪgəreɪt] *vt person [drink, food, thought]* fortifier; *[fresh air, snack]* revigorer; *[climate, air]* vivifier, tonifier, donner du tonus à; *[exercise]* tonifier; *campaign* animer.

invigorating [ɪnˈvɪgəreɪtɪŋ] *adj climate, air, walk* vivifiant, tonifiant; *speech* stimulant.

invincibility [ɪn,vɪnsɪˈbɪlɪtɪ] *n* invincibilité *f*.

invincible [ɪnˈvɪnsəbl] *adj* invincible.

inviolability [ɪn,vaɪələˈbɪlɪtɪ] *n* inviolabilité *f*.

inviolable [ɪnˈvaɪələbl] *adj* inviolable.

inviolably [ɪnˈvaɪələblɪ] *adv* inviolablement.

inviolate [ɪnˈvaɪəlɪt] *adj* inviolé.

invisibility [ɪn,vɪzəˈbɪlɪtɪ] *n* invisibilité *f*.

invisible [ɪnˈvɪzəbl] *adj* invisible. **~ ink** encre *f* sympathique; **~ mending** stoppage *m*.

invisibly [ɪnˈvɪzəblɪ] *adv* invisiblement. **I've had my coat ~ mended** j'ai fait stopper mon manteau.

invitation [,ɪnvɪˈteɪʃən] **1** *n* invitation *f*. **~ to dinner** invitation à dîner; **at sb's ~** à *or* sur l'invitation de qn; **by ~ (only)** sur invitation (seulement); (*iro*) **this lock is an ~ to burglars** cette serrure est une invite aux cambrioleurs!

2 *cpd*: **invitation card** (carte *f* d')invitation *f*, carton *m*.

invite [ɪnˈvaɪt] **1** *vt* **(a)** (*ask*) *person* inviter (*to do* à faire). **to ~ sb to dinner** inviter qn à dîner; **he ~d him for a drink** il l'a invité à prendre un verre; **I've never been ~d to their house** je n'ai jamais été invité chez eux; **they ~d him to give his opinion** ils l'ont invité à donner son avis; **he was ~d to the ceremony** il a été invité (à assister) à la cérémonie; **to ~ sb in/up/down** *etc* inviter qn à entrer/ monter/descendre *etc*; (*fig*) **a shop like that just ~s people to steal** ce magasin est une véritable incitation au vol.

(b) (*ask for*) *sb's attention, subscriptions etc* demander, solliciter. **he ~d our opinion on ...** il nous a demandé notre avis sur ...; **he ~d questions at the end of his talk** il a invité le public à poser des questions à la fin de sa causerie.

(c) (*lead to*) *confidences, questions, doubts, ridicule* appeler; *discussion, step* inviter à; *trouble, failure, defeat* chercher. **you're inviting a break-in if you leave that door open** en laissant cette porte ouverte vous invitez les cambrioleurs à entrer, laissser cette porte ouverte est une invite aux cambrioleurs.

2 [ˈɪnvaɪt] *n* (*) invitation *f*.

invite out *vt sep* inviter (à sortir). **he has invited her out several times** il l'a invitée à sortir (avec lui) *or* il lui a demandé de sortir (avec lui) plusieurs fois; **I've been invited out to dinner this evening** j'ai été invité à dîner ce soir.

invite over *vt sep* **(a)** inviter (à venir). **they often invite us over for a drink** ils nous invitent souvent à venir prendre un verre chez eux; **let's invite them over some time** invitons-les un de ces jours (à venir nous voir).

(b) he invited me over to his table il (m'appela et) m'invita à venir m'asseoir à sa table.

inviting [ɪnˈvaɪtɪŋ] *adj* invitant, engageant, attrayant; *gesture* encourageant; *meal, odour* appétissant, alléchant. **the sea looked very ~** la mer avait un aspect très tentant *or* engageant.

invitingly [ɪnˈvaɪtɪŋlɪ] *adv describe* d'une manière attrayante; *speak* d'un ton encourageant.

invocation [,ɪnvəʊˈkeɪʃən] *n* invocation *f*.

invoice [ˈɪnvɔɪs] **1** *n* facture *f*. **2** *vt goods* facturer. **3** *cpd*: **invoice clerk** facturier *m*, -ière *f*; **invoice typist** dactylofacturière *f*.

invoke [ɪnˈvəʊk] *vt* **(a)** (*call on*) *God, Muse, mercy, precedent, law* invoquer. **to ~ sb's help** invoquer *or* demander l'aide de qn; **to ~ vengeance on sb** appeler vengeance sur la tête de qn. **(b)** (*evoke*) *spirits, the devil* évoquer.

involuntarily [ɪnˈvɒləntərɪlɪ] *adv* involontairement.

involuntary [ɪnˈvɒləntərɪ] *adj* involontaire.

involve [ɪnˈvɒlv] *vt* **(a)** (*implicate, associate*) impliquer (*in, into* dans), mêler (*in, into* à), entraîner (*in, into* dans). **to ~ sb in a quarrel** mêler qn à une querelle; **to get ~d in a quarrel** se laisser entraîner dans une querelle; **to be ~d in a quarrel** être mêlé à une querelle; **they are trying to ~ him in the theft** ils essaient de l'impliquer dans le vol; **he wasn't ~d in the plot** il n'était pour rien dans le complot, il n'était pas impliqué dans le complot *or* mêlé au complot; **don't try to ~ me in this scheme** n'essaie pas de me mêler à ce projet; **we would prefer not to ~ Robert** nous préférerions ne pas mêler Robert à l'affaire *or* ne pas impliquer Robert; **to ~ sb in expense** entraîner qn à faire des frais; **to ~ o.s.** *or* **to get ~d in expense** se laisser entraîner à des dépenses *or* à la dépense; **how did you come to be ~d?** comment vous êtes-vous trouvé impliqué?; **he was so ~d in politics that he had no time to ...** il était tellement engagé dans la politique qu'il n'avait pas le temps de ...; **the police became ~d** la police est intervenue; **a question of principle is ~d** c'est une question de principe qui est en jeu; **the factors/forces/principles ~d** les facteurs/forces/principes en jeu; **the person ~d** l'intéressé(e) *m(f)*; **to feel personally ~d** se sentir concerné; **to get ~d with sb** (*gen*) se trouver mêlé aux affaires de qn; (*socially*) se trouver lié intimement à qn; (*fall in love with*) tomber amoureux de qn; **she likes him but she doesn't want to get (too) ~d*** elle a de l'affection pour lui mais elle ne veut pas (trop) s'engager.

(b) (*entail, imply*) entraîner, nécessiter. **does it ~ much trouble?** est-ce que cela nécessite *or* entraîne beaucoup de dérangement?; **it ~s a lot of expense** ceci entraîne beaucoup de frais; **the job ~s living in the country** le poste nécessite *or* exige qu'on réside (*subj*) à la campagne; **there's a good deal of work ~d** cela nécessite un gros travail.

involved [ɪnˈvɒlvd] *adj situation, relationship, question* compliqué, complexe; *style* contourné, compliqué; *V also* **involve.**

involvement [ɪnˈvɒlvmənt] *n* **(a)** (*U*) rôle *m* (*in* dans), participation *f* (*in* à). **we don't know the extent of his ~** nous ne savons pas dans quelle mesure il est impliqué; **his ~ in the affair/plot** *etc* son rôle dans l'affaire/le complot *etc*; **his ~ in politics** son engagement *m* dans la politique; **his ~ in social work** son action *f* en matière sociale; **one must avoid any ~ in their difficulties** il faut éviter de se trouver mêlé à leurs difficultés.

(b) (*difficulty*) problème *m*, difficulté *f*. **financial ~s** difficultés financières, problèmes *or* embarras financiers.

(c) (*U*) *[style etc]* complication(s) *f(pl)*.

invulnerability [ɪn,vʌlnərəˈbɪlɪtɪ] *n* invulnérabilité *f*.

invulnerable [ɪnˈvʌlnərəbl] *adj* invulnérable.

inward [ˈɪnwəd] **1** *adj movement* vers l'intérieur; *happiness, peace* intérieur (*f* -eure); *thoughts, desire, conviction* intime, profond. **2** *adv* = **inwards. 3** *cpd*: **inward-looking** replié sur soi(-même), introverti.

inwardly [ˈɪnwədlɪ] **1** *adv* **(a)** (*in the inside*) à l'intérieur, intérieurement, au-dedans. **the house was outwardly clean but ~ filthy** la maison était propre à l'extérieur mais dégoûtante à l'intérieur.

(b) (*secretly, privately*) *feel, think, know* secrètement, en son (*or* mon *etc*) for intérieur.

inwards [ˈɪnwədz] (*phr vb elem*) *adv move etc* vers l'intérieur. (*liter*) **his thoughts turned ~** il rentra en (dedans de) lui-même, il descendit en lui-même.

iodine [ˈaɪədiːn] *n* iode *m*.

iodize [ˈaɪədaɪz] *vt* ioder.

iodoform [aɪˈɒdəfɔːm] *n* iodoforme *m*.

ion [ˈaɪən] *n* ion *m*.

Ionian [aɪˈəʊnɪən] *adj* ionien. **the ~ Islands** les îles Ioniennes; **the ~ (Sea)** la mer Ionienne.

Ionic [aɪˈɒnɪk] *adj* (*Archit*) ionique.

ionic [aɪˈɒnɪk] *adj* (*Chem, Phys*) ionique.

ionize [ˈaɪənaɪz] *vt* ioniser.

ionosphere [aɪˈɒnəsfɪəʳ] *n* ionosphère *f*.

iota [aɪˈəʊtə] *n* (*letter*) iota *m*; (*fig: tiny amount*) brin *m*, grain *m*; (*in written matter*) iota. **he won't change an ~ (of what he has written)** il refuse de changer un iota (à ce qu'il a écrit); **if he had an ~ of sense** s'il avait un grain de bon sens; **not an ~ of truth** pas un brin de vérité, pas un mot de vrai.

IOU [,aɪəʊˈjuː] *n* (*abbr of* **I owe you**) reconnaissance *f* de dette(s). **he gave me an ~ for £2** il m'a signé un reçu *or* un billet pour 2 livres.

ipecac(uanha) [,ɪpɪkæk(jʊˈænə)] *n* ipéca(cuana) *m*.

Irak [ɪˈrɑːk] *n* = **Iraq.**

Iraki [ɪˈrɑːkɪ] = **Iraqi.**

Iran [ɪˈrɑːn] *n* Iran *m*.

Iranian [ɪˈreɪnɪən] **1** *adj* iranien. **2** *n* **(a)** Iranien(ne) *m(f)*. **(b)** (*Ling*) iranien *m*.

Iraq [ɪˈrɑːk] *n* Irak *m*.

Iraqi [ɪˈrɑːkɪ] **1** *adj* irakien. **2** *n* **(a)** Irakien(ne) *m(f)*. **(b)** (*Ling*) irakien *m*.

irascibility [ɪ,ræsɪˈbɪlɪtɪ] *n* irascibilité *f*.

irascible [ɪˈræsɪbl] *adj* irascible, coléreux, colérique.

irascibly [ɪˈræsɪblɪ] *adv* irasciblement.

irate [aɪˈreɪt] *adj* furieux, courroucé (*liter*).

ire [aɪəʳ] *n* (*liter*) colère *f*, courroux *m* (*liter*). **to rouse sb's ~** mettre qn dans une grande colère *or* en courroux (*liter*), provoquer le courroux de qn (*liter*).

Ireland [ˈaɪələnd] *n* Irlande *f*. **Northern ~** Irlande du Nord; (*Brit*) **Secretary (of State) for Northern ~** ministre *m* chargé de l'Irlande du Nord; (*Brit*) **Northern ~ Office** ministère *m* de l'Irlande du Nord; **Republic of ~** République *f* d'Irlande.

irides [ˈɪrɪdiːz] *npl of* **iris a.**

iridescence [,ɪrɪˈdesns] *n* irisation *f*; *[plumage etc]* chatoiement *m*.

iridescent [,ɪrɪˈdesnt] *adj* irisé, iridescent; *plumage* chatoyant.

iris [ˈaɪərɪs] *n* **(a)** (*pl* **irides**) *[eye]* iris *m*. **(b)** (*pl* **~es**) (*Bot*) iris *m*.

Irish [ˈaɪərɪʃ] **1** *adj* irlandais. **~ Free State** État *m* libre d'Irlande; **~man** Irlandais *m*; **~ Sea** mer *f* d'Irlande; (*Culin*) **~ stew** ragoût *m* de mouton (à l'irlandaise); **~woman** Irlandaise *f*.

2 *n* **(a) the ~** les Irlandais *mpl*.

(b) (*Ling*) irlandais *m*.

irk [ɜːk] *vt* contrarier, ennuyer.

irksome [ˈɜːksəm] *adj restriction, person* ennuyeux; *task* ingrat.

iron ['aɪən] **1** *n* **(a)** (*U: metal*) fer *m*. **old ~, scrap ~** ferraille *f* (*U*); (*fig*) **a man of ~** (*unyielding*) un homme de fer; (*cruel*) un homme au cœur de pierre; (*loc*) **to strike while the ~ is hot** battre le fer pendant qu'il est chaud; *V* **cast, rod, wrought** *etc*.
(b) (*tool*) fer *m*; (*for laundry: also* **flat ~**) fer (à repasser). **electric ~** fer électrique; (*fig*) **to have too many ~s in the fire** mener trop de choses *or* d'affaires de front; (*fig*) **I've got a lot of ~s in the fire** j'ai des quantités d'affaires en train; (*fig liter*) **the ~ had entered his soul** il avait la mort dans l'âme; **to give a dress an ~*** donner un coup de fer à une robe; *V* **fire, grapple, solder** *etc*.
(c) (*fetters*) **~s** fers *mpl*, chaînes *fpl*; **to put** *or* **clap sb in ~s** mettre qn aux fers; (*Naut*) **to be in ~s** faire chapelle.
(d) (*Golf*) fer *m*.
(e) (*U: Med*) (sels *mpl* de) fer *m*.
(f) (*surgical appliance*) attelle-étrier *f*; *V* **leg**.
2 *cpd* (*lit*) *tool, bridge* de *or* en fer; (*fig*) *determination* de fer, d'acier. **the Iron Age** l'âge *m* de fer; **the iron and steel industry** l'industrie *f* sidérurgique; (*Naut*) **ironclad** cuirassé *m*; **to have an iron constitution** avoir une santé de fer, être bâti à chaux et à sable *or* à chaux et à ciment; (*Pol*) **iron curtain** rideau *m* de fer; (*Brit Hist*) **the Iron Duke** le duc de Wellington; (*loc*) **an iron fist** *or* **hand in a velvet glove** une main de fer dans un gant de velours; **iron foundry** fonderie *f* de fonte; **iron grey** gris *inv* de fer, gris fer *inv*; *hair* gris acier *inv*; **to rule with an iron hand** gouverner d'une main *or* poigne de fer; (*Med*) **iron lung** poumon *m* d'acier; **the man in the iron mask** l'homme *m* au masque de fer; **ironmonger** *V* **ironmonger**; **iron ore** minerai *m* de fer; **iron oxide** oxyde *m* de fer; **iron rations** vivres *mpl or* rations *fpl* de réserve; **iron will** volonté *f* de fer; (*U*) **ironwork** (*gates, railings etc*) ferronnerie *f*, serrurerie *f*; (*parts of construction*) ferronnerie, ferrures *fpl*; **heavy ironwork** grosse ferronnerie *or* serrurerie; **ironworks** (*pl inv*) usine *f* sidérurgique; *V* **minimum, non-**.
3 *vt clothes etc* repasser; (*more sketchily*) donner un coup de fer à. **to ~ under a damp cloth** repasser à la pattemouille.
4 *vi [clothes etc]* se repasser.
iron out *vt sep creases* faire disparaître au fer; (*fig*) *difficulties* aplanir; *problems* faire disparaître.
ironic(al) [aɪ'rɒnɪk(əl)] *adj* ironique.
ironically [aɪ'rɒnɪkəlɪ] *adv* ironiquement.
ironing ['aɪənɪŋ] **1** *n* repassage *m*. **to do the ~** repasser, faire le repassage; **it needs no ~** cela n'a pas besoin d'être repassé, cela ne nécessite aucun repassage. **2** *cpd*: **ironing board** planche *f* à repasser.
ironmonger ['aɪən,mʌŋgəʳ] *n* (*Brit*) quincaillier *m*. **~'s (shop)** quincaillerie *f*.
ironmongery ['aɪən,mʌŋgərɪ] *n* (*Brit*) quincaillerie *f*.
irony ['aɪərənɪ] *n* ironie *f*. **the ~ of fate** l'ironie du sort; **the ~ of it is that ...** ce qu'il y a d'ironique (là-dedans) c'est que ...; *V* **dramatic**.
Iroquois ['ɪrəkwɔɪ] **1** *adj* iroquois. **2** *n* **(a)** (*also* **~ Indian**) Iroquois(e) *m(f)*. **(b)** (*Ling*) iroquois *m*.
irradiate [ɪ'reɪdɪeɪt] **1** *vt* **(a)** (*illuminate: lit, fig*) illuminer. **(b) to ~ light** émettre de la lumière; **to ~ heat** dégager de la chaleur. **(c)** (*expose to radiation*) irradier. **2** *vi* irradier.
irradiation [ɪ,reɪdɪ'eɪʃən] *n* (*V* **irradiate**) illumination *f*; irradiation *f*.
irrational [ɪ'ræʃənl] *adj person* pas rationnel; *animal* dépourvu de raison; *belief* déraisonnable, absurde; *conduct* irrationnel; (*Math*) irrationnel. **she had become quite ~ about it** elle n'était plus du tout capable d'y penser rationnellement.
irrationally [ɪ'ræʃnəlɪ] *adv believe* déraisonnablement; *behave* irrationnellement.
irreconcilable [ɪ,rekən'saɪləbl] *adj enemy, enemies* irréconciliable; *hatred* implacable; *belief, opinion* inconciliable, incompatible (*with* avec).
irrecoverable [,ɪrɪ'kʌvərəbl] *adj object* irrécupérable; (*Fin*) irrécouvrable; (*fig*) *loss* irréparable, irrémédiable.
irredeemable [,ɪrɪ'di:məbl] *adj* **(a)** *person* incorrigible, incurable; *error* irréparable; *disaster* irrémédiable. **(b)** (*Fin*) *loan* non amortissable, non remboursable; *bond* irremboursable.
irreducible [,ɪrɪ'dju:səbl] *adj* irréductible.
irrefutable [,ɪrɪ'fju:təbl] *adj argument* irréfutable; *testimony* irrécusable.
irregular [ɪ'regjʊləʳ] **1** *adj* **(a)** *marriage, troops, situation, hours, behaviour* irrégulier. **to be ~ in one's attendance** assister *or* être présent de façon peu régulière *or* intermittente; **he leads a very ~ life** il mène une vie très déréglée; **all this is very ~** tout cela n'est pas du tout régulier.
(b) *shape, pulse, handwriting* irrégulier; *surface* inégal; *object, outline* irrégulier, asymétrique.
(c) (*Ling*) irrégulier.
2 *npl* (*Mil*) **the ~s** les irréguliers *mpl*.
irregularity [ɪ,regjʊ'lærɪtɪ] *n* (*V* **irregular**) irrégularité *f*; asymétrie *f*. **the ~ of the ground** les accidents *mpl* du terrain.
irrelevance [ɪ'reləvəns] *n*, **irrelevancy** [ɪ'reləvənsɪ] *n* **(a)** (*U*) manque *m* de rapport, manque d'à-propos (*to* avec). **(b) a report full of ~s** *or* **irrelevancies** un compte rendu qui s'écarte sans cesse du sujet.
irrelevant [ɪ'reləvənt] *adj* sans rapport; *question, remark* hors de propos. **that's ~** cela n'a rien à voir avec *or* cela est sans rapport avec la question; **~ to the subject** hors du sujet.
irreligion [,ɪrɪ'lɪdʒən] *n* irréligion *f*.
irreligious [,ɪrɪ'lɪdʒəs] *adj* irréligieux.
irremediable [,ɪrɪ'mi:dɪəbl] *adj* irrémédiable, sans remède.
irremediably [,ɪrɪ'mi:dɪəblɪ] *adv* irrémédiablement.
irremovable [,ɪrɪ'mu:vəbl] *adj thing* immuable; *difficulty* invincible; *judge etc* inamovible.
irreparable [ɪ'repərəbl] *adj harm, wrong* irréparable; *loss* irréparable, irrémédiable.
irreparably [ɪ'repərəblɪ] *adv* irréparablement, irrémédiablement.
irreplaceable [,ɪrɪ'pleɪsəbl] *adj* irremplaçable.
irrepressible [,ɪrɪ'presəbl] *adj envy, laughter* irrépressible, irrésistible. **she's quite ~** elle pétille d'entrain, elle fait preuve d'un entrain débridé *or* irrépressible; (*of child*) c'est un vrai petit diable.
irreproachable [,ɪrɪ'prəʊtʃəbl] *adj* irréprochable.
irresistible [,ɪrɪ'zɪstəbl] *adj* irrésistible.
irresistibly [,ɪrɪ'zɪstəblɪ] *adv* irrésistiblement.
irresolute [ɪ'rezəlu:t] *adj* irrésolu, indécis, hésitant.
irresoluteness [ɪ'rezəlu:tnɪs] *n* irrésolution *f*, indécision *f*.
irrespective [,ɪrɪ'spektɪv] *adj*: **~ of** sans tenir compte de.
irresponsibility ['ɪrɪs,pɒnsə'bɪlɪtɪ] *n* (*also Jur*) irresponsabilité *f*.
irresponsible [,ɪrɪs'pɒnsəbl] *adj person* qui n'a pas le sens des responsabilités, irréfléchi; *act, remark* irréfléchi, inconsidéré; (*Jur*) irresponsable.
irretrievable [,ɪrɪ'tri:vəbl] *adj loss, damage* irréparable, irrémédiable; *object* introuvable.
irretrievably [,ɪrɪ'tri:vəblɪ] *adv* irréparablement, irrémédiablement.
irreverence [ɪ'revərəns] *n* irrévérence *f*.
irreverent [ɪ'revərənt] *adj* irrévérencieux.
irreverently [ɪ'revərəntlɪ] *adv* irrévérencieusement, avec irrévérence.
irreversible [,ɪrɪ'vɜ:səbl] *adj movement, operation* irréversible; *decision, judgment* irrévocable.
irrevocable [ɪ'revəkəbl] *adj* irrévocable.
irrevocably [ɪ'revəkəblɪ] *adv* irrévocablement.
irrigable ['ɪrɪgəbl] *adj* irrigable.
irrigate ['ɪrɪgeɪt] *vt* (*Agr, Med*) irriguer.
irrigation [,ɪrɪ'geɪʃən] *n* (*Agr, Med*) irrigation *f*.
irritability [,ɪrɪtə'bɪlɪtɪ] *n* (*V* **irritable**) irritabilité *f*; (*irascibility*) mauvais caractère, irascibilité *f* (*liter*).
irritable ['ɪrɪtəbl] *adj person* (*cross*) irritable; (*irascible*) irascible, coléreux; *look, mood* irritable; *temperament, nature* irascible. **to get** *or* **grow ~** devenir irritable.
irritably ['ɪrɪtəblɪ] *adv behave, nod* avec humeur; *speak* d'un ton irrité.
irritant ['ɪrɪtənt] *adj, n* (*esp Med*) irritant (*m*).
irritate ['ɪrɪteɪt] *vt* **(a)** (*annoy*) irriter, agacer. **(b)** (*Med*) irriter.
irritating ['ɪrɪteɪtɪŋ] *adj* **(a)** (*annoying*) irritant, agaçant. **(b)** (*Med*) irritant.
irritation [,ɪrɪ'teɪʃən] *n* (*also Med*) irritation *f*.
irruption [ɪ'rʌpʃən] *n* irruption *f*.
is [ɪz] *V* **be**.
...ish [ɪʃ] *suf* **(a)** ...âtre. **blackish** noirâtre. **(b) she came at threeish** elle est venue vers trois heures *or* sur les trois heures; **it's coldish** il fait un peu froid *or* frisquet*; **she's fortyish** elle a dans les quarante ans*.
isinglass ['aɪzɪŋglɑ:s] *n* ichtyocolle *f*; (*Culin*) gélatine *f*.
Islam ['ɪzlɑ:m] *n* Islam *m*.
Islamic [ɪz'læmɪk] *adj* islamique.
Islamism ['ɪzləmɪzəm] *n* Islamisme *m*.
island ['aɪlənd] **1** *n* **(a)** (*lit, fig*) île *f*. **small ~** îlot *m*. **(b)** (*also* **traffic** *or* **street ~**) refuge *m* (*pour piétons*). **2** *cpd people, community* des îles, insulaire; (*of specific ~*) de l'île.
islander ['aɪləndəʳ] *n* insulaire *mf*, habitant(e) *m(f)* d'une île *or* de l'île.
isle [aɪl] *n* **(a)** (*liter*) île *f*. **(b)** (*Geog*) **I~ of Man** île de Man; **I~ of Wight** île de Wight; *V* **British**.
islet ['aɪlɪt] *n* îlot *m*.
ism ['ɪzəm] *n* doctrine *f*, théorie *f*. **all the ~s of today** tous les mots en 'isme' actuels.
...ism ['ɪzəm] *suf* ...isme.
isn't ['ɪznt] = **is not**; *V* **be**.
iso... ['aɪsəʊ] *pref* iso... .
isobar ['aɪsəʊbɑ:ʳ] *n* isobare *f*.
isolate ['aɪsəʊleɪt] *vt* (*all senses*) isoler (*from* de).
isolated ['aɪsəʊleɪtɪd] *adj* (*Chem, Med etc*) isolé; *village* isolé, écarté. **~ case** cas isolé; **to feel ~** se sentir isolé.
isolation [,aɪsəʊ'leɪʃən] **1** *n* **(a)** (*gen, Med*) isolement *m*; *[village etc]* isolement, solitude *f*. **splendid ~** splendide isolement.
(b) (*Chem etc*) (*action*) isolation *f*; (*state*) isolement *m*.
2 *cpd*: **isolation hospital** hôpital *m* d'isolement *or* de contagieux; **isolation ward** salle *f* des contagieux.
isolationism [,aɪsəʊ'leɪʃənɪzəm] *n* isolationnisme *m*.
isolationist [,aɪsəʊ'leɪʃənɪst] *adj, n* isolationniste (*mf*).
Isolde [ɪ'zɒldə] *n* Iseut *f*.
isosceles [aɪ'sɒsɪli:z] *adj* isocèle.
isotherm ['aɪsəʊθɜ:m] *n* isotherme *f*.
isotope ['aɪsəʊtəʊp] *adj, n* isotope (*m*).
Israel ['ɪzreɪl] *n* Israël *m*.
Israeli [ɪz'reɪlɪ] **1** *adj* israélien. **2** *n* Israélien(ne) *m(f)*.
Israelite ['ɪzrɪəlaɪt] *n* Israélite *mf*.
issue ['ɪʃu:] **1** *n* **(a)** (*matter, question*) question *f*, sujet *m*, problème *m*. **it is a very difficult ~** c'est une question *or* un sujet *or* un problème très complexe, c'est un point très délicat; **he raised several new ~s** il a soulevé plusieurs points nouveaux; **the ~ is whether ...** la question consiste à savoir si ...; **the main ~ is to discover if ...** la question centrale est de découvrir si ...; **that's the main ~** voilà la question *or* le problème principal(e); **it's not a political ~** ce n'est pas un problème politique; **to cloud** *or* **confuse** *or* **obscure the ~** brouiller les cartes; **to face the ~** regarder le problème en face; **to force the ~** forcer une décision; **to evade** *or* **avoid the ~** prendre la tangente, s'échapper

par la tangente; **to make an ~ of sth** faire de qch un sujet de controverse, faire un problème de qch, monter qch en épingle; **he makes an ~ of every tiny detail** il fait une montagne du moindre détail; **I don't want to make an ~ of it but ...** je ne veux pas trop insister là-dessus mais ...; **the matter/factors at ~** l'affaire/les facteurs en jeu; **the point at ~** le point controversé, la question en litige *or* qui pose un problème; **his integrity is not at ~** son intégrité n'est pas (mise) en doute *or* en cause; **his political future is at ~** son avenir politique est (mis) en question *or* en cause; **they were at ~ over ...** ils étaient en désaccord sur ...; **to take** *or* **join ~ with sb** engager une controverse avec qn; **I feel I must take ~ with you on this** je me permets de ne pas partager votre avis là-dessus; *V* **side.**

(b) (*outcome*) résultat *m*, aboutissement *m*, issue *f*. **in the ~** en fin de compte, à la fin; **until the ~ is known** jusqu'à ce qu'on sache le résultat; **favourable ~** résultat heureux, heureuse issue; **we brought the matter to a successful ~** nous avons mené l'affaire à une heureuse conclusion.

(c) *[book]* publication *f*, parution *f*, sortie *f*; *[magazine, newspaper]* livraison *f*; *[goods, tickets]* distribution *f*; *[passport, document]* délivrance *f*; *[banknote, cheque, shares, stamp]* émission *f*, mise *f* en circulation; *[proclamation]* parution; (*Jur*) *[warrant, writ, summons]* lancement *m*. **there has been a new ~ of banknotes/stamps/shares** il y a eu une nouvelle émission de billets/de timbres/d'actions; **there were several ~s of clothing to refugees** il y a eu plusieurs distributions de vêtements aux réfugiés; **these coins are a new ~** ces pièces viennent d'être émises.

(d) (*copy*) *[newspaper, magazine]* numéro *m*. **in this ~** dans ce numéro; **back ~** vieux numéro.

(e) (*Med*) écoulement *m*.

(f) (*U: Jur: offspring*) descendance *f*, progéniture *f* (*liter*). **without ~** sans enfants, sans progéniture (*liter*), sans descendance; **X and his ~** X et sa descendance *or* ses descendants.

2 *cpd* (*esp Mil*) *clothing etc* réglementaire, d'ordonnance.

3 *vt book* publier, faire paraître; *order* donner; *goods, tickets* distribuer; *passport, document* délivrer; *banknote, cheque, shares, stamps* émettre, mettre en circulation; *proclamation* faire; (*Jur*) *warrant, warning, writ* lancer; (*Jur*) *verdict* rendre. **to ~ a statement** publier une mise au point, faire une déclaration; (*Jur*) **to ~ a summons** lancer une assignation; (*Fin*) **~d to bearer** émis au porteur; **to ~ sth to sb, to ~ sb with sth** fournir *or* donner qch à qn; **the children were ~d with pencils** on distribua *or* fournit *or* donna des crayons aux enfants.

Istanbul [ˌɪstænˈbuːl] *n* Istamboul.

isthmus [ˈɪsməs] *n* isthme *m*.

it[1] [ɪt] *pron* **(a)** (*specific*) (*nominative*) il, elle; (*accusative*) le, la, (*before vowel*) l'; (*dative*) lui. **where is the book? — ~'s on the table** où est le livre? — il est sur la table; **my machine is old but ~ works** ma machine est vieille mais elle marche; **here's the pencil — give ~ to me** voici le crayon — donne-le-moi; **if you can find the watch give ~ to him** si tu peux trouver la montre donne-la-lui; **he found the book and brought ~ to me** il a trouvé le livre et me l'a apporté; **let the dog in and give ~ a drink** fais entrer le chien et donne-lui à boire.

(b) of ~, from ~, about ~, for ~ *etc* en; **he's afraid of ~** il en a peur; **I took the letter out of ~** j'en ai sorti la lettre; **I feel the better for ~** je m'en trouve mieux; **I don't care about ~** je ne m'en soucie pas, je m'en fiche*; **speak to him about ~** parlez-lui-en; **he didn't speak to me about ~** il ne m'en a pas parlé; (*following French verbs with 'de'*) **I doubt ~** j'en doute.

(c) in ~, to ~, at ~ *etc* y; **I'll see to ~** j'y veillerai; **he fell in ~** il y est tombé; (*meeting etc*) **he'll be at ~** il y sera; **he agreed to ~** il y a consenti; (*following French verbs with 'à'*) **taste ~!** goutez-y!; **don't touch ~** n'y touche pas.

(d) above ~, over ~ (au-)dessus; **below ~, beneath ~, under ~** (au-)dessous, (en-)dessous; **there's the table and your book is on ~** voilà la table et votre livre est dessus; **a table with a cloth over ~** une table avec une nappe dessus; **he drew a house with a cloud above ~** il a dessiné une maison avec un nuage au-dessus; **there is a fence but you can get under ~** il y a une barrière mais vous pouvez passer (en-)dessous.

(e) (*impers: non-specific*) il, ce, cela, ça. **~ is raining** il pleut; **~'s hot today** il fait chaud aujourd'hui; **~ was a warm evening** il faisait doux ce soir-là; **~ all frightens me** tout cela m'effraie; **~'s very pleasant here** c'est agréable *or* bien ici; **~'s Wednesday 16th October** nous sommes (le) mercredi 16 octobre; **~'s 3 o'clock** il est 3 heures; **who is ~?** qui est-ce?; **~'s me** c'est moi; **what is ~?** qu'est-ce que c'est?; **what's ~ all about?** qu'est-ce qui se passe?, de quoi s'agit-il?, de quoi est-il question?; **where is ~?** où est-ce?, où est-ce que c'est?; **that's ~!** (*approval*) c'est ça!; (*agreement*) c'est bien ça!, exactement!, tout à fait!; (*achievement*) ça y est!, c'est fait!; (*dismay*) ça y est!; **how was ~?** comment ça s'est(-il) passé?, comment c'était?*; **what was that noise? — ~ was the cat** qu'est-ce que c'était que ce bruit? — c'était le chat; **~ isn't worth while** ce n'est pas la peine; **~'s no use trying to see him** ce n'est pas la peine de *or* ça ne sert à rien d'essayer de le voir; **~'s difficult to understand** c'est difficile à comprendre; **~'s difficult to understand why** il est difficile de comprendre pourquoi; **~'s a pity** c'est dommage; **I considered ~ pointless to protest** j'ai jugé (qu'il était) inutile de protester; **~'s fun to go for a swim** c'est amusant d'aller nager; **~ was your father who phoned** c'est ton père qui a téléphoné; **~ was Anne I gave it to** c'est à Anne que je l'ai donné; **~ can't be helped** on n'y peut rien, on ne peut rien y faire; **the best of ~ is that ...** ce qu'il y a de mieux (là-dedans) c'est que ...; **he's not got ~ in him to do this job properly** il est incapable de faire ce travail comme il faut, il n'a pas l'étoffe de mener la chose à bien; **he's got what ~ takes*** il est à la hauteur*; **keep at ~!** continuez!; **they made ~ up** ils se sont réconciliés; **let's face ~** regardons les choses en face; **now you've done ~!** ça y est, regarde ce que tu as fait!; **you'll catch ~!** tu vas écoper!*; **he's had ~*** il est fichu*; **to be with ~*** être dans le vent* *or* à la page; **to get with ~‡** se mettre à la page; **he's got ~ bad‡** il est pincé*; **he's got ~ bad for her‡** il en pince pour elle*, il l'a dans la peau‡; **she's got ~ in for me** elle m'en veut, elle a une dent contre moi*.

(f) (*in games*) **you're ~!** c'est toi le chat!; **she really thinks she's ~*** elle se prend vraiment pour le nombril du monde*.

(g) she's got ~‡ elle est sexy*.

it[2] [ɪt] *n* (*abbr of* **Italian**) **gin and ~** vermouth-gin *m*.

Italian [ɪˈtæljən] **1** *adj* italien, d'Italie. **2** *n* **(a)** Italien(ne) *m(f)*. **(b)** (*Ling*) italien *m*; *V* **Switzerland.**

italic [ɪˈtælɪk] **1** *adj* (*Typ*) italique. **~ script** écriture *f* italique. **2** *npl*: **~s** italique *m*; **to put a word in ~s** mettre un mot en italique; **'my ~s'** 'les italiques sont de moi'.

italicize [ɪˈtælɪsaɪz] *vt* (*Typ*) mettre *or* imprimer en italique.

Italy [ˈɪtəlɪ] *n* Italie *f*.

itch [ɪtʃ] **1** *n* (*lit*) démangeaison *f*. **I've got an ~ in my leg** ma jambe me démange; (*Med, Vet*) **the ~** la gale; (*fig*) **I've got an ~* to travel** l'envie de voyager me démange, je meurs d'envie de voyager.

2 *vi* **(a)** *[person]* éprouver des démangeaisons. **his legs ~** ses jambes le *or* lui démangent; **my back ~es** j'ai des démangeaisons dans le dos, le dos me démange.

(b) (**fig*) **to be ~ing to do sth** avoir une envie qui vous démange de faire qch; **I am ~ing to tell him the news** la langue me démange de lui annoncer la nouvelle; **he's ~ing for a fight** ça le démange de se battre; **my hand is ~ing (to slap him)** la main me démange *or* j'ai la main qui me démange (de le gifler).

3 *vt* démanger.

itching [ˈɪtʃɪŋ] *n* démangeaison *f*. **~ powder** poil *m* à gratter.

itchy [ˈɪtʃɪ] *adj* qui démange. **I've got an ~ back** j'ai le dos qui me démange, j'ai des démangeaisons dans le dos; (*fig*) **he's got ~ feet*** il a la bougeotte*; (*fig*) **he's got ~ fingers*** il est chapardeur, il a les doigts collants*.

it'd [ˈɪtd] = **it had, it would**; *V* **have, would.**

item [ˈaɪtəm] **1** *n* (*in list, at meeting*) question *f*, point *m*; (*in programme*) numéro *m*; (*in catalogue, newspaper; also Comm*) article *m*; (*Jur: in contract*) article; (*Book-keeping*) poste *m*. **~s on the agenda** questions à l'ordre du jour; **the first ~ on the programme** le premier numéro du programme; **to list the ~s** cataloguer les articles; **the first ~ on the list** le premier article de *or* sur la liste; (*Rad, TV*) **the main ~ in the news** le titre principal des informations, la grosse nouvelle, le fait du jour; **it's an important ~ in our policy** c'est un point important de notre politique.

2 *adv* de plus, en outre; (*Comm etc*) item.

itemize [ˈaɪtəmaɪz] *vt bill etc* détailler, spécifier.

itinerant [ɪˈtɪnərənt] *adj preacher* itinérant; *actors, musician* ambulant. **~ lace-seller** colporteur *m*, -euse *f* de dentelle.

itinerary [aɪˈtɪnərərɪ] *n* itinéraire *m*.

it'll [ˈɪtl] = **it will**; *V* **will.**

its [ɪts] **1** *poss adj* son *m* (*also f before vowel*), sa *f*, ses *pl*. **2** *poss pron* le sien, la sienne, les siens, les siennes.

it's [ɪts] = **it is, it has**; *V* **be, have.**

itself [ɪtˈself] *pron* **(a)** (*emphatic*) lui-même *m*, elle-même *f*. **the book ~ is not valuable** le livre (en) lui-même n'est pas de grande valeur; **the chair ~ was covered with ink** la chaise elle-même était couverte d'encre; **she is goodness ~** elle est la bonté même; **she fainted in the theatre ~** elle s'est évanouie en plein théâtre *or* dans le théâtre même; **the door closes by ~** la porte se ferme automatiquement *or* toute seule; **by ~** isolément, en soi; **this by** *or* **in ~ is not bad** ceci n'est pas un mal en soi.

(b) (*reflexive*) se. **the dog hurt ~** le chien s'est fait mal.

I've [aɪv] = **I have**; *V* **have.**

ivory [ˈaɪvərɪ] **1** *n* **(a)** (*U*) ivoire *m*.

(b) (objet *m* d')ivoire *m*. **an ~ of great worth** un ivoire de grande valeur; **ivories** (*: *piano keys*) touches *fpl*; (*Billiards*‡) boules *fpl* de billard; (*dice*) dés *mpl*; (‡: *teeth*) dents *fpl*.

2 *cpd statue, figure* en ivoire, d'ivoire; (*also* **ivory-coloured**) ivoire *inv*. **Ivory Coast** Côte *f* d'Ivoire; (*fig*) **ivory tower** tour *f* d'ivoire.

ivy [ˈaɪvɪ] *n* lierre *m*. (*US*) **I~ League** (*n*) *ensemble des grandes universités du nord-est*; (*adj*) typique des grandes universités du nord-est.

J

J, j [dʒeɪ] *n* (*letter*) J, j *m*.
jab [dʒæb] **1** *vt knife, stick* enfoncer, planter (*into* dans). **he ~bed his elbow into my side** il m'a donné un coup de coude dans les côtes; **he ~bed the cushion with his stick** il a enfoncé son bâton dans le coussin; **he ~bed a finger at the map** il a planté son doigt sur la carte.
2 *vi* (*Boxing*) lancer un coup droit, envoyer un direct (*at* à).
3 *n* **(a)** coup *m* (*donné avec un objet pointu*), coup de pointe.
(b) (*Brit Med**) piqûre *f*. **I've had my ~** on m'a fait ma piqûre.
(c) (*Boxing*) coup droit, direct *m*.
jabber ['dʒæbəʳ] **1** *vt excuse, explanation* bafouiller. **to ~ (out) one's prayers** bredouiller *or* marmotter ses prières. **2** *vi* (*also* **~ away**) (*chatter*) bavarder, jacasser. **they were ~ing (away) in Chinese** ils baragouinaient en chinois.
jabbering ['dʒæbərɪŋ] *n* bavardage *m*, jacasserie *f*; baragouinage *m*.
jacaranda [ˌdʒækə'rændə] *n* jacaranda *m*.
jack [dʒæk] **1** *n* **(a)** (*Aut*) cric *m*.
(b) (*Bowling*) cochonnet *m*, bouchon* *m*.
(c) (*Cards*) valet *m*.
(d) (*flag*) *V* **union**.
(e) (*dim of* **John**) **J~** Jeannot *m*; **J~ Frost** (le) Bonhomme Hiver; **before you could say J~ Robinson*** en moins de temps qu'il n'en faut pour le dire.
(f) every man ~ chacun; **every man ~ of them** tous tant qu'ils sont (*or* étaient *etc*).
2 *cpd*: **jackass** âne *m*, baudet* *m*; (*fig*) crétin* *m* (*V* **laughing**); (*Mil etc*) **jackboots** (*n*) bottes *fpl* à l'écuyère; (*cpd*) *discipline, method* autoritaire, dictatorial; **jackdaw** choucas *m*; (*pej*) **jack-in-office*** gratte-papier *m or* rond-de-cuir *m* (qui joue à l'important); **jack-in-the-box** diable *m* (à ressort); **jack-knife** couteau *m* de poche; **the lorry jack-knifed** la remorque (du camion) s'est mise en travers; **jack-knife dive** saut carpé *or* de carpe; **jack-of-all-trades** bricoleur *m*, homme *m* à tout faire; **jack-o'-lantern** feu follet *m*; **jackpot** (*Betting*) gros lot; (*Cards*) pot *m*; (*lit, fig*) **to hit the jackpot** gagner le gros lot; **their last disc hit the jackpot** leur dernier disque a fait un malheur* *or* un tabac* (*fig*); **jack rabbit** gros lièvre (*de l'Ouest américain*); (*fig*) **jackstraw** nullité *f*; (*game*) **jackstraws** (jeu *m* de) jonchets *mpl*; (*Naut**) **jack tar, Jack Tar** marin *m*, matelot *m*.
jack in‡ *vt sep* plaquer‡.
jack up *vt sep car* soulever avec un cric; (*: *raise*) *prices, wages* faire grimper. **the car was jacked up** la voiture était sur le cric.
jackal ['dʒækɔːl] *n* chacal *m*.
jackanapes ['dʒækəneɪps] *n* polisson(ne) *m(f)*.
jacket ['dʒækɪt] *n* **(a)** *[man]* veston *m*; *[woman]* jaquette *f*; *[child]* paletot *m*; *V* **life**.
(b) *[boiler etc]* enveloppe *f*, chemise *f*; *[book]* couverture *f*; *[fruit, potato etc]* peau *f*, pelure *f*. **potatoes baked in their ~s** pommes de terre en robe des champs *or* en robe de chambre *or* au four.
Jacob ['dʒeɪkəb] *n* Jacob *m*.
Jacobean [ˌdʒækə'biːən] *adj* de l'époque de Jacques Ier *(1603-1625)*.
Jacobite ['dʒækəbaɪt] *n* Jacobite *mf*.
jade[1] [dʒeɪd] **1** *n* jade *m*. **2** *adj* (*colour*) (couleur de) jade *inv*. **3** *cpd*: **jade-green** vert (de) jade *inv*.
jade[2] [dʒeɪd] *n* (*horse*) haridelle *f*, rossinante *f*; († *pej: prostitute*) traînée‡ *f*; (†: *pert girl*) coquine *f*.
jaded ['dʒeɪdɪd] *adj person* épuisé, éreinté, rompu; *palate* blasé. **his appetite was ~** il avait l'estomac fatigué.
jag [dʒæg] **1** *n* **(a)** pointe *f*, saillie *f*, aspérité *f*. **(b)** (‡) cuite* *f*. **they were on a ~ last night** ils se sont bien cuités* *or* ils ont pris une fameuse cuite* hier soir; **he's on the ~ again** il est de nouveau en train de boire. **2** *vt* déchirer, déchiqueter, denteler.
jagged ['dʒægɪd] *adj tear, edge, hole* irrégulier, déchiqueté, dentelé.
jaguar ['dʒægjʊəʳ] *n* jaguar *m*.
jail [dʒeɪl] **1** *n* prison *f*. **he is in ~** il est en prison; **he was in ~ for 5 years** il a fait 5 ans de prison; **to put sb in ~** mettre qn en prison, emprisonner qn, incarcérer qn; **to send sb to ~** condamner qn à la prison; **to send sb to ~ for 5 years** condamner qn à 5 ans de prison.
2 *vt* emprisonner, mettre en prison. **to ~ sb for life** condamner qn (à la réclusion) à perpétuité; **to ~ sb for murder** condamner qn à la prison pour meurtre.
3 *cpd*: **jailbird** récidiviste *mf*; **jailbreak** évasion *f* (de prison); **jailbreaker** évadé(e) *m(f)*.
jailer ['dʒeɪləʳ] *n* geôlier *m*, -ière *f*.
jalopy* [dʒə'lɒpɪ] *n* vieux tacot*, guimbarde *f*.
jalousie ['ʒælu(ː)ziː] *n* jalousie *f* (*store*).
jam[1] [dʒæm] **1** *n* **(a)** (*crowd*) foule *f*, cohue *f*; *[logs, vehicles etc]* embouteillage *m*, encombrement *m*; *V* **traffic**.
(b) (*) pétrin *m*. **to get into a ~** se mettre dans le pétrin; **to get sb out of a ~** tirer qn du pétrin.
2 *cpd*: **jam-full, jam-packed** *vehicle, place* comble, plein à craquer*; *container* plein à ras bord.
3 *vt* **(a)** (*crush, squeeze*) serrer, comprimer, écraser; (*wedge*) coincer. **to be ~med between the wall and the door** être coincé entre le mur et la porte; **ship ~med in the ice** navire bloqué par les glaces; **he got his finger ~med** *or* **he ~med his finger in the door** il s'est coincé le doigt dans la porte.
(b) (*make unworkable*) *brake, door* bloquer, coincer; *gun, machine* enrayer; (*Rad*) *station, broadcast* brouiller; (*Telec*) *line* encombrer.
(c) (*cram*) enfoncer, fourrer en forçant, tasser, entasser (*into* dans). **to ~ clothes into a suitcase** tasser des vêtements dans une valise; **the prisoners were ~med into a small cell** les prisonniers ont été entassés dans une petite cellule; **to ~ one's hat on one's head** enfoncer son chapeau sur sa tête; **to ~ one's foot on the brake** écraser le frein, freiner à bloc *or* à mort*.
(d) (*block*) *[crowd, cars etc] street, corridor* encombrer, embouteiller, obstruer; *door* encombrer. **a street ~med with cars** une rue embouteillée; **the street was ~med with people** la rue était noire de monde.
4 *vi* **(a)** (*press tightly*) *[crowd]* s'entasser (*into* dans).
(b) (*become stuck*) *[brake]* se bloquer; *[gun]* s'enrayer; *[door]* se coincer.
jam in *vt sep* serrer, écraser, coincer. **the crowd jammed him in so that he couldn't move** la foule le bloquait *or* le coinçait tellement qu'il lui était impossible de bouger; **to be jammed in by the crowd** être écrasé *or* compressé par *or* dans la foule; **my car is jammed in** ma voiture est coincée *or* bloquée (entre deux autres).
jam on *vt sep* **(a)** (*Aut*) **to jam on the brakes** bloquer les freins, freiner à bloc *or* à mort*.
(b) to jam on one's hat enfoncer son chapeau sur sa tête.
jam[2] [dʒæm] **1** *n* confiture *f*. **cherry ~** confiture de cerises; (*Brit*) **it's real ~‡** c'est du gâteau*; (*Brit*) **you want ~ on it!*** tu te contentes de peu! (*iro*), t'es pas difficile!* (*iro*), et avec ça?* (*iro*); *V* **money**.
2 *cpd tart* à la confiture. **jamjar, jampot** pot *m* à confitures; **jam puff** feuilleté *m* à la confiture; **jam roll** roulé *m* à la confiture; (*Mus*) **jam session** séance *f* de jazz improvisé, bœuf *m* (*Jazz sl*).
Jamaica [dʒə'meɪkə] *n* Jamaïque *f*. **in ~** à la Jamaïque.
Jamaican [dʒə'meɪkən] **1** *adj* jamaïquain. **2** *n* Jamaïquain(e) *m(f)*.
jamb [dʒæm] *n [door etc]* jambage *m*, montant *m*.
jamboree [ˌdʒæmbə'riː] *n* grand rassemblement; (*merry-making*) festivités *fpl*; (*fig*) réjouissances *fpl*; (*Scouts*) jamboree *m*.
James [dʒeɪmz] *n* Jacques *m*.
jamming ['dʒæmɪŋ] *n* (*Rad*) brouillage *m*.
jammy‡ ['dʒæmɪ] *adj* (*fig*) verni*. **it was ~** c'était un coup de veine* *or* de pot*.
Jane [dʒeɪn] *n* **(a)** Jeanne *f*; *V* **plain**. **(b) j~‡** pépée‡ *f*, nana‡ *f*.
jangle ['dʒæŋgl] **1** *vi [bells, saucepans]* retentir avec un bruit de ferraille *or* de casserole; *[bracelets, chains]* cliqueter. **2** *vt* faire retentir d'une façon discordante; faire cliqueter. **3** *n* bruit discordant; cliquetis *m*.
jangling ['dʒæŋglɪŋ] **1** *adj* (qui fait un bruit) discordant, cacophonique. **2** *n* bruit(s) discordant(s); cliquetis *m*.
janitor ['dʒænɪtəʳ] *n* (*doorkeeper*) portier *m*; (*US, Scot: caretaker*) concierge *m*, gardien *m*.
January ['dʒænjʊərɪ] *n* janvier *m*; *for phrases V* **September**.
Jap [dʒæp] *n* (*abbr of* **Japanese**: *often pej*) Japonais(e) *m(f)*.
Japan [dʒə'pæn] *n* Japon *m*.
japan [dʒə'pæn] **1** *n* laque *f*. **2** *vt* laquer, vernir.
Japanese [ˌdʒæpə'niːz] **1** *adj* japonais, nippon. **2** *n* **(a)** (*pl inv*) Japonais(e) *m(f)*. **(b)** (*Ling*) japonais *m*.
jape [dʒeɪp] *n* (*trick*) farce *f*, tour *m*; (*joke*) blague* *f*.
japonica [dʒə'pɒnɪkə] *n* cognassier *m* du Japon.
jar[1] [dʒɑːʳ] **1** *n* (*harsh sound*) son discordant; (*jolt: lit, fig*) secousse *f*, choc *m*. **that gave him a nasty ~** cela l'a sérieusement ébranlé *or* secoué.
2 *vi* **(a)** (*sound discordant*) rendre un son discordant, grincer, crisser; (*rattle, vibrate*) vibrer, trembler. **to ~ on** *or* **against sth** cogner sur qch *or* heurter qch (avec un bruit discordant).
(b) (*be out of harmony*) *[note]* détonner; *[colours]* jurer (*with* avec); (*fig*) *[ideas, opinions]* ne pas s'accorder (*with* avec), se heurter.
3 *vt structure* ébranler; *person* cogner, heurter; (*fig*) commotionner, choquer. **the explosion ~red the whole building** l'explosion a ébranlé tout le bâtiment; **he was badly ~red by the blow** il a été sérieusement commotionné par le choc; **you ~red my elbow** tu m'as cogné le coude.
jar (up)on *vt fus* irriter, agacer. **this noise jars (up)on my nerves** ce bruit me met les nerfs en boule* *or* me porte sur les nerfs*; **her screams jar (up)on my ears** ses cris m'écorchent *or* me percent les oreilles.
jar[2] [dʒɑːʳ] *n* **(a)** (*of stone, earthenware*) pot *m*, jarre *f*; (*of glass*) bocal *m*; *V* **jam**[2]. **(b)** (*Brit‡: drink*) pot* *m*.

jargon ['dʒɑːgən] *n (technical language)* jargon *m*; *(pompous nonsense)* jargon, charabia* *m*, baragouin *m*.
jarring ['dʒɑːrɪŋ] *adj sound* discordant; *colour* qui jure.
jasmine ['dʒæzmɪn] *n* jasmin *m*.
jasper ['dʒæspəʳ] *n* jaspe *m*.
jaundice ['dʒɔːndɪs] *n (Med)* jaunisse *f*; *(fig)* jalousie *f*, amertume *f*.
jaundiced ['dʒɔːndɪst] *adj (fig) (bitter)* amer, aigri; *(critical)* désapprobateur (*f* -trice). **to look on sth with a ~ eye, to take a ~ view of sth** voir qch d'un mauvais œil; **he has a fairly ~ view of things** il voit les choses en noir; **to give sb a ~ look** regarder qn d'un œil torve.
jaunt [dʒɔːnt] *n* balade* *f*. **to go for a ~** aller faire un tour, aller se balader*; **~ing car** carriole irlandaise (à deux roues).
jauntily ['dʒɔːntɪlɪ] *adv (V* **jaunty**) d'un pas vif; de façon désinvolte; d'un air crâneur*.
jauntiness ['dʒɔːntɪnɪs] *n (sprightliness)* insouciance *f*, légèreté *f*; *(offhand manner)* sans-gêne *m inv*, désinvolture *f*, allure *f* désinvolte *or* cavalière; *(swaggering)* crânerie* *f*, bravade *f*.
jaunty ['dʒɔːntɪ] *adj (sprightly) step* enjoué, vif (*f* vive); *(carefree) smile, air* désinvolte; *(swaggering)* crâneur*.
Java ['dʒɑːvə] *n* Java *f*.
Javanese [ˌdʒɑːvə'niːz] **1** *adj* javanais. **2** *n* **(a)** *(pl inv)* Javanais(e) *m(f)*. **(b)** *(Ling)* javanais *m*.
javelin ['dʒævlɪn] **1** *n (Mil)* javelot *m*, javeline *f*; *(Sport)* javelot. **2** *cpd*: *(Sport)* **javelin thrower** lanceur *m*, -euse *f* de javelot; **javelin throwing** le lancement *or* le lancer du javelot.
jaw [dʒɔː] **1** *n (Anat)* mâchoire *f*; *[pincer, vice]* mâchoire; (‡: *moralizing*) sermon* *m*; (‡: *long-winded talk*) laïus* *m*. *(fig)* **the ~s of the valley** l'entrée *f* de la vallée; **the ~s of death** les griffes *fpl or* l'étreinte *f* de la mort; **the ~s of hell** les portes *fpl* de l'enfer; **I'll break your ~ for you!*** je vais te casser la figure!*; **we had a good old ~** on a bien papoté*; **hold your ~!‡** ferme-là!‡; *V* **lock**[1], **lower**[1].
2 *vi* (‡) *(moralize)* faire un sermon*; *(talk at length)* laïusser*.
3 *vt* (‡) *(moralize at)* sermonner; *(scold)* enguirlander*.
4 *cpd*: **jawbone** (os *m*) maxillaire *m*.
jay [dʒeɪ] **1** *n (Orn)* geai *m*. **2** *cpd*: **jaywalk** marcher *or* se promener sur la chaussée; **jaywalker** piéton indiscipliné.
jazz [dʒæz] **1** *n (Mus)* jazz *m*; (‡: *liveliness*) entrain *m*, allant *m*; (‡: *pretentious talk*) baratin* *m*. **he gave them a lot of ~ about his marvellous job‡** il leur en a mis plein la vue* avec *or* il leur a fait tout un baratin* sur sa magnifique situation; **... and all that ~‡** ... et tout le bataclan*; *V* **hot**.
2 *cpd band, music* de jazz.
3 *vi (dance)* danser (sur un rythme de jazz).
jazz up *vt sep* **(a)** *(Mus)* **to jazz up the classics** *(play)* jouer les classiques en jazz; *(arrange)* adapter les classiques pour le jazz, jazzifier* les classiques.
(b) (‡) animer. **to jazz up a party** mettre de l'entrain *or* de l'animation dans une soirée; **to jazz up an old dress** égayer *or* rajeunir une vieille robe.
jazzy ['dʒæzɪ] *adj colour* tapageur; *pattern* bariolé; *dress* voyant.
jealous ['dʒeləs] *adj* **(a)** *(envious) person, look* jaloux (*of* de). **(b)** *(watchful, careful)* vigilant. **to keep a ~ watch over** *or* **a ~ eye on sb** surveiller qn avec un soin *or* d'un œil jaloux.
jealously ['dʒeləslɪ] *adv (enviously)* jalousement; *(attentively) guard etc* avec vigilance, avec un soin jaloux.
jealousy ['dʒeləsɪ] *n* jalousie *f*.
jeans [dʒiːnz] *npl (trousers)* blue-jean *m*, jean *m*; *(overalls)* bleu *m* de travail.
jeep [dʒiːp] *n* jeep *f*.
jeer [dʒɪəʳ] **1** *n* raillerie *f*, sarcasme *m*; *(from a crowd)* quolibet *m*, huée *f*. **2** *vi [individual]* railler; *[crowd]* huer, conspuer. **to ~ at sb** se moquer de qn, railler qn. **3** *vt* huer, conspuer.
jeering ['dʒɪərɪŋ] **1** *adj* railleur, moqueur, goguenard. **2** *n* sarcasmes *mpl*; *[crowd]* huées *fpl*.
Jehovah [dʒɪ'həʊvə] *n* Jéhovah *m*. **~'s Witness** Témoin *m* de Jéhovah.
jejune [dʒɪ'dʒuːn] *adj* ennuyeux, plat.
jell [dʒel] *vi (Culin) [jelly etc]* épaissir, prendre; (*) *[plan etc]* prendre tournure.
jello ['dʒeləʊ] *n* ® *(US Culin)* gelée *f*.
jelly ['dʒelɪ] **1** *n* **(a)** *(gen, Culin etc)* gelée *f*. **blackcurrant ~** gelée de cassis; *V* **petroleum**. **(b)** (‡) = **gelignite**. **2** *cpd*: **jellyfish** méduse *f*; *(US Culin)* **jelly roll** gâteau roulé.
jemmy ['dʒemɪ] *n (Brit)* pince-monseigneur *f*.
jeopardize ['dʒepədaɪz] *vt* mettre en danger, compromettre.
jeopardy ['dʒepədɪ] *n (U)* danger *m*, péril *m*. **his life is in ~** sa vie est *or* ses jours sont en danger; **his happiness is in ~** son bonheur est menacé *or* en péril; **my business is in ~** mes affaires sont en mauvaise posture.
jeremiad [ˌdʒerɪ'maɪəd] *n* jérémiade *f*.
jerk [dʒɜːk] **1** *n (push, pull, twist etc)* secousse *f*, saccade *f*, à-coup *m*; *(Med)* réflexe tendineux, crispation nerveuse; (‡*pej: person*) pauvre type* *m*. **the car moved along in a series of ~s** la voiture a avancé par saccades *or* par à-coups *or* par soubresauts; **the train started with a series of ~s** le train s'est ébranlé avec une série de secousses *or* de saccades; *V* **physical**.
2 *vt (pull)* tirer brusquement; *(shake)* secouer (par saccades), donner une secousse à. **she ~ed her head up** elle a brusquement redressé la tête; **he ~ed the book out of my hand** d'une secousse il m'a fait lâcher le livre; **he ~ed himself free** il s'est libéré d'une secousse; **to ~ out one's words** parler d'une façon saccadée.
3 *vi* **(a)** se mouvoir par saccades, cahoter. **the car ~ed along** la voiture roulait en cahotant; **he ~ed away (from me)** il a reculé brusquement.
(b) *[person, muscle]* se contracter, se crisper.
jerkily ['dʒɜːkɪlɪ] *adv move* par saccades, par à-coups; *speak* d'une voix saccadée.
jerkin ['dʒɜːkɪn] *n* blouson *m*; *(Hist)* justaucorps *m*, pourpoint *m*.
jerky ['dʒɜːkɪ] *adj motion* saccadé; *(fig) style* haché, heurté.
jerry[1]**‡** ['dʒerɪ] *n (Brit: chamberpot)* pot *m* (de chambre), Jules‡ *m*.
jerry[2] ['dʒerɪ] *cpd*: *(U)* **jerry-building** construction *f* bon marché; **jerry-built** (construit) en carton-pâte; **jerry-can** jerrycan *m*.
Jerry* ['dʒerɪ] *n* Fritz‡ *m inv*, Fridolin* *m*.
jersey ['dʒɜːzɪ] *n (garment)* tricot *m*; *(material)* jersey *m*.
Jersey ['dʒɜːzɪ] *n* **(a)** *(Geog)* (île *f* de) Jersey *f*. **(b)** *(Zool)* race *f* Jersey. **a ~ (cow)** une vache jersiaise *or* de Jersey.
Jerusalem [dʒə'ruːsələm] *n* Jérusalem. **~ artichoke** topinambour *m*.
jessamine ['dʒesəmɪn] *n* = **jasmine**.
jest [dʒest] **1** *n* plaisanterie *f*. **in ~** pour rire, en plaisantant. **2** *vi* plaisanter, se moquer.
jester ['dʒestəʳ] *n (Hist)* bouffon *m*; *(joker)* plaisantin *m*, farceur *m*, -euse *f*. **the King's ~** le fou du Roi.
jesting ['dʒestɪŋ] **1** *adj person* porté à la plaisanterie; *remark* (fait) en plaisantant *or* pour plaisanter. **2** *n* plaisanterie(s) *f(pl)*.
Jesuit ['dʒezjʊɪt] *n (Rel, fig)* Jésuite *m*.
jesuitic(al) [ˌdʒezjʊ'ɪtɪk(əl)] *adj (Rel, fig)* jésuitique.
Jesus ['dʒiːzəs] *n* Jésus *m*. **~ Christ** Jésus-Christ; *(excl)* **~!‡** nom de Dieu!‡; *V* **society**.
jet[1] [dʒet] **1** *n* **(a)** *[liquids]* jet *m*, giclée *f*; *[gas]* jet.
(b) *(Aviat: also* **~ plane)** avion *m* à réaction, jet *m*.
(c) *(nozzle)* brûleur *m*; *(Aut)* gicleur *m*.
2 *cpd (Aviat) travel* en jet. *(Aviat)* **jet engine** moteur *m* à réaction, réacteur *m*, jet *m*; *(Aviat)* **jet fighter** chasseur *m* à réaction; **jet fuel** kérosène *m*; **jet lag** (les troubles dûs au) décalage *m* horaire; **jet-powered, jet-propelled** à réaction; **jet propulsion** propulsion *f* par réaction; **the jet set*** la clientèle des Boeing, le monde des playboys.
3 *vi* **(a)** *[liquids]* gicler, jaillir.
(b) *(Aviat)* voyager en avion *or* en jet.
4 *vt* faire gicler, faire jaillir.
jet[2] [dʒet] *n* jais *m*. **~-black** de jais, noir comme jais.
jetsam ['dʒetsəm] *n* **(a)** *(U) objets jetés à la mer etc rejetés sur la côte*; *V* **flotsam**. **(b)** *(fig: down-and-outs)* épaves *fpl (fig)*.
jettison ['dʒetɪsn] *vt* **(a)** *(Naut)* jeter par-dessus bord, jeter à la mer *(pour alléger le navire)*, se délester de. **(b)** *(Aviat) bombs, fuel, cargo* larguer. **(c)** *(fig) hopes, chances* abandonner, renoncer à; *burden* se délester de.
jetty ['dʒetɪ] *n (breakwater)* jetée *f*, digue *f*; *(landing pier)* embarcadère *m*, débarcadère *m*; *(of wood)* appontement *m*.
Jew [dʒuː] *n* Juif *m*. **~-baiting** persécution *f* des Juifs; **~'s harp** guimbarde *f*.
jewel ['dʒuːəl] *n* bijou *m*, joyau *m*; *(gem)* pierre précieuse; *(Tech: in watch)* rubis *m*; *(fig)* bijou *m*, trésor *m*, perle *f*. **~ box, ~ case** coffret *m* à bijoux.
jewelled, *(US)* **jeweled** ['dʒuːəld] *adj* orné *or* paré de bijoux *or* de pierreries; *watch* monté sur rubis.
jeweller, *(US)* **jeweler** ['dʒuːələʳ] *n* bijoutier *m*, joaillier *m*. **~'s (shop)** bijouterie *f*, joaillerie *f*.
jewellery, *(US)* **jewelry** ['dʒuːəlrɪ] *n (U)* bijoux *mpl*, joyaux *mpl*, bijouterie *f*. **a piece of ~** un bijou.
Jewess ['dʒuːɪs] *n* Juive *f*.
Jewish ['dʒuːɪʃ] *adj* juif.
Jewry ['dʒʊərɪ] *n* la communauté juive, les Juifs *mpl*.
jib [dʒɪb] **1** *n* **(a)** *(Naut)* foc *m*. *(fig)* **the cut of his ~*** son allure, sa tournure. **(b)** *[crane]* flèche *f*, bras *m*. **2** *vi [person]* regimber, renâcler (*at sth* devant qch), répugner (*at sth* à qch), se refuser (*at doing* à faire); *[horse]* refuser d'avancer, regimber, se dérober. **the horse ~bed at the fence** le cheval a refusé la barrière.
jibe[1] [dʒaɪb] = **gibe**.
jibe[2]* [dʒaɪb] *vi (US: agree)* coller *(fig)*.
jiffy* ['dʒɪfɪ] *n*: **wait a ~** attends une minute *or* une seconde; **half a ~!** une seconde!; **in a ~** en moins de deux*.
jig [dʒɪg] **1** *n* **(a)** *(dance)* gigue *f*.
(b) *(Tech)* calibre *m*, gabarit *m*.
2 *vi (dance)* danser la gigue; *(fig: also* **~ about, ~ around)** sautiller, gigoter*, se trémousser. **to ~ up and down** sautiller, se trémousser.
3 *cpd*: *(Tech)* **jigsaw** scie *f* à chantourner; **jigsaw (puzzle)** puzzle *m*.
jigger[1] ['dʒɪgəʳ] *n (sieve)* tamis *m*, crible *m*.
jigger[2] ['dʒɪgəʳ] *n (sand flea)* pou *m* des sables.
jiggered‡ ['dʒɪgəd] *adj (Brit)* **(a)** *(astonished)* étonné. **well, I'm ~!** nom d'un chien!* **(b)** *(exhausted)* éreinté, crevé*.
jiggery-pokery‡ ['dʒɪgərɪ'pəʊkərɪ] *n (Brit: U)* entourloupettes* *fpl*, manigances *fpl*, micmac(s)* *m(pl)*.
jiggle ['dʒɪgl] *vt* secouer légèrement.
jilt [dʒɪlt] *vt* rompre avec, laisser tomber* *(un(e) fiancé(e))*.
Jim [dʒɪm] *n (dim of* **James**) Jacquot *m*, Jim *m*. *(US)* **~ Crow** *(policy)* politique *f* raciste *(envers les noirs)*; *(pej: Negro)* nègre *m (pej)*.
jimjams‡ ['dʒɪmdʒæmz] *n*: **to have the ~** *(from revulsion)* avoir des frissons *or* la chair de poule; *(from fear)* avoir les chocottes‡.
Jimmy ['dʒɪmɪ] *n* **(a)** *(dim of* **James**) Jacquot *m*, Jimmy *m*. **(b)** *(US)* **j~** = **jemmy**.
jingle ['dʒɪŋgl] **1** *n [keys etc]* tintement *m*, cliquetis *m*; *(fig: catchy verse)* petit couplet. **advertising ~** couplet *m* publicitaire. **2** *vi* tinter, cliqueter. **3** *vt keys, coins* faire tinter, faire sonner.

jingo ['dʒɪŋɡəʊ] *n* chauvin *m*. **by ~!*** ça alors!, nom d'une pipe!*

jingoism ['dʒɪŋɡəʊɪzəm] *n* chauvinisme *m*.

jingoistic [ˌdʒɪŋɡəʊ'ɪstɪk] *adj* chauvin.

jinks [dʒɪŋks] *npl V* **high 4.**

jinx* [dʒɪŋks] *n* porte-guigne* *m*, porte-poisse* *m*. **there's a ~ on this watch** on a jeté un sort à cette montre, cette montre est ensorcelée.

jitney‡ ['dʒɪtniː] *n* (*US*) **(a)** pièce *f* de cinq 'cents'. **(b)** *autobus m à itinéraire fixe et à prix modique.*

jitterbug ['dʒɪtəbʌɡ] **1** *n* (*dance*) boogie-woogie *m*; (*dancer*) fana* *mf* du boogie-woogie; (*: *panicky person*) froussard(e)* *m(f)*, trouillard(e)‡ *m(f)*, paniquard‡ *m*. **2** *vi* (*dance*) danser le boogie-woogie.

jitters* ['dʒɪtəz] *npl* frousse* *f*, trouille‡ *f*. **to have the ~** avoir la frousse*; **to give sb the ~** flanquer la frousse à qn*.

jittery* ['dʒɪtərɪ] *adj* froussard*, trouillard‡. **to be ~** avoir la frousse* *or* la trouille‡.

jiujitsu [dʒuː'dʒɪtsuː] *n* jiu-jitsu *m*.

jive [dʒaɪv] **1** *n* swing *m*. **2** *vi* danser le swing.

Joan [dʒəʊn] *n* Jeanne *f*. **~ of Arc** Jeanne d'Arc.

job [dʒɒb] **1** *n* **(a)** (*piece of work*) travail *m*, besogne *f*, tâche *f*, boulot* *m*. **I have a little ~ for you** j'ai un petit travail pour vous; **he's on the ~*** rien ne lui échappe; **he has made a good ~ of it** il a fait du bon travail *or* de la bonne besogne *or* du bon boulot*; **he has made a bad ~ of it** il a saboté son travail*, il a fait du sale boulot*; **he's done a good ~ of work** il a fait du bon travail; **this new airliner is a lovely ~*** ce nouvel avion c'est vraiment du beau travail*; **who's the blonde ~‡ in the red dress?** qui est la nana blonde fringuée en rouge?‡; *V* **odd.**

(b) (*post, situation*) travail *m*, poste *m*, boulot* *m*, job* *m*. **he found a ~ as a librarian** il a trouvé un poste de bibliothécaire; **he has a ~ for the vacation** il a un travail *or* un boulot* *or* un job* pour les vacances; **to look for a ~** chercher du travail; **to be out of a ~** être au *or* en chômage; **he has a very good ~** il a une belle situation; **~s for the boys*** des planques pour les (petits) copains*; *V* **cushy.**

(c) (*duty, responsibility*) travail *m*, boulot* *m*. **it's not my ~ to supervise him** ce n'est pas à moi *or* ce n'est pas mon travail de le surveiller; **he's got a ~ to do, he's only doing his ~** il ne fait que son boulot*; **he knows his ~** il connaît son affaire; **that's not his ~** ce n'est pas de son ressort, ce n'est pas son boulot*; **I had the ~ of telling them** c'est moi qui ai été obligé de le leur dire.

(d) (*state of affairs*) **it's a good ~ (that) he managed to meet you** c'est heureux *or* c'est une chance qu'il ait pu vous rencontrer; **that's a good ~!** à la bonne heure!; **it's a bad ~** c'est une sale affaire, c'est une affaire enquiquinante*; **to give sth/sb up as a bad ~** renoncer à qch/qn en désespoir de cause; **this is just the ~*** c'est juste *or* exactement ce qu'il faut.

(e) (*difficulty*) **to have a ~ to do sth** *or* **doing sth** avoir du mal à faire qch; **I had a ~ to finish this letter** j'ai eu du mal à venir à bout de cette lettre; **it was a ~** *or* **an awful ~ to organize this party** ça a été un sacré* travail *or* tout un travail pour organiser cette soirée; **it's been quite a ~ getting him back home** ça a été toute une affaire pour le ramener chez lui; **you've got a real ~ there!** tu n'es pas au bout de tes peines!

(f) (*dishonest business*) combine* *f*, tripotage* *m*. **a put-up ~** un coup monté; **remember that bank ~?** tu te rappelles le coup de la banque?

2 *cpd*: (*Ind*) **job analysis** analyse *f* des tâches, analyse statique *or* par poste de travail; (*Brit*) **job centre** agence *f* pour l'emploi; **job creation** création *f* d'emplois nouveaux; **job evaluation** qualification *f* du travail; **job hunting** chasse *f* à l'emploi; **job lot** lot *m* d'articles divers; **to sell/buy as a job lot** vendre/acheter par *or* en lot; **job satisfaction** satisfaction *f* au travail.

3 *vi* (*do casual work*) faire des petits travaux; (*St Ex*) négocier, faire des transactions; (*profit from public position*) tripoter*.

4 *vt* (*also* **~ out**) *work* sous-traiter.

jobber ['dʒɒbəʳ] *n* (*Brit St Ex*) *intermédiaire m qui traite directement avec l'agent de change*; (*pieceworker*) ouvrier *m*, -ière *f* à la tâche; (*dishonest person*) tripoteur* *m*, -euse* *f*.

jobbery ['dʒɒbərɪ] *n* (*Brit: U*) tripotage* *m*, maquignonnage *m*.

jobbing ['dʒɒbɪŋ] **1** *adj gardener* à la journée; *workman* à la tâche. **2** *n* (*U*) (*St Ex*) transactions boursières; (*odd jobs*) tripotage* *m*, maquignonnage *m*.

jobless ['dʒɒblɪs] *adj* sans travail, sans emploi, au *or* en chômage. **the ~** les chômeurs *mpl*, les sans-travail *mpl*.

Job's comforter ['dʒəʊbz'kʌmfətəʳ] *n* piètre consolateur *m*, -trice *f*.

Jock [dʒɒk] *n* (*Mil sl*) soldat écossais; (*gen*) Écossais *m*.

jockey ['dʒɒkɪ] **1** *n* jockey *m*. **J~ club** Jockey-Club *m*.

2 *vi*: **to ~ about** se bousculer; (*lit, fig*) **to ~ for position** manœuvrer pour se placer avantageusement; **they were ~ing for office in the new government** ils intriguaient pour se faire donner des postes dans le nouveau gouvernement.

3 *vt*: **to ~ sb into doing** inciter sournoisement qn à faire; **to ~ sb out of a job** réussir à (faire) évincer qn.

jockstrap ['dʒɒkstræp] *n* suspensoir *m*.

jocose [dʒə'kəʊs] *adj* (*merry*) joyeux, enjoué, jovial; (*jesting*) facétieux.

jocular ['dʒɒkjʊləʳ] *adj* (*merry*) joyeux, enjoué, jovial; (*humorous*) facétieux, badin, divertissant.

jocund ['dʒɒkənd] *adj* gai, joyeux, jovial.

jodhpurs ['dʒɒdpɜːz] *npl* jodhpurs *mpl*, culotte *f* de cheval.

Joe [dʒəʊ] *n* (*dim of* **Joseph**) Jo-Jo *m*.

jog [dʒɒɡ] **1** *n* **(a)** (*jerk*) secousse *f*, cahot *m*; (*nudge*) légère poussée; (*with elbow*) coup *m* de coude.

(b) (*also* **~-trot**) petit trot. **to go along at a ~(-trot)** aller au petit trot.

2 *vt* (*shake*) secouer, bringuebaler*; (*jerk*) faire cahoter; (*nudge*) pousser. **to ~ sb's elbow** pousser le coude de qn; (*fig*) **to ~ sb's memory** rafraîchir la mémoire de qn; (*fig*) **to ~ sb into action** secouer qn, inciter qn à agir.

3 *vi* **(a)** cahoter. **the cart ~s along the path** la charrette cahote sur le chemin.

(b) (*Sport*) faire du footing.

jog about 1 *vi* sautiller.

2 *vt sep* remuer.

jog along *vi* (*lit*) *[person, vehicle]* aller son petit bonhomme de chemin, cheminer; (*fig*) *[person]* aller cahin-caha*; *[piece of work, course of action]* aller tant bien que mal.

jog around *vti* = **jog about.**

jog on *vi* = **jog along.**

jogging ['dʒɒɡɪŋ] *n* (*Sport*) footing *m*.

joggle ['dʒɒɡl] **1** *vt* secouer. **2** *vi* branler, se mouvoir par saccades. **3** *n* légère secousse.

John [dʒɒn] *n* **(a)** Jean *m*. **~ the Baptist** saint Jean-Baptiste; **~ Bull** John Bull (*l'Anglais type; la nation anglaise*); (*US*) **~ Doe** M Dupont, M Durand. **(b)** (*US*‡) **the j~** les cabinets *mpl*.

Johnny ['dʒɒnɪ] *n* **(a)** (*dim of* **John**) Jeannot *m*. **(b) j~‡** type* *m*; *V* **onion.**

join [dʒɔɪn] **1** *vt* **(a)** (*lit, fig: also* **~ together**) (*unite*) joindre, unir; (*link*) relier (*to* à); (*Carpentry*) *2 bits of wood* joindre; *broken halves of stick etc* raccorder; (*Elec*) *batteries* accoupler, connecter. **to ~ 2 things (together)** joindre *or* réunir 2 choses; **to ~ sth to sth** unir qch à qch; **the island was ~ed to the mainland by a bridge** l'île était reliée à la terre par un pont; (*Mil, fig*) **to ~ battle (with)** entrer en lutte *or* engager le combat (avec); **to ~ hands** se donner la main; (*Mil, fig*) **to ~ forces** unir leurs forces; (*fig*) **to ~ forces (with sb) to do** s'unir (à qn) pour faire; **~ed in marriage** *or* **matrimony** unis par les liens du mariage; *V* **issue.**

(b) (*become member of*) *club* devenir membre de; *political party* entrer à, s'inscrire à, adhérer à; *university* entrer à, s'inscrire à; *procession* se joindre à. **to ~ the army** *etc* s'engager *or* s'enrôler dans l'armée *etc*; **to ~ one's regiment** rejoindre son régiment; **to ~ a religious order** entrer dans un ordre religieux; **to ~ one's ship** rallier *or* rejoindre son bâtiment; **to ~ the queue** prendre la queue.

(c) *person* rejoindre, retrouver. **I'll ~ you in 5 minutes** je vous rejoins *or* retrouve dans 5 minutes; **Paul ~s me in wishing you ...** Paul se joint à moi pour vous souhaiter ...; **will you ~ us?** (*come with us*) voulez-vous venir avec nous?; (*be one of our number*) voulez-vous être des nôtres?; (*in restaurant etc*) voulez-vous vous asseoir à notre table?; (*in restaurant etc*) **may I ~ you?** je peux *or* puis-je m'asseoir avec vous?; **will you ~ me in a drink?** vous prendrez un verre avec moi?

(d) *[river] another river, the sea* rejoindre, se jeter dans; *[road] another road* rejoindre.

2 *vi* **(a)** (*also* **~ together**; *V* **1a**) se joindre, s'unir; s'associer, se joindre, s'unir (*with* à); *[lines]* se rejoindre, se rencontrer; *[roads]* se rejoindre; *[rivers]* se joindre, avoir leur confluent.

(b) (*Mil: also* **~ up**) entrer dans l'armée.

(c) *[club member]* se faire membre, devenir membre.

3 *n* (*in mended crockery etc*) ligne *f* de raccord; (*Sewing*) couture *f*.

join in 1 *vi* participer, se mettre de la partie*. (*in singing etc*) **join in!** chantez *etc* avec nous!

2 *vt fus game, activity* se mêler à, participer à; *conversation* se mêler à, prendre part à; *protest(s), shouts* joindre sa voix à; *thanks, wishes* s'associer à; *V* **chorus.**

join on 1 *vi [person]* prendre son rang dans la queue *or* dans la file; *[links, parts of structure]* se joindre (*to* à).

2 *vt sep* fixer; (*by tying*) attacher.

join together 1 *vi* = **join 2a.**

2 *vt sep* = **join 1a.**

join up 1 *vi* (*Mil*) s'engager, s'enrôler.

2 *vt sep* joindre, assembler; *pieces of wood or metal* abouter, rabouter; (*Elec*) *wires etc* connecter, accoupler.

joiner ['dʒɔɪnəʳ] *n* menuisier *m*.

joinery ['dʒɔɪnərɪ] *n* menuiserie *f*.

joint [dʒɔɪnt] **1** *n* **(a)** (*Anat*) articulation *f*. **out of ~** *shoulder* démis, déboîté; *wrist* luxé; (*fig*) disloqué, de travers; **to put one's shoulder out of ~** se démettre *or* se déboîter l'épaule; **to put one's wrist out of ~** se luxer le poignet; *V* **ball, finger, nose.**

(b) (*Carpentry*) articulation *f*, jointure *f*; (*in armour*) joint *m*, jointure, articulation; *V* **mitre, universal.**

(c) (*Culin*) rôti *m*. **a cut off the ~** une tranche de rôti.

(d) (‡) (*place*) boîte* *f*; (*night club*) boîte de nuit; (*low pub*) bistro(t)* mal famé; (*gambling den*) tripot *m*.

(e) (*Drugs sl: reefer*) joint *m* (*sl*).

2 *adj* commun, conjugué, réuni. (*Fin*) **~ account** compte joint *or* commun; **~ author** coauteur *m*; **~ committee** commission *f* mixte, comité *m* paritaire; **~ communiqué** communiqué commun; **~ consultations** consultations bilatérales; **~ effort(s)** effort(s) conjugué(s); (*Jur*) **~ estate** biens communs; (*Jur*) **~ heir** cohéritier *m*, -ière *f*; (*Comm*) **~ manager** codirecteur *m*, -trice *f*, cogérant(e) *m(f)*; **~ obligation** coobligation *f*; **~ ownership** copropriété *f*; **~ partner** coassocié(e) *m(f)*; **~ responsibility** coresponsabilité *f*; (*Fin*) **~-stock company** société *f* par actions.

3 *vt* **(a)** (*Culin*) découper (aux jointures).

(b) *pipes* joindre, articuler, emboîter.

jointed ['dʒɔɪntɪd] *adj doll etc* articulé; *fishing rod, tent pole* démontable.

jointly ['dʒɔɪntlɪ] *adv* en commun, conjointement. (*Jur*) **to be ~ liable (for)** être solidaire (de).

jointure ['dʒɔɪntʃəʳ] *n* douaire *m*.

joist [dʒɔɪst] *n* solive *f*.

joke [dʒəʊk] 1 *n* **(a)** (*sth causing amusement*) plaisanterie *f*, blague* *f*. **for a ~** par plaisanterie, pour rire, pour blaguer*; **to make a ~ about** plaisanter sur; **he can't take a ~** il ne comprend pas la plaisanterie; **it's no ~!** (*it's not easy*) ce n'est pas une petite affaire!*; (*it's not enjoyable*) ce n'est pas drôle *or* rigolo* *or* marrant‡; **what a ~!** ce que c'est drôle!; **it's (getting) beyond a ~*** ça cesse d'être drôle; **the ~ is that ...** le plus drôle c'est que ..., ce qu'il y a de drôle *or* de rigolo* *or* de marrant‡ c'est que ...; *V* **standing.**
(b) (*trick*) tour *m*, farce *f*. **to play a ~ on sb** faire une farce à qn, jouer un tour à qn; *V* **practical.**
(c) (*object of amusement*) risée *f*. **he is the ~ of the village** il est la risée du village.
2 *vi* plaisanter, blaguer*. **you're joking!** vous voulez rire!, sans blague!*; **I am not joking** je ne plaisante pas, je suis parfaitement sérieux; **I was only joking** ce n'était qu'une plaisanterie; **you mustn't ~ about his accent** il ne faut pas se moquer de son accent.
joker [ˈdʒəʊkəʳ] *n* **(a)** blagueur* *m*, -euse* *f*. **(b)** (‡: *person*) type* *m*. **(c)** (*Cards*) joker *m*.
joking [ˈdʒəʊkɪŋ] 1 *adj tone* de plaisanterie. 2 *n* (*U*) plaisanterie *f*, blague* *f*. **~ apart** plaisanterie *or* blague* à part.
jokingly [ˈdʒəʊkɪŋlɪ] *adv* en plaisantant, à la blague*. **it was ~ called a luxury hotel** on l'avait baptisé, avec le plus grand sérieux, hôtel de luxe.
jollification* [ˌdʒɒlɪfɪˈkeɪʃən] *n* partie *f* de plaisir *or* de rigolade*, réjouissances *fpl*.
jollity [ˈdʒɒlɪtɪ] *n* gaieté *f or* gaîté *f*, joyeuse humeur.
jolly [ˈdʒɒlɪ] 1 *adj* **(a)** (*merry*) enjoué, jovial.
(b) (*pleasant*) agréable, amusant, plaisant.
2 *cpd*: (*Naut*) **jolly boat** canot *m*; **Jolly Roger** pavillon noir.
3 *adv* (*Brit**) drôlement*, rudement*, vachement‡. **he was ~ glad to come** il était drôlement* content de venir; **you are ~ lucky** tu as une drôle de veine*, tu as une sacrée veine*; **you ~ well will go!** pas question que tu n'y ailles pas!
4 *vt* enjôler, flatter. **they jollied him into joining them, they jollied him along until he agreed to join them** ils l'ont si bien enjôlé qu'il a fini par se joindre à eux.
jolt [dʒəʊlt] 1 *vi* [*vehicle*] cahoter, tressauter. **to ~ along** avancer en cahotant; **to ~ to a stop** faire un arrêt brutal.
2 *vt* (*lit, fig*) secouer, cahoter. (*fig*) **to ~ sb into action** secouer qn, inciter qn à agir.
3 *n* **(a)** (*jerk*) secousse *f*, cahot *m*, à-coup *m*. **the train started with a series of ~s** le train s'est ébranlé avec une série de secousses *or* de saccades; **the car moved along in a series of ~s** la voiture a avancé par saccades *or* par à-coups *or* par soubresauts.
(b) (*fig*) choc *m*. **it gave me a ~** ça m'a fait *or* donné un coup*.
jolting [ˈdʒəʊltɪŋ] 1 *adj* cahotant. 2 *n* (*U*) cahots *mpl*.
jolty [ˈdʒəʊltɪ] *adj car* cahotant, bringuebalant*; *road* cahoteux.
Jonah [ˈdʒəʊnə] *n* Jonas *m*; (*fig*) porte-malheur *m inv*, oiseau *m* de malheur.
jonquil [ˈdʒɒŋkwɪl] 1 *n* jonquille *f*, narcisse *m*. 2 *adj* jonquille *inv*.
Jordan [ˈdʒɔːdn] *n* (*country*) Jordanie *f*; (*river*) Jourdain *m*.
Joseph [ˈdʒəʊzɪf] *n* Joseph *m*.
Josephine [ˈdʒəʊzɪfiːn] *n* Joséphine *f*.
josh‡ [dʒɒʃ] (*US*) 1 *vt* taquiner, mettre en boîte*. 2 *vi* blaguer*. 3 *n* mise *f* en boîte*.
joss stick [ˈdʒɒsstɪk] *n* bâton *m* d'encens.
jostle [ˈdʒɒsl] 1 *vi* se cogner (*against* à), se bousculer. **he ~d against me** il m'a bousculé, il s'est cogné à moi; **to ~ through the crowd** se frayer un chemin (à coups de coudes) à travers la foule; **to ~ for sth** jouer des coudes pour obtenir qch. 2 *vt* bousculer. 3 *n* bousculade *f*.
jot [dʒɒt] *n* brin *m*, iota *m*. **there is not a ~ of truth in this** il n'y a pas un grain de vérité là-dedans; **not one ~ or tittle** pas un iota, pas un brin.
jot down *vt sep* noter, prendre note de. **to jot down notes** prendre *or* griffonner des notes; **to jot down a few points** prendre note de *or* noter quelques points.
jotter [ˈdʒɒtəʳ] *n* (*Brit*) (*exercise book*) cahier *m* (de brouillon); (*pad*) bloc-notes *m*.
jottings [ˈdʒɒtɪŋz] *npl* notes *fpl*.
journal [ˈdʒɜːnl] 1 *n* **(a)** (*periodical*) revue *f*; (*newspaper*) journal *m*. **(b)** (*Naut*) livre *m* de bord; (*Comm*) livre de comptes; (*Jur*) compte rendu. **(c)** (*diary*) journal *m*. 2 *cpd*: (*Tech*) **journal bearing** palier *m*.
journalese [ˌdʒɜːnəˈliːz] *n* (*U*: *pej*) jargon *m* journalistique.
journalism [ˈdʒɜːnəlɪzəm] *n* journalisme *m*.
journalist [ˈdʒɜːnəlɪst] *n* journaliste *mf*.
journalistic [ˌdʒɜːnəˈlɪstɪk] *adj* journalistique.
journey [ˈdʒɜːnɪ] 1 *n* (*travelling*) voyage *m*; (*distance covered*) trajet *m*, parcours *m*. **to go on a ~** partir en voyage; **to set out on one's ~** se mettre en route; **a 2 days' ~** un voyage de 2 jours; **to reach one's ~'s end** arriver à destination; **the ~ from home to office** le trajet de la maison au bureau; **the return ~, the ~ home** le (voyage de) retour; **a car ~** un voyage en voiture; **a long bus ~** un long trajet en autobus; *V* **outward.**
2 *vi* voyager. **to ~ on** continuer son voyage.
3 *cpd*: **journeyman** ouvrier *m*, compagnon *m* (*qui a fini son apprentissage*); **journeyman baker** ouvrier boulanger; **journeyman joiner** compagnon charpentier.
joust [dʒaʊst] 1 *n* joute *f*. 2 *vi* jouter.
Jove [dʒəʊv] *n* Jupiter *m*. **by ~!*** sapristi!*, 'cré nom!‡
jovial [ˈdʒəʊvɪəl] *adj* jovial.
joviality [ˌdʒəʊvɪˈælɪtɪ] *n* jovialité *f*.
jowl [dʒaʊl] *n* (*jaw*) mâchoire *f*; (*cheek*) bajoue *f*; *V* **cheek.**
-jowled [dʒaʊld] *adj ending in cpds*: **square-jowled** à la mâchoire carrée.
joy [dʒɔɪ] 1 *n* **(a)** (*U*) joie *f*. **to my great ~** à ma grande joie; (*iro*) **I wish you ~ of it!** je vous souhaite du plaisir!; (*iro*) **I wish you ~ (of that job)** je vous souhaite bien du plaisir (avec ce travail).
(b) (*gen pl*) **~s** plaisirs *mpl*; **the ~s of the seaside** les plaisirs *or* les charmes *mpl* du bord de la mer; **it's a ~ to hear him** c'est un (vrai) plaisir *or* délice de l'entendre.
2 *cpd*: **to go for a joy ride** faire une virée* *or* une balade* (en voiture) (*parfois volée*); (*Aviat*) **joystick** manche *m* à balai.
joyful [ˈdʒɔɪfʊl] *adj* joyeux.
joyfully [ˈdʒɔɪfəlɪ] *adv* joyeusement.
joyfulness [ˈdʒɔɪfʊlnɪs] *n* grande joie, allégresse *f*, humeur joyeuse.
joyless [ˈdʒɔɪlɪs] *adj* sans joie.
joyous [ˈdʒɔɪəs] *adj* joyeux.
jubilant [ˈdʒuːbɪlənt] *adj person, voice* débordant de joie; *face* épanoui, radieux. **he was ~** il jubilait.
jubilation [ˌdʒuːbɪˈleɪʃən] *n* **(a)** (*emotion*) allégresse *f*, exultation *f*, jubilation *f*. **(b)** (*celebration*) fête *f*, réjouissance(s) *f(pl)*.
jubilee [ˈdʒuːbɪliː] *n* jubilé *m*, cinquantenaire *m*; *V* **diamond** *etc*.
Judaea [dʒuːˈdiːə] *n* Judée *f*.
Judah [ˈdʒuːdə] *n* Juda *m*.
Judaic [dʒuːˈdeɪɪk] *adj* judaïque.
Judaism [ˈdʒuːdeɪɪzəm] *n* judaïsme *m*.
Judas [ˈdʒuːdəs] *n* **(a)** (*name*) Judas *m*. **(b)** (*traitor*) judas *m*, traître *m*. **(c)** (*peephole*) j~ judas *m*.
judder [ˈdʒʌdəʳ] 1 *vi* (*Brit*) vibrer, (*stronger*) trépider. 2 *n* vibration *f*, trépidation *f*.
judge [dʒʌdʒ] 1 *n* **(a)** (*Jur, Sport*) juge *m*. (*Jur*) **~ of appeal** conseiller *m* à la cour d'appel; (*Mil Jur*) **~-advocate** assesseur *m* (*auprès d'un tribunal militaire*).
(b) (*fig*) connaisseur *m*, juge *m*. **to be a good ~ of character** être bon psychologue, savoir juger les gens; **to be a good ~ of wine** être bon juge en vins, s'y connaître en vins; **you are no ~ in this case** tu n'es pas à même de juger cette affaire.
2 *vt* **(a)** (*assess*) *person, conduct, competition* juger; *qualities* apprécier.
(b) (*consider*) juger, estimer. **to ~ it necessary to do** juger *or* estimer nécessaire de faire; **he ~d the moment well (to do)** il a bien su choisir son moment (pour faire).
3 *vi* juger, rendre un jugement. **to ~ for oneself** juger par soi-même; **as far as one can ~** autant qu'on puisse en juger; **judging by** *or* **from** à en juger par *or* d'après.
judg(e)ment [ˈdʒʌdʒmənt] 1 *n* **(a)** (*Jur, Rel*) jugement *m*. **to sit in ~ on** juger; **to give** *or* **pass ~ (on)** prononcer *or* rendre un jugement (sur); *V* **last**[1].
(b) (*fig: opinion*) jugement *m*, opinion *f*, avis *m*. **to give one's ~ (on)** donner son avis (sur).
(c) (*U: good sense*) discernement *m*, bon sens, jugement *m*.
2 *cpd*: (*Rel*) **Judg(e)ment Day** le jour du Jugement.
judicature [ˈdʒuːdɪkətʃəʳ] *n* **(a)** (*process of justice*) justice *f*. **(b)** (*body of judges*) magistrature *f*. **(c)** (*judicial system*) organisation *f* judiciaire.
judicial [dʒuːˈdɪʃəl] *adj* **(a)** (*Jur*) *power, function* judiciaire. **~ proceedings** poursuites *fpl* judiciaires; **~ murder** assassinat *m* juridique *or* légal. **(b)** (*critical*) *mind* critique, impartial. **~ faculty** sens *m* critique.
judiciary [dʒuːˈdɪʃɪərɪ] 1 *adj* judiciaire. 2 *n* **(a)** (*system*) organisation *f* judiciaire. **(b)** (*body of judges*) magistrature *f*. **(c)** (*branch of government*) pouvoir *m* judiciaire.
judicious [dʒuːˈdɪʃəs] *adj* judicieux.
judiciously [dʒuːˈdɪʃəslɪ] *adv* judicieusement.
Judith [ˈdʒuːdɪθ] *n* Judith *f*.
judo [ˈdʒuːdəʊ] *n* judo *m*.
Judy [ˈdʒuːdɪ] *n* (*dim of* **Judith**) Judith *f*; *V* **Punch.**
jug [dʒʌg] 1 *n* **(a)** (*for milk etc*) pot *m*; (*of earthenware*) cruche *f*; (*of metal*) broc *m*.
(b) (*Prison sl: prison*) taule‡ *f or* tôle‡ *f*, bloc‡ *m*. **in ~** en taule‡, au bloc‡.
2 *vt* **(a)** (*Culin*) cuire à l'étuvée *or* à l'étouffée *or* en civet. **~ged hare** civet *m* de lièvre.
(b) (*Prison sl: imprison*) coffrer*.
juggernaut [ˈdʒʌgənɔːt] *n* **(a)** (*fig: destructive force*) force *f or* poussée *f* irrésistible, forces aveugles. **the ~ of war** la force meurtrière de la guerre.
(b) (*fig: cause, belief*) cause *f or* conviction *f* pour laquelle on est sacrifié *or* on se sacrifie soi-même.
(c) (*truck*) mastodonte *m*, monstre *m*.
(d) (*Rel*) J~ Jagannâth *m*.
juggins‡ [ˈdʒʌgɪnz] *n* niais(e) *m(f)*, jobard(e) *m(f)*, cruche* *f*.
juggle [ˈdʒʌgl] 1 *vi* (*lit, fig*) jongler (*with* avec). 2 *vt balls, plates, facts, figures* jongler avec.
juggler [ˈdʒʌgləʳ] *n* jongleur *m*, -euse *f*, prestidigitateur *m*, -trice *f*.
jugglery [ˈdʒʌglərɪ] *n*, **juggling** [ˈdʒʌglɪŋ] *n* (*U*) (*lit*) jonglerie *f*, tours *mpl* de prestidigitation *or* de passe-passe; (*fig: trickery*) tours de passe-passe.
Jugoslav [ˈjuːgəʊˈslɑːv] 1 *adj* yougoslave. 2 *n* Yougoslave *mf*.
Jugoslavia [ˈjuːgəʊˈslɑːvɪə] *n* Yougoslavie *f*.
jugular [ˈdʒʌgjʊləʳ] 1 *adj* jugulaire. 2 *n* (veine *f*) jugulaire *f*.
juice [dʒuːs] *n* **(a)** [*fruit, meat*] jus *m*. **orange ~** jus d'orange.
(b) (*Physiol*) suc *m*. **digestive ~s** sucs digestifs. **(c)** (‡: *electricity, gas etc*) jus‡ *m*.
juicer [ˈdʒuːsəʳ] *n* (*US*) centrifugeuse *f*.
juiciness [ˈdʒuːsɪnɪs] *n* juteux *m*.
juicy [ˈdʒuːsɪ] *adj fruit* juteux; *meat* moelleux; (*fig*) *story* savoureux.
jujube [ˈdʒuːdʒuːb] *n* jujube *m*.
jujutsu [dʒuːˈdʒɪtsʊ] *n* = **jiujitsu.**
jukebox [ˈdʒuːkbɒks] *n* juke-box *m*.
julep [ˈdʒuːlep] *n* boisson sucrée, sirop *m*, julep *m*; *V* **mint**[2].

Julian [ˈdʒuːlɪən] 1 n Julien m. 2 adj julien.
Juliet [ˈdʒuːlɪet] n Juliette f.
Julius [ˈdʒuːlɪəs] n Jules m. ~ Caesar Jules César.
July [dʒuːˈlaɪ] n juillet m; for phrases V September.
jumble [ˈdʒʌmbl] 1 vt (also ~ up) (a) (lit) brouiller, emmêler, mélanger. to ~ everything (up) tout mélanger; ~d (up) en vrac; his clothes are ~d (up) together on his bed ses habits sont pêle-mêle sur son lit.
(b) (fig) facts, details brouiller, embrouiller.
2 n (a) [objects] mélange m, fouillis m, salade* f, méli-mélo* m; [ideas etc] confusion f, enchevêtrement m, fouillis m.
(b) (U: junk; goods at ~ sale) bric-à-brac m.
3 cpd: (Brit) jumble sale vente f de charité (d'objets d'occasion).
jumbo [ˈdʒʌmbəʊ] 1 n (*) éléphant m. 2 cpd: (Aviat) jumbo jet jumbo-jet m, avion géant, avion gros porteur.
jump [dʒʌmp] 1 n (a) saut m; (of fear, nervousness) sursaut m. to give a ~ faire un saut, sauter; (nervously) sursauter; at one ~ d'un (seul) bond; (fig) the ~ in prices la montée en flèche des prix, la hausse brutale des prix; V high, running etc.
(b) (fig: in nervousness) sursaut m. it gave him a ~ ça l'a fait sursauter; to have the ~s‡ avoir les nerfs à vif.
2 cpd: jumped-up* (pej: pushing) parvenu; (cheeky) effronté; (conceited) prétentieux; (fig) they used the agreement as a jumping-off place for further negotiations ils se sont servis de l'accord comme d'un tremplin pour de plus amples négociations; jump-jet avion m à décollage vertical; (Equitation) jump-off (épreuve f) finale f (d'un concours hippique); (Aviat) jump suit combinaison f de saut.
3 vi (a) (leap) sauter, bondir. to ~ up and down sautiller; to ~ in/out/across etc entrer/sortir/traverser etc d'un bond; to ~ into the bus/the river sauter dans l'autobus/la rivière; to ~ across the stream franchir le ruisseau d'un bond; to ~ off a bus/train sauter d'un autobus/d'un train; to ~ off a wall sauter (du haut) d'un mur; he ~ed over the wall il a sauté par-dessus le mur; he ~ed over the fence d'un bond il a franchi la barrière; ~ to it!* et plus vite que ça!*, et que ça saute!*
(b) (fig) sauter. to ~ from one subject to another sauter sans transition d'un sujet à un autre, passer du coq à l'âne; to ~ to a conclusion conclure sans réflexion; he ~ed to the conclusion that ... il en a conclu tout de suite que ...; you mustn't ~ to conclusions il ne faut pas tirer des conclusions trop hâtives; to ~ down sb's throat* rabrouer qn.
(c) (from nervousness) sursauter, tressauter. the shout made him ~ le cri l'a fait sursauter or tressauter; it (almost) made him ~ out of his skin* cela l'a fait sauter au plafond*; his heart ~ed when ... son cœur a fait or n'a fait qu'un bond quand ... .
(d) [prices, shares] monter en flèche, faire un bond.
4 vt (a) ditch etc sauter, franchir (d'un bond).
(b) horse faire sauter. he ~ed his horse over the fence il a fait sauter la barrière à son cheval; he ~ed his son (up and down) on his knee il faisait sauter son fils sur ses genoux.
(c) (phrases) [train] to ~ the rails dérailler; to ~ the points dérailler à l'aiguillage; [pickup] to ~ (a groove) sauter; (Draughts) to ~ a man prendre or souffler un pion; (Jur) to ~ bail ne pas comparaître; to ~ a claim s'emparer illégalement d'une concession minière; to ~ the gun (Sport) partir avant le départ; (*fig) agir prématurément; (Aut) to ~ the lights* passer au rouge; to ~ the queue* passer avant son tour, resquiller; (Naut) to ~ ship déserter le navire; to ~ sb‡ rouler qn*; to ~ a train (get on) sauter dans un train en marche (pour voyager sans payer); (get off) sauter d'un train en marche.
jump about, jump around vi sautiller.
jump at vt fus object, person, offer, suggestion sauter sur.
jump down vi descendre d'un bond. (from wall, bicycle etc) jump down! sautez!
jump in vi sauter dedans. he came to the river and jumped in arrivé à la rivière il a sauté dedans; jump in! (into vehicle) montez vite!; (into swimming pool) sautez!
jump off 1 vi sauter. he jumped off il a sauté; (from bicycle, wall etc) jump off! sautez!
2 jumping-off adj V jump 2.
3 jump-off n V jump 2.
jump on 1 vi: to jump on(to) a bus sauter dans un autobus; (onto truck, bus) jump on! montez vite!; to jump on(to) one's bicycle sauter sur son vélo.
2 vt fus (*: reprimand) s'attaquer à, prendre à partie.
jump out vi sauter (of de). to jump out of bed sauter (à bas) du lit; to jump out of the window sauter par la fenêtre; to jump out of a car/train sauter d'une voiture/d'un train; (from car etc) jump out! sortez or descendez (vite)!
jump up 1 vi sauter sur ses pieds, se (re)lever d'un bond. (to fallen child) jump up now! lève-toi!
2 jumped-up* adj V jump 2.
jumper [ˈdʒʌmpəʳ] n (Brit) pull(over) m; [sailor] vareuse f; (US: dress) robe-chasuble f.
jumpy* [ˈdʒʌmpɪ] adj person nerveux; (St Ex) market instable.
junction [ˈdʒʌŋkʃən] 1 n (a) (U: also Mil) jonction f. (b) (meeting place) [roads] bifurcation f, (crossroads) carrefour m; [rivers] confluent m; [railway lines] embranchement m; (station) gare f de jonction. 2 cpd: (Elec) junction box boîte f de dérivation.
juncture [ˈdʒʌŋktʃəʳ] n (joining place) jointure f, point m de jonction; (fig: state of affairs) conjoncture f. (fig: point) at this ~ à ce moment-là.
June [dʒuːn] n juin m; for phrases V September.
jungle [ˈdʒʌŋgl] 1 n (lit, fig) jungle f. 2 cpd animal, bird de la jungle. jungle warfare combat m de jungle.
junior [ˈdʒuːnɪəʳ] 1 adj (a) (younger) (plus) jeune, cadet. he is ~ to me by 2 years il est mon cadet de 2 ans, il est plus jeune que moi de 2 ans; John Smith, J~ John Smith fils or junior; (Scol) the ~ classes les petites classes (de 8 à 11 ans); (Brit) ~ school école f primaire (de 8 à 11 ans), cours moyen; (Comm) ~ miss fillette f (de 11 à 14 ans); (US) ~ college collège m universitaire (du premier cycle); (US) ~ high school collège m d'enseignement secondaire or d'enseignement court (de 12 à 15 ans); (Brit††) ~ secondary school collège m d'enseignement général.
(b) (subordinate) employee, officer, job subalterne. ~ clerk petit commis; ~ executive jeune cadre m; (Parl) J~ Minister ≈ (sous-)secrétaire m d'État; ~ partner associé(-adjoint) m; he is ~ to me in the business il est au-dessous de moi dans l'affaire.
(c) (Sport) ≈ cadet, minime. ~ championship championnat m des cadets or des minimes.
2 n (a) cadet(te) m(f). he is my ~ by 2 years il est plus jeune que moi de 2 ans, il est mon cadet de 2 ans.
(b) (Brit Scol) petit(e) élève m(f) (de 8 à 11 ans); (US Univ) étudiant(e) m(f) de troisième année.
(c) (Sport) ≈ cadet(te) m(f), minime mf.
juniper [ˈdʒuːnɪpəʳ] n genévrier m. ~ berry baie f de genièvre; ~ berries genièvre m (U).
junk¹ [dʒʌŋk] 1 n (U) (discarded objects) bric-à-brac m inv, vieilleries fpl; (metal) ferraille f; (*: bad quality goods) camelote* f; (*: worthless objects) pacotille f; (‡: nonsense) âneries fpl; (Drugs sl) came f (sl).
2 cpd: junk heap dépotoir m; junk market marché m aux puces; junkshop (boutique f de) brocanteur m; junk yard dépotoir m.
3 vt (US*) balancer*.
junk² [dʒʌŋk] n (boat) jonque f.
junket [ˈdʒʌŋkɪt] 1 n (Culin) (lait m) caillé m. 2 vi faire bombance.
junketing [ˈdʒʌŋkɪtɪŋ] n (U) (merrymaking) bombance f, bringue‡ f; (*: trip, banquet etc at public expense) voyage m or banquet m etc aux frais de la princesse*.
junkie [ˈdʒʌŋkɪ] n (Drugs sl) drogué(e) m(f), camé(e) m(f) (sl).
junta [ˈdʒʌntə] n junte f.
Jupiter [ˈdʒuːpɪtəʳ] n (Myth) Jupiter m; (Astron) Jupiter f.
juridical [dʒʊəˈrɪdɪkəl] adj juridique.
jurisdiction [ˌdʒʊərɪsˈdɪkʃən] n juridiction f.
jurisdictional [ˌdʒʊərɪsˈdɪkʃənl] adj: (US) ~ dispute conflit m d'attributions.
jurisprudence [ˌdʒʊərɪsˈpruːdəns] n jurisprudence f; V medical.
jurist [ˈdʒʊərɪst] n juriste m, légiste m.
juror [ˈdʒʊərəʳ] n juré m. woman ~ femme f juré.
jury¹ [ˈdʒʊərɪ] 1 n (Jur) jury m, jurés mpl; [examination, exhibition etc] jury m. to sit on the ~ faire partie du jury; Gentlemen of the ~ Messieurs les jurés; V coroner, grand. 2 cpd: jury box banc m des jurés; juryman juré m.
jury² [ˈdʒʊərɪ] adj (Naut) de fortune, improvisé.
just¹ [dʒʌst] adv (a) (exactly) juste, exactement, justement, précisément. it's ~ 9 o'clock il est juste 9 heures, il est 9 heures juste(s) or sonnant(es) or tapant(es) (V also j); it's ~ on 9 il est tout juste 9 heures; it took me ~ 2 hours il m'a fallu juste or exactement 2 heures; it cost ~ on 50 francs cela a coûté tout juste 50 F; this is ~ what I want c'est exactement or juste ce qu'il me faut; that's ~ what I was going to say c'est juste or justement or exactement ce que j'allais dire; ~ what did he say? qu'est-ce qu'il a dit exactement? or précisément?; a doctor? — that's ~ what I am! un docteur? — mais je suis justement or précisément docteur!; that's ~ what I thought c'est exactement ce que je pensais; leave everything ~ as you find it laissez tout exactement comme vous l'avez trouvé; (fig) come ~ as you are* venez comme vous êtes; ~ as I thought, you aren't ready c'est bien ce que je pensais, or je m'en doutais bien, tu n'es pas prêt; ~ as you wish (c'est) comme vous voulez or voudrez; ~ at that moment à ce moment même; ~ when everything is going so well! juste quand tout va si bien!; that's ~ it!, that's ~ the point! justement!; that's ~ Robert, always late c'est bien Robert, toujours en retard; ~ how many came we don't know nous ne savons pas exactement or au juste combien de gens sont venus; it's ~ the same to me cela m'est tout à fait égal; ~ so! exactement!; everything was ~ so* tout était bien en ordre.
(b) (indicating immediate past) to have ~ done venir de faire; he had ~ left il venait de partir; I have only ~ heard about it je viens seulement de l'apprendre; I've ~ this minute or ~ this instant done it je viens de le faire à l'instant; this book is ~ out ce livre vient de paraître; ~ painted fraîchement peint.
(c) (at this or that moment) juste. we're ~ off nous partons (à l'instant); (I'm) ~ coming! j'arrive!; we're ~ about to start nous sommes sur le point de commencer; you're not interrupting us, I was ~ leaving vous ne nous interrompez pas, je partais; ~ as we arrived it began to rain juste comme nous arrivions, il s'est mis à pleuvoir.
(d) (almost not) juste, de justesse. we (only) ~ caught the train nous avons eu le train de justesse, c'est tout juste si nous avons eu le train; I'll ~ catch the train if I hurry j'aurai tout juste le train si je me presse; we only ~ missed the train nous avons manqué le train de très peu; you're ~ in time vous arrivez juste à temps; I will only ~ get there on time j'arriverai tout juste à l'heure; I have only ~ enough money j'ai tout juste assez d'argent; he passed the exam but only ~ il a été reçu à l'examen mais de justesse or mais cela a été juste or mais il s'en est fallu de peu.
(e) (with expressions of place) juste. ~ here juste ici, à cet endroit même; ~ over there/here juste là/ici; ~ by the church juste à côté de l'église; ~ past the station juste après la gare.
(f) ~ about à peu près; ~ about here à peu près ici; I've had ~

about enough!* *or* ~ **about as much as I can stand!*** j'en ai pardessus la tête!*; **it's ~ about 3 o'clock** il est à peu près 3 heures; **it's ~ about 5 kilos** cela pèse 5 kilos à peu de chose près; **have you finished? — ~ about*** avez-vous fini? — à peu près *or* presque; **the incident ~ about ruined him** l'incident l'a ruiné ou presque *or* l'a quasiment* ruiné.

(g) (*in comparison*) ~ as tout aussi; **this one is ~ as big as that** celui-ci est tout aussi grand que celui-là; **you sing ~ as well as I do** vous chantez tout aussi bien que moi.

(h) (+*imper*) donc, un peu. ~ **taste this!** goûte un peu à ça!*, goûte-moi ça!*; ~ **come here a moment** viens ici un instant; ~ **imagine!**, ~ **fancy!*** tu te rends compte!*, tu t'imagines un peu!*; ~ **look at that!** regarde-moi ça!*; ~ **you do!***, ~ **you try it!***, ~ **you dare!*** ose voir un peu!*; ~ **shut up!*** veux-tu te taire!; ~ **let me get my hands on him!*** que je l'attrape (*subj*) un peu!*

(i) (*slightly, immediately*) peu, juste. ~ **over £10** un peu plus de 10 livres, 10 livres et des poussières*; ~ **under £10** un peu moins de 10 livres; ~ **after 9 o'clock he came in** peu *or* juste après 9 heures il est entré; **it's ~ after 9 o'clock** il est un peu plus de 9 heures, il est 9 heures et quelques; ~ **after he came** juste après son arrivée; ~ **before Christmas** juste avant Noël; ~ **afterwards** juste après, tout de suite après; ~ **before it rained** peu *or* juste avant la pluie, peu *or* juste avant qu'il (ne) pleuve; **that's ~ over the kilo** cela fait tout juste un peu plus du kilo; **it's ~ to the left of the bookcase** c'est juste à gauche de la bibliothèque; **it's ~ on the left as you go in** c'est juste *or* tout de suite à gauche en entrant.

(j) (*only*) juste. ~ **a moment please** un instant s'il vous plaît; **he's ~ a lad** c'est un gamin, ce n'est qu'un gamin; **don't go yet, it's ~ 9 o'clock** ne partez pas encore, il n'est que 9 heures; **I've come ~ to see you** je suis venu exprès pour te voir; **he did it ~ for a laugh*** il l'a fait histoire de rire*; **there will be ~ the two of us** il n'y aura que nous deux, il y aura juste nous deux; ~ **a few** juste quelques-uns; **do you want any? — ~ a little bit** tu en veux? — juste un petit peu *or* rien qu'un petit peu; ~ **a line to let you know that ...** juste un petit mot pour vous dire que ... .

(k) (*simply*) (tout) simplement, seulement. **I ~ told him to go away** je lui ai tout simplement dit de s'en aller; **you should ~ send it back** vous n'avez qu'à le renvoyer; **I would ~ like to say this** je voudrais seulement *or* simplement dire ceci; **I ~ can't imagine what's happened to him** je ne peux vraiment pas m'imaginer *or* je n'arrive pas à imaginer ce qui lui est arrivé; **we shall ~ drop in on him** nous ne ferons que passer chez lui; **I was ~ wondering if you knew ...** je me demandais simplement *or* seulement si vous saviez ...; **it's ~ one of those things*** c'est comme ça*, c'est la vie.

(l) (*positively*) absolument, tout simplement. **it was ~ marvellous!** c'était absolument merveilleux!; **it's ~ fine!** c'est parfait!

(m) (*emphatic*) **did you enjoy it? — did we ~!*** *or* **I should ~ say we did!*** cela vous a plu? — et comment!*

(n) (*other uses*) **it's ~ as well it's insured** heureusement que c'est assuré; **it would be ~ as well if he took it** il ferait aussi bien de le prendre; **we brought the umbrellas, and ~ as well** on a bien fait d'apporter les parapluies; **I'm busy ~ now** je suis occupé pour l'instant; **I saw him ~ now** je l'ai vu tout à l'heure; **not ~ yet** pas tout de suite, pas pour l'instant (*V also* **yet**); ~ **in case it rains** juste au cas où il pleuvrait, si jamais il pleuvait; **I'm taking my umbrella, ~ in case** je prends mon parapluie, on ne sait jamais; ~ **the same***, **you shouldn't have done it** tout de même, tu n'aurais pas dû le faire; **I'd ~ as soon you kept quiet about it** j'aimerais autant que vous n'en disiez rien à personne.

just[2] [dʒʌst] *adj person, decision* juste, équitable (*to, towards* envers, avec); *punishment, reward* juste, mérité; *cause* juste; *anger* juste, légitime; *suspicion* justifié, bien fondé; *calculation* juste, exact. **it is only ~ to point out that ...** ce n'est que justice de faire remarquer que ...

justice [ˈdʒʌstɪs] *n* **(a)** (*U: Jur*) justice *f*. **to bring sb to ~** amener qn devant les tribunaux; (*US*) **Department of J~** ministère *m* de la Justice; *V* **poetic**.

(b) (*U: fairness*) équité *f*. **I must, in (all) ~, say ...** pour être juste, je dois dire ...; **in ~ to him he ..., to do him ~ he ...** pour être juste envers lui il ..., il faut lui rendre cette justice qu'il ...; **this photograph doesn't do him ~** cette photo ne le flatte pas *or* ne l'avantage pas; **she never does herself ~** elle ne se montre jamais à sa juste valeur; **to do ~ to a meal** faire honneur à un repas.

(c) (*judge*) juge *m*. (*Brit*) **Lord Chief J~** premier président de la Cour d'Appel; **J~ of the Peace** juge de paix.

(d) (*U*) = **justness**.

justifiable [ˌdʒʌstɪˈfaɪəbl] *adj* justifiable.

justifiably [ˌdʒʌstɪˈfaɪəblɪ] *adv* légitimement, avec raison.

justification [ˌdʒʌstɪfɪˈkeɪʃən] *n* (*also Rel*) justification *f* (*of, for* de, à, pour). **as a ~ for his action** comme justification de *or* à son acte; **he had no ~ for lying** son mensonge n'avait aucune justification, il n'avait aucune raison valable de mentir.

justify [ˈdʒʌstɪfaɪ] *vt behaviour, action* justifier, légitimer; *decision* prouver le bien fondé de. **this does not ~ his being late** cela ne justifie pas son retard; **to be justified in doing** être en droit de faire, avoir de bonnes raisons pour faire; **you're not justified in talking to her like that** rien ne vous autorise à lui parler de cette façon; **am I justified in thinking ...?** est-ce que j'ai raison de penser ...?

justly [ˈdʒʌstlɪ] *adv* avec raison, tout à fait justement.

justness [ˈdʒʌstnɪs] *n [cause]* justice *f*; *[idea, calculation]* justesse *f*.

jut [dʒʌt] *vi* (*also* ~ **out**) faire saillie, saillir, dépasser. **he saw a gun ~ting (out) from behind a wall** il a vu le canon d'un fusil dépasser de derrière un mur; **the cliff ~s (out) into the sea** la falaise avance dans la mer; **to ~ (out) over the street/the sea** surplomber la rue/la mer.

Jute [dʒuːt] *n* Jute *m*.

jute [dʒuːt] *n* jute *m*.

juvenile [ˈdʒuːvənaɪl] **1** *n* adolescent(e) *m(f)*, jeune *mf*.

2 *adj* juvénile; (*pej*) *behaviour, attitude* puéril (*f* puérile), juvénile. ~ **books** livres *mpl* pour enfants; (*Jur*) ~ **court** tribunal *m* pour enfants; ~ **delinquency** délinquance *f* juvénile; ~ **delinquent** mineur(e) *m(f)* délinquant(e), jeune délinquant(e) *m(f)*; ~ **delinquents** l'enfance *or* la jeunesse délinquante; *V* **lead**[1].

juxtapose [ˈdʒʌkstəpəʊz] *vt* juxtaposer.

juxtaposition [ˌdʒʌkstəpəˈzɪʃən] *n* juxtaposition *f*. **to be in ~** se juxtaposer.

K

K, k [keɪ] *n* (*letter*) K, k *m*.

kabob [kəˈbɒb] *n* = **kebab**.

Kaffir [ˈkæfə^r] **1** *n* Cafre *mf*. **2** *adj* cafre.

kaftan [ˈkæftæn] *n* kaftan *m*.

kail [keɪl] *n* = **kale**.

Kaiser [ˈkaɪzə^r] *n* Kaiser *m*.

kale [keɪl] *n* chou frisé.

kaleidoscope [kəˈlaɪdəskəʊp] *n* kaléidoscope *m*.

kaleidoscopic [kəˌlaɪdəˈskɒpɪk] *adj* kaléidoscopique.

kangaroo [ˌkæŋgəˈruː] *n* kangourou *m*. ~ **court** tribunal irrégulier.

kaolin [ˈkeɪəlɪn] *n* kaolin *m*.

kapok [ˈkeɪpɒk] **1** *n* kapok *m*. **2** *cpd cushion* rembourré de kapok.

kaput‡ [kəˈpʊt] *adj watch, car* fichu*, foutu‡, kaput‡ *inv*; *plan etc* fichu*, foutu‡, dans le lac*.

karat [ˈkærət] *n* = **carat**.

karate [kəˈrɑːtɪ] *n* (*U*) karaté *m*.

kart [kɑːt] **1** *n* kart *m*. **2** *vi*: **to go ~ing** faire du karting.

karting [ˈkɑːtɪŋ] *n* karting *m*.

Kashmir [kæʃˈmɪə^r] *n* Cachemire *m*.

Kate [keɪt] *n dim of* **Katharine**.

Katharine, Katherine [ˈkæθərɪn] *n*, **Kathleen** [ˈkæθliːn] *n* Catherine *f*.

katydid [ˈkeɪtɪdɪd] *n* sauterelle *f* d'Amérique.

kayak [ˈkaɪæk] *n* kayak *m*.

kebab [kəˈbæb] *n* kébab *m*, brochette *f* (de viande).

kedge [kedʒ] (*Naut*) **1** *n* ancre *f* à jet. **2** *vt* haler (sur une ancre à jet).

kedgeree [ˌkedʒəˈriː] *n* pilaf *m* de poisson.

keel [kiːl] **1** *n* (*Naut*) quille *f*. **on an even ~** (*Naut*) dans ses lignes, à égal tirant d'eau; (*fig*) stable; (*fig*) **to keep sth on an even ~** maintenir qch en équilibre.

2 *cpd*: **keelhaul** (*Naut*) faire passer sous la quille (*en guise de châtiment*); (*fig) passer un savon à*.

keel over 1 *vi* (*Naut*) chavirer; (*fig*) *[person]* tomber dans les pommes*, tourner de l'œil*.

2 *vt* (*Naut*) (faire) chavirer.

keen[1] [kiːn] *adj* **(a)** (*sharp*) *blade* aiguisé, affilé, tranchant; *point* aigu (*f* -guë); (*fig*) *wind, cold* piquant, cinglant; *air* vif; *sarcasm* mordant, caustique, âpre; *interest* vif; *pleasure, desire, feeling* vif, intense; *appetite* aiguisé; *grief, pain* cuisant, poignant; *sight, eye* pénétrant, perçant; *hearing, ear* fin; (*Brit*) *price* étudié (de près), serré; *competition* serré, acharné; *intelligence* vif, aigu, fin, pénétrant; *judgment* pénétrant. **he's a**

~ **judge of character** il a la pénétration *or* la finesse qui permet de juger les gens.

(b) (*enthusiastic*) *person* ardent, zélé, enthousiaste. **to be as ~ as mustard** déborder d'enthousiasme, être plein de zèle; **he tried not to seem too ~** il a essayé de ne pas se montrer trop enthousiaste *or* de ne pas montrer trop d'enthousiasme; **he's a ~ footballer** c'est un passionné du football; **she's a very ~ socialist** c'est une socialiste passionnée; **to be ~ to do** tenir (absolument) à faire; **to be ~ on music** avoir la passion de la musique; **to be ~ on an idea** être enthousiasmé par une idée; **to become** *or* **grow ~ on sth/sb** s'enthousiasmer *or* se passionner pour qch/qn; **I'm not too ~ on him** il ne me plaît pas beaucoup; **he's ~ on her*** il a un béguin* pour elle; **he's very ~ on Mozart** c'est un passionné de Mozart; **to be ~ on doing sth** aimer beaucoup faire qch; **he's not ~ on her coming** il ne tient pas tellement à ce qu'elle vienne; **he's very ~ that she should come** il tient beaucoup à ce qu'elle vienne; *V* **mad, madly.**

keen² [ki:n] **1** *n* (*Ir Mus*) mélopée *f* funèbre (*irlandaise*). **2** *vi* chanter une mélopée funèbre.

keenly ['ki:nlɪ] *adv* **(a)** (*acutely*) *interest, feel* vivement, profondément; *wish, desire* ardemment, profondément; *notice, remark, observe* astucieusement. **he looked at me ~** il m'a jeté un regard pénétrant.

(b) (*enthusiastically*) avec zèle, avec enthousiasme, ardemment.

keenness ['ki:nnɪs] *n* **(a)** *[blade]* finesse *f*; *[cold, wind]* âpreté *f*; *[interest, pleasure, grief]* intensité *f*; *[pain]* violence *f*, acuité *f*; *[hearing]* finesse; *[intelligence, mind]* finesse, pénétration *f*, vivacité *f*. **~ of sight** acuité visuelle.

(b) (*eagerness*) ardeur *f*, enthousiasme *m*. **his ~ to leave** son empressement à partir.

keep [ki:p] *pret, ptp* **kept 1** *vt* **(a)** (*retain*) *object* garder, retenir; *control, powers, right* garder, conserver. **you can ~ this book** tu peux garder ce livre; **you must ~ the receipt** il faut garder *or* conserver le reçu; **~ the change!** gardez la monnaie!; **to ~ one's job** garder son travail; **this material will ~ its colour/texture** *etc* ce tissu gardera ses couleurs/sa texture *etc*; **I can't ~ that tune in my head** je n'arrive pas à retenir cet air; **to ~ to one's bed/one's room** *etc* garder le lit/la chambre *etc*; **she ~s herself to herself** elle fuit la compagnie, elle se tient à l'écart; **they ~ themselves to themselves** *[group]* ils font bande à part, ils restent entre eux; *[couple]* ils se tiennent à l'écart; *V* **cool, foot, goal** *etc.*

(b) (+ *adj, vb etc: maintain*) tenir, garder. **to ~ sth clean** tenir *or* garder qch propre; **to ~ o.s. clean** être toujours propre; **exercise will ~ you fit** l'exercice physique vous maintiendra en forme; **to ~ sth tidy** tenir qch en état; **the garden was well kept** le jardin était bien tenu *or* entretenu; **'~ Britain tidy'** 'pour une Grande-Bretagne propre'; **he kept them working** *or* **at work all night** il les a forcés à continuer de travailler toute la nuit; **they kept him at it** ils l'ont tenu attelé à la tâche *or* au travail; **to ~ a machine running** maintenir une machine en activité; **he kept the (car) engine running** il a laissé le moteur (de la voiture) en marche; **to ~ sb waiting** faire attendre qn; **~ him talking while I ...** fais-lui la conversation pendant que je ...; **she managed to ~ the conversation going** elle a réussi à entretenir la conversation; **she kept him to his promise** elle l'a forcé à tenir sa promesse; **~ me informed (of)** tenez-moi au courant (de); **to ~ a piece of news from sb** cacher une nouvelle à qn; **~ it to yourself, ~ it under your hat*** garde-le pour toi, ne le dis à personne; *V* **alive, quiet, warm** *etc.*

(c) (*preserve, put aside*) garder, mettre de côté, mettre en réserve; (*store, hold in readiness*) avoir (en réserve); (*Comm: stock, sell*) vendre, avoir, stocker. **I've kept some for you** je vous en ai gardé; **I kept it for just this purpose** je l'ai gardé *or* mis de côté pour cela; **I'm ~ing some sugar in case there's a shortage** j'ai du sucre en réserve *or* une provision de sucre au cas où il viendrait à manquer; **~ it somewhere safe** mettez-le en lieu sûr; **you must ~ it in a cold place** il faut le garder *or* le conserver au froid; **where does he ~ his money?** où est-ce qu'il met son argent?; **where do you ~ your shoe polish?** où est-ce que tu ranges ton cirage?; (*in supermarket etc*) **where do you ~ the sugar?** où est-ce que vous mettez le sucre?

(d) (*detain*) garder, retenir; *prisoner* détenir. **to ~ sb in prison** détenir qn, garder qn en prison; **they kept him prisoner for some time** ils l'ont gardé prisonnier quelque temps; **what kept you?** qu'est-ce qui vous a retenu?; **I mustn't ~ you** je ne veux pas vous retarder *or* vous retenir; **they wanted to ~ me to dinner** ils ont voulu me garder à dîner; **illness kept her in bed** la maladie l'a forcée à rester au lit *or* à garder le lit.

(e) (*own; maintain; look after*) *shop, hotel, restaurant* tenir, avoir; *house, servant, dog, car* avoir; (*Agr*) *cattle, pigs, bees, chickens* élever, faire l'élevage de. **he ~s a good cellar** il a une bonne cave; *V* **house** *etc.*

(f) *accounts, diary* tenir. **I've kept a note of his name** j'ai pris note de *or* j'ai noté son nom; *V* **count¹, track** *etc.*

(g) (*support*) faire vivre, entretenir, subvenir aux besoins de. **I earn enough to ~ myself** je gagne assez pour vivre *or* pour subvenir à mes (propres) besoins; **I have 6 children to ~** j'ai 6 enfants à ma charge *or* à entretenir *or* à nourrir; **he ~s a mistress in Paris** il entretient une maîtresse à Paris; **to ~ sb in food/clothing** nourrir/habiller qn; **I can't afford to ~ you in cigarettes** je ne peux pas (me payer le luxe de) te fournir en cigarettes.

(h) (*restrain, prevent*) **to ~ sb from doing** empêcher qn de faire; **to ~ o.s. from doing** se retenir *or* s'empêcher de faire; **~ him from school for just now** ne l'envoyez pas à l'école pour le moment; **it kept him from despair** cela l'a sauvé *or* gardé (*frm*) du désespoir.

(i) (*observe, fulfil*) *promise* tenir; *law, rule* observer, respecter; *treaty* respecter; *vow* rester fidèle à; *obligations* remplir; *feast day* célébrer. **to ~ an appointment** se rendre à un rendez-vous; **she did not ~ her appointment with them** elle n'est pas venue à *or* elle n'a pas tenu son rendez-vous avec eux, elle leur a fait faux bond; **to ~ Lent/the Sabbath** observer le carême/le jour du sabbat; **to ~ sb's birthday** fêter l'anniversaire de qn; *V* **peace, word** *etc.*

(j) (†: *guard, protect*) garder, protéger; *sheep etc* garder. **God ~ you!** Dieu vous garde!

2 *vi* **(a)** (*continue*) garder, suivre, continuer. **~ on this road until you come to ...** suivez cette route jusqu'à ce que vous arriviez (*subj*) à ...; **to ~ (to the) left/right** garder sa gauche/droite; (*Aut*) tenir sa gauche/droite; **to ~ to** *or* **in the middle of the road** rester au *or* garder le milieu de la route; **to ~ straight on** continuer *or* suivre tout droit; **~ north till you get to ...** continuez vers le nord jusqu'à ce que vous arriviez (*subj*) à ...; **to ~ doing** continuer à *or* de faire, ne pas cesser de faire; **if you ~ complaining** si vous continuez à vous plaindre; **she ~s talking** elle n'arrête pas de parler; **he would ~ objecting** il ne cessait pas de faire des objections; **I ~ hoping she'll come back** j'espère toujours qu'elle reviendra; **to ~ standing** rester debout; **~ going!** allez-y!, continuez toujours!; **~ smiling!** gardez le sourire!

(b) (*remain*) rester, se tenir. **to ~ fit** se maintenir en forme (*V also* 4); **he ~s in good health** il est toujours en bonne santé; **to ~ still** rester *or* se tenir tranquille; **to ~ silent** se taire, garder le silence, rester silencieux; **~ calm!** reste calme!, du calme!; **~ there for a minute** restez là une minute; **'~ off the grass'** 'défense de marcher sur les pelouses'; **she kept inside for 3 days** elle est restée chez elle *or* elle n'est pas sortie pendant 3 jours; **she ~s to herself** elle fuit la compagnie, elle ne fréquente presque personne; **they ~ to themselves** *[group]* ils font bande à part, ils restent entre eux; *[couple]* ils se tiennent à l'écart; *V* **alive, cool, quiet** *etc.*

(c) (*in health*) aller, se porter (*frm*). **how are you ~ing?** comment allez-vous?, comment vous portez-vous? (*frm*); **to ~ well** aller bien; **she's not ~ing very well** elle ne va pas très bien; **he's ~ing better** il va mieux.

(d) *[food etc]* se garder, se conserver, garder sa fraîcheur. **apples that ~ all winter** des pommes qui se gardent *or* se conservent tout l'hiver; **this ham will ~ up to 3 days in the fridge** ce jambon conservera sa fraîcheur 3 jours au réfrigérateur; (*fig*) **this business can ~** cette affaire peut attendre; **that will ~ till tomorrow** cela attendra demain, cela tiendra jusqu'à demain.

3 *n* **(a)** (*U: livelihood, food*) **I got £15 a week and my ~** j'ai gagné 15 livres par semaine logé et nourri; **he's not worth his ~** il ne vaut pas ce qu'on dépense pour lui *or* ce qu'on dépense pour l'entretenir, il ne vaut pas la dépense.

(b) (*Archit, Hist*) donjon *m*.

(c) for ~s* pour de bon.

4 *cpd*: **she does keep-fit once a week** elle fait de la culture physique *or* de la gymnastique une fois par semaine; **keep-fit classes** cours *mpl* de gymnastique; **keep-fit exercises** culture *f* physique; **keepsake** souvenir *m* (*objet*).

keep at *vt fus* **(a)** (*continue*) continuer; (*work with persistence at*) travailler d'arrache-pied à, s'acharner à. **keep at it!** continuez!

(b) (*nag at*) harceler, s'acharner sur. **she keeps at him all the time** elle le harcèle, elle est toujours après lui*; **you'll have to keep at him till he pays you** il va falloir le harceler jusqu'à ce qu'il vous paie (*subj*).

keep away 1 *vi* (*lit*) ne pas s'approcher (*from* de). **keep away from the fire** ne t'approche pas du feu; (*fig*) **to keep away from drink** s'abstenir de boire, ne pas boire.

2 *vt sep person* tenir éloigné (*from* de). **keep them away from each other!** empêchez-les de se rencontrer!

keep back 1 *vi* rester en arrière, ne pas avancer, ne pas approcher. **keep back!** restez en arrière! *or* où vous êtes!, n'approchez pas!

2 *vt sep* **(a)** (*withhold*) retenir. **they keep back 5% of my wages for national insurance** on me retient 5% de mon salaire pour la Sécurité sociale.

(b) (*conceal*) cacher, ne pas dire, ne pas révéler; *secrets* taire. **they are keeping back the names of the victims** ils ne communiquent pas les noms des victimes; **don't keep anything back** ne nous (*or* me *etc*) cachez rien, racontez tout.

(c) (*hinder, make late*) retarder. **I don't want to keep you back** je ne veux pas vous retarder; **have I kept you back in your work?** vous ai-je retardé dans votre travail?

keep down 1 *vi* rester assis (*or* allongé *etc*). **keep down!** ne bougez pas!, restez assis (*or* allongé *etc*)!

2 *vt sep* **(a)** (*control*) retenir, maîtriser; *revolt, one's anger* réprimer, contenir; *dog* retenir, maîtriser. **you can't keep her down** elle ne se laisse jamais abattre; (*loc*) **you can't keep a good man down** un homme de valeur reprendra toujours le dessus.

(b) *spending* restreindre, limiter. **to keep prices down** maintenir les prix bas, empêcher les prix de monter, empêcher la hausse des prix.

(c) (*Scol*) **to keep a pupil down** faire redoubler une classe à un élève.

(d) (*Med*) **the sick man can't keep anything down** le malade ne garde rien, le malade vomit *or* rend tout ce qu'il prend.

keep from *vt fus*: **to keep from doing** s'abstenir *or* s'empêcher *or* se retenir de faire; **to keep from drink** s'abstenir de boire, ne pas boire.

keep in 1 *vi*: **to keep in with sb** rester en bons termes avec qn; (*for one's own purposes*) cultiver qn.

2 *vt sep* **(a)** *anger, feelings* contenir, réprimer.

(b) *person* empêcher de sortir. (*Scol*) **to keep a child in** garder un enfant en retenue, consigner un enfant.

(c) keep your tummy in! rentre ton *or* le ventre!; *V* **hand.**

keep off 1 *vi [person]* se tenir éloigné, rester à l'écart *or* à distance. **keep off!** n'approchez pas!; **if the rain keeps off** s'il ne pleut pas.

2 *vt sep dog* éloigner; *person* éloigner, écarter, tenir à distance. **this weather will keep the crowds off** ce temps fera rester les gens chez eux; **keep your hands off!** ne touchez pas!; keep your hat off ne (re)mettez pas votre chapeau.

keep on 1 *vi* **(a)** continuer, ne pas cesser. **he kept on reading** il a continué à *or* de lire, il n'a pas cessé de lire; **don't keep on so!** arrête! (*V also* **1c**); **she does keep on about her rich friends** elle n'arrête pas de parler de ses riches amis; **the child kept on crying the whole night** l'enfant n'a fait que pleurer toute la nuit.

(b) (*keep going*) continuer (à avancer). **keep on past the church till you get to the school** continuez après l'église jusqu'à (ce que vous arriviez (*subj*) à) l'école; (*fig*) **if you keep on as you're doing now you'll pass the exam** si tu continues dans cette voie tu seras reçu à l'examen.

(c) (*Brit*) **to keep on at sb** harceler qn; **don't keep on so!** cesse de me (*or* le *etc*) harceler!

2 *vt sep* **(a)** *servant, employee* garder.

(b) to keep one's hat on garder son chapeau; *[man]* rester couvert; *V* **hair.**

keep out 1 *vi* rester en dehors. **'keep out'** 'défense d'entrer', 'accès interdit'; **to keep out of danger** rester *or* se tenir à l'abri du danger; **to keep out of a quarrel** ne pas se mêler d'une dispute; **keep out of this!, you keep out of it!** mêlez-vous de ce qui vous regarde! *or* de vos (propres) affaires! *or* de vos oignons!*

2 *vt sep person, dog* empêcher d'entrer, ne pas laisser entrer. **that coat will keep out the cold** ce manteau protégera bien du froid.

keep to *vt fus*: **to keep to one's promise** tenir sa promesse, être fidèle à sa promesse; **to keep to the subject** ne pas s'écarter du sujet, rester dans le sujet; **to keep to the text** serrer le texte; **to keep to one's bed** garder le lit; *V also* **keep 2b.**

keep together 1 *vi [people]* rester ensemble, ne pas se séparer.

2 *vt sep objects* garder ensemble, (*fixed*) maintenir ensemble; *people* garder ensemble *or* unis.

keep under *vt sep anger, feelings* contenir, maîtriser; *passions* dominer; *people, race* soumettre, assujettir, asservir; *subordinates* dominer; *unruly pupils etc* tenir, mater.

keep up 1 *vi* **(a)** continuer, se maintenir; *[prices]* se maintenir. **their spirits are keeping up** ils ne se découragent pas; **I hope the good weather will keep up** j'espère que le beau temps va continuer *or* se maintenir.

(b) to keep up with sb (*in race, walk etc*) aller aussi vite que qn, se maintenir à la hauteur de qn; (*in work, achievement*) se maintenir au niveau de qn; (*in comprehension*) suivre qn; **I couldn't keep up with what he was saying** je n'ai pas pu suivre ce qu'il disait; (*Scol*) **to keep up with the class** bien suivre (en classe); (*fig*) **to keep up with the Joneses** ne pas se trouver en reste avec les voisins; **to keep up with the times** être de son temps *or* époque.

(c) (*stay friends with*) **to keep up with sb** rester en relations avec qn; **we haven't kept up at all since she went abroad** nous avons complètement perdu le contact depuis qu'elle est partie à l'étranger.

2 *vt sep* **(a)** continuer; *correspondence* entretenir; *study etc* continuer, ne pas interrompre *or* abandonner. **to keep up a subscription** maintenir un abonnement, continuer à payer une cotisation; **I try to keep up my Latin** j'essaie d'entretenir mon latin; **to keep up a custom** maintenir *or* respecter une tradition; **keep it up!** continuez!

(b) (*maintain*) *house, paintwork* maintenir en bon état; *engine, road* entretenir, maintenir en bon état.

keeper ['ki:pəʳ] *n* (*person*) gardien(ne) *m(f)*, surveillant(e) *m(f)*; (*in museum etc*) conservateur *m*, -trice *f*; (*in park, zoo etc*) gardien; (*gamekeeper*) garde-chasse *m*. **am I my brother's ~?** suis-je le gardien de mon frère?; *V* **bee, goal, shop** *etc.*

keeping ['ki:pɪŋ] *n* (*U*) **(a)** (*care*) garde *f*. **to put sb in sb's ~** confier qn à (la garde de) qn; **to put sth in sb's ~** confier qch à qn; *V* **safe** *etc.*

(b) (*observing*) *[rule]* observation *f*; *[festival etc]* célébration *f*.

(c) to be in ~ with s'accorder avec, être en rapport avec; **out of ~ with** en désaccord avec.

keg [keg] *n* **(a)** (*barrel*) *[beer, brandy etc]* tonnelet *m*, baril *m*, petit fût; *[fish]* caque *f*. **(b)** (*also* **~ beer**) bière *f* en tonnelet.

kelp [kelp] *n* (*U*) varech *m*.

ken [ken] **1** *n*: **that is beyond** *or* **outside my ~** cela dépasse ma compétence, ce n'est pas dans mes cordes. **2** *vt* (*Scot*) = **know.**

kennel ['kenl] **1** *n* **(a)** *[dog]* niche *f*; *[hound]* chenil *m*; (*fig pej*) chenil (*fig*), tanière *f* (*fig*). **~s** (*for breeding*) élevage *m* (de chiens), chenil; (*for boarding*) chenil; **to put a dog in ~s** mettre un chien en chenil.

(b) *[fox]* repaire *m*, tanière *f*.

2 *cpd*: **kennel maid** aide *f* de chenil.

Kenya ['kenjə] *n* Kenya *m*.

kepi ['keɪpɪ] *n* képi *m*.

kept [kept] *pret, ptp of* **keep.**

kerb [kɜ:b] (*Brit*) **1** *n* bordure *f* *or* bord *m* du trottoir. **along the ~** le long du trottoir; (*St Ex*) **on the ~** en coulisse, après la clôture (*de la Bourse*).

2 *cpd*: (*St Ex*) **kerb broker** courtier *m* en valeurs mobilières, coulissier *m*; **kerbstone** pierre *f* *or* pavé *m* de bordure (*de trottoir*).

kerchief ['kɜ:tʃɪf] *n* fanchon *f*, fichu *m*.

kerfuffle* [kə'fʌfl] *n* (*Brit*) histoire* *f*, affaire* *f*. **what a ~!** quelle histoire *or* que d'histoires pour si peu!*

kernel ['kɜ:nl] *n [nut, fruitstone]* amande *f*; (*seed*) grain *m*. (*fig*) **there's a ~ of truth in what he says** il y a un grain de vérité dans ce qu'il dit.

kerosene ['kerəsi:n] **1** *n* kérosène *m*. **2** *cpd lamp* à pétrole.

kestrel ['kestrəl] *n* crécerelle *f*.

ketch [ketʃ] *n* ketch *m*.

ketchup ['ketʃəp] *n* ketchup *m*.

kettle ['ketl] **1** *n* **(a)** (*for water: also* (*US*) **tea~**) bouilloire *f*. **the ~'s boiling** l'eau bout (dans la bouilloire); **I'll just put the ~ on (for some tea)** je vais mettre l'eau à chauffer (pour le thé).

(b) (*also* **fish ~**) poissonnière *f*. (*fig*) **that's a fine** *or* **a pretty ~ of fish** nous voilà dans de beaux draps *or* dans un joli pétrin.

2 *cpd*: (*Mus*) **kettledrum** timbale *f*.

key [ki:] **1** *n* **(a)** *[door etc]* clef *f* *or* clé *f*. **to turn the ~** donner un tour de clef; *V* **latch, lock¹, master** *etc.*

(b) *[clock]* clef *f* *or* clé *f* de pendule, remontoir *m*; *[clockwork toy etc]* remontoir; (*Tech*) clef de serrage *or* à écrous.

(c) (*fig: to problem etc*) clef *f* *or* clé *f*. **the ~ to the mystery** la clef du mystère.

(d) (*answers*) solutions *fpl*; (*Scol*) (*crib*) corrigé *m*; (*translation*) traduction *f* (*toute faite*).

(e) *[piano, typewriter etc]* touche *f*; *[wind instrument]* clef *f* *or* clé *f*.

(f) (*Mus*) ton *m*. **to be in/off ~** être/n'être pas dans le ton; **to go off ~** sortir du ton; **to sing in/off ~** chanter juste/faux; **to play in/off ~** jouer dans le ton/dans le mauvais ton; **in the ~ of C** en do; **change of ~** changement *m* de ton; *V* **low¹, minor.**

2 *adj* (*vital*) clef (*f inv*) *or* clé (*f inv*). **~ industry/position/question** industrie *f*/position *f*/question *f* clef; **~ jobs** postes *mpl* clefs; **~ man** pivot *m*, cheville *f* (ouvrière); *[argument etc]* **~ point** point capital *or* essentiel; **~ speech** discours *m* clef; (*Ind*) **~ workers** travailleurs *mpl* clefs.

3 *cpd*: *[piano, typewriter etc]* **keyboard** clavier *m*; **keyhole** trou *m* de serrure; **through the keyhole** par le trou de la serrure; **keyhole saw** scie *f* à guichet; **key money** pas *m* de porte (*fig*); **keynote** (*Mus*) tonique *f*; (*fig*) *[speech etc]* note dominante; (*Pol etc*) **keynote speech** discours-programme *m*; **key ring** porte-clefs *m inv*; (*Mus*) **key signature** armature *f*; (*Archit, fig*) **keystone** clef *f* de voûte.

4 *vt speech etc* adapter (*to or for one's audience* à son auditoire). **the colour scheme was ~ed to brown** les coloris s'harmonisaient autour du brun *or* étaient dans les bruns.

key up *vt sep* (*fig*) surexciter, tendre. **she was (all) keyed up about the interview** elle était surexcitée *or* tendue à la pensée de *or* dans l'attente de l'entrevue.

khaki ['kɑ:kɪ] **1** *adj* kaki *inv*. **2** *n* kaki *m*.

Khartoum [kɑ:'tu:m] *n* Khartoum.

Khmer [kmɛəʳ] **1** *adj* khmer (*f* khmère). **2** *n* **(a)** Khmer *m*, Khmère *f*. **(b)** (*Ling*) khmer *m*, cambodgien *m*.

kibbutz [kɪ'bʊts] *n, pl* **kibbutzim** [kɪ'bʊtsɪm] kibboutz *m*.

kibitz* ['kɪbɪts] *vi* (*Cards*) regarder le jeu de quelqu'un par-dessus son épaule.

kibitzer* ['kɪbɪtsəʳ] *n* (*Cards*) spectateur *m*, -trice *f* (*qui regarde le jeu de quelqu'un par-dessus son épaule*); (*busybody*) mouche *f* du coche; (*pej: disruptive wisecracker*) petit malin, petite maligne.

kibosh ['kaɪbɒʃ] *n*: **to put the ~ on sth**‡ mettre le holà à qch, mettre fin à qch.

kick [kɪk] **1** *n* **(a)** (*action*) coup *m* de pied. **to give the door a ~** donner un coup de pied dans la porte; **to aim** *or* **take a ~ at sb/sth** lancer un coup de pied à qn/qch *or* dans la direction de qn/qch; **to get a ~ on the leg** recevoir un coup de pied à la jambe; **to give sb a ~ in the pants*** donner un coup de pied au derrière à *or* de qn, botter* le derrière à *or* de qn; (*fig*) **this refusal was a ~ in the teeth‡ for her** ce refus a été pour elle (comme) une gifle en pleine figure; *V* **free.**

(b) (** fig: thrill etc*) **she got quite a ~ out of seeing Paris** elle a été tout émoustillée *or* excitée de voir Paris; **he gets a ~ out of making his sister cry** il prend un malin plaisir à faire pleurer sa sœur; **I get a ~ out of it** je trouve ça stimulant *or* excitant; **he did it for ~s** il l'a fait pour le plaisir, (*stronger*) il l'a fait parce que ça l'excitait *or* ça le bottait*; **he has no ~ left, there's no ~ left in him** il ne lui reste plus aucune énergie *or* aucun allant; **this drink hasn't much ~ in it** cette boisson n'est pas très corsée, ça n'est pas cette boisson qui te (*or* me *etc*) montera à la tête; **a drink with plenty of ~ in it** une boisson qui vous donne un coup de fouet.

(c) *[gun]* recul *m*. (*Aut*) **a ~ of the starting handle** un retour de manivelle.

(d) (*Ftbl etc*) **he's a good ~*** il a un bon dégagement.

2 *cpd*: **kickback*** (*reaction*) réaction *f*, contrecoup *m*; (*percentage of money made, money paid as bribe or for information etc*) pourcentage *m* (*reçu*); (*rebate on sale*) ristourne *f*, rabais *m*; **kick-off** (*Ftbl etc*) coup *m* d'envoi; (** fig: of meeting, ceremony etc*) démarrage* *m*; (*Ftbl*) **the kick-off is at 3 p.m.** le coup d'envoi est à 15h; (*fig*) **when's the kick-off?*** à quelle heure ça démarre?*; (*US*) *[motorcycle etc]* **kick-stand** béquille *f*; *[motorcycle]* **kick start(er)** démarreur *m* au pied, kick *m*.

3 *vi* **(a)** *[person]* donner *or* lancer un coup de pied; *[baby]* gigoter*; *[horse etc]* ruer. **to ~ at sb/sth** *[person]* lancer un coup de pied à qn/qch *or* en direction de qn/qch; *[horse]* lancer une ruade à qn/qch *or* en direction de qn/qch (*V also* **3b**); (*fig*) **to ~ against the pricks** regimber en pure perte; (*fig*) **to ~ over the traces** ruer dans les brancards (*fig*), regimber (*fig*), se cabrer (*fig*).

(b) (*: *object*) ruer dans les brancards, se rebiffer*. **to ~ at sth** se rebiffer contre qch*, regimber devant qch.

(c) *[gun]* reculer.

4 *vt ball, table, person [person]* donner un coup de pied à; *[horse etc]* lancer une ruade à. **to ~ sb's bottom** botter* le derrière *or* les fesses à *or* de qn; **to ~ sb downstairs** faire descendre qn à coups de pied dans le derrière; **to ~ sb upstairs** (*lit*) faire monter qn à coups de pied dans le derrière; (**fig*) catapulter *or* bombarder* *or* balancer‡ qn à un poste supérieur (pour s'en débarrasser); (*Brit Pol**) catapulter qn à la Chambre des lords (*un député dont on ne veut plus aux Communes*); (*Rugby*) **to ~ a goal** marquer un but; (*fig*) **to ~ the bucket‡** casser sa pipe*; **I could have ~ed myself*** je me serais flanqué* des coups *or* des gifles; (*fig*) **to ~ one's heels** faire le poireau* *or* le pied de grue, se morfondre, poireauter*.

kick about, kick around 1 *vi* (‡) *[books, clothes etc]* traîner; *[person]* traîner, traînasser (*pej*).

2 *vt sep*: **to kick a ball about** jouer au ballon, s'amuser avec un ballon; **he can't find anything better to do than kicking a ball about** tout ce qu'il sait faire c'est donner des coups de pied dans un ballon; (*fig*) **don't kick that book about** ne maltraite pas ce livre.

kick away *vt sep* **(a)** *object on ground* repousser du pied.

(b) he kicked away the last part of the fence il a démoli à coups de pied ce qui restait de la clôture.

kick back 1 *vi [engine]* avoir un retour de manivelle.

2 *vt sep ball etc* renvoyer (du pied).

3 kickback* *n V* **kick 2**.

kick down *vt sep door, hedge, barrier* démolir à coups de pied.

kick in *vt sep door* enfoncer à coups de pied. (*fig*) **to kick sb's teeth in‡** casser la figure* *or* la gueule‡ à qn.

kick off 1 *vi* (*Ftbl*) donner le coup d'envoi; (**fig*) démarrer*. **the party kicked off in great style** la soirée a démarré* en beauté.

2 *vt sep* enlever (du pied *or* d'un coup de pied).

3 kick-off *n V* **kick 2**.

kick out 1 *vi [horse]* ruer. **the man kicked out at his assailants** l'homme envoyait de grands coups de pied à ses assaillants.

2 *vt sep* (*lit*) chasser à coups de pied, flanquer dehors* *or* vider* à coups de pied; (**fig*) mettre à la porte (*fig*), flanquer dehors* (*fig*), vider* (*fig*).

kick up *vt sep dust* faire voler. (*fig*) **to kick up a row*** *or* **a din*** *or* **a racket*** faire du chahut *or* du tapage *or* du boucan‡; **to kick up a fuss*** faire des histoires *or* toute une histoire; **he kicked up a stink‡ about it** il en a fait tout un plat* *or* tout un foin‡.

kid [kɪd] **1** *n* **(a)** (*goat*) chevreau *m*, chevrette *f*.

(b) (*U: leather*) chevreau *m* (*U*).

(c) (*: *child*) gosse* *mf*, gamin(e)* *m(f)*. **when I was a ~** quand j'étais gosse*; **that's ~'s stuff** (*easy to do*) un gamin* *or* un gosse* saurait faire ça; (*suitable for children*) c'est (tout juste) bon pour des gosses*.

2 *cpd*: **my kid brother*** mon petit frère; **kid gloves/shoes** *etc* gants *mpl*/chaussures *fpl etc* de chevreau; (*fig*) **to handle with kid gloves** *person* ménager, traiter avec ménagements, prendre des gants avec*; *subject* traiter avec précaution.

3 *vt* (*) **to ~ sb** faire marcher qn*; **no ~ding!** sans blague!*; **you can't ~ me** tu ne me la feras pas‡, je ne marche pas*; **don't ~ yourself!** ne te fais pas d'illusions!

4 *vi* (*) (*also* **~ on**) raconter des blagues*. **he's just ~ding (on)** il te (*or* nous *etc*) fait marcher*, il te (*or* nous *etc*) raconte des blagues*; **I was only ~ding (on)** j'ai dit ça pour plaisanter *or* pour rigoler*.

kid on 1 *vi* = **kid 4**.

2 *vt sep* **(a) to kid sb on*** faire marcher qn*, raconter des blagues à qn*.

(b) (*pretend*) **he was kidding on* that he was hurt** il essayait de faire croire qu'il était blessé.

kiddy* [ˈkɪdɪ] *n* gosse* *mf*, gamin(e)* *m(f)*, mioche* *mf*, mouflet(te)* *m(f)*.

kidnap [ˈkɪdnæp] *vt* kidnapper, enlever.

kidnapper [ˈkɪdnæpə^{r}] *n* kidnappeur *m*, -euse *f*, ravisseur *m*, -euse *f*.

kidnapping [ˈkɪdnæpɪŋ] *n* enlèvement *m*, kidnapping *m*, rapt *m*.

kidney [ˈkɪdnɪ] **1** *n* (*Anat*) rein *m*; (*Culin*) rognon *m*. (*fig*) **of the same ~** du même acabit.

2 *cpd disease etc* rénal, de(s) reins. **kidney bean** haricot *m* rouge *or* de Soissons; (*Med*) **kidney machine** rein artificiel; **to be on a kidney machine** être sous rein artificiel *or* en hémodialyse, être en épuration extrarénale; **kidney-shaped** en forme de haricot; **kidney stone** calcul rénal *or* du rein; **kidney transplant** greffe *f* du rein.

kill [kɪl] **1** *n* **(a)** (*at bullfight, hunt*) mise *f* à mort. **the wolves gathered round for the ~** les loups se sont rassemblés pour tuer leur proie; **the tiger had made a ~** le tigre avait tué; (*fig*) **to be in at the ~** assister au dénouement; (*for unpleasant event*) assister au coup de grâce (*fig*).

(b) (*U: animal(s) killed: Hunting*) pièces tuées, tableau *m* de chasse. **the lion crouched over his ~** le lion s'est accroupi sur la proie qu'il venait de tuer *or* sur sa proie.

2 *cpd*: **killjoy** rabat-joie *m inv*.

3 *vt* **(a)** tuer; (*murder*) assassiner; (*gun down*) abattre; *animal* tuer; (*Hunting, Shooting; also in slaughterhouse*) abattre. **to be ~ed in action/battle** tomber au champ d'honneur/au combat; **thou shalt not ~** tu ne tueras point; (*Prov*) **to ~ two birds with one stone** faire d'une pierre deux coups (*Prov*); **her son's death/the shock ~ed her** c'est la mort de son fils/le choc qui l'a tuée; (*hum*) **it was ~ or cure** c'était un remède de cheval* (*fig*).

(b) (*fig*) *parliamentary bill, proposal, attempt* faire échouer; (*Press etc*) *paragraph, line* (faire) supprimer; *story* interdire la publication de; *rumour* étouffer, mettre fin à; *feeling, hope* détruire; *flavour, smell* tuer; *sound* étouffer, amortir; *engine, motor* arrêter. **to ~ time** tuer le temps; **the frost has ~ed my trees** le gel a tué *or* a fait mourir mes arbres; **this red ~s the other colours** ce rouge tue les autres couleurs; **to ~* a bottle of whisky** liquider* une bouteille de whisky.

(c) to ~ o.s. with work se tuer au *or* de travail; **he certainly wasn't ~ing himself*** le moins qu'on puisse dire c'est qu'il ne se tuait pas au *or* de travail; (*iro*) **don't ~ yourself!*** surtout ne te surmène pas!; (*iro*); **this heat is ~ing me*** cette chaleur me tue *or* me crève*; **my feet are ~ing me*** j'ai affreusement mal aux pieds; **she was laughing fit to ~ (herself)*, she was ~ing herself (laughing)*** elle riait comme une folle, elle était pliée en deux de rire; **this will ~ you!*** tu vas (mourir de) rire!; *V* **dress**.

kill off *vt sep* (*lit*) exterminer; (*fig*) éliminer.

killer [ˈkɪlə^{r}] **1** *n* tueur *m*, -euse *f*; (*murderer*) assassin *m*, meurtrier *m*, -ière *f*. **diphtheria was once a ~** autrefois la diphtérie tuait; *V* **lady**.

2 *cpd*: **a killer disease** une maladie qui tue; (*lit*) **the killer instinct** l'instinct *m* qui pousse à tuer; (*fig*) **he's got the killer instinct** il sait se montrer impitoyable; **killer whale** épaulard *m*.

killing [ˈkɪlɪŋ] **1** *n* **(a)** *[person]* meurtre *m*; *[people, group]* tuerie *f*, massacre *m*; *[animal]* (*Hunting*) mise *f* à mort; (*at abattoir*) abattage *m*. **the ~ of stags is forbidden** il est interdit de tuer les cerfs; **all the ~ sickened him of war** le massacre *or* la tuerie lui fit prendre la guerre en horreur; (*during disturbances etc*) **there were 3 separate ~s during the night** 3 personnes ont été tuées pendant la nuit, il y a eu 3 morts pendant la nuit.

(b) (*Fin*) **to make a ~** réussir un beau coup (de filet).

2 *adj* **(a)** *blow, disease, shot* meurtrier.

(b) (*: *exhausting*) *work* tuant, crevant*.

(c) (‡: *funny*) tordant*, crevant*. **it was ~** c'était tordant* *or* crevant*, c'était à mourir de rire.

killingly [ˈkɪlɪŋlɪ] *adv*: **~ funny** crevant*, tordant*; **it was ~ funny** c'était crevant* *or* tordant*, c'était à mourir de rire.

kiln [kɪln] *n* four *m*. **pottery ~** four céramique; *V* **lime**[1].

kilo [ˈkiːləʊ] *n* kilo *m*.

kiloampère [ˈkɪləʊˌæmpɛə^{r}] *n* kiloampère *m*.

kilocycle [ˈkɪləʊˌsaɪkl] *n* kilocycle *m*.

kilogramme, (*US*) **kilogram** [ˈkɪləʊgræm] *n* kilogramme *m*.

kilolitre, (*US*) **kiloliter** [ˈkɪləʊˌliːtə^{r}] *n* kilolitre *m*.

kilometre, (*US*) **kilometer** [ˈkɪləʊˌmiːtə^{r}] *n* kilomètre *m*.

kilometric [ˌkɪləʊˈmetrɪk] *adj* kilométrique.

kilovolt [ˈkɪləʊˌvəʊlt] *n* kilovolt *m*.

kilowatt [ˈkɪləʊwɒt] *n* kilowatt *m*. **~-hour** kilowatt-heure *m*.

kilt [kɪlt] *n* kilt *m*.

kilted [ˈkɪltɪd] *adj man* en kilt. **~ skirt** jupe-kilt *f*, kilt *m*.

kilter [ˈkɪltə^{r}] *n* (*esp US*) **out of ~*** détraqué, déglingué*.

kiltie* [ˈkɪltɪ] *n* homme *m* en kilt, Écossais *m* (en kilt); (*soldier*) soldat *m* en kilt.

kimono [kɪˈməʊnəʊ] *n* kimono *m*.

kin [kɪn] **1** *n* (*U*) parents *mpl*, famille *f*; *V* **kith, next**. **2** *cpd*: (*U*) **kin(s)folk** parents *mpl*, famille *f*; **kinship** *V* **kinship**; **kinsman** parent *m*; **kinswoman** parente *f*.

kind [kaɪnd] **1** *n* **(a)** (*class, variety, sort, type*) genre *m*, espèce *f*, sorte *f*; (*make: of car, coffee etc*) marque *f*. **this ~ of book** ce genre *or* cette espèce *or* cette sorte de livre; **books of all ~s** des livres de tous genres *or* de toutes espèces *or* de toutes sortes; **this ~ of thing(s)** ce genre de chose(s); **what ~ of flour do you want? — the ~ you gave me last time** quelle sorte *or* quelle espèce *or* quel genre de farine voulez-vous? — la même que vous m'avez donnée (*or* le même que vous m'avez donné) la dernière fois; **what ~ do you want?** vous en (*or* le *or* la *etc*) voulez de quelle sorte?; **what ~ of car is it?** quelle marque de voiture est-ce?; **what ~ of dog is he?** qu'est-ce que c'est comme (race de) chien?; **what ~ of man is he?** quel genre *or* quel type d'homme est-ce?; **he is not the ~ of man to refuse** ce n'est pas le genre d'homme à refuser, il n'est pas homme à refuser; **he's not that ~ of person** ce n'est pas son genre; **I'm not that ~ of girl!*** ce n'est pas mon genre!, mais pour qui me prenez-vous?, je ne suis pas celle que vous croyez!; **that's the ~ of person I am** c'est comme ça que je suis (fait); **what ~ of people does he think we are?** (mais enfin,) pour qui nous prend-il?; **what ~ of a fool does he take me for?** (non mais*,) il me prend pour un imbécile!; **what ~ of behaviour is this?** qu'est-ce que c'est que cette façon de se conduire?; **what ~ of an answer do you call that?** vous appelez ça une réponse?; **classical music is the ~ she likes most** c'est la musique classique qu'elle préfère; **and all that ~ of thing** et autres choses du même genre, et tout ça*; **you know the ~ of thing I mean** vous voyez (à peu près) ce que je veux dire; **I don't like that ~ of talk** je n'aime pas ce genre de conversation; **he's the ~ that will cheat** il est du genre à tricher; **I know his ~!** je connais les gens de son genre *or* espèce; **your ~* never do any good** les gens de votre genre *or* espèce ne font rien de bien; **he's not my ~*** je n'aime pas les gens de son genre *or* de son espèce; **it's my ~* of film** c'est le genre de film que j'aime *or* qui me plaît.

(b) (*in phrases*) **something of the ~** quelque chose de ce genre(-là) *or* d'approchant; **this is wrong — nothing of the ~!** c'est faux — pas le moins du monde! *or* absolument pas!; **I shall do nothing of the ~!** je n'en ferai rien!, certainement pas!; **I will have nothing of the ~!** je ne tolérerai pas cela!; (*pej*) **it was beef of a ~** c'était quelque chose qui pouvait passer pour du bœuf.

(c) a ~ of une sorte *or* espèce de, un genre de; **there was a ~ of box in the middle of the room** il y avait une sorte *or* une espèce *or* un genre de boîte au milieu de la pièce, il y avait quelque chose qui ressemblait à une boîte au milieu de la pièce; **there was a ~ of tinkling sound** il y avait une sorte *or* une espèce de bruit de grelot, on entendait quelque chose qui ressemblait à un bruit de grelot; **in a ~ of way* I'm sorry** d'une certaine façon je le regrette; **I had a ~ of fear that, I was ~ of* frightened that** j'avais comme peur que + ne + *subj*; **I ~ of***

thought that he would come j'avais un peu l'idée qu'il viendrait; he was ~ of* worried-looking il avait l'air un peu inquiet, il avait l'air comme qui dirait* inquiet; it's ~ of* blue c'est plutôt bleu; aren't you pleased? — ~ of!* tu n'es pas content? — assez! *or* ben si!‡

(d) (*race, species*) genre *m*, espèce *f*. human ~ le genre humain; they differ in ~ ils sont de genres différents *or* de natures différentes; they're two of a ~ ils sont du même genre *or* acabit; this painting is perfect of/the only one of its ~ ce tableau est parfait dans/unique en son genre; *V* man *etc.*

(e) (*U: goods as opposed to money*) nature *f*. to pay/payment in ~ payer/paiement *m* en nature; (*fig*) I shall repay you in ~ (*after good deed*) je vous le rendrai; (*after bad deed*) je vous rendrai la monnaie de votre pièce.

2 *adj person* gentil, bon, aimable. they were ~ people c'étaient de braves gens; to be ~ to sb être gentil avec qn, être bon pour *or* envers qn; we must be ~ to animals il faut être bon pour *or* envers les animaux; they were ~ to the play in New York ils ont fait bon accueil à la pièce à New York; would you be ~ enough to *or* would you be so ~ as to open the door? voulez-vous avoir l'amabilité d'ouvrir la porte?, voulez-vous être assez aimable *or* gentil pour ouvrir la porte?; he was ~ enough to say il a eu la gentillesse *or* l'amabilité *or* la bonté de dire; it was very ~ of you to help me vous avez été bien aimable *or* bien bon de m'aider, ça a été bien gentil à vous de m'aider; that's very ~ of you c'est très aimable *or* gentil à vous *or* de votre part; you're too ~ vous êtes trop aimable *or* gentil; how ~ of you! comme c'est gentil *or* aimable à vous!; that wasn't a very ~ thing to say ce n'était pas très gentil de dire cela.

3 *cpd*: kind-hearted bon, qui a bon cœur; kind-heartedness bonté *f*, bon cœur, grand cœur.

kindergarten ['kɪndə,gɑːtn] *n* jardin *m* d'enfants.

kindle ['kɪndl] 1 *vt fire* allumer; *wood* enflammer; (*fig*) *passion, desire* allumer, enflammer; *heart* enflammer. 2 *vi* s'allumer; s'enflammer.

kindliness ['kaɪndlɪnɪs] *n* bienveillance *f*, bonté *f*.

kindling ['kɪndlɪŋ] *n* (*U: wood*) petit bois, bois d'allumage.

kindly ['kaɪndlɪ] 1 *adv* (a) *speak, act* avec bonté, avec gentillesse.

(b) will you ~ do ... voulez-vous avoir la bonté *or* l'obligeance de faire ..., je vous prie de (bien vouloir) faire ...; ~ shut the door voulez-vous (bien) *or* veuillez (*frm*) fermer la porte, fermez la porte je vous prie; ~ be quiet! voulez-vous *or* allez-vous vous taire!

(c) I don't take ~ to his doing that je n'aime pas du tout qu'il fasse cela; she didn't take it ~ when I said that elle ne l'a pas bien pris *or* elle l'a mal pris quand j'ai dit cela; I would take it ~ if you would do so j'aimerais beaucoup que vous fassiez ainsi, vous m'obligeriez en agissant de la sorte (*frm*).

2 *adj person, advice* bienveillant; *voice* plein de bonté; *letter* gentil; *treatment* plein de gentillesse.

kindness ['kaɪndnɪs] *n* (a) (*U*) bonté *f* (*towards* pour), gentillesse *f* (*towards* pour, envers), bienveillance *f* (*towards* à l'égard de), amabilité *f* (*towards* envers). to treat sb with ~, to show ~ to sb être gentil avec *or* envers qn, avoir de la gentillesse pour qn; out of the ~ of his heart par (pure) bonté d'âme; will you have the ~ to give me it? voulez-vous avoir la bonté de *or* être assez gentil pour me le donner?

(b) (*act of* ~) bonté *f*, gentillesse *f*, service *m*. to do sb a ~ rendre service à qn; thank you for all your ~es merci de toutes vos gentillesses; it would be a ~ to tell him so ce serait lui rendre service que de le lui dire.

kindred ['kɪndrɪd] 1 *n* (*U*) (*relatives*) parents *mpl*, famille *f*; (*relationship*) parenté *f*.

2 *adj* (a) (*related*) *languages, tribes* apparenté, de la même famille.

(b) (*similar*) similaire, semblable, analogue. ~ spirits âmes sœurs *fpl*; to have a ~ feeling for sb sympathiser avec qn.

kinetic [kɪ'netɪk] *adj* cinétique.

king [kɪŋ] 1 *n* (a) (*lit, fig*) roi *m*. K~ David le roi David; (*Bible*) K~s le livre des Rois; the ~ of beasts le roi des animaux; (*fig*) it cost a ~'s ransom ça a coûté des sommes fabuleuses; an oil ~ un roi *or* un magnat du pétrole.

(b) (*Brit*) (*Jur*) K~'s Bench cour supérieure de justice; (*Jur*) K~'s Counsel avocat *m* de la Couronne; (*Jur*) to turn K~'s evidence dénoncer ses complices; the K~'s highway la voie publique; K~'s Messenger courrier *m* diplomatique.

(c) (*Cards, Chess*) roi *m*; (*Draughts*) dame *f*.

2 *cpd*: kingbolt pivot central, cheville ouvrière; king cobra cobra royal; kingcup (*buttercup*) bouton *m* d'or; (*marsh marigold*) souci *m* d'eau; kingdom *V* kingdom; kingfisher martin-pêcheur *m*; kingmaker homme *m* qui fait et défait les rois; king penguin manchot royal; kingpin (*Tech*) pivot central, cheville ouvrière; (*fig*) pivot, cheville ouvrière; kingship *V* kingship; (*Comm*) king-size(d) *cigarette* long (*f* longue); *packet* géant; I've got a king-size(d) headache* j'ai un mal de crâne à tout casser*.

kingdom ['kɪŋdəm] *n* royaume *m*; (*Bot, Zool*) règne *m*. the plant ~ le règne végétal; the K~ of God le royaume de Dieu; the K~ of Heaven le royaume des cieux, le royaume céleste; he's gone to ~ come* il est parti dans l'autre monde *or* dans un monde meilleur; to send sb to ~ come* envoyer qn dans l'autre monde *or* dans un monde meilleur *or* 'ad patres'*; till ~ come* jusqu'à la fin des siècles; *V* animal, united *etc.*

kingly ['kɪŋlɪ] *adj* (*lit, fig*) royal, de roi.

kingship ['kɪŋʃɪp] *n* royauté *f*.

kink [kɪŋk] 1 *n* (*in rope etc*) entortillement *m*; (*in hair*) crêpelure *f*; (*in paper etc*) défaut *m*; (*fig*) anomalie *f*, aberration *f*, déséquilibre *m*; (*sexual*) aberration. 2 *vi* [*rope etc*] s'entortiller.

kinky ['kɪŋkɪ] *adj* (a) *hair* crêpelé; (*tighter*) crépu. (b) (‡) *person* bizarre; (*unpleasantly so*) malade (*fig pej*); (*sexually*) qui a des goûts spéciaux, vicieux, cochon*; *idea* biscornu*; *dress, fashion* bizarre, excentrique.

kinship ['kɪnʃɪp] *n* (*U*) parenté *f*.

kiosk ['kiːɒsk] *n* (*for selling; also bandstand*) kiosque *m*; (*Brit Telec*) cabine *f* téléphonique.

kip‡ [kɪp] 1 *n* (*bed*) plumard‡ *m*, pieu‡ *m*; (*sleep*) roupillon* *m*. to get some ~ piquer un somme *or* un roupillon*. 2 *vi* (*also* ~ down) se pieuter‡.

kipper ['kɪpəʳ] 1 *n* hareng fumé et salé, kipper *m*. 2 *vt herring* fumer et saler. (*fig*) the room was so smoky we were nearly ~ed‡ la pièce était si enfumée qu'on a failli être transformés en harengs saurs.

kirk [kɜːk] *n* (*Scot*) église *f*. the K~ l'Église presbytérienne (d'Écosse).

kiss [kɪs] 1 *n* baiser *m*. to give sb a ~ donner un baiser à qn, embrasser qn; give me a ~ embrasse-moi; (*to child*) fais-moi une bise*; (*Med*) ~ of life bouche à bouche *m*; (*fig*) ~ of death coup fatal (*fig*); (*liter*) the wind's ~ on her hair le baiser du vent sur ses cheveux; (*in letter*) love and ~es bons baisers, grosses bises*; *V* blow[1].

2 *cpd*: (*Brit*) kiss curl accroche-cœur *m inv*.

3 *vt* embrasser, donner un baiser à. to ~ sb's cheek embrasser qn sur la joue; to ~ sb's hand baiser la main de qn; (*Diplomacy etc*) to ~ hands être admis au baisemain (du roi *or* de la reine); they ~ed each other ils se sont embrassés; to ~ sb good night/good-bye embrasser qn en lui souhaitant bonne nuit/en lui disant au revoir, souhaiter bonne nuit/dire au revoir à qn en l'embrassant; (*fig*) to ~ the dust *or* ground mordre la poussière.

4 *vi* s'embrasser. to ~ and make up faire la paix.

kiss away *vt sep*: she kissed away the child's tears elle a essuyé de ses baisers les larmes de l'enfant.

kiss back *vt sep person* rendre un baiser à.

kisser‡ ['kɪsəʳ] *n* gueule‡ *f*.

kit [kɪt] 1 *n* (a) (*U*) (*equipment, gear*) [*camping, skiing, climbing, photography etc*] matériel *m*, équipement *m*; (*Mil*) fourniment *m*, barda‡ *m*, fourbi* *m*; (*tools*) outils *mpl*; (*luggage*) bagages *mpl*. fishing *etc* ~ matériel *or* attirail *m or* équipement de pêche *etc.*

(b) (*U: belongings, gear*) effets *mpl* (personnels), affaires *fpl*.

(c) (*U: gen Sport: clothes*) équipement *m*, affaires *fpl*. have you got your gym/football ~? tu as tes affaires de gym/de football?

(d) (*set of items*) tool~ trousse *f* à outils; puncture-repair ~ trousse de réparations; first-aid ~ trousse d'urgence *or* de premiers secours; *V* survival *etc.*

(e) (*parts for assembly*) kit *m*. car/harpsichord sold in ~ voiture *f*/clavecin *m* vendu(e) en kit; he built it from a ~ il l'a assemblé à partir d'un kit; model aeroplane ~ maquette *f* d'avion (à assembler).

2 *cpd*: kitbag sac *m* (*de voyage, de sportif, de soldat, de marin etc*); (*Mil*) kit inspection revue *f* de détail.

kit out, kit up *vt sep* (a) (*Mil*) équiper (*with* de).

(b) to kit sb out with sth équiper qn de qch; he arrived kitted out in oilskins il est arrivé équipé d'un ciré; he had kitted himself out in a bright blue suit il avait mis *or* il s'était acheté un costume bleu vif.

kitchen ['kɪtʃɪn] 1 *n* cuisine *f* (*pièce*); *V* thief.

2 *cpd table, cutlery, scissors etc* de cuisine. kitchen cabinet buffet *m* de cuisine; kitchen-dinette cuisine *f* avec coin-repas; kitchen foil papier *m* d'aluminium *or* d'alu*; kitchen garden (jardin *m*) potager *m*; kitchenmaid fille *f* de cuisine; kitchen range fourneau *m* (de cuisine), cuisinière *f*; kitchen salt sel *m* de cuisine, gros sel; kitchen scales balance *f* (de cuisine); kitchen sink évier *m*; I've packed everything but the kitchen sink* j'ai tout empaqueté sauf les murs; (*Theat*) kitchen-sink* drama théâtre *m* naturaliste; kitchen soap savon *m* de Marseille; kitchen unit élément *m* de cuisine; kitchen utensil ustensile *m* de cuisine; (*U*) kitchenware (*dishes*) vaisselle *f or* faïence *f* (de cuisine); (*equipment*) ustensiles *mpl* de cuisine.

kitchenette [,kɪtʃɪ'net] *n* kitchenette *f*.

kite [kaɪt] *n* (*Orn*) milan *m*; (*toy*) cerf-volant *m*; *V* fly[3]. 2 *cpd*: (*Mil*) kite balloon ballon *m* d'observation, saucisse *f*.

kith [kɪθ] *n*: ~ and kin amis *mpl* et parents *mpl*.

kitsch [kɪtʃ] 1 *n* (*U*) kitsch *m*, art kitsch *or* pompier. 2 *adj* kitsch *inv*, pompier.

kitten ['kɪtn] *n* chaton *m*, petit chat. (*Brit fig*) to have ~s‡ piquer une crise*, être dans tous ses états.

kittenish ['kɪtənɪʃ] *adj* (*lit*) de chaton; (*fig*) de chaton, mutin.

kittiwake ['kɪtɪweɪk] *n* mouette *f* tridactyle.

kitty ['kɪtɪ] *n* (a) (*Cards etc*) cagnotte *f*; (**fig*) caisse *f*, cagnotte. there's nothing left in the ~ il n'y a plus un sou dans la caisse *or* dans la cagnotte. (b) (*: *cat*) minet* *m*, minou* *m*.

kiwi ['kiːwiː] *n* kiwi *m*.

klaxon ['klæksn] *n* klaxon *m*.

Kleenex ['kliːneks] *n* ® Kleenex *m* ®.

kleptomania [,kleptəʊ'meɪnɪə] *n* kleptomanie *f*.

kleptomaniac [,kleptəʊ'meɪnɪæk] *adj, n* kleptomane (*mf*).

Klondike ['klɒndaɪk] *n* Klondike *m*.

knack [næk] *n* tour *m* de main, truc* *m*. to learn *or* get the ~ of doing attraper *or* saisir le tour de main *or* le truc* pour faire; to have the ~ of doing avoir le talent *or* le chic pour faire; I've lost the ~ j'ai perdu le tour de main, j'ai perdu la main; she's got a ~ of saying the wrong thing elle a le chic pour dire *or* le don de dire ce qu'il ne faut pas; there's a ~ in it il y a un truc* *or* un tour de main à prendre; you'll soon get the ~ of it vous aurez vite fait d'attraper le truc* *or* le tour de main.

knacker ['nækəʳ] *(Brit)* **1** *n* **(a)** *[horses]* équarrisseur *m.* **to send a horse to the ~'s yard** envoyer un cheval à l'équarrissage. **(b)** *[boats, houses]* entrepreneur *m* de démolition, démolisseur *m.* **2** *vt*: **to be ~ed‡** être crevé* *or* éreinté.
knapsack ['næpsæk] *n* sac *m* à dos, havresac *m.*
knave [neɪv] *n* (†*pej*) filou *m*, fripon† *m*, coquin† *m*; *(Cards)* valet *m.*
knavery ['neɪvərɪ] *n* *(U: pej)* filouterie *f*, friponnerie† *f*, coquinerie† *f.*
knavish ['neɪvɪʃ] *adj (pej)* de filou, de coquin†.
knead [niːd] *vt dough etc* pétrir, travailler; *muscles* masser.
knee [niː] **1** *n* genou *m.* **on one's ~s**, *(liter or hum)* **on bended ~(s)** à genoux; **to go (down) on one's ~s** s'agenouiller, tomber *or* se mettre à genoux; **to go down on one's ~s to sb** *(lit)* tomber *or* se mettre à genoux devant qn; *(fig)* se mettre à genoux devant qn *(fig)*, supplier qn à genoux; *(fig)* **to bring sb to his ~s** forcer qn à capituler *or* à se rendre *or* à se soumettre; **he sank in up to the ~s** il s'est enfoncé jusqu'aux genoux; **these trousers are out at** *or* **have gone at the ~(s)** ce pantalon est usé aux genoux; **to put a child over one's ~** donner une fessée à un enfant.
2 *cpd*: **knee breeches** culotte courte; *(Anat)* **kneecap** rotule *f*; **the water was knee-deep** l'eau arrivait aux genoux; **he was knee-deep in mud** la boue lui arrivait *or* venait (jusqu')aux genoux, il était dans la boue jusqu'aux genoux; **knee-high** à hauteur de genou; *(esp US)* **knee-high to a grasshopper*** haut comme trois pommes; **knee jerk** = **knee reflex**; *(Anat)* **knee joint** articulation *f* du genou; **at knee level** à (la) hauteur du genou; **kneepad** genouillère *f*; **knee reflex** réflexe rotulien.
kneel [niːl] *pret, ptp* **knelt** *vi (also* **~ down**) s'agenouiller, se mettre à genoux. **he had to ~ on his case to shut it** il a dû se mettre à genoux sur sa valise pour la fermer; *(lit, fig)* **to ~ (down) to** *or* **before sb** se mettre à genoux devant qn.
knell [nel] *n* glas *m.* **to sound** *or* **toll the ~** sonner le glas.
knelt [nelt] *pret, ptp of* **kneel.**
knew [njuː] *pret of* **know.**
knickerbockers† ['nɪkəbɒkəz] *npl* knickerbockers *mpl*, culotte *f* de golf.
knickers ['nɪkəz] *npl* **(a)** *(Brit: woman's)* culotte *f*, slip *m (de femme. (excl)* **~!‡** merde!‡. **(b)** (†) = **knickerbockers.**
knick-knack ['nɪknæk] *n* bibelot *m*, babiole *f*; *(on dress)* colifichet *m.*
knife [naɪf] **1** *n, pl* **knives** *(at table, in kitchen etc; also weapon)* couteau *m*; *(pocket ~)* canif *m.* **~, fork and spoon** couvert *m*; *(fig)* **to turn** *or* **twist the ~ in the wound** retourner le couteau dans la plaie *(fig)*; *(fig)* **he's got his ~ into me*** il en a après moi*, il a une dent contre moi, il m'en veut; *(fig)* **it's war to the ~ between them** ils sont à couteaux tirés *(fig)*, c'est la guerre ouverte entre eux *(fig)*; *(Med)* **under the ~*** sur le billard*; **before you could say ~*** en moins de temps qu'il n'en faut pour le dire.
2 *vt person* donner un coup de couteau à. **she had been ~d** elle avait reçu un coup de couteau; *(to death)* elle avait été tuée à coups de couteau.
3 *cpd*: **knife box** boîte *f* à couteaux; **knife edge** fil *m* d'un couteau; *(Tech)* couteau; *(fig: tense, anxious) person* **on a knife edge** sur des charbons ardents *(fig)*; **the success of the scheme/the result was balanced on a knife edge** la réussite du projet/le résultat ne tenait qu'à un fil; **knife-edge(d)** *blade* tranchant, aiguisé; *crease* bien repassé, en lame de rasoir; **knife-grinder** rémouleur *m*, repasseur *m* de couteaux; **knife-sharpener** *(on wall, on wheel etc)* affiloir *m*, aiguisoir *m*; *(long, gen with handle)* fusil *m* à repasser les couteaux.
knight [naɪt] **1** *n* chevalier *m*; *(Chess)* cavalier *m.* *(Brit)* **K~ of the Garter** Chevalier de (l'ordre de) la Jarretière.
2 *cpd*: *(Hist)* **knight-errant** chevalier errant; *(U)* **knight-errantry** chevalerie errante; **Knight Templar** chevalier *m* de l'ordre du Temple, Templier *m.*
3 *vt* **(a)** *(Hist) squire etc* adouber, armer chevalier.
(b) *(Brit) [sovereign]* donner l'accolade (de chevalier) à, faire chevalier. **he was ~ed for services to industry** il a été fait chevalier pour services rendus dans l'industrie.
knighthood ['naɪthʊd] *n* **(a)** *(knights collectively)* chevalerie *f.* **(b)** *(rank)* titre *m* de chevalier. **to get** *or* **receive a ~** être fait chevalier, recevoir le titre de chevalier.
knightly ['naɪtlɪ] *adj courtesy* chevaleresque; *armour* de chevalier.
knit [nɪt] *pret, ptp* **knitted** *or* **knit 1** *vt* **(a)** tricoter. **'~ three, purl one'** 'trois mailles à l'endroit, une maille à l'envers'; **~ted jacket** veste tricotée *or* en tricot; *(Comm)* **~ted goods,** *(U)* **~wear** tricots *mpl*, articles *mpl* en tricot; *V* **thick** *etc.*
(b) *(fig: also* **~ together**) lier, unir. **to ~ one's brows** froncer les sourcils; *V* **close**[1] *etc.*
2 *vi* tricoter; *[bone etc] (also* **~ together, ~ up**) se souder. **to ~ tightly** tricoter serré.
knit together 1 *vi* = **knit 2.**
2 *vt sep* **(a) 'knit two together'** 'tricoter deux mailles ensemble'.
(b) *(fig)* = **knit 1b.**
knit up 1 *vi* **(a)** = **knit 2.**
(b) this wool knits up very quickly cette laine monte très vite, le tricot monte très vite avec cette laine.
2 *vt sep jersey* tricoter.
knitting ['nɪtɪŋ] **1** *n (U)* **(a)** tricot *m*; *(Ind)* tricotage *m*; *V* **double. (b)** *[bone etc]* soudure *f.* **2** *cpd*: **knitting machine** machine *f* à tricoter, tricoteuse *f*; **knitting needle, knitting pin** aiguille *f* à tricoter; **knitting wool** laine *f* à tricoter.
knives [naɪvz] *npl of* **knife.**
knob [nɒb] *n* **(a)** *[door, instrument etc]* bouton *m*; *[cane, walking stick]* pommeau *m*; *(small swelling)* bosse *f*, protubérance *f*; *(on tree)* nœud *m.* **(b)** *(small piece) [cheese etc]* petit morceau. **~ of butter** noix *f* de beurre.
knobbly ['nɒblɪ] *adj*, **knobby** ['nɒbɪ] *adj* noueux.
knock [nɒk] **1** *n* **(a)** *(blow)* coup *m*; *(collision)* heurt *m*, choc *m*; *(in engine etc)* cognement *m.* **there was a ~ at the door** on a frappé (à la porte); **after several ~s at the door he went away** après avoir frappé plusieurs fois à la porte il s'est éloigné; **I heard a ~ (at the door)** j'ai entendu (quelqu'un) frapper (à la porte); **~, ~!** toc, toc, toc!; **I'll give you a ~ at 7 o'clock** je viendrai taper à la porte à 7 heures; **he got a ~ (on the head** *etc***)** il a reçu *or* attrapé *or* pris* un coup (sur la tête *etc*); **he gave himself a nasty ~ (on the head** *etc***)** il s'est cogné très fort (à la tête *etc*); **he gave the car a ~** il a cabossé la voiture.
(b) *(fig: setback etc)* revers *m.* *(criticism)* **~s*** critiques *fpl*; **to take a ~** recevoir un coup *(fig)*; **that was a hard ~ for him** ça a été un coup pour lui; **his pride has taken a ~** son orgueil a été atteint, son orgueil en a pris un coup*.
2 *cpd*: **knockabout** *(n: Naut: esp US)* dériveur *m*, petit voilier; *(adj: boisterous)* turbulent, violent; **knockabout clothes** vieux vêtements (qui ne craignent rien); *(Theat)* **knockabout comedy** (grosse) farce *f*; **knockdown** *V* **knockdown**; *(Ind etc)* **knocking-off time*** heure *f* de la sortie; **to be knock-kneed, to have knock-knees** avoir les genoux cagneux; **knockout** *V* **knockout**; *(Tennis)* **to have a knock-up** faire des balles.
3 *vt* **(a)** *(hit, strike)* frapper. **to ~ a nail into a plank** planter *or* enfoncer un clou dans une planche; **to ~ a nail in (with a hammer/shoe** *etc***)** enfoncer un clou (d'un coup *or* à coups de marteau/de chaussure *etc*); **he ~ed the ball into the hedge** il a envoyé la balle dans la haie; **to ~ the bottom out of a box** défoncer (le fond d')une boîte; **to ~ holes in sth** faire des trous dans qch, trouer qch, percer qch; *(fig)* **to ~ the bottom out of an argument, to ~ holes in an argument** démolir un argument; **to ~ sb on the head** frapper qn sur la tête; *(stun)* assommer qn; **that ~ed his plans on the head*** cela a flanqué* par terre *or* démoli ses projets; **to ~ sb to the ground** jeter qn à terre, faire tomber qn; *(stun)* assommer qn; **to ~ sb unconscious** *or* **cold** *or* **senseless** *or* **silly** assommer qn; **she ~ed the knife out of his hand** elle lui a fait tomber le couteau des mains; **he ~ed the child out of the way** il a écarté brutalement l'enfant de son chemin; **to ~ a glass off a table** faire tomber un verre d'une table; **she ~ed the cup to the floor** elle a fait tomber la tasse (par terre); **I'll ~ the smile off your face!*** je vais te flanquer une raclée* qui t'enlèvera l'envie de sourire!; *(Brit)* **to ~ sb for six*** démolir* qn; **to ~ sb into the middle of next week*** faire voir trente-six chandelles à qn; **to ~ spots off sb*, to ~ sb into a cocked hat*** battre qn à plate(s) couture(s); *(astonish)* **to ~ sb sideways*** ébahir *or* ahurir qn; **to ~ some sense into sb, to ~ the nonsense out of sb** ramener qn à la raison (par la manière forte); *V* **stuffing.**
(b) *(collide with, strike) [vehicle]* heurter; *[person]* se cogner dans, heurter. **to ~ one's head on** *or* **against** se cogner la tête contre; **he ~ed his foot against a stone** il a donné du pied *or* a buté contre une pierre; **the car ~ed the gatepost** la voiture a heurté le poteau *or* est rentrée* dans le poteau; **I ~ed the car against the gatepost, I ~ed the gatepost with the car** je suis rentré* dans le poteau avec la voiture, j'ai heurté le poteau avec la voiture.
(c) (‡: *denigrate*) dire du mal de, critiquer, déblatérer contre; *(in advertising)* faire de la contre-publicité à.
4 *vi* **(a)** *(strike, hit)* frapper, cogner. **to ~ at the door/window** *etc* frapper *or* cogner à la porte/la fenêtre *etc*; **he ~ed on the table** il a frappé la table, il a cogné sur la table; **he's ~ing on‡ fifty** il frise la cinquantaine; **his knees were ~ing** il tremblait de peur, il avait les chocottes‡.
(b) *(bump, collide)* **to ~ against** *or* **into sb/sth** se cogner *or* se heurter contre qn/qch, heurter qn/qch; **my hand ~ed against the shelf** ma main a heurté l'étagère, je me suis cogné la main contre l'étagère; **the car ~ed against** *or* **into the lamppost** la voiture a heurté le réverbère; **he ~ed into the table** il s'est cogné dans *or* contre la table, il s'est heurté contre la table, il a heurté la table; *V also* **knock into.**
(c) *[car engine etc]* cogner.
knock about, knock around 1 *vi* **(a)** *(travel, wander)* vagabonder, vadrouiller*, bourlinguer*; *[sailor]* bourlinguer. **he has knocked about a bit** il a beaucoup bourlingué* *(fig)*, il a roulé sa bosse*.
(b) (*) traîner. **your socks are knocking about in the bedroom** tes chaussettes traînent dans la chambre.
2 *vt fus*: **to knock about the world** vadrouiller* *or* vagabonder de par le monde; **he's knocking about France somewhere*** il vadrouille* *or* il se balade* quelque part en France.
3 *vt sep* **(a)** *(ill-treat)* maltraiter, malmener. **he knocks her about** il lui flanque des coups*, il lui tape dessus*.
(b) ravager. **the harvest was badly knocked about by the storm** la récolte a été ravagée par l'orage.
4 knockabout *n, adj V* **knock 2.**
knock back 1 *vi (lit)* **he knocked on the wall and she knocked back** il a frappé *or* cogné au mur et elle a répondu de la même façon.
2 *vt sep* **(a)** (* *fig: drink*) s'enfiler (derrière la cravate)*, s'envoyer*.
(b) (‡: *cost*) **this watch knocked me back £20** cette montre a fait un trou de 20 livres dans mes finances.
(c) (* *fig: shock*) sonner*, ahurir, ébahir. **the news knocked her back a bit** la nouvelle l'a un peu sonnée*.
knock down 1 *vt sep* **(a)** *object* renverser; *building etc* abattre, démolir; *tree* abattre; *door* démolir. **he knocked me down with one blow** il m'a jeté à terre *or* étendu* d'un seul coup; **you could have knocked me down with a feather!** les bras m'en sont tombés!, j'en étais comme deux ronds de flan!‡

(b) (*Aut etc*) renverser. **he got knocked down by a bus** il a été renversé par un autobus.
(c) *price* baisser, abaisser. **he knocked the price down by 10%** il a baissé le prix de 10%, il a fait une remise de 10% sur le prix.
(d) (*at auction*) **to knock down sth to sb** adjuger qch à qn; **it was knocked down for £10** ça a été adjugé et vendu 10 livres.
2 knockdown *adj, n V* **knockdown.**

knock in *vt sep nail* enfoncer.

knock into* *vt fus* (*meet*) tomber sur.

knock off 1 *vi* (*: *stop work*) s'arrêter (de travailler), cesser le travail; *[striker]* débrayer*.
2 *vt sep* **(a)** (*lit*) *vase on shelf etc* faire tomber. **to knock sb's block off**: casser la figure* *or* la gueule: à qn.
(b) (*reduce price by*) baisser. **I'll knock off £10** je vais baisser (le prix) de 10 livres, je vais rabattre 10 livres du prix.
(c) (*) *homework, correspondence, piece of work* (*do quickly*) expédier; (*do quickly and well*) trousser; (*do quickly and badly*) bâcler.
(d) (*Brit*: *steal*) piquer:.
(e) (: *stop*) **to knock off smoking** arrêter de *or* cesser de fumer; **knock it off!** arrête!, suffit!*
3 knocking-off *adj V* **knock 2.**

knock out 1 *vt sep* **(a)** *nail etc* faire sortir (*of* de); (**fig*) *word, phrase, paragraph* barrer, biffer. **to knock out one's pipe** débourrer *or* éteindre sa pipe.
(b) (*stun*) assommer; (*Boxing*) mettre knock-out.
(c) (: *shock, overwhelm*) sonner*, ahurir, abasourdir.
(d) (*from competition etc*) éliminer (*of* de).
2 knockout *n, adj V* **knockout.**

knock over *vt sep table, stool etc* renverser, faire tomber; *object on shelf or table etc* faire tomber; (*Aut*) *pedestrian* renverser; *gatepost* faire tomber. **he was knocked over by a taxi** il a été renversé par un taxi.

knock together 1 *vi [glasses, knees]* s'entrechoquer.
2 *vt sep* **(a)** (*lit*) *two objects* cogner l'un contre l'autre. **I'd like to knock their heads together!*** j'aimerais prendre l'un pour taper sur l'autre!
(b) (*make hurriedly*) *table, shed etc* faire *or* bricoler à la hâte.

knock up 1 *vi* (*Tennis*) faire des balles.
2 *vt sep* **(a)** (*lit*) faire lever d'un coup. **to knock sb's arm up** faire voler le bras de qn en l'air.
(b) (*Brit: waken*) réveiller (en frappant à la porte).
(c) (*make hurriedly*) *meal* préparer en vitesse; *building* construire à la hâte *or* à la va-vite; *furniture, toy* faire *or* fabriquer en un rien de temps.
(d) (*Brit*: exhaust*) *person* éreinter, crever*.
(e) (*Brit*: make ill*) rendre malade. **you'll knock yourself up if you go on like this** tu vas te rendre malade *or* t'esquinter* si tu continues comme ça.
(f) (: *make pregnant*) mettre enceinte*, engrosser:.
3 knock-up *n V* **knock 2.**
4 knocker-up *n V* **knocker 2.**

knock up against *vt fus* **(a)** (*bump into*) *table, chair* se cogner dans, se heurter contre, heurter.
(b) (*: *meet*) tomber sur.

knockdown ['nɒkdaʊn] **1** *adj* **(a) a ~ blow** un coup qui assommerait un bœuf, un coup de boutoir.
(b) (*Brit*) **~ price** (*Comm*) prix imbattable; (*at auction*) prix minimum.
(c) (*capable of being taken apart*) *table, shed* démontable.
2 *n* (*price reduction*) réduction *f*, rabais *m*, remise *f*.

knocker ['nɒkə^r] **1** *n* (*also* **door-~**) marteau *m* (de porte), heurtoir *m*. **~s**: nichons: *mpl*, nénés: *mpl*, roberts: *mpl*. **2** *cpd*: (*Brit*) **knocker-up** *personne f qui réveille les gens en frappant à leur porte.*

knocking ['nɒkɪŋ] **1** *n* (*U*) **(a)** coups *mpl*. **I can hear ~ at the door** j'entends frapper à la porte. **(b)** (*in engine*) cognement *m*. **2** *adj* (*Advertising*) **~ copy** contre-publicité *f* (*dénigrant le concurrent*); **~-shop**: bordel: *m*.

knockout ['nɒkaʊt] **1** *n* **(a)** (*Boxing etc*) knock-out *m*.
(b) (: *overwhelming success*) *[person, record, achievement]* **to be a ~** être sensationnel* *or* formidable* *or* sensass:.
2 *adj* **(a) ~ blow** (*Boxing etc*) coup *m* qui (vous) met K.-O.; (*fig*) coup de grâce; (*Boxing*) **the ~ blow came in round 6** il a été mis knock-out au 6e round.
(b) (*) *pill, drug* qui (vous) assomme*. **~ drops** soporifique *m*, narcotique *m*.
(c) (*Sport*) **~ competition** compétition *f* (avec épreuves éliminatoires).

knoll [nəʊl] *n* **(a)** (*hillock*) tertre *m*, monticule *m*. **(b)** (††: *bell stroke*) son *m* de cloche.

knot [nɒt] **1** *n* **(a)** nœud *m*. **to tie/untie a ~** faire/défaire un nœud; **tight/slack ~** nœud serré/lâche; (*fig*) **the marriage ~** le lien du mariage; **Gordian ~** nœud gordien; *V* **granny, reef^2, slip, tie** *etc*.
(b) (*Naut*) nœud *m*. **to make 20 ~s** filer 20 nœuds; *V* **rate^1**.
(c) (*in wood*) nœud *m*; (*fig*) *[problem etc]* nœud. **a ~ of people** un petit groupe de gens.
2 *vt rope* faire un nœud à, nouer. **he ~ted the piece of string to the rope** il a noué la ficelle à la corde; **get ~ted!**: va te faire voir!* *or* foutre!:
3 *vi* faire un *or* des nœud(s).

knot together *vt sep* attacher, nouer.

knotty ['nɒtɪ] *adj wood, hand* noueux; *rope* plein de nœuds; *problem* épineux, difficile.

knout [naʊt] *n* knout *m*.

know [nəʊ] *pret* **knew**, *ptp* **known 1** *vt* **(a)** *facts, details, dates, results* savoir. **to ~ French** savoir le français; **I ~ (that) you're wrong** je sais que vous avez tort; **I ~ why he is angry** je sais pourquoi il est en colère; **do you ~ whether she's coming?** est-ce que tu sais si elle doit venir?; (*frm*) **I would have you ~ that ...** sachez que ...; **to ~ a lot about sth/sb** en savoir long sur qch/qn; **I don't ~ much about it/him** je ne sais pas grand-chose là-dessus/sur lui; **I'd like to ~ more (about it)** je voudrais en savoir davantage *or* plus long (là-dessus); **to ~ by heart** *text, song, poem* savoir par cœur; *subject, plan, route* connaître par cœur; **to get to ~ sth** apprendre qch (*V also* **1b**); **to ~ how to do sth** savoir faire qch; **I don't ~ where to begin** je ne sais pas par où commencer; **he ~s all the answers** il s'y connaît; (*pej*) c'est un (monsieur) je-sais-tout*; **he thinks he ~s all the answers** *or* **everything** il croit qu'il sait tout; **to ~ one's business, to ~ what's what*** connaître son affaire, s'y connaître, en connaître un bon bout*; **to ~ the difference between** connaître la différence entre; **to ~ one's mind** savoir ce qu'on veut; **he ~s a thing or two*** il sait pas mal de choses; **he ~s what he's talking about*** il sait de quoi il parle, il connaît son sujet; **you ~ what I mean ...** tu vois ce que je veux dire ...; **that's worth ~ing** ça vaut la peine de le savoir, c'est bon à savoir; **for all I ~** (autant) que je sache; **is he dead? — not that I ~** il est mort? — pas que je sache *or* pas à ma connaissance; **there's no ~ing what he'll do** impossible de savoir ce qu'il va faire, on ne peut pas savoir ce qu'il va faire (*V also* **2a**); **I don't ~ if I can do it** je ne sais pas si je peux le faire; **I don't ~ that that is a very good idea** je ne sais pas si c'est une très bonne idée; **what do you ~!*** dites donc!, eh bien!, ça alors!; **I've been a fool and don't I ~ it!*** j'ai agi comme un idiot et je suis bien placé pour le savoir!; **she's angry! — don't I ~ it!*** *or* **I ~ all about that!*** elle est en colère! — à qui le dis-tu! *or* je suis bien placé pour le savoir!; **not if I ~ it!*** c'est ce qu'on va voir!, ça m'étonnerait!; **the Channel was rough, as I well ~!** *or* **as well I ~!** la Manche était houleuse, j'en sais quelque chose!; **it's no good lying, I ~ all about it** ce n'est pas la peine de mentir, je sais tout; **she ~s all about sewing** elle s'y connaît *or* elle est très forte *or* elle est très calée* en couture; **that's all you ~ (about it)!*** c'est ce que tu crois!; **I ~ nothing about it** je n'en sais rien, je ne suis pas au courant; **it soon became ~n that ...** on a bientôt appris que ...; **it is well ~n that ...** il est (bien) connu que ..., tout le monde sait (bien) que ...; **to make sth ~n to sb** faire savoir qch à qn; **to make one's presence ~n to sb** manifester sa présence à qn; **he is ~n to have been there/to be dishonest** on sait qu'il y a été/qu'il est malhonnête; **I ~ him to be a liar, I ~ him for a liar** je sais que c'est un menteur; **he knew himself (to be) guilty** il se savait coupable; **he soon let me ~ what he thought of it** il m'a fait bientôt savoir ce qu'il en pensait; **I'll let you ~** je vous le ferai savoir, je vous préviendrai; **when can you let me ~?** quand pourrez-vous me le dire? *or* me prévenir?; **let me ~ if I can help** si je peux me rendre utile dites-le-moi; *V* **rope**.
(b) (*be acquainted with*) *person, place, book, author* connaître. **I ~ him well** je le connais bien; **I don't ~ him from Adam** je ne le connais ni d'Ève ni d'Adam; **do you ~ Paris?** connaissez-vous Paris?; **to ~ sb by sight/by name/by reputation** connaître qn de vue/de nom/de réputation; **I don't ~ her to speak to** je ne la connais pas (assez) pour lui parler; (*liter*) **~ thyself** connais-toi toi-même; **I was glad to see someone I knew** j'étais content de voir une personne de connaissance; **to get to ~ sb** arriver à (mieux) connaître qn; **to make o.s. ~n to sb** se présenter à qn; **he is ~n as X** on le connaît sous le nom de X; **she wishes to be ~n as Mrs X** elle veut se faire appeler Mme X.
(c) (*be aware of*) **I have never ~n him to smile** je ne l'ai jamais vu sourire; **you have never ~n them to tell a lie** vous ne leur avez jamais entendu dire un mensonge; **I've ~n such things to happen before** j'ai déjà vu cela se produire; **I've never ~n it to rain like this** je n'ai jamais vu pleuvoir comme ça.
(d) (*recognize*) reconnaître. **to ~ sb by his voice/his walk** reconnaître qn à sa voix/à sa démarche; **I knew him at once** je l'ai reconnu tout de suite; **you won't ~ him** tu ne le reconnaîtras pas; **he ~s a good horse when he sees one** il sait reconnaître un bon cheval; (*fig*) **she ~s a good thing when she sees it*** elle sait profiter des bonnes occasions, elle ne laisse pas échapper les bonnes occasions.
(e) (*distinguish*) reconnaître, distinguer. **I wouldn't ~ a spanner from a screwdriver** je ne sais pas reconnaître une clef à molette d'un tournevis; **he doesn't ~ one end of a horse/hammer** *etc* **from the other** c'est à peine s'il sait ce que c'est qu'un cheval/marteau *etc*; **you wouldn't ~ him from his brother** on le prendrait pour son frère.
2 *vi* **(a)** savoir. **as far as I ~** (autant) que je sache; **not as far as I ~** pas que je sache, pas à ma connaissance; **who ~s?** qui sait?; **is she nice? — I don't ~** *or* **I wouldn't ~*** est-ce qu'elle est gentille? — je ne sais pas *or* je n'en sais rien; **how should I ~?** est-ce que je sais (moi)!, comment voulez-vous que je le sache?; **it's raining, you ~** il pleut, tu sais; **will he help us? — there's no ~ing** va-t-il nous aider? — on ne peut pas savoir; **and afterwards they just don't want to ~*** et après ça ils font ceux qui n'en ont jamais entendu parler; **mummy ~s best!** maman a toujours raison!; **you ~ best, I suppose!** bien sûr, tu sais ce que tu dis!; **to ~ about** *or* **of sth** savoir qch, connaître qch, avoir entendu parler de qch; **I didn't ~ about that** je ne savais pas ça; **I'm going swimming — I don't ~ about that!*** je vais nager — c'est à voir!; **she ~s about cats** elle s'y connaît en (matière de) chats; **I knew of his death through a friend** j'ai appris sa mort par un ami; **I'd ~n of his death for some time** je savais depuis quelque temps qu'il était mort; **do you ~ about John?** tu es au courant pour Jean?*; **there were 10 in favour, 6 against, and 5 'don't ~s'** il y avait 10 pour, 6 contre et 5 'sans opinion'.
(b) I ~ better than to offer advice je me garde bien de donner des conseils; **he ~s better than to touch his capital** il est trop prudent *or* avisé pour entamer son capital; **you ought to ~ better than to go out without a coat** tu ne devrais pas avoir la stupidité de sortir sans manteau; **you ought to have ~n better**

tu aurais dû réfléchir; **he should ~ better at his age** à son âge il ne devrait pas être aussi bête *or* il devrait avoir un peu plus de bon sens; **they don't ~ any better** ils ne savent pas ce qu'ils font (*or* ce qu'il faut faire); **he says he didn't do it but I ~ better** il dit que ce n'est pas lui mais je ne suis pas dupe.

(c) do you ~ of a good hairdresser? connaissez-vous un bon coiffeur?; **I ~ of a nice little café** je connais un petit café sympathique; **I ~ of you through your sister** j'ai entendu parler de vous par votre sœur; **I don't know him but I ~ OF him** je ne le connais pas mais j'ai entendu parler de lui.

3 *cpd*: **a know-all*** un (monsieur) je-sais-tout*, une je-sais-tout*; **they have the materials to make the missile but they haven't got the know-how*** ils ont le matériel nécessaire à la fabrication du missile mais ils n'ont pas la technique; **after years in the job he has acquired a lot of know-how*** après des années dans cet emploi il a acquis beaucoup de technique *or* de savoir-faire *or* de métier; **you need quite a bit of know-how* to operate this machine** il faut pas mal de* compétence pour faire marcher cette machine; (*US*) **a know-it-all* = a know-all***.

4 *n*: **to be in the ~*** être au courant *or* au parfum‡.

knowable [ˈnəʊəbl] *adj* connaissable.

knowing [ˈnəʊɪŋ] *adj* (*shrewd*) fin, malin (*f* -igne); (*wise*) sage; *look, smile* entendu.

knowingly [ˈnəʊɪŋlɪ] *adv* **(a)** (*consciously*) sciemment. **(b)** (*in knowing way*) *look, smile* d'un air entendu.

knowledge [ˈnɒlɪdʒ] *n* (*U*) **(a)** (*understanding, awareness*) connaissance *f*. **to have ~ of** avoir connaissance de; **to have no ~ of** ne pas savoir, ignorer; **to (the best of) my ~** à ma connaissance, autant que je sache; **not to my ~** pas à ma connaissance, pas que je sache; **they had never to her ~ complained before** à sa connaissance ils ne s'étaient jamais plaints auparavant; **without his ~** à son insu; **without the ~ of her mother** à l'insu de sa mère; **it has come to my ~ that ...** j'ai appris que ...; **~ of the facts** la connaissance des faits; **it's common *or* public ~ that ...** il est de notoriété publique que ..., chacun sait que ... .

(b) (*learning, facts learnt*) connaissances *fpl*, science *f*, savoir *m*. **the advance of ~** le progrès du savoir *or* de la science *or* des connaissances; **his ~ will die with him** son savoir mourra avec lui; **my ~ of English is elementary** mes connaissances d'anglais sont élémentaires; **he has a working ~ of Japanese** il possède les éléments de base du japonais; **he has a thorough ~ of geography** il possède la géographie à fond.

knowledgeable [ˈnɒlɪdʒəbl] *adj person* bien informé; *report* bien documenté.

known [nəʊn] **1** *ptp of* **know.**

2 *adj* connu, reconnu. **he is a ~ thief/troublemaker** *etc* c'est un voleur/agitateur *etc* connu; **the ~ experts on this subject** les experts reconnus en la matière; **the ~ facts lead us to believe ...** les faits constatés *or* établis nous amènent à croire ... .

knuckle [ˈnʌkl] **1** *n* articulation *f or* jointure *f* du doigt. **to graze one's ~s** s'écorcher les articulations des doigts; *V* **rap.**

2 *cpd*: **knuckle-bone** (*Anat*) articulation *f* du doigt; (*Culin*) os *m* de jarret; **knuckleduster** coup-de-poing américain; **knucklehead‡** crétin(e)* *m(f)*, nouille* *f*.

knuckle down* *vi* s'y mettre. **to knuckle down to work** s'atteler au travail.

knuckle under* *vi* céder.

knurl [nɜːl] **1** *n* (*in wood*) nœud *m*; (*Tech*) moletage *m*. **2** *vt* (*Tech*) moleter.

K.O.* [ˈkeɪˈəʊ] (*vb: pret, ptp* **K.O.'d** [ˈkeɪˈəʊd]) (*abbr of* **knockout**) **1** *n* (*blow*) K.-O. *m*, knock-out *m*. **2** *vt* (*Boxing*) mettre knock-out, battre par knock-out; (*gen*) mettre K.-O.* *or* knock-out*.

koala [kəʊˈɑːlə] *n* (*also* **~ bear**) koala *m*.

Koran [kɒˈrɑːn] *n* Coran *m*.

Koranic [kɒˈrænɪk] *adj* coranique.

Korea [kəˈrɪə] *n* Corée *f*. **North/South ~** Corée du Nord/du Sud.

Korean [kəˈrɪən] **1** *adj* coréen. **North/South ~** nord-/sud-coréen. **2** *n* **(a)** Coréen(ne) *m(f)*. **North/South ~** Nord-/Sud-Coréen(ne). **(b)** (*Ling*) coréen *m*.

kosher [ˈkəʊʃəʳ] *adj* kascher *inv*. (*fig*) **it's ~‡** c'est O.K.*

kowtow [ˈkaʊˈtaʊ] *vi* se prosterner. **to ~ to sb** courber l'échine devant qn, faire des courbettes devant qn.

kraal [krɑːl] *n* kraal *m*.

Kremlin [ˈkremlɪn] *n* Kremlin *m*.

kremlinologist [ˈkremlɪˈnɒlədʒɪst] *n* kremlinologue *mf*, kremlinologiste *mf*.

kremlinology [ˈkremlɪˈnɒlədʒɪ] *n* kremlinologie *f*.

kudos* [ˈkjuːdɒs] *n* (*U*) gloire *f*, lauriers *mpl*. **he got all the ~** c'est lui qui a récolté toute la gloire *or* tous les lauriers.

kummel [ˈkɪməl] *n* kummel *m*.

Kuwait [kʊˈweɪt] *n* Koweit *f or* Kuwait *f*.

kwashiorkor [ˌkwɑːʃɪˈɔːkɔːʳ] *n* kwashiorkor *m*.

L

L, l [el] *n* (*letter*) L, l *m or f*. **L-shaped room** pièce *f* en (forme de) L; (*Brit Aut*) **L-plate** plaque *f* d'apprenti conducteur.

lab* [læb] *n* (*abbr of* **laboratory**) labo* *m*, laboratoire *m*.

label [ˈleɪbl] **1** *n* (*lit, fig*) étiquette *f*. **record on the Deltaphone ~** disque *m* (sorti chez) Deltaphone; *V* **luggage.**

2 *vt* **(a)** *parcel, bottle* coller une *or* des étiquette(s) sur; (*Comm*) *goods for sale* étiqueter. **every packet must be clearly ~led** tout paquet doit porter une *or* des étiquette(s) lisible(s) et précise(s); **the bottle was not ~led** il n'y avait pas d'étiquette sur la bouteille; **the bottle was ~led poison** sur la bouteille il y avait marqué poison.

(b) (*fig*) *person, group* étiqueter, cataloguer (*pej*) (*as* comme). **he was ~led (as) a revolutionary** on l'a étiqueté (comme) révolutionnaire.

labial [ˈleɪbɪəl] (*Ling*) **1** *adj* labial. **2** *n* labiale *f*.

labor [ˈleɪbəʳ] *etc* (*US*) = **labour** *etc.*

laboratory [ləˈbɒrətərɪ] **1** *n* laboratoire *m*; *V* **language. 2** *cpd experiment, instrument, product* de laboratoire. **laboratory assistant** assistant(e) *m(f)* de laboratoire, laborantin(e) *m(f)*; **laboratory equipment** équipement *m* de laboratoire.

laborious [ləˈbɔːrɪəs] *adj* laborieux.

laboriously [ləˈbɔːrɪəslɪ] *adv* laborieusement.

labour, (*US*) **labor** [ˈleɪbəʳ] **1** *n* **(a)** (*hard work; task*) travail *m*. **~ of love** travail fait par plaisir; **~s of Hercules** travaux *mpl* d'Hercule; *V* **hard, manual.**

(b) (*U: Ind: workers*) main-d'œuvre *f*, ouvriers *mpl*, travailleurs *mpl*. **Minister/Ministry of L~**, (*US*) **Secretary/Department of L~** ministre *m*/ministère *m* du Travail; *V* **skilled** *etc.*

(c) (*Pol*) **L~** les travaillistes *mpl*; **he votes L~** il vote travailliste.

(d) (*Med*) travail *m*. **in ~** en travail, en train d'accoucher.

2 *cpd* (*Ind*) *dispute, trouble* ouvrier; *relations* ouvriers-patronat *inv*. (*Brit Pol*) **Labour** *leader, movement, party* travailliste; **labour camp** camp *m* de travaux forcés; **Labour Day** fête *f* du travail; (*Brit*) **Labour Exchange** ≈ bourse *f* de l'emploi, Agence *f* pour l'emploi; (*Ind*) **labour force** (*number employed*) effectif(s) *m(pl)* en ouvriers; (*personnel*) main-d'œuvre *f*; **labour-intensive** qui nécessite l'emploi de beaucoup d'ouvriers *or* de main-d'œuvre; (*US*) **labor laws** législation industrielle *or* du travail; **labour market** marché *m* du travail; (*Med*) **labour pains** douleurs *fpl* de l'accouchement; **labour-saving** qui allège le travail; (*in household*) **labour-saving device** appareil ménager; (*Ind*) **labour shortage** pénurie *f* de main-d'œuvre; (*US*) **labor union** syndicat *m*.

3 *vi* **(a)** (*work with effort*) travailler dur (*at* à); (*work with difficulty*) peiner (*at* sur). **to ~ to do** travailler dur *or* peiner pour faire.

(b) *[engine, motor]* peiner; *[ship, boat]* fatiguer. **to ~ under a delusion** être victime d'une illusion; **to ~ up a hill** *[person]* gravir *or* monter péniblement une côte; *[car]* peiner dans une montée; *V* **misapprehension.**

4 *vt* insister sur, s'étendre sur. **I won't ~ the point** je n'insisterai pas (lourdement) sur ce point, je ne m'étendrai pas là-dessus.

laboured, (*US*) **labored** [ˈleɪbəd] *adj style* (*clumsy*) lourd; (*showing effort*) laborieux; (*overelaborate*) ampoulé. **~ breathing** respiration *f* pénible *or* difficile.

labourer, (*US*) **laborer** [ˈleɪbərəʳ] *n* ouvrier *m*, travailleur *m*; (*on farm*) ouvrier agricole; (*on roads, building sites etc*) manœuvre *m*; *V* **dock¹**.

labouring, (*US*) **laboring** [ˈleɪbərɪŋ] *adj class* ouvrier.

labourite, (*US*) **laborite** [ˈleɪbəraɪt] *n* (*Pol*) travailliste *mf*.

laburnum [ləˈbɜːnəm] *n* cytise *m*, faux ébénier.

labyrinth [ˈlæbɪrɪnθ] *n* labyrinthe *m*, dédale *m*.

labyrinthine [ˌlæbɪˈrɪnθaɪn] *adj* labyrinthique, labyrinthien.

lace [leɪs] **1** *n* **(a)** (*U: Tex*) dentelle *f*; (*pillow ~*) guipure *f*. **dress trimmed with ~** robe bordée de dentelle(s); (*Mil*) **gold ~** galon *m*.

(b) *[shoe, corset]* lacet *m*.

2 *cpd collar, curtains* de *or* en dentelle. **lacemaker** dentellière *f*; **lacemaking** fabrication *f* de la dentelle, dentellerie *f* (*rare*); **lace-up shoes, lace-ups*** chaussures *fpl* à lacets.

3 *vt* **(a)** (*also* **~ up**) *shoe, corset* lacer.

(b) *drink* arroser (*with* de), corser.

4 *vi* (*also* **~ up**) se lacer.

lace into: *vt fus* (*thrash*) rosser*; (*criticize*) éreinter, démolir.
lacerate [ˈlæsəreɪt] *vt* (*lit*) *face, skin, clothes* lacérer; (*fig*) *person* déchirer, fendre le cœur de. **body ~d by pain** corps lacéré par la douleur.
laceration [ˌlæsəˈreɪʃən] *n* (*act*) lacération *f*; (*tear: also Med*) déchirure *f*.
lachrymose [ˈlækrɪməʊs] *adj* (*liter*) larmoyant.
lack [læk] **1** *n* manque *m*. **through** *or* **for ~ of** faute de, par manque de; **there is a ~ of money** l'argent manque.
2 *vt confidence, friends, strength, interest* manquer de. **we ~ (the) time to do it** nous n'avons pas le temps de le faire, nous manquons de temps pour le faire; **he doesn't ~ talent** ce n'est pas le talent qui lui manque *or* qui lui fait défaut.
3 *vi* **(a)** *[food, money]* **to be ~ing** manquer, faire défaut.
(b) *[person]* **to be ~ing in, to ~ for** manquer de.
lackadaisical [ˌlækəˈdeɪzɪkəl] *adj* (*listless*) nonchalant, apathique; (*lazy*) indolent; *work* fait à la va-comme-je-te-pousse*.
lackey [ˈlækɪ] *n* laquais *m* (*also pej*), larbin* *m* (*pej*).
lacking* [ˈlækɪŋ] *adj* (*stupid*) simplet, demeuré*, débile*.
lacklustre, (*US*) **lackluster** [ˈlækˌlʌstəʳ] *adj* terne.
laconic [ləˈkɒnɪk] *adj* laconique.
laconically [ləˈkɒnɪkəlɪ] *adv* laconiquement.
lacquer [ˈlækəʳ] **1** *n* (*substance: for wood, hair etc*) laque *f*; (*object*) laque *m*. **~ ware** laques *mpl*. **2** *vt wood* laquer; *hair* mettre de la laque sur.
lacrosse [ləˈkrɒs] *n* lacrosse *m*. **~ stick** crosse *f*.
lactate [ˈlækteɪt] **1** *n* (*Chem*) lactate *m*. **2** *vi* produire du lait.
lactation [lækˈteɪʃən] *n* lactation *f*.
lacteal [ˈlæktɪəl] **1** *adj* lacté. **2** *npl*: **~s** veines lactées.
lactic [ˈlæktɪk] *adj* lacté. (*Chem*) **~ acid** acide *m* lactique.
lactose [ˈlæktəʊs] *n* lactose *m*.
lacuna [ləˈkjuːnə] *n, pl* **lacunae** [ləˈkjuːniː] lacune *f*.
lacustrine [ləˈkʌstraɪn] *adj* lacustre.
lacy [ˈleɪsɪ] *adj* qui ressemble à la dentelle. **the frost made a ~ pattern** il y avait une dentelle de givre.
lad [læd] *n* garçon *m*, gars* *m*. **when I was a ~** quand j'étais jeune, dans mon jeune temps; **he's only a ~** ce n'est qu'un gosse* *or* un gamin*; **I'm going for a drink with the ~s*** je vais boire un pot avec les copains*; **come on ~s!** allez les gars!*; **he's a bit of a ~** il est un peu noceur*; *V* **stable**[2].
ladder [ˈlædəʳ] **1** *n* **(a)** (*lit, fig*) échelle *f*. (*fig*) **to be at the top of the ~** être arrivé au sommet de l'échelle; *V* **rope, step.**
(b) (*esp Brit: in stocking*) échelle *f*, maille filée. **to have a ~ in one's stocking** avoir une échelle à son bas, avoir un bas filé.
2 *cpd*: (*esp Brit*) **ladderproof** indémaillable.
3 *vt* (*esp Brit*) *stocking* filer, faire une échelle à.
4 *vi* (*esp Brit*) *[stocking]* filer.
laddie* [ˈlædɪ] *n* (*esp Scot and dial*) garçon *m*, (petit) gars* *m*. **look here, ~!** dis donc, mon petit!*, dis donc, fiston!:
lade [leɪd] *pret* **laded,** *ptp* **laden** *vt* charger.
laden [ˈleɪdn] **1** *ptp of* **lade. 2** *adj* chargé (*with* de). **fully ~ truck/ship** camion *m*/navire *m* en pleine charge.
la-di-da* [ˈlɑːdɪˈdɑː] *adj person* bêcheur*; *voice* maniéré, apprêté. **she's very ~** elle fait la prétentieuse; **in a ~ way** de façon maniérée.
lading [ˈleɪdɪŋ] *n* cargaison *f*, chargement *m*.
ladle [ˈleɪdl] **1** *n* louche *f*. **2** *vt soup* servir (à la louche).
ladle out *vt sep soup* servir (à la louche); (**fig*) *money* répandre à gogo*; *advice* prodiguer à foison *or* en masse*.
lady [ˈleɪdɪ] **1** *n* dame *f*. **the ~ of the house** la maîtresse de maison; **Ladies and Gentlemen!** Mesdames, (Mesdemoiselles,) Messieurs!, Messieurs dames!: (*also hum*); **good morning, ladies and gentlemen** bonjour mesdames, bonjour mesdemoiselles, bonjour messieurs; **she's a real ~** c'est une vraie dame; **she's no ~** elle est très commune *or* fort peu distinguée; **your good ~*** votre dame: (*also hum*); **the headmaster and his ~†** le directeur et sa dame†; **young ~** (*married*) jeune femme *f*; (*unmarried*) jeune fille *f*; **look here, young ~!** dites donc, jeune fille!*; **this is the ~/the young ~ who served me** voilà la dame/la demoiselle qui m'a servi; **his young ~*†** (*girlfriend*) sa bonne amie†, sa petite amie; (*fiancée*) sa fiancée; **ladies' hairdresser** coiffeur *m*, -euse *f* pour dames; **~'s umbrella** parapluie *m* de dame *or* de femme; **he's a ladies' man** il plaît aux femmes; (*fig*) **a L~ Bountiful** une généreuse bienfaitrice; (*Rel*) **Our L~** Notre-Dame *f*; **listen here, ~:** écoutez un peu, ma petite dame:; (*public lavatory*) **Ladies** Dames; **where is the Ladies?*** où sont les toilettes?; (*Brit: in titles*) **L~ Davenport** lady Davenport; **Sir John and L~ Smith** sir John Smith et lady Smith; *V* **first, leading.**
2 *cpd*: **ladybird,** (*US*) **ladybug** coccinelle *f*, bête *f* à bon Dieu; (*Rel*) **Lady Chapel** chapelle *f* de la (Sainte) Vierge ; (*Brit*) **Lady Day** la fête de l'Annonciation; **lady doctor** femme *f* médecin, doctoresse *f*; **lady friend*** petite amie; **lady-in-waiting** dame *f* d'honneur; (*fig*) **ladykiller** don Juan *m*, tombeur* *m*, bourreau *m* des cœurs (*hum*); **ladylike** *person* bien élevée, distinguée; *manners* distingué; **it's not ladylike to yawn** une jeune fille bien élevée ne bâille pas, ce n'est pas poli *or* bien élevé de bâiller; († *or hum*) **his lady-love** sa bien-aimée†, la dame de ses pensées (*hum*); (*Brit*) **Lady Mayoress** femme *f* (*or* fille *f etc*) du Lord Mayor; **lady's maid** femme *f* de chambre (*attachée au service particulier d'une dame*).
ladyship [ˈleɪdɪʃɪp] *n*: **Her/Your L~** Madame *f* (la comtesse *or* la baronne *etc*).
lag[1] [læg] **1** *n* (*delay*) retard *m*; (*between two events*) décalage *m*; *V* **jet**[1], **time.**
2 *vi* rester en arrière, traîner. **he was ~ging behind the others** il traînait derrière les autres, il était à la traîne; (*fig*) **their country ~s behind ours in car exports** leur pays a du retard *or* est en retard sur le nôtre dans l'exportation automobile.
lag behind *vi* rester en arrière, traîner. (*fig*) **we lag behind in space exploration** nous sommes en retard *or* à la traîne* dans l'exploration spatiale.
lag[2] [læg] *vt pipes* calorifuger.
lag[3] [læg] *n* (*esp Brit*) **old ~*** récidiviste *mf*, (vieux) cheval *m* de retour.
lager [ˈlɑːgəʳ] *n* bière blonde.
laggard [ˈlægəd] *n* traînard(e) *m(f)*.
lagging [ˈlægɪŋ] *n* (*U*) (*material*) calorifuge *m*; (*act*) calorifugeage *m*.
lagoon [ləˈguːn] *n* (*gen*) lagune *f*; (*coral*) lagon *m*.
lah [lɑː] *n* (*Mus*) la *m*.
laicize [ˈleɪɪsaɪz] *vt* laïciser.
laid [leɪd] *pret, ptp of* **lay**[1]; *V* **new.**
lain [leɪn] *ptp of* **lie**[1].
lair [leəʳ] *n* (*lit, fig*) tanière *f*, repaire *m*.
laird [lɛəd] *n* (*Scot*) laird *m*, propriétaire foncier.
laity [ˈleɪɪtɪ] *collective n* **the ~** les laïcs *mpl*.
lake[1] [leɪk] **1** *n* lac *m*.
2 *cpd*: (*Brit Geog*) **the Lake District** la région des lacs; (*Hist*) **lake dwellers** habitants *mpl* d'un village *or* d'une cité lacustre; (*Hist*) **lake dwelling** habitation *f* lacustre; (*Literat*) **the Lake poets** les lakistes *mpl*; (*Brit Geog*) **the Lakes = the Lake District.**
lake[2] [leɪk] *n* (*Art*) laque *f*.
Lallans [ˈlælənz] **1** *n* Lallans *m* (*forme f littéraire du dialecte parlé dans les Basses Terres d'Écosse*). **2** *adj* en Lallans.
lam: [læm] **1** *vt* tabasser:. **2** *vi*: **to ~ into sb** (*thrash*) rentrer dans qn*; (*scold*) engueuler qn:.
lama [ˈlɑːmə] *n* lama *m* (*Rel*).
lamb [læm] **1** *n* (*Culin, Zool*) agneau *m*. (*Rel*) **L~ of God** Agneau de Dieu; **my little ~!*** mon trésor!, mon agneau!, mon ange!; **poor ~!*** le (*or* la) pauvre!; (*fig*) **he took it like a ~** il l'a pris sans broncher, il s'est laissé faire, il n'a pas protesté; **like a ~ to the slaughter** comme un agneau qu'on mène à l'abattoir.
2 *vi* agneler, mettre bas.
3 *cpd*: **lamb chop, lamb cutlet** côtelette *f* d'agneau; **lambskin** (*n*) (*skin itself*) peau *f* d'agneau; (*material*) agneau *m* (*U*); (*adj*) en agneau, d'agneau; **lamb's wool** *or* **lambswool sweater** tricot *m* en laine d'agneau.
lambast* [læmˈbæst] *vt*, **lambaste*** [læmˈbeɪst] *vt* (*beat*) rosser*; (*scold*) sonner les cloches à:; (*criticize severely*) éreinter, démolir.
lambing [ˈlæmɪŋ] *n* agnelage *m*. **~ time** (période *f* d')agnelage.
lambkin [ˈlæmkɪn] *n* jeune agneau *m*, agnelet *m*.
lame [leɪm] **1** *adj* **(a)** *animal, person* boiteux, estropié, éclopé. **to be ~** boiter; **to be slightly ~** boitiller; *[horse]* **to go ~** se mettre à boiter; **this horse is ~ in one leg** ce cheval boite d'une jambe; **~ duck** (*fig*) canard boiteux (*fig*); (*US Pol*) *officiel non réélu qui siège à titre provisoire jusqu'à l'instauration de son successeur.*
(b) (*fig*) *excuse* faible, piètre; *argument* faible, boiteux; (*Poetry*) *metre* boiteux, faux (*f* fausse).
2 *vt person, animal* estropier.
lamely [ˈleɪmlɪ] *adv say, argue* maladroitement, sans conviction.
lameness [ˈleɪmnɪs] *n* (*lit*) claudication *f* (*frm*), boiterie *f*; (*fig*) faiblesse *f*, pauvreté *f*, maladresse *f*.
lament [ləˈment] **1** *n* **(a)** lamentation *f*.
(b) (*poem*) élégie *f*; (*song*) complainte *f*; (*at funerals*) chant *m* funèbre; (*for bagpipes etc*) plainte *f*.
2 *vt* pleurer, regretter, se lamenter sur. **our (late) ~ed sister** notre regrettée sœur (*frm*), notre pauvre sœur, la sœur que nous avons perdue.
3 *vi* se lamenter (*for, over* sur), s'affliger (*for, over* de).
lamentable [ˈlæməntəbl] *adj state, condition, situation* déplorable, lamentable; *incident* fâcheux, regrettable; *results, performance* lamentable, déplorable.
lamentably [ˈlæməntəblɪ] *adv* lamentablement.
lamentation [ˌlæmənˈteɪʃən] *n* lamentation *f*.
laminate [ˈlæmɪneɪt] **1** *vt* laminer. **2** *n* laminé *m*.
laminated [ˈlæmɪneɪtɪd] *adj metal* laminé; *windscreen* en verre feuilleté. **~ glass** verre *m* feuilleté; **~ wood** contre-plaqué *m*.
lamp [læmp] **1** *n* **(a)** (*light*) lampe *f*; (*Aut*) feu *m*; *V* **blow**[1], **safety, street** *etc.*
(b) (*bulb*) ampoule *f*. **100-watt ~** ampoule de 100 watts.
2 *cpd*: **lampblack** noir *m* de fumée *or* de carbone; **lamp bracket** applique *f*; **by lamplight** à la lumière de la lampe; **lamplighter** allumeur *m* de réverbères; **lamppost** réverbère *m*; (*fig*) **between you, me and the lamppost*** tout à fait entre nous, entre quat'z'yeux:; **lampshade** abat-jour *m inv*; **lampstand** pied *m* de lampe; **lamp standard** lampadaire *m* (*dans la rue*).
lampoon [læmˈpuːn] **1** *n* (*gen*) virulente satire; (*written*) pamphlet *m*, libelle *m*; (*spoken*) diatribe *f*. **2** *vt person, action, quality* railler, tourner en dérision, faire la satire de; (*in song*) chansonner.
lampoonist [læmˈpuːnɪst] *n* (*gen*) satiriste *m*; (*writer*) pamphlétaire *m*; (*singer*) chansonnier *m*.
lamprey [ˈlæmprɪ] *n* lamproie *f*.
lance [lɑːns] **1** *n* (*weapon*) lance *f*; (*soldier*) lancier *m*; (*Med*) lancette *f*. **2** *vt abscess* percer, ouvrir; *finger* ouvrir. **3** *cpd*: **lance corporal** (*Brit Mil*) *[infantry]* caporal *m*; *[cavalry]* brigadier *m*; (*US Marines*) fusilier marin.
lancer [ˈlɑːnsəʳ] *n* (*soldier*) lancier *m*.
lancet [ˈlɑːnsɪt] **1** *n* (*Med*) lancette *f*. **2** *cpd*: (*Archit*) **lancet window** fenêtre *f* en ogive.
land [lænd] **1** *n* **(a)** (*U: opp of* **sea**) terre *f*. **dry ~** terre ferme; **on ~** à terre; **to go by ~** voyager par (voie de) terre; **over ~ and sea** sur terre et sur mer; (*Naut*) **to make ~** accoster; **we saw ~ for the first time in 3 months** pour la première fois en 3 mois nous sommes arrivés en vue d'une terre; (*fig*) **to see how the ~**

lies, to find out the lie of the ~ tâter le terrain, voir de quoi il retourne.

(b) (*U: Agr*) terre *f*. **fertile** ~ terre fertile; **to live off the** ~ vivre de la terre; **to work on the** ~ travailler la terre; **many people left the** ~ beaucoup de gens ont quitté *or* déserté la campagne; **he bought** ~ **in Devon** il a acheté une terre dans le Devon.

(c) (*property*) (*gen large*) terre(s) *f(pl)*; (*not so large*) terrain *m*. **get off my** ~! sortez de mes terres! *or* de mon terrain!; **the** ~ **on which this house is built** le terrain sur lequel cette maison est construite.

(d) (*country, nation*) pays *m*. **people of many** ~**s** des gens de nationalités diverses; **throughout the** ~ dans tout le pays; ~ **of milk and honey** pays de cocagne; (*fig*) **the L**~ **of Nod** le pays des rêves; **to be in the** ~ **of the living** être encore de ce monde; *V* **law, native, promised** *etc*.

2 *cpd breeze* de terre; *defences* terrestre; *law, policy, reform* agraire; *tax* foncier. **land agent** (*steward*) régisseur *m* d'un domaine; (*estate agent*) expert foncier; (*Brit*) **land army** corps *m* de travailleuses agricoles; **to make landfall** accoster; **land forces** armée *f* de terre, forces *fpl* terrestres; (*Brit*) **land girl** membre *m* du corps des travailleuses agricoles; **landlady** *[flat etc]* propriétaire *f*, logeuse *f*; *[boarding house etc]* patronne *f*; **landlocked** (*totally enclosed*) enfermé dans les terres, sans accès à la mer; (*almost totally enclosed*) entouré par les terres; **landlord** *[flat etc]* propriétaire *m*, logeur *m*; *[pub, boarding house]* patron *m*; **landlubber*** terrien(ne) *m(f)*; **he's a real landlubber*** pour lui, il n'y a que le plancher des vaches* (qui compte); **landmark** point *m* de repère; (*fig*) **to be a landmark in** faire date *or* faire époque dans; (*Mil*) **landmine** mine *f* terrestre; **landowner** propriétaire foncier *or* terrien; (*Geog*) **Land's End** cap *m* Land's End; **landslide** (*lit: also* **landslip**) *[mass of earth etc]* glissement *m* de terrain; *[loose rocks etc]* éboulement *m*; (*fig Pol*) raz-de-marée électoral; (*Pol etc*) **landslide victory** victoire écrasante; **land worker** ouvrier *m*, -ière *f* agricole.

3 *vt* **(a)** *cargo* décharger, débarquer; *passengers* débarquer; *aircraft* poser; *fish* (*on deck*) amener à bord, hisser sur le pont; (*on shore, bank*) amener sur le rivage. **to** ~ **a blow** infliger un coup.

(b) (*: *obtain*) *job, contract, prize* décrocher*.

(c) (*Brit* fig*) **that will** ~ **you in trouble** ça va vous attirer des ennuis *or* vous mettre dans le pétrin; **to** ~ **sb in a mess/in debt** mettre qn dans de beaux draps/dans les dettes; **that's what** ~**ed him in jail** c'est comme ça qu'il s'est retrouvé en prison.

(d) (*Brit**) **to be** ~**ed with sth** (*left with*) avoir qch *or* rester avec qch sur les bras; (*forced to take on*) récolter qch*, devoir se coltiner qch*; **now we're** ~**ed with all this extra work** maintenant il faut qu'on s'envoie (*subj*) tout ce boulot* en plus; **I've got** ~**ed with this job** on m'a collé* ce travail; **I got** ~**ed with him for 2 hours** je me le suis farci‡ pendant 2 heures.

4 *vi* **(a)** *[aircraft etc]* atterrir, se poser; (*on sea*) amerrir; (*on ship's deck*) apponter. **to** ~ **on the moon** *[rocket, spacecraft]* alunir, se poser sur la lune; *[person]* atterrir sur la lune; **we** ~**ed at Orly** nous sommes arrivés *or* nous avons atterri à Orly; **as the plane was coming in to** ~ comme l'avion s'apprêtait à atterrir.

(b) *[person, object]* (re)tomber, arriver, atterrir*. **the bomb** ~**ed square on target** la bombe est tombée en plein sur l'objectif; (*lit, fig*) **to** ~ **on one's feet** retomber sur ses pieds.

(c) (*from boat*) débarquer.

land up* *vi* atterrir*, échouer, (finir par) se retrouver. **to land up in Paris/in jail** atterrir* *or* finir par se retrouver à Paris/en prison; **the report landed up on my desk** le rapport a atterri* *or* a fini par arriver sur mon bureau; **he landed up with only £2** il s'est retrouvé avec 2 livres seulement; **we finally landed up in a small café** nous avons finalement échoué dans un petit café.

landau ['lændɔː] *n* landau *m* (*véhicule*).

landed ['lændɪd] *adj proprietor* foncier, terrien; *property* foncier. ~ **gentry** aristocratie terrienne.

landing[1] ['lændɪŋ] **1** *n* **(a)** *[aircraft, spacecraft etc]* atterrissage *m*; (*on sea*) amerrissage *m*; (*on moon*) alunissage *m*; (*on deck*) appontage *m*; *V* **crash, pancake, soft** *etc*.

(b) (*from ship*) débarquement *m*. (*Mil Hist*) **the Normandy** ~**s** le débarquement (du 6 juin 1944).

2 *cpd*: **landing card** carte *f* de débarquement; (*Mil*) **landing craft** chaland *m or* navire *m* de débarquement; (*Mil*) **landing force** troupes *fpl* de débarquement; (*Aviat*) **landing gear** train *m* d'atterrissage, atterrisseur *m*; **landing ground** terrain *m* d'atterrissage; **landing lights** (*on aircraft*) phares *mpl* d'atterrissage; (*on ground*) balises *fpl* (d'atterrissage); (*Fishing*) **landing net** épuisette *f*; (*Naut*) **landing party** détachement *m* de débarquement; **landing stage** débarcadère *m*, appontement *m*; **landing strip** piste *f* d'atterrissage; **landing wheels** roues *fpl* du train d'atterrissage.

landing[2] ['lændɪŋ] *n* (*between stairs*) palier *m*; (*floor*) étage *m*.

landscape ['lænskeɪp] **1** *n* (*land, view, picture*) paysage *m*.

2 *vt garden* dessiner; *bomb site, dirty place etc* aménager.

3 *cpd*: **landscape gardener** jardinier *m*, -ière *f* paysagiste; **landscape gardening** jardinage *m* paysagiste, paysagisme *m*; **landscape painter** paysagiste *m*.

landscaping ['læn,skeɪpɪŋ] *n* (*U*) aménagements paysagers.

landward ['lændwəd] **1** *adj* (situé *or* dirigé) du côté de la terre. ~ **breeze** brise *f* de mer; ~ **side** côté terre. **2** *adv* (*also* ~**s**) vers *or* en direction de la terre, vers l'intérieur.

lane [leɪn] **1** *n* **(a)** (*in country*) chemin *m*, petite route; (*in town*) ruelle *f*.

(b) (*Aut*) (*part of road*) voie *f*; (*line of traffic*) file *f*. **'keep in** ~**'** 'ne changez pas de file'; **'get into** ~**'** 'mettez-vous dans *or* sur la bonne file'; **to take the left-hand** ~ emprunter la voie de gauche, rouler sur la file de gauche; **3-**~ **road** route *f* à 3 voies; **I'm in the wrong** ~ je suis dans *or* sur la mauvaise file; **traffic was reduced to a single** ~ on ne circulait plus que sur une seule file; *V* **near** *etc*.

(c) (*Aviat*) couloir aérien; (*Sport: on track, in swimming pool*) couloir. (*Naut*) **shipping** ~ route *f* maritime.

2 *cpd*: (*Aut*) **lane markings** signalisation horizontale.

language ['læŋgwɪdʒ] **1** *n* **(a)** (*U*) (*means of communication; specialized terminology; way of expressing things*) langage *m*; (*abstract linguistic system*) langue *f*. **the origin of** ~ l'origine *f* du langage; **a child's use of** ~ le langage de l'enfant, la façon dont l'enfant se sert du langage; **the** ~ **of birds/mathematics/flowers** le langage des oiseaux/des mathématiques/des fleurs; (*Ling*) ~, **speaking and speech** la langue, la parole et le langage; (*Ling*) **speaking is one aspect of** ~ la parole est l'un des aspects du langage; **he is studying** ~ il fait de la linguistique; **scientific/legal** ~ langage scientifique/juridique; (*fig*) **they do not speak the same** ~ ils ne parlent pas le même langage; **try to express it in your own** ~ essayez d'exprimer cela en votre propre langage *or* en vous servant de vos propres mots; **the formal** ~ **of official documents** le langage conventionnel des documents officiels; **bad** *or* **strong** ~ gros mots, grossièretés *fpl*; **that's no** ~ **to use to your mother!** on ne parle pas comme ça à sa mère!; **(watch your)** ~! surveille ton langage!; *V* **sign**.

(b) (*national etc tongue*) langue *f*. **the French** ~ la langue française; **modern** ~**s** langues vivantes; **he studies** ~**s** il fait des (études de) langues; *V* **dead, source** *etc*.

2 *cpd studies* de *or* du langage, de langue(s). **language laboratory** laboratoire *m* de langues.

languid ['læŋgwɪd] *adj* languissant.

languidly ['læŋgwɪdlɪ] *adv* languissamment.

languidness ['læŋgwɪdnɪs] *n* langueur *f*.

languish ['læŋgwɪʃ] *vi* (se) languir (*for, over* après).

languishing ['læŋgwɪʃɪŋ] *adj* langoureux.

languishingly ['læŋgwɪʃɪŋlɪ] *adv* langoureusement.

languor ['læŋgə^r] *n* langueur *f*.

languorous ['læŋgərəs] *adj* alangui.

lank [læŋk] *adj hair* raide et terne; *grass, plant* long (*f* longue) et grêle.

lanky ['læŋkɪ] *adj* grand et maigre, dégingandé.

lanolin ['lænəʊlɪn] *n* lanoline *f*.

lantern ['læntən] **1** *n* (*all senses*) lanterne *f*; (*in paper*) lanterne vénitienne, lampion *m*; *V* **Chinese, magic**. **2** *cpd*: **lantern-jawed** aux joues creuses; **lantern slide** plaque *f* de lanterne magique.

lanyard ['lænjəd] *n* (*gen, Mil*) cordon *m*; (*Naut*) ride *f* (de hauban).

Laos [laʊs] *n* Laos *m*.

Laotian ['laʊʃɪən] **1** *adj* laotien. **2** *n* Laotien(ne) *m(f)*.

lap[1] [læp] **1** *n* genoux *mpl*, giron *m* (*gen hum*). **sitting on his mother's** ~ assis sur les genoux de sa mère; (*fig*) **it fell right into his** ~* ça lui est tombé tout cuit dans le bec*; (*fig*) **they dropped the problem in his** ~ ils lui ont laissé *or* collé* le problème (à résoudre); (*fig*) **it's in the** ~ **of the gods** c'est entre les mains des dieux; (*fig*) **in the** ~ **of luxury** dans le plus grand luxe, dans un luxe inouï.

2 *cpd*: (*Aut*) **lap and shoulder belt** ceinture *f* trois points; **lapdog** petit chien d'appartement, chien de manchon†.

lap[2] [læp] **1** *n* (*Sport*) tour *m* de piste. **to run a** ~ faire un tour de piste; **10-**~ **race** course *f* en *or* sur 10 tours; **on the 10th** ~ au 10e tour; ~ **of honour** tour d'honneur; (*fig*) **we're on the last** ~ on a fait le plus gros *or* le plus difficile, on tient le bon bout*.

2 *vt* (*Sport*) *runner, car* prendre un tour d'avance sur.

3 *vi* (*Racing*) **the car was** ~**ping at 200 km/h** la voiture faisait le circuit à 200 km/h de moyenne.

lap[3] [læp] **1** *vt milk* laper. **2** *vi [waves]* clapoter (*against* contre).

lap up *vt sep milk etc* laper; (**fig*) *compliments* accueillir *or* accepter béatement, boire comme du petit-lait*. (*fig*) **he laps up everything you say** il gobe* tout ce qu'on lui dit; (*fig*) **he fairly lapped it up** il buvait du petit-lait*.

lap[4] [læp] *vt* (*wrap*) enrouler (*round* autour de); envelopper (*in* de).

lap over *vi [tiles etc]* se chevaucher.

laparotomy [,læpə'rɒtəmɪ] *n* laparotomie *f*.

lapel [lə'pel] *n* revers *m* (*de veston etc*).

lapin ['læpɪn] *n* (*US*) (fourrure *f or* peau *f* de) lapin *m*.

lapis lazuli ['læpɪs'læzjʊlaɪ] *n* (*stone*) lapis(-lazuli) *m*; (*colour*) bleu *m* lapis(-lazuli).

Lapland ['læplænd] *n* Laponie *f*.

Laplander ['læplændə^r] *n* = **Lapp 2a**.

Lapp [læp] **1** *adj* lapon. **2** *n* **(a)** Lapon(ne) *m(f)*. **(b)** (*Ling*) lapon *m*.

lapping ['læpɪŋ] *n [waves]* clapotis *m*.

lapse [læps] **1** *n* **(a)** (*fault*) faute légère, défaillance *f*; (*in behaviour*) écart *m* (de conduite). ~ **of memory** trou *m* de mémoire; ~ **from truth/a diet** entorse *f* à la vérité/à un régime; **a** ~ **into bad habits** un retour à de mauvaises habitudes; **she behaved very well, with only a few** ~**s** elle s'est très bien conduite, à part quelques défaillances.

(b) (*passage of time*) intervalle *m*. **a** ~ **of time** un laps de temps; **after a** ~ **of 10 weeks** au bout de 10 semaines, après un intervalle de 10 semaines.

(c) (*falling into disuse*) *[custom etc]* disparition *f*, oubli *m*; *[right, privilege]* déchéance *f*.

2 *vi* **(a)** (*err*) faire un *or* des écart(s) (de conduite); faire une *or* des erreur(s) passagère(s).

(b) (*fall gradually*) tomber (*into* dans). **to** ~ **from grace** (*Rel*) perdre l'état de grâce; (*fig*) déchoir, démériter; **to** ~ **into bad habits** prendre de mauvaises habitudes *or* un mauvais pli; **to** ~ **into silence** se taire, s'enfermer dans le mutisme; **to** ~ **into**

unconsciousness (re)perdre connaissance; **he ~d into the vernacular** il retomba dans le patois.

(c) *[act, law]* être caduc (*f* -uque), tomber en désuétude; *[contract]* expirer, venir à expiration; *[ticket, passport]* se périmer; *[insurance policy]* se périmer, ne plus être valable; *[subscription]* prendre fin. **his membership ~d last month** son abonnement est venu à expiration *or* a pris fin le mois dernier, il n'est plus membre depuis le mois dernier.

lapsed [læpst] *adj contract, law* caduc (*f* -uque); *ticket, passport* périmé. **a ~ Catholic** un(e) catholique qui n'est plus pratiquant(e).

lapwing ['læpwɪŋ] *n* vanneau *m.*

larboard ['lɑːbəd] (*Naut*††) **1** *n* bâbord *m.* **2** *adj* de bâbord.

larceny ['lɑːsənɪ] *n* (*Jur*) vol *m* simple; *V* **grand, petty.**

larch [lɑːtʃ] *n* mélèze *m.*

lard [lɑːd] **1** *n* saindoux *m.* **2** *vt* (*Culin*) larder (*with* de). (*fig*) **to ~ one's speech with quotations** truffer son discours de citations.

larder ['lɑːdə^r] *n* (*cupboard*) garde-manger *m inv*; (*small room*) cellier *m.*

large [lɑːdʒ] **1** *adj* **(a)** (*in size*) *town, house, parcel* grand; *garden, room* grand, vaste; *person, animal, slice, hand* gros (*f* grosse); *sum, loss* fort, gros; *amount* grand, important; *family* nombreux; *population* nombreux, élevé; *meal* copieux. (*Anat*) **~ intestine** gros intestin; **a ~ number of them refused** beaucoup d'entre eux ont refusé, un grand nombre parmi eux a *or* ont refusé; **a ~ slice of his savings** une bonne partie de ses économies; **a ~ proportion of the business** une part importante des affaires; (*Comm: of packet, tube*) **the ~ size** le grand modèle; (*Comm*) **a ~ size/the largest size of this dress** une grande taille/la plus grande taille dans ce modèle; (*fig*) **there he was (as) ~ as life** c'était lui se conduisant comme si de rien n'était; **to grow** *or* **get ~(r)** grossir, grandir, s'agrandir; **to make ~r** agrandir.

(b) (*extensive*) **to do sth on a ~ scale** faire qch en grand *or* sur une grande échelle (*V also* **4**); **to a ~ extent** en grande mesure; **in (a) ~ measure** en grande mesure *or* partie, dans une large mesure; (*fig*) **to have ~ views** avoir des vues larges.

2 *n*: **at ~** (*at liberty*) en liberté; (*as a whole*) en général; (*at length*) tout au long; (*at random*) au hasard, sans (trop) préciser; **the prisoner is still at ~** le prisonnier est toujours en liberté *or* n'a pas encore été repris; **the country at ~** le pays dans son ensemble; **he treated the subject at ~** il a traité le sujet dans son ensemble; **to scatter accusations at ~** lancer des accusations au hasard; *V* **ambassador.**

3 *adv*: **by and ~** *V* **by 1d.**

4 *cpd*: (*fig*) **large-handed** généreux; (*fig*) **large-hearted** au grand cœur; (*fig*) **large-minded** qui a l'esprit large; **large-scale** *drawing, map* à grande échelle; *business activities, reforms, relations* (fait) sur une grande échelle; *powers* étendu; **large-size(d)** grand.

largely ['lɑːdʒlɪ] *adv* (*to a great extent*) en grande mesure *or* partie, dans une large mesure; (*principally*) pour la plupart, surtout; (*in general*) en général.

largeness ['lɑːdʒnɪs] *n* (*V* **large**) grande taille; grandeur *f*; grosseur *f*; importance *f.*

largesse [lɑː'ʒes] *n* (*U*) (*generosity*) largesse *f*; (*gifts*) largesses.

largish ['lɑːdʒɪʃ] *adj* (*V* **large**) assez grand; assez gros (*f* grosse); de bonne taille; assez important; assez nombreux; assez copieux.

largo ['lɑːgəʊ] *adv, n* largo (*m inv*).

lariat ['lærɪət] *n* (*lasso*) lasso *m*; (*tether*) longe *f.*

lark[1] [lɑːk] **1** *n* (*Orn*) alouette *f.* **to rise with the ~** se lever au chant du coq; *V* **happy, sing. 2** *cpd*: (*Bot*) **larkspur** pied *m* d'alouette, delphinium *m.*

lark[2]* [lɑːk] *n* blague* *f*, niche* *f.* **we only did it for a ~** on l'a seulement fait pour rigoler*, on l'a seulement fait histoire de rigoler*; **what a ~!** quelle rigolade!*, la bonne blague!*; **what do you think of this dinner jacket ~?** qu'est-ce que tu penses de cette histoire de smoking?

lark about*, lark around* *vi* faire le petit fou (*f* la petite folle)*. **to lark about with sth** jouer avec qch.

larva ['lɑːvə] *n, pl* **larvae** ['lɑːviː] larve *f* (*Zool*).

larval ['lɑːvəl] *adj* larvaire (*Zool*).

laryngitis [ˌlærɪn'dʒaɪtɪs] *n* laryngite *f.*

larynx ['lærɪŋks] *n* larynx *m.*

lascivious [lə'sɪvɪəs] *adj* lascif, luxurieux.

lasciviously [lə'sɪvɪəslɪ] *adv* lascivement.

lasciviousness [lə'sɪvɪəsnɪs] *n* luxure *f*, lasciveté *f or* lascivité *f.*

laser ['leɪzə^r] *n* laser *m.* **~ beam** rayon *m* laser *inv.*

lash [læʃ] **1** *n* **(a)** (*thong*) mèche *f*, lanière *f*; (*blow from whip*) coup *m* de fouet. **sentenced to 10 ~es** condamné à 10 coups de fouet; *V* **whip.**

(b) (*also* **eye~**) cil *m.*

2 *vt* **(a)** (*beat*) frapper (d'un grand coup de fouet), fouetter violemment; (*flog*) flageller. (*fig*) **to ~ sb with one's tongue** faire des remarques cinglantes à qn; (*fig*) **to ~ o.s. into a fury** s'emporter violemment; (*fig*) **the wind ~ed the sea into a fury** le vent a déchaîné *or* démonté la mer; **the sea ~es (against) the cliffs** la mer bat *or* fouette les falaises; **the hailstones ~ed (against) my face** la grêle me cinglait le visage; **the rain was ~ing (at** *or* **against) the windows** la pluie fouettait *or* cinglait les carreaux; **the crocodile ~ed its tail** le crocodile a donné de grands coups de queue; **the lion ~ed its tail** le lion a fouetté l'air de sa queue.

(b) (*fasten*) attacher *or* fixer fermement; *cargo* arrimer; *load* attacher, amarrer. **to ~ sth to a post** attacher solidement qch à un piquet.

3 *vi*: **to ~ against** *or* **at** *V* **2a.**

lash about *vi* (*in bonds, in pain etc*) se débattre violemment.

lash down 1 *vi [rain]* tomber avec violence.

2 *vt sep cargo* amarrer, arrimer.

lash out 1 *vi* **(a) to lash out at sb** (*with fists*) envoyer un *or* de violent(s) coup(s) de poing à qn; (*with feet*) envoyer un *or* de violent(s) coup(s) de pied à qn; (*with both*) jouer violemment des pieds et des poings contre qn; (*fig: verbally*) se répandre en invectives contre qn, fustiger qn (*liter*).

(b) (*: *spend a lot of money*) les lâcher*, les allonger*. **he lashed out and bought a car** il a lâché le paquet* et s'est payé une voiture; **now we can really lash out** maintenant on peut les faire valser*.

2 *vt sep* (*) *money* lâcher*, allonger*.

lash up *vt sep* attacher, amarrer, arrimer.

lashing ['læʃɪŋ] *n* **(a)** (*flogging*) flagellation *f.* **to give sb a ~** (*lit*) donner le fouet à qn; (*fig: verbally*) faire de vertes réprimandes à qn, tancer vertement qn.

(b) (*rope*) corde *f*; (*Naut*) amarre *f.*

(c) (*: *esp Brit: a lot*) **~s of** des tas de*, des masses de*; **with ~s of cream** avec des masses* *or* une montagne de crème.

lass [læs] *n* (*esp Scot and dial: girl*) jeune fille *f*; (††: *sweetheart*) bonne amie†.

lassie ['læsɪ] *n* (*esp Scot and dial*) gamine* *f*, gosse* *f.*

lassitude ['læsɪtjuːd] *n* lassitude *f.*

lasso [læ'suː] **1** *n* lasso *m.* **2** *vt* prendre au lasso.

last[1] [lɑːst] **1** *adj* **(a)** (*in series*) dernier. **the ~ Saturday of the month** le dernier samedi du mois; **the ~ 10 pages** les 10 dernières pages; **~ but one, second ~** avant-dernier, pénultième; **the ~ time but one** l'avant-dernière fois; **it's the ~ round but 3** il y a encore *or* il n'y a plus que 3 rounds après celui-ci; **his office is the second ~** son bureau est l'avant-dernier; **the third and ~ point is that ...** le troisième et dernier point est que ...; **and ~ but not least** et en dernier mais non par ordre d'importance.

(b) (*past, most recent*) dernier. **~ night** (*evening*) hier soir; (*night*) cette nuit, la nuit dernière; **~ week/year** la semaine/l'année dernière *or* passée; **~ month/summer** le mois/l'été dernier *or* passé; **~ Monday, on Monday ~** lundi dernier; **for the ~ few days** ces derniers jours, ces jours-ci, dernièrement; **for the ~ few weeks** ces dernières semaines, dernièrement; **he hasn't been seen these ~ 2 years** on ne l'a pas vu ces 2 dernières années; **for the ~ 2 years** depuis 2 ans; **the day before ~** avant-hier *m*; **the night/morning before ~** avant-hier soir/matin; **the week before ~** l'avant-dernière semaine; **what did you do ~ time?** qu'avez-vous fait la dernière fois?; **he was rather ill (the) ~ time I saw him** il était plutôt malade la dernière fois que je l'ai vu; **this time ~ year** (*last year about this time*) l'an dernier à pareille époque *or* à cette époque-ci; (*a year ago today*) il y a un an aujourd'hui.

(c) (*final*) *chance, hope* dernier. (*lit, fig*) **to fight to the ~ ditch** se battre dans ses derniers retranchements (*V also* **4**); **at one's ~ gasp** (*dying*) sur le point de mourir, à l'agonie; (*: *exhausted*) à bout; **he was on his ~ legs*** il était à bout; **the company is on its ~ legs*** la compagnie est au bord de la faillite; **the washing machine is on its ~ legs*** la machine à laver va bientôt nous lâcher* *or* rendre l'âme*; **at the ~ minute** à la dernière minute (*V also* **4**); (*Mil*) **~ post** retraite *f*; (*at funerals*) sonnerie *f* aux morts; **in the ~ resort** *or* **resource** en dernier ressort, en désespoir de cause; (*Rel*) **~ rites** les derniers sacrements; (*fig*) **that's the ~ straw!** c'est la goutte qui fait déborder le vase!; (*that's too much*) c'est le comble!; (*Rel*) **L~ Supper** Cène *f*; **~ thing at night** juste avant de se coucher; **for the ~ time, shut up!** pour la dernière fois, tais-toi!; **that was the ~ time I saw him** c'est la dernière fois que je l'ai vu; **that's the ~ time I lend you anything!** c'est la dernière fois que je te prête quelque chose; (*Rel*) **~ trump** *or* **trumpet** trompettes *fpl* du Jugement dernier; (*Rel*) **at the L~ Judgment** au Jugement dernier; **she always wants to have the ~ word** elle veut toujours avoir le dernier mot; **it's the ~ word in comfort** c'est ce qu'on fait de mieux *or* c'est le dernier cri en matière de confort; **I'm down to my ~ pound note** je n'ai plus *or* il ne me reste plus qu'une seule livre; *V* **first, laugh, stand.**

(d) (*least likely or desirable*) dernier. **he's the ~ person to ask** c'est la dernière personne à qui demander; **that's the ~ thing to worry about** c'est le dernier *or* le moindre *or* le cadet de mes (*or* tes *etc*) soucis.

2 *adv* **(a)** (*at the end*) en dernier. **she arrived ~** elle est arrivée en dernier *or* la dernière; **he arrived ~ of all** il est arrivé le tout dernier; **his horse came in ~** son cheval est arrivé (bon) dernier.

(b) (*most recently*) la dernière fois. **when I ~ saw him** quand je l'ai vu la dernière fois, la dernière fois que je l'ai vu; (*Cards*) **who dealt ~?** qui a donné en dernier?

(c) (*finally*) finalement, pour terminer. **~, I would like to say...** pour terminer *or* enfin je voudrais dire ... .

3 *n* **(a)** dernier *m*, -ière *f.* **he was the ~ of the Tudors** ce fut lui le dernier des Tudors; **this is the ~ of the pears** (*one*) voici la dernière poire; (*several*) voici les dernières poires, voici le reste des poires; **this is the ~ of the cider** voici le reste du cidre, voici tout ce qui reste de *or* comme cidre; **the ~ but one** l'avant-dernier *m*, -ière *f*, pénultième *mf*; **I'd be the ~ to criticize, but ...** bien que je sois le dernier à faire des critiques ..., j'ai horreur de critiquer, mais...; **each one better than the ~** tous meilleurs les uns que les autres.

(b) (*phrases*) **at ~** enfin, à la fin; **at (long) ~** enfin; **at long ~ he came** il a enfin fini par arriver; **here he is! — at ~!** le voici! — enfin! *or* ce n'est pas trop tôt!; **to the ~** jusqu'au bout, jusqu'à la fin; **that was the ~ I saw of him** c'est la dernière fois que je l'ai vu, je ne l'ai pas revu depuis; **we shall never hear the ~ of this** on n'a pas fini d'en entendre parler; **you haven't heard the ~ of this!** vous aurez de mes nouvelles! (*fig*); **I shall be glad to see the ~ of this** je serai content de voir tout ceci terminé *or* de voir la fin de tout ceci; **we were glad to see the ~ of him** nous avons été contents de le voir partir; *V* **breathe.**

4 *cpd*: **last-ditch*** (*adj*) désespéré, ultime; **last-minute** (*adj*) de dernière minute.

last[2] [lɑːst] **1** *vi* **(a)** (*continue*) *[pain, film, toffees etc]* durer. **it's too good to ~** c'est trop beau pour durer *or* pour que ça dure (*subj*); **will this good weather ~ till Saturday?** est-ce que le beau temps va durer *or* tenir jusqu'à samedi?; **it ~ed 2 hours** cela a duré 2 heures.

(b) (*hold out*) tenir. **no one ~s long in this job** personne ne reste longtemps dans ce poste; **after he got pneumonia he didn't ~ long** après sa pneumonie il n'a pas fait long feu* *or* il n'a pas traîné*; **that whisky didn't ~ long** ce whisky n'a pas fait long feu *or* n'a pas duré longtemps.

(c) (*esp Comm: remain usable*) durer. **this table will ~ a lifetime** cette table vous fera toute une vie; **will this material ~?** ce tissu fera-t-il de l'usage?; **made to ~** fait pour durer.

2 *vt* durer. **this amount should ~ you (for) a week** cela devrait vous durer *or* vous faire huit jours; **the car ~ed me 8 years** la voiture m'a fait *or* duré 8 ans; **I have enough money to ~ me a lifetime** l'argent que j'ai me fera bien *or* me conduira bien jusqu'à la fin de mes jours; **she must have got enough chocolates to ~ her a lifetime** elle a dû recevoir des chocolats pour jusqu'à la fin de ses jours.

last out 1 *vi [person]* tenir (le coup); *[money]* suffire.

2 *vt sep* faire. **he won't last the winter out** il ne passera pas *or* ne fera pas l'hiver, il ne verra pas la fin de l'hiver; **my money doesn't last out the month** mon argent ne me fait pas le mois.

last[3] [lɑːst] *n [cobbler]* forme *f*.

lasting [ˈlɑːstɪŋ] *adj benefit, friendship, good, peace* durable. **to his ~ shame** à sa plus grande honte.

lastly [ˈlɑːstlɪ] *adv* (enfin) pour terminer, en dernier lieu.

latch [lætʃ] **1** *n* loquet *m*. **the door is on the ~** la porte n'est pas fermée à clef; **~key** clef *f* (de la porte d'entrée); **~key child** enfant *mf* dont la mère travaille.

2 *vt* fermer au loquet.

latch on* *vi* **(a)** (*grab*) s'accrocher (*to* à).

(b) (*understand*) saisir, piger‡.

latch on to* *vt fus* **(a)** (*get possession of*) prendre possession de; (*catch hold of*) saisir; (*US: obtain*) se procurer. **he latched on to me as soon as I arrived** il s'est accroché *or* collé* à moi dès que je suis arrivé; **he latches on to the slightest mistake** il ne laisse pas passer la moindre erreur.

(b) (*understand*) saisir, piger‡; (*realize*) se rendre compte de, réaliser*.

late [leɪt] **1** *adj* **(a)** (*not on time*) en retard. *[person, vehicle]* **to be ~** être en retard, avoir du retard; **he's ~r than ever** il a encore plus de retard *or* il est encore plus en retard que d'habitude; **spring was ~** le printemps était en retard *or* était tardif; **your essay is ~** vous rendez votre dissertation en retard; **his ~ arrival** le fait qu'il est arrivé en retard; **we apologize for the ~ arrival of flight XY 709** nous vous prions d'excuser le retard du vol XY 709; **~ arrivals must sit at the back** les gens (qui arrivent) en retard doivent s'asseoir au fond; **to make sb ~** retarder qn, mettre qn en retard; **to be 2 hours ~** avoir 2 heures de retard; **~ for school/work** en retard à l'école/au travail; **to be ~ in arriving** arriver avec du retard *or* en retard; **to be ~ with payments** avoir des paiements en retard *or* des arriérés.

(b) (*far on in day, season etc*) *delivery, edition, performance* dernier. **to have a ~ meal** manger tard; **~ hours** heures avancées *or* tardives; **to keep ~ hours** se coucher tard, être couche-tard *inv*; **at this ~ hour** à cette heure tardive; **at this ~ stage** à ce stade avancé; **at a ~r stage in the discussions** à une étape plus avancée des discussions; **Easter is ~ this year** Pâques est tard cette année; **in ~ October** vers la fin (du mois) d'octobre, fin octobre; **in the ~ afternoon** en fin d'après-midi, vers la fin de l'après-midi; **he is in his ~ sixties** il est plus près de soixante-dix ans que de soixante, il approche des soixante-dix ans; **in the ~ 1920s** vers la fin des années 1920; **in ~r life** plus tard dans la vie; **in his ~r years** vers la fin de sa vie, dans ses dernières années; **one of his ~(r) symphonies** une de ses dernières symphonies; **at a ~r date** à une date ultérieure; **we'll discuss it at a ~r meeting** nous en discuterons au cours d'une réunion ultérieure; **at a ~r meeting they decided** au cours d'une réunion qui eut lieu plus tard ils décidèrent; (*Press*) **a ~r edition** une édition postérieure *or* plus tardive (*V also* **1d**); **a ~r train** un train plus tard; **the ~r train** le deuxième train; **the latest time you may come is 4 o'clock** l'heure limite à laquelle vous pouvez arriver est 4 heures; **when *or* what is the latest you can come?** quand pouvez-vous venir, au plus tard?; **I'll be there by noon at the latest** j'y serai à midi au plus tard; **give me your essay by noon at the latest** rendez-moi votre dissertation à midi dernier délai *or* dernière limite *or* au plus tard; **the latest time for doing it is April** c'est en avril dernière limite qu'il faut le faire; **the latest date he could do it was 31st July** la dernière date à laquelle il pouvait le faire était le 31 juillet; **the latest date for applications** la date limite de dépôt de candidatures.

(c) (*former*) ancien (*before n*). **the ~ Prime Minister** l'ancien Premier ministre, l'ex-Premier ministre.

(d) (*recent*) récent, de ces derniers temps. (*Press*) **a ~r edition** une édition plus récente; (*Press*) **the latest edition** la dernière (édition); **the latest fashion** la dernière mode; **the latest news** les dernières nouvelles; (*Rad, TV*) **the latest news (bulletin)** les dernières informations; **of ~** récemment, dernièrement, ces derniers temps; **this version is ~r than that one** cette version est postérieure à celle-là *or* plus récente que celle-là; **this is the latest in a series of murders** c'est le dernier en date d'une série de meurtres; **his latest statement** sa dernière déclaration (en date).

(e) (*dead*) **the ~ Mr X** feu M X; **our ~ colleague** notre regretté (*frm*) *or* défunt (*frm*) *or* pauvre collègue.

2 *adv* **(a)** (*not on time*) *arrive etc* en retard. **even ~r** encore plus en retard; **he arrived 10 minutes ~** il est arrivé 10 minutes en retard *or* avec 10 minutes de retard; (*Prov*) **better ~ than never** mieux vaut tard que jamais (*Prov*).

(b) (*far into day etc*) *get up etc* tard. **to work ~ at the office** rester tard au bureau pour travailler; **it's getting ~** il se fait tard; **~ at night** tard le soir; **~ into the night** tard dans la nuit; **~ in the afternoon** tard dans l'après-midi, vers la fin de l'après-midi; **~ in 1960** vers la fin de 1960, fin 1960; **~ in the year** tard dans l'année, vers la fin de l'année; **he decided ~ in life to become ...** sur le tard il a décidé de devenir ...; **2 weeks ~r** 2 semaines après *or* plus tard; **~r on** plus tard; (*fig*) **it is rather ~ in the day to change your mind** c'est un peu tard pour changer d'avis; **not *or* no ~r than** pas plus tard que; **essays must be handed in not ~r than Monday morning** les dissertations devront être remises lundi matin dernier délai *or* dernière limite *or* au plus tard; **see you ~r!*** à tout à l'heure!, à plus tard!; (*when interrupted etc*) **~r!** tout à l'heure!

(c) (*recently*) **as ~ as last week** pas plus tard que la semaine dernière, la semaine dernière encore; **as ~ as 1950** en 1950 encore.

(d) (*formerly*) **Mr X, ~ of Paris** M X, autrefois domicilié à Paris; **Acacia Avenue, ~ North Street** Acacia Avenue, anciennement North Street; **X, ~ of the Diplomatic Service** X, ancien membre du corps diplomatique.

3 *cpd*: (*lit*) **latecomer** retardataire *mf*; (*fig*) **he is a latecomer to politics** c'est un tard venu *or* il est venu tard à la politique.

lateen [ləˈtiːn] *n* (*also* **~ sail**) voile latine.

lately [ˈleɪtlɪ] *adv* (*recently*) dernièrement, récemment; (*these last few days*) ces jours-ci, ces derniers jours. **it's only ~ that** c'est seulement récemment que *or* depuis peu que; **till ~** jusqu'à ces derniers temps.

latency [ˈleɪtənsɪ] *n* (*Med*) latence *f*.

lateness [ˈleɪtnɪs] *n* **(a)** (*not being on time*) *[person, vehicle]* retard *m*. **punished for persistent ~** puni pour retards trop fréquents.

(b) the ~ of the hour prevented us from going vu l'heure tardive *or* avancée, nous n'avons pas pu y aller; **the ~ of the concert lets us dine first** l'heure tardive du concert nous permet de dîner avant.

latent [ˈleɪtənt] *adj* latent. (*Med*) **~ period** période *f* de latence; (*Phys*) **~ heat** chaleur latente.

lateral [ˈlætərəl] *adj* latéral. **~ thinking** la pensée latérale.

laterally [ˈlætərəlɪ] *adv* latéralement.

latest [ˈleɪtɪst] **1** *adj, adv, superl of* **late.**

2 *n* (*: *news*) **have you heard the ~?** tu connais la dernière?*; **what's the ~ on this affair?** qu'y a-t-il de nouveau dans cette affaire?; (*Rad, TV*) **for the ~ on the riots, over to X** pour les dernières informations sur les émeutes, à vous, X; (*girlfriend*) **have you seen his ~?** tu as vu sa nouvelle?*; (*joke*) **have you heard his ~?** tu connais sa dernière?*; (*exploit*) **did you hear about his ~?** on t'a raconté son dernier exploit? *or* sa dernière prouesse? (*iro*).

latex [ˈleɪteks] *n* latex *m*.

lath [læθ] *n, pl* **~s** [lɑːðz] (*Constr*) latte *f*; *[Venetian blind]* lame *f*.

lathe [leɪð] *n* (*Tech*) tour *m*; *V* **capstan, power** *etc*.

lather [ˈlɑːðəʳ] **1** *n* **(a)** *[soap]* mousse *f* (de savon).

(b) (*sweat*) *[horse]* écume *f*. **in a ~** *horse* couvert d'écume; *person* (*: *perspiring*) en nage; (‡: *nervous, anxious*) paniqué‡.

2 *vt* **(a)** *one's face etc* savonner.

(b) (*: *thrash*) rosser*, tanner (le cuir à)‡.

3 *vi [soap]* mousser.

latifundia [ˌlætɪˈfʊndɪə] *npl* latifundia *mpl*.

Latin [ˈlætɪn] **1** *adj peoples, temperament* latin. **~ quarter** quartier latin; **~ America** Amérique latine; **~-American** (*adj*) latino-américain, d'Amérique latine; (*n*) Latino-Américain(e) *m(f)*.

2 *n* **(a)** Latin(e) *m(f)*.

(b) (*Ling*) latin *m*. **late ~** latin décadent; **low ~** bas latin; **vulgar ~** latin vulgaire.

Latinist [ˈlætɪnɪst] *n* latiniste *mf*.

Latinization [ˌlætɪnaɪˈzeɪʃən] *n* latinisation *f*.

Latinize [ˈlætɪnaɪz] *vt* latiniser.

latish [ˈleɪtɪʃ] **1** *adj hour* assez avancé, assez tardif. **it's getting ~** il commence à se faire assez tard. **2** *adv* assez tard, plutôt tard.

latitude [ˈlætɪtjuːd] *n* **(a)** (*Geog*) latitude *f*. **at a ~ of 48° north** à *or* par 48° de latitude Nord; **in these ~s** à *or* sous ces latitudes.

(b) (*U: freedom*) latitude *f*.

latitudinal [ˌlætɪˈtjuːdɪnl] *adj* latitudinal.

latrine [ləˈtriːn] *n* latrine(s) *f(pl)* (*gen pl*).

latter [ˈlætəʳ] **1** *adj* **(a)** (*second*) deuxième, dernier. **the ~ proposition was accepted** cette dernière *or* la deuxième proposition fut acceptée.

(b) (*later*) dernier, deuxième. **the ~ half** la deuxième moitié; **the ~ half of the month** la deuxième quinzaine du mois; **the ~ part of the evening was quite pleasant** la fin de la soirée a été assez agréable; **in the ~ part of the century** vers la fin du siècle; **in the ~ years of his life** dans les dernières années de sa vie, tard dans sa vie.

2 *n*: **the ~ is the more expensive of the two systems** ce dernier système est le plus coûteux des deux; **of these two books the former is expensive but the ~ is not** le premier de ces deux livres est cher mais le second *or* le deuxième ne l'est pas, de ces

deux livres celui-là est cher mais celui-ci ne l'est pas.
3 *cpd*: **latter-day** moderne, d'aujourd'hui; (*Rel*) **Latter-Day Saints** Mormons *mpl*.
latterly ['lætəlɪ] *adv* **(a)** (*recently*) dernièrement, récemment, depuis quelque temps. **(b)** (*towards the end of a period*) vers la fin, sur le tard. **he was a farmer but ~ became a writer** il était cultivateur mais devint écrivain sur le tard.
lattice ['lætɪs] 1 *n* treillis *m*; (*fence*) treillage *m*, claire-voie *f*; (*climbing-plant frame*) treillage. 2 *cpd*: **lattice girder** poutre *f* à treillis; **lattice window** fenêtre treillissée; **lattice work** treillis *m*.
latticed ['lætɪst] *adj window* treillissé; *fence, wall* treillagé.
Latvia ['lætvɪə] *n* Lettonie *f*.
Latvian ['lætvɪən] 1 *adj* lette *or* letton (*f* -on(n)e). 2 *n* **(a)** Lette *mf or* Letton((n)e) *m(f)*, Latvien(ne) *m(f)*. **(b)** (*Ling*) lette *m or* letton *m*.
laud [lɔːd] *vt* (*liter*) louanger (*liter*); (*Rel*) louer, glorifier, chanter les louanges de.
laudable ['lɔːdəbl] *adj* louable, digne de louanges.
laudably ['lɔːdəblɪ] *adv* de manière louable *or* méritoire. **he was ~ calm** son calme était digne de louanges.
laudanum ['lɔːdnəm] *n* laudanum *m*.
laudatory ['lɔːdətərɪ] *adj* élogieux.
laugh [lɑːf] 1 *n* (*brief*) éclat *m* de rire; (*longer*) rire *m*. **with a ~** (*brief*) dans un éclat de rire; (*longer*) en riant; **with a scornful ~** avec un rire méprisant; **to give a ~** rire; **to give** *or* **laugh a scornful ~** rire dédaigneusement; **he has a very distinctive ~** il a un rire très caractéristique; (*fig*) **he had the last ~** finalement c'est lui qui a bien ri; **we'll see who has the last ~** on verra bien qui rira le dernier; **to have the ~ over sb** l'emporter finalement sur qn; **to have a good ~ at** *or* **over sth/at sb** bien rire de qch/qn; **that got a ~** cela a fait rire; **if you want a ~ go to her German class!** si tu veux t'amuser *or* rigoler* va assister à son cours d'allemand!; **the ~ is on you*** c'est toi qui fais les frais de la plaisanterie; **what a ~!*** comme on a ri!, qu'est-ce qu'on a ri!*, quelle rigolade!*; (**iro*) **that's a ~ anyway!** ça me fait bien rigoler!*; **just for a ~, for ~s*** rien que pour rire, histoire de rire*; **it was** *or* **we had a good ~** on a bien ri, on s'est bien amusés; **he likes a (good) ~** il aime bien rire *or* s'amuser; **he's always good for a ~*** il nous fera toujours bien rire; *V* **play, raise** *etc*.
2 *vi* rire. **to ~ at a joke** rire d'une plaisanterie; **he was so amusing he soon had them all ~ing at him** il était si drôle que bientôt tous riaient de ses plaisanteries (*V also* **laugh at**); **to ~ about** *or* **over sth** rire de qch; **there's nothing to ~ about** *or* **at** il n'y a pas de quoi rire; **to ~ out loud** rire tout haut, rire ouvertement; **to ~ inwardly** rire intérieurement; **he ~ed to himself** il a ri dans sa barbe *or* en lui-même; **he ~ed until he cried** il riait aux larmes, il pleurait de rire; **to ~ one's head off*** rire comme un fou *or* une baleine*; **she was ~ing fit to burst‡** elle riait comme une baleine*, elle riait à se faire mal aux côtes* *or* à en crever*; **he (nearly) split his sides ~ing** il se tordait de rire; (*Prov*) **he who ~s last ~s longest** rira bien qui rira le dernier (*Prov*); **to ~ in sb's face** rire au nez de qn; **he'll soon be ~ing on the other side of his face** il n'aura bientôt plus envie de rire, il va bientôt rire jaune; **I'll make you ~ on the other side of your face!** je vais t'apprendre à rire!; (*fig*) **to ~ up one's sleeve** rire sous cape; *[man]* rire dans sa barbe; **it's all very well for you to ~!** tu peux toujours rire!; **he makes me ~*** il me fait rire; (*iro*) **don't make me ~*** laisse-moi rire, ne me fais pas rire; **it's all right for him, he's ~ing*** lui il s'en fiche*, il est tranquille *or* il est peinard‡; **once we get this contract signed we're ~ing*** une fois ce contrat signé, on est tranquille *or* on tient le bon bout; *V* **burst out**.
3 *vt*: **he ~ed a jolly laugh** il eut un rire jovial; **they ~ed him to scorn** ils l'ont tourné en dérision; **his brothers ~ed him out of that idea** ses frères se sont tant moqués de lui qu'il a abandonné cette idée; (*fig*) **to ~ sb/sth out of court** tourner qn/qch en ridicule; **he ~ed himself silly*** il a ri comme un bossu* *or* comme une baleine*.
laugh at *vt fus* (*lit*) *person, sb's behaviour* rire de, se moquer de; (*fig*) *difficulty, danger* se rire de.
laugh down *vt sep*: **they laughed the speaker down** leurs moqueries ont réduit l'orateur au silence.
laugh off *vt sep accusation* écarter d'une plaisanterie *or* d'une boutade. **to laugh off an embarrassing situation** se tirer d'une situation embarrassante par une boutade *or* par une plaisanterie; **you can't laugh this one off** cette fois tu ne t'en tireras pas par la plaisanterie.
laughable ['lɑːfəbl] *adj suggestion* ridicule; *amount* dérisoire. **it is ~ to hope that ...** il est ridicule d'espérer que ... .
laughing ['lɑːfɪŋ] *adj* riant, rieur. **this is no ~ matter** il n'y a pas de quoi rire; **I'm in no ~ mood** (*angry*) je ne suis pas d'humeur à rire; (*sad*) je n'ai pas le cœur à rire; **~ gas** gaz hilarant; (*Zool*) **~ hyena** hyène *f* (*africaine*); (*Orn*) **~ jackass** dacélo *m*; **he was the ~ stock of the class** il était la risée de la classe; **he made himself a ~ stock** il s'est couvert de ridicule.
laughingly ['lɑːfɪŋlɪ] *adv say etc* en riant. **it is ~ called ...** on l'appelle par plaisanterie ... .
laughter ['lɑːftəʳ] *n* (*U*) rire(s) *m(pl)*. **~ is good for you** cela fait du bien de rire; **at this there was ~** à ces mots il y a eu des rires *or* des rires ont fusé; **he said amid ~ that ...** il dit au milieu des *or* parmi les rires que ...; **their ~ could be heard in the next room** on les entendait rire dans la pièce à côté; **to roar with ~** rire aux éclats; **to burst into ~** éclater de rire.
launch [lɔːntʃ] 1 *n* **(a)** (*also* **motor ~**) (*for patrol duties etc*) vedette *f*, canot *m* automobile; (*pleasure boat*) bateau *m* de plaisance. **police ~** vedette de la police.
(b) (*boat carried by warship*) chaloupe *f*.
(c) = **launching**.
2 *vt ship, satellite, missile, company* lancer; *shore lifeboat etc* faire sortir; *ship's boat* mettre à la mer; *product* lancer; *scheme, plan* mettre en action *or* en vigueur; *attack, offensive* lancer, déclencher. (*Fin*) **to ~ a share issue** émettre des actions, faire une émission d'actions; **to ~ sb on a career** lancer qn dans une carrière; **it would take £5,000 to ~ him as an architect** il faudrait 5.000 livres pour le lancer comme architecte; **once he is ~ed on this subject you can't stop him** une fois qu'il est lancé sur ce sujet on ne peut plus l'arrêter.
3 *vi* (*fig: also* **~ forth**) se lancer (*into, on* dans).
launch forth *vi* = **launch 3.**
launch out *vi* se lancer (*into, on* dans); se développer, prendre de l'extension.
launcher ['lɔːntʃəʳ] *n* (*Space*) lanceur *m*; *V* **missile, rocket.**
launching ['lɔːntʃɪŋ] 1 *n [new ship, missile, satellite, company, product]* lancement *m*; *[shore lifeboat]* sortie *f*; *[ship's boat]* mise *f* à la mer.
2 *cpd*: **launching ceremony** cérémonie *f* de lancement; (*Space*) **launching pad** rampe *f* de lancement; (*Mil, Space*) **launching site** aire *f* de lancement.
launder ['lɔːndəʳ] 1 *vt* blanchir. **to send sth to be ~ed** envoyer qch à la blanchisserie *or* au blanchissage. 2 *vi [shirt etc]* se laver.
launderette [ˌlɔːndə'ret] *n* laverie *f* automatique (*à libre-service*).
laundering ['lɔːndərɪŋ] *n* blanchissage *m*.
laundress ['lɔːndrɪs] *n* blanchisseuse *f*.
Laundromat ['lɔːndrəmæt] *n* ® (*US*) = **launderette.**
laundry ['lɔːndrɪ] 1 *n* **(a)** (*clean clothes*) linge *m*; (*dirty clothes*) linge (sale). **to do the ~** faire la lessive, laver le linge (sale).
(b) (*place*) blanchisserie *f*.
2 *cpd*: **laundry basket** panier *m* à linge; **laundry list** liste *f* de blanchissage; **laundry mark** marque *f* de la blanchisserie *or* du blanchissage; **laundry van** camionnette *f* du blanchisseur; **laundry worker** blanchisseur *m*, -euse *f*.
laureate ['lɔːrɪɪt] *adj, n* lauréat(e) *m(f)*. (*Brit*) **(poet) ~** poète lauréat.
laurel ['lɒrəl] 1 *n* (*Bot, fig*) laurier *m*. **to win one's ~s** se couvrir de lauriers; **to rest on one's ~s** se reposer sur ses lauriers; **you must look to your ~s** ne t'endors pas sur tes lauriers. 2 *cpd*: **laurel wreath** couronne *f* de lauriers.
lav‡ [læv] *n* (*abbr of* **lavatory**) cabs‡ *mpl*, cabinets *mpl*.
lava ['lɑːvə] 1 *n* lave *f*. 2 *cpd*: **lava bed/flow** champ *m*/coulée *f* de lave.
lavalier(e) [ˌlævə'lɪəʳ] *n* (*US*) pendentif *m*.
lavatory ['lævətrɪ] 1 *n* (*room*) toilettes *fpl*, W.-C. *mpl*, cabinets *mpl*; (*Brit: utensil*) (cuvette *f* et siège *m* de) W.-C. **to put sth down the ~** jeter qch dans les W.-C. *or* cabinets; *V* **public.**
2 *cpd*: **lavatory bowl** cuvette *f* des W.-C. *or* cabinets; (*fig pej*) **lavatory humour*** humour *m* scatologique; **lavatory pan** = **lavatory bowl**; **lavatory paper** papier *m* hygiénique; **lavatory seat** siège *m* des W.-C. *or* cabinets.
lavender ['lævɪndəʳ] 1 *n* lavande *f*. 2 *cpd* (*colour*) lavande *inv*. **lavender bag** sachet *m* de lavande; **lavender blue** bleu lavande *inv*; **lavender water** eau *f* de lavande.
lavish ['lævɪʃ] 1 *adj* **(a)** *person* prodigue (*of, with* de). **to be ~ with one's money** dépenser sans compter, se montrer prodigue.
(b) (*abundant*) *expenditure* considérable; *amount* gigantesque; *meal* plantureux, copieux; *helping, hospitality* généreux; *flat, surroundings* somptueux, luxueux. **to bestow ~ praise on sb** se répandre en éloges sur qn.
2 *vt* prodiguer (*sth on sb* qch à qn).
lavishly ['lævɪʃlɪ] *adv spend* sans compter; *give* généreusement, à profusion; *furnish* somptueusement, luxueusement.
lavishness ['lævɪʃnɪs] *n [spending]* extravagance *f*; *[furniture, surroundings etc]* luxe *m*, somptuosité *f*; (*prodigality*) prodigalité *f*.
law [lɔː] 1 *n* **(a)** (*U*) loi *f*. **the ~** la loi; **it's the ~** c'est la loi; **the ~ of the land** la législation *or* les lois du pays; **the ~ of the jungle** la loi de la jungle; **the L~ (of Moses)** la loi de Moïse; **the ~ as it stands** la législation en vigueur; **they are trying to change the ~ on this** ils essaient de changer la loi *or* la législation sur ce point; **~ and order** l'ordre public; **forces of ~ and order** forces *fpl* de l'ordre; (*Parl*) **a bill becomes ~** un projet de loi devient loi; **by ~** conformément à la loi; **by** *or* **under French ~** selon la loi *or* la législation française; **to be above the ~** être au-dessus des lois; **to have the ~ on one's side** avoir la loi pour soi; **to keep within the ~** rester dans (se) les limites de) la légalité; **to take the ~ into one's own hands** (se) faire justice soi-même; **he's a ~ unto himself** il ne connaît d'autre loi que la sienne, il fait ce qu'il veut; **his word is ~** sa parole fait loi; *V* **break, lay down, rule** *etc*.
(b) (*U: operation of the ~*) justice *f*. **court of ~** cour *f* de justice, tribunal *m*; **to go to ~** recourir à la justice; **to take a case to ~** porter une affaire devant les tribunaux; **to take sb to ~, to have the ~ on sb*** faire un procès à qn; **I'll have the ~ on you!*** je vous emmènerai devant la justice!, je vous traînerai devant les tribunaux!*; **here's the ~ arriving!‡** voilà les flics!‡; *V* **arm¹, officer.**
(c) (*U: system, science, profession*) droit *m*. **to study** *or* **read ~** faire son *or* du droit; **he practises ~** il est homme de loi; (*Univ*) **Faculty of L~** faculté *f* de droit; **civil/criminal** *etc* **~** le droit civil/criminel *etc*; *V* **common, martial, point** *etc*.
(d) (*legal ruling*) loi *f*. **several ~s have been passed against pollution** plusieurs lois ont été votées pour combattre la pollution; **is there a ~ against it?** y a-t-il une loi qui l'interdit? *or* l'interdise?; **there's no ~ against it!*** ce n'est pas interdit!, il n'y a rien qui l'interdit!*
(e) (*principle, rule*) (*gen, Phys*) loi *f*; (*Sport*) règle *f*. **moral ~** principe *m*; **the ~s of nature** les lois de la nature; **~ of gravity**

loi de la chute des corps *or* de la pesanteur; ~ **of supply and demand** loi de l'offre et de la demande; ~ **of diminishing returns** loi des rendements décroissants.

2 *cpd*: **law-abiding** respectueux des lois; **lawbreaker** personne *f* qui viole *or* transgresse la loi; **lawbreakers** ceux *mpl* qui violent la loi *or* qui ne respectent pas la loi; **law court** cour *f* de justice, tribunal *m*; **Law Courts** ≃ Palais *m* de Justice; (*Univ*) **Law Faculty** faculté *f* de droit; **lawgiver** législateur *m*, -trice *f*; (*Brit*) **Law Lords** *juges mpl siégeant à la Chambre des Lords*; **lawmaker** = **lawgiver**; (*Univ*) **law school** faculté *f* de droit; **he's at law school** il fait son droit; **law student** étudiant(e) *m(f)* en droit; **lawsuit** procès *m*; **to bring a lawsuit against sb** intenter un procès à qn, poursuivre qn en justice.

lawful ['lɔːfʊl] *adj action* légal, licite, permis; *marriage, child* légitime; *contract* valide. **it is not ~ to do that** il n'est pas légal de *or* il est illégal de faire cela; **to go about one's ~ business** vaquer à ses occupations.

lawfully ['lɔːfəlɪ] *adv* légalement.

lawless ['lɔːlɪs] *adj country* sans loi, anarchique; *person* qui ne respecte aucune loi; *activity* illégal, contraire à la loi.

lawlessness ['lɔːlɪsnɪs] *n [person]* manque *m* de respect envers la loi; *[country]* anarchie *f*; *[activity]* illégalité *f*.

lawn[1] [lɔːn] **1** *n* pelouse *f*. **2** *cpd*: **lawnmower** tondeuse *f* (à gazon); **lawn tennis** (*on grass*) tennis *m* sur gazon; (*on hard surface*) tennis.

lawn[2] [lɔːn] *n* (*Tex*) batiste *f*, linon *m*.

Lawrence ['lɒrəns] *n* Laurent *m*.

lawyer ['lɔːjə^r] *n* (*gen*) homme *m* de loi, juriste *m*; (*solicitor*) (*for sales, wills etc*) notaire *m*; (*in court*) avocat *m*; (*barrister*) avocat. **he is a ~** il est homme de loi *or* juriste; **... or I shall put the matter in the hands of my ~** ... sinon je mets l'affaire entre les mains de mon avocat.

lax [læks] *adj behaviour, discipline, morals* relâché; *person* négligent; (*Med*) *bowels* relâché; (*Ling*) *vowel* non tendu, relâché. **to be ~ in doing sth** faire qch avec négligence *or* sans soin; **to be ~ about one's work/duties** négliger son travail/ses devoirs; **he's become very ~ recently** il s'est beaucoup relâché récemment.

laxative ['læksətɪv] *adj, n* laxatif (*m*).

laxity ['læksɪtɪ] *n*, **laxness** ['læksnɪs] *n* (*V* **lax**) relâchement *m*; négligence *f*.

lay[1] [leɪ] (*vb: pret, ptp* **laid**) **1** *n* **(a)** *[countryside, district etc]* disposition *f*, configuration *f*. (*fig*) **to find out the ~ of the land** tâter le terrain.

(b) (*:*) **she's an easy ~** elle couche* avec n'importe qui, c'est une fille facile, elle a la cuisse légère*.

2 *cpd*: (*Brit*) **layabout*** fainéant(e) *m(f)*, feignant(e)* *m(f)*; (*Brit Aut*) **lay-by** petite aire de stationnement (*sur bas-côté*); (*Ind*) **lay-off** licenciement *m*, débauchage *m*; **layout** *[house, school]* disposition *f*, agencement *m*; *[garden]* plan *m*, dessin *m*, disposition; *[district]* disposition; *[essay]* plan; *[advertisement, newspaper article etc]* agencement, mise *f* en page; (*Press etc*) **the layout of page 4** la mise en page de la (page) 4; (*Cards*) **I don't like the layout of my hand** je n'aime pas la texture *or* la composition de mon jeu; (*US*) **layover** halte *f*.

3 *vt* **(a)** (*put, place, set*) mettre, poser; (*stretch out*) étendre. **he laid his briefcase on the table** il a posé *or* mis sa serviette à plat sur la table; (*euph: buried*) **to be laid to rest** être enterré; **he laid his head on the table** il a appuyé son front sur la table; **she laid her head on the pillow** elle a posé sa tête sur l'oreiller; **she laid her hand on my shoulder** elle a posé *or* mis la main sur mon épaule; **I wish I could ~ my hands on a good dictionary** si seulement je pouvais mettre la main sur *or* dénicher un bon dictionnaire; (*Rel*) **to ~ hands on sb** faire l'imposition des mains à qn; (*seize*) **to ~ hands on a territory** *etc* s'emparer d'un territoire *etc*; (*strike*) **to ~ a hand** *or* **hands on sb** porter *or* lever la main sur qn; **I didn't ~ a finger on him** je ne l'ai même pas touché; **if you so much as ~ a finger on me ...** si tu oses (seulement) lever la main sur moi ...; (*fig*) **to ~ sb by the heels** attraper qn; **the scene/story is laid in Paris** l'action/l'histoire se passe *or* se situe *or* se déroule à Paris; (*fig*) **to ~ sth at sb's door** tenir qn pour responsable de qch, faire porter la responsabilité de qch à qn; *V* **eye, hold, siege** *etc*.

(b) (*put down into position*) poser, mettre; *bricks, carpet, cable, pipe* poser; *mine* poser, mouiller. **to ~ the foundations of** (*lit*) faire *or* jeter les fondations de; (*fig*) poser les bases de; **to ~ the foundation stone** poser la première pierre; **to ~ a road** faire une route; **to ~ a floor with carpet** poser une moquette sur un sol.

(c) *eggs* pondre. **this bird ~s its eggs in the sand** cet oiseau pond (ses œufs) dans le sable; *V* **new**.

(d) (*prepare*) *fire* préparer; *snare, trap* tendre, dresser (*for* à); *tablecloth* mettre; *plans* former, élaborer. **to ~ the table for lunch** mettre la table *or* le couvert pour le déjeuner; **she laid the table for 5** elle a mis *or* dressé la table pour 5, elle a mis 5 couverts; **all our carefully-laid plans went wrong** tous nos plans si bien élaborés ont échoué.

(e) (*impose, place*) *tax* mettre, faire payer (*on sth* sur qch); *burden* imposer (*on sb* à qn); *V* **blame, emphasis, responsibility** *etc*.

(f) (*+adj*) (*fig*) **to ~ bare one's innermost thoughts/feelings** mettre à nu *or* dévoiler ses pensées les plus profondes/ses sentiments les plus secrets; (*liter*) **to ~ bare one's soul** mettre son âme à nu; **the blow laid him flat** *or* **low** le coup l'étendit par terre *or* l'abattit *or* l'envoya au tapis; **the storm laid the town flat** la tempête a rasé la ville; **he was laid low with flu** la grippe l'obligeait à garder le lit; **to ~ sb/to ~ o.s. open to criticism** *etc* exposer qn/s'exposer à la critique *etc*; **to ~ waste a town** ravager *or* dévaster une ville.

(g) (*wager*) *money* parier, miser (*on* sur). **to ~ a bet (on sth)** parier (sur qch); **I'll ~ you a fiver that ...** je vous parie cinq livres que ... .

(h) (*register, bring to sb's attention*) *accusation, charge* porter. (*Jur*) **to ~ a complaint** porter plainte (*against* contre, *with* auprès de); (*Police*) **to ~ information** donner des informations, servir d'indicateur (*f* -trice); (*Jur*) **to ~ a matter before the court** saisir le tribunal d'une affaire; **he laid his case before the commission** il a porté son cas devant *or* soumis son cas à la commission; **we shall ~ the facts before him** nous lui exposerons les faits; **they laid their plan before him** ils lui ont soumis leur projet; *V* **claim** *etc*.

(i) (*suppress*) *ghost* exorciser, conjurer; *doubt, fear* dissiper. **to ~ the dust** empêcher la poussière de voler, faire tomber la poussière.

(j) (*:*) *woman* baiser*.

4 *vi* **(a)** *[bird, fish, insect]* pondre.

(b) he laid about him with a stick il a distribué des coups de bâton tout autour de lui.

lay alongside (*Naut*) *vi, vt sep* accoster.

lay aside *vt sep* **(a)** (*save*) *money, supplies* mettre de côté.

(b) (*put away temporarily*) *object* mettre de côté. **he laid aside his book to greet me** il a mis son livre de côté pour me recevoir.

(c) (*abandon*) *prejudice, scruples* abandonner, oublier; *principles* se départir de. **we must lay aside our own feelings** nous devons faire abstraction de nos propres sentiments.

lay away *vt sep* (*US*) = **lay aside a.**

lay by 1 *vt sep* = **lay aside a.**

2 lay-by *n V* **lay**[1] **2.**

lay down 1 *vi* (*Cards*) étaler son jeu *or* ses cartes, montrer son jeu.

2 *vt sep* **(a)** (*deposit*) *object, parcel, burden* poser, déposer. **to lay down one's cards** étaler son jeu *or* ses cartes, montrer son jeu (*also fig*).

(b) *wine* mettre en cave.

(c) (*give up*) **to lay down one's arms** déposer ses *or* les armes; **to lay down one's life for sb** sacrifier sa vie pour qn; **to lay down (one's) office** se démettre de ses fonctions.

(d) (*establish, decide*) *rule* établir, poser; *condition, price* imposer, fixer. **he laid it down that ...** il décréta *or* stipula que ...; **it is laid down in the rules that ...** il est stipulé dans le règlement que ...; **to lay down a policy** dicter une politique; (*fig*) **to lay down the law to sb about sth** (essayer de) faire la loi à qn sur qch; **in our house it's my mother who lays down the law** c'est ma mère qui fait la loi à la maison.

lay in *vt sep goods, reserves* amasser, emmagasiner, entasser. **to lay in provisions** faire des provisions; **I must lay in some fruit** il faut que je m'approvisionne (*subj*) en fruits *or* que je prenne des fruits*.

lay into* *vt fus* (*attack physically*) foncer sur, tomber sur; (*attack verbally*) prendre à partie; (*scold*) passer un savon à*.

lay off 1 *vt sep* (*Ind*) *workers* licencier, débaucher.

2 *vt fus* (*) **lay off (it)!** (*stop*) tu veux t'arrêter?*; (*don't touch*) touche pas!*, pas touche!:, bas les pattes!:; **lay off him!** fiche-lui la paix!*; **I told him to lay off (it)** je lui ai dit d'arrêter.

3 lay-off *n V* **lay**[1] **2.**

lay on *vt sep* **(a)** *tax* mettre. **they lay on an extra charge for tea** ils ajoutent à la note le prix du thé.

(b) (*Brit*) (*install*) *water, gas* installer, mettre; (*provide*) *facilities, entertainment* fournir. **a house with water/gas/electricity laid on** une maison qui a l'eau courante/le gaz/l'électricité; **I'll have a car laid on for you** je tiendrai une voiture à votre disposition; **everything will be laid on** il y aura tout ce qu'il faut; **it was all laid on (for us) so that we didn't have to buy anything** tout (nous) était fourni si bien qu'on n'a rien eu à acheter.

(c) *varnish, paint* étaler. (*fig) **he laid it on thick** *or* **with a shovel** *or* **with a trowel** (*flattered*) il a passé de la pommade*, il a manié l'encensoir*; (*exaggerated*) il y est allé un peu fort*, il n'y a pas été avec le dos de la cuiller*.

lay out 1 *vt sep* **(a)** (*plan, design*) *garden* dessiner; *house* concevoir (le plan de); *essay* faire le plan de. **well-laid-out flat** appartement bien conçu; (*Typ*) **to lay out page 4** faire la mise en page de la (page) 4, monter la (page) 4.

(b) (*get ready, display*) *clothes* sortir, préparer; *goods for sale* disposer, étaler. **the meal that was laid out for them** le repas qui leur avait été préparé; **to lay out a body** faire la toilette d'un mort.

(c) (*spend*) *money* dépenser (*on* pour).

(d) (*knock out*) mettre knock-out *or* K.-O.*

(e) (*do one's utmost*) **to lay o.s. out to do** faire tout son possible pour faire, se mettre en peine *or* en quatre pour faire.

2 layout *n V* **lay**[1] **2.**

lay over (*US*) **1** *vi* s'arrêter, faire une halte.

2 layover *n V* **lay**[1] **2.**

lay to (*Naut*) **1** *vi* être en panne.

2 *vt sep* mettre en panne.

lay up *vt sep* **(a)** *store, provisions* amasser, entasser, emmagasiner. **to lay up trouble for o.s.** se préparer des ennuis.

(b) *car* remiser; *ship* désarmer. **he is laid up with flu** il est au lit avec la grippe, la grippe l'a forcé à s'aliter; **you'll lay yourself up if you carry on like this** tu vas te retrouver au lit si tu continues comme ça.

lay[2] [leɪ] *pret of* **lie**[1].

lay[3] [leɪ] *n* (*Mus, Poetry*) lai *m*.

lay[4] [leɪ] **1** *adj missionary, school, education* laïque. **~ brother** frère convers; **~ reader** prédicateur *m* laïque; **~ sister** sœur converse; (*fig*) **to the ~ mind** aux yeux du profane, pour le profane; **~ opinion on this** l'opinion des profanes sur la question.

2 *cpd*: **layman** (*Rel*) laïc *m*; (*fig*) profane *m*; (*fig*) **to the layman it would appear that ...** aux yeux du profane il semblerait que ... .

lay[5] [leɪ] *adj* (*Art*) ~ **figure** mannequin *m*.

layer [ˈleɪəʳ] **1** *n* **(a)** *[atmosphere, paint, dust, sand]* couche *f*; (*Geol*) couche, strate *f*.
(b) (*hen*) **a good ~** une bonne pondeuse.
(c) (*Horticulture*) marcotte *f*.
2 *vt* **(a)** (*Horticulture*) marcotter.
(b) *hair* couper en dégradé.
3 *cpd*: **layer cake** gâteau fourré.

layette [leɪˈet] *n* layette *f*.

laying [ˈleɪɪŋ] **1** *n [carpet]* pose *f*. (*Rel*) **the ~ on of hands** l'imposition *f* des mains. **2** *adj*: ~ **hen** poule pondeuse.

Lazarus [ˈlæzərəs] *n* Lazare *m*.

laze [leɪz] *vi* (*also* ~ **about,** ~ **around**) (*relax*) se reposer; (*be idle*) paresser, ne rien faire, traînasser (*pej*). **we ~d (about** *or* **around) in the sun for a week** nous avons passé une semaine au soleil à ne rien faire, nous avons eu une semaine de farniente au soleil; **stop lazing about** *or* **around and do some work!** cesse de perdre ton temps (à ne rien faire) et mets-toi au travail!

laze away *vt sep*: **to laze the time away** passer son temps à ne rien faire.

lazily [ˈleɪzɪlɪ] *adv* (*V* **lazy**) paresseusement, nonchalamment, avec indolence.

laziness [ˈleɪzɪnɪs] *n* paresse *f*, indolence *f*, fainéantise *f* (*pej*).

lazy [ˈleɪzɪ] **1** *adj person* paresseux, indolent, fainéant (*pej*); *attitude, gesture, smile* nonchalant, paresseux; *hour, afternoon* de paresse. **we had a ~ holiday** nous avons passé les vacances à ne rien faire. **2** *cpd*: **lazybones** feignant(e)* *m(f)*.

lea [liː] *n* (*liter*) pré *m*.

leach [liːtʃ] **1** *vt liquid* filtrer; *particles* lessiver. **2** *vi [ashes, soil]* être éliminé par filtration *or* filtrage; *[liquid]* filtrer.

lead[1] [liːd] (*vb: pret, ptp* **led**) **1** *n* **(a)** (*esp Sport*) (*front position*) tête *f*; (*distance or time ahead*) avance *f*. **to be in the ~** (*in match*) mener; (*in race, league*) être en tête; **to go into** *or* **take the ~** (*in race*) prendre la tête; (*in match*) mener; **to have a 3-point ~** avoir 3 points d'avance; **to have a 2-minute/10-metre ~ over sb** avoir 2 minutes/10 mètres d'avance sur qn.
(b) initiative *f*, exemple *m*. **to take the ~ in doing sth** être le premier à faire qch; **thanks to his ~ the rest were able to ...** grâce à son initiative les autres ont pu ...; **to follow sb's ~** suivre l'exemple de qn; **to give sb a ~** montrer le chemin à qn (*fig*); *V also* **1c**.
(c) (*clue*) piste *f*. **the police have a ~** la police tient une piste; **the footprint gave them a ~** l'empreinte de pas les a mis sur la voie *or* sur la piste.
(d) (*Cards*) **whose ~ is it?** à qui est-ce de jouer?
(e) (*Theat*) rôle principal. **to play the ~** tenir *or* jouer *or* avoir le rôle principal; **to sing the ~** chanter le rôle principal; **male/female ~** premier rôle masculin/féminin; **juvenile ~** jeune premier *m*.
(f) (*leash*) laisse *f*. **dogs must be kept on a ~** les chiens doivent être tenus en laisse.
(g) (*Elec*) fil *m*.
(h) (*Press: also* ~ **story**) article *m* de tête. **what is the ~?** quel est l'article de tête?; **the financial crisis is the ~ (story) in this morning's papers** la crise financière est le gros titre des *or* est à la une des journaux de ce matin.
2 *cpd*: **lead-in** introduction *f*, entrée *f* en matière; (*Press*) **lead story** *V* **1h**.
3 *vt* **(a)** (*conduct, show the way*) conduire, mener (*to* à). **to ~ sb in/out/across** *etc* faire entrer/sortir/traverser *etc* qn; **they led him into the king's presence** on le conduisit devant le roi; **to ~ sb into a room** faire entrer qn dans une pièce; **the guide led them through the courtyard** le guide leur a fait traverser la cour *or* les a fait passer par la cour; **the first street on the left will ~ you to the church** la première rue à gauche vous mènera à l'église; **what led you to Venice?** qu'est-ce qui vous a amené à Venise?; **each clue led him to another** chaque indice le menait à un autre; (*fig*) **he is easily led** il est très influençable; (*Jur*) **to ~ a witness** poser des questions tendancieuses à un témoin; (*lit, fig*) **to ~ the way** montrer le chemin; **he led the way to the garage** il nous (*or* les *etc*) a menés jusqu'au garage; **will you ~ the way?** vous passez devant et on vous suit; (*fig*) **to ~ sb astray** détourner qn du droit chemin, dévoyer qn (*liter*); (*fig*) **to ~ sb by the nose** mener qn par le bout du nez; **to ~ an army into battle** mener une armée au combat; **to ~ a team on to the field** conduire une équipe sur le terrain; **he led the party to victory** il a mené le parti à la victoire; **he will ~ us in prayer** il va diriger nos prières; *V* **garden**.
(b) (*be leader of*) *procession* (*be in charge of*) être à la tête de; (*be at head of*) être en tête de; *government, movement, party, team* être à la tête de, diriger; *expedition* être à la tête de, mener; *regiment* être à la tête de, commander; (*Ftbl etc*) *league* être en tête de; *orchestra* (*Brit*) être le premier violon de; (*US*) diriger.
(c) (*be ahead of: Sport, fig*) être en tête de. **they were ~ing us by 10 metres** ils avaient un avantage *or* une avance de 10 mètres sur nous; (*Sport, fig*) **to ~ the field** venir *or* être en tête; **this country ~s the world in textiles** ce pays est au *or* tient le premier rang mondial pour les textiles.
(d) (*Cards*) jouer; (*Bridge etc: at first trick*) attaquer de, entamer. **what is led?** qu'est-ce qui est joué? *or* demandé?
(e) *life, existence* mener. (*fig*) **to ~ sb a dance** faire la vie à qn*; *V* **dog** *etc*.
(f) (*induce, bring*) porter, amener. **I am led to the conclusion that ...** je suis amené à conclure que ...; **he led me to believe that he would help me** il m'a amené à croire qu'il m'aiderait; **what led you to think that?** qu'est-ce qui vous a porté à penser ça?; **his financial problems led him to steal** ses problèmes financiers l'ont poussé au vol.
4 *vi* **(a)** (*be ahead: esp Sport*) (*in match*) mener; (*in race*) être en tête. **which horse is ~ing?** quel est le cheval de tête?; **to ~ by half a length/3 points** avoir une demi-longueur/3 points d'avance; **to ~ by 4 goals to 3** mener (par) 4 buts à 3.
(b) (*go ahead*) aller devant. **you ~, I'll follow** passez *or* allez devant, je vous suis.
(c) (*Jur*) **to ~ for the defence** être l'avocat principal de la défense.
(d) (*Cards*) **who is it to ~?** c'est à qui de jouer?; (*Bridge*) **South to ~** sud joue.
(e) *[street, corridor]* mener, conduire; *[door]* mener (*to* à), donner, s'ouvrir (*to* sur). **the streets that ~ into/off the square** les rues qui débouchent sur/partent de la place; **the rooms which ~ off the corridor** les pièces qui donnent sur le couloir.
(f) (*fig*) conduire, aboutir (*to* à). **it led to war** cela a conduit à la guerre; **it led to his arrest** cela aboutit à son arrestation; **that will ~ to his undoing** cela causera *or* sera sa perte; **it led to nothing** cela n'a mené à rien; **this led to their asking to see the president** ceci les a amenés à demander à voir le président; **it could ~ to some confusion** cela pourrait créer *or* occasionner une certaine confusion; **it led to a change in his attitude** cela a amené *or* causé un changement dans son attitude; **one story led to another** une histoire en a amené une autre; **one thing led to another and we ...** une chose en amenant une autre, nous ... .

lead away *vt sep* emmener. **he was led away by the soldiers** il a été emmené par les soldats; **they led him away to the cells** ils l'ont conduit en cellule.

lead back *vt sep* ramener, reconduire. **they led us back to the house** ils nous ont ramenés *or* reconduits à la maison; **this road leads (you) back to the town hall** cette route vous ramène à l'hôtel de ville.

lead off **1** *vi* (*begin*) commencer, débuter.
2 *vt sep* = **lead away**.

lead on **1** *vi* marcher devant. **lead on!**, (*hum*) **lead on, Macduff!*** allez-y, je vous suis!
2 *vt sep* **(a)** (*tease*) taquiner, faire marcher*; (*fool*) duper, avoir*.
(b) (*raise hopes of*) donner de faux espoirs à.
(c) (*induce*) amener. **they led him on to talk about his experiences** ils l'ont amené à parler de ses expériences; **this led him on to say that ...** ceci l'amena à dire que ... .

lead up *vi* **(a)** conduire. **this road leads up to the castle** cette route conduit *or* mène au château; **this staircase leads up to the roof** cet escalier conduit au *or* donne accès au toit; (*fig*) **his speech led up to a discussion of war** son discours nous (*or* les *etc*) a amenés *or* entraînés à parler de la guerre; **he led up carefully to his proposal** il a soigneusement amené sa proposition; **what are you leading up to?** où voulez-vous en venir?; **what's all this leading up to?** où est-ce qu'on veut en venir avec tout ça?
(b) (*precede*) précéder. **the years that led up to the war** les années qui ont précédé la guerre; **the events that led up to the revolution** les événements qui ont conduit à la révolution.

lead[2] [led] **1** *n* **(a)** (*U: metal*) plomb *m*. **they filled him full of ~**‡ ils l'ont truffé de pruneaux‡, ils l'ont transformé en écumoire*; *V* **red** *etc*.
(b) (*U: graphite: also* **black ~**) mine *f* de plomb.
(c) *[pencil]* mine *f*; *[fishing line]* plomb *m*; (*for sounding*) plomb (de sonde).
(d) (*Typ*) interligne *f*, blanc *m*.
(e) (*Brit*) *[roof]* ~**s** couverture *f* de plomb; **(window)** ~**s** plombures *fpl*.
2 *cpd object, weight etc* de *or* en plomb. **lead acetate** acétate *m* de plomb; **lead-free paint** peinture *f* (garantie) sans plomb; **lead oxyde** oxyde *m* de plomb; **lead paint** peinture *f* à base de carbonate de plomb; **lead pencil** crayon *m* à mine de plomb *or* à papier; **lead piping** tuyauterie *f* de plomb; **lead poisoning** saturnisme *m*, coliques *fpl* de plomb; **lead shot** grenaille *f* de plomb; **lead works** fonderie *f* de plomb.

leaded [ˈledɪd] *adj* **(a)** ~ **window** fenêtre *f* à tout petits carreaux; ~ **lights** petits carreaux. **(b)** (*Typ*) interligné.

leaden [ˈledn] **1** *adj* (*made of lead*) de *or* en plomb; (*in colour*) *sky* de plomb, plombé; (*fig: heavy*) lourd, pesant; *silence* de mort; *atmosphere* chargé. **2** *cpd*: **leaden-eyed** aux yeux ternes; **to feel leaden-limbed** se sentir les membres en plomb.

leader [ˈliːdəʳ] *n* **(a)** *[expedition, gang, tribe]* chef *m*; *[club]* dirigeant(e) *m(f)*; (*guide*) guide *m*; *[riot, strike]* meneur *m*, -euse *f*; (*Mil*) commandant *m*; (*Pol*) dirigeant(e), leader *m*, chef (de file). (*Brit Parl*) **L~ of the House** chef de la majorité ministérielle à la Chambre; (*Pol*) **the ~ of the Socialist Party** le leader *or* le chef (du parti) socialiste, le dirigeant socialiste; **the national ~s** les dirigeants *or* leaders nationaux; **political ~s** chefs politiques; **one of the ~s of the trade union movement** un des dirigeants *or* chefs de file *or* leaders du mouvement syndical; **he's a born ~** il est né pour commander; **the ~ of the orchestra** (*Brit*) le premier violon; (*US*) le chef d'orchestre; **she was a ~ of fashion** elle était de celles qui créent *or* font la mode; **one of the ~s in the scientific field** une des sommités du monde scientifique; (*Jur*) **the ~ for the defence** l'avocat principal de la défense; *V* **follow, youth** *etc*.
(b) (*Sport*) (*in race*) coureur *m* de tête; (*Horse-racing*) cheval *m* de tête; (*in league*) leader *m*. **he managed to stay up with the ~s** il a réussi à rester dans les premiers *or* dans le peloton de tête.
(c) (*Press*) (*Brit*) éditorial *m*; (*US*) article *m* de tête. (*Brit*) ~ **writer** éditorialiste *mf*.
(d) *[film, tape etc]* amorce *f*.

leadership [ˈliːdəʃɪp] *n* **(a)** (*U*) (*position*) direction *f*, tête *f*; (*action*) direction; (*quality*) qualités *fpl* de chef. **during** *or* under his ~ sous sa direction; to take over the ~ of the country prendre la succession à la tête du pays; they were rivals for the party ~ ils étaient candidats rivaux à la direction du parti; to resign the party ~ démissionner de la tête du parti; he has ~ potential *or* qualities of ~ il a des qualités de chef *or* l'étoffe d'un chef.

(b) (*collective n: leaders*) dirigeants *mpl.* the union ~ agreed to arbitration les dirigeants du syndicat ont accepté l'arbitrage.

leading ['li:dɪŋ] *adj* (a) (*chief*) *person* de (tout) premier plan, principal; *part* prépondérant, majeur (*f* -eure), de premier plan; (*Theat*) *role* premier, principal; *topic, theme* principal; *idea* majeur, dominant, principal. he is one of the ~ writers in the country c'est un des écrivains les plus importants *or* les plus en vue du pays; he was one of the ~ figures of the twenties c'était un personnage marquant *or* une figure marquante des années vingt; he played a ~ part in getting the gang arrested il a joué un rôle majeur dans l'arrestation du gang; one of the ~ industries une des industries de pointe; (*Press*) ~ article (*Brit*) éditorial *m*; (*US*) article *m* de tête; (*Jur*) ~ case précédent *m*; (*Cine*) the ~ lady/man in the film la vedette féminine/masculine du film; (*Cine*) his ~ lady in that film was X il avait X pour co-vedette dans ce film; (*Theat*) the ~ lady/man was X c'est X qui tenait le rôle principal féminin/masculin; he is one of the ~ lights in the town* c'est un des gros bonnets* *or* une des huiles* de la ville; she was one of the ~ lights in the local drama society* c'était une des étoiles du groupe d'art dramatique local.

(b) (*front*) *horse* de tête; *car* (*in procession*) de tête; (*in race*) en tête. (*Aviat*) the ~ edge le bord d'attaque.

(c) ~ question (*Jur*) question tendancieuse; (*gen*) question insidieuse; [*horse*] ~ rein longe *f*; [*toddler*] ~ reins *or* strings guides *mpl* (*pour bébé*).

leaf [li:f] *pl* **leaves** 1 *n* (a) [*tree,plant*] feuille *f*. the leaves les feuilles, le feuillage; in ~ en feuilles; to come into ~ se couvrir de feuilles; (*fig*) to shake like a ~ trembler comme une feuille; *V* fig.

(b) [*book*] feuillet *m*, page *f*. (*fig*) you should take a ~ out of his book vous devriez prendre exemple sur lui; (*fig*) to turn over a new ~ changer de conduite; *V* fly[3].

(c) [*table*] (*on hinges*) rabat *m*, abattant *m*; (*in groove, removable*) rallonge *f*.

(d) [*metal*] feuille *f*; *V* gold.

2 *cpd*: leaf bud bourgeon *m* (à feuilles); (*U*) (*US*) leaf mold, (*Brit*) leaf mould terreau *m* (de feuilles); leaf tobacco tabac *m* en feuilles.

leaf through *vt fus book* feuilleter, parcourir.

leafless ['li:flɪs] *adj* sans feuilles, dénudé.

leaflet ['li:flɪt] *n* prospectus *m*; (*Pol, Rel*) tract *m*; (*for publicity*) brochure *f*, dépliant *m*, prospectus; (*with instructions*) notice explicative, mode *m* d'emploi.

leafy ['li:fɪ] *adj glade* entouré d'arbres feuillus; *tree* feuillu.

league[1] [li:g] 1 *n* (a) (*association*) ligue *f*. to form a ~ against se liguer contre; to be in ~ with être en coalition avec; L~ of Nations Société *f* des Nations.

(b) (*Sport*) championnat *m*. (*Brit Ftbl*) ~ division one première division du championnat; *V* rugby *etc*.

2 *cpd*: (*Brit Ftbl*) they were the league champions last year ils ont été champions l'année dernière; they are the league leaders now pour le moment ils sont en tête du championnat.

league[2] [li:g] *n* lieue *f*. seven- ~ boots bottes *fpl* de sept lieues.

leak [li:k] 1 *n* (*in bucket, pipe, roof, balloon*) fuite *f*; (*in boat*) voie *f* d'eau; (*fig: of information etc*) fuite. to spring a ~ [*boat*] commencer à faire eau; the ship sprang a ~ in the bow une voie d'eau s'est déclarée à l'avant du navire; [*bucket, pipe*] se mettre à fuir; a gas ~ une fuite de gaz; budget/security ~ fuite concernant le budget/la sécurité.

2 *vi* (a) [*bucket, pen, pipe, bottle*] fuir; [*ship*] faire eau; [*shoes*] prendre l'eau. the roof ~s le toit fuit, il y a des fuites dans le toit.

(b) [*gas, liquid*] fuir, s'échapper. the acid ~ed (through) on to the carpet l'acide a filtré jusque dans le tapis.

3 *vt liquid* répandre, faire couler; (*fig*) *information* divulguer, révéler (*to* à). it's ~ing acid all over the place l'acide est en train de se répandre partout.

leak in *vi* [*spilt liquid*] filtrer; [*water*] suinter, s'infiltrer. the water is leaking in through the roof l'eau entre *or* s'infiltre par le toit.

leak out 1 *vi* [*gas, liquid*] fuir, s'échapper; [*secret, news*] s'ébruiter, transpirer, être divulgué. it finally leaked out that on a fini par savoir *or* apprendre que, il a fini par transpirer que.

2 *vt sep facts, news* divulguer, révéler (*to* à).

leakage ['li:kɪdʒ] *n* (*leak*) [*gas, liquid, information*] fuite *f*; (*amount lost*) perte *f*. some of the acid was lost through ~ un peu d'acide a été perdu par (suite d'une) fuite.

leaky ['li:kɪ] *adj bucket, kettle* percé, qui fuit; *roof* qui a une fuite; *shoe* qui prend l'eau; *boat* qui fait eau.

lean[1] [li:n] *pret, ptp* **leaned** *or* **leant** 1 *vi* (a) (*slope*) [*wall, construction etc*] pencher. (*fig*) I ~ towards the belief that ... je tends à *or* j'incline à croire que ...; to ~ towards sb's opinion tendre à partager l'opinion de qn; (*Pol*) to ~ towards the left pencher vers la gauche, avoir des sympathies pour la gauche *or* à gauche.

(b) (*support o.s., rest*) [*person*] s'appuyer (*against, up against* contre, à, *on* sur), prendre appui (*against, up against* contre, *on* sur); (*with one's back*) s'adosser (*against, up against* à), s'appuyer (*against, up against* contre, à); (*with elbows*) s'accouder (*on* à). to be ~ing être appuyé *or* adossé *or* accoudé; [*ladder, cycle etc*] to be ~ing (up) against the wall être appuyé contre le mur, être adossé au mur; to ~ on one's elbows s'appuyer *or* prendre appui sur les coudes; (*fig*) to ~ on sb for help *or* support s'appuyer sur qn (*fig*); (*fig*) to ~ (heavily) on sb for advice compter (beaucoup) sur qn pour ses conseils.

(c) (*: *put pressure on*) faire pression (*on* sur), forcer la main (*on* à). they ~ed on him for payment ils ont fait pression sur lui *or* ils lui ont forcé la main pour qu'il paie (*subj*); the editor was ~ing on him for the article l'éditeur faisait pression sur lui pour qu'il écrive l'article.

2 *vt ladder, cycle etc* appuyer (*against, up against* contre), adosser (*against, up against* à). to ~ one's head on sb's shoulder incliner *or* pencher la tête sur l'épaule de qn.

3 *n* inclinaison *f*.

4 *cpd*: lean-to appentis *m*; lean-to garage/shed *etc* garage *m*/cabane *f etc* en appentis.

lean back 1 *vi* se pencher en arrière. to lean back in an armchair se laisser aller en arrière dans un fauteuil; to lean back against sth s'adosser contre *or* à qch.

2 *vt sep chair* pencher en arrière. to lean one's head back pencher la tête en arrière, renverser la tête (en arrière).

lean forward 1 *vi* se pencher en avant.

2 *vt sep* pencher en avant.

lean out 1 *vi* se pencher au dehors. to lean out of the window se pencher par la fenêtre; 'do not lean out' 'ne pas se pencher au dehors'.

2 *vt sep* pencher au dehors. he leant his head out of the window il a passé *or* penché la tête par la fenêtre.

lean over *vi* [*person*] (*forward*) se pencher *or* se courber en avant; (*sideways*) se pencher sur le côté; [*object, tree*] pencher, être penché. to lean over backwards se pencher en arrière; (*fig*) to lean over backwards to help sb* se mettre en quatre *or* se décarcasser* *or* faire des pieds et des mains* pour aider qn.

lean up *vi, vt sep V* lean[1] 1b, 2.

lean[2] [li:n] 1 *adj* (a) *person, animal, meat* maigre.

(b) (*unproductive*) *harvest* maigre, pauvre. this is a ~ year for corn c'est une mauvaise année pour le blé; those were ~ years c'étaient des années de vaches maigres; ~ diet régime *m* maigre; we had a ~ time on a mangé de la vache enragée.

2 *n* [*meat*] maigre *m*.

leaning ['li:nɪŋ] 1 *n* tendance *f* (*towards* à), penchant *m* (*towards* pour). he has artistic ~s il a un penchant pour les arts, il a des tendances artistiques; what are his political ~s? quelles sont ses tendances politiques?

2 *adj wall, building* penché. the L~ Tower of Pisa la tour penchée de Pise.

leanness ['li:nnɪs] *n* maigreur *f*.

leant [lent] *pret, ptp of* lean[1].

leap [li:p] (*vb: pret, ptp* **leaped** *or* **leapt**) 1 *n* (a) (*lit*) saut *m*, bond *m*; (*fig*) bond, pas *m*. to take a ~ bondir, sauter; at one ~ d'un bond; (*fig*) by ~s and bounds à pas de géant; (*fig*) a ~ in the dark un saut dans l'inconnu; (*fig*) a great ~ forward un bond en avant; (*fig*) a giant ~ for mankind un pas de géant pour l'humanité; (*fig*) there has been a ~ in profits this year les profits ont fait un bond cette année.

(b) (*in place-names*) saut *m*; (*also* salmon ~) saut à saumons.

2 *cpd*: leapfrog saute-mouton *m*; to leapfrog over sth franchir qch à saute-mouton; to leapfrog over sb sauter par-dessus qn à saute-mouton; leap year année *f* bissextile.

3 *vi* [*person, animal, fish*] sauter, bondir; [*flames*] jaillir. to ~ in/out *etc* sortir/entrer *etc* d'un bond; he leapt into/out of the car il sauta dans/de la voiture; to ~ over a ditch franchir un fossé d'un bond, sauter (par-dessus) un fossé; to ~ to one's feet se lever d'un bond; (*Mil etc*) to ~ to attention se mettre vivement au garde-à-vous; he leapt into the air il fit un bond (en l'air); the flames leapt into the air les flammes ont jailli *or* se sont élevées dans l'air; he leapt for joy il sauta *or* bondit de joie; (*fig*) her heart leapt son cœur a bondi dans sa poitrine; (*fig*) to ~ to the conclusion that ... conclure immédiatement que ...; you mustn't ~ to conclusions il ne faut pas conclure trop hâtivement; to ~ at the chance sauter sur *or* saisir l'occasion, saisir la balle au bond; to ~ at an offer sauter sur *or* saisir une offre, saisir la balle au bond; *V* look.

4 *vt* (a) *stream, hedge etc* sauter (par-dessus), franchir d'un bond.

(b) *horse* faire sauter.

leap about *vi* gambader. to leap about with excitement sauter de joie.

leap up *vi* (*off ground*) sauter en l'air; (*to one's feet*) se lever d'un bond; [*flame*] jaillir; [*prices etc*] faire un bond. the dog leapt up at him affectionately le chien a sauté affectueusement après lui; the dog leapt up at him and bit him le chien lui a sauté dessus et l'a mordu; he leapt up indignantly il a bondi d'indignation.

leapt [lept] *pret, ptp of* leap.

learn [lɜ:n] *pret, ptp* **learned** *or* **learnt** 1 *vt* (a) (*by study*) *language, lesson, musical instrument* apprendre. to ~ (how) to do sth apprendre à faire qch; to ~ sth by heart apprendre qch par cœur; (*fig*) he's ~t his lesson cela lui a servi de leçon, il vient d'avoir une bonne leçon.

(b) (*find out*) *facts, news, results etc* apprendre. I was sorry to ~ (that) you had been ill j'ai appris avec regret que vous aviez été malade; we haven't yet ~ed whether he recovered nous ne savons toujours pas s'il est guéri.

(c) (‡: *teach*) apprendre. I'll ~ you! je vais t'apprendre, moi!*; that'll ~ you! ça t'apprendra!*

2 *vi* (a) apprendre. we are ~ing about the Revolution at school en classe on étudie *or* fait* la Révolution; it's never too late to ~ il n'est jamais trop tard pour apprendre, on apprend à tout âge; to ~ from experience apprendre par l'expérience; to ~ from one's mistakes tirer la leçon de ses erreurs; (*fig iro*) he'll ~! un jour il comprendra!; (*fig*) I've ~t better *or* a lot since

then je sais à quoi m'en tenir maintenant, maintenant j'ai compris; *V* live[1].

(b) (*hear*) apprendre. **I was sorry to ~ of** *or* **about your illness** j'ai appris avec regret votre maladie.

learn off *vt sep* apprendre par cœur.

learn up *vt sep maths etc* travailler, bûcher*, bosser*. **she learnt up all she could about the district** elle a appris tout ce qu'elle a pu sur la région.

learned ['lɜ:nɪd] *adj person* (*in humanities*) érudit, savant; (*in sciences*) savant; *journal, society, remark, speech* savant; *profession* intellectuel. (*Brit Jur*) **my ~ friend** mon éminent confrère.

learnedly ['lɜ:nɪdlɪ] *adv* avec érudition, savamment.

learner ['lɜ:nə^r] *n* débutant(e) *m(f)*. (*Aut*) **~ (driver)** (conducteur *m*, -trice *f*) débutant(e); **you are a quick ~** vous apprenez vite.

learning ['lɜ:nɪŋ] *n* (*U*) **(a)** (*fund of knowledge*) érudition *f*, savoir *m*, science *f*. **man of (great) ~** (*in humanities*) érudit *m*; (*in sciences*) savant *m*; *V* **little[2], seat.**

(b) (*act*) *[language]* apprentissage *m* (*of* de); *[lesson]* étude *f* (*of* de). **~ develops the memory** apprendre développe la mémoire.

learnt [lɜ:nt] **1** *pret, ptp of* **learn. 2** *adj* (*Psych*) **~ behaviour** traits acquis.

lease [li:s] **1** *n* **(a)** (*Jur: contract, duration*) bail *m*. **long ~** bail à long terme; **99-year ~** bail de 99 ans; **to take a house on ~** prendre une maison à bail.

(b) (*fig*) **the antibiotics have given him a new ~ of life** les antibiotiques lui ont rendu sa vitalité; **the news gave him a new ~ of life** la nouvelle lui a donné un regain de vie, cela lui a donné une nouvelle vigueur; **to take on a new ~ of life** retrouver une nouvelle jeunesse.

2 *vt* **(a)** *[tenant]* louer à bail.

(b) (*also* **~ out**) *[owner]* louer à bail.

3 *cpd*: **leasehold** (*n*) (*contract*) bail *m*; (*property*) propriété louée à bail; (*adj*) *property* loué à bail; (*adv*) à bail; **leaseholder** preneur *m*, -euse *f*; **leasehold reform** révision *f* du bail; (*Econ*) **lease-lend,** (*US*) **lend-lease** prêt-bail *m*.

leash [li:ʃ] *n* (*for dog*) laisse *f*; (*for hawk*) filière *f*, créance *f*. **to keep on a ~** tenir en laisse.

least [li:st] *superl of* **little[2] 1** *adj* (*smallest amount of*) le moins de; (*smallest*) le moindre, la moindre, le plus petit, la plus petite. **he has (the) ~ money** c'est lui qui a le moins d'argent; **the ~ thing upsets her** la moindre chose *or* la plus petite chose la contrarie; **principle of ~ effort** principe *m* du moindre effort; **with the ~ possible expenditure** avec le moins de dépenses possible; **that's the ~ of our worries** c'est le cadet de nos soucis; *V* **line[1]**.

2 *pron* **(a)** le moins. **you've given me the ~** c'est à moi que tu en as donné le moins; **it's the ~ I can do** c'est le moins que je puisse faire, c'est la moindre des choses; **it's the ~ one can expect** c'est la moindre des choses; **what's the ~ you are willing to accept?** quel prix minimum êtes-vous prêt à accepter?; *V* **say.**

(b) (*in phrases*) **at ~** (*with quantity, comparison*) au moins; (*parenthetically*) du moins, tout au moins; **it costs £5 at ~** cela coûte au moins *or* au bas mot 5 livres; **there were at ~ 8 books** il y avait au moins 8 livres; **he's at ~ as old as you** il a au moins votre âge; **he eats at ~ as much as I do** il mange au moins autant que moi; **at ~ it's not raining** du moins *or* au moins il ne pleut pas; **you could at ~ have told me!** tu aurais pu au moins me le dire!; **I can at ~ try** je peux toujours *or* du moins essayer; **he's ill, at ~ that's what he says** il est malade, du moins c'est ce qu'il dit; **at the very ~** au moins, au minimum; **not in the ~!** pas du tout!; **he was not in the ~ tired** *or* **not tired in the ~** il n'était pas le moins du monde fatigué; **it didn't surprise me in the ~** cela ne m'a pas surpris le moins du monde; **it doesn't matter in the ~** cela n'a aucune importance *or* pas la moindre importance; (*Prov*) **~ said soonest mended** moins on en dit mieux on se porte, moins on en dit et mieux ça vaut.

3 *adv* le moins. **the ~ expensive** le moins cher, la moins chère; **the ~ expensive car** la voiture la moins chère; **he did it ~ easily of all** il l'a fait le moins facilement de tous; **she is ~ able to afford it** c'est elle qui peut le moins se l'offrir; **when you are ~ expecting it** quand vous vous y attendez le moins; **he deserves it ~ of all** c'est lui qui le mérite le moins de tous; **~ of all would I wish to offend him** je ne voudrais surtout pas le froisser.

leastways* ['li:stweɪz] *adv*, **leastwise*** ['li:stwaɪz] *adv* du moins, ou plutôt.

leather ['leðə^r] **1** *n* **(a)** (*U*) cuir *m*; *V* **hell, patent** *etc.*

(b) (*also* **wash ~**) peau *f* de chamois; *V* **chamois.**

2 *cpd boots, seat* de *or* en cuir. **leatherbound** *book* relié (en) cuir; **leather goods** articles *mpl* en cuir, maroquinerie *f*; **leatherjacket** larve *f* de la tipule; (*US*) **leatherneck‡** marine *m*, fusilier marin américain.

3 *vt* (*) tanner le cuir à‡.

leatherette [ˌleðə'ret] *n* similicuir *m*.

leathering* ['leðərɪŋ] *n*: **to give sb a ~** tanner le cuir à qn‡.

leathern ['leðən] *adj* (*of leather*) de *or* en cuir; (*like leather*) tanné.

leathery ['leðərɪ] *adj meat, substance* coriace; *skin* parcheminé, tanné.

leave [li:v] (*vb: pret, ptp* **left**) **1** *n* **(a)** (*U: consent*) permission *f*. **by** *or* **with your ~** avec votre permission; **without so much as a by-your-~*** sans même demander la permission; **to ask ~ (from sb) to do sth** demander (à qn) la permission de faire qch.

(b) (*gen: holiday*) congé *m*; (*Mil*) permission *f*. **to be on ~** être en permission *or* en congé; **6 weeks' ~** permission *or* congé de 6 semaines; **on ~ of absence** en congé exceptionnel; (*Mil*) en permission spéciale; *V* **absent, French, sick** *etc.*

(c) (*departure*) congé *m*. **to take (one's) ~ of sb** prendre congé de qn; **I must take my ~** il faut que je prenne congé; (*fig*) **have you taken ~ of your senses?** êtes-vous fou (*f* folle)?, avez-vous perdu la tête?

2 *cpd*: **leavetaking** adieux *mpl*.

3 *vt* **(a)** (*go away from*) *town* quitter, partir de, (*permanently*) quitter; *room, building* sortir de, quitter; *job* quitter. **he left Paris in 1974** il a quitté Paris en 1974; **we left Paris at 6 o'clock** nous sommes partis de Paris *or* nous avons quitté Paris à 6 heures; **he left school in 1974** il a terminé ses études *or* fini sa scolarité en 1974; **he left school at 4 p.m.** il est sorti de l'école *or* il a quitté l'école à 16 heures; **he left home in 1969** il est parti de la maison en 1969; **I left home at 6 o'clock** je suis sorti de chez moi *or* j'ai quitté la maison à 6 heures; **he has left this address** il n'habite plus à cette adresse; **to ~ prison** sortir de prison; **to ~ hospital** sortir de *or* quitter l'hôpital; **to ~ the room** (*go out*) sortir de la pièce; (*Scol euph: go to toilet*) sortir (*euph*); **to ~ the table** se lever de table, quitter la table; **the ship left port** le navire a quitté le port; **the train left the station** le train est sorti de *or* a quitté la gare; (*Rail*) **to ~ the track** dérailler; **the car left the road** la voiture a quitté la route; **I must ~ you** il faut que je vous quitte (*subj*); (*frm*) **you may ~ us** vous pouvez vous retirer (*frm*); **to ~ one's wife** quitter sa femme; *V* **lurch[2]**.

(b) (*forget*) laisser, oublier. **he left his umbrella on the train** il a laissé *or* oublié son parapluie dans le train.

(c) (*deposit, put*) laisser. **I'll ~ the book for you with my neighbour** je laisserai le livre pour vous chez mon voisin; **to ~ the waiter a tip** laisser un pourboire au garçon; **has the postman left anything?** est-ce que le facteur a apporté *or* laissé quelque chose?; *[parcel]* **'to be left till called for'** 'en consigne', 'on passera prendre'; **can I ~ my camera with you?** puis-je vous confier mon appareil-photo?; **he left the children with a neighbour** il a laissé *or* confié les enfants à un voisin; **he ~s a widow and one son** il laisse une veuve et un fils; **to ~ a message for sb** laisser un message à qn; **to ~ word** laisser un mot *or* un message (*with sb for sb* à qn pour qn, *that* que); **he left word with me for Paul to go and see him** il m'a chargé de dire à Paul d'aller le voir; **he left word for Paul to go and see him** il a fait dire à Paul d'aller le voir.

(d) (*allow to remain*) laisser. **to ~ the door open** laisser la porte ouverte; **to ~ 2 pages blank** laisser 2 pages en blanc; **~ it where it is** laisse-le là où il est; **he left it lying on the floor** il l'a laissé par terre; **don't ~ that letter lying around** ne laissez pas traîner cette lettre; **to ~ the phone off the hook** laisser le téléphone décroché; **some things are better left unsaid** il vaut mieux passer certaines choses sous silence; **it left a good impression on me** cela m'a fait bonne impression; **let's ~ it at that** tenons-nous-en là; **I'll ~ it to you to decide** je te laisse le soin de décider; **I('ll) ~ you to judge** je vous laisse juger; **I'll ~ the matter in your hands** je vous laisse vous occuper de l'affaire, je vous laisse le soin d'arranger cela; **shall we go via Paris? — I'll ~ it to you** passerons-nous par Paris? — je m'en remets à vous; **~ it to me!** laissez-moi faire!, je m'en charge!; **I'll ~ you to it*** je vous laisse (à vos occupations); **we left nothing to chance** nous n'avons rien laissé au hasard; **it ~s a lot to be desired** cela laisse beaucoup à désirer; **it left me free for the afternoon** cela m'a laissé l'après-midi de libre, cela m'a libéré pour l'après-midi; **this deal has left me in debt** cette affaire m'a laissé des dettes; **it ~s me cold*** cela me laisse froid *or* de marbre; **~ it alone** n'y touchez pas, laissez ça tranquille*; **~ me alone** laissez-moi tranquille; (*Prov*) **~ well alone** le mieux est l'ennemi du bien (*Prov*); **he was left a widower** il est resté veuf; **to ~ sb on his own** *or* **to himself** laisser qn tout seul; **to ~ sb in peace** *or* **to himself** laisser qn tranquille; **left to himself** *or* **left to his own devices, he'd never have finished** (tout) seul *or* laissé à lui-même, il n'aurait jamais fini; **where gardening's concerned, he ~s us all standing*** pour ce qui est du jardinage, il nous bat tous à plate(s) couture(s)*; **to ~ sb in charge of a house/shop** *etc* laisser à qn la garde d'une maison/d'une boutique *etc*; **the boss is out and he's left me in charge** le patron est sorti et m'a laissé la charge de tout; (*Typ etc*) **to ~ a space** laisser un blanc *or* un espace; **he left half his meal** il a laissé la moitié de son repas; **take it or ~ it** c'est à prendre ou à laisser; *V* **baby, go, shelf, stone.**

(e) (*Math*) **3 from 6 ~s 3** 3 ôté de 6 égale *or* reste 3; **if you take 4 from 7, what are you left with?** si tu enlèves 4 de 7, qu'est-ce qu'il te reste?

(f) to be left rester; **what's left?** qu'est-ce qui reste?; **who's left?** qui est-ce qui reste?; **there'll be none left** il n'en restera pas; **how many are (there) left?** combien est-ce qu'il en reste?; **I've no money left** il ne me reste plus d'argent, je n'ai plus d'argent; **I shall have nothing left** il ne me restera plus rien; **there are 3 cakes left** il reste 3 gâteaux; **are there any left?** est-ce qu'il en reste?; **have you (got) any left?** est-ce qu'il vous en reste?; **nothing was left for me but to sell the house** il ne me restait plus qu'à vendre la maison.

(g) (*in will*) *money* laisser (*to* à); *object, property* laisser, léguer (*to* à).

4 *vi* (*go away*) *[person, train, ship etc]* partir, s'en aller; (*resign*) partir, démissionner, s'en aller. **it's time we left, it's time for us to ~** il est l'heure de partir *or* que nous partions (*subj*); **he left for Paris** il est parti pour Paris; **the ship left for Australia** le bateau est parti *or* a appareillé pour l'Australie; **the train ~s at 4 o'clock** le train part à 4 heures; **he's just left** il sort d'ici, il vient de partir.

leave about, leave around *vt sep clothes, possessions etc* laisser traîner.

leave behind *vt sep* **(a)** (*not take*) *person* laisser, ne pas emmener; *object* laisser, ne pas prendre, ne pas emporter. **he**

left the children behind in Paris il a laissé les enfants à Paris; **you'll get left behind if you don't hurry up** on va te laisser si tu ne te dépêches pas.

(b) (*outdistance*) *opponent in race* distancer; *fellow students etc* dépasser.

(c) (*forget*) *gloves, umbrella etc* laisser, oublier.

leave in *vt sep paragraph, words etc* garder, laisser; *plug* laisser, ne pas enlever. (*Culin*) **leave the cake in for 50 minutes** laisser cuire le gâteau pendant 50 minutes.

leave off 1 *vi* (*: *stop*) s'arrêter. (*in work, reading*) **where did we leave off?** où en étions-nous?, où nous sommes-nous arrêtés?; **leave off!** arrête!, ça suffit!*

2 *vt sep* **(a)** (*: *stop*) cesser, arrêter (*doing* de faire).

(b) *lid* ne pas remettre; *clothes* (*not put back on*) ne pas remettre; (*stop wearing*) cesser de porter, abandonner; (*not put on*) ne pas mettre.

(c) *gas, heating, tap* laisser fermé; *light* laisser éteint.

leave on *vt sep* **(a)** *one's hat, coat etc* garder, ne pas enlever.

(b) *gas, heating, tap* laisser ouvert; *light* laisser allumé.

leave out *vt sep* **(a)** (*omit*) (*accidentally*) oublier, omettre; (*deliberately*) exclure; *line in text, (Mus) note* sauter. **they left him out** ils l'ont exclu, ils ne l'ont pas pris.

(b) (*not put back*) laisser sorti, ne pas ranger. **I left the box out on the table** j'ai laissé la boîte sortie sur la table; **to leave sth out in the rain** laisser qch dehors sous la pluie; **to leave sb out in the cold** (*lit*) laisser qn dans le froid; (*fig*) laisser qn à l'écart.

leave over 1 *vt sep* **(a) this is all the meat that was left over** c'est toute la viande qui reste; **there's nothing left over** il ne reste plus rien; **there's never anything left over** il n'y a jamais de restes; **after each child has 3 there are 2 left over** quand chaque enfant en a pris 3 il en reste 2; **if there's any money left over** s'il reste de l'argent.

(b) (*postpone*) remettre (à plus tard). **let's leave this over till tomorrow** remettons cela à demain.

2 left-overs *npl V* **left[1] 2.**

leaven ['levn] **1** *n* levain *m*. **2** *vt* (*lit*) faire lever. (*fig*) **his speech was ~ed by a few witty stories** son discours était relevé par quelques histoires spirituelles.

leavening ['levnıŋ] *n* (*lit, fig*) levain *m*.

leaves [li:vz] *npl of* **leaf.**

leavings ['li:vıŋz] *npl* restes *mpl*.

Lebanese [ˌlebəˈni:z] **1** *adj* libanais. **2** *n, pl inv* Libanais(e) *m(f)*.

Lebanon ['lebənən] *n* Liban *m*; *V* **cedar.**

lecher ['letʃəʳ] *n* débauché *m*.

lecherous ['letʃərəs] *adj* lubrique, luxurieux, libidineux (*hum*); *look* lascif.

lecherously ['letʃərəslı] *adv* lubriquement, lascivement.

lechery ['letʃərı] *n* (*U*) luxure *f*, lubricité *f*.

lectern ['lektɜ(:)n] *n* lutrin *m*.

lecture ['lektʃəʳ] **1** *n* **(a)** (*gen single occurrence*) conférence *f*; (*gen one of a series*) cours *m* (magistral). **to give a ~** faire *or* donner une conférence, faire un cours (*on* sur); **I went to the ~s on French poetry** j'ai suivi le cours de poésie française; *V* **inaugural.**

(b) (*fig: reproof*) réprimande *f*, sermon *m* (*pej*). **to give** *or* **read sb a ~** sermonner qn.

2 *vi* faire *or* donner une conférence (*to* à, *on* sur), faire un cours (*to* à, *on* sur). (*Univ etc*) **he ~s at 10 o'clock** il fait son cours à 10 heures; **he ~s at Oxford** il est professeur à Oxford; (*Univ*) **he ~s in law** il est professeur de droit; (*Univ etc*) **he's lecturing at the moment** il fait (son) cours en ce moment.

3 *vt* (*reprove*) réprimander, sermonner (*pej*) (*sb for having done* qn pour avoir fait). **he ~d me for my clumsiness** il m'a réprimandé pour ma maladresse.

4 *cpd*: (*Univ*) **lecture course** cours *m*; **lecture hall** amphithéâtre *m*; **lecture notes** notes *fpl* de cours; **lecture room** salle *f* de conférences.

lecturer ['lektʃərəʳ] *n* **(a)** (*speaker*) conférencier *m*, -ière *f*. **(b)** (*Brit Univ*) ≃ maître assistant *m*, maître *m* de conférences. **assistant ~** ≃ assistant(e) *m(f)*; **senior ~** ≃ chargé(e) *m(f)* d'enseignement.

lectureship ['lektʃəʃıp] *n* (*V* **lecturer b**) poste *m* de maître assistant *etc*; (*function*) assistanat *m*, maîtrise *f* de conférences. **he got a ~ at the university** il a été nommé maître assistant *etc* à l'Université.

led [led] *pret, ptp of* **lead[1].**

ledge [ledʒ] *n* (*on wall*) rebord *m*, saillie *f*; (*also* **window ~**) rebord (de la fenêtre); (*on mountain*) saillie, (*bigger*) corniche *f*; (*under sea*) (*ridge*) haut-fond *m*; (*reef*) récif *m*.

ledger ['ledʒəʳ] *n* (*Fin*) grand livre.

lee [li:] **1** *n* côté *m* sous le vent. **in** *or* **under the ~ of** à l'abri de. **2** *adj side of ship, shore* sous le vent.

leech [li:tʃ] *n* (*lit, also fig pej*) sangsue *f*. **he clung like a ~ to me all evening** il m'a collé* comme une sangsue toute la soirée.

leek [li:k] *n* poireau *m*.

leer [lıəʳ] **1** *vi* lorgner. **to ~ at sb** lorgner qn. **2** *n* (*evil*) regard mauvais; (*lustful*) regard concupiscent.

lees [li:z] *npl* [*wine*] lie *f* (*U*).

leeward ['li:wəd] (*esp Naut*) **1** *adj, adv* sous le vent. (*Geog*) **L~ Islands** îles *fpl* Sous-le-Vent. **2** *n* côté *m* sous le vent. **to ~** sous le vent.

leeway ['li:weı] *n* (*Naut*) dérive *f*. (*fig*) **that gives him a certain (amount of) ~** cela lui donne une certaine liberté d'action; (*fig*) **we had 10 minutes' ~ to catch the train** nous avions une marge (de sécurité) de 10 minutes pour attraper le train; (*fig*) **there's a lot of ~ to make up** il y a beaucoup de retard à rattraper.

left[1] [left] **1** *pret, ptp of* **leave. 2** *cpd* (*Brit*) **~ luggage** bagages *mpl* en consigne; **~-luggage (office)** consigne *f*; **~-luggage locker** casier *m* à consigne automatique; **~-overs** restes *mpl*; *V* **leave.**

left[2] [left] **1** *adj bank, side, hand, ear etc* gauche. (*Aut*) **~ hand down!** braquez à gauche!; *V also* **4.**

2 *adv turn, look* à gauche. (*Mil*) **eyes ~!** tête gauche!; **go** *or* **bear** *or* **take** *or* **turn ~ at the church** tournez *or* prenez à gauche à l'église; *V* **right.**

3 *n* **(a)** gauche *f*. **on your ~** à *or* sur votre gauche; **on the ~** sur la gauche, à gauche; **the door on the ~** la porte de gauche; **to drive on the ~** conduire à gauche; (*Aut*) **to keep to the ~** tenir sa gauche; **turn it to the ~** tournez-le vers la gauche *or* à gauche.

(b) (*Pol*) **the L~** la gauche; **he's further to the L~ than I am** il est plus à gauche que moi; **the parties of the L~** (les partis *mpl* de) la gauche.

(c) (*Boxing: punch*) gauche *m*.

4 *cpd*: (*Sport*) **left back** arrière *m* gauche; (*Sport*) **left half** demi *m* gauche; **left-hand** (*adj*) à *or* de gauche; **the left-hand door/page** *etc* la porte/page *etc* de gauche; **left-hand drive car** conduite *f* à gauche (*véhicule*); **this car is left-hand drive** cette voiture a la conduite à gauche; **on the left-hand side** à gauche; **a left-hand turn** un virage à gauche; **left-handed** *person* gaucher; *screw* filetée à gauche; *scissors etc* pour gaucher; (*fig*) **left-handed compliment** (*insincere*) compliment *m* hypocrite; (*ambiguous*) compliment ambigu; **left-hander** (*person*) gaucher *m*, -ère *f*; (*: *blow*) gifle *f or* claque* *f* (assenée de la main gauche); **left wing** (*Mil, Sport*) aile *f* gauche; (*Pol*) gauche *f*; **left-wing** *newspaper, view* de gauche; **he's very left-wing** il est très à gauche; **left-winger** (*Pol*) homme *m or* femme *f* de gauche; (*Sport*) ailier *m* gauche.

leftist ['leftıst] (*Pol*) **1** *n* homme *m or* femme *f* de gauche. **2** *adj* de gauche.

leg [leg] **1** *n* **(a)** [*person, horse*] jambe *f*; [*other animal, bird, insect*] patte *f*. **my ~s won't carry me any further!** je ne tiens plus sur mes jambes!; **to stand on one ~** se tenir sur un pied *or* une jambe; **she's got nice** *or* **good ~s** elle a les jambes bien faites; **to give sb a ~ up** (*lit*) faire la courte échelle à qn; (**fig*) donner un coup de pouce à qn; (*fig*) **he hasn't got a ~ to stand on** il ne peut s'appuyer sur rien, il n'a aucun argument valable; *V* **fast[1], hind[2], last[1], pull** *etc*.

(b) (*Culin*) [*lamb*] gigot *m*; [*beef*] gîte *m*, crosse *f*; [*veal*] sous-noix *f*; [*pork, chicken, frog*] cuisse *f*; [*venison*] cuissot *m*.

(c) [*table etc*] pied *m*; [*trousers, stocking etc*] jambe *f*; *V* **inside.**

(d) (*stage*) [*journey*] étape *f*. (*Ftbl etc*) **first ~ match** *m* aller; **second** *or* **return ~ match** retour; (*Sport: in relay*) **to run/swim the first ~** courir/nager la première distance *or* le premier relai.

2 *cpd*: **leg bone** tibia *m*; (*Med*) **leg iron** appareil *m* (orthopédique); **leg muscle** muscle *m* de la jambe, muscle jambier (*frm*); **leg-pull*** canular *m*; **leg-pulling*** mise *f* en boîte*, canulars *mpl*; **leg-room** place *f* pour les (*or* mes *etc*) jambes; **leg shield** protège-jambe *m*.

3 *vt* (*) **to ~ it** aller à pied, faire le chemin à pied.

legacy ['legəsı] *n* (*Jur*) legs *m*; (*fig*) legs, héritage *m*. (*Jur*) **to leave a ~ to sb** laisser un héritage à qn, faire un legs à qn; (*fig*) **this law is a ~ from medieval times** cette loi est un legs de l'époque médiévale; (*hum*) **this vase is a ~ from the previous tenants** on a hérité ce vase des précédents locataires.

legal ['li:gəl] *adj* **(a)** (*lawful*) *act, decision* légal; *requirements* légitime; *right* légal, légitime. **to acquire ~ status** acquérir un statut légal *or* judiciaire; (*Fin*) **~ currency, ~ tender** monnaie légale; **this note is no longer ~ currency** *or* **tender** ce billet n'a plus cours; **~ document** titre *m* authentique; (*US*) **~ holiday** jour férié.

(b) (*concerning the law*) judiciaire, juridique. **to take ~ action against** intenter un procès à *or* contre; **I am considering taking ~ action** j'envisage d'intenter une action; **to take ~ advice** consulter un homme de loi; **~ adviser** conseiller *m*, -ère *f* juridique; (*Brit*) **~ aid** assistance *f* judiciaire; **~ costs** frais *mpl* de justice; [*bank, firm etc*] **~ department** service *m* du contentieux; **it's a ~ matter** c'est une question juridique *or* de droit; **in ~ matters** en ce qui concerne le droit; **the ~ mind** l'esprit *m* juridique; **a ~ offence** une infraction à la loi; **~ proceedings** procès *m*, poursuites *fpl*; **the ~ process** la procédure; **the ~ profession** les hommes *mpl* de loi; **to go into the ~ profession** faire une carrière juridique *or* de juriste.

legality [lıˈgælıtı] *n* légalité *f*.

legalization [ˌli:gəlaıˈzeıʃən] *n* légalisation *f*.

legalize ['li:gəlaız] *vt* légaliser.

legally ['li:gəlı] *adv* (*lawfully*) légalement; (*in law*) juridiquement. **this contract is ~ binding** c'est un contrat qui lie; **~ valid** légalement valide; **~ responsible** légalement responsable, responsable aux yeux de la loi.

legate ['legıt] *n* légat *m*.

legatee [ˌlegəˈti:] *n* légataire *mf*.

legation [lıˈgeıʃən] *n* légation *f*.

legend ['ledʒənd] *n* (*all senses*) légende *f*.

legendary ['ledʒəndərı] *adj* légendaire.

legerdemain ['ledʒədəˈmeın] *n* prestidigitation *f*.

-legged ['legıd] *adj ending in cpds*: **four-legged** à quatre pattes, quadrupède (*frm*); **bare-legged** aux jambes nues; *V* **three** *etc*.

leggings ['legıŋz] *n* jambières *fpl*, leggings *mpl or fpl or* leggins *mpl or fpl*; (*for baby*) culotte *f* (longue); (*thigh boots*) cuissardes *fpl*. **waterproof ~** jambières imperméables.

leggo‡ [ˌleˈgəʊ] *excl* = **let go;** *V* **go 1b.**

leggy* ['legı] *adj person* aux longues jambes; *animal* aux longues pattes, haut sur pattes. **a gorgeous ~ blonde** une magnifique blonde toute en jambes.

legibility [ˌledʒıˈbılıtı] *n* lisibilité *f*.

legible ['ledʒəbl] *adj* lisible.

legibly ['ledʒəblı] *adv* lisiblement.

legion ['li:dʒən] *n* légion *f* (*also fig*); *V* **foreign.**
legionary ['li:dʒənəri] **1** *n* légionnaire *m.* **2** *adj* de la légion.
legionnaire [ˌli:dʒə'nεəʳ] *n* légionnaire *m.*
legislate ['ledʒısleıt] *vi* légiférer, faire des lois. **to ~ against** faire des lois contre.
legislation [ˌledʒıs'leıʃən] *n* **(a)** (*U*) (*making*) élaboration *f* des lois; (*enacting*) promulgation *f* des lois.
(b) (*law*) loi *f*; (*body of laws*) législation *f*. **to bring in** *or* **introduce ~** faire des lois; **the government is considering ~ against ...** le gouvernement envisage de créer une législation contre ...; **we are in favour of ~ to abolish ...** nous sommes partisans d'une législation qui abolirait ...; **under the present ~** sous la législation actuelle; **that is a ridiculous piece of ~** c'est une loi stupide.
legislative ['ledʒıslətıv] *adj* législatif. **the ~ body** le (corps) législatif.
legislator ['ledʒısleıtəʳ] *n* législateur *m*, -trice *f*.
legislature ['ledʒıslətʃəʳ] *n* (corps *m*) législatif *m.*
legist ['li:dʒıst] *n* légiste *mf.*
legit: [lə'dʒıt] *adj abbr of* **legitimate 1.**
legitimacy [lı'dʒıtıməsı] *n* légitimité *f.*
legitimate [lı'dʒıtımıt] **1** *adj* **(a)** (*Jur etc: lawful*) *action, right, ruler, child, authority* légitime. **for ~ purposes** dans un but légitime, pour des motifs valables.
(b) (*fig*) *argument, cause* juste, bon, valable; *excuse, complaint* légitime, fondé; *reasoning, conclusion* logique. **it would be ~ to think that ...** on serait en droit de penser que ...; **the ~ theatre** le théâtre littéraire.
2 [lı'dʒıtımeıt] *vt* légitimer.
legitimize [lı'dʒıtımaız] *vt* légitimer.
leguminous [le'gju:mınəs] *adj* légumineux.
Leipzig ['laıpzıg] *n* Leipzig.
leisure ['leʒəʳ] **1** *n* (*U*) loisir *m*, temps *m* libre. **he had the ~ in which to go fishing** il avait le loisir d'aller à la pêche; (*hum*) **she's a lady of ~** elle est rentière (*fig hum*); **a life of ~** une vie pleine de loisirs, une vie d'oisiveté (*pej*); **do it at your ~** faites-le quand vous en aurez le temps *or* le loisir, faites-le quand vous aurez du temps libre; **he is not often at ~** il n'a pas souvent de temps libre; **think about it at ~** réfléchissez-y à tête reposée.
2 *cpd*: **in my leisure moments** à mes moments de loisir, pendant mes loisirs; **leisure occupations** loisirs *mpl*; **leisure time** loisir *m*, temps *m* libre.
leisured ['leʒəd] *adj person* qui a beaucoup de loisirs, qui n'a rien à faire; *life, existence* doux (*f* douce), peu fatigant. **the ~ classes** la classe oisive, le beau monde (*pej*).
leisurely ['leʒəlı] **1** *adj pace, movement* lent, mesuré, tranquille; *person* placide, calme, pondéré; *journey, stroll* peu fatigant, fait sans se presser; *occupation* qui ne demande pas beaucoup d'efforts, peu fatigant. **he moved in a ~ way towards the door** il se dirigea vers la porte sans se presser; **to work in a ~ way** travailler sans se dépenser *or* sans faire de gros efforts *or* sans se fouler*.
2 *adv* (*without hurrying*) sans se presser, en prenant tout son temps; (*without exerting o.s.*) sans faire d'effort, sans se fouler*.
leitmotiv ['laıtməʊˌti:f] *n* (*Mus, fig*) leitmotiv *m.*
lem [lem] *n* (*Space*) lem *m*, module *m* lunaire.
lemming ['lemıŋ] *n* lemming *m.*
lemon ['lemən] **1** *n* **(a)** (*fruit*) citron *m*; (*tree*) citronnier *m*; (*colour*) citron; *V* **bitter.**
(b) (:) (*nasty trick*) vacherie: *f*, rosserie* *f*; (*unpleasant woman*) vache: *f*, rosse* *f*; (*ugly girl*) mocheté: *f*. **his car wouldn't go, it was a real ~** sa voiture était une vraie saloperie:, elle ne voulait pas démarrer.
2 *adj* (*in colour*) citron *inv.*
3 *cpd*: (*Brit*) **lemon cheese, lemon curd** (sorte *f* de) crème *f* de citron; **lemon drink** citronnade *f*; **lemon drop** bonbon *m* (acidulé) au citron; **lemon grove** plantation *f* de citronniers; **lemon juice** jus *m* de citron; (*drink*) citron pressé; (*Brit*) **lemon sole** limande-sole *f*; **lemon squash** citronnade *f*, jus *m* de citron; **lemon squeezer** presse-citron *m inv*; **lemon tea** thé *m* au citron; **lemon tree** citronnier *m*; **lemon yellow** (*adj, n*) jaune citron (*m*) *inv.*
lemonade [ˌlemə'neıd] *n* (*still*) citronnade *f*; (*fizzy*) limonade *f.*
lemur ['li:məʳ] *n* maki *m.*
lend [lend] *pret, ptp* **lent 1** *vt* **(a)** *money, possessions* prêter (*to sb* à qn). **to ~ money at 10%** prêter de l'argent à 10%; *V* **lease.**
(b) (*fig*) *importance* prêter, accorder (*to* à); *probability, mystery* donner, conférer (*to* à). **to ~ an ear** écouter, prêter l'oreille; **to ~ one's name to** accorder son patronage à; **he refused to ~ his name to** il a refusé de prêter son nom *or* d'accorder son patronage à; **it would ~ itself to a different treatment** cela se prêterait à un autre traitement; **it doesn't ~ itself to being filmed** cela ne donnerait pas matière à un film; **I shall not ~ myself to your scheme** je ne me prêterai pas à votre projet; *V* **hand, support** *etc.*
2 *cpd*: (*US*) **lend-lease = lease-lend**; *V* **lease 3.**
lend out *vt sep object, book* prêter.
lender ['lendəʳ] *n* prêteur *m*, -euse *f*; *V* **money.**
lending ['lendıŋ] **1** *n* prêt *m*. **bank ~** prêt bancaire. **2** *cpd*: **lending library** bibliothèque *f* de prêt.
length [leŋθ] **1** *n* **(a)** (*U: in space*) longueur *f*. **its ~ was 6 metres, it was 6 metres in ~** cela avait 6 mètres de long; **what is the ~ of the field?, what ~ is the field?** quelle est la longueur du champ?; **overall ~** longueur totale, longueur hors tout; **along the whole ~ of the river** tout au long de la rivière; **what ~ do you want?** quelle longueur vous faut-il?, il vous en faut combien de long?; **what ~ (of cloth) did you buy?** quel métrage (de tissu) as-tu acheté?; **the ship turns in its own ~** le navire vire sur place; (*fig*) **over the ~ and breadth of England** partout dans l'Angleterre, dans toute l'Angleterre; **to go** *or* **measure one's ~ (on the ground), to fall full ~** tomber *or* s'étaler* de tout son long; *V* **arm**[1], **full** *etc.*
(b) (*U*) (*in time etc*) durée *f*; *[book, essay, letter, film, speech]* longueur *f*. **what ~ is the film?** combien dure le film?; **~ of life** durée de vie; **for the whole ~ of his life** pendant toute la durée de sa vie; **for what ~ of time?** pour combien de temps?, pour quelle durée?; **for some ~ of time** pendant un certain temps, pendant quelque temps; **the ~ of time he took to do it** le temps qu'il a mis à le faire; (*Ling*) **the ~ of a syllable** la longueur d'une syllabe; (*Admin*) **~ of service** ancienneté *f*; **4,000 words in ~** de 4.000 mots; **at ~** enfin, à la fin; **at (great) ~** (*for a long time*) fort longuement; (*in detail*) dans le détail, à fond, en long et en large; (*fig*) **he went to the ~ of asking my advice** il est allé jusqu'à me demander conseil; **I've gone to great ~s to get it finished** je me suis donné beaucoup de mal pour le terminer; **he would go to any ~(s) to succeed** il ne reculerait devant rien pour réussir; **I didn't think he would go to such ~s to get the job** je n'aurais pas cru qu'il serait allé jusque-là pour avoir le poste.
(c) (*Sport*) longueur *f*. **to win by a ~** gagner d'une longueur; **he was 2 ~s behind** il avait un retard de 2 longueurs; **the race will be swum over 6 ~s** la course se nagera sur 6 longueurs; **4 ~s of the pool** 4 longueurs de piscine, 4 fois la longueur de la piscine; **he was about 3 car ~s behind me** il était à 3 longueurs de voiture derrière moi.
(d) (*section*) *[rope, wire]* morceau *m*, bout *m*; *[wallpaper]* lé *m*, laize *f*; *[cloth]* pièce *f*, morceau; *[tubing]* morceau, bout, tronçon *m*; *[track]* tronçon. **cut into metre ~s** coupé en morceaux d'un mètre; **I bought several ~s of dress material** j'ai acheté plusieurs métrages *mpl or* hauteurs *fpl* de tissu pour faire une robe; (*Sewing*) **dress/skirt ~** hauteur de robe/de jupe.
2 *cpd*: (*Ling*) **length mark** signe *m* diacritique de longueur.
lengthen ['leŋθən] **1** *vt object* allonger, rallonger; *visit, life* prolonger; (*Ling*) *vowel* allonger.
2 *vi* allonger, rallonger, s'allonger; *[skirts]* rallonger; *[visit etc]* se prolonger. **the days/nights are ~ing** les jours/nuits rallongent; **the intervals between his visits were ~ing** ses visites s'espaçaient.
lengthily ['leŋθılı] *adv* longuement.
lengthways ['leŋθweız], **lengthwise** ['leŋθwaız] **1** *adv* dans le sens de la longueur, en long, longitudinalement. **2** *adj* longitudinal, en longueur.
lengthy ['leŋθı] *adj* (très) long (*f* longue); (*tedious*) interminable. **the book is ~ in places** ce livre a des longueurs.
lenience ['li:nıəns] *n*, **leniency** ['li:nıənsı] *n* (*gen, Jur*) indulgence *f*; (*Pol etc*) clémence *f*.
lenient ['li:nıənt] *adj* (*V* **lenience**) indulgent (*to* envers, pour); clément (*to* envers).
leniently ['li:nıəntlı] *adv* (*V* **lenience**) avec indulgence; avec clémence (*liter*).
Leningrad ['lenıngræd] *n* Leningrad.
lens [lenz] **1** *n* (*for magnifying*) lentille *f*; *[camera]* objectif *m*; *[spectacles]* verre *m*; *[eye]* cristallin *m*; *V* **contact, telephoto, wide. 2** *cpd*: (*Phot*) **lens holder** porte-objectif *m inv*; **lens hood** parasoleil *m.*
lent [lent] *pret, ptp of* **lend.**
Lent [lent] *n* (*Rel*) Carême *m*. **in** *or* **during ~** pendant le Carême, en Carême; **to keep ~** observer le carême, faire carême; **I gave it up for ~** j'y ai renoncé pour le Carême.
Lenten ['lentən] *adj* de carême.
lentil ['lentl] *n* (*Bot, Culin*) lentille *f*. **~ soup** soupe *f* aux lentilles.
leonine ['li:ənaın] *adj* léonin.
leopard ['lepəd] **1** *n* léopard *m*. (*loc*) **the ~ cannot change its spots** on ne peut pas changer sa nature. **2** *cpd*: **leopardskin** peau *f* de léopard; **leopardskin coat** manteau *m* de léopard.
leopardess [ˌlepə(:)'des] *n* léopard *m* femelle.
leotard ['li:ətɑ:d] *n* collant *m* (*de danseur, d'acrobate*).
leper ['lepəʳ] *n* (*Med, fig*) lépreux *m*, -euse *f*. **~ colony** léproserie *f*.
lepidoptera [ˌlepı'dɒptərə] *npl* lépidoptères *mpl.*
leprechaun ['leprəkɔ:n] *n* (*Ir*) lutin *m*, farfadet *m.*
leprosy ['leprəsı] *n* lèpre *f*.
leprous ['leprəs] *adj* lépreux.
lesbian ['lezbıən] **1** *adj* lesbien. **2** *n* lesbienne *f*.
lesbianism ['lezbıənızəm] *n* lesbianisme *m*, homosexualité féminine.
lesion ['li:ʒən] *n* (*Med*) lésion *f*.
less [les] *comp of* **little**[2] **1** *adj, pron* **(a)** (*in amount, size, degree*) moins (de). **~ butter** moins de beurre; **I have ~ than you** j'en ai moins que vous; **I need ~ than that** il m'en faut moins que cela; **even ~** encore moins; **even** *or* **still ~ butter** encore moins de beurre; **I have ~ money than you** j'ai moins d'argent que vous; **much ~ milk** beaucoup moins de lait; **a little ~ cream** un peu moins de crème; **~ and ~** de moins en moins; **~ and ~ money** de moins en moins d'argent; **it costs ~ than the export model** il coûte moins cher que le modèle d'exportation; **it was ~ money than I expected** c'était moins (d'argent) que je n'escomptais; **~ than half the audience** moins de la moitié de l'assistance *or* des auditeurs; **he has little but I have ~** il n'a pas grand-chose mais j'en ai encore moins; **he did ~ to help them than his brother did** il a moins fait *or* fait moins pour les aider que son frère; (*fig*) **he couldn't have done ~ if he'd tried** même en essayant il n'aurait pas pu faire moins *or* moins faire; **I got ~ out of it than you did** j'en ai tiré moins de profit que toi; **of ~ importance** de moindre importance, de moins d'importance; **it took ~ time than I expected** cela a pris moins de temps que je ne pensais; **I have ~ time for reading** j'ai moins le temps de lire, j'ai moins de temps pour lire; **we eat ~ bread than we used to** nous mangeons moins de pain qu'avant; **~ noise please!**

moins de bruit s'il vous plaît!; **with ~ trouble** avec moins de mal; **he knows little German and ~ Russian** il ne sait pas bien l'allemand et encore moins le russe; **we must see ~ of her** il faut que nous la voyions (*subj*) moins souvent; **it is ~ than perfect** on ne peut pas dire que ce soit parfait; **in ~ than a month** en moins d'un mois; **in ~ than no time*** en un rien de temps, en moins de deux*; **not ~ than one kilo** pas moins d'un kilo; **a sum ~ than 10 francs** une somme de moins de 10 F; **it's ~ than you think** c'est moins que vous ne croyez; **I won't sell it for ~ than £10** je ne le vendrai pas à *or* pour moins de 10 livres; **can't you let me have it for ~?** vous ne pouvez pas me le laisser à moins?; **~ of your cheek!*** un peu moins de toupet!*

(b) (*in phrases*) **with no ~ skill than enthusiasm** avec non moins d'habileté que d'enthousiasme; **no ~ a person than the Prime Minister** rien moins que le Premier ministre; **he's bought a car, no ~*** il s'est payé une voiture, rien que ça*; **I was told the news by the bishop, no ~*** c'est l'évêque, s'il vous plaît*, qui m'a appris la nouvelle; **he has no ~ than 4 months' holiday a year** il a au moins *or* au bas mot 4 mois de vacances par an; **it costs no ~ than £100** ça ne coûte pas moins de 100 livres; **I think no ~ of him** *or* **I think none the ~ of him** *or* **I don't think any (the) ~ of him for that** il n'est pas descendu dans mon estime pour autant; **I have so much ~ money nowadays** j'ai tellement moins d'argent maintenant; **there will be so much the ~ to pay** il y aura autant de moins à payer; **the ~ said about it the better** mieux vaut ne pas en parler; **the ~ you buy the ~ you spend** moins vous achetez moins vous dépensez; **nothing ~ than** rien moins que, tout simplement; **he's nothing ~ than a thief** il n'est rien moins qu'un voleur, ce n'est qu'un voleur; **nothing ~ than a bomb would move them** il faudrait au moins une bombe pour les faire bouger; **nothing ~ than a public apology will satisfy him** il ne lui faudra rien moins que des excuses publiques pour le satisfaire; **it's nothing ~ than disgraceful** le moins qu'on puisse dire c'est que c'est une honte.

2 *adv* **(a)** moins. **you must eat ~** vous devez moins manger, il faut que vous mangiez (*subj*) moins; **I must see you ~** il faut que je vous voie moins souvent; **to grow ~** diminuer; **that's ~ important** c'est moins important, ça n'est pas si important; **~ and ~** de moins en moins; **~ regularly/often** moins régulièrement/souvent; **it's ~ expensive than you think** c'est moins cher que vous ne croyez; **whichever is the ~ expensive** le moins cher quel qu'il soit; **he is ~ well known** il est moins (bien) connu; **he was ~ hurt than frightened** il a eu plus de peur que de mal; **the problem is ~ one of capital than of personnel** ce n'est pas tant *or* c'est moins un problème de capital qu'un problème de personnel.

(b) (*in phrases*) **the ~ he works the ~ he earns** moins il travaille moins il gagne; **the ~ you worry about it the better** le moins vous vous ferez du souci à ce sujet et le mieux ça vaudra; **he was (all) the ~ pleased as he'd refused to give his permission** il était d'autant moins content qu'il avait refusé son autorisation; **he wasn't expecting me but he was none the ~ pleased to see me** il ne m'attendait pas mais il n'en fut pas moins content de me voir; **she is no ~ intelligent than you** elle n'est pas moins intelligente que vous; **he criticized the director no ~ than the caretaker** il a critiqué le directeur tout autant que le concierge; **he was ~ annoyed than amused** il était moins fâché qu'amusé; **it is ~ a short story than a novel** c'est moins une nouvelle qu'un roman; *V* **more**.

3 *prep* moins. **~ 10% discount** moins 10% de remise; **in a year ~ 4 days** dans un an moins 4 jours.

...less [lɪs] *adj ending in cpds*: **hatless** sans chapeau; **childless** sans enfants.

lessee [leˈsiː] *n* preneur *m*, -euse *f* (à bail).

lessen [ˈlesn] **1** *vt* (*gen*) diminuer; *cost* réduire; *anxiety, pain* atténuer; *effect, shock* amortir; (*Pol*) *tension* relâcher. **2** *vi* diminuer, s'amoindrir; *[pain]* s'atténuer; *[tension]* se relâcher.

lessening [ˈlesnɪŋ] *n* (*U*) diminution *f*, amoindrissement *m*. (*Pol*) **~ of tension** détente *f*.

lesser [ˈlesəʳ] *adj* moindre. **to a ~ degree** *or* **extent** à un moindre degré, à un degré moindre; **the ~ of two evils** le moindre de deux maux; (*hum*) **we ~ mortals*** *or* **beings*** nous (autres) simples mortels (*hum*).

lesson [ˈlesn] *n* **(a)** (*lit*) leçon *f*, cours *m*, classe *f*, (*fig*) leçon. **a French/geography** *etc* **~** une leçon *or* un cours de français/de géographie *etc*; **to have** *or* **take ~s in** prendre des leçons de; **to give ~s in** donner des leçons de; **we have ~s from 9 to midday** nous avons classe *or* cours de 9 heures à midi; **~s start at 9 o'clock** la classe commence à 9 heures; (*fig*) **I'll teach you a ~!** je vais t'apprendre!; **that will teach him a ~** cela lui donnera une bonne leçon, cela lui servira de leçon; **let that be a ~ to you!** que cela vous serve de leçon!; *V* **driving, learn, private** *etc*.

(b) (*Rel*) leçon *f*; *V* **read**[1].

lessor [leˈsɔːʳ] *n* bailleur *m*, -eresse *f*.

lest [lest] *conj* **(a)** (*for fear that*) de peur *or* de crainte de + *infin*, de peur *or* de crainte que (+ne) + *subj*. **he took the map ~ he should get lost** il a pris la carte de peur *or* crainte de se perdre; **I gave him the map ~ he should get lost** je lui ai donné la carte de peur *or* de crainte qu'il (ne) se perde; (*on war memorial etc*) **'~ we forget'** 'In memoriam'.

(b) (*liter*) **I was afraid ~ he should** *or* **might fall** je craignais qu'il ne tombe (*subj*) *or* ne tombât (*frm*).

let[1] [let] *pret, ptp* **let 1** *vt* **(a)** (*allow*) laisser, permettre; (*cause to*) laisser, faire. **to ~ sb do sth** laisser qn faire qch; **he wouldn't ~ us** il n'a pas voulu (nous le permettre); **she wanted to help but her mother wouldn't ~ her** elle voulait aider mais sa mère ne l'a pas laissée faire; **I won't ~ you be treated like that** je ne permettrai pas qu'on vous traite (*subj*) de cette façon; **I won't ~ it be said that ...** je ne permettrai pas que l'on dise que ...; **who ~ you into the house?** qui vous a fait entrer dans la maison?; **to ~ sb into a secret** faire entrer qn dans un secret, mettre qn au courant d'un secret; (*fig*) **to ~ sb off (doing) sth** dispenser qn de (faire) qch; **don't ~ it get you down*** n'aie pas le cafard *or* ne te laisse pas démoraliser pour autant*; **don't ~ me forget** rappelle-moi, fais-moi penser; **don't ~ the fire go out** ne laisse pas s'éteindre le feu; **~ me have a look** laissez-moi regarder *or* voir, faites voir; **~ me help you** laissez-moi vous aider, attendez que je vous aide* (*subj*); **~ me tell you ...** que je vous dise ... *or* raconte (*subj*) ...; **when can you ~ me have it?** quand est-ce que je pourrai l'avoir? *or* le prendre?; **~ him have it!** (*give*) donnez-le-lui!; (*‡:shoot*) règle-lui son compte!*; **~ him be!** laisse-le (tranquille)!; **(just you) ~ me catch you stealing again*** que je t'attrape (*subj*) *or* t'y prenne encore à voler; **the hunted man ~ himself be seen** l'homme traqué s'est laissé repérer; **I ~ myself be persuaded** je me suis laissé convaincre; *V* **alone, fly**[3], **go, know** *etc*.

(b) (*used to form imper of 1st person*) **~ us** *or* **~'s go for a walk** allons nous promener; **~'s go!** allons-y!; **~'s get out of here!** filons!, fichons le camp (d'ici)!*; **don't ~'s** *or* **~'s not start yet** ne commençons pas encore; **don't ~ me keep you** que je ne vous retienne pas; (*Rel*) **~ us pray** prions; **~ me see (now) ...** voyons ...; **~ me think** laissez-moi réfléchir, que je réfléchisse*.

(c) (*used to form imper of 3rd person*) **if he wants the book, ~ him come and get it himself** s'il veut le livre, qu'il vienne le chercher lui-même *or* il n'a qu'à venir le chercher lui-même; **~ him say what he likes, I don't care** qu'il dise ce qu'il veut, ça m'est égal; **~ no one believe that I will change my mind** que personne ne s'imagine (*subj*) que je vais changer d'avis; **~ that be a warning to you** que cela vous serve d'avertissement; **~ there be light** que la lumière soit; **just ~ them try!** qu'ils essaient (*subj*) un peu!; (*Math*) **~ x equal 2y** soit x égal à 2y.

(d) (*Med*) **to ~ blood** tirer du sang, faire une saignée.

(e) to ~ a window/door into a wall percer *or* ouvrir une fenêtre/porte dans un mur.

(f) (*hire out*) *house etc* louer, mettre en location. **'flat to ~'** 'appartement à louer'; **'to ~', 'to be ~'** 'à louer'.

2 *n [house etc]* location *f*. **I'm looking for a long/short ~ for my villa** je cherche à louer ma villa pour une longue/brève période.

3 *cpd*: **let alone** (*used as conj*) *V* **alone d**; **let-down*** déception *f*; **what a let-down!*** quelle déception!, cela promettait pourtant bien!; **the film was a let-down* after the book** voir le film après avoir lu le livre, quelle déception!; **let-up*** (*decrease*) diminution *f*; (*stop*) arrêt *m*; (*respite*) relâchement *m*, répit *m*; **if there is a let-up* in the rain** si la pluie s'arrête un peu; **he worked 5 hours without (a) let-up*** il a travaillé 5 heures d'affilée *or* sans s'arrêter; **he needs a let-up*** il a besoin d'une détente *or* de se détendre un peu; **there will be no let-up* in my efforts** je ne relâcherai pas mes efforts.

let away *vt sep* (*allow to leave*) laisser partir. **the headmaster let the children away early today** le directeur a laissé partir *or* a renvoyé les enfants tôt aujourd'hui; (*fig*) **you can't let him away with that!** tu ne peux pas le laisser s'en tirer comme ça!

let down 1 *vt sep* **(a)** *window* baisser; *one's hair* dénouer, défaire; *dress* rallonger; *hem* lâcher; *tyre* dégonfler; (*on rope etc*) *person, object* descendre. (*fig: not punish too hard*) **he let me down gently** il n'a pas été trop sévère avec moi; *V also* **hair**.

(b) (*disappoint, fail*) faire faux bond à, décevoir. **we're expecting you on Sunday, don't let us down** nous vous attendons dimanche, ne nous faites pas faux bond *or* nous comptons sur vous; **he's let me down several times** il m'a déçu plusieurs fois *or* à plusieurs reprises; **that shop has let me down before** j'ai déjà été déçu par cette boutique; **the car let me down** la voiture m'a joué un *or* des tour(s); **my watch never lets me down** ma montre ne se détraque jamais; **you've let the team down** ta façon de jouer a beaucoup déçu *or* desservi l'équipe; (*fig*) **you've let the side down** tu ne nous (*or* leur) as pas fait honneur; **the weather let us down** le beau temps n'a pas été de la partie.

2 let-down* *n V* **let**[1] **3**.

let in *vt sep* **(a)** *person, cat* faire entrer, laisser entrer, ouvrir (la porte) à. **can you let him in?** pouvez-vous lui ouvrir (la porte)?; **the maid let him in** la bonne lui a ouvert la porte *or* l'a fait entrer; **he pleaded with us to let him in** il nous a suppliés de le laisser entrer *or* de lui ouvrir (la porte); **he let himself in with a key** il a ouvert (la porte) *or* il est entré avec une clef; **to let in water** *[shoes, tent]* prendre l'eau; *[roof]* laisser entrer *or* passer la pluie; **the curtains let the light in** les rideaux laissent entrer la lumière; **this camera lets the light in** cet appareil-photo laisse passer la lumière; (*Aut*) **to let the clutch in** embrayer.

(b) (*fig*) **see what you've let me in for now!** tu vois dans quelle situation tu me mets maintenant!; **if I'd known what you were letting me in for I'd never have come** si j'avais su dans quoi tu allais m'entraîner je ne serais jamais venu; **you're letting yourself in for trouble** tu te prépares des ennuis; **you don't know what you're letting yourself in for** tu ne sais pas à quoi tu t'engages; **he let me in for helping at the camp** je me suis retrouvé à cause de lui contraint d'aider au camp; **I let myself in for doing the washing-up** je me suis laissé coincer pour la corvée de vaisselle; **I got let in for a £5 donation** j'ai dû donner 5 livres.

(c) to let sb in on a secret/a plan faire entrer qn dans un secret/un plan, mettre qn au courant d'un secret/d'un plan; **can't we let him in on it?** ne peut-on pas le mettre au courant?

let off *vt sep* **(a)** (*cause to explode, fire etc*) *bomb* faire éclater; *firework* tirer, faire partir; *firearm* faire partir.

(b) (*release*) dégager, lâcher. **to let off steam** *[boiler, engine]* lâcher *or* dégager de la vapeur; (**fig*) *[person]* (*anger*) décharger sa bile; (*excitement*) se défouler*.

(c) (*allow to leave*) laisser partir. **they let the children off early today** aujourd'hui ils ont laissé partir *or* renvoyé les enfants de bonne heure; **will you please let me off at 3 o'clock?** pourriez-vous s'il vous plaît me laisser partir à 3 heures?; (*fig*) **if you don't want to do it, I'll let you off** si tu ne veux pas le faire, je t'en dispense.

(d) (*not punish*) ne pas punir, faire grâce à. **he let me off** il ne m'a pas puni; **I'll let you off this time** je vous fais grâce *or* je ferme les yeux pour cette fois; **the headmaster let him off with a warning** le directeur lui a seulement donné un avertissement; **he was let off with a fine** il s'en est tiré avec une amende, il en a été quitte pour une amende; **to let sb off lightly** laisser qn s'en tirer à bon compte.

(e) *rooms etc* louer. **the house has been let off in flats** la maison a été louée en plusieurs appartements.

let on* **1** *vi* (*admit, acknowledge*) dire, avouer, vendre la mèche. **don't let on about what they did** ne va pas raconter *or* dire ce qu'ils ont fait; **I won't let on** je ne dirai rien, je garderai ça pour moi; **they knew the answer but they didn't let on** ils connaissaient la réponse mais ils n'ont pas pipé; **don't let on!** motus!; **he passed me in the street but he didn't let on** il m'a croisé dans la rue mais il a fait comme s'il ne m'avait pas vu.

2 *vt sep* **(a)** (*admit, acknowledge*) dire, avouer, aller raconter (*that* que). **don't let on that you've spoken to her** ne va pas raconter *or* dire que tu lui as parlé.

(b) (*pretend*) prétendre, raconter (*that* que).

let out **1** *vi*: **to let out at sb** (*with fists, stick etc*) envoyer des coups à qn; (*abuse*) injurier qn; (*speak angrily to*) attaquer qn; (*scold*) réprimander qn sévèrement.

2 *vt sep* **(a)** (*allow to leave*) *person, cat* faire *or* laisser sortir; (*release*) *prisoner* relâcher; *sheep, cattle* faire sortir (*of* de); *caged bird* lâcher. **let me out!** laissez-moi sortir!; **I'll let you out** je vais vous ouvrir la porte; **the maid let me out** la bonne m'a ouvert la porte *or* m'a reconduit à la porte; **the watchman let me out** le veilleur m'a fait sortir; **he let himself out quietly** il est sorti sans faire de bruit; **can you let yourself out?** vous m'excuserez de ne pas vous reconduire?; **they are let out of school at 4** on les fait sortir de l'école *or* on les libère à 16 heures; **to let the air out of a tyre** dégonfler un pneu; **to let the water out of the bath** vider l'eau de la baignoire; *V* **cat.**

(b) *fire, candle* laisser s'éteindre.

(c) (*reveal*) *secret, news* laisser échapper, révéler. **don't let it out that ...** ne va pas raconter que ... .

(d) *shout, cry* laisser échapper. **to let out a laugh** faire entendre un rire.

(e) *dress* élargir; *seam* lâcher. **to let one's belt out by 2 holes** desserrer sa ceinture de 2 crans.

(f) (*remove suspicion from*) disculper, mettre hors de cause; (*exclude*) exclure, éliminer. **his alibi lets him out** son alibi le met hors de cause; **if it's a bachelor you need that lets me out** si c'est un célibataire qu'il vous faut ça me met hors du coup* *or* je ne peux pas faire votre affaire.

(g) *house etc* louer.

let past *vt sep person, vehicle, animal, mistake* laisser passer.

let through *vt sep vehicle, person, light* laisser passer.

let up **1** *vi [rain]* diminuer; *[cold weather]* s'adoucir. **he didn't let up until he'd finished** il ne s'est accordé aucun répit avant d'avoir fini; **she worked all night without letting up** elle a travaillé toute la nuit sans relâche; **what a talker she is, she never lets up!** quelle bavarde, elle n'arrête pas!; **to let up on sb*** lâcher la bride à qn.

2 *vt sep* (*allow to rise*) **to let sb up** permettre à qn de se lever.

3 let-up* *n V* **let[1] 3.**

let[2] [let] *n* **(a)** (*Tennis: also* ~ **ball**) balle *f* let. ~! net!, let! **(b)** (*Jur*) **without ~ or hindrance** librement, sans empêchement aucun.

lethal ['li:θəl] *adj poison, dose, blow, wound* mortel, fatal; *effect* fatal; *weapon* meurtrier. (*fig*) **don't touch this coffee, it's ~!*** ne bois pas ce café, il est atroce!*

lethargic [le'θɑ:dʒɪk] *adj person, movement* léthargique; *atmosphere, heat* qui endort.

lethargy ['leθədʒɪ] *n* léthargie *f.*

Lett [let] = **Latvian.**

letter ['letə[r]] **1** *n* **(a)** (*of alphabet*) lettre *f.* **the ~ L** la lettre L; **it was printed in ~s 15 cm high** c'était écrit en lettres de 15 cm de haut; **he's got a lot of ~s after his name*** il a des tas* de diplômes (*or* de décorations *etc*); (*fig*) **the ~ of the law** la lettre de la loi; **he followed the instructions to the ~** il a suivi les instructions à la lettre *or* au pied de la lettre; *V* **block, capital, red** *etc.*

(b) (*written communication*) lettre *f.* **I wrote her a ~ yesterday** je lui ai écrit une lettre hier; **have you any ~s to post?** avez-vous des lettres à poster?; **were there any ~s for me?** y avait-il du courrier *or* des lettres pour moi?; **he was invited by ~** il a reçu une invitation écrite; **the news came in a ~ from her brother** une lettre de son frère annonçait la nouvelle; (*Comm*) **~ of acknowledgement** lettre accusant réception; (*Admin*) **~s of credence** lettres de créance; (*Fin*) **~ of credit** lettre de crédit; **~ of introduction** lettre de recommandation; **~s patent** lettres patentes; (*as publication*) **'The L~s of Virginia Woolf'** 'La correspondance *or* Les lettres de Virginia Woolf'; *V* **covering, love, open** *etc.*

(c) (*learning*) **~s** (belles-)lettres *fpl*; **man of ~s** homme *m* de lettres.

(d) (*US Scol*) distinctions *fpl* (*pour succès sportifs*).

2 *vt* **(a)** (*put ~ on*) **I've ~ed the packets according to the order they arrived in** j'ai inscrit des lettres sur les paquets selon leur ordre d'arrivée; **she ~ed the envelopes from A to M** elle a marqué les enveloppes de A à M.

(b) (*engrave*) graver (des lettres sur). **the book cover was ~ed in gold** la couverture du livre portait une inscription en lettres d'or; **the case is ~ed with my initials** l'étui est gravé à mes initiales, mes initiales sont gravées sur l'étui.

3 *cpd*: **letter bomb** lettre piégée; (*esp Brit*) **letterbox** boîte *f* aux *or* à lettres; (*Brit*) **letter-card** carte-lettre *f*; **letterhead** en-tête *m*; **letter opener** coupe-papier *m inv*; **letter paper** papier *m* à lettres; (*US*) **to be letter-perfect in sth** savoir qch sur le bout du doigt; (*Typ*) **letterpress** (*method*) typographie *f*; (*text*) texte imprimé; **he's a good/bad letter-writer** c'est un bon/mauvais correspondant *or* épistolier (*hum*).

lettered ['letəd] *adj person* lettré; *V also* **letter.**

lettering ['letərɪŋ] *n* (*U*) (*engraving*) gravure *f*; (*letters*) caractère *m* (*U*).

letting ['letɪŋ] *n* **(a)** *[flat etc]* location *f.* **(b)** *V* **blood 3.**

lettuce ['letɪs] *n* (*Bot*) laitue *f*; (*Culin*) laitue, salade *f.* **would you like some more ~?** veux-tu reprendre de la laitue? *or* de la salade?

leukaemia, (*US*) **leukemia** [lu:'ki:mɪə] *n* leucémie *f.*

Levant [lɪ'vænt] *n* Levant *m.*

levee[1] ['levɪ] *n* (*raised riverside of silt*) levée naturelle; (*man-made embankment*) levée, digue *f*; (*ridge surrounding field*) digue; (*landing place*) quai *m.*

levee[2] [le'veɪ] *n* (*Hist*) réception royale (*pour hommes*); (*at royal bedside*) lever *m* (du roi). (*US*) **a presidential ~** une réception présidentielle.

level ['levl] **1** *n* **(a)** (*height: lit, fig*) niveau *m*, hauteur *f*; (*scale*) niveau, échelon *m.* **the water reached a ~ of 10 metres** l'eau a atteint une hauteur de 10 mètres; **water finds its own ~** l'eau trouve son niveau; **the child will find his own ~** l'enfant trouvera son niveau; **at roof ~** au niveau du toit; (*fig*) **the teacher came down to their ~** le professeur s'est mis à leur niveau; (*fig*) **he's far above my ~** il est d'un niveau bien supérieur au mien; **I'm not on his ~ at all** je ne suis pas du tout à son niveau; **his ability is on a ~ with** *or* **on the same ~ as that of his schoolmates** ses capacités sont du même niveau que celles de ses camarades de classe; **that dirty trick is on a ~ with the other one he played** ce mauvais coup est (bien) à la hauteur du *or* vaut le précédent; **social/intellectual ~** niveau social/intellectuel; (*Admin, Pol etc*) **at a higher/lower ~** à un niveau *or* échelon supérieur/inférieur; **top-~ talks** conférence *f* au sommet; **at departmental ~** à l'échelon départemental; *V* **eye, knee, sea** *etc.*

(b) (*Aut, Rail*) palier *m.* **speed on the ~** vitesse *f* en palier; (*fig*) **I'm telling you on the ~*** je te le dis franchement; (*fig*) **is this on the ~?*** est-ce que c'est régulier? *or* réglo?‡; (*fig*) **is he on the ~?*** est-ce qu'il joue franc jeu?, est-ce qu'il est fair-play?

(c) (*also* **spirit ~**) niveau *m* à bulle (d'air).

(d) (*flat place*) terrain plat.

2 *adj* **(a)** (*flat; not bumpy; not sloping*) *surface* plat, plan, uni. **~ ground** terrain plat *or* plan *or* uni; **it's dead ~** c'est parfaitement plat; **the tray must be absolutely ~** il faut que le plateau soit absolument horizontal; **hold the stick ~** tiens le bâton horizontal *or* à l'horizontale; **a ~ spoonful** une cuillerée rase; **to do one's ~ best (to do sth)*** faire tout son possible *or* faire de son mieux (pour faire qch).

(b) (*at same standard, equal*) à égalité. **the 2 contestants are dead ~** les 2 participants sont exactement à égalité; **to be ~ with** (*in race*) être à la hauteur de *or* à la même hauteur que; (*in league*) être à égalité avec, avoir le même nombre de points que; (*in one's studies, achievements etc*) être au niveau de *or* au même niveau que; (*in salary, rank*) être à l'échelon de *or* au même échelon que; **to draw ~ with** (*in race*) arriver à la hauteur de *or* à la même hauteur que, rejoindre, rattraper; (*in league*) arriver dans la même position que, arriver au même score que; (*in one's studies, achievements etc*) arriver au niveau de *or* au même niveau que; (*in salary, rank*) arriver au niveau de *or* au même niveau que, arriver au même échelon que; **to be ~ in seniority with** avoir la même ancienneté que, être au même niveau d'ancienneté que; **the dining room is ~ with the garden** la salle à manger est de plain-pied avec le jardin; **~ with the ground** au niveau du sol, à ras du sol; **hold the 2 sticks absolutely ~** tiens les 2 bâtons exactement à la même hauteur.

(c) (*steady*) *voice, tones* calme, assuré; *judgment* sain, raisonné. (*fig*) **to keep a ~ head** garder tout son sang-froid; *V also* **3.**

3 *cpd*: (*Brit Rail*) **level crossing** passage *m* à niveau; **level-headed** équilibré; (*Brit*) **they were level-pegging** ils étaient à égalité.

4 *vt* **(a)** (*make level*) *site, ground* niveler, aplanir; *quantities* répartir également; (*demolish*) *building, town* raser. **to ~ sth to the ground** raser qch.

(b) **to ~ a blow at sb** allonger un coup de poing à qn; **to ~ a gun at sb** braquer *or* pointer un pistolet sur qn; **to ~ an accusation at sb** lancer *or* porter une accusation contre qn.

5 *vi* (*US**) **I'll ~ with you** je vais être franc (*f* franche) avec vous, je ne vais rien vous cacher; **you're not ~ling with me about what you bought** tu ne me dis pas tout ce que tu as acheté.

level down **1** *vt sep* (*lit*) *surface* aplanir, raboter; (*fig*) *standards* niveler par le bas.

2 levelling down *n V* **levelling 3.**

level off **1** *vi [curve on graph, statistics, results, prices etc]* se stabiliser; *[aircraft]* amorcer le vol en palier.

2 levelling off *n V* **levelling 3.**

level out **1** *vi [curve on graph, statistics, results, prices etc]* se stabiliser.

2 *vt sep* niveler, égaliser.

level up **1** *vt sep* (*lit*) *ground* niveler; (*fig*) *standards* niveler par le haut.

2 levelling up *n V* **levelling 3.**

leveller, (*US*) **leveler** ['levlə[r]] *n*: **poverty is a great ~** tous les hommes sont égaux dans la misère.

levelling ['levlɪŋ] 1 *n* (*U: lit, fig*) nivellement *m*.
2 *adj* (*fig*) *process, effect* de nivellement.
3 *cpd*: **levelling down** nivellement *m* par le bas; **levelling off** égalisation *f*, nivellement *m*; **levelling rod, levelling staff** mire *f*, jalon-mire *m*; **levelling up** nivellement *m* par le haut.

lever ['li:vəʳ] 1 *n* (*lit, fig*) levier *m*; *V* **gear**.
2 *vt*: to ~ sth into position mettre qch en place (à l'aide d'un levier).

lever out *vt sep*: **to lever sth out** extraire qch au moyen d'un levier; (*fig*) **he levered himself out of the chair** il s'est extirpé* du fauteuil; **they're trying to lever him out of his position as manager*** ils essaient de le déloger de son poste de directeur.

lever up *vt sep* soulever au moyen d'un levier. (*fig*) **he levered himself up on one elbow** il s'est soulevé sur un coude.

leverage ['li:vərɪdʒ] *n* (*lit*) force *f* (de levier); (*fig: influence*) influence *f*, prise *f* (*on or with sb* sur qn).

leveret ['levərɪt] *n* levraut *m*.

leviathan [lɪ'vaɪəθən] *n* (*Bible*) Léviathan *m*; (*fig: ship/organization etc*) navire/organisme *etc* géant.

Levis ['li:vaɪz] *npl* ® Levis *m* ®.

levitate ['levɪteɪt] 1 *vi* se soulever *or* être soulevé par lévitation.
2 *vt* soulever *or* élever par lévitation.

levitation [ˌlevɪ'teɪʃən] *n* lévitation *f*.

levity ['levɪtɪ] *n* **(a)** (*frivolity*) manque *m* de sérieux, légèreté *f*. **(b)** (*fickleness*) inconstance *f*.

levy ['levɪ] 1 *n* **(a)** (*Fin*) (*act*) taxation *f*; (*tax*) impôt *m*, taxe *f*; (*amount*) taxation; *V* **capital**.
(b) (*Mil*) (*act*) levée *f*, enrôlement *m*; (*troops*) troupes enrôlées, levée.
2 *vt* **(a)** (*impose*) *tax* prélever, mettre (*on sth* sur qch); *fine* infliger, imposer (*on sb* à qn).
(b) (*collect*) *taxes, contributions* percevoir, recueillir.
(c) (*Mil*) **to ~ troops/an army** lever des troupes/une armée; **to ~ war (on or against)** faire la guerre (à).

levy on *vt fus* (*Jur*) **to levy on sb's property** saisir (les biens de) qn.

lewd [lu:d] *adj* obscène, lubrique.

lewdly ['lu:dlɪ] *adv* de façon obscène.

lewdness ['lu:dnɪs] *n* obscénité *f*, lubricité *f*.

lexical ['leksɪkəl] *adj* lexical.

lexicographer [ˌleksɪ'kɒgrəfəʳ] *n* lexicographe *mf*.

lexicographical [ˌleksɪkəʊ'græfɪkəl] *adj* lexicographique.

lexicography [ˌleksɪ'kɒgrəfɪ] *n* lexicographie *f*.

lexicologist [ˌleksɪ'kɒlədʒɪst] *n* lexicologue *mf*.

lexicology [ˌleksɪ'kɒlədʒɪ] *n* lexicologie *f*.

lexicon ['leksɪkən] *n* lexique *m*.

liability [ˌlaɪə'bɪlɪtɪ] *n* **(a)** (*U*) responsabilité *f*. **don't admit ~ for the accident** n'acceptez pas la responsabilité de l'accident; **his ~ for the company's debts was limited to £50,000** sa responsabilité quant aux dettes de la compagnie était limitée à 50.000 livres; *V* **limited**.
(b) (*U*) **~ for tax/for paying tax** assujettissement *m* à l'impôt/au paiement de l'impôt; **~ for military service** obligations *fpl* militaires.
(c) (*Fin: debts*) **liabilities** obligations *fpl*, engagements *mpl*, passif *m*; **assets and liabilities** actif *m* et passif; **to meet one's liabilities** faire face à ses engagements.
(d) (*handicap*) handicap *m*, poids mort. **this car is a ~ for us** cette voiture nous coûte plus qu'elle ne nous sert; **he's a real ~** il nous handicape plutôt qu'autre chose*, c'est un vrai boulet.

liable ['laɪəbl] *adj* **(a)** (*likely*) **to be ~ to do** risquer de faire, avoir des chances de faire; **the pond is ~ to freeze** l'étang risque de *or* a tendance à geler; **it's ~ to explode** cela risque d'exploser; **he's ~ to refuse to do it** il est possible qu'il refuse (*subj*) de le faire; **he is ~ not to come** il est probable qu'il ne viendra pas; **we are ~ to get shot at** on risque de se faire tirer dessus; **we are ~ to be in London next week** nous pourrions bien nous trouver à Londres la semaine prochaine; **it's ~ to be hot** il se peut qu'il fasse *or* il pourrait faire très chaud.
(b) (*subject*) sujet, passible. **to be ~ to** *or* **for tax** *[person]* être imposable; *[thing]* être sujet à la taxation; **~ to a fine/imprisonment** passible d'une amende/d'emprisonnement; **to be ~ to prosecution** s'exposer à des poursuites; **he is ~ to seasickness** il est sujet au mal de mer; **every man of 20 is ~ for military service** tout homme de 20 ans est astreint au service militaire; **not ~ for military service** exempt d'obligations militaires; **the plan is ~ to changes** le projet est susceptible de changer; **the programme is ~ to alteration without notice** le programme peut être modifié sans préavis; *V* **damage**.
(c) (*Jur: responsible*) (civilement) responsable. **to be ~ for sb** être (civilement) responsable de qn; **to be ~ for sb's debts** répondre des dettes de qn.

liaise* [li:'eɪz] *vi* (*Brit*) **to ~ with sb** assurer la *or* rester en liaison avec qn.

liaison [li:'eɪzɒn] 1 *n* (*Ling, Mil, gen*) liaison *f*. 2 *cpd*: **liaison committee** comité *m* de liaison; (*Mil, gen*) **liaison officer** officier *m* de liaison.

liana [li:'ɑ:nə] *n* liane *f*.

liar ['laɪəʳ] *n* menteur *m*, -euse *f*.

lib‡ [lɪb] *n abbr of* **liberation**.

libation [laɪ'beɪʃən] *n* libation *f*.

libel ['laɪbəl] 1 *n* (*Jur*) (*act*) diffamation *f* (par écrit); (*document*) libelle *m*, pamphlet *m*, écrit *m* diffamatoire. **to sue sb for ~, to bring an action for ~ against sb** intenter un procès en diffamation à qn; (*fig*) **that's (a) ~!** c'est une calomnie!
2 *cpd*: (*Jur*) **libel laws** lois *fpl* contre la diffamation; **libel proceedings, libel suit** procès *m* en diffamation.
3 *vt* (*Jur*) diffamer (par écrit); (*gen*) calomnier, médire de.

libellous, (*US*) **libelous** ['laɪbələs] *adj* diffamatoire.

liberal ['lɪbərəl] 1 *adj* **(a)** (*broad-minded*) *education* libéral; *ideas, mind, interpretation* libéral, large. **~ arts** arts libéraux; **~-minded** libéral, large d'esprit.
(b) (*generous*) *offer* généreux; *person* prodigue (*with* de), généreux, libéral; (*copious*) *supply* ample, abondant.
(c) (*Pol*) **L~** libéral.
2 *n* (*Pol*) **L~** libéral(e) *m(f)*.

liberalism ['lɪbərəlɪzəm] *n* (*Pol, gen*) libéralisme *m*.

liberality [ˌlɪbə'rælɪtɪ] *n* (*broad-mindedness*) libéralisme *m*; (*generosity*) libéralité *f*, générosité *f*.

liberalize ['lɪbərəlaɪz] *vt* libéraliser.

liberally ['lɪbərəlɪ] *adv* libéralement.

liberate ['lɪbəreɪt] *vt* *prisoner, slave* libérer; (*Chem*) *gas* libérer, dégager; (*Fin*) *capital* dégager.

liberation [ˌlɪbə'reɪʃən] *n* libération *f*; (*Fin*) dégagement *m*.

liberator ['lɪbəreɪtəʳ] *n* libérateur *m*, -trice *f*.

Liberia [laɪ'bɪərɪə] *n* Libéria *m or* Liberia *m*.

Liberian [laɪ'bɪərɪən] 1 *adj* libérien. 2 *n* Libérien(ne) *m(f)*.

libertinage ['lɪbətɪnɪdʒ] *n* libertinage *m*.

libertine ['lɪbəti:n] *adj, n* libertin(e) *m(f)*.

liberty ['lɪbətɪ] *n* **(a)** (*freedom*) liberté *f*. **at ~** (*not detained*) en liberté; (*not busy*) libre; **you are at ~ to choose** vous êtes libre de choisir, libre à vous de choisir; **you are not at ~ to change the wording** vous n'avez pas le droit de changer le texte; **~ of the press** liberté de la presse; **~ of conscience** liberté de conscience; *V* **civil**.
(b) (*presumption*) liberté *f*. **to take liberties (with sb)** prendre *or* se permettre des libertés (avec qn); **to take the ~ of doing** prendre la liberté *or* se permettre de faire; **that was rather a ~ on his part** il ne s'est pas gêné; **what a ~!*** quel toupet!*

libidinous [lɪ'bɪdɪnəs] *adj* libidineux.

libido [lɪ'bi:dəʊ] *n* libido *f*.

Libra ['li:brə] *n* (*Astron*) la Balance.

librarian [laɪ'brɛərɪən] *n* bibliothécaire *mf*.

librarianship [laɪ'brɛərɪənʃɪp] *n* (*job*) poste *m* de bibliothécaire; (*esp Brit: science*) bibliothéconomie *f*; (*knowledge*) connaissances *fpl* de bibliothécaire. **to do or study ~** faire des études de bibliothécaire *or* de bibliothéconomie.

library ['laɪbrərɪ] 1 *n* **(a)** (*building, room*) bibliothèque *f*; *V* **public, reference**.
(b) (*private collection*) bibliothèque *f*; (*published series*) collection *f*, série *f*, bibliothèque.
2 *cpd*: **library book** livre *m* de bibliothèque; **library card = library ticket**; **library edition** édition reliée pour bibliothèque; (*esp US*) **library science** bibliothéconomie *f*; **library ticket** carte *f* de lecteur *or* de bibliothèque.

librettist [lɪ'bretɪst] *n* librettiste *mf*.

libretto [lɪ'bretəʊ] *n* libretto *m*, livret *m*.

Librium ['lɪbrɪəm] *n* ® Librium *m* ®.

Libya ['lɪbɪə] *n* Libye *f*.

Libyan ['lɪbɪən] 1 *n* Libyen(ne) *m(f)*. 2 *adj* libyen, de Libye.

lice [laɪs] *npl of* **louse**.

licence, (*US*) **license**[1] ['laɪsəns] 1 *n* **(a)** (*permit*) autorisation *f*, permis *m*; (*Comm*) licence *f*; (*Aut*) (*for driver*) permis; (*for car*) vignette *f*. **driving ~** permis de conduire; **export/import ~** permis d'exporter/d'importer; **pilot's ~** brevet *m* de pilote; **have you got a ~ for this radio?** est-ce que vous avez payé la redevance pour cette radio?; **you need a ~ for a television set** on a besoin de payer une redevance pour un poste de télévision; **they were married by special ~** ils se sont mariés avec dispense (de bans); **to manufacture sth under ~** fabriquer qch sous licence; *V* **marriage, off** *etc*.
(b) (*U*) (*freedom*) licence *f*, liberté *f*; (*excess*) licence. **you can allow some ~ in translation** on peut tolérer une certaine liberté dans la traduction; *V* **poetic**.
2 *cpd*: (*Aut*) **licence number** *[licence]* numéro *m* de permis de conduire; *[car]* numéro minéralogique *or* d'immatriculation *or* de police; **licence plate** plaque *f* minéralogique *or* d'immatriculation *or* de police.

license[2] ['laɪsəns] *vt* **(a)** (*give licence to*) donner une licence à; *car [licensing authority]* délivrer la vignette de; *[owner]* acheter la vignette de *or* pour. **the shop is ~d to sell tobacco** le magasin détient une licence de bureau de tabac; **the shop is ~d for the sale of alcoholic liquor** le magasin détient une licence de débit de boissons; **~d victualler** patron *m or* gérant *m* d'un pub; **(on) ~d premises** (dans un) établissement *m* ayant une licence de débit de boissons.
(b) (*permit*) autoriser (*sb to do* qn à faire), permettre (*sb to do* à qn de faire).

licensee [ˌlaɪsən'si:] *n* détenteur *m*, -trice *f* d'une licence; *[pub]* patron(ne) *m(f)*.

licentiate [laɪ'senʃɪɪt] *n* diplômé(e) *m(f)* (*pour pratiquer une profession libérale*).

licentious [laɪ'senʃəs] *adj* licencieux.

lichen ['laɪkən] *n* lichen *m*.

lichgate ['lɪtʃgeɪt] *n* porche *m* de cimetière.

licit ['lɪsɪt] *adj* licite.

lick [lɪk] 1 *n* **(a)** coup *m* de langue. **give me or let me have a ~** laisse-moi lécher un coup*; **give me a ~ of your lollipop** laisse-moi sucer ta sucette un coup*; **to give o.s. a ~ and a promise*** faire un (petit) brin de toilette; **a ~ of paint** un (petit) coup de peinture.
(b) (*: *speed*) vitesse *f*. **at full ~** en quatrième vitesse*, à toute vapeur*; (*Aut*) pleins gaz*; **at a fair or good ~** à toute vapeur*, à toute blinde‡.
(c) (*also* **salt ~**) (*natural deposit*) dépôt (naturel) de sel (*que les animaux viennent lécher*); (*block of rock salt*) pierre *f* à lécher, salègre *m*.
2 *cpd*: (*pej*) **lickspittle** lèche-bottes* *mf inv*.
3 *vt* **(a)** *[person, animal, flames]* lécher. **to ~ one's lips** (*lit*) se

lécher les lèvres; (*fig*) se frotter les mains (*fig*); to ~ one's chops se lécher *or* se pourlécher les babines*; she ~ed the cream off her fingers elle a léché la crème qu'elle avait sur les doigts; to ~ sth clean nettoyer qch à coups de langue; (*fig*) to ~ sb's boots jouer les lèche-bottes* envers qn; to ~ sb's arse** lécher le cul à qn**; (*fig*) to ~ one's wounds panser ses blessures (*fig*); *V* shape.

(b) (*) (*defeat*) écraser*, battre à plate(s) couture(s); (*outdo, surpass*) battre; (*thrash*) flanquer une correction à, tabasser‡. [*problem etc*] it's got me ~ed cela me dépasse.

lick off *vt sep* enlever à coups de langue, lécher. lick it off! lèche-le!

lick up *vt sep* lécher; [*cat*] laper.

licking* ['lɪkɪŋ] *n* (*whipping*) rossée* *f*, raclée* *f*; (*defeat*) déculottée‡ *f*.

licorice ['lɪkərɪs] *n* = liquorice.

lid [lɪd] *n* (a) [*pan, box, jar, piano*] couvercle *m*. (*fig*) the newspaper articles took *or* blew the ~ off his illegal activities les articles de presse ont étalé au grand jour ses activités illégales; that puts the ~ on it!* ça c'est un comble! *or* le pompon!*; *V* skid. (b) (*also* eye~) paupière *f*.

lido ['li:dəʊ] *n* (*resort*) complexe *m* balnéaire; (*swimming pool*) piscine *f* (*en plein air*).

lie[1] [laɪ] *pret* lay, *ptp* lain 1 *vi* (a) [*person etc*] (*act*) s'allonger, s'étendre, se coucher; (*state: gen* to be lying) être allongé *or* étendu *or* couché; (*in grave etc*) être enterré. go and ~ on the bed allez vous allonger *or* vous étendre sur le lit; don't ~ on the grass ne t'allonge pas *or* ne te couche pas sur l'herbe; he was lying on the floor (*resting etc*) il était allongé *or* étendu *or* couché par terre; (*unable to move*) il était étendu *or* il gisait par terre; she lay in bed until 10 o'clock elle est restée *or* a traîné (*pej*) au lit jusqu'à 10 heures; she was lying in bed reading elle lisait au lit; ~ on your side couche-toi *or* mets-toi *or* allonge-toi sur le côté; she was lying face downwards elle était (couchée *or* allongée *or* étendue) à plat ventre; he was lying asleep il était allongé et il dormait, il était allongé endormi; he lay asleep on the bed il dormait étendu *or* allongé sur le lit; he lay dead il était étendu mort; he lay dead at her feet il était étendu mort à ses pieds, il gisait à ses pieds; he lay helpless on the floor il était étendu par terre sans défense *or* sans pouvoir faire quoi que ce soit; he was lying still il était étendu immobile; ~ still! ne bouge pas!, reste tranquille!; his body was lying on the ground son corps gisait sur le sol; he ~s in the churchyard il repose dans le *or* est enterré au cimetière; the body lay in the coffin/the tomb le corps reposait dans le cercueil/la tombe; to ~ in state être exposé solennellement; (*on tombstone*) here ~s ... ci-gît ...; (*fig*) he lay in prison for many years il est resté en prison pendant de nombreuses années; (*fig*) to ~ low se cacher, rester caché; *V* ambush, sleeping, wait.

(b) [*object*] être; [*place, road*] se trouver, être; [*land, sea etc*] s'étendre; (*remain*) rester, être. the book lay on the table le livre était sur la table; the book lay unopened all day le livre est resté fermé toute la journée; the book lay open on the table le livre était ouvert sur la table; his food lay untouched while he told us the story il ne touchait pas à son assiette pendant qu'il nous racontait l'histoire; his clothes were lying on the floor ses vêtements étaient par terre; the whole contents of the box lay scattered on the carpet tout le contenu de la boîte était éparpillé *or* gisait éparpillé sur le tapis; our road lay along the river notre itinéraire longeait la rivière; the road ~s over the hills la route traverse les collines; the ship was lying in the harbour le navire était au port *or* avait mouillé dans le port; [*ship*] to ~ at anchor être à l'ancre, avoir mouillé; (*fig*) obstacles ~ in the way la route est semée d'embûches; the money is lying in the bank l'argent est en dépôt à la banque; the factory lay idle personne ne travaillait dans l'usine; the machines lay idle les machines étaient arrêtées; the money is lying idle in the bank l'argent dort à la banque; the snow lay 2 metres deep il y avait 2 mètres (d'épaisseur) de neige; the snow lay thick *or* deep on the ground il y avait une épaisse couche de neige sur le sol; the snow will not ~ la neige ne tiendra pas; the town lay in ruins la ville était en ruines; the meal lay heavy on his stomach le repas lui pesait sur l'estomac; the crime lay heavy on his conscience le crime lui pesait sur la conscience; the valley/lake/sea lay before us la vallée/le lac/la mer s'étendait devant nous; during the years that ~ before us pendant les années qui sont devant nous; a brilliant future ~s before you vous avez devant vous un brillant avenir; (*fig*) the (whole) world lay at her feet toutes les portes lui étaient ouvertes; *V* land.

(c) (*with abstract subject*) être, résider. he knows where his interests ~ il sait où sont *or* résident ses intérêts; the trouble ~s in the engine le problème vient du moteur; the trouble ~s in his inability to be strict le problème provient de *or* réside dans son incapacité d'être sévère; the difference ~s in the fact that ... la différence vient de ce que ...; the real remedy ~s in education le vrai remède se trouve dans *or* réside dans l'enseignement; the blame ~s with you c'est vous qui êtes à blâmer, c'est à vous que revient la faute *or* que la faute est imputable; it does not ~ within my power to decide il n'est pas en mon pouvoir de décider; it ~s with you to decide il vous appartient de décider, c'est à vous (qu'il incombe) de décider; (*liter, frm*) as far as in me ~s au mieux de mes possibilités, du mieux que je peux.

(d) (*Jur*) [*evidence, appeal*] être recevable.

2 *n* (a) (*Golf*) [*ball*] position *f*.

(b) [*land*] configuration *f*; *V* land.

3 *cpd*: lie-abed* flemmard(e)* *m(f)* (qui traîne au lit); (*Brit*) to have a lie-down* s'allonger, se reposer; (*Brit*) to have a lie-in* faire la grasse matinée.

lie about, lie around *vi* (a) [*objects, clothes, books*] traîner. don't leave that money lying about ne laissez pas traîner cet argent.

(b) [*person*] traînasser*. don't just lie about all day! tâche de ne pas traînasser toute la journée!

lie back *vi* (*in chair, on bed*) se renverser (en arrière). (*fig*) just lie back and enjoy yourself! laisse-toi (donc) vivre!

lie down 1 *vi* [*person, animal*] se coucher, s'allonger, s'étendre. she lay down for a while elle s'est allongée quelques instants; when I arrived she was lying down quand je suis arrivé elle était allongée; (*to dog*) lie down! couché!; to lie down on the job* tirer au flanc*, flemmarder*; (*fig*) to lie down under an insult courber la tête sous l'insulte; (*fig*) to take sth lying down encaisser qch* sans broncher, accepter qch sans protester, avaler des couleuvres; he won't take that lying down* il va se rebiffer*; I won't take it lying down* ça ne va pas se passer comme ça, je vais protester; he's not one to take things lying down* il n'est pas du genre à tout avaler* *or* encaisser sans rien dire.

2 lie-down* *n V* lie[1] 3.

lie in 1 *vi* (a) (*stay in bed*) rester au lit, faire la grasse matinée.

(b) (†: *in childbirth*) être en couches.

2 lie-in* *n V* lie[1] 3.

lie off *vi* (*Naut*) rester au large.

lie over *vi* (*be postponed*) être ajourné, être remis (à plus tard).

lie to *vi* (*Naut*) être *or* se tenir à la cape.

lie up *vi* (a) (*stay in bed*) garder le lit *or* la chambre.

(b) (*hide*) se cacher, rester caché.

lie[2] [laɪ] (*vb: pret, ptp* lied) 1 *n* mensonge *m*. to tell ~s mentir, dire des mensonges; that's a ~! vous mentez!, c'est un mensonge!; to give the ~ to *person* accuser de mentir; *claim, account* démentir, contredire; *V* pack, white.

2 *vi* mentir. he's lying in his teeth* il ment effrontément *or* comme un arracheur de dents.

3 *vt*: he tried to ~ his way out of it il a essayé de s'en sortir par des mensonges; he managed to ~ his way into the director's office il a réussi à s'introduire dans le bureau du directeur sous un prétexte mensonger; he ~d his way into the job il a obtenu le poste grâce à des mensonges.

4 *cpd*: lie detector détecteur *m* de mensonges.

lief [li:f] *adv* (†† *or liter*) I would as ~ die as tell a lie j'aimerais autant mourir que mentir.

liege [li:dʒ] *n* (*Hist*) (a) (*also* ~ lord) seigneur *m*, suzerain *m*. yes, my ~! oui, Sire! (b) (*also* ~ man) vassal *m* (lige).

lien [lɪən] *n* (*Jur*) droit *m* de rétention.

lieu [lu:] *n*: in ~ of au lieu de, à la place de; one month's notice or £24 in ~ un mois de préavis ou bien 24 livres.

lieutenant [lef'tenənt, (*US*) lu:'tenənt] 1 *n* (*in army*) lieutenant *m*; (*in navy*) [lə'tenənt, (*US*) lu:'tenənt] lieutenant de vaisseau; (*fig*) second *m*; *V* lord.

2 *cpd*: (*Mil*) lieutenant-colonel lieutenant-colonel *m*; (*Naut*) lieutenant-commander capitaine *m* de corvette; (*Mil*) lieutenant-general général *m* de corps d'armée; (*Can*) Lieutenant-Governor lieutenant-gouverneur *m*.

life [laɪf] *pl* lives 1 *n* (a) (*U: in general*) vie *f*. is there ~ on Mars? la vie existe-t-elle sur Mars?; animal and plant ~ vie animale et végétale; bird ~ les oiseaux *mpl*; insect ~ les insectes *mpl*; there was no sign of ~ il n'y avait pas signe de vie; a matter of ~ and death une question de vie ou de mort (*V also* 2); he came to ~ again il a repris conscience; the town came to ~ when the sailors arrived la ville s'éveillait à l'arrivée des marins; to bring sb back to ~ ranimer qn; *V* large, still[2] *etc*.

(b) (*existence*) vie *f*. he lived in France all his ~ il a vécu toute sa vie en France; for the rest of his ~ pour le restant de ses jours; (*Jur*) to be sent to prison for ~ être condamné à la prison à vie; to be on trial for one's ~ risquer la peine capitale; it will last you for ~ *or* (for) all your ~ cela vous durera toute votre vie; to have the time of one's ~ s'amuser follement; at my time of ~ à mon âge; she began ~ as a teacher elle a débuté comme professeur; never in (all) my ~ have I seen such stupidity jamais de ma vie je n'ai vu une telle stupidité; in early ~, early in ~ de bonne heure, tôt dans la vie; in her early ~ dans sa jeunesse; in later ~ plus tard; in his later ~ plus tard dans sa vie; late in ~ sur le tard, à un âge avancé; loss of ~ perte *f* de vies humaines; how many lives were lost? combien de vies cela a-t-il coûté?; many lives were lost beaucoup ont péri *or* trouvé la mort; no lives were lost il n'y a eu aucun mort *or* aucune victime; to lose one's ~ perdre la vie, périr; he ran for dear ~* *or* for his ~* il a pris ses jambes à son cou, il a foncé à bride abattue; run for your lives! sauve qui peut!; (*Rel*) in this ~ en cette vie; (*on tombstone etc*) departed this ~, May 10th 1842 qui a été enlevé(e) aux siens le 10 mai 1842; is there (a) ~ after death? y a-t-il une vie après la mort?; ~ isn't worth living la vie ne vaut pas la peine d'être vécue; the cat has nine lives le chat a neuf vies; to take sb's ~ donner la mort à qn; to take one's (own) ~ se donner la mort; to take one's ~ in one's hands jouer sa vie; (*liter*) to lay down one's ~ se sacrifier, donner sa vie; true to ~ vraisemblable, conforme à la réalité; (*Art*) a portrait taken from ~ un portrait d'après nature; it was Paul to the ~ c'était Paul tout craché; ~ begins at forty la vie commence à quarante ans; I couldn't for the ~ of me tell you his name* je ne pourrais absolument pas vous dire son nom; I couldn't for the ~ of me understand ...* je n'arrivais absolument pas à comprendre ..., j'avais beau m'évertuer, je ne pouvais comprendre ...; upon *or* 'pon my ~!† seigneur!, diantre!†; what a ~! quelle vie!, quel métier!*; how's ~?* comment (ça) va?*; such is ~!, that's ~! c'est la vie!; this is the ~!* voilà comment je comprends la vie!; not on your ~!* jamais de la vie!; I couldn't do it to save my ~* je ne pourrais le faire pour rien au monde; *V* after, rose[2] *etc*.

(c) (*U: way of living*) vie *f.* **which do you prefer, town or country ~?** que préférez-vous, la vie à la ville ou la vie à la campagne?; **his ~ was very unexciting** sa vie n'avait rien de passionnant; **high ~** la vie mondaine; **the good ~** (*pleasant*) la belle vie; (*Rel*) la vie d'un saint, une vie sainte; **it's a good ~** c'est la belle vie; **home ~** vie de famille; **the private ~ of Henry VIII** la vie privée d'Henri VIII; **he is known in private ~ as ...** dans le privé *or* dans l'intimité on l'appelle ...; **to lead a charmed ~** avoir la chance avec soi; **to lead a quiet ~** mener une vie tranquille; *V* **married, night, see[1]** *etc.*

(d) (*U: liveliness*) vie *f.* **to be full of ~** être plein de vie; **you need to put a bit of ~ into it** il faut y mettre plus d'ardeur, il faut y aller avec plus d'entrain; **he's the ~ and soul of the party** c'est un boute-en-train, c'est lui qui met l'ambiance*; **it put new ~ into me** ça m'a fait revivre, ça m'a ragaillardi *or* revigoré; **there isn't much ~ in our village** notre village n'est pas très vivant *or* est plutôt mort; **there's ~ in the old dog yet*** le bonhomme a encore du ressort.

(e) (*biography*) vie *f.* **the lives of the Saints** la vie des saints.

(f) (*fig: validity, usefulness*) *[car, ship, government, licence, battery etc]* durée *f.*

(g) (*: *imprisonment*). **he got ~** il a été condamné à perpétuité *or* à perpète‡; **he's doing ~** il tire une condamnation à perpétuité.

2 *cpd*: **a life-and-death struggle** un combat à mort; **life annuity** rente viagère; (*esp Brit*) **life assurance** assurance-vie *f*; **lifebelt** bouée *f* de sauvetage; (*fig*) **lifeblood** élément vital *or* moteur, âme *f*; **lifeboat** (*from shore*) bateau *m or* canot *m* de sauvetage; (*from ship*) chaloupe *f* de sauvetage; **lifeboatman** sauveteur *m* (en mer); **lifeboat station** centre *m or* poste *m* de secours en mer; **lifebuoy** bouée *f* de sauvetage; **life cycle** cycle *m* de (la) vie; **life expectancy** espérance *f* de vie; **life expectancy table** table *f* de survie; **the life force** la force vitale; **life-giving** vivifiant; **lifeguard** (*on beach*) surveillant *m* de plage *or* de baignade; (*Mil: bodyguard*) garde *m* du corps; (*Brit Mil*) **Life Guards** cavalerie *f* de la Garde (royale); **life imprisonment** (*gen*) prison *f* à vie; (*Jur*) réclusion *f* à perpétuité; **life insurance = life assurance**; (*Jur*) **life interest** usufruit *m*; **life jacket** gilet *m or* ceinture *f* de sauvetage; (*Navy*) brassière *f* (de sauvetage); **lifelike** qui semble vivant *or* vrai; **lifeline** (*on ship*) main courante; (*in palmistry*) ligne *f* de vie; (*for diver*) corde *f* de sécurité; (*fig*) **it was his lifeline** c'était vital pour lui; **lifelong** *ambition* de toute ma (*or* sa *etc*) vie; *friend, friendship* de toujours; **it is a lifelong task** c'est le travail de toute une vie; (*Brit*) **life peer** pair *m* à vie; (*Brit*) **life peerage** pairie *f* à vie; **life preserver** (*US: life jacket*) gilet *m or* ceinture *f* de sauvetage; (*Navy*) brassière *f* de sauvetage; (*Brit‡: bludgeon*) matraque *f*; **life raft** radeau *m* de sauvetage; **life-saver** (*person*) surveillant(e) *m(f)* de baignade; (*fig*) **that money was a life-saver** cet argent m'a (*or* lui a *etc*) sauvé la vie; **life-saving** (*n*) (*rescuing*) sauvetage *m*; (*first aid*) secourisme *m*; (*adj*) de sauvetage; (*Jur*) **life sentence** condamnation *f* à perpétuité *or* à vie; **life-sized** grandeur nature *inv*; **life span** durée *f or* espérance *f* de vie; **life story** biographie *f*; **his life story** sa biographie, l'histoire *f* de sa vie; **life style** style *m* de vie; **life support system** (*Space*) équipement *m* de vie; (*Med*) respirateur artificiel (pour traitement de survie); **to hold a life tenancy of a house** être locataire d'une maison à vie; **lifetime** *V* **lifetime**; (*US*) **life-vest = life jacket**; **lifework** œuvre *f* de toute une (*or* ma *etc*) vie.

lifeless ['laɪflɪs] *adj body* sans vie, inanimé; *matter* inanimé; (*fig*) *style* sans vie, sans vigueur, mou (*f* molle).

lifelessness ['laɪflɪsnɪs] *n* (*lit*) absence *f* de vie; (*fig*) manque *m* de vigueur *or* d'entrain.

lifer‡ ['laɪfəʳ] *n* condamné(e) *m(f)* à perpétuité.

lifetime ['laɪftaɪm] *n* **(a)** vie *f.* **it won't happen in *or* during my ~** je ne verrai pas cela de mon vivant; **the chance of a ~** la chance de sa (*or* ma *etc*) vie; **once in a ~** une fois dans la *or* une vie; **the work of a ~** l'œuvre de toute une vie; **a ~'s experience** l'expérience de toute une vie; *V* **last[2]**. **(b)** (*fig: eternity*) éternité *f.* **it seemed a ~** cela a semblé une éternité.

lift [lɪft] **1** *n* **(a)** (*Brit*) (*elevator*) ascenseur *m*; (*for goods*) monte-charge *m inv*; *V* **service**.

(b) give the box a ~ soulève la boîte; **give me a ~ with this trunk** aide-moi à soulever cette malle; **can you give me a ~ up, I can't reach the shelf** soulève-moi s'il te plaît, je n'arrive pas à atteindre l'étagère; *V* **air, face**.

(c) (*transport*) **can I give you a ~?** est-ce que je peux vous déposer quelque part?; **I gave him a ~ to Paris** je l'ai pris en voiture *or* je l'ai emmené jusqu'à Paris; **we didn't get any ~s** personne ne s'est arrêté pour nous prendre; **he stood there hoping for a ~** il était là (debout) dans l'espoir d'être pris en stop; *V* **hitch**.

(d) (*Aviat*) portance *f.*

(e) (*fig: boost*) **it gave us a ~** cela nous a remonté le moral *or* nous a encouragés.

2 *cpd*: (*Brit*) **liftboy, liftman** liftier *m*, garçon *m* d'ascenseur; (*Space*) **lift-off** décollage *m*; **we have lift-off!** décollage!; (*Brit*) **lift shaft** cage *f* d'ascenseur.

3 *vt* **(a)** (*raise*) lever, soulever; (*Agr*) *potatoes etc* arracher. **to ~ sth into the air** lever qch en l'air; **to ~ sb/sth onto a table** soulever qn/qch pour le poser sur une table; **to ~ sb/sth off a table** descendre qn/qch d'une table; **to ~ sb over a wall** faire passer qn par-dessus un mur; **this suitcase is too heavy for me to ~** cette valise est trop lourde pour que je la soulève (*subj*); (*fig*) **he didn't ~ a finger to help** il n'a pas levé le petit doigt pour aider; **he ~ed his fork to his mouth** il a porté la fourchette à sa bouche; *V* **face**.

(b) (*fig*) *restrictions* supprimer, abolir; *ban, blockade, siege* lever.

(c) (*: *steal*) chiper*, barboter‡; *V* **shop**.

(d) *quotation, passage* prendre, voler. **he ~ed that idea from Sartre** il a volé *or* pris cette idée à Sartre, il a plagié Sartre.

4 *vi [lid etc]* se soulever; *[fog]* se lever.

lift down *vt sep box, person* descendre. **to lift sth down from a shelf** descendre qch d'une étagère.

lift off 1 *vi* (*Space*) décoller.

2 *vt sep lid* enlever; *person* descendre.

3 lift-off *n V* **lift 2**.

lift out *vt sep object* sortir; (*Mil*) *troops* (*by plane*) évacuer par avion, aéroporter, (*by helicopter*) héliporter, évacuer par hélicoptère. **he lifted the child out of his playpen** il a sorti l'enfant de son parc.

lift up 1 *vi [drawbridge etc]* se soulever, basculer.

2 *vt sep object, carpet, skirt, person* soulever. **to lift up one's eyes** lever les yeux; **to lift up one's head** lever *or* redresser la tête; (*liter*) **he lifted up his voice** il a élevé la voix.

ligament ['lɪgəmənt] *n* ligament *m.*

ligature ['lɪgətʃəʳ] *n* (*Surg, Typ: act, object*) ligature *f*; (*Mus*) coulé *m*, liaison *f.*

light[1] [laɪt] (*vb: pret, ptp* **lit** *or* **lighted**) **1** *n* **(a)** (*U: gen*) lumière *f*; *[lamp]* lumière, éclairage *m*; *[sun]* lumière; (*daylight*) lumière, jour *m.* **electric ~** éclairage *or* lumière électrique; **to put on *or* turn on *or* switch on the ~** allumer (la lumière); **to put off *or* put out *or* turn off *or* turn out *or* switch off *or* switch out the ~** éteindre (la lumière); **by the ~ of a candle/the fire/a torch** à la lumière *or* lueur d'une bougie/du feu/d'une lampe de poche; **with the ~ of battle in his eyes** (avec) une lueur belliqueuse dans le regard; **at first ~** au point du jour; **the ~ was beginning to fail** le jour commençait à baisser; **she was sitting with her back to the ~ *or* with the ~ behind her** elle tournait le dos à la lumière; **to stand sth in the ~** mettre qch à la lumière; **you're holding it against the ~** vous le tenez à contre-jour; **to stand in one's own ~** se faire de l'ombre; **you're in my *or* the ~** (*daylight*) vous me cachez *or* bouchez le jour; (*electric*) vous me cachez la lumière; **get out of my *or* the ~!** pousse-toi, tu me fais de l'ombre!; **the ~ isn't good enough to take photographs** il ne fait pas assez clair *or* il n'y a pas assez de lumière pour prendre des photos; (*Art, Phot*) **~ and shade** les clairs *mpl* et les ombres *fpl*; (*fig*) **to see the ~** (*be born*) venir au monde; (*Rel*) se convertir; (*be published etc*) paraître; (*: *understand*) comprendre; *V* **fire, hide[1], moon** *etc.*

(b) (*fig*) lumière *f*, jour *m.* **to bring to ~** mettre en lumière, révéler; **to come to ~** être dévoilé *or* découvert; **new facts have come to ~** on a découvert des faits nouveaux; **can you throw any ~ on this question?** pouvez-vous éclaircir cette question?; **to shed *or* cast a new ~ on a subject** jeter un jour nouveau sur un sujet; **the incident revealed him in a new ~** l'incident l'a montré sous un jour nouveau; **in the ~ of what you say** à la lumière de *or* tenant compte de ce que vous dites; **I don't see things in that ~** je ne vois pas les choses sous cet angle-là *or* sous ce jour-là; **in the cold ~ of day** à tête reposée.

(c) (*gen*) lumière *f*; (*Aut*) (*gen*) feu *m*; (*headlamp*) phare *m*; *[cycle]* feu. **we saw several ~s on the horizon** nous avons vu plusieurs lumières à l'horizon; **there were ~s on in several of the rooms** il y avait de la lumière dans plusieurs pièces; **he put out the ~s one by one** il a éteint les lumières une à une; **~s out at 9 o'clock** extinction *f* des feux à 21 heures; **~s out!** extinction des feux!, on éteint!; (*Aut*) **the ~s were at red** le feu était (au) rouge; **he saw the ~s of several cars** (*rear*) il a vu les feux de plusieurs voitures; (*front*) il a vu les phares de plusieurs voitures; (*fig*) **according to *or* in his ~s** d'après ce qu'il a (*or* avait *etc*) compris; *V* **green, leading, pilot** *etc.*

(d) (*for cigarette etc*) feu *m.* **have you got a ~?** avez-vous du feu?; **to put a ~ to sth, to set ~ to sth** mettre le feu à qch; *V* **strike**.

(e) (*Archit: window*) fenêtre *f*, ouverture *f*, jour *m*; *V* **fan[1], leaded, sky**.

2 *adj* **(a)** *evening, room* clair. **it was growing ~** il commençait à faire jour *or* clair; **while it's still ~** pendant qu'il fait encore jour.

(b) *hair* clair, blond; *colour, complexion, skin* clair. **~ green eyes** yeux *mpl* vert clair *inv*; **a ~ blue dress** une robe bleu clair *inv.*

3 *cpd*: **light bulb** ampoule *f*, lampe *f*; **light-coloured** clair, de couleur claire; **light effects** effets *mpl or* jeux *mpl* de lumière; **light fitting** appareil *m* d'éclairage; **light-haired** blond; **lighthouse** phare *m*; **lighthouse keeper** gardien *m* de phare; (*Phot*) **light meter** photomètre *m*, cellule *f* (photoélectrique); **lightship** bateau-phare *m*, bateau-feu *m*; **light wave** onde lumineuse; **light-year** année-lumière *f*; **3,000 light-years away** distant de 3.000 années-lumière.

4 *vt* **(a)** *candle, cigarette, gas* allumer. **to ~ a match** frotter *or* craquer une allumette; **he lit the fire** il a allumé le feu; **he lit a fire** il a fait du feu.

(b) *room* éclairer. **this torch will ~ your way *or* the way for you** cette lampe de poche vous éclairera le chemin.

5 *vi* **(a)** *[match]* s'allumer; *[coal, wood]* prendre (feu).

(b) to ~ into sb‡ tomber sur qn (à bras raccourcis).

light out‡ *vi* foncer à toute pompe* (*for* vers).

light up 1 *vi* **(a)** *[lamp]* s'allumer; (*fig*) s'allumer, s'éclairer. **her eyes/face lit up** son regard/visage s'est éclairé.

(b) (*: *smoke*) allumer une cigarette *or* une pipe *etc.*

2 *vt sep [lighting, sun] room* éclairer. (*fig*) **a smile lit up her face** un sourire a éclairé *or* illuminé son visage; *V also* **lighting, lit**.

3 lit up *adj V* **lit 2**.

4 lighting-up *n V* **lighting 2**.

light[2] [laɪt] **1** *adj* **(a)** (*not heavy*) *parcel, weapon, clothes, sleep, meal, wine, soil* léger. **~er than air** plus léger que l'air; **as ~ as**

a feather léger comme une plume; **to be ~ on one's feet** avoir la démarche légère; **to be a ~ sleeper** avoir le sommeil léger; (*Brit*) **~ ale** *sorte f de bière blonde légère*; (*Mil*) **~ infantry** infanterie légère; (*Boxing*) **~ heavyweight** (*adj*) (poids) mi-lourd; (*n*) (poids *m*) mi-lourd *m*; **you've given me ~ weight** vous ne m'avez pas mis le poids (*V also* 4); **~ vehicles** véhicules légers.

(b) (*fig*) *play, music, breeze, punishment, shower* léger; *rain* petit, fin; *work, task* (*easy*) facile; (*not strenuous*) peu fatigant. **~ comedy** comédie légère; **~ opera** opérette *f*; **~ reading** lecture distrayante; **~ verse** poésie légère; **it is no ~ matter** c'est sérieux, ça n'est pas une plaisanterie; **a ~ fall of snow** une légère chute de neige; **with a ~ heart** le cœur léger; **'woman wanted for ~ work'** 'on demande employée de maison pour travaux légers'; **to make ~ work of sth** faire qch aisément *or* sans difficulté; **to make ~ of sth** prendre *or* traiter qch à la légère.

2 *adv*: **to sleep ~** avoir le sommeil léger; **to travel ~** voyager avec peu de bagages; **he got off ~*** il s'en est tiré à bon compte.

3 *npl*: **~s** mou *m* (*abats*).

4 *cpd*: **to be light-fingered** être chapardeur; **light-footed** au pas léger, à la démarche légère *or* gracieuse; **light-headed** (*dizzy*) étourdi, pris de vertige; (*unable to think clearly*) étourdi, hébété; (*excited*) exalté, grisé; (*thoughtless*) étourdi, écervelé; **light-hearted** *person* gai, aimable, enjoué; *laugh* joyeux, gai; *atmosphere* joyeux, gai, plaisant; *discussion* enjoué; **light-heartedly** (*happily*) joyeusement, allègrement; (*jokingly*) en plaisantant; (*cheerfully*) de bon cœur, avec bonne humeur; **lightweight** (*adj*) *jacket, shoes* léger; (*Boxing*) poids léger *inv*; (*n: Boxing*) poids léger; (*Boxing*) **European lightweight champion/championship** champion *m*/championnat *m* d'Europe des poids légers.

light[3] [laɪt] *pret, ptp* **lighted** *or* **lit** *vi*: **to ~ (up)on sth** trouver qch par hasard, tomber par chance sur qch; **his eyes lit upon the jewels** son regard est tombé sur les bijoux.

lighten[1] [ˈlaɪtn] **1** *vt* **(a)** (*light up*) *darkness, face* éclairer, illuminer. **(b)** (*make lighter*) *colour, hair* éclaircir. **2** *vi [sky]* s'éclaircir; (*fig*) *[face]* s'éclairer. (*Met*) **it is ~ing** il fait *or* il y a des éclairs.

lighten[2] [ˈlaɪtn] **1** *vt* (*make less heavy*) *cargo, burden* alléger; *tax* alléger, réduire. **2** *vi [load]* se réduire. **her heart ~ed at the news** la nouvelle lui a enlevé le poids qu'elle avait sur le cœur *or* lui a ôté un grand poids.

lighter[1] [ˈlaɪtəʳ] **1** *n* (*for gas cooker*) allume-gaz *m inv*; (*also* **cigarette ~**) briquet *m*; (*Aut: on dashboard*) allume-cigare *m inv*, allume-cigarette *m inv*; *V* **cigar, fire, lamp** *etc*.

2 *cpd*: **lighter flint** pierre *f* à briquet; **lighter fuel** gaz *m* (*or* essence *f*) à briquet.

lighter[2] [ˈlaɪtəʳ] *n* (*Naut*) péniche *f*, chaland *m*.

lighterage [ˈlaɪtərɪdʒ] *n* (transport *m* par) ac(c)onage *m*; (*fee*) droit *m* d'ac(c)onage.

lighting [ˈlaɪtɪŋ] **1** *n* (*U*) **(a)** (*Elec*) éclairage *m*; (*Theat*) éclairages.

(b) (*act*) *[lamp, candle etc]* allumage *m*.

2 *cpd*: **lighting effects** effets *mpl or* jeux *mpl* d'éclairage, éclairages *mpl*; **lighting engineer** éclairagiste *m*; **lighting fixture** appareil *m* d'éclairage; (*Brit Aut*) **lighting-up time** heure *f* de l'éclairage obligatoire des véhicules, tombée *f* du jour; (*duration*) heures d'obscurité.

lightly [ˈlaɪtlɪ] *adv* **(a)** *walk, clothe* légèrement. **she touched his brow ~ with her hand** elle lui a effleuré le front de la main. **(b)** *behave, speak* légèrement, à la légère; *laugh* légèrement. **(c) to get off ~** s'en tirer à bon compte.

lightness[1] [ˈlaɪtnɪs] *n* (*brightness*) clarté *f*.

lightness[2] [ˈlaɪtnɪs] *n* (*in weight, Culin*) légèreté *f*.

lightning [ˈlaɪtnɪŋ] **1** *n* éclair *m*, foudre *f*. **we saw ~** nous avons vu un éclair *or* des éclairs; **there was a lot of ~** il y avait beaucoup d'éclairs; **a flash of ~** un éclair; **struck by ~** frappé par la foudre, foudroyé; **~ never strikes twice in the same place** la foudre ne frappe *or* ne tombe jamais deux fois à la même place; **like ~*** avec la vitesse de l'éclair; *V* **forked, grease, sheet.**

2 *cpd attack* foudroyant; (*Ind*) *strike* surprise *inv*; *visit* éclair *inv*. **lightning conductor,** (*US*) **lightning rod** paratonnerre *m*.

ligneous [ˈlɪgnɪəs] *adj* ligneux.

lignite [ˈlɪgnaɪt] *n* lignite *m*.

lignum vitae [ˈlɪgnəmˈviːtaɪ] *n* (*tree*) gaïac *m*; (*wood*) bois *m* de gaïac.

like[1] [laɪk] **1** *adj* semblable, pareil, du même ordre, du même genre; (*stronger*) similaire, analogue. **they are as ~ as two peas (in a pod)** ils se ressemblent comme deux gouttes d'eau.

2 *prep* **(a)** comme, en. **he spoke ~ an aristocrat** il parlait comme un aristocrate; **he spoke ~ the aristocrat he was** il parlait comme l'aristocrate qu'il était, il parlait en aristocrate; **~ the fool he is, he ...** imbécile comme il l'est *or* (en) imbécile qu'il est, il ...; **he behaved ~ a fool** il s'est conduit comme un imbécile *or* en imbécile; **~ an animal in a trap he ...** tel une bête prise au piège, il ...; **the news spread ~ wildfire** la nouvelle s'est répandue comme une traînée de poudre; **it wasn't ~ that at all** ce n'était pas du tout comme ça; **it happened ~ this ...** voici comment ça s'est passé ..., ça s'est passé comme ceci ...; **it was ~ this, I'd just got home ...** voilà, je venais juste de rentrer ...; **I'm sorry I didn't come but it was ~ this ...** je m'excuse de ne pas être venu mais c'est que ...; *V* **anything, hell, mad** *etc*.

(b) (*resembling*) comme, du même genre que, semblable à, pareil à. **to be ~ sb/sth** ressembler à qn/qch; **who is he ~?** à qui ressemble-t-il?; **they are very (much) ~ one another** ils se ressemblent beaucoup; **he is ~ his father** (*in appearance*) il ressemble à son père; (*in character*) il est comme son père, il ressemble à son père; **the portrait is not ~ him** le portrait ne lui ressemble pas *or* n'est pas ressemblant; **his work is rather ~ Van Gogh's** son œuvre est un peu dans le genre *or* le style de celle de Van Gogh, son œuvre ressemble un peu à celle de Van Gogh; **your writing is rather ~ mine** vous avez un peu la même écriture que moi, votre écriture ressemble assez à la mienne; **a house ~ mine** une maison pareille à *or* comme la mienne; **an idiot ~ you** un imbécile comme vous; **a hat rather** *or* **something ~ yours** un chapeau un peu comme le vôtre *or* dans le genre du vôtre; **I found one ~ it** j'en ai trouvé un pareil, j'ai trouvé le même; **I never saw anything ~ it!** je n'ai jamais rien vu de pareil!; **we heard a noise ~ a car backfiring** on a entendu comme une pétarade de voiture; **she was ~ a sister to me** elle était comme une sœur pour moi; **that's just ~ him!** c'est bien de lui!; **it's not ~ him to be late** ça ne lui ressemble pas *or* ça n'est pas son genre d'être en retard; **that's just ~ a woman!** voilà bien les femmes!; **he's just ~ anybody else** il est comme tout le monde *or* comme n'importe qui; **can't you just accept it ~ everyone else?** tu ne peux pas simplement l'accepter comme tout le monde?; **it cost something ~ £100** cela a coûté dans les 100 livres, cela a coûté quelque chose comme 100 livres; **he's called Middlewick or something ~ that** il s'appelle Middlewick ou quelque chose comme ça*; **I was thinking of giving her something ~ a necklace** je pensais lui offrir un collier ou quelque chose dans ce genre-là *or* quelque chose comme ça*; **that's something ~ a steak!*** voilà ce que j'appelle *or* ce qui s'appelle un bifteck!; **that's something ~ it!*** c'est ça!, voilà!; **that's more ~ it!** voilà qui est mieux!, il y a du progrès!; **that's nothing ~ it!** ça n'est pas du tout ça!; **there's nothing ~ real silk** rien de tel que la soie véritable, rien ne vaut la soie véritable; **some people are ~ that** il y a des gens comme ça; **people ~ that can't be trusted** on ne peut pas se fier à des gens pareils *or* à des gens comme ça; **his father is ~ that** son père est ainsi fait *or* est comme ça*; **you know what she's ~** vous savez comment elle est; **what's he ~?** comment est-il?; **what's he ~ as a teacher?** comment est-il *or* que vaut-il comme professeur?; **what's the film ~?** comment as-tu trouvé le film?; **what's the weather ~ in Paris?** quel temps fait-il à Paris?; *V* **feel, look, sound**[1] *etc*.

(c) comme, de même que. (*Prov*) **~ father, ~ son** tel père, tel fils (*Prov*); **~ me, he is fond of Brahms** comme moi *or* de même que moi, il aime Brahms; **he, ~ me, thinks that ...** comme moi *or* de même que moi, il pense que ...; **he thinks ~ us*** il pense comme nous; **do it ~ me*** fais-le comme moi.

(d) comme, tel que, par exemple. **there are many hobbies you might take up, ~ painting, gardening and so on** il y a beaucoup d'activités que tu pourrais entreprendre, par exemple *or* comme la peinture, le jardinage et cætera; **the basic necessities of life, ~ food and drink** les éléments indispensables à la vie, tels que *or* comme la nourriture et la boisson.

3 *adv* **(a)** (*) **~ enough, as ~ as not, very ~** probablement.

(b) (*near*) **that record's nothing ~ as good as this one** ce disque-là est loin d'être aussi bon que celui-ci; **she's more ~ 30 than 25** elle a plutôt 30 ans que 25, elle est plus près de 30 ans que de 25.

(c) (*Brit*:) **he felt tired, ~** il se sentait comme qui dirait* fatigué; **I had a fortnight's holiday, ~, so I did a bit of gardening** j'avais quinze jours de vacances, alors comme ça* j'ai fait un peu de jardinage.

4 *conj* **(a)** (*: *as*) comme. **he did it ~ I did** il l'a fait comme moi; **he can't play poker ~ his brother can** il ne sait pas jouer au poker comme *or* aussi bien que son frère; **~ we used to** ainsi qu'on *or* comme on le faisait autrefois; **it's just ~ I say**: c'est comme je vous le dis.

(b) (*: *as if*) comme si. **he behaved ~ he was afraid** il s'est conduit comme s'il avait eu peur.

5 *n* (*similar thing*) chose pareille *or* semblable; (*person*) pareil *m*. **did you ever see the ~ (of it)?** a-t-on jamais vu chose pareille?; **oranges, lemons and the ~** *or* **and such~** des oranges, des citrons et autres fruits de ce genre; **the ~ of which we'll never see again** comme on n'en reverra plus jamais; **we shall not see his ~ again** jamais nous ne reverrons son pareil; **the ~s of him*** des gens comme lui *or* de son acabit (*pej*).

6 *cpd*: **like-minded** de même opinion, animés des mêmes sentiments; **you and other like-minded individuals** vous et d'autres (gens) qui pensent comme vous.

like[2] [laɪk] **1** *vt* **(a)** *person* aimer (bien). **I ~ him** (*of relative, friend etc*) je l'aime bien; (*of casual acquaintance, colleague etc*) il me plaît; **I don't ~ him** je ne l'aime pas beaucoup, il me déplaît; **he is well ~d here** on l'aime bien ici, on le trouve sympathique ici; **how do you ~ him?** comment le trouvez-vous?; **I don't ~ the look of him** son allure ne me dit rien (qui vaille).

(b) *object, food, activity* aimer (bien). **I ~ that hat** j'aime bien ce chapeau, ce chapeau me plaît; **which do you ~ best?** lequel aimes-tu le mieux?, lequel préfères-tu?; **this plant doesn't ~ sunlight** cette plante ne se plaît pas à la lumière du soleil; **I ~ oysters but they don't ~ me*** j'aime bien les huîtres mais c'est elles qui ne m'aiment pas*; **I ~ music/Beethoven/football** j'aime bien la musique/Beethoven/le football; **I ~ having** *or* **to have a rest after lunch** j'aime (bien) me reposer après déjeuner; **he ~s to be** *or* **being obeyed** il aime être obéi *or* qu'on lui obéisse; **I ~ people to be punctual** j'aime (bien) que les gens soient à l'heure, j'aime les gens ponctuels; (*iro*) **well, I ~ that!*** ah ça, par exemple!; (*iro*) **I ~ your cheek!*** tu as quand même du toupet!*; **how do you ~ Paris?** comment trouvez-vous Paris?, que pensez-vous de Paris?, est-ce que Paris vous plaît?; **how do you ~ it here?** (est-ce que) vous vous plaisez ici?; **your father won't ~ it** cela ne plaira pas à votre père; **whether he ~s it or not** que cela lui plaise ou non; **~ it or lump it*, you'll have to go** que tu le veuilles ou non *or* que ça te plaise ou non il faudra que tu y ailles; **if you don't ~ it, you can lump it*** si cela ne vous plaît pas, tant pis pour vous *or* c'est le même prix*.

(c) (*want, wish*) aimer (bien), vouloir, souhaiter. **I should ~ to go home** j'aimerais (bien) *or* je voudrais (bien) rentrer chez moi; **I should have ~d to be there** j'aurais (bien) aimé être là; **I didn't ~ to disturb you** je ne voulais pas vous déranger; **I thought of asking him but I didn't ~ to** j'ai bien pensé (à) le lui demander mais je n'ai pas osé; **would you ~ a drink?** voulez-vous boire quelque chose?; **I should ~ more time** je voudrais un peu plus de temps; **which one would you ~?** lequel voudriez-vous?; **I would ~ you to speak to him** je voudrais que tu lui parles (*subj*); **would you ~ me to go and get it?** veux-tu que j'aille le chercher?; **would you ~ to go to Paris?** aimerais-tu aller à Paris?; **how would you ~ to go to Paris?** est-ce que cela te plairait *or* te dirait* d'aller à Paris?; **how would you ~ me to phrase it?** comment voudriez-vous que je le dise?; **how do you ~ your steak?** comment aimez-vous votre bifteck?; **how would you ~ a steak?** est-ce que ça te dirait* de manger un bifteck?; **I can do it when/where/as much as/how I ~** je peux le faire quand/où/autant que/comme je veux; **whenever you ~** quand vous voudrez; **'As You L~ It'** 'Comme il vous plaira'; **don't think you can do as you ~** ne croyez pas que vous pouvez *or* puissiez faire comme vous voulez *or* comme bon vous semble; **I shall go out as much as I ~** je sortirai autant qu'il me plaira *or* autant que je voudrai; **come on Sunday if you ~** venez dimanche si vous voulez; **she can do what she ~s with him** elle fait tout ce qu'elle veut de lui; **(you can) shout as much as you ~, I won't open the door** crie tant que tu veux *or* voudras, je n'ouvrirai pas la porte; **he can say *or* let him say what he ~s, I won't change my mind** il peut dire ce qu'il veut, je ne changerai pas d'avis.

2 *n*: **~s** goûts *mpl*, préférences *fpl*; **he knows all my ~s and dislikes** il sait tout ce que j'aime et (tout) ce que je n'aime pas.

...like [laɪk] *adj ending in cpds*: **childlike** enfantin; **statesmanlike** d'homme d'État; *V* **cat** *etc*.

likeable [ˈlaɪkəbl] *adj* sympathique, agréable.

likeableness [ˈlaɪkəblnɪs] *n* caractère *m* sympathique *or* agréable.

likelihood [ˈlaɪklɪhʊd] *n* probabilité *f*, chance *f*. **there is little ~ of his coming *or* that he will come** il y a peu de chances *or* il est peu probable qu'il vienne; **there is a strong ~ of his coming *or* that he will come** il y a de fortes chances pour qu'il vienne, il est très probable qu'il viendra; **there is no ~ of that** cela ne risque pas d'arriver; **in all ~** selon toute probabilité.

likely [ˈlaɪklɪ] **1** *adj* **(a)** *happening, outcome* probable; *explanation* plausible, vraisemblable. **which is the likeliest time to find him at home?** à quelle heure a-t-on le plus de chances de le trouver chez lui?; **this looks a ~ place for mushrooms** ça me paraît être un endroit à champignons; **the likeliest place to set up camp** l'endroit le plus propice où dresser la tente; (*iro*) **a ~ story!** comme si j'allais croire ça!, elle est bien bonne! (*iro*); (*iro*) **a ~ excuse!** belle excuse!; **the most ~ candidates** les candidats qui ont le plus de chances de réussir; **I asked 6 ~ people** j'ai demandé à 6 personnes susceptibles de convenir *or* qui me semblaient pouvoir convenir; **he's a ~ young man** c'est un jeune homme qui promet; **it is ~ that** il est probable que + *fut indic*, il y a des chances pour que + *subj*; **it is not ~ that** il est peu probable que + *subj*, il y a peu de chances que + *subj*; **it is very ~ that** il est très possible que + *subj*, il y a de grandes chances que + *subj*; **it's hardly ~ that** il n'est guère probable que + *subj*; **is it ~ that he would forget?** risque-t-il d'oublier?; (*iro*) **is it ~ that I did?** aurais-je pu faire cela, moi? (*iro*).

(b) (*liable*) **to be ~ to do** avoir des chances de faire, risquer de faire; **she is ~ to arrive at any time** elle va probablement arriver *or* elle risque d'arriver d'une minute à l'autre; **she is not ~ to come** il est peu probable *or* il y a peu de chances qu'elle vienne; **he is not ~ to succeed** il a peu de chances de réussir; **the man most ~ to succeed** l'homme qui a le plus de chances de réussir; **this incident is ~ to cause trouble** cet incident pourrait (bien) amener des ennuis; **that is not ~ to happen** cela ne risque guère d'arriver.

2 *adv* probablement. **very *or* most ~** très probablement; **as ~ as not** sûrement, probablement; **are you going? — not ~!** tu y vas? — pas de danger!*; **I expect he'll let me off with a warning — (*iro*) not ~!** je pense qu'il me laissera m'en tirer avec un avertissement — tu crois ça!

liken [ˈlaɪkən] *vt* comparer (*to* à), assimiler (*to* à). **to ~ sb to a fox** comparer qn à un renard; **X can be ~ed to Y** on peut comparer *or* assimiler X et Y.

likeness [ˈlaɪknɪs] *n* **(a)** (*resemblance*) ressemblance *f* (*to* avec). **I can't see much ~ between them** je ne vois guère de ressemblance entre eux, je ne trouve pas qu'ils se ressemblent (*subj*) beaucoup; **a strong family ~** un air de famille très marqué; **to bear a ~ to** ressembler à.

(b) (*appearance*) forme *f*, aspect *m*, apparence *f*. **in the ~ of** sous la forme *or* l'aspect de; **to assume the ~ of** prendre la forme *or* l'aspect *or* l'apparence de.

(c) (*Art, Phot etc*) **to draw sb's ~** faire le portrait de qn; **to have one's ~ taken** se faire faire son portrait; **it is a good ~** c'est très ressemblant.

likewise [ˈlaɪkwaɪz] *adv* (*similarly*) de même, également, pareillement; (*also*) aussi; (*moreover*) de plus, en outre. **to do ~** en faire autant, faire pareil *or* de même; **he suggested it, but I wish it ~** c'est lui qui l'a suggéré mais je le souhaite pareillement *or* également *or* aussi; **my wife is well, the children ~** ma femme va bien, les enfants aussi *or* également; **and ~, it cannot be denied that ...** et en outre *or* de plus, on ne peut nier que ... .

liking [ˈlaɪkɪŋ] *n* (*for person*) sympathie *f*, affection *f* (*for* pour); (*for thing*) goût *m* (*for* pour), penchant *m* (*for* pour). **to take a ~ to sb** se prendre d'amitié pour qn; **to take a ~ to (doing) sth** se mettre à aimer (faire) qch; **to have a ~ for sb** tenir qn en affection, avoir de la sympathie pour qn; **to have a ~ for sth** avoir un penchant *or* du goût pour qch, aimer qch; **is it to your ~?** est-ce à votre goût?, est-ce que cela vous plaît?

lilac [ˈlaɪlək] **1** *n* (*bush, colour, flower*) lilas *m*. **an avenue of mauve ~s** une avenue bordée de lilas mauves; **a bunch of white ~** un bouquet de lilas blanc. **2** *adj* (*in colour*) lilas *inv*.

Lilliputian [ˌlɪlɪˈpjuːʃɪən] **1** *adj* lilliputien. **2** *n* Lilliputien(ne) *m(f)*.

lilt [lɪlt] *n [speech, song]* rythme *m*, cadence *f*. **a song with a ~ to it** une chanson bien rythmée; **her voice had a pleasant ~ (to it)** sa voix avait des cadences mélodieuses.

lilting [ˈlɪltɪŋ] *adj song* cadencé; *voice* aux intonations mélodieuses.

lily [ˈlɪlɪ] **1** *n* lis *m*. **~ of the valley** muguet *m*; *V* **water**. **2** *cpd*: (*liter*) **lily-livered** poltron (*liter*); **lily pad** feuille *f* de nénuphar; **lily-white** d'une blancheur de lis, blanc (*f* blanche) comme (un) lis.

Lima bean [ˈliːməˈbiːn] *n* haricot *m* de Lima.

limb [lɪm] *n* (*Anat, Zool, also fig*) membre *m*; *[tree]* grosse branche; *[cross]* bras *m*. **to tear ~ from ~** *person* mettre en pièces; *animal* démembrer; (*fig*) **to be out on a ~** (*isolated*) être isolé; (*vulnerable*) être dans une situation délicate; **~ of Satan** suppôt *m* de Satan.

-limbed [lɪmd] *adj ending in cpds*: **long-limbed** aux membres longs; **strong-limbed** aux membres forts.

limber[1] [ˈlɪmbəʳ] *adj person* souple, agile, leste; *thing* souple, flexible.

limber up *vi* (*Sport etc*) se dégourdir, faire des exercices d'assouplissement; (*fig*) se préparer, se mettre en train. **limbering-up exercises** exercices *mpl* d'assouplissement.

limber[2] [ˈlɪmbəʳ] *n [gun carriage]* avant-train *m*.

limbless [ˈlɪmlɪs] *adj tree* sans branches. **~ man** (*no limbs*) homme *m* sans membres, homme tronc; (*limb missing*) homme estropié, homme à qui il manque un bras *or* une jambe; (*after amputation*) amputé *m* (d'un membre); **~ ex-servicemen** ≃ (grands) mutilés *mpl* de guerre.

limbo[1] [ˈlɪmbəʊ] *n* (*Rel*) limbes *mpl*; (*fig*) oubli *m*. (*fig*) **to be in ~** être tombé dans l'oubli.

limbo[2] [ˈlɪmbəʊ] *n*: **~ dancer** danseur *m*, -euse *f* de limbo.

lime[1] [laɪm] **1** *n* **(a)** (*Chem*) chaux *f*; *V* **quick** *etc*. **(b)** (*bird~*) glu *f*. **2** *vt* **(a)** *ground* chauler. **(b)** *twig* engluer; *bird* prendre à la glu, engluer. **3** *cpd*: **lime kiln** four *m* à chaux; **limelight** *V* **limelight**; **limestone** pierre *f* à chaux.

lime[2] [laɪm] *n* (*fruit*) lime *f*, limette *f*; (*tree*) limettier *m*. **~ green** vert jaune *inv*; **~ juice** jus *m* de citron vert.

lime[3] [laɪm] *n* (*linden: also ~ tree*) tilleul *m*.

limelight [ˈlaɪmlaɪt] *n* (*Theat*) feux *mpl* de la rampe. (*fig*) **to be in the ~** être en vedette *or* au premier plan.

limerick [ˈlɪmərɪk] *n* poème *m* humoristique (*de 5 vers*).

limey [ˈlaɪmɪ] *n* (*Australia:*) Anglais *m*; (*sailor*) marin anglais.

limit [ˈlɪmɪt] **1** *n* (*furthest point*) *[territory, experience, vision etc]* limite *f*; (*fig*) limite, borne *f*; (*restriction on amount, number etc*) limitation *f*, restriction *f*; (*permitted maximum*) limite. **outside/within the ~s of** en dehors des/dans les limites de; **it is true within ~s** c'est vrai dans une certaine limite *or* mesure; **without ~** sans limitation, sans limite; **weight ~** limitation de poids; (*US*) **off ~s** *area, district* d'accès interdit; (*on sign*) 'accès interdit'; **we must set a ~ to the expense** il faut limiter *or* restreindre les dépenses; (*Aut*) **the 60-km ~** la limitation (de vitesse) de 60 km à l'heure; (*Aut*) **there is a 60 km/h ~ on this road** la vitesse est limitée à 60 km/h sur cette route; (*Aut*) **to keep within/go over the speed ~** respecter/dépasser la limitation de vitesse; **over the ~** (*of lorry in weight*) en surcharge, surchargé; (*of driver on Breathalyser*) qui excède le taux légal (*de l'alcootest*); **to go to the ~ to help sb** faire tout son possible pour aider qn; **he is at the ~ of his patience/endurance** il est à bout de patience/de forces; **there is a ~ to my patience** ma patience a des limites *or* des bornes; **his anger knows no ~s** sa colère ne connaît pas de limites, sa colère est sans borne(s); **there are ~s!*** quand même il y a des limites!, il y a une limite à tout!; **there is no ~ on the amount you can import** la quantité que l'on peut importer n'est pas limitée; **there is a ~ to what one can do** il y a une limite à ce qu'on peut faire, on ne peut (quand même) pas faire l'impossible; **that's the ~!*** c'est le comble!, ça dépasse les bornes!; **he's the ~!*** (*goes too far*) il dépasse les bornes!; (*amusing*) il est impayable!*

2 *vt* **(a)** (*restrict*) *speed, time* limiter (*to* à); *expense, power* limiter, restreindre (*to* à); *person* limiter. **he ~ed questions to those dealing with education** il a accepté seulement les questions portant sur l'éducation; **he ~ed questions to 25 minutes** il a limité les questions à 25 minutes; **to ~ o.s. to a few remarks** se borner à (faire) quelques remarques; **to ~ o.s. to 10 cigarettes a day** se limiter à 10 cigarettes par jour; **we are ~ed in what we can do** nous sommes limités dans ce que nous pouvons faire.

(b) (*confine*) limiter. **that plant is ~ed to Spain** cette plante ne se trouve qu'en Espagne; **our reorganization plans are ~ed to Africa** nos projets de réorganisation se limitent à *or* ne concernent que l'Afrique.

limitation [ˌlɪmɪˈteɪʃən] *n* **(a)** (*restriction*) limitation *f*, restriction *f*. **the ~ on imports** la limitation *or* la restriction des importations; **there is no ~ on the amount of currency you may take** il n'y a aucune restriction sur les devises que vous pouvez emporter; **he has/knows his ~s** il a/connaît ses limites.

(b) (*Jur*) prescription *f*.

limited [ˈlɪmɪtɪd] *adj* **(a)** (*small*) *choice, means, resources* restreint, limité. **this book is written for a ~ readership** ce livre est destiné à un public restreint.

(b) (*restricted*) *number* limité, restreint. **~ edition** édition *f* à tirage limité; **to a ~ extent** jusqu'à un certain point; **~-stop *or* (*US*) ~ bus** autobus semi-direct.

(c) (*narrow*) *intelligence, person* borné.

(d) (*esp Brit*) (*Comm, Jur*) **Smith and Sons L~** (*abbr* **Ltd**) ≃ Smith et fils, Société anonyme (*abbr* **S.A.**); (*Fin*) **~ (liability) company** société *f* à responsabilité limitée.

limitless ['lɪmɪtlɪs] *adj power* sans borne(s), illimité; *opportunities* illimité.

limousine ['lɪməziːn] *n* limousine *f*.

limp[1] [lɪmp] *adj* mou (*f* molle); (*pej*) *flesh, skin, body* flasque; (*pej*) *dress, hat* avachi, informe; *movement* mou, sans énergie; *handshake* mou; *voice* faible; *style* mou, sans fermeté. *[book]* **~ cover(s)** reliure *f* souple; **to let one's body go ~** se décontracter; **let your arm go ~** décontractez votre bras; **I feel very ~ in this hot weather** je me sens tout ramolli *or* avachi par cette chaleur.

limp[2] [lɪmp] **1** *vi [person]* boiter; (*fig*) *[vehicle etc]* marcher tant bien que mal. **to ~ in/out** *etc* entrer/sortir *etc* en boitant; **to ~ along** avancer en boitant, aller clopinant *or* clopin-clopant*; **he ~ed to the door** il est allé à la porte en boitant, il a clopiné jusqu'à la porte; **the plane managed to ~ home** l'avion a réussi à regagner sa base tant bien que mal.

2 *n* claudication *f*. **to have a ~, to walk with a ~** boiter, clopiner.

limpet ['lɪmpɪt] *n* **(a)** (*Zool*) patelle *f*, bernicle *f*; (*fig: person*) crampon *m*. **to cling** *or* **stick to sth like a ~** s'accrocher à qch comme une moule au rocher. **(b)** (*Mil: also* **~ mine**) mine-ventouse *f*.

limpid ['lɪmpɪd] *adj* (*lit, fig*) limpide.

limply ['lɪmplɪ] *adv* mollement, sans énergie. **he said ~** dit-il mollement.

limpness ['lɪmpnɪs] *n* (*V* **limp**[1]) mollesse *f*; flaccidité *f* (*frm*); avachissement *m*, manque *m* d'énergie *or* de fermeté.

limy ['laɪmɪ] *adj* (*V* **lime**[1]) calcaire; englué.

linchpin ['lɪntʃpɪn] *n* (*Aut*) esse *f*; (*fig*) pivot *m*.

linden ['lɪndən] *n* (*also* **~ tree**) tilleul *m*.

line[1] [laɪn] **1** *n* **(a)** (*mark*) ligne *f*, trait *m*; (*Math, TV*) ligne; (*pen stroke*) trait; (*on face, palm*) ligne; (*wrinkle*) ride *f*; (*boundary*) frontière *f*; (*Ftbl, Tennis*) ligne. (*Geog*) **the L~** l'équateur *m*, la ligne; **to draw a ~ under sth** tirer *or* tracer un trait sous qch; **to put a ~ through sth** barrer *or* rayer qch; **the teacher put a red ~ through my translation** le professeur a barré *or* rayé ma traduction d'un trait rouge; (*Bridge*) **above/below the ~** (marqué) en points d'honneur/en points de marche; (*Math*) **a straight ~** une (ligne) droite; (*Math*) **a curved ~** une (ligne) courbe; (*Mus*) **on the ~** sur la ligne; (*Aut*) **yellow/white ~** ligne jaune/blanche; *V* **dot, draw, hard, state** *etc*.

(b) (*rope*) corde *f*; (*wire*) fil *m*; (*Fishing*) ligne *f*, fil; (*Elec*) ligne; *[diver]* corde *f* (de sûreté); (*also* **clothes ~, washing ~**) corde (à linge). **the view was hidden by a ~ of washing** la vue était cachée par du linge étendu sur une corde; **to get a ~ to sb fallen overboard** lancer une corde *or* un bout à qn qui est tombé par-dessus bord; *V* **air, pipe** *etc*.

(c) (*Telec*) ligne *f*. **the ~s are out of order** les lignes sont en dérangement; **the ~s are down** les lignes ont été abattues; **the ~'s gone dead** (*cut off*) on nous a coupés; (*no dialling tone*) il n'y a plus de tonalité; **give me a ~** donnez-moi une ligne; **can you get me a ~ to Chicago?** pouvez-vous m'avoir Chicago (au téléphone)?; **the ~s are open from 6 o'clock onwards** on peut téléphoner *or* appeler à partir de 6 heures; **the ~ is engaged** *or* (*US*) **busy** la ligne est occupée, c'est occupé; **Mr Smith is on the ~** (c'est) M Smith au téléphone; **Mr Smith's ~ is engaged** la ligne de M Smith est occupée; **he's on the ~ to the manager** il téléphone au directeur; **663-1111 5 ~s** 663-1111 5 lignes groupées; *V* **hold, hot** *etc*.

(d) *[print, writing]* ligne *f*; *[poem]* vers *m*; (*: *letter*) mot *m*. (*esp Brit*) **(marriage) ~s** acte *m* de mariage; **a 6-~ stanza** une strophe de 6 vers; **30 ~s to a page** 30 lignes par page; **page 20, ~ 18** page 20, ligne 18; (*fig*) **to read between the ~s** lire entre les lignes; (*in dictation*) **new ~** à la ligne; **it's one of the best ~s in 'Hamlet'** c'est l'un des meilleurs vers de 'Hamlet'; (*Theat*) **to learn/forget one's ~s** apprendre/oublier son texte *or* son rôle; (*Scol*) **take 100 ~s** vous (me) ferez 100 lignes; **drop me a ~** envoyez-moi un (petit) mot.

(e) (*row*) *[trees, parked cars]* rangée *f*; *[cars in traffic etc]* file *f*; *[hills]* chaîne *f*; *[people]* (*side by side*) rang *m*, rangée; (*behind one another*) file, colonne *f*; (*esp US: queue*) file, queue *f*; (*in factory*) chaîne. (*US*) **to stand in ~, to make a ~** faire la queue; **they were waiting in ~** ils attendaient en file *or* en colonne; **they were standing in a ~** ils étaient alignés *or* en ligne; **they were waiting in ~s** ils attendaient en rangs; **they moved along quietly in ~** ils avançaient tranquillement à la queue leu leu *or* les uns derrière les autres; **he got into ~** (*beside others*) il s'est mis dans le rang; (*behind others*) il s'est mis dans la file *or* la colonne; (*fig*) **to bring sb into ~** mettre qn au pas; (*fig*) **to come** *or* **fall into ~** se conformer (*with sth* à qch), tomber d'accord (*with sb* avec qn); (*fig*) **to keep the party in ~** maintenir la discipline dans le parti; (*in drill etc*) **that man is out of ~** cet homme n'est pas à l'alignement; (*fig*) **he stepped out of ~** il a fait l'indépendant, il a refusé de se conformer, il a fait cavalier seul; (*fig*) **all along the ~** sur toute la ligne, complètement; *V* **assembly, bread, production** *etc*.

(f) (*direction*) ligne *f*, direction *f*. (*Mil*) **~ of fire** ligne de tir; **right in the ~ of fire** en plein champ de tir; (*Mil*) **~ of sight** ligne de visée; **~ of sight, ~ of vision** ligne de vision; (*fig*) **that's the ~ of least resistance** c'est la solution de facilité; (*fig*) **to take the ~ of least resistance** choisir la solution de facilité; *[policeman, ambassador etc]* **in the ~ of duty** dans l'exercice de ses (*or* mes *etc*) fonctions; **the soldier met his death in the ~ of duty** le soldat est tombé au champ d'honneur; **it's all in the ~ of duty** ça fait partie du travail *or* du boulot*; **~ of attack** (*Mil*) plan *m* d'attaque; (*fig*) plan d'action, ligne de conduite; **that is not my ~ of argument** ce n'est pas ce que je cherche à démontrer; **his ~ of argument was that ...** son raisonnement était que ...; **~ of research** ligne de recherche(s); **what is your ~ of thought?** qu'envisagez-vous de faire?, quels sont vos plans?; **to take a strong ~ on** adopter une attitude ferme sur; **this is not in ~ with company policy** ce n'est pas en accord avec *or* n'est pas conforme à la politique de la société; **we are all thinking along the same ~s** nous pensons tous de la même façon, nous sommes tous d'accord; **the president and those who think along the same ~s** le président et ceux qui partagent son opinion; **your essay is more or less along the same ~s** votre dissertation suit plus ou moins le même plan; **I was thinking of something along** *or* **on those ~s** je pensais à quelque chose dans cet ordre d'idées *or* dans ce genre-là *or* dans ce style; **you're on the right ~s** vous êtes sur la bonne voie; *V* **bee, inquiry, party** *etc*.

(g) (*descent*) ligne *f*, lignée *f*. **in a direct ~ from** en droite ligne de, en ligne directe de; **in the male ~** par les hommes; **he comes from a long ~ of artists** il vient d'une longue lignée d'artistes; **the royal ~** la lignée royale.

(h) (*) (*information*) renseignement *m*, tuyau* *m*; (*clue*) indice *m*, tuyau*. **we've got a ~ on where he's gone to** nous croyons savoir où il est allé; **the police have got a ~ on the criminal** la police a une idée de *or* des indices sur l'identité du coupable; **I've got a ~ on a good used car** j'ai un tuyau* pour une voiture d'occasion en bon état; *V* **hand, shoot**.

(i) (*also* **shipping ~**) (*company*) compagnie *f*; (*route*) ligne *f* (maritime). **the Cunard L~** la compagnie Cunard; **the New York-Southampton ~** la ligne New York-Southampton; *V* **air** *etc*.

(j) (*Rail*) (*route*) ligne *f* (de chemin de fer); *[underground]* ligne (de métro); (*track*) voie *f*. **the Brighton ~** la ligne de Brighton; **the ~ was blocked for several hours** la voie a été bloquée *or* la ligne a été interrompue pendant plusieurs heures; **cross the ~ by the footbridge** utilisez la passerelle pour traverser la voie; **the train left the ~** le train a déraillé; *V* **down**[1], **main, tram** *etc*.

(k) (*Art etc*) ligne *f* (*gen sg*). **I like the ~(s) of this car** j'aime la ligne de cette voiture; **the graceful ~s of Gothic churches** la ligne gracieuse des églises gothiques.

(l) (*Mil*) ligne *f*. (*Mil, fig*) **in the front ~** en première ligne; **behind the enemy ~s** derrière les lignes ennemies; **the Maginot ~** la ligne Maginot; **~ of battle** ligne de combat; (*Brit Mil*) **regiment of the ~** ≃ régiment *m* d'infanterie; (*Navy*) **~ abreast** ligne de front; **~ astern** ligne de file; **ship of the ~** vaisseau *m* de ligne, navire *m* de haut bord.

(m) (*business*) affaires *fpl*; (*occupation*) métier *m*, partie *f*. **what ~ are you in?, what's your ~ (of business)?** que faites-vous (dans la vie)?, quelle est votre partie?, dans quel genre d'affaires êtes-vous?; **he's in the grocery ~** il est dans l'épicerie; **cocktail parties are not (in) my ~** les cocktails ne sont pas mon genre; **fishing's more (in) my ~ (of country)** la pêche est davantage mon rayon* *or* dans mes cordes.

(n) (*Comm: series of goods*) article(s) *m(pl)*. **that ~ doesn't sell very well** cet article ne se vend pas bien; **they've brought out a new ~ in felt hats** ils ont sorti une nouveauté dans les chapeaux de feutre.

2 *cpd*: (*Art*) **line drawing** dessin *m* (au trait); (*Sport*) **line fishing** pêche *f* à la ligne; **lineman** (*Rail*) poseur *m* de rails; (*Telec*) ouvrier *m* de ligne; (*Rugby*) **line-out** touche *f*; (*Sport*) **linesman** (*Tennis*) juge *m* de ligne; (*Ftbl*) juge de touche; **line-up** (*row: of people etc*) file *f*; (*Police*) séance *f* d'identification (d'un suspect); (*Ftbl etc*) (composition *f* de l')équipe *f*; (*fig*) **the line-up of African powers** le front des puissances africaines.

3 *vt paper* régler, ligner; (*wrinkle*) *face* rider, marquer. **~d paper** papier réglé; **face ~d with sorrow** visage marqué par le chagrin; **the streets were ~d with cheering crowds** les rues étaient bordées d'une (double) haie de spectateurs enthousiastes; **cheering crowds ~d the route** une foule enthousiaste faisait la haie tout le long du parcours; **the road was ~d with trees** la route était bordée d'arbres; **the walls were ~d with books and pictures** les murs étaient couverts *or* tapissés de livres et de tableaux.

line up 1 *vi* (*stand in row*) se mettre en rang(s), s'aligner; (*US: stand in queue*) faire la queue. **the teams lined up and waited for the whistle** les équipes se sont alignées et ont attendu le coup de sifflet; (*Sport fig*) **the teams lined up as follows ...** les équipes étaient constituées comme suit ... .

2 *vt sep* **(a)** *people* aligner, mettre en ligne. **line them up against the wall** alignez-les le long du mur.

(b) (*: *find*) trouver, dénicher*; (*have in mind*) prévoir, avoir en vue. **we must line up a chairman for the meeting** il faut que nous trouvions (*subj*) *or* dénichions* (*subj*) un président pour la réunion; **have you got someone lined up?** avez-vous quelqu'un en vue?; **I wonder what he's got lined up for us** je me demande ce qu'il nous prépare.

3 line-up *n V* **line**[1] **2**.

line[2] [laɪn] *vt clothes* doubler (*with* de); *[bird] nest* garnir, tapisser; (*Tech*) revêtir, chemiser; *brakes* garnir. (*fig*) **to ~ one's pockets** se garnir *or* se remplir les poches; **to ~ one's stomach*** se mettre quelque chose dans le ventre:; *V* **wool** *etc*.

lineage ['lɪnɪɪdʒ] *n* (*ancestry*) lignage†† *m*; famille *f*; (*descendants*) lignée *f*. **she can trace her ~ back to the 17th century** sa famille remonte au 17e siècle.

lineal ['lɪnɪəl] *adj* en ligne directe.

lineament ['lɪnɪəmənt] *n* (*feature*) trait *m*, linéament *m*. (*characteristics*) **~s** caractéristiques *fpl*, particularités *fpl*.

linear ['lɪnɪə^r] *adj* linéaire.

linen ['lɪnɪn] **1** *n* **(a)** (*U: Tex*) (toile *f* de) lin *m*.

(b) (*collective n*) (*sheets, tablecloths etc: often US* **~s**) linge *m* (de maison); (*underwear*) linge (de corps). **dirty** *or* **soiled ~** linge sale; *V* **household, wash.**

2 *cpd sheet* de fil, pur fil; *suit, thread* de lin. **linen basket** panier *m* à linge; **linen closet, linen cupboard** armoire *f or* placard *m* à linge; **linen paper** papier *m* de lin.

liner ['laɪnəʳ] *n* **(a)** (*Naut*) paquebot *m* de grande ligne, liner *m*; *V* **air. (b) dustbin ~** sac *m* à poubelle. **(c)** *V* **eye 3.**

ling[1] [lɪŋ] *n* (*Bot*) brande *f.*

ling[2] [lɪŋ] *n* (*sea fish*) lingue *f*, morue longue, julienne *f*; (*freshwater fish*) lotte *f* de rivière.

linger ['lɪŋgəʳ] *vi* **(a)** (*also* **~ on**) *[person]* s'attarder, rester (en arrière); *[smell, pain]* persister; *[tradition, memory]* persister, subsister; *[doubt]* subsister. **the others had gone, but he ~ed (on)** les autres étaient partis, lui restait en arrière *or* s'attardait; **after the accident he ~ed (on) for several months** après l'accident il a traîné quelques mois avant de mourir.

(b) (*take one's time*) prendre son temps; (*dawdle*) traîner, lambiner*. **he always ~s behind everyone else** il est toujours derrière tout le monde, il est toujours à la traîne; **don't ~ about** *or* **around** ne lambine pas*, ne traîne pas; **to ~ over a meal** rester longtemps à table, manger sans se presser; **I let my eye ~ on the scene** j'ai laissé mon regard s'attarder sur la scène; **to ~ on a subject** s'attarder *or* s'étendre sur un sujet.

lingerie ['lænʒəriː] *n* (*U*) lingerie *f.*

lingering ['lɪŋgərɪŋ] *adj look* long (*f* longue), insistant; *doubt* qui subsiste (encore); *hope* faible; *death* lent.

lingo* ['lɪŋgəʊ] *n* (*pej*) (*language*) baragouin *m*, jargon* *m*; (*jargon*) jargon (*pej*). **I had a hard time in Spain because I don't speak the ~** j'ai eu du mal en Espagne parce que je ne comprends pas leur baragouin *or* parce que je ne cause: pas espagnol.

lingua franca ['lɪŋgwə'fræŋkə] *n* sabir *m*, langue franque.

linguist ['lɪŋgwɪst] *n* linguiste *mf*. **I'm no great ~** je ne suis guère doué pour les langues.

linguistic [lɪŋ'gwɪstɪk] *adj* linguistique.

linguistics [lɪŋ'gwɪstɪks] 1 *n* (*U*) linguistique *f*; *V* **comparative** *etc.* 2 *cpd book, degree, professor* de linguistique; *student* en linguistique.

liniment ['lɪnɪmənt] *n* liniment *m.*

lining ['laɪnɪŋ] *n [clothes, handbag]* doublure *f*; (*Tech*) revêtement *m*; *[brakes]* garniture *f*. **~ paper** papier peint de base; (*for drawers*) papier à tapisser; *V* **silver.**

link [lɪŋk] 1 *n [chain]* maillon *m*, chaînon *m*, anneau *m*; (*connection*) lien *m*, liaison *f*; (*interrelation*) rapport *m*, lien; (*bonds*) lien, relation *f*. **a new rail ~** une nouvelle liaison ferroviaire; **there must be a ~ between the 2 phenomena** il doit y avoir un lien *or* un rapport entre les 2 phénomènes; **he served as ~ between management and workers** il a servi de lien *or* d'intermédiaire entre la direction et les ouvriers; **cultural ~s** liens culturels, relations culturelles; **~s of friendship** liens d'amitié; **he broke off all ~s with his friends** il a cessé toutes relations avec ses amis, il a rompu les liens qui l'unissaient à ses amis; *V* **cuff, missing.**

2 *cpd*: (*Ling*) **linking verb** verbe copulatif; **link-up** (*gen*) lien *m*, rapport *m*; (*Rad, TV: connection*) liaison *f*; (*Rad, TV: programme*) émission *f* duplex; (*Space*) jonction *f*; **there is no apparent link-up between the 2 cases** il n'y a pas de rapport apparent *or* de lien apparent entre les 2 affaires; **is there any link-up between our company and theirs?** y a-t-il un lien entre notre compagnie et la leur?

3 *vt* **(a)** (*connect*) relier; (*fig*) lier. **~ed by rail/by telephone** reliés par (la) voie ferrée/par téléphone; **this is closely ~ed to our sales figures** ceci est étroitement lié à nos chiffres de vente.

(b) (*join*) lier, unir, joindre; *spacecraft* opérer l'arrimage de. **to ~ arms** se donner le bras; **~ed (together) in friendship** liés d'amitié; **the 2 companies are now ~ed (together)** les 2 compagnies sont maintenant liées *or* associées.

link together 1 *vi* s'unir, se rejoindre.

2 *vt sep two objects* unir, joindre; (*by means of a third*) relier; *V also* **link 3b.**

link up 1 *vi [persons]* se rejoindre; (*Comm*) *[firms, organizations etc]* s'associer; *[spacecraft]* opérer l'arrimage; *[roads, railway lines]* se rejoindre, se réunir, se rencontrer. **they linked up with the other group** ils ont rejoint l'autre groupe.

2 *vt sep* **(a)** (*Rad, Telec, TV*) relier, assurer la liaison entre. **(b)** *spacecraft* opérer l'arrimage de.

3 **link-up** *n V* **link 2.**

linkage ['lɪŋkɪdʒ] *n* **(a)** (*tie*) lien *m*, relation *f*. **(b)** (*Tech*) tringlerie *f*, transmission *f* par tringlerie. **(c)** (*Bio*) linkage *m.*

links [lɪŋks] *npl* (terrain *m* de) golf *m*, links *mpl.*

linnet ['lɪnɪt] *n* linotte *f.*

lino ['laɪnəʊ] *n* (*Brit** *abbr of* **linoleum**) lino *m*. **~cut** gravure *f* sur linoléum.

linoleum [lɪ'nəʊlɪəm] *n* linoléum *m.*

linotype ['laɪnəʊtaɪp] *n* linotype *f.*

linseed ['lɪnsiːd] *n* (*U*) graines *fpl* de lin. **~ oil** huile *f* de lin.

lint [lɪnt] *n* (*U*) **(a)** (*Med*) tissu ouaté (*pour pansements*). **a small piece of ~** une compresse, un petit pansement ouaté. **(b)** (*US: fluff*) peluches *fpl.*

lintel ['lɪntl] *n* linteau *m.*

lion ['laɪən] 1 *n* lion *m*; (*fig: person*) personnage *m* en vue, célébrité *f*. (*fig*) **to get** *or* **take the ~'s share** se tailler la part du lion; (*fig*) **to put one's head in the ~'s mouth** se jeter *or* se précipiter dans la gueule du loup; *V* **beard, mountain, Richard.**

2 *cpd*: **lion cub** lionceau *m*; **lion-hearted** d'un courage de lion; (*fig*) **she is a lion-hunter** elle cherche toujours à avoir des célébrités comme invités; **lion-tamer** dompteur *m*, -euse *f* de lions, belluaire *m.*

lioness ['laɪənɪs] *n* lionne *f.*

lionize ['laɪənaɪz] *vt person* faire fête à, faire un accueil délirant à, fêter comme une célébrité.

lip [lɪp] 1 *n* (*Anat*) lèvre *f*; *[jug]* bec *m*; *[cup, saucer]* rebord *m*; *[crater]* bord *m*; *[wound]* bord, lèvre; (*: *insolence*) culot* *m*, insolences *fpl*. **none of your ~!*** ne fais pas l'insolent! *or* le répondeur!*; *V* **bite, stiff** *etc.*

2 *cpd*: **lipread** lire sur les lèvres; **lip-reading** lecture *f* sur les lèvres; (*Brit*) **lip salve** pommade *f* rosat *or* pour les lèvres; **he pays lip service to socialism but ...** à l'écouter on dirait qu'il est socialiste mais ...; **he only pays lip service to socialism** il n'est socialiste qu'en paroles; **that was merely lip service on his part** il ne l'a dit que pour la forme, il l'a dit du bout des lèvres; **lipstick** (*U: substance*) rouge *m* à lèvres; (*stick*) bâton *m or* tube *m* de rouge à lèvres.

-lipped [lɪpt] *adj ending in cpds*: **dry-lipped** aux lèvres sèches; *V* **thick** *etc.*

liquefaction [ˌlɪkwɪ'fækʃən] *n* liquéfaction *f.*

liquefy ['lɪkwɪfaɪ] 1 *vt* liquéfier. 2 *vi* se liquéfier.

liqueur [lɪ'kjʊəʳ] *n* liqueur *f.*

liquid ['lɪkwɪd] 1 *adj* **(a)** (*not solid etc*) *substance* liquide; *container* pour (les) liquides. **~ air/oxygen** air *m*/oxygène *m* liquide; **~ ammonia** ammoniaque *m* (liquide); **~ diet** régime *m* (exclusivement) liquide; **~ measure** mesure *f* de capacité pour les liquides; (*Pharm*) **~ paraffin** huile *f* de paraffine.

(b) (*fig*) *eyes, sky* limpide, clair; *sound, voice* limpide, harmonieux; (*Ling*) liquide. (*Fin*) **~ assets** liquidités *fpl*, disponibilités *fpl.*

2 *n* (*fluid*) liquide *m*; (*Ling*) liquide *f.*

liquidate ['lɪkwɪdeɪt] *vt* (*Fin, Jur*) liquider; (*: *kill*) liquider*.

liquidation [ˌlɪkwɪ'deɪʃən] *n* (*Fin, Jur, also* *) liquidation *f*. **to go into ~** déposer son bilan.

liquidize ['lɪkwɪdaɪz] *vt* liquéfier; (*Culin*) passer à la centrifugeuse.

liquidizer ['lɪkwɪdaɪzəʳ] *n* (*Culin*) centrifugeuse *f.*

liquor ['lɪkəʳ] *n* (*alcohol*) spiritueux *m*, alcool *m*; (*Culin*) liquide *m*. **to be the worse for ~** être soûl *or* ivre; (*US*) **~ store** marchand *m* de vins et spiritueux; *V* **hard.**

liquorice ['lɪkərɪs] 1 *n* (*Bot*) réglisse *f*; (*sweet*) réglisse *m*. 2 *cpd*: (*gen Brit*) **liquorice allsorts** bonbons assortis au réglisse; **liquorice stick/root** bâton *m*/bois *m* de réglisse.

Lisbon ['lɪzbən] *n* Lisbonne.

lisle [laɪl] *n* (*also* **~ thread**) fil *m* d'Écosse.

lisp [lɪsp] 1 *vi* zézayer, zozoter*.

2 *vt* (*also* **~ out**) dire en zézayant. **'please don't say that,' she ~ed coyly** 's'il vous plaît ne dites pas cela,' dit-elle en faisant des manières.

3 *n* zézaiement *m*. **... she said with a ~** ... dit-elle en zézayant; **to speak with** *or* **have a ~** zézayer, zozoter*, avoir un cheveu sur la langue*.

lissom ['lɪsəm] *adj* souple, agile.

list[1] [lɪst] 1 *n* liste *f*. **your name isn't on the ~** votre nom ne figure pas *or* n'est pas couché (*frm*) sur la liste; **you can take me off the ~** vous pouvez me rayer de la liste; **you're (at the) top/bottom of the ~** vous êtes en tête/en fin *or* en queue de liste; *V* **active, civil, danger** *etc.*

2 *cpd*: (*Comm*) **list price** prix *m* de catalogue.

3 *vt* (*make list of*) faire *or* dresser la liste de; (*write down*) inscrire; (*enumerate*) énumérer. **your name isn't ~ed** votre nom n'est pas inscrit, votre nom n'est pas (porté) sur la liste; (*Comm*) **it isn't ~ed** cela ne figure pas au catalogue; **an airgun is ~ed as a weapon** un fusil à air comprimé est classé *or* catalogué parmi les armes; **'airgun' is ~ed under 'air'** 'airgun' se trouve sous 'air'; (*St Ex*) **the shares are ~ed at 85 francs** les actions sont cotées à 85 F; (*Brit*) **~ed building** monument classé *or* historique.

list[2] [lɪst] (*Naut etc*) 1 *vi* donner de la bande, gîter. **the ship is ~ing badly** le bateau gîte dangereusement; **to ~ to port** gîter *or* donner de la bande sur bâbord.

2 *n* inclinaison *f*. **to have a ~** gîter; **to have a ~ of 20°** gîter de 20°, donner 20° de gîte *or* de bande.

listen ['lɪsn] *vi* **(a)** écouter. **~ to me** écoute-moi (*V also* **b**); **~!** écoute!; **you never ~ to a word I say!** tu n'écoutes jamais ce que je dis!; **to ~ to the radio** écouter la radio; **you are ~ing to the BBC** vous êtes à l'écoute de la BBC; **I love ~ing to the rain** j'aime écouter la pluie (tomber); **to ~ for sth** prêter l'oreille à qch, essayer d'entendre qch; **~ for the telephone while I'm out** surveille le téléphone pendant que je suis sorti; **hush, I'm ~ing for the phone chut!** j'essaie d'entendre si le téléphone ne sonne pas; **he was ~ing for his father's return** il écoutait si son père ne rentrait pas; *V* **half.**

(b) (*heed*) écouter. **~ to your father** écoute ton père; (*as threat*) **~ to me!** écoute-moi bien!; **~*, I can't stop to talk now but ...** écoute, je n'ai pas le temps de parler tout de suite mais ...; **he wouldn't ~ to reason** il n'a pas voulu entendre raison.

listen in *vi* **(a)** (*Rad*) être à l'écoute, écouter.

(b) (*eavesdrop*) écouter. **I should like to listen in to your discussion** j'aimerais assister à votre discussion.

listener ['lɪsnəʳ] *n* personne *f* qui écoute; (*to speaker, radio etc*) auditeur *m*, -trice *f*. **the ~s** l'auditoire *m*, le public; **his ~s were enthralled** son auditoire était *or* son public était *or* ses auditeurs étaient sous le charme; **she's a good ~** elle sait écouter (avec patience et sympathie).

listening ['lɪsnɪŋ] *n* écoute *f*. (*Rad*) **goodbye and good ~!** au revoir et bonne soirée *etc* à l'écoute de nos programmes!; (*Rad*) **we don't do much ~** nous n'écoutons pas beaucoup *or* souvent la radio; (*Mil*) **~ post** poste *m* d'écoute.

listless ['lɪstlɪs] *adj* (*uninterested*) indifférent; (*apathetic*) indolent, apathique, amorphe; (*without energy*) sans énergie, mou (*f* molle); *wave* indolent; *handshake* mou. **to feel ~** se

sentir apathique *or* sans ressort; **the heat made him ~** la chaleur lui enlevait son énergie.
listlessly [ˈlɪstlɪslɪ] *adv* (*V* **listless**) avec indifférence; avec indolence, avec apathie; sans énergie, mollement.
listlessness [ˈlɪstlɪsnɪs] *n* (*V* **listless**) indifférence *f*; indolence *f*, apathie *f*; manque *m* d'énergie, mollesse *f*.
lists [lɪsts] *npl* (*Hist*) lice *f*. (*lit, fig*) **to enter the ~** entrer en lice.
lit [lɪt] **1** *pret, ptp of* **light**[1]. **2** *adj* éclairé, illuminé. **the street was very badly ~** la rue était très mal éclairée; (*drunk*) **~ up*** soûl, paf* *inv*.
litany [ˈlɪtənɪ] *n* (*Rel, fig*) litanie *f*.
liter [ˈliːtəʳ] *n* (*US*) = **litre.**
literacy [ˈlɪtərəsɪ] **1** *n* (*ability*) fait *m* de savoir lire et écrire, degré *m* d'alphabétisation. **his ~ was not in doubt** personne ne doutait du fait qu'il savait lire et écrire; **I am beginning to doubt even his ~** je commence même à douter qu'il sache lire et écrire; **universal ~ is one of the principal aims** l'un des buts principaux est de donner à tous la capacité de lire et d'écrire; **there is a high/low degree of ~ in that country** le degré d'alphabétisation est élevé/bas dans ce pays, le taux d'analphabétisme est bas/élevé dans ce pays.
2 *cpd*: **literacy campaign** campagne *f* d'alphabétisation; **literacy test** test *m* mesurant le niveau d'alphabétisation.
literal [ˈlɪtərəl] **1** *adj* **(a)** (*textual*) *translation* littéral, mot pour mot; *interpretation* au pied de la lettre; (*not fig*) *meaning* littéral, propre; (*unexaggerated*) réel, conforme à la réalité. **it was a ~ statement of fact** c'était un simple énoncé des faits; **the drought has meant ~ starvation for millions** la sécheresse a réduit littéralement à la famine des millions de gens.
(b) (*unimaginative*) *person* prosaïque.
2 *cpd*: **literal-minded** prosaïque, sans imagination; **literal-mindedness** manque *m* d'imagination, caractère *m* prosaïque.
literally [ˈlɪtərəlɪ] *adv* **(a)** *translate* littéralement, mot à mot; *mean* littéralement, au sens propre. **he interpreted the message ~** il a interprété le message dans son sens littéral *or* au pied de la lettre; **to carry out an order ~** exécuter un ordre à la lettre; **I was exaggerating but he took it ~** j'exagérais mais il a pris tout ce que je disais au pied de la lettre; **I was joking but he took me ~** je plaisantais mais il m'a pris au sérieux; **~ (speaking)** à proprement parler.
(b) (*really*) réellement, bel et bien. **it's ~ true** c'est bel et bien vrai; **it had ~ ceased to exist** cela avait bel et bien *or* réellement cessé d'exister.
(c) (*: *absolutely*) littéralement*. **the town was ~ bulging with sailors** la ville grouillait littéralement* de marins.
literary [ˈlɪtərərɪ] *adj history, studies, appreciation etc* littéraire. **he is a ~ man** (*well-read*) c'est un homme cultivé; (*writer etc*) c'est un homme de lettres; **~ critic/criticism** critique *m*/critique *f* littéraire.
literate [ˈlɪtərɪt] *adj* (*able to read etc*) qui sait lire et écrire; (*educated*) instruit; (*cultured*) cultivé. **few of them are ~** peu d'entre eux savent lire et écrire; **highly ~** très instruit *or* cultivé.
literati [ˌlɪtəˈrɑːtiː] *npl* gens *mpl* de lettres, lettrés *mpl*.
literature [ˈlɪtərɪtʃəʳ] *n* (*U*) **(a)** littérature *f*. **18th-century French ~** la littérature française du 18e siècle; **the ~ of ornithology** la littérature de l'ornithologie.
(b) (*brochures: about travel, school etc*) documentation *f*, brochure(s) *f(pl)*. **travel/educational ~** documentation *or* brochure(s) sur les voyages/l'éducation.
lithe [laɪð] *adj person* agile; *body, muscle* souple.
lithium [ˈlɪθɪəm] *n* lithium *m*.
lithograph [ˈlɪθəʊgrɑːf] **1** *n* lithographie *f* (*estampe*). **2** *vt* lithographier.
lithography [lɪˈθɒgrəfɪ] *n* lithographie *f* (*procédé*).
Lithuania [ˌlɪθjʊˈeɪnɪə] *n* Lit(h)uanie *f*.
Lithuanian [ˌlɪθjʊˈeɪnɪən] **1** *adj* lit(h)uanien. **2** *n* **(a)** Lit(h)uanien(ne) *m(f)*. **(b)** (*Ling*) lit(h)uanien *m*.
litigant [ˈlɪtɪgənt] *n* (*Jur*) plaideur *m*, -euse *f*.
litigate [ˈlɪtɪgeɪt] **1** *vi* plaider. **2** *vt* mettre en litige, contester.
litigation [ˌlɪtɪˈgeɪʃən] *n* litige *m*.
litigious [lɪˈtɪdʒəs] *adj* (*Jur*) litigieux; *person* (*given to litigation*) procédurier, chicaneur; (*argumentative etc*) chicanier.
litmus [ˈlɪtməs] *n* (*Chem*) tournesol *m*. **~ (paper)** papier *m* de tournesol.
litre, (*US*) **liter** [ˈliːtəʳ] *n* litre *m*. **~ bottle** (bouteille *f* d'un) litre.
litter [ˈlɪtəʳ] **1** *n* **(a)** (*U*) (*rubbish*) détritus *mpl*; (*dirtier*) ordures *fpl*; (*papers*) vieux papiers *mpl*. (*on basket etc*) '~' 'papiers S.V.P.'; **'take your ~ home'** 'ne jetez pas de papiers par *or* à terre'; **don't leave ~** ne jette pas de détritus *or* de papiers; (*on notice*) 'prière de ne pas laisser de détritus'.
(b) (*untidy mass*) fouillis *m*, désordre *m*. **in a ~** en désordre, en fouillis; **a ~ of books** un fouillis *or* un fatras de livres; (*fig*) **a ~ of caravans along the shore** des caravanes dispersées en désordre le long du rivage.
(c) (*Zool*) portée *f*. **10 little pigs at a ~** 10 cochonnets d'une même portée.
(d) (*Agr: bedding*) litière *f*.
(e) (*stretcher*) civière *f*; (*couch*) litière *f*.
2 *vt* **(a)** (*also* **~ up**) *[person] room* mettre du désordre dans, mettre en désordre; *countryside* laisser des détritus dans. **he ~ed the floor with all his football gear** il a éparpillé ses affaires de football sur le plancher; **he had ~ed papers all about the room** il avait laissé traîner des papiers dans toute la pièce.
(b) (*gen pass*) *[rubbish, papers]* joncher, couvrir. **the floor was ~ed with paper** des papiers jonchaient *or* couvraient le sol; **a street ~ed with broken bottles** une rue jonchée de débris de bouteilles; **the desk was ~ed with books** le bureau était couvert *or* encombré de livres; **the field was ~ed with caravans*** le champ était couvert de caravanes mal rangées.
3 *vi* (*Zool*) mettre bas.
4 *cpd*: **litter basket, litter bin** (*in street, playground, kitchen*) boîte *f* à ordures; (*dustbin*) poubelle *f*; (*pej*) **litterbug, litter-lout** *personne qui jette des détritus dans la rue ou dans la campagne*; **litterbugs should be fined** on devrait mettre à l'amende ces gens mal élevés qui jettent des détritus n'importe où; **all these litter-louts who foul up camp sites** tous ces cochons* qui jettent leurs détritus sur les terrains de camping.
little[1] [ˈlɪtl] *adj* (*small*) *house, group, gift, person* (*in height*) petit; (*short*) *stick, piece of string* petit, court; (*brief*) *period, holiday, visit* court, bref (*f* brève), petit; (*young*) *child, animal* petit, jeune; (*weak*) *voice, noise* petit, faible; *smell* petit, léger; (*small-scale*) *shopkeeper* petit; (*unimportant*) *detail, discomfort* petit, insignifiant, sans importance. **~ girl** petite fille, fillette *f*; **~ boy** petit garçon, garçonnet *m*; **my ~ brother** mon petit frère; **a ~ old woman** une petite vieille; **~ finger** petit doigt, auriculaire *m*; **~ toe** petit orteil; *[clock]* **~ hand** petite aiguille; (*Aut*) **~ end** pied *m* de bielle; **for a ~ while, for a ~ time** pendant *or* pour un petit moment; (*children*) **the ~ ones** les petits; (*Ir: fairies*) **the ~ people** les fées *fpl*, les lutins *mpl*; **it's ~ things like that which impress people** ce sont des petites choses comme ça qui font bonne impression (sur les gens); **he's quite a ~ gentleman!** qu'il est bien élevé ce petit!; **he's a ~ tyrant** c'est un (vrai) petit tyran; **a tiny ~ baby** un tout petit bébé; **here's a ~ something for yourself*** voilà un petit quelque chose* pour vous; **poor ~ thing!** pauvre petit(e)!; **she's a nice ~ thing** (*of child*) c'est un beau bébé, c'est une belle enfant; (*of woman*) c'est une gentille petite; **he's got a ~ place in the country** il a une petite maison de campagne; (*Comm*) **it's always the ~ man who suffers** ce sont toujours les petits (commerçants) qui souffrent; **the ~ farmers were nearly bankrupt** les petits cultivateurs étaient au bord de la faillite; **I know your ~ game** je connais votre petit jeu; (*pej*) **he's got a very ~ mind** il est très mesquin, il est très petit d'esprit; **all his dirty ~ jokes** toutes ses petites plaisanteries cochonnes*; *V* **bless** *etc*.
little[2] [ˈlɪtl] *comp* **less**, *superl* **least** **1** *adj, pron* **(a)** (*not much*) peu (de). **I have ~ money left** il me reste peu d'argent, il ne me reste pas beaucoup *or* il ne me reste guère d'argent; **I have very ~ money** j'ai très peu d'argent; **there is ~ hope of finding survivors** il y a peu d'espoir *or* il n'y a guère d'espoir de retrouver des survivants; **I have ~ time for reading** je n'ai pas beaucoup *or* je n'ai guère le temps de lire; **with no ~ trouble** non sans mal; **he reads ~** il lit peu, il ne lit guère; **he knows ~** il ne sait pas grand-chose; **he did ~ to help** il n'a pas fait grand-chose pour aider; **he did very ~** il a fait très peu de chose; **there was ~ I** (*or* **you, he** *etc*) **could do** il n'y avait pas grand-chose à faire; **I got ~ out of it** je n'en ai pas tiré grand-chose; **he had ~ to say** il n'avait pas grand-chose à dire; **it says (very) ~ for him** cela n'est guère en sa faveur *or* à son honneur; **it says ~ for his honesty** cela en dit long sur son honnêteté (*iro*); **I had ~ to do with it** je n'ai pas eu grand-chose à voir là-dedans; **that has very ~ to do with it!** ça a très peu à voir (avec ça)!; **I see ~ of her nowadays** je ne la vois plus beaucoup *or* plus guère maintenant; **he had ~ or nothing to say about it** il n'avait rien ou presque rien *or* il n'avait pratiquement rien à dire là-dessus; **to make ~ of sth** (*not stress*) faire peu de cas de qch, ne pas attacher grande importance à qch; (*belittle*) rabaisser qch, déprécier qch; (*fail to understand*) ne pas comprendre grand-chose à qch.
(b) (*in phrases*) **as ~ as possible** le moins possible; **I need as ~ money as he does** j'ai besoin d'aussi peu d'argent que lui; **you could pay as ~ as 20 francs for that** vous pourriez ne payer que 20 F pour cela; **he's got very ~ money — how ~?** il a très peu d'argent — très peu c'est-à-dire? *or* qu'entendez-vous (au juste) par très peu?; **however ~ you do** si peu que vous fassiez; **so ~ pleasure** si peu de plaisir; **so ~ of the cheese was mouldy that** ... une si petite partie du fromage était moisie que ...; **so ~ of what he says is true** il y a si peu de vrai dans ce qu'il dit; **he had eaten so ~** il avait mangé si peu; **I know too ~ about him to decide** j'en sais trop peu à son sujet pour décider; **he gave me too ~ money** il m'a donné trop peu d'argent.
(c) (*small amount*) **a ~** un peu (de); **the ~** le peu (de); **I have a ~ money left** il me reste un peu d'argent; **we're having a ~ trouble** nous avons un petit ennui *or* quelques difficultés; (*Prov*) **a ~ learning is a dangerous thing** avoir de vagues connaissances est une chose dangereuse; **would you like a ~ milk in your tea?** voulez-vous un peu *or* une goutte de lait dans votre thé?; **give me a ~** donne-m'en un peu; **I'd like a ~ of everything** je voudrais un peu de tout; **I know a ~ about stamp collecting** j'ai quelques connaissances en philatélie; **I know a ~ about what happened to him** je sais vaguement ce qui lui est arrivé; **the ~ I have seen is excellent** le peu que j'ai vu est excellent; **~ by ~** petit à petit, peu à peu; **I did what ~ I could** j'ai fait le peu que j'ai pu; (*Prov*) **every ~ helps** les petits ruisseaux font les grandes rivières (*Prov*); **it's all I can do — every ~ helps!** c'est tout ce que je peux faire — c'est toujours ça! *or* c'est toujours utile!; **stay here a ~** restez ici quelques instants *or* un petit moment; **she stayed only a ~** elle n'est restée que peu de temps *or* qu'un petit moment; **for a ~ (time** *or* **while)** pendant un petit moment, pendant quelques instants; **after a ~ (time** *or* **while)** au bout d'un petit moment *or* de quelques instants.
2 *adv* **(a)** (*slightly, somewhat*) **a ~** un peu; **a ~ too big** un peu trop grand; **she is a ~ tired** elle est un peu *or* légèrement fatiguée; **he spoke a ~ harshly** il a parlé avec une certaine dureté; **a ~ more slowly** un peu plus lentement; **he was not a ~ surprised** il n'a pas été peu surpris; **a ~ later** un peu plus tard, peu de temps après; **a ~ more/less cream** un peu plus/moins de crème.
(b) (*hardly, scarcely, not much*) **it's ~ better now he's**

rewritten it ça n'est guère mieux maintenant qu'il l'a récrit; **it's ~ short of folly** ça frise la folie; **~ more than a month ago** il y a à peine plus d'un mois; a **~-known work by Corelli** un morceau peu connu de Corelli; **his work is ~ performed these days** on ne joue plus guère ses œuvres aujourd'hui.

(c) (*in phrases*) **I like him as ~ as you do** je ne l'aime guère plus que vous, je l'aime aussi peu que vous l'aimez; **I like him as ~ as I used to** je l'aime aussi peu qu'auparavant; **however ~ you like him** si peu que vous l'aimiez (*subj*); **I felt so ~ encouraged by this** je me suis senti si peu encouragé par ceci; **~ as I know him** si peu que je le connaisse.

(d) (*rarely*) rarement, peu souvent. **I see him/it happens very ~** je le vois/cela arrive très rarement *or* très peu souvent; **I watch television very ~ nowadays** je ne regarde presque plus *or* plus beaucoup *or* plus très souvent la télévision maintenant.

(e) (+ *vb: not at all*) **he ~ supposed that ...** il était loin de supposer que ...; **~ did he know that ...** il était (bien) loin de se douter que ...; **~ do you know!** si seulement vous saviez!, vous ne savez pas tout!

littleness ['lɪtlnɪs] *n* **(a)** (*in size*) petitesse *f*. **(b)** (*morally*) petitesse *f*, mesquinerie *f*.

littoral ['lɪtərəl] *adj, n* littoral (*m*).

liturgical [lɪ'tɜːdʒɪkəl] *adj* liturgique.

liturgy ['lɪtədʒɪ] *n* liturgie *f*.

livable ['lɪvəbl] *adj climate* supportable; *life* supportable, tolérable; *house* habitable. **this house is not ~(-in)** cette maison est inhabitable; **he is/is not ~(-with)** il est facile à vivre/insupportable *or* invivable*; **her life is not ~** elle mène une vie impossible *or* insupportable.

live[1] [lɪv] 1 *vi* **(a)** (*be alive*) vivre; (*survive*) survivre. **he was still living when his daughter got married** il était encore en vie quand sa fille s'est mariée; **while his uncle ~d** du vivant de son oncle; **as long as I ~ I shall never leave you** je ne te quitterai pas tant que je vivrai; **I shall remember it as long as I ~** je m'en souviendrai jusqu'à mon dernier jour; **to ~ to be 90** vivre jusqu'à (l'âge de) 90 ans; **you'll ~ to be a hundred** vous serez centenaire; **she'll never ~ to see it** elle ne vivra pas assez longtemps pour le voir, elle mourra avant de le voir; **she has only 6 months to ~** il ne lui reste plus que 6 mois à vivre; **he didn't ~ long after his wife died** il n'a pas survécu longtemps à sa femme; **long ~ the King!** vive le roi!; **nothing could ~ in such a storm** rien ne pourrait survivre à pareille tempête; **the doctor said she would ~** le docteur a dit qu'elle s'en sortirait; **you'll ~!*** tu n'en mourras pas!; **the author makes his characters ~** l'auteur donne de la vie à ses personnages *or* fait vivre ses personnages.

(b) (*conduct o.s.*) vivre; (*exist*) vivre, exister. **to ~ honestly** vivre honnêtement, mener une vie honnête; **to ~ in luxury** vivre dans le luxe; **to ~ in style, to ~ well, to ~ like a king** *or* **a lord** mener grand train, vivre sur un grand pied; **to ~ according to one's means** vivre selon ses moyens; **they ~d happily ever after** après cela ils vécurent toujours heureux; (*in fairy tales*) ils furent heureux et ils eurent beaucoup d'enfants; **to ~ by one's pen** vivre de sa plume; **to ~ by journalism** gagner sa vie en étant *or* comme journaliste; **to ~ by buying and selling used cars** gagner sa vie en achetant et vendant des voitures d'occasion; **she ~s for her children** elle ne vit que pour ses enfants; **he is living for the day when he will see his son again** il ne vit que pour le jour où il reverra son fils; **I've got nothing left to ~ for** je n'ai plus de raison de vivre; **you must learn to ~ with it** il faut que tu t'y fasses *or* que tu t'en accommodes (*subj*); **he will have to ~ with that awful memory all his life** il lui faudra vivre avec cet horrible souvenir jusqu'à la fin de ses jours; (*Prov*) **~ and let ~** il faut se montrer tolérant; **(we** *or* **you) ~ and learn** on apprend à tout âge; *V* **hand** *etc*.

(c) (*reside*) vivre, habiter, résider. **to ~ in London** habiter (à) Londres; **to ~ in a flat** vivre en appartement, habiter un appartement; **where do you ~?** où habitez-vous?; **she ~s in the rue de Rivoli** elle habite rue de Rivoli; **this house isn't fit to ~ in** cette maison n'est pas habitable *or* est inhabitable; **a house fit for a queen to ~ in** une maison princière; **it's a nice place to ~ in** il fait bon vivre ici; **he's not an easy person to ~ with** il n'est pas facile à vivre; **he ~s with his mother** il vit *or* habite avec sa mère; (*in her house*) il vit chez sa mère; (*as man and wife*) **he's been living with Anne for over a year** il vit avec Anne depuis plus d'un an; **to ~ in sin** vivre dans le péché *or* en concubinage.

2 *vt* vivre, mener. **to ~ a healthy life** mener une vie saine; **to ~ a life of ease** avoir une vie facile; **to ~ a life of luxury/crime** vivre dans le luxe/le crime; **to ~ one's faith/one's socialism** *etc* vivre pleinement sa foi/son socialisme *etc*; **he just ~s* sailing/stamp collecting** *etc* il ne vit que pour la voile/pour sa collection de timbres *etc*; **to ~ a lie** vivre dans le mensonge; (*Theat, fig*) **to ~ the part** entrer dans la peau du personnage.

3 *cpd*: **all the livelong day** tout au long du jour (*liter*), toute la journée, toute la sainte journée* (*often pej*).

live down *vt sep disgrace, scandal* faire oublier (acec le temps). **you'll never live it down!** jamais tu ne feras oublier ça!

live in *vi [servant]* être logé et nourri; *[student, doctor]* être interne.

live off *vt fus* **(a)** *fruit, rice* vivre de, se nourrir de. **to live off the land** vivre des ressources naturelles, vivre du pays.

(b) = **live on 2c**.

live on 1 *vi [person]* continuer à vivre; *[tradition, memory]* rester, survivre.

2 *vt fus* **(a)** *fruit, rice* vivre de, se nourrir de. **you can't live on air*** on ne vit pas de l'air du temps; **she absolutely lives on chocolate*** elle se nourrit exclusivement de chocolat; (*fig*) **to live on hope** vivre d'espérance.

(b) to live on £3,000 a year vivre avec 3.000 livres par an; **we have just enough to live on** nous avons juste de quoi vivre; **what does he live on?** de quoi vit-il?, qu'est-ce qu'il a pour vivre?; **to live on one's salary** vivre de son salaire; **to live on one's capital** vivre de *or* manger son capital; **to live on borrowed time** être en sursis (*fig*).

(c) (*depend financially on*) vivre aux dépens *or* aux crochets de.

live out 1 *vi [servant]* ne pas être logé; *[student, doctor]* être externe.

2 *vt sep* passer. **she won't live the year out** elle ne passera pas l'année; **he lived out the war in the country** il a passé la durée de la guerre à la campagne.

live through *vt fus* **(a)** (*experience*) vivre, voir. **she has lived through two world wars** elle a vu deux guerres mondiales; **the difficult years he has lived through** les années difficiles qu'il a vécues.

(b) (*survive*) supporter, survivre à, passer. **he can't live through the winter** il ne passera pas l'hiver; **I couldn't live through another day like that** je ne pourrais pas supporter *or* passer une deuxième journée comme ça.

live together *vi* (*as man and wife*) vivre ensemble.

live up *vt sep*: **to live it up‡** (*live in luxury*) mener la grande vie; (*have fun*) mener une vie de bâton de chaise.

live up to *vt fus* **(a)** (*be true to*) *one's principles* vivre en accord avec, vivre selon; *one's promises* être fidèle à.

(b) (*be equal to*) être *or* se montrer à la hauteur de; (*be worthy of*) répondre à, se montrer digne de. **to live up to sb's expectations** être *or* se montrer à la hauteur des espérances de qn; **the holiday didn't live up to expectations** les vacances n'ont pas été ce qu'on avait espéré; **we must try to live up to our new surroundings** nous devons essayer d'avoir un train de vie en rapport avec *or* de nous montrer dignes de notre nouveau cadre; **his brother's success will give him something to live up to** la réussite de son frère lui fera un sujet d'émulation.

live[2] [laɪv] 1 *adj* **(a)** *person, animal* vivant, en vie; (*fig*) dynamique. (*Fishing*) **~ bait** vif *m* (*appât*); **a real ~ spaceman** un astronaute en chair et en os; (*fig*) **they're a really ~ group** c'est un groupe très dynamique; (*fig*) **this is a ~ problem today** c'est un problème brûlant aujourd'hui.

(b) (*Rad, TV*) (transmis *or* diffusé) en direct. **that programme was ~** cette émission était (transmise *or* diffusée) en direct; **performed before a ~ audience** joué en public.

(c) *coal* ardent; *ammunition, shell, cartridge* de combat; (*unexploded*) non explosé. (*Elec*) **that's ~!** c'est branché!; (*Elec*) **~ rail** rail conducteur; (*Elec*) **~ wire** fil *m* sous tension; (*fig*) **he's a ~ wire*** il a un dynamisme fou, il pète du *or* le feu*; **the switch/hair-drier was ~** l'interrupteur/ le séchoir à cheveux était mal isolé (et dangereux).

2 *adv* (*Rad, TV*) en direct. **it was broadcast ~** c'était (transmis *or* diffusé) en direct; **the match is brought to you ~ from ...** le match vous est transmis en direct depuis ...; **here, ~ from New York, is our reporter X** voici, en direct de New York, notre envoyé spécial X.

3 *cpd*: (*U*) **livestock** bétail *m*, cheptel *m*.

livelihood ['laɪvlɪhʊd] *n* (*U*) moyens *mpl* d'existence, gagne-pain *m inv*. **to earn a** *or* **one's ~** gagner sa vie; **his ~ depends on ...** son gagne-pain dépend de ...; **their principal ~ is tourism/rice** ils vivent du tourisme/de la culture du riz.

liveliness ['laɪvlɪnɪs] *n* (*V* **lively**) vivacité *f*, entrain *m*, allant *m*, pétulance *f*; vie *f*; animation *f*; vigueur *f*; gaieté *f* *or* gaîté *f*.

lively ['laɪvlɪ] *adj person, character* vif (*f* vive), plein d'entrain, plein d'allant, pétulant; *imagination, interest, colour* vif; *description, account, style* vivant; *party, discussion, conversation* animé, plein d'entrain; *performance, expression, instance, example, argument* frappant, percutant, vigoureux; *campaign* percutant, vigoureux; *tune* entraînant, allègre, gai. **he is very ~** il est plein d'entrain *or* de vie; **at a ~ pace** *or* **speed** à vive allure, à toute vitesse; **we had a ~ week** nous avons eu une semaine mouvementée; **we had a ~ time of it** nous avons eu des instants mouvementés; **things are getting a bit too ~** le rythme s'accélère un peu trop, les choses vont un peu trop vite; (*pej*) ça commence à barder‡.

liven ['laɪvn] 1 *vt*: **to ~ up** *person* égayer, réjouir; *evening, discussion, party etc* animer; **a bit of paint should ~ the room up** un peu de peinture égayerait la pièce. **2** *vi*: **to ~ up** s'animer; **things are beginning to ~ up** ça commence à s'animer.

liver[1] ['lɪvə^r] (*Anat*) 1 *n* foie *m*; *V* **lily**. 2 *cpd*: **liver complaint** maladie *f* de foie; (*Vet*) **liver fluke** douve *f* du foie; **liver paste** *pâte préparée au foie*; **liver pâté** pâté *m* de foie; **liver sausage**, (*esp US*) **liverwurst** saucisse *f* au pâté de foie.

liver[2] ['lɪvə^r] *n* (*person*) **clean ~** vertueux *m*, -euse *f*; **fast ~** débauché(e) *m(f)*.

liveried ['lɪvərɪd] *adj* en livrée.

liverish* ['lɪvərɪʃ] *adj* **(a)** (*bilious*) qui a mal au foie. **(b)** (*irritable*) de mauvais poil*, grincheux.

Liverpudlian [ˌlɪvə'pʌdlɪən] 1 *n*: **he's a ~** (*living there*) c'est un habitant de Liverpool, il habite Liverpool; (*born there*) il est originaire de Liverpool. 2 *adj* de Liverpool.

livery ['lɪvərɪ] 1 *n* livrée *f*. 2 *cpd*: (*Brit*) **livery company** corporation londonienne; **livery stable** (*boarding*) écurie *f* (qui prend les chevaux en garde); (*hiring out*) écurie de louage.

lives [laɪvz] *npl of* **life**.

livid ['lɪvɪd] *adj* **(a)** (*in colour*) *complexion, scar* livide, blafard; *sky* plombé, de plomb. **he was ~ with cold** il était tout blanc de froid; **she had a ~ bruise on her forehead** elle avait une vilaine ecchymose au front.

(b) (*furious: also* **~ with anger** *or* **rage** *or* **fury**) *person* furieux, furibond, en rage; *expression, appearance, gesture, glare* furieux, furibond.

living ['lɪvɪŋ] 1 *adj person* vivant, en vie; *language, example, faith* vivant; *coal* ardent; *water* vif (*f* vive). **he is still ~** il vit toujours, il est encore en vie; ~ **or dead** mort ou vif; **he's the greatest ~ pianist** c'est le plus grand pianiste actuellement vivant; **there wasn't a ~ soul** il n'y avait pas âme qui vive; **a ~ skeleton** un cadavre ambulant; **'the L~ Desert'** 'Le désert vivant'; **within ~ memory** de mémoire d'homme; **a ~ death** un enfer, un calvaire; **he's the ~ image of his father*** c'est le portrait (tout craché) de son père; **to beat** *or* **thrash the ~ daylights out of sb**‡ tabasser qn‡, rosser* qn; **to scare** *or* **frighten the ~ daylights out of sb**‡ faire *or* flanquer* une peur bleue à qn, flanquer la frousse* *or* la trouille‡ à qn; **the ~ rock** le roc; **carved out of the ~ rock** taillé à même *or* dans le roc.

2 *n* **(a)** (*means of livelihood*) vie *f*. **to earn** *or* **make a ~ by painting portraits/as an artist** gagner sa vie en peignant *or* à peindre des portraits/en tant qu'artiste; **they have to work for a ~** ils doivent travailler pour vivre; *V* **cost**.

(b) (*way of life*) vie *f*. **gracious ~** vie élégante *or* raffinée; **loose ~** vie de débauche; **~ was not easy in those days** la vie n'était pas facile en ce temps-là; *V* **standard**.

(c) (*Brit Rel*) cure *f*, bénéfice *m*.

(d) (*pl: people*) **the ~** les vivants *mpl*; *V* **land**.

3 *cpd*: **living conditions** conditions *fpl* de vie; **living quarters** logement(s) *m(pl)*; **living room** salle *f* de séjour, séjour *m*; **living space** espace vital; **living standards** niveau *m* de vie; **they were asking for a living wage** ils demandaient un salaire leur permettant de vivre décemment; **£20 a week isn't a living wage** on ne peut pas vivre avec 20 livres par semaine.

Livy ['lɪvɪ] *n* Tite-Live *m*.

lizard ['lɪzəd] **1** *n* lézard *m*; (*also* **~skin**) (peau *f* de) lézard. **2** *cpd bag etc* en lézard.

llama ['lɑːmə] *n* lama *m* (*Zool*).

lo [ləʊ] *excl* regardez! **when ~ and behold, in he walked!** et c'est alors qu'il est entré!; **~ and behold the result!** et voilà le résultat!

loach [ləʊtʃ] *n* loche *f* (*poisson*).

load [ləʊd] **1** *n* **(a)** (*thing carried*) *[person, animal, washing machine]* charge *f*; *[lorry]* chargement *m*, charge; *[ship]* cargaison *f*; (*weight*) (gros) poids *m*; (*pressure*) poids, pression *f*; (*fig*) (*burden*) fardeau *m*; (*mental strain*) poids. **he was carrying a heavy ~** il était lourdement chargé; **the ~ slipped off the lorry** le chargement *or* la charge a glissé du camion; **the lorry had a full ~** le camion avait un chargement complet; **the ship had a full ~** le navire avait une cargaison complète; **under (full) ~** chargé (à plein); **a ~ of coal** *[ship]* une cargaison de charbon; *[lorry]* un chargement *or* une charge de charbon; **I had 3 ~s of coal (delivered) last autumn** on m'a livré du charbon en 3 fois l'automne dernier; **tree weighed down by its ~ of fruit** arbre *m* ployant sous le poids des fruits; **supporting his brother's family was a heavy ~ for him** c'était pour lui une lourde charge (que) de faire vivre la famille de son frère; **he finds his new responsibilities a heavy ~** il trouve ses nouvelles responsabilités pesantes *or* lourdes; **to take a ~ off sb's mind** débarrasser qn de ce qui lui pèse (*fig*); **that's a ~ off my mind!** c'est un poids en moins!; quel soulagement!; *V* **bus, pay, shed**[2], **work** *etc*.

(b) (*Constr, Elec, Tech*; *also of firearm*) charge *f*. (*Elec*) **the new regulations spread the ~ on the power stations more evenly** les nouveaux règlements répartissent la charge plus uniformément sur les centrales électriques.

(c) (**fig*) **a ~ of** un tas de, des masses de*; **~s of** des tas de*, des masses de*; **that's a ~ of rubbish!** tout ça c'est de la blague!*; **we've got ~s of time** on a tout notre temps*, on a largement le temps; **he's got ~s of money** il est plein de fric‡; **we've got ~s (of them) at home** nous en avons (tout) plein* *or* des masses* *or* des tonnes* à la maison; **there were ~s of people** il y avait plein de monde* *or* des tas de gens* *or* des masses de gens*.

(d) get a ~ of this!‡ (*look*) regarde un peu ça!*; (*listen*) écoute un peu ça!*

2 *cpd*: (*Elec*) **load factor** facteur *m* d'utilisation; (*Naut*) **load line** ligne *f* de charge; **loadstar** = **lodestar** (*V* **lode 2**); **loadstone** = **lodestone** (*V* **lode 2**).

3 *vt* **(a)** *lorry, ship, washing machine etc* charger (*with* de); *person* charger; (*overwhelm*) accabler. **the branch was ~ed (down) with pears** la branche était chargée de poires, la branche ployait sous les poires; **she was ~ed (down) with her shopping** elle pliait sous le poids de ses achats; **his pockets were ~ed with sweets and toys** ses poches étaient bourrées de bonbons et de jouets; **they arrived ~ed (down) with presents for us** ils sont arrivés chargés de cadeaux pour nous; **to ~ sb (down) with gifts** couvrir qn de cadeaux; **to ~ sb with honours** combler *or* couvrir qn d'honneurs; **we are ~ed (down) with debts** nous sommes couverts *or* criblés de dettes; **~ed (down) with cares** accablé de soucis; **a heart ~ed (down) with sorrow** un cœur lourd *or* accablé de chagrin; **the whole business is ~ed (down) with problems** toute cette affaire présente des monceaux de difficultés.

(b) *[ship etc]* **to ~ coal/grain** *etc* charger du charbon/du grain *etc*.

(c) *gun, camera etc* charger.

(d) *cane etc* plomber; *dice* piper. (*lit*) **the dice were ~ed** les dés étaient pipés; (*fig*) **the dice were ~ed against him/in his favour** les cartes étaient truquées à son désavantage/à son avantage (*fig*); (*fig*) **to ~ the dice against sb** truquer les cartes pour desservir qn (*fig*); **the situation is ~ed in our favour** les faits jouent en notre faveur.

(e) *insurance premium* majorer.

4 *vi* *[lorry]* prendre un chargement; *[ship]* embarquer une cargaison; *[camera, gun]* se charger.

load down *vt sep* charger (*with* de); *V* **load 3a**.

load up 1 *vi* *[ship]* recevoir une cargaison; *[lorry]* prendre un chargement; *[person]* ramasser son chargement.

2 *vt sep lorry, animal, person* charger (*with* de).

loaded ['ləʊdɪd] *adj* **(a)** *lorry, ship, gun, camera* chargé; *dice* pipé; *cane* plombé; *V also* **load**.

(b) *word, statement* insidieux. **that's a ~ question!** c'est une question insidieuse!, c'est une question-piège!

(c) (‡) (*rich*) bourré de fric‡, plein aux as‡; (*drunk*) bourré‡; (*drugged*) défoncé‡.

loader ['ləʊdəʳ] *n* (*person, instrument*) chargeur *m*; *V* **low**[1].

loading ['ləʊdɪŋ] **1** *n* chargement *m*. (*street sign*) **'no ~ or unloading'** 'interdiction de charger et de décharger'. **2** *cpd*: **loading bay** aire *f* de chargement.

loaf[1] [ləʊf] *pl* **loaves 1** *n* **(a)** (*also* **~ of bread**) pain *m*, miche *f* de pain. (*Prov*) **half a ~ is better than no bread** mieux vaut peu que pas du tout (*loc*); (*Brit*) **use your ~!**‡ fais marcher tes méninges!*; *V* **cottage, sandwich, slice** *etc*. **(b) sugar ~** pain *m* de sucre; *V* **meat** *etc*. **2** *cpd*: **loaf sugar** sucre *m* en pain.

loaf[2] [ləʊf] *vi* (*also* **~ about, ~ around**) fainéanter, traîner, traînasser.

loafer ['ləʊfəʳ] *n* **(a)** (*person*) flemmard(e)* *m(f)*, tire-au-flanc* *m inv*. **(b)** (*shoe*) mocassin *m*.

loam [ləʊm] *n* (*U*) **(a)** (*soil*) terreau *m*. **(b)** *[moulds]* terre *f* de moulage.

loamy ['ləʊmɪ] *adj soil* riche en terreau.

loan [ləʊn] **1** *n* **(a)** (*money*) (*lent*) prêt *m*; (*advanced*) avance *f*; (*borrowed*) emprunt *m*. **can I ask you for a ~?** pouvez-vous m'accorder un prêt?; **'~s without security'** 'prêts sans garantie'; *V* **raise**.

(b) prêt *m*. **this picture is on ~** *or* **is a ~ from the city museum** ce tableau est prêté par le *or* est un prêt du musée municipal; **I have a car on ~ from the company** la compagnie me prête une voiture *or* met une voiture à ma disposition; **my assistant is on ~ to another department at the moment** mon assistant prête ses services *or* est détaché à une autre division en ce moment; (*in library*) **the book is out on ~** le livre est sorti; **I have this book out on ~ from the library** j'ai emprunté ce livre à la bibliothèque; **I asked for the ~ of the lawnmower** j'ai demandé à emprunter *or* à ce qu'on me prête (*subj*) la tondeuse à gazon; **may I have the ~ of your record player?** pouvez-vous me prêter votre électrophone?; **I can give you the ~ of it for a few days** je peux vous le prêter pour quelques jours.

2 *vt* (*US, also Brit**) prêter (*sth to sb* qch à qn).

3 *cpd*: (*Fin*) **loan capital** capital-obligations *m*, capital *m* d'emprunt; (*Art etc*) **loan collection** collection *f* de tableaux (*or* d'objets *etc*) prêtés; **loan fund** caisse *f* de prêt; **loan office** bureau *m* de prêt; **loan shark*** usurier *m*; (*Ling*) **loan word** (mot *m* d')emprunt *m*.

loath [ləʊθ] *adj*: **to be (very) ~ to do sth** répugner à faire qch; **he was ~ to see her again** il n'était pas du tout disposé à la revoir; **I am ~ to add to your difficulties but ...** je ne voudrais surtout pas ajouter à vos difficultés mais ...; **nothing ~** très volontiers.

loathe [ləʊð] *vt person* détester, haïr; *thing* détester, avoir en horreur, abhorrer (*frm*). **to ~ doing sth** avoir horreur de *or* détester faire qch; **he ~s being told off** il a horreur *or* il déteste qu'on le reprenne.

loathing ['ləʊðɪŋ] *n* (*U*) dégoût *m*, répugnance *f*. **he/it fills me with ~** il/cela me répugne *or* dégoûte.

loathsome ['ləʊðsəm] *adj* détestable, répugnant, écœurant.

loathsomeness ['ləʊðsəmnɪs] *n* caractère répugnant, nature détestable *or* écœurante.

loaves [ləʊvz] *npl of* **loaf**.

lob [lɒb] **1** *vt stone etc* lancer (haut *or* en chandelle). (*Tennis*) **to ~ a ball** faire un lob, lober; **he ~bed the book (over) to me** il m'a lancé *or* balancé* le livre; (*Ftbl*) **to ~ the goalkeeper** lober le gardien de but.

2 *vi* (*Tennis*) lober, faire un lob.

3 *n* (*Tennis*) lob *m*.

lobby ['lɒbɪ] **1** *n* **(a)** (*entrance hall*) *[hotel]* hall *m*; (*smaller*) vestibule *m*, entrée *f*; *[private house]* vestibule, entrée; *[theatre]* foyer *m* (des spectateurs).

(b) (*Brit Parl*) (*where Members meet public*) hall *m* (*de la Chambre des communes où le public rencontre les députés*), ≃ salle *f* des pas perdus; (*where Members vote: also* **division ~**) vestibule *m* (*où les députés se répartissent pour voter*).

(c) (*Pol: pressure group*) groupe *m* de pression, lobby *m*. **the antivivisection ~** le groupe de pression *or* le lobby antivivisectionniste.

2 *cpd*: (*Brit Press*) **lobby correspondent** journaliste *mf* parlementaire.

3 *vt* (*Pol*) faire pression sur.

4 *vi* (*Pol*) **they are ~ing for a stricter control of firearms** ils font pression pour obtenir un contrôle plus étroit des armes à feu.

lobbying ['lɒbɪɪŋ] *n* (*Pol*) sollicitations *fpl* (*d'un groupe de pression*), pressions *fpl*.

lobbyist ['lɒbɪɪst] *n* (*Pol*) membre *m* d'un groupe de pression; *V* **lobby**.

lobe [ləʊb] *n* (*Anat, Bot*) lobe *m*.

lobster ['lɒbstəʳ] *n* homard *m*. **~ pot** casier *m* à homards.

local ['ləʊkəl] **1** *adj belief, custom, saying, weather forecast, newspaper, radio* local, (*wider*) régional; *shops, library* du *or* de quartier; *wine, speciality* du pays, local; *time, train, branch, church, showers, fog, anaesthetic* local; (*Med*) *pain* localisé. (*Telec*) **a ~ call** une communication urbaine; **of ~ interest** d'intérêt local; **what is the ~ situation?** (*here*) quelle est la situation ici?; (*there*) quelle est la situation là-bas?; **he's a ~ man** il est du pays *or* du coin*; **the ~ doctor** (*gen*) le médecin le plus proche; (*in town*) le médecin du quartier; **it adds a bit of ~ colour** ça met un peu de couleur locale; **~ authority** (*n*) autorité locale; (*cpd*) des autorités locales; ~ **education authority** ≃ office régional de l'enseignement; ~ **government** administration locale; ~ **government elections** élections municipales; ~ **government officer** *or* **official** administrateur local, ≃ fonctionnaire *mf.*

2 *n* **(a)** (*: *person*) personne *f* du pays *or* du coin*. **the ~s** les gens du pays *or* du coin*; **he's one of the ~s** il est du pays *or* du coin*.

(b) (*Brit**: *pub*) café *m* du coin, bistro(t)* *m* du coin.

(c) (*US Rail*) (train *m*) omnibus *m.*

locale [ləʊˈkɑːl] *n* lieu *m*, scène *f* (*fig*), théâtre *m* (*frm*).

locality [ləʊˈkælɪtɪ] *n* **(a)** (*neighbourhood*) environs *mpl*, voisinage *m*; (*district*) région *f*. **in the ~** dans les environs, dans la région; **we are new to this ~** nous sommes nouveaux dans la région.

(b) (*place, position*) lieu *m*, endroit *m*, emplacement *m*. **the ~ of the murder** le lieu *or* la scène *or* le théâtre (*frm*) du meurtre; **I don't know the ~ of the church** je ne sais pas où se trouve l'église; **she has a good/has no sense of ~** elle a/n'a pas le sens de l'orientation; *V* **bump.**

localize [ˈləʊkəlaɪz] *vt* localiser. **~d pain** douleur localisée.

locally [ˈləʊkəlɪ] *adv* **(a)** (*in specific area*) localement. (*Met*) **showers ~** des averses locales, temps localement pluvieux; **onions are in short supply ~** les oignons manquent dans certaines régions.

(b) (*nearby*) dans les environs *or* la région *or* le coin*; (*near here*) par ici; (*out there*) là-bas. **we deliver free ~** nous livrons gratuitement dans les environs; **you will find mushrooms ~** vous allez trouver des champignons dans la région *or* dans le coin*; **I had it made ~** (*when I was there*) je l'ai fait faire sur place; (*around here*) je l'ai fait faire par ici; **~ appointed staff** personnel recruté localement.

locate [ləʊˈkeɪt] **1** *vt* **(a)** (*find*) *place, person* repérer, trouver; *noise, leak* localiser; *cause* localiser, repérer, trouver. **I can't ~ the school on this map** je n'arrive pas à repérer *or* à trouver l'école sur cette carte; **have you ~d the briefcase I left yesterday?** avez-vous retrouvé la serviette que j'ai oubliée hier?; **the doctors have ~d the cause of the pain/the source of the infection** les médecins ont localisé *or* déterminé la cause de la douleur/la source de l'infection.

(b) (*situate*) *factory, school etc* situer. **they decided to ~ the factory in Manchester** ils ont décidé d'implanter *or* de construire l'usine à Manchester; **where is the hospital to be ~d?** où va-t-on mettre *or* construire l'hôpital?; **the college is ~d in London** le collège est situé *or* se trouve à Londres.

(c) (*assume to be*) situer, placer. **many scholars ~ the Garden of Eden there** c'est là que de nombreux érudits situent *or* placent le Paradis terrestre.

2 *vi* (*US**) s'installer.

location [ləʊˈkeɪʃən] **1** *n* **(a)** (*position*) emplacement *m*, situation *f*. **suitable ~s for a shoe factory** emplacements convenant à une usine de chaussures.

(b) (*Cine*) extérieur(s) *m(pl)*. **on ~** en extérieur.

(c) (*U*: *V* **locate 1a**) repérage *m*; localisation *f*.

2 *cpd* (*Cine*) *scene, shot* en extérieur.

locative [ˈlɒkətɪv] *adj, n* locatif (*m*) (*Ling*).

loch [lɒx] *n* (*Scot*) lac *m*, loch *m*. **L~ Lomond** le loch Lomond; *V* **sea.**

lock¹ [lɒk] **1** *n* **(a)** [*door, box etc*] serrure *f*; [*steering wheel*] antivol *m*. **under ~ and key** *possessions* sous clef; *prisoner* sous les verrous, écroué; **to put/keep sth under ~ and key** mettre/garder qch sous clef; **to put sb under ~ and key** enfermer qn à clef; (*prisoner*) écrouer qn; **to keep sb under ~ and key** garder qn enfermé à clef; (*prisoner*) garder qn sous les verrous; *V* **combination, pick** *etc.*

(b) [*gun*] (*safety lock*) cran *m* de sûreté; (*gunlock*) percuteur *m*. (*fig*) **he sold the factory ~, stock and barrel** il a vendu l'usine en bloc; **they rejected the proposals ~, stock and barrel** ils ont rejeté les suggestions en bloc *or* toutes les suggestions sans exception; **he has moved out ~, stock and barrel** il a déménagé en emportant tout son fourbi*.

(c) [*canal*] écluse *f*; *V* **air.**

(d) (*Wrestling*) clef *f or* clé *f*.

(e) (*Aut*) rayon *m* de braquage. **this car has a good ~** cette voiture braque bien *or* a un bon rayon de braquage; **3.5 turns from ~ to ~** 3,5 tours d'une butée à l'autre.

(f) (*Rugby*: *also* **~ forward**) (avant *m* de) deuxième ligne *m*.

2 *cpd*: **lock gate** porte *f* d'écluse; (*Med*) **lockjaw** tétanos *m*, trisme *m*; **lock keeper** éclusier *m*, -ière *f*; **locknut** (*washer*) contre-écrou *m*; (*self-locking*) écrou auto-bloquant; (*Ind*) **lockout** lock-out *m inv*; **locksmith** serrurier *m*; **lock-up** (*Brit*: *garage*) box *m*; (*Brit*: *shop*) boutique *f* (*sans logement*); (*prison*) prison *f*, lieu *m* de détention provisoire, cellule *f* provisoire.

3 *vt* **(a)** (*fasten*) *door, suitcase, safe* fermer à clef. **behind ~ed doors** à huis clos; (*fig*) **to ~ the stable door after the horse has bolted** prendre ses précautions trop tard.

(b) *person* enfermer (*in* dans). **he got ~ed in the bathroom** il s'est trouvé enfermé dans la salle de bains.

(c) (*prevent movement in*) *mechanism* bloquer. **he ~ed the steering wheel on his car** il a bloqué la direction de sa voiture (en mettant l'antivol); (*Aut*: *by braking*) **to ~ the wheels** bloquer les roues.

(d) (*squeeze, also fig*) *person* étreindre, serrer. **she was ~ed in his arms** elle était serrée dans ses bras; **they were ~ed in a close embrace** ils étaient unis dans une étreinte passionnée; **the armies were ~ed in combat** les deux armées étaient aux prises.

4 *vi* **(a)** [*door*] fermer à clef.

(b) (*Aut*) [*wheel, steering wheel*] se bloquer.

lock away *vt sep object, jewels* mettre sous clef; *criminal* mettre sous les verrous; *mental patient etc* enfermer.

lock in *vt sep person, dog* enfermer (à l'intérieur). **to lock o.s. in** s'enfermer (à l'intérieur).

lock on to *vt fus* (*Space*) s'arrimer à, se raccorder à.

lock out **1** *vt sep* **(a)** *person* (*deliberately*) mettre à la porte; (*by mistake*) enfermer dehors, laisser dehors (sans clef). **to find o.s. locked out** (*by mistake*) se trouver enfermé dehors; (*as punishment*) se trouver mis à la porte; **to lock o.s. out** s'enfermer dehors; **to lock o.s. out of one's car** fermer la voiture en laissant les clefs à l'intérieur.

(b) (*Ind*) *workers* fermer l'usine à, lockouter.

2 lockout *n V* **lock¹ 2.**

lock up **1** *vi* fermer à clef (toutes les portes). **will you lock up when you leave?** voulez-vous tout fermer en partant?; **to lock up for the night** tout fermer pour la nuit.

2 *vt sep* **(a)** *object, jewels* enfermer, mettre sous clef; *house* fermer (à clef); *criminal* mettre sous les verrous; *mental patient etc* enfermer. **you ought to be locked up!*** on devrait t'enfermer!, tu es bon à enfermer!

(b) *capital, funds* immobiliser, bloquer (*in* dans).

3 lock-up *n V* **lock¹ 2.**

lock² [lɒk] *n* [*hair*] mèche *f*; (*ringlet*) boucle *f*. **his ~s** sa chevelure, ses cheveux *mpl*; **her curly ~s** ses boucles.

locker [ˈlɒkəʳ] *n* casier *m*, (petite) armoire *f*.

locket [ˈlɒkɪt] *n* médaillon *m* (*bijou*).

loci [ˈlɒkiː] *npl of* **locus.**

loco‡ [ˈləʊkəʊ] *adj* toqué*, timbré*, cinglé‡.

locomotion [ˌləʊkəˈməʊʃən] *n* locomotion *f*.

locomotive [ˌləʊkəˈməʊtɪv] **1** *n* (*Rail*) locomotive *f*. **~ shed** hangar *m* à locomotives. **2** *adj* locomotif.

locum (tenens) [ˈləʊkəm(ˈtenenz)] *n* (*esp Brit*) remplaçant(e) *m(f)* (*de prêtre ou de médecin etc*).

locus [ˈlɒkəs] *n, pl* **loci** lieu *m*, point *m*; (*Math*) lieu géométrique.

locust [ˈləʊkəst] **1** *n* locuste *f*, sauterelle *f*. **2** *cpd*: **locust bean** caroube *f*; **locust tree** caroubier *m*.

locution [ləˈkjuːʃən] *n* locution *f*.

lode [ləʊd] **1** *n* (*Miner*) filon *m*, veine *f*. **2** *cpd*: **lodestar** (*lit*) étoile *f* polaire; (*fig*) principe directeur; **lodestone** magnétite *f*, aimant naturel.

lodge [lɒdʒ] **1** *n* (*small house in grounds*) maison *f or* pavillon *m* de gardien; (*porter's room in building*) loge *f*; (*Freemasonry*) loge; [*beaver*] abri *m*, gîte *m*; *V* **hunting.**

2 *vt person* loger, héberger; *bullet* loger; *money* déposer; *statement, report* présenter (*with sb* à qn). (*Jur*) **to ~ an appeal** interjeter appel, se pourvoir en cassation; **to ~ a complaint against** porter plainte contre.

3 *vi* [*person*] être logé, être en pension (*with* chez); [*bullet*] se loger.

lodger [ˈlɒdʒəʳ] *n* (*room only*) locataire *mf*; (*room and meals*) pensionnaire *mf*. **to take (in) ~s** (*room only*) louer des chambres; (*room and meals*) prendre des pensionnaires.

lodging [ˈlɒdʒɪŋ] **1** *n* **(a)** (*U*: *accommodation*) logement *m*, hébergement *m*. **they gave us a night's ~** ils nous ont logés *or* hébergés une nuit; *V* **board.**

(b) **~s** (*room*) chambre *f*; (*flatlet*) logement *m*; **he took ~s with Mrs Smith†** (*with meals*) il a pris pension chez Mme Smith; (*without meals*) il a pris une chambre *or* un logement chez Mme Smith; **he's in ~s** il vit en meublé *or* en garni (*pej*); **to look for ~s** (*room*) chercher une chambre meublée; (*flatlet*) chercher un logement meublé; (*with meals*) chercher à prendre pension.

2 *cpd*: **lodging house** pension *f*.

loft [lɒft] **1** *n* **(a)** [*house, stable, barn*] grenier *m*; *V* **hay, pigeon** *etc.* **(b)** [*church, hall*] galerie *f*; *V* **organ.** **2** *vt ball* lancer en chandelle.

loftily [ˈlɒftɪlɪ] *adv* hautainement, avec hauteur *or* condescendance.

loftiness [ˈlɒftɪnɪs] *n* (*great height*) hauteur *f*; (*fig*) (*grandiosity*) grandeur *f*, noblesse *f*; (*haughtiness*) hauteur, condescendance *f*, dédain *m*.

lofty [ˈlɒftɪ] *adj* (*high*) *mountain, tower* haut, élevé; (*fig*) (*grandiose*) *feelings, aims, style* élevé, noble; (*haughty*) *behaviour, tone, look, remark* hautain, condescendant, dédaigneux.

log¹ [lɒg] **1** *n* **(a)** (*felled tree trunk*) rondin *m*; (*for fire*) bûche *f*. **he lay like a ~** il ne bougeait pas plus qu'une souche; *V* **sleep.**

(b) (*Naut*: *device*) loch *m*.

(c) (*also* **~book**) (*Naut*) livre *m or* journal *m* de bord; (*Aviat*) carnet *m* de vol; [*lorry driver etc*] carnet de route; (*gen*) registre *m*. **to write up** *or* **keep the ~(book)** tenir le livre de bord *or* le carnet de vol *etc*; **let's keep a ~ of everything we do today** notons *or* consignons tout ce que nous allons faire aujourd'hui.

2 *cpd*: **logbook** (*Aviat, Naut etc*) *V* **1c**; (*Brit Aut*) ≃ carte grise; **log cabin** cabane *f* en rondins; **log fire** feu *m* de bois; **log jam** (*lit*) train *m* de flottage bloqué; (*fig*) impasse *f* (*fig*); (*fig*) **log rolling** échange *m* de concessions *or* de faveurs mutuelles.

3 *vt* **(a)** *trees* tronçonner, débiter *or* tailler en rondins.

(b) (*record*) (*gen*) noter, consigner; (*Naut*) inscrire au journal de bord *or* au livre de bord; (*Aviat*) inscrire sur le *or* au carnet de vol.

(c) **the ship was ~ging 18 knots** le navire filait 18 nœuds; **the plane was ~ging 300 mph** l'avion volait à *or* faisait 500 km/h.

(d) (*also* **~ up**) **he has ~ged (up) 5,000 hours' flying time** il a à son actif *or* il compte 5.000 heures de vol; **we ~ged (up) 50 km that day** nous avons parcouru *or* couvert 50 km ce jour-là; **I've ~ged (up) 8 hours' work each day*** je me suis envoyé* *or* tapé* 8 heures de travail par jour.

log² [lɒg] *n* (*Math*: *abbr of* **logarithm**) log* *m*. **~ tables** tables *fpl* de logarithmes.

loganberry [ˈləʊgənbərɪ] *n* framboise *f* de Logan.

logarithm ['lɒgərɪθəm] *n* logarithme *m*.
loge [ləʊʒ] *n* (*Theat*) loge *f*.
loggerheads ['lɒgəhedz] *npl*: **to be at ~ (with)** être en désaccord *or* à couteaux tirés (avec).
loggia ['lɒdʒɪə] *n* loggia *f*.
logic ['lɒdʒɪk] *n* (*all senses*) logique *f*.
logical ['lɒdʒɪkəl] *adj* (*all senses*) logique. (*Philos*) **~ positivism** positivisme *m* logique; **to take sth to its ~ conclusion** amener qch à sa conclusion logique.
logically ['lɒdʒɪkəlɪ] *adv* logiquement.
logician [lɒ'dʒɪʃən] *n* logicien(ne) *m(f)*.
logistic [lɒ'dʒɪstɪk] **1** *adj* logistique. **2** *n* (*U*) **~s** logistique *f*.
logy* ['ləʊgɪ] *adj* (*US*) apathique, léthargique.
loin [lɔɪn] **1** *n* **(a)** **~s** (*Anat*) reins *mpl*, lombes *mpl*; (*liter*) reins; *V* **gird up**. **(b)** (*Culin*) (*gen*) filet *m*; *[veal, venison]* longe *f*; *[beef]* aloyau *m*. **2** *cpd*: (*Culin*) **loin chop** côte première; **loin cloth** pagne *m* (*d'étoffe*).
loiter ['lɔɪtəʳ] *vi* **(a)** (*also* **~ about**) (*dawdle*) s'attarder, traîner en route; (*loaf, stand around*) traîner, flâner, musarder.
(b) (*Jur*) **to ~ with intent** = commettre un délit d'intention; (*Jur*) **to be charged with ~ing with intent** être accusé d'un délit d'intention.
loiter away *vt sep*: **to loiter away one's time/days** passer son temps/ses journées à ne rien faire.
loll [lɒl] *vi [person]* se prélasser; *[head]* pendre.
loll about, loll around *vi* fainéanter, flâner.
loll back *vi [person]* se prélasser; *[head]* pendre en arrière. **to loll back in an armchair** se prélasser dans un fauteuil.
loll out **1** *vi [tongue]* pendre. **2** *vt sep tongue* laisser pendre.
lollipop ['lɒlɪpɒp] *n* sucette *f* (*bonbon*). (*Brit*) **~ man***, **~ lady*** contractuel(le) *m(f)* (*qui fait traverser la rue aux enfants*).
lollop ['lɒləp] *vi* (*esp Brit*) *[large dog]* galoper; *[person]* courir gauchement *or* à grandes enjambées maladroites. **to ~ in/out** *etc* entrer/sortir *etc* à grandes enjambées maladroites.
lolly ['lɒlɪ] *n* (*Brit*) **(a)** (*) = **lollipop**; *V* **ice**. **(b)** (*‡U: money*) fric‡, pognon‡ *m*.
Lombardy ['lɒmbədɪ] *n* Lombardie *f*. **~ poplar** peuplier *m* d'Italie.
London ['lʌndən] **1** *n* Londres *m*. **2** *cpd life* londonien, à Londres; *people* de Londres; *shopkeeper, taxi* londonien; *street* londonien, de Londres. **London Bridge** Pont *m* de Londres; (*Bot*) **London pride** saxifrage ombreuse, désespoir *m* des peintres.
Londoner ['lʌndənəʳ] *n* Londonien(ne) *m(f)*.
lone [ləʊn] *adj person* solitaire; *village, house* isolé; (*unique*) seul, unique. (*fig*) **to play a ~ hand** mener une action solitaire; (*fig*) **he's a ~ wolf** c'est un solitaire, c'est quelqu'un qui fait cavalier seul.
loneliness ['ləʊnlɪnɪs] *n [person]* solitude *f*, isolement *m*; *[house, road]* (*isolated position*) isolement; (*atmosphere*) solitude; *[life]* solitude.
lonely ['ləʊnlɪ] *adj person* seul, solitaire, isolé; *life, journey, job, house, road* solitaire; (*isolated*) isolé, perdu. **to feel ~** se sentir seul; **it's ~ out there** on se sent seul là-bas; **a small ~ figure on the horizon** une petite silhouette seule *or* solitaire à l'horizon; **~ hearts' club** club *m* de rencontres (pour personnes seules).
loner* ['ləʊnəʳ] *n* solitaire *mf*.
lonesome ['ləʊnsəm] **1** *adj* = **lonely**. **2** *n*: **all on my** (*or* **your** *etc*) **~*** tout seul (*f* toute seule).
long¹ [lɒŋ] **1** *adj* **(a)** (*in size*) *dress, hair, rope, distance, journey* long (*f* longue). **how ~ is the field?** quelle est la longueur du champ?; **10 metres ~** (long) de 10 mètres; **~ trousers** pantalon *m* (long); **to be ~ in the leg** *[person, horse]* avoir les jambes longues; *[other animal]* avoir les pattes longues; *[trousers]* être trop long; **he's (a bit) ~ in the tooth*** il n'est plus tout jeune, il n'est plus de la première jeunesse; (*fig*) **to have a ~ arm** avoir le bras long; (*fig*) **the ~ arm of the law** la justice toute puissante; **he has a ~ reach** il peut allonger le bras loin; *[boxer]* il a de l'allonge; (*fig*) **to have a ~ face** avoir la mine longue *or* allongée, faire triste mine; **to make** *or* **pull a ~ face** faire une *or* la grimace; **his face was as ~ as a fiddle** il faisait une mine de dix pieds de long *or* une tête d'enterrement; (*fig*) **the biggest by a ~ chalk** *or* shot de beaucoup le plus grand; (*fig*) **not by a ~ chalk** loin de là; (*Math*) **~ division** division écrite complète (*avec indication des restes partiels*); (*Sport*) **~ jump** saut *m* en longueur; (*Cine*) **~ shot** plan général *or* d'ensemble; (*fig*) **it's a ~ shot** *or* **chance but we might be lucky** c'est très risqué mais nous aurons peut-être de la chance; (*fig*) **it was just a ~ shot** *or* **a ~ chance** c'était un coup à tenter, il y avait peu de chances pour que cela réussisse; (*Rad*) **on the ~ wave** sur les grandes ondes; *V* **broad, daddy, way** *etc*.
(b) (*in time*) *visit, wait, look, film etc* long (*f* longue); (*Ling*) *vowel* long. **6 months ~** qui dure 6 mois, de 6 mois; **a ~ time** longtemps; **you took a ~ time to get here** *or* **getting here** tu as mis longtemps pour *or* à venir; **it takes a ~ time for that drug to act** ce médicament met du temps à agir; **it will be a ~ time before I see her again** je ne la reverrai pas de longtemps; **it'll be a ~ time before I do that again!** je ne recommencerai pas de si tôt!; **for a ~ time I had to stay in bed** j'ai dû rester au lit longtemps; **I have been learning English for a ~ time** j'apprends l'anglais depuis longtemps; **a ~ time ago** il y a longtemps; **a ~, ~ time ago** il y a bien longtemps; **it's a ~ time since I last saw him** ça fait longtemps que je ne l'ai vu; **~ time no see!‡** tiens, un revenant!* (*fig*); **at ~ last** enfin; **he's not ~ for this world** il n'en a plus pour longtemps (à vivre); **the days are getting ~er** les jours rallongent; **friends of ~ standing** des amis de longue date; **he wasn't ~ in coming** il n'a pas mis longtemps pour venir; **how ~ are the holidays?** les vacances durent combien de temps?; (*Brit Scol, Univ*) **~ vacation** grandes vacances; **I find the days very ~** je trouve les jours bien longs; **to take a ~ look at sb** regarder longuement qn; (*fig*) **to take a ~ (hard) look at sth** regarder qch bien en face; (*fig*) **to take a ~ (hard) look at o.s.** s'examiner honnêtement; **he took a ~ drink of water** il a bu une grande gorgée d'eau; **a ~ drink** un long drink; (*fig*) **in the ~ run** à la longue, finalement, en fin de compte; **it will be a ~ job** cela demandera du temps; **to take the ~ view** prévoir les choses de loin; **taking the ~ view** si on prévoit les choses de loin, si on pense à l'avenir; **to have a ~ memory** avoir bonne mémoire, avoir de la mémoire; **he's ~ on advice‡** il est toujours là pour donner des conseils, pour donner des conseils il est un peu là*; **he's ~ on brains‡** c'est une grosse tête‡, il en a dans la cervelle*; **there are ~ odds against your doing that** il y a très peu de chances pour que tu fasses cela; *V* **let¹**, **term**.
2 *adv* **(a)** depuis longtemps. **this method has ~ been used in industry** cette méthode est employée depuis longtemps dans l'industrie; **I have ~ wished to say...** il y a longtemps que je souhaite dire ...; **these are ~-needed changes** ce sont des changements dont on a besoin depuis longtemps; **his ~-awaited reply** sa réponse (si) longtemps attendue.
(b) longtemps. **~ ago** il y a longtemps; **how ~ ago was it?** il y a combien de temps de ça?; **as ~ ago as 1930** déjà en 1930; **of ~ ago** d'il y a longtemps; **not ~ ago** il y a peu de temps, il n'y a pas longtemps; **he arrived not ~ ago** il est arrivé depuis peu de temps, il n'y a pas longtemps qu'il est arrivé; **~ before** (*adv*) longtemps avant; (*conj*) longtemps avant que + *subj*; **~ before the war** longtemps *or* bien avant la guerre; **you should have done it ~ before now** vous auriez dû le faire il y a longtemps; **not ~ before** (*adv*) peu de temps avant; (*conj*) peu de temps avant que + *subj*; **~ after** (*adv*) longtemps après; (*conj*) longtemps après que + *indic*; **not ~ since** il n'y a pas longtemps; **~ since** il y a longtemps; **he thought of friends ~ since dead** il a pensé à des amis morts depuis longtemps; **how ~ is it since you saw him?** cela fait combien de temps que tu ne l'as pas vu?; **they didn't stay ~** ils ne sont pas restés longtemps; **he hasn't been gone ~** il n'y a pas longtemps qu'il est parti; **it didn't take him ~** ça ne lui a pas pris longtemps; **it didn't take him ~ to realize that ...** il n'a pas mis longtemps à se rendre compte que ...; **have you been here/been waiting ~?** il y a longtemps que vous êtes ici?/que vous attendez?; **he didn't live ~ after that** il n'a pas longtemps survécu à ça; **women live ~er than men** les femmes vivent plus longtemps que les hommes; **~ live the King!** vive le roi!; **I only had ~ enough to buy a paper** je n'ai eu que le temps d'acheter un journal; **wait a little ~er** attendez encore un peu; **do we have to wait any ~er?** est-ce qu'il nous faut encore attendre?; **will you be ~?** tu en as pour longtemps?; **don't be ~** dépêche-toi, ne prends pas trop de temps; **I shan't be ~** je n'en ai pas pour longtemps, je me dépêche; **how ~ did they stay?** combien de temps sont-ils restés?; **how ~ will you be?** ça va te demander combien de temps?, tu vas mettre combien de temps?; **how ~ have you been learning Greek?** depuis combien de temps apprenez-vous le grec?; **how ~ had you been living in Paris?** depuis combien de temps viviez-vous à Paris?, cela faisait combien de temps que vous viviez à Paris?; **I shan't forget him as ~ as I live** je ne l'oublierai pas aussi longtemps que je vivrai; **stay as ~ as you like** restez autant que *or* aussi longtemps que vous voulez; **as ~ as the war lasted** tant que dura la guerre; **as ~ as the war lasts** tant que la guerre durera; **as ~ as necessary** aussi longtemps que c'est nécessaire *or* qu'il le faut.
(c) **all night ~** toute la nuit; **all summer ~** tout l'été; **his whole life ~** toute sa vie, sa vie durant; **so ~ as, as ~ as** pourvu que + *subj*; **you can borrow it so** *or* **as ~ as you keep it clean** vous pouvez l'emprunter pourvu que vous ne le salissiez (*subj*) pas *or* à condition de ne pas le salir; **so ~!*** au revoir!, à bientôt!, salut!*; **I can't stay any ~er, I can stay no ~er** je ne peux pas rester plus longtemps; **she no ~er wishes to do it** elle ne veut plus le faire; **he is no ~er living there** il n'habite plus là; *V* **last²**.
3 *n* **(a)** (*a long time*) **before ~** (+*future*) avant peu, dans peu de temps; (+ *past*) peu de temps après; **are you going away for ~?** partez-vous pour longtemps?; **I'm not here for ~** je ne suis pas ici pour longtemps; **at (the) ~est** au plus; **he hasn't ~ to live** il n'(en) a plus pour longtemps à vivre.
(b) (*fig*) **the ~ and the short of it is that ...** le fin mot de l'histoire, c'est que ... .
(c) (*Mus, Poetry*) longue *f*.
4 *cpd*: **longboat** (grande) chaloupe *f*; **longbow** arc *m* (anglais); (*Fin*) **long-dated** à longue échéance; **long-distance** *race, runner* de fond; (*Telec*) **long-distance call** communication interurbaine; **long-distance flight** (vol *m*) long-courrier *m*; **long-drawn-out** long (*f* longue), interminable; **long-eared** aux longues oreilles; **long-forgotten** oublié depuis longtemps; **long-haired** *person* aux cheveux longs; *animal* à longs poils; **longhand** (*n*) écriture normale *or* courante; (*adj*) en écriture normale *or* courante; **long-headed** (*lit*) à tête allongée; (*fig*) avisé, perspicace, prévoyant; **longhorn cattle** bovins *mpl* longhorn *inv or* à longues cornes; **long johns*** caleçon *m* (long); **long-legged** *person, horse* aux jambes longues; *other animal, insect* à longues pattes; **long-limbed** aux membres longs; **long-lived** d'une grande longévité; **women are longer-lived** *or* **more long-lived than men** les femmes vivent plus longtemps que les hommes; **long-lost** perdu depuis longtemps; **long-nosed** au nez long; **long-playing record** (disque *m*) 33 tours *m inv*, microsillon *m*; **long-range** *gun* à longue portée; **long-range plane** (*Mil*) avion *m* à grand rayon d'action; (*civil*) long-courrier *m*; **long-range weather forecast** prévisions *fpl* météorologiques à long terme; *[Vikings]* **longship** drakkar *m*; (*Naut*) **longshoreman** débardeur *m*, docker *m*; **long-sighted** (*lit*) hypermétrope; (*in old age*) presbyte; (*fig*) *person* prévoyant, qui voit loin; *decision* pris avec prévoyance; *attitude* prévoyant; **long-sightedness** (*lit*) hypermétropie *f*; (*in old age*)

presbytie *f*; (*fig*) prévoyance *f*; **long-sleeved** à manches longues; **long-standing** de longue date; **long-suffering** très patient, d'une patience à toute épreuve; **long-tailed** à longue queue; **long-term** à long terme; **longways** en longueur, en long; **longways on** dans le sens de la longueur; **long-winded** *person* intarissable, prolixe; *speech* interminable; **long-windedly** intarissablement.

long[2] [lɒŋ] *vi*: to ~ **to do** avoir très envie de faire, mourir d'envie de faire; **I am ~ing to see you** j'ai hâte *or* il me tarde de vous voir; **to ~ for sth** désirer (ardemment) qch, avoir très envie de qch; **the ~ed-for news** la nouvelle tant désirée; **to ~ for sb** se languir de qn; **to ~ for sb to do sth** mourir d'envie que qn fasse qch.

longevity [lɒn'dʒevɪtɪ] *n* longévité *f*.

longing ['lɒŋɪŋ] **1** *n* **(a)** (*urge*) désir *m*, envie *f*. **to have a sudden ~ to do** avoir un désir soudain *or* une envie soudaine de faire.
(b) (*nostalgia*) nostalgie *f*, regret *m*, désir *m*.
(c) (*for food*) envie *f*, convoitise *f*.
2 *adj look* plein de désir *or* d'envie *or* de nostalgie *or* de regret *or* de convoitise.

longingly ['lɒŋɪŋlɪ] *adv* (*V* **longing**) *look, speak, think* avec désir *or* envie *or* nostalgie *or* regret *or* convoitise.

longish ['lɒŋɪʃ] *adj* assez long (*f* longue); *book, play etc* assez long, longuet* (*slightly pej*). **(for) a ~ time** assez longtemps.

longitude ['lɒŋgɪtju:d] *n* longitude *f*. **at a ~ of 48°** par 48° de longitude.

longitudinal [ˌlɒŋgɪ'tju:dɪnl] *adj* longitudinal.

longitudinally [ˌlɒŋgɪ'tju:dɪnəlɪ] *adv* longitudinalement.

loo* [lu:] *n* (*Brit*) cabinets *mpl*, waters *mpl*, petit coin*. **the ~'s blocked** les waters *or* cabinets sont bouchés; **he's in the ~** il est au petit coin* *or* aux waters *or* aux cabinets.

loofah ['lu:fə^{r}] *n* luffa *m or* loofa *m*.

look [lʊk] **1** *n* **(a) to have** *or* **take a ~ at sth** regarder qch, jeter un coup d'œil à qch; (*in order to repair it etc*) jeter un coup d'œil à qch, s'occuper de qch; **to take a good ~ at sth** regarder qch de près, examiner qch; **to take a good ~ at sb** regarder qn avec attention, observer qn; **take a good ~ at it!** *or* **him!** regarde-le bien!; **let me have a ~** faites voir, laissez-moi regarder; **let me have another ~** laissez-moi regarder encore une fois; **do you want a ~?** tu veux voir? *or* regarder? *or* jeter un coup d'œil?; **take** *or* **have a ~ at this!** regarde-moi ça!, regarde un peu ça!*; **have a ~ through the telescope** regarde dans *or* avec le télescope; **I've had a ~ inside the house** j'ai visité la maison; **to have a ~ round the house** faire un tour dans la maison; **I just want to have a ~ round** (*in town*) je veux simplement faire un tour; (*in a shop*) je ne fais que regarder; **a good long ~ at the car revealed that ...** un examen *or* une inspection de la voiture a révélé que ....
(b) regard *m*. **an inquiring ~** un regard interrogateur; **with a nasty ~ in his eye** avec un regard méchant; **he gave me a furious ~** il m'a jeté un regard furieux, il m'a regardé d'un air furieux; **we got some very odd ~s** les gens nous regardaient d'un drôle d'air; **I told her what I thought and if ~s could kill* I'd be dead** je lui ai dit mon opinion et elle m'a fusillé *or* foudroyé du regard; *V* **black, dirty, long**[1] *etc*.
(c) (*search*) **to have a ~ for sth** chercher qch; **have another ~!** cherche encore une fois!; **I've had a good ~ for it already** je l'ai déjà cherché partout.
(d) (*appearance etc*) aspect *m*, air *m*, allure *f*. **he had the ~ of a sailor** il avait l'air d'un marin; **she has a ~ of her mother (about her)** elle a quelque chose de sa mère (dans son apparence); **there was a sad ~ about him** il avait l'air triste, son allure avait quelque chose de triste; **I like the ~ of her** je lui trouve l'air sympathique *or* une bonne tête*; **I don't like the ~ of him** je n'aime pas son allure *or* son air, il a une tête qui ne me revient pas*; **I don't like the ~ of this at all** ça ne me plaît pas du tout, ça ne me dit rien qui vaille; **you can't go by ~s** on ne peut pas se fier aux apparences, l'habit ne fait pas le moine (*Prov*); **by the ~ of him** à le voir, à voir sa tête*; **by the ~(s) of it, by the ~(s) of things*** de toute apparence; **(good) ~s** beauté *f*; **she has kept her ~s** elle est restée belle; **she's losing her ~s** sa beauté se fane, elle n'est plus aussi belle qu'autrefois; **~s aren't everything** la beauté n'est pas tout; (*Fashion*) **the leather ~** la mode du cuir.
2 *cpd*: **looked-for** *result* attendu, prévu; *effect* escompté, recherché; (*: *visit*) **to give sb a look-in** passer voir qn, faire une visite éclair *or* un saut chez qn; (*: *chance*) **with such competition we shan't get a look-in** avec de tels concurrents nous n'avons pas le moindre espoir *or* nous n'avons pas l'ombre d'un espoir; **our team didn't have** *or* **get a look-in** notre équipe n'a jamais eu le moindre espoir *or* la moindre chance de gagner; **look-out** *V* **look-out**; **to have** *or* **to take a look-see*** jeter un coup d'œil, donner un œil*.
3 *vi* **(a)** (*see, glance*) regarder. **~ over there!** regarde là-bas! *or* par là!; **~!** regarde!; **just ~!** regarde un peu!; **~ and see if it's still there** regarde voir un peu* si c'est encore là; **let me ~** laisse-moi voir; **~ who's here!** regarde qui est là!; **~ what a mess you've made!** regarde le gâchis que tu as fait!; **~ here, we must discuss it first** écoutez, il faut d'abord en discuter; **~ here, I didn't say that at all!** dites donc, je n'ai jamais dit ça!; **to ~ the other way** (*lit*) regarder ailleurs *or* de l'autre côté; (*fig*) fermer les yeux (*fig*); **you must ~ on the bright side** il faut avoir de l'optimisme, il faut voir les bons côtés de la situation; (*Prov*) **~ before you leap** il ne faut pas se lancer à l'aveuglette *or* s'engager les yeux fermés; **to ~ about** *or* **around** regarder autour de soi; **he ~ed around him for an ashtray** il a cherché un cendrier (des yeux); **to ~ ahead** (*in front*) regarder devant soi; (*to future*) se tourner vers l'avenir, considérer l'avenir; **~ing ahead to the future ...** si nous nous tournons vers l'avenir ...; **to ~ down one's nose at sb*** regarder qn de haut; **she ~s down her nose at suburban houses*** elle fait la moue devant *or* elle dédaigne les pavillons de banlieue; **to ~ down the list** parcourir la liste; **she ~ed into his eyes** elle a plongé son regard dans le sien; **to ~ over sb's shoulder** (*lit*) regarder par-dessus l'épaule de qn; (*fig*) surveiller qn constamment.
(b) [*building*] donner, regarder. **the house ~s east** la maison donne *or* regarde à l'est; **the house ~s on to the main street** la maison donne sur la grand-rue.
(c) (*search*) chercher, regarder. **you should have ~ed more carefully** tu aurais dû chercher plus soigneusement, tu aurais dû mieux regarder; **you can't have ~ed far** tu n'as pas dû beaucoup chercher *or* bien regarder.
(d) (+ *adj or n complement: seem*) sembler, paraître, avoir l'air. **she ~s (as if she's) tired** elle semble fatiguée, elle a l'air fatigué(e), on dirait qu'elle est fatiguée; **that story ~s interesting** cette histoire a l'air intéressante *or* semble intéressante; **how pretty you ~!** que vous êtes jolie!; **he ~s older than that** il a l'air plus vieux que ça; **you ~** *or* **you're ~ing well** vous avez bonne mine; **she doesn't ~ well** elle n'a pas bonne mine, elle a mauvaise mine; **he doesn't ~ himself, he doesn't ~ very great*** il n'a pas l'air bien, il n'a pas l'air en forme *or* dans son assiette*; **he ~s (about) 40** il a l'air d'avoir 40 ans, on lui donnerait 40 ans; **he ~s about 75 kilos/1 metre 80** il a l'air de faire environ 75 kilos/1 mètre 80; **she ~s her age** elle fait son âge; **she doesn't ~ her age** elle ne fait pas son âge, elle porte bien son âge; **she's tired and she ~s it** elle est fatiguée et ça se voit; **he's a soldier and he ~s it** il est soldat et il en a bien l'air; **she ~s her best in blue** c'est le bleu qui lui va le mieux; **you must ~ your best for this interview** il faut que tu sois à ton avantage *or* sur ton trente et un* pour cette interview; **they made me ~ a fool** *or* **foolish** ils m'ont fait paraître ridicule, à cause d'eux j'ai eu l'air ridicule; (*fig*) **to make sb ~ small** rabaisser qn, diminuer qn; (*fig*) **it made me ~ small** j'ai eu l'air fin!* *or* malin!* (*iro*); (*fig*) **he just does it to ~ big** il fait cela uniquement pour se donner de l'importance; (*fig*) **to ~ the part** avoir le physique *or* la tête* de l'emploi; **don't ~ like that!** (*sad, cross*) n'ayez pas cet air-là!, ne faites pas cette tête-là!*; (*surprised*) ne faites pas des yeux comme ça!; **try to ~ as if you're glad to see them!** essaie d'avoir l'air content de les voir!; **~ alive!*** magne-toi!:; **~ smart*** *or* **~ snappy* (about it)!, ~ sharp about it!*** dépêche-toi!, grouille-toi!:; **he ~s good in uniform** l'uniforme lui va bien *or* lui sied; **that dress ~s good** *or* **well on her** cette robe lui va bien; **that hat makes her ~ old** ce chapeau la vieillit; **how did she ~?, what did she ~ like?** (*health*) est-ce qu'elle avait bonne mine?; (*on hearing news etc*) quelle tête* *or* quelle mine faisait-elle?; **how do I ~?** (*in these clothes*) est-ce que ça va *or* ça ira?; (*in this new dress etc*) est-ce que ça me va?; **that ~s good** [*food*] cela a l'air bon; [*brooch, picture etc*] cela fait très bien *or* très joli; [*plan, book, idea*] ça a l'air intéressant *or* prometteur; **it doesn't ~ right** (on dirait qu')il y a quelque chose qui ne va pas; **it ~s all right to me** ça m'a l'air d'aller, je trouve que ça va, à mon avis ça va; **how does it ~ to you?** qu'en pensez-vous?, ça va à votre avis?; **it ~s promising** c'est prometteur; **it will ~ bad** cela fera mauvais effet; **it ~s good on paper** c'est *or* cela fait très bien sur le papier *or* en théorie; **it ~s as if it's going to snow** j'ai l'impression *or* on dirait qu'il va neiger; **it ~s as if he isn't coming, it doesn't ~ as if he's coming** il n'a pas l'air de venir; **it ~s to me as if he isn't coming, it doesn't ~ to me as if he's coming** j'ai l'impression qu'il ne va pas venir; **what does it ~ like?** comment est-ce?, cela ressemble à quoi?, ça a l'air de quoi?*; **what does he ~ like?** comment est-il?; **he ~s like his brother** il ressemble à son frère; **he ~s like a soldier** il a l'air d'un soldat, on dirait un soldat; (*pej*) **she ~ed like nothing on earth*** (*badly dressed*) elle avait l'air d'un épouvantail *or* de Dieu sait quoi; (*ill, depressed*) elle avait une tête* épouvantable; **the picture doesn't ~ like him at all** le portrait n'est pas du tout ressemblant *or* ne lui ressemble pas du tout; **it ~s like salt** ça a l'air d'être du sel, on dirait du sel; **this ~s to me like the shop** cela m'a l'air d'être le magasin; **it ~s like rain** j'ai l'impression *or* on dirait qu'il va pleuvoir; **the rain doesn't ~ like stopping** la pluie n'a pas l'air de (vouloir) s'arrêter; **it certainly ~s like it** c'est bien probable, ça m'en a tout l'air; **the evening ~ed like being interesting** la soirée promettait d'être intéressante.
4 *vt* **(a)** regarder. **to ~ sb in the face** *or* **in the eye(s)** regarder qn en face *or* dans les yeux; **she ~ed him full in the face/straight in the eye** elle l'a regardé bien en face/droit dans les yeux; (*fig*) **I couldn't ~ him in the face** *or* **in the eye** je n'osais (*or* je n'oserais) pas le regarder en face; (*Prov*) **never ~ a gift horse in the mouth** à cheval donné on ne regarde pas la bride (*Prov*); **to ~ sb up and down** toiser qn, regarder qn de haut en bas; **to ~ daggers at sb** fusiller *or* foudroyer qn du regard; (*liter*) **to ~ one's last on sth** jeter un ultime regard sur qch.
(b) (*pay attention to*) regarder, faire attention à. **~ where you're going!** regarde *or* fais attention où tu vas!; **~ what you've done now!** regarde ce que tu as fait! *or* ce que tu viens de faire!

look about *vi* regarder autour de soi. **to look about for sb/sth** chercher qn/qch (des yeux).

look after *vt fus* **(a)** (*take care of*) *invalid, animal, plant* s'occuper de, soigner; *possessions* faire attention à, prendre soin de. **she doesn't look after herself very well** elle ne se soigne pas assez, elle néglige sa santé; **look after yourself!*** fais bien attention à toi!*, prends soin de toi!; **she's quite old enough to look after herself** elle est bien assez grande pour se défendre* *or* se débrouiller* toute seule; **he certainly looks after his car** il entretient bien sa voiture; **we're well looked after here** on s'occupe bien de nous ici, on nous soigne bien ici.
(b) (*take responsibility for*) *child* garder, s'occuper de; *shop, business* s'occuper de; *book, house, jewels* surveiller, avoir

l'œil sur. **to look after one's own interests** protéger ses propres intérêts.
look around *vi* = **look about.**
look at *vt fus* **(a)** (*observe*) *person, object* regarder. **just look at this mess!** regarde un peu ce fouillis!*; **just look at you!** regarde de quoi tu as l'air!; **to look at him you would never think (that)** ... à le voir on ne penserait jamais que ...; **it isn't much to look at, it's nothing to look at** ça ne paie pas de mine.
(b) (*consider*) *situation, problem* considérer, voir. **that's one way of looking at it** c'est une façon de voir les choses, c'est un point de vue parmi d'autres; **that's his way of looking at things** c'est comme ça qu'il voit les choses; **it depends (on) how you look at it** tout dépend comment on voit *or* envisage la chose; **just look at him now!** regarde où il en est aujourd'hui!; **let's look at the facts** considérons les faits; **they wouldn't look at my proposal** ils n'ont pas pris ma proposition en considération, ils n'ont pas considéré ma proposition; **I wouldn't look at the job** je n'accepterais ce poste pour rien au monde; **the landlady won't look at foreigners** la propriétaire ne veut pas avoir affaire à des étrangers.
(c) (*check*) vérifier; (*see to*) s'occuper de. **will you look at the carburettor?** pourriez-vous vérifier le carburateur?; **I'll look at it tomorrow** je m'en occuperai demain.
look away *vi* détourner les yeux *or* le regard (*from* de), regarder ailleurs.
look back *vi* **(a)** regarder derrière soi. **he looked back at the church** il s'est retourné pour regarder l'église.
(b) (*in memory*) regarder en arrière, revenir sur le passé. **to look back on** revoir en esprit, évoquer; **we can look back on 20 years of happy marriage** nous avons derrière nous 20 ans de bonheur conjugal; **after that he never looked back*** après, ça n'a fait qu'aller de mieux en mieux.
look down *vi* baisser les yeux. **to look down at the ground** regarder à terre; **don't look down, or you'll fall** ne regarde pas par terre *or* en bas, tu vas tomber; **he looked down on** *or* **at the town from the hilltop** il a regardé la ville du haut de la colline; **the castle looks down on the valley** le château domine la vallée.
look down on *vt fus person* regarder de haut, mépriser; *thing, habit* mépriser, faire fi de.
look for 1 *vt fus* **(a)** (*seek*) *object, work* chercher. **he goes around looking for trouble*** il cherche toujours les embêtements.
(b) (*expect*) *praise, reward* attendre, espérer.
2 looked-for *adj V* **look 2.**
look forward to *vt fus event, meal, trip, holiday* attendre avec impatience. **I'm looking forward to seeing you** j'attends avec impatience le plaisir de vous voir, je suis impatient de vous voir; (*in letter*) **looking forward to hearing from you** en espérant avoir bientôt une lettre de vous, dans l'attente de votre réponse (*frm*); **I look forward to the day when** j'attends avec impatience le jour où, je pense d'avance au jour où; **are you looking forward to it?** est-ce que vous êtes content à cette perspective?; **we've been looking forward to it for weeks** nous y pensons avec impatience depuis des semaines; **I'm so (much) looking forward to it** je m'en réjouis à l'avance, je m'en fais déjà une fête.
look in 1 *vi* **(a)** (*lit*) regarder à l'intérieur. **to look in at the window** regarder par la fenêtre (*vers l'intérieur*).
(b) (*: *pay visit*) passer (voir). **we looked in at Robert's** nous sommes passés chez Robert, nous avons fait un saut *or* un tour* chez Robert; **to look in on sb** passer voir qn; **the doctor will look in again tomorrow** le docteur repassera demain.
(c) (*: *watch television*) regarder la télévision. **we look in every evening** nous regardons la télé* tous les soirs.
2 look-in *n V* **look 2.**
look into *vt fus* (*examine*) examiner, étudier; (*investigate*) se renseigner sur. **I shall look into it** je vais me renseigner là-dessus, je vais m'en occuper; **we must look into what happened to the money** il va falloir que nous enquêtions (*subj*) sur ce qui est arrivé à cet argent; **the complaint is being looked into** on examine la plainte; **we shall look into the question/the possibility of** ... nous allons étudier *or* examiner la question/la possibilité de ... .
look on 1 *vi* regarder, être un spectateur (*or* une spectatrice). **they all looked on while the raiders escaped** ils se sont tous contentés de regarder *or* d'être spectateurs alors que les bandits s'enfuyaient; **he wrote the letter while I looked on** il a écrit la lettre tandis que je le regardais faire; **I've forgotten my book, may I look on with you?** j'ai oublié mon livre, puis-je suivre avec vous?
2 *vt fus* considérer. **I shall look favourably on your son's application** j'examinerai d'un œil favorable la demande de votre fils; **I do not look on the matter like that** je ne vois *or* ne considère *or* n'envisage pas la chose de cette façon-là; **I look on the French as our rivals** je considère les Français comme *or* je tiens les Français pour nos rivaux.
look out 1 *vi* **(a)** (*lit*) regarder dehors. **to look out of the window** regarder par la fenêtre.
(b) (*fig*) **I am looking out for a suitable house** je suis à la recherche d'une maison qui convienne, je cherche une maison qui convienne; **look out for the butcher's van and tell me when it's coming** guette la camionnette du boucher et préviens-moi; **look out for a good place to picnic** essaie de repérer un bon endroit pour le pique-nique.
(c) (*take care*) faire attention, prendre garde. **look out!** attention!, gare!; **I told you to look out!** je t'avais bien dit de faire attention!; **look out for sharks** soyez sur vos gardes *or* méfiez-vous, il y a peut-être des requins; **look out for ice on the road** faites attention au cas où il y aurait du verglas, méfiez-vous du verglas; **look out for the low ceiling** faites attention, *or* prenez garde, le plafond est bas.
2 *vt sep* (*Brit*) chercher et trouver. **I shall look out some old magazines for them** je vais essayer de leur trouver quelques vieux magazines.
3 look-out *V* **look-out.**
look over *vt sep essay* jeter un coup d'œil à, parcourir; *book* parcourir, feuilleter; *town, building* visiter; *person* (*quickly*) jeter un coup d'œil à; (*slowly*) regarder de la tête aux pieds.
look round 1 *vi* **(a)** regarder (autour de soi). (*in shop*) **we just want to look round** on veut seulement regarder, on ne fait que regarder; **I looked round for you after the concert** je vous ai cherché *or* j'ai essayé de vous voir après le concert; **I'm looking round for an assistant** je suis à la recherche d'un assistant, je cherche un assistant.
(b) (*look back*) regarder derrière soi. **I looked round to see where he was** je me suis retourné pour voir où il était; **don't look round!** ne vous retournez pas!
2 *vt fus town, factory* visiter, faire le tour de.
look through *vt fus* **(a)** (*examine*) *papers, book* examiner; (*briefly*) *papers* parcourir; *book* parcourir, feuilleter.
(b) (*revise*) *lesson* réviser, repasser; (*reread*) *notes* revoir, relire.
look to *vt fus* **(a)** (*attend to*) faire attention à, veiller à. **look to it that it doesn't happen again** faites attention que *or* veillez à ce que cela ne se reproduise pas; (*fig*) **to look to one's laurels** ne pas se laisser éclipser.
(b) (*look after*) s'occuper de. **look to the children** occupe-toi des enfants.
(c) (*rely on*) compter sur. **I look to you for help** je compte sur votre aide; **I always look to my mother for advice** quand j'ai besoin d'un conseil je me tourne vers ma mère.
look up 1 *vi* **(a)** regarder en haut; (*from reading etc*) lever les yeux.
(b) (*improve*) *[prospects]* s'améliorer; *[business]* reprendre; *[weather]* se lever. **things are looking up (for you)** ça a l'air d'aller mieux *or* de s'améliorer (pour vous); **oil shares are looking up** les actions pétrolières remontent *or* sont en hausse.
2 *vt sep* **(a)** *person* aller *or* venir voir. **look me up the next time you are in London** venez *or* passez me voir la prochaine fois que vous serez à Londres.
(b) (*search*) *name, word* chercher. **to look sb up in the phone book** chercher qn dans l'annuaire (du téléphone); **to look up a name on a list** chercher un nom sur une liste; **to look up a word in the dictionary** chercher un mot dans le dictionnaire; **you'll have to look that one up** il faut que tu cherches (*subj*) (ce que cela veut dire *or* ce que c'est *etc*).
3 *vt fus reference book* consulter, chercher *or* vérifier dans. **I looked up the dictionary** j'ai consulté le dictionnaire; **go and look up the dictionary** va chercher *or* vérifier dans le dictionnaire.
look upon *vt fus* = **look on 2.**
look up to *vt fus* respecter, avoir du respect pour.
looker ['lʊkəʳ] **1** *n* (*) **she's a good ~, she's a (real) ~** c'est une jolie fille, c'est un beau brin de fille; **he's a (good) ~** c'est un beau gars*. **2** *cpd*: **looker-on** spectateur *m*, -trice *f*.
-looking ['lʊkɪŋ] *adj ending in cpds*: **ugly-looking** laid (d'aspect); **sinister-looking** à l'air sinistre; *V* **good** *etc.*
looking-glass ['lʊkɪŋglɑːs] *n* glace *f*, miroir *m*.
look-out ['lʊkaʊt] **1** *n* **(a)** (*observation*) surveillance *f*, guet *m*. **to keep a ~, to be on the ~** faire le guet, guetter; **to keep a ~ for sb/sth** guetter qn/qch; **to be on the ~ for bargains** être à l'affût des bonnes affaires; **to be on the ~ for danger** être sur ses gardes à cause d'un danger éventuel; **to be on ~ (duty)** (*Mil*) être au guet; (*Naut*) être en vigie; *V* **sharp.**
(b) (*observer*) (*gen*) guetteur *m*; (*Mil*) homme *m* de guet, guetteur; (*Naut*) homme de veille *or* de vigie, vigie *f*.
(c) (*observation post*) (*gen, Mil*) poste *m* de guet; (*Naut*) vigie *f*.
(d) (*: *esp Brit: outlook*) perspective *f*. **it's a poor ~ for cotton** les perspectives pour le coton ne sont pas brillantes; **it's a grim ~ for people like us** la situation *or* ça s'annonce mal pour les gens comme nous; **that's your ~!** cela vous regarde!, c'est votre affaire!
2 *cpd tower* d'observation. (*Mil*) **look-out post** poste *m* de guet *or* d'observation.
loom[1] [luːm] *vi* (*also* ~ **up**) (*appear*) apparaître indistinctement, se dessiner; (*fig*) menacer, paraître imminent. **the ship ~ed (up) out of the mist** le navire a surgi de *or* dans la brume; **the skyscraper ~ed up out of the fog** le gratte-ciel est apparu indistinctement dans le brouillard; **the dark mountains ~ed (up) in front of us** les sombres montagnes sont apparues *or* se sont dressées menaçantes devant nous; **the probability of defeat ~ed (up) before him** la possibilité de la défaite s'est présentée à son esprit; **disaster is ~ing ahead** le désastre paraît imminent; **the threat of an epidemic ~ed large in their minds** la menace d'une épidémie était au premier plan de leurs préoccupations; **the exams are ~ing large*** les examens sont dangereusement proches.
loom[2] [luːm] *n* (*Tex*) métier *m* à tisser.
loon [luːn] *n* **(a)** (*†: *dial*) (*fool*) imbécile *m*, idiot *m*; (*good-for-nothing*) vaurien *m*. **(b)** (*US Orn*) plongeon *m*, plongeur *m*.
loony‡ ['luːnɪ] **1** *n* imbécile *mf*, idiot(e) *m(f)*, andouille‡ *f*. ~ **bin** maison *f* de fous, asile *m* (d'aliénés); **in the ~ bin** chez les fous. **2** *adj* timbré*, cinglé‡.
loop [luːp] **1** *n* **(a)** (*in string, ribbon, writing*) boucle *f*; (*in river*) méandre *m*, boucle. **the string has a ~ in it** la ficelle fait une boucle; **to put a ~ in sth** faire une boucle à qch.
(b) (*Elec*) circuit fermé; (*Computers*) boucle *f*; (*Rail: also* ~ **line**) voie *f* d'évitement; (*by motorway etc*) bretelle *f*.

(c) (*Med: contraceptive*) **the ~** le stérilet.
(d) (*curtain fastener*) embrasse *f.*
2 *cpd*: **loophole** (*Archit*) meurtrière *f*; (*fig: in law, argument, regulations*) point *m* faible, lacune *f*; (*fig*) **we must try to find a loophole** il faut que nous trouvions (*subj*) une échappatoire *or* une porte de sortie*.
3 *vt string etc* faire une boucle à, boucler. **he ~ed the rope round the post** il a passé la corde autour du poteau; (*Aviat*) **to ~ the loop** faire un looping, boucler la boucle.
4 *vi* former une boucle.
loop back 1 *vi [road, river]* former une boucle.
2 *vt sep curtain* retenir *or* relever avec une embrasse.
loop up *vt sep* = **loop back 2.**
loose [lu:s] **1** *adj* **(a)** (*not firmly attached*) *knot, shoelace* qui se défait, desserré; *screw* desserré, qui a du jeu; *stone, brick* branlant; *tooth* qui branle, qui bouge; *page from book* qui se détache; *hair* dénoué, flottant; *animal etc* (*free*) en liberté; (*escaped*) échappé; (*freed*) lâché. **to be coming** *or* **getting** *or* **working ~** *[knot]* se desserrer, se défaire; *[screw]* se desserrer, avoir du jeu; *[stone, brick]* branler; *[tooth]* branler, bouger; *[page]* se détacher; *[hair]* se dénouer, se défaire; **to be ~, to have come ~** *[knot]* s'être défait; *[screw]* s'être desserré; *[stone, brick]* branler; *[tooth]* branler, bouger; *[page]* s'être détaché; *[hair]* s'être dénoué; *[animal etc]* **to get ~** s'échapper; **to let** *or* **set** *or* **turn an animal ~** libérer *or* lâcher un animal; **to let the dogs ~ on sb** lâcher les chiens sur qn; **we can't let him ~ on that class** on ne peut pas le lâcher dans cette classe; **one of your buttons is very ~** l'un de tes boutons va tomber *or* se découd; **write it on a ~ sheet of paper** écrivez-le sur une feuille volante; (*to pupil*) écrivez-le sur une (feuille de) copie; (*on roadway*) **~ chippings** gravillons *mpl*; (*Elec*) **~ connection** mauvais contact; (*Brit*) *[furniture]* **~ covers** housses *fpl*; **the reins hung ~** les rênes n'étaient pas tenues *or* tendues, les rênes étaient sur le cou; **~ end of a rope** bout pendant *or* ballant d'une corde; (*fig*) **to be at a ~ end** ne pas trop savoir quoi faire, ne pas savoir quoi faire de sa peau*; (*fig*) **to tie up ~ ends** régler les détails qui restent; *V* **break, cut, hell, screw** *etc.*
(b) (*Comm: not packed*) *biscuits, carrots etc* en vrac; *butter, cheese* au poids. **the potatoes were ~ in the bottom of the basket** les pommes de terre étaient à même au fond du panier; **just put them ~ into the basket** mettez-les à même *or* tels quels dans le panier; **~ change** petite *or* menue monnaie.
(c) (*not tight*) *coat, dress* vague, ample; *skin* flasque, mou (*f* molle); *collar* lâche. **these trousers are too ~ round the waist** ce pantalon est trop large *or* lâche à la taille; **~ clothes are better for summer wear** l'été il vaut mieux porter des vêtements lâches *or* flottants *or* pas trop ajustés; **the rope round the dog's neck was quite ~** la corde passée au cou du chien était toute lâche; *V* **play.**
(d) (*pej*) *woman* facile, de mœurs légères; *morals* relâché, douteux. **to lead a ~ life** mener une vie dissolue; **~ living** vie dissolue, débauche *f*; **~ talk** propos grossiers.
(e) (*not strict*) *discipline* relâché; *reasoning, thinking* confus, vague, imprécis; *style* lâche, relâché; *translation* approximatif, assez libre. **a ~ interpretation of the rules** une interprétation peu rigoureuse du règlement.
(f) (*available*) *funds* disponible, liquide.
(g) (*not compact*) *soil* meuble; (*fig*) *association* vague. **there is a ~ connection between the two theories** il y a un vague lien entre les deux théories; (*Rugby*) **~ scrum** mêlée ouverte, regroupement *m*; **a ~ weave** un tissu lâche (*V also* 2); (*Med*) **his bowels are ~** ses intestins sont relâchés.
2 *cpd*: (*Brit: for horses*) **loose box** fourgon *m* à chevaux; **loose-fitting** ample, qui n'est pas ajusté; **loose-leaf(ed)** à feuilles volantes, à feuilles *or* feuillets mobiles; **loose-limbed** agile; **loose-weave** *material* lâche; *curtains* en tissu lâche.
3 *n*: **to be on the ~** (*free*) être en liberté; (*: *on a spree*) mener joyeuse vie, faire la bringue‡.
4 *vt* **(a)** (*undo*) défaire; (*untie*) délier, dénouer; *screw etc* desserrer; (*free*) *animal* lâcher; *prisoner* relâcher, mettre en liberté; **to ~ a boat (from its moorings)** démarrer une embarcation, larguer les amarres; **they ~d the dogs on him** ils ont lâché les chiens après *or* sur lui.
(b) (*also* **~ off**) *gun* décharger (*on or at sb* sur qn); *arrow* tirer (*on or at sb* sur qn). **they ~d (off) missiles at the invaders** ils ont fait pleuvoir des projectiles sur les envahisseurs; (*fig*) **to ~ (off) a volley of abuse at sb** déverser un torrent *or* lâcher une bordée d'injures sur qn.
loose off 1 *vi* (*shoot*) tirer (*at sb* sur qn).
2 *vt sep* = **loose 4b.**
loosely ['lu:slı] *adv* **(a)** (*not tightly*) *attach, tie, hold* sans serrer; *be fixed* lâchement, sans être serré; *weave* lâchement; *associate* vaguement. **the reins hung ~** les rênes pendaient sur le cou.
(b) (*imprecisely*) *translate* sans trop de rigueur, assez librement, approximativement. **this is ~ translated as ...** ceci est traduit approximativement *or* de façon assez libre par ...; **that word is ~ used to mean ...** on emploie ce mot de façon plutôt impropre pour dire ... .
loosen ['lu:sn] **1** *vt* **(a)** (*slacken*) *screw, belt, knot* desserrer; *rope* détendre, relâcher; (*untie*) *knot, shoelace* défaire. **first ~ the part then remove it gently** il faut d'abord donner du jeu à *or* ébranler la pièce puis tirer doucement; **to ~ one's grip on sth** relâcher son étreinte sur qch; (*fig*) **to ~ sb's tongue** délier la langue à qn.
(b) (*Agr*) *soil* rendre meuble, ameublir. (*Med*) **to ~ the bowels** relâcher les intestins.
2 *vi [fastening]* se défaire; *[screw]* se desserrer, jouer; *[knot]* (*slacken*) se desserrer; (*come undone*) se défaire; *[rope]* se détendre.
loosen up 1 *vi* **(a)** (*limber up*) faire des exercices d'assouplissement; (*before race etc*) s'échauffer.
(b) (*become less shy*) se dégeler, perdre sa timidité.
(c) (*become less strict with*) **to loosen up on sb*** se montrer plus coulant* *or* moins strict envers qn.
2 *vt sep*: **to loosen up one's muscles** faire des exercices d'assouplissement; (*before race etc*) s'échauffer.
looseness ['lu:snıs] *n* **(a)** *[knot]* desserrement *m*; *[screw, tooth]* jeu *m*; *[rope]* relâchement *m*; *[clothes]* ampleur *f*, flou *m*. **the ~ of the knot caused the accident** l'accident est arrivé parce que le nœud n'était pas assez serré.
(b) *[translation]* imprécision *f*, inexactitude *f*; *[thought, style]* manque *m* de rigueur *or* de précision.
(c) (*immorality*) *[behaviour]* licence *f*; *[morals]* relâchement *m.*
(d) *[soil]* ameublissement *m*. (*Med*) **~ of the bowels** relâchement *m* des intestins.
loot [lu:t] **1** *n* (*plunder*) butin *m*; (‡*fig: prizes, gifts, etc*) butin; (‡: *money*) pognon‡ *m*, fric‡ *m*, oseille‡ *f*. **2** *vt town* piller, mettre à sac; *shop, goods* piller. **3** *vi*: **to go ~ing** se livrer au pillage.
looter ['lu:təʳ] *n* pillard *m.*
looting ['lu:tıŋ] *n* pillage *m.*
lop [lɒp] *vt tree* tailler, élaguer, émonder; *branch* couper.
lop off *vt sep branch, piece* couper; *head* trancher.
lope [ləʊp] *vi* courir en bondissant. **to ~ along/in/out** *etc* avancer/entrer/sortir *etc* en bondissant.
lop-eared ['lɒpˌıəd] *adj* aux oreilles pendantes.
lop-sided ['lɒp'saıdıd] *adj* (*not straight*) de travers, de guingois, de traviole‡; (*asymmetric*) asymétrique, disproportionné.
loquacious [lə'kweıʃəs] *adj* loquace, bavard.
loquacity [lə'kwæsıtı] *n* loquacité *f*, volubilité *f.*
lord [lɔ:d] **1** *n* **(a)** seigneur *m*. **~ of the manor** châtelain *m*; (*hum*) **~ and master** seigneur et maître (*hum*); (*Brit*) **L~ (John) Smith** lord (John) Smith; **the (House of) L~s** la Chambre des Lords; **my L~ Bishop of Tooting** (Monseigneur) l'évêque de Tooting; **my L~** Monsieur le baron (*or* comte *etc*); (*to judge*) Monsieur le Juge; (*to bishop*) Excellence; *V* **law, live[1], sea** *etc.*
(b) (*Rel*) **the L~** le Seigneur; **Our L~** Notre Seigneur; **the L~ Jesus** le Seigneur Jésus; **the L~'s supper** l'eucharistie *f*, la sainte Cène; **the L~'s prayer** le Notre-Père; **the L~'s day** le jour du Seigneur; **good L~!*** Seigneur!, mon Dieu!, bon sang!*; **oh L~!*** Seigneur!, zut!*; **L~ knows what/who** *etc** Dieu sait quoi/qui *etc.*
2 *vt* (*) **to ~ it** vivre en grand seigneur, mener la grande vie; **to ~ it over sb** traiter qn avec arrogance.
3 *cpd*: (*Brit*) (*Scot Jur*) **Lord Advocate** ≃ Procureur *m* de la République; (*Jur*) **Lord Chief Justice (of England)** Président *m* de la Haute Cour de Justice; (*Jur, Parl*) **Lord (High) Chancellor** Grand Chancelier d'Angleterre; **Lord High Commissioner** *représentant de la Couronne à l'Assemblée générale de l'église d'Écosse*; (*Jur*) **Lord Justice of Appeal** juge *m* à la Cour d'appel; **Lord Lieutenant** *représentant de la Couronne dans un comté*; **Lord Mayor** *titre du maire des principales villes anglaises et galloises*; (*Jur*) **Lord of Appeal (in Ordinary)** juge *m* de la Cour de cassation (*siégeant à la Chambre des Lords*); (*Parl*) **First Lord of the Admiralty** ≃ ministre *m* de la Marine; (*Parl*) **Lord President of the Council** Président *m* du Conseil privé de la reine; (*Parl*) **Lord Privy Seal** lord *m* du Sceau privé; **Lord Provost** *titre du maire des principales villes écossaises*; (*Parl*) **Lord spiritual/temporal** *membre ecclésiastique/laïque de la Chambre des Lords.*
lordliness ['lɔ:dlınıs] *n* (*V* **lordly**) noblesse *f*, majesté *f*; magnificence *f*; (*pej*) hauteur *f*, arrogance *f*, morgue *f.*
lordly ['lɔ:dlı] *adj* (*dignified*) *bearing* noble, majestueux; (*magnificent*) *castle* seigneurial, magnifique; (*pej: arrogant*) *person, manner* hautain, arrogant, plein de morgue. **~ contempt** mépris souverain.
lordship ['lɔ:dʃıp] *n* (*rights, property*) seigneurie *f*; (*power*) autorité *f* (*over* sur). **Your L~** Monsieur le comte (*or* le baron *etc*); (*to judge*) Monsieur le Juge; (*to bishop*) Excellence.
lore [lɔ:ʳ] *n* (*U*) **(a)** (*traditions*) tradition(s) *f(pl)*, coutumes *fpl*, usages *mpl*; *V* **folk** *etc.* **(b)** (*knowledge: gen in cpds*) **his bird/wood ~** sa (grande) connaissance des oiseaux/de la vie dans les forêts.
lorgnette [lɔ:'njet] *n* (*eyeglasses*) face-à-main *m*; (*opera glasses*) lorgnette *f*, jumelles *fpl* de spectacle.
lorry ['lɒrı] (*Brit*) **1** *n* camion *m*. **to transport by ~** transporter par camion, camionner; *V* **articulate. 2** *cpd*: **lorry driver** camionneur *m*; (*long-distance*) routier *m*; **lorry load** chargement *m.*
lose [lu:z] *pret, ptp* **lost 1** *vt* **(a)** *person, job, limb, game, book, key, plane, enthusiasm* perdre; (*mislay*) *glove, key etc* égarer; *opportunity* manquer, perdre. **he got lost in the wood** il s'est perdu *or* égaré dans le bois; **the key got lost during the removal** on a perdu la clef au cours du déménagement; **get lost!‡** fiche le camp!*, barre-toi!‡; **I lost him in the crowd** je l'ai perdu dans la foule; **I lost my father when I was 10** j'ai perdu mon père à l'âge de 10 ans; *[doctor]* **to ~ a patient** perdre un malade; **to ~ the use of an arm** perdre l'usage d'un bras; **to ~ a bet** perdre un pari; (*in business, gambling etc*) **how much did you ~?** combien avez-vous perdu?; **he lost £1,000 on that deal** il a perdu 1.000 livres dans cette affaire; **you've nothing to ~ (by it)** tu n'as rien à perdre, tu ne risques rien; (*fig*) **you've nothing to ~ by helping him** tu ne perds rien *or* tu n'as rien à perdre *or* tu ne risques rien à l'aider; **100 men were lost** 100 hommes ont péri, on a perdu 100 hommes; **20 lives were lost in the explosion** 20 personnes ont péri dans l'explosion; **the ship was lost with all hands** le navire a été perdu corps et biens; *[person]* **to be lost at sea** périr *or* être perdu en mer; **not to ~ a word of** ne pas perdre un mot

de; **what he said was lost in the applause** ses paroles se sont perdues dans les applaudissements; **I lost his last sentence** je n'ai pas entendu sa dernière phrase; **the poem lost a lot in translation** le poème a beaucoup perdu à la traduction; (*after explanation etc*) **you've lost me there*** je ne vous suis plus, je n'y suis plus; *V also* **lost.**

(b) (*phrases*) **to ~ one's balance** perdre l'équilibre; (*lit, fig*) **to ~ one's bearings** être désorienté; **to ~ one's breath** perdre haleine, s'essouffler; **to have lost one's breath** être hors d'haleine, être à bout de souffle; **to ~ consciousness** perdre connaissance; **to ~ face** perdre la face; **she's lost her figure** elle s'est épaissie, elle a perdu sa ligne; (*Mil, fig*) **to ~ ground** perdre du terrain; **to ~ heart** perdre courage, se décourager; **to ~ one's heart to sb** tomber amoureux de qn; **to ~ interest in sth** se désintéresser de qch; (*Aut*) **he's lost his licence** on lui a retiré *or* il s'est fait retirer son permis de conduire; **to ~ one's life** perdre la vie, mourir; **she's losing her looks** sa beauté se fane, elle n'est plus aussi belle qu'autrefois; **to ~ patience with sb** perdre patience avec qn, s'impatienter contre qn; **to ~ one's rag‡** se mettre en rogne*, piquer une rogne*; (*lit, fig*) **to ~ sight of sb/sth** perdre qn/qch de vue; **he didn't ~ any sleep over it** il n'en a pas perdu le sommeil pour autant, ce n'est pas ça qui l'a empêché de dormir; **don't ~ any sleep over it!** ne vous en faites pas!, dormez sur vos deux oreilles!; **to ~ one's temper** se fâcher, se mettre en colère; **to ~ one's voice because of a cold** avoir une extinction de voix *or* être aphone à cause d'un rhume; **to ~ one's way** perdre son chemin, se perdre, s'égarer; **to ~ weight** perdre du poids, maigrir; **I lost 2 kilos** j'ai maigri de *or* j'ai perdu 2 kilos; *[clock etc]* **to ~ 10 minutes a day** retarder de 10 minutes par jour; **we mustn't ~ any time** il ne faut pas perdre de temps; **we must ~ no time in preventing this** nous devons empêcher cela au plus vite; **there's not a minute to ~** il n'y a pas une minute à perdre; *V* **cool, lost** *etc.*

(c) (*go too fast for*) *competitors, pursuers* devancer, distancer, semer. **he managed to ~ the detective who was following him** il a réussi à semer le détective qui le suivait; **try to ~ him before you come to see us*** essaie de le semer *or* le perdre en route avant de venir nous voir.

(d) (*cause loss of*) faire perdre, coûter. **that will ~ you your job** cela va vous faire perdre *or* vous coûter votre place; **that lost us the war/the match** cela nous a fait perdre la guerre/le match.

2 *vi* **(a)** *[player, team]* perdre, être perdant. (*Ftbl etc*) **they lost 6-1** ils ont perdu *or* ils se sont fait battre 6-1; **they lost to the new team** ils se sont fait battre par la nouvelle équipe; **our team is losing today** notre équipe est en train de perdre aujourd'hui; (*fig*) **he lost on the deal** il a été perdant dans l'affaire; **you can't ~*** tu n'as rien à perdre (mais tout à gagner), tu ne risques rien; (*fig*) **it ~s in translation** cela perd à la traduction; (*fig*) **the story did not ~ in the telling** l'histoire n'a rien perdu à être racontée.

(b) *[watch, clock]* retarder.

lose out *vi* être perdant. **to lose out on a deal** être perdant dans une affaire; **he lost out on it** il y a été perdant.

loser ['lu:zəʳ] *n* perdant(e) *m(f)*. **good/bad ~** bon/mauvais joueur, bonne/mauvaise joueuse; **to come off the ~** être perdant; **he is the ~ by it** il y perd; **he's a born ~** il est né perdant, il est né avec la poisse*, il n'a jamais de veine*; *V* **back.**

losing ['lu:zɪŋ] **1** *adj team, number* perdant; *business, concern* mauvais. **to be on a ~ streak*** être en période de déveine*, avoir une série de pertes; (*fig*) **it's a ~ battle** c'est une bataille perdue d'avance, c'est perdu d'avance. **2** *n*: **~s** pertes *fpl*.

loss [lɒs] *n* **(a)** (*V* **lose 1a**) perte *f*. **~ of blood** perte de sang, hémorragie *f*; **~ of heat** perte de chaleur; **there was great ~ of life** il y a eu beaucoup de victimes *or* de nombreuses victimes; **the coup succeeded without ~ of life** le coup (d'État) a réussi sans faire de victimes; (*Mil*) **to suffer heavy ~es** subir des pertes élevées *or* sévères; **it was a comfort to her in her great ~** c'était un réconfort pour elle dans son grand malheur *or* sa grande épreuve; **his death was a great ~ to the company** sa mort a été *or* a représenté une grande perte pour la compagnie; **without ~ of time** sans perte *or* perdre de temps; **to sell at a ~** *[salesman]* vendre à perte; *[goods]* se vendre à perte; **selling at a ~** vente *f* à perte; **the car was a total ~** la voiture était bonne pour la ferraille *or* la casse; **he's no great ~** ce n'est pas une grande *or* une grosse perte, on peut très bien se passer de lui; *V* **cut, dead, profit** *etc.*

(b) to be at a ~ être perplexe *or* embarrassé; **to be at a ~ to explain sth** être incapable d'expliquer qch, être embarrassé pour expliquer qch; **we are at a ~ to know why he did it** nous ne savons absolument pas *or* il est impossible de savoir pourquoi il l'a fait; **to be at a ~ for words** chercher *or* ne pas trouver ses mots; **he's never at a ~ for words** il n'est jamais à court de mots.

lost [lɒst] **1** *pret, ptp of* **lose.**

2 *adj* **(a)** (*V* **lose 1a**) perdu; égaré. **all is ~** tout est perdu; **~ cause** cause perdue; **several ~ children were reported** on a signalé plusieurs enfants qui s'étaient perdus; **the ~ generation** la génération sacrifiée; **a ~ opportunity** une occasion manquée *or* perdue; **a ~ soul** une âme en peine; **he was wandering around like a ~ soul** il errait comme une âme en peine; **the ~ sheep** la brebis égarée; **to make up for ~ time** rattraper le temps perdu; **~ property,** (*US*) **~ and found** objets trouvés; **~ property office,** (*US*) **~-and-found department** (bureau *m* des) objets trouvés; (*Press*) **~-and-found columns** (page *f* des) objets perdus et trouvés.

(b) (*bewildered*) perdu, désorienté; (*uncomprehending*) perdu, perplexe. **it was too difficult for me, I was ~** c'était trop compliqué pour moi, je ne suivais plus *or* j'étais perdu *or* je n'y étais plus; **after his death I felt ~** après sa mort j'étais complètement perdu *or* désorienté; **he had a ~ look in his eyes** *or* **a ~ expression on his face** il avait l'air complètement désorienté.

(c) (*dead, gone, wasted etc*) perdu. **to give sb/sth up for ~** considérer qn/qch comme perdu; **he was ~ to British science forever** ses dons ont été perdus à jamais pour la science britannique; **he is ~ to all finer feelings** tous les sentiments délicats le dépassent, dans le domaine des sentiments les finesses lui échappent; **my advice was ~ on him** il n'a pas écouté mes conseils, mes conseils ont été en pure perte; **modern music is ~ on me** je ne comprends pas la musique moderne, la musique moderne me laisse froid; **the remark was ~ on him** il n'a pas compris la remarque.

(d) (*absorbed*) perdu, plongé (*in* dans), absorbé (*in* par). **to be ~ in one's reading** être plongé dans son livre, être absorbé par sa lecture; **he was ~ in thought** il était plongé dans la réflexion *or* perdu dans ses pensées *or* absorbé par ses pensées; **she is ~ to the world** elle est ailleurs, plus rien n'existe pour elle.

lot [lɒt] *n* **(a)** (*destiny*) sort *m*, destinée *f*, lot *m* (*liter*); (*responsibility*) sort, responsabilité *f*. **it is the common ~** c'est le sort *or* le lot commun; **the hardships that are the ~ of the poor** la dure vie qui est le partage *or* le sort *or* le lot des pauvres; **it was not his ~ to make a fortune** il n'était pas destiné à faire fortune; **her ~ (in life) had not been a happy one** elle n'avait pas eu une vie heureuse; **it fell to my ~ to break the news to her** il m'incomba de *or* il me revint de lui annoncer la nouvelle; **it fell to my ~ to be wounded early in the battle** le sort a voulu que je sois blessé au début de la bataille; **to cast in** *or* **throw in one's ~ with sb** partager volontairement le sort de qn, unir sa destinée à celle de qn.

(b) (*random selection*) tirage *m* au sort, sort *m*. **by ~** par tirage au sort; **the ~ fell on me** le sort est tombé sur moi; *V* **draw.**

(c) (*at auctions etc*) lot *m*. (*Comm*) **there are 3 further ~s of hats to be delivered** il y a encore 3 lots de chapeaux à livrer; **there was only one ~ of recruits still to arrive** il ne manquait plus qu'un lot de recrues; **he's a bad ~*** il ne vaut pas cher*, c'est un mauvais sujet; **you rotten ~!‡** vous êtes vaches!‡, vous n'êtes pas chic!*; *V* **job.**

(d) (*plot of land*) lot *m* (de terrain), parcelle *f*, lotissement *m*. **building ~** lotissement; **parking ~** parking *m*.

(e) the ~ (*everything*) (le) tout; (*everyone*) tous *mpl*, toutes *fpl*; **that's the ~** c'est tout, c'est le tout, tout y est; **here are some apples, take the (whole) ~** voici des pommes, prends-les toutes; **can I have some milk? — take the ~** est-ce que je peux avoir du lait? — prends tout (ce qu'il y a); **the ~ cost £1** le tout coûtait une livre, cela coûtait une livre en tout; **big ones, little ones, the ~!** les grands, les petits, tous!; **the ~ of you** vous tous; **they went off, the whole ~ of them** ils sont tous partis, ils sont partis tous tant qu'ils étaient.

(f) (*large amount*) **a ~ of, ~s of** *butter, wine, honey* beaucoup de; *cars, dogs, flowers* beaucoup de, un tas de*; **a ~ of** *or* **~s of time/money** beaucoup de temps/d'argent, un temps/un argent fou; **there were a ~** *or* **~s of people** il y avait beaucoup de monde *or* un tas* de gens; **a ~** *or* **~s of people think that ...** beaucoup *or* des tas* de gens pensent que ...; **what a ~ of people!** que de monde! *or* de gens!; **what a ~ of time you take to dress!** tu en mets du temps à t'habiller!; **what a ~!** quelle quantité!; **there wasn't a ~ we could do** nous ne pouvions pas faire grand-chose; **I'd give a ~ to know ...** je donnerais cher pour savoir ...; **quite a ~ of** *people, cars* un assez grand nombre de, pas mal de; *honey, cream* une assez grande quantité de, pas mal de; **such a ~ of** tellement de, tant de; **there's an awful ~ of people/cars/cream*** *etc* c'est fou* ce qu'il y a comme gens/voitures/crème *etc*; **I have an awful ~ of things to do*** j'ai énormément* de *or* un tas* de choses à faire; **~s and ~s (of)** (*people, cars*) des tas (de)*; (*flowers, butter, honey*) des masses (de)*; (*milk, wine*) des flots (de).

(g) (*adv phrase*) **a ~** (*a great deal*) beaucoup; (*often*) beaucoup, souvent; **that's a ~** *or* **~s better** c'est (vraiment) beaucoup *or* (vraiment) bien mieux; **he's a ~ better** il va beaucoup *or* bien mieux; **we don't go out a ~** nous ne sortons pas beaucoup *or* pas souvent; **he cries such a ~** il pleure tellement; **he drinks an awful ~*** *or* **a tremendous ~*** il boit énormément *or* comme un trou*; **things have changed quite a ~** les choses ont beaucoup *or* pas mal* changé; **we see a ~ of her** nous la voyons souvent *or* beaucoup; **thanks a ~!*** merci beaucoup!; (*iro*) merci beaucoup!, grand merci!; (*iro*) **a ~ you care!*** comme si ça te faisait quelque chose!; (*iro*) **a ~ that'll help!*** comme si ça allait être utile!; *V* **fat.**

loth [ləʊθ] *adj* = **loath.**

lotion ['ləʊʃən] *n* lotion *f*; *V* **hand** *etc.*

lotos ['ləʊtəs] *n* = **lotus.**

lottery ['lɒtərɪ] *n* (*lit, fig*) loterie *f*. **~ ticket** billet *m* de loterie.

lotto ['lɒtəʊ] *n* loto *m*.

lotus ['ləʊtəs] *n* lotus *m*. (*Myth*) **~-eater** mangeur *m*, -euse *f* de lotus, lotophage *m*.

loud [laʊd] **1** *adj* **(a)** (*noisy*) *voice* fort, sonore, grand; *laugh* grand, bruyant, sonore; *noise, cry* sonore, grand; *music* bruyant, sonore; *thunder* fracassant; *applause* vif (*f* vive); *protests* vigoureux; (*pej*) *behaviour* tapageur. **the radio/orchestra/brass section is too ~** la radio/l'orchestre/les cuivres joue(nt) trop fort; **the music is too ~** la musique est trop bruyante; **in a ~ voice** d'une voix forte; **... he said in a ~ whisper ...** chuchota-t-il bruyamment; (*Mus*) **~ pedal** pédale forte.

(b) (*pej: gaudy*) *colour* voyant, criard; *clothes* voyant, tapageur.

2 *adv speak etc* fort, haut. **turn the radio up a little ~er** mets la radio un peu plus fort, augmente le volume; **out ~** tout haut;

(*Telec*) **I am reading** *or* **receiving you ~ and clear** je vous reçois cinq sur cinq.

3 *cpd*: (*Brit*) **loudhailer** porte-voix *m inv*, mégaphone *m*; (*pej*) **loud-mouth*** grande gueule‡; (*pej*) **loud-mouthed** braillard, fort en gueule‡; **loudspeaker** haut-parleur *m*; *[stereo]* baffle *m*.

loudly [ˈlaʊdlɪ] *adv* **(a)** *shout, speak* fort, d'une voix forte; *laugh* bruyamment; *proclaim* vigoureusement; *knock* fort, bruyamment. **don't say it too ~** ne le dites pas trop haut *or* trop fort. **(b)** (*pej*) *dress* d'une façon voyante *or* tapageuse.

loudness [ˈlaʊdnɪs] *n [voice, tone, music, thunder]* force *f*; *[applause]* bruit *m*; *[protests]* vigueur *f*.

Louisiana [luːˌiːzɪˈænə] *n* Louisiane *f*.

lounge [laʊndʒ] **1** *n* (*esp Brit*) *[house, hotel]* salon *m*; *V* **sun, television** *etc*.

2 *cpd*: **lounge bar** *[pub]* ≃ salle *f* de café; *[hotel]* ≃ (salle de) bar *m*; **lounge suit** complet(-veston) *m*; (*on invitation*) **'lounge suit'** 'tenue de ville'.

3 *vi* (*recline*) (*on bed etc*) se prélasser; (*sprawl*) être allongé paresseusement; (*in chair*) être vautré; (*stroll*) flâner; (*idle*) paresser, être oisif. **to ~ against a wall** s'appuyer paresseusement contre un mur; **we spent a week lounging in Biarritz** nous avons passé une semaine à flâner *or* à nous reposer à Biarritz.

lounge about, lounge around *vi* paresser, flâner, flemmarder*.

lounge back *vi*: **to lounge back in a chair** se prélasser dans un fauteuil.

lounger [ˈlaʊndʒəʳ] *n* **(a)** (*sun-bed etc*) lit *m* de plage. **(b)** (*pej: person*) fainéant(e) *m(f)*, flemmard(e)* *m(f)*.

louse [laʊs] *n, pl* **lice** **(a)** (*insect*) pou *m*.

(b) (‡*pej: person*) salaud‡ *m*, (peau *f* de) vache‡ *f* (*'louse' dans ce sens est utilisé au singulier seulement*).

louse up‡ *vt sep deal, event* bousiller*, foutre en l'air‡.

lousy [ˈlaʊzɪ] *adj* **(a)** (*lit*) pouilleux.

(b) (‡: *terrible*) *play, book, car* moche*. **it's ~ weather** il fait un temps dégueulasse‡; **we had a ~ weekend** nous avons passé un week-end infect *or* dégueulasse‡; **I'm ~ at maths** je suis complètement bouché* en maths; **he's a ~ teacher** il est nul *or* zéro* comme prof; **a ~ trick** un tour de cochon*, une crasse*, une vacherie‡; **I feel ~** je suis mal fichu* *or* mal foutu‡; **I've got a ~ headache** j'ai un sacré* mal de tête, j'ai vachement‡ mal à la tête.

(c) (‡) **~ with** plein de, bourré de; **the town is ~ with tourists** la ville est bourrée *or* grouille de touristes; **he is ~ with money** il est bourré de fric‡, il est plein aux as.

lout [laʊt] *n* rustre *m*, butor *m*; *V* **litter**.

loutish [ˈlaʊtɪʃ] *adj manners* de rustre, de butor. **his ~ behaviour** la grossièreté de sa conduite.

louver, louvre [ˈluːvəʳ] *n* (*in roof*) lucarne *f*; (*on window*) persienne *f*, jalousie *f*. **louvered** *or* **louvred door** porte *f* à claire-voie.

lovable [ˈlʌvəbl] *adj person* très sympathique; *child, animal* adorable.

love [lʌv] **1** *n* **(a)** (*for person*) amour *m* (*of* de, pour, *for* pour). **her ~ for** *or* **of her children** son amour pour ses enfants, l'amour qu'elle porte (*or* portait *etc*) à ses enfants; **her children's ~ (for her)** l'amour que lui portent (*or* portaient *etc*) ses enfants; **I feel no ~ for** *or* **towards him any longer** je n'éprouve plus d'amour pour lui; **they are in ~ (with each other)** ils s'aiment; **she's in ~** elle est amoureuse; **to be/fall in ~ with** être/tomber amoureux de; **it was ~ at first sight** ça a été le coup de foudre; **to make ~** faire l'amour (*with* avec, *to* à); **he was the ~ of her life** c'était l'homme de sa vie; **he thought of his first ~** il pensait à son premier amour (*V also* **1b**); (*fig*) **there's no ~ lost between them** ils ne peuvent pas se sentir; **for the ~ of God** pour l'amour de Dieu; (*: *indignantly*) pour l'amour du Ciel!, bon sang!*; **for the ~ of Mike*** pour l'amour du Ciel; **to marry for ~** faire un mariage d'amour; **for ~ of her son, out of ~ for her son** par amour pour son fils; **don't give me any money, I'm doing it for ~** ne me donnez pas d'argent, je le fais gratuitement *or* pour l'amour de l'art; **I won't do it for ~ nor money** je ne le ferai pour rien au monde, je ne le ferai ni pour or ni pour argent (*frm*); **it wasn't to be had for ~ nor money** c'était introuvable, on ne pouvait se le procurer à aucun prix; **give her my ~** dis-lui bien des choses de ma part, (*stronger*) embrasse-la pour moi; **he sends (you) his ~** il t'envoie bien des choses, (*stronger*) il t'embrasse; (*in letter*) **(with) ~ (from) Jim** affectueusement, Jim; (*stronger*) bons baisers, Jim; (*Brit: in shops etc*) **thanks ~*** (*to woman*) merci madame, merci ma jolie* *or* ma chérie*; (*to man*) merci monsieur; (*to child*) merci mon petit *or* mon chou*; **yes (my) ~** oui mon amour; **he's a little ~!** qu'il est mignon!, c'est un amour!; *V* **brotherly, labour, lady** *etc*.

(b) (*for country, music, horses*) amour *m* (*of* de, *for* pour); (*stronger*) passion *f* (*of* de, *for* pour). **the theatre was her great ~** le théâtre était sa grande passion; **his first ~ was football** sa première passion a été le football; **he studies history for the ~ of it** il étudie l'histoire pour son *or* le plaisir.

(c) (*Tennis etc*) rien *m*, zéro *m*. **~ 30** rien à 30, zéro 30.

2 *vt* **(a)** *spouse, child* aimer; *relative, friend* aimer (beaucoup). **~ thy neighbour as thyself** tu aimeras ton prochain comme toi-même; **he didn't just like her, he LOVED her** il ne l'aimait pas d'amitié, mais d'amour; **she ~d him dearly** elle l'aimait tendrement; **she ~s me, she ~s me not** elle m'aime, un peu, beaucoup, passionnément, à la folie, pas du tout; (*loc*) **~ me, ~ my dog** qui m'aime aime mon chien.

(b) *music, food, activity, place* aimer (beaucoup); (*stronger*) adorer. **to ~ to do** *or* **doing sth** aimer (beaucoup) *or* adorer faire qch; **she ~s riding** elle aime *or* adore monter à cheval, elle est passionnée d'équitation; **I'd ~ to come** j'aimerais beaucoup venir, je serais enchanté *or* ravi de venir, cela me ferait très plaisir de venir; **I'd ~ to!** je ne demande pas mieux!, cela me fera(it) très plaisir!; **I'd ~ to but unfortunately ...** cela me ferait très plaisir mais malheureusement ... .

3 *cpd*: **love affair** liaison *f* (amoureuse); (*Orn*) **lovebirds** perruches *fpl* inséparables; (*fig: people*) **the lovebirds** les tourtereaux *mpl* (*fig*); **love child** enfant *mf* de l'amour, enfant illégitime *or* naturel(le); (*Bot*) **love-in-a-mist** nigelle *f* de Damas; **love letter** lettre *f* d'amour, billet doux (*often hum*); **how's your love life these days?*** comment vont les amours?; **his love life is bothering him*** il a des problèmes de cœur *or* sentimentaux; († *or hum*) **lovelorn** qui languit d'amour; **lovemaking** amour *m*; **love match** mariage *m* d'amour; **love nest** nid *m* d'amoureux *or* d'amour; (*Theat*) **love scene** scène *f* d'amour; **lovesick** amoureux, qui languit d'amour; **lovesong** chanson *f* d'amour; **love story** histoire *f* d'amour; **love token** gage *m* d'amour.

loveless [ˈlʌvlɪs] *adj* (*not loved*) qui n'est pas aimé; (*not loving*) sans amour.

loveliness [ˈlʌvlɪnɪs] *n* beauté *f*, charme *m*.

lovely [ˈlʌvlɪ] **1** *adj* (*pretty*) *girl, flower, hat, house, view, voice* (très) joli, ravissant; *baby* mignon, joli; (*pleasant*) *girl, house, sense of humour, suggestion, view* charmant; *meal, evening, party* charmant, agréable; *voice* agréable; *night, sunshine, weather* beau (*f* belle); *holiday* (très) bon (*f* bonne), excellent, formidable*; *story* joli, charmant; *idea, suggestion* merveilleux, charmant; *smell* bon, agréable; *food* bon. **she's a ~ person** c'est une personne charmante *or* très agréable, elle est charmante; **she has a ~ nature** elle a vraiment bon caractère; **this dress looks ~ on you** cette robe vous va vraiment bien *or* vous va à merveille; **we had a ~ time** nous nous sommes bien amusés, nous avons passé un moment *or* une semaine *etc* excellent(e) *or* très agréable; **I hope you have a ~ time** j'espère que vous vous amuserez bien; **it's been ~ to see** *or* **seeing you** j'ai été ravi *or* vraiment content de vous voir, ça m'a fait vraiment plaisir de vous voir; **all this ~ money** tout ce bel argent; **this cloth feels ~** ce drap est très agréable au toucher; **it felt ~ to be warm again** c'était bien agréable d'avoir chaud de nouveau; **~ and cool/warm** *etc* délicieusement *or* bien frais/chaud *etc*; **we're ~ and early*** c'est bien, on est en avance.

2 *n* (*: *girl*) belle fille, beau brin de fille, mignonne *f*.

lover [ˈlʌvəʳ] **1** *n* **(a)** amant *m*; (*suitor*) amoureux *m*. **~s' vows** promesses *fpl* d'amoureux; **they have been ~s for 2 years** leur liaison dure depuis 2 ans; **she took a ~** elle a pris un amant; **Casanova was a great ~** Casanova fut un grand séducteur.

(b) *[hobby, wine etc]* amateur *m*. **he's a ~ of good food** il est grand amateur de bonne cuisine, il aime beaucoup la bonne cuisine; **he's a great ~ of Brahms** *or* **a great Brahms ~** c'est un fervent de Brahms, il aime beaucoup (la musique de) Brahms; **art/theatre ~** amateur d'art/de théâtre; **music ~** amateur de musique, mélomane *mf*; **he's a nature ~** il aime la nature, c'est un amoureux de la nature; **football ~s everywhere** tous les amateurs *or* passionnés de football.

2 *cpd*: (*hum or iro*) **lover boy*** (*male idol*) apollon* *m*; (*womanizer*) don Juan *m*, homme *m* à femmes, tombeur* *m*.

lovey-dovey* [ˈlʌvɪˈdʌvɪ] *adj* (*hum*) (trop) tendre.

loving [ˈlʌvɪŋ] **1** *adj* (*affectionate*) affectueux; (*tender*) tendre; (*dutiful*) *wife, son* aimant, bon (*f* bonne). **~ kindness** bonté *f*, charité *f*; **~ cup** coupe *f* de l'amitié.

2 **-loving** *adj ending in cpds*: **art-loving** qui aime l'art, qui est amateur d'art; **money-loving** qui aime l'argent, avare.

lovingly [ˈlʌvɪŋlɪ] *adv* affectueusement, tendrement, (*stronger*) avec amour.

low[1] [ləʊ] **1** *adj* **(a)** *wall* bas (*f* basse), peu élevé; *shelf, seat, ceiling, level, tide* bas. **she is rather ~ down in that chair** elle est bien bas dans ce fauteuil, elle est assise bien bas; (*Met*) **~ cloud** nuages bas; **the sun is ~ in the sky** le soleil est bas dans le ciel *or* bas sur l'horizon; **~er down the hill/the page** plus bas sur la colline/la page; **dress with a ~ neck** robe décolletée; (*Boxing*) **~ blow** coup bas; (*Geog*) **the L~ Countries** les Pays-Bas; **fog on ~ ground** brouillard *m* à basse altitude; **the ~ ground near the sea** les basses terres près de la mer; **the house/town is on low ground** la maison/ville est bâtie dans une dépression; **the river is very ~ just now** la rivière est très basse en ce moment; **at ~ tide** à marée basse; **~ water** marée basse, basses eaux; (*lit*) **~ watermark** laisse *f* de basse mer; (*fig*) **their morale had reached ~ watermark** leur moral était on ne peut plus bas, ils avaient le moral à zéro*; **sales had reached ~ watermark** les ventes n'avaient jamais été aussi mauvaises; **his spirits were at a ~ ebb** il avait le moral très bas *or* bien bas *or* à zéro*; **his funds were at a ~ ebb** ses fonds étaient bien bas *or* bien dégarnis; **to make a ~ bow** saluer *or* s'incliner bien bas; *V also* **4** *and* **lower**[1].

(b) *voice* (*soft*) bas (*f* basse); (*deep*) bas, profond; (*Mus*) *note* bas. **in a ~ voice** (*softly*) à voix basse; (*in deep tones*) d'une voix basse *or* profonde; **a ~ murmur** un murmure sourd *or* étouffé; **they were talking in a ~ murmur** ils chuchotaient le plus bas possible; **he gave a ~ groan** il a gémi faiblement, il a poussé un faible gémissement; (*of radio etc*) **it's a bit ~** on n'entend pas, ça n'est pas assez fort, c'est trop bas; *V also* **4**.

(c) *wage, rate* bas (*f* basse), faible; *price* bas, modéré, modique; (*Scol*) *mark* bas, faible; *latitude, number,* (*Elec*) *frequency* bas; (*Chem, Phys*) *density* faible; (*Aut*) *compression* faible, bas; *temperature* bas, peu élevé; *speed* petit, faible; *visibility* mauvais, limité; *standard* bas, faible; *quality* inférieur (*f* -eure). **a ~ card** une basse carte; (*Cards*) **a ~ diamond** un petit carreau; (*Aut*) **in ~ (gear)** en première ou seconde (vitesse); (*Math*) **~est common multiple** plus petit commun multiple; **~-calorie diet** régime *m* à basses calories; (*Culin*) **at a ~ heat** à feu doux; **the fire is getting ~/is ~** le feu baisse/est bas; **it has never fallen below £100/20° *etc* at the ~est** cela n'est jamais tombé à moins de 100 livres/20° *etc*; **activity is at its ~est in the summer** c'est en été que l'activité est particulièrement réduite;

people of ~ intelligence les gens de faible intelligence; people of ~ income les gens aux faibles revenus; supplies are getting ~ les provisions baissent; (*Comm etc*) their stock of soap was very ~ leur stock de savon était presque épuisé; they were ~ on water ils étaient à court d'eau; we're a bit ~ on petrol nous n'avons plus *or* il ne nous reste plus beaucoup d'essence; I'm ~ on funds je suis à court (d'argent); ~-quality goods marchandises *fpl* de qualité inférieure; to have a ~ opinion of sb ne pas avoir bonne opinion de qn, avoir (une) piètre opinion de qn; to have a ~ opinion of sth ne pas avoir bonne opinion de qch; to keep a ~ profile essayer de ne pas trop se faire remarquer; *V also* 4 *and* lower[1].

(d) (*feeble*) *person* faible, affaibli; *health* mauvais; (*depressed*) déprimé, démoralisé, cafardeux*. to be in ~ spirits, to be *or* feel ~ être déprimé *or* démoralisé, ne pas avoir le moral*, avoir le cafard*; the patient is very ~ le (*or* la) malade est bien bas(se).

(e) (*Bio, Zool: primitive*) inférieur (*f* -eure), peu évolué. the ~ forms of life les formes de vie inférieures *or* les moins évoluées.

(f) (*humble*) *rank, origin* bas (*f* basse); (*vulgar*) *company* mauvais, bas; *character* grossier; bas; *taste* mauvais; *café etc* de bas étage; (*shameful*) *behaviour* ignoble, vil (*f* vile), odieux. the ~est of the ~ le dernier des derniers; that's a ~ trick c'est un sale tour*; with ~ cunning avec une ruse ignoble; *V also* 4 *and* lower[1].

2 *adv* (a) (*in low position*) *aim, fly* bas. to bow ~ s'incliner profondément, saluer bien bas; a dress cut ~ in the back une robe très décolletée dans le dos; the plane came down ~ over the town l'avion est descendu et a survolé la ville à basse altitude; the plane flew ~ over the town l'avion a survolé la ville à basse altitude; *V* lay[1], lie[1].

(b) (*fig*) to turn the heating/lights/music/radio (down) ~ baisser le chauffage/l'éclairage/la musique/la radio; the fire was burning ~ le feu était bas; supplies are running ~ les provisions baissent; (*St Ex*) to buy ~ acheter quand le cours est bas; (*Cards*) to play ~ jouer une basse carte; to fall *or* sink ~ tomber bien bas; I wouldn't stoop so ~ as to do that je ne m'abaisserais pas jusqu'à faire cela; to speak ~ parler à voix basse *or* doucement; to sing ~ chanter bas; the song is pitched too ~ for me le ton de cette chanson est trop bas pour moi; (*in singing*) I can't get as ~ as that ma voix ne descend pas si bas que cela.

3 *n* (a) (*Met*) dépression *f*.

(b) (*Aut*) = low gear; *V* 1c.

(c) (*low point: esp Fin*) niveau bas, point bas. prices/temperatures have reached a new ~ *or* an all-time ~ les prix/les températures n'ont jamais été aussi bas(ses) *or* ne sont jamais tombé(e)s aussi bas; this is really a new ~ in vulgarity cela bat tous les records de vulgarité; the pound has sunk *or* fallen to a new ~ la livre a atteint son niveau le plus bas.

4 *cpd*: lowborn de basse origine *or* extraction; lowbrow (*n*) personne peu intellectuelle *or* sans prétentions intellectuelles; (*adj*) *person* terre à terre *inv*, peu intellectuel; *book, film* sans prétentions intellectuelles; Low Church Basse Église (*Anglicane*); low-cost (*adj*) (à) bon marché; (*U*) low-cost housing habitations *fpl* à loyer modéré, H.L.M. *mpl*; (*Dress*) low-cut décolleté; low-down *V* low-down; low-flying (*adj*) volant à basse altitude; (*n: U*) low flying vol(s) *m(pl)* à basse altitude; Low German bas allemand; low-grade de qualité *or* de catégorie inférieure; low-grade mental defective débile *mf* mental(e); low-heeled à talons plats, plat; low-key (*adj*) modéré; it was a low-key operation l'opération a été conduite de façon très discrète; to keep sth low-key faire qch avec modération *or* d'une façon modérée; Low Latin bas latin; low-level (*adj*) bas (*f* basse), à basse altitude; (*Aviat*) low-level flying vol *m* *or* navigation *f* à basse altitude; low-loader (*Aut*) semi-remorque *f* à plate-forme surbaissée; (*Rail*) wagon *m* (de marchandises) à plate-forme surbaissée; low-lying à basse altitude; (*Rel*) Low Mass messe basse; low-minded d'esprit vulgaire; low-necked décolleté; low-paid *job* mal payé, qui paie mal; *worker* mal payé, qui ne gagne pas beaucoup; the low-paid (*workers*) les petits salaires, les petits salariés (*V also* lower[1] 2); low-pitched *ball* bas (*f* basse); *sound* bas, grave; low-pressure à *or* de basse pression; low-priced à bas prix, (à) bon marché *inv*; low-principled sans grands principes; low-profile = low-key; (*Archit*) low-rise à *or* de hauteur limitée, bas (*f* basse); low-spirited déprimé, démoralisé; Low Sunday dimanche *m* de Quasimodo; low-tension à basse tension; (*Ling*) low vowel voyelle basse; *V also* lower[1].

low[2] [ləʊ] *vi [cattle]* meugler, beugler, mugir.

low-down ['ləʊdaʊn] 1 *adj* (*mean*) *action* bas (*f* basse), honteux, méprisable; *person* méprisable, vil (*f* vile); (*spiteful*) mesquin. a ~ trick un sale tour*.

2 *n* (‡) to get the ~ on sb/sth se tuyauter* sur qn/qch, se renseigner sur qn/qch; to give sb the ~ on sth tuyauter* qn sur qch, mettre qn au courant *or* au parfum‡ de qch.

lower[1] ['ləʊəʳ] *comp of* low[1] 1 *adj* inférieur (*f* -eure). (*Typ*) ~ case bas *m* de casse; ~-class de la classe inférieure; ~ middle class (*n*) petite bourgeoisie; (*adj*) petit bourgeois; the ~ classes (*socially*) les classes inférieures; (*Scol: also* the ~ school) le premier cycle; the ~ income groups les économiquement faibles *mpl*; (*Naut*) ~ deck pont inférieur; (*personnel*) gradés *mpl* et matelots *mpl*; (*Brit Parl*) the L~ House la Chambre basse, la Chambre des communes; ~ jaw mâchoire inférieure; the ~ valley of the Rhine la vallée inférieure du Rhin; ~ vertebrates vertébrés inférieurs; *V* second[1].

2 *adv*: the ~ paid la tranche inférieure des salariés *or* du salariat.

lower[2] ['ləʊəʳ] 1 *vt* (a) *blind, window, construction* baisser, abaisser; *sail, flag* abaisser, amener; *boat, lifeboat* mettre *or* amener à la mer. to ~ the boats mettre les embarcations à la mer; to ~ sb/sth on a rope (faire) descendre qn/descendre qch au bout d'une corde; to ~ one's guard (*Boxing*) baisser sa garde; (*fig*) ne plus être sur ses gardes.

(b) (*fig*) *pressure, heating, price, voice* baisser. (*Med*) to ~ sb's resistance diminuer la résistance de qn; to ~ sb's morale démoraliser qn, saper le moral de qn; ~ your voice! baisse la voix!, (parle) moins fort!; he ~ed his voice to a whisper il a baissé la voix jusqu'à en chuchoter, il s'est mis à chuchoter; to ~ o.s. to do sth s'abaisser à faire qch; I refuse to ~ myself je refuse de m'abaisser *or* de m'avilir ainsi.

2 *vi* (*lit*) baisser; *[pressure, price etc]* baisser, diminuer.

lower[3] ['laʊəʳ] *vi [sky]* se couvrir, s'assombrir; *[clouds]* être menaçant; *[person]* prendre un air sombre *or* menaçant. to ~ at sb jeter un regard menaçant à qn, regarder qn de travers.

lowering[1] ['ləʊərɪŋ] 1 *n* (a) *[window, flag]* abaissement *m*; *[boat]* mise *f* à la mer.

(b) *[temperature]* baisse *f*, abaissement *m*; *[price, value]* baisse, diminution *f*; *[pressure]* baisse; (*Med*) *[resistance]* diminution. the ~ of morale la baisse du moral, la démoralisation.

2 *adj* abaissant, dégradant, humiliant.

lowering[2] ['laʊərɪŋ] *adj look, sky* sombre, menaçant.

lowing ['ləʊɪŋ] *n [cattle]* meuglement *m*, beuglement *m*, mugissement *m*.

lowland ['ləʊlənd] 1 *n* plaine *f*. the L~s (of Scotland) la Basse Écosse, les Basses-Terres (d'Écosse). 2 *adj* (*Ling*) L~ Scots = Lallans.

lowliness ['ləʊlɪnɪs] *n* humilité *f*.

lowly ['ləʊlɪ] *n* (*humble*) humble, modeste; (*lowborn*) d'origine modeste.

lowness ['ləʊnɪs] *n* (*in height*) manque *m* de hauteur; *[price, wages]* modicité *f*; *[temperature]* peu *m* d'élévation. the ~ of the ceiling made him stoop la maison était si basse de plafond qu'il a dû se baisser.

loyal ['lɔɪəl] *adj* (*faithful*) *friend, supporter* loyal, fidèle; *servant* fidèle, dévoué, loyal†; (*respectful*) *subject* loyal. (*Brit*) the ~ toast le toast (porté) au souverain; he has been ~ to me il a été loyal envers moi, il m'a été fidèle.

loyalist ['lɔɪəlɪst] *adj, n* loyaliste (*mf*).

loyally ['lɔɪəlɪ] *adv* fidèlement, loyalement, avec loyauté.

loyalty ['lɔɪəltɪ] *n* (*V* loyal) loyauté *f*, fidélité *f*, dévouement *m*. (*Pol etc*) his ~ is not in question son loyalisme n'est pas en doute; a man of fierce loyalties un homme d'une loyauté à toute épreuve *or* d'une loyauté absolue.

lozenge ['lɒzɪndʒ] *n* (a) (*Med*) pastille *f*; *V* cough. (b) (*Her, Math*) losange *m*.

lubricant ['lu:brɪkənt] *adj, n* lubrifiant (*m*).

lubricate ['lu:brɪkeɪt] *vt* lubrifier; (*Aut*) graisser. lubricating oil huile *f* (de graissage), lubrifiant *m*.

lubricated‡ ['lu:brɪkeɪtɪd] *adj* (*drunk*) paf‡ *inv*, beurré‡.

lubrication [,lu:brɪ'keɪʃən] *n* lubrification *f*; (*Aut*) graissage *m*.

lubricator ['lu:brɪkeɪtəʳ] *n* (*person, device*) graisseur *m*.

lubricity [lu:'brɪsɪtɪ] *n* (a) (*slipperiness*) caractère glissant. (b) (*lewdness*) lubricité *f*.

lucerne [lu:'sɜ:n] *n* (*esp Brit*) luzerne *f*.

lucid ['lu:sɪd] *adj* (a) (*understandable*) *style, explanation* lucide. (b) (*sane*) lucide. ~ interval intervalle *m* lucide *or* de lucidité. (c) (*bright*) brillant, clair, lumineux.

lucidity [lu:'sɪdɪtɪ] *n* (*V* lucid) lucidité *f*, clarté *f*, luminosité *f*.

lucidly ['lu:sɪdlɪ] *adv explain, argue* lucidement, clairement.

Lucifer ['lu:sɪfəʳ] *n* Lucifer *m*.

luck [lʌk] *n* (a) (*chance, fortune*) hasard *m*, chance *f*. good ~ (bonne) chance, bonheur *m*, veine* *f*, pot* *m*; bad ~ malchance *f*, malheur *m*, déveine* *f*; to bring (sb) good/bad *or* ill ~ porter bonheur/malheur (à qn); it brought us nothing but bad ~ cela ne nous a vraiment pas porté chance; good ~! bonne chance!; bad *or* hard ~! pas *or* manque de chance!, manque de pot!*, pas de veine!*; better ~ next time! ça ira mieux la prochaine fois!; worse ~ malheureusement; to have the good/bad ~ to do sth avoir la chance *or* la bonne fortune/la malchance *or* la mauvaise fortune de faire qch; ~ favoured him, ~ was with him, ~ was on his side la fortune lui souriait, il était favorisé par la fortune *or* le destin; as ~ would have it comme par hasard; (*fig*) it's the ~ of the draw c'est une question de chance; it's good/bad ~ to see a black cat cela porte bonheur/malheur de voir un chat noir; (it's) just my ~! c'est bien ma chance! *or* ma veine!*; it was just his ~ to meet the boss par malchance *or* par malheur il a rencontré le patron, il a eu la malchance *or* la déveine* de rencontrer le patron; to be down on one's ~ avoir la déveine* *or* la poisse*; *V* beginner, chance, push *etc.*

(b) (*good fortune*) (bonne) chance *f*, bonheur *m*, veine* *f*, pot* *m*. you're in ~, your ~'s in tu as de la chance *or* de la veine* *or* du pot*; you're out of ~, your ~'s out tu n'as pas de chance *or* de veine* *or* de pot*; that's a bit of ~! quelle chance!, quelle veine!*; coup de pot!*; he had the ~ to meet her in the street il a eu la chance de la rencontrer dans la rue; here's (wishing you) ~! bonne chance!; (*drinking*) à votre santé!; no such ~!* ç'aurait été trop beau! *or* trop de chance!, penses-tu!; with any ~ ... avec un peu de chance ... *or* de veine*...; to keep a horseshoe for ~ avoir un fer à cheval comme porte-bonheur; (*iro*) and the best of (British) ~!* je vous (*or* leur *etc*) souhaite bien du plaisir!* (*iro*); he's got the ~ of the devil*, he's got the devil's own ~* il a une veine de pendu*.

luck out* *vi* (*US*) avoir de la veine* *or* du pot*.

luckily ['lʌkɪlɪ] *adv* heureusement, par bonheur. ~ for me ... heureusement pour moi ... .

luckless ['lʌklɪs] *adj person* malchanceux, qui n'a pas de

chance; *event, action* malencontreux; *day* fatal.
lucky ['lʌkɪ] *adj person* qui a de la chance, favorisé par la chance *or* la fortune, veinard*; *day* de chance, de veine*; *shot, guess, coincidence* heureux; *horseshoe, charm* porte-bonheur *inv*. **you are ~ to be alive** tu as de la chance *or* de la veine* de t'en sortir vivant; **he was ~ enough to get a seat** il a eu la chance *or* la veine* de trouver une place; **~ you!** (*in admiration*) veinard!*, tu en as de la chance! *or* de la veine!*; (*iro*) tu es verni!*; **(you) ~ dog!‡** veinard!*; **(he's a) ~ dog!‡** le veinard!*; **it was ~ for him that he got out of the way** heureusement (pour lui) qu'il s'est écarté; **it was ~ you got here in time** heureusement que vous êtes arrivé à temps; **how ~!** quelle chance!; **we had a ~ escape** nous l'avons échappé belle; **to have a ~ break*** avoir un coup de veine*; (*Brit: at fair etc*) **~ dip** pêche miraculeuse; (*Brit fig*) **it's a ~ dip** c'est une loterie, c'est une question de chance; *V* **star**[1], **third** *etc*.
lucrative ['lu:krətɪv] *adj business* lucratif, rentable; *employment* lucratif, qui paie bien, bien rémunéré.
lucre ['lu:kəʳ] *n* (*U: pej: gain*) lucre *m*. (**hum: money*) **(filthy) ~** fric‡ *m*, pognon‡ *m*.
ludicrous ['lu:dɪkrəs] *adj* ridicule, risible, absurde.
ludo ['lu:dəʊ] *n* (*Brit*) jeu *m* des petits chevaux.
luff [lʌf] (*Naut*) **1** *n* aulof(f)ée *f*. **2** *vi* lofer, venir au lof.
luffa ['lʌfə] *n* = **loofah.**
lug[1] [lʌg] *n* (*Constr*) tenon *m*; *[dish, saucepan etc]* oreille *f* (*d'une casserole etc*). (*Brit: ear*) **~hole‡** esgourde‡ *f*.
lug[2] [lʌg] *vt* traîner, tirer. **to ~ sth up/down** monter/descendre qch en le traînant; **to ~ sth out** traîner qch dehors; **why are you ~ging that parcel around?** pourquoi est-ce que tu trimbales* ce paquet?; (**fig*) **they ~ged him off to the theatre** ils l'ont traîné *or* embarqué* au théâtre (malgré lui).
luggage ['lʌgɪdʒ] **1** *n* (*U*) bagages *mpl*. (*Rail*) **~ in advance** bagages non accompagnés; *V* **hand, left**[1], **piece.**
2 *cpd*: (*Brit Aut*) **luggage boot** coffre *m*; **luggage carrier** porte-bagages *m inv*; (*at airport etc*) **luggage handler** bagagiste *m*; **luggage label** étiquette *f* à bagages; **luggage rack** (*Rail*) porte-bagages *m inv*, filet *m*; (*Aut*) galerie *f*; (*esp Brit Rail*) **luggage van** fourgon *m* (à bagages).
lugger ['lʌgəʳ] *n* lougre *m*.
lugubrious [lu:'gu:brɪəs] *adj* lugubre.
lugubriously [lu:'gu:brɪəslɪ] *adv* lugubrement.
Luke [lu:k] *n* Luc *m*.
lukewarm ['lu:kwɔ:m] *adj* (*lit*) tiède; (*fig*) tiède, peu enthousiaste.
lull [lʌl] **1** *n [storm]* accalmie *f*; *[hostilities, shooting]* arrêt *m*; *[conversation]* arrêt, pause *f*.
2 *vt person, fear* apaiser, calmer. **to ~ a child to sleep** endormir un enfant en le berçant; (*fig*) **to be ~ed into a false sense of security** s'endormir dans une fausse sécurité.
lullaby ['lʌləbaɪ] *n* berceuse *f*. **~ my baby** dors (mon) bébé, dors.
lumbago [lʌm'beɪgəʊ] *n* lumbago *m*.
lumbar ['lʌmbəʳ] *adj* lombaire.
lumber[1] ['lʌmbəʳ] **1** *n* (*U*) **(a)** (*wood*) bois *m* de charpente.
(b) (*junk*) bric-à-brac *m inv*.
2 *vt* **(a)** *room* encombrer. **~ all those books together in the corner** entassez *or* empilez tous ces livres dans le coin.
(b) (*US Forestry*) (*fell*) abattre; (*saw up*) débiter.
(c) (*Brit**: *burden*) **to ~ sb with sth** coller* *or* flanquer* qch à qn; **he got ~ed with the job of making the list** il s'est tapé* *or* appuyé* *or* farci‡ le boulot de dresser la liste; **I got ~ed with the girl for the evening** j'ai dû me coltiner* *or* m'appuyer* la fille toute la soirée; **now we're ~ed with it ...** maintenant qu'on a ça sur les bras ... *or* qu'on nous a collé* ça ... .
3 *cpd*: **lumberjack** bûcheron *m*; **lumber jacket** blouson *m*; **lumberman** = **lumberjack**; **lumber mill** scierie *f*; (*Brit*) **lumber room** (cabinet *m* de) débarras *m*; **lumber yard** chantier *m* de scierie.
lumber[2] ['lʌmbəʳ] *vi* (*also* **~ about, ~ along**) *[person, animal]* marcher pesamment; *[vehicle]* rouler pesamment. *[person]* **to ~ in/out** *etc* entrer/sortir *etc* d'un pas pesant *or* lourd.
lumbering[1] ['lʌmbərɪŋ] *n* (*US*) débit *m or* débitage *m or* tronçonnage *m* de bois.
lumbering[2] ['lʌmbərɪŋ] *adj step* lourd, pesant.
luminary ['lu:mɪnərɪ] *n* (*star*) astre *m*, corps *m* céleste; (*fig: person*) lumière *f*, sommité *f*.
luminescence [ˌlu:mɪ'nesns] *n* luminescence *f*.
luminosity [ˌlu:mɪ'nɒsɪtɪ] *n* luminosité *f*.
luminous ['lu:mɪnəs] *adj* lumineux. **my watch is ~** le cadran de ma montre est lumineux.
lumme‡ ['lʌmɪ] *excl* (*Brit*) = **lummy‡.**
lummox ['lʌməks] *n* (*US*) idiot(e) *m(f)*, lourdaud(e) *m(f)*.
lummy‡ ['lʌmɪ] *excl* (*Brit*) ça alors!, sapristi!*
lump[1] [lʌmp] **1** *n* **(a)** (*piece*) morceau *m*; (*larger*) gros morceau, masse *f*; *[metal, rock, stone]* morceau, masse; *[coal, cheese, sugar]* morceau; *[clay, earth]* motte *f*; (*in sauce etc*) grumeau *m*. **after the explosion there were large ~s of rock everywhere** après l'explosion il y avait de gros éclats de pierre partout.
(b) (*Med*) grosseur *f*; (*swelling*) protubérance *f*; (*from bump etc*) bosse *f*. (*fig*) **to have a ~ in one's throat** avoir une boule dans la gorge, avoir la gorge serrée.
(c) (**pej: person*) lourdaud(e) *m(f)*, empoté(e)* *m(f)*. **fat ~!** gros lourdaud!, espèce d'empoté(e)!*
2 *cpd*: **lump sugar** sucre *m* en morceaux; **lump sum** somme globale *or* forfaitaire; (*payment*) paiement *m* unique; **he was working for a lump sum** il travaillait à forfait.
3 *vt* (*also* **~ together**) *books, objects* réunir, mettre en tas; *persons* réunir; *subjects* réunir, considérer en bloc.
lump together 1 *vi* (*) **if we lumped together we could buy a car** si nous nous y mettions à plusieurs, nous pourrions acheter une voiture.
2 *vt sep* réunir; (*fig*) *people, cases* mettre dans la même catégorie *or* dans le même sac* (*pej*), considérer en bloc; *V also* **lump**[1] **3.**
lump[2]* [lʌmp] *vt* (*endure*) **you'll just have to ~ it** il faut bien que tu acceptes (*subj*) sans rien dire; *V* **like**[2].
lumpish ['lʌmpɪʃ] *adj* **(a)** (*) (*clumsy*) gauche, maladroit, pataud; (*stupid*) idiot, godiche*. **(b)** (*shapeless*) *mass, piece* informe.
lumpy ['lʌmpɪ] *adj gravy* grumeleux, qui a des grumeaux; *bed* défoncé, bosselé.
lunacy ['lu:nəsɪ] *n* (*Med*) aliénation mentale, folie *f*, démence *f*; (*fig*) démence, folie. **that's sheer ~!** c'est de la pure folie!, c'est démentiel! *or* de la démence!
lunar ['lu:nəʳ] *adj month, rock* lunaire; *eclipse* de la lune. (*Space*) **in ~ orbit** en orbite lunaire *or* autour de la lune; (*Space*) **~ module** module *m* lunaire; (*Space*) **~ landing** alunissage *m*.
lunatic ['lu:nətɪk] **1** *n* (*Med*) fou *m*, folle *f*, aliéné(e) *m(f)*, dément(e) *m(f)*; (*Jur*) dément(e); (*fig*) fou, folle, cinglé(e)‡ *m(f)*. **he's a ~!** il est fou à lier!, il est cinglé!‡
2 *adj* (*Med*) *person* fou (*f* folle), dément; (*fig*) fou, dément, cinglé‡; *idea, action* (*crazy*) absurde, extravagant, démentiel; (*stupid*) stupide, idiot. **~ asylum** asile *m* d'aliénés; **the ~ fringe** les enragés* *mpl*, les cinglés‡ *mpl*, les dingues‡ *mpl*.
lunch [lʌntʃ] **1** *n* déjeuner *m*. **light/quick ~** déjeuner léger/rapide; **we're having pork for ~** nous allons manger *or* nous avons du porc pour déjeuner *or* à midi; **to have ~** déjeuner; **he was at ~ when I called at his office** il était parti déjeuner quand je suis passé à son bureau; **come for ~ on Sunday** venez déjeuner dimanche; **we had him to ~ yesterday** il est venu déjeuner (chez nous) hier; *V* **working** *etc*.
2 *vi* déjeuner. **we ~ed on sandwiches** nous avons déjeuné de sandwiches, nous avons eu des sandwiches pour déjeuner.
3 *vt person* offrir un déjeuner à.
4 *cpd*: **lunch basket** panier-repas *m*; **lunch break** pause *f* de midi, heure *f* du déjeuner; **it's his lunch hour** *or* **lunchtime just now** c'est l'heure à laquelle il déjeune, c'est l'heure de son déjeuner; **it's lunchtime** c'est l'heure de déjeuner; **at lunchtime** à l'heure du déjeuner.
luncheon ['lʌntʃən] **1** *n* déjeuner *m* (*gén de cérémonie*). **2** *cpd*: **luncheon basket** panier-repas *m*; **luncheon meat** (sorte *f* de) mortadelle *f*; (*Brit*) **luncheon voucher** chèque-déjeuner *m*, ticket-restaurant *m*.
lung [lʌŋ] **1** *n* poumon *m*. (*fig*) **at the top of one's ~s** à pleins poumons, à tue-tête; *V* **iron. 2** *cpd disease* pulmonaire. **lung cancer** cancer *m* du poumon; **lung transplant** greffe *f* du poumon.
lunge [lʌndʒ] **1** *n* (*thrust*) (brusque) coup *m or* mouvement *m* en avant; (*Fencing*) botte *f*.
2 *vi* **(a)** (*also* **~ forward**) faire un mouvement brusque en avant; (*Fencing*) se fendre.
(b) to ~ at sb envoyer *or* assener un coup à qn; (*Fencing*) porter *or* allonger une botte à qn.
lupin ['lu:pɪn] *n* lupin *m*.
lurch[1] [lɜ:tʃ] **1** *n [person]* écart *m* brusque, vacillement *m*; *[car, ship]* embardée *f*. **to give a ~** *[car, ship]* faire une embardée; *[person]* vaciller, tituber.
2 *vi [person]* vaciller, tituber; *[car, ship]* faire une embardée. *[person]* **to ~ in/out/along** *etc* entrer/sortir/avancer *etc* en titubant; **the car ~ed along** la voiture avançait en faisant des embardées.
lurch[2] [lɜ:tʃ] *n*: **to leave sb in the ~** faire faux bond à qn, planter là qn*, laisser qn le bec dans l'eau.
lure [ljʊəʳ] **1** *n* **(a)** (*U*) (*charm*) attrait *m*, charme *m*; (*false attraction*) appât *m*, piège *m*, leurre *m*.
(b) (*decoy*) leurre *m*.
2 *vt* tromper, attirer *or* persuader par la ruse. **to ~ sb into a trap** attirer qn dans un piège; **to ~ sb into a house** attirer qn dans une maison (par la ruse); **to ~ sb in/out** *etc* persuader qn par la ruse d'entrer/de sortir *etc*.
lure away *vt sep*: **to lure sb away from the house** éloigner qn *or* faire sortir qn de la maison par la ruse; **to lure sb away from the path of duty** détourner qn de son devoir par la ruse.
lure on *vt sep* entraîner par la ruse, séduire.
lurid ['ljʊərɪd] *adj* **(a)** (*gruesome*) *details* affreux, atroce; *account, tale* effrayant, terrifiant; *crime* horrible, épouvantable; (*sensational*) *account, tale* à sensation. **a ~ description of the riot** une terrible *or* une saisissante description de l'émeute; **he gave us a ~ description of what lunch was like*** il nous a fait une description pittoresque *or* haute en couleur du déjeuner.
(b) (*fiery*) *colour* feu *inv*, sanglant; *sky, sunset* empourpré, sanglant.
(c) (*pallid, ghastly in colour*) livide, blafard; *light* effrayant, surnaturel.
lurk [lɜ:k] *vi [person]* se cacher (*dans un but malveillant*), se tapir; *[danger]* menacer; *[doubt]* persister. **he was ~ing behind the bush** il se cachait *or* il était tapi derrière le buisson; **there's someone ~ing (about) in the garden** quelqu'un rôde dans le jardin, il y a un rôdeur dans le jardin.
lurking ['lɜ:kɪŋ] *adj fear, doubt* vague. **a ~ idea** une idée de derrière la tête.
luscious ['lʌʃəs] *adj food* succulent; (**fig*) *blonde* appétissant, affriolant.
lush [lʌʃ] *adj* **(a)** *vegetation* luxuriant; *plant* plein de sève; *pasture* riche. **(b)** (*opulent*) *house, surroundings* luxueux.
lust [lʌst] *n* (*sexual*) luxure *f*, lubricité *f*; (*for fame, power etc*) soif *f* (*for* de). **the ~ for life** la soif *or* la rage de vivre.

lust after, lust for *vt fus woman* désirer, convoiter; *revenge, power* avoir soif de; *riches* convoiter.
luster ['lʌstəʳ] *n* (*US*) = **lustre.**
lustful ['lʌstfʊl] *adj* (*sexually*) lascif, luxurieux; (*greedy*) avide (*of* de).
lustfully ['lʌstfəlɪ] *adv* (*V* **lustful**) lascivement; avidement.
lustfulness ['lʌstfʊlnɪs] *n* lubricité *f*, lasciveté *f*.
lustre, (*US*) **luster** ['lʌstəʳ] *n* (*gloss*) lustre *m*, brillant *m*; (*substance*) lustre; (*fig: renown*) éclat *m*. ~**ware** poterie mordorée.
lustreless ['lʌstəlɪs] *adj* terne; *look, eyes* terne, vitreux.
lustrous ['lʌstrəs] *adj* (*shining*) *material* lustré, brillant; *eyes* brillant; *pearls* chatoyant; (*fig: splendid*) splendide, magnifique.
lusty ['lʌstɪ] *adj* (*healthy*) *person, infant* vigoureux, robuste; (*hearty*) *cheer, voice* vigoureux, vif (*f* vive).
lute [luːt] *n* luth *m*.
Lutheran ['luːθərən] **1** *n* Luthérien(ne) *m(f)*. **2** *adj* luthérien.
Lutheranism ['luːθərənɪzəm] *n* luthéranisme *m*.
Luxembourg ['lʌksəmbɜːg] *n* Luxembourg *m*.
luxuriance [lʌg'zjʊərɪəns] *n* (*V* **luxuriant**) luxuriance *f*; exubérance *f*; richesse *f*, fertilité *f*; surabondance *f*.
luxuriant [lʌg'zjʊərɪənt] *adj vegetation, hair* luxuriant, exubérant; *beard* exubérant; *soil, country, valley* riche, fertile; *crops* surabondant; *style, imagery* luxuriant.
luxuriate [lʌg'zjʊərɪeɪt] *vi* **(a)** (*revel*) **to ~ in** s'abandonner *or* se livrer avec délices à. **(b)** (*grow profusely*) pousser avec exubérance *or* à profusion.
luxurious [lʌg'zjʊərɪəs] *adj hotel, surroundings* luxueux, somptueux; *tastes* de luxe.
luxuriously [lʌg'zjʊərɪəslɪ] *adv furnish, decorate* luxueusement; *live* dans le luxe; *yawn, stretch* voluptueusement.
luxuriousness [lʌg'zjʊərɪəsnɪs] *n [hotel etc]* luxe *m*, somptuosité *f*. **the ~ of his tastes** ses goûts de luxe *or* pour le grand luxe.
luxury ['lʌkʃərɪ] **1** *n* **(a)** (*U*) luxe *m*. **to live in ~** vivre dans le luxe; *V* **lap**[1].
(b) (*object, commodity etc*) luxe *m*. **beef is becoming a ~** le bœuf devient un (produit de) luxe; **it's quite a ~ for me to go to the theatre** c'est du luxe pour moi que d'aller au théâtre; **what a ~ to have a bath at last!*** quel luxe *or* quelle volupté que de pouvoir enfin prendre un bain!
2 *cpd goods* de luxe; *flat, hotel* de grand luxe, de grand standing.
lyceum [laɪ'siːəm] *n* ≈ maison *f* de la culture.
lychgate ['lɪtʃgeɪt] *n* = **lichgate.**
lye [laɪ] *n* lessive *f* (*substance*).
lying[1] ['laɪɪŋ] **1** *n* (*U*) mensonge(s) *m(pl)*. **~ will get you nowhere** ça ne te servira à rien de mentir. **2** *adj person* menteur; *statement, story* mensonger, faux (*f* fausse).
lying[2] ['laɪɪŋ] *n [body]* **~ in state** exposition *f* (solennelle); (*Med*:†) **~-in** accouchement *m*, couches *fpl*; **~-in ward** salle *f* de travail *or* d'accouchement.
lymph [lɪmf] *n* (*Anat*) lymphe *f*. **~ gland** ganglion *m* lymphatique.
lymphatic [lɪm'fætɪk] *adj* (*Anat, fig*) lymphatique.
lynch [lɪntʃ] *vt* (*lit, fig*) lyncher. **~ law** loi *f* de lynch.
lynching ['lɪntʃɪŋ] *n* (*action, result*) lynchage *m*.
lynx [lɪŋks] *n* lynx *m inv*. **~-eyed** aux yeux de lynx.
Lyons ['laɪənz] *n* Lyon.
lyre ['laɪəʳ] *n* lyre *f*. **~bird** oiseau-lyre *m*, ménure *m*.
lyric ['lɪrɪk] **1** *n* **(a)** (*Poetry*) poème *m* lyrique. **(b)** *[song]* **~s** paroles *fpl*. **2** *adj poem, poet* lyrique.
lyrical ['lɪrɪkəl] *adj* **(a)** (*Poetry*) lyrique. **(b)** (*: *enthusiastic*) lyrique, passionné, enthousiaste. **he got** *or* **waxed ~ about Louis Armstrong** il est devenu lyrique quand il a parlé de Louis Armstrong.
lyrically ['lɪrɪkəlɪ] *adv* (*Poetry*) lyriquement, avec lyrisme; (*enthusiastically*) avec lyrisme, avec enthousiasme.
lyricism ['lɪrɪsɪzəm] *n* lyrisme *m*.
lyricist ['lɪrɪsɪst] *n* (*poet*) poète *m* lyrique; (*song-writer*) parolier *m*, -ière *f*.

M

M, m [em] *n* (*letter*) M, m *m or f*. (*Brit Aut*) **on the M6** sur l'autoroute M6, ≈ sur l'A6.
maː [mɑː] *n* maman *f*. (*pej*) **M~ Smith** la mère Smith.
ma'am [mæm] *n* (*abbr of* **madam a**) madame *f*, mademoiselle *f*.
mac [mæk] *n* **(a)** (*Brit* abbr of* **mackintosh**) imperméable *m*, imper* *m*. **(b)** (ː *form of address*) **hurry up M~!** hé! dépêchez-vous!; (*to friend*) dépêche-toi mon vieux! *or* mon pote!ː
macabre [mə'kɑːbrə] *adj* macabre.
macadam [mə'kædəm] **1** *n* macadam *m*; *V* **tar**[1]. **2** *cpd surface* en macadam; *road* macadamisé.
macadamize [mə'kædəmaɪz] *vt* macadamiser.
macaroni [ˌmækə'rəʊnɪ] *n* (*U*) macaroni(s) *m(pl)*. **~ cheese** macaroni au gratin.
macaronic [ˌmækə'rɒnɪk] **1** *adj* macaronique. **2** *n* vers *m* macaronique.
macaroon [ˌmækə'ruːn] *n* macaron *m*.
macaw [mə'kɔː] *n* ara *m*.
mace[1] [meɪs] *n* (*U: spice*) macis *m*.
mace[2] [meɪs] *n* (*weapon*) massue *f*; (*ceremonial staff*) masse *f*. **~bearer** massier *m*.
macerate ['mæsəreɪt] *vti* macérer.
Mach [mæk] *n* (*Aviat: also* **~ number**) (nombre *m* de) Mach *m*. **to fly at ~ 2** voler à Mach 2.
machete [mə'tʃeɪtɪ] *n* machette *f*.
Machiavelli [ˌmækɪə'velɪ] *n* Machiavel *m*.
Machiavellian [ˌmækɪə'velɪən] *adj* machiavélique.
machination [ˌmækɪ'neɪʃən] *n* machination *f*, intrigue *f*, manœuvre *f*.
machine [mə'ʃiːn] **1** *n* **(a)** (*gen, Tech, Theat*) machine *f*. **adding/translating** *etc* **~** machine à calculer/à traduire *etc*; *V* **knitting, washing** *etc*.
(b) (*plane*) appareil *m*; (*car, cycle*) machine *f*; *V* **flying.**
(c) (*fig*) machine *f*, appareil *m*, organisation *f*. **the ~ of government** la machine politique *or* de l'État; **the military ~** la machine *or* l'appareil militaire *or* de l'armée.
(d) (*US Pol*) **the democratic ~** la machine administrative *or* l'appareil *m* du parti démocrate; *V* **party.**
(e) (*pej: person*) machine *f*, automate *m*.
2 *vt* (*Tech*) façonner à la machine, usiner; (*Sewing*) coudre à la machine, piquer (à la machine).
3 *cpd* de la machine, des machines. **the machine age** le siècle de la machine *or* des machines; **machine gun** mitrailleuse *f*; **machine-gun** mitrailler; **machine gunner** mitrailleur *m*; **machine-gunning** mitraillage *m*; **machine language** langage-machine *m*; **machine-made** fait à la machine; (*Ind*) **machine operator** = **machinist; machine shop** atelier *m* d'usinage; **machine-stitch** piquer à la machine; **machine stitch** point *m* (de piqûre) à la machine; **machine tool** machine-outil *f*; **machine-tool operator** opérateur *m* sur machine-outil, usineur *m*.
machinery [mə'ʃiːnərɪ] *n* (*U*) (*machines collectively*) machinerie *f*, machines *fpl*; (*parts of machine*) mécanisme *m*, rouages *mpl*. **a piece of ~** un mécanisme; (*fig*) **the ~ of government** les rouages de l'État; (*fig Pol etc*) **we need the ~ to introduce these reforms** nous avons besoin de rouages qui nous permettent (*subj*) d'introduire ces réformes.
machinist [mə'ʃiːnɪst] *n* machiniste *mf*, opérateur *m*, -trice *f* (sur machine); (*on sewing, knitting machines*) mécanicienne *f*.
machismo [mæ'tʃiːzməʊ] *n* (*U*) masculinité *f* (agressive).
mackerel ['mækrəl] **1** *n, pl inv* maquereau *m*. **2** *cpd*: **mackerel sky** ciel pommelé.
mackintosh ['mækɪntɒʃ] *n* imperméable *m*.
macro... ['mækrəʊ] *pref* macro... . (*U*) **~linguistics** macrolinguistique *f*; **~molecule** macromolécule *f*.
macrocosm ['mækrəʊkɒzəm] *n* macrocosme *m*.
macron ['mækrɒn] *n* macron *m*.
macroscopic [ˌmækrə'skɒpɪk] *adj* macroscopique.
mad [mæd] **1** *adj* **(a)** (*deranged*) fou (*f* folle), dément, cinglé*ː*, dingueː; *bull* furieux; *dog* enragé; (*rash*) *person* fou, insensé; *hope, plan* insensé; *race, gallop* effréné. **to go ~** devenir fou; (*fig*) **this is idealism gone ~** c'est de l'idéalisme qui dépasse les bornes *or* (*stronger*) qui vire à la folie; **to drive sb ~** (*lit*) rendre qn fou (*V also* **1b**); (*exasperate*) exaspérer qn, rendre qn malade* (*fig*); **he is as ~ as a hatter** *or* **a March hare** il travaille du chapeauː, il a un grain*, il a le timbre fêlé*; **(stark) raving ~, stark staring ~** fou à lier *or* à enfermer; **~ with grief** fou de douleur; **that was a ~ thing to do** il fallait être fou pour faire cela; **what a ~ idea!** c'est une idée insensée!; **you're ~ to think of it!** tu es fou d'y songer!; **are you ~?** ça ne va pas?* (*iro*); **you must be ~!** ça ne va pas, non!* (*iro*); **to run like ~*** courir comme un dératé *or* un perdu; **to shout like ~*** crier à tue-tête *or* comme un forcené; **to be working like ~*** travailler d'arrache-pied; **this plant grows like ~*** cette plante pousse comme du chiendent; **we had a ~ dash for the bus** nous avons dû foncer* pour attraper le bus; **I'm in a ~ rush** c'est une vraie course contre la montre.
(b) (*: *angry*) furieux. **to be ~ at** *or* **with sb** être furieux contre qn; **to get ~ at** *or* **with sb** s'emporter contre qn; **don't get ~ with** *or* **at me!** ne te fâche pas contre moi!; **he makes me ~!** ce

qu'il peut m'agacer! *or* m'énerver!; **to drive sb ~** faire enrager qn, mettre qn en fureur; **he was ~ at me for spilling the tea** il était furieux contre moi pour avoir renversé le thé; **he's hopping** *or* **spitting ~** il est fou furieux; **he was really ~ about the mistake** l'erreur l'avait vraiment mis hors de lui (*V also* **1c**).
(c) (*: *enthusiastic: also* **~ keen**) **~ about** *or* **on** fou (*f* folle) de, entiché de*, mordu de*; **to be ~ about sb** être engoué (*fig*) de qn; (*in love*) être fou *or* toqué* de qn; **I'm ~ about you** je suis follement amoureux de vous; **I'm not ~ about him** (*not in love*) ce n'est pas la passion, on ne peut pas dire que je sois folle de lui; (*not enthusiastic, impressed*) il ne m'emballe pas*; **to be ~ on** *or* **about swimming** être un enragé *or* un mordu* de la natation; **I'm not ~ about it** ça ne m'emballe pas*, ça ne me remplit pas d'enthousiasme.
2 *adv only in* **~ keen** *V* **1c**.
3 *cpd*: **madcap** (*adj, n*) écervelé(e) *m(f)*; (*lit, also *fig*) **madhouse** maison *f* de fous; **madman** fou *m*, aliéné *m*; **madwoman** folle *f*, aliénée *f*.
madam [ˈmædəm] *n* **(a)** madame *f*; (*unmarried*) mademoiselle *f*. (*in letters*) **Dear M~** Madame; Mademoiselle; (*frm*) **M~ Chairman** Madame la Présidente. **(b)** mijaurée *f*, pimbêche *f*. **she's a little ~** c'est une petite pimbêche *or* mijaurée. **(c)** (*brothelkeeper*) sous-maîtresse *f*.
madden [ˈmædn] *vt* rendre fou (*f* folle); (*infuriate*) exaspérer. **~ed by pain** fou de douleur, exaspéré par la souffrance.
maddening [ˈmædnɪŋ] *adj* exaspérant, à rendre fou, rageant*.
maddeningly [ˈmædnɪŋlɪ] *adv* à un degré exaspérant, à vous rendre fou. **he is ~ well-organized** il est exaspérant d'organisation; **~ slow** d'une lenteur exaspérante.
made [meɪd] 1 *ptp of* **make**. 2 *cpd*: **made-to-measure** fait sur mesure; **made-to-order** fait sur commande; **made-up** *story* inventé, factice; (*pej*) faux (*f* fausse); *face* maquillé; *eyes, nails* fait; **she is too made-up** elle est trop fardée.
Madeira [məˈdɪərə] 1 *n* (*Geog*) Madère *f*; (*wine*) (vin *m* de) madère *m*. 2 *cpd*: **Madeira cake** (sorte *f* de) quatre-quarts *m*; **Madeira sauce** sauce *f* madère.
madly [ˈmædlɪ] *adv* **(a)** (*lit, also *fig*) comme un fou, follement, éperdument. **to be ~ in love with sb, to love sb ~** être éperdument amoureux de qn, aimer qn à la folie; **he's ~ interested in sport, he's ~ keen on sport** il est fou *or* passionné *or* mordu* de sport; **I ~ offered to help her** j'ai eu la folie de lui offrir mon aide.
(b) (*: *hurriedly*) désespérément, avec acharnement. **I was ~ trying to open it** j'essayais désespérément de l'ouvrir; **we were ~ rushing for the train** c'était la course pour attraper le train.
madness [ˈmædnɪs] *n* (*Med*) folie *f*, démence *f*, aliénation *f* (mentale); (*in animals*) rage *f*; (*rashness*) folie, démence. **it is sheer ~ to say so** c'est de la pure folie *or* de la démence de le dire; **what ~!** c'est de la pure folie!, il faut être fou!
Madonna [məˈdɒnə] *n* (*Rel*) Madone *f*; (*fig*) madone *f*.
madrigal [ˈmædrɪgəl] *n* madrigal *m*.
maelstrom [ˈmeɪlstrəʊm] *n* (*lit, fig*) tourbillon *m*, maelstrom *m*.
maestro [ˈmaɪstrəʊ] *n* maestro *m*.
Mae West* [ˌmeɪˈwest] *n* gilet *m* de sauvetage (gonflable).
mafia [ˈmæfɪə] *n* maf(f)ia *f*.
mag* [mæg] *n* (*abbr of* **magazine a**) (*Press*) revue *f*, périodique *m*, magazine *m*.
magazine [ˌmægəˈziːn] *n* **(a)** (*Press*) revue *f*, magazine *m*, périodique *m*; (*Rad, TV: also* **~ programme**) magazine. **(b)** (*Mil*) (*store*) magasin *m* (du corps); (*part of gun*) magasin.
magenta [məˈdʒentə] 1 *n* magenta *m*. 2 *adj* magenta *inv*.
Maggie [ˈmægɪ] *n* (*dim of* **Margaret**) Maguy *f*.
maggot [ˈmægət] *n* ver *m*, asticot *m*.
maggoty [ˈmægətɪ] *adj fruit* véreux.
Magi [ˈmeɪdʒaɪ] *npl* (rois *mpl*) mages *mpl*.
magic [ˈmædʒɪk] 1 *n* (*U*) magie *f*, enchantement *m*. **(as if) by ~** (comme) par enchantement *or* magie; **the ~ of that moment** la magie de cet instant.
2 *adj* (*lit*) magique, enchanté; (*fig*) surnaturel, merveilleux, prodigieux; *beauty* enchanteur (*f* -teresse). **~ lantern** lanterne *f* magique; **~ spell** sort *m*, sortilège *m*; **~ square** carré *m* magique; **to say the ~ word** prononcer la formule magique.
magical [ˈmædʒɪkəl] *adj* magique.
magically [ˈmædʒɪkəlɪ] *adv* magiquement, comme par enchantement *or* magie.
magician [məˈdʒɪʃən] *n* magicien(ne) *m(f)*; (*Theat etc*) illusionniste *mf*.
magisterial [ˌmædʒɪsˈtɪərɪəl] *adj* (*lit*) de magistrat; (*fig*) magistral, formidable.
magistracy [ˈmædʒɪstrəsɪ] *n* (*U*) magistrature *f*.
magistrate [ˈmædʒɪstreɪt] *n* magistrat *m*, juge *m*.
Magna C(h)arta [ˌmægnəˈkɑːtə] *n* (*Brit Hist*) Grande Charte.
magnanimity [ˌmægnəˈnɪmɪtɪ] *n* magnanimité *f*.
magnanimous [mægˈnænɪməs] *adj* magnanime.
magnanimously [mægˈnænɪməslɪ] *adv* magnanimement.
magnate [ˈmægneɪt] *n* magnat *m*, roi *m*. **industrial/financial ~** magnat de l'industrie/de la finance; **oil ~** roi du pétrole.
magnesia [mægˈniːʃə] *n* magnésie *f*; *V* **milk**.
magnesium [mægˈniːzɪəm] *n* magnésium *m*.
magnet [ˈmægnɪt] *n* (*lit, fig*) aimant *m*.
magnetic [mægˈnetɪk] *adj* (*lit, fig*) magnétique.
magnetically [mægˈnetɪkəlɪ] *adv* magnétiquement.
magnetism [ˈmægnɪtɪzəm] *n* (*lit, fig*) magnétisme *m*.
magnetize [ˈmægnɪtaɪz] *vt* (*lit*) aimanter, magnétiser; (*fig*) magnétiser.
magneto [mægˈniːtəʊ] *n* magnéto *f*.
magneto... [mægˈniːtəʊ] *pref* magnéto... .
magnification [ˌmægnɪfɪˈkeɪʃən] *n* (*V* **magnify**) grossissement *m*; amplification *f*; exagération *f*; (*Rel*) glorification *f*.
magnificence [mægˈnɪfɪsəns] *n* magnificence *f*, splendeur *f*.
magnificent [mægˈnɪfɪsənt] *adj* magnifique, splendide, superbe; (*sumptuous*) somptueux.
magnificently [mægˈnɪfɪsəntlɪ] *adv* magnifiquement.
magnify [ˈmægnɪfaɪ] *vt* **(a)** *image* grossir; *sound* amplifier (*fig*); *incident etc* exagérer, grossir. **to ~ sth 4 times** grossir qch 4 fois; **~ing glass** loupe *f*, verre grossissant. **(b)** (*Rel: praise*) glorifier.
magnitude [ˈmægnɪtjuːd] *n* ampleur *f*; (*Astron*) magnitude *f*.
magnolia [mægˈnəʊlɪə] *n* (*also* **~ tree**) magnolia *m*, magnolier *m*.
magnum [ˈmægnəm] 1 *n* magnum *m*. 2 *cpd*: (*Art, Literat, fig*) **magnum opus** œuvre maîtresse.
magpie [ˈmægpaɪ] *n* (*Orn*) pie *f*; (*petty thief*) chapardeur *m*, -euse *f*; (*: *chatterbox*) pie. **to chatter like a ~** jacasser comme une pie, être un vrai moulin à paroles*.
Magyar [ˈmægjɑːʳ] 1 *adj* magyar. 2 *n* Magyar(e) *m(f)*.
maharaja(h) [ˌmɑːhəˈrɑːdʒə] *n* mahara(d)jah *m*.
maharanee [ˌmɑːhəˈrɑːniː] *n* maharani *f*.
mahogany [məˈhɒgənɪ] 1 *n* acajou *m*. 2 *cpd* (*made of* **~**) en acajou; (**~-*coloured***) acajou *inv*.
Mahomet [məˈhɒmɪt] *n* Mahomet *m*.
Mahometan [məˈhɒmɪtən] 1 *adj* musulman, mahométan. 2 *n* Mahométan(e) *m(f)*.
maid [meɪd] 1 *n* **(a)** (*servant*) bonne *f*, domestique *f*; (*in hotel*) bonne; femme *f* de chambre; *V* **bar¹, house, lady** *etc*.
(b) (††) (*young girl*) jeune fille *f*; (*virgin*) vierge *f*. (*pej*) **old ~** vieille fille; (*Hist*) **the M~ (of Orleans)** la Pucelle (d'Orléans).
2 *cpd*: **maid-of-all-work** bonne *f* à tout faire; **maid of honour** demoiselle *f* d'honneur; **maidservant††** servante *f*.
maiden [ˈmeɪdn] 1 *n* (*liter*) (*girl*) jeune fille *f*; (*virgin*) vierge *f*.
2 *cpd flight, voyage* premier (*before n*), inaugural. **maiden aunt** tante *f* célibataire, tante vieille fille (*pej*); **maidenhair (fern)** capillaire *m*, cheveu *m* de Vénus; **maidenhead** (*Anat*) hymen *m*; (*state*) virginité *f*; **maiden lady** demoiselle *f*; **maiden name** nom *m* de jeune fille; (*Parl*) **maiden speech** premier discours (*d'un député etc*).
maidenhood [ˈmeɪdnhʊd] *n* virginité *f*.
maidenly [ˈmeɪdnlɪ] *adj* de jeune fille, virginal, modeste.
mail¹ [meɪl] 1 *n* (*U*) poste *f*; (*letters*) courrier *m*. **by ~** par la poste; **here's your ~** voici votre courrier; *V* **first-class** *etc*.
2 *vt* (*esp US*) envoyer *or* expédier (par la poste), poster.
3 *cpd*: **mailbag** sac postal; **mailboat** paquebot(-poste) *m*; (*US*) **mailbox** boîte *f* aux lettres; (*US Rail*) **mail car** wagon-poste *m*; (*US*) **mail carrier** facteur *m*, préposé(e) *m(f)*; **mail coach** (*Rail*) wagon-poste *m*; (*horse-drawn*) malle-poste *f*; **mail(ing) clerk** (employé(e) *m(f)*) préposé(e) *m(f)* au courrier; (*Comm*) **mailing list** liste *f* d'adresses; (*US*) **mailman** facteur *m*, préposé *m*; **mail-order** vente *f or* achat *m* par correspondance; **we got it by mail-order** nous l'avons acheté par correspondance; **mail-order firm, mail-order house** maison *f* de vente par correspondance; **mail train** train-poste *m*; (*Brit*) **mail van** (*Aut*) voiture *f or* fourgon *m* des postes; (*Rail*) wagon-poste *m*.
mail² [meɪl] *n* (*U*) mailles *fpl*. **coat of ~** cotte *f* de mailles; (*fig*) **the ~ed fist** la manière forte; *V* **chain**.
maim [meɪm] *vt* estropier, mutiler. **to be ~ed for life** être estropié pour la vie *or* à vie.
main [meɪn] 1 *adj* **(a)** *feature, idea, objective* principal, premier, essentiel; *door, entrance, shop* principal; *pipe, beam* maître (*f* maîtresse). **the ~ body of the army/the crowd** le gros de l'armée/de la foule; **my ~ idea was to establish ...** mon idée directrice était d'établir ...; **the ~ point of his speech** le point fondamental de son discours; **the ~ point** *or* **the ~ object** *or* **the ~ objective of the meeting** l'objet principal *or* le premier objectif de la réunion; **the ~ thing is to keep quiet** l'essentiel est de se taire; **the ~ thing to remember is ...** ce qu'il ne faut surtout pas oublier c'est ...; *V also* **3** *and* **eye, issue** *etc*.
(b) by ~ force de vive force.
2 *n* **(a)** (*principal pipe, wire*) canalisation *or* conduite maîtresse. **(electricity) ~** conducteur principal; **(gas) ~** (*in street*) conduite principale; (*in house*) conduite de gaz; **~ (sewer)** (égout *m*) collecteur *m*; **(water) ~** (*in street or house*) conduite d'eau de la ville; **the water in this tap comes from the ~s** l'eau de/ce robinet vient directement de la conduite; (*Elec*) **the ~s** le secteur; **connected to the ~s** branché sur (le) secteur; **this radio works by battery or from the ~s** ce poste de radio marche sur piles ou sur (le) secteur; **to turn off the electricity/gas/water at the ~(s)** couper le courant/le gaz/l'eau au compteur.
(b) in the ~ dans l'ensemble, en général, en gros; *V* **might²**.
(c) (*liter: sea*) **the ~** l'océan *m*, le (grand) large; *V* **Spanish**.
3 *cpd*: (*Archit*) **main beam** maîtresse poutre; (*Aut etc*) **main bearing** palier *m*; (*Naut*) **mainbrace** bras *m* (de grand-vergue) (*V* **splice 1**); (*Gram*) **main clause** proposition principale; (*Culin*) **main course** plat principal, plat de résistance; (*Naut*) **main deck** pont principal; (*Brit*) **main door (flat)** appartement *m* avec porte d'entrée particulière sur la rue; **mainland** continent *m* (*opposé à une île*); **the mainland of Greece, the Greek mainland** la Grèce continentale; (*Drugs sl: inject heroin etc*) **mainline** se piquer (par injection intraveineuse); (*Rail*) **main line** grande ligne, voie principale; **main-line station/train** gare *f*/train *m* de grande ligne; (*Drugs sl*) **mainliner** personne *f* qui se pique (dans la veine), piquouseur‡ *m*, -euse‡ *f*; (*Naut*) **mainmast** grand mât; (*Comm etc*) **main office** bureau principal; *[political party, newspaper, agency etc]* siège *m* (social); **a main road** une grande route, une route à grande circulation; **the main road** la grand-route; **it is one of the main roads into Edinburgh** c'est une des grandes voies d'accès à Édimbourg; (*Naut*) **mainsail** grand-voile *f*; (*Naut*) **main sheet** écoute *f* de (la) grand-voile; **mainspring** *[clock etc]* ressort principal; (*fig*) mobile principal; *[radio, tape recorder etc]* **mains set** poste-

secteur *m*; **to be on the mains supply** *(for electricity/gas/water)* être raccordé au réseau (de distribution) d'électricité/de gaz/d'eau; **mainstay** *(Naut)* étai *m* (de grand mât); *(fig)* soutien *m*, point *m* d'appui; **he was the mainstay of the organization** c'était lui le pilier *or* le pivot de l'organisation; **main street** grand-rue *f*, rue principale.

mainly ['meɪnlɪ] *adv* principalement, en grande partie; *(especially)* surtout.

maintain [meɪn'teɪn] *vt* **(a)** *(continue) order, progress* maintenir; *silence* garder; *friendship, correspondence* entretenir; *attitude, advantage* conserver, garder; *war* continuer, soutenir; *cause, rights, one's strength* soutenir. **he ~ed his opposition to** il continua à s'opposer à; **if the improvement is ~ed** si l'on (*or* s'il *etc*) continue à faire des progrès, si l'amélioration se maintient.

(b) *(support) army etc* entretenir; *family, wife, child* subvenir aux besoins de.

(c) *road, building, car, machine* entretenir.

(d) *(assert) opinion, fact* soutenir, maintenir. **I ~ that** je soutiens *or* je maintiens que.

maintenance ['meɪntɪnəns] **1** *n (U) [order etc]* maintien *m*; *[army, family]* entretien *m*; *[road, building, car, machine]* entretien, maintenance *f (Tech)*. **car ~** entretien des voitures; *(Jur)* **he pays £15 per week ~** il verse une pension alimentaire de 15 livres par semaine.

2 *cpd*: **maintenance allowance** *[student]* bourse *f* (d'études); *[worker away from home]* indemnité *f* (pour frais) de déplacement; **maintenance costs** frais *mpl* d'entretien; **maintenance crew** équipe *f* d'entretien; **maintenance grant = maintenance allowance**; *(Tech etc)* **maintenance man** employé chargé de l'entretien; *(Jur)* **maintenance order** obligation *f* alimentaire.

maisonette [,meɪzə'net] *n (esp Brit)* duplex *m*, appartement *m* (en duplex).

maize [meɪz] *n* maïs *m*. **~ field** champ *m* de maïs.

majestic [mə'dʒestɪk] *adj* majestueux, auguste.

majestically [mə'dʒestɪkəlɪ] *adv* majestueusement.

majesty ['mædʒɪstɪ] *n* majesté *f*. **His M~ the King** Sa Majesté le Roi; **Your M~** Votre Majesté; *V* **ship**.

major ['meɪdʒə^r] **1** *adj (gen, Jur, Mus, Philos etc)* majeur. **of ~ importance** d'une importance majeure *or* exceptionnelle; **of ~ interest** d'intérêt majeur; **for the ~ part** en grande partie; **the ~ portion** la majeure partie; *(Med)* **~ operation** opération majeure; *(Cards)* **~ suit** majeure *f*; *(Brit Scol)* **Smith M~** Smith aîné.

2 *cpd*: **majordomo** *V* **majordomo**; **majorette** *V* **majorette**; *(Mil)* **major-general** général *m* de division.

3 *n* **(a)** *(Mil, also US Air Force)* commandant *m*; *(cavalry)* chef *m* d'escadron; *(infantry)* chef de bataillon.

(b) *(Jur)* majeur(e) *m(f)*.

(c) *(US Univ)* matière principale.

4 *vi (US Univ)* **to ~ in chemistry** se spécialiser en chimie.

Majorca [mə'jɔːkə] *n* Majorque *f*.

Majorcan [mə'jɔːkən] **1** *adj* majorquin. **2** *n* Majorquin(e) *m(f)*.

majordomo [,meɪdʒə'dəʊməʊ] *n* majordome *m*.

majorette [,meɪdʒə'ret] *n* majorette *f*.

majority [mə'dʒɒrɪtɪ] **1** *n* **(a)** *(greater part)* majorité *f*. **to be in the ~** être majoritaire *or* en majorité; **elected by a ~ of 9** élu avec une majorité de 9 voix; **a four-fifths ~** une majorité des quatre cinquièmes; **in the ~ of cases** dans la majorité *or* la plupart des cas; **the ~ (of people)** la plupart (des gens); **the vast ~ of them believe** dans leur immense majorité ils croient; *V* **silent**.

(b) *(in age)* majorité *f*. **to reach one's ~** atteindre sa majorité.

2 *cpd (Pol) government, rule* majoritaire. *(Jur)* **a majority verdict** un verdict majoritaire *or* rendu à la majorité.

make [meɪk] *pret, ptp* **made 1** *vt* **(a)** *(gen: create, produce, form) bed, bread, clothes, coffee, fire, noise, peace, remark, one's will etc* faire; *building* construire; *toys, tools* faire, fabriquer; *pot, model* faire, façonner; *speech* faire, prononcer; *mistake* faire, commettre; *payment* faire, effectuer *(Comm)*; *(Sport etc) points, score* marquer. **God made Man** Dieu a créé l'homme; **made in France** fabriqué en France; **watch made of gold** montre en or; **you were made for me** tu es fait pour moi; *(fig)* **to show what one is made of** donner sa mesure; **this car wasn't made to carry 8 people** cette voiture n'est pas faite pour transporter 8 personnes; **I'm not made for running*** je ne suis pas fait pour la course à pied *or* pour courir; **he's as clever as they ~ 'em*** *or* **as they're made*** il est malin comme pas un*; **to ~ an attempt to do** essayer de faire, faire une tentative *or* un essai pour faire; **to ~ a bow to sb** faire un salut à qn, saluer qn; **to ~ a start on sth** commencer qch, se mettre à qch; *V* **difference, offer, promise** *etc*.

(b) *(cause to be)* rendre; faire. **to ~ sb sad** rendre qn triste, attrister qn; **to ~ o.s. useful/ill** *etc* se rendre utile/malade *etc*; **to ~ o.s. understood** se faire comprendre; **that smell ~s me hungry** cette odeur me donne faim; **~ yourself comfortable** mettez-vous à l'aise; **~ yourself at home** faites comme chez vous; **to ~ sth ready** préparer qch; **to ~ sth yellow** jaunir qch; **to ~ sb king** faire qn roi; **he made John his assistant** il a pris Jean comme assistant, il a fait de Jean son assistant; **this actor ~s the hero a tragic figure** cet acteur fait du héros un personnage tragique; **he made her his wife** il en a fait sa femme, il l'a épousée; **I'll ~ a tennis player (out) of him yet!*** il n'est pas dit que je n'en ferai pas un joueur de tennis!; **to ~ a friend of sb** se faire un ami de qn; **I ~ it a rule to rise early** je me fais une règle de me lever tôt; **to ~ sth into something else** transformer qch en quelque chose d'autre; **let's ~ it 5 o'clock/£3** si on disait 5 heures/3 livres; **I'm coming tomorrow — ~ it the afternoon** je viendrai demain — oui, mais dans l'après-midi *or* plutôt dans l'après-midi; *V* **best, habit, little²** *etc*.

(c) *(force, oblige)* faire; *(stronger)* obliger, forcer. **to ~ sb do sth** faire faire qch à qn, obliger *or* forcer qn à faire qch; **I was made to speak** on m'a fait prendre la parole; *(stronger)* on m'a obligé *or* forcé à parler; **what made you believe that ...?** qu'est-ce qui vous a fait croire que ...?; **what ~s you do that?** qu'est-ce qui te fait faire ça?; **I don't know what ~s him do it** je ne sais pas ce qui le pousse à le faire; **you can't ~ me!** tu ne peux pas m'y forcer! *or* obliger!; **to ~ sb laugh** faire rire qn; **the author ~s him die in the last chapter** l'auteur le fait mourir au dernier chapitre; **the children were making believe they were on a boat** les enfants faisaient semblant *or* jouaient à faire semblant d'être sur un bateau; **let's ~ believe we're on a desert island** on serait sur une île déserte (*V also* 4); **to ~ do with sth/sb, to ~ sth/sb do** *(be satisfied)* se contenter *or* s'arranger de qch/qn; *(manage)* se débrouiller avec qch/qn, se tirer d'affaire avec qch/qn; **to ~ do as best one can** s'arranger *or* se débrouiller de son mieux; *(fig)* **she had to ~ do and mend for many years** elle a dû se débrouiller pendant des années avec ce qu'elle avait; *V* **shift** *etc*.

(d) *(earn etc) money [person]* (se) faire, gagner; *[business deal etc]* rapporter; *profits* faire. **he ~s £50 a week** il se fait 50 livres par semaine; **how much do you ~?** combien gagnez-vous?; **to ~ a fortune** faire fortune; **I ~ a living (by) teaching music** je gagne ma vie en donnant des leçons de musique; **the deal made him £500** cette affaire lui a rapporté 500 livres; **what did you ~ by** *or* **on it?** qu'est-ce que ça t'a rapporté?; **how much do you stand to ~?** combien pensez-vous y gagner?; **he ~s a bit on the side** il se fait des (petits) à-côtés; *V* **profit** *etc*.

(e) *(equal; constitute; complete)* **2 and 2 ~ 4** 2 et 2 font *or* égalent 4; **100 centimetres ~ one metre** 100 centimètres font *or* égalent un mètre; **that ~s 20** ça fait 20; *(in shop etc)* **how much does that ~ (altogether)?** combien cela fait(-il)?; **to ~ a quorum** atteindre le quorum; **these books ~ a set** ces livres forment une collection; **it made a nice surprise** cela nous (*or* lui *etc*) a fait une bonne surprise; **partridges ~ good eating** les perdreaux sont très bons à manger; **it ~s pleasant reading** c'est d'une lecture agréable, c'est agréable à lire; **this cloth will ~ a dress** ce tissu va me (*or* te *etc*) faire une robe; **they ~ a handsome pair** ils forment un beau couple; **he made a good husband** il s'est montré bon mari; **she made him a good wife** elle a été une bonne épouse pour lui; **he'll ~ a good footballer** il fera un bon joueur de football; **'man' ~s 'men' in the plural** 'man' fait 'men' au pluriel; **I made one of their group** j'ai fait partie de leur groupe; **will you ~ one of us?** voulez-vous vous joindre à nous? *or* être des nôtres?; *(Cards etc)* **to ~ a fourth** faire le quatrième; **that ~s the third time I've rung him** ça fait la troisième fois *or* trois fois que je lui téléphone.

(f) *(reach, attain) destination* arriver à, se rendre à; *(catch) train etc* attraper, avoir. **will we ~ (it to) Paris before lunch?** est-ce que nous arriverons à Paris avant le déjeuner?; *(Naut)* **to ~ port** arriver au port; **do you think he'll ~ (it to) university?** croyez-vous qu'il arrivera à entrer à la faculté?; **the novel made the bestseller list** le roman a réussi à se placer sur la liste des best-sellers; **he made the first team** il a réussi à être sélectionné dans la première équipe; **to ~ it** *(arrive)* arriver; *(achieve sth)* parvenir à qch; *(succeed)* réussir, y parvenir, arriver; **eventually we made it** au bout du compte nous y sommes parvenus *or* arrivés; **you'll never ~ it!** vous n'y arriverez jamais! *or* ne réussirez jamais!; **he made it just in time** il est arrivé juste à temps; **can you ~ it by 3 o'clock?** est-ce que tu peux y être pour 3 heures?; **to ~ 100 km/h** faire 100 km/h, faire du cent*; *(Naut)* **to ~ 10 knots** filer 10 nœuds; **we made 100 km in one hour** nous avons fait 100 km en une heure; **we made good time** *(gen)* nous avons bien marché; *(in vehicle)* nous avons fait une bonne moyenne, nous avons bien roulé *or* bien marché*; (‡: *have intercourse with*) **to ~ (it with) a girl** s'envoyer‡ *or* se taper‡ une fille.

(g) *(reckon, estimate; consider, believe)* **what time do you ~ it?** quelle heure as-tu?, quelle heure (est-ce que) tu as?; **I ~ the total 70 francs** selon mes calculs cela fait 70 F; **how many do you ~ it?** combien tu en comptes?; **I ~ it 100 km from here to Paris** selon moi *or* d'après moi il y a 100 km d'ici à Paris; **what did you ~ of the film?** comment avez-vous compris ce film?; **what do you ~ of him?** qu'est-ce que tu penses de lui?; **I don't know what to ~ of it all** je ne sais pas quoi penser de tout ça; **I can't ~ anything of this letter, I can ~ nothing of this letter** je ne comprends rien à cette lettre.

(h) *(Cards)* **to ~ the cards** battre les cartes; **to ~ a trick** faire un pli; **he made 10 and lost 3 (tricks)** il en a fait 10 et en a perdu 3; *(Bridge)* **to bid and ~ 3 hearts** demander et faire 3 cœurs, faire 3 cœurs demandés; **he managed to ~ his queen of diamonds** il a réussi à faire sa dame de carreau.

(i) *(secure success or future of)* **this business has made him** cette affaire a fait sa fortune *or* son succès; **that film made her** ce film l'a consacrée; **he was made for life** son avenir était assuré; **you're made!*** pas de soucis à vous faire pour votre avenir!; **he's got it made‡** il n'a pas à s'en faire, pour lui c'est du tout cuit*; **to ~ or mar sth** faire la fortune ou la ruine de qch; **to ~ or break sb** assurer ou briser la carrière de qn; **his visit made my day!*** sa visite a transformé ma journée!; *(iro)* il ne manquait plus que sa visite pour compléter ma journée!

2 *vi* **(a)** **to ~ sure of sth** s'assurer de qch; **to ~ so bold as to suggest** se permettre de suggérer; *V* **free, good, merry** *etc*.

(b) **he made as if to strike me** il leva la main comme pour me frapper, il fit mine de me frapper; **the child made as if to cry** l'enfant a fait mine de pleurer; **she made (as if) to touch the book** elle a avancé la main vers le livre.

(c) *(go)* aller, se diriger. **they made after him** ils se sont mis à sa poursuite; **he made at me** *or* **for me with a knife** il s'est jeté sur moi avec un couteau; **to ~ for** aller vers, se diriger vers;

[ship etc] faire route pour (*V also* **2d**); **to ~ for home** rentrer, prendre le chemin du retour; *V also* **make off.**

(d) *[facts, evidence]* **to ~ in sb's favour/against sb** militer en faveur de qn/contre qn; **this will ~ against your chances of success** cela va nuire à vos chances de succès; **to ~ for sth** (*tend to result in*) tendre à qch; (*contribute to*) contribuer à qch; (*conduce to*) être favorable à qch, être à l'avantage de qch.

(e) *[tide, flood]* monter.

3 *n* **(a)** (*Comm*) (*brand*) marque *f*; (*manufacture*) fabrication *f*. **it's a good ~** c'est une bonne marque; **French ~ of car** marque française de voiture; **car of French ~** voiture *f* de construction française; **what ~ of car have you got?** qu'est-ce que vous avez comme (marque de) voiture?; **these are our own ~** ceux-ci sont fabriqués par nous *or* sont faits maison.

(b) (*) **he's on the ~** il cherche à s'enrichir; (*pej*) il est prêt à tout pour faire fortune.

4 *cpd*: **to play at make-believe** jouer à faire semblant; **the land of make-believe** le pays des chimères; **don't worry it's just make-believe** ne vous en faites pas, c'est pour faire semblant; **his story is pure make-believe** son histoire est de l'invention pure *or* (de la) pure fantaisie; **they were on a make-believe island** ils jouaient à faire semblant d'être sur une île; **the child made a make-believe boat out of the chair** l'enfant faisait comme si la chaise était un bateau; **makeshift** (*n*) expédient *m*; (*adj*) de fortune; **make-up** *V* **make-up**; **makeweight** (*lit*) complément *m* de poids; (*fig: person*) bouche-trou *m*.

make away *vi* = **make off.**

make away with *vt fus* (*murder*) supprimer. **to make away with o.s.** se supprimer.

make off *vi* se sauver, filer*, décamper*. **to make off with sth** filer avec qch.

make out 1 *vi* (*) (*get on*) se débrouiller; (*do well*) se tirer bien d'affaire, réussir. **how are you making out?** comment ça va?, comment vous débrouillez-vous?; **we're making out** ça va, on se débrouille; **we're just making out** on fait aller*; **the firm is making out all right** l'affaire marche bien; **he's making out very well in London** il se débrouille très bien à Londres; **I've got enough to make out** j'ai assez pour vivre, je me débrouille.

2 *vt sep* **(a)** (*draw up, write*) *list, account* faire; dresser; *cheque, will, document* faire, écrire. **to make out a bill** faire une facture; **he made out a good case for not doing it** il a présenté de bons arguments pour ne pas le faire.

(b) (*see, distinguish*) *object, person* discerner, reconnaître, distinguer; (*decipher*) *handwriting* déchiffrer; (*understand*) *ideas, reasons, sb's motives* comprendre, discerner. **I couldn't make out where the road was in the fog** je n'arrivais pas à voir où était la route dans le brouillard; **I can't make it out at all** je n'y comprends rien; **how do you make that out?** qu'est-ce qui vous fait penser cela?; **I can't make out what he wants/why he is here** je n'arrive pas à voir *or* comprendre ce qu'il veut/pourquoi il est ici.

(c) (*claim*) prétendre (*that* que); (*imply*) faire paraître. **the play makes her out to be naïve** la pièce la fait passer pour naïve; **they made him out to be a fool** ils ont dit que c'était un imbécile; **you make him out to be better than he is** vous le faites paraître mieux qu'il n'est; **he made himself out to be a doctor, he made out that he was a doctor** il se faisait passer pour (un) médecin, il prétendait être médecin; **he's not as stupid as he makes (himself) out** il n'est pas aussi stupide qu'il le prétend; **he isn't as rich as people make out** il n'est pas aussi riche que les gens le prétendent.

make over *vt sep* **(a)** (*assign*) *money, land* céder, transférer (*to* à).

(b) (*remake*) *dress, coat* refaire, reprendre. **she made his jacket over to fit his son** elle a repris sa veste pour (qu'elle aille à) son fils.

make up 1 *vi* **(a)** (*make friends again*) se réconcilier, se raccommoder*.

(b) (*apply cosmetics*) se maquiller, se farder; (*Theat*) se maquiller, se grimer.

2 *vt sep* **(a)** (*invent*) *story, excuse, explanation* inventer, fabriquer. **you're making it up!** tu l'inventes (de toutes pièces)!

(b) (*put together*) *packet, parcel* faire; *dress etc* assembler; *medicine, lotion, solution* faire, préparer; *list* faire, dresser. **to make sth up into a bundle** faire un paquet de qch; **to make up a collection of** faire une collection de; (*Typ*) **to make up a book** mettre un livre en pages; (*Pharm*) **to make up a prescription** exécuter *or* préparer une ordonnance; **she made up a bed for him on the sofa** elle lui a fait *or* préparé un lit sur le canapé; **have you made up the beds?** as-tu fait les lits?; **customers' accounts are made up monthly** les relevés de compte des clients sont établis chaque mois; **I've made up an outline of what we ought to do** j'ai établi les grandes lignes de ce que nous devons faire; **they make up clothes as well as sell material** ils vendent du tissu et font aussi la confection; **'customers' own material made up'** 'travail à façon'; *V* **mind** *etc.*

(c) (*counterbalance; replace*) compenser; *loss, deficit* combler, suppléer à; *sum of money, numbers, quantity, total* compléter. **he made it up to £100** il a complété les 100 livres; **to make up lost time** rattraper le temps perdu; (*lit, fig*) **to make up lost ground** regagner le terrain perdu.

(d) (*compensate for*) **to make sth up to sb, to make it up to sb for sth** compenser qn pour qch.

(e) (*settle*) *dispute, difference of opinion* mettre fin à. **to make up a quarrel, to make it up** se réconcilier, se raccommoder*; **let's make it up** faisons la paix.

(f) (*apply cosmetics to*) *person, face* maquiller, farder; (*Theat*) maquiller, grimer. **to make o.s. up** se maquiller, se farder; (*Theat*) se maquiller, se grimer.

(g) (*compose, form*) former, composer; (*represent*) représenter. **these parts make up the whole** ces parties forment *or* composent le tout; **the group was made up of 6 teachers** le groupe était fait *or* formé *or* composé de 6 professeurs; **how many people make up the team?** combien y a-t-il de personnes dans l'équipe?

3 make-up *n, cpd V* **make-up.**

4 made-up *adj V* **made 2.**

make up for *vt fus* compenser. **I'll make up for all you've suffered** je vous compenserai pour ce que vous avez souffert; **to make up for lost time** récupérer *or* rattraper *or* regagner le temps perdu; **he tried to make up for all the trouble he'd caused** il essaya de se faire pardonner les ennuis qu'il avait causés; **she said that nothing would make up for her husband's death** elle dit que rien ne compenserait la mort de son mari; **he has made up for last year's losses** il a rattrapé les pertes de l'année dernière; **he made up for all the mistakes he'd made** il s'est rattrapé pour toutes les erreurs qu'il avait commises.

make up on *vt fus* (*catch up with: gen, Sport*) rattraper.

make up to* *vt fus* (*curry favour with*) faire des avances à, essayer de se faire bien voir par; (*flatter*) flatter.

maker ['meɪkəʳ] *n* (*Comm*) fabricant *m*. (*Rel*) **our M~** le Créateur; (**hum*) **he's gone to meet his M~** il est allé voir saint Pierre* (*hum*); *V* **book, dress, trouble** *etc.*

make-up ['meɪkʌp] **1** *n* **(a)** (*U: nature etc*) *[object, group etc]* constitution *f*; *[person]* tempérament *m*, caractère *m*.

(b) (*U: cosmetics*) maquillage *m*, fard *m*. **she wears too much ~** elle se maquille trop, elle est trop fardée.

(c) (*US* Scol etc*) examen *m* de rattrapage.

2 *cpd*: **make-up artist** (*also* **make-up man**) maquilleur *m*; (*also* **make-up girl**) maquilleuse *f*; **make-up bag** trousse *f* de maquillage; **make-up base** base *f* (de maquillage); **make-up case** nécessaire *m or* boîte *f* de maquillage; **make-up remover** démaquillant *m*.

making ['meɪkɪŋ] *n* **(a)** (*U*) (*Comm, gen*) fabrication *f*; *[dress]* façon *f*, confection *f*; *[machines]* fabrication, construction *f*; *[food]* confection. **in the ~** en formation, en gestation; **it's still in the ~** c'est encore en cours de développement *or* en chantier; **it's history in the ~** c'est l'histoire en train de se faire; **it's civil war in the ~** c'est la guerre civile qui se prépare; **all his troubles are of his own ~** tous ses ennuis sont de sa faute; **it was the ~ of him/her** cela en a fait un homme/une femme.

(b) ~s éléments essentiels; **we have the ~s of a library** nous avons un début de bibliothèque; **he has the ~s of a footballer** il a l'étoffe d'un joueur de football; **the situation has the ~s of a civil war** dans cette situation tout présage une guerre civile.

maladjusted [ˌmælə'dʒʌstɪd] *adj* (*Psych etc*) inadapté; (*Tech*) mal ajusté, mal réglé.

maladjustment [ˌmælə'dʒʌstmənt] *n* (*Psych*) inadaptation *f*, déséquilibre *m*; (*Tech*) dérèglement *m*, mauvais ajustement.

maladministration ['mælədˌmɪnɪs'treɪʃən] *n* mauvaise gestion.

maladroit [ˌmælə'drɔɪt] *adj* maladroit.

maladroitly [ˌmælə'drɔɪtlɪ] *adv* maladroitement.

maladroitness [ˌmælə'drɔɪtnɪs] *n* maladresse *f*.

malady ['mælədɪ] *n* maladie *f*, mal *m*.

malapropism ['mæləprɒpɪzəm] *n* pataquès *m*.

malaria [mə'lɛərɪə] *n* malaria *f*, paludisme *m*.

malarial [mə'lɛərɪəl] *adj fever* paludéen; *mosquito* de la malaria, du paludisme.

Malawi [mə'lɑːwɪ] *n* Malawi *m*.

Malay [mə'leɪ] **1** *adj* malais. **2** *n* **(a)** Malais(e) *m(f)*. **(b)** (*Ling*) malais *m*.

Malaya [mə'leɪə] *n* Malaisie *f*.

Malayan [mə'leɪən] = **Malay.**

Malaysia [mə'leɪzɪə] *n* Malaysia *f*.

malcontent ['mælkənˌtent] *adj, n* mécontent(e) *m(f)*.

male [meɪl] **1** *adj* (*Anat, Bio, Bot, Tech etc*) mâle; (*fig: manly*) mâle, viril (*f* virile); *clothes* d'homme. **~ child** enfant mâle; (*pej*) **~ chauvinist pig*** sale phallocrate* *m*; **~ sex** sexe masculin; **~-voice choir** chœur *m* d'hommes, chœur de voix mâles. **2** *n* mâle *m*.

malediction [ˌmælɪ'dɪkʃən] *n* malédiction *f*.

malefactor ['mælɪfæktəʳ] *n* malfaiteur *m*, -trice *f*.

malevolence [mə'levələns] *n* malveillance *f* (*towards* envers).

malevolent [mə'levələnt] *adj* malveillant.

malevolently [mə'levələntlɪ] *adv* avec malveillance.

malformation [ˌmælfɔː'meɪʃən] *n* malformation *f*, difformité *f*.

malfunction [ˌmæl'fʌŋkʃən] **1** *n* mauvaise fonction. **2** *vi* mal fonctionner.

malice ['mælɪs] *n* malice *f*, méchanceté *f*; (*stronger*) malveillance *f*. **to bear sb ~** vouloir du mal à qn; (*Jur*) **with ~ aforethought** avec préméditation, avec intention criminelle *or* délictueuse.

malicious [mə'lɪʃəs] *adj* méchant; (*stronger*) malveillant; (*Jur*) délictueux, criminel. (*Jur*) **~ damage** dommage causé avec intention de nuire.

maliciously [mə'lɪʃəslɪ] *adv* avec méchanceté; (*stronger*) avec malveillance; (*Jur*) avec préméditation, avec intention criminelle *or* délictueuse.

malign [mə'laɪn] **1** *adj* pernicieux, nuisible. **2** *vt* calomnier, diffamer. **you ~ me** vous me calomniez.

malignancy [mə'lɪgnənsɪ] *n* malveillance *f*, malfaisance *f*; (*Med*) malignité *f*.

malignant [mə'lɪgnənt] *adj person* malfaisant, malveillant; *look, intention* malveillant; *action, effect* malfaisant; (*Med*) malin (*f* -igne).

malignity [mə'lɪgnɪtɪ] *n* = **malignancy.**

malinger [mə'lɪŋgəʳ] *vi* faire le (*or* la) malade.

malingerer [mə'lɪŋgərəʳ] *n* faux (*f* fausse) malade; (*Admin, Mil* *etc*) simulateur *m*, -trice *f*. **he's a ~** il se fait passer pour malade.

mall [mɔːl] *n* allée *f*, mail *m*.

mallard ['mæləd] *n* canard *m* sauvage, col-vert *m*.

malleability [ˌmælɪə'bɪlɪtɪ] *n* malléabilité *f*.

malleable ['mælɪəbl] *adj* malléable.

mallet ['mælɪt] *n* (*all senses*) maillet *m*.

mallow ['mæləʊ] *n* (*Bot*) mauve *f*; *V* **marsh.**

malnutrition [ˌmælnjʊ'trɪʃən] *n* sous-alimentation *f*, insuffisance *f* alimentaire.

malodorous [mæl'əʊdərəs] *adj* malodorant.

malpractice [ˌmæl'præktɪs] *n* (*wrongdoing*) faute professionnelle; (*neglect of duty*) négligence *or* incurie professionnelle.

malt [mɔːlt] **1** *n* malt *m*. **2** *cpd vinegar* de malt. **malted milk** lait malté; **malt extract** extrait *m* de malt; **malt whisky** (whisky *m*) pur malt.

Malta ['mɔːltə] *n* Malte *f*. **in ~** à Malte.

Maltese [ˌmɔːl'tiːz] **1** *adj* maltais. **~ cross** croix *f* de Malte; **~ fever** fièvre *f* de Malte. **2** *n* **(a)** Maltais(e) *m(f)*. **(b)** (*Ling*) maltais *m*.

maltreat [ˌmæl'triːt] *vt* maltraiter, malmener.

maltreatment [ˌmæl'triːtmənt] *n* mauvais traitement.

mam(m)a* [mə'mɑː] *n* maman *f*.

mammal ['mæməl] *n* mammifère *m*.

mammalian [mæ'meɪlɪən] *adj* mammifère.

mammary ['mæmərɪ] *adj* mammaire.

Mammon ['mæmən] *n* le dieu Argent, le Veau d'or (*fig*).

mammoth ['mæməθ] **1** *n* mammouth *m*. **2** *adj* géant, monstre, énorme.

mammy ['mæmɪ] *n* **(a)** (*) maman *f*. **(b)** (*US: Negro nurse*) nourrice noire.

man [mæn] *pl* **men 1** *n* **(a)** (*gen*) homme *m*; (*servant*) domestique *m*, valet *m*; (*in factory etc*) ouvrier *m*; (*in office, shop etc*) employé *m*; (*Mil*) homme (de troupe), soldat *m*; (*Naut*) homme (d'équipage), matelot *m*; (*Sport: player*) joueur *m*, équipier *m*; (*husband*) homme, type* *m*. **men and women** les hommes et les femmes; **he's a nice ~** c'est un homme très agréable, il est sympathique; **an old ~** un vieillard; **a blind ~** un aveugle; **that ~ Smith** ce (type*) Smith; (*Police etc* †) **the ~ Jones** le sieur *or* le nommé Jones; **the ~ in the moon** l'homme dans la lune; **as one ~** comme un seul homme; **they're communists to a ~** *or* **to the last ~** ils sont tous communistes sans exception; **they fought to the last ~** ils se sont battus jusqu'au dernier; **every ~ jack of them** tous autant qu'ils sont, tous sans exception; **he's been with this firm ~ and boy for 30 years** cela fait 30 ans qu'il est entré tout jeune encore dans la maison; (*liter*) **to grow to ~'s estate** atteindre sa maturité; **officers and men** (*Aviat, Mil*) officiers et soldats, officiers et hommes de troupe; (*Naut*) officiers et matelots; **the corporal and his men** le caporal et ses hommes; **the employers and the men** les patrons et les ouvriers; **~ and wife** mari et femme; **to live as ~ and wife** vivre maritalement; **her ~*** son homme, son type*; **my old ~*** (*father*) mon paternel*; (*husband*) mon homme*; **her young ~**† son amoureux†, son futur (*hum*); **it will make a ~ of him** cela en fera un homme; **be a ~!** sois un homme!; **he took it like a ~** il a pris ça vaillamment; **he was ~ enough to apologize** il a eu le courage de s'excuser; **if you're looking for someone to help you, then I'm your ~** si vous cherchez quelqu'un pour vous aider, je suis votre homme; **he's his own ~ again** (*not subordinate to anyone*) il est de nouveau son propre maître; (*in control of his emotions etc*) il est de nouveau maître de lui; *V* **best.**

(b) (*sort, type*) **I'm not a drinking ~** je ne bois pas (beaucoup); **he's not a football ~** ce n'est pas un amateur de football; **I'm a whisky ~ myself** moi, je préfère le whisky; **he's a Leeds ~** il est *or* vient de Leeds; **it's got to be a local ~** il faut que ce soit un homme du pays (*or* de la ville *or* du quartier *etc*); **he's not the ~ to fail** il n'est pas homme à échouer; **he's not the ~ for that** il n'est pas fait pour cela; **he's the ~ for the job** c'est l'homme qu'il (nous *or* leur *etc*) faut pour ce travail; **a medical ~** un docteur; **the ~ in the street** l'homme de la rue; **a ~ of the world** un homme d'expérience; **a ~ of letters** un homme de lettres; **a ~ about town** un homme du monde; *V* **property** *etc.*

(c) (*U: humanity in general*) **M~** l'homme *m*; (*Prov*) **M~ proposes, God disposes** l'homme propose et Dieu dispose (*Prov*).

(d) (*person*) homme *m*. **all men must die** tous les hommes sont mortels, nous sommes tous mortels; **men say that ...** on dit que ..., certains disent que ...; **any ~ would have done the same** n'importe qui aurait fait de même; **no ~ could blame him** personne ne pouvait le blâmer; **what else could a ~ do?** qu'est-ce qu'on aurait pu faire d'autre?

(e) (*in direct address*) **hurry up, ~!*** dépêchez-vous!; (*to friend etc*) dépêche-toi mon vieux!; **~, was I terrified!‡** j't'assure, j'en menais pas large!‡; **look here young ~!** dites donc jeune homme!; **(my) little ~!** mon grand!; **old ~** mon vieux; **my (good) ~** mon brave; **good ~!** bravo!

(f) (*Chess*) pièce *f*; (*Draughts*) pion *m*.

2 *cpd*: **man-at-arms** homme *m* d'armes, cuirassier *m*; (*liter*) **man-child** enfant *m* mâle; (*Comm, Ind etc*) **man-day** jour *m* de main-d'œuvre; **man-eater** (*animal*) mangeur *m* d'hommes; (*person*) cannibale *m*, anthropophage *m*; **man-eating** *animal* mangeur d'hommes; *tribe etc* anthropophage; **man Friday** (*lit*) Vendredi *m*; (*fig*) fidèle serviteur *m*; **manful** *V* **manful; manfully** *V* **manfully; manhandle** (*treat roughly*) maltraiter, malmener; (*esp Brit: move by hand*) *goods etc* manutentionner; [*woman*] **to be a man-hater** avoir les hommes en horreur; **manhole** trou *m* (d'homme), regard *m*; **manhole cover** plaque *f* d'égout; **manhood** *V* **manhood;** (*Comm, Ind etc*) **man-hour** heure *f* de main-d'œuvre; **manhunt** chasse *f* à l'homme; (*U*) **mankind** (*the human race*) l'homme *m*, le genre humain; (*the male sex*) les hommes; **manlike** *appearance* à l'aspect humain; *qualities* humain, d'homme; (*pej*) *woman* hommasse (*pej*); **manliness** *V* **manliness; manly** *V* **manly; man-made** *fibre, fabric* synthétique; *lake, barrier* artificiel; (*Naut*) **man-of-war, man-o'-war** vaisseau *m or* navire *m or* bâtiment *m* de guerre (*V* **Portuguese**); **manpower** *V* **manpower; manservant** valet *m* de chambre; (**fig*) **man-sized** grand, de taille, de grande personne*; (*Jur*) **manslaughter** homicide *m* involontaire; **man-to-man** (*adj, adv*) d'homme à homme; **mantrap** piège *m* à hommes; **men-at-arms** hommes *mpl* d'armes, cuirassiers *mpl*, grosse cavalerie (*U*).

3 *vt ship, fortress* armer, garnir d'hommes. (*Naut*) **to ~ the boats** armer les bateaux; (*Mil*) **to ~ the guns** servir les canons; **to ~ the pumps** armer les pompes; **the ship was ~ned mainly by Chinese** l'équipage était composé principalement de Chinois; **the telephone is ~ned twenty-four hours a day** il y a une permanence au téléphone vingt-quatre heures sur vingt-quatre.

manacle ['mænəkl] **1** *n*: **~s** menottes *fpl*. **2** *vt* mettre les menottes à.

manage ['mænɪdʒ] **1** *vt* **(a)** (*direct*) *business, estate, theatre, restaurant, hotel, shop* gérer; *institution, organization* administrer, diriger, mener; *farm* exploiter; (*pej*) *election etc* truquer. **you ~d the situation very well** tu as très bien arrangé les choses, tu t'en es très bien tiré.

(b) (*handle, deal with*) *boat, vehicle* manœuvrer, manier; *tool* manier; *animal, person* se faire écouter de, savoir s'y prendre avec.

(c) (*succeed, contrive*) **to ~ to do** réussir *or* arriver *or* parvenir à faire, trouver moyen de faire, s'arranger pour faire; **how did you ~ to do it?** comment t'y es-tu pris *or* t'es-tu arrangé pour le faire?; **how did you ~ not to spill it?** comment as-tu fait pour ne pas le renverser?; **he ~d not to get his feet wet** il a réussi à ne pas se mouiller les pieds; (*iro*) **he ~d to annoy everybody** il a trouvé le moyen de mécontenter tout le monde; **you'll ~ it next time!** tu y arriveras *or* parviendras la prochaine fois!; **will you come? — I can't ~ (it) just now** tu vas venir? — je ne peux pas pour l'instant.

(d) (*with noun object*) **how much will you give? — I can ~ 10 francs** combien allez-vous donner? — je peux aller jusqu'à 10 F *or* je peux y mettre 10 F; **surely you could ~ another biscuit?** tu mangerais bien encore un autre biscuit?; **I couldn't ~ another thing!*** je n'en peux plus!; **can you ~ the suitcases?** pouvez-vous porter les valises?; **can you ~ 8 o'clock?** 8 heures, ça vous convient?; **can you ~ 2 more in the car?** peux-tu encore en prendre 2 *or* as-tu de la place pour 2 de plus dans la voiture?

2 *vi* **(a)** (*succeed etc*) **can you ~?** tu y arrives?; **thanks, I can ~** merci, ça va; **I can ~ without him** je peux me passer de lui.

(b) (*financially etc*) se débrouiller. **she ~s on her pension/on £20 a week** elle se débrouille avec seulement sa pension/avec seulement 20 livres par semaine; **how will you ~?** comment allez-vous faire? *or* vous débrouiller?

manageable ['mænɪdʒəbl] *adj vehicle, boat* facile à manœuvrer, manœuvrable, maniable; *person, child, animal* docile, maniable; *size, proportions, amount* maniable. **~ hair** cheveux *mpl* faciles à coiffer *or* souples.

management ['mænɪdʒmənt] **1** *n* **(a)** (*U*) *[company, estate, theatre]* gestion *f*; *[institution, organization]* administration *f*, direction *f*; *[farm]* exploitation *f*. **his skilful ~ of his staff** l'habileté avec laquelle il dirige son personnel; (*Comm*) **'under new ~'** 'changement de direction'.

(b) (*collective: people*) *[business, firm]* cadres *mpl*, direction *f*, administration *f*; *[hotel, shop, cinema, theatre]* direction. **~ and workers** les cadres et les ouvriers; **he's (one of the) ~ now** il fait partie des cadres maintenant; **'the ~ regrets ...'** 'la direction regrette ...'.

2 *cpd*: **management committee** comité *m* de direction; **management consultant** conseiller *m* de *or* en gestion d'entreprise; **management selection procedures** (formalités *fpl* de) sélection *f* des cadres; **management trainee** cadre *m* stagiaire.

manager ['mænɪdʒə^r] *n [company, business]* directeur *m*, administrateur *m*; *[theatre, cinema]* directeur; *[restaurant, hotel, shop]* gérant *m*; *[farm]* exploitant *m*; *[actor, singer, boxer etc]* manager *m*. **general ~** directeur général; (*in household matters etc*) **she's a good ~** elle est bonne ménagère; (*in personal finances etc*) **he's a bad ~** il ne sait pas s'organiser; *V* **business, sale** *etc.*

manageress [ˌmænɪdʒə'res] *n [hotel, café, shop]* gérante *f*; *[theatre, cinema]* directrice *f*.

managerial [ˌmænə'dʒɪərɪəl] *adj* directorial. **the ~ class** la classe des cadres, les cadres *mpl*.

managing ['mænɪdʒɪŋ] *adj* **(a)** (*Brit: Comm, Ind*) **~ director** directeur général, ≃ P.-D.G. *m*. **(b)** (*bossy*) autoritaire.

manatee [ˌmænə'tiː] *n* lamantin *m*.

Manchuria [mæn'tʃʊərɪə] *n* Mandchourie *f*.

Manchurian [mæn'tʃʊərɪən] **1** *adj* mandchou. **2** *n* Mandchou(e) *m(f)*.

Mancunian [mæŋ'kjuːnɪən] **1** *adj* de (la ville de) Manchester. **2** *n* habitant(e) *m(f) or* natif *m*, -ive *f* de Manchester.

mandarin ['mændərɪn] *n* **(a)** (*person: lit, fig*) mandarin *m*. **(b)** (*Ling*) **M~** mandarin *m*. **(c)** (*also* **~ orange**) mandarine *f*; (*tree*) mandarinier *m*.

mandate ['mændeɪt] **1** *n* (*authority*) mandat *m*; (*country*) pays *m* sous mandat. **under French ~** sous mandat français; (*Parl*) **we have a ~ to do this** nous avons reçu le mandat de faire cela. **2** *vt country* mettre sous le mandat (*to* de).

mandatory ['mændətərɪ] *adj* **(a)** obligatoire. **it is ~ upon him to do so** il a l'obligation formelle de le faire. **(b)** *functions, powers* mandataire. **(c)** (*Pol*) mandataire.

mandible [ˈmændɪbl] *n [bird, insect]* mandibule *f*; *[mammal, fish]* mâchoire *f* (inférieure).
mandolin(e) [ˈmændəlɪn] *n* mandoline *f*.
mandrake [ˈmændreɪk] *n* mandragore *f*.
mandrill [ˈmændrɪl] *n* mandrill *m*.
mane [meɪn] *n* (*lit, fig*) crinière *f*.
maneuver [məˈnuːvəʳ] *etc* (*US*) = **manoeuvre** *etc*.
manful [ˈmænfʊl] *adj* vaillant.
manfully [ˈmænfəlɪ] *adv* vaillamment.
manganese [ˌmæŋgəˈniːz] 1 *n* manganèse *m*. 2 *cpd*: **manganese bronze** bronze *m* au manganèse; **manganese oxide** oxyde *m* de manganèse; **manganese steel** acier *m* au manganèse.
mange [meɪndʒ] *n* gale *f*.
mangel(-wurzel) [ˈmæŋgl(ˌwɜːzl)] *n* betterave fourragère.
manger [ˈmeɪndʒəʳ] *n* (*Agr*) mangeoire *f*; (*Rel*) crèche *f*; *V* **dog**.
mangle[1] [ˈmæŋgl] 1 *n* (*for wringing*) essoreuse *f*; (*for smoothing*) calandre *f*. 2 *vt* essorer; calandrer.
mangle[2] [ˈmæŋgl] *vt* (*also* ~ **up**) *object, body* déchirer, mutiler; (*fig*) *text* mutiler; *quotation* estropier; *message* estropier, mutiler.
mango [ˈmæŋgəʊ] *n* (*fruit*) mangue *f*; (*tree*) manguier *m*. ~ **chutney** condiment *m* à la mangue.
mangold(-wurzel) [ˈmæŋgəld(ˌwɜːzl)] *n* = **mangel(-wurzel)**.
mangrove [ˈmæŋgrəʊv] *n* palétuvier *m*, manglier *m*. ~ **swamp** mangrove *f*.
mangy [ˈmeɪndʒɪ] *adj animal* galeux; (*) *room, hat* pelé, miteux; *act* minable, moche*. **what a ~ trick!*** quel sale coup!*
manhattan [mænˈhætən] *n* (*US*) manhattan *m* (*cocktail m de whisky et de vermouth doux*).
manhood [ˈmænhʊd] *n* **(a)** (*age, state*) âge *m* d'homme, âge viril. **to reach ~** atteindre l'âge d'homme; **during his early ~** quand il était jeune homme.
(b) (*manliness*) virilité *f*, caractère viril.
(c) (*collective n*) **Scotland's ~** tous les hommes d'Écosse.
mania [ˈmeɪnɪə] *n* (*Psych*) manie *f*, penchant *m* morbide; (*) manie, passion *f*. **persecution ~** manie *or* folie *f* de la persécution; **to have a ~ for (doing) sth*** avoir la manie de (faire) qch.
...mania [ˈmeɪnɪə] *suf* ...manie *f*.
maniac [ˈmeɪnɪæk] 1 *n* (*Psych*) maniaque *mf*; (*) fou *m*, folle *f*, dément(e) *m(f)*. **these football ~s*** ces mordus* *mpl or* toqués* *mpl* du football; **he drives like a ~*** il conduit comme un fou; **he's a ~!*** il est fou à lier!, il est bon à enfermer!
2 *adj* maniaque, fou (*f* folle), dément.
maniacal [məˈnaɪəkəl] *adj* (*Psych*) maniaque; (*fig*) fou (*f* folle).
manic [ˈmænɪk] 1 *adj* (*Psych*) maniaque. 2 *cpd*: **manic depression** psychose maniaque dépressive, cyclothymie *f*; **manic-depressive** (*adj, n*) maniaque (*mf*) dépressif (*f* -ive), cyclothymique (*mf*).
manicure [ˈmænɪˌkjʊəʳ] 1 *n* soin *m* des mains.
2 *vt person* faire les mains *or* les ongles à; *nails* faire.
3 *cpd*: **manicure case** trousse *f* à ongles *or* de manucure; **manicure scissors** ciseaux *mpl* de manucure *or* à ongles; **manicure set** = **manicure case**.
manicurist [ˈmænɪˌkjʊərɪst] *n* manucure *mf*.
manifest [ˈmænɪfest] 1 *adj* manifeste, clair, évident. 2 *vt* manifester. 3 *n* (*Aviat, Naut*) manifeste *m*.
manifestation [ˌmænɪfesˈteɪʃən] *n* manifestation *f*.
manifestly [ˈmænɪfestlɪ] *adv* manifestement.
manifesto [ˌmænɪˈfestəʊ] *n* (*Pol etc*) manifeste *m*.
manifold [ˈmænɪfəʊld] 1 *adj collection* divers, varié; *duties* multiple, nombreux. ~ **wisdom** sagesse infinie. 2 *n* (*Aut etc*) **inlet/exhaust ~** collecteur *m* d'admission/d'échappement.
manioc [ˈmænɪɒk] *n* manioc *m*.
manipulate [məˈnɪpjʊleɪt] *vt* **(a)** *tool etc* manipuler, manœuvrer; *vehicle* manœuvrer; *person* manœuvrer. **(b)** (*pej*) *facts, figures, accounts* tripoter, trafiquer*. **to ~ a situation** faire son jeu des circonstances.
manipulation [məˌnɪpjʊˈleɪʃən] *n* (*U: V* **manipulate**) manipulation *f*; manœuvre *f*; (*pej*) tripotage *m*.
manliness [ˈmænlɪnɪs] *n* virilité *f*, caractère viril.
manly [ˈmænlɪ] *adj* viril (*f* virile), mâle.
manna [ˈmænə] *n* manne *f*.
mannequin [ˈmænɪkɪn] *n* mannequin *m*.
manner [ˈmænəʳ] *n* **(a)** (*mode, way*) manière *f*, façon *f*. **the ~ in which he did it** la manière *or* façon dont il l'a fait; **in such a ~ that** de telle sorte que + *indic* (*actual result*) *or* + *subj* (*intended result*); **in this ~**, (*frm*) **after this ~** de cette manière *or* façon; **in** *or* **after the ~ of Van Gogh** à la manière de Van Gogh; **in the same ~**, (*frm*) **in like ~** de la même manière; **in a (certain) ~** en quelque sorte; **in a ~ of speaking** pour ainsi dire; **it's a ~ of speaking** c'est une façon de parler; ~ **of payment** mode *m* de paiement; **(as) to the ~ born** comme s'il (*or* elle *etc*) avait cela dans le sang.
(b) (*behaviour, attitude*) façon *f* de se conduire *or* de se comporter, attitude *f*, comportement *m*. **his ~ to his mother** son attitude envers sa mère, sa manière de se conduire avec sa mère; **I don't like his ~** je n'aime pas son attitude; **there's something odd about his ~** il y a quelque chose de bizarre dans son comportement.
(c) (*social behaviour*) ~**s** manières *fpl*; **good ~s** bonnes manières, savoir-vivre *m*; **bad ~s** mauvaises manières; **it's good/bad ~s (to do)** cela se fait/ne se fait pas (de faire); **he has no ~s, his ~s are terrible** il ne sait pas se conduire, il a de très mauvaises manières, il n'a aucun savoir-vivre; (*to child*) **aren't you forgetting your ~s?** est-ce que c'est comme ça qu'on se tient?; **road ~s** politesse routière *or* au volant.
(d) (*social customs*) ~**s** mœurs *fpl*, usages *mpl*; **novel of ~s** roman *m* de mœurs; *V* **comedy**.
(e) (*class, sort, type*) sorte *f*, genre *m*. **all ~ of birds** toutes sortes d'oiseaux; **no ~ of doubt** aucun doute; *V* **mean**[2].
mannered [ˈmænəd] *adj person, style, book etc* maniéré, affecté.
-mannered [ˈmænəd] *adj ending in cpds*: **well-mannered** bien élevé; **rough-mannered** brusque, aux manières rudes; *V* **bad** *etc*.
mannerism [ˈmænərɪzəm] *n* **(a)** (*habit, trick of speech etc*) trait particulier; (*pej*) tic *m*, manie *f*. **(b)** (*U: Art, Literat etc*) maniérisme *m*.
mannerist [ˈmænərɪst] *adj, n* maniériste (*mf*).
mannerliness [ˈmænəlɪnɪs] *n* politesse *f*, courtoisie *f*, savoir-vivre *m*.
mannerly [ˈmænəlɪ] *adj* poli, bien élevé, courtois.
man(n)ikin [ˈmænɪkɪn] *n* **(a)** (*dwarf etc*) homoncule *m*, nabot *m*. **(b)** (*Art, Dressmaking*) mannequin *m* (*objet*).
mannish [ˈmænɪʃ] *adj woman* masculin, hommasse (*pej*); *style, clothes* masculin.
manœuvrability, (*US*) **maneuverability** [məˌnuːvrəˈbɪlɪtɪ] *n* manœuvrabilité *f*, maniabilité *f*.
manœuvrable, (*US*) **maneuverable** [məˈnuːvrəbl] *adj* manœuvrable, maniable.
manœuvre, (*US*) **maneuver** [məˈnuːvəʳ] 1 *n* (*all senses*) manœuvre *f*. (*Mil etc*) **to be on ~s** faire des *or* être en manœuvres.
2 *vt* (*all senses*) manœuvrer. **they ~d the gun into position** ils ont manœuvré le canon pour le mettre en position; **they ~d the enemy away from the city** leur manœuvre a réussi à éloigner l'ennemi de la ville; **he ~d the car through the gate** il a pu à force de manœuvres faire passer la voiture par le portail; **to ~ sth out/in/through** *etc* faire sortir/entrer/traverser *etc* qch en manœuvrant; **to ~ sb into doing sth** manœuvrer qn pour qu'il fasse qch; **can you ~ him into another job?** pouvez-vous user de votre influence pour lui faire changer son emploi?
3 *vi* (*all senses*) manœuvrer.
manor [ˈmænəʳ] *n* **(a)** (*also* ~ **house**) manoir *m*, gentilhommière *f*. **(b)** (*Hist: estate*) domaine seigneurial; *V* **lord**. **(c)** (*Brit: Police etc sl*) fief *m*.
manorial [məˈnɔːrɪəl] *adj* seigneurial.
manpower [ˈmænˌpaʊəʳ] *n* (*U*) **(a)** (*men available*) (*gen, Ind*) main-d'œuvre *f*; (*Mil etc*) effectifs *mpl*. **(b)** (*physical exertion*) force *f* physique. **he did it by sheer ~** il l'a fait uniquement par la force.
manse [mæns] *n* presbytère *m* (*d'un pasteur presbytérien*).
mansion [ˈmænʃən] *n* (*in town*) hôtel particulier; (*in country*) château *m*, manoir *m*. **the M~ House** *la résidence officielle du Lord Mayor de Londres*.
mansuetude [ˈmænswɪtjuːd] *n* mansuétude *f*, douceur *f*.
mantel [ˈmæntl] *n* **(a)** (*also* ~**piece**, ~**shelf**) (dessus *m or* tablette *f* de) cheminée *f*. **(b)** (*structure round fireplace*) manteau *m*, chambranle *m* (de cheminée).
mantilla [mænˈtɪlə] *n* mantille *f*.
mantis [ˈmæntɪs] *n* mante *f*; *V* **praying**.
mantle [ˈmæntl] 1 *n* **(a)** (*cloak*) cape *f*; *[lady]* (†) mante *f*. (*liter*) ~ **of snow** manteau *m* de neige. **(b)** *[gas lamp]* manchon *m*; *V* **gas**. 2 *vt* (*liter*) (re)couvrir.
manual [ˈmænjʊəl] 1 *adj labour, skill, controls* manuel. ~ **worker** travailleur manuel. 2 *n* **(a)** (*book*) manuel *m*. **(b)** *[organ]* clavier *m*.
manually [ˈmænjʊəlɪ] *adv* à la main, manuellement.
manufacture [ˌmænjʊˈfæktʃəʳ] 1 *n* **(a)** (*U*) fabrication *f*; *[clothes]* confection *f*.
(b) ~**s** produits manufacturés.
2 *vt* fabriquer; *clothes* confectionner; (*fig*) *story, excuse* fabriquer. **~d goods** produits manufacturés; **the manufacturing industries** les industries *fpl* de fabrication.
manufacturer [ˌmænjʊˈfæktʃərəʳ] *n* fabricant *m*.
manure [məˈnjʊəʳ] 1 *n* (*U*) (*farmyard* ~) fumier *m*; (*artificial* ~) engrais *m*. **liquid ~** purin *m*; *V* **horse**. 2 *cpd*: **manure heap** (tas *m* de) fumier *m*. 3 *vt* fumer, répandre des engrais sur.
manuscript [ˈmænjʊskrɪpt] 1 *n* manuscrit *m*. **in ~** (*not yet printed*) sous forme de manuscrit; (*handwritten*) écrit à la main. 2 *adj* manuscrit, écrit à la main.
Manx [mæŋks] 1 *adj* de l'île de Man. ~ **cat** chat *m* de l'île de Man; **~man** natif *m or* habitant *m* de l'île de Man. 2 *n* **(a) the ~** les habitants *mpl or* les natifs *mpl* de l'île de Man. **(b)** (*Ling*) mannois *m*.
many [ˈmenɪ] 1 *adj, pron, comp* **more,** *superl* **most** **(a)** beaucoup (de), un grand nombre (de). ~ **books** beaucoup de livres, un grand nombre de livres, de nombreux livres; **very ~ books** un très grand nombre de livres, de très nombreux livres; ~ **of those books** un grand nombre de ces livres; **a good ~ of those books** (un) bon nombre de ces livres; ~ **people** beaucoup de gens *or* de monde, bien des gens; ~ **came** beaucoup sont venus; ~ **believe that to be true** bien des gens croient que c'est vrai; ~ **of them** un grand nombre d'entre eux; **the ~** (*the masses*) la multitude, la foule; **the ~ who admire him** le grand nombre de gens qui l'admirent; ~ **times** bien des fois; ~ **a time, ~'s the time*** maintes fois, souvent; **before ~ days** avant qu'il soit longtemps, avant peu de jours; **I've lived here for ~ years** j'habite ici depuis des années *or* depuis (bien) longtemps; **he lived there for ~ years** il vécut là de nombreuses années *or* de longues années; **people of ~ kinds** des gens de toutes sortes; **a good** *or* **great ~ things** pas mal de choses*; **in ~ cases** dans bien des cas, dans de nombreux cas; ~ **a man would be grateful** il y en a plus d'un qui serait reconnaissant; **a woman of ~ moods** une femme d'humeur changeante; **a man of ~ parts** un homme qui a des talents très divers; ~ **happy returns (of the day)!** bon *or* joyeux anniversaire!
(b) (*in phrases*) **I have as ~ books as you** j'ai autant de livres que vous; **I have as ~ as you** j'en ai autant que vous; **as ~ as wish to come** tous ceux qui désirent venir; **as ~ as 100 people**

are expected on attend jusqu'à 100 personnes; **there were as ~ again outside the hall** il y en avait encore autant dehors que dans la salle; **how ~?** combien?; **how ~ people?** combien de gens?; **how ~ there are!** qu'ils sont nombreux!; **however ~ books you have** quel que soit le nombre de livres que vous ayez; **however ~ there may be** quel que soit leur nombre; **so ~ have said it** il y en a tant qui l'ont dit; **I've got so ~ already (that ...)** j'en ai déjà tant (que ...); **there were so ~ (that ...)** il y en avait tant (que ...); **so ~ dresses** tant de robes; **ever so ~ times** je ne sais combien de fois; **they ran away like so ~ sheep** ils se sont sauvés comme un troupeau de moutons; **he did not say that in so ~ words** il n'a pas dit cela explicitement; **there were too ~** il y en avait trop; **too ~ cakes** trop de gâteaux; **3 too ~** 3 de trop; **20 would not be too ~** il n'y en aurait pas trop de 20; (*fig*) **he's had one too ~*** il a bu un coup de trop; **I've got too ~ already** j'en ai déjà trop; **there are too ~ of you** vous êtes trop nombreux; **too ~ of these books** trop de ces livres; **I've told too ~ of the children** j'ai mis trop d'enfants au courant; **too ~ of us know that ...** nous sommes trop (nombreux) à savoir que ....

2 *cpd*: **many-coloured,** (*liter*) **many-hued** multicolore; **many-sided** *object* qui a de nombreux côtés; (*fig*) *person* aux intérêts (*or* talents) variés *or* multiples; *problem* complexe, qui a de nombreuses facettes.

Maoist ['maʊɪst] *adj, n* maoïste (*mf*).

Maori ['maʊrɪ] 1 *adj* maori. 2 *n* (a) Maori(e) *m(f)*. (b) (*Ling*) maori *m*.

map [mæp] 1 *n* carte *f*; plan *m*. **geological/historical/linguistic ~** carte géologique/historique/linguistique; **~ of France** carte de la France; **~ of Paris/the Underground** plan *m* de Paris/du métro; (*fig*) **this will put Tooting on the ~** cela fera connaître Tooting, cela mettra Tooting en vedette; (*fig*) **the whole town was wiped off the ~** la ville entière fut rasée; (*fig*) **off the ~*** (*distant*) à l'autre bout du monde; (*unimportant*) perdu; *V* **relief.**

2 *cpd*: **mapmaker** cartographe *m*; **mapmaking** cartographie *f*; **mapping pen** plume *f* de dessinateur *or* à dessin.

3 *vt country, district etc* faire *or* dresser la carte de; *route* tracer.

map out *vt sep route, plans* tracer; *book, essay* établir les grandes lignes de; *one's time, career, day* organiser. **he hasn't yet mapped out what he will do** il n'a pas encore de plan précis de ce qu'il va faire.

maple ['meɪpl] 1 *n* érable *m*. 2 *cpd*: **maple leaf/sugar/syrup** feuille *f*/sucre *m*/sirop *m* d'érable.

mar [mɑːʳ] *vt* gâter, gâcher; *V* **make.**

maraschino [ˌmærəs'kiːnəʊ] *n* marasquin *m*. **~ cherries** cerises *fpl* au marasquin.

marathon ['mærəθən] 1 *n* (*Sport, fig*) marathon *m*. 2 *adj* marathon *inv*. **a ~ session** une séance-marathon.

maraud [mə'rɔːd] *vi* marauder, être en maraude. **to go ~ing** aller à la maraude.

marauder [mə'rɔːdəʳ] *n* maraudeur *m*, -euse *f*.

marauding [mə'rɔːdɪŋ] 1 *adj* maraudeur, en maraude. 2 *n* maraude *f*.

marble ['mɑːbl] 1 *n* (a) marbre *m*. **the Elgin ~s** *partie de la frise du Parthénon conservée au British Museum.*

(b) (*toy*) bille *f*. **to play ~s** jouer aux billes.

2 *cpd staircase* de *or* en marbre; *industry* marbrier. **marble quarry** marbrière *f*.

3 *vt* marbrer.

March [mɑːtʃ] *n* mars *m*; *V* **mad**; *for other phrases V* **September.**

march[1] [mɑːtʃ] 1 *n* (a) (*Mil etc*) marche *f*. **on the ~** en marche; **quick/slow ~** marche rapide/lente; **a day's ~** une journée de marche; **a 10-km ~, a ~ of 10 km** une marche de 10 km; **the ~ on Rome** la marche sur Rome; (*fig*) **~ of time/progress** la marche du temps/progrès; *V* **forced, route, steal** *etc.*

(b) (*Mus*) marche *f*; *V* **dead.**

2 *cpd*: (*Mil*) **marching orders** feuille *f* de route (*V also* **order**); (*fig*) **to give sb his marching orders*** flanquer* qn à la porte, envoyer promener qn; (*fig*) **to get one's marching orders** se faire mettre à la porte; **marching song** chanson *f* de route; (*Mil etc*) **march-past** défilé *m*.

3 *vi* (a) (*Mil etc*) marcher au pas. **to ~ into battle** marcher au combat; **the army ~ed in/out/through** *etc* l'armée entra/sortit/traversa *etc* (au pas); **to ~ past** défiler; **to ~ past sb** défiler devant qn; **~!** marche!; *V* **forward, quick** *etc.*

(b) (*gen*) **to ~ in/out/up** *etc* entrer/sortir/monter *etc* (*briskly*) d'un pas énergique *or* (*angrily*) d'un air furieux; **he ~ed up to me** il s'est approché de moi d'un air décidé; **to ~ up and down the room** faire les cent pas dans la pièce, arpenter la pièce.

4 *vt* (a) (*Mil*) faire marcher (au pas). **to ~ troops in/out** *etc* faire entrer/faire sortir *etc* des troupes (au pas).

(b) (*fig*) **to ~ sb in/out/away** faire entrer/faire sortir/emmener qn tambour battant; **to ~ sb off to prison** embarquer qn en prison*.

march[2] [mɑːtʃ] *n* (*gen pl*) **~es** (*border*) frontière *f*; (*borderlands*) marche *f*.

marchioness ['mɑːʃənɪs] *n* marquise *f* (*personne*).

mare [mɛəʳ] *n* jument *f*. (*fig*) **his discovery turned out to be a ~'s nest** sa découverte s'est révélée très décevante.

Margaret ['mɑːgərɪt] *n* Marguerite *f*.

margarine [ˌmɑːdʒə'riːn] *n* margarine *f*. **whipped** *or* **soft ~** margarine ultra-légère.

marge* [mɑːdʒ] *n Brit abbr of* **margarine.**

margin ['mɑːdʒɪn] *n [book, page]* marge *f*; *[river, lake]* bord *m*; *[wood]* lisière *f*; (*fig: Comm, Econ, gen*) marge. **notes in the ~** notes en marge *or* marginales; **do not write in the ~** n'écrivez pas dans la marge; (*Typ*) **wide/narrow ~** grande/petite marge; (*fig*) **to win by a wide/narrow ~** gagner de loin/de peu; **elected by a narrow ~** élu avec peu de voix de majorité; **to allow a ~ for** laisser une marge pour; **to allow for a ~ of error** prévoir une marge d'erreur; **~ of profit** marge (bénéficiaire); **~ of safety** marge de sécurité.

marginal ['mɑːdʒɪnl] 1 *adj comments, benefit, profit, business* marginal. **he's of ~ ability** il est tout juste compétent; **a ~ case** un cas limite; (*Agr*) **~ land** terre *f* difficilement cultivable et de faible rendement; (*Parl*) **~ seat** siège disputé. 2 *n* (*Parl*) siège disputé.

marginally ['mɑːdʒɪnəlɪ] *adv* très légèrement, de très peu.

marguerite [ˌmɑːgə'riːt] *n* marguerite *f*.

Maria [mə'raɪə] *n* Marie *f*; *V* **black.**

marigold ['mærɪgəʊld] *n* (*Bot*) souci *m*.

marihuana, marijuana [ˌmærɪ'hwɑːnə] *n* marihuana *f or* marijuana *f*.

marina [mə'riːnə] *n* marina *f*.

marinade [ˌmærɪ'neɪd] 1 *n* marinade *f*. 2 *vt* mariner.

marinate ['mærɪneɪt] *vt* mariner.

marine [mə'riːn] 1 *adj* (*in the sea*) *plant, animal* marin; (*from the sea*) *products* de mer; (*by the sea*) *vegetation, forces, stores* maritime. **~ engineer** ingénieur *m* du génie maritime; **~ engineering** génie *m* maritime; **~ insurance** assurance *f* maritime; **~ life** vie marine.

2 *n* (a) (*Naut*) **mercantile ~, merchant ~** marine marchande.

(b) (*Mil*) fusilier marin. **M~s** (*Brit*) fusiliers marins; (*US*) marines *mpl* (américains); (*fig*) **tell that to the ~s!** à d'autres!

mariner ['mærɪnəʳ] *n* (*liter*) marin *m*. **~'s compass** boussole *f*, compas *m*; *V* **master.**

mariolatry [ˌmɛərɪ'ɒlətrɪ] *n* (*Rel*) vénération excessive de la Vierge.

marionette [ˌmærɪə'net] *n* marionnette *f*.

marital ['mærɪtl] *adj* (a) *problems* matrimonial; *happiness* conjugal. (*Jur*) **~ relations** rapports conjugaux; (*Admin*) **~ status** situation *f* de famille. (b) (*concerning husband*) marital.

maritime ['mærɪtaɪm] *adj* maritime. **~ law** droit *m* maritime.

marjoram ['mɑːdʒərəm] *n* marjolaine *f*.

Mark [mɑːk] *n* Marc *m*.

mark[1] [mɑːk] *n* (*currency*) mark *m*; (††: *weight*) marc *m*.

mark[2] [mɑːk] 1 *n* (a) (*written symbol on paper, cloth etc*) marque *f*, signe *m*; (*as signature*) marque, signe, croix *f*; (*on animal, body etc*) tache *f*, marque; (*Comm: label*) marque, étiquette *f*; (*stain*) marque, tache, trace *f*. **I have made a ~ on the pages I want to keep** j'ai marqué les pages que je veux garder; (*as signature*) **to make one's ~** faire une marque *or* une croix; (*fig*) **to make one's ~ as a poet** se faire un nom en tant que poète, s'imposer comme poète; (*fig*) **he has certainly made his ~** il s'est certainement imposé; **the ~s of his shoes in the soil** l'empreinte *f* de ses souliers sur le sol; **without a ~ on his body** sans trace de coups *or* de blessures sur le corps; **the ~ on this farmer's cattle** la marque (au fer rouge) sur le bétail de ce fermier; (*fig*) **to leave one's ~ on sth** laisser son empreinte sur qch; (*fig*) **it is the ~ of a gentleman** c'est un signe de bonne éducation; **the ~s of violence were visible everywhere** les marques *or* traces de violence étaient visibles partout; **it bears the ~(s) of genius** cela porte la marque du génie; **as a ~ of my gratitude** en témoignage de ma gratitude; **as a ~ of respect** en signe de respect; **as a ~ of our disapproval** pour marquer notre désapprobation; **printer's ~** marque de l'imprimeur; **punctuation ~** signe de ponctuation; **that will leave a ~** cela laissera une marque; **this ~ won't come out** cette marque *or* tache ne partira pas; **finger ~** marque *or* trace de doigt; *V* **foot, hall, trade** *etc.*

(b) (*Scol*) note *f*; point *m*. **good/bad ~** bonne/mauvaise note; **the ~ is out of 20** c'est une note sur 20; **you need 50 ~s to pass** il faut avoir 50 points pour être reçu; **to fail by 2 ~s** échouer à 2 points; **she got a good ~ in French** elle a eu une bonne note en français; (*fig*) **you get no ~s at all as a cook** tu mérites (un) zéro comme cuisinière; (*fig iro*) **there are no ~s for guessing his name** il n'y a pas besoin d'être un génie pour savoir de qui je parle.

(c) (*Sport etc: target*) but *m*, cible *f*. **to hit the ~** (*lit*) atteindre *or* toucher le but; (*fig*) mettre le doigt dessus*; (*lit*) **to miss the ~** manquer le but; (*fig*) **to miss the ~, to be wide of the ~** *or* **off the ~** *or* **far from the ~** être loin de la vérité; (*fig*) **that's beside the ~** c'est à côté de la question; (*pej*) **he's an easy ~** il se fait avoir* facilement.

(d) (*Sport*) ligne *f* de départ; (*Rugby*) arrêt *m* de volée. **on your ~s! get set! go!** à vos marques! prêts! partez!; (*lit, fig*) **to get off the ~** démarrer; (*fig*) **to be quick off the ~** (*quick on the uptake*) avoir l'esprit vif; (*quick reactions*) avoir des réactions rapides; (*fig*) **to be quick off the ~ in doing sth** ne pas perdre de temps pour faire qch; (*fig*) **I don't feel up to the ~** je ne suis pas dans mon assiette, je ne suis pas en forme; **he is not up to the ~ for this job** il n'est pas à la hauteur de ce travail; **this work is hardly up to the ~** cet ouvrage laisse beaucoup à désirer; **to come up to the ~** répondre à l'attente; *V* **overstep.**

(e) (*Mil, Tech: model, type*) **M~** série *f*; **Concorde M~ I** Concorde première série.

2 *cpd*: **marksman** *V* **marksman**; (*Comm*) **mark-up** (*profit*) marge *f* bénéficiaire (*du détaillant*); (*increase*) hausse *f*.

3 *vt* (a) (*make a ~ on*) marquer, mettre une marque à *or* sur; *paragraph, item, linen, suitcase* marquer; (*stain*) tacher, marquer. **to ~ the cards** maquiller *or* marquer les cartes; **to ~ a shirt with one's name** marquer son nom sur une chemise; **I hope your dress isn't ~ed** j'espère que ta robe n'est pas tachée; **the accident ~ed him for life** l'accident l'a marqué pour la vie; **suffering had ~ed him** la douleur l'avait marqué; **a bird ~ed with red** un oiseau tacheté de rouge.

(b) (*indicate*) marquer; *price etc* marquer, indiquer; (*St Ex*) coter; (*Sport*) *score* marquer. **X ~s the spot** l'endroit est marqué d'une croix; **this flag ~s the frontier** ce drapeau marque la frontière; **it ~s a change of policy** cela indique un changement de politique; **in order to ~ the occasion** pour marquer l'occasion; **this ~s him as a future manager** ceci fait présager pour lui une carrière de cadre; **his reign was ~ed by civil wars** son règne fut marqué par des guerres civiles; **to ~ time** (*Mil*) marquer le pas; (*fig*) faire du sur place, piétiner; (*by choice*) attendre son heure; *V also* **marked**.

(c) (*Scol etc*) *essay, exam* corriger, noter; *candidate* noter, donner une note à. **to ~ sth right/wrong** marquer qch juste/faux.

(d) (*note, pay attention to*) noter, faire attention à; (*Sport*) *opposing player* marquer. **~ my words!** écoutez-moi bien!, notez bien ce que je vous dis!; **~ you, he may have been right** remarquez qu'il avait peut-être raison; **~ him well**† observez-le bien.

4 *vi*: **this material ~s easily/will not ~** tout marque *or* se voit/rien ne se voit sur ce tissu.

mark down *vt sep* **(a)** (*write down*) inscrire, noter.

(b) (*reduce*) *price* baisser; *goods* baisser le prix de; (*Scol*) *exercise, pupil* baisser la note de. **all these items have been marked down for the sales** tous ces articles ont été démarqués pour les soldes; (*St Ex*) **to be marked down** s'inscrire en baisse, reculer.

(c) (*single out*) *person* désigner, prévoir (*for* pour).

mark off *vt sep* **(a)** (*separate*) séparer, distinguer (*from* de).

(b) (*Surv etc*) (*divide by boundary*) délimiter; *distance* mesurer; *road, boundary* tracer.

(c) *list* cocher. **he marked the names off as the people went in** il cochait les noms (sur la liste) à mesure que les gens entraient.

mark out *vt sep* **(a)** *zone, etc* délimiter, tracer les limites de; (*with stakes etc*) jalonner; *field* borner. **to mark out a tennis court** tracer les lignes d'un (court de) tennis; **the road is marked out with flags** la route est balisée de drapeaux.

(b) (*single out*) désigner, distinguer. **to mark sb out for promotion** désigner qn pour l'avancement; **he was marked out long ago for that job** il y a longtemps qu'on l'avait prévu pour ce poste; **his red hair marked him out from the others** ses cheveux roux le distinguaient des autres.

mark up 1 *vt sep* **(a)** (*on board, wall etc*) *price, score* marquer.

(b) (*Comm: put a price on*) indiquer *or* marquer le prix de. **these items have not been marked up** le prix n'est pas marqué sur ces articles; (*St Ex*) **to be marked up** s'inscrire en hausse, avancer.

(c) (*increase*) *price* hausser, augmenter, majorer; *goods* majorer le prix de. **all these chairs have been marked up** toutes ces chaises ont augmenté.

2 mark-up *n V* **mark²2.**

marked [mɑːkt] *adj difference, accent, bias* marqué, prononcé; *improvement, increase* sensible, manifeste. **it is becoming more ~** cela s'accentue; **he is a ~ man** (*Police etc*) c'est un homme marqué, c'est un suspect; (* *hum*) on l'a à l'œil*.

markedly ['mɑːkɪdlɪ] *adv* (*V* **marked**) d'une façon marquée *or* prononcée; sensiblement, visiblement, manifestement.

marker ['mɑːkəʳ] *n* (*person*) marqueur *m*, -euse *f*; (*Sport*) marqueur; (*flag, stake*) marque *f*, jalon *m*; *[ski course etc]* jalon; (*bookmark*) signet *m*; (*tool, also for linen*) marquoir *m*; (*pen*) (crayon *m*) feutre *m*, marker *m*.

market ['mɑːkɪt] **1** *n* **(a)** (*trade; place; also St Ex*) marché *m*. **to go to ~** aller au marché; **the wholesale ~** le marché de gros; **cattle ~** marché *or* foire *f* aux bestiaux; **the sugar ~, the ~ in sugar** le marché du *or* des sucre(s); **the world coffee ~** le marché mondial du *or* des café(s); **free ~** marché libre; (*St Ex*) **a dull/lively ~** un marché lourd/actif; (*St Ex*) **the ~ is rising/falling** les cours *mpl* sont en hausse/en baisse; *V* **black, buyer, common** *etc*.

(b) (*fig*) marché *m*, débouché *m*, clientèle *f*. **to have a good ~ for sth** avoir une grosse demande pour qch; **to find a ready ~ for sth** trouver facilement un marché *or* des débouchés pour qch; **there is a (ready) ~ for small cars** les petites voitures se vendent bien *or* sont d'une vente facile; **there's no ~ for pink socks** les chaussettes roses ne se vendent pas; **this appeals to the French ~** cela plaît à la clientèle française, cela se vend bien en France; **home/overseas/world ~** marché intérieur/d'outre-mer/mondial; **to be in the ~ for sth** être acheteur de qch; **to put sth/to be on the ~** mettre qch/être en vente *or* dans le commerce *or* sur le marché; **it's the dearest car on the ~** c'est la voiture la plus chère sur le marché; **on the open ~** en vente libre; *V* **flood** *etc*.

2 *cpd*: **market analysis** analyse *f* de marché; **market cross** croix *f* sur la place du marché; **market day** jour *m* de marché; (*Brit*) **market garden** jardin maraîcher; (*Brit*) **market gardener** maraîcher *m*, -ère *f*; (*Brit*) **market gardening** culture maraîchère; **market place** place *f* du marché; (*Comm*) **market price** prix marchand; **at market price** au cours, au prix courant; (*St Ex*) **market prices** cours *m* du marché; **market rates** taux *m* du cours libre; **market research** étude *f* de marché (*in* de); **market square = market place**; (*St Ex*) **market trends** tendances *fpl* du marché; **market value** valeur marchande.

3 *vt* (*sell*) vendre; (*launch*) lancer sur le marché; (*find outlet for*) trouver un *or* des débouché(s) pour.

4 *vi*: **to go ~ing** aller faire son marché.

marketability [ˌmɑːkɪtəˈbɪlɪtɪ] *n* possibilité *f* de commercialisation.

marketable ['mɑːkɪtəbl] *adj* vendable. **very ~** de bonne vente.

marketeer [ˌmɑːkəˈtɪəʳ] *n* **(a)** *V* **black. (b)** (*Brit Pol*) **(pro-) M~s** ceux qui sont en faveur du Marché Commun; **anti-M~s** ceux qui s'opposent au Marché Commun.

marketing ['mɑːkɪtɪŋ] *n* commercialisation *f*, marketing *m*.

marking ['mɑːkɪŋ] **1** *n* **(a)** (*U [animals, trees, goods]* marquage *m*. **(b)** (*Scol*) correction *f* (de copies). **(c)** *[animal]* marques *fpl*, taches *fpl*. **the ~s on the road** la signalisation horizontale. **2** *cpd*: **marking ink** encre *f* à marquer.

marksman ['mɑːksmən] *n* bon tireur, tireur d'élite.

marksmanship ['mɑːksmənʃɪp] *n* adresse *f* au tir.

marl [mɑːl] (*Geol*) **1** *n* marne *f*. **2** *vt* marner.

marlin ['mɑːlɪn] *n* (*fish*) makaire *m*.

marlin(e) ['mɑːlɪn] *n* (*Naut*) lusin *m*. **~spike** épissoir *m*.

marly ['mɑːlɪ] *adj* marneux.

marmalade ['mɑːməleɪd] *n* confiture *f* d'orange (*or* de citron *etc*). **~ orange** orange amère, bigarade *f*.

marmoreal [mɑːˈmɔːrɪəl] *adj* (*liter*) marmoréen.

marmoset ['mɑːməʊzet] *n* ouistiti *m*.

marmot ['mɑːmət] *n* marmotte *f*.

maroon¹ [məˈruːn] *adj* (*colour*) bordeaux *inv*.

maroon² [məˈruːn] *n* (*firework; signal*) pétard *m*.

maroon³ [məˈruːn] *vt* abandonner (sur une île *or* une côte déserte); (*fig*) bloquer.

marquee [mɑːˈkiː] *n* **(a)** (*esp Brit*) (*tent*) grande tente; (*in circus*) chapiteau *m*. **(b)** (*awning*) auvent *m*.

marquess ['mɑːkwɪs] *n* marquis *m*.

marquetry ['mɑːkɪtrɪ] **1** *n* marqueterie *f*. **2** *cpd table etc* de *or* en marqueterie.

marquis ['mɑːkwɪs] *n* = **marquess.**

marriage ['mærɪdʒ] **1** *n* mariage *m*; (*fig*) mariage, alliance *f*. **to give in ~** donner en mariage; **to take in ~** épouser; **civil ~** mariage civil; **~ of convenience** mariage de convenance; **aunt by ~** tante par alliance; **they are related by ~** ils sont parents par alliance; *V* **offer, shot** *etc*.

2 *cpd*: **marriage bed** lit conjugal; **marriage bonds** liens conjugaux; **marriage broker** agent matrimonial; **marriage bureau** agence matrimoniale; **marriage ceremony** mariage *m*; (*Rel*) bénédiction nuptiale; **marriage certificate** extrait *m* d'acte de mariage; **marriage customs** traditions *fpl* de mariage; **marriage guidance counsellor** conseiller *m*, -ère *f* conjugal(e); **marriage licence** ≃ dispense *f* de bans; (*Brit*) **marriage lines = marriage certificate**; **marriage partner** conjoint(e) *m(f)*, époux *m*, épouse *f*; **marriage rate** taux *m* de nuptialité; **marriage settlement** ≃ constitution *f* de rente sur la tête de l'épouse survivante; **marriage vows** vœux *mpl* de mariage.

marriageable ['mærɪdʒəbl] *adj* mariable, nubile. **of ~ age** en âge de se marier; **he's very ~** c'est un très bon parti.

married ['mærɪd] *adj man, woman* marié; *life, love* conjugal. **he is a ~ man** il est marié; **~ couple** couple *m* (marié); **the newly ~ couple** les (nouveaux) mariés; **~ name** nom *m* de femme mariée; (*Mil etc*) **~ quarters** appartements *mpl* pour familles (*dans une caserne*); *V also* **marry.**

marrow ['mærəʊ] *n* **(a)** *[bone]* moelle *f*; (*fig*) essence *f*, moelle. **~bone** os *m* à moelle; **to be chilled *or* frozen to the ~** être gelé jusqu'à la moelle des os. **(b)** (*Brit: vegetable*) courge *f*. **baby ~** courgette *f*.

marry ['mærɪ] **1** *vt* **(a)** (*take in marriage*) épouser, se marier avec. **will you ~ me?** voulez-vous m'épouser?; **to get *or* be married** se marier; **they've been married for 10 years** ils sont mariés depuis 10 ans; **to ~ money** épouser une fortune.

(b) (*give or join in marriage*) marier. **he has 3 daughters to ~ (off)** il a 3 filles à marier; **she married (off) her daughter to a lawyer** elle a marié sa fille avec *or* à un avocat.

2 *vi* se marier. **to ~ into a family** s'allier à une famille par le mariage, s'apparenter à une famille; **to ~ beneath o.s.** se mésallier; **to ~ again** se remarier.

marry off *vt sep [parent etc]* marier; *V* **marry 1b.**

Mars [mɑːz] *n* (*Astron*) Mars *f*; (*Myth*) Mars *m*.

Marseillaise [ˌmɑːsəˈleɪz] *n* Marseillaise *f*.

Marseilles [mɑːˈseɪlz] *n* Marseille.

marsh [mɑːʃ] **1** *n* marais *m*, marécage *m*; *V* **salt.**

2 *cpd*: **marsh fever** paludisme *m*; **marsh gas** gaz *m* des marais; **marshland** marécage *m*, marais *m*, région marécageuse; **marshmallow** (*Bot*) guimauve *f*; (*sweet*) (pâte *f* de) guimauve *f*; **marsh marigold** souci *m* d'eau.

marshal ['mɑːʃəl] **1** *n* **(a)** (*Mil etc*) maréchal *m*; *V* **air, field.**

(b) (*Brit: at demonstrations, sports meeting etc*) membre *m* du service d'ordre.

(c) (*US*) (*in police/fire department*) ≃ capitaine *m* de gendarmerie/des pompiers; (*law officer*) *officier fédéral chargé d'exécuter des jugements*.

(d) (*Brit: at Court etc*) chef *m* du protocole.

2 *vt troops* rassembler; *crowd* canaliser; (*Rail*) *wagons* trier; (*fig*) *facts, one's wits* rassembler. **the police ~led the procession into the town** la police a fait entrer le cortège en bon ordre dans la ville.

marshalling ['mɑːʃəlɪŋ] *n* **(a)** *[crowd, demonstrators]* maintien *m* de l'ordre (*of* parmi). **(b)** (*Rail*) triage *m*. **~ yard** gare *f or* centre *m* de triage.

marshy ['mɑːʃɪ] *adj* marécageux.

marsupial [mɑːˈsuːpɪəl] *adj, n* marsupial (*m*).

mart [mɑːt] *n* (*trade centre*) centre commercial; (*market*) marché *m*; (*auction room*) salle *f* des ventes; *V* **property.**

marten ['mɑːtɪn] *n* martre *f or* marte *f*.

martial ['mɑːʃəl] *adj bearing* martial; *music, speech* martial, guerrier. **~ law** loi martiale.

Martian ['mɑːʃɪən] **1** *n* Martien(ne) *m(f)*. **2** *adj* martien.

martin ['mɑːtɪn] *n* (*Orn*) martinet *m*.

martinet [ˌmɑːtɪˈnet] *n*: **to be a ~** être impitoyable *or* intraitable en matière de discipline.

Martinmas ['mɑːtɪnməs] *n* la Saint-Martin.

martyr ['mɑːtəʳ] **1** *n* (*Rel, fig*) martyr(e) *m(f)* (*to* de). **a ~'s crown** la couronne du martyre; **he is a ~ to migraine** ses mi-

graines lui font souffrir le martyre; **don't be such a ~!** cesse de jouer les martyrs! 2 *vt* (*Rel, fig*) martyriser.
martyrdom ['mɑːtədəm] *n* (*U*) (*Rel*) martyre *m*; (*fig*) martyre, calvaire *m*, supplice(s) *m(pl)*.
martyrize ['mɑːtɪraɪz] *vt* (*Rel, fig*) martyriser.
marvel ['mɑːvəl] 1 *n* merveille *f*, prodige *m*, miracle *m*. **the ~s of modern science** les prodiges de la science moderne; **his work is a ~ of patience** son œuvre est une merveille de patience; **if he gets there it will be a ~** ce sera (un) miracle s'il y arrive; **it's a ~ to me how he does it** je ne sais vraiment pas comment il peut le faire; **it's a ~ to me that** cela me paraît un miracle que + *subj*, je n'en reviens pas que + *subj*; **it's a ~ that** c'est un miracle que + *subj*; *V* **work**.
2 *vi* s'émerveiller, s'étonner (*at* de).
3 *vt* s'étonner (*that* de ce que + *indic or subj*). **to ~ how/why** se demander avec stupéfaction comment/pourquoi.
marvellous, (*US*) **marvelous** ['mɑːvələs] *adj* (*astonishing*) merveilleux, étonnant, extraordinaire; (*miraculous*) miraculeux; (*excellent*) merveilleux, magnifique, formidable*, sensationnel*. (*iro*) **isn't it ~!** ce n'est pas extraordinaire, ça?* (*iro*).
marvellously, (*US*) **marvelously** ['mɑːvələslɪ] *adv* merveilleusement, à merveille.
Marxian ['mɑːksɪən] *adj* marxien.
Marxism ['mɑːksɪzəm] *n* marxisme *m*.
Marxist ['mɑːksɪst] *adj, n* marxiste (*mf*).
Mary ['mɛərɪ] *n* Marie *f*. **~ Queen of Scots, ~ Stuart** Marie Stuart; *V* **bloody**.
marzipan [ˌmɑːzɪ'pæn] 1 *n* pâte *f* d'amandes, massepain *m*. 2 *cpd sweet etc* à la pâte d'amandes.
mascara [mæs'kɑːrə] *n* mascara *m*.
mascot ['mæskət] *n* mascotte *f*, porte-bonheur *m inv*.
masculine ['mæskjʊlɪn] 1 *adj sex, voice, courage* masculin, mâle; *woman* masculin, hommasse (*pej*); *gender, rhyme* masculin. **this word is ~** ce mot est (du) masculin. 2 *n* (*Gram*) masculin *m*.
masculinity [ˌmæskjʊ'lɪnɪtɪ] *n* masculinité *f*.
maser ['meɪzəʳ] *n* maser *m*.
mash [mæʃ] 1 *n* (*for horses*) mash *m*; (*for pigs, hens etc*) pâtée *f*; (*Brit Culin: potatoes*) purée *f* (de pommes de terre); (*Brewing*) pâte *f*; (*soft mixture*) bouillie *f*; (*pulp*) pulpe *f*. 2 *vt* **(a)** (*crush: also ~ up*) écraser, broyer; (*Culin*) *potatoes* faire en purée, faire une purée de; (*injure, damage*) écraser. **~ed potatoes** purée *f* (de pommes de terre). **(b)** (*Brewing*) brasser.
masher ['mæʃəʳ] *n* (*Tech*) broyeur *m*; (*in kitchen*) presse-purée *m inv*.
mashie ['mæʃɪ] *n* (*Golf*) mashie *m*.
mask [mɑːsk] 1 *n* (*all senses*) masque *m*; (*in silk or velvet*) masque, loup *m*; *V* **death, gas, iron** *etc*.
2 *vt* **(a)** *person, face* masquer. **~ed ball** bal masqué.
(b) (*hide*) *house, object* masquer, cacher; *truth, motives* masquer, cacher, dissimuler, voiler; *taste, smell* masquer, recouvrir.
(c) (*during painting, spraying*) **~ing tape** papier-cache adhésif.
3 *vi* [*surgeon etc*] se masquer.
masochism ['mæsəʊkɪzəm] *n* masochisme *m*.
masochist ['mæsəʊkɪst] *n* masochiste *mf*.
masochistic [ˌmæsəʊ'kɪstɪk] *adj* masochiste.
mason ['meɪsn] *n* **(a)** (*stoneworker*) maçon *m*; *V* **monumental**. **(b)** (*free~*) (franc-)maçon *m*.
masonic [mə'sɒnɪk] *adj* (franc-)maçonnique.
masonry ['meɪsnrɪ] *n* (*U*) **(a)** (*stonework*) maçonnerie *f*. **(b)** (*free~*) (franc-)maçonnerie *f*.
masque [mɑːsk] *n* (*Theat*) mascarade *f*, comédie-masque *f*.
masquerade [ˌmæskə'reɪd] 1 *n* (*ball*) bal masqué; (*fig*) mascarade *f* (*fig*). 2 *vi*: **to ~ as** se faire passer pour, se déguiser en.
mass¹ [mæs] 1 *n* **(a)** (*U: bulk, size; also Art, Phys*) masse *f*.
(b) [*matter, dough, rocks, air, snow, water etc*] masse *f*. **a ~ of daisies** une multitude de pâquerettes; **the garden was a (solid) ~ of colour** le jardin n'était qu'une masse de couleurs; **he was a ~ of bruises** il était couvert de bleus; **in the ~** dans l'ensemble; **the great ~ of people** la (grande) masse des gens, la (grande) majorité des gens; **~es of*** des masses de*, des tas de*.
(c) (*people*) **the ~(es)** la masse, le peuple, les masses (populaires); **Shakespeare for the ~es** Shakespeare à l'usage des masses.
2 *cpd culture* de masse; *psychology, education* des masses; *resignations* en masse; *demonstration* en masse, massif. **mass funeral** obsèques collectives; **mass grave** fosse commune, charnier *m*; **mass hysteria** hystérie collective; **mass media** media *mpl*, moyens *mpl* de diffusion de l'information; **mass meeting** (*of everyone concerned*) réunion générale; (*huge*) grand rassemblement, meeting *m* monstre; **mass murders** tuerie(s) *f(pl)*; (*Ind*) **mass-produce** fabriquer en série; (*Ind*) **mass production** production *f* or fabrication *f* en série; **mass protests** protestations générales *or* collectives.
3 *vt troops etc* masser.
4 *vi* [*troops, people*] se masser; [*clouds*] s'amonceler.
mass² [mæs] *n* (*Rel*) messe *f*. **to say ~** dire *or* célébrer la messe; **to go to ~** aller à la messe; *V* **black** *etc*.
massacre ['mæsəkəʳ] 1 *n* massacre *m*. **a ~ on the roads** une hécatombe sur les routes. 2 *vt* (*lit, fig*) massacrer.
massage ['mæsɑːʒ] 1 *n* massage *m*. 2 *vt* masser.
masseur [mæ'sɜːʳ] *n* masseur *m*.
masseuse [mæ'sɜːz] *n* masseuse *f*.
massif [mæ'siːf] *n* massif *m*.
massive ['mæsɪv] *adj rock, building, attack, dose, contribution* massif; *suitcase, parcel* énorme; *features* épais (*f* -aisse), lourd; *sound* retentissant.
massively ['mæsɪvlɪ] *adv* massivement.
massiveness ['mæsɪvnɪs] *n* aspect *or* caractère massif.
mast¹ [mɑːst] 1 *n* (*on ship, also flagpole*) mât *m*; (*for radio*) pylône *m*. **the ~s of a ship** la mâture d'un navire; (*Naut*) **to sail before the ~** servir comme simple matelot. 2 *cpd*: (*Naut*) **masthead** tête *f* de mât.
mast² [mɑːst] *n* (*Agr*) *V* **beech**.
-masted ['mɑːstɪd] *adj ending in cpds*: **3-masted** à 3 mâts.
master ['mɑːstəʳ] 1 *n* **(a)** [*household, institution, animal*] maître *m*; [*servant*] maître, employeur *m*; (*Art etc*) maître. **the ~ of the house** le maître de maison; **to be ~ in one's own house** être maître chez soi; **the ~ is not at home**† Monsieur n'est pas là; (*Prov*) **like ~ like man** tel maître tel valet (*Prov*); **I am the ~ now** c'est moi qui commande *or* qui donne les ordres maintenant; (*fig*) **he has met his ~** il a trouvé son maître; **to be one's own ~** être son (propre) maître; **to be ~ of o.s./of the situation** être maître de soi/de la situation; **to be (the) ~ of one's fate** disposer de *or* être (le) maître de son destin; **he is a ~ of the violin** c'est un maître du violon; (*Rel*) **the M~** Jésus-Christ, le Christ; *V* **old, past** *etc*.
(b) (*teacher*) (*in secondary school*) professeur *m*; (*in primary school*) instituteur *m*, maître *m*. **music ~** (*in school*) professeur de musique; (*private tutor*) professeur *or* maître de musique; *V* **fencing** *etc*.
(c) (*Naut*) [*ship*] capitaine *m*; [*liner*] (capitaine) commandant *m*; [*fishing boat*] patron *m*.
(d) (*Univ*) **M~ of Arts/Science** *etc* titulaire *mf* d'une maîtrise ès lettres/sciences *etc*; **a ~'s degree** une maîtrise.
(e) (*Brit Univ*) [*Oxford etc college*] = directeur *m*, principal *m*.
(f) (*title for boys*) monsieur *m*.
2 *cpd scheme, idea* directeur (*f* -trice), maître (*f* maîtresse), principal; *beam* maître; *control, cylinder, switch* principal. (*Naut*) **master-at-arms** capitaine *m* d'armes; **master baker/butcher** *etc* maître boulanger/boucher *etc*; **master bedroom** chambre principale; **master builder** entrepreneur *m* (de bâtiments); (*lit, fig*) **master card** carte maîtresse; **master class** cours *m* de (grand) maître; **master copy** original *m*; **masterful** *V* **masterful**; **masterfully** *V* **masterfully**; **master hand** (*expert*) maître *m*, expert *m*; (*skill*) main *f* de maître; **to be a master hand at (doing) sth** être maître dans l'art de (faire) qch; **master key** passe-partout *m inv*; **masterly** *V* **masterly**; (*Naut*) **master mariner** (*foreign-going*) = capitaine *m* au long cours; (*home trade*) = capitaine de la marine marchande; **mastermind** (*n*) (*genius*) intelligence *f* or esprit *m* supérieur(e), cerveau *m*; (*of plan, crime etc*) cerveau; (*vt*) *operation etc* diriger, organiser; **master of ceremonies** maître *m* des cérémonies; **master of (fox)hounds** grand veneur; **masterpiece** chef-d'œuvre *m*; **master plan** stratégie *f* d'ensemble; **the master race** la race supérieure; **'The Mastersingers'** 'les Maîtres chanteurs' *mpl*; **master stroke** coup magistral *or* de maître.
3 *vt* **(a)** *person, animal, emotion* maîtriser, dompter, mater; *one's defects* surmonter; *difficulty* venir à bout de, surmonter; *situation* se rendre maître de.
(b) (*understand*) *theory* saisir. **to have ~ed sth** posséder qch à fond.
(c) (*learn*) *subject, skill, craft* apprendre (à fond). **he has ~ed Greek** il connaît *or* possède le grec à fond; **he'll never ~ the violin** il ne saura jamais bien jouer du violon; **he has ~ed the trumpet** il est devenu très bon trompettiste *or* un trompettiste accompli; **it's so difficult that I'll never ~ it** c'est si difficile que je n'y parviendrai jamais.
masterful ['mɑːstəfʊl] *adj* **(a)** (*imperious*) dominateur (*f* -trice), autoritaire, impérieux. **(b)** (*expert*) = **masterly**.
masterfully ['mɑːstəfəlɪ] *adv* **(a)** (*imperiously*) *act, decide* en maître, avec autorité, impérieusement; *speak, announce* d'un ton décisif, sur un ton d'autorité. **(b)** (*expertly*) magistralement, de main de maître.
masterly ['mɑːstəlɪ] *adj* magistral. **in a ~ way** magistralement.
mastery ['mɑːstərɪ] *n* [*subject, musical instrument*] connaissance *f* (approfondie) (*of* de); (*skill*) virtuosité *f*, maestria *f*; (*sway, power*) maîtrise *f*, domination *f*, souveraineté *f*, autorité *f*; (*over opponent, competitor etc*) supériorité *f* (*over* sur), domination (*over* de). **to gain ~ over** *person* avoir le dessus sur, l'emporter sur; *animal* dompter, mater; *nation, country* s'assurer la domination de; *the seas* s'assurer la maîtrise de.
masticate ['mæstɪkeɪt] *vti* mastiquer, mâcher.
mastiff ['mæstɪf] *n* mastiff *m*.
mastodon ['mæstədɒn] *n* mastodonte *m* (*lit*).
mastoid ['mæstɔɪd] 1 *adj* mastoïde. 2 *n* (*bone*) apophyse *f* mastoïde; (*Med**: *inflammation*) mastoïdite *f*.
mastoiditis [ˌmæstɔɪd'aɪtɪs] *n* mastoïdite *f*.
masturbate ['mæstəbeɪt] *vi* se masturber.
masturbation [ˌmæstə'beɪʃən] *n* masturbation *f*.
mat¹ [mæt] 1 *n* (*for floors etc*) (petit) tapis *m*, carpette *f*; (*of straw etc*) natte *f*; (*at door*) paillasson *m*, tapis-brosse *m inv*, essuie-pieds *m inv*; (*in car, gymnasium*) tapis; (*for dressing table etc*) napperon *m*; (*hard table~*) dessous-de-plat *m inv*; (*linen etc table~*) napperon. (*fig*) **to have sb on the ~*** passer un savon à qn*; **a ~ of hair** des cheveux emmêlés; *V* **drip, place, rush²** *etc*.
2 *vi* **(a)** [*hair etc*] s'emmêler; *V* **matted**.
(b) [*woollens*] (se) feutrer.
mat² [mæt] *adj* = **matt**.
matador ['mætədɔːʳ] *n* matador *m*.
match¹ [mætʃ] 1 *n* allumette *f*. **box/book of ~es** boîte *f*/pochette *f* d'allumettes; **have you got a ~?** avez-vous une allumette? *or* du feu?; **to strike** *or* **light a ~** gratter *or* frotter *or* faire craquer une allumette; **to put** *or* **set a ~ to sth** mettre le feu à qch; *V* **safety**.

2 *cpd*: **matchbox** boîte *f* à allumettes; **matchwood** bois *m* d'allumettes; **to smash sth to matchwood** réduire qch en miettes, pulvériser qch.

match[2] [mætʃ] **1** *n* **(a)** (*Sport*) match *m*; (*game*) partie *f*. **to play a ~ against sb** disputer un match contre qn, jouer contre qn; **international ~** match international, rencontre internationale; **~ abandoned** match suspendu; *V* **away, home, return** *etc*.

(b) (*equal*) égal(e) *m(f)*. **to meet one's ~ (in sb)** trouver à qui parler (avec qn), avoir affaire à forte partie (avec qn); **he's a ~ for anybody** il est de taille à faire face à n'importe qui; **he's no ~ for Paul** il n'est pas de taille à lutter contre Paul, il ne fait pas le poids* contre Paul; **he was more than a ~ for Paul** Paul n'était pas à sa mesure, il a mis Paul dans sa poche.

(c) *[clothes, colours etc]* **to be a good ~** aller bien ensemble, s'assortir bien; **I'm looking for a ~ for these curtains** je cherche quelque chose pour aller avec ces rideaux.

(d) (*marriage*) mariage *m*. **he's a good ~** c'est un bon parti; **they're a good ~** ils sont bien assortis.

2 *cpd*: **matchless** *V* **matchless**; **matchmaker** marieur *m*, -euse *f*; **she is a great matchmaker, she's always matchmaking** c'est une marieuse enragée*, elle veut toujours marier les gens; (*Tennis*) **match point** balle *f* de match.

3 *vt* **(a)** (*be equal etc to: also* **~ up to**) égaler, être l'égal de. **his essay didn't ~ (up to) Paul's in originality** sa dissertation n'égalait pas *or* ne valait pas celle de Paul en originalité; **she doesn't ~ (up to) her sister in intelligence** elle n'a pas l'intelligence de sa sœur; **the result didn't ~ (up to) our hopes** le résultat a déçu nos espérances.

(b) *[clothes, colours etc]* s'assortir à, aller bien avec. **his tie doesn't ~ his shirt** sa cravate ne va pas avec *or* n'est pas assortie à sa chemise; **his looks ~ his character** son physique va de pair avec sa personnalité.

(c) (*find similar piece etc to: also* **~ up**) *cups etc* assortir, appareiller. **can you ~ (up) this material?** avez-vous du tissu identique à celui-ci?

(d) (*pair off*) **to ~ sb against sb** opposer qn à qn; **she ~ed her wits against his strength** elle opposait son intelligence à sa force; **they are well ~ed** *[opponents]* ils sont de force égale; *[married couple etc]* ils sont bien assortis.

4 *vi [colours, materials]* être bien assortis, aller bien ensemble; *[cups]* être appareillés; *[gloves, socks]* s'apparier, faire la paire; *[two identical objects]* se faire pendant(s). **with (a) skirt to ~, with (a) ~ing skirt** avec (une) jupe assortie.

match up 1 *vi [colours etc]* s'harmoniser, aller bien ensemble, être assortis.

2 *vt sep* = **match 3c.**

match up to *vt fus* = **match 3a.**

matchless ['mætʃlɪs] *adj* sans égal, sans pareil, incomparable.

mate[1] [meɪt] **1** *n* **(a)** (*at work*) camarade *mf* (de travail); (*: *friend*) copain* *m*, copine* *f*, camarade. **hey, ~!**‡ eh, mon vieux!; *V* **class, play, work** *etc*.

(b) (*assistant*) aide *mf*. **plumber's ~** aide-plombier *m*.

(c) (*animal*) mâle *m*, femelle *f*; (**hum: spouse*) époux *m*, épouse *f*.

(d) (*Merchant Navy*) ≃ second *m* (capitaine); *V* **first.**

2 *vt* accoupler (*with* à).

3 *vi* s'accoupler (*with* à, avec).

mate[2] [meɪt] (*Chess*) **1** *n* mat *m*; *V* **check**[2], **stalemate. 2** *vt* mettre échec et mat, mater.

material [mə'tɪərɪəl] **1** *adj* **(a)** *force, success, object, world* matériel; *comforts, well-being, needs, pleasures* matériel, physique. **from a ~ point of view** du point de vue matériel.

(b) (*important*) essentiel, important; (*relevant*) qui importe (*to* à), qui présente de l'intérêt (*to* pour); (*Jur*) *fact, evidence* pertinent; *witness* direct.

2 *n* **(a)** (*substance: stone, wood, concrete etc*) matière *f*; (*cloth etc*) tissu *m*, étoffe *f*. **dress ~(s)** tissus pour robes; (*fig*) **he is officer ~** il a l'étoffe d'un officier; *V* **raw.**

(b) (*equipment etc*) **~s** fournitures *fpl*, articles *mpl*; **building ~s** matériaux *mpl* de construction; **the desk held all his writing ~s** le bureau contenait tout son matériel nécessaire pour écrire; **have you got any writing ~s?** avez-vous de quoi écrire?

(c) (*U: for book, lecture*) matériaux *mpl*, documentation *f*. **he is looking for ~ for a TV programme** il cherche des matériaux pour une émission télévisée; **this is exactly the kind of ~ he needs** c'est exactement le genre de documentation dont il a besoin; **~ for thought** matière *f* à réflexion.

materialism [mə'tɪərɪəlɪzəm] *n* matérialisme *m*.

materialist [mə'tɪərɪəlɪst] *adj, n* matérialiste (*mf*).

materialistic [mə,tɪərɪə'lɪstɪk] *adj* matérialiste.

materialize [mə'tɪərɪəlaɪz] **1** *vi* **(a)** *[plan, wish]* se matérialiser, se réaliser; *[offer, loan etc]* se concrétiser, se matérialiser; *[idea]* prendre forme. **the promised cash didn't ~** l'argent promis ne s'est pas concrétisé *or* matérialisé; **at last the bus ~d*** le bus a enfin fait son apparition *or* est enfin arrivé.

(b) (*Spiritualism etc*) prendre une forme matérielle, se matérialiser.

2 *vt* matérialiser, concrétiser.

materially [mə'tɪərɪəlɪ] *adv* réellement; (*Philos*) matériellement, essentiellement.

maternal [mə'tɜːnl] *adj* maternel. (*Psych*) **~ deprivation** carence maternelle.

maternity [mə'tɜːnɪtɪ] **1** *n* maternité *f*. **2** *cpd clothes* de grossesse. (*Brit*) **maternity benefit** ≃ allocation *f* de maternité; **maternity home, maternity hospital** maternité *f*; (*private*) clinique *f* d'accouchement, clinique obstétrique.

matey‡ ['meɪtɪ] *adj* (*Brit*) familier, copain-copain‡ (*f inv*). **he's very ~ with everyone** il est à tu et à toi avec tout le monde.

math* [mæθ] *n* (*US abbr of* **mathematics**) math(s)* *fpl*.

mathematical [,mæθə'mætɪkəl] *adj process etc* mathématique. **I'm not ~, I haven't got a ~ mind** je n'ai pas le sens des mathématiques, je ne suis pas (un) matheux*; **he's a ~ genius** c'est un mathématicien de génie.

mathematically [,mæθə'mætɪkəlɪ] *adv* mathématiquement.

mathematician [,mæθəmə'tɪʃən] *n* mathématicien(ne) *m(f)*.

mathematics [,mæθə'mætɪks] *n* (*U*) mathématiques *fpl*.

Mat(h)ilda [mə'tɪldə] *n* Mathilde *f*.

maths* [mæθs] *n*, (*US*) **math*** *n* (*abbr of* **mathematics**) math(s)* *fpl*.

matinée ['mætɪneɪ] **1** *n* (*Theat*) matinée *f*. **2** *cpd*: (*Brit*) **matinée coat** veste *f* (de bébé); (*Theat*) **matinée idol** idole *f* du public féminin.

mating ['meɪtɪŋ] **1** *n [animals]* accouplement *m*. **2** *cpd*: **mating call** appel *m* du mâle; **mating season** saison *f* des amours.

matins ['mætɪnz] *n sg or pl* = **mattins.**

matri... ['meɪtrɪ] *pref* matri... .

matriarch ['meɪtrɪɑːk] *n* matrone *f*, femme *f* chef de tribu *or* de famille.

matriarchal [,meɪtrɪ'ɑːkl] *adj* matriarcal.

matriarchy ['meɪtrɪɑːkɪ] *n* matriarcat *m*.

matric [mə'trɪk] *n* (*Brit Scol sl*) *abbr of* **matriculation 1b.**

matricide ['meɪtrɪsaɪd] *n* (*crime*) matricide *m*; (*person*) matricide *mf*.

matriculate [mə'trɪkjʊleɪt] *vi* s'inscrire, se faire immatriculer; (*Brit Scol*††) *être reçu à l'examen de 'matriculation'*.

matriculation [mə,trɪkjʊ'leɪʃən] **1** *n* **(a)** (*Univ*) inscription *f*, immatriculation *f*. **(b)** (*Brit Scol*††) *examen donnant droit à l'inscription universitaire*. **2** *cpd* (*Univ*) *card, fee* d'inscription.

matrimonial [,mætrɪ'məʊnɪəl] *adj* matrimonial, conjugal.

matrimony ['mætrɪmənɪ] *n* (*U*) mariage *m*.

matrix ['meɪtrɪks] *n* matrice *f*.

matron ['meɪtrən] **1** *n* **(a)** matrone *f*, mère *f* de famille. **(b)** *[hospital]* infirmière *f* en chef; (*in school*) infirmière; *[orphanage, old people's home etc]* directrice *f*. **2** *cpd*: **matron-of-honour** dame *f* d'honneur.

matronly ['meɪtrənlɪ] *adj* de matrone. **she was a ~ person** elle faisait très digne *or* matrone (*pej*).

matt [mæt] *adj* mat. **paint with a ~ finish** peinture mate.

matted ['mætɪd] *adj hair* emmêlé; *weeds* enchevêtré; *cloth, sweater* feutré.

matter ['mætə^r] **1** *n* **(a)** (*U*) (*physical substance*) matière *f*, substance *f*; (*Philos, Phys*) matière; (*Typ*) matière, copie *f*; (*Med: pus*) pus *m*. **vegetable/inanimate ~** matière végétale/inanimée; **colouring ~** substance colorante; **reading ~** choses *fpl* à lire, de quoi lire; **advertising ~** publicité *f*, réclames *fpl*; *V* **grey, mind** *etc*.

(b) (*U: content*) *[book etc]* fond *m*, contenu *m*. **~ and form** le fond et la forme; **the ~ of his essay was good but the style poor** le contenu de sa dissertation était bon mais le style laissait à désirer.

(c) (*affair, concern, business*) affaire *f*, question *f*, sujet *m*, matière *f*. **the ~ in hand** l'affaire en question; **business ~s** (questions d')affaires *fpl*; **there's the ~ of my expenses** il y a la question de mes frais; **that's quite another ~, that's another ~ altogether, that's a very different ~** c'est tout autre chose, ça c'est une autre affaire; **that will only make ~s worse** cela ne fera qu'aggraver la situation; **then to make ~s worse he ...** puis pour ne rien arranger *or* qui pis est, il ...; **in this ~** à cet égard; **the ~ is closed** l'affaire est close, c'est une affaire classée; **it is a ~ of great concern to us** c'est une source de profonde inquiétude pour nous; **it's not a laughing ~** il n'y a pas de quoi rire; **it's a small ~ which we shan't discuss now** c'est une question insignifiante *or* une bagatelle dont nous ne discuterons pas maintenant; **there's the small ~ of that £200 I lent you** il y a la petite question *or* le petit problème des 200 livres que je vous ai prêtées; **it will be no easy ~** cela ne sera pas facile; **in the ~ of** en matière de, en *or* pour ce qui concerne; **it's a ~ of habit/opinion** c'est (une) question *or* (une) affaire d'habitude/d'opinion; **in all ~s of education** pour tout ce qui touche à *or* concerne l'éducation; **as ~s stand** vu l'état actuel des choses; **let's see how ~s stand** voyons où en sont les choses; **for that ~** pour ce qui est de cela, quant à cela; **as a ~ of course** automatiquement, tout naturellement; **as a ~ of fact** à vrai dire, en réalité, en fait (*V also* **2**); **it took a ~ of days (to do it)** cela a été l'affaire de quelques jours (pour le faire); **in a ~ of 10 minutes** en l'affaire de 10 minutes; *V* **mince.**

(d) (*importance*) **no ~!** peu importe!, tant pis!; (*liter*) **what ~?** qu'importe?; **what ~ if ...** qu'importe si ...; **it is of no ~** *or* (*frm*) **it makes no ~ whether ...** peu importe si ...; **it is (of) no great ~** c'est peu de chose, cela n'a pas grande importance; **get one, no ~ how** débrouille-toi (comme tu veux) pour en trouver un; **it must be done, no ~ how** cela doit être fait par n'importe quel moyen; **ring me no ~ how late** téléphonez-moi même tard *or* à n'importe quelle heure; **no ~ when he comes** quelle que soit l'heure (*or* quel que soit le jour *or* quelle que soit la date) de son arrivée, quelle que soit l'heure *etc* à laquelle il arrive (*subj*); **no ~ how big it is** quelque *or* si grand qu'il soit; **no ~ what he says** quoi qu'il dise; **no ~ where/who** où/qui que ce soit.

(e) (*U: difficulty, problem*) **what's the ~?** qu'est-ce qu'il y a?, qu'y a-t-il?; **what's the ~ with him?** qu'est-ce qu'il a?, qu'est-ce qui lui prend?; **what's the ~ with your hand?** qu'est-ce que vous avez à la main?; **what's the ~ with my hat?** qu'est-ce qu'il a, mon chapeau?*; **what's the ~ with trying to help him?** quel inconvénient *or* quelle objection y a-t-il à ce qu'on l'aide (*subj*)?; **there's something the ~ with my arm** j'ai quelque chose au bras; **there's something the ~ with the engine** il y a quelque chose qui cloche* *or* qui ne va pas dans le moteur; **as if nothing was the ~** comme si de rien n'était; **nothing's the ~*** il n'y a rien; **there's nothing the ~ with me!** moi, je vais tout à fait bien!; **there's nothing the ~ with the car** la voiture marche très bien; **there's**

nothing the ~ with that idea il n'y a rien à redire à cette idée.

2 *cpd*: **matter-of-fact** *tone, voice* neutre; *style* prosaïque; *attitude, person* terre à terre *or* terre-à-terre; *assessment, account* neutre, qui se limite aux faits; **in a very matter-of-fact way** sans avoir l'air de rien.

3 *vi* importer (*to* à). **it doesn't ~** cela n'a pas d'importance, cela ne fait rien; **it doesn't ~ whether** peu importe que + *subj*, cela ne fait rien si, peu importe si; **it doesn't ~ who/where** *etc* peu importe qui/où *etc*; **what does it ~?** qu'est-ce que cela peut faire?; **what does it ~ to you (if ...)?** qu'est-ce que cela peut bien vous faire (si ...)?, que vous importe (*frm*) (si ...)?; **why should it ~ to me?** pourquoi est-ce que cela me ferait quelque chose?; **it ~s little** cela importe peu, peu importe; **some things ~ more than others** il y a des choses qui importent plus que d'autres; **I shouldn't let what he says ~** je ne m'en ferais pas pour ce qu'il dit*.

Matterhorn ['mætəhɔːn] *n*: **the ~** le (mont) Cervin.

Matthew ['mæθjuː] *n* Mat(t)hieu *m*.

matting ['mætɪŋ] *n* (*U*) sparterie *f*, pièces *fpl* de natte; *V* **rush**[2] *etc.*

mattins ['mætɪnz] *n sg or pl* (*Rel*) matines *fpl*.

mattock ['mætək] *n* pioche *f*.

mattress ['mætrɪs] *n* matelas *m*.

mature [mə'tjʊəʳ] **1** *adj person, age, reflection, plan* mûr; *wine* qui est arrivé à maturité; *cheese* fait; (*Fin*) *bill* échu. **he's got much more ~ since then** il a beaucoup mûri depuis. **2** *vt* faire mûrir. **3** *vi [person]* mûrir; *[wine, cheese]* se faire; (*Fin*) venir à échéance, échoir.

maturity [mə'tjʊərɪtɪ] *n* maturité *f*. (*Fin*) **date of ~** échéance *f*.

maudlin ['mɔːdlɪn] *adj* larmoyant.

maul [mɔːl] *vt [tiger etc]* mutiler, lacérer; *[person]* malmener, brutaliser; (*fig*) *author, book etc* éreinter, malmener.

maunder ['mɔːndəʳ] *vi* (*talk*) divaguer; (*move*) errer; (*act*) agir de façon incohérente.

Maundy ['mɔːndɪ] *n*: **~ Thursday** le jeudi saint; (*Brit*) **~ money** aumône royale du jeudi saint.

Mauritania [ˌmɔːrɪ'teɪnɪə] *n* Mauritanie *f*.

Mauritius [mə'rɪʃəs] *n* l'île *f* Maurice.

mausoleum [ˌmɔːsə'lɪəm] *n* mausolée *m*.

mauve [məʊv] *adj, n* mauve (*m*).

maverick ['mævərɪk] **1** *n* (*calf*) veau non marqué; (*fig: person*) dissident(e) *m(f)*, non-conformiste *mf*, franc-tireur *m* (*fig*). **2** *adj* dissident, non-conformiste.

maw [mɔː] *n [cow]* caillette *f*; *[bird]* jabot *m*; (*fig*) gueule *f*.

mawkish ['mɔːkɪʃ] *adj* (*sentimental*) d'une sentimentalité excessive *or* exagérée; (*insipid*) insipide, fade; (*nauseating*) écœurant.

mawkishness ['mɔːkɪʃnɪs] *n* (*V* **mawkish**) sentimentalité excessive *or* exagérée; insipidité *f*, fadeur *f*; caractère écœurant.

maxi* ['mæksɪ] *n* (*coat/skirt*) (manteau *m*/jupe *f*) maxi *m*. **~ single (record *or* disc)** disque *m* double durée.

maxim ['mæksɪm] *n* maxime *f*.

maxima ['mæksɪmə] *npl of* **maximum 1**.

maximize ['mæksɪmaɪz] *vt* porter au maximum, maximiser. **to ~ the advantages of sth** tirer le maximum de qch.

maximum ['mæksɪməm] **1** *n, pl* **maxima** maximum *m*. **a ~ of £8** un maximum de 8 livres, 8 livres au maximum.

2 *adj* maximum (*f inv or* maxima). **~ prices** prix *mpl* maximums *or* maxima; (*Aut etc*) **~ speed** (*highest permitted*) vitesse *f* limite *or* maximum; (*highest possible*) plafond *m*; (*on truck*) **~ load** charge *f* limite; **~ temperatures** températures maximales.

may[1] [meɪ] *modal aux vb* (*pret and cond* **might**) **(a)** (*indicating possibility*) **he may arrive** il arrivera peut-être, il peut arriver; **he might arrive** il se peut qu'il arrive (*subj*), il pourrait arriver; **I said that he might arrive** j'ai dit qu'il arriverait peut-être; **you may *or* might be making a big mistake** tu fais peut-être *or* tu es peut-être en train de faire une grosse erreur; **might they have left already?** se peut-il qu'ils soient déjà partis?; **I might have left it behind** il se peut que je l'aie oublié, je l'ai peut-être bien oublié; **you might have killed me!** tu aurais pu me tuer!; **that's as may be but,** (*frm*) **that may well be but** peut-être bien *or* c'est bien possible mais; **as soon as may be** aussitôt que possible; (*frm*) **be that as it may** quoi qu'il en soit; **one might well ask whether ...** on est en droit de demander si ...; **what might your name be?** (*abrupt*) et vous comment vous appelez-vous?; (*polite*) puis-je savoir votre nom?; **how old might he be, I wonder?** je me demande quel âge il peut bien avoir.

(b) (*indicating permission*) **may I have a word with you? — yes, you may** puis-je vous parler un instant? — (mais) oui bien sûr; **may I help you?** puis-je vous aider?; (*in shop*) vous désirez (quelque chose)?; **might I see it?** est-ce que je pourrais le voir?, vous permettez que je le voie?; **might I suggest that ...?** puis-je me permettre de suggérer que ...?; **may I tell her now? — you may *or* might as well** est-ce que je peux le lui dire maintenant? — après tout pourquoi pas?; **may I sit here?** vous permettez que je m'assoie ici?; **may I?** vous permettez?; **you may go now** (*permission; also polite order*) vous pouvez partir; (*to subordinate*) vous pouvez disposer; **he said I might leave** il a dit que je pouvais partir, il m'a permis de partir.

(c) (*indicating suggestion: with 'might' only*) (*polite*) **you might try writing to him** tu pourrais toujours lui écrire; **you might give me a lift home if you've got time** tu pourrais peut-être me ramener si tu as le temps; **mightn't it be an idea to go and see him?** on ferait (*or* tu ferais *etc*) peut-être bien d'aller le voir?; (*abrupt*) **you might have told me you weren't coming!** tu aurais (tout de même) pu me prévenir que tu ne viendrais pas!; **you might at least say 'thank you'** tu pourrais au moins dire 'merci'.

(d) (*phrases*) **one might as well say £5 million** autant dire 5 millions de livres; **we might as well not buy that newspaper at all since no one ever reads it** je me demande bien pourquoi nous achetons ce journal puisque personne ne le lit; **I may *or* might as well tell you all about it** après tout je peux bien vous le raconter, je ferais aussi bien de tout vous dire; **you may *or* might as well leave now as wait any longer** vous feriez aussi bien de partir tout de suite plutôt que d'attendre encore; **they might (just) as well not have gone** ils auraient tout aussi bien pu ne pas y aller, ce n'était pas la peine qu'ils y aillent; **she blushed, as well she might!** elle a rougi, et pour cause!

(e) (*frm, liter: in exclamations expressing wishes, hopes etc*) **may God bless you!** (que) Dieu vous bénisse!; **may he rest in peace** qu'il repose (*subj*) en paix; **o might I see her but once again!** oh que je puisse la revoir ne fût-ce qu'une fois!; **much good may it do you!** grand bien vous fasse!

(f) (*frm, liter: subj use*) **O Lord, grant that we may always obey** Seigneur, accorde-nous *or* donne-nous de toujours obéir; **lest he may *or* might be anxious** de crainte qu'il n'éprouve (*subj*) de l'anxiété; **in order that they may *or* might know** afin qu'ils sachent.

may[2] [meɪ] **1** *n* **(a)** (*month*) **M~** mai *m*; **the merry month of M~** le joli mois de mai; *for other phrases V* **September**.

(b) (*hawthorn*) aubépine *f*.

2 *cpd branch etc* d'aubépine. **May beetle** hanneton *m*; **May Day** le Premier mai (*fête f du Travail*); **mayday** *V* **mayday**; **mayfly** éphémère *m*; **maypole** mât enrubanné (*autour duquel on danse*), ≃ mai *m*; **May queen** reine *f* de mai; **may tree** aubépine *f*.

maybe ['meɪbiː] *adv* peut-être. **~ he'll be there** peut-être qu'il sera là, peut-être sera-t-il là, il sera peut-être là.

mayday ['meɪdeɪ] *n* (*Aviat, Naut*) mayday *m*, S.O.S. *m*.

mayhem ['meɪhem] *n* **(a)** (*Jur†† or US*) mutilation *f* du corps humain. **(b)** (*havoc*) grabuge* *m*; (*destruction*) destruction *f*.

mayn't [meɪnt] *abbr of* **may not**; *V* **may**[1].

mayonnaise [ˌmeɪə'neɪz] *n* mayonnaise *f*.

mayor [mɛəʳ] *n* maire *m*. **Mr/Madam M~** Monsieur/Madame le maire; *V* **lord**.

mayoralty ['mɛərəltɪ] *n* mandat *m* de maire.

mayoress ['mɛəres] *n* ≃ mairesse *f*; *V* **lady**.

maze [meɪz] *n* labyrinthe *m*, dédale *m*. (*fig*) **a ~ of little streets** un labyrinthe *or* un dédale de ruelles; **to be in a ~** être complètement désorienté.

me [miː] *pers pron* **(a)** (*direct*) (*unstressed*) me; (*before vowel*) m'; (*stressed*) moi. **he can see ~** il me voit; **he saw ~** il m'a vu; **you saw ME!** vous m'avez vu, moi!

(b) (*indirect*) me, moi; (*before vowel*) m'. **he gave ~ the book** il me donna *or* m'a donné le livre; **give it to ~** donnez-le-moi; **he was speaking to ~** il me parlait.

(c) (*after prep etc*) moi. **without ~** sans moi; **it's ~** c'est moi; **it's ~ he's speaking to** c'est à moi qu'il parle; **you're smaller than ~** tu es plus petit que moi; **poor (little) ~!*** pauvre de moi!; **dear ~!*** mon Dieu!, oh là là!*

mead[1] [miːd] *n* (*drink*) hydromel *m*.

mead[2] [miːd] *n* (*liter: meadow*) pré *m*, prairie *f*.

meadow ['medəʊ] **1** *n* pré *m*, prairie *f*; *V* **water**. **2** *cpd*: **meadowsweet** reine *f* des prés.

meagre, (*US*) **meager** ['miːgəʳ] *adj* (*all senses*) maigre (*before n*).

meal[1] [miːl] **1** *n* repas *m*. **to have a ~** prendre un repas, manger; **to have *or* get a good ~** bien manger; **come and have a ~** venez manger, venez déjeuner (*or* dîner); **that was a lovely ~!** nous avons très bien déjeuné (*or* dîné); **he made a ~ of bread and cheese** il a déjeuné (*or* dîné) de pain et de fromage; (*fig*) **to make a ~ of sth*** faire tout un plat de qch*; *V* **square** *etc.*

2 *cpd*: **meals on wheels** *repas livrés à domicile aux personnes âgées ou handicapées;* **meal ticket** (*lit*) ticket *m or* coupon *m* de repas; (**fig: job, person etc*) gagne-pain *m inv*; **mealtime** heure *f* du repas.

meal[2] [miːl] *n* (*U: flour etc*) farine *f* (*d'avoine, de seigle, de maïs etc*); *V* **oat, wheat** *etc.*

mealies ['miːlɪz] *npl* maïs *m*.

mealy ['miːlɪ] **1** *adj substance, mixture, potato* farineux; *complexion* blême. **2** *cpd*: **mealy-mouthed** mielleux, doucereux.

mean[1] [miːn] *pret, ptp* **meant** *vt* **(a)** (*signify*) vouloir dire, signifier; (*imply*) vouloir dire. **what does 'media' ~?, what is meant by 'media'?** que veut dire *or* que signifie 'media'?; **'homely' ~s something different in America** 'homely' a un sens différent en Amérique; **what do you ~ (by that)?** que voulez-vous dire (par là)?, qu'entendez-vous par là?; **you don't really ~ that?** vous n'êtes pas sérieux?, vous plaisantez?; **I always ~ what I say** je pense toujours ce que je dis; **the name ~s nothing to me** ce nom ne me dit rien; **the play didn't ~ a thing to her** la pièce n'avait aucun sens pour elle; **what does this ~?** qu'est-ce que cela signifie? *or* veut dire?; **it ~s he won't be coming** cela veut dire qu'il ne viendra pas; **this ~s war** c'est la guerre à coup sûr; **it will ~ a lot of expense** cela entraînera beaucoup de dépenses; **catching the train ~s getting up early** pour avoir ce train il faut se lever tôt; **a pound ~s a lot to him** une livre représente une grosse somme pour lui; **holidays don't ~ much to me** les vacances comptent peu pour moi; **I can't tell you what your gift has meant to me!** je ne saurais vous dire à quel point votre cadeau m'a touché!; **don't I ~ anything to you at all?** je ne suis donc rien pour toi?; **what it ~s to be free!** quelle belle chose que la liberté!; **money doesn't ~ happiness** l'argent ne fait pas le bonheur.

(b) (*intend, purpose*) avoir l'intention (*to do* de faire), compter, vouloir (*to do* faire); (*intend, destine*) *gift etc* destiner (*for* à); *remark* adresser (*for* à). **I meant to come yesterday** j'avais l'intention de *or* je voulais venir hier; **what does he ~ to do now?**

que compte-t-il faire maintenant?; I didn't ~ to break it je n'ai pas fait exprès de le casser, je ne l'ai pas cassé exprès; I didn't ~ to! je ne l'ai pas fait exprès! *or* de propos délibéré!; I touched it without ~ing to je l'ai touché sans le vouloir; I ~ to succeed j'ai bien l'intention de réussir; despite what he says I ~ to go je partirai quoi qu'il dise; I ~ you to leave, (*US*) I ~ for you to leave je veux que vous partiez (*subj*); I really ~ it je ne plaisante pas, je suis sérieux; I'm sure he didn't ~ it je suis sûr que ce n'était pas intentionnel *or* délibéré; he said it as if he meant it il a dit cela d'un air sérieux *or* sans avoir l'air de plaisanter; I meant it as a joke j'ai dit (*or* fait) cela par plaisanterie *or* pour rire; we were meant to arrive at 6 nous étions censés arriver *or* nous devions arriver à 6 heures; she ~s well elle est pleine de bonnes intentions; he looks as if he ~s trouble il a une mine qui n'annonce rien de bon *or* qui vaille; do you ~ me? (*are you speaking to me*) c'est à moi que vous parlez?; (*are you speaking about me*) c'est de moi que vous parlez?; he meant you when he said ... c'est vous qu'il visait *or* c'est à vous qu'il faisait allusion lorsqu'il disait ...; I meant the book for Paul je destinais le livre à Paul; that book is meant for children ce livre est destiné aux enfants *or* est à l'intention des enfants; this cupboard was never meant to be *or* meant for a larder ce placard n'a jamais été conçu pour servir de garde-manger *or* n'a jamais été censé être un garde-manger; this portrait is meant to be Anne ce portrait est censé être celui d'Anne *or* représenter Anne; *V* business, harm, offence *etc.*

mean² [miːn] 1 *n* (a) (*middle term*) milieu *m*, moyen terme; (*Math*) moyenne *f*. the golden *or* happy ~ le juste milieu; *V* geometric.

(b) (*method, way*) ~s moyen(s) *m(pl)*; to find the ~s to do *or* of doing trouver le(s) moyen(s) de faire; to find (a) ~s of doing trouver moyen de faire; the only ~s of contacting him is ... le seul moyen de le joindre, c'est ...; there's no ~s of getting in il n'y a pas moyen d'y entrer; he has been the ~s of my success c'est grâce à lui que j'ai réussi; the ~s to an end le moyen d'arriver à ses fins; (*Rel*) the ~s of salvation les voies *fpl* du salut; by ~s of a penknife au moyen *or* à l'aide d'un canif; by ~s of his brother par l'entremise de son frère; by ~s of hard work à force de travail; come in by all ~s! je vous en prie, entrez!; by all ~s! certainement!, bien sûr!; by all manner of ~s par tous les moyens; by any (manner of) ~s n'importe comment, à n'importe quel prix; by no (manner of) ~s nullement, pas du tout, pas le moins du monde; she is by no ~s stupid elle est loin d'être stupide; by some ~s or (an)other d'une façon ou d'une autre; by this ~s de cette façon; *V* fair¹ *etc.*

(c) (*wealth etc*) ~s moyens *mpl*, ressources *fpl*; he is a man of ~s il a une belle fortune *or* de gros moyens*; to live within/beyond one's ~s vivre selon ses moyens/au-dessus de ses moyens; private ~s fortune personnelle; slender ~s ressources très modestes; we have no ~s *or* we haven't the ~s to do it nous n'avons pas les moyens de le faire.

2 *adj distance, temperature, price* moyen.

3 *cpd*: (*Admin*) means test enquête *f* (financière) sur les ressources (*d'une personne qui demande une aide pécuniaire*); meantime, meanwhile *V* meantime.

mean³ [miːn] *adj* (a) (*stingy*) avare, mesquin, chiche, radin*. ~ with one's time/money avare de son temps/argent; don't be so ~! ne sois pas si radin!*

(b) (*unpleasant, unkind*) *person, behaviour* mesquin, méchant. a ~ trick un sale tour, une crasse; you ~ thing!* chameau!*; (*to a child*) méchant!; you were ~ to me tu n'as vraiment pas été chic* *or* sympa: avec moi, tu as été plutôt rosse *or* chameau* avec moi; that was ~ of them c'était bien mesquin de leur part, ce n'était pas chic* de leur part; to feel ~ about sth* avoir un peu honte de qch, ne pas être très fier de qch.

(c) (*US**: *vicious*) *horse, dog etc* méchant, vicieux; *person* sadique, salaud:.

(d) (*inferior, poor*) *appearance, existence* misérable, minable. the ~est citizen le dernier des citoyens; the ~est intelligence l'esprit le plus borné; he is no ~ scholar c'est un savant d'envergure; he's no ~ singer c'est un chanteur de talent.

meander [mɪ'ændəʳ] 1 *vi* (a) [*river*] faire des méandres, serpenter. (b) [*person*] errer, vagabonder. she ~ed in elle entra sans se presser. 2 *n* méandre *m*, détour *m*, sinuosité *f*.

meaning ['miːnɪŋ] 1 *n* [*word*] sens *m*, signification *f*; [*phrase, action*] signification. with a double ~ à double sens; literal ~ sens propre *or* littéral; what is the ~ of this word? quel est le sens de ce mot?, que signifie ce mot?; (*in anger, disapproval etc*) what is the ~ of this? qu'est-ce que cela signifie?; you haven't got my ~ vous m'avez mal compris; look/gesture full of ~ regard/geste significatif *or* éloquent; 'really?' he said with ~ son 'vraiment?' fut significatif *or* éloquent.

2 *adj* significatif, éloquent, expressif.

meaningful ['miːnɪŋfʊl] *adj* significatif, éloquent, expressif.

meaningless ['miːnɪŋlɪs] *adj word, action* dénué de sens, sans signification; *waste, suffering* insensé.

meanness ['miːnnɪs] *n* (*V* mean³) avarice *f*, mesquinerie *f*; méchanceté *f*, manque *m* de cœur; pauvreté *f*, médiocrité *f*.

meant [ment] *pret, ptp of* mean¹.

meantime ['miːntaɪm] *adv*, **meanwhile** ['miːnwaɪl] *adv*: (in the) ~ en attendant, pendant ce temps, dans l'intervalle.

measles ['miːzlz] *n* rougeole *f*; *V* German.

measly* ['miːzlɪ] *adj* minable, misérable, piètre (*before n*).

measurable ['meʒərəbl] *adj* mesurable; (*Pharm etc*) dosable.

measure ['meʒəʳ] 1 *n* (a) (*system, unit, container*) mesure *f*; (*ruler etc*) règle *f*, mètre *m*; (*fig*) mesure. to give good *or* full ~ faire bonne mesure *or* bon poids; to give short ~ voler *or* rogner sur la quantité *or* sur le poids; (*fig*) for good ~ pour faire bonne mesure, pour la bonne mesure; suit made to ~ complet fait sur mesure; I've got his ~ je sais ce qu'il vaut; 10 ~s of wheat 10 mesures de blé; liquid ~ mesure de capacité pour les liquides; a pint ~ une mesure d'un demi-litre; (*Brit Math*) greatest common ~ le plus grand commun diviseur; happiness beyond ~ bonheur sans bornes; in some ~ dans une certaine mesure, jusqu'à un certain point; in great *or* large ~ dans une large mesure, en grande partie; *V* standard, tape *etc.*

(b) (*step*) mesure *f*, démarche *f*; (*Parl*) (*bill*) projet *m* de loi; (*act*) loi *f*. strong/drastic ~s mesures énergiques/draconiennes; to take ~s against prendre des mesures contre.

(c) (*Mus, Poetry etc*) mesure *f*.

2 *vt* (*lit*) *child, length, time* mesurer; (*fig*) *strength, courage* mesurer, estimer, évaluer, jauger. to ~ the height of sth mesurer *or* prendre la hauteur de qch; to be ~d for a dress faire prendre ses mesures pour une robe; what does it ~? quelles sont ses dimensions?; the room ~s 4 metres across la pièce a *or* fait *or* mesure 4 mètres de large; the carpet ~s 3 metres by 2 le tapis fait *or* mesure 3 mètres sur 2; (*fig: fall*) to ~ one's length tomber *or* s'étaler* de tout son long.

measure off *vt sep lengths of fabric etc* mesurer.

measure out *vt sep* (a) *ingredients, piece of ground* mesurer. (b) (*issue*) distribuer.

measure up *vt sep wood* mesurer; (*fig*) *sb's intentions* jauger; *person* évaluer, jauger.

measure up to *vt fus task* être au niveau de, être à la hauteur de; *person* être l'égal de.

measured ['meʒəd] *adj time, distance* mesuré; (*fig*) *words, language, statement* modéré, mesuré, circonspect; *tone* mesuré, avisé, modéré; *verse* mesuré, rythmique. (*Sport etc*) over a ~ kilometre sur un kilomètre exactement, sur une distance d'un kilomètre; with ~ steps à pas comptés *or* mesurés.

measureless ['meʒəlɪs] *adj power etc* incommensurable, infini, immense, sans bornes; *wrath* démesuré.

measurement ['meʒəmənt] *n* (a) (*dimensions: gen pl*) ~s mesures *fpl*, dimensions *fpl*; to take the ~s of a room prendre les mesures d'une pièce; what are your ~s? quelles sont vos mesures? (b) (*U*) mesurage *m*.

measuring ['meʒərɪŋ] 1 *adj*: ~ chain chaîne *f* d'arpenteur; ~ glass/jug verre/pot gradué; ~ rod règle *f*, mètre *m*; ~ tape mètre à ruban. 2 *n* (*U*) mesurage *m*.

meat [miːt] 1 *n* viande *f*; (*fig*) substance *f*; (††: *food*) nourriture *f*, aliment *m*. cold ~ viande froide; (*fig*) there's not much ~ in his book son livre n'a pas beaucoup de substance; (*lit*) ~ and drink de quoi manger et boire; (*fig*) this is ~ and drink to them c'est une (bonne) aubaine pour eux; (*Prov*) one man's ~ is another man's poison ce qui guérit l'un tue l'autre.

2 *cpd*: meatball boulette *f* de viande; meat diet régime carné; (*animal*) meat-eater carnivore *m*; he's a big meat-eater c'est un gros mangeur de viande; meat-eating carnivore; meat extract concentré *m* de viande; meatless *V* meatless; meat loaf (sorte *f* de) pâté *m* de viande; meat pie pâté *m* en croûte; (*Brit*) meat safe garde-manger *m inv*.

meatless ['miːtlɪs] *adj* sans viande, maigre.

meaty ['miːtɪ] *adj flavour* de viande; (*fig*) *argument, book* étoffé, substantiel.

Mecca ['mekə] *n* la Mecque. (*fig*) it was a ~ for tourists c'était un haut lieu du tourisme.

mechanic [mɪ'kænɪk] *n* mécanicien *m*. motor ~ mécanicien garagiste.

mechanical [mɪ'kænɪkəl] *adj power, process* mécanique; (*fig*) *action, reply* machinal, automatique, mécanique. ~ engineer ingénieur mécanicien; ~ engineering (*science*) mécanique *f*; (*industry*) construction *f* mécanique.

mechanically [mɪ'kænɪkəlɪ] *adv* mécaniquement; (*fig*) machinalement, mécaniquement.

mechanics [mɪ'kænɪks] *n* (a) (*U: science*) mécanique *f*.

(b) (*pl*) (*technical aspect*) mécanisme *m*, processus *m*; (*mechanism; working parts*) mécanisme, mécanique *f*. (*fig*) the ~ of running an office le processus *or* l'aspect *m* pratique de la gestion d'un bureau.

mechanism ['mekənɪzəm] *n* (*all senses*) mécanisme *m*. defence ~ mécanisme de défense; *V* safety *etc.*

mechanistic [ˌmekə'nɪstɪk] *adj* mécaniste.

mechanization [ˌmekənaɪ'zeɪʃən] *n* mécanisation *f*.

mechanize ['mekənaɪz] *vt process, production* mécaniser; *army* motoriser. ~d industry industrie mécanisée; ~d troops troupes motorisées.

medal ['medl] *n* (*Mil, Sport, gen*) médaille *f*. swimming ~ médaille de natation.

medalist ['medəlɪst] *n* (*US*) = **medallist**.

medallion [mɪ'dæljən] *n* (*gen, Archit*) médaillon *m*.

medallist, (*US*) **medalist** ['medəlɪst] *n* médaillé(e) *m(f)*. gold/silver ~ médaillé d'or/d'argent.

meddle ['medl] *vi* (a) (*interfere*) se mêler, s'occuper (*in* de), s'ingérer (*in* dans) (*frm*). stop meddling! cesse de t'occuper *or* de te mêler de ce qui ne te regarde pas! (b) (*tamper*) toucher (*with* à).

meddler ['medləʳ] *n* (a) (*busybody*) mouche *f* du coche, fâcheux *m*, -euse *f*. he's a dreadful ~ il est toujours à fourrer son nez partout. (b) (*touching things*) touche-à-tout *m inv*.

meddlesome ['medlsəm] *adj*, **meddling** ['medlɪŋ] *adj* (a) (*interfering*) qui fourre son nez partout, indiscret (*f* -ète). (b) (*touching*) qui touche à tout.

media ['miːdɪə] 1 *npl of* **medium** (*souvent employé au sg*) the ~ (*Press, Rad, TV*) (les journalistes *mpl* et reporters *mpl* de) la presse écrite et parlée, les media *mpl*; (*means of communication*) les media, les moyens *mpl* de diffusion de l'information. he claimed the ~ were all against him il prétendait qu'il avait tous les media contre lui; I heard it on the ~* je l'ai entendu à la radio (*or* à la télé); the ~ were waiting for him at the airport*

les journalistes et les photographes l'attendaient à l'aéroport.
2 *cpd*: **media man** (*Press, Rad, TV*) journaliste *m*, reporter *m*; (*Publicity*) agent *m* publicitaire.
mediaeval [ˌmedɪ'i:vəl] *adj* médiéval, du moyen âge; *streets, aspect, charm* moyenâgeux (*also pej*).
mediaevalism [ˌmedɪ'i:vəlɪzəm] *n* médiévisme *m*, médiévalisme *m*.
mediaevalist [ˌmedɪ'i:vəlɪst] *n* médiéviste *mf*.
medial ['mi:dɪəl] **1** *adj* **(a)** (*middle*) (*gen*) médian; (*Ling*) médial, médian. **(b)** (*average*) moyen. **2** *n* (*Ling*) médiale *f*.
median ['mi:dɪən] **1** *adj* médian. **2** *n* **(a)** (*Math, Statistics*) médiane *f*. **(b)** (*US Aut: also* ~ **strip**) bande médiane.
mediant ['mi:dɪənt] *n* médiante *f*.
mediate ['mi:dɪeɪt] **1** *vi* s'entremettre, s'interposer (*in* dans). **to ~ between** servir d'intermédiaire entre. **2** *vt peace, settlement* obtenir par médiation; *dispute* se faire le médiateur de. **3** *adj* médiat.
mediating ['mi:dɪeɪtɪŋ] *adj* médiateur (*f* -trice).
mediation [ˌmi:dɪ'eɪʃən] *n* médiation *f*, intervention *f*, entremise *f*.
mediator ['mi:dɪeɪtəʳ] *n* médiateur *m*, -trice *f*.
medic* ['medɪk] *n* (*abbr of* **medical**) (*student*) carabin* *m*; (*doctor*) toubib* *m*.
medical ['medɪkəl] **1** *adj subject, certificate, treatment* médical. ~ **board** commission médicale, conseil *m* de santé; (*Mil*) conseil de révision; ~ **examination** = **medical 2**; ~ **jurisprudence** médecine légale; ~ **officer** (*Ind*) médecin *m* du travail; (*Mil*) médecin militaire; **M~ Officer of Health** directeur *m* de la santé publique; ~ **practitioner** médecin *m* (de médecine générale), généraliste *mf*; **the ~ profession** (*career*) la carrière médicale; (*personnel*) le corps médical; (*Univ*) ~ **school** école *f or* faculté *f* de médecine; ~ **student** étudiant(e) *m(f)* en médecine; ~ **studies** études *fpl* de médecine *or* médicales; ~ **unit/ward** service *m*/salle *f* de médecine générale.
2 *n* (*also* ~ **examination**) (*in hospital, school, army etc*) visite médicale; (*private*) examen médical.
medically ['medɪkəlɪ] *adv* médicalement. **to be ~ examined** subir un examen médical.
medicament [me'dɪkəmənt] *n* médicament *m*.
Medicare ['medɪkɛəʳ] *n* (*US*) assistance médicale aux personnes âgées.
medicate ['medɪkeɪt] *vt* médicamenter. **~d shampoo** shampooing médical *or* traitant; **~d soap** savon médical *or* médicamenteux.
medication [ˌmedɪ'keɪʃən] *n* médication *f*.
medicinal [me'dɪsɪnl] *adj* médicinal. ~ **herbs** herbes médicinales, simples *mpl*.
medicine ['medsɪn, 'medɪsɪn] **1** *n* **(a)** (*U: science*) médecine *f*. **to study ~** faire (sa) médecine; (*Univ*) **Doctor of M~** docteur *m* en médecine; *V* **forensic** *etc*.
(b) (*drug etc*) médicament *m*, remède *m*. **he takes too many ~s** il prend *or* absorbe trop de médicaments, il se drogue trop; **to take one's ~** (*lit*) prendre son médicament; (*fig*) avaler la pilule; **let's give him a taste** *or* **dose of his own ~** on va lui rendre la monnaie de sa pièce; *V* **patent**.
2 *cpd*: **medicine box, medicine chest** pharmacie *f* (portative); **medicine cabinet, medicine chest, medicine cupboard** (armoire *f* à) pharmacie *f*; **medicine man** sorcier *m*.
medico* ['medɪkəʊ] *n* = **medic**.
medieval [ˌmedɪ'i:vəl] *adj* = **mediaeval**.
medievalism [ˌmedɪ'i:vəlɪzəm] *n* = **mediaevalism**.
medievalist [ˌmedɪ'i:vəlɪst] *n* = **mediaevalist**.
mediocre [ˌmi:dɪ'əʊkəʳ] *adj* médiocre.
mediocrity [ˌmi:dɪ'ɒkrɪtɪ] *n* médiocrité *f*.
meditate ['medɪteɪt] **1** *vt* méditer (*sth* qch, *doing* de faire). **2** *vi* méditer (*on, about* sur), réfléchir (*on, about* à).
meditation [ˌmedɪ'teɪʃən] *n* méditation *f*, réflexion *f* (*on, about* sur). **the fruit of long ~** le fruit de longues méditations; (*Literat etc*) **~s** méditations (*on* sur).
meditative ['medɪtətɪv] *adj* méditatif.
meditatively ['medɪtətɪvlɪ] *adv* d'un air méditatif.
Mediterranean [ˌmedɪtə'reɪnɪən] *adj* méditerranéen. **the ~ (Sea)** la (mer) Méditerranée.
medium ['mi:dɪəm] **1** *n, pl* **media (a)** (*Phys etc*) véhicule *m*; (*Bio, gen: environment, surrounding substance*) milieu *m*; (*fig: means, agency, channel*) moyen *m*, intermédiaire *m*, voie *f*. (*fig*) **through the ~ of the press** par voie de presse; **advertising ~** support *m* publicitaire; **artist's ~** moyens *mpl* d'expression d'un artiste; **television is the best ~ for this type of humour** c'est à la télévision que ce genre d'humour passe le mieux, c'est la télévision qui rend le mieux ce genre d'humour; *V* **culture**.
(b) (*mean*) milieu *m*. **the happy ~** le juste milieu.
(c) (*pl* **mediums**: *Spiritualism*) médium *m*.
2 *adj* moyen (*V also* 3).
3 *cpd*: **medium-dry** *wine, champagne* demi-sec; **medium-fine pen** stylo *m* à pointe moyenne; **medium-sized** de grandeur *or* de taille moyenne; (*Rad*) **on the medium wavelength** sur les ondes moyennes; (*Rad*) **medium waves** ondes moyennes.
medlar ['medləʳ] *n* (*fruit*) nèfle *f*; (*also* ~ **tree**) néflier *m*.
medley ['medlɪ] *n* mélange *m*; (*Mus*) pot-pourri *m*.
medulla [me'dʌlə] *n* (*Anat*) moelle *f*.
meek [mi:k] *adj* doux (*f* douce), humble. ~ **and mild** doux comme un agneau.
meekly ['mi:klɪ] *adv* doucement, humblement.
meekness ['mi:knɪs] *n* douceur *f*, humilité *f*.
meerschaum ['mɪəʃəm] *n* (*pipe*) pipe *f* en écume (de mer); (*clay*) écume *f* de mer.
meet[1] [mi:t] (*pret, ptp* **met**) **1** *vt* **(a)** *person* (*by chance*) rencontrer, tomber sur; (*coming in opposite direction*) croiser; (*by arrangement*) retrouver, rejoindre, revoir; (*go to* ~) (aller) chercher, (aller) attendre. **to arrange to ~ sb at 3 o'clock** donner rendez-vous à qn pour 3 heures; **I am ~ing the chairman at the airport** j'irai attendre le président à l'aéroport; **I am being met at the airport** on *or* quelqu'un viendra m'attendre à l'aéroport; **I'll ~ you outside the cinema** je te *or* on se retrouve devant le cinéma; **don't bother to ~ me** ne prenez pas la peine de venir me chercher; **the car will ~ the train** la voiture attendra *or* sera là à l'arrivée du train; **the bus for Aix ~s the 10 o'clock train** l'autobus d'Aix assure la correspondance avec le train de 10 heures; **he went out to ~ them** il s'avança à leur rencontre, il alla au-devant d'eux; **candidates will be required to ~ the committee** les candidats devront se présenter devant les membres du comité; **I'll ~ you halfway** (*lit*) j'irai à votre rencontre, je vous rencontrerai à mi-chemin; (*fig*) faisons un compromis (*V also* **1c**); *V* **match**[2] *etc*.
(b) (*get to know*) rencontrer, faire la connaissance de, connaître. ~ **Mr Jones** je vous présente M Jones; **I am very pleased to ~ you** enchanté de faire votre connaissance; **glad** *or* **pleased to ~ you!** enchanté!
(c) (*encounter*) *opponent, opposing team, obstacle* rencontrer; (*face*) *enemy, danger* faire face à, affronter; (*in duel*) se battre avec. **he met his death** *or* **his end in 1880** il trouva la mort en 1880; **to ~ death calmly** affronter la mort avec calme *or* sérénité; **to ~ trouble halfway** (aller) chercher les ennuis, aller au-devant des ennuis.
(d) (*satisfy etc*) *expenses, responsibilities, bill, debt* faire face à; *deficit* combler; *demand, need, want* satisfaire à, répondre à; *charge, objection* réfuter. **this will ~ the case** ceci fera l'affaire.
(e) the sound which met his ears le bruit qui frappa ses oreilles; **the sight which met my eye(s)** le spectacle qui me frappa les yeux *or* qui s'offrit à mes yeux; **I met his eye** mon regard rencontra le sien, nos regards se croisèrent; **I dared not** *or* **couldn't ~ her eye** je n'osais pas la regarder en face; **there's more to this than ~s the eye** on ne voit pas *or* on ne connaît pas les dessous de cette affaire.
2 *vi* **(a)** [*people*] (*by chance*) se rencontrer; (*by arrangement*) se retrouver, se rejoindre, se revoir; (*more than once*) se voir; (*get to know each other*) se rencontrer, se connaître, faire connaissance. **to ~ again** se revoir; **until we ~ again!** au revoir!, à la prochaine fois!; **keep it until we ~ again** *or* **until we next ~** garde-le jusqu'à la prochaine fois; **have you met before?** vous vous connaissez déjà?, vous vous êtes déjà rencontrés?; **they arranged to ~ at 10 o'clock** ils se sont donné rendez-vous pour 10 heures.
(b) [*Parliament etc*] se réunir, tenir séance; [*committee, society etc*] se réunir, s'assembler. **the class ~s in the art room** le cours a lieu dans la salle de dessin.
(c) [*armies*] se rencontrer, s'affronter; [*opposing teams*] se rencontrer.
(d) [*lines, roads etc*] (*join*) se rencontrer; (*cross*) se croiser; [*rivers*] se rencontrer, confluer. **our eyes met** nos regards se croisèrent; *V* **end**.
3 *n* **(a)** (*Hunting*) rendez-vous *m* (de chasse); (*huntsmen*) chasse *f*.
(b) (*US Sport etc*) réunion *f*, meeting *m*.
meet up *vi* (*by chance*) se rencontrer; (*by arrangement*) se retrouver, se rejoindre, se revoir. **to meet up with sb** rencontrer *or* rejoindre *or* retrouver *or* revoir qn.
meet with *vt fus* **(a)** *difficulties, obstacles* rencontrer; *refusal, losses, storm, gale* essuyer; *welcome, reception* recevoir. **he met with an accident** il lui est arrivé un accident; **we met with great kindness** on nous a traités avec une grande gentillesse.
(b) (*US*) *person* (*by chance*) rencontrer, tomber sur; (*coming in opposite direction*) croiser; (*by arrangement*) retrouver, rejoindre, revoir.
meet[2] [mi:t] *adj* († *or liter: suitable*) convenable, séant†.
meeting ['mi:tɪŋ] **1** *n* **(a)** (*assembly*) [*political party, club etc*] réunion *f*; (*large, formal*) assemblée *f*; (*Pol, Sport*) meeting *m*. **to hold a ~** tenir une assemblée *or* une réunion *or* un meeting; **to call a ~ of shareholders** convoquer les actionnaires; **to call a ~ to discuss sth** convoquer une réunion pour débattre qch; *V* **annual, mass**[1], **open** *etc*.
(b) (*between individuals*) rencontre *f*; (*arranged*) rendez-vous *m*; (*formal*) entrevue *f*. **the minister had a ~ with the ambassador** le ministre s'est entretenu avec l'ambassadeur, le ministre a eu une entrevue avec l'ambassadeur.
(c) (*Quakers*) culte *m*. **to go to ~** aller au culte.
2 *cpd*: **(Quakers') meeting house** temple *m*; **meeting place** lieu *m* de réunion.
mega... ['megə] *pref* méga... .
megacycle ['megəˌsaɪkl] *n* mégacycle *m*.
megalith ['megəlɪθ] *n* mégalithe *m*.
megalithic [ˌmegə'lɪθɪk] *adj* mégalithique.
megalomania [ˌmegələʊ'meɪnɪə] *n* mégalomanie *f*.
megalomaniac [ˌmegələʊ'meɪnɪæk] *adj, n* mégalomane (*mf*).
megaphone ['megəfəʊn] *n* porte-voix *m inv*.
megaton ['megətʌn] *n* mégatonne *f*.
meiosis [maɪ'əʊsɪs] *n* (*Bio*) méiose *f*; (*Literat*) litote *f*.
melamine ['meləmi:n] *n* mélamine *f*.
melancholia [ˌmelən'kəʊlɪə] *n* (*Psych*) mélancolie *f*.
melancholic [ˌmelən'kɒlɪk] *adj* (*gen, Psych*) mélancolique.
melancholy ['melənkəlɪ] **1** *n* (*U*) mélancolie *f*. **2** *adj person, look* mélancolique; *news, duty, event* triste, attristant.
melanic [mə'lænɪk] *adj* mélanique.
melanism ['melənɪzəm] *n* mélanisme *m*.
mellifluous [me'lɪflʊəs] *adj* mélodieux, doux (*f* douce) (à l'oreille).

mellow ['meləʊ] **1** *adj fruit* mûr, fondant; *wine* moelleux, velouté; *colour* doux, velouté; *light* doux (*f* douce), velouté; *earth, soil* meuble, riche; *voice, tone* moelleux, harmonieux, mélodieux; *building* patiné (par l'âge); *person* mûri et tranquille; *character* mûri par l'expérience. **to grow ~** mûrir, s'adoucir.

2 *vt fruit* (faire) mûrir; *wine* rendre moelleux, donner du velouté *or* du moelleux à; *voice, sound* adoucir, rendre plus moelleux; *colour* fondre, velouter; *person, character* adoucir, arrondir les angles de (*fig*). **the years have ~ed him** les angles de son caractère se sont arrondis avec l'âge, il s'est adouci avec les années.

3 *vi [fruit]* mûrir; *[wine]* se velouter; *[colour]* se velouter, se patiner; *[voice]* prendre du moelleux, se velouter; *[person, character]* s'adoucir.

mellowing ['meləʊɪŋ] **1** *n [fruit, wine]* maturation *f*; *[voice, colours, person, attitude]* adoucissement *m*. **2** *adj effect etc* adoucissant.

mellowness ['meləʊnɪs] *n [fruit]* douceur *f* (fondante); *[wine]* moelleux *m*, velouté *m*; *[colour]* douceur, velouté; *[voice, tone]* timbre moelleux *or* velouté; *[building]* patine *f*; *[light, character, attitude]* douceur.

melodic [mɪ'lɒdɪk] *adj* mélodique.

melodious [mɪ'ləʊdɪəs] *adj* mélodieux.

melodiously [mɪ'ləʊdɪəslɪ] *adv* mélodieusement.

melodrama ['meləʊˌdrɑːmə] *n* (*lit, fig*) mélodrame *m*, mélo* *m* (*pej*).

melodramatic [ˌmeləʊdrə'mætɪk] *adj* mélodramatique.

melodramatically [ˌmeləʊdrə'mætɪkəlɪ] *adv* d'un air *or* d'une façon mélodramatique.

melody ['melədɪ] *n* mélodie *f*.

melon ['melən] *n* melon *m*.

melt [melt] **1** *vi* **(a)** *[ice, butter, metal]* fondre; *[solid in liquid]* fondre, se dissoudre. **these cakes ~ in the mouth** ces pâtisseries fondent dans la bouche; (*fig*) **he looks as if butter wouldn't ~ in his mouth** on lui donnerait le bon Dieu sans confession* (*fig*); *V also* **melting.**

(b) (*fig*) *[colours, sounds]* se fondre, s'estomper (*into* dans); *[person]* se fondre, s'attendrir; *[anger]* tomber; *[resolution, determination]* fléchir, fondre. **to ~ into tears** fondre en larmes; **her heart ~ed with pity** son cœur s'est fondu de pitié; **night ~ed into day** la nuit a fait insensiblement place au jour; **one colour ~ed into another** les couleurs se fondaient les unes dans les autres; **the thief ~ed into the crowd** le voleur s'est fondu *or* a disparu dans la foule.

(c) (*: *be too hot*) fondre, être en nage.

2 *vt ice, butter* (faire) fondre; *metal* fondre. (*fig*) **to ~ sb's heart** attendrir *or* émouvoir (le cœur de) qn; (*Culin*) **~ed butter** beurre fondu; *V also* **melting.**

melt away *vi* **(a)** *[ice etc]* fondre complètement, disparaître.

(b) (*fig*) *[money, savings]* fondre; *[anger]* se dissiper, tomber; *[confidence]* disparaître; *[fog]* se dissiper; *[crowd]* se disperser; *[person]* se volatiliser, s'évaporer*, s'envoler*.

melt down *vt sep* fondre; *scrap iron, coins* remettre à la fonte.

melting ['meltɪŋ] **1** *adj snow* fondant; (*fig*) *voice, look* attendri; *words, sentiments* attendrissant.

2 *n [snow]* fonte *f*; *[metal]* fusion *f*, fonte.

3 *cpd*: **melting point** point *m* de fusion; (*lit*) **melting pot** creuset *m*; (*fig*) **the country was a melting pot of many nationalities** le pays était le creuset de bien des nationalités; **the scheme was back in the melting pot again** le projet a été remis en question une fois de plus; **it's still all in the melting pot** c'est encore en pleine discussion *or* au stade des discussions.

member ['membə^r^] **1** *n* **(a)** *[society, political party etc]* membre *m*, adhérent(e) *m(f)*; *[family, tribe]* membre. (*on notice etc*) **'~s only'** 'réservé aux adhérents'; **a ~ of the audience** un membre de l'assistance, l'un des assistants; (*hearer*) un auditeur; (*spectator*) un spectateur; (*US Pol*) **M~ of Congress** membre du Congrès; **a ~ of the congress** un(e) congressiste; **they treated her like a ~ of the family** ils l'ont traitée comme si elle faisait partie *or* était de la famille; (*Brit Pol*) **M~ of Parliament** ≈ député *m*; **the M~ (of Parliament) for Woodford** le député de Woodford; **a ~ of the public** un simple particulier, une simple particulière, un(e) simple citoyen(ne); (*Scol, Univ*) **a ~ of staff** un professeur; *V* **full, honorary, private** *etc.*

(b) (*Anat, Bot, Math etc*) membre *m*. (*Anat*) **(male) ~** membre (viril).

2 *cpd*: **the member nations** *or* **countries** *or* **states** les États *mpl or* pays *mpl* membres.

membership ['membəʃɪp] **1** *n* **(a)** (*state*) adhésion *f*. **Britain's ~ of the Common Market** l'adhésion de la Grande-Bretagne au Marché Commun; **when I applied for ~ of the club** quand j'ai fait ma demande d'adhésion au club; **he has given up his ~ of the party** il a rendu sa carte du parti; **~ carries certain privileges** l'adhésion donne droit à certains privilèges, les membres jouissent de certains privilèges.

(b) (*number of members*) **this society has a ~ of over 800** cette société a plus de 800 membres.

2 *cpd*: **membership card** carte *f* d'adhérent *or* de membre; **membership fee** cotisation *f*, droits *mpl* d'inscription; **membership qualifications** conditions *fpl* d'éligibilité.

membrane ['membreɪn] *n* membrane *f*.

membranous [mem'breɪnəs] *adj* membraneux.

memento [mə'mentəʊ] *n* (*keepsake*) souvenir *m*; (*note, mark etc*) mémento *m*; (*scar*) souvenir. **as a ~ of** en souvenir de.

memo ['meməʊ] **1** *n* (*) *abbr of* **memorandum a** *and* **b. 2** *cpd*: **memo pad** bloc-notes *m*.

memoir ['memwɑː^r^] *n* (*essay*) mémoire *m*, étude *f* (*on* sur); (*short biography*) notice *f* biographique. **~s** (*autobiographical*) mémoires; *[learned society]* actes *mpl*.

memorable ['memərəbl] *adj* mémorable.

memorably ['memərəblɪ] *adv* mémorablement.

memorandum [ˌmemə'rændəm] *n, pl* **memoranda** [ˌmemə'rændə] **(a)** (*reminder, note*) mémorandum *m*, note *f*. **to make a ~ of sth** prendre note de qch, noter qch.

(b) (*Comm etc: informal communication*) note *f*. **he sent a ~ round about the drop in sales** il a fait circuler une note *or* il a fait passer une circulaire à propos de la baisse des ventes.

(c) (*Diplomacy*) mémorandum *m*.

(d) (*Jur*) sommaire *m* des statuts (d'un contrat).

memorial [mɪ'mɔːrɪəl] **1** *adj plaque, service* commémoratif. (*US*) **M~ Day** le jour des morts au champ d'honneur (*dernier lundi de mai*).

2 *n* **(a)** (*sth serving as reminder*) **this scholarship is a ~ to John F. Kennedy** cette bourse d'études est en mémoire de John F. Kennedy.

(b) (*monument*) monument *m* (commémoratif), mémorial *m*; (*over grave*) monument (funéraire). **a ~ to the victims** un monument aux victimes.

(c) (*also* **war ~**) monument *m* aux morts.

(d) (*Hist: chronicles*) **~s** chroniques *fpl*, mémoires *mpl*, mémorial *m*.

(e) (*Admin etc: petition*) pétition *f*, requête *f* (officielle).

memorize ['meməraɪz] *vt facts, figures, names* retenir, graver dans sa mémoire; *poem, speech* apprendre par cœur.

memory ['memərɪ] *n* **(a)** (*faculty; also Computers*) mémoire *f*. **to have a good/bad ~** avoir (une) bonne/mauvaise mémoire; **to have a ~ for faces** avoir la mémoire des visages, être physionomiste; **to play/quote from ~** jouer/citer de mémoire; **to commit to ~** *poem* apprendre par cœur; *facts, figures* enregistrer dans sa mémoire, retenir; **to the best of my ~** autant que je m'en souvienne; **loss of ~** perte *f* de mémoire; (*Med*) amnésie *f*; *V* **living.**

(b) (*recollection*) souvenir *m*. **childhood memories** souvenirs d'enfance; **'memories of a country childhood'** 'souvenirs d'une enfance à la campagne'; **the ~ of the accident remained with him all his life** il a conservé toute sa vie le souvenir de l'accident, le souvenir de l'accident est resté gravé dans sa mémoire toute sa vie; **to keep sb's ~ alive** *or* **green** garder vivant le souvenir de qn, entretenir la mémoire de qn; **in ~ of** en souvenir de, à la mémoire de; **sacred to the ~ of** à la mémoire de; **of blessed ~** de glorieuse mémoire.

men [men] **1** *npl of* **man. 2** *cpd*: **the menfolk*** les hommes *mpl*; (*Comm*) **menswear** (*clothing*) habillement masculin; (*department*) rayon *m* hommes; *V also* **man.**

menace ['menɪs] **1** *n* menace *f*. **he drives so badly he's a ~ to the public** il conduit si mal qu'il est un danger public; **that child/dog/motorbike is a ~*** cet enfant/ce chien/cette motocyclette est une plaie*. **2** *vt* menacer.

menacing ['menɪsɪŋ] *adj* menaçant.

menacingly ['menɪsɪŋlɪ] *adv act* d'un air menaçant; *say* d'un ton menaçant.

ménage [me'nɑːʒ] *n* (*often pej*) ménage *m*.

menagerie [mɪ'nædʒərɪ] *n* ménagerie *f*.

mend [mend] **1** *vt* **(a)** (*repair*) *clothes etc* raccommoder; *watch, wall, vehicle, shoes etc* réparer; (*darn*) *sock, stocking* repriser; *laddered stocking* remmailler; *V* **invisibly.**

(b) (*fig*) *mistake etc* corriger, rectifier, réparer. **that won't ~ matters** cela ne va pas arranger les choses; **to ~ one's ways, to ~ one's manners** s'amender; *V* **least.**

2 *vi* **(a)** (*darn etc*) faire le raccommodage.

(b) (*) = **to be on the ~**; *V* **3b.**

3 *n* **(a)** (*on clothes*) raccommodage *m*; (*patch*) pièce *f*; (*darn*) reprise *f*.

(b) to be on the ~ *[invalid]* être en voie de guérison, aller mieux; *[business, sales]* prendre une meilleure tournure, reprendre, s'améliorer; *[conditions, situation, weather]* s'améliorer.

mendacious [men'deɪʃəs] *adj report* mensonger, fallacieux; *person* menteur.

mendacity [men'dæsɪtɪ] *n* **(a)** (*U*) (*habit*) fausseté *f*, habitude *f* de mentir; (*tendency*) propension *f* au mensonge; *[report]* caractère mensonger. **(b)** (*lie*) mensonge *m*.

Mendelian [men'diːlɪən] *adj* mendélien.

Mendelianism [men'diːlɪənɪzəm] *n*, **Mendelism** ['mendəlɪzəm] *n* mendélisme *m*.

mendicancy ['mendɪkənsɪ] *n* mendicité *f*.

mendicant ['mendɪkənt] *adj, n* mendiant(e) *m(f)*.

mendicity [men'dɪsɪtɪ] *n* mendicité *f*.

mending ['mendɪŋ] *n* raccommodage *m*; *V* **invisible.**

Menelaus [ˌmenɪ'leɪəs] *n* Ménélas *m*.

menial ['miːnɪəl] **1** *adj person* servile; *task* de domestique, inférieur; *position* subalterne. **2** *n* domestique *mf*, laquais *m* (*pej*).

meningitis [ˌmenɪn'dʒaɪtɪs] *n* méningite *f*.

menopausal ['menəʊpɔːzəl] *adj symptom* dû (*f* due) à la ménopause; *woman* à la ménopause.

menopause ['menəʊpɔːz] *n* ménopause *f*.

menses ['mensiːz] *npl* menstrues *fpl*.

menstrual ['menstrʊəl] *adj* menstruel. **pre-~ tension** syndrome prémenstruel.

menstruate ['menstrʊeɪt] *vi* avoir ses règles.

menstruation [ˌmenstrʊ'eɪʃən] *n* menstruation *f*.

mensuration [ˌmensjʊə'reɪʃən] *n* (*also Math*) mesurage *m*.

mental ['mentl] *adj* **(a)** *ability, process* mental, intellectuel; *illness* mental. **~ age** âge mental; **he's a ~ case*** il a le cerveau dérangé*, il est timbré*; (*Psych*) **~ defective** débile *mf* mental(e); (*Psych*) **~ deficiency** débilité *or* déficience mentale; (*US Med*) **~ healing** thérapeutique *f* par la suggestion; **~ home, ~ hospital, ~ institution** hôpital *m or* clinique *f* psychiatrique; **~**

patient malade *mf* mental(e); ~ **powers** facultés intellectuelles; (*Psych*) ~ **retardation** arriération mentale; ~ **strain** (*tension*) tension nerveuse; (*overwork*) surmenage *m* (intellectuel); **she's been under a great deal of ~ strain** ses nerfs ont été mis à rude épreuve.

(b) *calculation* mental, de tête; *prayer* intérieur. ~ **arithmetic** calcul mental; **he made a ~ note to do it** il prit note mentalement de le faire; **to have ~ reservations about sth** avoir des doutes sur qch.

(c) (*: *mad*) fou (*f* folle), malade*, timbré*.

mentality [men'tælɪtɪ] *n* mentalité *f*.

mentally ['mentəlɪ] *adv calculate, formulate* mentalement. (*Psych*) ~ **defective** mentalement déficient; ~ **disturbed** déséquilibré; ~ **disabled**, ~ **handicapped** anormal; **a ~ handicapped person** un(e) anormal(e); ~ **ill** atteint de maladie mentale; **a ~ ill person** un(e) malade mental(e); (*Psych*) ~ **retarded** (mentalement) arriéré.

menthol ['menθɒl] *n* menthol *m*. ~ **cigarettes** cigarettes mentholées.

mentholated ['menθəleɪtɪd] *adj* mentholé.

mention ['menʃən] **1** *vt* mentionner, faire mention de, signaler, parler de; (*quote*) citer. **he ~ed to me that you were coming** il m'a mentionné votre venue *or* que vous alliez venir; **I'll ~ it to him** je lui en toucherai un mot, je le lui signalerai; **I've never heard him ~ his father** je ne l'ai jamais entendu parler de son père; **to ~ sb in one's will** coucher qn sur son testament; **he didn't ~ the accident** il n'a pas fait mention de l'accident, il n'a pas soufflé mot de l'accident; **just ~ my name** dites que c'est de ma part; **he ~ed several names** il a cité plusieurs noms; **without ~ing any names** sans nommer *or* citer personne; **I ~ this fact only because ...** je relève ce fait uniquement parce que ...; **they are too numerous to ~** ils sont trop nombreux pour qu'on les mentionne (*subj*) *or* cite (*subj*) (tous); **don't ~ it!** il n'y a pas de quoi!, de rien!*, je vous en prie!; **I need hardly ~ that ...** il va sans dire que ...; **it must be ~ed that ...** il faut signaler que ...; **not to ~ ..., without ~ing ...** sans compter ...; **it is not worth ~ing** cela ne vaut pas la peine d'en parler; **I have no jazz records worth ~ing** je n'ai pour ainsi dire pas de disques de jazz; *V* **dispatch.**

2 *n* mention *f*. **to make ~ of** faire mention de, signaler; **honourable ~** mention honorable; **it got a ~ in the news*** on en a parlé *or* on l'a mentionné aux informations.

mentor ['mentɔːʳ] *n* mentor *m*.

menu ['menjuː] *n* menu *m*; (*printed, written*) menu, carte *f*; *V* **fixed.**

meow [miː'aʊ] = **miaow.**

Mephistopheles [ˌmefɪs'tɒfɪliːz] *n* Méphistophélès *m*.

mephistophelian [ˌmefɪstɒ'fiːlɪən] *adj* méphistophélique.

mercantile ['mɜːkəntaɪl] *adj* **(a)** *navy, vessel* marchand; *affairs* commercial; *nation* commerçant; *firm, establishment* de commerce; (*pej*) *person, attitude* mercantile. ~ **law** droit commercial; ~ **marine** marine marchande. **(b)** (*Econ*) mercantile.

mercantilism ['mɜːkəntɪlɪzəm] *n* (*Econ, also pej*) mercantilisme *m*.

mercantilist ['mɜːkəntɪlɪst] *adj, n* (*Econ*) mercantiliste (*m*).

mercenary ['mɜːsɪnərɪ] **1** *adj* **(a)** (*pej*) *person, attitude* intéressé, mercenaire. **(b)** (*Mil*) mercenaire. **2** *n* (*Mil*) mercenaire *m*.

mercer ['mɜːsəʳ] *n* (*Brit*) marchand *m* de tissus.

merchandise ['mɜːtʃəndaɪz] **1** *n* (*U*) marchandises *fpl*. **2** *vi* commercer, faire du commerce. **3** *vt* promouvoir la vente de.

merchandizer ['mɜːtʃəndaɪzəʳ] *n* spécialiste *mf* des techniques marchandes, merchandiser *m*.

merchandizing ['mɜːtʃəndaɪzɪŋ] *n* techniques marchandes, merchandising *m*.

merchant ['mɜːtʃənt] **1** *n* (*trader, dealer*) négociant *m*; (*wholesaler*) marchand *m* en gros, grossiste *m*; (*retailer*) marchand au détail, détaillant *m*; (*shopkeeper*) commerçant *m*. **'The M~ of Venice'** 'le Marchand de Venise'; *V* **coal, speed, wine** *etc*.

2 *cpd*: (*Brit Fin*) **merchant bank** banque *f* de commerce *or* d'affaires; (*Naut*) **merchantman** = **merchant ship**; (*US*) **merchant marine**, (*Brit*) **merchant navy** marine marchande; **merchant seaman** marin *m* de la marine marchande; **merchant ship** navire marchand *or* de commerce; (*U*) **merchant shipping** navires marchands; **merchant vessel** vaisseau marchand *or* de commerce.

merciful ['mɜːsɪfʊl] *adj* miséricordieux (*to, towards* pour), clément (*to, towards* envers). **his death was a ~ release** sa mort a été une délivrance.

mercifully ['mɜːsɪfəlɪ] *adv judge, act* miséricordieusement, avec clémence. ~ **it didn't rain*** Dieu merci *or* par bonheur il n'a pas plu.

merciless ['mɜːsɪlɪs] *adj person, judgment* impitoyable, implacable, sans pitié; *rain, storm, heat* implacable, impitoyable.

mercilessly ['mɜːsɪlɪslɪ] *adv* (*V* **merciless**) impitoyablement, implacablement, sans pitié.

mercurial [mɜː'kjʊərɪəl] *adj* (*Chem*) mercuriel; (*changeable*) d'humeur inégale *or* changeante; (*lively*) vif (*f* vive), plein d'entrain.

mercury ['mɜːkjʊrɪ] *n* **(a)** (*Chem*) mercure *m*. **(b)** **M~** (*Astron*) Mercure *f*; (*Myth*) Mercure *m*.

mercy ['mɜːsɪ] **1** *n* **(a)** indulgence *f*, pitié *f*, grâce *f*, merci *f*; (*Rel*) miséricorde *f*. **without ~** sans pitié; **for ~'s sake** par pitié; **God in his ~** Dieu en sa miséricorde; **no ~ was shown to the revolutionaries** les révolutionnaires furent impitoyablement traités *or* traités sans merci; **to have ~ on sb** avoir pitié de qn; **to beg for ~** demander grâce; **to show ~ towards** *or* **to sb** montrer de l'indulgence pour *or* envers qn; (*Jur*) **with a recommendation to ~** ≈ avec avis en faveur d'une commutation de peine; **to throw o.s. on sb's ~** s'en remettre à la merci de qn; **at the ~ of sb/the weather** *etc* à la merci de qn/du temps *etc*; (*iro*) **to leave sb to the tender ~** *or* **mercies of** abandonner qn aux bons soins (*iro*) *or* au bon vouloir (*iro*) de; (*excl*) ~ **(me)!*** Seigneur!, miséricorde!

(b) (*piece of good fortune*) **to be thankful for small mercies** être reconnaissant du peu qui s'offre; **it's a ~ that** heureusement que + *indic*, c'est une chance que + *subj*; **his death was a ~** sa mort a été une délivrance.

2 *cpd*: **mercy killing** euthanasie *f*.

mere[1] [mɪəʳ] *n* étang *m*, (petit) lac *m*.

mere[2] [mɪəʳ] *adj* simple, pur, seul. **he's a ~ child** ce n'est qu'un enfant; **he's a ~ clerk** c'est un simple employé de bureau, il n'est qu'employé de bureau; **by a ~ chance** par pur hasard; **the ~ sight of him makes me shiver** sa seule vue me fait frissonner, rien qu'à le voir je frissonne; **they quarrelled over a ~ nothing** ils se sont disputés pour une vétille; **he's a ~ nobody** il est moins que rien; **it's a ~ kilometre away** ce n'est qu'à un kilomètre (de distance).

merely ['mɪəlɪ] *adv* purement, simplement, seulement. **I ~ said that she was coming** j'ai tout simplement dit *or* je n'ai fait que dire qu'elle arrivait; **he ~ nodded** il se contenta de faire un signe de tête; **he's ~ a clerk** il n'est qu'employé de bureau; **I did it ~ to please her** je ne l'ai fait que pour lui faire plaisir; ~ **to look at him makes me shiver** rien que de le regarder me fait frissonner; **it's ~ a formality** ce n'est qu'une formalité, c'est une simple formalité; **it's not ~ broken, it's ruined** ce n'est pas seulement cassé, c'est fichu*.

meretricious [ˌmerɪ'trɪʃəs] *adj charm, attraction* factice; *style* plein d'artifices, ampoulé; *jewellery, decoration* clinquant.

merge [mɜːdʒ] **1** *vi* **(a)** *[colours, shapes]* se mêler (*into, with* à), se fondre (*into, with* dans); *[sounds]* se mêler (*into, with* à), se perdre (*into, with* dans); *[roads]* se rencontrer (*with* avec), se joindre (*with* à); *[river]* confluer (*with* avec).

(b) (*Comm, Fin*) fusionner (*with* avec).

2 *vt* **(a)** unifier, unir. **the states were ~d (into one) in 1976** les États se sont unifiés en 1976, l'unification des États s'est réalisée en 1976.

(b) (*Comm, Fin*) fusionner, amalgamer. **the firms were ~d** les entreprises ont fusionné; **they decided to ~ the companies into a single unit** ils décidèrent d'amalgamer *or* de fusionner les compagnies.

merger ['mɜːdʒəʳ] *n* (*Comm, Fin*) fusion *f*, fusionnement *m*.

meridian [mə'rɪdɪən] **1** *n* (*Astron, Geog*) méridien *m*; (*fig*) apogée *m*, zénith *m*. **2** *adj* méridien.

meridional [mə'rɪdɪənl] **1** *adj* méridional. **2** *n* Méridional(e) *m(f)*.

meringue [mə'ræŋ] *n* meringue *f*.

merino [mə'riːnəʊ] *n* mérinos *m*.

merit ['merɪt] **1** *n* mérite *m*, valeur *f*. **people of ~** gens de valeur *or* de mérite; **the great ~ of this scheme** le grand mérite de ce projet; **to treat sb according to his ~s** traiter qn selon ses mérites; **to decide a case on its ~s** décider d'un cas en toute objectivité; **they went into the ~s of the new plan** ils ont discuté le pour et le contre de ce nouveau projet.

2 *cpd*: **merit list** tableau *m* d'honneur; (*US Admin*) **merit system** système *m* de recrutement et de promotion par voie de concours.

3 *vt* mériter. **this ~s fuller discussion** ceci mérite plus ample discussion *or* d'être plus amplement discuté.

meritocracy [ˌmerɪ'tɒkrəsɪ] *n* méritocratie *f*.

meritorious [ˌmerɪ'tɔːrɪəs] *adj person* méritant; *work, deed* méritoire.

meritoriously [ˌmerɪ'tɔːrɪəslɪ] *adv* d'une façon méritoire.

merlin ['mɜːlɪn] *n* (*Orn*) émerillon *m*.

mermaid ['mɜːmeɪd] *n* (*Myth*) sirène *f*.

merman ['mɜːmæn] *n* (*Myth*) triton *m*.

merovingian [ˌmerəʊ'vɪndʒɪən] **1** *adj* mérovingien. **2** *n* Mérovingien(ne) *m(f)*.

merrily ['merɪlɪ] *adv* joyeusement, gaiement *or* gaîment.

merriment ['merɪmənt] *n* (*U*) gaieté *f or* gaîté *f*, joie *f*; (*laughter*) hilarité *f*. **this remark caused a lot of ~** cette remarque a provoqué l'hilarité générale.

merry ['merɪ] **1** *adj* **(a)** gai, joyeux. **to make ~**† s'amuser, se divertir; **M~ Christmas!** Joyeux Noël!; **M~ England** l'Angleterre du bon vieux temps; **Robin Hood and his ~ men** Robin des Bois et ses joyeux lurons; *V* **may**[2], **more** *etc*.

(b) (*: *tipsy*) éméché*, pompette*. **to grow** *or* **get ~** se griser; **he's getting ~** il a un verre dans le nez*.

2 *cpd*: **merry-go-round** (*in fairground*) manège *m* (*de chevaux de bois etc*); (*fig*) tourbillon *m*; (*U*) **merrymaking** réjouissances *fpl*.

mescaline ['meskəlɪn] *n* mescaline *f*.

mesh [meʃ] **1** *n* **(a)** *[net, sieve etc]* (*space*) maille *f*; (*fig*) (*network*) réseau *m*, rets *mpl*; (*snare*) rets, filets *mpl*. **netting with 5-cm ~** filet à mailles de 5 cm; **~es** (*threads*) mailles *fpl*; *[spider's web]* fils *mpl*, toile *f*; (*fig*) **trapped in the ~ of circumstances** pris dans l'engrenage des circonstances; (*fig*) **caught in the ~es of the law** pris dans les mailles de la justice; **the ~(es) of intrigue** le réseau d'intrigues; *V* **micro...**.

(b) (*U*) (*fabric*) tissu *m* à mailles. **nylon ~** tulle *m* de nylon; **wire ~** treillis *m*, grillage *m*; **a belt of fine gold ~** une ceinture tressée de fils d'or.

(c) *[gears etc]* engrenage *m*. **in ~** en prise.

2 *cpd*: **mesh bag** filet *m* (à provisions); **mesh stockings** (*nonrun*) bas *mpl* indémaillables; (*in cabaret, circus etc*) bas *mpl* filet.

3 *vi [wheels, gears]* s'engrener; *[dates, plans]* concorder, cadrer.

4 *vt fish etc* prendre au filet.

mesmeric [mezˈmerɪk] *adj* hypnotique, magnétique.

mesmerism [ˈmezmərɪzəm] *n* mesmérisme *m.*

mesmerize [ˈmezməraɪz] *vt* hypnotiser, magnétiser; *[snake]* fasciner. (*fig*) **to ~ sb into doing sth** amener qn à faire qch par hypnotisme *or* en faisant usage de (son) pouvoir magnétique.

meson [ˈmiːzɒn] *n* (*Phys*) méson *m.*

mess [mes] **1** *n* **(a)** (*confusion of objects etc*) désordre *m,* pagaïe* *f or* pagaille* *f,* fouillis* *m,* fatras *m;* (*dirt*) saleté *f;* (*muddle*) gâchis *m;* (*fig*) gâchis, pétrin *m,* cafouillage* *m,* cafouillis* *m.* **what a ~ the children have made!** quel désordre *or* gâchis les enfants ont fait!, les enfants ont mis un beau désordre!; **what a ~ your room is in!** quel fouillis* *or* quelle pagaïe* il y a dans ta chambre!; **get this ~ cleared up at once!** range-moi ce fouillis* tout de suite!; **the house was in a terrible ~** (*untidy*) la maison était dans un désordre épouvantable; (*dirty*) la maison était d'une saleté épouvantable; (*after warfare etc*) la maison était dans un triste état *or* un état épouvantable; **his shirt was in a ~** sa chemise était dans un triste état; **the toys were in a ~** les jouets étaient en pagaïe* *or* en désordre; **they left everything in a ~** ils ont tout laissé en pagaïe* *or* en désordre; **this page is (in) a ~, rewrite it** cette page est un vrai torchon, recopiez-la; (*after fight, accident etc*) **his face was in a dreadful ~** il avait le visage dans un état épouvantable; **she made a ~ of her new skirt** (*dirty*) elle a sali *or* tout taché sa jupe neuve; (*tear*) elle a déchiré sa jupe neuve; **the dog has made a ~ of the flowerbeds** le chien a saccagé les plates-bandes; **your boots have made an awful ~ on the carpet** tu as fait des saletés sur le tapis avec tes bottes; **the cat has made a ~ in the kitchen** le chat a fait des saletés dans la cuisine; (*fig*) **to make a ~ of** *essay, sewing, one's life, career* gâcher; **to make a ~ of things*** tout bousiller*, tout gâcher; (**fig: difficulties*) **to be/get (o.s.) in a ~** être/se mettre dans de beaux draps *or* dans le pétrin; **his life is in a ~** sa vie est un vrai gâchis; **to get (o.s.) out of a ~** se sortir d'un mauvais pas, se dépatouiller*; **to get sb out of a ~** sortir qn d'un mauvais pas; **what a ~ it all is!** quel pétrin!, quel gâchis!

(b) (*Mil*) (*place*) mess *m,* cantine *f,* popote* *f;* (*Naut*) carré *m,* gamelle *f;* (*food*) ordinaire *m,* gamelle; (*members*) mess.

(c) (*animal food*) pâtée *f;* (††: *dish*) mets *m,* plat *m.* (*Bible*) **a ~ of pottage** un plat de lentilles.

2 *cpd:* (*Naut*) **mess deck** poste *m* d'équipage; (*Mil etc*) **mess dress** tenue *f* de soirée; (*Brit*) **mess gear* = mess dress;** (*US*) **mess hall = mess room; mess jacket** (*Mil etc*) veston *m* de tenue de soirée; *[civilian waiter]* veste courte; **mess kit** (*US*) gamelle *f;* (*Brit**) tenue *f* de soirée; (*Naut*) **mess mate** camarade *m* de plat; **mess room** (*Mil*) (salle *f* de) mess *m;* (*Naut*) carré *m;* (*Mil*) **mess tin** gamelle *f;* (*Brit*) **mess-up*** gâchis *m.*

3 *vt* salir, souiller.

4 *vi* (*Mil etc*) manger au mess, manger en commun (*with* avec).

mess about, mess around 1 *vi* **(a)** (*in water, mud*) patouiller*, (*with feet*) patauger, (*with hands*) tripoter.

(b) (*) (*waste time*) gaspiller *or* perdre son temps; (*dawdle*) lambiner, lanterner. **he was messing about with his friends** il traînait *or* (se) baguenaudait avec ses copains; **what were you doing? — just messing about** que faisais-tu? — rien de particulier *or* de spécial; **I love messing about in boats** j'aime (m'amuser à) faire de la voile.

2 *vt sep* (*: *disturb, upset*) *person* créer des complications à, embêter*; *plans, arrangements* chambarder*, chambouler*.

mess about with*, mess around with* *vt fus* **(a)** (*fiddle with*) *pen, ornament etc* tripoter.

(b) (*amuse o.s. with*) **they were messing about with a ball** ils s'amusaient à taper *or* ils tapaient dans un ballon.

(c) = mess about 2.

(d) stop messing about with him and tell him the truth arrête de t'amuser avec lui et dis-lui la vérité.

(e) (*sexually*) peloter*.

mess together *vi* (*Mil etc*) manger ensemble au mess; (**gen*) faire popote* ensemble.

mess up 1 *vt sep clothes* salir, gâcher; *room* mettre en désordre, semer la pagaïe dans*; *hair* ébouriffer; *task, situation, plans, life etc* gâcher. **to mess sb's hair up** décoiffer qn; **that's messed everything up!** cela a tout gâché!

2 mess-up *n V* **mess 2.**

message [ˈmesɪdʒ] **1** *n* **(a)** (*communication: by speech, writing, signals etc*) message *m.* **telephone ~** message téléphonique; **to leave a ~ (for sb)** laisser un mot (pour qn); **would you give him this ~?** voudriez-vous lui faire cette commission?

(b) (*official or diplomatic etc communication*) message *m.* **the President's ~ to Congress** le message du Président au Congrès.

(c) *[prophet, writer, artist, book etc]* message *m.* **to get the ~*** comprendre, saisir*, piger*.

(d) (*Scot: errand*) course *f,* commission *f.* **to go on a ~ for sb** faire une course pour qn; **to go for** *or* **get the ~s** faire les courses *or* les commissions.

2 *cpd:* (*Scot*) **message basket** panier *m* à provisions; **message-boy** garçon *m* de courses.

messenger [ˈmesɪndʒəʳ] **1** *n* messager *m,* -ère *f;* (*in office*) commissionnaire *m,* coursier *m;* (*in hotel etc*) chasseur *m,* coursier; (*Post*) (petit) télégraphiste *m; V* **king** *etc.* **2** *cpd:* **messenger boy** garçon *m* de courses.

Messiah [mɪˈsaɪə] *n* Messie *m.*

messianic [ˌmesɪˈænɪk] *adj* messianique.

Messrs [ˈmesəz] *n* (*abbr*) messieurs *mpl* (*abbr* MM).

messy [ˈmesɪ] *adj clothes, room* (*dirty*) sale, malpropre; (*untidy*) en désordre, désordonné; *hair* en désordre, ébouriffé; *text, essay* sale; *job* salissant; (*) *situation* embrouillé, compliqué. (*fig*) **what a ~ business!*** quelle salade!*, quel embrouillamini!*

met[1] [met] *pret, ptp of* **meet**[1].

met[2] [met] *adj* (*Brit abbr of* **meteorological**) **the M~ Office** ≃ l'O.N.M. *m;* **~ report** bulletin *m* (de la) météo*.

meta... [ˈmetə] *pref* mét(a)... .

metabolic [ˌmetəˈbɒlɪk] *adj* métabolique.

metabolism [meˈtæbəlɪzəm] *n* métabolisme *m.*

metabolize [meˈtæbəlaɪz] *vt* transformer par le métabolisme.

metacarpal [ˌmetəˈkɑːpl] *adj, n* métacarpien (*m*).

metal [ˈmetl] **1** *n* **(a)** (*Miner*) métal *m.*

(b) (*Brit*) (*also* **road ~**) empierrement *m,* cailloutis *m;* (*for railway*) ballast *m.*

(c) (*Brit Rail*) **~s** rails *mpl.*

(d) (*Glassware*) pâte *f* de verre.

(e) (*Typ*) (*composed type*) caractère *m;* (*also* **type ~**) plomb *m.*

(f) = mettle.

2 *cpd* de métal, en métal. **metal polish** produit *m* d'entretien (*pour faire reluire les métaux*); **metalwork** (*articles*) ferronnerie *f;* (*craft*) travail *m* des métaux; **metalworker** ferronnier *m,* (*Ind*) (ouvrier *m*) métallurgiste *m.*

3 *vt* (*Brit*) *road* empierrer, caillouter.

metalanguage [ˈmetəlæŋgwɪdʒ] *n* métalangue *f,* métalangage *m.*

metalinguistics [ˌmetəlɪŋˈgwɪstɪks] *n* (*U*) métalinguistique *f.*

metallic [mɪˈtælɪk] *adj* métallique.

metallurgic(al) [ˌmetəˈlɜːdʒɪk(əl)] *adj* métallurgique.

metallurgist [meˈtælədʒɪst] *n* métallurgiste *m.*

metallurgy [meˈtælədʒɪ] *n* métallurgie *f.*

metamorphic [ˌmetəˈmɔːfɪk] *adj* métamorphique.

metamorphose [ˌmetəˈmɔːfəʊz] **1** *vt* métamorphoser, transformer (*into* en). **2** *vi* se métamorphoser (*into* en).

metamorphosis [ˌmetəˈmɔːfəsɪs] *n* métamorphose *f.*

metaphor [ˈmetəfəʳ] *n* métaphore *f,* image *f; V* **mixed.**

metaphorical [ˌmetəˈfɒrɪkəl] *adj* métaphorique.

metaphysical [ˌmetəˈfɪzɪkəl] *adj* métaphysique.

metaphysics [ˌmetəˈfɪzɪks] *n* (*U*) métaphysique *f.*

metatarsal [ˌmetəˈtɑːsl] *adj, n* métatarsien (*m*).

metathesis [meˈtæθəsɪs] *n* métathèse *f.*

mete [miːt] *vt:* **to ~ out** *punishment* infliger, donner; *reward* décerner; **to ~ justice** rendre la justice.

meteor [ˈmiːtɪəʳ] *n* météore *m.*

meteoric [ˌmiːtɪˈɒrɪk] *adj* **(a)** météorique; (*fig*) brillant et rapide, fulgurant. **his ~ rise in the firm** sa montée en flèche dans l'entreprise. **(b)** atmosphérique.

meteorite [ˈmiːtɪəraɪt] *n* météorite *m or f.*

meteorological [ˌmiːtɪərəˈlɒdʒɪkəl] *adj* météorologique. (*Brit*) **M~ Office** = Office National Météorologique, O.N.M. *m.*

meteorologist [ˌmiːtɪəˈrɒlədʒɪst] *n* météorologue *mf,* météorologiste *mf.*

meteorology [ˌmiːtɪəˈrɒlədʒɪ] *n* météorologie *f.*

meter [ˈmiːtəʳ] **1** *n* **(a)** compteur *m.* **electricity/gas/water ~** compteur d'électricité/à gaz/à eau; **to turn water** (*or* **gas** *or* **electricity**) **off at the ~** fermer l'eau (*or* le gaz *or* l'électricité) au compteur; *V* **light**[1], **parking** *etc.*

(b) (*US*) = **metre.**

2 *cpd:* (*US Aut*) **meter maid** contractuelle *f;* **meter reader** releveur *m* de compteurs.

meterage [ˈmiːtərɪdʒ] *n* métrage *m.*

methane [ˈmiːθeɪn] *n* méthane *m.*

method [ˈmeθəd] **1** *n* **(a)** (*U: orderliness*) méthode *f,* ordre *m.* **lack of ~** manque *m* de méthode; **there's ~ in his madness** sa folie ne manque pas d'une certaine logique.

(b) (*manner, fashion*) méthode *f;* manière *f,* façon *f.* **modern ~s of teaching languages** méthodes modernes d'enseignement des langues; **his ~ of working** sa méthode de travail; **there are several ~s of doing this** il y a plusieurs manières *or* façons de faire cela.

(c) (*Cine, Theat*) **the M~** le système *or* la méthode de Stanislavski.

2 *cpd:* (*Cine, Theat*) **method actor** *or* **actress** adepte *mf* du système *or* de la méthode de Stanislavski.

methodical [mɪˈθɒdɪkəl] *adj* méthodique.

Methodism [ˈmeθədɪzəm] *n* méthodisme *m.*

Methodist [ˈmeθədɪst] *adj, n* méthodiste (*mf*).

methodology [ˌmeθəˈdɒlədʒɪ] *n* méthodologie *f.*

meths* [meθs] (*Brit*) **1** *n abbr of* **methylated spirit(s). 2** *cpd:* **meths drinker*** alcoolique *mf* (qui se soûle à l'alcool à brûler).

Methuselah [məˈθuːzələ] *n* Mathusalem *m; V* **old.**

methyl [ˈmeθɪl] *n* méthyle *m.* **~ acetate/bromide/chloride** acétate *m*/bromure *m*/chlorure *m* de méthyle.

methylated [ˈmeθɪleɪtɪd] *adj:* **~ spirit(s)** alcool *m* à brûler *or* dénaturé.

methylene [ˈmeθɪliːn] *n* méthylène *m.*

meticulous [mɪˈtɪkjʊləs] *adj* méticuleux.

meticulously [mɪˈtɪkjʊləslɪ] *adv* méticuleusement. **~ clean** d'une propreté méticuleuse.

meticulousness [mɪˈtɪkjʊləsnɪs] *n* soin méticuleux.

métier [ˈmeɪtɪeɪ] *n* (*trade etc*) métier *m;* (*one's particular work etc*) partie *f,* rayon* *m,* domaine *m;* (*strong point*) point fort.

metre, (*US*) **meter** [ˈmiːtəʳ] *n* (*all senses*) mètre *m.*

metric [ˈmetrɪk] *adj* métrique. **~ system** système *m* métrique; **to go ~*** adopter le système métrique.

metrical [ˈmetrɪkəl] *adj* métrique.

metrication [ˌmetrɪˈkeɪʃən] *n* conversion *f* au système métrique.

metrics ['metrɪks] *n* (*U*) métrique *f*.
metrological [ˌmetrə'lɒdʒɪkəl] *adj* métrologique.
metrology [mɪ'trɒlədʒɪ] *n* métrologie *f*.
metronome ['metrənəʊm] *n* métronome *m*.
metropolis [mɪ'trɒpəlɪs] *n* métropole *f*.
metropolitan [ˌmetrə'pɒlɪtən] 1 *adj* (*Geog, Rel*) métropolitain. (*Brit*) **M~ Police** police *f* de Londres. 2 *n* (*Rel*) métropolitain *m*; (*in Orthodox Church*) métropolite *m*.
mettle ['metl] *n* [*person*] courage *m*, ardeur *f*, fougue *f*; [*horse*] fougue. **to be on one's ~** être prêt à donner le meilleur de soi-même, être d'attaque, être sur le qui-vive; **to show one's ~** faire ses preuves.
mettlesome ['metlsəm] *adj* ardent, fougueux.
mew [mju:] [*cat etc*] 1 *n* miaulement *m*. 2 *vi* miauler.
mews [mju:z] (*Brit*) 1 *npl* (*souvent employé comme sg*) **(a)** (*small street*) ruelle *f*, venelle *f*. **(b)** (††: *stables*) écuries *fpl*. 2 *cpd*: **mews flat** petit appartement assez chic (*aménagé dans le local d'une ancienne écurie, remise etc*).
Mexican ['meksɪkən] 1 *adj* mexicain. 2 *n* Mexicain(e) *m(f)*.
Mexico ['meksɪkəʊ] *n* Mexique *m*. **~ City** Mexico.
mezcaline ['mezkəlɪn] *n* = **mescaline.**
mezzanine ['mezəni:n] *n* mezzanine *f* (*also Theat*), entresol *m*.
mezzo-soprano [ˌmetsəʊsə'prɑ:nəʊ] *n* (*voice*) mezzo-soprano *m*; (*singer*) mezzo(-soprano) *f*.
mezzotint ['metsəʊtɪnt] *n* mezzo-tinto *m inv*.
mi [mi:] *n* (*Mus*) mi *m*.
miaow [mi:'aʊ] 1 *n* miaulement *m*, miaou *m*. 2 *vi* miauler.
miasma [mɪ'æzmə] *n* miasme *m*.
mica ['maɪkə] *n* mica *m*.
mice [maɪs] *npl of* **mouse.**
Michael ['maɪkl] *n* Michel *m*.
Michaelmas ['mɪklməs] 1 *n* (*also* **~ Day**) la Saint-Michel. 2 *cpd*: **Michaelmas daisy** aster *m* d'automne; (*Brit: Jur, Univ*) **Michaelmas term** trimestre *m* d'automne.
Michelangelo [ˌmaɪkəl'ændʒɪləʊ] *n* Michel-Ange *m*.
Mickey ['mɪkɪ] *n* (*dim of* **Michael**) Mimi *m*, Michou *m*. **~ Mouse** (*n*) Mickey *m*; (*adj*: ‡ *pej*) bébête*; **a ~ (Finn)**‡ une boisson droguée; (*Brit*) **to take the mickey out of sb**‡ faire marcher qn, charrier‡ qn; (*stronger*) se payer la tête de qn*; (*Brit*) **he's always taking the mickey**‡ il n'arrête pas de charrier‡ les gens *or* de se payer la tête des gens*.
micro... ['maɪkrəʊ] *pref* micro... . **~analysis** micro-analyse *f*; **~biology** microbiologie *f*; **~dot** microimage-point *m*; **~film** (*n*) microfilm *m*; (*vt*) microfilmer; **~film reader** = **~reader**; **~groove** microsillon *m*; **~mesh stockings** bas super-fins; **~meter** micromètre *m*; **~organism** micro-organisme *m*; **~reader** microliseuse *f*, microlecteur *m*; **~second** microseconde *f*; **~wave** micro-onde *f*; *V* **microcosm** *etc*.
microbe ['maɪkrəʊb] *n* microbe *m*.
microbial [maɪ'krəʊbɪəl] *adj*, **microbian** [maɪ'krəʊbɪən] *adj*, **microbic** [maɪ'krɒbɪk] *adj* microbien.
microbiologist [ˌmaɪkrəʊbaɪ'ɒlədʒɪst] *n* microbiologiste *mf*.
microcosm ['maɪkrəʊkɒzəm] *n* microcosme *m*.
microfiche ['maɪkrəʊfi:ʃ] *n* microfiche *f*.
micrograph ['maɪkrəʊgrɑ:f] *n* micrographe *m*.
micrography [maɪ'krɒgrəfɪ] *n* micrographie *f*.
micron ['maɪkrɒn] *n* micron *m*.
microphone ['maɪkrəfəʊn] *n* microphone *m*.
microscope ['maɪkrəskəʊp] *n* microscope *m*. **under the ~** au microscope.
microscopic [ˌmaɪkrə'skɒpɪk] *adj detail, mark* microscopique; *examination* microscopique, au microscope. **~ section** coupe *f* histologique.
microscopy [maɪ'krɒskəpɪ] *n* microscopie *f*.
micturate ['mɪktjʊəreɪt] *vt* uriner.
micturition [ˌmɪktjʊə'rɪʃən] *n* miction *f*.
mid[1] [mɪd] *adj* du milieu. **~ May** la mi-mai; **in ~ May** à la mi-mai, au milieu (du mois) de mai; **in ~ morning** au milieu de la matinée; **~-morning coffee break** pause café *f* du matin; **collision in ~ air** collision en plein ciel; (*fig*) **to leave sth in ~ air** laisser qch en suspens; **in ~ course** à mi-course; **in ~ ocean** en plein océan, au milieu de l'océan; **in ~ Atlantic** en plein Atlantique, au milieu de l'Atlantique; **a ~-Channel collision** une collision au milieu de la Manche; (*Brit*) **~-Victorian furniture** mobilier *m* du milieu de l'époque victorienne; *V* **midday, midstream** *etc*.
mid[2] [mɪd] *prep* (*liter*) = **amid.**
Midas ['maɪdəs] *n* Midas *m*. (*fig*) **to have the ~ touch** faire de l'or de tout ce que l'on touche.
midday [ˌmɪd'deɪ] 1 *n* midi *m*. **at ~** à midi. 2 ['mɪddeɪ] *cpd sun, heat* de midi.
midden ['mɪdn] *n* (*dunghill*) fumier *m*; (*refuse-heap*) tas *m* d'ordures. **this place is (like) a ~!*** c'est une vraie écurie! *or* porcherie!, on se croirait dans une écurie! *or* porcherie!
middle ['mɪdl] 1 *adj chair, period etc* du milieu. (*fig*) **to take the ~ course** choisir le moyen terme *or* la solution intermédiaire; **these grapes are of ~ quality** ces raisins sont de qualité moyenne; **a man of ~ size** un homme de taille moyenne; *V also* 3.

2 *n* **(a)** milieu *m*. **in the ~ of the room** au milieu de la pièce; **in the very ~ (of), right in the ~ (of)** au beau milieu (de); **the shot hit him in the ~ of his chest** le coup de feu l'a atteint en pleine poitrine; **in the ~ of the morning/year/century** au milieu de la matinée/de l'année/du siècle; **in the ~ of June** au milieu (du mois) de juin, à la mi-juin; **it's in the ~ of nowhere*** c'est en plein bled* *or* en pleine brousse*; **a village in the ~ of nowhere*** un petit trou perdu*; **I was in the ~ of my work** j'étais en plein travail; **I'm in the ~ of reading it** je suis justement en train de le lire.

(b) (*: *waist*) taille *f*. **he wore it round his ~** il le portait à la taille *or* autour de la taille; **in the water up to his ~** dans l'eau jusqu'à mi-corps *or* la ceinture *or* la taille.

3 *cpd*: **middle age** un certain âge; **during his middle age** quand il n'était (déjà) plus jeune; **middle-aged** d'un certain âge, entre deux âges; **the Middle Ages** le moyen âge; **middlebrow*** (*n*) personne *f* qui ne se pique *or* ne se targue pas d'intellectualisme, bourgeois(e) *m(f)* (*pej*); (*adj*) ne se piquant pas d'intellectualisme, bourgeois (*pej*); (*Mus*) **middle C** do *m* en dessous du la du diapason; **middle-class** bourgeois; **the middle class(es)** les classes moyennes, la classe moyenne, la bourgeoisie; **in the middle distance** (*Art etc*) au second plan; (*gen*) à mi-distance; (*Sport*) **middle-distance runner/race** coureur *m*, -euse *f*/course *f* de demi-fond; (*Anat*) **middle ear** oreille moyenne; **Middle East** Moyen-Orient *m*; **Middle Eastern** du Moyen-Orient; (*Ling*) **Middle English** moyen anglais; **middle finger** médius *m*, majeur *m*; (*Ling*) **Middle French** moyen français; (*Hist*) **the Middle Kingdom** [*Egypt*] le Moyen Empire; [*China*] l'Empire du Milieu; **middleman** (*gen*) intermédiaire *m*; (*Comm*) intermédiaire, revendeur *m*; **middlemost** = **midmost; middle name** deuxième nom *m*; (*Brit* fig*) **his middle name is Scrooge** il pourrait aussi bien s'appeler Harpagon; (*fig*) **middle-of-the-road** modéré; **middle school** ≃ premier cycle du secondaire; **middle-sized** *tree, building* de grandeur moyenne; *stick* de grosseur moyenne; *person* de taille moyenne; (*Ling*) **middle voice** voix moyenne; (*Boxing*) **middleweight** (*n*) poids moyen; (*adj*) *championship, boxer* de poids moyen.
middling ['mɪdlɪŋ] 1 *adj performance, result* moyen, passable. **of ~ size** de grandeur moyenne; **business is ~** les affaires vont comme ci comme ça *or* ne vont ni bien ni mal; **how are you? — ~*** comment ça va? — moyennement *or* comme ci comme ça.

2 *adv* (*) assez, moyennement. **~ well** assez bien; **~ big** assez grand.
middy* ['mɪdɪ] *n* (*Naut abbr of* **midshipman**) midship* *m*, aspirant *m*.
midge [mɪdʒ] *n* moucheron *m*.
midget ['mɪdʒɪt] 1 *n* nain(e) *m(f)*. 2 *adj* minuscule.
midland ['mɪdlənd] 1 *n* (*Brit Geog*) **the M~s** les comtés *mpl* du centre de l'Angleterre. 2 *cpd* du centre (du pays). **the midland regions** les régions centrales; (*Brit*) **a Midland town** une ville du centre de l'Angleterre.
midmost ['mɪdməʊst] *adj* le plus proche du milieu *or* centre.
midnight ['mɪdnaɪt] 1 *n* minuit *m*. **at ~** à minuit. 2 *cpd* de minuit. **to burn the midnight oil** travailler (*or* lire *etc*) fort avant dans la nuit; **his essay smells of the midnight oil*** on dirait qu'il a passé la moitié de la nuit sur sa dissertation; **the midnight sun** le soleil de minuit.
midriff ['mɪdrɪf] *n* (*diaphragm*) diaphragme *m*; (*stomach*) estomac *m*; [*dress*] taille *f*. **dress with a bare ~** robe découpée à la taille, robe (deux-pièces) laissant la taille nue.
midshipman ['mɪdʃɪpmən] *n* (*Naut*) midshipman *m*, midship* *m*, aspirant *m*.
midships ['mɪdʃɪps] *adv* = **amidships.**
midst [mɪdst] 1 *n*: **in the ~ of** (*in the middle of*) au milieu de; (*surrounded by*) entouré de; (*among*) parmi; (*during*) pendant, au cours de, au milieu de; **in our ~** parmi nous; (*liter*) **in the ~ of plenty** dans l'abondance; **in the ~ of life** au milieu de la vie; **I was in the ~ of saying*** j'étais en train de dire.

2 *prep* (*liter*) = **amidst.**
midstream ['mɪd'stri:m] *n*: **in ~** au milieu du courant.
midsummer ['mɪdˌsʌməʳ] 1 *n* (*height of summer*) milieu *m or* cœur *m* de l'été; (*solstice*) solstice *m* d'été. **in ~** au cœur de l'été, en plein été; **at ~** à la Saint-Jean. 2 *cpd heat, weather, storm etc* estival, de plein été. **Midsummer Day** la Saint-Jean; (*fig*) **midsummer madness** pure démence; **'A Midsummer Night's Dream'** 'le Songe d'une nuit d'été'.
midterm ['mɪd'tɜ:m] *n* **(a)** le milieu du trimestre. **(b)** (*also* **~ holiday**) ≃ vacances *fpl* de (la) Toussaint (*or* de février *or* de Pentecôte).
midway [ˌmɪd'weɪ] 1 *adj place* (situé) à mi-chemin. 2 *adv stop, pause* à mi-chemin, à mi-route. **~ between** à mi-chemin entre.
midweek [ˌmɪd'wi:k] *n* milieu *m* de la semaine. (*Rail*) **~ return (ticket)** (billet *m*) aller et retour *m* de milieu de semaine.
Midwest [ˌmɪd'west] *n* (*US*) (les grands plateaux du) Middle West *m or* Midwest *m*.
Midwestern [ˌmɪd'westən] *adj* (*US*) du Middle West, du Midwest.
midwife ['mɪdwaɪf] *n* sage-femme *f*.
midwifery ['mɪdwɪfərɪ] *n* (*U*) obstétrique *f*.
midwinter [ˌmɪd'wɪntəʳ] 1 *n* (*heart of winter*) milieu *m or* fort *m* de l'hiver; (*solstice*) solstice *m* d'hiver. **in ~** au cœur de l'hiver, en plein hiver; **at ~** au solstice d'hiver. 2 *cpd cold, snow, temperature* hivernal, de plein hiver.
mien [mi:n] *n* (*frm, liter*) contenance *f*, air *m*, mine *f*.
miff‡ [mɪf] 1 *n* (*quarrel*) fâcherie *f*; (*sulks*) bouderie *f*. 2 *vt* fâcher, mettre en boule*. **to be ~ed about** *or* **at sth** être fâché *or* vexé de qch.
might[1] [maɪt] 1 *modal aux vb V* **may**[1]. 2 *cpd*: **might-have-been** ce qui aurait pu être, espoir déçu, vœu non comblé; (*person*) raté(e) *m(f)*, fruit sec.
might[2] [maɪt] *n* (*U*) puissance *f*, force(s) *f(pl)*. (*Prov*) **~ is right** la force prime le droit; **with ~ and main, with all one's ~** de toutes ses forces.
mightily ['maɪtɪlɪ] *adv* (*powerfully*) puissamment, vigoureusement; (*†: *very*) rudement*, bigrement*.
mightiness ['maɪtɪnɪs] *n* puissance *f*, pouvoir *m*, grandeur *f*.
mightn't ['maɪtnt] = **might not**; *V* **may**[1].
mighty ['maɪtɪ] 1 *adj* **(a)** *nation, king, tree* puissant, fort; *achievement* formidable, considérable; *ocean* vaste, grandiose; *V* **high.**

(b) (*) sacré*. **he was in a ~ rage** il était sacrément* en colère; **there was a ~ row about it** cela a provoqué une sacrée bagarre* *or* un sacré chambard‡.

2 *adv* (*) rudement*, sacrément*, bigrement*, bougrement‡. **you think yourself ~ clever!** tu te crois très fin! *or* malin!; **I'm ~ sorry that ...** je regrette rudement* *or* sacrément* que ...; **you've got to be ~ careful** il faut faire rudement* *or* sacrément* attention.

mignonette [ˌmɪnjəˈnet] *n* réséda *m*.

migraine [ˈmiːgreɪn] *n* (*Med*) migraine *f*.

migrant [ˈmaɪgrənt] 1 *adj bird, animal* migrateur (*f* -trice); *tribe* nomade, migrateur. (*Agr, Ind*) **~ worker** (*Ind*) (travailleur *m*) migrant *m*; (*foreign*) travailleur étranger *or* immigré; (*Agr*) (travailleur) saisonnier *m*; (*Ind*) **~ labour** main-d'œuvre migrante (*or* saisonnière *or* étrangère).

2 *n* **(a)** (*bird, animal*) migrateur *m*; (*person*) nomade *mf*.

(b) = **~ worker**; *V* 1.

migrate [maɪˈgreɪt] *vi [bird, animal]* émigrer; *[person]* émigrer, immigrer.

migration [maɪˈgreɪʃən] *n [birds, animals]* migration *f*; *[person]* migration, émigration *f*, immigration *f*.

migratory [maɪˈgreɪtərɪ] *adj bird, tribe* migrateur (*f* -trice); *movement, journey* migratoire.

mikado [mɪˈkɑːdəʊ] *n* mikado *m*.

mike* [maɪk] *n* (*abbr of* **microphone**) micro *m*.

Mike [maɪk] *n* (*dim of* **Michael**) Mic *m*. **for the love of ~*** pour l'amour du ciel.

milady† [mɪˈleɪdɪ] *n* madame la comtesse *etc*.

milch [mɪltʃ] *adj*: **~ cow** vache laitière.

mild [maɪld] *adj person* doux (*f* douce), peu *or* pas sévère; *voice, temper* doux; *reproach, punishment* léger; *exercise, effect* modéré; *climate* doux, tempéré; *winter* doux, clément; *breeze* doux, faible; *flavour, cheese, tobacco* doux; *beer* léger; *sauce* peu épicé *or* relevé; *medicine* bénin (*f* -igne), anodin; *illness* bénin. **it's ~ today** il fait doux aujourd'hui; **he had a ~ form of polio** il a eu la poliomyélite sous une forme bénigne *or* atténuée; **a ~ sedative** un sédatif léger; (*Culin*) **a ~ curry** un curry pas trop fort *or* pimenté.

mildew [ˈmɪldjuː] 1 *n* (*U*) (*on wheat, roses etc*) rouille *f*; (*on vine*) mildiou *m*; (*on cloth, paper*) piqûres *fpl* d'humidité, moisissure *f*.

2 *vt plant* rouiller; *vine* frapper de mildiou; *paper, cloth* piquer (d'humidité). **~ed vine** vigne mildiousée.

3 *vi [roses, wheat etc]* se rouiller; *[vine]* devenir mildiousé, être attaqué par le mildiou; *[paper, cloth]* se piquer.

mildly [ˈmaɪldlɪ] *adv* doucement, avec douceur; (*Med*) bénignement, légèrement. **he's not very clever to put it ~*** pour ne pas dire plus il n'est pas très intelligent; **that's putting it ~!*** c'est le moins qu'on puisse (en) dire!, c'est un euphémisme!

mildness [ˈmaɪldnɪs] *n* (*V* **mild**) douceur *f*; clémence *f*; bénignité *f*; modération *f*; légèreté *f*; saveur peu relevée.

mile [maɪl] 1 *n* mile *m or* mille *m* (= *1.609,33 m*). **a 50-~ journey** un trajet de 80 km; (*Aut*) **~s per gallon** ≃ litres aux cent (km); **there was nothing but sand for ~s and ~s** il n'y avait que du sable sur des kilomètres (et des kilomètres); (*fig*) **not a hundred ~s from here** sans aller chercher bien loin; **we've walked (for) ~s!** on a marché pendant des kilomètres!, on a fait des kilomètres!; **they live ~s away** ils habitent à cent lieues d'ici; **you could see/smell it a ~ off*** ça se voyait/se sentait d'une lieue; **you were ~s off (the) target*** vous n'étiez pas près de toucher la cible, vous étiez bien loin du but; **he's ~s bigger than you*** il est bien plus grand que toi; **she's ~s better than I am at maths*** elle est bien plus calée que moi en maths*.

2 *cpd*: **mile post** ≃ poteau *m* kilométrique; **milestone** (*lit*) borne *f* (milliaire), ≃ borne kilométrique; (*fig: in life, career etc*) jalon *m*, événement marquant *or* déterminant.

mileage [ˈmaɪlɪdʒ] 1 *n* (*Aut etc*) (*distance covered*) distance *f* or parcours *m* en milles, ≃ kilométrage *m*; (*distance per gallon etc*) consommation *f* (de carburant) aux cent (km). **the indicator showed a very low ~** le compteur marquait peu de kilomètres; **the car had a low ~** la voiture avait peu roulé *or* avait peu de kilomètres; **what ~ has this car done?** quel est le kilométrage de cette voiture?, combien de kilomètres a cette voiture?; **for a car of that size the ~ was very good** pour une voiture aussi puissante elle consommait peu.

2 *cpd*: (*Admin etc*) **mileage allowance** ≃ indemnité *f* kilométrique; (*Aut*) **mileage indicator** ≃ compteur *m* kilométrique.

mileometer [maɪˈlɒmɪtə^r] *n* = **milometer**.

milieu [ˈmiːljɜː] *n* milieu *m* (social).

militant [ˈmɪlɪtənt] *adj, n* (*all senses*) militant(e) *m(f)*.

militarism [ˈmɪlɪtərɪzəm] *n* militarisme *m*.

militarist [ˈmɪlɪtərɪst] *adj, n* militariste (*mf*).

militaristic [ˌmɪlɪtəˈrɪstɪk] *adj* militariste.

militarize [ˈmɪlɪtəraɪz] *vt* militariser.

military [ˈmɪlɪtərɪ] 1 *adj government, life, uniform* militaire. **of ~ age** d'âge à faire son service (militaire *or* national); **~ police** police *f* militaire; **~ training** préparation *f* militaire; **to do one's ~ service** faire son service (militaire *or* national).

2 *collective n*: **the ~** l'armée *f*, le(s) militaire(s) *m(pl)*.

militate [ˈmɪlɪteɪt] *vi* militer (*against* contre).

militia [mɪˈlɪʃə] *collective n* milice(s) *f(pl)*. **~man** milicien *m*.

milk [mɪlk] 1 *n* lait *m*. **coconut ~** lait de coco; (*fig*) **the ~ of human kindness** le lait de la tendresse humaine; (*fig*) **a land flowing with ~ and honey** un pays de cocagne; (*hum*) **he came home with the ~*** il est rentré avec le jour *or* à potron-minet*; *V* **condense, cry, skim** *etc*.

2 *vt* **(a)** *cow* traire.

(b) (*fig: extract*) dépouiller (*of* de), plumer (*fig*). **his son ~ed him of all his savings** son fils l'a dépouillé de toutes ses économies, il s'est laissé plumer par son fils; **it ~ed (him of) his strength** cela a sapé *or* miné ses forces; **to ~ sb of ideas/information** soutirer des idées/des renseignements à qn.

3 *vi*: **to go ~ing** (s'en) aller traire ses vaches.

4 *cpd*: (*fig pej*) **milk-and-water** dilué, insipide; **milk bar** milk-bar *m*; **milk can** boîte *f* à lait, pot *m* à lait; (*larger: also* **milk churn**) bidon *m* à lait; **milk chocolate** chocolat *m* au lait; **milk diet** régime lacté; (*Brit*) **milk float** voiture *f* de laitier; **milkmaid** trayeuse *f*; **milkman** laitier *m*; **milk of magnesia** lait *m* de magnésie, magnésie hydratée; **milk products** produits laitiers; **milk pudding** entremets *m* au lait; **milk shake** lait parfumé fouetté; (*pej*) **milksop*** chiffe molle* (*fig*), lavette* *f* (*fig*), mollusque* *m* (*fig*); **milk tooth** dent *f* de lait; (*Bot*) **milkweed** laiteron *m*; (*liter*) **milk-white** d'une blancheur de lait, blanc (*f* blanche) comme le *or* du lait.

milking [ˈmɪlkɪŋ] 1 *n* traite *f*. 2 *cpd pail, stool* à traire. **milking machine** trayeuse *f* (mécanique); **milking time** l'heure *f* de la traite.

milky [ˈmɪlkɪ] *adj* (*lit*) *diet, product* lacté; (*fig: in colour etc*) laiteux. **~ coffee/tea** café *m*/thé *m* au lait; **a ~ drink** une boisson à base de lait; (*Astron*) **M~ Way** Voie lactée.

mill [mɪl] 1 *n* **(a)** (*wind~ or water ~*) moulin *m*; (*Ind: for grain*) minoterie *f*; (*small: for coffee etc*) moulin. **wind~** moulin à vent; **pepper-~** moulin à poivre; (*fig*) **to go through the ~** passer par de dures épreuves, en voir de dures*; (*fig*) **to put sb through the ~** mettre qn à l'épreuve, en faire voir de dures à qn*; *V* **coffee, run** *etc*.

(b) (*factory*) usine *f*, fabrique *f*; (*spinning ~*) filature *f*; (*weaving ~*) tissage *m*; (*steel ~*) aciérie *f*. **paper ~** (usine *f* de) papeterie *f*; **cotton ~** filature de coton; *V* **saw**[1] *etc*.

2 *cpd*: (*Ind*) **mill girl** ouvrière *f* des tissages *or* des filatures; (*Ind*) **millhand** = **mill worker**; (*Ind*) **mill owner** industriel *m* (du textile); **millpond** bief *m or* retenue *f* d'un moulin; **the sea was like a millpond** la mer était d'huile, la mer était (comme) un lac; **mill race** bief *m* d'amont *or* de moulin; (*lit*) **millstone** meule *f*; (*fig*) **it's a millstone round his neck** c'est un boulet qu'il traîne avec lui; **mill stream** courant *m* du bief; **mill wheel** roue *f* d'un moulin; (*Ind*) **mill worker** ouvrier *m*, -ière *f* des filatures (*or* tissages *or* aciéries); **millwright** constructeur *m or* installateur *m* de moulins.

3 *vt* **(a)** *flour, coffee, pepper* moudre; *vegetables* broyer.

(b) (*Tech*) *screw, nut* moleter; *wheel, edge of coin* créneler. *[coin]* **~ed edge** crénelage *m*, grènetis *m*.

4 *vi [crowd etc]* **to ~ round sth** grouiller autour de qch.

mill about, mill around *vi [crowd]* grouiller, fourmiller; *[cattle etc]* tourner sur place *or* en rond.

millenary [mɪˈlenərɪ] *adj, n*, **millennial** [mɪˈlenɪəl] *adj, n* millénaire (*m*).

millennium [mɪˈlenɪəm] *n* millénaire *m*. (*Rel, also fig*) **the ~** le millénium.

millepede [ˈmɪlɪpiːd] *n* = **millipede**.

miller [ˈmɪlə^r] *n* meunier *m*; (*Ind: large-scale*) minotier *m*.

millet [ˈmɪlɪt] *n* (*U*) millet *m*.

milli... [ˈmɪlɪ] *pref* milli... .

milliard [ˈmɪlɪɑːd] *n* (*Brit*) milliard *m*.

millibar [ˈmɪlɪbɑː^r] *n* millibar *m*.

milligram(me) [ˈmɪlɪgræm] *n* milligramme *m*.

millilitre, (*US*) **milliliter** [ˈmɪlɪˌliːtə^r] *n* millilitre *m*.

millimetre, (*US*) **millimeter** [ˈmɪlɪˌmiːtə^r] *n* millimètre *m*.

milliner [ˈmɪlɪnə^r] *n* modiste *f*, chapelier *m*, -ière *f*.

millinery [ˈmɪlɪnərɪ] *n* (*U*) modes *fpl*, chapellerie féminine.

milling [ˈmɪlɪŋ] 1 *n* (*U*) *[flour etc]* moulure *f*; *[screw etc]* moletage *m*; *[coin]* crénelage *m*. 2 *adj*: **the ~ crowd** la foule en remous.

million [ˈmɪljən] *n* million *m*. **a ~ men** un million d'hommes; **he's one in a ~*** c'est la crème *or* la perle des hommes; (*fig*) **~s of*** des milliers de; **thanks a ~!*** merci mille fois!; (*US*) **to feel like a ~ (dollars)*** se sentir dans une forme époustouflante*.

millionaire [ˌmɪljəˈnɛə^r] *n* millionnaire *m*, ≃ milliardaire *m*.

millionth [ˈmɪljənθ] 1 *adj* millionième. 2 *n* millionième *mf*; (*fraction*) millionième *m*.

millipede [ˈmɪlɪpiːd] *n* mille-pattes *m inv*.

milometer [maɪˈlɒmɪtə^r] *n* compteur *m* de milles, ≃ compteur kilométrique.

milord [mɪˈlɔːd] *n* milord *m*.

milt [mɪlt] *n* laitance *f*, laite *f*.

mime [maɪm] 1 *n* (*Theat*) (*skill, classical play*) mime *m*; (*actor*) mime *m*; (*modern play*) mimodrame *m*; (*fig: gestures etc*) mimique *f*. 2 *vti* mimer.

mimeograph [ˈmɪmɪəgrɑːf] ® 1 *n* machine *f* à polycopier (au stencil). 2 *vt* polycopier.

mimic [ˈmɪmɪk] 1 *n* imitateur *m*, -trice *f*; (*burlesquing*) imitateur, -trice, singe *m*.

2 *adj* **(a)** (*imitating*) imitateur (*f* -trice), singe.

(b) (*sham*) factice, simulé. **~ battle** bataille simulée.

3 *vt* (*copy*) imiter; (*burlesque*) imiter, singer, contrefaire.

mimicry [ˈmɪmɪkrɪ] *n* (*U*) imitation *f*; (*Zool: also* **protective ~**) mimétisme *m*.

mimosa [mɪˈməʊzə] *n* mimosa *m*.

minaret [ˈmɪnəret] *n* minaret *m*.

minatory [ˈmɪnətərɪ] *adj* comminatoire, menaçant.

mince [mɪns] 1 *n* (*Culin*) bifteck haché, hachis *m* de viande.

2 *cpd*: (*Culin*) **mincemeat** *hachis de fruits secs, de pommes et de graisse imbibé de cognac*; (*fig*) **to make mincemeat of** *opponent, enemy* battre à plate(s) couture(s)*, pulvériser; *theories, arguments* pulvériser; (*Culin*) **mince pie** tarte anglaise (au mincemeat).

3 *vt meat, vegetables* hacher. (*fig*) **he didn't ~ (his) words, he didn't ~ matters** il n'a pas mâché ses mots, il n'y est pas allé par quatre chemins; **he didn't ~ matters with me** il ne m'a pas mâché ses mots, il n'y est pas allé par quatre chemins avec moi,

il m'a parlé sans ambages; **not to ~ matters she just wasn't good enough** pour parler carrément *or* sans ambages elle n'était pas à la hauteur.

4 *vi* (*in talking*) parler du bout des lèvres; (*in walking*) marcher à petits pas maniérés. **to ~ in/out** entrer/sortir à petits pas maniérés.

mince up *vt sep* (*Culin etc*) hacher.

mincer ['mɪnsər] *n* hachoir *m* (*appareil*).

mincing ['mɪnsɪŋ] **1** *adj* affecté, minaudier. **with ~ steps** à petits pas maniérés. **2** *cpd*: **mincing machine** hachoir *m*.

mincingly ['mɪnsɪŋlɪ] *adv* d'une manière affectée, en minaudant.

mind [maɪnd] **1** *n* **(a)** esprit *m*; (*intellect*) esprit, intelligence *f*; (*as opposed to matter*) esprit; (*sanity*) raison *f*; (*memory*) souvenir *m*, mémoire *f*; (*opinion*) avis *m*, idée *f*; (*intention*) intention *f*. **in one's ~'s eye** en imagination; **his ~ is going** il n'a plus tout à fait sa tête, il baisse; **his ~ went blank** il a eu un trou *or* un passage à vide, ça a été le vide complet dans sa tête; **I'm not clear in my own ~ about it** je ne sais pas qu'en penser moi-même; **to be easy in one's ~** avoir l'esprit tranquille; **to be uneasy in one's ~ (about sth)** avoir des doutes (sur qch), être inquiet (*f* -ète) (au sujet de qch); **he is one of the great ~s of the century** c'est un des (grands) cerveaux du siècle; (*Prov*) **great ~s think alike** les grands esprits se rencontrent; **it was a case of ~ over matter** c'était la victoire de l'esprit sur la matière; **of sound ~** sain d'esprit; **of unsound ~** ne jouissant plus de toutes ses facultés (mentales); **to be in one's right ~** avoir toute sa raison *or* sa tête; **to be out of one's (right) ~** ne plus avoir toute sa raison *or* sa tête; **you must be out of your ~!*** ça ne va pas!*; **he went out of his ~** il a perdu la tête *or* la raison; **with one ~** comme un seul homme; **they were of one ~** ils étaient d'accord *or* du même avis; **to be in two ~s about sth/about doing** se tâter (*fig*) *or* être irrésolu pour ce qui est de qch/de faire; **I'm still of the same ~** je n'ai pas changé d'avis; **I was of the same ~ as my brother** j'étais du même avis que mon frère, je partageais l'opinion de mon frère; **what's on your ~?** qu'est-ce qui vous préoccupe? *or* vous tracasse?; **that's a load** *or* **a weight off my ~** c'est un gros souci de moins, cela m'ôte un poids; **I was of a ~** *or* **it was in my ~ to go and see him** je pensais aller le voir; **to my ~** à mon avis; **nothing is further from my ~!** (bien) loin de moi cette pensée!; **nothing was further from my ~ than going to see her** (bien) loin de moi la pensée d'aller la voir, je n'avais nullement l'intention d'aller la voir; *V* **frame, sight, state** *etc*.

(b) (*in verbal phrases*) **to bear sth in ~** (*take account of*) tenir compte de qch; (*remember*) ne pas oublier qch; **I'll bear you in ~** je songerai *or* penserai à vous; **bear it in ~!** songez-y bien!; **to bring one's ~ to bear on sth** porter *or* concentrer son attention sur qch, appliquer son esprit à l'étude de qch; **to bring** *or* **call sth to ~** rappeler qch, évoquer qch; **it came (in)to my ~ that ...** il m'est venu à l'esprit que ..., l'idée m'est venue que ...; **you must get it into your ~ that ...** tu dois te mettre en tête *or* dans la tête que ...; **I can't get it out of my ~** je ne peux m'empêcher d'y penser; **to give one's ~ to sth** appliquer son esprit à qch, se concentrer sur qch; **he can't give his whole ~ to his work** il n'arrive pas à se concentrer sur son travail; **it went quite** *or* **right** *or* **clean* out of my ~** je l'ai complètement oublié, cela m'est complètement sorti de la tête*; **you can do it if you have a ~ (to)** vous pouvez le faire si vous le voulez *or* désirez vraiment; **I have no ~ to offend him** je n'ai aucune envie de l'offenser; **to have (it) in ~ to do** avoir dans l'idée de faire; **I've a good ~ to do it*** j'ai bien envie de le faire, je crois bien que je vais le faire; **I've half a ~ to do it*** j'ai presque envie de le faire, ça me tente de le faire; **have you (got) anything particular in ~?** avez-vous quelque chose de particulier dans l'idée?; **whom have you in ~ for the job?** à qui songez-vous *or* qui avez-vous en vue pour le poste?; **to have sth on one's ~** avoir l'esprit préoccupé de qch; **to keep sth in ~** ne pas oublier qch; **to keep one's ~ on sth** se concentrer sur qch; **to know one's own ~** avoir des idées bien arrêtées, savoir ce que l'on veut; **to let one's ~ run on sth** se laisser aller à penser à qch, laisser ses pensées s'attarder sur qch; **to let one's ~ wander** laisser flotter ses pensées *or* son attention; **to make up one's ~ to do sth** prendre la décision *or* décider de faire qch; **we can't make up our ~s about the house** nous ne savons à quoi nous résoudre *or* nous ne savons quelle décision prendre pour la maison; **I can't make up my ~ about him** (*form opinion of*) je ne sais que penser de lui; (*decide about*) je n'arrive pas à me décider sur son compte; (*liter*) **to pass out of ~** tomber dans l'oubli; **that puts me in ~ of ...** cela me rappelle ...; **you can put that right out of your ~!** tu peux te dépêcher d'oublier tout ça!; **try to put it out of your ~** essayez de ne plus y penser; **to put** *or* **set one's ~ to a problem** s'attaquer à un problème; **you can do it if you put** *or* **set your ~ to it** tu peux le faire si tu t'y appliques; **to read sb's ~, to see into sb's ~** lire (jusqu'au fond de) la pensée de qn; **to set one's ~ on (doing) sth** vouloir fermement (faire) qch; **to set sb's ~ at rest** rassurer qn; **this will take her ~ off her troubles** cela lui changera les idées, cela la distraira de ses ennuis; **the noise takes my ~ off my work** le bruit m'empêche de me concentrer sur mon travail; *V* **cross, improve, piece, slip, speak** *etc*.

2 *cpd*: **mind-bending*** renversant; **mind-blowing*** hallucinant; **mindful** *V* **mindful**; (*lit*) **mind reader** liseur *m*, -euse *f* de pensées; (*fig*) **he's a mind reader!** il lit dans la pensée des gens!; **I'm not a mind reader!*** je ne suis pas devin!*; **mind reading** divination *f* par télépathie.

3 *vt* **(a)** (*pay attention to*) faire *or* prêter attention à; (*beware of*) prendre garde à. **never ~!** (*don't worry*) ne t'en fais pas!, ne t'inquiète pas!; (*it makes no odds*) ça ne fait rien!, peu importe!; **never ~ that now!** (*soothingly*) n'y pense plus (maintenant)!; (*irritably*) tu ne vas pas m'ennuyer avec ça maintenant!; **never ~ him!** ne t'occupe pas de lui!, ignore-le!; (*iro*) **don't ~ me!*** ne vous gênez surtout pas (pour moi)!* (*iro*); **never ~ the expense!** tant pis pour le prix!, ne regarde pas à la dépense!; **~ your language!** surveille ton langage!; **to ~ one's Ps and Qs** surveiller son langage *or* son comportement; **~ what I say!** écoute bien ce que je te dis!, fais bien attention à ce que je te dis!; **~ what you're doing!** (fais) attention à ce que tu fais!; **~ the step!** attention *or* gare à la marche!; **~ your head!** attention *or* gare à votre tête!; **~ your backs!** gare à vous!, dégagez!; **~ yourself!, ~ your eye!‡** prends garde!, fais gaffe!‡; **~ you don't fall!** prenez garde de ne pas tomber!; **~ you tell her!** ne manquez pas de le lui dire!; **~ and come to see us!*** n'oublie pas de venir nous voir!; **be there at 10, ~*** fais en sorte d'être là *or* tâche d'être là à 10 heures; **~ you, I didn't know he was going to Paris*** remarquez, je ne savais pas qu'il allait à Paris; **~ you, it isn't easy*** ce n'est pas facile, vous savez *or* je vous assure; **~ you he could be right*, he could be right ~*** peut-être qu'il a raison après tout; **I sold the car for £600 and ~ you* I had had it 4 years** j'ai vendu la voiture 600 livres et avec ça* *or* remarque, je l'avais gardée 4 ans; *V* **business**.

(b) (*object to*) **do you ~ if I take this book? — I don't ~ at all** cela ne vous fait rien que je prenne ce livre? — mais non, je vous en prie!; **which do you want? — I don't ~** lequel voulez-vous? — ça m'est égal; **did you ~ my** *or* **me* telling you that?** auriez-vous préféré que je ne vous le dise pas?; **did she ~ (it) when he got married?** a-t-elle été malheureuse quand il s'est marié?; **if you don't ~** si cela ne vous fait rien; (*iro: indignantly*) non, mais!; **I don't ~ going with you** je veux bien vous accompagner; **I don't ~ the cold** je ne crains pas le froid; **I don't ~ country life but I prefer the town** vivre à la campagne ne me déplaît pas, mais je préfère la ville; **would you ~ opening the door?** cela vous ennuierait d'ouvrir la porte?; **would you ~ coming with me?** cela vous dérangerait de m'accompagner?; (*abruptly*) je vous prie de m'accompagner; **do you ~ the noise?** le bruit vous gêne-t-il?; **I don't ~ what people say** je me moque du qu'en-dira-t-on; **I don't ~ him but I hate her!** lui passe encore, mais elle je la déteste!; **cigarette? — I don't ~ (if I do)*** une cigarette? — c'est pas de refus!*; **I wouldn't ~ a cup of coffee** une tasse de café ne serait pas de refus*, je prendrais bien une tasse de café.

(c) (*take charge of*) *children* garder, surveiller, prendre soin de; *animals* garder; *shop, business* garder, tenir.

(d) († *or dial: remember*) se souvenir de, se rappeler.

mind out* *vi* faire attention, faire gaffe‡. **mind out!** attention!; **mind out of the way!** ôtez-vous de là!, dégagez!*; **mind out or you'll break it** faites attention de ne pas le casser.

minded ['maɪndɪd] *adj*: **if you are so ~** si le cœur vous en dit, si vous y êtes disposé; **~ to do sth** disposé *or* enclin à faire qch.

-minded ['maɪndɪd] *adj ending in cpds*: **feeble-minded** faible d'esprit; **business-minded** qui a le sens des affaires; **he's become very ecology-minded** il est très sensibilisé sur l'écologie maintenant; **an industrially-minded nation** une nation orientée vers l'industrie, une nation aux options industrielles; **a romantically-minded girl** une jeune fille aux idées romantiques; *V* **high, like[1], strong-minded** *etc*.

minder ['maɪndər] *n* (*also* **baby-~, child-~**) gardienne *f*.

mindful ['maɪndfʊl] *adj*: **~ of** attentif à, soucieux de; **be ~ of what I said** songez à ce que j'ai dit.

mindless ['maɪndlɪs] *adj* **(a)** (*stupid*) stupide, idiot. **(b)** (*unmindful*) **~ of** oublieux de, indifférent à, inattentif à.

mine[1] [maɪn] **1** *poss pron* le mien, la mienne, les mien(ne)s. **this pencil is ~** ce crayon est le mien *or* à moi; **the house became ~** la maison est devenue (la) mienne; **no advice of ~ could prevent him** aucun conseil de ma part ne pouvait l'empêcher; **no it's ~** non c'est à moi *or* le mien; **which dress do you prefer, hers or ~?** quelle robe préférez-vous, la sienne ou la mienne?; **a friend of ~** un de mes amis, un ami à moi; **it's no fault of ~** ce n'est pas (de) ma faute; **what is ~ is yours** ce qui est à moi est à toi, ce qui m'appartient t'appartient; (*frm*) **it is not ~ to decide** ce n'est pas à moi de décider, il ne m'appartient pas de décider; **~ is a specialized department** ma section est une section spécialisée.

2 *poss adj* (†† *or liter*) mon, ma, mes; *V* **host[1]**.

mine[2] [maɪn] **1** *n* **(a)** (*Min*) mine *f*. **coal~** mine de charbon; **to go down the ~s** travailler *or* descendre à la mine; **to work a ~** exploiter une mine; (*fig*) **a real ~ of information** une véritable mine *or* une source inépuisable de renseignements.

(b) (*Mil, Naut etc*) mine *f*. **to lay a ~** poser une mine; **to clear a beach of ~s** déminer une plage; *V* **land** *etc*.

2 *vt* **(a)** (*Min*) *coal, ore* extraire.

(b) (*Mil, Naut etc*) *sea, beach* miner, semer de mines; *ship, tank* miner.

3 *vi* exploiter un gisement. **to ~ for coal** extraire du charbon, exploiter une mine (de charbon).

4 *cpd*: (*Mil*) **mine detector** détecteur *m* de mines; (*Mil, Naut*) **minefield** champ *m* de mines; (*Naut*) **minehunter** chasseur *m* de mines; (*Naut*) **minelayer** mouilleur *m* de mines; (*Min*) **mineshaft** puits *m* de mine; (*Naut*) **minesweeper** dragueur *m* de mines; (*Naut*) **mine-sweeping** dragage *m* de mines.

miner ['maɪnər] *n* mineur *m*. **~'s lamp** lampe *f* de mineur.

mineral ['mɪnərəl] **1** *n* **(a)** (*Geol*) minéral *m*. **(b)** (*Brit: soft drinks*) **~s** boissons gazeuses. **2** *adj* minéral. **the ~ kingdom** le règne minéral; **~ water** (*natural*) eau minérale; (*soft drink*) boisson gazeuse.

mineralogist [ˌmɪnəˈrælədʒɪst] *n* minéralogiste *mf*.

mineralogy [ˌmɪnəˈrælədʒɪ] *n* minéralogie *f*.

mingle ['mɪŋgl] **1** *vt* mêler (*with* à), mélanger, confondre (*with* avec). **2** *vi* se mêler, se mélanger; (*become indistinguishable*) se confondre (*with* avec). **to ~ with the crowd** se mêler à la foule; **he ~s with all sorts of people** il fraye avec toutes sortes de gens.

mingy* ['mɪndʒɪ] *adj person* radin*, pingre; *share* misérable.
mini... ['mɪnɪ] *pref* mini... . ~**bus** minibus *m*; (*Brit*) ~**cab** minitaxi *m*; ~**market**, ~**mart** minilibre-service *m*; ~**skirt** mini-jupe *f*; (*iro*) **he's a kind of ~-dictator*** c'est une sorte de mini-dictateur.
mini* ['mɪnɪ] *n* (*fashion*) mini *m*.
miniature ['mɪnɪtʃəʳ] 1 *n* (*also Art*) miniature *f*. (*lit, fig*) **in** ~ en miniature.
2 *adj* (en) miniature; (*tiny*) minuscule. **her doll had a ~ handbag** sa poupée avait un sac à main minuscule; ~ **bottle of whisky** mini-bouteille *f* de whisky; ~ **camera** appareil *m* de petit format; ~ **golf** golf-miniature *m*; ~ **poodle** caniche nain; ~ **railway** chemin de fer *m* miniature; ~ **submarine** sous-marin *m* de poche.
miniaturize ['mɪnɪtʃəraɪz] *vt* miniaturiser.
minim ['mɪnɪm] *n* (a) (*Mus: esp Brit*) blanche *f*. ~ **rest** demi-pause *f*. (b) (*Measure*) (= 0,5 *ml*) ≈ goutte *f*.
minima ['mɪnɪmə] *npl of* **minimum**.
minimal ['mɪnɪml] *adj* minimal.
minimize ['mɪnɪmaɪz] *vt* minimiser, réduire au minimum.
minimum ['mɪnɪməm] 1 *n, pl* **minima** minimum *m*. **to reduce to a** ~ réduire au minimum; **keep interruptions to a** ~ limitez les interruptions autant que possible; **a ~ of £100** un minimum de 100 livres; **with a ~ of common sense one could ...** avec un minimum de bon sens *or* le moindre bon sens on pourrait ... .
2 *adj age, price* minimum (*f inv or* minima, *pl* minimums *or* minima). (*Econ, Ind*) ~ **wage** salaire minimum garanti.
3 *cpd*: **minimum iron fabric** tissu *m* ne demandant qu'un repassage minimum.
mining ['maɪnɪŋ] 1 *n* (*U*) (a) (*Min*) exploitation minière.
(b) (*Mil, Naut*) pose *f or* mouillage *m* de mines.
2 *cpd village, industry* minier. **mining area** région (d'industrie) minière; **mining engineer** ingénieur *m* des mines; **he comes from a mining family** il est d'une famille de mineurs.
minion ['mɪnjən] *n* (*servant*) laquais *m*, serviteur *m*, larbin *m*; (*favourite*) favori(te) *m(f)*. (*hum, iro*) ~**s of the law** serviteurs de la loi.
minister ['mɪnɪstəʳ] 1 *n* (a) (*Brit: Diplomacy, Parl, Pol*) ministre *m*. **M~ of State** ≈ secrétaire *m* d'État; **M~ of Health** ministre de la Santé publique; *V* **defence, foreign etc.** (b) (*Rel: also* ~ **of religion**) pasteur *m*, ministre *m*. 2 *vi* (*frm*) **to ~ to sb's needs** pourvoir aux besoins de qn; **to ~ to sb** donner ses soins à qn; (*Rel*) **to ~ to a parish** desservir une paroisse.
ministerial [,mɪnɪs'tɪərɪəl] *adj* (a) (*Parl*) *decision, crisis* ministériel. **the ~ benches** le banc des ministres. (b) (*Rel*) de ministre, sacerdotal.
ministration [,mɪnɪs'treɪʃən] *n* (a) (*services, help*) ~**s** soins *mpl*. (b) (*Rel*) ministère *m*.
ministry ['mɪnɪstrɪ] *n* (a) (*government department*) ministère *m*. **M~ of Health** ministère de la Santé publique; (*Parl*) **to form a** ~ former un ministère *or* un gouvernement; **the coalition ~ lasted 2 years** le ministère de coalition a duré 2 ans.
(b) (*period of office*) ministère *m*.
(c) (*body of clergy*) **the** ~ le saint ministère; **to go into** *or* **enter the** ~ devenir *or* se faire pasteur *or* ministre.
mink [mɪŋk] 1 *n* (*animal, fur*) vison *m*. 2 *cpd coat etc* de vison.
minnow ['mɪnəʊ] *n* vairon *m*; (*any small fish*) fretin *m*; (*fig: unimportant person*) menu fretin (*sg or collective*).
minor ['maɪnəʳ] 1 *adj* (*Jur, Mus, Philos, Rel*) mineur; *detail, expenses, repairs* petit, menu; *importance, interest, position, role* secondaire. ~ **poet** poète mineur; ~ **problem/worry** problème/souci mineur; (*Mus*) **G** ~ sol mineur; (*Mus*) ~ **key** ton mineur; **in the ~ key** en mineur; (*Jur*) ~ **offence** ≈ contravention *f* de simple police; (*Med*) ~ **operation** opération bénigne; (*Theat, fig*) **to play a ~ part** jouer un rôle accessoire *or* un petit rôle; **the ~ planets** les petites planètes; (*Cards*) ~ **suit** (couleur *f*) mineure *f*; (*Brit Scol*) **Smith** ~ Smith junior.
2 *n* (a) (*Jur*) mineur(e) *m(f)*.
(b) (*US Univ*) matière *f* secondaire.
3 *vi* (*US Univ*) **to ~ in chemistry** étudier la chimie comme matière secondaire.
Minorca [mɪ'nɔːkə] *n* Minorque *f*.
minority [maɪ'nɒrɪtɪ] 1 *n* (*also Jur*) minorité *f*. **in the** ~ en minorité; **you are in a ~ of one** vous êtes le seul à penser ainsi, personne ne partage vos vues *or* votre opinion.
2 *cpd party, opinion, government* minoritaire. (*Rad, TV*) **minority programme** émission *f* à l'intention d'un auditoire restreint; (*Admin*) **minority report** rapport soumis par un groupe minoritaire.
Minotaur ['maɪnətɔːʳ] *n* Minotaure *m*.
minster ['mɪnstəʳ] *n* cathédrale *f*; *[monastery]* église abbatiale. **York M~** cathédrale de York.
minstrel ['mɪnstrəl] *n* (*Hist etc*) ménestrel *m*, trouvère *m*, troubadour *m*. (*Archit*) ~ **gallery** tribune *f* des musiciens.
minstrelsy ['mɪnstrəlsɪ] *n* (*U*) (*art*) art *m* du ménestrel *or* trouvère *or* troubadour; (*songs*) chants *mpl*.
mint¹ [mɪnt] 1 *n* (*also Brit*: **Royal M~**) (hôtel *m* de la) Monnaie *f*; (*fig: large sum*) une *or* des somme(s) folle(s). **he made a ~ of money** *or* **a ~* in oil** il a fait fortune dans le pétrole.
2 *cpd*: **in mint condition** à l'état (de) neuf, en parfaite condition; (*Philately*) **mint stamp** timbre non oblitéré.
3 *vt coins* battre; *gold* monnayer (*into* pour obtenir); (*fig*) *word, expression* forger, inventer. (*fig*) **he ~s money** il fait des affaires d'or, il ramasse l'argent à la pelle.
mint² [mɪnt] 1 *n* (*Bot, Culin*) menthe *f*; (*sweet*) bonbon *m* à la menthe. 2 *cpd chocolate, sauce* à la menthe. **mint julep** whisky *etc* glacé à la menthe.
minuet [,mɪnjʊ'et] *n* menuet *m*.
minus ['maɪnəs] 1 *prep* (a) (*Math etc*) moins. **5 ~ 3 equals 2** 5 moins 3 égale(nt) 2.
(b) (*: *without*) sans, avec ... en moins *or* de moins. **he arrived ~ his coat** il est arrivé sans son manteau; **they found his wallet ~ the money** ils ont retrouvé son portefeuille avec l'argent en moins; ~ **a finger** avec un doigt en *or* de moins.
2 *cpd*: **minus quantity** (*Math*) quantité négative; (*) quantité négligeable; (*Math*) **minus sign** moins *m*.
3 *n* (*Math*) (*sign*) moins *m*; (*amount*) quantité négative.
minute¹ ['mɪnɪt] 1 *n* (a) (*of time*) minute *f*; (*fig*) minute, instant *m*, moment *m*. **it is 20 ~s past 2** il est 2 heures 20 (minutes); **at 4 o'clock to the** ~ à 4 heures pile *or* tapant(es); **we got the train without a ~ to spare** une minute de plus et nous manquions le train; **I'll do it in a** ~ je le ferai dans une minute; **I'll do it the ~ he comes** je le ferai dès qu'il arrivera; **do it this** ~! fais-le tout de suite! *or* à la minute!; **he went out this (very)** ~ il vient tout juste de sortir; **any ~ now** d'une minute à l'autre; **I shan't be a** ~ j'en ai pour deux secondes; **it won't take five ~s** ce sera fait en un rien de temps; **wait a** ~ attendez une minute *or* un instant *or* un moment; (*indignantly*) minute!; **up to the** ~ *equipment* dernier modèle *inv*; *fashion* dernier cri *inv*; *news* de (la) dernière heure; **there's one born every ~!*** il faut vraiment le faire!.
(b) (*Geog, Math: part of degree*) minute *f*.
(c) (*official record*) compte rendu *m*, procès-verbal *m*; (*Comm etc: memorandum*) note *f*, circulaire *f*. **to take the ~s of a meeting** rédiger le procès-verbal *or* le compte rendu d'une réunion; **who will take the ~s?** qui sera le rapporteur de la réunion?
2 *cpd*: (*Admin, Comm etc*) **minute book** registre *m* des délibérations; *[clock etc]* **minute hand** grande aiguille; (*Culin*) **minute steak** entrecôte *f* minute.
3 *vt fact, detail* prendre note de; *meeting* rédiger le compte rendu de, dresser le procès-verbal de; *person* faire passer une note à (*about* au sujet de).
minute² [maɪ'njuːt] *adj* (*tiny*) *particles, amount* minuscule, infime, infinitésimal; *change, differences* minime, infime; (*detailed*) *report, examination, description* minutieux, détaillé. **in ~ detail** par le menu; **the ~st details** les moindres détails.
minutely [maɪ'njuːtlɪ] *adv* minutieusement, dans les moindres détails. **a ~ detailed account** un compte rendu extrêmement détaillé *or* circonstancié; **anything ~ resembling a fish** quelque chose ayant vaguement l'apparence d'un poisson.
minutiae [mɪ'njuːʃɪiː] *npl* menus détails, minuties *fpl*, vétilles *fpl* (*pej*).
minx [mɪŋks] *n* (petite) espiègle *f*, friponne *f*.
miracle ['mɪrəkl] 1 *n* miracle *m*; (*fig*) miracle, prodige *m*, merveille *f*. **by a ~, by some ~** par miracle; **it is a ~ of ingenuity** c'est un miracle *or* un prodige *or* une merveille d'ingéniosité; **it is a ~ that ...** c'est miracle que ... + *subj*; **it will be a ~ if ...** ce sera (un) miracle si ... . 2 *cpd*: **miracle cure, miracle drug** remède-miracle *m*; **miracle-man** homme-miracle *m*; (*Rel Theat*) **miracle play** miracle *m*.
miraculous [mɪ'rækjʊləs] *adj* (*lit*) miraculeux; (*fig*) miraculeux, prodigieux, merveilleux.
miraculously [mɪ'rækjʊləslɪ] *adv* (*lit, fig*) miraculeusement, par miracle.
mirage ['mɪrɑːʒ] *n* (*lit, fig*) mirage *m*.
mire ['maɪəʳ] *n* (*liter*) (*mud*) fange *f* (*liter*), bourbe *f*, boue *f*; (*swampy ground*) bourbier *m*. (*fig*) **to drag sb's name through the** ~ traîner (le nom de) qn dans la fange *or* la boue.
mirror ['mɪrəʳ] 1 *n* miroir *m*, glace *f*; (*Aut*) rétroviseur *m*; (*fig*) miroir. **hand** ~ glace à main; **pocket** ~ miroir de poche; **to look at o.s. in the** ~ se regarder dans le miroir *or* dans la glace; (*fig*) **it holds a ~ (up) to ...** cela reflète ... . 2 *cpd*: **mirror image** image invertie. 3 *vt* (*lit, fig*) refléter. (*lit, fig*) **to be ~ed in** se refléter dans.
mirth [mɜːθ] *n* (*U*) hilarité *f*, gaieté *f or* gaîté *f*, rires *mpl*. **this remark caused some** ~ cette remarque a déclenché des rires *or* une certaine hilarité.
mirthful ['mɜːθfʊl] *adj* gai, joyeux.
mirthless ['mɜːθlɪs] *adj* sans gaieté, triste.
miry ['maɪərɪ] *adj* (*liter*) fangeux (*liter*), bourbeux.
misadventure [,mɪsəd'ventʃəʳ] *n* mésaventure *f*; (*less serious*) contretemps *m*. (*Jur*) **death by** ~ mort accidentelle.
misalliance [,mɪsə'laɪəns] *n* mésalliance *f*.
misanthrope ['mɪzənθrəʊp] *n* misanthrope *mf*.
misanthropic [,mɪzən'θrɒpɪk] *adj person* misanthrope; *mood* misanthropique.
misanthropist [mɪ'zænθrəpɪst] *n* misanthrope *mf*.
misanthropy [mɪ'zænθrəpɪ] *n* misanthropie *f*.
misapply ['mɪsə'plaɪ] *vt discovery, knowledge* mal employer, mal appliquer; *abilities, intelligence* mal employer, mal diriger; *money, funds* détourner.
misapprehend ['mɪs,æprɪ'hend] *vt* mal comprendre, se faire une idée fausse de *or* sur, se méprendre sur.
misapprehension ['mɪs,æprɪ'henʃən] *n* erreur *f*, malentendu *m*, méprise *f*. **there seems to be some** ~ il semble y avoir erreur *or* malentendu *or* méprise; **he's (labouring) under a** ~ il n'a pas bien compris, il se fait une idée fausse.
misappropriate ['mɪsə'prəʊprɪeɪt] *vt money, funds* détourner.
misappropriation ['mɪsə,prəʊprɪ'eɪʃən] *n* détournement *m*.
misbegotten ['mɪsbɪ'gɒtn] *adj* (*lit: liter*) illégitime, bâtard; (*fig*) *plan, scheme* mal conçu, malencontreux.
misbehave ['mɪsbɪ'heɪv] *vi* se conduire mal; *[child]* ne pas être sage, se tenir mal.
misbehaviour, (*US*) **misbehavior** ['mɪsbɪ'heɪvjəʳ] *n [person, child]* mauvaise conduite *or* tenue; (*stronger*) inconduite *f*.
misbelief ['mɪsbɪ'liːf] *n* (*Rel*) croyance fausse.
misbeliever ['mɪsbɪ'liːvəʳ] *n* (*Rel*) mécréant(e) *m(f)*, infidèle *mf*.
miscalculate ['mɪs'kælkjʊleɪt] 1 *vt* mal calculer. 2 *vi* (*fig*) se tromper.

miscalculation ['mɪsˌkælkjʊ'leɪʃən] *n* (*lit, fig*) erreur *f* de calcul, mauvais calcul.
miscall ['mɪs'kɔːl] *vt* mal nommer, appeler à tort.
miscarriage ['mɪs'kærɪdʒ] *n* **(a)** *[plan etc]* insuccès *m*, échec *m*; *[letter, goods]* perte *f*, égarement *m*. ~ **of justice** erreur *f* judiciaire. **(b)** (*Med*) fausse couche. **to have a** ~ faire une fausse couche.
miscarry [ˌmɪs'kærɪ] *vi* **(a)** *[plan, scheme]* échouer, avorter, mal tourner; *[letter, goods]* s'égarer, ne pas arriver à destination. **(b)** (*Med*) faire une fausse couche.
miscast ['mɪs'kɑːst] *pret, ptp* **miscast** *vt* (*Cine, Theat etc*) *play* donner une mauvaise distribution à. **he was** ~ on n'aurait jamais dû lui donner *or* attribuer ce rôle.
miscegenation [ˌmɪsɪdʒɪ'neɪʃən] *n* croisement *m* entre races (*humaines*).
miscellaneous [ˌmɪsɪ'leɪnɪəs] *adj objects, collection* varié, divers, disparate (*pej*). ~ **conversation** conversation *f* sur des sujets divers; ~ **expenses** frais *mpl* divers; ~ **items** (*Comm*) articles divers; (*Press*) faits divers; (*on agenda*) '~' 'divers'.
miscellany [mɪ'selənɪ] *n [objects etc]* collection *f*; (*Literat*) recueil *m*, sélection *f*, choix *m*, anthologie *f*; (*Rad, TV*) sélection, choix. (*Literat*) **miscellanies** miscellanées *fpl*, (volume *m* de) mélanges *mpl*.
mischance [ˌmɪs'tʃɑːns] *n* mésaventure *f*, malchance *f*. **by (a)** ~ par malheur.
mischief ['mɪstʃɪf] **1** *n* **(a)** (*roguishness*) malice *f*, espièglerie *f*; (*naughtiness*) sottises *fpl*, polissonnerie *f*; (*maliciousness*) méchanceté *f*. **he's up to (some)** ~ *[child]* il (nous) prépare une *or* quelque sottise; *[adult]* (*in fun*) il (nous) prépare quelque farce *or* niche; (*from malice*) il médite un mauvais tour *or* coup; **he's always up to some** ~ il trouve toujours une sottise *or* niche à faire; *[child only]* **to get into** ~ faire des sottises, faire des siennes; **to keep sb out of** ~ empêcher qn de faire des sottises *or* des bêtises, garder qn sur le droit chemin (*hum*); **the children managed to keep out of** ~ les enfants sont arrivés à ne pas faire de sottises, les enfants ont même été sages; **he means** ~ *[child]* il va sûrement faire une sottise; *[adult]* (*in fun*) il va sûrement faire une farce; (*from malice*) il est mal intentionné; **out of sheer** ~ (*for fun*) par pure espièglerie; (*from malice*) par pure méchanceté; **full of** ~ espiègle, plein de malice; **bubbling over with** ~ pétillant de malice; **to make** ~ **(for sb)** créer des ennuis (à qn); **to make** ~ **between 2 people** semer la zizanie *or* la discorde entre 2 personnes.
(b) (*: *child*) petit(e) vilain(e) *m(f)*, polisson(ne) *m(f)*.
(c) (*U: injury, damage*) (*physical*) mal *m*; (*mental etc*) tort *m*; (*to ship, building etc*) dommage *m*, dégât(s) *m(pl)*. **to do sb a** ~ (*physically*) faire mal à qn, blesser qn; (*mentally etc*) faire du tort à qn; **to do o.s. a** ~ (*physically*) se faire mal, se blesser; (*mentally etc*) se faire du tort.
2 *cpd*: **mischief-maker** semeur *m*, -euse *f or* brandon *m* de discorde; (*esp gossip*) mauvaise langue, langue de vipère.
mischievous ['mɪstʃɪvəs] *adj* **(a)** (*playful, naughty*) *child, kitten* espiègle, malicieux, coquin; *adult* farceur; *glance etc* malicieux, espiègle. **he's as** ~ **as a monkey** c'est un vrai petit diable.
(b) (*harmful*) *person* méchant, malveillant; *attempt, report, rumour* malveillant, malin (*f* -igne).
mischievously ['mɪstʃɪvəslɪ] *adv* **(a)** (*naughtily etc*) malicieusement, par espièglerie. **(b)** (*harmfully*) méchamment, avec malveillance.
mischievousness ['mɪstʃɪvəsnɪs] *n* (*roguishness*) malice *f*, espièglerie *f*; (*maliciousness*) méchanceté *f*; (*naughtiness*) polissonnerie *f*.
misconceive ['mɪskən'siːv] **1** *vt* mal comprendre, mal interpréter. **2** *vi* se tromper, se méprendre (*of* sur).
misconception ['mɪskən'sepʃən] *n* (*wrong idea/opinion*) idée/opinion fausse; (*misunderstanding*) malentendu *m*, méprise *f*.
misconduct [ˌmɪs'kɒndʌkt] **1** *n* **(a)** (*bad behaviour*) inconduite *f*; (*Jur: sexual*) adultère *m*.
(b) (*bad management*) *[business etc]* mauvaise administration *or* gestion.
2 [ˌmɪskən'dʌkt] *vt business* mal diriger, mal gérer, mal administrer. **to** ~ **o.s.**† se conduire mal.
misconstruction ['mɪskən'strʌkʃən] *n* fausse interprétation. **words open to** ~ mots qui prêtent à méprise *or* contresens.
misconstrue ['mɪskən'struː] *vt acts, words* mal interpréter.
miscount ['mɪs'kaʊnt] **1** *n* (*gen*) mécompte *m*; (*Pol: during election*) erreur *f* dans le compte (des suffrages exprimés). **2** *vti* mal compter.
miscreant ['mɪskrɪənt] *n* († *or liter*) scélérat(e) *m(f)*, gredin(e) *m(f)*.
misdeal ['mɪs'diːl] (*vb: pret, ptp* **misdealt**) (*Cards*) **1** *n* maldonne *f*. **2** *vti*: **to** ~ **(the cards)** faire maldonne.
misdeed ['mɪs'diːd] *n* méfait *m*, mauvaise action; (*stronger*) crime *m*.
misdemeanour, (*US*) **misdemeanor** [ˌmɪsdɪ'miːnəʳ] *n* incartade *f*, écart *m* de conduite; (*more serious*) méfait *m*; (*Jur*) infraction *f*, contravention *f*.
misdirect ['mɪsdɪ'rekt] *vt letter etc* mal adresser; *person* mal renseigner, fourvoyer; *blow, efforts* mal diriger, mal orienter; *operation, scheme* mener mal. (*Jur*) **to** ~ **the jury** mal instruire le jury.
misdirection ['mɪsdɪ'rekʃən] *n [letter etc]* erreur *f* d'adresse *or* d'acheminement; *[blow, efforts]* mauvaise orientation; *[operation, scheme]* mauvaise conduite.
miser ['maɪzəʳ] *n* avare *mf*, grippe-sou *m*.
miserable ['mɪzərəbl] *adj* **(a)** (*unhappy*) *person, life, look* malheureux, triste; (*deplorable*) *sight, failure* pitoyable, lamentable. **to feel** ~ avoir le cafard* *or* des idées noires; **to make sb** ~ peiner *or* chagriner qn; (*stronger*) affliger qn; **to make sb's life** ~ faire *or* mener la vie dure à qn, rendre qn (constamment) malheureux; **don't look so** ~**!** ne fais pas cette tête d'enterrement!
(b) (*filthy, wretched*) misérable, miteux, minable. **they were living in** ~ **conditions** ils vivaient dans des conditions misérables *or* dans la misère.
(c) (*: *unpleasant*) *climate, weather* maussade; (*stronger*) détestable, sale*. **what a** ~ **day!, what** ~ **weather!** quel temps maussade!; (*stronger*) quel sale temps!*
(d) (*contemptible*) *meal, gift* méchant (*before n*), misérable, piteux; *amount, offer* dérisoire; *salary* dérisoire, de misère. **a** ~ **50 francs** une misérable *or* malheureuse somme de 50 F.
miserably ['mɪzərəblɪ] *adv live* misérablement, pauvrement; *look, smile, answer* pitoyablement; *pay* misérablement, chichement; *fail* lamentablement, pitoyablement. **it was raining** ~ une pluie maussade tombait; **they played** ~* ils ont joué minablement*, ils ont été minables*.
misère [mɪ'zɛəʳ] *n* (*Cards*) grande misère.
miserliness ['maɪzəlɪnɪs] *n* avarice *f*.
miserly ['maɪzəlɪ] *adj* avare, pingre, radin*.
misery ['mɪzərɪ] *n* **(a)** (*unhappiness*) tristesse *f*, douleur *f*; (*suffering*) souffrances *fpl*, supplice *m*; (*wretchedness*) misère *f*, détresse *f*. **the miseries of mankind** la misère de l'homme; **a life of** ~ une vie de misère; **to make sb's life a** ~ faire *or* mener la vie dure à qn, rendre qn (constamment) malheureux; **to put an animal out of its** ~ achever un animal; **put him out of his** ~* **and tell him the results** abrégez son supplice et donnez-lui les résultats.
(b) (*: *gloomy person*) (*child*) pleurnicheur* *m*, -euse* *f*; (*adult*) grincheux *m*, -euse *f*, rabat-joie *m inv*. **what a** ~ **you are!** quel grincheux tu fais!, ce que tu peux être pleurnicheur!* *or* grincheux! *or* rabat-joie!
misfire ['mɪs'faɪəʳ] *vi [gun]* faire long feu, rater; *[plan]* rater, foirer*; *[joke]* manquer son but, foirer*; *[car engine]* avoir des ratés.
misfit ['mɪsfɪt] *n* (*Dress*) vêtement mal réussi *or* qui ne va pas bien; (*fig: person*) inadapté(e) *m(f)*. **he's always been a** ~ **here** il ne s'est jamais intégré ici, il n'a jamais su s'adapter ici.
misfortune [mɪs'fɔːtʃən] *n* malheur *m*, malchance *f*, infortune *f* (*liter*). (*loc*) ~**s never come singly** un malheur n'arrive jamais seul; ~ **dogs his footsteps** il joue de malchance; **companion in** ~ compagnon *m or* compagne *f* d'infortune; **it is his** ~ **that he is deaf** pour son malheur il est sourd; **I had the** ~ **to meet him** par malheur *or* par malchance *or* pour mon malheur je l'ai rencontré; **that's** YOUR ~**!*** tant pis pour toi!
misgiving [mɪs'gɪvɪŋ] *n* crainte(s) *f(pl)*, doute(s) *m(pl)*, appréhension *f*. **not without some** ~**(s)** non sans appréhension *or* inquiétude; **I had** ~**s about the scheme** j'avais des doutes quant au projet.
misgovern ['mɪs'gʌvən] *vti* mal gouverner, mal administrer.
misgovernment ['mɪs'gʌvənmənt] *n* mauvais gouvernement, mauvaise administration.
misguided ['mɪs'gaɪdɪd] *adj person* abusé, malavisé (*liter*); *attempt* malencontreux; *decision, conduct, action* peu judicieux.
misguidedly ['mɪs'gaɪdɪdlɪ] *adv* malencontreusement, peu judicieusement, à mauvais escient.
mishandle ['mɪs'hændl] *vt* **(a)** (*treat roughly*) *person* maltraiter, malmener; *object* manier *or* manipuler sans précaution.
(b) (*mismanage*) *person* mal prendre, mal s'y prendre avec; *problem* mal traiter. **he** ~**d the whole situation** il a totalement manqué de sagacité *or* de finesse, il a été tout à fait maladroit.
mishap ['mɪshæp] *n* mésaventure *f*. **slight** ~ contretemps *m*; **without** ~ sans encombre; **he had a** ~ il lui est arrivé une (petite) mésaventure.
mishear ['mɪs'hɪəʳ] *pret, ptp* **misheard** *vt* mal entendre.
mishmash* ['mɪʃmæʃ] *n* méli-mélo* *m*.
misinform ['mɪsɪn'fɔːm] *vt* mal renseigner.
misinterpret ['mɪsɪn'tɜːprɪt] *vt* mal interpréter.
misinterpretation ['mɪsɪnˌtɜːprɪ'teɪʃən] *n* interprétation erronée (*of* de), contresens *m*. **open to** ~ qui prête à contresens.
misjudge ['mɪs'dʒʌdʒ] *vt amount, numbers, time* mal évaluer, (*underestimate*) sous-estimer; *person* méjuger, se méprendre sur le compte de.
misjudg(e)ment [ˌmɪs'dʒʌdʒmənt] *n* mauvaise évaluation; sous-estimation *f*.
mislay [ˌmɪs'leɪ] *pret, ptp* **mislaid** *vt* égarer.
mislead [ˌmɪs'liːd] *pret, ptp* **misled** *vt* (*accidentally*) induire en erreur, tromper; (*deliberately*) tromper, égarer, fourvoyer.
misleading [ˌmɪs'liːdɪŋ] *adj notice, suggestion* trompeur.
mislike†† [mɪs'laɪk] *vt* ne pas aimer, détester.
mismanage ['mɪs'mænɪdʒ] *vt* mal administrer, mal gérer.
mismanagement ['mɪs'mænɪdʒmənt] *n* mauvaise administration *or* gestion.
misname ['mɪs'neɪm] *vt* donner un nom inexact *or* impropre à, mal nommer.
misnomer ['mɪs'nəʊməʳ] *n* fausse appellation, erreur *f* d'appellation *or* de nom. **that is a** ~ c'est un nom vraiment mal approprié, c'est se moquer du monde* que de l'appeler (*or* les appeler *etc*) ainsi.
misogamist [mɪ'sɒgəmɪst] *n* misogame *mf*.
misogamy [mɪ'sɒgəmɪ] *n* misogamie *f*.
misogynist [mɪ'sɒdʒɪnɪst] *n* misogyne *mf*.
misogyny [mɪ'sɒdʒɪnɪ] *n* misogynie *f*.
misplace ['mɪs'pleɪs] *vt* **(a)** *object, word* mal placer, ne pas mettre où il faudrait; *affection, trust* mal placer. ~**d remark** remarque déplacée *or* hors de propos. **(b)** (*lose*) égarer.

misprint ['mɪsprɪnt] 1 *n* faute *f* d'impression *or* typographique, coquille *f*. 2 [ˌmɪs'prɪnt] *vt* imprimer mal *or* incorrectement.
mispronounce ['mɪsprə'naʊns] *vt* prononcer de travers, estropier, écorcher.
mispronunciation ['mɪsprəˌnʌnsɪ'eɪʃən] *n* prononciation incorrecte (*of* de), faute *f* de prononciation.
misquotation ['mɪskwəʊ'teɪʃən] *n* citation inexacte.
misquote ['mɪs'kwəʊt] *vt* citer faussement *or* inexactement. **he was ~d in the press as having said ...** les journalistes lui ont incorrectement fait dire que ...
misread ['mɪs'ri:d] *pret, ptp* **misread** ['mɪs'red] *vt* (*lit*) mal lire; (*fig: misinterpret*) mal interpréter, se tromper sur.
misrepresent ['mɪsˌreprɪ'zent] *vt facts* dénaturer, déformer; *person* présenter sous un faux jour, donner une impression incorrecte de. **he was ~ed in the press** ce qu'on a dit de lui dans les journaux est faux *or* incorrect.
misrepresentation ['mɪsˌreprɪzen'teɪʃən] *n* déformation *f*, présentation déformée.
misrule ['mɪs'ru:l] 1 *n* (*bad government*) mauvaise administration; (*disorder etc*) désordre *m*, anarchie *f*. 2 *vt* gouverner mal.
miss[1] [mɪs] 1 *n* **(a)** (*shot etc*) coup manqué *or* raté; (*: *omission*) manque *m*, lacune *f*; (*: *mistake*) erreur *f*, faute *f*; (*failure*) four *m*, bide* *m* (*fig*). (*Prov*) **a ~ is as good as a mile** rater c'est rater (même de justesse); **that shot was a near ~** le coup a failli toucher; (*lit, fig*) **that was a near ~** il s'en est fallu de peu *or* d'un cheveu; **we had a near ~ with that truck** ce camion a failli nous percuter, nous l'avons échappé belle avec ce camion; **to give a concert/lecture** *etc* **a ~*** s'abstenir d'assister à *or* ne pas aller à un concert/une conférence *etc*; **to give Paris/the Louvre** *etc* **a ~*** ne pas aller à Paris/au Louvre *etc*; **I'll give the wine a ~ this evening*** je m'abstiendrai de boire du vin *or* je me passerai de vin ce soir; **I'll give my evening class a ~ this week*** tant pis pour mon cours du soir cette semaine; **I'm giving my aunt a ~ this year*** pour une fois je ne vais pas aller voir ma tante cette année; **oh give it a ~!‡** ça suffit!, en voilà assez!, arrête!; **they voted the record a ~*** le disque a été jugé minable*; *V* **hit.**
(b) (*Med*: abbr of* **miscarriage b**) fausse couche.
2 *vt* **(a)** (*fail to hit*) *target, goal* manquer, rater, louper*. **the shot just ~ed me** la balle m'a manqué de justesse *or* d'un cheveu; **the plane just ~ed the tower** l'avion a failli toucher la tour.
(b) (*fail to find, catch, use etc*) *vocation, opportunity, appointment, train, person or thing sought, road, turning* manquer, rater; *house, thing looked out for, solution* ne pas trouver, ne pas voir; *meal* sauter; *class, lecture* manquer, sécher (*Scol sl*). (*iro*) **you haven't ~ed much!** vous n'avez pas manqué *or* perdu grand chose!; **we ~ed the tide** nous avons manqué la marée; (*fig*) **to ~ the boat*** *or* **the bus*** manquer le coche* (*fig*); **to ~ one's cue** (*Theat*) manquer sa réplique; (*fig*) rater l'occasion, manquer le coche*; **to ~ one's footing** glisser; **she doesn't ~ a trick*** rien ne lui échappe; **to ~ one's way** perdre son chemin, s'égarer; **you can't ~ our house** vous trouverez tout de suite notre maison; **you mustn't ~ (seeing) this film** ne manquez pas (de voir) *or* ne ratez pas ce film, c'est un film à ne pas manquer *or* rater; **don't ~ the Louvre** ne manquez pas d'aller au Louvre; **if we go that way we shall ~ Bourges** si nous prenons cette route nous ne verrons pas Bourges; **I ~ed him at the station by 5 minutes** je l'ai manqué *or* raté de 5 minutes à la gare.
(c) *remark, joke, meaning* (*not hear*) manquer, ne pas entendre; (*not understand*) ne pas comprendre, ne pas saisir*. **I ~ed what you said** je n'ai pas entendu ce que vous avez dit; **I ~ed that** je n'ai pas entendu, je n'ai pas compris; **you're ~ing the point** l'essentiel vous échappe, vous ne saisissez pas.
(d) (*escape, avoid*) *accident, bad weather* échapper à. **he narrowly ~ed being killed** il a manqué *or* il a bien failli se (faire) tuer, il l'a échappé belle.
(e) (*long for*) *person* regretter (l'absence de). **I do ~ Paris** Paris me manque beaucoup; **we ~ you very much** nous regrettons beaucoup ton absence, tu nous manques beaucoup; **are you ~ing me?** est-ce que je te manque?; **they're ~ing one another** ils se manquent l'un à l'autre; **he will be greatly ~ed** on le regrettera beaucoup; **he won't be ~ed** personne ne le regrettera; **I ~ the old trams** je regrette les vieux trams; **I ~ the sunshine/the freedom** le soleil/la liberté me manque.
(f) (*notice loss of*) *money, valuables* remarquer l'absence *or* la disparition de. **I suddenly ~ed my wallet** tout d'un coup je me suis aperçu que je n'avais plus mon portefeuille; **I'm ~ing 8 dollars*** il me manque 8 dollars, j'avais 8 dollars de plus; **here's your hat back — I hadn't even ~ed it!** je vous rends votre chapeau — je ne m'étais même pas aperçu *or* n'avais même pas remarqué que je ne l'avais plus!; **you can keep that pen, I shan't ~ it** vous pouvez garder ce stylo, il ne me fera pas défaut.
3 *vi* **(a)** [*shot, person*] manquer, rater. **you can't ~!** vous ne pouvez pas ne pas réussir!
(b) to be ~ing faire défaut, avoir disparu; **there is one plate ~ing, one plate is ~ing** il manque une assiette; **how many are ~ing?** combien en manque-t-il?; **there's nothing ~ing** il ne manque rien, tout y est; **one of our aircraft is ~ing** un de nos avions n'est pas rentré; *V also* **missing.**
miss out *vt sep* **(a)** (*accidentally*) *name, word, line of verse, page* passer, sauter, oublier; (*in distributing sth*) *person* sauter, oublier.
(b) (*on purpose*) *course at meal* ne pas prendre, sauter*; *name on list* omettre; *word, line of verse, page* laisser de côté, sauter; *concert, lecture, museum* ne pas aller à; (*in distributing sth*) *person* omettre.
miss out on* *vt fus* **(a)** *opportunity, bargain* laisser passer, louper*, ne pas profiter de; *one's share* ne pas recevoir, perdre. **he missed out on several good deals** il a raté *or* loupé* plusieurs occasions de faire une bonne affaire.
(b) he missed out on the deal il n'a pas obtenu tout ce qu'il aurait pu de l'affaire; **make sure you don't miss out on anything** vérifie que tu reçois ton dû.
miss[2] [mɪs] *n* **(a)** mademoiselle *f*. **M~ Smith** mademoiselle Smith, Mlle Smith; († *or frm*) **the M~es Smith** les demoiselles *fpl* Smith; (*on letter*) Mesdemoiselles Smith; (*in letter*) **Dear M~ Smith** Chère Mademoiselle; **yes M~ Smith** oui mademoiselle; **yes ~*** oui mademoiselle *or* mam'selle* (*l'anglais ne s'emploie que pour un professeur*); **M~ France 1980** Miss France 1980.
(b) (*: *often hum*) petite *or* jeune fille. **the modern ~** la jeune fille moderne; **she's a cheeky little ~** c'est une petite effrontée.
missal ['mɪsəl] *n* missel *m*.
misshapen ['mɪs'ʃeɪpən] *adj object, body, limbs* difforme, contrefait.
missile ['mɪsaɪl] 1 *n* (*gen*) projectile *m*; (*Mil*) missile *m*; *V* **ballistic, ground**[1], **guided** *etc*. 2 *cpd*: **missile launcher** lance-missiles *m*.
missing ['mɪsɪŋ] *adj* **(a)** *person* absent, disparu; *object* manquant, égaré, perdu. (*Admin, Police etc*) **~ person** personne absente (*Jur*); **the 3 ~ students are safe** les 3 étudiants dont on était sans nouvelles sont sains et saufs; **fill in the ~ words** ≃ complétez les phrases suivantes, donnez les mots qui manquent; (*fig*) **the ~ link** (*gen*) le maillon qui manque à la chaîne; (*between ape and man*) le chaînon manquant.
(b) (*Mil*) disparu. **~ in action** disparu au champ d'honneur; **~ believed killed** disparu présumé tué; **to be reported ~** être porté disparu.
mission ['mɪʃən] *n* (*all senses*) mission *f*. **trade ~** mission de commerce; (*Rel*) **foreign ~s** missions étrangères; **to send sb on a ~ to sb** envoyer qn en mission auprès de qn; **his ~ in life is to help others** il s'est donné pour mission d'aider autrui.
missionary ['mɪʃənrɪ] 1 *n* missionnaire *mf*. 2 *cpd work, duties* missionnaire; *society* de missionnaires.
missis‡ ['mɪsɪz] *n* (*wife*) **the/my ~** la/ma bourgeoise‡; (*boss*) **the ~** la patronne‡; **hey ~!** dites m'dame! *or* ma petite dame!*
missive ['mɪsɪv] *n* missive *f*.
misspell ['mɪs'spel] *pret, ptp* **misspelled** *or* **misspelt** *vt* mal écrire, mal orthographier.
misspelling ['mɪs'spelɪŋ] *n* faute *f* d'orthographe.
misspend ['mɪs'spend] *pret, ptp* **misspent** *vt money* dépenser à tort et à travers, gaspiller; *time, strength, talents* mal employer, gaspiller. **misspent youth** folle jeunesse.
misstate ['mɪs'steɪt] *vt* rapporter incorrectement.
misstatement ['mɪs'steɪtmənt] *n* rapport inexact.
missus‡ ['mɪsɪz] *n* = **missis‡**.
missy*† ['mɪsɪ] *n* ma petite demoiselle*.
mist [mɪst] 1 *n* (*Met*) brume *f*; (*on glass*) buée *f*; (*before eyes*) brouillard *m*; [*perfume, dust etc*] nuage *m*; [*ignorance, tears*] voile *m*. **morning/sea ~** brume matinale/ de mer; (*fig liter*) **lost in the ~s of time** perdu dans la nuit des temps; *V* **Scotch** *etc*.
2 *vt* (*also* **~ over, ~ up**) *mirror, windscreen, eyes* embuer.
3 *vi* (*also* **~ over, ~ up**) [*scene, landscape, view*] se couvrir de brume, devenir brumeux; [*mirror, windscreen, eyes*] s'embuer.
mistakable [mɪs'teɪkəbl] *adj* facile à confondre (*with, for* avec).
mistake [mɪs'teɪk] (*vb: pret* **mistook**, *ptp* **mistaken**) 1 *n* erreur *f*, faute *f*; (*misunderstanding*) méprise *f*. **to make a ~ in a dictation/problem** faire une faute dans une dictée/une erreur dans un problème; **I made a ~ about the book/about him** je me suis trompé sur le livre/sur son compte; **I made a ~ about** *or* **over the road to take/about** *or* **over the dates** je me suis trompé de route/de dates, j'ai fait une erreur en ce qui concerne la route qu'il fallait prendre/les dates; **make no ~ about it** ne vous y trompez pas; **you're making a big ~** tu fais une grave *or* lourde erreur; **to make the ~ of doing** avoir le tort de faire, commettre l'erreur de faire; **by ~** par erreur; (*carelessly*) par inadvertance, par mégarde; **I took his umbrella in ~ for mine** j'ai pris son parapluie par erreur *or* en croyant prendre le mien; **there must be some ~** il doit y avoir erreur; **there must be** *or* **let there be no ~ about it** qu'on ne s'y méprenne pas *or* trompe (*subj*) pas; **it's cold today and no ~!*** décidément il fait froid aujourd'hui!; **my ~!*** c'est (de) ma faute!, mea-culpa!
2 *vt* **(a)** *meaning* mal comprendre, mal interpréter; *intentions* se méprendre sur; *time, road* se tromper de. **there's no mistaking her voice** il est impossible de ne pas reconnaître sa voix; **there's no mistaking that ...** il est indubitable que ...; **to ~ A for B** prendre A pour B, confondre A avec B; *V also* **mistaken.**
(b) to be ~n faire erreur (*about* en ce qui concerne), se tromper (*about* sur); **if I'm not ~n** sauf erreur, si je ne me trompe; **that's just where you're ~n!** c'est ce qui vous trompe!, c'est en quoi vous faites erreur!; *V also* **mistaken.**
mistaken [mɪs'teɪkən] 1 *ptp of* **mistake**. 2 *adj idea, opinion* erroné, faux (*f* fausse); *conclusion* erroné, mal fondé; *generosity* mal placé. **in the ~ belief that ...** croyant à tort que ...; *V* **identity.**
mistakenly [mɪs'teɪkənlɪ] *adv* par erreur; (*carelessly*) par inadvertance, par mégarde.
mister ['mɪstəʳ] *n* **(a)** (*toujours abrégé en* **Mr**) monsieur *m*. **Mr Smith** Monsieur Smith, M Smith; **yes Mr Smith** oui Monsieur; **Mr Chairman** monsieur le président. **(b)** (‡) **hey ~!** dites m'sieu!*
mistime ['mɪs'taɪm] *vt act, blow* mal calculer. **to ~ one's arrival** (*arrive inopportunely*) arriver à contretemps; (*miscalculate time*) se tromper sur *or* mal calculer son (heure d')arrivée; **~d remark** remarque inopportune.
mistiness ['mɪstɪnɪs] *n* [*morning etc*] bruine *f*, état brumeux; (*on windscreen etc*) condensation *f*.
mistle thrush ['mɪslθrʌʃ] *n* draine *f*.
mistletoe ['mɪsltəʊ] *n* (*U*) gui *m*.

mistook [mɪsˈtʊk] *pret of* **mistake.**
mistranslate [ˈmɪstrænzˈleɪt] *vt* mal traduire, faire un (*or* des) contresens en traduisant.
mistranslation [ˈmɪstrænzˈleɪʃən] *n* **(a)** erreur *f* de traduction, contresens *m*. **(b)** (*U*) *[text etc]* mauvaise traduction, traduction inexacte.
mistreat [ˌmɪsˈtriːt] *vt* maltraiter.
mistreatment [ˌmɪsˈtriːtmənt] *n* mauvais traitement.
mistress [ˈmɪstrɪs] *n* **(a)** *[household, institution etc]* (*also fig*) maîtresse *f*. (†) **is your ~ *or* the ~ at home?** Madame est-elle là?; (*fig*) **to be ~ of oneself** être maîtresse de soi; **to be one's own ~** être sa propre maîtresse, être indépendante.
(b) (*Brit: teacher*) (*in primary school*) maîtresse *f*, institutrice *f*; (*in secondary school*) professeur *m*. **the English ~** le professeur d'anglais; **they have a ~ for geography** ils ont un professeur femme en géographie.
(c) (*lover; also*†‡: *sweetheart*) maîtresse *f*, amante†† *f*.
(d) [ˈmɪsɪz] (*term of address: abrév* **Mrs** *sauf* †† *et dial*) madame *f*. **Mrs Smith** Madame Smith, Mme Smith; **yes Mrs Smith** oui Madame.
mistrial [ˌmɪsˈtraɪəl] *n* (*Jur*) procès entaché d'un vice de procédure.
mistrust [ˈmɪsˈtrʌst] **1** *n* méfiance *f*, défiance *f* (*of* à l'égard de).
2 *vt person, sb's motives, suggestion* se méfier de, se défier de (*liter*); *abilities* douter de, ne pas avoir confiance en.
mistrustful [mɪsˈtrʌstfʊl] *adj* méfiant, défiant (*of* à l'égard de).
mistrustfully [mɪsˈtrʌstfəlɪ] *adv* avec méfiance; *look, say* d'un air méfiant.
misty [ˈmɪstɪ] **1** *adj weather* brumeux; *day* de brume, brumeux; *mirror, windscreen* embué; (*fig*) *eyes, look* embrumé, embué; (*fig*) *outline, recollection, idea* nébuleux, flou.
2 *cpd*: **misty-eyed** (*near tears*) qui a les yeux voilés de larmes; (*fig: sentimental*) qui a la larme à l'œil.
misunderstand [ˈmɪsʌndəˈstænd] *pret, ptp* **misunderstood** *vt words, action, reason* mal comprendre, comprendre de travers, mal interpréter. **you ~ me** vous m'avez mal compris, ce n'est pas ce que j'ai voulu dire; **she was misunderstood all her life** toute sa vie elle est restée incomprise *or* méconnue.
misunderstanding [ˈmɪsʌndəˈstændɪŋ] *n* erreur *f*, méprise *f*; (*disagreement*) malentendu *m*, mésentente *f*. **there must be some ~** il doit y avoir méprise *or* une erreur; **they had a slight ~** il y a eu une légère mésentente entre eux.
misunderstood [ˈmɪsʌndəˈstʊd] *pret, ptp of* **misunderstand.**
misuse [ˈmɪsˈjuːs] **1** *n [power, authority]* abus *m*; *[word, tool]* usage *m* impropre *or* abusif; *[money, resources, energies, one's time]* mauvais emploi. (*Jur*) **~ of funds** détournement *m* de fonds.
2 [ˈmɪsˈjuːz] *vt power, authority* abuser de; *word, tool* employer improprement *or* abusivement; *money, resources, energies, one's time* mal employer; *funds* détourner.
mite [maɪt] *n* **(a)** (††: *coin*) denier *m*; (*as contribution*) obole *f*. **the widow's ~** le denier de la veuve; **he gave his ~ to the collection** il a apporté son obole à la souscription.
(b) (*small amount*) grain *m*, brin *m*, atome *m*, parcelle *f*, tantinet *m*. **there's not a ~ of bread left** il ne reste plus une miette de pain; **not a ~ of truth** pas une parcelle *or* un atome de vérité; **a ~ of consolation** une toute petite consolation; **well, just a ~ then** bon, mais alors un tantinet seulement; **we were a ~ surprised*** nous avons été un tantinet *or* un rien surpris.
(c) (*small child*) petit(e) *m(f)*. **poor little ~** le pauvre petit.
(d) (*Zool*) mite *f*. **cheese ~** mite de fromage.
miter [ˈmaɪtəʳ] (*US*) = **mitre.**
mitigate [ˈmɪtɪgeɪt] *vt punishment, sentence* atténuer, réduire, mitiger; *suffering, sorrow* adoucir, alléger, atténuer; *effect, evil* atténuer, mitiger. **mitigating circumstances** circonstances atténuantes.
mitigation [ˌmɪtɪˈgeɪʃən] *n* (*V* **mitigate**) atténuation *f*, réduction *f*, mitigation *f*, adoucissement *m*, allégement *m*.
mitre, (*US*) **miter** [ˈmaɪtəʳ] **1** *n* (*Rel*) mitre *f*; (*Carpentry*) onglet *m*. **2** *vt* (*Carpentry*) (*join*) assembler à *or* en onglet; (*cut*) tailler à onglet. **3** *cpd*: (*Carpentry*) **mitre joint** (assemblage *m* à) onglet *m*.
mitt [mɪt] *n* **(a)** = **mitten. (b)** (*Baseball*) gant *m*. **(c)** (‡: *hand*) patte* *f*, patoche‡ *f*.
mitten [ˈmɪtn] *n* (*with cut-off fingers*) mitaine *f*; (*with no separate fingers*) moufle *f*; (*Boxing**) gant *m*, mitaine*.
mix [mɪks] **1** *n [cement, concrete etc]* mélange *m*, mortier *m*; *[metals]* alliage *m*, amalgame *m*; (*Culin*) *[ingredients]* mélange; (*commercially prepared*) préparation *f*. **a packet of cake ~** un paquet de préparation pour gâteau.
2 *cpd*: **mix-up** confusion *f*; **there was a mix-up over tickets** il y a eu confusion en ce qui concerne les billets; **we got in a mix-up over the dates** nous nous sommes embrouillés dans les dates; **he got into a mix-up with the police** il a eu un démêlé avec la police.
3 *vt substances, elements, things, ingredients, colours* mélanger, mêler; *metals* allier; *cement, mortar* malaxer; *cake, sauce* préparer, faire; *cocktails etc* préparer; *salad* remuer, retourner. **to ~ one thing with another** mélanger une chose à une autre *or* avec une autre *or* et une autre; **to ~ to a smooth paste** battre pour obtenir une pâte homogène; **~ the eggs into the sugar** incorporez les œufs au sucre; **he ~ed the drinks** il a préparé les boissons; **can I ~ you a drink?** je vous sers un cocktail?; **never ~ your drinks!** évitez toujours les mélanges!; **to ~ business and *or* with pleasure** combiner les affaires et le plaisir; **to ~ one's metaphors** faire des métaphores incohérentes; *V also* **mixed.**
4 *vi* (*V* **1**) se mélanger, se mêler, s'amalgamer, s'allier. **these colours just don't ~** ces couleurs ne s'harmonisent pas *or* ne vont pas bien ensemble; **he ~es with all kinds of people** il fraye avec *or* il fréquente toutes sortes de gens; **he doesn't ~ well** il est peu sociable; **these groups of children just won't ~** ces groupes d'enfants ne fraternisent pas.
mix in 1 *vi*: **he doesn't want to mix in** il préfère rester à l'écart; **you must try to mix in** il faut essayer de vous mêler un peu aux autres.
2 *vt sep*: **mix in the eggs (with)** incorporez les œufs (à).
mix round *vt sep* mélanger, remuer.
mix together *vt sep* mélanger, amalgamer.
mix up 1 *vt sep* **(a)** (*prepare*) *drink, medicine* mélanger, préparer.
(b) (*put in disorder*) *documents, garments* mêler, mélanger.
(c) (*confuse*) *two objects, two people* confondre. **to mix sth/sb up with sth/sb else** confondre qch...qn avec qch/qn d'autre.
(d) to mix sb up in sth impliquer qn dans qch; **to be/get mixed up in an affair** être/se trouver mêlé à une affaire; **don't get mixed up in it!** restez à l'écart!; **he is/he has got mixed up with a lot of criminals** il fréquente/il s'est mis à fréquenter un tas de malfaiteurs*.
(e) *person* embrouiller. **to be mixed up** *[person]* être (tout) désorienté *or* déboussolé*; *[account, facts]* être embrouillé *or* confus; **I am all mixed up about it** je ne sais plus où j'en suis, je ne m'y reconnais plus; **you've got me all mixed up** vous m'avez embrouillé.
2 mix-up *n V* **mix 2.**
3 mixed-up *adj V* **mixed** 2.
mixed [mɪkst] **1** *adj marriage, school* mixte; *biscuits, nuts* assortis. **the weather was ~** le temps était inégal *or* variable; (*fig*) **it's a ~ bag*** il y a un peu de tout; **it's a ~ blessing** c'est une bonne chose qui a son mauvais côté, cette médaille a son revers; **man/woman of ~ blood** un/une sang-mêlé; **in ~ company** en présence d'hommes et de femmes; (*Tennis*) **~ doubles** double *m* mixte; (*Pol Econ*) **~ economy** économie *f* mixte; **~ farming** polyculture *f*; **~ feelings** sentiments *mpl* contraires *or* contradictoires; **she had ~ feelings about it** elle était partagée à ce sujet; **she agreed with ~ feelings** elle a consenti sans enthousiasme; **~ grill** assortiment *m* de grillades, mixed grill *m*; **~ metaphor** métaphore incohérente; **~ motives** intentions qui ne sont pas entièrement pures; **to meet with a ~ reception** recevoir un accueil mitigé.
2 *cpd*: **mixed-up** *person* désorienté, déboussolé*; *account* embrouillé, confus; **he's a mixed-up kid*** c'est un gosse* qui a des problèmes.
mixer [ˈmɪksəʳ] **1** *n* **(a)** (*Culin*) **hand ~** batteur *m* à main; **electric ~** batteur électrique, mixer *m*, mixeur *m*.
(b) *[cement, mortar etc]* malaxeur *m*; *[industrial liquids]* agitateur *m*. **cement ~** bétonnière *f*, malaxeur à béton.
(c) (*Cine etc: also* **sound ~**) (*person*) ingénieur *m* du son; (*machine*) mélangeur *m* du son.
(d) he's a good ~ il est très sociable *or* liant.
2 *cpd*: (*Brit*) **mixer tap** (robinet *m*) mélangeur *m*.
mixing [ˈmɪksɪŋ] **1** *n* (*V* **mix 3**) mélange *m*; préparation *f*; incorporation *f*; alliage *m*; malaxage *m*; (*Cine etc: also* **sound ~**) mixage *m*. **2** *cpd*: (*Culin*) **mixing bowl** grand bol (de cuisine); (*US*) **mixing faucet** (robinet *m*) mélangeur *m*.
mixture [ˈmɪkstʃəʳ] *n* mélange *m*; (*Med*) préparation *f*, mixture *f*. **the family is an odd ~** cette famille est un mélange bizarre *or* curieux; (*fig*) **it's just the ~ as before** c'est toujours la même chose, il n'y a rien de nouveau; *V* **cough.**
mizzen [ˈmɪzn] *n* (*Naut*) artimon *m*. **~mast** mât *m* d'artimon.
mizzle [ˈmɪzl] (* *or dial*) **1** *vi* bruiner. **2** *n* bruine *f*.
mnemonic [nɪˈmɒnɪk] *adj, n* mnémotechnique (*f*), mnémonique (*f*).
mnemonics [nɪˈmɒnɪks] *n* (*U*) mnémotechnique *f*.
mo'* [məʊ] *n* (*abbr of* **moment** a) moment *m*, instant *m*. **half a ~!, just a ~!** un instant!; (*interrupting*) minute!*
moan [məʊn] **1** *n* (*groan: also of wind etc*) gémissement *m*, plainte *f*; (*: *complaint*) plainte, récrimination *f*.
2 *vi* (*groan*) gémir, pousser des gémissements, geindre; *[wind etc]* gémir; (*: *complain*) maugréer, rouspéter*, râler‡.
3 *vt* dire en gémissant.
moaning [ˈməʊnɪŋ] **1** *n* gémissements *mpl*, plainte(s) *f(pl)*; (*: *complaints*) plaintes, jérémiades *fpl*. **2** *adj* gémissant; (*: *complaining*) rouspéteur*, râleur‡.
moat [məʊt] *n* douves *fpl*, fossés *mpl*.
mob [mɒb] **1** *n* **(a)** *[people]* foule *f*, masse *f*, (*disorderly*) cohue *f*. (†*pej: the common people*) **the ~** la populace; **a ~ of soldiers/supporters** une cohue de soldats/de supporters; **the embassy was burnt by the ~** les émeutiers ont brûlé l'ambassade; **they went in a ~ to the town hall** ils se rendirent en masse *or* en foule à la mairie; **a whole ~ of cars*** toute une cohue de voitures.
(b) (*) bande *f*, clique *f* (*pej*). **Paul and his ~** Paul et sa bande, Paul et sa clique (*pej*); **I had nothing to do with that ~** je n'avais rien à voir avec cette clique.
(c) *[criminals, bandits etc]* gang *m*.
2 *cpd*: **mob oratory** l'éloquence *f* démagogique; (*pej*) **mob rule** la loi de la populace *or* de la rue.
3 *vt person* assaillir, faire foule autour de; *place* assiéger. **the shops were ~bed*** les magasins étaient pris d'assaut *or* assiégés.
mobcap [ˈmɒbkæp] *n* charlotte *f* (*bonnet*).
mobile [ˈməʊbaɪl] **1** *adj troops, population* mobile; (*Soc*) mobile; *features, face* mobile, expressif. (*fig*) **I'm not ~ this week*** je n'ai pas de voiture *or* je ne suis pas motorisé cette semaine; **~ canteen** (cuisine) roulante *f*; **~ home** grande caravane *f* (*utilisée comme domicile*); (*Rad, TV*) **~ studio** car *m* de reportage; *V* **shop.**
2 *n* (*Art*) mobile *m*.

mobility [məʊ'bɪlɪtɪ] *n* mobilité *f.*
mobilization [ˌməʊbɪlaɪ'zeɪʃən] *n* (*all senses*) mobilisation *f.*
mobilize ['məʊbɪlaɪz] *vti* (*all senses*) mobiliser.
mobster ['mɒbstəʳ] *n* émeutier *m.*
moccasin ['mɒkəsɪn] *n* mocassin *m.*
mocha ['mɒkə] *n* moka *m.*
mock [mɒk] **1** *n*: **to make a ~ of sth/sb** tourner qch/qn en ridicule.
2 *adj* **(a)** (*imitation*) *leather etc* faux (*f* fausse) (*before n*), imitation *inv* (*before n*), simili- *inv.* **~ turtle soup** potage *m* (fausse) tortue.
(b) (*pretended*) *anger, modesty* simulé, feint. **a ~ battle/trial** un simulacre de bataille/de procès; (*Scol etc*) **~ examination** examen blanc.
(c) (*Literat*) burlesque; *V also* **3.**
3 *cpd*: **mock-heroic** (*gen*) burlesque; (*Literat*) héroï-comique, burlesque; (*Bot*) **mock orange** seringa *m*; **mock-up** maquette *f.*
4 *vt* **(a)** (*ridicule*) ridiculiser; (*scoff at*) se moquer de, railler; (*mimic, burlesque*) singer, parodier.
(b) (*liter: defy*) *sb's plans, attempts* narguer.
5 *vi* se moquer (*at* de).
mock up 1 *vt sep* faire la maquette de.
2 mock-up *n V* **mock 3.**
mocker ['mɒkəʳ] *n* moqueur *m,* -euse *f.*
mockery ['mɒkərɪ] *n* (*mocking*) moquerie *f,* raillerie *f;* (*person, thing*) sujet *m* de moquerie *or* de raillerie, objet *m* de risée; (*travesty*) parodie *f,* travestissement *m,* caricature *f.* **to make a ~ of sb/sth** tourner qn/qch en dérision, bafouer qn/qch; **he had to put up with a lot of ~** il a dû endurer beaucoup de railleries *or* de persiflages; **it is a ~ of justice** c'est une parodie de (la) justice, c'est un travestissement de la justice; **a ~ of a trial** une parodie *or* une caricature de procès; **what a ~ it was!** c'était grotesque!
mocking ['mɒkɪŋ] **1** *n* (*U*) moquerie *f,* raillerie *f.* **2** *adj person, smile, voice* moqueur, railleur; (*malicious*) narquois. **3** *cpd*: **mockingbird** moqueur *m.*
mockingly ['mɒkɪŋlɪ] *adv say* d'un ton moqueur *or* railleur *or* narquois, par moquerie *or* dérision; *smile* d'une façon moqueuse *or* narquoise.
mod[1] [mɒd] (*abbr of* **modern**) **1** *adj* **(a)** (*:†*) *person* dans le vent*; *clothes* à la mode. **(b)** (*) **~ cons** = **modern conveniences**; *V* **modern 1. 2** *n* (*Brit*) **~s and rockers** ≃ blousons noirs.
mod[2] [mɒd] *n* (*Scot*) concours *m* de musique et de poésie (*en gaélique*).
modal ['məʊdl] *adj* (*Ling, Mus etc*) modal.
modality [məʊ'dælɪtɪ] *n* modalité *f.*
mode [məʊd] *n* mode *m,* façon *f,* manière *f;* (*Gram, Mus, Philos*) mode *m;* (*Fashion*) mode *f.* **~ of life** façon *or* manière de vivre, mode *m* de vie.
model ['mɒdl] **1** *n* **(a)** (*small-scale representation of boat etc*) modèle *m* (réduit); (*Archit, Tech, Town Planning etc*) maquette *f; V* **scale**[1] *etc.*
(b) (*standard, example*) modèle *m,* exemple *m.* **he was a ~ of discretion** c'était un modèle de discrétion; **on the ~ of** sur le modèle de, à l'image de; **to take sb/sth as one's ~** prendre modèle *or* prendre exemple sur qn/qch; **to hold sb out** *or* **up as a ~** citer *or* donner qn en exemple.
(c) (*person*) (*Art, Phot, Sculp etc*) modèle *m;* (*Fashion*) mannequin *m.*
(d) (*Comm*) modèle *m.* (*garments, hats*) **the latest ~s** les derniers modèles; (*Aut*) **a 1978 ~** un modèle 1978; (*Aut*) **sports ~** modèle sport; **factory ~** modèle de fabrique.
2 *adj* **(a)** (*designed as ~*) (*gen*) modèle; *prison, factory, school* -pilote, modèle; (*exemplary*) *behaviour, conditions* modèle, exemplaire.
(b) (*small-scale*) *tram, plane, car etc* modèle réduit *inv; railway, village* en miniature.
3 *vt* **(a)** (*make ~ of*) modeler (*in* en). **~ling clay** pâte *f* à modeler.
(b) to ~ sth on sth else modeler qch sur qch d'autre; **to ~ o.s. on sb** se modeler sur qn, prendre modèle *or* exemple sur qn.
(c) (*Fashion*) **to ~ clothes** être mannequin, présenter les modèles de collection; **she was ~ling swimwear** elle présentait les modèles de maillots de bain.
4 *vi* (*Art, Phot, Sculp*) poser (*for* pour); (*Fashion*) être mannequin (*for* chez). **she does a bit of ~ling** elle travaille comme modèle *or* comme mannequin de temps en temps.
modeller, (*US*) **modeler** ['mɒdləʳ] *n* modeleur *m,* -euse *f.*
modelling, (*US*) **modeling** ['mɒdlɪŋ] *n* (*Art etc*) modelage *m.*
moderate ['mɒdərɪt] **1** *adj opinions, demands* modéré (*also Pol*); *person* modéré (*in* dans); *price, income, amount, size, appetite* modéré, raisonnable, moyen; *heat* modéré; *climate* tempéré; *language, terms* mesuré; *talent, capabilities* modéré, moyen, ordinaire; *results* passable, modéré, moyen.
2 *cpd*: **moderate-sized** de grandeur *or* de grosseur *or* de taille moyenne.
3 *n* (*esp Pol*) modéré(e) *m(f).*
4 ['mɒdəreɪt] *vt* **(a)** (*restrain, diminish*) modérer. **moderating influence** influence modératrice.
(b) (*preside over*) présider.
5 *vi* [*storm, wind etc*] se modérer, s'apaiser, se calmer.
moderately ['mɒdərɪtlɪ] *adv* modérément, avec modération. **this book is ~ priced** ce livre est d'un prix raisonnable; **~ pleased** plus ou moins *or* raisonnablement satisfait.
moderation [ˌmɒdə'reɪʃən] *n* (*U*) modération *f,* mesure *f.* **in ~** modérément; **with ~** avec mesure *or* modération; **to advise ~ in drinking** conseiller la modération dans le boire, conseiller de boire modérément *or* avec modération.
moderator ['mɒdəreɪtəʳ] *n* **(a)** (*Rel*) **M~** président *m* (*de l'Assemblée générale de l'Église presbytérienne*). **(b)** (*Phys, Tech*) modérateur *m.*
modern ['mɒdən] **1** *adj* moderne. **house with all ~ conveniences** (*abbr* **mod cons**) maison *f* tout confort; **it has all ~ conveniences** il y a tout le confort (moderne); **~ languages** langues vivantes; **in ~ times** dans les temps modernes, à l'époque moderne.
2 *n* (*artist, poet etc*) moderne *mf.*
modernism ['mɒdənɪzəm] *n* **(a)** (*U: Art, Rel*) modernisme *m.* **(b)** (*word*) néologisme *m.*
modernist ['mɒdənɪst] *adj, n* moderniste (*mf*).
modernistic [ˌmɒdə'nɪstɪk] *adj* moderniste.
modernity [mɒ'dɜːnɪtɪ] *n* modernité *f.*
modernization [ˌmɒdənaɪ'zeɪʃən] *n* modernisation *f.*
modernize ['mɒdənaɪz] **1** *vt* moderniser. **2** *vi* se moderniser.
modest ['mɒdɪst] *adj* **(a)** (*not boastful*) modeste, effacé, réservé; (*†: chaste*) pudique, modeste. **to be ~ about one's achievements** ne pas se faire gloire de ses réussites *or* exploits; **don't be so ~!** ne fais pas le modeste!, tu es trop modeste!
(b) (*fairly small; simple*) *success, achievement, amount, origin* modeste; *demands, needs* modeste, très modéré; *wage, price, sum* (*moderate*) modeste; (*very small*) modique. **a ~ little house** une modeste maisonnette, une maisonnette sans prétention(s).
modestly ['mɒdɪstlɪ] *adv* **(a)** (*without boasting*) modestement, avec modestie; (*†: chastely*) modestement, pudiquement, avec pudeur. **(b)** (*simply*) modestement, simplement, sans prétention(s).
modesty ['mɒdɪstɪ] *n* (*V* **modest**) **(a)** modestie *f;* (*†: chasteness*) pudeur *f,* modestie. **false ~** fausse modestie; **may I say with all due ~ ...** soit dit en toute modestie ... . **(b)** [*request etc*] modération *f;* [*sum of money, price*] modicité *f.*
modicum ['mɒdɪkəm] *n*: **a ~ of** un minimum de.
modifiable ['mɒdɪfaɪəbl] *adj* modifiable.
modification [ˌmɒdɪfɪ'keɪʃən] *n* modification *f* (*to, in* à). **to make ~s (in** *or* **to)** faire *or* apporter des modifications (à).
modifier ['mɒdɪfaɪəʳ] *n* modificateur *m;* (*Gram*) modificatif *m.*
modify ['mɒdɪfaɪ] *vt* **(a)** (*change*) *plans, design* modifier, apporter des modifications à; *customs, society* transformer, modifier; (*Gram*) modifier.
(b) (*make less strong*) modérer. **he'll have to ~ his demands** il faudra qu'il modère (*subj*) ses exigences *or* qu'il en rabatte; **he modified his statement** il modéra les termes de sa déclaration.
modifying ['mɒdɪfaɪɪŋ] **1** *n* modification *f.* **2** *adj note, term* modificatif (*also Gram*); *factor* modifiant.
modish ['məʊdɪʃ] *adj* à la mode, mode *inv.*
modishly ['məʊdɪʃlɪ] *adv* à la mode.
modiste [məʊ'diːst] *n* modiste *f.*
Mods* [mɒdz] *n* (*Oxford Univ abbr of* **moderations**) premier examen (pour le grade de bachelier ès arts).
modular ['mɒdjʊləʳ] *adj* (*Archit, Math*) modulaire; *furniture* modulaire, à éléments (composables).
modulate ['mɒdjʊleɪt] *vt* (*all senses*) moduler.
modulation [ˌmɒdjʊ'leɪʃən] *n* modulation *f.* **frequency ~** modulation de fréquence.
module ['mɒdjuːl] *n* (*Archit, Math, Measure, Space*) module *m; V* **lunar.**
modulus ['mɒdjʊləs] *n* (*Math, Phys*) module *m,* coefficient *m.*
mogul ['məʊgəl] *n* manitou *m* (*fig*). **a ~ of the film industry** un grand manitou du cinéma.
mohair ['məʊhɛəʳ] **1** *n* mohair *m.* **2** *cpd* en *or* de mohair.
Mohammed [məʊ'hæmed] *n* Mahomet *m.*
Mohammedan [məʊ'hæmɪdən] = **Mahometan.**
Mohican ['məʊhɪkən] *n* (*also* **~ Indian**) Mohican *mf.*
moist [mɔɪst] *adj hand, atmosphere* moite; *climate, wind, surface* humide; *heat* moite, humide. **eyes ~ with tears** des yeux humides *or* mouillés de larmes.
moisten ['mɔɪsn] **1** *vt* humecter, mouiller légèrement; (*Culin*) mouiller légèrement. **to ~ one's lips** s'humecter les lèvres. **2** *vi* devenir humide *or* moite.
moistness ['mɔɪstnɪs] *n* (*V* **moist**) moiteur *f,* humidité *f.*
moisture ['mɔɪstʃəʳ] *n* (*on grass etc*) humidité *f;* (*on glass etc*) buée *f.*
moisturize ['mɔɪstʃəraɪz] *vt air, atmosphere* humidifier; *skin* hydrater.
moisturizer ['mɔɪstʃəraɪzəʳ] *n* (*for skin*) crème *f or* lait *m* hydratant(e).
moke‡ [məʊk] *n* (*Brit*) bourricot *m,* baudet *m.*
molar ['məʊləʳ] **1** *n* (*tooth*) molaire *f.* **2** *adj* (*Dentistry, Phys*) molaire.
molasses [məʊ'læsɪz] *n* (*U*) mélasse *f.*
mold [məʊld] *etc* (*US*) = **mould** *etc.*
mole[1] [məʊl] **1** *n* (*Zool*) taupe *f.* **2** *cpd*: **mole-catcher** taupier *m;* **molehill** taupinière *f* (*V* **mountain 1**); **moleskin** (*n*) (*lit*) (peau *f* de) taupe *f;* (*Tex*) velours *m* de coton; (*adj*) de *or* en (peau de) taupe; de *or* en velours de coton.
mole[2] [məʊl] *n* (*on skin*) grain *m* de beauté.
mole[3] [məʊl] *n* (*breakwater*) môle *m,* digue *f.*
molecular [məʊ'lekjʊləʳ] *adj* moléculaire.
molecule ['mɒlɪkjuːl] *n* molécule *f.*
molest [məʊ'lest] *vt* (*trouble*) importuner, tracasser; (*harm*) molester, rudoyer, brutaliser; (*Jur: sexually*) attenter à la pudeur de.
molestation [ˌməʊles'teɪʃən] *n* (*V* **molest**) tracasserie(s) *f(pl);* brutalités *fpl;* attentat *m* à la pudeur.
moll* [mɒl] *n* (*pej*) nana‡ *f* (de gangster).
mollify ['mɒlɪfaɪ] *vt person, anger* apaiser, calmer; *demands* modérer, tempérer. **~ing remarks** propos lénifiants.
mollusc, (*US*) **mollusk** ['mɒləsk] *n* mollusque *m.*

mollycoddle ['mɒlɪkɒdl] *vt* élever dans du coton, chouchouter.
molt [məʊlt] (*US*) = **moult.**
molten ['məʊltən] *adj metal, glass* en fusion, fondu.
molybdenum [mɒ'lɪbdɪnəm] *n* molybdène *m.*
mom* [mɒm] *n* (*US*) maman *f.*
moment ['məʊmənt] *n* **(a)** moment *m*, instant *m*. **man of the ~** homme *m* du moment; **the psychological ~** le moment psychologique; **the ~ of truth** l'instant *or* la minute de vérité; **wait a ~!, just a ~!, one ~!, half a ~!*** (attendez) un instant! *or* une minute!; (*objecting to sth*) minute!, pas si vite!*; **I shan't be a ~, I'll just** *or* **only be a ~** j'en ai pour un instant; **a ~ ago** il y a un instant; **a ~ later** un instant plus tard; **that very ~** à cet instant *or* ce moment précis; **the ~ he arrives** dès *or* aussitôt qu'il arrivera; **the ~ he arrived** dès *or* aussitôt qu'il arriva, dès son arrivée; **do it this ~!** fais-le à l'instant! *or* sur-le-champ!; **I've just this ~ heard of it** je viens de l'apprendre à l'instant (même); **it won't take a ~** c'est l'affaire d'un instant; **at the (present) ~, at this ~ in time** en ce moment (même), à l'heure qu'il est; **at that ~** à ce moment(-là); **at any ~** d'un moment *or* instant à l'autre; **at the right ~** au bon moment, à point nommé; **at the last ~** au dernier moment; **to leave things till the last ~** attendre le dernier moment; **for a ~** un instant; **for a brief ~** l'espace d'un instant; **not for a ~!** jamais de la vie!; **for the ~** pour le moment; **from the ~ I saw him** dès l'instant où je l'ai vu; **from that ~** dès ce moment, dès cet instant; **I'll come in a ~** j'arrive dans un instant; **it was all over in a ~** tout s'est passé en un instant *or* en un clin d'œil *or* en un tournemain; *V* **spur.**
(b) (*importance*) importance *f.* **of little ~** de peu d'importance; **of (great) ~** de grande *or* haute importance.
(c) (*Tech*) moment *m.* **~ of inertia** moment d'inertie.
momentarily ['məʊməntərɪlɪ] *adv* (*briefly*) momentanément; (*at any moment*) d'un moment à l'autre; (*US: now*) en ce moment.
momentary ['məʊməntərɪ] *adj* (*brief*) momentané, passager; (*constant*) constant, continuel.
momentous [məʊ'mentəs] *adj* très important, considérable, capital.
momentousness [məʊ'mentəsnɪs] *n* (*U*) importance capitale, portée *f.*
momentum [məʊ'mentəm] *n* (*Phys etc*) moment *m* (*des quantités de mouvement*); (*fig*) élan *m*, vitesse *f* (acquise). **to gather ~** *[spacecraft, car etc]* prendre de la vitesse; (*fig*) gagner du terrain; (*Aut, Space etc, also fig*) **to lose ~** être en perte de vitesse.
Monacan [mɒ'nɑːkən] **1** *adj* monégasque. **2** *n* Monégasque *mf.*
Monaco ['mɒnəkəʊ] *n* Monaco *f.*
monad ['mɒnæd] *n* (*Chem, Philos*) monade *f.*
Mona Lisa ['məʊnə'liːzə] *n* la Joconde.
monarch ['mɒnək] *n* (*lit, fig*) monarque *m.*
monarchic(al) [mɒ'nɑːkɪk(əl)] *adj* monarchique.
monarchism ['mɒnəkɪzəm] *n* monarchisme *m.*
monarchist ['mɒnəkɪst] *adj, n* monarchiste (*mf*).
monarchy ['mɒnəkɪ] *n* monarchie *f.*
monastery ['mɒnəstərɪ] *n* monastère *m.*
monastic [mə'næstɪk] *adj life* monastique, monacal; *vows, architecture* monastique.
monasticism [mə'næstɪsɪzəm] *n* monachisme *m.*
monaural [ˌmɒn'ɔːrəl] *adj instrument* monophonique, monaural; *hearing* monauriculaire.
Monday ['mʌndɪ] *n* lundi *m*; *for phrases V* **Saturday**; *V also* **Easter, Whit** *etc.*
monetary ['mʌnɪtərɪ] *adj* monétaire.
money ['mʌnɪ] **1** *n* **(a)** (*U*) argent *m*; (*Fin*) monnaie *f.* **French ~** argent français; **paper ~** papier-monnaie *m*, monnaie de papier (*often pej*); (*Prov*) **~ is the root of all evil** l'argent est la racine de tous les maux; **lack of ~** manque *m* d'argent; **your ~ or your life!** la bourse ou la vie!; (*Brit*) **it's ~ for jam*** *or* **for old rope*** c'est de l'argent vite gagné *or* gagné sans peine; **to make ~** *[person]* gagner de l'argent; *[business etc]* rapporter, être lucratif (*V also* **1b**); **to come into ~** (*by inheritance*) hériter (d'une somme d'argent); (*gen*) recevoir une somme d'argent; **he's earning good ~** il gagne bien sa vie, il gagne gros (*V also* **1b**); **he gets his ~ on Fridays** il touche son argent *or* sa paie le vendredi, il est payé le vendredi; **when do I get my ~?** quand est-ce que j'aurai mon argent?; (*lit, fig*) **to get one's ~'s worth** en avoir pour son argent; **to get one's ~ back** être remboursé; **I want my ~ back!** remboursez!; **to put ~ into sth** placer son argent dans qch; **is there ~ in it?** est-ce que ça rapporte?, est-ce que c'est lucratif?; **it's a bargain for the ~!** à ce prix-là c'est une occasion!; *V* **big, coin, counterfeit, ready** *etc.*
(b) (*fig phrases*) **that's the one for my ~!** c'est juste ce qu'il me faut!; **that's the team for my ~** je serais prêt à parier pour cette équipe; **for my ~ we should do it now** à mon avis nous devrions le faire maintenant; **he's made of ~*, he's rolling in ~*, he has pots of ~*** il est cousu d'or, il roule sur l'or*; **he's got ~ to burn** il a de l'argent à ne savoir qu'en faire *or* à jeter par la fenêtre; **we're in the ~ now!‡** nous roulons sur l'or* maintenant; **he's in the big ~‡** il récolte un fric fou‡; (*Prov*) **~ makes ~** l'argent va où est l'argent; (*Prov*) **~ talks** l'argent est roi; (*loc*) **~ doesn't grow on trees** l'argent ne se trouve pas sous le pas d'un cheval; **put your ~ where your mouth is*** un placement d'argent convainc plus qu'un beau discours, tes grands discours ne te coûtent rien; **to throw** *or* **send good ~ after bad** s'enfoncer dans une mauvaise affaire; (*loc*) **bad ~ drives out good** des capitaux douteux font fuir les investissements sains; **this ~ burns a hole in his pocket** il brûle de dépenser cet argent; **~ runs through his fingers like water** l'argent lui fond dans les mains; *V* **even²**.
(c) (*Jur*) **~s, monies** sommes *fpl* d'argent; **~s paid out** versements *mpl*; **~s received** recettes *fpl*, rentrées *fpl*; **public ~s** deniers publics.
2 *cpd difficulties, problems, questions* d'argent, financier. **moneybag** sac *m* d'argent; **he's a moneybags‡** il est plein aux as‡; **moneybox** tirelire *f*; **moneychanger** changeur *m*; **money expert** expert *m* en matières financières; (*pej*) **moneygrubber** grippe-sou *m*; (*pej*) **moneygrubbing** (*n*) thésaurisation *f*, rapacité *f*; (*adj*) rapace, grippe-sou *inv*; **moneylender** prêteur *m*, -euse *f* sur gages; **moneylending** (*n*) prêt *m* à intérêt; (*adj*) prêteur; **moneymaker** affaire lucrative; **moneymaking** (*n*) acquisition *f* d'argent; (*adj*) lucratif, qui rapporte; (*Fin*) **money market** marché *m* monétaire; **money matters** questions *fpl* d'argent *or* financières; (*Fin*) **money order** mandat *m*; **money spider*** araignée *f* porte-bonheur *inv*; (*Brit*) **money spinner** mine *f* d'or (*fig*).
moneyed ['mʌnɪd] *adj* riche, cossu, argenté*. **the ~ classes** les classes possédantes, les nantis *mpl.*
...monger ['mʌŋgə^r] *suf* marchand de...; *V* **fish, scandal, war** *etc.*
Mongol ['mɒŋgəl] **1** *adj* **(a)** (*Geog, Ling*) mongol. **(b)** (*Med*) **m~** mongolien. **2** *n* **(a)** Mongol(e) *m(f).* **(b)** (*Ling*) mongol *m.* **(c)** (*Med*) **m~** mongolien(ne) *m(f).*
Mongolia [mɒŋ'gəʊlɪə] *n* Mongolie *f.*
Mongolian [mɒŋ'gəʊlɪən] = **Mongol 1a, 2a, 2b.**
mongolism ['mɒŋgəlɪzəm] *n* (*Med*) mongolisme *m.*
mongoose ['mɒŋguːs] *n* (*Zool*) mangouste *f.*
mongrel ['mʌŋgrəl] **1** *n* (*dog*) (chien *m*) bâtard *m*; (*animal, plant*) hybride *m*, métis(se) *m(f).* **2** *adj* hybride, bâtard, (de race) indéfinissable.
monies ['mʌnɪz] *npl of* **money**; *V* **money 1c.**
monitor ['mɒnɪtə^r] **1** *n* **(a)** (*Scol*) ≃ chef *m* de classe.
(b) (*Rad*) (*person*) rédacteur *m*, -trice *f* d'un service d'écoute; (*TV set*) moniteur *m*, écran *m* de contrôle; (*Med, Tech: device etc*) moniteur.
2 *vt* **(a)** (*Rad*) *foreign broadcast, station* être à l'écoute de.
(b) (*Tech etc*) *machine, system* contrôler (les performances de).
(c) *discussion, group* diriger.
monitory ['mɒnɪtərɪ] *adj* monitoire, d'avertissement, d'admonition.
monk [mʌŋk] *n* moine *m*, religieux *m.* (*Bot*) **~'s hood** aconit *m.*
monkey ['mʌŋkɪ] **1** *n* singe *m*; (*fig: child*) galopin(e) *m(f)*, polisson(ne) *m(f)*; (*Brit‡*) cinq cents livres. **female ~** guenon *f*; **to make a ~ out of sb** tourner qn en ridicule.
2 *cpd*: (*fig*) **monkey business*** (*dishonest*) quelque chose de louche, combine(s) *f(pl)*; (*mischievous*) singeries *fpl*; **no monkey business now!*** pas de blagues!*; **monkey house** maison *f* des singes, singerie *f*; (*Naut*) **monkey jacket** vareuse ajustée; **monkey nut** cacahouète *f* *or* cacahuète *f*; (*Bot: tree*) **monkey puzzle** araucaria *m*; (*fig*) **monkey tricks*** = **monkey business***; **monkey wrench** clef anglaise *or* à molette.
monkey about*, monkey around* *vi* **(a)** (*waste time*) perdre son temps. **stop monkeying about and get on with your work** cesse de perdre ton temps et fais ton travail.
(b) (*play the fool*) faire l'idiot *or* l'imbécile. **to monkey about with sth** tripoter qch, faire l'imbécile avec qch.
monkish ['mʌŋkɪʃ] *adj* de moine.
mono... ['mɒnəʊ] *pref* mon(o)... .
mono ['mɒnəʊ] *adj* (*abbr of* **monophonic**) mono* *inv*, monophonique, monaural. **recorded in ~** enregistré en monophonie.
monochrome ['mɒnəkrəʊm] **1** *n* camaïeu *m.* **landscape in ~** paysage *m* en camaïeu. **2** *adj* monochrome, en camaïeu.
monocle ['mɒnəkl] *n* monocle *m.*
monogamous [mɒ'nɒgəməs] *adj* monogame.
monogamy [mɒ'nɒgəmɪ] *n* monogamie *f.*
monogram ['mɒnəgræm] *n* monogramme *m.*
monograph ['mɒnəgræf] *n* monographie *f.*
monolingual [ˌmɒnəʊ'lɪŋgwəl] *adj* monolingue.
monolith ['mɒnəʊlɪθ] *n* monolithe *m.*
monolithic [ˌmɒnəʊ'lɪθɪk] *adj* monolithe.
monologue ['mɒnəlɒg] *n* monologue *m.*
monomania [ˌmɒnəʊ'meɪnɪə] *n* monomanie *f.*
monomial [mɒ'nəʊmɪəl] (*Math*) **1** *n* monôme *m.* **2** *adj* de *or* en monôme.
mononucleosis [ˌmɒnəʊnjuːklɪ'əʊsɪs] *n* mononucléose *f.*
monophonic [ˌmɒnəʊ'fɒnɪk] *adj* monophonique, monaural.
monoplane ['mɒnəʊpleɪn] *n* monoplan *m.*
monopolize [mə'nɒpəlaɪz] *vt* (*Comm*) monopoliser, avoir le monopole de; (*fig*) monopoliser, accaparer.
monopoly [mə'nɒpəlɪ] *n* **(a)** monopole *m* (*of, in* de). **(b)** (*game*) ® **M~** Monopoly *m* ®.
monorail ['mɒnəʊreɪl] *n* monorail *m.*
monosyllabic ['mɒnəʊsɪ'læbɪk] *adj word* monosyllabe; *language, reply* monosyllabique. **he was ~** il a parlé par monosyllabes.
monosyllable ['mɒnəˌsɪləbl] *n* monosyllabe *m.* **to answer in ~s** répondre par monosyllabes.
monotheism ['mɒnəʊˌθiːɪzəm] *n* monothéisme *m.*
monotheist ['mɒnəʊˌθiːɪst] *n* monothéiste *mf.*
monotheistic [ˌmɒnəʊθiː'ɪstɪk] *adj* monothéiste.
monotone ['mɒnətəʊn] *n* (*voice/tone etc*) voix *f*/ton *m etc* monocorde. **to speak in a ~** parler sur un ton monocorde.
monotonous [mə'nɒtənəs] *adj music, routine* monotone; *landscape, scenery* monotone, uniforme; *voice* monotone, monocorde.
monotony [mə'nɒtənɪ] *n* monotonie *f.*
monotype ['mɒnəʊtaɪp] *n* (*Art, Engraving*) monotype *m.* (*Typ: machine*) **M~** Monotype *f* ®.
monoxide [mɒ'nɒksaɪd] *n* protoxyde *m.*
Monroe doctrine [mən'rəʊ'dɒktrɪn] *n* doctrine *f* de Monroe.

monseigneur [ˌmɒnsenˈjɜːʳ] *n* monseigneur *m.*
monsignor [mɒnˈsiːnjəʳ] *n* (*Rel*) monsignor *m.*
monsoon [mɒnˈsuːn] *n* mousson *f.* **the ~ season** la mousson d'été.
monster [ˈmɒnstəʳ] **1** *n* (*all senses*) monstre *m.* **2** *adj* colossal, monstre*.
monstrance [ˈmɒnstrəns] *n* ostensoir *m.*
monstrosity [mɒnsˈtrɒsɪtɪ] *n* **(a)** (*U*) monstruosité *f*, atrocité *f.* **(b)** (*thing*) monstruosité *f*, chose monstrueuse; (*person*) monstre *m* de laideur.
monstrous [ˈmɒnstrəs] *adj* **(a)** (*huge*) *animal, fish, building* colossal, énorme, gigantesque. **(b)** (*atrocious*) *crime, behaviour* monstrueux, abominable. **it is quite ~ that** ... il est monstrueux *or* scandaleux que ... + *subj.*
monstrously [ˈmɒnstrəslɪ] *adv* monstrueusement.
montage [mɒnˈtɑːʒ] *n* (*Cine, Phot*) montage *m.*
Monte Carlo [ˈmɒntɪˈkɑːləʊ] *n* Monte-Carlo.
month [mʌnθ] *n* mois *m.* **it went on for ~s** cela a duré des mois (et des mois); **in the ~ of May** au mois de mai, en mai; **to be paid by the ~** être payé au mois *or* mensualisé; **every ~** *happen* tous les mois; *pay* mensuellement; **which day of the ~ is it?** le combien sommes-nous?; **at the end of this ~** *or* (*Comm*) **of the current ~** fin courant (*Comm*); **he owes his landlady two ~s' rent** il doit deux mois à sa propriétaire; **six ~s pregnant** enceinte de six mois; **he'll never do it in a ~ of Sundays** il le fera la semaine des quatre jeudis* *or* à la saint-glinglin*; *V* **calendar, lunar** *etc.*
monthly [ˈmʌnθlɪ] **1** *adj publication* mensuel. **~ instalment, ~ payment** mensualité *f*; (*Med*) **~ period** règles *fpl*; **~ salary** salaire mensuel, mensualité; **~ ticket** billet *m* valable pour un mois.
2 *n* (*Press*) revue *or* publication mensuelle.
3 *adv pay* au mois, mensuellement; *happen* tous les mois.
Montreal [ˌmɒntrɪˈɔːl] *n* Montréal.
monument [ˈmɒnjʊmənt] *n* (*all senses*) monument *m* (*to* à).
monumental [ˌmɒnjʊˈmentl] *adj* (*all senses*) monumental. **~ mason** marbrier *m.*
moo [muː] **1** *n* meuglement *m*, beuglement *m*, mugissement *m.* **2** *vi* meugler, beugler, mugir.
moochꜝ [muːtʃ] **1** *vt* (*US: cadge*) **to ~ sth from sb** taper qn de qchꜝ. **2** *vi*: **to ~ in/out** *etc* entrer/sortir *etc* en traînant*.
mooch aboutꜝ, **mooch around**ꜝ *vi* traînasser, flemmarder*.
mood [muːd] **1** *n* **(a)** humeur *f*, disposition *f.* **to be in a good/bad ~** être de bonne/mauvaise humeur, être de bon/mauvais poil*; **to be in a nasty** *or* **ugly ~** *[person]* être d'une humeur massacrante *or* exécrable; *[crowd]* être menaçant; **to be in a forgiving ~** être en veine de générosité *or* d'indulgence; **I'm in the ~ for dancing** je danserais volontiers, j'ai envie de danser; **I'm not in the ~** *or* **I'm in no ~ for laughing** je ne suis pas d'humeur à rire, je n'ai aucune envie de rire; **I'm in no ~ to listen to him** je ne suis pas d'humeur à l'écouter; **are you in the ~ for chess?** une partie d'échecs ça vous dit?; **he plays well when he's in the ~** quand il est d'humeur *or* quand ça lui chante* il joue bien; **I'm not in the ~** ça ne me dit rien; **as the ~ takes him** selon son humeur, comme ça lui chante*; **that depends on his ~** cela dépend de son humeur; **he's in one of his ~s** il est encore mal luné; **she has ~s** elle a des sautes d'humeur; **the ~ of the meeting** l'état *m* d'esprit de l'assemblée.
(b) (*Gram, Mus*) mode *m.*
2 *cpd*: **mood music** musique *f* d'ambiance.
moodily [ˈmuːdɪlɪ] *adv* (*bad-temperedly*) *reply* d'un ton maussade, maussadement; (*gloomily*) *stare* d'un air morose.
moodiness [ˈmuːdɪnɪs] *n* (*sulkiness*) humeur *f* maussade; (*changeability*) humeur changeante.
moody [ˈmuːdɪ] *adj* (*variable*) d'humeur changeante, lunatique; (*sulky*) maussade, de mauvaise humeur, mal luné.
moon [muːn] **1** *n* lune *f.* **full/new ~** pleine/nouvelle lune; **there was no ~** c'était une nuit sans lune; **there was a ~ that night** il y avait *or* il faisait clair de lune cette nuit-là; **by the light of the ~** à la clarté de la lune, au clair de (la) lune; (*fig*) **to ask** *or* **cry for the ~** demander la lune; *V* **blue, land, man** *etc.*
2 *cpd*: **moonbeam** rayon *m* de lune; **moon buggy** jeep *f* lunaire; **moon landing** alunissage *m*; **moonless** *V* **moonless**; **moonlight(ing)** *V* **moonlight(ing)**; **moonlit** éclairé par la lune; **moonlit night** nuit *f* de lune; **moonrise** lever *m* de (la) lune; **moonrover** = **moon buggy**; (*fig*) **moonshine*** (*rubbish*) balivernes *fpl*, fadaises *fpl*, sornettes *fpl*; (*US: illegal spirits*) alcool *m* de contrebande; (*US*) **moonshiner** contrebandier *m* de l'alcool; (*Space*) **moon shot** tir *m* lunaire; **moonstone** pierre *f* de lune; (*fig*) **moonstruck** dans la lune; **moon walk** marche *f* lunaire.
moon about, moon around *vi* musarder en rêvassant.
moonless [ˈmuːnlɪs] *adj* sans lune.
moonlight [ˈmuːnlaɪt] **1** *n* clair *m* de lune. **by ~** au clair de (la) lune. **2** *cpd walk, encounter* au clair de lune. (*Brit fig*) **to do a moonlight flit** déménager à la cloche de bois; **moonlight night** nuit *f* de lune. **3** *vi* (*) faire du travail noir.
moonlighting* [ˈmuːnlaɪtɪŋ] *n* (*U*) travail noir.
Moor [mʊəʳ] *n* Maure *m or* More *m*, Mauresque *f or* Moresque *f.*
moor[1] [mʊəʳ] **1** *n* lande *f.* **2** *cpd*: **moorhen** poule *f* d'eau; **moorland** lande *f*, bruyère *f.*
moor[2] [mʊəʳ] **1** *vt ship* amarrer. **2** *vi* mouiller.
mooring [ˈmʊərɪŋ] *n* (*Naut*) (*place*) mouillage *m*; (*ropes etc*) amarres *fpl.* **at her ~s** sur ses amarres; **~ buoy** coffre *m* (d'amarrage), bouée *f* de corps-mort.
Moorish [ˈmʊərɪʃ] *adj* maure (*f inv or* mauresque) *or* more (*f inv or* moresque).
moose [muːs] *n* (*Canada*) orignac *m or* orignal *m*; (*Europe*) élan *m.*
moot [muːt] **1** *adj point, question* discutable. **2** *vt question* soulever, mettre sur le tapis. **it has been ~ed that** ... on a suggéré que ... .
mop [mɒp] **1** *n* (*for floor*) balai *m* laveur; (*Naut*) faubert *m*; (*for dishes*) lavette *f* (à vaisselle); (*fig: also* **~ of hair**) tignasse *f.* **~ of curls** toison bouclée.
2 *cpd*: (*Mil*) **mopping-up operations** nettoyage *m.*
3 *vt floor, surface* essuyer. **to ~ one's brow** s'éponger le front; (*fig*) **to ~ the floor with sb*** battre qn à plate(s) couture(s).
mop down *vt sep* passer un coup de balai à.
mop up 1 *vt sep* **(a)** *liquid* éponger; *floor, surface* essuyer.
(b) (*fig*) *profits* rafler, absorber.
(c) (*Mil*) *terrain* nettoyer; *remnants* éliminer.
(d) (ꜝ: *drink*) siffler*.
2 mopping-up *adj V* **mop 2.**
mope [məʊp] *vi* se morfondre, avoir le cafard* *or* des idées noires. **she ~d about it all day** toute la journée elle a broyé du noir en y pensant.
mope about, mope around *vi* passer son temps à se morfondre, traîner son ennui.
moped [ˈməʊped] *n* cyclomoteur *m*, mobylette *f* ®.
moquette [mɒˈket] *n* moquette *f* (*étoffe*).
moraine [mɒˈreɪn] *n* moraine *f.*
moral [ˈmɒrəl] **1** *adj* (*all senses*) moral. **it is a ~ certainty** c'est une certitude morale; **to be under** *or* **have a ~ obligation to do** être moralement obligé de faire, être dans l'obligation morale de faire; **~ support** soutien moral; **~ philosopher** moraliste *mf*; **~ philosophy** la morale, l'éthique *f*; **~ suasion** pression morale.
2 *n* **(a)** *[story]* morale *f.* **to point the ~** faire ressortir la morale.
(b) *[person, act, attitude]* **~s** moralité *f*; **of loose ~s** d'une moralité relâchée; **he has no ~s** il est sans moralité.
morale [mɒˈrɑːl] *n* (*U*) moral *m.* **high ~** bon moral; **his ~ was very low** il avait le moral très bas *or* à zéro; **to raise sb's ~** remonter le moral à qn; **to lower** *or* **undermine sb's ~** démoraliser qn.
moralist [ˈmɒrəlɪst] *n* moraliste *mf.*
morality [məˈrælɪtɪ] *n* **(a)** (*U*) moralité *f.* **(b)** (*Theat: also* **~ play**) moralité *f.*
moralize [ˈmɒrəlaɪz] **1** *vi* moraliser (*about* sur), faire le moraliste. **2** *vt* moraliser, faire la morale à.
moralizing [ˈmɒrəlaɪzɪŋ] *adj* moralisateur (*f* -trice).
morally [ˈmɒrəlɪ] *adv act* moralement. **~ certain** moralement certain; **~ speaking** du point de vue de la morale, moralement parlant; **~ wrong** immoral, contraire à la morale.
morass [məˈræs] *n* marais *m*, marécage *m.* (*fig*) **a ~ of problems** des problèmes à ne plus s'y retrouver *or* à ne plus s'en sortir; **a ~ of figures** un fatras de chiffres; **a ~ of paperwork** de la paperasserie, un monceau de paperasserie.
moratorium [ˌmɒrəˈtɔːrɪəm] *n* moratoire *m*, moratorium *m.*
morbid [ˈmɔːbɪd] *adj* **(a)** *interest, curiosity, imagination* morbide, malsain; *details* morbide, horrifiant; *fear, dislike* maladif; (*gloomy*) lugubre. **don't be so ~!** ne te complais pas dans ces pensées! *or* ces idées!
(b) (*Med*) *growth* morbide; *anatomy* pathologique.
morbidity [mɔːˈbɪdɪtɪ] *n* (*V* **morbid**) **(a)** morbidité *f*; état maladif; (*gloom*) abattement maladif, neurasthénie *f.* **(b)** (*Med*) morbidité *f.*
morbidly [ˈmɔːbɪdlɪ] *adv* (*abnormally*) d'une façon morbide *or* malsaine *or* maladive; (*gloomily*) sombrement, sinistrement. **~ obsessed by** morbidement *or* maladivement obsédé *or* hanté par.
morbidness [ˈmɔːbɪdnɪs] *n* = **morbidity.**
mordacity [mɔːˈdæsɪtɪ] *n* mordacité *f* (*liter*), causticité *f.*
mordant [ˈmɔːdənt] *adj* mordant, caustique.
more [mɔːʳ] *comp of* **many, much 1** *adj, pron* (*greater in number etc*) plus (de), davantage (de); (*additional*) encore (de); (*other*) d'autres. **I've got ~ money/books than you** j'ai plus d'argent/de livres que vous; **he's got ~ than you** il en a plus que vous; **~ people than seats/than usual/than we expected** plus de gens que de places/que de coutume/que prévu *or* que nous ne l'escomptions; **many came but ~ stayed away** beaucoup de gens sont venus mais davantage *or* un plus grand nombre se sont abstenus; **many ~** *or* **a lot ~ books/time** beaucoup plus de livres/de temps; **I need a lot ~** il m'en faut beaucoup plus *or* bien davantage; **I need a few ~ books** il me faut encore quelques livres *or* quelques livres de plus; **some were talking and a few ~ were reading** il y en avait qui parlaient et d'autres qui lisaient; **a little ~** un peu plus (de); **several ~ days** quelques jours de plus, encore quelques jours; **I'd like (some) ~ meat** je voudrais encore de la viande *or* un peu plus de viande; **there's no ~ meat** il n'y a plus de viande; **is there (any) ~ wine?** y a-t-il encore du vin?, est-ce qu'il reste du vin?; **have some ~ ice cream** reprenez de la glace; **has she any ~ children?** a-t-elle d'autres enfants?; **no ~ shouting!** assez de cris!; **I've got no ~, I haven't any ~** je n'en ai plus, il ne m'en reste plus; **I've no ~ time** je n'ai plus le temps; **he can't afford ~ than a small house** il ne peut se payer qu'une petite maison; **I shan't say any ~, I shall say no ~** je n'en dirai pas davantage; (*threat*) tenez-le-vous pour dit; **it cost ~ than I expected** c'était plus cher que je ne l'escomptais; **have you heard any ~ about him?** avez-vous d'autres nouvelles de lui?; **one pound is ~ than 50p** une livre est plus que 50 pence; **~ than half the audience** plus de la moitié de l'assistance *or* des auditeurs; **not ~ than a kilo** pas plus d'un kilo; **~ than 20 came** plus de 20 personnes sont venues; **no ~ than a dozen** une douzaine au plus; **~ than enough** plus que suffisant, amplement *or* bien suffisant; **I've got ~ like these** j'en ai d'autres comme ça, j'en ai encore comme ça; (*fig*) **you couldn't ask for ~** on ne peut guère en demander plus *or* davantage; **we must see ~ of her** il faut que nous la voyions (*subj*) davantage *or* plus souvent; **I want to know ~ about it** je veux en savoir plus

long, je veux en savoir davantage; (*loc*) **the ~ the merrier** plus on est de fous plus on rit (*Prov*); **and what's ~ ...** et qui plus est ...; **his speech, of which ~ later** son discours, sur lequel nous reviendrons; **let's say no ~ about it** n'en parlons plus; **I shall have ~ to say about that** je reviendrai sur ce sujet (plus tard), ce n'est pas tout sur ce sujet; **I've nothing ~ to say** je n'ai rien à ajouter; **nothing ~** rien de plus; **something ~** autre chose, quelque chose d'autre *or* de plus.

2 *adv* **(a)** (*forming comp of adjs and advs*) plus. **~ difficult** plus difficile; **~ easily** plus facilement; **~ and ~ difficult** de plus en plus difficile; **even ~ difficult** encore plus difficile.

(b) *exercise, sleep etc* plus, davantage. **you must rest ~** vous devez vous reposer davantage; **he talks ~ than I do** il parle plus *or* davantage que moi; **she talks even ~ than he does** elle parle encore plus *or* davantage que lui; **he sleeps ~ and ~** il dort de plus en plus; **I like apples ~ than oranges** j'aime les pommes plus que les oranges.

(c) (*in phrases*) **~ amused than annoyed** plus amusé que fâché; **he was ~ frightened than hurt** il a eu plus de peur que de mal; **it's ~ a short story than a novel** c'est une nouvelle plus qu'un roman; **he's no ~ a duke than I am** il n'est pas plus duc que moi; **he could no ~ pay me than fly in the air*** il ne pourrait pas plus me payer que devenir pape*; **~ or less** plus ou moins; **neither ~ nor less (than)** ni plus ni moins (que); **it will ~ than cover the cost** cela couvrira largement *or* amplement les frais; **the house is ~ than half built** la maison est plus qu'à moitié bâtie; **I had ~ than kept my promise** j'avais fait plus que tenir ma promesse; **I can't bear him! — no ~ can I!** je ne peux pas le souffrir! — ni moi non plus!; **I shan't go there again! — no ~ you shall** je ne veux pas y retourner! — c'est entendu.

(d) (*the ~*) **the ~ you rest the quicker you'll get better** plus vous vous reposerez plus vous vous rétablirez rapidement; **the ~ I think of it the ~ ashamed I feel** plus j'y pense plus j'ai honte; **the ~'s the pity!** c'est d'autant plus dommage!, c'est bien dommage!; **(the) ~ fool you to go!** tu es d'autant plus idiot d'y aller!; **he is all the ~ happy** il est d'autant plus heureux (*as* que); **(all) the ~ so as** *or* **because ...** d'autant plus que ....

(e) (*again etc*) **I won't do it any ~** je ne le ferai plus; **don't do it any ~!** ne recommence pas!; **he doesn't live here any ~** il n'habite plus ici; **I can't stay any ~** je ne peux pas rester plus longtemps *or* davantage; (*frm*) **we shall see him no ~** nous ne le reverrons jamais plus *or* plus jamais; (*frm*) **he is no ~** il n'est plus; **once ~** une fois de plus, encore une fois; **only once ~** une dernière fois; (*liter*) **never~** (ne ...) plus jamais, (ne ...) jamais plus.

moreover [mɔː'rəʊvəʳ] *adv* (*further*) de plus, en outre; (*besides*) d'ailleurs, du reste.

mores ['mɔːreɪz] *npl* mœurs *fpl*.

morganatic [ˌmɔːgə'nætɪk] *adj* morganatique.

morganatically [ˌmɔːgə'nætɪkəlɪ] *adv* morganatiquement.

morgue [mɔːg] *n* morgue *f*.

moribund ['mɒrɪbʌnd] *adj* moribond.

Mormon ['mɔːmən] 1 *n* mormon(e) *m(f)*. 2 *adj* mormon.

Mormonism ['mɔːmənɪzəm] *n* mormonisme *m*.

morn [mɔːn] *n* (*liter*) (*morning*) matin *m*; (*dawn*) aube *f*.

morning ['mɔːnɪŋ] 1 *n* matin *m*; matinée *f*. **good ~!** (*hallo*) bonjour!; (*goodbye*) au revoir!; **he came in the ~** il est arrivé dans la matinée; **I'll do it in the ~** je le ferai le matin *or* dans la matinée; (*tomorrow*) je le ferai demain matin; **it happened first thing in the ~** c'est arrivé tout au début de la matinée; **I'll do it first thing in the ~** je le ferai demain à la première heure; **I work in the ~(s)** je travaille le matin; **she's working ~s** *or* **she's on ~s* this week** elle travaille le matin, cette semaine; **a ~'s work** une matinée de travail; **she's got the ~ off** elle a congé ce matin; **I have a ~ off every week** j'ai un matin *or* une matinée de libre par semaine; **during (the course of) the ~** pendant la matinée; **I was busy all (the) ~** j'ai été occupé toute la matinée; **on the ~ of January 23rd** le 23 janvier au matin, le matin du 23 janvier; **what a beautiful ~!** quelle belle matinée!; **at 7 (o'clock) in the ~** à 7 heures du matin; **in the early ~** au (petit) matin; **to get up very early in the ~** se lever de très bonne heure *or* très tôt (le matin), se lever de bon *or* de grand matin; **this ~** ce matin; **tomorrow ~** demain matin; **the ~ before** la veille au matin; **yesterday ~** hier matin; **the next** *or* **following ~, the ~ after** le lendemain matin; **the ~ after (the night before)*** un lendemain de cuite*; **every Sunday ~** tous les dimanches matin; **one summer ~** (par) un matin d'été.

2 *adj walk, swim* matinal, du matin.

3 *cpd*: **morning coat** jaquette *f*; **morning dress** jaquette *f* et pantalon rayé, habit *m*, frac *m*; (*Bot*) **morning-glory** belle-de-jour *f*; **morning paper** journal *m* (du matin); **morning prayer(s)**, **morning service** office *m* du matin; **morning sickness** nausée *f* (du matin), nausées matinales; **morning star** étoile *f* du matin; (*Naut*) **morning watch** premier quart du jour.

Moroccan [mə'rɒkən] 1 *adj* marocain. 2 *n* Marocain(e) *m(f)*.

Morocco [mə'rɒkəʊ] *n* **(a)** Maroc *m*. **(b) m~ (leather)** maroquin *m*; **m~-bound** relié en maroquin.

moron ['mɔːrɒn] *n* (*gen*) idiot(e) *m(f)*, crétin(e) *m(f)*, minus (habens)* *m inv*; (*Med*††) faible *mf* d'esprit. **he's a ~!*** c'est un crétin!, il est bouché!

moronic [mə'rɒnɪk] *adj* crétin, idiot.

morose [mə'rəʊs] *adj* (*gloomy*) morose, sombre; (*sullen*) maussade, renfrogné.

morpheme ['mɔːfiːm] *n* morphème *m*.

Morpheus ['mɔːfɪəs] *n* Morphée *m*; *V* **arm**[1].

morphia ['mɔːfɪə] *n*, **morphine** ['mɔːfiːn] *n* morphine *f*. **~ addict** morphinomane *mf*.

morphological [ˌmɔːfə'lɒdʒɪkəl] *adj* morphologique.

morphologist [mɔː'fɒlədʒɪst] *n* morphologue *mf*.

morphology [mɔː'fɒlədʒɪ] *n* morphologie *f*.

morrow ['mɒrəʊ] *n* (†† *or liter*) (*morning*) matin *m*; (*next day*) lendemain *m*.

Morse [mɔːs] 1 *n* (*also* **~ code**) morse *m*. 2 *cpd*: **Morse alphabet** alphabet *m* morse; **Morse signals** signaux *mpl* en morse.

morsel ['mɔːsl] *n* (petit) morceau *m*; (*of food*) bouchée *f*.

mortadella [ˌmɔːtə'delə] *n* mortadelle *f*.

mortal ['mɔːtl] 1 *adj life, hatred, enemy, fear* mortel; *injury* mortel, fatal. **~ combat** combat *m* à mort; **~ remains** dépouille mortelle; **~ sin** péché mortel; **it's no ~ good to him*** cela ne lui sert strictement à rien. 2 *n* (*also* *) mortel *m*.

mortality [mɔː'tælɪtɪ] *n* mortalité *f*. **infant ~** (taux *m* de) mortalité infantile.

mortally ['mɔːtəlɪ] *adv* (*lit, fig*) mortellement.

mortar ['mɔːtəʳ] 1 *n* (*Constr, Mil, Pharm*) mortier *m*. 2 *cpd*: **mortarboard** mortier *m* (*coiffure universitaire*).

mortgage ['mɔːgɪdʒ] 1 *n* (*in house buying etc*) emprunt-logement *m*; (*second loan etc*) hypothèque *f*. **to take out** *or* **raise a ~** obtenir un emprunt-logement (*on, for* pour); prendre une hypothèque; **to pay off** *or* **clear a ~** rembourser un emprunt-logement; purger une hypothèque. 2 *vt house, one's future* hypothéquer.

mortgagee [ˌmɔːgə'dʒiː] *n* créancier *m*, -ière *f* hypothécaire.

mortgagor [ˌmɔːgə'dʒɔːʳ] *n* débiteur *m*, -trice *f* hypothécaire.

mortice ['mɔːtɪs] *n* = **mortise**.

mortification [ˌmɔːtɪfɪ'keɪʃən] *n* mortification *f* (*also Rel*), humiliation *f*.

mortify ['mɔːtɪfaɪ] *vt* mortifier (*also Rel*), humilier. **I was mortified to learn that ...** j'ai été mortifié d'apprendre que ...; (*Rel*) **to ~ the flesh** se mortifier, mortifier sa chair.

mortifying ['mɔːtɪfaɪɪŋ] *adj* mortifiant, humiliant.

mortise ['mɔːtɪs] *n* mortaise *f*. **~ lock** serrure encastrée.

mortuary ['mɔːtjʊərɪ] 1 *n* morgue *f*, dépôt *m* mortuaire. 2 *adj* mortuaire.

Mosaic [məʊ'zeɪɪk] *adj* (*Bible Hist*) mosaïque, de Moïse.

mosaic [məʊ'zeɪɪk] 1 *n* mosaïque *f*. 2 *cpd* (en) mosaïque.

Moscow ['mɒskəʊ] *n* Moscou. **the ~ team** l'équipe *f* moscovite.

Moses ['məʊzɪs] 1 *n* Moïse *m*. **Holy ~!‡** Seigneur Dieu! 2 *cpd*: **Moses basket** moïse *m*.

mosey‡ ['məʊzɪ] *vi*: **to ~ along** aller *or* marcher sans se presser.

Moslem ['mɒzlem] = **Muslim**.

mosque [mɒsk] *n* mosquée *f*.

mosquito [mɒs'kiːtəʊ] 1 *n, pl* **~es** moustique *m*. 2 *cpd*: **mosquito bite** piqûre *f* de moustique; **mosquito net** moustiquaire *f*; **mosquito netting** mousseline *f* *or* gaze *f* pour moustiquaire.

moss [mɒs] 1 *n* mousse *f*; *V* **rolling**. 2 *cpd*: **moss rose** rose moussue; (*Knitting*) **moss stitch** point *m* de riz.

mossy ['mɒsɪ] *adj* moussu.

most [məʊst] *superl of* **many, much** 1 *adj, pron* **(a)** (*greatest in amount etc*) le plus (de), la plus grande quantité (de), le plus grand nombre (de). **he earns (the) ~ money** c'est lui qui gagne le plus d'argent; **I've got (the) ~ records** c'est moi qui ai le plus (grand nombre) de disques; **(the) ~** le plus, le maximum; **who has got (the) ~?** qui en a le plus?; **do the ~ you can** fais-en le plus que tu pourras; **at (the) ~, at the very ~** au maximum, (tout) au plus; **to make the ~ of** *one's time* ne pas perdre, bien employer; *respite, opportunity, sunshine, sb's absence* profiter (au maximum) de; *one's talents, business offer, money* tirer le meilleur parti de; *one's resources, remaining food* utiliser au mieux, faire durer; **make the ~ of it!** profitez-en bien!, tâchez de bien en profiter!; **he certainly made the ~ of the story** il a vraiment exploité cette histoire à fond; **to make the ~ of o.s.** se faire valoir, se mettre en valeur; **they're the ~!‡** ils sont champions!*; **the girl with the ~(est)‡** la fille la mieux roulée‡.

(b) (*largest part*) la plus grande partie (de), la majeure *or* la meilleure partie (de); (*greatest number*) la majorité (de), la plupart (de). **~ (of the) people/books** *etc* la plupart *or* la majorité des gens/des livres *etc*; **~ honey is expensive** le miel en général coûte cher, la plupart des marques de miel coûtent cher; **~ of the butter** presque tout le beurre; **~ of the money** la plus grande *or* la majeure partie de l'argent, presque tout l'argent; **~ of it** presque tout; **~ of them** la plupart d'entre eux; **~ of the day** la plus grande *or* la majeure partie de la journée; **~ of the time** la plupart du temps; **for the ~ part** pour la plupart, en général; **in ~ cases** dans la plupart *or* la majorité des cas.

2 *adv* **(a)** (*forming superl of adjs and advs*) le plus. **the ~ intelligent boy** le garçon le plus intelligent; **the ~ beautiful woman of all** la plus belle femme *or* la femme la plus belle de toutes; **~ easily** le plus facilement.

(b) *work, sleep etc* le plus. **he talked ~** c'est lui qui a le plus parlé *or* parlé le plus; **what he wants ~ (of all)** ce qu'il désire le plus *or* par-dessus tout *or* avant tout; **the book he wanted ~ (of all)** le livre qu'il voulait le plus *or* entre tous; **that's what annoyed me ~ (of all)** c'est ce qui m'a contrarié le plus *or* par-dessus tout.

(c) (*very*) bien, très, fort. **~ likely** très probablement; **a ~ delightful day** une journée on ne peut plus agréable *or* des plus agréables *or* bien agréable; **you are ~ kind** vous êtes (vraiment) très aimable; **it's a ~ useful gadget** c'est un gadget des plus utiles *or* tout ce qu'il y a de plus utile; **the M~ High** le Très-Haut; **M~ Reverend** révérendissime.

(d) (*US**: *almost*) presque.

...most [məʊst] *suf* le plus. **northern~** le plus au nord; *V* **foremost, inner** *etc*.

mostly ['məʊstlɪ] *adv* (*chiefly*) principalement, surtout; (*almost all*) pour la plupart; (*most often*) le plus souvent, la plupart du temps, en général. **it is ~ water** c'est presque entièrement composé d'eau; **they're ~ women** ce sont surtout des femmes, pour la plupart ce sont des femmes; **~ because** principalement *or* surtout parce que; **it's ~ raining there** il y pleut la plupart du temps *or* presque constamment; **he ~ comes on Mondays** en général il vient le lundi.

mote [məʊt] *n* atome *m*; *[dust]* grain *m*. (*Bible*) **the ~ in thy brother's eye** la paille dans l'œil du voisin.

motel [məʊ'tel] *n* motel *m*.

motet [məʊ'tet] *n* motet *m*.

moth [mɒθ] **1** *n* papillon *m* de nuit, phalène *m or f*; (*in clothes*) mite *f*.

2 *cpd*: **mothball** boule *f* de naphtaline; (*fig*) **in mothballs*** *object* en conserve (*hum*); *ship, plan* en réserve; **moth-eaten** mangé des mites, mité; (**fig*) mangé aux mites*; **to become moth-eaten** se miter; **moth-hole** trou *m* de mite; **mothproof** (*adj*) traité à l'antimite; (*vt*) traiter à l'antimite.

mother ['mʌðəʳ] **1** *n* **(a)** (*lit, fig*) mère *f*. **she was (like) a ~ to me** elle était une vraie mère pour moi; (*Rel*) **M~ Superior** Mère supérieure; (*Rel*) **the Reverend M~** la Révérende Mère; **every ~'s son of them was drunk:** ils étaient soûls tous tant qu'ils étaient*; *V* **foster, house, necessity** *etc*.

(b) († *or liter*) **old M~ Jones** la mère Jones; *V also* **3**.

2 *vt* (*act as ~ to*) servir de mère à, entourer de soins maternels; (*indulge, protect*) dorloter, chouchouter; (††: *give birth to*) donner naissance à. **she always ~s her lodgers** elle est une vraie mère pour ses locataires.

3 *cpd*: **our Mother Church** notre sainte mère l'Église; **mother country** mère patrie *f*; **mothercraft** puériculture *f*; **Mother Goose** ma Mère l'Oie; **mother hen** mère poule *f*; **mother-in-law** belle-mère *f*; **motherland** patrie *f*; **mother love** amour maternel; **mother-naked** tout nu, nu comme un ver; **Mother Nature** Dame Nature *f*; **Mother of God** Marie, mère de Dieu; **mother-of-pearl** nacre *f* (de perle); **Mother's Day** la fête des Mères; **mother's help** aide maternelle; (*Naut*) **mother ship** ravitailleur *m*; **mother-to-be** future maman; **mother tongue** langue maternelle; **mother wit** bon sens inné.

motherhood ['mʌðəhʊd] *n* maternité *f*.

mothering ['mʌðərɪŋ] *n* soins maternels, amour maternel. **he needs ~** il a besoin d'une mère qui s'occupe de lui *or* de la tendresse d'une mère; (*Brit*) **M~ Sunday** la fête des Mères.

motherless ['mʌðəlɪs] *adj* orphelin de mère, sans mère.

motherly ['mʌðəlɪ] *adj* maternel.

motif [məʊ'tiːf] *n* (*Art, Mus*) motif *m*.

motion ['məʊʃən] **1** *n* **(a)** (*U*) mouvement *m*, marche *f*. **perpetual ~** mouvement perpétuel; **to be in ~** *[vehicle]* être en marche; *[machine]* être en mouvement *or* en marche; **to set in ~** *machine* mettre en mouvement *or* en marche; *vehicle* mettre en marche; (*fig*) *process etc* mettre en branle.

(b) mouvement *m*, geste *m*. **he made a ~ to close the door** il a esquissé le geste d'aller fermer la porte; **to go through the ~s of doing sth** (*mechanically*) faire qch en ayant l'esprit ailleurs; (*insincerely*) faire mine *or* semblant de faire qch.

(c) (*at meeting etc*) motion *f*; (*Parl*) proposition *f*. **~ carried/rejected** motion adoptée/rejetée.

(d) (*Med*) selles *fpl*. **to have *or* pass a ~** aller à la selle.

(e) *[watch]* mouvement *m*.

2 *cpd*: **motionless** *V* **motionless**; (*Cine*) **motion picture** film *m* (de cinéma); **motion-picture camera** caméra *f*; **the motion-picture industry** l'industrie *f* cinématographique, le cinéma; **motion sickness** mal *m* de la route (*or* de mer *or* de l'air); (*Ind etc*) **motion study** étude *f* des cadences.

3 *vti*: **to ~ (to) sb to do** faire signe à qn de faire; **he ~ed me in/out/to a chair** il me fit signe d'entrer/de sortir/de m'asseoir, il m'invita d'un geste à entrer/à sortir/à m'asseoir.

motionless ['məʊʃənlɪs] *adj* immobile, sans mouvement, sans bouger.

motivate ['məʊtɪveɪt] *vt act, decision* motiver; *person* pousser, inciter (*to do* à faire).

motivation [ˌməʊtɪ'veɪʃən] *n* motivation *f*. **~ research** études *fpl* de motivation.

motive ['məʊtɪv] **1** *n* **(a)** motif *m*, intention *f*, raison *f*; (*Jur*) mobile *m*. **I did it from the best ~s** je l'ai fait avec les meilleures intentions *or* avec les motifs les plus louables; **his ~ for saying that** la raison pour laquelle il a dit cela; **he had no ~ for killing her** il l'a tuée sans raisons *or* sans mobile; **what was the ~ for the murder?** quel était le mobile du meurtre?; **the only suspect with a ~** le seul suspect à avoir un mobile; *V* **profit, ulterior.**

(b) = **motif.**

2 *adj* moteur (*f* -trice). **~ power** force motrice.

motiveless ['məʊtɪvlɪs] *adj act, crime* immotivé, gratuit.

motley ['mɒtlɪ] **1** *adj* (*many-coloured*) bigarré, bariolé; (*mixed*) bigarré, hétéroclite. **a ~ collection of ...** une collection hétéroclite de ...; **they were a ~ crew** ils formaient une bande hétéroclite *or* curieusement assortie.

2 *n* (*garment*) habit bigarré (*du bouffon*).

motor ['məʊtəʳ] **1** *n* **(a)** (*engine*) moteur *m*.

(b) (*Brit Aut*) = **~car**; *V* **2**.

2 *cpd accident* de voiture, d'auto. **motor-assisted** à moteur; **motorbike*** moto* *f*; **motorboat** canot *m* automobile; **motor bus**† autobus *m*; **motorcade** *V* **motorcade**; (*Brit*) **motorcar** auto(mobile) *f*, voiture *f*; **motor coach** car *m*; **motorcycle** motocyclette *f*; **motorcycle combination** (motocyclette *f* à) side-car *m*; **motorcycling** motocyclisme *m*; **motorcyclist** motocycliste *mf*; (*Tech*) **motor drive** entraînement *m* par moteur; **motor-driven** à entraînement par moteur; **motor insurance** assurance-automobile *f*; (*Naut*) **motor launch** vedette *f*; (*Brit*) **motor lorry** = **motor truck**; (*US*) **motorman** conducteur *m* (*d'un train etc électrique*); **motor mechanic** mécanicien *m* garagiste; **motor mower** tondeuse *f* (à gazon) à moteur; **motor oil** huile *f* (de graissage); (*U*) **motor racing** course *f* automobile; **motor road** route ouverte à la circulation automobile; **motor scooter** scooter *m*; **motor ship** = **motor vessel**; **motor show** exposition *f* d'autos; **the Motor Show** le Salon de l'Automobile; **motor torpedo boat** vedette *f* lance-torpilles; **motor truck** camion *m* (automobile); **motor vehicle** véhicule *m* automobile; (*Naut*) **motor vessel** navire *m* à moteur (diesel), motorship *m*; (*Brit Aut*) **motorway** autoroute *f*.

3 *adj muscle, nerve* moteur (*f* -trice).

4 *vi* (†) aller en auto. **to go ~ing** faire de l'auto; **to ~ away/back** *etc* partir/revenir *etc* en auto.

5 *vt* (*Brit*†) conduire en auto. **to ~ sb away/back** *etc* emmener/ramener *etc* qn en auto.

motorcade ['məʊtəkeɪd] *n* (*US*) cortège *m* d'automobiles.

-motored ['məʊtəd] *adj ending in cpds*: **four-motored** quadrimoteur (*f* -trice).

motoring ['məʊtərɪŋ] **1** *n* tourisme *m* automobile. **2** *cpd accident* de voiture, d'auto; *holiday* en voiture, en auto. **the motoring public** les automobilistes *mpl*; **motoring school** auto-école *f*.

motorist ['məʊtərɪst] *n* automobiliste *mf*.

motorization [ˌməʊtəraɪ'zeɪʃən] *n* motorisation *f*.

motorize ['məʊtəraɪz] *vt* (*esp Mil*) motoriser. (*) **if you are not ~d I can run you home** si vous n'êtes pas motorisé* *or* en voiture je peux vous reconduire chez vous.

mottle ['mɒtl] *vt* tacheter, moucheter, marbrer (*with* de).

mottled ['mɒtld] *adj* tacheté; (*different colours*) bigarré; *horse* moucheté, pommelé; *skin* marbré; *sky* pommelé; *material* chiné; *porcelain* truité. **~ complexion** teint brouillé.

motto ['mɒtəʊ] *n* **(a)** *[family, school etc]* devise *f*. **(b)** (*in cracker*) (*riddle*) devinette *f*; (*joke*) blague *f*.

mould[1], (*US*) **mold**[1] [məʊld] **1** *n* (*Art, Culin, Metal, Tech etc*) (*container, core, frame*) moule *m*; (*model for design*) modèle *m*, gabarit *m*. **to cast metal in a ~** couler *or* jeter du métal dans un moule; **to cast a figure in a ~** jeter une figure en moule, mouler une figure; (*fig*) **cast in a heroic ~** de la trempe des héros; (*fig*) **cast in the same ~** fait sur *or* coulé dans le même moule; (*fig*) **men of his ~** des hommes de sa trempe *or* de son calibre*; (*Culin*) **rice ~** gâteau *m* de riz.

2 *vt* (*cast*) *metals* fondre, mouler; *plaster, clay* mouler; (*fashion*) *figure etc* modeler (*in, out of* en); (*fig*) *sb's character, public opinion etc* former, façonner.

mould[2], (*US*) **mold**[2] [məʊld] **1** *n* (*fungus*) moisissure *f*. **2** *vi* moisir.

mould[3], (*US*) **mold**[3] [məʊld] *n* (*soil*) humus *m*, terreau *m*; *V* **leaf.**

moulder, (*US*) **molder** ['məʊldəʳ] *vi* (*also ~ away*) *[building]* tomber en poussière, se désagréger; (**fig*) *[person, object]* moisir.

moulding, (*US*) **molding** ['məʊldɪŋ] *n* **(a)** (*U*: *V* **mould**[1] **2**) (*gen*) moulage *m*; *[metal]* coulée *f*; *[statue]* coulage *m*; (*fig*) formation *f*, modelage *m*. **(b)** (*Archit*: *ornament*) moulure *f*.

mouldy, (*US*) **moldy** ['məʊldɪ] *adj* (*lit*) moisi; (**fig*: *unpleasant*) moche*, minable*. **to go ~** moisir; **to smell ~** sentir le moisi; (*fig*) **all he gave me was a ~ £5*** il s'est tout juste fendu* d'un malheureux billet de 5 livres.

moult, (*US*) **molt** [məʊlt] **1** *n* mue *f*. **2** *vi* muer. **3** *vt feathers, hair* perdre.

mound [maʊnd] *n* **(a)** *[earth]* (*natural*) tertre *m*, butte *f*, monticule *m*; (*artificial*) levée *f* de terre, remblai *m*; (*Archeol*) tertre artificiel, mound *m*; (*burial ~*) tumulus *m*. **(b)** (*pile*) tas *m*, monceau *m*.

mount [maʊnt] **1** *n* **(a)** (*liter*) mont *m*, montagne *f*. **M~ Everest** le mont Everest; **the M~ of Olives** le mont des Oliviers; **the Sermon on the M~** le Sermon sur la Montagne.

(b) (*horse*) monture *f*.

(c) (*support*) *[machine]* support *m*; *[jewel, lens, specimen]* monture *f*; *[microscope slide]* lame *f*; *[transparency]* cadre *m* en carton *or* en plastique; *[painting, photo]* carton *m* de montage; *[stamp in album]* charnière *f*.

2 *vt* **(a)** (*climb on or up*) *hill, stairs* monter, (*with effort*) gravir; *horse* monter (sur), enfourcher; *cycle* monter sur, enfourcher; *ladder* monter à *or* sur; *platform, throne* monter sur. **the car ~ed the pavement** l'auto est montée sur le trottoir.

(b) *[stallion etc]* monter.

(c) *machine, specimen, jewel* monter (*on, in* sur); *map* monter, entoiler; *picture, photo* monter *or* coller sur carton; *exhibit* fixer sur un support; *gun* mettre en position. **to ~ stamps in an album** coller *or* mettre des timbres dans un album.

(d) *play, demonstration, plot* monter. (*Mil*) **to ~ guard (on *or* over)** monter la garde (sur *or* auprès de); **to ~ an offensive** monter une attaque.

(e) (*provide with horse*) monter; *V* **mounted.**

3 *vi* **(a)** *[prices, temperature]* monter, augmenter.

(b) (*get on horse*) se mettre en selle.

(c) (*fig*) **the blood ~ed to his cheeks** le sang lui monta au visage.

mount up *vi* (*increase*) monter, s'élever; (*accumulate*) s'accumuler. **it all mounts up** tout cela finit par chiffrer.

mountain ['maʊntɪn] **1** *n* montagne *f*; (*fig*) montagne, monceau *m*, tas *m*. **to go to/live in the ~s** aller à/habiter la montagne; (*fig*) **to make a ~ out of a molehill** (se) faire une montagne d'un rien; (*Econ*) **beef/butter ~** montagne de bœuf/de beurre; (*fig*) **a ~ of dirty washing** un monceau de linge sale; **a ~ of work** un travail fou *or* monstre.

2 *cpd tribe, people* montagnard; *animal, plant* de(s) montagne(s); *air* de la montagne; *path, scenery, shoes, chalet* de montagne. **mountain ash** sorbier *m* (d'Amérique); **mountain cat** puma *m*, couguar *m or* cougouar *m*; **mountain chain** chaîne *f* de montagnes; **mountain dew*** whisky *m* (*gén illicitement distillé*); (*US*) **mountain lion** = **mountain cat**; **mountain range** chaîne *f* de montagnes; **mountain sickness** mal *m* des montagnes; **mountainside** flanc *m or* versant *m* d'une montagne.

mountaineer [ˌmaʊntɪˈnɪəʳ] 1 *n* alpiniste *mf.* 2 *vi* faire de l'alpinisme.
mountaineering [ˌmaʊntɪˈnɪərɪŋ] *n* alpinisme *m.*
mountainous [ˈmaʊntɪnəs] *adj country* montagneux; (*fig*) gigantesque, énorme.
mountebank [ˈmaʊntɪbæŋk] *n* charlatan *m*, imposteur *m.*
mounted [ˈmaʊntɪd] *adj troops* monté, à cheval. ~ **police** police *f* à cheval *or* montée.
Mountie* [ˈmaʊntɪ] *n* membre *m* de la police montée canadienne. **the** ~**s** la police montée canadienne.
mourn [mɔːn] 1 *vi* pleurer. **to** ~ **for sb** pleurer (la mort de) qn; **to** ~ **for sth** pleurer la perte (*or* la disparition *etc*) de qch; **it's no good** ~**ing over it** rien ne sert de se lamenter à ce sujet. 2 *vt* pleurer, se lamenter sur.
mourner [ˈmɔːnəʳ] *n* parent(e) *m(f) or* allié(e) *m(f) or* ami(e) *m(f)* du défunt. **the** ~**s** le convoi *or* le cortège funèbre; **to be the chief** ~ mener le deuil.
mournful [ˈmɔːnfʊl] *adj person* mélancolique, triste; (*stronger*) affligé, éploré; *tone, sound, occasion* lugubre, funèbre. **what a** ~ **expression!** quelle tête *or* mine d'enterrement!
mournfully [ˈmɔːnfəlɪ] *adv* lugubrement, mélancoliquement.
mournfulness [ˈmɔːnfʊlnɪs] *n* tristesse *f*, air *m or* aspect *m* lugubre *or* désolé.
mourning [ˈmɔːnɪŋ] 1 *n* affliction *f*, deuil *m*; (*clothes*) vêtements *mpl* de deuil. **in deep** ~ en grand deuil; **to be in** ~ **(for sb)** porter le deuil (de qn), être en deuil (de qn); **to go into/come out of** ~ prendre/ quitter le deuil.
2 *cpd clothes* de deuil. **mourning band** crêpe *m.*
mouse [maʊs] *pl* **mice** 1 *n* souris *f*; (*fig*) timide *mf*, souris; *V* **field, white.** 2 *adj* = **mousy.** 3 *cpd*: **mousehole** trou *m* de souris; **mousetrap** souricière *f*; (*pej*) **mousetrap (cheese)*** fromage *m* ordinaire. 4 *vi* chasser les souris.
mouser [ˈmaʊsəʳ] *n* souricier *m.*
mousse [muːs] *n* (*Culin*) mousse *f.* **chocolate** ~ mousse au chocolat.
moustache, (*US*) **mustache** [məsˈtɑːʃ] *n* moustache(s) *f(pl).* **man with a** ~ homme moustachu *or* à moustache.
moustachio, (*US*) **mustachio** [məsˈtɑːʃɪəʊ] *n* moustache *f* à la gauloise.
moustachioed, (*US*) **mustachioed** [məsˈtɑːʃɪəʊd] *adj* moustachu.
mousy [ˈmaʊsɪ] *adj smell, noise* de souris; (*fig*) *person, character* timide, effacé. ~ **hair** cheveux *mpl* châtain clair (sans éclat).
mouth [maʊθ] *pl* **mouths** [maʊðz] 1 *n* **(a)** *[person, horse, sheep, cow etc]* bouche *f*; *[dog, cat, lion, tiger etc]* gueule *f.* **with one's** ~ **wide open** bouche bée, bouche béante; **she didn't dare open her** ~ elle n'a pas osé ouvrir la bouche *or* dire un mot; **he never opened his** ~ **all evening** il n'a pas ouvert la bouche *or* il n'a pas desserré les dents de la soirée; **he didn't open his** ~ **about it, he kept his** ~ **shut about it** il n'en a pas soufflé mot, il est resté bouche cousue sur la question; **keep your** ~ **shut about this!** n'en parle à personne!, garde-le pour toi!, bouche cousue!; **shut your** ~**!‡** ferme-la!‡, boucle-la!‡; (*fig*) **to shut** *or* **close sb's** ~ **(for him)*, to stop sb's** ~ (*silence*) fermer la bouche à qn*; (*kill*) supprimer qn; **(you've got a) big** ~**!‡** tu ne pouvais pas la fermer!‡; **he's a big** ~ c'est un fort en gueule‡, c'est une grande gueule‡; **it makes my** ~ **water** cela me fait venir l'eau à la bouche; *V* **down**[1], **heart, word** *etc.*
(b) *[river]* embouchure *f*; *[bag]* ouverture *f*; *[hole, cave, harbour etc]* entrée *f*; *[bottle]* goulot *m*; *[cannon, gun]* bouche *f*, gueule *f*; *[well]* trou *m*; *[volcano]* bouche; *[letterbox]* ouverture, fente *f.*
2 *cpd*: **mouthful** *V* **mouthful**; **mouth organ** harmonica *m*; **mouthpiece** *[musical instrument]* bec *m*, embouchure *f*; *[telephone]* microphone *m*; (*fig: spokesman*) porte-parole *m inv*; **mouth-to-mouth (resuscitation)** bouche à bouche *m inv*; **mouthwash** eau *f* dentifrice, élixir *m* dentaire; (*for gargling*) gargarisme *m*; **mouth-watering** appétissant, alléchant.
3 [maʊð] *vt* (*soundlessly*) dire du bout des lèvres *or* d'une manière inaudible; (*affectedly*) dire avec affectation.
-mouthed [maʊðd] *adj ending in cpds* à la bouche ..., qui a la bouche ... . **wide-mouthed** qui a la bouche grande; *V* **loud, mealy** *etc.*
mouthful [ˈmaʊθfʊl] *n [food]* bouchée *f.* ~ **of tea/wine** (grande) gorgée *f* de thé/de vin; **he swallowed it at one** ~ il n'en a fait qu'une bouchée *or* gorgée; (*fig*) **it's a real** ~ **of a name!*** quel nom à coucher dehors!, quel nom! on en a plein la bouche!
movable [ˈmuːvəbl] 1 *adj* mobile. (*Rel*) ~ **feast** fête *f* mobile. 2 *npl* (*Jur*) ~s effets mobiliers, biens *mpl* meubles.
move [muːv] 1 *n* **(a)** mouvement *m.* **to be always on the** ~ *[gipsies etc]* se déplacer continuellement, être toujours par monts et par vaux; *[military or diplomatic personnel etc]* être toujours en déplacement; *[child, animal]* ne jamais rester en place; (*: *be busy*) ne jamais (s')arrêter; **the circus is on the** ~ **again** le cirque a repris la route; *[troops, army]* **to be on the** ~ être en marche *or* en mouvement; (*fig*) **it is a country on the** ~ c'est un pays en marche; **it was midnight and no one had made a** ~ il était minuit et personne n'avait manifesté l'intention *or* fait mine de partir; **it's time we made a** ~ il est temps que nous partions (*subj*); **he made a** ~ **towards the door** il esquissa un mouvement vers la porte; **get a** ~ **on!*** remue-toi!*, grouille-toi!‡
(b) (*change of house*) déménagement *m*; (*change of job*) changement *m* d'emploi. **he made a** ~ **to Paris** il est parti s'installer à Paris; **it's our third** ~ **in 2 years** c'est notre troisième déménagement en 2 ans; **it's time he had a** ~ il a besoin de changer d'air *or* d'horizon.
(c) (*Chess, Draughts etc*) *[chessman etc]* coup *m*; (*player's turn*) tour *m*; (*fig*) pas *m*, démarche *f*, manœuvre *f*, mesure *f.* **knight's** ~ marche *f* du cavalier; **that was a silly** ~ (*in game*) ça c'était un coup stupide; (*fig*) c'était une démarche *or* une manœuvre stupide; **it's your** ~ c'est à vous de jouer; (*fig*) **he knows every** ~ **in the game** il connaît toutes les astuces; **one false** ~ **and he's ruined** un faux pas et il est ruiné; **his first** ~ **after the election was to announce ...** son premier acte après son élection fut d'annoncer ...; **what's our** *or* **the next** ~? et maintenant qu'est-ce qu'on fait?; **it's a** ~ **in the right direction** c'est un pas dans la bonne direction; **let him make the first** ~ laisse-lui faire les premiers pas; **we must watch his every** ~ il nous faut surveiller tous ses faits et gestes; **without making the least** ~ **to do** so sans manifester la moindre intention de le faire; **there was a** ~ **to defeat the proposal** il y a eu une tentative pour faire échec à la proposition.
2 *vt* **(a)** (*change position of*) *object, furniture* changer de place, déplacer, bouger*; *limbs* mouvoir, remuer; *troops, animals* transporter. **you've** ~**d the stick!** tu as bougé le bâton!; **he hadn't** ~**d his chair** il n'avait pas déplacé sa chaise *or* changé sa chaise de place; ~ **your chair nearer the fire** approchez votre chaise du feu; ~ **your books over here** mets tes livres par ici; **can you** ~ **your fingers?** pouvez-vous remuer *or* mouvoir vos doigts?; **he** ~**d his family out of the war zone** il a évacué sa famille hors de la zone de guerre; **they** ~**d the crowd off the grass** ils ont fait partir la foule de sur la pelouse; ~ **your arm off my book** ôte ton bras de sur mon livre; **to** ~ **house** déménager; **to** ~ **one's job** changer d'emploi; **his firm want to** ~ **him** son entreprise veut l'envoyer ailleurs; **he's asked to be** ~**d to London/to a new department/to an easier job** il a demandé à être muté à Londres/affecté à une autre section/affecté à un emploi plus facile; (*fig*) **to** ~ **heaven and earth to do sth** remuer ciel et terre pour faire qch, se mettre en quatre pour faire qch; (*Chess*) **to** ~ **a piece** jouer une pièce; (*fig*) **he didn't** ~ **a muscle** il n'a pas bronché, il n'a pas sourcillé; (*Comm*) **we must try to** ~ **this old stock** nous devons essayer d'écouler ce vieux stock.
(b) (*set in motion*) **the wind** ~**s the leaves** le vent agite *or* fait remuer les feuilles; (*Med*) **to** ~ **one's bowels** aller à la selle.
(c) (*fig*) pousser, inciter (*sb to do* qn à faire). **I am** ~**d to ask why ...** je suis incité à demander pourquoi ...; **if I feel** ~**d to do it,** (*hum*) **if the spirit** ~**s me** si le cœur m'en dit; **he won't be** ~**d** il est inébranlable; **even this did not** ~ **him** même ceci n'a pas réussi à l'ébranler.
(d) (*emotionally*) émouvoir. **she's easily** ~**d** elle s'émeut facilement; **this did not** ~ **him** ceci n'a pas réussi à l'émouvoir, ceci l'a trouvé impassible; **to** ~ **sb to tears** émouvoir qn jusqu'aux larmes; **to** ~ **sb to laughter** faire rire qn; **to** ~ **sb to anger** mettre qn en colère; **to** ~ **sb to pity** attendrir qn.
(e) (*Admin, Parl etc*) proposer. **to** ~ **a resolution** proposer une motion; **to** ~ **that sth be done** proposer que qch soit fait; **he** ~**d the adjournment of the meeting** *or* **that the meeting be adjourned** il a proposé que la séance soit levée.
3 *vi* **(a)** *[person, animal]* (*stir*) bouger, remuer; (*go*) aller, se déplacer; *[limb]* bouger, remuer, se mouvoir; *[lips, trees, leaves, curtains, door]* bouger, remuer; *[clouds]* passer, avancer; *[vehicle, ship, plane, procession]* aller, passer; *[troops, army]* se déplacer. **don't** ~**!** ne bougez pas!; **he** ~**d slowly towards the door** il se dirigea lentement vers la porte; **let's** ~ **into the garden** passons dans le jardin; **she** ~**s well** elle a une démarche aisée; **troops are moving near the frontier** il y a des mouvements de troupes près de la frontière; **they** ~**d rapidly across the lawn** ils ont traversé la pelouse rapidement; **the procession** ~**d slowly out of sight** petit à petit la procession a disparu; **the car** ~**d round the corner** la voiture a tourné au coin de la rue; **I saw something moving over there** j'ai vu quelque chose bouger là-bas; **I'll not** ~ **from here** je ne bougerai pas d'ici; **keep moving!** (*to keep warm etc*) ne restez pas sans bouger!; (*pass along etc*) circulez!; **he has** ~**d into class three** il est passé dans la troisième classe; (*fig*) **to** ~ **in high society** fréquenter la haute société; **to** ~ **freely** *[piece of machinery]* jouer librement; *[people, cars]* circuler aisément; *[traffic]* être fluide; **to keep the traffic moving** assurer la circulation ininterrompue des véhicules; **the car in front isn't moving** la voiture devant nous est à l'arrêt; **do not get out while the bus is moving** ne descendez pas de l'autobus en marche, attendez l'arrêt complet de l'autobus pour descendre; **the coach was moving at 30 km/h** le car faisait 30 km/h *or* roulait à 30 (km) à l'heure; **he was certainly moving!** il ne traînait pas!, il gazait!*; **that horse can certainly** ~ quand il s'agit de foncer ce cheval se défend!*; (*Comm*) **these goods** ~ **very fast** ces marchandises se vendent très rapidement; (*Comm*) **these toys won't** ~ ces jouets ne se vendent pas; **you can't** ~ **for books in that room*** on ne peut plus se retourner dans cette pièce tellement il y a de livres.
(b) (*depart*) **it's time we were moving** il est temps que nous partions (*subj*), il est temps de partir; **let's** ~**!** partons!, en route!
(c) (~ *house*) déménager. **to** ~ **to a bigger house** aller habiter une maison plus grande, emménager dans une maison plus grande; **to** ~ **to the country** aller habiter (à) la campagne, aller s'installer à la campagne.
(d) (*progress*) *[plans, talks etc]* progresser, avancer. **things are moving at last!** enfin ça avance! *or* ça progresse!; **he got things moving** avec lui ça a bien démarré *or* c'est bien parti; **your roses are certainly moving!*** vos roses sont bien parties! *or* poussent bien!
(e) (*act, take steps*) agir. **the government won't** ~ **until ...** le gouvernement ne bougera pas *or* ne fera rien tant que ...; **we must** ~ **first** nous devons prendre l'initiative; **we'll have to** ~ **quickly if we want to avoid ...** il nous faudra agir sans tarder si nous voulons éviter ...; **the committee** ~**d to stop the abuse** le

comité a pris des mesures pour mettre fin aux abus.

(f) (*in games*) *[player]* jouer; *[chesspiece]* marcher. **it's you to ~** (c'est) votre tour de jouer; (*Chess*) **white ~s** les blancs jouent; (*Chess*) **the knight ~s like this** le cavalier marche *or* se déplace comme cela.

move about 1 *vi* (*fidget*) remuer; (*travel*) voyager. **he can move about only with difficulty** il ne se déplace qu'avec peine; **stop moving about!** tiens-toi tranquille!; (*change residence*) **we've moved about a good deal** nous ne sommes jamais restés longtemps au même endroit.

2 *vt sep object, furniture, employee* déplacer.

move along 1 *vi [people or vehicles in line]* avancer, circuler. **move along there!** *[bus conductor]* avancez vers l'intérieur!; *[policeman]* circulez!; (*on bench etc*) **can you move along a few places?** pouvez-vous vous pousser un peu?

2 *vt sep crowd* faire circuler, faire avancer; *animals* faire avancer.

move around = move about.

move away 1 *vi* **(a)** (*depart*) partir, s'éloigner (*from* de).

(b) (*move house*) déménager. **they've moved away from here** ils n'habitent plus par ici.

2 *vt sep person, object* éloigner, écarter (*from* de).

move back 1 *vi* **(a)** (*withdraw*) reculer, se retirer.

(b) (*to original position*) retourner, revenir. **he moved back to the desk** il retourna au bureau.

(c) (*move house*) **they've moved back to London** ils sont retournés *or* revenus habiter (à) Londres.

2 *vt sep* **(a)** *person, crowd, animals* faire reculer; *troops* replier; *object, furniture* reculer.

(b) (*to original position*) *person* faire revenir *or* retourner; *object* remettre. **his firm moved him back to London** son entreprise l'a fait revenir *or* retourner à Londres; **move the table back to where it was before** remets la table là où elle était.

move down 1 *vi* **(a)** *[person, object, lift]* descendre. **he moved down from the top floor** il est descendu du dernier étage; (*on bench etc*) **can you move down a few places?** pouvez-vous vous pousser un peu?

(b) (*Sport: in league*) reculer. (*Scol*) **he has had to move down one class** il a dû descendre d'une classe.

2 *vt sep* **(a)** *person* faire descendre; *object* descendre.

(b) (*demote*) *pupil* faire descendre (dans une classe inférieure); *employee* rétrograder.

move forward 1 *vi [person, animal, vehicle]* avancer; *[troops]* se porter en avant.

2 *vt sep person, vehicle* faire avancer; *troops* porter en avant; *object, chair* avancer.

move in 1 *vi* **(a)** *[police etc]* avancer (*on* sur), intervenir.

(b) (*to a house*) emménager. **to move in on sb for the night*** se faire héberger par qn pour la nuit.

(c) (**fig: try for control of*) **to move in on a firm** essayer d'accaparer une compagnie, essayer de mettre le grappin* sur une compagnie.

2 *vt sep person* faire entrer; *furniture etc* rentrer, mettre *or* remettre à l'intérieur; (*on removal day*) installer.

move off 1 *vi [person]* s'en aller, s'éloigner, partir; *[car]* démarrer; *[train, army, procession]* s'ébranler, partir.

2 *vt sep object* enlever.

move on 1 *vi [person, vehicle]* avancer; (*after stopping*) se remettre en route; *[time]* passer, s'écouler. **the gipsies moved on to another site** les bohémiens sont allés s'installer plus loin; *[policeman etc]* **move on please!** circulez s'il vous plaît!; **and now we move on to a later episode** et maintenant nous passons à un épisode ultérieur.

2 *vt sep crowd* faire circuler; *hands of clock* avancer.

move out 1 *vi* (*of house, office, room etc*) déménager. **to move out of a flat** déménager d'un appartement, quitter un appartement.

2 *vt sep person, animal* faire sortir; *troops* retirer, dégager; *object, furniture* sortir; (*on removal day*) déménager.

move over 1 *vi* s'écarter, se déplacer, se pousser. **move over!** pousse-toi!

2 *vt sep* déplacer, écarter.

move up 1 *vi* **(a)** *[person, flag etc]* monter. **can you move up a few seats?** pouvez-vous vous pousser un peu?; **I want to move up nearer the platform** je veux m'approcher de l'estrade.

(b) *[employee]* avoir de l'avancement; (*Sport: in league*) avancer. *[pupil]* **to move up a class** passer dans la classe supérieure.

2 *vt sep* **(a)** *person* faire monter; *object* monter.

(b) (*promote*) *employee* donner de l'avancement à; *pupil* faire passer dans une classe supérieure.

movement ['mu:vmənt] *n* **(a)** (*act*) *[person, troops, army, population, vehicles, goods, capital]* mouvement *m*; (*gesture*) mouvement, geste *m*; (*St Ex: activity*) activité *f* (*in* dans); (*St Ex: price changes*) mouvement. **he lay without ~** il était étendu sans mouvement; **upward/downward ~ of the hand** mouvement ascendant/descendant de la main; **troop ~s** mouvements de troupes; **upward ~ in the price of butter** hausse *f* du prix du beurre; (*fig*) **there has been little ~ in the political situation** la situation politique demeure à peu près inchangée; **the film lacks ~** le film manque de mouvement, le rythme du film est trop lent; **there was a ~ towards the exit** il y eut un mouvement vers la sortie, on se dirigea vers la sortie; (*fig*) **there has been some ~ towards fewer customs restrictions** on va *or* s'aiguille vers une réduction des restrictions douanières; **to study sb's ~s** épier les allées et venues de qn; **the police are watching his ~s** la police a l'œil sur tous ses déplacements; **~ of traffic** circulation *f*.

(b) (*Pol etc*) mouvement *m*. **the Women's Liberation M~** le mouvement de libération de la femme.

(c) (*Mus*) mouvement *m*. **in 4 ~s** en 4 mouvements.

(d) (*Tech*) *[machine, clock, watch etc]* mouvement *m*.

(e) (*Med: also* **bowel ~**) selles *fpl*. **to have a ~** aller à la selle.

mover ['mu:vəʳ] *n* **(a)** (*Admin, Parl etc: of motion*) motionnaire *mf*, auteur *m* d'une motion; *V* **prime**. **(b)** (*US*) déménageur *m*.

movie* ['mu:vɪ] (*esp US*) **1** *n* film *m* (*de cinéma*). **to go to the ~s** aller au cinéma *or* au ciné*.

2 *cpd*: **movie camera** caméra *f*; **moviegoer** amateur *m* de cinéma, cinéphile *mf*; **movie house** cinéma *m*; **the movie industry** l'industrie *f* cinématographique, le cinéma; **movieland** le (monde du) cinéma.

moving ['mu:vɪŋ] *adj* **(a)** *vehicle, object, crowd* en mouvement, en marche; *power* moteur (*f*-trice). (*in machine*) **~ part** pièce *f* mobile; (*Cine*) **~ picture** film *m* (*de cinéma*); **~ pavement**, (*US*) **~ sidewalk** tapis roulant; **~ staircase** escalier *m* mécanique *or* roulant; **he was the ~ spirit in the whole affair** il était l'âme de toute l'affaire.

(b) (*touching*) *sight, plea* émouvant, touchant.

movingly ['mu:vɪŋlɪ] *adv* d'une manière émouvante *or* touchante.

mow [məʊ] *pret* **mowed**, *ptp* **mowed** *or* **mown** *vt corn* faucher. **to ~ the lawn** tondre le gazon.

mow down *vt sep* (*fig*) *people, troops* faucher.

mower ['məʊəʳ] *n* **(a)** (*person*) faucheur *m*, -euse *f*. **(b)** (*machine*) (*Agr*) faucheuse *f*; (*lawn~*) tondeuse *f* (à gazon); *V* **motor**.

mowing ['məʊɪŋ] *n* (*Agr*) fauchage *m*. **~ machine** (*Agr*) faucheuse *f*; (*in garden*) tondeuse *f* (à gazon).

mown [məʊn] *ptp of* **mow**.

Mr ['mɪstəʳ] *n V* **mister a.**

Mrs ['mɪsɪz] *n V* **mistress d.**

much [mʌtʃ] *comp* **more**, *superl* **most 1** *adj, pron* **(a)** (*a great deal, a lot*) beaucoup (de). **~ money** beaucoup d'argent; **he hasn't (very) ~ time** il n'a pas beaucoup de temps; **~ trouble** beaucoup d'ennuis, bien des ennuis; (*fig*) **it's a bit ~!*** c'est un peu fort!; **I haven't got ~ left** il ne m'en reste pas beaucoup *or* pas grand-chose; **does it cost ~?** est-ce que ça coûte cher?; **~ of the town/night** une bonne partie de la ville/de la nuit; **~ of what you say** une bonne partie de ce que vous dites; **he hadn't ~ to say about it** il n'avait pas grand-chose à dire à ce sujet; **there's not ~ anyone can do about it** personne n'y peut grand-chose; **we don't see ~ of each other** nous ne nous voyons guère *or* pas souvent; **we have ~ to be thankful for** nous avons tout lieu d'être reconnaissants; (*iro*) **~ you know about it!** comme si tu t'y connaissais!, comme si tu y connaissais quelque chose!; **it isn't up to ~*** ça ne vaut pas grand-chose, ce n'est pas fameux; **he's not ~ to look at** il ne paie pas de mine; **he is not ~ of a writer** il n'est pas extraordinaire comme écrivain, comme écrivain il y a mieux; **it wasn't ~ of an evening** ce n'était pas une soirée très réussie; **he didn't think ~ of that** cela ne lui a pas dit grand-chose; **I don't think ~ of that film** à mon avis ce film ne vaut pas grand-chose, je ne trouve pas ce film bien fameux; **there isn't ~ to choose between them** ils se valent plus ou moins; (*in choice, competition etc*) **there isn't ~ in it** ils se valent, c'est kif-kif*; (*in race etc*) **there wasn't ~ in it** il a (*or* elle a etc) gagné de justesse; **to make ~ of sb** faire grand cas de qn; **he made ~ of the fact that ...** il a fait grand cas du fait que ..., il a attaché beaucoup d'importance au fait que ...; **I couldn't make ~ of what he was saying** je n'ai pas bien compris *or* saisi ce qu'il disait.

(b) (*in phrases*) **as ~ time as ...** autant de temps que ...; **as ~ as possible** autant que possible; **I've got as ~ as you** j'en ai autant que vous; **take as ~ as you can** prenez-en autant que vous pouvez; **as ~ again** encore autant; **twice as ~** deux fois autant *or* plus; **twice as ~ money** deux fois plus *or* deux fois autant d'argent; **half as ~ again** la moitié en plus; **it's as ~ as he can do to stand up** c'est tout juste s'il peut se lever; **you could pay as ~ as 20 francs for that** vous pourriez payer jusqu'à 20 F pour cela; **there was as ~ as 4 kg of butter** il y avait bien *or* jusqu'à 4 kg de beurre; **I thought as ~!** c'est bien ce que je pensais!, je m'y attendais!; **as ~ as to say** comme pour dire; **how ~?** combien?; **how ~ does it cost?** combien cela coûte-t-il?, qu'est-ce que cela coûte?; **how ~ money have you got?** combien d'argent as-tu?, qu'est-ce que tu as comme argent?; **however ~ you protest** vous avez beau protester; **so ~ pleasure** tant de plaisir; **so ~ of the cheese was mouldy that ...** une si grande partie du fromage était moisie que ..., comme presque tout le fromage était moisi ...; **I've read so ~** *or* **this ~** *or* **that ~** j'en ai lu (tout) ça; **so ~ of what he says is untrue** il y a tellement *or* tant de mensonges dans ce qu'il dit; **he'd drunk so ~ that ...** il avait tellement *or* tant bu que ...; **I haven't so ~ as a penny on me** je n'ai pas un sou sur moi; **without so ~ as a word** sans même (dire) un mot; **so ~ for that!** (*resignedly*) tant pis!; (*and now for the next*) et d'une!*; **so ~ for his help!** voilà ce qu'il *or* c'est ça qu'il appelle aider!; **so ~ for his promises!** voilà ce qui reste de ses promesses!, voilà ce que valaient ses promesses!; **he beat me by so ~** *or* **by this ~** il m'a battu de ça; **this** *or* **that ~ bread** ça de pain; **I'd like about this** *or* **that ~** j'en voudrais comme ça; **I know this ~** je sais tout au moins ceci; **this ~ is true** il y a ceci de vrai; **too ~ sugar** trop de sucre; **I've eaten too ~** j'ai trop mangé; **that's too ~!** (*lit*) c'est trop!; (*fig*) c'est trop fort!; **£500 is too ~** 500 livres c'est trop; **that was too ~ for me** ce n'était trop pour moi; **he was too ~ for his opponent** il était trop fort pour son adversaire; **the child was too ~ for his grandparents** l'enfant était trop fatigant pour ses grands-parents; **this work is too ~ for me** ce travail est trop fatigant *or* difficile pour moi; (*: *disapproving*) **that film was really too ~** *or* **a bit ~ for me** pour moi ce film dépassait vraiment les bornes; **he made too ~ of it** il y a attaché trop d'importance, il en a fait trop de cas.

2 *adv* **(a)** (*with vb*) beaucoup, fort, très; (*with comp* *and superl)* beaucoup. **thank you very ~** merci beaucoup, merci bien; *(frm)* **he ~ regrets** il regrette vivement; *(frm)* **you are ~ to be envied** vous êtes fort digne d'envie; *(frm)* **he was ~ surprised** il fut fort *or* bien surpris; **it doesn't ~ matter** cela ne fait pas grand-chose, cela n'a pas beaucoup d'importance; **she doesn't go out ~** elle ne sort pas beaucoup *or* pas souvent; **are you going? — not ~!‡** tu y vas? — mon œil!‡; **~ bigger** beaucoup plus grand; **~ more easily** beaucoup plus facilement; **he's not ~ cleverer than you** il n'est guère plus intelligent que vous; **~ the cleverest** de beaucoup *or* de loin le plus intelligent.

(b) *(in phrases)* **I like you as ~ as him** je vous aime autant que lui; **I don't like him as ~ as I used to** je ne l'aime pas autant qu'auparavant; **I love him as ~ as ever** je l'aime toujours autant; **I don't like it as ~ as all that, I don't like it all that ~** je ne l'aime pas tant que ça; **however ~ you like him** quelle que soit votre affection pour lui; **the problem is not so ~ one of money as of staff** il ne s'agit pas tant d'un problème d'argent que d'un problème de personnel; **she wasn't so ~ helping as hindering** elle gênait plus qu'elle n'aidait; **I liked the film so ~ that I went back again** j'ai tellement *or* tant aimé le film que je suis retourné le voir; **I felt so ~ encouraged by this** je me suis senti tellement encouragé par ceci; **so ~ the less to do** autant de moins à faire; **so ~ so that ...** à tel point que ...; **it's that ~ too long** c'est trop long de (tout) ça; **he talks too ~** il parle trop; **did you like the film? — not too ~** le film vous a plu? — pas trop; **he didn't even smile, ~ less speak** il n'a même pas souri et encore moins parlé; **I don't know him, ~ less his father** lui, je ne le connais pas, et son père encore moins; **(very *or* pretty) ~ the same** presque le même; **they are (very *or* pretty) ~ of an age** ils sont à peu près du même âge; **~ as *or* ~ though I would like to go** bien que je désire *(subj)* beaucoup y aller, malgré tout mon désir d'y aller; **~ as I like you** en dépit de *or* malgré *or* quelle que soit mon affection pour vous; **~ as she protested** en dépit de *or* malgré ses protestations; **~ as I dislike doing this** si peu que j'aime *(subj)* faire ceci; **~ to my amazement** à ma grande *or* profonde stupéfaction.

muchness* ['mʌtʃnɪs] *n*: **they're much of a ~** c'est blanc bonnet et bonnet blanc.

mucilage ['mju:sɪlɪdʒ] *n* mucilage *m*.

muck [mʌk] **1** *n (U) (manure)* fumier *m*; *(mud)* boue *f*, gadoue *f*; *(dirt)* saletés *fpl*; *(fig)* ordure(s) *f(pl)*, saleté(s) *f(pl)*, cochonnerie(s) *f(pl)*. **dog ~** crotte *f* de chien; **that article is just ~** cet article est une ordure; *(bungle)* **to make a ~ of sth‡** gâcher *or* saloper‡ qch; **she thinks she is Lady M~*** ce qu'elle peut se croire!*

2 *cpd*: **muck heap** tas *m* de fumier *or* d'ordures; *(fig)* **muckraker** déterreur *m* de scandales *or* d'ordures; **muckraking** déterrement *m* de scandales *or* d'ordures; *(bungle)* **muck-up‡** gâchis *m*.

muck about, muck around *(Brit)* **1** *vi* (*) **(a)** *(spend time aimlessly)* traîner, perdre son temps. **stop mucking about and get on with your work** cesse de perdre ton temps et fais ton travail; **he enjoys mucking about in the garden** il aime bricoler dans le jardin.

(b) *(play the fool)* faire l'idiot *or* l'imbécile. **he will muck about with my watch!** il faut toujours qu'il joue *(subj)* avec *or* qu'il tripote *(subj)* ma montre, il ne peut pas laisser ma montre tranquille; **he keeps mucking about with matters he doesn't understand** il n'arrête pas de fourrer son nez dans des choses qui le dépassent.

2 *vt sep* (‡) *person* créer des complications *or* des embarras à.

muck in‡ *vi (Brit) (share money etc)* faire bourse commune *(with* avec); *(share room)* crécher‡ *(with* avec). **everyone mucks in here** tout le monde met la main à la pâte* ici; **come on, muck in!** allons, donne un coup de main! *or* mets la main à la pâte!*

muck out *vt sep stable* nettoyer, curer.

muck up‡ *(Brit)* **1** *vt sep* **(a)** *(ruin) task, plans, deal, life* gâcher; *car, machine* bousiller*.

(b) *(untidy) room* semer la pagaïe dans; *(dirty) room, clothes* salir.

2 muck-up *n V* **muck 2**.

muckiness ['mʌkɪnɪs] *n* saleté *f*, malpropreté *f*.

mucky ['mʌkɪ] *adj (muddy)* boueux, bourbeux; *(filthy)* sale, crotté. **what ~ weather!*** quel sale temps!; **you ~ pup!‡** petit goret!

mucous ['mju:kəs] *adj* muqueux. **~ membrane** (membrane *f*) muqueuse *f*.

mucus ['mju:kəs] *n* mucus *m*.

mud [mʌd] **1** *n* boue *f*, gadoue *f*, fange *f (liter)*; *(in river, sea)* boue, vase *f*; *(in swamp)* bourbe *f*. **car stuck in the ~** voiture embourbée; *(fig)* **to drag sb's name in the ~** traîner qn dans la boue; *(fig)* **to throw *or* sling ~ at sb** couvrir qn de boue; **her name is ~*** elle est l'objet de la réprobation générale; **if I do that my name will be ~* in the office** si je fais ça ma réputation est finie *or* je peux dire adieu à ma réputation dans le bureau; *(hum)* **here's ~ in your eye!‡** à la tienne Étienne! *(hum)*; *V* **clear, stick**.

2 *cpd*: **mudbank** banc *m* de vase; **mudbath** bain *m* de boue; *(Aut)* **mud flap** pare-boue *m*; **mud flat(s)** laisse *f* de vase; *(Aut etc)* **mudguard** garde-boue *m inv*; **mud hut** hutte *f* de terre; **mudlark†** gamin(e) *m(f)* des rues; **mudpack** masque *m* de beauté; **mud pie** pâté *m* (de terre); *(U)* **mud-slinging** médisance *f*, dénigrement *m*.

muddle ['mʌdl] **1** *n (disorder)* désordre *m*, fouillis *m*, pagaïe *f or* pagaille *f*; *(perplexity)* perplexité *f*, confusion *f*; *(mix-up)* confusion, embrouillamini* *m*. **what a ~!** *(disorder)* quel fouillis!; *(mix-up)* quel embrouillamini!*; **to be in a ~** *[room, books, clothes]* être en désordre *or* en pagaïe, être sens dessus dessous; *[person]* ne plus s'y retrouver *(over sth* dans qch); *[ideas]* être brouillé *or* embrouillé *or* confus; *[plans, arrangements]* être confus *or* incertain *or* sens dessus dessous; **to get into a ~** *[ideas]* se brouiller, s'embrouiller; *[person]* s'embrouiller *(over sth* dans qch, au sujet de qch); **the books have got into a ~** les livres sont en désordre; **there's been a ~ over the seats** il y a eu confusion en ce qui concerne les places.

2 *cpd*: **muddle-headed** *person* aux idées confuses, brouillon; *plan, ideas* confus; **muddle-up** confusion *f*, embrouillamini* *m*.

3 *vt (also* **~ up) (a) to ~ (up) A and B, to ~ (up) A with B** confondre A avec B.

(b) *(perplex) person* embrouiller; *sb's ideas* brouiller, embrouiller. **he was ~d by the whisky** le whisky lui avait brouillé l'esprit; **to get ~d (up)** s'embrouiller, se brouiller; **to be ~d (up)** être embrouillé.

(c) *facts, story, details* brouiller, embrouiller.

muddle along, muddle on *vi* aller son chemin tant bien que mal.

muddle through *vi* se tirer d'affaire *or* se débrouiller *or* s'en sortir tant bien que mal. **I expect we'll muddle through** je suppose que nous nous en sortirons d'une façon ou d'une autre.

muddle up 1 *vt sep* = **muddle 3**.

2 muddle-up *n V* **muddle 2**.

muddler ['mʌdləʳ] *n* esprit brouillon *(personne)*.

muddy ['mʌdɪ] **1** *adj road* boueux, bourbeux; *water* boueux; *river* vaseux, boueux; *clothes, shoes, hands* crotté, couvert de boue; *(fig) light* grisâtre, terne; *liquid* trouble; *complexion* terreux, brouillé; *ideas* brouillé, confus.

2 *vt hands, clothes, shoes* crotter, salir; *road* rendre boueux; *water, river* troubler.

muezzin [mu:'ezɪn] *n* muezzin *m*.

muff [mʌf] **1** *n (Dress, Tech)* manchon *m*. **2** *vt* (*) rater, louper*; *(Sport) ball, shot* rater, louper*; *chance, opportunity* rater, laisser passer. *(Theat)* **to ~ one's lines** se tromper dans son texte; **to ~ it*** rater son coup. **3** *vi* (*) rater son coup.

muffin ['mʌfɪn] *n* muffin *m (petit pain rond et plat)*.

muffle ['mʌfl] *vt* **(a)** *sound, noise* assourdir, étouffer, amortir; *noisy thing, bell, drum* assourdir. **to ~ the oars** assourdir les avirons; **in a ~d voice** d'une voix sourde *or* voilée *or* étouffée.

(b) *(also* **~ up**: *wrap up) object* envelopper; *person* emmitoufler*. **~d (up) in a blanket** enveloppé *or* emmitouflé* *or* enroulé dans une couverture; **to ~ o.s. (up)** s'emmitoufler*; **he was all ~d up** il était emmitouflé* des pieds à la tête.

muffle up 1 *vi* s'emmitoufler*.

2 *vt sep* = **muffle b**.

muffler ['mʌfləʳ] *n (scarf)* cache-nez *m inv*, cache-col *m inv*; *(US Aut)* silencieux *m*.

mufti ['mʌftɪ] *n* **(a)** *(Dress)* tenue civile. **in ~** en civil, en pékin *(Mil sl)*. **(b)** *(Muslim)* mufti *m or* muphti *m*.

mug [mʌg] **1** *n* **(a)** *(for coffee, tea) (grande)* tasse *f (sans soucoupe)*, chope *f*; *(for beer)* chope *f*, pot *m* à bière; *(made of metal)* gobelet *m*, timbale *f*.

(b) (‡: *face*) bouille* *f*, bille‡ *f*. **ugly ~** gueule *f* d'empeigne*.

(c) *(Brit‡: fool)* nigaud(e) *m(f)*, jobard(e) *m(f)*. **what a ~!** quelle poire!*; **what sort of a ~ do you take me for?** tu me prends pour une andouille?‡; **they're looking for a ~ to help** ils cherchent une bonne poire* pour aider.

2 *vt (assault)* agresser.

mug up‡ *vt sep (Brit Scol)* bûcher*, potasser*, piocher*.

mugger ['mʌgəʳ] *n* agresseur *m (Jur)*.

mugging ['mʌgɪŋ] *n* agression *f (Jur)*.

muggins‡ ['mʌgɪnz] *n (Brit)* idiot(e) *m(f)*, niais(e) *m(f)*. *(oneself)* **~ had to pay for it** c'est encore ma pomme‡ qui a payé.

muggy ['mʌgɪ] *adj room* qui sent le renfermé; *climate, weather* mou *(f* molle). **it's ~ today** il fait lourd aujourd'hui.

mugwump ['mʌgwʌmp] *n (US Pol)* non-inscrit *m*, indépendant *m*.

mulatto [mju:'lætəʊ] **1** *n* mulâtre(sse) *m(f)*. **2** *adj* mulâtre *(f inv)*.

mulberry ['mʌlbərɪ] *n (fruit)* mûre *f*; *(also* **~ tree)** mûrier *m*.

mulch [mʌltʃ] **1** *n* paillis *m*. **2** *vt* pailler *(des semis etc)*.

mulct [mʌlkt] **1** *n (fine)* amende *f*. **2** *vt* **(a)** *(fine)* frapper d'une amende. **(b)** *(by fraud etc)* **to ~ sb of sth, to ~ sth from sb** extorquer qch à qn.

mule¹ [mju:l] *n* **(a)** mulet *m*; *(female)* mule *f*; *(fig: person)* mule. **obstinate *or* stubborn as a ~** têtu comme une mule *or* un mulet. **(b)** *(Spinning)* renvideur *m*.

mule² [mju:l] *n (slipper)* mule *f*.

muleteer [,mju:lɪ'tɪəʳ] *n* muletier *m*, -ière *f*.

mulish ['mju:lɪʃ] *adj look, air* buté, têtu; *person* entêté *or* têtu (comme un mulet).

mulishness ['mju:lɪʃnɪs] *n* entêtement *m*.

mull [mʌl] *vt wine, ale* chauffer et épicer. **(a glass of) ~ed wine** (un) vin chaud.

mull over *vt sep* ruminer, retourner dans sa tête, réfléchir à.

mullet ['mʌlɪt] *n*: **grey ~** mulet *m*; **red ~** rouget *m*.

mulligatawny [,mʌlɪgə'tɔ:nɪ] *n* soupe *f* au curry.

mullion ['mʌlɪən] *n* meneau *m*. **~ed window** fenêtre *f* à meneaux.

multi... ['mʌltɪ] *pref* multi... **~coloured** multicolore; **~directional** multidirectionnel; **~family** pour *or* destiné à *or* occupé par plusieurs familles; **~form** multiforme; **~lateral** multilatéral; **~lingual** polyglotte, multilingue; **~millionaire** multimilliardaire *mf*; **~national** *(adj)* multinational; *(n)* multinationale *f*; **~purpose** polyvalent, multi-usages *inv*; **~racial** multiracial; *(Space)* **~stage** à étages multiples; **~storeyed, ~storey** à étages; *V* **multifarious** *etc*.

multifarious [,mʌltɪ'fɛərɪəs] *adj* très varié, divers.

multiple ['mʌltɪpl] **1** *n (Math)* multiple *m*; *V* **low¹**. **2** *adj* multiple. *(Med)* **~ sclerosis** sclérose *f* en plaques; *(Brit)* **~ store** grand magasin (à succursales multiples).

multiplication [ˌmʌltɪplɪˈkeɪʃən] *n* multiplication *f*. (*Scol*) ~ **tables** tables *fpl* de multiplication.
multiplicity [ˌmʌltɪˈplɪsɪtɪ] *n* multiplicité *f*.
multiply [ˈmʌltɪplaɪ] **1** *vt* multiplier (*by* par). **2** *vi* se multiplier.
multitude [ˈmʌltɪtjuːd] *n* multitude *f*. **the** ~ la multitude, la foule; **for a** ~ **of reasons** pour une multitude *or* une multiplicité *or* une foule de raisons.
multitudinous [ˌmʌltɪˈtjuːdɪnəs] *adj* innombrable.
mum[1]* [mʌm] *n* (*Brit: mother*) maman *f*.
mum[2] [mʌm] *adj*: **to keep** ~ **(about sth)** ne pas piper mot (de qch), ne pas souffler mot (de qch); ~**'s the word!** motus!, bouche cousue!
mumble [ˈmʌmbl] **1** *vi* marmotter. **stop mumbling** arrête de marmotter *or* de parler entre tes dents.
2 *vt* marmonner, marmotter. **to** ~ **one's words** manger ses mots; **to** ~ **an answer** répondre entre ses dents, marmonner une réponse.
3 *n* marmonnement *m*, marmottement *m*. **he said in a** ~ dit-il entre ses dents.
mumbo jumbo [ˌmʌmbəʊˈdʒʌmbəʊ] *n* (*pej*) **(a)** (*Rel*) (*idol etc*) fétiche *m*; (*cult*) momerie *f* (*liter*); (*words*) jargon *m*. **(b)** (*gen: gibberish*) baragouin* *m*, charabia* *m*.
mummer [ˈmʌməʳ] *n* (*Theat*) mime *m*.
mummery [ˈmʌmərɪ] *n* (*Theat, fig*) momerie *f*.
mummification [ˌmʌmɪfɪˈkeɪʃən] *n* momification *f*.
mummify [ˈmʌmɪfaɪ] *vt* momifier.
mummy[1] [ˈmʌmɪ] *n* (*embalmed*) momie *f*.
mummy[2]* [ˈmʌmɪ] *n* (*Brit: mother*) maman *f*. (*pej*) ~**'s boy** fils *m* à sa mère.
mump [mʌmp] *vi* grogner, grommeler.
mumps [mʌmps] *n* (*U*) oreillons *mpl*.
munch [mʌntʃ] **1** *vt* (*also* ~ **up**) mastiquer. **2** *vi* mâcher, mastiquer. **to** ~ **(away) on** *or* **at sth** dévorer qch à belles dents.
mundane [ˌmʌnˈdeɪn] *adj* (*worldly*) de ce monde, mondain, terrestre (*fig*); (*humdrum*) banal.
municipal [mjuːˈnɪsɪpəl] *adj* municipal.
municipality [mjuːˌnɪsɪˈpælɪtɪ] *n* municipalité *f*.
munificence [mjuːˈnɪfɪsns] *n* munificence *f*.
munificent [mjuːˈnɪfɪsnt] *adj* munificent.
muniments [ˈmjuːnɪmənts] *npl* (*Jur*) titres *mpl* (*concernant la propriété d'un bien-fonds*).
munition [mjuːˈnɪʃən] **1** *npl*: ~**s** munitions *fpl*. **2** *cpd*: **munitions dump** entrepôt *m* de munitions.
mural [ˈmjʊərəl] **1** *adj* mural. **2** *n* peinture murale.
murder [ˈmɜːdəʳ] **1** *n* **(a)** (*gen*) meurtre *m*; (*Jur*) meurtre, (*premeditated*) assassinat *m*. **4** ~**s in one week** 4 meurtres en une semaine; (*Prov*) ~ **will out** tôt ou tard la vérité se fait jour; (*fig*) **he was shouting blue** ~* il criait comme un putois *or* comme si on l'écorchait; (*fig*) **she lets the children get away with** ~* elle passe tout aux enfants; (*fig*) **they get away with** ~* ils peuvent faire n'importe quoi impunément.
(b) (*: fig*) **the noise/heat in here is** ~ le bruit/la chaleur ici est infernal(e); **did you have a good holiday? — no, it was** ~ avez-vous passé de bonnes vacances? — non, des vacances tuantes *or* c'était tuant; **the roads were** ~ les routes étaient un cauchemar.
2 *cpd*: **murder case** [*barrister*] procès *m* en homicide; [*detective*] affaire *f* d'homicide; (*Police*) **Murder Squad** ≃ brigade criminelle de la police judiciaire; **murder trial** ≃ procès capital; **the murder weapon** l'arme *f* du meurtre.
3 *vt person* assassiner; (*fig*) *song, music, language* massacrer.
murderer [ˈmɜːdərəʳ] *n* meurtrier *m*, assassin *m*.
murderess [ˈmɜːdərɪs] *n* meurtrière *f*.
murderous [ˈmɜːdərəs] *adj act, rage, person, climate, road* meurtrier; (*cruel*) féroce, cruel. **a** ~**-looking individual** un individu à tête d'assassin; (*fig*) **this heat is** ~* cette chaleur est infernale.
murk [mɜːk] *n* obscurité *f*.
murkiness [ˈmɜːkɪnɪs] *n* obscurité *f*.
murky [ˈmɜːkɪ] *adj* obscur, sombre, ténébreux; *sky* sombre; *darkness* épais (*f* -aisse); *water* trouble. (*hum*) **his** ~ **past** son passé trouble.
murmur [ˈmɜːməʳ] **1** *n* murmure *m*; [*bees, traffic etc*] bourdonnement *m*; (*fig: protest*) murmure. **there wasn't a** ~ **in the classroom** il n'y avait pas un murmure dans la classe; **to speak in a** ~ parler à voix basse, chuchoter; **a** ~ **of conversation** un bourdonnement de voix; **there were** ~**s of disagreement** il y eut des murmures de désapprobation; **he agreed without a** ~ il accepta sans murmure; (*Med*) **a heart** ~ un souffle au cœur.
2 *vt* murmurer.
3 *vi* [*person, stream*] murmurer; (*complain*) murmurer (*against, about* contre).
muscatel [ˌmʌskəˈtel] *n* (*grape, wine*) muscat *m*.
muscle [ˈmʌsl] *n* muscle *m*; *V* **move**.
muscle in: *vi* intervenir, s'immiscer. **to muscle in on a group/a discussion** essayer de s'imposer dans un groupe/une discussion; **stop muscling in!** occupe-toi de tes oignons!*
Muscovite [ˈmʌskəvaɪt] **1** *adj* moscovite. **2** *n* Moscovite *mf*.
muscular [ˈmʌskjʊləʳ] *adj tissue, disease* musculaire; *person, arm* musclé. ~ **dystrophy** dystrophie *f* musculaire.
musculature [ˈmʌskjʊlətjʊəʳ] *n* musculature *f*.
muse [mjuːz] **1** *vi* méditer (*on, about, over* sur); songer, réfléchir (*on, about, over* à). **2** *vt*: **'they might accept' he** ~**d** 'il se pourrait qu'ils acceptent' songeait-il. **3** *n* (*Myth, fig: also* **M**~) muse *f*.
museum [mjuːˈzɪəm] *n* musée *m*. ~ **piece** pièce *f* de musée; (*fig*) vieillerie *f*, antiquaille *f*.
mush [mʌʃ] *n* (*U*) bouillie *f*; (*fig*) sentimentalité *f* de guimauve *or* à l'eau de rose.
mushroom [ˈmʌʃrʊm] **1** *n* champignon *m* (comestible). **a great** ~ **of smoke** un nuage de fumée en forme de champignon; **that child grows like a** ~ cet enfant pousse comme un champignon; **houses sprang up like** ~**s** les maisons ont poussé comme des champignons.
2 *cpd soup, omelette* aux champignons; *flavour* de champignons; (*colour*) *carpet etc* beige rosé *inv*. **mushroom cloud** champignon *m* atomique; **mushroom growth** poussée soudaine; **mushroom town** ville *f* champignon *inv*.
3 *vi* **(a)** (*grow quickly*) [*town etc*] pousser comme un champignon. **the village** ~**ed into a town** le village est rapidement devenu ville; **shops** ~**ed all over the place** des magasins se sont multipliés un peu partout.
(b) a cloud of smoke went ~**ing up** un nuage de fumée en forme de champignon s'est élevé dans le ciel.
(c) to go ~**ing** aller aux champignons.
mushy [ˈmʌʃɪ] *adj vegetables, food* en bouillie; *fruit* blet; *ground* spongieux; (*fig pej*) fleur bleue *inv*, à la guimauve, à l'eau de rose.
music [ˈmjuːzɪk] **1** *n* (*all senses*) musique *f*. **to set to** ~ mettre en musique; (*fig*) **it was** ~ **to his ears** c'était doux à son oreille; (*Univ*) **the Faculty of M**~ la faculté de Musique; *V* **ear**[1], **face, pop**[2] *etc*.
2 *cpd teacher, lesson, exam* de musique. **music box** boîte *f* à musique; **music case** porte-musique *m inv*; **music centre** chaîne compacte stéréo; (*Press*) **music critic** critique musical; **music festival** festival *m*; (*Brit*) **music hall** (*n*) music-hall *m*; (*cpd*) de music-hall; **music lover** mélomane *mf*; **music paper** papier *m* à musique; **music stand** pupitre *m* à musique; **music stool** tabouret *m* de musique.
musical [ˈmjuːzɪkəl] **1** *adj* (*lit, fig*) *voice, sound, criticism, studies* musical. **he comes from a** ~ **family** il sort d'une famille musicienne; **she's very** ~ (*gifted*) elle est musicienne, elle est très douée pour la musique; (*fond of it*) elle est mélomane; ~ **box** boîte *f* à musique; (*game*) ~ **chairs** chaises musicales; (*fig*) **they were playing at** ~ **chairs** ils changeaient tout le temps de place; ~ **comedy** comédie musicale, opérette *f*; ~ **evening** soirée musicale; ~ **instrument** instrument *m* de musique.
2 *n* (*Cine, Theat*) comédie musicale.
musically [ˈmjuːzɪkəlɪ] *adv* musicalement.
musician [mjuːˈzɪʃən] *n* musicien(ne) *m(f)*.
musicianship [mjuːˈzɪʃənʃɪp] *n* maestria *f* (de musicien), sens *m* de la musique.
musicologist [ˌmjuːzɪˈkɒlədʒɪst] *n* musicologue *mf*.
musicology [ˌmjuːzɪˈkɒlədʒɪ] *n* musicologie *f*.
musing [ˈmjuːzɪŋ] **1** *adj* songeur, pensif, rêveur. **2** *n* songerie *f*, rêverie *f*. **idle** ~**s** rêvasseries *fpl*.
musingly [ˈmjuːzɪŋlɪ] *adv* d'un air songeur *or* rêveur, pensivement.
musk [mʌsk] **1** *n* musc *m*. **2** *cpd*: **muskmelon** cantaloup *m*; **musk ox** bœuf musqué; **muskrat** rat musqué, ondatra *m*; **musk rose** rose *f* muscade.
musket [ˈmʌskɪt] *n* mousquet *m*.
musketeer [ˌmʌskɪˈtɪəʳ] *n* mousquetaire *m*.
musketry [ˈmʌskɪtrɪ] **1** *n* tir *m* (au fusil *etc*). **2** *cpd range, training* de tir (au fusil *etc*).
musky [ˈmʌskɪ] *adj* musqué, de musc.
Muslim [ˈmʊslɪm] **1** *n* musulman(e) *m(f)*; *V* **black**. **2** *adj* musulman.
muslin [ˈmʌzlɪn] **1** *n* mousseline *f*. **2** *cpd* de *or* en mousseline.
musquash [ˈmʌskwɒʃ] **1** *n* (*animal*) rat musqué, ondatra *m*; (*fur*) rat d'Amérique, ondatra. **2** *cpd coat* d'ondatra.
muss* [mʌs] *vt* (*also* ~ **up**) *dress, clothes* chiffonner, froisser. **to** ~ **sb's hair** décoiffer qn.
mussel [ˈmʌsl] *n* moule *f*. ~ **bed** parc *m* à moules, moulière *f*.
must [mʌst] **1** *modal aux vb* **(a)** (*indicating obligation*) **you must leave now** vous devez partir *or* il faut que vous partiez (*subj*) maintenant; (†† *or hum*) **I must away** je dois partir, il faut que je parte; (*on notice*) **'the windows must not be opened'** 'défense d'ouvrir les fenêtres'; **I (simply** *or* **absolutely) MUST see him!** il faut absolument que je le voie!; **you mustn't touch it** il ne faut pas *or* tu ne dois pas y toucher, c'est défendu d'y toucher; **what must we do now?** que faut-il *or* que devons-nous faire à présent?; **why must you always be so rude?** pourquoi faut-il toujours que tu sois si grossier?; (*frm*) **you must know that ...** il faut que vous sachiez que ...; **I must ask you not to touch that** je dois vous prier *or* je vous prie de ne pas toucher à cela; **if you MUST leave then go at once** s'il faut vraiment que vous partiez (*subj*), partez tout de suite; **sit down if you must** asseyez-vous si c'est indispensable *or* si vous y tenez; **I MUST say, he's very irritating** il n'y a pas à dire *or* franchement il est très agaçant; **you look well, I must say!** je dois dire que *or* vraiment tu as très bonne mine!; (*iro*) **that's brilliant, I MUST say!** pour être réussi, c'est réussi (je dois dire)!* (*iro*); **well I MUST say!*** eh bien vraiment!, ça alors!*; **what must he do but bang the door just when ..., he must bang the door just when ...** il a (bien) fallu qu'il claque (*subj*) la porte juste au moment où ... .
(b) (*indicating certainty*) **he must be wrong** il doit se tromper, il se trompe certainement; **I realized he must be wrong** j'ai compris qu'il devait se tromper *or* qu'il se trompait certainement; **he must be clever, mustn't he?** il doit être intelligent *or* il est bien intelligent, n'est-ce pas?; **he must be mad!** il doit être fou!, il est fou!; **is he mad? — he MUST be!** est-ce qu'il est fou? — il faut le croire! *or* sûrement!; **I must have made a mistake** j'ai dû me tromper; **you must be joking!** vous devez plaisanter!, vous plaisantez!; **you must know my aunt** vous devez connaître ma tante, vous connaissez sans doute ma tante; **that must be John** ça doit être Jean.

2 *n* (*) impératif *m*, chose *f* indispensable *or* obligatoire. **this book is a ~** c'est un livre qu'il faut absolument avoir *or* lire; **a car is a ~ in the country** une voiture est absolument indispensable à la campagne; **a ~ for all housewives!** ce que toutes les ménagères doivent posséder!, indispensable à toutes les ménagères!
mustache ['mʌstæʃ] *etc* (*US*) = **moustache** *etc*.
mustang ['mʌstæŋ] *n* mustang *m*.
mustard ['mʌstəd] **1** *n* (*Bot, Culin*) moutarde *f*; *V* **keen**.
2 *cpd*: **mustard and cress** moutarde blanche et cresson alénois; **mustard bath** bain sinapisé *or* à la moutarde; **mustard gas** ypérite *f*, gaz *m* moutarde; **mustard plaster** sinapisme *m*, cataplasme sinapisé; **mustard pot** moutardier *m*.
muster ['mʌstəʳ] **1** *n* (*gathering*) assemblée *f*; (*Mil, Naut*: *also* **~ roll**) rassemblement *m*; (*roll-call*) appel *m*. (*fig*) **to pass ~** (pouvoir) passer, être acceptable.
2 *vt* (*call together*) rassembler; (*call roll of*) battre le rappel de; (*collect*) *number, sum* réunir; (*also* **~ up**) *strength, courage, energy* rassembler. **he ~ed (up) the courage to say so** il prit son courage à deux mains pour le dire; **I couldn't ~ up enough energy to protest** je n'ai pas eu l'énergie de protester; **I could only ~ 50p** je n'ai pu réunir en tout et pour tout que 50 pence; **they could only ~ 5 volunteers** ils n'ont pu trouver *or* réunir que 5 volontaires; **the club can only ~ 20 members** le club ne compte que 20 membres.
3 *vi* se réunir, se rassembler.
mustiness ['mʌstɪnɪs] *n* (goût *m or* odeur *f* de) moisi *m*.
mustn't ['mʌsnt] = **must not**; *V* **must**.
musty ['mʌstɪ] *adj taste, smell* de moisi; *room* qui sent le moisi *or* le renfermé; (**fig*) *ideas, methods* vieux jeu *inv*. **to grow ~** moisir; **to smell ~** *[room, air]* avoir une odeur de renfermé; *[book, clothes]* avoir une odeur de moisi *or* de vieux.
mutability [ˌmju:tə'bɪlɪtɪ] *n* mutabilité *f*.
mutable ['mju:təbl] *adj* muable, mutable; (*Ling*) sujet à la mutation.
mutant ['mju:tənt] *adj, n* mutant (*m*).
mutate [mju:'teɪt] *vi* subir une mutation.
mutation [mju:'teɪʃən] *n* mutation *f*.
mute [mju:t] **1** *adj person, reproach* muet. **~ with admiration, in ~ admiration** muet d'admiration; (*Ling*) **H ~** H muet.
2 *n* **(a)** (*Med*) muet(te) *m(f)*.
(b) (*Mus*) sourdine *f*.
3 *vt* **(a)** (*Mus*) mettre la sourdine à.
(b) *sound* assourdir, rendre moins sonore; *colour* adoucir, atténuer, assourdir.
muted ['mju:tɪd] *adj voice, sound* sourd, assourdi; *colour* sourd; (*Mus*) *violin* en sourdine; *criticism, protest* voilé.
mutilate ['mju:tɪleɪt] *vt person, limb* mutiler, estropier; *object* mutiler, dégrader; (*fig*) *text* mutiler, tronquer.
mutilation [ˌmju:tɪ'leɪʃən] *n* mutilation *f*.
mutineer [ˌmju:tɪ'nɪəʳ] *n* (*Mil, Naut*) mutiné *m*, mutin *m*.
mutinous ['mju:tɪnəs] *adj* (*Mil, Naut*) *crew, troops* mutiné; (*fig*) *attitude* rebelle. **a ~ look** un regard noir; **the children were already fairly ~** les enfants regimbaient *or* se rebiffaient* déjà.
mutiny ['mju:tɪnɪ] **1** *n* (*Mil, Naut*) mutinerie *f*; (*fig*) révolte *f*. **2** *vi* se mutiner, se révolter.
mutt‡ [mʌt] *n* crétin(e)* *m(f)*, andouille‡ *f*.
mutter ['mʌtəʳ] **1** *n* marmottement *m*, marmonnement *m*; (*grumbling*) grommellement *m*.
2 *vt threat, wish* marmotter, marmonner. **'no' he ~ed** 'non' marmonna-t-il *or* dit-il entre ses dents.
3 *vi* marmonner, murmurer; (*grumble*) grommeler, grogner; *[thunder]* gronder.
mutton ['mʌtn] **1** *n* (*Culin*) mouton *m*. **leg of ~** gigot *m*; **shoulder of ~** épaule *f* de mouton; *V* **dead**. **2** *cpd*: (*Culin*) **mutton chop** côtelette *f* de mouton; (*whiskers*) **mutton chops*** (favoris *mpl* en) côtelettes *fpl*; **muttonhead‡** cornichon* *m*.
mutual ['mju:tjʊəl] *adj* **(a)** (*reciprocal*) *affection, help* mutuel, réciproque; (*Comm*) mutuel. **~ aid** entraide *f*, aide mutuelle *or* réciproque; **by ~ consent** par consentement mutuel; **the feeling is ~** c'est réciproque; **~ insurance company** (compagnie *f* d'assurance) mutuelle *f*; (*US Fin*) **~ fund** société *f* d'investissement.
(b) (*common*) *friend, cousin, share* commun.
mutuality [ˌmju:tjʊ'ælɪtɪ] *n* mutualité *f*.
mutually ['mju:tjʊəlɪ] *adv* mutuellement, réciproquement.
muzzle ['mʌzl] **1** *n [dog, fox etc]* museau *m*; *[gun]* bouche *f*, gueule *f*; (*anti-biting device*) muselière *f*; (*fig*) muselière, bâillon *m*.
2 *cpd*: **muzzle loader** arme *f* qu'on charge par le canon; **muzzle velocity** vitesse initiale.
3 *vt dog* museler; (*fig*) museler, bâillonner.
muzzy ['mʌzɪ] *adj* dans les vapes*, tout chose*; (*tipsy*) éméché; *ideas* confus, nébuleux; *outline* estompé, flou. **this cold makes me feel ~** ce rhume me brouille la cervelle *or* m'abrutit.
my [maɪ] **1** *poss adj* mon, ma, mes. **~ book** mon livre; **~ table** ma table; **~ friend** mon ami(e); **~ clothes** mes vêtements; **MY book** mon livre à moi; **I've broken ~ leg** je me suis cassé la jambe. **2** *excl*: **(oh) ~!*, ~, ~!*** ça, par exemple!
mycology [maɪ'kɒlədʒɪ] *n* mycologie *f*.
myopia [maɪ'əʊpɪə] *n* myopie *f*.
myopic [maɪ'ɒpɪk] *adj* myope.
myriad ['mɪrɪəd] **1** *n* myriade *f*. **2** *adj* (*liter*) innombrable, sans nombre.
myrmidon ['mɜ:mɪdən] *n* (*pej hum*) sbire *m*.
myrrh [mɜ:ʳ] *n* myrrhe *f*.
myrtle ['mɜ:tl] *n* myrte *m*.
myself [maɪ'self] *pers pron* (*reflexive: direct and indirect*) me; (*emphatic*) moi-même; (*after prep*) moi. **I've hurt ~** je me suis blessé; **I said to ~** je me suis dit; **I spoke to him ~** je lui ai parlé moi-même; **he asked me for a photo of ~** il m'a demandé une photo de moi *or* une de mes photos; **all by ~** tout seul; **I'm not ~ today** je ne suis pas dans mon état normal *or* dans mon assiette* aujourd'hui.
mysterious [mɪs'tɪərɪəs] *adj* mystérieux.
mysteriously [mɪs'tɪərɪəslɪ] *adv* mystérieusement.
mystery ['mɪstərɪ] **1** *n* **(a)** (*also Rel*) mystère *m*. **there's no ~ about it** ça n'a rien de mystérieux; **it's a ~ to me how he did it** je n'arrive pas à comprendre comment il l'a fait; **to make a great ~ of sth** faire grand mystère de qch.
(b) (*Theat*: *also* **~ play**) mystère *m*.
(c) (*Literat*: *also* **~ story**) roman *m* à suspense.
2 *cpd ship, man* mystérieux.
mystic ['mɪstɪk] **1** *adj* (*Rel*) mystique; *power* occulte; *rite* ésotérique; *truth* surnaturel; *formula* magique. **2** *n* mystique *mf*.
mystical ['mɪstɪkəl] *adj* mystique.
mysticism ['mɪstɪsɪzəm] *n* mysticisme *m*.
mystification [ˌmɪstɪfɪ'keɪʃən] *n* (*bewildering*) mystification *f*; (*bewilderment*) perplexité *f*. **why all the ~?** pourquoi tout ce mystère?
mystify ['mɪstɪfaɪ] *vt* rendre *or* laisser perplexe; (*deliberately deceive*) mystifier.
mystique [mɪs'ti:k] *n* mystique *f*.
myth [mɪθ] *n* mythe *m*.
mythical ['mɪθɪkəl] *adj* mythique.
mythological [ˌmɪθə'lɒdʒɪkəl] *adj* mythologique.
mythology [mɪ'θɒlədʒɪ] *n* mythologie *f*.
myxomatosis [ˌmɪksəʊmə'təʊsɪs] *n* myxomatose *f*.

N

N, n [en] *n* **(a)** (*letter*) N, n *m*. **(b)** (*Math*) **to the nth (power)**, (*fig*) **to the nth degree*** à la puissance n; **I told him for the nth time* to stop talking** je lui ai dit pour la énième fois de se taire.
'n'‡ [ən] *conj* = **and**.
nab* [næb] *vt* **(a)** (*catch in wrongdoing*) pincer*, choper‡, poisser‡. **(b)** (*catch to speak to etc*) attraper, coincer*.
nabob ['neɪbɒb] *n* (*lit, fig*) nabab *m*.
nacelle [næ'sel] *n* (*Aviat*) nacelle *f*.
nacre ['neɪkəʳ] *n* nacre *f*.
nacred ['neɪkəd] *adj*, **nacreous** ['neɪkrɪəs] *adj* nacré.
nadir ['neɪdɪəʳ] *n* (*Astron*) nadir *m*; (*fig*) point le plus bas. **in the ~ of despair** dans le plus profond désespoir; **his fortunes reached their ~ when ...** il atteignit le comble de l'infortune quand ... .
nag[1] [næg] **1** *vt* (*also* **~ at**) *[person]* reprendre tout le temps, être toujours après*; *[doubt etc]* harceler. **he was ~ging (at) me to keep my room tidy** il me harcelait *or* m'asticotait* pour que je tienne ma chambre en ordre; **to ~ sb into doing sth** harceler qn jusqu'à ce qu'il fasse qch; **his conscience was ~ging (at) him** sa conscience le travaillait; **~ged by doubts** assailli *or* harcelé *or* poursuivi par le doute. **2** *vi [person]* (*scold*) faire des remarques continuelles; *[pain, doubts]* être harcelant. **to ~ at sb** = **to ~ sb**; *V* **1**. **3** *n*: **he's a dreadful ~*** (*scolding*) il n'arrête pas de faire des remarques; (*pestering*) il n'arrête pas de nous (*or* le *etc*) harceler.
nag[2]* [næg] *n* (*horse*) bidet *m*; (*pej*) canasson* *m* (*pej*).
nagger ['nægəʳ] *n* = **nag[1] 3**.
nagging ['nægɪŋ] **1** *adj person* qui n'arrête pas de faire des remarques; *pain, worry, doubt* harcelant. **2** *n* (*U*) remarques continuelles, criailleries *fpl*.

naiad ['naɪæd] *n* naïade *f.*

nail [neɪl] **1** *n* **(a)** (*Anat*) ongle *m.* **finger~** ongle (de doigt de la main); *V* **bite, toe, tooth** *etc.*

(b) (*Tech*) clou *m.* (*fig*) **to pay on the ~** payer rubis sur l'ongle; **he was offered the job on the ~*** on lui a offert le poste sur-le-champ *or* illico*; (*fig*) **that decision was a** *or* **another ~ in his coffin** cette décision n'a fait que le pousser davantage vers le précipice; *V* **bed, hard, hit.**

2 *cpd*: **nail-biting** habitude *f* de se ronger les ongles; **nail-brush** brosse *f* à ongles; **nail clippers** pince *f* à ongles; **nailfile** lime *f* à ongles; **nail lacquer, nail polish** vernis *m* à ongles; **nail polish remover** dissolvant *m*; **nail scissors** ciseaux *mpl* à ongles; **nail varnish** = **nail lacquer; nail varnish remover** = **nail polish remover.**

3 *vt* **(a)** (*fix with ~s*) clouer. **to ~ the lid on a crate** clouer le couvercle d'une caisse; (*fig*) **to ~ one's colours to the mast** proclamer une fois pour toutes sa position; (*fig*) **to be ~ed to the spot** *or* **ground** rester cloué sur place.

(b) (*put ~s into*) clouter. **~ed shoes** chaussures cloutées.

(c) (*: *catch in crime etc*) *person* pincer*, choper‡; (*expose*) *lie* démasquer; *rumour* démentir.

nail down *vt sep* **(a)** *lid* clouer.

(b) (*fig*) *person* mettre au pied du mur, coincer*. **I nailed him down to coming at 6 o'clock** je l'ai réduit *or* contraint à accepter de venir à 6 heures.

nail up *vt sep* **(a)** *picture etc* fixer par des clous.

(b) *door, window* condamner (*en clouant*).

(c) *box, crate* clouer. **to nail up goods in a crate** empaqueter des marchandises dans une caisse clouée.

naïve [naɪ'iːv] *adj* naïf (*f* naïve), ingénu.

naïvely [naɪ'iːvlɪ] *adv* naïvement, ingénument.

naïveté [naɪ'iːvteɪ] *n*, **naïvety** [naɪ'iːvtɪ] *n* naïveté *f*, ingénuité *f.*

naked ['neɪkɪd] *adj* **(a)** *person* (tout) nu. **to go ~** se promener (tout) nu; *V* **stark, strip.**

(b) *branch* dénudé, dépouillé; *countryside* pelé, dénudé; *sword* nu. **~ flame** *or* **light** flamme nue; **visible to the ~ eye** visible à l'œil nu; **you can't see it with the ~ eye** on ne peut pas le voir à l'œil nu; **the ~ truth** la vérité toute nue; **~ facts** faits bruts; **a ~ outline of the events** un aperçu des événements réduit à sa plus simple expression; **it was a ~ attempt at fraud** c'était une tentative de fraude non déguisée.

nakedness ['neɪkɪdnɪs] *n* nudité *f.*

namby-pamby* ['næmbɪ'pæmbɪ] **1** *n* gnangnan* *mf or* gnian-gnian* *mf.* **2** *adj person* gnangnan* *inv or* gnian-gnian* *inv*; *style* à l'eau de rose.

name [neɪm] **1** *n* **(a)** nom *m.* **what's your ~?** comment vous appelez-vous?, quel est votre nom?; **my ~ is Robert** je m'appelle Robert; **I'll do it or my ~'s not Robert Smith!*** je le ferai, foi de Robert Smith!; **I haven't a ha'penny** *or* **a penny to my ~*** je n'ai pas un sou vaillant, je n'ai pas le sou; **what ~ are they giving the child?** comment vont-ils appeler l'enfant?; **they married to give the child a ~** ils se sont mariés pour que l'enfant soit légitime; **what ~ shall I say?** (*Telec*) c'est de la part de qui?; (*announcing arrival*) qui dois-je annoncer?; **please fill in your ~ and address** prière d'inscrire vos nom(, prénom) et adresse; **to take sb's ~ and address** noter *or* prendre les nom (, prénom) et adresse de qn; (*Ftbl etc*) **to have one's ~ taken** recevoir un avertissement; **this man, Smith by ~** *or* **by the ~ of Smith** cet homme, qui répond au nom de Smith; **we know it by** *or* **under another ~** nous le connaissons sous un autre nom; **to go by** *or* **under the ~ of** se faire appeler; **he writes under the ~ of X** il écrit sous le pseudonyme de X; **but his real ~ is Y** mais il s'appelle Y de son vrai nom, mais son vrai nom est Y; **I know him only by ~** *or* **by ~ alone** je ne le connais que de nom; **he knows all his customers by ~** il connaît tous ses clients par leur(s) nom(s); **in ~ only** de nom seulement; **to exist in ~ only** *or* **in ~ alone** n'exister que de nom; *[power, rights]* être nominal; **a marriage in ~ only** *or* **in ~ alone** un mariage (tout) nominal; **he is king in ~ only** il n'est roi que de nom, il n'a de roi que le nom; **to refer to sb by ~** désigner qn par son nom; **to name** *or* **mention no ~s, naming** *or* **mentioning no ~s** pour ne nommer personne; **to put one's ~ down for a job** poser sa candidature à un poste; **to put one's ~ down for a competition/for a class** s'inscrire à une compétition/à un cours; **I'll put my ~ down for a company car** je vais faire une demande pour avoir une voiture de fonction; **to call sb ~s** injurier qn, traiter qn de tous les noms; **~s cannot hurt me** les injures ne me touchent pas; **she was surprised to hear the child use those ~s** elle a été surprise d'entendre l'enfant employer de si vilains mots; (*fig*) **in the ~ of ...** au nom de ...; **in God's ~** au nom de Dieu, pour l'amour de Dieu; **in the king's ~** de par le roi; **what in the ~ of goodness* are you doing?** pour l'amour de Dieu, qu'est-ce que vous faites?, que diable faites-vous?; **all the great** *or* **big ~s were there** tout ce qui a un nom (connu) était là; **he's one of the big ~s in show business** il est un des grands noms du monde du spectacle; *V* **first, maiden, pet[1]** *etc.*

(b) (*reputation*) réputation *f*, renom *m.* **he has a ~ for honesty** il est réputé honnête, il a la réputation d'être honnête; **he has a ~ for carelessness** il a la réputation d'être négligent; **to protect one's (good) ~** protéger sa réputation; **this firm has a good ~** cette maison a (une) bonne réputation; **to get a bad ~** se faire une mauvaise réputation *or* un mauvais renom; **this book made his ~** ce livre l'a rendu célèbre; **to make one's ~** se faire un nom; **he made his ~ as a singer** il s'est fait un nom en tant que chanteur; **to make a ~ for o.s. (as)** se faire une réputation *or* un nom (comme *or* en tant que); **my ~ is mud* in this place** je ne suis pas en odeur de sainteté ici, je suis très mal vu ici; *V* **dog, vain.**

2 *vt* **(a)** (*call by a ~, give a ~ to*) nommer, appeler, donner un nom à; *ship* baptiser; *comet, star* donner un nom à. **a person ~d Smith** un(e) nommé(e) Smith; **the child was ~d Peter** on a appelé l'enfant Pierre; **to ~ a child after** *or* **for sb** donner à un enfant le nom de qn; **the child was ~d after his father** l'enfant a reçu le nom de son père; **they ~d him Winston after Churchill** ils l'ont appelé Winston en souvenir de Churchill; **tell me how plants are ~d** expliquez-moi l'appellation des plantes.

(b) (*give ~ of; list*) nommer, citer (le nom de); (*designate*) nommer, désigner (par son nom *or* nominalement); (*fix*) *date, price* fixer. **he was ~d as chairman** il a été nommé président; **he was ~d for the chairmanship** son nom a été présenté pour la présidence; **he ~d his son (as) his heir** il a désigné son fils comme héritier; **he has been ~d as the leader of the expedition** on l'a désigné pour diriger l'expédition; **he was ~d as the thief** on l'a désigné comme étant le voleur; **he refused to ~ his accomplices** il a refusé de nommer ses complices *or* de citer les noms de ses complices; **naming no names** pour ne nommer personne; **they have been ~d as witnesses** ils ont été cités comme témoins; **my collaborators are ~d in the preface** mes collaborateurs sont mentionnés dans l'avant-propos; **~ the presidents** donnez *or* citez le nom des *or* les noms des présidents, nommez les présidents; **~ the chief works of Shakespeare** citez les principaux ouvrages de Shakespeare; **~ your price** fixez votre prix; (*wedding*) **to ~ the day** fixer la date du mariage; **you ~ it, they have it!*** tout ce que vous pouvez imaginer, ils l'ont!

3 *cpd*: **name day** fête *f* (*d'une personne*); **he's a dreadful name-dropper*** il émaille toujours sa conversation de noms de gens en vue (*qu'il connaît*), à l'entendre il connaît la terre entière; **there was so much name dropping* in his speech** son discours était truffé de noms de gens en vue (*qu'il connaît*); (*Theat*) **name part** rôle *m* titulaire; **nameplate** (*on door etc*) plaque *f*, écusson *m*; (*on manufactured goods*) plaque du fabricant *or* du constructeur; **namesake** homonyme *m* (*personne*).

-named [neɪmd] *adj ending in cpds*: **the first-named** le premier, la première; **the last-named** ce dernier, cette dernière.

nameless ['neɪmlɪs] *adj* **(a)** (*unknown*) *person* sans nom, inconnu; (*anonymous*) anonyme. **a certain person who shall be ~** une (certaine) personne que je ne nommerai pas; **a ~ grave** une tombe sans inscription *or* anonyme.

(b) (*undefined*) *sensation, emotion, fear* indéfinissable, inexprimable; (*too hideous to name*) *vice, crime* innommable.

namely ['neɪmlɪ] *adv* à savoir, c'est-à-dire.

nance‡ [næns] *n*, **nancy‡** ['nænsɪ] *n*, **nancy-boy‡** ['nænsɪbɔɪ] *n* (*pej*) tante‡ *f*, tapette‡ *f.*

nankeen [næn'kiːn] *n* (*Tex*) nankin *m.*

nanny ['nænɪ] *n* (*Brit*) bonne *f* d'enfants, nounou* *f*, nurse *f.* **yes ~** oui nounou.

nanny-goat ['nænɪgəʊt] *n* chèvre *f*, bique* *f*, biquette* *f.*

nap[1] [næp] **1** *n* (*sleep*) petit somme. **afternoon ~** sieste *f*; **to have** *or* **take a ~** faire un petit somme; (*after lunch*) faire la sieste.

2 *vi* faire un (petit) somme, sommeiller. (*fig*) **to catch sb ~ping** (*unawares*) prendre qn à l'improviste *or* au dépourvu; (*in error etc*) surprendre qn en défaut.

nap[2] [næp] *n* (*Tex*) poil *m.* **cloth that has lost its ~** tissu râpé *or* élimé.

nap[3] [næp] *n* (*Cards*) = manille *f* aux enchères.

nap[4] [næp] *vt* (*Brit Racing*) **to ~ the winner** donner le cheval gagnant.

napalm ['neɪpɑːm] *n* napalm *m.* **~ bomb/bombing** bombe *f*/bombardement *m* au napalm.

nape [neɪp] *n* nuque *f.*

naphtha ['næfθə] *n* (*gen*) naphte *m.* **petroleum ~** naphta *m.*

naphthalene ['næfθəliːn] *n* naphtaline *f.*

napkin ['næpkɪn] *n* **(a)** serviette *f* (de table). **~ ring** rond *m* de serviette. **(b)** (*Brit: for babies*) couche *f.*

Napoleon [nə'pəʊlɪən] *n* **(a)** Napoléon *m.* **(b)** (*coin*) **n~** napoléon *m.* **(c)** (*US: pastry*) **n~** millefeuille *m.*

Napoleonic [nə,pəʊlɪ'ɒnɪk] *adj* napoléonien.

napper‡† ['næpə^r] *n* (*head*) caboche‡ *f.*

nappy ['næpɪ] *n* (*Brit*) = **napkin b.**

narcissi [nɑː'sɪsaɪ] *npl of* **narcissus.**

narcissism [nɑː'sɪsɪzəm] *n* narcissisme *m.*

narcissistic [,nɑːsɪ'sɪstɪk] *adj* narcissique.

narcissus [nɑː'sɪsəs] *n, pl* **narcissi** narcisse *m*, jonquille *f.*

narcosis [nɑː'kəʊsɪs] *n* narcose *f.*

narcotic [nɑː'kɒtɪk] *adj, n* (*lit, fig*) narcotique (*m*).

narcotize ['nɑːkətaɪz] *vt* donner *or* administrer un narcotique à, narcotiser.

nark‡ [nɑːk] (*Brit*) **1** *vt* **(a)** (*infuriate*) ficher en boule*, foutre en rogne‡. **(to get) ~ed** (se ficher) en boule*, (se foutre) en rogne‡. **(b) to ~ it** arrêter (de faire qch); **~ it!** suffit!*, écrase!‡ **2** *vi* (*inform police*) moucharder*. **3** *n* (*also* **copper's ~**) indic‡ *m*, mouchard* *m.*

narky‡ ['nɑːkɪ] *adj* (*Brit*) de mauvais poil*, en boule*, en rogne*.

narrate [nə'reɪt] *vt* raconter, narrer (*liter*).

narration [nə'reɪʃən] *n* narration *f.*

narrative ['nærətɪv] **1** *n* **(a)** (*story, account*) récit *m*, narration *f*, histoire *f.* **(b)** (*U*) narration *f.* **he has a gift for ~** il est doué pour la narration. **2** *adj poem, painting* narratif; *skill* de conteur. **~ writer** narrateur *m*, -trice *f.*

narrator [nə'reɪtə^r] *n* narrateur *m*, -trice *f*; (*Mus*) récitant(e) *m(f).*

narrow ['nærəʊ] **1** *adj* **(a)** *road, path* étroit; *valley* étroit, encaissé; *passage* étranglé; *garment* étroit, étriqué; *boundary, limits* restreint, étroit. **within a ~ compass** dans d'étroites limites, dans un champ restreint; **to grow** *or* **become ~(er)** se rétrécir, se resserrer.

(b) (*fig*) *outlook, mind* étroit, restreint, borné; *person* aux vues étroites, à l'esprit étroit, borné; *existence* limité, circonscrit; *scrutiny* serré, poussé; *means, resources, income* limité, juste (*fig*); *majority* faible, petit; *advantage* petit. **in the ~est sense (of the word)** au sens le plus restreint (du terme); **a ~ victory** une victoire remportée de justesse; **to have a ~ escape** s'en tirer de justesse, l'échapper belle; **that was a ~ shave!*** *or* **squeak!*** on l'a échappé belle!, il était moins une!; (*Ling*) **~ vowel** voyelle tendue.

2 *npl*: **~s** passage étroit; *[harbour]* passe *f*, goulet *m*; *[river]* pertuis *m*, étranglement *m*.

3 *cpd*: (*Rail*) **narrow-gauge line** *or* **track** voie étroite; **narrow-minded** *person* aux vues étroites, à l'esprit étroit, borné; *ideas, outlook* étroit, restreint, borné; **narrow-mindedness** étroitesse *f* *or* petitesse *f* d'esprit; **narrow-shouldered** étroit de carrure.

4 *vi* **(a)** *[road, path, valley]* se rétrécir. **his eyes ~ed** il plissa les yeux.

(b) (*fig: also* **~ down**) *[majority]* s'amenuiser, se rétrécir; *[opinions, outlook]* se restreindre. **the search has now ~ed (down) to Soho** les recherches se limitent maintenant à Soho; **the field of inquiry/the choice has ~ed (down) to 5 people** le champ d'investigation/le choix se ramène *or* se limite *or* se réduit maintenant à 5 personnes; **the question ~s (down) to this** la question se ramène *or* se réduit à ceci; **his outlook has ~ed (down) considerably since then** son horizon s'est beaucoup restreint *or* rétréci depuis lors.

5 *vt* (*also* **~ down**) **(a)** rétrécir.

(b) (*fig*) *person* limiter; *mind, ideas* rétrécir. (*fig*) **to ~ the field (down)** restreindre le champ; **with ~ed eyes** en plissant les yeux (*de méfiance etc*).

narrow down 1 *vi* **(a)** *[road, path, valley]* se rétrécir.

(b) (*fig*) = **narrow 4b.**

2 *vt sep* = **narrow 5.**

narrowly ['nærəʊlɪ] *adv* **(a)** (*by a small margin*) de justesse. **he ~ escaped being killed** il a bien failli être tué, il était à deux doigts d'être tué; **the bullet ~ missed him** la balle l'a raté de justesse *or* de peu.

(b) (*strictly*) *interpret rules etc* strictement, rigoureusement, étroitement.

(c) (*closely*) *examine* de près, minutieusement, méticuleusement.

narwhal ['nɑːwəl] *n* narval *m*.

nasal ['neɪzəl] **1** *adj* (*Anat*) nasal; (*Ling*) *sound* nasal; *accent* nasillard. **to speak in a ~ voice** parler du nez, nasiller. **2** *n* (*Ling*) nasale *f*.

nasality [neɪ'zælɪtɪ] *n* nasalité *f*.

nasalization [ˌneɪzəlaɪ'zeɪʃən] *n* nasalisation *f*.

nasalize ['neɪzəlaɪz] *vt* nasaliser.

nasally ['neɪzəlɪ] *adv whine, complain* sur un ton nasillard. **to speak ~** parler du nez, nasiller.

nascent ['næsnt] *adj* naissant; (*Chem etc*) à l'état naissant.

nastily ['nɑːstɪlɪ] *adv* (*unpleasantly*) désagréablement; (*spitefully*) méchamment; (*obscenely*) indécemment, d'une manière obscène. **it rained quite ~** il est tombé une sale pluie.

nastiness ['nɑːstɪnɪs] *n* (*V* **nasty**) (*unpleasantness*) caractère *m* désagréable; (*spitefulness*) méchanceté *f*; (*indecency*) indécence *f*, obscénité *f*; (*in taste*) mauvais goût; (*in odour*) mauvaise odeur; (*dirtiness*) saleté *f*.

nasturtium [nəs'tɜːʃəm] *n* (*Bot*) capucine *f*. **climbing/dwarf ~** capucine grimpante/naine.

nasty ['nɑːstɪ] *adj* **(a)** (*unpleasant*) *person, event, experience* déplaisant, désagréable; *cough, cold, weather* vilain, mauvais, sale (*before n*); *accident* vilain, sale*; *smell, taste* mauvais, désagréable. **the weather turned ~** le temps s'est gâté (*V also* **b, d**); **to taste ~** avoir un mauvais goût; **to smell ~** sentir mauvais, avoir une mauvaise odeur; **he's a ~ piece of work*** c'est un vilain bonhomme* *or* un sale type*; **to be ~ to sb** être *or* se montrer désagréable envers *or* avec qn; **to have a ~ temper** avoir très mauvais caractère, avoir un caractère de cochon*; **a ~ job** un sale travail, un sale *or* fichu boulot*; **what a ~ man!** quel horrible bonhomme!*; **he had a ~ time of it!** (*short spell*) il a passé un mauvais quart d'heure!; (*longer period*) il a passé de mauvais moments; (*fig*) **what a ~ mess!** quel gâchis épouvantable!

(b) (*spiteful*) *person, remark* méchant, mauvais. **a ~ rumour** une rumeur dictée par la méchanceté; **he turned ~ when I told him that ...** il est devenu mauvais *or* méchant quand je lui ai dit que ... (*V also* **d**); **that was a ~ trick** c'était un sale tour.

(c) (*indecent*) *book, story* indécent, obscène. **to have a ~ mind** avoir l'esprit mal tourné *or* malsain.

(d) (*dangerous, difficult*) *experience* dangereux, mauvais; *wound* dangereux. **to have a ~ look in one's eye** avoir l'œil mauvais *or* menaçant; (*Aut*) **a ~ corner** un sale *or* mauvais virage; **it was a ~ few moments** ce furent quelques moments très pénibles; **events took a ~ turn, the situation turned ~** la situation tourna très mal.

natal ['neɪtl] *adj* natal. (*liter*) **~ day** jour *m* de (la) naissance; *V* **antenatal, postnatal.**

natality [nə'tælɪtɪ] *n* natalité *f*.

nation ['neɪʃən] **1** *n* nation *f*, peuple *m*. **the French ~** la nation française; **people of all ~s** des gens de toutes les nationalités; **the voice of the ~** la voix de la nation *or* du peuple; **in the service of the ~** au service de la nation; **the whole ~ watched while he did it** il l'a fait sous les yeux de la nation tout entière; *V* **league[1], united.**

2 *cpd*: **nation-wide** (*adj*) *strike, protest* intéressant l'ensemble du pays; (*adv*) à travers tout le pays, dans l'ensemble du territoire; **there was a nation-wide search for the killers** on recherchait les assassins à travers tout le pays.

national ['næʃənl] **1** *adj* **(a)** (*of one nation*) national. **~ anthem** hymne national; (*Brit Admin*) **N~ Assistance**† Sécurité sociale; **~ costume** = **~ dress**; **~ debt** dette publique *or* nationale; **~ dress** costume national; **~ flag** drapeau national; (*Naut*) pavillon national; (*US*) **N~ Guard** garde nationale; (*Brit*) **N~ Health Service** ≃ Sécurité sociale; (*Brit*) **I got it on the N~ Health*** je l'ai eu par la Sécurité sociale; **~ holiday** fête nationale; **~ income** revenu national; (*Brit*) **N~ Insurance** ≃ Sécurité sociale; (*Brit*) **N~ Insurance benefits** prestations *fpl* de la Sécurité sociale; **~ monument** monument national; **~ park** parc national; (*Brit*) **N~ Savings** épargne nationale; (*Brit*) **N~ Savings Certificate** bon *m* d'épargne; (*Brit Mil*) **(to do one's) ~ service** (faire son) service national *or* militaire; (*Brit Mil*) **~ serviceman** appelé *m*, conscrit *m*; **N~ Socialism** national-socialisme *m*; **~ status** nationalité *f*; (*Brit*) **N~ Trust** ≃ Caisse Nationale des Monuments Historiques et des Sites.

(b) (*nation-wide*) national, à l'échelon national, dans l'ensemble du pays. **on a ~ scale** à l'échelon national; **there was ~ opposition to ...** la nation (entière) s'est opposée à ...; **~ strike of miners** grève *f* des mineurs intéressant l'ensemble du pays; (*Press*) **the ~ and local papers** la grande presse et la presse locale.

2 *n* **(a)** (*person*) ressortissant(e) *m(f)*, national(e) *m(f)*. **he's a French ~** (*in France*) il est de nationalité française; (*elsewhere*) c'est un ressortissant *or* un national français; **foreign ~s** ressortissants étrangers.

(b) (*Brit Racing*) **the Grand N~** le Grand National (*grande course de haies réputée pour sa difficulté*).

nationalism ['næʃnəlɪzəm] *n* (*also Pol*) nationalisme *m*; *V* **Scottish** *etc.*

nationalist ['næʃnəlɪst] *adj, n* nationaliste (*mf*); *V* **Scottish** *etc.*

nationalistic [ˌnæʃnə'lɪstɪk] *adj* nationaliste.

nationality [ˌnæʃə'nælɪtɪ] *n* nationalité *f*; *V* **dual.**

nationalization [ˌnæʃnəlaɪ'zeɪʃən] *n* **(a)** (*Ind, Pol*) nationalisation *f*. **(b)** *[person]* = **naturalization a.**

nationalize ['næʃnəlaɪz] *vt* **(a)** (*Ind, Pol*) nationaliser. **(b)** *person* = **naturalize 1a.**

nationally ['næʃnəlɪ] *adv* nationalement, du point de vue national, sous l'angle national; (*Rad*) *broadcast* dans le pays tout entier. **it is ~ known/felt that ...** on sait/sent dans tout le pays que ... .

nationhood ['neɪʃənhʊd] *n* nationalité *f* (*existence en tant que nation*).

native ['neɪtɪv] **1** *adj* **(a)** *country, town* natal; *language* maternel. **~ land** pays natal, patrie *f*.

(b) (*innate*) *charm, talent, ability* inné, naturel. **~ wit** bon sens inné.

(c) (*indigenous*) *plant, animal* indigène; *product, resources* naturel, du pays, de la région. **plant/animal ~ to** plante *f*/animal *m* originaire de; **French ~ speaker** personne *f* dont la langue maternelle est le français *or* de langue maternelle française; (*Ling*) **you should ask a ~ speaker** il faudrait (le) demander à un locuteur natif.

(d) *customs, costume* du pays; *matters, rights, knowledge* du pays, des autochtones. **Minister of N~ Affairs** ministre chargé des Affaires indigènes; **Ministry of N~ Affairs** ministère *m* des Affaires indigènes; **~ labour** main-d'œuvre *f* indigène; **~ quarter** quartier *m* indigène; **to go ~*** adopter le mode de vie indigène; *V* **informant.**

2 *n* **(a)** (*person*) autochtone *mf*; (*esp of colony*) indigène *mf*. **a ~ of France** un(e) Français(e) de naissance; **he is a ~ of Bourges** il est originaire de *or* natif de Bourges; **she speaks French like a ~** elle parle français comme si c'était sa langue maternelle; **the ~s** les habitants *mpl or* gens *mpl* du pays, les autochtones *mpl* (*also hum*).

(b) (*Bot, Zool*) indigène *mf*. **this plant/animal is a ~ of Australia** cette plante/cet animal est originaire d'Australie.

nativity [nə'tɪvɪtɪ] **1** *n* **(a)** (*Rel*) **N~** Nativité *f*; **Festival of the N~** (fête *f* de la) Nativité. **(b)** (*Astrol*) horoscope *m*. **2** *cpd*: **nativity play** miracle *m or* mystère *m* de la Nativité.

natter* ['nætə^{r}] (*Brit*) **1** *vi* (*chat*) causer, bavarder; (*chatter*) bavarder, jacasser; (*continuously*) bavarder *or* jacasser sans arrêt; (*grumble*) grommeler, bougonner*. **we ~ed (away) for hours** nous avons bavardé pendant des heures; **she does ~!** elle n'arrête pas de jacasser!

2 *n* **(a)** (*chat*) causerie *f*, causette* *f*. **we had a good ~** nous avons bien bavardé, nous avons taillé une bonne bavette*.

(b) (*chatterbox*) moulin *m* à paroles*.

natterer* ['nætərə^{r}] *n* = **natter 2b.**

natty* ['nætɪ] *adj* **(a)** (*neat*) *dress* pimpant, coquet, chic *inv*; *person* chic *inv*. **(b)** (*handy*) *tool, gadget* astucieux, bien trouvé.

natural ['nætʃrəl] **1** *adj* **(a)** (*normal*) naturel, normal. **it seems quite ~ to me** ça me semble tout à fait normal *or* naturel; **it is ~ for this animal to hibernate** il est dans la nature de cet animal d'hiberner, il est naturel *or* normal que cet animal hiberne (*subj*); **it is ~ for you to think ..., it is ~ that you should think ...** il est naturel *or* normal *or* logique que vous pensiez (*subj*) ...; **~ childbirth** accouchement *m* sans douleur; (*Jur*) **death from ~ causes** mort naturelle; **to die a ~ death** mourir de sa belle mort; **~ gas** gaz naturel; **~ history** histoire naturelle; **~ law** la loi de la nature; (*Jur*) **for (the rest of) his ~ life** à vie; (*Math*) **~ number** nombre naturel; **~ philosophy** physique *f*; **~ philosopher** physicien(ne) *m(f)*; **~ science** sciences naturelles; **~ selection** sélection naturelle.

(b) (*inborn*) inné, naturel. **to have a ~ talent for** avoir une facilité innée pour; **he's a ~ painter** il est né peintre, c'est un peintre né; **playing the piano comes ~* to her** elle est naturellement douée pour le piano.

(c) (*unaffected*) *manner* simple, naturel, sans affectation.

(d) (*Mus*) naturel. **~ key** ton naturel.

(e) (†) *child* naturel.

2 *n* **(a)** (*Mus*) (*sign*) bécarre *m*; (*note*) note *f* dans son ton naturel.

(b) (*: *ideal*) **he's a ~ for this part** il est fait pour ce rôle, il joue ce rôle au naturel; **did you see him act? — he's a ~!** vous l'avez vu jouer? — il est sur scène comme un poisson dans l'eau!

(c) (††: *simpleton*) idiot(e) *m(f)* (de naissance), demeuré(e) *m(f)*.

(d) (‡: *life*) **for the rest of one's ~** pour le restant de ses jours.

naturalism ['nætʃrəlɪzəm] *n* naturalisme *m*.

naturalist ['nætʃrəlɪst] *adj, n* naturaliste *(mf)*.

naturalistic [ˌnætʃrə'lɪstɪk] *adj* naturaliste.

naturalization [ˌnætʃrəlaɪ'zeɪʃən] *n* (a) *[person]* naturalisation *f*. **letters of ~, ~ papers** déclaration *f* de naturalisation. (b) *[plant, animal]* acclimatation *f*.

naturalize ['nætʃrəlaɪz] 1 *vt* (a) *person* naturaliser. **to be ~d** se faire naturaliser.

(b) *animal, plant* acclimater; *word, sport* naturaliser.

2 *vi* (a) *[person]* se faire naturaliser.

(b) *[plant, animal]* s'acclimater.

(c) (*study natural history*) faire de l'histoire naturelle.

naturally ['nætʃrəlɪ] *adv* (a) (*as is normal*) naturellement; (*of course*) naturellement, bien sûr, bien entendu, comme de juste. **will you do it? — ~ not!** tu le feras? — sûrement pas! *or* bien sûr que non!

(b) (*by nature*) de nature, par tempérament. **he is ~ lazy** il est paresseux de nature *or* par tempérament; **a ~ optimistic person** un(e) optimiste né(e); **her hair is ~ curly** elle frise naturellement; **it comes ~ to him to do this** il fait cela tout naturellement; **playing the piano comes ~ to her** elle a un don (naturel) pour le piano.

(c) (*unaffectedly*) *accept, behave, laugh* simplement, sans affectation, avec naturel. **she said it quite ~** elle l'a dit avec un grand naturel.

naturalness ['nætʃrəlnɪs] *n* (*natural appearance, behaviour etc*) naturel *m*; (*simplicity*) simplicité *f*.

nature ['neɪtʃəʳ] 1 *n* (a) (*U*) nature *f*. **he loves ~** il aime la nature; **the laws of ~** les lois *fpl* de la nature; **a freak of ~** un caprice de la nature; **to paint from ~** peindre d'après nature; **against ~** contre nature; **~ abhors a vacuum** la nature a horreur du vide; (*hum*) **in a state of ~** à l'état naturel, dans le costume d'Adam*; **return to ~** retour *m* à l'état de nature *or* à la nature; *V* **mother**.

(b) (*character etc*) *[person, animal]* nature *f*, naturel *m*, tempérament *m*, caractère *m*. **by ~** de nature, par tempérament; **he has a nice ~** il a un naturel *or* un tempérament *or* un caractère facile, il est d'un naturel facile, c'est une bonne nature; **she hid a loving ~ under ...** elle cachait une nature aimante *or* un caractère aimant sous ...; **the ~ of birds is to fly, it is in the ~ of birds to fly** il est de *or* dans la nature des oiseaux de voler; **it is not in his ~ to lie** il n'est pas de *or* dans sa nature de mentir; **that's very much in his ~** c'est tout à fait dans sa nature; *V* **good, human, second**[1] *etc*.

(c) (*essential quality*) nature *f*, essence *f*. **the ~ of the soil** la nature du sol; **it is in the ~ of things** il est dans l'ordre des choses, il est de *or* dans la nature des choses; **the true ~ of things** l'essence des choses; **in the ~ of this case it is clear that ...** vu la nature de ce cas il est clair que ... .

(d) (*type, sort*) espèce *f*, genre *m*, sorte *f*, nature *f*. **things of this ~** les choses de cette nature *or* de ce genre; **his comment was in the ~ of a compliment** sa remarque était en quelque sorte un compliment; **invitation in the ~ of a threat** invitation qui tient de la menace; **something in the ~ of an apology** une sorte d'excuse, une vague excuse.

2 *cpd*: **nature conservancy** protection *f* de la nature; (*Brit*) **Nature Conservancy Board** ≃ Direction Générale de la Protection de la Nature et de l'Environnement; (*Med*) **nature cure** naturisme *m*; **nature lover** amoureux *m*, -euse *f* de la nature; **nature reserve** réserve naturelle; **nature study** histoire naturelle; (*Scol*) sciences naturelles; **nature trail** circuit forestier éducatif; **nature worship** adoration *f* de la nature.

-natured ['neɪtʃəd] *adj ending in cpds* de nature. **jealous-natured** jaloux de nature, d'un naturel jaloux; *V* **good, ill**.

naturism ['neɪtʃərɪzəm] *n* naturisme *m*.

naturist ['neɪtʃərɪst] *n* naturiste *mf*.

naught [nɔːt] *n* (a) (*Math*) zéro *m*. **~s and crosses** ≃ morpion *m*.

(b) († *or liter: nothing*) rien *m*. **to bring to ~** faire échouer, faire avorter; **to come to ~** échouer, n'aboutir à rien; **to care ~ for, to set at ~** ne faire aucun cas de, ne tenir aucun compte de.

naughtily ['nɔːtɪlɪ] *adv say, remark* avec malice. **to behave ~** se conduire mal; *[child]* être vilain.

naughtiness ['nɔːtɪnɪs] *n* (a) *[child etc]* désobéissance *f*, mauvaise conduite. **a piece of ~** une désobéissance. (b) *[story, joke, play]* grivoiserie *f*.

naughty ['nɔːtɪ] *adj* (a) méchant, vilain, pas sage. **a ~ child** un vilain *or* méchant (enfant), un enfant pas sage; **that was a ~ thing to do!** ce n'est pas beau ce que tu as fait!

(b) *joke, story* grivois, risqué, leste. **the N~ Nineties** ≃ la Belle Époque; **~ word** vilain mot.

nausea ['nɔːsɪə] *n* (*Med*) nausée *f*; (*fig*) dégoût *m*, écœurement *m*. (*Med*) **a feeling of ~** un haut-le-cœur, un mal au cœur, une envie de vomir.

nauseate ['nɔːsɪeɪt] *vt* (*Med, fig*) écœurer.

nauseating ['nɔːsɪeɪtɪŋ] *adj* (*Med*) écœurant, qui soulève le cœur; (*fig*) écœurant, dégoûtant.

nauseatingly ['nɔːsɪeɪtɪŋlɪ] *adv* (*Med, fig*) d'une façon dégoûtante *or* écœurante.

nauseous ['nɔːsɪəs] *adj* (*Med*) nauséeux; (*fig*) dégoûtant, écœurant.

nautical ['nɔːtɪkəl] *adj* nautique, naval. **~ almanac** almanach *m* nautique; **~ matters** questions navales; **~ mile** mille marin *or* nautique; **~ term** terme *m* nautique *or* de marine *or* de navigation; **the music has a slight ~ flavour** la musique évoque un peu la mer.

nautilus ['nɔːtɪləs] *n* (*Zool*) nautile *m*.

Navaho ['nævəhəʊ] *n* (*also* **~ Indian**) Navaho *mf or* Navajo *mf*.

naval ['neɪvəl] *adj battle, strength* naval; *affairs, matters* de la marine. **~ architect** ingénieur *m* du génie maritime *or* des constructions navales; **~ architecture** construction navale; **~ aviation** aéronavale *f*; **~ barracks** caserne *f* maritime; **~ base** base navale, port *m* de guerre; **~ college** école navale; **~ dockyard** arsenal *m* (maritime); **~ forces** marine *f* de guerre, marine militaire; **~ hospital** hôpital *m* maritime; **~ officer** officier *m* de marine; **~ power** puissance *f* maritime; **~ station** = **~ base**; **~ stores** entrepôts *mpl* maritimes; **~ warfare** combat naval.

nave[1] [neɪv] *n [church]* nef *f*.

nave[2] [neɪv] *n [wheel]* moyeu *m*. (*Aut*) **~ plate** enjoliveur *m*.

navel ['neɪvəl] 1 *n* (*Anat*) nombril *m*, ombilic *m*. 2 *cpd*: **navel orange** (orange *f*) navel *f*.

navigable ['nævɪgəbl] *adj* (a) *river, channel* navigable. (b) *missile, balloon, airship* dirigeable.

navigate ['nævɪgeɪt] 1 *vi* naviguer.

2 *vt* (a) (*plot course of*) **to ~ a ship** *or* **a plane** *or* **a car** *etc* naviguer.

(b) (*steer*) *dinghy* être à la barre de; *steamer etc* gouverner; *aircraft* piloter; *missile* diriger. **he ~d the ship through the dangerous channel** il a dirigé le navire dans le dangereux chenal.

(c) *seas, ocean* naviguer sur.

navigation [ˌnævɪ'geɪʃən] 1 *n* navigation *f*. 2 *cpd*: **navigation laws** code *m* maritime; **navigation lights** feux *mpl* de bord; *V* **coastal** *etc*.

navigator ['nævɪgeɪtəʳ] *n* (a) (*Aut, Aviat, Naut*) navigateur *m*. (b) (*sailor-explorer*) navigateur *m*, marin *m*.

navvy ['nævɪ] *n* (*Brit*) terrassier *m*.

navy ['neɪvɪ] 1 *n* marine *f* (militaire *or* de guerre). **he's in the ~** il est dans la marine, il est marin; (*US*) **Department of the N~, N~ Department** ministère *m* de la Marine; **Secretary for the N~** ministre *m* de la Marine; **to serve in the ~** servir dans la marine; *V* **merchant, royal**.

2 *cpd*: **navy(-blue)** bleu marine *inv*; (*US*) **Navy Register** liste navale; (*US*) **navy yard** arsenal *m* (maritime).

nay [neɪ] (†† *or liter*) 1 *particle* non. **do not say me ~** ne me dites pas non; *V* **yea**. 2 *adv* (et) même, voire. **surprised, ~ astonished** surpris et même abasourdi; **for months, ~ for years ...** pendant des mois, voire des années ... .

Nazi ['nɑːtsɪ] 1 *n* Nazi(e) *m(f)*. 2 *adj* nazi.

Nazism ['nɑːtsɪzəm] *n* nazisme *m*.

Neanderthal [nɪ'ændətɑːl] 1 *n* (*Geog*) Néandert(h)al *m*. 2 *adj* néandert(h)alien. **~ man** homme *m* de Néandert(h)al.

neap [niːp] *n* (*also* **~tide**) marée *f* de morte-eau. **~(tide) season** époque *f* des mortes-eaux.

Neapolitan [nɪə'pɒlɪtən] 1 *adj* napolitain. **a ~ ice (cream)** une tranche napolitaine. 2 *n* Napolitain(e) *m(f)*.

near [nɪəʳ] 1 *adv* (a) (*in space*) près, à proximité, proche; (*in time*) près, proche. **he lives quite ~** il habite tout près *or* tout à côté; **~ at hand** *object* tout près, à proximité, à portée de la main; *event* tout proche; *place* non loin, dans le voisinage; **to draw** *or* **come ~ (to)** s'approcher (de); **to draw** *or* **come ~er (to)** s'approcher davantage (de); **to draw** *or* **bring sth ~er** rapprocher qch; **it was drawing** *or* **getting ~ to Christmas, Christmas was drawing** *or* **getting ~** on était à l'approche *or* aux approches de Noël, Noël approchait; **it was ~ to 6 o'clock** il était près de *or* presque 6 heures; **~ to where I had seen him** près de l'endroit où je l'avais vu; **she was ~ to tears** elle était au bord des larmes.

(b) (*gen* **~ly**: *in degree*) presque. **this train is nowhere ~ full** ce train est loin d'être plein, il s'en faut de beaucoup que ce train (ne) soit plein.

(c) (*close*) **as ~ as I can judge** autant que je puisse juger; **the more you look at this portrait, the ~er it resembles him** plus on regarde ce portrait, plus il lui ressemble; **you won't get any ~er than that to what you want** vous ne trouverez pas mieux; **that's ~ enough*** ça pourra aller; **there were 60 people, ~ enough*** il y avait 60 personnes, à peu près *or* grosso modo; **as ~ as dammit*** ou presque, ou c'est tout comme.

(d) (*Naut*) près du vent, en serrant le vent. **as ~ as she can** au plus près.

2 *prep* (a) (*in space*) près de, auprès de, dans le voisinage de; (*in time*) près de, vers. **~ here/there** près d'ici/de là; **~ the church** près de l'église, dans le voisinage de l'église; **he was standing ~ the table** il se tenait (au)près de la table; **regions ~ the Equator** les régions avoisinant l'équateur; **keep ~ me** restez près de moi; **don't come ~ me** ne vous approchez pas de moi; **the sun was ~ setting** le soleil était près de se coucher; (*liter*) **the evening was drawing ~ its close** la soirée tirait à sa fin; **the passage is ~ the end of the book** le passage se trouve vers la fin du livre; **her birthday is ~ mine** son anniversaire est proche du mien; (*fig*) **the steak is so tough the knife won't go ~ it*** le bifteck est si dur que le couteau n'arrive pas à l'entamer*; **he won't go ~ anything illegal*** il ne se risquera jamais à faire quoi que ce soit d'illégal*.

(b) (*on the point of*) près de, sur le point de. **~ tears** au bord des larmes; **~ death** près de *or* sur le point de mourir; **he was very ~ refusing** il était sur le point de *or* à deux doigts de refuser.

(c) (*on the same level, in the same degree*) au niveau de, près de. **to come** *or* **be ~ sth** se rapprocher de qch; (*fig*) ressembler à qch; **French is ~er Latin than English is** le français ressemble plus au latin *or* est plus près du latin que l'anglais; it's the same thing or ~ it c'est la même chose ou presque *or* à peu près; it's as ~ snowing as makes no difference il neige ou peu s'en faut; nobody comes anywhere ~ him at swimming il n'y a personne à son niveau pour la natation, personne ne lui arrive à la cheville en natation; that's ~er it, that's ~er the thing* voilà qui est mieux; *V* nowhere.

3 *adj* (a) (*close in space*) *building, town, tree* proche, voisin; *neighbour* proche. to get a ~ view of sth examiner qch de près; these glasses make things look ~er ces lunettes rapprochent les objets; (*Math*) to the ~est decimal place à la plus proche décimale près; to the ~est pound à une livre près; the ~est way la route la plus courte *or* la plus directe; this is very ~ work ce travail est très minutieux *or* délicat.

(b) (*close in time*) proche, prochain, rapproché. the hour is ~ (when) l'heure est proche (où); in the ~ future dans un proche avenir, dans un avenir prochain; these events are still very ~ ces événements sont encore très proches *or* très rapprochés de nous.

(c) (*fig*) *relative, relationship* proche; *friend* cher, intime; *friendship* intime; *guess* près de la vérité, à peu près juste; *resemblance* exact; *portrait* ressemblant; *offer* approchant; *race, contest* disputé, serré; *result* serré. my ~est and dearest* mes proches (parents), ceux qui me touchent de près; the ~est (in line) to the throne l'héritier *m*, -ière *f* le (*or* la) plus proche du trône; a very ~ concern of mine une chose qui me touche de très près; the ~est equivalent ce qui s'en rapproche le plus; (*lit, fig*) a ~ miss un coup manqué de peu; (*lit*) that was a ~ miss le coup est passé très près; (*fig*) that was a ~ miss *or* a ~ thing* il s'en est fallu de peu, il était moins une*; the translation is fairly ~ la traduction est assez fidèle; that's the ~est thing to a compliment ça pourrait passer pour un compliment.

(d) (*: *mean*) radin*, pingre.

4 *vt place* approcher de; *person* approcher, s'approcher de. (*liter*) to be ~ing one's end toucher à *or* être près de sa fin; my book is ~ing completion mon livre est près d'être achevé; the book is ~ing publication le livre approche de sa date de publication; the country is ~ing disaster le pays est au bord de la catastrophe.

5 *cpd*: (*US*) near beer bière légère; nearby (*adv*) près, tout près; (*adj*) proche, avoisinant, tout près de là (*or* d'ici); the Near East le Proche-Orient; near gold similor *m*; near-nudity nudité presque totale, quasi-nudité; (*Brit Aut*) nearside (*in Britain*) côté *m* gauche; (*in France, US etc*) côté droit; (*Aut*) nearside lane/verge (*in Britain*) voie *f*/accotement *m* de gauche; (*in France, US etc*) voie/accotement de droite; to be near-sighted être myope, avoir la vue basse; near-sightedness myopie *f*; near silk soie artificielle.

nearly ['nɪəlɪ] *adv* (a) (*almost*) presque, à peu près, près de. it's ~ complete c'est presque terminé; ~ black presque noir; I've ~ finished j'ai presque fini; we are ~ there nous sommes presque arrivés; it's ~ 2 o'clock il est près de *or* presque 2 heures; it's ~ time to go il est presque l'heure de partir; she is ~ 60 elle a près de 60 ans, elle va sur ses 60 ans; their marks are ~ the same leurs notes sont à peu près les mêmes; ~ all my money presque tout mon argent, la presque totalité de mon argent; he ~ laughed il a failli rire; I very ~ lost my place j'ai bien failli perdre ma place; she was ~ crying elle était sur le point de pleurer, elle était au bord des larmes; it's the same or very ~ so c'est la même chose ou presque.

(b) not ~ loin de; she is not ~ so old as you elle est loin d'être aussi âgée que vous; that's not ~ enough c'est loin d'être suffisant; it's not ~ good enough c'est loin d'être satisfaisant.

(c) (*closely*) près, de près. this concerns me very ~ cela me touche de très près.

nearness ['nɪənɪs] *n* (a) (*in time, place*) proximité *f*; [*friendship, relationship*] intimité *f*; [*translation*] fidélité *f*; [*resemblance*] exactitude *f*. (b) (*meanness*) parcimonie *f*, radinerie* *f*.

neat [ni:t] *adj* (a) (*clean and tidy*) *person, clothes* soigné, propre, net (*f* nette); *sb's appearance, garden, sewing, stitches* soigné, net; *house, room* net, ordonné, bien tenu. her hair is always very ~ elle est toujours bien coiffée; ~ as a new pin propre comme un sou neuf; he is a ~ worker il est soigneux dans son travail; his work is very ~ son travail est très soigné; his desk is always very ~ son bureau est toujours bien rangé; ~ handwriting une écriture nette; she is very ~ in her dress elle est très soignée dans sa mise, elle s'habille de façon très soignée; a ~ little suit un petit tailleur de coupe nette.

(b) (*pleasing to eye*) ~ ankles chevilles fines; ~ legs jambes bien faites; she has a ~ figure elle est bien faite, elle a une jolie ligne; a ~ little horse un beau petit cheval; a ~ little car une belle *or* jolie petite voiture.

(c) (*skilful*) *phrase, style* élégant, net (*f* nette); *solution* élégant; *plan* habile, ingénieux; (*: *wonderful*) très bien, sensass‡ *inv*. a ~ little speech un petit discours bien tourné; that's ~! c'est du beau travail!, c'est du beau boulot!‡; to make a ~ job of sth bien faire qch, réussir qch; he's very ~ with his hands il est très adroit, il est très habile (de ses mains).

(d) (*undiluted*) *spirits* pur, sans eau, sec. he drinks his whisky/brandy ~ il prend son whisky/son cognac sec *or* sans eau; he had a glass of ~ whisky il a pris un verre de whisky pur *or* sec; I'll take it ~ je le prendrai sec.

neaten ['ni:tn] *vt dress* ajuster; *desk* ranger. to ~ one's hair se recoiffer.

'neath [ni:θ] *prep* (*liter*) = beneath 1.

neatly ['ni:tlɪ] *adv* (a) (*tidily*) avec ordre, d'une manière ordonnée *or* soignée; *dress* avec soin; *write* proprement. to put sth away ~ ranger qch avec soin.

(b) (*skilfully*) habilement, adroitement. he avoided the question very ~ il a éludé la question très habilement *or* adroitement; ~ put joliment dit; a ~ turned sentence une phrase bien tournée *or* joliment tournée; you got out of that very ~ vous vous en êtes adroitement *or* très bien tiré.

neatness ['ni:tnɪs] *n* (a) (*tidiness*) [*person, clothes*] netteté *f*, propreté *f*; [*house, room*] netteté, belle ordonnance; [*garden, sewing, stitches*] netteté. the ~ of her work/appearance son travail/sa tenue soigné(e), le soin qu'elle apporte à son travail/sa tenue. (b) [*ankles*] finesse *f*; [*legs, figure*] finesse, galbe *m*. (c) (*skilfulness*) adresse *f*, habileté *f*, dextérité *f*; [*style etc*] adresse.

nebula ['nebjʊlə] *n, pl* ~e ['nebjʊli:] nébuleuse *f*.

nebulous ['nebjʊləs] *adj* (*Astron*) nébuleux; (*fig*) nébuleux, vague, flou.

necessarily ['nesɪsərɪlɪ] *adv* nécessairement, forcément, inévitablement. they must ~ leave tomorrow ils devront nécessairement *or* inévitablement partir demain; this is not ~ the case ce n'est pas forcément *or* nécessairement le cas; you don't ~ have to believe it vous n'êtes pas forcé *or* obligé de le croire.

necessary ['nesɪsərɪ] 1 *adj* (a) (*essential*) nécessaire, essentiel (*to, for* à). it is ~ to do il faut faire, il est nécessaire de faire; it is ~ for him to be there il faut qu'il soit là, il est nécessaire *or* essentiel qu'il soit là; it is ~ that ... il faut que ... + *subj*, il est nécessaire que ... + *subj*; if ~ s'il le faut, en cas de *or* au besoin, si besoin est; to do everything *or* what is ~ (for) faire tout ce qu'il faut (pour), faire le nécessaire (pour); to make the ~ arrangements (for sth to be done) prendre les dispositions nécessaires *or* faire le nécessaire (pour que qch se fasse); to make it ~ for sb to do mettre qn dans la nécessité de faire; to do more than is ~ faire plus qu'il ne faut, faire plus que le nécessaire; don't do any more than is ~ n'en faites pas plus qu'il ne faut *or* qu'il n'est nécessaire; to do no more than is ~ ne faire que le nécessaire; good food is ~ to health une bonne alimentation est nécessaire *or* essentielle à la santé; all the ~ qualifications for this job toutes les qualités requises pour (obtenir) ce poste; the law was clearly ~ la loi était de toute évidence nécessaire.

(b) (*unavoidable*) *corollary* nécessaire; *result* inévitable. a ~ evil un mal nécessaire.

2 *n* (a) to do the ~* faire le nécessaire.

(b) (*money*) the ~* le fric‡, les fonds *mpl*.

(c) (*Jur: necessities*) necessaries nécessaire *m*.

necessitate [nɪ'sesɪteɪt] *vt* nécessiter, rendre nécessaire. the situation ~d his immediate return la situation l'a obligé à revenir immédiatement, la situation a nécessité son retour immédiat.

necessitous [nɪ'sesɪtəs] *adj* nécessiteux. in ~ circumstances dans le besoin, dans la nécessité.

necessity [nɪ'sesɪtɪ] *n* (a) (*U: compelling circumstances*) nécessité *f*; (*need, compulsion*) besoin *m*, nécessité. to be under the ~ of doing être dans la nécessité de faire; from *or* out of ~ par nécessité, par la force des choses; of ~ de (toute) nécessité, nécessairement; (*Prov*) ~ knows no law nécessité fait loi (*Prov*); (*Prov*) ~ is the mother of invention de la nécessité naît l'invention, la nécessité rend ingénieux; case of absolute ~ cas *m* de force majeure; there is no ~ for you to do that vous n'avez pas besoin de faire cela, il n'est pas nécessaire que vous fassiez cela; in case of ~ au besoin, en cas de besoin; the ~ of doing le besoin *or* la nécessité de faire; she realized the ~ of going to see him elle comprit qu'il était nécessaire d'aller le voir, elle comprit la nécessité dans laquelle elle se trouvait d'aller le voir; is there any ~? est-ce nécessaire?; there's no ~ for tears/apologies vous n'avez pas besoin de pleurer/de vous excuser; *V* virtue.

(b) (*U: poverty*) besoin *m*, dénuement *m*, nécessité *f*. to live in ~ vivre dans le besoin *or* le dénuement *or* la nécessité.

(c) (*necessary object etc*) chose nécessaire *or* essentielle. the bare necessities of life les choses nécessaires *or* essentielles à la vie; a dishwasher is a ~ nowadays un lave-vaisselle est une chose essentielle de nos jours.

neck [nek] 1 *n* (a) cou *m*; [*horse etc*] encolure *f*. to have a sore ~ avoir mal au cou; (*fig*) to risk one's ~ risquer sa vie *or* sa peau*; (*fig*) to save one's ~ sauver sa peau*; to fall on sb's ~, to fling one's arms round sb's ~ se jeter *or* sauter au cou de qn; (*Racing*) to win by a ~ gagner d'une encolure; to be up to one's ~ in work avoir du travail par-dessus la tête*; to be up to one's ~ in a crime être totalement impliqué dans un crime; he's up to his ~ in it* il est dans le bain* jusqu'au cou; he got it in the ~‡ il en a pris pour son compte *or* grade*, il a dérouillé‡; to stick *or* shoot one's ~ out* se mouiller‡, s'avancer (*fig*), prendre un *or* des risque(s); I don't want (to have) him round my ~* je ne veux pas l'avoir sur le dos (*fig*); to throw sb out ~ and crop jeter qn dehors sans appel; (*Brit*) it's ~ or nothing* il faut jouer le tout pour le tout; ~ of mutton collet *m* de mouton; ~ of beef collier *m* de bœuf; (*Culin*) best end of ~ côtelettes premières; *V* break, pain, stiff *etc*.

(b) [*dress, shirt etc*] encolure *f*. high ~ col montant; square ~ décolleté *m or* encolure *f* carré(e); dress with a low ~ robe décolletée; shirt with a 38 cm ~ chemise qui fait 38 cm d'encolure *or* de tour de cou; *V* polo, roll *etc*.

(c) [*bottle*] col *m*, goulot *m*; [*vase*] col; [*screw etc*] collet *m*; [*land*] isthme *m*; [*guitar, violin*] manche *m*; *V* bottle.

(d) (*Brit‡: impertinence*) toupet* *m*, culot‡ *m*.

2 *vi* (‡) se peloter‡. to ~ with sb peloter qn.

3 *cpd*: neck and neck à égalité; neckband col *m*, tour *m* du cou; necklace *V* necklace; neckline encolure *f*; plunging neckline décolleté *or* décolletage plongeant; necktie cravate *f*.

-necked [nekt] *adj ending in cpds V* low[1] 4, round 5, stiff 2 *etc*.

neckerchief ['nekətʃi:f] *n* (*scarf*) foulard *m*, tour *m* de cou; (*on dress*) fichu *m*.

necking: [ˈnekɪŋ] *n* pelotage: *m.*
necklace [ˈneklɪs] *n* collier *m*; (*long*) sautoir *m.* **diamond/pearl ~** collier de diamants/de perles.
necklet [ˈneklɪt] *n* collier *m*; (*fur*) collet *m* (en fourrure).
necrological [ˌnekrəʊˈlɒdʒɪkəl] *adj* nécrologique.
necrologist [neˈkrɒlədʒɪst] *n* nécrologue *m.*
necrology [neˈkrɒlədʒɪ] *n* **(a)** nécrologie *f.* **(b)** (*Rel*) nécrologe *m.*
necromancer [ˈnekrəʊmænsəʳ] *n* nécromancien(ne) *m(f).*
necromancy [ˈnekrəʊmænsɪ] *n* nécromancie *f.*
necrophilia [ˌnekrəʊˈfɪlɪə] *n,* **necrophilism** [neˈkrɒfɪlɪzəm] *n* nécrophilie *f.*
necropolis [neˈkrɒpəlɪs] *n* nécropole *f.*
nectar [ˈnektəʳ] *n* nectar *m.*
nectarine [ˈnektərɪn] *n* (*fruit*) brugnon *m,* nectarine *f*; (*tree*) brugnonnier *m.*
née [neɪ] *adj* née. **Mrs Smith, ~ Jones** Mme Smith, née Jones.
need [ni:d] **1** *n* **(a)** (*U: necessity, obligation*) besoin *m.* **if ~ be** si besoin est, s'il le faut; **in case of ~** en cas de besoin; **there is no ~ for tears** vous n'avez pas besoin de pleurer; **there's no ~ to hurry** on n'a pas besoin de se presser; **no ~ to worry!** pas besoin de s'en faire!*; **no ~ to tell him** pas besoin de lui dire; **there's no ~ for you to come, you have no ~ to come** vous n'êtes pas obligé de venir; **to have no ~ to do sth** ne pas avoir besoin de *or* ne pas être obligé de *or* ne pas avoir à faire qch.
(b) (*U*) (*want, lack*) besoin *m*; (*poverty*) besoin, indigence *f,* dénuement *m,* gêne *f.* **there is much ~ of food** il y a un grand besoin de vivres; **to have ~ of, to be in ~ of** avoir besoin de; **to be badly** *or* **greatly in ~ of** avoir grand besoin de; **I have no ~ of advice** je n'ai pas *or* aucun besoin de conseils; **I'm in ~ of a drink** il me faut à boire; **the house is in ~ of repainting** la maison a besoin d'être repeinte; **those most in ~ of help** ceux qui ont le plus besoin de secours; **to be in ~** être dans le besoin; **his ~ is great** son dénuement est grand; **your ~ is greater than mine** vous êtes plus dans le besoin que moi; (**hum*) vous en avez plus besoin que moi; *V* **serve.**
(c) (*U: misfortune*) adversité *f,* difficulté *f.* **in times of ~** aux heures *or* aux moments difficiles; **do not fail me in my hour of ~** ne m'abandonnez pas dans l'adversité.
(d) (*thing needed*) besoin *m.* **to supply sb's ~s** subvenir aux besoins de qn; **his ~s are few** il a peu de besoins; **give me a list of your ~s** donnez-moi une liste de ce dont vous avez besoin *or* de ce qu'il vous faut; **the greatest ~s of industry** ce dont l'industrie a le plus besoin.
2 *pret, ptp* **needed** *vt* **(a)** (*require*) *[person, thing]* avoir besoin de. **they ~ one another** ils ont besoin l'un de l'autre; **I ~ money** j'ai besoin d'argent, il me faut de l'argent; **I ~ more money** il me faut davantage d'argent; **I ~ it** j'en ai besoin, il me le faut; **do you ~ more time?** avez-vous besoin qu'on vous accorde (*subj*) plus de *or* davantage de temps?; **have you got all that you ~?** vous avez tout ce qu'il vous faut?; **it's just what I ~ed** c'est tout à fait ce qu'il me fallait; **I ~ 2 more to complete the series** il m'en faut encore 2 pour compléter la série; **he ~ed no second invitation** il n'a pas eu besoin qu'on lui répète (*subj*) l'invitation; **the house ~s repainting** *or* **to be repainted** la maison a besoin d'être repeinte; **her hair ~s brushing** *or* **to be brushed** ses cheveux ont besoin d'un coup de brosse; **a visa is ~ed** il faut un visa; **a much ~ed holiday** des vacances dont on a (*or* j'ai *etc*) grand besoin; **I gave it a much ~ed wash** je l'ai lavé, ce dont il avait grand besoin; **it ~ed a war to alter that** il a fallu une guerre pour changer ça; **it** *or* **he doesn't ~ me to tell him** il n'a pas besoin que je le lui dise; **she ~s watching** *or* **to be watched** elle a besoin d'être surveillée; **he ~s to have everything explained to him in detail** il faut tout lui expliquer en détail; **you will hardly ~ to be reminded that ...** vous n'avez sûrement pas besoin qu'on (*or* que je *etc*) vous rappelle (*subj*) que ...; **you only ~ed to ask** tu n'avais qu'à demander; *V* **hole.**
(b) (*demand*) demander, nécessiter, exiger. **this book ~s careful reading** ce livre demande à être lu attentivement *or* nécessite une lecture attentive; **this coat ~s to be cleaned regularly** ce manteau doit être nettoyé régulièrement; **this plant ~s care** cette plante exige qu'on en prenne soin; **the situation ~s detailed consideration** la situation doit être considérée dans le détail; **this will ~ some explaining** il va falloir fournir de sérieuses explications là-dessus; **it shouldn't ~ a famine to make us realize that ...** nous ne devrions pas avoir besoin d'une famine pour nous apercevoir que ... .
3 *pret* **need** (*suivi de l'infin sans 'to'*), **needed** (*suivi de 'to' + infin*) *modal auxiliary vb* (*ne s'emploie qu'à la forme interrogative, négative et avec 'hardly', 'scarcely' etc: les formes du type 'no one needs to do' sont moins littéraires que celles du type 'no one need do'*). **(a)** (*indicating obligation*) **need he go?** a-t-il besoin *or* est-il obligé d'y aller?, faut-il qu'il y aille?; **you needn't wait** vous n'avez pas besoin *or* vous n'êtes pas obligé d'attendre; **you needn't bother to write to me** ce n'est pas la peine *or* ne vous donnez pas la peine de m'écrire; **I told her she needn't reply** *or* **she didn't need to reply** je lui ai dit qu'elle n'était pas obligée *or* forcée de répondre; **we needn't have hurried** ce n'était pas la peine de nous presser; **need I finish the book now?** faut-il que je termine (*subj*) le livre maintenant?; **need we go into all this now?** est-il nécessaire de *or* faut-il discuter de tout cela maintenant?; **I need hardly say that ...** je n'ai guère besoin de dire que ..., inutile de dire que ...; **need I say more?** ai-je besoin d'en dire plus (long)?; **you needn't say any more** inutile d'en dire plus (long); **there need be no questions asked** personne n'aura besoin de poser de questions; **no one need go** *or* **needs to go hungry nowadays** de nos jours personne n'est obligé d'avoir *or* n'est condamné à avoir faim; **why need you always remind me of that?, why do you always need to remind me of that?** pourquoi faut-il toujours que tu me rappelles (*subj*) cela?
(b) (*indicating logical necessity*) **need that be true?** est-ce nécessairement vrai?; **that needn't be the case** ce n'est pas nécessairement *or* forcément le cas; **it need not follow that they are all affected** il ne s'ensuit pas nécessairement *or* forcément qu'ils soient tous affectés.
needful [ˈni:dfʊl] **1** *adj* nécessaire. **to do what is ~** faire ce qui est nécessaire, faire le nécessaire; **as much as is ~** autant qu'il en faut. **2** *n* **(a) to do the ~** * faire ce qu'il faut. **(b)** (*: money*) **the ~** le fric:, les fonds *mpl.*
neediness [ˈni:dɪnɪs] *n* indigence *f,* dénuement *m,* nécessité *f.*
needle [ˈni:dl] **1** *n* **(a)** (*most senses*) aiguille *f.* **knitting/darning** *etc* **~** aiguille à tricoter/à repriser *etc*; **record-player ~** saphir *m* de tourne-disque; **gramophone ~** aiguille de phonographe; (*Bot*) **pine ~** aiguille de pin; (*fig*) **to look for a ~ in a haystack** chercher une aiguille dans une botte de foin; *V* **pin, sharp** *etc.*
(b) he gives me the ~: (*tease*) il me charrie:; (*annoy*) il me tape sur les nerfs* *or* sur le système*; (*Brit*) **to get the ~:** se ficher en boule:.
2 *vt* **(a)** (*) (*annoy*) asticoter, agacer; (*hurt*) piquer *or* toucher au vif; (*nag*) harceler. **she was ~d into replying sharply** touchée au vif *or* agacée elle a répondu avec brusquerie.
(b) (*US*) **to ~ a drink:** corser une boisson.
3 *cpd*: **needle book, needle case** porte-aiguilles *m inv*; **needlecraft** travaux *mpl* d'aiguille; **needlepoint** tapisserie *f* à l'aiguille; (*fig*) **needle sharp** (*alert*) malin (*f* -igne) comme un singe; (*penetrating*) perspicace; **she is a good needlewoman** elle coud bien; **needlework** (*gen*) travaux *mpl* d'aiguille; (*mending etc; also Scol*) couture *f*; **bring your needlework with you** apportez votre ouvrage.
needless [ˈni:dlɪs] *adj expense, inconvenience* inutile, superflu; *action* inutile, qui ne sert à rien; *remark* déplacé. **~ to say it then began to rain** inutile de dire que la pluie s'est mise alors à tomber.
needlessly [ˈni:dlɪslɪ] *adv* inutilement. **you're worrying quite ~** vous vous inquiétez tout à fait inutilement *or* sans raison.
needlessness [ˈni:dlɪsnɪs] *n* inutilité *f*; *[remark]* inopportunité *f.*
needs [ni:dz] *adv* (*ne s'emploie qu'avec 'must'*) absolument, de toute nécessité. **I must ~ leave tomorrow** il me faut absolument partir demain, je dois de toute nécessité partir demain; **if ~ must** s'il le faut absolument, si c'est absolument nécessaire; (*Prov*) **~ must when the devil drives** nécessité fait loi (*Prov*).
needy [ˈni:dɪ] **1** *adj person* nécessiteux, indigent. **in ~ circumstances** dans le besoin, dans l'indigence. **2** *n*: **the ~** les nécessiteux *mpl,* les indigents *mpl.*
ne'er [nɛəʳ] **1** *adv* (*liter*) = **never 1. 2** *cpd*: **ne'er-do-well** (*n*) vaurien(ne) *m(f),* bon(ne) *m(f) or* propre *mf* à rien; (*adj*) bon *or* propre à rien; (*liter*) **ne'ertheless** = **nevertheless.**
nefarious [nɪˈfɛərɪəs] *adj* abominable, infâme, vil (*f* vile) (*liter*).
nefariousness [nɪˈfɛərɪəsnɪs] *n* scélératesse *f.*
negate [nɪˈgeɪt] *vt* (*frm*) (*nullify*) annuler; (*deny truth of*) nier la vérité de; (*deny existence of*) nier (l'existence de). **this ~d all the good that we had achieved** cela a réduit à rien tout le bien que nous avions fait.
negation [nɪˈgeɪʃən] *n* (*all senses*) négation *f.*
negative [ˈnegətɪv] **1** *adj* (*all senses*) négatif.
2 *n* **(a)** réponse négative. **his answer was a curt ~** il a répondu par un non fort sec; **the answer was in the ~** la réponse était négative; **to answer in the ~** répondre négativement *or* par la négative, faire une réponse négative.
(b) (*Gram*) négation *f.* **double ~** double négation; **two ~s make a positive** deux négations équivalent à une affirmation; **put this sentence into the ~** mettez cette phrase à la forme négative.
(c) (*Phot*) négatif *m,* cliché *m.*
(d) (*Elec*) (pôle *m*) négatif *m.*
3 *vt* **(a)** (*veto*) *plan* rejeter, s'opposer à, repousser. **the amendment was ~d** l'amendement fut repoussé.
(b) (*contradict, refute*) *statement* contredire, réfuter.
(c) (*nullify*) *effect* neutraliser.
negatively [ˈnegətɪvlɪ] *adv* négativement.
neglect [nɪˈglekt] **1** *vt child* négliger, laisser à l'abandon, délaisser; *animal, invalid* négliger, ne pas s'occuper de; *one's wife, one's friends* négliger, délaisser; *garden* laisser à l'abandon, ne pas s'occuper de, ne prendre aucun soin de; *house, car, machinery* ne pas s'occuper de, ne prendre aucun soin de; *rule, law* ne tenir aucun compte de, ne faire aucun cas de; *duty, obligation* manquer à, négliger, oublier; *business, work, hobby* négliger, délaisser, se désintéresser de; *opportunity* laisser échapper, négliger; *promise* manquer à, ne pas tenir; *one's health* négliger; *advice* négliger, ne tenir aucun compte de, ne faire aucun cas de. **to ~ o.s., to ~ one's appearance** *or* **person** se négliger; **to ~ to do** négliger *or* omettre de faire; *V also* **neglected.**
2 *n* (*U*) *[person]* manque *m* de soins *or* d'égards *or* d'attention (*of* envers); *[duty, obligation]* manquement *m* (*of* à); *[work]* désintérêt *m* (*of* pour). **~ of one's appearance** manque de soins apportés à son apparence; **his ~ of his promise** son manquement à sa promesse, le fait de ne pas tenir sa promesse; **his ~ of his house/garden/car** le fait qu'il ne s'occupe pas de sa maison/de son jardin/de sa voiture; **the garden was in a state of ~** le jardin était mal tenu *or* était à l'abandon; **children left in utter ~** enfants laissés complètement à l'abandon; **the fire happened through ~** l'incendie est dû à la négligence.
neglected [nɪˈglektɪd] *adj appearance* négligé, peu soigné; *wife, family* abandonné, délaissé; *house* mal tenu; *garden* mal tenu, laissé à l'abandon. **to feel ~** se sentir abandonné *or* délaissé *or* oublié; **this district of the town is very ~** ce quartier de la ville est laissé complètement à l'abandon.

neglectful [nɪ'glektfʊl] *adj* négligent. **to be ~ of** négliger.
neglectfully [nɪ'glektfəlɪ] *adv* avec négligence.
négligé, negligee ['neglɪʒeɪ] *n* négligé *m*, déshabillé *m*.
negligence ['neglɪdʒəns] *n (U)* négligence *f*, manque *m* de soins *or* de précautions. **through ~** par négligence; *(Rel)* **sin of ~** faute *f or* péché *m* d'omission; *V* **contributory**.
negligent ['neglɪdʒənt] *adj* **(a)** *(neglectful)* négligent. **to be ~ of one's duties** être oublieux de *or* négliger ses devoirs; **he was ~ in his work** il négligeait son travail. **(b)** *(offhand) gesture, look* négligent. **with a ~ air** d'un air négligent *or* détaché.
negligently ['neglɪdʒəntlɪ] *adv* **(a)** *(offhandedly)* négligemment, avec insouciance. **(b)** *(neglectfully)* par négligence.
negligible ['neglɪdʒəbl] *adj* négligeable.
negotiable [nɪ'gəʊʃɪəbl] *adj* **(a)** *(Fin)* négociable. **~ securities** fonds *mpl* négociables; **not ~** non négociable. **(b)** *road* praticable; *mountain, obstacle* franchissable; *river (can be sailed)* navigable, *(can be crossed)* franchissable.
negotiate [nɪ'gəʊʃɪeɪt] **1** *vt* **(a)** *sale, loan, settlement* négocier. **(b)** *obstacle, hill* franchir; *river (sail on)* naviguer, *(cross)* franchir, traverser; *rapids, falls* franchir; *bend in road* prendre, négocier; *difficulty* surmonter, franchir.
(c) *bill, cheque, bond* négocier.
2 *vi* négocier, traiter *(with sb for sth* avec qn pour obtenir qch). **they are negotiating with the employers for more pay** ils sont en pourparler(s) *or* ils négocient *or* ils traitent avec les patrons pour obtenir des augmentations.
negotiation [nɪ,gəʊʃɪ'eɪʃən] *n (discussion)* négociation *f*, pourparler *m*. **to begin ~s with** engager *or* entamer des négociations *or* des pourparlers avec; **to be in ~ with** être en pourparler(s) avec; **~s are proceeding** des négociations *or* des pourparlers sont en cours.
negotiator [nɪ'gəʊʃɪeɪtə'] *n* négociateur *m*, -trice *f*.
Negress ['ni:gres] *n* négresse *f*.
Negro ['ni:grəʊ] **1** *adj* nègre; *V* **spiritual**. **2** *n, pl* **~es** nègre *m*.
negroid ['ni:grɔɪd] *adj* négroïde.
neigh [neɪ] **1** *vi* hennir. **2** *n* hennissement *m*.
neighbour, *(US)* **neighbor** ['neɪbə'] **1** *n* voisin(e) *m(f)*; *(Bible etc)* prochain(e) *m(f)*. **she is my ~** c'est ma voisine; **she is a good ~** c'est une bonne voisine; **Britain's nearest ~ is France** la France est la plus proche voisine de la Grande-Bretagne; *V* **next door**.
2 *cpd*: *(US Pol)* **Good Neighbour Policy** politique *f* de bon voisinage.
3 *vi (US)* **to ~ with sb** se montrer bon voisin envers qn.
neighbourhood, *(US)* **neighborhood** ['neɪbəhʊd] *n* **(a)** *(district)* voisinage *m*, quartier *m*; *(area nearby)* voisinage, alentours *mpl*, environs *mpl*. **all the children of the ~** tous les enfants du voisinage; **it's not a nice ~** ce n'est pas un quartier bien; **the whole ~ knows him** tout le voisinage *or* le quartier le connaît; **the soil in this ~ is very rich** la terre de cette région est très riche; **the cinema is in his ~** le cinéma est près de *or* à proximité de chez lui; **in the ~ of the church** aux alentours de *or* aux environs de l'église, dans le voisinage de l'église; **(something) in the ~ of £100** dans les 100 livres, environ 100 livres, à peu près 100 livres; **anyone in the ~ of the crime** toute personne se trouvant dans les parages du crime.
(b) *(U)* voisinage *m*. **good ~** rapports *mpl* de bon voisinage.
neighbouring, *(US)* **neighboring** ['neɪbərɪŋ] *adj* avoisinant, voisin.
neighbourly, *(US)* **neighborly** ['neɪbəlɪ] *adj person* bon voisin, amical, obligeant; *feelings* de bon voisin, amical; *action* de bon voisin. **they are ~ people** ils sont bons voisins; **to behave in a ~ way** agir en bon voisin; **~ relations** rapports *mpl* de bon voisinage.
neighing ['neɪɪŋ] **1** *n* hennissement(s) *m(pl)*. **2** *adj* hennissant.
neither ['naɪðə'] **1** *adv* ni. **~ ... nor** ni ... ni (+ *ne before vb*); **~ you nor I know** ni vous ni moi ne (le) savons; **the book is ~ good nor bad** le livre n'est ni bon ni mauvais; **I've seen ~ him nor her** je n'ai vu ni lui ni elle; **he can ~ read nor write** il ne sait ni lire ni écrire; **he ~ knows nor cares** il ne le sait pas et ne s'en soucie point; *(fig)* **that's ~ here nor there** ce n'est pas la question, cela n'a rien à voir (avec la question).
2 *conj* **(a)** ne ... non plus, (et ...) non plus, ni. **if you don't go, ~ shall I** si tu n'y vas pas je n'irai pas non plus; **I'm not going — ~ am I** je n'y vais pas — (et) moi non plus *or* ni moi *or* ni moi non plus†; **he didn't do it — ~ did his brother** ce n'est pas lui qui l'a fait — son frère non plus *or* ni son frère.
(b) *(liter: moreover ... not)* d'ailleurs ... ne ... pas. **I can't go, ~ do I want to** je ne peux pas y aller et d'ailleurs je ne le veux pas.
3 *adj*: **~ story is true** ni l'une ni l'autre des deux histoires n'est vraie, aucune des deux histoires n'est vraie; **in ~ way** ni d'une manière ni de l'autre; **in ~ case** ni dans un cas ni dans l'autre.
4 *pron* aucun(e) *m(f)*, ni l'un(e) ni l'autre (+ *ne before vb*). **~ of them knows** ni l'un ni l'autre ne le sait, ils ne le savent ni l'un ni l'autre; **I know ~ of them** je ne (les) connais ni l'un ni l'autre; **which (of the two) do you prefer? — ~** lequel (des deux) préférez-vous? — ni l'un ni l'autre.
Nelly ['nelɪ] *n (dim of* **Helen, Ellen***)* Hélène *f*, Éléonore *f*. **not on your ~!‡** jamais de la vie!
nelson ['nelsən] *n (Wrestling)* **full ~** nelson *m*; **half ~** clef *f* du cou; *(fig)* **to put a half ~ on sb*** attraper qn *(pour l'empêcher de faire qch)*.
nemesis ['nemɪsɪs] *n* châtiment *or* sort mérité.
neo... ['ni:əʊ] *pref* néo-. **~classical** néo-classique; **~classicism** néo-classicisme *m*; **~fascism** néo-fascisme *m*; **~fascist** *(adj, n)* néo-fasciste *(mf)*; **~nazi** *(adj, n)* néo-nazi(e) *m(f)*; **~platonic** néo-platonicien; **~platonism** néo-platonisme *m*; **~platonist** *(adj, n)* néo-platonicien(ne) *m(f)*.
neolithic [,ni:əʊ'lɪθɪk] *adj* néolithique. **~ age** âge *m* néolithique *or* de la pierre polie.
neologism [nɪ'ɒlədʒɪzəm] *n*, **neology** [nɪ'ɒlədʒɪ] *n* néologisme *m*.
neon ['ni:ɒn] **1** *n (gaz m)* néon *m*. **2** *cpd lamp, lighting* au néon. **neon sign** enseigne *f* (lumineuse) au néon.
neonatal [ni:əʊ'neɪtl] *adj* néo-natal.
neophyte ['ni:əʊfaɪt] *n* néophyte *mf*.
neoplasm ['ni:əʊplæzəm] *n* néoplasme *m*.
Nepal [nɪ'pɔ:l] *n* Népal *m*.
Nepalese [,nepɔ:'li:z] **1** *adj* népalais. **2** *n* **(a)** *(pl inv)* Népalais(e) *m(f)*. **(b)** *(Ling)* népalais *m*.
nephew ['nevju:, *(esp US)* 'nefju:] *n* neveu *m*.
nephritic [ne'frɪtɪk] *adj* néphrétique.
nephritis [ne'fraɪtɪs] *n* néphrite *f*.
nepotism ['nepətɪzəm] *n* népotisme *m*.
nereid ['nɪərɪɪd] *n (Myth, Zool)* néréide *f*.
Nero ['nɪərəʊ] *n* Néron *m*.
nerve [nɜ:v] **1** *n* **(a)** *(Anat, Dentistry)* nerf *m*; *(Bot)* nervure *f*. **to kill the ~ of a tooth** dévitaliser une dent.
(b) *(fig)* **~s** nerfs *mpl*, nervosité *f*; **her ~s are bad** elle est très nerveuse; **she suffers from ~s** elle a les nerfs fragiles; *(before performance)* **to have a fit** *or* **an attack of ~s** avoir le trac*; **it's only ~s** c'est de la nervosité; **to be all ~s, to be a bundle of ~s** être un paquet de nerfs; **he was in a state of ~s, his ~s were on edge** il était sur les nerfs, il avait les nerfs tendus *or* à vif; **he/that noise gets on my ~s** il/ce bruit me porte *or* me tape sur les nerfs* *or* sur le système*; **to live on one's ~s** vivre sur les nerfs; **to have ~s of steel** *or* **of iron** avoir les nerfs très solides *or* à toute épreuve; **war of ~s** guerre *f* des nerfs; *V* **strain**[1].
(c) *(U: fig) (courage)* courage *m*; *(self-confidence)* assurance *f*, confiance *f* en soi(-même). **it was a test of ~ and stamina** c'était une épreuve de sang-froid et d'endurance; **try to keep your ~** essayez de conserver votre sang-froid; **after the accident he never got his ~ back** *or* **never regained his ~** après l'accident il n'a jamais retrouvé son assurance *or* sa confiance en lui-même; **I haven't the ~ to do that** je n'ai pas le courage *or* le cran* de faire ça *(V also* 1d); **his ~ failed him, he lost his ~** il s'est dégonflé*.
(d) (*: *cheek*) toupet* *m*, culot‡ *m*. **you've got a ~!** tu es gonflé!*, tu as du culot!‡ *or* du toupet!*; **you've got a bloody‡ ~!** tu charries!‡; **what a ~!, of all the ~!, the ~ of it!** quel culot!‡, quel toupet!*, en voilà un culot!‡ *or* un toupet!*; **he had the ~ to say that ...** il a eu le culot‡ *or* le toupet* de dire que ... .
2 *vt*: **to ~ sb to do** donner à qn le courage *or* l'assurance de faire; **to ~ o.s. to do** prendre son courage à deux mains *or* faire appel à son courage pour faire; **I can't ~ myself to do it** je n'ai pas le courage de le faire.
3 *cpd*: **nerve cell** cellule nerveuse; **nerve centre** *(Anat)* centre nerveux; *(fig)* centre *m* d'opérations *(fig)*; **nerve ending** terminaison nerveuse; **nerve gas** gaz asphyxiant; **nerve-racking** éprouvant (pour les nerfs); **nerve specialist** neurologue *mf*.
nerveless ['nɜ:vlɪs] *adj* **(a)** *(Anat)* sans nerfs; *(Bot)* sans nervures. **(fig) it fell from his ~ grasp** sa main, inerte, l'a lâché.
(b) *(fig: calm, collected)* maître *(f* maîtresse) de soi, (plein) de sang-froid.
nervelessness ['nɜ:vlɪsnɪs] *n* *(fig: feebleness)* inertie *f*, manque *m* de vigueur *or* d'énergie; *(calmness)* sang-froid *m*.
nerviness* ['nɜ:vɪnɪs] *n* **(a)** énervement *m*, nervosité *f*. **(b)** *(US: cheek)* culot‡ *m*, toupet* *m*.
nervous ['nɜ:vəs] *adj* **(a)** *(Anat)* nerveux. **(to have a) ~ breakdown** (avoir *or* faire* une) dépression nerveuse; **~ disease** maladie nerveuse; **full of ~ energy** plein de vitalité *or* d'énergie; **~ exhaustion** fatigue nerveuse, *(serious)* surmenage mental; **~ system** système nerveux; **~ tension** tension nerveuse.
(b) *(easily excited)* nerveux, excitable; *(tense)* nerveux, tendu; *(apprehensive)* inquiet *(f* -ète), intimidé, troublé. **in a ~ state** très agité; **to feel ~** se sentir mal à l'aise; *(before performance etc)* avoir le trac*; **he makes me (feel) ~** *(fearful)* il m'intimide; *(tense)* il m'énerve; **I was ~ about him** *or* **on his account** j'avais peur *or* j'étais inquiet pour lui; **I'm rather ~ about diving** j'ai un peu peur de plonger, j'ai une certaine appréhension à plonger; **don't be ~, it'll be all right** n'aie pas peur *or* ne t'inquiète pas, tout se passera bien; **he's a ~ wreck*** il est à bout de nerfs.
nervously ['nɜ:vəslɪ] *adv* *(tensely)* nerveusement; *(apprehensively)* avec inquiétude.
nervousness ['nɜ:vəsnɪs] *n* **(a)** *(excitement)* nervosité *f*, état nerveux, état d'agitation; *(apprehension)* crainte *f*, trac* *m*. **(b)** *[style etc]* nervosité *f*.
nervy* ['nɜ:vɪ] *adj* **(a)** *(Brit: tense)* énervé, irrité. **to be in a ~ state** avoir les nerfs en boule *or* à fleur de peau *or* à vif. **(b)** *(US: cheeky)* effronté, qui a du toupet* *or* du culot‡.
nest [nest] **1** *n* **(a)** *[birds, mice, turtles, ants etc]* nid *m*; *(contents)* nichée *f*. *(lit, fig)* **to leave the ~** quitter le nid; *V* **hornet**.
(b) *(fig)* nid *m*. **~ of brigands/machine guns** nid de brigands/mitrailleuses.
(c) *[boxes etc]* jeu *m*. **~ of tables** table *f* gigogne.
2 *vi* **(a)** *[bird etc]* (se) nicher, faire son nid.
(b) to go (bird) ~ing aller dénicher les oiseaux *or* les œufs.
(c) *[boxes etc]* s'emboîter.
3 *cpd*: *(fig)* **nest egg** pécule *m*; **nesting box** *(for hens)* pondoir *m*; *(for blue tits etc)* nichoir *m*.
nestle ['nesl] *vi* se nicher, se pelotonner, se blottir. **to ~ down in bed** se pelotonner dans son lit; **to ~ up to** *or* **(up) against sb** se serrer *or* se blottir contre qn; **to ~ against sb's shoulder** se blottir contre l'épaule de qn; **a house nestling among the trees** une maison nichée parmi les arbres *or* blottie dans la verdure.

nestling ['neslɪŋ] *n* oisillon *m*.

net[1] [net] **1** *n* **(a)** (*gen, Ftbl, Tennis etc; also fig*) filet *m*. (*fig*) **to walk into the ~** donner *or* tomber dans le panneau; (*fig*) **to be caught in the ~** être pris au piège *or* au filet; **hair~** résille *f*, filet à cheveux; (*Tennis*) **to come up to the ~** monter au filet; (*Ftbl etc*) **the ball's in the ~!** c'est un but!; *V* **butterfly, mosquito, safety** *etc*.

(b) (*U: Tex*) tulle *m*.

2 *vt* **(a)** *fish, game* prendre au filet. (*fig*) **the police ~ted several wanted men** la police a ramassé dans ses filets plusieurs des hommes qu'elle recherchait.

(b) *river* tendre des filets dans; *fruit bushes* poser un filet sur.

(c) (*Sport*) **to ~ the ball** envoyer la balle dans le filet; **to ~ a goal** marquer un but.

(d) (*make out of ~*) faire au filet.

3 *cpd*: (*Brit*) **netball** netball *m*; **net curtains** voilage *m*, (*half-length*) brise-bise *m inv*; **net fishing** pêche *f* au filet; (*Tennis etc*) **net play** jeu *m* au filet; **network** *V* **network**.

net[2] [net] **1** *adj price, income, weight* net. **~ loss** perte sèche; **~ profit** bénéfice net; **the price is £15 ~** le prix est de 15 livres net; **'terms strictly ~'** 'prix nets'. **2** *vt [business deal etc]* rapporter *or* produire net; *[person]* gagner *or* toucher net.

nether ['neðə^r] **1** *adj* († *or liter*) bas (*f* basse), inférieur (*f* -eure). **~ regions, ~ world** enfers *mpl*. **2** *cpd*: **nethermost** le plus bas, le plus profond; **in the nethermost parts of the earth** dans les profondeurs de la terre.

Netherlands ['neðələndz] *npl*: **the ~** les Pays-Bas *mpl*; **in the ~** aux Pays-Bas.

nett [net] = **net**[2].

netting ['netɪŋ] *n* (*U*) **(a)** (*nets*) filets *mpl*; (*mesh*) mailles *fpl*; (*for fence etc*) treillis *m* métallique; (*Tex*) voile *m*, tulle *m* (*pour rideaux*); *V* **mosquito, wire** *etc*.

(b) (*net-making*) fabrication *f* de filets.

(c) (*action*) (*Fishing*) pêche *f* au filet; (*for catching game etc*) pose *f* de filets.

nettle ['netl] **1** *n* (*Bot*) ortie *f*. **stinging ~** ortie brûlante *or* romaine; **dead ~** ortie blanche; (*fig*) **to seize** *or* **grasp the ~** prendre le taureau par les cornes. **2** *vt* (*fig*) agacer, irriter, faire monter la moutarde au nez de. **he was ~d into replying sharply** agacé, il a répondu avec brusquerie. **3** *cpd*: **nettlerash** urticaire *f*; **nettle sting** piqûre *f* d'ortie.

nettlesome ['netlsəm] *adj* (*annoying*) irritant; (*touchy*) susceptible.

network ['netwɜːk] *n* réseau *m*, lacis *m*, enchevêtrement *m*; (*Elec, Rad, TV*) réseau. **rail ~** réseau ferré *or* ferroviaire *or* de chemin de fer; **road ~** réseau *or* système routier; **~ of narrow streets** lacis *or* enchevêtrement de ruelles; **~ of veins** lacis de veines; **~ of spies/contacts/salesmen** réseau d'espions/de contacts/de représentants de commerce; **~ of lies** tissu *m* de mensonges; (*Rad, TV*) **the programme went out over the whole ~** le programme a été diffusé sur l'ensemble du réseau.

neural ['njʊərəl] *adj* neural.

neuralgia [njʊə'rældʒə] *n* névralgie *f*.

neurasthenia [ˌnjʊərəs'θiːnɪə] *n* neurasthénie *f*.

neurasthenic [ˌnjʊərəs'θenɪk] *adj, n* neurasthénique (*mf*).

neuritis [njʊə'raɪtɪs] *n* névrite *f*.

neuro... ['njʊərəʊ] *pref* névro..., neuro... . **~pathology** névropathologie *f*, neuropathologie *f*; **~surgeon** neurochirurgien(ne) *m(f)*; **~surgery** neurochirurgie *f*; **~surgical** neurochirurgique.

neurological [ˌnjʊərə'lɒdʒɪkəl] *adj* neurologique.

neurologist [njʊə'rɒlədʒɪst] *n* neurologue *mf*.

neurology [njʊə'rɒlədʒɪ] *n* neurologie *f*.

neuron ['njʊərɒn] *n* neurone *m*.

neuropath ['njʊərəpæθ] *n* névropathe *mf*.

neuropathic [njʊərə'pæθɪk] *adj* névropathique.

neurosis [njʊə'rəʊsɪs] *n, pl* **neuroses** [njʊə'rəʊsiːz] névrose *f*.

neurotic [njʊə'rɒtɪk] **1** *adj person* névrosé; *disease, disturbance* névrotique. (*fig*) **she's getting quite ~ about slimming** son désir de maigrir prend des proportions de névrose; **she's getting ~ about the whole business** elle fait une véritable maladie de toute cette histoire.

2 *n* névrosé(e) *m(f)*, névropathe *mf*, neurasthénique *mf*.

neuter ['njuːtə^r] **1** *adj* **(a)** neutre. **(b)** (*Bot, Zool*) neutre; (*Zool: castrated*) châtré. **2** *n* **(a)** (*Gram*) neutre *m*. **in the ~** au neutre. **(b)** (*Zool*) animal châtré. **3** *vt* (*Vet*) châtrer.

neutral ['njuːtrəl] **1** *adj* (*all senses*) neutre. **to remain ~** garder la neutralité, rester neutre; (*Pol*) **the ~ powers** les puissances *fpl* neutres; **~ policy** politique *f* neutraliste *or* de neutralité.

2 *n* **(a)** (*Pol*) habitant(e) *m(f)* d'un pays neutre.

(b) (*Aut*) point mort. **to put the gear in ~** mettre l'embrayage au point mort; **the car** *or* **the engine was in ~** la voiture était au point mort.

neutralism ['njuːtrəlɪzəm] *n* neutralisme *m*.

neutralist ['njuːtrəlɪst] *adj, n* neutraliste (*mf*).

neutrality [njuː'trælɪtɪ] *n* (*gen, Chem, Pol etc*) neutralité *f*; *V* **armed**.

neutralization [ˌnjuːtrəlaɪ'zeɪʃən] *n* neutralisation *f*.

neutralize ['njuːtrəlaɪz] *vt* neutraliser.

neutron ['njuːtrɒn] *n* neutron *m*. **~ bomb** bombe *f* à neutrons; **~ number** nombre *m* de neutrons.

never ['nevə^r] **1** *adv* **(a)** (ne ...) jamais. **I ~ eat it** je n'en mange jamais; **I have ~ seen him** je ne l'ai jamais vu; **I've ~ seen him before** je ne l'ai jamais vu (jusqu'à aujourd'hui); **I'd ~ seen him before** je ne l'avais jamais vu auparavant; **~ before had there been such a disaster** jamais on n'avait connu tel désastre; **he will ~ come back** il ne reviendra jamais *or* plus (jamais); **~ again!** jamais plus!, plus jamais!; **~ say that again** ne répète jamais ça; **we shall ~ see her again** on ne la reverra (plus) jamais; **I have ~ yet been able to find ...** je n'ai encore jamais pu trouver ..., jusqu'ici je n'ai jamais pu trouver ...; **~ in all my life** jamais de ma vie; **I ~ heard such a thing!** (de ma vie) je n'ai jamais entendu une telle histoire!; *V* **now**.

(b) (*emphatic* = *not*) **that will ~ do!** c'est inadmissible!; **I ~ slept a wink** je n'ai pas fermé l'œil; **he ~ so much as smiled** il n'a pas même souri; **he ~ said a word**, (*liter*) **he said ~ a word** il n'a pas dit le moindre mot, il n'a pas soufflé mot; **~ a one** pas un seul; **~ was a child more loved** jamais enfant ne fut plus aimé; **(surely) you've ~ left it behind!*** ne me dites pas que vous l'avez oublié!; **I've left it behind! — ~!** je l'ai oublié! — ça n'est pas vrai! *or* pas possible!; **well I ~ (did)!*** (ça) par exemple!, pas possible!, mince alors!*; **~ mind!** ça ne fait rien!, ne vous en faites pas!; **~ fear!** n'ayez pas peur!, soyez tranquille!

2 *cpd*: **never-ending** qui n'en finit plus, sans fin, interminable; **never-failing** *method* infaillible; *source, spring* inépuisable, intarissable; **nevermore** ne ... plus jamais, ne ... jamais plus; **nevermore!** jamais plus!, plus jamais!; (*Brit*) **to buy on the never-never*** acheter à crédit *or* à tempérament; **never-never land** pays *m* imaginaire *or* de légende *or* de cocagne; **nevertheless** *V* **nevertheless**; **never-to-be-forgotten** inoubliable, qu'on n'oubliera jamais.

nevertheless [ˌnevəðə'les] *adv* néanmoins, toutefois, quand même, (et) pourtant, cependant, malgré tout. **it is ~ true that ...** il est néanmoins *or* toutefois *or* quand même *or* pourtant *or* cependant *or* malgré tout vrai que ...; **I shall go ~** j'irai quand même *or* malgré tout, et pourtant j'irai; **he is ~ my brother** c'est quand même mon frère, malgré tout c'est mon frère; **she has had no news, (yet) ~ she goes on hoping** elle n'a pas reçu de nouvelles, et pourtant *or* et malgré tout elle continue à espérer.

new [njuː] **1** *adj* **(a)** (*not previously known etc*) nouveau (*before vowel* nouvel, *f* nouvelle); (*brand-new*) neuf (*f* neuve); (*different*) nouveau, autre. **I've got a ~ car** (*different*) j'ai une nouvelle *or* une autre voiture; (*brand-new*) j'ai une voiture neuve; **he has written a ~ book/article** il a écrit un nouveau livre/un nouvel article; **this is X's ~ book** c'est le nouveau *or* dernier livre de X; **I've got a ~ library book** j'ai emprunté un nouveau livre à la bibliothèque; **~ potatoes** pommes (de terre) nouvelles; **~ carrots** carottes *fpl* de primeur *or* nouvelles; **there are several ~ plays on in London** on donne plusieurs nouvelles pièces à Londres; **~ fashion** dernière *or* nouvelle mode; **~ theory/invention** nouvelle théorie/invention; **the ~ moon** la nouvelle lune; **there's a ~ moon tonight** c'est la nouvelle lune ce soir; **to break ~ ground** (*Agr*) défricher une terre, mettre en culture un terrain vierge; (*fig*) innover, faire œuvre de pionnier; **I need a ~ notebook** il me faut un nouveau carnet *or* un carnet neuf; **don't get your ~ shoes wet** ne mouille pas tes chaussures neuves; **dressed in ~ clothes** vêtu *or* habillé de neuf; **as good as ~** comme neuf, à l'état de neuf; **he made the bike as good as ~** il a remis le vélo à neuf; **'as ~'** 'état neuf'; **I don't like all these ~ paintings** je n'aime pas tous ces tableaux modernes; **I've got several ~ ideas** j'ai plusieurs idées nouvelles *or* neuves; **this idea is not ~** ce n'est pas une idée nouvelle *or* neuve; **the ~ nations** les pays neufs; **a ~ town** une ville nouvelle; **this is a completely ~ subject** c'est un sujet tout à fait neuf; **this sort of work is ~ to me** ce genre de travail est (quelque chose de) nouveau pour moi; **I'm ~ to this kind of work** je n'ai jamais fait ce genre de travail, je suis novice dans ce genre de travail; **he came ~ to the firm last year** il est arrivé dans la compagnie l'an dernier; **he's ~ to the trade** il est nouveau *or* novice dans le métier; **he's quite ~ to the town** il est tout nouvellement arrivé dans la ville; **the ~ people at number 5** les nouveaux habitants du *or* au 5; **~ recruit** nouvelle recrue, bleu* *m*; **the ~ students** les nouveaux *mpl*, les nouvelles *fpl*; (*Scol*) **a ~ boy** un nouveau; (*Scol*) **a ~ girl** une nouvelle; **she's ~, poor thing** elle est nouvelle, la pauvre; **are you ~ here?** (*gen*) vous venez d'arriver ici?; (*in school, firm etc*) vous êtes nouveau ici?; **the ~ woman** la femme moderne; **the ~ diplomacy** la diplomatie moderne *or* nouvelle manière; **~ style** nouveau style (*V also* 3); **the ~ rich** les nouveaux riches; **bring me a ~ glass for this one is dirty** apportez-moi un autre verre car celui-ci est sale; **there was a ~ waiter today** il y avait un autre *or* un nouveau serveur aujourd'hui; (*fig*) **he's a ~ man since he remarried** il est transformé depuis qu'il s'est remarié; (*Prov*) **there's nothing ~ under the sun** il n'y a rien de nouveau sous le soleil (*Prov*); **that's nothing ~!** ce *or* ça n'est pas nouveau!, il n'y a rien de neuf là-dedans!; **that's a ~ one on me!*** première nouvelle!*; on en apprend tous les jours! (*iro*); **that's something ~!** ça c'est nouveau!; **what's ~?*** quoi de neuf?; *V* **brand, broom, leaf, split** *etc*.

(b) (*fresh*) *bread* frais (*f* fraîche); *milk* frais, fraîchement trait; *cheese* frais, pas (encore) fait; *wine* nouveau (*f* nouvelle), jeune.

2 *adv* (*gen in cpds*) nouvellement, récemment. **he's ~ out of college** il est frais émoulu du collège, il sort tout juste du collège; *V* 3.

3 *cpd*: **newborn** nouveau-né(e) *m(f)*; **new-built** nouvellement construit, tout neuf (*f* toute neuve); **New Canadian** Néo-Canadien(ne) *m(f)*; **newcomer** nouveau venu *m*, nouvelle venue *f*, nouvel(le) arrivé(e) *m(f)*, nouvel(le) arrivant(e) *m(f)*; **they are newcomers to this town** ce sont des nouveaux venus dans cette ville; **New Delhi** New Delhi; **New England** Nouvelle-Angleterre *f*; (*pej*) **new-fangled** trop moderne, nouveau genre; **new-found** tout neuf (*f* toute neuve); **Newfoundland** *V* **Newfoundland**; **New Guinea** Nouvelle-Guinée *f*; **New Hebrides** Nouvelles-Hébrides *fpl*; **new-laid egg** œuf *m* du jour *or* tout frais (pondu); **new look** new-look *m*; **new-look** (*adj*) new-look *inv*; **New Mexico** Nouveau-Mexique *m*; **new-mown** *grass* frais coupé; *hay* frais fauché; **New Orleans** la Nouvelle-Orléans; **New South Wales** Nouvelle-Galles *f* du Sud; **the**

new(-style) calendar le nouveau calendrier, le calendrier grégorien; **New Testament** Nouveau Testament; **the New World** le Nouveau Monde; **New Year** *V* **New Year**; **New York** (*n*) New York *m*; (*adj*) new-yorkais; **New Yorker** New-Yorkais(e) *m(f)*; **New Zealand** (*n*) Nouvelle-Zélande *f*; (*adj*) néo-zélandais; **New Zealander** Néo-Zélandais(e) *m(f)*.

newel ['nju:əl] *n* noyau *m* (d'escalier).

Newfoundland ['nju:fəndlənd] **1** *n* Terre-Neuve *f*. **2** *adj* terre-neuvien. **~ dog** chien *m* de Terre-Neuve, terre-neuve *m inv*; **~ fisherman** terre-neuvas *m*.

Newfoundlander [nju:'faʊndləndəʳ] *n* habitant(e) *m(f)* de Terre-Neuve, Terre-Neuvien(ne) *m(f)*.

newish ['nju:ɪʃ] *adj* assez neuf (*f* neuve), assez nouveau (*f* nouvelle).

newly ['nju:lɪ] **1** *adv* nouvellement, récemment, fraîchement. **~ arrived** nouvellement *or* récemment *or* fraîchement arrivé; **~ shaved** rasé de frais; **the ~-elected members** les membres nouvellement élus, les nouveaux élus; **~-formed friendship** amitié *f* de fraîche date; **~-found happiness** bonheur tout neuf; **her ~-awakened curiosity** sa curiosité récemment éveillée; **~ rich** nouveau riche; **~ made** neuf (*f* neuve), nouveau (*f* nouvelle), de fabrication toute récente; **a ~-dug grave** une tombe fraîchement creusée *or* ouverte.

2 *cpd*: **the newly-weds** les jeunes *or* les nouveaux mariés.

newness ['nju:nɪs] *n* [*fashion, ideas etc*] nouveauté *f*; [*clothes etc*] état *m* (de) neuf; [*person*] inexpérience *f*; [*bread*] fraîcheur *f*; [*cheese*] manque *m* de maturité; [*wine*] jeunesse *f*.

news [nju:z] **1** *n* (*U*) **(a)** nouvelle(s) *f(pl)*. **a piece** *or* **an item of ~** (*gen*) une nouvelle; (*Press*) une information; **have you heard the ~?** vous connaissez la nouvelle?; **have you heard the ~ about John?** vous savez ce qui est arrivé à Jean?; **have you any ~ of him?** avez-vous de ses nouvelles?; **I have no ~ of her** je n'ai pas de ses nouvelles, je n'ai pas de nouvelles d'elle; **do let me have your ~** surtout donnez-moi de vos nouvelles; **what's your ~?** quoi de neuf *or* de nouveau (chez vous)?; **is there any ~?** y a-t-il du nouveau?; **I've got ~ for you!** j'ai du nouveau à vous annoncer!; **this is ~ to me!** première nouvelle!*, on en apprend tous les jours! (*iro*); **it will be ~ to him that we are here** ça va le surprendre d'apprendre que nous sommes ici; **good ~** bonnes nouvelles; **bad** *or* **sad ~** tristes nouvelles; (*loc*) **bad ~ travels fast** les malheurs s'apprennent vite; **no ~ is good ~!** pas de nouvelles, bonnes nouvelles! (*loc*); **when the ~ broke** quand on a su la nouvelle; **'dog bites man' isn't ~** 'un homme mordu par un chien' n'est pas (ce qu'on peut appeler) une nouvelle; **to make ~** faire parler de soi; (*fig*) **he's in the ~ again** le voilà qui refait parler de lui; *V* **break**.

(b) (*Press, Rad, TV*) informations *fpl*; (*Cine, TV*) actualités *fpl*. **I missed the ~ (broadcast** *or* **bulletin)** j'ai raté les informations *or* le bulletin d'informations *or* les actualités; **official ~** communiqué officiel; **financial/sporting** *etc* **~** chronique *or* rubrique financière/sportive *etc*; (*Press*) **'N~ in Brief'** 'Nouvelles brèves'; (*name of paper*) **'Birmingham N~'** 'Nouvelles de Birmingham'.

2 *cpd*: **news agency** agence *f* de presse; (*esp Brit*) **newsagent** marchand(e) *m(f)* de *or* dépositaire *mf* de journaux; **newsboy** vendeur *m or* crieur *m* de journaux; **news bulletin**, (*US*) **newscast** (*Rad*) (bulletin *m* d')informations *fpl*; (*TV*) actualités *fpl* (télévisées); (*Rad, TV*) **newscaster** = **newsreader**; (*US*) **newsdealer** = **newsagent**; **news editor** rédacteur *m*; **news film** film *m* d'actualités; **news flash** flash *m* (d'information); **newshawk** = **newshound**; **news headlines** titres *mpl* de l'actualité; **newshound** reporter *m*; (*pej*) **there was a crowd of newshounds around him** il y avait une meute de journalistes acharnés après lui; (*Press etc*) **news item** information *f*; **newsletter** bulletin *m* (*de société, de compagnie etc*); **newsman** journaliste *m*; (*pej*) **newsmonger** colporteur *m*, -euse *f* de ragots *or* de potins; **newspaper** *V* **newspaper**; **news pictures** reportage *m* photographique; (*U*) **newsprint** papier *m* de journal, papier journal; (*Rad, TV*) **newsreader** speaker(ine) *m(f)*; **newsreel** actualités *fpl* (filmées); **newsroom** (*Press*) salles *fpl* de rédaction; (*Rad, TV*) studio *m*; **news sheet** feuille *f* d'informations; **news stand** kiosque *m* (à journaux); **news theatre** cinéma *m or* salle *f* d'actualités; **to have news value = to be newsworthy**; **newsvendor** vendeur *m* de journaux; **to be newsworthy** présenter un intérêt pour le public.

newspaper ['nju:sˌpeɪpəʳ] **1** *n* journal *m*; (*minor*) feuille *f*. **daily ~** (journal) quotidien *m*; **weekly ~** (journal) hebdomadaire *m*; **he works on a ~** il travaille pour un journal.

2 *cpd*: **newspaper clippings, newspaper cuttings** coupures *fpl* de journaux *or* de presse; **newspaperman** journaliste *m*; **newspaper office** (bureaux *mpl* de la) rédaction *f*; **newspaper photographer** reporter *m* photographe; **newspaper report** reportage *m*.

newsy* ['nju:zɪ] *adj* plein de nouvelles.

newt [nju:t] *n* triton *m*.

New Year ['nju:'jɪəʳ] **1** *n* nouvel an, nouvelle année. **to bring in** *or* **see in the ~** faire le réveillon (de la Saint-Sylvestre *or* du jour de l'an), réveillonner (à la Saint-Sylvestre); **Happy ~!** bonne année!; **to wish sb a happy ~** souhaiter une *or* la bonne année à qn.

2 *cpd*: **New Year gift** étrennes *fpl*; **New Year resolution** résolution *f* de nouvel an; **New Year's Day** jour *m or* premier *m* de l'an, nouvel an; **New Year's Eve** la Saint-Sylvestre; *V* **honour**.

next [nekst] **1** *adj* **(a)** (*of place*) prochain, le (*or* la) plus proche, voisin, (d')à côté. **the ~ room** la pièce voisine *or* (d')à côté; **~ to** à côté de, contigu (*f* -guë) à, attenant à, jouxtant.

(b) (*of time*) (*in future*) prochain; (*in past*) suivant. **come back ~ week/month** revenez la semaine prochaine/le mois prochain; **he came back the ~ week** il revint la semaine suivante *or* d'après; **he came back the ~ day** il revint le lendemain *or* le jour suivant *or* le jour d'après; **the ~ day but one** le surlendemain; **during the ~ 5 days he did not go out** il n'est pas sorti pendant les 5 jours suivants *or* qui ont suivi; **I will finish this in the ~ 5 days** je finirai ceci dans les 5 jours qui viennent *or* à venir; **the ~ morning** le lendemain matin; **(the) ~ time I see him** la prochaine fois que je le verrai; **the ~ time I saw him** la première fois où *or* que je l'ai revu, quand je l'ai revu; **I'll come back ~ week and the ~ again** je reviendrai la semaine prochaine et la suivante; **this time ~ week** d'ici huit jours; **the ~ moment** l'instant d'après; **from one moment to the ~** d'un moment à l'autre; **the year after ~** dans deux ans.

(c) (*of order*) **who's ~?** à qui le tour?, c'est à qui?; **you're ~** c'est votre tour, c'est à vous (maintenant); **~ please!** au suivant!; **I come ~ after you** je viens après vous, je vous suis (immédiatement); **I was the ~ person** *or* **I was ~ to speak** ce fut ensuite à mon tour de parler (*V also* 4a); **I'll ask the very ~ person I see** je vais demander à la première personne que je verrai; **in the ~ place** ensuite; **on the ~ page** à la page suivante; **'continued in the ~ column'** 'voir colonne ci-contre'; **the ~ thing to do is ...** la première chose à faire maintenant est de ...; **he saw that the ~ thing to do was ...** il vit que ce qu'il devait faire ensuite (c')était ...; **I'll try the ~ size** je vais essayer la taille au-dessus.

2 *adv* **(a)** ensuite, après; la prochaine fois. **~ we had lunch** ensuite *or* après nous avons déjeuné; **what shall we do ~?** qu'allons-nous faire maintenant?; **when ~ you come to see us** la prochaine fois que vous viendrez nous voir; **when I ~ saw him** quand je l'ai revu (la fois suivante); **when shall we meet ~?** quand nous reverrons-nous?; **a new dress! what ~?** une nouvelle robe! et puis quoi encore?

(b) the ~ best thing would be to speak to his brother à défaut le mieux serait de parler à son frère; **she's my ~ best friend** à part une autre c'est ma meilleure amie; **this is my ~ oldest daughter after Mary** c'est la plus âgée de mes filles après Marie; **she's the ~ youngest** elle suit (par ordre d'âge); **who's the ~ tallest boy?** quel est le plus grand après?

(c) ~ to (*beside*) auprès de, à côté de; (*almost*) presque; **his room is ~ (to) mine** sa chambre est à côté de *or* contiguë à *or* attenante à la mienne; **the church stands ~ (to) the school** l'église est à côté de l'école; **he was sitting ~ (to) me** il était assis à côté de moi *or* auprès de moi; **to wear wool ~ (to) the skin** porter de la laine sur la peau *or* à même la peau; **the thing ~ (to) my heart** la chose qui me tient le plus à cœur; (*US*) **to get ~ to sb‡** se mettre bien* avec qn; **the ~ to last row** l'avant-dernier *or* le pénultième rang; **he was ~ to last** il était avant-dernier; **~ to nothing** presque rien; **I got it for ~ to nothing** je l'ai payé trois fois rien; **~ to nobody** presque personne; **there's ~ to no news** il n'y a presque rien de neuf; **the ~ to top/bottom shelf** le deuxième rayon (en partant) du haut/du bas.

3 *prep* (*Brit*) près de, auprès de, à côté de; *V* **2c**.

4 *n* **(a)** prochain(e) *m(f)*. **the ~ to speak is John** c'est Jean qui parle ensuite, c'est Jean qui est le prochain à parler; **the ~ to arrive was Robert** c'est Robert qui est arrivé ensuite *or* le suivant; **I hope my ~ will be a boy** j'espère que mon prochain (enfant) sera un garçon.

(b) to be continued in our ~ suite au prochain numéro.

5 *cpd*: **next door** *V* **next door**; (*on forms etc*) **'next-of-kin'** 'nom et prénom de votre plus proche parent'; **who is your next-of-kin?** qui est votre plus proche parent?; **the police will inform the next-of-kin** la police préviendra la famille.

next door ['neks'dɔ:ʳ] **1** *n* la maison d'à côté. **it's the man from ~** c'est le monsieur d'à côté *or* qui habite à côté.

2 *adv* **(a) they live ~ to us** ils habitent à côté de chez nous, ils habitent la maison voisine (de la nôtre); **we live ~ to each other** nous habitons porte à porte; **the boy/girl ~** le garçon/la fille d'à côté *or* qui habite à côté; **despite her wealth she's just like the girl ~** malgré sa fortune elle est restée très simple; **the people/house ~** les gens/la maison d'à côté.

(b) (*fig*) **that is ~ to madness** cela frise la folie; **if he isn't mad he's ~ to it** s'il n'est pas fou il s'en faut de peu *or* c'est tout comme*; **we were ~ to being ruined** nous avons été au bord de la ruine, nous avons frôlé la ruine.

3 next-door *cpd*: **next-door house** maison voisine *or* d'à côté; **next-door neighbour** voisin(e) *m(f)* (d'à côté).

nexus ['neksəs] *n* connection *f*, liaison *f*, lien *m*.

Niagara [naɪ'ægrə] *n* Niagara *m*. **~ Falls** les chutes *fpl* du Niagara.

nib [nɪb] *n* **(a)** [*pen*] (bec *m* de) plume *f*. **fine ~** plume fine *or* à bec fin; **broad ~** grosse plume, plume à gros bec. **(b)** [*tool*] pointe *f*.

-nibbed [nɪbd] *adj ending in cpds*: **fine-nibbed** à plume fine; **gold-nibbed** à plume en or.

nibble ['nɪbl] **1** *vti* (*gen*) grignoter, mordiller; [*sheep, goats etc*] brouter; [*fish*] toucher, mordiller l'èche. (*fig*) **to ~ (at) an offer** se montrer tenté par une offre; **to ~ (at) one's food** chipoter; **she was nibbling (at) some chocolate** elle grignotait un morceau de chocolat.

2 *n* **(a)** (*Fishing*) touche *f*.

(b) (**:**) **I feel like a ~** je grignoterais bien quelque chose.

nibs [nɪbz] *n* (*hum*) **his ~‡** Son Altesse (*iro*).

Nicaragua [ˌnɪkə'rægjʊə] *n* Nicaragua *m*.

Nicaraguan [ˌnɪkə'rægjʊən] **1** *adj* nicaraguayen. **2** *n* Nicaraguayen(ne) *m(f)*.

nice [naɪs] **1** *adj* **(a)** (*pleasant*) *person* agréable, aimable, gentil, charmant, sympathique; *holiday, weather* beau (*f* belle), agréable; *dress, smile, voice* joli, charmant; *view, visit* charmant, agréable; *meal* bon, délicieux; *smell, taste* bon, agréable; (*iro*) joli, beau. **that's a ~ ring/photo** elle est jolie *or* belle, cette bague/photo; **what a ~ face she's got** quel joli *or* charmant visage elle a; **how ~ you look!** vous êtes vraiment bien!; **Barcombe's a ~ place** Barcombe est un joli coin *or* un coin agréable; **be ~ to him** soyez gentil *or* aimable avec lui; **that wasn't ~ of you** vous n'avez pas été gentil *or* aimable; **we had a ~ evening** nous avons passé une bonne soirée *or* une soirée agréable; **they had a ~ time** ils se sont bien amusés; **to say ~ things** dire des choses aimables *or* gentilles, dire des gentillesses; **how ~ of you to ...** comme c'est gentil *or* aimable à vous de ...; **it's ~ here** on est bien ici; (*iro*) **here's a ~ state of affairs!** (eh bien) voilà du joli!; (*iro*) **you're in a ~ mess** vous voilà dans un beau *or* joli pétrin, vous voilà dans de beaux *or* jolis draps; (*iro*) **that's a ~ way to talk!** c'est du joli ce que vous dites là!

(b) (*intensive*) **~ and warm** bien chaud; **~ and easy** très facile, tout à fait facile; **~ and sweet** bien sucré; **to have a ~ cold drink** boire quelque chose de bien frais; **he gets ~ long holidays** ce qui est bien c'est qu'il a de longues vacances.

(c) (*respectable, refined*) convenable, bien *inv*, comme il faut. **not ~** peu convenable, pas beau* (*f* belle); **she's a ~ girl** c'est une jeune fille (très) bien *or* très comme il faut*; **our neighbours are not very ~ people** nos voisins ne sont pas des gens très bien; **the play/film/book was not very ~** la pièce/le film/le livre n'était pas très convenable.

(d) (*hard to please*) *person* difficile, méticuleux; (*tricky*) *job, task* délicat; (*subtle*) *distinction, shade of meaning* délicat, subtil (*f* subtile). **she's not very ~ in her methods** elle n'a pas beaucoup de scrupules quant à ses méthodes; **to be ~ about one's food** être difficile *or* exigeant pour *or* sur la nourriture; **~ point** point délicat, question délicate *or* subtile; **he has a ~ taste in ...** il a un goût fin *or* raffiné en... .

2 *cpd*: **nice-looking** joli, beau (*f* belle); **he's nice-looking** il est joli garçon *or* beau garçon.

nicely ['naɪslɪ] *adv* **(a)** (*kindly*) gentiment, aimablement; (*pleasantly*) agréablement, joliment, bien. **a ~ situated house** une maison bien *or* agréablement située; **we are ~ placed to judge what has been going on** nous sommes parfaitement bien placés pour juger de ce qui s'est passé; **~ done** bien fait; **that will do ~** cela fera très bien l'affaire; **~, thank you** très bien merci; **the child behaved very ~** l'enfant s'est très bien conduit *or* a été très gentil.

(b) (*carefully*) minutieusement; (*exactly*) exactement.

niceness ['naɪsnɪs] *n* **(a)** (*pleasantness*) *[person]* gentillesse *f*, amabilité *f*; *[place, thing]* agrément *m*, caractère *m* agréable.

(b) (*fastidiousness*) délicatesse *f*; (*punctiliousness*) caractère *or* côté méticuleux; *[distinction, taste etc]* subtilité *f*, finesse *f*; *[experiment, point etc]* délicatesse.

nicety ['naɪsɪtɪ] *n* **(a)** (*of one's judgment*) exactitude *f*, justesse *f*, précision *f*. **a point of great ~** une question très délicate *or* subtile; **to a ~** à la perfection, exactement, à point. **(b) niceties** (*subtleties*) finesses *fpl*; (*refinements*) raffinements *mpl*.

niche [niːʃ] *n* (*Archit*) niche *f*. (*fig*) **he found his ~ (in life)** il a trouvé sa voie (dans la vie).

Nicholas ['nɪkələs] *n* Nicolas *m*.

Nick [nɪk] *n* (*dim of* **Nicholas**) **Old ~** le diable, le malin.

nick [nɪk] **1** *n* **(a)** (*in wood*) encoche *f*; (*in blade, dish*) brèche *f*; (*on face, skin*) entaille *f*, coupure *f*. (*fig*) **in the ~ of time** juste à temps.

(b) (*Brit: Prison etc sl*) taule‡ *f or* tôle‡ *f*. **to be in the ~** être en taule‡, faire de la taule‡.

(c) (*Brit*) **in good ~‡** en bonne condition, impec‡.

2 *vt* **(a)** *plank, stick* entailler, faire une *or* des encoche(s) sur; *blade, dish* ébrécher; *cards* biseauter. **he ~ed his chin while shaving** il s'est fait une entaille *or* une coupure au menton en se rasant.

(b) (*Brit‡: arrest*) pincer‡, choper‡. **to get ~ed** se faire pincer‡ *or* choper‡.

(c) (*Brit‡: steal*) piquer‡, faucher‡, barboter‡.

(d) (*US*) **how much did they ~ you for that suit?‡** tu t'es fait avoir* de combien pour *or* sur ce costume?

nickel ['nɪkl] **1** *n* **(a)** (*U*) nickel *m*. **(b)** (*Can, US*) pièce *f* de cinq cents. **2** *cpd*: (*US*) **nickel-in-the-slot machine** appareil *m* à sous; **nickel-plated** nickelé; **nickel silver** argentan *m*, maillechort *m*. **3** *vt* nickeler.

nicker‡ ['nɪkəʳ] *n, pl inv* (*Brit*) livre *f* (sterling).

nickname ['nɪkneɪm] **1** *n* surnom *m*; (*esp humorous or malicious*) sobriquet *m*; (*short form of name*) diminutif *m*.

2 *vt* surnommer, donner un sobriquet à. **John, ~d 'Taffy'** John, surnommé 'Taffy'; **they ~d their teacher 'Goggles'** ils ont surnommé leur professeur 'Carreaux'; ils ont donné à leur professeur le sobriquet (de) 'Carreaux'.

nicotine ['nɪkətiːn] **1** *n* nicotine *f*. **2** *cpd*: **nicotine poisoning** nicotinisme *m*; **nicotine-stained** jauni *or* taché de nicotine.

niece [niːs] *n* nièce *f*.

niff‡ [nɪf] *n* (*Brit*) puanteur *f*. **what a ~!** ce que ça cocotte!‡ *or* schlingue!‡

niffy‡ ['nɪfɪ] *adj* (*Brit*) puant. **it's ~ in here** ça pue *or* cocotte‡ ici!

nifty‡ ['nɪftɪ] *adj* (*stylish*) coquet, pimpant, chic *inv*; (*clever*) dégourdi, débrouillard; (*skilful*) habile. **that's a ~ car** voilà une (petite) voiture qui a de la classe; **that was a ~ piece of work** ça a été vite fait; **you'd better be ~ about it!** il faudrait faire vite!

Niger ['naɪdʒəʳ] *n* Niger *m*.

Nigeria [naɪ'dʒɪərɪə] *n* Nigéria *m or f*.

Nigerian [naɪ'dʒɪərɪən] **1** *adj* nigérien. **2** *n* Nigérien(ne) *m(f)*.

niggardliness ['nɪgədlɪnɪs] *n* avarice *f*, pingrerie *f*.

niggardly ['nɪgədlɪ] **1** *adj person* chiche, pingre, avare; *amount, portion* mesquin, piètre. **2** *adv* chichement, mesquinement, parcimonieusement.

nigger ['nɪgəʳ] **1** *n* (∵ *pej: Negro*) nègre *m*, négresse *f*. (*Brit fig*) **there's a ~ in the woodpile** il se trame quelque chose, il y a anguille sous roche; (*Brit fig*) **to be the ~ in the woodpile** faire le trouble-fête. **2** *cpd*: (*Brit*) **nigger brown** tête de nègre *inv*.

niggle ['nɪgl] **1** *vi [person]* tatillonner, couper les cheveux en quatre. **2** *vt*: **his conscience was niggling him** sa conscience le travaillait*.

niggling ['nɪglɪŋ] **1** *adj person* tatillon; *details* insignifiant. **a ~ doubt** un petit doute insinuant; **a ~ little pain** une petite douleur persistante. **2** *n* (*U*) chicanerie *f*.

nigh [naɪ] *adj, adv, prep* (*liter*) = **near 1, 2, 3.**

night [naɪt] **1** *n* **(a)** nuit *f*; soir *m*. **at ~, in the ~** la nuit; **by ~, in the ~** de nuit; **last ~** hier soir, la nuit dernière, cette nuit; **tomorrow ~** demain soir; **the ~ before** la veille au soir; **the ~ before last** avant-hier soir; **in the ~, during the ~** pendant la nuit; **Monday ~** lundi soir, la nuit de lundi à mardi; **6 o'clock at ~** 6 heures du soir; **far into the ~** jusqu'à une heure avancée de la nuit, (très) tard dans la nuit; **to spend the ~** passer la nuit; **to have a good/bad ~** bien/mal dormir, passer une bonne/mauvaise nuit; **I've had several bad ~s in a row** j'ai mal dormi plusieurs nuits de suite; **~ and day** nuit et jour; **~ after ~** des nuits durant; **all ~ (long)** toute la nuit; **to sit up all ~ talking** passer la nuit (entière) à bavarder; **to have a ~ out** sortir le soir; **the maid's ~ out** le soir de sortie de la bonne; **let's make a ~ of it** (*gen*) autant y passer la soirée *or* nuit; (*in entertainment etc*) il est trop tôt pour aller se coucher; **he's working ~s** *or* **he's on ~s this week** il est de nuit cette semaine; **I've had too many late ~s** je me suis couché tard trop souvent; **she's used to late ~s** elle a l'habitude de se coucher tard; **he needs a ~'s sleep** il a besoin d'une bonne nuit de sommeil; **a ~'s lodging** un toit *or* un gîte pour la nuit; *V* **Arabian, good** *etc*.

(b) (*U: darkness*) nuit *f*, obscurité *f*, ténèbres *fpl* (*liter*). **~ is falling** la nuit *or* le soir tombe; **he went out into the ~** il partit dans la nuit *or* les ténèbres (*liter*); **he's afraid of the ~** il a peur du noir.

(c) (*Theat*) soirée *f*, représentation *f*. **the last 3 ~s of ...** les 3 dernières (représentations) de ...; **Mozart ~** soirée Mozart *or* consacrée à Mozart; *V* **first** *etc*.

2 *adv* (*US*) **I can't sleep ~s** je ne peux pas dormir la nuit.

3 *cpd clothes, work, flight* de nuit. **night-bird** (*lit*) oiseau *m* nocturne; (*fig*) couche-tard *mf inv*, noctambule *mf* (*hum*); **night blindness** héméralopie *f*; **nightcap** (*Dress*) bonnet *m* de nuit; (*drink*) boisson *f* (*gén alcoolisée, prise avant le coucher*); **would you like a nightcap?** voulez-vous boire quelque chose avant de vous coucher?; **night club** boîte *f* de nuit; **nightdress** chemise *f* de nuit (*de femme*); (*Press*) **night editor** secrétaire *mf* de rédaction de nuit; **nightfall** tombée *f* du jour *or* de la nuit; **at nightfall** au tomber du jour, à la nuit tombante; (*Aviat*) **night-fighter** chasseur *m* de nuit; **nightgown** chemise *f* de nuit (*de femme*); **nighthawk** engoulevent *m* d'Amérique; **nightjar** engoulevent *m* d'Europe, tête-chèvre *m*, crapaud volant; **night life** vie *f* nocturne; **night light** (*child's*) veilleuse *f*; (*Naut*) feu *m* de position; (*lit, fig*) **nightmare** cauchemar *m*; **the very thought was a nightmare to me** rien qu'à y penser j'en avais des cauchemars; **nightmarish** de cauchemar, cauchemardesque; **night nurse** infirmier *m*, -ière *f* de nuit; (*fig*) **night owl*** couche-tard *mf inv*, noctambule *mf* (*hum*); **night porter** gardien *m* de nuit, concierge *mf* de service la nuit; **night school** cours *mpl* du soir; **nightshade** *V* **nightshade**; **nightshift** (*workers*) équipe *f* de nuit; (*work*) poste *m* de nuit; **to be** *or* **to work on nightshift** être (au poste) de nuit; **nightshirt** chemise *f* de nuit (*d'homme*); **night spot*** = **night club**; **night storage heater/heating** radiateur *m*/chauffage *m* par accumulation (*fonctionnant au tarif de nuit*); (*U*) **night-time** nuit *f*, **at night-time** la nuit; **in the night-time** pendant la nuit, de nuit; **night watchman** veilleur *m or* gardien *m* de nuit; (*U*) **nightwear** vêtements *mpl* de nuit; **night work** travail *m* de nuit.

nightie* ['naɪtɪ] *n* chemise *f* de nuit (*de femme*), nuisette* *f*.

nightingale ['naɪtɪŋgeɪl] *n* rossignol *m*.

nightly ['naɪtlɪ] **1** *adj* (*every night*) de tous les soirs, de toutes les nuits. (*Theat*) **~ performance** représentation *f* (de) tous les soirs.

2 *adv* tous les soirs, chaque soir, chaque nuit. (*Theat*) **performances ~** représentations tous les soirs; **twice ~** deux fois par soir *or* nuit.

nightshade ['naɪtʃeɪd] *n*: **black ~** morelle noire; **deadly ~** belladone *f*; **woody ~** douce-amère *f*.

nihilism ['naɪɪlɪzəm] *n* nihilisme *m*.

nihilist ['naɪɪlɪst] *n* nihiliste *mf*.

nihilistic [,naɪɪ'lɪstɪk] *adj* nihiliste.

nil [nɪl] *n* rien *m*; (*Brit: in form-filling etc*) néant *m*; (*Brit Sport*) zéro *m*.

Nile [naɪl] *n* Nil *m*. (*Hist*) **the Battle of the ~** la bataille d'Aboukir.

nimbi ['nɪmbaɪ] *npl of* **nimbus.**

nimble ['nɪmbl] **1** *adj person, fingers* agile, leste, preste; *mind* vif, prompt. **you have to be fairly ~ to get over this hedge** il faut être assez agile *or* leste pour passer par-dessus cette haie; *[old person]* **she is still ~** elle est encore alerte.

2 *cpd*: **nimble-fingered/-footed** aux doigts/pieds agiles *or* lestes *or* prestes; **nimble-minded, nimble-witted** à l'esprit vif *or* prompt.

nimbleness ['nɪmblnɪs] *n [person, fingers]* agilité *f*; *[limbs etc]* agilité, souplesse *f*; *[mind]* vivacité *f*.

nimbly ['nɪmblɪ] *adv* agilement, lestement, prestement.

nimbus ['nɪmbəs] *n, pl* **nimbi** *or* **~es** **(a)** (*halo*) nimbe *m*, halo *m*. **(b)** (*cloud*) nimbus *m*.

nincompoop* ['nɪŋkəmpuːp] *n* cornichon* *m*, serin(e)* *m(f)*, gourde* *f*.

nine [naɪn] **1** *adj* neuf *inv*. **~ times out of ten** neuf fois sur dix; (*fig*) **he's got ~ lives** il a l'âme chevillée au corps; **a ~ days' wonder** la merveille d'un jour; **a ~-hole golf course** un (parcours de) neuf trous.

2 n neuf *m inv.* (*fig*) **dressed (up) to the ~s** en grand tralala, sur son trente et un; *for other phrases V* **six.**
3 *cpd*: **ninepins** (jeu *m* de) quilles *fpl*; **they went down like ninepins** ils sont tombés comme des mouches.
nineteen [ˈnaɪnˈtiːn] **1** *adj* dix-neuf *inv.* **2** *n* dix-neuf *m inv.* (*Brit fig*) **he talks ~ to the dozen*** c'est un vrai moulin à paroles *or* une vraie pie; **they were talking ~ to the dozen** ils jacassaient à qui mieux mieux; *for other phrases V* **six.**
nineteenth [ˈnaɪnˈtiːnθ] **1** *adj* dix-neuvième. (*Golf hum*) **the ~ (hole)** le bar, la buvette. **2** *n* dix-neuvième *mf*; (*fraction*) dix-neuvième *m*; *for other phrases V* **sixth.**
ninetieth [ˈnaɪntɪɪθ] **1** *adj* quatre-vingt-dixième. **2** *n* quatre-vingt-dixième *mf*; (*fraction*) quatre-vingt-dixième *m*.
ninety [ˈnaɪntɪ] **1** *adj* quatre-vingt-dix *inv*.
2 *n* quatre-vingt-dix *m inv.* **~-one** quatre-vingt-onze; **~-nine** quatre-vingt-dix-neuf; **to be in one's nineties** être nonagénaire, avoir passé quatre-vingt-dix ans; (*at doctor's*) **'say ~-nine!'** = 'dites trente-trois!'; *V* **naughty**; *for other phrases V* **sixty.**
ninny* [ˈnɪnɪ] *n* cornichon* *m*, serin(e)* *m(f)*, gourde* *f*.
ninth [naɪnθ] **1** *adj* neuvième. **2** *n* neuvième *mf*; (*fraction*) neuvième *m*; *for phrases V* **sixth.**
nip[1] [nɪp] **1** *n* (*pinch*) pinçon *m*; (*bite*) morsure *f*. **the dog gave him a ~** le chien lui a donné un (petit) coup de dent; (*US*) **~ and tuck*** serré, au quart de poil près*; **there's a ~ in the air today** ça pince aujourd'hui, l'air est piquant aujourd'hui.
2 *vt* **(a)** (*pinch*) pincer; (*bite*) donner un (petit) coup de dent à; *[cold, frost] plants* brûler; (*prune*) *bud, shoot* pincer; (*fig*) *plan, ambition* faire échec à. **I've ~ped my finger** je me suis pincé le doigt; (*fig*) **to ~ in the bud** faire avorter, tuer *or* écraser dans l'œuf; **the cold air ~ped our faces** l'air froid nous pinçait le *or* au visage; **all the plants had been ~ped by the frost** toutes les plantes avaient été brûlées par la gelée.
(b) (‡: *steal*) piquer‡, faucher‡.
3 *vi* (*Brit**) **to ~ up/down/out** *etc* monter/descendre/sortir *etc* en courant *or* d'un pas allègre; **he ~ped into the café** il a fait un saut au café.
nip along* *vi* (*Brit*) *[person]* aller d'un bon pas; *[car]* filer. **nip along to John's house** cours vite *or* fais un saut chez Jean.
nip in* *vi* (*Brit*) entrer en courant; entrer un instant. **I've just nipped in for a minute** je ne fais qu'entrer et sortir; **to nip in and out of the traffic** se faufiler entre les voitures.
nip off **1** *vi* (*Brit**) filer*, se sauver*.
2 *vt sep bud, shoot* pincer.
nip[2] [nɪp] *n* (*drink*) goutte *f*, petit verre. **to take a ~** boire une goutte *or* un petit verre; **have a ~ of whisky!** une goutte de whisky?
nipper [ˈnɪpəʳ] *n* **(a)** (*Brit*‡) gosse* *mf*, mioche* *mf*. **(b) (pair of) ~s** pince *f*, tenaille(s) *f(pl)*. **(c)** (*Zool*) pince *f*.
nipple [ˈnɪpl] *n* (*Anat*) mamelon *m*, bout *m* de sein; *[baby's bottle]* tétine *f*; (*Geog*) mamelon; (*Aut*) graisseur *m*.
nippy* [ˈnɪpɪ] *adj* **(a)** (*Brit*) alerte, vif, preste. **be ~ about it!** fais vite!, grouille-toi!‡ **(b)** (*sharp, cold*) *wind* coupant, cuisant, âpre. **it's ~ today** ça pince aujourd'hui, l'air est piquant aujourd'hui. **(c)** *flavour* fort, piquant.
nisi [ˈnaɪsaɪ] *adj V* **decree 1.**
Nissen hut [ˈnɪsnˌhʌt] *n* hutte préfabriquée (*en tôle, cylindrique*).
nit [nɪt] **1** *n* **(a)** (*Zool*) lente *f*. **(b)** (*Brit*‡: *fool*) crétin(e)* *m(f)*. **2** *cpd*: **he's always nit-picking*** il coupe toujours les cheveux en quatre.
niter [ˈnaɪtəʳ] *n* (*US*) = **nitre.**
nitrate [ˈnaɪtreɪt] *n* nitrate *m*, azotate *m*.
nitration [naɪˈtreɪʃən] *n* nitration *f*.
nitre, (*US*) **niter** [ˈnaɪtəʳ] *n* nitre *m*, salpêtre *m*.
nitric [ˈnaɪtrɪk] *adj* nitrique, azotique. **~ acid** acide *m* nitrique *or* azotique; **~ oxide** oxyde *m* azotique *or* nitrique, bioxyde *m* d'azote, nitrosyle *m*.
nitrogen [ˈnaɪtrədʒən] *n* azote *m*. **~ gas** (gaz *m*) azote.
nitrogenous [naɪˈtrɒdʒɪnəs] *adj* azoté.
nitroglycerin(e) [ˈnaɪtrəʊˈglɪsəriːn] *n* nitroglycérine *f*.
nitrous [ˈnaɪtrəs] *adj* nitreux, azoteux, d'azote. **~ acid** acide azoteux *or* nitreux; **~ oxide** oxyde azoteux *or* nitreux, protoxyde *m* d'azote.
nitty-gritty* [ˈnɪtɪˈgrɪtɪ] *n*: **let's get down to the ~** venons-en au fond du problème *or* aux choses sérieuses (*iro*); **the ~ of life** les dures réalités de la vie (*iro*).
nitwit* [ˈnɪtwɪt] *n* imbécile *mf*, nigaud(e)* *m(f)*.
nix‡ [nɪks] *n* (*nothing*) rien *m*, que dalle‡, peau *f* de balle‡.
no [nəʊ] **1** *particle* (*opp of* **yes**) non. **oh ~!** mais non!; **to say/answer ~** dire/répondre non; **the answer is ~** la réponse est non *or* négative; **I won't take ~ for an answer** (il n'est) pas question de me dire non; **I wouldn't do it, ~ not for £100** je ne le ferais pas, même pas pour 100 livres.
2 *n, pl* **~es** non *m inv.* **the ~es have it** les non l'emportent, les voix contre l'emportent; **there were 7 ~es** il y avait 7 non *or* 7 voix contre; *V* **ay(e).**
3 *adj* **(a)** (*not any*) aucun, nul (*f* nulle), pas de, point de. **she had ~ coat** elle n'avait pas de manteau; **I have ~ idea** je n'ai aucune idée; **I have ~ more money** je n'ai plus d'argent; **~ man could do more** aucun homme *or* personne *or* nul ne pourrait faire davantage; **~ one man could do it** aucun homme ne pourrait le faire (à lui) seul; **~ two men would agree on this** il n'y a pas deux hommes qui seraient d'accord là-dessus; **~ other man** aucun autre homme, personne d'autre; **~ sensible man would have done that** aucun homme de bon sens n'aurait fait ça, un homme de bon sens n'aurait pas fait ça; **~ Frenchman would say that** aucun Français ne dirait ça, un Français ne dirait pas ça; **it's of ~ interest** c'est sans intérêt; **a man of ~ intelligence** un homme sans intelligence *or* dénué d'intelligence; **~ go!*** pas moyen!, pas mèche!*; **it's ~ go* trying to get him to help us** pas moyen d'obtenir qu'il nous aide (*subj*) (*V also* **5**); **it's ~ good waiting for him** cela ne sert à rien *or* ce n'est pas la peine de l'attendre; **it's ~ wonder (that)** (ce n'est) pas étonnant (que + *subj or* si + *indic*); **~ wonder!** pas étonnant!*
(b) (*emphatic*) peu, pas de, nullement. **by ~ means** aucunement, nullement, pas du tout; **he's ~ friend of mine** il n'est pas de mes amis; **he's ~ genius** ce n'est certes pas un génie, il n'a rien d'un génie; **this is ~ place for children** ce n'est pas un endroit pour les enfants; **in ~ time** en un rien de temps; **it's ~ small matter** ce n'est pas rien, ce n'est pas une petite affaire; **theirs is ~ easy task** ils n'ont pas la tâche facile, leur tâche n'est pas (du tout) facile; **there's ~ such thing** cela n'existe pas; **and ~ mistake!*** ça il n'y a pas de doute!*; *V* **end.**
(c) (*forbidding*) **~ smoking** défense de fumer; **~ entry, ~ admittance** entrée interdite, défense d'entrer; **~ parking** stationnement interdit; **~ surrender!** on ne se rend pas!; **~ nonsense!** pas d'histoires!, pas de blagues!*
(d) (*with gerund*) **there's ~ saying what he'll do next** impossible de dire ce qu'il fera après; **there's ~ pleasing him** (quoi qu'on fasse) il n'est jamais satisfait.
4 *adv* **(a)** non. **whether he comes or ~** qu'il vienne ou non; **hungry or ~ you'll eat it** que tu aies faim ou non, tu le mangeras.
(b) (*with comp*) ne ... pas, ne ... plus. **the invalid is ~ better** le malade ne va pas mieux; **I can go ~ farther** je ne peux pas aller plus loin, je n'en peux plus; **I can bear it ~ longer** je ne peux plus le supporter; **she took ~ less than 4 weeks to do it** il ne lui a pas fallu moins de 4 semaines pour le faire; **she came herself, ~ less!** elle est venue en personne, voyez-vous ça! (*iro*).
5 *cpd*: **nobody** *V* **nobody; no-claim(s) bonus** bonification *f* pour non-sinistre; (*Brit Mil*) **no-go area** zone interdite (*à la police et à l'armée*); **no-good*** (*adj*) nul (*f* nulle), propre *or* bon (*f* bonne) à rien; (*n*) propre *mf* à rien; **nohow*** aucunement, en aucune façon; **no man's land** (*Mil*) no man's land *m*; (*wasteland*) terrain *m* vague; (*indefinite area*) zone mal définie; **no one** = **nobody 1**; (*Comm*) **no sale** non-vente *f*; **no-trump(s)** sans-atout *m inv*; **to call no-trump(s)** annoncer sans-atout.
Noah [ˈnəʊə] *n* Noé *m*. **~'s ark** l'arche *f* de Noé.
nob[1]**‡** [nɒb] *n* (*esp Brit*) aristo‡ *m*; richard‡ *m*. **the ~s** (les gens de) la haute‡, les rupins‡ *mpl*.
nob[2]**‡** [nɒb] *n* (*head*) caboche* *f*, fiole‡ *f*.
nobble* [ˈnɒbl] *vt* (*Brit*) **(a)** (*bribe, corrupt*) *person* acheter, soudoyer.
(b) (*obtain dishonestly*) *votes etc* acheter; *money* faucher‡, rafler*.
(c) (*Racing*) *horse, dog* droguer (*pour l'empêcher de gagner*).
(d) (*catch*) *wrongdoer* pincer‡, choper‡. **the reporters ~d him as he left his hotel** les reporters l'ont happé *or* lui ont mis la main dessus au moment où il quittait son hôtel.
Nobel [ˈnəʊbel] *n*: **~ prize** prix *m* Nobel; **~ prizewinner** (lauréat *m* du) prix Nobel.
nobility [nəʊˈbɪlɪtɪ] *n* (*U*) **(a)** (*nobles*) (haute) noblesse *f*. **the old ~** la noblesse d'extraction *or* d'épée, la vieille noblesse. **(b)** (*quality*) noblesse *f*. **~ of mind** grandeur *f* d'âme, magnanimité *f*.
noble [ˈnəʊbl] **1** *adj* **(a)** *person, appearance, matter* noble; *soul, sentiment* noble, grand; *monument, edifice* majestueux, imposant. **of ~ birth** de haute naissance, de naissance noble; **the ~ art of self-defence** le noble art, la boxe; **a ~ wine** un grand vin, un vin noble.
(b) (*: *unselfish*) magnanime. **I was very ~ and gave her my share** dans un geste magnanime je lui ai donné ma part, je lui ai généreusement donné ma part; **don't be so ~!** ne fais pas le (*or* la) magnanime!
(c) *metal* noble, précieux.
2 *n* noble *m*.
3 *cpd*: **nobleman** noble *m*, aristocrate *m*; **noble-minded** magnanime, généreux; **noblewoman** aristocrate *f*, femme *f* de la noblesse, noble *f*.
nobleness [ˈnəʊblnɪs] *n [person, birth]* noblesse *f*; *[spirit, action etc]* noblesse, magnanimité *f*, générosité *f*; *[animal, statue etc]* belles proportions, noblesse de proportions; *[building etc]* majesté *f*. **~ of mind** grandeur *f* d'âme, magnanimité, générosité.
nobly [ˈnəʊblɪ] *adv* **(a)** (*aristocratically*) noblement. **~ born** de haute naissance. **(b)** (*magnificently*) *proportioned* majestueusement. **(c)** (*: *selflessly*) généreusement, noblement. **he ~ gave her his seat** il lui céda généreusement sa place; **you've done ~!** vous avez été magnifique!, vous avez bien mérité de la patrie! (*hum*).
nobody [ˈnəʊbədɪ] **1** *pron* personne, nul, aucun (+ *ne before vb*). **I saw ~** je n'ai vu personne; **~ knows** nul *or* personne ne le sait; **~ spoke to me** personne ne m'a parlé; **who saw him?** — **~** qui l'a vu? — personne; **~ knows better than I** personne ne sait mieux que moi; **~ (that was) there will ever forget ...** personne parmi ceux qui étaient là n'oubliera jamais ...; **this is ~'s business** cela ne regarde personne; (*fig*) **he's ~'s fool** il n'est pas né d'hier, il est loin d'être un imbécile.
2 *n* nullité *f*, zéro *m*, rien *m* du tout. **he's a mere ~, he's just a ~** c'est un rien du tout; **they are nobodies** ce sont des moins que rien; **I worked with him when he was ~** j'ai travaillé avec lui alors qu'il était encore inconnu.
nocturnal [nɒkˈtɜːnl] *adj* nocturne, de nuit.
nocturne [ˈnɒktɜːn] *n* (*Mus*) nocturne *m*.
nod [nɒd] **1** *n* **(a)** signe *m or* inclination *f* de (la) tête. **he gave me a ~** il m'a fait un signe de (la) tête; (*in greeting*) il m'a salué de la tête; **he rose with a ~ of agreement** il s'est levé, signifiant son accord d'un signe de (la) tête; **to answer with a ~** répondre d'un signe de (la) tête; (*loc*) **a ~ is as good as a wink (to a blind man)** c'est bien *or* ça va*, on a compris.
(b) the land of N~ le pays des rêves *or* des songes.

2 *vi* **(a)** (*move head down*) faire un signe de (la) tête, incliner la tête; (*as sign of assent*) hocher la tête, faire signe que oui, faire un signe de tête affirmatif. **to ~ to sb** faire un signe de tête à qn; (*in greeting*) saluer qn d'un signe de tête, saluer qn de la tête; **he ~ded to me to go** de la tête il me fit signe de m'en aller; **we have a ~ding acquaintance** nous nous disons bonjour, nous nous saluons.

(b) (*doze*) sommeiller, somnoler. **he was ~ding over a book** il dodelinait de la tête *or* il somnolait sur un livre; (*loc*) **even Homer ~s** tout le monde peut faire une erreur, personne n'est infaillible; (*fig*) **to catch sb ~ding** prendre qn en défaut.

(c) *[flowers, plumes]* se balancer, danser; *[trees]* onduler, se balancer.

3 *vt*: **to ~ one's head** (*move head down*) faire un signe de (la) tête, incliner la tête; (*as sign of assent*) faire signe que oui, faire un signe de tête affirmatif; **to ~ one's agreement/approval** manifester son assentiment/son approbation par un *or* d'un signe de tête; **to ~ assent** faire signe que oui, manifester son assentiment par un *or* d'un signe de tête.

nod off *vi* s'endormir. **I nodded off for a moment** je me suis endormi un instant.

nodal ['nəʊdl] *adj* nodal.

noddle‡† ['nɒdl] *n* (*head*) caboche* *f*, fiole‡ *f*.

node [nəʊd] *n* (*gen, Astron, Geom, Ling, Phys*) nœud *m*; (*Bot*) nœud, nodosité *f*; (*Anat*) nodus *m*, nodosité.

nodular ['nɒdjʊləʳ] *adj* nodulaire.

nodule ['nɒdjuːl] *n* (*Anat, Bot, Geol*) nodule *m*.

Noel ['nəʊəl] *n* Noël *m* (*prénom*).

noggin ['nɒgɪn] *n* (*container*) (petit) pot *m*; (*amount*) quart *m* (de pinte). **let's have a ~** allons boire *or* prendre un pot.

noise [nɔɪz] **1** *n* **(a)** (*sound*) bruit *m*, son *m*. **I heard a small ~** j'ai entendu un petit bruit; **the ~ of bells** le son des cloches; **~s in the ears** bourdonnements *mpl* (d'oreilles); **a hammering ~** un martellement; **a clanging ~** un bruit métallique.

(b) (*loud sound*) bruit *m*, tapage *m* (*U*), vacarme *m* (*U*). **the ~ of the traffic** le bruit *or* le vacarme de la circulation; **I hate ~** j'ai horreur du bruit; **to make a ~** faire du bruit *or* du tapage *or* du vacarme; (*fig*) **the book made a lot of ~ when it came out** le livre a fait beaucoup de bruit *or* beaucoup de tapage *or* beaucoup parler de lui quand il est sorti; (*fig*) **to make a lot of ~ about sth*** faire du tapage autour de qch; **she made ~s* about wanting to go home early** elle a marmonné qu'elle voulait rentrer tôt; **stop that ~!** arrêtez(-moi) ce tapage! *or* ce vacarme! *or* ce tintamarre!; **hold your ~!**‡ ferme-la!‡; (*person*) **a big ~*** une huile*, une grosse légume*.

(c) (*U*) (*Rad, TV*) interférences *fpl*, parasites *mpl*; (*Telec*) friture *f*; (*Computers*) bruit *m*.

2 *vt*: **to ~ sth abroad** *or* **about** ébruiter qch.

3 *cpd*: **noise abatement** lutte *f* anti-bruit; **noise-abatement campaign/society** campagne *f*/société *f* pour la lutte contre le bruit.

noiseless ['nɔɪzlɪs] *adj* silencieux. **with ~ tread** à pas feutrés.

noiselessly ['nɔɪzlɪslɪ] *adv* sans bruit, en silence, silencieusement.

noiselessness ['nɔɪzlɪsnɪs] *n* silence *m*, absence *f* de bruit.

noisily ['nɔɪzɪlɪ] *adv* bruyamment.

noisiness ['nɔɪzɪnɪs] *n* caractère bruyant; *[children]* turbulence *f*.

noisome ['nɔɪsəm] *adj* (*disgusting*) repoussant, répugnant; (*smelly*) puant, fétide, infect; (*harmful*) nocif, nuisible.

noisy ['nɔɪzɪ] *adj* **(a)** *child etc* bruyant, tapageur; *protest, street* bruyant; *discussion, meeting, welcome* bruyant, tumultueux. *[person, machine]* **to be ~** faire du bruit *or* du tapage. **(b)** *colour* criard, voyant.

nomad ['nəʊmæd] *n* nomade *mf*.

nomadic [nəʊ'mædɪk] *adj* nomade.

nomadism ['nəʊmədɪzəm] *n* nomadisme *m*.

nom de plume ['nɒmdə'pluːm] *n* (*Literat*) pseudonyme *m*.

nomenclature [nəʊ'menklətʃəʳ] *n* nomenclature *f*.

nominal ['nɒmɪnl] *adj* **(a)** (*in name only*) *ruler* de nom (seulement); *agreement, power, rights* nominal. **he was the ~ head of state** il était chef d'État de nom.

(b) (*for form only*) *salary, fee* nominal, insignifiant. **a ~ amount** une somme nominale *or* insignifiante; **~ value** valeur nominale *or* fictive; **~ rent** loyer insignifiant. **(c)** (*Gram*) nominal.

nominalism ['nɒmɪnəlɪzəm] *n* nominalisme *m*.

nominalist ['nɒmɪnəlɪst] *n* nominaliste *mf*.

nominalization [ˌnɒmməlaɪ'zeɪʃən] *n* (*Ling*) nominalisation *f*.

nominally ['nɒmɪnəlɪ] *adv* (*in name only*) nominalement, de nom; (*as a matter of form*) pour la forme.

nominate ['nɒmɪneɪt] *vt* **(a)** (*appoint*) nommer, désigner. **he was ~d chairman, he was ~d to the chairmanship** il a été nommé président; **~d and elected members of a committee** membres désignés et membres élus d'un comité.

(b) (*propose*) proposer, présenter. **he was ~d for the presidency** il a été proposé comme candidat à la présidence; **they ~d Mr X for mayor** ils ont proposé M X comme candidat à la mairie.

nomination [ˌnɒmɪ'neɪʃən] *n* **(a)** (*appointment*) nomination *f* (*to* à).

(b) proposition *f* de candidat. **~s must be received by ...** toutes propositions de candidats doivent être reçues avant ... .

nominative ['nɒmɪnətɪv] *adj, n* (*Gram*) nominatif (*m*). **in the ~ (case)** au nominatif, au cas sujet.

nominator ['nɒmɪneɪtəʳ] *n* présentateur *m*.

nominee [ˌnɒmɪ'niː] *n* (*for post*) personne désignée *or* nommée, candidat(e) agréé(e); (*for annuity etc*) personne dénommée.

non- [nɒn] *pref* non-, in... . **non-absorbent** non-absorbant; (*Comm, Fin*) **non-acceptance** non-acceptation *f*; **non-accomplishment** inaccomplissement *m*, inachèvement *m*; **non-adjustable** non-réglable; **non-admission** non-admission *f*; **non-affiliated** *business* non-affilié; *industry* non confédéré; **non-aggression** non-agression *f*; **non-aggression pact** pacte *m* de non-agression; **non-alcoholic** non alcoolisé, sans alcool; (*Pol*) **non-aligned** neutraliste, non-aligné; (*Pol*) **non-alignment** neutralisme *m*, non-alignement *m*; **non-alignment policy** politique *f* neutraliste; (*Jur*) **non-appearance** non-comparution *f*; **non-arrival** non-arrivée *f*; **non-attendance** absence *f*; **non-availability** non-disponibilité *f*; **non-available** non-disponible; (*Rel*) **non-believer** incroyant(e) *m(f)*; **non-belligerent** (*adj, n*) non-belligérant (*m*); **non-breakable** incassable; **non-Catholic** (*adj, n*) non-catholique (*mf*); **non-collegiate** *student* qui n'appartient à aucun collège (*d'une université*); **non-collegiate university** université *f* qui n'est pas divisée en collèges; (*US Mil*) **non-com*** (*abbr of* **non-commissioned officer**) sous-off* *m*, gradé *m*; **non-combatant** (*adj, n*) non-combattant (*m*); **non-combustible** non-combustible; (*Mil*) **non-commissioned** non-breveté, sans brevet; **non-commissioned officer** sous-officier *m*, gradé *m*; (*Rel*) **non-communicant** (*adj, n*) non-communiant(e) *m(f)*; **non-completion** *[work]* non-achèvement *m*; *[contract]* non-exécution *f*; **non-compliance** refus *m* d'obéissance (*with an order* à un ordre); **non-conductor** (*Phys*) non-conducteur *m*, mauvais conducteur; *[heat]* isolant *m*, calorifuge *m*; (*Elec*) isolant; **non-contributory pension scheme** régime *m* de retraite sans retenues *or* cotisations; **non-cooperation** refus *m* de coopération; **non-cumulative** non-cumulatif; **non-dazzle** anti-éblouissant; **non-detachable** *handle etc* fixe, indémontable; *lining, hood* non-détachable; **non-directional** omnidirectionnel; (*Psych*) **non-directive therapy** psychothérapie non directive, non-directivisme *m*; (*Ling*) **non-distinctive** non-distinctif; **non-essential** non essentiel, peu important, accessoire; **non-essentials** accessoires *mpl*; **the meeting was a non-event*** la réunion n'a jamais démarré; **non-existence** non-existence *f*; **non-existent** non-existant, inexistant; **non-explosive** inexplosible; **non-ferrous** non-ferreux; **non-fiction** littérature *f* non-romanesque; **he only reads non-fiction** il ne lit jamais de romans; **non-finite verb** verbe *m* au mode impersonnel; **non-finite forms** formes *fpl* des modes impersonnels; **non-fulfilment** non-exécution *f*, inexécution *f*; **non-grammatical** non-grammatical; **non-greasy** *ointment, lotion* qui ne graisse pas; *skin, hair* qui n'est pas gras (*f* grasse); (*Elec*) **non-inductive** non-inductif; **non-inflammable** ininflammable; **non-interference** non-intervention *f*; (*Pol etc*) **non-intervention** non-intervention *f*, laisser-faire *m*; **non-iron** qui ne nécessite aucun repassage; (*on label*) **'non-iron'** 'ne pas repasser'; **non-laddering** = **non-run**; **non-literate** non-lettré; qui ne possède pas de langue écrite; **non-material** immatériel; **non-medical** non-médical; *[club etc]* **non-member** personne étrangère (au club *etc*); **open to non-members** ouvert au public; (*Chem*) **non-metal** métalloïde *m*; **non-metallic** (*relating to non-metals*) métalloïdique; (*not of metallic quality*) non métallique; **non negotiable** non négociable; **non-participant** (*adj, n*) non-participant(e) *m(f)*; **non-partisan** impartial, sans parti pris; (*Pol*) **non-party** *vote, decision* indépendant (de tout parti politique); **non-payment** non-paiement *m*, défaut *m* de paiement; **non-poisonous** *snake* non venimeux; *mixture* non toxique; (*Chem*) **non-polar** non polaire; **non-productive** improductif; **non-professional** (*adj*) *player etc* amateur; (*n: Sport etc*) amateur *mf*; **non-professional conduct** manquement *m* aux devoirs de la profession; **non-profitmaking**, (*US*) **non-profit** sans but lucratif; **non-resident** (*adj*) non résident; (*n*) non-résident(e) *m(f)*; (*Brit: in hotel*) client(e) *m(f)* de passage; (*Pol etc*) **non-resistance** non-résistance *f*; (*Pol etc*) **non-resistant** non-résistant(e) *m(f)*; **non-run** indémaillable; **non-sectarian** qui n'est pas sectaire; **non-shrink** irrétrécissable; **non-skid** antidérapant; **non-smoker** (*person*) non-fumeur *m*, personne *f* qui ne fume pas; (*Rail*) compartiment *m* 'non-fumeurs'; **he is a non-smoker** il ne fume pas; (*Chem*) **non-solvent** non-dissolvant; (*Ling*) **non-standard** non conforme à la langue correcte; **non-starter** (*horse: lit, fig*) non-partant *m*; (*worthless person*) non-valeur *f*; **this proposal is a non-starter** cette proposition est hors de question; **non-stick** *saucepan* qui n'attache pas; **non-stop** *V* **non-stop**; **non-taxable** non-imposable; (*Ind*) **non-union** *workers, labour* non syndiqué; **non-viable** non-viable; **non-violence** non-violence *f*; **non-violent** non-violent; (*Pol etc*) **non-white** (*n*) personne *f* de couleur; (*adj*) de couleur; **non-woven** non-tissé.

nonagenarian [ˌnɒnədʒɪ'neərɪən] *adj, n* nonagénaire (*mf*).

nonce [nɒns] *n*: **for the ~** pour la circonstance, pour l'occasion; **~-word** mot créé pour l'occasion, mot de circonstance.

nonchalance ['nɒnʃələns] *n* nonchalance *f*.

nonchalant ['nɒnʃələnt] *adj* nonchalant.

nonchalantly ['nɒnʃələntlɪ] *adv* nonchalamment.

non-committal ['nɒnkə'mɪtl] *adj person, attitude* réservé, qui ne se compromet pas; *statement* qui n'engage à rien. **a ~ answer** une réponse diplomatique *or* de Normand; **I'll be very ~** je ne m'avancerai pas, je ne m'engagerai à rien, je resterai réservé; **he was very ~ about it** il a été *or* s'est montré très réservé là-dessus.

nonconformism ['nɒnkən'fɔːmɪzəm] *n* non-conformisme *m*.

nonconformist ['nɒnkən'fɔːmɪst] **1** *n* non-conformiste *mf*. **2** *adj* non-conformiste, dissident.

nonconformity ['nɒnkən'fɔːmɪtɪ] *n* non-conformité *f*.

nondescript ['nɒndɪskrɪpt] *adj colour* indéfinissable; *person* sans trait distinctif, quelconque; *appearance* insignifiant, quelconque.

none [nʌn] **1** *pron* **(a)** (*not one thing*) aucun(e) *m(f)*. **~ of the books** aucun livre, aucun des livres; **~ of this** rien de ceci; **~ of that!** pas de ça!; **I want ~ of your excuses!** vos excuses ne m'intéressent pas!; **he would have ~ of it** il ne *or* n'en voulait rien savoir; **~ at all** pas un(e) seul(e); **I need money but have ~ at all** j'ai besoin d'argent mais je n'en ai pas du tout; **~ of this money** pas un centime de cet argent; **~ of this cheese** pas un gramme de ce fromage; **~ of this milk** pas une goutte de ce lait; **~ of this land** pas un mètre carré *or* pas un pouce de ce terrain; **there's ~ left** il n'en reste plus; **is there any bread left? — ~ at all** y a-t-il encore du pain? — pas une miette; (*liter or hum*) **money have I ~** d'argent, je n'en ai point; (*liter or hum*) **traces there were ~** de traces, aucune *or* point (*liter or hum*).

(b) (*not one person*) personne, aucun(e) *m(f)*, nul(le) *m(f)*. **~ of them** aucun d'entre eux; **~ of us** aucun de nous *or* d'entre nous, personne parmi nous; **~ can tell** personne *or* nul ne peut le dire; **~ but you can do it** vous seul êtes capable de le faire; **I have told ~ but you** je ne l'ai dit à personne d'autre que vous; **~ but a fool would do it** il n'y a qu'un imbécile pour le faire; **I know, ~ better, that ...** je sais mieux que personne que ...; **their guest was ~ other than the president himself** leur invité n'était autre que le président en personne.

(c) (*in form-filling etc*) néant *m*.

2 *adv*: **he's ~ the worse for it** il ne s'en porte pas plus mal; **I'm ~ the worse for having eaten it** je ne me ressens pas de l'avoir mangé; **I like him ~ the worse for it** je ne l'en aime pas moins pour cela; **he was ~ the wiser** il n'en savait pas plus pour autant, il n'était pas plus avancé; **it's ~ too warm** il ne fait pas tellement chaud; **and ~ too soon either!** et ce n'est pas trop tôt!; **at last he arrived and ~ too soon** il arriva enfin et il était grand temps *or* ce n'était pas trop tôt; **it was ~ too easy** ce n'était pas tellement facile; **I was ~ too sure that he would come** j'étais loin d'être sûr qu'il viendrait; **we were ~ too comfortable** notre situation n'était pas ce qu'on peut appeler confortable.

3 *cpd*: **nonesuch = nonsuch; nonetheless = nevertheless.**

nonentity [nɒ'nentɪtɪ] *n* personne insignifiante *or* sans intérêt. **he's a complete ~** c'est une nullité.

nonpareil ['nɒnpərəl] (*frm, liter*) **1** *n* personne *f or* chose *f* sans pareille. **2** *adj* incomparable, sans égal.

nonplus ['nɒn'plʌs] *vt* déconcerter, dérouter, rendre perplexe. **I was utterly ~sed** j'étais complètement perplexe *or* dérouté.

nonsense ['nɒnsəns] **1** *n* (*U*) absurdités *fpl*, inepties *fpl*, sottises *fpl*, idioties *fpl*, non-sens *m*. **to talk ~** dire *or* débiter des absurdités *or* des inepties; **that's a piece of ~!** c'est une absurdité! *or* sottise! *or* idiotie!, c'est un non-sens!; **that's (a lot of) ~!** tout ça ce sont des absurdités *or* des inepties *or* des sottises *or* des idioties; **but that's ~** mais c'est absurde; **oh, ~!** oh, ne dis pas d'absurdités! *or* de sottises! *or* d'idioties!; **all this ~ about them not being able to pay** toutes ces histoires idiotes comme quoi* *or* selon lesquelles ils seraient incapables de payer; **it is ~ to say** il est absurde *or* idiot de dire, c'est un non-sens de dire; **it's just his ~** il dit des sottises (comme d'habitude); **he will stand no ~ from anybody** il ne se laissera pas faire par qui que ce soit, il ne se laissera marcher sur les pieds par personne; **he won't stand any ~ about that** il ne plaisante pas là-dessus; **I've had enough of this ~!** j'en ai assez de ces histoires! *or* idioties!; **stop this ~!, no more of your ~!** cesse ces idioties!; **there's no ~ about him** c'est un homme très carré; **to knock the ~ out of sb*** ramener qn à la raison; **to make a ~ out of sth** (complètement) saboter qch; *V* **stuff.**

2 *cpd*: **nonsense verse** vers *mpl* amphigouriques.

nonsensical [nɒn'sensɪkəl] *adj idea, action* absurde, inepte, qui n'a pas de sens; *person* absurde, idiot. **don't be so ~** ne soyez pas si absurde *or* idiot, ne dites pas tant d'absurdités *or* de sottises.

nonsensically [nɒn'sensɪkəlɪ] *adv* absurdement.

non sequitur [ˌnɒn'sekwɪtə'] *n* manque *m* de suite (*dans un raisonnement*), conclusion *f* illogique.

non-stop ['nɒn'stɒp] **1** *adj* sans arrêt; *train* direct; *journey* sans arrêt; *flight* direct, sans escale. (*Cine, Theat etc*) **~ performance** spectacle permanent. **2** *adv talk* sans arrêt. **to fly ~ from London to Chicago** faire Londres-Chicago sans escale.

nonsuch ['nʌnsʌtʃ] *n* personne *f or* chose *f* sans pareille.

noodle ['nu:dl] *n* **(a)** (*Culin*) **~s** nouilles *fpl*; **~ soup** potage *m* au vermicelle. **(b)** (‡: *person*) nouille‡ *f*, nigaud(e) *m(f)*.

nook [nʊk] *n* (*corner*) coin *m*, recoin *m*; (*remote spot*) retraite *f*. **~s and crannies, ~s and corners** coins et recoins; **breakfast ~** coin-repas *m*; **a shady ~** une retraite ombragée, un coin ombragé.

noon [nu:n] **1** *n* midi *m*. **at/about ~** à/vers midi; *V* **high. 2** *cpd*: **noonday, noontide** (*n*) midi *m*; (*adj*) de midi; (*fig liter*) **at the noonday** *or* **noontide of his fame** au sommet de sa gloire.

noose [nu:s] **1** *n* nœud coulant; (*in animal trapping*) collet *m*; *[cowboy]* lasso *m*; *[hangman]* corde *f*. (*fig*) **to put one's head in the ~, to put a ~ round one's neck** se jeter dans la gueule du loup.

2 *vt* **(a)** *rope* faire un nœud coulant à.

(b) (*in trapping*) prendre au collet; *[cowboy]* prendre *or* attraper au lasso.

nope‡ [nəʊp] *particle* (*US*) non.

nor [nɔ:'] *conj* **(a)** (*following 'neither'*) ni. **neither you ~ I can do it** ni vous ni moi (nous) ne pouvons le faire; **she neither eats ~ drinks** elle ne mange ni ne boit; **neither here ~ elsewhere does he stop working** ici comme ailleurs il ne cesse pas de travailler; *V* **neither.**

(b) (*= and not*) **I don't know, ~ do I care** je ne sais pas et d'ailleurs je m'en moque; **that's not funny, ~ is it true** ce n'est ni drôle ni vrai; **that's not funny, ~ do I believe it's true** cela n'est pas drôle et je ne crois pas non plus que ce soit vrai; **I shan't go and ~ will you** je n'irai pas et vous non plus; **I don't like him — ~ do I** je ne l'aime pas — moi non plus; **~ was this all** et ce n'était pas tout; **~ will I deny that ...** et je ne nie pas non plus que ... + *subj*; **~ was he disappointed** et il ne fut pas déçu non plus; *V* **yet.**

nor' [nɔ:'] *adj* (*Naut: in cpds*) = **north. nor'east** *etc* = **north-east** *etc*; *V* **north 4.**

Nordic ['nɔ:dɪk] *adj* nordique.

norm [nɔ:m] *n* norme *f*.

normal ['nɔ:məl] **1** *adj* **(a)** *person, situation, performance* normal; *habit* ordinaire, commun. **the child is not ~** l'enfant n'est pas normal; **it is quite ~ to believe ...** il est tout à fait normal *or* naturel de croire ...; **it was quite ~ for him to object** il était tout à fait normal *or* naturel qu'il fasse des objections; **it's quite a ~ thing for children to fight** c'est une chose très normale que les enfants se battent (*subj*); **with old people this is quite ~** chez les gens âgés c'est très normal *or* commun; **beyond ~ experience** au-delà de l'expérience ordinaire; (*Engineering, Tech*) **~ working** régime *m*; **~ speed** vitesse *f* de régime; (*Med*) **~ temperature** température normale.

(b) (*Math*) normal, perpendiculaire.

(c) (*Chem*) neutre.

(d) (*US etc*) **~ school** école normale (d'instituteurs *or* d'institutrices).

2 *n* **(a)** normale *f*, état normal, condition normale. **temperatures below ~** des températures au-dessous de la normale.

(b) (*Math*) normale *f*, perpendiculaire *f*.

normalcy ['nɔ:məlsɪ] *n*, **normality** [nɔ:'mælɪtɪ] *n* normalité *f*.

normalization [ˌnɔ:məlaɪ'zeɪʃən] *n* normalisation *f*.

normalize ['nɔ:məlaɪz] *vt* normaliser, régulariser.

normally ['nɔ:məlɪ] *adv* normalement, en temps normal.

Norman ['nɔ:mən] **1** *adj* normand; (*Archit*) roman. **the ~ Conquest** la conquête normande; (*Ling*) **~ French** anglo-normand *m*. **2** *n* Normand(e) *m(f)*.

Normandy ['nɔ:məndɪ] *n* Normandie *f*.

Norse [nɔ:s] **1** *adj* (*Hist*) nordique, scandinave. **~man** Scandinave *m*. **2** *n* (*Ling*) nordique *m*, norrois *m*. **Old ~** vieux norrois.

north [nɔ:θ] **1** *n* nord *m*. **magnetic ~** nord *or* pôle *m* magnétique; **(to the) ~ of** au nord de; **house facing the ~** maison exposée au nord; *[wind]* **to veer to the ~, to go into the ~** tourner au nord, anordir (*Naut*); **the wind is in the ~** le vent est au nord; **the wind is from the ~** le vent vient *or* souffle du nord; **to live in the ~** habiter dans le nord; **in the ~ of Scotland** dans le nord de l'Écosse; (*US Hist*) **the N~** les États *mpl* antiesclavagistes *or* du nord.

2 *adj* nord *inv*, au *or* du nord, septentrional. **~ wind** vent *m* du nord, bise *f*; **~ coast** côte *f* nord; **on the ~ side** du côté nord; **studio with a ~ light** atelier *m* qui reçoit la lumière du nord; **a ~ aspect** une exposition au nord; **room with a ~ aspect** pièce exposée au nord; **~ wall** mur exposé au nord; (*Archit*) **~ transept/door** transept/portail nord *or* septentrional; **in the N~ Atlantic** dans l'Atlantique Nord; *V also* **4.**

3 *adv* au nord, vers le nord. **the town lies ~ of the border** la ville est située au nord de la frontière; **we drove ~ for 100 km** nous avons roulé pendant 100 km en direction du nord; **go ~ till you get to Crewe** allez en direction du nord jusqu'à Crewe; **to sail due ~** aller droit vers le nord; avoir le cap au nord (*Naut*).

4 *cpd*: **North Africa** Afrique *f* du Nord; **North African** (*adj*) nord-africain, d'Afrique du Nord; (*n*) Africain(e) *m(f)* du Nord, Nord-Africain(e) *m(f)*; **North America** Amérique *f* du Nord; **North American** (*adj*) nord-américain, d'Amérique du Nord; (*n*) Nord-Américain(e) *m(f)*; **northbound** *traffic, vehicles* (se déplaçant) en direction du nord; *carriageway* nord *inv*; **North Carolina** Caroline *f* du Nord; **north-country** (*adj*) du Nord (de l'Angleterre); **North Dakota** Dakota *m* du Nord; **north-east** (*n*) nord-est *m*; (*adj*) (du *or* au) nord-est *inv*; (*adv*) vers le nord-est; **north-easter** vent *m* du nord-est; **north-easterly** (*adj*) *wind, direction* du nord-est; *situation* au nord-est; (*adv*) vers le nord-est; **north-eastern** (du) nord-est; **north-eastward(s)** vers le nord-est; **north-facing** exposé au nord; **the Northlands** les pays *mpl* du Nord; (*Hist*) **Northman** Scandinave *m*; **north-north-east** (*n*) nord-nord-est *m*; (*adj*) (du *or* au) nord-nord-est *inv*; (*adv*) vers le nord-nord-est; **north-north-west** (*n*) nord-nord-ouest *m*; (*adj*) (du *or* au) nord-nord-ouest *inv*; (*adv*) vers le nord-nord-ouest; **North Pole** pôle *m* Nord; **North Sea** la mer du Nord; (*Brit*) **North Sea gas** gaz naturel (de la mer du Nord); **North Sea oil** pétrole *m* de la mer du Nord; **North Star** étoile *f* polaire; **north-west** (*n*) nord-ouest *m*; (*adj*) (du *or* au) nord-ouest *inv*; (*adv*) vers le nord-ouest; **north-wester** noroît *m*, vent *m* du nord-ouest; **north-westerly** (*adj*) *wind, direction* du nord-ouest; *situation* au nord-ouest; (*adv*) vers le nord-ouest; **north-western** nord-ouest *inv*, du nord-ouest; **North-West Passage** passage *m* du Nord-Ouest; **North-west Territories** (territoires *mpl* du) Nord-Ouest *m*; **north-westward(s)** vers le nord-ouest; *V* **Korea, Vietnam** *etc.*

northerly ['nɔ:ðəlɪ] **1** *adj wind* du nord; *situation* au nord; *direction* vers le nord. **~ latitudes** latitudes boréales; **~ aspect** exposition *f* au nord; **in a ~ direction** vers le nord. **2** *adv* vers le nord.

northern ['nɔ:ðən] **1** *adj* du nord, septentrional. **house with a ~ outlook** maison exposée au nord; **~ wall** mur exposé au nord; **in ~ Spain** dans le nord de l'Espagne; **~ hemisphere** hémisphère nord *or* boréal; **~ lights** aurore boréale; *[Australia]* **N~ Territory** Territoire *m* du Nord; *V* **Ireland** *etc.*

2 *cpd*: **northernmost** le plus au nord, à l'extrême nord.

northerner ['nɔ:ðənə'] *n* **(a)** homme *m or* femme *f* du Nord, habitant(e) *m(f)* du Nord. **he is a ~** il vient du Nord; **the ~s** les gens *mpl* du Nord, les septentrionaux *mpl*. **(b)** (*US Hist*) Nordiste *mf*, antiesclavagiste *mf*.

northward ['nɔ:θwəd] **1** *adj* au nord. **2** *adv* (*also* **~s**) vers le nord.

Norway ['nɔ:weɪ] *n* Norvège *f*.

Norwegian [nɔ:'wi:dʒən] **1** *adj* norvégien. **2** *n* **(a)** Norvégien(ne) *m(f)*. **(b)** (*Ling*) norvégien *m*.

nose [nəʊz] 1 *n* **(a)** *[person]* nez *m*; *[dog]* nez, truffe *f*. **his ~ was bleeding** il saignait du nez; **he has a nice ~** il a un joli nez; **the horse won by a ~** le cheval a gagné d'une demi-tête; **to speak through one's ~** nasiller, parler du nez; **it was there under his very ~** *or* **right under his ~ all the time** c'était là juste *or* en plein sous son nez; **she did it under his very ~** *or* **right under his ~** elle l'a fait à sa barbe *or* sous son nez; (*fig*) **his ~ is out of joint** il est dépité; **that put his ~ out of joint** ça l'a défrisé*; (*fig*) **to lead sb by the ~** mener qn par le bout du nez; (*fig*) **to look down one's ~ at sb/sth** faire le nez à qn/devant qch; (*fig*) **to turn up one's ~** faire le dégoûté (*at* devant); (*fig*) **to keep one's ~ to the grindstone** travailler sans répit *or* relâche; (*fig*) **to keep sb's ~ to the grindstone** faire travailler qn sans répit *or* relâche, ne laisser aucun répit à qn; **to poke** *or* **stick one's ~ into sth** mettre *or* fourrer son nez dans qch; (**fig*) **you'd better keep your ~ clean** il vaut mieux que tu te tiennes à carreau*; *V* **blow**[1], **follow, snub**[2], **thumb** *etc*.

(b) (*sense of smell*) odorat *m*, nez *m*. **to have a good ~** avoir l'odorat *or* le nez fin; (*fig*) **to have a (good) ~ for ...** avoir du flair pour ... .

(c) *[wine etc]* arôme *m*, bouquet *m*.

(d) *[boat etc]* nez *m*; *[tool etc]* bec *m*. (*Brit*) **a line of cars ~ to tail** une file de voitures pare-choc contre pare-choc; **he put the car's ~ towards the town** il tourna la voiture en direction de la ville.

2 *cpd*: **nosebag** musette *f* mangeoire; **nosebleed** saignement *m* de nez; **to have a nosebleed** saigner du nez; (*Space*) **nose cone** ogive *f*; (*Aviat*) **nose-dive** (*n*) piqué *m*; (*vi*) descendre en piqué; **nose drops** gouttes nasales, gouttes pour le nez*; **nosegay** petit bouquet; **nose ring** anneau *m* de nez.

3 *vt* (*smell*) flairer, renifler.

4 *vi [ship, vehicle]* s'avancer avec précaution. **the ship ~d (her way) through the fog** le navire progressait avec précaution dans le brouillard.

nose about, nose around *vi* fouiller, fureter, fouiner*.

nose at *vt fus* flairer, renifler.

nose in *vi* **(a)** *[car]* se glisser dans une file. **(b)** (*) *[person]* s'immiscer *or* s'insinuer (dans un groupe).

nose out 1 *vi [car]* sortir d'une file. 2 *vt sep* **(a)** *[dog]* flairer. **(b) to nose out a secret*** découvrir *or* flairer un secret; **to nose sb out*** dénicher *or* dépister qn.

-nosed [nəʊzd] *adj ending in cpds* au nez ... . **red-nosed** au nez rouge; *V* **long** *etc*.

nos(e)y* ['nəʊzɪ] *adj* curieux, fouinard*, fureteur. **to be ~** mettre *or* fourrer* son nez partout; **don't be so ~** mêlez-vous de vos affaires! *or* de ce qui vous regarde!; (*pej*) **N~ Parker** fouinard(e)* *m(f)*.

nosh‡ [nɒʃ] (*Brit*) 1 *n* bouffe‡ *f*. **to have some ~, to have a ~-up** boulotter*, bouffer‡. 2 *vi* boulotter*, bouffer.

nostalgia [nɒs'tældʒɪə] *n* nostalgie *f*; (*homesickness*) nostalgie, mal *m* du pays.

nostalgic [nɒs'tældʒɪk] *adj* nostalgique.

nostril ['nɒstrəl] *n [person, dog etc]* narine *f*; *[horse etc]* naseau *m*.

nostrum ['nɒstrəm] *n* (*patent medicine, also fig*) panacée *f*, remède universel; (*quack medicine*) remède de charlatan.

not [nɒt] *adv* **(a)** (*with vb*) ne ... pas, ne ... point (*liter, also hum*). **he is ~ here** il n'est pas ici; **he has ~** *or* **hasn't come** il n'est pas venu; **he will ~** *or* **won't stay** il ne restera pas; **is it ~?, isn't it?** non?, n'est-ce pas?; **you have got it, haven't you?** vous l'avez (bien), non? *or* n'est-ce pas?; **he told me ~ to come** il m'a dit de ne pas venir; **~ to mention ...** sans compter ..., pour ne pas parler de ...; **~ wanting to be heard he removed his shoes** ne voulant pas qu'on l'entende il ôta ses chaussures.

(b) (*as substitute for clause*) non. **is he coming? — I believe ~** est-ce qu'il vient? — je crois que non; **is it going to rain? — I hope ~** va-t-il pleuvoir? — j'espère que non; **it would appear ~** il semble que non; **I am going whether he comes or ~** j'y vais qu'il vienne ou non; **believe it or ~, she has gone** le croiriez-vous, elle est partie.

(c) (*elliptically*) **are you cold? — ~ at all** avez-vous froid? — pas du tout; **thank you very much — ~ at all** merci beaucoup — je vous en prie *or* de rien *or* il n'y a pas de quoi; **~ in the least** pas du tout, nullement; **I wish it were ~ so** je voudrais bien qu'il en soit autrement; **big, ~ to say enormous** gros pour ne pas dire énorme; **~ that I care** non pas que cela me fasse quelque chose*; **~ that I know of** pas (autant) que je sache; **~ that they haven't been useful, ~ but what they have been useful*** on ne peut pas dire qu'ils *or* ce n'est pas qu'ils n'aient pas été utiles; **will he come? — as likely as ~** est-ce qu'il viendra? — ça se peut; **as likely as ~ he'll come** il y a une chance sur deux *or* il y a des chances (pour) qu'il vienne; **why ~?** pourquoi pas?

(d) (*understatement*) **~ a few ...** bien des ..., pas mal de ...; **~ without reason** et pour cause, non sans raison; **~ without some regrets** non sans quelques regrets; **I shall ~ be sorry to ...** je ne serai pas mécontent de ...; **it is ~ unlikely that ...** il n'est pas du tout impossible que ...; **a ~ inconsiderable number of ...** un nombre non négligeable de ...; **~ half!‡** tu parles!‡, et comment!‡

(e) (*with pron etc*) **~ I!** moi pas!, pas moi!; **~ one book** pas un livre; **~ one man knew** pas un (homme) ne savait; **~ everyone can do that** tout le monde ne peut pas faire cela; **~ any more** plus (maintenant); **~ yet** pas encore.

(f) (*with adj*) non, pas. **~ guilty** non coupable; **~ negotiable** non négociable.

notability [ˌnəʊtə'bɪlɪtɪ] *n* **(a)** (*U: quality*) prééminence *f*. **(b)** (*person*) notabilité *f*, notable *m*.

notable ['nəʊtəbl] 1 *adj person* notable, éminent; *thing, fact* notable, remarquable. **it is ~ that ...** il est remarquable que ... + *subj*. 2 *n* notable *m*.

notably ['nəʊtəblɪ] *adv* **(a)** (*in particular*) notamment, particulièrement, spécialement. **(b)** (*outstandingly*) notablement, remarquablement.

notarial [nəʊ'tɛərɪəl] *adj seal* notarial; *deed* notarié; *style* de notaire.

notary ['nəʊtərɪ] *n* (*also* **~ public**) notaire *m*. **before a ~** par-devant notaire.

notation [nəʊ'teɪʃən] *n* notation *f*; (*Math*) numération *f*.

notch [nɒtʃ] 1 *n* (*in wood, stick etc*) entaille *f*, encoche *f*, coche *f*; (*in belt etc*) cran *m*; (*in wheel, board etc*) dent *f*, cran; (*in saw*) dent; (*in blade*) ébréchure *f*; (*US Geog*) défilé *m*; (*Sewing*) cran. **he pulled his belt in one ~** il resserra sa ceinture d'un cran.

2 *vt stick etc* encocher, cocher; *wheel etc* cranter, denteler; *blade* ébrécher; (*Sewing*) *seam* cranter.

notch together *vt sep* (*Carpentry*) assembler à entailles.

notch up *vt sep score, point etc* marquer.

note [nəʊt] 1 *n* **(a)** (*short record of facts etc*) note *f*. **to take** *or* **make a ~ of sth** prendre qch en note, prendre note de qch; **please make a ~ of her name** prenez note de son nom s'il vous plaît; (*fig*) **I must make a ~ to buy some more** il faut que je me souvienne d'en racheter; *[student, policeman, secretary etc]* **to take** *or* **make ~s** prendre des notes; **lecture ~s** notes de cours; **to speak from ~s** parler en consultant ses notes; **to speak without ~s** parler sans notes *or* papiers; *V* **compare**.

(b) (*Diplomacy*) note *f*. **diplomatic ~** note diplomatique, mémorandum *m*; **official ~ from the government** note officielle du gouvernement.

(c) (*short commentary*) note *f*, annotation *f*, commentaire *m*. **author's ~** note de l'auteur; **translator's ~s** (*footnotes etc*) remarques *fpl or* notes du traducteur; (*foreword*) 'préface *f* du traducteur'; **'N~s on Gibbon'** 'Remarques *or* Notes sur Gibbon'; **~s on a literary work** commentaire sur un ouvrage littéraire; **to put ~s into a text** annoter un texte.

(d) (*informal letter*) mot *m*. **take a ~ to Mr X, Miss Jones** je vais vous dicter un mot pour M X, Mlle Jones; **just a quick ~ to tell you ...** un petit mot à la hâte *or* en vitesse pour te dire ... .

(e) (*Mus*) note *f*; *[piano]* touche *f*; *[bird]* note. **to give the ~** donner la note; **to hold a ~** tenir *or* prolonger une note; **to play a false ~, to sing a false ~** faire une fausse note; (*fig*) **his speech struck the right/wrong ~** son discours était bien dans la note/n'était pas dans la note.

(f) (*quality, tone*) note *f*, ton *m*, accent *m*. **with a ~ of anxiety in his voice** avec une note d'anxiété dans la voix; **his voice held a ~ of desperation** sa voix avait un accent de désespoir; **a ~ of nostalgia** une note *or* touche nostalgique; **a ~ of warning** un avertissement discret.

(g) (*Brit: also* **bank~**) billet *m* (de banque). **one-pound ~** billet d'une livre (sterling).

(h) (*Comm*) billet *m*, bon *m*. **~ of hand** reconnaissance *f* (de dette); *V* **advice, promissory**.

(i) (*U: notability*) **a man of ~** un homme éminent *or* de marque; **a family of ~** une famille éminente; **all the people of ~** toutes les notabilités; **nothing of ~** rien d'important.

(j) (*U: notice*) **to take ~ of** prendre (bonne) note de, remarquer; **take ~!** prenez bonne note!; **the critics took ~ of the book** les critiques ont remarqué le livre; **they will take ~ of what you say** ils feront *or* prêteront attention à ce que vous dites; **worthy of ~** remarquable, digne d'attention.

2 *cpd*: **notebook** carnet *m*, calepin *m*, agenda *m*; (*Scol*) cahier *m*; *[stenographer]* bloc-notes *m*; (*Brit*) **note-case** portefeuille *m*, porte-billets *m inv*; (*Brit*) **notepad** bloc-notes *m*; **notepaper** papier *m* à lettres; **noteworthiness** importance *f*; **noteworthy** notable, remarquable, digne d'attention; **it is noteworthy that ...** il convient de noter que ... .

3 *vt* **(a)** (*Admin, Jur etc*) noter, prendre (bonne) note de. **to ~ a fact** prendre acte d'un fait; (*Jur*) **'which fact is duly ~d'** 'dont acte'; **we have ~d your remarks** nous avons pris (bonne) note de vos remarques.

(b) (*notice*) remarquer, constater. **to ~ an error** relever une faute; **~ that the matter is not closed yet** notez *or* remarquez bien que l'affaire n'est pas encore close; **she ~d that his hands were dirty** elle remarqua qu'il avait les mains sales; **she ~d that they hadn't arrived** elle constata qu'ils n'étaient pas arrivés.

(c) (*also* **~ down**) noter, inscrire, écrire. **let me ~ it (down)** laissez-moi le noter *or* l'écrire; **to ~ (down) sb's remarks** noter les remarques de qn; **to ~ (down) an appointment in one's diary** noter *or* inscrire un rendez-vous dans son agenda.

note down *vt sep* = **note 3c**.

noted ['nəʊtɪd] *adj person* éminent, illustre, célèbre; *thing, fact* réputé, célèbre. **to be ~ for one's generosity** être (bien) connu pour sa générosité, avoir une réputation de générosité; (*iro*) **he's not ~ for his broad-mindedness** il n'est pas connu pour la largeur de ses vues; **a town ~ for its beauty** une ville connue *or* célèbre pour sa beauté; **a place ~ for its wine** un endroit célèbre *or* réputé pour son vin.

nothing ['nʌθɪŋ] 1 *n* **(a)** rien *m*. **I saw ~** je n'ai rien vu; **~ happened** il n'est rien arrivé, il ne s'est rien passé; **to eat ~** ne rien manger; **~ to eat/read** rien à manger/à lire; **he's had ~ to eat yet** il n'a pas encore mangé; **he's eaten ~ yet** il n'a encore rien mangé; **~ could be easier** rien de plus simple; **~ pleases him** rien ne le satisfait, il n'est jamais content; **there is ~ that pleases him** il n'y a rien qui lui plaise.

(b) (+ *adj*) rien de. **~ new/interesting** *etc* rien de nouveau/d'intéressant *etc*.

(c) (*in phrases*) **he's five foot ~** il ne fait qu'un mètre cinquante; **~ on earth** rien au monde; **you look like ~ on earth*** tu as l'air de je ne sais quoi; **as if ~ had happened** comme si de rien n'était; **fit for ~** propre *or* bon (*f* bonne) à rien; **to say ~ of ...** sans parler de ...; **I can do ~ (about it)** je n'y peux rien; **he is**

~ **if not polite** il est avant tout poli; **for** ~ (*in vain*) en vain, inutilement; (*without payment*) pour rien, gratuitement; (*for no reason*) sans raison; **he was working for** ~ il travaillait gratuitement *or* sans se faire payer *or* bénévolement; **he got** ~ **out of it** il n'en a rien retiré, il n'y a rien gagné; **all his fame was as** ~, **all his fame stood** *or* **counted for** ~ toute sa gloire ne comptait pour rien; **to think** ~ **of doing sth** (*do as matter of course*) trouver naturel de faire qch, n'attacher aucune importance à faire qch; (*do unscrupulously*) n'avoir aucun scrupule à faire qch; **think** ~ **of it!** mais je vous en prie!, mais pas du tout!; **don't apologize, it's** ~ ne vous excusez pas, ce n'est rien; **that is** ~ **to you** (*it's easy for you*) pour vous ce n'est rien; (*it's not your business*) cela ne vous regarde pas; **she is** *or* **means** ~ **to him** elle n'est rien pour lui; **it's** ~ *or* **it means** ~ **to me whether he comes or not** il m'est indifférent qu'il vienne ou non; **as a secretary she is** ~ **to** *or* ~ **compared with her sister** comme secrétaire elle ne vaut pas sa sœur; **I can make** ~ **of it** je n'y comprends rien; **to have** ~ **on** (*be naked*) être nu; **I have** ~ **on (for) this evening** je ne suis pas pris ce soir, je n'ai rien (de prévu) ce soir; **there's** ~ **in it** (*not interesting*) c'est sans intérêt; (*not true*) ce n'est absolument pas vrai; **there's** ~ **in these rumours** il n'y a rien de vrai *or* pas un grain de vérité dans ces rumeurs; **there's** ~ **in it for us** nous n'avons rien à y gagner; **there's** ~ **to it*** c'est facile (comme bonjour*); **I love swimming, there's** ~ **like it!** j'adore la natation, il n'y a rien de tel! *or* de mieux!; **there's** ~ **like exercise for keeping one fit** il n'y a rien de tel que l'exercice pour garder la forme, rien ne vaut l'exercice pour rester en forme; (*Prov*) ~ **venture** ~ **gain** *or* **have** *or* **win** qui ne risque rien n'a rien (*Prov*); **you get** ~ **for** ~ on n'a rien pour rien; **to come to** ~ ne pas aboutir, ne rien donner, faire fiasco; **to reduce to** ~ réduire à néant *or* à rien; **there's** ~ **wrong with that sentence** cette phrase est tout à fait correcte; **he looks ill but there's** ~ **wrong with him** il a mauvaise mine mais il va très bien; ~ **much** pas grand-chose; ~ **but** rien que; **he does** ~ **but eat** il ne fait que manger; **I get** ~ **but complaints all day** je n'entends que des plaintes à longueur de journée; (*Brit*) **there's** ~ **for it but to go** il n'y a qu'à *or* il ne nous reste qu'à partir; ~ **less than** rien moins que; ~ **more** rien de plus; ~ **else** rien d'autre; **there's** ~ **else for it** c'est inévitable; **we could do** ~ **else** (*nothing more*) nous ne pouvions rien faire de plus; (*no other thing*) nous ne pouvions rien faire d'autre; **that has** ~ **to do with us** nous n'avons rien à voir là-dedans; **I've got** ~ **to do with it** je n'y suis pour rien; **have** ~ **to do with it!** ne vous en mêlez pas!; **that has** ~ **to do with it** cela n'entre pas en ligne de compte; **there is** ~ **to laugh at** il n'y a pas de quoi rire; **he had** ~ **to say for himself** (*no explanation*) il se trouvait sans excuse; (*no conversation*) il n'avait pas de conversation; **I have** ~ **against him/the idea** je n'ai rien contre lui/cette idée; **there was** ~ **doing* at the club so I went home** il ne se passait rien d'intéressant au club, alors je suis rentré; **will you come?** — ~ **doing!*** tu vas venir? — rien à faire! *or* pas question!

(d) (*Math*) zéro *m*.

(e) (*U: nothingness*) néant *m*, rien *m*.

(f) (*person*) zéro *m*, nullité *f*; (*thing*) vétille *f*, rien *m*. **it's a mere** ~ **compared with what he spent last year** ça n'est rien *or* c'est une paille en comparaison de ce qu'il a dépensé l'an dernier; **to say sweet** ~**s to sb** conter fleurette à qn; **he's just a** ~ c'est une nullité *or* un zéro.

2 *adv* aucunement, nullement, pas du tout. ~ **less than** rien moins que; **he is** ~ **the worse for it** il ne s'en porte pas plus mal; **it was** ~ **like as big as we thought** c'était loin d'être aussi grand qu'on avait cru; *V* **loath.**

nothingness ['nʌθɪŋnɪs] *n* (*U*) néant *m*.

notice ['nəʊtɪs] **1** *n* **(a)** (*U*) (*warning, intimation*) avis *m*, notification *f*; (*period*) délai *m*. ~ **is hereby given that ...** il est porté à la connaissance du public par la présente que ...; **advance** ~ préavis *m*; **final** ~ dernier avertissement; ~ **to pay** avis d'avoir à payer; (*Comm*) ~ **of receipt** avis de réception; (*to tenant etc*) ~ **to quit** congé *m*; **to give** ~ **to** (*to tenant*) donner congé à; (*to landlord etc*) donner un préavis de départ à (*V also* **1b**); **to give sb** ~ **to do sth** aviser qn d'avoir à faire qch; **to give sb** ~ **that ...**, (*frm*) **to serve** ~ **on sb that ...** aviser qn que ..., faire savoir à qn que ...; **to give** ~ **that ...** faire savoir que ...; (*Admin etc: officially*) donner acte que ... (*Admin*); **to give** ~ **of sth** annoncer qch; **to give sb** ~ **of sth** avertir *or* prévenir qn de qch; (*Admin etc: officially*) donner acte à qn de qch; **I must have (some)** ~ **of what you intend to do** il faut que je sois prévenu *or* avisé à l'avance de ce que vous avez l'intention de faire; **we require 6 days'** ~ nous demandons un préavis de 6 jours; **you must give me at least a week's** ~ **if you want to do ...** il faut me prévenir *or* m'avertir au moins une semaine à l'avance si vous voulez faire ...; **we had no** ~ **(of it)** nous n'(en) avons pas été prévenus à l'avance, nous n'avons pas eu de préavis (à ce sujet); (*Admin frm*) **without (previous)** ~ sans préavis, sans avis préalable; **without any** ~, **with no** ~ sans en aviser personne; **until further** ~ jusqu'à nouvel ordre; **at short** ~ à bref délai; (*Fin*) à court terme; **you must be ready to leave at very short** ~ il faut que vous soyiez prêt à partir dans les plus brefs délais; **at a moment's** ~ sur-le-champ, immédiatement; **at 3 days'** ~ dans un délai de 3 jours.

(b) (*U: end of work contract*) (*by employer*) congé *m*; (*by employee*) démission *f*. **to give sb** ~ **of dismissal** (*employee*) licencier qn, renvoyer qn; (*servant etc*) donner son congé à qn, congédier qn; **to give** ~, **to give in** *or* **hand in one's** ~ *[professional or office worker]* donner sa démission; *[servant]* donner ses huit jours; **he was dismissed without (any)** ~ *or* **with no** ~ il a été renvoyé sans préavis; **to get one's** ~ recevoir son licenciement *or* son congé; **he's under** ~ **(to leave)** il a reçu son congé; **a week's** ~ une semaine de préavis, un préavis d'une semaine.

(c) (*announcement*) avis *m*, annonce *f*; (*esp in newspaper*) entrefilet *m*, notice *f*; (*poster*) affiche *f*, placard *m*; (*sign*) pancarte *f*, écriteau *m*. **public** ~ avis au public; **to put a** ~ **in the paper** mettre *or* faire insérer une annonce *or* un entrefilet dans le journal; (*Press*) **birth/marriage/death** ~ annonce de naissance/mariage/décès; **I saw a** ~ **in the paper about the concert** j'ai vu une annonce *or* un entrefilet *or* une notice dans le journal à propos du concert; **the** ~ **says 'keep out'** la pancarte *or* l'écriteau porte l'inscription 'défense d'entrer'; **the** ~ **of the meeting was published in ...** l'annonce de la réunion *or* la notice annonçant la réunion a été publiée dans ... .

(d) (*review*) *[book, film, play etc]* compte rendu *m*, critique *f*. **the book/film/play got good** ~**s** le livre/le film/la pièce a eu de bonnes critiques.

(e) (*U*) **to take** ~ **of sb/sth** observer qn/qch, tenir compte de qn/qch, prêter attention à qn/qch; **to take no** ~ **of sb/sth** ne tenir aucun compte de qn/qch, ne prêter aucune attention à qn/qch; **take no** ~**!** ne faites pas attention!; **he took no** ~ **of her remarks** il ne tint aucun compte de ses remarques; **he took no** ~ **of her** il ne fit aucune attention à elle; **a lot of** ~ **he takes of me!** pour lui c'est comme si je n'existais pas!; **I wasn't taking much** ~ **at the time** je ne faisais pas très attention à ce moment-là; **it has attracted a lot of** ~ cela a suscité un grand intérêt; **it escaped his** ~ **that ...** il ne s'est pas aperçu que ..., il n'a pas remarqué que ...; **to attract** ~ se faire remarquer, s'afficher (*pej*); **to avoid** ~ (essayer de) passer inaperçu; **to bring to sb's** ~ faire observer *or* faire remarquer à qn, porter à la connaissance de qn; **it came to his** ~ **that ...** il s'est aperçu que ..., son attention a été attirée sur le fait que ...; **it has come** *or* **it has been brought to my** ~ **that ...** il a été porté à ma connaissance que ..., il m'a été signalé que ...; **that is beneath my** ~ c'est indigne de mon attention; *V* **sit up, slip.**

2 *vt* **(a)** (*perceive*) s'apercevoir de, remarquer; (*heed*) faire attention à. **I** ~**d a tear in his coat** j'ai remarqué un accroc dans son manteau; **when he** ~**d me he called out to me** quand il m'a vu *or* s'est aperçu que j'étais là il m'a appelé; **to** ~ **a mistake** remarquer une *or* s'apercevoir d'une faute; **without my noticing it** sans que je le remarque (*subj*) *or* m'en aperçoive, sans que j'y fasse attention; **I'm afraid I didn't** ~ malheureusement je n'ai pas remarqué; **I never** ~ **such things** je ne remarque jamais ces choses-là, je ne fais jamais attention à ces choses-là; **I** ~**d her hesitating** j'ai remarqué *or* je me suis aperçu qu'elle hésitait; **I** ~ **you have a new dress** je vois que vous avez une nouvelle robe.

(b) (*review*) *book, film, play* faire le compte rendu *or* la critique de.

3 *cpd*: (*Brit*) **notice board** (*printed or painted sign*) écriteau *m*, pancarte *f*; (*for holding announcements*) panneau *m* d'affichage.

noticeable ['nəʊtɪsəbl] *adj* (*perceptible*) perceptible, visible; (*obvious*) évident, net (*f* nette), clair. **it isn't really** ~ ça ne se voit pas vraiment; **his lack of enthusiasm was very** ~ son manque d'enthousiasme était très visible *or* perceptible; **she was** ~ **on account of her large hat** elle se faisait remarquer par son énorme chapeau; **it is** ~ **that ...** il est évident *or* net *or* clair que ... .

noticeably ['nəʊtɪsəblɪ] *adv* sensiblement, perceptiblement, visiblement.

notifiable ['nəʊtɪfaɪəbl] *adj* (*Admin etc*) *disease* à déclarer obligatoirement. **all changes of address are** ~ **immediately** tout changement d'adresse doit être signalé immédiatement aux autorités.

notification [ˌnəʊtɪfɪ'keɪʃən] *n* avis *m*, annonce *f*, notification *f*; *[marriage, engagement]* annonce; *[birth, death]* déclaration *f*. (*Press*) **'please accept this as the only** ~**'** 'le présent avis tient lieu de faire-part'.

notify ['nəʊtɪfaɪ] *vt*: **to** ~ **sth to sb** signaler *or* notifier qch à qn; **to** ~ **sb of sth** aviser *or* avertir qn de qch; **any change of address must be notified** tout changement d'adresse doit être signalé *or* notifié; **you will be notified later of the result** on vous communiquera le résultat ultérieurement *or* plus tard.

notion ['nəʊʃən] *n* **(a)** (*thought, project*) idée *f*. **brilliant** ~ idée géniale *or* de génie; **what a** ~**!** quelle idée!, en voilà une idée!; **what a funny** ~**!** quelle drôle d'idée!; **I can't bear the** ~ **(of it)** je n'ose pas y penser; **he has** *or* **gets some wonderful** ~**s** il a de merveilleuses idées; **I've got a** ~ **for a play** j'ai l'idée d'une pièce; **I hit (up)on** *or* **suddenly had the** ~ **of going to see her** tout à coup l'idée m'est venue d'aller la voir; **that** ~ **never entered my head** cette idée ne m'est jamais venue, je n'y ai jamais pensé; **he got the** ~ **(into his head)** *or* **he somehow got hold of the** ~ **that she wouldn't help him** il s'est mis en tête (l'idée) qu'elle ne l'aiderait pas; **where did you get the** ~ *or* **what gave you the** ~ **that I couldn't come?** où as-tu pris l'idée que *or* qu'est-ce qui t'a fait penser que je ne pourrais pas venir?; **to put** ~**s into sb's head, to give sb** ~**s** mettre *or* fourrer* des idées dans la tête de qn; **that gave me the** ~ **of inviting her** cela m'a donné l'idée de l'inviter.

(b) (*opinion*) idée *f*, opinion *f*; (*way of thinking*) conception *f*, façon *f* de penser. **he has some odd** ~**s** il a de drôles d'idées; **she has some odd** ~**s about how to bring up children** elle a de drôles d'idées sur la façon d'élever les enfants; **according to his** ~ selon sa façon de penser; **if that's your** ~ **of fun ...** si c'est ça que tu appelles t'amuser ...; **it wasn't my** ~ **of a holiday** ce n'était pas ce que j'appelle des vacances.

(c) (*vague knowledge*) idée *f*, notion *f*. **I've got some** ~ **of physics** j'ai quelques notions de physique; **have you any** ~ **of what he meant to do?** avez-vous la moindre idée de ce qu'il voulait faire?; **I haven't the least** *or* **slightest** *or* **foggiest*** ~ je n'en ai pas la moindre idée; **I have a** ~ **that he was going to Paris** j'ai idée *or* j'ai dans l'idée qu'il allait à Paris; **I had no** ~ **they knew each other** je n'avais aucune idée *or* j'ignorais absolument qu'ils se connaissaient; **can you give me a rough ~ of how many you want?** pouvez-vous m'indiquer en gros combien vous en voulez?

(d) (*US: ribbons, thread etc*) **~s** (articles *mpl* de) mercerie *f*.

notional [ˈnəʊʃənl] *adj* **(a)** (*not real*) imaginaire, irréel. **(b)** (*Ling*) **~ grammar** grammaire notionnelle; **~ word** mot plein. **(c)** (*Philos*) notionnel, conceptuel. **(d)** (*US: whimsical*) *person* capricieux, fantasque.

notoriety [ˌnəʊtəˈraɪətɪ] *n* **(a)** (*U*) (triste) notoriété *f*, triste réputation *f*. **(b)** (*person*) individu *m* au nom tristement célèbre.

notorious [nəʊˈtɔːrɪəs] *adj event, act* d'une triste notoriété; *crime* notoire, célèbre; *person* (au nom) tristement célèbre; *place* mal famé. **a ~ liar** un menteur *or* une menteuse notoire; **a ~ woman** une femme de mauvaise réputation; **the ~ case of ...** le cas tristement célèbre de ...; **he is ~ for his dishonesty** il est d'une malhonnêteté notoire; **it is ~ that ...** c'est un fait notoire que ..., il est de notoriété publique que ... .

notoriously [nəʊˈtɔːrɪəslɪ] *adv* notoirement. **this office is ~ inefficient** ce bureau est notoirement incompétent *or* est bien connu pour son incompétence; **it is ~ difficult to do that** il est notoire qu'il est difficile de faire cela, il est notoirement difficile de faire cela.

notwithstanding [ˌnɒtwɪθˈstændɪŋ] **1** *prep* malgré, en dépit de. **2** *adv* néanmoins, malgré tout, quand même, tout de même, pourtant. **3** *conj* (*gen* **~ that**) quoique + *subj*, bien que + *subj*.

nougat [ˈnuːgɑː] *n* nougat *m*.

nought [nɔːt] *n* = **naught**.

noun [naʊn] **1** *n* nom *m*, substantif *m*. **2** *cpd*: **noun clause** proposition substantive; **noun phrase** groupe nominal.

nourish [ˈnʌrɪʃ] *vt person* nourrir (*with* de); *leather etc* entretenir; (*fig*) *hopes etc* nourrir, entretenir; *V* **ill, under, well**[2].

nourishing [ˈnʌrɪʃɪŋ] *adj* nourrissant, nutritif.

nourishment [ˈnʌrɪʃmənt] *n* (*U: food*) nourriture *f*, aliments *mpl*. **he has taken (some) ~** il s'est (un peu) alimenté.

nous* [naʊs] *n* (*Brit: U*) bon sens. **he's got a lot of ~** il a du plomb dans la cervelle*.

nova [ˈnəʊvə] *n, pl* **~e** [ˈnəʊviː] *or* **~s** nova *f*.

Nova Scotia [ˈnəʊvəˈskəʊʃə] *n* Nouvelle-Écosse *f*.

novel [ˈnɒvəl] **1** *n* (*Literat*) roman *m*. **2** *adj* nouveau (*f* nouvelle) (*after n*), original, singulier. **this is something ~** voici quelque chose de neuf.

novelette [ˌnɒvəˈlet] *n* (*Literat*) nouvelle *f*; (*slightly pej*) roman *m* à bon marché, roman à deux sous; (*love story*) (petit) roman à l'eau de rose.

novelettish [ˌnɒvəˈletɪʃ] *adj* (*pej*) de roman à deux sous; (*sentimental*) à l'eau de rose.

novelist [ˈnɒvəlɪst] *n* romancier *m*, -ière *f*.

novelty [ˈnɒvəltɪ] *n* **(a)** (*U*) (*newness*) nouveauté *f*; (*unusualness*) étrangeté *f*. **once the ~ has worn off** une fois passée la nouveauté.

(b) (*idea, thing*) innovation *f*. **it was quite a ~** c'était une innovation *or* du nouveau *or* de l'inédit.

(c) (*Comm*) (article *m* de) nouveauté *f*, fantaisie *f*.

November [nəʊˈvembəʳ] *n* novembre *m*; *for phrases V* **September.**

novena [nəʊˈviːnə] *n* neuvaine *f*.

novice [ˈnɒvɪs] *n* novice *mf*, apprenti(e) *m(f)*, débutant(e) *m(f)*; (*Rel*) novice. **to be a ~ at sth** être novice en qch; **he's a ~ in politics, he's a political ~** c'est un novice *or* débutant en politique; **he's no ~** il n'est pas novice, il n'en est pas à son coup d'essai.

noviciate, novitiate [nəʊˈvɪʃɪɪt] *n* (*Rel*) (*period*) (temps *m* du) noviciat *m*; (*place*) maison *f* des novices, noviciat; (*fig*) noviciat, apprentissage *m*.

novocain(e) [ˈnəʊvəʊkeɪn] *n* ® novocaïne *f* ®.

now [naʊ] **1** *adv* **(a)** (*at this time*) maintenant, à présent, actuellement, en ce moment; (*at that time*) alors, à ce moment-là; (*in these circumstances*) maintenant, dans ces circonstances, à ce moment-là. **I'm writing it (right) ~** j'écris ceci actuellement *or* en ce moment *or* à présent *or* à l'instant même; **he ~ understood why she had left him** alors il comprit *or* il comprit alors pourquoi elle l'avait quitté; **how can I believe you ~?** comment puis-je te croire maintenant? *or* dans ces circonstances?; **~ is the time to do it** c'est le moment de le faire; **~ is the best time to go to Scotland** c'est maintenant *or* en ce moment le meilleur moment pour aller en Écosse; **apples are in season just ~** c'est la saison des pommes maintenant *or* à présent *or* en ce moment; **I saw him come in just ~** je l'ai vu arriver à l'instant, je viens de le voir arriver; **I'll do it just ~** *or* **right ~** je vais le faire dès maintenant *or* à l'instant; **I must be off ~** sur ce *or* maintenant il faut que je me sauve (*subj*); **they won't be long ~** ils ne vont plus tarder (maintenant); **~ I'm ready** maintenant *or* à présent je suis prêt; **here and ~** sur-le-champ; **(every) ~ and again, (every) ~ and then** de temps en temps, de temps à autre, par moments; **it's ~ or never!** c'est le moment ou jamais!; **even ~ there's time to change your mind** il est encore temps (maintenant) de changer d'avis; **people do that even ~** les gens font ça encore aujourd'hui *or* maintenant; **even ~ we have no rifles** encore actuellement *or* à l'heure actuelle nous n'avons pas de fusils.

(b) (*with prep*) **you should have done that before ~** vous auriez dû déjà l'avoir fait; **before ~ people thought that ...** auparavant les gens pensaient que ...; **you should have finished long before ~** il y a longtemps que vous auriez dû avoir fini; **long before ~ it was realized that ...** il y a longtemps déjà on comprenait que ...; **between ~ and next Tuesday** d'ici (à) mardi prochain; **they should have arrived by ~** ils devraient être déjà arrivés, ils devraient être arrivés à l'heure qu'il est; **haven't you finished by ~?** vous n'avez toujours pas fini?, vous n'avez pas encore fini?; **by ~ it was clear that ...** déjà à ce moment-là il était évident que ...; **that will do for ~** ça ira pour l'instant *or* pour le moment; **from ~ on(wards)** (*with present tense*) à partir de maintenant; (*with future tense*) à partir de maintenant, dorénavant, désormais; (*with past tense*) dès lors, dès ce moment-là; **(in) 3 weeks from ~** d'ici (à) 3 semaines; **from ~ until then** d'ici là; **till ~, until ~, up to ~** (*till this moment*) jusqu'à présent, jusqu'ici; (*till that moment*) jusque-là.

(c) (*showing alternation*) **~ walking, ~ running** tantôt (en) marchant, tantôt (en) courant; **~ here, ~ there** tantôt par ici, tantôt par là.

(d) (*without temporal force*) **~!** bon!, alors!, bon alors!; **~, ~!** allons, allons!; (*warning*) **~, Johnny!** allons, Jeannot!; **come ~!** allons!; **well, ~!** eh bien!; **~ then, let's start!** bon, commençons!; **~ then, what's all this?** alors *or* allons, qu'est-ce que c'est que ça?; **~, they had been looking for him all morning** or, ils avaient passé toute la matinée à sa recherche; **~ he was a fisherman** or il était pêcheur; **~ do be quiet for a minute** allons, taisez-vous une minute.

2 *conj* maintenant que, à présent que. **~ (that) you've seen him** maintenant que *or* à présent que vous l'avez vu.

nowadays [ˈnaʊədeɪz] *adv* aujourd'hui, de nos jours, actuellement.

noway(s) [ˈnəʊweɪ(z)] *adv* (*US*) aucunement, nullement, en aucune façon.

nowhere [ˈnəʊwɛəʳ] *adv* **(a)** nulle part. **he went ~** il n'est allé nulle part; **~ in Europe** nulle part en Europe; **it's ~ you'll ever find it** c'est dans un endroit où tu ne le trouveras jamais; **it's ~ you know** ce n'est pas un endroit que tu connais; **where are you going? — ~ special** où vas-tu? — nulle part en particulier; **~ else** nulle part ailleurs; **she was ~ to be found** elle était introuvable; **she is ~ to be seen** on ne la voit *or* trouve nulle part; **they appeared from ~** *or* **out of ~** ils apparurent comme par miracle; **he seemed to come from ~** on aurait dit qu'il était tombé du ciel; **they came up from ~ and won the championship** ils sont revenus de loin pour gagner le championnat; **the rest of the runners came ~** les autres concurrents sont arrivés (bien) loin derrière; **lying will get you ~** tu ne gagneras rien à mentir, ça ne te servira à rien de mentir; **we're getting ~ (fast)*** ça ne nous mène strictement à rien.

(b) his house is ~ near the church sa maison n'est pas du tout vers l'église; **she is ~ near as clever as he is** il s'en faut de beaucoup qu'elle soit aussi intelligente que lui; **you are ~ near the truth** vous êtes à mille lieues de la vérité; **you're ~ near it!, you're ~ near right!** tu n'y es pas du tout!; **£10 is ~ near enough** 10 livres sont (très) loin du compte.

nowise [ˈnəʊwaɪz] *adv* (*US*) = **noway(s).**

nowt [naʊt] *n* (*Brit dial*) = **nothing.**

noxious [ˈnɒkʃəs] *adj fumes, gas* délétère, nocif; *substance, habit, influence* nocif. **to have a ~ effect on** avoir un effet nocif sur.

nozzle [ˈnɒzl] *n* **(a)** *[hose etc]* ajutage *m*, jet *m*; *[syringe]* canule *f*; *[bellows]* bec *m*; *[vacuum cleaner]* suceur *m*; *[flamethrower]* ajutage *m*. **(b)** (*: nose*) pif* *m*, blair* *m*.

nth [enθ] *adj V* **N b.**

nuance [ˈnjuːɑ̃ːns] *n* nuance *f*.

nub [nʌb] *n* (*small lump*) petit morceau. (*fig*) **the ~ of the matter** le cœur *or* le noyau *or* l'essentiel *m* de l'affaire.

nubile [ˈnjuːbaɪl] *adj* nubile.

nubility [njuːˈbɪlɪtɪ] *n* nubilité *f*.

nuclear [ˈnjuːklɪəʳ] *adj* **(a)** (*Phys*) *charge, energy* nucléaire; *war, missile* nucléaire, atomique. **~ deterrent** force *f* de dissuasion nucléaire; **~ disarmament** désarmement *m* nucléaire; **~ fission** fission *f* nucléaire *or* de l'atome; **~ fusion** fusion *f* de l'atome; **~ physicist** physicien(ne) *m(f)* atomiste; **~ physics** physique *f* nucléaire *or* atomique; **~ power station** centrale *f* nucléaire; **~ reaction** réaction *f* nucléaire *or* atomique; **~ reactor** réacteur *m* nucléaire, pile *f* atomique; **~(-powered) submarine** sous-marin *m* atomique; **~ scientist** (savant *m*) atomiste *m*; **~ test(ing)** essai *m* *or* expérience *f* nucléaire; **~ warhead** ogive *f* *or* tête *f* nucléaire.

(b) (*Soc*) **~ family** famille *f* nucléaire.

nuclei [ˈnjuːklɪaɪ] *npl of* **nucleus.**

nucleic [ˈnjuːklɪɪk] *adj*: **~ acid** acide *m* nucléique.

nucleo... [ˈnjuːklɪəʊ] *pref* nucléo... .

nucleus [ˈnjuːklɪəs] *n, pl* **nuclei** (*Astron, Phys*) noyau *m*; (*Bio*) *[cell]* nucléus *m*. **atomic ~** noyau atomique; (*fig*) **the ~ of a library/university/crew** les éléments *mpl* de base d'une bibliothèque/d'une université/d'un équipage; **the ~ of the affair** le noyau *or* le fond de l'affaire.

nude [njuːd] **1** *adj* nu. (*Art*) **~ figures, ~ studies** nus *mpl*. **2** *n* **(a)** (*Art*) nu(e) *m(f)*, figure nue, nudité *f*. **a Goya ~** un nu de Goya. **(b) the ~** le nu; **in the ~** nu.

nudge [nʌdʒ] **1** *vt* pousser du coude, donner un (petit) coup de coude à. (*fig*) **to ~ sb's memory** rafraîchir la mémoire à qn. **2** *n* coup *m* de coude.

nudism [ˈnjuːdɪzəm] *n* nudisme *m*.

nudist [ˈnjuːdɪst] *adj, n* nudiste (*mf*). **~ colony/camp** colonie *f*/camp *m* de nudistes.

nudity [ˈnjuːdɪtɪ] *n* nudité *f*.

nugatory [ˈnjuːgətərɪ] *adj* (*frm*) (*worthless*) futile, sans valeur; (*trivial*) insignifiant; (*ineffectual*) inefficace, inopérant; (*not valid*) non valable.

nugget [ˈnʌgɪt] *n* pépite *f*. **gold ~** pépite d'or.

nuisance [ˈnjuːsns] **1** *n* **(a)** (*thing, event*) ennui *m*, embêtement* *m*. **what a ~ he is not coming** que c'est ennuyeux *or* comme c'est embêtant* qu'il ne vienne pas; **it's a ~ having to shave** c'est assommant* d'avoir à se raser; **the ~ of having to shave each morning** l'embêtement* d'avoir à se raser tous les matins; **this wind is a ~** ce vent est bien embêtant* *or* gênant;

this hat is a ~ ce chapeau m'embête*; what a ~! quelle barbe!*, quelle plaie!*; these mosquitoes are a ~ ces moustiques sont une plaie* *or* sont assommants*.

(b) (*person*) peste *f*, fléau *m*. **that child is a perfect** ~ cet enfant est une vraie peste *or* un vrai fléau; **what a ~ you are!** ce que tu peux être empoisonnant!*; **you're being a** ~ tu nous embêtes*, tu nous casses les pieds‡; **to make a ~ of o.s.** embêter le monde*, être une peste *or* un fléau; **he's really a public** ~*, **he's public ~ number one*** c'est une calamité publique*, il empoisonne le monde*; *V also* **1c.**

(c) (*Jur*) infraction *f* simple, dommage *m* simple. **for causing a public** ~ pour dommage simple à autrui; **'commit no ~'** (*no litter*) 'défense de déposer des ordures'; (*do not urinate*) 'défense d'uriner'.

2 *cpd*: **it has a certain nuisance value** cela sert à gêner *or* embêter* le monde.

null [nʌl] *adj* **(a)** (*Jur*) *act, decree* nul (*f* nulle), invalide; *legacy* caduc (*f* -uque). ~ **and void** nul et non avenu; **to render** ~ annuler, infirmer, invalider. **(b)** (*ineffectual*) *thing* inefficace, inopérant, sans effet; *person* insignifiant.

nullification [ˌnʌlɪfɪˈkeɪʃən] *n* infirmation *f*, invalidation *f*.

nullify [ˈnʌlɪfaɪ] *vt* infirmer, invalider.

nullity [ˈnʌlɪtɪ] **1** *n* (*U: Jur*) *[act, decree]* nullité *f*, invalidité *f*; *[legacy]* caducité *f*. **2** *cpd*: (*Jur*) **nullity suit** demande *f* en nullité de mariage.

numb [nʌm] **1** *adj* engourdi, gourd; (*fig*) paralysé. **hands ~ with cold** mains engourdies par le froid; **my fingers have gone** ~ mes doigts se sont engourdis; **to be ~ with fright** être paralysé par la peur, être transi *or* glacé de peur.

2 *vt* engourdir; (*fig*) *[fear etc]* transir, glacer. **~ed with grief** muet (*f* muette) *or* figé de douleur; **~ed with fear** paralysé par la peur, transi *or* glacé de peur.

number [ˈnʌmbəʳ] **1** *n* **(a)** (*Math*) nombre *m*, chiffre *m*. **even/odd/whole/cardinal/ordinal** ~ nombre pair/impair/entier/cardinal/ordinal; **round** ~ chiffre rond; **in round ~s** en chiffres ronds; (*Bible*) **the Book of N~s** les Nombres.

(b) (*quantity, amount*) nombre *m*, quantité *f*. **a ~ of people** un certain nombre de gens, plusieurs personnes; **(large) ~s of people** (un grand) nombre de gens, de nombreuses personnes; **a great ~ of books/chairs** une grande quantité de livres/chaises; **in a small ~ of cases** dans un petit nombre de cas; **on a ~ of occasions** à plusieurs occasions, à maintes occasions; **there were a ~ of faults in the machine** la machine avait un (certain) nombre de défauts; **a fair** ~ un assez grand nombre; **boys and girls in equal ~s** garçons et filles en nombre égal; **~s being equal** à nombre égal; **10 in** ~ au nombre de 10; **they were 10 in** ~ ils étaient (au nombre de) 10; **to the ~ of some 200** au nombre de 200 environ; **few in ~, in small ~s** en petit nombre; **many in ~, in large ~s** en grand nombre; **to swell the ~ of** grossir le nombre de; **he was brought in to swell the ~s** on l'a amené pour grossir l'effectif; **without** ~ innombrable, sans nombre; **times without** ~ à maintes reprises, mille et mille fois; **any ~ can play** le nombre de joueurs est illimité; **there were any ~ of cards in the box** il y avait une quantité *or* un tas* de cartes dans la boîte; **I've told you any ~ of times** je ne sais pas combien de fois je te l'ai dit; **they are found in ~s in Africa** on les trouve en grand nombre en Afrique; **they came in their ~s** ils sont venus en grand nombre; **there were flies in such ~s that ...** les mouches étaient en si grand nombre que ...; **the power of ~s** le pouvoir du nombre; **to win by force of ~s** *or* **by sheer ~s** l'emporter par le nombre *or* par la force du nombre; **one of their** ~ un d'entre eux; **one of our** ~ un des nôtres; **he was of our** ~ il était des nôtres, il était avec nous.

(c) *[house, page etc]* (*also Telec*) numéro *m*. (*Telec*) **wrong** ~ faux numéro; **at ~ 4** au (numéro) 4; (*Brit Pol*) **N~ 10** 10 Downing Street (*résidence du Premier ministre*); **reference** ~ numéro de référence; (*Aut, Mil*) **(registration)** ~ (numéro d')immatriculation *f*, numéro minéralogique; **to take a car's** ~ relever le numéro d'une voiture; (*fig*) **I've got his ~!*** je le connais, lui! (*pej*); **his ~'s up*** il est fichu*, son compte est bon; **that bullet had his ~ on it!*** (il était dit que) cette balle était pour lui!; ~ **one*** moi, bibi‡, ma pomme‡, mézigue‡; **he only thinks of ~ one*** il ne pense qu'à lui *or* à cézigue‡ *or* à sa pomme‡; **to take care of** *or* **look after ~ one*** penser avant tout à son propre intérêt; **the ~ one English player** le meilleur *or* premier joueur anglais; **he's my ~ two*** il est mon second; *V* **opposite.**

(d) *[manufactured goods, clothes, car]* modèle *m*; *[newspaper, journal]* numéro *m*. **the January** ~ le numéro de janvier; **this car's a nice little ~*** c'est une chouette* petite voiture; **she's a pretty little ~*** c'est une jolie fille, c'est une belle nénette‡; *V* **back.**

(e) *[music hall, circus]* numéro *m*; *[pianist, dance band]* morceau *m*; *[singer]* chanson *f*; *[dancer]* danse *f*. **there were several dance ~s on the programme** le programme comprenait plusieurs numéros de danse; *[singer]* **my next ~ will be ...** je vais maintenant chanter ... .

(f) (*U: Gram etc*) nombre *m*. ~ **is one of the basic concepts** le (concept de) nombre est un des concepts de base.

(g) (*Mus*) rythme *m*. **~s** (*Poetry*) vers *mpl*, poésie *f*; (*Mus*) mesures *fpl*.

2 *cpd*: (*Brit Aut*) **number plate** plaque *f* minéralogique *or* d'immatriculation *or* de police.

3 *vt* **(a)** (*give a number to*) numéroter. **the houses are not ~ed** les maisons n'ont pas de numéro.

(b) (*include*) compter, comprendre. **the library ~s 30,000 volumes** la bibliothèque compte *or* comporte 30.000 volumes; **I ~ him among my friends** je le compte parmi mes amis; **to be ~ed with the heroes** compter au nombre des *or* parmi les héros.

(c) (*amount to*) compter. **the crew ~s 50 men** l'équipage compte 50 hommes; **they ~ed 700** leur nombre s'élevait *or* se montait à 700, ils étaient au nombre de 700.

(d) (*count*) compter. (*fig*) **his days were ~ed** ses jours étaient comptés; **your chances of trying again are ~ed** il ne te reste plus beaucoup d'occasions de tenter ta chance; **he was ~ing the hours till the attack began** il comptait les heures qui le séparaient de l'assaut.

4 *vi* (*Mil etc: also* ~ **off**) **to ~ (off) (from the right)** se numéroter (en partant de la droite).

numbering [ˈnʌmbərɪŋ] *n* (*U*) compte *m*, comptage *m*, dénombrement *m*; *[houses etc]* numérotage *m*.

numberless [ˈnʌmbəlɪs] *adj* innombrable, sans nombre.

numbness [ˈnʌmnɪs] *n [hand, finger, senses]* engourdissement *m*; *[mind]* torpeur *f*, engourdissement.

numerable [ˈnjuːmərəbl] *adj* nombrable, dénombrable.

numeracy [ˈnjuːmərəsɪ] *n* (*U*) notions *fpl* de calcul, capacités *fpl* au calcul.

numeral [ˈnjuːmərəl] **1** *n* chiffre *m*, nombre *m*. **Arabic/Roman** ~ chiffre arabe/romain. **2** *adj* numéral.

numerate [ˈnjuːmərɪt] *adj* qui a le sens de l'arithmétique. **he is hardly** ~ il sait à peine compter.

numeration [ˌnjuːməˈreɪʃən] *n* (*Math*) numération *f*.

numerator [ˈnjuːməreɪtəʳ] *n* (*Math*) numérateur *m*; (*instrument*) numéroteur *m*.

numerical [njuːˈmerɪkəl] *adj* numérique. **in ~ order** dans l'ordre numérique.

numerically [njuːˈmerɪkəlɪ] *adv* numériquement. ~ **superior to the enemy** supérieur (*f* -eure) en nombre *or* numériquement supérieur à l'ennemi.

numerous [ˈnjuːmərəs] *adj* nombreux. **a ~ family** une famille nombreuse; **in ~ cases** dans de nombreux cas, dans beaucoup de cas.

numismatic [ˌnjuːmɪzˈmætɪk] *adj* numismatique.

numismatics [ˌnjuːmɪzˈmætɪks] *n* (*U*) numismatique *f*.

numismatist [njuːˈmɪzmətɪst] *n* numismate *mf*.

numskull [ˈnʌmskʌl] *n* imbécile *mf*, gourde‡ *f*.

nun [nʌn] *n* religieuse *f*, bonne sœur*. **to become a** ~ entrer en religion, prendre le voile.

nunciature [ˈnʌnʃɪətjʊəʳ] *n* nonciature *f*.

nuncio [ˈnʌnʃɪəʊ] *n* nonce *m*; *V* **papal.**

nunnery† [ˈnʌnərɪ] *n* couvent *m*.

nuptial [ˈnʌpʃəl] (*liter or hum*) **1** *adj* nuptial. **the ~ day** le jour des noces. **2** *npl*: **~s** noce *f*.

nurse [nɜːs] **1** *n* **(a)** (*in hospital*) infirmière *f*; (*at home*) infirmière, garde-malade *f*. **male** ~ infirmier *m*, garde-malade *m*; *V* **night.**

(b) (*children's* ~) nurse *f*, bonne *f* d'enfants. **yes** ~ oui nounou.

(c) (*wet-*~) nourrice *f*.

2 *cpd*: **nursemaid** bonne *f* d'enfants.

3 *vt* **(a)** (*Med*) soigner; (*suckle*) nourrir, allaiter; (*cradle in arms*) bercer (dans ses bras). **she ~d him through pneumonia** elle l'a soigné pendant sa pneumonie; **she ~d him back to health** il a guéri grâce à ses soins; **to ~ a cold** soigner un rhume.

(b) (*fig*) *plant* soigner; *hope, one's wrath etc* nourrir, entretenir; *plan, plot* mijoter, couver; *horse, car engine* ménager; *a fire* entretenir. (*Brit Pol*) **to ~ a constituency** soigner les électeurs; **he was nursing the contact till he needed it** il cultivait cette relation pour s'en servir quand il en aurait besoin; **to ~ the business along** (essayer de) maintenir la compagnie à flot.

nurseling [ˈnɜːslɪŋ] *n* = **nursling.**

nursery [ˈnɜːsərɪ] **1** *n* **(a)** (*room*) nursery *f*, chambre *f* d'enfants. **day** ~ nursery; **night** ~ chambre des enfants *or* d'enfants.

(b) (*institution*) (*daytime only*) crèche *f*, garderie *f*; (*daytime or residential*) pouponnière *f*.

(c) (*Agr*) pépinière *f*.

(d) (*fig*) pépinière *f*. **this town is the ~ of the province's cultural life** cette ville est la pépinière de la vie culturelle de la province.

2 *cpd*: **nursery education** enseignement *m* de la maternelle; **nurseryman** pépiniériste *m*; **nursery rhyme** comptine *f*; **nursery school** (*state-run*) école maternelle; (*gen private*) jardin *m* d'enfants; **nursery-school teacher** (*state-run*) institutrice *f* de maternelle; (*private*) jardinière *f* d'enfants; (*Ski*) **nursery slopes** pentes *fpl or* pistes *fpl* pour débutants.

nursing [ˈnɜːsɪŋ] **1** *adj* **(a)** allaitant. ~ **mother** mère *f* qui allaite. (*in stations etc*) **room for ~ mothers** salle réservée aux mères qui allaitent.

(b) (*Med*) *[hospital]* **the ~ staff** le personnel soignant *or* infirmier, les infirmières.

2 *n* (*suckling*) allaitement *m*; (*care of invalids*) soins *mpl*; (*profession of nurse*) profession *f* d'infirmière. **she's going in for** ~ elle va être infirmière.

3 *cpd*: (*Brit*) **nursing auxiliary** aide soignante; **nursing home** (*esp Brit: for medical, surgical cases*) clinique *f*, polyclinique *f*; (*for mental cases, disabled etc*) maison *f* de santé; (*for convalescence/rest cure*) maison de convalescence/de repos; (*US: for old people*) maison de retraite; (*Brit Mil*) **nursing orderly** infirmier *m* (militaire); **nursing studies** études *fpl* d'infirmière *or* d'infirmier.

nursling [ˈnɜːslɪŋ] *n* nourrisson(ne) *m(f)*.

nurture [ˈnɜːtʃəʳ] **1** *n* (*frm: lit, fig*) nourriture *f*. **2** *vt* (*lit, fig*) (*rear*) élever, éduquer; (*feed*) nourrir (*on* de).

nut [nʌt] **1** *n* **(a)** (*Bot*) *terme générique pour fruits à écale* (*no generic term in French*). **a bag of mixed ~s** un sachet de noisettes, cacahuètes, amandes *etc* panachées; **~s and raisins**

mendiants *mpl*; (*fig*) **he's a tough ~** c'est un dur à cuire*; (*fig*) a **hard ~ to crack** (*problem*) un problème difficile à résoudre; (*person*) un(e) dur(e) à cuire*; **he can't paint for ~s‡** il peint comme une savate‡; *V* **beech, walnut** *etc.*

(b) (*Tech*) écrou *m.*

(c) (**coal**) **~s, ~ coal** noix *fpl*, tête(s)-de-moineau *f(pl) or* tête(s) de moineau *f(pl)*; **anthracite ~s** noix *or* tête(s)-de-moineau d'anthracite.

(d) (*Culin*) *V* **ginger.**

(e) (‡: *head*) caboche* *f.* **use your ~!** réfléchis donc un peu!, creuse-toi un peu les méninges!‡; **to be off one's ~** être tombé sur la tête*, être cinglé‡; **you must be off your ~!** mais ça (ne) va plus!‡, mais tu es tombé sur la tête!*; **to go off one's ~** perdre la boule‡; (*Brit*) **to do one's ~** être dans tous ses états.

(f) (‡: *mad person*) **he's a real ~** c'est un fou, il est cinglé‡ *or* toqué*.

(g) (*US excl*) **~s!*** des clous!‡

2 *cpd*: **nut-brown** *eyes* noisette *inv*; *complexion* brun; *hair* châtain; **nutcase‡** dingue‡ *mf*, cinglé(e)‡ *m(f)*; **he's a nutcase‡** il est bon à enfermer*, il est dingue‡; **nut chocolate** chocolat *m* aux amandes (*or* aux noisettes *etc*); **nutcracker chin** menton *m* en galoche *or* en casse-noisette; **nutcracker(s)** casse-noix *m inv*, casse-noisette(s) *m*; (*Orn*) **nuthatch** sitelle *f*, grimpereau *m*; (*Brit*) **nuthouse‡** asile *m* (d'aliénés), maison *f* de fous *or* de dingues‡; **he's in the nuthouse‡** il est chez les dingues‡; **nutmeg** (*nut*) (noix *f*) muscade *f*; (*tree*) muscadier *m*; **nutmeg-grater** râpe *f* à muscade; **nutshell** coquille *f* de noix *or* noisette *etc*; (*fig*) **in a nutshell** ... en un mot ..., bref ...; (*fig*) **to put the matter in a nutshell** résumer l'affaire en un mot.

nutrient [ˈnjuːtrɪənt] **1** *adj* nutritif. **2** *n* substance nutritive, élément nutritif.

nutriment [ˈnjuːtrɪmənt] *n* nourriture *f*, éléments nourrissants *or* nutritifs, aliments *mpl.*

nutrition [njuːˈtrɪʃən] *n* nutrition *f*, alimentation *f.*

nutritional [njuːˈtrɪʃənl] *adj* alimentaire.

nutritious [njuːˈtrɪʃəs] *adj* nutritif, nourrissant.

nutritiousness [njuːˈtrɪʃəsnɪs] *n* caractère nutritif.

nutritive [ˈnjuːtrɪtɪv] *adj* = **nutritious.**

nuts‡ [nʌts] *adj* dingue‡, cinglé‡, toqué*. **he's ~** il est dingue‡ *or* cinglé‡, il est bon à enfermer*; **to go ~** perdre la boule‡; **to be ~ about sb/sth** être dingue‡ de qn/qch.

nutter‡ [ˈnʌtəʳ] *n* (*Brit*) cinglé(e)‡ *m(f)*, dingue‡ *mf.*

nutty [ˈnʌtɪ] *adj* **(a)** (*V* **nut**) *chocolate etc* aux noisettes (*or* amandes *or* noix *etc*); *flavour* au goût de noisette *etc*, à la noisette *etc.* **(b)** (*Brit: coal*) **~ slack** charbonnaille *f.* **(c)** (‡: *mad*) = **nuts.**

nuzzle [ˈnʌzl] *vi* [*pig*] fouiller du groin, fouiner; [*dog*] flairer, renifler. **the dog ~d up to my leg** le chien est venu me renifler la jambe.

nylon [ˈnaɪlɒn] **1** *n* **(a)** (*U*) nylon *m.* **(b)** = **~ stocking**; *V* **2. 2** *cpd* de *or* en nylon. **nylon stockings** bas *mpl* nylon.

nymph [nɪmf] *n* nymphe *f*; (*water ~*) naïade *f*; (*wood ~*) (hama)dryade *f*; (*sea ~*) néréide *f*; (*mountain ~*) oréade *f.*

nymphet [nɪmˈfet] *n* nymphette *f.*

nympho‡ [ˈnɪmfəʊ] *adj, n* (*abbr of* **nymphomaniac**) nymphomane (*f*).

nymphomania [ˌnɪmfəʊˈmeɪnɪə] *n* nymphomanie *f.*

nymphomaniac [ˌnɪmfəʊˈmeɪnɪæk] *adj, n* nymphomane (*f*).

O

O, o¹ [əʊ] *n* **(a)** (*letter*) O, o *m.* **O.K.*** *V* **O.K.***; **O-shaped** en forme de O *or* de cercle. **(b)** (*number: Telec etc*) zéro *m.*

o² [əʊ] *excl* (*liter*) ô.

o' [əʊ] *prep* (*abbr of* **of**) de; *V* **o'clock** *etc.*

oaf [əʊf] *n* (*awkward*) balourd(e) *m(f)*; (*bad-mannered*) malotru(e) *m(f)*, mufle *m.*

oafish [ˈəʊfɪʃ] *adj person* mufle; *behaviour* de mufle, de malotru.

oak [əʊk] **1** *n* chêne *m.* **light/dark ~** chêne clair/foncé.

2 *cpd* (*made of ~*) de *or* en (bois de) chêne; (*~-coloured*) (couleur) chêne *inv.* **oak apple** noix *f* de galle, galle *f* du chêne; (*US*) **oak leaf cluster** ≈ barrette *f* (*portée sur le ruban d'une médaille*); **oakwood** (*forest*) chênaie *f*, bois *m* de chênes; (*U: material*) (bois *m* de) chêne *m.*

oaken [ˈəʊkən] *adj* de *or* en (bois de) chêne.

oakum [ˈəʊkəm] *n* étoupe *f.* **to pick ~** faire de l'étoupe.

oar [ɔːʳ] **1** *n* **(a)** aviron *m*, rame *f.* **he always puts** *or* **pushes** *or* **sticks** *or* **shoves his ~ in** il faut toujours qu'il s'en mêle (*subj*) *or* qu'il y mette son grain de sel; *V* **rest, ship** *etc.*

(b) (*person*) rameur *m*, -euse *f.*

2 *cpd*: **oarlock** dame *f* (de nage), tolet *m*; **oarsman** rameur *m*; (*Naut, also Sport*) nageur *m*; **oarsmanship** (*art of rowing*) art *m* de ramer; (*skill as rower*) qualités *fpl* de rameur; **oarswoman** rameuse *f.*

-oared [ɔːd] *adj ending in cpds*: **four-oared** à quatre rames *or* avirons.

oasis [əʊˈeɪsɪs] *n, pl* **oases** [əʊˈeɪsiːz] (*lit, fig*) oasis *f.* **an ~ of peace** un havre *or* une oasis de paix.

oast [əʊst] *n* four *m* à (sécher le) houblon. **~-house** sécherie *f or* séchoir *m* à houblon.

oat [əʊt] **1** *n* (*plant, food*) **~s** avoine *f* (*U*); **to be off one's ~s‡** avoir perdu l'appétit; *V* **rolled, wild** *etc.*

2 *cpd*: **oatcake** biscuit *m or* galette *f* d'avoine; **oatmeal** (*n: U*) flocons *mpl* d'avoine; (*cpd: colour*) *dress etc* beige, grège; **oatmeal porridge** bouillie *f* d'avoine, porridge *m.*

oath [əʊθ] *pl* **~s** [əʊðz] **1** *n* **(a)** (*Jur etc*) serment *m.* (*Jur*) **to take the ~** prêter serment; **he took** *or* **swore an ~ to avenge himself** il fit (le) serment *or* il jura de se venger; (*Jur*) **on** *or* **under ~** sous serment; (*Jur*) **witness on** *or* **under ~** témoin assermenté; (*Jur*) **to put sb on** *or* **under ~, to administer the ~ to sb** faire prêter serment à qn; (*Jur*) **to put sb on** *or* **under ~ to do sth** faire promettre à qn sous serment de faire qch; **he swore on his ~ that he had never been there** il jura n'y avoir jamais été *or* qu'il n'y avait jamais été; **on my ~!, I'll take my ~ on it!** je vous le jure!; *V* **allegiance.**

(b) (*bad language*) juron *m.* **to let out** *or* **utter an ~** lâcher *or* pousser un juron.

2 *cpd*: (*Jur etc*) **oath-taking** prestation *f* de serment.

obbligato [ˌɒblɪˈgɑːtəʊ] (*Mus*) **1** *adj* obligé. **2** *n* partie obligée.

obduracy [ˈɒbdjʊrəsɪ] *n* (*V* **obdurate**) opiniâtreté *f*, obstination *f*; inflexibilité *f*; dureté *f*; impénitence *f.*

obdurate [ˈɒbdjʊrɪt] *adj* (*stubborn*) obstiné, opiniâtre; (*unyielding*) inflexible; (*hard-hearted*) endurci; (*unrepentant*) impénitent.

obedience [əˈbiːdɪəns] *n* (*U*) obéissance *f*, soumission *f* (*to* à), obédience *f* (*liter*); (*Rel*) obédience (*to* à). **in ~ to the law/his orders** conformément à la loi/ses ordres; (*frm*) **to owe ~ to sb** devoir obéissance *or* obédience (*liter*) à qn; **to show ~ to sb/sth** obéir à qn/qch; **to compel ~ from sb** se faire obéir par qn; **he commands ~** il sait se faire obéir; *V* **blind.**

obedient [əˈbiːdɪənt] *adj person, child* obéissant; *dog etc* obéissant, docile; (*submissive*) docile, soumis. **to be ~ to sb/sth** obéir à qn/qch, être *or* se montrer obéissant envers qn/à qch; (*frm: in letters*) **your ~ servant** ≈ je vous prie d'agréer Monsieur (*or* Madame *etc*) l'expression de ma considération distinguée.

obediently [əˈbiːdɪəntlɪ] *adv* docilement; d'une manière soumise, avec soumission. **he ~ sat down** il s'est assis docilement; **she smiled ~** elle a souri d'un air soumis.

obeisance [əʊˈbeɪsəns] *n* (*frm*) **(a)** (*U: homage*) hommage *m.* **(b)** (*bow*) révérence *f*, salut cérémonieux.

obelisk [ˈɒbɪlɪsk] *n* **(a)** (*Archit*) obélisque *m.* **(b)** (*Typ:* †) obel *m or* obèle *m.*

obese [əʊˈbiːs] *adj* obèse.

obeseness [əʊˈbiːsnɪs] *n*, **obesity** [əʊˈbiːsɪtɪ] *n* obésité *f.*

obey [əˈbeɪ] **1** *vt person, instinct, order* obéir à; *the law* se conformer à, obéir à; *instructions* se conformer à, observer; (*Jur*) *summons, order* obtempérer à. **the machine was no longer ~ing the controls** la machine ne répondait plus aux commandes. **2** *vi* obéir.

obfuscate [ˈɒbfəskeɪt] *vt* (*frm*) *mind, judgment* obscurcir; *person* dérouter, déconcerter.

obituary [əˈbɪtjʊərɪ] **1** *n* (*also* **~ notice**) notice *f* nécrologique, nécrologie *f.* **2** *adj announcement* nécrologique; *register* obituaire. **~ column** nécrologie *f*, rubrique *f* nécrologique.

object [ˈɒbdʒɪkt] **1** *n* **(a)** (*thing in general*) objet *m*, chose *f*; (*pej: thing*) bizarrerie *f*; (*pej: person*) personne *f* ridicule. **~ of pity/ridicule** objet de pitié/de risée; **the ~ of one's love** l'objet aimé; (*pej*) **what an ~ she looks in that dress!*** de quoi elle a l'air dans cette robe!* (*pej*).

(b) (*Gram*) complément *m* (d'objet). **direct/indirect ~** complément (d'objet) direct/indirect.

(c) (*aim*) but *m*, objectif *m*, objet *m*, fin *f*; (*Philos*) objet. **he has no ~ in life** il n'a aucun but dans la vie; **with this ~ (in view** *or* **in mind)** dans ce but, à cette fin; **with the ~ of doing** dans le but de faire; **with the sole ~ of doing** à seule fin *or* dans le seul but de faire; **what ~ is there in** *or* **what's the ~ of doing that?** à quoi bon faire cela?; **'distance no ~'** 'toutes distances'; *V* **defeat.**

2 *cpd*: (*Gram*) **object clause** proposition *f* complément d'objet, complétive *f* d'objet; (*Scol etc*) **object lesson** leçon *f* de choses; (*fig*) **it was an object lesson in good manners** c'était une démonstration de bonnes manières; **it was an object lesson in**

how not to drive a car c'était une illustration de ce que l'on ne doit pas faire au volant.

3 [əb'dʒekt] *vi* élever une objection (*to* contre), trouver à redire. **I ~ to that remark** je désapprouve tout à fait cette remarque; (*frm*) je proteste *or* je m'élève contre cette remarque; **I ~ to your rudeness** votre grossièreté est inadmissible, je ne tolérerai pas votre grossièreté; (*excl*) **I ~!** je proteste!, je regrette!; **I ~ most strongly!** je proteste catégoriquement! *or* énergiquement!; **if you don't ~** si vous n'y voyez pas d'inconvénient *or* d'objection; **I shall not come if you ~** je ne viendrai pas si vous vous y opposez *or* si vous y voyez une objection *or* si vous y voyez un inconvénient; **he didn't ~ when ...** il n'a élevé *or* formulé aucune objection quand ...; **he ~s to her drinking** il désapprouve qu'elle boive; **do you ~ to my smoking?** cela vous ennuie que je fume? (*subj*), est-ce que cela vous gêne si je fume?; **she ~s to all this noise** elle ne peut tolérer tout ce bruit; **I don't ~ to helping you** je veux bien vous aider; **I would ~ to Paul but not to Robert as chairman** je serais contre Paul mais je n'ai rien contre Robert comme président; **they ~ed to him because he was too young** on lui a objecté son jeune âge; (*Jur*) **to ~ to a witness** récuser un témoin; **I wouldn't ~ to a bite to eat*** je mangerais bien un morceau.

4 [əb'dʒekt] *vt*: **to ~ that** objecter que, faire valoir que.

objection [əb'dʒekʃən] *n* objection *f*; (*drawback*) inconvénient *m*, obstacle *m*. **I have no ~** je n'ai pas d'objection, je ne m'y oppose pas; **if you have no ~** si cela ne vous fait rien, si vous n'y voyez pas d'inconvénient *or* d'objection; **I have no ~ to him** je n'ai rien contre lui, je ne trouve rien à redire sur son compte; **I have a strong ~ to dogs in shops** j'ai horreur des chiens dans les magasins; **have you any ~ to my smoking?** cela ne vous ennuie pas que je fume? (*subj*), est-ce que cela vous gêne si je fume?; **I have no ~ to the idea/to his leaving** je ne vois pas d'objection *or* je ne m'oppose pas à cette idée/à ce qu'il parte; **there is no ~ to our leaving** il n'y a pas d'obstacle *or* d'inconvénient à ce que nous partions (*subj*); **to make** *or* **raise an ~** soulever *or* élever *or* formuler une objection; (*excl*) **~!** (*Jur*) objection!; (*gen*) je proteste!; (*Jur*) **~ overruled!** objection rejetée!

objectionable [əb'dʒekʃnəbl] *adj* **(a)** (*disagreeable*) *person, behaviour* extrêmement désagréable, impossible, insupportable; *smell* nauséabond; *remark* désobligeant, choquant; *language* grossier, choquant.

(b) (*open to objection*) *conduct* répréhensible, blâmable, condamnable; *proposal* inadmissible, inacceptable.

objective [əb'dʒektɪv] **1** *adj* **(a)** (*impartial*) objectif, impartial (*about* en ce qui concerne); (*Philos*) objectif. (*Press etc*) **he is very ~ in his reporting** ses reportages sont très objectifs *or* impartiaux. **(b)** (*Gram*) *case* accusatif; *pronoun* complément d'objet; *genitive* objectif. **~ case** (cas *m*) accusatif *m*, cas régime. **2** *n* (*all senses*) objectif *m*.

objectively [əb'dʒektɪvlɪ] *adv* (*gen*) objectivement, impartialement, sans parti pris; (*Gram, Philos*) objectivement.

objectivism [əb'dʒektɪvɪzəm] *n* objectivisme *m*.

objectivity [ˌɒbdʒɪk'tɪvɪtɪ] *n* objectivité *f*, impartialité *f*.

objector [əb'dʒektəʳ] *n* opposant(e) *m(f)*. **the ~s to this scheme** ceux qui s'opposent à ce projet; *V* **conscientious**.

objurgate ['ɒbdʒɜːgeɪt] *vt* (*frm*) réprimander; (*stronger*) accabler de reproches.

objurgation [ˌɒbdʒɜː'geɪʃən] *n* (*frm*) objurgation *f*, réprimande *f*.

oblate ['ɒbleɪt] **1** *n* (*Rel*) oblat(e) *m(f)*. **2** *adj* (*Geom*) aplati aux pôles.

oblation [əʊ'bleɪʃən] *n* (*Rel*) (*act*) oblation *f*; (*offering: also* **~s**) oblats *mpl*.

obligate ['ɒblɪgeɪt] *vt* obliger, contraindre (*sb to do* qn à faire). **to be ~d to do** être obligé de *or* contraint à faire.

obligation [ˌɒblɪ'geɪʃən] *n* **(a)** (*compulsion; duty etc*) obligation *f*, devoir *m*, engagement *m*. **to be under an ~ to do** être tenu de faire, être dans l'obligation de faire; **to put** *or* **lay an ~ on sb to do, to put** *or* **lay sb under an ~ to do** mettre qn dans l'obligation de faire; **it is your ~ to see that ...** il est de votre devoir de veiller à ce que ... + *subj*; (*in advert*) **'without ~'** 'sans engagement'; **'no ~ to buy'** (*in advert*) 'aucune obligation d'achat'; (*in shop*) 'entrée libre'.

(b) (*debt etc*) devoir *m*, dette *f* (de reconnaissance). **to meet one's ~s** faire honneur à *or* satisfaire à ses obligations *or* ses engagements; **to be under an ~ to sb for sth** être redevable à qn de qch; **to lay** *or* **put sb under an ~** créer une obligation à qn; **to repay an ~** acquitter une dette de reconnaissance.

obligatory [ɒ'blɪgətərɪ] *adj* (*compulsory*) obligatoire; (*imposed by custom*) de rigueur. **to make it ~ for sb to do** imposer à qn l'obligation de faire.

oblige [ə'blaɪdʒ] *vt* **(a)** (*compel*) obliger, forcer, astreindre, contraindre (*sb to do* qn à faire). **to be ~d to do** être obligé *or* forcé de faire, être astreint *or* contraint à faire, devoir faire.

(b) (*do a favour to*) rendre service à, obliger. **he did it to ~ us** il l'a fait par gentillesse pour nous *or* pour nous rendre service; **she is always ready to ~** elle est toujours prête à rendre service *or* toujours très obligeante; **anything to ~!*** toujours prêt à rendre service!; (*frm*) **can you ~ me with a pen?** auriez-vous l'amabilité *or* l'obligeance de me prêter un stylo?; (*frm*) **~ me by leaving the room** faites-moi le plaisir de quitter la pièce; (*Comm*) **a prompt answer will ~** une réponse rapide nous obligerait; **to be ~d to sb for sth** être reconnaissant *or* savoir gré à qn de qch; **I am much ~d to you** je vous remercie infiniment; **much ~d!** merci beaucoup!, merci mille fois!

obliging [ə'blaɪdʒɪŋ] *adj* obligeant, serviable, complaisant. **it is very ~ of them** c'est très gentil *or* aimable de leur part.

obligingly [ə'blaɪdʒɪŋlɪ] *adv* obligeamment, aimablement. **the books which you ~ gave me** les livres que vous avez eu l'obligeance *or* l'amabilité de me donner.

oblique [ə'bliːk] **1** *adj* oblique; *look* en biais, oblique; *allusion, reference, style* indirect; *route, method* indirect, détourné. (*Gram*) **~ case** cas *m* oblique. **2** *n* (*Anat*) oblique *m*; (*Brit Typ: also* **~ stroke**) trait *m* oblique, oblique *f*.

obliquely [ə'bliːklɪ] *adv* obliquement, en oblique, de *or* en biais; (*fig*) indirectement. **the car was hit ~ by the lorry** la voiture a été prise en écharpe par le camion.

obliqueness [ə'bliːknɪs] *n*, **obliquity** [ə'blɪkwɪtɪ] *n* (*V* **oblique**) obliquité *f*; caractère détourné *or* indirect.

obliterate [ə'blɪtəreɪt] *vt* (*erase*) effacer, enlever; (*cross out*) rayer, raturer; (*by progressive wear*) effacer, oblitérer†; *memory, impressions* effacer, oblitérer (*liter*); *the past* faire table rase de; (*Post*) *stamp* oblitérer.

obliteration [əˌblɪtə'reɪʃən] *n* (*V* **obliterate**) effacement *m*; rature *f*; (*Post*) oblitération *f*.

oblivion [ə'blɪvɪən] *n* (état *m* d')oubli *m*. **to sink** *or* **fall into ~** tomber dans l'oubli.

oblivious [ə'blɪvɪəs] *adj* (*forgetful*) oublieux (*to, of* de); (*unaware*) inconscient (*to, of* de).

oblong ['ɒblɒŋ] **1** *adj* (*rectangular*) oblong (*f* oblongue); (*elongated*) allongé. **~ dish** plat *m* rectangulaire. **2** *n* rectangle *m*.

obloquy ['ɒbləkwɪ] *n* opprobre *m*.

obnoxious [əb'nɒkʃəs] *adj person* odieux, infect; *child, dog* détestable, insupportable; *smell* nauséabond; *behaviour* odieux, abominable.

oboe ['əʊbəʊ] *n* hautbois *m*.

oboist ['əʊbəʊɪst] *n* hautboïste *mf*.

obscene [əb'siːn] *adj* obscène.

obscenely [əb'siːnlɪ] *adv* d'une manière obscène. **to talk ~** dire des obscénités.

obscenity [əb'senɪtɪ] *n* obscénité *f*.

obscurantism [ˌɒbskjʊə'ræntɪzəm] *n* obscurantisme *m*.

obscurantist [ˌɒbskjʊə'ræntɪst] *adj, n* obscurantiste (*mf*).

obscure [əb'skjʊəʳ] **1** *adj* (*dark*) obscur, sombre; (*fig*) *book, reason, origin, birth* obscur; *poem, style* obscur, abscons (*liter*); *feeling, memory* indistinct, vague; *life, village, poet* obscur, inconnu, ignoré.

2 *vt* (*darken*) obscurcir, assombrir; (*hide*) *sun* voiler, cacher, éclipser; *view* cacher, masquer; (*fig*) *argument, idea* rendre obscur, embrouiller, obscurcir; *mind* obscurcir, obnubiler. **to ~ the issue** embrouiller la question.

obscurely [əb'skjʊəlɪ] *adv* obscurément.

obscurity [əb'skjʊərɪtɪ] *n* (*darkness*) obscurité *f*, ténèbres *fpl* (*liter*); (*fig*) obscurité.

obsequies ['ɒbsɪkwɪz] *npl* (*frm*) obsèques *fpl*, funérailles *fpl*.

obsequious [əb'siːkwɪəs] *adj* obséquieux, servile (*to, towards* devant).

obsequiously [əb'siːkwɪəslɪ] *adv* obséquieusement.

obsequiousness [əb'siːkwɪəsnɪs] *n* obséquiosité *f*, servilité *f*.

observable [əb'zɜːvəbl] *adj* (*visible*) observable, visible, perceptible; (*appreciable*) notable, appréciable. **as is ~ in rabbits** ainsi qu'on peut l'observer chez les lapins.

observance [əb'zɜːvəns] *n* **(a)** (*U*) *[rule]* observation *f*; *[rite, custom, Sabbath]* observance *f*; *[anniversary]* célébration *f*. **(b)** (*rule, practice, custom*) observance *f*. **religious ~s** observances religieuses.

observant [əb'zɜːvənt] *adj person, mind* observateur (*f* -trice), perspicace. **the child is very ~** cet enfant est très observateur *or* fait preuve d'un grand don d'observation.

observation [ˌɒbzə'veɪʃən] **1** *n* **(a)** (*U*) observation *f*, surveillance *f*. **to keep sb under ~** (*Med*) garder qn en observation; (*Police etc*) surveiller qn; (*Police etc*) **he came under ~ when ...** on s'est mis à le surveiller quand ...; **he kept the valley under ~** il surveillait la vallée; **~ of birds/bats** observation des oiseaux/des chauves-souris; **his powers of ~** ses facultés *fpl* d'observation; *V* **escape**.

(b) (*remark*) observation *f*, remarque *f*. **his ~s on 'Hamlet'** ses réflexions *fpl* sur 'Hamlet'.

2 *cpd*: **observation balloon** ballon *m* d'observation *or* d'aérostation; (*US Rail*) **observation car** wagon *m or* voiture *f* panoramique; (*Mil*) **observation post** poste *m* d'observation, observatoire *m*; **observation tower** mirador *m*; (*Med*) **observation ward** salle *f* des malades en observation.

observatory [əb'zɜːvətrɪ] *n* observatoire *m*.

observe [əb'zɜːv] *vt* **(a)** (*obey etc*) *rule, custom* observer, se conformer à, respecter; *anniversary* célébrer; *silence* garder, observer. (*Jur*) **failure to ~ the law** inobservation *f* de la loi.

(b) (*take note of*) observer, remarquer; (*study*) observer. **to ~ sth closely** observer qch attentivement, scruter qch.

(c) (*say, remark*) (faire) remarquer, faire observer. **he ~d that it was cold** il fit observer *or* fit remarquer qu'il faisait froid; **as I was about to ~** comme j'allais le dire *or* le faire remarquer; **I ~d to him that ...** je lui ai fait remarquer *or* observer que ...; **'he has gone' she ~d** 'il est parti' dit-elle *or* remarqua-t-elle; **as Eliot ~d** comme l'a remarqué *or* relevé Eliot.

observer [əb'zɜːvəʳ] *n* (*all senses*) observateur *m*, -trice *f*.

obsess [əb'ses] *vt* obséder, hanter. **~ed by** obsédé *or* hanté par.

obsession [əb'seʃən] *n* (*state*) obsession *f*; (*fixed idea*) obsession, idée *f* fixe; (*of sth unpleasant*) hantise *f*. **he's got an ~ with sport, sport is an ~ with him** le sport c'est son idée fixe, le sport tient de l'obsession chez lui; **he has an ~ about cleanliness** c'est un obsédé de la propreté, il a l'obsession de la propreté; **his ~ with her** la manière dont elle l'obsède; **his ~ with death** son obsession *or* sa hantise de la mort.

obsessive [əb'sesɪv] *adj memory, thought* obsédant; (*Psych*) obsessionnel.

obsessively [əb'sesɪvlɪ] *adv* d'une manière obsédante. **~ keen to get married** obsédé par le désir de se marier; **~ anxious not to be seen** ayant la hantise d'être vu.

obsidian [ɒbˈsɪdɪən] *n* obsidienne *f.*

obsolescence [ˌɒbsəˈlesns] *n [goods, words]* vieillissement *m*; *[machinery]* obsolescence *f*; (*Bio*) atrophie *f*, myopathie *f.* (*Comm*) **planned** *or* **built-in ~** désuétude calculée.

obsolescent [ˌɒbsəˈlesnt] *adj machinery* obsolescent; *word* vieilli, qui tombe en désuétude; (*Bio*) *organ* en voie d'atrophie.

obsolete [ˈɒbsəliːt] *adj* (*no longer valid*) dépassé, périmé; (*out of fashion*) démodé, désuet (*f* -ète); (*out-of-date*) suranné; *machine* dépassé; (*Ling*) obsolète; (*Bio*) atrophié. **to become ~** tomber en désuétude.

obstacle [ˈɒbstəkl] **1** *n* obstacle *m*; (*fig*) obstacle, empêchement *m* (*to* à). **to be an ~ to sth** faire obstacle à qch, entraver qch, être un obstacle à qch; **agriculture is the main ~ in the negotiations** l'agriculture constitue la pierre d'achoppement des négociations; **to put an ~ in the way of sth/in sb's way** faire obstacle à qch/qn.

2 *cpd*: (*Sport*) **obstacle race** course *f* d'obstacles.

obstetric(al) [ɒbˈstetrɪk(əl)] *adj techniques etc* obstétrical; *clinic* obstétrique.

obstetrician [ˌɒbstəˈtrɪʃən] *n* obstétricien(ne) *m(f)*, (médecin *m*) accoucheur *m.*

obstetrics [ɒbˈstetrɪks] *n* (*U*) obstétrique *f.*

obstinacy [ˈɒbstɪnəsɪ] *n* obstination *f*, entêtement *m*, opiniâtreté *f* (*in doing* à faire); *[illness]* persistance *f*; *[resistance]* obstination, persévérance *f*, détermination *f.*

obstinate [ˈɒbstɪnɪt] *adj person* obstiné, têtu, entêté, opiniâtre; *effort, work, resistance* obstiné, acharné; *pain, illness* persistant; *fever* rebelle; *fight* acharné. **to be as ~ as a mule** être têtu comme une mule *or* comme une bourrique*, avoir une tête de mule* *or* de cochon*; **he's very ~ about it** il n'en démord pas.

obstinately [ˈɒbstɪnɪtlɪ] *adv* obstinément, opiniâtrement; *struggle* avec acharnement. **to refuse ~** refuser obstinément, s'obstiner à refuser; **he ~ insisted on leaving** il a absolument tenu à partir; **he tried ~ to do it by himself** il s'est obstiné *or* entêté à le faire tout seul.

obstreperous [əbˈstrepərəs] *adj* (*noisy*) bruyant, tapageur; (*unruly*) turbulent, chahuteur; (*rebellious*) récalcitrant, rebelle, rouspéteur*. **the crowd grew ~** la foule s'est mise à protester bruyamment *or* à rouspéter* bruyamment.

obstreperously [əbˈstrepərəslɪ] *adv* (*noisily*) bruyamment, tapageusement; (*rebelliously*) avec force protestations, en rouspétant*.

obstruct [əbˈstrʌkt] **1** *vt* **(a)** (*block*) *road* encombrer, obstruer (*with* de), barrer, boucher (*with* avec); *pipe* boucher (*with* avec, *by* par), engorger; *artery* obstruer, oblitérer; *view* boucher, cacher.

(b) (*halt*) *traffic* bloquer; *progress* arrêter, enrayer.

(c) (*hinder*) *progress, traffic* entraver, gêner; *plan* entraver, faire obstacle à; *person* gêner, entraver; (*Sport*) *player* faire obstruction à. (*Pol*) **to ~ (the passage of) a bill** faire de l'obstruction parlementaire; (*Jur*) **to ~ a policeman in the execution of his duty** gêner *or* entraver un agent de police dans l'exercice de ses fonctions.

2 *vi* (*Sport*) faire de l'obstruction.

obstruction [əbˈstrʌkʃən] *n* **(a)** (*U: act, state: V* **obstruct 1**) obstruction *f*, encombrement *m*; engorgement *m*; arrêt *m*; interruption *f.* (*Jur*) **he was charged with ~ of the police in the course of their duties** ≃ il a été inculpé d'avoir refusé d'aider les policiers dans l'exercice de leurs fonctions.

(b) (*sth which obstructs*) (*to road, passage, plan, progress, view*) obstacle *m*; (*to pipe*) bouchon *m*; (*to traffic*) embouteillage *m*, bouchon; (*to artery*) caillot *m.* (*Jur etc*) **to cause an ~** (*gen*) encombrer *or* obstruer la voie publique; (*Aut*) bloquer la circulation, provoquer un embouteillage.

obstructionism [əbˈstrʌkʃənɪzəm] *n* obstructionnisme *m.*

obstructionist [əbˈstrʌkʃənɪst] *adj, n* obstructionniste (*mf*). **to adopt ~ tactics** faire de l'obstruction, pratiquer l'obstruction.

obstructive [əbˈstrʌktɪv] *adj* **(a)** *measures, policy* d'obstruction, obstructionniste; *person* (*Pol etc*) obstructionniste, qui fait de l'obstruction; (*gen*) qui se met en travers, qui suscite des obstacles. **you're being ~** vous ne pensez qu'à mettre des bâtons dans les roues. **(b)** (*Med*) obstructif, obstruant.

obtain [əbˈteɪn] **1** *vt goods* procurer (*for sb* à qn); (*for o.s.*) se procurer; *information, job* obtenir; *money* obtenir, (se) procurer; *votes* obtenir, recueillir; *prize* obtenir, remporter; (*Fin*) *shares* acquérir. **this gas is ~ed from coal** on obtient ce gaz à partir du charbon; **these goods may be ~ed from any large store** on peut se procurer ces articles dans tous les grands magasins.

2 *vi [rule, custom etc]* avoir cours; *[fashion]* être en vogue; *[method]* être courant.

obtainable [əbˈteɪnəbl] *adj* qu'on peut se procurer. **where is that book ~?** où peut-on se procurer *or* trouver *or* acheter ce livre?; '**~ at all good chemists**' 'en vente dans toutes les bonnes pharmacies'.

obtrude [əbˈtruːd] **1** *vt* imposer (*sth on sb* qch à qn). **2** *vi [person]* s'imposer, imposer sa présence. **the author's opinions do not ~** l'auteur n'impose pas ses opinions.

obtrusion [əbˈtruːʒən] *n* intrusion *f.*

obtrusive [əbˈtruːsɪv] *adj person* importun, indiscret (*f* -ète); *opinions* ostentatoire, affiché; *smell* pénétrant; *building etc* trop en évidence, qui accroche *or* qui heurte le regard.

obtrusively [əbˈtruːsɪvlɪ] *adv* importunément, avec indiscrétion.

obtuse [əbˈtjuːs] *adj* (*blunt*) obtus; (*Geom*) obtus; *person* obtus, borné. **you're just being ~!** tu fais exprès de ne pas comprendre!

obtuseness [əbˈtjuːsnɪs] *n* stupidité *f.*

obverse [ˈɒbvɜːs] **1** *n [coin]* face *f*, côté *m* face; *[statement, truth]* contrepartie *f*, contre-pied *m.*

2 *adj* **(a)** *side of coin etc* de face, qui fait face; (*fig*) correspondant, faisant contrepartie.

(b) (*in shape*) *leaf* renversé, plus large au sommet qu'à la base.

obviate [ˈɒbvɪeɪt] *vt difficulty* obvier à, parer à; *necessity* parer à; *danger, objection* prévenir.

obvious [ˈɒbvɪəs] **1** *adj* évident, manifeste. **it's an ~ fact, it's quite ~** c'est bien évident, c'est l'évidence même; **it's ~ that** il est évident que, il est de toute évidence que; **the ~ thing to do is to leave** la chose à faire c'est évidemment de partir; **that's the ~ one to choose** c'est bien évidemment celui-là qu'il faut choisir; **~ statement** truisme *m*, lapalissade *f*; **with ~ shyness** avec une timidité évidente *or* visible; **his ~ good faith** sa bonne foi évidente *or* incontestable; **we must not be too ~ about it** il va falloir ne pas trop montrer notre jeu.

2 *n*: **you are merely stating the ~** il n'y a rien de nouveau dans ce que vous dites, vous enfoncez une porte ouverte.

obviously [ˈɒbvɪəslɪ] *adv* évidemment, manifestement, bien sûr. **it's ~ true** c'est de toute évidence vrai; **he was ~ not drunk** il était évident qu'il n'était pas ivre; **he was not ~ drunk** il n'était pas visiblement ivre; **~!** bien sûr!, évidemment!; **~ not!** bien sûr que non!

ocarina [ˌɒkəˈriːnə] *n* ocarina *m.*

occasion [əˈkeɪʒən] **1** *n* **(a)** (*juncture; suitable time*) occasion *f*, circonstance *f.* **on the ~ of** à l'occasion de; **(on) the first ~ (that) it happened** la première fois que cela s'est passé; **on that ~** à cette occasion, cette fois-là; **on several ~s** à plusieurs occasions *or* reprises; **on rare ~s** en de rares occasions; **on just such an ~** dans une occasion tout à fait semblable; **on great ~s** dans les grandes occasions *or* circonstances; **I'll do it on the first possible ~** je le ferai à la première occasion (possible) *or* dès que l'occasion se présentera; **(up)on ~** à l'occasion, quand l'occasion se présente (*or* se présentait); **should the ~ arise** le cas échéant; **should the ~ so demand** si les circonstances l'exigent; **as the ~ requires** selon le cas; **he has had few ~s to speak Italian** il n'a pas eu souvent l'occasion de parler italien; **he took (the) ~ to say ...** il en a profité pour dire ...; **he was waiting for a suitable ~ to apologize** il attendait une occasion *or* circonstance favorable pour présenter ses excuses; **this would be a good ~ to try it out** c'est l'occasion tout indiquée pour l'essayer; **to rise to/to be equal to the ~** se montrer/être à la hauteur des circonstances *or* de la situation.

(b) (*event, function*) événement *m.* **a big ~** un grand événement; **it was quite an ~** cela n'a pas été une petite affaire *or* un petit événement; **play/music written for the ~** pièce spécialement écrite/musique spécialement composée pour l'occasion.

(c) (*reason*) motif *m*, occasion *f.* **there is no ~ for alarm** *or* **to be alarmed** il n'y a pas lieu de s'alarmer, il n'y a pas de quoi s'alarmer; **there was no ~ for it** ce n'était pas nécessaire; **I have no ~ for complaint** je n'ai pas sujet de me plaindre, je n'ai aucun motif de plainte; **you had no ~ to say that** vous n'aviez aucune raison de dire cela; **I had ~ to reprimand him** j'ai eu l'occasion de *or* j'ai eu à le réprimander.

(d) (*frm*) **to go about one's lawful ~s** vaquer à ses occupations.

2 *vt* occasionner, causer.

occasional [əˈkeɪʒənl] *adj* **(a)** *event* qui a lieu de temps en temps *or* de temps à autre; *visits* espacés; *rain, showers* intermittent. **we have an ~ visitor** il nous arrive d'avoir quelqu'un (de temps en temps); **we're just ~ visitors** nous ne venons ici qu'occasionnellement; **they had passed an ~ car on the road** ils avaient croisé quelques rares voitures; **~ table** table volante; (*esp round*) guéridon *m.*

(b) *verses, music* de circonstance.

occasionally [əˈkeɪʒnəlɪ] *adv* de temps en temps, de temps à autre, quelquefois, parfois. **very ~** à intervalles très espacés; **only very ~** très peu souvent, rarement, presque jamais.

occident [ˈɒksɪdənt] *n* (*liter*) occident *m*, couchant *m.* **the O~** l'Occident *m.*

occidental [ˌɒksɪˈdentl] *adj* (*liter*) occidental.

occiput [ˈɒksɪpʌt] *n* occiput *m.*

occlude [ɒˈkluːd] **1** *vt* (*all senses*) occlure. (*Met*) **~d front** front occlus. **2** *vi* (*Dentistry*) s'emboîter.

occlusion [ɒˈkluːʒən] *n* (*all senses*) occlusion *f.*

occlusive [ɒˈkluːsɪv] **1** *adj* (*also Ling*) occlusif. **2** *n* (*Ling*) (consonne *f*) occlusive *f.*

occult [ɒˈkʌlt] **1** *adj* occulte. **2** *n*: **the ~** le surnaturel; **to study the ~** étudier les sciences occultes.

occultism [ˈɒkəltɪzəm] *n* occultisme *m.*

occupancy [ˈɒkjʊpənsɪ] *n* occupation *f* (*d'une maison etc*).

occupant [ˈɒkjʊpənt] *n [house]* occupant(e) *m(f)*, habitant(e) *m(f)*; *[land, vehicle etc]* occupant(e); *[job, post]* titulaire *mf.*

occupation [ˌɒkjʊˈpeɪʃən] **1** *n* **(a)** (*U*) *[house etc]* occupation *f*; (*Jur*) prise *f* de possession. **unfit for ~** impropre à l'habitation; **the house is ready for ~** la maison est prête à être habitée; **we found them already in ~** nous les avons trouvés déjà installés.

(b) (*U: Mil etc*) occupation *f.* **army of ~** armée *f* d'occupation; **under military ~** sous occupation militaire; **during the O~** pendant *or* sous l'occupation.

(c) (*trade*) métier *m*; (*profession*) profession *f*; (*work*) emploi *m*, travail *m*; (*activity, pastime*) occupation *f.* **he is a plumber by ~** il est plombier de son métier; **he needs some ~ for his spare time** il lui faut une occupation *or* de quoi occuper ses loisirs; **his only ~ was helping his father** sa seule occupation était *or* il avait pour seule occupation d'aider son père.

2 *cpd troops* d'occupation.

occupational [ˌɒkjʊˈpeɪʃənl] *adj* qui a rapport au métier *or* à la profession. **~ disease** maladie *f* du travail; **~ hazard** *or* **risk** risque *m* du métier; **~ therapist** ergothérapeute *mf*; **~ therapy** thérapeutique occupationnelle, ergothérapie *f.*

occupier ['ɒkjʊpaɪəʳ] *n [house]* occupant(e) *m(f)*, habitant(e) *m(f)*; *[land]* occupant(e); *V* **owner.**

occupy ['ɒkjʊpaɪ] *vt* **(a)** *house* occuper, habiter, résider dans; *room, chair* occuper; *post, position* remplir, occuper.

(b) *[troops, demonstrators]* occuper. (*Mil*) **occupied territory** territoire occupé.

(c) *space* occuper, tenir; *time* occuper, prendre.

(d) *attention, mind, person* occuper. **occupied with the thought of** absorbé par la pensée de; **to be occupied in** *or* **with doing** être occupé à faire; **to ~ o.s.** *or* **one's time (with** *or* **by doing)** s'occuper (à faire); **how do you keep occupied all day?** qu'est-ce que vous trouvez à faire toute la journée?; **to keep one's mind occupied** s'occuper l'esprit.

occur [ə'kɜːʳ] *vi* **(a)** *[event]* avoir lieu, arriver, survenir, se produire; *[word, error]* se rencontrer, se trouver; *[difficulty, opportunity]* se présenter; *[change]* s'opérer; *[disease]* se produire, se rencontrer; *[plant etc]* se trouver. **don't let it ~ again!** que cela ne se reproduise plus! *or* ne se répète (*subj*) pas!; **if a vacancy ~s** en cas de poste vacant; **should the case ~** le cas échéant.

(b) (*come to mind*) se présenter *or* venir à l'esprit (*to sb* de qn). **an idea ~red to me** une idée m'est venue; **it ~s to me that he is wrong** il me vient à l'esprit qu'il a tort, l'idée me vient qu'il a tort; **it didn't ~ to him to refuse** il n'a pas eu l'idée de refuser; **did it never ~ to you to ask?** il ne t'est jamais venu à l'esprit de demander?, tu n'as jamais eu l'idée de demander?

occurrence [ə'kʌrəns] *n* **(a)** (*event*) événement *m*, circonstance *f*. **an everyday ~** un fait journalier; **this is a common ~** ceci arrive *or* se produit souvent.

(b) fait *m* de se produire *or* d'arriver. *[plant etc]* **its ~ in the south is well-known** son existence est bien constatée dans le sud; **to be of frequent ~** se produire *or* arriver souvent.

ocean ['əʊʃən] **1** *n* (*lit, fig*) océan *m*. (*fig*) **~s of*** énormément de*. **2** *cpd climate, region* océanique; *cruise* sur l'océan. **ocean bed** fond sous-marin; **ocean-going** de haute mer; **ocean-going ship** (navire *m*) long-courrier *m*; **ocean liner** paquebot *m*.

Oceania [ˌəʊʃɪ'eɪnɪə] *n* Océanie *f*.

oceanic [ˌəʊʃɪ'ænɪk] *adj current* océanique, pélagique; *fauna* pélagique.

oceanographer [ˌəʊʃə'nɒgrəfəʳ] *n* océanographe *mf*.

oceanography [ˌəʊʃə'nɒgrəfɪ] *n* océanographie *f*.

ocelot ['əʊsɪlɒt] *n* ocelot *m*.

ochre, (*US*) **ocher** ['əʊkəʳ] *n* (*substance*) ocre *f*; (*colour*) ocre *m*.

ochreous ['əʊkrɪəs] *adj* ocreux.

o'clock [ə'klɒk] *adv*: **it is one ~** il est une heure; **what ~ is it?** quelle heure est-il?; **at 5 ~** à 5 heures; **at exactly 9 ~** à 9 heures précises *or* justes; **at twelve ~** (*midday*) à midi; (*midnight*) à minuit; (*Aviat, Mil: direction*) **aircraft approaching at 5 ~** avion *m* à 5 heures.

octagon ['ɒktəgən] *n* octogone *m*.

octagonal [ɒk'tægənl] *adj* octogonal.

octahedron ['ɒktə'hiːdrən] *n* octaèdre *m*.

octane ['ɒkteɪn] **1** *n* octane *m*. **2** *cpd* d'octane. **octane number** indice *m* d'octane; **high-octane petrol** carburant *m* à indice d'octane élevé; **octane rating** = **octane number.**

octave ['ɒktɪv] *n* (*Fencing, Mus, Rel*) octave *f*; (*Poetry*) huitain *m*.

octavo [ɒk'teɪvəʊ] *n* in-octavo *m*.

octet [ɒk'tet] *n* (*Mus*) octuor *m*; (*Poetry*) huitain *m*.

October [ɒk'təʊbəʳ] *n* octobre *m*; *for phrases V* **September.**

octogenarian [ˌɒktəʊdʒɪ'neərɪən] *adj, n* octogénaire (*mf*).

octopus ['ɒktəpəs] **1** *n* (*Zool*) pieuvre *f*, poulpe *m*; (*Brit Aut: for luggage etc*) pieuvre, fixe-bagages *m inv*. **2** *cpd organization* ramifié, à ramifications (multiples).

octosyllabic ['ɒktəʊsɪ'læbɪk] **1** *adj* octosyllabique. **2** *n* octosyllabe *m*, vers *m* octosyllabique.

octosyllable ['ɒktəʊ'sɪləbl] *n* (*line*) octosyllabe *m*, vers *m* octosyllabique; (*word*) mot *m* octosyllabique.

ocular ['ɒkjʊləʳ] *adj, n* oculaire (*m*).

oculist ['ɒkjʊlɪst] *n* oculiste *mf*.

odalisque ['əʊdəlɪsk] *n* odalisque *f*.

odd [ɒd] **1** *adj* **(a)** (*strange*) bizarre, étrange, singulier, curieux. **(how) ~!** bizarre!, étrange!, curieux!; **how ~ that we should meet him** comme c'est curieux que nous l'ayons rencontré; **what an ~ thing for him to do!** c'est curieux *or* bizarre qu'il ait fait cela!; **he says some very ~ things** il dit de drôles de choses parfois; **the ~ thing about it is** ce qui est bizarre *or* étrange à ce sujet c'est, le plus curieux de l'affaire c'est; **he's got rather ~ lately** il est bizarre depuis quelque temps.

(b) (*Math*) *number* impair.

(c) (*extra, left over*) qui reste(nt); (*from pair*) *shoe, sock* dépareillé; (*from set*) dépareillé. **I've got it all but the ~ penny** il me manque un penny pour avoir le compte; **£5 and some ~ pennies** 5 livres et quelques pennies; **any ~ piece of wood** un morceau de bois quelconque; **any ~ piece of bread you can spare** n'importe quel morceau de pain dont vous n'ayez pas besoin; **a few ~ hats** deux ou trois chapeaux; (*Brit*) **this is an ~ size that we don't stock** c'est une taille peu courante que nous n'avons pas (en stock); **to be the ~ one over** être en surnombre; **the ~ man out, the ~ one out** l'exception *f*; *V also* **odds.**

(d) (*and a few more*) **60-~** 60 et quelques; **forty-~ years** une quarantaine d'années, quarante et quelques années; **£20-~** 20 et quelques livres, 20 livres et quelques.

(e) (*occasional, not regular*) **in ~ moments he ...** à ses moments perdus il ...; **at ~ times** de temps en temps; **in ~ corners all over the house** dans les coins et recoins de la maison; **~ jobs** menus travaux, travaux divers (*V also* **2**); **to do ~ jobs about the house** (*housework*) faire de menus travaux domestiques; (*do-it-yourself*) bricoler dans la maison; **he does ~ jobs around the garden** il fait de petits travaux de jardinage; **I've got one or two ~ jobs for you to do** j'ai deux ou trois choses *or* bricoles à te faire faire; **I don't grudge her the ~ meal (or two)** je ne lui fais pas grief d'un repas par-ci par-là; **he has written the ~ article** il a écrit un ou deux articles; **I get the ~ letter from him** de temps en temps je reçois une lettre de lui.

2 *cpd*: (*esp US*) **oddball‡** (*n*) excentrique *mf*; (*adj*) rare, excentrique; **oddbod‡** (*person*) individu *m*, type *m*; (*peculiar person*) drôle *m* d'oiseau*; **odd-job man** homme *m* à tout faire; **odd-looking** à l'air bizarre.

oddity ['ɒdɪtɪ] *n* **(a)** (*strangeness*) = **oddness.**

(b) (*odd person*) personne *f* bizarre, excentrique *mf*; (*odd thing*) curiosité *f*; (*odd trait*) singularité *f*. **he's a real ~** il a vraiment un genre très spécial; **one of the oddities of the situation** un des aspects insolites de la situation.

oddly ['ɒdlɪ] *adv* singulièrement, bizarrement, curieusement; de façon étrange *or* bizarre. **~ enough she was at home** chose curieuse *or* singulière elle était chez elle; **she was ~ attractive** elle avait un charme insolite.

oddment ['ɒdmənt] *n* (*Comm*) fin *f* de série; article dépareillé; *[cloth]* coupon *m*.

oddness ['ɒdnɪs] *n* (*U*) bizarrerie *f*, étrangeté *f*, singularité *f*.

odds [ɒdz] **1** *npl* **(a)** (*Betting*) cote *f*. **he gave him ~ of 5 to 1 (for Jupiter)** il lui a donné une cote de 5 contre 1 (sur Jupiter); **he gave him ~ of 5 to 1 that he would fail his exams** il lui a parié à 5 contre 1 qu'il échouerait à ses examens; **I got good/short/long ~** on m'a donné une bonne/faible/forte cote; **the ~ on** *or* **against a horse** la cote d'un cheval; **the ~ are 7 to 2 against Lucifer** (la cote de) Lucifer est à 7 contre 2; **the ~ are 6 to 4 on** la cote est à 4 contre 6; **the ~ are 6 to 4 against** la cote est à 6 contre 4; **what ~ will you give me?** quelle est votre cote?

(b) (*fig: balance of advantage*) chances *fpl* (*for* pour, *against* contre), avantage *m*. **the ~ are against his** *or* **him* coming** il est pratiquement certain qu'il ne viendra pas, il y a gros à parier qu'il ne viendra pas, il y a peu de chances qu'il vienne; **the ~ are on him coming** *or* **that he will come** il est pratiquement sûr *or* certain qu'il viendra, il y a de fortes chances (pour) qu'il vienne; **the ~ are even that he will come** il y a cinquante pour cent de chances qu'il vienne; **to fight against heavy** *or* **great ~** avoir affaire à plus fort que soi, combattre *or* lutter contre des forces supérieures; **he managed to succeed against overwhelming ~** *or* **against all the ~** il a réussi alors que tout était contre lui; **the ~ are too great** le succès est trop improbable; **by all the ~** (*unquestionably*) sans aucun doute; (*by far*) de loin; (*judging from past experience*) à en juger par l'expérience, d'après ce que l'on sait.

(c) (*difference*) **it makes no ~** cela n'a pas d'importance, ça ne fait rien*; **it makes no ~ to me** ça m'est complètement égal, ça ne me fait rien, je m'en moque, je m'en fiche*; **what's the ~?*** qu'est-ce que ça fait?, qu'est-ce que ça peut bien faire?

(d) to be at ~ (with sb over sth) être brouillé (avec qn pour qch), ne pas être d'accord (avec qn sur qch); **to set 2 people at ~** brouiller 2 personnes, semer la discorde entre 2 personnes.

2 *cpd*: **odds and ends** (*gen*) des petites choses qui restent; *[cloth]* bouts *mpl*; *[food]* restes *mpl*; **there were a few odds and ends lying about the house** quelques objets traînaient çà et là dans la maison; (*fig*) **we still have a few odds and ends to settle** il nous reste encore quelques points à régler; (*Racing*) **odds-on favourite** grand favori; (*fig*) **he's the odds-on favourite for the job** c'est le grand favori pour avoir le poste; **it's odds-on that he'll come** il y a toutes les chances pour qu'il vienne.

ode [əʊd] *n* ode *f* (*to* à, *on* sur).

odious ['əʊdɪəs] *adj* détestable, odieux.

odium ['əʊdɪəm] *n* (*U*) réprobation générale, anathème *m*.

odometer [ɒ'dɒmɪtəʳ] *n* odomètre *m*.

odont(o)... [ɒ'dɒnt(əʊ)] *pref* odont(o)... .

odontologist [ˌɒdɒn'tɒlədʒɪst] *n* odontologiste *mf*.

odontology [ˌɒdɒn'tɒlədʒɪ] *n* odontologie *f*.

odor ['əʊdəʳ] *n* (*US*) = **odour.**

odoriferous [ˌəʊdə'rɪfərəs] *adj* odoriférant, parfumé.

odorless ['əʊdəlɪs] *adj* (*US*) = **odourless.**

odorous ['əʊdərəs] *adj* (*liter*) odorant, parfumé.

odour, (*US*) **odor** ['əʊdəʳ] *n* odeur *f*; (*pleasant*) odeur (agréable), parfum *m*; (*unpleasant*) (mauvaise) odeur; (*fig*) trace *f*, parfum (*liter*). (*fig*) **to be in good/bad ~ with sb** être/ne pas être en faveur auprès de qn, être bien/mal vu de qn; **~ of sanctity** odeur de sainteté.

odourless, (*US*) **odorless** ['əʊdəlɪs] *adj* inodore.

odyssey ['ɒdɪsɪ] *n* odyssée *f*.

oecology [ɪ'kɒlədʒɪ] *n* = **ecology.**

oecumenical [ˌiːkjuː'menɪkəl] *adj* = **ecumenical.**

oedema [ɪ'diːmə] *n* = **edema.**

Oedipus ['iːdɪpəs] *n* Œdipe *m*. (*Psych*) **~ complex** complexe *m* d'Œdipe.

oenologist [iː'nɒlədʒɪst] *n* œnologue *mf*.

oenology [iː'nɒlədʒɪ] *n* œnologie *f*.

o'er ['əʊəʳ] (*liter*) = **over.**

oesophagus [iː'sɒfəgəs] *n* = **esophagus.**

oestrogen, (*US*) **estrogen** ['iːstrəʊdʒən] *n* œstrogène *m*.

oestrus, (*US*) **estrus** ['iːstrəs] *n* œstrus *m*.

of [ɒv,əv] *prep* **(a)** (*possession*) de. **the wife ~ the doctor** la femme du médecin; **a painting ~ the queen's** un tableau de la reine *or* qui appartient à la reine; **a friend ~ ours** un de nos amis; **that funny nose ~ hers** son drôle de nez, ce drôle de nez qu'elle a.

(b) (*objective and subjective genitive*) de; pour. **his love ~ his father** son amour pour son père; **love ~ money** amour de l'argent; **a painting ~ the queen** un tableau de la reine *or* qui représente la reine; **a leader ~ men** un meneur d'hommes; **writer ~ legal articles** auteur d'articles de droit.

(c) (*partitive*) de; entre. **the whole ~ the house** toute la maison; **how much ~ this do you want?** combien *or* quelle quantité en voulez-vous?; **there were 6 ~ us** nous étions 6; **he asked the six ~ us to lunch** il nous a invités tous les six à déjeuner; **~ the ten only one was absent** sur les dix un seul était absent; **he is not one ~ us** il n'est pas des nôtres; **the 2nd ~ June** le 2 juin; **today ~ all days** ce jour entre tous; **you ~ all people ought to know** vous devriez le savoir mieux que personne; (*liter*) **he is the bravest ~ the brave** c'est un brave entre les braves; **the quality ~ (all) qualities** la qualité qui domine toutes les autres; (*liter*) **he drank ~ the wine** il but du vin; *V* **best, first, most, some** *etc.*

(d) (*concerning, in respect of*) de. **what do you think ~ him?** que pensez-vous de lui?; **what ~ it?** et alors?; **hard ~ hearing** dur d'oreille; **20 years ~ age** âgé de 20 ans; *V* **bachelor, capable, warn** *etc.*

(e) (*separation in space or time*) de. **south ~ Paris** au sud de Paris; **within a month/a kilometre ~** à moins d'un mois/d'un kilomètre de; (*US*) **a quarter ~ 6** 6 heures moins le quart.

(f) (*origin*) de. **~ noble birth** de naissance noble; **~ royal origin** d'origine royale; **a book ~ Dante's** un livre de Dante.

(g) (*cause*) de. **to die ~ hunger** mourir de faim; **because ~** à cause de; **it did not happen ~ itself** ce n'est pas arrivé tout seul; **for fear ~** de peur de; *V* **ashamed, choice, necessity** *etc.*

(h) (*with certain verbs*) **it tastes ~ garlic** cela a un goût d'ail; *V* **smell** *etc.*

(i) (*deprivation, riddance*) de. **to get rid ~** se débarrasser de; **loss ~ appetite** perte d'appétit; **cured ~** guéri de; *V* **free, irrespective, short** *etc.*

(j) (*material*) de, en. **dress (made) ~ wool** robe en *or* de laine.

(k) (*descriptive*) de. **house ~ 10 rooms** maison de 10 pièces; **man ~ courage** homme courageux; **girl ~ 10** petite fille de 10 ans; **question ~ no importance** question sans importance; **the city ~ Paris** la ville de Paris; **town ~ narrow streets** ville aux rues étroites; **fruit ~ his own growing** fruits qu'il a cultivés lui-même; **that idiot ~ a doctor** cet imbécile de docteur; **he has a real palace ~ a house** c'est un véritable palais que sa maison; *V* **extraction, make, name** *etc.*

(l) (*agent etc*) de. **beloved ~ all** bien-aimé de tous; **it was horrid ~ him to say so** c'était méchant de sa part (que) de dire cela; *V* **kind** *etc.*

(m) (*in temporal phrases*) **~ late** depuis quelque temps; (*liter*) **it was often fine ~ a morning** il faisait souvent beau le matin; *V* **old** *etc.*

off [ɒf] (*phr vb elem*) **1** *adv* **(a)** (*distance*) **the house is 5 km ~** la maison est à 5 km; **it fell not 50 metres ~** c'est tombé à moins de 50 mètres; **some way ~ (from)** à quelque distance (de); **my holiday is a week ~** je serai en vacances dans une semaine; (*Theat*) **noises/voices ~** bruits/voix dans les coulisses; *V* **far, keep off, ward off** *etc.*

(b) (*departure*) **to be ~** partir, s'en aller; **~ with you!, ~ you go!** va-t'en!, sauve-toi!*, file!*; **I must be ~, it's time I was ~** je dois m'en aller *or* filer* *or* me sauver*; (*Sport*) **they're ~!** et les voilà partis!; **where are you ~ to?** où allez-vous?; **we're ~ to France today** nous partons pour la France aujourd'hui; **I'm ~ fishing** je vais à la pêche; **he's gone ~ to school** il est parti pour l'école; **he's (gone) ~ fishing** il est (parti) à la pêche; **he's ~ fishing every Saturday** il va à la pêche tous les samedis; **he's ~ on his favourite subject*** le voilà lancé* sur son thème favori; *V* **go off, run off** *etc.*

(c) (*absence*) **he's ~ on Tuesdays** il n'est pas là le mardi; **she's ~ at 4 o'clock** elle termine à 4 heures, elle est libre à 4 heures; **to take a day ~** prendre un jour de congé; **I've got this afternoon ~** j'ai congé cet après-midi; **to be ~ sick** être absent pour cause de maladie; **he's ~ sick** (il n'est pas là,) il est malade; **he's been ~ for 3 weeks** cela fait 3 semaines qu'il est absent; *V* **day, time** *etc.*

(d) (*removal*) **he had his coat ~** il avait enlevé son manteau; **with his hat ~** sans chapeau; **~ with those socks!** enlève tes chaussettes!; **the lid was ~** on avait enlevé le couvercle; **~ with his head!** qu'on lui coupe (*subj*) la tête!; **hands ~!** bas les pattes!*; **the handle is ~** *or* **has come ~** la poignée s'est détachée; **there are 2 buttons ~** il manque 2 boutons; (*Comm*) **10% ~** 10% de remise *or* de réduction *or* de rabais; **I'll give you 5% ~** je vais vous faire une remise *or* une réduction *or* un rabais de 5%; *V* **help, take off** etc.

(e) (*not functioning*) **to be ~** *[brakes]* être desserré; *[machine, television, light]* être éteint; *[engine, gas at main, electricity, water]* être coupé; *[tap, gas-tap]* être fermé; (*at cooker etc*) **the gas is ~** le gaz est fermé; **the light/TV/radio is ~** la lumière/la télé*/la radio est éteinte; **the tap is ~** le robinet est fermé; *V* **put off, turn off** *etc.*

(f) (*cancelled etc*) **the play is ~** (*cancelled*) la pièce est annulée *or* n'aura pas lieu; (*no longer running*) la pièce a quitté l'affiche; **the party's ~** (*cancelled*) la soirée est annulée; (*postponed*) la soirée est remise; **their engagement is ~** ils ont rompu leurs fiançailles; (*in restaurant etc*) **the cutlets are ~** il n'y a plus de côtelettes; *V* **put off** *etc.*

(g) (*stale etc*) **to be ~** *[meat]* être mauvais *or* avancé *or* faisandé; *[fish]* être mauvais *or* avancé; *[milk]* être tourné; *[butter]* être rance; *[cheese]* être trop fait; (*Brit fig*) **that's a bit ~!*** c'est un peu exagéré!* *or* moche!*

(h) (*phrases*) **~ and on, on and ~** de temps à autre, par intervalles, par intermittence; **they are badly ~** ils sont dans la gêne; **we're badly ~ for sugar** nous sommes à court de sucre; **the family is comfortably ~** *or* **well ~** la famille vit bien, c'est une famille aisée; **he is better ~ where he is** il est mieux là où il est; **right ~*, straight ~*** tout de suite, à l'instant, sur-le-champ.

2 *prep* **(a)** de; sur; dans; à. **he fell/jumped ~ the wall** il est tombé/a sauté du mur; **he took the book ~ the table** il a pris le livre sur la table; **there are 2 buttons ~ my coat** il manque 2 boutons à mon manteau; **the lid was ~ the tin** le couvercle de la boîte n'était pas mis, on avait ôté le couvercle de la boîte; **they eat ~ chipped plates** ils mangent dans des assiettes ébréchées; **they dined ~ a chicken** ils ont dîné d'un poulet; **he cut a slice ~ the cake** il a coupé une tranche du gâteau; **I'll take something ~ the price for you** je vais vous faire une réduction *or* une remise (sur le prix); *V* **get off, keep off, road** *etc.*

(b) (*distant from*) éloigné de, écarté de. (*Naut*) **~ Portland Bill** au large de Portland Bill; **he was a yard ~ me** il était à un mètre de moi; **height ~ the ground** hauteur (à partir) du sol; **street ~ the square** rue qui part de la place; **house ~ the main road** maison éloignée *or* à l'écart de la grand-route; **I'm ~ sausages*** je n'aime plus les saucisses; **I'm ~ smoking*** je ne fume plus; *V* **duty, food, work** *etc.*

3 *cpd*: **offbeat** (*adj*) *clothes, music, person, behaviour* excentrique, original; (*Mus*) à temps faible; (*n: Mus*) temps *m* faible; **off-centre** désaxé, déséquilibré, décentré; *construction* en porte-à-faux; **I came on the off chance of seeing her** je suis venu avec l'espoir de la voir; **he bought it on the off chance that it would come in useful** il l'a acheté au cas *or* pour le cas où cela pourrait servir (un jour); **I did it on the off chance*** je l'ai fait à tout hasard *or* au cas où*; (*Brit*) **he's off-colour today** il est mal fichu* *or* il n'est pas dans son assiette aujourd'hui; **an off-colour* story** une histoire scabreuse; **he was having an off day** il n'était pas en forme *or* en train ce jour-là; **offhand** (*adj: also* **offhanded**) (*casual*) *manner* dégagé, désinvolte; *behaviour, person* sans-gêne *inv*; *tone, behaviour* cavalier, désinvolte; (*curt*) brusque; (*adv*) spontanément; **I can't just say offhand** je ne peux vous le dire à l'improviste *or* comme ça*; **offhandedly** *V* **offhandedly**; **offhandedness** *V* **offhandedness**; (*Mus*) **off-key** (*adj*) faux (*f* fausse); (*adv*) faux; (*Brit*) **off-licence** (*permit*) licence *f* (*permettant la vente de boissons alcooliques à emporter*); (*shop*) magasin *m* de vins et spiritueux; (*US Mil*) **off-limits (to troops)** interdit (au personnel militaire); **off-load** *goods* décharger, débarquer; *passengers* débarquer; *task* passer (*on or onto sb* à qn); (*Brit*) **off-peak** aux heures creuses; (*Elec*) **off-peak charges** tarif réduit (aux heures creuses); (*Elec*) **off-peak heating** chauffage *m* par accumulation (*ne consommant d'électricité qu'aux heures creuses*); (*Comm, Rail, Traffic etc*) **off-peak hours** heures creuses; (*Rail etc*) **off-peak ticket** billet *m* bénéficiant du tarif réduit heures creuses; **offprint** tirage *m* *or* tiré *m* à part; (*Brit*) **off-putting*** *task* rebutant; *food* peu ragoûtant; *person, manner* rébarbatif, peu engageant; *welcome, reception* peu engageant, décourageant; (*Brit*) **off sales** débit *m* de boissons (à emporter); **off-season** (*n*) morte-saison *f*, morte saison; (*adj, adv*) hors-saison; **in the off-season** à la morte-saison; **offset** *V* **offset**; **offshoot** *[plant, tree]* rejeton *m*; *[organization]* ramification *f*; *[discussion, action etc]* conséquence *f*; **offshore** *breeze* de terre; *island* proche du littoral; *waters* côtier, proche du littoral; *fishing* côtier; (*Brit Aut*) **offside** (*in Britain*) côté droit; (*in France, US etc*) côté gauche; (*Aut*) **offside verge** (*in Britain*) accotement *m* de droite; (*in France, US etc*) accotement de gauche; (*Sport*) **offside** hors-jeu *m inv*; **to be offside** être hors jeu; **the offside rule** la règle du hors-jeu; **offspring** (*pl inv*) progéniture *f* (*U*); (*fig*) fruit *m*, résultat *m*; (*hum*) **how are your offspring?*** comment vont vos rejetons?* (*hum*), comment va votre progéniture?; (*Theat*) **offstage** (*adv, adj*) dans les coulisses; **off-street parking** le stationnement hors de la voie publique; **off the cuff** (*adv*) à l'improviste, au pied levé; **off-the-cuff** (*adj*) *remark, speech* impromptu, au pied levé; (*Brit*) **off the peg** (*adv*) en confection, en prêt-à-porter; (*Brit*) **off-the-peg** (*adj*) prêt à porter, de confection; **off the record** (*adv*) confidentiellement, entre nous; **this is strictly off the record** ceci doit rester strictement entre nous; **off-the-record** (*adj*) (*unofficial*) sans caractère officiel; (*secret*) confidentiel; **to buy sth off the shelf** acheter qch tout fait; **off-white** (*adj, n*) blanc cassé *inv*.

4 *n* (*: *beginning*) **from the ~** dès le départ.

offal [ˈɒfəl] *n* (*U*) (*Culin*) abats *mpl*; (*garbage*) déchets *mpl*, ordures *fpl*, détritus *mpl*.

offence, (US) offense [əˈfens] *n* **(a)** (*Jur*) délit *m* (*against* contre), infraction *f* (*against* à), violation *f* (*against* de); (*Rel etc: sin*) offense *f*, péché *m*. (*Jur etc*) **it is an ~ to do that** il est contraire à la loi *or* il est illégal de faire cela; **first ~** premier délit; **second ~** récidive *f*; **political ~** délit *or* crime politique; **capital ~** crime capital; **to commit an ~** commettre un délit, commettre une infraction (à la loi); **~ against common decency** outrage *m* aux bonnes mœurs; **he was charged with an ~ against ...** il a été inculpé d'avoir enfreint ...; **~ against God** offense faite à Dieu; (*fig*) **it is an ~ to the eye** cela choque *or* offense la vue; *V* **indictable** *etc.*

(b) (*U: hurting of sb's feelings*) **to give** *or* **cause ~ to sb** blesser *or* froisser *or* offenser qn; **to take ~ (at)** se vexer (de), se froisser (de), s'offenser (de), s'offusquer (de); **no ~ taken!** il n'y a pas de mal, il n'y a pas d'offense (*fig*); **no ~ meant!** je ne voulais pas vous blesser *or* froisser; **no ~ meant but ...** soit dit sans offense ... .

(c) (*U: Mil: as opposed to defence*) attaque *f*. (*US Sport*) **the ~** les attaquants *mpl*; *V* **weapon.**

offend [əˈfend] **1** *vt person* blesser, froisser, offenser; *ears, eyes* offusquer, choquer; *reason* choquer, heurter, outrager. **to be** *or* **become ~ed (at)** se vexer (de), se froisser (de), s'offenser (de), s'offusquer (de), se formaliser (de); **she was ~ed by** *or* **at my remark** mon observation l'a blessée *or* froissée *or* offensée; **it ~s my sense of justice** cela va à l'encontre de *or* cela choque mon sens de la justice.

2 *vi* commettre une infraction. (*fig*) **the ~ing word/object** le mot/l'objet incriminé.

offend against *vt fus law, rule* enfreindre, violer; *good taste* offenser; *common sense* aller à l'encontre de, être une insulte *or* un outrage à.

offender [əˈfendəʳ] *n* **(a)** (*lawbreaker*) délinquant(e) *m(f)*; (*against traffic regulations etc*) contrevenant(e) *m(f)*. (*Jur*) **first ~** délinquant(e) primaire; **previous ~** récidiviste *mf*; **persistent** *or* **habitual ~** récidiviste invétéré(e); **~s against the parking regulations** les contrevenants (aux règlements du stationnement); **who left this book here? — I was the ~** qui a laissé ce livre ici? — c'est moi le coupable *or* le fautif.
(b) (*insulter*) offenseur *m*; (*aggressor*) agresseur *m*.

offense [əˈfens] *n* (*US*) = **offence.**

offensive [əˈfensɪv] **1** *adj* **(a)** (*shocking*) offensant, choquant; (*hurtful*) blessant; (*disgusting*) repoussant; (*insulting*) grossier, injurieux; (*rude, unpleasant*) déplaisant. **to be ~ to sb** insulter *or* injurier qn; **~ language** propos choquants, grossièretés *fpl*; **they found his behaviour very ~** sa conduite les a profondément choqués.
(b) (*Mil etc*) *action, tactics* offensif. (*Jur*) **~ weapon** arme offensive.
2 *n* (*Mil: action, state*) offensive *f*. **to be on the ~** être en position d'attaque, avoir pris l'offensive; **to go over to/take the ~** passer à/prendre l'offensive; *V* **peace.**

offensively [əˈfensɪvlɪ] *adv* (*V* **offensive 1a**) *behave* d'une manière offensante *or* choquante *or* inconvenante; *say* d'une manière blessante *or* injurieuse, désagréablement.

offer [ˈɒfəʳ] **1** *n* (*also Comm*) offre *f* (*of* de, *for* pour, *to do* de faire), proposition *f* (*of* de); (*of marriage*) demande *f* (en mariage). **to make a peace ~** faire une proposition *or* offre de paix; **make me an ~!** faites-moi une proposition! *or* offre!; **I'm open to ~s** je suis disposé *or* prêt à recevoir des offres; **it's my best ~** c'est mon dernier mot; **~s over/around £9,000** offres au-dessus/autour de 9.000 livres; (*in advertisement*) **£5 or nearest ~** 5 livres ou au plus offrant; **he's had a good ~ for the house** on lui a fait une offre avantageuse *or* une proposition intéressante pour la maison; (*Comm*) **this brand is on ~** cette marque est en promotion *or* en (vente-)réclame; (*Comm*) **'on ~ this week', 'this week's special ~'** 'articles en promotion cette semaine'.
2 *vt* **(a)** *job, gift, prayers* offrir (*to* à); *help, object, money* proposer (*to* à). **to ~ to do** offrir *or* proposer de faire; **she ~ed me her house for the week** elle m'a proposé sa maison *or* elle a mis sa maison à ma disposition pour la semaine; **to ~ o.s. for a mission** être volontaire *or* se proposer pour exécuter une mission; (*Rel*) **to ~ a sacrifice** offrir un sacrifice, faire l'offrande d'un sacrifice; (*Mil*) **to ~ one's flank to the enemy** présenter le flanc à l'ennemi.
(b) (*fig*) *apology, difficulty, opportunity, view* offrir, présenter; *remark, opinion* proposer, suggérer, émettre; *V* **resistance.**
3 *vi [opportunity etc]* s'offrir, se présenter.

offer up *vt sep* (*liter*) *prayers* offrir; *sacrifice etc* offrir, faire l'offrande de.

offering [ˈɒfərɪŋ] *n* (*act; also thing offered*) offre *f*, don *m*, offrande *f*; (*Rel*) offrande, sacrifice *m*; *V* **burnt, peace, thank** *etc.*

offertory [ˈɒfətərɪ] *n* (*Rel*) (*part of service*) offertoire *m*, oblation *f*; (*collection*) quête *f*. **~ box** tronc *m*.

offhanded [ˈɒfˈhændɪd] *adj* = **offhand**; *V* **off 3.**

offhandedly [ˈɒfˈhændɪdlɪ] *adv* (*casually*) avec désinvolture, avec sans-gêne, cavalièrement; (*curtly*) avec brusquerie.

offhandedness [ˈɒfˈhændɪdnɪs] *n* désinvolture *f*, sans-gêne *m*; brusquerie *f*.

office [ˈɒfɪs] **1** *n* **(a)** (*place, room*) bureau *m*; (*part of organization*) section *f*. **lawyer's ~** étude *f* de notaire; (*US*) **doctor's ~** cabinet *m* (médical); **our London ~** notre siège *or* notre bureau de Londres; **he works in an ~** il travaille dans un bureau, il est employé de bureau; (*esp Brit*) *[house etc]* **'usual ~s'** 'cuisine, sanitaires'; *V* **box office, foreign, head, home, newspaper** *etc.*
(b) (*function*) charge *f*, fonction *f*, poste *m*; (*duty*) fonctions, devoir *m*. (*frm*) **it is my ~ to ensure ...** j'ai charge d'assurer ..., il m'incombe d'assurer ...; **he performs the ~ of treasurer** il fait fonction de trésorier; **to be in ~, to hold ~** *[mayor, chairman]* occuper sa charge, remplir sa fonction, être en fonction; *[minister]* détenir *or* avoir un portefeuille; *[political party]* être au pouvoir *or* au gouvernement; **to take ~** *[chairman, mayor, minister]* entrer en fonctions; *[political party]* arriver au *or* prendre le pouvoir; **he took ~ as prime minister in January** il est entré dans ses fonctions de premier ministre au mois de janvier; **to go out of ~** *[mayor, chairman]* quitter ses fonctions; *[minister]* quitter le ministère, abandonner *or* perdre son portefeuille; *[political party]* perdre le pouvoir; **public ~** fonctions officielles; *V* **jack.**
(c) **~s** offices *mpl*, service(s) *m(pl)*, aide *f*; **through his good ~s** par ses bons offices; **through the ~s of** par l'entremise de; **to offer one's good ~s** offrir ses bons offices.
(d) (*Rel*) office *m*. **O~ for the dead** office funèbre *or* des morts; *V* **divine**[1] *etc.*
2 *cpd staff, furniture, work* de bureau. *[club, society]* **office bearer** membre *m* du bureau *or* comité directeur; (*Brit*) **office block** immeuble *m* de bureaux; **office boy** garçon *m* de bureau; **office building = office block; office hours** heures *fpl* de bureau; **to work office hours** avoir des heures de bureau; **he's got an office job** il travaille dans un bureau; **office manager** directeur *m* de bureau; **office-worker** employé(e) *m(f)* de bureau.

officer [ˈɒfɪsəʳ] **1** *n* **(a)** (*Aviat, Mil, Naut*) officier *m*. **~s' mess** mess *m*; (*Mil*) **~ of the day** officier *or* service *m* de jour; (*Naut*) **~ of the watch** officier de quart; *V* **commission, man, petty** *etc.*
(b) (*official*) *[local government]* fonctionnaire *m*, officier *m*; *[company, institution, organization, club]* membre *m* du bureau *or* comité directeur. **police ~**, (*frm*) **~ of the law** agent *m* (de police); (*to policeman*) **yes ~** oui monsieur l'agent.
2 *vt* (*Mil etc*) (*command*) commander; (*provide with ~s*) pourvoir d'officiers *or* de cadres.

official [əˈfɪʃəl] **1** *adj document, news, ceremony, circles, capacity, responsibilities* officiel; *language, style* administratif; *uniform* réglementaire. **it's not yet ~** ce n'est pas encore officiel.
2 *n* (*gen, Sport etc: person in authority*) officiel *m*; *[civil service]* fonctionnaire *mf*; *[railways, post office etc]* employé(e) *m(f)*. **town hall ~** employé(e) de mairie; **local government ~** ≃ fonctionnaire (de l'administration locale); **government ~** fonctionnaire (de l'Administration); **an ~ of the Ministry** un représentant *or* personnage officiel du ministère.

officialdom [əˈfɪʃəldəm] *n* (*U*) administration *f*, bureaucratie *f* (*also pej*).

officialese [əˌfɪʃəˈliːz] *n* (*U: pej*) jargon administratif.

officially [əˈfɪʃəlɪ] *adv* (*Admin etc*) officiellement; *announce, appoint, recognize* officiellement, à titre officiel; (*) officiellement, en principe.

officiate [əˈfɪʃɪeɪt] *vi* **(a)** (*Rel*) officier. **to ~ at a wedding** célébrer un mariage. **(b)** assister en sa capacité officielle (*at* à). **to ~ as** remplir *or* exercer les fonctions de.

officious [əˈfɪʃəs] *adj person, behaviour* trop empressé, trop zélé. **to be ~** faire l'officieux *or* l'empressé.

officiously [əˈfɪʃəslɪ] *adv* avec un empressement *or* un zèle excessif.

officiousness [əˈfɪʃəsnɪs] *n* excès *m* d'empressement.

offing [ˈɒfɪŋ] *n*: **in the ~** (*Naut*) au large; (*fig*) en vue, en perspective.

offset [ˈɒfset] (*vb: pret, ptp* **offset**) **1** *n* **(a)** (*counterbalancing factor*) compensation *f*. **as an ~ to sth** pour compenser qch.
(b) (*Typ*) (*process*) offset *m*; (*smudge etc*) maculage *m*.
(c) (*Bot*) rejeton *m*; (*in pipe etc*) coude *m*, courbure *f*.
(d) (*start*) début *m*, commencement *m*.
2 *cpd*: (*Typ*) **offset lithography = offset printing; offset paper** papier *m* offset; **offset press** presse *f* offset; **offset printing** offset *m*.
3 *vt* **(a)** (*counteract, compensate for*) contrebalancer, compenser.
(b) (*weigh up*) **to ~ one factor against another** mettre en balance deux facteurs.
(c) (*Typ*) (*print*) imprimer en offset; (*smudge*) maculer.

oft [ɒft] *adv* (*liter*) maintes fois, souvent. **many a time and ~** maintes et maintes fois; **~-times**†† souventes fois††.

often [ˈɒfən] *adv* souvent, fréquemment, à maintes reprises. **very ~** très souvent, bien des fois; **as ~ as he did it** toutes les fois qu'il l'a fait; **as ~ as not, more ~ than not** la plupart du temps, le plus souvent; **so ~** si souvent, tant de fois; **every so ~** (*in time*) de temps en temps, de temps à autre, parfois; (*in spacing, distance etc*) çà et là; **too ~** trop souvent; **once too ~** une fois de trop; **it cannot be said too ~ that ...** on ne dira *or* répétera jamais assez que ...; **how ~ have you seen her?** combien de fois l'avez-vous vue?; **how ~ do the boats leave?** les bateaux partent tous les combien?

ogival [əʊˈdʒaɪvəl] *adj* ogival, en ogive.

ogive [ˈəʊdʒaɪv] *n* ogive *f* (*Archit*).

ogle [ˈəʊgl] *vt* reluquer, lorgner.

ogre [ˈəʊgəʳ] *n* ogre *m*.

ogress [ˈəʊgrɪs] *n* ogresse *f*.

oh [əʊ] *excl* **(a)** ô!, oh!, ah! **~ dear!** oh là là!, (oh) mon Dieu!; **~ what a waste of time!** ah, quelle perte de temps!; **~ for some fresh air!** si seulement on pouvait avoir un peu d'air frais!; **~ to be in France!** que ne suis-je en France!; **~ really?** non, c'est vrai?; **he's going with her — ~ is he!** il y va avec elle — (*surprise*) tiens, tiens!, vraiment! *or* (*interest or acceptance*) ah bon! *or* (*disapproval*) je vois! *or* (*denial*) on verra!; **~ no you don't! — ~ yes I do!** ah mais non! — ah mais si! *or* oh que si!; **~, just a minute ...** euh, une minute ... .
(b) (*cry of pain*) aïe!

ohm [əʊm] *n* ohm *m*.

oil [ɔɪl] **1** *n* **(a)** (*U: Comm, Geol, Ind etc*) pétrole *m*. (*fig*) **to pour ~ on troubled waters** ramener le calme; *V* **crude.**
(b) (*Art, Aut, Culin, Pharm etc*) huile *f*. **fried in ~** frit à l'huile; (*Culin*) **~ and vinegar (dressing)** vinaigrette *f*; **~ of cloves** essence *f* de girofle; (*Aut*) **to check the ~** vérifier le niveau d'huile; **to paint in ~s** faire de la peinture à l'huile; **an ~ by Picasso** une huile de Picasso; *V* **hair, midnight.**
2 *vt machine* graisser, lubrifier. (*fig*) **to ~ the wheels** *or* **works** mettre de l'huile dans les rouages; (*fig*) **to be well-~ed**‡ être beurré‡, être paf‡ *inv*; *V* **palm**[1].
3 *cpd industry, shares* pétrolier; *king, magnate, millionaire* du pétrole. **oil-burning** *lamp* à pétrole, à huile; *stove* (*paraffin*) à pétrole, (*fuel oil*) à mazout; *boiler* à mazout; **oilcake** tourteau *m* (*pour bétail*); **oilcan** (*for lubricating*) burette *f* à huile *or* de graissage; (*for storage*) bidon *m* à huile; **oilcloth** toile cirée; **oil colour** peinture *f* à l'huile; **oil deposits** gisements *mpl* de pétrole; **oil drill** trépan *m*; **oilfield** gisement *m or* champ *m* pétrolifère; (*Aut*) **oil filter** filtre *m* à huile; **oil-fired** *boiler* à mazout; *central heating* au mazout; **oil gauge** jauge *f* de niveau d'huile *or* de pression d'huile; **oil installation** installation pétrolière; **oil lamp** lampe *f* à huile *or* à pétrole; (*Aut etc*) **oil level** niveau *m* d'huile; **oil paint** peinture *f* à l'huile; (*Art*) couleur *f* à l'huile; **oil painting** (*picture, occupation*) peinture *f* à l'huile; (*fig*) **she's no oil painting*** ce n'est vraiment pas une beauté; **oilpaper** papier huilé; **oil pipeline** oléoduc *m*, pipe-line *m*; **oil pollution** pollution *f* aux hydrocarbures; **oil pressure** pression *f* d'huile; **oil refinery** raffinerie *f* (de pétrole); **oil rig** (*land*) derrick *m*; (*sea*) plate-forme pétrolière; **oil sheik** émir *m* du pé-

trole; **oilskin** (*n*) toile cirée; (*adj*) en toile cirée; (*Dress*) **oilskin(s)** ciré *m*; **oil slick** nappe *f* de pétrole; (*larger*) marée noire; **oilstone** pierre *f* à l'huile; **oil storage tank** (*Ind*) réservoir *m* de stockage de pétrole; (*for central heating*) cuve *f* à mazout; **oil stove** (*paraffin*) poêle *m* à pétrole; (*fuel oil*) poêle à mazout; **oil tanker** (*ship*) pétrolier *m*, tanker *m*; (*truck*) camion-citerne *m* (à pétrole); **oil terminal** port *m* d'arrivée *or* de départ pour le pétrole; **oil well** puits *m* de pétrole.

oiler ['ɔɪləʳ] *n* (*ship*) pétrolier *m*; (*can*) burette *f* à huile *or* de graissage; (*person*) graisseur *m*.

oiliness ['ɔɪlɪnɪs] *n [liquid, consistency, stain]* aspect huileux; *[cooking, food]* aspect gras; (*fig pej*) *[manners, tone etc]* onction *f*.

oily ['ɔɪlɪ] *adj liquid, consistency* huileux; *stain* d'huile; *rag, clothes, hands* graisseux; *cooking, food* gras (*f* grasse); (*fig pej*) *manners, tone* onctueux, mielleux.

ointment ['ɔɪntmənt] *n* onguent *m*, pommade *f*.

O.K.* ['əʊ'keɪ] (*vb: pret, ptp* **O.K.'d**) **1** *excl* d'accord!, parfait!, O.K.! (*don't fuss*) ~, ~! ça va, ça va!

2 *adj* (*agreed*) parfait, très bien; (*in order*) en règle; (*on draft etc as approval*) (lu et) approuvé. **that's ~ with me!** (je suis) d'accord!, ça me va!, parfait!; **is it ~ with you if I come too?** ça ne vous ennuie pas que je vous accompagne? (*subj*); **I'm coming too, ~?** je viens aussi, d'accord?; **I'm ~** je vais bien, ça va (bien); **fortunately the car is ~** (*undamaged*) heureusement la voiture est intacte; (*repaired etc*) heureusement la voiture marche *or* est en bon état; **this car is ~ but I prefer the other** cette voiture n'est pas mal mais je préfère l'autre; **it's the ~ thing to do these days** c'est ce qui se fait de nos jours.

3 *vt order, suggestion* approuver; *document, draft* (*lit*) parafer *or* parapher; (*fig*) approuver.

4 *n*: **to give one's ~** donner son accord *or* approbation.

okapi [əʊ'kɑːpɪ] *n* okapi *m*.

okay* ['əʊ'keɪ] = **O.K.***

okra ['əʊkrə] *n* okra *m*.

old [əʊld] **1** *adj* **(a)** (*aged; not young*) vieux (*f* vieille), âgé. **an ~ man** un vieil homme, un vieillard, un vieux († *or slightly pej*); **an ~ lady** (*gen*) une vieille dame; (*specifically unmarried*) une vieille demoiselle; **an ~ woman** une vieille femme, une vieille († *or slightly pej*); (*pej*) **he's a real ~ woman** il a des manies de petite vieille; **a poor ~ man** un pauvre vieillard, un pauvre vieux; **~ people, ~ folk, ~ folks*** personnes âgées, vieux *mpl*, vieillards *mpl*, vieilles gens; **~ people's home, ~ folks' home** hospice *m* de vieillards; (*private or specific groups*) maison *f* de retraite; **he's as ~ as Methuselah** il est vieux comme Mathusalem; **to have an ~ head on young shoulders** être mûr pour son âge, faire preuve d'une maturité précoce; **~ for his age** *or* **for his years** mûr pour son âge; **to be/grow ~ before one's time** être vieux/vieillir avant l'âge; **to grow** *or* **get ~(er)** vieillir, se faire vieux; **he's getting ~** il vieillit, il se fait vieux, il prend de l'âge; **in his ~ age he ...** sur ses vieux jours *or* dans sa vieillesse il ... (*V also* 2); **that dress is too ~ for you** cette robe fait trop vieux pour toi; **~ Mr Smith** le vieux M Smith; **~ Smith*, ~ man Smith‡** le vieux Smith, le (vieux) père Smith*; *V also* 2 *and* **fogey, ripe, salt** *etc*.

(b) (**fig*) **~ Paul here** ce bon vieux Paul; **he's a good ~ dog** c'est un brave (vieux) chien; **you ~ scoundrel!** sacré vieux!; **I say, ~ man** *or* **~ fellow** *or* **~ chap** *or* **~ boy** dites donc mon vieux; **my** *or* **the ~ man‡** (*husband*) le patron‡; (*father*) le paternel (*hum*), le pater (*hum*), le vieux‡; (*boss*) **the ~ man** le patron; **my** *or* **the ~ woman‡** (*wife*) la patronne‡, ma bourgeoise* (*hum*); (*mother*) la maternelle‡ (*hum*), la mater* (*hum*), la vieille‡; *V* **Harry** *etc*.

(c) (*of specified age*) **how ~ are you?** quel âge avez-vous?; **he is 10 years ~** il a 10 ans, il est âgé de 10 ans; **at 10 years ~** à (l'âge de) 10 ans; **a 6-year-~ boy, a boy (of) 6 years ~** un garçon de 6 ans; **a 3-year-~** (*child*) un(e) enfant de 3 ans; (*horse*) un (cheval de) 3 ans; **the firm is 80 years ~** la compagnie a 80 ans; **he is ~ enough to dress himself** il est assez grand pour s'habiller tout seul; **they are ~ enough to vote** ils sont en âge de *or* d'âge à voter; **you're ~ enough to know better!** à ton âge tu devrais avoir plus de bon sens!; **too ~ for that sort of work** trop âgé pour ce genre de travail; **I didn't know he was as ~ as that** je ne savais pas qu'il avait cet âge-là; **if I live to be as ~ as that** si je vis jusqu'à cet âge-là; (*to child*) **when you're ~er** quand tu seras plus grand; **if I were ~er** si j'étais plus âgé; **if I were 10 years ~er** si j'avais 10 ans de plus; **he is ~er than you** il est plus âgé que toi; **he's 6 years ~er than you** il a 6 ans de plus que toi; **~er brother/son** frère/fils aîné; **his ~est son** son fils aîné; **she's the ~est** elle est *or* c'est elle la plus âgée, elle est l'aînée; **the ~er generation** la génération antérieure.

(d) (*not new*) *gold, clothes, custom, carrots, bread, moon* vieux (*f* vieille); *building, furniture, debt* vieux, ancien (*after n*); (*of long standing*) vieux, ancien (*after n*), établi (depuis longtemps). **an ~ staircase** un vieil escalier, un escalier ancien; **~ wine** vin vieux; **that's an ~ one!** *[story etc]* elle n'est pas nouvelle!, elle est connue!; *[trick etc]* ce n'est pas nouveau!; **as ~ as the hills** vieux comme le monde *or* comme Hérode; **it's as ~ as Adam** c'est vieux comme le monde, ça remonte au déluge; **the ~ part of Nice** le vieux Nice; **we're ~ friends** nous sommes de vieux amis *or* des amis de longue date; **an ~ family** une vieille famille, une famille de vieille souche; *V also* 2 *and* **brigade, hand, lag[3], school[1]** *etc*.

(e) (*former*) *school, mayor, home* ancien (*before n*). (*Brit Scol*) **~ boy** ancien élève; **in the ~ days** dans le temps, autrefois, jadis; **in the good ~ days** *or* **times** dans le bon vieux temps; **this is the ~ way of doing it** on s'y prenait comme cela autrefois; (*Mil*) **~ campaigner** vétéran *m*; *V also* 2 *and* **school[1], soldier** *etc*.

(f) (**: as intensifier*) **any ~ how/where** *etc* n'importe comment/où *etc*; **any ~ thing** n'importe quoi; **we had a great ~ time** on s'est vraiment bien amusé; (*fig*) **it's the same ~ story** c'est toujours la même histoire.

2 *cpd*: **old age** vieillesse *f*; **in his old age** dans sa vieillesse, sur ses vieux jours; **old-age pension** pension *f* vieillesse (*de la Sécurité sociale*); **old-age pensioner** retraité(e) *m(f)*; (*Brit Jur*) **Old Bailey** *cour f d'assises de Londres*; **old-clothes dealer** fripier *m*, -ière *f*; **the old country** la mère patrie; (*Ling*) **Old English** vieil anglais; **Old English sheepdog** ≃ briard *m*; **old-established** ancien (*after n*), établi (depuis longtemps); **old-fashioned** *V* **old-fashioned**; (*Ling*) **Old French** ancien *or* vieux français; (*US*) **Old Glory** la Bannière étoilée (*drapeau m des États-Unis*); (*colour*) **old gold** vieil or *inv*; (*fig*) **old hat** *V* **hat 1**; **oldish** *V* **oldish**; (*Pol etc*) **old-line** ultra(-conservateur (*f* -trice)), ultra-traditionaliste; **old-looking** qui a l'air vieux; (*pej*) **old maid** vieille fille; (*pej*) **old-maidish** *habits* de vieille fille; *person* maniaque (comme une vieille fille); (*Art*) **old master** (*artist*) grand peintre, grand maître (de la peinture); (*painting*) tableau *m* de maître; (*Brit*) **old school tie** (*lit*) cravate *f* aux couleurs de son ancienne école; (*fig*) favoritisme *m* de clan, piston *m*; **old stager** vétéran *m*, vieux routier; **oldster** *V* **oldster**; **old-style** à l'ancienne (mode); **old-style calendar** calendrier julien, vieux calendrier; **Old Testament** Ancien Testament; **old-time** du temps jadis, (*older*) ancien (*before n*); **old-time dancing** danses anciennes; **old-timer*** vieillard *m*, ancien *m*; (*as term of address*) le vieux, l'ancien; **old wives' tale** conte *m* de bonne femme; (*pej*) **old-womanish** *person* qui a des manies de petite vieille; *behaviour, remark* de petite vieille; **the Old World** l'ancien monde; **old-world** *V* **old-world**.

3 *n* **(a) the ~** les vieux *mpl*, les vieillards *mpl*, les vieilles gens. **it will appeal to ~ and young (alike)** cela plaira aux vieux comme aux jeunes, cela plaira à tous les âges.

(b) (in days) of ~ autrefois, (au temps) jadis; **the men of ~** les hommes d'antan (*liter*) *or* de jadis; **I know him of ~** je le connais depuis longtemps.

olden ['əʊldən] *adj* (*liter*) vieux (*f* vieille), d'autrefois, de jadis. **in ~ times** *or* **days** (au temps) jadis, autrefois; **city of ~ times** ville *f* antique.

olde-worlde ['əʊldɪ'wɜːldɪ] *adj* (*hum or pej*) **(a)** = **old-world.** **(b)** (*pseudo*) vieillot (*f* -otte), faussement ancien (*after n*).

old-fashioned ['əʊld'fæʃnd] *adj* **(a)** (*old, from past times*) *attitude, idea, outlook* ancien (*after n*), d'autrefois; *clothes, furniture, tools* à l'ancienne mode, d'autrefois. **in the ~ way** à la manière ancienne; (*fig*) **she is a good ~ kind of teacher** c'est un professeur de la vieille école *or* comme on n'en trouve plus; (*fig*) **good ~ discipline** la bonne discipline d'autrefois; (*fig*) **to give sb/sth an ~ look*** regarder qn/qch de travers.

(b) (*out-of-date*) démodé, passé de mode, suranné; *person, attitude* vieux jeu *inv*.

oldie* ['əʊldɪ] *n* (*film etc*) vieux succès*; (*person*) croulant(e)* *m(f)*.

oldish ['əʊldɪʃ] *adj* (*V* **old**) assez vieux (*f* vieille), assez ancien (*after n*).

oldster* ['əʊldstəʳ] *n* (*US*) ancien *m*, vieillard *m*.

old-world ['əʊld'wɜːld] *adj village, cottage* très vieux (*f* vieille) et pittoresque; (*from past times*) d'antan, d'autrefois; (*outdated*) démodé, suranné. **with ~ lettering** avec une inscription archaïque; **an ~ interior** un intérieur de style antique; **Stratford is very ~** Stratford fait très petite ville d'antan.

oleaginous [,əʊlɪ'ædʒɪnəs] *adj* oléagineux.

oleander [,əʊlɪ'ændəʳ] *n* laurier-rose *m*.

oleo... ['əʊlɪəʊ] *pref* olé(i)..., olé(o)... .

oleo* ['əʊlɪəʊ] *n* (*US*) *abbr of* **oleomargarine.**

oleomargarine ['əʊlɪəʊ'mɑːdʒəriːn] *n* (*US*) margarine *f*.

olfactory [ɒl'fæktərɪ] *adj* olfactif.

oligarchic(al) [,ɒlɪ'gɑːkɪk(əl)] *adj* oligarchique.

oligarchy ['ɒlɪgɑːkɪ] *n* oligarchie *f*.

olive ['ɒlɪv] **1** *n* olive *f*; (*also* **~ tree**) olivier *m*; (*also* **~ wood**) (bois *m* d')olivier; (*colour*) (vert *m*) olive *m*; *V* **mount** *etc*.

2 *adj* (*also* **~-coloured**) *paint, cloth* (vert) olive *inv*; *complexion, skin* olivâtre.

3 *cpd*: (*fig*) **to hold out the olive branch to sb** se présenter à qn le rameau d'olivier à la main; (*US*) **olive drab** (*adj*) gris-vert (olive) *inv*; (*n*) toile *f* de couleur gris-vert (olive) (*utilisée pour les uniformes de l'armée des U.S.A.*); **olive-green** (*adj*) vert olive *inv*; (*n*) vert *m* olive; **olive grove** olivaie *f* *or* oliveraie *f*; **olive oil** huile *f* d'olive.

Oliver ['ɒlɪvəʳ] *n* Olivier *m*.

Olympiad [əʊ'lɪmpɪæd] *n* olympiade *f*.

Olympian [əʊ'lɪmpɪən] **1** *adj* (*Myth, fig*) olympien. **2** *n* (*Myth*) dieu *m* de l'Olympe, Olympien *m*; (*US Sport*) athlète *mf* olympique.

Olympic [əʊ'lɪmpɪk] **1** *adj champion, medal, stadium* olympique. **~ flame** flambeau *m* *or* flamme *f* olympique; **~ Games** Jeux *mpl* olympiques; **~ torch** flambeau *m* *or* torche *f* olympique. **2** *n*: **the ~s** les Jeux *mpl* olympiques.

Olympus [əʊ'lɪmpəs] *n* (*Geog, Myth*) l'Olympe *m*.

ombudsman ['ɒmbʊdzmən] *n* médiateur *m* (*Admin*), protecteur *m* du citoyen (*Can*).

omega ['əʊmɪgə] *n* oméga *m*.

omelet(te) ['ɒmlɪt] *n* omelette *f*. **cheese ~** omelette au fromage; (*Prov*) **you can't make an ~ without breaking eggs** on ne fait pas d'omelette sans casser les œufs (*Prov*).

omen ['əʊmen] **1** *n* présage *m*, augure *m*, auspice *m*. **it is a good ~ that ...** il est de bon augure *or* c'est un bon présage que ... + *subj*; **of ill** *or* **bad ~** de mauvais augure *or* présage; *V* **bird**. **2** *vt* présager, augurer.

ominous ['ɒmɪnəs] *adj event, appearance* de mauvais augure, de sinistre présage; *look, tone, cloud, voice* menaçant; *sound* sinistre; *sign* (très) inquiétant, alarmant. **the silence was ~** le silence ne présageait rien de bon, (*stronger*) le silence était lourd de menaces; **that's ~!** c'est de bien mauvais augure!

ominously [ˈɒmɪnəslɪ] *adv* (*V* **ominous**) d'une façon menaçante; sinistrement; d'une façon très inquiétante; *speak, say* d'un ton menaçant. **he was ~ silent** son silence ne présageait rien de bon.

omission [əʊˈmɪʃən] *n* (*thing omitted*) omission *f*, lacune *f*; (*Typ: word(s) omitted*) bourdon *m*; (*act of omitting*) omission, oubli *m*. **it was an ~ on my part** c'est un oubli de ma part; *V* **sin.**

omit [əʊˈmɪt] *vt* (*accidentally*) omettre, oublier (*to do* de faire); (*deliberately*) omettre, négliger (*to do* de faire). **to ~ any reference to sth** passer qch sous silence.

omni... [ˈɒmnɪ] *pref* omni... .

omnibus [ˈɒmnɪbəs] **1** *n* **(a)** (†: *bus*) omnibus† *m*. **(b)** (*book*) recueil *m*. **2** *adj* à usage multiple. (*US Pol*) **~ bill** projet *m* de loi qui comprend plusieurs mesures.

omnidirectional [ˌɒmnɪdɪˈrekʃənl] *adj* omnidirectionnel.

omnipotence [ɒmˈnɪpətəns] *n* omnipotence *f*, toute-puissance *f*.

omnipotent [ɒmˈnɪpətənt] **1** *adj* omnipotent, tout-puissant. **2** *n*: **the O~** le Tout-Puissant.

omnipresence [ˈɒmnɪˈprezəns] *n* omniprésence *f*.

omnipresent [ˈɒmnɪˈprezənt] *adj* omniprésent.

omniscience [ɒmˈnɪsɪəns] *n* omniscience *f*.

omniscient [ɒmˈnɪsɪənt] *adj* omniscient.

omnivorous [ɒmˈnɪvərəs] *adj* omnivore; (*fig*) *reader* insatiable.

on [ɒn] (*phr vb elem*) **1** *adv* **(a)** (*indicating idea of covering*) **he had his coat ~** il avait mis son manteau; **~ with your pyjamas!** allez, mets ton pyjama!; **she had nothing ~** elle était toute nue; **what had he got ~?** qu'est-ce qu'il portait?; **the lid is ~** le couvercle est mis; **it was not ~ properly** cela avait été mal mis; *V* **glove, put on, shoe, try on** *etc.*

(b) (*indicating forward movement*) **~!** en avant!; **he put/threw it ~ to the table** il l'a mis/jeté sur la table; **he climbed (up) ~ to the wall** il a grimpé sur le mur; **from that time ~** à partir de ce moment-là; **it was getting ~ for 2 o'clock** il n'était pas loin de 2 heures; **it was well ~ in the night** la nuit était bien avancée, il était tard dans la nuit; **well ~ in September** bien avant dans le mois de septembre; **it was well ~ into September** septembre était déjà bien avancé; *V* **broadside, farther, pass on, year** *etc.*

(c) (*indicating continuation*) **go ~ with your work** continuez votre travail; **let's drive ~ a bit** continuons un peu (*en voiture*); **and so ~** et ainsi de suite; **life must go ~** la vie continue; **they talked ~ and ~ for hours** ils ont parlé sans discontinuer *or* sans arrêt pendant des heures; *V* **off, keep on, read on, show** *etc.*

(d) (*functioning, in action*) **to be ~** *[machine, engine]* être en marche, marcher; *[light]* être allumé; *[TV, radio]* être branché *or* allumé, marcher; *[tap]* être ouvert; *[brake]* être serré *or* mis; *V* **put on, switch on, turn on** *etc.*

(e) (*taking place*) *[meeting, programme etc]* **to be ~** être en train *or* en cours; **while the meeting was ~** pendant la réunion; **the show is ~ already** le spectacle a déjà commencé; **the play is still ~** la pièce est encore à l'affiche; **what's ~ at the cinema?** qu'est-ce qu'on donne *or* joue au cinéma?; (*Rad/TV*) **what's ~?** quel est le programme?, qu'y a-t-il à la radio/à la télé?; (*Rad, TV*) **X is ~ tonight** il y a X ce soir; **what film is ~ tonight?** quel film est-ce qu'on passe *or* donne ce soir?; (*Rad, TV*) **you're ~ now!** (c'est) à vous maintenant!; *V* **put on** *etc.*

(f) (*phrases*) **I've nothing ~ this evening** je ne suis pas pris *or* je n'ai rien ce soir; **we are going out, are you ~?*** nous sortons, vous venez?; **you're ~!*** tope (là)!; **it's not ~*** (*refusing*) (il n'en est) pas question!; (*not done*) cela ne se fait pas; **he is always ~ at me*** il est toujours après moi*; **I'll get ~ to him tomorrow** je vais me mettre en rapport avec lui demain; **he's been ~ to me about the broken window** il m'a déjà parlé du carreau cassé; **I've been ~ to him on the phone** je lui ai parlé *or* je l'ai eu au téléphone; **I'm ~ to something** je suis sur une piste intéressante; **the police are ~ to him** la police est sur sa piste; **he was ~ to it at last** (*had found it*) il l'avait enfin trouvé *or* découvert; (*had understood*) il l'avait enfin compris *or* saisi; **he's ~ to a good thing** il a trouvé un filon*; **she's ~ to the fact that we met yesterday** elle sait que nous nous sommes vus hier; *V* **have on** *etc.*

2 *prep* **(a)** (*indicating position, direction*) sur. **~ the table** sur la table; **~ an island** sur une île; **~ the Continent** sur le continent; **~ the high seas** en haute *or* pleine mer; **with sandals ~ her feet** des sandales aux pieds; **with a coat ~ his arm** un manteau sur le bras; **with a ring ~ her finger** une bague au doigt; **the ring ~ her finger** la bague qu'elle avait au doigt; **I have no money ~ me** je n'ai pas d'argent sur moi; **the balcony looks ~ (to) the bay** le balcon donne sur la baie; **they advanced ~ the fort** ils avancèrent sur le fort; **he turned his back ~ us** il nous a tourné le dos; **~ the right** à droite; **~ the blackboard/wall/ceiling** au tableau/mur/plafond; **he hung his hat ~ the nail** il a suspendu son chapeau au clou; **Southend-~-Sea** Southend-sur-mer; **house ~ the main road** maison sur *or* au bord de la grand-route; *V* **stage** *etc.*

(b) (*fig*) **he played the tune ~ his violin** il a joué l'air sur son violon; **he played it ~ the violin** il l'a joué au violon; **he played ~ the violin** il jouait du violon; **with Louis Armstrong ~ the trumpet** avec Louis Armstrong à la trompette; **he swore it ~ the Bible** il l'a juré sur la Bible; **an attack ~ the government** une attaque contre le gouvernement; **the heating works ~ oil** le chauffage marche au mazout; **~ the radio** à la radio; **~ the BBC** (*TV*) sur (la chaîne de) la B.B.C.; (*Rad*) à la B.B.C.; (*Rad*) **~ France-Inter** sur France-Inter; (*Rad, TV*) **you're ~ the air** vous avez l'antenne; **I'm ~ £3,000 a year** je gagne 3.000 livres par an; **a student ~ a grant** un (étudiant) boursier; **he's ~ a course** il suit un cours; **to be ~ pills** prendre des pilules; **to be ~ drugs** se droguer; **he's ~ heroin** il se drogue à l'héroïne; **I'm back ~ cigarettes** je me suis remis à fumer (des cigarettes); **we're ~ irregular verbs** nous en sommes aux verbes irréguliers; **he's got nothing ~ me*** (*not as good as*) je pourrais lui en remontrer n'importe quand, (*stronger*) il ne me vient pas à la cheville; (*no hold over*) il n'a pas barre *or* de prise sur moi; *V* **air, condition, fire, live on** *etc.*

(c) (*indicating means of travel*) **~ the train/bus/plane** dans le train/l'autobus/l'avion; **~ the boat** dans *or* sur le bateau; *V* **foot, horse** *etc.*

(d) (*in expressions of time*) **~ Sunday** dimanche; **~ Sundays** le dimanche; **~ December 1st** le 1er décembre; **~ the evening of December 3rd** le 3 décembre au soir; **~ or about the 20th** vers le 20; **~ and after the 20th** à partir *or* à dater du 20; **~ Easter Day** le jour de Pâques; **it's just ~ 5 o'clock** il est bientôt *or* il va être 5 heures; *V* **clear, day, occasion** *etc.*

(e) (*at the time etc of*) **~ my arrival home** à mon arrivée chez moi; **~ the death of his son** à la mort de son fils; **~ my refusal to go away** lorsque je refusai de partir; **~ hearing this** en entendant cela; *V* **application, production, receipt** *etc.*

(f) (*about, concerning*) sur, de. **he lectures ~ Dante** il fait un cours sur Dante; **a book ~ grammar** un livre de grammaire; **an essay ~ this subject** une dissertation sur ce sujet; **he spoke ~ atomic energy** il a parlé de l'énergie atomique; **have you heard him ~ V.A.T.?** vous l'avez entendu parler de la T.V.A.?; **we've read Jones ~ Marx** nous avons lu ce que Jones a écrit sur Marx; *V* **congratulate, keen**[1] etc.

(g) (*indicating membership*) **to be ~ the team/committee** faire partie de l'équipe/du comité, être (membre) de l'équipe/du comité; **he is ~ the 'Evening News'** il est *or* travaille à l' 'Evening News'; *V* **side, staff** *etc.*

(h) (*engaged upon*) **I'm ~ a new project** je travaille à un nouveau projet; **he was away ~ an errand** il était parti faire une course; **while we're ~ the subject** pendant que nous y sommes; *V* **business, holiday, tour** *etc.*

(i) (*at the expense of*) **we had a drink ~ the house** nous avons bu un verre aux frais du patron *or* de la maison; **this round's ~ me** c'est ma tournée, c'est moi qui paie cette tournée; **have the ticket ~ me** je vous paie le billet.

(j) (*as against*) **prices are up/down ~ last year's** les prix sont en hausse/en baisse par rapport à *or* sur (ceux de) l'année dernière.

3 *adj*: **switch in the ~ position** interrupteur *m or* bouton *m* en position de marche; **it wasn't one of his ~ days*** il n'était pas en forme *or* en train ce jour-là.

4 *cpd*: **oncoming** (*adj*) *car etc* qui approche, qui arrive, venant en sens inverse; *danger* imminent; (*n*) *[winter etc]* approche *f*, arrivée *f*; (*Brit Comm*) **on-costs** frais généraux; **ongoing projects** projets *mpl* en cours; **they have an ongoing relationship** ils entretiennent des relations suivies; **the onlookers** les spectateurs *mpl*, l'assistance *f*, les assistants *mpl*; **onrush** *[people]* ruée *f*; *[water]* torrent *m*; **onset** *V* **onset**; **onshore wind** vent *m* de mer *or* du large; **onslaught** *V* **onslaught**; **onto** (*prep*) = **on to** (*V* **on 1, 2**); **onward(s)** *V* **onward.**

once [wʌns] **1** *adv* **(a)** (*on one occasion*) une fois. **only ~, ~ only** une seule fois; **~ before** déjà une fois; **~ again, ~ more** encore une fois, une fois de plus; **~ (and) for all** une fois pour toutes, une bonne fois, définitivement; **~ a week** tous les huit jours, une fois par semaine; **~ a month** une fois par mois; **~ and again, ~ in a while, ~ in a way** de temps en temps, de temps à autre; **more than ~** plus d'une fois, à plusieurs reprises, plusieurs fois; **~ or twice** une fois ou deux, une ou deux fois; **for ~** pour une fois; **(just) this ~** (juste) pour cette fois(-ci), (juste) pour une fois; **not ~, never ~** pas une seule fois; **~ punished, he ...** une fois puni, il ...; **if ~ you begin to hesitate** si jamais vous commencez à hésiter; **~ is enough** une fois suffit, une fois c'est suffisant; **~ a journalist always a journalist** qui a été journaliste le reste toute sa vie; *V* **thief** *etc.*

(b) (*formerly*) jadis, autrefois, une fois, à un moment donné. **he was ~ famous** il était jadis *or* autrefois *or* à un moment donné bien connu; **~ upon a time there was a prince** il y avait une fois *or* il était une fois un prince; **a ~ powerful nation** une nation puissante dans le passé, une nation jadis *or* autrefois puissante.

(c) at ~ (*immediately*) tout de suite, immédiatement; (*simultaneously*) à la fois, d'un seul coup; **all at ~** (*suddenly*) tout à coup, tout d'un coup, soudain, soudainement; (*simultaneously*) à la fois.

2 *conj* une fois que. **~ she'd seen him she left** l'ayant vu *or* une fois qu'elle l'eut vu elle s'en alla; **~ you give him the chance** si jamais on lui en donne l'occasion.

3 *cpd*: (*: *quick look*) **to give sb the once-over** jauger qn d'un coup d'œil; **to give sth the once-over** vérifier qch très rapidement *or* d'un coup d'œil; (*: *quick clean*) **I gave the room the once-over with the duster** j'ai donné *or* passé un coup (de chiffon *or* de torchon) à la pièce.

one [wʌn] **1** *adj* **(a)** (*numerical*) un, une. **~ woman out of *or* in two** une femme sur deux; **~ or two people** une ou deux personnes; **~ girl was pretty, the other was ugly** une des filles était jolie, l'autre était laide; **~ hundred and twenty** cent vingt; **God is ~** Dieu est un; **that's ~ way of doing it** c'est une façon (entre autres) de le faire, on peut aussi le faire comme ça; **she is ~ (year old)** elle a un an; **it's ~ o'clock** il est une heure; **for ~ thing I've got no money** d'abord *or* pour commencer je n'ai pas d'argent; **as ~ man** comme un seul homme; **with ~ voice** d'une seule voix.

(b) (*indefinite*) un, une. **~ day** un jour; **~ Sunday morning** un (certain) dimanche matin; **~ hot summer afternoon she went ...**

par un chaud après-midi d'été elle partit ...; ~ **moment she's laughing, the next she's in tears** une minute elle rit, l'autre elle pleure.

(c) (*sole*) (un(e)) seul(e), unique. **the ~ man who could do it** le seul qui pourrait *or* puisse le faire; **no ~ man could do it** un homme ne pourrait pas le faire (à lui) seul; **my ~ and only pleasure** mon seul et unique plaisir; **the ~ and only Charlie Chaplin!** le seul, l'unique Charlot!

(d) (*same*) (le) même, identique. **they all went in the ~ car** ils sont tous partis dans la même voiture; **they are ~ (and the same) person** ils sont une seule et même personne; **it's ~ and the same thing** c'est exactement la même chose.

2 *n* **(a)** (*numeral*) un(e) *m(f)*. **~, two, three** un(e), deux, trois; **twenty-~** vingt et un; **there are three ~s in her phone number** il y a trois uns dans son numéro de téléphone; **~ of them** (*people*) l'un d'eux, l'une d'elles; (*things*) (l')un, (l')une; **any ~ of them** (*people*) n'importe lequel d'entre eux, n'importe laquelle d'entre elles; (*things*) n'importe lequel, n'importe laquelle; **the last but ~** l'avant-dernier *m*, -ière *f*; **chapter ~** chapitre un; (*Comm*) **price of ~** prix à la pièce; **these items are sold in ~s** ces articles se vendent à la pièce.

(b) (*phrases*) **I for ~ don't believe it** pour ma part je ne le crois pas; **who doesn't agree? — I for ~!** qui n'est pas d'accord? — moi par exemple! *or* pour commencer!; **never (a) ~** pas un (seul); **~ by ~** un à un, un par un; **by** *or* **in ~s and twos** par petits groupes; **~ after the other** l'un après l'autre; **~ and all** tous tant qu'ils étaient, tous sans exception; **it's all ~** c'est tout un; **it's all ~ to me** cela m'est égal *or* indifférent; (*Brit Fin*††) **~ and sixpence** un shilling et six pence; **he's president and secretary (all) in ~** il est à la fois président et secrétaire; **it's made all in ~** c'est fait d'une seule pièce *or* tout d'une pièce; **to be ~ up (on sb)*** avoir l'avantage (sur qn) (*V also* **4**); **to go ~ better than sb** faire mieux que qn; **he's had ~ too many*** il a bu un coup de trop*; *V* **number, road** *etc.*

3 *pron* **(a)** (*indefinite*) un(e) *m(f)*. **would you like ~?** en voulez-vous (un)?; **have you got ~?** en avez-vous (un)?; **the problem is ~ of money** c'est une question d'argent; **~ of these days** un de ces jours; **he's ~ of my best friends** c'est un de mes meilleurs amis; **she's ~ of the family** elle fait partie de la famille; **he's ~ of us** il est des nôtres; **the book is ~ which** *or* **that I've never read** c'est un livre que je n'ai jamais lu; **he's a teacher and I want to be ~ too** il est professeur et je veux l'être aussi; **every ~ of the boys/books** tous les garçons/les livres sans exception; **you can't have ~ without the other** on ne peut avoir l'un sans l'autre; **sit in ~ or other of the chairs** asseyez-vous sur l'une des chaises; *V* **anyone, no, someone** *etc.*

(b) (*specific*) **this ~** celui-ci, celle-ci; **these ~s*** ceux-ci, celles-ci; **that ~** celui-là, celle-là; **those ~s*** ceux-là, celles-là; **the ~ who** *or* **that** celui qui, celle qui; **the ~ whom** *or* **that** celui que, celle que; **the ~ that** *or* **which is lying on the table** celui *or* celle qui se trouve sur la table; **the ~ on the floor** celui *or* celle qui est par terre; **here's my brother's ~*** voici celui *or* celle de mon frère; **he's the ~ with brown hair** c'est celui qui a les cheveux bruns; **which is the ~ you want?** lequel voulez-vous?; **which ~?** lequel?, laquelle?; **which ~s?*** lesquels?, lesquelles?; **he hit her ~ on the nose*** il lui a flanqué un coup sur le nez*; **I want the red ~/the grey ~s** je veux le rouge/les gris; **this grey ~ will do** ce gris-ci fera l'affaire; **mine's a better ~** le mien *or* la mienne est meilleur(e); **you've taken the wrong ~** vous n'avez pas pris le bon; **that's a difficult ~!** ça c'est difficile!; *V* **eye, quick** *etc.*

(c) (*personal*) **they thought of the absent ~** ils ont pensé à l'absent; **the little ~s** les petits; **my dearest ~** mon chéri, ma chérie; **our dear ~s** ceux qui nous sont chers; († *or frm*) **~ John Smith** un certain *or* un nommé John Smith; **he's a clever ~** c'est un malin; **for ~ who claims to know the language, he ...** pour quelqu'un qui prétend connaître la langue, il ...; **he looked like ~ who had seen a ghost** il avait l'air de quelqu'un qui aurait vu un fantôme; **to ~ who can read between the lines** à celui qui sait lire entre les lignes; **he's not ~ to agree to that sort of thing** il n'est pas de ceux qui acceptent ce genre de choses; **he's a great ~ for chess** c'est un mordu* des échecs; **I'm not ~** *or* **much of a ~* for sweets** je ne suis pas (grand) amateur de bonbons; **you are a ~!‡** tu en as de bonnes!*

(d) **~ another = each other**; *V* **each 2c.**

(e) (*impersonal*) (*nominative*) on; (*accusative, dative*) vous. **~ must try to remember** on doit *or* il faut se souvenir; **it tires ~ too much** cela (vous) fatigue trop; **~ likes to see ~'s friends happy** on aime voir ses amis heureux, on aime que ses amis soient heureux.

4 *cpd*: **one-...** d'un (seul) ..., à un seul ..., à ... unique; **one-act play** pièce *f* en un (seul) acte; **one-armed** manchot; **one-armed bandit*** machine *f* à sous; **one-eyed** *person* borgne; (*Zool*) unioculé; **one-handed** (*adj*) *person* manchot, qui a une (seule) main; *tool* utilisable d'une (seule) main; (*adv*) d'une (seule) main; **one-horse town** *or* **place** bled* *m*, trou* *m*; **one-legged** unijambiste; **one-line message** message *m* d'une (seule) ligne; **one-liner** mot *m*, plaisanterie *f* express; **one-man** *V* **one-man**; (*Theat*) **one-night stand** soirée *f* *or* représentation *f* unique; (*Brit*) **one-off*** rarissime, exceptionnel; (*US*) **one-one = one-to-one**; (*Aut etc*) **one-owner** qui n'a eu qu'un propriétaire; (*Pol*) **one-party system** système *m* à parti unique; (*Dress*) **one-piece** (*adj*) une pièce *inv*, d'une seule pièce; (*n*) vêtement *m* une pièce; **one-piece swimsuit** maillot *m* une pièce; **one-room(ed) flat** *or* **apartment** studio *m*, appartement *m* d'une pièce; **oneself** *V* **oneself**; (*US*) **one-shot* = one-off***; **one-sided** *decision* unilatéral; *contest, game* inégal; *judgment, account* partial; *bargain, contract* inéquitable; **one-time** ancien (*before n*), d'autrefois, de jadis; **one-to-one** univoque; (*Rail*) **one-track** à voie unique; (*fig*) **to have a one-track mind** n'avoir qu'une idée en tête, avoir une idée fixe; (*hum*) **one-upmanship*** art *m* de faire mieux que les autres; **one-way** *street* à sens unique; *traffic* en sens unique; (*Rail etc*) *ticket* simple; (*fig*) *friendship, emotion etc* non partagé; **he's a one-woman man** c'est l'homme d'une seule femme, c'est un homme qui n'aimera jamais qu'une seule femme.

one-man ['wʌn'mæn] *adj job* fait *or* à faire par un seul homme, pour lequel un seul homme suffit; *business, office* que fait marcher un seul homme; *woman, dog etc* qui n'aime qu'un seul homme. (*Mus, also fig*) **~ band** homme-orchestre *m*; **~ show** (*Art etc*) exposition consacrée à un seul artiste; (*Rad, Theat, TV*) one man show *m*; (*fig*) **this business is a ~ band*** *or* **~ show*** un seul homme fait marcher toute l'affaire.

oneness ['wʌnnɪs] *n* unité *f*; (*sameness*) identité *f*; (*agreement*) accord *m*, entente *f*.

onerous ['ɒnərəs] *adj task* pénible; *responsibility* lourd.

oneself [wʌn'self] *pron* se, soi-même; (*after prep*) soi(-même); (*emphatic*) soi-même. **to hurt ~** se blesser; **to dress ~** s'habiller; **to speak to ~** se parler (à soi-même); **to be sure of ~** être sûr de soi(-même); **one must do it ~** il faut le faire soi-même; **(all) by ~** (tout) seul.

onion ['ʌnjən] **1** *n* oignon *m*. (*Brit*) **to know one's ~s*** connaître son affaire, s'y connaître; *V* **cocktail, spring** *etc.*

2 *cpd soup* à l'oignon; *skin* d'oignon; *stew* aux oignons. (*Archit*) **onion dome** dôme bulbeux; **onion johnny** vendeur *m* d'oignons (ambulant); **onion-shaped** bulbeux; **onionskin** pelure *f* d'oignon.

only ['əʊnlɪ] **1** *adj* seul, unique. **~ child** enfant *mf* unique; **you're the ~ one to think of that** vous êtes le seul à y avoir pensé, vous seul y avez pensé; **I'm tired! — you're not the ~ one!*** je suis fatigué! — vous n'êtes pas le seul!; **it's the ~ one left** c'est le seul qui reste (*subj*); **he is not the ~ one here** il n'est pas le seul ici, il n'y a pas que lui ici; **his ~ friend was his dog** son chien était son seul ami; **his ~ answer was to shake his head** pour toute réponse il a hoché la tête de droite à gauche; **your ~ hope is to find another one** votre unique espoir est d'en trouver un autre; **the ~ thing is that it's too late** seulement *or* malheureusement il est trop tard; **that's the ~ way to do it** c'est la seule façon de le faire, on ne peut pas le faire autrement; *V* **one, pebble** *etc.*

2 *adv* seulement, simplement, ne ... (plus) que. **~ Paul can wait** Paul seul peut attendre, il n'y a que Paul qui puisse attendre; **he can ~ wait** il ne peut qu'attendre; **God ~ knows!** Dieu seul le sait!; **I can ~ say how sorry I am** tout ce que je peux dire c'est combien je suis désolé; **it's ~ that I thought he might ...** c'est que, simplement, je pensais qu'il pourrait ...; **I will ~ say that ...** je me bornerai à dire *or* je dirai simplement que ...; **~ time will tell** c'est l'avenir qui le dira; **it will ~ take a minute** ça ne prendra qu'une minute; **I'm ~ the secretary** je ne suis que le secrétaire; **a ticket for one person ~** un billet pour une seule personne; **'ladies ~'** 'réservé aux dames'; **I ~ looked at it** je n'ai fait que le regarder; **you've ~ to ask** vous n'avez qu'à demander; **~ think of the situation!** imaginez un peu la situation!; **~ to think of it** rien que d'y penser; **he was ~ too pleased to come** il n'a été que trop content de venir, il ne demandait pas mieux que de venir; **it's ~ too true** ce n'est que trop vrai; **not ~ A but also B** non seulement A mais aussi B; **not ~ was it dark, but it was also foggy** non seulement il faisait noir, mais il y avait aussi du brouillard; **~ yesterday** hier encore, pas plus tard qu'hier; **it seems like ~ yesterday** il semble que c'était hier; **he has ~ just arrived** il vient tout juste d'arriver; **but I've ~ just bought it!** mais je viens seulement de l'acheter!; **I caught the train but ~ just** j'ai eu le train mais (c'était) de justesse; **if ~** si seulement.

3 *conj* seulement, mais. **I would buy it, ~ it's too dear** je l'achèterais bien, seulement *or* mais il est trop cher; **he would come too, ~ he's ill** il viendrait bien aussi, si ce n'est qu'il est malade *or* seulement il est malade.

onomastic [ˌɒnəʊ'mæstɪk] *adj* onomastique.

onomatopoeia [ˌɒnəʊmætəʊ'piːə] *n* onomatopée *f*.

onomatopoeic [ˌɒnəʊmætəʊ'piːɪk] *adj*, **onomatopoetic** [ˌɒnəʊmætəʊpəʊ'etɪk] *adj* onomatopéique.

onset ['ɒnset] *n* **(a)** (*attack*) attaque *f*, assaut *m*. **(b)** [*illness etc*] début *m*, commencement *m*; [*old age, winter etc*] approche *f*. **at the ~** d'emblée.

onslaught ['ɒnslɔːt] *n* attaque *f*, assaut *m*, charge *f*. (*fig*) **he made a furious ~ on the chairman** il s'en prit violemment au président.

onto ['ɒntʊ] *prep* = **on to**; *V* **on 1b, 1f, 2a.**

ontological [ˌɒntə'lɒdʒɪkəl] *adj* ontologique.

ontology [ɒn'tɒlədʒɪ] *n* ontologie *f*.

onus ['əʊnəs] *n* (*no pl*) responsabilité *f*, charge *f*, obligation *f*. **the ~ of proof rests with him** il a la charge de (le) prouver, c'est à lui de faire la preuve; **the ~ is on him to do it** il lui incombe de le faire; **the ~ is on the manufacturers** c'est la responsabilité des fabricants.

onward ['ɒnwəd] (*phr vb elem*) **1** *adv* en avant, plus loin. (*excl*) **~!** en avant!; **to walk ~** avancer; **from this time ~** désormais, dorénavant; **from today ~** à partir d'aujourd'hui, désormais, dorénavant. **2** *adj step, march* en avant.

onwards ['ɒnwədz] *adv* = **onward 1.**

onyx ['ɒnɪks] **1** *n* onyx *m*. **2** *cpd* en onyx, d'onyx.

oodles‡ ['uːdlz] *npl* un tas*, des masses* *fpl*, des quantités *fpl*.

oolite ['əʊəlaɪt] *n* oolithe *m*.

oolitic [ˌəʊə'lɪtɪk] *adj* oolithique.

oompah ['uːmpɑː] *n* flonflon *m*.

oomph‡ [ʊmf] *n* (*energy*) énergie *f*, allant *m*, dynamisme *m*; (*sex appeal*) sex-appeal *m*, chien *m*.

oops* [ʊps] *excl* houp! **~-a-daisy!** hop-là!

ooze [u:z] **1** *n* vase *f*, limon *m*, boue *f*.
2 *vi [water, pus, walls etc]* suinter; *[resin, gum]* exsuder.
3 *vt*: **his wounds ~d pus** le pus suintait de ses blessures; (*fig pej*) **she was oozing charm/self-complacency** le charme/la suffisance lui sortait par tous les pores.
ooze away *vi [liquids]* s'en aller, suinter; *[strength, courage, enthusiasm]* disparaître, se dérober. **his strength** *etc* **was oozing away** ses forces *etc* l'abandonnaient.
ooze out *vi [liquids]* sortir, suinter; *[news, secret]* transpirer.
opacity [əʊ'pæsɪtɪ] *n* (*V* **opaque**) opacité *f*; obscurité *f*; stupidité *f*.
opal ['əʊpəl] **1** *n* opale *f*. **2** *cpd ring, necklace* d'opale; (*also* **opal-coloured**) opalin.
opalescence [ˌəʊpə'lesns] *n* opalescence *f*.
opalescent [ˌəʊpə'lesnt] *adj* opalescent, opalin.
opaque [əʊ'peɪk] *adj substance, darkness* opaque; (*fig*) (*unclear*) obscur; (*stupid*) stupide, obtus.
open ['əʊpən] **1** *adj* **(a)** (*not closed*) *door, box, envelope, book, handbag, parcel, grave, wound, eyes, flower etc* ouvert; *bottle, jar* ouvert, débouché; *map, newspaper* ouvert, déplié; *shirt, coat, collar* ouvert, déboutonné. **wide ~** grand ouvert; **the door was slightly ~** la porte était entrouverte *or* entrebâillée; (*fig*) **he is** *or* **his thoughts are** *or* **his mind is an ~ book** ses pensées sont un véritable livre ouvert, on peut lire en lui comme dans un livre; **a dress ~ at the neck** une robe à col ouvert *or* échancrée (à l'encolure); (*Brit Banking*) **~ cheque** chèque ouvert *or* non barré; (*Ling*) **~ vowel** voyelle ouverte; (*Elec*) **~ circuit** circuit ouvert; **to welcome sb with ~ arms** accueillir qn à bras ouverts; (*fig*) **to welcome sth with ~ arms** accueillir qch avec joie; (*fig*) **it's an ~-and-shut case** c'est un cas transparent *or* clair comme le jour; (*Pol Econ*) **the ~ door** la porte ouverte; **the window flew ~** la fenêtre s'ouvrit brusquement; *V* **break, cut, eye, mouth** *etc.*
(b) *shop, museum* ouvert. **our grocer is ~ on Mondays** notre épicier ouvre *or* est ouvert le lundi; **gardens ~ to the public** jardins ouverts au public; (*fig*) **to keep ~ house** tenir table ouverte; (*Brit*) **~ day** journée *f* portes ouvertes *or* du public; *V* **throw.**
(c) *river, water, canal* (*not obstructed*) ouvert à la navigation; (*not frozen*) non gelé; *road, corridor* dégagé; *pipe* ouvert, non bouché; (*Med*) *bowels* relâché; *pores* dilaté. **road ~ to traffic** route ouverte à la circulation; **the way to Paris lay ~** la route de Paris était libre; **the road to anarchy lay wide ~** on allait tout droit à l'anarchie; **the ~ road** la grand-route.
(d) (*unrestricted*) **the ~ air** le plein air (*V also* **2**); **in the ~ air** *live, walk, eat* au grand air, en plein air; *sleep* à la belle étoile; *swimming pool* à ciel ouvert, en plein air; **in ~ country** en rase campagne, en plein champ; **when you reach ~ country** *or* **~ ground** quand vous gagnerez la campagne; **patch of ~ ground** (*between trees*) clairière *f*; (*in town*) terrain *m* vague; **beyond the woods he found the ~ fields** au-delà des bois il trouva les champs qui s'étendaient; **the ~ sea** la haute mer, le large; **on the ~ sea(s)** en haute mer, au large, de par les mers (*liter*); **~ space** espace *m* libre; **the (wide) ~ spaces** les grands espaces vides; **~ view** *or* **aspect** vue dégagée.
(e) (*not enclosed*) *car, carriage* découvert, décapoté; *boat* ouvert, non ponté; *drain, sewer* à ciel ouvert. **~ sandwich** canapé *m* (froid).
(f) (*exposed*) *coast etc* ouvert, exposé. **(wide) ~ to the winds/the elements** exposé à tous les vents/aux éléments; (*Mil, Pol*) **~ city** ville ouverte; (*Mil*) **a position ~ to attack** une position exposée à l'attaque; **~ to persuasion** accessible *or* ouvert à la persuasion; **I'm ~ to advice** je me laisserais volontiers conseiller; **I'm ~ to correction, but I believe he said ...** dites-moi si je me trompe mais je crois qu'il a dit ..., si je ne me trompe (*frm*) il a dit ...; **the decision is ~ to criticism** cette décision prête le flanc à la critique; **it is ~ to doubt whether ...** on peut douter que ... + *subj*; *V* **lay**[1], **offer** *etc.*
(g) (*accessible to public*) *market, meeting, trial, discussion* public (*f* -ique); *competition* ouvert à tous, open *inv*. **membership is not ~ to women** les femmes ne peuvent pas être membres; **the course is not ~ to schoolchildren** ce cours n'est pas ouvert aux lycéens, les lycéens ne peuvent pas choisir ce cours; **it is ~ to you to refuse** libre à vous de refuser, vous pouvez parfaitement refuser; **several methods/choices were ~ to them** plusieurs méthodes/choix s'offraient *or* se présentaient à eux; **this post is still ~** ce poste est encore vacant; (*Jur*) **in ~ court** en audience publique; **~ letter** lettre ouverte; **~ scholarship** bourse *f* (*décernée par un concours ouvert à tous*); (*Hunting*) **~ season** saison *f* de la chasse; (*Ind Pol*) **~ shop** atelier ouvert aux non-syndiqués; (*Brit*) **the O~ University** le Centre de Télé-enseignement universitaire.
(h) (*frank*) *person, character, face, manner* ouvert, franc (*f* franche); (*declared*) *enemy* déclaré; *admiration, envy* manifeste; *campaign* ouvert; *attempt* non dissimulé, patent; *scandal* public (*f* -ique). **in ~ revolt (against)** en rébellion ouverte (contre); **~ secret** secret *m* de Polichinelle; **it's an ~ secret that ...** ce n'est un secret pour personne que ...; **he was not very ~ with us** il ne nous a pas tout dit, il nous a parlé avec réticence.
(i) (*undecided*) *question* non résolu, non tranché. **the race was still wide ~** l'issue de la course était encore indécise; **it's an ~ question whether he would have come if ...** on ne saura jamais s'il serait venu si ...; **they left the matter ~** ils n'ont pas tranché la question, ils ont laissé la question en suspens; **let's leave the date/arrangements ~** n'arrêtons pas *or* ne précisons pas la date/les dispositions; **to keep an ~ mind on sth** réserver son jugement *or* son opinion sur qch (*V also* **2**); **I've got an ~ mind about it** je n'ai pas encore formé d'opinion à ce sujet (*V also* **2**); (*Jur*) **~ verdict** (*not stating cause of death*) *verdict m de décès par mort violente sans que les causes aient été réellement déterminées*; (*where guilty party unknown*) verdict sans désignation de coupable; **~ ticket** billet *m* open; *V* **option** *etc.*
2 *cpd*: **open-air** *games, activities* de plein air; *swimming pool, market, meeting* en plein air, à ciel ouvert; **open-air theatre** théâtre *m* de verdure; (*Med*) **open-air treatment** cure *f* d'air; (*Brit Min*) **opencast** à ciel ouvert; **open-ended,** (*US*) **open-end** *box, tube* à deux ouvertures; *discussion, meeting* sans limite de durée; *offer* flexible; **open-eyed** (*lit*) les yeux ouverts; (*in surprise, wonder*) les yeux écarquillés; **in open-eyed astonishment** béant d'étonnement; (*US*) **open-faced sandwich** canapé *m* (froid); **to be open-handed** être généreux, avoir le cœur sur la main; (*Med*) **open-heart surgery** chirurgie *f* à cœur ouvert; **open-hearted** franc (*f* franche), sincère; **open-minded** à l'esprit ouvert *or* large, sans parti pris, sans préjugés; (*fig*) **open-mouthed** (*adj, adv*) bouche bée; **in open-mouthed admiration** béant *or* béat d'admiration; **open-necked** à col ouvert, échancré; (*Archit*) **open-plan** *design* qui élimine les cloisons; *house, school, office* à aire ouverte, sans cloisons, non cloisonné; **openwork** (*n*) (*Sewing*) (a)jours *mpl*; (*Archit*) claire-voie *f*, ajours; (*cpd*) *stockings etc* ajouré, à jour; (*Archit*) à claire-voie.
3 *n* **(a) to be out in the ~** (*out of doors*) être dehors *or* en plein air; (*in the country*) être au grand air *or* en plein champ; **to sleep in the ~** dormir à la belle étoile; **to come out into the ~** (*lit*) émerger au grand jour *or* en plein jour; (*fig*) se faire jour, se manifester; **he came (out) into the ~ about what had been going on** il a dévoilé *or* révélé ce qui s'était passé; **why don't you come into the ~ about it?** pourquoi n'en parlez-vous pas franchement?, pourquoi ne le dites-vous pas ouvertement?; **to bring a dispute (out) into the ~** divulguer une querelle.
(b) (*Golf*) **the O~** le tournoi open.
4 *vt* **(a)** *door, box, book, shop, grave, eyes* ouvrir; *letter, envelope* ouvrir, décacheter; *parcel* ouvrir, défaire; *bottle, jar* ouvrir, déboucher; *jacket, coat, collar* ouvrir, déboutonner; *map, newspaper* ouvrir, déplier; (*Elec*) *circuit* ouvrir; (*Med*) *abscess* ouvrir; *bowels* relâcher; *pores* dilater; *wound* (r)ouvrir; *legs* écarter; (*fig*) *horizon, career, one's heart etc* ouvrir. **to ~ wide** ouvrir tout grand; **to ~ slightly** *door, window* entrebâiller, entrouvrir; *eyes* entrouvrir; **to ~ again** rouvrir; *V* **eye, mouth** *etc.*
(b) (*drive*) *passage, road* ouvrir, pratiquer, frayer; *hole* percer.
(c) (*begin*) *meeting, account, debate,* (*Jur*) *case, trial* ouvrir; *conversation* entamer, engager; *negotiations* ouvrir, engager; (*inaugurate*) *exhibition, new hospital, factory* ouvrir, inaugurer; (*found*) *institution, school, business* ouvrir, fonder. **the Queen ~ed Parliament** la reine a ouvert la session parlementaire; (*Mil*) **to ~ fire (at** *or* **on)** ouvrir le feu (sur); (*Bridge*) **to ~ the bidding** ouvrir (les enchères).
5 *vi* **(a)** *[door]* (s')ouvrir; *[book, eyes]* s'ouvrir; *[flower]* s'ouvrir, s'épanouir, éclore; *[shop, museum, bank etc]* ouvrir; *[gulf, crevasse]* s'ouvrir, se former. **this door never ~s** cette porte n'ouvre jamais; **the door ~ed** la porte s'ouvrit; **the door ~ed slightly** la porte s'entrouvrit *or* s'entrebâilla; **to ~ again** se rouvrir; **door that ~s on to the garden** porte qui donne sur le jardin; **the kitchen ~s into the dining room** la cuisine donne sur la salle à manger; **the two rooms ~ into one another** les deux pièces communiquent *or* se commandent; **~ sesame!** sésame ouvre-toi!
(b) (*begin*) *[class, debate, meeting, play, book]* (s')ouvrir, commencer (*with* par); (*Bridge*) ouvrir. **he ~ed with a warning about inflation** il commença par donner un avertissement sur l'inflation; (*Theat*) **the play ~s next week** la première a lieu la semaine prochaine; (*Theat*) **they ~ next week** ils donnent la première la semaine prochaine; (*Bridge*) **to ~ (with) 2 hearts** ouvrir de 2 cœurs.
open out 1 *vi* **(a)** *[flower]* s'ouvrir, s'épanouir, éclore; *[view, countryside]* s'ouvrir; (*fig*) *[person]* (*become less shy etc*) s'ouvrir; *[company, business]* étendre le champ de ses activités; *[team, player etc]* s'affirmer.
(b) (*widen*) *[passage, tunnel, street]* s'élargir. **to open out on to** déboucher sur.
2 *vt sep* ouvrir; *map, newspaper* ouvrir, déplier; (*fig*) *business* développer.
open up 1 *vi* **(a)** *[shop, business, new career, opportunity]* s'ouvrir.
(b) (*Mil etc: start shooting*) ouvrir le feu, se mettre à tirer.
(c) *[flower]* s'ouvrir, s'épanouir, éclore.
(d) (*fig*) s'ouvrir (*to sb* à qn, *about sth* de qch). **I couldn't get him to open up at all** je ne suis pas arrivé à le faire s'épancher *or* se déboutonner*; **we got him to open up about his plans** il a fini par nous communiquer ses projets.
2 *vt sep* **(a)** *box, suitcase, parcel* ouvrir, défaire; *map, newspaper* ouvrir, déplier; *jacket, coat* ouvrir, déboutonner; *abscess, wound* ouvrir. **the owner opened up the shop for the police** le propriétaire a ouvert le magasin spécialement pour la police; **to open up again** rouvrir.
(b) (*start*) *business, branch etc* ouvrir.
(c) *oilfield, mine* ouvrir, commencer l'exploitation de; *route* ouvrir; *road through jungle etc* frayer, ouvrir (*through* à travers); *virgin country, jungle* rendre accessible; *blocked road* dégager; *blocked pipe* déboucher; (*fig*) *prospects, vistas, possibility* découvrir, révéler; *horizons, career* ouvrir. **to open up a country for trade** ouvrir un pays au commerce; **to open up a country for development** développer le potentiel d'un pays; **to open up a new market for one's products** établir de nouveaux débouchés pour ses produits.
opener ['əʊpnəʳ] *n* **(a)** (*surtout dans les composés*) *personne ou dispositif qui ouvre*; *V* **bottle, eye, tin** *etc.* **(b)** (*Theat*) (*artiste*)

artiste *mf* en lever de rideau; (*act*) lever *m* de rideau. **(c)** (*Bridge*) ouvreur *m*.

opening ['əʊpnɪŋ] **1** *n* **(a)** ouverture *f*; (*in wall*) brèche *f*; *[door, window]* embrasure *f*; (*in trees*) échappée *f*, trouée *f*; (*in forest, roof*) percée *f*; (*in clouds*) éclaircie *f*; *[tunnel]* entrée *f*, ouverture, début *m*.

(b) (*beginning*) *[meeting, debate, play, speech]* ouverture *f*, début *m*, commencement *m*; *[negotiations]* ouverture, amorce *f*.

(c) (*U: act of* ~) *[door, road, letter]* ouverture *f*; *[shooting, war]* déclenchement *m*; *[flower]* épanouissement *m*, éclosion *f*; (*Jur*) exposition *f* des faits; (*Cards, Chess*) ouverture; *[ceremony, exhibition]* inauguration *f*. (*Brit*) **O~ of Parliament** ouverture de la session parlementaire.

(d) (*opportunity*) occasion *f* (*to do* de faire, pour faire); (*trade outlet*) débouché *m* (*for* pour); (*job*) poste vacant; (*work*) travail *m*. **to give one's opponent/the enemy an** ~ prêter le flanc à son adversaire/à l'ennemi.

2 *adj ceremony, speech* d'inauguration, inaugural; *remark* préliminaire; (*St Ex*) *price* d'ouverture. ~ **gambit** (*Chess*) gambit *m*; (*fig*) manœuvre *f or* ruse *f* (stratégique); (*Theat*) ~ **night** première *f*, soirée *f* d'ouverture; (*Brit*) ~ **time** l'heure *f* d'ouverture (*des pubs*).

openly ['əʊpənlɪ] *adv* ouvertement, franchement; publiquement.

openness ['əʊpnnɪs] *n* **(a)** (*candour*) franchise *f*. ~ **of mind** largeur *f* d'esprit. **(b)** *[land, countryside]* aspect découvert *or* exposé.

opera ['ɒpərə] **1** *n* opéra *m*. ~ **bouffe** opéra bouffe; *V* **comic, grand, light**[2].

2 *cpd*: **opera glasses** jumelles *fpl* de théâtre, lorgnette *f*; **opera-goer** amateur *m* d'opéra; **opera hat** (chapeau *m*) claque *m*, gibus *m*; **opera house** (théâtre *m* de l')opéra *m*; **opera-lover** = **opera-goer**; **opera singer** chanteur *m*, -euse *f* d'opéra.

operable ['ɒpərəbl] *adj* opérable.

operate ['ɒpəreɪt] **1** *vi* **(a)** *[machine, vehicle]* marcher, fonctionner (*by electricity etc* à l'électricité *etc*); *[system, sb's mind]* fonctionner; *[law]* jouer. **several factors ~d to produce this situation** plusieurs facteurs ont joué pour produire cette situation.

(b) *[drug, medicine, propaganda]* opérer, faire effet (*on, upon* sur).

(c) *[fleet, regiment, thief etc]* opérer; (*St Ex*) faire des opérations (de bourse), spéculer. **they can't ~ efficiently on so little money** le manque d'argent les empêche d'opérer *or* de procéder avec efficacité.

(d) (*Med*) opérer (*on sb for sth* qn de qch). **he ~d/was ~d on for appendicitis** il a opéré/a été opéré de l'appendicite; **to ~ on sb's eyes** opérer qn aux *or* des yeux, opérer les yeux de qn; **he has still not been ~d on** il n'a pas encore été opéré, il n'a pas encore subi l'opération.

2 *vt* **(a)** *[person] machine, tool, vehicle, switchboard, telephone, brakes etc* faire marcher, faire fonctionner. **a machine ~d by electricity** une machine qui marche à l'électricité; **this switch ~s a fan** ce bouton commande *or* actionne un ventilateur; (*fig*) **such a law will ~ considerable changes** une telle loi opérera des changements considérables.

(b) *business, factory* diriger, gérer; *coalmine, oil well, canal, quarry* exploiter, faire valoir.

(c) *system* opérer, pratiquer. **he has ~d several clever swindles** il a réalisé plusieurs belles escroqueries.

operatic [,ɒpə'rætɪk] **1** *adj* d'opéra. **2** *n*: **(amateur) ~s** opéra *m* d'amateurs.

operating ['ɒpəreɪtɪŋ] *adj* **(a)** (*Comm*) ~ **costs** coût opérationnel. **(b)** (*Med*) (*US*) ~ **room** = ~ **theatre**; ~ **table** table *f* d'opération, billard* *m*; (*Brit*) ~ **theatre** salle *f* d'opération.

operation [,ɒpə'reɪʃən] *n* **(a)** (*U*) *[machine, vehicle]* marche *f*, fonctionnement *m*; *[mind, digestion]* fonctionnement; *[drug etc]* action *f*, effet *m* (*on* sur); *[business]* gestion *f*; *[mine, oil well, quarry, canal]* exploitation *f*; *[system]* application *f*. **in full** ~ *machine* fonctionnant à plein (rendement); *business, factory etc* en pleine activité; *mine etc* en pleine exploitation; *law* pleinement en vigueur; **to be in** ~ *[machine]* être en service; *[business etc]* fonctionner; *[mine etc]* être en exploitation; *[law, system]* être en vigueur; **to come into** ~ *[law, system]* entrer en vigueur; *[machine]* entrer en service; *[business]* se mettre à fonctionner; **to put into** ~ *machine* mettre en service; *law* mettre *or* faire entrer en vigueur; *plan* mettre en application.

(b) (*gen, Comm, Fin, Math, Mil, Pol etc*) opération *f*. **rebuilding ~s began at once** les opérations de reconstruction ont commencé immédiatement; (*Mil*) **O~ Overlord** Opération Overlord; (*Mil*) **~s research** recherche opérationnelle.

(c) (*Med*) opération *f*, intervention (chirurgicale). **to have an ~ (for appendicitis)** se faire opérer (de l'appendicite); **a lung ~** une opération au poumon; **to perform an ~ on sb (for sth)** opérer qn (de qch).

operational [,ɒpə'reɪʃənl] *adj* **(a)** *base, research, unit, soldiers, cost, dangers* opérationnel.

(b) (*ready for use*) *machine, vehicle* en état de marche *or* de fonctionnement, opérationnel; *system etc* opérationnel. **when the service is fully ~** quand le service sera pleinement opérationnel *or* à même de fonctionner à plein.

operative ['ɒpərətɪv] **1** *adj* **(a)** *law, measure, system* en vigueur. **to become ~** entrer en vigueur; **the ~ words** les mots clefs. **(b)** (*Med*) opératoire. **2** *n* (*worker*) ouvrier *m*, -ière *f*; (*machine operator*) opérateur *m*, -trice *f*; (*detective*) détective *m* (privé); (*spy*) espion(ne) *m(f)*; (*secret agent*) agent secret. **the steel ~s** la main-d'œuvre des aciéries.

operator ['ɒpəreɪtə[r]] *n* **(a)** (*person*) *[machine etc]* opérateur *m*, -trice *f*; (*Cine*) opérateur, -trice (de prise de vues); *[telephones]* téléphoniste *mf*, standardiste *mf*; (*Telegraphy*) radio *m*; *[business, factory]* dirigeant(e) *m(f)*, directeur *m*, -trice *f*. **tour ~** organisateur *m*, -trice *f* de voyages; **~s in this section of the industry** ceux qui travaillent dans ce secteur de l'industrie; (*criminal*) **a big-time ~** un escroc d'envergure; (*pej*) **he is a smooth ~*** c'est quelqu'un qui sait y faire*.

(b) (*Math*) opérateur *m*.

operetta [,ɒpə'retə] *n* opérette *f*.

ophthalmia [ɒf'θælmɪə] *n* ophtalmie *f*.

ophthalmic [ɒf'θælmɪk] *adj nerve, vein* ophtalmique; *clinic, surgeon, surgery* ophtalmologique.

ophthalmologist [,ɒfθæl'mɒlədʒɪst] *n* ophtalmologiste *mf*, ophtalmologue *mf*.

ophthalmology [,ɒfθæl'mɒlədʒɪ] *n* ophtalmologie *f*.

opiate ['əʊpɪɪt] **1** *n* opiat *m*. **2** *adj* opiacé.

opine [əʊ'paɪn] *vt* (*think*) être d'avis (*that* que); (*say*) émettre l'avis (*that* que).

opinion [ə'pɪnjən] **1** *n* (*point of view*) avis *m*, opinion *f*; (*belief*) opinion, conviction *f*; (*judgment*) opinion, jugement *m*, appréciation *f*; (*professional advice*) avis. **in my ~** à mon avis, pour moi, d'après moi; **in the ~ of** d'après, selon; **that's my ~ for what it's worth** c'est mon humble avis; **it's a matter of ~ whether ...** c'est (une) affaire d'opinion pour ce qui est de savoir si ...; **I'm entirely of your ~** je suis tout à fait de votre avis *or* opinion, je partage tout à fait votre opinion; **to be of the ~ that** être d'avis que, estimer que; **political ~s** opinions politiques; **to have a good *or* high ~ of sb/sth** avoir bonne opinion de qn/qch, estimer qn/qch; **what is your ~ of this book?** que pensez-vous de ce livre?; **I haven't much of an ~ of him, I've got a low ~ *or* no ~ of him** j'ai mauvaise opinion *or* une piètre opinion de lui; (*Jur*) **to take counsel's ~** consulter un avocat; (*Jur*) **~ of the court** jugement rendu par le tribunal; (*Med*) **to take a second ~** consulter un autre médecin, prendre l'avis d'un autre médecin; *V* **public, strong.**

2 *cpd*: **opinion poll** sondage *m* d'opinion.

opinionated [ə'pɪnjəneɪtɪd] *adj* arrêté dans ses opinions, dogmatique.

opium ['əʊpɪəm] **1** *n* opium *m*. **2** *cpd*: **opium addict** opiomane *mf*; **opium den** fumerie *f* d'opium.

opossum [ə'pɒsəm] *n* opossum *m*.

opponent [ə'pəʊnənt] *n* (*Mil, Sport*) adversaire *mf*; (*in discussion, debate*) antagoniste *mf*; (*of government, ideas etc*) adversaire, opposant(e) *m(f)* (*of* de). **he has always been an ~ of nationalization** il a toujours été contre les nationalisations, il s'est toujours opposé aux nationalisations.

opportune ['ɒpətju:n] *adj time* opportun, propice, convenable; *action, event, remark* à propos, opportun. **you have come at the ~ moment** vous arrivez à point (nommé) *or* à propos.

opportunely ['ɒpətju:nlɪ] *adv* opportunément, au moment opportun, à propos.

opportuneness [,ɒpə'tju:nnɪs] *n* opportunité *f*.

opportunism [,ɒpə'tju:nɪzəm] *n* opportunisme *m*.

opportunist [,ɒpə'tju:nɪst] *adj, n* opportuniste (*mf*).

opportunity [,ɒpə'tju:nɪtɪ] *n* occasion *f*. **to have the *or* an ~ to do *or* of doing** avoir l'occasion de faire; **to take the ~ of doing *or* to do** profiter de l'occasion pour faire; **you really missed your ~ there!** tu as vraiment laissé passer ta chance! *or* l'occasion!; **at the first *or* earliest ~** à la première occasion, dès que l'occasion se présentera; **when the ~ occurs** à l'occasion; **if the ~ should occur** si l'occasion se présente; **if you get the ~** si vous en avez l'occasion; **equality of ~** chances égales, égalité *f* de chances; **to make the most of one's opportunities** profiter pleinement de ses chances; **this job offers great opportunities** ce poste a des débouchés, ce poste ouvre *or* offre des perspectives d'avenir.

oppose [ə'pəʊz] *vt* **(a)** *person, argument, opinion* s'opposer à, combattre; *sb's will, desires, suggestion* s'opposer à, faire opposition à; *decision, plan* s'opposer à, mettre opposition à, contrecarrer, contrarier; *motion, resolution* (*Pol*) faire opposition à; (*in debate*) parler contre. **he ~s our coming** il s'oppose à ce que nous venions (*subj*); **but he ~d it** mais il s'y est opposé.

(b) (*set against*) opposer (*sth to sth else* qch à qch d'autre).

opposed [ə'pəʊzd] *adj* opposé, hostile (*to* à). **to be ~ to sth** être opposé *or* hostile à qch, s'opposer à qch; **I'm ~ to your marrying him** je m'oppose à ce que vous l'épousiez (*subj*); **as ~ to** par opposition à; **as ~ to that, there is the question of ...** par contre, il y a la question de ... .

opposing [ə'pəʊzɪŋ] *adj army* opposé; *minority* opposant; (*Jur*) adverse. (*Sport*) **~ team** adversaire(s) *m(pl)*; **the ~ votes** les voix 'contre'.

opposite ['ɒpəzɪt] **1** *adj house etc* d'en face; *bank, side, end* opposé, autre; *direction, pole* opposé; (*fig*) *attitude, point of view* opposé, contraire. **'see map on ~ page'** 'voir plan ci-contre'; **the ~ sex** l'autre sexe *m*; **we take the ~ view (to his)** nous pensons le contraire (de ce qu'il pense), notre opinion est diamétralement opposée (à la sienne); **his ~ number** son homologue *mf*.

2 *adv* (d')en face. **the house ~** la maison d'en face; **the house is immediately *or* directly ~** la maison est directement en face.

3 *prep* (*also* **~ to**) en face de. **the house is ~ the church** la maison est en face de l'église; **the house and the church are ~ one another** la maison et l'église sont en vis-à-vis; **they sat ~ one another** ils étaient assis face à face *or* en vis-à-vis; **they live ~ us** ils habitent en face de chez nous; (*Cine, Theat etc*) **to play ~ sb** partager la vedette avec qn; (*Naut*) **~ Calais** à la hauteur de Calais.

4 *n* opposé *m*, contraire *m*, inverse *m*. **quite the ~!** au contraire!; **he told me just the ~ *or* the exact ~** il m'a dit

l'inverse *or* tout le contraire *or* l'opposé; **he says the ~ of everything I say** il prend le contre-pied de tout ce que je dis.
opposition [ˌɒpəˈzɪʃən] **1** *n* **(a)** opposition *f* (*also Astron, Pol*). **his ~ to the scheme** son opposition au projet; **in ~ (to)** en opposition (avec); (*Pol*) **the party in ~** le parti de l'opposition; (*Pol*) **to be in ~** être dans l'opposition; (*Pol*) **the leader of the O~** le chef de l'opposition; **the ~*** (*opposing team, rival political faction*) l'adversaire *m*; (*business competitors*) la concurrence.
(b) (*Mil etc*) opposition *f*, résistance *f*. **they put up** *or* **offered considerable ~** ils opposèrent une vive résistance; **the army met with little or no ~** l'armée a rencontré peu sinon point de résistance.
2 *cpd*: (*Pol*) **Opposition** *speaker, member, motion, party* de l'opposition; **the Opposition benches** les bancs *mpl* de l'opposition.
oppress [əˈpres] *vt* **(a)** (*Mil, Pol etc*) opprimer. **(b)** *[anxiety, heat etc]* oppresser, accabler.
oppression [əˈpreʃən] *n* (*all senses*) oppression *f*.
oppressive [əˈpresɪv] *adj* **(a)** (*Mil, Pol etc*) tyrannique; *law, tax, measure* oppressif. **(b)** *anxiety, suffering* accablant; *heat* accablant, étouffant; *weather* lourd.
oppressively [əˈpresɪvlɪ] *adv* (*V* **oppressive**) **(a)** d'une manière oppressive; (*Mil, Pol etc*) tyranniquement. **(b)** d'une manière accablante. **it was ~ hot** il faisait une chaleur accablante *or* étouffante.
oppressor [əˈpresəʳ] *n* oppresseur *m*.
opprobrious [əˈprəʊbrɪəs] *adj* (*frm*) chargé d'opprobre.
opprobrium [əˈprəʊbrɪəm] *n* opprobre *m* (*liter*).
opt [ɒpt] *vi*: **to ~ for sth** opter pour qch (*also Jur*); **to ~ to do** choisir de faire.
opt in* *vi* choisir de participer (*to* à).
opt out* *vi* choisir de ne pas participer (*of* à); (*Soc*) s'évader de *or* rejeter la société (de consommation). **he opted out of going** il a choisi de ne pas y aller; **you can always opt out** tu peux toujours abandonner *or* te retirer *or* te récuser.
optative [ˈɒptətɪv] *adj, n* optatif (*m*).
optic [ˈɒptɪk] **1** *adj* optique. **2** *n* (*U*) **~s** optique *f*.
optical [ˈɒptɪkəl] *adj glass, lens* optique; *instrument* d'optique. **~ illusion** illusion *f* d'optique.
optician [ɒpˈtɪʃən] *n* opticien(ne) *m(f)*.
optimal [ˈɒptɪml] *adj* optimal.
optimism [ˈɒptɪmɪzəm] *n* optimisme *m*.
optimist [ˈɒptɪmɪst] *n* optimiste *mf*.
optimistic [ˌɒptɪˈmɪstɪk] *adj* optimiste.
optimistically [ˌɒptɪˈmɪstɪklɪ] *adv* avec optimisme, d'une manière optimiste.
optimum [ˈɒptɪməm] **1** *adj* optimum. **~ conditions** conditions *fpl* optimums *or* optima. **2** *n, pl* **optima** [ˈɒptɪmə] *or* **~s** optimum *m*.
option [ˈɒpʃən] *n* choix *m*, option *f*; (*Comm, Fin*) option (*on* sur). **to take up the ~** lever l'option; **at the ~ of the purchaser** au gré de l'acheteur; (*Jur*) **6 months with/without the ~ of a fine** 6 mois avec/sans substitution d'amende; **Latin is one of the ~s** le latin est une des matières à option; **I have no ~** je n'ai pas le choix; **he had no ~ but to come** il n'a pas pu faire autrement que de venir; **you have the ~ of remaining here** vous pouvez rester ici si vous voulez; **it's left to your ~** c'est à vous de choisir *or* de décider; (*fig*) **he left** *or* **kept his ~s open** il n'a pas voulu s'engager (irrévocablement).
optional [ˈɒpʃənl] *adj* (*gen, Scol etc*) facultatif. **'dress ~'** 'la tenue de soirée n'est pas de rigueur'; (*Comm*) **~ extras** accessoires *mpl* en supplément *or* en option; **the sun roof is ~** *or* **an ~ extra** le toit ouvrant est en option.
optometrist [ɒpˈtɒmətrɪst] *n* optométriste *mf*.
opulence [ˈɒpjʊləns] *n* (*U: V* **opulent**) opulence *f*, richesse(s) *f(pl)*; abondance *f*; luxuriance *f*.
opulent [ˈɒpjʊlənt] *adj person, life* opulent, riche; *hair* abondant; *vegetation* abondant, luxuriant.
opus [ˈəʊpəs] *n* opus *m*; *V* **magnum**.
or [ɔːʳ] *conj* ou (bien); (*with neg*) ni. **red ~ black?** rouge ou noir?; **~ else** ou bien; **do it ~ else!*** fais-le, sinon (tu vas voir)!; **without tears ~ sighs** sans larmes ni soupirs; **he could not read ~ write** il ne savait ni lire ni écrire; **an hour ~ so** environ *or* à peu près une heure; **botany, ~ the science of plants** la botanique, ou la science des plantes, la botanique, autrement dit la science des plantes; *V* **either**.
oracle [ˈɒrəkl] *n* (*Hist, fig*) oracle *m*. (*fig*) **he managed to work the ~ and got 3 days' leave** il s'est mystérieusement débrouillé pour obtenir 3 jours de congé.
oracular [ɒˈrækjʊləʳ] *adj* (*lit, fig*) d'oracle; (*mysterious*) sibyllin (*liter*).
oral [ˈɔːrəl] **1** *adj* **(a)** *examination, teaching methods* oral; *testimony, message, account* oral, verbal.
(b) (*Anat*) *cavity* buccal, oral; (*Pharm etc*) *dose* par voie orale. (*Ling*) **~ vowel** voyelle orale.
2 *n* (examen *m*) oral *m*, épreuve orale.
orally [ˈɔːrəlɪ] *adv testify, communicate* oralement, de vive voix; (*Pharm*) par voie orale.
orange [ˈɒrɪndʒ] **1** *n* (*fruit*) orange *f*; (*also* **~-tree**) oranger *m*; (*colour*) orange *m*, orangé *m*. **'~s and lemons'** *chanson et jeu d'enfants*; *V* **blood** *etc*.
2 *adj* (*colour*) orangé, orange *inv*; *drink, flavour* d'orange; *liqueur* à l'orange.
3 *cpd*: **orange blossom** fleur(s) *f(pl)* d'oranger; (*Ir*) **Orange Day** le 12 juillet (*procession annuelle des orangistes de l'Irlande du Nord*); **orange grove** orangeraie *f*; (*Ir*) **Orangeman** orangiste *m*; **orange marmalade** confiture *f* d'oranges; **orange stick** bâtonnet *m* (*pour manucure etc*).
orangeade [ˈɒrɪndʒˈeɪd] *n* orangeade *f*.
orang-outang, orang-utan [ɔːˌræŋuːˈtæn] *n* orang-outan(g) *m*.
orate [ɒˈreɪt] *vi* discourir, faire un discours; (*speechify*) pérorer.
oration [ɔːˈreɪʃən] *n* discours solennel; *V* **funeral**.
orator [ˈɒrətəʳ] *n* orateur *m*, -trice *f*.
oratorical [ˌɒrəˈtɒrɪkəl] *adj* oratoire.
oratorio [ˌɒrəˈtɔːrɪəʊ] *n* oratorio *m*.
oratory[1] [ˈɒrətərɪ] *n* (*art*) art *m* oratoire; (*what is said*) éloquence *f*, rhétorique *f*. **brilliant piece of ~** brillant discours.
oratory[2] [ˈɒrətərɪ] *n* (*Rel*) oratoire *m*.
orbit [ˈɔːbɪt] **1** *n* (*Anat, Astron*) orbite *f*. **to be in/go into/put into ~ (around)** être/entrer/mettre en orbite (autour de); (*fig*) **that doesn't come within my ~** ceci n'est pas de mon domaine *or* de mon rayon.
2 *vt* graviter autour de, décrire une *or* des orbite(s) autour de.
3 *vi* orbiter, être *or* rester en orbite (*round* autour de).
orbital [ˈɔːbɪtl] *adj* (*Astron*) orbital; (*Anat*) orbitaire; *road* périphérique.
orchard [ˈɔːtʃəd] *n* verger *m*. **apple ~** verger de pommiers.
orchestra [ˈɔːkɪstrə] **1** *n* orchestre *m*; *V* **leader, string** *etc*. **2** *cpd*: (*Theat*) **orchestra pit** fosse *f* d'orchestre; **orchestra stalls** (fauteuils *mpl* d')orchestre *m*.
orchestral [ɔːˈkestrəl] *adj music, style* orchestral; *concert* symphonique.
orchestrate [ˈɔːkɪstreɪt] *vt* orchestrer.
orchestration [ˌɔːkɪsˈtreɪʃən] *n* orchestration *f*, instrumentation *f*.
orchid [ˈɔːkɪd] *n* orchidée *f*. **wild ~** orchis *m*.
orchis [ˈɔːkɪs] *n* orchis *m*.
ordain [ɔːˈdeɪn] *vt* **(a)** *[God, fate]* décréter (*that* que); *[law]* décréter (*that* que), prescrire (*that* que + *subj*); *[judge]* ordonner (*that* que + *subj*). **it was ~ed that he should die young** il était destiné à mourir jeune, le sort *or* le destin a voulu qu'il meure jeune.
(b) (*Rel*) *priest* ordonner. **he was ~ed (priest)** il a reçu l'ordination, il a été ordonné prêtre.
ordeal [ɔːˈdiːl] *n* **(a)** supplice *m*, (rude) épreuve *f*. **they suffered terrible ~s** ils sont passés par *or* ils ont subi d'atroces épreuves; **speaking in public was an ~ for him** il était au supplice quand il devait parler en public, parler en public le mettait au supplice.
(b) (*Hist Jur*) ordalie *f*. **~ by fire** épreuve *f* du feu.
order [ˈɔːdəʳ] **1** *n* **(a)** (*U: disposition, sequence*) ordre *m*. **word ~** ordre des mots; **what ~ should these cards be in?** dans quel ordre ces cartes devraient-elles être?; **in ~ of merit** par ordre de mérite; (*Theat*) **in ~ of appearance** par ordre *or* dans l'ordre d'entrée en scène; **the cards were out of ~** les cartes n'étaient pas en ordre; **to put in(to) ~** mettre en ordre, agencer, classer; *[papers etc]* **to get out of ~** se déclasser; **it is in the ~ of things** c'est dans l'ordre des choses; **the old ~ is changing** l'ancien état de choses change; *V* **battle, close**[1] *etc*.
(b) (*U: good ~*) ordre *m*. **he's got no sense of ~** il n'a aucun (sens de l')ordre; **in ~** *room etc* en ordre; *passport, documents* en règle; **to put one's room/one's affairs in ~** mettre de l'ordre dans sa chambre/ses affaires, mettre sa chambre/ses affaires en ordre; (*US*) **in short ~** sans délai, tout de suite; **machine out of ~** *or* **not in (working** *or* **running) ~** machine en panne *or* détraquée; (*Telec*) **the line is out of ~** la ligne est en dérangement; **to be in running** *or* **working ~** marcher bien, être en bon état *or* en état de marche.
(c) in ~ to do pour faire, afin de faire; **in ~ that** afin que + *subj*, pour que + *subj*.
(d) (*correct procedure: also Parl*) ordre *m*. (*Parl*) **~, ~!** à l'ordre!; (*Parl etc*) **to call sb to ~** rappeler qn à l'ordre; (*Parl etc*) **(on a) point of ~** (sur une) question de droit *or* de forme, (sur un) point de droit *or* de procédure; **is it in ~ to do that?** est-il permis de faire cela?; **would it be in ~ for me to speak to her?** serait-il approprié que je lui parle? (*subj*); **his request is quite in ~** sa demande est tout à fait normale *or* dans les règles; (*hum*) **a drink seems in ~** un verre (de quelque chose) me semble tout indiqué.
(e) (*peace, control*) ordre *m*. **to keep ~** *[police etc]* faire régner l'ordre, maintenir l'ordre; *[teacher]* faire régner la discipline; **she can't keep her class in ~** elle n'arrive pas à tenir sa classe; **keep your dog in ~!** surveillez *or* tenez votre chien!; *V* **law** *etc*.
(f) (*Bio*) ordre *m*; (*social position*) classe *f*; (*kind*) ordre, sorte *f*, genre *m*. (*social rank*) **the lower/higher ~s** les classes inférieures/supérieures; (*fig*) **of a high ~** de premier ordre; **of the ~ of 500** de l'ordre de 500.
(g) (*Archit*) ordre *m*.
(h) (*society, association etc*) ordre *m*; (*fig: medal*) décoration *f*, insigne *m*. **Benedictine O~** ordre des bénédictins; (*Brit*) **the O~ of the Bath** l'ordre du Bain; *V* **boot**[1], **garter** *etc*.
(i) (*Rel*) **(holy) ~s** ordres *mpl* (majeurs); **to be in/take (holy) ~s** être/entrer dans les ordres.
(j) (*command*) ordre *m*, commandement *m*, consigne *f* (*Mil*). **sealed ~s** instructions secrètes; **to obey ~s** obéir aux ordres, observer *or* respecter la consigne; **to give sb ~s to do sth** ordonner à qn de faire qch; **you can't give me ~s!, I don't take ~s from you!** je ne suis pas à vos ordres!, ce n'est pas à vous de me donner des ordres!; **I don't take ~s from anyone** je n'ai d'ordres à recevoir de personne; **~s are ~s** la consigne c'est la consigne, les ordres sont les ordres; **that's an ~!** c'est un ordre!; **he gave the ~ for it to be done** il ordonna qu'on le fasse, il a donné (l')ordre de le faire; **on the ~s of** sur l'ordre de; **by ~ of** par ordre de; **to be under the ~s of** être sous les ordres de; **to be under ~s to do** avoir (reçu l')ordre de faire; **till further ~s** jusqu'à nouvel ordre; **~ of the day** ordre du jour; (*fig*) **strikes**

were the ~ of the day les grèves étaient à l'ordre du jour; (*Brit Parl*) **O~ in Council** ordonnance prise en Conseil privé, ≈ décret-loi *m*; (*Jur*) **judge's ~** ordonnance *f*; (*Jur*) **~ of the Court** injonction *f* de la cour; *V* **march¹, starter, tall** *etc*.

(k) (*Comm*) commande *f*. **made to ~** fait sur commande; **to give an ~ to sb (for sth), to place an ~ with sb (for sth)** passer une commande (de qch) à qn; **we have the shelves on ~ for you** vos étagères sont commandées; (*Comm, fig*) **to do sth to ~** faire qch sur commande; *V* **repeat, rush** *etc*.

(l) (*warrant, permit*) permis *m*. **~ to view** permis de visiter.

(m) (*Fin etc: money ~*) mandat *m*. **pay to the ~ of** payer à l'ordre de; **pay X or ~** payez X ou à son ordre; *V* **banker, postal** *etc*.

2 *cpd*: (*Comm, Ind*) **order book** carnet *m* de commandes; (*Ind*) **the company's order books were full** les carnets de commandes de la compagnie étaient complets; (*Comm*) **order form** billet *m or* bon *m* de commande; (*Brit Parl*) **order paper** ordre *m* du jour.

3 *vt* **(a)** (*command*) ordonner (*sb to do* à qn de faire, *that* que + *subj*), donner l'ordre (*that* que + *subj*). **he was ~ed to be quiet** on lui ordonna de se taire; **to ~ sb in/out/up** *etc* ordonner à qn d'entrer/de sortir/de monter *etc*; **to ~ a regiment abroad** envoyer un régiment à l'étranger; **the regiment was ~ed to Berlin** le régiment a reçu l'ordre d'aller à Berlin.

(b) (*Comm*) *goods, meal* commander; *taxi* retenir.

(c) (*put in ~*) *one's affairs etc* organiser, régler.

4 *vi* (*in restaurant etc*) passer sa commande.

order about, order around *vt sep* commander. **he likes ordering people about** il aime commander les gens, il aime donner des ordres à droite et à gauche; **I won't be ordered about by him!** je ne suis pas à ses ordres!

orderliness [ˈɔːdəlɪnɪs] *n* (habitude *f* d')ordre *m*.

orderly [ˈɔːdəlɪ] **1** *adj room* ordonné, en ordre; *mind* méthodique; *life* rangé, réglé; *person* qui a de l'ordre *or* de la méthode; *crowd* discipliné. **in an ~ way** avec ordre, méthodiquement, d'une façon disciplinée.

2 *n* **(a)** (*Mil*) planton *m*, ordonnance *f*.

(b) (*Med*) garçon *m* de salle; *V* **nursing**.

3 *cpd*: (*Mil*) **orderly officer** officier *m* de service *or* de semaine; (*Mil*) **orderly room** salle *f* de rapport.

ordinal [ˈɔːdɪnl] **1** *adj number* ordinal. **2** *n* nombre ordinal.

ordinance [ˈɔːdɪnəns] *n* ordonnance *f*, arrêté *m*.

ordinarily [ˈɔːdnrɪlɪ] *adv* ordinairement, d'habitude, normalement, d'ordinaire, généralement. **more than ~ polite** d'une politesse qui sort de l'ordinaire.

ordinary [ˈɔːdnrɪ] **1** *adj* **(a)** (*usual*) ordinaire, normal, habituel, courant. **in the ~ way, in the ~ course of events** en temps normal, dans des circonstances normales; **in ~ use** d'usage *or* d'emploi courant; **for all ~ purposes** pour l'usage courant; (*Naut*) **~ seaman** matelot breveté; (*Brit Fin*) **~ share** action *f* ordinaire; **my ~ grocer's** mon épicerie habituelle; **it's not what you would call an ~ present** c'est vraiment un cadeau peu ordinaire *or* peu banal.

(b) (*average*) *intelligence, knowledge, reader etc* moyen. **I'm just an ~ fellow** je suis un homme comme les autres.

(c) (*pej*) *person, meal etc* ordinaire, quelconque, médiocre.

2 *n* **(a)** ordinaire *m*. **out of the ~** hors du commun, exceptionnel, qui sort de l'ordinaire; **above the ~** au-dessus du commun *or* de l'ordinaire.

(b) (*US*††) bicycle†† *m*.

ordination [ˌɔːdɪˈneɪʃən] *n* (*Rel*) ordination *f*.

ordnance [ˈɔːdnəns] (*Mil*) **1** *n* (*guns*) (pièces *fpl* d')artillerie *f*; (*unit*) service *m* du matériel et des dépôts.

2 *cpd*: **Ordnance Corps** Service *m* du matériel; **ordnance factory** usine *f* d'artillerie; (*Brit*) **Ordnance Survey** service *m* cartographique de l'État; (*Brit*) **Ordnance Survey map** ≈ carte *f* d'État-Major.

ordure [ˈɔːdjʊəʳ] *n* ordure *f*.

ore [ɔːʳ] *n* minerai *m*. **iron ~** minerai de fer.

oregano [ˌɒrɪˈgɑːnəʊ] *n* origan *m*.

organ [ˈɔːgən] **1** *n* **(a)** (*Mus*) orgue *m*, orgues *fpl*. **grand ~** grandes orgues; *V* **barrel, mouth** *etc*.

(b) (*Press: mouthpiece*) organe *m*, porte-parole *m inv*.

(c) (*Anat*) organe *m*. **vocal ~s, ~s of speech** organes vocaux, appareil vocal; **sexual ~s** organes génitaux *or* sexuels.

(d) (*fig: instrument*) organe *m*. **the chief ~ of the administration** l'organe principal de l'administration.

2 *cpd*: **organ-builder** facteur *m* d'orgue; **organ-grinder** joueur *m*, -euse *f* d'orgue de Barbarie; **organ loft** tribune *f* d'orgue; **organ pipe/stop** tuyau *m*/jeu *m* d'orgue.

organdie [ˈɔːgəndɪ] **1** *n* organdi *m*. **2** *cpd* en organdi, d'organdi.

organic [ɔːˈgænɪk] *adj disease, life, substance, chemistry, law* organique; *part* fondamental. **~ being** être organisé; **~ whole** tout *m* systématique.

organically [ɔːˈgænɪkəlɪ] *adv* (*Bio, Physiol etc*) organiquement; (*basically*) foncièrement, fondamentalement.

organism [ˈɔːgənɪzəm] *n* (*Bio*) organisme *m*.

organist [ˈɔːgənɪst] *n* organiste *mf*. **~ at X cathedral** titulaire *mf* des (grandes) orgues de la cathédrale de X.

organization [ˌɔːgənaɪˈzeɪʃən] **1** *n* **(a)** (*gen*) organisation *f*; (*statutory body*) organisme *m*, organisation; (*society*) organisation, association *f*. **youth ~** organisation *or* organisme de jeunesse; **she belongs to several ~s** elle est membre de plusieurs organisations *or* associations; **a charitable ~ to help the needy** une œuvre *or* une fondation charitable de secours aux indigents; *V* **travel**.

(b) (*executives etc*) [*business firm, political party*] cadres *mpl*.

(c) (*U*) organisation *f*. **his work lacks ~** son travail manque d'organisation.

2 *cpd*: **organization chart** organigramme *m*; (*pej*) **organization man** fantoche *m* de l'administration.

organize [ˈɔːgənaɪz] *vt* organiser. **to get ~d** s'organiser; **organizing committee** comité chargé de l'organisation.

organized [ˈɔːgənaɪzd] *adj resistance, society, tour* organisé (*also Bio etc*). **~ labour** main d'œuvre syndiquée *or* organisée en syndicats; **to get ~** s'organiser; **he's not very ~** il n'est pas très organisé, il ne sait pas s'organiser.

organizer [ˈɔːgənaɪzəʳ] *n* organisateur *m*, -trice *f*.

orgasm [ˈɔːgæzəm] *n* orgasme *m*.

orgiastic [ˌɔːdʒɪˈæstɪk] *adj* orgiaque.

orgy [ˈɔːdʒɪ] *n* (*lit, fig*) orgie *f*.

oriel [ˈɔːrɪəl] *n* encorbellement *m*; (*window*) fenêtre *f* en encorbellement.

orient [ˈɔːrɪənt] **1** *n* (*liter*) orient *m*, levant *m*. **the O~** l'Orient. **2** *vt* = **orientate**.

oriental [ˌɔːrɪˈentəl] **1** *adj peoples, civilization* oriental; *carpet* d'Orient. **2** *n*: **O~** Oriental(e) *m(f)*.

orientate [ˈɔːrɪənteɪt] *vt* (*lit, fig*) orienter.

orientation [ˌɔːrɪənˈteɪʃən] *n* orientation *f*.

orienteering [ˌɔːrɪənˈtɪərɪŋ] *n* (*Sport*) exercice *m* d'orientation sur le terrain.

orifice [ˈɒrɪfɪs] *n* orifice *m*.

origami [ˌɒrɪˈgɑːmɪ] *n* (*art*) art *m* du pliage; (*object*) pliage *m*.

origin [ˈɒrɪdʒɪn] *n* (*parentage, source*) origine *f*; [*manufactured goods etc*] origine, provenance *f*. **to have humble ~s, to be of humble ~** être d'origine modeste; **his family had its ~ in France** sa famille était originaire de France; **country of ~** pays *m* d'origine.

original [əˈrɪdʒɪnl] **1** *adj* **(a)** (*first, earliest*) *sin* originel; *inhabitant, member* originel, premier, originaire; *purpose, suggestion, meaning* originel, initial, premier; *shape, colour* primitif; *edition* original, princeps *inv*.

(b) (*not copied etc*) *painting, idea, writer* original; *play* inédit, original.

(c) (*unconventional*) *character, person* singulier, original, excentrique.

2 *n* **(a)** [*painting, language, document*] original *m*. **to read Dante in the ~** lire Dante dans l'original.

(b) (*person*) original(e) *m(f)*, phénomène* *m*.

originality [əˌrɪdʒɪˈnælɪtɪ] *n* originalité *f*.

originally [əˈrɪdʒənəlɪ] *adv* **(a)** (*in the beginning*) originairement, à l'origine; (*at first*) originellement. **(b)** (*not copying*) originalement, d'une manière originale.

originate [əˈrɪdʒɪneɪt] **1** *vt* [*person*] être l'auteur de, être à l'origine de; *event, effect* donner naissance à, produire, créer.

2 *vi* **(a)** (*from thing or place*) [*person*] être originaire (*from* de); [*stream, custom*] prendre naissance *or* sa source (*in* dans); [*goods*] provenir (*from* de).

(b) (*from person*) [*suggestion, idea*] émaner (*from* de).

originator [əˈrɪdʒɪneɪtəʳ] *n* auteur *m*, créateur *m*, -trice *f*; initiateur *m*, -trice *f*.

oriole [ˈɔːrɪəʊl] *n* loriot *m*; *V* **golden**.

Orkney Islands [ˈɔːknɪˌaɪləndz] *npl*, **Orkneys** [ˈɔːknɪz] *npl* Orcades *fpl*.

orlon [ˈɔːlɒn] **1** *n* ® orlon *m* ®. **2** *cpd* en orlon.

ormolu [ˈɔːməʊluː] **1** *n* similor *m*, chrysocale *m*. **2** *cpd* en similor, en chrysocale.

ornament [ˈɔːnəmənt] **1** *n* **(a)** (*on building, ceiling, dress etc*) ornement *m*; (*vase etc*) objet décoratif, bibelot *m*; (*fig, liter: person, quality*) ornement (*fig, liter*). **a row of ~s on the shelf** une rangée de bibelots sur l'étagère.

(b) (*U: Archit, Dress etc*) ornement *m*. **rich in ~** richement orné.

(c) (*Mus*) ornement *m*.

2 [ˈɔːnəment] *vt style* orner, embellir (*with* de); *room, building, ceiling* décorer, ornementer (*with* de); *dress* agrémenter, orner (*with* de).

ornamental [ˌɔːnəˈmentl] *adj* ornemental; *garden, lake* d'agrément; *design* décoratif.

ornamentation [ˌɔːnəmenˈteɪʃən] *n* ornementation *f*, décoration *f*.

ornate [ɔːˈneɪt] *adj vase* très orné; *style* très orné, fleuri.

ornately [ɔːˈneɪtlɪ] *adv decorate, design* avec une profusion d'ornements; *write etc* dans un style très orné *or* fleuri.

ornery* [ˈɔːnərɪ] *adj* (*US*) (*nasty*) méchant; (*obstinate*) entêté, têtu comme un âne; (*base*) vil (*f* vile).

ornithological [ˌɔːnɪθəˈlɒdʒɪkəl] *adj* ornithologique.

ornithologist [ˌɔːnɪˈθɒlədʒɪst] *n* ornithologiste *mf*, ornithologue *mf*.

ornithology [ˌɔːnɪˈθɒlədʒɪ] *n* ornithologie *f*.

orphan [ˈɔːfən] **1** *n* orphelin(e) *m(f)*. **2** *adj* orphelin. **3** *vt*: **to be ~ed** devenir orphelin(e); **the children were ~ed by the accident** l'accident a laissé *or* rendu les enfants orphelins.

orphanage [ˈɔːfənɪdʒ] *n* orphelinat *m*.

Orpheus [ˈɔːfjuːs] *n* Orphée *m*.

ortho... [ˈɔːθəʊ] *pref* orth(o)...

orthodontics [ˌɔːθəʊˈdɒntɪks] *n* (*U*) orthodontie *f*.

orthodox [ˈɔːθədɒks] *adj* (*Rel, also fig*) orthodoxe.

orthodoxy [ˈɔːθədɒksɪ] *n* orthodoxie *f*.

orthographic(al) [ˌɔːθəˈgræfɪk(əl)] *adj* orthographique.

orthography [ɔːˈθɒgrəfɪ] *n* orthographe *f*.

orthopaedic, (*US***) orthopedic** [ˌɔːθəʊˈpiːdɪk] *adj* orthopédique. **~ surgeon** chirurgien(ne) orthopédiste *m(f)*; **~ surgery** chirurgie *f* orthopédique.

orthopaedics, (*US***) orthopedics** [ˌɔːθəʊˈpiːdɪks] *n* orthopédie *f*.

orthopaedist, (*US***) orthopedist** [ˌɔːθəʊˈpiːdɪst] *n* orthopédiste *mf*.

orthopaedy, (*US*) **orthopedy** [ˈɔːθəʊpiːdɪ] *n* = **orthopaedics.**
oscillate [ˈɒsɪleɪt] **1** *vi* (*gen, Elec, Phys etc*) osciller; (*fig*) *[ideas, opinions]* fluctuer, varier; *[person]* osciller, balancer (*between* entre). **2** *vt* faire osciller.
oscillation [ˌɒsɪˈleɪʃən] *n* oscillation *f.*
oscillator [ˈɒsɪleɪtəʳ] *n* oscillateur *m.*
oscillatory [ˌɒsɪˈleɪtərɪ] *adj* oscillatoire.
osculate [ˈɒskjʊleɪt] (*hum*) **1** *vi* s'embrasser. **2** *vt* embrasser.
osier [ˈəʊʒəʳ] **1** *n* osier *m.* **2** *cpd branch* d'osier; *basket* en osier, d'osier.
osmosis [ɒzˈməʊsɪs] *n* (*Phys, fig*) osmose *f.* **by ~** par osmose.
osmotic [ɒzˈmɒtɪk] *adj* osmotique.
osprey [ˈɒspreɪ] *n* (*Orn*) orfraie *f*; (*on hat*) aigrette *f.*
osseous [ˈɒsɪəs] *adj* **(a)** (*Anat, Zool*) osseux. **(b)** = **ossiferous.**
ossiferous [ɒˈsɪfərəs] *adj* ossifère.
ossification [ˌɒsɪfɪˈkeɪʃən] *n* ossification *f.*
ossify [ˈɒsɪfaɪ] (*lit, fig*) **1** *vt* ossifier. **2** *vi* s'ossifier.
ossuary [ˈɒsjʊərɪ] *n* ossuaire *m.*
Ostend [ɒsˈtend] *n* Ostende.
ostensible [ɒsˈtensəbl] *adj* prétendu, feint, apparent.
ostensibly [ɒsˈtensəblɪ] *adv* en apparence. **he was ~ a student** il était soi-disant étudiant, il était censé être étudiant; **he went out ~ to telephone** il est sorti sous prétexte de téléphoner.
ostentation [ˌɒstenˈteɪʃən] *n* (*U*) ostentation *f*, étalage *m*, parade *f.*
ostentatious [ˌɒstenˈteɪʃəs] *adj surroundings* prétentieux, plein d'ostentation; *person, manner* prétentieux, ostentatoire (*liter*); *dislike, concern, attempt* exagéré, ostentatoire (*liter*).
ostentatiously [ˌɒstenˈteɪʃəslɪ] *adv* avec ostentation, d'une manière exagérée *or* ostentatoire.
osteo... [ˈɒstɪəʊ] *pref* ostéo... .
osteoarthritis [ˈɒstɪəʊɑːˈθraɪtɪs] *n* ostéoarthrite *f.*
osteopath [ˈɒstɪəpæθ] *n* ostéopathe *mf.*
osteopathy [ˌɒstɪˈɒpəθɪ] *n* ostéopathie *f.*
ostler†† [ˈɒsləʳ] *n* (*esp Brit*) valet *m* d'écurie.
ostracism [ˈɒstrəsɪzəm] *n* ostracisme *m.*
ostracize [ˈɒstrəsaɪz] *vt* frapper d'ostracisme, mettre au ban de la société, mettre en quarantaine.
ostrich [ˈɒstrɪtʃ] *n* autruche *f.*
other [ˈʌðəʳ] **1** *adj* autre. **the ~ one** l'autre *mf*; **the ~ 5** les 5 autres; **~ people have done it** d'autres l'ont fait; **~ people's property** la propriété d'autrui; **it always happens to ~ people** ça arrive toujours aux autres; (*fig*) **the ~ world** l'au-delà *m*, l'autre monde *m* (*V also* **4**); **the ~ day/week** l'autre jour/semaine; **come back some ~ day** revenez un autre jour; **I wouldn't wish him ~ than he is** je ne le voudrais pas autre qu'il est, je ne souhaiterais pas qu'il soit différent; **someone or ~ said that ...** je ne sais qui a dit que ...; **some writer or ~ said that ...** je ne sais quel écrivain a dit que ..., un écrivain, je ne sais plus lequel, a dit que ...; **some fool or ~** un idiot quelconque; **there must be some ~ way of doing it** on doit pouvoir le faire d'une autre manière; *V* **every, hand, time, word** *etc.*
2 *pron* autre *mf.* **and these 5 ~s** et ces 5 autres; **there are some ~s** il y en a d'autres; **several ~s have mentioned it** plusieurs autres l'ont mentionné; **one after the ~** l'un après l'autre; **~s have spoken of him** il y en a d'autres qui ont parlé de lui; **he doesn't like hurting ~s** il n'aime pas faire de mal aux autres *or* à autrui; **some like flying, ~s prefer the train** les uns aiment prendre l'avion, les autres préfèrent le train; **some do, ~s don't** il y en a qui le font, d'autres qui ne le font pas; **one or ~ of them will come** il y en aura bien un qui viendra; **somebody or ~ suggested that ...** je ne sais qui a suggéré que ..., quelqu'un, je ne sais qui, a suggéré que ...; **that man of all ~s** cet homme entre tous; **you and no ~** vous et personne d'autre; **no ~ than** nul autre que; *V* **each, none.**
3 *adv* autrement. **he could not have acted ~ than he did** il n'aurait pas pu agir autrement; **I've never seen her ~ than with her husband** je ne l'ai jamais vue (autrement) qu'avec son mari; **I couldn't do ~ than come, I could do no ~ than come** je ne pouvais faire autrement que de venir, je ne pouvais que venir; **no one ~ than a member of the family** nul autre qu'un membre de la famille; *V* **somehow** *etc.*
4 *cpd*: **other-worldly** *attitude* détaché des contingences (de ce monde); *person* qui n'a pas les pieds sur terre.
otherwise [ˈʌðəwaɪz] **1** *adv* **(a)** (*in another way*) autrement, différemment, d'une autre manière. **I could not do ~ than agree** je ne pouvais faire autrement que de consentir; **it cannot be ~** il ne peut en être autrement; **he was ~ engaged** il était occupé à (faire) autre chose; **except where ~ stated** sauf indication contraire; (*frm*) **should it be ~** dans le cas contraire; **Montgomery ~ (known as) Monty** Montgomery autrement (dit *or* appelé) Monty.
(b) (*in other respects*) autrement, à part cela. **~ it's a very good car** autrement *or* à part ça c'est une excellente voiture.
2 *conj* autrement, sans quoi, sans cela, sinon.
otiose [ˈəʊʃɪəʊs] *adj* (*frm*) (*idle*) oisif; (*useless*) oiseux, inutile, vain.
otitis [əʊˈtaɪtɪs] *n* otite *f.*
otter [ˈɒtəʳ] *n* loutre *f*; *V* **sea.**
ottoman [ˈɒtəmən] *n* ottomane *f.*
Ottoman [ˈɒtəmən] **1** *adj* ottoman. **2** *n* Ottoman(e) *m(f).*
ouch [aʊtʃ] *excl* aïe!
ought[1] [ɔːt] *pret* **ought** *modal aux vb* **(a)** (*indicating obligation, advisability, desirability*) **I ought to do it** je devrais le faire, il faudrait *or* il faut que je le fasse; **I really ought to go and see him** je devrais bien aller le voir; **he thought he ought to tell you** il a pensé qu'il devait vous le dire; **if they behave as they ought** s'ils se conduisent comme ils le doivent, s'ils se conduisent correctement; **this ought to have been finished long ago** cela aurait dû être terminé il y a longtemps; **oughtn't you to have left by now?** est-ce que vous n'auriez pas dû déjà être parti?
(b) (*indicating probability*) **they ought to be arriving soon** ils devraient bientôt arriver; **he ought to have got there by now I expect** je pense qu'il est arrivé *or* qu'il a dû arriver (à l'heure qu'il est); **that ought to do** ça devrait aller; **that ought to be very enjoyable** cela devrait être très agréable.
ought[2] [ɔːt] *n* = **aught.**
ouija [ˈwiːdʒə] *n*: **~ board** oui-ja *m inv.*
ounce [aʊns] *n* once *f* (= *28,35 grammes*); (*fig: of truth etc*) grain *m*, once, gramme *m.*
our [ˈaʊəʳ] *poss adj* notre, *pl* nos.
ours [ˈaʊəz] *poss pron* le nôtre, la nôtre, les nôtres. **this car is ~** cette voiture est à nous *or* nous appartient *or* est la nôtre; **a friend of ~** un de nos amis (à nous), un ami à nous*; **I think it's one of ~** je crois que c'est un des nôtres; **your house is better than ~** votre maison est mieux que la nôtre; **it's no fault of ~** ce n'est pas de notre faute (à nous); (*pej*) **that car of ~** notre fichue* voiture; **that stupid son of ~** notre idiot de fils; **the house became ~** la maison est devenue la nôtre; **no advice of ~ could prevent him** aucun conseil de notre part ne pouvait l'empêcher; (*frm*) **it is not ~ to decide** ce n'est pas à nous de décider, il ne nous appartient pas de décider; **~ is a specialized department** notre section est une section spécialisée.
ourself [ˌaʊəˈself] *pers pron* (*frm, liter: of royal or editorial 'we'*) nous-même.
ourselves [ˌaʊəˈselvz] *pers pron* (*reflexive: direct and indirect*) nous; (*emphatic*) nous-mêmes; (*after prep*) nous. **we've hurt ~** nous nous sommes blessés; **we said to ~** nous nous sommes dit, on s'est dit*; **we saw it ~** nous l'avons vu nous-mêmes; **we've kept 3 for ~** nous nous en sommes réservé 3; **we were talking amongst ~** nous discutions entre nous; **(all) by ~** tout seuls, toutes seules.
oust [aʊst] *vt* évincer (*sb from sth* qn de qch). **they ~ed him from the chairmanship** ils l'ont évincé de la présidence, ils l'ont forcé à démissionner; **X soon ~ed Y as the teenagers' idol** X a bientôt supplanté Y comme idole des jeunes.
out [aʊt] (*phr vb elem*) **1** *adv* **(a)** (*away, not inside etc*) dehors. **he's ~ in the garden** il est dans le jardin; **Paul is ~** Paul est sorti *or* n'est pas là; **he's ~ a good deal** il sort beaucoup, il n'est pas souvent chez lui; (*in library*) **that book is ~** ce livre est sorti; **he's ~ fishing** il est (parti) à la pêche; **to be ~ and about again** être de nouveau sur pied; **to go ~** sortir; **get ~!** sortez!, dehors!; **~ you go!** sortez!, décampez!, filez!*; **can you find your own way ~?** pouvez-vous trouver la sortie *or* la porte tout seul?; (*above exit*) '~' 'sortie'; **to lunch ~** déjeuner dehors *or* en ville; **to have a day ~** sortir pour la journée; **it's her evening ~** c'est sa soirée de sortie; **let's have a night ~ tonight** si on sortait ce soir?; **~ there** là-bas; **look ~ there** regardez là-bas (dehors), regardez (là-bas) dehors; **~ here** ici; **come in! — no, I like it ~ here** rentrez! — non, je suis bien dehors; **when he was ~ in Iran** lorsqu'il était en Iran; **he went ~ to China** il est parti pour la *or* en Chine; **the voyage ~** l'aller *m*; **to be ~ at sea** être en mer *or* au large; **the current carried him ~ (to sea)** le courant l'a entraîné vers le large; **the boat was 10 km ~ (to sea)** le bateau était à 10 km du rivage; **5 days ~ from Liverpool** à 5 jours (de voyage) de Liverpool; (*Sport*) **the ball is ~** le ballon est sorti; (*Tennis*) '~!' 'out!', 'dehors!'; *V* **come out, run out, throw out** *etc.*
(b) (*loudly, clearly*) **~ loud** tout haut, à haute voix; **~ with it!** vas-y, parle!, dis-le donc!, accouche!‡; **I couldn't get his name ~** je ne suis pas arrivé à prononcer *or* à sortir* son nom; *V* **shout out, speak out** *etc.*
(c) (*fig*) **the roses are ~** les roses sont ouvertes *or* épanouies, les rosiers sont en fleur(s); **the trees were ~** (*in leaf*) les arbres étaient verts; (*in flower*) les arbres étaient en fleur(s); **the sun was ~** il faisait (du) soleil; **the moon was ~** la lune s'était levée, il y avait clair de lune; **the stars were ~** les étoiles brillaient; **the secret is ~** le secret est connu (maintenant), le secret n'en est plus un; **wait till the news gets ~!** attends que la nouvelle soit ébruitée!; **his book is ~** son livre vient de paraître; **the tide is ~** la marée est basse; **there's a warrant ~ for his arrest** un mandat d'arrêt a été délivré contre lui; **the steelworkers are ~ (on strike)** les ouvriers des aciéries sont en grève *or* ont débrayé*; **long skirts are ~** les jupes longues sont démodées *or* ne se font plus; **the socialists are ~** les socialistes ne sont plus au pouvoir; **these trousers are ~ at the knees, the knees are ~ on these trousers** ce pantalon est troué aux genoux; (*unconscious*) **he was ~ for 10 minutes** il est resté évanoui *or* sans connaissance pendant 10 minutes; **3 gins and he's ~ (cold)*** 3 gins et il n'y a plus personne; (*Boxing*) **he was ~ (for the count)** il était K.-O.; **before the month was** (*or* **is**) **~** avant la fin du mois; (*in cards, games etc*) **you're ~** tu es éliminé; *V* **come out, have out, knock out** *etc.*
(d) (*extinguished*) *[light, fire, gas etc]* **to be ~** être éteint; **'lights ~ at 10 p.m.'** 'extinction des feux à 22 heures'; *V* **blow out, burn out, go out, put out** *etc.*
(e) (*wrong, incorrect*) **he was ~ in his calculations, his calculations were ~** il s'est trompé dans ses calculs *or* ses comptes; **you were ~ by 20 cm, you were 20 cm ~** vous vous êtes trompé *or* vous avez fait une erreur de 20 cm; **you're not far ~** tu ne te trompes pas de beaucoup, tu n'es pas loin du compte, tu n'es pas tombé loin*; **my watch is 10 minutes ~** (*fast*) ma montre avance de 10 minutes; (*slow*) ma montre retarde de 10 minutes.
(f) (*indicating purpose etc*) **he was ~ to pass the exam** il voulait à tout prix réussir à l'examen, il était résolu à réussir à l'examen; **she was just ~ for a good time** elle ne voulait que s'amuser; **he's ~ for trouble** il cherche les ennuis; **he's ~ for all he**

can get toutes les chances de s'enrichir sont bonnes pour lui; **she's ~ for** *or* **to get a husband** elle fait la chasse au mari, elle veut à tout prix se marier; **they were ~ to get him** ils avaient résolu sa perte; **to be ~ to find sth** chercher qch.

(g) (*phrases*) **to be worn ~** *or* **tired ~** *or* **all ~*** être épuisé *or* éreinté *or* à bout de forces; **the car was going all ~** *or* **flat ~** la voiture fonçait *or* allait à toute vitesse; **he was going all ~ to pass the exam** il travaillait d'arrache-pied *or* sans désemparer pour réussir à l'examen; (*unequivocally*) **right ~, straight ~, ~ straight*** franchement, sans détours, sans ambages; **it's the best car ~*** c'est la meilleure voiture qu'il y ait; **it's the biggest swindle ~*** c'est l'escroquerie de l'année; **he's the best footballer ~*** c'est le meilleur joueur de football du moment; **she was ~ and away the youngest** elle était de beaucoup *or* de loin la plus jeune.

2 out of *prep* **(a)** (*outside*) en dehors de, hors de. **he lives ~ of town** il habite en dehors de la ville; **he is ~ of town this week** il n'est pas en ville cette semaine; **they were 100 km ~ of Paris** ils étaient à 100 km de Paris; **fish cannot live ~ of water** les poissons ne peuvent vivre hors de l'eau; **to go ~ of the room** sortir de la pièce; **he went ~ of the door** il sortit (par la porte); **come ~ of there!** sortez de là!; **let's get ~ of here!** ne restons pas ici!, partons!; **he jumped ~ of bed** il sauta du lit; **~ of the window** par la fenêtre; **(get) ~ of my** *or* **the way!** écartez-vous!, ne restez pas sur mon chemin! (*V also* **5**); **you're well ~ of it** c'est une chance *or* c'est aussi bien que vous ne soyez pas *or* plus concerné *or* dans le coup*; **to feel ~ of it** se sentir en marge, se sentir de trop *or* en trop; **Paul looks rather ~ of it** Paul n'a pas l'air d'être dans le coup*; **get ~ of it!** (*: *go away*) sortez-vous de là!*; (‡: *I don't believe you*) tu charries!‡; **~ of danger** hors de danger; *V* **bound**[1], **place, sight, way** *etc.*

(b) (*cause, motive*) par. **~ of curiosity/necessity** *etc* par curiosité/nécessité *etc.*

(c) (*origin, source*) de; dans. **one chapter ~ of a novel** un chapitre d'un roman; **like a princess ~ of a fairy tale** comme une princesse sortie d'un conte de fée; **he read to her ~ of a book by Balzac** il lui a lu un extrait d'un livre de Balzac; **a box made ~ of onyx** une boîte en onyx; **he made the table ~ of a crate** il a fait la table avec une caisse; **carved ~ of wood** sculpté dans le bois; **to drink ~ of a glass** boire dans un verre; **they ate ~ of the same plate** ils mangeaient dans la même assiette; **to take sth ~ of a drawer** prendre qch dans un tiroir; **he copied the poem ~ of a book** il a copié le poème dans un livre; **it was like something ~ of a nightmare** on aurait dit un cauchemar, c'était comme dans un cauchemar; **she looks like something ~ of 'Madame Butterfly'** on dirait qu'elle est sortie tout droit de 'Madame Butterfly'; (*Horse-racing*) **Lexicon by Hercules ~ of Alphabet** Lexicon issu d'Hercule et d'Alphabet.

(d) (*from among*) sur. **in 9 cases ~ of 10** dans 9 cas sur 10; **one ~ of (every) 5 smokers** un fumeur sur 5.

(e) (*without*) sans, démuni de. **to be ~ of money** être sans *or* démuni d'argent; **we were ~ of bread** nous n'avions plus de pain; **~ of work** sans emploi, en chômage; *V* **mind, print, stock** *etc.*

3 *n V* **in 4a**.

4 *adj* (*in office*) **the ~ tray** la corbeille pour le courrier à expédier.

5 *cpd*: **out-and-out** *fool, liar, crook* fieffé, consommé, achevé; *revolutionary, believer, reactionary* à tout crin, à tous crins; *defeat* total, écrasant; *victory, success* éclatant, retentissant; **outback** (*Australia*) intérieur *m* du pays (*plus ou moins inculte*); (*gen*) campagne isolée *or* presque déserte, cambrousse* *f*; **outbid** (*vt*) enchérir sur; (*vi*) surenchérir; (*Naut*) **outboard (motor)** (moteur *m*) hors-bord *m*; **to outbox sb** dominer qn par la technique de la boxe; **outbreak** *V* **outbreak**; **outbuilding** dépendance *f*; (*separate*) appentis *m*, remise *f*; (*gen*) **the outbuildings** les communs *mpl*; **outburst** *V* **outburst**; **outcast** exilé(e) *m(f)*, proscrit(e) *m(f)*, banni(e) *m(f)*; **social outcast** paria *m*, réprouvé(e) *m(f)*; **outclass** (*Sport*) surclasser; (*gen*) surclasser, surpasser; **outcome** *[meeting, work, discussions]* issue *f*, aboutissement *m*, résultat *m*; *[decision etc]* conséquence *f*; (*Geol*) **outcrop** (*n*) affleurement *m*; (*vi*) affleurer; **outcry** *V* **outcry**; **outdated** *custom* suranné, désuet (*f* -ète); *clothes* démodé; *theory, concept* périmé, démodé; *word* vieilli; **outdistance** distancer; **outdo** *V* **outdo**; **outdoor(s)** *V* **outdoor(s)**; **to outface sb** (*stare out*) dévisager qn; (*fig*) faire perdre contenance à qn; **outfall** *[river]* embouchure *f*; *[sewer]* déversoir *m*; **outfit** *V* **outfit**; **outfitter** *V* **outfitter**; **outflank** (*Mil*) déborder; (*fig*) déjouer les manœuvres de; **outflow** *[water]* écoulement *m*, débit *m*; *[funds, emigrants etc]* exode *m*; (*Mil*) **outgeneral** surpasser en tactique; **outgoing** *tenant, president* sortant; *train, boat, plane, mail* en partance; *tide* descendant; *person, personality* ouvert; (*Brit*) **outgoings** (*npl*) dépenses *fpl*, débours *mpl*; **outgrow** *V* **outgrow**; **outgrowth** excroissance *f*; (*esp US*) **outguess** devancer; **to out-Herod Herod** dépasser Hérode en cruauté *or* violence *etc*; **outhouse** appentis *m*, remise *f*; (*US*) cabinets extérieurs; **the outhouses** les communs *mpl*; **outlandish** *V* **outlandish**; **outlast** survivre à; **outlaw** (*n*) hors-la-loi *m inv*; (*vt*) *person* mettre hors la loi; *conduct* proscrire, bannir; **outlay** *V* **outlay**; **outlet** *V* **outlet**; **outline** *V* **outline**; **outlive** *V* **outlive**; **outlook** *V* **outlook**; **outlying** (*peripheral*) périphérique, excentrique; (*remote*) écarté, isolé; **the outlying suburbs** la grande banlieue; **outmanoeuvre** (*Mil, fig*) dominer en manœuvrant plus habilement; **outmoded = outdated**; **outnumber** surpasser en nombre, être plus nombreux que; **we were outnumbered five to one** nous étions à un contre cinq; **out-of-date** *passport, ticket* périmé; *custom* suranné, désuet (*f* -ète); *clothes* démodé; *theory, concept* périmé, démodé; *word* vieilli; **out-of-doors = outdoors**; **out-of-pocket expenses** débours *mpl*; **out-of-the-way** (*remote*) *spot* écarté, peu fréquenté, perdu; (*unusual: also* **out-of-the-ordinary**) *theory, approach, film, book* insolite; **outpace** devancer, distancer; (*Med*) **outpatient** malade *mf* en consultation externe; **outpatients department** service *m* (hospitalier) de consultation externe; (*Sport*) **outplay** dominer (par son jeu); (*Mil, fig*) **outpost** avant-poste *m*; (*fig*) **outpourings** épanchement(s) *m(pl)*; effusion(s) *f(pl)*; **output** *V* **output**; **outrage** *V* **outrage**; (*Mil*) **outrank** avoir un rang supérieur à; **outrider** (*on horseback*) cavalier *m*; (*on motorcycle*) motocycliste *m*, motard* *m* (*faisant partie d'une escorte*); **there were 4 outriders** il y avait une escorte de 4 motocyclistes (*or* cavaliers *etc*); (*Naut: all senses*) **outrigger** outrigger *m*; **outright** *V* **outright**; **outrun** *opponent, pursuer etc* distancer; (*fig*) *resources, abilities* excéder; **outset** début *m*, commencement *m*; (*fig*) **outshine** éclipser, surpasser; **outside** *V* **outside**; **outsize** (*gen*) énorme, colossal, gigantesque; *clothes* grande taille *inv*; **outsize shop** magasin spécialisé (dans les) grandes tailles; **outskirts** *[town]* faubourgs *mpl*, banlieue *f*, approches *fpl*; *[forest]* lisière *f*, bord *m*, orée *f*; **outsmart*** se montrer plus malin (*f* -igne) que; **to outspend sb** dépenser plus que qn; **outspoken** *V* **outspoken**; **outspread wings** ailes déployées; **outstanding** *V* **outstanding**; **to outstay sb** rester plus longtemps que qn; **I hope I have not outstayed my welcome** j'espère que je n'ai pas abusé de votre hospitalité; **outstretched** *body, leg* étendu; *arm* tendu; *wings* déployé; **to welcome sb with outstretched arms** accueillir qn à bras ouverts; (*Sport, fig*) **outstrip** devancer; (*US*) **outturn** *[factory]* production *f*; *[machine, worker]* rendement *m*; **outvote** *V* **outvote**; **outward(s)** *V* **outward(s)**; **outweigh** (*be more important than*) l'emporter sur; (*compensate for*) compenser; **outwit** (*gen*) se montrer plus malin (*f* -igne) que; *pursuer* dépister, semer*; **outworn** *clothes* usé; *custom, doctrine* périmé; *idea* périmé, rebattu; *subject, expression* usé, rebattu.

outage ['aʊtɪdʒ] *n* (*US*) interruption *f* de service; (*Elec*) coupure *f* de courant.

outbreak ['aʊtbreɪk] *n [war, fighting etc]* début *m*, déclenchement *m*; *[violence]* éruption *f*; *[emotion]* débordement *m*; *[anger etc]* explosion *f*, bouffée *f*, accès *m*; *[fever]* accès; *[spots]* éruption, poussée *f*; *[disease, epidemic]* commencement *m*, début; *[demonstrations]* vague *f*; *[revolt]* déclenchement *m*. **at the ~ of the disease** lorsque la maladie se déclara; **at the ~ of war** lorsque la guerre éclata; **the ~ of hostilities** l'ouverture *f* des hostilités.

outburst ['aʊtbɜːst] *n* explosion *f*, éruption *f*; *[anger]* explosion, bouffée *f*, accès *m*; *[energy]* accès. **he was ashamed of his ~** il avait honte de l'éclat *or* de la scène qu'il venait de faire.

outcry ['aʊtkraɪ] *n* tollé *m* (général), huées *fpl*, protestations *fpl*. **to raise an ~ about sth** crier haro sur qch, ameuter l'opinion sur qch; **there was a general ~ against ...** un tollé général s'éleva contre ... .

outdo [aʊt'duː] *pret* **outdid** [aʊt'dɪd], *ptp* **outdone** [aʊt'dʌn] *vt* surpasser, l'emporter sur, (r)enchérir sur (*sb in sth* qn en qch). **but he was not to be outdone** mais il ne serait pas dit qu'il serait vaincu *or* battu, mais il refusait de s'avouer vaincu *or* battu; **and I, not to be outdone, said that ...** et moi, pour ne pas être en reste, je dis que ... .

outdoor ['aʊtdɔː^r] *adj activity, games* de plein air; *swimming pool* en plein air, à ciel ouvert. **~ clothes** vêtements chauds (*or* imperméables *etc*); **to lead an ~ life** vivre au grand air; **he likes the ~ life** il aime la vie au grand air *or* en plein air.

outdoors ['aʊt'dɔːz] **1** *adv* (*also* **out-of-doors**) *stay, play* dehors; *live* au grand air; *sleep* dehors, à la belle étoile. **2** *n*: **the great ~** le grand air.

outer ['aʊtə^r] **1** *adj door, wrapping* extérieur(*f* -eure). **~ garments** vêtements *mpl* de dessus; **~ space** espace *m* (cosmique *or* intersidéral), cosmos *m*; **the ~ suburbs** la grande banlieue.

2 *cpd*: **outermost** (*furthest out*) le plus à l'extérieur, le plus en dehors; (*most isolated*) le plus écarté; **outermost parts of the earth** extrémités *fpl* de la terre.

outfit ['aʊtfɪt] **1** *n* **(a)** (*clothes and equipment*) équipement *m*, attirail* *m*; (*tools*) matériel *m*, outillage *m*. **camping ~** matériel *or* équipement *or* attirail* de camping; **he wants a Red Indian ~ for Christmas** il veut une panoplie d'Indien pour Noël; **puncture repair ~** trousse *f* de réparation (de pneus).

(b) (*set of clothes*) tenue *f*. **travelling/skiing ~** tenue *f* de voyage/de ski; **she's got a new spring ~** elle a une nouvelle toilette de demi-saison; **did you see the ~ she was wearing?** (*in admiration*) avez-vous remarqué sa toilette?; (*pej*) avez-vous remarqué son accoutrement *or* comment elle était accoutrée?

(c) (*: *organization etc*) équipe* *f*. **he's not in our ~** il n'est pas de chez nous, il n'est pas un des nôtres; **when I joined this ~** quand je me suis retrouvé avec cette bande*.

2 *vt* équiper.

outfitter ['aʊtfɪtə^r] *n* (*Brit: also* **gents' ~**) spécialiste *mf* de confection (pour) hommes. **(gents') ~'s** maison *f* d'habillement *or* de confection pour hommes; **sports ~'s** maison de sports.

outgrow [aʊt'grəʊ] *pret* **outgrew** [aʊt'gruː], *ptp* **outgrown** [aʊt'grəʊn] *vt clothes* devenir trop grand pour; (*fig*) *hobby, sport* ne plus s'intéresser à (qch) en grandissant; *habit, defect* perdre *or* se défaire de (qch) en prenant de l'âge; *friends* se détacher de (qn) en grandissant; *opinion, way of life* abandonner en prenant de l'âge. **we've ~n all that now** nous avons dépassé ce stade, nous n'en sommes plus là.

outing ['aʊtɪŋ] *n* sortie *f*, excursion *f*. **the school ~** la sortie annuelle de l'école; **the annual ~ to Blackpool** l'excursion annuelle à Blackpool; **let's go for an ~ tomorrow** faisons une sortie demain; **to go for an ~ in the car** partir faire une randonnée *or* un tour en voiture; **a birthday ~ to the theatre** une sortie au théâtre pour (fêter) un anniversaire.

outlandish [aʊt'lændɪʃ] *adj* exotique; (*pej*) étrange, bizarre, (*stronger*) barbare.
outlay ['aʊtleɪ] *n* (*expenses*) frais *mpl*, dépenses *fpl*, débours *mpl*; (*investment*) mise *f* de fonds. **national ~ on education** dépenses nationales pour l'éducation.
outlet ['aʊtlet] **1** *n* (*for water etc*) issue *f*, sortie *f*; (*US Elec*) prise *f* de courant; *[lake]* dégorgeoir *m*, déversoir *m*; *[river, stream]* embouchure *f*; *[tunnel]* sortie; (*fig*) (*for talents etc*) débouché *m*; (*for energy, emotions*) exutoire *m* (*for* à); (*Comm*) débouché; *V* **retail**.
2 *cpd* (*Tech*) *pipe* d'échappement, d'écoulement; *valve* d'échappement.
outline ['aʊtlaɪn] **1** *n* **(a)** *[object]* contour *m*, configuration *f*; *[building, tree etc]* profil *m*, silhouette *f*; *[face]* profil *m*; (*shorthand*) sténogramme *m*. **he drew the ~ of the house** il traça le contour de la maison; **to draw sth in ~** dessiner qch au trait; (*Art*) **rough ~** premier jet, ébauche *f*.
(b) (*fig: summary*) esquisse *f*, idée *f*. (*main features*) **~s** grandes lignes, grands traits; **rough ~ of an article** canevas *m* d'un article; **to give the broad** *or* **main** *or* **general ~s of sth** décrire *or* esquisser qch à grands traits; **in broad ~ the plan is as follows** dans ses grandes lignes *or* en gros, le plan est le suivant; **I'll give you a quick ~ of what we mean to do** je vous donnerai un aperçu de ce que nous avons l'intention de faire; (*as title*) **'O~s of Botany'** 'Éléments *mpl* de Botanique'.
2 *cpd*: **outline drawing** dessin *m* au trait; **outline map** tracé *m* des contours (d'un pays), carte muette.
3 *vt* **(a)** délinéer, tracer le contour de. **she ~d her eyes with a dark pencil** elle a souligné *or* dessiné le contour de ses yeux avec un crayon foncé; **the mountain was ~d against the sky** la montagne se profilait *or* se dessinait *or* se découpait sur le ciel.
(b) (*summarize*) *theory, plan, idea* exposer à grands traits *or* dans ses lignes générales, exposer les grandes lignes de; *book, event* faire un bref compte rendu de; *facts, details* passer brièvement en revue. **to ~ the situation** brosser un tableau *or* donner un aperçu de la situation.
outlive [aʊt'lɪv] *vt* **(a)** (*survive*) *person, era, war etc* survivre à. **he ~d her by 10 years** il lui a survécu de 10 ans; *[person, object, scheme]* **to have ~d one's usefulness** avoir fait son temps, ne plus servir à rien. **(b)** (*live down*) *disgrace etc* survivre à.
outlook ['aʊtlʊk] *n* **(a)** (*view*) vue *f* (*on, over* sur), perspective *f* (*on, over* de); (*fig: prospect*) perspective (d'avenir), horizon *m* (*fig*). **the ~ for June is wet** on annonce *or* prévoit de la pluie pour juin; **the economic ~** les perspectives *or* les horizons économiques; **the ~ for the wheat crop is good** la récolte de blé s'annonce bonne; **the ~ (for us) is rather rosy*** les choses se présentent *or* s'annoncent assez bien (pour nous); **it's a grim** *or* **bleak ~** l'horizon est sombre *or* bouché, les perspectives sont fort sombres.
(b) (*point of view*) attitude *f* (*on* à l'égard de), point *m* de vue (*on* sur), conception *f* (*on* de). **he has a pessimistic ~** il voit les choses en noir.
output ['aʊtpʊt] *n* **(a)** *[factory, mine, oilfield, writer]* production *f*; (*Agr*) *[land]* rendement *m*, production; *[machine, factory worker]* rendement. **~ fell/rose** le rendement *or* la production a diminué/augmenté; **this factory has an ~ of 600 radios per day** cette usine débite 600 radios par jour.
(b) (*Computers*) sortie *f*.
(c) (*Elec*) puissance fournie *or* de sortie.
outrage ['aʊtreɪdʒ] **1** *n* atrocité *f*; (*during riot etc*) acte *m* de violence; (*public scandal*) scandale *m*. **the prisoners suffered ~s at the hands of ...** les prisonniers ont été atrocement maltraités par ...; **it's an ~ against humanity** c'est un crime de lèse-humanité; **an ~ against justice** un outrage à la justice; **several ~s occurred** *or* **were committed in the course of the night** plusieurs actes de violence ont été commis au cours de la nuit; **bomb ~** attentat *m* au plastic *or* à la bombe; **it's an ~!** c'est un scandale!
2 *vt* [aʊt'reɪdʒ] *morals, sense of decency* outrager, faire outrage à. **to be ~d by sth** trouver qch monstrueux, être outré de *or* par qch.
outrageous [aʊt'reɪdʒəs] *adj crime, suffering* atroce, terrible, monstrueux; *conduct, action* scandaleux, monstrueux; *remark* outrageant, injurieux, (*weaker*) choquant; *sense of humour* outré, scabreux; *price* scandaleux*, exorbitant; *hat, fashion* impossible, extravagant. **it's ~!** c'est un scandale!, cela dépasse les bornes! *or* la mesure!; **it's absolutely ~ that ...** il est absolument monstrueux *or* scandaleux que ... + *subj*.
outrageously [aʊt'reɪdʒəslɪ] *adv suffer* atrocement, terriblement; *behave, speak* outrageusement, scandaleusement, (*weaker*) de façon choquante; *lie* outrageusement, effrontément; *dress* de manière ridicule *or* grotesque. **it is ~ expensive** c'est atrocement cher.
outré ['u:treɪ] *adj* outré, outrancier, qui dépasse la mesure *or* les bornes.
outright [aʊt'raɪt] **1** *adv* (*at one time*) sur-le-champ, sur le coup; (*completely*) entièrement, complètement; *reject, refuse, deny* catégoriquement; (*forthrightly*) *say, tell* carrément, (tout) net, franchement. **the bullet killed him ~** la balle l'a tué net *or* sur le coup; **to buy sth ~** (*buy and pay immediately*) acheter qch au comptant; (*buy all of sth*) acheter qch en bloc; **he won the prize ~** il a été le gagnant incontesté du prix; **to laugh ~ at sth** rire franchement *or* ouvertement de qch.
2 ['aʊtraɪt] *adj* (*complete*) complet (*f* -ète), total, absolu; *sale* (*paying immediately*) au comptant; (*selling all of sth*) en bloc; *selfishness, arrogance* pur; *denial, refusal, rejection* catégorique; *explanation* franc (*f* franche); *supporter* inconditionnel. **to be an ~ opponent of sth** s'opposer totalement à qch; **the ~ winner** le gagnant incontesté.
outside ['aʊt'saɪd] (*phr vb elem*) **1** *adv* (au) dehors, à l'extérieur. **go and play ~** va jouer dehors; (*Cine etc*) **we must shoot this scene ~** cette scène doit être tournée en extérieur; **the box was clean ~ but dirty inside** la boîte était propre à l'extérieur *or* au dehors mais sale à l'intérieur; (*lit, fig*) **seen from ~** vu du dehors *or* de l'extérieur; **he left the car ~** il a laissé la voiture dans la rue; (*at night*) il a laissé la voiture passer la nuit dehors*; **there's a man ~ asking for Paul** il y a un homme dehors qui demande Paul; **to go ~** sortir; (*on bus*) **to ride ~** voyager sur l'impériale.
2 *prep* (*also* **~ of***) **(a)** (*lit*) à l'extérieur de, hors de. **~ the house** dehors, à l'extérieur de la maison, hors de la maison; **he was waiting ~ the door** il attendait à la porte; **don't go ~ the garden** ne sors pas du jardin; **the ball landed ~ this line** la balle a atterri de l'autre côté de cette ligne; **~ the harbour** au large du port.
(b) (*fig: beyond, apart from*) en dehors de. **~ the question** en dehors du problème; **~ the festival proper** en dehors du *or* en marge du vrai festival; **it's ~ the normal range** ceci sort de la gamme normale; **it's ~ our scheme** ça ne fait pas partie de notre projet; **that is ~ the committee's terms of reference** ceci n'est pas de la compétence de la commission; **she doesn't see anyone ~ her immediate family** elle ne voit personne en dehors de *or* hors ses proches parents.
3 *n [house, car, object]* extérieur *m*, dehors *m*; (*appearance*) aspect extérieur, apparence *f*; (*fig*) (monde *m*) extérieur. **on the ~ of** sur l'extérieur de; (*beyond*) à l'extérieur de, hors de, en dehors de; **he opened the door from the ~** il a ouvert la porte du dehors; **there's no window on to the ~** il n'y a pas de fenêtre qui donne sur l'extérieur; **the box was dirty on the ~** la boîte était sale à l'extérieur; **the ~ of the box was dirty** l'extérieur *or* le dehors de la boîte était sale; **~ in = inside out** (*V* **inside 3b**); (*lit, fig*) **to look at sth from the ~** regarder qch de l'extérieur *or* du dehors; (*fig*) **(judging) from the ~** à en juger par les apparences; **he passed the car on the ~** (*Brit*) il a doublé la voiture sur la droite; (*US, Europe etc*) il a doublé la voiture sur la gauche; **at the (very) ~** (tout) au plus, au maximum.
4 *adj* **(a)** (*lit*) *measurements, repairs, aerial* extérieur (*f* -eure). (*in bus, plane etc*) **would you like an ~ seat or an inside one?** voulez-vous une place côté couloir ou côté fenêtre?; (*Aut*) **the ~ lane** (*Brit*) la voie de droite; (*US, Europe etc*) la voie de gauche; (*Rad, TV*) **~ broadcast** émission réalisée à l'extérieur; (*Rad, TV*) **~ broadcasting van** *or* **unit** car *m* de reportage.
(b) (*fig*) *world, help, influence* extérieur (*f* -eure); (*maximum*) *price, figure, amount* maximum, le plus haut *or* élevé. **to get an ~ opinion** demander l'avis d'une personne indépendante *or* non intéressée; (*fig*) **there is an ~ possibility that he will come** il n'est pas impossible qu'il vienne; (*fig*) **he has an ~ chance of succeeding** il a une très faible chance de réussir.
5 *cpd*: (*Ftbl*) **outside-left/-right** ailier gauche/droit.
outsider ['aʊt'saɪdə^r] *n* **(a)** (*stranger*) étranger *m*, -ère *f*. **we don't want some ~ coming in and telling us what to do** nous ne voulons pas que quelqu'un d'étranger *or* du dehors *or* d'inconnu vienne nous dire ce qu'il faut faire; (*pej*) **he is an ~** il n'est pas des nôtres.
(b) (*horse or person unlikely to win*) outsider *m*.
outspoken [aʊt'spəʊkən] *adj person, answer* franc (*f* franche), carré. **to be ~** avoir son franc-parler, ne pas mâcher ses mots.
outspokenly [aʊt'spəʊkənlɪ] *adv* franchement, carrément.
outspokenness [aʊt'spəʊkənnɪs] *n* franc-parler *m*, franchise *f*.
outstanding [aʊt'stændɪŋ] *adj* **(a)** (*exceptional*) *person* éminent, remarquable, exceptionnel; *talent, beauty* remarquable, exceptionnel, hors ligne; *detail, event* marquant, frappant, mémorable; *feature* dominant; *interest, importance* exceptionnel.
(b) (*unfinished etc*) *business* non encore réglé, en suspens, en souffrance; *account* arriéré, impayé; *debt* impayé; *interest* à échoir; *problem* non résolu. **a lot of work is still ~** beaucoup de travail reste à faire.
outstandingly [aʊt'stændɪŋlɪ] *adv* remarquablement, exceptionnellement, éminemment.
outvote [aʊt'vəʊt] *vt person* mettre en minorité, battre. **his project was ~d** son projet a été rejeté à la majorité des voix *or* n'a pas obtenu la majorité.
outward ['aʊtwəd] **1** *adv* vers l'extérieur. (*Naut*) **~ bound (for/from)** en partance (pour/de).
2 *adj movement* vers l'extérieur; *ship, freight* en partance; (*fig*) *appearance etc* extérieur (*f* -eure). **~ journey** (voyage *m* d')aller *m*; **with an ~ show of pleasure** en faisant mine d'être ravi.
outwardly ['aʊtwədlɪ] *adv* à l'extérieur, extérieurement, du *or* au dehors; (*apparently*) en apparence. **he was ~ pleased but inwardly furious** il avait l'air content *or* il faisait mine d'être content mais il était secrètement furieux.
outwards ['aʊtwədz] *adv* = **outward 1**.
ouzo ['u:zəʊ] *n* ouzo *m*.
ova ['əʊvə] *npl of* **ovum**.
oval ['əʊvəl] **1** *adj* (en) ovale. **2** *n* ovale *m*.
ovary ['əʊvərɪ] *n* (*Anat, Bot*) ovaire *m*.
ovate ['əʊveɪt] *adj* ové.
ovation [əʊ'veɪʃən] *n* ovation *f*, acclamations *fpl*. **to give sb an ~** ovationner qn, faire une ovation à qn; *V* **standing**.
oven ['ʌvn] **1** *n* (*Culin*) four *m*; (*Tech*) four, étuve *f*. **in the ~** au four; **in a hot ~** à four vif *or* chaud; **in a cool** *or* **slow ~** à four doux; **this room/Tangiers is (like) an ~** cette pièce/Tanger est une fournaise *or* une étuve; *V* **Dutch, gas** *etc*.
2 *cpd*: (*Brit*) **oven glove** gant isolant; **ovenproof** allant au four; **oven-ready** prêt à cuire; (*U*) **ovenware** plats *mpl* allant au four.

over ['əʊvə^r] (*phr vb elem*) **1** *adv* **(a)** (*above*) (par-)dessus. **this one goes ~ and that one under** celui-ci passe par-dessus *or* se met dessus et celui-là dessous; **we often see jets fly ~** nous voyons souvent des avions à réaction passer dans le ciel; **the ball went ~ into the field** le ballon est passé par-dessus la haie (*or* le mur *etc*) et il est tombé dans le champ; **children of 8 and ~** enfants à partir de 8 ans; **if it is 2 metres or ~, then ...** si ça fait 2 mètres ou plus, alors ...; *V* **boil over** *etc.*

(b) (*across*) **~ here** ici; **~ there** là-bas; **he has gone ~ to Belgium** il est parti en Belgique; **~ in France** là-bas en France; **they're ~ from Canada** ils arrivent du Canada; **he drove us ~ to the other side of town** il nous a conduits de l'autre côté de la ville; (*Telec etc*) **~ to you!** à vous!; (*Rad, TV*) **and now ~ to our Birmingham studio** et maintenant nous passons l'antenne à notre studio de Birmingham; **they swam ~ to us** ils sont venus vers nous (à la nage); **he went ~ to his mother's** il est passé chez sa mère; **let's ask Paul ~** si on invitait Paul à venir nous voir; **I'll be ~ at 7 o'clock** je serai là *or* je passerai à 7 heures; **we had them ~ last week** ils sont venus chez nous la semaine dernière; **when you're next ~ this way** la prochaine fois que vous passerez par ici; **they were ~ for the day** ils sont venus passer la journée; (*fig*) **he went ~ to the enemy** il est passé à l'ennemi; (*fig*) **I've gone ~ to a new brand of coffee** j'ai changé de marque de café; **~ against the wall** là-bas contre le mur; **yes, but ~ against that ...** oui, mais en contrepartie ... *or* par contre ...; *V* **cross over, hand over, win over** *etc.*

(c) (*everywhere*) partout. **the world ~** dans le monde entier, aux quatre coins du monde; **I looked for you all ~** je vous ai cherché partout; **they searched the house ~** ils ont cherché dans toute la maison; **covered all ~ with dust** tout couvert de poussière; **she was flour all ~, she was all ~ flour*** elle était couverte de farine, elle avait de la farine partout; **embroidered all ~** tout brodé; **he was trembling all ~** il tremblait de tous ses membres; (*fig*) **that's him all ~!** c'est bien de lui!, on le reconnaît bien là!; *V* **look over, read over** *etc.*

(d) (*down, round, sideways etc*) **he hit her and ~ she went** il la frappa et elle bascula; **he turned the watch ~ and ~** il a retourné la montre dans tous les sens; **to turn ~ in bed** se retourner dans son lit; *V* **bend over, fall over, knock over** *etc.*

(e) (*again*) encore (une fois). **~ and ~ (again)** à maintes reprises, maintes et maintes fois; **he makes the same mistake ~ and ~ (again)** il n'arrête pas de faire la même erreur; **you'll have to do it ~** il faut que tu le refasses, il te faudra le refaire; **he did it 5 times ~** il l'a fait 5 fois de suite; **start all ~ (again)** recommencez au début *or* à partir du début, reprenez au commencement; **he had to count them ~ (again)** il a dû les recompter.

(f) (*finished*) fini. **the rain is ~** la pluie s'est arrêtée, il a cessé de pleuvoir; **the danger was ~** le danger était passé; **autumn/the war/the meeting was just ~** l'automne/la guerre/la réunion venait de finir *or* de s'achever; **after the war is ~** quand la guerre sera finie; **when this is all ~** quand tout cela sera fini *or* terminé; **it's all ~!** c'est fini!; **it's all ~ between us** tout est fini entre nous; **it's all ~ with him** (*he's finished*) il est tout à fait fini *or* fichu*, c'en est fait de lui; (*we're through*) nous avons rompu.

(g) (*too*) trop, très. **he was not ~ pleased with himself** il n'était pas trop content de lui; **I'm not ~ glad to see him again** le revoir ne m'enchante guère; **there's not ~ much** il n'y en a pas tant que cela; **she's not ~ strong** elle n'est pas trop *or* tellement solide; **you haven't done it ~ well** vous ne l'avez pas trop *or* très bien fait; *V also* **3.**

(h) (*remaining*) en plus. **if there is any meat (left) ~** s'il reste de la viande; **there's nothing ~** il ne reste plus rien; **there are 3 ~** il en reste 3; **there were 2 apples each and one ~** il y avait 2 pommes pour chacun et une en plus; **four into twenty-nine goes seven and one ~** vingt-neuf divisé par quatre fait sept et il reste un; **I've got one card ~** il me reste une carte, j'ai une carte en trop; **6 metres and a bit ~** un peu plus de 6 mètres; *V* **leave over** *etc.*

2 *prep* **(a)** (*on top of*) sur, par-dessus. **he spread the blanket ~ the bed** il a étendu la couverture sur le lit; **I spilled coffee ~ it** j'ai renversé du café dessus; **with his hat ~ one ear** le chapeau sur l'oreille; **tie a piece of paper ~ (the top of) the jar** couvrez le pot avec un morceau de papier et attachez; **she put on a cardigan ~ her blouse** elle a mis un gilet par-dessus son corsage; *V* **fall, trip** *etc.*

(b) (*above*) au-dessus de. **there was a lamp ~ the table** il y avait une lampe au-dessus de la table; **the water came ~ his knees** l'eau lui arrivait au-dessus du genou, l'eau lui recouvrait les genoux.

(c) (*across*) par-dessus; de l'autre côté de. **the house ~ the way** *or* **~ the road** la maison d'en face; **there is a café ~ the road** il y a un café en face; **the bridge ~ the river** le pont qui traverse la rivière; **it's just ~ the river** c'est juste de l'autre côté de la rivière; (*liter*) **from ~ the seas** de par delà les mers; **tourists from ~ the Atlantic/the Channel** touristes *mpl* d'outre-Atlantique/d'outre-Manche; **the noise came from ~ the wall** le bruit venait de l'autre côté du mur; **to look ~ the wall** regarder par-dessus le mur; **he looked ~ my shoulder** il a regardé par-dessus mon épaule; **to jump ~ a wall** sauter un mur; **he escaped ~ the border** il s'est enfui au-delà de la frontière; *V* **climb, leap** *etc.*

(d) (*fig*) **~ the summer** au cours de l'été, pendant l'été; **~ Christmas** au cours des fêtes *or* pendant les fêtes de Noël; **he stayed ~ Christmas with us** il a passé Noël chez nous; **may I stay ~ Friday?** puis-je rester jusqu'à vendredi soir (*or* samedi)?; **~ a period of** sur une période de; **their visits were spread ~ several months** leurs visites se sont échelonnées sur une période de plusieurs mois; **~ the last few years** pendant les *or* au cours des quelques dernières années; **they were sitting ~ the fire** ils étaient assis tout près du feu; **they talked ~ a cup of coffee** ils ont bavardé (tout) en prenant *or* buvant une tasse de café; **~ the phone** au téléphone; **~ the radio** à la radio; **how long will you be ~ it?** combien de temps cela te prendra-t-il?; **he'll be a long time ~ that letter** cette lettre va lui prendre longtemps; **he ruled ~ the English** il a régné sur les Anglais; **you have an advantage ~ me** vous avez un avantage sur moi; **a sudden change came ~ him** il changea soudain; **what came ~ you?** qu'est-ce qui t'a pris?; **he's ~ me in the firm** il est au-dessus de moi dans la compagnie; **to pause ~ a difficulty** marquer un temps d'arrêt sur un point difficile; **they fell out ~ money** ils se sont brouillés pour une question d'argent; **an increase of 5% ~ last year's total** une augmentation de 5% par rapport au total de l'année dernière; **~ and above what he has already done for us** sans compter *or* en plus de ce qu'il a déjà fait pour nous; **yes, but ~ and above that ...** oui, mais en outre *or* par-dessus le marché ...; **Celtic were all ~ Rangers*** le Celtic dominait complètement les Rangers; **she was all ~ me* in her efforts to make me stay with her** elle était aux petits soins pour moi dans l'espoir de me convaincre de rester avec elle; **they were all ~ him* when he told them the news** quand il leur a annoncé la nouvelle, ils lui ont fait fête; *V* **look over, think over** *etc.*

(e) (*everywhere in*) **it was raining ~ Paris** il pleuvait sur Paris, **it snowed all ~ the country** il a neigé sur toute l'étendue du pays *or* sur tout le pays; **all ~ France** partout en France; **all ~ the world** dans le monde entier, aux quatre coins du monde; **I'll show you ~ the house** je vais vous faire visiter la maison.

(f) (*more than*) plus de, au-dessus de. **they stayed for ~ 3 hours** ils sont restés plus de 3 heures; **she is ~ sixty** elle a plus de soixante ans, elle a passé la soixantaine; **the boat is ~ 10 metres long** le bateau a plus de 10 mètres de long; **well ~ 200** bien plus de 200; **all numbers ~ 20** tous les chiffres au-dessus de 20.

3 *cpd*: **over...** sur...; **overabundant** surabondant; (*Theat*) **overact** charger *or* outrer *or* exagérer son rôle; **overactive** trop actif; (*Med*) **he has an overactive thyroid** il souffre d'hyperthyroïdie; **overall** *V* **overall**; **overanxious** trop inquiet (*f*-ète) *or* anxieux (*f*-euse); **I'm not overanxious to go** je n'ai pas trop *or* tellement envie d'y aller, je ne suis pas trop pressé d'y aller; **overarm** *throw, serve* par en-dessus; **overawe** *[person]* intimider, impressionner; *[sight etc]* impressionner; **overbalance** *V* **overbalance**; **overbearing** autoritaire, impérieux, arrogant; (*at auction etc*) **overbid** (*vt*) enchérir sur; (*vi*) surenchérir; **overblown** *flower* trop ouvert; *woman* plantureux; *style* ampoulé; **overboard** *V* **overboard**; **overbold** *person, remark* impudent; *action* trop audacieux; **overburden** (*lit*) surcharger; (*fig*) surcharger, accabler (*with* de);**overcast** *sky* couvert, sombre; *weather* couvert, bouché; **to grow overcast** se couvrir; **overcautious** trop prudent *or* circonspect, prudent *or* circonspect à l'excès; **overcautiously** avec un excès de prudence *or* circonspection, avec trop de prudence *or* circonspection; **overcautiousness** excès *m* de prudence *or* circonspection; **overcharge** *V* **overcharge**; **overcoat** pardessus *m*, manteau *m*; *[soldier]* capote *f*; *[sailor]* caban *m*; **overcome** *V* **overcome**; (*Econ, Psych*) **overcompensation** surcompensation *f*; **overcompress** surcomprimer; **overconfidence** (*assurance*) suffisance *f*, présomption *f*; (*trust*) confiance *f* aveugle (*in* en); **overconfident** (*assured*) suffisant, présomptueux; (*trusting*) trop confiant (*in* en); **overconsumption** surconsommation *f*; **overcook** trop cuire; **overcrowded** *room, bus* bondé, comble; *house, town* surpeuplé; *class* surchargé, pléthorique; *shelf* surchargé, encombré (*with* de); **the room was overcrowded** il y avait trop de monde dans la pièce, la pièce était bondée; **room overcrowded with furniture** pièce encombrée (de meubles); **overcrowding** (*in housing etc*) surpeuplement *m*, entassement *m*; (*in classroom*) effectif(s) surchargé(s); (*in bus etc*) encombrement *m*; (*in town, district*) surpeuplement *m*, surpopulation *f*; (*Phot, gen*) **overdeveloped** trop développé; **overdo** *V* **overdo**; **overdose** dose trop forte *or* excessive, surdose *f*; **to take an overdose** prendre une dose excessive *or* une surdose de sédatifs (*or* barbituriques *etc*); **she died from an overdose** elle est morte pour avoir absorbé une dose excessive *or* une surdose de sédatifs (*or* barbituriques *etc*); (*Banking*) **overdraft** découvert *m*; **I've got an overdraft** mon compte est à découvert; **I've got an overdraft of £50** j'ai un découvert de 50 livres; **to overdraw one's account** mettre son compte à découvert, dépasser son crédit; **overdrawn account** crédit *m or* compte *m* à découvert; **I am** *or* **my account is overdrawn** mon compte est à découvert; **I am** *or* **my account is overdrawn by £50** j'ai un découvert de 50 livres; **overdress** (*n*) robe-chasuble *f*; (*vi: also* **to be overdressed**) s'habiller avec trop de recherche; (*Aut*) **overdrive** (vitesse *f*) surmultipliée *f*; **overdue** *V* **overdue**; **overeager** trop zélé, trop empressé; **he was not overeager to leave** il n'avait pas une envie folle de partir, il n'était pas trop pressé de partir; **overeat** (*on one occasion*) trop manger; (*regularly*) trop manger, se suralimenter; **overeating** excès *mpl* de table; **overelaborate** *design, plan* trop compliqué; *style* trop travaillé, contourné, tarabiscoté; *excuse* contourné; *dress* trop recherché; **overemployment** suremploi *m*; **overenthusiastic** trop enthousiaste, fanatique; **overenthusiastically** avec trop d'enthousiasme; **overestimate** *price, costs, importance* surestimer; *strength* trop présumer de; *danger* exagérer; **overexcite** surexciter; **to get overexcited** se mettre dans un état de surexcitation, devenir surexcité; **overexcitement** surexcitation *f*; **to overexert o.s.** se surmener, s'éreinter; **overexertion** surmenage *m*;(*Phot*) **overexpose** surexposer; (*Phot; also* *fig*) **overexposure** surexposition *f*; **overfamiliar** trop familier; **overfeed** (*vt*) suralimenter, donner trop à manger à; (*vi*) trop manger, se suralimenter; **overfeeding** suralimentation *f*; **overflow** *V* **overflow**; **overfly** survoler; **overfull** trop plein (*of* de); **overgenerous** *person* prodigue (*with* de); *helping* excessif; **overgrown** *V* **overgrown**; (*US*) **overhand** *throw, serve* par en-dessus; **overhang** *V* **overhang**; **overhaul** *V* **overhaul**; **overhead** *V* **overhead**; **overhear** *V* **overhear**; **overheat** (*vt*) surchauffer; (*vi*) *[engine]* chauffer; **overheated** *room* surchauffé; *brakes, engine* qui chauffe; **overindulge** (*vt*) *person* trop gâter, satisfaire tous les caprices de; *passion, appetite* céder trop facilement à; (*vi*) abuser (*in* de); (*hum*) **I rather overindulged last night** je me suis laissé aller à faire des excès hier soir; **overindulgence** indulgence excessive (*of or towards sb* des caprices *or* envers les caprices de qn); abus *m* (*in sth* de qch); **overindulgent** trop indulgent (*to, towards* envers); **overjoyed** *V* **overjoyed**; **overkill** (capacité *f* de) surextermination *f*; (*gen, Elec*) **overladen** surchargé; **overland** par voie de terre; **overland route** itinéraire *m* par voie de terre (*to* pour aller à); **overlap** *V* **overlap**; **overlay** (*vt*) (re)couvrir (*with* de); (*n*) revêtement *m*; **overleaf** au verso, au dos (de la page); **overload** (*n*) surcharge *f*; (*vt*) *circuit, truck, animal* surcharger (*with* de); *engine* surmener; **overlook** *V* **overlook**; **overlord** (*Hist*) suzerain *m*; (*leader*) chef *m* suprême; **overmuch** (*adv*) trop, excessivement, à l'excès; (*adj*) trop de, excessif; **overnice** *person* trop pointilleux, trop scrupuleux; *distinction* trop subtil; **overnight** *V* **overnight**; **overparticular** *person* trop pointilleux, trop scrupuleux; *examination* trop minutieux; **not to be overparticular about discipline/principles** ne pas être à cheval sur la discipline/les principes; **I'm not overparticular (about it)** ça m'est égal, je ne suis pas maniaque (sur ce point); (*US Aut*) **overpass** pont autoroutier; **overpay** *person, job* trop payer, surpayer; **he was overpaid by £5** on lui a payé 5 livres de trop; **overpayment** surpaye *f*, paiement excessif; (*fig*) **to overplay one's hand** aller trop loin, prendre trop de risques; **overpopulated** surpeuplé; **overpopulation** surpopulation *f* (*in* dans), surpeuplement *m* (*of* de); **overpower** *etc V* **overpower** *etc*; **overpraise** faire des éloges excessifs de; **overprint** (*vt*) surcharger; (*n*) surcharge *f*; (*Ind*) **overproduce** surproduire; (*Ind*) **overproduction** surproduction *f*; **overprotect** *child* protéger excessivement, surprotéger; **overprotective** protecteur (*f* -trice) à l'excès; **overrate** surestimer, surévaluer, faire trop grand cas de; **that book is very overrated** ce livre est très surfait; (*fig*) **to overreach o.s.** (vouloir) trop entreprendre; **overreact** *etc V* **overreact** *etc*; **override** *etc V* **override** *etc*; **overripe** *fruit* trop mûr, blet (*f* blette); *cheese* trop fait; **overrule** *V* **overrule**; **overrun** *V* **overrun**; **overscrupulous** trop pointilleux, trop scrupuleux; **overseas** *V* **overseas**; **oversee** surveiller; **overseer** (*in factory, on roadworks etc*) contremaître *m*, chef *m* d'équipe; (*in coalmine*) porion *m*; *[prisoners, slaves]* surveillant *m*; **to oversell** faire trop valoir, mettre trop en avant; (*Comm*) **the match/show was oversold** on a vendu plus de tickets qu'il n'y avait de places pour le match/le spectacle; **oversensitive** trop sensible, trop susceptible; **he's really oversexed*** c'est un obsédé sexuel (*iro*); **overshadow** *[leaves etc]* ombrager; *[clouds]* obscurcir, voiler; (*fig*) éclipser; **overshoe** galoche *f*; (*of rubber*) caoutchouc *m*; **overshoot** *V* **overshoot**; **oversight** *V* **oversight**; **oversimplification** simplification excessive; **oversimplify** trop simplifier, simplifier à l'extrême; **oversize(d)** (*gen*) trop grand; *class* trop nombreux, pléthorique; *family* trop nombreux; (*huge*) gigantesque, énorme; **oversleep** dormir trop longtemps, se réveiller (trop) tard, ne pas se réveiller à temps; **overspend** *allowance, resources* dépenser au-dessus de *or* au-delà de; **to overspend by £10** dépenser 10 livres de trop; (*Brit*) **overspill** excédent *m* de population; (*Brit*) **an overspill town** ≈ une ville(-)satellite; **this office is overstaffed** il y a trop de personnel dans ce bureau; **overstate** exagérer; **overstatement** exagération *f*; **to overstay one's leave** (*Mil*) excéder la durée fixée de sa permission; (*gen*) excéder la durée fixée de son congé; **I hope I have not overstayed my welcome** j'espère que je n'ai pas abusé de votre hospitalité; **overstep** *V* **overstep**; **overstocked** *market* encombré (*with* de); *shop* approvisionné *or* fourni à l'excès (*with* en); *pond, river* surchargé de poissons; *farm* qui a un excès de cheptel; **overstrain** *person* surmener; *heart* fatiguer; *strength* abuser de; *horse, metal* forcer; *resources, reserves* user avec excès; **to overstrain o.s.** se surmener; **overstrung** *piano* à cordes croisées; (*tense*) *person* surexcité; **overstuffed** rembourré; (*St Ex*) **oversubscribed** sursouscrit; **this outing was oversubscribed** il y a eu trop d'inscriptions pour cette sortie; **overtake** *etc V* **overtake** *etc*; **overtax** (*Fin*) surimposer; (*fig*) *sb's strength, patience* abuser de; *person* surmener; **to overtax one's strength** abuser de ses forces, se surmener; **overthrow** *V* **overthrow**; **overtime** *V* **overtime**; **overtone** *V* **overtone**; (*Bridge*) **overtrick** levée *f* de mieux; (*Cards*) **overtrump** surcouper; **overturn** *V* **overturn**; **overuse** abuser de; **overvalue** surestimer; **overweight** *V* **overweight**; **overwork** *V* **overwork**; **overwrought** excédé; **overzealous** trop zélé; **to be overzealous** faire du zèle *or* de l'excès de zèle.

overage ['əʊvərɪdʒ] *n* (*US Comm*) excédent *m* (*de marchandises etc*).

overall [ˌəʊvər'ɔːl] **1** *adv view, survey, grasp* en général; *measure, paint, decorate* d'un bout à l'autre, de bout en bout.

2 ['əʊvərɔːl] *adj study, survey* global, d'ensemble; *width, length* total, hors tout; (*total*) total, complet (*f* -ète). (*Aut*) ~ **measurements** encombrement *m*.

3 ['əʊvərɔːl] *n* (*Brit*) (*woman's*) blouse *f*; (*child's*) tablier *m*, blouse; (*painter's*) blouse, sarrau *m*. (*Ind etc*) ~**s** salopette *f*, combinaison *f*, bleus *mpl* (de travail).

overbalance [ˌəʊvə'bæləns] **1** *vi [person]* perdre l'équilibre, basculer; *[object]* se renverser, basculer. **2** *vt object, boat* (faire) basculer, renverser; *person* faire perdre l'équilibre à.

overboard ['əʊvəbɔːd] *adv* (*Naut*) *jump, fall, push* à la mer; *cast* par-dessus bord. **man** ~! un homme à la mer!; (*lit, fig*) **to throw** ~ jeter par-dessus bord; **the crate was washed** ~ la caisse a été entraînée par-dessus bord par une lame; (*fig*) **to go** ~ **for sth** s'enthousiasmer *or* s'emballer* pour qch.

overcharge [ˌəʊvə'tʃɑːdʒ] **1** *vt* **(a) to** ~ **sb for sth** faire payer qch trop cher à qn, faire payer un prix excessif à qn pour qch, (*in selling*) vendre qch trop cher à qn; **you were** ~**d** vous avez payé un prix excessif, vous avez été estampé*.

(b) *electric circuit* surcharger. (*fig*) **speech** ~**d with emotion** discours débordant *or* excessivement empreint d'émotion.

2 *vi* demander un prix excessif.

overcome [ˌəʊvə'kʌm] *pret* **overcame,** *ptp* **overcome** *vt enemy* vaincre, triompher de; *temptation* surmonter; *difficulty, obstacle* venir à bout de, franchir, surmonter; *one's rage, disgust, dislike etc* maîtriser, dominer; *opposition* triompher de. **we shall** ~! nous vaincrons!; **to be** ~ **by temptation/remorse/grief** succomber à la tentation/au remords/à la douleur; **sleep overcame him** il a succombé au sommeil; ~ **with fear** paralysé par la peur, transi de peur; ~ **with cold** transi (de froid); **she was quite** ~ elle fut saisie, elle resta muette de saisissement.

overdo [ˌəʊvə'duː] *pret* **overdid** [ˌəʊvə'dɪd], *ptp* **overdone** *vt* **(a)** (*exaggerate*) *attitude, accent* exagérer, outrer; *concern, interest* exagérer; (*eat or drink to excess*) prendre *or* consommer trop de. **don't** ~ **the smoking/the drink** ne fume/bois pas trop; **to** ~ **it, to** ~ **things** (*exaggerate*) exagérer; (*in description, sentiment etc*) dépasser la mesure, forcer la note*; (*go too far*) exagérer, pousser*; (*work etc too hard*) s'éreinter, se surmener, s'épuiser; **she rather overdoes the scent** elle se met un peu trop de parfum, elle y va un peu fort* avec le parfum; **she rather overdoes the loving wife*** elle fait un peu trop la petite épouse dévouée.

(b) (*overcook*) trop cuire, faire cuire trop longtemps.

overdone [ˌəʊvə'dʌn] **1** *ptp of* **overdo. 2** *adj* (*exaggerated*) exagéré, excessif, outré; (*overcooked*) trop cuit.

overdue [ˌəʊvə'djuː] *adj train, bus* en retard; *reform* qui tarde (à être réalisé); *acknowledgement, recognition, apology* tardif; *account* arriéré, impayé, en souffrance. **the plane is 20 minutes** ~ l'avion a 20 minutes de retard; **that change is long** ~ ce changement se fait attendre depuis longtemps.

overflow ['əʊvəfləʊ] **1** *n* **(a)** (*pipe, outlet*) *[bath, sink etc]* trop-plein *m*; *[canal, reservoir etc]* déversoir *m*, dégorgeoir *m*.

(b) (*flooding*) inondation *f*; (*excess liquid*) débordement *m*, trop-plein *m*.

(c) (*excess*) *[people, population]* excédent *m*; *[objects]* excédent, surplus *m*.

2 [ˌəʊvə'fləʊ] *vt container* déborder de. **the river has** ~**ed its banks** la rivière a débordé *or* est sortie de son lit.

3 [ˌəʊvə'fləʊ] *vi* **(a)** *[liquid, river etc]* déborder; (*fig: of people, objects*) déborder. **to fill a cup to** ~**ing** remplir une tasse à ras bords; **the river** ~**ed into the fields** la rivière a inondé les champs; **the crowd** ~**ed into the next room** la foule a débordé dans la pièce voisine.

(b) *[container]* déborder (*with* de); *[room, vehicle]* regorger (*with* de). **full to** ~**ing** (*cup, jug*) plein à ras bords *or* à déborder; (*room, vehicle*) plein à craquer.

(c) (*fig: be full of*) déborder, regorger (*with* de), abonder (*with* en). **his heart was** ~**ing with love** son cœur débordait d'amour; **the town was** ~**ing with visitors** la ville regorgeait de visiteurs; **he** ~**ed with suggestions** il abondait en suggestions.

4 *cpd pipe* d'écoulement.

overgrown ['əʊvə'grəʊn] *adj* **(a) the path is** ~ **(with grass)** le chemin est envahi par l'herbe; ~ **with weeds** recouvert de mauvaises herbes, envahi par les mauvaises herbes; **wall** ~ **with ivy/moss** mur recouvert *or* tapissé de lierre/de mousse; **the garden is quite** ~ le jardin est une vraie forêt vierge *or* est complètement envahi (par la végétation).

(b) *child* qui a trop grandi, qui a grandi trop vite. **he's just an** ~ **schoolboy** il a gardé une mentalité d'écolier.

overhang ['əʊvə'hæŋ] *pret, ptp* **overhung** ['əʊvə'hʌŋ] **1** *vt [rocks, balcony]* surplomber, faire saillie au-dessus de; *[mist, smoke]* planer sur; *[danger etc]* menacer.

2 *vi [cliff, balcony]* faire saillie, être en surplomb.

3 ['əʊvəhæŋ] *n [cliff, rock, balcony, building]* surplomb *m*.

overhanging ['əʊvə'hæŋɪŋ] *adj cliff, balcony, wall* en saillie, en surplomb.

overhaul ['əʊvəhɔːl] **1** *n [vehicle, machine]* révision *f*; *[ship]* radoub *m*.

2 [ˌəʊvə'hɔːl] *vt* **(a)** (*check*) *vehicle, machine* réviser; *ship* radouber. **(b)** (*catch up with*) rattraper, gagner de vitesse; (*overtake*) dépasser.

overhead [ˌəʊvə'hed] **1** *adv* (*up above*) au-dessus (de nos têtes *etc*); (*in the sky*) dans le ciel; (*on the floor above*) (à l'étage) au-dessus, en haut.

2 ['əʊvəhed] *adj* **(a)** *wires, cables, railway* aérien. ~ **lighting** éclairage vertical.

(b) (*Comm*) ~ **charges** *or* **costs** *or* **expenses** frais généraux.

3 ['əʊvəhed] *n* (*US*)~, (*Brit*) ~**s** frais généraux.

overhear [ˌəʊvə'hɪəʳ] *pret, ptp* **overheard** [ˌəʊvə'hɜːd] *vt* (*accidentally*) surprendre, entendre par hasard; (*deliberately*) entendre. **he was overheard to say that ...** on lui a entendu dire *or* on l'a surpris à dire que ...; **I overheard your conversation** j'ai entendu votre conversation malgré moi, j'ai surpris votre conversation.

overjoyed [ˌəʊvə'dʒɔɪd] *adj* ravi, enchanté (*at, by* de, *that* que + *subj*), transporté de joie (*at, by* par). **I was** ~ **to see you** j'étais ravi *or* enchanté de vous voir; **she was** ~ **at the news** la nouvelle la transporta de joie *or* la mit au comble de la joie.

overlap ['əʊvəlæp] **1** *n* empiètement *m*, chevauchement *m*; *[tiles]* embronchement *m*.

2 [ˌəʊvə'læp] *vi* (*also* ~ **each other**) se recouvrir partiellement; *[teeth, boards]* se chevaucher; *[tiles]* se chevaucher, s'imbriquer (les uns dans les autres); (*fig*) se chevaucher. **his work and ours** ~ son travail et le nôtre se chevauchent, son travail empiète sur le nôtre; **our holidays** ~ nos vacances coïncident en partie *or* (se) chevauchent.

3 [ˌəʊvə'læp] *vt tiles, slates* enchevaucher, embroncher; *edges* dépasser, déborder de; (*fig*) empiéter sur. **to** ~ **each other** *V* **2**.

overlook [ˌəʊvə'lʊk] *vt* **(a)** (*have a view over*) *[house etc]* donner sur, avoir vue sur; *[window, door]* s'ouvrir sur, donner sur; *[castle etc]* dominer. **our garden is not** ~**ed** les voisins n'ont pas vue sur notre jardin, personne ne voit dans *or* n'a vue sur notre jardin.

(b) (*miss*) *fact, detail* oublier, laisser échapper; *problem, difficulty* oublier, négliger. **I** ~**ed that** j'ai oublié cela, cela m'a échappé; **it is easy to** ~ **the fact that ...** on oublie facilement que ...; **this plant is so small that it is easily** ~**ed** cette plante est si petite qu'il est facile de ne pas la remarquer.

(c) (*wink at, ignore*) *mistake etc* laisser passer, passer sur, fermer les yeux sur. **we'll** ~ **it this time** nous passerons là-dessus cette fois-ci, nous fermerons les yeux (pour) cette fois.

(d) (*supervise*) surveiller.

overly ['əʊvəlɪ] *adv* (*liter*) trop.

overnight ['əʊvə'naɪt] **1** *adv* (*during the night*) (pendant) la nuit; (*until next day*) jusqu'au lendemain; (*fig: suddenly*) du jour au lendemain. **to stay** ~ **with sb** passer la nuit chez qn; **we drove** ~ nous avons conduit toute la nuit; **will it keep** ~? est-ce que cela se gardera jusqu'à demain?; **the town had changed** ~ la ville avait changé du jour au lendemain.

2 *adj stay* d'une nuit; *journey* de nuit; (*fig: sudden*) soudain. ~ **bag** nécessaire *m* de voyage; (*fig*) **there had been an** ~ **change of plans** depuis la veille au soir *or* en une nuit un changement de projets était intervenu.

overpower [ˌəʊvə'paʊəʳ] *vt* (*defeat*) vaincre, subjuguer; (*subdue physically*) dominer, maîtriser; (*fig*) accabler, terrasser.

overpowering [ˌəʊvə'paʊərɪŋ] *adj strength, forces* irrésistible, écrasant; *passion* irrésistible; *smell* suffocant; *heat* accablant, suffocant. **I had an** ~ **desire to tell him everything** j'éprouvais une envie irrésistible de tout lui dire.

overreact [ˌəʊvəriː'ækt] *vi* (*also Psych*) réagir avec excès *or* excessivement. **observers considered that the government had** ~**ed** les observateurs ont trouvé excessive *or* trop forte la réaction gouvernementale.

overreaction [ˌəʊvəriː'ækʃən] *n* réaction excessive *or* disproportionnée.

override [ˌəʊvə'raɪd] *pret* **overrode** [ˌəʊvə'rəʊd], *ptp* **overridden** [ˌəʊvə'rɪdn] *vt law, duty, sb's rights* fouler aux pieds; *order, instructions* outrepasser; *decision* annuler, casser; *opinion, objection, protests, sb's wishes, claims* passer outre à, ne pas tenir compte de; *person* passer outre aux désirs de. **this fact** ~**s all others** ce fait l'emporte sur tous les autres; **this** ~**s what we decided before** ceci annule ce que nous avions décidé auparavant.

overriding [ˌəʊvə'raɪdɪŋ] *adj importance* primordial; *factor, item* prépondérant; (*Jur*) *act, clause* dérogatoire. **his** ~ **desire was to leave as soon as possible** il était dominé par le désir de partir le plus vite possible.

overrule [ˌəʊvə'ruːl] *vt judgment, decision* annuler, casser; *claim, objection* rejeter. **he was** ~**d by the chairman** la décision du président a prévalu contre lui; *V* **objection**.

overrun [ˌəʊvə'rʌn] *pret* **overran** [ˌəʊvə'ræn], *ptp* **overrun** **1** *vt* **(a)** *[rats, weeds]* envahir, infester; *[troops, army]* se rendre maître de, occuper. **the town is overrun with tourists** la ville est envahie par les touristes *or* de touristes.

(b) *line, edge etc* dépasser, aller au-delà de. (*Rail*) **to** ~ **a signal** brûler un signal; **the train overran the platform** le train s'est arrêté au-delà du quai; **to** ~ **one's time** *V* **2**.

2 *vi* (*also* ~ **one's time**) *[speaker]* dépasser le temps alloué (*by 10 minutes* de 10 minutes); *[programme, concert etc]* dépasser l'heure prévue (*by 10 minutes* de 10 minutes).

overseas ['əʊvə'siːz] **1** *adv* outre-mer; (*abroad*) à l'étranger. **he's just back from** ~ il revient ces jours-ci d'outre-mer *or* de l'étranger; **visitors from** ~ visiteurs *mpl* (venus) d'outre-mer, étrangers *mpl*.

2 *adj colony, market* d'outre-mer; *trade* extérieur (*f* -eure); *visitor* (venu) d'outre-mer, étranger; *aid* aux pays étrangers. (*Admin, Ind etc*) **he got an** ~ **posting** il a été détaché à l'étranger *or* outre-mer; (*Brit*) **Minister/Ministry of O**~ **Development** ≃ ministre *m*/ministère *m* de la Coopération.

overshoot [ˌəʊvə'ʃuːt] *pret, ptp* **overshot** [ˌəʊvə'ʃɒt] *vt* dépasser, aller au-delà de. (*lit, fig*) **to** ~ **the mark** dépasser le but; **the plane overshot the runway** l'avion a dépassé la piste d'atterrissage.

oversight ['əʊvəsaɪt] *n* **(a)** (*omission*) omission *f*, oubli *m*. **by** *or* **through an** ~ par mégarde, par inadvertance, par négligence; **it was an** ~ c'était une erreur. **(b)** (*supervision*) surveillance *f*. **under the** ~ **of** sous la surveillance de.

overstep [ˌəʊvə'step] *vt limits* dépasser, outrepasser. **to** ~ **one's authority** excéder *or* outrepasser son pouvoir; (*fig*) **to** ~ **the line** *or* **mark** exagérer (*fig*), dépasser la mesure.

overt [əʊ'vɜːt] *adj* déclaré, non déguisé.

overtake [ˌəʊvə'teɪk] *pret* **overtook** [ˌəʊvə'tʊk], *ptp* **overtaken** [ˌəʊvə'teɪkən] *vt* (*catch up*) rattraper, rejoindre; (*Brit: pass*) *car* doubler, dépasser; *competitor, runner* devancer, dépasser; *[storm, night]* surprendre; *[fate]* s'abattre sur, frapper. ~**n by fear** frappé d'effroi; **to be** ~**n by events** être dépassé par les événements; (*Brit Aut*) **'no overtaking'** 'défense de doubler'.

overthrow [ˌəʊvə'θrəʊ] *pret* **overthrew** [ˌəʊvə'θruː], *ptp* **overthrown** [ˌəʊvə'θrəʊn] **1** *vt enemy, country, empire* vaincre (définitivement); *dictator, government, system* renverser. **2** ['əʊvəθrəʊ] *n [enemy etc]* défaite *f*; *[empire, government etc]* chute *f*, renversement *m*.

overtime ['əʊvətaɪm] **1** *n* heures *fpl* supplémentaires. **I am on** ~, **I'm doing** *or* **working** ~ je fais des heures supplémentaires; **£60 per week with** ~ 60 livres par semaine heures supplémentaires comprises; **to work** ~ faire des heures supplémentaires; (*fig*) **his conscience was working** ~ sa conscience le travaillait sérieusement*; (*fig*) **we shall have to work** ~ **to regain the advantage we have lost** il nous faudra mettre les bouchées doubles pour reprendre l'avantage perdu.

2 *cpd*: **overtime pay** (rémunération *f* pour) heures *fpl* supplémentaires; **overtime work(ing)** heures *fpl* supplémentaires.

overtly [əʊ'vɜːtlɪ] *adv* ouvertement.

overtone ['əʊvətəʊn] *n* (*Mus*) harmonique *m or f*; (*fig*) note *f*, accent *m*, sous-entendu *m*. **there were** ~**s** *or* **there was an** ~ **of hostility in his voice** on sentait une note *or* des accents d'hostilité dans sa voix; **his speech had political** ~**s** il y avait des sous-entendus politiques dans son discours.

overture ['əʊvətjʊəʳ] *n* (*Mus*) ouverture *f*; (*fig*) ouverture, avance *f*. **to make** ~**s to sb** faire des ouvertures à qn; **peace** ~**s** ouvertures de paix; **friendly** ~**s** avances amicales.

overturn [ˌəʊvə'tɜːn] **1** *vt car, chair* renverser; *boat* faire chavirer *or* capoter; (*fig*) *government, plans* renverser. **2** *vi [chair]* se renverser; *[car, plane]* se retourner, capoter; *[railway coach]* se retourner, verser; *[boat]* chavirer, capoter.

overweening [ˌəʊvə'wiːnɪŋ] *adj person* outrecuidant; *pride, ambition, self-confidence* démesuré.

overweight ['əʊvə'weɪt] **1** *adj*: **to be** ~ *[person]* peser trop, avoir des kilos en trop; *[suitcase etc]* peser trop lourd, être en excès du poids réglementaire; **your luggage is** ~ vous avez un excédent de bagages; **to be 5 kilos** ~ peser 5 kilos de trop.

2 *n* poids *m* en excès; *[person]* embonpoint *m*.

overwhelm [ˌəʊvə'welm] *vt [person]* (*in war, game, argument*) écraser; *[flood, waves, sea]* submerger, engloutir; *[earth, lava, avalanche]* engloutir, ensevelir; *[emotions]* accabler, submerger; *[misfortunes]* atterrer, accabler; *[shame, praise, kindness]* confondre, rendre confus. **to** ~ **sb with questions** accabler qn de questions; **to** ~ **sb with favours** combler qn de faveurs; **I am** ~**ed by his kindness** je suis tout confus de sa bonté; **to be** ~**ed (with joy)** être au comble de la joie; **to be** ~**ed (with grief)** être accablé (par la douleur); **to be** ~**ed with work** être débordé *or* accablé *or* submergé de travail; **we have been** ~**ed with offers of help** nous avons été submergés *or* inondés d'offres d'aide; **Venice quite** ~**ed me** Venise m'a bouleversé.

overwhelming [ˌəʊvə'welmɪŋ] *adj victory, majority, defeat* écrasant; *desire, power, pressure* irrésistible; *misfortune, sorrow, heat* accablant; *bad news* affligeant, atterrant; *good news* extrêmement réjouissant; *welcome, reception* extrêmement chaleureux. **one's** ~ **impression is of heat** l'impression dominante est celle de la chaleur, on est avant tout saisi par la chaleur.

overwhelmingly [ˌəʊvə'welmɪŋlɪ] *adv win, defeat* d'une manière écrasante *or* accablante; *vote, accept, reject* en masse. **he was** ~ **polite** il était d'une politesse embarrassante.

overwork [ˌəʊvə'wɜːk] **1** *n* surmenage *m*. **to be ill from** ~ être malade d'avoir trop travaillé *or* de s'être surmené.

2 *vt person* surmener, surcharger de travail; *horse* forcer. **to** ~ **o.s.** se surmener; (*iro*) **he did not** ~ **himself** il ne s'est pas fatigué *or* foulé* *or* cassé*.

3 *vi* trop travailler, se surmener.

Ovid ['ɒvɪd] *n* Ovide *m*.

oviduct ['əʊvɪdʌkt] *n* oviducte *m*.

oviform ['əʊvɪfɔːm] *adj* oviforme.

ovine ['əʊvaɪn] *adj* ovin.

oviparous [əʊ'vɪpərəs] *adj* ovipare.

ovoid ['əʊvɔɪd] **1** *adj* ovoïde. **2** *n* forme *f* ovoïde.

ovulation [ˌəʊvjʊ'leɪʃən] *n* ovulation *f*.

ovule ['əʊvjuːl] *n* (*Bot, Zool*) ovule *m*.

ovum ['əʊvəm] *n, pl* **ova** (*Bio*) ovule *m*.

owe [əʊ] *vt* **(a)** *money etc* devoir (*to sb* à qn). **he** ~**s me £5** il me doit 5 livres; **I'll** ~ **it to you** je vous le devrai; **I still** ~ **him for the meal** je lui dois toujours le (prix du) repas.

(b) (*fig*) *respect, obedience, one's life etc* devoir (*to sb* à qn). **I** ~ **you a lunch** je vous dois un déjeuner; **to** ~ **sb a grudge** garder rancune à qn, en vouloir à qn (*for* de); **I** ~ **you thanks for ...** je ne vous ai pas encore remercié pour ... (*or* de ...); **you** ~ **him nothing** vous ne lui devez rien, vous ne lui êtes redevable de rien; **he** ~**s his talent to his father** il tient son talent de son père; **he** ~**s his failure to his own carelessness** il doit son échec à sa propre négligence; (*frm*) **to what do I** ~ **the honour of ...?** qu'est-ce qui me vaut l'honneur de ...? (*frm*); **they** ~ **it to you that they succeeded** ils vous doivent leur succès *or* d'avoir réussi, c'est grâce à vous qu'ils ont réussi; **I** ~ **it to him to do that** je lui dois (bien) de faire cela; **you** ~ **it to yourself to make a success of it** vous vous devez de réussir.

owing ['əʊɪŋ] **1** *adj* dû. **the amount** ~ **on the house** ce qui reste dû sur le prix de la maison; **a lot of money is** ~ **to me** on me doit beaucoup d'argent; **the money still** ~ **to me** la somme qu'on me doit encore, la somme qui m'est redue (*Comm*).

2 owing to *prep* à cause de, par suite de, en raison de, vu.

owl [aʊl] *n* hibou *m*. (*fig: person*) **a wise old** ~ un vieux hibou; *V* **barn** *etc*.

owlish ['aʊlɪʃ] *adj appearance* de hibou. **he gave me an** ~ **stare** il m'a regardé fixement comme un hibou.

owlishly ['aʊlɪʃlɪ] *adv look, stare* (fixement) comme un hibou.
own [əʊn] **1** *adj* propre (*before n*). **his ~ car** sa propre voiture, sa voiture à lui; **this is my ~ book** ce livre est à moi *or* m'appartient; **it's my very ~ book** c'est mon livre à moi; **I saw it with my ~ eyes** je l'ai vu de mes propres yeux; **but your ~ brother said so** mais votre propre frère l'a dit; **all my ~ work!** c'est moi qui ai fait tout (le travail) moi-même!; **it was his ~ idea** c'était son idée à lui, l'idée venait de lui; **he does his ~ cooking** il fait sa cuisine lui-même; **the house has its ~ garage** la maison a son garage particulier; **my ~ one** mon chéri, ma chérie; *V* **accord, sake[1], sweet, thing** *etc.*

2 *pron* **(a) that's my ~** c'est à moi, c'est le mien; **those are his ~** ceux-là sont à lui, ceux-là sont les siens; **my time is my ~** je suis maître *or* libre de mon temps; **it's all my ~** c'est tout à moi; **a style all his ~** un style bien à lui; **it has a charm all (of) its ~** *or* **of its ~** cela possède un charme tout particulier *or* qui lui est propre; **for reasons of his ~** pour des raisons qui lui étaient propres *or* particulières, pour des raisons personnelles; **a copy of your ~** votre propre exemplaire; **can I have it for my very ~?** puis-je l'avoir pour moi tout seul?; **it's my very ~** c'est à moi tout seul; **a house of your very ~** une maison bien à vous; **she wants a room of her ~** elle veut sa propre chambre *or* sa chambre à elle; **I have money of my ~** j'ai de l'argent à moi *or* des ressources personnelles; **he gave me one of his ~** il m'a donné un des siens, il m'en a donné un qui lui appartenait.

(b) (*phrases*) **to be on one's ~** être tout seul; **did you do it (all) on your ~?** est-ce que vous l'avez fait tout seul? *or* sans aucune aide?; **if I can get him on his ~** si je réussis à le voir seul à seul; (*fig*) **you're on your ~ now!** à toi de jouer (maintenant)!; **he's got nothing to call his ~** *or* **nothing that he can call his ~** il n'a rien à lui, il n'a rien qui lui appartienne réellement; **I'm so busy I can scarcely call my time my ~** je suis si pris que je n'ai pas de temps à moi; (*fig*) **to come into one's ~** réaliser sa destinée, trouver sa justification; **to get one's ~ back (on sb for sth)** prendre sa revanche (sur qn de qch).

3 *vt* **(a)** (*possess*) posséder. **he ~s 2 tractors** il possède 2 tracteurs; **he ~s 3 houses/3 newspapers** il est le propriétaire de 3 maisons/3 journaux; **who ~s this pen/house/paper?** à qui appartient ce stylo/cette maison/ce journal?; **he looks as if he ~s the place*** on dirait qu'il est chez lui.

(b) (*acknowledge*) avouer, reconnaître (*that* que). **I ~ it** je le reconnais, je l'avoue; **he ~ed his mistake** il a reconnu *or* avoué son erreur; **he ~ed himself defeated** il s'est avoué vaincu; **he ~ed the child as his** il a reconnu l'enfant.

4 *vi*: **to ~ to a mistake** avouer *or* reconnaître avoir commis une erreur; **he ~ed to debts of £75** il a avoué *or* reconnu avoir 75 livres de dettes; **he ~ed to having done it** il a avoué l'avoir fait *or* qu'il l'avait fait.
own up *vi* avouer, confesser, faire des aveux. **to own up to sth** admettre qch; **he owned up to having stolen it** il a avoué *or* confessé l'avoir volé *or* qu'il l'avait volé; **come on, own up!** allons, avoue!

owner ['əʊnəʳ] **1** *n* propriétaire *mf.* (*Comm*) **at ~'s risk** aux risques et périls du propriétaire; **who is the ~ of this book?** à qui appartient ce livre?; **the ~ of car number CUF 457L** le propriétaire de la voiture immatriculée CUF 457L; **all dog ~s will agree that ...** tous ceux qui ont un chien conviendront que ...; *V* **land** *etc.*

2 *cpd*: **owner-driver** conducteur *m* propriétaire; **owner-occupied house** maison occupée par son propriétaire; **owner-occupier** occupant *m* propriétaire.
ownerless ['əʊnəlɪs] *adj* sans propriétaire.
ownership ['əʊnəʃɪp] *n* possession *f*, droit *m* de propriété. (*Comm*) **'under new ~'** 'changement de propriétaire'; **under his ~ business looked up** lui propriétaire, le commerce reprit.
ownsome‡ ['əʊnsəm] *n*, **owny-o‡** ['əʊnɪəʊ] *n* (*hum*) **on one's ~** tout seul.
owt [aʊt] *n* (*Brit dial*) quelque chose.
ox [ɒks] *pl* **oxen 1** *n* bœuf *m.* **as strong as an ~** fort comme un bœuf; (*pej*) **he's a big ~*** c'est un gros balourd.

2 *cpd*: (*colour*) **oxblood** rouge foncé (*m*) *inv*; (*Geog*) **oxbow** méandre *m*; **oxbow lake** bras mort; **oxcart** char *m* à bœufs; **ox-eye daisy** marguerite *f*; **oxhide** cuir *m* de bœuf; **oxtail** queue *f* de bœuf; **oxtail soup** soupe *f* à la queue de bœuf.
oxalic [ɒk'sælɪk] *adj* oxalique.
Oxbridge ['ɒksbrɪdʒ] (*Brit*) **1** *n l'université d'Oxford ou de Cambridge (ou les deux)*. **2** *cpd education* à l'université d'Oxford ou de Cambridge; *accent, attitude* typique des universitaires *or* des anciens d'Oxford ou de Cambridge.
oxen ['ɒksən] *npl of* **ox.**
oxidation [ˌɒksɪ'deɪʃən] *n* (*Chem*) oxydation *f*, combustion *f*; (*Metal*) calcination *f.*
oxide ['ɒksaɪd] *n* oxyde *m.*
oxidize ['ɒksɪdaɪz] **1** *vt* oxyder. **2** *vi* s'oxyder.
oxyacetylene ['ɒksɪə'setɪliːn] *adj* oxyacétylénique. **~ burner** *or* **lamp** *or* **torch** chalumeau *m* oxyacétylénique; **~ welding** soudure *f* (au chalumeau) oxyacétylénique.
oxygen ['ɒksɪdʒən] **1** *n* oxygène *m.* **2** *cpd*: **oxygen bottle, oxygen cylinder** bouteille *f* d'oxygène; **oxygen mask** masque *m* à oxygène; **oxygen tank** ballon *m* d'oxygène; **oxygen tent** tente *f* à oxygène.
oxygenate [ɒk'sɪdʒəneɪt] *vt* oxygéner.
oxygenation [ˌɒksɪdʒə'neɪʃən] *n* oxygénation *f.*
oyez [əʊ'jez] *excl* oyez! (*cri du crieur public ou d'un huissier*).
oyster ['ɔɪstəʳ] **1** *n* huître *f.* (*fig*) **the world is his ~** le monde est à lui; (*fig*) **to shut up like an ~*** (en) rester muet comme une carpe.

2 *cpd industry* ostréicole, huîtrier; *knife* à huître. **oyster bed** banc *m* d'huîtres, huîtrière *f*; (*Orn*) **oystercatcher** huîtrier *m*; **oyster farm** huîtrière *f*, parc *m* à huîtres; **oyster shell** écaille *f* *or* coquille *f* d'huître.
ozone ['əʊzəʊn] *n* ozone *m.*

P

P, p [piː] *n* **(a)** (*letter*) P, p *m.* **to mind** *or* **watch one's Ps and Qs*** faire attention à ce qu'on fait *or* à ce qu'on dit, se surveiller. **(b)** (**abbr of* **penny** *or* **pence**) (nouveau) penny *m*, (nouveaux) pence *mpl.*
pa* [pɑː] *n* papa *m.*
pace [peɪs] **1** *n* **(a)** (*measure*) pas *m.* **20 ~s away** à 20 pas.

(b) (*speed*) pas *m*, allure *f.* **to go at a quick** *or* **good** *or* **smart ~** aller d'un bon pas *or* à vive allure; **to go at a slow ~** aller à pas lents *or* lentement *or* à (une) petite allure; **at a walking ~** au pas; **to quicken one's ~** hâter *or* presser le pas; **to set the ~** (*Sport*) mener le train, donner l'allure; (*fig*) donner le ton; **to keep ~ with sb** (*lit*) aller à la même allure que qn; (*fig*) marcher de pair avec qn; (*fig*) **he can't keep ~ with things** il est dépassé par les événements.

(c) to put a horse through its ~s faire parader un cheval; (*fig*) **to put sb through his ~s** mettre qn à l'épreuve, voir ce dont qn est capable.

2 *cpd*: **pacemaker** (*Med*) pacemaker *m*, stimulateur *m* cardiaque; (*Sport: also* **pace-setter**) meneur *m*, -euse *f* de train.

3 *vi* marcher à pas mesurés. **to ~ up and down** faire les cent pas.

4 *vt* **(a)** *room, street* arpenter.

(b) (*Sport*) *runner* régler l'allure de.
pace out *vt sep distance* mesurer au pas.
pacer ['peɪsəʳ] *n* (*US Sport*) meneur *m*, -euse *f* de train.
pachyderm ['pækɪdɜːm] *n* pachyderme *m.*
pacific [pə'sɪfɪk] *adj* pacifique. **the P~ (Ocean)** le Pacifique, l'océan *m* Pacifique.

pacifically [pə'sɪfɪkəlɪ] *adv* pacifiquement.
pacification [ˌpæsɪfɪ'keɪʃən] *n* (*V* **pacify**) apaisement *m*; pacification *f.*
pacifier ['pæsɪfaɪəʳ] *n* **(a)** (*dummy-teat*) tétine *f*, sucette *f.* **(b)** (*person*) pacificateur *m*, -trice *f.*
pacifism ['pæsɪfɪzəm] *n* pacifisme *m.*
pacifist ['pæsɪfɪst] *adj, n* pacifiste (*mf*).
pacify ['pæsɪfaɪ] *vt person, fears* calmer, apaiser; *country, creditors* pacifier.
pack [pæk] **1** *n* **(a)** *[goods, cotton]* balle *f*; *[pedlar]* ballot *m*; *[pack animal]* bât *m*; (*Mil*) sac *m* (d'ordonnance).

(b) (*group*) *[hounds]* meute *f*; *[wolves, thieves]* bande *f.* **~ of fools*** tas* *m or* bande* *f* d'imbéciles; **~ of lies** tissu *m* de mensonges.

(c) *[cards]* jeu *m.*

(d) (*Comm*) paquet *m.* (*US*) **~ of cigarettes** paquet de cigarettes; *V* **economy.**

(e) (*Rugby*) (*forwards*) pack *m*; (*scrum*) mêlée *f.*

(f) (*Med*) **cold/wet ~** enveloppement froid/humide.

2 *cpd*: **pack animal** bête *f* de somme; **packhorse** cheval *m* de charge; **pack ice** banquise *f*, pack *m*; **packsaddle** bât *m*; **pack trail** sentier muletier.

3 *vt* **(a)** (*put into box etc*) empaqueter, emballer; (*put into suitcase etc*) mettre dans une valise *etc*, emballer; (*Comm*) *goods etc* emballer; *wool* mettre en balles. (*Comm*) **they come ~ed in dozens** on les reçoit par paquets de douze; **~ed lunch** repas froid, panier-repas *m*; **to ~ a vase in straw** envelopper un vase dans de la paille.

(b) *(fill) trunk, suitcase* faire; *box* remplir (*with* de). **to ~ a suitcase with clothes** remplir une valise de vêtements; **to ~ one's bags** (*lit*) faire ses bagages *or* ses valises; (*fig*) plier bagage, faire son baluchon*.
(c) *(crush together) earth, objects* tasser (*into* dans); *people* entasser (*into* dans). (*fig*) **~ed like sardines** serrés comme des sardines.
(d) *(fill tightly) room, vehicle* remplir, bourrer (*with* de); (*fig*) *mind, memory* bourrer (*with* de). **the bus was ~ed (with people)** l'autobus était bondé, l'autobus regorgeait de monde; **~ed room** salle comble *or* bondée.
(e) to ~ a jury* composer un jury favorable.
(f) *[boxer, fighter]* **he ~s a good punch** il a du punch; (*US*) **to ~ a gun:** porter un revolver.
4 *vi* **(a)** (*do one's luggage*) faire ses bagages *or* sa valise; *V* **send.**
(b) these books ~ easily into that box ces livres tiennent bien dans cette boîte.
(c) *[people]* se serrer, s'entasser. **they ~ed into the hall to see him** ils se pressaient dans la salle pour le voir; **the crowd ~ed round him** la foule se pressait autour de lui.
pack away *vt sep* ranger.
pack in: **1** *vi [car, watch etc]* tomber en panne.
2 *vt sep person, job* plaquer:. **pack it in!** laisse tomber!*, écrase!:; **let's pack it in for the day** assez *or* on arrête pour aujourd'hui.
pack off* *vt sep* envoyer promener*. **to pack a child off to bed** envoyer un enfant au lit; **they packed John off to London** ils ont expédié* Jean à Londres.
pack up 1 *vi* **(a)** (*do one's luggage*) faire sa valise *or* ses bagages.
(b) (*: *give up and go*) plier bagage.
(c) (*: *break down, stop working*) tomber en panne, rendre l'âme (*hum*).
2 *vt sep* **(a)** *clothes, belongings* mettre dans une valise; *object, book* emballer, empaqueter. **he packed up his bits and pieces** il a rassemblé ses affaires; *V* **bag.**
(b) (:: *give up*) *work, school* laisser tomber*. **pack it up now!** laisse tomber!*, arrête!
package ['pækɪdʒ] **1** *n* (*parcel*) paquet *m*, colis *m*. **2** *cpd*: **package deal** marché global; (*contract*) contrat global; (*purchase*) achat *m* forfaitaire; **package holiday** vacances organisées; **package tour** voyage organisé. **3** *vt* (*Comm*) emballer.
packaging ['pækɪdʒɪŋ] *n* (*Comm*) *[goods]* conditionnement *m*; (*wrapping materials*) emballage *m*.
packer ['pækəʳ] *n* (*person*) emballeur *m*, -euse *f*; (*device*) emballeuse *f*.
packet ['pækɪt] *n* **(a)** (*parcel*) paquet *m*, colis *m*; *[needles, sweets]* sachet *m*; *[cigarettes, seeds]* paquet; (*paper bag*) pochette *f*. **that must have cost a ~!*** cela a dû coûter les yeux de la tête! **(b)** (*Naut: also* **~ boat**) paquebot *m*, malle *f*. **the Dover ~** la malle de Douvres.
packing ['pækɪŋ] **1** *n* **(a)** (*making up*) *[parcel]* emballage *m*, empaquetage *m*. **to do one's ~** faire sa valise *or* ses bagages.
(b) (*act of filling*) *[space]* remplissage *m*.
(c) (*Tech*) *[piston, joint]* garniture *f*.
(d) (*material used*) (fournitures *fpl or* matériaux *mpl* pour) emballage *m*; (*Tech*) (matière *f* pour) garnitures *fpl*.
2 *cpd*: **packing case** caisse *f* d'emballage.
pact [pækt] *n* pacte *m*, traité *m*. **France made a ~ with England** la France conclut *or* signa un pacte avec l'Angleterre; **they made a ~ not to tell their mother** ils se sont mis d'accord pour n'en rien dire à leur mère.
pad [pæd] **1** *n* **(a)** (*to prevent friction, damage*) bourrelet *m*, coussinet *m*; (*Tech*) tampon *m* (amortisseur).
(b) (*Ftbl*) protège-cheville *m inv*; (*Hockey etc*) jambière *f*; (*Fencing*) plastron *m*.
(c) (*block of paper*) bloc *m*; (*writing* ~) bloc (de papier à lettres); (*note*~) bloc-notes *m*; *V* **blotting.**
(d) (*for inking*) tampon encreur.
(e) *[rabbit]* patte *f*; *[cat, dog]* coussin charnu.
(f) (*fig*) **the ~ of footsteps** des pas feutrés.
(g) (*Space: also* **launching ~**) rampe *f* (de lancement).
(h) *[water lily]* feuille *f* de nénuphar.
(i) (*: *sanitary towel*) serviette *f* hygiénique.
(j) (:) (*bed*) pieu: *m*; (*room*) piaule: *f*.
2 *vi* aller à pas feutrés. **to ~ along** marcher à pas de loup *or* à pas feutrés; **to ~ about** aller et venir à pas de loup *or* à pas feutrés.
3 *vt* **(a)** *cushion, clothing, shoulders* rembourrer; *furniture* capitonner; *door* matelasser, capitonner. **~ded shoulders** épaules rembourrées; **~ded cell** cellule matelassée, cabanon *m*; **to ~ with cotton wool** ouater.
(b) (*fig: also* **~ out**) *speech* délayer. **he ~ded his essay (out) a good deal** il y a beaucoup de délayage *or* de remplissage dans sa dissertation, il a bien allongé la sauce* dans sa dissertation.
pad out *vt sep clothes, shoulders* rembourrer; *V also* **pad 3b.**
padding ['pædɪŋ] *n* **(a)** (*action*) rembourrage *m*. **(b)** (*material*) bourre *f*, ouate *f*; (*fig: in book, speech*) délayage *m*, remplissage *m*.
paddle ['pædl] **1** *n* **(a)** *[canoe]* pagaie *f*; *[waterwheel]* aube *f*, palette *f*.
(b) the child went for a ~ l'enfant est allé barboter *or* faire trempette.
2 *cpd*: **paddle boat, paddle steamer** bateau *m* à aubes *or* à roues; **paddle wheel** roue *f* à aubes *or* à palettes; **paddling pool** (*in park etc*) (petit) bassin *m* pour enfants; (*for garden*) petite piscine (*démontable*).
3 *vt*: **to ~ a canoe** pagayer; (*fig*) **to ~ one's own canoe** se débrouiller tout seul, diriger seul sa barque.
4 *vi* **(a)** (*walk*) (*in water*) barboter, faire trempette; (*in mud*) patauger.
(b) (*in canoe*) **to ~ up/down the river** remonter/descendre la rivière en pagayant.
paddock ['pædək] *n* enclos *m* (*pour chevaux*); (*Racing*) paddock *m*.
Paddy ['pædɪ] *n* (*surnom des Irlandais*) *dim of* **Patrick.**
paddy[1] ['pædɪ] *n* paddy *m*, riz non décortiqué. **~ field** rizière *f*.
paddy[2]* ['pædɪ] *n* (*anger*) rogne* *f*. **to be in a ~** être en rogne*.
paddy waggon: ['pædɪ,wægən] *n* (*US*) panier *m* à salade* (*fig*).
padlock ['pædlɒk] **1** *n [door, chain]* cadenas *m*; *[cycle]* antivol *m*. **2** *vt door* cadenasser; *cycle* mettre un antivol à.
padre ['pɑːdrɪ] *n* **(a)** (*Mil, Naut etc*) aumônier *m*. **(b)** (*: *clergyman*) (*Catholic*) prêtre *m*, curé *m*; (*Protestant*) pasteur *m*.
paean ['piːən] *n* péan *m*. **~s of praise** louanges *fpl*, dithyrambe *m*.
paediatric, (*US*) **pediatric** [,piːdɪ'ætrɪk] *adj department* de pédiatrie; *illness, medicine, surgery* infantile.
paediatrician, (*US*) **pediatrician** [,piːdɪə'trɪʃən] *n* pédiatre *mf*.
paediatrics, (*US*) **pediatrics** [,piːdɪ'ætrɪks] *n* (*U*) pédiatrie *f*.
pagan ['peɪgən] *adj, n* (*lit, fig*) païen(ne) *m(f)*.
paganism ['peɪgənɪzəm] *n* paganisme *m*.
page[1] [peɪdʒ] **1** *n* page *f*. **on ~ 10** (à la) page 10; **continued on ~ 20** suite (en) page 20; (*Typ*) **~ proofs** épreuves *fpl* en pages. **2** *vt book* paginer; *printed sheets* mettre en pages.
page[2] [peɪdʒ] **1** *n* (*also* **~ boy**) (*in hotel*) groom *m*, chasseur *m*; (*at court*) page *m*. **2** *vt person* faire appeler (*par un chasseur*); *[page boy]* appeler.
pageant ['pædʒənt] *n* (*historical*) spectacle *m or* reconstitution *f* historique; (*fig*) spectacle pompeux, pompe *f*. **air ~** fête *f* de l'air.
pageantry ['pædʒəntrɪ] *n* apparat *m*, pompe *f*.
paginate ['pædʒɪneɪt] *vt* paginer.
pagination [,pædʒɪ'neɪʃən] *n* pagination *f*.
pagoda [pə'gəʊdə] *n* pagode *f*.
paid [peɪd] **1** *pret, ptp of* **pay. 2** *adj gunman* à gages. **a ~ hack** un nègre (*fig*). **3** *cpd*: (*Fin*) **paid-up** libéré; **paid-up member** membre *m* qui a payé sa cotisation.
pail [peɪl] *n* seau *m*. **~(ful) of water** seau d'eau.
paillasse ['pælıæs] *n* paillasse *f*.
pain [peɪn] **1** *n* **(a)** (*U*) (*physical*) douleur *f*, souffrance *f*; (*mental*) peine *f*, (*stronger*) douleur, souffrance. **to be in (great) ~** souffrir (beaucoup); **to cause ~ to** (*physically*) faire mal à, faire souffrir; (*mentally*) faire de la peine à, peiner, affliger; **cry of ~** cri *m* de douleur.
(b) (*localized*) douleur *f*. **I have a ~ in my shoulder** j'ai une douleur à l'épaule, j'ai mal à l'épaule, mon épaule me fait mal; **to have rheumatic ~s** souffrir de rhumatismes; **where have you got a ~?** où as-tu mal?; **to give sb a ~ in the neck*** enquiquiner qn*; **he's a ~ (in the neck)*** il est casse-pieds*.
(c) (*trouble*) **~s** peine *f*; **to take ~s** *or* **to be at ~s to do sth** faire qch très soigneusement; **to take ~s over sth** se donner beaucoup de mal pour (faire) qch; **to spare no ~s** ne pas ménager ses efforts (*to do* pour faire).
(d) (††: *punishment*) peine *f*, punition *f*. (*frm*) **on ~ of death** sous peine de mort.
2 *cpd*: **painkiller** calmant *m*, analgésique *m*.
3 *vt* faire souffrir, peiner, faire de la peine à.
pained [peɪnd] *adj smile, expression, voice* froissé, peiné.
painful ['peɪnfʊl] *adj* **(a)** (*causing physical pain*) *wound* douloureux. **my hand is ~** j'ai mal à la main. **(b)** (*distressing*) *sight, duty* pénible. **it is ~ to see her now** maintenant elle fait peine à voir. **(c)** (*laborious*) *climb, task* pénible, difficile.
painfully ['peɪnfəlɪ] *adv throb* douloureusement; *walk* péniblement, avec difficulté; (*) terriblement*. **it was ~ clear that ...** il n'était que trop évident que ...; **he was ~ shy/slow** *etc* sa timidité/sa lenteur *etc* faisait peine à voir.
painless ['peɪnlɪs] *adj operation* indolore; *extraction, childbirth* sans douleur; (*fig*) *experience* inoffensif, bénin (*f* -igne). **the exam was fairly ~*** l'examen n'avait rien de bien méchant*.
painlessly ['peɪnlɪslɪ] *adv* (*lit*) sans douleur; (*: *easily*) sans peine, sans difficulté.
painstaking ['peɪnz,teɪkɪŋ] *adj work* soigné; *person* assidu, appliqué, soigneux.
painstakingly ['peɪnz,teɪkɪŋlɪ] *adv* assidûment, avec soin, laborieusement.
paint [peɪnt] **1** *n* **(a)** (*U*) peinture *f*; *V* **coat, wet.**
(b) ~s couleurs *fpl*; **box of ~s** boîte *f* de couleurs.
(c) (*pej: make-up*) peinture *f* (*pej*); *V* **grease.**
2 *cpd*: **paintbox** boîte *f* de couleurs; **paintbrush** (*Art*) pinceau *m*; (*for decorating*) brosse *f*, pinceau *m*; **paintpot** pot *m* de peinture (*lit*); **paint remover** décapant *m* (pour peinture); **paint roller** rouleau *m* à peinture; **paint spray** pulvérisateur *m* (de peinture); **paint-stripper** (*chemical*) décapant *m*; (*tool*) racloir *m*; **the paintwork** les peintures *fpl*.
3 *vt* **(a)** *wall etc* peindre, couvrir de peinture. **to ~ a wall red** peindre un mur en rouge; (*fig*) **to ~ the town red** faire la noce*, faire la bringue:.
(b) (*Art*) *picture, portrait* peindre; (*fig: describe*) dépeindre, décrire. (*fig*) **he ~ed the situation in very black colours** il brossa un tableau très sombre de la situation.
(c) (*Med*) *throat, wound* badigeonner.
4 *vi* (*Art*) peindre, faire de la peinture. **to ~ in oils** peindre à l'huile, faire de la peinture à l'huile; **to ~ in watercolours** faire de l'aquarelle.
paint in *vt sep* peindre.
paint out *vt sep* effacer d'une couche de peinture.
paint over *vt sep* repeindre.
painter[1] ['peɪntəʳ] *n* **(a)** (*Art*) peintre *m*. **portrait ~** portraitiste

mf; *V* **landscape. (b)** (*also* **house** ~) peintre *m* (en bâtiments). ~ **and decorator** peintre décorateur.
painter[2] [ˈpeɪntəʳ] *n* (*Naut*) amarre *f*.
painting [ˈpeɪntɪŋ] *n* **(a)** (*U*) (*Art*) peinture *f*; *[buildings]* décoration *f*; (*fig: description*) peinture, description *f*. ~ **in oils** peinture à l'huile; **to study** ~ étudier la peinture. **(b)** (*picture*) tableau *m*, toile *f*.
pair [pɛəʳ] **1** *n* **(a)** (*two*) *[shoes etc]* paire *f*. **these gloves make** *or* **are a** ~ ces gants font la paire; **a** ~ **of trousers** un pantalon; **a** ~ **of scissors** une paire de ciseaux; **a** ~ **of steps** un escabeau.
(b) (*man and wife*) couple *m*. **the happy** ~ l'heureux couple.
(c) *[animals]* paire *f*; (*mated*) couple *m*; *V* **carriage.**
(d) (*Brit Parl*) *un de deux députés de partis opposés qui se sont entendus pour s'absenter lors d'un vote.*
2 *vt* **(a)** *socks* appareiller.
(b) *animals* accoupler, apparier.
3 *vi* **(a)** *[glove etc]* faire la paire (*with* avec).
(b) *[animals]* s'accoupler, s'apparier.
pair off 1 *vi* **(a)** *[people]* s'arranger deux par deux.
(b) (*Brit Parl*) *s'entendre avec un adversaire pour s'absenter lors d'un vote.*
2 *vt sep objects* mettre par paires; *animals* accoupler. **John was paired off with her at the dance** on lui a attribué Jean comme cavalier.
pajamas [pəˈdʒɑːməz] *npl* (*US*) = **pyjamas.**
Paki [ˈpækɪ] (*pej*) *abbr of* **Pakistani.**
Pakistan [ˌpɑːkɪsˈtɑːn] *n* Pakistan *m*.
Pakistani [ˌpɑːkɪsˈtɑːnɪ] **1** *adj* pakistanais. **2** *n* Pakistanais(e) *m(f)*.
pal* [pæl] *n* copain* *m*, copine* *f*. **they're great** ~**s** ils sont très copains, ce sont de grands copains.
pal up‡ *vi* devenir copain(s)* (*with* avec).
palace [ˈpælɪs] *n* palais *m*. **bishop's** ~ évêché *m*, palais épiscopal; **royal** ~ palais royal.
paladin [ˈpælədɪn] *n* paladin *m*.
palaeo... [ˈpælɪəʊ] *pref* = **paleo...** .
palatable [ˈpælətəbl] *adj food* agréable au goût; (*fig: fact etc*) acceptable.
palatal [ˈpælətl] **1** *adj* palatal. (*Ling*) ~ **l** l mouillé. **2** *n* palatale *f*.
palatalize [ˈpælətəlaɪz] *vt* palataliser, mouiller.
palate [ˈpælɪt] *n* (*Anat, also fig*) palais *m*; *V* **soft.**
palatial [pəˈleɪʃəl] *adj* grandiose, magnifique, comme un palais. **this hotel is** ~ cet hôtel est un palace; **the house is** ~ la maison est un palais.
palatinate [pəˈlætɪnɪt] *n* palatinat *m*.
palaver [pəˈlɑːvəʳ] **1** *n* **(a)** (*parley*) palabre *f*. **(b)** (*) (*idle talk*) palabres *fpl*; (*fuss*) histoire *f*, affaire *f*. **what a** ~**!** quelle histoire pour si peu! **2** *vi* palabrer.
pale[1] [peɪl] **1** *adj face, person* (*naturally*) pâle; (*from sickness, fear*) blême; *colour* pâle. **to grow** ~ pâlir; ~ **blue eyes** yeux *mpl* bleu pâle; ~ **ale** *sorte f de bière blonde légère*, pale-ale *m*.
2 *cpd*: **paleface** Visage pâle *mf*; **pale-faced** (*naturally*) au teint pâle; (*from sickness, fear etc*) blême.
3 *vi [person]* pâlir, devenir blême. (*fig*) **it** ~**s into insignificance beside ...** cela perd toute importance *or* cela n'a rien d'important comparé à ... .
pale[2] [peɪl] *n* (*stake*) pieu *m*. **he's quite beyond the** ~ (*politically etc*) il est à mettre à l'index; (*socially*) il n'est absolument pas fréquentable.
paleness [ˈpeɪlnɪs] *n* pâleur *f*.
paleo... [ˈpælɪəʊ] *pref* palé(o)... .
paleographer [ˌpælɪˈɒgrəfəʳ] *n* paléographe *mf*.
paleography [ˌpælɪˈɒgrəfɪ] *n* paléographie *f*.
paleolithic [ˌpælɪəʊˈlɪθɪk] *adj* paléolithique. **the** ~ **age** l'âge *m* paléolithique *or* de la pierre taillée.
paleontology [ˌpælɪɒnˈtɒlədʒɪ] *n* paléontologie *f*.
Palestine [ˈpælɪstaɪn] *n* Palestine *f*.
Palestinian [ˌpæləsˈtɪnɪən] **1** *adj* palestinien. **2** *n* Palestinien(ne) *m(f)*.
palette [ˈpælɪt] *n* palette *f*. ~ **knife** (*Art*) couteau *m* (à palette); (*for cakes*) pelle *f* (à tarte); (*for cooking*) spatule *f*.
palfrey [ˈpɔːlfrɪ] *n* palefroi *m*.
palimpsest [ˈpælɪmpsest] *n* palimpseste *m*.
palindrome [ˈpælɪndrəʊm] *n* palindrome *m*.
paling [ˈpeɪlɪŋ] *n* (*fence*) palissade *f*; (*stake*) palis *m*.
palisade [ˌpælɪˈseɪd] *n* palissade *f*.
pall[1] [pɔːl] *vi* perdre son charme (*on sb* pour qn). **it never** ~**s on you** on ne s'en lasse jamais; **his speech** ~**ed on the audience** son discours a fini par lasser l'auditoire.
pall[2] [pɔːl] *n* drap *m* mortuaire; (*Rel*) pallium *m*; (*fig*) *[smoke]* voile *m*; *[snow]* manteau *m*. **to be a** ~**bearer** tenir les cordons du poêle.
pallet [ˈpælɪt] *n* (*mattress*) paillasse *f*; (*bed*) grabat *m*.
palliasse [ˈpælɪæs] *n* = **paillasse.**
palliate [ˈpælɪeɪt] *vt* (*Med, fig*) pallier. **palliating circumstances** circonstances atténuantes.
palliative [ˈpælɪətɪv] *adj, n* palliatif (*m*).
pallid [ˈpælɪd] *adj person, complexion* pâle, blême, blafard; *light* blafard.
pallidness [ˈpælɪdnɪs] *n*, **pallor** [ˈpæləʳ] *n* pâleur *f*; *[face]* teint blafard, pâleur.
pally‡ [ˈpælɪ] *adj* (très) copain (*f* copine)* (*with* avec).
palm[1] [pɑːm] **1** *n [hand]* paume *f*. (*fig*) **to have sb in the** ~ **of one's hand** tenir qn, faire de qn ce qu'on veut; (*fig*) **to grease** *or* **oil sb's** ~ graisser la patte* à qn. **2** *vt* (*conceal*) cacher au creux de la main; (*pick up*) subtiliser, escamoter.
palm off *vt sep sth worthless* refiler* (*on, onto* à).
palm[2] [pɑːm] **1** *n* (*also* ~ **tree**) palmier *m*; (*branch*) palme *f*; (*Rel*) rameau *m*. **2** *cpd*: **Palm Sunday** (dimanche *m* or fête *f* des) Rameaux *mpl*.
palmist [ˈpɑːmɪst] *n* chiromancien(ne) *m(f)*.
palmistry [ˈpɑːmɪstrɪ] *n* chiromancie *f*.
palmy [ˈpɑːmɪ] *adj* (*fig*) heureux; *era* florissant, glorieux, triomphant.
palpable [ˈpælpəbl] *adj* (*lit*) palpable; (*fig*) *error* évident, manifeste.
palpably [ˈpælpəblɪ] *adv* manifestement, d'une façon évidente.
palpitate [ˈpælpɪteɪt] *vi* palpiter.
palpitating [ˈpælpɪteɪtɪŋ] *adj* palpitant.
palpitation [ˌpælpɪˈteɪʃən] *n* palpitation *f*.
palsied [ˈpɔːlzɪd] *adj* (*paralyzed*) paralysé, paralytique; (*trembling*) tremblotant.
palsy [ˈpɔːlzɪ] *n* (*Med*) (*trembling*) paralysie agitante; (*paralysis*) paralysie.
paltry [ˈpɔːltrɪ] *adj amount* misérable, dérisoire; *excuse* piètre.
pampas [ˈpæmpəs] *npl* pampa(s) *f(pl)*. ~ **grass** herbe *f* des pampas.
pamper [ˈpæmpəʳ] *vt* choyer, dorloter, gâter. **to** ~ **o.s.** se dorloter.
pamphlet [ˈpæmflɪt] *n* brochure *f*; (*Literat*) opuscule *m*; (*scurrilous tract*) pamphlet *m*.
pamphleteer [ˌpæmflɪˈtɪəʳ] *n* auteur *m* de brochures; *[tracts]* pamphlétaire *mf*.
pan[1] [pæn] **1** *n* **(a)** (*Culin*) casserole *f*, poêlon *m*. **frying** ~ poêle *f*; **roasting** ~ plat *m* à rôtir; *V* **pot.**
(b) *[scales]* plateau *m*, bassin *m*; *[lavatory]* cuvette *f*; (*Miner*) batée *f*; *V* **brain, flash, salt.**
(c) (*US‡: face*) binette‡ *f*, bille *f* (de clown)‡; *V* **dead.**
2 *cpd*: **pan scrubber** tampon *m* à récurer, éponge *f* métallique.
3 *vt* **(a)** *sand* laver à la batée.
(b) (‡: *criticize harshly*) *film, book* taper sur*.
4 *vi*: **to** ~ **for gold** laver le sable aurifère (*à la batée pour en extraire de l'or*).
pan out *vi* (‡: *turn out*) tourner, se passer; (*turn out well*) bien tourner, réussir. **it all panned out in the long run** ça s'est (bien) arrangé en fin de compte; **events didn't pan out as he'd hoped** les événements n'ont pas tourné comme il l'avait espéré.
pan[2] [pæn] **1** *vi* (*Cine, TV*) *[camera]* faire un panoramique, panoramiquer. **2** *vt*: **to** ~ **the camera** panoramiquer.
pan... [pæn] *pref* pan... .
panacea [ˌpænəˈsɪə] *n* panacée *f*.
panache [pəˈnæʃ] *n* panache *m*.
Pan-African [ˈpænˈæfrɪkən] *adj* panafricain.
Panama [ˈpænəˌmɑː] *n* Panama *m*. ~ **Canal** canal *m* de Panama; **p**~ **(hat)** panama *m*.
Panamanian [ˌpænəˈmeɪnɪən] **1** *adj* panamien *or* panaméen. **2** *n* Panamien(ne) *m(f) or* Panaméen(ne) *m(f)*.
Pan-American [ˈpænəˈmerɪkən] *adj* panaméricain. ~ **Union** Union panaméricaine.
Pan-Americanism [ˈpænəˈmerɪkənɪzəm] *n* panaméricanisme *m*.
Pan-Asian [ˈpænˈeɪʃən] *adj* panasiatique.
Pan-Asianism [ˈpænˈeɪʃənɪzəm] *n* panasiatisme *m*.
pancake [ˈpænkeɪk] **1** *n* **(a)** (*Culin*) crêpe *f*. **as flat as a** ~ plat comme une galette. **(b)** (*Aviat: also* ~ **landing**) atterrissage *m* à plat. **2** *cpd*: (*Elec*) **pancake coil** galette *f*; **Pancake Day, Pancake Tuesday** mardi gras. **3** vi (*Aviat*) se plaquer, atterrir à plat.
panchromatic [ˈpænkrəʊˈmætɪk] *adj* panchromatique.
pancreas [ˈpæŋkrɪəs] *n* pancréas *m*.
pancreatic [ˌpæŋkrɪˈætɪk] *adj* pancréatique.
panda [ˈpændə] *n* panda *m*. (*Brit*) ~ **car** ≈ voiture *f* pie *inv* (*de la police*).
pandemic [pænˈdemɪk] **1** *adj* universel. **2** *n* pandémie *f*.
pandemonium [ˌpændɪˈməʊnɪəm] *n* tohu-bohu *m*, chahut *m* (monstre). **it's sheer** ~**!** c'est un véritable charivari!, quel tohu-bohu!
pander [ˈpændəʳ] *vi*: **to** ~ **to** *person* se prêter aux exigences de; *whims, desires* se plier à; *tastes, weaknesses* flatter bassement.
Pandora [pænˈdɔːrə] *n*: ~**'s box** boîte *f* de Pandore.
pane [peɪn] *n* vitre *f*, carreau *m*.
panegyric [ˌpænɪˈdʒɪrɪk] *adj, n* panégyrique (*m*).
panel [ˈpænl] **1** *n* **(a)** *[door, wall]* panneau *m*; *[ceiling]* caisson *m*.
(b) (*Aut, Aviat: also* **instrument** ~) tableau *m* de bord.
(c) (*Dress*) pan *m*.
(d) (*Jur*) (*list*) liste *f* (des jurés); (*jury*) jury *m*. (*Admin, Scol etc*) ~ **of examiners** jury (d'examinateurs).
(e) (*Brit Med*) **to be on a doctor's** ~ être inscrit sur le registre d'un médecin conventionné.
(f) (*Rad, TV etc: group of speakers*) (*gen*) invités *mpl*; (*for debate*) invités, experts *mpl*, tribune *f*; (*for game*) jury *m*.
2 *cpd*: (*Rad, TV etc*) **panel discussion** réunion-débat *f*; **panel doctor** médecin conventionné; (*Rad, TV*) **panel game** jeu radiophonique *or* télévisé; **panel patient** malade *mf* assuré(e) social(e).
3 *vt surface* plaquer; *room, wall* recouvrir de panneaux *or* de boiseries, lambrisser. ~**led door** porte *f* à panneaux; **oak-**~**led** lambrissé de chêne, garni de boiseries de chêne.
paneling [ˈpænəlɪŋ] *n* (*US*) = **panelling.**
panelist [ˈpænəlɪst] *n* (*Rad, TV etc: V* **panel 1f**) invité(e) *m(f)*, expert *m*; membre *m* d'une tribune *or* d'un jury.
panelling, (*US*) **paneling** [ˈpænəlɪŋ] *n* (*U*) panneaux *mpl*, lambris *m*, boiseries *fpl*.
pang [pæŋ] *n* serrement *m or* pincement *m* de cœur. ~**s of death** affres *fpl or* angoisses de la mort; ~ **of conscience** remords *mpl* de conscience; **he saw her go without a** ~ il l'a vue partir sans regret, cela ne lui a fait ni chaud ni froid* de la voir partir; **to**

feel the ~s of hunger commencer à ressentir des tiraillements d'estomac.

panhandle ['pænhændl] **1** *n* manche *m* (de casserole); (*US fig: strip of land*) enclave *f*. **2** *vi* (*US*:) mendier. **3** *vt* (*US*:) demander l'aumône à.

panic ['pænɪk] **1** *n* (*U*) panique *f*, terreur *f*, affolement *m*. **to throw a crowd into a ~** semer la panique dans une foule; **to get into a ~** s'affoler, paniquer*; **to throw sb into a ~** affoler *or* paniquer* qn.

2 *cpd fear* panique; *decision* de panique. **it was panic stations**: ça a été la panique générale*; **panic-stricken** affolé, pris de panique, paniqué*.

3 *vi* s'affoler, être pris de panique, paniquer*. **don't ~!*** pas d'affolement!

4 *vt crowd* jeter *or* semer la panique dans; *person* affoler. **she was ~ked into burning the letter** affolée elle brûla la lettre.

panicky ['pænɪkɪ] *adj report, newspaper* alarmiste; *decision, action* de panique; *person* qui s'affole facilement, paniquard*.

panjandrum [pæn'dʒændrəm] *n* grand ponte*, gros bonnet*, gros manitou*.

pannier ['pænɪəʳ] *n* panier *m*, corbeille *f*; *[pack animal]* panier de bât; (*on motorcycle etc: also* **~ bag**) sacoche *f*.

panoply ['pænəplɪ] *n* panoplie *f*.

panorama [,pænə'rɑːmə] *n* panorama *m*.

panoramic [,pænə'ræmɪk] *adj* panoramique. (*Cine*) **~ screen** écran *m* panoramique; **~ view** vue *f* panoramique.

pansy ['pænzɪ] *n* **(a)** (*Bot*) pensée *f*. **(b)** (:*pej*) tante: *f*, tapette: *f*.

pant [pænt] **1** *vi* **(a)** (*gasp*) *[person]* haleter; *[animal]* battre du flanc, haleter. **to ~ for breath** chercher (à reprendre) son souffle; **the boy/the dog ~ed along after him** le garçon/le chien s'essoufflait à sa suite; **he ~ed up the hill** il grimpa la colline en haletant.

(b) (*throb*) *[heart]* palpiter.

2 *vt* (*also* **~ out**) *words, phrases* dire d'une voix haletante, dire en haletant.

3 *n* (*V* 1) halètement *m*; palpitation *f*.

pant after *vt fus* (*liter*) *knowledge etc* aspirer à.

pant for *vt fus* **(a)** (*liter*) = **pant after**.

(b) (:) *cigarette, drink* mourir d'envie de.

pantaloon [,pæntə'luːn] *n* **(a)** **(pair of) ~s** culotte *f*. **(b)** (*Theat*) **P~** Pantalon *m*.

pantechnicon [pæn'teknɪkən] *n* (*van*) grand camion de déménagement; (*warehouse*) entrepôt *m* (*pour meubles*).

pantheism ['pænθiːɪzəm] *n* panthéisme *m*.

pantheist ['pænθiːɪst] *n* panthéiste *mf*.

pantheistic [,pænθiː'ɪstɪk] *adj* panthéiste.

pantheon ['pænθɪən] *n* panthéon *m*.

panther ['pænθəʳ] *n* panthère *f*; *V* **black**.

panties* ['pæntɪz] *npl* slip *m* (*de femme*).

panting ['pæntɪŋ] *n [person, animal]* essoufflement *m*, halètement *m*; *[heart]* palpitation *f*.

pantograph ['pæntəgrɑːf] *n* (*Rail, Tech*) pantographe *m*.

pantomime ['pæntəmaɪm] *n* **(a)** (*Brit Theat: show*) spectacle *m* de Noël (*tiré d'un conte de fée*). **(b)** (*mime*) pantomime *f*, mime *m*. **in ~** en mimant. **(c)** (*fig pej*) comédie *f* (*fig pej*).

pantry ['pæntrɪ] *n* (*in hotel, mansion*) office *f*; (*in house*) garde-manger *m inv*.

pants [pænts] *npl* **(a)** (*underwear*) (*for women*) culotte *f*, slip *m*; (*for men*) caleçon *m*, slip. **(b)** (*: *trousers*) pantalon *m*. **she's the one who wears the ~*** c'est elle qui porte la culotte*; **to catch sb with his ~ down**: prendre qn au dépourvu.

panzer ['pæntsəʳ] *n* panzer *m*. **~ division** division blindée (allemande).

pap[1] [pæp] *n* (*Culin*) bouillie *f*.

pap[2]†† [pæp] *n* (*breast*) mamelon *m*.

papa [pə'pɑː] *n* papa *m*.

papacy ['peɪpəsɪ] *n* papauté *f*.

papal ['peɪpəl] *adj* papal; *bull, legate* du Pape. **~ nuncio** nonce *m* du Pape.

paper ['peɪpəʳ] **1** *n* **(a)** (*U*) papier *m*. **a piece of ~** (*odd bit*) un bout *or* un morceau de papier; (*sheet*) une feuille de papier; (*document etc*) un papier; **old ~** paperasses *fpl*; (*frm*) **to commit to ~** coucher (par écrit); **to put sth down on ~** mettre qch par écrit; **it's a good plan on ~** c'est un bon plan sur le papier; *V* **brown, carbon, rice** *etc*.

(b) (*newspaper*) journal *m*. **to write for the ~s** faire du journalisme; **it was in the ~s yesterday** c'était dans les journaux hier; **I saw it in the ~** je l'ai vu dans le journal; *V* **illustrate** *etc*.

(c) (*document: gen pl*) **~s** pièces *fpl*, documents *mpl*, papiers *mpl*; **show me your (identity) ~s** montrez-moi vos papiers (d'identité); (*Mil*) **(call-up) ~s** ordre *m* d'appel; **ship's ~s** papiers de bord.

(d) (*Scol, Univ*) (*set of exam questions*) (sujets *mpl* de l')épreuve *f* (écrite); (*student's written answers*) copie *f*. **geography ~** épreuve de géographie; **she did a good ~ in French** elle a rendu une bonne copie de français.

(e) (*scholarly work*) article *m*, exposé *m*. **to write a ~ on** écrire un article sur; **to give** *or* **read a ~ on** faire une communication sur.

2 *cpd doll, towel* en papier, de papier. **paperback** livre broché, (*cheaper*) livre de poche; **paperback(ed) edition** édition brochée *or* de poche; **paper bag** sac *m* en papier, (*small*) pochette *f*; **paperbound** = **paperbacked**; **paperboy** (*delivering*) (petit) livreur *m* de journaux; (*selling*) vendeur *m* de journaux; **paper chain** chaîne *f* de papier; **paper chase** rallye-papier *m*; **paper clip** trombone *m*; (*staple*) agrafe *f*; (*bulldog clip*) pince *f*; **paper currency** billets *mpl* (de banque); **paper fastener** attache *f* métallique (*à tête*); (*clip*) trombone *m*; **paper handkerchief** mouchoir *m* en papier; **paper industry** industrie *f* du papier; **paper knife** coupe-papier *m inv*; **paper lantern** lampion *m*; **paper mill** (usine *f* de) papeterie *f*; **paper money** papier-monnaie *m*; **paper shop*** marchand *m* de journaux; **paperweight** presse-papiers *m inv*; **paper work** écritures *fpl*, paperasserie *f* (*pej*).

3 *vt room* tapisser.

paper over *vt fus crack etc* recouvrir de papier. (*fig*) **as the situation deteriorated they tried to paper over the cracks** à mesure que la situation se dégradait ils essayaient de la replâtrer (*fig*).

papery ['peɪpərɪ] *adj* (fin) comme du papier.

papist ['peɪpɪst] (*pej*) **1** *n* papiste *mf* (*pej*). **2** *adj* de(s) papiste(s) (*pej*).

papistry ['peɪpɪstrɪ] *n* (*pej*) papisme *m* (*pej*).

papoose [pə'puːs] *n* bébé *m* peau-rouge.

paprika ['pæprɪkə] *n* paprika *m*.

papyrus [pə'paɪərəs] *n, pl* **papyri** [pə'paɪəraɪ] papyrus *m inv*.

par[1] [pɑːʳ] *n* **(a)** (*equality of value*) égalité *f*, pair *m*; (*Fin*) [*currency*] pair. **to be on a ~ with** aller de pair avec, être l'égal de, être au niveau de; (*Fin*) **above/below ~** au-dessus/au-dessous du pair; (*Fin*) **at ~** au pair.

(b) (*average*) moyenne *f*. (*fig*) **to feel below ~** ne pas se sentir en forme.

(c) (*Golf*) normale *f* du parcours.

par[2]* [pɑːʳ] *n* (*Press*) *abbr of* **paragraph**.

para* ['pærə] *n abbr of* **paragraph 1a**.

para... ['pærə] *pref* para... .

parable ['pærəbl] *n* parabole *f*. **in ~s** par paraboles.

parabola [pə'ræbələ] *n* parabole *f* (*Math*).

parabolic [,pærə'bɒlɪk] *adj* parabolique.

parachute ['pærəʃuːt] **1** *n* parachute *m*. **2** *cpd cords* de parachute. **parachute drop** parachutage *m*; **parachute jump** saut *m* en parachute; **parachute landing** = **parachute drop**. **3** *vi* descendre en parachute. **4** *vt* parachuter.

parachutist ['pærəʃuːtɪst] *n* parachutiste *mf*.

parade [pə'reɪd] **1** *n* **(a)** (*Mil*) (*procession*) défilé *m*; (*ceremony*) parade *f*, revue *f*. **to be on ~** (*drilling*) être à l'exercice; (*for review*) défiler.

(b) fashion ~ présentation *f* de collections; **mannequin ~** défilé *m* de mannequins.

(c) (*fig: exhibition*) étalage *m*. **to make a ~ of one's wealth** faire étalage de sa richesse.

(d) (*road*) boulevard *m* (*souvent au bord de la mer*).

(e) (*Mil: also* **~ ground**) terrain *m* de manœuvres.

2 *vt troops* faire défiler; (*fig: display*) faire étalage de, afficher.

3 *vi* (*Mil etc*) défiler.

parade about*, **parade around*** *vi* se balader*, circuler*. **don't parade about with nothing on!** ne te promène pas *or* ne te balade* pas tout nu!

paradigm ['pærədaɪm] *n* (*Ling etc*) paradigme *m*.

paradigmatic [,pærədɪg'mætɪk] *adj* (*Ling*) paradigmatique.

paradise ['pærədaɪs] *n* paradis *m*. (*fig*) **earthly ~** paradis terrestre; **bird of ~** oiseau *m* de paradis; *V* **fool**[1].

paradox ['pærədɒks] *n* paradoxe *m*.

paradoxical [,pærə'dɒksɪkəl] *adj* paradoxal.

paradoxically [,pærə'dɒksɪkəlɪ] *adv* paradoxalement.

paraffin ['pærəfɪn] **1** *n* (*Chem*) paraffine *f*. (*fuel*) **~ (oil)** pétrole *m* (lampant); (*Med*) **liquid ~** huile *f* de paraffine. **2** *cpd*: **paraffin lamp** lampe *f* à pétrole; **paraffin wax** paraffine *f*.

paragon ['pærəgən] *n* modèle *m or* parangon *m* de vertu. **~ of politeness** modèle de politesse.

paragraph ['pærəgrɑːf] **1** *n* **(a)** paragraphe *m*, alinéa m. **'new ~'** 'à la ligne'; **to begin a new ~** aller à la ligne. **(b)** (*newspaper item*) entrefilet *m*. **2** *cpd*: (*Typ*) **paragraph mark** pied *m* de mouche. **3** *vt* diviser en paragraphes *or* en alinéas.

Paraguay ['pærəgwaɪ] *n* Paraguay *m*.

Paraguayan [,pærə'gwaɪən] **1** *adj* paraguayen. **2** *n* Paraguayen(ne) *m(f)*.

parakeet ['pærəkiːt] *n* perruche *f* (ondulée).

parallel ['pærəlel] **1** *adj* **(a)** (*Math etc*) parallèle (*with, to* à). **the road runs ~ to the railway** la route est parallèle à la voie de chemin de fer; **~ bars** barres *fpl* parallèles.

(b) (*fig*) analogue, parallèle (*with, to* à).

2 *n* **(a)** (*Geog*) parallèle *m*.

(b) (*Math*) (ligne *f*) parallèle *f*.

(c) (*fig*) parallèle *m*, comparaison *f*. **to draw a ~ between** établir *or* faire un parallèle entre; **he/she is without ~** il/elle est sans pareil(le).

3 *vt* (*Math*) être parallèle à; (*fig*) (*find equivalent to*) trouver un équivalent à; (*be ~ to*) être équivalent à.

parallelism ['pærəlelɪzəm] *n* (*Math, fig*) parallélisme *m*.

parallelogram [,pærə'leləugræm] *n* parallélogramme *m*.

paralysis [pə'ræləsɪs] *n* **(a)** (*Med*) paralysie *f*, *V* **creeping, infantile**. **(b)** (*fig*) *[traffic etc]* immobilisation *f*.

paralytic [,pærə'lɪtɪk] **1** *adj* **(a)** (*Med*) paralytique. **(b)** (*Brit*: *drunk*) ivre mort. **2** *n* paralytique *mf*.

paralyzation [,pærəlaɪ'zeɪʃən] *n* immobilisation *f*.

paralyze ['pærəlaɪz] *vt* (*Med*) paralyser; (*fig*) *person* paralyser, pétrifier, méduser; *traffic, communications* paralyser. **his arm is ~d** il est paralysé du bras; **~d with fear** paralysé *or* transi de peur.

paramilitary [,pærə'mɪlɪtərɪ] *adj* paramilitaire.

paramount ['pærəmaunt] *adj chief* souverain. **of ~ importance** d'une suprême importance.

paramour ['pærəmuəʳ] *n* amant *m*; maîtresse *f*.

paranoia [,pærə'nɔɪə] *n* paranoïa *f*.

paranoiac [,pærə'nɔɪɪk] *adj, n* paranoïaque (*mf*).

paranoid ['pærənɔɪd] *adj* paranoïde.

parapet ['pærəpɪt] *n* **(a)** *[bridge etc]* parapet *m*, garde-fou *m*. **(b)** (*Mil*) parapet *m*.

paraphernalia ['pærəfə'neɪlɪə] *npl* (*belongings, also for hobbies, sports etc*) attirail *m*; (*bits and pieces*) bazar* *m*.
paraphrase ['pærəfreɪz] 1 *n* paraphrase *f*. 2 *vt* paraphraser.
paraplegia [ˌpærə'pli:dʒə] *n* paraplégie *f*.
paraplegic [ˌpærə'pli:dʒɪk] *adj, n* paraplégique (*mf*).
paras* ['pærəz] *npl* (*abbr of* **paratroops**) paras* *mpl*.
parasite ['pærəsaɪt] *n* (*Bot, Zool, fig*) parasite *m*.
parasitic(al) [ˌpærə'sɪtɪk(əl)] *adj* **(a)** parasite (*on* de). **(b)** (*Med*) *disease* parasitaire.
parasitism ['pærəsɪtɪzəm] *n* parasitisme *m*.
parasitology [ˌpærəsɪ'tɒlədʒɪ] *n* parasitologie *f*.
parasol [ˌpærə'sɒl] *n* ombrelle *f*; (*over table etc*) parasol *m*.
paratrooper ['pærətru:pə^r] *n* parachutiste *m* (*soldat*).
paratroops ['pærətru:ps] *npl* parachutistes *mpl* (*soldats*).
paratyphoid ['pærə'taɪfɔɪd] *n* paratyphoïde *f*.
parboil ['pɑ:bɔɪl] *vt* (*Culin*) faire bouillir *or* faire cuire à demi.
parcel ['pɑ:sl] 1 *n* **(a)** (*package*) colis *m*, paquet *m*.
(b) (*portion*) *[land]* parcelle *f*; *[shares]* paquet *m*; *[goods]* lot *m*; *V* **part**.
(c) (*fig*) ~ **of lies** tas *m* de mensonges; ~ **of liars/of fools** tas* *or* bande* *f* de menteurs/de sots.
2 *cpd*: **parcel bomb** paquet piégé; **parcel net** filet *m* à bagages; **parcel office** bureau *m* de messageries; **parcel post** service *m* de colis postaux, service de messageries; **to send sth by parcel post** envoyer qch par colis postal.
3 *vt* (*also* ~ **up**) *object, purchases* emballer, empaqueter, faire un paquet de.
parcel out *vt sep* distribuer; *inheritance* partager; *land* lotir.
parch [pɑ:tʃ] *vt* **(a)** *crops, land* dessécher, brûler. **(b)** *person* altérer. **to be ~ed with thirst** avoir une soif dévorante; **to be ~ed*** mourir de soif*. **(c)** (*toast*) griller légèrement.
parchment ['pɑ:tʃmənt] *n* parchemin *m*. **~-like** parcheminé; ~ **paper** papier-parchemin *m*.
pardon ['pɑ:dn] 1 *n* **(a)** (*U*) pardon *m*; *V* **beg**.
(b) (*Rel*) indulgence *f*.
(c) (*Jur*: *also* **free** ~) grâce *f*. **letter of** ~ lettre *f* de grâce; **general** ~ amnistie *f*.
2 *vt* **(a)** *mistake, person* pardonner. **to ~ sb for sth** pardonner qch à qn; ~ **me for troubling you** pardonnez-moi de vous déranger.
(b) (*Jur*) gracier; amnistier.
3 *excl* (*apologizing*) pardon!, excusez-moi!; (*not hearing*) comment?, vous dites?
pardonable ['pɑ:dnəbl] *adj mistake* pardonnable; (*Jur*) graciable.
pardonably ['pɑ:dnəblɪ] *adv* de façon bien excusable *or* bien pardonnable.
pare [pɛə^r] *vt* **(a)** *fruit* peler, éplucher; *nails* rogner, couper. **(b)** (*reduce*: *also* ~ **down**) *expenses* réduire.
parent ['pɛərənt] 1 *n* père *m or* mère *f*. **his ~s** ses parents *mpl*, son père et sa mère, ses père et mère.
2 *cpd*: **the parent animals, the parent birds** *etc* les parents *mpl*; (*Comm, Fin*) **parent company** maison *f or* société *f* mère; (*Scol*) **parent-teacher association** association *f* des parents d'élèves et des professeurs; **parent tree** souche *f*.
parentage ['pɛərəntɪdʒ] *n* naissance *f*, lignée *f*, origine *f*. **of unknown** ~ de parents inconnus.
parental [pə'rentl] *adj* des parents, parental (*frm*).
parenthesis [pə'renθɪsɪs] *n, pl* **parentheses** [pə'renθɪsi:z] parenthèse *f*. **in** ~ entre parenthèses.
parenthetic(al) [ˌpærən'θetɪk(əl)] *adj* (placé) entre parenthèses.
parenthetically [ˌpærən'θetɪkəlɪ] *adv* par parenthèse, entre parenthèses.
parenthood ['pɛərənthʊd] *n* condition *f* de parent(s), paternité *f or* maternité *f*. **the joys of** ~ les joies de la paternité *or* de la maternité.
pariah ['pærɪə] *n* paria *m*.
paring ['pɛərɪŋ] *n* **(a)** (*V* **pare**) action *f* d'éplucher *or* de peler *etc*; *V* **cheese**. **(b)** **~s** *[fruit, vegetable]* épluchures *fpl*, pelures *fpl*; *[nails]* rognures *fpl*; *[metal]* cisaille *f*.
pari passu ['pærɪ'pæsu:] *adv* (*liter*) de pair.
Paris ['pærɪs] *n* Paris; *V* **plaster**.
parish ['pærɪʃ] 1 *n* (*Rel*) paroisse *f*; (*civil*) commune *f*.
2 *cpd*: **parish church** église paroissiale; **parish council** ≃ conseil municipal; **parish hall** salle paroissiale *or* municipale; **parish priest** (*Catholic*) curé *m*; (*Protestant*) pasteur *m*; (*pej*) **parish-pump** *subject* d'intérêt purement local; *point of view* borné; **parish-pump mentality/politics** esprit *m*/politique *f* de clocher; **parish register** registre paroissial; **parish school** école communale.
parishioner [pə'rɪʃənə^r] *n* paroissien(ne) *m(f)*.
Parisian [pə'rɪzɪən] 1 *adj* parisien. 2 *n* Parisien(ne) *m(f)*.
parity ['pærɪtɪ] *n* égalité *f*, parité *f*; (*Fin*) parité. (*Fin*) **exchange at** ~ change *m* au pair *or* à (la) parité.
park [pɑ:k] 1 *n* (*public*) jardin public, parc *m*; *[country house]* parc; *V* **car, national, safari**.
2 *cpd*: **park keeper** gardien *m* de parc; (*US*) **parkway** avenue *f*.
3 *vt* garer, parquer. **he was ~ed near the theatre** il était garé *or* parqué près du théâtre; **to ~ the car** garer la voiture, se garer.
4 *vi* stationner, se garer. **I was ~ing when I caught sight of him** j'étais en train de me garer quand je l'aperçus; **do not ~ here** ne stationnez pas ici.
parka ['pɑ:kə] *n* parka *m*.
parking ['pɑ:kɪŋ] 1 *n* stationnement *m*. '~' 'parking', 'stationnement autorisé'; **'no ~'** 'défense de stationner', 'stationnement interdit'; ~ **is very difficult** il est très difficile de trouver à se garer.
2 *cpd*: **parking attendant** gardien *m* de parking, gardien de parc de stationnement; **parking bay** lieu *m* de stationnement (autorisé); **parking lights** feux *mpl* de position; (*US*) **parking lot** parking *m*, parc *m* de stationnement; **parking meter** parcomètre *m*; **parking place** lieu *m or* créneau *m* de stationnement; **I couldn't find a parking place** je n'ai pas pu trouver à me garer; **parking ticket** P.-V.* *m*, procès-verbal *m*.
parky‡ ['pɑ:kɪ] *adj* (*Brit*) **it's** ~ il fait frisquet*.
parlance ['pɑ:ləns] *n* langage *m*, parler *m*. **in common** ~ en langage courant *or* ordinaire *or* de tous les jours.
parlay ['pɑ:lɪ] *vt* (*US*) (*Betting*) réemployer (*les gains d'un précédent pari et le pari originel*); (*fig*) *talent, inheritance* faire fructifier.
parley ['pɑ:lɪ] 1 *n* conférence *f*, pourparlers *mpl*; (*Mil*) pourparlers. 2 *vi* (*also Mil*) parlementer (*with* avec); (*more formally*) entrer *or* être en pourparlers (*with* avec).
parliament ['pɑ:ləmənt] *n* **(a)** (*Brit*) **P~** (*institution*) Parlement *m*, Chambres *fpl*; (*building*) Parlement; (*Hist*) Parlement. **to go into** *or* **enter** ~ se faire élire député, entrer au Parlement; *V* **house, member**. **(b)** parlement *m*.
parliamentarian [ˌpɑ:ləmen'tɛərɪən] 1 *n* **(a)** (*Parl*) parlementaire *mf*, membre *m* du Parlement. **(b)** (*Brit Hist*) parlementaire *mf*. 2 *adj* (*Brit Hist*) parlementaire.
parliamentary [ˌpɑ:lə'mentərɪ] *adj business, language, behaviour* parlementaire. ~ **election** élection législative; (*Brit*) **P~ Secretary to the Minister of Transport/of Defence** *etc* ≃ chef *m* de Cabinet du ministre des Transports/de la Défense *etc*.
parlour, (US) parlor ['pɑ:lə^r] 1 *n* (*in house*:†) petit salon; (*in convent*) parloir *m*; (*in bar*) arrière-salle *f*.
2 *cpd*: (*US Rail*) **parlor car** wagon-salon *m*; **parlour game** jeu *m* de salon *or* de société; **parlourmaid** femme *f* de chambre (*chez des particuliers*).
parlous ['pɑ:ləs] *adj* (*liter, frm*, †) précaire, périlleux, alarmant.
Parma ['pɑ:mə] *n* Parme. ~ **ham** jambon *m* de Parme; ~ **violet** violette *f* de Parme.
Parmesan [ˌpɑ:mɪ'zæn] *n* (*cheese*) parmesan *m*.
Parnassus [pɑ:'næsəs] *n* Parnasse *m*.
parochial [pə'rəʊkɪəl] *adj* (*Rel*) paroissial; (*fig pej*) de clocher.
parochialism [pə'rəʊkɪəlɪzəm] *n* esprit *m* de clocher.
parodist ['pærədɪst] *n* parodiste *mf*.
parody ['pærədɪ] 1 *n* (*lit, fig*) parodie *f*. 2 *vt* parodier.
parole [pə'rəʊl] 1 *n* (*Mil etc*) parole *f* d'honneur; (*Jur*) liberté conditionnelle. **on** ~ (*Mil*) sur parole; (*Jur*) en liberté conditionnelle; (*Jur*) **to release sb on** ~ mettre qn en liberté conditionnelle; (*Jur*) **to break** ~ se rendre coupable d'un délit entraînant la révocation de sa mise en liberté conditionnelle.
2 *vt prisoner* mettre en liberté conditionnelle.
paroquet ['pærəkɪt] *n* = **parakeet**.
paroxysm ['pærəksɪzəm] *n* (*Med*) paroxysme *m*; (*fig*) *[grief, pain]* paroxysme *m*; *[anger]* accès *m*. **in a ~ of delight** dans un transport de joie; ~ **of tears/laughter** crise *f* de larmes/de fou rire.
parquet ['pɑ:keɪ] 1 *n* **(a)** parquet *m*. (*U*) ~ **flooring** parquet.
(b) (*US Theat*) parterre *m*. 2 *vt* parqueter.
parquetry ['pɑ:kɪtrɪ] *n* parquetage *m*, parqueterie *f*.
parricidal ['pærɪsaɪdl] *adj* parricide.
parricide ['pærɪsaɪd] *n* (*act*) parricide *m*; (*person*) parricide *mf*.
parrot ['pærət] 1 *n* (*Orn*) perroquet *m*, perruche *f*; (*fig*) perroquet. 2 *cpd*: **parrot disease** psittacose *f*; **parrot fashion** comme un perroquet; **parrot fever** = **parrot disease**; **parrot fish** perroquet *m* de mer.
parry ['pærɪ] 1 *vt blow* parer, détourner; *question* éluder; *attack* parer; *difficulty* tourner, éviter. 2 *n* (*Sport*) parade *f*.
parse [pɑ:z] *vt* faire l'analyse grammaticale de.
parsec ['pɑ:sek] *n* parsec *m*.
parsimonious [ˌpɑ:sɪ'məʊnɪəs] *adj* parcimonieux.
parsimoniously [ˌpɑ:sɪ'məʊnɪəslɪ] *adv* avec parcimonie, parcimonieusement.
parsimony ['pɑ:sɪmənɪ] *n* parcimonie *f*.
parsley ['pɑ:slɪ] *n* persil *m*. ~ **sauce** sauce persillée.
parsnip ['pɑ:snɪp] *n* panais *m*.
parson ['pɑ:sn] *n* (*Church of England etc*) pasteur *m*; (*clergyman in general*) prêtre *m*, ecclésiastique *m*. (*Culin*) **~'s nose** croupion *m*.
parsonage ['pɑ:sənɪdʒ] *n* presbytère *m*.
part [pɑ:t] 1 *n* **(a)** (*section, division*) partie *f*. **only (a) ~ of the play is good** il n'y a qu'une partie de la pièce qui soit bonne; **the play is good in ~s, ~s of the play are good** il y a de bons passages dans la pièce; **in ~** en partie, partiellement; **for the most ~** dans l'ensemble; **to be ~ and parcel of** faire partie (intégrante) de; **a penny is the hundredth ~ of £1** un penny est le centième d'une livre; (*liter*) **a man of ~s** un homme très doué; **the funny ~ of it is that ...** le plus drôle dans l'histoire c'est que ...; *V* **moving, private, spare**.
(b) *[book, play]* partie *f*; (*Publishing*: *instalment*) livraison *f*, fascicule *m*; (*Press, Rad, TV*: *of serial*) épisode *m*.
(c) (*esp Culin*) mesure *f*. **three ~s water to one ~ milk** trois mesures d'eau pour une mesure de lait.
(d) (*Gram*) *[verb]* **principal ~s** temps principaux; **~s of speech** parties *fpl* du discours, catégories grammaticales; **what ~ of speech is 'of'?** à quelle catégorie grammaticale estce que 'of' appartient?
(e) (*share*) participation *f*, rôle *m*; (*Cine, Theat*) rôle. **he had a large ~ in the organization of ...** il a joué un grand rôle dans l'organisation de ...; **she had some ~ in it** elle y fut pour quelque chose; **we all have our ~ to play** nous avons tous notre rôle à jouer; **to take ~ in** participer à; **I'll have** *or* **I want no ~ in it** je ne veux pas m'en mêler; *V* **act, play**.

(f) (*side, behalf*) parti *m*, part *f*. **to take sb's ~ (in a quarrel)** prendre le parti de qn *or* prendre parti pour qn (dans une dispute); **for my ~** pour ma part, quant à moi; **an error on the ~ of his secretary** une erreur de la part de sa secrétaire; **to take sth in good ~** prendre qch du bon côté.

(g) (*Mus*) partie *f*; *[song, fugue]* voix *f*. **the violin ~** la partie de violon; **two-~ song** chant *m* à deux voix.

(h) (*region*) **in these ~s** dans cette région, dans ce coin*; **in this ~ of the world** dans ce coin*, par ici; **in foreign ~s** à l'étranger.

2 *cpd*: **part exchange** reprise *f* en compte; **to take a car** *etc* **in part exchange** reprendre une voiture *etc* en compte; **part owner** copropriétaire *mf*; **part payment** (*exchange*) règlement partiel; (*deposit*) arrhes *fpl*; **part song** chant *m* à plusieurs voix *or* polyphonique; **part-time** *V* **part-time; part-timer** travailleur *m*, -euse *f or* employé(e) *m(f)* à temps partiel.

3 *adv* en partie. **she is ~ French** elle est en partie française.

4 *vt* **(a)** *crowd* ouvrir un passage dans; *people, boxers* séparer. **they were ~ed during the war years** ils sont restés séparés pendant toute la guerre.

(b) to ~ one's hair se faire une raie; **his hair was ~ed at the side** il portait une raie sur le côté.

(c) to ~ company with (*leave*) fausser compagnie à, quitter; (*disagree*) ne plus être d'accord avec; **they ~ed company** (*lit*) ils se quittèrent; (*fig*) ils se trouvèrent en désaccord; (*hum*) **the trailer ~ed company with the car** la remorque a faussé compagnie à la voiture.

5 *vi [crowd]* s'ouvrir; *[boxers etc]* se séparer; *[friends]* se quitter; *[rope]* se rompre. **to ~ from sb** se séparer de qn; **to ~ with** *money* débourser; *possessions* se défaire de, renoncer à.

partake [pɑː'teɪk] *pret* **partook** [pɑː'tʊk], *ptp* **partaken** [pɑː'teɪkən] *vi* (*frm*) **to ~ in** prendre part à, participer à; **to ~ of** *meal, refreshment* prendre; (*fig*) tenir de, avoir quelque chose de.

parthenogenesis ['pɑːθɪnəʊ'dʒenɪsɪs] *n* parthénogénèse *f*.

partial ['pɑːʃəl] *adj* **(a)** (*in part*) *success, eclipse* partiel. **(b)** (*biased*) partial (*to, towards* envers), injuste. (*: *like*) **to be ~ to sth** avoir un faible pour qch; **to be ~ to doing** avoir un penchant à faire.

partiality [ˌpɑːʃɪ'ælɪtɪ] *n* **(a)** (*bias*) partialité *f* (*for, to, towards* pour, envers), préjugé *m* (favorable) (*for, to* pour, en faveur de), favoritisme *m*. **(b)** (*liking*) prédilection *f*, penchant *m*, faible *m* (*for* pour).

partially ['pɑːʃəlɪ] *adv* **(a)** (*partly*) en partie, partiellement. **(b)** (*with bias*) avec partialité, partialement.

participant [pɑː'tɪsɪpənt] *n* participant(e) *m(f)* (*in* à).

participate [pɑː'tɪsɪpeɪt] *vi* participer, prendre part (*in* à).

participation [pɑːˌtɪsɪ'peɪʃən] *n* participation *f* (*in* à).

participial [ˌpɑːtɪ'sɪpɪəl] *adj* participial.

participle ['pɑːtɪsɪpl] *n* participe *m*. **past/present ~** participe passé/présent.

particle ['pɑːtɪkl] *n* parcelle *f*, particule *f*; *[dust, flour etc]* grain *m*; *[metal]* paillette *f*; (*Ling, Phys*) particule; (*fig*) brin *m*, grain. **a ~ of truth/of sense** un grain de vérité/de bon sens; **not a ~ of evidence** pas l'ombre d'une preuve, pas la moindre preuve.

parti-coloured, (*US*) **parti-colored** ['pɑːtɪˌkʌləd] *adj* bariolé.

particular [pə'tɪkjʊlə^r] 1 *adj* **(a)** (*distinct from others*) particulier, distinct des autres; (*characteristic*) particulier; (*personal*) personnel. **in this ~ case** dans ce cas particulier; **for no ~ reason** sans raison précise *or* bien définie; **that ~ brand** cette marque-là (*et non pas une autre*); **her ~ type of humour** son genre particulier d'humour, son humour personnel; **my ~ choice** mon choix personnel.

(b) (*outstanding*) particulier, spécial. **nothing ~ happened** rien de particulier *or* de spécial n'est arrivé; **he took ~ care over it** il y mit un soin particulier; **to pay ~ attention to sth** faire bien attention à qch; **a ~ friend of his** un de ses meilleurs amis, un de ses amis intimes; **she didn't say anything ~** elle n'a rien dit de spécial.

(c) (*having high standards*) minutieux, méticuleux; (*over cleanliness*) méticuleux; (*hard to please*) pointilleux, difficile, exigeant. **she is ~ about whom she talks to** elle ne parle pas à n'importe qui; **he is ~ about his food** il est difficile pour la nourriture; **which do you want? — I'm not ~*** lequel voulez-vous? — cela m'est égal *or* je n'ai pas de préférence.

(d) (*very exact*) *account* détaillé, circonstancié.

2 *n* **(a) in ~** en particulier, notamment; **nothing in ~** rien en *or* de particulier.

(b) (*gen pl: detail*) détail(s) *m(pl)*. **in every ~** en tout point; **he is wrong in one ~** il se trompe sur un point; **~s** (*information*) détails, renseignements *mpl*; (*description*) description *f*; *[person]* (*description*) signalement *m*; (*name, address etc*) coordonnées* *fpl*; **full ~s** tous les détails, tous les renseignements; **for further ~s apply to ...** pour plus amples renseignements s'adresser à ... .

particularity [pəˌtɪkjʊ'lærɪtɪ] *n* **(a)** (*special feature*) particularité *f*. **(b)** (*meticulousness*) minutie *f*.

particularize [pə'tɪkjʊləraɪz] 1 *vt* particulariser, spécifier, détailler, préciser. 2 *vi* spécifier, préciser.

particularly [pə'tɪkjʊləlɪ] *adv* (*in particular*) en particulier, particulièrement, spécialement; (*notably*) notamment, particulièrement; (*very carefully*) méticuleusement, avec grand soin.

parting ['pɑːtɪŋ] 1 *n* **(a)** séparation *f*; *[waters]* partage *m*. (*lit, fig*) **the ~ of the ways** la croisée des chemins. **(b)** *[hair]* raie *f*; *[mane]* épi *m*. 2 *adj gift* d'adieu. **~ words** paroles *fpl* d'adieu; (*fig*) **~ shot** flèche *f* du Parthe.

partisan [ˌpɑːtɪ'zæn] 1 *n* (*supporter; fighter*) partisan *m*. 2 *adj*: **~ politics** politique partisane; (*Pol etc*) **~ spirit** esprit *m* de parti; (*Mil*) **~ warfare** guerre *f* de partisans.

partisanship [ˌpɑːtɪ'zænʃɪp] *n* esprit *m* de parti, partialité *f*; appartenance *f* à un parti.

partition [pɑː'tɪʃən] 1 *n* **(a)** (*also* **~ wall**) cloison *f*. **glass ~** cloison vitrée.

(b) (*dividing*) division *f*; *[country]* partition *f*, partage *m*, démembrement *m*; *[land]* morcellement *m*.

2 *vt* diviser; *country* partager, démembrer; *land* morceler; *room* cloisonner.

partition off *vt sep room, part of room* cloisonner.

partitive ['pɑːtɪtɪv] *adj, n* partitif (*m*).

partly ['pɑːtlɪ] *adv* partiellement, en partie. **~ blue, ~ green** moitié bleu, moitié vert.

partner ['pɑːtnə^r] 1 *n* **(a)** (*Comm, Fin, Jur, Med etc*) associé(e) *m(f)*. **senior ~** associé principal; **junior ~** associé adjoint; (*fig*) **~s in crime** associés *or* complices *mpl* dans le crime; *V* **sleeping.**

(b) (*Sport*) partenaire *mf*; (*co-driver*) coéquipier *m*, -ière *f*; (*Dancing*) cavalier *m*, -ière *f*; (*in marriage*) époux *m*, épouse *f*, conjoint(e) *m(f)*.

2 *vt* (*Comm, Fin etc*) être l'associé (de), s'associer à; (*Sport*) être le partenaire de, être le coéquipier de; (*Dancing*) danser avec.

partnership ['pɑːtnəʃɪp] *n* association *f*. (*Comm, Fin*) **limited ~** (société *f* en) commandite *f*; **to be in ~** être en association, être associé; **to enter** *or* **go into ~ (with)** s'associer (avec); **to take sb into ~** prendre qn comme associé; **a doctors' ~** une association de médecins, un cabinet de groupe (*médical*).

partridge ['pɑːtrɪdʒ] *n* perdrix *f*; (*young bird, also Culin*) perdreau *m*.

part-time ['pɑːt'taɪm] 1 *adj* **(a)** *job, employment* à temps partiel; (*half-time*) à mi-temps. **to do ~ work** travailler à temps partiel *or* à mi-temps.

(b) *employee, staff* (qui travaille) à temps partiel, à mi-temps.

2 *n* (*Ind*) **to be on ~*** être en chômage partiel.

3 *adv* à temps partiel.

parturition [ˌpɑːtjʊə'rɪʃən] *n* parturition *f*.

party ['pɑːtɪ] 1 *n* **(a)** (*Pol etc*) parti *m*. **political/Conservative/Labour ~** parti politique/conservateur/travailliste.

(b) (*group*) *[travellers]* groupe *m*, troupe* *f*; *[workmen]* équipe *f*, brigade *f*; (*Mil*) détachement *m*, escouade *f*. (*lit, fig*) **advance ~** éclaireurs *mpl*; **rescue ~** équipe de secours.

(c) (*Jur etc*) partie *f*. **all parties concerned** tous les intéressés; **to be ~ to a suit** être en cause; **to become a ~ to a contract** signer un contrat; **third ~** tierce personne, tiers *m* (*V also* **third**); **innocent ~** innocent(e) *m(f)*; (*fig*) **I will not be (a) ~ to any dishonesty** je ne me ferai le *or* la complice d'aucune malhonnêteté; (*fig*) **to be a ~ to a crime** être complice d'un crime.

(d) (*celebration*) réunion *f*, réception *f*; fête *f*. **to give a ~** donner une surprise-partie *or* une petite réception, inviter des amis; (*more formally*) donner une réception *or* une soirée, recevoir (du monde); **birthday ~** fête *f* d'anniversaire; **dinner ~** dîner *m*; **evening ~** soirée *f*; **private ~** réunion intime; **tea ~** thé *m*; **let's keep the ~ clean*** pas d'inconvenances!, un peu de tenue!; *V* **bottle, Christmas.**

(e) (‡*hum: person*) individu *m*.

2 *cpd politics, leader* de parti, du parti; *disputes* de partis. **party dress** robe habillée; (*evening dress*) toilette *f* de soirée; **party line** (*Pol*) politique *f or* ligne *f* du parti; (*Telec*) ligne commune à deux abonnés; (*Pol*) **to follow** *or* **to toe the party line** suivre la ligne du parti, être dans la ligne du parti; **his party manners were terrible** sa façon de se tenir en société était abominable; **the children were on their party manners*** les enfants ont été d'une tenue exemplaire; (*Pol*) **party machine** machine *f or* administration *f* du parti; (*Rad, TV*) **party political broadcast** *émission réservée à un parti politique*, ≃ 'tribune libre'; **this is not a party political question** ce n'est pas une question qui relève de la ligne du parti; **party spirit** (*Pol*) esprit *m* de parti; (*: *gaiety*) entrain *m*; **party wall** mur mitoyen.

pasha ['pæʃə] *n* pacha *m*.

pass [pɑːs] 1 *n* **(a)** (*permit*) *[journalist, worker etc]* coupe-file *m*, laissez-passer *m inv*; (*Rail etc*) carte *f* d'abonnement; (*Theat*) billet *m* de faveur; (*Naut*) lettre *f* de mer; (*Mil etc: safe conduct*) sauf-conduit *m*.

(b) (*in mountains*) col *m*, défilé *m*; *V* **sell.**

(c) (*in exam*) moyenne *f*, mention *f* passable. **did you get a ~?** avez-vous eu la moyenne?, avez-vous été reçu?; **to get a ~ in history** être reçu en histoire.

(d) (*U: situation*) situation *f*, état *m*. (*iro*) **things have come to a pretty ~!** voilà à quoi on en est arrivé!; **to bring sb to a pretty ~** mettre qn dans de beaux draps; **things have reached such a ~ that ...** les choses en sont arrivées à un tel point que ... .

(e) (*Ftbl etc*) passe *f*; (*Fencing*) botte *f*, attaque *f*. **to make a ~* at a woman** faire du plat* à une femme.

(f) *[conjuror]* passe *f*.

2 *cpd*: (*Fin*) **passbook** livret *m* (bancaire); (*Univ*) **pass degree** licence *f* libre; **passkey** passe-partout *m inv*, passe *m*; (*Scol, Univ*) **passmark** moyenne *f*; **password** mot *m* de passe.

3 *vi* **(a)** (*come, go*) passer (*through* par); *[procession]* défiler; (*Aut: overtake*) dépasser, doubler. **to let sb ~** laisser passer qn; **to ~ down the street** descendre la rue; **~ down the bus please!** avançons s'il vous plaît!; **to ~ behind/in front of** passer derrière/devant; **to ~ into oblivion** tomber dans l'oubli; **to ~ out of sight** disparaître; **letters ~ed between them** ils ont échangé des lettres.

(b) *[time]* (se) passer, s'écouler. **the afternoon ~ed pleasantly** l'après-midi a passé *or* s'est passé(e) agréablement; **how time ~es!** que le temps passe vite!

(c) (*esp Chem: change*) se transformer (*into* en).

(d) (*esp Jur: transfer*) passer, être transmis. **the estate ~ed to my brother** la propriété est revenue à mon frère.
(e) (*also* ~ **away**) *[memory, opportunity]* s'effacer, disparaître; *[pain]* passer.
(f) (*in exam*) être reçu (*in* en).
(g) (*take place*) se passer, avoir lieu. **all that ~ed between them** tout ce qui s'est passé entre eux; (*liter, frm*) **to bring sth to ~** accomplir qch, réaliser qch; (*liter*) **it came to ~ that** il advint que.
(h) (*be accepted*) *[coins]* avoir cours; *[behaviour]* convenir, être acceptable; *[project]* passer. **to ~ under the name of** être connu sous le nom de; **what ~es for a hat these days** ce qui de nos jours passe pour un chapeau; **she would ~ for 20** on lui donnerait 20 ans; **will this do? — oh it'll ~** est-ce que ceci convient? — oh ça peut aller; **let it ~!** laisse couler!*; **he let it ~** il l'a laissé passer, il ne l'a pas relevé; **he couldn't let it ~** il ne pouvait pas laisser passer ça comme ça.
(i) (*Cards*) passer. **(I) ~!** (je) passe!
(j) (*Sport*) faire une passe.
4 *vt* **(a)** (*go past*) *building* passer devant; *person* croiser, rencontrer; *barrier, frontier* passer; (*Aut: overtake*) dépasser, doubler; (*go beyond: also Sport*) dépasser. **when you have ~ed the town hall** quand vous serez passé devant *or* quand vous aurez dépassé la mairie; **they ~ed each other on the way** ils se sont croisés en chemin; (*frm*) **no remark ~ed his lips** il ne souffla *or* ne dit pas mot; *V* **muster.**
(b) (*get through*) *customs* passer; *exam* être reçu à *or* admis à, réussir. **the film ~ed the censors** le film a reçu le visa de la censure.
(c) *time* passer. **just to ~ the time** pour passer le temps, histoire de passer le temps*; **to ~ the evening reading** passer la soirée à lire; *V* **time.**
(d) (*hand over*) (faire) passer. **please ~ the salt** faites passer le sel s'il vous plaît; **~ me the box** passez-moi la boîte; **to ~ a dish round the table** faire passer un plat autour de la table; **the telegram was ~ed round the room** on fit passer le télégramme dans la salle; **to ~ sth down the line** faire passer qch (de main en main); **~ the word that it's time to go** faites passer la consigne que c'est l'heure de partir; **to play at ~-the-parcel** ≃ jouer au furet; *V* **buck.**
(e) (*accept, allow*) *candidate* recevoir, admettre; (*Parl*) *bill* voter, faire passer. **the censors ~ed the film** le film a été autorisé par la censure; **the censors haven't ~ed the film** le film a été interdit par la censure; (*Scol, Univ*) **they didn't ~ him** ils l'ont refusé *or* recalé*; **the doctor ~ed him fit for work** le docteur l'a déclaré en état de reprendre le travail; (*Typ*) **to ~ the proofs (for press)** donner le bon à tirer.
(f) (*utter*) *comment* faire; *opinion* émettre, formuler. **to ~ remarks about sb/sth** faire des observations sur qn/qch; (*Jur, fig*) **to ~ judgment** prononcer *or* rendre un jugement (*on* sur); (*Jur*) **to ~ sentence** prononcer une condamnation (*on sb* contre qn); *V also* **sentence.**
(g) (*move*) passer. **he ~ed his hand over his brow** il se passa la main sur le front; **he ~ed his handkerchief over his face** il passa son mouchoir sur son visage; **to ~ a rope through a ring** passer une corde dans un anneau; **to ~ a cloth over a table** donner *or* passer un coup de chiffon à une table; **to ~ a knife through sth** enfoncer un couteau dans qch; (*Culin*) **to ~ sth through a sieve** passer qch (au tamis); (*Mil, fig*) **to ~ in review** passer en revue.
(h) (*Sport*) *ball* passer.
(i) *forged money* (faire) passer, écouler; *stolen goods* faire passer.
(j) (*surpass*) **to ~ comprehension** dépasser l'entendement; **to ~ belief** être incroyable.
(k) (*Med*) **to ~ blood** avoir du sang dans les urines; **to ~ a stone** évacuer un calcul; **to ~ water** uriner.
pass along 1 *vi* passer, circuler, passer son chemin.
2 *vt sep* faire passer (de main en main).
pass away *vi* **(a)** (*euph: die*) mourir, s'éteindre (*euph*), décéder (*frm*). **(b) = pass 3e.**
pass back *vt sep object* rendre, retourner. (*Rad, TV*) **I will now pass you back to the studio** je vais rendre l'antenne au studio.
pass by 1 *vi* passer (à côté); *[procession]* défiler. **I saw him passing by** je l'ai vu passer.
2 *vt sep* ne pas faire attention à, négliger, ignorer. **life has passed me by** je n'ai vraiment pas vécu.
pass down 1 *vi [inheritance etc]* être transmis, revenir (*to* à).
2 *vt sep* transmettre. **to pass sth down (in a family)** transmettre qch par héritage (dans une famille); **passed down from father to son** transmis de père en fils.
pass in *vt sep* (faire) passer. **to pass a parcel in through a window** (faire) passer un colis par la fenêtre.
pass off 1 *vi* **(a)** (*subside*) *[faintness etc]* passer, se dissiper.
(b) (*take place*) *[events]* se passer, se dérouler, s'accomplir. **everything passed off smoothly** tout s'est passé sans accroc.
2 *vt sep* **(a)** faire passer, faire prendre. **to pass someone off as someone else** faire passer une personne pour une autre; **to pass o.s. off as a doctor** se faire passer pour (un) médecin.
(b) to pass sth off on sb repasser *or* refiler* qch à qn.
pass on 1 *vi* **(a)** (*euph: die*) s'éteindre (*euph*).
(b) (*continue one's way*) passer son chemin, ne pas s'arrêter. (*fig*) **to pass on to a new subject** passer à un nouveau sujet.
2 *vt sep* (*hand on*) *object* faire passer (*to* à); *news* faire circuler, faire savoir; *message* transmettre. **take it and pass it on** prenez et faites passer; **to pass on old clothes to sb** repasser de vieux vêtements à qn; **you've passed your cold on to me** tu m'as passé ton rhume.
pass out 1 *vi* **(a)** (*faint*) s'évanouir, perdre connaissance, tomber dans les pommes*; (*from drink*) tomber ivre mort. **he passed out on us** il nous a fait le coup de tomber dans les pommes* (*or* ivre mort).
(b) (*US Scol*) **to pass out of high school** sortir du lycée, quitter le lycée (*à la fin des études*).
2 *vt sep leaflets etc* distribuer.
pass over 1 *vi* (*euph*) **= pass on 1a.**
2 *vt* **(a)** (*sep: neglect*) omettre, négliger, ignorer. **to pass over Paul in favour of Robert** donner la préférence à Robert au détriment de Paul; **he was passed over in favour of his brother** on lui a préféré son frère.
(b) (*fus: ignore*) passer sous silence, ne pas relever.
pass round *vt sep bottle* faire passer; *sweets, leaflets* distribuer. (*fig*) **to pass round the hat** faire la quête.
pass through 1 *vi* passer. **I can't stop I'm only passing through** je ne peux pas rester je ne fais que passer.
2 *vt fus* **(a)** *hardships* subir, endurer.
(b) (*travel through*) traverser.
pass up *vt sep* **(a)** (*lit*) passer.
(b) (*: *forego*) *chance, opportunity* laisser passer.
passable ['pɑːsəbl] *adj* **(a)** (*tolerable*) passable, assez bon. **(b)** *road* praticable, carrossable; *river* franchissable.
passably ['pɑːsəblɪ] *adv* passablement, assez.
passage ['pæsɪdʒ] **1** *n* **(a)** (*passing*) (*lit*) passage *m*; *[bill, law]* adoption *f*; (*fig*) passage, transition *f* (*from... to* de ... à). **with the ~ of time he understood** avec le temps il finit par comprendre; (*fig, liter*) **~ of** *or* **at arms** passe *f* d'armes; *V* **bird.**
(b) (*Naut*) voyage *m*, traversée *f*.
(c) (*way through: also* **~way**) passage *m*. **to force a ~way through** se frayer un passage *or* un chemin (à travers); **to leave a ~way** laisser un passage, laisser le passage libre.
(d) (*also* **~way**) (*indoors*) couloir *m*, corridor *m*; (*outdoors*) ruelle *f*, passage *m*.
(e) (*Mus*) passage *m*; *[text]* passage. (*Literat*) **selected ~s** morceaux choisis.
2 *cpd*: **passageway = passage 1c, 1d.**
passé ['pæseɪ] *adj play, book, person* vieux jeu *inv*, démodé, dépassé*; *woman* défraîchi, fané.
passenger ['pæsɪndʒəʳ] **1** *n* (*in train*) voyageur *m*, -euse *f*; (*in boat, plane, car*) passager *m*, -ère *f*. (*pej*) **he's just a ~** il n'est vraiment qu'un poids mort.
2 *cpd*: (*Rail*) **passenger coach,** (*US*) **passenger car** voiture *f* *or* wagon *m* de voyageurs; (*Aviat, Naut*) **passenger list** liste *f* des passagers; **passenger mile** (*Aviat*) kilomètre-passager *m*; (*Rail etc*) kilomètre-voyageur *m*, voyageur *m* kilométrique; (*Aut*) **passenger seat** siège *m* (de passagers); (*Rail*) **passenger station** gare *f* de voyageurs; **passenger train** train *m* de voyageurs.
passe-partout ['pæspɑːtuː] *n* **(a)** (*master key*) passe-partout *m inv* (*clef*), passe *m* . **(b)** (*Art*) **~ (frame)** (encadrement *m* en) sous-verre *m*.
passer-by ['pɑːsə'baɪ] *n* passant(e) *m(f)*.
passing ['pɑːsɪŋ] **1** *adj* (*lit*) *person, car* qui passe (*or* passait *etc*); (*fig: brief*) éphémère, passager. **~ desire** désir fugitif; **~ remark** remarque en passant.
2 *adv* (*†† or liter*) extrêmement. **~ fair** de toute beauté.
3 *n* **(a)** *[time]* écoulement *m*; *[train, car]* passage *m*; (*Aut: overtaking*) dépassement *m*. **with the ~ of time** avec le temps.
(b) (*euph: death*) mort *f*, trépas *m* (*liter*). **~ bell** glas *m*.
4 *cpd*: (*Mil*) **passing-out parade** défilé *m* de promotion.
passion ['pæʃən] **1** *n* **(a)** (*love*) passion *f*, amour *m*; (*fig*) passion (*for* de). **to have a ~ for music** avoir la passion de la musique; **ruling ~** passion dominante.
(b) (*burst of anger*) colère *f*, emportement *m*. **fit of ~** accès *m* de colère; **to be in a ~** être furieux; *V* **fly³.**
(c) (*strong emotion*) passion *f*, émotion violente.
(d) (*Rel*) **the P~** la Passion.
2 *cpd*: (*Bot*) **passionflower** passiflore *f*; (*Bot*) **passion fruit** fruit *m* de la passiflore; (*Rel*) **Passion play/Sunday/week** mystère *m*/dimanche *m*/semaine *f* de la Passion.
passionate ['pæʃənɪt] *adj person, plea, love, embrace* passionné; *speech* véhément.
passionately ['pæʃənɪtlɪ] *adv* passionnément, avec passion. **to be ~ fond of sth/sb** adorer qch/qn.
passionless ['pæʃənlɪs] *adj* sans passion, détaché.
passive ['pæsɪv] **1** *adj* **(a)** (*motionless*) passif, inactif, inerte; (*resigned*) passif, soumis. (*Pol*) **~ resistance** résistance passive; (*Pol*) **~ disobedience** désobéissance passive. **(b)** (*Gram*) passif. **2** *n* (*Gram*) passif *m*. **in the ~** au passif.
passively ['pæsɪvlɪ] *adv* passivement; (*Gram*) au passif.
passiveness ['pæsɪvnɪs] *n*, **passivity** [pæ'sɪvɪtɪ] *n* passivité *f*.
Passover ['pɑːsəʊvəʳ] *n* Pâque *f* des Juifs.
passport ['pɑːspɔːt] *n* passeport *m*. **no-~ day trip to France** une journée en France sans passeport; **~ section** service *m* des passeports; (*fig*) **~ to success** clef *f* de la réussite.
past [pɑːst] **1** *n* **(a)** passé *m*. **in the ~** dans le temps, dans le passé, autrefois; **as in the ~** comme par le passé; **she lives in the ~** elle vit dans le passé; **it's a thing of the ~** cela ne se fait plus, cela n'existe plus, c'est du passé, c'est de l'histoire ancienne; **domestic servants are a thing of the ~** les domestiques, cela n'existe plus; **I thought you'd quarrelled? — that's a thing of the ~** je croyais que vous étiez fâchés? — c'est de l'histoire ancienne; **do you know his ~?** vous connaissez son passé?; **a woman with a ~** une femme au passé chargé.
(b) (*Gram*) passé *m*. **in the ~** au passé; **~ definite** passé simple, passé défini, prétérit *m*.
2 *adj* **(a)** passé. **for some time ~** depuis quelque temps; **in times ~** autrefois, (au temps) jadis; **in ~ centuries** pendant les siècles passés; **the ~ week** la semaine dernière *or* passée; **the ~ few days** ces derniers jours; **all that is now ~** tout cela c'est

du passé; ~ **president** ancien président; (*fig*) **to be a ~ master of sth** être expert en qch; **to be a ~ master at doing sth** avoir l'art de faire qch.

(b) (*Gram*) passé. **in the ~ tense** au passé; **~ participle** participe passé.

3 *prep* **(a)** (*beyond in time*) plus de. **it is ~ 11 o'clock** il est plus de 11 heures, il est 11 heures passées; (*Brit*) **half ~ 3** 3 heures et demie; **quarter ~ 3** 3 heures et quart; **at 20 ~ 3** à 3 heures 20; (*Brit*) **the train goes at 5 ~*** le train part à 5*; **she is ~ 60** elle a plus de 60 ans, elle a 60 ans passés, elle a dépassé la soixantaine.

(b) (*beyond in space*) au delà de, plus loin que. **just ~ the post office** un peu plus loin que la poste, juste après la poste.

(c) (*in front of*) devant. **he goes ~ the house every day** tous les jours il passe devant la maison; **he rushed ~ me** il est passé devant moi *or* (*overtook*) m'a dépassé à toute allure.

(d) (*beyond limits of*) au delà de. **~ endurance** insupportable; **it is ~ all understanding** cela dépasse l'entendement; **that is ~ all belief** cela n'est pas croyable, c'est incroyable; **I'm ~ caring** je ne m'en fais plus, j'ai cessé de m'en faire; **he is ~ praying for** on ne peut plus rien pour lui; **he is ~ work** il n'est plus en état de travailler; **he's a bit ~ it now*** il n'est plus dans la course*; **that cake is ~ its best** ce gâteau n'est plus si bon; **I wouldn't put it ~ her to have done it** je la croirais bien capable de l'avoir fait, cela ne m'étonnerait pas d'elle qu'elle l'ait fait; **I wouldn't put it ~ him** cela ne m'étonnerait pas de lui, il en est bien capable.

4 *adv* (*phr vb elem*) auprès, devant. **to go** *or* **walk ~** passer; *V* **march**[1] *etc.*

pasta ['pæstə] *n* (*Culin*) pâtes *fpl.*

paste [peɪst] **1** *n* **(a)** (*Culin*) (*pastry, dough*) pâte *f*; *[meat etc]* pâté *m*. **liver ~** pâté *or* crème *f* de foie; **tomato ~** concentré *m or* purée *f* de tomate; **almond ~** pâte d'amandes; **anchovy ~** beurre *m* d'anchois.

(b) (*gen cpd*) pâte *f*. **tooth~** pâte dentifrice, dentifrice *m*.

(c) (*glue*) colle *f* (de pâte).

(d) (*jewellery*) strass *m*.

2 *cpd jewellery* en strass. **pasteboard** carton *m*; (*US: pastry board*) planche *f* à pâtisserie.

3 *vt* **(a)** coller; *wallpaper* enduire de colle. **to ~ photos into an album** coller des photos dans un album; **he ~d the pages together** il colla les pages ensemble.

(b) (‡: *thrash*) rosser*.

paste up *vt sep notice, list* afficher.

pastel ['pæstəl] *n* (crayon *m*) pastel *m*. **~ drawing** (dessin *m* au) pastel; **~ shade** ton *m* pastel *inv*.

pasteurization [ˌpæstəraɪ'zeɪʃən] *n* pasteurisation *f.*

pasteurize ['pæstəraɪz] *vt* pasteuriser.

pasteurized ['pæstəraɪzd] *adj* pasteurisé.

pastiche [pæs'ti:ʃ] *n* pastiche *m.*

pastille ['pæstɪl] *n* pastille *f.*

pastime ['pɑ:staɪm] *n* passe-temps *m inv*, divertissement *m*, distraction *f*.

pasting‡ ['peɪstɪŋ] *n* (*thrashing*) rossée* *f*. **to give sb a ~** flanquer une rossée à qn*.

pastor ['pɑ:stəʳ] *n* pasteur *m.*

pastoral ['pɑ:stərəl] **1** *adj* **(a)** (*rural*) pastoral, champêtre; (*Agr*) de pâture; (*Literat etc*) pastoral. **~ land** pâturages *mpl*. **(b)** (*Rel*) pastoral. **2** *n* (*Literat, Rel*) pastorale *f.*

pastry ['peɪstrɪ] **1** *n* **(a)** (*U*) pâte *f*; *V* **puff, short. (b)** (*cake*) pâtisserie *f*. **2** *cpd*: **pastryboard** planche *f* à pâtisserie; **pastrybrush** pinceau *m* à pâtisserie; **pastrycase** croûte *f*; **pastrycook** pâtissier *m*, -ière *f.*

pasturage ['pɑ:stjʊrɪdʒ] *n* pâturage *m.*

pasture ['pɑ:stʃəʳ] **1** *n* (*Agr*) (lieu *m* de) pâture *f*, pré *m*, pâturage *m*. **2** *vi* paître. **3** *vt* (faire) paître. **4** *cpd*: **pasture land** herbage *m*, pâturage(s) *m(pl)*.

pasty ['peɪstɪ] **1** *adj* pâteux; (*pej*) *face, complexion* terreux. (*pej*) **~-faced** au teint terreux *or* de papier mâché*. **2** ['pæstɪ] *n* (*Culin*) petit pâté *m*, feuilleté *m.*

Pat [pæt] *n* **(a)** *dim of* **Patrick** *or* **Patricia. (b)** *au masculin surnom de l'Irlandais.*

pat[1] [pæt] **1** *vt ball etc* taper, tapoter, donner une tape à; *animal* flatter de la main, caresser. **he ~ted my hand** il me tapota la main.

2 *n* **(a)** (*tap*) coup léger, petite tape; (*on animal*) caresse *f*. **to give sb a ~ on the back** (*lit*) tapoter qn dans le dos; (*fig*) complimenter qn, congratuler qn; **he deserves a ~ on the back for that** cela mérite qu'on lui fasse un petit compliment; **to give o.s. a ~ on the back** se congratuler, s'applaudir.

(b) ~ of butter noix *f* de beurre; (*larger*) motte *f* de beurre.

pat[2] [pæt] **1** *adv* à propos, à point. **to answer ~** (*immediately*) répondre sur-le-champ; (*with repartee*) répondre du tac au tac; **to know sth off ~** savoir qch sur le bout du doigt.

2 *adj example* à propos, à point; *answer* tout prêt, bien envoyé. **he had his explanation ~** il avait son explication toute prête.

patch [pætʃ] **1** *n* **(a)** (*for clothes*) pièce *f*; (*for inner tube, airbed*) rustine *f*; (*over eye*) bandeau *m*; (*cosmetic: on face*) mouche *f.*

(b) (*small area*) *[colour]* tache *f*; *[sky]* morceau *m*, échappée *f*, pan *m*; *[land]* parcelle *f*; *[vegetables]* carré *m*; *[ice]* plaque *f*; *[mist]* nappe *f*; *[water]* flaque *f*; (*on dog's back etc*) tache.

(c) (*fig*) **he isn't a ~ on his brother*** son frère pourrait lui en remontrer n'importe quand, (*stronger*) il n'arrive pas à la cheville de son frère; **to strike a bad ~** être dans la déveine*; **we've had our bad ~es** nous avons eu nos moments difficiles.

2 *cpd*: **patch pocket** poche rapportée.

3 *vt clothes* rapiécer; *tyre* réparer, poser une rustine à.

patch up *vt sep clothes* rapiécer, rapetasser*; *machine* rafistoler*. **to patch up a quarrel** se raccommoder.

patchwork ['pætʃwɜ:k] **1** *n* (*lit, fig*) patchwork *m*. **2** *cpd quilt* en patchwork; *landscape* bigarré; (*pej: lacking in unity*) fait de pièces et de morceaux, disparate.

patchy ['pætʃɪ] *adj* (*lit; also fig pej*) inégal.

pate [peɪt] *n* tête *f*. **a bald ~** un crâne chauve.

patella [pə'telə] *n* rotule *f.*

paten ['pætən] *n* patène *f.*

patent ['peɪtənt] **1** *adj* **(a)** (*obvious*) *fact, dishonesty* patent, manifeste, évident.

(b) *invention* breveté. **~ medicine** spécialité *f* pharmaceutique; **letters ~** lettres patentes.

(c) ~ leather cuir verni; **~ (leather) shoes** souliers vernis *or* en cuir verni.

2 *n* (*licence*) brevet *m* d'invention; (*invention*) invention brevetée. **to take out a ~** prendre un brevet; **~(s) applied for** demande *f* de brevet déposée.

3 *cpd*: (*Brit*) **Patent Office/Rolls** bureau *m*/registre *m* des brevets d'invention.

4 *vt* faire breveter.

patentee [ˌpeɪtən'ti:] *n* détenteur *m*, -trice *f* d'un brevet.

patently ['peɪtəntlɪ] *adv* manifestement, clairement.

pater‡ ['peɪtəʳ] **1** *n* (*esp Brit*) pater‡ *m*, paternel‡ *m*. **2** *cpd*: **paterfamilias** pater familias *m*; (*Rel*) **paternoster** pater *m* (noster).

paternal [pə'tɜ:nl] *adj* paternel.

paternalism [pə'tɜ:nəlɪzəm] *n* paternalisme *m.*

paternalist [pə'tɜ:nəlɪst] *adj* paternaliste.

paternally [pə'tɜ:nəlɪ] *adv* paternellement.

paternity [pə'tɜ:nɪtɪ] *n* (*lit, fig*) paternité *f*. (*Jur*) **~ order** reconnaissance *f* de paternité judiciaire.

path [pɑ:θ] **1** *n* **(a)** (*also* **~way**) (*in woods etc*) sentier *m*, chemin *m*; (*in garden*) allée *f*; (*also* **foot~**: *beside road*) sentier (pour les piétons); (*fig*) sentier, chemin, voie *f*; *V* **primrose** *etc.*

(b) *[river]* cours *m*; *[sun]* route *f*; *[bullet, missile, spacecraft, planet]* trajectoire *f.*

2 *cpd*: **pathfinder** pionnier *m*, éclaireur *m.*

pathetic [pə'θetɪk] *adj* **(a)** *sight, grief* pitoyable, navrant. **~ attempt** tentative désespérée; **it was ~ to see it** cela faisait peine à voir, c'était un spectacle navrant. **(b)** (*) *piece of work, performance* pitoyable, piteux, minable.

pathetically [pə'θetɪklɪ] *adv* pitoyablement. **~ thin** d'une maigreur pitoyable; **she was ~ glad to find him** son plaisir à le retrouver vous serrait le cœur.

pathological [ˌpæθə'lɒdʒɪkəl] *adj* pathologique.

pathologist [pə'θɒlədʒɪst] *n* pathologiste *mf.*

pathology [pə'θɒlədʒɪ] *n* pathologie *f.*

pathos ['peɪθɒs] *n* pathétique *m.*

patience ['peɪʃəns] *n* **(a)** patience *f*. **to have ~** prendre patience, patienter; **to lose ~** perdre patience, s'impatienter; **I am out of ~, my ~ is exhausted** ma patience est à bout, je suis à bout de patience; **I have no ~ with these people** ces gens m'exaspèrent; *V* **possess, tax, try** *etc.*

(b) (*Brit Cards*) réussite *f*. **to play ~** faire des réussites.

patient ['peɪʃənt] **1** *adj* patient, endurant. **(you must) be ~!** patientez!, (un peu de) patience!*; **he's been ~ long enough** il a assez patienté *or* attendu, sa patience a des limites.

2 *n* (*gen*) malade *mf*; *[dentist etc]* patient(e) *m(f)*; (*post-operative*) opéré(e) *m(f)*. **a doctor's ~s** (*undergoing treatment*) les patients *or* les malades d'un médecin; (*on his list*) les clients *mpl* d'un médecin; *V* **in, out.**

patiently ['peɪʃəntlɪ] *adv* patiemment, avec patience.

patina ['pætɪnə] *n* patine *f.*

patio ['pætɪəʊ] *n* patio *m.*

patois ['pætwɑ:] *n* patois *m.*

patriarch ['peɪtrɪɑ:k] *n* patriarche *m.*

patriarchal [ˌpeɪtrɪ'ɑ:kəl] *adj* patriarcal.

patriarchy [ˌpeɪtrɪ'ɑ:kɪ] *n* patriarcat *m*, gouvernement patriarcal.

Patricia [pə'trɪʃə] *n* Patricia *f.*

patrician [pə'trɪʃən] *adj, n* patricien(ne) *m(f)*.

Patrick ['pætrɪk] *n* Patrice *m*, Patrick *m.*

patrimony ['pætrɪmənɪ] *n* **(a)** patrimoine *m*, héritage *m*. **(b)** (*Rel*) biens-fonds *mpl* (*d'une église*).

patriot ['peɪtrɪət] *n* patriote *mf.*

patriotic [ˌpætrɪ'ɒtɪk] *adj deed, speech* patriotique; *person* patriote.

patriotically [ˌpætrɪ'ɒtɪkəlɪ] *adv* patriotiquement, en patriote.

patriotism ['pætrɪətɪzəm] *n* patriotisme *m.*

patrol [pə'trəʊl] **1** *n* **(a)** (*U*) patrouille *f*. **to go on ~** aller en patrouille, faire une ronde; **to be on ~** être de patrouille.

(b) (*group of troops, police, Scouts etc*) patrouille *f*; (*ship, aircraft on ~*) patrouilleur *m.*

2 *cpd helicopter, vehicle* de patrouille. **patrolboat** patrouilleur *m*; (*Police*) **patrol car** voiture *f* de police; (*Mil, Scouting*) **patrol leader** chef *m* de patrouille; **patrolman** *V* **patrolman**; (*US*) **patrol wagon** voiture *f* cellulaire.

3 *vt [police, troops etc] district, town* patrouiller dans, faire une patrouille dans.

4 *vi [troops, police]* patrouiller, faire une patrouille. (*fig*) **to ~ up and down*** faire les cent pas.

patrolman [pə'trəʊlmən] *n* **(a)** (*US*) agent *m* de police. **(b)** (*Aut*) agent *m* de la sécurité routière.

patron ['peɪtrən] *n* **(a)** *[artist]* protecteur *m*, -trice *f*; *[a charity]* patron(ne) *m(f)*; (*also* **~ saint**) saint(e) patron(ne) *m(f)*. **~ of the arts** protecteur des arts, mécène *m.*

(b) *[hotel, shop]* client(e) *m(f)*; *[theatre]* habitué(e) *m(f)*. **our ~s** (*Comm*) notre clientèle *f*; (*Theat*) notre public *m.*

patronage ['pætrənɪdʒ] *n* **(a)** *[artist etc]* patronage *m*, appui *m*. **under the ~ of** sous le patronage de, sous les auspices de; **~ of the arts** mécénat *m*, protection *f* des arts.

(b) (*Comm*) clientèle *f*, pratique *f*.
(c) (*Rel*) droit *m* de disposer d'un bénéfice; (*Pol*) droit de présentation.
(d) (*Pol pej*) népotisme *m*.

patronize ['pætrənaɪz] *vt* **(a)** (*pej*) traiter avec condescendance. **(b)** (*Comm*) *shop, firm* donner *or* accorder sa clientèle à, se fournir chez; *dress shop* s'habiller chez.

patronizing ['pætrənaɪzɪŋ] *adj person* condescendant; *look, tone, smile, manner* condescendant, de condescendance.

patronizingly ['pætrənaɪzɪŋlɪ] *adv* d'un air *or* d'un ton condescendant.

patronymic [,pætrə'nɪmɪk] **1** *n* patronyme *m*, nom *m* patronymique. **2** *adj* patronymique.

patter[1] ['pætəʳ] **1** *n [comedian, conjurer]* bavardage *m*, baratin‡ *m*; *[salesman etc]* boniment *m*, bagou* *m*; (*jargon*) jargon *m*. **2** *vi* (*also* ~ **away,** ~ **on**) jacasser, baratiner‡.

patter[2] ['pætəʳ] **1** *n [rain]* crépitement *m*, bruit *m*; *[hail]* crépitement. **a** ~ **of footsteps** un petit bruit de pas pressés. **2** *vi [footsteps]* trottiner; *[rain]* frapper, battre (*on* contre); *[hail]* crépiter.

patter about, patter around *vi* trottiner çà et là.

pattern ['pætən] **1** *n* **(a)** (*design: on material, wallpaper etc*) dessin(s) *m(pl)*, motif *m*. **floral** ~ motif de fleurs *or* floral.
(b) (*Sewing: also* **paper** ~) patron *m*; (*fig*) exemple *m*, modèle *m*. (*fig*) ~ **of living** mode *m* de vie; **on the** ~ **of** sur le modèle de; **it set a** ~ **for other meetings** cela a institué une marche à suivre pour les autres séances; **it followed the usual** ~ cela s'est passé selon la formule habituelle; **behaviour** ~**s of teenagers** les types de comportement chez les adolescents.
(c) (*sample*) *[material etc]* échantillon *m*.
2 *cpd*: **pattern book** *[material, wallpaper etc]* liasse *f or* album *m* d'échantillons; (*Sewing*) catalogue *m or* album *m* de modes; (*Metal*) **pattern maker** modeleur *m*.
3 *vt* **(a)** modeler (*on* sur).
(b) (*decorate*) orner de motifs. ~**ed material** tissu *m* à motifs.

patty ['pætɪ] *n* petit pâté *m*. ~ **pan** petit moule.

paucity ['pɔːsɪtɪ] *n [crops, coal, oil]* pénurie *f*; *[money]* manque *m*; *[news, supplies, water]* disette *f*; *[ideas]* indigence *f*, disette.

Paul [pɔːl] *n* Paul *m*; *V* **rob.**

paunch [pɔːntʃ] *n [person]* ventre *m*, panse *f*, bedaine* *f*; *[ruminants]* panse.

pauper ['pɔːpəʳ] *n* indigent(e) *m(f)*, pauvre *m*, -esse *f*. ~**'s grave** fosse commune.

pause [pɔːz] **1** *n* **(a)** (*temporary halt*) pause *f*, arrêt *m*. **to give** ~ **to sb** faire hésiter qn, donner à réfléchir à qn; **a** ~ **in the conversation** un petit *or* bref silence dans la conversation; **after a** ~ **he added ...** après une pause il ajouta ...; **there was a** ~ **for discussion/for refreshments** on s'arrêta pour discuter/pour prendre des rafraîchissements.
(b) (*Mus*) (*rest*) repos *m*, silence *m*; (*sign*) point *m* d'orgue, silence; (*Poetry*) césure *f*.
2 *vi* **(a)** (*stop*) faire une pause, marquer un temps d'arrêt, s'arrêter un instant. **to** ~ **for breath** s'arrêter pour reprendre haleine.
(b) (*hesitate*) hésiter. **it made him** ~ **(for thought)** cela lui a donné à réfléchir.
(c) (*linger over*) s'arrêter (*on* sur).

pave [peɪv] *vt street* paver; *yard* carreler, paver. ~**d with gold** pavé d'or; (*fig*) **to** ~ **the way (for)** frayer *or* ouvrir la voie (à), préparer le chemin (pour).

pavement ['peɪvmənt] **1** *n* **(a)** (*Brit*) trottoir *m*. **(b)** (*road surface*) (*of stone, wood*) pavé *m*, pavage *m*; (*stone slabs*) dallage *m*; (*ornate*) pavement *m*. **(c)** (*US: roadway*) chaussée *f*. **2** *cpd*: **pavement artist** artiste *mf* des rues (*qui dessine à la craie à même le trottoir*).

pavilion [pə'vɪlɪən] *n* (*tent, building*) pavillon *m* (*tente, construction*).

paving ['peɪvɪŋ] **1** *n* **(a)** (*material; stone*) pavé *m*; (*flagstones*) dalles *fpl*; (*tiles*) carreaux *mpl*. **(b)** (*paved ground*) pavage *m*; dallage *m*; carrelage *m*; *V* **crazy. 2** *cpd*: **paving stone** pavé *m*.

paw [pɔː] **1** *n* **(a)** *[animal]* patte *f*.
(b) (‡: *hand*) patte* *f*. **keep your** ~**s off!** bas les pattes!*
2 *vt* **(a)** *[animal]* donner un coup de patte à. *[horse]* **to** ~ **the ground** piaffer.
(b) (‡: *pej*) *[person]* tripoter*; (*amorously: also* ~ **about**) tripoter*, peloter‡.

pawky ['pɔːkɪ] *adj* (*Scot*) narquois.

pawn[1] [pɔːn] *n* (*Chess*) pion *m*. (*fig*) **to be sb's** ~ être le jouet de qn, se laisser manœuvrer par qn; (*fig*) **he's a mere** ~ **(in the game)** il n'est qu'un pion sur l'échiquier.

pawn[2] [pɔːn] **1** *vt one's watch etc* mettre en gage *or* au mont-de-piété, mettre au clou*.
2 *n* **(a)** (*thing pledged*) gage *m*, nantissement *m*.
(b) (*U*) **in** ~ en gage, au mont-de-piété, au clou*; **to get sth out of** ~ dégager qch du mont-de-piété.
3 *cpd*: **pawnbroker** prêteur *m*, -euse *f* sur gages; **pawnbroker's, pawnshop** bureau *m* de prêteur sur gages, mont-de-piété *m*; **pawn ticket** reconnaissance *f* (du mont-de-piété) (*de dépôt de gage*).

pax [pæks] *n* **(a)** (*Brit Scol sl*) pouce! **(b)** (*Rel*) paix *f*.

pay [peɪ] (*vb: pret, ptp* **paid**) **1** *n* (*gen*) salaire *m*; *[manual worker]* paie *f or* paye *f*; *[office worker]* appointements *mpl*; *[civil servant]* traitement *m*; *[servant]* gages *mpl*; (*Mil, Naut*) solde *f*, paie. **in the** ~ **of** à la solde de, aux gages de; **the** ~**'s not very good** ce n'est pas très bien payé; **holidays with** ~ congés payés; *V* **equal, half etc.**
2 *cpd*: **pay day** jour *m* de paie; **pay desk** caisse *f*; (*Theat*) caisse, guichet *m*; (*Min*) **pay dirt** (gisement *m* d')alluvions *fpl* exploitables; (*US*) **to hit pay dirt*** trouver un (bon) filon*; **pay increase** = **pay rise**; (*Banking*) **pay-in slip** bordereau *m* de versement; **pay load** (*weight carried*) (*by aircraft*) emport *m*; (*by rocket, missile*) poids *m* utile en charge; (*explosive energy: of warhead, bombload*) puissance *f*; (*Naut: of cargo*) charge payante; **paymaster** (*gen*) intendant *m*, caissier *m*, payeur *m*; (*Naut*) commissaire *m*; (*Mil*) trésorier *m*; (*Brit*) **Paymaster General** *trésorier-payeur de l'Échiquier*; **payoff** *[person]* remboursement *m* (total); *[debt etc]* règlement *m* (total); (*: *reward*) récompense *f*; (*: *outcome*) résultat final; (*: *climax*) comble *m*, bouquet* *m*; (*Brit*) **pay packet** = **wage packet** (*V* **wage**); **pay rise** augmentation *f* de salaire; (*Ind*) **payroll** (*list*) registre *m* du personnel; (*money*) paie *f* (de tout le personnel); (*all the employees*) ensemble *m* du personnel; **the factory has 60 people on the payroll** *or* **a payroll of 60** l'usine a 60 membres de personnel *or* un personnel de 60; **to be on a firm's payroll** être employé par une société; **payslip** feuille *f or* bulletin *m* de paie; (*US*) **pay station** cabine *f* téléphonique, téléphone public; **pay-TV** télé-banque *f*.
3 *vt* **(a)** *person* payer (*to do, for doing* à faire, pour faire); *tradesman, bill, fee* payer, régler; *instalments, money* payer; *deposit* verser; *debt* acquitter, s'acquitter de, régler; *loan* rembourser; (*Fin*) *interest* rapporter; (*Fin*) *dividend* distribuer. **to** ~ **sb £10** payer 10 livres à qn; **he paid me for the book** il m'a payé le livre; **he paid me £2 for the ticket** il m'a payé le billet 2 livres; **he paid £2 for the ticket** il a payé le billet 2 livres; **he paid a lot for his suit** son costume lui a coûté cher, il a payé son costume très cher; **he paid me for my trouble** il m'a dédommagé de mes peines; **I don't** ~ **you to ask questions** je ne vous paie pas pour poser des questions; **we're not paid for that** on n'est pas payé pour cela, on n'est pas payé pour‡; **that's what you're paid for** c'est pour cela qu'on vous paye; **they** ~ **good wages** ils paient bien; **I get paid on Fridays** on me paie *or* je touche ma paie le vendredi; **to** ~ **cash (down)** payer comptant; (*Prov*) **he who** ~**s the piper calls the tune** qui paie les violons choisit la musique; (*fig*) **to** ~ **the penalty** subir *or* payer les conséquences; (*fig*) **to** ~ **the price of** payer le prix de; (*Fin*) **shares that** ~ **5%** des actions qui rapportent 5%; (*Banking*) **to** ~ **money into an account** verser de l'argent à un compte; (*fig*) **his generosity paid dividends** sa générosité porta ses fruits; (*fig*) **the business is** ~**ing its way now** l'affaire couvre ses frais maintenant; (*fig*) **he likes to** ~ **his way** il aime payer sa part *or* participer aux frais; (*fig*) **to put paid to sb's plans** mettre les projets de qn par terre; **I'll soon put paid to him!*** j'aurai vite fait de l'envoyer promener!* *or* de lui régler son compte!; *V* **rob.**
(b) (*fig: be profitable to*) rapporter à. **it would** ~ **him to employ an accountant** il aurait avantage à *or* cela lui rapporterait d'employer un comptable; **it will** ~ **you to be nice to him** vous gagnerez à *or* vous avez intérêt à être aimable avec lui; **it won't** ~ **him to tell the truth** il ne gagnera rien à dire la vérité; **it doesn't** ~ **to be polite these days** on ne gagne rien à *or* on n'a pas intérêt à *or* cela ne paie pas d'être poli de nos jours; **... but it paid him in the long run** ... mais il y a gagné en fin de compte.
(c) to ~ **attention** *or* **heed** to faire attention à, prêter attention à; ~ **no heed to it!** il ne faut pas y faire attention; **to** ~ **compliments to** faire des compliments à; **to** ~ **court to**† faire la cour à; **to** ~ **hommage to** rendre hommage à; **to** ~ **the last honours to** rendre un dernier hommage à; **to** ~ **sb a visit** rendre visite à qn; **we paid a visit to Paris on our way south** nous avons fait un petit tour à Paris en descendant vers le sud; (*euph*) **to** ~ **a visit*** *or* **a call*** aller au petit coin*.
4 *vi* **(a)** payer. **to** ~ **for the meal** payer le repas; (*fig*) **he paid dearly for it** il l'a payé cher (*fig*); **we'll have to** ~ **through the nose for it*** cela va nous coûter les yeux de la tête*; (*fig*) **you'll** ~ **for this!** vous (me) le payerez!; (*fig*) **I'll make him** ~ **for that** je lui ferai payer cela; (*Fin*) '~ **as you earn' system** système fiscal de prélèvement à la source; (*on bus*) '~ **on entry**' 'paiement à l'entrée'; *V* **cash, instalment, nail etc.**
(b) (*fig*) être avantageux, rapporter un profit *or* un bénéfice. **we need to sell 600 copies to make it** ~ nous devons vendre 600 exemplaires pour faire un bénéfice *or* pour que ce soit rentable; **does it** ~**?** est-ce que ça paie?, c'est payant?, c'est rentable?; **this business doesn't** ~ cette affaire n'est pas rentable; **it** ~**s to advertise** la publicité rapporte; **it doesn't** ~ **to tell lies** cela ne sert à rien de mentir, mentir ne sert à rien; **crime doesn't** ~ le crime ne paie pas.

pay away *vt sep* **(a)** (*Naut*) *rope* laisser filer.
(b) *money* dépenser.

pay back *vt sep* **(a)** *stolen money* rendre, restituer; *loan* rembourser; *person* rembourser. **I paid my brother back the £10 I owed him** j'ai remboursé à mon frère les 10 livres que je lui devais.
(b) (*fig*) (*get even with*) **to pay sb back for doing sth** faire payer (*fig*) à qn qch qu'il a fait; **I'll pay you back for that!** je vous le revaudrai!

pay down *vt sep*: **he paid £10 down** (*whole amount in cash*) il paya 10 livres comptant; (*as deposit*) il versa un acompte de 10 livres.

pay in *vt sep* verser (*to* à). **to pay in money at the bank** verser de l'argent à son compte (bancaire); **to pay a sum in to an account** verser une somme à un compte; **to pay in a cheque** verser un chèque.

pay off 1 *vi* rapporter, être avantageux, être rentable. **that trick didn't pay off** cette ruse n'a pas été payante; **his patience paid off in the long run** finalement il a été récompensé de sa patience.
2 *vt sep* **(a)** *debts* régler, acquitter, s'acquitter de; *creditor* rembourser. (*fig*) **to pay off an old score** régler un vieux compte; (*fig*) **to pay off a grudge against sb** prendre sa revanche sur qn.

(b) (*discharge*) *worker, staff* licencier; *servant* donner son compte à, congédier; (*Naut*) *crew* débarquer.
pay out *vt sep* **(a)** *rope* laisser filer.
(b) *money* (*spend*) débourser, dépenser; *[cashier etc]* payer.
(c) (*fig*) **I paid him out for reporting me to the boss** il m'a dénoncé au patron mais je le lui ai fait payer; **I'll pay him out for that!** je lui ferai payer ça!, je le lui revaudrai!
pay up 1 *vi* payer. **pay up!** payez!
2 *vt sep amount* payer, verser; *debts, arrears* régler, s'acquitter de. **the instalments will be paid up over 2 years** les versements vont s'échelonner sur 2 ans; *V* **paid.**
payable ['peɪəbl] *adj* **(a)** (*due, owed*) payable (*in/over 3 months* dans/en 3 mois). ~ **to bearer/on demand/at sight** payable au porteur/sur présentation/à vue; **to make a cheque ~ to sb** faire un chèque à l'ordre de qn.
(b) (*profitable*) rentable, payant. **it's not a ~ proposition** ce n'est pas (une proposition) rentable, ce n'est pas payant.
payee [peɪ'iː] *n [cheque]* bénéficiaire *mf*; *[postal order]* destinataire *mf*, bénéficiaire.
payer ['peɪəʳ] *n* celui qui paie; *[cheque]* tireur *m*, -euse *f*. **he's a slow** *or* **bad ~** c'est un mauvais payeur.
paying ['peɪɪŋ] **1** *adj* **(a)** (*who pays*) payant. ~ **guest** pensionnaire *mf*, hôte payant.
(b) (*profitable*) *business* rémunérateur (*f* -trice), qui rapporte, rentable; *scheme* rentable. **it's not a ~ proposition** ce n'est pas (une proposition) rentable.
2 *n [debt]* règlement *m*, acquittement *m*; *[creditor]* remboursement *m*; *[money]* paiement *m*, versement *m*.
payment ['peɪmənt] *n* **(a)** (*V* **pay**) paiement *m*; versement *m*; règlement *m*; acquittement *m*; remboursement *m*. **on ~ of £50** moyennant (la somme de) 50 livres; **as** *or* **in ~ for the item you sold me** en règlement de l'article que vous m'avez vendu; **as** *or* **in ~ for the sum I owe you** en remboursement de la somme que je vous dois; **as** *or* **in ~ for your help** en paiement de l'aide que vous m'avez apportée; **method of ~** mode *m* de règlement; **without ~** à titre gracieux; **cash ~** (*not credit*) paiement comptant; (*in cash*) paiement en liquide; **~ in full** règlement complet; **~ by instalments** paiement par traites *or* à tempérament; **in monthly ~s of £10** payable en mensualités de 10 livres *or* en versements de 10 livres par mois; **to make a ~** faire *or* effectuer un paiement; **~ of interest** service *m* d'intérêt; **to present sth for ~** présenter qch pour paiement; *V* **down¹, easy, stop** *etc.*
(b) (*reward*) récompense *f*. **as ~ for** en récompense de.
pea [piː] **1** *n* (*Bot, Culin*) (petit) pois *m*. (*fig*) **they are as like as two ~s (in a pod)** ils se ressemblent comme deux gouttes d'eau; *V* **shell, split, sweet** *etc.* **2** *cpd*: **peagreen** vert pomme *inv*; (*Naut*) **pea jacket** caban *m*; **peapod** cosse *f* de pois; **peashooter** sarbacane *f*; **pea soup** soupe *f* aux pois; (*from split peas*) soupe aux pois cassés; **pea soup fog, pea souper*** purée *f* de pois (*fig*).
peace [piːs] **1** *n* **(a)** (*U*) (*not war*) paix *f*; (*treaty*) (traité *m* de) paix. **to be at ~** être en paix; **to live in** *or* **at ~ with** vivre en paix avec; **to make ~** faire la paix; **to make ~ with** signer *or* conclure la paix avec; (*fig*) **to make one's ~ with** se réconcilier avec; **after a long (period of) ~ war broke out** après une longue période de paix la guerre éclata.
(b) (*calm*) paix *f*, tranquillité *f*, calme *m*. **to be at ~ with oneself** avoir la conscience tranquille *or* en paix; **~ of mind** tranquillité d'esprit; **to disturb sb's ~ of mind** troubler l'esprit de qn; **leave him in ~** laisse-le tranquille, fiche-lui la paix*; **he gives them no ~** il ne les laisse pas en paix; **anything for the sake of ~ and quiet** n'importe quoi pour avoir la paix; **to hold one's ~** garder le silence, se taire; *V* **rest.**
(c) (*Jur etc: civil order*) paix *f*, ordre public. **to disturb** *or* **break the ~** troubler *or* violer l'ordre public; **to keep the ~** *[citizen]* ne pas troubler l'ordre public; *[police]* veiller à l'ordre public; (*fig: stop disagreement*) maintenir le calme *or* la paix; **you two try to keep the ~!** essayez de ne pas vous disputer, vous deux!; *V* **breach, justice.**
2 *cpd*: (*US*) **Peace Corps** (organisation américaine de) Coopération *f* (*pour l'aide aux pays en voie de développement*); **peace-keeping force** forces *fpl* de maintien de la paix; **peace-keeping operation/policy** opération *f*/politique *f* de pacification; **peace-loving** pacifique; **peacemaker** pacificateur *m*, -trice *f*, conciliateur *m*, -trice *f*; **peace offensive** offensive *f* de paix; **peace offering** (*Rel: sacrifice*) offrande *f* propitiatoire; (*fig*) cadeau *m* *or* gage *m* de réconciliation; **peace pipe** calumet *m* de la paix; **peace talks** pourparlers *mpl* de paix; **in peacetime** en temps de paix; **peace treaty** (traité *m* de) paix *f*.
peaceable ['piːsəbl] *adj person, nature* pacifique, paisible; *period* paisible, tranquille, calme; *discussion* calme; *settlement* amiable.
peaceably ['piːsəblɪ] *adv* (*V* **peaceable**) pacifiquement; paisiblement; tranquillement; calmement; à l'amiable.
peaceful ['piːsfʊl] *adj* **(a)** (*quiet: not violent*) *reign, period* paisible; *life, place, sleep* paisible, tranquille; *meeting* calme; *demonstration* non-violent. **~ coexistence** coexistence *f* pacifique.
(b) (*for peacetime*) pacifique. **the ~ uses of atomic energy** l'utilisation pacifique de l'énergie nucléaire.
(c) (*not quarrelsome*) *person, disposition* pacifique, paisible.
peacefully ['piːsfəlɪ] *adv demonstrate, reign* paisiblement; *work, lie, sleep* paisiblement, tranquillement. **the demonstration passed off ~** la manifestation s'est déroulée dans le calme *or* paisiblement.
peacefulness ['piːsfʊlnɪs] *n* paix *f*, tranquillité *f*, calme *m*.
peach¹ [piːtʃ] **1** *n* **(a)** pêche *f*; (*also* **~ tree**) pêcher *m*.
(b) (:) **she's a ~!** elle est jolie comme un cœur!*; (*Sport*) **that was a ~ of a shot!** quel beau coup!; **what a ~ of a car!** quelle voiture sensationnelle!*; **what a ~ of a dress!** quel amour* de robe!
2 *adj* (couleur) pêche *inv*.
3 *cpd*: **a peaches and cream complexion** un teint de lis et de rose; **peach blossom** fleur *f* de pêcher; **peach stone** noyau *m* de pêche.
peach² [piːtʃ] *vti* (*Prison sl*) **to ~ (on) sb** moucharder qn*.
peacock ['piːkɒk] *n* paon *m*. **~ blue** bleu paon *inv*; *V* **proud.**
peahen ['piːhen] *n* paonne *f*.
peak [piːk] **1** *n [mountain]* pic *m*, cime *f*, sommet *m*; (*mountain itself*) pic; *[roof etc]* arête *f*, faîte *m*; *[cap]* visière *f*; (*on graph*) sommet; (*fig*) *[career]* sommet, apogée *m*. **when the Empire was at its ~** quand l'Empire était à son apogée; (*Comm*) **when demand was at its ~** quand la demande était à son maximum; **business was at its ~ in 1970** les affaires ont atteint un point culminant en 1970; **at the ~ of his fame** à l'apogée *or* au sommet de sa gloire; **discontent reached its ~** le mécontentement était à son comble; **traffic reaches its ~ about 5** la circulation est à son maximum (d'intensité) vers 17 heures, l'heure de pointe (de la circulation) est vers 17 heures; *V* **off, widow.**
2 *cpd*: **peak demand** (*Comm*) demande *f* maximum *or* record *inv*; (*Elec*) période *f* de consommation de pointe; **peak hours** (*for shops*) heures *fpl* d'affluence; (*for traffic*) heures d'affluence *or* de pointe; **peak period** (*for shops, business*) période *f* de pointe; (*for traffic*) période d'affluence *or* de pointe; (*Ind*) **peak production** production *f* maximum; **peak season** pleine saison; **peak traffic** circulation *f* aux heures d'affluence *or* de pointe; **peak year** année *f* record *inv*.
peaked [piːkt] *adj cap* à visière; *roof* pointu.
peaky ['piːkɪ] *adj* fatigué. **to look ~** avoir les traits un peu tirés, ne pas avoir l'air très en forme*; **to feel ~** ne pas se sentir très en forme*, se sentir mal fichu*.
peal [piːl] **1** *n*: **~ of bells** (*sound*) sonnerie *f* de cloches, carillon *m*; (*set*) carillon; **~ of thunder** coup *m* de tonnerre; **the ~s of the organ** le ronflement de l'orgue; **~ of laughter** éclat *m* de rire; **to go (off) into ~s of laughter** rire aux éclats *or* à gorge déployée.
2 *vi* (*also* **~ out**) *[bells]* carillonner; *[thunder]* gronder; *[organ]* ronfler; *[laughter]* éclater.
3 *vt bells* sonner (à toute volée).
peanut ['piːnʌt] **1** *n* (*nut*) cacahouète *f* *or* cacahuète *f*; (*plant*) arachide *f*. **£300 is ~s for him:** pour lui 300 livres représentent une bagatelle; **what you're offering is just ~s:** ce que vous offrez est une bagatelle *or* est trois fois rien.
2 *cpd*: **peanut butter** beurre *m* de cacahouètes; (*US*) **peanut gallery*** poulailler* *m* (*dans un théâtre*); **peanut oil** huile *f* d'arachide.
pear [pɛəʳ] *n* poire *f*; (*also* **~ tree**) poirier *m*. **~-shaped** en forme de poire, piriforme; *V* **prickly.**
pearl [pɜːl] **1** *n* perle *f*. **(mother of) ~** nacre *f*; **real/cultured ~s** perles fines/de culture; (*fig*) **~s of wisdom** trésors *mpl* de sagesse; (*liter*) **a ~ among women** la perle des femmes; (*fig*) **to cast ~s before swine** jeter des perles aux pourceaux; *V* **seed, string** *etc.*
2 *cpd*: **pearl barley** orge perlé; **pearl button** bouton *m* de nacre; **pearl diver** pêcheur *m*, -euse *f* de perles; **pearl diving** pêche *f* des perles; **pearl grey** gris perle *inv*; **pearl-handled** *knife* à manche de nacre; *revolver* à crosse de nacre; **pearl necklace** collier *m* de perles; **pearl oyster** huître perlière.
3 *vi* **(a)** *[water]* perler, former des gouttelettes.
(b) (*dive for ~s*) pêcher les perles.
pearly ['pɜːlɪ] *adj* (*made of pearl*) en *or* de nacre; (*in colour*) nacré. (*hum*) **the P~ Gates** les portes du Paradis; (*Brit*) **~ king, ~ queen** *marchand(e) des quatre saisons de Londres qui porte des vêtements couverts de boutons de nacre*; **~ teeth** dents nacrées *or* de perle.
peasant ['pezənt] **1** *n* paysan(ne) *m(f)*; (*pej*) paysan, péquenaud(e)* *m(f)*, rustre *m*. **the ~s** (*Hist, Soc*) les paysans; (*Econ: small farmers*) les agriculteurs *mpl*, les ruraux *mpl*.
2 *adj crafts, life* rural, paysan. **~ farmer** petit propriétaire paysan; **~ farming** petite propriété paysanne.
peasantry ['pezəntrɪ] *n*: **the ~** la paysannerie, les paysans *mpl*; (*countrymen*) les campagnards *mpl*.
pease [piːz] *adj*: **~ pudding** purée *f* de pois cassés.
peat [piːt] *n* (*U*) tourbe *f*; (*one piece*) motte *f* de tourbe. **to dig** *or* **cut ~** extraire de la tourbe; **~ bog** tourbière *f*.
peaty ['piːtɪ] *adj soil* tourbeux; *smell* de tourbe.
pebble ['pebl] **1** *n* **(a)** (*stone*) caillou *m*; (*on beach*) galet *m*. (*fig*) **he's not the only ~ on the beach** il n'est pas unique au monde, il n'y a pas que lui.
(b) (*Opt*) lentille *f* en cristal de roche.
2 *cpd*: **pebbledash** crépi moucheté; (*Tex*) **pebbleweave (cloth)** granité *m*.
pebbly ['peblɪ] *adj surface, road* caillouteux. **~ beach** plage *f* de galets.
pecan [pɪ'kæn] *n* (*nut*) (noix *f*) pacane *f*; (*tree*) pacanier *m*.
peccadillo [ˌpekə'dɪləʊ] *n* peccadille *f*, vétille *f*.
peccary ['pekərɪ] *n* pécari *m*.
peck¹ [pek] **1** *n* **(a)** *[bird]* coup *m* de bec.
(b) (*hasty kiss*) bise* *f*. **to give sb a ~ on the cheek** donner à qn une bise sur la joue.
2 *vt [bird] object, ground* becqueter, picoter; *food* picorer; *person, attacker* donner un coup de bec à. **to ~ a hole in sth** faire un trou dans qch à (force de) coups de bec; **the bird ~ed his eyes out** l'oiseau lui a crevé les yeux à coups de bec.
3 *vi*: **the bird ~ed at him furiously** l'oiseau lui donnait des coups de bec furieux; **the bird ~ed at the bread** l'oiseau picora le pain; *[person]* **to ~ at one's food** manger du bout des dents, chipoter*; **~ing order,** (*US*) **~ order** *[birds]* ordre *m* hiérarchique; (*fig*) hiérarchie *f*, ordre *m* des préséances.
peck² [pek] *n* (*Measure*) picotin *m*. **a ~ of troubles** bien des ennuis.

pecker ['pekəʳ] *n* (*Brit*) **to keep one's ~ up‡** ne pas se laisser abattre *or* démonter.
peckish* ['pekɪʃ] *adj* qui a de l'appétit, qui a envie de manger. **I'm feeling ~** j'ai la dent*, je mangerais bien un morceau*.
pectin ['pektɪn] *n* pectine *f*.
pectoral ['pektərəl] **1** *adj* pectoral. **2** *n* pectoral *m* (*ornement*).
peculate ['pekjʊleɪt] *vi* détourner des fonds (publics).
peculation [ˌpekjʊ'leɪʃən] *n* détournement *m* de fonds (publics), péculat *m*.
peculiar [pɪ'kju:lɪəʳ] *adj* **(a)** (*odd*) bizarre, curieux, étrange. **a most ~ flavour** un goût très curieux *or* bizarre; **he's rather ~** il est un peu bizarre, il est plutôt excentrique; **it's really most ~!** c'est vraiment très bizarre! *or* curieux! *or* étrange!
(b) (*special*) particulier, spécial. **a matter of ~ importance** une question d'une importance particulière.
(c) (*belonging exclusively*) particulier. **the ~ properties of this drug** les propriétés particulières de ce médicament; **the region has its ~ dialect** cette région a son dialecte particulier *or* son propre dialecte; **~ to** particulier à, propre à; **an animal ~ to Africa** un animal qui n'existe qu'en Afrique; **it is a phrase ~ to him** c'est une expression qui lui est particulière *or* propre.
peculiarity [pɪˌkjʊlɪ'ærɪtɪ] *n* **(a)** (*distinctive feature*) particularité *f*, trait distinctif. **it has the ~ that ...** cela a *or* présente la particularité de ... *+infin*; (*on passport etc*) **'special peculiarities'** 'signes particuliers'.
(b) (*oddity*) bizarrerie *f*, singularité *f* (*liter*). **she's got her little peculiarities** elle a ses petites manies; **there is some ~ which I cannot define** il y a quelque chose d'étrange *or* de bizarre que je n'arrive pas à définir.
peculiarly [pɪ'kju:lɪəlɪ] *adv* **(a)** (*specially*) particulièrement.
(b) (*oddly*) étrangement, singulièrement.
pecuniary [pɪ'kju:nɪərə] *adj* pécuniaire, financier. **~ difficulties** ennuis *mpl* d'argent, embarras *mpl* pécuniaires.
pedagogic(al) [ˌpedə'gɒdʒɪk(əl)] *adj* pédagogique.
pedagogue ['pedəgɒg] *n* pédagogue *mf*.
pedagogy ['pedəgɒgɪ] *n* pédagogie *f*.
pedal ['pedl] **1** *n* (*all types*) pédale *f*. *[piano]* **loud ~** pédale forte *or* de droite; **soft ~** pédale douce *or* sourde *or* de gauche; *V* **clutch** *etc*.
2 *cpd*: **pedalbin** poubelle *f* à pédale; **pedalcar** voiture *f* à pédales; **pedalboat** pédalo *m*.
3 *vi [cyclist]* pédaler. **he ~led through the town** il traversa la ville (à bicyclette); *V* **soft**.
4 *vt machine, cycle* appuyer sur la *or* les pédale(s) de.
pedant ['pedənt] *n* pédant(e) *m(f)*.
pedantic [pɪ'dæntɪk] *adj* pédant, pédantesque (*liter*).
pedantically [pɪ'dæntɪkəlɪ] *adv* de façon pédante, avec pédantisme.
pedantry ['pedəntrɪ] *n* pédantisme *m*, pédanterie *f* (*liter*).
peddle ['pedl] **1** *vi* faire du colportage. **2** *vt goods* colporter; (*fig pej*) *gossip* colporter, répandre; *ideas* propager; *drugs* faire le trafic de.
peddler ['pedləʳ] *n* (*US*) = **pedlar.**
pederast ['pedəræst] *n* pédéraste *m*.
pederasty ['pedəræstɪ] *n* pédérastie *f*.
pedestal ['pedɪstl] **1** *n* piédestal *m*, socle *m*; (*fig*) piédestal. (*fig*) **to put** *or* **set sb on a ~** mettre qn sur un piédestal. **2** *cpd*: **pedestal desk** bureau *m* ministre *inv*; **pedestal table** guéridon *m*.
pedestrian [pɪ'destrɪən] **1** *n* piéton *m*.
2 *adj style, speech* prosaïque, plat, terre à terre *inv*; *exercise, activity* (qui se fait) à pied, pédestre.
3 *cpd*: **pedestrian crossing** passage *m* pour piétons, passage clouté; **pedestrian precinct** zone piétonnière; **pedestrian traffic** piétons *mpl*; **pedestrian traffic is increasing here** les piétons deviennent de plus en plus nombreux ici; **'pedestrian traffic only'** 'réservé aux piétons'.
pediatrician [ˌpi:dɪə'trɪʃən] *n* (*US*) = **paediatrician.**
pediatric [ˌpi:dɪ'ætrɪk] *adj* (*US*) = **paediatric.**
pediatrics [ˌpi:dɪ'ætrɪks] *n* (*US*) = **paediatrics.**
pedicure ['pedɪkjʊəʳ] *n* **(a)** (*treatment*) pédicurie *f*, podologie *f*, soins *mpl* du pied *or* des pieds (*donnés par un pédicure*). **to have a ~** se faire soigner les pieds (*par un pédicure*). **(b)** (*chiropodist*) pédicure *mf*.
pedigree ['pedɪgri:] **1** *n* **(a)** (*lineage*) *[animal]* pedigree *m*; *[person]* ascendance *f*, lignée *f*. **to be proud of one's ~** être fier de son ascendance *or* de sa lignée.
(b) (*tree*) *[person, animal]* arbre *m* généalogique.
(c) (*document*) *[dogs, horses etc]* pedigree *m*; *[person]* pièce *f* *or* document *m* généalogique.
2 *cpd dog, cattle* de (pure) race.
pediment ['pedɪmənt] *n* fronton *m*.
pedlar, (*US*) peddler ['pedləʳ] *n* (*door to door*) colporteur *m*; (*in street*) camelot *m*; *V* **drug.**
pedometer [pɪ'dɒmɪtəʳ] *n* podomètre *m*.
pee‡ [pi:] **1** *vi* pisser‡, faire pipi*. **2** *n* pisse‡ *f*, pipi* *m*.
peek [pi:k] **1** *n* coup *m* d'œil (furtif). **to take a ~ at** jeter un coup d'œil (furtif) à *or* sur; **~-a-boo!** coucou! **2** *vi* jeter un coup d'œil (furtif) (*at* sur, à).
peel [pi:l] **1** *n [apple, potato]* pelure *f*, épluchure *f*; *[orange]* écorce *f*, peau *m*; (*Culin, also in drink*) zeste *m*; (*also* **candied ~**) écorce confite.
2 *vt fruit* peler, éplucher; *potato* éplucher; *stick* écorcer; *shrimps* décortiquer, éplucher. **to keep one's eyes ~ed‡** ouvrir l'œil*, faire gaffe‡; **keep your eyes ~ed for a signpost!** ouvre l'œil* et tâche d'apercevoir un panneau!
3 *vi [fruit]* se peler; *[paint]* s'écailler; *[skin]* peler.
peel away 1 *vi [skin]* peler; (*Med*) se desquamer; *[paint]* s'écailler; *[wallpaper]* se décoller.
2 *vt sep rind, skin* peler; *film, covering* détacher, décoller.
peel back *vt sep film, covering* détacher, décoller.
peel off 1 *vi* **(a)** = **peel away 1.** **(b)** (*Aviat: leave formation*) s'écarter de la formation. **2** *vt* **(a)** = **peel away 2.** **(b)** (*fig*) **to peel off one's clothes*** enlever ses vêtements, se déshabiller.
peeler ['pi:ləʳ] *n* **(a)** (*gadget*) (couteau-)éplucheur *m*; (*electric*) éplucheur électrique. **(b)** (*Brit*†† : *policeman*) sergent *m* de ville, sergot‡† *m*.
peeling ['pi:lɪŋ] *n* **(a)** *[face etc]* (*Med*) desquamation *f*; (*cosmetic trade*) peeling *m*. **(b) ~s** *[fruit, vegetables]* pelures *fpl*, épluchures *fpl*.
peep[1] [pi:p] **1** *n* **(a)** coup *m* d'œil, regard furtif. **have a ~!** jette un coup d'œil!, regarde vite!; **to have** *or* **take a ~ at sth** jeter un coup d'œil à *or* sur qch, regarder qch à la dérobée *or* en cachette; **she had a ~ at her present** elle jeta un (petit) coup d'œil à son cadeau; **to get** *or* **have a ~ at the exam papers** jeter un (petit) coup d'œil discret sur les sujets d'examen.
(b) *[gas]* veilleuse *f*, (toute) petite flamme. **a ~ of light showed through the curtains** un rayon de lumière filtrait entre les rideaux.
2 *cpd*: **peep-bo!** coucou!; **peephole** trou *m* (pour épier); **peeping Tom** voyeur *m*; **peep show** (*box*) visionneuse *f*; (*pictures*) vues *fpl* stéréoscopiques; (*fig*) spectacle osé *or* risqué; **peeptoe shoe** *or* **sandal** chaussure *f* *or* sandale *f* à bout découpé.
3 *vi* jeter un coup d'œil, regarder furtivement. **to ~ at sth** jeter un coup d'œil à qch, regarder qch furtivement *or* à la dérobée; **she ~ed into the box** elle jeta un coup d'œil *or* elle regarda furtivement à l'intérieur de la boîte; **he was ~ing at us from behind a tree** il nous regardait furtivement *or* à la dérobée de derrière un arbre; **to ~ over a wall** regarder à la dérobée *or* furtivement par-dessus un mur, passer la tête par-dessus un mur; **to ~ through a window** regarder furtivement *or* jeter un coup d'œil par la fenêtre; **I'll just go and ~ down the stairs** je vais seulement jeter un coup d'œil dans l'escalier.
peep out 1 *vi [person]* se montrer, apparaître. **she was peeping out from behind the curtains** elle passait le nez de derrière les rideaux; **the sun peeped out from behind the clouds** le soleil se montra entre les nuages.
2 *vt*: **she peeped her head out** elle passa la tête.
peep[2] [pi:p] **1** *n [bird]* pépiement *m*, piaulement *m*; *[mouse]* petit cri aigu. **one ~ out of you and I'll send you to bed!‡** si tu ouvres la bouche je t'envoie te coucher! **2** *vi [bird]* pépier, piauler; *[mouse]* pousser de petits cris aigus.
peepers‡ ['pi:pəz] quinquets‡ *mpl*.
peer[1] [pɪəʳ] *n* **(a)** (*equal*) pair *m*, égal(e) *m(f)*. **to be tried by one's ~s** être jugé par ses pairs; **it will not be easy to find her ~** il sera difficile de trouver son égale *or* sa pareille; **as a musician he has no ~** comme musicien il est hors pair *or* il n'a pas son pareil.
(b) (*noble*: *also* **~ of the realm**) pair *m* (du royaume); *V* **life.**
peer[2] [pɪəʳ] *vi*: **to ~ at sb** regarder qn; (*inquiringly*) regarder qn d'un air interrogateur; (*doubtfully*) regarder qn d'un air dubitatif; (*anxiously*) regarder qn d'un air inquiet; (*short-sightedly*) regarder qn avec des yeux de myope; **to ~ at a book/photograph** scruter (du regard) *or* regarder attentivement un livre/une photographie; **she ~ed into the room** elle regarda dans la pièce d'un air interrogateur *or* dubitatif *etc*; **to ~ out of the window/over the wall** regarder par la fenêtre/par-dessus le mur d'un air interrogateur *etc*; **to ~ into sb's face** regarder qn d'un air interrogateur *etc*, dévisager qn; **she ~ed around over her spectacles** elle regarda autour d'elle par-dessus ses lunettes.
peerage ['pɪərɪdʒ] *n* (*rank*) pairie *f*; (*collective: the peers*) pairs *mpl*, noblesse *f*; (*list of peers*) nobiliaire *m*. **to inherit a ~** hériter d'une pairie; **to be given a ~** être anobli; *V* **life.**
peeress ['pɪərɪs] *n* pairesse *f*.
peerless ['pɪəlɪs] *adj* sans pareil, sans égal.
peeve‡ [pi:v] *vt* mettre en rogne*.
peeved‡ [pi:vd] *adj* fâché, irrité, en rogne*.
peevish ['pi:vɪʃ] *adj* grincheux, maussade; *child* grognon, de mauvaise humeur.
peevishly ['pi:vɪʃlɪ] *adv* maussadement, avec maussaderie, avec (mauvaise) humeur.
peevishness ['pi:vɪʃnɪs] *n* maussaderie *f*, mauvaise humeur.
peewit ['pi:wɪt] *n* vanneau *m*.
peg [peg] **1** *n* **(a)** (*wooden*) cheville *f*; (*metal*) fiche *f*; (*for coat, hat*) patère *f*; (*tent* ~) piquet *m*; *[violin]* cheville; *[cask]* fausset *m*; (*Croquet*) piquet; (*fig*) prétexte *m*, excuse *f*. (*Brit*) **clothes ~** pince *f* à linge; **to buy a dress off the ~** acheter une robe de prêt-à-porter *or* de confection; **I bought this off the ~** c'est du prêt-à-porter, j'ai acheté ça tout fait; (*fig*) **to take sb down a ~ (or two)** remettre qn à sa place, rabattre *or* rabaisser le caquet à qn; (*fig*) **a ~ to hang a complaint on** un prétexte de plainte, un prétexte *or* une excuse pour se plaindre; *V* **level, square.**
(b) (*Brit*) **a ~ of whisky** un whisky-soda.
2 *cpd*: **pegboard** panneau alvéolé; **pegleg‡** jambe *f* de bois, pilon *m*.
3 *vt* **(a)** (*Tech*) cheviller. **to ~ clothes (out) on the line** étendre du linge sur la corde (à l'aide de pinces).
(b) (*Econ*) *prices, wages* stabiliser.
peg away‡ *vi* bosser‡. **he is pegging away at his maths** il pioche* ses maths.
peg down *vt sep* **(a)** *tent* fixer avec des piquets.
(b) (*fig*) **I pegged him down to saying how much he wanted for it/to 50p an hour** j'ai réussi à le décider à fixer son prix/à accepter 50 pence de l'heure.
peg out 1 *vi* (‡: *die*) claquer‡, casser sa pipe*.
2 *vt sep piece of land* piqueter, délimiter; *V also* **peg 3a.**
pejorative [pɪ'dʒɒrɪtɪv] *adj* péjoratif.
peke* [pi:k] *n abbr of* **pekin(g)ese.**
Pekin [pi:'kɪn] *n*, **Peking** [pi:'kɪŋ] *n* Pékin.

pekin(g)ese [ˌpiːkɪ'niːz] *n* pékinois *m* (*chien*).
pelagic [pɪ'lædʒɪk] *adj* pélagique.
pelargonium [ˌpelə'gəʊnɪəm] *n* pélargonium *m*.
pelf [pelf] *n* (*pej*) lucre *m* (*pej*), richesses *fpl*.
pelican ['pelɪkən] *n* pélican *m*.
pellet ['pelɪt] *n [paper, bread]* boulette *f*; (*for gun*) (grain *m* de) plomb *m*; (*Med*) pilule *f*; *[owl etc]* boulette (de résidus regorgés); *[chemicals]* pastille *f*.
pell-mell ['pel'mel] *adv* pêle-mêle, en désordre, en vrac.
pellucid [pe'luːsɪd] *adj* pellucide (*liter*), transparent; (*fig*) *style* clair, limpide; *mind* lucide, clair.
pelmet ['pelmɪt] *n* (*wooden*) lambrequin *m*; (*cloth*) cantonnière *f*.
pelota [pɪ'ləʊtə] *n* pelote *f* basque.
pelt[1] [pelt] **1** *vt* bombarder, cribler (*with* de). **to ~ sb with stones** lancer une volée *or* une grêle de pierres à qn; **to ~ sb with arrows** cribler qn de flèches; **to ~ sb with tomatoes** bombarder qn de tomates.
2 *vi* **(a) the rain is** *or* **it's ~ing (down)*, it's ~ing with rain*** il tombe des cordes*, il pleut à torrents *or* à seaux; **~ing rain** pluie battante.
(b) (*: *run*) courir à toutes jambes, galoper*. **to ~ down the street** descendre la rue au grand galop *or* à fond de train *or* à toute blinde‡.
3 *n*: **(at) full ~** à toute vitesse, à fond de train.
pelt[2] [pelt] *n* (*skin*) peau *f*; (*fur*) fourrure *f*.
pelvic ['pelvɪk] *adj* pelvien. **~ girdle** ceinture pelvienne.
pelvis ['pelvɪs] *n* bassin *m*, pelvis *m*.
pen[1] [pen] **1** *n* plume *f*; (*ball-point*) stylo *m* à bille; (*felt-tip*) (crayon *m*) feutre *m*; (*fountain ~*) stylo. **he's usually too lazy to put ~ to paper** il est généralement trop paresseux pour prendre la plume *or* pour écrire; **don't put ~ to paper till you're quite sure** ne faites rien par écrit avant d'être certain; **to run** *or* **put one's ~ through sth** barrer *or* rayer qch (d'un trait de plume); **to live by one's ~** vivre de sa plume; *V* **quill** *etc*.
2 *cpd*: **pen-and-ink drawing** dessin *m* à la plume; **penfriend** correspondant(e) *m(f)*; **penholder** porte-plume *m inv*; **penknife** canif *m*; **penmanship** calligraphie *f*; **pen name** pseudonyme *m* (littéraire); **pen nib** bec *m* de plume; (*pej*) **penpusher** gratte-papier* *m inv*, rond-de-cuir* *m*; **penpushing** (travail *m* d')écritures *fpl*; **penwiper** essuie-plume *m inv*.
3 *vt letter* écrire; *article* rédiger.
pen[2] [pen] (*vb: pret* **penned**, *ptp* **penned** *or* **pent**) **1** *n [animals]* parc *m*, enclos *m*; (*also* **play~**) parc (d'enfant). **2** *vt* (*also* **~ in, ~ up**) *animals* parquer; *people* enfermer, parquer (*pej*).
pen[3] [pen] *n* (*Orn*) cygne *m* femelle.
pen[4]**‡** [pen] *n* (*US abbr of* **penitentiary a**) taule‡ *f or* tôle‡ *f*, trou‡ *m*.
penal ['piːnl] *adj law, clause* pénal; *offence* punissable. **~ code** code pénal; **~ colony, ~ settlement** colonie *f* pénitentiaire; (*Jur*) **~ servitude (for life)** travaux forcés (à perpétuité).
penalization [ˌpiːnəlaɪ'zeɪʃən] *n* sanction *f*, pénalité *f*; (*Sport*) pénalisation *f*.
penalize ['piːnəlaɪz] *vt* **(a)** (*punish*) *person* pénaliser, infliger une pénalité à; *action, mistake* pénaliser; (*Sport*) *player, competitor* pénaliser, infliger une pénalisation à. **he was ~d for refusing** il a été pénalisé pour son refus; (*Sport*) **to be ~d for a foul** être pénalisé *or* recevoir une pénalisation pour une infraction.
(b) (*handicap*) handicaper, désavantager. **he was greatly ~d by his deafness** il était sérieusement handicapé par sa surdité; **the rail strike ~s those who haven't got a car** la grève des chemins de fer touche les gens qui n'ont pas de voiture.
penalty ['penəltɪ] **1** *n* (*punishment*) pénalité *f*, peine *f*; (*fine*) amende *f*; (*Sport*) pénalisation *f*; (*Ftbl etc*) penalty *m*. **'~ for breaking these rules: £10'** 'pénalité pour infraction au règlement: 10 livres'; **the ~ for this crime is 10 years' imprisonment** pour ce crime la peine est 10 ans de réclusion; **on ~ of** sous peine de; **under ~ of death** sous peine de mort; **the ~ for not doing this is ...** si on ne fait pas cela la pénalité est ...; (*fig*) **to pay the ~** supporter les conséquences; (*fig*) **to pay the ~ of wealth** payer la rançon de la fortune; (*in games*) **a 5-point ~ for a wrong answer** une pénalisation *or* une amende de 5 points pour chaque erreur.
2 *cpd*: (*Ftbl*) **penalty area, penalty box** surface *f* de réparation; (*Rugby etc*) **penalty goal** but *m* sur pénalité; (*Ftbl*) **penalty kick** coup *m* de pied de pénalité; (*Ftbl*) **penalty spot** point *m* de réparation.
penance ['penəns] *n* (*Rel, fig*) pénitence *f* (*for* de, pour). **to do ~ for** faire pénitence de *or* pour.
pence [pens] *n* **(a)** *pl of* **penny**. **(b) one (new) ~*** un (nouveau) penny.
penchant ['pɑ̃ːŋʃɑ̃ːŋ] *n* penchant *m* (*for* pour), inclination *f* (*for* pour).
pencil ['pensl] **1** *n* **(a)** crayon *m*. **to write in ~** écrire au crayon; **coloured ~** crayon de couleur; **(eyebrow) ~** crayon à sourcils; *V* **indelible, lead**[2], **propel** *etc*.
(b) a ~ of light shone from his torch sa lampe (de poche) projetait un pinceau lumineux.
2 *cpd note, line, mark* au crayon. **pencil box** plumier *m*; **pencil case** trousse *f* (d'écolier); **pencil drawing** dessin *m* au crayon, crayonnage *m*; **pencil rubber** gomme *f* (à crayon); **pencil sharpener** taille-crayon *m*.
3 *vt note* crayonner, écrire au crayon. **to ~ one's eyebrows** se faire les sourcils (au crayon).
pendant ['pendənt] *n* (*on necklace*) pendentif *m*; (*earring*) pendant *m* (d'oreille); (*ceiling lamp*) lustre *m*; (*on chandelier etc*) pendeloque *f*.
pending ['pendɪŋ] **1** *adj business, question* pendant, en suspens, en souffrance; (*Jur*) *case* pendant, en instance. **the ~ tray** le casier des affaires en souffrance; **other matters ~ will be dealt with next week** les affaires en suspens seront réglées la semaine prochaine.
2 *prep* (*until*) en attendant; (*during*) pendant, durant.
pendulous ['pendjʊləs] *adj* **(a)** (*hanging*) *lips, cheeks, nest* pendant; *flowers* pendant, qui retombe. **(b)** (*swinging*) *movement* de balancement, oscillant.
pendulum ['pendjʊləm] *n* (*gen*) pendule *m*; *[clock]* balancier *m*. (*fig*) **the swing of the ~ will bring the socialists back to power** le mouvement du pendule ramènera les socialistes au pouvoir.
penetrable ['penɪtrəbl] *adj* pénétrable.
penetrate ['penɪtreɪt] **1** *vt* pénétrer (dans). **the bullet ~d his heart** la balle lui a pénétré le cœur *or* lui est entrée dans le cœur; **to ~ a forest** pénétrer dans *or* entrer dans une forêt; **to ~ enemy territory** pénétrer en *or* entrer en territoire ennemi; **the car's lights ~d the darkness** les phares de la voiture perçaient l'obscurité; **to ~ a mystery/sb's mind** pénétrer *or* comprendre un mystère/les pensées de qn; **to ~ sb's disguise** percer le déguisement de qn; **to ~ sb's plans** pénétrer *or* découvrir les plans de qn; (*Pol*) **subversive elements have ~d the party** des éléments subversifs se sont infiltrés dans le parti; (*Comm*) **they managed to ~ the sugar market** ils ont réussi à s'infiltrer dans le marché du sucre.
2 *vi*: **to ~ (into)** *[person, flames]* pénétrer (dans); *[light, water]* pénétrer (dans), filtrer (dans); **to ~ through** traverser.
penetrating ['penɪtreɪtɪŋ] *adj* **(a)** *wind, rain* pénétrant; *cold* pénétrant, mordant; *sound, voice* pénétrant, perçant; *look* pénétrant, perçant.
(b) (*acute, discerning*) *mind, remark* pénétrant, perspicace; *person, assessment* clairvoyant, perspicace, intelligent.
penetratingly ['penɪtreɪtɪŋlɪ] *adv* **(a)** *speak, shriek* d'une voix perçante. **(b)** *assess, observe* avec pénétration, avec perspicacité, avec intelligence.
penetration [ˌpenɪ'treɪʃən] *n* (*U*) pénétration *f*; (*discernment*) pénétration *f*, perspicacité *f*.
penetrative ['penɪtrətɪv] *ad* pénétrant.
penguin ['peŋgwɪn] *n* pingouin *m*.
penicillin [ˌpenɪ'sɪlɪn] *n* pénicilline *f*.
peninsula [pɪ'nɪnsjʊlə] *n* péninsule *f*.
peninsular [pɪ'nɪnsjʊlə^{r}] *adj* péninsulaire. **the P~ War** la guerre (*napoléonienne*) d'Espagne.
penis ['piːnɪs] *n* pénis *m*. (*Psych*) **~ envy** revendication subconsciente du phallus.
penitence ['penɪtəns] *n* pénitence *f*, repentir *m*.
penitent ['penɪtənt] *adj, n* pénitent(e) *m(f)*.
penitential [ˌpenɪ'tenʃəl] **1** *adj* contrit. (*Rel*) **~ psalm** psaume *m* de la pénitence *or* pénitentiel. **2** *n* (*code*) pénitentiel *m*.
penitentiary [ˌpenɪ'tenʃərɪ] *n* **(a)** (*Jur*) (*Brit*) pénitencier *m*; (*US*) prison *f*. **(b)** (*Rel*) pénitencerie *f*.
penitently ['penɪtəntlɪ] *adv* d'un air *or* d'un ton contrit.
pennant ['penənt] *n* flamme *f*, banderole *f*; (*Naut*) flamme, guidon *m*.
penniless ['penɪlɪs] *adj* sans le sou, sans ressources. **he's quite ~** il n'a pas le sou, il est sans le sou *or* sans ressources; **she was left ~** elle s'est retrouvée sans le sou *or* sans ressources.
pennon ['penən] *n* flamme *f*, banderole *f*; (*Naut*) flamme, guidon *m*.
Pennsylvania [ˌpensɪl'veɪnɪə] *n* Pennsylvanie *f*.
penny ['penɪ] **1** *n, pl* **pence** (*valeur*), **pennies** (*pièces*) penny *m* (*avant 1971, douzième du shilling; depuis 1971, centième de la livre*). **one old/new ~** un ancien/un nouveau penny; **it costs 5 pence** cela coûte 5 pence; **I have 5 pennies** j'ai 5 pennies, j'ai 5 pièces de un penny; (*fig*) **nobody was a ~ the worse** personne n'en a souffert, cela n'a fait de tort à personne; (*fig*) **he is not a ~ the wiser (for it)** il n'en sait pas plus long qu'avant, il n'est pas plus avancé*; **he hasn't a ~ (to his name), he hasn't got two pennies to rub together** il est sans le sou, il n'a pas un sou vaillant, il n'a pas le sou *or* un radis‡; **(a) ~ for your thoughts!** à quoi pensez-vous?; **the ~ has dropped!*** il a (*or* j'ai *etc*) enfin pigé!‡, ça y est!*, ça a fait tilt!‡; (*fig*) **he keeps turning up like a bad ~** pas moyen de se débarrasser de lui; (*Prov*) **a ~ saved is a ~ gained** un sou est un sou; (*Prov*) **in for a ~ in for a pound** (au point où on en est) autant faire les choses jusqu'au bout; (*Prov*) **take care of the pennies and the pounds will take care of themselves** les petits ruisseaux font les grandes rivières (*Prov*), il n'y a pas de petites économies; *V* **honest, pretty, spend** *etc*.
2 *cpd book, pencil* de deux sous. **penny-a-liner*** pigiste *mf*, journaliste *mf* à la pige *or* à deux sous la ligne; (*Brit*) **penny dreadful** roman *m* à deux sous, (petit) roman à sensation; (*Brit*) **penny farthing (bicycle)** bicycle *m*; **penny-in-the-slot machine** (*for amusements*) machine *f* à sous; (*for selling*) distributeur *m* automatique; **pennyweight** un gramme et demi; **penny whistle** flûteau *m*; (*Prov*) **to be ~ wise and pound foolish** économiser un franc et en prodiguer mille; **I want a pennyworth of sweets** je voudrais pour un penny de bonbons.
penologist [piː'nɒlədʒɪst] *n* pénologiste *mf*, pénologue *mf*.
penology [piː'nɒlədʒɪ] *n* pénologie *f*.
pension ['penʃən] **1** *n* **(a)** (*state payment*) pension *f*. **(old age) ~** pension vieillesse (de la Sécurité sociale); **retirement ~** (pension de) retraite *f*; **war/widow's/disablement ~** pension de guerre/de veuve/d'invalidité.
(b) (*Ind: from company etc*) retraite *f*. **he retired at 60 but got no ~** il s'est retiré à 60 ans mais n'a pas touché de retraite; **it is possible to retire on a ~ at 55** il est possible de toucher une retraite à partir de 55 ans.
(c) (*to artist, former servant etc*) pension *f*.
2 *cpd*: **pension book** livret *m* de retraite; **pension fund** fonds *m* vieillesse, assurance *f* vieillesse; (*Ind*) **pension scheme** caisse *f* de retraite.
3 *vt* pensionner.

pension off *vt sep* mettre à la retraite.
pensionable ['penʃnəbl] *adj post* qui donne droit à une pension. **to be of ~ age** avoir (atteint) l'âge de la retraite.
pensioner ['penʃənə^r] *n* (*also* **old age ~**) retraité(e) *m(f)*; (*any kind of pension*) pensionné(e) *m(f)*; (*also* **war ~**) militaire retraité, (*disabled*) invalide *m* de guerre.
pensive ['pensɪv] *adj person, look* pensif, songeur; *music etc* méditatif.
pensively ['pensɪvlɪ] *adv* pensivement, d'un air *or* d'un ton pensif *or* songeur.
pent [pent] **1** *ptp of* **pen²**. **2** *adj* (*liter*) emprisonné. **3** *cpd*: **pent-up** *emotions, rage* refoulé, réprimé; *energy* refoulé, contenu; **she was very pent-up** elle était très tendue, elle était sur les nerfs.
pentagon ['pentəgən] *n* pentagone *m*. (*US*) **the P~** le Pentagone.
pentagonal [pen'tægənl] *adj* pentagonal.
pentameter [pen'tæmɪtə^r] *n* pentamètre *m*; *V* **iambic**.
Pentateuch ['pentətju:k] *n* Pentateuque *m*.
pentathlon [pen'tæθlən] *n* pentathlon *m*.
pentatonic [,pentə'tɒnɪk] *adj* pentatonique.
Pentecost ['pentɪkɒst] *n* Pentecôte *f*.
Pentecostal [,pentɪ'kɒstl] *adj* de (la) Pentecôte.
penthouse ['penthaʊs] *n* **(a)** (*also* **~ flat**) appartement *m* de grand standing (*construit sur le toit d'un immeuble*). **(b)** (*Archit*) auvent *m*, abri extérieur. **~ roof** appentis *m*, toit *m* en auvent.
penultimatt [pɪ'nʌltɪmɪt] **1** *adj* avant-dernier, pénultième. **2** *n* (*Ling*) pénultième *f*, avant-dernière syllabe.
penumbra [pɪ'nʌmbrə] *n* (*Astron*) pénombre *f*.
penurious [pɪ'njʊərɪəs] *adj* (*indigent*) indigent, misérable; (*stingy*) parcimonieux, ladre.
penury ['penjʊrɪ] *n* misère *f*, indigence *f*.
peon ['pi:ən] *n* (*in India*) péon *m*, fantassin *m*; (*in South America*) péon, journalier *m*.
peony (rose) ['pɪənɪ('rəʊz)] *n* pivoine *f*.
people ['pi:pl] **1** *n* **(a)** (*pl*: *persons*) gens *pl*, personnes *fpl*; (*crowd*) monde *m* (*no pl*). **old ~** les personnes âgées, les vieilles gens, les vieux *mpl*; **young ~** les jeunes gens *mpl*, les jeunes *mpl*, la jeunesse; **clever ~** les gens intelligents; **all these good ~** toutes ces bonnes gens, tous ces braves gens; **old ~ are often lonely** les vieilles gens sont souvent très seuls; **all the old experienced ~** toutes ces vieilles gens pleins d'expérience; **~ are more important than animals** les gens *or* les êtres humains sont plus importants que les animaux; **a lot of ~** beaucoup de gens *or* de monde, un tas de gens*; **what a lot of ~!** que de monde!; **the place was full of ~** il y avait beaucoup de monde, il y avait un monde fou*; **several ~ said ...** plusieurs personnes ont dit ...; **how many ~?** combien de personnes?; **there were several English ~ in the hotel** il y avait plusieurs Anglais à l'hôtel; **they're strange ~** ce sont de drôles de gens; **I like the ~ in the hotel** j'aime les gens à l'hôtel; **what do you ~ think?** qu'est-ce que vous en pensez, vous (tous)? *or* vous autres?; *V* **little¹, other.**
(b) (*pl*: *in general*) **what will ~ think?** qu'est-ce que vont penser les gens?, que va-t-on penser?; **~ say ... on dit ...**; **~ get worried when they see that** on s'inquiète quand on voit cela, les gens s'inquiètent quand ils voient cela; **~ quarrel a lot here** on se dispute beaucoup ici.
(c) (*pl*: *inhabitants*) *[a country]* peuple *m*, nation *f*, population *f*; *[district, town]* habitants *mpl*, population. **country ~** les gens de la campagne, les populations rurales; **town ~** les habitants des villes, les citadins *mpl*; **the French ~** les Français, le peuple français, la nation française; **English ~ often say ...** les Anglais disent souvent ... .
(d) (*pl*) (*Pol*: *citizens*) peuple *m*; (*general public*) public *m*. **government by the ~** gouvernement *m* par le peuple; **the king and his ~** le roi et ses sujets *or* son peuple; **~ of the Republic!** citoyens!; **the ~ at large** le grand public; **man of the ~** homme *m* du peuple; *V* **common.**
(e) (*sg*: *nation, race etc*) peuple *m*, nation *f*, race *f*. **the Jewish ~** la race juive, les Juifs *mpl*; **the ~s of the East** les nations de l'Orient, les Orientaux *mpl*.
(f) (*pl*: *: family*) famille *f*, parents *mpl*. **I am writing to my ~** j'écris à ma famille; **how are your ~?** comment va votre famille?, comment ça va chez vous?*
2 *vt* peupler (*with* de).
pep [pep] **1** *n* (*:U*) entrain *m*, dynamisme *m*, allant *m*. **full of ~** très dynamique, plein d'entrain *or* d'allant. **2** *cpd*: **pep pill*** excitant *m*, stimulant *m*; **peptalk*** laïus* *m* d'encouragement.
pep up* **1** *vi [person]* s'animer, être ragaillardi; *[business, trade]* reprendre, remonter.
2 *vt sep person* remonter le moral à, ragaillardir; *party, conversation* animer; *drink, plot* corser.
pepper ['pepə^r] **1** *n* **(a)** (*spice*) poivre *m*. **white/black ~** poivre blanc/gris; *V* **cayenne** *etc*.
(b) (*vegetable*) poivron *m*. **red/green ~** poivron rouge/vert.
2 *cpd*: **pepper-and-salt** *cloth* marengo; *hair* poivre et sel; **peppercorn** grain *m* de poivre; (*Jur*) **peppercorn rent** loyer nominal; **pepper mill** moulin *m* à poivre; **peppermint** (*sweet*) pastille *f* de menthe; (*plant*) menthe poivrée; **peppermint (-flavoured)** à la menthe; **pepperpot** poivrier *m*, poivrière *f*.
3 *vt* (*Culin*) poivrer. (*fig*) **to ~ sb with shot** cribler qn de plombs; **to ~ sb with questions** assaillir *or* mitrailler qn de questions.
peppery ['pepərɪ] *adj food, taste* poivré; (*fig*) *person* irascible, emporté; *speech* irrité.
pepsin ['pepsɪn] *n* pepsine *f*.
peptic ['peptɪk] *adj* digestif. **~ ulcer** ulcère gastro-duodénal.
peptone ['peptəʊn] *n* peptone *f*.
per [pɜ:^r] *prep* **(a)** par. **~ annum** par an; **~ capita** par personne; **~ cent** pour cent; **a 10 ~ cent discount/increase** un rabais/une augmentation de 10 pour cent; **~ diem, ~ day** par jour; **~ head** par tête, par personne; **to drive at 100 km ~ hour** rouler à 100 (km) à l'heure; **she is paid 5 francs ~ hour** on la paie 5 F (de) l'heure; **3 francs ~ kilo** 3 F le kilo; **4 hours ~ person** 4 heures par personne.
(b) (*Comm*) **~ post** par la poste; **as ~ invoice** suivant facture; **as ~ usual*** comme d'habitude.
peradventure [,pərəd'ventʃə^r] *adv* (*liter*) par hasard, d'aventure (*liter*).
perambulate [pə'ræmbjʊleɪt] **1** *vt* parcourir (*un terrain, surtout en vue de l'inspecter*). **2** *vi* marcher, faire les cent pas.
perambulation [pə,ræmbjʊ'leɪʃən] *n* marche *f*, promenade(s) *f(pl)*, déambulation *f*.
perambulator ['præmbjʊleɪtə^r] *n* (*Brit*: †, *frm*) voiture *f* d'enfant, landau *m*.
perceive [pə'si:v] *vt* **(a)** (*see, hear*) *sound, light* percevoir. **(b)** (*notice*) remarquer, apercevoir, s'apercevoir de. **he ~d that ...** il remarqua *or* s'aperçut que ... . **(c)** (*understand*) percevoir, comprendre, saisir.
percentage [pə'sentɪdʒ] *n* pourcentage *m*. **the figure is expressed as a ~** le chiffre donné est un pourcentage; (*Comm*) **to get a ~ on all sales** recevoir un pourcentage sur chaque vente; **a high ~ were girls** les filles constituaient un fort pourcentage.
perceptible [pə'septəbl] *adj sound, movement* perceptible; *difference, increase* perceptible, sensible, appréciable.
perceptibly [pə'septɪblɪ] *adv move* d'une manière perceptible; *change, increase* sensiblement.
perception [pə'sepʃən] *n* **(a)** *[sound, sight etc]* perception *f*. **one's powers of ~ decrease with age** la faculté de perception diminue avec l'âge.
(b) (*sensitiveness*) sensibilité *f*, intuition *f*; (*insight*) perspicacité *f*, pénétration *f*.
(c) (*Psych*) perception *f*.
(d) *[rents, taxes, profits]* perception *f*.
perceptive [pə'septɪv] *adj faculty* percepteur (*f* -trice), de (la) perception; *analysis, assessment* pénétrant; *person* fin, perspicace. **how very ~ of you!** vous êtes très perspicace!
perceptiveness [pə'septɪvnɪs] *n* = **perception b.**
perch¹ [pɜ:tʃ] *n* (*fish*) perche *f*.
perch² [pɜ:tʃ] **1** *n* **(a)** *[bird]* perchoir *m*, juchoir *m*. (*fig*) **to knock sb off his ~** détrôner qn*.
(b) (*measure*) perche *f*.
2 *vi [bird]* (se) percher; *[person]* se percher, se jucher. **we ~ed in a tree to see the procession** nous nous sommes perchés dans un arbre pour voir le défilé; **she ~ed on the arm of my chair** elle se percha *or* se jucha sur le bras de mon fauteuil.
3 *vt* percher, jucher. **to ~ a vase on a pedestal** percher *or* jucher un vase sur un piédestal; **we ~ed the child on the wall** nous avons perché *or* juché l'enfant sur le mur; **a chalet ~ed on top of a mountain** un chalet perché *or* juché sur le sommet d'une montagne.
perchance [pə'tʃɑ:ns] *adv* (*liter*) (*by chance*) par hasard, d'aventure (*liter*); (*perhaps*) peut-être.
percipient [pə'sɪpɪənt] **1** *adj faculty* percepteur (*f* -trice); *person* fin, perspicace; *choice* éclairé. **2** *n* personne *f* qui perçoit.
percolate ['pɜ:kəleɪt] **1** *vt coffee* passer. **I am going to ~ the coffee** je vais passer le café; **I don't like ~d coffee** je n'aime pas le café fait dans une cafetière à pression.
2 *vi [coffee, water]* passer (*through* par). (*fig*) **the news ~d through from the front** la nouvelle a filtré du front.
percolator ['pɜ:kəleɪtə^r] *n* cafetière *f* à pression; (*in café*) percolateur *m*. **electric ~** cafetière électrique.
percussion [pə'kʌʃən] **1** *n* **(a)** (*impact; noise*) percussion *f*, choc *m*. **(b)** (*Mus*) percussion *f*, batterie *f*. **2** *cpd*: **percussion bullet** balle explosive; **percussion cap** capsule fulminante; (*Mus*) **percussion instrument** instrument *m* à *or* de percussion.
percussive [pə'kʌsɪv] *adj* percutant.
perdition [pə'dɪʃən] *n* perdition *f*, ruine *f*, perte *f*; (*Rel*) perdition, damnation *f*.
peregrination [,perɪgrɪ'neɪʃən] *n* (†, *frm*) pérégrination *f*. **~s** voyage *m*, pérégrinations.
peregrine ['perɪgrɪn] *adj*: **~ falcon** faucon *m* pèlerin.
peremptorily [pə'remptərɪlɪ] *adv* péremptoirement, d'un ton *or* d'une manière péremptoire, impérieusement.
peremptory [pə'remptərɪ] *adj instruction, order* péremptoire, formel; *argument* décisif, sans réplique; *tone* tranchant, péremptoire.
perennial [pə'renɪəl] **1** *adj* (*long lasting, enduring*) perpétuel, éternel; (*perpetual, recurrent*) perpétuel, continuel; *plant* vivace. **2** *n* plante *f* vivace; *V* **hardy.**
perennially [pə'renɪəlɪ] *adv* (*everlastingly*) éternellement; (*continually*) perpétuellement, continuellement.
perfect ['pɜ:fɪkt] **1** *adj* **(a)** *person, work of art, meal, weather, crime* parfait; *love* parfait, idéal; *harmony* parfait, complet (*f* -ète), total; *wife, hostess, teacher etc* parfait, exemplaire, modèle. **no one is ~** personne n'est parfait, la perfection n'est pas de ce monde; **his English is ~** son anglais est parfait *or* impeccable; **his Spanish is far from ~** son espagnol est loin d'être parfait *or* laisse beaucoup à désirer; **it was the ~ moment to speak to him about it** c'était le moment idéal *or* le meilleur moment possible pour lui en parler; (*Mus*) **~ pitch** le la absolu, l'oreille absolue; (*Gram*) **~ tense** parfait *m*; *V* **word.**
(b) (*emphatic*) véritable, parfait. **he's a ~ stranger** personne ne le connaît; **he's a ~ stranger to me** il m'est complètement inconnu; **I am a ~ stranger here** je ne connais absolument

personne ici; a ~ **pest** un véritable fléau; a ~ **fool** un parfait imbécile, un imbécile fini.
2 *n* (*Gram*) parfait *m*. **in the** ~ au parfait.
3 [pəˈfekt] *vt work of art* achever, parachever, parfaire; *skill, technique* mettre au point. **to** ~ **one's French** parfaire ses connaissances de français.
perfectibility [pəˌfektɪˈbɪlɪtɪ] *n* perfectibilité *f*.
perfectible [pəˈfektɪbl] *adj* perfectible.
perfection [pəˈfekʃən] *n* (*completion*) achèvement *m*; (*faultlessness*) perfection *f*; (*perfecting*) perfectionnement *m*. **to** ~ à la perfection.
perfectionist [pəˈfekʃənɪst] *adj, n* perfectionniste (*mf*).
perfective [pəˈfektɪv] (*Gram*) **1** *adj* perfectif. **2** *n* (*aspect*) aspect perfectif; (*verb*) verbe perfectif.
perfectly [ˈpɜːfɪktlɪ] *adv* parfaitement.
perfidious [pɜːˈfɪdɪəs] *adj* perfide, traître (*f* traîtresse).
perfidiously [pɜːˈfɪdɪəslɪ] *adv* perfidement, traîtreusement; *act* en traître, perfidement.
perfidy [ˈpɜːfɪdɪ] *n* perfidie *f*.
perforate [ˈpɜːfəreɪt] *vt paper, metal* perforer, percer; *ticket* perforer, poinçonner. **tear along the** ~**d line** détachez suivant le pointillé.
perforation [ˌpɜːfəˈreɪʃən] *n* perforation *f*.
perforce [pəˈfɔːs] *adv* forcément, nécessairement.
perform [pəˈfɔːm] **1** *vt* **(a)** *task* exécuter, accomplir; *duty* remplir, accomplir, s'acquitter de; *function* remplir; *miracle* accomplir; *rite* célébrer. **to** ~ **an operation** (*gen*) accomplir *or* exécuter une opération; (*Med*) pratiquer une opération, opérer.
(b) (*Theat etc*) *play* jouer, représenter, donner; *ballet, opera* donner; *symphony* exécuter, jouer. **to** ~ **a part** (*in play*) jouer *or* tenir un rôle; (*in ballet*) danser un rôle; (*in opera*) chanter un rôle; **to** ~ **a solo/acrobatics** exécuter un solo/un numéro d'acrobatie.
2 *vi* **(a)** (*gen*) donner une *or* des représentation(s); *[actor]* jouer; *[singer]* chanter; *[dancer]* danser; *[acrobat, trained animal]* exécuter un *or* des numéro(s). **to** ~ **on the violin** jouer du violon, exécuter un morceau au violon; **he** ~**ed brilliantly as Hamlet** il a brillamment joué *or* interprété Hamlet; (*Theat*) **when we** ~**ed in Edinburgh** quand nous avons donné une *or* des représentation(s) à Édimbourg, quand nous avons joué à Édimbourg; **the elephants** ~**ed well** les éléphants ont bien exécuté leur numéro; ~**ing seals/dogs** *etc* phoques/chiens *etc* savants.
(b) *[machine, vehicle]* marcher, fonctionner. **the car is not** ~**ing properly** la voiture ne marche pas bien.
performance [pəˈfɔːməns] *n* **(a)** (*session, presentation*) (*Theat*) représentation *f*; (*Cine*) séance *f*; *[opera, ballet, circus]* représentation, spectacle *m*; *[concert]* séance, audition *f*. (*Theat*) **2** ~**s nightly** 2 représentations chaque soir; **'no** ~ **tonight'** 'ce soir relâche'; (*Theat etc*) **the late** ~ la dernière représentation *or* séance de la journée; (*Theat etc*) **first** ~ première *f* (représentation); **the play had 300** ~**s** la pièce a eu 300 représentations; (*Cine*) **continuous** ~ spectacle permanent.
(b) *[actor, singer, dancer]* interprétation *f*; *[musician]* interprétation, exécution *f*; *[acrobat]* numéro *m*; *[racehorse, athlete etc]* performance *f*. (*Sport*) **after several poor** ~**s he finally managed to ...** après plusieurs performances médiocres il a enfin réussi à ...; (*Sport*) **the team's** ~ **left much to be desired** la performance de l'équipe a beaucoup laissé à désirer; **his** ~ **of Bach was outstanding** son interprétation de Bach était tout à fait remarquable; **the pianist gave a splendid** ~ le pianiste a joué de façon remarquable; **I didn't like her** ~ **of Giselle** je n'ai pas aimé son interprétation de Giselle.
(c) *[machine]* fonctionnement *m*; *[vehicle]* performance *f*. **the machine has given a consistently fine** ~ le fonctionnement de la machine s'est révélé uniformément excellent.
(d) (*U: V* **perform 1a**) exécution *f*; accomplissement *m*; célébration *f*. **in the** ~ **of his duties** dans l'exercice de ses fonctions.
(e) (*: *fuss*) affaire *f*, histoire* *f*. **it was a whole** ~ **to get her to agree to see him!** ça a été toute une affaire *or* toute une histoire* pour la décider à le voir!; **what a** ~**!** quelle affaire!, quelle histoire!*; **it's such a** ~ **getting ready that it's hardly worth while going for a picnic** c'est une telle affaire *or* une telle histoire* de tout préparer que ça ne vaut guère la peine d'aller piqueniquer.
performer [pəˈfɔːməʳ] *n* (*Theat*) (*gen*) artiste *mf*; (*actor*) interprète *mf*, acteur *m*, -trice *f*; (*pianist etc*) exécutant(e) *m(f)*, interprète; (*dancer*) interprète.
perfume [ˈpɜːfjuːm] **1** *n* parfum *m*.
2 [pəˈfjuːm] *vt* parfumer.
perfumery [pəˈfjuːmərɪ] *n* parfumerie *f*.
perfunctorily [pəˈfʌŋktərɪlɪ] *adv bow, greet* négligemment; *answer, agree* sans conviction, pour la forme; *perform* avec négligence, sommairement, par-dessous la jambe.
perfunctory [pəˈfʌŋktərɪ] *adj nod, bow, greeting* négligent, pour la forme; *agreement* superficiel, fait pour la forme.
pergola [ˈpɜːgələ] *n* pergola *f*.
perhaps [pəˈhæps, præps] *adv* peut-être. ~ **so/not** peut-être que oui/que non; ~ **he will come** peut-être viendra-t-il, il viendra peut-être, peut-être qu'il viendra.
perigee [ˈperɪdʒiː] *n* périgée *m*.
peril [ˈperɪl] *n* péril *m*, danger *m*. **in** ~ **of** en danger de; **at the** ~ **of** au péril de; **at your** ~ à vos risques et périls.
perilous [ˈperɪləs] *adj* périlleux, dangereux.
perilously [ˈperɪləslɪ] *adv* périlleusement, dangereusement. **they were** ~ **near disaster/death** *etc* ils frôlaient la catastrophe/la mort *etc*.
perimeter [pəˈrɪmɪtəʳ] *n* périmètre *m*.
period [ˈpɪərɪəd] **1** *n* **(a)** (*epoch*) période *f*, époque *f*; (*stage: in career, development etc*) époque, moment *m*; (*length of time*) période. **the classical** ~ la période classique; **costumes/ furniture of the** ~ costumes/meubles de l'époque; **Picasso's blue** ~ la période bleue de Picasso; **the** ~ **from 1600 to 1750** la période allant de 1600 à 1750; **the post-war** ~ (la période de) l'après-guerre *m*; **during the whole** ~ **of the negotiations** pendant toute la période *or* durée des négociations; **at a later** ~ plus tard; **at that** ~ **in** *or* **of his life** à cette époque *or* à ce moment de sa vie; **a** ~ **of social upheaval** une période *or* une époque de bouleversements sociaux; **he had several** ~**s of illness** il a été malade à plusieurs reprises; (*Astron*) ~ **of revolution** *or* **rotation** période de rotation; (*Med*) **incubation** ~ période d'incubation; **the holiday** ~ la période des vacances; (*Met*) **bright/rainy** ~**s** périodes ensoleillées/de pluie; **in the** ~ **of a year** en l'espace d'une année; **it must be done within a 3-month** ~ il faut le faire dans un délai de 3 mois; *V* **safe.**
(b) (*Scol*) cours *m*, leçon *f*. **2 geography** ~**s** 2 cours *or* leçons de géographie.
(c) (*Gram: full stop*) point *m*. (*impressive sentences*) ~**s** périodes *fpl*, phrases bien tournées.
(d) (*menstruation: also* **monthly** ~) règles *fpl*.
2 *cpd*: **period costume, period dress** costume *m* de l'époque; **period furniture** (*genuine*) meuble *m* d'époque; (*copy*) meuble de style ancien; (*fig*) **period piece** curiosité *f*.
periodic [ˌpɪərɪˈɒdɪk] *adj* périodique.
periodical [ˌpɪərɪˈɒdɪkəl] **1** *adj* périodique. **2** *n* (journal *m*) périodique *m*, publication *f* périodique.
periodically [ˌpɪərɪˈɒdɪkəlɪ] *adv* périodiquement.
periodicity [ˌpɪərɪəˈdɪsɪtɪ] *n* périodicité *f*.
peripatetic [ˌperɪpəˈtetɪk] *adj* (*itinerant*) ambulant; (*Philos*) péripatéticque.
peripheral [pəˈrɪfərəl] *adj* périphérique.
periphery [pəˈrɪfərɪ] *n* périphérie *f*.
periphrasis [pəˈrɪfrəsɪs] *n, pl* **periphrases** [pəˈrɪfrəsiːz] périphrase *f*, circonlocution *f*.
periscope [ˈperɪskəʊp] *n* périscope *m*.
perish [ˈperɪʃ] **1** *vi* **(a)** (*die*) périr, mourir. **we shall do it or** ~ **in the attempt!** nous réussirons ou nous y laisserons la vie!; (*hum*) ~ **the thought!** jamais de la vie!, loin de moi cette pensée! (*hum*).
(b) (*) **to be** ~**ing** *or* ~**ed** avoir très froid, être frigorifié; **I'm absolutely** ~**ed!** *or* ~**ing!** je suis frigorifié!, je crève* de froid!
(c) *[rubber, material, leather]* se détériorer, s'abîmer; *[foods etc]* (*be spoilt*) se détériorer, s'abîmer; (*be lost*) être détruit, être perdu.
2 *vt rubber, foods etc* abîmer, détériorer.
perishable [ˈperɪʃəbl] **1** *adj* périssable. **2** *n*: ~**s** denrées *fpl* périssables.
perisher‡ [ˈperɪʃəʳ] *n* (*Brit*) enquiquineur* *m*, -euse* *f*. **little** ~! (espèce *f* de) petit poison!*
perishing [ˈperɪʃɪŋ] *adj* **(a)** très froid. **outside in the** ~ **cold** dehors dans le froid glacial *or* intense; **it was** ~* il faisait un froid de loup *or* de canard*; *V* **perish. (b)** (*Brit*‡) sacré* (*before n*), fichu* (*before n*), foutu‡ (*before n*). **it's a** ~ **nuisance!** c'est vraiment enquiquinant!*
perishingly* [ˈperɪʃɪŋlɪ] *adv* (*Brit*) ~ **cold** terriblement froid.
peristyle [ˈperɪstaɪl] *n* péristyle *m*.
peritoneum [ˌperɪtəˈniːəm] *n* péritoine *m*.
peritonitis [ˌperɪtəˈnaɪtɪs] *n* péritonite *f*.
periwig [ˈperɪwɪg] *n* perruque *f*.
periwinkle [ˈperɪˌwɪŋkl] *n* (*Bot*) pervenche *f*; (*Zool*) bigorneau *m*.
perjure [ˈpɜːdʒəʳ] *vt*: **to** ~ **o.s.** se parjurer, (*Jur*) faire un faux serment; (*Jur*) ~**d evidence** faux serment, faux témoignage (volontaire).
perjurer [ˈpɜːdʒərəʳ] *n* parjure *mf*.
perjury [ˈpɜːdʒərɪ] *n* parjure *m*; (*Jur*) faux serment. **to commit** ~ se parjurer; (*Jur*) faire un faux serment.
perk[1] [pɜːk] **1** *vi*: **to** ~ **up** (*cheer up*) se ragaillardir; (*after illness*) se remonter, se retaper*; (*show interest*) s'animer, dresser l'oreille (*fig*).
2 *vt*: **to** ~ **sb up** ragaillardir qn, retaper qn*; **to** ~ **o.s. up** se faire beau; (*lit, fig*) **to** ~ **one's ears up** dresser l'oreille; **to** ~ **one's head up** relever *or* dresser la tête.
perk[2]* [pɜːk] *n* (*Brit: gen pl*) à-côté *m*, avantage *m* accessoire. ~**s** gratte* *f*, petits bénéfices *or* bénefs‡.
perkily [ˈpɜːkɪlɪ] *adv* (*V* **perky**) d'un air *or* d'un ton guilleret; vivement, avec entrain; avec désinvolture.
perkiness [ˈpɜːkɪnɪs] *n* (*V* **perky**) gaieté *f*; entrain *m*; désinvolture *f*.
perky [ˈpɜːkɪ] *adj* (*gay*) guilleret, gai; (*lively*) vif, éveillé, plein d'entrain; (*cheeky*) désinvolte, effronté.
perm[1] [pɜːm] **1** *n* (*abbr of* **permanent 2**) permanente *f*. **to have a** ~ se faire faire une permanente. **2** *vt*: **to** ~ **sb's hair** faire une permanente à qn; **to have one's hair** ~**ed** se faire faire une permanente.
perm[2]* [pɜːm] *n abbr of* **permutation.**
permanence [ˈpɜːmənəns] *n* permanence *f*.
permanency [ˈpɜːmənənsɪ] *n* **(a)** (*U*) permanence *f*, stabilité *f*. **(b)** (*job*) emploi permanent, poste *m* fixe.
permanent [ˈpɜːmənənt] **1** *adj* permanent. **we cannot make any** ~ **arrangements** nous ne pouvons pas prendre de dispositions permanentes *or* fixes; **I'm not** ~ **here** je ne suis pas ici à titre définitif; ~ **address** résidence *f or* adresse *f* fixe; (*Brit Admin*) **P**~ **Under-secretary** ≃ secrétaire général (de ministère); ~ **wave** permanente *f*; (*Brit Rail*) ~ **way** voie ferrée.
2 *n* (*for hair*) permanente *f*.
permanently [ˈpɜːmənəntlɪ] *adj* en permanence, de façon permanente, à titre définitif. **he was** ~ **appointed last September** en septembre dernier il a été nommé à titre définitif.

permanganate [pɜːˈmæŋgənɪt] *n* permanganate *m*.

permeability [ˌpɜːmɪəˈbɪlɪtɪ] *n* perméabilité *f*.

permeable [ˈpɜːmɪəbl] *adj* perméable, pénétrable.

permeate [ˈpɜːmɪeɪt] **1** *vt [liquid]* pénétrer, filtrer à travers; *[ideas]* pénétrer dans *or* parmi, se répandre dans *or* parmi. (*lit, fig*) **~d with** saturé de, imprégné de. **2** *vi* (*pass through*) pénétrer, s'infiltrer; (*fig: spread*) se répandre, pénétrer.

permissible [pəˈmɪsɪbl] *adj action* permis, acceptable. **it is ~ to refuse** il est permis de refuser; **would it be ~ to say that ...?** serait-il acceptable de dire que ...?; **the degree of ~ error is 2%** la marge d'erreur acceptable *or* tolérable est de 2%.

permission [pəˈmɪʃən] *n* permission *f*; (*official*) autorisation *f*. **without ~** sans permission, sans autorisation; **with your ~** avec votre permission; **'by kind ~ of'** 'avec l'aimable consentement de'; **no ~ is needed** il n'est pas nécessaire d'avoir une autorisation; **she gave ~ for her daughter's marriage** elle consentit au mariage de sa fille; **she gave her daughter ~ to marry** elle autorisa sa fille à se marier; **~ is required in writing from the committee** il est nécessaire d'obtenir l'autorisation écrite du comité; **who gave you ~ to do that?** qui vous a autorisé à *or* qui vous a permis de faire cela?; **you have my ~ to do that** je vous permets de *or* vous autorise à faire cela, je vous accorde la permission *or* l'autorisation de faire cela.

permissive [pəˈmɪsɪv] *adj* **(a)** (*tolerant*) *person, parent* tolérant, (*pej*) trop tolérant; *morals, law* laxiste. **the ~ society** la société de tolérance. **(b)** (*optional*) facultatif.

permissively [pəˈmɪsɪvlɪ] *adv* de façon laxiste *or* trop tolérante, peu strictement.

permissiveness [pəˈmɪsɪvnɪs] *n* (*V* **permissive a**) tolérance *f*; (*pej*) excès *m* de tolérance; laxisme *m*.

permit [ˈpɜːmɪt] **1** *n* autorisation écrite; (*for specific activity*) permis *m*; (*for goods at Customs*) passavant *m*. **building ~** permis de bâtir *or* de construire; **fishing ~** permis *or* licence *f* de pêche; **residence ~** permis de séjour; **you need a ~ to go into the laboratory** pour entrer dans le laboratoire il vous faut une autorisation écrite *or* un laissez-passer; **please show your ~ at the gate** prière de montrer son laissez-passer à l'entrée; *V* **entry** *etc*.

2 [pəˈmɪt] *vt* permettre (*sb to do* à qn de faire); autoriser (*sb to do* qn à faire). **is it ~ted to smoke?** est-il permis de fumer?; **it is not ~ted to smoke** il n'est pas permis *or* il est interdit de fumer; **we could never ~ it to happen** nous ne pourrions jamais permettre que cela se produise, nous ne pourrions jamais laisser cela se produire; **I won't ~ it** je ne le permettrai pas; **her mother will not ~ her to sell the house** sa mère ne lui permet pas de *or* ne l'autorise pas à vendre la maison; **her mother will never ~ the sale of the house** sa mère n'autorisera jamais la vente de la maison; **the law ~s the sale of this substance** la loi autorise la vente de cette substance; **the vent ~s the escape of gas** l'orifice permet l'échappement du gaz.

3 [pəˈmɪt] *vi*: **to ~ of sth** permettre qch; **it does not ~ of doubt** cela ne permet pas le moindre doute; **weather ~ting** si le temps le permet.

permutation [ˌpɜːmjʊˈteɪʃən] *n* permutation *f*.

permute [pəˈmjuːt] *vt* permuter.

pernicious [pɜːˈnɪʃəs] *adj* (*injurious*) nuisible, préjudiciable; (*Med*) pernicieux. **~ anaemia** anémie pernicieuse.

pernickety* [pəˈnɪkɪtɪ] *adj* (*stickler for detail*) pointilleux, formaliste; (*hard to please*) difficile. **he's very ~** il est très pointilleux, il cherche toujours la petite bête, il est très difficile; **he's very ~ about what he wears/about his food** il est très difficile pour ses vêtements/pour sa nourriture.

peroration [ˌperəˈreɪʃən] *n* péroraison *f*.

peroxide [pəˈrɒksaɪd] *n* (*Chem*) peroxyde *m*. **~ blonde*** blonde décolorée *or* oxygénée*; *V* **hydrogen.**

perpendicular [ˌpɜːpənˈdɪkjʊləʳ] **1** *adj* (*also Archit, Math*) perpendiculaire (*to* à); *cliff, slope* à pic. (*Archit*) **~ Gothic** gothique perpendiculaire anglais. **2** *n* perpendiculaire *f*. **to be out of ~** être hors d'aplomb, sortir de la perpendiculaire.

perpendicularly [ˌpɜːpənˈdɪkjʊləlɪ] *adv* perpendiculairement.

perpetrate [ˈpɜːpɪtreɪt] *vt crime* perpétrer, commettre; *blunder, hoax* faire.

perpetration [ˌpɜːpɪˈtreɪʃən] *n* perpétration *f*.

perpetrator [ˈpɜːpɪtreɪtəʳ] *n* auteur *m* (*d'un crime etc*). **~ of a crime** auteur d'un crime, coupable *mf*, criminel(le) *m(f)*.

perpetual [pəˈpetjʊəl] *adj movement, calendar* perpétuel; *nuisance, worry* perpétuel, constant; *noise, questions* perpétuel, continuel; *flower* perpétuel. **a ~ stream of visitors** un flot continu *or* perpétuel *or* ininterrompu de visiteurs; **he's a ~ nuisance** il ne cesse d'enquiquiner* le monde.

perpetually [pəˈpetjʊəlɪ] *adv* perpétuellement, continuellement, sans cesse.

perpetuate [pəˈpetjʊeɪt] *vt* perpétuer.

perpetuation [pəˌpetjʊˈeɪʃən] *n* perpétuation *f*.

perpetuity [ˌpɜːpɪˈtjuːɪtɪ] *n* perpétuité *f*. **in ~** à perpétuité.

perplex [pəˈpleks] *vt* **(a)** (*puzzle*) plonger dans la perplexité, rendre perplexe. **I was ~ed by his refusal to help** son refus d'aider m'a rendu perplexe.

(b) (*complicate*) *matter, question* compliquer, embrouiller. **to ~ the issue** compliquer *or* embrouiller la question.

perplexed [pəˈplekst] *adj person* embarrassé, perplexe; *tone, glance* perplexe. **I'm ~** je suis perplexe, je ne sais pas trop quoi faire; **to look ~** avoir l'air perplexe *or* embarrassé.

perplexedly [pəˈpleksɪdlɪ] *adv* avec perplexité, d'un air *or* d'un ton perplexe, d'un air embarrassé.

perplexing [pəˈpleksɪŋ] *adj matter, question* embarrassant, compliqué; *situation* embarrassant, confus.

perplexity [pəˈpleksɪtɪ] *n* (*bewilderment*) embarras *m*, perplexité *f*; (*complexity*) complexité *f*.

perquisite [ˈpɜːkwɪzɪt] *n* à-côté *m*; (*in money*) à-côté, gratification *f*.

perry [ˈperɪ] *n* poiré *m*.

persecute [ˈpɜːsɪkjuːt] *vt* (*harass, oppress*) *minorities etc* persécuter; (*annoy*) harceler (*with* de), tourmenter, persécuter.

persecution [ˌpɜːsɪˈkjuːʃən] *n* persécution *f*. **he has got a ~ mania** *or* **complex** il a la manie *or* la folie de la persécution.

persecutor [ˈpɜːsɪkjuːtəʳ] *n* persécuteur *m*, -trice *f*.

perseverance [ˌpɜːsɪˈvɪərəns] *n* persévérance *f*, ténacité *f*. **by sheer ~** à force de persévérance *or* de persévérer.

persevere [ˌpɜːsɪˈvɪəʳ] *vi* persévérer (*in sth* dans qch), persister (*in sth* dans qch, *at doing sth* à faire qch).

persevering [ˌpɜːsɪˈvɪərɪŋ] *adj* (*determined*) persévérant, obstiné; (*hard-working*) assidu.

perseveringly [ˌpɜːsɪˈvɪərɪŋlɪ] *adv* (*V* **persevering**) avec persévérance, avec obstination; assidûment, avec assiduité.

Persia [ˈpɜːʃə] *n* Perse *f*.

Persian [ˈpɜːʃən] **1** *adj* (*Hist*) *empire, army* perse; (*modern*) *cat, art, language* persan. **~ carpet** tapis *m* de Perse; **~ Gulf** golfe *m* Persique; **~ lamb** astrakan *m*, agneau rasé. **2** *n* **(a)** Persan(e) *m(f)*; (*Hist*) Perse *mf*. **(b)** (*Ling*) persan *m*.

persiflage [ˌpɜːsɪˈflɑːʒ] *n* persiflage *m*, ironie *f*, raillerie *f*.

persimmon [pɜːˈsɪmən] *n* (*tree*) plaqueminier *m* de Virginie *or* du Japon, kaki *m*; (*fruit*) kaki *m*.

persist [pəˈsɪst] *vi* persister, s'obstiner (*in sth* dans qch, *in doing* à faire); *[pain, opinion]* persister.

persistence [pəˈsɪstəns] *n*, **persistency** [pəˈsɪstənsɪ] *n* (*U*) *[person]* (*perseverance*) persistance *f*, persévérance *f*; (*obstinacy*) persistance, obstination *f*; *[pain]* persistance. **his ~ in talking** sa persistance *or* son obstination à parler; **as a reward for her ~** pour la récompenser de sa persistance *or* de sa persévérance.

persistent [pəˈsɪstənt] *adj person* (*persevering*) persévérant; (*obstinate*) obstiné; *smell* persistant; *warnings, complaints, interruptions* continuel, répété; *noise, nuisance* continuel, incessant. (*Jur*) **~ offender** multi-récidiviste *mf*.

persistently [pəˈsɪstəntlɪ] *adv* (*constantly*) constamment; (*obstinately*) avec persistance, obstinément. **he ~ refused to help us** il refusait obstinément *or* il persistait à refuser de nous aider.

person [ˈpɜːsn] *n* **(a)** personne *f*, individu *m* (*often pej*); (*Jur*) personne. **I know no such ~** (*no one of that name*) je ne connais personne de ce nom; (*no one like that*) je ne connais personne de ce genre; **in ~** en personne; **give it to him in ~** remettez-le-lui en mains propres; **in the ~ of** dans *or* en la personne de; **a certain ~ who shall be nameless** une certaine personne qui restera anonyme *or* qu'il vaut mieux ne pas nommer; (*Telec*) **a ~ to ~ call** une communication (téléphonique) avec préavis; (*Police etc*) **he had a knife on his ~** il avait un couteau sur lui; (*Jur*) **acting with ~ or ~s unknown** (agissant) de concert *or* en complicité avec un ou des tiers non-identifiés; *V* **displaced, per, private** *etc*.

(b) (*Gram*) personne *f*. **in the first ~ singular** à la première personne du singulier.

persona [pɜːˈsəʊnə] *n* (*Psych etc*) personnage *m*. **~ grata/non grata** persona grata/non grata.

personable [ˈpɜːsnəbl] *adj* de belle mine, de belle prestance.

personage [ˈpɜːsnɪdʒ] *n* (*Theat, gen*) personnage *m*.

personal [ˈpɜːsnl] *adj* (*private*) *opinion, matter* personnel; (*individual*) *style* personnel, particulier; *liberty etc* personnel, individuel; (*for one's own use*) *luggage, belongings* personnel; (*to do with the body*) *habits* intime; (*in person*) *call, visit* personnel; *application* (fait) en personne; (*Gram*) personnel; (*slightly pej*) *remark, question* indiscret (*f* -ète). **my ~ belief is ...** personnellement *or* pour ma part *or* en ce qui me concerne je crois ...; **I have no ~ knowledge of this** personnellement *or* moi-même je ne sais rien à ce sujet; **a letter marked '~'** une lettre marquée 'personnelle'; **his ~ interests were at stake** ses intérêts personnels *or* particuliers étaient en jeu; **the conversation/argument grew ~** la conversation/la discussion prit un ton *or* un tour personnel; **don't be ~!** ne sois pas si indiscret!, ne fais pas de remarques désobligeantes!; **don't let's get ~!** abstenons-nous de remarques désobligeantes!; **his ~ appearance leaves much to be desired** son apparence (personnelle) *or* sa tenue laisse beaucoup à désirer; **to make a ~ appearance** apparaître en personne; **~ cleanliness** hygiène *f* intime; (*Brit Telec*) **~ call** (*person-to-person*) communication *f* (téléphonique) avec préavis; (*private*) communication téléphonique privée; (*Press*) **~ column** annonces personnelles; (*Customs etc*) **~ effects** effets personnels; (*Jur*) **~ estate, ~ property** biens personnels; **do me a ~ favour and ...** rendez-moi service *or* faites-moi plaisir et ...; **~ friend** ami(e) *m(f)* intime; **his ~ life** sa vie privée; (*Gram*) **~ pronoun** pronom *m* personnel *m*; **~ stationery** papier *m* à lettres à en-tête personnel; **to give sth the ~ touch** ajouter une note personnelle *or* originale à qch.

personality [ˌpɜːsəˈnælɪtɪ] *n* **(a)** (*U: also Psych*) personnalité *f*. **you must allow him to express his ~** vous devez lui permettre d'exprimer sa personnalité; **he has a pleasant/strong ~** il a une personnalité sympathique/forte; **he has a lot of ~** il a beaucoup de personnalité; **the house seemed to have a ~ of its own** la maison semblait avoir un caractère bien à elle; *V* **dual, split.**

(b) (*celebrity*) personnalité *f*, personnage connu; (*high-ranking person*) notabilité *f*. **~ cult** culte *m* de la personnalité; **a well-known television ~** une vedette de la télévision *or* du petit écran.

(c) to indulge in personalities faire des personnalités, faire des remarques désobligeantes; **let's keep personalities out of**

this ne faisons pas de personnalités, abstenons-nous de remarques désobligeantes.

personally ['pɜːsnəlɪ] *adv* **(a)** (*in person*) en personne. **I spoke to him ~** je lui ai parlé en personne; **hand it over to him ~** remettez-le-lui en mains propres.

(b) personnellement, quant à moi (*or* toi *etc*), pour ma (*or* ta *etc*) part. **~ I believe that it is possible** personnellement *or* pour ma part je crois que c'est possible; **others may refuse but ~ I am willing to help you** d'autres refuseront peut-être, quant à moi *or* mais pour ma part *or* mais personnellement je suis prêt à vous aider.

(c) don't take it ~! ne croyez pas que vous soyez personnellement visé!; **I like him ~ but not as an employer** je l'aime en tant que personne mais pas en tant que patron.

personalty ['pɜːsnltɪ] *n* (*Jur*) biens personnels.

personate ['pɜːsəneɪt] *vt* **(a)** (*Theat*) jouer le rôle de. **(b)** (*personify*) personnifier; (*impersonate*) se faire passer pour.

personification [pɜːˌsɒnɪfɪ'keɪʃən] *n* (*all senses*) personnification *f*. **he is the ~ of good taste** il est la personnification *or* l'incarnation *f* du bon goût, il est le bon goût personnifié.

personify [pɜː'sɒnɪfaɪ] *vt* personnifier. **she's kindness personified** c'est la bonté personnifiée *or* en personne; **he's fascism personified** il est le fascisme personnifié.

personnel [ˌpɜːsə'nel] **1** *n* personnel *m*.

2 *cpd*: **personnel agency** agence *f* pour l'emploi, bureau *m* de placement; (*Mil*) **personnel carrier** véhicule *m* transport de troupes; **personnel department** service *m* du personnel; **personnel management** gestion *f or* direction *f* de *or* du personnel; **personnel manager** chef *m* du personnel; **personnel officer** cadre *m or* attaché *m* de gestion du personnel, responsable *mf* du personnel.

perspective [pə'spektɪv] *n* **(a)** (*Archit, Art, Surv, gen*) perspective *f*. (*Art etc*) **he has no sense of ~** il n'a aucun sens de la perspective; (*fig*) **to see sth in its true ~** voir qch dans son contexte; **let's get this into ~** ne perdons pas le sens des proportions; (*fig*) **in historical ~** dans une perspective historique.

(b) (*prospect*) perspective *f*. **we have the ~ of much unemployment ahead** nous avons devant nous la perspective d'un chômage considérable; **they had in ~ a great industrial expansion** ils avaient une grande expansion industrielle en perspective.

perspex ['pɜːspeks] *n* (*esp Brit*) ® plexiglas *m* ®.

perspicacious [ˌpɜːspɪ'keɪʃəs] *adj person* perspicace; *analysis* pénétrant.

perspicacity [ˌpɜːspɪ'kæsɪtɪ] *n* perspicacité *f*, clairvoyance *f*.

perspicuous [ˌpə'spɪkjuəs] *adj* clair, net.

perspicuity [ˌpɜːspɪ'kjuːɪtɪ] *n* **(a)** = **perspicacity. (b)** *[explanation, statement]* clarté *f*, netteté *f*.

perspiration [ˌpɜːspə'reɪʃən] *n* transpiration *f*, sueur *f*. **bathed in ~, dripping with ~** en nage, tout en sueur; **beads of ~** gouttes *fpl* de sueur *or* de transpiration.

perspire [pəs'paɪəʳ] *vi* transpirer. **he was perspiring profusely** il était en sueur *or* en nage, il transpirait abondamment.

persuadable [pə'sweɪdəbl] *adj* qui peut être persuadé.

persuade [pə'sweɪd] *vt* persuader (*sb of sth* qn de qch, *sb that* qn que), convaincre (*sb of sth* qn de qch). **to ~ sb to do** persuader qn de faire, amener *or* décider qn à faire; **to ~ sb not to do** persuader qn de ne pas faire, dissuader qn de faire; **I wanted to help but they ~d me not to** je voulais aider mais on m'en a dissuadé; **they ~d me that I ought to see him** ils m'ont persuadé que je devais le voir; **to ~ sb of the truth of a theory** convaincre qn de la vérité d'une théorie; **she is easily ~d** elle se laisse facilement persuader *or* convaincre; **it doesn't take much to ~ him** il n'en faut pas beaucoup pour le persuader *or* le convaincre; **I am (quite) ~d that he is wrong** je suis (tout à fait) persuadé qu'il a tort.

persuasion [pə'sweɪʒən] *n* **(a)** (*U*) persuasion *f*. **a little gentle ~ will get him to help** si nous le persuadons en douceur il nous aidera; **he needed a lot of ~** il a fallu beaucoup de persuasion pour le convaincre; **I don't need much ~ to stop working** il n'en faut pas beaucoup pour me persuader de m'arrêter de travailler.

(b) (*frm*: *conviction*) persuasion *f*, conviction *f*. **it is my ~ that ...** je suis persuadé que ... .

(c) (*Rel*) religion *f*, confession *f*. **people of all ~s** des gens de toutes les religions *or* confessions; **I am not of that ~ myself** personnellement je ne partage pas cette croyance; **the Mahometan ~** la religion mahométane; **and others of that ~** et d'autres de la même confession.

persuasive [pə'sweɪsɪv] *adj person, voice* persuasif; *evidence, argument* convaincant.

persuasively [pə'sweɪsɪvlɪ] *adv speak* d'un ton persuasif; *behave, smile* d'une manière persuasive.

persuasiveness [pə'sweɪsɪvnɪs] *n* pouvoir *m or* force *f* de persuasion.

pert [pɜːt] *adj* impertinent, effronté. **a ~ little hat** un petit chapeau coquin.

pertain [pɜː'teɪn] *vi* **(a)** (*relate*) se rapporter, avoir rapport, se rattacher (*to* à). **documents ~ing to the case** documents se rapportant à *or* relatifs à l'affaire. **(b)** (*Jur etc*) *[land]* appartenir (*to* à).

pertinacious [ˌpɜːtɪ'neɪʃəs] *adj* (*stubborn*) entêté, obstiné; (*in opinions etc*) opiniâtre.

pertinaciously [ˌpɜːtɪ'neɪʃəslɪ] *adv* (*V* **pertinacious**) avec entêtement, obstinément; opiniâtrement.

pertinacity [ˌpɜːtɪ'næsɪtɪ] *n* (*V* **pertinacious**) entêtement *m*, obstination *f*; opiniâtreté *f*.

pertinence ['pɜːtɪnəns] *n* justesse *f*, à-propos *m*, pertinence *f*; (*Ling*) pertinence.

pertinent ['pɜːtɪnənt] *adj answer, remark* pertinent, approprié, judicieux; (*Ling*) pertinent. **~ to** approprié à, qui a rapport à.

pertinently ['pɜːtɪnəntlɪ] *adv* pertinemment, avec justesse, à propos.

pertly ['pɜːtlɪ] *adv* avec effronterie, avec impertinence.

pertness ['pɜːtnɪs] *n* effronterie *f*, impertinence *f*.

perturb [pə'tɜːb] *vt* perturber, inquiéter, agiter. **I was ~ed to hear that ...** j'ai appris avec inquiétude que ... .

perturbation [ˌpɜːtɜː'beɪʃən] *n* (*U*) perturbation *f*, inquiétude *f*, agitation *f*.

perturbing [pə'tɜːbɪŋ] *adj* troublant, inquiétant.

Peru [pə'ruː] *n* Pérou *m*.

perusal [pə'ruːzəl] *n* lecture *f*; (*thorough*) lecture attentive.

peruse [pə'ruːz] *vt* lire; (*thoroughly*) lire attentivement.

Peruvian [pə'ruːvɪən] **1** *adj* péruvien. **2** *n* Péruvien(ne) *m(f)*.

pervade [pɜː'veɪd] *vt [smell]* se répandre dans; *[influence]* s'étendre dans; *[ideas]* s'insinuer dans, pénétrer dans; *[gloom]* envahir. **the feeling/the atmosphere ~s the whole book** ce sentiment/cette atmosphère se retrouve dans tout le livre.

pervasive [pɜː'veɪsɪv] *adj smell, ideas* pénétrant; *gloom* envahissant; *influence* qui se fait sentir un peu partout.

perverse [pə'vɜːs] *adj* (*wicked*) pervers, mauvais; (*stubborn*) obstiné, têtu, entêté; (*contrary*) contrariant. **driven by a ~ desire to hurt himself** poussé par un désir pervers de se faire souffrir; **how ~ of him!** qu'il est contrariant!, quel esprit de contradiction!

perversely [pə'vɜːslɪ] *adv* (*wickedly*) avec perversité, par pure méchanceté; (*stubbornly*) par pur entêtement; (*contrarily*) par esprit de contradiction.

perverseness [pə'vɜːsnɪs] *n* = **perversity.**

perversion [pə'vɜːʃən] *n* (*also Psych*) perversion *f*; *[facts]* déformation *f*, travestissement *m*. **sexual ~s** perversions sexuelles; (*Med etc*) **~ of a function** perversion *or* altération *f* d'une fonction; **a ~ of justice/of truth** un travestissement de la justice/de la vérité.

perversity [pə'vɜːsɪtɪ] *n* (*wickedness*) perversité *f*, méchanceté *f*; (*stubbornness*) obstination *f*, entêtement *m*; (*contrariness*) caractère contrariant, esprit *m* de contradiction.

pervert [pə'vɜːt] **1** *vt person* pervertir, dépraver; (*Psych*) pervertir; (*Rel*) détourner de ses croyances; *habits* dénaturer, dépraver; *fact* fausser, travestir; *sb's words* dénaturer, déformer; *justice, truth* travestir.

2 ['pɜːvɜːt] *n* **(a)** (*Psych: also* **sexual ~**) perverti(e) *m(f)* sexuel(le).

(b) (*Rel: pej*) apostat *m*.

pervious ['pɜːvɪəs] *adj* perméable, pénétrable; (*fig*) accessible (*to* à).

peseta [pə'setə] *n* peseta *f*.

peskyː ['peskɪ] *adj* (*US*) fichu* (*before n*), sacréː (*before n*).

pessary ['pesərɪ] *n* pessaire *m*.

pessimism ['pesɪmɪzəm] *n* pessimisme *m*.

pessimist ['pesɪmɪst] *n* pessimiste *mf*.

pessimistic [ˌpesɪ'mɪstɪk] *adj* pessimiste (*about* au sujet de, sur). **I'm very ~ about it** je suis très pessimiste à ce sujet *or* là-dessus; **I feel** *or* **I am fairly ~ about his coming** je n'ai pas grand espoir qu'il vienne.

pessimistically [ˌpesɪ'mɪstɪkəlɪ] *adv* avec pessimisme, d'un ton *or* d'un air pessimiste.

pest [pest] **1** *n* **(a)** (*insect*) insecte *m* nuisible; (*animal*) animal *m* nuisible. **rabbits are (officially) a ~ in Australia** en Australie les lapins sont classés comme animaux nuisibles.

(b) (*person*) casse-pieds* *m*, empoisonneur* *m*, -euse* *f*. **what a ~ that meeting is!** quelle barbeː cette réunion!; **it's a ~ having to go** c'est embêtant* *or* barbantː d'avoir à y aller; **you're a perfect ~!** tu n'es qu'un empoisonneur public!*, si tu savais ce que tu es embêtant!*

2 *cpd*: **pest control** (*insects*) lutte *f* contre les insectes; (*rats*) dératisation *f*; (*Admin*) **pest control officer** agent préposé à la lutte antiparasitaire.

pester ['pestəʳ] *vt* importuner, harceler. **to ~ sb with questions** harceler qn de questions; **he ~ed me to go to the cinema with him but I refused** il m'a harcelé *or* il m'a cassé les pieds* pour que j'aille au cinéma avec lui mais j'ai refusé; **he ~ed me to go to the cinema with him and I went, he went on ~ing me until I went to the cinema with him** il n'a eu de cesse que j'aille au cinéma avec lui, il m'a tellement cassé les pieds* que je suis allé au cinéma avec lui; **she has been ~ing me for an answer** elle n'arrête pas de me réclamer une réponse; **he ~ed his father into lending him the car** à force d'insister auprès de son père il a fini par se faire prêter la voiture; **he ~s the life out of me*** il me casse les pieds*; **stop ~ing me** laisse-moi tranquille, fiche-moi la paix*; **stop ~ing me about your bike** fiche-moi la paix* avec ton vélo; **is this man ~ing you?** est-ce que cet homme vous importune?

pesticide ['pestɪsaɪd] *n* (*gen*) pesticide *m*; *[insects]* insecticide *m*; *[rodents]* mort-aux-rats *f*.

pestiferous [pes'tɪfərəs] *adj* = **pestilent.**

pestilence ['pestɪləns] *n* peste *f* (*also fig*).

pestilent ['pestɪlənt] *adj*, **pestilential** [ˌpestɪ'lenʃəl] *adj* (*causing disease*) pestilentiel; (*pernicious*) nuisible; (*: *annoying*) fichu* (*before n*), sacréː (*before n*).

pestle ['pesl] *n* pilon *m*.

pet[1] [pet] **1** *n* **(a)** (*animal*) animal familier. **we have 6 ~s** nous avons 6 animaux chez nous *or* à la maison; **he hasn't got any ~s** il n'a pas d'animaux chez lui; **she keeps a goldfish as a ~** en fait d'animal elle a un poisson rouge; **'no ~s allowed'** 'les animaux sont interdits'.

(b) (*: *favourite*) chouchou(te)* *m(f)*. **the teacher's ~** le chouchou* du professeur; **to make a ~ of sb** chouchouter qn*.

(c) (*) **be a ~** sois chou*, sois gentil; **he's rather a ~** c'est un chou*, il est adorable; **come here (my)** ~ viens ici mon chou* *or* mon lapin*.

2 *cpd cat, dog* favori(te); *lion, snake* apprivoisé. **pet aversion*, pet hate*** bête noire; **pet name** petit nom (d'amitié); **pet shop** boutique *f* d'animaux; **pet subject** marotte *f*, dada* *m*; **it's his pet subject** c'est sa marotte, c'est son dada*; **once he gets on his pet subject ...** quand il enfourche son cheval de bataille ... *or* son dada favori* ... .

3 *vt* (*indulge*) chouchouter*; (*fondle*) câliner; (*sexually*) peloter‡.

4 *vi* se peloter‡.

pet²* [pet] *n*: **to be in a** ~ être d'une humeur de dogue, être de mauvais poil*, être en rogne*.

petal ['petl] *n* pétale *m*. **~-shaped** en forme de pétale.

petard [pe'tɑːd] *n* pétard *m*; *V* **hoist.**

Pete [piːt] *n* (*dim of* Peter) Pierrot *m*. **for ~'s sake!*** mais enfin!, bon sang!*

Peter ['piːtəʳ] *n* Pierre *m*. (*Rel*) **~'s pence** denier *m* de saint-Pierre; *V* **blue, rob.**

peter ['piːtəʳ] *vi*: **to ~ out** *[supplies]* s'épuiser; *[stream, conversation]* tarir; *[plans]* tomber à l'eau; *[story, plot, play, book]* tourner court; *[fire, flame]* mourir; *[road]* se perdre.

petite [pə'tiːt] *adj woman* menue, gracile.

petition [pə'tɪʃən] **1** *n* **(a)** (*list of signatures*) pétition *f*. **to get up a ~ for/against sth** organiser une pétition en faveur de/contre qch.

(b) (*prayer*) prière *f*; (*request*) requête *f*, supplique *f*.

(c) (*Jur*) requête *f*, pétition *f*. **~ for divorce** demande *f* en divorce; **right of ~** droit *m* de pétition; *V* **file².**

2 *vt* **(a)** adresser une pétition à, pétitionner. **they ~ed the king for the release of the prisoner** ils adressèrent une pétition au roi pour demander la libération du prisonnier.

(b) (*beg*) implorer, prier (*sb to do* qn de faire).

(c) (*Jur*) **to ~ the court** adresser *or* présenter une pétition en justice.

3 *vi* adresser une pétition, pétitionner. (*Jur*) **to ~ for divorce** faire une demande en divorce.

petitioner [pə'tɪʃnəʳ] *n* pétitionnaire *mf*; (*Jur*) requérant(e) *m(f)*, pétitionnaire *mf*; (*in divorce*) demandeur *m*, -eresse *f* (en divorce).

petrel ['petrəl] *n* pétrel *m*; *V* **stormy.**

petrifaction [ˌpetrɪ'fækʃən] *n* (*lit, fig*) pétrification *f*.

petrified ['petrɪfaɪd] *adj* (*lit*) pétrifié; (*fig: also* **~ with fear**) pétrifié de peur, paralysé de peur, cloué (sur place) de peur. **I was absolutely ~!** j'étais terrifié!, j'étais pétrifié de peur!

petrify ['petrɪfaɪ] **1** *vt* (*lit*) pétrifier; (*fig*) pétrifier *or* paralyser de peur, clouer (sur place) de peur.

2 *vi* se pétrifier (*lit*).

petro... ['petrəʊ] *pref* pétro... . **~chemical** (*n*) produit *m* pétrochimique; (*adj*) pétrochimique; **~dollar** pétrodollar *m*.

petrol ['petrəl] (*Brit*) **1** *n* essence *f*. **high-octane ~** supercarburant *m*, super* *m*; **this car is heavy on ~** cette voiture consomme beaucoup (d'essence); **we've run out of ~** *[driver]* nous sommes en panne d'essence; *[garage owner]* nous n'avons plus d'essence; *V* **star.**

2 *cpd*: **petrol can** bidon *m* à essence; **petrol engine** moteur *m* à essence; **petrol (filler) cap** bouchon *m* de réservoir d'essence; **petrol gauge** jauge *f* d'essence; **petrol pump** (*at garage*) pompe *f* d'essence; (*in engine*) pompe à essence; **petrol rationing** rationnement *m* d'essence; **petrol station** station-service *f*, station *f* *or* poste *m* d'essence; **petrol tank** réservoir *m* (d'essence); **petrol tanker** (*ship*) pétrolier *m*, tanker *m*; (*lorry*) camion-citerne *m* (*transportant de l'essence*).

petroleum [pɪ'trəʊlɪəm] *n* pétrole *m*. **~ jelly** vaseline *f*.

petroliferous [ˌpetrə'lɪfərəs] *adj* pétrolifère.

petrology [pe'trɒlədʒɪ] *n* pétrologie *f*.

petticoat ['petɪkəʊt] *n* (*underskirt*) jupon *m*; (*slip*) combinaison *f*. **the rustle of ~s** le bruissement *or* le froufrou des jupons.

pettifogging ['petɪfɒgɪŋ] *adj* **(a)** (*insignificant*) *details* insignifiant; *objections* chicanier.

(b) (*slightly dishonest*) *person* plutôt louche; *dealings* plutôt douteux, plutôt louche.

pettiness ['petɪnɪs] *n* (*U*) (*V* **petty b, c**) insignifiance *f*, manque *m* d'importance; mesquinerie *f*, petitesse *f*; méchanceté *f*, malveillance *f*; caractère pointilleux; manie *f* de critiquer; intolérance *f*, étroitesse *f*.

petting ['petɪŋ] *n* (*U*) pelotage‡ *m*. **heavy ~** pelotage poussé‡.

pettish ['petɪʃ] *adj person* de mauvaise humeur, irritable; *remark* maussade; *child* grognon.

pettishly ['petɪʃlɪ] *adv* avec mauvaise humeur, d'un air *or* d'un ton maussade.

petty ['petɪ] *adj* **(a)** (*on a small scale*) *farmer, shopkeeper* petit. **~ cash** petite *or* menue monnaie; **~ expenses** menues dépenses; (*Jur*) **~ larceny** larcin *m*; **~ official** fonctionnaire *mf* subalterne, petit fonctionnaire; (*Brit Jur*) **P~ Sessions** sessions *fpl* des juges de paix.

(b) (*trivial*) *detail, complaint* petit, insignifiant, sans importance. **~ annoyances** désagréments mineurs, tracasseries *fpl*; **~ regulations** règlement tracassier.

(c) (*small-minded*) mesquin, petit; (*spiteful*) méchant, mauvais, malveillant; (*preoccupied with detail*) (trop) pointilleux; (*faultfinding*) critique; (*intolerant*) intolérant, étroit. **~-minded** mesquin.

(d) (*Naut*) **~ officer** second maître.

petulance ['petjʊləns] *n* irritabilité *f*, irascibilité *f*.

petulant ['petjʊlənt] *adj person* irritable, irascible. **in a ~ mood** de mauvaise humeur.

petulantly ['petjʊləntlɪ] *adv speak* d'un ton irrité, avec irritation, avec humeur; *behave* avec mauvaise humeur.

petunia [pɪ'tjuːnɪə] *n* pétunia *m*.

pew [pjuː] *n* (*Rel*) banc *m* (d'église); (*) siège *m*. (*hum*) **take a ~** prends donc un siège.

pewter ['pjuːtəʳ] *n* (*U*) étain *m*. **to collect ~** collectionner les étains; **~ pot** pot *m* en *or* d'étain.

phalanx ['fælæŋks] *n, pl* **~es** phalange *f*; (*pl* **phalanges** [fæ'lændʒiːz]) (*Anat*) phalange; (*Bot*) faisceau *m* d'étamines.

phallic ['fælɪk] *adj* phallique.

phallus ['fæləs] *n* phallus *m*.

phantasm ['fæntæzəm] *n* (*ghost*) fantôme *m*; (*illusion*) illusion *f*, fantasme *m*, chimère *f*; (*hallucination*) hallucination *f*.

phantasmagoria [ˌfæntæzmə'gɔːrɪə] *n* fantasmagorie *f*.

phantasmagoric [ˌfæntæzmə'gɒrɪk] *adj* fantasmagorique.

phantasmal [fæn'tæzməl] *adj* fantomatique.

phantasy ['fæntəzɪ] *n* = **fantasy.**

phantom ['fæntəm] *n* (*ghost*) fantôme *m*; (*vision*) fantasme *m*.

Pharaoh ['fɛərəʊ] *n* Pharaon *m*.

Pharisaic(al) [ˌfærɪ'seɪɪk(əl)] *adj* pharisaïque.

Pharisee ['færɪsiː] *n* Pharisien(ne) *m(f)*.

pharmaceutical [ˌfɑːmə'sjuːtɪkəl] *adj* pharmaceutique.

pharmacist ['fɑːməsɪst] *n* pharmacien(ne) *m(f)*.

pharmacological [ˌfɑːməkə'lɒdʒɪkəl] *adj* pharmacologique.

pharmacology [ˌfɑːmə'kɒlədʒɪ] *n* pharmacologie *f*.

pharmacopoeia [ˌfɑːməkə'piːə] *n* pharmacopée *f*, Codex *m*.

pharmacy ['fɑːməsɪ] *n* pharmacie *f*.

pharyngitis [ˌfærɪn'dʒaɪtɪs] *n* pharyngite *f*.

pharynx ['færɪŋks] *n* pharynx *m*.

phase [feɪz] **1** *n* (*stage in process*) phase *f*, période *f*; (*aspect, side*) aspect *m*; (*Astron, Chem, Elec, Phys etc*) phase. **the adolescent ~ in the development of the individual** la période *or* la phase de l'adolescence dans le développement de l'individu; **every child goes through a difficult ~** tout enfant passe par une période difficile; **it's just a ~ (he's going through)** ça lui passera; **a critical ~ in the negotiations** une phase *or* une période *or* un stade critique des négociations; **the ~s of a disease** les phases d'une maladie; **the ~s of the moon** les phases de la lune; (*Elec*) **in ~** en phase; (*Elec, fig*) **out of ~** déphasé.

2 *vt innovations, developments* introduire graduellement; *execution of plan* procéder par étapes à. **they ~d the modernization of the factory** on a procédé par étapes à la modernisation de l'usine; **the modernization of the factory was ~d over 3 years** la modernisation de l'usine s'est effectuée en 3 ans par étapes; **the changes were ~d carefully so as to avoid unemployment** on a pris soin d'introduire les changements graduellement afin d'éviter le chômage; **we must ~ the various processes so as to lose as little time as possible** nous devons arranger *or* organiser les diverses opérations de façon à perdre le moins de temps possible; **~d changes** changements organisés de façon progressive; **a ~d withdrawal of troops** un retrait progressif des troupes.

phase in *vt sep new machinery* introduire progressivement *or* graduellement.

phase out *vt sep machinery* retirer progressivement; *jobs* supprimer graduellement.

pheasant ['feznt] *n* faisan *m*; (*hen ~*) faisane *f*; (*young ~*) faisandeau *m*.

phenobarbitone ['fiːnəʊ'bɑːbɪtəʊn] *n* phénobarbital *m*.

phenol ['fiːnɒl] *n* phénol *m*.

phenomena [fɪ'nɒmɪnə] *npl of* **phenomenon.**

phenomenal [fɪ'nɒmɪnl] *adj* (*lit, fig*) phénoménal.

phenomenally [fɪ'nɒmɪnəlɪ] *adv* phénoménalement.

phenomenon [fɪ'nɒmɪnən] *n, pl* **phenomena** (*lit, fig*) phénomène *m*.

phew [fjuː] *excl* (*from disgust*) pouah!; (*surprise*) oh!; (*relief*) ouf!; (*heat*) pfff!

phial ['faɪəl] *n* fiole *f*.

philander [fɪ'lændəʳ] *vi* courir (après les femmes), faire la cour aux femmes.

philanderer [fɪ'lændərəʳ] *n* coureur *m* (de jupons), don Juan *m*.

philanthropic [ˌfɪlən'θrɒpɪk] *adj* philanthropique.

philanthropist [fɪ'lænθrəpɪst] *n* philanthrope *mf*.

philanthropy [fɪ'lænθrəpɪ] *n* philanthropie *f*.

philatelic [ˌfɪlə'telɪk] *adj* philatélique.

philatelist [fɪ'lætəlɪst] *n* philatéliste *mf*.

philately [fɪ'lætəlɪ] *n* philatélie *f*.

...phile [faɪl] *suf* ...phile. **franco~** (*adj, n*) francophile (*mf*).

philharmonic [ˌfɪlɑː'mɒnɪk] *adj* philharmonique.

...philia ['fɪlɪə] *suf* ...philie *f*. **franco~** francophilie *f*.

Philip ['fɪlɪp] *n* Philippe *m*.

Philippine ['fɪlɪpiːn] **1** *adj* philippin. **2** *n* Philippin(e) *m(f)*. **the ~ Islands, the ~s** les Philippines *fpl*.

Philistine ['fɪlɪstaɪn] **1** *adj* philistin; (*fig*) béotien. **2** *n* Philistin *m*; (*fig*) philistin *m*, béotien(ne) *m(f)*.

Philistinism ['fɪlɪstɪnɪzəm] *n* philistinisme *m*.

philological [ˌfɪlə'lɒdʒɪkəl] *adj* philologique.

philologist [fɪ'lɒlədʒɪst] *n* philologue *mf*.

philology [fɪ'lɒlədʒɪ] *n* philologie *f*.

philosopher [fɪ'lɒsəfəʳ] *n* philosophe *mf*. (*fig*) **he's something of a ~** il est du genre philosophe; **~'s stone** pierre philosophale.

philosophic(al) [ˌfɪlə'sɒfɪk(əl)] *adj* **(a)** *subject, debate* philosophique.

(b) (*fig: calm, resigned*) philosophe, calme, résigné. **in a ~ tone** d'un ton philosophe; **I felt fairly ~ about it all** j'ai pris tout cela assez philosophiquement *or* avec une certaine philosophie.

philosophically [ˌfɪlə'sɒfɪkəlɪ] *adv* philosophiquement, avec philosophie.

philosophize [fɪ'lɒsəfaɪz] *vi* philosopher (*about, on* sur).

philosophy [fɪ'lɒsəfɪ] *n* philosophie *f*. **Aristotle's ~** la philosophie d'Aristote; **his ~ of life** sa philosophie, sa conception de la vie; **he took the news with ~** il reçut la nouvelle avec philosophie *or* philosophiquement; *V* **moral, natural.**

philtre, (*US*) **philter** [ˈfɪltəʳ] *n* philtre *m*.

phiz‡ [fɪz] *n*, **phizog**‡ [fɪˈzɒg] *n* (*abbr of* **physiognomy**) binette‡ *f*, bouille‡ *f*.

phlebitis [flɪˈbaɪtɪs] *n* phlébite *f*.

phlebotomy [flɪˈbɒtəmɪ] *n* phlébotomie *f*.

phlegm [flem] *n* (*Med, fig*) flegme *m*.

phlegmatic [flegˈmætɪk] *adj* flegmatique.

phlegmatically [flegˈmætɪkəlɪ] *adv* flegmatiquement, avec flegme.

phlox [flɒks] *n* phlox *m inv*.

...phobe [fəʊb] *suf* ...phobe. **franco~** (*adj, n*) francophobe (*mf*).

phobia [ˈfəʊbɪə] *n* phobie *f*.

...phobia [ˈfəʊbɪə] *suf* ...phobie *f*. **anglo~** anglophobie *f*.

phoenix [ˈfiːnɪks] *n* phénix *m*.

phone[1] [fəʊn] (*abbr of* **telephone**) **1** *n* téléphone *m*. **I'm on the ~** (*subscriber*) j'ai le téléphone; (*speaking*) je suis au téléphone; **to have sb on the ~** avoir qn au bout du fil.

2 *cpd*: **phone book** annuaire *m*; **phone box** cabine *f* téléphonique; **phone call** coup *m* de fil *or* de téléphone; (*Rad*) **phone-in (programme)** programme *m* à ligne ouverte; **phone number** numéro *m* de téléphone.

3 *vt* téléphoner à, passer un coup de fil à.

4 *vi* téléphoner.

phone[2] [fəʊn] *n* (*Ling*) phone *m*.

phoneme [ˈfəʊniːm] *n* phonème *m*.

phonemic [fəʊˈniːmɪk] **1** *adj* phonémique.

2 *n* (*U*) **~s** phonématique *f*.

phonetic [fəʊˈnetɪk] **1** *adj* phonétique. **the ~ alphabet** l'alphabet *m* phonétique; **~ law** loi *f* phonétique.

2 *n* (*U*) **~s** phonétique *f*; **the ~s of Russian** la phonétique russe.

phonetician [ˌfəʊnɪˈtɪʃən] *n* phonéticien(ne) *m(f)*.

phoney* [ˈfəʊnɪ] **1** *adj name* faux (*f* fausse); *jewels* en toc*; *emotion* factice, simulé; *excuse, story, report* bidon* *inv*, à la noix*. (*in 1939*) **the ~ war*** la drôle de guerre; **this diamond is ~** ce diamant c'est du toc*; **apparently he was a ~ doctor** il paraît que c'était un charlatan *or* un médecin marron; **a ~ company** une société bidon*; **it sounds ~** cela a l'air d'être de la frime* *or* de la blague*.

2 *n* (*person*) charlatan *m*, fumiste* *mf*, farceur *m*, -euse *f*. **that diamond is a ~** ce diamant est du toc*.

phonic [ˈfɒnɪk] *adj* phonique.

phono... [ˈfəʊnəʊ] *pref* phono... .

phonograph [ˈfəʊnəgrɑːf] *n* (*US, also Brit*†) électrophone *m*, phonographe† *m*.

phonological [ˌfəʊnəˈlɒdʒɪkəl] *adj* phonologique.

phonology [fəʊˈnɒlədʒɪ] *n* phonologie *f*.

phony* [ˈfəʊnɪ] = **phoney***.

phosgene [ˈfɒzdʒiːn] *n* phosgène *m*.

phosphate [ˈfɒsfeɪt] *n* (*Chem*) phosphate *m*. (*Agr*) **~s** phosphates, engrais phosphatés.

phosphoresce [ˌfɒsfəˈres] *vi* être phosphorescent.

phosphorescence [ˌfɒsfəˈresns] *n* phosphorescence *f*.

phosphorescent [ˌfɒsfəˈresnt] *adj* phosphorescent.

phosphoric [fɒsˈfɒrɪk] *adj* phosphorique.

phosphorous [ˈfɒsfərəs] *adj* phosphoreux.

phosphorus [ˈfɒsfərəs] *n* phosphore *m*.

photo [ˈfəʊtəʊ] **1** *n* (*: *abbr of* **photograph**) photo *f*; *for phrases V* **photograph**.

2 *cpd*: **photo album** album *m* de photos; **photocopier** photocopieur *m*; **photocopy** (*n*) photocopie *f*; (*vt*) photocopier; **photocopying** reprographie *f*, xérographie *f* ®; **photoelectric** photoélectrique; **photoengraving** photogravure *f*; (*Sport*) **photo finish** photo-finish *f*; **photoflash** flash *m*; **photogravure** photogravure *f*, héliogravure *f*; **photometer** [fəˈtɒmɪtəʳ] photomètre *m*; **photostat** = **photocopy**; **photosynthesis** photosynthèse *f*.

photo... [ˈfəʊtəʊ] *pref* photo... .

photogenic [ˌfəʊtəʊˈdʒenɪk] *adj* photogénique.

photograph [ˈfəʊtəgræf] **1** *n* photo(graphie) *f*. **to take a ~ of sb/sth** prendre une photo de qn/qch, prendre qn/qch en photo; **he takes good ~s** il fait de bonnes photos; **he takes a good ~*** (*is photogenic*) il est photogénique, il est bien en photo*; *V* **aerial, colour.**

2 *cpd*: **photograph album** album *m* de photos *or* de photographies.

3 *vt* photographier, prendre en photo.

4 *vi*: **to ~ well** être photogénique, être bien en photo*.

photographer [fəˈtɒgrəfəʳ] *n* (*also Press etc*) photographe *mf*. **newspaper ~** reporter *m* photographe; **street ~** photostoppeur *m*; **he's a keen ~** il est passionné de photo.

photographic [ˌfəʊtəˈgræfɪk] *adj* photographique.

photographically [ˌfəʊtəˈgræfɪkəlɪ] *adv* photographiquement.

photography [fəˈtɒgrəfɪ] *n* (*U*) photographie *f* (*U*); *V* **colour, trick.**

photon [ˈfəʊtɒn] *n* photon *m*.

phototropism [ˈfəʊtəʊˈtrəʊpɪzəm] *n* phototropisme *m*.

phrasal [ˈfreɪzəl] *adj*: **~ verb** verbe *m* à postposition.

phrase [freɪz] **1** *n* **(a)** (*saying*) expression *f*. **as the ~ is** *or* **goes** comme on dit, selon l'expression consacrée; **that's exactly the ~ I'm looking for** voilà exactement l'expression que je cherche; *V* **set.**

(b) (*Gram*) locution *f*; (*Ling*) syntagme *m*. **verb ~** syntagme verbal.

(c) (*Mus*) phrase *f*.

2 *vt* **(a)** *thought* exprimer; *letter* rédiger. **a neatly ~d letter** une lettre bien tournée; **can we ~ it differently?** pouvons-nous l'exprimer différemment? *or* en d'autres termes?

(b) (*Mus*) phraser.

3 *cpd*: **phrasebook** recueil *m* d'expressions; (*Ling*) **phrase marker** indicateur *m* syntagmatique; (*Ling*) **phrase structure analysis** analyse *f* en constituants immédiats; (*Ling*) **phrase structure grammar** grammaire *f* syntagmatique; (*Ling*) **phrase structure tree** arbre *m* syntagmatique.

phraseology [ˌfreɪzɪˈɒlədʒɪ] *n* phraséologie *f*.

phrasing [ˈfreɪzɪŋ] *n* **(a)** *[ideas]* expression *f*, *[text]* rédaction *f*, style *m*; phraséologie *f*. **the ~ is unfortunate** les termes sont mal choisis. **(b)** (*Mus*) phrasé *m*.

phrenetic [frɪˈnetɪk] *adj* = **frenetic.**

phrenologist [frɪˈnɒlədʒɪst] *n* phrénologue *mf*, phrénologiste *mf*.

phrenology [frɪˈnɒlədʒɪ] *n* phrénologie *f*.

phthisis [ˈθaɪsɪs] *n* phtisie *f*.

phut‡ [fʌt] *adv*: **to go ~** *[machine, object]* péter‡, rendre l'âme*; *[scheme, plan]* tomber à l'eau.

phylloxera [ˌfɪlɒkˈsɪərə] *n* phylloxéra *m*.

phylum [ˈfaɪləm] *n* phylum *m*.

physic [ˈfɪzɪk] *n* **(a)** (*U*) **~s** physique *f*; **experimental ~s** physique expérimentale; *V* **atomic, nuclear** *etc.* **(b)** (††) médicament *m*.

physical [ˈfɪzɪkəl] **1** *adj* **(a)** (*of the body*) physique. **~ culture** culture *f* physique; **~ examination, ~ check-up** examen médical, bilan *m* de santé, check-up* *m inv*; **~ exercise** exercice *m* physique; **~ exercises,** (*Brit*) **~ jerks*** exercices *mpl* d'assouplissement, gymnastique *f*; **~ handicap** handicap *m* physique; **it's a ~ impossibility for him to get there on time** il lui est physiquement *or* matériellement impossible d'arriver là-bas à l'heure.

(b) *geography, properties, sciences* physique; *world, universe, object* matériel.

2 *n* (*) examen médical, bilan *m* de santé, check-up* *m inv*. **to go for a ~** aller passer une visite médicale.

physically [ˈfɪzɪkəlɪ] *adv* physiquement. **he is ~ handicapped** c'est un handicapé physique.

physician [fɪˈzɪʃən] *n* médecin *m*.

physicist [ˈfɪzɪsɪst] *n* physicien(ne) *m(f)*. **experimental ~** physicien(ne) de physique expérimentale; *V* **atomic** *etc.*

physio... [ˈfɪzɪəʊ] *pref* physio...

physiognomy [ˌfɪzɪˈɒnəmɪ] *n* (*all senses*) physionomie *f*; (**hum: face*) bobine‡ *f*, bouille‡ *f*.

physiological [ˌfɪzɪəˈlɒdʒɪkəl] *adj* physiologique.

physiologist [ˌfɪzɪˈɒlədʒɪst] *n* physiologiste *mf*.

physiology [ˌfɪzɪˈɒlədʒɪ] *n* physiologie *f*.

physiotherapist [ˌfɪzɪəˈθerəpɪst] *n* kinésithérapeute *mf*.

physiotherapy [ˌfɪzɪəˈθerəpɪ] *n* kinésithérapie *f*.

physique [fɪˈziːk] *n* (*strength, health etc*) constitution *f*. (*appearance*) physique *m*. **he has a fine/poor ~** il a une bonne/mauvaise constitution.

pi[1]* [paɪ] *adj* (*pej abbr of* **pious**) *person* satisfait de soi, suffisant; *expression* suffisant, béat.

pi[2] [paɪ] *n* (*Math*) pi *m*.

pianist [ˈpɪənɪst] *n* pianiste *mf*.

piano [ˈpjɑːnəʊ] **1** *n* piano *m*; *V* **baby, grand, upright** *etc.*

2 *cpd*: **piano-accordion** accordéon *m* à clavier; **piano duet** morceau *m* pour quatre mains; **piano lesson** leçon *f* de piano; **piano organ** piano *m* mécanique; **piano piece** morceau *m* pour piano; **piano stool** tabouret *m*; **piano teacher** professeur *m* de piano; **piano tuner** accordeur *m* (de piano).

3 *adv* (*Mus*) piano.

pianoforte [ˌpjɑːnəʊˈfɔːtɪ] *n* (*frm*) = **piano 1.**

pianola [pɪəˈnəʊlə] *n* ® piano *m* mécanique, pianola *m* ®.

piazza [pɪˈætsə] *n* **(a)** (*square*) place *f*. **(b)** (*US*) véranda *f*.

pibroch [ˈpiːbrɒx] *n* pibrock *m*.

pica [ˈpaɪkə] *n* (*Typ*) douze *m*, cicéro *m*.

picador [ˈpɪkədɔː] *n* picador *m*.

Picardy [ˈpɪkədɪ] *n* Picardie *f*.

picaresque [ˌpɪkəˈresk] *adj* picaresque.

picayune* [ˌpɪkəˈjuːn] *adj* (*US*) insignifiant, mesquin.

piccalilli [ˈpɪkəˌlɪlɪ] (espèce *f* de) pickles *mpl*.

piccaninny [ˈpɪkəˌnɪnɪ] *n* négrillon(ne) *m(f)*.

piccolo [ˈpɪkələʊ] *n* piccolo *m*.

pick [pɪk] **1** *n* **(a)** (*also* **~axe**) pioche *f*, pic *m*; *[mason]* smille *f*; *[miner]* rivelaine *f*; *V* **ice, tooth.**

(b) (*choice*) choix *m*. **to take one's ~** faire son choix; **take your ~** choisissez, vous avez le choix, à votre choix; **whose ~ is it now?** à qui de choisir?; **he is our ~ for the most popular boy** c'est lui que nous avons choisi comme étant le garçon le plus populaire.

(c) (*best*) meilleur(e) *m(f)*. **the ~ of the bunch** le meilleur de tous; (*TV etc*) **~ of the pops** palmarès *m* de la chanson, hit-parade *m*.

2 *cpd*: **picklock** (*key*) crochet *m*, rossignol *m*; (*thief*) crocheteur *m*; **pick-me-up*** remontant *m*; **pick-pocket** pick-pocket *m*, voleur *m* à la tire; **pickup** *V* **pickup.**

3 *vt* **(a)** (*choose*) choisir. **you can ~ whichever you like** vous pouvez choisir celui que vous voulez; (*Sport*) **to ~ (the) sides** former *or* sélectionner les équipes; (*Racing*) **he ~ed the winner** il a pronostiqué le (cheval) gagnant; (*Racing*) **I'm not very good at ~ing the winner** je ne suis pas très doué pour choisir le gagnant; (*fig*) **they certainly ~ed a winner in Colin Smith** avec Colin Smith ils ont vraiment tiré le bon numéro; to **~ one's way through/among** avancer avec précaution à travers/parmi; **to ~ a quarrel with** chercher querelle *or* noise à; **to ~ a fight with sb** chercher la bagarre* avec qn, se bagarrer* avec qn.

(b) (*gather*) *fruit, flower* cueillir.

(c) (*take out, remove*) *spot, scab* gratter, écorcher. **to ~ one's nose** se mettre les doigts dans le nez; **to ~ a splinter from one's hand** s'enlever une écharde de la main; **to ~ the bones of a chicken** sucer les os d'un poulet; **the dog was ~ing the bone**

le chien rongeait l'os; **to ~ one's teeth** se curer les dents; **you've ~ed a hole in your jersey** à force de tirailler tu as fait un trou à ton pull; (*fig*) **to ~ holes in an argument** relever les défauts *or* les failles d'un raisonnement; **he's always ~ing holes in everything** il trouve toujours à redire; **to ~ sb's brains*** faire appel aux lumières de qn; **I want to ~ your brains*** j'ai besoin de vos lumières; **to ~ a lock** crocheter une serrure; **to ~ pockets** pratiquer le vol à la tire; **I've had my pocket ~ed** on m'a fait les poches; *V also* **bone.**

4 *vi*: **to ~ and choose** faire le (*or* la) difficile; **I like to ~ and choose** j'aime bien prendre mon temps pour choisir; **to ~ at one's food** manger du bout des dents, chipoter*, pignocher*; **the bird ~ed at the bread** l'oiseau picorait le pain; **don't ~ at that spot** ne gratte pas ce bouton.

pick at *vt fus* (*US**) = **pick on a.**

pick off *vt sep* **(a)** *paint* gratter, enlever; *flower, leaf* cueillir, enlever.

(b) (*shoot*) abattre après avoir visé soigneusement. **he picked off the sentry** il visa soigneusement et abattit la sentinelle; **he picked off the 3 sentries** il abattit les 3 sentinelles l'une après l'autre.

pick on *vt fus* **(a)** (*: *nag at, harass*) harceler. **to pick on sb** harceler qn, être toujours sur le dos de qn*; **he is always picking on Robert** il est toujours sur le dos de Robert*, c'est toujours après Robert qu'il rouspète*; **stop picking on me!** fiche-moi la paix!*, arrête de rouspéter après moi!*

(b) (*single out*) choisir, désigner. **the teacher picked on him to collect the books** le professeur le choisit *or* le désigna pour ramasser les livres; **why pick on me? all the rest did the same** pourquoi t'en (*or* s'en) prendre à moi? les autres ont fait la même chose.

pick out *vt sep* **(a)** (*choose*) choisir, désigner. **pick out two or three you would like to keep** choisissez-en deux ou trois que vous aimeriez garder; **she picked 2 apples out of the basket** elle choisit 2 pommes dans le panier; **he had already picked out his successor** il avait déjà choisi son successeur.

(b) (*distinguish*) distinguer; (*in identification parade*) identifier. **I couldn't pick out anyone I knew in the crowd** je ne pouvais repérer *or* distinguer personne de ma connaissance dans la foule; **can you pick out the melody in this passage?** pouvez-vous distinguer la mélodie dans ce passage?; **can you pick me out in this photo?** pouvez-vous me reconnaître sur cette photo?

(c) to pick out a tune on the piano retrouver un air au piano.

(d) (*highlight*) **to pick out a colour** rehausser *or* mettre en valeur une couleur; **letters picked out in gold on a black background** lettres rehaussées d'or sur fond noir.

pick over *vt sep collection of fruit, goods etc* trier, examiner (pour choisir). **to pick some books over** examiner quelques livres; **he picked the rags over** il tria les chiffons; **she was picking over the shirts in the sale** elle examinait les chemises en solde les unes après les autres.

pick through *vt fus* = **pick over.**

pick up 1 *vi* **(a)** (*improve*) *[conditions, programme, weather]* s'améliorer; *[prices, wages]* remonter; *[invalid]* se rétablir, se remettre. **business has picked up recently** les affaires ont repris récemment; (*Comm, Fin*) **the market will pick up soon** le marché va bientôt remonter; (*Sport*) **the team is picking up now** l'équipe est en progrès maintenant; (*Rad, TV etc*) **the sound picked up towards the end** le son s'améliora vers la fin; **things are picking up a bit*** ça commence à aller mieux.

(b) (*put on speed*) *[vehicle]* prendre de la vitesse. **the car picked up once we got out of town** dès la sortie de la ville la voiture prit de la vitesse.

(c) (*: *continue*) continuer, reprendre. **after dinner we picked up where we'd left off** après le dîner nous avons repris la conversation (*or* le travail *etc*) où nous l'avions laissé(e).

2 *vt sep* **(a)** (*lift*) *sth dropped, book, clothes etc* ramasser. **to pick o.s. up after a fall** se relever *or* se remettre sur pieds après une chute; **he picked up the child** il prit l'enfant dans ses bras; **he picked up the telephone and dialled a number** il décrocha le téléphone et composa un numéro; **pick up all your clothes before you go out!** ramasse tous tes vêtements avant de sortir!

(b) (*collect*) (passer) prendre. **can you pick up my coat from the cleaners?** pourrais-tu (passer) prendre mon manteau chez le teinturier?; **I'll pick up the books next week** je passerai prendre les livres la semaine prochaine; **I'll pick you up at 6 o'clock** je passerai vous prendre à 6 heures, je viendrai vous chercher à 6 heures.

(c) (*Aut: give lift to*) *passenger, hitchhiker* prendre. **I'll pick you up at the shop** je vous prendrai devant le magasin.

(d) (*pej*) ramasser. **he picked up a girl at the cinema** il a ramassé une fille au cinéma.

(e) (*buy, obtain*) découvrir, dénicher. **to pick up a bargain at a sale** tomber sur *or* trouver une occasion dans une vente; **where did you pick up that record?** où avez-vous déniché ce disque?; **it's a book you can pick up anywhere** c'est un livre que l'on trouve partout.

(f) (*acquire, learn*) apprendre. **he picked up French very quickly** il n'a pas mis longtemps à apprendre le français; **you'll soon pick it up again** vous vous y remettrez vite; **to pick up an accent** prendre un accent; **to pick up bad habits** prendre de mauvaises habitudes; **I picked up a bit of news about him today** j'ai appris quelque chose sur lui aujourd'hui; **see what you can pick up about their export scheme** essayez d'avoir des renseignements *or* des tuyaux* sur leur plan d'exportations; **our agents have picked up something about it** nos agents ont appris *or* découvert quelque chose là-dessus.

(g) (*Rad, Telec*) *station, programme, message* capter.

(h) (*Naut: rescue*) recueillir. **to pick up survivors from the sea** repêcher des survivants; **the helicopter/lifeboat picked up 10 survivors** l'hélicoptère/le canot de sauvetage a recueilli 10 survivants.

(i) (*catch, arrest*) *wanted man* arrêter, cueillir*, pincer*. **they picked him up for questioning** on l'a arrêté pour l'interroger.

(j) (*focus on*) *[lights, camera]* saisir dans le champ. **we picked up a rabbit in the car headlights** nous avons aperçu un lapin dans la lumière des phares; **the cameras picked him up as he left the hall** en sortant du hall il est entré dans le champ des caméras.

(k) (*: *reprimand*) faire une remarque *or* une observation à, reprendre. **to pick sb up for having made a mistake** reprendre qn pour une faute.

(l) *[car, boat]* **to pick up speed** prendre de la vitesse; (*Sport*) **he managed to pick up a few points in the later events** il a réussi à gagner *or* rattraper quelques points dans les épreuves suivantes.

(m) (‡: *steal*) faucher*, piquer‡.

3 pickup *V* **pickup.**

4 pick-me-up* *n V* **pick 2.**

pickaback ['pɪkəbæk] **1** *adv* sur le dos. **2** *n*: **to give sb a ~** porter qn sur son dos; **give me a ~ daddy!** fais-moi faire un tour (à dada) sur ton dos papa!

pickaninny ['pɪkəˌnɪnɪ] *n* = **piccaninny.**

picked [pɪkt] *adj* (*also* **hand-~**) *goods, objects* sélectionné; *men* trié sur le volet. **a group of (hand-)~ soldiers** un groupe de soldats d'élite *or* de soldats triés sur le volet.

picker ['pɪkəʳ] *n* (*gen in cpds*) cueilleur *m*, -euse *f*. **apple-~** cueilleur, -euse de pommes.

picket ['pɪkɪt] **1** *n* **(a)** (*Ind: also* **strike-~**) piquet *m* de grève.

(b) (*at civil demonstrations*) piquet *m* (de manifestants).

(c) (*Mil*) détachement *m* (de soldats). **fire ~** piquet *m* d'incendie.

(d) (*stake*) pieu *m*, piquet *m*.

2 *cpd*: (*Ind*) **to be on picket duty** faire partie d'un piquet de grève; **picket line** (cordon *m* de) piquet *m* de grève; **to cross a picket line** traverser un cordon de piquet de grève.

3 *vt* **(a)** (*Ind*) **to ~ a factory** mettre un piquet de grève aux portes d'une usine; **the demonstrators ~ed the embassy** les manifestants ont formé un cordon devant l'ambassade.

(b) *field* clôturer.

4 *vi [strikers]* organiser un piquet de grève. **there was no ~ing** il n'y a pas eu de piquet de grève.

picking ['pɪkɪŋ] *n* **(a)** *[object from group]* choix *m*; *[candidate]* choix, sélection *f*; *[fruit, vegetables]* cueillette *f*; *[lock]* crochetage *m*; (*careful choosing*) triage *m*.

(b) ~s (*left-overs*) restes *mpl*, débris *mpl*; (*dishonest profits*) gratte* *f*, grapillage* *m*.

pickle ['pɪkl] **1** *n* **(a)** (*U: Culin*) (*brine*) saumure *f*; (*wine, spices*) marinade *f*; (*vinegar*) vinaigre *m*. **~(s)** pickles *mpl*, petits légumes macérés dans du vinaigre.

(b) (*) **to be in a (pretty *or* fine) ~** être dans de beaux draps, être dans le pétrin; **I'm in rather a ~** je suis plutôt dans le pétrin.

2 *vt* (*V* **1a**) conserver dans de la saumure *or* dans du vinaigre.

pickup ['pɪkʌp] **1** *n* **(a)** *[record-player]* pick-up *m inv*, lecteur *m*; (*microphone*) microphone *m*.

(b) (*Aut: passenger*) passager *m*, -ère *f* ramassé(e) en route. **the bus made 3 ~s** l'autobus s'est arrêté 3 fois pour prendre *or* laisser monter des passagers.

(c) (*: *casual lover*) partenaire *mf* de rencontre.

(d) (*Aut: acceleration*) reprise(s) *f(pl)*.

(e) (*Med: recovery*) rétablissement *m*.

(f) (*: *pick-me-up*) remontant *m*.

2 *adj* **(a)** (*US*) **~ (truck),** (*Brit*) **~ van** pick-up *m inv*.

(b) (*Sport*) *game* impromptu, improvisé. **~ side** équipe *f* de fortune.

picnic ['pɪknɪk] (*vb: pret, ptp* **picnicked**) **1** *n* pique-nique *m*. **it's no ~*** ça n'est pas une partie de plaisir*; **~ basket, ~ hamper** panier *m* à pique-nique. **2** *vi* pique-niquer, faire un pique-nique.

picnicker ['pɪknɪkəʳ] *n* pique-niqueur *m*, -euse *f*.

pics‡ [pɪks] *npl* (*abbr of* **pictures**) ciné* *m*.

Pict [pɪkt] *n* Picte *mf*.

Pictish ['pɪktɪʃ] *adj* picte.

pictograph ['pɪktəgrɑːf] *n* **(a)** (*record, chart etc*) pictogramme *m*. **(b)** (*Ling*) (*symbol*) idéogramme *m*; (*writing*) idéographie *f*.

pictorial [pɪk'tɔːrɪəl] **1** *adj magazine, calendar* illustré; *record* en images; *masterpiece* pictural, de peinture. **2** *n* illustré *m*.

pictorially [pɪk'tɔːrɪəlɪ] *adv* en images, au moyen d'images, à l'aide d'images.

picture ['pɪktʃəʳ] **1** *n* **(a)** (*gen*) image *f*; (*illustration*) image, illustration *f*; (*photograph*) photo(graphie) *f*; (*TV*) image; (*painting*) tableau *m*, peinture *f*; (*portrait*) portrait *m*; (*engraving*) gravure *f*; (*reproduction*) reproduction *f*; (*drawing*) dessin *m*. **~s made by reflections in the water** images produites par les reflets sur l'eau; **I took a good ~ of him** j'ai pris une bonne photo de lui; **I must get a ~ of that fountain!** je veux absolument prendre une vue de *or* photographier cette fontaine!; (*TV*) **we have the sound but no ~** nous avons le son mais pas l'image; **to paint a ~** faire un tableau; **to draw a ~** faire un dessin; **to paint/draw a ~ of sth** peindre/dessiner qch; *V* **pretty.**

(b) (*Cine*) film *m*. **they made a ~ about it** on en a fait *or* tiré un film; (*esp Brit*) **to go to the ~s** aller au cinéma, aller voir un film; (*esp Brit*) **what's on at the ~s?** qu'est-ce qu'on donne au cinéma?; **there's a good ~ on this week** on donne *or* on passe un bon film cette semaine; *V* **motion** *etc*.

(c) (*fig*) (*spoken*) description *f*, tableau *m*, image *f*; (*mental* *image*) image, représentation *f*. **he gave us a ~ of the scenes at the front line** il nous présenta un tableau de *or* nous décrivit la situation au front; **his ~ of ancient Greece** le tableau *or* l'image qu'il présente (*or* présentait *etc*) de la Grèce antique; **he painted a black ~ of the future** il nous peignit un sombre tableau de l'avenir; **I have a clear ~ of him as he was when I saw him last** je le revois clairement *or* je me souviens très bien de lui tel qu'il était la dernière fois que je l'ai vu; **I have no very clear ~ of the room** je ne me représente pas très bien la pièce; **these figures give the general ~** ces chiffres donnent un tableau général de la situation; **do you get the ~?*** tu vois la situation?, tu vois le tableau?*, tu piges?‡; **to put sb in the ~** mettre qn au courant.

(d) (*phrases*) **she was a ~ in her new dress** elle était ravissante dans sa nouvelle robe; **the garden is a ~ in June** le jardin est magnifique en juin; **he is** *or* **looks the ~ of health/happiness** il respire la santé/le bonheur; **you're the ~ of your mother!** vous êtes (tout) le portrait de votre mère!; (*fig*) **the other side of the ~** le revers de la médaille; **his face was a ~!*** son expression en disait long!, si vous aviez vu sa tête!*

2 *cpd*: **picture book** livre *m* d'images; **picture frame** cadre *m*; **picture gallery** (*public*) musée *m* (de peinture); (*private*) galerie *f* (de peinture); **picturegoer** habitué(e) *m(f)* du cinéma, amateur *m* de cinéma; **picture hat** capeline *f*; **picture house**† cinéma *m*; **picture postcard** carte postale (illustrée); **picture rail** cimaise *f*; (*TV*) **picture tube** tube-image *m*; **picture window** fenêtre *f* panoramique; **picture writing** écriture *f* pictographique.

3 *vt* **(a)** (*imagine*) s'imaginer, se représenter. **just ~ yourself lying on the beach** imaginez-vous étendu sur la plage.

(b) (*describe*) dépeindre, décrire, représenter.

(c) (*by drawing etc*) représenter.

picturesque [ˌpɪktʃəˈresk] *adj* pittoresque.

picturesquely [ˌpɪktʃəˈresklɪ] *adv* d'une manière pittoresque, avec pittoresque.

picturesqueness [ˌpɪktʃəˈresknɪs] *n* pittoresque *m*.

piddle‡ [ˈpɪdl] *vi* faire pipi*.

piddling* [ˈpɪdlɪŋ] *adj* (*insignificant*) insignifiant, futile; (*small*) négligeable, de rien.

pidgin [ˈpɪdʒɪn] *n* **(a)** (*language*) sabir *m*, petit nègre. **(b)** (*also* **~ English**) pidgin *m*. **(c)** (*) *V* **pigeon 1b**.

pie [paɪ] **1** *n* [*fruit, fish, meat with gravy etc*] tourte *f*; [*compact filling*] pâté *m* en croûte. **apple ~** tourte aux pommes; **rabbit/chicken ~** tourte au lapin/au poulet; **pork ~** pâté de porc en croûte; **it's ~ in the sky‡** ce sont des promesses pour l'avenir, ce sont des châteaux en Espagne; *V* **finger, humble, mud** *etc*.

2 *cpd*: **piecrust** croûte *f* de *or* pour pâté; **pie dish** plat *m* allant au four, terrine *f*; **pie-eyed‡** parti*, rond*; **pie plate** moule *m* à tarte, tourtière *f*.

piebald [ˈpaɪbɔːld] **1** *adj horse* pie *inv*. **2** *n* cheval *m or* jument *f* pie.

piece [piːs] **1** *n* **(a)** morceau *m*; [*cloth, chocolate, glass, paper*] morceau, bout *m*; [*bread, cake*] morceau, tranche *f*; [*wood*] bout, morceau, (*large*) pièce *f*; [*ribbon, string*] bout; (*broken or detached part*) morceau, fragment *m*; (*Comm, Ind*) pièce; (*item, section, also Chess*) pièce; (*Draughts*) pion *m*. (*fig*) **it's a ~ of cake!‡** c'est du gâteau!*; **a ~ of land** (*for agriculture*) une pièce *or* parcelle de terre; (*for building*) un lotissement; **a ~ of meat** un morceau *or* une pièce de viande; (*left over*) un morceau *or* un bout de viande; **I bought a nice ~ of beef** j'ai acheté un beau morceau de bœuf; **a sizeable ~ of beef** une belle pièce de bœuf; **I've got a ~ of grit in my eye** j'ai une poussière *or* une escarbille dans l'œil; **a ~ of advice** un conseil; **a ~ of carelessness** de la négligence; **it's a ~ of folly** c'est de la folie; **a ~ of furniture** un meuble; **a ~ of information** un renseignement; **by a ~ of luck** par (un coup de) chance; **a ~ of music** un morceau de musique; **a ~ of news** une nouvelle; **a ~ of poetry** un poème, une poésie, une pièce de vers (*liter*); **a good ~ of work** du bon travail; (*Mus*) **that nice ~ in the third movement** ce joli passage dans le troisième mouvement; **read me a ~ out of 'Ivanhoe'** lisez-moi un passage *or* un extrait d''Ivanhoé'; **it is made (all) in one ~** c'est fait d'une seule pièce *or* tout d'une pièce; **we got back in one ~*** nous sommes rentrés sains et saufs; **the vase is still in one ~** le vase ne s'est pas cassé *or* est intact; **he had a nasty fall but he's still in one ~*** il a fait une mauvaise chute mais il est entier* *or* indemne; **the back is (all) of a ~ with the seat** le dossier et le siège sont d'un seul tenant; **it is (all) of a ~ with what he said before** cela s'accorde tout à fait avec ce qu'il a dit auparavant; **to give sb a ~ of one's mind*** dire ses quatre vérités à qn*, dire son fait à qn; **he got a ~ of my mind** je lui ai dit son fait, il a eu de mes nouvelles*; (*Comm*) **sold by the ~** vendu à la pièce *or* au détail; (*Ind*) **paid by the ~** payé à la pièce; **a 5-franc ~** une pièce de 5 F; **~ of eight** dollar espagnol; **a 30-~ tea set** un service à thé de 30 pièces; (*Mus*) **10-~ band** orchestre *m* de 10 exécutants; **3 ~s of luggage** 3 valises *fpl or* sacs *mpl etc*; **how many ~s of luggage have you got?** qu'est-ce que vous avez comme bagages?; **~ by ~** pièce à pièce, morceau par morceau; [*jigsaw, game*] **there's a ~ missing** il y a une pièce qui manque; **to put** *or* **fit together the ~s of a mystery** résoudre un mystère en rassemblant les éléments; *V* **bit²**, **museum, paper, set** *etc*.

(b) (*phrases*) **in ~s** (*broken*) en pièces, en morceaux, en fragments; (*not yet assembled*) *furniture etc* en pièces détachées; **it just came to ~s** c'est parti en morceaux *or* en pièces détachées (*hum*); **it fell to ~s** c'est tombé en morceaux; **the chair comes to ~s if you unscrew the screws** la chaise se démonte si on desserre les vis; (*fig*) **to go to ~s*** [*person*] (*collapse*) s'effondrer; (*lose one's grip*) lâcher pied (*fig*), lâcher les pédales‡; [*team etc*] se désintégrer; **to take sth to ~s** démonter qch, désassembler qch; **it takes to ~s** c'est démontable; **to cut** *or* **hack sth to ~s** couper *or* mettre qch en pièces; **to smash sth to ~s** briser qch en mille morceaux, mettre qch en miettes; **the boat was smashed to ~s** le bateau vola en éclats; *V* **pull, tear** *etc*.

(c) (*Mus*) morceau *m*; (*poem*) poème *m*, (pièce *f* de) vers *mpl*. **piano ~** morceau pour piano; **a ~ by Grieg** un morceau de Grieg.

(d) (*gun*) pièce *f* (d'artillerie).

(e) (‡: *girl*) **she's a nice ~** c'est un beau brin de fille.

2 *cpd*: (*Ind*) **piecework** travail *m* à la pièce *or* aux pièces; **to be on piecework, to do piecework** travailler à la pièce; **pieceworker** ouvrier *m*, -ière *f* payé(e) à la pièce.

piece together *vt sep broken object* rassembler; *jigsaw* assembler; (*fig*) *story* reconstituer; (*fig*) *facts* rassembler, faire concorder. **I managed to piece together what had happened from what he said** à partir de ce qu'il a dit, j'ai réussi à reconstituer les événements.

piecemeal [ˈpiːsmiːl] **1** *adv* (*bit by bit*) *tell, explain, recount* par bribes; *construct* petit à petit, par bouts; (*haphazardly*) sans plan *or* système véritable, sans trop d'ordre; **he tossed the books ~ into the box** il jeta les livres en vrac dans la caisse.

2 *adj* (*V* 1) raconté par bribes; fait petit à petit, fait par bouts; peu systématique, peu ordonné. **he gave me a ~ account/description of it** il m'en a donné par bribes un compte rendu/une description; **the construction was ~** la construction a été réalisée petit à petit *or* par étapes; **this essay is ~** cette dissertation est décousue *or* manque de plan; **a ~ argument** un raisonnement peu systématique *or* qui manque de rigueur.

pied [paɪd] *adj* bariolé, bigarré, panaché; *animal* pie *inv*. **the P~ Piper** le joueur de flûte d'Hameln.

pied-à-terre [ˌpɪeɪdæˈtɛəʳ] *n* pied-à-terre *m inv*.

Piedmont [ˈpiːdmɒnt] *n* Piémont *m*.

pier [pɪəʳ] **1** *n* **(a)** (*with amusements etc*) jetée *f* (*promenade*); (*landing stage*) appontement *m*, embarcadère *m*; (*breakwater*) brise-lames *m*; (*in airport*) jetée d'embarquement (*or* de débarquement).

(b) (*Archit*) (*column*) pilier *m*, colonne *f*; [*bridge*] pile *f*; (*brickwork*) pied-droit *m or* piédroit *m*.

2 *cpd*: **pier glass** trumeau *m*; **pierhead** musoir *m*.

pierce [pɪəs] *vt* **(a)** (*make hole in, go through*) percer, transpercer. **to have one's ears ~d** se faire percer les oreilles; **the arrow ~d his armour** la flèche transperça son armure; **the bullet ~d his arm** la balle lui transperça le bras.

(b) [*sound*] percer; [*cold, wind*] transpercer. (*liter*) **the words ~d his heart** ces paroles lui percèrent le cœur.

piercing [ˈpɪəsɪŋ] *adj sound, voice* aigu (*f* -guë), perçant; *look* perçant; *cold, wind* glacial, pénétrant.

piercingly [ˈpɪəsɪŋlɪ] *adv scream* d'une voix perçante. **~ cold wind** vent d'un froid pénétrant, vent glacial.

pierrot [ˈpɪərəʊ] *n* pierrot *m*.

piety [ˈpaɪətɪ] *n* piété *f*.

piffle* [ˈpɪfl] *n* balivernes *fpl*, fadaises *fpl*.

piffling [ˈpɪflɪŋ] *adj* (*trivial*) futile, frivole; (*worthless*) insignifiant.

pig [pɪg] **1** *n* **(a)** cochon *m*, porc *m*. (*fig*) **to buy a ~ in a poke** acheter chat en poche; **~s might fly!*** c'est (*or* ce sera *etc*) la semaine des quatre jeudis!*, c'est (*or* ce sera *etc*) le jour où les poules auront des dents!*; **they were living like ~s** ils vivaient comme des porcs *or* dans une (vraie) porcherie; *V* **Guinea, suck** *etc*.

(b) (‡*pej: person*) cochon* *m*, sale type* *m*. **to make a ~ of o.s.** manger comme un goinfre, se goinfrer*.

(c) (‡*pej: policeman*) flicard‡ *m*. **the ~s** la flicaille‡.

2 *cpd*: **pig breeding** élevage porcin; **pig industry** industrie porcine; **pig iron** saumon *m* de fonte; **pigman** porcher *m*; **pigskin** peau *f* de porc; (*Brit: lit, fig*) **pigsty** porcherie *f*; **your room is like a pigsty!** ta chambre est une vraie porcherie!; **pigswill** pâtée *f* pour les porcs; [*hair*] **pigtail** natte *f*.

3 *vi* [*sow*] mettre bas, cochonner.

4 *vt*: **to ~ it‡** vivre comme un cochon* (*or* des cochons).

pigeon [ˈpɪdʒən] **1** *n* **(a)** (*also Culin*) pigeon *m*. **wood-~** ramier *m*; *V* **carrier, clay, homing** *etc*.

(b) (*: *also* **pidgin**) affaire *f*. **that's not my ~** ça n'est pas mes oignons*; **that's your ~** c'est toi que ça regarde, c'est tes oignons*.

2 *cpd*: **pigeon-fancier** colombophile *mf*; **pigeonhole** (*n*) (*in desk*) case *f*, casier *m*; (*on wall etc*) casier; (*vt*) (*store away*) *papers* classer, ranger; (*shelve*) *project, problem* enterrer temporairement; (*classify*) *person* étiqueter (*as* comme), cataloguer (*as* comme), classer (*as* comme); **pigeon house, pigeon loft** pigeonnier *m*; **pigeon shooting** tir *m* aux pigeons; **to be pigeon-toed** avoir *or* marcher les pieds tournés en dedans.

piggery [ˈpɪgərɪ] *n* porcherie *f*.

piggish* [ˈpɪgɪʃ] *adj* (*pej*) (*in manners*) sale, grossier; (*greedy*) goinfre; (*stubborn*) têtu.

piggy [ˈpɪgɪ] **1** *n* (*child language*) cochon *m*. **2** *adj* porcin, comme un cochon. **3** *cpd*: **piggyback** = **pickaback**; **piggy bank** tirelire *f* (*souvent en forme de cochon*).

pigheaded [ˈpɪgˈhedɪd] *adj* (*pej*) entêté, obstiné, têtu.

pigheadedly [ˈpɪgˈhedɪdlɪ] *adv* (*pej*) obstinément, avec entêtement.

pigheadedness [ˈpɪgˈhedɪdnɪs] *n* (*pej*) entêtement *m*, obstination *f*.

piglet [ˈpɪglɪt] *n* porcelet *m*, petit cochon.

pigment [ˈpɪgmənt] *n* pigment *m*.

pigmentation [ˌpɪgmənˈteɪʃən] *n* pigmentation *f*.

pigmented [pɪgˈmentɪd] *adj* pigmenté.

pigmy [ˈpɪgmɪ] = **pygmy**.

pike¹ [paɪk] *n* (*spear*) pique *f*.

pike[2] [paɪk] *n* (*fish*) brochet *m*.
pike[3] [paɪk] *n* = **turnpike;** *V* **turn 2.**
pike[4] [paɪk] *n* (*Brit dial: peak*) pic *m*.
piker: [paɪkəʳ] *n* (*US*) (*small gambler*) thunard: *m*; (*small speculator*) boursicoteur *m*, -euse *f*; (*contemptible person*) minable *mf*.
pikestaff [ˈpaɪkstɑːf] *n V* **plain.**
pilaster [pɪˈlæstəʳ] *n* pilastre *m*.
Pilate [ˈpaɪlət] *n*: **Pontius ~** Ponce Pilate *m*.
pilchard [ˈpɪltʃəd] *n* pilchard *m*, célan *m*.
pile[1] [paɪl] **1** *n* **(a)** (*Constr etc*) pieu *m* de fondation, pilot *m*. **~ driver** sonnette *f*. **(b)** (*pointed stake*) pieu *m*. **2** *vt land* enfoncer des pieux *or* des pilots dans.
pile[2] [paɪl] **1** *n* **(a)** (*heap*) *[bricks, books etc]* pile *f*; (*less tidy*) tas *m*. **his clothes lay in a ~** ses vêtements étaient en tas; **the linen was in a neat ~** le linge était rangé en une pile bien nette; **to make a ~ of books, to put books in a ~** empiler des livres, mettre des livres en tas *or* en pile.
(b) (*: *fortune*) fortune *f*. **to make one's ~** faire fortune; **he made a ~ on this deal** il a ramassé un joli paquet* avec cette affaire.
(c) (*) **~s of, a ~ of** *butter, honey* beaucoup de, des masses de*; *cars, flowers* beaucoup de, un tas de*; **to have a ~ of** *or* **~s of money** avoir beaucoup d'argent *or* un argent fou *or* plein d'argent*.
(d) (*Phys*) pile *f*; *V* **atomic.**
(e) (*liter: imposing building*) édifice *m*. **the Louvre, that impressive ~** le Louvre, cet édifice impressionnant.
(f) (*Med*) **~s** hémorroïdes *fpl*.
2 *cpd*: (*Hist*) **pile dwelling** maison *f* sur pilotis; (*Aut*) **pileup** carambolage *m*; **there was a 10-car pileup on the motorway** 10 voitures se sont carambolées sur l'autoroute.
3 *vt* **(a)** (*also* **~ up**) empiler, entasser. **he ~d the books (up) one on top of the other** il empila les livres les uns sur les autres; **don't ~ them (up) too high** ne les empile pas trop haut; **a table ~d (high) with books** une table couverte de piles de livres; **to ~ coal on the fire, to ~ the fire up with coal** entasser du charbon sur le feu.
(b) he ~d the books into the box il empila *or* entassa les livres dans la caisse; **I ~d the children into the car*** j'ai entassé *or* enfourné* *or* empilé* les enfants dans la voiture.
4 *vi* (*) **we all ~d into the car** nous nous sommes tous entassés *or* empilés* dans la voiture; **we ~d off the train** nous sommes descendus du train en nous bousculant; **they ~d through the door** ils sont entrés *or* sortis en se bousculant.
pile in* *vi [people]* s'entasser, s'empiler*. **the bus arrived and we all piled in** l'autobus est arrivé et nous nous sommes tous entassés *or* empilés* dedans; **pile in, all of you!** empilez-vous* là-dedans!
pile off* *vi [people]* descendre en désordre.
pile on: *vt sep*: **to pile it on** exagérer, en rajouter, en remettre*; **he does tend to pile it on** il a tendance à en rajouter *or* à en remettre*; **stop piling it on** arrête de forcer la dose!*, n'en rajoute pas!; **to pile on the agony** dramatiser, faire du mélo*.
pile out* *vi* sortir en désordre *or* en se bousculant.
pile up 1 *vi* **(a)** *[snow etc]* s'amonceler; *[reasons etc]* s'amonceler, s'accumuler; (*) *[work, business]* s'accumuler. **he had to let the work pile up while his colleague was away** pendant que son collègue était parti il a dû laisser le travail s'accumuler *or* il a dû accumuler du travail en retard; **the evidence piled up against him** les preuves s'amoncelaient *or* s'accumulaient contre lui.
(b) (*: *crash*) **the car piled up against the wall** la voiture est rentrée* dans le mur *or* s'est écrasée contre le mur *or* a tamponné le mur; **the ship piled up on the rocks** le bateau s'est fracassé sur les rochers.
2 *vt sep* **(a)** (*lit*) *V* **pile**[2] **3a.**
(b) *evidence* accumuler, amonceler; *reasons* accumuler.
(c) (*: *crash*) **he piled up the car/the motorbike last night** hier soir il a bousillé: la voiture/la moto.
3 pileup *n V* **pile**[2] **2.**
pile[3] [paɪl] *n* (*Tex*) poils *mpl*. **the ~ of a carpet** les poils d'un tapis; **carpet with a deep ~** tapis de haute laine.
pilfer [ˈpɪlfəʳ] **1** *vt* chaparder*. **2** *vi* se livrer au chapardage*.
pilferer [ˈpɪlfərəʳ] *n* chapardeur *m*, -euse *f*.
pilfering [ˈpɪlfərɪŋ] *n* chapardage* *m*.
pilgrim [ˈpɪlgrɪm] *n* pèlerin *m*. **the ~s to Lourdes** les pèlerins de Lourdes; (*Hist*) **the P~ Fathers** les (Pères) Pèlerins; **'P~'s Progress'** 'Le Voyage du Pèlerin'.
pilgrimage [ˈpɪlgrɪmɪdʒ] *n* pèlerinage *m*. **to make a ~, to go on a ~** faire un pèlerinage.
pill [pɪl] **1** *n* **(a)** (*Med, fig*) pilule *f*. **to sugar** *or* **sweeten the ~** dorer la pilule (*for sb* à qn); *V* **bitter. (b)** (*also* **birth ~**) pilule *f*. **to be on the ~** prendre la pilule. **2** *cpd*: **pillbox** (*Med*) boîte *f* à pilules; (*Mil*) blockhaus *m inv*; (*hat*) toque *f*.
pillage [ˈpɪlɪdʒ] **1** *n* pillage *m*, saccage *m*. **2** *vt* piller, mettre à sac. **3** *vi* se livrer au pillage *or* au saccage.
pillar [ˈpɪləʳ] **1** *n* (*Archit*) pilier *m*, colonne *f*; (*Min*) pilier; (*fig*) *[fire, smoke]* colonne; (*fig: support*) pilier, soutien *m*. **he was pushed around from ~ to post** on se le renvoyait de l'un à l'autre; **after giving up his job he went from ~ to post until ...** après avoir quitté son emploi il a erré à droite et à gauche jusqu'au jour où ...; **~ of water** trombe *f* d'eau; **~ of salt** statue *f* de sel; **~ of the Church** pilier de l'Église; **he was a ~ of strength** il a été ferme comme le roc; (*Geog*) **the P~s of Hercules** les Colonnes d'Hercule.
2 *cpd*: (*Brit*) **pillar box** boîte *f* aux *or* à lettres; **pillar-box red** rouge sang *inv*.
pillion [ˈpɪljən] **1** *n [motorcycle]* siège *m* arrière, tan-sad *m*; *[horse]* selle *f* de derrière. **~ passenger** passager *m* de derrière.
2 *adv*: **to ride ~** (*on horse*) monter en croupe; (*on motorcycle*) monter sur le siège arrière.
pillory [ˈpɪlərɪ] **1** *n* pilori *m*. **2** *vt* (*Hist, fig*) mettre au pilori.
pillow [ˈpɪləʊ] **1** *n* **(a)** oreiller *m*. **he rested his head on a ~ of moss** il reposa sa tête sur un coussin de mousse.
(b) (*Tech: also* **lace ~**) carreau *m* (de dentellière).
2 *cpd*: **pillowcase** taie *f* d'oreiller; **pillow fight** bataille *f* d'oreillers *or* de polochons*; **pillow slip** = **pillowcase;** *V* **lace.**
3 *vt head* reposer. **she ~ed her head on my shoulder** elle reposa *or* appuya la tête sur mon épaule; **she ~ed her head in her arms** elle a reposé sa tête sur ses bras.
pilot [ˈpaɪlət] **1** *n* (*Aviat, Naut*) pilote *m*. **co-~** copilote *m*; *V* **automatic.**
2 *cpd*: **pilot boat** bateau-pilote *m*; (*TV*) **pilot film** film-pilote *m*; **pilot house** poste *m* de pilotage; **pilot jet, pilot light** veilleuse *f* (*de cuisinière, de chauffe-eau etc*); **pilot officer** sous-lieutenant *m* (de l'armée de l'air); **pilot scheme** projet expérimental *or* d'essai, projet-pilote *m*.
3 *vt* (*Aviat, Naut*) piloter. **he ~ed us through the crowd** il nous guida *or* pilota à travers la foule; **he ~ed the country through the difficult post-war period** il guida *or* dirigea le pays à travers les difficultés de l'après-guerre; (*Parl*) **to ~ a bill through the House** assurer le passage d'un projet de loi.
pimento [pɪˈmentəʊ] *n* piment *m*.
pimp [pɪmp] **1** *n* souteneur *m*, maquereau: *m*. **2** *vi* être souteneur, faire le maquereau:.
pimpernel [ˈpɪmpənel] *n* mouron *m*; *V* **scarlet.**
pimple [ˈpɪmpl] *n* bouton *m* (*Med*).
pimply [ˈpɪmplɪ] *adj face, person* boutonneux.
pin [pɪn] **1** *n* **(a)** (*Sewing: also for hair, tie etc*) épingle *f*; (*also* **drawing ~**) punaise *f*. **(hat)~** épingle à chapeau; **the room was like** *or* **was as neat as a new ~** la pièce était impeccable; **he was as neat as a new ~** (*clean*) il était propre comme un sou neuf*; (*tidy*) il était tiré à quatre épingles; **you could have heard a ~ drop** on aurait entendu voler une mouche; **I've got ~s and needles (in my foot)** j'ai des fourmis (au pied); (*fig*) **to be on ~s** être sur des charbons ardents; **for two ~s I'd smack his face*** pour un peu je lui donnerais une gifle; *V* **rolling, safety** *etc.*
(b) (*Tech*) goupille *f*, goujon *m*; *[hand grenade]* goupille; *[pulley]* essieu *m*; (*Elec*) fiche *f or* broche *f* (de prise de courant); (*Med: in limb*) broche. (*Elec*) **3-~ plug** prise *f* à 3 fiches *or* broches.
(c) (*Bowling*) quille *f*; (*Golf*) drapeau *m* de trou.
(d) (*: *leg*) **~s** guibolles: *fpl or* guiboles: *fpl*, quilles: *fpl*; **he's not very steady on his ~s** il a les guibolles: en coton, il ne tient pas sur ses guibolles:.
2 *cpd*: **pinball** flipper *m*; **pinball machine** flipper *m*; **pincushion** pelote *f* à épingles; **pinhead** (*lit*) tête *f* d'épingle; (*:*pej: idiot*) imbécile *mf*, andouille: *f*; **pinhole** trou *m* d'épingle; (*Phot*) sténopé *m*; **pin money** argent *m* de poche; **pinpoint** (*n*) (*lit*) pointe *f* d'épingle; (*vt*) *place* localiser avec précision; *problem* mettre le doigt sur, définir; **pinprick** (*lit*) piqûre *f* d'épingle; (*fig: annoyance*) coup *m* d'épingle; **pinstripe** rayure très fine; **black material with a white pinstripe** tissu noir finement rayé de blanc; **pinstripe suit** costume rayé; **pin table** = **pinball machine; pinup (girl)*** pin-up *f inv*.
3 *vt* **(a)** (*put pin in*) *dress* épingler; *papers* (*together*) attacher *or* réunir *or* assembler avec une épingle; (*to wall etc*) attacher avec une punaise. **he ~ned the medal to his uniform** il épingla la médaille sur son uniforme; **he ~ned the calendar on the wall** il attacha *or* fixa le calendrier au mur (avec une punaise).
(b) (*fig*) **to ~ sb's arms (to his side)** lier les bras de qn (contre son corps); **to ~ sb against a wall** clouer qn à un mur, immobiliser qn contre un mur; **the fallen tree ~ned him against the house** l'arbre abattu le cloua *or* le coinça *or* l'immobilisa contre la maison; **the battalion was ~ned (down) against the river** le bataillon était bloqué sur la berge du fleuve; **to ~ one's hopes on sth** mettre tous ses espoirs dans qch; **they tried to ~ the crime on him*** ils ont essayé de lui mettre le crime sur le dos *or* de lui coller* la responsabilité du crime; **you can't ~ it on me!*** vous ne pouvez rien prouver contre moi!
(c) (*Tech*) cheviller, goupiller.
pin back *vt sep* (*lit*) retenir (avec une épingle). (*fig*) **to pin one's ears back*** ouvrir ses oreilles (toutes grandes) *or* ses esgourdes*.
pin down *vt sep* **(a)** (*secure*) attacher *or* fixer avec une épingle *or* une punaise.
(b) (*trap*) immobiliser, coincer. **to be pinned down by a fallen tree** être immobilisé par *or* coincé sous un arbre tombé.
(c) (*fig*) **to pin sb down to a promise** obliger qn à tenir sa promesse; **I can't manage to pin him down** je n'arrive pas à le coincer* (*fig*); **see if you can pin him down to naming a price** essaie de le décider à fixer un prix; **there's something wrong but I can't pin it down** il y a quelque chose qui ne va pas mais je n'arrive pas à définir exactement ce que c'est *or* à mettre le doigt dessus.
pin on *vt sep* attacher avec une punaise *or* une épingle, épingler.
pin up 1 *vt sep notice* attacher (au mur) avec une punaise, afficher; *hem* épingler; *hair* épingler, relever avec des épingles.
2 pinup *n, adj V* **pin 2.**
pinafore [ˈpɪnəfɔːʳ] *n* (*apron*) tablier *m*; (*overall*) blouse *f* (*de travail*). **~ dress** robe-chasuble *f*.
pincer [ˈpɪnsəʳ] *n* **(a)** *[crab]* pince *f*. **~ movement** (*fig, Mil*) mouvement *m* de tenailles. **(b)** (*tool*) **~s** tenailles *fpl*.
pinch [pɪntʃ] **1** *n* **(a)** (*action*) pincement *m*; (*mark*) pinçon *m*. **to give sb a ~ (on the arm)** pincer qn (au bras); (*fig*) **people are beginning to feel the ~** les gens commencent à être serrés *or* à

court; (*fig*) at a ~, (*US*) **in a ~** au besoin, en cas de besoin, à la rigueur; **it'll do at a ~** cela fera l'affaire à la rigueur *or* faute de mieux; **when it comes to the ~** au moment critique.

(b) *[salt]* pincée *f*; *[snuff]* prise *f*. (*fig*) **to take sth with a ~ of salt** ne pas prendre qch pour argent comptant *or* au pied de la lettre.

2 *vt* **(a)** pincer; *[shoes]* serrer. **he ~ed her arm** il lui a pincé le bras, il l'a pincée au bras.

(b) (*: *steal*) chiper*, piquer‡, faucher‡. **I had my car ~ed** on m'a fauché‡ ma voiture; **he ~ed that idea from Shaw** il a chipé* *or* piqué‡ cette idée à Shaw; **Robert ~ed John's girlfriend** Robert a piqué‡ sa petite amie à Jean.

(c) (‡: *arrest*) pincer*. **to get ~ed** se faire pincer*; **they ~ed him with the jewels on him** on l'a pincé* *or* piqué‡ en possession des bijoux; **he got ~ed for speeding** il s'est fait pincer* pour excès de vitesse.

3 *vi* **(a)** *[shoe]* être étroit, serrer. (*fig*) **that's where the shoe ~es** c'est là que le bât blesse.

(b) to ~ and scrape rogner sur tout, se serrer la ceinture*.

pinch back, pinch off *vt sep bud* épincer.

pinchbeck ['pɪntʃbek] **1** *n* toc *m*. **2** *adj* en toc.

pinched ['pɪntʃt] *adj* **(a)** (*drawn*) **to look ~** avoir les traits tirés; **to look ~ with cold/with hunger** avoir l'air transi de froid/ tenaillé par la faim. **(b) ~ for money** à court d'argent; **~ for space** à l'étroit.

pinch-hit ['pɪntʃhɪt] *vi* (*US Baseball*) jouer en remplaçant.

Pindar ['pɪndəʳ] *n* Pindare *m*.

Pindaric [pɪn'dærɪk] *adj* pindarique.

pine[1] [paɪn] **1** *n* (*also* **~ tree**) pin *m*.

2 *cpd*: **pinecone** pomme *f* de pin; **pine grove** pinède *f*; **pine kernel** pigne *f*; **pine marten** martre *f*; **pine needle** aiguille *f* de pin; **pine nut** = **pine kernel**; **pinewood** (*grove*) bois *m* de pins, pinède *f*; (*U: material*) bois de pin, pin *m*.

pine[2] [paɪn] *vi* **(a)** (*long*) **to ~ for sth** soupirer après qch (*liter*), désirer ardemment *or* vivement qch; **to ~ for one's family** s'ennuyer de sa famille, désirer ardemment retrouver sa famille; **after 6 months in London she began to ~ for home** après 6 mois passés à Londres elle ne pensait qu'à *or* aspirait à *or* désirait ardemment rentrer chez elle; **exiles pining for home** des exilés qui ont la nostalgie du pays natal.

(b) (*be sad*) languir, dépérir.

pine away *vi* languir, dépérir.

pineapple ['paɪn,æpl] *n* ananas *m*.

ping [pɪŋ] **1** *n* bruit *m* métallique; *[bell, clock]* tintement *m*. **2** *vi* faire un bruit métallique, tinter. **3** *cpd*: **ping-pong** ping-pong *m*; **ping-pong ball** balle *f* de ping-pong; **ping-pong player** pongiste *mf*.

pinion[1] ['pɪnjən] **1** *n [bird]* aileron *m*. **2** *vt* **(a)** *person* lier. **to ~ sb's arms** lier les bras à qn; **he was ~ed against the wall** il était cloué au mur, il était coincé contre le mur. **(b)** *bird* rogner les ailes à.

pinion[2] ['pɪnjən] *n* (*Tech*) pignon *m*. **~ wheel** roue *f* à pignon; *V* **rack**[1].

pink[1] [pɪŋk] **1** *n* **(a)** (*colour*) rose *m*. (*fig*) **to be in the ~** se porter comme un charme; **in the ~ of condition** en excellente *or* pleine forme; *V* **hunting, salmon**.

(b) (*Bot*) œillet *m*, mignardise *f*.

2 *adj cheek, clothes, paper* rose; (*Pol*) gauchisant. **the petals turn ~** les pétales rosissent; **she turned ~ with pleasure** elle rosit *or* rougit de plaisir; **he turned ~ with embarrassment** il rougit de confusion; *V* **strike, tickle**.

3 *cpd*: (*Med*) **pink eye** conjonctivite aiguë contagieuse; **pink gin** cocktail *m* de gin et d'angusture.

pink[2] [pɪŋk] *vt* **(a)** (*Sewing*) denteler les bords de. **~ing shears** ciseaux *mpl* à denteler. **(b)** (*put holes in*) perforer. **(c)** (*pierce*) percer.

pink[3] [pɪŋk] *vi [car engine etc]* cliqueter.

pinkie* ['pɪŋkɪ] *n* petit doigt, auriculaire *m*.

pinkish ['pɪŋkɪʃ] *adj* rosâtre, rosé; (*Pol*) gauchisant.

pinnace ['pɪnɪs] *n* chaloupe *f*, grand canot.

pinnacle ['pɪnəkl] *n* (*Archit*) pinacle *m*; (*mountain peak*) pic *m*, cime *f*; (*fig*) apogée *m*, sommet *m*, pinacle.

pinny‡ ['pɪnɪ] *n* (*abbr of* **pinafore**) tablier *m*.

pint [paɪnt] **1** *n* **(a)** pinte *f*, ≃ demi-litre *m* (*Brit* = *0,57 litre; US* = *0,47 litre*).

(b) (*: *beer*) ≃ demi *m* (de bière). **let's go for a ~** allons boire un demi *or* prendre un pot*; **he had a few ~s** il but quelques demis; **he likes his ~** il aime son verre de bière; **he likes his ~ every evening** il aime boire son demi *or* son pot chaque soir.

2 *cpd*: **a pint-size(d) man/woman*** un petit bout d'homme/de femme.

pinta* ['paɪntə] *n* (*abbr of* **pint of milk**: *terme publicitaire*) ≃ demi-litre *m* de lait.

pioneer [,paɪə'nɪəʳ] **1** *n* (*explorer*) explorateur *m*, -trice *f*; (*early settler*) pionnier *m*, colon *m*; (*Mil*) pionnier, sapeur *m*; *[scheme, science, method]* pionnier, promoteur *m*, -trice *f*. **he was one of the ~s in this field** il a été l'un des pionniers *or* novateurs *or* précurseurs dans ce domaine; **he was a ~ in the study of bats** il a été un pionnier de l'étude des chauves-souris, il a été l'un des premiers à étudier les chauves-souris; **one of the ~s of aviation/scientific research** l'un des pionniers de l'aviation/de la recherche scientifique.

2 *vt*: **to ~ the study of sth** être l'un des premiers (*or* l'une des premières) à étudier qch; **she ~ed research in this field** elle fut à l'avant-garde de la recherche dans ce domaine, elle ouvrit la voie dans ce domaine; **he ~ed the use of this drug** il a été l'un des premiers à utiliser ce médicament, il a lancé l'usage de ce médicament.

3 *cpd research, study* complètement nouveau *or* original. **to do pioneer work in a subject** défricher un sujet.

pious ['paɪəs] *adj person, deed* pieux. **a ~ deed** une action pieuse, une œuvre pie; (*iro*) **~ hope** espoir légitime.

piously ['paɪəslɪ] *adv* avec piété, pieusement.

pip[1] [pɪp] **1** *n* **(a)** *[fruit]* pépin *m*.

(b) *[card, dice]* point *m*.

(c) (*Brit Mil**: *on uniform*) ≃ galon *m*.

(d) (*Telec*) top *m*. **the ~s** le bip-bip; **at the third ~ it will be 6.49 and 20 seconds** au troisième top il sera exactement 6 heures 49 minutes 20 secondes; **put more money in when you hear the ~s** introduisez des pièces supplémentaires quand vous entendrez le bip-bip.

(e) (*Radar*) spot *m*.

2 *cpd*: **he's a pipsqueak‡** c'est un rien du tout*.

pip[2] [pɪp] *n* (*Vet*) pépie *f*. **he gives me the ~‡** il me hérisse le poil*.

pip[3]***** [pɪp] *vt* **(a)** (*hit*) atteindre d'une balle. **(b) to be ~ped at the post** se faire coiffer au poteau, se faire battre *or* griller* de justesse. **(c)** (*fail*) se faire recaler* *or* coller*.

pipe [paɪp] **1** *n* **(a)** (*tube*) tube *m*; (*for water, gas*) tuyau *m*, conduit *m*, conduite *f*. **to lay water ~s** poser des conduites d'eau *or* une canalisation d'eau; *V* **drain, wind**[1].

(b) (*Mus*) pipeau *m*, chalumeau *m*; *[organ]* tuyau *m*; (*boatswain's*) sifflet *m*. **(bag)~s** cornemuse *f*; **~s of Pan** flûte *f* de Pan.

(c) (*sound*) *[bird]* chant *m*.

(d) pipe *f*. **he smokes a ~** il fume la pipe; **he smoked a ~ before he left** il fuma une pipe avant de partir; **to fill a ~** bourrer une pipe; **~ of peace** calumet *m* de (la) paix; **a ~(ful) of tobacco** une pipe de tabac; **put that in your ~ and smoke it!‡** si ça ne te plaît pas c'est le même prix!*, mets ça dans ta poche et ton mouchoir par-dessus!

2 *cpd*: **pipeclay** terre *f* de pipe; **pipe cleaner** cure-pipe *m*; **pipe dream** château *m* en Espagne (*fig*); **pipeline** (*gen*) pipeline *m*; *[oil]* oléoduc *m*; *[natural gas]* gazoduc *m*; (*fig*) **the goods you ordered are in the pipeline** les marchandises que vous avez commandées sont en route; (*fig*) **the trade unions have got a new pay increase in the pipeline** les syndicats ont introduit une nouvelle demande de hausse des salaires; **pipe organ** grandes orgues; **pipe rack** porte-pipes *m inv*; **pipe tobacco** tabac *m* à pipe.

3 *vt* **(a)** transporter par tuyau *or* conduite *or* canalisation *etc*. **water is ~d to the farm** l'eau est amenée jusqu'à la ferme par une canalisation; **to ~ oil across the desert** transporter du pétrole à travers le désert par pipe-line *or* oléoduc; **to ~ oil into a tank** verser *or* faire passer du pétrole dans un réservoir à l'aide d'un tuyau; (*TV*) **~d music** musique *f* de fond enregistrée.

(b) (*Mus*) *tune* jouer (sur un pipeau *etc*); (*Naut*) *order* siffler. **to ~ all hands on deck** rassembler l'équipage sur le pont (au son du sifflet); **to ~ sb in/out** saluer l'arrivée/le départ de qn (au son du sifflet); **the commander was ~d aboard** le commandant a reçu les honneurs du sifflet en montant à bord.

(c) (*Sewing*) passepoiler, garnir d'un passepoil. **~d with blue** passepoilé de bleu, garni d'un passepoil bleu.

(d) (*Culin*) **to ~ icing/cream** *etc* **on a cake** décorer un gâteau de fondant/de crème fouettée *etc* (à l'aide d'une douille).

(e) (*say*) dire d'une voix flûtée; (*sing*) chanter d'une voix flûtée.

4 *vi* **(a)** (*Mus*) jouer du pipeau *or* du chalumeau *or* de la flûte *or* de la cornemuse.

(b) (*Naut*) donner un coup de sifflet.

pipe down‡ *vi* mettre la sourdine*, se taire. **(do) pipe down!** un peu de calme!, mets-y une sourdine!*, baisse un peu le ton!*

pipe up* *vi* se faire entendre.

piper ['paɪpəʳ] *n* joueur *m*, -euse *f* de pipeau *or* de chalumeau; (*bagpiper*) cornemuseur *m*; *V* **pay**.

pipette [pɪ'pet] *n* pipette *f*.

piping ['paɪpɪŋ] **1** *n* (*U*) **(a)** (*in house*) tuyauterie *f*, canalisation *f*, conduites *fpl*.

(b) (*Mus*) son *m* du pipeau *or* du chalumeau *or* de la cornemuse.

(c) (*Sewing*) passepoil *m*. **~ cord** ganse *f*.

(d) (*on cake etc*) décorations (appliquées) à la douille.

2 *adj voice, tone* flûté.

3 *adv*: **~ hot** tout chaud, tout bouillant.

pipit ['pɪpɪt] *n* (*Orn*) pipi(t) *m*.

pipkin ['pɪpkɪn] *n* poêlon *m* (en terre).

pippin ['pɪpɪn] *n* (pomme *f*) reinette *f*.

piquancy ['pi:kənsɪ] *n* (*flavour*) goût piquant; *[story]* sel *m*, piquant *m*.

piquant ['pi:kənt] *adj flavour, story* piquant.

piquantly ['pi:kəntlɪ] *adv* d'une manière piquante.

pique [pi:k] **1** *vt* **(a)** *person* dépiter, irriter, froisser. **(b)** *sb's curiosity, interest* piquer, exciter. **2** *n* ressentiment *m*, dépit *m*. **in a fit of ~** dans un accès de dépit.

piquet [pɪ'ket] *n* piquet *m* (*jeu de cartes*).

piracy ['paɪərəsɪ] *n* (*U*) piraterie *f*; (*fig*) *[book]* plagiat *m*; *[idea]* pillage *m*, vol *m*; (*Comm*) contrefaçon *f*. **a tale of ~** une histoire de pirates.

piranha [pɪ'rɑ:njə] *n* piranha *m or* piraya *m*.

pirate ['paɪərɪt] **1** *n* **(a)** (*Hist*) pirate *m*, corsaire *m*, flibustier *m*.

(b) (*Comm*) (*gen*) contrefacteur *m*; (*in publishing*) plagiaire *mf*, démarqueur *m*; *[ideas]* voleur *m*, -euse *f*.

2 *cpd flag, ship* de pirates. **pirate radio** radio *f or* émetteur *m* pirate.

3 *vt book* publier en édition pirate, démarquer, plagier; *product* contrefaire; *invention, idea* s'approprier, piller, voler.

pirated ['paɪərɪtɪd] *adj* (*Comm*) contrefait. **~ edition** édition pirate *or* plagiée.

piratical [paɪ'rætɪkəl] *adj* (*V* **pirate**) de pirate; de contrefacteur; de plagiaire.

pirouette [ˌpɪrʊˈet] **1** *n* pirouette *f*. **2** *vi* faire la pirouette, pirouetter.
Pisa [ˈpiːzə] *n* Pise.
Pisces [ˈpaɪsiːz] *n* (*Astron*) les Poissons *mpl*.
piss⁂ [pɪs] **1** *n* pisse⁂ *f*. **2** *vi* pisser⁂.
piss off⁂ **1** *vi* foutre le camp⁑. **piss off!** fous(-moi) le camp!⁑ **2** *vt*: **I'm pissed off** j'en ai marre⁑, j'en ai ras le bol⁑.
pissed⁂ [pɪst] *adj* bituré⁑, bourré⁑, blindé⁑. **to get ~** se soûler la gueule⁑.
pistachio [pɪsˈtɑːʃɪəʊ] *n* **(a)** (*nut*) pistache *f*; (*tree*) pistachier *m*. **~-flavoured ice cream** glace *f* à la pistache. **(b)** (*colour*) (vert *m*) pistache *m inv*.
pistil [ˈpɪstɪl] *n* pistil *m*.
pistol [ˈpɪstl] **1** *n* pistolet *m*, colt *m*. **2** *cpd*: **at pistol point** sous la menace du pistolet; **pistol shot** coup *m* de pistolet.
piston [ˈpɪstən] **1** *n* piston *m* (*lit*). **2** *cpd*: **piston engine** moteur *m* à pistons; **piston-engined** à moteur à pistons; **piston ring** segment *m* (de pistons); **piston rod** tige *f* de piston.
pit[1] [pɪt] **1** *n* **(a)** (*large hole*) trou *m*; (*on moon's surface etc*) cratère *m*, dépression *f*; (*also* **coal~**) mine *f*, puits *m* de mine; (*as game trap etc*) trappe *f*, fosse *f*; (*quarry*) carrière *f*; (*in garage*) fosse; (*in motor racing*) stand *m*. **chalk~** carrière à chaux; **he works in the ~s** il travaille à la mine; **the men in the ~s** les mineurs *mpl* (de fond); (*fig: hell*) **the ~** l'enfer *m*.
(b) (*small depression*) (*in metal, glass*) petit trou; (*on face*) (petite) marque *f or* cicatrice *f*.
(c) (*Anat*) creux *m*. **the ball hit him in the ~ of his stomach/back** la balle l'a touché au creux de l'estomac/des reins; *V* **arm**[1].
(d) (*Brit Theat*) (fauteuils *mpl* d')orchestre *m*; (*for cock-fighting*) arène *f*; (*US St Ex*) parquet *m* de la Bourse. (*US St Ex*) **the wheat ~** la Bourse du blé.
2 *cpd*: (*Min*) **pithead** carreau *m* de la mine; (*Min*) **pit pony** cheval *m* de mine; (*Min*) **pit prop** poteau *m or* étai *m* de mine; (*Min*) **pit worker** mineur *m* de fond.
3 *vt* **(a)** opposer (*sb against sb* qn à qn). **to ~ o.s. against sb** se mesurer avec *or* à qn; **to be ~ted against sb** avoir qn comme *or* pour adversaire; **to ~ one's wits against** jouer au plus fin avec, se mesurer avec.
(b) *metal* trouer, piqueter; *face, skin* grêler, marquer. **a car ~ted with rust** une voiture piquée de rouille; **his face was ~ted with pockmarks** son visage était grêlé par la petite vérole; **the ~ted surface of the glass** la surface piquetée du verre.
pit[2] [pɪt] **1** *n* (*fruit-stone*) noyau *m*. **2** *vt* dénoyauter.
pitapat [ˈpɪtəˈpæt] *adv*: **to go ~** *[feet]* trottiner; *[heart]* palpiter, battre; *[rain]* crépiter.
pitch[1] [pɪtʃ] **1** *n* **(a)** (*throw*) acte *m* de lancer, lancement *m*. **the ball went full ~ over the fence** le ballon vola par-dessus la barrière.
(b) (*degree*) degré *m*, point *m*; *[voice]* hauteur *f*. **at its (highest) ~** à son comble; **excitement was at fever ~** l'excitation allait jusqu'à la fièvre; **things have reached such a ~ that ...** les choses en sont arrivées à un point tel que ... .
(c) (*Mus*) ton *m*, diapason *m*. **to give the ~** donner le ton; *V* **concert**.
(d) (*Brit Sport*) terrain *m*. **football/cricket** *etc* **~** terrain de football/de cricket *etc*.
(e) (*Brit*) *[trader]* place *f* (habituelle); *V* **queer**.
(f) *[roof]* degré *m* de pente.
(g) (*movement of boat*) tangage *m*.
(h) (*Aviat, Naut*) *[propeller]* pas *m*. **variable ~ propeller** hélice *f* à pas variable.
2 *cpd*: (*Golf*) **pitch-and-putt** pitch-and-putt *m* (*genre de golf limité à deux clubs*); **pitch-and-toss** *sorte f de jeu de pile ou face*; **pitchfork** (*n*) fourche *f* (à foin); (*vt*) (*Agr*) fourcher, lancer avec une fourche; (*fig*) **he was pitchforked into the job** on l'a bombardé* à ce poste; (*fig*) **I was pitchforked into it** j'ai été bien forcé de le faire; (*Mus*) **pitch pipe** diapason *m* (*en forme de sifflet*).
3 *vt* **(a)** (*throw*) *ball* (*also Baseball*) lancer; *object* jeter, lancer; (*Agr*) *hay* lancer avec une fourche; (*discard*) jeter, bazarder*. **~ it over here!** jette-le *or* lance-le par ici!; **he was ~ed off his horse** il fut jeté à bas de son cheval, il fut désarçonné; **the horse ~ed him off** le cheval le jeta à bas *or* à terre; **to ~ over/through/under** *etc* lancer *or* jeter par-dessus/à travers/par-dessous *etc*.
(b) (*Mus*) *note* donner; *melody* donner le ton de *or* à. **she can't ~ a note properly** elle ne sait pas trouver la note juste (*lit*); **I'll ~ you a note** je vous donne une note pour commencer; **to ~ the voice higher/lower** hausser/baisser le ton de la voix; **this song is ~ed too low** cette chanson est dans un ton trop bas; **to ~ one's aspirations too high** aspirer *or* viser trop haut, placer ses aspirations trop haut; **it is ~ed in rather high-flown terms** c'est exprimé en des termes assez ronflants; **the speech must be ~ed at the right level for the audience** le ton du discours doit être adapté au public; (*fig*) **you're ~ing it a bit high!** *or* **strong!** tu exagères un peu!, tu y vas un peu fort!; **he ~ed me a story about*** ... il m'a débité *or* m'a sorti* une histoire sur ... .
(c) (*set up*) **to ~ a tent** dresser une tente; **to ~ camp** établir un camp.
4 *vi* **(a)** (*fall*) tomber; (*be jerked*) être projeté; *[ball]* rebondir, tomber. **she slipped and ~ed forward** elle glissa et tomba le nez en avant *or* et piqua du nez; **he ~ed forward as the bus stopped** il fut projeté en avant quand l'autobus s'arrêta; **to ~ into the lake** tomber la tête la première dans le lac; **to ~ off a horse** tomber de cheval; **the aircraft ~ed into the sea** l'avion plongea dans la mer; **he ~ed over** il tomba; **he ~ed over backwards** il tomba à la renverse; **the ball ~ed (down) at his feet** la balle tomba *or* rebondit à ses pieds.
(b) (*Naut*) tanguer. **the ship ~ed and tossed** le navire tanguait.
pitch in* *vi* s'atteler *or* s'attaquer au boulot*, s'y coller*. **they all pitched in to help him** ils s'y sont tous collés* pour l'aider; **come on, pitch in all of you!** allez, mettez-vous-y *or* collez-vous-y* tous!
pitch into* *vt fus* **(a)** (*attack*) tomber sur; (*abuse*) tomber sur, taper sur*, éreinter*.
(b) s'attaquer à. **they pitched into the work** ils se sont attaqués *or* collés* au travail; **they pitched into the meal** ils se sont attaqués au repas, ils y sont allés d'un bon coup de fourchette.
pitch out *vt sep* (*get rid of*) *person* expulser, éjecter*, vider*; *thing* jeter, bazarder*. **the car overturned and the driver was pitched out** la voiture fit un tonneau et le conducteur fut éjecté.
pitch (up)on *vt fus* arrêter son choix sur.
pitch[2] [pɪtʃ] **1** *n* (*tar*) poix *f*, brai *m*. **mineral ~** asphalte minéral, bitume *m*.
2 *cpd*: **pitch-black** noir comme poix, noir ébène *inv*; **pitchblende** pechblende *f*; **it's a pitch-dark night** il fait nuit noire; **it's pitch-dark** il fait noir comme dans un four; **pitch pine** pitchpin *m*.
3 *vt* brayer, enduire de poix *or* de brai.
pitched [pɪtʃt] *adj*: **~ battle** (*Mil*) bataille rangée; (*fig*) véritable bataille.
pitcher[1] [ˈpɪtʃəʳ] *n* cruche *f*; (*bigger*) broc *m*.
pitcher[2] [ˈpɪtʃəʳ] *n* (*Baseball*) lanceur *m*.
piteous [ˈpɪtɪəs] *adj* (*pathetic*) pitoyable. **a ~ sight** un spectacle pitoyable *or* à faire pitié.
piteously [ˈpɪtɪəslɪ] *adv* pitoyablement.
pitfall [ˈpɪtfɔːl] *n* (*lit*) trappe *f*, piège *m*; (*fig*) piège, embûche *f*. **the ~s of English** les pièges de l'anglais; (*fig*) **there are many ~s ahead** de nombreuses embûches nous (*or* les *etc*) guettent.
pith [pɪθ] *n* **(a)** *[bone, plant]* moelle *f*; *[orange]* peau blanche. **~ helmet** casque colonial. **(b)** (*fig*) (*essence*) essence *f*, moelle *f* (*fig*); (*force*) force *f*, vigueur *f*.
pithiness [ˈpɪθɪnɪs] *n* *[style]* vigueur *f*, concision *f*.
pithy [ˈpɪθɪ] *adj* (*forceful*) nerveux, vigoureux; (*terse*) concis; (*pointed*) savoureux, piquant. **a ~ saying** une remarque piquante.
pitiable [ˈpɪtɪəbl] *adj* *hovel* pitoyable; *income* misérable, de misère; *appearance* piteux, minable; *attempt* piteux. **a ~ situation** une situation pitoyable *or* navrante.
pitiful [ˈpɪtɪfʊl] *adj* **(a)** (*touching*) *appearance, sight, cripple* pitoyable. **(b)** (*deplorable*) *cowardice* lamentable, déplorable. **his ~ efforts to speak French** ses lamentables efforts pour parler français.
pitifully [ˈpɪtɪfəlɪ] *adv* (*pathetically*) pitoyablement, à faire pitié; (*contemptibly*) lamentablement. **he was ~ thin** il était maigre à faire pitié; **a ~ bad play** une pièce lamentable.
pitiless [ˈpɪtɪlɪs] *adj* sans pitié, impitoyable.
pitilessly [ˈpɪtɪlɪslɪ] *adv* sans pitié, impitoyablement.
pittance [ˈpɪtəns] *n* maigre revenu *m*. **she's living on a ~** elle n'a presque rien pour vivre; **they're offering a mere ~** ils offrent un salaire de misère.
pitter-patter [ˈpɪtəˈpætəʳ] **1** *adv* = **pitapat**. **2** *n* = **patter**[2] **1**.
pituitary [pɪˈtjuːɪtərɪ] *adj* pituitaire. **~ gland** glande *f* pituitaire, hypophyse *f*.
pity [ˈpɪtɪ] **1** *n* **(a)** pitié *f*, compassion *f*. **for ~'s sake** par pitié, de grâce; **to have** *or* **take ~ on sb** prendre *or* avoir pitié de qn, prendre qn en pitié; **have ~ on him!** ayez pitié de lui!; **to feel ~ for sb** avoir pitié de qn, s'apitoyer sur qn; **to move sb to ~** exciter la compassion de qn, apitoyer qn; **out of ~ (for him)** par pitié (pour lui).
(b) (*misfortune*) dommage *m*. **it is a ~/a great ~** c'est dommage/bien dommage; **it is a thousand pities that ...** il est mille fois *or* extrêmement dommage que ... + *subj*; **it's a ~ (that) you can't come** il est *or* quel dommage que vous ne puissiez (pas) venir; **what a ~!** quel dommage!; **(the) more's the ~!** c'est bien dommage!, c'est d'autant plus dommage!; **the ~ of it is that ...** le plus malheureux c'est que ... .
2 *vt* plaindre, s'apitoyer sur, avoir pitié de. **he is to be pitied** il est à plaindre.
pitying [ˈpɪtɪɪŋ] *adj* compatissant, plein de pitié.
pityingly [ˈpɪtɪɪŋlɪ] *adv* avec compassion, avec pitié.
Pius [ˈpaɪəs] *n* Pie *m*.
pivot [ˈpɪvət] **1** *n* (*Mil, Tech, fig*) pivot *m*.
2 *vt* (*turn*) faire pivoter; (*mount on ~*) monter sur pivot. **he ~ed it on his hand** il le fit pivoter *or* tourner sur sa main.
3 *vi* (*Tech*) pivoter, tourner. **she ~ed round and round** elle tournoyait sans s'arrêter; **he ~ed on his heel** il tourna sur ses talons; **his whole argument ~s on this point** son argument repose entièrement sur ce point.
pivotal [ˈpɪvətl] *adj* essentiel, central.
pixie [ˈpɪksɪ] *n* lutin *m*, fée *f*. **~ hood** bonnet pointu.
placard [ˈplækɑːd] **1** *n* affiche *f*, placard *m*. **2** *vt* *wall* placarder; *announcement* afficher. **the town is ~ed with slogans** la ville est placardée de slogans.
placate [pləˈkeɪt] *vt* calmer, apaiser.
place [pleɪs] **1** *n* **(a)** (*gen*) endroit *m*, lieu *m* (*gen frm*). **to take ~** avoir lieu; **this is the ~** c'est ici, voici l'endroit; **we came to a ~ where ...** nous sommes arrivés à un endroit où ...; **any ~ will do** n'importe où fera l'affaire; (*US*) **I couldn't find it any ~*** je n'ai pu le trouver nulle part; (*US*) **it must be some ~ in the house*** ça doit être quelque part dans la maison; (*US*) **some ~ else*** quelque part ailleurs; **he was in another ~ altogether** il était dans un tout autre endroit *or* un tout autre lieu; **this is no ~ for children** cela n'est pas un endroit (convenable) pour des enfants; **can't you find a better ~ to sit down?** est-ce que tu ne pourrais pas trouver un meilleur *or* un autre endroit où t'asseoir?; **it's not a very nice ~ here for a picnic** ça n'est pas un bien joli endroit pour pique-niquer; **this is no ~** *or* **this isn't the ~ to start an argument** nous ne pouvons pas commencer à dis-

cuter ici, ce n'est pas un lieu pour discuter; **from ~ to ~** d'un endroit à l'autre, de lieu en lieu; **he went from ~ to ~ looking for her** il la chercha de ville en ville (*or* de village en village *etc*); **she moved around the room from ~ to ~** elle allait d'un coin de la pièce à un autre *or* de-ci de-là dans la pièce; **his clothes were all over the ~** ses vêtements traînaient partout; **I've looked for him all over the ~** je l'ai cherché partout; **to find/lose one's ~ in a book** trouver/perdre sa page dans un livre (*V also* 1h); **to laugh at the right ~** rire quand il faut, rire au bon endroit *or* moment; (*: *travel*) **to go ~s** voyager, voir du pays; **we like to go ~s at weekends*** nous aimons faire un tour *or* bouger* pendant les week-ends; (*: *make good*) **he'll go ~s all right!** il ira loin!, il fera son chemin!; **he's going ~s*** il fait son chemin; (*: *make progress*) **we're going ~s at last** nous avançons enfin (*fig*), ça démarre* (*fig*); **I can't be in two ~s at once!*** je ne peux pas être dans deux endroits (différents) à la fois!

(b) (*specific spot*) lieu *m*, endroit *m*. **~ of amusement/birth/death/residence/work** lieu de distraction(s)/de naissance/de décès/de résidence/de travail; **~ of refuge** (lieu de) refuge *m*; **he is at his ~ of business** il est à son lieu de travail; **this building is a ~ of business** cet immeuble est occupé par des locaux commerciaux; **~ of worship** édifice religieux, lieu de culte; **the time and ~ of the crime** l'heure et le lieu du crime; **do you remember the ~ where we met?** te souviens-tu de l'endroit où nous nous sommes rencontrés?; *V* **fortify, market, watering** *etc*.

(c) (*district, area*) endroit *m*, coin *m*; (*building*) endroit, bâtiment *m*, immeuble *m*; (*town*) endroit, ville *f*; (*village*) endroit, village *m*, localité *f*. **it's a small ~** (*village*) c'est un petit village *or* coin; (*house*) c'est une petite maison; **it's just a little country ~** ce n'est qu'un petit village de campagne; **he has a ~ in the country** il a une maison *or* une résidence à la campagne; **the house is a vast great ~** la maison est immense; **the town is such a big ~ now that ...** la ville s'est tellement agrandie *or* étendue que ...; **we tried to find a native of the ~** nous avons essayé de trouver un natif du lieu; **the train doesn't stop at that ~ any more** le train ne s'arrête plus là *or* à cet endroit; **house prices are high in every ~ round here** le prix des maisons est élevé partout par ici *or* dans tout le coin* *or* secteur*; **his family is growing, he needs a bigger ~** sa famille s'agrandit, il lui faut quelque chose de plus grand *or* une maison plus grande; **his business is growing, he needs a bigger ~** son affaire s'agrandit, il lui faut quelque chose de plus grand *or* des locaux plus étendus; **we were at Peter's ~*** nous étions chez Pierre; **come over to our ~*** venez à la maison *or* chez nous.

(d) (*in street names*) rue *f*. **Washington P~** rue de Washington.

(e) (*seat*) place *f*; (*at table*) place, couvert *m*. **a theatre with 2,000 ~s** un théâtre de 2.000 places; **are there any ~s left?** est-ce qu'il reste des places?; **keep a ~ for me** gardez-moi une place; (*in restaurant, theatre etc*) **is this ~ taken?** est-ce que cette place est prise? *or* occupée?; **to lay** *or* **set an extra ~** (*at table*) mettre un couvert supplémentaire; *V* **change**.

(f) (*position, situation; circumstance; function*) place *f*; *[star, planet]* position *f*. **in ~ of** à la place de, au lieu de; **to take the ~ of sb/sth** remplacer qn/qch; **to take sb's ~** remplacer qn; **out of ~** *object* déplacé; *remark* (*inopportune*) hors de propos, (*improper*) déplacé; **it looks out of ~ there** ça n'a pas l'air à sa place là-bas; **I feel rather out of ~ here** je ne me sens pas à ma place ici; **in ~** *object* à sa place; *remark* à propos; **put the book back in its ~** remets le livre à sa place; **it wasn't in its ~** ça n'était pas à sa place, ça avait été déplacé; **a ~ for everything and everything in its ~** une place pour chaque chose et chaque chose à sa place; (*Scol etc*) **he was not in his ~** il n'était pas à sa place (*lit*); (*fig*) **to put sb in his ~** remettre qn à sa place, reprendre qn; **that certainly put him in his ~!** ça l'a bien remis à sa place!; (*Scol*) **go back to your ~s** retournez à *or* reprenez vos places; **take your ~s for a quadrille** mettez-vous à *or* prenez vos places pour un quadrille; **(if I were) in your ~ ...** (si j'étais) à votre place ...; **to know one's ~** savoir se tenir à sa place; **it's not your ~ to criticize** ce n'est pas à vous de critiquer; **it's my ~ to tell him** c'est à moi de le lui dire; **can you find a ~ for this vase?** pouvez-vous trouver une place *or* un endroit où mettre ce vase?; **to give ~ to** céder la place à; **there's a ~ in this town for a good administrator** cette ville a besoin d'un bon administrateur, il manque à cette ville un bon administrateur.

(g) (*job, position, post, vacancy*) place *f*, situation *f*, poste *m*. **~s for 500 workers** des places *or* de l'emploi pour 500 ouvriers; **we have a ~ for a typist** nous avons une place pour une dactylo; **we have a ~ for a teacher** nous avons un poste pour un professeur; **he's looking for a ~ in publishing** il cherche une situation dans l'édition; **we will try to find a ~ for him** on va essayer de lui trouver une place *or* une situation, on va essayer de le caser* quelque part; **the school will offer 10 ~s next term** l'école disposera de 10 places le trimestre prochain; **this school must have a further 80 ~s** cette école a besoin de 80 places supplémentaires; (*Univ etc*) **I have got a ~ on the sociology course** j'ai une place pour faire sociologie, j'ai été admis à faire sociologie.

(h) (*rank*) rang *m*, place *f*; (*in series*) place; (*in exam results*) place. **in the first ~** en premier lieu, premièrement, primo; **in the second ~** en second lieu, deuxièmement; **in the next ~** ensuite; **in the last ~** enfin; (*Math*) **to 5 decimal ~s, to 5 ~s of decimals** jusqu'à la 5e décimale; **John won the race with Robert in second ~** Jean a gagné la course et Robert s'est placé *or* a terminé second; **Robert took second ~ in the race** Robert a été second dans la course; (*Ftbl etc*) **the team was in third ~** l'équipe était placée troisième *or* était en troisième position; **he took second ~ in history/in the history exam** il a été deuxième en histoire/à l'examen d'histoire; (*Scol etc*) **a high/low ~** une bonne/mauvaise place; (*Scol*) **he took first ~ in class last year** l'année dernière il a été (le) premier de sa classe; (*Racing*) **to back a horse for a ~** jouer un cheval placé; **to keep/lose one's ~ in the queue** garder/perdre sa place dans la queue; **people in high ~s** les gens haut placés *or* en haut lieu.

2 *cpd*: **place card** carte *f* marque-place; (*Rugby*) **place kick** coup de pied placé; **place mat** set *m*, napperon individuel; **place-name** nom *m* de lieu; (*as study, as group*) **place-names** toponymie *f*; **place setting** couvert *m*.

3 *vt* **(a)** (*put*) placer, mettre. **~ it on the table** mets-le *or* place-le *or* pose-le sur la table; **the picture is ~d rather high up** le tableau est placé un peu trop haut; **to ~ an advertisement in the paper** placer *or* mettre *or* passer une annonce dans le journal; **she ~d the matter in the hands of her solicitor** elle remit l'affaire entre les mains de son avocat; **to ~ confidence in sb/sth** placer sa confiance en qn/qch; **to ~ trust in sb** faire confiance à qn; **he ~s good health among his greatest assets** il considère *or* place une robuste santé parmi ses meilleurs atouts.

(b) (*situate: gen pass*) placer, situer. **the house is well ~d** la maison est bien située; **he ~d his house high on the hill** il fit construire sa maison près du sommet de la colline; **the shop is awkwardly ~d** le magasin est mal situé *or* mal placé; **the town is ~d in the valley** la ville est située dans la vallée; (*Mil etc*) **they were well ~d to attack** ils étaient en bonne position *or* bien placés pour attaquer; (*fig*) **I am rather awkwardly ~d at the moment** je me trouve dans une situation assez délicate en ce moment; **he is well ~d to decide** il est bien placé pour décider; **we are better ~d than we were a month ago** notre situation est meilleure qu'il y a un mois.

(c) (*in exam*) placer, classer; (*in race*) placer. **he was ~d first in French** il s'est placé *or* classé premier en français; **he was ~d first in the race** il s'est placé premier dans la course; **he wasn't ~d in the race** il n'a pas été placé dans la course; **my horse wasn't ~d** mon cheval n'a pas été placé; (*Ftbl etc*) **our team is well ~d in the league** notre équipe a une bonne position dans le classement.

(d) (*Fin*) *money* placer, investir. **to ~ money at interest** placer de l'argent à intérêt; (*Comm*) **he ~d an order for wood with that firm** il a passé une commande de bois à cette firme; **to ~ a bet with sb** placer un pari chez qn; **to ~ a contract for machinery with a firm** passer un contrat d'achat avec une firme pour de l'outillage; (*Comm*) **these goods are difficult to ~** ces marchandises sont difficiles à placer; (*Comm*) **we are trying to ~ our surplus butter production** nous essayons de placer *or* d'écouler le surplus de notre production de beurre; **to ~ a book with a publisher** faire accepter un livre par un éditeur.

(e) (*appoint; find a job for*) placer, trouver une place *or* un emploi pour. **they ~d him in the accounts department** on l'a mis *or* placé à la comptabilité; **the agency is trying to ~ him with a building firm** l'agence essaie de lui trouver une place *or* de le placer dans une entreprise de construction.

(f) (*remember; identify*) se rappeler, remettre. **I just can't ~ him at all** je n'arrive absolument pas à le remettre *or* à le situer; **he ~d her at once** il la reconnut aussitôt, il se la rappela immédiatement; **to ~ a face** remettre un visage; **to ~ an accent** situer *or* reconnaître un accent.

placebo [plə'siːbəʊ] *n* (*Med, fig*) placebo *m*.

placement ['pleɪsmənt] *n* (*Fin*) placement *m*, investissement *m*; (*Univ etc: during studies*) stage *m*.

placenta [plə'sentə] *n* placenta *m*.

placid ['plæsɪd] *adj person, smile* placide, calme, serein; *waters* tranquille, calme.

placidity [plə'sɪdɪtɪ] *n* placidité *f*, calme *m*, tranquillité *f*.

placidly ['plæsɪdlɪ] *adv* avec placidité, avec calme, placidement.

placing ['pleɪsɪŋ] *n [money, funds]* placement *m*, investissement *m*; *[ball, players]* position *f*.

plagiarism ['pleɪdʒjərɪzəm] *n* plagiat *m*, démarquage *m*.

plagiarist ['pleɪdʒjərɪst] *n* plagiaire *mf*, démarqueur *m*, -euse *f*.

plagiarize ['pleɪdʒjəraɪz] *vt* plagier, démarquer.

plague [pleɪg] **1** *n* (*Med*) peste *f*; (*fig*) fléau *m*, plaie *f*. **to avoid/hate like the ~** fuir/haïr comme la peste; **what a ~ he is!*** c'est une vraie plaie!; *V* **bubonic** *etc*.

2 *cpd*: **plague-ridden, plague-stricken** *region, household* frappé de la peste; *person* pestiféré.

3 *vt [person, fear etc]* tourmenter, harceler, tracasser. **to ~ sb with questions** harceler qn de questions; **to ~ the life out of sb** rendre la vie impossible à qn.

plaguey*†† ['pleɪgɪ] *adj* fâcheux, assommant.

plaice [pleɪs] *n* carrelet *m*, plie *f*.

plaid [plæd] **1** *n* (*U: cloth, pattern*) tissu écossais; (*over shoulder*) plaid *m*. **2** *adj* (en tissu) écossais.

plain [pleɪn] **1** *adj* **(a)** (*manifest*) clair, évident. **the path is quite ~** la voie est clairement tracée; **in ~ view** à la vue de tous; **it must be ~ to everyone that ...** il est clair pour tout le monde que ..., il ne doit échapper à personne que ...; **it's as ~ as a pikestaff** *or* **as the nose on your face*** c'est clair comme le jour *or* comme de l'eau de roche; **a ~ case of jealousy** un cas manifeste *or* évident de jalousie; **I must make it ~ that ...** vous devez bien comprendre que ...; **he made his feelings ~** il ne cacha pas ce qu'il ressentait *or* pensait; **to make sth ~ to sb** faire comprendre qch à qn.

(b) (*unambiguous*) clair, franc (*f* franche); *statement, assessment* clair. **~ talk** propos *mpl* sans équivoque; **I like ~ speaking** j'aime le franc-parler *or* la franchise; **to use ~ language** parler sans ambages, appeler les choses par leur nom; **in ~ words** *or* **in ~ English, I think you made a mistake** je vous le dis *or* pour vous le dire carrément, je pense que vous vous êtes trompé; **I explained it all in ~ words** *or* **in ~ English** j'ai tout expliqué très clairement; **I gave him a ~ answer** je lui ai répondu carrément *or* sans détours *or* sans ambages; **~ dealing(s)** procédés *mpl* honnêtes; **the ~ truth of the matter is (that)** ... à dire vrai ..., à la vérité ...; **let me be quite ~ with you** je serai franc avec vous; **do I make myself ~?** est-ce que je me fais bien comprendre?

(c) (*sheer, utter*) pur, tout pur, pur et simple. **it's ~ folly** *or* **madness** c'est pure folie, c'est de la folie toute pure.

(d) (*simple; unadorned*) *dress, style, diet, food* simple; (*in one colour*) *fabric, suit, colour* uni. **~ living** mode *m* de vie tout simple *or* sans luxe; **I'm a ~ man** je suis un homme tout simple, je ne suis pas un homme compliqué; **they used to be called ~ Smith** dans le temps ils s'appelaient Smith tout court; (*Knitting*) **~ stitch** maille *f* à l'endroit; (*Knitting*) **one ~, one purl** une maille à l'endroit, une maille à l'envers; **a row of ~, a ~ row** un rang à l'endroit; **~ chocolate** chocolat *m* (à croquer); **to send under ~ cover** envoyer sous pli discret; (*fig*) **it's ~ sailing from now on** maintenant ça va aller comme sur des roulettes.

(e) (*not pretty*) sans beauté, quelconque, ordinaire (*pej*). **she's very ~** elle a un visage ingrat, elle n'a rien d'une beauté; **she's rather a ~ Jane*** ce n'est pas une Vénus.

2 *adv* **(a)** (*clearly*) **I told him quite ~ what I thought of him** je lui ai dit franchement *or* carrément *or* sans ambages ce que je pensais de lui; **I can't put it ~er than this** je ne peux pas m'exprimer plus clairement que cela *or* en termes plus explicites.

(b) (*: *in truth*) tout bonnement. **she's just ~ shy** elle est tout bonnement timide.

3 *n* plaine *f*. (*US*) **the (Great) P~s** les Prairies *fpl*, la Grande Prairie.

4 *cpd*: **plain chant** plain-chant *m*; **in plain clothes** en civil; **a plain-clothes (police)man** un policier en civil; **plainsman** habitant *m* de la plaine; **plainsong = plain chant**; **plain-spoken** qui a son franc-parler, qui appelle les choses par leur nom.

plainly ['pleɪnlɪ] *adv* **(a)** (*manifestly*) clairement, manifestement; (*unambiguously*) carrément, sans détours. **there has ~ been a mistake** il y a eu manifestement erreur, il est clair qu'il y a eu erreur; **he explained it ~** il l'a expliqué clairement *or* en termes clairs; **I can see the answer ~** la réponse saute aux yeux; **I remember it ~** je m'en souviens distinctement *or* clairement; **to speak ~ to sb** parler à qn sans détours *or* sans ambages.

(b) (*simply*) *dress* simplement, sobrement, sans recherche.

plainness ['pleɪnnɪs] *n* (*clarity*) clarté *f*; (*simplicity*) simplicité *f*, sobriété *f*; (*lack of beauty*) manque *m* de beauté.

plaintiff ['pleɪntɪf] *n* (*Jur*) demandeur *m*, -eresse *f*, plaignant(e) *m(f)*.

plaintive ['pleɪntɪv] *adj voice* plaintif.

plaintively ['pleɪntɪvlɪ] *adv* plaintivement, d'un ton plaintif.

plait [plæt] **1** *n [hair]* natte *f*, tresse *f*. **she wears her hair in ~s** elle porte des tresses. **2** *vt hair, string* natter, tresser; *wicker* tresser; *straw* ourdir.

plan [plæn] **1** *n* **(a)** (*drawing, map*) *[building, estate, district etc]* plan *m*; *V* **seating.**

(b) (*Econ, Pol, gen: project*) plan *m*, projet *m*. **~ of campaign** plan de campagne; (*Pol*) **five-year ~** plan de cinq ans, plan quinquennal; **development ~** plan *or* projet de développement; **to draw up a ~** dresser un plan; **everything is going according to ~** tout se passe selon les prévisions *or* comme prévu; **to make ~s** faire des projets; **to upset** *or* **spoil sb's ~s** déranger les projets de qn; **to change one's ~s** changer d'idée, prendre d'autres dispositions; **the best ~ would be to leave tomorrow** le mieux serait de partir demain; **the ~ is to come back here after the show** notre idée est *or* nous prévoyons de revenir ici après le spectacle; **what ~s have you for the holiday/for your son?** quels sont vos projets pour les vacances/pour votre fils?; **I haven't any particular ~s** je n'ai aucun projet précis; **have you got any ~s for tonight?** est-ce que vous avez prévu quelque chose pour ce soir?

2 *vt* **(a)** (*devise scheme for, make plans for*) *house, estate, garden etc* concevoir, dresser les plans de; *programme, holiday, journey* préparer à l'avance, organiser; *crime* préméditer, combiner; *essay* faire le plan de; (*Mil*) *campaign, attack* organiser. **who ~ned the house/garden?** qui a dressé les plans de la maison/du jardin?; **well-~ned house** maison bien conçue; **they ~ned the attack together** ils ont concerté l'attaque; **he has got it all ~ned** il a tout prévu, il a pensé à tout; **that wasn't ~ned** cela n'était pas prévu; **we shall go on as ~ned** nous continuerons comme prévu; **couples can now ~ their families** les couples peuvent maintenant contrôler les naissances dans leur foyer; **~ned parenthood** contrôle *m or* régulation *f* des naissances; (*Econ*) **~ned economy** économie planifiée; **to ~ the future of an industry** planifier l'avenir d'une industrie.

(b) (*have in mind*) *visit, holiday* projeter. **to ~ to do** projeter de *or* se proposer de *or* avoir l'intention de faire, former *or* concevoir le projet de faire (*frm*); **how long do you ~ to be away for?** combien de temps avez-vous l'intention de vous absenter?; **will you stay for a while? — I wasn't ~ning to** resterez-vous un peu? — ce n'était pas dans mes intentions.

3 *vi* faire des projets. **one has to ~ months ahead** il faut s'y prendre des mois à l'avance; **we are ~ning for the future/the holidays** *etc* nous faisons des projets *or* nous prenons nos dispositions pour l'avenir/les vacances *etc*; **we didn't ~ for such a large number of visitors** nous n'avions pas prévu un si grand nombre de visiteurs.

plan out *vt sep* préparer *or* organiser dans tous les détails.

planchette [plɑːn'ʃet] *n* planchette *f*.

plane[1] [pleɪn] *n* (*abbr of* **aeroplane** *or* **airplane**) avion *m*. **by ~** par avion.

plane[2] [pleɪn] (*Carpentry*) **1** *n* rabot *m*. **2** *vt* (*also* **~ down**) raboter.

plane[3] [pleɪn] *n* (*also* **~ tree**) platane *m*.

plane[4] [pleɪn] **1** *n* (*Archit, Art, Math etc*) plan *m*; (*fig*) plan, niveau *m*. **horizontal ~** plan horizontal; (*fig*) **on the same ~ as** sur le même plan que, au même niveau que; **he seems to exist on another ~ altogether** il semble vivre dans un autre monde *or* un autre univers.

2 *adj* plan, uni, plat; (*Math*) plan. **~ geometry** géométrie plane.

plane[5] [pleɪn] *vi [bird, glider, boat]* planer; *[car]* faire de l'aquaplanage.

plane down *vi [bird, glider]* descendre en vol plané.

planet ['plænɪt] *n* planète *f*.

planetarium [ˌplænɪ'tɛərɪəm] *n* planétarium *m*.

planetary ['plænɪtərɪ] *adj* planétaire.

plangent ['plændʒənt] *adj* (*liter*) retentissant.

planisphere ['plænɪsfɪəʳ] *n [world]* planisphère *m*; *[stars]* planisphère céleste.

plank [plæŋk] **1** *n* planche *f*; (*fig Pol*) article *m or* point *m* (d'un programme politique *or* électoral); *V* **walk.** **2** *vt* (*: *also* **~ down**) déposer avec poigne, planter.

planking ['plæŋkɪŋ] *n* (*U*) planchéiage *m*; (*Naut*) planches *fpl*, bordages *mpl*, revêtement *m*.

plankton ['plæŋktən] *n* plancton *m*.

planner ['plænəʳ] *n* (*Econ*) planificateur *m*, -trice *f*; *V* **town.**

planning ['plænɪŋ] **1** *n* (*U*) planification *f*, organisation *f*; (*Comm, Ind*) planning *m*. **we must do some ~ for the holidays** il faut dresser des plans pour les vacances; *V* **family, town.**

2 *cpd*: **planning board, planning committee** (*Econ, Ind*) service *m or* bureau *m* de planning; (*in local government*) ≃ service *m* de l'urbanisme; **planning permission** permis *m* de construire.

plant [plɑːnt] **1** *n* **(a)** (*Bot*) plante *f*.

(b) (*Ind, Tech*) (*U: machinery, equipment*) matériel *m*, équipement *m*; (*fixed*) installation *f*; (*U: equipment and buildings*) bâtiments *mpl* et matériel; (*factory*) usine *f*, fabrique *f*. **the heating ~** l'installation de chauffage; **he had to hire the ~ to do it** il a dû louer le matériel *or* l'équipement pour le faire; **a steel ~** une aciérie.

(c) (*: *frame-up*) coup monté.

2 *cpd*: (*Ind, Tech*) **plant-hire firm** entreprise *f* de location de matériel; (*Bot*) **the plant kingdom** le règne végétal; **plant life** flore *f*; **plant louse** puceron *m*; **plant pot** pot *m* (de fleurs).

3 *vt* **(a)** *seeds, plants, bulbs* planter; *field etc* planter (*with* en). **a field ~ed with wheat** un champ planté de *or* en blé.

(b) (*place*) *flag, stick etc* planter, enfoncer; *box, chair, suitcase etc* planter, camper; *people, colonists etc* établir, installer; *blow* appliquer, envoyer, flanquer*; *kiss* planter; *idea* implanter (*in sb's head* dans la tête de qn). **he ~ed himself in the middle of the road** il se planta *or* se campa au milieu de la route; (*fig*) **to ~ a revolver on sb** cacher un revolver sur qn (pour le faire incriminer).

plant down *vt sep* planter, camper.

plant out *vt sep seedlings* repiquer.

plantain ['plæntɪn] *n* plantain *m*.

plantation [plæn'teɪʃən] *n* (*all senses*) plantation *f*. **coffee/rubber ~** plantation de café/de caoutchouc.

planter ['plɑːntəʳ] *n* (*person*) planteur *m*; (*machine*) planteuse *f*. **coffee/rubber ~** planteur de café/de caoutchouc.

plaque [plæk] *n* plaque *f*.

plash [plæʃ] **1** *n [waves]* clapotis, clapotement *m*; *[object falling into water]* floc *m*. **2** *vi* clapoter; faire floc *or* flac.

plasm ['plæzəm] *n* protoplasme *m*.

plasma ['plæzmə] *n* plasma *m*; *V* **blood.**

plaster ['plɑːstəʳ] **1** *n* **(a)** (*Constr*) plâtre *m*.

(b) (*Med*) (*U: for broken bones*) plâtre *m*; (*for wounds*) pansement adhésif. **~ of Paris** plâtre de moulage; **he had his leg in ~** il avait la jambe dans le plâtre *or* la jambe plâtrée; **adhesive** *or* **sticking ~** sparadrap *m*; **to put a (piece o) ~ on a cut** mettre un pansement adhésif sur une coupure; *V* **mustard.**

2 *cpd mould etc* de *or* en plâtre. (*U*) **plasterboard** carreau *m* de plâtre; **plaster cast** (*Med*) plâtre *m*; (*Sculp*) moule *m* (en plâtre); (*U: Constr*) **plaster work** plâtre(s) *m(pl)*.

3 *vt* **(a)** (*Constr, Med*) plâtrer; (*fig: cover*) couvrir (*with* de). (*fig*) **~ed with** couvert de; **to ~ a wall with posters, to ~ posters on** *or* **over a wall** couvrir *or* tapisser un mur d'affiches.

(b) (*Mil**: *with bombs, shells*) pilonner; (‡: *bash up*) tabasser‡, battre comme plâtre*.

plaster on* *vt sep butter, hair cream, make-up etc* étaler *or* mettre une couche épaisse de.

plaster over, plaster up *vt sep crack, hole* boucher.

plastered‡ ['plɑːstəd] *adj* (*drunk*) beurré‡, bourré‡.

plasterer ['plɑːstərəʳ] *n* plâtrier *m*.

plastic ['plæstɪk] **1** *adj toy, box, jacket etc* en *or* de (matière) plastique; *art, substance* plastique; (*flexible*) plastique, malléable, flexible. **2** *n* (matière *f*) plastique *m*. **~s** matières plastiques. **3** *cpd dish, cup* de *or* en (matière) plastique. **plastic explosive** plastic *m* (*U*); **plastic(s) industry** industrie *f* plastique; **plastic surgeon** spécialiste *mf* de chirurgie esthétique; **plastic surgery** chirurgie *f* esthétique.

plasticine ['plæstɪsiːn] *n* ® (*U*) pâte *f* à modeler.

plasticity [plæs'tɪsɪtɪ] *n* plasticité *f*.

plate [pleɪt] **1** *n* **(a)** assiette *f*; (*Rel: also* **collection ~**) plateau *m* de quête. **a ~ of soup** une assiette de soupe; (*fig*) **he wants to be handed everything on a ~** il voudrait qu'on lui apporte (*subj*) tout sur un plateau *or* sur un plat d'argent; (*fig*) **to have a lot on one's ~*** avoir du pain sur la planche; (*fig*) **he's got too much on his ~ already*** il ne sait déjà plus où donner de la tête; *V* **dinner, soup, tea** *etc*.

(b) (*U*) (*gold* ~) orfèvrerie *f*, vaisselle *f* d'or; (*silver* ~) argenterie *f*, vaisselle d'argent.

(c) (*of metal etc*) plaque *f*, lame *f*, feuille *f*; (*on wall, door, battery, armour*) plaque; (*Aut: number* ~) plaque minéralogique *or* d'immatriculation; (*Phot*) plaque; (*Typ*) cliché *m*; (*for engraving*) planche *f*; (*book illustration*) gravure *f*; (*dental* ~) dentier *m*; (*racing prize*) prix *m*. (*in book*) **full-page** ~ gravure hors-texte, planche; *V* **clutch, fashion, number** *etc.*

2 *cpd*: (*U*) **plate armour** blindage *m*; (*U*) **plate glass** verre *m* à vitre très épais, verre double *or* triple; **plate-glass window** baie vitrée; (*Brit Rail*) **platelayer** poseur *m* de rails; **plate rack** égouttoir *m*; **plate warmer** chauffe-assiettes *m inv*.

3 *vt* **(a)** (*with metal*) plaquer; (*with gold*) dorer; (*with silver*) argenter; (*with nickel*) nickeler; *V* **armour** *etc.*

(b) *ship etc* blinder.

plateau ['plætəʊ] *n* plateau *m* (*Geog*).

plateful ['pleɪtfʊl] *n* assiettée *f*, assiette *f*.

platform ['plætfɔːm] **1** *n* (*on bus, scales, in scaffolding etc*) plate-forme *f*; (*for band, in hall*) estrade *f*; (*at meeting etc*) tribune *f*; (*Rail*) quai *m*; (*fig Pol*) plate-forme (électorale). (*Rail*) ~ **(number) six** quai (numéro) six; **he was on the ~ at the last meeting** il était sur l'estrade *or* il était à la tribune (d'honneur) lors de la dernière réunion.

2 *cpd*: (*at meeting*) **the platform party** la tribune; **platform scales** (balance *f* à) bascule *f*; **platform-soled shoes, platform soles*** chaussures *fpl* à semelles compensées; (*Rail*) **platform ticket** billet *m* de quai.

plating ['pleɪtɪŋ] *n* (*V* **plate 3**) placage *m*; dorage *m*, dorure *f*; argentage *m*, argenture *f*; nickelage *m*; blindage *m*; *V* **armour** *etc.*

platinum ['plætɪnəm] **1** *n* (*U*) platine *m*. **2** *cpd jewellery* en *or* de platine. **platinum blonde** blonde platinée; **platinum blond(e) hair** cheveux platinés *or* blond platiné.

platitude ['plætɪtjuːd] *n* platitude *f*, lieu commun.

platitudinize [ˌplætɪ'tjuːdɪnaɪz] *vi* débiter des platitudes *or* des lieux communs.

platitudinous [ˌplætɪ'tjuːdɪnəs] *adj* banal, d'une grande platitude, rebattu.

Plato ['pleɪtəʊ] *n* Platon *m*.

Platonic [plə'tɒnɪk] *adj* **(a)** *philosophy* platonicien. **(b)** **p~** *relationship, love* platonique.

Platonist ['pleɪtənɪst] *adj, n* platonicien(ne) *m(f)*.

platoon [plə'tuːn] *n* (*Mil*) section *f*; *[policemen, firemen etc]* peloton *m*.

platter ['plætəʳ] *n* plat *m*.

platypus ['plætɪpəs] *n* ornithorynque *m*.

plaudits ['plɔːdɪts] *npl* applaudissements *mpl*, acclamations *fpl*.

plausibility [ˌplɔːzə'bɪlɪtɪ] *n [argument, excuse]* plausibilité *f*. **his** ~ le fait qu'il est si convaincant.

plausible ['plɔːzəbl] *adj argument, excuse* plausible, vraisemblable; *person* convaincant.

plausibly ['plɔːzəblɪ] *adv* plausiblement, d'une manière plausible *or* convaincante.

play [pleɪ] **1** *n* **(a)** (*U: amusement*) jeu *m*, divertissement *m*, amusement *m*. **the children were at ~** les enfants jouaient *or* s'amusaient; **to say sth in ~** dire qch par jeu *or* par plaisanterie; **a ~ on words** un jeu de mots, un calembour; (*fig*) **the ~ of light on water** le jeu de la lumière sur l'eau; (*Sport*) **there was some good ~ in the second half** il y a eu du beau jeu à la deuxième mi-temps; **that was a clever piece of ~** c'était finement *or* astucieusement joué; **ball in/out of ~** ballon *or* balle en/hors jeu; **~ starts at 11 o'clock** le(s) match(s) commence(nt) à 11 heures; (*fig*) **to make a ~ for sth** tout faire pour avoir *or* obtenir qch; **he made a ~ for her** il lui a fait des avances; (*fig*) **to bring sth into ~** mettre *or* faire entrer qch en jeu; (*fig*) **to come into ~** entrer en jeu; (*fig*) **to make great ~ with sth** faire grand cas de qch, faire tout un plat* de qch; *V* **child, fair[1], foul** *etc.*

b) (*U: Tech etc: movement, scope*) jeu *m*. **there's too much ~ in the clutch** il y a trop de jeu dans l'embrayage; (*fig*) **to give full** *or* **free ~ to one's imagination/emotions** donner libre cours à son imagination/à ses émotions.

(c) (*Theat*) pièce *f* (de théâtre); (*performance*) représentation *f*, spectacle *m*. **the ~s of Molière** les pièces *or* le théâtre de Molière; **to go to (see) a ~** aller au théâtre; **radio ~** pièce radiophonique; **television ~** dramatique *f*.

2 *cpd*: **playact** jouer la comédie, faire du théâtre; (*fig*) **it's only playacting** c'est de la (pure) comédie *or* du cinéma*; (*fig*) **he's a playactor** il est comédien, il joue continuellement la comédie; **play-back** réécoute *f*; **playbill** affiche *f* (de théâtre); (*US*) programme *m*; **play box** coffre *m* à jouets; **playboy** playboy *m*; **play clothes** vêtements *mpl* qui ne craignent rien (*pour jouer*); **playfellow**† = **playmate; playgoer** amateur *m* de théâtre; **he is a regular playgoer** il va régulièrement au théâtre; **playground** cour *f* de récréation; **playgroup** = garderie *f*; **playhouse** (*Theat*) théâtre *m*; (*for children*) maison *f* (pliante); **playmate** (petit(e)) camarade *mf*, (petit) copain *m*, (petite) copine *f*; (*Sport*) **play-off** belle *f*; **playpen** parc *m* (pour petits enfants); **play reading** lecture *f* d'une pièce (de théâtre); **playroom** salle *f* de jeux (*pour enfants*); **playschool** = **playgroup**; (*lit, fig*) **plaything** jouet *m*; (*Scol*) **playtime** récréation *f*; **playwright** dramaturge *m*, auteur *m* dramatique.

3 *vt* **(a)** *game, cards* jouer à; *card, chesspiece* jouer; *opponent, opposing team* jouer contre. **to ~ football/bridge/chess** jouer au football/au bridge/aux échecs; **will you ~ tennis with me?** voulez-vous faire une partie de tennis avec moi?; **I'll ~ you for the drinks** jouons la tournée; **England are ~ing Scotland on Saturday** l'Angleterre joue contre *or* rencontre l'Écosse samedi; **England will be ~ing Smith (in the team)** l'Angleterre a sélectionné Smith (pour l'équipe); **to ~ a match against sb** disputer un match avec qn; **the match will be ~ed on Saturday** le match aura lieu samedi; **to ~ the game** (*Sport etc*) jouer franc jeu, jouer selon les règles; (*fig*) jouer le jeu, être loyal; **don't ~ games with me!** ne me faites pas marcher!, ne vous moquez pas de moi!; (*fig*) **he's ~ing a safe game** il ne prend pas de risques; **the boys were ~ing soldiers** les garçons jouaient aux soldats; (*Tennis*) **he ~ed the ball into the net** il mit *or* envoya la balle dans le filet; (*fig*) **to ~ ball with sb** entrer dans le jeu de qn; **he just won't ~ ball** il refuse de jouer le jeu; (*Cards*) **to ~ hearts/trumps** jouer cœur/atout; **he ~ed a heart** il a joué (un) cœur; **he ~ed his ace** (*lit*) il a joué son as; (*fig*) il a joué sa carte maîtresse; (*fig*) **to ~ one's cards well** *or* **right** bien jouer son jeu; **to ~ a fish** fatiguer un poisson; (*St Ex*) **to ~ the market** jouer à la Bourse; (*fig*) **to ~ the field*** jouer sur plusieurs tableaux; (*fig*) **to ~ it cool*** garder son sang-froid, ne pas s'énerver; (*fig*) **we'll have to ~ it by ear** il nous faudra aviser selon les circonstances *or* sur le tas; **to ~ a joke** *or* **trick on sb** jouer un tour à qn, faire une farce à qn; **my eyesight is ~ing tricks with** *or* **on me** ma vue me joue des tours; **his memory is ~ing him tricks** sa mémoire lui joue des tours; (*liter*) **to ~ sb false, to ~ false with sb** agir déloyalement avec qn; *V* **cat, Harry, truant, waiting** *etc.*

(b) (*Theat etc*) *part* jouer, interpréter; *play* jouer, présenter, donner. **they ~ed it as a comedy** ils en ont donné une interprétation comique, ils l'ont joué en comédie; **we ~ed Brighton last week** nous avons joué à Brighton la semaine dernière; **let's ~ it for laughs*** jouons-le en farce; **he ~ed (the part of) Macbeth** il a joué *or* il a incarné Macbeth; **he ~ed Macbeth as a well-meaning fool** il a fait de Macbeth un sot plein de bonnes intentions; **what did you ~ in 'Macbeth'?** quel rôle jouiez-vous *or* interprétiez-vous dans 'Macbeth'?; (*lit, fig*) **to ~ one's part well** bien jouer; (*fig*) **he was only ~ing a part** il jouait la comédie; (*fig*) **to ~ a part in sth** *[person]* prendre part à qch, contribuer à qch; *[quality, object]* contribuer à qch; (*fig*) **he ~ed no part in it** il n'y était pour rien; **to ~ the fool*** faire l'imbécile; **it ~ed the devil*** *or* **merry hell* with our plans** ça a chamboulé* *or* flanqué en l'air* nos projets.

(c) (*Mus*) *instrument* jouer de; *note, tune, concerto* jouer; *record* passer, jouer*. **to ~ the piano** jouer du piano; **they were ~ing Beethoven** ils jouaient du Beethoven; *V* **ear[1], second[1]**.

(d) (*direct*) *hose, searchlight* diriger (*on* sur). **they ~ed the searchlights over the front of the building** ils promenèrent les projecteurs sur la façade du bâtiment.

4 *vi* **(a)** (*gen, Cards, Sport etc*) jouer; *[lambs etc]* s'ébattre, folâtrer. **to ~ at chess** jouer aux échecs; **it's you** *or* **your turn to ~** c'est votre tour de jouer; **is Paul coming out to ~?** est-ce que Paul vient jouer? *or* s'amuser?; **what are you doing? — just ~ing** que faites-vous? — rien, on s'amuse; (*fig*) **he just ~s at being a soldier** il ne prend pas au sérieux son métier de soldat; **the boys were ~ing at soldiers** les garçons jouaient aux soldats; **the little girl was ~ing at being a lady** la petite fille jouait à la dame; **they were ~ing with a gun** ils jouaient avec un fusil; **stop ~ing with that pencil and listen to me** laisse ce crayon tranquille *or* arrête de tripoter ce crayon, et écoute-moi; (*Golf*) **he ~ed into the trees** il envoya sa balle dans les arbres; **to ~ for money/matches** jouer de l'argent/des allumettes; (*lit, fig*) **to ~ for high stakes** jouer gros jeu; **to ~ fair** (*Sport etc*) jouer franc jeu, jouer selon les règles; (*fig*) jouer le jeu, être loyal.

(b) (*fig*) **to ~ with fire** jouer avec le feu; (*fig*) **to ~ for time** essayer de gagner du temps; **to ~ hard to get*** se faire désirer; **to ~ fast and loose with sb** se jouer de qn, traiter qn à la légère; **to ~ into sb's hands** faire le jeu de qn, se faire avoir* par qn; **it's not a question to be ~ed with** ce n'est pas une question qui se traite à la légère; **he's not a man to be ~ed with** ce n'est pas un homme avec qui plaisanter; **he's just ~ing with you** il vous fait marcher; **to ~ with an idea** caresser une idée.

(c) *[light, fountain]* jouer (*on* sur).

(d) (*Mus*) *[person, organ, orchestra]* jouer. **to ~ on the piano** jouer du piano; **piece to be ~ed on two pianos** morceau exécuté *or* se jouant sur deux pianos; **to ~ by ear** jouer d'oreille; **will you ~ for us?** (*perform*) voulez-vous nous jouer quelque chose *or* nous faire un peu de musique?; (*accompany*) voulez-vous nous accompagner?

(e) (*Theat etc*) jouer. **he ~ed in a film with Greta Garbo** il a joué dans un film avec Greta Garbo; **we have ~ed all over the South** nous avons fait une tournée dans le sud; (*fig*) **to ~ dead** faire le mort; *V* **gallery**.

play about *vi* **(a)** *[children etc]* jouer, s'amuser.

(b) (*toy, fiddle*) jouer, s'amuser (*with* avec). **he was playing about with the gun when it went off** il s'amusait avec *or* il jouait avec *or* il tripotait le fusil quand le coup est parti; **stop playing about with that watch** arrête de tripoter cette montre, laisse cette montre tranquille; **he's just playing about with you*** il vous fait marcher.

play along 1 *vi* (*fig*) **to play along with sb** entrer dans le jeu de qn.

2 *vt sep* (*fig*) **to play sb along** tenir qn en haleine.

play around *vi* = **play about.**

play back 1 *vt sep tape* (ré)écouter, repasser.

2 play-back *n V* **play 2.**

play down *vt sep* (*fig*) minimiser.

play in *vt sep* **(a)** (*fig*) **to play o.s. in** prendre la température* (*fig*), se faire la main*.

(b) the band played the procession in le défilé entra aux sons de la fanfare.

play off 1 *vt sep* **(a)** **to play off A against B** monter A contre B (pour en tirer profit).

(b) (*Sport*) **to play a match off** jouer la belle.

2 play-off *n V* **play 2.**
play on *vt fus sb's emotions, credulity, good nature* jouer sur, miser sur. **to play on words** jouer sur les mots, faire des calembours; **the noise began to play on her nerves** le bruit commençait à l'agacer *or* à lui taper sur les nerfs*.
play out *vt sep* **(a) the band played the procession out** le défilé sortit aux sons de la fanfare.
(b) to be played out* *[person]* être épuisé *or* éreinté* *or* vanné*; *[argument]* être périmé, avoir fait son temps.
play over, play through *vt sep piece of music* jouer.
play up 1 *vi* **(a)** (*Sport*) bien jouer. **play up!** allez-y!
(b) (*: *give trouble*) **the engine is playing up** le moteur fait des siennes *or* ne tourne pas rond; **his rheumatism/his leg is playing up** son rhumatisme/sa jambe lui joue des tours; **the children have been playing up all day** les enfants ont été insupportables *or* ont fait des leurs toute la journée.
(c) (*: *curry favour with*) **to play up to sb** chercher à se faire bien voir de qn, faire de la lèche à qn*.
2 *vt sep* **(a) his rheumatism/his leg is playing him up** son rhumatisme/sa jambe le tracasse; **that boy plays his father up** ce garçon en fait voir à son père.
(b) (*magnify importance of*) insister sur (l'importance de).
play upon *vt fus* = **play on.**
player ['pleɪə^r] **1** *n* **(a)** (*Sport*) joueur *m*, -euse *f*. **football ~** joueur de football; **he's a very good ~** il joue très bien, c'est un excellent joueur.
(b) (*Theat*) acteur *m*, -trice *f*.
(c) (*Mus*) musicien(ne) *m(f)*, exécutant(e) *m(f)*. **flute ~** joueur *m*, -euse *f* de flûte, flûtiste *mf*; **he's a good ~** c'est un bon musicien, il joue bien.
2 *cpd*: **player piano** piano *m* mécanique.
playful ['pleɪfʊl] *adj person* enjoué, espiègle, taquin; *animal* joueur, espiègle; *mood, tone, remark* badin, enjoué.
playfully ['pleɪfəlɪ] *adv* en badinant, en jouant; *smile* d'une manière taquine; *say* en badinant, d'un ton taquin.
playfulness ['pleɪfʊlnɪs] *n* (*V* **playful**) enjouement *m*, espièglerie *f*, esprit taquin, badinage *m*.
playing ['pleɪɪŋ] **1** *n* (*U*) **(a)** (*Sport*) jeu *m*. **there was some good ~ in the second half** il y a eu du beau jeu à la deuxième mi-temps.
(b) (*Mus*) **the orchestra's ~ of the symphony was uninspired** l'orchestre manquait d'inspiration dans l'interprétation de la symphonie; **there was some fine ~ in the violin concerto** il y a eu des passages bien joués dans le concerto pour violon.
2 *cpd*: **playing card** carte *f* à jouer; **playing field** terrain *m* de jeu *or* de sport.
plea [pliː] *n* **(a)** (*excuse*) excuse *f*; (*claim*) allégation *f*. **on the ~ of** en alléguant, en invoquant; **on the ~ that** en alléguant *or* en invoquant que.
(b) (*Jur*) (*statement*) argument *m*; (*defence*) défense *f*. **to put forward** *or* **make a ~ of self-defence** plaider la légitime défense; **to enter a ~ of guilty/not guilty** plaider coupable/non coupable.
(c) (*entreaty*) appel *m* (*for* à), supplication *f*. **to make a ~ for mercy** implorer la clémence.
plead [pliːd] *pret, ptp* **pleaded** *or* (*: *esp US*) **pled 1** *vi* **(a) to ~ with sb to do** supplier *or* implorer qn de faire; **he ~ed for help** il a imploré *or* supplié qu'on l'aide (*subj*); **he ~ed with them for help** il a imploré leur aide; **to ~ for mercy** implorer la clémence; **he ~ed for mercy for his brother** (*begged*) il a imploré la clémence pour son frère; (*spoke eloquently*) il a plaidé la clémence envers son frère; **to ~ for a scheme/programme** *etc* plaider pour un projet/un programme *etc*.
(b) (*Jur*) plaider (*for* pour, en faveur de, *against* contre). **to ~ guilty/not guilty** plaider coupable/non coupable; **how do you ~?** plaidez-vous coupable ou non coupable?
2 *vt* **(a)** (*Jur etc: argue*) plaider. (*Jur*) **to ~ sb's case,** (*fig*) **to ~ sb's cause** plaider la cause de qn (*Jur, fig*).
(b) (*give as excuse*) alléguer, invoquer; (*Jur*) plaider. **to ~ ignorance** alléguer *or* invoquer son ignorance; **he ~ed unemployment as a reason for ...** il invoqua *or* il allégua le chômage pour expliquer ...; (*Jur*) **to ~ insanity** plaider la démence.
pleading ['pliːdɪŋ] **1** *n* prières *fpl* (*for sb* en faveur de qn), intercession *f* (*liter*); (*Jur*) plaidoirie *f*, plaidoyer *m*. **2** *adj* implorant, suppliant.
pleadingly ['pliːdɪŋlɪ] *adv* d'un air *or* d'un ton suppliant *or* implorant.
pleasant ['pleznt] *adj person* agréable, plaisant, charmant, sympathique, aimable; *house, town* agréable, attrayant, plaisant; *smell, taste* agréable, bon (*f* bonne); *style* agréable; *weather, summer* agréable, beau (*f* belle); *surprise* agréable, heureux, bon. **they had a ~ time** ils ont passé un bon moment, ils se sont bien amusés; **they spent a ~ afternoon** ils ont passé un bon *or* un agréable après-midi; **it's very ~ here** on est bien ici, il fait bon ici; **Barcombe is a ~ place** Barcombe est un coin agréable *or* un joli coin; **he was** *or* **he made himself very ~ to us** il s'est montré très aimable *or* charmant avec nous; **~ dreams!** fais de beaux rêves!
pleasantly ['plezntlɪ] *adv behave, smile, answer* aimablement. **~ surprised** agréablement surpris; **the garden was ~ laid out** le jardin était agréablement *or* plaisamment arrangé; **it was ~ warm** il faisait une chaleur agréable.
pleasantness ['plezntnɪs] *n [person, manner, welcome]* amabilité *f*; *[place, house]* agrément *m*, attrait *m*, charme *m*.
pleasantry ['plezntrɪ] *n* (*joke*) plaisanterie *f*. (*polite remarks*) **pleasantries** civilités *fpl*, propos *mpl* aimables.
please [pliːz] **1** *vi* **(a)** (*abbr of* **if you ~**) s'il vous plaît, s'il te plaît. **yes ~** oui s'il vous (*or* te) plaît; **~ come in, come in ~** entrez, je vous prie; (*frm*) **~ be seated** veuillez vous asseoir (*frm*); **~ do not smoke** (*notice*) prière de ne pas fumer; (*spoken*) ne fumez pas s'il vous plaît, je vous prie de ne pas fumer; **~ let me know if I can help you** ne manquez pas de me faire savoir si je peux vous aider; **may I smoke?** — **~ do!** je peux fumer? — faites donc! *or* je vous en prie! *or* mais bien sûr!; **shall I tell him?** — **~ do!** je le lui dis? — mais oui dites-le-lui *or* mais oui bien sûr *or* mais oui allez-y*; (*excl*) **~!** (*entreating*) s'il vous plaît!; (*protesting*) (ah non!) je vous en prie! *or* s'il vous plaît!; **~ don't!** ne faites pas ça s'il vous plaît!
(b) (*think fit*) **I shall do as I ~** je ferai comme il me plaira *or* comme je veux; **do as you ~!** faites comme vous voulez *or* comme bon vous semble; **as you ~!** comme vous voulez!, à votre guise!; **you may take as many as you ~** vous pouvez en prendre autant qu'il vous plaira; **if you ~** s'il vous plaît; (*iro*) **he wanted £5 if you ~!** il voulait 5 livres, rien que ça! *or* s'il vous plaît!
(c) plaire, faire plaisir. (*esp Comm*) **our aim is to ~** nous ne cherchons qu'à satisfaire; **he is very anxious to ~** il est très désireux de plaire; **a gift that is sure to ~** un cadeau qui ne peut que faire plaisir *or* que plaire.
2 *vt* **(a)** (*give pleasure to*) plaire à, faire plaisir à; (*satisfy*) satisfaire, contenter. **the gift ~d him** le cadeau lui a plu *or* lui a fait plaisir; **I did it just to ~ you** je ne l'ai fait que pour te faire plaisir; **that will ~ him** ça va lui faire plaisir, il va être content; **he is easily ~d/hard to ~** il est facile/difficile à contenter *or* à satisfaire; **there's no pleasing him** il n'y a jamais moyen de le contenter *or* de le satisfaire; (*loc*) **you can't ~ all (of) the people all (of) the time** on ne saurait contenter tout le monde; **music that ~s the ear** musique plaisante à l'oreille *or* qui flatte l'oreille; (*frm*) **it ~d him to refuse permission ...** il lui a plu de ne pas consentir ..., il a trouvé bon de ne pas consentir ... .
(b) to ~ oneself faire comme on veut; **~ yourself!** comme vous voulez!, à votre guise!; **you must ~ yourself whether you do it or not** c'est à vous de décider si vous voulez le faire ou non; **~ God he comes!** plaise à Dieu qu'il vienne!
pleased [pliːzd] *adj* content, heureux (*with* de). **as ~ as Punch** heureux comme un roi, aux anges; **he looked very ~ at the news** la nouvelle a eu l'air de lui faire grand plaisir; **he was ~ to hear that ...** il a été heureux *or* content d'apprendre que ...; **~ to meet you!*** enchanté!; **I am ~ that you can come** je suis heureux *or* content que vous puissiez venir; (*frm*) **we are ~ to inform you that ...** nous avons l'honneur de *or* (*less frm*) le plaisir de vous informer que ...; **to be ~ with o.s./sb/sth** être content de soi/qn/qch; **they were anything but ~ with the decision** la décision était loin de leur faire plaisir; *V* **graciously.**
pleasing ['pliːzɪŋ] *adj personality* sympathique, aimable, plaisant; *sight, news, results, effect* plaisant, qui fait plaisir. **it was very ~ to him** cela lui a fait grand plaisir.
pleasingly ['pliːzɪŋlɪ] *adv* agréablement.
pleasurable ['pleʒərəbl] *adj* (très) agréable.
pleasurably ['pleʒərəblɪ] *adv* (très) agréablement.
pleasure ['pleʒə^r] **1** *n* **(a)** (*satisfaction*) plaisir *m*. **with ~** avec plaisir, volontiers; **one of my greatest ~s** un de mes plus grands plaisirs, une de mes plus grandes joies; **it's a ~!, the ~ is mine!** je vous en prie!; **it's a ~ to see you** quel plaisir de vous voir!; **it gave me much ~ to hear that ...** cela m'a fait grand plaisir d'apprendre que ...; **if it gives you any ~** si ça peut vous faire plaisir; (*frm: at dance*) **may I have the ~?** voulez-vous m'accorder cette danse?; (*frm*) **may we have the ~ of your company at dinner?** voulez-vous nous faire le plaisir de dîner avec nous?; (*frm*) **Mrs A requests the ~ of Mr B's company at dinner** Mme A prie M B de lui faire l'honneur de venir dîner; **he finds** *or* **takes great ~ in chess** il trouve *or* prend beaucoup de plaisir aux échecs; **what ~ can you find in doing that?** quel plaisir pouvez-vous trouver à faire cela?; **to take great ~ in doing** éprouver *or* avoir *or* prendre *or* trouver beaucoup de plaisir à faire; (*pej*) se complaire à faire; **they took great ~ in his success** ils se sont réjouis de son succès; **it takes all the ~ out of it** ça vous gâche le plaisir; **has he gone to Paris on business or for ~?** est-il allé à Paris pour affaires ou pour son plaisir?; **a life of ~** une vie de plaisirs; *V* **business.**
(b) (*U: will, desire*) bon plaisir, volonté *f*. **at ~** à volonté; **at your ~** à votre gré; (*Jur*) **during the Queen's ~** aussi longtemps qu'il plaira à Sa Majesté, pendant le bon plaisir de la reine; (*Comm*) **we await your ~** nous attendons votre décision.
2 *cpd*: **pleasure boat** bateau *m* de plaisance; (*collective*) **pleasure craft** bateaux *mpl* de plaisance; **pleasure cruise** voyage *m* d'agrément; **pleasure-loving** qui aime le(s) plaisir(s); (*Psych*) **the pleasure principle** le principe hédonistique; **pleasure-seeker** hédoniste *mf*; **pleasure-seeking** hédoniste; **pleasure steamer** vapeur *m* de plaisance; **pleasure trip** excursion *f*.
pleat [pliːt] **1** *n* pli *m*. **2** *vt* plisser.
pleb* [pleb] *n* (*pej*) plébéien(ne) *m(f)*, roturier *m*, -ière *f*. **the ~s** le commun (des mortels).
plebeian [plɪ'biːən] *adj, n* plébéien(ne) *m(f)*.
plebiscite ['plebɪsɪt] *n* plébiscite *m*. **to hold a ~** faire un plébiscite.
plectrum ['plektrəm] *n* plectre *m*.
pled* [pled] (*esp US*) *pret, ptp of* **plead.**
pledge [pledʒ] **1** *n* **(a)** (*security, token; also in pawnshop*) gage *m*. **as a ~ of his love** en gage *or* témoignage de son amour.
(b) (*promise*) promesse *f*, engagement *m*; (*agreement*) pacte *m*. **I give you this ~** je vous fais cette promesse; **he made a ~ of secrecy** il a promis de *or* il s'est engagé à garder le secret; **the government did not honour its ~ to cut taxes** le gouvernement n'a pas honoré son engagement *or* n'a pas tenu sa promesse de réduire les impôts; **the countries signed a ~ to help each other** les pays ont signé un pacte d'aide mutuelle; (*fig*) **to sign** *or* **take the ~** faire vœu de tempérance.
(c) (*toast*) toast *m* (*to* à).

2 *vt* **(a)** (*pawn*) engager, mettre en gage.

(b) (*promise*) *one's help, support, allegiance* promettre. **to ~ o.s. to do** promettre de faire, s'engager à faire; **to ~ sb to secrecy** faire promettre le secret à qn; **he is ~d to secrecy** il a promis de garder le secret; **to ~ one's word (that)** donner sa parole (que).

(c) (*toast*) boire à la santé de.

Pleiades ['plaɪədiːz] *npl* Pléiades *fpl*.

plenary ['pliːnərɪ] *adj power* absolu; *assembly* plénier; (*Rel*) plénier. **(in) ~ session** (en) séance plénière.

plenipotentiary [ˌplenɪpə'tenʃərɪ] *adj, n* plénipotentiaire (*mf*). **ambassador ~** ambassadeur *m* plénipotentiaire.

plenitude ['plenɪtjuːd] *n* plénitude *f*.

plenteous ['plentɪəs] *adj*, **plentiful** ['plentɪfʊl] *adj harvest, food* abondant; *meal, amount* copieux. **a ~ supply of** une abondance *or* une profusion de; **eggs are ~ just now** il y a (une) abondance d'œufs en ce moment.

plentifully ['plentɪfəlɪ] *adv* abondamment, copieusement.

plenty ['plentɪ] **1** *n* **(a)** abondance *f*. **it grows here in ~** cela pousse en abondance *or* à foison ici; **he had friends in ~** il ne manquait pas d'amis; **to live in ~** vivre dans l'abondance; **land of ~** pays *m* de cocagne; *V* **horn.**

(b) ~ of (bien) assez de; **I've got ~** j'en ai bien assez; **he's got ~ of friends** il ne manque pas d'amis; **he's got ~ of money** il n'est pas pauvre; **10 is ~** 10 suffisent (largement *or* amplement); **that's ~** ça suffit (amplement); **there's ~ to go on** nous avons toutes les données nécessaires pour le moment.

2 *adj* (*: or dial*) = **~ of**; *V* **1b.**

3 *adv* (*) assez. **it's ~ big enough!** c'est bien assez grand!; (*US*) **it sure rained ~!** qu'est-ce qu'il est tombé!*

pleonasm ['pliːənæzəm] *n* pléonasme *m*.

pleonastic [pliːə'næstɪk] *adj* pléonastique.

plethora ['pleθərə] *n* pléthore *f*, surabondance *f* (*of* de); (*Med*) pléthore.

plethoric [ple'θɒrɪk] *adj* pléthorique.

pleurisy ['plʊərɪsɪ] *n* (*U*) pleurésie *f*.

plexus ['pleksəs] *n* plexus *m*; *V* **solar.**

pliability [ˌplaɪə'bɪlɪtɪ] *n* (*V* **pliable**) flexibilité *f*; souplesse *f*, docilité *f*, malléabilité *f*.

pliable ['plaɪəbl] *adj*, **pliant** ['plaɪənt] *adj substance* flexible; *character, person* souple, docile, malléable.

pliers ['plaɪəz] *npl* (*also* **pair of ~**) pince(s) *f(pl)*, tenaille(s) *f(pl)*.

plight[1] [plaɪt] *n* situation *f* critique, état *m* critique. **the country's economic ~** la crise *or* les difficultés *fpl* économique(s) du pays; **in a sad** *or* **sorry ~** dans un triste état; **what a dreadful ~ (to be in)!** quelles circonstances désespérées!, quelle situation lamentable!

plight[2] [plaɪt] *vt* (*liter*, ††) **to ~ one's word** engager sa parole; (†† *or hum*) **to ~ one's troth** engager sa foi†, se fiancer.

plimsoll ['plɪmsəl] **1** *n* (*Brit*) (chaussure *f* de) tennis *m*. **2** *cpd*: (*Naut*) **Plimsoll line, Plimsoll mark** marque *f* de Plimsoll.

plinth [plɪnθ] *n* [*column, pedestal*] plinthe *f*; [*statue, record player*] socle *m*.

Pliny ['plɪnɪ] *n* Pline *m*.

plod [plɒd] **1** *n*: **they went at a steady ~** ils cheminaient d'un pas égal; **the slow ~ of the horses on the cobbles** le lent martellement des sabots sur les pavés.

2 *vi* **(a)** (*also* **~ along**) cheminer, avancer d'un pas lent *or* égal *or* lourd. **to ~ in/out** *etc* entrer/sortir *etc* d'un pas lent *or* égal *or* lourd.

(b) (*fig: work*) bosser*, bûcher*. **he was ~ding through his maths** il peinait sur ses maths, il bûchait* ses maths; **I'm ~ding through that book** je lis ce livre mais c'est laborieux; **you'll have to ~ through it** il faudra (faire l'effort de) persévérer jusqu'au bout.

3 *vt*: **we ~ded the road for another hour** nous avons poursuivi notre lente marche pendant une heure.

plod along *vi V* **plod 2a.**

plod on *vi* (*lit*) continuer *or* poursuivre son chemin; (*fig*) persévérer *or* progresser (laborieusement).

plodder ['plɒdəʳ] *n* travailleur *m*, -euse *f* assidu(e), bûcheur *m*, -euse *f*.

plodding ['plɒdɪŋ] *adj step* lourd, pesant; *student, worker* bûcheur.

plonk [plɒŋk] **1** *n* **(a)** (*sound*) plouf *m*, floc *m*. **(b)** (*: *cheap wine*) vin *m* ordinaire, gros rouge. **2** *adv* (*) **it fell ~ in the middle of the table** c'est tombé au beau milieu de la table. **3** *vt* (*also* **~ down**) poser (bruyamment). **he ~ed the book (down) on to the table** il posa (bruyamment) le livre sur la table; **he ~ed himself (down) into the chair** il s'est laissé tomber dans le fauteuil.

plop [plɒp] **1** *n* ploc *m*, plouf *m*, floc *m*, flac *m*. **2** *adv*: **it went ~ into the water** c'est tombé dans l'eau (en faisant ploc *or* plouf). **3** *vi* [*stone*] faire ploc *or* floc *or* flac *or* plouf; [*single drop*] faire flac *or* floc; [*raindrops*] faire flic flac.

plosive ['pləʊsɪv] (*Ling*) **1** *adj* explosif. **2** *n* consonne explosive.

plot [plɒt] **1** *n* **(a)** (*of ground*) (lot *m* de) terrain *m*, lotissement *m*. **~ of grass** gazon *m*; **building ~** terrain à bâtir; **the vegetable ~** le coin des légumes.

(b) (*plan, conspiracy*) complot *m*, conspiration *f* (*against* contre, *to do* pour faire).

(c) (*Literat, Theat*) intrigue *f*. (*fig*) **the ~ thickens** l'affaire *or* l'histoire se corse.

2 *vt* **(a)** (*mark out: also* **~ out**) (*Aviat, Naut etc*) *course, route* déterminer; *graph, curve, diagram* tracer point par point; *boundary, piece of land* relever. (*Naut*) **to ~ one's position on the map** pointer la carte.

(b) *sb's death, ruin etc* comploter. **to ~ to do** comploter de faire.

3 *vi* (*conspire*) comploter, conspirer (*against* contre).

plotter ['plɒtəʳ] *n* conspirateur *m*, -trice *f*; (*against the government*) conjuré(e) *m(f)*.

plotting ['plɒtɪŋ] *n* (*U*) complots *mpl*, conspirations *fpl*.

plough, (*US*) **plow** [plaʊ] **1** *n* (*Agr*) charrue *f*. (*Astron*) **the P~** la Grande Ourse, le Grand Chariot; *V* **snow** *etc*.

2 *cpd*: **plough horse** cheval *m* de labour; **ploughland** terre *f* de labour, terre arable; **ploughman** laboureur *m*; **ploughshare** soc *m* (de charrue).

3 *vt* **(a)** (*Agr*) *field* labourer; *furrow* creuser, tracer. (*fig*) **to ~ one's way** *V* **4b.**

(b) (*Brit* *†: *fail*) *candidate* recaler*, coller*.

4 *vi* **(a)** (*Agr*) labourer.

(b) (*fig: also* **~ one's way**) **to ~ through the mud/snow** avancer péniblement dans la boue/la neige; **the ship ~ed through the heavy swell** le navire avançait en luttant contre la forte houle; **the car ~ed through the fence** la voiture a défoncé la barrière; **to ~ through a book** lire un livre d'une manière laborieuse, peiner sur un livre.

plough back **1** *vt sep profits* réinvestir, reverser (*into* dans). **2 ploughing back** *n V* **ploughing.**

plough in, plough under *vt sep crops, grass* recouvrir *or* enterrer en labourant; *path, right of way* labourer (pour faire disparaître).

plough up *vt sep* **(a)** *field, bushes, path, right of way* labourer.

(b) (*fig*) **the tanks ploughed up the field** les tanks ont labouré *or* défoncé le champ; **the train ploughed up the track for 40 metres** le train a labouré *or* défoncé la voie sur 40 mètres.

ploughing ['plaʊɪŋ] *n* (*U*) labour *m*; [*field etc*] labourage *m*. (*fig*) **the ~ back of profits** le réinvestissement des bénéfices.

plover ['plʌvəʳ] *n* pluvier *m*.

plow [plaʊ] (*US*) = **plough.**

ploy* [plɔɪ] *n* stratagème *m*, truc* *m* (*to do* pour faire).

pluck [plʌk] **1** *n* **(a)** (*U: courage*) courage *m*, cran* *m*, estomac *m*. **(b)** (*U: Culin*) fressure *f*. **(c)** (*tug*) petit coup. **2** *vt fruit, flower* cueillir; (*Mus*) *strings* pincer; *guitar* pincer les cordes de; (*Culin*) *bird* plumer. **to ~ one's eyebrows** s'épiler les sourcils.

pluck at *vt fus*: **to pluck at sb's sleeve** tirer qn doucement par la manche.

pluck off *vt sep feathers* arracher; *fluff etc* détacher, enlever.

pluck out *vt sep* arracher.

pluck up *vt sep* **(a)** *weed* arracher, extirper.

(b) to pluck up courage prendre son courage à deux mains; **he plucked up (the) courage to tell her** il trouva (enfin) le courage de *or* il se décida (enfin) à le lui dire.

pluckily ['plʌkɪlɪ] *adv* avec cran*, courageusement.

pluckiness ['plʌkɪnɪs] *n* (*U*) courage *m*, cran* *m*.

plucky ['plʌkɪ] *adj* courageux, qui a du cran* *or* de l'estomac.

plug [plʌg] **1** *n* **(a)** (*for draining*) [*bath, basin*] bonde *f*, vidange *f*; [*barrel*] bonde; (*to stop a leak*) tampon *m*; (*stopper*) bouchon *m*; (*Geol: in volcano*) culot *m*. **a ~ of cotton wool** un tampon de coton; **~ of tobacco** (*for smoking*) carotte *f*; (*for chewing*) chique *f*; **to put in/pull out the ~** mettre/enlever *or* ôter la bonde; (*in lavatory*) **to pull the ~** tirer la chasse d'eau.

(b) (*Elec*) (*on flex, apparatus*) fiche *f*; (*wall* **~**) prise *f* (de courant); (*Aut: sparking* **~**) bougie *f*; *V* **amp, fused, pin.**

(c) (*US: fire* **~**) bouche *f* d'incendie.

(d) (*: *publicity*) coup *m* de pouce (publicitaire), réclame *f* *or* publicité *f* (clandestine *or* indirecte). **to give sth/sb a ~, to put in a ~ for sth/sb** donner un coup de pouce (publicitaire) à qch/qn, faire de la réclame *or* de la publicité indirecte pour qch/qn.

2 *cpd*: **plughole** trou *m* (d'écoulement *or* de vidange), bonde *f*, vidange *f*; **it went down the plughole** il est tombé dans le trou (du lavabo *or* de l'évier *etc*); (*Elec*) **plug-in** qui se branche sur le secteur; (*US*) **plugugly*** gueule *f* d'empeigne*.

3 *vt* **(a)** (*also* **~ up**) *hole, crack* boucher, obturer; *barrel, jar* boucher; *leak* colmater, (*on boat*) aveugler; *tooth* obturer (*with* avec). (*fig*) **to ~ the gap in the tax laws** mettre fin aux échappatoires en matière de fiscalité; (*fig*) **to ~ the drain on gold reserves** arrêter l'hémorragie *or* la fuite des réserves d'or.

(b) to ~ sth into a hole enfoncer qch dans un trou; **~ the TV into the wall** branchez le téléviseur sur le secteur.

(c) (*: *publicize*) (*on one occasion*) faire de la réclame *or* de la publicité pour; (*repeatedly*) matraquer*.

(d) (*) (*shoot*) flinguer*, ficher* *or* flanquer* une balle dans la peau à; (*punch*) ficher* *or* flanquer* un *or* des coup(s) de poing à.

plug away* *vi* bosser*, travailler dur (*at doing* pour faire). **he was plugging away at his maths** il bûchait* *or* piochait* ses maths.

plug in **1** *vi* se brancher. **the TV plugs in over there** la télé se branche là-bas; **does your radio plug in?** est-ce que votre radio peut se brancher sur le secteur?

2 *vt sep lead, apparatus* brancher.

3 plug-in *adj V* **plug 2.**

plug up *vt sep* = **plug 3a.**

plum [plʌm] **1** *n* **(a)** (*fruit*) prune *f*; (*also* **~ tree**) prunier *m*.

(b) (**fig*) (*choice thing*) meilleur morceau (*fig*), meilleure part (*fig*); (*choice job*) boulot* *m* en or.

2 *adj* **(a)** (*also* **~-coloured**) lie de vin *inv*.

(b) (*: *best, choice*) de choix, le plus chouette*. **he got the ~ job** c'est lui qui a décroché le meilleur travail *or* le travail le plus chouette*; **he has a ~ job** il a un boulot* en or.

3 *cpd*: **plumcake** (plum-)cake *m*; **plum duff, plum pudding** (plum-)pudding *m*.

plumage ['pluːmɪdʒ] *n* plumage *m*.

plumb [plʌm] **1** *n* plomb *m*. **out of ~** hors d'aplomb.

2 *cpd*: **plumbline** fil *m* à plomb; (*Naut*) sonde *f*.

3 *adj* vertical, à plomb, d'aplomb.

4 *adv* **(a)** en plein, exactement. ~ **in the middle of** en plein milieu de, au beau milieu de.
(b) (*US**) complètement, absolument, tout à fait.
5 *vt* sonder. **to ~ the depths** (*lit*) sonder les profondeurs; (*fig*) toucher le fond (du désespoir).
plumb in *vt sep washing machine etc* faire le raccordement de.
plumbago [plʌm'beɪgəʊ] *n* plombagine *f*.
plumber ['plʌməʳ] *n* plombier *m*.
plumbic ['plʌmbɪk] *adj* plombifère.
plumbing ['plʌmɪŋ] *n* (*trade*) (travail *m* de) plomberie *f*; (*system*) plomberie, tuyauterie *f*.
plume [plu:m] **1** *n* (*large feather*) plume *f* (*d'autruche etc*); (*cluster of feathers*) plumes; (*on hat, helmet*) plumet *m*, (*larger*) panache *m*; (*fig: of smoke*) panache. (*fig*) **in borrowed ~s** paré d'atours d'emprunt, paré des plumes du paon (*fig*).
2 *vt [bird] wing, feather* lisser. **the bird was pluming itself** l'oiseau se lissait les plumes; (*fig*) **to ~ o.s. on sth** se targuer de qch.
plumed [plu:md] *adj* (*V* **plume**) à plumet, empanaché.
plummet ['plʌmɪt] **1** *n* plomb *m*. **2** *vi [aircraft, bird]* plonger, descendre *or* tomber à pic; *[temperature]* baisser *or* descendre brusquement; *[price, sales]* dégringoler; *[spirits, morale]* tomber à zéro.
plummy* ['plʌmɪ] *adj accent* de la haute‡. ~ **job** (bonne) planque* *f* (*fig*), sinécure *f*.
plump[1] [plʌmp] **1** *adj person* grassouillet, rondelet; *child, hand* potelé; *cheek, face* rebondi, plein; *arm, leg* dodu, potelé; *chicken* dodu, charnu; *cushion* rebondi, bien rembourré. **2** *vt poultry* engraisser; (*also* ~ **up**) *pillow* tapoter, faire bouffer. **3** *vi* (*also* ~ **out**) devenir rondelet, grossir.
plump[2] [plʌmp] **1** *vt* laisser tomber lourdement, flanquer*. **2** *vi* tomber lourdement. **3** *adv* **(a)** en plein, exactement. ~ **in the middle of** en plein milieu de, au beau milieu de. **(b)** (*in plain words*) carrément, sans mâcher ses mots.
plump down 1 *vi* s'affaler.
2 *vt sep* laisser tomber lourdement. **to plump o.s. down on the sofa** s'affaler sur le sofa.
plump for *vt fus* fixer son choix sur, se décider pour, jeter son dévolu sur.
plumpness ['plʌmpnɪs] *n [person]* rondeur *f*, embonpoint *m*.
plunder ['plʌndəʳ] **1** *n* (*U*) (*act*) pillage *m*; (*loot*) butin *m*. **2** *vt* piller.
plunderer ['plʌndərəʳ] *n* pillard *m*.
plundering ['plʌndərɪŋ] **1** *n* (*U*) pillage *m*. **2** *adj* pillard.
plunge [plʌndʒ] **1** *n [bird, diver, goalkeeper]* plongeon *m*; (*quick bathe*) (petit) plongeon; (*steep fall*) chute *f*, (*fig: fall*) chute, dégringolade* *f* (*in* de); (*Fin: rash investment*) spéculation hasardeuse (*on* sur). **to take a ~** *[diver etc]* plonger; *[bather]* faire un (petit) plongeon; *[shares, prices etc]* dégringoler*; **his ~ into debt** son endettement soudain; (*fig*) **to take the ~** se jeter à l'eau, franchir *or* sauter le pas.
2 *vt hand, knife, dagger* plonger, enfoncer (*into* dans); (*into water*) plonger (*into* dans); (*fig*) plonger (*into war/darkness/despair etc* dans la guerre/les ténèbres/le désespoir *etc*).
3 *vi* **(a)** (*dive*) *[diver, goalkeeper, penguin, submarine]* plonger (*into* dans, *from* de); *[horse]* piquer une tête, piquer du nez; *[ship]* piquer de l'avant *or* du nez; *[road, cliff]* plonger (*into* dans); (*fig*) *[person]* se jeter, se lancer (*into* dans). **he ~d into the argument** il se lança dans la discussion; (*fig*) **the stream/road ~d down the mountainside** le ruisseau/la route dévalait le flanc de la colline; **the neckline ~s at the back** le décolleté est plongeant dans le dos.
(b) (*fall*) *[person]* tomber, faire une chute (*from* de); *[vehicle]* dégringoler, tomber (*from* de); *[prices etc]* dégringoler, tomber. **he ~d to his death** il fit une chute mortelle; **the plane ~d to the ground/into the sea** l'avion s'est écrasé au sol/abîmé dans la mer; **the car ~d over the cliff** la voiture plongea pardessus la falaise; **the truck ~d across the road** le camion fit une embardée en travers de la route.
(c) (*rush*) se jeter, se lancer, se précipiter. **to ~ in/out/across** *etc* entrer/sortir/traverser *etc* précipitamment *or* à toute allure *or* en quatrième vitesse*; **he ~d down the stairs** il dégringola *or* dévala l'escalier quatre à quatre; **he ~d through the hedge** il piqua brusquement *or* se jeta au travers de la haie.
(d) (*) (*gamble*) jouer gros jeu, flamber; (*St Ex: speculate*) spéculer imprudemment. **he ~d and bought a car** il a sauté le pas et s'est offert une voiture.
plunge in 1 *vi [diver etc]* plonger; (*fig: into work etc*) s'y mettre de grand cœur; *V* **deep**.
2 *vt sep* (y) plonger.
plunger ['plʌndʒəʳ] *n* **(a)** (*piston*) piston *m*; (*for blocked pipe*) ventouse *f*. **(b)** (*gambler*) flambeur *m*; (*St Ex*) (spéculateur *m*) risque-tout *m inv*.
plunging ['plʌndʒɪŋ] **1** *n* (*action*) plongement *m*; *[diver etc]* plongées *fpl*; *[boat]* tangage *m*. **2** *adj*: ~ **neckline** décolleté plongeant.
plunk [plʌŋk] = **plonk 1a, 2, 3.**
pluperfect ['plu:'pɜ:fɪkt] *n* plus-que-parfait *m*.
plural ['plʊərəl] **1** *adj* **(a)** (*Gram*) *form, number, ending, person* pluriel, du pluriel; *verb, noun* au pluriel. **(b)** *vote* plural. **2** *n* (*Gram*) pluriel *m*. **in the ~** au pluriel.
pluralism ['plʊərəlɪzəm] *n* (*Philos*) pluralisme *m*; (*Rel*) cumul *m*.
plurality [ˌplʊə'rælɪtɪ] *n* pluralité *f*; *[benefices etc]* cumul *m*; (*US Pol*) majorité *f*.
plus [plʌs] **1** *prep* plus. **3 ~ 4** 3 plus *or* et 4; **~ what I've done already** plus ce que j'ai déjà fait; (*Bridge etc*) **we are ~ 5** nous menons par 5 points.
2 *adj* **(a)** (*Elec, Math*) positif. (*lit*) **on the ~ side of the account** à l'actif du compte; (*fig*) **we have his support on the ~ side of the account** l'aspect positif c'est que nous avons son appui; **his languages are a ~ factor** sa connaissance des langues est un atout.
(b) 10-~ hours a week un minimum de 10 heures *or* plus de 10 heures par semaine; (*Scol etc*) **beta ~** bêta plus; **we've sold 100 ~** nous en avons vendu 100 et quelques *or* plus de 100.
3 *n* (*Math: sign*) (signe *m*) plus *m*; (*fig: extra advantage*) avantage additionnel, atout *m*.
4 *cpd*: **plus fours** culotte *f* de golf; (*Math*) **plus sign** signe *m* plus.
plush [plʌʃ] **1** *n* (*Tex*) peluche *f*. **2** *adj* (*made of ~*) de *or* en peluche; (*~-like*) pelucheux; (*: *sumptuous*) rupin‡, somptueux.
plushy* ['plʌʃɪ] *adj* rupin‡, somptueux.
Plutarch ['plu:tɑ:k] *n* Plutarque *m*.
Pluto ['plu:təʊ] *n* (*Astron*) Pluton *f*; (*Myth*) Pluton *m*.
plutocracy [plu:'tɒkrəsɪ] *n* ploutocratie *f*.
plutocrat ['plu:təʊkræt] *n* ploutocrate *m*.
plutocratic [ˌplu:təʊ'krætɪk] *adj* ploutocratique.
plutonium [plu:'təʊnɪəm] *n* plutonium *m*.
pluviometer [ˌplu:vɪ'ɒmɪtəʳ] *n* pluviomètre *m*.
ply[1] [plaɪ] **1** *n [wood]* feuille *f*, épaisseur *f*; *[wool]* fil *m*, brin *m*; *[rope]* toron *m*, brin. **three-~ (wool)** laine *f* trois fils. **2** *cpd*: **plywood** contre-plaqué *m*.
ply[2] [plaɪ] **1** *vt* **(a)** *needle, tool* manier, jouer (habilement) de; *oar* manier; *ship, river* naviguer sur, voguer sur (*liter*). **they plied their oars** ils faisaient force de rames; **to ~ one's trade (as)** exercer son métier (de).
(b) to ~ sb with questions presser qn de questions; **to ~ sb for information** demander continuellement des renseignements à qn; **he plied them with drink** il ne cessait de remplir leur verre.
2 *vi [ship, coach etc]* **to ~ between** faire la navette entre; **to ~ for hire** faire un service de taxi.
pneumatic [nju:'mætɪk] *adj* pneumatique. **~ drill** marteau-piqueur *m*; **~ tyre** pneu *m*.
pneumatically [nju:'mætɪkəlɪ] *adv* pneumatiquement.
pneumonia [nju:'məʊnɪə] *n* (*U: Med*) pneumonie *f*, fluxion *f* de poitrine.
po‡ [pəʊ] *n* pot *m* (de chambre). (*pej*) **~-faced‡** à l'air pincé.
poach[1] [pəʊtʃ] *vt* (*Culin*) pocher. **~ed eggs** œufs pochés.
poach[2] [pəʊtʃ] **1** *vt game* braconner, chasser illégalement; *fish* braconner, pêcher illégalement.
2 *vi* braconner. **to ~ for salmon** *etc* braconner du saumon; (*lit, fig*) **to ~ on sb's preserves** *or* **territory** braconner sur les terres de qn; (*fig*) **stop ~ing!*** (*in tennis*) arrête de me chiper la balle!*; (*in work*) arrête de marcher sur mes plates-bandes!*
poacher[1] ['pəʊtʃəʳ] *n* (*for eggs*) pocheuse *f*.
poacher[2] ['pəʊtʃəʳ] *n* (*of game etc*) braconnier *m*.
poaching ['pəʊtʃɪŋ] *n* braconnage *m*.
pock [pɒk] **1** *n* (*Med*) pustule *f* de petite vérole. **2** *cpd*: **pockmark** marque *f* de petite vérole; **pockmarked** *face* grêlé; *surface* criblé de (petits) trous.
pocket ['pɒkɪt] **1** *n* **(a)** (*in garment, suitcase, file, book cover*) poche *f*. **with his hands in his ~s** les mains dans les poches; **in his trouser ~** dans sa poche de pantalon; (*fig*) **he is always putting his hand in his ~** il n'arrête pas de débourser; **he had to put his hand in his ~ and pay their bills** il a dû payer leurs factures de sa poche; (*fig*) **the deal put £100 in his ~** l'affaire lui a rapporté 100 livres; **it is a drain on his ~** ça grève son budget; **that will hurt his ~** ça fera mal à son porte-monnaie; (*fig*) **to have sb in one's ~** avoir qn dans sa manche *or* dans sa poche; **he has the game in his ~** il a le jeu dans sa poche; **to fill** *or* **line one's ~s** se remplir les poches; **to be in ~** avoir une marge de bénéfice; **to be out of ~** en être de sa poche; **out-of-~** *V* **out 5**; **I was £5 in/out of ~** j'avais fait un bénéfice/essuyé une perte de 5 livres; **it left me £5 in/out of ~** ça m'a rapporté/coûté 5 livres.
(b) (*fig*) poche *f*; (*Aviat: air ~*) trou *m* d'air; (*Billiards*) blouse *f*. **~ of gas/pus/resistance** poche de gaz/de pus/de résistance; **~ of infection** foyer *m* de contagion; **there are still some ~s of unemployment** il reste quelques petites zones de chômage.
2 *cpd flask, torch, dictionary, edition etc* de poche. **pocket battleship** cuirassé *m* de poche; (*US*) **pocket billiards** billard *m* à blouses; **pocketbook** (*wallet*) portefeuille *m*; (*notebook*) calepin *m*, carnet *m*; (*US: handbag*) sac *m* à main; **pocket calculator** calculatrice *f* de poche; **pocket-handkerchief** (*n*) mouchoir *m* de poche; (*adj: fig*) grand comme un mouchoir de poche; **pocket knife** couteau *m* de poche, canif *m*; **pocket money** argent *m* de poche; **pocket-size(d)** (*lit*) de poche; (*fig*) *person, house, garden etc* tout petit; (*US Pol*) **pocket veto** véto présidentiel (*opposé sans explications*).
3 *vt* (*lit*) empocher, mettre dans sa poche; (*fig*) (*gain*) empocher; (*steal*) empocher, barboter‡. (*fig*) **to ~ one's pride** *etc* mettre son amour-propre *etc* dans sa poche.
pocketful ['pɒkɪtfʊl] *n* poche pleine.
pod [pɒd] *n [bean, pea etc]* cosse *f*. (*fig*) **to be in ~‡** être enceinte, avoir un polichinelle dans le tiroir‡.
podgy* ['pɒdʒɪ] *adj* rondelet.
podiatrist [pɒ'di:ətrɪst] *n* (*US*) pédicure *mf*.
podiatry [pɒ'di:ətrɪ] *n* (*US*) (*science*) podologie *f*, (*treatment*) soins *mpl* du pied, traitement *m* des maladies du pied.
podium ['pəʊdɪəm] *n*, *pl* **podia** ['pəʊdɪə] podium *m*.
poem ['pəʊɪm] *n* poème *m*. **the ~s of Keats** les poèmes *or* les poésies *fpl* de Keats.
poet ['pəʊɪt] *n* poète *m*. (*Brit*) **~ laureate** poète lauréat.
poetaster [ˌpəʊɪ'tæstəʳ] *n* mauvais poète, rimailleur *m*.
poetess ['pəʊɪtes] *n* poétesse *f*.

poetic [pəʊ'etɪk] **1** *adj* poétique. ~ **licence** licence *f* poétique; **it's ~ justice** c'est bonne justice. **2** *n*: ~**s** poétique *f*.
poetical [pəʊ'etɪkəl] *adj* poétique.
poetically [pəʊ'etɪkəlɪ] *adv* poétiquement.
poeticize [pəʊ'etɪsaɪz] *vt* poétiser.
poetry ['pəʊɪtrɪ] **1** *n* (*U: lit, fig*) poésie *f*. **the ~ of Keats** la poésie de Keats; **he writes ~** il écrit *or* fait des vers, il fait de la poésie. **2** *cpd*: **poetry reading** lecture *f* de poèmes.
pogo-stick ['pəʊgəʊ,stɪk] *n* échasse sauteuse.
pogrom ['pɒgrəm] *n* pogrom *m*.
poignancy ['pɔɪnjənsɪ] *n* (*V* **poignant**) caractère poignant, intensité *f*.
poignant ['pɔɪnjənt] *adj emotion, grief* poignant, intense, vif (*f* vive); *look, entreaty* poignant.
poignantly ['pɔɪnjəntlɪ] *adv feel* d'une manière poignante, intensément, vivement; *look, entreat* d'une manière poignante.
poinsettia [pɔɪn'setɪə] *n* poinsettia *m*.
point [pɔɪnt] **1** *n* **(a)** (*sharp end*) *[pencil, needle, knife, jaw etc]* pointe *f*; (*Geog*) pointe, promontoire *m*, cap *m*. **knife with a sharp ~** couteau très pointu; **to put a ~ on a pencil** tailler un crayon (en pointe); (*fig*) **not to put too fine a ~ on it** pour ne pas y aller par quatre chemins, pour dire les choses comme elles sont; **star with 5 ~s** étoile à 5 branches; **stag with 8 ~s** cerf (de) 8 cors; (*Ballet*) **to be** *or* **dance on ~s** faire des pointes; **at the ~ of a sword** à la pointe de l'épée; **at the ~ of a revolver** sous la menace du revolver; *V* **gun, pistol** *etc*.
(b) (*dot*) (*Geom, Typ*) point *m*; (*Math: decimal ~*) virgule *f* (décimale). **3 ~ 6 (3.6)** 3 virgule 6 (3,6); (*Geom*) **~ A** le point A.
(c) (*position*) (*on scale*) point *m*; (*in space*) point, endroit *m*; (*in time*) point, moment *m*. **~ of the compass** point du compas; **the (thirty-two) ~s of the compass** la rose des vents; **from all ~s (of the compass)** de toutes parts, de tous côtés; **all ~s east** toute ville (*or* escale *etc*) à l'est; **the train stops at Slough, and all ~s west** le train s'arrête à Slough et dans toutes les gares à l'ouest de Slough; **~ of departure** point de départ; **~ of entry (into a country)** point d'arrivée (dans un pays); (*fig*) **there was no ~ of contact between them** il n'y avait aucun point de contact *or* point commun entre eux; **~ of view** point de vue; **from that/my ~ of view** de ce/mon point de vue; **from the social ~ of view** du point de vue social; **the highest ~ in the district** le point culminant de la région; **at that ~ in the road** à cet endroit de la route; **at the ~ where the road forks** là où la route bifurque; (*Brit Elec*) **(wall** *or* **power) ~** prise *f* de courant; *[pipe etc]* **outlet ~** point de sortie; **boiling/freezing ~** point d'ébullition/de congélation; **the bag was full to bursting ~** le sac était plein à craquer; **from that ~ onwards** (*in space*) à partir de là; (*in time*) à partir de ce moment, désormais; **at this** *or* **that ~** (*in space*) là, à cet endroit; (*in time*) à cet instant précis, à ce moment-là; **at this ~ in time** à l'heure qu'il est, en ce moment.
(d) (*in phrases*) **to be on the ~ of doing** être sur le point de faire; **he had reached the ~ of resigning** il en était au point de donner sa démission; (*lit, fig*) **he had reached the ~ of no return** il avait atteint le point de non-retour; (*fig*) **up to a ~** jusqu'à un certain point, dans une certaine mesure; **at the ~ of death** à l'article de la mort; **when it comes to the ~** en fin de compte, quand tout est dit (*V also* **1g**); **when it came to the ~ of paying** quand le moment de payer est arrivé; **severe to the ~ of cruelty** sévère au point d'être cruel; **they provoked him to the ~ of losing his temper** *or* **to the ~ where he lost his temper** ils l'ont provoqué au point de le mettre hors de lui; *V* **focal, turning** *etc*.
(e) (*counting unit: Scol, Sport, St Ex; also on scale*) point *m*; (*on thermometer*) degré *m*. (*Boxing*) **on ~s** aux points; **the cost-of-living index went up 2 ~s** l'indice du coût de la vie a augmenté de 2 points; (*St Ex*) **to rise** *or* **gain 3 ~s** gagner 3 points, enregistrer une hausse de 3 points; (*Typ*) **8-~ type** caractères *mpl* de 8 points; *V* **score**.
(f) (*idea, subject, item, detail*) point *m*. **the ~ at issue** notre (*or* leur *etc*) propos, la question qui nous (*or* les *etc*) concerne; **~ of interest/of no importance** point intéressant/sans importance; **just as a ~ of interest, did you ...?** histoire de savoir, est-ce que vous ...?; **on this ~ we are agreed** sur ce point *or* là-dessus nous sommes d'accord, c'est un point acquis; **on all ~s** en tous points; **12-~ plan** plan *m* en 12 points; **it's a ~ of detail** c'est un point de détail; **on a ~ of principle** sur une question de principe; **a ~ of law** un point de droit; **it was a ~ of honour with him never to refuse** il se faisait un point d'honneur de ne jamais refuser, il mettait son point d'honneur à ne jamais refuser; **in ~ of fact** en fait, à vrai dire; **the main ~s to remember** les principaux points à ne pas oublier; **~ by ~** point par point (*V also* **2**); **he made the ~ that ...** il fit remarquer que ...; **he made a good ~ when he said that ...** il a fait une remarque pertinente *or* judicieuse en disant que ...; **I'd like to make a ~ if I may** j'aurais une remarque à faire si vous le permettez; **you've made your ~!** vous avez dit ce que vous aviez à dire!; **I take your ~** je vois ce que vous voulez dire *or* où vous voulez en venir; **~ taken!** très juste!; **you have a ~ there!** c'est juste!, il y a du vrai dans ce que vous dites!; **to carry** *or* **gain** *or* **win one's ~** avoir gain de cause; **he gave me a few ~s on what to do** il m'a donné quelques conseils *or* il m'a donné quelques tuyaux* *or* il m'a tuyauté* sur ce que je devais faire; *V* **case**[1], **moot, order** *etc*.
(g) (*important part, main idea etc*) *[argument etc]* (point *m*) essentiel *m*; *[joke etc]* astuce *f*, sel *m*, piquant *m*; (*meaning, purpose*) intérêt *m*, sens *m*. **there's no ~ in waiting** cela ne sert à rien d'attendre; **what's the ~ of** *or* **in waiting?** à quoi bon attendre?; **what's the ~?** à quoi bon?; **I don't see any ~ in doing that** je ne vois aucun intérêt *or* sens à faire cela; **what was the ~ of his visit?** quel était le sens de *or* à quoi rimait sa visite?; **the ~ is that you had promised it for today!** le fait est que *or* c'est que vous l'aviez promis pour aujourd'hui!; **the whole ~ was to have it today** tout l'intérêt était de l'avoir aujourd'hui; **that's the (whole) ~!** justement!; **that's not the ~** il ne s'agit pas de cela, là n'est pas la question; **that is beside the ~** c'est à côté de la question, cela n'a rien à voir; **that is hardly the ~!** comme s'il s'agissait de cela!; **off the ~** hors de propos; **(very much) to the ~** (très) pertinent; **the ~ of this story is that ...** là où je veux (*or* il veut *etc*) en venir avec cette histoire, c'est que ...; **a long story that seemed to have no ~ at all** une longue histoire sans rime ni raison; **I missed the ~ of that joke** je n'ai pas compris ce que ça avait de drôle, je n'ai pas saisi l'astuce; **you've missed the whole ~!** vous n'avez rien compris!; **to see** *or* **get the ~** comprendre, piger*; **you get the ~?** vous saisissez?*; **to come to the ~** (en) venir au fait; **come to the ~!** au fait!, venez-en à l'essentiel!; **let's get back to the ~** revenons à nos moutons (*fig*); **to keep** *or* **stick to the ~** rester dans le sujet; **to make a ~ of doing** ne pas manquer de faire; **the news gave ~ to his arguments** les nouvelles ont souligné la pertinence de ses arguments; **his remarks lack ~** ses remarques ne sont pas très pertinentes.
(h) (*characteristic*) *[horse etc]* caractéristique *f*. **good ~s** qualités *fpl*; **bad ~s** défauts *mpl*; **it is not his strong ~** ce n'est pas son fort; **he has his ~s** il a ses bons côtés, il n'est pas sans qualités; **the ~s to look for when buying a car** les détails *mpl* que vous devez prendre en considération lors de l'achat d'une voiture.
(i) (*Rail*) **~s** aiguilles *fpl*.
2 *cpd*: **point-blank** *V* **point-blank; point-by-point** méthodique; (*Police etc*) **to be on point duty** diriger la circulation; (*Rail*) **pointsman** aiguilleur *m*; (*Boxing*) **points decision** décision *f* aux points; **points system** système *m* des points; **points win** victoire *f* aux points; (*Racing*) **point-to-point (race)** *course f de chevaux dans laquelle la liberté est laissée au cavalier de choisir son parcours d'un point à un autre.*
3 *vt* **(a)** (*aim, direct*) *telescope, hosepipe etc* pointer, braquer, diriger (*on* sur). **to ~ a gun at sb** braquer un revolver sur qn; **he ~ed his stick towards the house** il tendit *or* pointa son bâton vers la maison; **he ~ed the boat towards the harbour** il a mis le cap sur le port; **he ~ed the car towards the town** il a tourné la voiture en direction de la ville; **he ~ed his finger at me** il pointa *or* tendit son doigt vers moi, il me montra du doigt; *V also* **finger**.
(b) (*mark, show*) montrer, indiquer. **the signs ~ the way to London** les panneaux de signalisation indiquent *or* montrent la direction de Londres; (*fig*) **it ~s the way to closer cooperation** cela montre la voie pour *or* ouvre la voie à une plus grande coopération; (*fig*) **to ~ the moral** souligner *or* faire ressortir la morale.
(c) (*sharpen*) *pencil, stick* tailler (en pointe); *tool* aiguiser, affûter.
(d) (*Constr*) *wall* jointoyer (*with* de).
(e) (*punctuate*) ponctuer; *Hebrew* mettre les points-voyelles à; *psalm* marquer de points.
4 *vi* **(a)** *[person]* montrer *or* indiquer du doigt. **it's rude to ~** ce n'est pas poli de montrer du doigt; **to ~ at** *or* **towards sth/sb** montrer *or* indiquer qch/qn du doigt; **he ~ed at the house with his stick** il montra *or* indiqua la maison avec sa canne; (*fig*) **I want to ~ to one or two facts** je veux attirer votre attention sur un ou deux faits; (*fig*) **all the evidence ~s to him** *or* **to his guilt** tous les témoignages l'accusent; **everything ~s to a brilliant career for him** tout annonce *or* indique qu'il aura une brillante carrière; **it all ~s to the fact that ...** tout laisse à penser que ...; **everything ~s to murder/suicide** tout laisse à penser qu'il s'agit d'un meurtre/d'un suicide; (*fig*) **everything ~s that way** tout nous amène à cette conclusion.
(b) *[signpost]* indiquer la direction (*towards* de); *[gun]* être braqué (*at* sur); *[vehicle etc]* être dirigé, être tourné (*towards* vers). **the needle is ~ing north** l'aiguille indique le nord; **the hour hand is ~ing to 4** la petite aiguille indique 4 heures; **the car isn't ~ing in the right direction** la voiture n'est pas tournée dans la bonne direction *or* dans le bon sens.
(c) *[dog]* tomber en arrêt.
point out *vt sep* **(a)** (*show*) *person, object, place* montrer, indiquer, désigner.
(b) (*mention*) signaler, attirer l'attention sur; faire remarquer (*that* que). **to point sth out to sb** signaler qch à qn, attirer l'attention de qn sur qch; **he pointed out to me that I was wrong** il m'a signalé *or* il m'a fait remarquer que j'avais tort; **I should point out that ...** je dois vous dire *or signaler que ...* .
point up *vt sep* faire ressortir, mettre en évidence, souligner. **to point up a story** illustrer une histoire.
point-blank ['pɔɪnt'blæŋk] **1** *adj shot* à bout portant; (*fig*) *refusal* net, catégorique; *request* de but en blanc, à brûle-pourpoint.
2 *adv fire, shoot* à bout portant; (*fig*) *refuse* tout net, catégoriquement; *request, demand* de but en blanc, à brûle-pourpoint. **at ~ range** à bout portant.
pointed ['pɔɪntɪd] *adj* **(a)** *knife, stick, pencil, roof, chin, nose* pointu; *beard* en pointe; (*Archit*) *window, arch* en ogive. **the ~ end** le bout pointu.
(b) (*fig*) *remark* lourd de sens, plein de sous-entendus. **her rather ~ silence** son silence lourd de sens *or* significatif.
pointedly ['pɔɪntɪdlɪ] *adv reply* d'une manière significative. **... she said ~ ...** dit-elle avec intention *or* d'un ton plein de sous-entendus; **rather ~ she refused to comment** sa façon de se refuser à tout commentaire disait bien ce qu'elle voulait dire.
pointer ['pɔɪntə'] *n* (*stick*) baguette *f*; (*on scale*) (*indicator*) index *m*, (*needle*) aiguille *f*; (*dog*) chien *m* d'arrêt; (*clue, indication*) indice *m* (*to* de); (*piece of advice*) tuyau* *m*. **he gave me some ~s on what to do*** il m'a donné quelques conseils *mpl* (pratiques) *or* indications *fpl or* tuyaux* sur ce que je devais faire; **there is at present no ~ to the outcome** rien ne permet de présumer *or* de conjecturer l'issue pour le moment; **they are**

looking for ~s on how the situation will develop ils cherchent des indices permettant d'établir comment la situation va évoluer; his remarks are a possible ~ to a solution ses remarques pourraient bien laisser entrevoir une solution.

pointing [ˈpɔɪntɪŋ] *n* (*Constr*) jointoiement *m*.

pointillism [ˈpwæntɪlɪzəm] *n* pointillisme *m*.

pointless [ˈpɔɪntlɪs] *adj attempt, task* inutile, vain, futile; *murder* gratuit; *suffering* inutile, vain, injustifié; *explanation, joke, story* sans rime ni raison, qui ne rime à rien. **it is ~ to complain** il ne sert à rien de se plaindre, c'est peine perdue que de se plaindre; **life seemed ~ to her** la vie lui paraissait dénuée de sens.

pointlessly [ˈpɔɪntlɪslɪ] *adv try, work, suffer* inutilement, vainement; *kill* gratuitement, sans raison.

pointlessness [ˈpɔɪntlɪsnɪs] *n* (*V* **pointless**) inutilité *f*, futilité *f*; gratuité *f*.

poise [pɔɪz] **1** *n* (*balance*) équilibre *m*; (*carriage*) maintien *m*; *[head, body etc]* port *m*; (*fig*) (*composure etc*) calme *m*, sang-froid *m*; (*self-confidence*) (calme) assurance *f*; (*grace*) grâce *f*. **they walked with books on their heads to improve their ~** elles marchaient en portant des livres sur la tête pour perfectionner leur maintien; **a woman of great ~** une femme pleine de grâce *or* empreinte d'une tranquille assurance; **he is young and lacks ~** il est jeune et manque d'assurance *or* d'aisance.

2 *vt* (*balance*) mettre en équilibre; (*hold balanced*) tenir en équilibre, maintenir en équilibre. **she ~d her pen *or* held her pen ~d over her notebook** elle tenait son stylo suspendu audessus du bloc-notes (prête à écrire); **he ~d himself on his toes** il se tint sur la pointe des pieds (sans bouger); **to be ~d** (*balanced*) être en équilibre; (*held, hanging*) être suspendu immobile; (*hovering*) être immobile *or* suspendu (en l'air); **the diver was ~d at the edge of the pool** le plongeur se tenait sur le rebord de la piscine prêt à plonger; **the tiger was ~d ready to spring** le tigre se tenait (immobile) prêt à bondir; **~d (ready) to attack/for the attack** (tout) prêt à attaquer/pour l'attaque; (*fig*) **~d on the brink of success/ruin** au bord de la réussite/de la ruine.

poison [ˈpɔɪzn] **1** *n* (*lit, fig*) poison *m*; *[snake]* venin *m*. **to take ~** s'empoisonner; **to die of ~** mourir empoisonné; **they hate each other like ~** ils ne peuvent pas se sentir; *V* **rat**.

2 *cpd*: **poison fang** dent venimeuse; **poison gas** gaz toxique *or* asphyxiant; **poison gland** glande *f* à venin; (*Bot*) **poison ivy** sumac vénéneux; **poison-pen letter** lettre *f* anonyme venimeuse.

3 *vt [person] person, food, well, arrow* empoisonner; *[noxious substance] person* empoisonner, intoxiquer; *rivers etc* empoisonner. **the drugs are ~ing his system** les drogues l'intoxiquent; (*fig*) **it is ~ing their friendship** cela empoisonne *or* gâche *or* gâte leur amitié; **to ~ sb's mind** (*corrupt*) corrompre qn; (*instil doubts*) faire douter qn; **he ~ed her mind against her husband** il l'a fait douter de son mari.

poisoner [ˈpɔɪznəʳ] *n* empoisonneur *m*, -euse *f* (*lit*).

poisoning [ˈpɔɪznɪŋ] *n* (*V* **poison 3**) empoisonnement *m*; intoxication *f*. **to die of ~** mourir empoisonné; *V* **food, lead**[2].

poisonous [ˈpɔɪznəs] *adj snake* venimeux; *plant* vénéneux; *gas, fumes* toxique, asphyxiant; *substance* toxique; (*fig*) *propaganda, rumours, doctrine* pernicieux, diabolique. **he is quite ~*** il est absolument ignoble; **this coffee is ~*** ce café est infect.

poke[1] [pəʊk] *n* (*dial, esp Scot*) sac *m*; *V* **pig**.

poke[2] [pəʊk] **1** *n* **(a)** (*push*) poussée *f*; (*jab*) (petit) coup *m* (*de coude, de canne, avec le doigt etc*); (*US*: punch*) coup de poing. **to give the fire a ~** donner un coup de tisonnier au feu; **to give sb a ~ in the ribs** enfoncer son coude (*or* son doigt *etc*) dans les côtes de qn, pousser qn dans les côtes avec son coude (*or* son doigt *etc*), pousser qn du coude; **I got a ~ in the eye from his umbrella** j'ai reçu son parapluie dans l'œil; **he gave the ground a ~ with his stick** il a enfoncé sa canne dans le sol.

(b) (*Brit***) coït *m*, coup** *m*.

2 *vt* **(a)** (*jab with finger, stick etc*) pousser, donner un coup de coude (*or* de canne *or* avec le doigt) à; (*US*: punch*) donner un coup de poing à; (*thrust*) *stick, finger etc* enfoncer (*into* dans, *through* à travers); *rag etc* fourrer (*into* dans). **to ~ the fire** tisonner le feu; **he ~d me with his umbrella** il m'a donné un petit coup de parapluie, il m'a poussé avec son parapluie; **he ~d his finger in her eye** il lui a mis le doigt dans l'œil; **he ~d the ground with his stick, he ~d his stick into the ground** il a enfoncé sa canne dans le sol; **he ~d me in the ribs** il m'a enfoncé son coude (*or* son doigt *etc*) dans les côtes, il m'a poussé dans les côtes avec son coude (*or* son doigt), il m'a poussé du coude; (*US*) **he ~d me one in the stomach*** il m'a envoyé son poing dans l'estomac; **he ~d his finger at me** il pointa son index vers moi; **he ~d his finger up his nose** il s'est fourré le doigt dans le nez; **to ~ one's head out of the window** passer la tête hors de *or* par la fenêtre; **to ~ a hole in sth (with one's finger/stick etc)** faire un trou dans qch *or* percer qch (avec le doigt/sa canne *etc*); *V* **fun, nose**.

(b) (*Brit***) faire l'amour avec, tirer son coup avec**, tringler**.

3 *vi* **(a)** (*also* **~ out**) *[elbows, stomach, stick]* sortir, dépasser (*from, through* de).

(b) he ~d at me with his finger il pointa son index vers moi; **he ~d at the suitcase with his stick** il poussa la valise avec sa canne; **the children were poking at their food** les enfants chipotaient (en mangeant); (*fig*) **to ~ into sth*** fourrer le nez dans qch, fourgonner dans qch.

poke about, poke around *vi* **(a)** (*lit*) fourrager; fureter. **to poke about in a drawer/a dustbin** fourrager dans un tiroir/une poubelle; **I spent the morning poking about in antique shops** j'ai passé la matinée à fureter dans les magasins d'antiquités.

(b) (*pej*) fouiner. **he was poking about in my study** il fouinait dans mon bureau.

poke in *vt sep head* passer à l'intérieur; *stick etc* enfoncer; *rag* fourrer. (*fig*) **to poke one's nose in*** fourrer son nez dans les affaires des autres, se mêler de ce qui ne vous regarde pas.

poke out 1 *vi* **(a)** = **poke 3a**.

(b) (*bulge*) *[stomach, chest, bottom]* être protubérant *or* proéminent.

2 *vt sep* **(a)** sortir. **the tortoise poked its head out** la tortue sortit la tête.

(b) (*remove etc*) faire partir, déloger. **he poked the ants out with a stick** il a délogé les fourmis avec un bâton; **to poke sb's eye out** crever l'œil à qn.

poker[1] [ˈpəʊkəʳ] *n* (*for fire etc*) tisonnier *m*. (*U*) **~ work** (*craft*) pyrogravure *f*; (*objects*) pyrogravures *fpl*; *V* **stiff**.

poker[2] [ˈpəʊkəʳ] **1** *n* (*Cards*) poker *m*. **2** *cpd*: **poker-face** visage *m* impassible; **poker-faced** au visage impassible.

poky [ˈpəʊkɪ] *adj* (*pej*) *house, room* exigu (*f* -guë) et sombre.

Poland [ˈpəʊlənd] *n* Pologne *f*.

polar [ˈpəʊləʳ] *adj* (*Elec, Geog*) polaire. **~ bear** ours blanc; **P~ Circle** cercle *m* polaire; **~ lights** aurore *f* polaire.

polarimeter [ˌpəʊləˈrɪmɪtəʳ] *n* polarimètre *m*.

polariscope [pəʊˈlærɪskəʊp] *n* polariscope *m*.

polarity [pəʊˈlærɪtɪ] *n* polarité *f*.

polarization [ˌpəʊləraɪˈzeɪʃən] *n* (*lit, fig*) polarisation *f*.

polarize [ˈpəʊləraɪz] *vt* (*lit, fig*) polariser.

Pole [pəʊl] *n* Polonais(e) *m(f)*.

pole[1] [pəʊl] **1** *n* **(a)** (*rod*) perche *f*; (*fixed*) poteau *m*, mât *m*; (*flag~, tent ~; also in gymnastics, for climbing*) mât; (*telegraph ~*) poteau télégraphique; (*curtain ~*) tringle *f*; (*barber's ~*) ≃ enseigne *f* de barbier; (*in fire station*) perche *f*; (*for vaulting, punting*) perche. **their only weapons were wooden ~s** leurs seules armes étaient de longs bâtons; (*fig*) **to be up the ~*** dérailler* (*fig*); (*fig*) **to send *or* drive sb up the ~*** rendre qn fou (*f* folle), faire perdre la tête à qn; *V* **greasy, ski** *etc*.

(b) (††: *Measure*) = 5,029 mètres.

2 *cpd*: **poleax(e)** (*n*) (*weapon*) hache *f* d'armes; *[butcher etc]* merlin *m*; (*vt*) *cattle etc* abattre, assommer; (*fig*) *person* terrasser; (*Sport*) **pole jump, pole vault** (*n*) saut *m* à la perche; (*vi*) sauter à la perche; **pole jumper, pole vaulter** sauteur *m*, -euse *f* à la perche, perchiste *mf*.

3 *vt punt etc* faire avancer (à l'aide d'une perche).

pole[2] [pəʊl] **1** *n* (*Elec, Geog*) pôle *m*. **North/South P~** pôle Nord/Sud; **from ~ to ~** d'un pôle à l'autre; (*fig*) **they are ~s apart** ils sont aux antipodes (l'un de l'autre). **2** *cpd*: **pole star** étoile *f* polaire.

polecat [ˈpəʊlkæt] *n* putois *m*.

polemic [pɒˈlemɪk] **1** *adj* polémique. **2** *n* (*argument*) polémique *f*. **~s** polémique (*U*).

polemical [pɒˈlemɪkəl] *adj* polémique.

police [pəˈliːs] **1** *n* (*U*) (*organization*) ≃ police *f* (*under Ministry of the Interior: gen in towns*); gendarmerie *f* (*under Ministry of War: throughout France*). (*collective*) **the ~** la police, les gendarmes *mpl*; **to join the ~** entrer dans la police, se faire policier *or* gendarme; **he is in the ~, he is a member of the ~** il est dans la police, il est policier, il est gendarme; **extra ~ were called in** on fit venir des renforts de police; **river/railway ~** police fluviale/des chemins de fer; *V* **mounted** *etc*.

2 *cpd escort, leave, vehicle, members* de la police *or* de la gendarmerie; *campaign, control, inquiry* policier, de la police *or* de la gendarmerie. **police car** voiture *f* de police *or* de la gendarmerie; (*Brit*) **police constable** ≃ agent *m* de police, gendarme *m*; **police court** tribunal *m* de simple police; **police dog** chien policier; **the police force** la police, les gendarmes *mpl*, les forces *fpl* de l'ordre; **police inspector** ≃ inspecteur *m* de police, capitaine *m* de gendarmerie; **policeman, police officer** agent *m* de police, gardien *m* de la paix, gendarme *m*; **police protection** protection *f* de la police *or* de la gendarmerie; **to have a police record** avoir un casier judiciaire; **he hasn't a police record** il a un casier judiciaire vierge; **police state** état policier; **police station** poste *m* *or* commissariat *m* de police, gendarmerie *f*; **policewoman** femme-agent *f*.

3 *vt* **(a)** (*lit: with policemen*) **it was decided to ~ the streets** on décida d'envoyer des agents de police (*or* des gendarmes) pour maintenir l'ordre dans les rues.

(b) *[vigilantes, volunteers etc] district, road, football match etc* faire la police dans (*or* à, sur *etc*); (*Mil*) *frontier, territory* contrôler, maintenir la paix dans (*or* à, sur *etc*); (*fig*) *agreements, controls* veiller à l'application de; *prices etc* contrôler. **the border is ~d by U.N. patrols** la frontière est sous la surveillance des patrouilles de l'O.N.U.

policy[1] [ˈpɒlɪsɪ] **1** *n* **(a)** (*aims, principles etc*) (*Pol*) politique *f*; *[newspaper, company, organisation]* politique (générale), ligne *f* (d'action); (*course of action*) règle *f*. **the government's policies** la politique du gouvernement; (*Pol*) **foreign/economic/social ~** politique étrangère/économique/sociale; **what is the company ~ on this matter?** quelle est la ligne suivie par la compagnie à ce sujet?; **the paper followed a ~ of attacking the Church** le journal attaquait systématiquement l'Église; **the Ruritanian ~ of expelling its critics** la politique d'expulsion pratiquée par les Ruritaniens à l'encontre de leurs critiques; **nationalisation is a matter of ~ for the Socialists** les nationalisations sont une question de principe pour les socialistes; **it has always been our ~ to deliver goods free** nous avons toujours eu pour règle de livrer les marchandises franco de port; **my ~ has always been to wait and see** j'ai toujours eu pour règle d'attendre et de voir venir; **it would be good/bad ~ to do that** ce serait une bonne/mauvaise politique que de faire cela; **complete frankness is the best ~** la franchise totale est la meilleure politique; *V* **honesty**.

(b) (*U: prudence*) (bonne) politique *f*. **it would not be ~ to refuse** il ne serait pas politique de refuser.

2 *cpd*: **policy decision** décision *f* de principe; **policy discussion** discussion *f* de politique générale *or* de ligne d'action; **policy matter** question *f* de politique générale *or* de principe; **to make a policy statement** faire une déclaration de principe.

policy² [ˈpɒlɪsɪ] *n* (*Insurance*) police *f* (d'assurance). **to take out a ~** souscrire à une police d'assurance; **~holder** assuré(e) *m(f)*.

polio [ˈpəʊlɪəʊ] *n* (*abbr of* **poliomyelitis**) polio *f*. **~ victim** polio *mf*.

poliomyelitis [ˈpəʊlɪəʊmaɪəˈlaɪtɪs] *n* poliomyélite *f*.

Polish [ˈpəʊlɪʃ] **1** *adj* polonais. **2** *n* (*Ling*) polonais *m*.

polish [ˈpɒlɪʃ] **1** *n* **(a)** (*substance*) (*for shoes*) cirage *m*, crème *f* (à chaussures); (*for floor, furniture*) encaustique *f*, cire *f*; (*for nails*) vernis *m* (à ongles). **metal ~** produit *m* d'entretien pour les métaux.

(b) (*act*) **to give sth a ~** faire briller qch; **my shoes need a ~** mes chaussures ont besoin d'être cirées.

(c) (*shine*) poli *m*, éclat *m*, brillant *m*; (*fig: refinement*) *[person]* raffinement *m*; *[style, work, performance]* perfection *f*, élégance *f*. **high ~** lustre *m*; **to put a ~ on sth** faire briller qch; **the buttons have lost their ~** les boutons ont perdu leur éclat *or* leur brillant, les boutons se sont ternis.

2 *vt* (*also* **~ up**) *stones, glass* polir; *shoes* cirer; *floor, furniture* cirer, astiquer, faire briller; *car* astiquer, briquer; *pans, metal* fourbir, astiquer, faire briller; *leather* lustrer; (*fig*) *person* parfaire l'éducation de; *manners* affiner; *style, language* polir, châtier. **to ~ (up) one's French** perfectionner *or* travailler son français; **the style needs ~ing** le style manque de poli *or* laisse à désirer *or* aurait besoin d'être plus soigné; *V also* **polished.**

polish off *vt sep food, drink* finir; *work, correspondence* expédier; *competitor, enemy* régler son compte à, en finir avec; (*‡: kill*) liquider*, nettoyer‡. **he polished off the meal** il a tout mangé jusqu'à la dernière miette.

polish up *vt sep* = **polish 2.**

polished [ˈpɒlɪʃt] *adj surface* poli, brillant; *floor, shoes* ciré, brillant; *silver, ornaments* brillant, fourbi, astiqué; *stone, glass* poli; (*fig*) *person* qui a de l'éducation *or* du savoir-vivre; *manners* raffiné; *style* poli, châtié; *performer* accompli; *performance* impeccable.

polisher [ˈpɒlɪʃəʳ] *n* (*person*) polisseur *m*, -euse *f*; (*machine*) polissoir *m*; (*for floors*) cireuse *f*.

polite [pəˈlaɪt] *adj person, remark* poli. **to be ~ to sb** être poli *or* correct avec *or* envers *or* à l'égard de qn; **when I said it was not his best work I was being ~** c'est par pure politesse que j'ai dit que ce n'était pas sa meilleure œuvre; **be ~ about his car!** ne dis pas de mal de sa voiture!; **in ~ society** dans la bonne société.

politely [pəˈlaɪtlɪ] *adv* poliment, avec politesse.

politeness [pəˈlaɪtnɪs] *n* politesse *f*. **to do sth out of ~** faire qch par politesse.

politic [ˈpɒlɪtɪk] **1** *adj* politique, diplomatique. **he thought** *or* **deemed it ~ to refuse** il a jugé politique de refuser; *V* **body.**

2 *n*: **~s** politique *f*; **to talk ~s** parler politique; **to go into ~s** choisir *or* embrasser une carrière politique; **foreign ~s** politique étrangère; *V* **party.**

political [pəˈlɪtɪkəl] *adj* (*all senses*) politique. **~ economy/geography/science** économie *f*/géographie *f*/sciences *fpl* politique(s); **to ask for ~ asylum** demander le droit d'asile (politique); *V* **party.**

politically [pəˈlɪtɪkəlɪ] *adv* politiquement.

politician [ˌpɒlɪˈtɪʃən] *n* homme *m* politique, femme *f* politique, politicien(ne) *m(f)* (*pej*).

politic(o)... [pəˈlɪtɪk(əʊ)] *pref* politico... .

polity [ˈpɒlɪtɪ] *n* (*system of government*) régime *m*, administration *f* politique; (*government organization*) constitution *f* politique; (*the State*) État *m*.

polka [ˈpɒlkə] *n* polka *f*. **~ dot** pois *m* (*sur tissu*).

poll [pəʊl] **1** *n* **(a)** (*Pol*) (*general vote*) vote *m*; (*voting at election*) scrutin *m*; (*election*) élection(s) *f(pl)*; (*list of voters*) liste électorale; (*voting place*) bureau *m* de vote; (*votes cast*) voix *fpl*, suffrages *mpl*. **to take a ~ on sth** procéder à un vote sur *or* au sujet de qch; **the result of the ~** le résultat de l'élection *or* du scrutin; **on the eve of the ~** à la veille de l'élection *or* du scrutin; **people under 18 are excluded from the ~** les jeunes de moins de 18 ans n'ont pas le droit de vote *or* ne peuvent pas voter; **to go to the ~s** aller aux urnes; **a crushing defeat at the ~s** une écrasante défaite aux élections; **to head the ~** arriver en tête de scrutin, avoir le plus grand nombre de voix; **there was an 84% ~, there was an 84% turnout at the ~s** 84% des inscrits ont voté, la participation électorale était de (l'ordre de) 84%; **the ~ was heavy/light** *or* **low** la participation électorale était importante *or* forte/faible; **he got 20% of the ~** il a obtenu 20% des suffrages exprimés; **he achieved a ~ of 5,000 votes** il a obtenu 5.000 voix.

(b) (*opinion survey*) sondage *m*. **(public) opinion ~** sondage d'opinion; **to take a ~** sonder l'opinion (*of* de); **the Gallup ~** le sondage Gallup.

(c) (*††: head*) chef† *m*.

2 *cpd*: **poll tax** capitation *f*.

3 *vt* **(a)** *votes* obtenir; *people* sonder l'opinion de. **they ~ed the students to find out whether ...** ils ont sondé l'opinion des étudiants pour savoir si ...; **40% of those ~ed supported the government** 40% de ceux qui ont participé au sondage d'opinion étaient pour le gouvernement.

(b) *cattle* décorner; *tree* étêter, écimer.

4 *vi* **(a) the party will ~ badly/heavily in Scotland** le parti obtiendra peu de/beaucoup de voix *or* de suffrages en Écosse.

(b) (*vote*) voter.

pollard [ˈpɒləd] **1** *n* (*animal*) animal *m* sans cornes; (*tree*) têtard *m*, arbre étêté *or* écimé. **2** *vt animal* décorner; *tree* étêter, écimer.

pollen [ˈpɒlən] *n* pollen *m*.

pollinate [ˈpɒlɪneɪt] *vt* féconder (avec du pollen).

pollination [ˌpɒlɪˈneɪʃən] *n* pollinisation *f*, fécondation *f*.

polling [ˈpəʊlɪŋ] **1** *n* élections *fpl*. **~ is on Thursday** les élections ont lieu jeudi, on vote jeudi; **~ was heavy** il y a eu une forte participation électorale, le nombre des votants a été élevé.

2 *cpd*: **polling booth** isoloir *m*; **polling day** jour *m* des élections; **polling station** bureau *m* de vote.

pollster [ˈpəʊlstəʳ] *n* enquêteur *m*, -euse *f*.

pollute [pəˈluːt] *vt* polluer; (*fig*) contaminer; (*corrupt*) corrompre; (*desecrate*) profaner, polluer (*liter*). **the river was ~d with chemicals** la rivière était polluée par des produits chimiques.

pollution [pəˈluːʃən] *n* (*V* **pollute**) pollution *f*; contamination *f*; profanation *f*. **air ~** pollution de l'air.

polo [ˈpəʊləʊ] **1** *n* polo *m*; *V* **water. 2** *cpd*: **poloneck** (*n*) col roulé; (*adj*) à col roulé; **polo stick** maillet *m* (de polo).

polonaise [ˌpɒləˈneɪz] *n* (*Mus*) polonaise *f*.

poltergeist [ˈpɔːltəgaɪst] *n* esprit frappeur.

poltroon† [pɒlˈtruːn] *n* poltron *m*.

poly... [ˈpɒlɪ] *pref* poly... .

polyandrous [ˌpɒlɪˈændrəs] *adj* polyandre.

polyandry [ˈpɒlɪændrɪ] *n* polyandrie *f*.

polyanthus [ˌpɒlɪˈænθəs] *n* primevère *f* (*multiflore*).

polychromatic [ˌpɒlɪkrəʊˈmætɪk] *adj* polychrome.

polychrome [ˈpɒlɪkrəʊm] **1** *adj* polychrome. **2** *n* statue *f* (*or* tableau *m etc*) polychrome.

polyclinic [ˈpɒlɪklɪnɪk] *n* polyclinique *f*.

polyester [ˌpɒlɪˈestəʳ] **1** *n* polyester *m*. **2** *cpd* de *or* en polyester.

polyethylene [ˌpɒlɪˈeθəliːn] *n* (*US*) polyéthylène *m*, polythène *m*.

polygamist [pɒˈlɪgəmɪst] *n* polygame *mf*.

polygamous [pɒˈlɪgəməs] *adj* polygame.

polygamy [pɒˈlɪgəmɪ] *n* polygamie *f*.

polygenesis [ˌpɒlɪˈdʒenɪsɪs] *n* polygénisme *m*.

polygenetic [ˌpɒlɪdʒɪˈnetɪk] *adj* polygénétique.

polyglot [ˈpɒlɪglɒt] *adj, n* polyglotte (*mf*).

polygon [ˈpɒlɪgən] *n* polygone *m*.

polygonal [pɒˈlɪgənl] *adj* polygonal.

polyhedral [ˌpɒlɪˈhiːdrəl] *adj* polyédrique.

polyhedron [ˌpɒlɪˈhiːdrən] *n* polyèdre *m*.

polymath [ˈpɒlɪmæθ] *n* polymathe *m*.

polymer [ˈpɒlɪməʳ] *n* polymère *m*.

polymerization [ˈpɒlɪməraɪˈzeɪʃən] *n* polymérisation *f*.

polymorphism [ˌpɒlɪˈmɔːfɪzəm] *n* polymorphisme *m*, polymorphie *f*.

polymorphous [ˌpɒlɪˈmɔːfəs] *adj* polymorphe.

Polynesia [ˌpɒlɪˈniːzɪə] *n* Polynésie *f*.

Polynesian [ˌpɒlɪˈniːzɪən] **1** *adj* polynésien. **2** *n* Polynésien(ne) *m(f)*.

polynomial [ˌpɒlɪˈnəʊmɪəl] *adj, n* polynôme (*m*).

polyp [ˈpɒlɪp] *n* polype *m*.

polyphase [ˈpɒlɪfeɪz] *adj* polyphase.

polyphonic [ˌpɒlɪˈfɒnɪk] *adj* polyphonique.

polyphony [pəˈlɪfənɪ] *n* polyphonie *f*.

polypropylene [ˌpɒlɪˈprɒpɪliːn] *n* polypropylène *m*.

polypus [ˈpɒlɪpəs] *n* (*Med*) polype *m*.

polysemous [pɒˈlɪsəməs] *adj* polysémique.

polysemy [pɒˈlɪsəmɪ] *n* polysémie *f*.

polystyrene [ˌpɒlɪˈstaɪriːn] **1** *n* polystyrène *m*. **2** *cpd*: **polystyrene cement** colle *f* polystyrène; **polystyrene chips** billes *fpl* (de) polystyrène.

polysyllabic [ˈpɒlɪsɪˈlæbɪk] *adj* polysyllabe, polysyllabique.

polysyllable [ˈpɒlɪˌsɪləbl] *n* polysyllabe *m*.

polytechnic [ˌpɒlɪˈteknɪk] *n* (*Brit*) ≃ IUT *m*, Institut *m* Universitaire de Technologie.

polytheism [ˈpɒlɪθiːɪzəm] *n* polythéisme *m*.

polytheistic [ˌpɒlɪθiːˈɪstɪk] *adj* polythéiste.

polythene [ˈpɒlɪθiːn] *n* (*Brit*) polyéthylène *m*, polythène *m*. **~ bag** sac *m* en plastique *or polyéthylène*.

polyurethane [ˌpɒlɪˈjʊərɪθeɪn] *n* polyuréthane *m*.

polyvalent [pəˈlɪvələnt] *adj* polyvalent.

polyvinyl [ˈpɒlɪvaɪnl] *n* polyvinyl *m*.

pom [pɒm] *n* = **pommy.**

pomade [pəˈmɑːd] **1** *n* pommade *f*. **2** *vt* pommader.

pomegranate [ˈpɒməˌgrænɪt] *n* (*fruit*) grenade *f*; (*tree*) grenadier *m*.

Pomeranian [ˌpɒməˈreɪnɪən] *n* (*dog*) loulou *m* (de Poméranie).

pommel [ˈpʌml] **1** *n* pommeau *m*. **2** *vt* = **pummel.**

pommy‡ [ˈpɒmɪ] (*Australia pej*) **1** *n* Anglais(e) *m(f)*. **2** *adj* anglais.

pomp [pɒmp] *n* pompe *f*, faste *m*, apparat *m*. **~ and circumstance** grand apparat, pompes (*liter*); **with great ~** en grande pompe.

Pompeii [pɒmˈpeɪɪ] *n* Pompéi *m*.

Pompey [ˈpɒmpɪ] *n* Pompée *m*.

pompom [ˈpɒmpɒm] *n* (*Mil*) canon-mitrailleuse *m* (de D.C.A.).

pompon [ˈpɒmpɒn] *n* pompon *m*.

pomposity [pɒmˈpɒsɪtɪ] *n* (*pej*) manières pompeuses, air *or* ton pompeux, solennité *f*.

pompous [ˈpɒmpəs] *adj* (*pej*) *person* pompeux, solennel, plein de son importance; *remark, speech, tone, voice* pompeux, pontifiant, solennel; *style* pompeux, ampoulé.

pompously [ˈpɒmpəslɪ] *adv* (*pej*) pompeusement, d'un ton *or* d'un air pompeux.

ponce‡ [pɒns] **1** *n* (*Brit*) maquereau‡ *m*, souteneur *m*. **2** *vi* faire le maquereau‡, être souteneur.

poncho [ˈpɒntʃəʊ] *n* poncho *m*.

pond [pɒnd] 1 *n* étang *m*; (*stagnant*) mare *f*; (*artificial*) bassin *m*; *V* **fish, mill** *etc.* 2 *cpd*: **pondlife** vie animale des eaux stagnantes; **pondweed** épi *m* d'eau, potamot *m*.
ponder ['pɒndəʳ] 1 *vt* considérer, peser, réfléchir à *or* sur. 2 *vi* méditer (*over, on* sur), réfléchir (*over, on* à, sur).
ponderable ['pɒndərəbl] *adj* pondérable.
ponderous ['pɒndərəs] *adj movement, object* lourd, pesant; *style, joke* lourd; *speech, tone, voice* pesant et solennel.
ponderously ['pɒndərəslɪ] *adv move* pesamment; *write* avec lourdeur; *say, declaim* d'une voix pesante et solennelle.
pone [pəʊn] *n* (*US*) pain *m* de maïs.
pong‡ [pɒŋ] (*Brit*) 1 *n* mauvaise odeur; puanteur *f*. **what a ~ in here!** ça pue ici! 2 *vi* puer.
pontiff ['pɒntɪf] *n* (*Rel*) (*dignitary*) pontife *m*; (*pope*) souverain pontife, pontife romain.
pontifical [pɒn'tɪfɪkəl] *adj* (*Rel*) pontifical; (*fig*) pontifiant.
pontificate [pɒn'tɪfɪkɪt] 1 *n* (*Rel*) pontificat *m*. 2 [pɒn'tɪfɪkeɪt] *vi* (*fig*) pontifier (*about* au sujet de, sur).
Pontius Pilate ['pɒnʃəs'paɪlət] *n* Ponce Pilate *m*.
pontoon [pɒn'tuːn] *n* ponton *m*; (*Brit Cards*) vingt-et-un *m*. **~ bridge** pont flottant.
pony ['pəʊnɪ] 1 *n* poney *m*; (*Brit‡*) 25 livres; (*US Scol‡: crib*) traduc* *f*, corrigé *m* (*utilisé illicitement*). 2 *cpd*: **hair in a ponytail** cheveux *mpl* en queue de cheval; **pony trekking** randonnée *f* équestre *or* à cheval.
pooch‡ [puːtʃ] *n* cabot‡ *m*, clebs‡ *m*.
poodle ['puːdl] *n* caniche *m*.
poof‡ [pʊf] *n* (*Brit pej*) tante‡ *f*, tapette‡ *f*.
poofy‡ ['pʊfɪ] *adj* (*Brit pej*) efféminé, du genre tapette‡. **it's ~** ça fait fille.
pooh [puː] 1 *excl* bah!, peuh! 2 *cpd*: **to pooh-pooh sth** faire fi de qch, dédaigner qch.
pool[1] [puːl] *n* **(a)** (*puddle*) *[water, rain]* flaque *f* (d'eau); *[spilt liquid]* flaque, (*larger*) mare *f*; (*fig*) *[sunlight, shadow]* flaque. **lying in a ~ of blood** étendu dans une mare de sang; **in a ~ of light** dans une flaque *or* (*smaller*) un rond de lumière.
(b) (*pond*) (*natural*) étang *m*; (*artificial*) bassin *m*, pièce *f* d'eau; (*in river*) plan *m* d'eau; (*water hole*) point *m* d'eau; (*swimming ~*) piscine *f*; *V* **paddle**.
pool[2] [puːl] 1 *n* **(a)** (*money*) (*Cards etc: stake*) poule *f*, cagnotte *f*; (*gen: common fund*) cagnotte.
(b) (*fig*) (*of things owned in common*) fonds commun; (*reserve, source*) *[ideas, experience, ability]* réservoir *m*; *[advisers, experts]* équipe *f*. **a ~ of vehicles** un parc de voitures; **(typing) ~** bureau *m* des dactylos, pool *m*, dactylo *f*.
(c) the ~s = the football ~s; *V* **football**.
(d) (*US: snooker*) billard américain. **to shoot ~** blouser une bille.
(e) (*Comm: consortium*) pool *m*; (*US: monopoly trust*) trust *m*. **the coal and steel ~** le pool du charbon et de l'acier.
2 *cpd*: (*Billiards*) **poolroom** (salle *f* de) billard *m*; **pool table** billard *m* (*table*).
3 *vt money, resources, objects* mettre en commun; *knowledge, efforts* unir.
poop [puːp] *n* (*Naut*) poupe *f*. **~ deck** dunette *f*.
pooped‡ [puːpt] *adj* (*exhausted*) épuisé, vanné, à plat*.
poor [pʊəʳ] 1 *adj* **(a)** (*not rich*) *person, family, nation* pauvre. **as ~ as a church-mouse** pauvre comme un rat *or* comme Job; **how ~ is he really?** jusqu'à quel point est-il pauvre?; **to become ~er** s'appauvrir; **in ~ circumstances** dans le besoin, dans la gêne; (*fig: lacking*) **~ in mineral resources** pauvre en minerais; *V also* **3**.
(b) (*inferior*) *amount, sales, harvest, output* maigre, médiocre; *work, worker, soldier, film, result, food, holiday, summer* médiocre, piètre (*before n*); *effort* insuffisant; *light* faible; *sight* faible, mauvais; *soil* pauvre, peu productif; *cards* médiocre. **he has a ~ chance of success** il a peu de chances de réussir; **to have ~ hearing** être dur d'oreille; **he has a ~ memory** il n'a pas bonne mémoire; **to be in ~ health** ne pas être en bonne santé, être en mauvaise santé; **a ~ meal of bread and water** un maigre *or* piètre repas de pain et d'eau; **it was a ~ evening** ce n'était pas une soirée réussie, la soirée n'était pas une réussite; **he showed a ~ grasp of the facts** il a manifesté un manque de compréhension des faits; **to be ~ at (doing) sth, to be a ~ hand at (doing) sth** ne pas être doué pour (faire) qch; **I'm a ~ sailor** je n'ai pas le pied marin; **he is a ~ traveller** il supporte mal les voyages; *V* **second**[1], **show** *etc.*
(c) (*pitiable*) pauvre. **~ little boy** pauvre petit garçon; **she's all alone, ~ woman** elle est toute seule, la pauvre; **~ Smith, he lost his money** ce pauvre Smith, il a perdu son argent; **~ things*, they look cold** les pauvres, ils ont l'air d'avoir froid; **you ~ old thing!*** mon pauvre vieux!, ma pauvre vieille!; **it's a ~ thing when ...** c'est malheureux que ...+*subj*; (*iro*) **in my ~ opinion** à mon humble avis.
2 *n*: **the ~** les pauvres *mpl*.
3 *cpd*: (*Rel*) **poorbox** tronc *m* des pauvres; (*Hist*) **poorhouse** hospice *m* (des pauvres); (*Hist*) **poor law** assistance *f* publique; (*Hist*) **the poor laws** les lois *fpl* sur l'assistance publique; **poor-spirited** timoré, pusillanime.
poorly ['pʊəlɪ] 1 *adj* malade, souffrant. 2 *adv live, dress* pauvrement; *perform, work, write, explain, swim, eat* médiocrement, mal. **~ lit/paid** *etc* mal éclairé/payé *etc*; **to be ~ off** être pauvre.
poorness ['pʊənɪs] *n* (*lack of wealth*) pauvreté *f*; (*badness*) pauvreté, mauvaise qualité, médiocrité *f*.
pop[1] [pɒp] 1 *n* **(a)** (*sound*) *[cork etc]* pan *m*; *[press stud etc]* bruit sec. (*excl*) **~!** pan!; **to go ~** faire pan.
(b) (**U: drink*) boisson gazeuse.
2 *cpd*: **popcorn** pop-corn *m*; **popeyed** les yeux écarquillés, ébahi; **popgun** pistolet *m* à bouchon.
3 *vt* **(a)** *balloon* crever; *cork* faire sauter; *corn* faire éclater; *press stud* fermer.
(b) (*put*) passer; mettre, fourrer; jeter. **to ~ one's head round the door/out of the window** passer brusquement la tête par la porte/par la fenêtre; **to ~ sth into the oven** passer *or* mettre qch au four; **he ~ped it into his mouth** il l'a fourré *or* l'a mis dans sa bouche; **could you ~ this letter into the postbox?** pourriez-vous jeter *or* mettre cette lettre à la boîte?; (*fig*) **to ~ the question** faire sa demande (en mariage).
(c) (‡†: *pawn*) mettre au clou*.
4 *vi* **(a)** *[balloon]* crever; *[cork]* sauter; *[corn]* éclater; *[press stud, buttons etc]* sauter. **my ears ~ped** mes oreilles se sont brusquement débouchées; **his eyes ~ped** il écarquilla les yeux, il ouvrit des yeux ronds *or* de grands yeux; **his eyes were ~ping out of his head** les yeux lui sortaient de la tête, il avait les yeux exorbités.
(b) (*go*) **I ~ped over (*or* round *or* across *or* out) to the grocer's** j'ai fait un saut à l'épicerie; **he ~ped into a café** il entra dans un café en vitesse.
pop back 1 *vi* revenir, retourner (en vitesse *or* pour un instant).
2 *vt sep lid etc* remettre, replacer.
pop in *vi* entrer en passant, ne faire que passer. **I popped in to say hullo to them** je suis entré (en passant) leur dire bonjour; **she kept popping in and out** elle n'a pas cessé d'entrer et de sortir.
pop off *vi* **(a)** (*leave*) partir. **they popped off to Spain for a few days** ils sont partis passer quelques jours en Espagne, ils ont filé* pour quelques jours en Espagne.
(b) (‡: *die*) mourir (subitement), claquer*.
pop out *vi [person]* sortir; *[cork]* sauter. **the rabbit popped out of its burrow** le lapin détala de son terrier.
pop up *vi* (*from water, above wall etc*) surgir. **he popped up unexpectedly in Tangiers** il a réapparu inopinément à Tanger.
pop[2] [pɒp] (*abbr of* **popular**) 1 *adj music, song, singer, concert, art* pop *inv*. 2 *n* (musique *f*) pop *m*. **it's top of the ~s just now** c'est en tête du hit-parade *or* du palmarès de la chanson en ce moment.
pop[3]* [pɒp] *n* (*esp US*) papa *m*. (*to old man*) **yes ~** oui grand-père*, oui pépé*.
pope [pəʊp] *n* pape *m*. **P~ John XXIII** le pape Jean XXIII.
popery ['pəʊpərɪ] *n* (*pej*) papisme *m* (*pej*). **no ~!** à bas le pape!
popinjay† ['pɒpɪndʒeɪ] *n* fat *m*, freluquet *m*.
popish ['pəʊpɪʃ] *adj* (*pej*) papiste (*pej*).
poplar ['pɒpləʳ] *n* peuplier *m*.
poplin ['pɒplɪn] 1 *n* popeline *f*. 2 *cpd* de *or* en popeline.
popper ['pɒpəʳ] *n* (*Brit*: press stud*) pression *f*, bouton-pression *m*.
poppet* ['pɒpɪt] *n* (*Brit*) **yes (my) ~** oui mon petit chou; **she's a ~** elle est à croquer, c'est un amour.
poppy ['pɒpɪ] 1 *n* **(a)** (*Bot*) pavot *m*; (*growing wild*) coquelicot *m*. **(b)** (*Brit*) coquelicot *m* (*artificiel vendu au bénéfice des mutilés de guerre*). 2 *adj* (*colour*) ponceau *inv*. 3 *cpd*: (*Brit*: *V* **1b**) **Poppy Day** anniversaire *m* de l'armistice; **poppy seed** graine *f* de pavot.
poppycock* ['pɒpɪkɒk] *n* (*U*) balivernes *fpl*, fariboles *fpl*. **~!** balivernes!
popsy‡ ['pɒpsɪ] *n* souris‡ *f* (*fig*).
populace ['pɒpjʊlɪs] *n* peuple *m*, foule *f*, populace *f* (*pej*).
popular ['pɒpjʊləʳ] *adj* **(a)** (*well-liked*) *person, decision, book, sport* populaire; (*fashionable*) *style, model* à la mode, en vogue. **he is ~ with his colleagues** ses collègues l'aiment beaucoup, il jouit d'une grande popularité auprès de ses collègues; **he is ~ with the girls** il a du succès *or* il a la cote* auprès des filles; **I'm not very ~ with the boss just now*** je ne suis pas très bien vu du patron *or* je n'ai pas la cote* auprès du patron en ce moment; (*Comm*) **this is a very ~ colour** cette couleur se vend beaucoup; **it is ~ to despise politicians** mépriser les hommes politiques est à la mode, c'est la mode de mépriser les hommes politiques.
(b) (*of, for, by the people*) *music, concert* populaire; *lecture, journal* de vulgarisation; *government, opinion, discontent* populaire, du peuple; *mistake, habit, practice* populaire, courant. (*Pol*) **~ front** front *m* populaire; **at ~ prices** à la portée de toutes les bourses; **by ~ request** à la demande générale.
popularity [ˌpɒpjʊ'lærɪtɪ] *n* popularité *f* (*with* auprès de, *among* parmi). **to grow in ~** être de plus en plus populaire, acquérir une popularité de plus en plus grande; **to decline in ~** être de moins en moins populaire, perdre de sa popularité; **it enjoyed a certain ~** cela a joui d'une certaine popularité *or* faveur.
popularization ['pɒpjʊləraɪ'zeɪʃən] *n* **(a)** (*U*: *V* **popularize**) popularisation *f*; vulgarisation *f*. **(b)** (*popularized work*) œuvre *f or* ouvrage *m* de vulgarisation.
popularize ['pɒpjʊləraɪz] *vt sport, music, fashion, product* populariser, rendre populaire; *science, ideas* vulgariser.
popularizer ['pɒpjʊləraɪzəʳ] *n [sport, fashion]* promoteur *m*, -trice *f*; *[science, ideas]* vulgarisateur *m*, -trice *f*. **he was the ~ of the new-style bicycle** c'est lui qui a popularisé *or* rendu populaire le nouveau modèle de bicyclette.
popularly ['pɒpjʊləlɪ] *adv*: **~ known as ...** communément connu *or* connu de tous sous le nom de ...; **it is ~ supposed that ...** il est communément *or* généralement présumé que ...; **he is ~ believed to be rich** il passe communément *or* généralement pour être riche.
populate ['pɒpjʊleɪt] *vt* peupler. **densely/sparsely ~d** très/peu peuplé, à forte/faible densité de population.
population [ˌpɒpjʊ'leɪʃən] 1 *n* population *f*. **a fall/rise in (the) ~** une diminution/un accroissement de la population; **the ~ of the town is 15,000** la population de la ville est de *or* la ville a une population de 15.000 habitants; **all the working ~** toute la population active.

2 *cpd increase* de la population, démographique. **the population explosion** l'explosion *f* démographique.
populous ['pɒpjʊləs] *adj* populeux, très peuplé, à forte densité de population.
porcelain ['pɔːsəlɪn] 1 *n* (*U: substance, objects*) porcelaine *f*. **a piece of ~** une porcelaine. 2 *cpd dish* de *or* en porcelaine; *clay, glaze* à porcelaine. (*U*) **porcelain ware** vaisselle *f* en *or* de porcelaine.
porch [pɔːtʃ] *n [house, church]* porche *m*; *[hotel]* marquise *f*; (*also* **sun ~**) véranda *f*.
porcine ['pɔːsaɪn] *adj* (*frm*) porcin, de porc.
porcupine ['pɔːkjʊpaɪn] *n* porc-épic *m*; *V* **prickly**.
pore[1] [pɔːʳ] *n* (*Physiol*) pore *m*.
pore[2] [pɔːʳ] *vi*: **to ~ over** *book* s'absorber dans; *letter, map* étudier de près; *problem* méditer longuement; **he was poring over the book** il était plongé dans *or* absorbé par le livre.
pork [pɔːk] (*Culin*) 1 *n* porc *m*. 2 *cpd chop etc* de porc. **pork butcher** ≈ charcutier *m*; **porkpie** ≈ pâté *m* en croûte; **porkpie hat** (chapeau *m*) feutre rond; **pork sausage** saucisse *f* (de porc).
porker ['pɔːkəʳ] *n* porc *m* à l'engrais, goret *m*.
porky* ['pɔːkɪ] *adj* (*pej*) gras comme un porc, bouffi.
porn* [pɔːn] *n* (*U: abbr of* **pornography**) porno* *m or f*. **it's just ~** c'est porno (*adj inv*); **~ shop** boutique *f* pornographique.
pornographic [ˌpɔːnəˈgræfɪk] *adj* pornographique.
pornography [pɔːˈnɒgrəfɪ] *n* pornographie *f*.
porosity [pɔːˈrɒsɪtɪ] *n* porosité *f*.
porous ['pɔːrəs] *adj* poreux, perméable.
porousness ['pɔːrəsnɪs] *n* porosité *f*.
porphyry ['pɔːfɪrɪ] *n* porphyre *m*.
porpoise ['pɔːpəs] *n* marsouin *m* (*Zool*).
porridge ['pɒrɪdʒ] *n* porridge *m*, bouillie *f* de flocons d'avoine. **~ oats** flocons *mpl* d'avoine.
porringer† ['pɒrɪndʒəʳ] *n* bol *m*, écuelle *f*.
port[1] [pɔːt] 1 *n* (*harbour, town*) port *m*. (*Naut*) **~ of call** (port d')escale *f*; (*fig*) **I've only one more ~ of call** il ne me reste plus qu'une course à faire; **~ of entry** port de débarquement *or* d'arrivée; **naval/fishing ~** port militaire/de pêche; **to come into ~** entrer dans le port; **they put into ~ at Dieppe** ils ont relâché dans le port de Dieppe; **to leave ~** appareiller, lever l'ancre; (*loc*) **any ~ in a storm** nécessité n'a pas de loi (*Prov*); *V* **sea, trading** *etc*.
2 *cpd facilities, security* portuaire, du port. **port authorities** autorités *fpl* portuaires; **port dues** droits *mpl* de port.
port[2] [pɔːt] *n* (*opening*) (*Aviat, Naut: also* **~hole**) hublot *m*; (*Naut: for guns, cargo*) sabord *m*.
port[3] [pɔːt] (*Naut: left*) 1 *n* (*also* **~ side**) bâbord *m*. **to ~** à bâbord; **land to ~!** terre par bâbord! 2 *adj guns, lights* de bâbord. 3 *vt*: **to ~ the helm** mettre la barre à bâbord.
port[4] [pɔːt] *n* (*wine*) porto *m*.
portable ['pɔːtəbl] *adj* portatif.
portage ['pɔːtɪdʒ] *n* (*action*) port *m*, transport *m*; (*cost*) frais *mpl* de port *or* de transport.
portal ['pɔːtl] *n* portail *m*.
portcullis [pɔːtˈkʌlɪs] *n* herse *f* (*de château fort*).
portend [pɔːˈtend] *vt* présager, laisser pressentir, laisser augurer, annoncer.
portent ['pɔːtent] *n* prodige *m*, présage *m*. **of evil ~** de mauvais présage.
portentous [pɔːˈtentəs] *adj* (*ominous*) de mauvais présage, de mauvais augure, sinistre; (*marvellous*) prodigieux, extraordinaire; (*grave*) solennel, grave; (*pej: pompous*) pompeux, pontifiant.
portentously [pɔːˈtentəslɪ] *adv say* d'un air *or* d'un ton solennel *or* grave *or* pompeux (*pej*) *or* pontifiant (*pej*).
porter ['pɔːtəʳ] 1 *n* (**a**) (*for luggage: in station, hotel etc, on expedition*) porteur *m*; (*US Rail: attendant*) employé(e) *m(f)* des wagons-lits; (*Brit: doorkeeper*) *[private housing]* concierge *mf*; *[public building]* portier *m*, gardien(ne) *m(f)*. **~'s lodge** loge *f* du *or* de la concierge.
(**b**) (*beer*) porter *m*, bière brune.
2 *cpd*: (*esp US*) **porterhouse (steak)** ≈ chateaubriand *m*.
porterage ['pɔːtərɪdʒ] *n* (*act*) portage *m*; (*cost*) frais *mpl* de portage.
portfolio [pɔːtˈfəʊlɪəʊ] *n* serviette *f*, portefeuille† *m*; (*Fin, Parl*) portefeuille. **minister without ~** ministre *m* sans portefeuille.
portico ['pɔːtɪkəʊ] *n* portique *m*.
portion ['pɔːʃən] 1 *n* (*part, percentage*) portion *f*, partie *f*; *[train, ticket etc]* partie; (*share*) portion, (quote-)part *f*; *[estate, inheritance etc]* portion, part; (*of food: helping*) portion; (†: *marriage ~*) dot *f*; (*liter: fate*) sort *m*, destin *m*.
2 *vti* (*also* **~ out**) répartir (*among, between* entre).
portliness ['pɔːtlɪnɪs] *n* embonpoint *m*, corpulence *f*.
portly ['pɔːtlɪ] *adj* corpulent.
portmanteau [pɔːtˈmæntəʊ] *n* grosse valise (*de cuir*). (*Ling*) **~ word** mot-portemanteau *m*, mot-valise *m*.
portrait ['pɔːtrɪt] 1 *n* (*Art, gen*) portrait *m*. **to paint sb's ~** peindre (le portrait de) qn. 2 *cpd*: **portrait gallery** galerie *f* de portraits; **portrait painter** portraitiste *mf*.
portraitist ['pɔːtrɪtɪst] *n* portraitiste *mf*.
portraiture ['pɔːtrɪtʃəʳ] *n* (*U*) (*art*) art *m* du portrait; (*portrait*) portrait; (*collectively*) portraits.
portray [pɔːˈtreɪ] *vt [painter]* peindre, faire le portrait de; *[painting]* représenter. **he ~ed him as an embittered man** *[painter]* il l'a peint *or* il en a fait le portrait sous les traits d'un homme aigri; *[writer, speaker, actor]* il en a fait un homme aigri.
portrayal [pɔːˈtreɪəl] *n* (*V* **portray**) peinture *f*, portrait *m*; représentation *f*.
Portugal ['pɔːtjʊgəl] *n* Portugal *m*.
Portuguese [ˌpɔːtjʊˈgiːz] 1 *adj* portugais. 2 *n* (**a**) (*pl inv*) Portugais(e) *m(f)*. (**b**) (*Ling*) portugais *m*. 3 *cpd*: **Portuguese man-of-war** galère *f* (*Zool*).
pose [pəʊz] 1 *n* (*body position*) pose *f*, attitude *f*; (*Art*) pose; (*fig*) pose; (*pej*) pose, attitude, affectation *f*. **to strike a ~** poser (pour la galerie); **it's only a ~** c'est de la pose, c'est pure affectation, ce n'est qu'une attitude.
2 *vi* (*Art, Phot*) poser (*for* pour, *as* en); (*fig: attitudinize*) poser, prendre des poses, se donner des airs. **to ~ as a doctor** se faire passer pour un docteur; **he ~s as an expert on old books** il se pose en expert en livres anciens.
3 *vt* (**a**) *artist's model* faire prendre une pose à; *person* faire poser.
(**b**) *problem, question* poser; *difficulties* créer; *argument, claim* présenter, formuler.
poser ['pəʊzəʳ] *n* question *f* difficile. **that's a ~!** ça c'est difficile, ça c'est un vrai casse-tête.
poseur [pəʊˈzɜːʳ] *n* (*pej*) poseur *m*, -euse *f* (*pej*).
posh [pɒʃ] 1 *adj* (*: *often pej*) *person* chic *inv*, snob (*f inv*), rupin‡; *accent* distingué, de la haute‡; *house, neighbourhood, hotel* chic, rupin‡; *car, school* chic, de riches, de rupins‡; *clothes* chic, élégant. **~ people** les snob(s) *mpl*, les gens chic, les gens bien, les rupins‡; **a ~ wedding** un grand mariage, un mariage à grand tralala*; **he was looking very ~** il s'était mis *or* il était sur son trente et un.
2 *adv* (‡ *pej*) **to talk ~** parler comme les gens bien *or* la haute‡.
posh up‡ *vt sep house* embellir; (*clean up*) briquer; *child* pomponner, bichonner. **to posh o.s. up** se pomponner; **he was all poshed up** il était sur son trente et un, il était bien sapé‡.
posit ['pɒzɪt] *vt* avancer, énoncer, poser en principe.
position [pəˈzɪʃən] 1 *n* (**a**) (*place, location*) *[person, object]* position *f* (*also Geog, Math, Mil, Mus, Naut, Phys etc*), place *f*; *[house, shop, town]* emplacement *m*, situation *f*; *[gun]* emplacement. **in(to) ~** en place, en position; **to change the ~ of sth** changer qch de place; **to take up (one's) ~** prendre position *or* place; **to be in a good ~** être bien placé (*V also* **1d**); (*Mil etc*) **the enemy ~s** les positions de l'ennemi; (*Sport*) **what ~ do you play in?** à quelle place jouez-vous?; (*lit, fig*) **to jockey** *or* **jostle** *or* **manoeuvre for ~** manœuvrer pour se placer avantageusement; (*in post office, bank*) **'~ closed'** 'guichet fermé'.
(**b**) (*attitude, angle: also Art, Ballet*) position *f*. **in a horizontal ~** en position horizontale; **in an uncomfortable ~** dans une position incommode; **to change (one's) ~** changer de position.
(**c**) (*in class, league*) position *f*, place *f*; (*socially*) position, condition *f*; (*job*) poste *m*, emploi *m*, situation *f*. **he finished in 3rd ~** il est arrivé en 3e position *or* place; **her ~ in class was 4th** elle était la 4e de sa classe; **his ~ in society** sa position dans la société; **a man of ~** un homme de condition; **a man in his ~ should not ...** un homme dans sa position *or* de sa condition ne devrait pas ... (*V also* **1d**); **his ~ in the government** son poste *or* sa fonction dans le gouvernement; **a high ~ in the Ministry** une haute fonction au ministère; **a ~ of trust** un poste de confiance.
(**d**) (*fig: situation, circumstances*) situation *f*, place *f*. **to be in a ~ to do sth** être en position *or* en mesure de faire qch; **he is in a good ~ to judge** il est bien placé pour juger; **he is in no ~ to decide** il n'est pas en position *or* en mesure de décider; **put yourself in my ~** mettez-vous à ma place; **a man in his ~ cannot expect mercy** un homme dans sa situation ne peut s'attendre à la clémence; **what would you do in my ~?** que feriez-vous à ma place?; **our ~ is desperate** notre situation est désespérée; **the economic ~** la situation économique, la conjoncture; **we were in a false/awkward ~** nous étions dans une situation fausse/délicate.
(**e**) (*fig: point of view, opinion*) position *f*, opinion *f*. **you must make your ~ clear** vous devez dire franchement quelle est votre position, vous devez donner votre opinion; **his ~ on foreign aid** sa position sur la question de l'aide aux pays en voie de développement; **to take up a ~ on sth** prendre position sur qch; **he took up the ~ that ...** il a adopté le point de vue selon lequel ... .
2 *vt* (**a**) (*adjust angle of*) *light, microscope, camera* mettre en position.
(**b**) (*put in place*) *gun, chair, camera* mettre en place, placer; *house, school* situer, placer; *guards, policemen* placer, poster; *army, ship* mettre en position. **he ~ed each item with great care** il a très soigneusement disposé chaque article; **to ~ o.s.** se mettre, se placer.
(**c**) (*find ~ of*) déterminer la position de.
positive ['pɒzɪtɪv] 1 *adj* (**a**) (*not negative: also Elec, Gram, Math, Phot, Typ*) positif; *test, result, reaction* positif; (*affirmative*) affirmatif; (*constructive*) *suggestion* positif, concret (*f* concrète); *attitude, criticism* positif. **they need some ~ help** ils ont besoin d'une aide concrète *or* effective.
(**b**) (*definite, indisputable*) *order, rule, instruction* catégorique, formel; *fact* indéniable, irréfutable; *change, increase, improvement* réel, tangible. **~ proof, proof ~** preuve formelle; **there is ~ evidence that ...** il y a des preuves indéniables du fait que ...; **~ progress has been made** un réel progrès *or* un progrès tangible a été fait; **he has made a ~ contribution to the scheme** il a apporté une contribution effective au projet, il a contribué de manière effective au projet; **it's a ~ miracle*** c'est pur miracle; **he's a ~ genius*** c'est un vrai *or* véritable génie; **he's a ~ fool*** il est complètement idiot *or* stupide, c'est un idiot fini.
(**c**) (*sure, certain*) *person* sûr, certain (*about, on, of* de). **are you quite ~?** en êtes-vous bien sûr? *or* certain?; **I'm absolutely ~ I put it back** je mettrais ma main au feu que je l'ai remis à sa place; ... **he said in a ~ tone of voice** ... dit-il d'un ton très assuré; **to my ~ knowledge he did not see it** je sais sans l'ombre d'un doute qu'il ne l'a pas vu; **she is a very ~ person** elle est très

résolue *or* tranchante, elle sait ce qu'elle veut.

2 *n* (*Elec*) pôle positif; (*Gram*) (degré *m*) positif *m*; (*Math*) nombre positif, quantité positive; (*Phot*) épreuve positive, positif.

positively ['pɒzɪtɪvlɪ] *adv* (*definitely, indisputably*) indéniablement, irréfutablement; (*categorically*) formellement, catégoriquement; (*affirmatively*) affirmativement; (*with certainty*) de façon certaine *or* sûre; (*emphatically*) positivement; (*absolutely*) complètement, absolument. **he was ~ rude to me** il a été positivement grossier avec moi; **he's ~ mad** il est complètement fou.

positivism ['pɒzɪtɪvɪzəm] *n* positivisme *m*.

positivist ['pɒzɪtɪvɪst] *adj, n* positiviste (*mf*).

posse ['pɒsɪ] *n* (*also fig hum*) petite troupe, détachement *m*.

possess [pə'zes] *vt* **(a)** (*own, have*) *property, qualities* posséder, avoir; *documents, money, proof* posséder, avoir, être en possession de. **all I ~** tout ce que je possède; **it ~es several advantages** cela présente plusieurs avantages; **to ~ o.s. of sth** s'emparer de qch; **to be ~ed of** posséder, avoir; **to ~ one's soul** *or* **o.s. in patience** s'armer de patience.

(b) *[demon, rage]* posséder; (*fig: obsess*) posséder, obséder. **like one ~ed** comme un possédé; **he was ~ed by the devil** il était possédé du démon; **~ed with** *or* **by jealousy** obsédé *or* dévoré par la jalousie, en proie à la jalousie; **one single aim ~ed him** il n'avait qu'un seul but en tête; **what can have ~ed him to say that?** qu'est-ce qui l'a pris de dire ça?*

possession [pə'zeʃən] *n* **(a)** (*U: act, state*) possession *f*; (*Jur: occupancy*) jouissance *f*. **in ~ of** en possession de; **to have ~ of** posséder, avoir la jouissance de; **to have in one's ~** avoir en sa possession; **to get ~ of** acquérir, obtenir; (*improperly*) s'emparer de, s'approprier; **to come into ~ of** entrer en possession de; **he was in full ~ of his senses** il était en pleine possession de ses facultés, il avait le plein usage de ses facultés; **to come into sb's ~** tomber en la possession de qn; **according to the information in my ~** selon les renseignements dont je dispose; **to take ~ of** prendre possession de; (*improperly*) s'approprier; (*confiscate*) confisquer; (*Jur*) **to take ~** prendre possession; (*Jur*) **to be in ~** occuper les lieux; (*Jur etc*) **a house with vacant ~** une maison avec jouissance immédiate; (*Prov*) **~ is nine points of the law** (en fait de meubles) possession vaut titre.

(b) (*object*) possession *f*, bien *m*; (*territory*) possession.

possessive [pə'zesɪv] 1 *adj* **(a)** *person, nature, attitude, love* possessif. **to be ~ about sth** ne pas vouloir partager qch; **to be ~ towards** *or* **with sb** être possessif avec *or* à l'égard de qn; **an over~ mother** une mère abusive.

(b) (*Gram*) possessif.

2 *n* (*Gram*) possessif *m*. **in the ~** au possessif.

possessively [pə'zesɪvlɪ] *adv* d'une façon possessive.

possessiveness [pə'zesɪvnɪs] *n* (*U*) possessivité *f*.

possessor [pə'zesəʳ] *n* possesseur *m*; (*owner*) propriétaire *mf*. **to be the ~ of** être possesseur de, posséder; **he was the proud ~ of** il était l'heureux propriétaire de.

posset ['pɒsɪt] *n boisson composée de lait chaud, de vin ou de bière et d'épices.*

possibility [ˌpɒsə'bɪlɪtɪ] *n* **(a)** (*U*) possibilité *f*. **within the bounds of ~** dans l'ordre des choses possibles, dans la limite du possible; **if by any ~ ...** si par impossible ..., si par hasard ...; **there is some ~/not much ~ of success** il y a quelques chances/peu de chances de succès; **there is no ~ of my leaving** il n'est pas possible que je parte; **there is some ~** *or* **a ~ that I might come** il est possible que je puisse venir, il n'est pas impossible que je vienne; **it's a distinct ~** c'est bien possible.

(b) (*possible event*) possibilité *f*, éventualité *f*. **to foresee all the possibilities** envisager toutes les possibilités *or* éventualités; **we must allow for the ~ that he may refuse** nous devons nous préparer à *or* nous devons envisager l'éventualité de son refus; **he is a ~ for the job** c'est un candidat possible* *or* acceptable.

(c) (*promise, potential*) **the firm saw good possibilities for expansion** la compagnie voyait de bonnes possibilités d'expansion; **the scheme/the job has real possibilities** c'est un projet/un emploi qui offre toutes sortes de possibilités; **it's got possibilities!** c'est possible!, c'est à voir! *or* à étudier!

possible ['pɒsəbl] 1 *adj* **(a)** possible; *event, reaction, victory, loss* possible, éventuel. **it's just ~** ce n'est pas impossible; **it's not ~!** ce n'est pas possible!, pas possible!*; **it is ~ that** il se peut que + *subj*, il est possible que + *subj*; **it's just ~ that** il n'est pas impossible que + *subj*, il y a une chance que + *subj*; **it's ~ to do so** il est possible de le faire, c'est faisable; **it is ~ for me to leave** il m'est possible de partir; **to make sth ~** rendre qch possible; **he made it ~ for me to go to Spain** il a rendu possible mon voyage en Espagne; **if ~** si possible; **as far as ~** dans la mesure du possible; **as much as ~** autant que possible; **he did as much as ~** il a fait tout ce qu'il pouvait; **as soon as ~** dès que possible, aussitôt que possible; **as quickly as ~** le plus vite possible; **the best ~ result** le meilleur résultat possible; **one ~ result** un résultat possible *or* éventuel; **what ~ interest can you have in it?** qu'est-ce qui peut bien vous intéresser là-dedans?; **there is no ~ excuse for his behaviour** sa conduite n'a aucune excuse *or* est tout à fait inexcusable.

(b) (*perhaps acceptable*) *candidate, successor* possible*, acceptable. **a ~ solution** une solution possible *or* à envisager; **it is a ~ solution to the problem** ce pourrait être une manière de résoudre le problème.

2 *n* (*) **that idea is a ~** c'est une idée à suivre *or* à approfondir *or* à voir, c'est une possibilité; **a list of ~s for the job** une liste de personnes susceptibles d'être retenues pour ce poste; **he's a ~ for the match on Saturday** c'est un joueur éventuel pour le match de samedi; (*Sport*) **the P~s versus the Probables** la sélection B contre la sélection A.

possibly ['pɒsəblɪ] *adv* **(a)** (*with 'can' etc*) **as often as I ~ can** aussi souvent qu'il m'est (*or* me sera) matériellement possible (de le faire); **he did all he ~ could to help them** il a fait tout son possible pour les aider; **if I ~ can** si cela m'est (le moins du monde) possible, dans la mesure du possible; **I cannot ~ come** il m'est absolument impossible de venir; **how can I ~ allow it?** comment puis-je en toute conscience le permettre?; **it can't ~ be true!** ça ne se peut pas!, ce n'est pas vrai!

(b) (*perhaps*) peut-être. **~ they've gone already** ils sont peut-être déjà partis, peut-être qu'ils sont déjà partis, il se peut qu'ils soient déjà partis; **(yes) ~** peut-être bien; **~ not** peut-être pas.

possum ['pɒsəm] *n* (*: *abbr of* **opossum**) opossum *m*. (*fig*) **to play ~*** faire le mort.

post¹ [pəʊst] 1 *n* (*of wood, metal*) poteau *m*; (*stake*) pieu *m*; (*for door etc: upright*) montant *m*. (*Sport*) **starting/finishing ~** poteau de départ/d'arrivée; (*fig*) **to be left at the ~** manquer le départ, rester sur la touche; (*Sport, fig*) **to be beaten at the ~** être battu *or* coiffé sur le poteau; *V* **deaf, gate, lamp** *etc.*

2 *vt* **(a)** (*also* **~ up**) *notice, list* afficher. **'~ no bills'** 'défense d'afficher'.

(b) (*announce*) annoncer. **to ~ a ship/a soldier missing** porter un navire/un soldat disparu.

(c) to ~ a wall with advertisements poser *or* coller des affiches publicitaires sur un mur.

post² [pəʊst] 1 *n* **(a)** (*Mil, gen*) poste *m*. **at one's ~** à son poste; (*Brit: bugle call*) **last ~** (sonnerie *f* de) l'extinction *f* des feux; (*at funerals*) sonnerie aux morts; *V* **forward** *etc.*

(b) (*esp Can, US: trading ~*) comptoir *m*.

(c) (*situation, job*) poste *m*, situation *f*; (*in civil service, government etc*) poste. **a ~ as a manager** un poste *or* une situation de directeur.

2 *cpd*: (*US Mil*) **post exchange** économat *m*, coopérative *f*.

3 *vt* **(a)** (*also Mil: position*) *sentry, guard* poster. **they ~ed a man by the stairs** ils postèrent un homme près de l'escalier.

(b) (*send, assign*) (*Mil*) affecter (*to* à); (*Admin, Comm*) affecter, nommer (*to* à).

post³ [pəʊst] 1 *n* **(a)** (*esp Brit: U*) poste *f*; (*letters*) courrier *m*. **by ~** par la poste; **by return (of) ~** par retour du courrier; **by first-/second-class ~** ≃ tarif normal/réduit; **your receipt is in the ~** votre reçu est déjà posté; **I'll put it in the ~ today** je le posterai aujourd'hui; **it went first ~ this morning** c'est parti ce matin par le premier courrier; **to catch/miss the ~** avoir/manquer la levée; **take this to the ~** allez poster ceci, portez ceci à la poste *or* à la boîte*; **drop it in the ~ on your way** mettez-le à la boîte en route; **the ~ was lifted** *or* **collected at 8 o'clock** la levée a eu lieu à 8 heures; **has the ~ been** *or* **come yet?** le courrier est-il arrivé?, le facteur est-il passé?; **the ~ is late** le courrier a du retard; **is there any ~ for me?** est-ce que j'ai du courrier?, y a-t-il une lettre pour moi?; (*cost*) **~ and packing** frais *mpl* de port et d'emballage; (*Brit*) **Minister/Ministry of P~s and Telecommunications** ministre *m*/ministère *m* des Postes et (des) Télécommunications; *V* **registered** *etc.*

(b) (*Hist: riders etc*) poste *f*; *V* **general.**

2 *cpd*: (*Brit*) **post-bag** sac postal; (*esp Brit*) **postbox** boîte *f* aux lettres, boîte postale; **postcard** carte postale; (*Hist*) **post chaise** chaise *f* de poste; **post code** code postal; **post-free** franco, franc de port, en franchise; **posthaste** à toute allure; **postman** facteur *m*, préposé *m* (*Admin*); (*game*) **postman's knock** ≃ mariage chinois; **postmark** (*n*) cachet *m* de la poste; (*vt*) tamponner, timbrer; **date as postmark** pour la date se référer au cachet de la poste; **letter with a French postmark** lettre timbrée de France; **it is postmarked Paris** il y a 'Paris' sur le cachet; **postmaster** receveur *m* des postes; **Postmaster General** ministre *m* des Postes et Télécommunications; **postmistress** receveuse *f* des postes; **post office** *V* **post office; post-paid** port payé.

3 *vt* **(a)** (*send by ~*) envoyer *or* expédier par la poste; (*Brit: put in mailbox*) mettre à la poste, poster, mettre à la boîte*. **~ early for Christmas** n'attendez pas la dernière minute pour poster vos cartes et colis de Noël.

(b) (*Book-keeping: also* **~ up**) *transaction* inscrire. **to ~ an entry to the ledger** passer une écriture dans le registre; **to ~ (up) a ledger** tenir un registre à jour; (*fig*) **to keep sb ~ed** tenir qn au courant.

4 *vi* (*Hist: travel by stages*) voyager par la poste; prendre le courrier; (††: *hasten*) courir la poste, faire diligence.

post on *vt sep letter, parcel* faire suivre.

post up *vt sep* = **post³ 3b.**

post... [pəʊst] *pref* post... . **~glacial** postglaciaire; **~-1950** (*adj*) postérieur (*f* -eure) à (l'année) 1950, d'après 1950; (*adv*) après 1950; *V* **postdate, post-impressionism** *etc.*

postage ['pəʊstɪdʒ] 1 *n* (*U*) tarifs postaux *or* d'affranchissement. **what is the ~ to Canada?** quels sont les tarifs d'affranchissement *or* les tarifs postaux pour le Canada?; (*in account etc*) **~: £2** frais *mpl* de port: 2 livres; **~ due 20p** surtaxe 20 pence.

2 *cpd*: **postage rates** tarifs postaux; **postage stamp** timbre-poste *m*.

postal ['pəʊstəl] *adj district, code, zone* postal; *application* par la poste. **~ charges, ~ rates** tarifs postaux; **~ order** mandat(-poste) *m*, mandat postal (*for 10 francs* de 10 F); **the ~ services** les services postaux; **2-tier ~ service** courrier *m* à 2 vitesses; **~ vote** vote *m* par correspondance; **~ worker** employé(e) *m(f)* des postes.

postdate ['pəʊst'deɪt] *vt* postdater.

poster ['pəʊstəʳ] *n* affiche *f*; (*decorative*) poster *m*. **~ paint** gouache *f*.

poste restante ['pəʊst'restɑ̃:nt] *n, adv* (*esp Brit*) poste restante.

posterior [pɒsˈtɪərɪəʳ] **1** *adj* postérieur (*f* -eure) (*to* à). **2** *n* (* *hum*) derrière *m*, postérieur* *m*.
posterity [pɒsˈterɪtɪ] *n* postérité *f*.
postern [ˈpəʊstɜːn] *n* poterne *f*.
postgraduate [ˈpəʊstˈgrædjʊɪt] **1** *adj studies, course, grant* ≃ de troisième cycle (universitaire). ~ **diploma** diplôme décerné après la licence (≃ *D.E.S., maîtrise etc*).
2 *n* ≃ étudiant(e) *m(f)* de troisième cycle.
posthumous [ˈpɒstjʊməs] *adj* posthume.
posthumously [ˈpɒstjʊməslɪ] *adv publish, appear* après la mort de l'auteur, après ma (*or* sa *etc*) mort; *award* à titre posthume.
postilion [pəsˈtɪlɪən] *n* postillon *m*.
post-impressionism [ˈpəʊstɪmˈpreʃənɪzəm] *n* post-impressionnisme *m*.
post-impressionist [ˈpəʊstɪmˈpreʃənɪst] *adj, n* post-impressionniste (*mf*).
posting [ˈpəʊstɪŋ] *n* **(a)** (*U: sending by post*) expédition *f or* envoi *m* par la poste.
(b) (*assignment*) affectation *f*. **he got a ~ to Paris** il a été affecté *or* nommé à Paris.
post-mortem [ˈpəʊstˈmɔːtəm] **1** *adj*: ~ **examination** autopsie *f*. **2** *n* (*Med, also fig*) autopsie *f*. **to hold a ~** faire une autopsie; **to carry out a ~ on** faire l'autopsie de, autopsier.
postnatal [ˈpəʊstˈneɪtl] *adj* post-natal.
post office [ˈpəʊstˌɒfɪs] **1** *n* (*place*) (bureau *m* de) poste *f*; (*organization*) administration *f* des postes, service *m* des postes. **he works *or* he is in the ~** il est postier, il est employé des postes; **the main ~** la grande poste; *V* **general** *etc*.
2 *cpd*: **post office Box No. 24** (*abbr* **P.O. Box 24**) boîte postale no. 24 (*abbr* B.P. 24); (*US*) **Post Office Department** ministère *m* des Postes et Télécommunications; **he has £100 in post office savings *or* in the Post Office Savings Bank** il a 100 livres sur son livret de Caisse d'Épargne, il a 100 livres à la Caisse (Nationale) d'Épargne; **post office worker** employé(e) *m(f)* des postes, postier *m*, -ière *f*.
postpone [pəʊstˈpəʊn] *vt* renvoyer (à plus tard), remettre, ajourner, reporter (*for* de, *until* à).
postponement [pəʊstˈpəʊnmənt] *n* ajournement *m*, renvoi *m* (à plus tard), remise *f* à plus tard.
postposition [ˈpəʊstpəˈzɪʃən] *n* postposition *f*.
postprandial [ˈpəʊstˈprændɪəl] *adj* (*liter or hum*) (d')après le repas.
postscript [ˈpəʊsskrɪpt] *n* (*to letter: abbr* **P.S.**) post-scriptum *m inv* (*abbr* P.S. *m*); (*to book*) postface *f*. (*fig*) **I'd like to add a ~ to what you have said** je voudrais ajouter un mot à ce que vous avez dit.
postulant [ˈpɒstjʊlənt] *n* (*Rel*) postulant(e) *m(f)*.
postulate [ˈpɒstjʊlɪt] **1** *n* postulat *m*. **2** [ˈpɒstjʊleɪt] *vt* poser comme principe; (*Philos*) postuler.
posture [ˈpɒstʃəʳ] **1** *n* posture *f*, position *f*, attitude *f*; (*fig*) attitude, position. **his ~ is very bad** il se tient très mal. **2** *vi* (*pej*) poser, prendre des attitudes.
postwar [ˈpəʊstˈwɔːʳ] *adj* de l'après-guerre. (*Brit Fin*) ~ **credits** *crédits gouvernementaux résultant d'une réduction dans l'abattement fiscal pendant la seconde guerre mondiale;* **the ~ period, the ~ years** l'après-guerre *m*.
posy [ˈpəʊzɪ] *n* petit bouquet (de fleurs).
pot [pɒt] **1** *n* **(a)** (*for flowers, jam, dry goods etc*) pot *m*; (†: *for beer*) chope *f*; (*piece of pottery*) poterie *f*; (*for cooking*) marmite *f*, pot†; (*saucepan*) casserole *f*; (*tea~*) théière *f*; (*coffee~*) cafetière *f*; (*potful*) marmite, pot, casserole; (*chamber~*) pot (de chambre), vase *m* de nuit. **jam ~** pot à confiture; **~ of jam** pot de confiture; **~s and pans** casseroles, batterie *f* de cuisine; (*Prov*) **it's the ~ calling the kettle black** c'est la Pitié qui se moque de la Charité, c'est la poêle qui se moque du chaudron; (*fig*) **he can just keep the ~ boiling** il arrive tout juste à faire bouillir la marmite, il gagne tout juste de quoi vivre; (*in game etc*) **keep the ~ boiling!** allez-y!, à votre tour!; *V* **flower** *etc*.
(b) (* *fig*) (*prize*) coupe *f*; (*large stomach*) brioche* *f*, bedaine* *f*; (‡ *U: marijuana*) marie-jeanne* *f*. (*important person*) **a big ~*** une huile‡, une grosse légume*; **to have ~s of money*** avoir un argent fou, rouler sur l'or; **to have ~s of time*** avoir tout son temps; **to go to ~*** *[person]* se laisser complètement aller; *[business]* aller à la dérive; *[plans]* aller à vau-l'eau; **to have gone to ~*** être fichu*.
2 *cpd*: **potbellied** (*from overeating*) ventru, bedonnant*; (*from malnutrition*) au ventre ballonné; **potbelly** (*from overeating*) gros ventre, bedaine* *f*; (*from malnutrition*) ventre ballonné; (*fig pej*) **potboiler** œuvre *f* alimentaire; **this plant is pot-bound** cette plante est (trop) à l'étroit dans son pot; **potherbs** herbes potagères; **pothole** (*in road*) nid *m* de poule, fondrière *f*; (*underground*) caverne *f*, (*larger*) grotte *f*, gouffre *m*; **potholer** spéléologue *mf*, spéléo* *mf*; **potholing** spéléologie *f*; **to go potholing** faire de la spéléologie; **pothook** (*lit*) crémaillère *f*; (*Handwriting*) boucle *f*; **pothunter*** chasseur acharné de trophées; (*fig*) **to take potluck** manger à la fortune du pot; (*US*) **potpie** tourte *f* à la viande; **potpourri** *V* **potpourri;** (*Culin*) **pot roast** rôti braisé, rôti à la cocotte; **pot scourer, pot scrubber** tampon *m* à récurer; (*Archeol*) **potsherd** tesson *m* (de poterie); **to take a potshot at sth** tirer qch à vue de nez *or* au pifomètre*; **pot-trained** *child* propre.
3 *vt* **(a)** *plant, jam etc* mettre en pot. **~ted meat** *sorte f de rillettes de viande;* **~ted plant** plante *f* en pot, plante d'appartement; **~ted shrimps** *crevettes conservées dans du beurre fondu;* (*fig*) **a ~ted version of 'Ivanhoe'** un abrégé *or* un condensé d''Ivanhoé'; **he gave me a ~ted account of what had happened** il m'a raconté en deux mots ce qui était arrivé, il m'a fait un bref résumé de ce qui était arrivé.
(b) (*Billiards*) **to ~ the ball** blouser la bille.
(c) (*: *shoot*) *duck, pheasant* abattre, descendre*.
(d) (*) *baby* mettre sur le pot.
4 *vi* **(a)** (*make pottery*) faire de la poterie.
(b) (*shoot*) **to ~ at sth** tirer qch, canarder qch.
potable [ˈpəʊtəbl] *adj* potable.
potash [ˈpɒtæʃ] *n* (carbonate *m* de) potasse *f*.
potassium [pəˈtæsɪəm] **1** *n* potassium *m*. **2** *cpd* de potassium.
potation [pəʊˈteɪʃən] *n* (*gen pl*) libation *f*.
potato [pəˈteɪtəʊ] *pl* **~es 1** *n* pomme *f* de terre. **sweet ~** patate *f* (douce); *V* **fry**^{2}, **hot, mash** *etc*.
2 *cpd field, salad* de pommes de terre. **potato beetle** doryphore *m*; **potato blight** maladie *f* des pommes de terre; **potato bug** = **potato beetle; potato cake** croquette *f* de pommes de terre; (*US*) **potato chips,** (*Brit*) **potato crisps** pommes chips *fpl*; **potato-masher** presse-purée *m inv*; **potato omelette** omelette aux pommes de terre *or* parmentière; **potato-peeler** couteau éplucheur, épluche-légumes *m inv*; **potato soup** soupe *f* de pommes de terre, potage parmentier; **with a potato topping** recouvert de pommes de terre au gratin.
poteen [pɒˈtiːn, pɒˈtʃiːn] *n* (*Ir*) whisky *m* (illicite).
potency [ˈpəʊtənsɪ] *n [remedy, drug, charm, argument]* puissance *f*, force *f*; *[drink]* forte teneur en alcool.
potent [ˈpəʊtənt] *adj remedy, drug, charm* puissant; *drink* fort; *argument, reason* convaincant, puissant.
potentate [ˈpəʊtənteɪt] *n* potentat *m*.
potential [pəʊˈtenʃəl] **1** *adj energy, resources* potentiel; *sales, uses* possible, éventuel; *success, danger, enemy* potentiel, en puissance; (*Gram*) potentiel. **he is a ~ prime minister** c'est un premier ministre en puissance.
2 *n* (*U*) **(a)** (*Elec, Gram, Math, Phys etc*) potentiel *m*. **military ~** potentiel militaire.
(b) (*fig: promise, possibilities*) potentialités *fpl*. **to have ~** être prometteur; **to have great ~** promettre beaucoup, avoir de l'avenir; **he hasn't yet realized his full ~** il n'a pas encore donné toute sa mesure.
potentiality [pəʊˌtenʃɪˈælɪtɪ] *n* potentialité *f*. **potentialities** = **potential 2b.**
potentially [pəʊˈtenʃəlɪ] *adv* potentiellement.
pother [ˈpɒðəʳ] *n* (*U*) (*fuss*) agitation *f*; (*noise*) vacarme *m*, tapage *m*.
potion [ˈpəʊʃən] *n* (*medicine*) potion *f*; (*magic drink*) philtre *m*, breuvage *m* magique. **love ~** philtre (d'amour).
potpourri [pəʊˈpʊrɪ] *n [flowers]* fleurs séchées (*dans un pot-pourri*); (*fig, Literat, Mus*) pot-pourri *m*.
potter^{1} [ˈpɒtəʳ] *vi* mener sa petite vie tranquille, bricoler*. **to ~ round the house** suivre son petit traintrain* *or* faire des petits travaux dans la maison; **to ~ round the shops** faire les magasins sans se presser.
potter about *vi* suivre son petit traintrain*, bricoler*.
potter along *vi* aller son petit bonhomme de chemin, poursuivre sa route sans se presser. **we potter along** nous continuons notre traintrain*.
potter around, potter away *vi* = **potter about.**
potter^{2} [ˈpɒtəʳ] *n* potier *f*. **~'s clay** argile *f or* terre *f* à *or* de potier; **~'s wheel** tour *m* de potier.
pottery [ˈpɒtərɪ] **1** *n* **(a)** (*U*) (*craft, occupation*) poterie *f*; (*objects*) poteries, vaisselle *f* (*U*) de terre; (*glazed*) faïencerie *f* (*U*); (*ceramics*) céramiques *fpl*. **a piece of ~** une poterie; **Etruscan ~** poterie(s) étrusque(s).
(b) (*place*) poterie *f*. (*Brit Geog*) **the Potteries** la région des Poteries (*dans le Staffordshire*).
2 *cpd jug, dish* de *or* en terre, de *or* en céramique, de *or* en faïence.
potty^{1}* [ˈpɒtɪ] *n* pot *m* (de bébé). **~-trained** propre.
potty^{2}* [ˈpɒtɪ] *adj* (*Brit*) **(a)** *person* toqué*; *idea* farfelu. **to be ~ about sb/sth** être toqué de qn/qch*. **(b)** (*slightly pej*) **a ~ little house** une maison de rien du tout.
pouch [paʊtʃ] *n* petit sac; (*for money*) bourse *f*; (*for ammunition*) étui *m*; (*for cartridges*) giberne *f*; (*for tobacco*) blague *f*; (*US Diplomacy*) valise *f* (diplomatique); *[kangaroo etc]* poche *f* (ventrale); (*under eye*) poche.
pouf(fe) [puːf] *n* **(a)** pouf *m*. **(b)** (*Brit* ‡) = **poof.**
poulterer [ˈpəʊltərəʳ] *n* marchand *m* de volailles, volailler *m*.
poultice [ˈpəʊltɪs] **1** *n* cataplasme *m*. **2** *vt* mettre un cataplasme à.
poultry [ˈpəʊltrɪ] **1** *n* (*U*) volaille *f* (*U*), volailles.
2 *cpd*: **poultry dealer** volailler *m*; **poultry farm** exploitation *f* pour l'élevage de la volaille, élevage *m* de volaille(s); **poultry farmer** volailleur *m*, -euse *f*; (*U*) **poultry farming** élevage *m* de volaille(s); aviculture *f*.
pounce [paʊns] **1** *n* bond *m*, attaque subite. **2** *vi* bondir, sauter. **to ~ on** *prey etc* bondir sur, sauter sur; *book, small object* se précipiter sur; (*fig*) *idea, suggestion* sauter sur.
pound^{1} [paʊnd] **1** *n* **(a)** (*weight*) livre *f* (= *453,6 grammes*). **sold by the ~** vendu à la livre; **30p a ~** 30 pence la livre; **to demand one's ~ of flesh** exiger impitoyablement pleine réparation.
(b) (*money*) livre *f*. **~ sterling** livre sterling; **10 ~s sterling** 10 livres sterling; *V* **penny.**
2 *cpd*: **pound cake** quatre-quarts *m inv*; **pound note** billet *m* d'une livre.
pound^{2} [paʊnd] **1** *vt drugs, spices, nuts* piler; *meat* attendrir; *dough* battre, taper sur; *rocks* concasser; *earth, paving slabs* pilonner; *[guns, bombs, shells]* pilonner, marteler. **to ~ sth to a pulp/to pieces** réduire *or* mettre qch en bouillie/en miettes; **to ~ sth to a powder** pulvériser qch, réduire *or* mettre qch en poudre; **the guns ~ed the walls to pieces** les canons ont pulvérisé les murs; **the bombs ~ed the city to rubble** les bombes n'ont laissé que des décombres dans la ville; **the artillery ~ed the enemy line** l'artillerie a pilonné *or* martelé la ligne ennemie; **the waves ~ed the boat to pieces** les vagues ont mis le

bateau en miettes; **the sea was ~ing the boat** la mer battait sans arrêt contre le bateau; **to ~ sb (with one's fists)** bourrer qn de coups; **he ~ed the door (with his fists) in a fury** furieux, il martela la porte (à coups de poing) *or* il tambourina contre la porte; **he ~ed the stake into the ground with a rock** il enfonça le pieu dans le sol à l'aide d'une grosse pierre; *(fig)* **I tried to ~ some sense into his head** j'ai essayé de faire entrer *or* d'enfoncer un peu de bon sens dans son crâne; **she was ~ing the dough vigorously** elle battait la pâte énergiquement à coups de poing; **he was ~ing the piano** il tapait (comme un sourd) sur le piano, il jouait comme un forcené; **he was ~ing the typewriter all evening** il n'a pas arrêté de taper sur sa machine toute la soirée.

2 *vi* **(a)** *[heart]* battre fort, *(with fear)* battre la chamade; *[sea, waves]* battre (*on, against* contre). **he ~ed at** *or* **on the door** il martela la porte (à coups de poing), il frappa de grands coups à la porte; **he ~ed on the table** il donna de grands coups sur la table, il frappa du poing sur la table; **he was ~ing on the piano** il tapait (comme un sourd) sur le piano, il jouait comme un forcené; **the drums were ~ing** les tambours battaient, on entendait battre le(s) tambour(s).

(b) *(move heavily)* **to ~ in/out** *etc (heavily)* entrer/sortir *etc* en martelant le pavé (*or* le plancher); *(at a run)* entrer/sortir *etc* en courant bruyamment; **he was ~ing up and down his room** il arpentait sa chambre à pas lourds.

pound away *vi*: **to pound away at** *or* **on the piano** taper à tours de bras sur le piano, jouer comme un forcené; **he was pounding away at** *or* **on the typewriter all evening** il a tapé sur sa machine à tours de bras toute la soirée.

pound down *vt sep drugs, spices, nuts* piler; *rocks* concasser; *earth, paving slabs* pilonner. **to pound sth down to a pulp** réduire *or* mettre qch en bouillie; **to pound sth down to a powder** pulvériser qch, réduire *or* mettre qch en poudre.

pound out *vt sep*: **to pound out a tune on the piano** marteler un air au piano; **to pound out a letter on the typewriter** taper énergiquement une lettre à la machine.

pound up *vt sep drugs, spices, nuts* piler; *rocks* concasser; *earth, paving slabs* pilonner.

pound^3 [paʊnd] *n (for dogs, cars)* fourrière *f*.

poundage ['paʊndɪdʒ] *n* **(a)** *(tax/commission)* impôt *m*/commission *f* de tant par livre (*sterling ou de poids*). **(b)** *(weight)* poids *m* (en livres).

-pounder ['paʊndəʳ] *n ending in cpds*: *(gun)* **thirty-pounder** pièce *f or* canon *m* de trente; *(fish)* **three-pounder** poisson *m* de trois livres.

pounding ['paʊndɪŋ] *n* **(a)** (*V* **pound**^{2}) pilage *m*; pilonnage *m*; concassage *m*. **(b)** *[guns etc]* pilonnage *m*; *[heart]* battement *m* frénétique; *[sea, waves]* coups *mpl* de boutoir; *[feet, hooves etc]* martellement *m*. **the boat took a ~ from the waves** le bateau a été battu par les vagues; **the city took a ~** la ville a été pilonnée; *(fig)* **our team took a ~ on Saturday*** notre équipe s'est fait battre à plate(s) couture(s) samedi.

pour [pɔːʳ] **1** *vt liquid* verser. **she ~ed him a cup of tea** elle lui versa *or* servit une tasse de thé; **~ yourself some tea** prenez du thé, servez-vous *or* versez-vous du thé; **shall I ~ the tea?** je sers le thé?; **he ~ed me a drink** il m'a versé *or* servi à boire; **she ~ed the water off the carrots** elle a vidé l'eau des carottes; **to ~ metal/wax into a mould** couler du métal/de la cire; *(fig)* **to ~ money into a scheme** investir énormément d'argent dans un projet; **they ~ed more and more men into the war** ils ont envoyé au front un nombre toujours croissant de troupes; **she looked as if she had been ~ed into her dress*** elle était *or* semblait moulée dans sa robe; *V* **oil, water.**

2 *vi* **(a)** *[water, blood etc]* couler à flots, se déverser, ruisseler (*from* de). **water came ~ing into the room** l'eau se déversa *or* entra à flots dans la pièce; **water was ~ing down the walls** l'eau ruisselait le long des murs; **smoke was ~ing from the chimney** des nuages de fumée s'échappaient de la cheminée; **sunshine ~ed into the room** le soleil entrait à flots dans la pièce; **the sweat ~ed off him** il ruisselait de sueur; *(fig)* **goods are ~ing out of the factories** les usines déversent des quantités de marchandises.

(b) it is ~ing (with rain), it's ~ing buckets* il pleut à verse *or* à flots *or* à torrents *or* à seaux; **it ~ed for 4 days** il n'a pas arrêté de pleuvoir à torrents pendant 4 jours; *V* **rain.**

(c) *[people, cars, animals]* affluer. **to ~ in/out** entrer/sortir en grand nombre *or* en masse; **tourists are ~ing into London** les touristes affluent à *or* se déversent dans Londres.

(d) this saucepan does not ~ well cette casserole verse mal.

(e) (*US: act as hostess*) jouer le rôle de maîtresse de maison.

pour away *vt sep dregs etc* vider.

pour down *vi*: **the rain** *or* **it was pouring down** il pleuvait à verse *or* à flots *or* à torrents.

pour forth *vt sep* = **pour out 2b.**

pour in 1 *vi [water, sunshine, rain]* entrer (à flots); *[people, cars, animals]* arriver de toutes parts *or* en masse. **complaints/letters poured in** il y a eu un déluge *or* une avalanche de réclamations/de lettres.

2 *vt sep liquid* verser. *(fig)* **they poured in capital** ils y ont investi d'énormes capitaux.

pour off *vt sep liquid* vider.

pour out 1 *vi [water]* sortir à flots; *[people, cars, animals]* sortir en masse. **the words came pouring out** ce fut une cascade *or* un flot de paroles.

2 *vt sep* **(a)** *tea, coffee, drinks* verser, servir (*for sb* à qn); *dregs, unwanted liquid* vider. **shall I pour out?** je sers?; **the factory pours out hundreds of cars a day** l'usine sort des centaines de voitures chaque jour; **the country is pouring out money on such projects** le pays engloutit des sommes folles dans de tels projets.

(b) *(fig) anger, emotion* donner libre cours à; *troubles* épancher; *complaint* déverser. **to pour out one's heart to sb** s'épancher avec qn, épancher son cœur avec qn; **he poured out his story to me** il m'a raconté *or* sorti* son histoire d'un seul jet.

pouring ['pɔːrɪŋ] *adj* **(a)** (*also* **of ~ consistency**) *sauce etc* liquide. **(b) (in) the ~ rain** (sous) la pluie torrentielle *or* battante; **a ~ wet day** une journée de pluie torrentielle.

pout [paʊt] **1** *n* moue *f*. **... she said with a ~ ...** dit-elle en faisant la moue. **2** *vi* faire la moue. **3** *vt*: **to ~ one's lips** faire la moue; **'no' she ~ed** 'non' dit-elle en faisant la moue.

poverty ['pɒvətɪ] **1** *n* pauvreté *f*. **to live in ~** vivre dans le besoin *or* dans la gêne; **to live in extreme ~** vivre dans la misère *or* l'indigence *f or* le dénuement; **~ of ideas** pauvreté *or* manque *m or* indigence d'idées; **~ of resources** manque de ressources.

2 *cpd*: **poverty-stricken** *person, family* dans le dénuement; (* *hum*) fauché*, sans le sou; *district* miséreux, misérable; *conditions* misérable.

powder ['paʊdəʳ] **1** *n* (*all senses*) poudre *f*. **gun~** poudre à canon; **face ~** poudre de riz; (*Culin*) **milk ~** lait *m* en poudre; **to reduce sth to a ~** pulvériser qch, réduire qch en poudre; **in the form of a ~** en poudre; *(fig)* **to keep one's ~ dry** être paré; (*US*) **to take a ~**‡ décamper; *V* **baking, talcum** *etc.*

2 *cpd*: **powder blue** bleu pastel (*m*) *inv*; **powder blue dress** robe *f* bleu pastel; **powder compact** poudrier *m*; **in powder form** en poudre; **powder keg** (*lit*) baril *m* de poudre; *(fig)* poudrière *f*; **powder magazine** poudrière *f*; **powder puff** houppette *f*, (*big, fluffy*) houppe *f*; **powder room** toilettes *fpl* (pour dames).

3 *vt* **(a)** *chalk, rocks* réduire en poudre, pulvériser; *milk, eggs* réduire en poudre. **~ed milk** lait *m* en poudre; (*US*) **~ed sugar** sucre *m* glace.

(b) *face, body* poudrer; (*Culin*) *cake etc* saupoudrer (*with* de). **to ~ one's nose** (*lit*) se mettre de la poudre; (* *euph*) (aller) se refaire une beauté (*euph*); **trees ~ed with snow** arbres saupoudrés de neige; *(fig)* **nose ~ed with freckles** nez couvert de taches de rousseur.

powdering ['paʊdərɪŋ] *n*: **a ~ of snow** une mince pellicule de neige; **a ~ of sugar** un saupoudrage de sucre.

powdery ['paʊdərɪ] *adj substance, snow* poudreux; *stone etc* friable; *surface* couvert de poudre.

power ['paʊəʳ] **1** *n* **(a)** (*ability, capacity*) pouvoir *m*, capacité *f*; (*faculty*) faculté *f*. **it is not (with)in my ~ to help you** il n'est pas en mon pouvoir de vous aider; **he did everything** *or* **all in his ~ to help us** il a fait tout son possible *or* tout ce qui était en son pouvoir pour nous aider; **it is quite beyond her ~ to save him** elle est tout à fait impuissante à le sauver, il n'est pas en son pouvoir de le sauver; **mental ~s** facultés mentales; **the ~ of movement/of hearing** la faculté de se mouvoir/d'entendre; **he lost the ~ of speech** il a perdu la parole; **his ~s are failing with age** ses facultés déclinent *or* baissent avec l'âge; **his ~s of persuasion** son pouvoir *or* sa force de persuasion; **his ~s of resistance** sa capacité de résistance; **his ~s of imagination** sa faculté d'imagination; **the body's recuperative ~** la capacité *or* la faculté régénératrice du corps.

(b) (*strength*) *[person, blow, sun, explosion]* puissance *f*, force *f*. **the ~ of love/thought** la toute-puissance de l'amour/de la pensée; **sea/air ~** puissance navale/aérienne; **more ~ to your elbow!** puissiez-vous réussir!

(c) (*authority*) pouvoir *m* (*also Pol*), autorité *f*. **the ~ of the President/the police/the army** l'autorité *or* le pouvoir du Président/de la police/de l'armée; **student/pupil** *etc* **~** le pouvoir des étudiants/lycéens *etc*; **absolute ~** pouvoir absolu; **he has the ~ to act** il a le pouvoir d'agir; **they have no ~ in economic matters** ils n'ont aucune autorité en matière économique; **that does not fall within my ~(s), that is beyond** *or* **outside my ~(s)** ceci n'est pas *or* ne relève pas de ma compétence; **he exceeded his ~s** il a outrepassé *or* excédé ses pouvoirs; **at the height of his ~** à l'apogée de son pouvoir; **the ~ of veto** le droit de veto; (*Jur*) **the ~ of attorney** la procuration, la délégation des pouvoirs; (*Pol*) **in ~** au pouvoir; **to come to ~** accéder au pouvoir; **to have ~ over sb** avoir autorité sur qn; **to have sb in one's ~** avoir qn en son pouvoir; **to fall into sb's ~** tomber au pouvoir de qn.

(d) *(fig)* **they are the real ~ in the government** ce sont eux qui détiennent le pouvoir réel dans le gouvernement; *(fig)* **the ~ behind the throne** celui (*or* celle) qui tire les ficelles; **the Church is no longer the ~ it was** l'Église n'est plus la puissance qu'elle était; **he is a ~ in the university** il est très influent à l'université; **he is a ~ in the land** c'est un homme très puissant *or* très influent; **the ~s of darkness/evil** les forces *fpl* des ténèbres/ du mal; **the ~s that be** les autorités constituées.

(e) (*nation*) puissance *f*. **the nuclear/world ~s** les puissances nucléaires/mondiales; **one of the great naval ~s** une des grandes puissances navales.

(f) *[engine, telescope etc]* puissance *f*; (*Elec, Phys, Tech etc*) puissance, force *f*; (*energy*) énergie *f*; (*Opt*) puissance; (*output*) rendement *m*; (*electricity*) électricité *f*, courant *m*. **it works by nuclear ~** ça marche *or* fonctionne à l'énergie nucléaire; (*Elec*) **they cut off the ~** ils ont coupé le courant; (*Elec*) **our consumption of ~ has risen** notre consommation d'électricité a augmenté; **a low-~ microscope** un microscope de faible puissance; **magnifying ~** grossissement *m*; **engines at half ~** moteurs à mi-régime; **the ship returned to port under her own ~** le navire est rentré au port par ses propres moyens; *V* **horse** *etc.*

(g) (*Math*) puissance *f*. **5 to the ~ of 3** 5 puissance 3; **to the nth ~** (à la) puissance n.

(h) (*) **a ~ of** un tas* de, énormément de; **it did me a ~ of good** ça m'a fait un bien immense, ça m'a rudement* fait du bien; **he made a ~ of money** il a gagné un argent fou.

2 *cpd saw, loom, lathe* mécanique. **power-assisted** assisté; **powerboat** hors-bord *m inv*; (*Elec*) **power cable** câble *m* électrique; (*Elec*) **power cut** coupure *f* de courant; (*Aviat*) **power dive** descente *f* en piqué; **power-driven** à moteur; (*Elec*) électrique; **powerhouse** (*lit*) centrale *f* électrique; (*fig*) personne *f or* groupe *m* très dynamique; (*fig*) **a powerhouse of new ideas** une mine d'idées nouvelles; (*Elec*) **power line** ligne *f* à haute tension; (*Brit Elec*) **power point** prise *f* de courant *or* de force; **they are engaged in power politics** ils manœuvrent pour s'assurer une place prépondérante; (*Pol*) **power sharing** le partage du pouvoir; (*Elec*) **power station** centrale *f* électrique; **power structure** répartition *f* des pouvoirs.

3 *vt* (*gen pass*) faire marcher, faire fonctionner, actionner; (*propel*) propulser. **~ed by nuclear energy** qui marche *or* fonctionne à l'énergie nucléaire; **~ed by jet engines** propulsé par des moteurs à réaction.

-powered ['paʊəd] *adj ending in cpds*: **nuclear-powered** qui marche *or* fonctionne à l'énergie nucléaire; *V* **high** *etc*.

powerful ['paʊəfʊl] *adj* (*all senses*) puissant. **he gave a ~ performance in 'Hamlet'** il a donné une représentation puissante *or* émouvante dans 'Hamlet'; **a ~ lot of*** beaucoup de, un tas de*.

powerfully ['paʊəfəlɪ] *adv hit, strike* avec force; *affect* fortement; *write etc* puissamment. **to be ~ built** avoir une carrure puissante.

powerless ['paʊəlɪs] *adj* impuissant. **he is ~ to help you** il est dans l'impossibilité de vous aider, il est impuissant à vous aider; **they are ~ in the matter** ceci n'est pas de leur compétence, ils n'ont aucun pouvoir en la matière.

powerlessly ['paʊəlɪslɪ] *adv* impuissamment, dans l'impuissance.

powwow ['paʊwaʊ] 1 *n* assemblée *f* (*de Peaux-Rouges*); (* *fig*) tête-à-tête *m inv*. 2 *vi* (* *fig*) s'entretenir, palabrer (*pej*).

pox [pɒks] *n* (*gen*:†) vérole† *f*; (*: *syphilis*) vérole‡ *f*. **a ~ on ...!**†† maudit soit ...!; *V* **chicken, cow**[1] *etc*.

practicability [ˌpræktɪkə'bɪlɪtɪ] *n [road, path]* praticabilité *f*; *[scheme, suggestion]* praticabilité, possibilité *f* de réalisation. **to doubt the ~ of a scheme** douter qu'un projet soit réalisable.

practicable ['præktɪkəbl] *adj scheme, solution, suggestion* praticable, réalisable, exécutable; *road* praticable.

practical ['præktɪkəl] *adj* (*all senses*) pratique. **~ joke** farce *f*; (*US*) **~ nurse** infirmier *m*, -ière *f* auxiliaire; aide-soignant(e) *m(f)*; **he's very ~** il a beaucoup de sens pratique, c'est un homme très pratique.

practicality [ˌpræktɪ'kælɪtɪ] *n* **(a)** (*U*) *[person]* sens *m or* esprit *m* pratique; *[scheme, suggestion]* aspect *m* pratique. **to doubt the ~ of a scheme** douter qu'un projet soit viable (dans la pratique). **(b) practicalities** détails *mpl* pratiques.

practically ['præktɪklɪ] *adv* (*in a practical way*) d'une manière pratique; *say, suggest* d'une manière pragmatique; (*in practice*) pratiquement, dans la pratique, en fait; (*almost*) presque, pratiquement.

practicalness ['præktɪkəlnɪs] *n* = **practicality a.**

practice ['præktɪs] 1 *n* **(a)** (*habits, usage*) pratique *f*, coutume *f*, usage *m*. **to make a ~ of doing, to make it a ~ to do** avoir l'habitude *or* se faire une habitude de faire; **it is not my ~ to do so** il n'est pas dans mes habitudes de le faire; **as is my (usual) ~** comme je fais d'habitude; **it's common ~** c'est courant; *V* **restrictive, sharp** *etc*.

(b) (*exercise, training*) entraînement *m*; (*rehearsal*) répétition *f*. **he does 6 hours' piano ~ a day** il s'exerce au *or* il travaille le piano (pendant) 6 heures par jour, il fait 6 heures de piano par jour; **it takes years of ~** il faut de longues années d'entraînement, il faut s'exercer pendant des années; **I need more ~** je manque d'entraînement, je ne me suis pas assez exercé; **in ~** bien entraîné *or* exercé; **out of ~** rouillé (*fig*); (*Prov*) **~ makes perfect** c'est en forgeant qu'on devient forgeron (*Prov*).

(c) (*U: as opposed to theory*) pratique *f*. **in(to) ~** en pratique.

(d) (*profession: of law, medicine etc*) exercice *m*; (*business, clients*) clientèle *f*, cabinet *m*. **to go into ~ or to set up in ~ as a doctor/lawyer** s'installer *or* s'établir docteur/avocat; **he is in ~ in Valence** il exerce à Valence; **he has a large ~** il a une nombreuse clientèle, il a un cabinet important; *V* **general**.

2 *cpd flight, run* d'entraînement.

3 *vt* (*US*) = **practise.**

practise, (*US*) **practice** ['præktɪs] 1 *vt* **(a)** (*put into practice*) *charity, self-denial, one's religion* pratiquer; *method* employer, appliquer. **to ~ medicine/law** exercer la médecine *or* la profession de médecin/la profession d'avocat; (*loc*) **to ~ what one preaches** mettre en pratique ce que l'on prêche, prêcher d'exemple.

(b) (*exercise in*) (*Sport*) s'entraîner à; *violin etc* s'exercer à, travailler; *song, chorus, recitation* travailler. **she was practising her scales** elle faisait ses gammes; **to ~ doing** s'entraîner *or* s'exercer à faire; **I'm practising my German on him** je m'exerce à parler allemand avec lui; *V also* **practised.**

2 *vi* **(a)** (*Mus*) s'exercer; (*Sport*) s'entraîner; *[beginner]* faire des exercices. **to ~ on the piano** s'exercer au piano, travailler le piano; **he ~s for 2 hours every day** il fait 2 heures d'entraînement *or* d'exercices par jour.

(b) *[doctor, lawyer]* exercer. **to ~ as a doctor/lawyer** exercer la médecine *or* la profession de médecin/la profession d'avocat.

practised, (*US*) **practiced** ['præktɪst] *adj teacher, nurse, soldier* expérimenté, chevronné; *eye, ear* exercé; *movement* expert.

practising, (*US*) **practicing** ['præktɪsɪŋ] *adj doctor* exerçant; *lawyer* en exercice; *Catholic, Buddhist* pratiquant. **a ~ Christian** un (chrétien) pratiquant; **he is not a ~ homosexual** son homosexualité demeure à l'état latent.

practitioner [præk'tɪʃənə^r] *n* (*of an art*) praticien *m*, -ienne *f*; (*Med: also* **medical ~**) médecin *m*; *V* **general** *etc*.

praesidium [prɪ'sɪdɪəm] *n* præsidium *m*.

praetorian [prɪ'tɔːrɪən] *adj* prétorien.

pragmatic [præg'mætɪk] 1 *adj* **(a)** (*Philos, gen*) pragmatique. **(b)** (*dogmatic*) dogmatique, positif; (*officious*) officieux. 2 *n* (*U*) **~s** la pragmatique.

pragmatical [præg'mætɪkl] *adj* = **pragmatic 1b.**

pragmatism ['prægmətɪzəm] *n* (*V* **pragmatic**) pragmatisme *m*; dogmatisme *m*; caractère officieux.

pragmatist ['prægmətɪst] *adj, n* pragmatiste (*mf*).

prairie ['prɛərɪ] 1 *n* plaine *f* (herbeuse). (*US*) **the ~(s)** la Grande Prairie, les Prairies. 2 *cpd*: (*US*) **prairie dog** chien *m* de prairie, cynomys *m*; **prairie wolf** coyote *m*.

praise [preɪz] 1 *n* **(a)** éloge(s) *m(pl)*, louange(s) *f(pl)*. **in ~ of** à la louange de; **to speak (or write etc) in ~ of sb/sth** faire l'éloge de qn/qch; **it is beyond ~** c'est au-dessus de tout éloge; **I have nothing but ~ for what he has done** je ne peux que le louer de ce qu'il a fait; **I have nothing but ~ for him** je n'ai qu'à me louer *or* me féliciter de lui; **all ~ to him for speaking out!** je lui tire mon chapeau (*fig*) d'avoir dit ce qu'il pensait; **he was loud *or* warm in his ~(s) of ...** il n'a pas tari d'éloges sur ..., il a chanté les louanges de ...; *V* **sing** *etc*.

(b) (*Rel*) **a hymn of ~** un cantique; **~ be to God!** Dieu soit loué!; **~ be!*** Dieu merci!

2 *cpd*: **praiseworthy** *V* **praiseworthy.**

3 *vt* **(a)** *person, action, sb's courage etc* louer, faire l'éloge de. **to ~ sb for sth/for doing** louer qn de *or* pour qch/d'avoir fait; **to ~ sb to the skies** porter qn aux nues, chanter les louanges de qn.

(b) (*Rel*) louer, glorifier.

praise up *vt sep* chanter les louanges de.

praiseworthily ['preɪzˌwɜːðɪlɪ] *adv* d'une manière louable *or* méritoire.

praiseworthiness ['preɪzˌwɜːðɪnɪs] *n* mérite *m*.

praiseworthy ['preɪzˌwɜːðɪ] *adj person* digne d'éloges; *cause, attempt* digne d'éloges, louable, méritoire.

pram [præm] *n* (*Brit*) (*gen*) voiture *f* d'enfant; (*large*) landau *m*.

prance [prɑːns] *vi [horse, dancer etc]* caracoler. **the horse was prancing about** le cheval caracolait; **she was prancing* around *or* about with nothing on** elle se baladait* toute nue; **to ~ in/out** *etc [horse]* entrer/sortir en caracolant; *[person]* (*arrogantly*) entrer/sortir en se pavanant; (*gaily*) entrer/sortir avec pétulance.

prang‡† [præŋ] *vt* (*Brit*) (*crash*) *plane, car* bousiller*; (*bomb*) pilonner.

prank [præŋk] *n* (*escapade*) frasque *f*, fredaine *f*, équipée *f*; (*joke*) farce *f*, tour *m*, niche *f*. **a childish ~** une gaminerie; **to play a ~ on sb** jouer un tour à qn, faire une farce *or* une niche à qn.

prankster† ['præŋkstə^r] *n* farceur *m*, -euse *f*.

prate [preɪt] *vi* jaser, babiller (*pej*). **to ~ on about sth** parler à n'en plus finir de qch.

prattle ['prætl] 1 *vi [one person]* jaser, babiller (*pej*); *[several people]* papoter, jacasser; *[child]* babiller, gazouiller. **to ~ on about sth** parler à n'en plus finir de qch; **he ~s on and on** c'est un vrai moulin à paroles.

2 *n [one person]* bavardage *m*, babil *m* (*pej*), babillage *m* (*pej*); *[several people]* jacasserie *f*, papotage *m*; *[child]* babil, babillage.

prawn [prɔːn] *n* crevette *f* rose, bouquet *m*. **~ cocktail** salade *f or* mayonnaise *f* de crevettes; *V* **Dublin.**

pray [preɪ] 1 *vi* **(a)** prier. **they ~ed to God to help them** ils prièrent Dieu de les secourir; **he ~ed to be released from his suffering** il pria le ciel de mettre fin à ses souffrances; **to ~ for sb/sb's soul/one's country** *etc* prier pour qn/l'âme de qn/son pays *etc*; **he ~ed for forgiveness** il pria Dieu de lui pardonner; **to ~ for rain** prier pour qu'il pleuve, faire des prières pour la pluie; (*fig*) **we're ~ing for fine weather** nous faisons des prières pour qu'il fasse beau; **he's past ~ing for*** il est perdu; (*also hum*) c'est un cas désespéré.

(b) (†, *liter*) **~ be seated** veuillez vous asseoir, asseyez-vous je vous prie; (*iro*) **what good is that, ~?** à quoi cela peut-il bien servir, je vous le demande?

2 *vt* (†, *liter*) prier (*sb to do* qn de faire, *that* que + *subj*). **they ~ed God to help him** ils prièrent Dieu de lui venir en aide; **I ~ you** je vous (en) prie.

prayer [prɛə^r] 1 *n* **(a)** (*Rel*) prière *f* (*also U*). **to be at ~ or at one's ~s** être en prière; **he was kneeling in ~** il priait à genoux; **to say one's ~s** faire sa prière; **they said a ~ for him** ils ont fait *or* dit une prière pour lui, ils ont prié pour lui; (*as service*) **~s** office *m*; *V* **common, evening, lord** *etc*.

(b) (*liter*) **it is our earnest ~ that ...** nous espérons de tout cœur que ... .

2 *cpd*: **prayer book** livre *m* de messe; **the Prayer Book** le rituel de l'Église anglicane; **prayer mat** tapis *m* de prière; **prayer meeting** service religieux non-conformiste; **prayer wheel** moulin *m* à prières.

praying ['preɪɪŋ] 1 *n* (*U*) prières *fpl*. 2 *adj* en prière. (*Zool*) **~ mantis** mante religieuse.

pre... [priː] *pref* pré... . **~-glacial** préglaciaire; **~-1950** (*adj*) antérieur (*f* -eure) à (l'année) 1950, d'avant 1950; (*adv*) avant 1950; *V* **predate, prerecord** *etc*.

preach [priːtʃ] 1 *vi* (*Rel*) prêcher (*also fig pej*), évangéliser; (*in church*) prêcher. **to ~ to sb** prêcher qn; (*fig pej*) **to ~ to *or* at sb** prêcher *or* sermonner qn; (*fig*) **you are ~ing to the converted** vous prêchez un converti; *V* **practise.**

2 *vt religion, the Gospel, crusade, doctrine* prêcher; (*fig*) *patience* prêcher, préconiser, prôner; *advantage* prôner. **to ~ a sermon** prêcher, faire un sermon.

preacher ['priːtʃə^r] *n* prédicateur *m*; (*US: clergyman*) pasteur *m*.

preachify* ['priːtʃɪfaɪ] *vi (pej)* prêcher, faire la morale.
preaching ['priːtʃɪŋ] *n (U)* prédication *f*, sermon *m*; *(fig pej)* prêchi-prêcha* *m (pej)*.
preachy* ['priːtʃɪ] *adj (pej)* prêcheur, sermonneur.
preamble [priː'æmbl] *n* préambule *m*; *(in book)* préface *f*.
preamplifier [ˌpriː'æmplɪfaɪəʳ] *n* préamplificateur *m*, préampli* *m*.
prearrange ['priːə'reɪndʒ] *vt* arranger *or* organiser *or* fixer à l'avance *or* au préalable.
prebend ['prebənd] *n* prébende *f*.
prebendary ['prebəndərɪ] *n* prébendier *m*.
precarious [prɪ'keərɪəs] *adj* précaire.
precariously [prɪ'keərɪəslɪ] *adv* précairement.
precast ['priː'kɑːst] *adj*: ~ **concrete** béton précoulé.
precaution [prɪ'kɔːʃən] *n* précaution *f* (*against* contre). **as a** ~ par précaution; **to take** ~**s** prendre ses précautions; **to take the** ~ **of doing** prendre la précaution de faire.
precautionary [prɪ'kɔːʃənərɪ] *adj* de précaution, préventif. **as a** ~ **measure** par mesure de précaution.
precede [prɪ'siːd] *vt* (*in space, time*) précéder; (*in rank*) avoir la préséance sur. **the week preceding his death** la semaine qui a précédé sa mort, la semaine avant sa mort.
precedence ['presɪdəns] *n* (*in rank*) préséance *f*; (*in importance*) priorité *f*. **to have** *or* **take** ~ **over sb** avoir la préséance *or* le pas sur qn; **this question must take** ~ **over the others** ce problème a la priorité sur les autres, ce problème passe en priorité *or* est prioritaire.
precedent ['presɪdənt] *n* précédent *m*. **without** ~ sans précédent; **to act as** *or* **form a** ~ constituer un précédent; **to set** *or* **create a** ~ créer un précédent.
preceding [prɪ'siːdɪŋ] *adj* précédent. **the** ~ **day** le jour précédent, la veille.
precentor [prɪ'sentəʳ] *n* premier chantre, maître *m* de chapelle.
precept ['priːsept] *n* précepte *m*.
preceptor [prɪ'septəʳ] *n* précepteur *m*, -trice *f*.
precinct ['priːsɪŋkt] *n* **(a)** (*round cathedral etc*) enceinte *f*; (*boundary*) pourtour *m*. (*fig*) **within the** ~**s of** dans les limites de; (*neighbourhood*) **the** ~**s** les alentours *mpl*, les environs *mpl*; *V* **pedestrian, shopping.**
(b) (*US Police*) circonscription administrative; (*US Pol*) circonscription électorale, arrondissement *m*.
preciosity [ˌpresɪ'ɒsɪtɪ] *n* préciosité *f*.
precious ['preʃəs] **1** *adj* **(a)** *metal, person, moment* précieux; *object, book, possession* précieux, de valeur; (* *iro*) chéri, cher (*f* chère). ~ **stone** pierre précieuse; **don't waste** ~ **time arguing** ne perds pas un temps précieux à discuter; **this book is very** ~ **to me** ce livre a une très grande valeur pour moi, ce livre m'est très précieux; **he is very** ~ **to me** il m'est très précieux; (*iro*) **your** ~ **son*** ton fils chéri *or* adoré, ton cher fils; (*iro*) **your** ~ **car** ta voiture chérie, ta chère voiture.
(b) *style, language* précieux, affecté.
(c) (*) **a** ~ **liar** un beau *or* joli *or* fameux menteur.
2 *adv* (*) ~ **few,** ~ **little** très *or* fort *or* bien peu.
3 *n*: **(my)** ~! mon trésor!
precipice ['presɪpɪs] *n* à-pic *m inv*. **to fall over a** ~ tomber dans un précipice.
precipitance [prɪ'sɪpɪtəns] *n*, **precipitancy** [prɪ'sɪpɪtənsɪ] *n* précipitation *f*.
precipitant [prɪ'sɪpɪtənt] **1** *adj* = **precipitate 4. 2** *n* (*Chem*) précipitant *m*.
precipitate [prɪ'sɪpɪteɪt] **1** *vt* **(a)** (*hasten*) *event, crisis* hâter; (*hurl*) *person* précipiter (*into* dans).
(b) (*Chem*) précipiter; (*Met*) condenser.
2 *vi* (*Chem*) (se) précipiter; (*Met*) se condenser.
3 *n* (*Chem*) précipité *m*.
4 [prɪ'sɪpɪtɪt] *adj* irréfléchi, hâtif.
precipitately [prɪ'sɪpɪtɪtlɪ] *adv* précipitamment, avec précipitation, à la hâte.
precipitation [prɪˌsɪpɪ'teɪʃən] *n* précipitation *f* (*also Chem, Met*).
precipitous [prɪ'sɪpɪtəs] *adj* **(a)** escarpé, abrupt, à pic. **(b)** = **precipitate 4.**
precipitously [prɪ'sɪpɪtəslɪ] *adv* à pic, abruptement.
précis ['preɪsiː] **1** *n, pl* **précis** ['preɪsiːz] résumé *m*, précis *m*. **2** *vt* faire un résumé *or* précis de.
precise [prɪ'saɪs] *adj* **(a)** *details, instructions, description* précis; *measurement, meaning, account* précis, exact. **be (more)** ~! soyez (plus) précis *or* explicite!, précisez!; **there were 8 to be** ~ il y en avait 8 pour être exact *or* précis; **it was the** ~ **amount I needed** c'était exactement la quantité (*or* somme) qu'il me fallait; **he gave me that** ~ **book** c'est ce livre même qu'il m'a donné; **at that** ~ **moment** à ce moment précis *or* même.
(b) (*meticulous*) *movement* précis; *person, manner* méticuleux, minutieux; (*pej: over-*~) pointilleux, maniaque. **he is a very** ~ **worker** c'est un travailleur très méticuleux *or* minutieux, il est extrêmement méticuleux dans son travail; **in that** ~ **voice of hers** de sa façon de parler si nette.
precisely [prɪ'saɪslɪ] *adv explain, instruct, describe, recount* précisément; *use instrument* avec précision; (*exactly*) précisément, exactement. **... he said very** ~ **...** dit-il d'une voix très nette *or* en détachant nettement les syllabes; **at 10 o'clock** ~ à 10 heures précises *or* sonnantes; **you have** ~ **2 minutes to get out** vous avez très précisément *or* exactement 2 minutes pour sortir; **he said** ~ **nothing** il n'a absolument rien dit; **what** ~ **does he do for a living?** que fait-il au juste pour gagner sa vie?; ~! justement!, précisément!, exactement!
preciseness [prɪ'saɪsnɪs] *n* = **precision 1.**
precision [prɪ'sɪʒən] **1** *n* (*V* **precise**) précision *f*; exactitude *f*; minutie *f*. **2** *cpd instrument, tool* de précision. **precision bombing** bombardement *m* de précision.
preclude [prɪ'kluːd] *vt doubt* écarter, dissiper; *misunderstanding* prévenir; *possibility* exclure. **to be** ~**d from doing** être empêché *or* dans l'impossibilité de faire; **that** ~**s his leaving** cela le met dans l'impossibilité de partir.
precocious [prɪ'kəʊʃəs] *adj* précoce.
precociously [prɪ'kəʊʃəslɪ] *adv* précocement, avec précocité.
precociousness [prɪ'kəʊʃəsnɪs] *n*, **precocity** [prə'kɒsɪtɪ] *n* précocité *f*.
precognition [ˌpriːkɒg'nɪʃən] *n* préconnaissance *f*.
precombustion ['priːkəm'bʌstʃən] *n* précombustion *f*.
preconceived ['priːkən'siːvd] *adj*: ~ **idea** idée préconçue.
preconception ['priːkən'sepʃən] *n* idée préconçue, préconception *f*.
preconcerted ['priːkən'sɜːtɪd] *adj* arrêté *or* concerté d'avance *or* au préalable.
precondition ['priːkən'dɪʃən] **1** *n* condition nécessaire *or* requise, condition sine qua non. **2** *vt* conditionner (*sb to do* qn à faire).
precool ['priː'kuːl] *vt* refroidir d'avance.
precursor [priː'kɜːsəʳ] *n* (*person*) précurseur *m*; (*thing, event*) annonce *f*, signe avant-coureur.
precursory [prɪ'kɜːsərɪ] *adj remark* préliminaire; *taste, glimpse* annonciateur (*f* -trice).
predaceous, predacious [prɪ'deɪʃəs] *adj* = **predatory.**
predate ['priː'deɪt] *vt* **(a)** (*put earlier date on*) *cheque, document* antidater. **(b)** (*come before in time*) *event* précéder, avoir lieu avant, venir avant; *document* être antérieur (*f* -eure) à, précéder.
predator ['predətəʳ] *n* prédateur *m*, rapace *m*.
predatory ['predətərɪ] *adj animal, bird, insect* de proie, prédateur, rapace; *habits* de prédateur(s); *person* rapace; *armies* pillard; *look* vorace, avide.
predecease ['priːdɪ'siːs] *vt* prédécéder.
predecessor ['priːdɪsesəʳ] *n* prédécesseur *m*.
predestination [priːˌdestɪ'neɪʃən] *n* prédestination *f*.
predestine [priː'destɪn] *vt* (*also Rel*) prédestiner (*to* à, *to do* à faire).
predetermination ['priːdɪˌtɜːmɪ'neɪʃən] *n* détermination antérieure; (*Philos, Rel*) prédétermination *f*.
predetermine ['priːdɪ'tɜːmɪn] *vt* déterminer *or* arrêter au préalable *or* d'avance; (*Philos, Rel*) prédéterminer.
predicable ['predɪkəbl] *adj, n* (*Philos*) prédicable (*m*).
predicament [prɪ'dɪkəmənt] *n* situation difficile *or* fâcheuse. **I'm in a real** ~! (*puzzled*) je ne sais vraiment pas que faire!; (*in a fix*) me voilà dans de beaux draps!
predicate ['predɪkeɪt] **1** *vt* (*also Philos*) affirmer. **2** ['predɪkɪt] *n* (*Gram*) prédicat *m*; (*Philos*) prédicat, attribut *m*. **3** ['predɪkɪt] *adj* (*Gram*) attribut *inv*; (*Philos*) attributif.
predicative [prɪ'dɪkətɪv] *adj* = **predicate 3.**
predicatively [prɪ'dɪkətɪvlɪ] *adv* (*Gram*) en tant qu'attribut.
predict [prɪ'dɪkt] *vt* prédire.
predictable [prɪ'dɪktəbl] *adj* prévisible. **his reaction was very** ~ sa réaction était tout à fait prévisible *or* était facile à prévoir, il a réagi comme on pouvait le prévoir.
predictably [prɪ'dɪktəblɪ] *adv* d'une manière prévisible. ~**, he did not appear** comme on pouvait le prévoir, il ne s'est pas montré.
prediction [prɪ'dɪkʃən] *n* prédiction *f*.
predictive [prɪ'dɪktɪv] *adj* prophétique.
predilection [ˌpriːdɪ'lekʃən] *n* prédilection *f*. **to have a** ~ **for sth** avoir une prédilection *or* une préférence marquée pour qch, affectionner qch.
predispose ['priːdɪs'pəʊz] *vt* prédisposer (*to sth* à qch, *to do* à faire).
predisposition ['priːˌdɪspə'zɪʃən] *n* prédisposition *f* (*to* à).
predominance [prɪ'dɒmɪnəns] *n* prédominance *f*.
predominant [prɪ'dɒmɪnənt] *adj* prédominant.
predominantly [prɪ'dɒmɪnəntlɪ] *adv* d'une manière prédominante. **they are** ~ **French** il y a une prédominance de Français parmi eux.
predominate [prɪ'dɒmɪneɪt] *vi* prédominer (*over* sur), prévaloir.
pre-eminence [priː'emɪnəns] *n* prééminence *f*.
pre-eminent [priː'emɪnənt] *adj* prééminent.
pre-eminently [priː'emɪnəntlɪ] *adv* à un degré prééminent, par excellence.
pre-empt [priː'empt] *vt* acquérir par droit de préemption.
pre-emption [priː'empʃən] *n* (droit *m* de) préemption *f*.
pre-emptive [pri(ː)'emptɪv] *adj* préemptif. (*Bridge*) ~ **bid** (demande *f* de) barrage *m*.
preen [priːn] *vt feathers, tail* lisser. **the bird was** ~**ing itself** l'oiseau se lissait les plumes; **she was** ~**ing herself in front of the mirror** elle se pomponnait *or* s'arrangeait complaisamment devant la glace; (*fig*) **to** ~ **o.s. on sth/on doing** s'enorgueillir de qch/de faire.
pre-establish ['priːɪs'tæblɪʃ] *vt* préétablir.
pre-exist ['priːɪg'zɪst] **1** *vi* préexister. **2** *vt* préexister à.
pre-existence ['priːɪg'zɪstəns] *n* préexistence *f*.
pre-existent ['priːɪg'zɪstənt] *adj* préexistant.
prefab* ['priːfæb] *n* (*abbr of* **prefabricated building**) maison (*or* salle de classe *etc*) préfabriquée.
prefabricate [ˌpriː'fæbrɪkeɪt] *vt* préfabriquer.
preface ['prefɪs] **1** *n* (*to book*) préface *f*, avant-propos *m inv*; (*to speech*) introduction *f*, exorde *m*, préambule *m*.
2 *vt book* faire précéder (*by* de). **he** ~**d his speech by asking for volunteers** en guise d'introduction à son discours il a demandé des volontaires; **he** ~**d this by saying ...** en avant-propos il a dit ..., il a commencé par dire ... .
prefatory ['prefətərɪ] *adj remarks* préliminaire; *page* liminaire.

prefect ['pri:fekt] n (*French Admin*) préfet *m*; (*Brit Scol*) *élève des grandes classes chargé(e) de la discipline.*
prefecture ['pri:fektjʊəʳ] n préfecture *f*.
prefer [prɪ'fɜ:ʳ] vt (a) to ~ A to B préférer A à B, aimer mieux A que B; to ~ doing *or* to do aimer mieux *or* préférer faire; I ~ to take the train rather than go by car, I ~ taking the train to going by car j'aime mieux *or* je préfère prendre le train que d'aller en voiture; I ~ you to leave at once je préfère *or* j'aime mieux que vous partiez (*subj*) tout de suite; I would ~ not to (do it) je préférerais *or* j'aimerais mieux ne pas le faire; I much ~ Scotland je préfère de beaucoup l'Écosse, j'aime beaucoup mieux l'Écosse; (*of envelope etc*) Post Office ~red size format recommandé *or* approuvé par le service des Postes; (*US Fin*) ~red stock = preference shares (*V* preference 2).
(b) (*Jur*) *charge* porter; *action* intenter; *request* formuler; *petition* adresser; *argument, reason* présenter. to ~ a complaint against sb déposer une plainte *or* porter plainte contre qn.
(c) (*esp Rel: promote*) élever (*to* à).
preferable ['prefərəbl] *adj* préférable (*to sth* à qch). it is ~ to refuse il est préférable de refuser, il vaut mieux refuser.
preferably ['prefərəblɪ] *adv* de préférence.
preference ['prefərəns] 1 *n* (*liking*) préférence *f* (*for* pour); (*priority: also Econ*) priorité *f* (*over* sur), préférence. what is your ~? que préférez-vous?; in ~ to +*n* de préférence à, plutôt que; in ~ to doing plutôt que de faire; to give A ~ (over B) accorder *or* donner la préférence à A (plutôt qu'à B).
2 *cpd*: (*Brit Fin*) preference shares, preference stock actions privilégiées *or* de priorité.
preferential [,prefə'renʃəl] *adj tariff, treatment, terms* préférentiel, de faveur; *trade, ballot, voting* préférentiel.
preferment [prɪ'fɜ:mənt] *n* (*esp Rel*) avancement *m*, élévation *f* (*to* à).
prefiguration [,pri:fɪgə'reɪʃən] *n* préfiguration *f*.
prefigure [pri:'fɪgəʳ] *vt* (*foreshadow*) préfigurer; (*imagine*) se figurer d'avance.
prefix ['pri:fɪks] 1 *n* préfixe *m*. 2 [pri:'fɪks] *vt* préfixer.
preflight ['pri:'flaɪt] *adj* d'avant le décollage.
preform ['pri:'fɔ:m] *vt* préformer.
preformation ['pri:fɔ:'meɪʃən] *n* préformation *f*.
prefrontal [,pri:'frʌntl] *adj* préfrontal.
pregnancy ['pregnənsɪ] *n* [*woman*] grossesse *f*; [*animal*] gestation *f*. ~ test test *m* de grossesse.
pregnant ['pregnənt] *adj woman* enceinte; *animal* pleine, gravide; (*fig*) *pause, silence* lourd de sens. 3 months ~ enceinte de 3 mois; (*fig*) ~ with gros (*f* grosse) de, riche de.
preheat ['pri:'hi:t] *vt* chauffer à l'avance. ~ed oven four chaud.
prehensile [prɪ'hensaɪl] *adj* préhensile.
prehistoric ['pri:hɪs'tɒrɪk] *adj* préhistorique.
prehistory ['pri:'hɪstərɪ] *n* préhistoire *f*.
preignition ['pri:ɪg'nɪʃən] *n* auto-allumage *m*.
prejudge ['pri:'dʒʌdʒ] *vt question* préjuger de; *person* condamner *or* juger d'avance.
prejudice ['predʒʊdɪs] 1 *n* (a) préjugé *m*, prévention *f*; (*U*) préjugés, prévention(s). he found a lot of ~ in that country il a trouvé beaucoup de préjugés *or* de prévention(s) dans ce pays; racial ~ préjugés raciaux; to have a ~ against/in favour of avoir un préjugé *or* des préjugés *or* une prévention *or* des préventions contre/en faveur de; he is quite without ~ in this matter il est sans parti pris dans cette affaire.
(b) (*esp Jur: detriment*) préjudice *m*. to the ~ of au préjudice de; without ~ (to) sans préjudice (de).
2 *vt* (a) *person* prévenir (*against* contre, *in favour of* en faveur de); *V also* prejudiced.
(b) (*also Jur*) *claim, chance* porter préjudice à.
prejudiced ['predʒʊdɪst] *adj person* plein de préjugés *or* de prévention(s); *idea, opinion* préconçu, partial. he is ~/not ~ in that matter il est de parti pris/sans parti pris dans cette affaire.
prejudicial [,predʒʊ'dɪʃəl] *adj* préjudiciable, nuisible (*to* à). to be ~ to nuire à.
prelacy ['preləsɪ] *n* (*office*) prélature *f*; (*prelates collectively*) prélats *mpl*.
prelate ['prelɪt] *n* prélat *m*.
prelim* ['pri:lɪm] *n* (*Univ abbr of* preliminary exam) examen *m* préliminaire.
preliminary [prɪ'lɪmɪnərɪ] 1 *adj exam, inquiry, remark* préliminaire; *stage* premier, initial. 2 *n* (*gen pl*) preliminaries préliminaires *mpl*.
prelude ['prelju:d] 1 *n* (*Mus, gen*) prélude *m* (*to* de). 2 *vt* préluder à.
premarital ['pri:'mærɪtl] *adj* avant le mariage.
premature ['premətʃʊəʳ] *adj decision etc* prématuré; *birth* prématuré, avant terme. ~ baby (enfant) prématuré(e) *m(f)*, enfant né(e) avant terme; you are a little ~ vous anticipez un peu.
prematurely ['premətʃʊəlɪ] *adv arrive, decide, age* prématurément; *be born* avant terme. ~ bald/lined chauve/ridé avant l'âge; he was ~ grey il avait blanchi avant l'âge *or* prématurément.
premeditate [pri:'medɪteɪt] *vt* préméditer.
premeditation [pri:,medɪ'teɪʃən] *n* préméditation *f*.
premier ['premɪəʳ] 1 *adj* premier, primordial. 2 *n* (*Pol*) premier ministre.
première ['premɪɛəʳ] (*Cine, Theat*) 1 *n* première *f*. the film had its London ~ last night la première londonienne du film a eu lieu hier soir. 2 *vt* donner la première de.
premiership ['premɪəʃɪp] *n* (*Pol*) fonction *f* de premier ministre. during his ~ sous son ministère, pendant qu'il était premier ministre; he was aiming at the ~ il voulait être *or* il aspirait à être premier ministre.
premise ['premɪs] *n* (a) (*Philos, gen: hypothesis*) prémisse *f*.
(b) (*property*) ~s locaux *mpl*, lieux *mpl*; business ~s locaux commerciaux; on the ~s sur les lieux, sur place; off the ~s à l'extérieur, hors des lieux; to see sb off the ~s accompagner qn jusqu'à la sortie; get off the ~s videz *or* évacuez les lieux.
premium ['pri:mɪəm] 1 *n* (*gen, Comm, Fin, Insurance*) prime *f*. (*St Ex*) to sell sth at a ~ vendre qch à prime; (*Comm, fig*) to be at a ~ faire prime; to set *or* put a ~ on [*person*] faire grand cas de; [*situation, event*] donner beaucoup de valeur à.
2 *cpd*: (*Brit*) premium bond bon *m* à lots.
premonition [,pri:mə'nɪʃən] *n* prémonition *f*, pressentiment *m*. to have a ~ that avoir le pressentiment que, pressentir que.
premonitory [prɪ'mɒnɪtərɪ] *adj* prémonitoire, précurseur.
prenatal ['pri:'neɪtl] *adj* prénatal.
prenuptial [,pri:'nʌpʃəl] *adj* prénuptial.
preoccupation [pri:,ɒkjʊ'peɪʃən] *n* préoccupation *f*. his greatest ~ was discovering the facts sa préoccupation majeure était de découvrir les faits; his ~ with money son obsession *f* de l'argent; his ~ with finishing the book stopped him from ... il était tellement préoccupé de l'idée de terminer le livre qu'il n'a pas ... .
preoccupy [pri:'ɒkjʊpaɪ] *vt person, mind* préoccuper. to be preoccupied être préoccupé (*by, with* de).
preordain ['pri:ɔ:'deɪn] *vt* ordonner *or* régler d'avance; (*Philos, Rel*) préordonner.
prep* [prep] *n* (*Scol*) (a) (*Brit abbr of* preparation) (*work*) devoirs *mpl*, préparation *f*; (*period*) étude *f*. (b) ~ (school) (*abbr of* preparatory (school)); *V* preparatory.
prepack ['pri:'pæk] *vt*, **prepackage** ['pri:'pækɪdʒ] *vt* (*Comm*) préconditionner.
prepaid ['pri:'peɪd] *pret, ptp of* prepay.
preparation [,prepə'reɪʃən] *n* (a) (*U: act*) préparation *f*; (*Culin, Pharm etc: thing prepared*) préparation. ~s préparatifs *mpl*; the country's ~s for war les préparatifs de guerre du pays; to make ~s for sth prendre ses dispositions pour qch, faire les préparatifs de qch; [*book, film etc*] to be in ~ être en préparation; in ~ for en vue de; Latin is a good ~ for Greek le latin prépare bien au grec, le latin est une bonne formation pour le grec.
(b) (*U: Scol**) (*work*) devoirs *mpl*, préparation *f*; (*period*) étude *f*.
preparatory [prɪ'pærətərɪ] *adj work* préparatoire; *measure, step* préliminaire, préalable. ~ school (*Brit*) école primaire privée; (*US*) lycée privé; ~ to avant, préalablement à; en vue de; ~ to sth/to doing en vue de qch/de faire, avant qch/de faire.
prepare [prɪ'pɛəʳ] 1 *vt plan, speech, lesson, work, medicine, sauce* préparer; *meal, dish* préparer, apprêter; *surprise* préparer, ménager (*for sb* à qn); *room, equipment* préparer (*for* pour); *person* préparer (*for an exam* à un examen, *for an operation* pour une opération). to ~ sb for a shock/for bad news préparer qn à un choc/à une mauvaise nouvelle; to ~ o.s. for = to ~ for (*V* 2); to ~ the way/ground for sth préparer la voie/le terrain pour qch; *V also* prepared.
2 *vi*: to ~ for (*make arrangements*) *journey, sb's arrival, event* faire des préparatifs pour, prendre ses dispositions pour; (*prepare o.s. for*) *storm, flood, meeting, discussion* se préparer pour; *war* se préparer à; *examination* préparer; to ~ to do sth s'apprêter *or* se préparer à faire qch.
prepared [prɪ'pɛəd] *adj person, army, country* prêt; *statement, answer* préparé à l'avance; (*Culin*) *sauce, soup* tout prêt. be ~! soyez toujours sur le qui-vive!; be ~ for bad news préparez-vous à une mauvaise nouvelle; I am ~ for anything (*can cope with anything*) j'ai tout prévu, je suis paré; (*won't be surprised at anything*) je m'attends à tout; to be ~ to do sth être prêt *or* disposé à faire qch.
preparedness [prɪ'pɛərɪdnɪs] *n* état *m* de préparation. (*Mil*) state of ~ état d'alerte préventive.
prepay ['pri:'peɪ] *pret, ptp* prepaid *vt* payer d'avance. reply prepaid réponse payée; carriage prepaid port payé.
prepayment ['pri:'peɪmənt] *n* paiement *m* d'avance.
preponderance [prɪ'pɒndərəns] *n* prépondérance *f* (*over* sur).
preponderant [prɪ'pɒndərənt] *adj* prépondérant.
preponderantly [prɪ'pɒndərəntlɪ] *adv* de façon prépondérante.
preponderate [prɪ'pɒndəreɪt] *vi* l'emporter (*over* sur), être prépondérant.
preposition [,prepə'zɪʃən] *n* préposition *f*.
prepositional [,prepə'zɪʃənl] *adj phrase* prépositif; *use* prépositionnel.
prepositionally [,prepə'zɪʃənəlɪ] *adv* prépositivement.
prepossess [,pri:pə'zes] *vt* (*preoccupy*) préoccuper; (*bias*) prévenir, influencer; (*impress favourably*) impressionner favorablement.
prepossessing [,pri:pə'zesɪŋ] *adj appearance* avenant. he is very ~ il est très avenant, il présente* bien, il fait très bonne impression; she married a very ~ young man elle a épousé un jeune homme très bien*.
preposterous [prɪ'pɒstərəs] *adj* absurde, ridicule, grotesque.
preposterously [prɪ'pɒstərəslɪ] *adv* absurdement, ridiculement.
preposterousness [prɪ'pɒstərəsnɪs] *n* (*U*) absurdité *f*, grotesque *m*.
prepuce ['pri:pju:s] *n* prépuce *m*.
Pre-Raphaelite ['pri:'ræfəlaɪt] *adj, n* préraphaélite (*mf*).
prerecord ['pri:rɪ'kɔ:d] *vt song, programme* enregistrer à l'avance. ~ed broadcast émission *f* en différé.
prerelease ['pri:rɪ'li:s] *adj* (*Cine*) ~ showing avant-première *f*.
prerequisite ['pri:'rekwɪzɪt] 1 *n* condition *f* préalable. 2 *adj* nécessaire au préalable, préalablement nécessaire.
prerogative [prɪ'rɒgətɪv] *n* prérogative *f*, privilège *m*, apanage

m. (*Brit*) **to exercise the Royal P~** faire acte de souverain.

presage ['presɪdʒ] **1** *n* (*omen*) présage *m*; (*foreboding*) pressentiment *m*. **2** *vt* présager, annoncer, laisser prévoir.

presbyopia [ˌprezbɪ'əʊpɪə] *n* presbytie *f*.

Presbyterian [ˌprezbɪ'tɪərɪən] *adj, n* presbytérien(ne) *m(f)*.

Presbyterianism [ˌprezbɪ'tɪərɪənɪzəm] *n* presbytérianisme *m*.

presbytery ['prezbɪtərɪ] *n* (*part of church*) chœur *m*; (*residence*) presbytère *m*; (*court*) consistoire *m*.

preschool ['priː'skuːl] *adj years, age* préscolaire; *child* d'âge préscolaire.

prescience ['presɪəns] *n* prescience *f*.

prescient ['presɪənt] *adj* prescient.

prescribe [prɪs'kraɪb] *vt* (*gen, Admin, Jur, Med*) prescrire (*sth for sb* qch pour qn). **the ~d dose/form/punishment** la dose/le formulaire/la punition prescrit(e); **~d books** œuvres *fpl* (inscrites) au programme; **this diet is ~d in some cases** ce régime se prescrit dans certains cas; **to ~ for boils** faire une ordonnance pour des furoncles; **he ~d complete rest** il a prescrit *or* ordonné le repos absolu; (*fig*) **what do you ~?** que me conseillez-vous?, que me recommandez-vous?

prescription [prɪs'krɪpʃən] **1** *n* **(a)** (*U: gen, Admin, Jur, Med*) prescription *f*.

(b) (*Med*) ordonnance *f*. **to make out *or* write out a ~ for sb** rédiger *or* faire une ordonnance pour qn; **to make up *or* (*US*) fill a ~** exécuter une ordonnance; **it can only be obtained on ~** c'est délivré *or* vendu seulement sur ordonnance.

2 *cpd* (*made according to ~*) prescrit; (*available only on ~*) vendu sur ordonnance seulement. (*Brit Med*) **prescription charges** *somme f fixe à payer lors de l'exécution de l'ordonnance.*

prescriptive [prɪs'krɪptɪv] *adj* (*giving precepts*) *method, science, grammar, dictionary* normatif; (*legalized by custom*) *rights etc* consacré par l'usage.

presence ['prezns] *n* **(a)** présence *f*. **~ of mind** présence d'esprit; **in the ~ of** en présence de; (*Jur*) par-devant; (*frm*) **your ~ is requested** vous êtes prié d'y assister; (*liter, frm*) **they were admitted to the king's ~** ils furent admis en présence du roi; **he certainly made his ~ felt*** il n'est vraiment pas passé inaperçu; **a ghostly ~** une présence surnaturelle; **this country will maintain a ~ in North Africa** ce pays maintiendra une présence en Afrique du Nord; **there was a massive police ~ at the match** il y avait un imposant service d'ordre au match.

(b) (*bearing etc*) présence *f*, prestance *f*, allure *f*. **to lack ~** manquer de présence; **he has a good stage ~** il a de la présence (sur scène); **a man of noble ~** un homme de belle prestance *or* de belle allure.

present ['preznt] **1** *adj* **(a)** (*in attendance; in existence*) présent. **~ at/in** présent à/dans; **to be ~ at sth** être présent à qch, assister à qch; **those ~** les personnes présentes, ceux qui étaient là, l'assistance *f*; **who was ~?** qui était là?; **is there a doctor ~?** y a-t-il un docteur ici? *or* dans l'assistance?; **all ~ and correct!** tous présents à l'appel!; **~ company excepted** les personnes ici présentes exceptées, à l'exception des personnes ici présentes.

(b) (*existing now*) *state, epoch, year, circumstances, techniques, residence* présent (*after n*), actuel; (*in question*) présent (*before n*), en question; (*Gram*) présent (*after n*). **her ~ husband** son mari actuel; **the ~ writer believes** l'auteur croit; **in the ~ case** dans la présente affaire, dans le cas présent *or* qui nous intéresse *or* en question; **at the ~ day *or* time** actuellement, à présent (*V also* 2); **at the ~ moment** actuellement, à présent; (*more precisely*) en ce moment même; **the ~ month** le mois courant, ce mois-ci.

2 *cpd*: **present-day** *adj* actuel, d'aujourd'hui, contemporain, d'à présent; (*Gram*) **present perfect** passé composé.

3 *n* **(a)** (*also Gram*) présent *m*. **up to the ~** jusqu'à présent; **for the ~** pour le moment; **at ~** actuellement, à présent, en ce moment; **as things are at ~** au point où en sont les choses; (*loc*) **there's no time like the ~!** il ne faut jamais remettre au lendemain ce que l'on peut faire le jour même; (*Gram*) **in the ~** au présent.

(b) (*gift*) cadeau *m*. **it's for a ~** c'est pour offrir; **she gave me the book as a ~** elle m'a offert le livre; (*lit, fig*) **to make sb a ~ of sth** faire cadeau *or* don de qch à qn; *V* **birthday, Christmas** *etc*.

4 [prɪ'zent] *vt* **(a) to ~ sb with sth, to ~ sth to sb** (*give as gift*) offrir qch à qn, faire don *or* cadeau de qch à qn; (*hand over*) *prize, medal* remettre qch à qn; **she ~ed him with a son** elle lui a donné un fils; **we were ~ed with a fait accompli** nous nous sommes trouvés devant un fait accompli; (*Mil*) **to ~ arms** présenter les armes; **~ arms!** présentez armes!

(b) *tickets, documents, credentials, one's compliments, apologies* présenter (*to* à); *plan, account, proposal, report, petition* présenter, soumettre (*to* à); *complaint* déposer; *proof, evidence* apporter, fournir; (*Parl*) *bill* introduire, présenter; (*Jur etc*) *case* exposer. **to ~ o.s. at the desk/for an interview** se présenter au bureau/à une entrevue; **to ~ a cheque (for payment)** encaisser *or* présenter un chèque; **his report ~s the matter in another light** son rapport présente la question sous un autre jour, son rapport jette une lumière différente sur la question.

(c) (*offer, provide*) *problem* présenter, poser; *difficulties, features* présenter; *opportunity* donner. **the bay ~s a magnificent sight** la baie présente un spectacle splendide; **the opportunity ~ed itself** l'occasion s'est présentée; **to ~ the appearance of sth** avoir *or* donner (toute) l'apparence de qch; **the patrol ~ed an easy target** la patrouille offrait *or* constituait une cible facile.

(d) *play, concert* donner; *film* donner, passer; (*Rad, TV*) *play, programme* donner, passer; (*act as presenter of*) présenter. **we are glad to ~ ...** nous sommes heureux de vous présenter ...; **'~ing Glenda Jackson as Lady Macbeth'** 'avec Glenda Jackson dans le rôle de Lady Macbeth'.

(e) (*introduce*) présenter (*sb to sb* qn à qn). **may I ~ Miss Smith?** permettez-moi de vous présenter Mademoiselle Smith; (*Brit*) **to be ~ed (at Court)** être présenté à la Cour.

presentable [prɪ'zentəbl] *adj person, appearance, room* présentable; *clothes* présentable, mettable, sortable*. **go and make yourself (look) ~** va t'arranger un peu; **I'm not very ~** je ne suis guère présentable, je ne peux guère me montrer.

presentation [ˌprezən'teɪʃən] **1** *n* **(a)** (*U*) *[plan, account, proposal, report, petition]* présentation *f*, soumission *f*; *[complaint]* déposition *f*; *[parliamentary bill]* présentation, introduction *f*; *[cheque]* encaissement *m*; *[case]* exposition *f*. **his ~ of the play** (*the fact that he did it*) le fait qu'il ait donné la pièce; (*the way he did it*) sa mise en scène de la pièce; **on ~ of this ticket** sur présentation de ce billet; **the subject matter is good but the ~ is poor** le fond est bon mais la présentation laisse à désirer.

(b) (*introduction*) présentation *f*.

(c) (*gift*) cadeau *m*; (*ceremony*) remise *f* du cadeau (*or* de la médaille *etc*), ≃ vin *m* d'honneur. **who made the ~?** qui a remis le cadeau (*or* la médaille *etc*)?; **to make a ~ of sth to sb** remettre qch à qn.

2 *cpd*: *[book]* **presentation copy** (*for inspection, review*) spécimen *m* (gratuit), exemplaire envoyé à titre gracieux; (*from author*) exemplaire offert en hommage.

presenter [prɪ'zentəʳ] *n* (*Rad, TV*) présentateur *m*, -trice *f*.

presentiment [prɪ'zentɪmənt] *n* pressentiment *m*.

presently ['prezntlɪ] *adv* (*in a little while*) tout à l'heure, bientôt; (*esp US: now*) à présent, en ce moment.

presentment [prɪ'zentmənt] *n* *[note, bill of exchange etc]* présentation *f*; (*Jur*) déclaration *f* émanant du jury.

preservation [ˌprezə'veɪʃən] **1** *n* conservation *f*; (*from harm*) préservation *f*. **in good ~, in a good state of ~** en bon état de conservation.

2 *cpd*: (*Brit Admin*) **to put a preservation order on a building** classer un édifice; (*Archit etc*) **preservation society** association *f* pour la sauvegarde et la conservation (*des sites etc*).

preservative [prɪ'zɜːvətɪv] *n* (*Culin*) agent *m* de conservation.

preserve [prɪ'zɜːv] **1** *vt* **(a)** (*keep, maintain*) *building, traditions, manuscript, eyesight, position* conserver; *leather, wood* entretenir; *memory* conserver, garder; *dignity, sense of humour, reputation* garder; *peace* maintenir; *silence* observer, garder. **well-/badly-~d** en bon/mauvais état de conservation; **she is very well-~d** elle est bien conservée (pour son âge); **to ~ one's looks** conserver sa beauté; **have you ~d the original?** avez-vous gardé *or* conservé l'original?

(b) (*from harm etc*) préserver, garantir (*from* de), protéger (*from* contre). **may God ~ you!** Dieu vous garde!, que Dieu vous protège!; **(heaven *or* the saints) ~ me from that!*** le ciel m'en préserve!

(c) (*Culin*) *fruit etc* conserver, mettre en conserve. **~d** en conserve; **~d food** (*in bottles, cans*) conserves *fpl*; (*frozen*) produits surgelés.

(d) (*Hunting*) **~d** *fishing* réservé; *land, river* privé.

2 *n* **(a)** (*Culin: often pl*) (*Brit: jam*) confiture *f*; (*Brit: chutney*) condiment *m* à base de fruits; (*Brit, US: bottled fruit/vegetables*) fruits *mpl*/légumes *mpl* en conserve.

(b) (*Hunting*) réserve *f*. **game ~** chasse gardée *or* interdite.

preserver [prɪ'zɜːvəʳ] *n* (*person*) sauveur *m*; *V* **life**.

preshrunk ['priː'ʃrʌŋk] *adj* irrétrécissable.

preside [prɪ'zaɪd] *vi* présider. **to ~ at *or* over a meeting** présider une réunion.

presidency ['prezɪdənsɪ] *n* présidence *f*.

president ['prezɪdənt] **1** *n* (*Pol etc*) président *m*; (*US Comm*) président-directeur général, P.-D.G. *m*; (*US Univ*) recteur *m*. (*Brit Parl*) **P~ of the Board of Trade** ≃ ministre *m* du Commerce. **2** *cpd*: **president-elect** président désigné.

presidential [ˌprezɪ'denʃəl] *adj* présidentiel.

presidentially [ˌprezɪ'denʃəlɪ] *adv* en tant que président.

presidium [prɪ'sɪdɪəm] *n* = **praesidium**.

press [pres] **1** *n* **(a)** (*apparatus*) (*for wine, olives, cheese etc*) pressoir *m*; (*for gluing, moulding etc*) presse *f*; (*trouser ~*) presse à pantalon; (*racket ~*) presse-raquette *m inv*. **cider ~** pressoir à cidre; **hydraulic ~** presse hydraulique.

(b) (*Typ*) (*machine: also* **printing ~**) presse *f* (typographique); (*place, publishing firm*) imprimerie *f*; (*newspapers collectively*) presse. **rotary ~** presse rotative; **in the ~** sous presse; **to go to ~** *[book etc]* être mis sous presse; *[newspaper]* aller à l'impression; **correct at time of going to ~** correct au moment de mettre sous presse; **to set the ~es rolling** mettre les presses en marche; **to pass sth for ~** donner le bon à tirer de qch; **the national ~** la grande presse; **I saw it in the ~** je l'ai lu dans la presse *or* dans les journaux; **the ~ reported that ...** la presse a relaté que ..., on a rapporté dans la presse que ...; **to advertise in the ~** (*Comm*) faire de la publicité dans la presse *or* dans les journaux; (*privately*) mettre une annonce dans les journaux; **a member of the ~** un(e) journaliste; **is the ~ *or* are any of the ~ present?** la presse est-elle représentée?; **to get a good/bad ~** avoir bonne/mauvaise presse; *V* **yellow**.

(c) (*pressure: with hand, instrument*) pression *f*. **he gave his trousers a ~** il a donné un coup de fer à son pantalon.

(d) (*cupboard*) armoire *f*, placard *m*.

(e) († *or liter: crowd*) foule *f*, presse *f* (*liter*). **he lost his hat in the ~ to get out** il a perdu son chapeau dans la bousculade à la sortie.

2 *cpd campaign, card etc* de presse. **press agency** agence *f* de presse; **press agent** agent *m* de publicité; **press baron** magnat *m* de la presse; **press box** tribune *f* de la presse; **press button** bouton(-poussoir) *m*; **press clipping** coupure *f* de presse *or* de journal; **press conference** conférence *f* de presse; **press**

cutting = **press clipping; press-cutting agency** argus *m* de la presse; (*Brit Parl*) **press gallery** tribune *f* de la presse; (*Hist*) **press-gang** racoleurs *mpl*; (*fig*) **to press-gang sb into doing sth** faire pression sur qn *or* forcer la main à qn pour qu'il fasse qch; **press lord** = **press baron;** (*Brit*) **pressman** journaliste *m*; (*Brit*) **pressmark** cote *f* (*d'un livre de bibliothèque*); **press photographer** photographe *mf* de la presse, reporter *m* photographe; **press release** communiqué *m* de presse; **press report** reportage *m*; (*Brit*) **press stud** bouton-pression *m*, pression *f*; (*Gymnastics*) **press-up** traction *f*; **to do press-ups** faire des tractions *or* des pompes*; (*Cine*) **press view** avant-première *f*.

3 *vt* **(a)** (*push, squeeze*) *button, knob, switch, trigger, accelerator* appuyer sur; *sb's hand etc* serrer, presser. **he ~ed his fingertips together** il pressa les extrémités de ses doigts les unes contre les autres; **he ~ed his nose against the window** il a collé son nez à la fenêtre; **he ~ed her to him** il la serra *or* pressa contre lui; **she ~ed the lid on to the box** elle a fait pression sur le couvercle de la boîte (pour la fermer); **as the crowd moved back he found himself ~ed (up) against a wall** comme la foule reculait il s'est trouvé acculé *or* pressé contre un mur.

(b) *grapes, olives, lemons, flowers* presser. **to ~ the juice out of an orange** presser une orange, exprimer le jus d'une orange.

(c) *clothes etc* repasser, donner un coup de fer à.

(d) (*make by ~ing*) *object, machine part* mouler, fabriquer.

(e) (*fig*) (*in battle, game*) presser, attaquer constamment; *[pursuer]* talonner, serrer de près; *[creditor]* poursuivre, harceler. **to ~ sb for payment/an answer** presser qn de payer/de répondre; **to be ~ed for time/money** être à court de temps/d'argent, manquer de temps/d'argent; **I am really ~ed today** je suis débordé (de travail) aujourd'hui; **to ~ a gift/money on sb** presser qn d'accepter *or* insister pour que qn accepte (*subj*) un cadeau/de l'argent, offrir avec insistance un cadeau/de l'argent à qn; **to ~ sb to do sth** presser qn de *or* pousser qn à faire qch, insister pour que qn fasse qch; **to ~ sb into doing sth** forcer qn à faire qch; **he didn't need much ~ing** il n'y a guère eu besoin d'insister, il ne s'est guère fait prier; **we were all ~ed into service** nous avons tous été obligés d'offrir nos services *or* de mettre la main à la pâte*; **the box was ~ed into service as a table** la caisse a fait office de table; († *or hum*) **to ~ one's suit** faire sa demande (en mariage); *V* **hard.**

(f) *attack, advantage* pousser, poursuivre; *claim, demand* renouveler; insister sur. (*Jur*) **to ~ charges against sb** engager des poursuites contre qn; **I shan't ~ the point** je n'insisterai pas.

4 *vi* **(a)** (*exert pressure*) (*with hand etc*) appuyer, presser (*on* sur); *[weight, burden]* faire pression, peser (*on* sur); *[debts, troubles]* peser (*on sb* à qn). **time ~es!** le temps presse!, l'heure tourne!; (*fig*) **to ~ for sth** faire pression pour obtenir qch, demander instamment qch; **they are ~ing to have the road diverted** ils font pression pour (obtenir) que la route soit déviée.

(b) he ~ed through the crowd il se fraya un chemin dans la foule; **he ~ed in/out** *etc* il est entré/sorti *etc* en jouant des coudes; **they ~ed in/out** *etc* ils entrèrent/sortirent *etc* en masse; **the people ~ed round his car** les gens se pressaient autour de sa voiture.

press back *vt sep* **(a)** *crowd, enemy* refouler.

(b) (*replace etc*) *lid* remettre en appuyant. **he pressed the box back into shape** il redonna sa forme à la boîte d'une pression de la main.

press down 1 *vi* appuyer (*on* sur).

2 *vt sep knob, button, switch* appuyer sur. **she pressed the clothes down into the suitcase** elle appuya sur les vêtements pour les faire entrer dans la valise.

press in *vt sep panel etc* enfoncer.

press on *vi* (*in work, journey etc*) continuer, persévérer. **press on!** persévérez!, continuez!, n'abandonnez pas!; **we've got to press on regardless!*** continuons quand même!, nous ne pouvons pas nous permettre de nous arrêter!; (*fig*) **to press on with sth** continuer (à faire) qch.

press out *vt sep* **(a)** *juice, liquid* exprimer.

(b) *crease, fold* aplatir; (*with iron*) aplatir au fer *or* en repassant.

pressing [ˈpresɪŋ] **1** *adj business, problem* urgent; *danger* pressant; *invitation* instant. **he was very ~ and I could not refuse** il a beaucoup insisté et je n'ai pas pu refuser.

2 *n* *[clothes]* repassage *m*. **to send sth for cleaning and ~** faire nettoyer et repasser qch, envoyer qch au pressing.

pressure [ˈpreʃəʳ] **1** *n* **(a)** (*gen, Met, Phys, Tech*) pression *f*; (*Aut: tyre ~*) pression (de gonflage). **atmospheric ~** pression atmosphérique; **water ~** pression de l'eau; **a ~ of 2 kg to the square cm** une pression de 2 kg par cm²; **to exert** *or* **put ~ on sth** faire pression *or* exercer une pression sur qch, presser *or* appuyer sur qch; (*Tech etc*) **at full ~** à pression maxima; (*fig*) **the factory is now working at full ~** l'usine fonctionne maintenant à plein rendement; **he was working at high** *or* **full ~** il travaillait à la limite de ses possibilités; *V* **blood pressure** *etc.*

(b) (*fig: influence, compulsion*) pression *f*, contrainte *f*. **because of parental ~** à cause de la pression des parents, parce que les parents ont fait pression; **to put ~ on sb, to bring ~ to bear on sb** faire pression *or* exercer une pression sur qn (*to do* pour qu'il fasse); **they're putting the ~ on now*** ils nous (*or* le *etc*) talonnent maintenant; **he was acting under ~ when he said ...** il agissait sous la contrainte *or* il n'agissait pas de son plein gré quand il a dit ... (*V also* 1c); **under ~ from his staff** sous la pression de son personnel; **to use ~ to obtain a confession** user de contrainte pour obtenir une confession.

(c) (*fig: stress, burden*) **the ~ of these events/of life today** la tension créée par ces événements/par la vie d'aujourd'hui; **~ of work prevented him from going** le travail l'a empêché d'y aller, il n'a pas pu y aller parce qu'il avait trop de travail; **he has had a lot of ~ on him recently, he has been under a lot of ~ recently** il est débordé, il est sous pression*; **I work badly under ~** je travaille mal quand je suis sous pression*; **I can't work well under such ~** je ne fais pas du bon travail quand je suis talonné de cette façon.

2 *cpd:* (*Aviat*) **pressure cabin** cabine pressurisée *or* sous pression; **pressure-cook** cuire à la cocotte-minute ® *or* en autocuiseur; **pressure cooker** autocuiseur *m*, cocotte-minute *f* ®; **pressure-feed** alimentation *f* sous pression; **pressure gauge** manomètre *m*, jauge *f* de pression; (*fig: Pol etc*) **pressure group** groupe *m* de pression; (*Anat*) **pressure point** point *m* de compression digitale de l'artère; (*Space etc*) **pressure suit** scaphandre pressurisé.

3 *vt* (*) **to ~ sb to do** faire pression sur qn pour qu'il fasse; **to ~ sb into doing** forcer qn à *or* contraindre qn de faire.

pressurization [ˌpreʃəraɪˈzeɪʃən] *n* pressurisation *f*, mise *f* en pression.

pressurize [ˈpreʃəraɪz] *vt* **(a)** *cabin, spacesuit* pressuriser. (*Aviat*) **~d cabin** cabine pressurisée *or* sous pression. **(b)** (* *fig*) = **pressure 3.**

prestidigitation [ˈprestɪˌdɪdʒɪˈteɪʃən] *n* prestidigitation *f*.

prestige [presˈtiːʒ] *n* prestige *m*.

prestigious [presˈtɪdʒəs] *adj* prestigieux.

presto [ˈprestəʊ] *adv* (*Mus, gen*) presto. **hey ~!** le tour est joué!

prestressed [ˈpriːˈstrest] *adj*: **~ concrete** (béton armé) précontraint *m*.

presumable [prɪˈzjuːməbl] *adj* présumable.

presumably [prɪˈzjuːməblɪ] *adv* vraisemblablement, probablement. **you are ~ his son** vous êtes son fils, je présume.

presume [prɪˈzjuːm] **1** *vt* **(a)** (*suppose*) présumer (*also Jur*), supposer (*that* que); *sb's death* présumer. **every man is ~d (to be) innocent** tout homme est présumé (être) innocent; **it may be ~d that ...** on peut présumer que ...; **I ~ so** je (le) présume, je (le) suppose; **you are presuming rather a lot** vous faites pas mal de suppositions, vous présumez pas mal de choses.

(b) (*venture, take liberty*) se permettre (*to do* de faire).

2 *vi*: **you ~ too much!** vous prenez bien des libertés!; **I hope I'm not presuming** je ne voudrais pas être impertinent; (*when asking a favour*) je ne voudrais pas abuser de votre gentillesse; **to ~ (up)on** abuser de.

presumption [prɪˈzʌmpʃən] *n* **(a)** (*supposition*) présomption *f*, supposition *f*. **the ~ is that** on présume que, on suppose que, il est à présumer que; **there is a strong ~ that** tout laisse à présumer que.

(b) (*U*) présomption *f*, audace *f*, impertinence *f*. **if you'll excuse my ~** si vous me le permettez, si vous voulez bien pardonner mon audace.

presumptive [prɪˈzʌmptɪv] *adj heir* présomptif; (*Jur*) *evidence* par présomption.

presumptuous [prɪˈzʌmptjʊəs] *adj person, letter, question* présomptueux, impertinent.

presumptuously [prɪˈzʌmptjʊəslɪ] *adv* présomptueusement.

presumptuousness [prɪˈzʌmptjʊəsnɪs] *n* (*U*) = **presumption b.**

presuppose [ˌpriːsəˈpəʊz] *vt* présupposer.

presupposition [ˌpriːsʌpəˈzɪʃən] *n* présupposition *f*.

pretence, (US) pretense [prɪˈtens] *n* **(a)** (*pretext*) prétexte *m*, excuse *f*; (*claim*) prétention *f*; (*U: affectation*) prétention. **he makes no ~ to learning** il n'a pas la prétention d'être savant; **under** *or* **on the ~ of (doing) sth** sous prétexte *or* sous couleur de (faire) qch; *V* **false.**

(b) (*make-believe*) **to make a ~ of doing** faire semblant *or* feindre de faire; **he made a ~ of friendship** il a feint l'amitié; **it's all (a) ~** tout cela est pure comédie *or* une feinte; **I'm tired of their ~ that all is well** je suis las de les voir faire comme si tout allait bien; **his ~ of sympathy did not impress me** sa feinte sympathie m'a laissé froid, ses démonstrations de feinte sympathie m'ont laissé froid.

pretend [prɪˈtend] **1** *vt* **(a)** (*feign*) faire semblant (*to do* de faire, *that* que); *ignorance, concern, illness* feindre, simuler. **let's ~ we're soldiers** jouons aux soldats; (*pej*) **he was ~ing to be a doctor** il se faisait passer pour un docteur.

(b) (*claim*) prétendre (*that* que). **I don't ~ to know everything about it** je ne prétends pas tout savoir là-dessus, je n'ai pas la prétention de tout savoir là-dessus.

2 *vi* **(a)** (*feign*) faire semblant. **the children were playing at let's ~** les enfants jouaient à faire semblant; **I was only ~ing!** c'était pour rire!, je plaisantais!; **let's stop ~ing!** assez joué la comédie!; **let's not ~ to each other** ne nous jouons pas la comédie, soyons francs l'un avec l'autre.

(b) (*claim*) **to ~ to sth** prétendre à qch, avoir des prétentions à qch.

3 *adj* (*) *money, house etc* pour (de) rire*. **it's only ~!** c'est pour rire!*

pretended [prɪˈtendɪd] *adj* prétendu, soi-disant *inv*.

pretender [prɪˈtendəʳ] *n* prétendant(e) *m(f)* (*to the throne* au trône). (*Hist*) **the Young P~** le Jeune Prétendant (*Charles Édouard Stuart*).

pretense [prɪˈtens] *n* (*US*) = **pretence.**

pretension [prɪˈtenʃən] *n* **(a)** (*claim: also pej*) prétention *f* (*to sth* à qch). **this work has serious literary ~s** cette œuvre peut à juste titre prétendre à *or* cette œuvre a droit à la reconnaissance littéraire; (*pej*) **he has social ~s** il a des prétentions sociales.

(b) (*U: pretentiousness*) prétention *f*.

pretentious [prɪˈtenʃəs] *adj* prétentieux.

pretentiously [prɪˈtenʃəslɪ] *adv* prétentieusement.

pretentiousness [prɪˈtenʃəsnɪs] *n* (*U*) prétention *f*.

preterite [ˈpretərɪt] *n* prétérit *m*, passé *m* simple.

preternatural [ˌpriːtəˈnætʃrəl] *adj* surnaturel.
pretext [ˈpriːtekst] *n* prétexte *m* (*to do* pour faire). **under** *or* **on the ~ of (doing) sth** sous prétexte de (faire) qch.
prettify [ˈprɪtɪfaɪ] *vt child* pomponner; *house, garden, dress* enjoliver. **to ~ o.s.** se faire une beauté*, se pomponner.
prettily [ˈprɪtɪlɪ] *adv* joliment.
pretty [ˈprɪtɪ] **1** *adj* **(a)** (*pleasing*) *child, flower, music etc* joli (*before n*). **as ~ as a picture** *person* joli comme un cœur *or* à croquer; *garden etc* ravissant; **she's not just a ~ face*** elle n'a pas seulement un joli minois, elle a d'autres atouts que son joli visage; **it wasn't a ~ sight** ce n'était pas beau à voir; (*to parrot*) **~ polly!** bonjour Jacquot!; **he has a ~ wit†** il est très spirituel, il a beaucoup d'esprit.
(b) (*iro*) joli, beau (*f* belle). **that's a ~ state of affairs!** c'est du joli!; **you've made a ~ mess of it!** vous avez fait là de la jolie besogne!
(c) (*: *considerable*) *sum, price* joli, coquet. **it will cost a ~ penny** cela coûtera une jolie somme *or* une somme coquette.
2 *adv* assez. **it's ~ cold!** il fait assez froid!, il ne fait pas chaud!; **~ well!** pas mal!; **we've ~ well finished** nous avons presque *or* pratiquement fini; **it's ~ much the same thing** c'est à peu près *or* pratiquement la même chose; **he's ~ nearly better** il est presque *or* pratiquement guéri; *V* **sit**.
3 *cpd*: (*pej*) **pretty-pretty*** un peu trop joli.
pretty up* *vt sep* = **prettify**.
pretzel [ˈpretsl] *n* bretzel *m*.
prevail [prɪˈveɪl] *vi* **(a)** (*gain victory*) prévaloir (*against* contre, *over* sur), l'emporter, avoir l'avantage (*against* contre, *over* sur). **common sense will ~** le bon sens prévaudra *or* s'imposera.
(b) *[conditions, attitude]* prédominer, avoir cours, régner; *[wind]* prédominer; *[fashion, style]* être en vogue. **the situation which now ~s** la situation actuelle.
(c) to ~ (up)on sb to do décider qn à faire, persuader qn de faire; **can I ~ on you to lend me some money?** accepteriez-vous de me prêter de l'argent?
prevailing [prɪˈveɪlɪŋ] *adj wind* dominant; *belief, opinion, attitude* courant, actuellement répandu; *conditions, situation, customs* actuel; *fashion, style* en vogue.
prevalence [ˈprevələns] *n [illness]* fréquence *f*; *[belief, opinion, attitude]* prédominance *f*, fréquence; *[conditions, situation, customs]* caractère généralisé; *[fashion, style]* vogue *f*. **I'm surprised by the ~ of that idea** cela m'étonne que cette idée soit si répandue.
prevalent [ˈprevələnt] *adj belief, opinion, attitude* courant, répandu, fréquent; *conditions, situation, customs* actuel; *illness* répandu; *fashion, style* en vogue. **that sort of thing is very ~** ce genre de chose se voit (*or* se fait) partout, ce genre de chose est très courant.
prevaricate [prɪˈværɪkeɪt] *vi* équivoquer, biaiser, tergiverser, user de faux-fuyants.
prevarication [prɪˌværɪˈkeɪʃən] *n* faux-fuyant(s) *m(pl)*.
prevent [prɪˈvent] *vt* empêcher (*sb from doing, sb's doing* qn de faire); *event, action* empêcher; *illness* prévenir; *accident, fire, war* empêcher, éviter. **nothing could ~ him** rien ne pouvait l'en empêcher; **she couldn't ~ his death** elle n'a pu empêcher qu'il ne meure *or* l'empêcher de mourir; **I couldn't ~ the door from closing** je n'ai pas pu empêcher la porte de se fermer *or* éviter que la porte ne se ferme (*subj*).
preventable [prɪˈventəbl] *adj* évitable.
preventative [prɪˈventətɪv] *adj* préventif.
prevention [prɪˈvenʃən] *n* (*U*) prévention *f*. (*Prov*) **~ is better than cure** mieux vaut prévenir que guérir; **Society for the P~ of Cruelty to Animals** Société Protectrice des Animaux; *V* **accident, fire** *etc*.
preventive [prɪˈventɪv] **1** *adj medicine, measures, detention* préventif. **2** *n* (*measure*) mesure préventive (*against* contre); (*medicine*) médicament préventif (*against* contre).
preview [ˈpriːvjuː] *n [film, exhibition]* avant-première *f*. (*fig*) **to give sb a ~ of sth** donner à qn un aperçu de qch; (*Rad, TV*) **for a ~ of today's main events over now to Jack Smith** et maintenant pour un tour d'horizon des principaux événements de la journée je passe l'antenne à Jack Smith.
previous [ˈpriːvɪəs] **1** *adj* **(a)** *occasion, job, letter* précédent, antérieur (*f*-eure). **the ~ letter** la précédente lettre, la lettre précédente; **a ~ letter** une lettre précédente *or* antérieure; **in a ~ life** dans une vie antérieure; **~ to** antérieur à; **have you made any ~ applications?** avez-vous déjà fait des demandes?; **I have a ~ engagement** je suis déjà pris; (*Comm*) **no ~ experience necessary** aucune expérience (préalable) exigée; (*Jur*) **to have no ~ convictions** avoir un casier judiciaire vierge; (*Jur*) **he has 3 ~ convictions** il a déjà 3 condamnations; **the car has had 2 ~ owners** la voiture a déjà eu 2 propriétaires.
(b) (*frm: hasty*) prématuré. **this seems somewhat ~** ceci semble quelque peu prématuré; **you have been rather ~ in inviting him** votre invitation est quelque peu prématurée, vous avez été bien pressé de l'inviter.
2 *adv*: **~ to** antérieurement à, préalablement à, avant; **~ to (his) leaving he ...** avant de partir *or* avant son départ il ...; **~ to his leaving we ...** avant son départ *or* avant qu'il ne parte nous ... .
previously [ˈpriːvɪəslɪ] *adv* (*before*) précédemment, avant, auparavant; (*in the past*) dans le temps, jadis; (*already*) déjà.
prewar [ˈpriːˈwɔːʳ] *adj* d'avant-guerre.
prewash [ˈpriːwɒʃ] *n* prélavage *m*.
prey [preɪ] **1** *n* (*lit, fig*) proie *f*. **bird of ~** oiseau *m* de proie; **to be a ~ to** *nightmares, illnesses* être en proie à; **to fall a ~ to** être la proie de, être la victime de.
2 *vi*: **to ~ on** *[animal etc]* faire sa proie de; *[person]* faire sa victime de, s'attaquer (continuellement) à; *[fear, anxiety]* ronger, miner; **something is ~ing on her mind** il y a quelque chose qui la travaille*.
price [praɪs] **1** *n* **(a)** (*Comm etc*) (*cost*) prix *m* (*also fig*); (*estimate*) devis *m*; (*St Ex*) cours *m*. **to go up** *or* **rise in ~** augmenter; **to go down** *or* **fall in ~** baisser; **what is the ~ of this book?** combien coûte *or* vaut ce livre?, à quel prix est ce livre?; **that's my ~ — take it or leave it** c'est mon dernier prix — c'est à prendre ou à laisser; **to put a ~ on sth** fixer le prix de qch; **we pay top ~s for gold and silver** nous achetons l'or et l'argent au prix fort; **he got a good ~ for it** il l'a vendu à un prix élevé; (*fig*) **he paid a high** *or* **big ~ for his success** il a payé chèrement son succès; (*fig*) **it's a high** *or* **big ~ to pay for it** c'est le payer chèrement, c'est l'obtenir au prix d'un grand sacrifice, c'est consentir un grand sacrifice pour l'avoir; (*fig*) **it's a small ~ to pay for it** c'est consentir un bien petit sacrifice pour l'avoir; (*fig*) **every man has his ~** tout homme est corruptible à condition d'y mettre le prix; **I wouldn't buy it at any ~** je ne l'achèterais à aucun prix; (*fig*) **I wouldn't help him at any ~!** je ne l'aiderais à aucun prix!; **they want peace at any ~** ils veulent la paix coûte que coûte *or* à tout prix; (*fig*) **will you do it? — not at any ~!** vous allez le faire? — pour rien au monde! *or* pas question!; **you can get it but at a ~!** vous pouvez l'avoir mais cela vous coûtera cher; (*fig*) **he's famous now but at what a ~!** il est célèbre maintenant mais à quel prix!; **he'll do it for a ~** il le fera si on y met le prix; **the ~ is right** c'est un prix normal; (*Brit*) **Secretary of State for/Department of P~s** ministre *m*/ministère *m* des prix, ≃ Direction générale de la concurrence et des prix; **ask him for a ~ for putting in a new window** demandez-lui un devis *or* combien ça coûterait *or* quel est son prix pour poser une nouvelle fenêtre; (*St Ex*) **to make a ~** fixer un cours; (*St Ex*) **market ~** cours *m* du marché; (*fig*) **there's a ~ on his head, he has got a ~ on his head** sa tête a été mise à prix; **to put a ~ on sb's head** mettre à prix la tête de qn; *V* **cheap, closing, reduced** *etc*.
(b) (*value*) prix *m*, valeur *f*. **to put a ~ on a jewel/picture** évaluer un bijou/un tableau; (*fig*) **I cannot put a ~ on his friendship** son amitié n'a pas de prix (pour moi), je ne saurais dire combien j'apprécie son amitié; **he sets** *or* **puts a high ~ on loyalty** il attache beaucoup de valeur *or* un grand prix à la loyauté, il fait très grand cas de la loyauté; (*liter*) **beyond ~, without ~** qui n'a pas de prix, hors de prix, sans prix.
(c) (*Betting*) cote *f*. **what ~ are they giving on Black Beauty?** quelle est la cote de Black Beauty?; (*fig*) **what ~* all his promises now?** que valent *or* que dites-vous de toutes ses promesses maintenant?; **what ~* he'll change his mind?** vous pariez combien qu'il va changer d'avis?
2 *cpd control, index, war* des prix; *reduction, rise* de(s) prix. **price bracket = price range; price cut** réduction *f*, rabais *m*; **price cutting** réductions *fpl* de prix; **price fixing** (*by government*) contrôle *m* des prix; (*pej: by firms*) alignement *m* des prix; **price freeze** blocage *m* des prix; **to put a price limit on sth** fixer le prix maximum de qch; **my price limit is £400** je n'irai pas au-dessus de 400 livres; **price list** tarif *m*, prix courant(s); **price range** éventail *m or* gamme *f* de prix; **within my price range** dans mes prix; **in the medium price range** d'un prix modéré, dans les prix moyens; (*pej: by firms*) **price-rigging** alignement *m* des prix; **price ring** cartel *m* des prix; **prices and incomes policy** politique *f* des prix et des revenus; (*lit*) **price tag** étiquette *f*; (*fig*) **it's got a heavy price tag** le prix est très élevé, ça coûte cher; **what's the price tag on that house?** quel prix demandent-ils pour cette maison?; **price ticket = price tag**.
3 *vt* (*fix ~ of*) fixer le prix de; (*mark ~ on*) marquer le prix de; (*ask ~ of*) demander le prix de, s'informer du prix de; (*fig: estimate value of*) évaluer. **it is ~d at £10** ça coûte 10 livres, ça se vend 10 livres; **it is ~d rather high** c'est plutôt cher; **it isn't ~d in the window** le prix n'est pas (marqué) en vitrine *or* à l'étalage.
price down *vt sep* (*Comm*) (*reduce price of*) réduire le prix de, solder; (*mark lower price on*) inscrire un prix réduit sur, changer l'étiquette de.
price out *vt sep*: **to price one's goods out of the market** perdre un marché à vouloir demander des prix trop élevés; **Japanese radios have priced ours out (of the market)** nos radios ne peuvent plus soutenir la concurrence des prix japonais; **the French have priced us out of that market** les bas prix pratiqués par les Français nous ont chassés de ce marché.
price up *vt sep* (*Comm*) (*raise price of*) augmenter; (*mark higher price on*) inscrire un prix plus élevé sur, changer l'étiquette de.
-priced [praɪst] *adj ending in cpds*: **high-priced** coûteux, cher; *V* **low**[1] *etc*.
priceless [ˈpraɪslɪs] *adj* **(a)** *picture, jewels* qui n'a pas de prix, sans prix, hors de prix, inestimable; *friendship, contribution, gift* inestimable, très précieux. **(b)** (*: *amusing*) impayable*.
pricey* [ˈpraɪsɪ] *adj* coûteux, cher, chérot* (*m only*).
prick [prɪk] **1** *n* **(a)** (*act, sensation, mark*) piqûre *f*. **to give sth a ~** piquer qch; (*fig*) **the ~s of conscience** les aiguillons *mpl* de la conscience, le remords; *V* **kick**.
(b) (**: *penis*) verge *f*, bitte** *f*.
2 *vt* **(a)** *[person, thorn, pin, hypodermic]* piquer; *balloon, blister* crever; *name on list etc* piquer, pointer. **she ~ed her finger with a pin** elle s'est piqué le doigt avec une épingle; **to ~ a hole in sth** faire un trou d'épingle (*or* d'aiguille *etc*) dans qch; (*fig*) **his conscience ~ed him** il avait mauvaise conscience, il n'avait pas la conscience tranquille.
(b) to ~ (up) one's ears *[animal]* dresser les oreilles; *[person]* (*fig*) dresser *or* tendre *or* prêter l'oreille.
3 *vi* **(a)** *[thorn etc]* piquer. (*fig*) **his conscience was ~ing** il avait mauvaise conscience.

(b) my eyes are ~ing les yeux me cuisent; **my toe is ~ing** j'ai des fourmis dans l'orteil.

prick out *vt sep* **(a)** *seedlings* repiquer.

(b) (*with pin etc*) *outline, design* piquer, tracer en piquant.

prick up 1 *vi* dresser l'oreille (*lit, fig*).

2 *vt sep* = **prick 2b.**

pricking ['prɪkɪŋ] *n* picotement *m*, sensation cuisante. (*fig*) **~s of conscience** remords *m(pl)*.

prickle ['prɪkl] **1** *n* **(a)** *[plant]* épine *f*, piquant *m*; *[hedgehog etc]* piquant. **(b)** (*sensation: on skin etc*) picotement *m*, sensation cuisante. **2** *vt* piquer. **3** *vi [skin, fingers etc]* fourmiller, picoter.

prickly ['prɪklɪ] *adj plant* épineux, hérissé; *animal* hérissé, armé de piquants; (*fig*) *person* irritable, hargneux; *subject* épineux, délicat. **his beard was ~** sa barbe piquait; **my arm feels ~** j'ai des fourmis *or* des fourmillements dans le bras; (*fig*) **he is as ~ as a porcupine** c'est un vrai hérisson; (*Med*) **~ heat** fièvre *f* miliaire; (*Bot*) **~ pear** (*fruit*) figue *f* de Barbarie; (*tree*) figuier *m* de Barbarie.

pride [praɪd] **1** *n* **(a)** (*U*) (*self-respect*) orgueil *m*, amour-propre *m*; (*satisfaction*) fierté *f*; (*pej: arrogance*) orgueil, arrogance *f*, vanité *f*. **his ~ was hurt** il était blessé dans son orgueil *or* dans son amour-propre; **he has too much ~ to ask for help** il est trop fier *or* il a trop d'amour-propre pour demander de l'aide; **she has no ~** elle n'a pas d'amour-propre; **false ~** vanité; (*Prov*) **~ comes** *or* **goes before a fall** péché d'orgueil ne va pas sans danger; (*Prov*) **~ feels no pain** il faut souffrir pour être belle (*Prov*); **her son's success is a great source of ~ to her** elle s'enorgueillit *or* elle est très fière du succès de son fils; **her ~ in her family** la fierté qu'elle tire de sa famille; **he spoke of them with ~** il parla d'eux avec fierté; **to take a ~ in** *children, achievements* être très fier de; *house, car etc* prendre (grand) soin de; **she takes a ~ in her appearance** elle prend soin de sa personne; **to take (a) ~ in doing** mettre sa fierté à faire; **to take** *or* **have ~ of place** avoir la place d'honneur.

(b) (*object of ~*) fierté *f*. **she is her father's ~ and joy** elle est la fierté de son père.

(c) a ~ of lions une troupe de lions.

2 *vt*: **to ~ o.s. (up)on (doing) sth** être fier *or* s'enorgueillir de (faire) qch.

priest [pri:st] **1** *n* (*Christian, pagan*) prêtre *m*; (*parish ~*) curé *m*. (*collectively*) **the ~s** le clergé; *V* **assistant, high** *etc*. **2** *cpd*: (*pej*) **priest-ridden** dominé par le clergé, sous la tutelle des curés (*pej*).

priestess ['pri:stɪs] *n* prêtresse *f*.

priesthood ['pri:sthʊd] *n* (*function*) prêtrise *f*, sacerdoce *m*; (*priests collectively*) clergé *m*. **to enter the ~** se faire prêtre, prendre la soutane.

priestly ['pri:stlɪ] *adj* sacerdotal, de prêtre.

prig [prɪg] *n* pharisien(ne) *m(f)*. **what a ~ she is!** ce qu'elle peut se prendre au sérieux!; **don't be such a ~!** ne fais pas le petit saint! (*or* la petite sainte!).

priggish ['prɪgɪʃ] *adj* pharisaïque, suffisant, fat (*m only*).

priggishness ['prɪgɪʃnɪs] *n* (*U*) pharisaïsme *m*, suffisance *f*, fatuité *f*.

prim [prɪm] *adj person* (*also* **~ and proper**) (*prudish*) collet monté, guindé; (*demure*) très convenable, comme il faut*; *manner, smile, look, expression* compassé, guindé, contraint; *dress, hat* très correct, très convenable; *house, garden* trop coquet *or* net *or* impeccable.

primacy ['praɪməsɪ] *n* (*supremacy*) primauté *f*; (*Rel*) primatie *f*.

primadonna ['pri:mə'dɒnə] *n* prima donna *f inv*.

prima facie ['praɪmə'feɪʃɪ] **1** *adv* à première vue, de prime abord.

2 *adj* (*Jur*) recevable, bien fondé; (*gen*) légitime (à première vue). **to have a ~ case** (*Jur*) avoir une affaire recevable; (*gen*) avoir raison à première vue; (*Jur*) **to be ~ evidence** avoir force probante; **there are ~ reasons why ...** il existe à première vue des raisons très légitimes qui expliquent que ... .

primal ['praɪməl] *adj* (*first in time*) primitif, des premiers âges, primordial; (*first in importance*) principal, primordial, premier (*before n*).

primarily ['praɪmərɪlɪ] *adv* (*chiefly*) essentiellement, principalement; (*originally*) primitivement, à l'origine.

primary ['praɪmərɪ] **1** *adj* **(a)** (*first in time or order*) primaire (*also Astron, Chem, Elec, Geol, Med etc*), premier, primitif, fondamental. (*Philos*) **~ cause** cause première; **~ colour** couleur fondamentale; **~ education** enseignement *m* primaire; (*US Pol*) **~ election** élection *f* primaire; **~ feather** rémige *f*; (*Ind*) **~ product** produit *m* de base; **~ school** école *f* primaire; **~ (school)teacher** instituteur *m*, -trice *f*; (*Gram*) **~ tense** temps primitif; (*Elec*) **~ winding** enroulement *m* primaire.

(b) (*first in importance, basic*) *cause, reason* principal, primordial, fondamental; *concern, aim* principal, premier (*before n*). **of ~ importance** d'une importance primordiale, de la plus haute *or* de toute première importance; **the ~ meaning of a word** le sens primitif d'un mot.

2 *n* (*school*) école *f* primaire; (*colour*) couleur fondamentale; (*feather*) rémige *f*; (*Elec*) enroulement *m* primaire; (*US Pol*) primaire *f*.

primate ['praɪmɪt] *n* (*Rel*) primat *m*; ['praɪmeɪt] (*Zool*) primate *m*.

prime [praɪm] **1** *adj* **(a)** (*chief, principal*) *cause, reason* principal, primordial, fondamental. **a ~ advantage** un avantage de premier ordre; **a ~ factor** un facteur primordial *or* fondamental; **of ~ importance** d'une importance primordiale, de la plus haute *or* de toute première importance.

(b) (*excellent*) *meat* de premier choix. **in ~ condition** *animal, athlete* en parfaite condition; *car* en excellent état; **~ cut** morceau *m* de premier choix; **a ~ example of what to avoid** un excellent exemple de ce qu'il faut éviter; **of ~ quality** de première qualité; **~ ribs** côtes premières.

(c) (*Math*) premier.

2 *cpd*: (*Comm, Ind*) **prime cost** prix coûtant; (*Math*) **prime factor** facteur premier, diviseur premier; **prime meridian** premier méridien; **prime minister** premier ministre; **prime mover** (*Phys, Tech*) force motrice; (*Philos*) moteur† *m*, cause première; (*fig: person*) instigateur *m*, -trice *f*; (*Math*) **prime number** nombre premier; (*Rad, TV*) **prime time** heure(s) *f(pl)* d'écoute maximum.

3 *n* **(a) in the ~ of life, in one's ~** dans *or* à la fleur de l'âge; **when the Renaissance was in its ~** quand la Renaissance était à son apogée, aux plus beaux jours de la Renaissance; **he is past his ~** il est sur le retour; (*hum*) **this grapefruit is past its ~*** ce pamplemousse n'est plus de la première fraîcheur, ce pamplemousse a vu des jours meilleurs (*hum*).

(b) (*Math*) nombre premier.

(c) (*Rel*) prime *f*.

4 *vt* **(a)** *gun, pump* amorcer. (*fig*) **to ~ the pump** renflouer une entreprise *or* une affaire; **to ~ sb with drink** faire boire qn (tant et plus); **he was well ~d (with drink)** il avait bu plus que de raison.

(b) *surface for painting* apprêter.

(c) (*fig*) *person* mettre au fait, mettre au courant. **they ~d him about what he should say** ils lui ont bien fait répéter ce qu'il avait à dire; **he was ~d to say that** ils lui ont fait la leçon pour qu'il dise cela; **she came well ~d for the interview** elle est arrivée à l'entrevue tout à fait préparée.

primer ['praɪməʳ] *n* (*textbook*) premier livre, livre élémentaire; (*reading book*) abécédaire *m*; (*paint*) apprêt *m*.

primeval [praɪ'mi:vəl] *adj* primitif, des premiers âges; primordial. **~ forest** forêt *f* vierge.

priming ['praɪmɪŋ] *n* **(a)** *[pump]* amorçage *m*; *[gun]* amorce *f*.

(b) (*Painting*) (*substance*) couche *f* d'apprêt; (*action*) apprêt *m*.

primitive ['prɪmɪtɪv] *adj, n* (*all senses*) primitif (*m*).

primly ['prɪmlɪ] *adv* (*prudishly*) d'une manière guindée *or* compassée *or* contrainte; (*demurely*) d'un petit air sage.

primness ['prɪmnɪs] *n [person]* (*prudishness*) façons guindées *or* compassées, air *m* collet monté; (*demureness*) façons très correctes *or* très convenables; *[house, garden]* aspect trop coquet *or* impeccable; *[dress, hat]* aspect très correct.

primogeniture [ˌpraɪməʊ'dʒenɪtʃəʳ] *n* (*Jur etc*) primogéniture *f*.

primordial [praɪ'mɔ:dɪəl] *adj* primordial.

primp [prɪmp] **1** *vi* se pomponner, se bichonner. **2** *vt* pomponner, bichonner.

primrose ['prɪmrəʊz] **1** *n* (*Bot*) primevère *f*. (*fig*) **the ~ path** le chemin *or* la voie de la facilité. **2** *adj* (*also* **~ yellow**) jaune pâle *inv*, (jaune) primevère *inv*.

primula ['prɪmjʊlə] *n* primevère *f*.

primus ['praɪməs] *n* ® (*also* **~ stove**) réchaud *m* de camping (à pétrole), Primus *m* ®.

prince [prɪns] *n* prince *m* (*also fig*). **P~ Charles** le prince Charles; **the P~ of Wales** le prince de Galles; **~ consort** prince consort; **~ regent** prince régent; **P~ Charming** le Prince Charmant; **the P~ of Darkness** le prince des ténèbres *or* des démons; (*fig*) **the ~s of this world** les princes de la terre, les grands *mpl* de ce monde.

princeling ['prɪnslɪŋ] *n* principicule *m*.

princely ['prɪnslɪ] *adj* (*lit, fig*) princier.

princess [prɪn'ses] *n* princesse *f*. **P~ Anne** la princesse Anne; **P~ Royal** princesse royale (*titre donné à la fille aînée du monarque*).

principal ['prɪnsɪpəl] **1** *adj* (*most senses*) principal. **the ~ horn in the orchestra** le premier cor dans l'orchestre; (*Brit Theat*) **~ boy** jeune héros *m* (*rôle tenu par une actrice dans les spectacles de Noël*); (*Gram*) **~ clause** (proposition *f*) principale *f*; (*Gram*) **~ parts of a verb** temps primitifs d'un verbe.

2 *n* **(a)** *[primary school, institution]* directeur *m*, -trice *f*; *[secondary school, college]* proviseur *m* (de lycée), directeur, -trice, principal† *m*; (*in orchestra*) chef *m* de pupitre; (*Theat*) vedette *f*; (*Jur: lawyer's client*) commettant *m*; (*Jur: chief perpetrator of crime*) auteur *m* (d'un crime), principal responsable.

(b) (*Fin*) principal *m*, capital *m*. **~ and interest** principal *or* capital et intérêts.

principality [ˌprɪnsɪ'pælɪtɪ] *n* principauté *f*.

principally ['prɪnsɪpəlɪ] *adv* principalement.

principle ['prɪnsəpl] *n* (*all senses*) principe *m*. **to go back to first ~s** remonter jusqu'au principe; **it is based on false ~s** cela repose sur de fausses prémisses *or* de faux principes; **in ~** en principe; **on ~, as a matter of ~** par principe; **I make it a ~ never to lend money, it's against my ~s to lend money** j'ai pour principe de ne jamais prêter d'argent; **that would be totally against my ~s** cela irait à l'encontre de tous mes principes; **for the ~ of the thing*** pour le principe; **he is a man of ~(s), he has high ~s** c'est un homme qui a des principes; **all these machines work on the same ~** toutes ces machines marchent sur *or* selon le même principe.

-principled ['prɪnsəpld] *adj ending in cpds V* **high, low**[1].

prink [prɪŋk] = **primp.**

print [prɪnt] **1** *n* **(a)** (*mark*) *[hand, foot, tyre etc]* empreinte *f*; (*finger~*) empreinte (digitale). **a thumb/paw** *etc* **~** l'empreinte d'un pouce/d'une patte *etc*; (*Police etc*) **to take sb's ~s** prendre les empreintes de qn; *V* **finger, foot** *etc*.

(b) (*U: Typ*) (*actual letters*) caractères *mpl*; (*printed material*) texte imprimé. **in small/large ~** en petits/gros caractères; **read the small** *or* **fine ~ before you sign** lisez toutes les clauses avant de signer; **the ~ is poor** les caractères ne sont pas nets; it

was there in cold ~! c'était là noir sur blanc!; **the book is out of ~/in ~** le livre est épuisé/n'est pas épuisé; **he wants to see himself in ~** il veut se faire imprimer; **I've got into ~ at last!** me voilà enfin imprimé!; **don't let that get into ~** n'allez pas imprimer *or* publier cela.

(c) (*Art: etching, woodcut etc*) estampe *f*, gravure *f*; (*Art: reproduction*) gravure; (*Phot*) épreuve *f*; (*Tex: material, design*) imprimé *m*; (*printed dress*) robe imprimée. (*Phot*) **to make a ~ from a negative** tirer une épreuve d'un cliché; **a cotton ~** une cotonnade imprimée; *V* **blue.**

2 *cpd dress etc* en (tissu) imprimé. **printmaker** graveur *m*; (*Computers*) **print-out** listage *m*; (*Typ*) **print shop** imprimerie *f*.

3 *vt* **(a)** (*Typ*) imprimer; (*publish*) imprimer, publier. **~ed in England** imprimé en Angleterre; **the book is being ~ed just now** le livre est sous presse *or* à l'impression en ce moment; **100 copies were ~ed** cela a été tiré *or* imprimé à 100 exemplaires, on en a tiré 100 exemplaires; **he has had several books ~ed** il a publié plusieurs livres; **they didn't dare ~ it** ils n'ont pas osé l'imprimer *or* le publier; **will you have your lectures ~ed?** publierez-vous *or* ferez-vous imprimer vos conférences?; *V also* **printed.**

(b) (*Tex*) imprimer; (*Phot*) tirer.

(c) (*write in block letters*) écrire en caractères d'imprimerie. **~ it in block capitals** écrivez-le en lettres majuscules.

(d) the mark of horses' hooves ~ed in the sand la marque de sabots de chevaux imprimée sur le sable, la trace *or* les empreintes *fpl* de sabots de chevaux sur le sable; (*fig*) **face ~ed in sb's memory** visage gravé dans la mémoire.

4 *vi [machine]* imprimer. **the book is ~ing now** le livre est à l'impression en ce moment; (*Phot*) **this negative won't ~** ce cliché ne donnera rien.

print off *vt sep* (*Typ*) tirer, imprimer; (*Phot*) tirer.

print out (*Computers*) **1** *vt sep* imprimer.

2 print-out *n V* **print 2.**

printable [ˈprɪntəbl] *adj* imprimable. (*hum*) **what he said is just not ~** on ne peut vraiment pas répéter ce qu'il a dit.

printed [ˈprɪntɪd] *adj notice, form, cotton, design, dress* imprimé; *writing paper* à en-tête. **~ matter, ~ papers** imprimés *mpl*; **the ~ word** tout ce qui est imprimé, la chose imprimée; (*Electronics*) **~ circuit** circuit imprimé.

printer [ˈprɪntəʳ] *n* imprimeur *m*; (*typographer*) typographe *mf*, imprimeur. **the text has gone to the ~** le texte est chez l'imprimeur; **~'s devil** apprenti imprimeur; **~'s error** faute *f* d'impression, coquille *f*; **~'s ink** encre *f* d'imprimerie; **~'s reader** correcteur *m*, -trice *f* (d'épreuves).

printing [ˈprɪntɪŋ] **1** *n* (*Press, Tex, Typ*) impression *f*; (*Phot*) tirage *m*; (*block writing*) écriture *f* en caractères d'imprimerie.

2 *cpd*: (*Phot*) **printing frame** châssis-presse *m*; **printing ink** encre *f* d'imprimerie; **printing office** imprimerie *f*; **printing press** presse *f* typographique; **printing works** imprimerie *f*.

prior [ˈpraɪəʳ] **1** *adj* précédent, antérieur (*f* -eure). **~ to** antérieur à; **without ~ notice** sans préavis, sans avertissement préalable; **to have a ~ claim to sth** avoir droit à qch par priorité.

2 *adv*: **~ to** antérieurement à, préalablement à, avant; **~ to (his) leaving he ...** avant de partir *or* avant son départ il ...; **~ to his leaving we ...** avant son départ *or* avant qu'il ne parte nous ... .

3 *n* (*Rel*) prieur *m*.

prioress [ˈpraɪərɪs] *n* prieure *f*.

priority [praɪˈɒrɪtɪ] **1** *n* priorité *f*. **to have or take ~ over** avoir la priorité sur; **housing must be given first or top ~** on doit donner la priorité absolue au logement; **schools were low on the list of priorities or the ~ list** les écoles venaient loin sur la liste des priorités *or* n'étaient pas une des priorités les plus pressantes; **you must get your priorities right** vous devez décider de ce qui compte le plus pour vous.

2 *cpd*: (*St Ex*) **priority share** action *f* de priorité.

priory [ˈpraɪərɪ] *n* prieuré *m*.

prise [praɪz] *vt* (*Brit*) **to ~ open a box** ouvrir une boîte en faisant levier, forcer une boîte; **to ~ the lid off a box** forcer le couvercle d'une boîte; (*fig*) **I ~d him out of his chair** je l'ai enfin fait décoller* de sa chaise; (*fig*) **I managed to ~ him out of the job** je suis arrivé à le faire sauter; (*fig*) **to ~ a secret out of sb** arracher un secret à qn.

prise off *vt sep* enlever en faisant levier.

prise up *vt sep* soulever en faisant levier.

prism [ˈprɪzəm] *n* prisme *m*; *V* **prune**[1].

prismatic [prɪzˈmætɪk] *adj surface, shape, colour* prismatique (*also fig*). **~ compass** boussole *f* topographique à prismes.

prison [ˈprɪzn] **1** *n* (*place*) prison *f*; (*imprisonment*) prison, réclusion *f*. **he is in ~** il est en prison, il fait de la prison; **to put sb in ~** mettre qn en prison, incarcérer qn, emprisonner qn; **to send sb to ~** condamner qn à la prison; **to send sb to ~ for 5 years** condamner qn à 5 ans de prison; **he was in ~ for 5 years** il a fait 5 ans de prison.

2 *cpd food, life, conditions* dans la *or* une *or* les prison(s), pénitentiaire; *system, organization, colony* pénitentiaire. **prison camp** camp *m* de prisonniers; **prison governor** directeur *m* de prison; **prison officer** gardien(ne) *m(f)* *or* surveillant(e) *m(f)* (de prison); **the prison population** la population pénitentiaire; **prison van** voiture *f* cellulaire, panier *m* à salade*; **prison yard** cour *f* *or* préau *m* de prison.

prisoner [ˈprɪznəʳ] *n* détenu(e) *m(f)*; prisonnier *m*, -ière *f*; (*Mil, fig*) prisonnier, -ière. **~ of war** prisonnier de guerre; (*Jur*) **~ at the bar** accusé(e) *m(f)*, inculpé(e) *m(f)*; **the enemy took him ~** il a été fait prisonnier par l'ennemi; **to hold sb ~** détenir qn, garder qn en captivité.

prissy* [ˈprɪsɪ] *adj* bégueule.

pristine [ˈprɪstaɪn] *adj* (*primitive*) primitif; (*unspoiled*) parfait, virginal.

prithee†† [ˈprɪðiː] *excl* je vous prie.

privacy [ˈprɪvəsɪ] *n* intimité *f*, solitude *f*. **his desire for ~** son désir d'être seul, son désir de solitude; *[public figure etc]* son désir de préserver sa vie privée; **there is no ~ in these flats** on ne peut avoir aucune vie privée dans ces appartements; **everyone needs some ~** tout le monde a besoin de solitude *or* a besoin d'être seul de temps en temps; **they were looking for ~** ils cherchaient un coin retiré; **he told me in strictest ~** il me l'a dit dans le plus grand secret; **in the ~ of his own home** dans l'intimité de son foyer; *V* **invasion.**

private [ˈpraɪvɪt] **1** *adj* **(a)** (*not public*) *conversation, meeting, interview* privé, en privé; *land, road* privé; (*confidential*) confidentiel, personnel, de caractère privé. '**~**' (*on door etc*) 'privé', 'interdit au public'; (*on envelope*) 'personnelle'; **mark the letter '~'** inscrivez 'personnelle' sur la lettre; **this matter is strictly ~** cette affaire est strictement confidentielle; **it's a ~ matter** *or* **affair** c'est une affaire privée; **they have a ~ agreement to help each other** ils ont convenu (entre eux) de s'aider mutuellement, ils se sont entendus *or* se sont mis d'accord pour s'aider mutuellement; '**~ fishing**' 'pêche réservée *or* gardée'; '**funeral ~**' 'les obsèques auront lieu dans la plus stricte intimité'; (*Admin, Jur*) **~ hearing** audience *f* à huis clos; **for your ~ information** à titre confidentiel *or* officieux; **I have ~ information that ...** je sais de source privée que ...; **~ letter** lettre de caractère privé; **in (his) ~ life** dans sa vie privée, dans le privé; (*Theat etc*) **~ performance** représentation *f* à bureaux fermés; **~ place** coin retiré, petit coin tranquille; **~ property** propriété privée; (*Art etc*) **~ view** vernissage *m*; **~ wedding** mariage célébré dans l'intimité.

(b) (*for use of one person*) *house, car, lesson, room* particulier; (*personal*) *bank account, advantage* personnel. **a ~ (bank) account** un compte en banque personnel; **room with ~ bath(room)** chambre *f* avec salle de bain particulière; **in his ~ capacity** à titre personnel; **~ car** voiture particulière; **~ house** domicile particulier; **he has a ~ income, he has ~ means** il a une fortune personnelle; **~ joke** plaisanterie personnelle; **it is my ~ opinion that ...** pour ma part je pense que ...; (*Anat*) **~ parts** les parties *fpl* (génitales); **~ pupil** élève *mf* en leçons particulières; **for ~ reasons** pour des raisons personnelles; **~ secretary** secrétaire particulier *or* privé, secrétaire particulière *or* privée; (*Parl*) secrétaire *mf* privé(e); **~ teacher, ~ tutor** (*for full education*) précepteur *m*, institutrice *f*; (*for one subject*) répétiteur *m*, -trice *f*; **he's got a ~ teacher for maths** il prend des leçons particulières en maths, il a un répétiteur en maths; **in his ~ thoughts** dans ses pensées secrètes *or* intimes; **~ tuition** leçons particulières; **for his ~ use** pour son usage personnel.

(c) (*not official; not state-controlled etc*) *company, institution, army* privé; *clinic, nursing home* privé, non conventionné. **~ school** école privée *or* libre; (*Econ*) **~ enterprise** entreprise privée; (*Econ, Ind*) **the ~ sector** le secteur privé; (*esp Brit Med*) **to be in ~ practice** ≈ être médecin non conventionné; (*esp Brit Med*) **~ treatment** ≈ traitement non remboursé; **~ detective, ~ investigator, ~ eye*** détective privé; **a ~ citizen, a ~ person** un particulier, un simple citoyen, une personne privée; (*Parl*) **~ member** simple député *m*; (*Parl*) **~ member's bill** proposition *f* de loi.

(d) (*Mil*) **~ soldier** (simple) soldat *m*, soldat de deuxième classe.

2 *n* **(a)** (*Mil*) (simple) soldat *m*, soldat de deuxième classe. **P~ Martin** le soldat Martin; **P~ Martin!** soldat Martin!; (*US*) **~ 1st class** soldat de 1ère classe.

(b) in ~ = **privately b.**

(c) (*Anat*) **~s** les parties *fpl* (génitales).

privateer [ˌpraɪvəˈtɪəʳ] *n* (*man, ship*) corsaire *m*.

privately [ˈpraɪvɪtlɪ] *adv* **(a)** (*secretly, personally*) dans son for intérieur. **~ he believes that ...** dans son for intérieur il croit que ...; **~ he was against the scheme** intérieurement *or* secrètement il était opposé au projet.

(b) (*not publicly*) **may I speak to you ~?** puis-je vous parler en privé?; **he told me ~ that ...** il m'a dit en confidence que ...; **he has said ~ that ...** il a dit en privé *or* en petit comité que ...; **the wedding was held ~** le mariage a eu lieu dans l'intimité; **the committee sat ~** le comité s'est réuni en séance privée *or* à huis clos.

(c) (*unofficially*) *write, apply, object* à titre personnel, en tant que particulier.

(d) he is being ~ educated (*private school*) il fait ses études dans une institution privée; (*private tutor*) il a un précepteur.

privation [praɪˈveɪʃən] *n* privation *f*.

privative [ˈprɪvətɪv] *adj, n* (*also Ling*) privatif (*m*).

privet [ˈprɪvɪt] *n* troène *m*. **~ hedge** haie *f* de troènes.

privilege [ˈprɪvɪlɪdʒ] **1** *n* privilège *m*; (*U: Parl etc*) prérogative *f*, immunité *f*. **to have the ~ of doing** avoir le privilège *or* jouir du privilège de faire; **I hate ~** je déteste les privilèges.

2 *vt* (*pass only*) **to be ~d to do** avoir le privilège de faire; **I was ~d to meet him once** j'ai eu le privilège de le rencontrer une fois.

privileged [ˈprɪvɪlɪdʒd] *adj person, group, situation, position* privilégié. a **~ few** quelques privilégiés; **the ~ few** la minorité privilégiée; **~ information** renseignements confidentiels (*obtenus dans l'exercice de ses fonctions*); *V* **under.**

privily†† [ˈprɪvɪlɪ] *adj* en secret.

privy [ˈprɪvɪ] **1** *adj* (†† *or Jur*) privé, secret (f -ète). **~ to** au courant de, dans le secret de. **2** *cpd*: (*Brit*) **Privy Council/Councillor** conseil/conseiller privé; **Privy Purse** cassette royale; **Privy Seal** petit sceau. **3** *n* cabinets *mpl*, W.-C. *mpl*.

prize[1] [praɪz] **1** *n* **(a)** (*gen, Scol, fig*) prix *m*; (*in lottery*) lot *m*. **to**

win first ~ (*Scol etc*) remporter le premier prix (*in* de); (*in lottery*) gagner le gros lot; **the Nobel P~** le prix Nobel; *V* **cash** *etc.*

(b) (*Naut*) prise *f* de navire (*or* de cargaison).

2 *adj sheep, novel, entry* primé. **that's a ~ example of official stupidity!** c'est un parfait exemple de la bêtise des milieux officiels; **she is a ~ idiot*** c'est une idiote finie *or* de premier ordre.

3 *cpd*: (*Scol*) **prize day** distribution *f* des prix; **prize draw** tombola *f*; (*Boxing*) **prize fight** combat professionnel; **prize fighter** boxeur professionnel; **prize fighting** boxe professionnelle; (*Scol etc*) **prize giving** distribution *f* des prix; **prize list** palmarès *m*; **prize money** (*gen, Sport*) argent *m* du prix; (*Naut*) part *f* de prise; (*Boxing*) **prize ring** ring *m*; **prizewinner** (*Scol, gen*) lauréat(e) *m(f)*; (*in lottery*) gagnant(e) *m(f)*; **prizewinning** *essay, novel, entry etc* primé, qui remporte le prix; *ticket* gagnant.

4 *vt* priser, attacher beaucoup de prix à, faire grand cas de. **to ~ sth very highly** faire très grand cas de qch, priser hautement qch; **~d possession** bien le plus précieux.

prize[2] [praɪz] *vt* = **prise.**

pro[1] [prəʊ] **1** *pref* **(a)** (*in favour of*) **pro-** pro...; **~-French** profrançais; **they are very ~-Moscow** ils sont prosoviétiques; **he was ~-Hitler** il était hitlérien, il était partisan d'Hitler.

(b) (*acting for*) **pro...** pro-, vice-; *V* **proconsul** *etc.*

2 *n*: **the ~s and the cons** le pour et le contre.

3 *cpd*: **pro forma** pour la forme; **pro forma invoice** facture pro forma; **pro rata** au prorata; **pro tempore, pro tem*** (*adj*) temporaire; (*adv*) temporairement.

pro[2]* [prəʊ] *n* (*abbr of* **professional**) (*Sport*) pro *mf.* (*fig hum*) **you can see he's a ~** on voit bien qu'on a affaire à un professionnel, on dirait qu'il a fait ça toute sa vie.

probability [ˌprɒbəˈbɪlɪtɪ] *n* probabilité *f.* **in all ~** selon toute probabilité; **the ~ is that** il est très probable que + *indic*, il y a de grandes chances pour que + *subj*; **there is little ~ that** il est peu probable que + *subj.*

probable [ˈprɒbəbl] **1** *adj* **(a)** (*likely*) *reason, success, event, election* probable. **it is ~ that he will succeed** il est probable qu'il réussira.

(b) (*credible*) vraisemblable. **his explanation did not sound very ~** son explication ne m'a pas paru très vraisemblable.

2 *n*: **he is one of the ~s for the job** il est un de ceux qui sont considérés très sérieusement pour le poste; *V* **possible.**

probably [ˈprɒbəblɪ] *adv* probablement, vraisemblablement, selon toute probabilité. **he ~ forgot** il a probablement *or* vraisemblablement oublié, selon toute probabilité il aura oublié; **very ~, but ...** c'est bien probable *or* peut-être bien, mais ...

probate [ˈprəʊbɪt] (*Jur*) **1** *n* homologation *f* (d'un testament). **to value sth for ~** évaluer *or* expertiser qch pour l'homologation d'un testament; **to grant/take out ~ of a will** homologuer/faire homologuer un testament.

2 *cpd*: **probate court** tribunal *m* des successions.

3 *vt* (*US*) *will* homologuer.

probation [prəˈbeɪʃən] **1** *n* (*Jur*) ≈ mise *f* à l'épreuve; (*for minors*) mise *f* en liberté surveillée. **he is on ~** (*Jur*) ≈ il est en sursis avec mise à l'épreuve *or* en liberté surveillée; (*gen: in employment etc*) il a été engagé à l'essai; (*Rel*) il est novice; (*Jur*) **to put sb on ~** mettre qn en sursis avec mise à l'épreuve *or* en liberté surveillée.

2 *cpd*: (*Jur*) **probation officer** agent *m* de probation; (*for minors*) ≈ délégué(e) *m(f)* à la liberté surveillée.

probationary [prəˈbeɪʃnərɪ] *adj* (*gen*) d'essai; (*Jur*) de sursis, avec mise à l'épreuve; (*Rel*) de probation, de noviciat.

probationer [prəˈbeɪʃnəʳ] *n* (*in business, factory etc*) employé(e) *m(f)* engagé(e) à l'essai; (*Rel*) novice *mf*; (*Jur*) ≈ condamné(e) *m(f)* sursitaire avec mise à l'épreuve, (*minor*) délinquant(e) *m(f)* en liberté surveillée.

probe [prəʊb] **1** *n* (*gen, Med, Space*) sonde *f*; (*fig: investigation*) enquête *f* (*into* sur), investigation *f* (*into* de).

2 *vt* **(a)** *hole, crack* explorer, examiner; (*Med*) sonder; (*Space*) explorer. **he ~d the ground with his stick** il fouilla la terre de sa canne.

(b) *sb's subconscious, past, private life* sonder, explorer, chercher à découvrir; *causes, crime, sb's death* chercher à éclaircir; *mystery* approfondir.

3 *vi* (*gen, Med etc*) faire un examen avec une sonde, faire un sondage; (*fig: inquire*) faire des recherches, poursuivre une investigation, fouiner (*pej*). **to ~ for sth** (*gen, Med*) chercher à localiser *or* à découvrir qch; (*fig: by investigation*) rechercher qch, fouiner à la recherche de qch; **the police should have ~d more deeply** la police aurait dû pousser plus loin ses investigations; **to ~ into sth = to probe sth;** *V* **2b.**

probing [ˈprəʊbɪŋ] **1** *adj instrument* pour sonder; (*fig*) *question, study* pénétrant; *interrogation* serré; *look* inquisiteur (*f*-trice).

2 *n* (*gen, Med*) sondage *m*; (*fig: investigations*) investigations *fpl* (*into* de).

probity [ˈprəʊbɪtɪ] *n* probité *f.*

problem [ˈprɒbləm] **1** *n* problème *m* (*also Math*). **the housing ~** le problème *or* (*more acute*) la crise du logement; **he is a great ~ to his mother** il pose de gros problèmes à sa mère; **we've got ~s with the car** nous avons des ennuis avec la voiture; **he's got drinking ~s** il a des tendances à l'alcoolisme, il est porté sur la boisson; **it's not my ~** ça ne me concerne pas; **that's no ~ to him** ça ne lui pose pas de problème, c'est simple comme tout pour lui; **that's no ~!, no ~!*** (ça ne pose) pas de problème!*; **what's the ~?** qu'est-ce qui ne va pas?; **I had no ~ in getting the money, it was no ~ to get the money** je n'ai eu aucun mal à obtenir l'argent.

2 *cpd child* difficile, caractériel; *family* en difficulté; (*Literat etc*) *novel, play* à thèse. (*Press*) **problem page** courrier *m* du cœur.

problematic(al) [ˌprɒblɪˈmætɪk(l)] *adj* problématique. **it is ~ whether ...** il n'est pas du tout certain que ... + *subj.*

proboscis [prəʊˈbɒsɪs] *n* (*Zool*) trompe *f*; (*hum: nose*) appendice *m* (*hum*).

procedural [prəˈsiːdjʊrəl] *adj* (*Admin, Insurance etc*) de procédure.

procedure [prəˈsiːdʒəʳ] *n* procédure *f.* **the correct ~ is to do it thus** c'est ainsi qu'on doit procéder; **the normal** *or* **usual ~ involves ...** la procédure normale implique ...; **what's the ~?*** comment doit-on procéder?, qu'est-ce qu'il faut faire?; (*Admin, Jur etc*) **order of ~** règles *fpl* de procédure.

proceed [prəˈsiːd] **1** *vi* **(a)** (*go*) aller, avancer, circuler. **he was ~ing along the road** il avançait sur la route; (*lit, fig*) **before we ~ any further** avant d'aller plus loin; **cars should ~ slowly** les autos devraient avancer *or* rouler lentement; **to ~ on one's way** poursuivre son chemin *or* sa route; **you must ~ cautiously** il faut avancer avec prudence; (*fig: act*) il faut agir *or* procéder avec prudence.

(b) (*go on*) aller, se rendre; (*fig*) passer (*to* à); (*continue*) continuer. **they then ~ed to London** ils se sont ensuite rendus à Londres; **let us ~ to the next item** passons à la question suivante; **I am not sure how to ~** je ne sais pas très bien comment m'y prendre; **to ~ to do sth** se mettre à faire qch; **they ~ed with their plan** ils ont donné suite à leur projet; (*Jur*) **they did not ~ with the charges against him** ils ont abandonné les poursuites engagées contre lui; **~ with your work** continuez *or* poursuivez votre travail; **please ~!** veuillez continuer *or* poursuivre; **everything is ~ing well** les choses suivent leur cours de manière satisfaisante; **it is all ~ing according to plan** tout se passe ainsi que prévu; **the discussions are ~ing normally** les discussions se poursuivent normalement; **the text ~s thus** le texte continue ainsi.

(c) (*originate*) **to ~ from** venir de, provenir de; (*fig*) provenir de, découler de.

(d) (*Jur*) **to ~ against sb** engager des poursuites contre qn.

2 *vt* continuer. **'well' she ~ed** 'eh bien' continua-t-elle.

3 ~s [ˈprəʊsiːdz] *npl* produit *m.*

proceeding [prəˈsiːdɪŋ] *n* **(a)** (*course of action*) procédé *m*, façon *f or* manière *f* d'agir. **it was a somewhat dubious ~** c'était une manière de procéder *or* une façon d'agir quelque peu douteuse; **the safest ~ would be to wait** la conduite la plus sage serait d'attendre; **there were some odd ~s** il se passait des choses bizarres, il y avait des agissements *mpl or* des menées *fpl* bizarres.

(b) ~s (*ceremony*) cérémonie *f*; (*meeting*) séance *f*, réunion *f*; (*discussions*) débats *mpl*; **the ~s begin at 7 o'clock** la réunion *or* la séance commencera à 19 heures; **the secretary recorded all the ~s** le secrétaire a enregistré *or* consigné tous les débats.

(c) (*esp Jur: measures*) **~s** mesures *fpl*; **to take ~s** prendre des mesures (*in order to do* pour faire, *against sb* contre qn); (*Jur*) **to take (legal) ~s against sb** engager des poursuites contre qn, intenter un procès à qn; **legal ~s** procès *m*; *V* **divorce.**

(d) (*records*) **~s** compte rendu, rapport *m.* **it was published in the Society's ~s** cela a été publié dans les actes de la Société; (*as title*) **P~s of the Historical Society** Actes *mpl* de la Société d'histoire.

process[1] [ˈprəʊses] **1** *n* **(a)** (*continuing action*) processus *m.* **the ~ of digestion/growing up** *etc* le processus de la digestion/de la croissance *etc*; **a natural/chemical ~** un processus naturel/chimique; **it's a slow** *or* **long ~** (*Chem etc*) c'est un processus lent; (*fig*) ça prend du temps, c'est un processus lent; **the ~es of the law** le processus de la justice; **he supervised the whole ~** il a supervisé l'opération du début à la fin; **in the ~ of cleaning the picture, they discovered ...** au cours du nettoyage du tableau *or* pendant qu'ils nettoyaient le tableau ils ont découvert ...; **in the ~ of time** avec le temps.

(b) to be in ~ *[discussions, examinations, work]* être en cours; *[building]* être en cours *or* en voie de construction; **while work is in ~** pendant les travaux, quand le travail est en cours; **it is in ~ of construction** c'est en cours *or* en voie de construction; **we are in (the) ~ of removal to Leeds** nous sommes en train de déménager pour aller à Leeds.

(c) (*specific method*) procédé *m*, méthode *f.* **the Bessemer ~** le procédé Bessemer; **he has devised a ~ for controlling weeds** il a mis au point un procédé pour venir à bout des mauvaises herbes.

(d) (*Jur*) (*action*) procès *m*; (*summons*) citation *f*, sommation *f* de comparaître. **to bring a ~ against sb** intenter un procès à qn; **to serve a ~ on sb** signifier une citation à qn.

(e) (*Anat, Bot, Zool*) excroissance *f*, protubérance *f.*

2 *cpd*: **process control** commande *f or* régulation *f* de processus; **process(ed) cheese** fromage *m* fondu, crème *f* de gruyère *etc*; (*Typ*) **process printing** quadrichromie *f.*

3 *vt* (*Ind*) *raw materials* traiter, transformer; *seeds* traiter; *food* traiter, faire subir un traitement à; (*Phot*) *film* développer; (*Computers*) *information, data* traiter; (*Computers*) *tape* faire passer en machine; (*Admin etc*) *an application, papers, records* s'occuper de. **they ~ 10,000 forms per day** 10.000 formulaires passent chaque jour entre leurs mains.

process[2] [prəˈses] *vi* (*Brit: go in procession*) défiler; avancer en cortège; (*Rel*) aller en procession.

processing [ˈprəʊsesɪŋ] *n* (*U: V* **process**[1] **3**) traitement *m*, transformation *f*, développement *m*; *V* **data.**

procession [prəˈseʃən] *n [people, cars]* cortège *m*, défilé *m*; (*Rel*) procession *f.* **to walk in (a) ~** défiler, aller en cortège *or* en procession; *V* **funeral.**

processional [prəˈseʃənl] (*Rel*) **1** *adj* processionnel.

2 *n* hymne processionnel.

proclaim [prəˈkleɪm] *vt* **(a)** (*announce*) proclamer, déclarer (*that* que); *holiday* proclamer, instituer; *one's independence* proclamer; *war, peace, one's love* déclarer; *edict* promulguer. **to ~ sb king** proclamer qn roi.
(b) (*reveal*) démontrer, révéler. **his tone ~ed his confidence** le ton de sa voix démontrait *or* révélait sa confiance; **their expressions ~ed their guilt** la culpabilité se lisait sur leurs visages.

proclamation [ˌprɒkləˈmeɪʃən] *n* proclamation *f*.

proclivity [prəˈklɪvɪtɪ] *n* (*frm*) propension *f*, inclination *f* (*to sth* à qch, *to do* à faire).

proconsul [ˈprəʊˈkɒnsəl] *n* proconsul *m*.

procrastinate [prəʊˈkræstɪneɪt] *vi* (avoir tendance à) tout remettre au lendemain.

procrastination [prəʊˌkræstɪˈneɪʃən] *n* procrastination *f*.

procreate [ˈprəʊkrɪeɪt] *vt* procréer, engendrer.

procreation [ˌprəʊkrɪˈeɪʃən] *n* procréation *f*.

Procrustean [prəʊˈkrʌstɪən] *adj* de Procuste.

proctor [ˈprɒktəʳ] *n* **(a)** (*Jur etc*) fondé *m* de pouvoir. **(b)** (*Univ*) (*Oxford, Cambridge*) personne *f* responsable de la discipline; (*US*) surveillant(e) *m(f)* (à un examen).

procurable [prəˈkjʊərəbl] *adj* que l'on peut se procurer. **it is easily ~** on peut se le procurer facilement.

procurator [ˈprɒkjʊreɪtəʳ] *n* (*Jur*) fondé *m* de pouvoir. (*Scot Jur*) **P~ Fiscal** ≈ procureur *m* (*de la République*).

procure [prəˈkjʊəʳ] **1** *vt* **(a)** (*obtain for o.s.*) se procurer, obtenir; *sb's release etc* obtenir. **to ~ sth for sb, to ~ sb sth** procurer qch à qn, faire obtenir qch à qn; **to ~ sb's death**† faire assassiner qn.
(b) (*Jur*) *prostitute etc* offrir les services de, procurer.
2 *vi* (*Jur*) faire du proxénétisme.

procurement [prəˈkjʊəmənt] *n* obtention *f*.

procurer [prəˈkjʊərəʳ] *n* (*Jur*) proxénète *m*.

procuress [prəˈkjʊərɪs] *n* (*Jur*) proxénète *f*.

procuring [prəˈkjʊərɪŋ] *n [goods, objects]* obtention *f*; (*Jur*) proxénétisme *m*.

prod [prɒd] **1** *n* (*push*) poussée *f*; (*jab*) (petit) coup *m* (*de canne, avec le doigt etc*). **to give sb a ~** pousser qn doucement (du doigt *or* du pied *or* avec la pointe d'un bâton *etc*); (*fig*) pousser *or* aiguillonner qn; (*fig*) **he needs a ~ from time to time** il a besoin d'être poussé *or* d'être aiguillonné *or* qu'on le secoue* (*subj*) un peu de temps en temps.
2 *vt* pousser doucement. **to ~ sb** pousser qn doucement (du doigt *or* du pied *or* avec la pointe d'un bâton *etc*); (*fig*) pousser *or* aiguillonner qn; **he ~ded the box with his umbrella** il poussa la boîte avec la pointe de son parapluie; **he ~ded the map with his finger** il planta son doigt sur la carte; **to ~ sb into doing sth** pousser *or* inciter qn à faire qch; **he needs ~ding** il a besoin d'être poussé *or* d'être aiguillonné *or* qu'on le secoue* (*subj*); **to ~ sb along/out** *etc* faire avancer/sortir *etc* qn en le poussant (du doigt *or* du pied *or* avec la pointe d'un bâton).
3 *vi*: **to ~ at sb/sth = to ~ sb/sth**; *V* **2**.

prodigal [ˈprɒdɪgəl] *adj* prodigue (*of* de). **the ~ (son)** (*Bible*) le fils prodigue; (*fig*) l'enfant *m* prodigue.

prodigality [ˌprɒdɪˈgælɪtɪ] *n* prodigalité *f*.

prodigally [ˈprɒdɪgəlɪ] *adv* avec prodigalité, prodigalement.

prodigious [prəˈdɪdʒəs] *adj* prodigieux, extraordinaire.

prodigiously [prəˈdɪdʒəslɪ] *adv* prodigieusement.

prodigy [ˈprɒdɪdʒɪ] *n* prodige *m*, merveille *f*. **child ~, infant ~** enfant *mf* prodige; **a ~ of learning** un puits de science.

produce [prəˈdjuːs] **1** *vt* **(a)** (*make, yield, manufacture*) *milk, oil, coal, ore, crops* produire; *cars, radios* produire, fabriquer; *[writer, artist, musician etc]* produire; (*Fin*) *interest, profit* rapporter; *offspring [animal]* produire, donner naissance à; *[woman]* donner naissance à. (*Fin*) **his shares ~ a yield of 7½%** ses actions rapportent 7½%; **that investment ~s no return** cet investissement ne rapporte rien; **Scotland ~s whisky** l'Écosse produit du whisky *or* est un pays producteur de whisky; **we must ~ more coal** nous devons produire plus de charbon; **coal ~s electricity** le charbon produit *or* donne de l'électricité; **he burned sticks to ~ some warmth** il a brûlé des brindilles pour faire un peu de chaleur; **these magazines are ~d by the same firm** ces revues sont éditées par la même maison; **he ~d a masterpiece** il a produit un chef-d'œuvre; **well- ~d** *book* bien présenté; *goods* bien fait (*V also* **1d**); **he has ~d a new pop record** il a sorti un nouveau disque pop.
(b) (*bring forward, show*) *gift, handkerchief, gun* sortir (*from* de), exhiber, produire; *ticket, documents etc* produire, présenter, exhiber; *witness* produire; *proof* fournir, apporter. **he suddenly ~d a large parcel** il a soudain sorti *or* produit *or* exhibé un gros paquet; **I can't ~ £100 just like that!** je ne peux pas trouver 100 livres comme ça!; **can you ~ a box to put this in?** vous n'auriez pas une boîte (à me donner) où je puisse mettre cela?; **he ~d a sudden burst of energy** il a eu un sursaut d'énergie.
(c) (*cause*) *famine, deaths* causer, provoquer; *dispute, bitterness* occasionner, provoquer, causer; *results* produire, donner; *impression* faire, donner; *pleasure, interest* susciter; (*Elec*) *current* engendrer; *spark* faire jaillir. **it ~d a sensation** cela a fait sensation.
(d) (*Theat*) mettre en scène; (*Cine*) produire; (*Rad*) *play* mettre en ondes; *programme* réaliser; (*TV*) *play, film* mettre en scène; *programme* réaliser. **well ~d** bien monté.
(e) (*Geom*) *line, plane* prolonger, continuer.
2 *vi* **(a)** *[mine, oil well, factory]* produire; *[land, trees, cows]* produire, rendre.
(b) (*Theat*) assurer la mise en scène; (*Cine*) assurer la production (*d'un film*); (*Rad, TV*) assurer la réalisation d'une émission.
3 [ˈprɒdjuːs] *n* (*U*) produit(s) *m(pl)* (alimentaire(s) *or* d'alimentation). **agricultural/garden/foreign ~** produits agricoles/maraîchers/étrangers; **'~ of France'** 'produit français', 'produit de France'; **we eat mostly our own ~** nous mangeons surtout nos propres produits *or* ce que nous produisons nous-mêmes.

producer [prəˈdjuːsəʳ] **1** *n* (*Agr, Ind etc*) producteur *m*, -trice *f*; (*Theat*) metteur *m* en scène; (*Cine*) producteur *m*, -trice *f*; (*Rad, TV*) réalisateur *m*, metteur en ondes. **one of the largest oil ~s** un des plus gros producteurs de pétrole.
2 *cpd*: **producer gas** gaz *m* fourni par gazogène; (*Econ*) **producer goods** biens *mpl* de production.

-producing [prəˈdjuːsɪŋ] *adj ending in cpds* producteur (*f* -trice) de ... . **oil-producing** producteur de pétrole; **one of the most important coal-producing countries** un des plus gros pays producteurs de charbon.

product [ˈprɒdʌkt] *n* **(a)** (*Comm, Ind etc*) produit *m*; (*fig*) produit, résultat *m*, fruit *m*. **food ~s** produits alimentaires *or* d'alimentation, denrées (alimentaires) *fpl*; **it is the ~ of his imagination** c'est le fruit de son imagination; (*fig*) **he is the ~ of our educational system** il est le produit de notre système d'enseignement; **she is the ~ of a broken home** elle est le résultat d'un foyer désuni; *V* **finished, gross, waste** *etc*.
(b) (*Math*) produit *m*.

production [prəˈdʌkʃən] **1** *n* **(a)** (*U: V* **produce 1a**) production *f*; fabrication *f*; (*output*) rendement *m*. **to put sth into ~** entreprendre la production *or* la fabrication de qch; **to take sth out of ~** retirer qch de la production; **the factory is in full ~** l'usine *f* tourne à plein rendement; **car ~ has risen recently** la production automobile a récemment augmenté.
(b) (*U: showing: V* **produce 1b**) production *f*, présentation *f*. **on ~ of this ticket** sur présentation de ce billet.
(c) (*act of producing: V* **produce 1d**) (*Theat*) mise *f* en scène; (*Cine*) production *f*; (*Rad*) mise en ondes, réalisation *f*; (*TV*) mise en scène, réalisation. (*Theat*) **'Macbeth': a new ~ by ...** 'Macbeth': une nouvelle mise en scène de ...; (*fig*) **he made a real ~ out of it*** il en a fait toute une affaire *or* tout un plat*.
(d) (*work produced*) (*Theat*) pièce *f*; (*Cine, Rad, TV*) production *f*; (*Art, Literat*) production, œuvre *f*.
2 *cpd*: (*Ind*) **production line** chaîne *f* de fabrication; **he works on the production line** il travaille à la chaîne; **production line work** travail *m* à la chaîne; **production manager** directeur *m* de la production.

productive [prəˈdʌktɪv] *adj land, imagination* fertile, fécond; *meeting, discussion, work* fructueux, fécond; (*Econ*) *employment, labour* productif; (*Ling*) productif. **to be ~ of sth** produire qch, engendrer qch, être générateur (*f*-trice) de qch; **I've had a very ~ day** j'ai eu une journée bien remplie, j'ai bien travaillé aujourd'hui.

productivity [ˌprɒdʌkˈtɪvɪtɪ] **1** *n* (*U: Econ, Ind*) productivité *f*.
2 *cpd fall, increase* de productivité. **productivity agreement** accord *m* de productivité; **productivity bonus** prime *f* à la productivité.

prof* [prɒf] *n* (*abbr of* **professor**) prof* *m*, professeur *m*.

profanation [ˌprɒfəˈneɪʃən] *n* profanation *f*.

profane [prəˈfeɪn] **1** *adj* (*secular, lay*) profane; (*pej*) *language etc* impie, sacrilège; *V* **sacred**. **2** *vt* profaner.

profanity [prəˈfænɪtɪ] *n* (*U: V* **profane**) nature *f* *or* caractère *m* profane; (*pej*) impiété *f*; (*oath*) juron *m*, blasphème *m*. **he uttered a stream of profanities** il proféra un chapelet de jurons.

profess [prəˈfes] *vt* **(a)** professer, déclarer, affirmer (*that* que); *faith, religion* professer; (*publicly*) professer, faire profession de; *an opinion, respect, hatred* professer. **she ~ed total ignorance** elle a affirmé ne rien savoir du tout; **he ~ed himself satisfied** il s'est déclaré satisfait; **she ~es to be 39** elle se donne 39 ans, elle prétend avoir 39 ans; **he ~es to know all about it** il déclare *or* prétend tout savoir sur ce sujet; **I don't ~ to be an expert** je ne prétends pas être expert en la matière.
(b) (*frmw; have as one's profession*) **to ~ law/medicine** exercer la profession d'avocat/de médecin.
(c) (*frm: Univ: teach*) professer.

professed [prəˈfest] *adj atheist, communist etc* déclaré; (*Rel*) *monk, nun* profès (*f* -esse).

professedly [prəˈfesɪdlɪ] *adv* de son (*or* leur *etc*) propre aveu, d'après lui (*or* eux *etc*); (*allegedly*) soi-disant, prétendument.

profession [prəˈfeʃən] *n* **(a)** (*calling*) profession *f*; (*body of people*) (membres *mpl* d'une) profession. **by ~** de son (*or* mon *etc*) métier; **the medical ~** (*calling*) la profession de médecin, la médecine; (*doctors collectively*) le corps médical, les médecins *mpl*; *V* **learned** *etc*.
(b) (*declaration*) profession *f*, déclaration *f*. **~ of faith** profession de foi; *[monk, nun]* **to make one's ~** faire sa profession, prononcer ses vœux.

professional [prəˈfeʃənl] **1** *adj* **(a)** *skill, organization, training, etiquette* professionnel. **he is a ~ man** il exerce une profession libérale; **the ~ classes** les (membres *mpl* des) professions libérales; **to take ~ advice** (*medical/legal*) consulter un médecin/un avocat; (*on practical problem*) consulter un professionnel *or* un homme de métier; **it is not ~ practice to do so** faire cela est contraire à l'usage professionnel.
(b) (*by profession*) *writer, politician* professionnel, de profession; *footballer, tennis player* professionnel; *diplomat, soldier* de carrière; (*fig: of high standard*) *play, piece of work* de haute qualité, excellent. **~ army** armée *f* de métier; **~ football/tennis** *etc* football/tennis *etc* professionnel; (*Sport*) **to turn** *or* **go ~** passer professionnel; **to have a very ~ attitude to one's work** prendre son travail très au sérieux; **it is well up to ~ standards** c'est d'un niveau de professionnel.
2 *n* (*all senses*) professionnel(le) *m(f)*.

professionalism [prəˈfeʃnəlɪzəm] *n [writer, actor etc]* professionnalisme *m*; (*Sport*) professionnalisme; *[play, piece of work]* excellence *f*, haute qualité.

professionally [prəˈfeʃnəlɪ] *adv* professionnellement, de manière professionnelle; (*Sport*) *play* en professionnel. **he is known ~ as Joe Bloggs** dans la profession *or* le métier il est connu sous le nom de Joe Bloggs; **I know him only ~** je n'ai que des rapports de travail avec lui, je ne suis en rapports avec lui que pour le travail; **I never met him ~** je n'ai jamais eu de rapports de travail avec lui; (*fig*) **he did that very ~** il a fait cela de manière très professionnelle; **to be ~ qualified** être diplômé; **he was acting ~ when he did that** il agissait dans le cadre de ses fonctions officielles *or* à titre officiel quand il a fait cela; **he had it ~ built** il l'a fait construire par un professionnel; **the play was ~ produced** la mise en scène (de la pièce) était d'un professionnel; **have you ever sung ~?** avez-vous jamais été chanteur professionnel?

professor [prəˈfesəʳ] *n* (*Univ: Brit, US*) professeur *m* (titulaire d'une chaire); (*US: teacher*) professeur. **~ of French, French ~** professeur (de la chaire) de français; *V* **assistant** *etc.*

professorial [ˌprɒfəˈsɔːrɪəl] *adj* professoral.

professorship [prəˈfesəʃɪp] *n* chaire *f* (*of* de). **he has got a ~** il est titulaire d'une chaire.

proffer [ˈprɒfəʳ] *vt object, arm* offrir, tendre; *a remark, suggestion* faire; *one's thanks, apologies* offrir, présenter. **to ~ one's hand to sb** tendre la main à qn.

proficiency [prəˈfɪʃənsɪ] *n* (grande) compétence *f* (*in* en).

proficient [prəˈfɪʃənt] *adj* (très) compétent (*in* en).

profile [ˈprəʊfaɪl] **1** *n* **(a)** *[head, building, hill etc]* profil *m* (*also Archit*). **in ~** de profil; *V* **low**[1]. **(b)** (*fig*) *[person]* portrait *m*; *[situation etc]* esquisse *f*, profil *m*. **2** *vt* (*show in ~*) profiler (*also Archit*); (*fig*) *person* faire le portrait de; *situation* tracer une esquisse de, établir le profil de.

profit [ˈprɒfɪt] **1** *n* (*Comm*) profit *m*, bénéfice *m*; (*fig*) profit, avantage *m*. **~ and loss** profits et pertes (*V also* **2**); **gross/net ~** bénéfice brut/net; **to make a ~/a ~ of £100** faire du *or* un bénéfice/un bénéfice de 100 livres (*on sth* sur qch); **to sell sth at a ~** vendre qch à profit; **to show** *or* **yield a ~** rapporter (un bénéfice); (*Insurance*) **with ~s policy** police *f* (d'assurance) avec participation aux bénéfices; (*fig*) **with ~** avec profit, avec fruit; (*fig*) **to turn sth to ~** mettre à profit qch, tirer parti de qch.

2 *cpd*: (*Book-keeping*) **profit and loss account** compte *m* de profits et pertes; **a profit-making/non-profit-making organization** une organisation à but lucratif/non lucratif; **profit margin** marge *f* bénéficiaire; **the profit motive** la recherche du profit; (*Ind*) **profit-sharing** participation *f* aux bénéfices; **profit-sharing scheme** système *m* de participation (aux bénéfices); (*St Ex*) **profit taking** vente *f* d'actions avec bénéfice.

3 *vi* (*fig*) tirer un profit *or* un avantage. **to ~ by** *or* **from sth** tirer avantage *or* profit de qch, bien profiter de qch; **I can't see how he hopes to ~ (by it)** je ne vois pas ce qu'il espère en retirer *or* y gagner.

4 *vt* (†† *or liter*) profiter à. **it will ~ him nothing** cela ne lui profitera en rien.

profitability [ˌprɒfɪtəˈbɪlɪtɪ] *n* (*Comm etc*) rentabilité *f*; (*fig*) rentabilité, caractère profitable *or* fructueux.

profitable [ˈprɒfɪtəbl] *adj* (*Comm etc*) *deal, sale, investment* rentable, lucratif, payant; (*fig*) *scheme, agreement, contract* avantageux, rentable; *meeting, discussion, visit* fructueux, payant (*fig*), profitable. **we don't stock them any more as they were not ~** nous ne les stockons plus parce qu'ils n'étaient pas rentables; **it was a very ~ half-hour** cela a été une demi-heure très fructueuse *or* payante *or* profitable; **you would find it ~ to read this** vous trouveriez la lecture de ceci utile *or* profitable, c'est avec profit que vous liriez ceci.

profitably [ˈprɒfɪtəblɪ] *adv sell* à profit; *deal* avec profit; (*fig*) avec profit, avec fruit, utilement.

profiteer [ˌprɒfɪˈtɪəʳ] (*pej*) **1** *n* profiteur *m* (*pej*), mercanti *m* (*pej*). **2** *vi* faire des bénéfices excessifs.

profitless [ˈprɒfɪtlɪs] *adj* (*lit, fig*) sans profit.

profitlessly [ˈprɒfɪtlɪslɪ] *adv* (*lit, fig*) sans profit.

profligacy [ˈprɒflɪgəsɪ] *n* (*debauchery*) débauche *f*, libertinage *m*; (*extravagance*) extrême prodigalité *f*.

profligate [ˈprɒflɪgɪt] **1** *adj* (*debauched*) *person, behaviour* débauché, libertin, dissolu; *life* de débauche, de libertinage; (*extravagant*) extrêmement prodigue. **2** *n* débauché(e) *m(f)*, libertin(e) *m(f)*.

profound [prəˈfaʊnd] *adj* (*all senses*) profond.

profoundly [prəˈfaʊndlɪ] *adv* profondément.

profundity [prəˈfʌndɪtɪ] *n* profondeur *f*.

profuse [prəˈfjuːs] *adj vegetation, bleeding* abondant; *thanks, praise, apologies* profus, multiple. **~ in** prodigue de; **to be ~ in one's thanks/excuses** se confondre en remerciements/excuses.

profusely [prəˈfjuːslɪ] *adv grow etc* à profusion, à foison, en abondance; *bleed, sweat* abondamment; *thank* avec effusion. **to apologize ~** se confondre en excuses; **to praise sb ~** se répandre en éloges sur qn.

profusion [prəˈfjuːʒən] *n* profusion *f*, abondance *f* (*of* de). **in ~** à profusion, à foison.

progenitor [prəʊˈdʒenɪtəʳ] *n* (*lit*) ancêtre *m*; (*fig*) auteur *m*.

progeny [ˈprɒdʒɪnɪ] *n* (*offspring*) progéniture *f*; (*descendants*) lignée *f*, descendants *mpl*.

progesterone [prəʊˈdʒestəˌrəʊn] *n* progestérone *f*.

prognathous [prɒgˈneɪθəs] *adj* prognathe.

prognosis [prɒgˈnəʊsɪs] *n, pl* **prognoses** [prɒgˈnəʊsiːz] pronostic *m*.

prognostic [prɒgˈnɒstɪk] *n* (*frm*) présage *m*, signe *m* avant-coureur.

prognosticate [prɒgˈnɒstɪkeɪt] *vt* pronostiquer, prédire, présager.

prognostication [prɒgˌnɒstɪˈkeɪʃən] *n* pronostic *m*.

programme, (US) program [ˈprəʊgræm] **1** *n* (*most senses*) programme *m*; (*Rad, TV: broadcast*) émission *f* (*on* sur, *about* au sujet de); (*Rad: station*) poste *m*; (*TV: station*) chaîne *f*. **what's the ~ for today?** (*during course etc*) quel est l'emploi du temps aujourd'hui?; (* *fig*) qu'est-ce qu'on fait aujourd'hui?, quel est le programme des réjouissances aujourd'hui?*; **what's on the ~?** qu'est-ce qu'il y a au programme?; **what's on the other ~?** (*TV*) qu'y a-t-il sur l'autre chaîne?; (*Rad*) qu'y a-t-il sur l'autre poste?; (*Rad, TV*) **details of the morning's ~s** le programme de la matinée, les détails des émissions de la matinée; *V* **request** *etc.*

2 *cpd*: (*Rad, TV*) **programme editor** éditorialiste *mf*; **programme music** musique *f* à programme; (*Mus*) **programme notes** notes *fpl* sur le programme; (*Theat*) **programme seller** vendeur *m*, -euse *f* de programmes.

3 *vt computer, washing machine etc* programmer (*to do* pour faire); *problem, task* programmer. **~d learning** enseignement programmé; **the broadcast was ~d for Sunday evening/for 8 o'clock** l'émission était programmée pour dimanche soir/pour 8 heures; **the meeting was ~d to start at 7** le début de la réunion était prévu pour 19 heures.

programmer [ˈprəʊgræməʳ] *n* (*person: also* **computer ~**) programmeur *m*, -euse *f*; (*device*) programmateur *m*.

programming [ˈprəʊgræmɪŋ] *n* (*also* **computer ~**) programmation *f*.

progress [ˈprəʊgres] **1** *n* **(a)** (*U: lit, fig*) progrès *m(pl)*. **in the name of ~** au nom du progrès; **we made slow ~ through the mud** nous avons avancé lentement dans la boue; **we are making good ~ in our search for a solution** nos travaux pour trouver une solution progressent de manière satisfaisante; **we have made little/no ~** nous n'avons guère fait de progrès/fait aucun progrès; **he is making ~** *[student etc]* il fait des progrès, il est en progrès; *[patient]* son état (de santé) s'améliore; **the ~ of events** le cours des événements; **the meeting is in ~** la réunion est en cours *or* a déjà commencé; **while the meeting was in ~** pendant que la réunion se déroulait; **the work in ~** les travaux en cours; **'silence: exam in ~'** 'silence: examen'.

(b) (††: *journey*) voyage *m*; *V* **pilgrim**.

2 *cpd*: **progress report** (*Med*) fiche *f or* bulletin *m* de santé; (*Admin etc*) état *m or* compte rendu des travaux.

3 *vi* [prəˈgres] (*lit, fig*) aller, avancer (*towards* vers); *[student etc]* faire des progrès, progresser; *[patient]* aller mieux; *[search, investigations, researches, studies etc]* progresser, avancer. **matters are ~ing slowly** les choses progressent lentement; **as the game ~ed** à mesure que la partie se déroulait; **while the discussions were ~ing** pendant que les discussions se déroulaient.

progression [prəˈgreʃən] *n* (*gen, Math*) progression *f*. **by arithmetical/geometrical ~** selon une progression arithmétique/géométrique; **it's a logical ~** c'est une suite logique.

progressive [prəˈgresɪv] **1** *adj movement, taxation, disease, improvement* progressif; *idea, party, person, outlook* progressiste (*also Pol*); *age* de *or* du progrès. **in ~ stages** par degrés, par étapes. **2** *n* (*Pol etc*) progressiste *mf*.

progressively [prəˈgresɪvlɪ] *adv* progressivement, par degrés, petit à petit, graduellement.

progressiveness [prəˈgresɪvnɪs] *n* progressivité *f*.

prohibit [prəˈhɪbɪt] *vt* **(a)** (*forbid*) interdire, défendre (*sb from doing* à qn de faire); (*Admin, Jur etc*) *weapons, drugs, swearing* prohiber. **smoking ~ed** défense de fumer; **feeding the animals is ~ed** il est interdit *or* défendu de donner à manger aux animaux; **pedestrians are ~ed from using this bridge** il est interdit aux piétons d'utiliser ce pont, l'usage de ce pont est interdit aux piétons.

(b) (*prevent*) empêcher (*sb from doing* qn de faire). **my health ~s me from swimming** ma santé m'empêche de nager, il m'est interdit *or* défendu de nager pour des raisons de santé.

prohibition [ˌprəʊɪˈbɪʃən] **1** *n* (*V* **prohibit**) prohibition *f*; interdiction *f*, défense *f*; (*esp US: against alcohol*) prohibition. **2** *cpd* (*US*) *laws, party* prohibitionniste.

prohibitionism [ˌprəʊɪˈbɪʃənɪzəm] *n* prohibitionnisme *m*.

prohibitionist [ˌprəʊɪˈbɪʃənɪst] *adj, n* prohibitionniste (*mf*).

prohibitive [prəˈhɪbɪtɪv] *adj price, tax, laws* prohibitif.

prohibitory [prəˈhɪbɪtərɪ] *adj* prohibitif.

project [ˈprɒdʒekt] **1** *n* **(a)** (*plan, scheme*) projet *m*, plan *m*, programme *m* (*to do, for doing* pour faire); (*undertaking*) opération *f*, entreprise *f*; (*study*) étude *f* (*on* de); (*Scol*) dossier *m* (*on* sur). **they are studying the ~ for the new road** ils étudient le projet de construction de la nouvelle route; **the whole ~ will cost 2 million** l'opération *or* l'entreprise tout entière coûtera 2 millions; **his ~ on asthma is almost finished** son étude de l'asthme est presque finie; (*Scol*) **they are doing a ~ on the Vikings** ils préparent un dossier sur les Vikings.

(b) (*US: also* **housing ~**) cité *f*, lotissement *m*.

2 *cpd budget, staff* de l'opération, de l'entreprise.

3 [prəˈdʒekt] *vt* (*all senses*) projeter.

4 [prəˈdʒekt] *vi* former *or* faire saillie, être en saillie, saillir. **to ~ over sth** surplomber qch; **to ~ into sth** s'avancer (en saillie) dans qch.

projectile [prəˈdʒektaɪl] *n* projectile *m*.

projecting [prəˈdʒektɪŋ] *adj construction* saillant, en saillie; *tooth* qui avance.

projection [prəˈdʒekʃən] **1** *n* **(a)** (*U: V* **project 3**) projection *f*. **(b)** (*overhang*) saillie *f*, ressaut *m*. **2** *cpd*: (*Cine*) **projection booth, projection room** cabine *f* de projection.

projectionist [prəˈdʒekʃnɪst] *n* projectionniste *mf*.

projective [prəˈdʒektɪv] *adj* projectif.

projector [prəˈdʒektəʳ] *n* (*Cine etc*) projecteur *m*.

prolactin [prəʊ'læktɪn] *n* prolactine *f*.
prolapse ['prəʊlæps] **1** *n* ptose *f*, prolapsus *m*. **2** *vi* descendre.
prole* [prəʊl] *adj, n* (*pej abbr of* **proletarian**) prolo* (*m*).
proletarian [ˌprəʊlə'tɛərɪən] **1** *n* prolétaire *m*. **2** *adj class, party* prolétarien; *life, ways, mentality* de prolétaire.
proletarianize [ˌprəʊlə'tɛərɪənaɪz] *vt* prolétariser.
proletariat [ˌprəʊlə'tɛərɪət] *n* prolétariat *m*.
proliferate [prə'lɪfəreɪt] *vi* proliférer.
proliferation [prəˌlɪfə'reɪʃən] *n* prolifération *f*.
proliferous [prə'lɪfərəs] *adj* prolifère.
prolific [prə'lɪfɪk] *adj* prolifique.
prolix ['prəʊlɪks] *adj* prolixe.
prolixity [prəʊ'lɪksɪtɪ] *n* prolixité *f*.
prologue ['prəʊlɒg] *n* (*Literat etc*) prologue *m* (*to* de); (*fig*) prologue (*to* à).
prolong [prə'lɒŋ] *vt* prolonger.
prolongation [ˌprəʊlɒŋ'geɪʃən] *n* (*in space*) prolongement *m*; (*in time*) prolongation *f*.
prom* [prɒm] *n* (*abbr of* **promenade**) **(a)** (*Brit: by sea*) promenade *f*, front *m* de mer. **(b)** (*Brit*) = **promenade concert**; *V* **promenade 2**. **(c)** (*US*) = **promenade 1c**.
promenade [ˌprɒmɪ'nɑːd] **1** *n* **(a)** (*walk*) promenade *f*.
(b) (*place*) (*by sea*) promenade *f*, front *m* de mer; (*in park etc*) avenue *f*; (*in theatre, hall etc*) promenoir *m*.
(c) (*US*) bal *m* d'étudiants.
2 *cpd*: (*Brit*) **promenade concert** concert *m* (promenade) (*donné dans une salle à promenoir*); (*Naut*) **promenade deck** pont *m* promenade.
3 *vi* (*walk*) se promener.
4 *vt person* promener; *avenue* se promener le long de.
promenader* [ˌprɒmɪ'nɑːdəʳ] *n* (*Brit Mus*) auditeur *m*, -trice *f* d'un 'promenade concert'; *V* **promenade**.
Prometheus [prə'miːθjuːs] *n* Prométhée *m*.
prominence ['prɒmɪnəns] *n* (*V* **prominent**) proéminence *f*, aspect saillant *or* frappant *or* marquant; importance *f*. **to bring sth/sb into ~** mettre qch/qn en vue, attirer l'attention sur qch/qn; **to come into ~** prendre de l'importance.
prominent ['prɒmɪnənt] *adj ridge, structure, nose* proéminent; *cheekbones* saillant; *tooth* qui avance; (*fig: striking*) *pattern, markings* frappant; *feature* marquant; (*fig: outstanding*) *person* important, bien en vue. **he is a ~ member of ...** c'est un membre important de ...; **she is ~ in London literary circles** elle est très en vue dans les cercles littéraires londoniens; **he was very ~ in ..., he played a ~ part in ...** il a joué un rôle important dans ...; **to put sth in a ~ position** mettre qch bien en vue *or* en valeur; (*fig*) **he occupies a ~ position in ...** il occupe une position importante *or* en vue dans ... .
prominently ['prɒmɪnəntlɪ] *adv display, place, set* bien en vue. **his name figured ~ in the case** on a beaucoup entendu parler de lui dans l'affaire.
promiscuity [ˌprɒmɪs'kjuːɪtɪ] *n* **(a)** (*pej: sexual*) promiscuité sexuelle. **(b)** (*gen*) promiscuité *f*.
promiscuous [prə'mɪskjʊəs] *adj* **(a)** (*pej: in sexual matters*) *person* de mœurs faciles *or* légères; *conduct* léger, libre, immoral. **(b)** (*disorderly, mixed*) *collection, heap* confus.
promiscuously [prə'mɪskjʊəslɪ] *adv* **(a)** (*pej*) *behave* immoralement. **(b)** *heap, collect* confusément.
promiscuousness [prə'mɪskjʊəsnɪs] *n* = **promiscuity**.
promise ['prɒmɪs] **1** *n* **(a)** (*undertaking*) promesse *f*. **~ of marriage** promesse de mariage; **under (a** *or* **the) ~ of** sous promesse de; **to make sb a ~** faire une promesse à qn (*to do* de faire); **is it a ~?** c'est promis?; **to keep one's ~** tenir sa promesse; **to hold** *or* **keep sb to his ~** contraindre qn à tenir sa promesse, faire tenir sa promesse à qn.
(b) (*hope*) promesse(s) *f(pl)*, espérance(s) *f(pl)*. **a young man of ~** un jeune homme plein de promesses *or* qui promet; **he shows great ~** il donne de grandes espérances; **it holds out a ~ of peace** cela promet *or* fait espérer la paix.
2 *vt* **(a)** promettre (*sth to sb* qch à qn, *sb to do* à qn de faire, *that* que). **I ~ (you)!** je vous le promets!; **'I will help you' she ~d** 'je vous aiderai' promit-elle; **I can't ~ (anything)** je ne peux rien (vous) promettre; (*fig*) **to ~ sb the earth** *or* **the moon** promettre monts et merveilles à qn, promettre la lune à qn; **to ~ o.s. (to do) sth** se promettre (de faire) qch.
(b) (*fig*) promettre, annoncer. **those clouds ~ rain** ces nuages annoncent la pluie; **they ~ us rain tomorrow** ils nous ont promis *or* annoncé de la pluie pour demain; **it ~s to be hot today** il va sûrement faire chaud aujourd'hui; **this ~s to be difficult** ça promet d'être *or* ça s'annonce difficile.
3 *vi* **(a)** promettre. **(will you) ~?** (c'est) promis?, juré?; **I can't ~ but I'll do my best** je ne vous promets rien mais je ferai de mon mieux.
(b) (*fig*) **to ~ well** *[person]* promettre, être plein de promesses; *[situation, event]* être plein de promesses, être prometteur; *[crop, business]* s'annoncer bien; *[first book]* promettre, être prometteur; **this doesn't ~ well** ce n'est guère prometteur, ça ne s'annonce pas bien.
promised ['prɒmɪst] *adj* promis. **the P~ Land** la Terre Promise.
promising ['prɒmɪsɪŋ] *adj* prometteur, qui promet, plein de promesses. **the future is ~** l'avenir s'annonce bien; **that's ~** c'est prometteur; (*iro*) ça promet!; (*iro*); **it doesn't look very ~** ça ne semble guère prometteur; (*of scheme, plan etc*) ça m'étonnerait que ça marche (*subj*), ça ne se présente pas bien; **he is a ~ young man** c'est un jeune homme plein de promesses *or* qui promet; **we have 2 ~ candidates** nous avons 2 candidats prometteurs; **he is a ~ pianist** c'est un pianiste d'avenir.
promisingly ['prɒmɪsɪŋlɪ] *adv* d'une façon prometteuse. **it's going quite ~** c'est prometteur, ça marche bien.
promissory ['prɒmɪsərɪ] *adj*: **~ note** billet *m* à ordre.
promontory ['prɒməntrɪ] *n* promontoire *m*.

promote [prə'məʊt] *vt* **(a)** *person* promouvoir (*to* à). **to be ~d** être promu, monter en grade; **he was ~d (to) colonel** *or* **to the rank of colonel** il a été promu colonel; (*Ftbl etc*) **they've been ~d to the first division** ils sont montés en première division.
(b) (*encourage*) *cause, cooperation, plan, sales, product* promouvoir; *trade* promouvoir, développer, favoriser, encourager; (*Comm*) *firm, company, business, campaign* lancer; (*Parl*) *bill* présenter.
promoter [prə'məʊtəʳ] *n [sport]* organisateur *m*, -trice *f*; (*Comm*) *[product]* promoteur *m* de vente; *[business, company]* fondateur *m*, -trice *f*.
promotion [prə'məʊʃən] *n* **(a)** promotion *f*, avancement *m*. **to get ~** obtenir de l'avancement, être promu.
(b) (*U: V* **promote b**) promotion *f*, développement *m*; lancement *m*; présentation *f*. **(sales) ~** promotion des ventes.
(c) (*advertising material*) réclames *fpl*, publicité *f*.
prompt [prɒmpt] **1** *adj* **(a)** (*speedy*) *action* rapide, prompt; *delivery, reply, service* rapide. **~ payment** paiement *m* rapide; (*Comm*) paiement dans les délais; **they were ~ to offer their services** ils ont été prompts à offrir leurs services, ils ont offert leurs services sans tarder.
(b) (*punctual*) ponctuel, à l'heure.
2 *adv* ponctuellement. **at 6 o'clock ~** à 6 heures pile *or* tapantes *or* sonnantes; **I want it on May 6th ~** je le veux le 6 mai sans faute *or* au plus tard.
3 *vt* **(a)** pousser, inciter (*sb to do* qn à faire). **I felt ~ed to protest** cela m'a incité à protester, je me suis senti obligé de protester; **he was ~ed by a desire to see justice done** il était animé *or* poussé par un désir de voir la justice triompher; **it ~s the thought that ...** cela incite à penser que ..., cela vous fait penser que ...; **a feeling of regret ~ed by the sight of ...** un sentiment de regret provoqué *or* déclenché par la vue de ... .
(b) (*Theat*) souffler.
4 *n* (*Theat*) **to give sb a ~** souffler une réplique à qn.
5 *cpd*: (*Theat*) **prompt box** trou *m* du souffleur; **prompt side/off prompt side** côté *m* cour/côté jardin.
prompter ['prɒmptəʳ] *n* (*Theat*) souffleur *m*, -euse *f*.
prompting ['prɒmptɪŋ] *n* incitation *f*. **he did it at my ~** il l'a fait à mon instigation; **he did it without (any) ~** il l'a fait de son propre chef.
promptitude ['prɒmptɪtjuːd] *n* promptitude *f*, empressement *m* (*in doing* à faire); (*punctuality*) ponctualité *f*.
promptly ['prɒmptlɪ] *adv* (*speedily*) rapidement, promptement, avec promptitude; (*punctually*) ponctuellement. **to pay ~** payer sans tarder; (*Comm*) payer recta *or* dans les délais.
promptness ['prɒmptnɪs] *n* = **promptitude**.
promulgate ['prɒməlgeɪt] *vt law* promulguer; *idea, doctrine, creed* répandre, disséminer.
promulgation [ˌprɒməl'geɪʃən] *n* (*V* **promulgate**) promulgation *f*; dissémination *f*.
prone [prəʊn] *adj* **(a)** (*face down*) (couché) sur le ventre, étendu face contre terre, prostré. **(b)** (*liable*) prédisposé, enclin, sujet (*to sth* à qch, *to do* à faire).
proneness ['prəʊnnɪs] *n* tendance *f*, prédisposition *f* (*to sth* à qch, *to do* à faire).
prong [prɒŋ] *n [fork]* dent *f*; *[antler]* pointe *f*.
pronged [prɒŋd] *adj* à dents.
-pronged [prɒŋd] *adj ending in cpds*: **three-pronged** *fork* à trois dents; (*Mil etc*) *attack, advance* sur trois fronts, triple.
pronominal [prəʊ'nɒmɪnl] *adj* pronominal.
pronoun ['prəʊnaʊn] *n* pronom *m*.
pronounce [prə'naʊns] **1** *vt* **(a)** *word etc* prononcer. **how is it ~d?** comment ça se prononce?; **the 'k' in 'knot' is not ~d** on ne prononce pas le 'k' dans 'knot', le 'k' dans 'knot' est muet.
(b) déclarer, prononcer (*that* que). (*Jur*) **to ~ sentence** prononcer une sentence; **they ~d him unfit to drive** ils l'ont déclaré inapte à la conduite; **he ~d himself in favour of the suggestion** il s'est prononcé *or* il s'est déclaré en faveur de la suggestion.
2 *vi* se prononcer (*on* sur, *for* en faveur de, *against* contre); (*Jur*) prononcer (*for* en faveur de, *against* contre), rendre un arrêt.
pronounceable [prə'naʊnsəbl] *adj* prononçable.
pronounced [prə'naʊnst] *adj* prononcé, marqué.
pronouncement [prə'naʊnsmənt] *n* déclaration *f*.
pronto* ['prɒntəʊ] *adv* tout de suite, illico*.
pronunciation [prəˌnʌnsɪ'eɪʃən] *n* prononciation *f*.
proof [pruːf] **1** *n* **(a)** (*gen, Jur, Math etc*) preuve *f*. (*Jur etc*) **~ of identity** papiers *mpl or* pièce(s) *f(pl)* d'identité; (*Jur*) **the burden of ~ lies with the prosecution** la charge de la preuve incombe au ministère public; **by way of ~** en guise de preuve, comme preuve, pour preuve; **as (a) ~ of, in ~ of** pour preuve de; **I've got ~ that he did it** j'ai la preuve *or* je peux prouver qu'il l'a fait; **it is ~ that he is honest** c'est la preuve qu'il est honnête; (*fig*) **he showed** *or* **gave ~ of great courage** il a fait preuve *or* il a témoigné de beaucoup de courage; *V* **positive**.
(b) (*test*) épreuve *f*. **to put sth/sb to the ~** mettre qch/qn à l'épreuve, éprouver qch/qn; (*Prov*) **the ~ of the pudding is in the eating** c'est à l'usage que l'on peut juger de la qualité d'une chose.
(c) *[book, pamphlet, engraving, photograph]* épreuve *f*. **to pass the ~s** donner le bon à tirer; **to read** *or* **correct the ~s** corriger les épreuves; **the book is in ~** le livre est au stade des épreuves; *V* **galley, page**[1] *etc*.
(d) (*of alcohol*) teneur *f* en alcool. **this whisky is 70° ~** ≃ ce whisky titre 40° d'alcool *or* 40° Gay Lussac; **under/over ~** moins de/plus de la teneur normale *or* exigée en alcool.
2 *cpd*: **proofread** corriger les épreuves de; **proofreader** correcteur *m*, -trice *f* d'épreuves; **proofreading** correction *f*

des épreuves; **proof sheets** épreuves *fpl*; **proof spirit** alcool *m* à 57°; **at proof stage** au stade des épreuves.

3 *adj*: ~ **against** *bullets, time, wear, erosion* à l'épreuve de; *temptation, suggestion* insensible à.

4 *vt* **(a)** *fabric, anorak, tent* imperméabiliser.

(b) (*Typ etc*) corriger les épreuves de.

...proof [pru:f] *adj endings in cpds* à l'épreuve de; *V* **bullet, fool**[1] *etc.*

prop[1] [prɒp] **1** *n* support *m*; (*for wall, in mine, tunnel etc*) étai *m*; (*for clothes-line*) perche *f*; (*for vines, hops etc*) échalas *m*; (*for beans, peas*) rame *f*; (*for seedlings*) tuteur *m*; (*fig*) soutien *m*, appui *m* (*to, for* de). **his presence was a great ~ to her morale** elle trouvait beaucoup de réconfort dans sa présence, sa présence lui était d'un grand réconfort (moral).

2 *vt* (*also* ~ **up**) (*lean*) *ladder, cycle* appuyer (*against* contre); (*support, shore up*) *tunnel, wall, building* étayer; *clothes-line, lid* caler; *vine, hops* échalasser; *beans, peas* mettre une rame à; *seedlings* mettre un tuteur à; (*fig*) *régime* maintenir; *business, company* soutenir, renflouer; *organization* soutenir, patronner; (*Fin*) *the pound* venir au secours de. **to ~ o.s. (up) against** se caler contre, s'adosser à; **he managed to ~ the box open** il réussit à maintenir la boîte ouverte.

prop[2]* [prɒp] *n* (*Theat*) *abbr of* **property 1c.**

prop[3]* [prɒp] *n* (*Aviat*) *abbr of* **propeller.**

propaganda [ˌprɒpəˈgændə] **1** *n* propagande *f*. **2** *cpd leaflet, campaign* de propagande.

propagandist [ˌprɒpəˈgændɪst] *adj, n* propagandiste (*mf*).

propagandize [ˌprɒpəˈgændaɪz] **1** *vi* faire de la propagande. **2** *vt doctrine* faire de la propagande pour; *person* soumettre à la propagande, faire de la propagande à.

propagate [ˈprɒpəgeɪt] (*lit, fig*) **1** *vt* propager. **2** *vi* se propager.

propagation [ˌprɒpəˈgeɪʃən] *n* propagation *f*.

propel [prəˈpel] **1** *vt* **(a)** *vehicle, boat, machine* propulser, faire avancer. **(b)** (*push*) pousser. **to ~ sth/sb along** faire avancer qch/qn (en le poussant); **they ~led him into the room** ils l'ont poussé dans la pièce, (*more violently*) ils l'ont propulsé dans la pièce. **2** *cpd*: **propelling pencil** porte-mine *m inv*.

propellant [prəˈpelənt] *n* (*gen*) combustible *m*.

propellent [prəˈpelənt] **1** *adj* propulseur, propulsif. **2** *n* = **propellant.**

propeller [prəˈpeləʳ] **1** *n* [*plane, ship*] hélice *f*. **2** *cpd*: **propeller shaft** (*Aut*) arbre *m* de transmission; (*Aviat, Naut*) arbre d'hélice.

propensity [prəˈpensɪtɪ] *n* propension *f*, tendance naturelle (*to or towards or for sth* à qch, *to do, for doing* à faire).

proper [ˈprɒpəʳ] **1** *adj* **(a)** (*appropriate, suitable, correct*) convenable, adéquat, indiqué, correct. **you'll have to put the lid on the ~ way** il faut que vous mettiez (*subj*) le couvercle comme il faut; **you'll have to apply for it (in) the ~ way** il faudra faire votre demande dans les règles; **you should be wearing ~ clothes** vous devriez porter une tenue adéquate *or* une tenue plus indiquée; **the ~ dress for the occasion** la tenue de rigueur pour l'occasion; **that is not the ~ tool for the job** ce n'est pas le bon outil *or* l'outil adéquat *or* l'outil indiqué *or* l'outil qu'il faut *or* l'outil qui convient pour ce travail; **the ~ spelling** l'orthographe correcte; **in the ~ meaning** *or* **sense of the word** au sens propre du mot; **if you had come at the ~ time** si vous étiez venu à la bonne heure *or* à l'heure dite; **2 a.m. isn't a ~ time to phone anyone** 2 heures du matin n'est pas une heure (convenable) pour téléphoner à qui que ce soit; (*Admin etc*) **you must go through the ~ channels** vous devez passer par la filière officielle; **the ~ reply would have been 'no'** la réponse qui aurait convenu c'est 'non'; **to make a ~ job of sth** bien réussir qch (*also iro*); **to do the ~ thing by sb** bien agir *or* agir honorablement envers qn; (*Math*) ~ **fraction** fraction *f* inférieure à l'unité; (*Gram*) ~ **noun** nom *m* propre; (*Rel*) ~ **psalm** psaume *m* du jour; **do as you think ~** faites ce qui vous semble bon; **if you think it ~ to do so** si vous jugez bon de faire ainsi; **in a manner ~ to his position** ainsi que l'exigeait sa position; **the qualities which are ~ to this substance** les qualités propres à *or* typiques de cette substance; *V* **right** *etc.*

(b) (*authentic*) vrai, véritable, authentique; (*after n: strictly speaking*) proprement dit, même. **he's not a ~ electrician** il n'est pas un véritable électricien; **I'm not a ~ Londoner** *or* **a Londoner ~** je ne suis pas à proprement parler londonien; **outside Paris ~** en dehors de Paris même *or* de Paris proprement dit.

(c) (*seemly*) *person* comme il faut*, convenable*; *book, behaviour* convenable, correct. **it isn't ~ to do that** cela ne se fait pas, faire cela n'est pas correct *or* convenable; *V* **prim.**

(d) (*: *intensive*) **he's a ~ fool** c'est un imbécile fini; **I felt a ~ idiot** je me suis senti vraiment idiot; **he's a ~ gentleman** c'est un monsieur très comme il faut*, c'est un vrai gentleman; **he made a ~ mess of it** il (en) a fait un beau gâchis; **it's a ~ mess in there!** c'est un beau désordre *or* la pagaïe* complète là-dedans!

2 *adv* (‡) **(a)** *behave, talk* comme il faut.

(b) vraiment, très. **he did it ~ quick** et comment qu'il l'a fait vite‡; **it's ~ cruel!** qu'est-ce que c'est cruel!‡

3 *n* (*Rel: often* **P~**) propre *m*.

properly [ˈprɒpəlɪ] *adv* **(a)** (*appropriately, correctly*) convenablement, correctement, comme il faut. **he was not ~ dressed for the reception** il n'était pas correctement vêtu pour la réception; **use the tool ~** sers-toi de l'outil correctement *or* comme il faut; **if you can't do it ~ I'll help you** si tu n'arrives pas à le faire comme il faut je t'aiderai; **he can't speak ~** il ne peut pas parler normalement; ~ **speaking** à proprement parler; **it's not ~ spelt** ce n'est pas orthographié correctement; **he very ~ refused** il a refusé et avec raison *or* à juste titre; (*Admin, Jur etc*) **he was behaving quite ~** il se conduisait d'une manière tout à fait correcte.

(b) (*in seemly way*) **to behave ~** se conduire convenablement *or* comme il faut; **behave/speak ~!** tiens-toi/parle comme il faut!; **he doesn't speak ~** il parle mal; **you're not even ~ dressed** tu n'es même pas vêtu comme il faut.

(c) (*: *completely*) vraiment. **we were ~ beaten** nous avons été battus à plate(s) couture(s); **I was ~ ashamed** j'avais vraiment *or* drôlement* honte; **I told him ~ what I thought of him** je lui ai dit carrément *or* sans mâcher mes mots ce que je pensais de lui.

propertied [ˈprɒpətɪd] *adj* possédant.

property [ˈprɒpətɪ] **1** *n* **(a)** (*possessions*) biens *mpl*, propriété *f*; (*land, building*) propriété, immeuble *m*; (*estate*) domaine *m*. (*Jur*) **personal ~** biens personnels *or* mobiliers; **is this your ~?** est-ce à vous?, cela vous appartient?; **a man of ~** un homme qui a des biens; *V* **common, lost** *etc.*

(b) (*Chem, Phys etc: quality*) propriété *f*.

(c) (*Theat*) accessoire *m*.

2 *cpd*: **property developer** promoteur *m* (de construction); (*Theat*) **property man** accessoiriste *m*; **the property market** *or* **mart** le marché immobilier; (*Theat*) **property mistress** accessoiriste *f*; **property owner** propriétaire foncier; **property tax** impôt foncier.

prophecy [ˈprɒfɪsɪ] *n* prophétie *f*.

prophesy [ˈprɒfɪsaɪ] **1** *vt* prédire (*that* que); *event* prédire, prophétiser. **2** *vi* prophétiser, faire des prophéties.

prophet [ˈprɒfɪt] *n* prophète *m*.

prophetess [ˈprɒfɪtɪs] *n* prophétesse *f*.

prophetic(al) [prəˈfetɪk(l)] *adj* prophétique.

prophetically [prəˈfetɪkəlɪ] *adv* prophétiquement.

prophylactic [ˌprɒfɪˈlæktɪk] **1** *adj* prophylactique. **2** *n* prophylactique *m*; (*US: contraceptive*) préservatif *m*.

prophylaxis [ˌprɒfɪˈlæksɪs] *n* prophylaxie *f*.

propinquity [prəˈpɪŋkwɪtɪ] *n* (*in time, space*) proximité *f*; (*in relationship*) parenté *f* proche, consanguinité *f*; [*ideas etc*] ressemblance *f*, affinité *f*.

propitiate [prəˈpɪʃɪeɪt] *vt* se concilier.

propitiation [prəˌpɪʃɪˈeɪʃən] *n* propitiation *f*.

propitiatory [prəˈpɪʃɪətərɪ] *adj* propitiatoire.

propitious [prəˈpɪʃəs] *adj* propice, favorable (*to* à).

propitiously [prəˈpɪʃəslɪ] *adv* d'une manière propice, favorablement.

proportion [prəˈpɔːʃən] **1** *n* **(a)** (*ratio, relationship: also Math*) proportion *f*. **the ~ of blacks to whites** la proportion *or* le pourcentage des noirs par rapport aux blancs; **in due ~** selon une proportion équitable *or* une juste proportion; **in perfect ~** parfaitement proportionné; **in ~ as** à mesure que; **add milk in ~ to the weight of flour** ajoutez du lait en proportion avec le poids de la farine; **her weight is not in ~ to her height** son poids n'est pas proportionné à sa taille; **contributions in ~ to one's earnings** contributions au prorata de *or* en proportion de ses revenus; **in ~ to what she earns, what she gives is enormous** en proportion de ce qu'elle gagne, ce qu'elle donne est énorme; **out of (all) ~** hors de (toute) proportion; **out of ~ to** hors de proportion avec, disproportionné à *or* avec; **he's got it out of ~** [*artist etc*] il n'a pas respecté les proportions, c'est mal proportionné; (*fig*) il a exagéré, c'est hors de proportion; (*lit, fig*) **he has no sense of ~** il n'a pas le sens des proportions.

(b) (*size*) ~**s** proportions *fpl*, dimensions *fpl*.

(c) (*portion, amount, share*) part *f*, partie *f*, pourcentage *m*. **in equal ~s** à parts égales; **a certain ~ of the staff** une certaine partie *or* un certain pourcentage du personnel; **your ~ of the work** votre part du travail; **what ~ is rented?** quel est le pourcentage de ce qui est loué?

2 *vt* proportionner (*to* à). **well-~ed** bien proportionné.

proportional [prəˈpɔːʃənl] *adj* proportionnel, proportionné (*to* à), en proportion (*to* de). (*Pol*) ~ **representation** représentation proportionnelle.

proportionally [prəˈpɔːʃnəlɪ] *adv* proportionnellement.

proportionate [prəˈpɔːʃnɪt] **1** *adj* = **proportional. 2** *vt* = **proportion 2.**

proportionately [prəˈpɔːʃnɪtlɪ] *adv* = **proportionally.**

proposal [prəˈpəʊzl] *n* **(a)** (*offer*) proposition *f*, offre *f*; (*of marriage*) demande *f* en mariage, offre de mariage. **(b)** (*plan*) projet *m*, plan *m* (*for sth* de *or* pour qch, *to do* pour faire); (*suggestion*) proposition *f*, suggestion *f* (*to do* de faire).

propose [prəˈpəʊz] **1** *vt* **(a)** (*suggest*) proposer, suggérer (*that* que + *subj*); *measures, course of action* proposer; *plan, motion, course* proposer, présenter, soumettre; *toast* porter; *candidate* proposer. **to ~ sb's health** porter un toast à la santé de qn; **to ~ marriage to sb** faire sa demande à qn, demander qn en mariage; **he ~d Smith as** *or* **for chairman** il a proposé Smith pour la présidence.

(b) (*have in mind*) **to ~ to do** *or* **doing** se proposer *or* avoir l'intention de faire, penser *or* compter faire.

2 *vi* (*offer marriage*) faire une demande en mariage, faire sa demande (*to sb* à qn).

proposer [prəˈpəʊzəʳ] *n* (*Admin, Parl etc*) auteur *m* de la proposition.

proposition [ˌprɒpəˈzɪʃən] **1** *n* **(a)** (*gen, Comm, Math, Philos etc: statement, offer*) proposition *f* (*also pej*).

(b) (*affair, enterprise*) **that's quite another ~** *or* **a different ~** ça c'est une tout autre affaire; **the journey alone is quite a ~** *or* **is a big ~** rien que le voyage n'est pas une petite affaire; **it's a tough ~** c'est ardu, ça présente de grandes difficultés; **he's a tough ~*** il est coriace, il n'est pas commode; *V* **economic, paying** *etc.*

2 *vt* faire des propositions (déshonnêtes) à.

propound [prəˈpaʊnd] *vt theory, idea* proposer, soumettre; *problem, question* poser.

proprietary [prəˈpraɪətərɪ] *adj* **(a)** (*Comm*) *article* de marque

déposée. ~ **brand** (produit *m* de) marque déposée; ~ **medicine** spécialité *f* pharmaceutique; ~ **name** marque déposée; ~ **rights** droit *m* de propriété. **(b)** *duties etc* de propriétaire.
proprietor [prə'praɪətəʳ] *n* propriétaire *m*.
proprietorship [prə'praɪətəʃɪp] *n* (*right*) droit *m* de propriété. **under his** ~ quand il en était (*or* sera) le propriétaire, lui (étant) propriétaire.
proprietress [prə'praɪətrɪs] *n* propriétaire *f*.
propriety [prə'praɪətɪ] *n* **(a)** (*decency*) bienséance *f*, convenance *f*, correction *f*. **to observe the proprieties** respecter *or* observer les bienséances *or* les convenances; **he threw ~ to the winds** il a envoyé promener les bienséances *or* les convenances.
(b) (*U: appropriateness, correctness etc*) *[behaviour, conduct, step]* justesse *f*, rectitude *f*; *[phrase, expression]* justesse, correction *f*.
propulsion [prə'pʌlʃən] *n* propulsion *f*.
propulsive [prə'pʌlsɪv] *adj* propulsif, propulseur, de propulsion.
prorate ['prəʊreɪt] *vt* (*US*) distribuer au prorata.
prorogation [ˌprəʊrə'geɪʃən] *n* prorogation *f*.
prorogue [prə'rəʊg] *vt* (*esp Parl*) proroger.
prosaic [prəʊ'zeɪɪk] *adj* prosaïque.
prosaically [prəʊ'zeɪɪkəlɪ] *adv* prosaïquement.
proscenium [prəʊ'si:nɪəm] *n* proscenium *m*.
proscribe [prəʊs'kraɪb] *vt* proscrire.
proscription [prəʊs'krɪpʃən] *n* proscription *f*.
prose [prəʊz] **1** *n* **(a)** (*U: Literat*) prose *f*. **in** ~ en prose. **(b)** (*Scol, Univ: also* ~ **translation**) thème *m*. **2** *cpd poem, comedy* en prose. **prose writer** prosateur *m*.
prosecute ['prɒsɪkju:t] *vt* **(a)** (*Jur etc*) poursuivre (en justice). **he was ~d for speeding** il a été poursuivi pour excès de vitesse; **to appear as prosecuting counsel** représenter le ministère public; *V* **trespasser.**
(b) (*further*) *enquiry, researches, a war* poursuivre.
prosecution [ˌprɒsɪ'kju:ʃən] *n* **(a)** (*Jur*) (*case*) accusation *f*; (*act, proceedings*) poursuites *fpl* judiciaires. **the** ~ (*side*) les plaignants, la partie plaignante; (*in crown court*) le ministère public; **you are liable to ~ if ...** vous pouvez être poursuivi si ...; vous pouvez être *or* faire l'objet de poursuites si ...; **to appear as counsel for the** ~ représenter le ministère public; **witness for the** ~ témoin *m* à charge; *V* **director.**
(b) (*furtherance: V* **prosecute b**) poursuite *f*.
prosecutor ['prɒsɪkju:təʳ] *n* plaignant *m*; (*also* **public** ~) procureur *m* (de la République), ministère public.
proselyte ['prɒsɪlaɪt] **1** *n* prosélyte *mf*. **2** *vti* = **proselytize.**
proselytism ['prɒsɪlɪtɪzəm] *n* prosélytisme *m*.
proselytize ['prɒsɪlɪtaɪz] **1** *vi* faire du prosélytisme. **2** *vt person* convertir, faire un(e) prosélyte de.
prosodic [prə'sɒdɪk] *adj* prosodique.
prosody ['prɒsədɪ] *n* prosodie *f*, métrique *f*.
prospect ['prɒspekt] **1** *n* **(a)** (*view*) vue *f*, perspective *f* (*of, from* de); (*fig*) (*outlook*) perspective; (*future*) (perspectives d')avenir *m*; (*hope*) espoir *m* (*of sth* de qch, *of doing* de faire). **this ~ cheered him up** cette perspective l'a réjoui; **to have sth in** ~ avoir qch en perspective *or* en vue; **the events in** ~ les événements en perspective; **there is little ~ of his coming** il y a peu de chances *or* d'espoir (pour) qu'il vienne; **he has little ~ of succeeding** il a peu de chances de réussir; **there is no ~ of that** rien ne laisse prévoir cela; **there is every ~ of success/of succeeding** tout laisse prévoir le succès/qu'on réussira; **the ~s for the harvest are good/poor** la récolte s'annonce bien/mal; **future ~s for the steel industry** les perspectives d'avenir de la sidérurgie; **what are his ~s?** quelles sont ses perspectives d'avenir?; **he has good ~s** il a de l'avenir; **he has no ~s** il n'a aucun avenir; **the job has no ~s** c'est un emploi sans avenir; **'good ~s of promotion'** 'nombreuses *or* réelles possibilités de développement', 'situation *f* d'avenir'; **the job offered the ~ of foreign travel** l'emploi offrait la possibilité de voyager à l'étranger.
(b) (*likely person, thing*) (*for marriage*) parti *m*. **he is a good ~ for the England team** c'est un bon espoir pour l'équipe anglaise; **this product is an exciting ~ for the European market** ce produit ouvre des perspectives passionnantes en ce qui concerne le marché européen; (*Comm etc*) **he seems quite a good** ~ il semble prometteur; **their offer/the deal seemed quite a good** ~ leur offre/l'affaire semblait prometteuse dans l'ensemble.
2 [prəs'pekt] *vi* prospecter. **to ~ for gold** *etc* prospecter pour trouver de l'or *etc*, chercher de l'or *etc*.
3 [prəs'pekt] *vt land, district* prospecter.
prospecting [prəs'pektɪŋ] *n* (*Min etc*) prospection *f*.
prospective [prəs'pektɪv] *adj son-in-law, home, legislation* futur; *journey* en perspective; *customer* éventuel, possible.
prospector [prəs'pektəʳ] *n* prospecteur *m*, -trice *f*. **gold** ~ chercheur *m* d'or.
prospectus [prəs'pektəs] *n* prospectus *m*.
prosper ['prɒspəʳ] **1** *vi [person]* prospérer; *[company, enterprise]* prospérer, réussir. **2** *vt* (†, *liter*) favoriser, faire prospérer, faire réussir.
prosperity [prɒs'perɪtɪ] *n* (*U*) prospérité *f*.
prosperous ['prɒspərəs] *adj person, city, business* prospère, florissant; *period, years* prospère; *undertaking* prospère, qui réussit; *look, appearance* prospère, de prospérité; (*liter*) *wind* favorable.
prosperously ['prɒspərəslɪ] *adv* de manière prospère *or* florissante.
prostate ['prɒsteɪt] *n* (*also* ~ **gland**) prostate *f*.
prosthesis [prɒs'θi:sɪs] *n* prosthèse *f or* prothèse *f*.
prosthetic [prɒs'θetɪk] *adj* prosthétique *or* prothétique.
prostitute ['prɒstɪtju:t] **1** *n* prostituée *f*. **male** ~ prostitué *m*, homme *m* se livrant à la prostitution. **2** *vt* (*lit, fig*) prostituer.
prostitution [ˌprɒstɪ'tju:ʃən] *n* (*U*) prostitution *f*.
prostrate ['prɒstreɪt] **1** *adj* (*lit*) à plat ventre; (*in respect, submission*) prosterné; (*in exhaustion*) prostré; (*fig: nervously, mentally*) prostré, accablé, abattu.
2 [prɒs'treɪt] *vt* **(a) to ~ o.s.** se prosterner.
(b) (*fig*) accabler. **the news ~d him** la nouvelle l'a accablé *or* abattu; **~d with grief/by the heat** accablé de chagrin/par la chaleur.
prostration [prɒs'treɪʃən] *n* (*act*) prosternation *f*, prosternement *m*; (*Rel*) prostration *f*; (*fig: nervous exhaustion*) prostration. **in a state of** ~ prostré.
prosy ['prəʊzɪ] *adj* ennuyeux, insipide.
protagonist [prəʊ'tægənɪst] *n* protagoniste *m*.
protean ['prəʊtɪən] *adj* changeant, inconstant.
protect [prə'tekt] *vt person, property, country, plants* protéger (*from* de, *against* contre); *interests, rights* sauvegarder; (*Econ*) *industry* protéger.
protection [prə'tekʃən] **1** *n* (*V* **protect**) protection *f* (*against* contre), sauvegarde *f*. **to be under sb's** ~ être sous la protection *or* sous l'aile de qn; **he wore a helmet for ~ against rock falls** il portait un casque pour se protéger des *or* contre les chutes de pierres; **it is some ~ against the cold** cela protège (un peu) contre le froid, cela donne une certaine protection contre le froid.
2 *cpd*: **he pays 200 dollars a week protection money** il paye 200 dollars par semaine pour ne pas être attaqué par le gang; **he pays protection money to Big Joe** il verse de l'argent à Big Joe pour qu'il le laisse (*subj*) en paix; **he's running a protection racket** il est à la tête d'un racket, il extorque des fonds par intimidation.
protectionism [prə'tekʃənɪzəm] *n* protectionnisme *m*.
protectionist [prə'tekʃənɪst] *adj, n* protectionniste (*mf*).
protective [prə'tektɪv] *adj layer, attitude, gesture* protecteur (*f* -trice), de protection; *clothing, covering* de protection; (*Econ*) *tariff, duty, system* protecteur. (*Zool*) ~ **colouring** *or* **coloration** camouflage *m*; (*Jur*) ~ **custody** détention préventive (*comme mesure de protection*).
protectively [prə'tektɪvlɪ] *adv* d'un geste *etc* protecteur.
protector [prə'tektəʳ] *n* (*person*) protecteur *m*; (*object, device*) dispositif *m* de protection. (*Brit Hist*) **the (Lord) P~** le Protecteur.
protectorate [prə'tektərɪt] *n* protectorat *m* (*also Brit Hist*).
protectress [prə'tektrɪs] *n* protectrice *f*.
protein ['prəʊti:n] *n* protéine *f*.
protest ['prəʊtest] **1** *n* protestation *f* (*against* contre, *about* à propos de). **to do sth under** ~ faire qch en protestant *or* contre son gré; **to make a** ~ protester, élever une protestation (*against* contre).
2 *cpd* (*Pol etc*) *meeting* de protestation. **protest march, protest demonstration** manifestation *f*.
3 [prə'test] *vt* protester (*that* que); *one's innocence, loyalty* protester de. **'I didn't do it' he ~ed** 'ce n'est pas moi qui l'ai fait' protesta-t-il.
4 [prə'test] *vi* protester, élever une *or* des protestation(s) (*against* contre, *about* à propos de, *to sb* auprès de qn).
Protestant ['prɒtɪstənt] *adj, n* protestant(e) *m(f)*.
Protestantism ['prɒtɪstəntɪzəm] *n* protestantisme *m*.
protestation [ˌprɒtes'teɪʃən] *n* protestation *f*.
protester [prə'testəʳ] *n* protestataire *mf*; (*on march, in demonstration etc*) manifestant(e) *m(f)*.
proto... ['prəʊtəʊ] *pref* proto... .
protocol ['prəʊtəkɒl] *n* protocole *m*.
proton ['prəʊtɒn] *n* proton *m*.
protoplasm ['prəʊtəʊplæzəm] *n* protoplasme *m*, protoplasma *m*.
prototype ['prəʊtəʊtaɪp] *n* prototype *m*.
protract [prə'trækt] *vt* prolonger, faire durer, faire traîner.
protracted [prə'træktɪd] *adj* prolongé, très long (*f* longue).
protraction [prə'trækʃən] *n* prolongation *f*.
protractor [prə'træktəʳ] *n* (*Geom*) rapporteur *m*.
protrude [prə'tru:d] **1** *vi [stick, gutter, rock, shelf]* dépasser, faire saillie, avancer; *[teeth]* avancer; *[eyes]* être globuleux. **2** *vt* faire dépasser.
protruding [prə'tru:dɪŋ] *adj teeth* qui avance; *eyes* globuleux; *chin* saillant; *shelf, rock* en saillie.
protrusion [prə'tru:ʒən] *n* saillie *f*, avancée *f*.
protrusive [prə'tru:sɪv] *adj* = **protruding.**
protuberance [prə'tju:bərəns] *n* protubérance *f*.
protuberant [prə'tju:bərənt] *adj* protubérant.
proud [praʊd] *adj* **(a)** *person* fier (*of sb/sth* de qn/qch, *that* que + *subj, to do* de faire); (*arrogant*) fier, orgueilleux, hautain. **that's nothing to be ~ of!** il n'y a pas de quoi être fier!; **I'm not very ~ of myself** je ne suis pas très fier de moi; **as ~ as a peacock** fier comme Artaban; (*pej*) vaniteux comme un paon; **it was a ~ day for us when ...** nous avons été remplis de fierté *or* très fiers le jour où ...; **to do o.s. ~*** ne se priver de rien; **to do sb ~*** se mettre en frais pour qn, recevoir qn comme un roi (*or* une reine); *V* **house, possessor** *etc*.
(b) (*splendid*) *building, ship* imposant, superbe, majestueux; *stallion* fier.
proudly ['praʊdlɪ] *adv* fièrement, avec fierté; (*pej: arrogantly*) fièrement, orgueilleusement; (*splendidly*) majestueusement, superbement, de manière imposante.
prove [pru:v] **1** *vt* **(a)** (*give proof of*) prouver (*also Jur*); (*show*) prouver, démontrer. **that ~s his innocence** *or* **him innocent** *or* **that he is innocent** cela prouve son innocence *or* qu'il est innocent; **you can't ~ anything against me** vous n'avez aucune preuve contre moi; **can you ~ it?** pouvez-vous le prouver?; **that**

~s it! c'est la preuve!; (*Scot Jur*) **verdict of not ~n** (ordonnance *f* de) non-lieu *m* (*en l'absence de charges suffisantes*); **the case was not ~n** il y a eu ordonnance de non-lieu.

(b) (*test*) mettre à l'épreuve; *will* homologuer. **to ~ o.s.** faire ses preuves.

2 *vi* s'avérer, se montrer, se révéler. **he ~d (to be) incapable of helping us** il s'est montré *or* révélé incapable de nous aider; **the information ~d (to be) correct** les renseignements se sont avérés *or* révélés justes; **the money ~d to be in his pocket** l'argent s'est trouvé être dans sa poche; **if it ~s otherwise** s'il en est autrement *or* différemment.

provenance ['prɒvɪnəns] *n* provenance *f.*

Provençal [ˌprɒvɑ̃:n'sɑ:l] **1** *adj* provençal. **2** *n* **(a)** Provençal(e) *m(f).* **(b)** (*Ling*) provençal *m.*

Provence [prɒ'vɑ̃:ns] *n* Provence *f.*

provender ['prɒvɪndər] *n* fourrage *m*, provende *f.*

proverb ['prɒvɜ:b] *n* proverbe *m.*

proverbial [prə'vɜ:bɪəl] *adj* proverbial.

proverbially [prə'vɜ:bɪəlɪ] *adv* proverbialement.

provide [prə'vaɪd] **1** *vt* **(a)** (*supply*) fournir (*sb with sth, sth for sb* qch à qn); (*equip*) munir, pourvoir (*sb with sth* qn de qch), fournir (*sb with sth* qch à qn). **to ~ o.s. with sth** se pourvoir *or* se munir de qch, se procurer qch; **I will ~ food for everyone** c'est moi qui fournirai la nourriture pour tout le monde; **he ~d the school with a new library** il a pourvu l'école d'une nouvelle bibliothèque; **candidates must ~ their own pencils** les candidats doivent être munis de leurs propres crayons; **can you ~ a substitute?** pouvez-vous trouver un remplaçant?; **it ~s accommodation for 5 families** cela loge 5 familles; **the field ~s plenty of space for a car park** le champ offre suffisamment d'espace pour un parc à autos; **I am already ~d with all I need** je suis déjà bien pourvu, j'ai déjà tout ce qu'il me faut; **the car is ~d with a radio** la voiture est pourvue d'une radio.

(b) *[legislation, treaty etc]* stipuler, prévoir (*that* que). **unless otherwise ~d** sauf conventions contraires.

2 *vi* **(a) to ~ for sb** pourvoir *or* subvenir aux besoins de qn; (*in the future*) assurer l'avenir de qn; **I'll see you well ~d for** je ferai le nécessaire pour que vous ne manquiez (*subj*) de rien; **the Lord will ~** Dieu y pourvoira.

(b) to ~ for sth prévoir qch; *[treaty, legislation]* prévoir *or* stipuler qch; **they hadn't ~d for such a lot of spectators** le nombre de spectateurs les a pris au dépourvu; **he had ~d for any eventuality** il avait paré à toute éventualité; **to ~ against** se prémunir contre prendre ses précautions contre.

provided [prə'vaɪdɪd] *conj*: **~ (that)** pourvu que + *subj*, à condition que + *subj*, à condition de + *infin*; **you can go ~ it doesn't rain** tu peux y aller pourvu qu'il *or* à condition qu'il ne pleuve pas; **you can go ~ you pass your exam** tu peux y aller à condition de réussir ton examen.

providence ['prɒvɪdəns] *n* **(a)** (*Rel etc*) providence *f.* **P~** la Providence.

(b) (†: *foresight*) prévoyance *f*, prudence *f.*

provident ['prɒvɪdənt] *adj person* prévoyant, prudent; (*Brit*) *fund, society* de prévoyance.

providential [ˌprɒvɪ'denʃəl] *adj* providentiel.

providentially [ˌprɒvɪ'denʃəlɪ] *adv* providentiellement.

providently ['prɒvɪdəntlɪ] *adv* avec prévoyance, prudemment.

provider [prə'vaɪdər] *n* pourvoyeur *m*, -euse *f*; (*Comm*) fournisseur *m*, -euse *f.*

providing [prə'vaɪdɪŋ] *conj* = **provided.**

province ['prɒvɪns] *n* **(a)** province *f.* **the ~s** la province; **in the ~s** en province.

(b) (*fig*) domaine *m*, compétence *f* (*esp Admin*). **that is not my ~, it is not within my ~** cela n'est pas de mon domaine *or* de ma compétence *or* de mon ressort; **his particular ~ is housing** le logement est son domaine *or* sa spécialité.

(c) (*Rel*) archevêché *m.*

provincial [prə'vɪnʃəl] **1** *adj* (*also pej*) provincial, de province. **2** *n* provincial(e) *m(f).*

provincialism [prə'vɪnʃəlɪzəm] *n* provincialisme *m.*

provision [prə'vɪʒən] **1** *n* **(a)** (*supply*) provision *f.* **to lay in** *or* **get in a ~ of coal** faire provision de charbon; (*food etc*) **~s** provisions *fpl*; **to get ~s in** faire des provisions.

(b) (*U: supplying*) fourniture *f*, approvisionnement *m.* **the ~ of housing** le logement; **~ of food to the soldiers** approvisionnement des soldats en nourriture; (*Fin*) **~ of capital** apport *m or* fourniture de capitaux; **to make ~ for** *one's family, dependents etc* pourvoir aux besoins de, assurer l'avenir de; *journey, siege, famine* prendre des dispositions *or* des précautions pour.

(c) (*Admin, Jur etc: stipulation*) disposition *f*, clause *f.* **according to the ~s of the treaty** selon les dispositions du traité; **it falls within the ~s of this law** cela tombe sous le coup de cette loi, c'est un cas prévu par cette loi; **~ to the contrary** clause contraire; **there is no ~ for this in the rules, the rules make no ~ for this** le règlement ne prévoit pas cela.

2 *cpd*: **provision merchant** marchand *m* de comestibles.

3 *vt* approvisionner, ravitailler.

provisional [prə'vɪʒənl] **1** *adj government, arrangement* provisoire; (*Admin*) *appointment* à titre provisoire; (*Jur*) provisionnel. (*Brit*) **~ driving licence** permis *m* de conduire provisoire (*obligatoire pour l'élève conducteur*).

2 *n* (*Ir Pol*) **the P~s** les Provisionals (*tendance activiste de l'IRA*).

provisionally [prə'vɪʒnəlɪ] *adv agree* provisoirement; *appoint* à titre provisoire.

proviso [prə'vaɪzəʊ] *n* stipulation *f*, condition *f*; (*Jur*) clause restrictive, condition formelle. **with the ~ that** à condition que + *subj.*

Provo* ['prɒvəʊ] *n* = **provisional 2.**

Provo* ['prɒvəʊ] *n* = **provisional 2.**

provocation [ˌprɒvə'keɪʃən] *n* provocation *f.* **under ~** en réponse à une provocation.

provocative [prə'vɒkətɪv] *adj* (*aggressive*) *gesture, remark* provocant, provocateur (*f* -trice); (*thought-provoking*) *book, title, talk* qui donne à penser, qui vise à provoquer des réactions; (*seductive*) *woman, movement, smile* provocant, aguichant. **now you're trying to be ~** là vous essayez de me (*or* le *etc*) provoquer, là vous me (*or* lui *etc*) cherchez querelle.

provocatively [prə'vɒkətɪvlɪ] *adv* (*V* **provocative**) d'un air *or* d'un ton provocant *or* provocateur; d'une manière apte à provoquer des réactions; d'un air aguichant.

provoke [prə'vəʊk] *vt* **(a)** (*rouse*) provoquer, pousser, inciter (*sb to do or into doing* qn à faire); *war, dispute, revolt* provoquer, faire naître; *reply* provoquer, susciter. **it ~d them to action** cela les a provoqués *or* incités *or* poussés à agir.

(b) to ~ sb, to ~ sb's anger *or* **sb to anger** provoquer qn.

provoking [prə'vəʊkɪŋ] *adj* contrariant, agaçant; *V* **thought.**

provost ['prɒvəst] **1** *n* (*Brit Univ*) principal *m*; (*US Univ*) ≃ doyen *m*; (*Scot*) maire *m*; (*Rel*) doyen *m*; *V* **lord. 2** *cpd*: (*Mil*) **provost court** tribunal prévôtal; **provost guard** prévôté *f*; **provost marshal** prévôt *m.*

prow [praʊ] *n* proue *f.*

prowess ['praʊɪs] *n* prouesse *f.*

prowl [praʊl] **1** *vi* (*also* **~ about, ~ around**) rôder. **2** *n*: **to be on the ~** rôder. **3** *cpd*: (*US Police*) **prowl car** voiture *f* de police.

prowler ['praʊlər] *n* rôdeur *m*, -euse *f.*

prowling ['praʊlɪŋ] *adj* rôdeur; *taxi* en maraude.

proximity [prɒk'sɪmɪtɪ] *n* proximité *f.* **in ~ to** à proximité de.

proximo ['prɒksɪməʊ] *adv* (*Comm*) (du mois) prochain.

proxy ['prɒksɪ] **1** *n* (*power*) procuration *f*, pouvoir *m*, mandat *m*; (*person*) mandataire *mf.* **by ~** par procuration. **2** *cpd*: **proxy vote** vote *m* par procuration.

prude [pru:d] *n* prude *f*, bégueule *f.* **he is a ~** il est prude *or* bégueule.

prudence ['pru:dəns] *n* prudence *f*, circonspection *f.*

prudent ['pru:dənt] *adj* prudent, circonspect.

prudential [pru(:)'denʃəl] *adj* prudent, de prudence.

prudently ['pru:dəntlɪ] *adv* prudemment, avec prudence.

prudery ['pru:dərɪ] *n* pruderie *f*, pudibonderie *f.*

prudish ['pru:dɪʃ] *adj* prude, pudibond, bégueule.

prudishness ['pru:dɪʃnɪs] *n* = **prudery.**

prune[1] [pru:n] *n* (*fruit*) pruneau *m*; (*US*‡: *pej: person*) repoussoir *m.* (*fig*) **~s and prisms** afféterie *f*, préciosité *f.*

prune[2] [pru:n] *vt tree* tailler, élaguer, émonder; (*fig: also* **~ down**) *article, essay* élaguer, faire des coupures dans.

prune away *vt sep branches* tailler, élaguer; (*fig*) *paragraph, words* élaguer.

pruning ['pru:nɪŋ] **1** *n* taille *f*, émondage *m*, élagage *m.* **2** *cpd*: **pruning hook** émondoir *m*, ébranchoir *m*; **pruning knife** serpette *f*; **pruning shears** cisailles *fpl.*

prurience ['prʊərɪəns] *n* lascivité *f*, luxure *f.*

prurient ['prʊərɪənt] *adj* lascif.

Prussia ['prʌʃə] *n* Prusse *f.*

Prussian ['prʌʃən] **1** *adj* prussien. **~ blue** bleu *m* de Prusse. **2** *n* Prussien(ne) *m(f).*

prussic ['prʌsɪk] *adj*: **~ acid** acide *m* prussique.

pry[1] [praɪ] *vi* fourrer son nez dans les affaires des autres, s'occuper de ce qui ne vous regarde pas. **I don't want to ~ but ...** je ne veux pas être indiscret mais ...; **stop ~ing!** occupez-vous de ce qui vous regarde!; **to ~ into sb's desk** fureter *or* fouiller *or* fouiner dans le bureau de qn; **to ~ into a secret** chercher à découvrir un secret.

pry[2] [praɪ] *vt* (*US*) = **prise.**

prying ['praɪɪŋ] *adj* fureteur, curieux, indiscret (*f* -ète).

psalm [sɑ:m] *n* psaume *m.*

psalmist ['sɑ:mɪst] *n* psalmiste *m.*

psalmody ['sælmədɪ] *n* psalmodie *f.*

psalter ['sɔ:ltər] *n* psautier *m.*

psephologist [se'fɒlədʒɪst] *n* spécialiste *mf* des élections.

psephology [se'fɒlədʒɪ] *n* étude *f* des élections.

pseud‡ [sju:d] *n* bêcheur* *m*, -euse* *f.*

pseudo- ['sju:dəʊ] *pref* pseudo-. **~antique** pseudo-antique; **~autobiography** pseudo-autobiographie *f*; **~apologetically** sous couleur de s'excuser.

pseudo* ['sju:dəʊ] *adj* insincère, faux (*f* fausse).

pseudonym ['sju:dənɪm] *n* pseudonyme *m.*

pseudonymous [sju:'dɒnɪməs] *adj* pseudonyme.

pshaw [pʃɔ:] *excl* peuh!

psittacosis [ˌpsɪtə'kəʊsɪs] *n* psittacose *f.*

psoriasis [sɒ'raɪəsɪs] *n* psoriasis *m.*

psyche ['saɪkɪ] *n* psychisme *m*, psyché *f.*

psychedelic [ˌsaɪkɪ'delɪk] *adj* psychédélique.

psychiatric [ˌsaɪkɪ'ætrɪk] *adj hospital, treatment* psychiatrique; *disease* mental.

psychiatrist [saɪ'kaɪətrɪst] *n* psychiatre *mf.*

psychiatry [saɪ'kaɪətrɪ] *n* psychiatrie *f.*

psychic ['saɪkɪk] **1** *adj* **(a)** (*supernatural*) *phenomenon* métapsychique, psychique*; (*telepathic*) télépathe. **~ research** recherches *fpl* métapsychiques; **I'm not ~*** je ne suis pas devin. **(b)** (*Psych*) psychique. **2** *n* médium *m.*

psychical ['saɪkɪkəl] *adj* = **psychic 1.**

psycho... ['saɪkəʊ] *pref* psych(o)... .

psycho‡ ['saɪkəʊ] *abbr of* **psychopath(ic), psychotic.**

psychoanalysis [ˌsaɪkəʊə'nælɪsɪs] *n* psychanalyse *f.*

psychoanalyst [ˌsaɪkəʊ'ænəlɪst] *n* psychanalyste *mf.*

psychoanalytic(al) ['saɪkəʊˌænə'lɪtɪk(əl)] *adj* psychanalytique.

psychoanalyze [ˌsaɪkəʊ'ænəlaɪz] *vt* psychanalyser.

psycholinguistic ['saɪkəʊlɪŋ'gwɪstɪk] **1** *adj* psycholinguistique. **2** *n* (*U*) **~s** psycholinguistique *f.*

psychological [ˌsaɪkəˈlɒdʒɪkəl] *adj method, study, state, moment, warfare* psychologique. **it's only ~*** c'est psychique *or* psychologique.

psychologically [ˌsaɪkəˈlɒdʒɪkəlɪ] *adv* psychologiquement.

psychologist [saɪˈkɒlədʒɪst] *n* psychologue *mf*; *V* **child** *etc.*

psychology [saɪˈkɒlədʒɪ] *n* psychologie *f*; *V* **child** *etc.*

psychometric [ˈsaɪkəʊˈmetrɪk] **1** *adj* psychométrique. **2** *n* (*U*) **~s** psychométrie *f*.

psychometry [saɪˈkɒmɪtrɪ] *n* psychométrie *f*.

psychomotor [ˈsaɪkəʊˈməʊtəʳ] *adj* psychomoteur (*f* -trice).

psychoneurosis [ˈsaɪkəʊnjʊəˈrəʊsɪs] *n* psychonévrose *f*, psychoneurasthénie *f*.

psychoneurotic [ˈsaɪkəʊnjʊəˈrɒtɪk] *adj* psychonévrotique.

psychopath [ˈsaɪkəʊpæθ] *n* psychopathe *mf*.

psychopathic [ˌsaɪkəʊˈpæθɪk] *adj person* psychopathe; *condition* psychopathique.

psychopathology [ˈsaɪkəʊpəˈθɒlədʒɪ] *n* psychopathologie *f*.

psychopharmacological [ˈsaɪkəʊfɑːməkəˈlɒdʒɪkəl] *adj* psychopharmacologique.

psychopharmacology [ˈsaɪkəʊfɑːməˈkɒlədʒɪ] *n* psychopharmacologie *f*.

psychophysical [ˈsaɪkəʊˈfɪzɪkəl] *adj* psychophysique.

psychophysics [ˈsaɪkəʊˈfɪzɪks] *n* (*U*) psychophysique *f*.

psychophysiological [ˈsaɪkəʊˌfɪzɪəˈlɒdʒɪkəl] *adj* psychophysiologique.

psychophysiology [ˈsaɪkəʊfɪzɪˈɒlədʒɪ] *n* psychophysiologie *f*.

psychosis [saɪˈkəʊsɪs] *n, pl* **psychoses** [saɪˈkəʊsiːz] psychose *f*.

psychosocial [ˈsaɪkəʊˈsəʊʃəl] *adj* psychosocial.

psychosociological [ˈsaɪkəʊˌsəʊsɪəˈlɒdʒɪkəl] *adj* psychosociologique.

psychosomatic [ˈsaɪkəʊsəʊˈmætɪk] *adj* psychosomatique.

psychosurgery [ˈsaɪkəʊˈsɜːdʒərɪ] *n* psychochirurgie *f*.

psychotherapist [ˈsaɪkəʊˈθerəpɪst] *n* (psycho)thérapeute *mf*.

psychotherapy [ˈsaɪkəʊˈθerəpɪ] *n* psychothérapie *f*.

psychotic [saɪˈkɒtɪk] *adj, n* psychotique (*mf*).

ptarmigan [ˈtɑːmɪgən] *n* lagopède *m*.

pterodactyl [ˌterəʊˈdæktɪl] *n* ptérodactyle *m*.

Ptolemaic [ˌtɒləˈmeɪɪk] *adj* ptolémaïque.

Ptolemy [ˈtɒləmɪ] *n* Ptolémée *m*.

ptomaine [ˈtəʊmeɪn] *n* ptomaïne *f*. **~ poisoning** intoxication *f* alimentaire.

ptosis [ˈtəʊsɪs] *n* ptose *f*.

pub [pʌb] (*Brit abbr of* **public house**) **1** *n* pub *m*. **2** *cpd*: **to go on a pub crawl*, to go pub-crawling*** faire la tournée des bistrots *or* des pubs.

puberty [ˈpjuːbətɪ] *n* puberté *f*.

pubescence [pjuːˈbesəns] *n* pubescence *f*.

pubescent [pjuːˈbesənt] *adj* pubescent.

pubic [ˈpjuːbɪk] *adj region etc* pubien. **~ hair** poils *mpl* du pubis.

pubis [ˈpjuːbɪs] *n* pubis *m*.

public [ˈpʌblɪk] **1** *adj meeting, park, indignation* public (*f* -ique); (*Econ: publicly owned*) *company* étatisé, nationalisé. **to make sth ~** rendre qch public, publier qch, porter qch à la connaissance du public; **it was all quite ~** ça n'avait rien de secret, c'était tout à fait officiel; **let's go over there, it's too ~ here** allons là-bas, c'est trop public ici; (*of copyright*) **in the ~ domain** dans le domaine public; (*Econ, Ind*) **the ~ sector** le secteur public; **his ~ support of the communists** son appui déclaré *or* ouvert aux communistes; **he made a ~ protest** il a protesté publiquement; **there was a ~ protest against ...** il y a eu une manifestation pour protester contre ...; **it is a matter of ~ interest** c'est une question d'intérêt public *or* général; **he has the ~ interest at heart** il a à cœur l'intérêt *or* le bien public; **the house has 2 ~ rooms and 3 bedrooms** la maison a 5 pièces dont 3 chambres; (*Fin*) **the company went ~ in 1978** la société a été cotée en Bourse en 1978; *V also* **2** *and* **image, nuisance** *etc.*

2 *cpd*: **public address system** (installation *f* de) sonorisation *f*; **public affairs** affaires *fpl* publiques; **public analyst** analyste *mf* d'État *or* officiel(le); **public assistance** = **public welfare**; (*Brit*) **public bar** bar *m*; **public building** édifice public; (*Brit*) **public convenience** = **public lavatory**; (*Econ*) **the public debt** la dette publique; (*US Jur*) **public defender** avocat *m* de l'assistance judiciaire; **public enemy** ennemi public; **public enemy number one*** ennemi public numéro un; **to be in the public eye** être très en vue; **he's a public figure** c'est une personnalité bien connue; (*Brit*) **public footpath** passage *m* public pour piétons, sentier *m* public; **public holiday** jour férié, fête légale; (*Brit*) **public house** pub *m*, ≈ café *m*, bistrot *m*; **public lavatory** toilettes *fpl*, W.-C. *mpl*; **public law** droit public; **public library** bibliothèque municipale; **a man in ~ life** un homme public; **he is active in ~ life** il prend une part active aux affaires publiques *or* du pays; (*Econ etc*) **public money** deniers *mpl* publics; **public opinion** opinion publique; **public opinion poll** sondage *m* d'opinion publique; (*Pol Econ*) **public ownership** étatisation *f*; **under public ownership** étatisé, nationalisé; **to take sth into public ownership** étatiser *or* nationaliser qch; (*Jur*) **public prosecutor** procureur *m* (de la République), ministère public; (*Econ*) **the public purse** le trésor public; (*Brit*) **Public Records Office** Archives nationales; **public relations** relations *fpl* publiques, public-relations* *fpl*; **public relations officer** public-relations* *m*, personne chargée des relations avec le public; **public school** (*Brit*) collège secondaire privé; (*US*) école publique; (*Brit*) **public schoolboy** *or* **schoolgirl** élève *mf* d'un collège secondaire privé; **public servant** fonctionnaire *mf*; **public service** service public; (*US*) **public service corporation** service public non étatisé; (*Brit Admin*) **public service vehicle** véhicule *m* de transport en commun; **he is a good public speaker** il parle bien en public; **public speaking** art *m* oratoire; **public spirit** civisme *m*; **to be public-spirited** faire preuve de civisme; **public transport** transport(s) *m(pl)* en commun; **public utility** service public; **public welfare** assistance publique; **public works** travaux publics.

3 *n* public *m*. **in ~** en public; **the reading/sporting ~** les amateurs *mpl* de lecture/de sport; (*hum*) **the great British ~** les sujets *mpl* de Sa (Gracieuse) Majesté; **he couldn't disappoint his ~** il ne pouvait (pas) décevoir son public; *V* **general** *etc.*

publican [ˈpʌblɪkən] *n* **(a)** (*Brit*) patron(ne) *m(f)* de bistrot. **(b)** (*Bible*) publicain *m*.

publication [ˌpʌblɪˈkeɪʃən] **1** *n* **(a)** (*U: act of publishing*) *[book etc]* publication *f*; (*Jur*) *[banns]* publication *f*; *[decree]* promulgation *f*, publication *f*. **after the ~ of the book** après la publication *or* la parution du livre; **this is not for ~** (*lit*) (*gen*) il ne faut pas publier ceci, (*by the press*) ceci ne doit pas être communiqué à la presse; (*fig*) ceci doit rester entre nous.

(b) (*published work*) publication *f*.

2 *cpd*: **publication date** date *f* de parution *or* de publication.

publicist [ˈpʌblɪsɪst] *n* (*Jur*) spécialiste *mf* de droit public international; (*Press*) journaliste *mf*; (*Advertising*) (agent *m*) publicitaire *m*, agent de publicité.

publicity [pʌbˈlɪsɪtɪ] **1** *n* (*U*) **(a)** publicité *f*. **can you give us some ~ for the concert?** pouvez-vous nous faire de la publicité pour le concert?

(b) (*posters, advertisements etc*) publicité *f*, réclame(s) *f(pl)*. **I've seen some of their ~** j'ai vu des exemples de leur publicité; **I got a lot of ~ in my mail for that new soap powder** j'ai reçu beaucoup de réclames pour cette nouvelle lessive dans mon courrier.

2 *cpd*: **publicity agency** agence *f* publicitaire *or* de publicité; **publicity agent** (agent *m*) publicitaire *m*, agent de publicité.

publicize [ˈpʌblɪsaɪz] *vt* **(a)** (*make public*) rendre public (*f* -ique), publier. **I don't ~ the fact, but ...** je ne le crie pas sur les toits mais... . **(b)** (*advertise*) faire de la publicité pour.

publicly [ˈpʌblɪklɪ] *adv* publiquement, en public. (*Econ*) **~-owned** étatisé, nationalisé.

publish [ˈpʌblɪʃ] *vt* **(a)** *news* publier, faire connaître. (*Jur*) **to ~ the banns** publier les bans. **(b)** *book* publier, éditer, faire paraître, sortir; *author* éditer. **'to be ~ed'** 'à paraître'; **'just ~ed'** 'vient de paraître'; **~ed monthly** paraît tous les mois.

publisher [ˈpʌblɪʃəʳ] *n* éditeur *m*, -trice *f*.

publishing [ˈpʌblɪʃɪŋ] *n* *[book etc]* publication *f*. **he's in ~** il travaille dans l'édition; **~ house** maison *f* d'édition.

puce [pjuːs] *adj* puce *inv*.

puck[1] [pʌk] *n* (*elf*) lutin *m*, farfadet *m*.

puck[2] [pʌk] *n* (*Ice Hockey*) palet *m*.

pucker [ˈpʌkəʳ] **1** *vi* (*also* **~ up**) *[face, feature, forehead]* se plisser; (*Sewing*) goder, faire un faux pli. **2** *vt* (*also* **~ up**) (*Sewing*) faire goder, donner un faux pli à. **to ~ (up) one's brow** *or* **forehead** plisser son front. **3** *n* (*Sewing*) faux pli *m*.

puckish [ˈpʌkɪʃ] *adj* de lutin, malicieux.

pud‡ [pʊd] *n abbr of* **pudding.**

pudding [ˈpʊdɪŋ] **1** *n* (*dessert*) dessert *m*; (* *pej: person*) patapouf* *m*, dondon* *f*. **rice ~** riz *m* au lait; (*sausage*) **black/white ~** boudin noir/blanc; *V* **milk, proof** *etc.*

2 *cpd*: **pudding basin** jatte *f*, bol *m*; (*fig pej*) **pudding-face‡** (face *f* de) lune‡ *f*, tête *f* de lard‡; (*fig pej*) **pudding-head‡** empoté(e)* *m(f)*; (*Geol*) **puddingstone** poudingue *m*, conglomérat *m*.

puddle [ˈpʌdl] *n* flaque *f* d'eau.

pudenda [puːˈdendə] *npl* parties *fpl* génitales.

pudgy [ˈpʌdʒɪ] *adj* = **podgy.**

puerile [ˈpjʊəraɪl] *adj* puéril (*f* puérile).

puerility [pjʊəˈrɪlɪtɪ] *n* puérilité *f*.

puerperal [pju(ː)ˈɜːpərəl] *adj* puerpéral.

Puerto Rican [ˈpwɜːtəʊˈriːkən] **1** *adj* portoricain. **2** *n* Portoricain(e) *m(f)*.

Puerto Rico [ˈpwɜːtəʊˈriːkəʊ] *n* Porto Rico *f*.

puff [pʌf] **1** *n* **(a)** *[air]* bouffée *f*, souffle *m*; (*from mouth*) souffle; *[wind, smoke]* bouffée; (*sound of engine*) teuf-teuf *m*. **our hopes vanished in a ~ of smoke** nos espoirs se sont évanouis *or* s'en sont allés en fumée; **he blew out the candles with one ~** il a éteint les bougies d'un seul souffle; **to be out of ~*** être à bout de souffle, être essoufflé; **to get one's ~* back** reprendre son souffle, reprendre haleine; **he took a ~ at his pipe/cigarette** il a tiré une bouffée de sa pipe/cigarette; **just time for a quick ~!*** juste le temps de griller* une cigarette en vitesse!

(b) (*powder ~*) houppe *f*, (*small*) houppette *f*; (*in dress*) bouillon *m*; (*pastry*) feuilleté *m*. **jam ~** feuilleté à la confiture.

(c) (*: *advertisement*) réclame *f* (*U*), boniment *m* (*U*); (*written article*) papier *m*. (*Press, Rad, TV*) **he gave the record a ~** il a fait de la réclame *or* du boniment pour le disque; **there's a ~ about his new book** il y a un papier sur son nouveau livre.

2 *cpd*: **puff adder** vipère heurtante; **puffball** vesse-de-loup *f*; **puff pastry**, (*US*) **puff paste** pâte feuilletée; (*baby talk*) **puff-puff*** teuf-teuf *m* (*baby talk*); **puff(ed) sleeves** manches bouffantes.

3 *vi* (*blow*) souffler; (*pant*) haleter; *[wind]* souffler. **smoke was ~ing from the ship's funnel** des bouffées de fumée sortaient de la cheminée du navire; **he was ~ing hard** *or* **~ing like a grampus** *or* **~ing and panting** il soufflait comme un phoque *or* un bœuf; to **~ (away) at one's pipe/cigarette** tirer des bouffées de sa pipe/cigarette; **he ~ed up to the top of the hill** soufflant et haletant il a grimpé jusqu'en haut de la colline; *[train]* **to ~ in/out** *etc* entrer/sortir *etc* en envoyant des bouffées de fumée.

4 *vt* **(a)** *[person, chimney, engine, boat]* **to ~ (out) smoke** envoyer des bouffées de fumée; **stop ~ing smoke into my face** arrête de m'envoyer ta fumée dans la figure; **he ~ed his pipe** il tirait des bouffées de sa pipe.

(b) *rice* faire gonfler; (*also* **~ out**) *sails etc* gonfler. **to ~ (out)**

one's cheeks gonfler ses joues; **to ~ out one's chest** gonfler *or* bomber sa poitrine; **the bird ~ed out** *or* **up its feathers** l'oiseau hérissa ses plumes; **his eyes are ~ed (up)** il a les yeux gonflés *or* bouffis.

(c) to be ~ed (out)* être à bout de souffle, être haletant.

puff away *vi V* **puff 3.**

puff out 1 *vi [sails etc]* se gonfler; *V also* **puff 3.**

2 *vt sep* **(a)** *V* **puff 4a, 4b, 4c.**

(b) (*utter breathlessly*) dire en haletant *or* tout essoufflé.

puff up 1 *vi [sails etc]* se gonfler; *[eye, face]* enfler.

2 *vt sep* (*inflate*) gonfler. (*fig*) **to be puffed up (with pride)** être bouffi d'orgueil; *V also* **puff 4b.**

puffer* ['pʌfər] *n* (*baby talk*) teuf-teuf *m* (*baby talk*), train *m*.

puffin ['pʌfɪn] *n* macareux *m*.

puffiness ['pʌfɪnɪs] *n* (*V* **puffy**) gonflement *m*, bouffissure *f*; boursouflure *f*.

puffy ['pʌfɪ] *adj eye* gonflé, bouffi; *face* gonflé, bouffi, boursouflé.

pug [pʌg] **1** *n* carlin *m*. **2** *cpd*: **pug nose** nez rond retroussé; **pugnosed** au nez rond retroussé.

pugilism ['pju:dʒɪlɪzəm] *n* boxe *f*.

pugilist ['pju:dʒɪlɪst] *n* pugiliste *m*, boxeur *m*.

pugnacious [pʌg'neɪʃəs] *adj* batailleur, pugnace, querelleur.

pugnaciously [pʌg'neɪʃəslɪ] *adv* avec pugnacité, d'un ton querelleur.

pugnacity [pʌg'næsɪtɪ] *n* pugnacité *f*.

puke‡ [pju:k] *vi* vomir, dégobiller‡. (*fig*) **it makes you ~** c'est à faire vomir, c'est dégueulasse‡.

pukka* ['pʌkə] *adj* (*genuine*) vrai, authentique, véritable; (*excellent*) de premier ordre; (*socially superior*) snob *inv*. (*Brit: fig*, †) **he's a ~ sahib** c'est ce qu'on appelle un gentleman.

pulchritude ['pʌlkrɪtju:d] *n* (*frm*) beauté *f*.

pull [pʊl] **1** *n* **(a)** (*act, effect*) traction *f*; *[moon]* attraction *f*; (*attraction: magnetic, fig*) (force *f* d')attraction, magnétisme *m*. **to give sth a ~, to give a ~ on** *or* **at sth** tirer (sur) qch; **one more ~ and we'll have it up** encore un coup et on l'aura; **I felt a ~ at my sleeve** j'ai senti quelqu'un qui tirait ma manche; **it was a long ~ up the hill** la montée était longue (et raide) pour aller jusqu'en haut de la colline; (*Rowing*) **it was a long ~ to the shore** il a fallu faire force de rames pour arriver jusqu'au rivage; **the ~ of the current** la force du courant; (*fig*) **the ~ of family ties** la force des liens familiaux; (*fig*) **the ~ of the South/the sea** *etc* l'attraction du Sud/de la mer *etc*; (*fig*) **to have a ~ over sb** (*have advantage over*) avoir l'avantage *or* le dessus sur qn; (*have a hold over*) avoir barre sur qn; (*fig*) **to have (some) ~ with sb** avoir de l'influence auprès de qn; (*fig*) **he's got ~*** il a le bras long; *V* **leg.**

(b) (*at bottle, glass, drink*) lampée *f*, gorgée *f*. **he took a ~ at the bottle** il a bu une gorgée *or* lampée à même la bouteille; **he took a long ~ at his cigarette/pipe** il a tiré longuement sur sa cigarette/pipe.

(c) (*handle*) poignée *f*; (*cord*) cordon *m*; *V* **bell.**

(d) (*Typ*) épreuve *f*.

(e) (*Golf*) coup hooké.

2 *cpd*: (*Brit*) **pull-in** (*lay-by*) parking *m*; (*café*) café *m*, snack *m*, auberge *f* de routiers; **pull-out** (*n: in magazine etc*) supplément *m* détachable; (*adj*) *magazine section* détachable; *table leaf, shelf* rétractable; **pullover** pull *m*, pullover *m*; **pull-up** (*Brit: by roadside*) = **pull-in**; (*Gymnastics*) traction *f* (*sur anneaux etc*).

3 *vt* **(a)** (*draw*) *cart, carriage, coach, caravan, curtains* tirer. **to ~ a door shut** tirer une porte derrière *or* après soi; **to ~ a door open** ouvrir une porte en la tirant; **~ your chair closer to the table** approchez votre chaise de la table; **he ~ed the box over to the window** il a traîné la caisse jusqu'à la fenêtre; **he ~ed her towards him** il l'attira vers lui.

(b) (*tug*) *bell, rope* tirer; *trigger* presser; *oars* manier. **he ~s a good oar** il est bon rameur; **to ~ to pieces** *or* **to bits** (*lit*) *toy, box etc* mettre en pièces *or* en morceaux, démolir; *daisy* effeuiller; (*fig*) *argument, scheme* démolir; *play, film* esquinter*; (*) *person* éreinter; **to ~ sb's hair** tirer les cheveux à qn; (*fig*) **to ~ sb's leg** faire marcher qn*, monter un bateau à qn* (*V also* **leg**); **~ the other one (it's got bells on)!*** à d'autres!; (*Horse-racing*) **to ~ a horse** retenir un cheval; (*Boxing, also fig*) **to ~ one's punches** ménager son adversaire; **he didn't ~ any punches** il n'y est pas allé de main morte; (*fig*) **she was the one ~ing the strings** c'était elle qui tirait les ficelles; (*fig*) **he had to ~ strings** *or* **wires to get the job** il a dû user de son influence *or* se faire pistonner *or* faire jouer le piston pour obtenir le poste; (*fig*) **to ~ strings** *or* **wires for sb** exercer son influence pour aider qn, pistonner qn; (*fig*) **to ~ one's weight** faire sa part du travail, fournir sa part d'effort; (*fig*) **to ~ rank on sb** en imposer hiérarchiquement à qn.

(c) (*draw out*) *tooth* arracher, extraire; *cork, stopper* ôter, enlever, retirer; *gun, knife* tirer, sortir; *flowers* cueillir; *weeds* arracher, extirper; *beer* tirer; (*Culin*) *chicken* vider. **he ~ed a gun on me** il a (soudain) braqué un revolver sur moi; **he's ~ing pints* somewhere in London** il est barman *or* garçon de café quelque part à Londres; (*Cards*) **to ~ trumps*** faire tomber les atouts.

(d) (*strain, tear*) *thread* tirer; *muscle, tendon, ligament* se déchirer, se froisser, se claquer.

(e) (*Typ*) tirer.

(f) (*Golf etc*) *ball* hooker. **to ~ a shot** hooker.

(g) (*fig: make, do*) faire, effectuer. **the gang ~ed several bank raids/several burglaries last month** le gang a effectué plusieurs hold-up de banques/plusieurs cambriolages le mois dernier; **to ~ a fast one on sb*** rouler qn*, avoir qn*; *V* **face, long**[1] *etc.*

4 *vi* **(a)** (*tug*) tirer (*at, on* sur). **stop ~ing!** arrêtez de tirer!; **he ~ed at her sleeve** il lui tira la manche, il la tira par la manche; **the car/the steering is ~ing to the left** la voiture/la direction tire *or* porte à gauche; **the brakes ~ to the left** quand on freine la voiture tire à gauche *or* porte à gauche *or* est déportée sur la gauche; **the rope won't ~, it must be stuck** la corde ne vient pas, elle doit être coincée.

(b) (*move*) **the coach ~ed slowly up the hill** le car a gravi lentement la colline; **the train ~ed into/out of the station** le train est entré en gare/est sorti de la gare; **he soon ~ed clear of the traffic** il a eu vite fait de laisser le gros de la circulation derrière lui; **he began to ~ ahead of his pursuers** il a commencé à prendre de l'avance sur *or* à se détacher de *or* à distancer ses poursuivants; **the car isn't ~ing very well** la voiture manque de reprises.

(c) to ~ at a cigarette/pipe *etc* tirer sur une cigarette/pipe *etc*; **he ~ed at his whisky** il a pris une gorgée *or* une lampée de son whisky.

(d) (*row*) ramer (*for* vers).

pull about, pull around *vt sep* **(a)** *wheeled object etc* tirer derrière soi.

(b) (*handle roughly*) *watch, ornament etc* tirailler; *person* malmener.

pull along *vt sep wheeled object etc* tirer derrière soi. **to pull o.s. along** se traîner.

pull apart 1 *vi*: **this box pulls apart** cette boîte est démontable *or* se démonte.

2 *vt sep* **(a)** (*pull to pieces*) démonter; (*break*) mettre en pièces *or* en morceaux. (*fig*) **the police pulled the whole house apart looking for drugs** la police a mis la maison sens dessus dessous en cherchant de la drogue.

(b) (*separate*) *dogs, adversaries* séparer; *sheets of paper etc* détacher, séparer.

pull away 1 *vi* **(a)** *[vehicle, ship]* démarrer; *[train]* démarrer, s'ébranler. **he pulled away from the kerb** il s'est éloigné du trottoir; **he began to pull away from his pursuers** il a commencé à se détacher de *or* à prendre de l'avance sur *or* à distancer ses poursuivants; **she suddenly pulled away from him** elle s'écarta soudain de lui.

(b) they were pulling away on the oars ils faisaient force de rames.

2 *vt sep* (*withdraw*) retirer brusquement (*from sb* à qn); (*snatch*) ôter, arracher (*from sb* à qn, des mains de qn). **he pulled the child away from the fire** il a éloigné *or* écarté l'enfant du feu.

pull back 1 *vi* (*Mil, gen, fig: withdraw*) se retirer.

2 *vt sep* **(a)** (*withdraw*) *object* retirer (*from* de); *person* tirer en arrière (*from* loin de); (*Mil*) retirer, ramener à *or* vers l'arrière. **to pull back the curtains** ouvrir les rideaux.

(b) *lever* tirer (sur).

pull down 1 *vi*: **the blind won't pull down** le store ne descend pas.

2 *vt sep* **(a)** *blind* baisser, descendre. **he pulled his opponent down (to the ground)** il a mis à terre son adversaire; **he pulled his hat down over his eyes** il ramena *or* rabattit son chapeau sur ses yeux; **pull your skirt down over your knees** ramène *or* tire ta jupe sur tes genoux; **she slipped and pulled everything down off the shelf with her** elle a glissé et entraîné dans sa chute tout ce qui était sur l'étagère.

(b) (*demolish*) *building* démolir, abattre; *tree* abattre. **the whole street has been pulled down** la rue a été complètement démolie; (*fig*) **to pull down the government** renverser le gouvernement.

(c) (*weaken, reduce*) affaiblir, abattre. **his illness has pulled him down a good deal** la maladie a sapé ses forces, la maladie l'a beaucoup affaibli *or* abattu; **his geography marks pulled him down** ses notes de géographie ont fait baisser sa moyenne *or* l'ont fait dégringoler*.

(d) (*US**: *earn*) *[person]* gagner; *[business, shop etc]* rapporter.

pull in 1 *vi* (*Aut etc*) (*arrive*) arriver; (*enter*) entrer; (*stop*) s'arrêter. **when the train pulled in (at the station)** quand le train est entré en gare.

2 *vt sep* **(a)** *rope, fishing line* ramener. **to pull sb in** (*into room, car*) faire entrer qn, tirer qn à l'intérieur; (*into pool etc*) faire piquer une tête dans l'eau à qn; **pull your chair in (to the table)** rentre ta chaise (sous la table); **pull your stomach in!** rentre le ventre!; (*fig*) **that film is certainly pulling people in** sans aucun doute ce film attire les foules; *V* **belt, horn.**

(b) (*detain*) **the police pulled him in for questioning** la police l'a appréhendé pour l'interroger.

(c) (*restrain*) *horse* retenir.

(d) (*: *earn*) *[person]* gagner; *[business, shop etc]* rapporter.

3 pull-in *n V* **pull 2.**

pull off *vt sep* **(a)** (*remove*) *handle, lid, cloth* enlever, ôter; *gloves, shoes, coat, hat* enlever, ôter, retirer.

(b) (*fig*) *plan, aim* réaliser; *deal* mener à bien, conclure; *attack, hoax* réussir. **he didn't manage to pull it off** il n'a pas réussi son coup.

pull on 1 *vi*: **the cover pulls on** la housse s'enfile.

2 *vt sep gloves, coat, cover* mettre, enfiler; *shoes, hat* mettre.

pull out 1 *vi* **(a)** (*leave*) *[train]* s'ébranler, démarrer; *[car, ship]* démarrer; (*withdraw: lit, fig*) se retirer (*of* de). (*Aviat*) **to pull out of a dive** se redresser; **he pulled out of the deal at the last minute** il a tiré son épingle du jeu *or* il s'est retiré à la dernière minute.

(b) (*Aut*) déboîter, sortir de la file. **he pulled out to overtake the truck** il a déboîté pour doubler le camion.

(c) the drawers pull out easily les tiroirs coulissent bien; **the table pulls out to seat 8** avec la rallonge 8 personnes peuvent s'asseoir à la table; **the centre pages pull out** les pages du milieu sont détachables *or* se détachent.

2 *vt sep* **(a)** (*extract, remove*) *nail, hair, page* arracher; *splinter* enlever; *cork, stopper* ôter, enlever, retirer; *tooth* arracher, extraire; *weeds* arracher, extirper; *gun, knife, cigarette lighter* sortir, tirer. **he pulled a rabbit out of his hat** il a sorti *or* tiré un lapin de son chapeau; **to pull sb out of a room** faire sortir qn d'une pièce, tirer qn à l'extérieur; **they pulled him out of the wreckage alive** ils l'ont tiré *or* sorti vivant des débris; *V* **finger, stop.**

(b) (*withdraw*) *troops, police etc* retirer (*of* de).

(c) (**fig: produce*) *reason, argument* sortir*, fournir, donner. (*fig*) **he pulled out one last trick** il a usé d'un dernier stratagème.

3 **pull-out** *adj, n V* **pull 2.**

pull over 1 *vi* (*Aut*) **he pulled over (to one side) to let the ambulance past** il s'est rangé *or* rabattu sur le côté pour laisser passer l'ambulance.

2 *vt sep* **(a) he pulled the box over to the window** il a traîné la caisse jusqu'à la fenêtre; **she pulled the chair over and stood on it** elle a tiré la chaise à elle pour grimper dessus; **they pulled him over to the door** ils l'ont entraîné vers la porte.

(b) they climbed the wall and pulled him over ils ont grimpé sur le mur et l'ont fait passer de l'autre côté.

(c) (*topple*) **he pulled the bookcase over on top of himself** il a entraîné la bibliothèque dans sa chute, il s'est renversé la bibliothèque dessus.

3 **pullover** *n V* **pull 2.**

pull round 1 *vi [unconscious person]* revenir à soi, reprendre conscience; *[sick person]* se remettre, se rétablir, s'en sortir.

2 *vt sep* **(a)** *chair etc* faire pivoter, tourner. **he pulled me round to face him** il m'a fait me retourner pour me forcer à lui faire face.

(b) *unconscious person* ranimer; *sick person* tirer *or* sortir de là.

pull through 1 *vi* **(a) the rope won't pull through** la corde ne passe pas.

(b) (*fig*) (*from illness*) s'en tirer, s'en sortir; (*from difficulties*) se tirer d'affaire *or* d'embarras, s'en sortir, s'en tirer.

2 *vt sep* **(a)** *rope etc* faire passer.

(b) (*fig*) *person* (*from illness*) guérir, tirer *or* sortir de là, tirer d'affaire; (*from difficulties*) sortir *or* tirer d'affaire *or* d'embarras.

pull together 1 *vi* (*on rope etc*) tirer ensemble *or* simultanément; (*row*) ramer simultanément *or* à l'unisson; (*fig: cooperate*) (s'entendre pour) faire un effort.

2 *vt sep* (*join*) *rope ends etc* joindre. (*fig*) **to pull o.s. together** se reprendre, se ressaisir; **pull yourself together!** ressaisissez-toi!, reprends-toi!, ne te laisse pas aller!

pull up 1 *vi* **(a)** (*stop*) *[vehicle]* s'arrêter, stopper; *[athlete, horse]* s'arrêter (net).

(b) (*draw level with*) **he pulled up with the leaders** il a rattrapé *or* rejoint ceux qui menaient.

2 *vt sep* **(a)** *object* remonter; (*haul up*) hisser; *stockings* remonter, tirer. **when the bucket was full he pulled it up** une fois le seau plein il l'a remonté; **he leaned down from the wall and pulled the child up** il se pencha du haut du mur et hissa l'enfant jusqu'à lui; **he pulled me up out of the armchair** il m'a tiré *or* fait sortir du fauteuil; (*fig*) **your geography mark has pulled you up** votre note de géographie vous a remonté*; *V* **sock[1].**

(b) *tree etc* arracher, déraciner; *weed* arracher, extirper. (*fig*) **to pull up one's roots** larguer ses amarres (*fig*), se déraciner.

(c) (*halt*) *vehicle* arrêter, stopper; *horse* arrêter. **the chairman pulled the speaker up (short)** le président a interrompu *or* a coupé la parole à l'orateur; **he pulled himself up (short)** il s'arrêta net *or* pile; **the police pulled him up for speeding** la police l'a stoppé pour excès de vitesse; (*fig*) **the headmaster pulled him up for using bad language** il a été repris *or* réprimandé par le directeur pour avoir été grossier.

3 **pull-up** *n V* **pull 2.**

pullet ['pʊlɪt] *n* jeune poule *f*, poulette *f*.

pulley ['pʊlɪ] *n* poulie *f*; (*for clothes-drying*) séchoir *m* à linge (suspendu).

Pullman ['pʊlmən] *n* (*Rail*) (*also* ~ **carriage**) pullman *m*, voiture-salon *f*, wagon-salon *m*; (*sleeper: also* ~ **car**) voiture-lit *f*, wagon-lit *m*.

pullulate ['pʌljʊleɪt] *vi* pulluler.

pulmonary ['pʌlmənərɪ] *adj* pulmonaire.

pulp [pʌlp] **1** *n* pulpe *f*; (*part of fruit*) pulpe, chair *f*; (*for paper*) pâte *f* à papier, pulpe (à papier). **to reduce** *or* **crush to a** ~ *wood* réduire en pâte *or* en pulpe; *fruit* réduire en pulpe *or* en purée *or* en marmelade; (*fig*) **his arm was crushed to a** ~ il a eu le bras complètement écrasé, il a eu le bras mis en bouillie *or* en marmelade; *V* **pound[2]** *etc.*

2 *cpd*: **pulp magazine** magazine *m* à sensation, torchon* *m*.

3 *vt wood, linen* réduire en pâte *or* en pulpe; *fruit* réduire en pulpe *or* en purée *or* en marmelade; *book* mettre au pilon, pilonner.

pulpit ['pʊlpɪt] *n* chaire *f* (*Rel*).

pulpy ['pʌlpɪ] *adj fruit* charnu, pulpeux; (*Bio*) *tissue* pulpeux.

pulsar ['pʌlsəʳ] *n* pulsar *m*.

pulsate [pʌl'seɪt] *vi* produire *or* émettre des pulsations; *[heart]* battre fort, palpiter; *[blood]* battre; *[music]* vibrer. **the pulsating rhythm of the drums** le battement rythmique des tambours.

pulsation [pʌl'seɪʃən] *n [heart]* battement *m*, pulsation *f*; (*Elec, Phys*) pulsation.

pulse[1] [pʌls] **1** *n* (*Med*) pouls *m*; (*Elec, Phys, Rad*) vibration *f*; *[radar]* impulsion *f*; (*fig*) *[drums etc]* battement *m* rythmique; *[emotion]* frémissement *m*, palpitation *f*. **to take sb's** ~ prendre le pouls de qn; **an event that stirred my** ~**s** un événement qui m'a remué le cœur *or* qui m'a fait palpiter d'émotion.

2 *cpd*: (*Med*) **pulsebeat** (battement *m or* pulsation *f* de) pouls *m*.

3 *vi [heart]* battre fort; *[blood]* battre. **it sent the blood pulsing through his veins** cela lui fouetta le sang, cela le fit palpiter d'émotion; **the life pulsing in a great city** la vie qui palpite au cœur d'une grande ville.

pulse[2] [pʌls] *n* légume *m* à gousse; (*dried*) légume sec; (*plant*) légumineuse *f*.

pulverization [,pʌlvəraɪ'zeɪʃən] *n* pulvérisation *f*.

pulverize ['pʌlvəraɪz] *vt* (*lit, fig*) pulvériser.

puma ['pju:mə] *n* puma *m*.

pumice ['pʌmɪs] *n* (*also* ~ **stone**) pierre *f* ponce.

pummel ['pʌml] *vt* bourrer *or* rouer de coups.

pummelling ['pʌməlɪŋ] *n* volée *f* de coups. **to take a** ~ (*lit*) se faire rouer de coups; (*Sport: be beaten*) se faire battre à plate(s) couture(s); (*be criticized/attacked*) se faire violemment critiquer/attaquer.

pump[1] [pʌmp] **1** *n* (*all senses*) pompe *f*; *V* **parish, petrol, prime** *etc.*

2 *cpd*: (*Brit*) **pump attendant** pompiste *mf*; **pump house, pumping station** station *f* d'épuisement *or* de pompage; **pump room** buvette *f* (*où l'on prend les eaux dans une station thermale*); **pump-water** eau *f* de la pompe.

3 *vt* **(a) to** ~ **sth out of sth** pomper qch de qch; **to** ~ **sth into sth** refouler qch dans qch (au moyen d'une pompe); **to** ~ **water into sth** pomper de l'eau dans qch; **to** ~ **air into a tyre** gonfler un pneu (avec une pompe); **the water is** ~**ed up to the house** l'eau est amenée jusqu'à la maison au moyen d'une pompe; **to** ~ **oil through a pipe** faire passer *or* faire couler du pétrole dans un pipe-line (à l'aide d'une pompe); **they** ~**ed the tank dry** ils ont vidé *or* asséché le réservoir (à la pompe); **the heart** ~**s the blood round the body** le cœur fait circuler le sang dans le corps; (*fig*) **they** ~**ed money into the project** ils ont injecté de plus en plus d'argent dans le projet; (*fig*) **he** ~**ed facts into their heads** il leur bourrait* la tête de faits précis; **to** ~ **sb full of lead**‡ trouer la peau‡ *or* faire la peau* à qn.

(b) (*fig: question*) **to** ~ **sb for sth** essayer de soutirer qch à qn; **they'll try to** ~ **you (for information)** ils essayeront de vous faire parler *or* de vous cuisiner* *or* de vous tirer les vers du nez; **he managed to** ~ **the figures out of me** il a réussi à me soutirer *or* à me faire dire les chiffres.

(c) *handle etc* lever et abaisser plusieurs fois *or* continuellement. **he** ~**ed my hand vigorously** il me secoua vigoureusement la main.

4 *vi [pump, machine, person]* pomper; *[heart]* battre fort. **blood** ~**ed from the artery** le sang coulait à flots de l'artère; **the oil was** ~**ing along the pipeline** le pétrole coulait dans le pipeline; **the piston was** ~**ing up and down** le piston montait et descendait régulièrement.

pump in *vt sep water, oil, gas etc* refouler (à l'aide d'une pompe). **pump some more air in** donnez plus d'air.

pump out 1 *vt sep water, oil, gas etc* pomper, aspirer (à l'aide d'une pompe).

2 *vi [blood, oil]* couler à flots (*of* de).

pump up *vt sep tyre, airbed* gonfler; *V also* **pump 3a.**

pump[2] [pʌmp] *n* (*slip-on shoe*) chaussure *f* sans lacet; (*Brit: dancing shoe*) escarpin *m*.

pumpernickel ['pʌmpənɪkl] *n* pumpernickel *m*, pain *m* de seigle noir.

pumpkin ['pʌmpkɪn] *n* citrouille *f*; (*bigger*) potiron *m*. ~ **pie** tarte *f* au potiron.

pun [pʌn] **1** *n* calembour *m*, jeu *m* de mots. **2** *vi* faire un *or* des calembour(s), faire un *or* des jeu(x) de mots.

Punch [pʌntʃ] *n* Polichinelle *m*. ~ **and Judy Show** (théâtre *m* de) guignol *m*; *V* **pleased.**

punch[1] [pʌntʃ] **1** *n* **(a)** (*blow*) coup *m* de poing. **to give sb a** ~ **on the nose** donner un coup de poing sur le nez à qn; (*Boxing*) **he's got a good** ~ il a du punch; *V* **pack, pull, rabbit** *etc.*

(b) (*U: fig: force*) *[person]* punch* *m*. **a phrase with more** ~ une expression plus frappante *or* plus incisive; **we need a presentation with some** ~ **to it** il nous faut une présentation (qui soit) énergique *or* vigoureuse; **a story with no** ~ **to it** une histoire qui manque de mordant.

(c) (*tool*) (*for tickets*) poinçonneuse *f*; (*for holes in paper*) perforateur *m*; (*Metalworking*) poinçonneuse, emporte-pièce *m inv*; (*for stamping design*) étampe *f*, (*smaller*) poinçon *m*; (*for driving in nails*) chasse-clou *m*.

2 *cpd*: **punch(ing) bag** (*lit*) sac *m* de sable, punching-bag *m*; (*fig*) souffre-douleur *m inv*; (*Brit*) **punchball** punching-ball *m*; **punch(ed) card** carte perforée; **punch-drunk** (*Boxing*) abruti par les coups, groggy, sonné*; (*fig*) abruti; **punching ball** = **punchball;** *[joke etc]* **punch-line** astuce *f*; **the punch-line of his speech** la phrase-clé à la fin de son discours; (*Computers*) ~**(ed) (paper) tape** bande perforée; (*Brit*) **punch-up*** bagarre* *f*; (*Brit*) **to have a punch-up** se bagarrer*.

3 *vt* **(a)** (*with fist*) *person* donner un coup de poing à; *ball, door* frapper d'un coup de poing. **to** ~ **sb's nose/face** donner un coup de poing sur le nez/sur la figure à qn; **he** ~**ed his fist through the glass** il a passé son poing à travers la vitre, il a brisé la vitre d'un coup de poing; **the goalkeeper** ~**ed the ball over the bar** d'un coup de poing le gardien de but a envoyé le ballon par-dessus la barre; **he** ~**ed his way through** il s'est ouvert un chemin à (force de) coups de poing *or* en frappant à droite et à gauche.

(b) (*US*) **to** ~ **cattle** conduire le bétail (à l'aiguillon).

(c) (*with tool*) *paper* poinçonner, perforer; *ticket* (*by hand*) poinçonner; (*automatically*) composter; *computer cards* perforer; *metal* poinçonner, découper à l'emporte-pièce; *design* estamper; *nails* enfoncer profondément (au chasse-clou). **to ~ a hole in sth** faire un trou dans qch; (*Ind*) **to ~ the time clock, to ~ one's card** pointer.

4 *vi* frapper (dur), cogner. (*Boxing*) **he ~es well** il sait frapper.

punch in 1 *vi* (*Ind: on time clock*) pointer (en arrivant).

2 *vt sep door, lid etc* ouvrir d'un coup de poing. **to punch sb's face or head in**: casser la gueule à qn:.

punch out 1 *vi* (*Ind: on time clock*) pointer (en partant).

2 *vt sep hole* faire au poinçon *or* à la poinçonneuse; *machine parts* découper à l'emporte-pièce; *design* estamper.

punch² [pʌntʃ] *n* (*drink*) punch *m*. **~ bowl** bol *m* à punch.

punchy* [pʌntʃɪ] *adj* **(a)** (*esp US: forceful*) *person* qui a du punch*, dynamique; *remark, reply* incisif, mordant. **(b)** = **punch-drunk**; *V* **punch¹ 2**.

punctilio [pʌŋk'tɪlɪəʊ] *n* (*frm*) (*U: formality*) formalisme *m*; (*point of etiquette*) point *m or* détail *m* d'étiquette.

punctilious [pʌŋk'tɪlɪəs] *adj* pointilleux.

punctiliously [pʌŋk'tɪlɪəslɪ] *adv* de façon pointilleuse.

punctual ['pʌŋktjʊəl] *adj person, train* à l'heure; *payment* ponctuel. **he is always ~** il est très ponctuel, il est toujours à l'heure; **be ~** soyez *or* arrivez à l'heure.

punctuality [,pʌŋktjʊ'ælɪtɪ] *n* (*V* **punctual**) *[person]* ponctualité *f*, exactitude *f*; *[train]* exactitude.

punctually ['pʌŋktjʊəlɪ] *adv* à l'heure; ponctuellement. **the train arrived ~** le train est arrivé *or* était à l'heure; **the train arrived ~ at 7 o'clock** le train est arrivé à 7 heures pile *or* précises; **he leaves ~ at 8 every morning** il part à 8 heures précises *or* ponctuellement à 8 heures tous les matins.

punctuate ['pʌŋktjʊeɪt] *vt* (*lit, fig*) ponctuer (*with* de).

punctuation [,pʌŋktjʊ'eɪʃən] *n* ponctuation *f*. **~ mark** signe *m* de ponctuation.

puncture ['pʌŋktʃəʳ] **1** *n* (*in tyre*) crevaison *f*; (*in skin, paper, leather*) piqûre *f*; (*Med*) ponction *f*. (*Aut etc*) **I've got a ~** j'ai (un pneu) crevé; **they had a ~ outside Limoges** ils ont crevé près de Limoges.

2 *cpd*: **puncture repair kit** trousse *f* de secours pour crevaisons.

3 *vt tyre, balloon* crever; *skin, leather, paper* piquer; (*Med*) *abscess* percer, ouvrir.

4 *vi [tyre etc]* crever.

pundit ['pʌndɪt] *n* (*iro*) expert *m*, pontife *m*.

pungency ['pʌndʒənsɪ] *n [smell, taste]* âcreté *f*; *[sauce]* goût piquant *or* relevé; *[remark, criticism]* mordant *m*, causticité *f*.

pungent ['pʌndʒənt] *adj smell, taste* âcre, piquant; *sauce* piquant, relevé; *remark, criticism* mordant, caustique, acerbe; *sorrow* déchirant.

pungently ['pʌndʒəntlɪ] *adv remark* d'un ton mordant *or* caustique *or* acerbe; *criticize* de façon mordante *or* caustique *or* acerbe.

Punic ['pju:nɪk] *adj* punique.

punish ['pʌnɪʃ] *vt* **(a)** *person* punir (*for sth* de qch, *for doing* pour avoir fait); *theft, fault* punir. **he was ~ed by having to clean it all up** pour le punir on lui a fait tout nettoyer, pour sa punition il a dû tout nettoyer.

(b) (*fig*) *opponent in fight, boxer, opposing team* malmener; *engine* fatiguer; *roast beef* faire honneur à; *bottle of whisky* taper dans*. **the jockey really ~ed his horse** le jockey a vraiment forcé *or* fatigué son cheval.

punishable ['pʌnɪʃəbl] *adj offence* punissable. **~ by death** passible de la peine de mort.

punishing ['pʌnɪʃɪŋ] **1** *n* (*act*) punition *f*. (*fig*) *[boxer, opponent, opposing team]* **to take a ~** se faire malmener; **the roast beef/the bottle of whisky took a ~** il n'est pas resté grand-chose du rosbif/de la bouteille de whisky, le rosbif/le whisky en a pris un coup*. **2** *adj speed, heat, game, work* épuisant, exténuant.

punishment ['pʌnɪʃmənt] *n* punition *f*, (*solemn*) châtiment *m*. **as a ~ (for)** en punition (de); **he took his ~ bravely** *or* **like a man** il a subi *or* encaissé* sa punition sans se plaindre; **to make the ~ fit the crime** adapter le châtiment au crime, proportionner la peine au délit; (*fig*) **to take a lot of ~** *[boxer, opponent in fight]* encaisser*; *[opposing team]* se faire malmener; *V* **capital, corporal² etc.**

punitive ['pju:nɪtɪv] *adj expedition* punitif; *measure* de punition.

punk [pʌŋk] **1** *n* **(a)** (:*pej: person*) con*: *m*, conne*: *f*; (*homosexual*) tapette: *f*. **(b)** (*:*nonsense*) foutaises: *fpl*. **(c)** (*Mus etc*) punk *m*. **~ rock** le rock punk, le punk rock. **2** *adj*(:) qui ne vaut rien, moche*.

punnet ['pʌnɪt] *n* (*Brit*) carton *m*, petit panier.

punster ['pʌnstəʳ] *n* personne *f* qui fait des calembours.

punt¹ [pʌnt] **1** *n* (*boat*) bachot *m or* bateau *m* à fond plat. **2** *vt boat* faire avancer à la perche; *goods* transporter en bachot. **3** *vi*: **to go ~ing** faire un tour de rivière, aller se promener en bachot.

punt² [pʌnt] (*Ftbl*) **1** *vt ball* envoyer d'un coup de volée. **2** *n* coup *m* de volée.

punt³ [pʌnt] *vi* (*Brit: bet*) parier; (*Brit, US: Cards*) ponter.

punter ['pʌntəʳ] *n* (*Brit: gen*) parieur *m*, -ieuse *f*; (*Brit, US: Cards*) ponte *m*.

puny ['pju:nɪ] *adj person, animal* chétif, malingre, frêle; *effort* faible, piteux.

pup [pʌp] **1** *n* (*dog*) chiot *m*, jeune chien(ne) *m(f)*; (*seal*) bébé-phoque *m*, jeune phoque *m*; (* *fig pej: youth*) freluquet *m*, godelureau *m*. **he's an insolent young ~** c'est un petit morveux*; *V* **sell. 2** *vi* mettre bas.

pupa ['pju:pə] *n, pl* **pupae** ['pju:pi:] chrysalide *f*, pupe *f*.

pupate ['pju:peɪt] *vi* devenir chrysalide *or* pupe.

pupil¹ ['pju:pl] **1** *n* (*Scol etc*) élève *mf*. **2** *cpd*: **pupil power** pouvoir *m* des lycéens; **pupil teacher** professeur *m* stagiaire.

pupil² ['pju:pl] *n [eye]* pupille *f*.

puppet ['pʌpɪt] **1** *n* (*lit*) marionnette *f*; (*flat cutout*) pantin *m*; (*fig*) marionnette, pantin, fantoche *m*. **he was like a ~ on a string** il n'était qu'une marionnette *or* qu'un pantin dont on tire les fils; *V* **glove etc.**

2 *cpd theatre, play* de marionnettes; (*fig, esp Pol*) *state, leader, cabinet* fantoche. **puppet show** (spectacle *m* de) marionnettes *fpl*.

puppeteer [pʌpɪ'tɪəʳ] *n* montreur *m*, -euse *f* de marionnettes, marionnettiste *mf*.

puppetry ['pʌpɪtrɪ] *n* art *m* des marionnettes.

puppy ['pʌpɪ] **1** *n* = **pup 1. 2** *cpd*: **puppy fat** rondeurs *fpl* d'adolescent(e); **puppy love** premier amour (d'adolescent).

purblind ['pɜ:blaɪnd] *adj* (*blind*) aveugle; (*poorly sighted*) qui voit très mal, qui a une vue très faible; (*fig: stupid*) aveugle, borné, obtus.

purchase ['pɜ:tʃɪs] **1** *n* **(a)** (*Comm etc*) achat *m*. **to make a ~** faire un achat.

(b) (*grip, hold*) prise *f*. **the wheels can't get a ~ on this surface** les roues n'ont pas de prise sur cette surface; **I can't get a ~ on this rock** je n'arrive pas à trouver un point d'appui *or* une prise sur ce rocher.

2 *cpd*: **purchase money** = **purchase price**; (*Ind etc*) **purchasing officer** acheteur *m*, -euse *f* (professionnel(le)); **purchasing power** pouvoir *m* d'achat; **purchase price** prix *m* d'achat; (*Brit*) **purchase tax** taxe *f* à l'achat.

3 *vt* acheter (*sth from sb* qch à qn, *sth for sb* pour *or* à qn).

purchaser ['pɜ:tʃɪsəʳ] *n* acheteur *m*, -euse *f*.

pure [pjʊəʳ] **1** *adj* (*all senses*) pur. **as ~ as the driven snow** innocent comme l'enfant qui vient de naître; (*Bible*) **~ in heart** au cœur pur; **~ science** science pure; (*Genetics*) **~ line** hérédité pure; **a ~ wool suit** un complet pure laine; **~ and simple** pur et simple; **it was ~ hypocrisy** c'était de la pure hypocrisie *or* de l'hypocrisie pure; **it was a ~ accident** c'était un pur accident; **a ~ waste of time** une pure *or* belle *or* vraie perte de temps.

2 *cpd*: **purebred** (*adj*) de race; (*n*) animal *m* de race; (*horse*) pur-sang *m inv*; **pure-hearted** (au cœur) pur; **pure-minded** pur (d'esprit).

purée ['pjʊəreɪ] *n* purée *f*.

purely ['pjʊəlɪ] *adv* purement. **~ and simply** purement et simplement.

pureness ['pjʊənɪs] *n* (*U*) pureté *f*.

purgation [pɜ:'geɪʃən] *n* (*Rel*) purgation *f*, purification *f*; (*Pol*) purge *f*, épuration *f*; (*Med*) purge.

purgative ['pɜ:gətɪv] *adj, n* purgatif (*m*).

purgatory ['pɜ:gətərɪ] *n* (*lit, fig*) purgatoire *m*. (*fig*) **it was ~!** c'était un vrai purgatoire! *or* supplice!

purge [pɜ:dʒ] **1** *n* (*act: gen, Med*) purge *f*; (*Pol*) purge, épuration *f*; (*medicament*) purge, purgatif *m*. **the political ~s which followed the revolution** les purges politiques qui ont *or* l'épuration politique qui a suivi la révolution; **a ~ of the dissidents** une purge des dissidents.

2 *vt* **(a)** (*gen*) purger (*of* de); (*Med*) *person, body* purger; (*Pol*) *state, nation, party* purger (*of* de); *traitors, bad elements* éliminer; *sins* purger, expier.

(b) (*Jur*) *person* disculper (*of* de); *accusation* se disculper de. **to ~ an offence** purger une peine; (*US*) **to ~ one's contempt (of Congress)** purger sa contumace.

purification [,pjʊərɪfɪ'keɪʃən] *n [air, water, metal etc]* épuration *f*; *[person]* purification *f*.

purifier ['pjʊərɪfaɪəʳ] *n* épurateur *m*, purificateur *m*. **air ~** purificateur d'air; *V* **water etc.**

purify ['pjʊərɪfaɪ] *vt substance* épurer, purifier; *person* purifier.

purist ['pjʊərɪst] *adj, n* puriste (*mf*).

puritan ['pjʊərɪtən] *adj, n* puritain(e) *m(f)*.

puritanical [,pjʊərɪ'tænɪkəl] *adj* puritain, de puritain.

puritanism ['pjʊərɪtənɪzəm] *n* puritanisme *m*.

purity ['pjʊərɪtɪ] *n* pureté *f*.

purl [pɜ:l] (*Knitting*) **1** *n* (*also* **~ stitch**) maille *f* à l'envers. **a row of ~ (stitches)** un rang à l'envers; *V* **plain. 2** *vt* tricoter à l'envers; *V* **knit.**

purlieus ['pɜ:lju:z] *npl* (*frm*) alentours *mpl*, abords *mpl*, environs *mpl*.

purloin [pɜ:'lɔɪn] *vt* dérober.

purple ['pɜ:pl] **1** *adj* cramoisi, violet, pourpre. **to go ~ (in the face)** devenir cramoisi *or* pourpre; (*Drugs sl*) **~ heart** pilule *f* du bonheur:; (*Literat*) **~ passage** morceau *m* de bravoure.

2 *n* (*colour*) pourpre *m*, violet *m*. (*Rel*) **the ~** la pourpre.

purplish ['pɜ:plɪʃ] *adj* violacé, qui tire sur le violet.

purport ['pɜ:pət] **1** *n* (*meaning*) signification *f*, portée *f*, teneur *f*; (*intention*) but *m*.

2 [pɜ:'pɔ:t] *vt*: **to ~ to be** *[person]* se présenter comme étant, se faire passer pour, se prétendre; *[book, film, statement etc]* se vouloir; **a man ~ing to come from the Ministry** un homme qui serait envoyé *or* qui prétend être envoyé par le ministère; **to ~ that ...** prétendre *or* suggérer *or* laisser entendre que ... .

purpose ['pɜ:pəs] **1** *n* **(a)** (*aim, intention*) but *m*, objet *m*; (*use*) usage *m*, utilité *f*. **he's a man with a ~ in life** c'est un homme qui a un but *or* un objectif dans la vie; **it's a film with a ~** c'est un film à thèse *or* qui contient un message; **what is the ~ of the meeting?** quel est le but *or* l'objet *or* l'utilité de la réunion?; **what was the ~ of his visit?** quel était le but *or* l'objet de sa visite?, dans quel but est-il venu?; **what is the ~ of this tool?** à quoi sert cet outil?; **my ~ in doing this is ...** la raison pour laquelle je fais ceci est ..., le but *or* l'objet que je me propose est ...; **for** *or* **with the ~ of doing ...** dans le but *or* l'intention de faire ..., afin de faire ...; **for this ~** dans ce but, à cet effet, à cette fin;

for my ~s pour ce que je veux faire; **for our ~s we may disregard this** en ce qui nous concerne *or* pour ce qui nous touche nous n'avons pas besoin de tenir compte de cela; **it is adequate for the ~** cela fait l'affaire, cela atteint son but, cela remplit son objet; **for all practical ~s** en pratique; **for the ~s of the meeting** pour (les besoins de) cette réunion; *V* **all, intent, serve** *etc.*

(b) (*phrases*) **on ~** exprès, à dessein, délibérément; **he did it on ~** il l'a fait exprès *or* à dessein; **he did it on ~ to annoy me** il l'a fait exprès pour me contrarier; **to no ~** en vain, inutilement; **to no ~ at all** en pure perte; **to some ~, to good ~** utilement, à profit; **the money will be used to good ~** l'argent sera bien *or* utilement employé; **to the ~** à propos; **not to the ~** hors de propos.

(c) (*U*) **(sense of) ~** résolution *f*; **he has no sense of ~** il vit sans but, il manque de résolution; **his activities seem to lack ~** il semble agir sans but précis; **he has great strength of ~** il est très résolu *or* déterminé, il a énormément de volonté; *V* **infirm, infirmity.**

2 *cpd*: **purpose-built** fonctionnalisé, construit spécialement; **it was purpose-built** c'était construit spécialement pour cet usage, c'était fonctionnalisé.

3 *vt* se proposer (*to do* de faire).

purposeful ['pɜːpəsfʊl] *adj* (*determined*) *person* résolu, déterminé, qui sait ce qu'il veut; *gesture, look* résolu, décidé; (*intentional*) *act* réfléchi, significatif.

purposefully ['pɜːpəsfəlɪ] *adv move, act* dans un but précis *or* réfléchi, avec une intention bien arrêtée, délibérément.

purposefulness ['pɜːpəsfʊlnɪs] *n* résolution *f*, détermination *f*, ténacité *f*.

purposeless ['pɜːpəslɪs] *adj person* qui manque de résolution, qui n'a pas de but, qui ne sait pas ce qu'il veut; *character* indécis, irrésolu; *act* sans but *or* objet (précis), inutile.

purposely ['pɜːpəslɪ] *adv* exprès, à dessein, de propos délibéré. **he made a ~ vague statement** il a fait exprès de faire une déclaration peu précise; **the government's statement was ~ vague** la déclaration du gouvernement a été délibérément vague *or* a été vague à dessein.

purr [pɜːʳ] **1** *vi [cat]* ronronner, faire ronron; *[person, engine, car]* ronronner. **2** *vt*: **'sit down, darling' she ~ed** 'assieds-toi, chéri' roucoula-t-elle. **3** *n [cat]* ronronnement *m*, ronron *m*; *[engine, car]* ronronnement.

purse [pɜːs] **1** *n* (*for coins*) porte-monnaie *m inv*, bourse *f*; (*wallet*) portefeuille *m*; (*US: handbag*) sac *m* à main; (*esp Sport: prize*) prix *m*, récompense *f*. (*fig*) **it's beyond my ~** c'est trop cher pour moi *or* pour ma bourse, c'est au-delà de mes moyens; *V* **public.**

2 *cpd*: **purse-proud** fier de sa fortune; (*fig*) **to hold/tighten the purse strings** tenir/serrer les cordons de la bourse.

3 *vt*: **to ~ (up) one's lips** faire la moue, se pincer les lèvres.

purser ['pɜːsəʳ] *n* (*Naut*) commissaire *m* du bord.

pursuance [pə'sjuːəns] *n* (*frm*) exécution *f*. **in ~ of** dans l'exécution de.

pursuant [pə'sjuːənt] *adj* (*frm*) **~ to** (*following on*) suivant; (*in accordance with*) conformément à.

pursue [pə'sjuː] *vt* **(a)** (*chase*) poursuivre; *thief, animal* poursuivre, pourchasser, (*track*) traquer; *pleasure* rechercher; *objective* poursuivre; *success, fame* rechercher, briguer; *[misfortune etc]* suivre, accompagner. **his eyes ~d me round the room** il me suivait du regard à travers la pièce; (*fig*) **he won't stop pursuing her** il n'arrête pas de la poursuivre *or* de lui courir après*.

(b) (*continue*) *studies, career* poursuivre, continuer; *profession* exercer; *course of action* suivre; *plan, theme, inquiry* poursuivre.

pursuer [pə'sjuːəʳ] *n* poursuivant(e) *m(f)*.

pursuit [pə'sjuːt] **1** *n* **(a)** (*chase*) poursuite *f*; (*fig: of pleasure, happiness*) poursuite, recherche *f*. **in ~ of** *thief* à la poursuite de; *happiness, success* à la poursuite de, à la recherche de; **to go in ~ of sb/sth** se mettre à la poursuite *or* à la recherche de qn/qch; **with two policemen in hot ~** avec deux agents à ses (*or* mes *etc*) trousses.

(b) (*occupation*) occupation *f*, travail *m*, activité *f*; (*pastime*) passe-temps *m inv*. **scientific ~s** travaux *mpl or* recherches *fpl* scientifiques.

2 *cpd*: **pursuit plane** avion *m* de chasse.

purulence ['pjʊərʊləns] *n* purulence *f*.

purulent ['pjʊərʊlənt] *adj* purulent.

purvey [pɜː'veɪ] *vt* (*Comm etc*) fournir (*sth to sb* qch à qn), approvisionner (*sth to sb* qn en qch).

purveyance [pɜː'veɪəns] *n* (*Comm etc*) approvisionnement *m*, fourniture *f* de provisions.

purveyor [pɜː'veɪəʳ] *n* (*Comm etc*) fournisseur *m*, -euse *f*, approvisionneur *m*, -euse *f* (*of sth* en qch, *to sb* de qn).

purview ['pɜːvjuː] *n* (*frm*) *[act, bill]* articles *mpl*; *[the law]* domaine *m*, limites *fpl*; *[inquiry]* champ *m*, limites; *[committee]* capacité *f*, compétence *f*; *[book, film]* limites, portée *f*.

pus [pʌs] *n* pus *m*.

push [pʊʃ] **1** *n* **(a)** (*shove*) poussée *f*. **with one ~** d'une (seule) poussée, en poussant une seule fois; **to give sb/sth a ~** pousser qn/qch; **the car needs a ~** il faut pousser la voiture; (*Brit fig*) **to give sb the ~‡** *[employer]* flanquer qn à la porte*; *[boyfriend, girlfriend etc]* laisser tomber qn*, plaquer qn‡; (*Brit fig*) **he got the ~‡** (*from employer*) il s'est fait flanquer à la porte*; (*from girlfriend*) elle l'a laissé tomber*, elle l'a plaqué‡; **there was a great ~ as the crowd emerged** quand la foule est sortie il y a eu une grande bousculade; *V* **bell**[1] *etc.*

(b) (*Mil: advance*) poussée *f*, avance *f*. (*Mil*) **they made a ~ to the coast** ils ont fait une poussée *or* ils ont avancé jusqu'à la côte.

(c) (*fig*) (*effort*) gros effort, coup *m* de collier; (*campaign*) campagne *f*. **they made a ~ to get everything finished in time** ils ont fait un gros effort *or* ils ont donné un coup de collier pour tout terminer à temps; **they were having a ~ on sales** *or* **a sales ~** ils avaient organisé une campagne de promotion des ventes; **we're having a ~ for more teachers** nous menons une campagne pour une augmentation du nombre d'enseignants; **at a ~*** au besoin, en cas de besoin, à la rigueur; **when it comes to the ~*** au moment critique *or* crucial.

(d) (**U: drive, energy*) dynamisme *m*, initiative *f*. **he's got plenty of ~** il est très dynamique, il est plein d'initiative.

2 *cpd*: (*Brit*) **push-bike*** vélo *m*, bécane* *f*; **push-button** bouton *m*, poussoir *m*; **push-button controls** commandes *fpl* presse-bouton; **push-button warfare** guerre *f* presse-bouton; **pushcart** charrette *f* à bras; (*Brit*) **push chair** poussette *f*; **it was a pushover*** c'était la facilité même, c'était un jeu d'enfant, c'était l'enfance de l'art*; **he was a pushover*** (*easily beaten*) il a été battu à plate(s) couture(s), il s'est fait enfoncer*; (*easily swindled*) il s'est laissé avoir*, il a donné dans le panneau; (*easily convinced*) il a marché* tout de suite; **pushpin** épingle *f* (à tête de couleur); (*Electronics*) **push-pull circuit** push-pull *m*; (*Gymnastics*) **push-up** traction *f*; **to do push-ups** faire des tractions *or* des pompes*.

3 *vt* **(a)** (*shove*) *car, barrow, door, person* pousser; (*press*) *knob, button* appuyer sur, presser sur; (*prod*) pousser; (*thrust*) *stick, finger etc* enfoncer (*into* dans, *between* entre); *rag etc* fourrer (*into* dans). **don't ~ me!** ne me poussez pas!, ne me bousculez pas!; **to ~ sb into a room** pousser qn dans une pièce; **to ~ sb against a wall** pousser *or* presser qn contre un mur; **to ~ sb off the pavement** pousser qn du trottoir, (*by jostling*) obliger qn à descendre du trottoir (en le bousculant); **to ~ sb in/out/up** *etc* faire entrer/sortir/monter *etc* qn en le poussant *or* d'une poussée; **he ~ed him down the stairs** il l'a poussé et l'a fait tomber dans l'escalier; **they ~ed him out of the car** ils l'ont poussé hors de la voiture; **to ~ sb/sth out of the way** écarter qn/qch en poussant, pousser qn/qch à l'écart; **he ~ed the box under the table** (*moved*) il a poussé *or* fourré* la boîte sous la table; (*hid*) il a vite caché la boîte sous la table; **they ~ed the car off the road** ils ont poussé la voiture sur le bas-côté; **she ~ed the books off the table** elle a poussé *or* balayé les livres de dessus la table; **he ~ed his finger into my eye** il m'a mis le doigt dans l'œil; **he ~ed his head through the window** il a mis *or* passé la tête par la fenêtre; **he ~ed the book into my hand** il m'a fourré* le livre dans la main; **to ~ a door open/shut** ouvrir/fermer une porte en poussant *or* d'une poussée, pousser une porte (pour l'ouvrir/la fermer); **to ~ one's way through a crowd** se frayer *or* s'ouvrir un chemin dans la foule (*V also* **4b** *and* **push in 1a** *etc*); (*fig*) **he ~ed the thought to the back of his mind** il a repoussé *or* écarté cette pensée pour le moment; (*fig*) **it ~ed the matter right out of my mind** cela m'a fait complètement oublier l'affaire; (*fig*) **he must be ~ing 40*** il ne doit pas avoir loin de 40 ans, il doit approcher de la quarantaine.

(b) (*fig: press, advance*) *advantage* poursuivre; *claim* présenter avec insistance; *one's views* mettre en avant, imposer; *product* pousser la vente de, faire de la réclame pour; *candidate etc* appuyer, soutenir. **he ~ed the bill through Parliament** il a réussi à faire voter le projet de loi; **to ~ home an attack** pousser à fond une attaque; **they are going to ~ the export side of the business** ils vont donner priorité aux exportations dans leur affaire; **to ~ drugs** revendre de la drogue; **he was ~ing drugs to students** il ravitaillait les étudiants en drogue, il revendait de la drogue aux étudiants; **don't ~ your luck*** vas-y doucement!; **he's ~ing his luck*** il y va un peu fort.

(c) (*put pressure on*) pousser; (*force*) forcer, obliger; (*harass*) importuner, harceler. **to ~ sb for payment/for an answer** presser *or* engager qn à payer/à répondre; **to ~ o.s. hard** se mener la vie dure; **he ~es himself too hard** il exige trop de lui-même; **don't ~ him too hard** *or* **too far** ne soyez pas trop dur envers lui, ne le poussez pas à bout; **they ~ed him to the limits of his endurance** on l'a poussé jusqu'à la limite de ses forces; **stop ~ing him and let him make up his own mind** arrêtez de le harceler *or* fichez-lui la paix* et laissez-le décider tout seul; **to ~ sb to do** pousser qn à faire, insister pour que qn fasse; **to ~ sb into doing** forcer *or* obliger qn à faire; **I was ~ed into it** on m'y a poussé *or* forcé, je n'ai pas eu le choix; **he was ~ed into teaching** on l'a poussé *or* forcé *or* obligé à faire de l'enseignement; **to be ~ed for time/money** être à court de temps/d'argent, manquer de temps/d'argent; **I'm really ~ed today** je suis vraiment bousculé *or* débordé aujourd'hui; **I'm rather ~ed for boxes just now** je n'ai pas beaucoup de boîtes en ce moment; **that's ~ing it a bit!*** c'est un peu fort!, tu y vas (*or* il y va *etc*) un peu fort!

(d) (*US Golf*) **to ~ the ball** couper la balle, faire dévier la balle.

4 *vi* **(a)** pousser; (*on bell*) appuyer (*on* sur). **you ~ and I'll pull** poussez et moi je vais tirer; (*in crowd etc*) **stop ~ing!** arrêtez de pousser!, ne bousculez pas!; '**~**' (*on door*) 'poussez'; (*on bell*) 'appuyez', 'sonnez'; (*fig*) **he ~es too much** il se met trop en avant; (*fig*) **to ~ for better conditions/higher wages** *etc* faire pression pour obtenir de meilleures conditions/une augmentation de salaire *etc.*

(b) (*move: also* **~ one's way**) **they ~ed (their way) into/out of the room** ils sont entrés dans la pièce/sortis de la pièce en se frayant un passage; **he ~ed (his way) past me** il a réussi à passer *or* il m'a dépassé en me bousculant; **she ~ed (her way) through the crowd** elle s'est frayé *or* ouvert un chemin dans la foule.

push about *vt sep* = **push around.**

push along 1 *vi* **(a)** (**: leave*) filer*, se sauver*.

(b) (*Aut etc: move quickly*) rouler bon train. **the coach was**

pushing along at 70 le car faisait facilement du 110 (à l'heure).

2 *vt sep person, cart, chair* pousser; (*fig: hasten*) *work* activer, accélérer.

push around *vt sep* **(a)** *cart, toy* pousser de-ci de-là, pousser à droite et à gauche.

(b) (* *fig: bully*) marcher sur les pieds à* (*fig*), être vache: avec. **stop pushing me around!** arrête de me donner des ordres! *or* de me marcher sur les pieds!*

push aside *vt sep person, chair* écarter (brusquement), pousser à l'écart; (*fig*) *objection, suggestion* écarter, rejeter.

push away *vt sep person, chair, one's plate* repousser; *gift* repousser, rejeter.

push back *vt sep cover, blankets, lock of hair* rejeter *or* repousser (en arrière); *curtains* ouvrir; *person, crowd, enemy* repousser, faire reculer; (*fig*) *desire, impulse* réprimer, contenir, refréner.

push down 1 *vi* appuyer (*on* sur).

2 *vt sep switch, lever* abaisser; *knob, button* appuyer sur; *pin, stick* enfoncer; (*knock over*) *fence, barrier, person* renverser. **he pushed the ball down off the roof** d'une poussée il a fait tomber le ballon du toit; **he pushed the books down into the box** il a entassé les livres dans la caisse.

push forward 1 *vi* (*also* **push one's way forward**) avancer, se frayer *or* s'ouvrir un chemin.

2 *vt sep person, box etc* pousser en avant, faire avancer. **he pushed himself forward** il s'est avancé, il s'est frayé *or* ouvert un chemin; (*fig*) il s'est mis en avant, il s'est fait valoir.

push in 1 *vi* **(a)** (*also* **push one's way in**) s'introduire de force.

(b) (*fig: interfere*) intervenir. **he's always pushing in where he's not wanted** il se mêle toujours de *or* il intervient toujours dans ce qui ne le regarde pas.

2 *vt sep* **(a)** *stick, pin, finger* enfoncer; *rag* fourrer dedans; *person* pousser dedans; *knob, button* appuyer sur. **they opened the door and pushed him in** ils ouvrirent la porte et le poussèrent dans la pièce; **they took him to the pond and pushed him in** ils l'ont conduit à l'étang et l'ont poussé dedans; *V* **oar.**

(b) (*break*) *window, door, sides of box* enfoncer.

push off 1 *vi* **(a)** (*Naut*) pousser au large.

(b) (*: *leave*) filer*, se sauver*, ficher le camp*. **I must push off** il faut que je file* (*subj*) *or* que je me sauve* (*subj*); **push off!** décampez!, fichez le camp!*, filez!*

(c) the top just pushes off il suffit de pousser le haut pour l'enlever.

2 *vt sep* **(a)** *top, lid* pousser, enlever en poussant; *vase from shelf etc* faire tomber (*from* de); *person from cliff etc* pousser, faire tomber (*from* de, du haut de).

(b) (*Naut*) déborder.

push on 1 *vi* (*in journey*) pousser (*to* jusqu'à), continuer son chemin; (*in work*) continuer, persévérer. **to push on with sth** continuer (à faire) qch.

2 *vt sep* **(a)** *lid, cover* placer *or* (re)mettre en place (en pressant *or* en appuyant).

(b) (*fig: incite*) pousser, inciter (*sb to do* qn à faire).

push out 1 *vi* **(a)** (*also* **push one's way out**) se frayer *or* s'ouvrir un chemin (à travers la foule).

(b) *[roots, branches]* pousser; *[shoots]* pointer, sortir; *[birds]* sortir.

2 *vt sep* **(a)** *person, object* pousser dehors; *stopper* faire sortir (en poussant); (*fig*) *employee, office-holder* évincer, se débarrasser de. **to push the boat out** (*lit*) pousser au large; (*fig*) faire la fête, célébrer.

(b) (*Bot*) *roots, shoots* produire.

push over 1 *vi*: **he pushed (his way) over towards her** il se fraya *or* s'ouvrit un chemin vers elle.

2 *vt sep* **(a)** *object* pousser (*to sb* vers qn); (*over cliff, bridge etc*) pousser, faire tomber.

(b) (*topple*) *chair, vase, person* renverser, faire tomber.

3 pushover* *n V* **push 2.**

push through 1 *vi* (*also* **push one's way through**) se frayer *or* s'ouvrir un chemin.

2 *vt sep* **(a)** *stick, hand etc* enfoncer, (faire) passer.

(b) (*fig*) *deal, business* conclure à la hâte; *decision* faire accepter à la hâte; (*Parl*) *bill* réussir à faire voter.

push to *vt sep door* fermer (en poussant), pousser (pour fermer).

push up 1 *vt sep* **(a)** *stick, hand, lever, switch* (re)lever; *spectacles* relever. (*fig*) **he's pushing up the daisies*** il mange les pissenlits par la racine*.

(b) (*fig: increase*) *numbers, taxes, sales* augmenter; *prices* augmenter, faire monter; *demand, speed* augmenter, accroître; *sb's temperature, blood pressure* faire monter. **that pushes up the total to over 100** cela fait monter le total à plus de 100.

2 push-up *n V* **push 2.**

pusher ['pʊʃəʳ] *n* **(a)** (*pej*) arriviste *mf*; *V* **pen**[1] *etc.* **(b)** (*Drugs sl: also* **drug-~**) revendeur *m*, -euse *f* (de drogue), ravitailleur *m*, -euse *f* (en drogue).

pushful* ['pʊʃfʊl] *adj* (*pej*) *person* arriviste, qui se fait valoir, qui se met trop en avant; *manner* arrogant.

pushfulness* ['pʊʃfʊlnɪs] *n* (*pej*) arrivisme *m*, excès *m* d'ambition; *[manner]* arrogance *f*.

pushing ['pʊʃɪŋ] *adj person* dynamique, entreprenant; (*pej*) arriviste, qui se fait valoir, qui se met trop en avant; *manner* arrogant.

pushy* ['pʊʃɪ] *adj* = **pushful.**

pusillanimity [ˌpjuːsɪləˈnɪmɪtɪ] *n* pusillanimité *f*.

pusillanimous [ˌpjuːsɪˈlænɪməs] *adj* pusillanime.

puss* [pʊs] *n* **(a)** (*cat*) minet *m*, -ette *f*, minou *m*. (*to cat*) **~, ~!** minet, minet!, minou, minou!; **P~ in Boots** le Chat Botté. **(b)** (:) (*girl*) nana: *f*, souris: *f*; (*face*) gueule: *f*; (*mouth*) margoulette: *f*.

pussy* ['pʊsɪ] **1** *n* (*also* **~-cat**) minet *m*, -ette *f*, minou *m*.

2 *cpd*: **pussyfoot*** (*vi*) marcher à pas de loup; (*fig*) ne pas se mouiller*, ménager la chèvre et le chou; **pussyfooting*** (*adj: fig*) *person* qui a peur de se mouiller*; *attitude* timoré; (*Bot*) **pussy willow** saule *m* (blanc).

pustule ['pʌstjuːl] *n* pustule *f*.

put [pʊt] *pret, ptp* **put 1** *vt* **(a)** (*place*) mettre; poser; placer. **~ it on the table/beside the window/over there** mettez-le *or* posez-le *or* placez-le sur la table/près de la fenêtre/là-bas; **~ it in the drawer** mettez-le *or* placez-le dans le tiroir; **to ~ sth in one's pocket/purse** *etc* mettre qch dans sa poche/son porte-monnaie *etc*; **you've ~ the picture rather high up** tu as mis *or* placé *or* accroché le tableau un peu trop haut; **he ~s sugar in his tea** il met *or* prend du sucre dans son thé; **he ~ some sugar in his tea** il a mis du sucre dans son thé, il a sucré son thé; **he ~ some more coal on the fire** il a remis *or* rajouté du charbon sur le feu; **~ the book in its proper place** (re)mets le livre à sa place; **to ~ one's arms round sb** prendre qn dans ses bras, entourer qn de ses bras; **he ~ his head through the window** il a passé la tête par la fenêtre; **he ~ his head round the door** il a passé la tête par la porte; **she ~ the shell to her ear** elle a mis le coquillage contre son oreille, elle a porté le coquillage à son oreille; **he ~ his rucksack over the fence** il a mis *or* passé son sac à dos de l'autre côté de la barrière; **they ~ a plank across the stream** ils ont mis *or* placé *or* posé une planche en travers du ruisseau; **he ~ the lid on the box** il a mis *or* placé le couvercle sur la boîte; **he ~ his hand over his mouth** il s'est mis la main devant la bouche; (*shaking hands*) **~ it there!*** tope là!; **to ~ a spacecraft into orbit** placer un vaisseau spatial sur orbite, mettre un vaisseau spatial en orbite; **to ~ a button on a shirt** mettre *or* coudre un bouton à une chemise; **to ~ a patch on a sheet** mettre une pièce à un drap, rapiécer un drap; **to ~ a new blade on a saw** mettre *or* fixer une nouvelle lame à une scie, remplacer la lame d'une scie; **to ~ an advertisement in the paper** placer *or* mettre *or* passer une annonce dans le journal; **he ~ me on the train** il m'a mis *or* accompagné au train; **he ~ me into a non-smoker** il m'a trouvé une place dans un compartiment non-fumeurs; **to ~ sb off a train/boat** *etc* débarquer qn d'un train/d'un bateau *etc*; **to ~ sb on to/off a committee** nommer qn à un/renvoyer qn d'un comité; (*fig*) **that ~ me in a mess!*** ça m'a mis *or* fourré dans le pétrin!; *for other phrases V* **bed, stay** *etc.*

(b) (*fig*) mettre; *signature* apposer (*on, to* à); *mark* faire (*on* sur, à). **he ~ the matter in the hands of his solicitor** il a remis l'affaire entre les mains de son avocat; **to ~ one's confidence in sb/sth** placer sa confiance en qn/qch; **what value do you ~ on this?** (*lit*) à quelle valeur *or* à quel prix estimez-vous cela?; (*fig*) quelle valeur accordez-vous *or* attribuez-vous *or* attachez-vous à cela?; **he ~ all his energy into his career** il a consacré toute son énergie à sa carrière; **you get out of life what you ~ into it** on ne retire de la vie que ce qu'on y met soi-même; **he has ~ a lot into his marriage** il a fait beaucoup d'efforts pour que son mariage soit une réussite; **I've ~ a lot of time and trouble into it** j'y ai consacré beaucoup de temps et d'efforts; **to ~ money into a company** placer *or* investir de l'argent dans une affaire; **he ~ all his savings into the project** il a placé *or* englouti toutes ses économies dans ce projet; **to ~ money on a horse** parier *or* miser sur un cheval; **he ~ £10 on Black Beauty** il a parié *or* misé 10 livres sur Black Beauty; **he ~s good health among his greatest assets** il estime que sa robuste santé est l'un de ses meilleurs atouts; **we should ~ happiness before** *or* **above wealth** on devrait placer le bonheur au-dessus de la richesse, on devrait préférer le bonheur à la richesse; **I ~ Milton above Tennyson** je place Milton au-dessus de Tennyson, je trouve Milton supérieur à Tennyson; **I shouldn't ~ him among the greatest poets** je ne le place *or* classe pas parmi les plus grands poètes, à mon avis ce n'est pas l'un des plus grands poètes; *for other phrases V* **blame, end, market, pay,** *etc.*

(c) (*thrust; direct*) enfoncer. **to ~ one's fist through a window** passer le poing à travers une vitre; **to ~ one's pen through a word** rayer *or* barrer *or* biffer un mot; **to ~ a knife into sb** poignarder qn, filer* un coup de poignard à qn; **to ~ a bullet into sb** atteindre qn d'une balle, coller une balle dans la peau de qn*; **I ~ a bullet through his head** je lui ai tiré une balle dans la tête; (*Sport*) **to ~ the shot** *or* **the weight** lancer le poids; (*Naut*) **to ~ the rudder to port** mettre la barre à bâbord.

(d) (*cause to be, do, begin etc*) **to ~ sb in a good/bad mood** mettre qn de bonne/mauvaise humeur; **to ~ sb on a diet** mettre qn au régime; **to ~ sb to great expense** occasionner de grosses dépenses à qn; **to ~ sb to some trouble** *or* **inconvenience** déranger qn; **to ~ one's time to good use** bien employer son temps, mettre son temps à profit, faire bon usage de son temps; **they ~ him to dig(ging) the garden** ils lui ont fait bêcher le jardin, ils lui ont donné la tâche de bêcher le jardin; **I ~ him to work at once** je l'ai mis au travail aussitôt; **they had to ~ 4 men on to this job** ils ont dû employer 4 hommes à ce travail *or* pour faire ce travail; **to ~ a watch to the right time** mettre une montre à l'heure; *for other phrases V* **death, sleep, wise** *etc.*

(e) (*prepositional usages*) **he tried to ~ one across** *or* **over on me*** il a essayé de me faire marcher* *or* de m'avoir*; **you'll never ~ anything across** *or* **over on him*** on ne la lui fait pas, on ne peut pas le faire marcher*; **she ~ my brother against me** elle a monté mon frère contre moi; **his remarks ~ me off my food** ses remarques m'ont coupé l'appétit; **it almost ~ me off opera for good** cela a failli me dégoûter de l'opéra pour toujours; **it certainly ~ me off going to Greece** cela m'a certainement ôté l'envie d'aller en Grèce; **the noise is ~ting me off my work** le bruit me distrait de mon travail, le bruit m'empêche de me concentrer sur mon travail; **someone has been ~ over him at the office** on a placé quelqu'un au-dessus de lui au bureau; **to ~ sb through an examination** faire subir un examen à qn; **they**

really ~ him through it* ils lui en ont fait voir de dures*, ils lui ont fait passer un mauvais quart d'heure; *for other phrases V* **pace, scent, stroke** *etc.*

(f) (*express*) dire, exprimer. **can you ~ it another way?** pouvez-vous vous exprimer autrement?; **to ~ it bluntly** pour parler franc, sans mâcher mes mots; **as he would ~ it** selon sa formule *or* son expression, pour employer sa formule *or* son expression; **as Shakespeare ~s it** comme le dit Shakespeare; **I don't quite know how to ~ it** je ne sais pas trop comment le dire; **let me ~ it another way** si je peux m'exprimer autrement, en d'autres mots; **how shall I ~ it?** comment dire?, comment dirais-je?; **~ it so as not to offend her** présente la chose de façon à ne pas la blesser; **how will you ~ it to him?** comment vas-tu le lui dire?, comment vas-tu lui présenter la chose?; **if I may ~ it so** si je puis dire, si je peux m'exprimer ainsi; **the compliment was gracefully ~** le compliment était bien tourné; **to ~ an expression into French** traduire *or* mettre une expression en français; **how would you ~ it in French?** comment le dirais-tu en français?; **to ~ into verse** mettre en vers; *for other phrases V* **mildly, word, writing** *etc.*

(g) (*submit, expound*) *case, problem* exposer, présenter; *proposal, resolution* présenter, soumettre; *question* poser. **he ~ the arguments for and against the project** il a présenté les arguments pour et contre le projet; **he ~ his own side of the argument very clearly** il a présenté *or* exposé très clairement son côté de l'affaire; **I ~ it to you that ...** n'est-il pas vrai que ...?, je maintiens que ...; **it was ~ to me in no uncertain terms that I should resign** on m'a déclaré en termes très clairs que je devrais donner ma démission.

(h) (*estimate*) estimer, évaluer. **they ~ the loss at £10,000** on estime *or* évalue *or* chiffre la perte à 10.000 livres; **the population was ~ at 50,000** on a évalué *or* estimé le nombre d'habitants à 50.000; **what would you ~ it at?** à combien l'estimez-vous? *or* l'évaluez-vous?; **I'd ~ her *or* her age at 50** je lui donnerais 50 ans.

2 *vi* (*Naut*) **to ~ into port** faire escale *or* relâche, entrer au port; **the ship ~ into Southampton** le navire est entré au port de Southampton; **to ~ to sea** appareiller, lever l'ancre, prendre le large.

3 *cpd*: **put-on*** (*n: pretence*) comédie *f*; (*hoax*) mystification *f*, farce *f*; (*adj: feigned*) affecté, feint, simulé; **a put-up job*** un coup monté; **to be put-upon*** se faire marcher sur les pieds* (*fig*); (*Brit*) **put-you-up** (*n*) canapé-lit *m*, divan *m*.

put about 1 *vi* (*Naut*) virer de bord.

2 *vt sep* **(a)** *rumour etc* faire courir, faire circuler. **he put it about that ...** il a fait courir *or* circuler le bruit que ....

(b) (†) = **put out 2g.**

(c) (*Naut*) **to put the ship about** virer de bord.

put across *vt sep* **(a)** (*communicate; get accepted*) *ideas, intentions, desires* faire comprendre, faire accepter, communiquer (*to sb* à qn). **to put sth across to sb** faire comprendre *or* faire accepter qch à qn; **the play puts the message across very well** l'auteur de la pièce communique très bien son message, le message de la pièce passe la rampe; **he knows his stuff but he can't put it across** il connaît son sujet à fond mais il n'arrive pas à le faire comprendre aux autres *or* à communiquer; **he can't put himself across** il n'arrive pas à se mettre en valeur; **there was a special campaign to put the new product across to the housewife** il y a eu une campagne spéciale pour faire accepter le nouveau produit aux ménagères; **she put the song across beautifully** elle a interprété la chanson à merveille.

(b) (*perform successfully*) **to put a deal across** réussir une affaire, conclure un marché; **he tried to put one *or* it across on me*** il a essayé de me faire marcher* *or* de m'avoir*; **you'll never put one *or* it across on him*** on ne la lui fait pas, on ne peut pas le faire marcher*.

put apart *vt sep* (*fig*) **that puts him apart from the others** cela le distingue des autres.

put around *vt sep* = **put about 2a.**

put aside *vt sep* **(a)** *object* mettre à part *or* de côté; (*keep, save*) *food, money* mettre de côté, garder en réserve. **she put her book aside when I came in** elle a posé son livre quand je suis entré; **he put aside the document to read later** il a mis le document à part *or* de côté pour le lire plus tard; (*Comm*) **I have had it put aside for you** je vous l'ai fait mettre de côté.

(b) (*fig*) *doubts, worries* écarter, éloigner de soi, chasser; *idea, hope* renoncer à, écarter.

put away *vt sep* **(a)** = **put aside a.**

(b) = **put aside b.**

(c) (*put in storage place*) *clothes, toys, books* ranger. **to put the car away** rentrer la voiture, mettre la voiture au garage.

(d) (*confine*) (*in prison*) mettre en prison, boucler*, coffrer*; (*in mental hospital*) (faire) enfermer, (faire) interner.

(e) (*: *consume*) *food* engloutir, avaler, bâfrer‡; *drink* siffler*.

(f) = **put down k.**

put back 1 *vi* (*Naut*) **to put back to port** rentrer au port; **they put back to Dieppe** ils sont rentrés *or* retournés à Dieppe.

2 *vt sep* **(a)** (*replace*) remettre (à sa place *or* en place). **put it back on the shelf** remettez-le *or* replacez-le sur l'étagère; **put it back!** remets-le à sa place!

(b) (*retard*) *development, progress* retarder, freiner; *clock* retarder (*by one hour* d'une heure); *clock hands* remettre en arrière. **the disaster put the project back (by) 10 years** le désastre a retardé de 10 ans la réalisation du projet; **this will put us back 10 years** cela nous fera perdre 10 ans, cela nous ramènera où nous en étions il y a 10 ans; *V also* **clock.**

(c) (*postpone*) remettre (*to* à).

put by *vt sep* = **put aside a.**

put down 1 *vi [aircraft]* se poser, atterrir; (*on carrier*) apponter.

2 *vt sep* **(a)** *parcel, book* poser, déposer; *child* poser, mettre à terre (*or* sur un lit *etc*); (*Aut*) *passenger* déposer, laisser. **put it down!** pose ça!; **she put her book down and rose to her feet** elle posa son livre et se leva; (*fig*) **I simply couldn't put that book down** je ne pouvais pas m'arracher à ce livre; (*Aut*) **put me down at the corner here** déposez-moi *or* laissez-moi *or* débarquez-moi* au coin; *V* **foot** *etc.*

(b) (*Aviat*) *aircraft* poser.

(c) *umbrella* fermer.

(d) (*pay*) *deposit, money* verser (*on* pour). **he put down £100 (as a deposit) on the car** il a versé 100 livres d'arrhes pour la voiture.

(e) *wine* mettre en cave.

(f) (*suppress*) *revolt* réprimer, étouffer; *custom, practice* faire cesser, abolir, supprimer. **there was a campaign to put down vandalism** il y avait une campagne pour la répression du vandalisme.

(g) (*silence*) réduire au silence, faire taire; (*snub*) rabrouer; (*humiliate*) humilier, rabaisser.

(h) (*record*) noter, inscrire. **to put sth down in writing *or* on paper** coucher *or* mettre qch par écrit; (*Comm*) **put it down on my account** mettez-le *or* portez-le sur mon compte; **I have put you down as a teacher/for £10** je vous ai inscrit comme professeur/pour 10 livres; **I'll put you down for the next vacancy** je vais inscrire votre nom pour la prochaine place disponible; *V* **name** *etc.*

(i) (*attribute*) attribuer (*sth to sth* qch à qch). **I put it down to his stupidity** je l'attribue à sa stupidité; **the accident must be put down to negligence** l'accident doit être imputé à la négligence; **we put it all down to the fact that he was tired** nous avons attribué tout cela à sa fatigue, nous avons mis tout cela sur le compte de sa fatigue.

(j) (*consider, assess*) considérer (*as* comme), tenir (*as* pour), prendre (*as* pour). **I had put him down as a complete fool** je l'avais pris pour *or* je le considérais comme *or* je le tenais pour un parfait imbécile; **I'd put her down as about forty** je lui donnerais la quarantaine *or* environ quarante ans.

(k) (*euph: kill*) *dog, cat* faire piquer; *horse* abattre, tuer.

put forth *vt sep* (*liter*) *leaves, roots, shoots* produire; *arm, hand* tendre, avancer; (*fig*) *idea, suggestion* avancer, émettre; *effort* fournir, déployer; *news, rumour* répandre, faire circuler.

put forward *vt sep* **(a)** (*propose*) *theory, argument, reason* avancer, présenter; *opinion* exprimer, émettre; *plan* proposer. **he put his name forward as a candidate** il s'est porté candidat, il a posé sa candidature; **he put himself forward for the job** il s'est porté candidat au poste, il a posé sa candidature au poste; **he put Jones forward for the job** il a proposé Jones pour le poste.

(b) (*advance*) *meeting, starting time, clock, schedule, programme* avancer (*by* de, *to, until* à).

put in 1 *vi* (*Naut*) faire relâche *or* escale (*at* à).

2 *vt sep* **(a)** (*into box, drawer, room etc*) mettre dedans *or* à l'intérieur; *seeds* planter, semer. **he put his head in at the window** il a passé la tête par la fenêtre; **I've put the car in for repairs** j'ai donné la voiture à réparer; (*into luggage etc*) **have you put in the camera?** est-ce que tu as pris l'appareil photo?; *V* **appearance, oar** *etc.*

(b) (*insert*) *word, paragraph* insérer, introduire; *remark* ajouter, glisser; (*include: in letter, publication*) inclure. **have you put in why you are not going?** est-ce que vous avez expliqué pourquoi vous n'y allez pas?; **'but it's cold' he put in** 'mais il fait froid' fit-il remarquer.

(c) (*enter*) *document* présenter, produire, fournir; *claim* présenter; *application* faire; *one's name* avancer, inscrire. (*Jur*) **to put in a plea** plaider; **to put in a protest** élever *or* formuler une protestation; **to put sb in for an exam** inscrire *or* présenter qn à un examen; **to put sb in for a job/promotion** proposer qn pour un poste/pour de l'avancement.

(d) (*esp Pol: install*) *political party, person* élire.

(e) *time* passer. **he put in the morning writing the report** il a passé la matinée à écrire le rapport; **they put in the time playing cards** ils ont passé le temps *or* ils se sont occupés en jouant aux cartes; **we have an hour to put in before the plane leaves** nous avons une heure à perdre *or* à occuper avant le départ de l'avion; **I've put in a lot of time on it** j'y ai passé *or* consacré beaucoup de temps; **he has put in a full day's work** il a bien rempli sa journée; **can you put in a few hours at the weekend?** pourrais-tu travailler quelques heures pendant le week-end?; **she puts in an hour a day at the piano** elle fait une heure de piano par jour.

put in for *vt fus job* poser sa candidature pour *or* à; *promotion, rise, new house, supplementary benefit* faire une demande de, solliciter.

put off 1 *vi* (*Naut*) démarrer (*from* de), pousser au large.

2 *vt sep* **(a)** (*postpone*) *departure, appointment, meeting* retarder, ajourner, repousser; *decision* remettre à plus tard, différer; *visitor* renvoyer à plus tard. **he put off writing the letter** il a remis la lettre à plus tard; **to put sth off for 10 days/until January** remettre qch de 10 jours/jusqu'à janvier; **I'm sorry to have to put you off** je suis désolé d'avoir à vous décommander (jusqu'à une autre fois), je suis désolé d'avoir à vous renvoyer à plus tard.

(b) (*dissuade, divert*) dissuader; (*hinder, distract*) démonter, dérouter; (*disconcert*) déconcerter, troubler. **he put her off with vague promises** il l'a dissuadée avec de vagues promesses; **he is not easily put off** il ne se laisse pas facilement démonter *or* dérouter *or* troubler; **he puts me off when he laughs like that** cela me déconcerte quand il rit de cette façon;

the colour of the drink quite put me off la couleur de la boisson m'a plutôt dégoûté; **don't let his abruptness put you off** ne vous laissez pas troubler par sa brusquerie.
(c) *coat, hat etc* enlever, retirer; *passenger* déposer, débarquer.
(d) (*extinguish etc*) *light, gas* éteindre; *radio, TV, heater* fermer.
put on 1 *vt sep* **(a)** *coat, skirt, trousers* mettre, passer, enfiler; *gloves, socks* mettre, enfiler; *hat, glasses* mettre. **to put on one's shoes** mettre ses chaussures, se chausser.
(b) (*add, increase*) *pressure, speed* augmenter, accroître. **to put on weight** prendre du poids, grossir; **he put on 3 kilos** il a pris 3 kilos, il a grossi de 3 kilos; **they put on two goals in the second half** ils ont encore marqué deux buts pendant la deuxième mi-temps.
(c) (*assume*) *indignation* affecter, feindre, simuler; *air, accent* prendre, se donner, emprunter; (*: *deceive*) *person* faire marcher*. **he's just putting it on** il fait seulement semblant, c'est un air qu'il se donne; **she really puts it on*** elle se donne des airs, c'est une poseuse *or* une crâneuse*; **you're only putting me on!*** tu me fais marcher!*; **he is always putting people on* about his rich relations** il raconte toujours des histoires sur ses riches parents.
(d) (*make available etc*) *concert, play, show* organiser; *film* projeter; *extra train, bus etc* mettre en service. **he put on a childish display of temper** il a manifesté sa mauvaise humeur de façon puérile; **when the veal was finished they put on beef** quand il n'y a plus eu de veau ils ont servi du bœuf; (*Telec*) **put me on to Mr Brown** passez-moi M Brown; (*Telec*) **would you put on Mrs Smith?** je voudrais parler à Mme Smith, passez-moi Mme Smith.
(e) (*start functioning etc*) *light, gas* allumer; *radio, TV* ouvrir; *radiator, heater* ouvrir, allumer. **put the kettle on** mets l'eau à chauffer; **I'll just put the soup on** je vais juste mettre la soupe à cuire (*or* chauffer); **to put the brakes on** freiner.
(f) (*advance*) *clock* avancer (*by* de).
(g) (*wager*) parier, miser, mettre (*on* sur).
(h) (*inform, indicate*) indiquer. **they put the police on to him** ils l'ont signalé à la police; **can you put me on to a good dentist?** pourriez-vous me donner l'adresse d'un bon dentiste? *or* m'indiquer un bon dentiste?; **Paul put us on to you** c'est Paul qui nous a dit de nous adresser à vous, c'est Paul qui nous envoie; **what put you on to it?** qu'est-ce qui vous en a donné l'idée?, qu'est-ce qui vous y a fait penser?
2 put-on* *adj, n V* **put 3.**
put out 1 *vi* (*Naut*) prendre le large. **to put out to sea** prendre le large, quitter le port; **to put out from Dieppe** quitter Dieppe.
2 *vt sep* **(a)** (*put outside*) *chair etc* sortir, mettre dehors; (*get rid of*) *rubbish* sortir; (*expel*) *person* expulser (*of* de), mettre dehors; *country, organization* expulser (*of* de). **he put the rug out to dry** il a mis *or* étendu la couverture dehors pour qu'elle sèche (*subj*); **he put the cat out for the night** il a fait sortir le chat *or* il a mis le chat dehors pour la nuit; **to put sb's eyes out** crever les yeux à qn; (*fig*) **to put sth out of one's head** *or* **mind** ne plus penser à qch; *for other phrases V* **grass** *etc.*
(b) (*Naut*) *boat* mettre à l'eau *or* à la mer.
(c)(*stretch out, extend*) *arm, leg* allonger, étendre; *foot* avancer; *tongue* tirer (*at sb* à qn); *leaves, shoots, roots* produire. **to put out one's hand** tendre *or* avancer la main; (*in greeting*) tendre la main; *[car driver, traffic policeman]* tendre le bras; **to put one's head out of the window** passer la tête par la fenêtre; **the snail put out its horns** l'escargot a sorti ses cornes; *for other phrases V* **feeler** *etc.*
(d) (*lay out in order*) *cards* étaler; *chessmen etc* disposer; *sb's clothes* sortir; *dishes, cutlery* sortir, disposer. **you can put the papers out on the table** vous pouvez étaler les papiers sur la table.
(e) (*extinguish*) *light, flames, gas, cigarette* éteindre; *heater* fermer. **put the fire out** (*heater*) fermez le radiateur; (*coal etc*) éteignez le feu.
(f) (*disconcert*) déconcerter, dérouter (*by, about* par), interloquer; (*vex*) fâcher, contrarier, ennuyer (*by, about* par). **she looked very put out** elle avait l'air très contrariée.
(g) (*inconvenience*) déranger, gêner. **I don't want to put you out** je ne voudrais pas vous déranger; **don't put yourself out** ne vous dérangez pas; (*iro*) surtout ne vous gênez pas!; **she really put herself out for us** elle s'est donné beaucoup de mal pour nous, elle s'est mise en quatre *or* en frais pour nous.
(h) (*issue*) *news* annoncer; *report, regulations* publier; *rumour* faire courir *or* circuler; *propaganda* faire; *book, edition* sortir, publier. **the government will put out a statement about it** le gouvernement va faire une déclaration *or* va publier un communiqué à ce sujet.
(i) (*spend*) dépenser. **they put out half a million on the project** ils ont dépensé un demi-million pour ce projet, ils ont investi un demi-million dans ce projet.
(j) (*lend at interest*) placer, prêter à intérêt. **he has £1,000 put out at 12%** il a placé 1.000 livres à 12%.
(k) *repairs, small jobs* donner au dehors; (*Ind: subcontract*) donner à un *or* des sous-traitant(s). **that shop puts out all its repair work** ce magasin donne toutes les réparations au dehors.
(l) (*exert*) *one's strength* déployer, user de. **they had to put out all their diplomacy to reach agreement** ils ont dû déployer *or* prodiguer tous leurs talents de diplomatie pour arriver à un accord.
(m) (*dislocate*) *shoulder* déboîter, disloquer, démettre; *ankle, knee, back* démettre.
put over *vt sep* = **put across.**
put through *vt sep* **(a)** (*make, complete*) *deal* conclure, mener à bien; *decision* prendre; *proposal* faire accepter, faire approuver.
(b) (*Telec: connect*) *call* passer; *caller* brancher, mettre en communication. **I'm putting you through now** je vous mets en communication, vous êtes en ligne; **put me through to Mr Smith** passez-moi M Smith.
put together *vt sep* **(a)** (*lit*) mettre ensemble. **you must not put two hamsters together in the same cage** il ne faut pas mettre deux hamsters ensemble dans une cage; **we don't want to put two men together at table** il vaut mieux ne pas placer deux hommes l'un à côté de l'autre à table; **he's worth more than the rest of the family put together** à lui tout seul il vaut largement le reste de la famille; *for other phrases V* **head, two** *etc.*
(b) (*assemble*) *table, bookcase, radio* assembler, monter; *jigsaw* assembler, faire; *book, story, account* composer; (*mend*) *broken vase etc* réparer, recoller, remettre ensemble les morceaux de. **she put together an excellent supper** elle a improvisé un délicieux dîner.
put up 1 *vi* **(a)** (*lodge*) descendre (*at* dans); (*for one night*) passer la nuit (*at* à).
(b) (*offer o.s.*) se porter candidat(e) (*for* à), se présenter comme candidat(e) (*for* pour). **to put up for president** se porter candidat à la présidence, poser sa candidature à la présidence; (*Parl*) **to put up for a constituency** chercher à se faire accepter comme candidat dans une circonscription électorale; **to put up for re-election** être candidat pour un nouveau mandat.
2 *vt sep* **(a)** (*raise*) *hand* lever; *flag, sail* hisser; *tent* dresser; *collar, window* remonter; *umbrella* ouvrir; *notice* mettre, afficher (*on* sur); *picture* mettre, accrocher (*on* sur); *missile, rocket, space probe* lancer; *building, bridge* construire, ériger; *fence, barrier* ériger, dresser. **to put a ladder up against a wall** poser *or* dresser une échelle contre un mur; **put them up!*** (*in robbery etc*) haut les mains!; (*challenge to fight*) défends-toi!; *for other phrases V* **back, foot** *etc.*
(b) (*increase*) *numbers, taxes, sales* augmenter; *prices* augmenter, faire monter; *demand, speed* augmenter, accroître; *sb's temperature, blood pressure* faire monter. **that puts up the total to over 1,000** cela fait monter le total à plus de 1.000.
(c) (*offer*) *proposal, suggestion, idea* présenter, soumettre; *plea, prayer, resistance* offrir; (*nominate*) proposer comme candidat (*for* à, *as* comme). **the plans were put up to the committee** les plans ont été présentés *or* soumis au comité; **the matter was put up to the board for a decision** l'affaire a été soumise au conseil d'administration pour qu'il décide (*subj*); **to put sth up for sale/auction** mettre qch en vente/aux enchères; **he was put up by his local branch** il a été présenté comme candidat par sa section locale; **they put him up for the chairmanship** on l'a présenté *or* proposé comme candidat à la présidence; **I'll put you up for the club** je vous proposerai comme membre du club; *for other phrases V* **fight, show, struggle** *etc.*
(d) (*provide*) *money, funds* fournir (*for* pour); *reward* offrir. **to put up money for a project** financer un projet, fournir les fonds pour un projet; **how much can you put up?** combien pouvez-vous (y) mettre?
(e) (*prepare, pack*) *picnic, sandwiches* préparer; (*Comm*) *order* exécuter; (*Pharm*) *prescription* préparer, exécuter. **the pills are put up in plastic tubes** les pilules sont présentées *or* emballées dans des tubes en plastique; **to put up apples for the winter** emmagasiner des pommes pour l'hiver, se constituer une réserve de pommes pour l'hiver.
(f) (*lodge*) loger, héberger. **I'm sorry I can't put you up** je suis désolé de ne pas pouvoir vous recevoir pour la nuit *or* vous coucher.
(g) (*incite*) **to put sb up to doing** pousser *or* inciter qn à faire; **someone must have put him up to it** quelqu'un a dû l'y pousser *or* l'y inciter *or* lui en donner l'idée.
(h) (*inform about*) **to put sb up to sth** mettre qn au courant de qch, renseigner qn sur qch; **I'll put you up to all his little tricks** je te mettrai au courant *or* je t'avertirai de tous ses petits tours; **he put her up to all the ways of avoiding tax** il l'a renseignée *or* tuyautée* sur tous les moyens d'éviter de payer des impôts.
3 put-up *adj*, **put-you-up** *n V* **put 3.**
put upon 1 *vt fus* (*gen pass*) **I won't be put upon any more!** je ne vais plus me laisser faire! *or* me laisser marcher sur les pieds!*
2 put-upon* *adj V* **put 3.**
put up with *vt fus* tolérer, supporter, encaisser*. **he has a lot to put up with** il a beaucoup de problèmes, il n'a pas la vie facile; **it is difficult to put up with** c'est difficile à supporter, c'est difficilement supportable.
putative ['pjuːtətɪv] *adj* (*frm*) putatif.
putrefaction [ˌpjuːtrɪ'fækʃən] *n* putréfaction *f.*
putrefy ['pjuːtrɪfaɪ] **1** *vt* putréfier. **2** *vi* se putréfier.
putrescence [pjuː'tresns] *n* putrescence *f.*
putrescent [pjuː'tresnt] *adj* putrescent, en voie de putréfaction.
putrid ['pjuːtrɪd] *adj* putride, pourrissant; (* *fig*) dégoûtant, dégueulasse‡.
putsch [pʊtʃ] *n* putsch *m*, coup *m* d'État.
putt [pʌt] (*Golf*) **1** *n* putt *m*, coup roulé. **2** *vti* putter.
puttee ['pʌtiː] *n* bande molletière.
putter[1] ['pʌtə^{r}] *n* (*golf club*) putter *m.*
putter[2] ['pʌtə^{r}] *vi* = **potter[1]**.
putting ['pʌtɪŋ] **1** *n* putting *m.* **2** *cpd*: **putting green** green *m.*
putty ['pʌtɪ] **1** *n* mastic *m* (*ciment*). **she's like ~ in my hands** c'est une pâte molle entre mes mains.
2 *cpd*: **putty knife** couteau *m* de vitrier.
3 *vt* mastiquer.
puzzle ['pʌzl] **1** *n* **(a)** (*mystery*) énigme *f*, mystère *m*;

(*bewilderment*) perplexité *f.* **he is a real ~ to me** c'est une énigme vivante pour moi; **it is a ~ to me how he ever got the job** je n'arriverai jamais à comprendre comment il a obtenu le poste; **to be in a ~ about sth** être perplexe au sujet de qch; **I'm in a ~ about what to do** je suis dans l'incertitude *or* la perplexité, je ne sais pas trop quoi faire.

(b) (*game*) casse-tête *m inv*; (*word game*) rébus *m*; (*crossword*) mots croisés; (*jigsaw*) puzzle *m*; (*riddle*) devinette *f.*

2 *cpd*: **puzzle book** livre *m* de jeux.

3 *vt* rendre *or* laisser perplexe. **that really ~d him** ça l'a vraiment rendu *or* laissé perplexe; **I am ~d to know why** je n'arrive pas à comprendre pourquoi; **he was ~d about what to say** il ne savait pas quoi dire.

4 *vi*: **to ~ over** *or* **about** *problem, mystery* essayer de résoudre; *event, sb's actions, intentions* essayer de comprendre; **I'm still puzzling over where he might have hidden it** j'en suis encore à me demander où il a bien pu le cacher.

puzzle out *vt sep problem* résoudre; *mystery* éclaircir, élucider; *writing* déchiffrer; *answer, solution* trouver, découvrir; *sb's actions, attitude* comprendre. **I'm trying to puzzle out why he did it** j'essaie de comprendre *or* découvrir pourquoi il l'a fait.

puzzled [ˈpʌzld] *adj* perplexe; *V also* **puzzle.**

puzzlement [ˈpʌzlmənt] *n* (*U*) perplexité *f.*

puzzler [ˈpʌzləʳ] *n* question *f* difficile, casse-tête *m inv.*

puzzling [ˈpʌzlɪŋ] *adj behaviour etc* curieux, inexplicable; *mechanism etc* mystérieux, incompréhensible.

pygmy [ˈpɪgmɪ] **1** *n* (*also fig*) pygmée *m.* **2** *adj* (*also fig*) pygmée (*f inv*), pygméen.

pyjama [pɪˈdʒɑːmə] (*Brit*) **1** *npl*: **~s** pyjama *m*; **in (one's) ~s** en pyjama. **2** *cpd jacket, trousers* de pyjama.

pylon [ˈpaɪlən] *n* pylône *m.*

pyorrhea [paɪəˈrɪə] *n* pyorrhée *f* alvéolaire.

pyramid [ˈpɪrəmɪd] **1** *n* pyramide *f.* **2** *cpd*: **pyramid selling** vente *f* à la boule de neige.

pyramidal [pɪˈræmɪdl] *adj* pyramidal.

pyre [ˈpaɪəʳ] *n* bûcher *m* funéraire.

Pyrenean [pɪrəˈniːən] *adj* pyrénéen, des Pyrénées.

Pyrenees [pɪrəˈniːz] *npl* Pyrénées *fpl.*

pyrethrum [paɪˈriːθrəm] *n* pyrèthre *m.*

pyretic [paɪˈretɪk] *adj* pyrétique.

Pyrex [ˈpaɪreks] ® **1** *n* pyrex *m* ®. **2** *cpd dish* en pyrex.

pyrites [paɪˈraɪtiːz] *n* pyrite *f.* **iron ~** sulfure *m* de fer, fer sulfuré.

pyritic [paɪˈrɪtɪk] *adj* pyriteux.

pyro... [ˈpaɪərəʊ] *pref* pyro... .

pyromaniac [ˌpaɪərəʊˈmeɪnɪæk] *n* pyromane *mf*, incendiaire *mf.*

pyrotechnic [ˌpaɪərəʊˈteknɪk] **1** *adj* pyrotechnique. **~ display** feu(x) *m(pl)* d'artifice. **2** *n*: **~s** (*U: Phys*) pyrotechnie *f*; (*pl: fig hum*) feux *mpl* d'artifice.

Pyrrhic [ˈpɪrɪk] *adj*: **~ victory** victoire *f* à la Pyrrhus, victoire coûteuse *or* aux conséquences désastreuses.

Pythagoras [paɪˈθægərəs] *n* Pythagore *m.*

Pythagorean [paɪˈθægəˈrɪən] *adj* pythagoricien.

python [ˈpaɪθən] *n* python *m.*

pyx [pɪks] *n* (*in church*) ciboire *m*; (*for sick communions*) pyxide *f.*

Q

Q, q [kjuː] *n* (*letter*) Q, q *m.* **on the q.t.*** = **on the quiet** (*V* **quiet** 2c); *V* **P.**

qua [kweɪ] *adv* en tant que, considéré comme, en (sa *etc*) qualité de.

quack[1] [kwæk] **1** *n* coin-coin *m* (*cri du canard*). **2** *vi* faire coin-coin. **3** *cpd*: (*baby talk*) **quack-quack** coin-coin *m.*

quack[2] [kwæk] **1** *n* (*Med, gen*) charlatan *m.* **2** *cpd* de charlatan.

quackery [ˈkwækərɪ] *n* (*U*) charlatanisme *m.*

quad[1] [kwɒd] *n abbr of* **quadruplet** *and* **quadrangle.**

quad[2] [kwɒd] *n* = **quod**[2].

Quadragesima [ˌkwɒdrəˈdʒesɪmə] *n* Quadragésime *f.*

quadrangle [ˈkwɒdræŋgl] *n* (*Math*) quadrilatère *m*; (*courtyard*) cour *f* (*d'un collège etc*).

quadrangular [kwɒˈdræŋgjʊləʳ] *adj* quadrangulaire.

quadrant [ˈkwɒdrənt] *n [circle]* quadrant *m*, quart *m* de cercle.

quadratic [kwɒˈdrætɪk] *adj* (*Math*) quadratique. **~ equation** équation *f* du second degré.

quadrature [ˈkwɒdrətʃəʳ] *n* quadrature *f.*

quadr(i)... [ˈkwɒdrɪ] *pref* quadr(i)... .

quadrilateral [ˌkwɒdrɪˈlætərəl] (*Math*) **1** *adj* quadrilatère, quadrilatéral.

2 *n* quadrilatère *m.*

quadrilingual [ˌkwɒdrɪˈlɪŋgwəl] *adj* quadrilingue.

quadrille [kwəˈdrɪl] *n* (*Dancing*) quadrille *m.*

quadripartite [ˈkwɒdrɪˈpɑːtaɪt] *adj* quadriparti (*f* -e *or* -te).

quadriphonic [ˈkwɒdrɪˈfɒnɪk] *adj* quadriphonique. **in ~ sound** en quadriphonie.

quadroon [kwɒˈdruːn] *n* quarteron(ne) *m(f).*

quadruped [ˈkwɒdruped] *adj, n* quadrupède (*m*).

quadruple [ˈkwɒdrʊpl] **1** *adj, n* quadruple (*m*). **2** [ˈkwɒˈdruːpl] *vti* quadrupler.

quadruplet [kwɒˈdruːplɪt] *n* quadruplé(e) *m(f).*

quadruplicate [kwɒˈdruːplɪkɪt] **1** *adj* quadruplé. **2** *n*: **in ~** en quatre exemplaires.

quaff [kwɒf] *vt* († *or hum*) *glass* vider à longs traits; *wine* lamper.

quagmire [ˈkwægmaɪəʳ] *n* (*lit, fig*) bourbier *m.*

quail[1] [kweɪl] *vi [person]* perdre courage, reculer (*before* devant). **his heart** *or* **spirit ~ed** son courage l'a trahi.

quail[2] [kweɪl] *n, pl inv or* **~s** (*Orn*) caille *f.*

quaint [kweɪnt] *adj* (*odd*) *person, dress, attitude, idea, custom* bizarre, original; (*picturesque*) pittoresque; (*old-fashioned etc*) au charme vieillot, qui a un petit cachet vieillot *or* désuet. **a ~ little village** un petit village au charme vieillot; **a ~ custom** une coutume pittoresque; **~ old countryman** vieux paysan pittoresque.

quaintly [ˈkweɪntlɪ] *adv* (*V* **quaint**) d'une manière originale *or* bizarre *or* pittoresque.

quaintness [ˈkweɪntnɪs] *n* (*V* **quaint**) originalité *f*, bizarrerie *f*; pittoresque *m*; cachet *or* caractère vieillot.

quake [kweɪk] **1** *vi [earth]* trembler; *[person etc]* trembler, frémir (*with* de). **I was quaking*** je tremblais comme une feuille. **2** *n* (*abbr of* **earthquake**) tremblement *m* de terre, séisme *m.*

Quaker [ˈkweɪkəʳ] **1** *n* quaker(esse) *m(f).* **2** *adj* de quaker(s). **~ meeting** réunion *f* de quakers.

Quakerism [ˈkweɪkərɪzəm] *n* quakerisme *m.*

qualification [ˌkwɒlɪfɪˈkeɪʃən] *n* **(a)** (*ability*) compétence *f* (*for* en, *to do* pour faire), aptitude *f* (*for* à), capacité *f* (*to do* pour faire). **I doubt his ~ to teach English** je doute qu'il ait qualité *or* qu'il ait les compétences requises *or* qu'il ait les capacités requises pour enseigner l'anglais; **we have never questioned his ~ for the job** nous n'avons jamais mis en doute son aptitude à remplir le poste.

(b) (*gen pl*) **~s** (*degrees, diplomas etc*) titres *mpl*, diplômes *mpl*; (*necessary conditions for a post etc*) conditions requises *or* nécessaires, conditions à remplir; **his only ~ for the job was his experience in similar work** seule son expérience dans des domaines similaires le qualifiait pour ce travail; **what are your ~s?** (*skill, degrees, experience etc*) quelle est votre formation?; (*paper* **~s**) qu'est-ce que vous avez comme diplômes?; **he has a lot of experience but no paper ~s** *or* **formal ~s** il a beaucoup d'expérience mais aucun diplôme *or* titre; **I have no teaching ~(s)** je n'ai pas le(s) diplôme(s) requis pour enseigner.

(c) (*limitation*) réserve *f*, restriction *f*, condition *f.* **to accept a plan with ~(s)** accepter un projet avec des réserves *or* avec des restrictions *or* à certaines conditions; **without ~(s)** sans réserves *or* restrictions *or* conditions.

(d) (*U: V* **qualify 1c**) qualification *f.*

qualified [ˈkwɒlɪfaɪd] *adj* **(a)** *person* compétent, qualifié (*for* pour, en matière de); *engineer, doctor, nurse, teacher* diplômé; *craftsman, player* qualifié. **we must find a ~ person to take charge of the project** il nous faut trouver une personne ayant qualité pour *or* ayant la compétence voulue pour prendre la direction du projet; **he was not ~ for this job** il ne remplissait pas les conditions requises pour ce poste, il n'avait pas le(s) diplôme(s) *or* les titres requis pour ce poste; **to be ~ to do** être qualifié *or* avoir la compétence voulue *or* avoir qualité pour faire, être habilité à faire (*esp Jur*); **he is ~ to teach** il a qualité pour enseigner; **they are not ~ to vote** ils ne sont pas habilités à voter; **I'm not ~ to speak for her** je ne suis pas qualifié pour parler en son nom; **I don't feel ~ to judge** je ne me sens pas qualifié pour juger.

(b) (*modified*) *praise* mitigé; *support, acceptance, approval* conditionnel. **a ~ success** une demi-réussite.

qualify [ˈkwɒlɪfaɪ] **1** *vt* **(a)** (*make competent*) qualifier, donner qualité à (*for* pour). **to ~ sb to do** qualifier qn pour faire, donner qualité à qn pour faire, donner à qn les compétences *or* qualités requises pour faire; (*Jur*) habiliter qn à faire; **this should ~ you for this post** ceci devrait vous qualifier pour ce poste, ceci devrait vous donner les compétences *or* qualités requises pour requises pour faire; (*Jur*) habiliter qn à faire; **this should ~ you for this post** ceci devrait vous qualifier pour ce poste, ceci devrait vous donner les compétences *or* qualités requises pour (occuper) ce poste; **that doesn't ~ him to speak on it** cela ne lui donne pas qualité pour en parler.

(b) (*modify*) *attitude, praise* mitiger, tempérer, atténuer; *approval, support* mettre des réserves à; *statement, opinion* nuancer. **to ~ one's acceptance of sth** accepter qch sous réserve *or* sous condition; **I think you should ~ that statement** je pense que vous devriez nuancer cette déclaration.

(c) (*describe*) qualifier (*as* de); (*Gram*) qualifier.

2 *vi* obtenir son diplôme *or* son brevet *etc.* **to ~ as a doctor** obtenir le *or* son diplôme de docteur (en médecine); **he has qualified as a teacher** il a obtenu le *or* son diplome de professeur; **while he was ~ing as a teacher** pendant qu'il faisait des études pour devenir professeur; **to ~ as a nurse/an engineer** obtenir son diplôme d'infirmière/d'ingénieur; **to ~ for a job** obtenir le(s) diplôme(s) *or* titre(s) nécessaire(s) pour un poste; **he doesn't ~ for that post** il n'a pas le(s) diplôme(s) *or* titre(s) nécessaire(s) pour (occuper) ce poste; **does he ~?** est-ce qu'il remplit les conditions requises?; (*Sport*) **to ~ for the final** se qualifier pour la finale; (*fig*) **he hardly qualifies as a poet** il ne mérite pas vraiment le nom de poète.

qualifying ['kwɒlɪfaɪɪŋ] *adj* **(a)** *mark* de passage, qui permet de passer; *examination* d'entrée; *score* qui permet de se qualifier. (*Sport*) **~ heat** éliminatoire *f*; **~ round** série *f* éliminatoire. **(b)** (*Gram*) qualificatif.

qualitative ['kwɒlɪtətɪv] *adj* qualitatif.

qualitatively ['kwɒlɪtətɪvlɪ] *adv* qualitativement.

quality ['kwɒlɪtɪ] **1** *n* **(a)** (*nature, kind*) qualité *f*. **of the best ~** de première qualité, de premier ordre *or* choix; **of good *or* high ~** de bonne qualité, de qualité supérieure; **of poor *or* bad *or* low ~** de mauvaise qualité, de qualité inférieure; **the ~ of life** la qualité de la vie.

(b) (*U: goodness*) qualité *f*. **guarantee of ~** garantie *f* de qualité; **it's ~ rather than quantity that counts** c'est la qualité qui compte plus que la quantité; **this wine has ~** ce vin a de la qualité *or* est de qualité; **he has real ~** il a de la classe.

(c) (*attribute*) qualité *f*. **natural qualities** qualités naturelles; **one of his (good) qualities** une de ses qualités; **one of his bad qualities** un de ses défauts; **he has many artistic qualities** il a beaucoup de qualités *or* de dons *mpl* artistiques.

(d) *[voice, sound]* qualité *f*, timbre *m*.

(e) († *or hum: high rank*) qualité† *f*.

2 *cpd car, film, product* de qualité. (*Ind*) **quality control** contrôle *m* de qualité (*auquel on soumet les produits manufacturés*); (*Press*) **the quality papers** les journaux sérieux.

qualm [kwɑːm] *n* (*nausea*) malaise *m*, nausée *f*, haut-le-cœur *m inv*; (*scruple*) doute *m*, scrupule *m*; (*misgiving*) appréhension *f*, inquiétude *f*. **~s of conscience** scrupules de conscience; **he did it without a ~** il l'a fait sans le moindre scrupule; **I would feel no ~s about doing that** je n'aurais pas le moindre scrupule à faire cela; **I had some ~s about his future** j'avais quelques inquiétudes sur *or* pour son avenir.

quandary ['kwɒndərɪ] *n* embarras *m*, dilemme *m*, difficulté *f*. **to be in a ~** être dans l'embarras, être pris dans un dilemme; **he was in a ~ about *or* as to *or* over what to do** il était bien embarrassé de savoir quoi faire; **that got him out of a ~** ça l'a sorti d'un dilemme, ça l'a tiré d'embarras.

quantifier ['kwɒntɪfaɪəʳ] *n* (*Ling, Philos*) terme quantitatif.

quantify ['kwɒntɪfaɪ] *vt* déterminer la quantité de, évaluer quantitativement; (*Philos*) quantifier.

quantitative ['kwɒntɪtətɪv] *adj* (*Chem etc*) quantitatif; (*Ling, Poetry*) de quantité. (*Chem*) **~ analysis** analyse quantitative.

quantitatively ['kwɒntɪtətɪvlɪ] *adv* quantitativement.

quantity ['kwɒntɪtɪ] *n* (*gen, Ling, Math, Poetry*) quantité *f*. **a small ~ of rice** une petite quantité de riz; **what ~ do you want?** quelle quantité (en) voulez-vous?; **in ~** en (grande) quantité; **in large quantities** en grandes quantités; **a ~ of, any ~ of, quantities of** une quantité de, (des) quantités de, un grand nombre de; *V* **quality, unknown.**

2 *cpd* (*Comm*) *production* sur une grande échelle, en série. (*Ling, Poet*) **quantity mark** signe *m* de quantité; (*Brit*) **quantity surveying** métrage *m*; (*Brit*) **quantity surveyor** métreur *m* (vérificateur).

quantum ['kwɒntəm] *pl* **quanta** ['kwɒntə] **1** *n* quantum *m*. **2** *cpd*: (*Phys*) **quantum mechanics** mécanique *f* quantique; **quantum number** nombre *m* quantique; **quantum theory** théorie *f* des quanta.

quarantine ['kwɒrəntiːn] **1** *n* quarantaine *f*. **in ~** en quarantaine. **2** *cpd regulations, period* de quarantaine. **3** *vt* mettre en quarantaine.

quark [kwɑːk] *n* quark *m*.

quarrel ['kwɒrəl] **1** *n* (*dispute*) querelle *f*, dispute *f*; (*more intellectual*) différend *m*; (*breach*) brouille *f*. **I had a ~ with him yesterday** je me suis disputé *or* querellé avec lui hier; **they've had a ~** (*argued*) ils se sont disputés *or* querellés; (*fallen out*) ils se sont brouillés; **they had a sudden ~** ils ont eu un accrochage*; **the children's little ~s** les disputes *or* chamailleries* *fpl* des enfants; **to start a ~** provoquer *or* susciter une querelle *or* dispute; **to pick a ~ with sb, to try to start a ~ with sb** chercher querelle à qn; (*fig*) **I have no ~ with you** je n'ai rien contre vous; **he had no ~ with what we had done** il n'avait rien à redire à ce que nous avions fait.

2 *vi* (*have a dispute*) se disputer, se quereller, se chamailler* (*with sb* avec qn, *about, over* à propos de); (*break off friendship*) se brouiller (*with sb* avec qn). (*fig*) **I cannot ~ with that** je n'ai rien à redire à cela; **what he ~s with is ...** ce contre quoi il s'insurge c'est ... .

quarrelling, (*US*) **quarreling** ['kwɒrəlɪŋ] **1** *n* (*U*) disputes *fpl*, querelles *fpl*; (*petty*) chamailleries* *fpl*. **2** *adj* qui se disputent.

quarrelsome ['kwɒrəlsəm] *adj* querelleur, batailleur, chamailleur, mauvais coucheur*.

quarrier ['kwɒrɪəʳ] *n* (ouvrier *m*) carrier *m*.

quarry¹ ['kwɒrɪ] **1** *n* carrière *f*; *V* **marble** *etc.*

2 *cpd*: **quarryman** (ouvrier *m*) carrier *m*; **quarry tile** carreau *m*; **quarry-tiled floor** sol carrelé.

3 *vt stone* extraire; *hillside* exploiter (*en carrière*).

4 *vi* exploiter une carrière. **they are ~ing for marble** ils exploitent une carrière de marbre.

quarry out *vt sep block, stone* extraire.

quarry² ['kwɒrɪ] *n* (*animal, bird etc*) proie *f*; (*Hunting: game*) gibier *m*. **the detectives lost their ~** les policiers ont perdu la trace de celui qu'ils pourchassaient.

quart [kwɔːt] *n* (*measure*) ≃ litre *m* (*Brit = 1,136 litres; US = 0,946 litre*). (*fig*) **it's like trying to put a ~ into a pint pot** c'est tenter l'impossible (il n'y a vraiment pas la place).

quarter ['kwɔːtəʳ] **1** *n* **(a)** (*fourth part*) quart *m*. **to divide sth into ~s** diviser qch en quatre (parties égales) *or* en (quatre) quartiers; **a ~ (of a pound) of tea** un quart (de livre) de thé; **a ~ full/empty** au quart plein/vide; **it's a ~ gone already** il y en a déjà un quart de parti; **a ~ as big as** quatre fois moins grand que; **I bought it for a ~ of the price *or* for ~ the price** je l'ai acheté au quart du prix *or* pour le quart de son prix.

(b) (*in expressions of time*) quart *m* (d'heure). **a ~ of an hour** un quart d'heure; **a ~ to 7,** (*US*) **a ~ of 7** 7 heures moins le quart *or* moins un quart; **a ~ past 6,** (*US*) **a ~ after 6** 6 heures un quart *or* et quart; (*Aut*) **to drive with one's hands at a ~ to three** conduire avec les mains à neuf heures et quart; **it wasn't the ~ yet** il n'était pas encore le quart; **the clock strikes the ~s** l'horloge sonne les quarts.

(c) (*specific fourth parts*) *[year]* trimestre *m*; (*US and Can money*) quart *m* de dollar, vingt-cinq cents; (*Brit weight*) = *28 livres* (= *12,7* kg); (*US weight*) = *25 livres* (= *11,34* kg); (*Her*) quartier *m*; *[beef, apple etc]* quartier; *[moon]* quartier. **to pay by the ~** payer tous les trois mois *or* par trimestre; **a ~'s rent** un terme (de loyer); *V* **forequarters, hindquarters** *etc.*

(d) (*direction*) direction *f*, part *f*, côté *m*; (*compass point*) point cardinal. (*Naut*) **on the port/starboard ~** par la hanche de bâbord/tribord; **from all ~s** de toutes parts, de tous côtés; **you must report that to the proper ~** vous devez signaler cela à qui de droit; **in responsible ~s** dans les milieux autorisés.

(e) (*part of town*) quartier *m*. **the Latin ~** le quartier latin.

(f) (*lodgings*) **~s** résidence *f*, domicile *m*; (*Mil*) quartiers *mpl*, (*temporary*) cantonnement *m*; **they are living in very cramped ~s** ils sont logés très à l'étroit; *V* **married** *etc.*

(g) (*U: liter: mercy*) quartier *m* (*liter*), grâce *f*. **to give/cry ~** faire/demander quartier.

2 *vt* **(a)** (*divide into four*) diviser en quatre (parts égales), diviser en (quatre) quartiers; *traitor's body* écarteler; (*Her*) écarteler; *V* **hang.**

(b) (*lodge*) (*Mil*) *troops* caserner, (*temporarily*) cantonner; (*gen*) loger (*on* chez).

(c) *[dogs]* **to ~ the ground** quêter; *[police etc]* **to ~ a town in search of sb** quadriller une ville à la recherche de qn.

3 *adj* d'un quart. **the ~ part of** le quart de; **a ~ share in sth** (une part d')un quart de qch; *V also* **4**.

4 *cpd*: (*Fin, Jur*) **quarter day** (jour *m* du) terme *m*; (*Naut*) **quarter-deck** plage *f* arrière; *[sailing ship]* gaillard *m* d'arrière; (*Sport*) **quarter final** quart *m* de finale; (*Brit Aut*) **quarter light** déflecteur *m*; **quartermaster** *V* **quartermaster;** (*Sport*) **quarter mile** (course *f* d'un) quart *m* de mille; (*Mus*) **quarter note** noire *f*; **quarter pound** quart *m* de livre; **quarter-pound** d'un quart de livre; (*Jur*) **quarter sessions** (*sessions*) ≃ assises trimestrielles (de tribunal de grande instance); (*court*) ≃ tribunal *m* de grande instance.

quartering ['kwɔːtərɪŋ] *n* (*U*) **(a)** division *f* en quatre; (*Her*) écartelure *f*. **(b)** (*Mil: lodging*) cantonnement *m*.

quarterly ['kwɔːtəlɪ] **1** *adj review, payment* trimestriel. **2** *n* (*periodical*) publication trimestrielle. **3** *adv* tous les trois mois; trimestriellement, (une fois) par trimestre.

quartermaster ['kwɔːtə,mɑːstəʳ] **1** *n* **(a)** (*Mil*) intendant *m* militaire de troisième classe. **(b)** (*Naut*) maître *m* de manœuvre. **2** *cpd*: (*Mil*) **quartermaster general** intendant général d'armée de première classe; (*Mil*) **quartermaster sergeant** intendant militaire adjoint.

quartet(te) [kwɔː'tet] *n* (*classical music; players*) quatuor *m*; (*jazz players*) quartette *m*; (*often hum: four people*) quatuor*.

quarto ['kwɔːtəʊ] **1** *n* in-quarto *m*. **2** *adj paper* in-quarto *inv*.

quartz ['kwɔːts] **1** *n* quartz *m*. **2** *cpd* de *or* en quartz. **quartz clock** pendule *f* à quartz.

quartzite ['kwɔːtsaɪt] *n* quartzite *m*.

quasar ['kweɪzɑːʳ] *n* quasar *m*.

quash ['kwɒʃ] *vt decision, verdict* casser, infirmer, annuler; *rebellion* réprimer, étouffer; *proposal, suggestion* rejeter, repousser.

quasi- ['kwɑːzɪ] *pref* (+*n*) quasi-; (+*adj*) quasi, presque. **~marriage** quasi-mariage *m*; **~revolutionary** quasi *or* presque révolutionnaire.

quatercentenary [,kwɒtəsen'tiːnərɪ] *n* quatrième centenaire *m*.

quaternary [kwə'tɜːnərɪ] **1** *adj* (*Chem, Geol, Math*) quaternaire. **2** *n* (*set of four*) ensemble *m* de quatre; (*number four*) quatre *m*. (*Geol*) **the Q~** le quaternaire.

quatrain ['kwɒtreɪn] *n* quatrain *m*.

quaver ['kweɪvəʳ] **1** *n* (*Mus: esp Brit: note*) croche *f*; (*gen: voice tremor*) tremblement *m*, chevrotement *m*. **2** *cpd*: (*Brit Mus*) **quaver rest** demi-soupir *m*. **3** *vi [voice]* chevroter, trembloter; *[person]* chevroter, parler d'une voix chevrotante *or* tremblotante. **4** *vt* (*also* **~ out**) chevroter.

quavering ['kweɪvərɪŋ] 1 *adj* tremblotant, chevrotant. 2 *n* tremblement *m*, tremblotement *m*, chevrotement *m*.
quaveringly ['kweɪvərɪŋlɪ] *adv* d'une voix chevrotante *or* tremblotante, avec des tremblements dans la voix.
quavery ['kweɪvərɪ] *adj* = **quavering 1.**
quay [ki:] *n* (*Naut etc*) quai *m*. **at** *or* **alongside the ~side** à quai.
queasiness ['kwi:zɪnɪs] *n* (*U*) mal *m* au cœur, malaise *m*.
queasy ['kwi:zɪ] *adj food* (*upsetting*) indigeste; (*nauseating*) écœurant; *stomach, digestion* délicat; *person* sujet aux nausées. **he was ~, he felt ~, his stomach was ~** il avait mal au cœur, il avait envie de vomir; (*fig*) **he's got a ~ conscience** il n'a pas la conscience tranquille.
Quebec [kwɪ'bek] 1 *n* Québec *m*. 2 *adj* québécois. (*Ling*) **~ French** (franco-)québécois *m*.
Quebec(k)er [kwɪ'bekəʳ] *n* Québécois(e) *m(f)*.
queen [kwi:n] 1 *n* **(a)** (*also fig*) reine *f*. **Q~ Elizabeth** la reine Élisabeth; **she was ~ to George III** elle était l'épouse de Georges III; (*iro*) **Q~ Anne's dead!*** ce n'est pas une nouvelle!, tu ne nous apprends rien!; **a Q~ Anne chair** une chaise (de l'époque de la) reine Anne; **~ of the ball** reine du bal; *V* **beauty, Mary, may² etc.**
(b) (*Brit*) (*Jur*) **Q~'s Bench** cour supérieure de justice; (*Jur*) **Q~'s Counsel** avocat *m* de la Couronne; (*Jur*) **to turn Q~'s evidence** dénoncer ses complices; **the Q~'s highway** la voie publique; **Q~'s Messenger** courrier *m* diplomatique.
(c) (*ant, bee, wasp*) reine *f*; (*Chess*) dame *f*, reine; (*Cards*) dame.
(d) (*‡ pej: homosexual*) tante‡ *f* (*pej*), pédale‡ *f* (*pej*).
2 *cpd*: **queen bee** reine *f* des abeilles; **Queen Mother** reine mère *f*.
3 *vt* **(a)** (*) **to ~ it** faire la grande dame; **to ~ it over sb** prendre des airs d'impératrice avec qn.
(b) (*Chess*) *pawn* damer.
queenly ['kwi:nlɪ] *adj* de reine.
queer [kwɪəʳ] 1 *adj* **(a)** (*odd*) étrange, bizarre, singulier. **a ~ fellow** un curieux personnage *or* bonhomme, un drôle de corps*; (*pej*) **a ~ customer** un drôle d'individu *or* de type*; **~ in the head*** dérangé, toqué*; (*Brit*) **to be in Q~ Street*** se trouver dans une mauvaise passe *or* en mauvaise posture.
(b) (*suspicious*) suspect, louche. **there's something ~ going on** il se passe quelque chose de louche; **there's something ~ about the way he always has money** il y a quelque chose de suspect dans le fait qu'il a toujours de l'argent.
(c) (*: *unwell*) mal fichu*, patraque*. **she suddenly felt ~** elle s'est soudain trouvée prise d'un malaise.
(d) (*: *homosexual*) homosexuel. **he's ~** c'est un pédé‡.
2 *cpd*: **queer-bashing‡** chasse *f* aux pédés‡; **he was a queer-looking man** il avait une drôle d'allure; **it was a queer-sounding name** c'était un nom (qui avait une consonance) bizarre.
3 *n* (*: *homosexual*) (*male*) pédéraste *m*, pédé‡ *m*; (*female*) lesbienne *f*.
4 *vt* gâter, abîmer. (*Brit fig*) **to ~ sb's pitch** couper l'herbe sous les pieds à *or* de qn.
queerly ['kwɪəlɪ] *adv* étrangement, bizarrement, singulièrement.
queerness ['kwɪənɪs] *n* étrangeté *f*, bizarrerie *f*, singularité *f*.
quell [kwel] *vt rebellion, rage, anxieties* réprimer, étouffer. **she ~ed him with a glance** elle l'a fait rentrer sous terre d'un regard, elle l'a foudroyé du regard.
quench [kwentʃ] *vt flames, fire* éteindre; *steel etc* tremper; *hope, desire* réprimer, étouffer; *enthusiasm* refroidir. **to ~ one's thirst** se désaltérer.
quenchless ['kwentʃlɪs] *adj* (*liter*) inextinguible.
quern [kwɜ:n] *n* moulin *m* à bras (*pour le grain*).
querulous ['kwerʊləs] *adj person* récriminateur (*f* -trice), bougon*, ronchonneur*; *tone* plaintif, bougon*.
querulously ['kwerʊləslɪ] *adv* en se lamentant, d'un ton plaintif *or* bougon*.
query ['kwɪərɪ] 1 *n* **(a)** (*question*) question *f*; (*doubt*) doute *m*. **readers' queries** questions des lecteurs; **this raises a ~ about the viability of the scheme** cela met en question la viabilité de ce projet.
(b) (*Gram: question mark(?)*) point *m* d'interrogation.
2 *vt* **(a)** *statement, motive, evidence* mettre en doute *or* en question. **I ~ that!** je me permets d'en douter!; **to ~ whether** demander si, chercher à savoir si.
(b) (*write ? against*) *part of text* marquer d'un point d'interrogation.
quest [kwest] *n* quête *f*, recherche *f*, poursuite *f* (*for* de). **in ~ of** en quête de.
question ['kwestʃən] 1 *n* **(a)** question *f* (*also Parl*). **to ask sb a ~, to put a ~ to sb**, (*Parl*) **to put down a ~ for sb** poser une question à qn; **what a ~ to ask!** quelle question!, belle question! (*iro*); (*Gram*) **indirect** *or* **oblique ~** interrogation indirecte; **to put sth to the ~** soumettre qch au vote; *V* **leading, pop¹, sixty** *etc*.
(b) (*U: doubt*) (mise *f* en) doute *m*. **beyond (all) ~, without ~, past ~** (*adj*) hors de doute, incontestable; (*adv*) incontestablement, sans aucun doute; **there is no ~ about it** il n'y a pas de question *or* pas de doute; **there is no ~ but that he has left** nul doute *or* il n'y a pas de doute qu'il ne soit parti; *V* **call.**
(c) (*matter, subject*) question *f*, sujet *m*, affaire *f*. **that's the ~!** là est la question!, c'est là (toute) la question!; **that's not the ~** là n'est pas la question, il ne s'agit pas de cela; **that's another ~ altogether** ça c'est une tout autre affaire; **the person in ~** la personne en question *or* dont il s'agit; **there's some/no ~ of closing the shop** il est/il n'est pas question de fermer *or* qu'on ferme (*subj*) le magasin; **there's no ~ of that, that is out of the ~** il ne peut en être question, il n'en est pas question, il ne saurait en être question (*frm*); **the ~ is how many** la question c'est de savoir combien, il s'agit de savoir combien; (*in concluding*) reste à savoir combien; **the ~ is to decide ...** il s'agit de décider ...; (*in concluding*) reste à décider ...; **the German ~** la question allemande, le problème allemand; **it is a ~ of sincerity** c'est une question de sincérité; **it's (all) a ~ of what you want to do eventually** tout dépend de ce que tu veux faire en fin de compte; **it's an open ~ (whether)** la question reste posée (de savoir si), personne ne sait (si); **success is a ~ of time** le succès n'est qu'une affaire de temps; *V* **burning** *etc*.
2 *cpd*: **question mark** point *m* d'interrogation; (*fig*) **there is a question mark over whether he meant to do it** on ne sait pas au juste s'il avait l'intention de le faire; (*fig*) **a big question mark hangs over his future** quant à son avenir c'est un point d'interrogation; **questionmaster** meneur *m* de jeu; (*Rad, TV*) animateur *m*; **question tag** queue *f* de phrase interrogative; (*Brit Parl*) **question time** heure réservée aux questions orales.
3 *vt* **(a)** interroger, poser des questions à, questionner (*on* sur, *about* au sujet de, à propos de). **we ~ed him closely to find out whether** nous l'avons interrogé de près pour savoir si; **I will not be ~ed about it** je refuse d'être l'objet de questions à ce sujet.
(b) *motive, account, sb's honesty* mettre en doute *or* en question, douter de; *claim* contester. **to ~ whether** douter que +*subj*.
questionable ['kwestʃənəbl] *adj statement, figures* discutable, douteux, contestable; (*pej*) *motive etc* louche, douteux, suspect; *taste* discutable, douteux. **it is ~ whether** il est douteux *or* discutable que + *subj*.
questioner ['kwestʃənəʳ] *n* personne *f* qui pose des questions; (*interrupting*) interpellateur *m*, -trice *f*. **she looked at her ~** elle regarda la personne qui l'interrogeait.
questioning ['kwestʃənɪŋ] 1 *adj* interrogateur (*f* -trice), questionneur. **he gave me a ~ look** il m'interrogea du regard. 2 *n* interrogation *f*.
questionnaire [,kwestʃə'nɛəʳ] *n* questionnaire *m*.
queue [kju:] 1 *n* **(a)** (*Brit*) *[people]* queue *f*, file *f* (d'attente); *[cars]* file. **to stand in a ~, to form a ~** faire la queue; **go to the end of the ~!** prenez la queue!; **he joined the theatre ~** il s'est joint aux personnes qui faisaient la queue au théâtre; **ticket ~** queue devant les guichets; *V* **jump** *etc*.
(b) (*pigtail*) natte *f* (*d'homme*).
2 *cpd*: (*Brit*) **queue-jumper** resquilleur *m*, -euse *f* (*qui passe avant son tour*).
3 *vi* (*Brit: also* **~ up**) *[people, cars]* faire la queue (*for* pour). **we ~d (up) for an hour** nous avons fait une heure de queue.
quibble ['kwɪbl] 1 *n* chicane *f*, argutie *f*. **that's just a ~** c'est couper les cheveux en quatre*. 2 *vi* chicaner, ergoter (*over* sur).
quibbler ['kwɪbləʳ] *n* chicaneur *m*, -euse *f*, chicanier *m*, -ière *f*, ergoteur *m*, -euse *f*.
quibbling ['kwɪblɪŋ] 1 *adj person* ergoteur, chicaneur, chicanier; *argument* captieux, spécieux; *objection* spécieux. 2 *n* (*U*) chicanerie *f*.
quick [kwɪk] 1 *adj* **(a)** (*rapid*) *pulse, train, movement, route, decision, method* rapide; *recovery, answer* prompt. **be ~!** dépêche-toi!, fais vite!; **try to be ~er next time** essaie de faire plus vite la prochaine fois; **at a ~ pace** d'un pas vif *or* rapide, d'un bon pas; (*Mil*) **~ march!** en avant, marche!; **I had a ~ chat with her** *or* **a few ~ words with her** j'ai échangé quelques mots (rapides) avec elle; **going cheap for a ~ sale** bradé *or* sacrifié pour vente rapide; **we had a ~ meal** nous avons mangé en vitesse *or* sur le pouce*; **to have a ~ one*** prendre un pot* en vitesse; **it's ~er by train** c'est plus rapide *or* ça va plus vite par le train; **he's a ~ worker** il travaille vite; (* *iro*) il ne perd pas de temps (*iro*); *V* **double, draw** *etc*.
(b) (*lively*) *mind* vif (*f* vive), rapide, éveillé, agile; *child* vif, éveillé. **he's too ~ for me** il est trop rapide pour moi, il va trop vite pour moi; **he has a ~ eye for mistakes** il repère vite les fautes; **to have a ~ ear** avoir l'oreille fine; **to have a ~ wit** avoir la repartie facile *or* de la repartie (*V also* **4**); **he was ~ to see that ...** il fut prompt à voir que ...; **to be ~ to take offence** être prompt à s'offenser, s'offenser pour un rien; **to have a ~ temper** s'emporter facilement, être soupe au lait* (*V also* **4**); (*liter*) **to be ~ to anger** avoir la tête chaude, être prompt à s'emporter; **he is ~ at figures** il calcule vite.
2 *n* **(a)** (*Anat*) vif *m*. **to bite one's nails to the ~** se ronger les ongles jusqu'au sang; (*fig*) **to cut** *or* **sting sb to the ~** piquer *or* blesser qn au vif.
(b) (††, *liter*) **the ~ and the dead** les vivants *mpl* et les morts *mpl*.
3 *adv* = **quickly. ~, over here!** vite, par ici!; **as ~ as lightning** *or* **as a flash** avec la rapidité de l'éclair.
4 *cpd*: (*Theat*) **quick-change artist** spécialiste *mf* des transformations rapides; **a series of quick-fire questions** un feu roulant de questions; **to shoot quick-fire questions at sb** mitrailler qn de questions; (*Mil*) **quick-firing** à tir rapide; **quick-freeze** surgeler; **quicklime** chaux vive; **quicksand** sable mouvant; **quicksands** sables mouvants; **to get stuck in quicksands** s'enliser; **quickset hedge** haie vive; (*hawthorn*) haie d'aubépine; **quick-setting** *cement, jelly* qui prend facilement; **quicksilver** vif-argent *m*, mercure *m*; (*Dancing*) **quickstep** fox(-trot) *m*; **to be quick-tempered** avoir la tête chaude, être prompt à s'emporter, être soupe au lait*; **quick-witted** à l'esprit vif *or* délié; (*in answering*) qui a la repartie facile *or* de la repartie.
quicken ['kwɪkən] 1 *vt* (*lit*) accélérer, presser, hâter; (*fig*) *feelings, imagination* exciter, stimuler; *appetite* stimuler, aiguiser. **to ~ one's pace** accélérer son allure, presser le pas; (*Mus*) **to ~ the tempo** presser l'allure *or* la cadence.

2 *vi [pace, movement]* s'accélérer, devenir *or* se faire plus rapide; *[hope]* se ranimer; *[foetus]* remuer.

quickie* ['kwɪkɪ] *n* chose faite en vitesse *or* à la hâte; (*drink*) pot* pris en vitesse; (*question*) question *f* éclair *inv*; (*Cine*) court métrage vite fait.

quickly ['kwɪklɪ] *adv* (*fast*) vite, rapidement; (*without delay*) promptement, sans tarder. **~!** vite!, dépêchez-vous!; **as ~ as possible** aussi vite que possible, au plus vite; **as ~ as I can** aussi vite que je peux; **the police were ~ on the spot** la police arriva sans tarder *or* promptement sur les lieux.

quickness ['kwɪknɪs] *n* vitesse *f*, rapidité *f*; *[intelligence, sight, gesture]* vivacité *f*; *[mind]* promptitude *f*, vivacité; *[pulse]* rapidité; *[hearing]* finesse *f*. **~ of temper** promptitude à s'emporter; **~ of wit** vivacité d'esprit.

quid[1]‡ [kwɪd] *n* (*pl inv: Brit: pound*) livre *f* (*sterling*).

quid[2] [kwɪd] *n [tobacco]* chique *f*.

quiddity ['kwɪdɪtɪ] *n* (*Philos*) quiddité *f*.

quid pro quo ['kwɪdprəʊ'kwəʊ] *n* (*sth in return*) compensation *f*; (*equivalent*) équivalent *m*.

quiescence [kwaɪ'esns] *n* quiétude *f*, calme *m*, tranquillité *f*.

quiescent [kwaɪ'esnt] *adj* passif, immobile, tranquille.

quiet ['kwaɪət] **1** *adj* **(a)** (*silent, not noisy, still*) *sea, street, evening, neighbour* tranquille; *person* silencieux, tranquille. **he was ~ for a long time** (*silent*) il est resté longtemps sans rien dire; (*still*) il est resté longtemps sans bouger; **you're very ~ today** tu ne dis rien *or* pas grand-chose aujourd'hui; **be ~!, keep ~!** taisez-vous!; **isn't it ~!** que c'est calme! *or* tranquille!; **it was ~ as the grave** il y avait un silence de mort; **try to be a little ~er** essayez de ne pas faire autant de bruit; **to keep** *or* **stay ~** (*still*) se tenir *or* rester tranquille; (*silent*) garder le silence; **to keep sb ~** (*still*) faire tenir qn tranquille, forcer qn à se tenir tranquille; (*silent*) faire taire qn, imposer silence à qn; **that book should keep him ~ for a while** ce livre devrait le faire se tenir tranquille un moment; **keep those bottles ~** empêchez ces bouteilles de tinter, ne faites pas de bruit avec ces bouteilles.

(b) (*not loud*) *music* doux (*f* douce); *voice, tone* bas (*f* basse); *footstep, sound* léger; *cough, laugh* petit (*V also* **1e**). **keep the radio ~** baisse le volume (de la radio).

(c) (*subdued*) *person, face, temperament* doux (*f* douce); *dog, horse* docile; *child* calme, facile, doux; *dress, colour* sobre, discret (*f* -ète); *style* simple. **a ~ old lady** une vieille dame tranquille; **my daughter is a very ~ girl** ma fille n'est pas expansive, ma fille est une silencieuse.

(d) (*peaceful, calm*) calme, paisible, tranquille. **the patient had a ~ night** le malade a passé une nuit tranquille *or* paisible; **he had a ~ sleep** il a dormi tranquillement *or* paisiblement; **those were ~ times** la vie était calme en ce temps-là; (*Mil etc*) **all ~** rien de nouveau; **all ~ on the western front** à l'ouest rien de nouveau; **they lead a ~ life** ils mènent une vie tranquille; **this town is too ~ for me** cette ville est trop endormie pour moi, pour moi cette ville manque d'animation; **they had a ~ wedding** ils se sont mariés dans l'intimité; **the wedding was very ~** le mariage a eu lieu dans la plus stricte intimité; **business is ~** les affaires sont calmes; (*St Ex*) **the market was ~** la Bourse était calme; **he went to sleep with a ~ mind** il s'endormit l'esprit tranquille.

(e) (*secret*) caché, dissimulé; (*private*) intime; *evening, dinner, discussion* intime; *irony* voilé, discret (*f* -ète); *resentment* sourd. **they had a ~ wedding** ils se sont mariés dans l'intimité; **I'll have a ~ word with her** je vais lui glisser discrètement un mot à l'oreille, je vais lui dire deux mots en particulier; **they had a ~ laugh over it** ils en ont ri doucement; **he said with a ~ smile** dit-il avec un petit sourire; **with ~ humour** avec une pointe d'humour; **he had a ~ dig* at his brother** il lança une pointe discrète à son frère; **he kept the whole thing ~** il n'a pas ébruité l'affaire; **keep it ~** gardez cela pour vous.

2 *n* (*U*) **(a)** (*silence*) silence *m*, tranquillité *f*. **in the ~ of the night** dans le silence de la nuit; **let's have complete ~ for a few minutes** faisons silence complet pendant quelques minutes.

(b) (*peace*) calme *m*, paix *f*, tranquillité *f*. **an hour of blessed ~** une heure de répit fort appréciée; **there was a period of ~ after the fighting** il y a eu une accalmie après les combats; *V* **peace**.

(c) (*) **on the ~** en cachette, en douce*; **to do sth on the ~** faire qch en cachette *or* en dessous; **she had a drink on the ~** elle a pris un verre en douce* *or* en suisse; **he told me on the ~** il me l'a dit en confidence.

3 *vt* = **quieten**.

quieten ['kwaɪətn] *vt* (*esp Brit*) *person, crowd, horse, suspicion* calmer, apaiser; *fear* calmer, dissiper; *pain* calmer; *conscience* tranquilliser, apaiser.

quiet(en) down **1** *vi* s'apaiser, se calmer, s'assagir; (*after unruly youth*) se ranger. **their children have quietened down a lot** leurs enfants se sont beaucoup assagis.

2 *vt sep person, dog, horse* calmer, apaiser.

quietism ['kwaɪɪtɪzəm] *n* quiétisme *m*.

quietist ['kwaɪɪtɪst] *adj, n* quiétiste (*mf*).

quietly ['kwaɪətlɪ] *adv* (*silently*) silencieusement, sans (faire de) bruit, en sourdine; (*not loudly*) *speak, sing* doucement; (*gently*) doucement, calmement; (*without fuss*) paisiblement, sobrement, discrètement, simplement; (*secretly*) en cachette, en douce*, secrètement. **they got married very ~** ils se sont mariés dans la plus stricte intimité.

quietness ['kwaɪətnɪs] *n* (*silence*) silence *m*; (*stillness*) calme *m*, tranquillité *f*, quiétude *f*; (*gentleness*) douceur *f*; (*peacefulness*) repos *m*, tranquillité, calme.

quietude ['kwaɪətju:d] *n* quiétude *f*.

quietus [kwaɪ'i:təs] *n* (*Jur*) quittance *f*; (*fig*) (*release*) coup *m* de grâce (*lit, fig*); (*death*) mort *f*.

quiff [kwɪf] *n* (*Brit: also* **~ of hair**) (*on forehead*) mèche *f*; (*kiss curl*) accroche-cœur *m*; (*at back of head*) épi *m*; (*on top of baby's head*) coque *f*.

quill [kwɪl] *n* (*feather*) penne *f*; (*part of feather*) tuyau *m* de plume; (*also* **~-pen**) plume *f* d'oie; *[porcupine etc]* piquant *m*.

quilt [kwɪlt] **1** *n* édredon *m* (piqué), courtepointe *f*. **continental ~** édredon *m*, couverture-édredon *f*. **2** *vt eiderdown, cover* ouater et piquer; *dressing gown* molletonner, ouatiner; *furniture, bedhead etc* capitonner.

quilting ['kwɪltɪŋ] *n* (*U*) (*process*) ouatage *m*, capitonnage *m*; (*material*) ouate *f*, molleton *m*, ouatine *f*, capitonnage.

quin [kwɪn] *n* (*Brit*) *abbr of* **quintuplet**.

quince [kwɪns] **1** *n* (*fruit*) coing *m*; (*tree*) cognassier *m*. **2** *cpd jam* de coings.

quincentenary [,kwɪnsen'ti:nərɪ] *n* cinquième centenaire *m*.

quinine [kwɪ'ni:n] *n* quinine *f*.

Quinquagesima [,kwɪŋkwə'dʒesɪmə] *n* Quinquagésime *f*.

quinquennial [kwɪŋ'kwenɪəl] *adj* quinquennal.

quinquennium [kwɪŋ'kwenɪəm] *n* quinquennat *m*.

quinsy ['kwɪnzɪ] *n* (*Med*††) amygdalite purulente.

quint [kwɪnt] *n* (*US*) *abbr of* **quintuplet**.

quintessence [kwɪn'tesns] *n* quintessence *f*.

quintessential [,kwɪntɪ'senʃəl] *adj* quintessenciel.

quintet(te) [kwɪn'tet] *n* quintette *m*.

quintuple ['kwɪntjʊpl] **1** *adj, n* quintuple (*m*). **2** ['kwɪn'tju:pl] *vti* quintupler.

quintuplet [kwɪn'tju:plɪt] *n* quintuplé(e) *m(f)*.

quip [kwɪp] **1** *n* raillerie *f*, quolibet *m*, otpiquant. **2** *vi* railler, lancer des pointes. **3** *vt*: **'never on a Sunday' she ~ped** 'jamais le dimanche' dit-elle avec piquant *or* avec esprit.

quire ['kwaɪə^r] *n* **(a)** (*Bookbinding*) (*part of book*) cahier *m* (d'un livre) (*4 feuilles*). **book in ~s** livre en feuilles (détachées) *or* en cahiers. **(b) ~ of paper** main *f*.

quirk [kwɜ:k] *n* **(a)** bizarrerie *f*, excentricité *f*. **it's just one of his ~s** (c'est) encore une de ses excentricités; **by a ~ of fate** par un caprice du destin; **by some ~ of nature/of circumstance** par une bizarrerie de la nature/de(s) circonstance(s).

(b) (*flourish*) (*Art, Mus*) arabesque *f*; (*in signature*) parafe *m* *or* paraphe *m*; (*in handwriting*) fioriture *f*.

quirky ['kwɜ:kɪ] *adj* capricieux, primesautier.

quisling ['kwɪzlɪŋ] *n* collaborateur *m*, -trice *f* (*pej*), collabo* *mf*.

quit [kwɪt] *pret, ptp* **quit** *or* **quitted** **1** *vt* **(a)** (*leave*) *place, premises* quitter, laisser, s'en aller de. **notice to ~** avis *m* de vider les lieux.

(b) (*give up*) lâcher, quitter, abandonner; (*esp US: stop*) cesser, arrêter (*doing* de faire). **to ~ school** quitter l'école *or* le collège *etc*; **to ~ one's job** quitter sa place; **to ~ hold** lâcher prise; **to ~ hold of sth** lâcher qch; **to ~ work** cesser le travail; **~ fooling!** arrête de faire l'idiot!

2 *vi* (*esp US*) (*give up: in game etc*) se rendre; (*accept defeat*) abandonner la partie, renoncer; (*resign*) démissionner. **I ~!** j'arrête!, j'abandonne!; **he ~s too easily** il se laisse décourager *or* il abandonne la partie trop facilement.

3 *adj*: **~ of** débarrassé de.

quite [kwaɪt] *adv* **(a)** (*entirely*) complètement, entièrement, tout à fait, tout. (*also iro*) **~ (so)!** exactement!; **I ~ agree with you** je suis entièrement *or* tout à fait de votre avis; **he ~ realizes that he must go** il se rend parfaitement compte qu'il doit partir; **I ~ understand** je comprends très bien; **I ~ believe it** je le crois volontiers *or* sans difficulté, je n'ai aucun mal à le croire; **I don't ~ know** je ne sais pas bien *or* trop; **I don't ~ see what he means** je ne vois pas tout à fait *or* pas trop ce qu'il veut dire; **that's ~ enough!** ça suffit comme ça!; **that's ~ enough for me** j'en ai vraiment assez; **it wasn't ~ what I wanted** ce n'était pas exactement ce que je voulais; **not ~ as many as last week** pas tout à fait autant que la semaine dernière; **that's ~ another matter** c'est une tout autre affaire; **~ 4 days ago** il y a bien 4 jours; **he was ~ right** il avait bien raison *or* tout à fait raison; **my watch is ~ right** ma montre a l'heure exacte; **~ new** tout (à fait) neuf (*f* neuve); **he was ~ alone** il était tout seul; **she was ~ a beauty** c'était une véritable beauté; **it is ~ splendid** c'est vraiment splendide!; *V* **thing**.

(b) (*to some degree, moderately*) plutôt, assez. **it was ~ dark for 6 o'clock** il faisait plutôt sombre pour 6 heures; **~ a long time** assez longtemps; **~ a few people** un bon *or* assez grand nombre de gens; **your essay was ~ good** votre dissertation n'était pas mal *inv* *or* mauvaise du tout; **he is ~ a good singer** c'est un assez bon chanteur; **I ~ like this painting** j'aime assez ce tableau.

quits [kwɪts] *adj* quitte. **to be ~ with sb** être quitte envers qn; **now they are ~** maintenant ils sont quittes; **let's call it ~** restons-en là; **to cry ~** se déclarer quittes, déclarer match nul (*fig*).

quittance ['kwɪtəns] *n* (*Fin etc*) quittance *f*.

quitter ['kwɪtə^r] *n* (*pej*) personne *f* qui abandonne facilement la partie *or* qui se laisse rebuter par les difficultés.

quiver[1] ['kwɪvə^r] **1** *vi [person]* frémir, frissonner, trembler (*with* de); *[voice]* trembler, trembloter, chevroter; *[leaves]* frémir, frissonner; *[flame]* vaciller; *[wings]* battre, palpiter; *[lips]* trembler, frémir; *[eyelids]* battre; *[flesh, heart]* frémir, palpiter; *[violin]* frémir.

2 *n* (*V* **1**) frémissement *m*; tremblement *m*; frisson *m*, frissonnement *m* (*liter*); vacillement *m*; battement *m*; palpitation *f*.

quiver[2] ['kwɪvə^r] *n* (*for arrows*) carquois *m*.

qui vive [ki:'vi:v] *n*: **on the ~** sur le qui-vive.

Quixote ['kwɪksət] *n*: **Don ~** don Quichotte *m*.

quixotic [kwɪk'sɒtɪk] *adj person* (*unselfish*) chevaleresque, généreux; (*visionary*) chimérique; *plan, idea* donquichottesque. **with a ~ disregard for his own safety** avec un mépris donquichottesque pour sa propre sécurité.

quixotically [kwɪkˈsɒtɪkəlɪ] *adv* à la (manière de) don Quichotte. **to behave ~** jouer les don Quichottes; **he volunteered ~ to go himself** en don Quichotte, il offrit d'y aller lui-même.
quixotism [ˈkwɪksətɪzəm] *n*, **quixotry** [ˈkwɪksətrɪ] *n* donquichottisme *m*.
quiz [kwɪz] **1** *n* (*Rad, TV*) quiz *m*, jeu-concours *m* (radiophonique *or* télévisé); (*in magazine etc*) série *f* de questions; (*puzzle*) devinette *f*.
2 *vt* interroger, questionner, presser de questions (*about* au sujet de).
3 *cpd*: (*US*) **quiz kid*** enfant *mf* prodige; **quizmaster** meneur *m* de jeu; (*Rad, TV*) animateur *m*; (*Rad, TV*) **quiz programme** quiz *m*.
quizzical [ˈkwɪzɪkəl] *adj* (*mocking, questioning*) moqueur, narquois, ironique; (*puzzled*) perplexe; (*amusing*) amusant; (*odd*) bizarre, étrange.
quizzically [ˈkwɪzɪkəlɪ] *adv* (*V* **quizzical**) d'un air narquois *or* ironique; d'un air perplexe; d'une manière amusante; bizarrement.
quod‡ [kwɒd] *n* (*Brit*) taule‡ *f or* tôle‡ *f*, bloc* *m*. **to be in ~** être au bloc* *or* à l'ombre*, faire de la taule‡.
quoin [kwɔɪn] *n* (*angle*) coin *m or* angle *m* d'un mur; (*stone*) pierre *f* d'angle.
quoit [kwɔɪt] *n* palet *m*. **~s** jeu *m* du palet; **to play ~s** jouer au palet.
quondam [ˈkwɒndæm] *adj* (*liter*) ancien (*before n*), d'autrefois.
Quonset hut [ˈkwɒnsɪtˈhʌt] *n* ® (*US*) baraque *or* hutte préfabriquée (*en tôle, cylindrique*).
quorum [ˈkwɔːrəm] *n* quorum *m*. **we have not got a ~** nous n'avons pas de quorum, le quorum n'est pas atteint.
quota [ˈkwəʊtə] *n* **(a)** (*share*) quote-part *f*, part *f*.
(b) (*permitted amount*) *[imports, immigrants]* quota *m*, contingent *m*.
quotable [ˈkwəʊtəbl] *adj* digne d'être cité, bon à citer.
quotation [kwəʊˈteɪʃən] **1** *n* **(a)** (*passage cited*) citation *f* (*from* de).
(b) (*St Ex*) cours *m*, cote *f*; (*Comm: estimate*) devis *m* (estimatif).
2 *cpd*: **quotation marks** guillemets *mpl*; **in quotation marks** entre guillemets; **to open/close the quotation marks** ouvrir/fermer les guillemets.
quote [kwəʊt] **1** *vt* **(a)** *author, poem, fact, text* citer; *words* rapporter, citer; *reference number etc* rappeler. **to ~ Shelley** citer Shelley; **to ~ sb as an example** citer *or* donner qn en exemple; **you can ~ me** vous pouvez me citer *or* citer ce que j'ai dit; **don't ~ me** ne dites pas que c'est moi qui vous l'ai dit; **he was ~d as saying that ...** il aurait dit que ...; **can you ~ (me) a recent instance of this?** pouvez-vous (me) citer un exemple récent de ceci?; (*Comm*) **when ordering please ~ this number** pour toute commande prière de rappeler ce numéro.
(b) (*Comm*) *price* indiquer, établir, spécifier; (*St Ex*) *price* coter (*at* à). **this was the best price he could ~ us** c'est le meilleur prix qu'il a pu nous faire *or* proposer.
2 *vi* **(a)** (*Literat etc*) faire des citations. **to ~ from the Bible** citer la Bible.
(b) (*Comm*) **to ~ for a job** établir *or* faire un devis pour un travail.
3 *n* **(a)** = **quotation 1a.**
(b) he said, ~ 'I will never do it' il a dit, (*in dictation*) ouvrez les guillemets *or* (*in lecture, report etc*) je cite 'je ne le ferai jamais'; **~s** = **quotation marks** (*V* **quotation 2**).
quoth [kwəʊθ] *defective vb* (†† *or hum*) **~ he** fit-il, dit-il.
quotient [ˈkwəʊʃənt] *n* (*esp Math*) quotient *m*; *V* **intelligence.**

R

R, r [ɑːʳ] *n* (*letter*) R, r *m*. **the three R's** *la lecture, l'écriture et l'arithmétique (les trois bases de l'enseignement).*
rabbet [ˈræbɪt] *n* feuillure *f*, rainure *f*.
rabbi [ˈræbaɪ] *n* rabbin *m*; *V* **chief.**
rabbinical [rəˈbɪnɪkəl] *adj* rabbinique.
rabbit [ˈræbɪt] **1** *n* lapin *m*; (* *fig: Sport etc*) nullard(e)* *m(f)*. **doe ~** lapine *f*; *V* **Welsh** *etc.*
2 *vi*: **to go ~ing** chasser le lapin.
3 *cpd*: **rabbit burrow, rabbit hole** terrier *m* (de lapin); **rabbit hutch** clapier *m*, cabane *f or* cage *f* à lapins; (*Boxing etc*) **rabbit punch** coup *m* du lapin *or* sur la nuque; **rabbit warren** garenne *f*.
rabble [ˈræbl] **1** *n* (*disorderly crowd*) cohue *f*, foule *f* (confuse); (*pej: lower classes*) populace *f* (*pej*).
2 *cpd*: (*pej*) **rabble-rouser** fomentateur *m*, -trice *f* de troubles, agitateur *m*, -trice *f*; (*pej*) **rabble-rousing** (*n*) incitation *f* à la révolte *or* à la violence; (*adj*) qui incite à la révolte *or* à la violence.
Rabelaisian [ˌræbəˈleɪzɪən] *adj* rabelaisien.
rabid [ˈræbɪd] *adj* (*animal*) enragé; (*person*) atteint de la rage; (*fig*) furieux, violent, forcené; *hate* féroce, farouche; *politician* enragé, fanatique.
rabies [ˈreɪbiːz] **1** *n* rage *f* (*Med*). **2** *cpd virus* rabiaque, de la rage; *injection* contre la rage.
raccoon [rəˈkuːn] *n* = **racoon.**
race¹ [reɪs] **1** *n* **(a)** (*Sport etc*) course *f*. **the 100 metres ~** la course sur *or* de 100 mètres, le 100 mètres; **horse ~** course de chevaux; **cycle ~** course cycliste; (*Horse-racing*) **the ~s** les courses (de chevaux); (*lit, fig*) **~ against time** course contre la montre; *V* **arm², long¹, relay.**
(b) (*swift current*) (*in sea*) raz *m*; (*in stream*) courant fort; *V* **mill.**
(c) (*fig, liter*) *[sun, moon]* cours *m*.
2 *vt* **(a)** *person* faire une course avec, s'efforcer de dépasser. **I'll ~ you to school!** à qui arrivera le premier à l'école!; **the car was racing the train** la voiture faisait la course avec le train *or* luttait de vitesse avec le train.
(b) (*cause to speed*) *car* lancer (à fond). (*Aut*) **to ~ the engine** emballer le moteur.
(c) (*Sport*) *horse* faire courir. **the champion ~s Ferraris** le champion court sur Ferrari.
3 *vi* **(a)** (*compete*) **to ~ against sb** faire la course avec qn; (*fig*) **to ~ against time** *or* **the clock** courir contre la montre.
(b) (*rush*) *[person]* aller *or* courir à toute allure *or* à toute vitesse. **to ~ in/out/across** *etc* entrer/sortir/traverser *etc* à toute allure; **to ~ for a taxi** courir pour avoir un taxi; **to ~ to the station** courir à la gare, foncer jusqu'à la gare; **to ~ along** filer (à toute allure); **he ~d down the street** il a descendu la rue à toute vitesse.
(c) *[engine]* s'emballer; *[propeller]* s'affoler; *[pulse]* être très rapide.
(d) *[horse owners]* **he ~s at Longchamp every week** il fait courir à Longchamp toutes les semaines.
4 *cpd*: **race card** programme *m* (des courses); (*esp Brit*) **racecourse** champ *m* de courses, hippodrome *m*; **racegoer** turfiste *mf*; **racehorse** cheval *m* de course; **race meeting** (réunion *f* de) courses *fpl*; **racetrack** (*for horses*) champ *m* de courses, piste *f*; (*for athletes*) piste.
race² [reɪs] **1** *n* (*lit, fig*) race *f*. **the human ~** la race *or* l'espèce humaine.
2 *cpd hatred, prejudice* racial. **race consciousness** racisme *m*; **race relations** rapports *mpl* entre (les) races; (*Brit*) **the Race Relations Board** *commission chargée de supprimer la discrimination raciale;* **race riot** bagarre(s) raciale(s).
raceme [ˈræsiːm] *n* racème *m* (*rare*), grappe *f*.
racer [ˈreɪsəʳ] *n* (*person*) coureur *m*, -euse *f*; (*car, yacht*) racer *m*; (*horse*) cheval *m* de course; (*cycle*) vélo *m or* bicyclette *f* de course.
rachitic [ræˈkɪtɪk] *adj* rachitique.
racial [ˈreɪʃəl] *adj discrimination etc* racial. **~ minorities** races *fpl* minoritaires; *V* **violence.**
racialism [ˈreɪʃəlɪzəm] *n* racisme *m*.
racialist [ˈreɪʃəlɪst] *adj, n* raciste (*mf*).
raciness [ˈreɪsɪnɪs] *n* (*V* **racy**) verve *f*, piquant *m*.
racing [ˈreɪsɪŋ] **1** *n*: **horse-~** courses *fpl* de chevaux, hippisme *m*; **motor ~** courses d'automobiles.
2 *cpd calendar, stable* de(s) courses. **racing bicycle** vélo *m or* bicyclette *f* de course; **racing car** voiture *f* de course; **racing colours** couleurs *fpl* d'une écurie (*portées par le jockey*); **racing cyclist** coureur *m* cycliste; **racing driver** coureur *m* automobile, pilote *m* de courses; **racing man** turfiste *m*, amateur *m* de courses; **the racing world** *[horses]* le monde hippique *or* du turf; *[cars]* le monde des courses (automobiles); **racing yacht** racer *m*, yacht *m* de course.
racism [ˈreɪsɪzəm] *n* racisme *m*.
racist [ˈreɪsɪst] *adj, n* raciste (*mf*).
rack¹ [ræk] *n* (*for fodder*) râtelier *m*; (*for bottles*) casier *m*; (*for documents, files*) classeur *m*; (*in shops*) étagère *f*, rayon *m*. (*Tech*) **~ and pinion** crémaillère *f*; *V* **bicycle, hat, luggage, roof, toast.**
rack² [ræk] **1** *n* (*Hist*) chevalet *m*. **to put sb on the ~** infliger *or* faire subir à qn le supplice du chevalet; (*fig*) mettre qn au supplice.
2 *cpd*: **rack rent** loyer exorbitant.
3 *vt* (*Hist*) faire subir le supplice du chevalet à; (*fig*) *[pain]* torturer, tourmenter. (*fig*) **~ed by remorse** tenaillé par le remords; **to ~ one's brains** se creuser la tête *or* la cervelle*.

rack[3] [ræk] *n*: **to go to ~ and ruin** *[building]* tomber en ruine; *[business, economy]* aller à vau-l'eau; *[person, country]* aller à la ruine.

racket[1] ['rækɪt] *n* (*Sport*) raquette *f.* (*game*) **~s** (jeu *m* de) paume *f*; **~ press** presse-raquette *m inv*, presse *f.*

racket[2] ['rækɪt] **1** *n* **(a)** (*noise*) *[people]* tapage *m*, raffut* *m*, boucan: *m*; *[machine]* vacarme *m*. **to make a ~** faire du raffut* *or* du boucan: *or* du vacarme.

(b) (*) (*organized crime*) racket *m*; (*dishonest scheme*) escroquerie *f.* **the drug ~** le trafic de la drogue; **that firm is on to quite a ~** cette firme a trouvé une jolie combine*; **that package tour was a dreadful ~** ce voyage organisé était du vol manifeste!; **he's in on the ~** il est dans le coup*.

(c) to stand the ~: (*take responsibility*) payer les pots cassés*; (*pay up*) payer, casquer:.

2 *vi* (*make a noise*) faire du raffut* *or* du boucan:; (*also* **~ about, ~ around**: *lead a gay life*) faire la bombe* *or* la bringue:.

racketeer [ˌrækɪ'tɪəʳ] *n* racketter *m*, racketteur *m*.

racketeering [ˌrækɪ'tɪərɪŋ] *n* racket *m*.

racking ['rækɪŋ] *adj pain* atroce, épouvantable.

raconteur [ˌrækɒn'tɜːʳ] *n* conteur *m*, -euse *f*.

racoon [rə'kuːn] **1** *n* raton *m* laveur. **2** *cpd* en fourrure de raton (laveur).

racquet ['rækɪt] *n* = **racket**[1].

racy ['reɪsɪ] *adj speech* plein de verve; *style* plein de verve, piquant; *story* savoureux, piquant; *wine* qui a un goût de terroir.

radar ['reɪdɑːʳ] **1** *n* radar *m*.

2 *cpd echo, screen, station* radar *inv*. **radar beacon** balise *f* radar; **radar operator** radariste *mf*; **radar scanner** déchiffreur *m* de radar; **radar sensor** détecteur *m* (radar); (*Aut Police*) **radar trap** piège *m* radar.

raddle ['rædl] **1** *n* ocre *f* rouge.

2 *vt* passer à l'ocre; *sheep* marquer à l'ocre. **~d face** visage peinturluré*.

radial ['reɪdɪəl] *adj* (*Med, Tech*) radial. **~ engine** moteur *m* en étoile; **~ tyre** pneu *m* à carcasse radiale.

radiance ['reɪdɪəns] *n*, **radiancy** ['reɪdɪənsɪ] *n [sun, lights etc]* éclat *m*, rayonnement *m*, splendeur *f* (*liter*); *[face, personality, beauty]* éclat, rayonnement.

radiant ['reɪdɪənt] **1** *adj sun* radieux, rayonnant; *colour* éclatant; *person, beauty, smile* radieux. **to be ~ with joy/health** rayonner de joie/de santé; (*Phys*) **~ heat** chaleur radiante; **~ heater** radiateur *m* à foyer rayonnant; **~ heating** chauffage direct *or* par rayonnement.

2 *n* (*Phys*) point radiant; (*Math*) radian *m*; (*Astron*) (point *m*) radiant *m*.

radiantly ['reɪdɪəntlɪ] *adv shine* d'un vif éclat; *smile* d'un air radieux. **to be ~ happy** rayonner de joie.

radiate ['reɪdɪeɪt] **1** *vi* (*emit rays*) irradier, rayonner (*liter*); (*emit heat*) rayonner; (*Phys*) irradier; (*fig*) *[lines, roads]* rayonner (*from* de), partir du même centre.

2 *vt heat* émettre, dégager, répandre. (*fig*) **to ~ happiness** être rayonnant *or* rayonner de bonheur; **he ~s enthusiasm** il respire l'enthousiasme.

radiation [ˌreɪdɪ'eɪʃən] **1** *n [light]* irradiation *f*; *[heat]* rayonnement *m*; (*radioactivity*) radiation *f*. **2** *cpd*: **radiation sickness** mal *m* des rayons; (*Med*) **radiation treatment*** radiothérapie *f*.

radiator ['reɪdɪeɪtəʳ] **1** *n* (*also Aut*) radiateur *m*. **2** *cpd*: (*Aut*) **radiator cap** bouchon *m* de radiateur; (*Aut*) **radiator grill** calandre *f*.

radical ['rædɪkəl] *adj, n* (*all senses*) radical (*m*).

radicalism ['rædɪkəlɪzəm] *n* radicalisme *m*.

radically ['rædɪkəlɪ] *adv* radicalement.

radices ['reɪdɪsiːz] *npl of* **radix**.

radicle ['rædɪkl] *n* (*Bot*) radicule *f*, radicelle *f*; (*Chem*) radical *m*.

radii ['reɪdɪaɪ] *npl of* **radius**.

radio ['reɪdɪəʊ] **1** *n* **(a)** (*also* **~ set**) poste *m* (de radio), radio *f*. **on the ~** à la radio; **he has got a ~** il a un poste de radio, il a la radio; **to put the ~ on/off** allumer/éteindre la radio *or* le poste; *V* **transistor**.

(b) (*U: Telec*) radio *f*, radiotélégraphie *f*. **to send a message by ~** envoyer un (message) radio; **they were communicating by ~** ils communiquaient par radio.

2 *vt person* appeler *or* joindre par radio; *one's position* signaler par radio. **to ~ a message** envoyer un (message) radio.

3 *vi*: **to ~ for help** appeler au secours par radio.

4 *cpd*: **radioactive** radioactif; **radioactive waste** déchets radioactifs; **radioactivity** radioactivité *f*; **radio announcer** speaker(ine) *m(f)*, annonceur *m*; **radio astronomy** radioastronomie *f*; (*Aviat, Naut*) **radio beacon** radiophare *m*, radiobalise *f*; **radio beam** faisceau *m* radio *inv*; **radio broadcast** émission *f* radiophonique; **radio communication** contact *m* radio *inv*; **radio compass** radiocompas *m*; **radio contact = radio communication**; **radio control** téléguidage *m*; **radio-controlled** téléguidé; **radio direction finding** radiogoniométrie *f*; **radio engineer** ingénieur *m* radio *inv*; **radioisotope** radio-isotope *m*; **radio link** liaison *f* radio *inv*; **radio mast** antenne *f* (radio); **radio operator** opérateur *m* (radio), radio *m*; **radio programme** émission *f* (de radio), programme *m* radiophonique; **radio set** poste *m* (de radio), radio *f*; **radio silence** silence *m* radio *inv*; **radio (sono-)buoy** bouée *f* sonore; **radio station** station *f* de radio, poste émetteur; **radio taxi** radio-taxi *m*; **radiotelephone** radiotéléphone *m*; **radiotelephony** radiotéléphonie *f*; **radio telescope** radiotélescope *m*; **radiotherapy** radiothérapie *f*; (*Rad, TV*) **radio van** studio *m* mobile (de radiodiffusion *or* d'enregistrement); **radio wave** onde hertzienne.

radiogram ['reɪdɪəʊgræm] *n* (*message*) radiogramme *m*, radio *m*; (*Brit: apparatus*) combiné *m* (*avec radio et pickup*).

radiograph ['reɪdɪəʊgrɑːf] *n* radio *f*, radiographie *f*.

radiographer [ˌreɪdɪ'ɒgrəfəʳ] *n* radiologue *mf* (*technicien*).

radiography [ˌreɪdɪ'ɒgrəfɪ] *n* radiographie *f*, radio *f*.

radiologist [ˌreɪdɪ'ɒlədʒɪst] *n* radiologue *mf* (*médecin*).

radiology [ˌreɪdɪ'ɒlədʒɪ] *n* radiologie *f*.

radioscopy [ˌreɪdɪ'ɒskəpɪ] *n* radioscopie *f*.

radish ['rædɪʃ] *n* radis *m*.

radium ['reɪdɪəm] *n* radium *m*. (*Med*) **~ treatment** radiumthérapie *f*, curiethérapie *f*.

radius ['reɪdɪəs] *n, pl* **radii** (*Math, fig*) rayon *m*; (*Anat*) radius *m*. **within a 6 km ~ of Paris** dans un rayon de 6 km autour de Paris.

radix ['reɪdɪks] *n, pl* **radices** (*Math*) base *f*; (*Ling*) radical *m*.

raffia ['ræfɪə] **1** *n* raphia *m*. **2** *cpd* en raphia.

raffish ['ræfɪʃ] *adj person* qui mène une vie dissolue *or* déréglée, libertin; *look* canaille.

raffle ['ræfl] **1** *n* tombola *f*, loterie *f*. **~ ticket** billet *m* de tombola *or* de loterie. **2** *vt* mettre en tombola *or* en loterie.

raft [rɑːft] *n* (*flat structure*) radeau *m*; (*logs*) train *m* de flottage; *V* **life**.

rafter ['rɑːftəʳ] *n* (*Archit*) chevron *m*.

rag[1] [ræg] **1** *n* **(a)** lambeau *m*, loque *f*; (*for wiping etc*) chiffon *m*. **a ~ to wipe the floor** un (bout de) chiffon pour essuyer le plancher; **I haven't a ~ to wear*** je n'ai rien à me mettre sur le dos*; **to feel like a wet ~*** (*emotionally*) se sentir mou (*f* molle) comme une chiffe; (*physically*) se sentir ramollo* *inv*; **~s** (*for paper-making*) chiffons, peilles *fpl*; (*old clothes*) guenilles *fpl*, haillons *mpl*; **his clothes were in ~s** ses vêtements étaient en lambeaux *or* tombaient en loques; **to be (dressed) in ~s** être vêtu de guenilles *or* de haillons, être déguenillé; **in ~s and tatters** tout en loques; **to go from ~s to riches** passer de la misère à la richesse; *V* **glad**.

(b) (*fig: of truth, self-respect*) brin *m*; (**pej: newspaper*) torchon* *m* (*pej*), feuille *f* de chou*.

2 *cpd*: **ragbag** (*lit*) sac *m* à chiffons; (*Brit fig*) ramassis *m*, pot-pourri *m*; **rag doll** poupée *f* de chiffon; (*Brit*) **rag(-and-bone) man, ragpicker** chiffonnier *m*; **rag, tag and bobtail** racaille *f*, populace *f*; **ragtime** rag-time *m*; **the rag trade:** la confection; (*Bot*) **ragwort** jacobée *f*.

rag[2]* [ræg] (*Brit*) **1** *n* (*joke*) farce *f*, blague* *f*. **for a ~** par plaisanterie, pour s'amuser, pour blaguer*; (*Univ*) **the ~, ~ week** *la semaine où les étudiants organisent des attractions au profit d'œuvres charitables.*

2 *vt* (*tease*) taquiner, mettre en boîte*; (*play trick on*) faire une blague* à.

ragamuffin ['rægəˌmʌfɪn] *n* (*urchin*) galopin* *m*; (*ragged fellow*) va-nu-pieds *m inv*.

rage [reɪdʒ] **1** *n* rage *f*, fureur *f*; *[sea]* furie *f*. **to be in a ~** être furieux *or* en fureur *or* en rage; **to put sb into a ~** mettre qn en rage *or* en fureur; **to fly into a ~** entrer en fureur, se mettre en rage, sortir de ses gonds; **fit of ~** accès *m or* crise *f* de fureur *or* rage; (*fig*) **to be (all) the ~** faire fureur.

2 *vi [person]* être furieux (*against* contre), rager*; *[battle]* faire rage; *[sea]* être démonté, être en furie; *[storm]* se déchaîner, faire rage; *[wind]* être déchaîné.

ragged ['rægɪd] *adj clothes* en lambeaux, en loques; *person* déguenillé, en haillons; *animal's coat* à poil long (et broussailleux); *edge of page, rock* déchiqueté; *cuff* usé, effiloché; (*fig*) *cloud* échevelé; *performance* inégal. (*Bot*) **~ robin** fleur *f* de coucou.

raging ['reɪdʒɪŋ] **1** *adj person* furieux; *thirst* ardent; *pain* atroce; *sea* démonté, en furie; *wind, storm* déchaîné. **to be in a ~ temper, to be ~ mad*** être dans une colère noire *or* une rage folle; **~ toothache** rage *f* de dents; **~ fever** fièvre violente *or* de cheval.

2 *n [person]* rage *f*, fureur *f*; *[elements]* déchaînement *m*. **the ~ of the sea** la mer en furie.

raglan ['ræglən] *adj, n* raglan (*m*) *inv*.

ragout ['rægu:] *n* ragoût *m*.

raid [reɪd] **1** *n* (*Mil*) raid *m*, incursion *f*; (*by police*) descente *f*, rafle *f*; (*by bandits*) razzia *f*; (*by thieves*) hold-up *m inv*. **air ~** raid (aérien), bombardement aérien.

2 *vt* (*Mil*) faire une incursion *or* un raid dans; (*Aviat*) bombarder, faire un raid sur; *[police]* faire une descente *or* une rafle dans; *[bandits]* razzier; *[thieves]* faire un hold-up à; (*fig*) *orchard* marauder dans; (*hum*) *cashbox, penny bank* puiser dans; *larder* dévaliser, faire une descente dans*.

raider ['reɪdəʳ] *n* (*bandit*) pillard *m*; (*criminal*) malfaiteur *m*, brigand *m*, pillard *m*; (*ship*) navire *m* qui accomplit un raid, raider *m*; (*plane*) bombardier *m*. (*Mil*) **~s** commando *m*.

rail[1] [reɪl] **1** *n* **(a)** (*bar*) *[bridge, quay]* garde-fou *m*; *[boat]* bastingage *m*, rambarde *f*; *[balcony, terrace]* balustrade *f*; (*handrail: on wall*) main courante; (*banister*) rampe *f*; (*for carpet, curtains, spotlights etc*) tringle *m*. (*Racing*) **the horse was close to the ~s** le cheval tenait la corde; (*fence*) **~s** grille *f*, barrière *f*; *V* **altar, towel** *etc*.

(b) (*for train, tram*) rail *m*. **to travel by ~** voyager en train; **to send by ~** envoyer par (le) train *or* par chemin de fer; **to go off the ~s** (*lit*) *[train etc]* dérailler; (*fig*) *[person]* (*err*) s'écarter du droit chemin; (*be confused*) être déboussolé*; *V* **live**[2].

2 *cpd*: **railhead** tête *f* de ligne; **rail strike** grève *f* des employés de chemin de fer; **rail traffic** trafic *m* ferroviaire.

rail in *vt sep* clôturer, entourer d'une clôture *or* d'une barrière.

rail off *vt sep* fermer au moyen d'une clôture *or* d'une barrière.

rail[2] [reɪl] *vi*: **to ~ at** *or* **against sb** se répandre en injures contre qn.

railing ['reɪlɪŋ] *n* **(a)** (*rail*) *[bridge, quay]* garde-fou *m*; *[balcony, terrace]* balustrade *f*; (*on stairs*) rampe *f*; (*on wall*) main

courante. **(b)** (*part of fence*) barreau *m*; (*fence: also* ~s) grille *f*.
raillery ['reɪlərɪ] *n* taquinerie *f*, badinage *m*.
railroad ['reɪlrəʊd] **1** *n* (*US*) = **railway 1.**
2 *vt* **(a)** (*US*) expédier par chemin de fer *or* par rail.
(b) (: *fig*) **to ~ a bill** faire voter un projet de loi (après un débat sommaire); **to ~ sb into doing sth** forcer qn à faire qch sans qu'il ait le temps de réfléchir *or* de faire ouf*.
railway ['reɪlweɪ] (*esp Brit*) **1** *n* (*system*) chemin *m* de fer; (*track*) voie ferrée; *V* **aerial, scenic, underground.**
2 *cpd bridge, ticket* de chemin de fer. **railway carriage** voiture *f*, wagon *m*; **railway engine** locomotive *f*; **railway guide** indicateur *m* des chemins de fer; **railway line** ligne *f* de chemin de fer; (*track*) voie ferrée; **railwayman** cheminot *m*; **railway network** réseau *m* ferroviaire; **railway porter** porteur *m*; **railway station** gare *f*; (*small*) station *f* *or* halte *f* de chemin de fer; **railway timetable** horaire *m* des chemins de fer, Chaix *m* ®; **railway yard** dépôt *m* (d'une gare).
raiment ['reɪmənt] *n* (*liter*) vêtements *mpl*.
rain [reɪn] **1** *n* **(a)** (*Met*) pluie *f*. **it looks like ~** le temps est à la pluie; **in the ~** sous la pluie; **heavy/light ~** pluie battante/fine; **the ~'s on** ça pleut*; **(come) ~ (hail) or shine** (*lit*) par tous les temps, qu'il pleuve ou qu'il vente; (*fig*) quoi qu'il arrive; **the ~s** la saison des pluies; *V* **right.**
(b) (*fig*) *[arrows, blows, bullets]* pluie *f*.
2 *cpd*: **rain belt** zone *f* des pluies; **rainbow** *V* **rainbow**; (*US fig*) **I'll take a rain check** je m'en souviendrai à l'occasion; **raincoat** imperméable *m*, imper* *m*; **rain cloud** nuage *m* de pluie; **raindrop** goutte *f* de pluie; **rainfall** (*shower*) chute *f* de pluie; (*depth*) hauteur *f* des précipitations; **rain gauge** pluviomètre *m*; **rainproof** (*adj*) imperméable; (*vt*) imperméabiliser; **rainstorm** pluie torrentielle, trombe *f* d'eau; **rainwater** eau *f* de pluie.
3 *vt blows* faire pleuvoir.
4 *vi* pleuvoir. **it is ~ing** il pleut; **it is ~ing heavily** il pleut à verse; **it's ~ing cats and dogs, it's ~ing buckets*** il pleut à seaux *or* à torrents, il pleut *or* il tombe des cordes*; (*Prov*) **it never ~s but it pours** un malheur n'arrive jamais seul.
rain down *vi [bullets, stones etc]* pleuvoir.
rain off, (*US*) **rain out** *vt sep*: **the match was rained off** *or* **out** le match a été annulé (*or* abandonné) à cause de la pluie.
rainbow ['reɪnbəʊ] *n* arc-en-ciel *m*. **of all colours of the ~** de toutes les couleurs de l'arc-en-ciel; **~ trout** truite *f* arc-en-ciel.
rainless ['reɪnlɪs] *adj* sec (*f* sèche), sans pluie.
rainy ['reɪnɪ] *adj* pluvieux. **the ~ season** (*in Tropics*) la saison des pluies, les pluies *fpl*; (*hum: in Britain etc*) la mauvaise saison; (*fig*) **to put something away for a ~ day** mettre de l'argent de côté, garder une poire pour la soif.
raise [reɪz] **1** *vt* **(a)** (*lift, cause to rise*) *arm, leg, eyes* lever; *object, weight* lever, soulever; *dust* soulever. **to ~ a blind** (re)lever un store; (*Theat*) **to ~ the curtain** lever le rideau; (*lit*) **to ~ one's eyebrows** lever les sourcils; (*fig*) **that will make him ~ his eyebrows** cela le fera tiquer; (*fig*) **he didn't ~ an eyebrow** il n'a pas sourcillé *or* tiqué; **to ~ one's hat to sb** donner un coup de chapeau à qn; (*fig*) tirer son chapeau à qn*; **to ~ one's glass to sb** lever son verre à qn, boire à la santé de qn; **to ~ one's hand to sb** lever la main sur qn; **to ~ one's fist to sb** menacer qn du poing; **to ~ sb from the dead** ressusciter qn (d'entre les morts); **to ~ one's voice** (*speak louder*) hausser la voix; (*get angry*) élever la voix, hausser le ton; **not a voice was ~d in protest** personne n'a élevé la voix pour protester; **to ~ sb's spirits** remonter le moral de qn; **to ~ sb's hopes** donner à espérer à qn; **he ~d the people to revolt** il souleva le peuple; (*fig*) **to ~ the roof*** faire un boucan monstre‡; (*in protest*) rouspéter ferme*; **to ~ the level of the ground** rehausser le niveau du sol; (*Naut*) **to ~ a sunken ship** renflouer un navire coulé; *V* **tone.**
(b) (*increase*) *salary* augmenter, relever (*Admin*); *price* majorer, augmenter; *standard, level* élever; *temperature* faire monter.
(c) (*build, erect*) *monument* élever, ériger; *building* construire, édifier, bâtir.
(d) (*produce*) *spirit* évoquer; *ghosts* faire apparaître; *problems, difficulties* soulever, provoquer. **to ~ a blister** provoquer une ampoule; **to ~ a laugh** provoquer le rire, faire rire; **to ~ a cheer** (*oneself*) crier 'hourra'; (*in others*) faire jaillir des hourras; **to ~ difficulties** soulever *or* faire des difficultés; **to ~ a smile** (*oneself*) ébaucher un sourire; (*in others*) faire sourire, donner à sourire; **to ~ suspicion in sb's mind** faire naître des soupçons dans l'esprit de qn; **to ~ Cain*** *or* **hell‡** faire un éclat *or* du boucan‡, faire une scène de tous les diables*.
(e) (*bring to notice*) *question* soulever; *objection, protest* élever.
(f) (*grow, breed*) *animals, children, family* élever; *corn, wheat* cultiver, faire pousser.
(g) (*get together*) *army, taxes* lever; *money* se procurer; *funds* réunir, rassembler. **to ~ a loan** *[government etc]* lancer *or* émettre un emprunt; *[person]* emprunter; **to ~ money on sth** emprunter de l'argent sur qch; **I can't ~ the £500 I need** je n'arrive pas à me procurer les 500 livres dont j'ai besoin; *V* **mortgage.**
(h) (*end*) *siege, embargo* lever.
(i) (*Cards*) (*Poker*) faire une mise supérieure, relancer; (*Bridge*) faire une annonce supérieure, monter, enchérir. **I'll ~ you 6** je fais une relance de 6; *V* **bid.**
(j) (*contact*) **have you managed to ~ sb on the radio?** avez-vous réussi à entrer en contact avec *or* à toucher qn par (la) radio?
2 *n* **(a)** (*US, also Brit**: *payrise*) augmentation *f* (de salaire).
(b) (*Cards*) (*Poker*) relance *f*, mise supérieure; (*Bridge*) annonce supérieure, enchère *f*.
raise up *vt sep* lever, soulever. **he raised himself up on his elbow** il s'est soulevé sur son coude.
raisin ['reɪzən] *n* raisin sec.
raj [rɑːdʒ] *n* empire *m* (*aux Indes*).
rajah ['rɑːdʒə] *n* raja(h) *m* *or* radja(h) *m*.
rake[1] [reɪk] **1** *n* (*for gardener, croupier*) râteau *m*; (*for grate*) râble *m*, ringard *m*.
2 *cpd*: **rake-off*** profit *m*, (*illegal*) dessous *m* de table.
3 *vt garden* ratisser; *hay, leaves* râteler. **to ~ a fire** tisonner un feu; **to ~ the stones off the lawn** enlever les cailloux de la pelouse (à l'aide d'un râteau); (*fig*) **to ~ one's memory** fouiller dans sa mémoire *or* dans ses souvenirs; (*fig*) **his glance ~d the crowd** il a parcouru la foule du regard; **to ~ sth with machine-gun fire** balayer qch avec une mitrailleuse.
4 *vi* (*fig: search*) **to ~ among** *or* **through** fouiller dans.
rake in* *vt sep money* amasser. **he's just raking it in!** il remue le fric à la pelle!‡
rake out *vt sep*: **to rake out a fire** éteindre un feu en faisant tomber la braise.
rake over *vt sep flower bed* ratisser; (*fig*) *memories* remuer.
rake up *vt sep fire* attiser; *leaves* ramasser avec un râteau, ratisser; (*fig*) *grievance* rappeler. **to rake up the past** revenir sur le passé; **to rake up sb's past** fouiller dans le passé de qn.
rake[2] [reɪk] *n* (*person*) débauché *m*, coureur *m*, roué† *m*.
rake[3] [reɪk] **1** *n* (*Naut*) *[mast]* quête *f*; (*Theat*) *[stage]* pente *f*; (*Aut*) *[seat]* inclinaison *f*. **2** *vi* (*Naut*) être incliné; (*Theat*) être en pente.
rakish[1] ['reɪkɪʃ] *adj person* débauché, libertin; *appearance* cavalier, désinvolte. **he wore his hat at a ~ angle** il portait *or* il avait campé son chapeau sur le coin de l'œil.
rakish[2] ['reɪkɪʃ] *adj* (*Naut*) élancé, à la ligne élancée.
rakishly ['reɪkɪʃlɪ] *adv behave* en libertin, en débauché; *speak, dress* avec désinvolture.
rally[1] ['rælɪ] **1** *n* **(a)** *[troops]* rassemblement *m*, ralliement *m*; *[people]* rassemblement; (*Pol*) rassemblement, meeting *m*; (*Aut*) rallye *m*; (*Tennis*) échange *m*. **youth/peace ~** rassemblement de la jeunesse/en faveur de la paix; **electoral ~** meeting de campagne électorale.
(b) (*in health*) amélioration *f*, mieux *m*; (*St Ex*) reprise *f*.
2 *vt troops* rassembler, rallier; *supporters* rallier; *one's strength* retrouver, reprendre.
3 *vi [troops, people]* se rallier; *[sick person]* aller mieux, reprendre des forces *or* le dessus. **~ing point** point *m* de ralliement; (*fig*) **to ~ to a movement/to the support of sb** se rallier à un mouvement/à la cause de qn; (*Aut*) **to go ~ing** faire un *or* des rallye(s); (*St Ex*) **the market rallied** les cours ont repris.
rally round 1 *vi* (*fig*) venir en aide.
2 *vt fus*: **during her husband's illness everyone rallied round her** elle a été très entourée pendant la maladie de son mari.
rally[2] ['rælɪ] *vt* (*tease*) taquiner, se moquer (gentiment) de.
ram [ræm] **1** *n* bélier *m* (*also Astron*); (*Tech*) hie *f*, dame *f*; *[pile driver]* mouton *m*; (*for water*) bélier hydraulique; *V* **battering.**
2 *cpd*: (*Aviat*) **ramjet** statoréacteur *m*.
3 *vt* **(a)** (*push down*) enfoncer, pilonner (*Tech*), damer (*Tech*); (*pack down*) tasser (*into* dans). **he ~med his umbrella down the pipe** il a enfoncé son parapluie dans le tuyau; **he ~med the clothes into the case** il a tassé les vêtements dans la valise, il a bourré la valise de vêtements; (*Mil, Min*) **to ~ a charge home** refouler une charge; (*fig*) **to ~ home an argument** développer un argument à fond; (*fig*) **to ~ sth down sb's throat** rebattre les oreilles à qn de qch; (*fig*) **to ~ sth into sb's head** enfoncer *or* fourrer* qch dans la tête *or* dans le crâne de qn.
(b) (*crash into*) (*Naut*) heurter de l'avant *or* par l'étrave, (*in battle*) éperonner; (*Aut: deliberately or accidentally*) *another vehicle* emboutir; *post, tree* percuter (contre).
ram down *vt sep earth* tasser; (*Tech*) damer; *piles* enfoncer. **his hat rammed down over his ears** le chapeau enfoncé jusqu'aux oreilles.
ram in *vt sep* enfoncer.
Ramadan [ˌræməˈdæn] *n* ramadan *m*.
ramble ['ræmbl] **1** *n* randonnée *f*, excursion *f* (à pied), balade* *f*. **to go for a ~** faire une randonnée *or* une excursion (à pied) *or* une balade*.
2 *vi* **(a)** (*wander about*) se promener au hasard; (*go on hike*) faire une randonnée, faire une *or* des excursion(s) à pied.
(b) (*pej: in speech: also* **~ on**) parler pour ne rien dire; *[old person]* radoter. **he ~d on for half an hour** il a discouru *or* n'a cessé de discourir pendant une demi-heure.
rambler ['ræmbləʳ] *n* **(a)** (*person*) promeneur *m*, -euse *f*, excursionniste *mf*. **(b)** (*also* **~ rose**) rosier grimpant.
rambling ['ræmblɪŋ] **1** *adj speech, writing* décousu; *person* qui radote; *town, building* construit au hasard *or* sans plan défini; *plant* grimpant. **2** *n* (*incoherent speech*) divagations *fpl*, radotages *mpl*.
rambunctious [ræmˈbʌŋkʃəs] *adj* (*US*) = **rumbustious.**
ramification [ˌræmɪfɪˈkeɪʃən] *n* ramification *f*.
ramify ['ræmɪfaɪ] **1** *vt* ramifier. **2** *vi* se ramifier.
rammer ['ræməʳ] *n* (*Tech*) dame *f*, hie *f*; (*Mil*) refouloir *m*.
ramp [ræmp] *n* **(a)** (*on road etc*) rampe *f*; (*in garage etc*) pont *m* de graissage; (*Mil: bank*) glacis *m*, talus *m*. (*Aviat*) **(approach** *or* **boarding) ~** passerelle *f*; (*in garage*) **hydraulic ~** pont élévateur; (*Aut*) '~' 'dénivellation'.
(b) (*Brit‡: swindle*) escroquerie *f*. **it's a ~** c'est du vol.
rampage [ræmˈpeɪdʒ] **1** *n*: **to be on the ~** se déchaîner; **to go on the ~** se déchaîner; (*looting etc*) se livrer au saccage. **2** *vi* (*also* **~ about, ~ around**) se déchaîner.
rampancy ['ræmpənsɪ] *n [plants]* exubérance *f*; (*fig*) *[evil etc]* déchaînement *m*.

rampant ['ræmpənt] *adj plants* exubérant, luxuriant; (*Her*) rampant. (*fig*) **to be ~** sévir, régner.
rampart ['ræmpɑːt] *n* (*lit, fig*) rempart *m*.
ramrod ['ræmrɒd] *n* [*gun*] baguette *f*; [*cannon*] refouloir *m*; *V* **stiff.**
ramshackle ['ræm,ʃækl] *adj building* délabré, branlant; *table* branlant; *machine* déglingué*. **~ old car** vieille guimbarde, vieux tacot*.
ran [ræn] *pret of* **run.**
ranch [rɑːntʃ] **1** *n* ranch *m*. **2** *cpd*: **ranch hand** ouvrier *m* de ranch; **ranch house** maison *f* rustique (en rez-de-chaussée).
rancher ['rɑːntʃəʳ] *n* (*US*) (*owner*) propriétaire *mf* de ranch; (*employee*) cowboy *m*.
rancid ['rænsɪd] *adj* rance. **to go ~** rancir; **to smell ~** sentir le rance.
rancidity [ræn'sɪdɪtɪ] *n*, **rancidness** ['rænsɪdnɪs] *n* rance *m*.
rancorous ['ræŋkərəs] *adj* plein de rancœur, rancunier.
rancour, (*US*) **rancor** ['ræŋkəʳ] *n* rancœur *f*, rancune *f*.
rand [rænd] *n* (*monetary unit*) rand *m*.
random ['rændəm] **1** *n*: **at ~** au hasard; **chosen at ~** choisi au hasard; **to walk about at ~** se promener à l'aventure; **to hit out at ~** lancer des coups à l'aveuglette. **2** *adj* fait au hasard. **~ bullet** balle perdue; **~ sample** échantillon prélevé au hasard.
randy ['rændɪ] *adj* excité, aguiché*.
ranee ['rɑːniː] *n* = **rani.**
rang [ræŋ] *pret of* **ring**[2].
range [reɪndʒ] **1** *n* **(a)** (*row*) rangée *f*, rang *m*; [*mountains*] chaîne *f*.
(b) (*scope, distance covered*) [*telescope, gun, missile*] portée *f*; [*plane, ship, mooncraft*] rayon *m* d'action, autonomie *f*. **at a ~ of** à une distance de; **at long ~** à longue portée; (*Mil*) **to find the ~** régler son tir; (*lit, fig*) **to be out of ~** être hors de portée; **within (firing) ~** à portée de tir; (*fig*) **within my ~** à ma portée; **~ of vision** champ visuel; *V* **free, long**[1], **shooting** *etc*.
(c) (*extent between limits*) [*temperature*] variations *fpl*; [*prices, salaries*] échelle *f*, éventail *m*; (*Mus*) [*instrument, voice*] étendue *f*, tessiture *f*, registre *m*; (*selection*) [*colours, feelings, speeds*] gamme *f*; [*patterns*] assortiment *m*, choix *m*. **there will be a wide ~ of subjects** il y aura un grand choix de sujets.
(d) [*animal, plant*] habitat *m*, région *f*.
(e) (*domain, sphere*) [*activity*] champ *m*, rayon *m*; [*influence*] sphère *f*; [*knowledge*] étendue *f*, cercle *m*, champ. **the ~ of his ideas is limited** le cercle de ses idées est restreint.
(f) (*US: grazing land*) prairie *f*, (grand) pâturage *m*.
(g) (*also* **shooting ~**) (*Mil*) champ *m* de tir; (*at fair*) stand *m* (de tir); *V* **rifle**[2].
(h) (*Surv*) direction *f*, alignement *m*. **in ~ with** dans l'alignement *or* le prolongement de.
(i) (*cooking stove*) fourneau *m* de cuisine.
2 *vt* **(a)** (*place in a row*) *objects* ranger, mettre en rang, disposer en ligne; *troops* aligner. (*fig*) **to ~ o.s. on the side of** se ranger du côté de; **they ~d themselves along the pavement to see the procession** ils se sont postés le long du trottoir pour regarder le défilé.
(b) (*classify*) ranger, classer (*among* parmi).
(c) (*roam over*) parcourir. **he ~d the whole country looking for ...** il a parcouru le pays en tous sens à la recherche de ...; **to ~ the seas** parcourir *or* sillonner les mers.
(d) (*direct*) *gun, telescope* braquer (*on* sur).
3 *vi* **(a)** (*extend*) [*discussion, quest*] s'étendre (*from ... to* de ... à, *over* sur); [*results, opinions*] aller (*from ... to* de ... à), varier (*from ... to* entre ... et). **the search ~d over the whole country** les recherches se sont étendues sur tout le pays; **the numbers ~ from 10 to 20** les numéros vont de 10 à 20; **the temperature ~s from 18° to 24°** *or* **between 18° and 24°** la température varie entre 18° et 24°; (*fig*) **researches ranging over a wide field** recherches qui embrassent un large domaine.
(b) (*roam*) errer, vagabonder. **to ~ over the area** parcourir la région; **animals ranging through the jungle** des animaux qui rôdent dans la jungle.
(c) [*guns, missiles, shells*] **to ~ over** avoir une portée de, porter à.
4 *cpd*: (*Mil, Naut, Phot*) **rangefinder** télémètre *m*.
ranger ['reɪndʒəʳ] *n* [*forest etc*] garde *m* forestier; (*US: mounted patrolman*) gendarme *m* à cheval. (*US*) **~s** gendarmerie *f* à cheval.
rani ['rɑːniː] *n* rani *f*.
rank[1] [ræŋk] **1** *n* **(a)** (*row*) rang *m*; (*also* **taxi ~**) station *f* de taxis. **the taxi at the head of the ~** le taxi en tête de file.
(b) (*Mil*) rang *m*. **to break ~s** rompre les rangs; **to serve in the ~s** servir dans les rangs; **the ~s**, (*Brit*) **other ~s** les sous-officiers *mpl* et hommes *mpl* de troupe; (*Mil*) **the ~ and file** les hommes de troupe; (*fig*) la masse, le peuple; (*Pol*) **the ~ and file of the party** les membres *mpl* ordinaires du parti; **the ~ and file workers** la base, les ouvriers *mpl*; **to rise from the ~s** sortir du rang; **to reduce to the ~s** casser; *V* **close**[2].
(c) (*Mil: grade*) grade *m*, rang *m*. **to reach the ~ of general** atteindre le grade de général; *V* **pull.**
(d) (*class, position*) rang *m* (social), condition *f*, classe *f*. **people of all ~s** gens de toutes conditions; **a person of ~** une personne de haut rang; **a singer of the first ~** un chanteur de (tout) premier ordre; **a second-~ painter** un peintre de seconde zone *or* de deuxième ordre.
2 *vt* **(a) I ~ it as one of the best red wines** je le classe parmi les meilleurs vins rouges; **I ~ Beethoven among the great** je compte Beethoven parmi les grands.
(b) (*US Mil*) = **outrank**; *V* **out 5.**
3 *vi* [*book etc*] se classer, compter; [*person*] compter. **he ~s among my friends** il compte parmi mes amis; **to ~ above/below sb** être supérieur/inférieur à qn; **to ~ high among** occuper un rang élevé parmi; (*Mil*) **the ~ing officer** l'officier responsable *or* le plus haut en grade.
rank[2] [ræŋk] *adj* **(a)** *plants* exubérant, luxuriant; *grass* dru, touffu; *soil* plantureux, trop fertile, trop riche. **it is ~ with weeds** les mauvaises herbes y poussent à foison.
(b) *smell* fétide, fort; *dustbin, drains* fétide; *fats* rance; *person* grossier, répugnant, ignoble.
(c) (*flagrant*) *disgrace* absolu, complet (*f* -ète); *poison, traitor* véritable; *injustice* criant, flagrant; *insolence* caractérisé; *liar* fieffé; *lie* grossier, flagrant.
ranker ['ræŋkəʳ] *n* (*Mil*) (*soldier*) simple soldat *m*; (*officer*) officier sorti du rang.
rankle ['ræŋkl] *vi* rester sur le cœur, laisser une rancœur. **it ~d with him** il en était ulcéré, il l'avait sur le cœur, ça lui était resté sur l'estomac*.
rankness ['ræŋknɪs] *n* **(a)** [*plants etc*] exubérance *f*, luxuriance *f*. **(b)** (*smell*) odeur *f* fétide; (*taste*) goût *m* rance.
ransack ['rænsæk] *vt* (*pillage*) *house, shop* saccager, piller; *town, region* mettre à sac; (*search*) *room* fouiller (à fond), mettre tout sens dessus dessous; *one's memory* fouiller dans (*for* pour trouver).
ransom ['rænsəm] **1** *n* (*lit, fig*) rançon *f*. **to hold sb to ~** rançonner qn, mettre qn à rançon; (*fig*) exercer un chantage sur qn; (*fig*) **they are being held to ~** ils ont le couteau sur la gorge; *V* **king. 2** *vt* racheter.
rant [rænt] *vi* **(a)** (*pej*) [*orator etc*] déclamer (de façon exagérée), parler avec emphase. **(b)** (*also* **~ on**) divaguer. **to ~ and rave** tempêter; **to ~ (and rave) at sb** tempêter *or* fulminer contre qn.
ranting ['ræntɪŋ] **1** *n* rodomontade(s) *f*(*pl*). **2** *adj* déclamatoire.
ranunculus [rə'nʌŋkjʊləs] *n* renoncule *f*.
rap [ræp] **1** *n* (*noise*) petit coup sec; (*blow*) tape *f*. **there was a ~ at the door** on a frappé bruyamment à la porte; **to give sb a ~ on the knuckles** donner sur les doigts à qn; (*fig: rebuke*) taper sur les doigts de qn; **to take the ~*** payer les pots cassés; **I don't care a ~*** je m'en fiche* éperdument.
2 *vt door* frapper bruyamment à; *table* frapper sur. **to ~ sb's knuckles, to ~ sb over the knuckles** donner sur les doigts de qn; (*fig: rebuke*) taper sur les doigts de qn.
3 *vi* frapper, cogner, donner un coup sec.
rap out *vt sep* **(a)** (*say curtly*) dire brusquement; *oath* lâcher; *order, retort* lancer.
(b) (*Spiritualism*) *message* communiquer *or* annoncer au moyen de coups.
rapacious [rə'peɪʃəs] *adj* rapace, avide.
rapaciously [rə'peɪʃəslɪ] *adv* avec rapacité *or* avidité.
rapacity [rə'pæsɪtɪ] *n* rapacité *f*, avidité *f*.
rape[1] [reɪp] **1** *n* (*also Jur*) viol *m*; (††: *abduction*) ravissement† *m*, rapt *m*. **2** *vt* violer.
rape[2] [reɪp] *n* (*Bot*) colza *m*. **~ oil/seed** huile *f*/graine *f* de colza.
rape[3] [reɪp] *n* (*grape pulp*) marc *m* de raisin; (*wine*) râpé *m*.
rapid ['ræpɪd] **1** *adj action* rapide, prompt; *river, pulse* rapide; *slope, descent* raide, rapide. (*Mil*) **~ fire** tir *m* rapide; (*fig*) **~ fire of questions** feu roulant de questions. **2** *n* (*Geog*) **~s** rapides *mpl*.
rapidity [rə'pɪdɪtɪ] *n* rapidité *f*.
rapidly ['ræpɪdlɪ] *adv* rapidement.
rapier ['reɪpɪəʳ] *n* rapière *f*. **~ thrust** (*lit*) coup *m* de pointe; (*fig*) remarque mordante.
rapine ['ræpaɪn] *n* rapine *f*.
rapist ['reɪpɪst] *n* (*Jur*) violeur *m*, auteur *m* d'un viol.
rapping ['ræpɪŋ] *n* coups secs et durs.
rapport [ræ'pɔːʳ] *n* rapport *m* (*with* avec, *between* entre). **in ~ with** en harmonie avec.
rapprochement [ræ'prɒʃmɑ̃ːŋ] *n* rapprochement *m* (*fig*).
rapscallion [ræp'skælɪən] *n* vaurien *m*, mauvais garnement.
rapt [ræpt] *adj interest, attention* profond, intense; *look* ravi, extasié, transporté. **~ in contemplation/in thought** plongé dans la contemplation/dans ses pensées.
rapture ['ræptʃəʳ] *n* (*delight*) ravissement *m*, enchantement *m*; (*ecstasy*) extase *f*, transport *m*. **to be in ~s over** *or* **about** *object* être ravi *or* enchanté de; *person* être en extase devant; **to go into ~s over** *or* **about sth/sb** s'extasier sur qch/qn.
rapturous ['ræptʃərəs] *adj exclamation* de ravissement, d'extase; *applause* frénétique, enthousiaste.
rapturously ['ræptʃərəslɪ] *adv greet, listen* avec ravissement; *applaud* avec frénésie.
rare [rɛəʳ] *adj occurrence, plant* rare; *atmosphere* raréfié; (*: *excellent*) fameux*; (*underdone*) *meat* saignant. (*Chem*) **~ earth** terre *f* rare; **with very ~ exceptions** à de rares exceptions près; **it is ~ for her to come** il est rare qu'elle vienne; **to grow ~(r)** [*plants, atmosphere*] se raréfier, [*visits*] devenir plus rares *or* moins fréquents; **we had a ~ (old) time* on holiday** nous avons passé de fameuses* vacances; **a very ~ steak** un bifteck bleu.
rarebit ['rɛəbɪt] *n V* **Welsh.**
rarefaction [,rɛərɪ'fækʃən] *n* raréfaction *f*.
rarefied ['rɛərɪfaɪd] *adj atmosphere* raréfié; (*fig*) trop raffiné. **to become ~** se raréfier.
rarefy ['rɛərɪfaɪ] **1** *vt* raréfier. **2** *vi* se raréfier.
rarely ['rɛəlɪ] *adv* rarement.
rareness ['rɛənɪs] *n* rareté *f* (*qualité*).
rarity ['rɛərɪtɪ] *n* rareté *f*. **rain is a ~ here** la pluie est un événement rare ici.
rascal ['rɑːskəl] *n* (*scoundrel*) coquin *m*, vaurien *m*; (*scamp*) polisson(ne) *m*(*f*), fripon(ne) *m*(*f*).
rascality [rɑːs'kælɪtɪ] *n* coquinerie *f*, friponnerie *f*.
rascally ['rɑːskəlɪ] *adj lawyer, merchant* retors; *trick* méchant, vilain, de coquin. **a ~ man** un vaurien, un coquin; **his ~ nephew**

son coquin de neveu; ~ **habits** habitudes *fpl* de vaurien *or* de coquin.

rash[1] [ræʃ] *n* (*Med: gen sense*) rougeur *f*, éruption *f*; (*from food etc*) (plaques *fpl* d')urticaire *f*; (*in measles etc*) éruption, taches *fpl* rouges. **to come out** *or* **break out in a** ~ avoir une éruption; *V* **heat, nettle.**

rash[2] [ræʃ] *adj person* imprudent, impétueux, qui manque de réflexion, qui agit à la légère; *promise, words, thoughts, judgment* irréfléchi, imprudent. **it was** ~ **of him to do that** il s'est montré très imprudent en faisant cela.

rasher ['ræʃəʳ] *n* (mince) tranche *f* (de lard).

rashly ['ræʃlɪ] *adv* imprudemment, sans réfléchir.

rashness ['ræʃnɪs] *n* (*V* **rash**[2]) imprudence *f*, impétuosité *f*, irréflexion *f*.

rasp [rɑːsp] **1** *n* (*tool*) râpe *f*; (*noise*) grincement *m*. **2** *vt* **(a)** (*Tech*) râper. **(b)** (*speak: also* ~ **out**) dire *or* crier d'une voix grinçante *or* âpre. **3** *vi* grincer, crisser.

raspberry ['rɑːzbərɪ] **1** *n* (*fruit*) framboise *f*. (*fig*) **to blow a** ~* faire pfft, faire un bruit de dérision; **to get a** ~* **from** se faire rabrouer *or* rembarrer* par. **2** *cpd ice cream* (à la) framboise *inv*; *jam* de framboise. **raspberry bush, raspberry cane** framboisier *m*.

rasping ['rɑːspɪŋ] **1** *adj sound* grinçant, crissant; *voice* âpre, rugueux. **2** *n* (*sound*) crissement *m*, grincement *m*.

rat [ræt] **1** *n* (*Zool*) rat *m*; (**pej: person*) salaud‡ *m*, vache* *f*; (‡: *informer*) mouchard(e) *m(f)*; (‡: *blackleg*) jaune *m*; (*: *abandoning friends*) lâcheur* *m*, -euse* *f*. **he's a dirty** ~* c'est un salaud‡ *or* un sale individu*; **you** ~!* espèce de salaud!‡; ~**s!*** mon œil!*

2 *cpd*: **ratcatcher** chasseur *m* de rats; **ratcatching** chasse *f* aux rats; (*extermination*) dératisation *f*; (*Naut*) **ratline** enfléchure *f*; **rat poison** mort-aux-rats *f*; **rat race** foire *f* d'empoigne; (*pej*) **her hair was in rats' tails*** ses cheveux étaient en queues de rat; **rattrap** piège *m* à rats, ratière *f*.

3 *vi* (*) **to** ~ **on sb** (*desert*) lâcher qn*; (*inform on*) donner qn, moucharder qn*.

ratable ['reɪtəbl] *adj* = **rateable.**

ratchet ['rætʃɪt] *n* cliquet *m*. ~ **wheel** roue *f* à rochet.

rate[1] [reɪt] **1** *n* **(a)** (*ratio, proportion*) proportion *f*, taux *m*; (*speed*) vitesse *f*, train *m*, allure *f*. **birth/death** ~ (taux *m* de) la natalité/la mortalité; **the failure** ~ **for this exam is high** il y a un pourcentage élevé d'échecs à cet examen; ~ **of consumption** taux de consommation; (*Elec, Water*) ~ **of flow** débit *m* (moyen); **at the** ~ **of 100 litres an hour** à raison de 100 litres par heure; **at a** ~ **of** à une vitesse de; (*Aviat*) ~ **of climb** vitesse ascensionnelle; (*Med*) **pulse** ~ fréquence *f* des pulsations; **to pay sb at the** ~ **of £4 per hour** payer qn à raison de 4 livres de l'heure; **at a great** ~, **at a** ~ **of knots*** à toute allure, au trot*, à fond de train*; **to go at a terrific** ~ aller à un train d'enfer; **if you continue at this** ~ si vous continuez à ce train-là *or* de cette façon; **at his** ~ **of working, he'll never finish** au rythme auquel il travaille, il n'aura jamais terminé; (*fig*) **at the** ~ **you're going, you'll be dead before long** du train où vous allez, vous ne ferez pas de vieux os; (*fig*) **at any** ~ en tout cas, de toute façon; **at that** ~ à ce compte-là, dans ce cas; *V* **first-rate** etc.

(b) (*Comm, Fin*) taux *m*, cours *m*, tarif *m*. ~ **of exchange** taux *or* cours du change; ~ **of interest/pay** taux d'intérêt/de rémunération; **postage/advertising** ~**s** tarifs postaux/de publicité; **insurance** ~**s** primes *fpl* d'assurance; **there is a reduced** ~ **for children** les enfants bénéficient d'un tarif réduit *or* d'une réduction; **basic salary** ~ traitement *m* de base.

(c) (*Brit Fin: municipal tax*) ~**s** impôts locaux; ~**s and taxes** impôts et contributions; **a penny on/off the** ~**s** une augmentation/réduction d'un pour cent des impôts locaux; *V* **water.**

2 *cpd*: (*Brit*) **rate collector** receveur municipal; **ratepayer** contribuable *mf* (*payant les impôts locaux*); **rate(s) office** recette municipale (*bureau*).

3 *vt* **(a)** (*estimate worth of, appraise*) évaluer; (*fig: consider*) considérer (*as* comme). **to** ~ **sb/sth highly** faire grand cas de qn/qch; **how does he** ~ **that film?** que pense-t-il de ce film?; **I** ~ **him amongst my best pupils** je le considère comme un de mes meilleurs élèves, je le compte parmi mes meilleurs élèves.

(b) (*Local Government*) fixer le loyer matriciel de. **house** ~**d at £100 per annum** ≈ maison *f* dont le loyer matriciel (*Admin*) *or* la valeur locative imposable est de 100 livres par an.

(c) (*deserve*) mériter. (*Scol*) **I think he** ~**s a pass (mark)** je crois qu'il mérite *or* vaut la moyenne*.

4 *vi* (*be classed*) être classé, se classer (*as* comme).

rate[2] [reɪt] *vt* (*liter*) = **berate.**

rateable ['reɪtəbl] *adj property* imposable. ~ **value** ≈ loyer matriciel (*Admin*), valeur locative imposable.

rather ['rɑːðəʳ] *adv* **(a)** (*for preference*) plutôt. ~ **than wait, he went away** plutôt que d'attendre, il est parti; **I would** ~ **have the blue dress** je préférerais *or* j'aimerais mieux *or* je prendrais plutôt la robe bleue; **I would much** ~ ... je préférerais de beaucoup ...; **I would** ~ **be happy than rich** j'aimerais mieux être heureux que riche, je préfère le bonheur à la richesse; **I would** ~ **you came yourself** je préférerais que vous veniez (*subj*) vous-même; **I'd** ~ **not** je préfère pas*, j'aime mieux pas*; **I'd** ~ **not go** j'aimerais mieux ne pas y aller; **I'd** ~ **die!** plutôt mourir!

(b) (*more accurately*) plus exactement, plutôt. **a car, or** ~ **an old banger** une voiture, ou plus exactement *or* ou plutôt une vieille guimbarde; **he isn't on holiday, but** ~ **out of work** plutôt qu'en vacances disons qu'il est en chômage.

(c) (*to a considerable degree*) plutôt; (*to some extent*) un peu; (*somewhat*) quelque peu; (*fairly*) assez; (*slightly*) légèrement. **he's a** ~ **clever person, he's** ~ **a clever person** il est plutôt intelligent; **he felt** ~ **better** il se sentait un peu mieux; **he looked** ~ **silly** il a eu l'air plutôt stupide; **it's** ~ **more difficult than you think** c'est un peu plus difficile que vous ne croyez; **Latin is** ~ **too difficult for me** le latin est un peu trop difficile pour moi; **it's** ~ **a pity** c'est plutôt dommage; **his book is** ~ **good** son livre n'est pas mauvais du tout; **that costs** ~ **a lot** cela coûte assez cher; **I** ~ **think he's wrong** je crois bien *or* j'ai l'impression qu'il a tort; (*excl*) ~**!*** et comment!*

ratification [ˌrætɪfɪ'keɪʃən] *n* ratification *f*.

ratify ['rætɪfaɪ] *vt* ratifier.

rating[1] ['reɪtɪŋ] *n* **(a)** (*assessment*) estimation *f*, évaluation *f*. **(b)** (*Fin*) *[property etc]* montant *m* des impôts locaux.

(c) (*placing*) classement *m*.

(d) (*Naut*) (*classification*) classe *f*; (*sailor*) marin *m*, matelot *m*. **the** ~**s** les matelots et gradés *mpl*.

rating[2] ['reɪtɪŋ] *n* réprimande *f*, semonce *f*, engueulade‡ *f*.

ratio ['reɪʃɪəʊ] *n* proportion *f*, raison *f*, rapport *m*. **in the** ~ **of 100 to 1** dans la proportion de 100 contre 1, dans le rapport de 100 contre *or* à 1; **inverse** *or* **indirect** ~ raison inverse; **in direct** ~ **to** en raison directe de.

ratiocinate [rætɪ'ɒsɪmeɪt] *vi* (*frm*) raisonner, ratiociner (*pej*).

ratiocination [ˌrætɪɒsɪ'neɪʃən] *n* (*frm*) raisonnement *m*, ratiocination *f* (*pej*).

ration ['ræʃən] **1** *n* (*allowance: of food, goods etc*) ration *f*. **it's off the** ~* ce n'est plus rationné; (*food*) ~**s** vivres *mpl*; **to put sb on short** ~**s** réduire les rations de qn; *V* **iron.**

2 *cpd*: **ration book, ration card** carte *f* de rationnement.

3 *vt goods, food, people* rationner. **he was** ~**ed to 1 kg** sa ration était 1 kg.

ration out *vt sep food etc* rationner.

rational ['ræʃənl] *adj creature, person* doué de raison, raisonnable; (*Med: lucid*) lucide; *faculty* rationnel; (*Math*) rationnel; *activity, thinking* rationnel, conforme à la raison; *action, argument, behaviour, person* raisonnable, sensé; *explanation* logique, raisonné; *solution* logique. **it was the only** ~ **thing to do** c'était la seule façon logique *or* rationnelle d'agir; **it wasn't very** ~ **of him to do that** il n'a pas agi de façon très logique *or* rationnelle.

rationale [ræʃə'nɑːl] *n* (*reasoning*) raisonnement *m*; (*statement*) exposé raisonné.

rationalism ['ræʃnəlɪzəm] *n* rationalisme *m*.

rationalist ['ræʃnəlɪst] *adj, n* rationaliste (*mf*).

rationalistic [ˌræʃnə'lɪstɪk] *adj* rationaliste.

rationality [ˌræʃə'nælɪtɪ] *n* rationalité *f*.

rationalization [ˌræʃnəlaɪ'zeɪʃən] *n* rationalisation *f*.

rationalize ['ræʃnəlaɪz] **1** *vt* **(a)** *event, conduct etc* (tenter de) trouver une explication logique à; (*Psych*) justifier *or* motiver après coup.

(b) (*organize efficiently*) *industry, production, problems* rationaliser.

(c) (*Math*) rendre rationnel.

2 *vi* (*Psych*) chercher une justification après coup.

rationally ['ræʃnəlɪ] *adv behave, discuss, speak* rationnellement, raisonnablement. ~, **it should be possible to do it** logiquement, il devrait être possible de le faire.

rationing ['ræʃnɪŋ] *n* rationnement *m*. **food** ~ rationnement de l'alimentation.

rat-tat-tat ['rætə'tæt] *n* (*on door*) toc-toc *m*; (*on drum*) ran-tan-plan *m*.

rattle ['rætl] **1** *n* **(a)** (*sound*) *[vehicle]* bruit *m* (de ferraille), fracas *m*; *[chains, bottles, typewriter]* cliquetis *m*; *[door]* claquement *m*; *[hailstones, machine gun]* crépitement *m*; *[rattlesnake]* sonnettes *fpl*; (*Med: also* **death** ~) râle *m*.

(b) (*object*) *[child]* hochet *m*; *[sports fan]* crécelle *f*.

2 *cpd*: **rattlebrained** écervelé, étourdi, sans cervelle; **rattlesnake** serpent *m* à sonnettes, crotale *m*; **rattletrap** guimbarde *f*, tacot* *m*.

3 *vi [box, container, object]* faire du bruit; *[articles in box]* s'entrechoquer, bringuebaler, ballotter; *[vehicle]* faire un bruit de ferraille; *[gunfire, hailstones]* crépiter; *[machinery]* cliqueter; *[window]* trembler. **to** ~ **at the door** cogner à la porte; **there is something rattling** il y a quelque chose qui cogne; *[vehicle]* **to** ~ **along/away** *etc* rouler/partir *etc* dans un bruit de ferraille.

4 *vt* **(a)** *box* agiter (avec bruit); *bottles, cans* faire s'entrechoquer; *dice* agiter, secouer; *keys* faire cliqueter.

(b) (*: *alarm*) *person* déconcerter, démonter, ébranler. **don't get** ~**d!** ne panique pas!*, pas de panique!*

rattle down *vi [falling stones etc]* dégringoler *or* tomber avec fracas.

rattle off *vt sep poem, speech, apology* débiter à toute allure.

rattle on* *vi* parler sans arrêt (*about sth* de qch), jacasser.

rattle through *vt fus* faire (*or* écrire *or* lire *etc*) à toute vitesse *or* au grand galop.

rattling ['rætlɪŋ] **1** *n* = **rattle 1a. 2** *adj* bruyant. **I heard a** ~ **noise** j'ai entendu un cliquetis, j'ai entendu quelque chose qui cognait; **at a** ~ **pace** *or* **speed** à grande vitesse, à vive allure. **3** *adv* (*†) ~ **good** formidable*, épatant*.

ratty* ['rætɪ] *adj* en rogne*, fâché.

raucous ['rɔːkəs] *adj* rauque.

raucously ['rɔːkəslɪ] *adv* d'une voix rauque.

raucousness ['rɔːkəsnɪs] *n* ton *m* rauque, raucité *f*.

ravage ['rævɪdʒ] **1** *n [war etc]* ravage *m*, dévastation *f*. **the** ~**s of time** les outrages *mpl* *or* les ravages du temps, l'injure *f* des ans.

2 *vt* (*ruin*) ravager, dévaster; (*plunder*) ravager, piller. **body** ~**d by disease** corps ravagé par la maladie.

rave [reɪv] **1** *vi* (*be delirious*) délirer, divaguer; (*talk wildly*) divaguer, déraisonner; (*speak furiously*) s'emporter, tempêter (*at, against* contre); (*speak enthusiastically*) s'extasier (*about, over* sur), parler avec enthousiasme (*about, over* de); *[storm]* faire rage; *[wind]* être déchaîné; *[sea]* être démonté *or* en furie; *V* **rant.**

2 *cpd*: **rave notice*, rave review*** critique *f* dithyrambique.
ravel ['rævəl] **1** *vt* **(a)** (*entangle: lit, fig*) emmêler, embrouiller, enchevêtrer.
(b) (*disentangle*) = **ravel out 2.**
2 *vi* (*become tangled*) s'embrouiller, s'enchevêtrer; (*fray*) s'effilocher.
ravel out 1 *vi* s'effilocher.
2 *vt sep material* effilocher; *threads* démêler; *knitting* défaire; (*fig*) *difficulty* débrouiller; *plot* dénouer.
raven ['reɪvn] **1** *n* corbeau *m*. **2** *cpd* (*colour*) noir comme (du) jais *or* comme l'ébène. **raven-haired** aux cheveux de jais.
ravening ['rævnɪŋ] *adj* vorace, rapace.
ravenous ['rævənəs] *adj animal* vorace, rapace; *person* affamé; *appetite* vorace, féroce; *hunger* dévorant. **I'm ~*** j'ai une faim de loup, j'ai l'estomac dans les talons*.
ravenously ['rævənəslɪ] *adv* voracement. **to be ~ hungry** avoir une faim de loup, avoir l'estomac dans les talons*.
ravine [rə'vi:n] *n* ravin *m*.
raving ['reɪvɪŋ] **1** *adj* délirant. **~ lunatic** fou furieux, folle furieuse; *V* **mad. 2** *n*: **~(s)** délire *m*, divagations *fpl*.
ravioli [,rævɪ'əʊlɪ] *n* ravioli *mpl*.
ravish ['rævɪʃ] *vt* **(a)** (*delight*) ravir, enchanter, transporter.
(b) (†† *or liter*) (*rape*) violer; (*abduct*) ravir.
ravisher ['rævɪʃər] *n* ravisseur *m*.
ravishing ['rævɪʃɪŋ] *adj woman, sight* ravissant, enchanteur (*f* -teresse); *beauty* enchanteur.
ravishingly ['rævɪʃɪŋlɪ] *adv* de façon *or* de manière ravissante. **she is ~ beautiful** elle est belle à ravir, elle est d'une beauté éblouissante.
ravishment ['rævɪʃmənt] *n* **(a)** (*delight*) enchantement *m*, ravissement *m*. **(b)** (†† *or liter*) (*rape*) viol *m*; (*abduction*) ravissement† *m*, rapt *m*.
raw [rɔ:] **1** *adj* **(a)** (*uncooked*) *meat, food* cru; (*unprocessed*) *cloth, leather* écru; *ore, sugar* brut; *silk* grège; *spirit, alcohol* pur. **~ colour** couleur crue; **a ~ deal*** un sale coup*; **to give sb a ~ deal*** faire un sale coup à qn*; **he got a ~ deal* when ...** on lui a fait un sale coup* quand ...; **the old get a ~ deal* nowadays** les vieux sont très mal traités de nos jours; *[cloth etc]* **~ edge** bord coupé; **~ material(s)** matières premières; **~ spirits** alcool pur.
(b) (*inexperienced*) inexpérimenté, novice; *troops* non aguerri; (*uncouth*) mal dégrossi; (*coarse*) *humour, story* cru. **~ recruit** bleu* *m*.
(c) (*sore*) sensible, irrité; *wound* à vif; *skin* écorché; *nerves* à fleur de peau, à vif.
(d) *climate* froid et humide, âpre; *wind* âpre, aigre; *air* vif.
2 *n*: **to get sb on the ~** toucher *or* piquer qn au vif; **life/nature in the ~** la vie/la nature telle qu'elle est; (*naked*) **in the ~*** nu, à poil*.
3 *cpd*: **rawboned** *person* maigre, décharné; *horse* efflanqué; **rawhide** (*n*) cuir brut *or* vert; (*adj*) de *or* en cuir brut *or* vert.
rawlplug ['rɔ:lplʌg] *n* cheville *f* (*Menuiserie*).
rawness ['rɔ:nɪs] *n* **(a) the ~ of this meat/colour** cette viande/couleur crue. **(b)** (*lack of experience*) inexpérience *f*. **(c)** (*on skin*) écorchure *f*. **(d)** *[climate]* froid *m* humide. **the ~ of the wind** l'âpreté *f* du vent, le vent aigre.
ray¹ [reɪ] *n [light, heat, sun etc]* rayon *m*; (*fig*) rayon *m*, lueur *f*. **~ of hope** lueur d'espoir; *V* **cathode, death, X-ray** *etc*.
ray² [reɪ] *n* (*fish*) raie *f*; *V* **sting.**
rayon ['reɪɒn] **1** *n* (*Tex*) rayonne *f*, soie artificielle. **2** *adj* en rayonne.
raze [reɪz] *vt* raser. **to ~ to the ground** *town* raser; *building* raser, abattre à ras de terre.
razor ['reɪzər] **1** *n* rasoir *m*. **electric ~** rasoir électrique; (*fig*) **on the ~'s edge** sur la corde raide; *V* **safety** *etc*.
2 *cpd*: **razor blade** lame *f* de rasoir; **razor-sharp** *knife etc* tranchant comme un rasoir; (*fig*) *person, mind* délié, vif; *wit* acéré; **razor-slashing** taillades *fpl* à coup de rasoir.
razz‡ [ræz] *vt* mettre en boîte*.
razzle(-dazzle)‡ ['ræzl(,dæzl)] *n*: **to go on the ~** faire la bringue‡ *or* la nouba‡.
re¹ [reɪ] *n* (*Mus*) ré *m*.
re² [ri:] *prep* (*Admin, Comm etc: referring to*) au sujet de, relativement à, concernant; (*Jur: also* **in ~**) en l'affaire de.
re... [ri:] *pref* (*before consonant*) re..., ré...; (*before vowel*) r..., ré... . **to ~do** refaire; **to ~heat** réchauffer; **to ~open** rouvrir; **to ~-elect** réélire.
reach [ri:tʃ] **1** *n* **(a)** (*accessibility*) portée *f*, atteinte *f*. **within ~** à portée; **out of ~** hors de portée *or* d'atteinte; **within sb's ~** à (la) portée de qn; **out of sb's ~** hors de (la) portée de qn; **within arm's ~** à portée de la main; **cars are within everyone's ~ nowadays** de nos jours les voitures sont à la portée de toutes les bourses *or* de tous; **out of the children's ~** hors de (la) portée des enfants; **I keep it within easy ~** *or* **within my ~** je le garde à portée de main *or* sous la main; **mountains not within easy ~** montagnes difficilement accessibles *or* d'accès difficile; **within easy ~ of the sea** à proximité de la mer, proche de la mer; **she was beyond (the) ~ of human help** elle était au-delà de tout secours humain; **beyond the ~ of the law** à l'abri de la justice; **this subject is beyond his ~** ce sujet le dépasse.
(b) (*length*) *[beach, river]* étendue *f*; *[canal]* bief *m*.
(c) (*esp Boxing*) allonge *f*. **he has a long ~** il a une bonne allonge.
2 *cpd*: **reach-me-downs*** (*ready-made*) vêtements *mpl* de confection; (*secondhand*) vêtements achetés au décrochez-moi-ça*.
3 *vt* **(a)** (*get as far as*) *place* atteindre, gagner, arriver à; *age, goal, limit* atteindre; *agreement, understanding* aboutir à, arriver à; *conclusion* arriver à; *perfection* atteindre. **when we ~ed him he was dead** quand nous sommes arrivés auprès de lui, il était mort; **to ~ the terrace you have to cross the garden** pour accéder à la terrasse, il faut traverser le jardin; **I hope this letter ~es him** j'espère que cette lettre lui parviendra; **the news ~ed us too late** nous avons appris *or* reçu la nouvelle trop tard; **to ~ page 50** arriver *or* en être à la page 50; **not a sound ~ed our ears** aucun bruit ne parvenait à nos oreilles; **you can ~ me at my hotel** vous pouvez me joindre à mon hôtel; **he is tall enough to ~ the top shelf** il est assez grand pour atteindre l'étagère d'en haut; **he ~es her shoulder** il lui arrive à l'épaule; **her dress ~es the floor** sa robe descend jusqu'à terre.
(b) (*get and give*) passer. **~ me (over) that book** passez-moi ce livre; **~ (over) the salt for Richard** passez le sel à Richard.
(c) (*US Jur*) *witness* corrompre, suborner.
4 *vi* **(a)** *[territory etc]* s'étendre; *[voice, sound]* porter (*to* jusqu'à); *V* **far.**
(b) (*stretch out hand, arm: also* **~ across, ~ out, ~ over**) étendre le bras (*for sth* pour prendre qch, *to grasp etc* pour saisir *etc*). (*US*) **~ for the sky!‡** haut les mains!
reach back *vi* (*fig*) remonter (*to* à). **to reach back to Victorian times** remonter à l'époque victorienne.
reach down 1 *vi [clothes, curtains etc]* descendre (*to* jusqu'à).
2 *vt sep* (*from hook*) décrocher; (*from shelf*) descendre. **will you reach me down the book?** voulez-vous me descendre le livre?, voulez-vous me passer le livre qui est là-haut?
reach out *vt sep* étendre. **he reached out his hand for the cup** il a étendu le bras pour prendre la tasse.
reach up *vi* **(a)** lever le bras. **he reached up to get the book on the shelf** il a levé le bras pour atteindre le livre sur le rayon.
(b) monter. **the flood water reached up to the windows** la crue (des eaux) est montée jusqu'aux fenêtres.
reachable ['ri:tʃəbl] *adj* accessible, à portée.
react [ri:'ækt] *vi* réagir (*against* contre, *on* sur, *to* à).
reaction [ri:'ækʃən] *n* (*all senses*) réaction *f*. **what was his ~ to your suggestion?** comment a-t-il réagi *or* quelle a été sa réaction à votre proposition?; **this decision was a ~ against violence** cette décision a été le contrecoup de la violence *or* a été la riposte à la violence *or* a été prise en réaction contre la violence; (*Pol*) **forces of ~** forces *fpl* de la réaction, forces réactionnaires; *V* **chain.**
reactionary [ri:'ækʃənrɪ] *adj, n* réactionnaire (*mf*).
reactive [ri:'æktɪv] *adj* (*Chem, Phys*) réactif.
reactor [ri:'æktər] *n* (*Chem, Elec, Phys*) réacteur *m*; *V* **nuclear.**
read¹ [ri:d] *pret, ptp* **read** [red] **1** *vt* **(a)** *book, letter etc* lire; *music, bad handwriting* déchiffrer, lire; *hieroglyphs* déchiffrer; *proofs* corriger. **I read him to sleep** je lui ai fait la lecture jusqu'à ce qu'il s'endorme; **I brought you something to ~** je vous ai apporté de la lecture; (*Jur*) **to ~ the Riot Act** ≃ faire les trois sommations; (*fig*) **he read them the riot act*** ils les a tancés vertement; (*fig*) **to ~ sb a lesson*** faire la leçon à qn, sermonner qn; (*fig*) **to take sth as read** (*as self-evident*) considérer qch comme allant de soi; (*as agreed*) considérer qch comme convenu; (*Admin*) **they took the minutes as read** ils sont passés à l'ordre du jour (sans revenir sur le procès-verbal de la dernière séance); (*in errata*) **for 'meet' ~ 'met'** au lieu de 'meet' prière de lire 'met'; (*Jur: on document*) **read and approved** lu et approuvé.
(b) (*interpret*) *dream* interpréter, expliquer; (*understand*) comprendre. **to ~ sb's hand** lire les lignes de la main de *or* à qn; **to ~ the tea leaves** *or* **the teacups** ≃ lire dans le marc de café; **these words can be read in several ways** ces mots peuvent s'interpréter de plusieurs façons; (*fig*) **to ~ between the lines** lire entre les ligne **to ~ something into a text** faire dire à un texte quelque chose qu'il ne dit pas, solliciter un texte; **to ~ sb's thoughts** lire (dans) la pensée de qn; **I can ~ him like a book** je sais *or* devine toujours ce qu'il pense; **I read disappointment in his eyes** j'ai lu la déception dans ses yeux.
(c) (*esp Univ: study*) étudier. **to ~ medicine/law** faire (des études de) médecine/droit, faire sa médecine/son droit; **he is ~ing English/geography** *etc* **at the Sorbonne** il fait de l'anglais/de la géographie *etc* à la Sorbonne.
(d) *thermometer, barometer etc* lire. **to ~ a meter** relever un compteur.
(e) *[instruments]* marquer, indiquer. **the thermometer ~s 37°** le thermomètre indique (une température de) 37° *or* marque 37°.
(f) (*Aviat, Mil etc*) recevoir. **do you ~ me?** est-ce que vous me recevez?; *V* **loud.**
2 *vi* **(a)** lire. **he can ~ and write** il sait lire et écrire; **she ~s well** elle lit bien, elle fait bien la lecture; *[learner, beginner]* elle sait bien lire; **he likes ~ing** il aime lire *or* bouquiner*, il aime la lecture; **to ~ aloud** lire à haute voix; **to ~ to oneself** lire tout bas; **do you like being read to?** aimez-vous qu'on vous fasse la lecture?; **I read about it in the paper** je l'ai lu *or* je l'ai vu dans le journal; **I've read about him** j'ai lu quelque chose à son sujet.
(b) the letter ~s thus voici ce que dit la lettre, voici comment la lettre est rédigée; **the quotation ~s as follows** voici les termes exacts de la citation; **this book ~s well/badly** ce livre se lit bien/mal; **his article ~s like an official report** le style de son article fait penser à celui d'un rapport officiel, son article a l'allure d'un rapport officiel.
(c) (*esp Univ: study*) étudier, faire des études. **to ~ for an examination** préparer un examen; *V* **bar¹.**
3 *n* (*) lecture *f*. **she enjoys a good ~** elle aime bien la lecture, elle aime bouquiner*; **to have a quiet/a little ~** lire *or* bouquiner* tranquillement/un peu.
read back *vt sep one's notes etc* relire.
read off *vt sep* **(a)** *text* (*without pause*) lire d'un trait; (*at sight*) lire à livre ouvert.
(b) *instrument readings* relever.
read on *vi* continuer à lire, poursuivre sa lecture. **'now read on'** 'et maintenant, à vous de lire'.

read out *vt sep text* lire à haute voix; *instrument readings* relever à haute voix.
read over *vt sep* relire.
read through *vt sep* (*rapidly*) parcourir; (*thoroughly*) lire en entier *or* d'un bout à l'autre.
read up *vt sep* étudier, bûcher*, potasser*. **I must read up the Revolution** il faut que j'étudie (*subj*) *or* que je potasse* (*subj*) la Révolution.
read up on *vt fus* = **read up.**
read[2] [red] **1** *pret, ptp of* **read**[1]. **2** *adj ending in cpds*: **he is well-/badly-read** il a/il n'a pas beaucoup lu.
readable ['ri:dəbl] *adj handwriting* lisible; *book* agréable *or* facile à lire. **not very ~** difficile à lire; **it's very ~** ça se lit facilement.
readdress [ˌri:ə'dres] *vt letter, parcel* réadresser.
reader ['ri:dəʳ] *n* **(a)** lecteur *m*, -trice *f*. **publisher's ~** lecteur, -trice dans une maison d'édition; **he's a great ~** il aime beaucoup lire, c'est un grand liseur; *V* **lay**[4], **proof** *etc.*
(b) (*Brit Univ*) ≃ maître *m* de conférences.
(c) (*schoolbook*) (*to teach reading*) livre *m* de lecture; (*anthology*) recueil *m* de textes. **first French ~** recueil de textes français pour première année.
readership ['ri:dəʃɪp] *n* **(a)** *[newspaper, magazine]* nombre *m* de lecteurs. **this paper has a big ~/a ~ of millions** ce journal a beaucoup de lecteurs/des millions de lecteurs.
(b) (*Brit Univ*) ≃ maîtrise *f* de conférences.
readily ['redɪlɪ] *adv* (*willingly*) volontiers, de bon cœur; (*easily*) facilement, aisément.
readiness ['redɪnɪs] *n* **(a)** (*preparedness*) **to be (kept) in ~** être (tenu) prêt (*for* à, pour). **(b)** (*willingness*) empressement *m*, bonne volonté. **his ~ to help us** son empressement à nous aider, l'empressement qu'il a montré à nous aider.
reading ['ri:dɪŋ] **1** *n* **(a)** (*U*) lecture *f*; *[proofs]* correction *f*. **she likes ~** elle aime bien lire *or* la lecture; **this book is** *or* **makes very interesting ~** ce livre est très intéressant (à lire); **I'd prefer some light ~** je préférerais un livre distrayant *or* délassant *or* d'une lecture facile.
(b) (*recital*) séance *f* de lecture; *V* **play, poetry.**
(c) (*interpretation*) interprétation *f*, explication *f*. **my ~ of the sentence** mon explication *or* interprétation de la phrase; (*Cine, Theat*) **his ~ of the part** son interprétation du rôle.
(d) (*variant*) variante *f*, leçon *f*.
(e) (*Elec, Med, Phys etc: from instrument*) **to take a ~** lire un instrument, relever les indications d'un instrument; **the ~ is ...** l'instrument indique ... .
(f) (*Parl*) *[bill]* discussion *f*, lecture *f*. **the House gave the bill its first ~** la Chambre a examiné le projet de loi en première lecture; **the third ~ of the bill was debated** le projet de loi a été discuté en troisième lecture.
(g) (*U: knowledge*) culture *f*, connaissances *fpl*. **of wide ~** instruit, cultivé.
2 *cpd*: **reading book** livre *m* de lecture; **reading desk** pupitre *m*; (*Rel*) lutrin *m*; **reading glass** loupe *f*; **reading glasses** lunettes *fpl* pour lire; **to have a reading knowledge of Spanish** savoir lire l'espagnol; **reading lamp** lampe *f* de travail *or* de bureau; **reading matter** choses *fpl* à lire, de quoi lire; **reading room** salle *f* de lecture *or* de travail.
readjust ['ri:ə'dʒʌst] **1** *vt* rajuster, réarranger, réadapter; (*correct*) rectifier; *salary* rajuster; *instrument* régler (de nouveau).
2 *vi* se réadapter (*to* à).
readjustment ['ri:ə'dʒʌstmənt] *n* réadaptation *f*; *[salary]* rajustement *m or* réajustement *m*.
ready ['redɪ] **1** *adj* **(a)** (*prepared*) *person, thing* prêt. **dinner is ~** le dîner est prêt; **'dinner's ~!'** 'à table!'; **everything is ~ for his visit** tout est prêt pour sa visite; **~ for anything** prêt à toute éventualité; **~ to use** *or* **for use** prêt à l'usage; **to be ~ to do** être prêt à faire; **to get ~ to do** se préparer *or* s'apprêter à faire; **to get (o.s.) ~** se préparer, s'apprêter; **to be ~ with an excuse** avoir une excuse toute prête *or* en réserve; **to make** *or* **get sth ~** préparer *or* apprêter qch; (*Sport*) **~, steady, go!** prêts? 1-2-3 partez!; (*Naut*) **~ about!** pare à virer!; **I'm ~ for him!** je l'attends de pied ferme!; **get ~ for it!** tenez-vous prêt!; (*before momentous news etc*) tenez-vous bien!; (*Publishing*) **'now ~'** 'vient de paraître'; (*Comm*) **we have the goods you ordered ~ to hand** nous tenons à votre disposition les marchandises que vous avez commandées; **~ money, ~ cash** (argent *m*) liquide *m*; **to pay in ~ cash** payer en espèces; **how much have you got in ~ money?** *or* **cash?** combien avez-vous en liquide?
(b) (*willing*) prêt, disposé (*to* à); (*inclined*) enclin, porté (*to* à); (*quick*) prompt (*to do* à faire); (*about to*) sur le point, près (*to do* de faire). **he is always ~ to help** il est toujours prêt à rendre service; **I am quite ~ to see him** je suis tout à fait disposé à le voir; **don't be so ~ to criticize** ne soyez pas si prompt à critiquer; **I'm ~ to believe it** je veux bien le croire, je suis prêt à le croire; **he was ~ to cry** il était sur le point de *or* près de pleurer.
(c) (*prompt*) *reply, wit* prompt. **to have a ~ tongue** avoir la langue déliée, avoir la parole facile; *[goods]* **to have a ~ sale** se vendre facilement, être de vente courante; **~ solution** solution tout indiquée.
2 *n* **(a)** (*Mil*) **to come to the ~** apprêter l'arme; **at the ~** (*Mil*) prêt à faire feu; (*Naut*) paré à faire feu; (*fig*) tout prêt.
(b) (*money*) **the ~**‡ le fric‡.
3 *adv* (*in cpds*) **ready-cooked/-furnished** tout cuit/tout meublé (d'avance).
4 *cpd*: **ready-made** *curtains* tout fait; *clothes* de confection, prêt à porter; *solution, answer* tout prêt; **ready-made ideas** des idées banales *or* toutes faites; (*Culin*) **ready-mix for cakes/pancakes** *etc* préparation *f* pour gâteaux/crêpes *etc*; **she made a ready-mix cake** elle a fait un gâteau à partir d'une préparation *or* d'un sachet; **ready reckoner** barème *m*; **ready-to-serve** prêt à servir; **ready-to-wear** prêt à porter.
reafforestation ['ri:əˌfɒrɪs'teɪʃən] *n*, (*US*) **reforestation** ['ri:fɒrɪs'teɪʃən] *n* reboisement *m*.
reagent [ri:'eɪdʒənt] *n* (*Chem*) réactif *m*.
real [rɪəl] **1** *adj* **(a)** (*as opposed to apparent*) véritable, vrai, réel; *gold, jewels* vrai, véritable; *flowers, silk* naturel; (*Philos*) réel. **in ~ life** dans la réalité, dans la vie réelle; **he is the ~ boss** c'est lui le véritable patron *or* le patron réel; **he has no ~ power** il n'a pas de pouvoir effectif; **what is the ~ reason?** quelle est la vraie *or* véritable raison?; **here in ~ terms is how inflation affects us** voici comment l'inflation nous touche dans la réalité *or* dans la pratique; **when you've tasted the ~ thing, this whisky ...** quand tu as (*or* auras) goûté du vrai whisky, celui-ci ...; **climbing this hill isn't much when you've done the ~ thing** si tu as vraiment fait de l'alpinisme, cette petite colline n'est rien du tout; **it's the ~ thing*** *or* **the ~ McCoy*** c'est de l'authentique, c'est du vrai de vrai*; (*Rel*) **R~ Presence** présence réelle.
(b) (*Jur*) **~ estate** biens fonciers *or* immeubles *or* immobiliers; (*US*) **~-estate developer** promoteur *m* (de construction); **~-estate office** agence immobilière; (*US*) **~-estate register** cadastre *m*; **~ property** propriété immobilière.
2 *adv* (‡) rudement*, vachement*. **we had a ~ good laugh** on a rudement bien ri*, on a vachement rigolé*, on s'est drôlement marré*.
3 *n* **(a) for ~*** pour de vrai*.
(b) (*Philos*) **the ~** le réel.
realism ['rɪəlɪzəm] *n* réalisme *m*.
realist ['rɪəlɪst] *adj, n* réaliste (*mf*).
realistic [rɪə'lɪstɪk] *adj* réaliste.
realistically [rɪə'lɪstɪkəlɪ] *adv* avec réalisme, d'une façon réaliste.
reality [ri:'ælɪtɪ] *n* **(a)** réalité *f*. **to bring sb back to ~** ramener qn à la réalité; **in ~** en réalité, en fait. **(b)** (*trueness to life*) réalisme *m*.
realizable ['rɪəlaɪzəbl] *adj assets, hope, plan* réalisable.
realization [ˌrɪəlaɪ'zeɪʃən] *n* **(a)** *[assets, hope, plan]* réalisation *f*. **(b)** (*awareness*) prise *f* de conscience. **the sudden ~ that ...** la découverte soudaine que ... .
realize ['rɪəlaɪz] *vt* **(a)** (*become aware of*) se rendre compte de, prendre conscience de; (*be aware of*) (bien) savoir; (*understand*) comprendre. **does he ~ the problems?** se rend-il compte des problèmes?; **the committee ~s the gravity of the situation** le comité a pris conscience de la gravité de la situation; **he had not fully ~d that she was dead** il n'avait pas (vraiment) réalisé qu'elle était morte; **I ~d it was raining** je me suis rendu compte qu'il pleuvait, j'ai réalisé* qu'il pleuvait; **I made her ~ that I was right** je lui ai bien fait comprendre que j'avais raison; **I ~ that ...** je me rends compte du fait que ...; **yes, I ~ that!** oui, je sais bien!, oui, je m'en rends bien compte!; **I ~d how he had done it** j'ai compris comment *or* je me suis rendu compte de la façon dont il l'avait fait; **I ~d why ...** j'ai compris pourquoi ...; **I ~ it's too late, but ...** je sais bien qu'il est trop tard, mais ... .
(b) *hope, plan* réaliser.
(c) (*Fin*) *assets* réaliser; *price* atteindre; *interest* rapporter. **how much did your Rembrandt ~?, how much did you ~ on your Rembrandt?** combien votre Rembrandt vous a-t-il rapporté?
really ['rɪəlɪ] **1** *adv* vraiment, réellement, véritablement. **I ~ don't know what to think** je ne sais vraiment pas quoi penser; **he ~ is an idiot** c'est un véritable imbécile, il est vraiment idiot; **you ~ MUST visit Paris** il faut absolument que vous visitiez (*subj*) Paris.
2 *excl* (*in doubt*) vraiment?, sans blague!*; (*in surprise*) c'est vrai?; (*in protest*) vraiment! **not ~!** pas vraiment!; (*in disbelief*) pas possible!
realm [relm] *n* (*liter: kingdom*) royaume *m*; (*fig*) domaine *m*; *V* **coin.**
realtor ['rɪəltɔ:ʳ] *n* (*US*) agent immobilier.
realty ['rɪəltɪ] *n* (*Jur*) biens immobiliers *or* immeubles.
ream [ri:m] *n [paper]* rame *f*. (*fig*) **he always writes ~s*** il écrit toujours des volumes *or* toute une tartine*.
reanimate [ˌri:'ænɪmeɪt] *vt* ranimer, raviver.
reanimation ['ri:ˌænɪ'meɪʃən] *n* (*Med*) réanimation *f*.
reap [ri:p] **1** *vt* (*Agr*) moissonner, faucher; (*fig*) *profit* récolter, tirer. **to ~ the fruit of one's labours** recueillir le fruit de son labeur; (*fig*) **to ~ what one has sown** récolter ce qu'on a semé; *V* **sow**[2]. **2** *vi* moissonner, faire la moisson.
reaper ['ri:pəʳ] *n* (*person*) moissonneur *m*, -euse *f*; (*machine*) moissonneuse *f*. **~ and binder** moissonneuse-lieuse *f*.
reaping ['ri:pɪŋ] **1** *n* moisson *f*. **2** *cpd*: **reaping hook** faucille *f*; **reaping machine** moissonneuse *f*.
reappear ['ri:ə'pɪəʳ] *vi* réapparaître, reparaître.
reappearance ['ri:ə'pɪərəns] *n* réapparition *f*.
reappoint ['ri:ə'pɔɪnt] *vt* renommer (*to* à).
reappointment ['ri:ə'pɔɪntmənt] *n* renouvellement *m* de nomination (*to* à).
reappraisal ['ri:ə'preɪzəl] *n [situation, problem]* réévaluation *f*, réexamen *m*; *[author, film etc]* réévaluation.
rear[1] [rɪəʳ] **1** *n* **(a)** (*back part*) arrière *m*, derrière *m*; (*: *buttocks*) derrière*. **in** *or* **at the ~** à l'arrière; **at the ~ of** derrière, à l'arrière de; **from the ~, he looks like Chaplin** (vu) de dos, il ressemble à Charlot; **from the ~ the car looks like ...** par l'arrière *or* vue de derrière la voiture ressemble à ... .
(b) (*Mil*) arrière-garde *f*, arrières *mpl*; *[squad]* dernier rang; *[column]* queue *f*. **to attack an army in the ~** attaquer une armée à revers; *V* **bring up.**
2 *adj* de derrière, arrière *inv*. **~ door** *[house]* porte *f* de derrière; (*Aut*) portière *f* arrière; (*Aut*) **~ wheel** roue *f* arrière *or* de derrière; (*Aut*) **~ window** glace *f* arrière.

3 *cpd*: **rear admiral** contre-amiral *m*; (*Aut*) **rear-engined** avec moteur *m* à l'arrière; **rear gunner** mitrailleur *m* arrière *inv*; **rear-mounted** installé à l'arrière; (*Cine*) **rear projection** projection *f* par transparence; (*Aut*) **rear-view mirror** rétroviseur *m*; (*Aut*) **rear-wheel drive** roues *fpl* arrière motrices.

rear[2] [rɪəʳ] **1** *vt* **(a)** *animals, family* élever.

(b) **to ~ one's head** relever *or* dresser la tête; **the snake ~ed its head** le serpent s'est dressé; **violence ~s its ugly head again** la violence fait sa réapparition (dans toute son horreur), on voit poindre à nouveau l'horrible violence.

(c) (*set up*) *monument* dresser, ériger.

2 *vi* (*also* ~ **up**) *[animal]* se cabrer.

rearguard ['rɪəgɑːd] *n* (*Mil*) arrière-garde *f*. ~ **action** combat *m* d'arrière-garde.

rearm [ˌriːˈɑːm] *vti* réarmer.

rearmament [ˌriːˈɑːməmənt] *n* réarmement *m*.

rearmost ['rɪəməʊst] *adj* dernier, de queue.

rearrange ['riːəˈreɪndʒ] *vt* réarranger.

rearrangement ['riːəˈreɪndʒmənt] *n* réarrangement *m*, nouvel arrangement.

rearward ['rɪəwəd] **1** *n* arrière *m*. **2** *adj part* arrière *inv*; *position* (situé) à l'arrière, de l'arrière; *movement* en arrière. **3** *adv* (*also* ~**s**) vers l'arrière, par derrière.

reason ['riːzn] **1** *n* **(a)** (*cause, justification*) *[behaviour]* raison *f*, motif *m*; *[event]* raison, cause *f*. **the ~ for my lateness/why I am late is that ...** la raison de mon retard/pour laquelle je suis en retard, c'est que ...; **my ~ for going, the ~ for my going** la raison de mon départ *or* pour laquelle je pars (*or* suis parti *etc*); **I want to know the ~ why** je veux savoir (le) pourquoi; **and that's the ~ why** et voilà pourquoi, et voilà la raison; **I have (good) ~ to believe that ...** j'ai (tout) lieu *or* j'ai de bonnes raisons de croire que ...; **there is ~ to believe that he is dead** il y a lieu de croire qu'il est mort; **for the simple ~ that ...** pour la simple *or* bonne raison que ...; **for the very ~ that ...** précisément parce que ...; **for that very ~** pour cette raison, pour cela même; **for no ~** sans raison, sans motif; **for some ~ or another** pour une raison ou pour une autre; **for ~s best known to himself** pour des raisons qu'il est seul à connaître, pour des raisons connues de lui seul; **all the more ~ for doing** *or* **to do** raison de plus pour faire; **with ~** avec (juste) raison, à juste titre; **by ~ of** en raison de, à cause de.

(b) (*U: mental faculty*) raison *f*. **to lose one's ~** perdre la raison.

(c) (*U: common sense*) raison *f*, bon sens. **he listened to ~** il s'est rendu à la raison; **he won't listen to ~** on ne peut pas lui faire entendre raison; **that stands to ~** cela va sans dire, cela va de soi; **it stands to ~ that** il va sans dire que; **I will do anything in** *or* **within ~** je ferai tout ce qu'il est raisonnablement possible de faire; *V* **rhyme.**

2 *vi* **(a)** (*think logically*) raisonner.

(b) (*argue*) **to ~ with sb** raisonner qn; **one can't ~ with her** il n'y a pas moyen de lui faire entendre raison.

3 *vt*: **to ~ sb out of his folly** ramener qn à la raison, faire renoncer qn à sa folie en le raisonnant; **to ~ sb into a sensible decision** faire prendre une décision intelligente à qn en le raisonnant; **he ~ed that we could get to Paris before noon** il a calculé que nous pourrions être à Paris avant midi.

reasonable ['riːznəbl] *adj person, attitude* raisonnable; *price* raisonnable, modéré, abordable; *offer* raisonnable, acceptable; *essay, results* acceptable, passable. (*Jur*) ~ **doubt** doute bien fondé; **there is a ~ chance that ...** il y a une bonne chance que ... + *subj*; **a ~ amount of** une certaine quantité de.

reasonableness ['riːznəblnɪs] *n* caractère *m or* nature *f* raisonnable.

reasonably ['riːznəblɪ] *adv* raisonnablement. **one can ~ think that ...** il est raisonnable de penser que ...; ~ **priced** à *or* d'un prix raisonnable.

reasoned ['riːznd] *adj* raisonné.

reasoning ['riːznɪŋ] **1** *n* raisonnement *m*, dialectique *f*. **2** *adj mind* doué de raison.

reassemble [ˌriːəˈsembl] **1** *vt people, troops* rassembler; *tool, machine* remonter. **2** *vi* se rassembler.

reassert ['riːəˈsɜːt] *vt* réaffirmer. **to ~ o.s.** s'imposer à nouveau.

reassess ['riːəˈses] *vt situation* réexaminer; (*for taxation*) *person* réviser la cote de; (*Jur*) *damages* réévaluer.

reassurance [ˌriːəˈʃʊərəns] *n* réconfort *m*.

reassure [ˌriːəˈʃʊəʳ] *vt* rassurer.

reassuring [ˌriːəˈʃʊərɪŋ] *adj* rassurant.

reassuringly [ˌriːəˈʃʊərɪŋlɪ] *adv* d'une manière rassurante.

reawaken ['riːəˈweɪkən] **1** *vt person* réveiller; *interest* réveiller, faire renaître. **2** *vi* se réveiller.

reawakening ['riːəˈweɪknɪŋ] *n* réveil *m*; *[ideas, interest]* renaissance *f*, réveil.

rebarbative [rɪˈbɑːbətɪv] *adj* rébarbatif, rebutant.

rebate ['riːbeɪt] *n* (*discount*) rabais *m*, remise *f*; (*money back*) remboursement *m*.

rebel ['rebl] **1** *n* rebelle *mf*, insurgé(e) *m(f)*, révolté(e) *m(f)*; (*fig*) rebelle. **2** *adj* rebelle. **3** [rɪˈbel] *vi* (*lit, fig*) se rebeller, se révolter, s'insurger (*against* contre).

rebellion [rɪˈbeljən] *n* rébellion *f*, révolte *f*. **to rise in ~** se rebeller, se révolter.

rebellious [rɪˈbeljəs] *adj* rebelle; (*Mil*) insubordonné; (*fig*) *child* désobéissant, indocile.

rebelliousness [rɪˈbeljəsnɪs] *n* esprit *m* de rébellion, disposition *f* à la rébellion, insubordination *f*.

rebirth ['riːˈbɜːθ] *n* renaissance *f*.

rebore ['riːˈbɔːʳ] (*Tech*) **1** *vt* réaléser. **2** *n* réalésage *m*. **this engine needs a ~** ce moteur a besoin d'être réalésé.

reborn ['riːˈbɔːn] *adj* réincarné. (*fig*) **to be ~ in** se réincarner dans.

rebound [rɪˈbaʊnd] **1** *vi [ball]* rebondir (*against* sur). (*fig*) **your violent methods will ~ (on you)** vos méthodes violentes retomberont sur vous *or* se retourneront contre vous.

2 ['riːbaʊnd] *n [ball]* rebond *m*; *[bullet]* ricochet *m*. **to hit a ball on the ~** frapper une balle après le premier rebond; (*fig*) **she was on the ~ when she married Robert*** elle était encore sous le coup d'une déception (sentimentale) quand elle a épousé Robert.

rebroadcast ['riːˈbrɔːdkɑːst] **1** *n* retransmission *f*. **2** *vt* retransmettre.

rebuff [rɪˈbʌf] **1** *n* rebuffade *f*. **to meet with a ~** essuyer une rebuffade. **2** *vt person* repousser, rabrouer; *offering, suggestion* repousser.

rebuild [ˌriːˈbɪld] *vt* rebâtir, reconstruire.

rebuilding [ˌriːˈbɪldɪŋ] *n* (*U*) reconstruction *f*.

rebuke [rɪˈbjuːk] **1** *n* reproche *m*, réprimande *f*, blâme *m*. **2** *vt* réprimander, faire des reproches à. **to ~ sb for sth** reprocher qch à qn; **to ~ sb for having done** reprocher à qn d'avoir fait.

rebus ['riːbəs] *n* rébus *m*.

rebut [rɪˈbʌt] *vt* réfuter.

rebuttal [rɪˈbʌtl] *n* réfutation *f*.

recalcitrance [rɪˈkælsɪtrəns] *n* caractère *or* esprit récalcitrant.

recalcitrant [rɪˈkælsɪtrənt] *adj* récalcitrant.

recall [rɪˈkɔːl] **1** *vt* **(a)** (*summon back*) *ambassador, library book* rappeler; (*Fin*) *capital* faire rentrer. (*fig*) **this music ~s the past** cette musique rappelle le passé; (*lit, fig*) **to ~ sb to life** rappeler qn à la vie; **to ~ Parliament** convoquer le Parlement (en session extraordinaire).

(b) (*remember*) se rappeler, se souvenir de. **I cannot ~ meeting him** *or* **whether I met him** je ne me rappelle pas l'avoir rencontré.

2 *n* rappel *m* (*also Mil*). *[library]* **this book is on ~** ce livre a été rappelé; (*fig*) **beyond** *or* **past ~** (*adj*) irrévocable; (*adv*) irrévocablement.

3 *cpd*: *[library]* **recall slip** fiche *f* de rappel.

recant [rɪˈkænt] **1** *vt statement* rétracter; *opinion* désavouer; *religious belief* abjurer. **to ~ one's opinion** se déjuger. **2** *vi* se rétracter; (*Rel*) abjurer.

recantation [ˌriːkænˈteɪʃən] *n* rétractation *f*, reniement *m*; (*Rel*) abjuration *f*.

recap[1]* ['riːkæp] **1** *n* (*abbr of* **recapitulation**) récapitulation *f*. **2** *vti* (*abbr of* **recapitulate**) **well, to ~, ...** eh bien, en résumé ... .

recap[2] ['riːkæp] (*US*) **1** *n* (*tyre*) pneu rechapé. **2** *vt* rechaper.

recapitulate [ˌriːkəˈpɪtjʊleɪt] **1** *vt argument* récapituler, faire le résumé de; *facts* reprendre. **2** *vi* récapituler, faire un résumé.

recapitulation ['riːkəˌpɪtjʊˈleɪʃən] *n* récapitulation *f*.

recapture ['riːˈkæptʃəʳ] **1** *vt animal, prisoner* reprendre, rattraper; *emotion, enthusiasm* retrouver; *[film, play, book] atmosphere, period* recréer. **2** *n [town, territory]* reprise *f*; *[escapee]* arrestation *f*.

recast ['riːˈkɑːst] **1** *vt* **(a)** (*Metal*) refondre. **(b)** *play, film* changer la distribution (des rôles) de; *actor* donner un nouveau rôle à. **(c)** (*rewrite*) refondre, remanier. **2** *n* (*Metal*) refonte *f*.

recce* ['rekɪ] (*Mil*) *abbr of* **reconnaissance, reconnoitre.**

recede [rɪˈsiːd] **1** *vi* **(a)** *[tide]* descendre; (*fig*) *[coast, person]* s'éloigner. **to ~ into the distance** s'éloigner, disparaître dans le lointain; **to ~ from an opinion** revenir sur une opinion.

(b) *[chin, forehead]* être fuyant. **his hair is receding** son front se dégarnit; **receding chin/forehead** menton/front fuyant; **receding hairline** front dégarni.

(c) *[price]* baisser.

receipt [rɪˈsiːt] **1** *n* **(a)** (*U: esp Comm*) réception *f*. **to acknowledge ~ of** accuser réception de; **on ~ of** au reçu de, dès réception de; **I am in ~ of ...** j'ai reçu ...; **to pay on ~** payer à la réception.

(b) (*paper*) (*for payment*) reçu *m*, quittance *f*, récépissé *m* (*for* de); (*for parcel, letter*) accusé *m* de réception. ~ **book** livre *m or* carnet *m* de quittances, quittancier *m*.

(c) (*Comm, Fin: money taken*) ~**s** recette(s) *f(pl)*, rentrées *fpl*.

(d) (*Culin* †) = **recipe.**

2 *vt bill* acquitter.

receivable [rɪˈsiːvəbl] *adj* recevable.

receive [rɪˈsiːv] **1** *vt* **(a)** (*get*) *letter, present* recevoir; *money, salary* recevoir, toucher; *punch* encaisser*; *refusal, setback* essuyer; (*Jur*) *stolen goods* recéler *or* receler. (*Jur*) **to ~ 2 years** *or* **2 years' imprisonment** être condamné à 2 ans de prison; **we ~d nothing but abuse** nous n'avons reçu que des insultes; (*Comm*) ~**d with thanks** pour acquit.

(b) (*welcome*) recevoir, accueillir. **to ~ sb with open arms** recevoir qn à bras ouverts; **his suggestion was well/not well ~d** sa suggestion a reçu un accueil favorable/défavorable; (*Rel*) **to be ~d into the Church** être reçu dans l'Église.

(c) (*Rad, TV*) *transmissions* capter, recevoir; *V* **loud.**

2 *vi* **(a)** recevoir. **Mrs X ~s on Mondays** Mme X reçoit le lundi.

(b) (*Jur*) être coupable de recel.

received [rɪˈsiːvd] *adj opinion* reçu, admis. (*Brit Ling*) ~ **pronunciation** prononciation *f* standard (de l'anglais).

receiver [rɪˈsiːvəʳ] *n* **(a)** receveur *m*, -euse *f*; *[letter]* destinataire *mf*; *[goods]* consignataire *mf*, réceptionnaire *mf*; *[stolen property]* receleur *m*, -euse *f*.

(b) (*Fin, Jur*) liquidateur *m*, -trice *f*. **official ~ (in bankruptcy)** administrateur *m* judiciaire (en matière de faillite).

(c) *[telephone]* récepteur *m*, combiné *m*. **to lift the ~** décrocher; **to replace the ~** raccrocher; ~ **rest** commutateur *m*.

(d) (*radio set*) (poste *m*) récepteur *m*.
receiving [rɪ'siːvɪŋ] **1** *adj* récepteur (*f* -trice), de réception. (*fig*) **to be on the ~ end* of a gift** recevoir un cadeau; **he blew his top and I was on the ~ end*** il s'est mis dans une colère noire, et c'est moi qui ai écopé* *or* qui en ai fait les frais*; (*Rad*) **~ set** poste récepteur.
2 *n [stolen goods]* recel *m*.
recension [rɪ'senʃən] *n* **(a)** (*U*) révision *f*. **(b)** (*text*) texte révisé.
recent ['riːsnt] *adj arrival, event, invention* récent; *development* nouveau (*f* nouvelle); *acquaintance etc* de fraîche date, nouveau. **in ~ years** ces dernières années.
recently ['riːsntlɪ] *adv* récemment, dernièrement. **as ~ as** pas plus tard que; **until (quite) ~** jusqu'à ces derniers temps.
receptacle [rɪ'septəkl] *n* récipient *m*; (*fig*) réceptacle *m*.
reception [rɪ'sepʃən] **1** *n* **(a)** (*U*) réception *f*.
(b) (*ceremony*) réception *f*.
(c) (*welcome*) réception *f*, accueil *m*. **to get a favourable ~** être bien accueilli *or* reçu; **to give sb a warm/chilly ~** faire un accueil chaleureux/froid à qn.
(d) (*Rad, TV*) réception *f*.
2 *cpd*: **reception centre** centre *m* d'accueil; **reception clerk** réceptionniste *mf*; **reception (desk)** (bureau *m* de) réception *f*.
receptionist [rɪ'sepʃənɪst] *n* réceptionniste *mf*.
receptive [rɪ'septɪv] *adj* réceptif (*to* à).
receptiveness [rɪ'septɪvnɪs] *n*, **receptivity** ['riːsep'tɪvɪtɪ] *n* réceptivité *f*.
recess [rɪ'ses] **1** *n* **(a)** (*cessation of business*) (*Jur*) vacances *fpl* (judiciaires); (*Parl*) vacances (parlementaires); (*US Jur*) suspension *f* d'audience; (*Scol, esp US*) récréation *f*.
(b) (*alcove*) renfoncement *m*; *[bed]* alcôve *f*; *[door, window]* embrasure *f*; *[statue]* niche *f*.
(c) (*lit: secret place*) recoin *m*; (*fig: depths*) recoin, repli *m*.
2 *vt* (*make an alcove in*) pratiquer un renfoncement dans.
3 *vi* (*US Jur, Parl*) suspendre les séances, être en vacances.
recession [rɪ'seʃən] *n* **(a)** (*U*) recul *m*, régression *f*.
(b) (*Econ*) récession *f*.
recessional [rɪ'seʃənl] (*Rel*) **1** *n* hymne *m* de sortie du clergé. **2** *adj* de sortie.
recessive [rɪ'sesɪv] *adj* rétrograde; (*Genetics*) récessif.
recharge ['riː'tʃɑːdʒ] *vt battery, gun* recharger.
recidivism [rɪ'sɪdɪvɪzəm] *n* récidive *f*.
recidivist [rɪ'sɪdɪvɪst] *adj, n* récidiviste (*mf*).
recipe ['resɪpɪ] *n* (*Culin, Pharm*) recette *f*; (*fig*) recette, secret *m* (*for* de).
recipient [rɪ'sɪpɪənt] *n [letter]* destinataire *mf*; *[cheque]* bénéficiaire *mf*; *[award, decoration]* récipiendaire *m*; (*Jur*) donataire *mf*.
reciprocal [rɪ'sɪprəkəl] **1** *adj* (*mutual*) réciproque, mutuel; (*Gram*) réciproque; (*Math*) réciproque, inverse. **2** *n* (*Math*) réciproque *f*.
reciprocally [rɪ'sɪprəkəlɪ] *adv* réciproquement, mutuellement; (*Math*) inversement.
reciprocate [rɪ'sɪprəkeɪt] **1** *vt* **(a)** *smiles, wishes* échanger; *help* donner *or* offrir en retour; *kindness* retourner.
(b) (*Tech*) donner un mouvement alternatif à.
2 *vi* **(a)** faire la même chose en retour, s'empresser d'en faire autant. **he insulted me and I ~d** il m'a injurié, et je lui ai rendu la pareille; **he called me a fool and I ~d** il m'a traité d'imbécile et je lui ai retourné le compliment.
(b) (*Tech*) avoir un mouvement alternatif *or* de va-et-vient. **reciprocating engine** moteur alternatif; **reciprocating device** dispositif *m* de va-et-vient.
reciprocation [rɪˌsɪprə'keɪʃən] *n* **(a)** *[help, kindness]* échange *m*. **(b)** (*Tech*) alternance *f*, va-et-vient *m inv*.
reciprocity [ˌresɪ'prɒsɪtɪ] *n* réciprocité *f*.
recital [rɪ'saɪtl] *n* **(a)** (*account*) récit *m*, compte rendu, narration *f*; *[details]* énumération *f*.
(b) *[poetry]* récitation *f*, récital *m*; *[music]* récital.
recitation [ˌresɪ'teɪʃən] *n* récitation *f*.
recitative [ˌresɪtə'tiːv] *n* récitatif *m*.
recite [rɪ'saɪt] **1** *vt* **(a)** *poetry* réciter, déclamer. **(b)** *facts* exposer; *details* énumérer. **2** *vi* réciter, déclamer.
reckless ['reklɪs] *adj* (*heedless*) insouciant; (*rash*) imprudent, téméraire, casse-cou* *inv*. (*Aut*) **~ driving** conduite imprudente; **~ driver** automobiliste *mf* imprudent(e).
recklessly ['reklɪslɪ] *adv* (*V* **reckless**) avec insouciance; imprudemment.
recklessness ['reklɪsnɪs] *n* (*V* **reckless**) insouciance *f*; imprudence *f*; témérité *f*.
reckon ['rekən] **1** *vt* **(a)** (*calculate*) *time, numbers, points* compter; *cost, surface* calculer.
(b) (*judge*) considérer, estimer. **I ~ him among my friends** je le compte parmi *or* au nombre de mes amis; **Mrs X is ~ed a beautiful woman** Mme X est considérée comme une femme très belle.
(c) (*) (*think*) penser, croire; (*estimate*) estimer, juger; (*suppose*) supposer, imaginer. **I ~ we can start** je pense qu'on peut commencer; **I ~ he must be about forty** j'estime qu'il a *or* je lui donnerais la quarantaine; **about thirty, I ~** une trentaine, à mon avis.
2 *vi* **(a)** calculer, compter. **~ing from tomorrow** en comptant à partir de demain, à compter de demain.
(b) (*fig*) **you can ~ on 30** tu peux compter sur 30; **I was ~ing on doing that tomorrow** j'avais prévu faire *or* je pensais faire ça demain; **I wasn't ~ing on having to do that** je ne m'attendais pas à devoir faire ça; **you'll have to ~ with 6 more** il faudra compter avec 6 de plus; **you'll have to ~ with an objection from them** il faut s'attendre à une objection de leur part; **he's a person to be ~ed with** c'est une personne avec laquelle il faut compter; **if you insult him you'll have to ~ with the whole family** si vous l'insultez, vous aurez affaire à toute la famille; **he was ~ing without his secretary** il avait compté sans sa secrétaire; **he ~ed without the fact that ...** il n'avait pas prévu que ..., il n'avait pas tenu compte du fait que ... .
reckoning ['reknɪŋ] *n* **(a)** (*Math etc*) (*evaluation*) compte *m*; (*calculation*) calcul *m*. **to be out in one's ~** s'être trompé dans ses calculs.
(b) (*Comm*) règlement *m* de compte(s) (*lit*); *[hotel]* note *f*; *[restaurant]* addition *f*. (*Rel, fig*) **the day of ~** le jour du Jugement.
(c) (*judgment*) estimation *f*. **to the best of my ~** (pour) autant que je puisse en juger; **in your ~** d'après vous, à votre avis.
(d) (*Naut*) estime *f*; *V* **dead**.
reclaim [rɪ'kleɪm] **1** *vt land* (*from forest, bush*) défricher; (*from sea*) assécher, conquérir par assèchement; (*with manure etc*) amender, bonifier; *person* amender, corriger (*from* de); (*Tech*) *by-product* récupérer; (*demand back*) réclamer (*sth from sb* qch à qn).
2 *n*: **past** *or* **beyond ~** perdu à tout jamais; **he is beyond ~** il ne se corrigera jamais.
reclaimable [rɪ'kleɪməbl] *adj land* amendable; *by-products* récupérable.
reclamation [ˌreklə'meɪʃən] *n* (*V* **reclaim**) défrichement *m*; assèchement *m*; amendement *m*; récupération *f*; réclamation *f*.
recline [rɪ'klaɪn] **1** *vt head, arm* reposer, appuyer.
2 *vi [person]* être couché, être allongé. **she was reclining in the armchair** elle s'était étendue sur le fauteuil; **reclining in his bath** étendu *or* allongé dans son bain; **the seat ~s** le dossier (du siège) est réglable.
reclining [rɪ'klaɪnɪŋ] *adj*: **~ chair** chaise longue; *[coach, plane]* **~ seat** siège *m* à dossier réglable.
recluse [rɪ'kluːs] *n* reclus(e) *m(f)*, ermite *m*.
recognition [ˌrekəg'nɪʃən] *n* **(a)** (*gen, Pol: acknowledgement*) reconnaissance *f*. **in ~ of** en reconnaissance de; **his exploits have gained world-wide ~** ses exploits ont été reconnus dans le monde entier; **to receive no ~** passer inaperçu.
(b) (*identification*) reconnaissance *f*; (*Aviat*) identification *f*. **he has changed beyond** *or* **out of all ~** il est devenu méconnaissable; **he has changed it beyond** *or* **out of all ~** il l'a rendu méconnaissable; **to improve beyond** *or* **out of (all) ~** s'améliorer jusqu'à en être méconnaissable.
recognizable ['rekəgnaɪzəbl] *adj* reconnaissable.
recognizance [rɪ'kɒgnɪzəns] *n* (*Jur*) engagement *m*; (*sum of money*) caution *f* (personnelle). **to enter into ~s (for sb)** donner *or* fournir *or* se porter caution (pour qn); **bail in his own ~ of £100** mise en liberté (provisoire) sous caution personnelle de 100 livres.
recognize ['rekəgnaɪz] *vt* (*all senses*) reconnaître (*by* à, *as* comme étant, *that* que).
recognized ['rekəgnaɪzd] *adj* **(a)** reconnu, admis, reçu. **a ~ fact** un fait reconnu *or* indiscuté. **(b)** (*Comm*) attitré.
recoil [rɪ'kɔɪl] **1** *vi* **(a)** *[person]* reculer, avoir un mouvement de recul (*from* devant). **to ~ in disgust** reculer de dégoût; **to ~ from doing** reculer devant l'idée de faire, se refuser à faire.
(b) *[gun]* reculer; *[spring]* se détendre; (*fig*) *[actions etc]* retomber (*on* sur).
2 *n [gun]* recul *m*; *[spring]* détente *f*; (*fig*) dégoût *m* (*from* pour, de), horreur *f* (*from* de), répugnance *f* (*from* pour).
recollect [ˌrekə'lekt] **1** *vt* se rappeler, se souvenir de. **to ~ o.s.** se recueillir. **2** *vi* se souvenir. **as far as I ~** autant que je m'en souvienne.
recollection [ˌrekə'lekʃən] *n* souvenir *m*. **to the best of my ~, within my ~** autant que je m'en souvienne; **his ~ of it is vague** il ne s'en souvient que vaguement; **I have some ~ of it** j'en ai un vague souvenir; **I have no ~ of it** je ne m'en souviens pas, je n'en ai aucun souvenir.
recommence ['riːkə'mens] *vti* recommencer (*doing* à faire).
recommend [ˌrekə'mend] *vt* **(a)** (*speak good of*) recommander. **to ~ sb for a job** recommander qn pour un emploi, appuyer la candidature de qn; **it is to be ~ed** c'est à conseiller; **it is not to be ~ed** c'est à déconseiller.
(b) (*advise*) recommander, conseiller (*sb to do* à qn de faire). **what do you ~ for curing a cough?** que recommandez-vous pour guérir une toux?; **he was ~ed to accept** on lui a recommandé *or* conseillé d'accepter.
(c) (*make acceptable*) prévenir en faveur de, rendre acceptable. **she has a lot to ~ her** elle a beaucoup de qualités en sa faveur, il y a beaucoup à dire en sa faveur; **she has little to ~ her** elle n'a pas grand-chose pour elle.
(d) (*commit*) *child, one's soul* recommander, confier (*to* à).
recommendable [ˌrekə'mendəbl] *adj* recommandable. **it is not ~** c'est à déconseiller.
recommendation [ˌrekəmen'deɪʃən] *n* recommandation *f*. **on the ~ of** sur la recommandation de.
recommendatory [ˌrekə'mendətərɪ] *adj* de recommandation.
recompense ['rekəmpens] **1** *n* **(a)** (*reward*) récompense *f*. **in ~ for** en récompense de.
(b) (*Jur: for damage*) dédommagement *m*, compensation *f*.
2 *vt* **(a)** (*reward*) récompenser (*for* de).
(b) (*Jur etc: repay*) *person* dédommager; *damage, loss* compenser, réparer.
recompose [ˌriːkəm'pəʊz] *vt* **(a)** (*rewrite*) recomposer. **(b)** (*calm*) **to ~ o.s.** se ressaisir, retrouver son calme *or* son sang-froid.
reconcilable ['rekənsaɪləbl] *adj ideas, opinions* conciliable, compatible (*with* avec).
reconcile ['rekənsaɪl] *vt person* réconcilier (*to* avec); *argument, dispute* arranger; *two facts or ideas* concilier, accorder (*with* avec, *and* et). **they became ~d** ils se sont réconciliés; **to ~**

o.s. to sth se résigner à qch, se faire à qch; what ~d him to it was ... ce qui le lui a fait accepter, c'était ... .
reconciliation [ˌrekənsɪlɪ'eɪʃən] n [persons] réconciliation f; [opinions, principles] conciliation f.
recondite [rɪ'kɒndaɪt] adj abstrus, obscur.
recondition ['riːkən'dɪʃən] vt remettre à neuf or en état, rénover; machine réviser. (Aut) ~ed engine moteur remis à neuf or révisé.
reconnaissance [rɪ'kɒnɪsəns] n (Aviat, Mil) reconnaissance f. ~ flight/patrol vol m/patrouille f de reconnaissance.
reconnoitre, (US) reconnoiter [ˌrekə'nɔɪtəʳ] (Aviat, Mil) 1 vt region reconnaître. 2 vi faire une reconnaissance.
reconquer [ˌriː'kɒŋkəʳ] vt reconquérir.
reconquest [ˌriː'kɒŋkwest] n reconquête f.
reconsider ['riːkən'sɪdəʳ] vt decision, opinion reconsidérer, remettre en cause, réexaminer; judgment réviser. won't you ~ it? est-ce que vous seriez prêt à reconsidérer la question?
reconsideration ['riːkənˌsɪdə'reɪʃən] n remise f en cause, nouvel examen.
reconstitute [ˌriː'kɒnstɪtjuːt] vt reconstituer.
reconstitution ['riːˌkɒnstɪ'tjuːʃən] n reconstitution f.
reconstruct ['riːkən'strʌkt] vt building reconstruire, rebâtir; crime reconstituer.
reconstruction ['riːkən'strʌkʃən] n [building] reconstruction f, réfection f; [crime] reconstitution f.
record [rɪ'kɔːd] 1 vt (a) (register) facts, story enregistrer; protest, disapproval prendre acte de; event etc (in journal, log) noter; (describe) décrire. to ~ the proceedings of a meeting tenir le procès-verbal d'une assemblée; (Parl) to ~ one's vote voter; his speech as ~ed in the newspapers ... son discours, tel que le rapportent les journaux ...; history/the author ~s that ... l'histoire/l'auteur rapporte que ...; it's not ~ed anywhere ce n'est pas attesté; to ~ the population recenser la population.
(b) [thermometer etc] enregistrer, marquer.
(c) speech, music enregistrer. to ~ on tape enregistrer sur bande; V tape.
2 vi enregistrer. he is ~ing at 5 o'clock il enregistre à 5 heures; his voice does not ~ well sa voix ne se prête pas bien à l'enregistrement.
3 ['rekɔːd] n (a) (account, report) rapport m, récit m; (of attendance) registre m; (of act, decision) minute f; (of evidence, meeting) procès-verbal m; (official report) rapport officiel; (Jur) enregistrement m; (historical report) document m. the society's ~s les actes mpl de la société; (public) ~s archives fpl, annales fpl; to make or keep a ~ of noter, consigner; (fig) it is on ~ that ... c'est un fait établi or il est établi que ...; there is no similar example on ~ aucun exemple semblable n'est attesté; to go on ~ as saying that ... déclarer publiquement que ...; to put on ~ consigner, mentionner (par écrit); there is no ~ of his having said it il n'est noté or consigné nulle part qu'il l'ait dit; there is no ~ of it in history l'histoire n'en fait pas mention; to put or set the ~ straight mettre les choses au clair, dissiper toute confusion possible; just to set the ~ straight, let me point out that ... pour qu'il n'y ait aucune confusion possible, disons bien que ...; this is strictly off the ~* ceci est à titre (purement) confidentiel or officieux; the interview was off the ~* l'interview n'était pas officielle; off the ~*, he did come! entre nous, il est venu!; (fig) this statue is a ~ of a past civilization cette statue est la marque d'une civilisation passée.
(b) (case history) dossier m; (card) fiche f. (Mil) service ~ états mpl de service; (Jur) (police) ~ casier m judiciaire; ~ of previous convictions dossier du prévenu; (Jur, Police) he's got a clean ~, he hasn't got a ~* il a un casier (judiciaire) vierge; France's splendid ~ les succès glorieux de la France; his past ~ sa conduite passée; (Scol) his attendance ~ is bad il a été souvent absent; to have a good ~ at school avoir un bon dossier scolaire; this airline has a good safety ~ cette compagnie aérienne a une bonne tradition de sécurité; he left a splendid ~ of achievements il avait à son compte de magnifiques réussites.
(c) (recording) [voice etc] enregistrement m; (also gramophone ~) disque m. to make or cut a ~ graver un disque.
(d) (Sport, fig) record m. to beat or break the ~ battre le record; to hold the ~ détenir le record; long-jump ~ record du saut en longueur; V world etc.
(e) [seismograph etc] courbe enregistrée.
4 cpd amount, attendance, result record inv. (Mus) record album album m de disques; (Sport) record breaker personne f (or performance f) qui bat le(s) record(s); (Sport, fig) record-breaking qui bat tous les records; record cabinet casier m à disques, discothèque f; record card fiche f; record changer changeur m de disques automatique; record dealer disquaire mf; (Sport) record holder détenteur m, -trice f du record; record library discothèque f (collection); record player tourne-disque m, électrophone m; (Rad) record programme programme m de disques; to do sth in record time faire qch en un temps record; record token bon-cadeau m (négociable contre un disque), chèque-disque m.
recorded [rɪ'kɔːdɪd] adj (a) music enregistré; (Rad, TV) programme enregistré à l'avance, transmis en différé. (Brit Post) to send by ~ delivery ≃ envoyer en recommandé or avec avis de réception. (b) fact, occurrence attesté, noté.
recorder [rɪ'kɔːdəʳ] n (a) [official facts] archiviste mf; (registrar) greffier m.
(b) (Brit Jur) ≃ avocat nommé à la fonction de juge; (US Jur) ≃ juge suppléant.
(c) [sounds] (apparatus) appareil enregistreur; (person) artiste mf qui enregistre; V tape.
(d) (Mus) flûte f à bec.
recording [rɪ'kɔːdɪŋ] 1 n [sound, facts] enregistrement m. (Rad, TV) 'this programme is a ~' 'ce programme est enregistré'.
2 adj (a) (Admin etc) official chargé du recensement. (Rel) the R~ Angel l'ange qui tient le grand livre des bienfaits et des méfaits.
(b) artist qui enregistre; apparatus enregistreur. (Mus) ~ session séance f d'enregistrement; (Mus) ~ studio studio m d'enregistrement; ~ tape bande f or ruban m magnétique; (Rad, TV) ~ van car m de reportage.
recount [rɪ'kaʊnt] vt (relate) raconter, narrer.
re-count [ˌriː'kaʊnt] 1 vt recompter, compter de nouveau. 2 ['riːkaʊnt] n [votes] pointage m.
recoup [rɪ'kuːp] 1 vt (a) (make good) losses récupérer. (b) (reimburse) dédommager (for de). to ~ o.s. se dédommager, se rattraper. (c) (Jur) déduire, défalquer. 2 vi récupérer ses pertes.
recourse [rɪ'kɔːs] n recours m (to à). to have ~ to avoir recours à, recourir à.
recover [rɪ'kʌvəʳ] 1 vt sth lost, one's appetite, reason, balance retrouver; sth lent reprendre (from sb à qn), récupérer; lost territory regagner, reconquérir; sth floating repêcher; space capsule, wreck récupérer; (Ind etc) materials récupérer; (Fin) debt recouvrer, récupérer; goods, property rentrer en possession de. to ~ one's breath reprendre haleine or sa respiration; [invalid] to ~ one's strength reprendre des forces; to ~ consciousness revenir à soi, reprendre connaissance; to ~ one's sight/health retrouver or recouvrer la vue/la santé; to ~ land from the sea conquérir du terrain sur la mer; (fig) to ~ lost ground se rattraper; to ~ o.s. or one's composure se ressaisir, se reprendre; (Med) to be quite ~ed être tout à fait rétabli; to ~ expenses rentrer dans ses frais, récupérer ses débours; to ~ one's losses réparer ses pertes; (Jur) to ~ damages obtenir des dommages-intérêts.
2 vi (a) (after shock, accident etc) se remettre (from de); (from illness) guérir, se rétablir (from de); (regain consciousness) revenir à soi, reprendre connaissance; [the economy, the dollar] se rétablir, se redresser; [stock market] reprendre; [shares] remonter. she has completely ~ed elle est tout à fait rétablie.
(b) (Jur) obtenir gain de cause. right to ~ droit m de reprise.
re-cover [ˌriː'kʌvəʳ] vt couvrir de nouveau, recouvrir; chair, umbrella recouvrir.
recoverable [rɪ'kʌvərəbl] adj (Fin) récupérable, recouvrable; losses réparable.
recovery [rɪ'kʌvərɪ] n (a) (V recover 1) récupération f; recouvrement m; reconquête f; (Jur: of damages) obtention f.
(b) (V recover 2a) guérison f; rétablissement m; redressement m; reprise f; remontée f. to be on the way to ~ être en voie de guérison; he is making a good ~ il est en bonne voie de guérison; past ~ sick person dans un état désespéré; situation sans remède, irrémédiable; (Sport) to make a ~ se ressaisir.
recreant ['rekrɪənt] adj, n (liter) lâche (m), traître(sse) m(f).
recreate ['riːkrɪ'eɪt] vt recréer.
recreation [ˌrekrɪ'eɪʃən] 1 n (a) (U) récréation f, détente f, délassement m. for ~ I go fishing je vais à la pêche pour me détendre. (b) (Scol) récréation f, récré* f. 2 cpd: recreation ground terrain m de jeux; recreation room salle f de récréation.
recreational [ˌrekrɪ'eɪʃənəl] adj facilities de récréation.
recreative ['rekrɪˌeɪtɪv] adj récréatif, divertissant.
recriminate [rɪ'krɪmɪneɪt] vi récriminer (against contre).
recrimination [rɪˌkrɪmɪ'neɪʃən] n récrimination f.
recrudesce [ˌriːkruː'des] vi être en recrudescence.
recrudescence [ˌriːkruː'desns] n recrudescence f.
recrudescent [ˌriːkruː'desnt] adj recrudescent.
recruit [rɪ'kruːt] 1 n (Mil, fig) recrue f. the party gained ~s from the middle classes le parti faisait des recrues dans la bourgeoisie; V raw etc.
2 vt member, soldier, staff recruter. the party was ~ed from the middle classes le parti se recrutait dans la bourgeoisie; he ~ed me to help il m'a embauché* pour aider.
recruiting [rɪ'kruːtɪŋ] 1 n recrutement m. 2 cpd: (Mil) recruiting office bureau m de recrutement; recruiting officer recruteur m.
recruitment [rɪ'kruːtmənt] n recrutement m.
rectal ['rektəl] adj rectal.
rectangle ['rekˌtæŋgl] n rectangle m.
rectangular [rek'tæŋgjʊləʳ] adj rectangulaire.
rectifiable ['rektɪfaɪəbl] adj rectifiable.
rectification [ˌrektɪfɪ'keɪʃən] n (Chem, Math, gen) rectification f; (Elec) redressement m.
rectifier ['rektɪfaɪəʳ] n (Elec) redresseur m.
rectify ['rektɪfaɪ] vt (a) error rectifier, corriger. to ~ an omission réparer une négligence or un oubli. (b) (Chem, Math) rectifier. (c) (Elec) redresser.
rectilineal [ˌrektɪ'lɪnɪəl] adj, **rectilinear** [ˌrektɪ'lɪnɪəʳ] adj rectiligne.
rectitude ['rektɪtjuːd] n rectitude f.
rector ['rektəʳ] n (a) (Rel) pasteur m (anglican). (b) (Scot) (Scol) proviseur m (de lycée); (Univ) président élu d'une université.
rectory ['rektərɪ] n presbytère m (anglican).
rectum ['rektəm] n rectum m.
recumbent [rɪ'kʌmbənt] adj couché, étendu. (Art) ~ figure gisant m.
recuperate [rɪ'kuːpəreɪt] 1 vi se rétablir, se remettre, récupérer. 2 vt object récupérer; losses réparer.
recuperation [rɪˌkuːpə'reɪʃən] n (Med) rétablissement m; [materials etc] récupération f.
recuperative [rɪ'kuːpərətɪv] adj régénérateur (f -trice). he has

amazing ~ **powers** il a des pouvoirs étonnants de récupération, il récupère à une vitesse étonnante.

recur [rɪˈkɜːʳ] *vi* **(a)** (*happen again*) *[error, event]* se reproduire; *[idea, theme]* se retrouver, revenir; *[illness, infection]* réapparaître; *[opportunity, problem]* se représenter.
(b) (*come to mind again*) revenir à la mémoire (*to sb* de qn).
(c) (*Math*) se reproduire périodiquement.

recurrence [rɪˈkʌrəns] *n [error, event, idea, theme]* répétition *f*; *[headaches, symptoms]* réapparition *f*; *[opportunity, problem]* réapparition, retour *m*. **a ~ of the illness** un nouvel accès de la maladie, une rechute; **let there be no ~ of this** que ceci ne se reproduise plus.

recurrent [rɪˈkʌrənt] *adj* **(a)** fréquent, périodique, qui revient souvent. (*Comm*) **~ expenses** frais généraux. **(b)** (*Anat*) récurrent.

recurring [rɪˈkɜːrɪŋ] *adj* (*Math*) périodique. **~ decimal** fraction *f* périodique.

recusant [ˈrekjʊzənt] *adj* réfractaire.

recycle [ˌriːˈsaɪkl] *vt* recycler, récupérer.

red [red] **1** *adj* (*in colour*) rouge; *hair* roux (*f* rousse); *lips* vermeil; (*Pol*) rouge. **~ with anger** rouge de colère; **~ as a beetroot** rouge comme une pivoine *or* un coquelicot *or* une tomate; (*lit*) **he was rather ~ in the face** il était rougeaud, il avait le teint rouge; (*fig*) **was I ~ in the face!*, was my face ~!*, did I have a ~ face!*** j'étais rouge de confusion, j'étais très embarrassé; **to go** *or* **turn ~** rougir; **to see ~** voir rouge, se fâcher tout rouge; **it's like a ~ rag to a bull** c'est comme le rouge pour les taureaux; **that is like a ~ rag to him** il voit rouge quand on lui parle de cela (*or* quand on lui montre cela *etc*); (*fig*) **to roll out the ~ carpet for sb** recevoir qn en grande pompe, se mettre en frais pour recevoir qn; **~ hat** chapeau *m* de cardinal; **~ light** (*lit*) feu *m* rouge; (*fig*) signe *m* de danger; **to see the ~ light*** se rendre compte du danger; (*Aut*) **to go through the ~ light** passer au rouge, brûler un feu rouge; *V also* **3**, *and* **paint** *etc.*
2 *n* (*colour*) rouge *m*; (*Pol: person*) rouge *mf*, communiste *mf*; (*Billiards*) bille *f* rouge; (*Roulette*) rouge *m*. (*fig*) **to be in the ~*** *[individual]* être à découvert; *[company]* être en déficit; **to get out of the ~** ne plus être à découvert, combler le déficit; **to be £100 in the ~** avoir un découvert *or* un déficit de 100 livres.
3 *cpd*: **red admiral (butterfly)** vulcain *m*; **the Red Army** l'Armée *f* rouge; **red-blooded** vigoureux; **redbreast** rouge-gorge *m*; (*Brit*) **red-brick university** université *f* de l'ère industrielle; **red cap** (*Brit Mil**) policier *m* militaire; (*US*) porteur *m*; (*Brit Hist*) **redcoat** soldat anglais; **Red Crescent** Croissant *m* Rouge; **Red Cross** Croix-Rouge *f*; **red currant** groseille *f* (rouge); **red deer** cerf commun; (*Naut*) **red duster*** = **red ensign**; (*Naut*) **red ensign** pavillon *m* de la marine marchande (britannique); **red-eyed** aux yeux rouges; **red-faced** (*lit*) rougeaud, rubicond; (*fig*) gêné, rouge de confusion; **Red Flag** drapeau *m* rouge; **red grouse** grouse *f*, lagopède *m* rouge d'Écosse; **to be caught red-handed** être pris en flagrant délit *or* la main dans le sac; **red-haired, red-headed** roux (*f* rousse); **redhead** roux *m*, rousse *f*, rouquin(e) *m(f)*; **to raise iron to red heat** chauffer le fer au rouge; (*lit*) **red herring** hareng saur; (*fig*) **that's a red herring** c'est pour brouiller les pistes, c'est une diversion; **red-hot** (*lit*) chauffé au rouge, brûlant; (*fig: enthusiastic*) ardent, enthousiaste; **Red Indian** peau-rouge *mf*; **red lead** minium *m*; **red-letter day** jour *m* mémorable, jour à marquer d'une pierre blanche; **red light** *V* **1**; **red-light district** quartier réservé (*où sont les maisons de prostitution*); **red pepper** poivron *m* rouge; **(Little) Red Riding Hood** le Petit Chaperon Rouge; (*Geog*) **Red Sea** mer *f* Rouge; **redskin** peau-rouge *mf*; (*Orn*) **redstart** rouge-queue *m*; **red tape** paperasserie *f*, bureaucratie tatillonne, chinoiseries administratives; (*Orn*) **redwing** mauvis *m*; (*Bot*) **redwood** séquoia *m*.

redact [rɪˈdækt] *vt* (*draw up*) rédiger; (*edit*) éditer.

redaction [rɪˈdækʃən] *n* (*V* **redact**) rédaction *f*; édition *f*.

redden [ˈredn] **1** *vt* rendre rouge, rougir. **2** *vi [person]* rougir; *[foliage]* roussir, devenir roux.

reddish [ˈredɪʃ] *adj* rougeâtre. **~ hair** cheveux qui tirent vers *or* sur le roux.

redecorate [ˌriːˈdekəreɪt] **1** *vt room, house* refaire, repeindre, retapisser. **2** *vi* refaire les peintures *or* les papiers peints.

redecoration [riːˌdekəˈreɪʃən] *n* remise *f* à neuf des peintures, remplacement *m* des papiers peints.

redeem [rɪˈdiːm] *vt* (*buy back*) racheter; (*from pawn*) dégager; (*Fin*) *debt* amortir, rembourser; *bill* honorer; *mortgage* purger; (*US*) *banknote* convertir en espèces; *promise* tenir; *obligation* s'acquitter de, satisfaire à; (*Rel*) *sinner* racheter, rédimer, sauver; (*compensate for*) *failing* racheter, compenser; *fault* réparer. **to ~ o.s.** *or* **one's honour** se racheter.

redeemable [rɪˈdiːməbl] *adj* rachetable; *debt* amortissable; *bill* remboursable; *mortgage* remboursable, amortissable; (*from pawn*) qui peut être dégagé.

Redeemer [rɪˈdiːməʳ] *n* (*Rel*) Rédempteur *m*.

redeeming [rɪˈdiːmɪŋ] *adj* rédempteur (*f* -trice); *quality* qui rachète les défauts. **it's a bad newspaper and its only ~ feature is that it is politically unbiased** c'est un mauvais journal qui ne se rachète que par son objectivité en politique *or* dont le seul bon côté est son objectivité en politique.

redemption [rɪˈdempʃən] *n* (*V* **redeem**) rachat *m*; dégagement *m*; amortissement *m*; remboursement *m*; purge *f*; (*Rel*) rédemption *f*. (*fig*) **beyond** *or* **past ~** *object* irréparable; *situation* irrémédiable; *person* qui ne peut plus être sauvé.

redemptive [rɪˈdemptɪv] *adj* rédempteur (*f* -trice).

redeploy [ˈriːdɪˈplɔɪ] *vt troops* redéployer; *workers, staff* réorganiser (de façon plus rationnelle).

redeployment [ˈriːdɪˈplɔɪmənt] *n* (*V* **redeploy**) redéploiement *m*, réorganisation *f*.

redirect [ˌriːdaɪˈrekt] *vt letter, parcel* faire suivre.

rediscover [ˈriːdɪsˈkʌvəʳ] *vt* redécouvrir.

redistribute [ˈriːdɪsˈtrɪbjuːt] *vt* redistribuer.

redness [ˈrednɪs] *n* rougeur *f*; *[hair]* rousseur *f*.

redo [ˈriːˈduː] *vt* refaire.

redolence [ˈredəʊləns] *n* parfum *m*, odeur *f* agréable.

redolent [ˈredəʊlənt] *adj* odorant, parfumé. **~ of lavender** qui sent la lavande; (*fig*) **~ of** qui évoque *or* suggère, évocateur (*f* -trice) de.

redouble [riːˈdʌbl] **1** *vt* **(a)** redoubler. **to ~ one's efforts** redoubler ses efforts *or* d'efforts. **(b)** (*Bridge*) surcontrer. **2** *vi* redoubler. **3** *n* (*Bridge*) surcontre *m*.

redoubt [rɪˈdaʊt] *n* (*Mil*) redoute *f*.

redoubtable [rɪˈdaʊtəbl] *adj* redoutable, formidable.

redound [rɪˈdaʊnd] *vi* contribuer (*to* à). **to ~ upon** retomber sur; **to ~ to sb's credit** être (tout) à l'honneur de qn.

redraft [ˌriːˈdrɑːft] *vt* rédiger de nouveau.

redress [rɪˈdres] **1** *vt wrong, errors* redresser, réparer; *situation* redresser. **to ~ the balance** redresser *or* rétablir l'équilibre; **to ~ a grievance** réparer un tort.
2 *n* (*V* **1**) redressement *m*, réparation *f*. **to seek ~ for** demander réparation de; **you have no ~** vous ne pouvez pas obtenir réparation.

reduce [rɪˈdjuːs] **1** *vt* **(a)** (*lessen*) réduire, diminuer; (*shorten*) raccourcir; (*weaken*) affaiblir; (*lower*) abaisser, ravaler; *drawing, plan* réduire; *expenses* réduire, restreindre; *price* baisser, diminuer; (*Med*) *swelling* résorber, résoudre; *temperature* faire descendre, abaisser; (*Culin*) *sauce* faire réduire; (*Ind*) *output* ralentir; (*Mil etc: in rank*) rétrograder, réduire à un grade inférieur. (*Mil*) **to ~ to the ranks** casser; (*Aut*) **to ~ speed** diminuer la vitesse, ralentir; **'~ speed now'** 'ralentir'; (*Jur*) **to ~ a prisoner's sentence** réduire la peine d'un prisonnier.
(b) (*Chem, Math, fig*) réduire (*to* en, à). **to ~ sth to a powder/to pieces/to ashes** réduire qch en poudre/ en morceaux/en cendres; **to ~ an argument to its simplest form** réduire un raisonnement à sa plus simple expression, simplifier un raisonnement au maximum; **it has been ~d to nothing** cela a été réduit à zéro; **he's ~d to a skeleton** il n'est plus qu'un squelette ambulant; **to ~ sb to silence/obedience/despair** réduire qn au silence/à l'obéissance/au désespoir; **to ~ sb to begging/to slavery** réduire qn à la mendicité/en esclavage; **to be ~d to begging** être réduit *or* contraint à mendier; **to ~ sb to submission** soumettre qn; **to ~ sb to tears** faire pleurer qn.
2 *vi* (*slim*) maigrir. **to be reducing** être au régime.

reduced [rɪˈdjuːst] *adj* réduit. **to buy at a ~ price** *rail, theatre ticket* acheter à prix réduit; *goods in shops* acheter au rabais *or* en solde; (*Comm*) **~ goods** soldes *mpl*; **on a ~ scale** à échelle réduite; (*fig*) sur une petite échelle, en petit; **in ~ circumstances** dans la gêne.

reducer [rɪˈdjuːsəʳ] *n* (*slimming device*) appareil *m* d'amaigrissement; (*Phot*) réducteur *m*.

reducible [rɪˈdjuːsəbl] *adj* réductible.

reduction [rɪˈdʌkʃən] *n* (*gen, Chem, Math etc*) réduction *f*; (*in length*) raccourcissement *m*; (*in width*) diminution *f*; *[expenses, staff]* réduction, compression *f*; *[prices, wages]* diminution, réduction, baisse *f*; *[temperature]* baisse; (*Elec: of voltage*) diminution; (*Jur: of sentence*) réduction, modération *f*; (*Med: of swelling*) résorption *f*, résolution *f*; (*Phot*) réduction *f*; (*Tech*) démultiplication *f*. (*Comm*) **to make a ~ on an article** faire une remise sur un article; (*Comm*) **this is a ~** c'est un rabais; **to sell sth at a ~** vendre qch au rabais; **~ for cash** escompte *m* au comptant; **~ of taxes** dégrèvement *m* d'impôts; **~ of speed** ralentissement *m*; (*Mil etc*) **~ in strength** réduction *or* diminution des effectifs; **~ in rank** rétrogradation *f*.

redundance [rɪˈdʌndəns], **redundancy** [rɪˈdʌndənsɪ] **1** *n* excès *m*, superfluité *f*, surabondance *f*; (*Literat*) redondance *f*, pléonasme *m*, tautologie *f*; (*Ind*) licenciement *m*, mise *f* en chômage (pour raisons économiques). **the depression caused a lot of ~** *or* **many redundancies** la dépression a causé de nombreux licenciements, la dépression a causé la mise en chômage de nombreux employés; **he feared ~** il craignait d'être licencié *or* mis en chômage.
2 *cpd*: (*Brit Ind*) **redundancy payment** prime *f* *or* indemnité *f* de licenciement.

redundant [rɪˈdʌndənt] *adj object, example, detail* superflu; *style, word* redondant; *person, helper, worker* en surnombre; (*Ind: out of work*) au chômage, qui a été licencié (pour raisons économiques). (*Ind*) **to be made ~, to become ~** être licencié, être mis en chômage; **he found himself ~** il s'est retrouvé au chômage.

reduplicate [rɪˈdjuːplɪkeɪt] **1** *vt* redoubler; (*Ling*) rédupliquer. **2** [rɪˈdjuːplɪkɪt] *adj* redoublé; rédupliqué.

reduplication [rɪˌdjuːplɪˈkeɪʃən] *n* redoublement *m*; (*Ling*) réduplication *f*.

reduplicative [rɪˈdjuːplɪkətɪv] *adj* (*Ling*) réduplicatif.

re-echo [ˈriːˈekəʊ] **1** *vi* retentir, résonner (de nouveau *or* plusieurs fois). **2** *vt* répéter, renvoyer en écho.

reed [riːd] **1** *n* (*Bot*) roseau *m*; *[wind instrument]* anche *f*; (*liter: pipe*) chalumeau *m*, pipeau *m*. (*Mus*) **the ~s** les instruments *mpl* à anche; *V* **broken**.
2 *cpd basket etc* de *or* en roseau(x). (*Orn*) **reed bunting** bruant *m* des roseaux; (*Mus*) **reed instrument** instrument *m* à anche; (*Mus*) **reed stop** jeu *m* d'anches *or* à anches.

re-educate [ˌriːˈedjʊkeɪt] *vt* rééduquer.

re-education [ˈriːˌedjʊˈkeɪʃən] *n* rééducation *f*.

reedy [ˈriːdɪ] *adj field, area* couvert de roseaux; (*fig*) *instrument, sound* nasillard, aigu (*f* -guë); *voice* flûté, ténu.

reef[1] [riːf] *n* **(a)** récif *m*, écueil *m*; (*fig*) écueil. **coral ~** récif de corail.
(b) (*Min*) reef *m*, veine *f*, filon *m*.

reef² [riːf] **1** *n* (*Naut*) ris *m*. **2** *vt* (*Naut*) *sail* prendre un ris dans. **3** *cpd*: **reef knot** nœud plat.

reefer [ˈriːfəʳ] *n* **(a)** (*jacket*) caban *m*. **(b)** (*:*) joint*: *m*, cigarette *f* de marijuana.

reek [riːk] **1** *n* puanteur *f*, relent *m*. **2** *vi* **(a)** (*smell*) puer, empester, sentir mauvais. **to ~ of sth** puer *or* empester qch. **(b)** (*Scot*) *[chimney]* fumer.

reel [riːl] **1** *n* **(a)** *[thread etc]* bobine *f*; (*Fishing*) moulinet *m*; (*Cine*) *[film]* bande *f*; (*Tech*) dévidoir *m*, touret *m*, bobine. (*US fig*) **off the ~*** tout d'un trait, sans s'arrêter; *V* **inertia**.
(b) (*dance*) reel *m* (*danse écossaise*).
2 *cpd*: **reel holder** porte-bobines *m inv*.
3 *vt* (*Tech*) *thread* bobiner.
4 *vi* chanceler, vaciller; *[drunken man]* tituber. **he ~ed back from the edge of the cliff** il s'est écarté en chancelant du bord de la falaise; **he went ~ing down the street** il a descendu la rue en vacillant *or* titubant; **the blow made him ~** le coup l'a fait chanceler, il a chancelé sous le coup; (*fig*) **the street ~ed before her eyes** la rue a vacillé *or* chaviré autour d'elle; (*fig*) **my head is ~ing** la tête me tourne; (*fig*) **the news made him** *or* **his mind ~** la nouvelle l'a ébranlé *or* bouleversé; (*fig*) **I ~ed at the very thought** cette pensée m'a donné le vertige.

reel in *vt sep* (*Fishing, Naut*) ramener, remonter.

reel off *vt sep verses, list* débiter; *thread* dévider.

reel up *vt sep* enrouler; *fishing line* enrouler, ramener.

re-embark [ˈriːɪmˈbɑːk] *vti* rembarquer.

re-embarkation [ˈriːˌembɑːˈkeɪʃən] *n* rembarquement *m*.

re-emerge [ˈriːɪˈmɜːdʒ] *vi* *[object, swimmer]* ressurgir; *[facts]* ressortir.

re-enact [ˈriːɪˈnækt] *vt* **(a)** (*Jur*) remettre en vigueur. **(b)** *scene, crime* reconstituer, reproduire.

re-enactment [ˈriːɪˈnæktmənt] *n* *[law etc]* remise *f* en vigueur; *[crime]* reconstitution *f*.

re-engage [ˈriːɪnˈgeɪdʒ] *vt employee* rengager, réembaucher (*Ind*); (*Tech*) rengrener. (*Aut*) **to ~ the clutch** rembrayer.

re-engagement [ˈriːɪnˈgeɪdʒmənt] *n* (*V* **re-engage**) rengagement *m*, réembauchage *m* (*Ind*); rengrènement *m*.

re-enlist [ˈriːɪnˈlɪst] **1** *vi* se rengager. **2** *vt* rengager.

re-enter [ˌriːˈentəʳ] **1** *vi* **(a)** rentrer.
(b) to ~ for an exam se représenter à *or* se réinscrire pour un examen. **2** *vt* rentrer dans. (*Space*) **to ~ the atmosphere** rentrer dans l'atmosphère.

re-entry [ˌriːˈentrɪ] *n* (*also Space*) rentrée *f*. (*Space*) **~ point** point *m* de rentrée.

re-erect [ˈriːɪˈrekt] *vt building, bridge* reconstruire; *scaffolding, toy* remonter.

re-establish [ˈriːɪsˈtæblɪʃ] *vt order* rétablir; *person* réhabiliter; *custom* restaurer.

re-establishment [ˌriːɪsˈtæblɪʃmənt] *n* (*V* **re-establish**) rétablissement *m*, réhabilitation *f*, restauration *f*.

reeve¹ [riːv] *n* (*Hist*) premier magistrat; (*Can*) président *m* du conseil municipal.

reeve² [riːv] *vt* (*Naut*) *rope* passer dans un anneau *or* une poulie, capeler; *shoal* passer au travers de.

re-examination [ˈriːɪgˌzæmɪˈneɪʃən] *n* nouvel examen; (*Jur: of witness*) nouvel interrogatoire.

re-examine [ˈriːɪgˈzæmɪn] *vt* examiner de nouveau; (*Jur*) *witness* interroger de nouveau.

ref* [ref] *n* (*Sport: abbr of* **referee**) arbitre *m*.

refection [rɪˈfekʃən] *n* (*light meal*) collation *f*, repas léger; (*refreshment*) rafraîchissements *mpl*.

refectory [rɪˈfektərɪ] *n* réfectoire *m*.

refer [rɪˈfɜːʳ] **1** *vt* **(a)** (*pass*) soumettre (*to* à). **the problem was ~red to the U.N.** le problème a été soumis *or* renvoyé à l'O.N.U.; **the dispute was ~red to arbitration** le litige a été soumis à l'arbitrage; **it was ~red to us for (a) decision** on nous a demandé de prendre une décision là-dessus; **I have to ~ it to my boss** je dois le soumettre à *or* en parler à mon patron; **I ~red him to the manager** je lui ai dit de s'adresser au gérant; **to ~ sb to the article on ...** renvoyer qn à l'article sur..., prier qn de se reporter *or* se référer à l'article sur ...; **'the reader is ~red to page 10'** 'prière de se reporter *or* se référer à la page 10'; (*Banking*) **to ~ a cheque to drawer** refuser d'honorer un chèque.
(b) (*liter, frm: ascribe*) attribuer (*to* à); (*relate*) rattacher (*to* à).
2 *vi* **(a)** (*allude*) (*directly*) parler, faire mention (*to* de); (*indirectly*) faire allusion (*to* à). **I am not ~ring to you** je ne parle pas de vous; **we shall not ~ to it again** nous n'en reparlerons pas, nous n'en parlerons plus; **he never ~s to that evening** il ne parle jamais de ce soir-là; **what can he be ~ring to?** de quoi parle-t-il?, à quoi peut-il bien faire allusion?; (*Comm*) **~ring to your letter** (comme) suite *or* en réponse à votre lettre.
(b) (*apply*) s'appliquer (*to* à). **does that remark ~ to me?** est-ce que cette remarque s'applique à moi?; **this ~s to you all** cela vous concerne tous.
(c) (*consult*) se reporter (*to sth* à qch). **to ~ to one's notes** consulter ses notes, se reporter à ses notes; **'please ~ to section 3'** 'prière de se reporter *or* se référer à la section 3'; **you must ~ to the original** vous devez vous reporter à l'original; **he ~red to the manager** il a consulté le gérant.

refer back *vt sep decision* remettre (à plus tard), ajourner. **to refer sth back to sb** consulter qn sur *or* au sujet de qch.

referable [rɪˈfɜːrəbl] *adj* attribuable (*to* à).

referee [ˌrefəˈriː] **1** *n* **(a)** (*Sport, also fig*) arbitre *m*.
(b) (*Brit: giving a reference*) répondant(e) *m(f)*. **to be ~ for sb** fournir des références *or* une attestation à qn.
2 *vt* (*Sport, fig*) arbitrer.
3 *vi* (*Sport, fig*) servir d'arbitre, être arbitre.

reference [ˈrefrəns] **1** *n* **(a)** (*U*) référence *f* (*to* à); *[question for judgment]* renvoi *m*; *[committee, tribunal]* compétence *f*. **outside the ~ of** hors de la compétence de; *V* **term**.
(b) (*allusion*) (*direct*) mention *f* (*to* de); (*indirect*) allusion *f* (*to* à). **a ~ was made to his illness** on a fait allusion à *or* on a fait mention de *or* on a parlé de sa maladie; **in** *or* **with ~ to** quant à, en ce qui concerne; (*Comm*) (comme) suite à; **without ~ to** sans tenir compte de, sans égard pour.
(c) (*testimonial*) **~(s)** références *fpl*; **to give sb a good ~** *or* **good ~s** fournir de bonnes références à qn; **a banker's ~** des références bancaires; **I've been asked for a ~ for him** on m'a demandé de fournir des renseignements sur lui.
(d) (*esp US*) = **referee 1b**.
(e) (*in book, article: note redirecting reader*) renvoi *m*, référence *f*; (*on map*) coordonnées *fpl*; (*Comm: on letter*) référence. **please quote this ~** prière de rappeler cette référence; *V* **cross**.
(f) (*connection*) rapport *m* (*to* avec). **this has no ~ to ...** cela n'a aucun rapport avec ... .
2 *cpd*: **reference book** ouvrage *m* de référence *or* à consulter; **reference library** bibliothèque *f* d'ouvrages à consulter; **reference mark** renvoi *m*; (*Comm*) **reference number** numéro *m* de référence; **reference point** point *m* de référence.

referendum [ˌrefəˈrendəm] *n*, *pl* **referenda** [ˌrefəˈrendə] référendum *m*. **to hold a ~** organiser un référendum; **a ~ will be held** un référendum aura lieu.

refill [ˌriːˈfɪl] **1** *vt glass, bottle* remplir à nouveau; *pen, lighter* recharger.
2 [ˈriːfɪl] *n* *[fountain pen]* cartouche *f*; *[ballpoint, lipstick]* recharge *f*; *[propelling pencil]* mine *f* de rechange; *[notebook]* feuilles *fpl* de rechange. (*: *of drink*) **would you like a ~?** encore un verre (*or* une tasse)?

refine [rɪˈfaɪn] **1** *vt metal* affiner; *oil* épurer; *crude oil, sugar* raffiner; *language* châtier; *manners* réformer; *taste* affiner. **2** *vi* **(a)** s'affiner; s'épurer.
(b) to ~ upon sth raffiner sur qch.

refined [rɪˈfaɪnd] *adj* **(a)** *crude oil, sugar* raffiné; *metal* affiné, pur; *oil* épuré.
(b) *person* raffiné, cultivé; *style, taste* raffiné, fin.

refinement [rɪˈfaɪnmənt] *n* **(a)** (*U: refining*) *[crude oil, sugar]* raffinage *m*; *[metal]* affinage *m*; *[oil]* épuration *f*.
(b) (*U*) *[person]* raffinement *m*, délicatesse *f*; *[language, style]* raffinement, subtilité *f*, recherche *f*.
(c) (*improvement: in technique, machine etc*) perfectionnement *m* (*in* de). (*fig*) **that is a ~ of cruelty** c'est la cruauté raffinée.

refiner [rɪˈfaɪnəʳ] *n* *[crude oil, sugar]* raffineur *m*; *[metals]* affineur *m*; *[oil]* épureur *m*.

refinery [rɪˈfaɪnərɪ] *n* *[crude oil, sugar]* raffinerie *f*; *[metals]* affinerie *f*.

refit [ˌriːˈfɪt] **1** *vt* remettre en état, réparer; *ship* réparer, remettre en état; *factory* équiper de nouveau, renouveler l'équipement de.
2 *vi* *[ship]* être réparé, être remis en état.
3 [ˈriːfɪt] *n* (*Naut*) réparation *f*, remise *f* en état, refonte *f*; *[factory]* nouvel équipement.

refitting [ˌriːˈfɪtɪŋ] *n*, **refitment** [ˈriːˈfɪtmənt] *n* = **refit 3**.

reflate [ˌriːˈfleɪt] *vt* (*Econ*) relancer.

reflation [riːˈfleɪʃn] *n* (*Econ*) relance *f*.

reflationary [riːˈfleɪʃnərɪ] *adj* (*Econ*) de relance.

reflect [rɪˈflekt] **1** *vt* **(a)** (*throw back*) *heat, sound* renvoyer; *light, image* refléter, *[mirror]* réfléchir; (*fig*) *credit, discredit* faire rejaillir, faire retomber (*on* sur). **the moon is ~ed in the lake** la lune se reflète dans le lac; **I saw him ~ed in the mirror** j'ai vu son image dans le miroir *or* réfléchie par le miroir; **he saw himself ~ed in the mirror** le miroir a réfléchi *or* lui a renvoyé son image; **~ing prism** prisme réflecteur; (*fig*) **he basked in the ~ed glory of his friend's success** il se chauffait aux rayons de la gloire de son ami; **the many difficulties are ~ed in his report** son rapport reflète les nombreuses difficultés; **his music ~s his love for her** sa musique reflète *or* exprime *or* traduit son amour pour elle.
(b) (*think*) se dire, penser, se faire la réflexion (*that* que).
2 *vi* (*meditate*) réfléchir, méditer (*on* sur), penser (*on* à).

reflect (up)on *vt fus* (*discredit*) *person* faire tort à; *reputation* nuire à, porter atteinte à; *motives, reasons* discréditer.

reflectingly [rɪˈflektɪŋlɪ] *adv* = **reflectively**.

reflection [rɪˈflekʃən] *n* **(a)** (*U: reflecting*) *[light, heat, sound]* réflexion *f*.
(b) (*image: in mirror etc*) reflet *m*, image *f*. **to see one's ~ in a mirror** voir son reflet dans un miroir; (*fig*) **a pale ~ of former glory** un pâle reflet de la gloire passée.
(c) (*U: consideration*) réflexion *f*. **on ~** (toute) réflexion faite, à la réflexion; **on serious ~** après mûre réflexion; **he did it without sufficient ~** il l'a fait sans avoir suffisamment réfléchi.
(d) (*thoughts, comments*) **~s** pensées *fpl*, réflexions *fpl*, remarques *fpl* (*on, upon* sur).
(e) (*adverse criticism*) critique *f* (*on* de), réflexion désobligeante (*on* sur); (*on sb's honour*) atteinte *f* (*on* à). **this is a ~ on your motives** cela fait douter de vos motifs; **this is no ~ on...** cela ne porte pas atteinte à... .

reflective [rɪˈflektɪv] *adj* **(a)** (*Phys etc*) *surface* réfléchissant, réflecteur (*f* -trice); *light* réfléchi. **(b)** *faculty, powers* de réflexion; *person* réfléchi. **(c)** (*Gram*) = **reflexive**.

reflectively [rɪˈflektɪvlɪ] *adv* d'un air *or* d'un ton réfléchi *or* pensif, avec réflexion.

reflectiveness [rɪˈflektɪvnɪs] *n* caractère réfléchi.

reflector [rɪˈflektəʳ] *n* (*gen*) réflecteur *m*; (*Aut*) réflecteur, cataphote *m*.

reflex [ˈriːfleks] **1** *adj* (*Physiol, Psych, fig*) réflexe; (*Math*) *angle* rentrant; (*Phys*) réfléchi. (*Phot*) ~ **camera** (appareil *m*) reflex *m*. 2 *n* réflexe *m*; *V* **condition.**

reflexion [rɪˈflekʃən] *n* = **reflection.**

reflexive [rɪˈfleksɪv] (*Gram*) 1 *adj* réfléchi. 2 *n* verbe réfléchi.

reflexively [rɪˈfleksɪvlɪ] *adv* (*Gram*) au sens réfléchi; à la forme réfléchie.

refloat [ˌriːˈfləʊt] 1 *vt ship, business etc* renflouer, remettre à flot. 2 *vi* être renfloué, être remis à flot.

reflux [ˈriːflʌks] *n* reflux *m*.

reforestation [ˌriːfɒrɪsˈteɪʃən] *n* (*US*) = **reafforestation.**

reform [rɪˈfɔːm] 1 *n* réforme *f*; *V* **land.**

2 *cpd measures etc* de réforme. (*Brit Hist*) **the Reform Laws** les lois *fpl* de réforme parlementaire; (*US*) **reform school** maison *f* de redressement.

3 *vt law* réformer; *institutions, services* réformer, faire des réformes dans; *conduct* corriger; *person* faire prendre de meilleures habitudes à. **to ~ spelling** faire une réforme de *or* réformer l'orthographe.

4 *vi [person]* se réformer, se corriger, s'amender.

re-form [ˈriːˈfɔːm] 1 *vt* **(a)** (*form again*) reformer, rendre sa première forme à; (*Mil*) *ranks* reformer; *troops* rallier, remettre en rangs.

(b) (*give new form to*) donner une nouvelle forme à.

2 *vi* se reformer; (*Mil*) se reformer, se remettre en rangs, reprendre sa formation.

reformable [rɪˈfɔːməbl] *adj* réformable.

reformation [ˌrefəˈmeɪʃən] *n* (*U*) *[church, spelling, conduct]* réforme *f*; *[person]* retour *m* à une vie honnête *or* à une conduite meilleure. (*Hist*) **the R~** la Réforme, la Réformation.

reformative [rɪˈfɔːmətɪv] *adj* de réforme, réformateur (*f* -trice).

reformatory [rɪˈfɔːmətərɪ] *n* (*Brit*††) maison *f* de correction *or* de redressement; (*US Jur*) centre *m* d'éducation surveillée.

reformed [rɪˈfɔːmd] *adj church, spelling* réformé; *behaviour, person* amendé. (*hum*) **he's a ~ character*** il s'est rangé *or* assagi.

reformer [rɪˈfɔːmə[r]] *n* réformateur *m*, -trice *f*.

reformist [rɪˈfɔːmɪst] *adj, n* réformiste (*mf*).

refract [rɪˈfrækt] *vt* réfracter.

refracting [rɪˈfræktɪŋ] *adj* (*Phys*) réfringent. ~ **angle** angle *m* de réfringence; ~ **telescope** lunette *f* d'approche.

refraction [rɪˈfrækʃən] *n* réfraction *f*.

refractive [rɪˈfræktɪv] *adj* réfractif, réfringent. ~ **index** indice *m* de réfraction.

refractor [rɪˈfræktə[r]] *n* **(a)** (*Phys*) milieu réfringent, dispositif *m* de réfraction. **(b)** (*telescope*) lunette *f* d'approche.

refractory [rɪˈfræktərɪ] *adj person* réfractaire, rebelle, insoumis; *disease* rebelle, opiniâtre; (*Chem, Miner*) réfractaire.

refrain[1] [rɪˈfreɪn] *vi* se retenir, s'abstenir (*from doing* de faire). **he ~ed from comment** il s'est abstenu de tout commentaire; **they ~ed from measures leading to...** ils se sont abstenus de toute mesure menant à...; **I couldn't ~ from laughing** je n'ai pas pu m'empêcher de rire; **please ~ from smoking** (*on notice*) prière de ne pas fumer; (*spoken*) ayez l'obligeance de ne pas fumer.

refrain[2] [rɪˈfreɪn] *n* (*Mus, Poetry, fig*) refrain *m*.

refrangible [rɪˈfrændʒəbl] *adj* réfrangible.

refresh [rɪˈfreʃ] *vt [drink, bath]* rafraîchir; *[food]* revigorer, redonner des forces à; *[sleep, rest etc]* délasser, détendre, reposer. **to ~ o.s.** (*with drink*) se rafraîchir; (*with food*) se restaurer; (*with sleep*) se reposer, se délasser; **to ~ one's memory** se rafraîchir la mémoire; **to ~ one's memory about sth** se remettre qch en mémoire; **let me ~ your memory!** je vais vous rafraîchir la mémoire!*

refresher [rɪˈfreʃə[r]] 1 *n* (*Jur*) honoraires *mpl* supplémentaires. 2 *cpd*: (*Univ etc*) ~ **course** cours *m* de recyclage.

refreshing [rɪˈfreʃɪŋ] *adj fruit, drink* rafraîchissant; *sleep* reposant, réparateur (*f* -trice); *sight, news* réconfortant; *change* agréable; *idea, approach, point of view* nouveau (*f* nouvelle), intéressant.

refreshment [rɪˈfreʃmənt] 1 *n* **(a)** *[mind, body]* repos *m*, délassement *m*.

(b) (*food, drink*) **(light) ~s** rafraîchissements *mpl*; (*place*) **~s** = **~ room** (*V* 2).

2 *cpd*: **refreshment bar** buvette *f*; (*Rail*) **refreshment room** buffet *m*; **refreshment stall** = **refreshment bar.**

refrigerant [rɪˈfrɪdʒərənt] *adj, n* réfrigérant (*m*); (*Med*) fébrifuge (*m*).

refrigerate [rɪˈfrɪdʒəreɪt] *vt* réfrigérer, (*in cold room etc*) frigorifier.

refrigeration [rɪˌfrɪdʒəˈreɪʃən] *n* réfrigération *f*; frigorification *f*.

refrigerator [rɪˈfrɪdʒəreɪtə[r]] 1 *n* (*cabinet*) réfrigérateur *m*, frigidaire *m* ®, frigo* *m*; (*room*) chambre *f* frigorifique; (*apparatus*) condenseur *m*. 2 *cpd truck etc* frigorifique.

refrigeratory [rɪˈfrɪdʒərətərɪ] *adj, n* (*Chem*) réfrigérant (*m*).

refringent [rɪˈfrɪndʒənt] *adj* réfringent.

refuel [ˈriːˈfjʊəl] 1 *vi* se ravitailler en carburant *or* en combustible. 2 *vt* ravitailler.

refuelling [ˈriːˈfjʊəlɪŋ] *n* ravitaillement *m* (en carburant *or* en combustible). (*Aviat*) ~ **stop** escale *f* technique.

refuge [ˈrefjuːdʒ] *n* (*lit, fig*) refuge *m*, abri *m* (*from* contre); (*for climbers, pedestrians etc*) refuge. **place of ~** asile *m*; **to seek ~** chercher refuge *or* asile; (*lit, fig*) **to take ~ in** se réfugier dans; **to take ~ in lying** se réfugier dans les mensonges; **God is my ~** Dieu est mon refuge.

refugee [ˌrefjʊˈdʒiː] *n* réfugié(e) *m(f)*. ~ **camp** camp *m* de réfugiés.

refulgence [rɪˈfʌldʒəns] *n* (*liter*) splendeur *f*, éclat *m*.

refulgent [rɪˈfʌldʒənt] *adj* (*liter*) resplendissant, éclatant.

refund [rɪˈfʌnd] 1 *vt* **(a)** rembourser. **to ~ sb's expenses** rembourser qn de ses frais *or* dépenses; **to ~ postage** rembourser les frais de port.

(b) (*Fin*) *excess payments* ristourner.

2 [ˈriːfʌnd] *n* remboursement *m*; (*Fin*) ristourne *f*. **tax ~** bonification *f* de trop-perçu.

refundable [rɪˈfʌndəbl] *adj* remboursable.

refurbish [ˌriːˈfɜːbɪʃ] *vt* remettre à neuf.

refurnish [ˌriːˈfɜːnɪʃ] *vt* remeubler.

refusal [rɪˈfjuːzəl] *n* refus *m* (*to do* de faire). (*Jur*) ~ **of justice** déni *m* de justice; **to get a ~, to meet with a ~** se heurter à *or* essuyer un refus; **to give a flat ~** refuser net; (*Equitation*) **3 ~s** 3 refus; **to give sb first ~ of sth** accorder à qn l'option sur qch; **to have (the) first ~ of sth** recevoir la première offre de qch, avoir le droit de préemption sur qch.

refuse[1] [rɪˈfjuːz] 1 *vt* refuser (*sb sth* qch à qn, *to do* de faire), se refuser (*to do* à faire); *offer, invitation* refuser, décliner; *request* refuser, rejeter, repousser; *candidate* refuser. **I absolutely ~ to do it** je me refuse catégoriquement à le faire; **to be ~d** essuyer un refus; **to be ~d sth** se voir refuser qch; **they were ~d permission to leave** on leur a refusé *or* ils se sont vu refuser la permission de partir; **she ~d him** elle l'a rejeté; **she ~d his proposal** elle a rejeté son offre de mariage; *[horse]* **to ~ a fence** refuser l'obstacle.

2 *vi* refuser, opposer un refus; *[horse]* refuser l'obstacle.

refuse[2] [ˈrefjuːs] 1 *n* détritus *mpl*, ordures *fpl*; (*industrial or food waste*) déchets *mpl*. **household ~** ordures ménagères; **garden ~** détritus de jardin.

2 *cpd*: **refuse bin** poubelle *f*, boîte *f* à ordures; **refuse chute** (*at dump*) dépotoir *m*; (*in building*) vide-ordures *m inv*; **refuse collection** ramassage *m* d'ordures; **refuse collector** éboueur *m*; **refuse destructor** incinérateur *m* (d'ordures); **refuse disposal** traitement *m* des ordures; **refuse disposal service** service *m* de voirie; **refuse disposal unit** broyeur *m* d'ordures; **refuse dump** (*public*) décharge *f* (publique), dépotoir *m*; (*in garden*) monceau *m* de détritus; **refuse lorry** voiture *f* d'éboueurs.

refutable [rɪˈfjuːtəbl] *adj* réfutable.

refutation [ˌrefjʊˈteɪʃən] *n* réfutation *f*.

refute [rɪˈfjuːt] *vt* réfuter.

regain [rɪˈgeɪn] *vt* regagner; *health, one's sight* recouvrer; *territory* reconquérir. **to ~ one's strength** récupérer (ses forces); **to ~ consciousness** revenir à soi, reprendre connaissance; **to ~ lost time** regagner *or* rattraper le temps perdu; **to ~ one's footing** reprendre pied; **to ~ possession (of)** rentrer en possession (de).

regal [ˈriːgəl] *adj* royal, digne d'un roi.

regale [rɪˈgeɪl] *vt* régaler (*sb with sth* qn de qch).

regalia [rɪˈgeɪlɪə] *n [monarch]* prérogatives *fpl* royales; (*insignia*) insignes royaux; *[Freemasons etc]* insignes. (*hum*) **she was in full ~** elle était dans ses plus beaux atours *or* en grand tra-la-la*.

regally [ˈriːgəlɪ] *adv* (*lit, fig*) royalement.

regard [rɪˈgɑːd] 1 *vt* **(a)** (*look at*) regarder, observer, considérer; (*consider*) considérer, regarder (*as* comme), tenir (*as* pour). **to ~ with favour/horror** regarder d'un œil favorable/avec horreur; **we ~ it as worth doing** à notre avis ça vaut la peine de le faire; **we don't ~ it as necessary** nous ne le considérons pas comme nécessaire; (*frm*) **I ~ him highly** je le tiens en grande estime; **without ~ing his wishes** sans tenir compte de ses souhaits.

(b) (*concern*) concerner, regarder. **as ~s ...** pour *or* en ce qui concerne..., pour ce qui regarde... .

2 *n* **(a)** (*attention, concern*) attention *f*, considération *f*. **to pay ~ to, to have ~ for** tenir compte de; **to have *or* show little ~ for** faire peu de cas de; **to have *or* show no ~ for** ne faire aucun cas de; **without ~ to *or* for** sans égard pour; **out of ~ for** par égard pour; **having ~ to** si l'on tient compte de; **in this ~** à cet égard, sous ce rapport; **with *or* in ~ to** pour *or* en ce qui concerne, quant à, relativement à.

(b) (*U: esteem*) respect *m*, estime *f*, considération *f*. (*frm*) **to hold sb in high ~** tenir qn en haute estime; **to have a great ~ for sb** avoir beaucoup d'estime pour qn.

(c) (*in messages*) **give him my ~s** faites-lui mes amitiés, dites-lui bien des choses de ma part; **Paul sends his kind ~s** Paul vous fait *or* vous envoie ses amitiés; (*as letter-ending*) **(kindest) ~s** amicalement, cordialement.

(d) (*liter: look*) regard *m*.

regardful [rɪˈgɑːdfʊl] *adj*: ~ **of** *feelings, duty* attentif à; *interests* soucieux de, soigneux de.

regarding [rɪˈgɑːdɪŋ] *prep* pour *or* en ce qui concerne, quant à, relativement à.

regardless [rɪˈgɑːdlɪs] 1 *adj*: ~ **of** *sb's feelings, fate* indifférent à; *future, danger* insouciant de; *sb's troubles* inattentif à; **~ of consequences** sans se soucier des conséquences; **~ of expense *or* cost** sans regarder à la dépense; **~ of rank** sans distinction de rang. 2 *adv* (*) quand même. **he did it ~** il l'a fait quand même.

regatta [rɪˈgætə] *n* régate *f*.

regency [ˈriːdʒənsɪ] 1 *n* régence *f*. 2 *cpd furniture, style* Régence (anglaise) *inv*.

regenerate [rɪˈdʒenəreɪt] 1 *vt* régénérer. 2 *vi* se régénérer. 3 [rɪˈdʒenərɪt] *adj* régénéré.

regeneration [rɪˌdʒenəˈreɪʃən] *n* régénération *f*.

regenerative [rɪˈdʒenərətɪv] *adj* régénérateur (*f* -trice).

regent [ˈriːdʒənt] *n* régent(e) *m(f)*; (*US Univ*) administrateur *m*, -trice *f*. **prince ~** prince régent.

regicide [ˈredʒɪsaɪd] *n* (*person*) régicide *mf*; (*act*) régicide *m*.

régime [reɪˈʒiːm] *n* régime *m* (*politique etc*).

regimen ['redʒɪmen] *n* (*frm*) régime *m* (*médical*).
regiment ['redʒɪmənt] **1** *n* (*Mil, fig*) régiment *m*.
2 *vt* (*fig*) **they are too ~ed at that college** la discipline est trop stricte dans ce collège.
regimental [ˌredʒɪ'mentl] **1** *adj* (*Mil*) *insignia, car* régimentaire; *traditions* du régiment. ~ **band** musique *f* du régiment; (*Mil*) ~ **sergeant-major** ≈ adjudant-chef *m*.
2 *n* (*Mil*) **~s** uniforme *m*; **in full ~s** en grand uniforme, en grande tenue.
regimentation [ˌredʒɪmen'teɪʃən] *n* (*pej*) discipline excessive.
region ['riːdʒən] *n* (*all senses*) région *f*. (*fig*) **the lower ~s** les enfers *mpl*; **in the ~ of 5 kg/10 francs** environ *or* dans les 5 kg/10 F, aux alentours de 5 kg/10 F.
regional ['riːdʒənl] *adj* régional. (*Brit Admin*) ~ **development** ≈ aménagement *m* du territoire.
regionalism ['riːdʒənəlɪzəm] *n* régionalisme *m*.
regionalist ['riːdʒənəlɪst] *adj, n* régionaliste (*mf*).
register ['redʒɪstəʳ] **1** *n* **(a)** (*gen, Ling, Mus, Typ; also at school, in hotel*) registre *m*; (*of members etc*) liste *f*. **electoral ~** liste électorale; ~ **of births, marriages and deaths** registre d'état civil.
(b) (*Tech: gauge of speed, numbers etc*) compteur *m*, enregistreur *m*; *V* **cash**.
2 *cpd*: (*Naut*) **register ton** tonneau *m* (de jauge).
3 *vt* **(a)** (*record formally*) *fact, figure* enregistrer; *birth, death* déclarer; *vehicle* (faire) immatriculer. **to ~ a trademark** déposer une marque de fabrique; **he is ~ed as disabled** il est officiellement reconnu comme handicapé; **he ~ed his disapproval by refusing ...** il a fait connaître sa désapprobation en refusant ...; **to ~ a protest** protester; *V also* **registered**.
(b) (*take note of*) *fact* enregistrer; (*: *realize*) se rendre compte de, réaliser*. **I ~ed the fact that he had gone** je me suis rendu compte *or* j'ai réalisé* qu'il était parti.
(c) (*indicate*) *[machines] speed, quantity* indiquer, marquer; *rainfall* enregistrer; *temperature* marquer; *[face, expression] happiness, sorrow* exprimer, refléter. **he ~ed surprise** son visage *or* il a exprimé l'étonnement, il a paru étonné; **he ~ed no emotion** il n'a pas exprimé d'émotion, il n'a pas paru ému.
(d) (*Post*) *letter* recommander; (*Rail*) *luggage* (faire) enregistrer. **to ~ one's luggage through to London** (faire) enregistrer ses bagages jusqu'à Londres; *V also* **registered.**
(e) (*Tech*) *parts* faire coïncider; (*Typ*) mettre en registre.
4 *vi* **(a)** (*on electoral list etc*) se faire inscrire, s'inscrire; (*in hotel*) s'inscrire sur *or* signer le registre. **to ~ with a doctor** se faire inscrire comme patient chez un médecin; **to ~ with the police** se déclarer à la police; **to ~ for military service** se faire recenser, se faire porter sur les tableaux de recensement; **to ~ for a course/for French literature** s'inscrire à un cours/en littérature française.
(b) (*Tech*) *[two parts of machine]* coïncider exactement; (*Typ*) être en registre.
(c) (*: *be understood*) être compris, pénétrer. **it hasn't ~ed (with him)** cela n'a pas encore pénétré, il n'a pas saisi, il n'a pas pigé‡; **her death hadn't ~ed with him** il n'avait pas vraiment réalisé qu'elle était morte.
registered ['redʒɪstəd] *adj* **(a)** *student, voter* inscrit; *vehicle* immatriculé; ~ **company** société inscrite au tribunal de commerce; ~ **name** nom déposé; (*US*) ~ **nurse** infirmière diplômée d'État; ~ **shareholder** ≈ actionnaire inscrit; ~ **stocks** actions *or* valeurs nominatives, titres nominatifs; ~ **trademark** marque déposée; *V* **state.**
(b) (*Post*) *letter* recommandé; (*Rail*) *luggage* enregistré. **by ~ post** par envoi recommandé.
registrar [ˌredʒɪs'trɑːʳ] *n* (*Admin*) officier *m* de l'état civil; (*Jur: in court*) greffier *m*; (*Univ*) secrétaire *m* (général); (*Med*) interne *mf*. (*Brit Admin*) **~'s office** bureau *m* de l'état civil; **to be married by the ~** se marier civilement *or* à la mairie.
registration [ˌredʒɪs'treɪʃən] **1** *n* enregistrement *m*, inscription *f*; *[trademark]* dépôt *m*; (*Post*) *[letter]* recommandation *f*; (*Rail*) *[luggage]* enregistrement.
2 *cpd*: **registration fee** (*Post*) taxe *f* de recommandation; (*Rail: for luggage*) frais *mpl* d'enregistrement; (*Univ*) droits *mpl* d'inscription; (*Aut*) **registration number** numéro *m* minéralogique *or* d'immatriculation; **car (with) registration number X** voiture immatriculée X.
registry ['redʒɪstrɪ] **1** *n* (*act*) enregistrement *m*, inscription *f*; (*office*) (*gen*) bureau *m* de l'enregistrement; (*Brit Admin*) bureau de l'état civil; (*Naut*) certificat *m* d'immatriculation. (*Naut*) **port of ~** port *m* d'attache.
2 *cpd*: (*Brit*) **registry office** bureau *m* de l'état civil; **to get married in a registry office** se marier civilement *or* à la mairie.
regius ['riːdʒəs] *adj* (*Brit Univ*) ~ **professor** professeur *m* (*titulaire d'une chaire de fondation royale*).
regnal ['regnl] *adj*: ~ **year** année *f* du règne.
regnant ['regnənt] *adj* (*lit, fig*) régnant.
regorge [rɪ'gɔːdʒ] **1** *vt* vomir, régurgiter. **2** *vi* refluer.
regress [rɪ'gres] **1** *vi* **(a)** (*Bio, Psych, fig*) régresser, rétrograder. **(b)** (*move backwards*) retourner en arrière, reculer. **2** ['riːgres] *n* = **regression.**
regression [rɪ'greʃən] *n* (*lit*) retour *m* en arrière, recul *m*; (*Bio, Psych, fig*) régression *f*.
regressive [rɪ'gresɪv] *adj* régressif.
regret [rɪ'gret] **1** *vt* regretter (*doing, to do* de faire; *that* que +*subj*); *mistake, words, event* regretter, être désolé *or* navré de; *one's youth, lost opportunity* regretter. **I ~ to say that ...** j'ai le regret de dire que ...; **he is very ill, I ~ to say** il est très malade, hélas *or* je regrette de le dire; **we ~ to hear that ...** nous sommes désolés d'apprendre que ...; **it is to be ~ted that ...** il est regrettable que ... +*subj*; **you won't ~ it!** vous ne le regretterez pas!; (*frm*) **the President ~s he cannot see you today** le Président est au regret *or* exprime ses regrets de ne pouvoir vous recevoir aujourd'hui; **he is much ~ted** on le regrette beaucoup.
2 *n* regret *m* (*for* de). **much to my ~** à mon grand regret; **I have no ~s** je ne regrette rien, je n'ai aucun regret; **to do sth with ~** (*sadly*) faire qch avec regret; (*against one's wishes*) faire qch à regret *or* à contrecœur; **to send ~s** envoyer ses regrets; **please give her my ~s that I cannot come** dites-lui, s'il vous plaît, combien je regrette de ne pouvoir venir.
regretful [rɪ'gretfʊl] *adj person* plein de regrets; désolé, navré; *look, attitude* de regret.
regretfully [rɪ'gretfəlɪ] *adv* (*sadly*) avec regret; (*unwillingly*) à regret, à contrecœur.
regrettable [rɪ'gretəbl] *adj* regrettable, fâcheux. **it is ~ that** il est à regretter *or* regrettable *or* fâcheux que +*subj*.
regrettably [rɪ'gretəblɪ] *adv late, poor* fâcheusement. **~, he refused** malheureusement, il a refusé.
regroup [ˌriː'gruːp] **1** *vt* regrouper. **2** *vi* se regrouper.
regrouping [ˌriː'gruːpɪŋ] *n* regroupement *m*.
regular ['regjʊləʳ] **1** *adj* **(a)** (*symmetrical*) régulier, symétrique; (*Math*) *figure* régulier; (*even*) *surface* uni. ~ **features** traits réguliers, visage régulier.
(b) (*recurring at even intervals*) *pulse, breathing, footsteps, reminders* régulier. **there is a ~ bus service to town** il y a un service régulier d'autobus allant en ville; **to be ~ in one's habits** être régulier dans ses habitudes; ~ **way of life** vie régulière *or* réglée; **to keep ~ hours** mener une vie réglée; **he is as ~ as clockwork** il est très ponctuel, il est réglé comme une horloge; **his visits are as ~ as clockwork** ses visites sont très régulières, ses visites sont réglées comme du papier à musique*; **he has no ~ employment** il est sans emploi régulier; (*Med*) ~ **bowel movements** selles régulières.
(c) (*habitual*) habituel, normal, ordinaire; (*Comm*) *size* ordinaire, standard *inv*; *price* normal, courant; *listener, reader* fidèle. **the ~ staff** le personnel permanent; **our ~ cleaning woman** notre femme de ménage habituelle; **my ~ dentist** mon dentiste habituel; **my ~ doctor** mon médecin traitant; **his ~ time for getting up** l'heure à laquelle il se lève habituellement *or* normalement.
(d) (*permissible, accepted*) *action, procedure* régulier, en règle. **to make ~** régulariser; **it is quite ~ to apply in person** il est tout à fait normal *or* régulier de faire sa demande en personne.
(e) (*Mil*) (*not conscripted*) *soldier, army* de métier; *officer* de carrière; (*not territorial*) d'active.
(f) (*Ling*) régulier.
(g) (*Rel*) ~ **clergy** clergé régulier.
(h) (*) vrai, véritable. **he's a ~ idiot** c'est un imbécile fini; (*US*) ~ **guy** chic type* *m*.
2 *n* (*Mil*) soldat *m* de métier; (*habitual customer etc*) habitué(e) *m(f)*, bon(ne) client(e) *m(f)*; (*Rel*) régulier *m*, religieux *m*. (*Rad, TV*) **he's one of the ~s on that programme** il participe *or* prend part régulièrement à ce programme.
regularity [ˌregjʊ'lærɪtɪ] *n* régularité *f*.
regularize ['regjʊləraɪz] *vt* régulariser.
regularly ['regjʊləlɪ] *adv* régulièrement.
regulate ['regjʊleɪt] *vt* **(a)** (*control systematically*) *amount, flow* régler; *expenditure* régler, calculer. **to ~ one's life by** se régler sur. **(b)** *machine* régler, ajuster.
regulation [ˌregjʊ'leɪʃən] **1** *n* (*rule*) règlement *m*; (*Admin*) règlement, arrêté *m*. **against ~s** contraire au règlement; *V* **fire, safety.**
2 *cpd style, size* réglementaire. (*Mil*) **regulation boots** brodequins *mpl* d'ordonnance; (*Mil*) **regulation dress** tenue *f* réglementaire.
regulative ['regjʊlətɪv] *adj* régulateur (*f* -trice).
regulator ['regjʊleɪtəʳ] *n* (*person*) régulateur *m*, -trice *f*; (*instrument*) régulateur *m*.
regurgitate [rɪ'gɜːdʒɪteɪt] **1** *vt [person]* régurgiter, rendre; *[drainpipe etc]* dégorger. **2** *vi* refluer.
regurgitation [rɪˌgɜːdʒɪ'teɪʃən] *n* régurgitation *f*.
rehabilitate [ˌriːə'bɪlɪteɪt] *vt* **(a)** (*restore respect, position to*) réhabiliter. **(b)** *the disabled* (*to everyday life*) rééduquer; (*to work*) réadapter; *refugees* réadapter; *demobilized troops* réintégrer (dans la vie civile).
rehabilitation ['riːəˌbɪlɪ'teɪʃən] *n* (*V* **rehabilitate**) réhabilitation *f*; rééducation *f*; réadaptation *f*; réintégration *f* (dans la vie civile). (*Admin*) ~ **centre** centre *m* de rééducation (professionnelle).
rehash [ˌriː'hæʃ] **1** *vt literary material etc* remanier, réarranger. **2** ['riːhæʃ] *n* réchauffé *m*, resucée* *f*.
rehearsal [rɪ'hɜːsəl] *n* **(a)** (*Theat*) répétition *f*. **this play is in ~** on répète cette pièce; *V* **dress.**
(b) (*U*) *[facts etc]* énumération *f*, récit détaillé.
rehearse [rɪ'hɜːs] *vt* (*Theat*) répéter; (*gen*) *facts, grievances* réciter, énumérer, raconter en détail. **to ~ what one is going to say** préparer ce qu'on va dire.
rehouse [ˌriː'haʊz] *vt* reloger.
reign [reɪn] **1** *n* (*lit, fig*) règne *m*. **in the ~ of** sous le règne de; (*Hist*) **the R~ of Terror** la Terreur; (*fig*) **~ of terror** régime *m* de terreur.
2 *vi* (*lit, fig*) régner. **silence ~s** le silence règne; **to ~ supreme** *[monarch etc]* régner en *or* être le maître absolu; *[champion etc]* être sans rival; *[justice, peace]* régner en souverain(e).
reigning ['reɪnɪŋ] *adj* (*lit, fig*) régnant.
reimburse [ˌriːɪm'bɜːs] *vt* rembourser (*sb for sth* qch à qn, qn de qch). **to ~ sb (for) his expenses** rembourser qn de ses dépenses.
reimbursement [ˌriːɪm'bɜːsmənt] *n* remboursement *m*.
reimpose ['riːɪm'pəʊz] *vt* réimposer.

rein [reɪn] *n (often pl: lit, fig)* rêne *f*; *[horse in harness]* guide *f*. *[child]* ~s rênes; (*lit, fig*) **to hold the** ~**s** tenir les rênes; (*lit, fig*) **to keep a** ~ **on** tenir en bride; (*lit, fig*) **to keep a tight** ~ **on** tenir la bride haute *or* serrée à; (*fig*) **to give free** ~ **to** *anger, passions* lâcher la bride à, donner libre cours à; *one's imagination* lâcher la bride à, se laisser entraîner par.
rein back 1 *vt sep horse* arrêter.
2 *vi* s'arrêter.
rein in *vt sep horse* serrer la bride à, ramener au pas; (*fig*) *passions* contenir, maîtriser.
reincarnate [ˌriːɪnˈkɑːneɪt] **1** *vt* réincarner. **2** [ˌriːɪnˈkɑːnɪt] *adj* réincarné.
reincarnation [ˈriːɪnkɑːˈneɪʃən] *n* réincarnation *f*.
reindeer [ˈreɪndɪəʳ] *n,pl inv* renne *m*.
reinforce [ˌriːɪnˈfɔːs] *vt* (*Mil*) renforcer; (*gen*) *wall, bridge, heel* renforcer; *beam* armer, renforcer; *one's demands etc* appuyer. ~**d concrete** béton armé.
reinforcement [ˌriːɪnˈfɔːsmənt] **1** *n* **(a)** (*action*) reinforcement *m*; (*thing*) armature *f*.
(b) (*Mil: action*) reinforcement *m*. (*also fig*) ~s renforts *mpl*.
2 *cpd troops, supplies* de renfort.
reinsert [ˈriːɪnˈsɜːt] *vt* réinsérer.
reinstate [ˈriːɪnˈsteɪt] *vt* réintégrer, rétablir (*in* dans).
reinstatement [ˈriːɪnˈsteɪtmənt] *n* réintégration *f*, rétablissement *m*.
reinsurance [ˈriːɪnˈʃʊərəns] *n* réassurance *f*; *[underwriter etc, against possible losses]* contre-assurance *f*.
reinsure [ˈriːɪnˈʃʊəʳ] *vt* (*V* **reinsurance**) réassurer; contracter une contre-assurance sur.
reintegrate [ˌriːˈɪntɪgreɪt] *vt* réintégrer.
reintegration [ˈriːˌɪntrˈgreɪʃən] *n* réintégration *f*.
reinvest [ˈriːɪnˈvest] *vt* (*Fin*) réinvestir.
reinvestment [ˈriːɪnˈvestmənt] *n* (*Fin*) nouveau placement, nouvel investissement.
reinvigorate [ˌriːɪnˈvɪgəreɪt] *vt* revigorer.
reissue [ˌriːˈɪʃjuː] **1** *vt book* donner une nouvelle édition de, rééditer; *film* ressortir, redistribuer.
2 *n* (*act*) réédition *f*, redistribution *f*. **it is a** ~ *[book]* il a été réédité; *[film]* il est ressorti.
reiterate [riːˈɪtəreɪt] *vt* réitérer, répéter.
reiteration [riːˌɪtəˈreɪʃən] *n* réitération *f*, répétition *f*.
reiterative [riːˈɪtərətɪv] *adj* réitératif.
reject [rɪˈdʒekt] **1** *vt* **(a)** *damaged goods etc [customer, shopkeeper]* refuser; *[maker, producer]* mettre au rebut; *suitor* éconduire; *candidate, manuscript* refuser; *offer, proposal, application* rejeter; *plea, advances* repousser; *possibility* rejeter, repousser.
(b) (*Med*) *[body] medicament, transplant* rejeter.
2 [ˈriːdʒekt] *n* (*Comm*) pièce *f* or article *m* de rebut; *V* **export**.
3 [ˈriːdʒekt] *cpd* (*Comm, Ind*) *goods* de rebut.
rejection [rɪˈdʒekʃən] **1** *n* (*V* **reject**) refus *m*; rejet *m*. **2** *cpd*: (*Publishing*) **rejection slip** lettre *f* de refus.
rejoice [rɪˈdʒɔɪs] **1** *vt* réjouir, ravir, enchanter. (*frm, liter*) **it** ~**d his heart to see ...** il s'est félicité du fond du cœur de voir ... .
2 *vi* se réjouir, être ravi, être enchanté (*at, over* de). **to** ~ **in sth** jouir de qch, posséder qch; (*hum, iro*) **he** ~**s in the name of Marmaduke** il a le privilège de s'appeler Marmaduke (*iro*).
rejoicing [rɪˈdʒɔɪsɪŋ] *n* **(a)** (*U*) réjouissance *f*, jubilation *f*. **(b)** ~s réjouissances *fpl*, fête *f*.
rejoin[1] [ˌriːˈdʒɔɪn] **1** *vt person, army* rejoindre. (*Naut*) **to** ~ **ship** rallier le bord; **the road** ~**s the motorway** la route rejoint l'autoroute. **2** *vi* se rejoindre.
rejoin[2] [rɪˈdʒɔɪn] *vi* (*reply*) répliquer, répondre.
rejoinder [rɪˈdʒɔɪndəʳ] *n* réplique *f*, repartie *f*, riposte *f*; (*Jur*) repartie.
rejuvenate [rɪˈdʒuːvɪneɪt] *vti* rajeunir.
rekindle [ˌriːˈkɪndl] **1** *vt fire* rallumer, attiser; (*fig*) *hope, enthusiasm* ranimer, raviver. **2** *vi* se rallumer, se ranimer.
relapse [rɪˈlæps] **1** *n* (*Med, fig*) rechute *f*. **to have a** ~ avoir *or* faire une rechute, rechuter.
2 *vi* (*Med*) rechuter. **to** ~ **into unconsciousness/crime** retomber dans le coma/le crime.
relate [rɪˈleɪt] **1** *vt* **(a)** (*recount*) *story* raconter, relater, faire le récit de; *details* rapporter. **strange to** ~ **...** chose curieuse (à dire) ... .
(b) (*associate*) établir un rapport entre, rapprocher; *breeds* apparenter; (*to a category*) rattacher, lier. **it is often difficult to** ~ **the cause to the effect** il est souvent difficile d'établir un rapport de cause à effet *or* d'établir un lien entre la cause et l'effet *or* de rattacher l'effet à la cause.
2 *vi* se rapporter, toucher (*to* à).
related [rɪˈleɪtɪd] *adj* **(a)** (*in family*) apparenté, allié (*to* à), parent (*to* de). **she is** ~ **to us** elle est notre parente; **to be closely/distantly** ~ être proche parent/parent éloigné; ~ **by marriage** to parent par alliance de, allié à.
(b) (*connected*) (*Chem*) apparenté; (*Philos*) connexe; (*Mus*) relatif. **French is** ~ **to Spanish** le français est parent de l'espagnol; **geometry and other** ~ **subjects** la géométrie et les sujets connexes *or* qui s'y rattachent.
relating [rɪˈleɪtɪŋ] *adj*: ~ **to** concernant, relatif à.
relation [rɪˈleɪʃən] *n* **(a)** (*family: person*) parent(e) *m(f)*; (*kinship*) parenté *f*. **is he any** ~ **to you?** est-il de vos parents?; **he is no** ~ **(of mine)** il n'est pas de ma famille, il n'y a aucun lien de parenté *or* aucune parenté entre nous; **what** ~ **is she to you?** quelle est sa parenté avec vous?
(b) (*relationship*) relation *f*, rapport *m*. **to bear a** ~ **to** avoir rapport à; **to bear no** ~ **to** n'avoir aucun rapport avec, être sans rapport avec; **in** ~ **to** par rapport à, relativement à; ~**s** relations, rapports; (*personal ties*) rapports; **to have business** ~**s with** être en rapports *or* relations d'affaires avec; **diplomatic/friendly/international** ~**s** relations diplomatiques/d'amitié/internationales; ~**s are rather strained** les relations *or* les rapports sont assez tendu(e)s; **sexual** ~**s** rapports (sexuels); *V* **public**.
(c) (*telling*) *[story]* récit *m*, relation *f*; *[details]* rapport *m*.
relationship [rɪˈleɪʃənʃɪp] *n* **(a)** (*family ties*) liens *mpl* de parenté. **what is your** ~ **to him?** quels sont les liens de parenté entre vous?, quels sont vos liens de parenté avec lui?
(b) (*connection*) rapport *m*; (*relations*) relations *fpl*, rapports; (*personal ties*) rapports. **to see a** ~ **between 2 events** voir un rapport *or* un lien entre 2 événements; **to have a** ~ **with sb** (*general*) avoir des relations *or* être en relations avec qn; (*sexual*) avoir une liaison avec qn; **he has a good** ~ **with his clients** il est en bons rapports avec ses clients; **they have a good** ~ ils s'entendent bien; **friendly/business** ~ relations d'amitié/d'affaires; **his** ~ **with his father was strained** ses rapports avec son père étaient tendus; **the** ~ **between mother and child** les rapports entre la mère et l'enfant.
relative [ˈrelətɪv] **1** *adj* **(a)** (*comparative*) relatif; (*respective*) respectif. **happiness is** ~ le bonheur est relatif; **fuel consumption is** ~ **to speed** la consommation d'essence est fonction de la vitesse; **to live in** ~ **luxury** vivre dans un luxe relatif; **the** ~ **merits of A and B** les mérites respectifs de A et de B.
(b) (*relevant*) ~ **to** relatif à, qui se rapporte à; **the documents** ~ **to the problem** les documents relatifs au *or* qui se rapportent au problème.
(c) (*Ling, Mus*) relatif.
2 *n* **(a)** (*person*) parent(e) *m(f)*.
(b) (*Ling*) relatif *m*.
relatively [ˈrelətɪvlɪ] *adv* (*V* **relative**) relativement; respectivement; (*fairly, rather*) assez. ~ **speaking** relativement parlant.
relativism [ˈrelətɪvɪzəm] *n* relativisme *m*.
relativist [ˈrelətɪvɪst] *adj, n* relativiste (*mf*).
relativistic [ˌrelətɪvˈɪstɪk] *adj* relativiste.
relativity [ˌreləˈtɪvɪtɪ] *n* (*Philos, Phys*) relativité *f*. **theory of** ~ théorie *f* de la relativité.
relax [rɪˈlæks] **1** *vt hold, grip* relâcher, desserrer; (*Med*) *bowels* relâcher; *muscles* relâcher, décontracter, relaxer; *discipline, attention, effort* relâcher; *restrictions* modérer; *person, one's mind* détendre, délasser; *V also* **relaxed**.
2 *vi* **(a)** (*rest*) se détendre, se délasser, se relaxer. (*: *calm down*) **let's just** ~! restons calmes!, ne nous énervons pas!, du calme!
(b) (*V* 1) se relâcher; se desserrer; se décontracter.
relaxation [ˌriːlækˈseɪʃən] *n* **(a)** (*U*) *[muscles, discipline, attention]* relâchement *m*; *[mind]* détente *f*, relaxation *f*; *[body]* décontraction *f*, relaxation.
(b) (*recreation*) détente *f*, délassement *m*; (*rest*) repos *m*. **you need some** ~ **after work** on a besoin d'une détente après le travail; **books are her** ~ pour se délasser *or* se détendre elle lit; **the** ~**s of the wealthy** les distractions *fpl* des riches.
relaxed [rɪˈlækst] *adj discipline, effort, attention* relâché; *muscle etc* relâché, relaxé; *smile, voice, attitude* détendu. (*Med*) ~ **throat** gorge irritée *or* enflammée; **to feel** ~ se sentir détendu *or* décontracté; (*fig: don't feel strongly one way or other*) **I feel fairly** ~ **about it*** ça m'est égal, ça ne me fait ni chaud ni froid*.
relaxing [rɪˈlæksɪŋ] *adj climate* reposant, amollissant (*pej*), débilitant (*pej*); *atmosphere, activity* délassant, relaxant, qui procure de la *or* une détente.
relay [ˈriːleɪ] **1** *n* **(a)** *[horses, men etc]* relais *m*. **to work in** ~**s** travailler par relais, se relayer.
(b) (*Rad, TV*) émission relayée.
(c) (*Sport*) = **relay race**; *V* **2**.
(d) (*Elec, Phys, Tech*) relais *m*.
2 *cpd*: **relay race** course *f* de relais; (*Rad, TV*) **relay station** relais *m*.
3 *vt* (*Elec, Rad, TV etc*) *programme, signal, message* relayer, retransmettre.
re-lay [ˌriːˈleɪ] *vt carpet* reposer.
release [rɪˈliːs] **1** *n* **(a)** (*U*) (*from captivity, obligation*) libération *f*; (*from prison*) libération, élargissement *m* (*frm*); (*Jur: from custody*) relaxe *f*; (*from obligation, responsibility*) libération; (*from service*) dispense *f*, exemption *f*; (*Comm: from customs, bond*) congé *m*. **on his** ~ **from prison he ...** dès sa sortie de prison, il ...; **the** ~ **of the prisoners by the allied forces** la libération des prisonniers par les forces alliées; **death was a happy** ~ **for him** pour lui la mort a été une délivrance.
(b) (*U*) (*Comm*) *[goods]* mise *f* en vente; (*Jur*) *[land]* cession *f*, transfert *m*; *[news]* autorisation *f* de publier; *[film, record]* sortie *f*; *[book]* parution *f*, sortie. **this film is now on general** ~ ce film n'est plus en exclusivité.
(c) (*record*) (nouveau) disque *m*; (*film*) (nouveau) film *m*; (*book*) nouveauté *f*; *V* **press**.
(d) (*U*) *[bomb]* lâchage *m*, largage *m*; (*Phot etc*) déclenchement *m*; *[brake]* dégagement *m*, desserrage *m*; *[steam]* échappement *m*. ~ **valve** soupape *f* de sûreté.
2 *vt* **(a)** (*set free*) *person* (*from prison*) libérer, relâcher (*from* de), mettre en liberté, relaxer (*Jur*); (*from chains*) libérer (*from* de); (*from rubble, wreckage*) dégager (*from* de); (*from obligation*) dégager, libérer (*from* de); (*from promise, vow*) relever (*from* de). (*Jur*) **to** ~ **sb on bail** mettre qn en liberté provisoire sous caution; **to** ~ **sb from a debt** faire la remise d'une dette à qn; **death** ~**d him from pain** la mort mit fin à ses souffrances; **his employer agreed to** ~ **him** son patron lui a permis de cesser son travail; **can you** ~ **him for a few hours each week?** pouvez-vous le libérer *or* le rendre disponible quelques heures par semaine?
(b) (*let go*) *object, sb's hand, pigeon* lâcher; *bomb* lâcher, lar-

guer; (*Chem*) *gas* dégager. to ~ one's grip *or* hold lâcher prise; to ~ one's hold of *or* one's grip on sth lâcher qch.
(c) (*Comm etc*) *book, record* sortir, faire paraître; *film* (faire) sortir; *goods* mettre en vente; *news* autoriser la publication de.
(d) (*Jur*) *property* céder.
(e) *spring, clasp, catch* faire jouer; (*Phot*) *shutter* déclencher; *handbrake* desserrer. (*Aut*) to ~ the clutch débrayer.
relegate ['relɪgeɪt] *vt* **(a)** (*demote*) *person* reléguer; (*Sport*) *team* reléguer (*to* à, en), déclasser. **to ~ old furniture to the attic** reléguer de vieux meubles au grenier. **(b)** (*hand over*) *matter, question* renvoyer (*to* à), se décharger de (*to* sur).
relegation [ˌrelɪ'geɪʃən] *n* relégation *f* (*also Sport*); *[matter, question]* renvoi *m* (*to* à).
relent [rɪ'lent] *vi* s'adoucir, se laisser toucher, se laisser fléchir; (*reverse one's decision*) revenir sur une décision.
relentless [rɪ'lentlɪs] *adj* implacable, impitoyable, inflexible.
relentlessly [rɪ'lentlɪslɪ] *adv* implacablement, impitoyablement.
relet ['riː'let] *vt* relouer.
relevance ['reləvəns] *n* pertinence *f*, à-propos *m inv*, rapport *m* (*to* avec). **what is the ~ of your question to the problem?** quel est le rapport entre votre question et le problème?
relevant ['reləvənt] *adj* ayant rapport (*to* à); *remark, argument* pertinent (*to* à); *regulation* applicable, approprié (*to* à); *fact* significatif; *information, course, study* utile; (*Jur*) *document* justificatif. **that is not ~** cela n'entre pas en ligne de compte, cela n'a rien à voir*; **you must refer to the ~ chapter** vous devez vous rapporter au chapitre approprié.
reliability [rɪˌlaɪə'bɪlɪtɪ] *n [person, character]* (esprit *m* de) sérieux *m*; *[memory, description]* sûreté *f*, précision *f*; *[device, machine]* qualité *f*, robustesse *f*, solidité *f*, fiabilité *f*.
reliable [rɪ'laɪəbl] *adj person* sérieux, digne de confiance, sûr; *employee* sérieux, efficace, sur qui l'on peut compter *or* se reposer; *firm, company* sérieux; *machine* bon, solide, fiable; *information* sérieux, sûr. **she's very ~** elle est très sérieuse, on peut toujours compter sur elle; **a ~ source of information** une source digne de foi, une source sûre; **her memory is not very ~** on ne peut pas vraiment se fier à sa mémoire.
reliably [rɪ'laɪəblɪ] *adv work* sérieusement. **I am ~ informed that ...** j'apprends de source sûre *or* de bonne source que ... .
reliance [rɪ'laɪəns] *n* (*trust*) confiance *f* (*on* en); (*dependence*) dépendance *f* (*on* de), besoin *m* (*on* de). **to place ~ on sb/in sth** avoir confiance en qn/en qch.
reliant [rɪ'laɪənt] *adj* (*trusting*) confiant (*on* en). (*dependent*) **~ on** dépendant de, qui compte sur, qui a besoin de; **self-~** indépendant.
relic ['relɪk] *n* relique *f* (*also Rel*). (*human remains*) **~s** restes *mpl*, dépouille *f* (mortelle).
relict†† ['relɪkt] *n* veuve *f*.
relief [rɪ'liːf] **1** *n* **(a)** (*from pain, anxiety*) soulagement *m*. **to bring ~** to apporter *or* procurer du soulagement à; **I felt great ~ when ...** j'ai éprouvé un grand *or* vif soulagement quand ...; **to my ~** à mon grand soulagement; **that's a ~!** quel soulagement!; **(to me) it was a ~ to find it** j'ai été soulagé de le retrouver; *V* **comic**.
(b) (*assistance*) secours *m*, aide *f*, assistance *f*. **to go to the ~ of** aller au secours de; **to come to the ~ of** venir en aide à; **to send ~ to** envoyer des secours à.
(c) (*Mil*) *[town]* délivrance *f*; *[guard]* relève *f*.
(d) (*exemption*) (*Jur*) exonération *f*; (*fiscal*) dégrèvement *m*.
(e) (*Art, Geog*) relief *m*. **high/low ~** haut-/bas-relief; **to stand out in ~ against** se détacher sur; (*lit, fig*) **to bring *or* throw sth into ~** mettre qch en relief, faire ressortir qch.
2 *cpd train, coach, typist, clerk* supplémentaire. **relief fund** caisse *f* de secours; **relief map** carte *f* en relief; *[refugees, earthquakes etc]* **relief organization** société *f* de secours; **relief road** route *f* de délestage; **relief supplies** secours *mpl*; **relief troops** relève *f*, troupes *fpl* de secours; **relief valve** soupape *f* de sûreté; **relief work** œuvres *fpl* de secours.
relieve [rɪ'liːv] *vt* **(a)** *person* soulager. **to feel ~d** se sentir soulagé; **he was ~d to learn that ...** il a été soulagé d'apprendre que ...; **to ~ sb of a burden** soulager qn d'un fardeau; **to ~ sb of a coat/suitcase** débarrasser qn d'un manteau/d'une valise; **to ~ sb of a duty** décharger qn d'une obligation; **to ~ sb of a post,** (*Mil*) **to ~ sb of a command** relever qn de ses fonctions; **the news ~d me of anxiety** la nouvelle a dissipé mes inquiétudes; (*hum*) **a thief has ~d me of my purse** un voleur m'a soulagé de (*hum*) *or* délesté de* mon porte-monnaie.
(b) (*mitigate*) *anxiety, pain* soulager, alléger; *fear, boredom* dissiper; *poverty* remédier à, pallier. **to ~ sb's mind** tranquilliser (l'esprit de) qn; **to ~ one's feelings** (*sorrow*) s'épancher, décharger son cœur; (*anger*) décharger sa colère *or* sa bile; **to ~ a situation** remédier à une situation; **the black of her dress was ~d by a white collar** un col blanc égayait sa robe noire; **the new road ~s peak-hour congestion** la nouvelle route facilite la circulation aux heures de pointe; **the new road ~s congestion in the town centre** la nouvelle route décongestionne le centre de la ville; (*Med*) **to ~ congestion** décongestionner; (*euph*) **to ~ o.s.** se soulager*, faire ses besoins*.
(c) (*help*) secourir, aider, venir en aide à.
(d) (*take over from*) relayer. **Paul will ~ you at 6** Paul vous relayera à 6 heures; (*Mil*) **to ~ the guard** relever la garde.
(e) (*Mil*) *town* délivrer, faire lever le siège de.
relievo [rɪ'liːvəʊ] *n* (*Art*) relief *m*.
religion [rɪ'lɪdʒən] *n* (*belief*) religion *f*; (*form of worship*) culte *m*. **the Christian ~** la religion chrétienne; **this new ~ already has many adherents** ce nouveau culte a déjà de nombreux adeptes; **wars of ~** guerres *fpl* de religion; (*fig*) **to make a ~ of doing** se faire une obligation (absolue) de faire; (*lit*) **it's against my ~ (to do that)** c'est contraire à ma religion (de faire cela); (*hum*) **it's against my ~ to clean windows*** je ne fais jamais les vitres, c'est contraire à ma religion (*hum*); **to enter ~** entrer en religion; **her name in ~** son nom de religion; **he's got ~*** il est devenu bigot *or* calotin*.
religiosity [rɪˌlɪdʒɪ'ɒsɪtɪ] *n* religiosité *f*.
religious [rɪ'lɪdʒəs] **1** *adj* **(a)** *person, teaching, order, life, freedom* religieux; *book* de piété; *wars* de religion. **to be very ~** être pieux *or* croyant *or* pratiquant.
(b) (*fig: conscientious, exact*) *care* scrupuleux, religieux; *silence* religieux.
2 *n* religieux *m*, -ieuse *f*.
religiously [rɪ'lɪdʒəslɪ] *adv* religieusement, pieusement; (*conscientiously*) scrupuleusement.
religiousness [rɪ'lɪdʒəsnɪs] *n* piété *f*, dévotion *f*.
reline ['riː'laɪn] *vt coat, jacket* mettre une nouvelle doublure à, redoubler.
relinquish [rɪ'lɪŋkwɪʃ] *vt* **(a)** (*give up*) *hope, power* abandonner; *plan, right* renoncer à (*to sb* en faveur de qn); *habit* renoncer à; *post* quitter, abandonner; *goods, property etc* se dessaisir de, abandonner.
(b) (*let go*) *object* lâcher. **to ~ one's hold on sth** lâcher qch.
relinquishment [rɪ'lɪŋkwɪʃmənt] *n* (*V* **relinquish**) abandon *m* (*of* de); renonciation *f* (*of* à).
reliquary ['relɪkwərɪ] *n* reliquaire *m*.
relish ['relɪʃ] **1** *n* **(a)** (*enjoyment*) goût *m* (*for* pour). **to do sth with (great) ~, to take ~ in doing sth** faire qch avec goût *or* délectation; **he ate with ~** il mangeait de bon appétit.
(b) (*Culin*) (*flavour*) goût *m*, saveur *f*; (*seasoning*) condiment *m*, assaisonnement *m*; (*trace: of spices etc*) soupçon *m*; (*fig: charm*) attrait *m*, charme *m*. (*fig*) **it had lost all ~** cela avait perdu tout attrait.
2 *vt food, wine* savourer. **to ~ doing** se délecter à faire, trouver du plaisir à faire; **I don't ~ the thought of getting up at 5** l'idée de me lever à 5 heures ne me sourit guère *or* ne me dit rien.
relive ['riː'lɪv] *vt* revivre.
reload ['riː'ləʊd] *vt* recharger.
reluctance [rɪ'lʌktəns] *n* **(a)** répugnance *f* (*to do* à faire). **to do sth with ~** faire qch à regret *or* avec répugnance *or* à contrecœur; **to make a show of ~** se faire prier, se faire tirer l'oreille. **(b)** (*Elec*) réluctance *f*.
reluctant [rɪ'lʌktənt] *adj* **(a)** (*unwilling, disinclined*) *person, animal* peu disposé (*to* à), peu enthousiaste. **he is ~ to do it** il hésite *or* il rechigne *or* il est peu disposé à le faire; **he is a ~ soldier** il est soldat mais il n'a pas le feu sacré.
(b) (*done unwillingly*) fait à regret *or* à contrecœur; *consent, praise* accordé à contrecœur.
reluctantly [rɪ'lʌktəntlɪ] *adv* à regret, à contrecœur, sans enthousiasme.
rely [rɪ'laɪ] *vi*: **to ~ (up)on sb/sth** compter sur qn/qch, avoir confiance en qn/qch, se fier à qn/qch; **she relied on the trains being on time** elle comptait *or* tablait sur le fait que les trains seraient à l'heure; **I ~ on him for my income** je dépends de lui pour mes revenus; **you can ~ upon it** vous pouvez y compter; **you can ~ on me not to say anything about it** vous pouvez compter sur moi pour ne pas en parler, comptez sur ma discrétion; **she is not to be relied upon** on ne peut pas compter sur elle; **he relies increasingly on his assistants** il se repose de plus en plus sur ses assistants.
remain [rɪ'meɪn] *vi* **(a)** (*be left*) rester. **much ~s to be done** il reste beaucoup à faire; **nothing ~s to be said** il ne reste plus rien à dire; **nothing ~s but to accept** il ne reste plus qu'à accepter; **it ~s to be seen whether ...** reste à savoir si ...; **that ~s to be seen** c'est ce que nous verrons, c'est ce qu'il reste à voir; **the fact ~s that he is wrong** il n'en est pas moins vrai *or* toujours est-il qu'il a tort; **take 2 from 4, 2 ~ 4** moins 2, il reste 2.
(b) (*stay*) rester, demeurer. **to ~ faithful** demeurer *or* rester fidèle; **~ seated** restez assis; **to ~ out/in** *etc* rester (en) dehors/(en) dedans *etc*; **to ~ up** rester levé; **let the matter ~ as it is** laissez l'affaire comme cela; **it ~s the same** ça ne change pas; **to ~ silent** garder le silence; **it ~s unsolved** ce n'est toujours pas résolu; **if the weather ~s fine** si le temps se maintient (au beau); (*in letters*) **I ~, yours faithfully** je vous prie d'agréer *or* veuillez agréer l'expression de mes sentiments distingués.
remain behind *vi* rester.
remainder [rɪ'meɪndəʳ] **1** *n* **(a)** (*part of thing left over*) reste *m*; (*remaining people*) autres *mfpl*; (*Math*) reste; (*Jur*) usufruit *m* avec réversibilité. **for the ~ of the week** pendant le reste *or* le restant de la semaine.
(b) **~s** (*Comm*) (*books etc*) invendus soldés; (*clothes, articles*) fin(s) *f(pl)* de série.
2 *vt books etc* solder.
remaining [rɪ'meɪnɪŋ] *adj* qui reste. **I have only one ~** il ne m'en reste qu'un, je n'en ai qu'un de reste; **the ~ cakes** le reste des gâteaux, les gâteaux qui restent.
remains [rɪ'meɪnz] *npl [meal]* restes *mpl*; *[fortune, army]* débris *mpl*; *[building]* restes, vestiges *mpl*, ruines *fpl*. **literary ~** œuvres *fpl* posthumes; **his (mortal) ~** ses restes, sa dépouille mortelle; **human ~** restes humains.
remake ['riː'meɪk] **1** *vt* refaire. **2** ['riːmeɪk] *n* (*Cine*) remake *m*.
remand [rɪ'mɑːnd] **1** *vt* (*Jur*) renvoyer (*to* à). **to ~ sb to a higher court** renvoyer qn à une instance supérieure; **to ~ in custody** renvoyer avec détention provisoire; **the man ~ed in custody** le détenu préventif; **case ~ed for a week** affaire renvoyée à huitaine.
2 *n* renvoi *m* (à une autre audience). **to be on ~** être en détention préventive *or* en prévention; (*Brit*) **~ home** ≃ maison *f* d'arrêt.
remark [rɪ'mɑːk] **1** *n* **(a)** (*comment*) remarque *f*, réflexion *f*, observation *f*, commentaire *m*. **to make *or* pass the ~ that**

remarquer que, faire observer que; **I have a few ~s to make on that subject** j'ai quelques remarques *or* réflexions *or* observations à vous communiquer à ce sujet; **~s were passed about your absence** on a fait des remarques *or* des réflexions sur votre absence.

(b) (*U*) remarque *f*, attention *f*. **worthy of ~** digne d'attention, remarquable.

2 *vt* **(a)** *(say)* (faire) remarquer, (faire) observer. **'I can't go' he ~ed** 'je ne peux pas y aller' dit-il.

(b) (*notice*) remarquer, observer.

3 *vi* faire des remarques *or* des observations (*on* sur). **he ~ed on it to me** il m'en a fait l'observation *or* la remarque.

remarkable [rɪ'mɑːkəbl] *adj* remarquable (*for* par); *event* remarquable, marquant; *pupil, mind* remarquable, brillant.

remarkably [rɪ'mɑːkəblɪ] *adv* remarquablement.

remarriage ['riː'mærɪdʒ] *n* remariage *m*.

remarry ['riː'mærɪ] *vi* se remarier.

remediable [rɪ'miːdɪəbl] *adj* remédiable.

remedial [rɪ'miːdɪəl] *adj action* réparateur (*f* -trice); *measures* de redressement; *class* de rattrapage. **~ (course in) English** cours *m* de rattrapage en anglais; **~ exercises** gymnastique médicale *or* corrective; **~ teaching** cours *mpl* de rattrapage; **~ treatment** traitement curatif.

remedy ['remədɪ] **1** *n* (*Med, fig*) remède *m* (*for* contre, à, de); (*Jur*) recours *m*. **past *or* beyond ~** sans remède; **we must provide a ~ for injustice** nous devons trouver un remède à l'injustice; **the ~ for boredom is work** le travail est le remède de *or* contre l'ennui; **the ~ for despair** le remède contre le désespoir.

2 *vt* (*Med*) remédier à; (*fig*) remédier à, porter remède à. **the situation cannot be remedied** la situation est sans remède.

remember [rɪ'membəʳ] **1** *vt* **(a)** (*recall*) *person, date, occasion* se souvenir de, se rappeler. **to ~ that** se rappeler que; **I ~ doing it** je me rappelle l'avoir fait *or* que je l'ai fait, je me souviens de l'avoir fait; **I ~ed to do it** j'ai pensé à le faire; **I ~ when an egg cost one penny** je me souviens de l'époque où un œuf coûtait un penny; **I cannot ~ your name** je ne me rappelle pas votre nom; **don't you ~ me?** (*face to face*) vous ne me reconnaissez pas?; (*phone*) vous ne vous souvenez pas de moi?; **I ~ your face** je me souviens de votre visage, je vous reconnais; **I don't ~ a thing about it** je n'en ai pas le moindre souvenir; **I can never ~ phone numbers** je n'ai aucune mémoire pour les numéros de téléphone; **let us ~ that ...** n'oublions pas que ...; **here's something to ~ him by** voici un souvenir de lui; **I can't ~ the word at the moment** le mot m'échappe pour le moment; **we can't always ~ everything** on ne peut pas toujours songer à tout; **~ where you are!** ressaisissez-vous!; **to ~ o.s.** se reprendre; **to ~ sb in one's prayers/one's will** ne pas oublier qn dans ses prières/son testament.

(b) (*commemorate*) *the fallen, a battle* commémorer.

(c) (*give good wishes to*) rappeler (*to* au bon souvenir de). **~ me to your mother** rappelez-moi au bon souvenir de votre mère; **he asks to be ~ed to you** il vous envoie son meilleur souvenir.

2 *vi* se souvenir. **I can't ~** je ne me souviens pas, je ne sais plus; **as far as I ~** autant qu'il m'en souvienne; **not as far as I ~** pas à ma connaissance, pas que je m'en souvienne; **if I ~ right(ly)** si j'ai bonne mémoire, si je m'en *or* me souviens bien.

remembrance [rɪ'membrəns] *n* (*memory, thing remembered*) souvenir *m*, mémoire *f*; (*act of remembering, keepsake*) souvenir. **R~ Day** (le jour de) l'Armistice *m*, le onze novembre; **in ~ of** en souvenir de; **to the best of my ~** autant qu'il m'en souvienne; **within the ~ of man** de mémoire d'homme; **to have no ~ of** ne pas se souvenir de, n'avoir aucun souvenir de; **give my kind ~s to your sister** rappelez-moi au bon souvenir de votre sœur.

remind [rɪ'maɪnd] *vt* rappeler (*sb of sth* qch à qn, *sb that* à qn que). **you are ~ed that ...** nous vous rappelons que ...; **to ~ sb to do** faire penser à qn à faire; **must I ~ you (again)?** faut-il que je (vous) le redise? *or* le rappelle (*subj*) encore une fois?; **she ~ed him of his mother** elle lui rappelait sa mère; **that ~s me!** à propos!

reminder [rɪ'maɪndəʳ] *n* (*note, knot etc*) mémento *m*, pense-bête *m*. **as a ~ that** pour (vous *or* lui *etc*) rappeler que; **his presence was a ~ of ...** sa présence rappelait ...; **a gentle ~** un rappel discret; **give him a gentle ~** rappelez-le-lui discrètement; (*Comm*) **(letter of) ~** lettre *f* de rappel.

reminisce [ˌremɪ'nɪs] *vi* raconter ses souvenirs (*about* de).

reminiscence [ˌremɪ'nɪsəns] *n* réminiscence *f*.

reminiscent [ˌremɪ'nɪsənt] *adj*: **~ of** qui rappelle, qui fait penser à, évocateur (*f* -trice) de; **style ~ of Shakespeare's** style qui rappelle (celui de) Shakespeare.

reminiscently [ˌremɪ'nɪsəntlɪ] *adv*: **to smile ~** sourire à un souvenir *or* à ce souvenir; **he talked ~ of the war** il rappelait ses souvenirs de (la) guerre, il évoquait des souvenirs de (la) guerre.

remiss [rɪ'mɪs] *adj* négligent, insouciant, peu zélé. **he has been ~ in not finishing his work** c'est négligent de sa part de ne pas avoir terminé son travail; **that was very ~ of you** vous vous êtes montré très négligent.

remission [rɪ'mɪʃən] *n* (*gen, Med, Rel*) rémission *f*; (*Jur*) remise *f*. **the ~ of sins** la rémission des péchés; (*Jur*) **he earned 3 years' ~ (for good conduct)** on lui a accordé 3 ans de remise (pour bonne conduite); (*Jur*) **~ from a debt** remise d'une dette; **there can be no ~ of registration fees** il ne peut y avoir de dispense *or* d'exemption des droits d'inscription.

remissness [rɪ'mɪsnɪs] *n* négligence *f*, manque *m* de zèle.

remit[1] [rɪ'mɪt] **1** *vt* **(a)** (*Rel*) *sins* pardonner, remettre; (*Jur etc*) *fee, debt, penalty* remettre. **the prisoner's sentence was ~ted** on a remis la peine du détenu, le détenu a reçu une remise de peine.

(b) (*send*) *money* envoyer, faire parvenir.

(c) (*lessen*) relâcher, se relâcher de.

(d) (*postpone*) différer.

(e) (*Jur*) renvoyer (à une instance inférieure).

2 *vi* (*become less*) diminuer; *[storm]* se calmer; *[effort]* se relâcher.

remit[2] ['riːmɪt] *n* attributions *fpl*.

remittal [rɪ'mɪtl] *n* (*Jur*) = **remitter b.**

remittance [rɪ'mɪtəns] *n* (*sending*) envoi *m or* remise *f* (*de fonds*); (*money sent*) versement *m*. **enclose your ~** joignez le paiement.

remittee [remɪ'tiː] *n* destinataire *mf* (*d'un envoi de fonds*).

remittent [rɪ'mɪtənt] *adj* (*Med*) rémittent; (*fig*) intermittent.

remitter [rɪ'mɪtəʳ] *n* **(a)** remetteur *m*, -euse *f*; *[money]* envoyeur *m*, -euse *f*; (*Comm*) remettant *m*. **(b)** (*Jur*) renvoi *m* (à une instance inférieure).

remnant ['remnənt] **1** *n* (*anything remaining*) reste *m*, restant *m*; (*piece*) débris *m*, bout *m*; *[custom, splendour]* vestige *m*; *[food, fortune]* bribe *f*, débris; *[cloth]* coupon *m*. (*Comm*) **~s** soldes *mpl* (de fins de série).

2 *cpd*: (*Comm*) **remnant day** jour *m* de soldes; **remnant sale** solde *m* (de coupons *or* d'invendus *or* de fins de série).

remodel [ˌriː'mɒdl] *vt* (*also Art, Tech*) remodeler; (*fig*) *society* réorganiser; *constitution* remanier.

remonstrance [rɪ'mɒnstrəns] *n* **(a)** (*U*) remontrance *f*.

(b) (*protest*) protestation *f*; (*reproof*) reproche *f*.

remonstrant [rɪ'mɒnstrənt] **1** *adj tone* de remontrance, de protestation. **2** *n* protestataire *mf*.

remonstrate ['remənstreɪt] **1** *vi* protester (*against* contre). **to ~ with sb about sth** faire des remontrances à qn au sujet de qch.

2 *vt* faire observer *or* remarquer (*that* que) (*avec l'idée de reproche ou de contradiction*).

remorse [rɪ'mɔːs] *n* (*U*) remords *m* (*at* de, *for* pour). **a feeling of ~** un remords; **without ~** sans pitié.

remorseful [rɪ'mɔːsfʊl] *adj* plein de remords.

remorsefully [rɪ'mɔːsfəlɪ] *adv* avec remords.

remorsefulness [rɪ'mɔːsfʊlnɪs] *n* (*U*) remords *m*.

remorseless [rɪ'mɔːslɪs] *adj* sans remords, dénué de remords; (*fig*) implacable.

remorselessly [rɪ'mɔːslɪslɪ] *adv* sans remords; (*fig*) sans pitié, impitoyablement, implacablement.

remorselessness [rɪ'mɔːslɪsnɪs] *n* absence *f or* manque *m* de pitié *or* de remords.

remote [rɪ'məʊt] **1** *adj* **(a)** *place* (*distant*) lointain, éloigné; (*isolated*) écarté, isolé; *past time* lointain, ancien, reculé; *future time* lointain; *person* distant, froid, réservé. **in ~ country districts** au (fin) fond de la campagne; **in the remotest parts of Africa** au fin fond de l'Afrique; **in a ~ spot** dans un lieu retiré *or* écarté *or* à l'écart; **house ~ from a main road** maison située loin *or* à l'écart d'une grand-route; **~ antiquity** antiquité reculée, haute antiquité; **in the ~ past/future** dans le passé/l'avenir lointain; **~ ancestor** ancêtre éloigné; **what he said was rather ~ from the subject in hand** ce qu'il a dit était plutôt éloigné de la question; **you will find her rather ~** vous la trouverez assez distante *or* d'un abord assez difficile.

(b) (*slight*) vague, petit. **very ~ resemblance** ressemblance très vague *or* lointaine; **I haven't the remotest idea** je n'ai pas la moindre idée; **he hasn't a ~ chance** il n'a pas le moindre espoir; **there is a ~ possibility that he will come** il y a une petite chance qu'il vienne.

2 *cpd*: **remote control** télécommande *f*, commande *f* à distance; **remote-controlled** télécommandé.

remotely [rɪ'məʊtlɪ] *adv* **(a)** (*distantly*) *situated* au loin, dans le lointain. **we are ~ related** nous sommes parents éloignés.

(b) (*haughtily*) *look, speak* de façon distante, avec froideur.

(c) (*slightly*) vaguement, faiblement. **it is ~ possible that** il est tout juste possible que + *subj*.

remoteness [rɪ'məʊtnɪs] *n* (*in space*) éloignement *m*, isolement *m*; (*in time*) éloignement. **his ~** son attitude distante *or* réservée (*from sb* envers qn); **his ~ from everyday life** son isolement de la vie ordinaire.

remould [ˌriː'məʊld] (*Brit*) **1** *vt* (*Tech*) remouler; *tyre* rechaper; (*fig*) *sb's character* corriger. **2** ['riːməʊld] *n* (*tyre*) pneu rechapé.

remount [ˌriː'maʊnt] **1** *vt* **(a)** *horse* remonter sur; *bicycle* enfourcher de nouveau; *hill* remonter; *ladder* grimper de nouveau sur. **(b)** *picture* rentoiler; *photo* faire un nouveau montage de. **2** *vi* remonter à cheval (*or* à bicyclette).

removable [rɪ'muːvəbl] *adj* (*detachable*) amovible, détachable; (*movable*) *object* mobile; *machine* transportable.

removal [rɪ'muːvəl] **1** *n* enlèvement *m*; *[furniture, household]* déménagement *m*; *[abuse, evil]* suppression *f*; *[pain]* soulagement *m*; (*from a job*) (*demotion*) déplacement *m*; (*sacking*) renvoi *m*, révocation *f*; (*Med*) ablation *f*. **stain ~** détachage *m*; **after our ~** après notre changement *m* de domicile; **our ~ to this house** notre emménagement *m* dans cette maison; **our ~ from London** notre déménagement de Londres.

2 *cpd*: **removal allowance** indemnité *f* de déménagement; **removal expenses** frais *mpl* de déménagement; **removal man** déménageur *m*; **removal van** voiture *f or* camion *m or* fourgon *m* de déménagement.

remove [rɪ'muːv] **1** *vt object* enlever (*from* de); *clothes* enlever, ôter; *furniture* enlever, *[removers]* déménager; *stain, graffiti* enlever, faire partir; *paragraph, word, item on list* rayer, barrer; *threat, tax, abuse* supprimer; *objection* réfuter; *difficulty, problem* résoudre; (*lit, fig*) *obstacle* écarter; *doubt* chasser; *suspicion, fear* dissiper; *employee* renvoyer, destituer; *official* déplacer; (*Med*) *lung, kidney* enlever, pratiquer l'ablation de, retirer; *tumour* extirper, enlever; *splint, bandage* enlever. **~ the lid** enlevez le couvercle; **he was ~d to**

the cells on l'a emmené en cellule; **to ~ sb to hospital** hospitaliser qn; **to ~ a child from school** retirer un enfant de l'école; **he ~d himself to another room** il s'est retiré dans une autre pièce; (*hum*) **I must ~ myself*** je dois filer*; **to ~ sb's name** rayer qn, radier qn; **to ~ one's make-up** se démaquiller; **make-up removing cream** crème démaquillante; **to ~ unwanted hair from the legs** épiler les jambes; (*fig*) **to be far ~d from** être loin de; **cousin once/twice ~d** cousin(e) *m(f)* au deuxième/troisième degré.

2 *vi* déménager, changer de domicile. **to ~ to London** aller habiter (à) Londres, aller s'installer à Londres.

3 *n* (*in relationship*) degré *m* de parenté. (*fig*) **to be only a few ~s from** être tout proche de; **this is but one ~ from disaster** nous frisons (*or* ils frisent *etc*) le désastre; **it's a far ~ from ...** c'est loin d'être ... .

remover [rɪ'muːvəʳ] *n* **(a)** (*removal man*) déménageur *m*.
(b) *[varnish]* dissolvant *m*; *[stains]* détachant *m*. **paint ~** décapant *m* (pour peintures); *V* **cuticle, hair, make-up.**

remunerate [rɪ'mjuːnəreɪt] *vt* rémunérer.

remuneration [rɪ,mjuːnə'reɪʃən] *n* rémunération *f* (*for* de).

remunerative [rɪ'mjuːnərətɪv] *adj* rémunérateur (*f* -trice), lucratif.

renaissance [rɪ'neɪsɑ̃ːns] **1** *n* renaissance *f*. (*Hist*) **the R~** la Renaissance. **2** *cpd*: **Renaissance** *art, scholar* de la Renaissance; *style, palace* Renaissance *inv*.

renal ['riːnl] *adj* rénal. **~ failure** défaillance *or* insuffisance rénale.

rename ['riː'neɪm] *vt person, street, town* rebaptiser (*fig*).

renascence [rɪ'næsns] *n* = **renaissance.**

renascent [rɪ'næsnt] *adj* renaissant.

rend [rend] *pret, ptp* **rent** *vt* (*liter*) *cloth* déchirer; *armour* fendre; (*fig*) déchirer, fendre. (*lit, fig*) **to ~ sth from** arracher qch à *or* de; **country rent by civil war** pays déchiré par la guerre civile; **a cry rent the silence** un cri a déchiré le silence; **to ~ sb's heart** fendre le cœur à qn.

render ['rendəʳ] *vt* **(a)** (*frm: give*) *service, homage, judgment* rendre; *help* donner; *explanation* donner, fournir. **~ unto Caesar the things which are Caesar's** rendez donc *or* il faut rendre à César ce qui est de César; **to ~ thanks to sb** remercier qn; **to ~ thanks to God** rendre grâce à Dieu; **to ~ assistance** prêter assistance *or* secours; **to ~ an account of sth** rendre compte de qch.
(b) (*Comm*) *account* remettre, présenter. **(to) account ~ed £10** rappel de compte *or* facture de rappel — 10 livres.
(c) *music* interpréter; *text* rendre, traduire (*into* en).
(d) (*make*) rendre. **his accident ~ed him helpless** son accident l'a rendu complètement infirme.
(e) (*Culin*) *fat* faire fondre, clarifier.
(f) (*Constr*) plâtrer.

render down *vt sep fat* faire fondre.

render up *vt sep* (*liter*) *fortress* rendre; *prisoner, treasure* livrer.

rendering ['rendərɪŋ] *n [piece of music, poem]* interprétation *f*; (*translation*) traduction *f* (*into* en).

rendez-vous ['rɒndɪvuː] **1** *n,pl* **rendez-vous** ['rɒndɪvuːz] rendez-vous *m*. **2** *vi* (*meet*) se retrouver; (*assemble*) se réunir. (*Mil etc*) **they rendez-voused with the patrol at dawn** ils ont rejoint la patrouille à l'aube.

rendition [ren'dɪʃən] *n* = **rendering.**

reneague [rɪ'niːg] *vi* = **renege.**

renegade ['renɪgeɪd] *n* renégat(e) *m(f)*.

renege [rɪ'niːg] *vi* manquer à sa parole; (*Cards*) renoncer. **to ~ on a promise** manquer à sa promesse.

renew [rɪ'njuː] *vt appointment, attack, contract, passport, promise, one's strength* renouveler; *lease* renouveler, reconduire; *supplies* remplacer, renouveler. **to ~ negotiations/discussions** reprendre des négociations/discussions; **to ~ one's subscription** renouveler son abonnement, se réabonner; **to ~ one's acquaintance with sb** renouer connaissance avec qn; **with ~ed enthusiasm** avec un regain d'enthousiasme; **~ed outbreaks of rioting** recrudescence *f* de troubles; **to make ~ed efforts to do** redoubler d'efforts pour faire.

renewable [rɪ'njuːəbl] *adj* renouvelable.

renewal [rɪ'njuːəl] *n* (*V* **renew**) renouvellement *m*; reconduction *f*; remplacement *m*; reprise *f*; *[strength]* regain *m*. **~ of subscription** réabonnement *m*.

rennet ['renɪt] *n* (*extract*) présure *f*; (*apple*) reinette *f*.

renounce [rɪ'naʊns] **1** *vt liberty, opinions, ideas, title* renoncer à; *religion* abjurer; *right* renoncer à, abandonner; *treaty* dénoncer; *friend* renier; *cause, party* renier, désavouer; *principles* répudier. **2** *vi* (*Cards*) renoncer.

renouncement [rɪ'naʊnsmənt] *n* = **renunciation.**

renovate ['renəʊveɪt] *vt clothes, house* remettre à neuf, rénover; *building, painting, statue* restaurer.

renovation [,renəʊ'veɪʃən] *n* (*V* **renovate**) remise *f* à neuf, rénovation *f*; restauration *f*.

renown [rɪ'naʊn] *n* renommée *f*, renom *m*, célébrité *f*. **of high ~** de grand renom.

renowned [rɪ'naʊnd] *adj* renommé (*for* pour), célèbre (*for* par), en renom, illustre.

rent[1] [rent] **1** *n [house, room]* loyer *m*; *[farm]* fermage *m*; *[television etc]* (prix *m* de) location *f*. (*US*) **for ~** à louer; **quarter's ~** terme *m*; **(one week) late** *or* **behind with one's ~** en retard (d'une semaine) sur son loyer; **to pay a high/low ~ for** payer un gros/petit loyer pour; **evicted for non-payment of ~** expulsé pour non-paiement de loyer.

2 *cpd*: **rent collector** receveur *m* de loyers; **rent control** contrôle *m* des loyers; **rent-controlled** au loyer contrôlé (par le gouvernement); **rent-free** (*adj*) exempt de loyer, gratuit; (*adv*) sans payer de loyer; **rent rebate** dégrèvement *m* de loyer.

3 *vt* **(a)** (*take for ~*) louer, prendre en location. **we don't own it, only ~ it** nous ne sommes pas propriétaires, mais locataires seulement.
(b) (*also ~ out*) louer, donner en location.

4 *vi [house etc]* se louer, être loué.

rent[2] [rent] **1** *pret, ptp of* **rend. 2** *n* (*tear*) *[cloth]* déchirure *f*, accroc *m*; *[rock]* fissure *f*; *[clouds]* déchirure, trouée *f*; (*fig*) *[party etc]* rupture *f*, scission *f*.

rental ['rentl] *n* (*amount paid*) *[house, land]* (montant *m* du) loyer *m*, prix *m* de location; *[television etc]* (prix de) location *f*; (*income from rents*) revenu *m* en loyers *or* fermages. (*US*) **~ library** bibliothèque *f* de prêt (*payante*).

renumber [,riː'nʌmbəʳ] *vt* numéroter de nouveau, renuméroter.

renunciation [rɪ,nʌnsɪ'eɪʃən] *n* (*V* **renounce**) renonciation *f* (*of* à); abjuration *f*; dénonciation *f*; reniement *m*, désaveu *m* (*of* de); (*Jur*) répudiation *f*.

reoccupy [,riː'ɒkjʊpaɪ] *vt* réoccuper.

reopen [,riː'əʊpən] **1** *vt box, door* rouvrir; *fight, battle, hostilities* reprendre; *debate, discussion* rouvrir. (*Jur*) **to ~ a case** rouvrir une affaire. **2** *vi [school]* reprendre; *[shop, theatre etc]* rouvrir; *[wound]* se rouvrir.

reopening [,riː'əʊpnɪŋ] *n* réouverture *f*.

reorder ['riː'ɔːdəʳ] *vt* **(a)** *goods, supplies* commander de nouveau. **(b)** (*reorganize*) reclasser, réorganiser.

reorganization ['riː,ɔːgənaɪ'zeɪʃən] *n* réorganisation *f*.

reorganize ['riː'ɔːgənaɪz] **1** *vt* réorganiser. **2** *vi* se réorganiser.

rep[1]* [rep] *n abbr of* **repertory b.**

rep[2] [rep] *n* (*Tex*) reps *m*.

rep[3]* [rep] *n* (*Comm abbr of* **representative**) représentant *m* (de commerce), agent commercial.

repaint ['riː'peɪnt] *vt* repeindre.

repair[1] [rɪ'pɛəʳ] **1** *vt tyre, shoes, chair* réparer; *clothes* réparer, raccommoder; *machine, watch* réparer, arranger; *roof, road* réparer, refaire; (*Naut*) *hull* radouber; (*fig*) *error, wrong* réparer, remédier à.

2 *n* **(a)** réparation *f*; *[clothes]* raccommodage *m*; *[roof, road]* réfection *f*; (*Naut*) *[hull]* radoub *m*. **to be under ~** être en réparation; (*lit, fig*) **(damaged) beyond ~** irréparable; **closed for ~s** fermé pour cause de travaux; **'road ~s'** 'chantier'; **'(shoe) ~s while you wait'** 'talon minute'.
(b) (*U: condition*) **to be in good/bad ~** être en bon/mauvais état; **to keep in (good) ~** entretenir.

3 *cpd*: **repair kit** trousse *f* de réparation *or* d'outils; **repair man** réparateur *m*; **repair outfit** = **repair kit; repair shop** atelier *m* de réparations.

repair[2] [rɪ'pɛəʳ] *vi* (*liter: go*) aller, se rendre.

repairable [rɪ'pɛərəbl] *adj* réparable.

repairer [rɪ'pɛərəʳ] *n* réparateur *m*, -trice *f*; *V* **clock, shoe** *etc*.

repaper [,riː'peɪpəʳ] *vt* retapisser, refaire les papiers peints de.

reparable ['repərəbl] *adj* réparable.

reparation [,repə'reɪʃən] *n* réparation *f*. **to make ~s for** réparer (*une injure etc*).

repartee [,repɑː'tiː] *n* repartie *f*, réplique *f*. **to be good at ~** avoir la réplique facile, avoir de la repartie.

repast [rɪ'pɑːst] *n* (*liter*) repas *m*, banquet *m*.

repatriate [riː'pætrɪeɪt] **1** *vt* rapatrier. **2** *n* [riː'pætrɪət] rapatrié(e) *m(f)*.

repatriation [riː,pætrɪ'eɪʃən] *n* rapatriement *m*.

repay [riː'peɪ] *pret, ptp* **repaid** *vt* **(a)** (*pay back*) *money* rendre, rembourser; *debt, obligation* s'acquitter de. **if you lend me £2 I'll ~ you on Saturday** si tu me prêtes 2 livres je te les rendrai *or* je te rembourserai samedi; **to ~ sb's expenses** rembourser *or* indemniser qn de ses frais.
(b) (*give in return*) récompenser. **to ~ sb's kindness** payer de retour la gentillesse de qn, récompenser qn de sa gentillesse; **to ~ sb with gratitude** payer qn de gratitude; **to be repaid for one's efforts** être récompensé de ses efforts; **it ~s obstinacy** la persévérance paie *or* est payante, cela vaut la peine de persévérer.

repayable [riː'peɪəbl] *adj* remboursable. **~ in 10 monthly instalments** remboursable en 10 mensualités.

repayment [riː'peɪmənt] *n [money]* remboursement *m*; *[effort]* récompense *f*. **~s can be spread over 3 years** les remboursements peuvent s'échelonner sur 3 ans.

repeal [rɪ'piːl] **1** *vt law* abroger, annuler; *sentence* annuler; *decree* révoquer. **2** *n* abrogation *f*, annulation *f*, révocation *f*.

repeat [rɪ'piːt] **1** *vt* (*say again*) répéter, redire, réitérer; *demand, promise* réitérer; (*Mus*) reprendre; (*recite*) *poem etc* réciter (par cœur); (*do again*) *action, attack* répéter, renouveler; *pattern, motif* répéter, reproduire; (*Comm*) *order* renouveler. (*Comm*) **this offer will never be ~ed** (c'est une) offre unique *or* exceptionnelle; **you must not ~ what I tell you** il ne faut pas répéter ce que je vous dis; **to ~ o.s.** se répéter; **to ~ one's efforts** renouveler ses efforts; (*Scol*) **to ~ a class** redoubler une classe.

2 *vi* **(a)** répéter. **I ~, it is impossible** je le répète, c'est impossible.
(b) (*Math*) se reproduire périodiquement. **0.054 ~ing** 0,054 périodique.
(c) (*) **radishes ~ on me** les radis me donnent des renvois*.

3 *n* répétition *f*; (*Mus*) reprise *f*; (*Rad, TV*) reprise *f*, nouvelle *or* deuxième retransmission.

4 *cpd*: (*Comm*) **repeat order** commande renouvelée; (*Theat*) **repeat performance** deuxième représentation *f*; (*fig*) **he gave a repeat performance** il a fait exactement la même chose; (*pej*) il a fait la même comédie.

repeated [rɪ'piːtɪd] *adj requests, criticism* répété; *efforts* renouvelé.

repeatedly [rɪˈpiːtɪdlɪ] *adv* à maintes reprises, très souvent. **I have ~ told you** je ne cesse de vous répéter; **he had ~ proclaimed his innocence** il n'avait pas cessé de proclamer son innocence.

repeater [rɪˈpiːtə^r] *n* (*gun/watch/alarm clock*) fusil *m*/montre *f*/réveil *m* à répétition; (*Math*) fraction *f* périodique.

repel [rɪˈpel] *vt enemy, sb's advances* repousser; (*fig: disgust*) repousser, rebuter, inspirer de la répulsion *or* de la répugnance à. (*fig*) **to be ~led by** éprouver de la répulsion pour.

repellent [rɪˈpelənt] *adj* repoussant, répugnant. **I find him ~** il me répugne, il me dégoûte, je le trouve très antipathique; *V* **insect, water** *etc.*

repent [rɪˈpent] **1** *vi* se repentir (*of* de).
2 *vt* se repentir de, regretter.

repentance [rɪˈpentəns] *n* repentir *m*.

repentant [rɪˈpentənt] *adj* repentant.

repercussion [ˌriːpəˈkʌʃən] *n [sounds]* répercussion *f*; *[shock]* répercussion, contrecoup *m*; (*fig*) répercussion *f*. **to have ~s on** se répercuter sur, avoir des répercussions sur *or* son contrecoup dans; **the ~(s) of this defeat** le contrecoup *or* les répercussions de cet échec; **there will be no ~s** il n'y aura pas de répercussions; **the ~ on prices of the rise in costs** la répercussion sur les prix de la hausse du coût.

repertoire [ˈrepətwɑː^r] *n* (*Theat, fig*) répertoire *m*.

repertory [ˈrepətərɪ] *n* **(a)** (*Theat, fig*) = **repertoire**.
(b) (*also* **~ theatre**) théâtre *m* de répertoire. **~ company** compagnie *f or* troupe *f* (de théâtre) de répertoire; **to act in ~, to play ~** faire partie d'une troupe de répertoire; **he did 3 years in ~** il a joué pendant 3 ans dans un théâtre de répertoire.

repetition [ˌrepɪˈtɪʃən] *n* **(a)** (*U: V* **repeat 1**) répétition *f*, redite *f*, réitération *f*; récitation *f*; renouvellement *m*; reproduction *f*.
(b) (*recurrence*) répétition *f*, retour *m*.

repetitious [ˌrepɪˈtɪʃəs] *adj* plein de répétitions *or* de redites.

repetitive [rɪˈpetɪtɪv] *adj person* rabâcheur; *writing* plein de redites; *work* monotone.

repine [rɪˈpaɪn] *vi* se plaindre, murmurer.

replace [rɪˈpleɪs] *vt* **(a)** (*put back*) replacer, remettre (à sa place *or* en place), ranger. (*Telec*) **to ~ the receiver** raccrocher.
(b) (*take the place of*) remplacer, tenir la place de.
(c) (*provide substitute for*) remplacer (*by, with* par).

replaceable [rɪˈpleɪsəbl] *adj* remplaçable.

replacement [rɪˈpleɪsmənt] **1** *n* **(a)** (*putting back*) remise *f* en place, replacement *m*. **(b)** (*substituting*) remplacement *m*, substitution *f*; (*person*) remplaçant(e) *m(f)*; (*product*) produit *m* de remplacement. **2** *cpd*: (*Aut*) **replacement engine** moteur *m* de rechange; **to fit a replacement engine/clutch** faire l'échange standard du moteur/de l'embrayage; (*Tech*) **replacement part** pièce *f* de rechange.

replant [ˈriːˈplɑːnt] *vt* replanter.

replay [ˈriːpleɪ] (*Sport*) **1** *n* match rejoué; *V* **action**. **2** [ˌriːˈpleɪ] *vt* rejouer.

replenish [rɪˈplenɪʃ] *vt* remplir (*with* de). **to ~ one's supplies of sth** se réapprovisionner en qch; **to ~ one's wardrobe** remonter sa garde-robe.

replenishment [rɪˈplenɪʃmənt] *n* remplissage *m*. **~ of supplies** réapprovisionnement *m*.

replete [rɪˈpliːt] *adj* rempli, plein (*with* de); (*well-fed*) *person* rassasié.

repletion [rɪˈpliːʃən] *n* satiété *f*.

replica [ˈreplɪkə] *n [painting]* réplique *f*; *[document]* fac-similé *m*, copie exacte.

reply [rɪˈplaɪ] **1** *n* réponse *f*; (*quick*) réplique *f*. **in ~ (to)** en réponse (à). **2** *vti* répondre; (*quickly*) répliquer. **3** *cpd*: (*Post*) **reply coupon** coupon-réponse *m*; **reply paid** réponse payée.

report [rɪˈpɔːt] **1** *n* **(a)** (*account, statement*) rapport *m*; *[speech]* compte rendu *m*; *[debate, meeting]* compte rendu, procès-verbal *m*; (*Press, Rad, TV*) reportage *m*; (*official*) rapport (d'enquête). **(Government) ~ on the motor industry** enquête *f* (parlementaire) sur l'industrie automobile; **monthly ~** bulletin mensuel; **school ~** bulletin *m* scolaire; **to make a progress ~ on** dresser un état périodique de; **to make a ~ on** faire un rapport sur; (*Press, Rad, TV*) faire un reportage sur; (*Comm*) **annual ~** rapport annuel (de gestion); **chairman's ~** rapport présidentiel; (*Jur*) **law ~s** recueil *m* de jurisprudence *or* de droit; (*Jur*) **to make a ~ against** dresser un procès-verbal à; *V* **weather**.
(b) (*rumour*) rumeur *f*. **there is a ~ that ...** le bruit court que ..., on dit que ...; **as ~ has it** selon les bruits qui courent, selon la rumeur publique; **to know sth only by ~** ne savoir qch que par ouï-dire; **I have heard a ~ that ...** j'ai entendu dire que ... .
(c) (*repute*) *[person]* réputation *f*; *[product]* renom *m*, renommée *f*. **of good ~** de bonne réputation, dont on dit du bien.
(d) (*explosion*) détonation *f*, explosion *f*; *[rifle, gun]* coup *m* de fusil. **with a loud ~** avec une forte détonation.
2 *cpd*: (*Scol*) **report card** bulletin *m* scolaire; (*Brit Parl*) **the bill has reached the ~ stage** le rapport de la Commission du projet de loi a été présenté.
3 *vt* **(a)** (*give account of*) rapporter, rendre compte de; (*bring to notice*) signaler; (*Press, Rad, TV*) faire un reportage sur. **to ~ a speech** faire le compte rendu d'un discours; **to ~ one's findings** *[scientist etc]* rendre compte de l'état de ses recherches; *[commission]* présenter ses conclusions; **to ~ progress** (*orally*) faire un exposé de l'état de la situation; (*in writing*) dresser un état sur la situation; **only one paper ~ed his death** un seul journal a signalé *or* mentionné sa mort; **the papers ~ed the crime as solved** les journaux ont présenté le crime comme résolu; **he is ~ed as having said** il aurait dit; **it is ~ed that a prisoner has escaped, a prisoner is ~ed to have escaped** un détenu se serait évadé; (*Gram*) **~ed speech** style *or* discours indirect; (*Parl*) **to ~ a Bill** présenter un projet de loi; (*Parl*) **to move to ~ progress** demander la clôture des débats.
(b) (*announce*) déclarer, annoncer. **it is ~ed from the White House that ...** on annonce à la Maison Blanche que ... .
(c) (*notify authorities of*) *accident, crime, suspect* signaler; *criminal, culprit* dénoncer (*often pej*). **all accidents must be ~ed to the police** tous les accidents doivent être signalés à la police; **to ~ sb for bad behaviour** signaler qn pour mauvaise conduite; **to ~ sb's bad behaviour** signaler la mauvaise conduite de qn; **her colleague ~ed her to the boss out of jealousy** sa collègue l'a dénoncée au patron par jalousie.
(d) (*Mil, Naut*) signaler. **to ~ sb sick** signaler que qn est malade; **~ed missing** porté manquant *or* disparu; **nothing to ~** rien à signaler; **to ~ one's position** signaler *or* donner sa position.
4 *vi* **(a)** (*announce o.s. ready*) se présenter. **~ to the director on Monday** présentez-vous chez le directeur lundi; **to ~ for duty** se présenter au travail, prendre son service.
(b) (*Mil*) **to ~ to one's unit** rallier son unité; **to ~ sick** se faire porter malade.
(c) (*give a report*) faire un rapport (*on* sur); (*Press, Rad, TV*) faire un reportage (*on* sur). **the committee is ready to ~** le comité est prêt à faire son rapport; (*Rad, TV*) **Michael Brown ~s from Rome** de Rome, (le reportage de) Michael Brown; **our correspondent ~s from Rome that ...** notre correspondant à Rome nous apprend que ... .

report back *vi* **(a)** (*Mil etc*) rentrer au quartier. (*gen*) **you must report back at 6 o'clock** il faut que vous soyez de retour à 6 heures.
(b) donner *or* présenter son rapport (*to* à). **the committee was asked to investigate the complaint and report back to the assembly** le comité a été chargé d'examiner la plainte et de présenter son rapport à l'assemblée.

reportage [ˌrepɔːˈtɑːʒ] *n* reportage *m*.

reporter [rɪˈpɔːtə^r] *n* **(a)** (*Press*) journaliste *mf*; (*on the spot*) reporter *m*; (*Rad, TV*) reporter. **special ~** envoyé(e) spécial(e) *m(f)*; (*Jur, Parl*) **~s' gallery** tribune *f* de la presse.
(b) (*Jur, Parl: stenographer*) sténographe *mf*.

repose [rɪˈpəʊz] **1** *n* (*rest*) repos *m*; (*sleep*) sommeil *m*; (*peace*) repos, tranquillité *f*, paix *f*. **in ~** en repos, au repos. **2** *vt* (*frm*) *confidence, trust* mettre, placer (*in* en). (*rest*) **to ~ o.s.** se reposer. **3** *vi* **(a)** (*rest*) se reposer; *[dead]* reposer. **(b)** (*be based*) reposer, être fondé (*on* sur).

repository [rɪˈpɒzɪtərɪ] *n* (*warehouse*) dépôt *m*, entrepôt *m*; (*fig*) *[facts etc]* répertoire *m*, mine *f*; (*person*) dépositaire *mf* (*d'un secret etc*).

repossess [ˈriːpəˈzes] *vt* reprendre possession de, rentrer en possession de.

repp [rep] *n* = **rep**^{2}.

reprehend [ˌreprɪˈhend] *vt person* réprimander; *action, behaviour* blâmer, condamner.

reprehensible [ˌreprɪˈhensɪbl] *adj* répréhensible, blâmable.

reprehensibly [ˌreprɪˈhensɪblɪ] *adv* de façon répréhensible.

reprehension [ˌreprɪˈhenʃən] *n* (*U*) réprimande *f*, blâme *m*.

represent [ˌreprɪˈzent] *vt* **(a)** (*stand for, symbolize*) représenter. **a drawing ~ing prehistoric man** un dessin représentant *or* qui représente l'homme préhistorique; **phonetic symbols ~ sounds** les symboles phonétiques représentent des sons; (*fig*) **he ~s all that is best in his country's culture** il représente *or* personnifie les meilleurs aspects de la culture de son pays; **£100 doesn't ~ a good salary these days** 100 livres ne représentent *or* ne constituent plus un bon salaire de nos jours.
(b) (*declare to be*) *person, event* représenter, dépeindre, décrire (*as* comme étant); *grievance, risk etc* présenter. **he ~ed me to be a fool** *or* **as a fool** il m'a représenté *or* dépeint comme un imbécile; **I am not what you ~ me to be** je ne suis pas tel que vous me décrivez *or* dépeignez; **he ~s himself as a doctor** il se fait passer pour (un) médecin; **it is exactly as ~ed in the advertisement** cela est exactement conforme à la description de l'annonce (publicitaire); **he ~ed the risks as being slight** il a présenté les risques comme négligeables.
(c) (*explain*) expliquer, exposer, représenter (*liter*); (*point out*) faire remarquer, signaler. **can you ~ to him how much we need his help?** pouvez-vous lui expliquer *or* lui faire comprendre à quel point nous avons besoin de son aide?
(d) (*act or speak for*) représenter (*also Parl*); (*Jur*) représenter (en justice), postuler pour. **he ~s Bogminster in Parliament** il représente Bogminster au Parlement, il est le député de Bogminster; **the delegation ~ed the mining industry** la délégation représentait l'industrie minière; **he ~s their firm in London** il représente leur maison à Londres; **many countries were ~ed at the ceremony** de nombreux pays s'étaient fait représenter à la cérémonie; **I ~ Mr X** je viens de la part de M X.
(e) (*Theat*) *character* jouer (le rôle de); *part* jouer, interpréter.

re-present [ˈriːprɪˈzent] *vt* présenter de nouveau.

representation [ˌreprɪzenˈteɪʃən] *n* **(a)** (*Theat, gen*) représentation *f*; *[role]* interprétation *f*. (*Parl*) **proportional ~** représentation proportionnelle.
(b) (*protest*) **~s** démarche *f*; **the ambassador made ~s to the government** l'ambassadeur a fait une démarche auprès du gouvernement.

representational [ˌreprɪzenˈteɪʃənəl] *adj* représentatif, qui représente; (*Painting*) figuratif.

representative [ˌreprɪˈzentətɪv] **1** *adj* **(a)** (*typical*) représentatif, caractéristique, typique (*of* de). **an attitude ~ of the younger generation** une attitude caractéristique de la jeune génération; **a ~ cross section of the public** une fraction représentative du public; **this is not a ~ sample** ceci ne constitue pas un échantillon représentatif.

(b) (*Parl*) **~ government** gouvernement représentatif.

2 *n* représentant(e) *m(f)*; (*Comm*) représentant (de commerce); (*US Pol*) député *m*; *V* **house.**

repress [rɪ'pres] *vt emotions* réprimer, contenir; *revolt* réprimer; *sneeze* étouffer; (*Psych*) refouler.

repressed [rɪ'prest] *adj* réprimé, contenu; (*Psych*) refoulé.

repression [rɪ'preʃən] *n* **(a)** répression *f*. **(b)** (*Psych*) (*voluntary*) répression *f*; (*involuntary*) refoulement *m*.

repressive [rɪ'presɪv] *adj* répressif. (*Pol*) **~ measures** mesures *fpl* de répression.

reprieve [rɪ'priːv] **1** *n* (*Jur*) (lettres *fpl* de) grâce *f*, commutation *f* de la peine capitale; (*delay*) sursis *m*; (*fig: respite*) répit *m*, sursis, délai *m*. **they won a ~ for the house** ils ont obtenu un sursis pour la maison.

2 *vt* (*Jur*) accorder une commutation de la peine capitale à; (*delay*) surseoir à l'exécution de; (*fig*) accorder du répit à. (*fig*) **the building has been ~d for a while** le bâtiment a bénéficié d'un sursis.

reprimand ['reprɪmɑːnd] **1** *n* réprimande *f*; (*Jur*) blâme *m*. **2** *vt* réprimander; (*Jur*) blâmer.

reprint [ˌriː'prɪnt] **1** *vt* réimprimer. **this book is being ~ed** ce livre est en réimpression. **2** *vi [book]* être en réimpression. **3** ['riːprɪnt] *n* réimpression *f*. **cheap ~** édition *f* à bon marché.

reprisal [rɪ'praɪzəl] *n*: **~s** représailles *fpl*; **to take ~s** user de représailles; **as a ~ for** en représailles de; **by way of ~** par représailles.

reproach [rɪ'prəʊtʃ] **1** *n* **(a)** (*rebuke*) reproche *m*. **to heap ~es on sb** accabler qn de reproches; (*fig*) **to be a ~ to** être la honte de.

(b) (*U: discredit*) honte *f*, opprobre *m*. **term of ~** parole *f* de reproche; **to bring ~ on** jeter le discrédit sur, discréditer; **above** *or* **beyond ~** sans reproche(s), irréprochable.

2 *vt* faire des reproches à, reprocher à. **to ~ sb for his mistake** reprocher son erreur à qn; **to ~ sb for having done** reprocher à qn d'avoir fait; **he has nothing to ~ himself with** il n'a rien à se reprocher.

reproachful [rɪ'prəʊtʃfʊl] *adj look, tone* réprobateur (*f* -trice); *words* de reproche.

reproachfully [rɪ'prəʊtʃfəlɪ] *adv* avec reproche, d'un air *or* ton de reproche.

reprobate ['reprəʊbeɪt] **1** *adj, n* dépravé(e) *m(f)*. **2** *vt* réprouver.

reprobation [ˌreprəʊ'beɪʃən] *n* réprobation *f*.

reproduce [ˌriːprə'djuːs] **1** *vt* reproduire. **2** *vi* se reproduire.

reproduction [ˌriːprə'dʌkʃən] **1** *n* **(a)** (*procreation*) reproduction *f*.

(b) (*Art*) reproduction *f*. **sound ~** reproduction sonore; **this picture is a ~** ce tableau est une reproduction *or* une copie.

2 *cpd*: **reproduction furniture** imitation(s) *f(pl)* de meuble(s) ancien(s).

reproductive [ˌriːprə'dʌktɪv] *adj* reproducteur (*f* -trice).

reproof[1] ['riː'pruːf] *vt garment* réimperméabiliser.

reproof[2] [rɪ'pruːf] *n* reproche *m*, réprimande *f*, désapprobation *f*.

reproval [rɪ'pruːvəl] *n* reproche *m*, blâme *m*.

reprove [rɪ'pruːv] *vt person* blâmer (*for* de), réprimander (*for* sur); *action* réprouver, condamner.

reproving [rɪ'pruːvɪŋ] *adj* réprobateur (*f* -trice).

reprovingly [rɪ'pruːvɪŋlɪ] *adv* d'un air *or* ton de reproche.

reptile ['reptaɪl] *adj, n* (*also fig pej*) reptile (*m*).

reptilian [rep'tɪlɪən] **1** *adj* (*Zool*) reptilien; (*fig pej*) reptile (*liter*), de reptile. **2** *n* reptile *m* (*also fig*).

republic [rɪ'pʌblɪk] *n* république *f*.

republican [rɪ'pʌblɪkən] *adj, n* républicain(e) *m(f)*.

republicanism [rɪ'pʌblɪkənɪzəm] *n* républicanisme *m*.

republication ['riːˌpʌblɪ'keɪʃən] *n [book]* réédition *f*, nouvelle édition; *[law, banns]* nouvelle publication.

republish ['riː'pʌblɪʃ] *vt book* rééditer; *banns* publier de nouveau.

repudiate [rɪ'pjuːdɪeɪt] *vt person* renier, désavouer; *accusation* répudier, repousser, rejeter; *[government etc] debt, obligation* refuser d'honorer. **to ~ one's wife** répudier sa femme.

repudiation [rɪˌpjuːdɪ'eɪʃən] *n* (*V* **repudiate**) reniement *m*, désaveu *m*; répudiation *f*, rejet *m*.

repugnance [rɪ'pʌgnəns] *n* répugnance *f*, aversion *f* (*to* pour). **he shows ~ to accepting charity** il répugne à accepter la charité.

repugnant [rɪ'pʌgnənt] *adj* répugnant, dégoûtant. **he finds her ~** elle lui répugne.

repulse [rɪ'pʌls] **1** *vt* (*Mil*) repousser, refouler; (*fig*) *help, offer* repousser, rejeter. **2** *n* (*Mil*) échec *m*; (*fig*) rebuffade *f*, refus *m*. **to meet with** *or* **suffer a ~** essuyer une rebuffade.

repulsion [rɪ'pʌlʃən] *n* (*also Phys*) répulsion *f*.

repulsive [rɪ'pʌlsɪv] *adj* répulsif, repoussant; (*Phys*) répulsif.

repulsively [rɪ'pʌlsɪvlɪ] *adv* d'une façon repoussante. **~ ugly** d'une laideur repoussante.

repulsiveness [rɪ'pʌlsɪvnɪs] *n* aspect *or* caractère repoussant; (*Phys*) force répulsive.

repurchase [ˌriː'pɜːtʃɪs] **1** *n* rachat *m*. **2** *vt* racheter.

reputable ['repjʊtəbl] *adj person* honorable, estimé, de bonne réputation; *occupation* honorable; *dealer, firm* de bonne réputation.

reputation [ˌrepjʊ'teɪʃən] *n* réputation *f*. **to have a good/bad ~** avoir (une) bonne/(une) mauvaise réputation; **a good ~ as a singer** une bonne réputation de chanteur; **to have a ~ for honesty** avoir la réputation d'être honnête, être réputé pour son honnêteté; **to live up to one's ~** soutenir sa réputation.

repute [rɪ'pjuːt] **1** *n* réputation *f*, renom *m*. **to know sb by ~** connaître qn de réputation; **to be of good ~** avoir (une) bonne réputation; **a restaurant of ~** un restaurant réputé *or* en renom; (*euph: brothel*) **a house of ill ~** une maison close; **to hold sb in high ~** avoir une très haute opinion de qn.

2 *vt* (*pass only*) **to be ~d rich** passer pour riche; **he is ~d to be the best player** il est réputé *or* censé être le meilleur joueur.

reputed [rɪ'pjuːtɪd] *adj* réputé. (*Jur*) **~ father** père putatif.

reputedly [rɪ'pjuːtɪdlɪ] *adv* à *or* d'après ce qu'on dit, selon la rumeur publique.

request [rɪ'kwest] **1** *n* demande *f*, requête *f*. **at sb's ~** sur *or* à la demande de qn, à la requête de qn; **by general** *or* **popular ~** à la demande générale; **on** *or* **by ~** sur demande; **to make a ~ for sth** faire une demande de qch; **to make a ~ to sb for sth** demander qch à qn; **to grant a ~** accéder à une demande *or* à une requête.

2 *vt* demander. **to ~ sth from sb** demander qch à qn; **to ~ sb to do** demander à qn de faire, prier qn de faire; **'you are ~ed not to smoke'** 'prière de ne pas fumer'; **it's all I ~ of you** c'est tout ce que je vous demande.

3 *cpd*: (*Rad*) **request programme** programme *m* des auditeurs; *[bus]* **request stop** arrêt facultatif.

requiem ['rekwɪem] *n* requiem *m*. **~ mass** messe *f* de requiem.

require [rɪ'kwaɪə[r]] *vt* **(a)** (*need*) *[person]* avoir besoin de; *[thing, action]* demander, nécessiter. **I have all I ~** j'ai tout ce qu'il me faut *or* tout ce dont j'ai besoin; **the journey will ~ 3 hours** le voyage prendra *or* demandera 3 heures; **it ~s great care** cela demande *or* nécessite *or* exige beaucoup de soin; **this plant ~s frequent watering** cette plante demande à être arrosée souvent; **if ~d** au besoin, si besoin est, s'il le faut; **when (it is) ~d** quand il le faut; **what qualifications are ~d?** quels sont les diplômes nécessaires? *or* exigés?

(b) (*order*) exiger, réclamer. **to ~ sb to do** exiger de qn qu'il fasse; **to ~ sth of sb** exiger qch de qn; **as ~d by law** comme la loi l'exige.

required [rɪ'kwaɪəd] *adj* exigé, demandé, requis. **to satisfy the ~ conditions** satisfaire aux conditions requises; **by the ~ date** en temps voulu; **in the ~ time** dans les délais prescrits; **the ~ amount** la quantité voulue.

requirement [rɪ'kwaɪəmənt] *n* **(a)** (*need*) exigence *f*, besoin *m*. **to meet sb's ~s** satisfaire aux exigences *or* aux besoins de qn; **there isn't enough bread to meet the ~** il n'y a pas assez de pain pour satisfaire *or* suffire à la demande.

(b) (*condition*) condition requise. **to fit the ~s** remplir les conditions.

requisite ['rekwɪzɪt] **1** *n* chose nécessaire *or* requise (*for* pour). **all the ~s** tout ce qui est nécessaire; **toilet ~s** accessoires *mpl* de toilette. **2** *adj* requis, nécessaire.

requisition [ˌrekwɪ'zɪʃən] **1** *n* demande *f*; (*gen Mil*) réquisition *f*. **to make a ~ for** faire une demande de; (*gen Mil*) réquisitionner. **2** *vt* (*gen Mil*) réquisitionner.

requital [rɪ'kwaɪtl] *n* (*repayment*) récompense *f*; (*revenge*) revanche *f*.

requite [rɪ'kwaɪt] *vt* **(a)** (*repay*) *person, action* récompenser, payer (*for* de). **~d love** amour partagé.

(b) (*avenge*) *action* venger; *person* se venger de.

reread ['riː'riːd] *pret, ptp* **reread** ['riː'red] *vt* relire.

reredos ['rɪədɒs] *n* retable *m*.

reroute ['riː'ruːt] *vt train, coach* changer l'itinéraire de, dérouter. **our train was ~d through Leeds** on a fait faire à notre train un détour par Leeds, notre train a été dérouté par Leeds.

rerun ['riːrʌn] **1** *n [film, tape]* reprise *f*. **2** ['riː'rʌn] *vt film, tape* passer de nouveau; *race* courir de nouveau.

resale ['riː'seɪl] *n* revente *f*.

rescind [rɪ'sɪnd] *vt judgment* rescinder, casser; *law* abroger; *act* révoquer; *contract* résilier, dissoudre; *decision, agreement* annuler.

rescission [rɪ'sɪʒən] *n* (*V* **rescind**) rescision *f*; abrogation *f*; révocation *f*; résiliation *f*; annulation *f*.

rescript ['riːskrɪpt] *n* (*Hist, Rel*) rescrit *m*.

rescue ['reskjuː] **1** *n* (*help*) secours *mpl*; (*saving*) sauvetage *m*; (*freeing*) délivrance *f*. **~ was difficult** le sauvetage a été difficile; **~ came too late** les secours sont arrivés trop tard; **to go to sb's ~** aller au secours *or* à la rescousse de qn; **to come to sb's ~** venir en aide à qn *or* à la rescousse de qn; **to the ~** à la rescousse; *V* **air.**

2 *vt* (*save*) sauver, secourir; (*free*) délivrer (*from* de). **you ~d me from a difficult situation** vous m'avez tiré d'une situation difficile; **the ~d were taken to hospital** les rescapés ont été emmenés à l'hôpital.

3 *cpd attempt* de sauvetage. **rescue operations/party** opérations *fpl*/équipe *f* de sauvetage.

rescuer ['reskjʊə[r]] *n* (*V* **rescue**) sauveteur *m*; libérateur *m*, -trice *f*.

research [rɪ'sɜːtʃ] **1** *n* recherche(s) *f(pl)*. **a piece of ~** un travail de recherche; **to do ~** faire des recherches *or* de la recherche; **to carry out ~ into the effects of ...** faire des recherches sur les effets de ... .

2 *vi* faire des recherches (*into, on* sur).

3 *vt article* faire des recherches pour *or* en vue de.

4 *cpd*: **research establishment** centre *m* de recherches; (*Univ*) **research fellow** ≃ chercheur *m*, -euse *f* attaché(e) à l'université; **research laboratory** laboratoire *m* de recherches; (*Univ*) **research student** étudiant(e) *m(f)* qui fait de la recherche; **research work** recherches *fpl*; **research worker** chercheur *m*, -euse *f*.

researcher [rɪ'sɜːtʃə[r]] *n* chercheur *m*, -euse *f*.

reseat ['riː'siːt] *vt* **(a)** *person* faire changer de place à. **to ~ o.s.** se rasseoir. **(b)** *chair* refaire le fond de; *trousers* mettre un fond à.

resection [riː'sekʃən] *n* résection *f*.

resell [ˌriːˈsel] *vt* revendre.
resemblance [rɪˈzembləns] *n* ressemblance *f*. **to bear a strong/faint ~** to avoir une grande/vague ressemblance avec; **there's not the slightest ~ between them** il n'y a pas la moindre ressemblance entre eux, ils ne se ressemblent pas du tout; **this bears no ~ to the facts** ceci n'a aucune ressemblance avec les faits.
resemble [rɪˈzembl] *vt [person]* ressembler à; *[thing]* ressembler à, être semblable à. **they ~ each other** ils se ressemblent.
resent [rɪˈzent] *vt* s'offusquer de, être froissé de, avoir sur le cœur, être indigné de. **I ~ that!** je vous en prie!, je proteste!; **I ~ your tone** votre ton me déplaît; **he ~ed your having seen her** il était très contrarié du fait que tu l'aies vue; **he may ~ my being here** il n'appréciera peut-être pas ma présence.
resentful [rɪˈzentfʊl] *adj* rancunier. **to be ~ of sb's success** envier à qn son succès; **to feel ~ about** éprouver du ressentiment de, être froissé *or* irrité de.
resentfully [rɪˈzentfəlɪ] *adv* avec ressentiment.
resentment [rɪˈzentmənt] *n* ressentiment *m*.
reservation [ˌrezəˈveɪʃən] *n* **(a)** réserve *f*; (*Jur*) réservation *f*. **mental ~** restriction mentale; **without ~** sans réserve, sans arrière-pensée; **with ~s** avec certaines réserves, sous réserve; **to have ~s about** avoir des doutes sur.
(b) (*booking*) réservation *f*, location *f*. **to make a ~ at the hotel/on the boat** réserver *or* retenir une chambre à l'hôtel/une place sur le bateau; **to have a ~** (*in train, coach, plane*) avoir une place réservée; (*in hotel*) avoir une chambre réservée; (*in restaurant*) avoir une table réservée.
(c) (*area of land*) réserve *f*; (*US*) réserve (indienne). (*on roadway*) **(central) ~** bande *f* médiane.
(d) (*Rel*) **R~ (of the Sacrament)** les Saintes Réserves.
reserve [rɪˈzɜːv] **1** *vt* **(a)** (*keep*) réserver, garder, mettre en réserve *or* de côté. **to ~ one's strength** ménager *or* garder ses forces; (*Sport*) se réserver; **to ~ the best wine for one's friends** réserver le meilleur vin pour ses amis; **to ~ judgment/one's decision** se réserver de prononcer un jugement/de prendre une décision; **to ~ the right to do** se réserver le droit de faire; **to ~ a warm welcome for sb** ménager *or* réserver un accueil chaleureux à qn; **to ~ o.s. for** se réserver pour.
(b) (*book in advance*) *room, seat* réserver, retenir.
2 *n* **(a)** (*sth stored*) réserve *f*, stock *m*. **to have great ~s of energy** avoir une grande réserve d'énergie; **cash ~** réserve de caisse; **gold ~s** réserves *fpl* d'or; **world ~s of pyrites** réserves mondiales de pyrite; **to keep** *or* **hold in ~** tenir en réserve.
(b) (*restriction*) réserve *f*, restriction *f*. **without ~** sans réserve, sans restriction; **with all ~** *or* **all proper ~s** sous toutes réserves.
(c) = **~ price**; *V* **3**.
(d) (*piece of land*) réserve *f*; *V* **game[1], nature.**
(e) (*U: attitude*) réserve *f*, retenue *f*. **he treated me with some ~** il s'est tenu sur la réserve avec moi; **to break through sb's ~** amener qn à se départir de sa réserve *or* retenue.
(f) (*Mil*) **the R~** la réserve; **the ~s** la réserve, les réservistes *mpl*.
(g) (*Sport*) remplaçant(e) *m(f)*.
3 *cpd currency, fund* de réserve. (*Mil*) **reserve list** cadre *m* de réserve; **reserve (petrol) tank** reservoir *m* (d'essence) de secours, nourrice *f*; (*Sport*) **reserve player** remplaçant(e) *m(f)*; **reserve price** prix *m* minimum; **reserve team** deuxième équipe *f*, équipe B.
reserved [rɪˈzɜːvd] *adj* **(a)** (*shy*) réservé, timide; (*uncommunicative*) renfermé. **he was very ~ about ...** il est resté sur la réserve quant à ... .
(b) *room* réservé. **~ seats** places réservées.
(c) (*Comm*) **all rights ~** tous droits de reproduction réservés; *V* **copyright.**
reservedly [rɪˈzɜːvɪdlɪ] *adv* avec réserve, avec retenue.
reservist [rɪˈzɜːvɪst] *n* (*Mil*) réserviste *m*.
reservoir [ˈrezəvwɑːʳ] *n* (*lit, fig*) réservoir *m*.
reset [ˈriːˈset] *vt precious stone* remonter; *saw* raffûter; *watch* remettre à l'heure; (*Med*) *limb* remettre; (*Typ*) recomposer. **to ~ a broken bone** réduire une fracture.
resettle [ˌriːˈsetl] *vt refugee* établir, implanter; *land* repeupler.
resettlement [ˌriːˈsetlmənt] *n* (*V* **resettle**) établissement *m*, implantation *f*; repeuplement *m*.
reshape [ˈriːˈʃeɪp] *vt dough, clay* refaçonner, modeler de nouveau; *text, policy* réorganiser.
reshuffle [ˌriːˈʃʌfl] **1** *vt cards* battre de nouveau; (*fig*) *cabinet, board of directors* remanier. **2** *n [cards]* **to have a ~** rebattre; (*Pol*) **Cabinet ~** remaniement ministériel.
reside [rɪˈzaɪd] *vi* (*lit, fig*) résider (*in* en, dans, *with sth* dans qch). **the power ~s in the President** le pouvoir est entre les mains du Président *or* réside dans le Président.
residence [ˈrezɪdəns] *n* **(a)** (*house: frm*) résidence *f*, demeure *f*; (*hostel: for students, nurses*) foyer *m*. **the President's official ~** la résidence officielle du Président; *V* **hall** *etc*.
(b) (*U: stay*) séjour *m*, résidence *f*. **after 5 years' ~ in Britain** après avoir résidé en Grande-Bretagne pendant 5 ans; **to take up ~ in the country** élire domicile *or* s'installer à la campagne; *[monarch, governor etc]* **to be in ~** être en résidence; **the students are now in ~** les étudiants sont maintenant rentrés; **there is always a doctor in ~** il y a toujours un médecin résidant; **~ permit** permis *m* de séjour.
residency [ˈrezɪdənsɪ] *n* résidence officielle.
resident [ˈrezɪdənt] **1** *n* habitant(e) *m(f)*; (*in foreign country*) résident(e) *m(f)*; (*in street*) riverain(e) *m(f)*; (*in hostel*) pensionnaire *mf*.
2 *adj* résidant; *chaplain, tutor* à demeure. **they are ~ in France** ils résident en France; **the ~ population** la population fixe, les habitants *mpl* du pays; (*Med*) **~ physician** interne *mf*.
residential [ˌrezɪˈdenʃəl] *adj area* résidentiel; *conditions* de résidence; *work, post* qui demande résidence.
residual [rɪˈzɪdjʊəl] **1** *adj* restant; (*Chem, Phys*) résiduaire, résiduel. **2** *n* (*Chem*) résidu *m*; (*Math*) reste *m*.
residuary [rɪˈzɪdjʊərɪ] *adj* restant; (*Chem, Phys*) résiduaire. (*Jur*) **~ legatee** ≈ légataire *mf* universel(le).
residue [ˈrezɪdjuː] *n* reste(s) *m(pl)*; (*Chem, Phys*) résidu *m*; (*Math*) reste; (*Jur*) reliquat *m*.
residuum [rɪˈzɪdjʊəm] *n* résidu *m*, reste *m*.
resign [rɪˈzaɪn] **1** *vt* (*give up*) *job* se démettre de, résigner (*liter*); (*hand over*) céder (*to* à). **he ~ed the leadership to his colleague** il a cédé la direction à son collègue; (*Mil etc*) **to ~ one's commission** démissionner (*se dit d'un officier*); **to ~ o.s. to (doing) sth** se résigner à (faire) qch.
2 *vi* démissionner, donner sa démission (*from* de).
resignation [ˌrezɪgˈneɪʃən] *n* **(a)** (*from job*) démission *f*. **to tender one's ~** donner sa démission. **(b)** (*mental state*) résignation *f*. **(c)** (*U*) *[a right]* abandon *m* (*of* de), renonciation *f* (*of* à).
resigned [rɪˈzaɪnd] *adj person, look, voice* résigné. **to become ~ to (doing) sth** se résigner à (faire) qch; **I was ~ to walking, when...** je m'étais résigné à y aller à pied, lorsque... .
resignedly [rɪˈzaɪnɪdlɪ] *adv* avec résignation, d'un ton *or* d'un air résigné.
resilience [rɪˈzɪlɪəns] *n [person, character]* élasticité *f*, ressort *m*; *[rubber]* élasticité.
resilient [rɪˈzɪlɪənt] *adj nature, character* qui réagit; *rubber, metal* élastique. **he's very ~** (*physically*) il a beaucoup de résistance, il récupère bien; (*mentally etc*) il a du ressort, il ne se laisse pas abattre *or* déprimer.
resin [ˈrezɪn] *n* résine *f*.
resinous [ˈrezɪnəs] *adj* résineux.
resist [rɪˈzɪst] **1** *vt attack, arrest* résister à, s'opposer à; *temptation* résister à; *person* repousser, résister à; *order* refuser d'obéir *or* d'obtempérer à; *change* s'opposer à. **I couldn't ~ (eating) another cake** je n'ai pas pu résister à l'envie de *or* je n'ai pas pu m'empêcher de manger encore un gâteau; **she can't ~ him** elle ne peut rien lui refuser.
2 *vi* résister, offrir de la résistance.
resistance [rɪˈzɪstəns] **1** *n* (*gen, Elec, Med, Mil, Phys*) résistance *f*. (*Hist*) **the R~** la Résistance; **to meet with ~** se heurter à une résistance; **to offer ~ to** résister à; **he offered no ~** il n'opposa aucune résistance; (*Med*) **his ~ was very low** il n'offrait presque plus de résistance (*au mal*); *V* **line[1], passive.**
2 *cpd*: **resistance fighter** résistant(e) *m(f)*; **the Resistance movement** la Résistance.
resistant [rɪˈzɪstənt] *adj* résistant, (*Med*) rebelle. (*of virus, strain*) **~ to** rebelle à; **~ to penicillin** pénicillo-résistant; *V* **water.**
resit [ˈriːˈsɪt] *pret, ptp* **resat** **1** *vt* se représenter à, repasser. **2** *vi* se présenter à la deuxième session. **3** [ˈriːsɪt] *n* deuxième session *f* (*d'un examen*).
resole [ˈriːˈsəʊl] *vt* ressemeler.
resolute [ˈrezəluːt] *adj* résolu, déterminé.
resolutely [ˈrezəluːtlɪ] *adv* résolument, avec détermination.
resoluteness [ˈrezəluːtnɪs] *n* résolution *f*, détermination *f*, fermeté *f*.
resolution [ˌrezəˈluːʃən] *n* **(a)** (*decision*) résolution *f*; (*Admin etc*) résolution, délibération *f*. **to make a ~** prendre une résolution; **to adopt/reject a ~** adopter/rejeter une résolution; **good ~s** bonnes résolutions; *V* **New Year. (b)** (*U: resoluteness*) fermeté *f*, résolution *f*. **to show ~** faire preuve de fermeté, faire preuve (d'esprit) de décision. **(c)** (*U: solving*) *[problem, puzzle]* solution *f*. **(d)** (*U: Chem, Med, Mus*) résolution *f* (*into* en).
resolvable [rɪˈzɒlvəbl] *adj* résoluble.
resolve [rɪˈzɒlv] **1** *vt* **(a)** (*break up*) résoudre, réduire (*into* en). **to ~ sth into its elements** ramener *or* réduire qch à ses éléments; **water ~s itself into steam** l'eau se résout *or* se transforme en vapeur; **the meeting ~d itself into a committee** l'assemblée se constitua en commission.
(b) *problem, difficulty* résoudre; *doubt* dissiper.
(c) (*Med, Mus*) résoudre.
2 *vi* **(a)** (*decide*) résoudre, décider (*to do* de faire); se résoudre, se décider (*to do* à faire). **to ~ (up)on sth** se résoudre à qch; **to ~ that ...** décider que ...; **it has been ~d that** il a été résolu que.
(b) (*break up*) se résoudre (*into* en). **the question ~s into 4 points** la question se divise en 4 points.
3 *n* **(a)** (*decision*) résolution *f*, décision *f*. **to make a ~ to do** prendre la résolution de faire, résoudre de faire.
(b) (*U: resoluteness*) résolution *f*, fermeté *f*. **to do sth with ~** faire qch avec détermination.
resolved [rɪˈzɒlvd] *adj* résolu, décidé (*to do* à faire).
resonance [ˈrezənəns] *n* (*Mus, Phys, gen*) résonance *f*; *[voice]* résonance, sonorité *f*.
resonant [ˈrezənənt] *adj* (*Phys*) résonant; *voice* sonore, résonant.
resonator [ˈrezəneɪtəʳ] *n* résonateur *m*.
resorption [rɪˈzɔːpʃən] *n* résorption *f*.
resort [rɪˈzɔːt] **1** *n* **(a)** (*recourse*) recours *m*; (*thing, action resorted to*) ressource *f*, recours, expédient *m* (*often pej*). **without ~ to violence** sans recourir *or* avoir recours à la violence; **as a last ~, in the last ~** en dernier ressort; **hiding was the only ~ left to them** se cacher était la seule ressource qui leur restait.
(b) (*place*) lieu *m* de séjour *or* de vacances. **coastal ~** plage *f*; **seaside/summer ~** station balnéaire/estivale; **winter sports ~** station de sports d'hiver; (*fig liter*) **a ~ of thieves** un repaire de voleurs; *V* **health, holiday.**
2 *vi* avoir recours (*to sth/sb* à qch/qn), recourir (*to sth* à qch), en venir (*to doing* à faire).

resound [rɪ'zaʊnd] **1** *vi* retentir, résonner (*with* de). (*fig*) **his speech will ~ throughout France** son discours aura du retentissement dans toute la France. **2** *vt* faire retentir *or* résonner.

resounding [rɪ'zaʊndɪŋ] *adj noise, shout* sonore, retentissant; *laugh* sonore; *voice* sonore, tonitruant (*pej*); *triumph, victory* retentissant. **~ success** succès retentissant *or* fou*; **~ defeat** défaite écrasante.

resoundingly [rɪ'zaʊndɪŋlɪ] *adv* d'une manière retentissante. **the play was ~ successful** la pièce a eu un succès retentissant.

resource [rɪ'sɔːs] *n* **(a)** (*wealth, supplies etc*) **~s** ressources *fpl*; **financial/mineral/natural ~s** ressources pécuniaires/en minerais/naturelles; **~s of men and materials** ressources en hommes et en matériel; (*Fin*) **the total ~s of a company** les ressources totales d'une société; (*fig*) **he has no ~s against boredom** il ne sait pas lutter *or* se défendre contre l'ennui; (*fig*) **left to his own ~s** livré à ses propres ressources *or* à lui-même.
(b) (*expedient*) ressource *f*. **as a last ~** en dernier ressort, en dernière ressource; **you are my last ~** vous êtes ma dernière ressource *or* mon dernier espoir.

resourceful [rɪ'sɔːsfʊl] *adj person* (plein) de ressources, ingénieux, débrouillard*; *scheme* ingénieux.

resourcefully [rɪ'sɔːsfəlɪ] *adv* d'une manière ingénieuse *or* débrouillarde*.

resourcefulness [rɪ'sɔːsfʊlnɪs] *n* (*U*) ressource *f*.

respect [rɪs'pekt] **1** *n* **(a)** (*U: esteem*) respect *m*, considération *f*, estime *f*. **to have ~ for** *person* avoir du respect pour, respecter; *the law, sb's intelligence* respecter; **I have the greatest ~ for him** j'ai infiniment de respect pour lui; **to treat with ~** traiter avec respect; **to be held in ~** être tenu en haute estime; **he can command ~** il impose le respect, il sait se faire respecter.
(b) (*U: consideration*) respect *m*, considération *f*, égard *m*. **she has no ~ for other people's feelings** elle n'a aucune considération *or* aucun respect pour les sentiments d'autrui; **out of ~ for** par respect *or* égard pour; **with (due) ~ I still think that** sans vouloir vous contredire *or* sauf votre respect je crois toujours que; (*frm*) **without ~ of persons** sans acception de personne; **without ~ to the consequences** sans tenir compte *or* se soucier des conséquences, sans s'arrêter aux conséquences.
(c) (*U: reference; aspect*) égard *m*, rapport *m*. **with ~ to** pour *or* en ce qui concerne, quant à, relativement à; **good in ~ of content** bon sous le rapport du contenu *or* quant au contenu; **in what ~?** sous quel rapport?, à quel égard?; **in some ~s** à certains égards, sous certains rapports; **in many ~s** à bien des égards; **in this ~** à cet égard, sous ce rapport; **in other ~s** à d'autres égards.
(d) (*regards*) **~s** respects *mpl*, hommages *mpl*; **to pay one's ~s to sb** présenter ses respects à qn; **give my ~s to** présentez mes respects *or* mes hommages à.
2 *vt* **(a)** *person, customs, sb's wishes, opinions, grief, the law* respecter. **to ~ o.s.** se respecter.
(b) as ~s quant à, en ce qui concerne.

respectability [rɪsˌpektə'bɪlɪtɪ] *n* respectabilité *f*.

respectable [rɪs'pektəbl] *adj* **(a)** (*estimable*) *person* respectable, honorable, estimable; *motives* respectable, honorable; (*socially approved*) *person* respectable, convenable; *clothes, behaviour* convenable, comme il faut. **a poor but ~ woman** une femme pauvre mais tout à fait respectable; **they are very ~ people** ce sont de très braves gens; **he was outwardly ~ but...** il avait l'apparence de la respectabilité mais...; **in ~ society** entre gens convenables *or* comme il faut; **that's not ~** ça ne se fait pas.
(b) (*of some size, importance*) *size, income* considérable, respectable. **a ~ writer** un écrivain qui n'est pas sans talent; **a ~ sum** une somme respectable *or* rondelette.

respectably [rɪs'pektəblɪ] *adv* **(a)** *dress, behave* convenablement, correctement, comme il faut*. **(b)** (*quite well*) passablement, pas mal*.

respecter [rɪs'pektəʳ] *n*: **death/the law is no ~ of persons** tout le monde est égal devant la mort/la loi; **death is no ~ of wealth** les riches et les pauvres sont égaux devant la mort; **he is no ~ of persons** il ne s'en laisse imposer par personne.

respectful [rɪs'pektfʊl] *adj person, behaviour, tone* respectueux (*of* de, *towards* envers, à l'égard de).

respectfully [rɪs'pektfəlɪ] *adv* respectueusement, avec respect. (*in letters*) **I remain ~ yours** *or* **yours ~** je vous prie d'agréer l'expression de mes sentiments respectueux *or* (*man to woman*) de mes très respectueux hommages.

respectfulness [rɪs'pektfʊlnɪs] *n* respect *m*, caractère respectueux.

respecting [rɪs'pektɪŋ] *prep* en ce qui concerne, quant à, concernant, touchant.

respective [rɪs'pektɪv] *adj* respectif.

respectively [rɪs'pektɪvlɪ] *adv* respectivement.

respiration [ˌrespɪ'reɪʃən] *n* (*Bot, Med*) respiration *f*.

respirator ['respɪreɪtəʳ] *n* (*Med*) respirateur *m*; (*Mil*) masque *m* à gaz.

respiratory [rɪs'paɪərətərɪ] *adj* respiratoire; *V* **tract**¹.

respire [rɪs'paɪəʳ] *vti* respirer.

respite ['respaɪt] *n* répit *m*, relâche *m or f*; (*Jur*) sursis *m*. **without (a) ~** sans répit, sans relâche, sans cesse.

resplendence [rɪs'plendəns] *n* resplendissement *m* (*liter*); splendeur *f*.

resplendent [rɪs'plendənt] *adj* resplendissant.

respond [rɪs'pɒnd] *vi* **(a)** (*reply*) répondre (*to* à, *with* par), faire une réponse (*to* à); (*Rel*) chanter les répons. **to ~ to a toast** répondre à un toast.
(b) (*show reaction to*) répondre (*to* à). **brakes that ~ well** freins qui répondent bien; **car that ~s well to controls** voiture qui a de bonnes réactions *or* qui répond bien aux commandes; **the patient ~ed to treatment** le malade a bien réagi au traitement; **the illness ~ed to treatment** le traitement a agi sur la maladie.

respondent [rɪs'pɒndənt] **1** *n* (*Jur*) défendeur *m*, -deresse *f*. **2** *adj* qui répond *or* réagit (*to* à).

response [rɪs'pɒns] *n* **(a)** (*lit, fig*) réponse *f*; (*to treatment*) réaction *f*. **in ~ to** en réponse à; **in ~ to the radio appeal, the sum of £1,000 was raised** par suite de *or* en réponse à l'appel radiodiffusé, on a recueilli la somme de 1.000 livres; **we had hoped for a bigger ~ from the public** nous n'avons pas reçu du public la réponse escomptée.
(b) (*Rel*) répons *m*.

responsibility [rɪsˌpɒnsə'bɪlɪtɪ] **1** *n* responsabilité *f*. **to lay** *or* **put** *or* **place the ~ for sth on sb** tenir qn pour responsable de qch, faire porter la responsabilité de qch à qn; **to take ~ for sth** prendre la responsabilité de qch; **'the company takes no ~ for objects left here'** ≃ 'la compagnie décline toute responsabilité pour les objets en dépôt'; **to take on the ~** accepter *or* assumer la responsabilité; **that's** HIS **~** c'est à lui de s'en occuper; **it's not** MY **~ to do that** ce n'est pas à moi de faire ça; **on my own ~** sous ma responsabilité; **he has too many responsibilities** il a *or* assume trop de responsabilités.
2 *cpd*: **responsibility payment** prime *f* de fonction.

responsible [rɪs'pɒnsəbl] *adj* **(a)** (*liable*) responsable (*for* de). **she is not ~ for her actions** elle n'est pas responsable de ses actes; **to be ~ to sb for sth** être responsable de qch envers qn *or* devant qn; **to be directly ~ to sb** relever directement de qn; **who is ~ for this mistake?** qui est l'auteur *or* le responsable de cette erreur?; **I hold you ~ for all that happened** je vous considère *or* rends responsable de tout ce qui est arrivé.
(b) (*trustworthy*) *person* digne de confiance, sur qui on peut compter. **he has a very ~ nature** il a un grand sens des responsabilités, on peut vraiment compter sur lui.
(c) *job, duty* comportant des responsabilités.

responsibly [rɪs'pɒnsəblɪ] *adv* avec sérieux.

responsive [rɪs'pɒnsɪv] *adj audience, class, pupil* qui réagit bien. **he is very ~** il n'est pas du tout timide *or* réservé; (*to affection*) il est très affectueux; **he wasn't very ~ when I spoke to him about it** quand je lui en ai parlé il n'a pas beaucoup réagi.

responsiveness [rɪs'pɒnsɪvnɪs] *n* (*V* **responsive**) bonne réaction (*to* à); manque *m* de réserve *or* de timidité; caractère affectueux.

rest [rest] **1** *n* **(a)** (*gen sense*) repos *m*; (*Mus*) silence *m*; (*Poetry*) césure *f*. **a day of ~** un jour de repos; **to need ~** avoir besoin de repos; **to need a ~** avoir besoin de se reposer; **to have a ~** se reposer; **she took** *or* **had an hour's ~** elle s'est reposée pendant une heure; **we had a couple of ~s during the walk** pendant la promenade nous nous sommes arrêtés deux fois pour nous reposer; **take a ~!** reposez-vous!; **to have a good night's ~** passer une bonne nuit; (*liter*) **to retire to ~** se retirer; **at ~** au repos; **to be at ~** (*peaceful*) être tranquille *or* calme; (*immobile*) rester immobile, ne pas bouger; (*euph: dead*) reposer en paix; **to lay to ~** porter en terre; **to set at ~** *fears, doubts* dissiper; **to put** *or* **set sb's mind at ~** tranquilliser qn, rassurer qn; **you can set** *or* **put your mind at ~** tu peux être tranquille; **to come to ~** *[ball, car etc]* s'arrêter, s'immobiliser; *[bird, insect]* se poser (*on* sur); **give it a ~!*** (*change the subject*) change de disque!*; (*stop working*) laisse tomber!*
(b) (*support*) support *m*, appui *m*; *V* **arm**¹, **receiver** *etc*.
(c) (*remainder*) **the ~ of the money** le reste *or* le restant *or* ce qui reste de l'argent, l'argent qui reste; **the ~ of the boys** les garçons qui restent, les autres garçons; **I will take half of the money and you keep the ~** je prends la moitié de l'argent et tu gardes le reste *or* le restant; **I will take this book and you keep the ~** je prends ce livre et tu gardes les autres; **you go off and the ~ of us will wait here** pars, nous (autres) nous resterons ici; **he was as drunk as the ~ of them** il était aussi ivre que (tous) les autres; **all the ~ of the money** tout ce qui reste de l'argent, tout l'argent qui reste; **all the ~ of the books** tous les autres livres; **and all the ~ of it*** et tout ça*, et tout ce qui s'ensuit; **for the ~** quant au reste.
2 *cpd*: (*Mil*) **rest camp** cantonnement *m* de repos; **rest centre** centre *m* d'accueil; **rest cure** cure *f* de repos; **rest day** jour *m* de repos; **rest home, rest house** maison *f* de repos; **resting place** lieu *m* de repos; *[the dead]* dernière demeure; (*US euph*) **rest room** toilettes *fpl*.
3 *vi* **(a)** (*repose*) se reposer; (*euph: be buried*) reposer. **she never ~s** elle ne se repose jamais, elle ne sait pas se reposer; **you must ~ for an hour** il faut vous reposer pendant une heure; (*fig*) **he won't ~ till he finds out the truth** il n'aura de cesse qu'il ne découvre (*subj*) la vérité; (*fig*) **to ~ easy** dormir sur ses deux oreilles; **to ~ on one's oars** (*lit*) lever les avirons *or* les rames; (*fig*) prendre un repos bien mérité; (*fig*) **to ~ on one's laurels** se reposer *or* s'endormir sur ses lauriers; *[actor]* (*euph*) **to be ~ing** se trouver sans engagement; **may he ~ in peace** qu'il repose (*subj*) en paix; (*Agr*) **to let a field ~** laisser reposer un champ, laisser un champ en jachère; **(the case for) the prosecution ~s** sur quoi l'accusation conclut.
(b) (*remain*) rester, demeurer. **~ assured that** soyez certain *or* assuré que; **the matter must not ~ there, things must not ~ like that** il n'est pas admissible que l'affaire en reste (*subj*) là; **and there the matter ~s for the moment** l'affaire en est là pour le moment; **the authority ~s with him** c'est lui qui détient l'autorité; **the decision ~s with him, it ~s with him to decide** il lui appartient de décider, c'est à lui de prendre la décision; **it doesn't ~ with me** cela ne dépend pas de moi.
(c) (*lean, be supported*) *[person]* s'appuyer (*on* sur, *against* contre); *[ladder]* appuyer (*on* sur, *against* contre); *[roof etc]* reposer, appuyer (*on* sur); (*fig*) *[argument, reputation, case]*

reposer (*on* sur); *[eyes, gaze]* se poser, s'arrêter (*on* sur). **her elbows were ~ing on the table** elle appuyait ses coudes sur la table; (*fig*) **a heavy responsibility ~s on him** il a de lourdes responsabilités.

4 *vt* **(a)** faire *or* laisser reposer, donner du repos à. **to ~ o.s.** se reposer; **I am quite ~ed** je me sens tout à fait reposé; **to ~ the horses** laisser reposer les chevaux; **God ~ his soul!** que Dieu ait son âme!, paix à son âme!; (*Jur*) **to ~ one's case** conclure son plaidoyer.

(b) (*lean*) poser, appuyer (*on* sur, *against* contre); (*fig: base*) *suspicions* fonder, faire reposer, baser (*on* sur). **to ~ one's hand on sb's shoulder** poser la main sur l'épaule de qn; **to ~ one's elbows on the table** appuyer *or* poser les coudes sur la table; **to ~ a ladder against a wall** appuyer une échelle contre un mur.

rest up* *vi* se reposer.

restart ['riː'stɑːt] **1** *vt work, activity* reprendre, recommencer; *engine* relancer, remettre en marche; *machine* remettre en marche.

2 *vi* reprendre, recommencer; *[engine, machine]* se remettre en marche.

restate ['riː'steɪt] *vt argument, reasons* répéter; *problem* énoncer de nouveau; *theory, case, one's position* exposer de nouveau.

restatement ['riː'steɪtmənt] *n* répétition *f*; *[plan, theory]* nouvel énoncé.

restaurant ['restərɔ̃ːŋ] **1** *n* restaurant *m*. **2** *cpd food, prices* de restaurant. (*Brit Rail*) **restaurant car** wagon-restaurant *m*.

restaurateur [ˌrestərə'tɜːʳ] *n* restaurateur *m*.

restful ['restfʊl] *adj occupation, pastime etc* reposant, qui procure du repos; *colour* reposant; *place* paisible, tranquille, reposant. **she is very ~ to be with** elle est très reposante.

restfully ['restfəlɪ] *adv* paisiblement, tranquillement.

restitution [ˌrestɪ'tjuːʃən] *n* **(a)** (*U*) restitution *f*. **to make ~ of sth** restituer qch; (*Jur*) **~ of conjugal rights** ordre *m* de réintégration du domicile conjugal. **(b)** (*reparation*) réparation *f*, compensation *f*, indemnité *f*.

restive ['restɪv] *adj horse* rétif; *person* agité, énervé; *manner* impatient, nerveux. **to get** *or* **grow ~** *[person]* s'agiter, s'énerver; *[horse]* devenir rétif.

restiveness ['restɪvnɪs] *n [horse]* état rétif; *[person]* agitation *f*, énervement *m*.

restless ['restlɪs] *adj person, manner, sea* agité; *child* agité, remuant. **I had a ~ night** j'ai mal dormi; **he is ~ in his sleep** il a le sommeil agité; *[audience, class etc]* **to get ~** s'impatienter, s'agiter, donner des signes d'agitation; (*fig*) **he is very ~ just now** il n'a pas encore trouvé sa voie, il ne sait pas quoi faire de sa peau*.

restlessly ['restlɪslɪ] *adv* avec agitation. **to walk ~ up and down** faire nerveusement les cent pas.

restlessness ['restlɪsnɪs] *n [sleep]* agitation *f*; *[manner]* agitation, nervosité *f*; *[crowd]* impatience *f*.

restock ['riː'stɒk] *vt shop* réapprovisionner; *pond, river* empoissonner.

restoration [ˌrestə'reɪʃən] *n* **(a)** (*U: return*) rétablissement *m*; (*Jur*) *[property]* restitution *f*. (*Brit Hist*) **the R~** la Restauration. **(b)** *[text]* rétablissement *m*; *[monument, work of art]* restauration *f*.

restorative [rɪs'tɔːrətɪv] *adj, n* fortifiant (*m*), reconstituant (*m*).

restore [rɪs'tɔːʳ] *vt* **(a)** (*give or bring back*) *sth lost, borrowed, stolen* rendre, restituer (*to* à); *sb's sight etc* rendre; (*Jur*) *rights* rétablir; *confidence* redonner (*to sb* à qn, *in* dans); *order, calm* rétablir, ramener. **to ~ sb's health** rétablir la santé de qn, rendre la santé à qn; **~d to health** rétabli, guéri; **to ~ sb to life** ramener qn à la vie; **to ~ sth to its former condition** remettre qch en état; **the brandy ~d my strength** *or* **me** le cognac m'a redonné des forces; **he was ~d to them safe and sound** il leur a été rendu sain et sauf; **to ~ to the throne** replacer sur le trône; **to ~ to power** ramener au pouvoir.

(b) (*repair*) *building, painting, furniture etc* restaurer; *text* restituer, rétablir.

restorer [rɪs'tɔːrəʳ] *n* (*Art etc*) restaurateur *m*, -trice *f*; *V* **hair**.

restrain [rɪs'treɪn] *vt* retenir; *sb's activities* limiter, restreindre; *anger* contenir, réprimer, maîtriser; *feelings* contenir, refréner, dominer. **to ~ sb from doing** empêcher *or* retenir qn de faire; **to ~ o.s.** se retenir; **please ~ yourself!** je vous en prie, maîtrisez-vous! *or* calmez-vous!; **the prisoner had to be ~ed** il a fallu maîtriser le prisonnier.

restrained [rɪs'treɪnd] *adj emotions* contenu; *tone, voice, words, manner* mesuré; *style* sobre. **he was very ~ when he heard the news** quand il a appris la nouvelle, il est resté très maître de lui-même *or* de soi.

restraint [rɪs'treɪnt] *n* **(a)** (*restriction*) contrainte *f*, entrave *f*, frein *m*. **without ~** sans contrainte; (*Jur*) **to place under ~** interner; **subject to many ~s** sujet à de nombreuses contraintes.

(b) (*U: moderation*) *[speech]* retenue *f*, mesure *f*; *[style]* sobriété *f*. **to show a lack of ~** manquer de maîtrise de soi; **he said with great ~ that** mesurant ses paroles, il a déclaré que.

restrict [rɪs'trɪkt] *vt* restreindre, limiter (*to* à). **visiting is ~ed to one hour per day** les visites sont limitées à une heure par jour; **to ~ sb's authority/freedom** restreindre *or* limiter l'autorité/la liberté de qn.

restricted [rɪs'trɪktɪd] *adj number, group, circulation, aim* restreint, limité; (*Admin, Mil*) *document* confidentiel; *point of view, horizon* étroit. **within a ~ area** dans une zone restreinte *or* limitée; (*fig*) dans certaines limites; (*Aut*) **~ area** zone à vitesse limitée.

restriction [rɪs'trɪkʃən] *n* restriction *f*, limitation *f*. **to place ~s** on apporter des restrictions à; (*Aut*) **speed ~** limitation de vitesse; (*Comm*) **price ~** contrôle *m* de prix.

restrictive [rɪs'trɪktɪv] *adj* restrictif. **~ practices** (*Ind*) pratiques restrictives de production; (*Comm*) entraves *fpl* à la libre concurrence *or* à la liberté du commerce.

re-string ['riː'strɪŋ] *pret, ptp* **re-strung** *vt* (*Mus*) *violin* remplacer les cordes de; (*Sport*) *racket* recorder; *bow* remplacer la corde de, remettre une corde à.

result [rɪ'zʌlt] **1** *n* **(a)** résultat *m*, conséquence *f*; (*Math*) résultat. **as a ~ he failed** en conséquence il a échoué, résultat – il a échoué*; **to be the ~ of** être la conséquence de, être dû à; **as a ~ of my inquiry** par suite de mon enquête; **without ~** sans résultat.

(b) *[election, exam, race]* résultat *m*. **to demand ~s** exiger des résultats; **to get ~s*** *[person]* obtenir de bons résultats, arriver à quelque chose*; *[action]* donner de bons résultats, aboutir à quelque chose*.

2 *vi* **(a)** (*follow*) résulter, provenir (*from* de). **it ~s that** il s'ensuit que.

(b) (*finish*) **that's going to ~ badly** cela va mal se terminer.

result in *vt fus* mener à, aboutir à, se terminer par.

resultant [rɪ'zʌltənt] **1** *adj* résultant, qui (en) résulte. **2** *n* (*Math*) résultante *f*.

resume [rɪ'zjuːm] **1** *vt* **(a)** (*restart etc*) *tale, account* reprendre; *activity* reprendre, recommencer. **to ~ work** reprendre le travail, se remettre au travail; **to ~ one's journey** reprendre la route, continuer son voyage; **'well' he ~d** 'eh bien' reprit-il; **to ~ one's seat** se rasseoir; (*frm*) **to ~ possession of** reprendre possession de. **(b)** (*sum up*) résumer. **2** *vi [classes, work etc]* reprendre, recommencer.

résumé ['reɪzjuːmeɪ] *n* résumé *m*; (*US*) curriculum vitæ *m inv*.

resumption [rɪ'zʌmpʃən] *n* reprise *f*.

resurface [ˌriː'sɜːfɪs] **1** *vt road* refaire la surface de. **2** *vi [diver, submarine]* remonter à la *or* en surface, faire surface.

resurgence [rɪ'sɜːdʒəns] *n* réapparition *f*.

resurgent [rɪ'sɜːdʒənt] *adj* renaissant.

resurrect [ˌrezə'rekt] *vt* ressusciter (des morts); (*fig*) *fashion, ideas* faire revivre; *memories* réveiller; (* *hum*) *dress, chair etc* remettre en service.

resurrection [ˌrezə'rekʃən] *n* (*Rel, fig*) résurrection *f*.

resuscitate [rɪ'sʌsɪteɪt] *vt* ranimer; (*Med*) réanimer.

resuscitation [rɪˌsʌsɪ'teɪʃən] *n* résurrection *f*, retour *m* à la vie; (*Med*) réanimation *f*.

retail ['riːteɪl] **1** *n* (vente *f* au) détail *m*.

2 *vt* vendre au détail, détailler; (*fig*) *gossip* colporter, répandre.

3 *vi [goods]* se vendre (au détail) (*at* à).

4 *adv*: **to sell ~** vendre au détail.

5 *cpd*: **retail business** commerce *m* de détail; **retail dealer** détaillant(e) *m(f)*; **they are looking for a retail outlet for ...** ils cherchent un débouché pour ...; **50 retail outlets** 50 points *mpl* de vente; **retail price** prix *m* de détail; **the retail trade** (*traders*) les détaillants *mpl*; (*selling*) la vente au détail.

retailer ['riːteɪləʳ] *n* détaillant(e) *m(f)*.

retain [rɪ'teɪn] *vt* **(a)** (*keep*) conserver, garder; (*hold*) retenir, maintenir. **~ing wall** mur *m* de soutènement; **to ~ control (of)** garder le contrôle (de).

(b) (*remember*) garder en mémoire.

(c) (*engage*) *lawyer* retenir, engager. **~ing fee** = **retainer b**.

retainer [rɪ'teɪnəʳ] *n* **(a)** (†, *liter: servant*) serviteur *m*. **(b)** (*fee*) acompte *m*; (*to lawyer*) provision *f*.

retake ['riːteɪk] (*vb: pret* **retook**, *ptp* **retaken**) **1** *n* (*Cine*) nouvelle prise de vues. **2** ['riː'teɪk] *vt* **(a)** reprendre; *prisoner* reprendre, rattraper. **(b)** (*Cine*) tourner de nouveau, refaire un take de.

retaliate [rɪ'tælɪeɪt] *vi* se venger (*against sb/sth* de qn/qch), user de représailles (*against sb* envers qn). **he ~d by breaking a window** pour se venger il a brisé une fenêtre; **he ~d by pointing out that ...** il a riposté *or* rétorqué que ..., pour sa part il a fait observer que ...; **to ~ (up)on sb** rendre la pareille à qn, user de représailles envers qn.

retaliation [rɪˌtælɪ'eɪʃən] *n* revanche *f*, vengeance *f*, représailles *fpl*. **in ~** par représailles; **in ~ for** pour venger, pour se venger de; **policy of ~** politique *f* de représailles.

retaliatory [rɪ'tælɪətərɪ] *adj* de représailles. **~ measures** représailles *fpl*.

retard [rɪ'tɑːd] **1** *vt* retarder; (*Aut*) *ignition* retarder. **2** *n* retard *m*.

retarded [rɪ'tɑːdɪd] *adj* (*Med*) retardé, arriéré; (*pej*) demeuré*. (*Aut*) **~ ignition** retard *m* à l'allumage; (*Tech*) **~ acceleration** accélération négative; **mentally ~** arriéré.

retch [retʃ] **1** *vi* avoir des haut-le-cœur. **2** *n* haut-le-cœur *m inv*.

retching ['retʃɪŋ] *n* haut-le-cœur *mpl*.

retell ['riː'tel] *pret, ptp* **retold** *vt* raconter de nouveau.

retention [rɪ'tenʃən] *n* conservation *f*, maintien *m*; (*Med*) rétention *f*; (*memory*) mémoire *f*.

retentive [rɪ'tentɪv] *adj memory* fidèle, sûr. **he is very ~** il a une très bonne mémoire.

retentiveness [rɪ'tentɪvnɪs] *n* faculté *f* de retenir, mémoire *f*.

rethink ['riː'θɪŋk] *pret, ptp* **rethought** **1** *vt* repenser. **2** *n* (*) **we'll have to have a ~** nous allons devoir y réfléchir encore un coup*.

reticence ['retɪsəns] *n* réticence *f*.

reticent ['retɪsənt] *adj* réticent, réservé. **to be ~ about** (*habitually*) ne pas parler beaucoup de; (*on one occasion*) ne pas dire grand-chose de.

reticently ['retɪsəntlɪ] *adv* avec réticence, avec réserve.

reticle ['retɪkl] *n* (*Opt*) réticule *m*.

reticulate [rɪ'tɪkjʊlɪt] *adj*, **reticulated** [rɪ'tɪkjʊleɪtɪd] *adj* réticulé.

reticule ['retɪkjuːl] *n* **(a)** = **reticle. (b)** (*handbag*) réticule *m*.
retina ['retɪnə] *n, pl* **retinæ** ['retɪniː] *or* ~**s** rétine *f*.
retinue ['retɪnjuː] *n* suite *f*, cortège *m*.
retire [rɪ'taɪəʳ] **1** *vi* **(a)** (*withdraw*) se retirer, partir; (*Mil*) reculer, se replier. **to ~ from the room** quitter la pièce; **to ~ to the lounge** se retirer au salon, passer au salon; (*Sport*) **to ~ hurt** abandonner à la suite d'une blessure; **to ~ into o.s.** rentrer en *or* se replier sur soi-même; **to ~ from the world/from public life** se retirer du monde/de la vie publique.
(b) (*go to bed*) (aller) se coucher.
(c) (*give up one's work*) prendre sa retraite. **he ~d on a good pension** il a pris sa retraite et il touche une bonne pension; **to ~ from business** se retirer des affaires.
2 *vt worker, employee* mettre à la retraite; (*Fin*) *bond* retirer de la circulation. **to be compulsorily ~d** être mis à la retraite d'office.
retired [rɪ'taɪəd] *adj* **(a)** (*no longer working*) retraité, à la retraite. **a ~ person** un(e) retraité(e); (*Mil*) **~ list** état *m* des mises à la retraite; **~ pay** pension *f* de retraite. **(b)** (*secluded*) *life, spot* retiré.
retirement [rɪ'taɪəmənt] **1** *n* **(a)** (*stopping work*) retraite *f*. **~ at 60** (mise *f* à la) retraite à 60 ans; **to announce one's ~** annoncer que l'on prend sa retraite; **to come out of ~** reprendre ses activités *or* une occupation *or* du service (*après avoir pris sa retraite*); **how will you spend your ~?** qu'est-ce que vous ferez quand vous aurez pris votre retraite?; *V* **compulsory.**
(b) (*seclusion*) isolement *m*, solitude *f*. **to live in ~** vivre retiré du monde.
(c) (*Mil*) retraite *f*, repli *m*; (*Sport*) abandon *m*.
2 *cpd*: **retirement age** âge *m* de (la) retraite; **retirement benefit** prime *f* de retraite; **retirement pay** retraite *f*; **retirement pension** (pension *f* de) retraite *f*; (*Mil*) solde *f* de retraite; *V also* **pension.**
retiring [rɪ'taɪərɪŋ] *adj* **(a)** (*shy*) réservé. **(b) ~ room** cabinet particulier. **(c) ~ age** âge *m* de (la) retraite.
retort [rɪ'tɔːt] **1** *n* **(a)** (*answer*) réplique *f*, riposte *f*. **(b)** (*Chem*) cornue *f*. **2** *vt* rétorquer, riposter, répliquer (*that* que). **'not at all' he ~ed** 'pas du tout' rétorqua-t-il *or* riposta-t-il *or* répliqua-t-il. **3** *vi* rétorquer, riposter.
retouch ['riː'tʌtʃ] *vt* (*Art, Phot*) retoucher.
retrace [rɪ'treɪs] *vt developments etc* (*research into*) reconstituer; (*give account of*) retracer. **to ~ one's path** *or* **steps** revenir sur ses pas, rebrousser chemin.
retract [rɪ'trækt] **1** *vt* **(a)** (*withdraw*) *offer* rétracter, retirer; *statement* rétracter, revenir sur, désavouer. **(b)** (*draw back*) *claws* rétracter, rentrer; (*Aviat*) *undercarriage* rentrer, escamoter. **2** *vi* **(a)** (*withdraw*) se rétracter, se désavouer. **(b)** (*draw back*) se rétracter; (*Aviat*) rentrer.
retractable [rɪ'træktəbl] *adj* (*lit*) rentrant, escamotable; (*fig*) *remark* que l'on peut rétracter *or* retirer.
retraction [rɪ'trækʃən] *n [offer]* rétractation *f*; *[declaration]* rétractation, désaveu *m*; *[claws etc]* rétraction *f*; *[undercarriage]* escamotage *m*.
retrain ['riː'treɪn] **1** *vt* recycler, donner une nouvelle formation (professionnelle) à. **2** *vi* se recycler.
retraining ['riː'treɪnɪŋ] *n* recyclage *m*.
retransmit ['riːtrænz'mɪt] *vt* réexpédier; (*Phys, Rad, TV*) retransmettre, rediffuser.
retread [ˌriː'tred] **1** *vt tyre* rechaper. **2** ['riːtred] *n* (*tyre*) pneu rechapé.
retreat [rɪ'triːt] **1** *n* **(a)** (*esp Mil*) retraite *f*, repli *m*, recul *m*. **the army is in ~** l'armée bat en retraite; **to sound the ~** battre la retraite; **to make** *or* **beat a hasty ~** partir en vitesse.
(b) (*place*) asile *m*, refuge *m*, retraite *f* (*liter*); (*Rel*) retraite. **a country ~** un endroit (*or* une maison *etc*) tranquille à la campagne.
2 *vi* (*Mil*) battre en retraite; (*withdraw*) se retirer (*from* de); *[flood, glacier]* reculer; *[chin, forehead]* être fuyant. **to ~ within o.s.** se replier sur soi-même.
3 *vt* (*Chess*) ramener.
retrench [rɪ'trentʃ] **1** *vt* restreindre, réduire; *book* faire des coupures dans. **2** *vi* faire des économies.
retrenchment [rɪ'trentʃmənt] *n* **(a)** *[expense]* réduction *f* (des dépenses). **(b)** (*Mil*) retranchement *m*.
retrial ['riː'traɪəl] *n* (*Jur*) nouveau procès.
retribution [ˌretrɪ'bjuːʃən] *n* châtiment *m*, récompense *f* (*d'une mauvaise action*).
retributive [rɪ'trɪbjʊtɪv] *adj person, action* vengeur (*f* -geresse); *justice* distributif.
retrievable [rɪ'triːvəbl] *adj object, material* récupérable; *money* recouvrable; *error, loss* réparable.
retrieval [rɪ'triːvəl] *n* (*V* **retrieve**) récupération *f*; recouvrement *m*; réparation *f*. **beyond** *or* **past ~** irréparable; *V* **information.**
retrieve [rɪ'triːv] **1** *vt* (*recover*) *object* récupérer (*from* de); *[dog]* rapporter; (*Fin*) recouvrer; *information* rechercher et extraire; *fortune, honour, position* rétablir; (*set to rights*) *error* réparer; *situation* redresser, sauver; (*rescue*) sauver, tirer (*from* de). (*lit, fig*) **we shall ~ nothing from this disaster** nous ne sauverons *or* récupérerons rien de ce désastre.
2 *vi [dog]* rapporter.
retriever [rɪ'triːvəʳ] *n* retriever *m*, chien *m* d'arrêt.
retro... ['retrəʊ] *pref* rétro... .
retroactive [ˌretrəʊ'æktɪv] *adj* rétroactif.
retroflex ['retrəʊfleks] *adj* (*Ling*) apical, rétroflexe.
retrograde ['retrəʊgreɪd] **1** *adj* rétrograde. **2** *vi* rétrograder.
retrogress [ˌretrəʊ'gres] *vi* rétrograder.
retrogression [ˌretrəʊ'greʃən] *n* rétrogradation *f*, régression *f*.
retrogressive [ˌretrəʊ'gresɪv] *adj* rétrogressif, rétrograde; (*Bio*) régressif.
retrorocket ['retrəʊ'rɒkɪt] *n* rétrofusée *f*.
retrospect ['retrəʊspekt] *n* examen *or* coup d'œil rétrospectif. **in ~** rétrospectivement, après coup.
retrospection [ˌretrəʊ'spekʃən] *n* examen rétrospectif.
retrospective [ˌretrəʊ'spektɪv] *adj glance, thought, wisdom* rétrospectif; (*Admin, Jur*) *pay rise, effect* rétroactif.
retrospectively [ˌretrəʊ'spektɪvlɪ] *adv* rétrospectivement; (*Admin, Jur*) rétroactivement.
retry ['riː'traɪ] *vt* (*Jur*) juger de nouveau.
return [rɪ'tɜːn] **1** *vi [person, vehicle etc]* (*come back*) revenir; (*go back*) retourner; *[property]* retourner, revenir, faire retour (*to* à); *[symptoms, doubts, fears]* réapparaître. **to ~ home** rentrer; **have they ~ed?** sont-ils revenus? *or* rentrés? *or* de retour?; **his good spirits ~ed** sa bonne humeur est revenue; **to ~ to one's work** reprendre *or* se remettre à son travail; **to ~ to school** rentrer (en classe); **to ~ to a subject/an idea** revenir à un sujet/une idée; **to ~ to what we were talking about, he...** pour en revenir à la question, il...; **to ~ to one's bad habits** reprendre ses mauvaises habitudes.
2 *vt* **(a)** (*give back*) (*gen*) rendre; *sth borrowed, stolen, lost* rendre, restituer; (*bring back*) rapporter; *goods to shop* rendre, rapporter; (*put back*) remettre; (*send back*) renvoyer, retourner; *ball, sound, light* renvoyer; *compliment, salute, blow, visit* rendre; *sb's love* répondre à. **to ~ money to sb** rembourser qn; **he ~ed the £5 to him** il lui a remboursé les 5 livres, il l'a remboursé des 5 livres; **to ~ a book to the library** rapporter *or* rendre un livre à la bibliothèque; **to ~ a book to the shelf** remettre un livre sur le rayon; **he ~ed it to his pocket** il l'a remis dans sa poche; (*on letter*) **'~ to sender'** 'retour à l'envoyeur'; (*liter*) **to ~ thanks** rendre grâce, remercier; **to ~ sb's favour** rendre service à qn (en échange); **I hope to ~ your kindness** j'espère pouvoir vous rendre service en retour; **his love was not ~ed** elle n'a pas répondu à son amour; **to ~ good for evil** rendre le bien pour le mal; **to ~ like for like** rendre la pareille; (*Bridge*) **to ~ hearts** rejouer du cœur, renvoyer cœur.
(b) (*reply*) répondre, répliquer, riposter.
(c) (*declare*) *income, details* déclarer. (*Jur*) **to ~ a verdict** rendre *or* prononcer un verdict; (*Jur*) **to ~ a verdict of guilty on sb** déclarer qn coupable; **to ~ a verdict of murder** conclure au meurtre.
(d) (*Fin*) *profit, income* rapporter, donner.
(e) (*Parl*) *candidate* élire. **he was ~ed by an overwhelming majority** il a été élu à *or* avec une très forte majorité.
3 *n* **(a)** (*coming, going back*) *[person, illness, seasons]* retour *m*. **on my ~** dès mon retour; **~ home** retour; **~ to school** rentrée *f* (des classes); **by ~ of post** par retour du courrier; **a ~ to one's old habits** un retour à ses vieilles habitudes; **many happy ~s (of the day)!** bon anniversaire!; *V* **point.**
(b) (*giving back*) retour *m*; (*sending back*) renvoi *m*; (*putting back*) remise *f* en place; *[sth lost, stolen, borrowed]* restitution *f*; *[money]* remboursement *m*; *V* **sale.**
(c) (*Brit: also* **~ ticket**) aller et retour *m*.
(d) (*recompense*) récompense *f* (*for* de), (*from land, business, mine*) rendement *m*, rapport *m*; (*from investments, shares*) rapport. **~s** (*profits*) bénéfice *m*, profit *m*; (*receipts*) rentrées *fpl*, recettes *fpl*; **small profits and quick ~s** de bas prix et un gros chiffre d'affaires; (*Fin*) **~ on capital** rapport *m* de capital; **~ on investments** rentabilité *f* des investissements; **to get a poor ~ for one's kindness** être mal récompensé *or* mal payé de sa gentillesse; **in ~** en revanche; **in ~ for** en récompense de, en échange de; *V* **diminish.**
(e) (*act of declaring*) *[verdict]* déclaration *f*; *[election results]* proclamation *f*; (*report*) rapport *m*, relevé *m*; (*statistics*) statistique *f*. **official ~s** statistique officielle; **the population ~s show that ...** le recensement montre que ...; **the election ~s** les résultats *mpl* de l'élection; **tax ~** (feuille *f* de) déclaration de revenus *or* d'impôts.
(f) (*Parl*) *[candidate]* élection *f*.
(g) (*Sport*) riposte *f*; (*Tennis*) retour *m*.
4 *cpd*: **return fare** (prix *m*) aller et retour *m*; **return flight** vol *m* de retour; *[ticket]* **return half** coupon *m* de retour; (*Pol*) **returning officer** scrutateur *m*; **return journey** (voyage *m or* trajet *m* de) retour *m*; **return match** revanche *f*, match *m* retour; (*Tech*) **return stroke** course *f* retour; (*Brit*) **return ticket** (billet *m* d')aller et retour *m*.
returnable [rɪ'tɜːnəbl] *adj* qu'on doit rendre; *bottle etc* consigné. **the bottles are non-~** ça n'est pas consigné, c'est du verre perdu.
reunification ['riːˌjuːnɪfɪ'keɪʃən] *n* réunification *f*.
reunify ['riː'juːnɪfaɪ] *vt* réunifier.
reunion [riː'juːnjən] *n* réunion *f*.
reunite ['riːjuː'naɪt] **1** *vt* réunir. **they were ~d at last** ils se sont enfin retrouvés. **2** *vi* se réunir.
rev* [rev] **1** *n* (*Aut: abbr of* **revolution**) tour *m*. **~ counter** compte-tours *m inv*; **4,000 ~s per minute** 4.000 tours minute. **2** *vt*: **to ~ (up) the engine** emballer le moteur. **3** *vi* (*also* **~up**) *[engine]* s'emballer; *[driver]* emballer le moteur.
revaluation [riːˌvælju'eɪʃən] *n* (*Fin*) réévaluation *f*.
revalue ['riː'væljuː] *vt* (*Fin*) réévaluer.
revamp* ['riː'væmp] *vt company, department* réorganiser; *house, room, object* retaper*.
reveal [rɪ'viːl] *vt* (*make visible*) découvrir, laisser voir; (*make known*) révéler (*that* que); *truth, facts* révéler, faire connaître; *corruption* révéler, mettre à jour. **I cannot ~ to you what he said** je ne peux pas vous révéler ce qu'il a dit; **he ~ed himself as being ...** il s'est révélé comme étant...; **~ed religion** religion révélée.
revealing [rɪ'viːlɪŋ] *adj* révélateur (*f* -trice); *dress* décolleté.
reveille [rɪ'vælɪ] *n* (*Mil*) réveil *m*; *V* **sound**[1].
revel ['revl] **1** *vi* **(a)** (*make merry*) s'amuser, se divertir;

(*carouse*) faire la fête. **(b)** (*delight*) se délecter (*in sth* de qch). **to ~ in doing** se délecter à faire, prendre grand plaisir à faire. **2** *n*: **~s** (*entertainment*) divertissements *mpl*; (*carousing*) festivités *fpl*.

revelation [ˌrevəˈleɪʃən] *n* révélation *f*. (*Rel*) **(the Book of) R~** l'Apocalypse *f*.

reveller [ˈrevlər] *n* fêtard *m*, noceur* *m*, -euse* *f*, bambocheur* *m*, -euse* *f* (*all slightly pej*). **the ~s** les gens *mpl* de la fête.

revelry [ˈrevlrɪ] *n* (*U*) festivités *fpl*.

revenge [rɪˈvendʒ] **1** *n* vengeance *f*; (*Sport etc*) revanche *f*. **to take ~ on sb for sth** se venger de qch sur qn; **to get one's ~** se venger; **to do sth out of ~** faire qch par vengeance; **in ~ he killed him** pour se venger il l'a tué.

2 *vt insult, murder* venger. **to ~ o.s., to be ~d** se venger; **to ~ o.s. on sb/on sb for sth** se venger de qn/de qch sur qn.

revengeful [rɪˈvendʒfʊl] *adj person* vindicatif; *act* vengeur (*f* -geresse).

revengefully [rɪˈvendʒfəlɪ] *adv* par (esprit de) vengeance.

revenger [rɪˈvendʒər] *n* vengeur *m*, -geresse *f*.

revenue [ˈrevənjuː] **1** *n* [*state*] revenu *m*; [*individual*] revenu, rentes *fpl*; *V* **inland** *etc*. **2** *cpd*: **revenue man** douanier *m*; **revenue officer** agent *m or* employé(e) *m(f)* des douanes; **revenue stamp** timbre fiscal.

reverberate [rɪˈvɜːbəreɪt] **1** *vi* [*sound*] retentir, résonner, se répercuter; [*light, heat*] se réverbérer. **2** *vt sound* renvoyer, répercuter; *light* réverbérer, réfléchir; *heat* réverbérer.

reverberation [rɪˌvɜːbəˈreɪʃən] *n* [*sound*] répercussion *f*; [*light, heat*] réverbération *f*.

reverberator [rɪˈvɜːbəreɪtər] *n* réflecteur *m*.

revere [rɪˈvɪər] *vt* révérer, vénérer.

reverence [ˈrevərəns] **1** *n* **(a)** respect *m* (religieux), vénération *f*. **to have ~ for sb, to hold sb in ~** révérer qn; **to show** *or* **pay ~ to** rendre hommage à. **(b) your R~** ≈ mon (révérend) père, monsieur l'abbé. **2** *vt* révérer.

reverend [ˈrevərənd] **1** *adj* vénérable. **the R~ Robert Martin** (*Anglican*) le révérend Robert Martin; (*Roman Catholic*) l'abbé (Robert) Martin; (*Nonconformist*) le pasteur (Robert) Martin; **the Most R~** le Révérendissime; **the Very** *or* **Right R~ Robert Martin** (*Anglican*) le très révérend Robert Martin; (*Roman Catholic*) monseigneur Martin; **R~ Mother** révérende mère.

2 *n* (*) (*Roman Catholic*) curé *m*; (*Protestant*) pasteur *m*.

reverent [ˈrevərənt] *adj* respectueux.

reverential [ˌrevəˈrenʃəl] *adj* révérenciel.

reverently [ˈrevərəntlɪ] *adv* avec respect, avec vénération.

reverie [ˈrevərɪ] *n* rêverie *f*.

revers [rɪˈvɪər] *n* revers *m* (*d'un vêtement*).

reversal [rɪˈvɜːsəl] *n* (*turning upside down*) renversement *m*; (*switching over of 2 objects*) interversion *f*; [*opinion, view etc*] revirement *m*; (*Jur*) [*judgment*] arrêt *m* d'annulation, réforme *f*.

reverse [rɪˈvɜːs] **1** *adj* **(a)** (*opposite*) contraire, inverse, opposé; *direction* contraire, opposé. **~ side** [*coin, medal*] revers *m*; [*sheet of paper*] verso *m*; [*cloth*] envers *m*; [*painting*] dos *m*; **in ~ order** en ordre inverse; **~ turn** (*Aut*) virage *m* en marche arrière; (*Dancing*) renversement *m*.

(b) (*Aut: backwards*) **~ gear** marche *f* arrière; (*Tech*) **~ motion** *or* **action** (*backwards*) mouvement renversé; (*opposite direction*) mouvement inverse.

2 *n* **(a)** (*opposite*) contraire *m*, opposé *m*, inverse *m*. **quite the ~!** tout *or* bien au contraire!; **it is quite the ~** c'est tout le contraire *or* tout l'opposé; **he is the ~ of polite** il n'est rien moins que poli, c'est tout le contraire d'un homme poli; (*fig*) **in ~** dans l'ordre inverse.

(b) (*back*) [*coin, medal*] revers *m*; [*sheet of paper*] verso *m*; [*cloth*] envers *m*; [*painting*] dos *m*.

(c) (*setback, loss*) revers *m*, échec *m*; (*defeat*) défaite *f*.

(d) (*Aut*) **in ~** en marche arrière.

3 *vt* **(a)** (*turn the other way round*) renverser, retourner; *garment* retourner; *situation* renverser, changer complètement; *photo, result* inverser. **to ~ the order of things** inverser l'ordre des choses; **to ~ one's policy** faire volte-face (*fig*); **to ~ a procedure** procéder par ordre inverse; **to ~ a trend** renverser une tendance; (*Brit Telec*) **to ~ the charges** téléphoner en P.C.V.; **~d charge call** communication *f* en P.C.V.; **to ~ the position(s) of two objects** intervertir *or* inverser deux objets.

(b) (*cause to move backwards*) *moving belt* renverser la direction *or* la marche de; *typewriter ribbon* changer de sens. (*Tech*) **to ~ the engine** faire machine arrière; **to ~ one's car into the garage/down the hill** rentrer dans le garage/descendre la côte en marche arrière; **he ~d the car into a tree** il a heurté un arbre en faisant une marche arrière; **to ~ one's car across the road** faire une marche arrière en travers de la route.

(c) (*Jur: annul*) *decision, verdict* réformer, annuler; *judgment* réformer, déjuger; *sentence* révoquer, casser.

4 *vi* (*move backwards*) [*car*] faire marche arrière; [*dancer*] renverser. (*Aut*) **to ~ into the garage/down the hill** rentrer dans le garage/descendre la côte en marche arrière; **to ~ into a tree** heurter un arbre en faisant une marche arrière; **to ~ across the road** faire une marche arrière en travers de la route; (*Aut*) **reversing lights** feux *mpl* de marche arrière.

reversibility [rɪˌvɜːsɪˈbɪlɪtɪ] *n* réversibilité *f*.

reversible [rɪˈvɜːsəbl] *adj* réversible; *garment, cloth* réversible, sans envers ni endroit; *decision* révocable.

reversion [rɪˈvɜːʃən] *n* **(a)** (*return to former state*) retour *m* (*to* à); (*Bio*) réversion *f*. **~ to type** réversion au type primitif. **(b)** (*Jur*) réversion *f*, droit *m* de retour. **(c)** (*Phot*) inversion *f*.

reversionary [rɪˈvɜːʃnərɪ] *adj* **(a)** (*Jur*) de réversion, réversible. **(b)** (*Bio*) atavique, régressif.

revert [rɪˈvɜːt] *vi* **(a)** (*return*) revenir (*to* à); (*Jur*) revenir, retourner (*to* à); [*property*] faire retour (*to* à). **to ~ to the question** pour en revenir à la question; (*Bio*) **to ~ to type** retourner *or* revenir au type primitif; (*fig*) **he has ~ed to type** le naturel a repris le dessus.

(b) (*become again*) **fields ~ing to woodland** des champs qui retournent à l'état de forêt.

review [rɪˈvjuː] **1** *n* **(a)** (*act*) révision *f*; (*instance of this*) revue *f*, examen *m*. **the agreement comes up for ~** *or* **comes under ~ next year** l'accord doit être révisé l'année prochaine; **I shall keep your case under ~** je suivrai votre cas de très près; **he gave a ~ of recent developments in photography** il passa en revue les progrès récents de la photographie.

(b) (*Mil, Naut: inspection*) revue *f*. **to hold a ~** passer une revue.

(c) (*critical article*) [*book, film, play etc*] critique *f*, compte rendu *m*. [*book*] **~ copy** exemplaire *m* de service de presse, exemplaire pour compte rendu.

(d) (*magazine*) revue *f*, périodique *m*.

2 *vt* **(a)** (*consider again*) *one's life, the past* passer en revue. **we shall ~ the situation next year** nous réexaminerons *or* reconsidérerons la situation l'année prochaine.

(b) *troops* passer en revue.

(c) *book, play, film* faire la critique de, donner *or* faire un compte rendu de.

reviewer [rɪˈvjuːər] *n* critique *m*. **book ~** critique littéraire.

revile [rɪˈvaɪl] **1** *vt* injurier, insulter. **2** *vi* proférer des injures (*at, against* contre).

revise [rɪˈvaɪz] **1** *vt* **(a)** (*change*) *opinion, estimate* réviser, modifier.

(b) (*correct*) *proof* corriger, revoir; *text* revoir, réviser, corriger. **~d edition** édition revue et corrigée; (*Brit*) [*Bible*] **R~d Version** traduction (anglaise) de la Bible de 1884.

(c) (*learn up*) revoir, repasser, réviser.

2 *vi* réviser. **to ~ for exams** réviser *or* faire des révisions pour des examens; **to start revising** commencer à réviser *or* (à faire) ses révisions.

3 *n* (*Typ*) (épreuve *f* de) mise *f* en pages, seconde épreuve.

reviser [rɪˈvaɪzər] *n* réviseur *m*; [*proof*] correcteur *m*, -trice *f*.

revision [rɪˈvɪʒən] *n* révision *f*.

revisionism [rɪˈvɪʒənɪzəm] *n* révisionnisme *m*.

revisionist [rɪˈvɪʒənɪst] *adj, n* révisionniste (*mf*).

revisit [ˈriːˈvɪzɪt] *vt place* revisiter; *person* retourner voir.

revitalize [ˌriːˈvaɪtəlaɪz] *vt* redonner de la vitalité à, revivifier (*liter*).

revival [rɪˈvaɪvəl] *n* **(a)** (*bringing back*) [*custom, ceremony*] reprise *f*; (*Jur*) remise *f* en vigueur. (*Hist*) **the R~ of Learning** la Renaissance. **(b)** (*Rel*) [*faith*] renouveau *m*, réveil *m*. **~ meeting** réunion *f* pour le renouveau de la foi.

revivalist [rɪˈvaɪvəlɪst] *adj, n* revivaliste (*mf*).

revive [rɪˈvaɪv] **1** *vt person* (*from fainting*) ranimer; (*from near death, esp Med*) réanimer; *fashion* remettre en vogue; *conversation, fire* ranimer; *hope* faire renaître; *courage* redonner; *custom, usage* rétablir; *play* reprendre. **a glass of brandy will ~ you** un verre de cognac vous remontera *or* vous requinquera*.

2 *vi* [*person*] reprendre connaissance; [*hope, feelings*] renaître; [*business, trade*] reprendre.

revivify [riːˈvɪvɪfaɪ] *vt* revivifier (*liter*).

revocation [ˌrevəˈkeɪʃən] *n* [*order, promise*] révocation *f*; [*law, bill*] abrogation *f*; [*licence*] retrait *m*; [*decision*] annulation *f*.

revoke [rɪˈvəʊk] **1** *vt law* rapporter, abroger; *order* révoquer; *promise* revenir sur, révoquer; *decision* revenir sur, annuler; *licence* retirer. **2** *vi* (*Bridge*) faire une (fausse) renonce. **3** *n* (*Bridge*) (fausse) renonce *f*.

revolt [rɪˈvəʊlt] **1** *n* révolte *f*. **to break out in ~, to rise in ~** se révolter, se soulever; **to be in ~ (against)** se révolter *or* être révolté (contre); *V* **stir**[1].

2 *vi* **(a)** (*rebel*) se révolter, se soulever, se rebeller (*against* contre).

(b) (*be disgusted*) se révolter (*at* contre), être dégoûté (*at* par).

3 *vt* révolter, dégoûter, répugner. **to be ~ed by** être révolté *or* dégoûté par.

revolting [rɪˈvəʊltɪŋ] *adj* (*repulsive, disgusting*) dégoûtant, écœurant, révoltant; *sight, story, meal* dégoûtant, répugnant; (*: *unpleasant*) *weather, colour* épouvantable, dégueulasse‡; *dress* affreux.

revoltingly [rɪˈvəʊltɪŋlɪ] *adv* d'une manière révoltante *or* écœurante.

revolution [ˌrevəˈluːʃən] *n* **(a)** (*turn*) [*planet*] révolution *f*; [*wheel*] révolution, tour *m*.

(b) (*Pol etc: uprising*) révolution *f*, coup *m* d'État; (*fig*) révolution. (*Hist*) **French R~** Révolution française; **~ in methods of farming** révolution dans les méthodes d'exploitation agricole; (*Hist*) **Industrial/Agricultural R~** Révolution industrielle/agricole.

revolutionary [ˌrevəˈluːʃnərɪ] *adj, n* (*lit, fig*) révolutionnaire (*mf*).

revolutionize [ˌrevəˈluːʃənaɪz] *vt* révolutionner, transformer radicalement.

revolve [rɪˈvɒlv] **1** *vt* (*lit*) faire tourner. (*fig*) **to ~ a problem in one's mind** tourner et retourner un problème dans son esprit.

2 *vi* tourner. **to ~ on an axis/around the sun** tourner sur un axe/autour du soleil; (*fig*) **everything ~s around him** tout dépend de lui.

revolver [rɪˈvɒlvər] *n* revolver *m*.

revolving [rɪˈvɒlvɪŋ] *adj* tournant; (*Astron*) en rotation, qui tourne; (*Tech*) rotatif, à rotation. **~ chair/bookcase** fauteuil *m*/bibliothèque *f* pivotant(e); **~ door** tambour *m*; **~ light** feu tournant *or* feu à éclats; **~ stage** scène tournante.

revue [rɪ'vjuː] *n* (*Theat*) (*satirical*) revue *f*; (*spectacular*) revue, spectacle *m* de music-hall. ~ **artist** artiste *mf* de music-hall.
revulsion [rɪ'vʌlʃən] *n* **(a)** (*disgust*) dégoût *m*, écœurement *m*, répugnance *f*. **(b)** (*sudden change*) revirement *m*; (*reaction*) réaction *f* (*against* contre).
reward [rɪ'wɔːd] **1** *n* récompense *f*. **as a ~ for your honesty** en récompense de votre honnêteté; **as a ~ for helping me** pour vous (*or* le *etc*) récompenser de m'avoir aidé; **1,000 francs ~** 1.000 F de récompense; **to offer a ~** offrir une récompense.
2 *vt* récompenser (*for* de); (*with money*) récompenser, rémunérer (*for* de). **'finder will be ~ed'** 'récompense à qui rapportera l'objet'; **to ~ sb with a smile** remercier qn d'un sourire.
rewarding [rɪ'wɔːdɪŋ] *adj* (*financially*) rémunérateur (*f* -trice); (*mentally, morally*) qui en vaut la peine. **this is a very ~ book** ce livre vaut la peine d'être lu; **a ~ film** un film qui vaut la peine d'être vu; **bringing up a child is exhausting but ~** élever un enfant est une occupation exténuante mais qui a sa récompense.
rewind ['riː'waɪnd] *pret, ptp* **rewound** *vt* (*Tex*) rebobiner; (*Cine*) réembobiner; *ribbon, tape* réembobiner; *watch* remonter.
rewinding ['riː'waɪndɪŋ] *n* (*V* **rewind**) rebobinage *m*; réembobinage *m*; remontage *m*.
rewire ['riː'waɪəʳ] *vt*: **to ~ a house** refaire l'installation électrique d'une maison.
reword ['riː'wɜːd] *vt paragraph, sentence* rédiger à nouveau, recomposer; *idea* exprimer en d'autres termes.
rewrite ['riː'raɪt] *pret* **rewrote**, *ptp* **rewritten** **1** *vt* récrire, remanier; (*copy*) recopier. **2** *n* (*) remaniement *m*.
rhapsodic [ræp'sɒdɪk] *adj* (*Mus*) r(h)apsodique; (*fig*) élogieux, dithyrambique (*often iro*).
rhapsodize ['ræpsədaɪz] *vi* s'extasier (*over, about* sur).
rhapsody ['ræpsədɪ] *n* (*Mus*) r(h)apsodie *f*; (*fig*) éloge *m* enthousiaste, dithyrambe *m* (*often iro*).
rhea ['riːə] *n* nandou *m*.
Rhenish ['renɪʃ] *adj wine* du Rhin.
rheostat ['riːəʊstæt] *n* rhéostat *m*.
rhesus ['riːsəs] **1** *n* rhésus *m*. **2** *cpd*: **rhesus factor** facteur *m* rhésus; **rhesus monkey** rhésus *m*; **rhesus negative/positive** rhésus négatif/positif.
rhetoric ['retərɪk] *n* rhétorique *f* (*also pej*), éloquence *f*.
rhetorical [rɪ'tɒrɪkəl] *adj* (de) rhétorique; *style* ampoulé (*pej*). ~ **question** question *f* pour la forme *or* l'effet.
rhetorically [rɪ'tɒrɪkəlɪ] *adv speak, declaim* en orateur, en rhéteur (*pej*); *ask* pour la forme, pour l'effet.
rhetorician [ˌretə'rɪʃən] *n* rhétoricien(ne) *m(f)*, rhéteur *m* (*pej*).
rheumatic [ruː'mætɪk] **1** *n* **(a)** (*person*) rhumatisant(e) *m(f)*. **(b)** **~s** = **rheumatism**. **2** *adj* rhumatismal. **~ fever** rhumatisme articulaire aigu.
rheumatism ['ruːmətɪzəm] *n* rhumatisme *m*.
rheumatoid ['ruːmətɔɪd] *adj*: **~ arthritis** polyarthrite chronique évolutive, rhumatisme *m* chronique polyarticulaire.
rheumy ['ruːmɪ] *adj* chassieux.
Rhine [raɪn] **1** *n* Rhin *m*. **2** *cpd*: **the Rhineland** la Rhénanie, les pays rhénans; **rhinestone** faux diamant.
rhino* ['raɪnəʊ] *n abbr of* **rhinoceros**.
rhinoceros [raɪ'nɒsərəs] *n* rhinocéros *m*.
rhizome ['raɪzəʊm] *n* rhizome *m*.
Rhodes [rəʊdz] *n* (*Geog*) Rhodes *f* **in ~** à Rhodes.
Rhodesia [rəʊ'diːʒə] *n* Rhodésie *f*.
Rhodesian [rəʊ'diːʒən] **1** *adj* rhodésien. **2** *n* Rhodésien(ne) *m(f)*.
rhododendron [ˌrəʊdə'dendrən] *n* rhododendron *m*.
rhomb [rɒm] *n* losange *m*, rhombe *m*.
rhombic ['rɒmbɪk] *adj* rhombique.
rhomboid ['rɒmbɔɪd] **1** *n* rhomboïde *m*. **2** *adj* rhombique, rhomboïdal.
rhombus ['rɒmbəs] *n* = **rhomb**.
Rhone [rəʊn] *n* Rhône *m*.
rhubarb ['ruːbɑːb] **1** *n* rhubarbe *f*. (*Theat*) '~, ~, ~' ≈ brouhaha *m* (*mot employé pour constituer un murmure de fond*). **2** *cpd jam* de rhubarbe; *pie* à la rhubarbe.
rhyme [raɪm] **1** *n* **(a)** (*identical sound*) rime *f*. **for (the sake of) the ~** pour la rime; (*fig*) **without ~ or reason** sans rime ni raison; (*fig*) **there seems to be neither ~ nor reason to it** cela ne rime à rien, cela n'a ni rime ni raison.
(b) (*U: poetry*) vers *mpl*, poème *m*. **in ~** en vers (rimés); **to put into ~** mettre en vers; *V* **nursery**.
2 *cpd*: **rhyme scheme** agencement *m* des rimes.
3 *vt* faire rimer (*with* avec).
4 *vi* **(a)** *[word]* rimer (*with* avec). **rhyming slang** *argot m des Cockneys qui substitue à un mot donné une locution qui rime avec ce mot.*
(b) (*pej: write verse*) faire de mauvais vers, rimailler (*pej*).
rhymer ['raɪməʳ] *n*, **rhymester** ['raɪmstəʳ] *n* (*pej*) rimailleur *m*, -euse *f* (*pej*).
rhythm ['rɪðəm] *n* rythme *m*. (*Med*) *[contraception]* **~ method** méthode *f* des températures.
rhythmic(al) ['rɪðmɪk(əl)] *adj movement, beat* rythmique; *music* rythmé, cadencé.
rhythmically ['rɪðmɪkəlɪ] *adv* de façon rythmée, avec rythme.
rib [rɪb] **1** *n* **(a)** (*Anat, Culin*) côte *f*. **to dig *or* poke sb in the ~s** pousser qn du coude. **(b)** *[leaf, ceiling]* nervure *f*; *[ship]* membre *m*, membrure *f*; *[shell]* strie *f*; *[umbrella]* baleine *f*; *[knitting]* côte *f*. **2** *vt* (*: *tease*) taquiner, mettre en boîte*.
ribald ['rɪbəld] *adj* grivois, paillard. **~ joke** grivoiserie *f*, paillardise *f*.
ribaldry ['rɪbəldrɪ] *n* (*U*) paillardises *fpl*.
riband†† ['rɪbənd] *n* = **ribbon**.
ribbed [rɪbd] *adj knitting* à *or* en côtes; *shell* strié; *ceiling* à nervures.
ribbon ['rɪbən] **1** *n* **(a)** *[dress, hair, typewriter, decoration]* ruban *m*. **velvet ~** ruban de velours; *V* **bunch**.
(b) (*tatters*) **in ~s** en lambeaux; **to tear sth to ~s** (*lit*) mettre qch en lambeaux; (*fig*) *play etc* éreinter.
(c) (*†: *reins*) **~s** guides *fpl*.
2 *cpd*: **ribbon development** extension urbaine linéaire en bordure de route.
ribonucleic ['raɪbəʊnjuː'kliːɪk] *adj*: **~ acid** acide *m* ribonucléique.
rice [raɪs] **1** *n* riz *m*. **2** *cpd*: **Rice Krispies** ® grains de riz soufflés, Rice Krispies *mpl* ®; **ricefield** rizière *f*; **rice growing** riziculture *f*; **rice-growing** producteur (*f* -trice) de riz; **rice paper** papier *m* de riz; **rice pudding** riz *m* au lait; **rice wine** saké *m*.
rich [rɪtʃ] **1** *adj person, nation, country, countryside* riche; *profit* gros (*f* grosse); *furniture, decoration, style* riche, magnifique, luxueux; *gift, clothes, banquet* riche, somptueux; *wine* généreux; *food* riche; *soil, land* riche, fertile; *colour, sound* riche, chaud, vif; *voice* chaud, ample, étoffé; (*: *amusing*) rigolo* (*f* -ote), amusant, marrant‡. **to grow *or* get ~(er)** s'enrichir; **to make sb ~** enrichir qn; **~ in corn/minerals/vitamins** riche en maïs/minerais/vitamines; (*fig*) **~ in detail** riche en *or* qui abonde en détails; **he lives in a very ~ district** il habite un quartier très chic; **~ tea biscuit** ≈ petit-beurre *m*; (*iro*) **that's ~!*** ça c'est pas mal!* (*iro*), c'est le comble!; *V* **get**.
2 *n* **(a) the ~** les riches *mpl*.
(b) ~es richesse(s) *f(pl)*.
Richard ['rɪtʃəd] *n* Richard *m*. **~ (the) Lionheart** Richard Cœur-de-Lion.
richly ['rɪtʃlɪ] *adv dress* richement, somptueusement; *decorate* richement, magnifiquement, luxueusement; *deserve* largement, grandement, joliment. (*lit, fig*) **he was ~ rewarded** il a été largement *or* richement récompensé.
richness ['rɪtʃnɪs] *n* (*V* **rich**) richesse *f*; somptuosité *f*; luxe *m*; fertilité *f*; ampleur *f*; *[colour]* éclat *m*. **~ in oil/vitamins** richesse en pétrole/vitamines.
rick[1] [rɪk] *n* (*Agr*) meule *f* (de foin *etc*).
rick[2] [rɪk] = **wrick**.
rickets ['rɪkɪts] *n* (*U*) rachitisme *m*. **to have ~** être rachitique.
rickety ['rɪkɪtɪ] *adj* (*Med*) rachitique; (*fig*) *furniture* bancal, boiteux, branlant; *stairs* délabré, branlant.
rickshaw ['rɪkʃɔː] *n* pousse(-pousse) *m inv*.
ricochet ['rɪkəʃeɪ] **1** *n* ricochet *m*. **2** *vi* ricocher.
rictus ['rɪktəs] *n* rictus *m*.
rid [rɪd] *pret, ptp* **rid *or* ridded** *vt* (*of pests, disease*) débarrasser; (*of bandits etc*) délivrer (*of* de). **to get ~ of, to ~ o.s. of** *fleas etc* se débarrasser de; *habit, illusion, desire, tendency* perdre, se défaire de; *fears, doubts* perdre; *spots, cold, cough* se débarrasser de; **to be ~ of sb/sth** être débarrassé de qn/qch; **to get ~ of one's debts** liquider *or* régler ses dettes; **the body gets ~ of waste** l'organisme élimine les déchets.
riddance ['rɪdəns] *n* débarras *m*. **good ~!*** bon débarras!*; **it was (a) good ~!*** quel débarras!*
ridden ['rɪdn] **1** *ptp of* **ride**. **2** *adj*: **~ by** tourmenté *or* hanté par; **~ by fears, fear-~** hanté par la peur; **~ by remorse, remorse-~** tourmenté par le remords; *V* **debt, hag *etc***.
riddle[1] ['rɪdl] **1** *n* crible *m*, claie *f*.
2 *vt* **(a)** *coal, soil etc* cribler, passer au crible; *stove* agiter la grille de.
(b) *person, target* cribler (*with bullets etc* de balles *etc*). **~d with holes** criblé de trous; **the council is ~d with corruption** la corruption règne au conseil; **the committee is ~d with troublemakers** le comité grouille de provocateurs.
riddle[2] ['rɪdl] *n* énigme *f*, devinette *f*; (*mystery*) énigme, mystère *m*. **to speak in ~s** parler par énigmes; **to ask sb a ~** poser une devinette à qn.
ride [raɪd] (*vb: pret* **rode**, *ptp* **ridden**) **1** *n* **(a)** (*outing*) promenade *f*, tour *m*, balade* *f*; (*distance covered*) trajet *m*. **horse ~, ~ on horseback** (*for pleasure*) promenade *or* tour *or* balade* à cheval; (*long journey*) chevauchée *f*; **the ~ of the Valkyries** la chevauchée des Valkyries; **after a hard ~ across country** après une chevauchée pénible à travers la campagne; **he gave the child a ~ on his back** il a promené l'enfant sur son dos; **cycle/car ~** tour *or* promenade *or* balade* à bicyclette/en voiture; **coach ~** tour *or* excursion *f* en car; **to go for a ~ in a car** faire un tour *or* une promenade en voiture, se promener en voiture; **to take sb for a ~** (*in car etc*) emmener qn en promenade; (*fig: make fool of*) faire marcher qn*, mener qn en bateau*; (*swindle*) rouler qn*, posséder qn*; **he gave me a ~ into town in his car** il m'a emmené en ville dans sa voiture; **it's my first ~ in a Rolls** c'est la première fois que je me promène en Rolls *or* que je roule dans une Rolls; **I've never had a ~ in a train** je n'ai jamais pris le train; **can I have a ~ on your bike?** est-ce que je peux monter sur ton vélo?; **3 ~s on the merry-go-round** 3 tours sur le manège; **to have a ~ in a helicopter** faire un tour en hélicoptère; **we had a ~ in a taxi** nous avons pris un taxi; **it was the taxi ~ they liked best** c'est le taxi qu'ils ont préféré; **it's a short taxi ~ to the airport** ce n'est pas loin en taxi jusqu'à l'aéroport; **he has a long (car/bus) ~ to work** il a un long trajet (en voiture/en autobus) jusqu'à son lieu de travail; **it's only a short ~ by bus/taxi** il n'y en a pas pour longtemps par l'autobus/en taxi; **it's a 20p ~ from the station** le trajet depuis la gare coûte 20 pence; **to steal a ~** voyager sans billet *or* sans payer; *V* **joy**.
(b) (*path for horses*) allée cavalière.
2 *vi* **(a)** (*Sport etc: ride a horse*) monter à cheval, faire du

cheval, monter. **can you ~?** savez-vous monter à cheval?; **he has ridden since childhood** il fait du cheval depuis son enfance; **to go riding** faire du cheval, monter (à cheval); **to ~ astride/sidesaddle** monter à califourchon/en amazone; **he ~s well** il monte bien, il est bon cavalier; **to ~ to hounds** chasser à courre, faire de la chasse à courre; **the jockey was riding just under 65 kilos** (en tenue) le jockey pesait un peu moins de 65 kilos.

(b) (*go on horseback/by bicycle/by motorcycle*) aller à cheval/à bicyclette/en *or* à moto. **to ~ down/away** *etc* descendre/s'éloigner *etc* à cheval (*or* à bicyclette *or* en moto *or* à moto); **he stopped then rode on** il s'est arrêté puis a repris sa route; **they had ridden all day** ils avaient passé toute la journée en selle; **he rode to London** il est allé à Londres à cheval (*or* à bicyclette *etc*); **he was riding on a bicycle/a camel** il était à bicyclette/à dos de chameau; **the child was riding on his father's back** l'enfant était à cheval sur le dos de son père; **he was riding on his father's shoulders** il était (assis à califourchon) sur les épaules de son père; **the witch was riding on a broomstick** la sorcière était à cheval *or* à califourchon sur un balai; **they were riding on a bus/in a car/in a train/in a cart** ils étaient en autobus/en voiture/en train/en charrette; **they rode in a bus to ...** ils sont allés en autobus à ...; (*fig*) **to be riding for a fall** courir à un échec; (*fig*) **to ~ roughshod over** *person* passer sur le corps *or* sur le ventre* de; *objection* passer outre à; (*fig liter*) **the seagull ~s on the wind** la mouette est portée par le vent; (*fig*) **the moon was riding high in the sky** la lune voguait dans le ciel; (*fig*) **he's riding high** il est dans une bonne passe, il a le vent en poupe; *[ship]* **to ~ at anchor** être à l'ancre *or* au mouillage; (*fig*) **we'll just have to let the matter** *or* **to let things ~ for a while** nous allons devoir laisser l'affaire suivre son cours *or* laisser courir* pendant un certain temps; (*fig*) **she had to let things ~** elle a dû laisser courir*; *V* **shank**.

(c) *[horse]* **to ~ well** être une bonne monture.

(d) (*Tech etc*) (*overlap*) chevaucher; (*work out of place*) travailler.

3 *vt* **(a) to ~ a horse** monter à cheval; **have you ever ridden a horse?** avez-vous jamais fait du cheval?; **I have never ridden Flash** je n'ai jamais monté Flash; **he rode Cass at Newmarket** il montait Cass à Newmarket; **he rode Buster into town** il a pris Buster pour aller en ville, il est allé en ville sur Buster; **Jason will be ridden by J. Bean** Jason sera monté par J. Bean; *[jockey]* **to ~ a race** monter dans une course; **to ~ a good race** faire une bonne course; **he rode his horse straight at me** il a dirigé son cheval droit sur moi; **he rode his horse up the stairs** il a fait monter l'escalier à son cheval; **he rode his horse away/back** *etc* il est parti/revenu *etc* à cheval; **he ~s his pony to school** il va à l'école à dos de poney; **have you ever ridden a donkey/camel?** êtes-vous jamais monté à dos d'âne/à dos de chameau?; **he was riding a donkey** il était à dos d'âne; **he was riding a motorbike** il était à *or* en moto; **he rode his motorbike to the station** il est allé à la gare en moto; **I have never ridden a bicycle/a motorbike** je ne suis jamais monté à bicyclette/à moto; **can I ~ your bike?** est-ce que je peux monter sur ton vélo?; **he was riding a bicycle** il était à bicyclette; **he rode his cycle into town** il est allé en ville à bicyclette; **he always ~s a bicycle** il va partout à *or* il se déplace toujours à bicyclette; **witches ~ broomsticks** les sorcières chevauchent des balais; **she was riding a broomstick** elle était à cheval *or* à califourchon sur un balai; **they had ridden 10 km** ils avaient fait 10 km à cheval (*or* à bicyclette *or* à *or* en moto); **they had ridden all the way** ils avaient fait tout le trajet *or* le voyage à cheval (*or* à bicyclette *etc*); **he rode the country looking for ...** il a parcouru tout le pays à cheval (*or* à bicyclette *etc*) à la recherche de ...; (*fig*) **the birds rode the wind** les oiseaux étaient portés par le vent; (*liter*) **the ship rode the waves** le bateau voguait sur les vagues.

(b) (*: *esp US: nag etc*) être toujours sur le dos de*, ne pas ficher la paix à* (*about* au sujet de). **don't ~ him too hard** ne soyez pas trop dur avec lui, ne le poussez pas trop loin.

ride about, ride around *vi* se déplacer *or* aller çà et là *or* faire un tour (à cheval *or* à bicyclette *or* en voiture *etc*).

ride behind *vi* (*on same horse*) monter en croupe; (*on motorcycle*) monter derrière *or* en croupe; (*in car*) s'asseoir *or* être assis à l'arrière.

ride down *vt sep* **(a)** (*trample*) renverser, piétiner.

(b) (*catch up with*) rattraper (*à cheval*).

ride out 1 *vi* sortir (à cheval *or* à bicyclette *etc*).

2 *vt sep* (*fig*) surmonter. **to ride out the storm** (*Naut*) étaler la tempête; (*fig*) surmonter la crise; **to ride out a difficult time** se tirer d'une *or* surmonter une mauvaise passe; **the company managed to ride out the depression** la société a réussi à survivre à la dépression.

ride up *vi* **(a)** *[horseman, motorcyclist etc]* arriver.

(b) *[skirt etc]* remonter.

rider ['raɪdəʳ] *n* **(a)** (*person*) *[horse]* cavalier *m*, -ière *f*; *[racehorse]* jockey *m*; *[circus horse]* écuyer *m*, -ère *f*; *[bicycle]* cycliste *mf*; *[motorcycle]* motocycliste *mf*. **a good ~** un bon cavalier, une bonne cavalière; *V* **dispatch, out**.

(b) (*addition: to document*) annexe *f*, acte *or* article additionnel; (*to bill*) clause additionnelle; (*to insurance policy, jury's verdict*) avenant *m*. **the committee added a ~ condemning ...** la commission ajouta un article *or* une annexe condamnant ... .

ridge [rɪdʒ] **1** *n* **(a)** (*top of a line of hills*) (ligne *f* de) faîte *m*; (*extended top of a hill*) faîte; (*ledge on hillside*) corniche *f*; (*chain of hills, mountains*) chaîne *f*; (*in sea: reef*) récif *m*.

(b) (*in roof, on nose*) arête *f*; (*on sand*) ride *f*; (*in ploughed land*) billon *m*; (*on cliff, rockface*) strie *f*. **alveolar ~, teeth~** arcade *f* alvéolaire; (*Met*) **a ~ of high pressure** une ligne de hautes pressions.

2 *cpd*: **ridge piece, ridge pole** (poutre *f* de) faîte *m*, faîtage *m*; **ridge tent** tente *f* (de camping); **ridge tile** (tuile *f*) faîtière *f*, enfaîteau *m*; **ridge way** chemin *m* de faîte, route *f* des crêtes.

3 *vt roof* enfaîter; *earth* billonner; *rockface* strier; *sand* rider.

ridicule ['rɪdɪkju:l] **1** *n* raillerie *f*, ridicule *m*. **to hold sb/sth up to ~** tourner qn/qch en ridicule *or* en dérision; **she's an object of ~** elle est un objet de risée.

2 *vt* ridiculiser, tourner en ridicule *or* en dérision.

ridiculous [rɪ'dɪkjʊləs] *adj* ridicule. **to make sth ~** ridiculiser qch; **to make o.s. (look) ~** se rendre ridicule, se ridiculiser; **to see the ~ side of sth** voir le ridicule de qch *or* le côté risible de qch; *V* **sublime**.

ridiculously [rɪ'dɪkjʊləslɪ] *adv* ridiculement.

ridiculousness [rɪ'dɪkjʊləsnɪs] *n* ridicule *m* (*état*).

riding ['raɪdɪŋ] **1** *n* (*horse-riding*) équitation *f*; (*horsemanship*) monte *f*. **2** *cpd*: **riding boots** bottes *fpl* (de cheval); **riding breeches** culotte *f* de cheval; **riding crop = riding whip**; **riding habit** (tenue *f* d')amazone *f*; **riding master** professeur *m* d'équitation; **riding school** manège *m*, école *f* d'équitation; **riding stable(s)** *V* **stable**[2]; **riding whip** cravache *f*.

rife [raɪf] *adj* **(a)** (*widespread*) *disease, corruption* répandu. **to be ~** sévir, être répandu, régner; **rumour is ~** des bruits courent. **(b)** (*full of*) **~ with** abondant en.

riffle ['rɪfl] *vt pages* feuilleter *or* tourner rapidement.

riffraff ['rɪfræf] *n* canaille *f*, racaille *f*.

rifle[1] ['raɪfl] *vt town* piller; *tomb* violer; *sb's pockets* puiser dans; *drawer, till* vider, dévaliser, rafler* le contenu de; *house* dévaliser, vider.

rifle[2] ['raɪfl] **1** *n* (*gun*) fusil *m* (rayé); (*for hunting*) carabine *f* de chasse. (*Mil*) **the R~s** ≈ les chasseurs *mpl* à pied, (le régiment de) l'infanterie légère.

2 *cpd*: **rifle butt** crosse *f* de fusil; **rifleman** fusilier *m*; **rifle range** (*outdoor*) champ *m* de tir; (*indoor*) stand *m* de tir; **rifle shot** coup *m* de fusil; (*marksman*) tireur *m*; **within rifle range** *or* **rifle shot** à portée de fusil.

rift [rɪft] *n* fente *f*, fissure *f*, crevasse *f*; (*in clouds*) éclaircie *f*, trouée *f*; (*fig: in friendship*) faille *f*, fissure; (*Pol: in party*) scission *f*; (*in cabinet, group*) division *f*, désaccord *m*. (*Geol*) **~ valley** graben *m*.

rig [rɪg] **1** *n* **(a)** (*Naut*) gréement *m*.

(b) (*oil ~*) (*land*) derrick *m*; (*sea*) plate-forme pétrolière.

(c) (*: *outfit: also* **~ out**) tenue *f*, accoutrement *m* (*pej*).

2 *vt* (*Naut*) gréer. (*fig*) **to ~ an election** truquer une élection; (*St Ex*) **to ~ the market** provoquer une hausse *or* une baisse factice dans les cours.

3 *vi* (*Naut*) être gréé.

rig out* *vt sep* (*clothe*) habiller, fringuer‡, nipper* (*with* de, *as* en).

rig up *vt ship* gréer; (*with mast*) mâter; *equipment* monter, installer; (*fig*) (*make hastily*) faire avec des moyens de fortune *or* avec les moyens du bord; (*arrange*) arranger.

rigger ['rɪgəʳ] *n* (*Naut*) gréeur *m*; (*Aviat*) monteur-régleur *m*.

rigging ['rɪgɪŋ] *n* **(a)** (*Naut*) (*ropes etc*) gréement *m*; (*action*) gréage *m*. **(b)** (*: *dishonest interference*) truquage *m*, tripotage* *m*.

right [raɪt] **1** *adj* **(a)** (*just, fair*) équitable, juste; (*morally good*) bien *inv*, conforme au devoir, conforme à la morale. **it isn't ~ to lie, lying isn't ~** ce n'est pas bien de mentir; **to do what is ~** faire ce qui est conforme au devoir *or* à la morale, faire ce qu'il faut, se conduire bien *or* honnêtement (*V also* **1c**); **he thought it ~ to warn me** il a cru *or* jugé bon de m'avertir; **it seemed only ~ to give him the money** il ne semblait que juste de lui donner l'argent; **it's only ~ and proper** ce n'est que justice, c'est bien le moins; **it is only ~ for her to go** *or* **that she should go** il n'est que juste qu'elle y aille; **it is only ~ to point out that ...** nous devons néanmoins signaler que..., en toute justice il faut signaler que...; **would it be ~ to tell him?** ferait-on bien de le lui dire?; **to do the ~ thing by sb** bien agir *or* agir honorablement envers qn.

(b) (*true, correct*) juste, exact, conforme à la vérité. **to be ~** *[person]* avoir raison; *[answer, solution]* être juste, être exact; **you're quite ~** vous avez parfaitement raison; **how ~ you are!*** (*approvingly*) vous avez cent fois raison!; (*iro*) et comment!*; **that's ~** c'est juste, c'est exact, c'est ça*; **the ~ answer** la bonne réponse; **the ~ time** l'heure exacte *or* juste; **is the clock ~?** est-ce que la pendule est à l'heure?; **you were ~ to refuse** *or* **in refusing** vous avez bien fait de *or* vous avez eu raison de refuser; (*lit*) **on the ~ road** sur le bon chemin; (*fig*) **on the ~ road, on the ~ track** sur la bonne voie; **is this the ~ road for Paris?** est-ce bien la route de Paris?, est-ce que c'est la bonne route pour Paris?; **you are on the ~ train now** vous êtes dans le bon train maintenant; **my guess was ~** j'avais deviné juste; **I got all my sums ~ at school** j'ai réussi toutes mes additions en classe; (*iro*) **the Chancellor didn't get his sums ~** le ministre des Finances n'est pas tombé juste dans ses calculs; **to get one's facts ~** être sûr de ce qu'on avance; **let's get it ~ this time!** essayons d'y arriver cette fois-ci!; **your opinions are ~** vos opinions sont bien fondées; **to put** *or* **set ~** *error* corriger, rectifier; *situation* redresser, rétablir; *clock* remettre à l'heure; **that can easily be put ~** on peut facilement arranger ça; **I tried to put things ~ after their quarrel** j'ai essayé d'arranger les choses *or* la situation après leur querelle; **the plumber came and put things ~** le plombier est venu et a fait la *or* les réparation(s); **to put** *or* **set sb ~** détromper qn, éclairer qn, tirer qn d'erreur; **put me ~ if I'm wrong** dites-moi si je me trompe (*V also* **1d**); *V* **all right**.

(c) (*most suitable, preferable*) *clothes* approprié, convenable; *document* bon, approprié; (*best*) meilleur (*f* -eure). **what's the ~ thing to do?** quelle est la meilleure chose à faire?, qu'est-ce qu'il vaut mieux faire?; **to come at the ~ time** arriver au bon moment, tomber bien; **to do sth at the ~ time** faire qch au bon moment *or* au moment voulu; **to do sth the ~ way** faire qch comme il faut, s'y prendre bien; **that is the ~ way of looking at it** c'est bien ainsi qu'il faut envisager la question; **the ~ word** le mot juste; **the ~ man for the job** l'homme de la situation, l'homme qu'il faut; **Mr R~*** l'homme *m* de ma (*or* sa *etc*) vie; **it is just the ~ size** c'est exactement la taille qu'il faut; **I don't know what's the ~ thing to do** je ne sais pas ce qu'il vaut mieux faire; **we will do what is ~ for the country** nous ferons ce qui est dans l'intérêt du pays; **she is on the ~ side of forty** elle n'a pas encore quarante ans, elle a moins de quarante ans; **to get on the ~ side of sb*** s'insinuer dans les bonnes grâces *or* dans les petits papiers* de qn; **the ~ side of the material** l'endroit *m* du tissu; **to know the ~ people** avoir des relations utiles; **more than is ~** plus que de raison; *V also* **side.**

(d) (*well*) *[person]* en bonne santé, bien portant; *[thing]* en bon état, en ordre, normal. **the medicine soon put *or* set him ~** le médicament l'a vite guéri; **I don't feel quite ~ today** je ne me sens pas très bien *or* pas très d'aplomb *or* pas dans mon assiette* aujourd'hui; (*Brit*) **to be as ~ as rain*** (*after illness*) se porter comme un charme; (*after fall*) être indemne; **he put the engine ~** il a remis le moteur en état; **to be in one's ~ mind** avoir toute sa raison; **he's not ~ in the head‡** il est un peu dingue‡; *V* **all right.**

(e) (*Math*) *angle, cone* droit. **at ~ angles** à angle droit (*to* avec), perpendiculaire (*to* à).

(f) (*phrases*) **~!,** (*Brit*) **~-oh!*, ~ you are!*** d'accord!, entendu!, convenu!; **that's ~!** mais oui!, c'est ça!; **is that ~?** vraiment?, c'est vrai?; **~ enough!** bien sûr!, c'est vrai!, effectivement!; **it's a ~ mess in there*** c'est la pagaïe* complète là-dedans; **he's a ~ fool!*** c'est un imbécile fini; **he's the ~ sort*** c'est un type bien*, c'est un chic type*.

(g) (*opposite of left*) droit, de droite. **~ hand** main droite (*V also* **5**); **I'd give my ~ hand to know the answer** je donnerais beaucoup *or* cher* pour connaître la réponse; **on my ~ hand you see the bridge** sur ma droite vous voyez le pont; *V* **hook.**

2 *adv* **(a)** (*straight, directly*) droit, tout droit, directement; (*exactly*) tout, tout à fait. **~ in front of you** (tout) droit devant vous; **~ ahead of you** directement devant vous; **go ~ on** continuez tout droit; **~ away, ~ off*** (*immediately*) tout de suite, sur-le-champ; (*at the first attempt*) du premier coup; **~ now** en ce moment; (*at once*) tout de suite; **~ here** ici même; **~ in the middle** au beau milieu, en plein milieu; **~ at the start** dès le (tout) début; **the blow hit me ~ on the face** j'ai reçu le coup en pleine figure; **you'll have the wind ~ behind you** vous aurez le vent juste dans le dos.

(b) (*completely, all the way*) tout à fait, complètement. **~ round the house** tout autour de la maison; **to fall ~ to the bottom** tomber droit au fond *or* tout au fond; (*lit, fig*) **rotten ~ through** complètement pourri; **pierced ~ through** transpercé *or* percé de part en part; **to turn ~ round** se retourner; **~ (up) against the wall** tout contre le mur; **~ at the top of the mountain** tout en haut *or* juste au sommet de la montagne; **~ at the back, ~ at the bottom** tout au fond; **push it ~ in** enfoncez-le complètement *or* jusqu'au bout.

(c) (*correctly*) bien, juste, correctement; (*well*) bien, comme il faut, d'une manière satisfaisante. **to guess ~** deviner juste; **to answer ~** répondre correctement; **if I remember ~** si je me souviens bien; **you did ~ to refuse** vous avez bien fait de refuser, vous avez eu raison de refuser; **if everything goes ~** si tout va bien; **nothing goes ~ for them** rien ne leur réussit; **if I get you ~*** si je comprends bien; **I'll see you ~‡** je veillerai à ce que vous n'y perdiez (*subj*) pas, vous n'en serez pas de votre poche*; *V* **serve.**

(d) (†, *dial: very*) fort, très, tout à fait. (*frm*) **the R~ Honourable** le Très Honorable; *V* **reverend.**

(e) (*opposite of left*) à droite. **to look ~ and left** regarder à droite et à gauche; **to be cheated ~ and left** être volé par tout le monde, être volé de tous les côtés; **to owe money ~ and left** devoir de l'argent à tout le monde; (*Mil*) **eyes ~!** tête droite!; (*Mil*) **~ about turn!** demi-tour *m* à droite!

3 *n* **(a)** (*moral*) bien *m*; (*intellectual*) vrai *m*. **he doesn't know ~ from wrong** il ne sait pas discerner le bien du mal; **to be in the ~** avoir raison, être dans le vrai.

(b) (*entitlement*) droit *m*. **to have a ~ to sth** avoir droit à qch; **to have a *or* the ~ to do** avoir le droit de faire, être en droit de faire; **he has no ~ to sit here** il n'a pas le droit de s'asseoir là; **what ~ have you to say that?** de quel droit dites-vous cela?; **by what ~?** à quel titre?, de quel droit?; **he has no ~ to the money** il n'a pas droit à cet argent; **he is within his ~s** il est dans son (bon) droit; **by ~s** en toute justice; **by ~ of conquest** par droit de conquête, à titre de conquérant; **I know my ~s** je sais quels sont mes droits; (*Jur*) **in one's own ~** de son propre chef; **she's a good actress in her own ~** elle est elle-même une bonne actrice; **to stand on *or* assert one's ~s** revendiquer *or* faire valoir ses droits; **divine ~** droit divin; **women's ~s** droits de la femme; **women's ~s movement** mouvement *m* pour les droits de la femme; (*Comm*) **to have the (sole) ~s of sth** avoir les droits (exclusifs) pour qch; (*Jur*) **~ of appeal** droit d'appel; *V* **civil.**

(c) (*proper state*) **to put *or* set sth to ~s** mettre qch en ordre; (*fig*) **to put the world *or* things to ~s** reconstruire *or* refaire le monde; **to know the ~s and wrongs of a question** connaître tous les détails d'une question, être tout à fait au courant d'une question; **I want to know the ~s and wrongs of it first** je veux d'abord savoir qui a tort et qui a raison là-dedans.

(d) (*not left*) droite *f*. **to drive on the ~** conduire à droite; **to keep to the ~** tenir la *or* sa droite; **on my ~** à ma droite; **on *or* to the ~ of the church** à droite de l'église; (*Pol*) **the R~** la droite.

4 *vt* **(a)** (*return to normal*) *car, ship* redresser. **the car ~ed itself** la voiture s'est redressée (toute seule); **the problem should ~ itself** le problème devrait s'arranger tout seul *or* se résoudre de lui-même.

(b) (*make amends for*) *wrong* redresser; *injustice* réparer.

5 *cpd*: **right angle** angle droit; **right-angled** à angle droit; **right-angled triangle** triangle *m* rectangle; **right-hand drive car** voiture *f* avec (la) conduite à droite; **right-handed** *person* droitier; *punch, throw* du droit; *screw* fileté à droite; **right-hander** (*Sport*) coup *m* du droit; (*person*) droitier *m*, -ière *f*; **the right-hand side** le côté droit; (*fig*) **his right-hand man** son bras droit (*fig*); **right-minded = right-thinking; right-of-way** (*across property*) droit *m* de passage; (*Aut: priority*) priorité *f*; (*Aut*) **it's his right-of-way** c'est lui qui a priorité; **he has (the) right-of-way** il a (la) priorité; **right-thinking** sensé, sain d'esprit; **right wing** (*Sport: also* **right-winger**) ailier droit; (*Pol*) droite *f*; **the right wing of the party** l'aile droite du parti; **right-wing** (*Pol*) de droite; (*Pol*) **to be right-wing** être de droite.

righteous [ˈraɪtʃəs] *adj* **(a)** *character, person* droit, vertueux; *V* **self. (b)** (*Bible*) juste; *anger, indignation* juste, justifié.

righteously [ˈraɪtʃəslɪ] *adv* vertueusement.

righteousness [ˈraɪtʃəsnɪs] *n* droiture *f*, vertu *f*.

rightful [ˈraɪtfʊl] *adj* **(a)** *heir, owner* légitime. **~ claimant** ayant droit *m*. **(b)** (*fair*) *action* juste.

rightfully [ˈraɪtfəlɪ] *adv* légitimement, à juste titre.

rightist [ˈraɪtɪst] (*Pol*) **1** *n* homme *m* de droite. **2** *adj* de droite.

rightly [ˈraɪtlɪ] *adv* **(a)** (*correctly*) bien, correctement. **I don't ~ know*** je ne sais pas très bien *or* pas au juste.

(b) (*justifiably*) avec justesse, à juste titre. **~ or wrongly** à tort ou à raison; **~ so** à juste titre, avec (juste) raison.

rigid [ˈrɪdʒɪd] *adj* (*lit*) *board, material* rigide, raide; (*fig*) *person, discipline, character* rigide, inflexible, sévère; *specifications, interpretation, principles* strict; *system* qui manque de flexibilité. **~ with fear** paralysé de peur; **he's quite ~ about it** il est inflexible là-dessus.

rigidity [rɪˈdʒɪdɪtɪ] *n* (*V* **rigid**) rigidité *f*; raideur *f*; inflexibilité *f*, sévérité *f*; caractère strict; manque *m* de flexibilité.

rigidly [ˈrɪdʒɪdlɪ] *adv* *stand etc* avec raideur, rigidement; (*fig*) *behave, treat* inflexiblement, rigoureusement; *oppose* absolument.

rigmarole [ˈrɪgmərəʊl] *n* (*speech*) galimatias *m*, discours incohérents *or* verbeux. **to go through the whole *or* same ~ again** recommencer la même comédie*.

rigor [ˈrɪgəʳ] *n* (*US*) = **rigour.**

rigor mortis [ˈrɪgəˈmɔːtɪs] *n* rigidité *f* cadavérique.

rigorous [ˈrɪgərəs] *adj* rigoureux.

rigorously [ˈrɪgərəslɪ] *adv* rigoureusement, avec rigueur.

rigour, (*US*) rigor [ˈrɪgəʳ] *n* rigueur *f*.

rile* [raɪl] *vt* agacer, mettre en boule*.

rill [rɪl] *n* (*liter*) ruisselet *m*.

rim [rɪm] **1** *n [wheel]* jante *f*; *[spectacles]* monture *f*; *[cup, bowl]* bord *m*. **2** *vt* border; *wheel* janter, cercler.

rime[1] [raɪm] *n* = **rhyme.**

rime[2] [raɪm] *n* (*liter*) givre *m*.

rimless [ˈrɪmlɪs] *adj* *spectacles* à monture invisible, à verres non cerclés.

rind [raɪnd] **1** *n [fruit]* peau *f*, pelure *f*; *[cheese]* croûte *f*; *[bacon]* couenne *f*. **melon ~** écorce *f* de melon. **2** *vt* peler; enlever la croûte *or* la couenne de; écorcer.

ring[1] [rɪŋ] **1** *n* **(a)** (*gen: also for curtain, in gym etc*) anneau *m*; (*on finger*) anneau, (*with stone*) bague *f*, *[bishop]* anneau; (*on bird's foot*) bague; (*for napkin*) rond *m*; (*for swimmer*) bouée *f* de natation; (*for invalid to sit on*) rond (pour malade); *[piston]* segment *m*; *[turbine]* couronne *f*. **diamond ~** bague de diamant(s); **wedding ~** alliance *f*, anneau de mariage; *V* **ear**[1], **key, signet** *etc*.

(b) (*circle*) cercle *m*, rond *m*; (*of people*) cercle; (*of smoke, in water etc*) rond; (*in treetrunk*) cercle; (*round sun, moon*) auréole *f*, halo *m*. **the ~s of Saturn** les anneaux de Saturne; **to have ~s round the eyes** avoir les yeux cernés *or* battus; **to stand in a ~** se tenir en cercle *or* en rond, former un cercle; (*fig*) **to run *or* make ~s round sb*** battre qn à plate(s) couture(s), enfoncer qn*.

(c) (*group*) (*gen, also Pol*) coterie *f*, clique *f* (*pej*); *[dealers]* groupe *m*, cartel *m*; *[gangsters]* bande *f*, gang *m*; *[spies]* réseau *m*.

(d) (*enclosure*) (*at circus*) piste *f*; (*at exhibition*) arène *f*, piste; (*Horse-racing*) enceinte *f* des bookmakers; (*Boxing*) ring *m*. (*boxing itself*) **the ~** la boxe, le ring.

2 *vt* (*surround*) entourer, encercler, cerner; (*with quoit, hoop*) jeter un anneau sur; (*put ~ on or round*) *item on list etc* entourer d'un cercle; *bird, tree* baguer; *bear, bull* mettre un anneau au nez de.

3 *cpd*: **ring-a-ring-a-roses** *ronde enfantine*; **ring binder** classeur *m* à anneaux; **ringbolt** (*Tech*) piton *m*; (*Naut*) anneau *m* (d'amarrage); **ringdove** ramier *m*; **ring finger** annulaire *m*; **ringleader** chef *m*, meneur *m*; **ringmaster** ≃ 'Monsieur Loyal'; **ring road** route *f* de ceinture, (*motorway-type*) périphérique *m*; **ringside seat** place *f* au premier rang; (*fig*) **to have a ringside seat** être aux premières loges (*fig*); **ring spanner** clef polygonale; **ring-tailed** à queue zébrée; **ringworm** teigne *f*.

ring[2] [rɪŋ] (*vb: pret* **rang,** *ptp* **rung**) **1** *n* **(a)** (*sound*) son *m*; *[bell]* sonnerie *f*, (*lighter*) tintement *m*; *[electric bell]* retentissement *m*; *[coins]* tintement. **there was a ~ at the door** on a sonné à la porte; **to hear a ~ at the door** entendre sonner à la porte; **give 2 ~s for the maid** sonne 2 coups *or* 2 fois pour (appeler) la bonne; **his voice had an angry ~ (in it)** il y avait un accent *or* une note de colère dans sa voix; **that has the ~ of truth (to it)** ça sonne juste.

(b) (*Telec*) coup *m* de téléphone *or* de fil*. **to give sb a ~** donner *or* passer un coup de téléphone *or* de fil* à qn.

(c) ~ of bells jeu *m* de cloches.

2 *vi* **(a)** *[bell]* sonner, retentir, (*lightly*) tinter; *[alarm clock, telephone]* sonner. **the bell rang** la cloche a sonné *or* tinté, la sonnette a retenti; **the bell rang for dinner** la cloche a sonné le dîner; **to ~ for sb** sonner qn; **to ~ for sth** sonner pour demander qch; **please ~ for attention** prière de sonner; **to ~ for the lift** appeler l'ascenseur; **to ~ at the door** sonner à la porte; **you rang, sir?** Monsieur a sonné?

(b) (*telephone*) téléphoner.

(c) (*sound*) *[words]* retentir, résonner; *[voice]* vibrer; *[coin]* sonner, tinter; (*resound*) résonner, retentir; *[ears]* tinter, bourdonner. *[coin]* **to ~ false/true** sonner faux/clair; (*fig*) **that ~s true** ça sonne juste; **that doesn't ~ true** ça sonne faux; **the room rang with their shouts** la pièce résonnait de leurs cris; **the town rang with his praises** la ville entière chantait ses louanges; **the news set the town ~ing** toute la ville parlait de la nouvelle, dans toute la ville il n'était bruit que de la nouvelle; **his voice rang with emotion** sa voix vibrait d'émotion; **his words still ~ in my ears** ses mots retentissent encore à mes oreilles.

3 *vt* **(a)** *bell* (faire) sonner; *coin* faire sonner, faire tinter. **to ~ the doorbell** sonner (à la porte); **to ~ the bell** (*lit*) sonner, donner un coup de sonnette; (*handbell*) agiter la sonnette; (**fig: succeed*) décrocher la timbale*, réussir magnifiquement; (*fig*) **his name ~s a bell*** son nom me dit quelque chose *or* me rappelle quelque chose; (*liter: lit, fig*) **to ~ the knell (of)** sonner le glas (de); **to ~ the hours** sonner les heures; *[bells]* **to ~ the changes** carillonner (*en variant l'ordre des cloches*); (*fig*) **to ~ the changes on the same speech** rabâcher le même discours avec des variantes; **to ~ the changes on an outfit/the menu** *etc* varier un ensemble/le menu *etc*.

(b) (*Telec: also* **~ up**) téléphoner à, donner *or* passer un coup de téléphone *or* de fil* à.

ring back (*Telec*) *vi, vt sep* rappeler.

ring down *vt sep* (*Theat*) **to ring down the curtain** (faire) baisser le rideau; (*fig*) **to ring down the curtain on sth** marquer la fin de qch.

ring in 1 *vi* **(a)** (*report by telephone*) téléphoner un reportage.

(b) (*US: clock on*) se pointer en arrivant.

2 *vt sep*: **to ring in the New Year** carillonner le Nouvel An.

ring off *vi* (*Telec*) raccrocher.

ring out *vi* **(a)** *[bell]* sonner; *[electric bell]* retentir; *[voice]* résonner; *[shot]* éclater, retentir.

(b) (*US: clock off*) se pointer en partant.

ring up *vt sep* **(a)** (*Telec*) donner un coup de téléphone *or* de fil* à.

(b) (*Theat*) **to ring up the curtain** frapper les trois coups, (sonner pour faire) lever le rideau; (*fig*) **to ring up the curtain on a new career** *etc* marquer le début d'une nouvelle carrière *etc*.

ringer ['rɪŋə^{r}] *n* **(a)** (*bell ~*) sonneur *m*, carillonneur *m*. **(b)** sosie *m*.

ringing ['rɪŋɪŋ] 1 *adj bell* qui résonne *or* tinte; *voice, tone* sonore, retentissant, vibrant. (*Brit Telec*) **~ tone** tonalité *f*. 2 *n* *[bell]* sonnerie *f*, son *m*, (*lighter*) tintement *m*; *[electric bell]* retentissement *m*; *[telephone]* sonnerie; (*in ears*) tintement, bourdonnement *m*.

ringlet ['rɪŋlɪt] *n* frisette *f*; (*long*) anglaise *f*.

rink [rɪŋk] *n [ice-skating]* patinoire *f*; *[roller-skating]* skating *m*.

rinse [rɪns] 1 *n* **(a)** (*act*) rinçage *m*. **give the cup a ~** rincez la tasse, passez la tasse sous le robinet.

(b) (*for hair*) rinçage *m*.

2 *vt* **(a)** *clothes etc* rincer. **to ~ one's hands** se passer les mains à l'eau; **to ~ the soap off one's hands** se rincer les mains.

(b) (*colour with a ~*) **to ~ one's hair** se faire un *or* des rinçage(s); **she ~d her hair black** elle s'est fait un rinçage noir.

rinse out *vt sep* **(a)** *hair tint, colour, dirt* faire partir à l'eau.

(b) *cup* rincer. **to rinse out one's mouth** se rincer la bouche.

riot ['raɪət] 1 *n* (*uprising*) émeute *f*, bagarre *f*. (*fig*) **a ~ of colour(s)** une débauche de couleurs; **a ~ of reds and blues** une profusion de rouges et de bleus; **a ~ of flowers** une profusion de fleurs; **he's a ~‡** c'est un (type) rigolo*; **she is a ~‡** elle est rigolote*; **the film is a ~‡** (*funny*) le film est tordant*; (*successful*) le film a un succès fou*; *V* **run**.

2 *cpd*: (*Hist*) **Riot Act** loi *f* contre les attroupements séditieux (*V also* **read**[1]); **the riot police** les forces *fpl* d'intervention (de police).

3 *vi* manifester avec violence, se livrer à des bagarres, (*stronger*) faire une émeute.

rioter ['raɪətə^{r}] *n* manifestant(e) *m(f)* (*violent*), (*stronger*) émeutier *m*, -ière *f*, insurgé(e) *m(f)*.

riotous ['raɪətəs] *adj person, assembly* tapageur; (*: *hilarious*) tordant*, marrant‡. **~ living** vie *f* de débauche, vie déréglée; **a ~ success** un succès fou* *or* monstre*; **we had a ~ time*** nous nous sommes bien marrés‡.

riotously ['raɪətəslɪ] *adv* tapageusement, bruyamment. **it was ~ funny‡** c'était à se tordre*, c'était rigolo* au possible.

rip [rɪp] 1 *n* déchirure *f*; (*in material*) déchirure, accroc *m*.

2 *cpd*: **ripcord** poignée *f* d'ouverture; **it's a rip-off‡** c'est du vol à main armée (*fig*), c'est du vol organisé (*fig*); **rip-roaring*** bruyant; exubérant; **ripsaw** scie *f* à refendre; **riptide** courant *m* de retour, contre-courant *m*, turbulence *f*.

3 *vt* déchirer, fendre. **to ~ open a letter** ouvrir une lettre en hâte, fendre une enveloppe; **to ~ the buttons from a shirt** arracher les boutons d'une chemise.

4 *vi* **(a)** *[cloth]* se déchirer, se fendre.

(b) (*) **the car ~s along** la voiture roule à toute vitesse *or* roule à toute biture*; **let her ~!** appuie!, fonce!*; **to let ~** (*gen*) laisser courir*; (*in anger*) éclater, exploser (*de colère etc*); **he let ~ a string of oaths** il a lâché un chapelet de jurons; **he let ~ at me** il m'a passé un bon savon*.

rip off 1 *vt sep* **(a)** (*lit*) arracher, déchirer, enlever à la hâte.

(b) (‡ *fig*) *object, goods* voler; *bank, shop, house* cambrioler.

2 **rip-off‡** *n V* **rip 2**.

rip out *vt sep* arracher.

rip up *vt sep* déchirer.

riparian [raɪ'pɛərɪən] *adj, n* riverain(e) *m(f)*.

ripe [raɪp] *adj fruit* mûr; *cheese* fait; *age, judgment* mûr. **to live to a ~ old age** vivre très vieux, vivre jusqu'à un bel âge *or* un âge avancé; (*fig*) **to be ~ for** être mûr *or* bon pour; (*fig iro*) **that's ~!‡** ça c'est pas mal!*, faut le faire!*; *V* **over**.

ripen ['raɪpən] 1 *vt* (faire) mûrir. 2 *vi* mûrir; *[cheese]* se faire.

ripeness ['raɪpnɪs] *n* maturité *f*.

riposte [rɪ'pɒst] 1 *n* (*Fencing: also fig*) riposte *f*. 2 *vi* riposter.

ripping‡† ['rɪpɪŋ] *adj* (*Brit*) épatant*, sensationnel*.

ripple ['rɪpl] 1 *n* **(a)** (*movement*) *[water]* ride *f*, ondulation *f*; *[crops]* ondulation.

(b) (*noise*) *[tide]* clapotis *m*; *[voices]* murmure(s) *m(pl)*, gazouillement *m*; *[laughter]* cascade *f*.

2 *vi [water]* se rider; *[crops, hair]* onduler; *[waves]* clapoter.

3 *vt* rider; faire onduler.

rise [raɪz] (*vb: pret* **rose**, *ptp* **risen**) 1 *n* **(a)** *[theatre curtain, sun]* lever *m*; (*Mus*) hausse *f*; (*increase*) (*in temperature*) élévation *f*, hausse; (*in pressure*) hausse; *[tide]* flux *m*, flot *m*; *[river]* crue *f*; (*in wages*) augmentation *f*, relèvement *m* (*Admin*); (*in prices*) hausse, augmentation, majoration *f*; (*in bank rate*) relèvement. **prices are on the ~** les prix sont en hausse; *[employee]* **to ask for a ~** demander une augmentation (de salaire); **there has been a ~ in the number of people who do this** le nombre de personnes qui font cela a augmenté; (*fig*) **his meteoric ~** son ascension rapide; **his ~ to power** sa montée au pouvoir; **his ~ to fame** la gloire à laquelle il est (*or* était) parvenu; **the ~ of Bristol/the steel industry** l'essor *m* de Bristol/de l'industrie de l'acier; **the ~ of the working classes** l'ascension du prolétariat; **the ~ and fall of an empire** l'essor et la chute d'un empire, la grandeur et la décadence d'un empire; (*fig*) **to get a ~ out of sb*** faire marcher qn*.

(b) (*small hill*) éminence *f*, hauteur *f*, élévation *f*; (*slope*) côte *f*, pente *f*.

(c) (*origin*) *[river]* source *f*; (*fig*) source, origine *f*, naissance *f*. **the river has** *or* **takes its ~ (in)** la rivière prend sa source *or* a son origine (dans); (*fig*) **to give ~ to** donner lieu *or* naissance à, engendrer, susciter.

2 *vi* **(a)** (*get up*) (*from sitting, lying*) se lever, se mettre debout; (*from bed*) se lever; (*after falling*) se relever. **he ~s early/late** il se lève tôt/tard; **he rose to go** il s'est levé pour partir; **to ~ to one's feet** se mettre debout, se lever; **to ~ on tiptoe** se mettre sur la pointe des pieds; **to ~ from (the) table** se lever de table; **he rose from his chair** il s'est levé de sa chaise; **he rose from his sickbed to go and see her** il a quitté son lit pour aller la voir; **to ~ from the dead** ressusciter (des morts); **the horse rose on its hind legs** le cheval s'est dressé (sur ses jambes de derrière) *or* s'est cabré.

(b) *[smoke, mist]* s'élever, monter; *[balloon]* s'élever; *[aircraft, lift]* monter; *[theatre curtain, sun, moon, wind, bread, dough]* se lever; *[hair]* se dresser; *[ground]* monter (en pente); *[voice]* monter, devenir plus aigu (*f* -guë); *[sea]* devenir houleux; *[water, river, tide, blood pressure, temperature, exchange rate]* monter; *[barometer]* remonter, être en hausse; *[hopes, anger]* croître, grandir; *[prices]* monter, augmenter; *[cost of living]* augmenter, être en hausse; *[stocks, shares]* monter, être en hausse. *[swimmer, object, fish]* **to ~ to the surface** remonter à la *or* en surface; **the fish are rising well** les poissons mordent bien; (*fig*) **he rose to the bait** il a mordu à l'hameçon; **he won't ~ to any of your taunts** il ne réagira à aucune de vos piques; **his eyebrows rose at the sight of her** quand il l'a vue il a levé les sourcils (d'étonnement); (*fig*) **the idea/image rose in his mind** l'idée/l'image s'est présentée à son esprit; **the mountain ~s to 3,000 metres** la montagne a une altitude de 3.000 mètres; **the mountains rising before him** les montagnes qui se dressaient *or* s'élevaient devant lui; **to ~ to the occasion** se montrer à la hauteur de la situation *or* des circonstances; **I can't ~ to £10** je ne peux pas aller jusqu'à 10 livres; **to ~ in price** augmenter (de prix); **to ~ above a certain temperature/a certain level** dépasser une température donnée/un niveau donné; **her spirits rose** son moral a remonté; **his gorge rose at this sight** son cœur s'est soulevé à ce spectacle; **the colour rose to her cheeks** ses joues se sont empourprées, le rouge lui est monté aux joues.

(c) (*fig: in society, rank*) s'élever. **to ~ in the world** réussir, faire son chemin dans le monde; **to ~ from nothing** partir de rien; (*Mil*) **to ~ from the ranks** sortir du rang; (*Mil*) **he rose to be President/a captain** il s'est élevé jusqu'à devenir Président/jusqu'au grade de capitaine.

(d) (*adjourn*) *[assembly]* clore la session; *[meeting]* lever la séance. (*Parl*) **the House rose at 2 a.m.** l'Assemblée a levé la séance à 2 heures du matin; **Parliament will ~ on Thursday next** les vacances parlementaires commenceront jeudi prochain.

(e) (*originate*) *[river]* prendre sa source *or* sa naissance (*in* dans).

(f) (*rebel: also* **~ up**) se soulever, se révolter (*against* contre). **to ~ (up) in revolt** se révolter (*against* contre); **they rose (up) in anger and assassinated the tyrant** emportés par la colère ils se sont soulevés et ont assassiné le tyran.

rise up *vi [person]* se lever; *V also* **rise 2**.

risen ['rɪzn] 1 *ptp of* **rise**. 2 *adj* (*Rel*) **the ~ Lord** le Christ ressuscité.

riser ['raɪzə^{r}] *n* **(a)** (*person*) **to be an early ~** (aimer) se lever tôt, être lève-tôt *inv or* matinal; **to be a late ~** (aimer) se lever tard, être lève-tard *inv*. **(b)** *[stair]* contremarche *f*.

risibility [ˌrɪzɪˈbɪlɪtɪ] *n* caractère *m* drôle.
risible [ˈrɪzɪbl] *adj* risible.
rising [ˈraɪzɪŋ] **1** *n* **(a)** (*rebellion*) soulèvement *m*, insurrection *f*.
(b) (*U*) *[sun, star]* lever *m*; *[barometer]* hausse *f*; *[prices]* augmentation *f*, hausse; *[river]* crue *f*; *[person from dead]* résurrection *f*; (*Theat*) *[curtain]* lever; *[ground]* élévation *f*. **the ~ and falling of the waves** le mouvement montant et descendant des vagues, les vagues s'élevant et s'abaissant; **the ~ and falling of the boat on the water** le mouvement du bateau qui danse sur les flots.
(c) *[Parliament, court]* ajournement *m*, clôture *f* de séance.
2 *adj* **(a)** *sun* levant; *barometer, prices, temperature* en hausse; *tide* montant; *wind* qui se lève; *tone* qui monte; *anger, fury* croissant; *ground* qui monte en pente. **~ damp** humidité *f* (par capillarité).
(b) (*fig*) nouveau (*f* nouvelle). **the ~ sap** la sève ascendante; **a ~ young doctor** un jeune médecin d'avenir; **the ~ generation** la nouvelle génération, les jeunes *mpl*.
3 *adv* (*) **she's ~ six** elle va sur ses six ans.
risk [rɪsk] **1** *n* **(a)** (*possible danger*) risque *m*. **to take** *or* **run ~s** courir des risques; **to take** *or* **run the ~ of doing** courir le risque de faire; **that's a ~ you'll have to take** c'est un risque à courir; **there's too much ~ involved** c'est trop risqué; **it's not worth the ~** ça ne vaut pas la peine de courir un tel risque; **there is no ~ of his coming** *or* **that he will come** il n'y a pas de risque qu'il vienne, il ne risque pas de venir; **you do it at your own ~** vous le faites à vos risques et périls; (*Comm*) **goods sent at sender's ~** envois faits aux risques de l'expéditeur; **at the ~ of seeming stupid** au risque de *or* quitte à paraître stupide; **at the ~ of his life** au péril de sa vie; **at ~** en danger, en péril, menacé; **children at ~** l'enfance *f* en danger; **some jobs are at ~** des emplois risquent d'être supprimés *or* sont menacés; *V* **occupational**.
(b) (*Insurance*) risque *m*. **fire ~** risque d'incendie; **he's a bad accident ~** il présente des risques élevés d'accident; *V* **security**.
2 *vt* **(a)** *life, career, future* risquer, aventurer, hasarder; *reputation, savings* risquer. **you ~ falling** vous risquez de tomber; *V* **neck**.
(b) *battle, defeat, quarrel* s'exposer aux risques de; *accident* risquer d'avoir, courir le risque de; (*venture*) *criticism, remark* risquer, aventurer, hasarder. **she won't ~ coming today** elle ne se risquera pas à venir aujourd'hui; **I'll ~ it** je vais risquer *or* tenter le coup*; **I can't ~ it** je ne peux pas prendre un tel risque.
riskiness [ˈrɪskɪnɪs] *n* (*U*) risques *mpl*, hasards *mpl*, aléas *mpl*.
risky [ˈrɪskɪ] *adj enterprise, deed* plein de risques, risqué, hasardeux; *joke, story* risqué, osé. **it's ~, it's a ~ business** c'est risqué.
risotto [rɪˈzɒtəʊ] *n* risotto *m*.
risqué [ˈriːskeɪ] *adj story, joke* risqué, osé.
rissole [ˈrɪsəʊl] *n* croquette *f*.
rite [raɪt] *n* rite *m*, cérémonie *f*. **funeral ~s** rites funèbres; **last ~s** derniers sacrements.
ritual [ˈrɪtjʊəl] **1** *adj* rituel. **2** *n* rituel *m*. (*fig*) **he went through the ~** il a fait les gestes rituels, il s'est conformé aux rites; **he went through the ~ of apologizing** il a fait les excuses rituelles, il s'est excusé comme de coutume.
ritualism [ˈrɪtjʊəlɪzəm] *n* ritualisme *m*.
ritualist [ˈrɪtjʊəlɪst] *adj, n* ritualiste (*mf*).
ritualistic [ˌrɪtjʊəˈlɪstɪk] *adj* ritualiste.
ritzy‡ [ˈrɪtsɪ] *adj* (*US*) luxueux.
rival [ˈraɪvəl] **1** *n* rival(e) *m(f)*.
2 *adj firm, enterprise* rival, qui fait concurrence (*to* à); *attraction, claim* opposé, antagonique. **two ~ firms** deux entreprises rivales, deux concurrents.
3 *vt* rivaliser avec (*in* de), égaler (*in* en); (*Comm*) être en concurrence avec. **he can't ~ her in intelligence** il ne peut pas l'égaler en intelligence, il ne peut pas rivaliser d'intelligence avec elle; **his achievements ~ even yours** ses réussites égalent même les vôtres.
rivalry [ˈraɪvəlrɪ] *n* rivalité *f* (*with* avec, *between* entre).
rive [raɪv] *pret* **rived**, *ptp* **riven** [ˈrɪvən] (*liter*) **1** *vt* fendre. **2** *vi* se fendre. **riven by** fendu par; (*fig*) déchiré par.
river [ˈrɪvəʳ] **1** *n* rivière *f*, (*major*) fleuve *m* (*also fig*), (*Admin, Econ, Geog etc*) cours *m* d'eau. **down ~** en aval; **up ~** en amont; (*Brit*) **the ~ Seine**, (*US*) **the Seine ~** la Seine; (*fig*) **~s of blood** des fleuves de sang; *V* **sell**.
2 *cpd police, port, system* fluvial. **riverbank** rive *f*, berge *f*, bord *m*; **river basin** bassin fluvial; **riverbed** lit *m* de rivière *or* de fleuve; **river fish** poisson *m* d'eau douce *or* de rivière; **river fishing** pêche fluviale *or* en eau douce; **river head** source *f* (de rivière *or* de fleuve); **river horse** hippopotame *m*; **rivermouth** bouche *f* d'une rivière *or* d'un fleuve, embouchure *f*; **riverside** (*n*) bord *m* de l'eau (*or* de la rivière *or* du fleuve), rive *f*; (*adj*) (situé) au bord de la rivière *etc*; **by the riverside** au bord de l'eau (*or* de la rivière *etc*); **along the riverside** le long de la rivière (*or* du fleuve); **river traffic** trafic fluvial, navigation fluviale.
riverine [ˈrɪvəraɪn] *adj* fluvial; *person* riverain.
rivet [ˈrɪvɪt] **1** *n* rivet *m*.
2 *vt* (*Tech*) riveter, river. (*fig*) **he ~ed his eyes on the door** il a fixé ses yeux sur la porte; **it ~ed our attention** ça nous a fascinés; **~ed with fear** rivé *or* cloué sur place par la peur.
3 *cpd*: **rivet joint** assemblage *m* par rivets.
riveter [ˈrɪvɪtəʳ] *n* (*person*) riveur *m*; (*machine*) riveuse *f*.
rivet(t)ing [ˈrɪvɪtɪŋ] **1** *n* rivetage *m*. **2** *adj* (*fig*) fascinant. **it was absolutely ~** c'était tout à fait fascinant, je ne pouvais pas (*or* il ne pouvait pas *etc*) détourner les yeux.
Riviera [ˌrɪvɪˈɛərə] *n*: **the (French) ~** la Côte d'Azur; **the Italian ~** la Riviera (italienne).
rivulet [ˈrɪvjʊlɪt] *n* (petit) ruisseau *m*.
roach [rəʊtʃ] *n* gardon *m*.
road [rəʊd] **1** *n* **(a)** (*gen*) route *f*; (*minor*) chemin *m*; (*in town*) rue *f*; (*fig*) chemin, voie *f*. **trunk ~** (route) nationale *f*, grande route; **country ~** route de campagne, petite route, (route) départementale *f*; **'~ up'** 'attention travaux'; **she lives across the ~ (from us)** elle habite en face de chez nous; **just across the ~ is a bakery** il y a une boulangerie juste en face; **my car is off the ~ just now** (*laid up*) ma voiture est sur cales pour le moment; (*being repaired*) ma voiture est en réparation; **I hope to put it back on the ~ soon** j'espère qu'elle sera bientôt en état (de rouler); **this vehicle shouldn't be on the ~** on ne devrait pas laisser circuler un véhicule dans cet état; **a spot of petrol will get us on the ~ again** un peu d'essence va nous dépanner; **he is a danger on the ~** (au volant) c'est un danger public; **to take the ~** se mettre en route; *[salesman, theatre company]* **to be on the ~** être en tournée; **we were on the ~ at 6 in the morning** nous étions sur la route à 6 heures du matin; **we've been on the ~ since this morning** nous voyageons depuis ce matin; **we were on the ~ to Paris** nous étions en route pour Paris; **is this the ~ to London?** *or* **the London ~?** c'est (bien) la route de Londres?; (*in towns*) **London R~** rue de Londres; **you're on the right ~** vous êtes sur la bonne route; (*fig*) vous êtes sur la bonne voie; **on the ~ to ruin/success** sur le chemin de la ruine/du succès; (*fig*) **somewhere along the ~ he changed his mind** à un moment donné *or* en cours de route* il a changé de nom; **you're in my ~*** vous me barrez le passage, vous m'empêchez de passer, vous êtes sur *or* dans mon chemin; **(get) out of the ~!*** dégagez!; (*dial*) **any ~‡** de toute façon; **to have one for the ~*** prendre un dernier verre avant de partir, boire le coup de l'étrier; (*Naut*) **~s** rade *f*; *V* **arterial, hit, main, Rome** *etc*.
(b) (*US*) *abbr of* **railroad**.
2 *cpd*: **road accident** accident *m* de la route *or* de la circulation; **roadblock** barrage routier; **road book** guide routier; **road-bridge** pont routier; **road construction** construction *f* des routes; **road haulage** transports routiers; **road haulier** entrepreneur *m* de transports routiers; **roadhog** chauffard *m*, écraseur* *m*, -euse* *f*; **roadhouse** hostellerie *f*, relais *m*; (*U*) **roadmaking** construction *f* de (la) route; **roadman** cantonnier *m*; **roadmap** carte routière; **roadmender** = **roadman**; **road metal** empierrement *m*; **roadroller** rouleau *m* compresseur; **road safety** sécurité routière; **road sense** sens *m* de la conduite (sur route); (*Theat*) **road show** spectacle *m* de tournée; **roadside** *V* **roadside**; **roadsign** panneau *m* (de signalisation), poteau indicateur; **international roadsigns** signalisation routière internationale; (*Naut*) **roadstead** rade *f*; **road surveyor** agent *m* voyer, agent des Ponts et Chaussées; **roadsweeper** (*person*) balayeur *m*, -euse *f*; (*vehicle*) balayeuse *f*; **road test** (*n*) essai *m* sur route; **they are road-testing the car tomorrow** ils vont faire les essais sur route demain; **road traffic** circulation routière; **road transport** transports routiers; **road-trials** (*road test*) essais *mpl* sur route; (*rally*) épreuves *fpl* sur route; **road-user** usager *m* de la route; **roadway** chaussée *f*; **roadworks** travaux *mpl* (d'entretien des routes); **a roadworthy car** une voiture en état de marche.
roadside [ˈrəʊdsaɪd] **1** *n* bord *m* de la route, accotement *m*, bas-côté *m*. **along** *or* **by the ~** au bord de la route. **2** *cpd inn* (situé) au bord de la route. **roadside repairs** (*professional*) dépannage *m*; (*done alone*) réparations *fpl* de fortune.
roadster [ˈrəʊdstəʳ] *n* (*car*) roadster *m*; (*cycle*) bicyclette routière.
roam [rəʊm] **1** *vt streets, countryside* parcourir, errer dans *or* par. **to ~ the (seven) seas** courir *or* parcourir les mers, bourlinguer; *[child, dog]* **to ~ the streets** traîner dans les rues.
2 *vi* errer, rôder; *[thoughts]* vagabonder. **to ~ about the house** errer dans la maison; **to ~ about the world** rouler *or* errer (de) par le monde; **to ~ about the streets** traîner dans les rues, traîner les rues (*pej*).
roam about, roam around *vi* errer de-ci de-là; (*wider*) vagabonder, bourlinguer*, rouler sa bosse*.
roamer [ˈrəʊməʳ] *n* vagabond *m*.
roaming [ˈrəʊmɪŋ] **1** *adj person* errant, vagabond; *dog* errant; *thoughts* vagabond. **2** *n* vagabondage *m*.
roan[1] [rəʊn] *adj, n* (*horse*) rouan (*m*); *V* **strawberry**.
roan[2] [rəʊn] *n* (*leather*) basane *f*.
roar [rɔːʳ] **1** *vi [person, crowd]* hurler, pousser de grands cris; (*with anger*) rugir; *[lion]* rugir; *[bull]* mugir, beugler; *[wind, sea]* mugir; *[thunder, gun, waterfall, storm, forest fire, engine, vehicle]* gronder; (*Aut: rev*) vrombir; *[fire in hearth]* ronfler. **to ~ with pain** hurler de douleur; **to ~ with laughter** rire à gorge déployée, éclater de rire, se tordre; **this will make you ~!*** tu vas te marrer!‡, tu vas rigoler!*; **the trucks ~ed past** les camions sont passés bruyamment à toute allure; **the car ~ed up the street** la voiture est passée dans la rue en vrombissant; **he ~ed away on his motorbike** il est parti en faisant vrombir sa moto.
2 *vt* **(a)** (*also* **~ out**) *order* vociférer; *song* chanter à tue-tête, brailler, beugler*; *one's disapproval* hurler.
(b) (*Aut*) **to ~ the engine*** faire ronfler *or* faire vrombir le moteur.
3 *n* hurlement(s) *m(pl)*; rugissement *m*; mugissement *m*; beuglement *m*; grondement *m*; vrombissement *m*; ronflement *m*. **~s of laughter** de gros éclats de rire; **the ~s of the crowd** les clameurs *fpl* de la foule.
roaring [ˈrɔːrɪŋ] **1** *adj* (*V* **roar 1**) hurlant; rugissant; mugissant; beuglant; grondant; vrombissant; ronflant. (*in hearth*) **a ~ fire** une belle flambée; (*Geog*) **the ~ forties** les quarantièmes rugissants *mpl*; (*fig*) **~ drunk** complètement bourré* *or* noir*; **a ~ success** un succès fou *or* monstre; **to do a ~ trade** faire un gros commerce (*in* de), faire des affaires d'or*.

2 *n* = roar 3.

roast [rəʊst] **1** *n* rôti *m*. ~ of beef rôti de bœuf, rosbif *m*; ~ of veal/pork *etc* rôti de veau/porc *etc*; a slice off the ~ une tranche de *or* du rôti.

2 *adj pork, veal, chicken* rôti. ~ beef rôti *m* de bœuf, rosbif *m*.

3 *vt* **(a)** *meat* (faire) rôtir; *chestnuts* griller, rôtir; *coffee beans* griller, torréfier; *minerals* calciner, griller. the sun was ~ing the city le soleil grillait la ville; to ~ o.s. by the fire se rôtir au coin du feu.

(b) (*US*‡: *criticize*) éreinter.

4 *vi [meat]* rôtir. I'm ~ing!* je crève* (de chaleur)!

roaster ['rəʊstəʳ] *n* (*device*) rôtissoire *f*; (*bird*) poulet *m etc* à rôtir.

roasting ['rəʊstɪŋ] **1** *n* (*lit*) rôtissage *m*. (*fig*) to give sb a ~‡ sonner les cloches à qn*; ~ jack, ~ spit tournebroche *m*.

2 *adj* **(a)** (*: *hot*) *day, weather* torride. it's ~ in here* on crève* (de chaleur) ici, on rôtit* ici.

(b) (*Culin*) *chicken etc* à rôtir.

rob [rɒb] *vt person* voler, dévaliser; *shop* dévaliser; *orchard* piller. to ~ sb of sth (*purse etc*) voler *or* dérober qch à qn; (*rights, privileges*) dépouiller *or* priver qn de qch; to ~ an orchard piller un verger; to ~ the till voler de l'argent dans la caisse; (*loc*) to ~ Peter to pay Paul déshabiller saint Pierre pour habiller saint Paul, faire un trou pour en boucher un autre; I've been ~bed of my watch on m'a volé ma montre; I've been ~bed! j'ai été volé!; the bank was ~bed la banque a été dévalisée, il y a eu un vol à la banque; (*fig*) he has been ~bed of the pleasure of seeing her il a été privé du plaisir de la voir; the shock ~bed him of speech (*briefly*) le choc lui a fait perdre la parole; (*long-term*) le choc lui a ôté l'usage de la parole.

robber ['rɒbəʳ] *n* bandit *m*, voleur *m*.

robbery ['rɒbərɪ] *n* vol *m*. (*Jur*) ~ with violence vol à main armée *or* avec violence; highway ~ vol de grand chemin, brigandage *m*; at that price it's sheer ~!* à ce prix-là c'est du vol manifeste! *or* de l'escroquerie!; *V* armed, daylight.

robe [rəʊb] **1** *n* **(a)** (*garment*) robe *f*; (*for house wear*) peignoir *m*. he was wearing his ~ of office il portait la robe *or* la toge de sa charge; ceremonial ~s vêtements *mpl* de cérémonie; christening ~ robe de baptême; *V* coronation. **(b)** (*US: rug*) couverture *f*. **2** *vt* revêtir (d'une robe); (*fig, liter*) parer, revêtir (*in* de). **3** *vi [judge etc]* revêtir sa robe.

Robert ['rɒbət] *n* Robert *m*.

robin ['rɒbɪn] *n* rouge-gorge *m*; *V* round.

robot ['rəʊbɒt] **1** *n* robot *m*; (*fig*) robot, automate *m*. **2** *cpd worker, guidance, pilot* automatique.

robust [rəʊ'bʌst] *adj person* robuste, vigoureux, solide; *defence* vigoureux, énergique; *material, structure, appetite* solide; *wine* robuste; *humour, style* robuste.

robustness [rəʊ'bʌstnɪs] *n* robustesse *f*, solidité *f*.

roc [rɒk] *n* rock *m*, roc *m*.

rock[1] [rɒk] **1** *vt* **(a)** (*swing to and fro*) *child* bercer; *cradle* balancer. to ~ a child to sleep endormir un enfant en le berçant; a boat ~ed by the waves un bateau bercé par les vagues (*V also* 1b); to ~ o.s. in a rocking chair se balancer dans un fauteuil à bascule.

(b) (*shake*) ébranler, secouer; *ship* ballotter; (**fig: startle*) ébranler, secouer. town ~ed by an earthquake ville ébranlée par un tremblement de terre; (*fig*) to ~ the boat* jouer les trouble-fête, semer le trouble *or* la perturbation; (*fig*) don't ~ the boat* ne compromets pas les choses, ne fais pas l'empêcheur de danser en rond*; that bit of news will ~ her!* cette nouvelle va la bouleverser! *or* lui donner un sale coup!*

2 *vi* **(a)** (*sway gently*) *[cradle, hammock]* (se) balancer; *[person, ship]* se balancer. he was ~ing back and forth il se balançait d'avant en arrière.

(b) (*sway violently*) *[person]* chanceler; *[building]* être ébranlé *or* secoué. the mast was ~ing in the wind le mât oscillait sous les coups du vent; the ground ~ed beneath our feet le sol a tremblé sous nos pieds; they ~ed with laughter* ils se sont tordus *or* gondolés‡.

3 *n* (*pop music*) rock *m*; *V* punk.

4 *cpd*: rock-and-roll rock (and roll) *m or* rock 'n' roll *m*; to do the rock-and-roll danser le rock (and roll); rocking chair fauteuil *m* à bascule; rocking horse cheval *m* à bascule.

rock[2] [rɒk] **1** *n* **(a)** (*substance*) (*any kind*) roche *f*; (*hard*) roc *m*; (*rock face*) rocher *m*, paroi rocheuse. caves hewn out of the ~ des cavernes taillées dans la roche *or* le roc *or* le rocher; hewn out of solid ~ creusé à même le roc, creusé dans le roc; (*lit, fig*) built on ~ bâti sur le roc; they were drilling into ~ and not clay ils foraient la roche *or* le roc et non l'argile; plants that grow in ~ plantes qui poussent sur la roche; porous/volcanic *etc* ~ roche poreuse/volcanique *etc*.

(b) the study of ~s l'étude des roches.

(c) (*large mass, huge boulder*) rocher *m*, roc *m* (*liter*); (*smaller*) roche *f*. a huge ~ blocked their way un énorme rocher leur bouchait le chemin; the entrance was blocked by a pile of fallen ~s l'entrée était bouchée par des éboulis de roches; (*Geog*) the R~ (of Gibraltar) le rocher de Gibraltar; (*fig*) as solid as a ~ solide comme le roc; the ship went on the ~s le bateau est allé donner sur les rochers *or* sur les écueils; *[drink]* on the ~s avec des glaçons; (*fig*) he's on the ~s‡ il n'a pas le sou, il est à sec* *or* dans la purée*; that firm went on the ~s last year* cette firme a fait faillite *or* est tombée en déconfiture* l'an dernier; their marriage is on the ~s* leur mariage est en train de craquer*.

(d) (‡) (*diamond*) bouchon *m* de carafe* (*hum*). (*jewels*) ~s quincaillerie* *f*.

(e) (*sweet*) ≈ sucre *m* d'orge. Brighton ~ *bâton de sucre d'orge marqué au nom de Brighton.*

2 *cpd*: rock bun, rock cake rocher *m* (*Culin*); rock carving sculpture *f* sur roc; rock-climber varappeur *m*, -euse *f*; rock-climbing varappe *f*, escalade *f*; rock crystal cristal *m* de roche; rock face paroi rocheuse; rock fall chute *f* de pierres *or* de rochers; rockfish gobie *m*, rascasse *f*, scorpène *f*; rock garden (jardin *m* de) rocaille *f*; (*Art*) rock painting peinture rupestre *or* pariétale; rock plant plante *f* alpestre *or* de rocaille; rock rose hélianthème *m*; rock salmon roussette *f*; rock salt sel *m* gemme.

rock-bottom ['rɒk'bɒtəm] *n* (*Geol*) fond rocheux. (*fig*) this is ~* c'est la fin de tout, c'est la catastrophe; her spirits reached ~* elle avait le moral au plus bas *or* à zéro*; prices were at ~ les prix étaient tombés aux niveaux les plus bas; (*Comm*) '~ prices' 'marchandises sacrifiées', 'prix défiant toute concurrence'.

rocker ['rɒkəʳ] *n [cradle etc]* bascule *f*; (*chair*) fauteuil *m* à bascule. to be off one's ~‡ être cinglé‡, avoir le cerveau détraqué*; to go off one's ~‡ perdre la boule*; *V* mod[1].

rockery ['rɒkərɪ] *n* (jardin *m* de) rocaille *f*.

rocket ['rɒkɪt] **1** *n* (*Mil*) fusée *f*, roquette *f*; (*Aviat, also firework*) fusée. to fire *or* send up a ~ lancer une fusée; distress ~ fusée *or* signal *m* de détresse; space ~ fusée interplanétaire; (*Brit: fig*) he's just had a ~* from the boss le patron vient de lui passer un savon* *or* de l'enguirlander*.

2 *vi [prices]* monter en flèche. (*fig*) to ~ to fame devenir célèbre du jour au lendemain; he went ~ing* past my door il est passé en trombe devant ma porte.

3 *cpd*: rocket gun fusil *m* lance-fusées *inv or* lance-roquettes *m inv*; rocket launcher lance-fusées *m inv*, lance-roquettes *m inv*; rocket plane avion-fusée *m*; rocket-propelled autopropulsé; rocket propulsion propulsion *f* par fusée, autopropulsion *f*; rocket range base *f* de lancement de missiles; within rocket-range à portée de missiles; rocket research recherches aérospatiales; rocket ship navire *m* lance-fusées *or* lance-missiles.

rocketry ['rɒkɪtrɪ] *n* (*science*) fuséologie *f*; (*rockets collectively*) (panoplie *f* de) fusées *fpl*.

rocky[1] ['rɒkɪ] *adj* (*unsteady*) *table* branlant; (* *fig*) *health, situation* chancelant; *government* branlant. his English is rather ~* son anglais est faiblard*; his finances are ~* sa situation financière est branlante *or* chancelante.

rocky[2] ['rɒkɪ] *adj mountain, hill* rocheux; *road, path* rocailleux. (*Geog*) the R~ Mountains, the Rockies les (montagnes *fpl*) Rocheuses *fpl*.

rococo [rəʊ'kəʊkəʊ] **1** *n* rococo *m*. **2** *adj* rococo *inv*.

rod [rɒd] **1** *n* **(a)** (*wooden*) baguette *f*; (*metallic*) tringle *f*; *[machinery]* tige *f*. curtain/stair ~ tringle à rideaux/d'escalier; *V* connect, piston *etc*.

(b) (*fishing* ~) canne *f* à pêche; (*for punishment*) baguette *f*, canne; (*symbol of authority*) verge *f*; (*measure*) perche *f* (= 5,03 *m*); (*US*‡: *gun*) flingue‡ *m*. to fish with ~ and line pêcher à la ligne; (*fig*) to make a ~ for one's own back se préparer *or* s'attirer des ennuis; to rule with a ~ of iron *country* gouverner d'une main de fer *or* avec une verge de fer (*liter*); *person, family* mener à la baguette *or* à la trique*; *V* black, spare *etc*.

2 *cpd*: (*Med*) rod bacterium bâtonnet *m*; (*Tech*) rod bearing manchon *m* de bielle.

rode [rəʊd] *pret of* ride.

rodent ['rəʊdənt] *adj, n* rongeur (*m*).

rodeo ['rəʊdɪəʊ] *n* rodeo *m*.

rodomontade [ˌrɒdəmɒn'teɪd] *n* rodomontade *f*.

roe[1] [rəʊ] *n* (*species*: also ~ deer) chevreuil *m*. ~ buck chevreuil mâle; (*female*) ~ deer chevreuil *m* femelle, chevrette *f*.

roe[2] [rəʊ] *n [fish]* hard ~ œufs *mpl* de poisson; soft ~ laitance *f*; herring ~ œufs *or* laitance de hareng.

roentgen ['rɒntjən] *n* Roentgen *m or* Röntgen *m*.

rogation [rəʊ'geɪʃən] (*Rel*) **1** *n* (*gen pl*) rogations *fpl*.

2 *cpd*: Rogation Days *les 3 jours qui précèdent l'Ascension*; Rogation Sunday dimanche *m* des Rogations; Rogation-tide période *f* des Rogations.

Roger ['rɒdʒəʳ] *n* Roger *m*. (*Telec*) 'r~' 'compris'; *V* jolly.

rogue [rəʊg] **1** *n* **(a)** (*scoundrel*) coquin *m*, gredin *m*; (*scamp*) polisson(ne) *m(f)*, coquin(e) *m(f)*, fripon(ne) *m(f)*. you little ~! petit coquin!

(b) (*Zool*) solitaire *m*.

2 *cpd*: rogue elephant éléphant *m* solitaire; rogues' gallery (*Police*) (collection *f* de) photographies *fpl* de repris de justice; (*fig*) they look like a rogues' gallery ils ont des têtes *or* des gueules‡ de repris de justice.

roguery ['rəʊgərɪ] *n* (*wickedness*) coquinerie *f*, malhonnêteté *f*; (*mischief*) espièglerie *f*, friponnerie *f*, polissonnerie *f*.

roguish ['rəʊgɪʃ] *adj* espiègle, coquin, polisson.

roguishly ['rəʊgɪʃlɪ] *adv behave, speak* avec espièglerie, malicieusement; *look* d'un œil coquin.

roister ['rɔɪstəʳ] *vi* s'amuser bruyamment.

roisterer ['rɔɪstərəʳ] *n* fêtard(e)* *m(f)*.

Roland ['rəʊlənd] *n* Roland *m*. (*loc*) a ~ for an Oliver un prêté pour un rendu.

role [rəʊl] **1** *n* (*Theat, fig*) rôle *m*; *V* leading *etc*. **2** *cpd*: (*Psych*) role-playing psychodrame *m*.

roll [rəʊl] **1** *n* **(a)** *[cloth, paper, netting, wire, hair etc]* rouleau *m*; *[banknotes]* liasse *f*; *[tobacco]* carotte *f*; *[butter]* coquille *f*; *[flesh, fat]* bourrelet *m*. (*Phot*) ~ of film (rouleau *m* de) pellicule *f*.

(b) (*also* bread ~) petit pain; *V* sausage, Swiss *etc*.

(c) (*movement*) *[ship]* roulis *m*; *[sea]* houle *f*; (*Aviat*) vol *m* en tonneau. to walk with a ~ rouler les hanches, se dandiner *or* se balancer en marchant; the ship gave a sudden ~ le bateau s'est mis à rouler; the horse was having a ~ on the grass le cheval se roulait dans l'herbe; to have a ~ in the hay with sb‡ batifoler* dans l'herbe avec qn.

(d) (*sound*) *[thunder, drums]* roulement *m*; *[organ]* ronflement *m*.
(e) (*list, register*) liste *f*, tableau *m*; (*for court, ship's crew etc*) rôle *m*. **we have 60 pupils on our ~(s)** nous avons 60 élèves inscrits; **to call the ~** faire l'appel; **~ of honour** (*Mil*) liste des combattants morts pour la patrie *or* tombés au champ d'honneur; (*Scol*) tableau d'honneur; (*Jur*) **to strike sb *or* sb's name off the ~s** radier qn des listes *or* du tableau; *V* **electoral.**
2 *cpd*: (*US Econ*) **rollback*** baisse forcée des prix (*sur ordre du gouvernement*); (*gen, Mil, Scol*) **roll call** appel *m*; **roll-collar** = **roll-neck; roll film** pellicule *f* (en rouleau); **rollmop (herring)** rollmops *m*; *[sweater]* **roll-neck** col roulé; **roll-neck(ed)** à col roulé; (*corset*) **roll-on** gaine *f*; **roll-on-roll-off** (manutention *f*) roll-on-roll-off *m*; **roll-on-roll-off port** port *m* roll-on-roll-off; **roll-on-roll-off ship** navire *or* cargo transroulier; **roll-top desk** bureau *m* à cylindre.
3 *vi* **(a)** (*turn over*) rouler. **to ~ over and over** rouler sur soi-même; **the coin ~ed under the table** la pièce a roulé sous la table; **stones ~ed down the hill** des pierres ont roulé *or* déboulé jusqu'au pied de la colline; **to ~ headlong down a slope** dégringoler une pente, rouler du haut en bas d'une pente; **the children were ~ing down the slope** les enfants roulaient le long de la pente; **tears were ~ing down her cheeks** les larmes roulaient sur ses joues; **the waves were ~ing on to the beach** les vagues déferlaient sur la plage; **the newspapers were ~ing off the presses** les journaux tombaient des rotatives; **the wheels kept ~ing** les roues continuaient à tourner; (*fig*) **heads will ~** il y aura des limogeages*, des têtes tomberont; (*Aut*) **we were ~ing along at 100 km/h** nous roulions à 100 (km) à l'heure; (*Theat*) **to keep the show ~ing*** s'arranger pour que le spectacle continue (*subj*); (*fig*) **you must keep the ball *or* things ~ing while I'm away*** arrangez-vous pour que ça tourne (*subj*) rond *or* pour que tout marche (*subj*) pendant mon absence; **the horse ~ed in the mud** le cheval s'est vautré dans la boue; (*fig*) **he's ~ing (in money *or* in it)*** il roule sur l'or; (*fig*) **they were ~ing in the aisles*** ils se tordaient, ils se tenaient les côtes*.
(b) *[ship]* rouler. **he ~ed from side to side as he walked** il se balançait en marchant; **his eyes were ~ing** ses yeux roulaient, il roulait les yeux.
(c) *[thunder]* gronder, rouler; *[drums, words]* rouler; *[voice]* retentir; *[noises]* se répercuter.
4 *vt barrel, hoop, ball* (faire) rouler; *umbrella, cigarette* rouler; *pastry, dough* étendre *or* abaisser au rouleau; *metal* laminer; *lawn* rouler; *road* cylindrer. **to ~ one's eyes** rouler les yeux; **to ~ one's r's** rouler les r; **to ~ sth between one's fingers** rouler qch en boule; **to ~ string into a ball** enrouler de la ficelle en pelote; **the hedgehog ~ed itself up into a ball** le hérisson s'est roulé en boule; **he ~ed himself in a blanket** il s'est roulé *or* enroulé dans une couverture; **they ~ed the car to the side of the road** ils ont poussé la voiture sur le bas-côté; *V also* **rolled.**

roll about *vi [coins, marbles]* rouler çà et là; *[ship]* rouler; *[person, dog]* se rouler par terre.
roll along 1 *vi* **(a)** *[ball, vehicle]* rouler.
(b) (*: *arrive*) s'amener‡, se pointer‡.
2 *vt sep ball* faire rouler; *car* pousser.
roll away 1 *vi [clouds, mist, vehicle]* s'éloigner; *[ball]* rouler au loin. **the ball rolled away from me** le ballon a roulé loin de moi.
2 *vt sep trolley, table* éloigner, emmener.
roll back 1 *vi [object]* rouler en arrière; *[eyes]* chavirer.
2 *vt sep object* rouler en arrière; *carpet* rouler; *sheet* enlever (en roulant). (*fig*) **if only we could roll back the years** si seulement nous pouvions ramener le temps passé.
3 **rollback*** *n V* **roll 2.**
roll by *vi [vehicle, procession]* passer; *[clouds]* être chassé; *[time, years]* s'écouler, passer.
roll down 1 *vi [ball, person]* rouler de haut en bas; *[tears]* couler.
2 *vt sep cart* descendre (en roulant).
roll in 1 *vi [waves]* déferler; (*) *[letters, contributions, suggestions]* affluer; (*) *[person]* s'amener‡, se pointer‡, entrer (avec désinvolture). **he rolled in* half an hour late** il s'est amené‡ avec une demi-heure de retard; **the money keeps rolling in*** l'argent continue à affluer.
2 *vt sep barrel, trolley* faire entrer (en roulant).
roll off 1 *vi* **(a)** *[vehicle, procession]* s'ébranler, se mettre en marche.
(b) (*fall off*) dégringoler.
2 **roll-on-roll-off** *n, adj V* **roll 2.**
roll on 1 *vi [vehicle etc]* continuer de rouler; *[time]* s'écouler. **roll on the holidays!*** vivement les vacances!; **roll on Tuesday!*** vivement qu'on soit mardi!
2 *vt sep stockings* enfiler.
3 **roll-on** *n*, **roll-on-roll-off** *n, adj V* **roll 2.**
roll out *vt sep* **(a)** *barrel, trolley* rouler *or* pousser dehors.
(b) *sentence, verse* débiter.
(c) *pastry* étendre *or* abaisser au rouleau; *metal* laminer.
roll over 1 *vi [person, animal]* (*once*) se retourner (sur soi-même); (*several times: also* **roll over and over**) se rouler.
2 *vt sep person, animal, object* retourner.
roll past *vi* = **roll by.**
roll up 1 *vi* **(a)** *[animal]* se rouler (*into* en).
(b) (*: *arrive*) arriver, s'amener‡. *[fairground]* **roll up and see the show!** approchez, venez voir le spectacle!
2 *vt sep cloth, paper, map* rouler. **to roll up one's sleeves** retrousser ses manches; *V also* **roll 4.**

rolled [rəʊld] *adj* (*in a roll*) *blanket etc* roulé, enroulé, en rouleau. **~ tobacco** tabac *m* en carotte; **~ gold** plaqué *m* or; **~-gold bracelet** bracelet *m* plaqué or; **~ oats** flocons *mpl* d'avoine.

roller ['rəʊləʳ] **1** *n* **(a)** (*for pressing, smoothing*) rouleau *m*; *[pastry]* rouleau à pâtisserie; *[roads]* rouleau compresseur; *[lawn]* rouleau de jardin; *[metal]* laminoir *m*, cylindre *m* lamineur; (*Papermaking, Tex*) calandre *f*; (*for inking*) rouleau encreur; *V* **paint.**
(b) (*for winding sth round*) rouleau *m*; *[blind]* enrouleur *m*; *[hair]* rouleau (à mise en plis). **to put one's hair in ~s** se mettre des rouleaux.
(c) (*for moving things*) rouleau *m*; (*wheel*) roulette *f*, galet *m*. **table on ~s** table *f* à roulettes.
(d) (*wave*) lame *f* de houle.
2 *cpd*: **roller bandage** bande roulée; **roller blind** store *m*; **roller coaster** montagnes *fpl* russes; **roller skate** patin *m* à roulettes; **roller-skate** faire du patin à roulettes; **roller-skating** patinage *m* à roulettes; **roller towel** essuie-main(s) *m* à *or* en rouleau.
rollick ['rɒlɪk] *vi* (*also* **~ about**) s'amuser bruyamment.
rollicking ['rɒlɪkɪŋ] *adj person* d'une gaieté exubérante, joyeux; *play, farce* bouffon; *occasion* (bruyant et) joyeux. **to lead a ~ life** mener joyeuse vie *or* une vie de patachon; **to have a ~ time** s'amuser follement *or* comme des fous; **it was a ~ party** nous nous sommes amusés comme des petits fous à la soirée.
rolling ['rəʊlɪŋ] **1** *adj ship* qui roule; *sea* houleux; *countryside, ground* onduleux, à ondulations. (*Prov*) **a ~ stone gathers no moss** pierre qui roule n'amasse pas mousse (*Prov*); (*fig*) **he's a ~ stone** il roule sa bosse*; **to have a ~ gait** rouler *or* balancer les hanches, se déhancher; **~ waves** grosses vagues, lames déferlantes.
2 *cpd*: **rolling mill** (*factory*) laminerie *f*, usine *f* de laminage; (*machine*) laminoir *m*; **rolling pin** rouleau *m* (à pâtisserie); (*Rail*) **rolling stock** matériel roulant.
roly-poly ['rəʊlɪ'pəʊlɪ] **1** *adj* (*) grassouillet, boulot (*f* -otte), rondelet.
2 *n* **(a)** (*Brit: also* **~ pudding**) roulé *m* à la confiture.
(b) (*: *plump child*) poupard *m*.
romaine [rəʊ'meɪn] *n* (*US: also* **~ lettuce**) (laitue *f*) romaine *f*.
Roman ['rəʊmən] **1** *n* **(a)** (*Hist*) Romain(e) *m(f)*.
(b) (*Typ*) romain *m*.
2 *adj* (*Archit, Geog, Hist, Rel, Typ*) romain. **~ candle** chandelle romaine; **~ Catholic** (*adj, n*) catholique (*mf*); **the ~ Catholic Church** l'Église catholique (et romaine); (*Typ*) **~ letters** caractères romains; **~ nose** nez aquilin; **~ numerals** chiffres romains; (*Rel*) **the ~ Rite** le rite romain.
romance [rəʊ'mæns] **1** *n* **(a)** (*tale of chivalry*) roman *m*; (*love story/film*) roman/film *m* à l'eau de rose; (*Mus*) romance *f*; (*love affair*) idylle *f*; (*love*) amour *m*; (*U: charm, attraction*) charme *m*. **it's quite a ~** c'est un vrai roman; (*fig: lies*) **it's pure ~** c'est de la pure invention, c'est du roman; **their ~ lasted six months** leur idylle a duré six mois; **he was her first ~** il était son premier amoureux *or* amour; **they had a beautiful ~** ils ont vécu un beau roman (d'amour); **the ~ of the sea/of foreign lands** la poésie de la mer/des pays étrangers.
(b) (*Ling*) **R~** roman *m*.
2 *adj* (*Ling*) **R~** roman.
3 *vi* enjoliver (à plaisir), broder (*fig*).
romancer [rəʊ'mænsəʳ] *n* conteur *m*, -euse *f*. (*fig*) **he's a ~** il enjolive toujours tout.
Romanesque [,rəʊmə'nesk] *adj language, architecture* roman.
Romania [rəʊ'meɪnɪə] *n* Roumanie *f*.
Romanian [rəʊ'meɪnɪən] **1** *adj* roumain.
2 *n* **(a)** Roumain(e) *m(f)*.
(b) (*Ling*) roumain *m*.
Romanic [rəʊ'mænɪk] *adj language* roman.
romanize ['rəʊmənaɪz] *vt* (*Hist*) romaniser; (*Rel*) convertir au catholicisme.
Romansh [rəʊ'mænʃ] *n* romanche *m*.
romantic [rəʊ'mæntɪk] **1** *adj appearance, landscape, building* romantique (*also Art, Hist, Literat, Mus*); *person, film, book* romantique, sentimental (*pej*); *adventure, setting* romanesque. (*Cine, Theat*) **~ lead** jeune premier *m*.
2 *n* romantique *mf*, sentimental(e) *m(f)*; (*Art, Literat, Mus*) romantique.
romantically [rəʊ'mæntɪkəlɪ] *adv write, describe* d'une façon romanesque; *sing, woo* en romantique. **castle ~ situated in a wood** château situé dans le cadre romantique d'un bois.
romanticism [rəʊ'mæntɪsɪzəm] *n* (*Art, Literat, Mus*) romantisme *m*.
romanticist [rəʊ'mæntɪsɪst] *n* (*Art, Literat, Mus*) romantique *mf*.
romanticize [rəʊ'mæntɪsaɪz] *vti* romancer.
Romany ['rɒmənɪ] **1** *n* **(a)** bohémien(ne) *m(f)*. **(b)** (*Ling*) romani *m*. **2** *adj* de bohémien.
Rome [rəʊm] *n* Rome. (*loc*) **when in ~ (do as the Romans do)** à Rome il faut vivre comme les Romains; (*Prov*) **~ wasn't built in a day** Paris *or* Rome ne s'est pas fait en un jour; (*Prov*) **all roads lead to ~** tous les chemins mènent à Rome; **the Church of ~** l'Église (catholique) romaine; (*Rel*) **to go over to ~** se convertir au catholicisme.
Romeo ['rəʊmɪəʊ] *n* Roméo *m* (*also fig*).
Romish ['rəʊmɪʃ] *adj* (*pej*) catholique.
romp [rɒmp] **1** *n* jeux bruyants, ébats *mpl*. **the play was just a ~** la pièce n'était (guère) qu'une farce.
2 *vi [children, puppies]* jouer bruyamment, s'ébattre. **the horse ~ed home** le cheval est arrivé dans un fauteuil*; (*fig*) **to ~ through an exam** passer un examen haut la main.
rompers ['rɒmpəz] *npl* barboteuse *f* (*pour enfant*).
rondeau ['rɒndəʊ] *n*, **rondel** ['rɒndl] *n* (*Mus, Poetry*) rondeau *m*.
rondo ['rɒndəʊ] *n* (*Mus*) rondeau *m*.
Roneo ['rəʊnɪəʊ] *vt* ® polycopier, ronéotyper, ronéoter.

rood [ruːd] n (a) (*Rel Archit*) crucifix m. ~ **screen** jubé m. (b) (*Brit: measure*) quart m d'arpent.

roof [ruːf] 1 n [*building, car*] toit m; [*cave, tunnel*] plafond m; (*fig: of sky, branches*) voûte f. (*Anat*) the ~ of the mouth la voûte du palais; without a ~ over one's head sans abri *or* toit; a room in the ~ une chambre sous les combles *or* sous les toits; I couldn't live under her ~ je ne pourrais pas vivre chez elle; to live under the same ~ as sb vivre sous le même toit avec *or* que qn; (*fig*) to go through the ~* [*person*] exploser, piquer une crise*; [*price, claim*] devenir excessif; V flat[1], raise, sunshine *etc*.

2 *cpd*: roof garden jardin m sur le toit; (*gen, Aut*) roof light plafonnier m; (*Aut*) roof rack galerie f; rooftop toit m.

3 vt *house* couvrir (d'un toit). red-~ed à toit rouge.

roof in vt sep couvrir d'un toit.

roof over vt sep recouvrir d'un toit.

roofing ['ruːfɪŋ] n (a) (*on house*) toiture f, couverture f. ~ felt couverture bitumée *or* goudronnée. (b) (*act*) pose f de la toiture *or* de la couverture.

rook[1] [rʊk] 1 n (*Orn*) corneille f, freux m.

2 vt (‡: *swindle*) rouler*, empiler*, escroquer.

rook[2] [rʊk] n (*Chess*) tour f.

rookery ['rʊkərɪ] n colonie f de freux *or* de corneilles; [*seals, penguins*] colonie; (*fig pej: overcrowded slum*) taudis surpeuplé.

rookie‡ ['rʊkɪ] n (*esp Mil*) bleu* m.

room [rʊm] 1 n (a) (*in house, building*) pièce f; (*large*) salle f; (*bedroom*) chambre f; (*office*) bureau m; (*in hotel*) chambre. ~s to let chambres fpl à louer; ~ and board pension f; his ~s son appartement m; come to my ~s for coffee venez prendre le café chez moi; they live in ~s ils habitent un meublé *or* un garni (*pej*); V double, lecture, roof *etc*.

(b) (*U: space*) place f. is there ~? y a-t-il de la place?; there is ~ for 2 people il y a de la place pour 2 personnes; there's no ~ il n'y a pas de place; (*fig*) there's no ~ to swing a cat* il n'y a pas la place de se retourner; to take up ~/ too much ~ prendre de la place/trop de place; to make ~ for sb faire une place pour qn; to make ~ for sth faire de la place pour qch; (*fig*) there is still ~ for hope il y a encore lieu d'espérer; there is little ~ for hope il ne reste pas beaucoup d'espoir; there is no ~ for doubt il n'y a pas de doute possible; there is ~ for improvement in your work votre travail laisse à désirer.

2 vi partager une chambre (*with* avec). to ~ with a landlady louer une chambre meublée; (*US*) ~ing house maison f *or* immeuble m de rapport.

3 *cpd*: (*US*) room clerk réceptionniste mf, réceptionnaire mf; room divider meuble m de séparation; roommate camarade mf de chambre; room service (*on bill etc*) service m des chambres (d'hôtel); ring for room service appelez le garçon d'étage; room temperature température ambiante; wine at room temperature vin chambré.

-roomed [rʊmd] adj *ending in cpds*: a 6-roomed house une maison de 6 pièces; a two-roomed flat un deux-pièces.

roomer ['rʊməʳ] n (*US*) locataire mf.

roomful ['rʊmfʊl] n pleine salle.

roominess ['rʊmɪnɪs] n dimensions spacieuses.

roomy ['rʊmɪ] adj *flat, handbag* spacieux; *garment* ample.

roost [ruːst] 1 n perchoir m, juchoir m; V rule. 2 vi (*settle*) se percher, se jucher; (*sleep*) jucher. (*fig*) to come home to ~ retomber sur *or* se retourner contre son auteur.

rooster ['ruːstəʳ] n coq m.

root [ruːt] 1 n (*Anat, Bot, Ling, Math*) racine f; (*fig*) [*trouble etc*] origine f, cause f. to pull up *or* out by the ~s déraciner, extirper; (*lit, fig*) to take ~ prendre racine; (*fig*) to pull up one's ~s se déraciner; her ~s are in France elle est française de cœur *or* d'esprit; she has no ~s c'est une déracinée; to put down ~s in a country s'enraciner dans un pays; (*fig*) ~ and branch entièrement, radicalement; the ~ of the matter la vraie raison; to get to the ~s of the problem trouver la cause *or* aller au fond du problème; that is at the ~ of ... cela est à l'origine de ...; what lies at the ~ of his attitude? quelle est la raison fondamentale de son attitude?; V cube, grass, square.

2 *cpd*: root cause cause première; root crops racines fpl alimentaires; (*Math*) root sign radical m; (*Bot*) rootstock rhizome m; (*Ling*) root word mot m racine *inv*, mot souche *inv*.

3 vt (*Bot*) enraciner. (*fig*) a deeply ~ed belief une croyance bien enracinée; (*fig*) to be ~ed to the spot être cloué sur place.

4 vi (a) [*plants etc*] s'enraciner, prendre racine.

(b) [*pigs*] fouiller (avec le groin).

root about, root around vi fouiller (*among* dans, *for sth* pour trouver qch).

root for vt fus (*: *esp US*) *team* encourager, applaudir.

root out vt sep (*fig*) (*find*) dénicher; (*remove*) extirper.

root up vt sep *plant* déraciner; [*pigs*] déterrer; (*fig*) extirper.

rootless ['ruːtlɪs] adj (*lit, fig*) sans racine(s).

rope [rəʊp] 1 n corde f; (*Naut*) cordage m; [*bell*] cordon m. (*fig*) to give sb more ~ lâcher la bride à qn; give him enough ~ and he'll hang himself si on le laisse faire il se passera lui-même la corde au cou *or* il creusera sa propre tombe; (*Boxing etc*) the ~s les cordes fpl; on the ~s (*Boxing*) dans les cordes; (* *fig*) *person* sur le flanc*; *business* ne battant que d'une aile*; (*fig*) to know the ~s* être au courant, connaître son affaire *or* les ficelles*; to show sb the ~s* mettre qn au courant; to learn the ~s* se mettre au courant; a ~ of pearls un collier de perles; a ~ of onions un chapelet d'oignons; a ~ of hair une torsade de cheveux; (*Alpinism*) a ~ of climbers une cordée d'alpinistes; [*climber*] to put on the ~ s'encorder; (*Alpinism*) there were 3 of them on the ~ ils formaient une cordée de 3; V clothes, skipping, tight *etc*.

2 *cpd*: ropedancer funambule mf, danseur m, -euse f de corde; rope ladder échelle f de corde; ropemaker cordier m; (Indian) rope trick tour m de la corde (*prestidigitation*); ropewalker = ropedancer.

3 vt (a) *box, case* corder. to ~ sb to a tree lier qn à un arbre; to ~ climbers (together) encorder des alpinistes.

(b) (*US: catch*) *cattle* prendre au lasso.

rope in vt sep *area* entourer de cordes, délimiter par une corde. (*fig*) to rope sb in* enrôler qn, embringuer qn*; he got himself roped in to help at the fête il s'est laissé embringuer* pour aider à la fête; I don't want to get roped in* for anything je ne veux pas me laisser embringuer*.

rope off vt sep réserver par une corde.

rope up (*Alpinism*) 1 vi s'encorder. 2 vt sep encorder. to be roped up être encordé.

rop(e)y ['rəʊpɪ] adj *liquid* visqueux; (* *fig: bad*) pas fameux.

rosary ['rəʊzərɪ] n (a) (*Rel*) chapelet m; (*fifteen decades*) rosaire m. (b) (*in garden*) roseraie f.

rose[1] [rəʊz] *pret of* rise.

rose[2] [rəʊz] 1 n (a) (*flower*) rose f; (*also* ~bush, ~ tree) rosier m. wild ~ églantine f; (*fig*) my life isn't all ~s* tout n'est pas rose dans ma vie; (*Prov*) there is no ~ without a thorn il n'y a pas de roses sans épines; (*fig*) she's an English ~ elle est belle comme une fleur *or* fraîche comme une rose; (*fig*) that will put ~s back in your cheeks cela va te rendre tes belles couleurs; (*fig liter*) under the ~ en confidence, sous le manteau; (*Brit Hist*) the Wars of the R~s la guerre des Deux-Roses; V bed, Christmas, rock[2].

(b) [*hose, watering can*] pomme f; (*on hat, shoe*) rosette f; [*pump*] crépine f; (*on ceiling*) rosace f (de plafond); V compass.

(c) (*colour*) rose m.

2 adj rose.

3 *cpd leaf, petal* de rose. rosebay laurier-rose m; rosebed massif m de rosiers; rosebowl coupe f à fleurs; rosebud bouton m de rose; rosebud mouth bouche f en cerise; rose-coloured rose, couleur de rose *inv*; (*fig*) to see everything/life through rose-coloured spectacles voir tout/la vie en rose; rose diamond rose f (*diamant*); rose garden roseraie f; rose grower rosiériste mf; rose hip gratte-cul m; roselike rosacé; rosemary V rosemary; rose pink rose, rosé; rose-red vermeil; rose water eau f de rose (*lit*); rose window rosace f, rose f; rosewood (*n*) bois m de rose; (*adj*) en bois de rose.

rosé ['rəʊzeɪ] n rosé m (*vin*).

roseate ['rəʊzɪɪt] adj rose.

rosemary ['rəʊzmərɪ] n romarin m.

roseola [rəʊ'zɪələ] n roséole f.

rosette [rəʊ'zet] n (*ribbons etc*) rosette f; (*Sport: as prize*) cocarde f; (*Archit*) rosace f.

rosin ['rɒzɪn] n colophane f.

roster ['rɒstəʳ] n liste f, tableau m; V duty.

rostrum ['rɒstrəm] n tribune f; (*Roman Hist*) rostres mpl.

rosy ['rəʊzɪ] adj rose, rosé. ~ cheeks joues fpl roses *or* vermeilles (*liter*); to have a ~ complexion avoir les joues roses; (*fig*) his future looks ~ il semble avoir un brillant avenir devant lui; the situation looks ~ la situation se présente bien; to paint a ~ picture of sth dépeindre *or* peindre qch en rose.

rot [rɒt] 1 n (*U*) (a) pourriture f; (*Bot, Med*) carie f. (*fig*) he worked well at the beginning then the ~ set in* au début il travaillait bien mais par la suite il a flanché* *or* les problèmes ont commencé; (*fig*) to stop the ~ redresser la situation; V dry.

(b) (*: *rubbish*) bêtises fpl, balivernes fpl, idioties fpl. to talk ~ dire des bêtises, débiter des blagues* *or* des foutaises‡; that's utter ~, that's a lot of ~ ça, c'est de la blague* *or* de la foutaise‡; (what) ~ quelle idiotie *or* blague*, c'est de la blague* *or* de la foutaise‡.

2 *cpd*: (*pej*) rotgut‡ tord-boyaux‡ m; rotproof imputrescible.

3 vi pourrir, se décomposer, se putréfier; (*fig*) [*person*] dépérir, pourrir, croupir. to ~ in jail pourrir *or* croupir en prison; let him ~!* qu'il aille se faire pendre!*

4 vt (faire) pourrir.

rot away vi tomber en pourriture.

rota ['rəʊtə] n (a) liste f, tableau m. (b) (*Rel*) R~ rote f.

Rotarian [rəʊ'tɛərɪən] adj, n rotarien (m).

rotary ['rəʊtərɪ] adj (a) rotatif, rotatoire. ~ (printing) press rotative f; ~ printer rotativiste m. (b) R~ (Club) Rotary Club m.

rotate [rəʊ'teɪt] 1 vt (*revolve*) faire tourner; (*on pivot*) faire pivoter; (*change round*) *crops* alterner; *work, jobs* faire à tour de rôle. 2 vi tourner; (*on pivot*) pivoter; [*crops*] être alterné.

rotating [rəʊ'teɪtɪŋ] adj (V rotate) tournant; rotatif; pivotant; alternant.

rotation [rəʊ'teɪʃən] n (*turning*) rotation f; (*turn*) rotation, tour m. in *or* by ~ à tour de rôle; ~ of crops assolement m, rotation f (des cultures).

rotatory [rəʊ'teɪtərɪ] adj rotatoire.

rotavate ['rəʊtəveɪt] vt labourer avec un motoculteur.

Rotavator ['rəʊtəveɪtəʳ] n ® motoculteur m.

rote [rəʊt] n: by ~ *learn* machinalement, sans essayer de comprendre; *recite* comme un perroquet.

rotogravure [ˌrəʊtəʊgrə'vjʊəʳ] n rotogravure f.

rotor ['rəʊtəʳ] 1 n (*Aviat, Elec*) rotor m. 2 *cpd*: rotor blade pale f de rotor.

rototill ['rəʊtəʊtɪl] vt (*US*) labourer avec un motoculteur.

Rototiller ['rəʊtəʊtɪləʳ] n ® (*US*) motoculteur m.

rotten ['rɒtn] adj (a) *wood, vegetation, egg* pourri; *tooth* carié, gâté; *fruit* gâté, pourri; (*fig: corrupt*) véreux, corrompu. (*lit, fig*) ~ to the core complètement pourri.

(b) (*: *bad*) mauvais, moche*. it's ~ weather! quel temps de chien!; to feel ~* se sentir patraque *or* mal fichu*; it's a ~ business c'est une sale affaire; what ~ luck! quelle guigne!*, quelle poisse!*; what a ~ trick! quel sale tour!*.

rottenness ['rɒtnnɪs] *n* (état *m* de) pourriture *f*.
rotter*† ['rɒtəʳ] *n* (*esp Brit*) sale type* *m*, vache: *f*.
rotting ['rɒtɪŋ] *adj* en pourriture, qui pourrit.
rotund [rəʊ'tʌnd] *adj person* replet (*f* -ète), rondelet; *object* rond, arrondi; (*fig*) *speech, literary style* emphatique, ampoulé, ronflant; *voice* sonore.
rotunda [rəʊ'tʌndə] *n* rotonde *f*.
rotundity [rəʊ'tʌndɪtɪ] *n [person]* embonpoint *m*, corpulence *f*, (*fig*) *[style]* grandiloquence *f*; *[voice]* sonorité *f*.
rouble, (*US*) **ruble** ['ru:bl] *n* rouble *m*.
roué ['ru:eɪ] *n* roué *m*, débauché *m*.
rouge [ru:ʒ] **1** *n* rouge *m* (à joues). **2** *vt*: **to ~ one's cheeks** se farder les joues, se mettre du rouge (à joues).
rough [rʌf] **1** *adj* **(a)** (*uneven*) *ground* accidenté, inégal; *skin, cloth* rêche, rugueux; *surface* rugueux; *path, road* raboteux, rocailleux. **~ to the touch** rude *or* rêche *or* rugueux au toucher; **~ hands** *[peasant]* mains rugueuses; *[housewife]* mains rêches.
(b) (*fig*) *sound* rude, âpre; *taste* âpre, âcre; *voice* rauque; rude; (*coarse, unrefined*) *person, manners* rude, fruste; *speech* rude; (*harsh etc*) *person* brutal, violent; *manners* grossier; *neighbourhood* mauvais; *life* dur, rude; *tongue* mauvais; *tone, voice* brusque. **~ handling of sth** manque *m* de soin envers qch; **a ~ sea, ~ seas** mer agitée *or* houleuse, grosse mer; **the waves were very ~** il y avait de très grosses vagues; **a ~ crossing** une mauvaise traversée; **~ weather** gros temps, mauvais temps; (*Sport etc*) **~ play** jeu brutal; **it's a ~ game** c'est un jeu brutal; **~ stuff*** brutalité *f* (gratuite); **there was a bit of ~ stuff* at the pub last night** il y a eu de la bagarre *or* ça a bardé* hier soir au café; **these boys are very ~** ces garçons sont des (petites) brutes *or* sont très durs; **a ~ customer*** un dur*; **to have a ~ time (of it)** en voir de rudes *or* de dures*; **to be ~ with sb, to give sb a ~ time (of it)** malmener qn; (*fig*) être dur avec qn, en faire voir de toutes les couleurs à qn*; (*fig*) **to make things ~ for sb*** mener la vie dure à qn; **it is ~ on him*** (*in this instance*) il n'a pas de veine*, c'est un coup dur* pour lui; (*generally*) ce n'est pas marrant: pour lui; (*fig: ill*) **to feel ~*** ne pas se sentir bien, être mal fichu*.
(c) (*approximate, unfinished*) *plan* non travaillé, ébauché; *calculation, translation* approximatif. **~ copy, ~ draft,** (*U*) **~ work** brouillon *m*; **~ sketch** croquis *m*, ébauche *f*; **~ paper** papier *m* de brouillon; **~ justice** justice *f* sommaire; **~ estimate, ~ guess** approximation *f*; **at a ~ estimate** *or* **guess** à vue d'œil, approximativement; **in its ~ state** à l'état brut; **~ diamond** diamant brut; (*fig*) **he's a ~ diamond** sous ses dehors frustes c'est un brave garçon.
2 *adv live* à la dure; *play* brutalement. **to sleep ~** coucher dehors *or* à la dure; (*fig*) **to cut up ~*** (*angry*) se mettre en rogne* *or* en boule*; (*violent*) devenir violent.
3 *n* **(a)** (*ground*) terrain accidenté *or* rocailleux; (*Golf*) rough *m*. (*fig*) **to take the ~ with the smooth** prendre les choses comme elles viennent.
(b) (*unfinished*) **in the ~** brut, à l'état brut *or* d'ébauche.
(c) (*: *person*) voyou *m*.
4 *cpd*: **rough-and-ready** *method* fruste, rudimentaire; *work* grossier, fait à la hâte; *installation, equipment* rudimentaire, de fortune; *person* sans façons; **rough-and-tumble** (*adj*) désordonné, confus; (*n*) mêlée *f*, bagarre *f*; **after the rough-and-tumble of his life in the navy** après sa vie mouvementée de marin; **roughcast** (*adj, n*) crépi (*m*); (*vt*) crépir; **rough-dry** (*vt*) sécher sans repasser; **rough-hewn** dégrossi, ébauché; **rough-house*** bagarre *f*; **roughneck:** voyou *m*, dur *m* à cuire*; **rough-rider** dresseur *m* *or* dompteur *m* de chevaux; **roughshod** *V* **ride 2b**; **rough-spoken** au langage grossier.
5 *vt*: **to ~ it*** vivre à la dure.
rough out *vt sep* dégrossir; *plan, drawing* ébaucher.
rough up *vt sep hair* ébouriffer. (*fig*) **to rough sb up*** malmener qn, (*stronger*) tabasser: qn.
roughage ['rʌfɪdʒ] *n* (*U*) aliments *mpl* qui font travailler les intestins *or* qui régularisent les fonctions intestinales.
roughen ['rʌfn] **1** *vt* rendre rude *or* rugueux. **2** *vi* devenir rude *or* rugueux.
roughly ['rʌflɪ] *adv* **(a)** (*not gently*) *push* rudement, brutalement; *play* brutalement; *answer, order* brusquement, avec brusquerie. **to treat sth/sb ~** malmener qch/qn.
(b) (*not finely*) *make, sew* grossièrement. **the table is very ~ made** la table est très grossière; **to sketch sth ~** faire un croquis de qch.
(c) (*approximately*) approximativement, en gros, à peu près. **~ speaking** en gros, approximativement; **it costs ~ 100 francs** cela coûte environ 100 F; **tell me ~ what it's all about** dites-moi grosso modo *or* en gros de quoi il s'agit; **she is ~ 40** elle a dans les *or* à peu près 40 ans.
roughness ['rʌfnɪs] *n* (*V* **rough**) inégalité *f*; rugosité *f*; rudesse *f*; âpreté *f*; violence *f*; brutalité *f*; grossièreté *f*; brusquerie *f*; dureté *f*; état brut; *[road]* inégalités *fpl*, mauvais état; *[sea]* agitation *f*.
roulette [ru:'let] *n* roulette *f* (*jeu, cuvette*); *V* **Russian 1**.
Roumania [ru:'meɪnɪə] *n* = **Romania**.
Roumanian [ru:'meɪnɪən] *adj* = **Romanian**.
round [raʊnd] (*phr vb elem*) **1** *adv*: **there was a wall right ~** *or* **all ~** il y avait un mur tout autour; **he went ~ by the bridge** il a fait le détour *or* il est passé par le pont; **you can't get through here, you'll have to go ~** vous ne pouvez pas passer par ici, il faut faire le tour; **the long way ~** le chemin le plus long; **it's a long way ~** ça fait un grand détour *or* un grand crochet; **she ran ~ to her mother's** elle a couru chez sa mère; **come ~ and see me** venez me voir; **I asked him ~ for a drink** je l'ai invité à prendre un verre chez moi; **I'll be ~ at 8 o'clock** je serai là à 8 heures; **spring will soon be ~ again** le printemps reviendra bientôt; **all (the) year ~** pendant toute l'année, d'un bout à l'autre de l'année; **drinks all ~!*** je paie une tournée!*; (*fig*) **taking things all ~, taken all ~** tout compte fait; *V* **gather round, look round** *etc*.
2 *prep* **(a)** (*of place etc*) autour de. **sitting ~ the table** assis autour de la table; **sitting ~ the fire** assis au coin du feu *or* auprès du feu; **all ~ the house** tout autour de la maison; **the villages ~ Lewes** les villages des environs *or* des alentours de Lewes; **the house is just ~ the corner** la maison est au coin de la rue *or* juste après le coin de la rue; (*fig*) la maison est tout près; **come and see me if you're ~ this way** viens me voir si tu passes par ici *or* si tu es dans le coin*; **to go ~ a corner** tourner un coin; (*Aut*) prendre un virage; **to go ~ an obstacle** contourner un obstacle; **to look ~ a house** visiter une maison; **to show sb ~ a town** faire visiter une ville à qn; **they went ~ the castle** ils ont visité le château; **they went ~ the cafés looking for ...** ils ont fait le tour des cafés à la recherche de ...; **she's 75 cm ~ the waist** elle fait 75 cm de tour de taille; **put a blanket ~ him** enveloppez-le d'une couverture; *V* **clock, world** *etc*.
(b) (*approximately*) autour de, environ. **~ (about) 7 o'clock** autour de *or* environ 7 heures, vers (les) 7 heures; **~ (about) £800** 800 livres environ, dans les 800 livres, autour de 800 livres.
3 *adj* (*circular*) rond, circulaire; (*rounded*) rond, arrondi. **to have ~ shoulders** avoir le dos rond *or* voûté; (*Ling*) **~ vowel** voyelle arrondie; **in rich ~ tones** d'une voix riche et sonore; (*Archit*) **~ arch** (arc *m* en) plein cintre, arc roman; **~ handwriting** écriture ronde; (*fig*) **a ~ dozen** une douzaine tout rond; **~ figure, ~ number** chiffre rond; **in ~ figures that will cost 20 million** cela coûtera 20 millions en chiffres ronds *or* pour donner un chiffre rond; **at a ~ pace** à vive allure; **a (good) ~ sum** une somme rondelette *or* coquette*; **he told me in ~ terms why ...** il m'a expliqué tout net pourquoi ...; **the cost of the ~ journey** *or* **the ~ trip** le prix du voyage aller et retour; **Concorde does 3 ~ trips a week** Concorde effectue 3 rotations *fpl* par semaine.
4 *n* **(a)** (*circle etc*) rond *m*, cercle *m*; (*slice: of bread, meat*) tranche *f*. **a ~ of toast** un toast, une tranche de pain grillé.
(b) to do *or* **make one's ~(s)** *[watchman, policeman]* faire sa ronde *or* sa tournée; *[postman, milkman]* faire sa tournée; *[doctor]* faire ses visites; **he has got a paper ~** il distribue des journaux; **to go the ~s** *[infection, a cold etc]* courir, circuler; *[news, story]* passer de bouche en bouche; **the story is going the ~s that ...** le bruit court que ..., on raconte *or* on dit que ...; **the story went the ~s of the club** l'histoire a fait le tour du club; **this coat has gone the ~s of the family*** ce manteau a fait le tour de la famille; (*fig*) **the daily ~** la routine quotidienne, le train-train quotidien; **one long ~ of pleasures** une longue suite de plaisirs.
(c) *[cards, golf]* partie *f*; (*Boxing*) round *m*, reprise *f*; (*Equitation*) tour *m* de piste, parcours *m*; *[competition, tournament]* partie, manche *f*; *[election]* manche; *[talks, discussions]* série *f*. (*Equitation*) **to have a clear ~** faire un tour de piste *or* un parcours sans fautes; **a new ~ of negotiations** une nouvelle série de négociations; **to pay for a ~ (of drinks)** payer une tournée*; **it's my ~** c'est ma tournée*; (*Mil*) **~ of ammunition** cartouche *f*; **a ~ of 5 shots** une salve de 5 coups; **a ~ of applause** une salve d'applaudissements; (*Theat*) **let's have a ~ of applause for Lucy!** applaudissons Lucy!, un ban* pour Lucy!
(d) (*Mus*) canon *m*; (*Dancing*) ronde *f*. **in the ~** (*Sculp*) en ronde-bosse; (*Theat*) en rond; (*fig*) en détail.
5 *cpd*: **roundabout** *V* **roundabout**; **round-cheeked** aux joues rondes, joufflu; **round dance** ronde *f*; **round-eyed** (avec) des yeux ronds, aux yeux ronds; **round-faced** au visage rond; **round-game** *jeu m pour un nombre indéterminé de joueurs*; (*Brit Hist*) **Roundhead** Tête ronde; (*US Rail*) **roundhouse** rotonde *f*; **round-necked pullover** pullover *m* ras du cou; **round robin** pétition *f* (*où les signatures sont disposées en rond*); **round-shouldered** voûté; **roundsman** *V* **roundsman**; (*Hist*) **Round Table** Table ronde; (*fig*) **round-table discussion** table ronde; **round-up** *[cattle, people]* rassemblement *m*; *[criminals, suspects]* rafle *f*.
6 *vt* **(a)** (*make round*) arrondir.
(b) (*go round*) *corner* tourner; *bend* prendre; (*Naut*) *cape* doubler; *obstacle* contourner.
round down *vt sep prices etc* arrondir (au chiffre inférieur).
round off *vt sep speech, list, series* terminer; *sentence* parachever; *debate, meeting* mettre fin à, clore. **and now, to round off, I must say ...** et maintenant, pour conclure *or* en dernier lieu, je dois dire ... .
round up 1 *vt sep* **(a)** (*bring together*) *people* rassembler, réunir; *cattle* rassembler; *criminals* effectuer une rafle de, ramasser*.
(b) *prices etc* arrondir (au chiffre supérieur).
2 round-up *n* *V* **round 5**.
round (up)on *vt fus* (*in words*) s'en prendre à; (*in actions*) sauter sur, attaquer.
roundabout ['raʊndəbaʊt] **1** *adj route* détourné, indirect. **we came (by) a ~ way** nous avons fait un détour; **by ~ means** par des moyens détournés; **~ phrase** circonlocution *f*; **what a ~ way of doing things!** quelle façon contournée *or* compliquée de faire les choses!
2 *n* (*Brit*) (*merry-go-round*) manège *m* (*dans une fête foraine*); (*at road junction*) rond-point *m* (à sens giratoire); (*on traffic sign*) sens *m* giratoire; *V* **swing**.
rounded ['raʊndɪd] *adj object, face* arrondi; *cheeks* rebondi, plein; (*fig*) *sentences, style* harmonieux, élégant.
roundelay ['raʊndɪleɪ] *n* (*Mus* ††) rondeau *m*.
rounders ['raʊndəz] *n* (*Brit*) *sorte f de baseball*.
roundly ['raʊndlɪ] *adv* (*fig*) tout net, franchement, carrément, rondement.
roundness ['raʊndnɪs] *n* rondeur *f*.

roundsman ['raʊndzmən] *n,pl* **roundsmen** ['raʊndzmən] (*Brit*) livreur *m*. **milk ~** laitier *m*.
rouse [raʊz] **1** *vt* (*awaken*) réveiller, éveiller; (*stimulate*) activer, éveiller; *feeling* exciter, stimuler; *admiration, interest* susciter; *indignation* provoquer, soulever; *suspicions* éveiller. **~ yourself!** secouez-vous!*; **to ~ the masses** soulever les masses; **to ~ sb to action** inciter *or* pousser qn à agir; **to ~ sb (to anger)** mettre qn en colère; **he's a terrible man when he's ~d** il est terrible quand il est en colère.
2 *vi* (*waken*) se réveiller; (*become active*) sortir de sa torpeur.
rousing ['raʊzɪŋ] *adj speech, sermon* vibrant, véhément; *cheers, applause* frénétique, enthousiaste; *music* entraînant.
roustabout ['raʊstəbaʊt] *n* (*US*) débardeur *m*; (*Australia*) manœuvre *m*, homme *m* à tout faire.
rout[1] [raʊt] **1** *n* **(a)** (*Mil: defeat*) déroute *f*, débâcle *f*. **to put to ~** mettre en déroute. **(b)** (††: *revels*) raout†† *m*, fête mondaine. **(c)** (*Jur: mob*) attroupement illégal. **2** *vt* (*defeat*) mettre en déroute.
rout[2] [raʊt] *vi* (*also* **~ about**) *[pig]* fouiller.
rout out *vt* (*find*) dénicher; (*force out*) déloger. **to rout sb out of bed** tirer qn de son lit.
route [ru:t] **1** *n* **(a)** (*gen, also of train, plane, ship etc*) itinéraire *m*; (*Alpinism*) itinéraire, voie *f*. **shipping/air ~s** routes maritimes/aériennes; (*Aut*) **all ~s** toutes directions; **what ~ does the 39 bus take?** par où passe le 39?, quel est le trajet *or* le parcours *or* l'itinéraire du 39?; **we're on a bus ~** nous sommes sur une ligne d'autobus; **the ~ to the coast goes through ...** pour aller à la côte on passe par...; **I know a good ~ to London** je connais un bon itinéraire pour aller à Londres; **en ~** en route (*for* pour); *V* **sea, trade.**
(b) (*often* [raʊt]: *Mil*) ordres *mpl* de marche, route *f* à suivre.
(c) (*US: often* [raʊt]: *delivery round*) livraison *f*. **he has a paper ~** il distribue les journaux.
2 *cpd*: **route map** carte routière; (*Mil*) **route march** marche *f* d'entraînement.
3 *vt* (*plan ~ of*) *train, coach, bus* fixer le parcours *or* l'itinéraire de. **my luggage was ~d through Amsterdam** mes bagages ont été expédiés via Amsterdam; **they've ~d the train by Leeds** le train passe maintenant par Leeds.
routine [ru:'ti:n] **1** *n* **(a)** routine *f*. **daily ~** (*Mil, Naut*) emploi *m* du temps; (*gen*) occupations journalières, train-train *m* de la vie quotidienne; **business** *or* **office ~** travail courant du bureau; **as a matter of ~** automatiquement, systématiquement.
(b) (*Theat*) numéro *m*. **dance ~** numéro de danse; (*fig*) **he gave me the old ~**: **about his wife not understanding him** il m'a sorti le laïus: d'usage comme quoi sa femme ne le comprenait pas, il a mis le disque* du mari incompris.
2 *adj procedure, enquiry* d'usage; *work etc* ordinaire, habituel; (*pej*) monotone, de routine. **~ duties** affaires *or* obligations courantes; **it was quite ~** ça n'avait rien d'anormal *or* de spécial.
rove [rəʊv] **1** *vi* errer, vagabonder, rôder; *[eyes]* errer. **2** *vt countryside* parcourir, errer dans *or* sur; *streets* errer dans, aller au hasard dans.
rover ['rəʊvə^r] *n* vagabond(e) *m(f)*.
roving ['rəʊvɪŋ] **1** *adj* vagabond, nomade. **he has a ~ eye** il aime reluquer* *or* lorgner les filles; **~ life** vie *f* nomade; **~ ambassador** ambassadeur itinérant; **~ reporter** reporter volant; **to have a ~ commission** avoir (toute) liberté de manœuvre.
2 *n* vagabondage *m*.
row[1] [rəʊ] **1** *n [objects, people]* (*beside one another*) rang *m*, rangée *f*; (*behind one another*) file *f*, ligne *f*; *[seeds, plants]* rayon *m*, rang; *[houses, trees, figures]* rangée; *[cars]* file; (*Knitting*) rang. **in the front ~** au premier rang; **they were sitting in a ~** ils étaient assis en rang; (*fig*) **4 failures in a ~** 4 échecs d'affilée *or* de suite *or* à la file*.
2 *cpd*: (*US*) **they live in a row-house** leur maison est attenante aux maisons voisines.
row[2] [rəʊ] **1** *vt boat* faire aller à la rame *or* à l'aviron; *person, object* transporter en canot. **to ~ sb across** faire traverser qn en canot; **to ~ a race** faire une course d'aviron; *V* **stroke.**
2 *vi* ramer. **to ~ away/back** s'éloigner/revenir à la rame; **he ~ed across the Atlantic** il a traversé l'Atlantique à la rame *or* à l'aviron; **to go ~ing** (*for pleasure*) canoter, faire du canotage; (*Sport*) faire de l'aviron.
3 *n* promenade *f* en canot. **to go for a ~** canoter, faire un tour en canot; **it will be a hard ~ upstream** ce sera dur de remonter la rivière à la rame *or* à l'aviron.
4 *cpd*: **rowboat** canot *m* (à rames); **rowlock** ['rɒlək] dame *f* de nage, tolet *m*.
row[3] [raʊ] **1** *n* (*noise*) tapage *m*, vacarme *m*, raffut* *m*, boucan: *m*; (*quarrel*) querelle *f*, dispute *f*; (*scolding*) réprimande *f*, savon* *m*, engueulade: *f*. **to make a ~** faire du raffut* *or* du boucan:; **what a ~!** quel boucan!:; **hold your ~!:** la ferme!:; **to have a ~ with sb** se disputer avec qn, s'engueuler avec qn:; **to give sb a ~** passer un savon à qn*, sonner les cloches à qn*, engueuler qn:; **to get (into) a ~** se faire passer un savon*, se faire laver la tête*, se faire sonner les cloches*.
2 *vt* passer un savon à*, sonner les cloches à*.
3 *vi* se quereller, se disputer, s'engueuler: (*with* avec).
rowan ['raʊən] *n* (*tree*) sorbier *m* des oiseleurs; (*berry*) sorbe *f*.
rowdiness ['raʊdɪnɪs] *n* (*noise*) tapage *m*, chahut *m*; (*fighting*) bagarre* *f*.
rowdy ['raʊdɪ] **1** *adj* (*noisy*) chahuteur; (*rough*) bagarreur*. **to be ~** (*make a din*) chahuter; (*fight*) se bagarrer*. **2** *n* (*) bagarreur* *m*, voyou *m*. **football rowdies** les voyous qui vont aux matchs de football.
rowdyism ['raʊdɪɪzəm] *n* (*V* **rowdy**) chahut *m*; bagarre* *f*, violence *f*.
rower ['rəʊə^r] *n* rameur *m*, -euse *f*; (*in navy*) nageur *m*.
rowing ['rəʊɪŋ] **1** *n* (*for pleasure*) canotage *m*; (*Sport*) aviron *m*; (*in navy*) nage *f*. **2** *cpd*: (*Brit*) **rowing boat** canot *m* (à rames); **rowing club** cercle *m* *or* club *m* d'aviron.
royal ['rɔɪəl] **1** *adj* **(a)** *person, age, family, palace, etiquette* royal; (*fig*) royal, princier, magnifique. (*Brit*) **R~ Academy** Académie Royale; (*Brit*) **R~ Air Force** Royal Air Force *f*, armée *f* de l'air; (*Brit Pol*) **R~ assent** assentiment royal (*accordé à un projet de loi*); **~ blue** bleu roi *inv*; **R~ Canadian Mounted Police** Gendarmerie royale du Canada; (*Brit*) **R~ Commission** Commission *f* extra-parlementaire; (*Brit Mil*) **R~ Engineers** génie *m*; (*Cards*) **~ flush** flush royal; **Your/His R~ Highness** Votre/Son Altesse Royale; **the ~ household** la maison du roi *or* de la reine; (*Brit*) **R~ Navy** marine nationale; (*fig*) **the ~ road to freedom/success** *etc* la voie *or* la route royale de la liberté/du succès *etc*; (*Brit*) **R~ Society** Académie *f* des Sciences; (*fig*) **they gave him a ~ welcome** ils l'ont reçu de façon royale.
(b) *paper* de format grand raisin. **~ octavo** in-huit raisin.
2 *n* (*) personne *f* de la famille royale. **the ~s** la famille royale.
royalism ['rɔɪəlɪzəm] *n* royalisme *m*.
royalist ['rɔɪəlɪst] *adj, n* royaliste (*mf*).
royally ['rɔɪəlɪ] *adv* (*lit, fig*) royalement.
royalty ['rɔɪəltɪ] *n* **(a)** (*position, dignity, rank*) royauté *f*; (*collectively: royal persons*) personnages royaux, (membres *mpl* de) la famille royale. **(b) royalties** (*from book*) droits *mpl* d'auteur; (*from oil well, patent*) royalties *fpl*.
rozzer: ['rɒzə^r] *n* (*Brit*) flic: *m*, poulet* *m*.
rub [rʌb] **1** *n* (*on thing*) frottement *m*; (*on person*) friction *f*; (*with duster etc*) coup *m* de chiffon *or* de torchon. **to give sth a ~** (*furniture, shoes, silver*) donner un coup de chiffon *or* de torchon à qch; (*sore place, one's arms*) frotter qch; (*fig*) **there's the ~!** c'est là la difficulté!, voilà le hic!*; **the ~ is that...** l'ennui *or* le hic*, c'est que... .
2 *cpd*: **rub-a-dub(-dub)** rataplan *m*; **to give a horse a rubdown** bouchonner un cheval; **to give sb a rub-down** faire une friction à qn, frictionner qn; **to give sth a rub-up** frotter *or* astiquer qch.
3 *vt* frotter; (*polish*) astiquer, frotter; (*Art*) *brass, inscription* prendre un frottis de. **~ yourself and you'll soon be dry** frictionne-toi *or* frotte-toi, tu seras bientôt sec; **to ~ one's nose** se frotter le nez; **to ~ one's hands (together)** se frotter les mains; **to ~ sth dry** sécher qch en le frottant; **to ~ a hole in sth** faire un trou dans qch à force de frotter; **to ~ sth through a sieve** passer qch au tamis; **to ~ lotion into the skin** faire pénétrer de la lotion dans la peau; (*fig*) **to ~ shoulders with all sorts of people** coudoyer toutes sortes de gens; *V* **salt.**
4 *vi [thing]* frotter (*against* contre); *[person, cat]* se frotter (*against* contre).
rub along *vi* (*) faire *or* poursuivre son petit bonhomme de chemin. *[two people]* **to rub along (together)** vivre *or* s'accorder tant bien que mal; (*fig*) **he can rub along in French, he knows enough French to rub along with** il sait assez de français pour se tirer d'affaire tant bien que mal *or* pour se débrouiller.
rub away *vt sep mark* faire disparaître (en frottant), effacer. **she rubbed her tears away** elle a essuyé ses larmes (de la main).
rub down 1 *vt sep horse* bouchonner; *person* frictionner (*with* à, avec); *wall, paintwork* (*clean*) frotter, nettoyer du haut en bas; (*sandpaper*) poncer, polir.
2 rub-down *n V* **rub 2.**
rub in *vt sep oil, liniment* faire pénétrer en frottant; (*fig*) *idea* insister sur; *lesson* faire entrer (*to* à). (*fig*) **don't rub it in!*** n'insistez pas lourdement!; **he's always rubbing in how rich he is** il ne vous laisse jamais oublier à quel point il est riche.
rub off 1 *vi [mark]* partir, s'en aller; *[writing]* s'effacer, disparaître. **the blue will rub off on to your hands** tu vas avoir les mains toutes bleues; (*fig*) **I hope some of his politeness will rub off on to his brother*** j'espère qu'il passera un peu de sa politesse à son frère.
2 *vt sep writing on blackboard* effacer; *dirt* enlever en frottant.
rub out 1 *vi [mark, writing]* s'effacer, s'en aller. **that ink won't rub out** cette encre ne s'effacera pas.
2 *vt sep* (*erase*) effacer; (*: kill*) descendre*, liquider*.
rub up 1 *vi* (*fig*) **to rub up against all sorts of people** côtoyer toutes sortes de gens.
2 *vt sep vase, table* frotter, astiquer. (*fig*) **to rub sb up the right way** savoir (comment) s'y prendre avec qn; (*fig*) **to rub sb up the wrong way** prendre qn à rebrousse-poil*; (*: *revise*) **to rub up one's French** dérouiller* son français.
3 rub-up *n V* **rub 2.**
rubber[1] ['rʌbə^r] **1** *n* (*material: U*) caoutchouc *m*; (*Brit: eraser*) gomme *f*; (*: *contraceptive*) préservatif *m*, capote anglaise:. **synthetic ~** caoutchouc synthétique; (*shoes*) **~s** caoutchoucs *mpl*; *V* **foam etc.**
2 *cpd goods, clothes* de *or* en caoutchouc. **rubber band** élastique *m*; **rubber boots** bottes *fpl* de caoutchouc; **rubber-covered** sous caoutchouc; (*US*) **rubberneck:†** (*n*) badaud(e) *m(f)*; (*vi*) baguenauder; **rubber plantation** plantation *f* de hévéas; **rubber ring** (*for sitting on*) rond *m* (pour malade); (*for swimming*) bouée *f* de natation; **rubber solution** dissolution *f*; **rubber stamp** tampon *m*; **rubber-stamp*** (*lit*) tamponner; (*fig*) approuver sans discussion; **rubber tree** arbre *m* à gomme, hévéa *m*; **rubber-tyred** sur pneus.
rubber[2] ['rʌbə^r] *n* (*Cards*) rob *m*, robre *m*. **to play a ~** faire un robre *or* une partie; (*Bridge*) **that's game and ~** c'est la partie.
rubberized ['rʌbəraɪzd] *adj* caoutchouté.
rubbery ['rʌbərɪ] *adj* caoutchouteux.
rubbing ['rʌbɪŋ] *n* (*action*) frottement *m*, frottage *m*; (*Art*)

frottis m reproduction f par frottage, V brass.

rubbish ['rʌbɪʃ] 1 n (a) (*waste material*) détritus *mpl*; (*Brit: household* ~) ordures *fpl*, immondices *fpl*; [*factory*] déchets *mpl*; [*building site*] décombres *mpl*; (*pej: worthless things*) choses *fpl* sans valeur, camelote* *f*, pacotille *f*. **household** ~ ordures ménagères; **garden** ~ détritus de jardin; **this shop sells a lot of** ~ ce magasin ne vend que de la camelote* *or* des saletés*; **it's just** ~ ça ne vaut rien (*V also* 1b).

(b) (*fig: nonsense*) bêtises *fpl*, absurdités *fpl*, stupidités *fpl*. **to talk** ~ débiter des bêtises *or* des absurdités; **he talked a lot of** ~ **about ...** il a raconté des bêtises *or* des absurdités au sujet de ...; **(what a lot of)** ~**!*** quelle blague!*; **this book is** ~ ce livre ne vaut strictement rien; **that's just** ~ ça ne veut rien (dire), ça n'a aucun sens; **it is** ~ **to say that ...** c'est idiot de dire que ... .

2 *cpd*: (*Brit*) **rubbish bin** poubelle *f*, boîte *f* à ordures; **rubbish cart** voiture *f* d'éboueurs; **rubbish chute** (*at dump*) dépotoir *m*; (*in building*) vide-ordures *m inv*; **rubbish collection** ramassage *m* d'ordures; **rubbish dump, rubbish heap** (*public*) décharge publique, dépotoir *m*; (*in garden*) monceau *m* de détritus.

rubbishy ['rʌbɪʃɪ] *adj goods* sans valeur, de pacotille; (*fig*) *ideas* sans valeur. ~ **shoes** chaussures de mauvaise qualité; **this is** ~ **stuff** c'est de la camelote* *or* de la saleté*.

rubble ['rʌbl] *n* [*ruined house, bomb site, demolition site*] décombres *mpl*, (*smaller pieces*) gravats *mpl*; (*in road-building*) blocaille *f*, blocage *m*. **the building was reduced to a heap of** ~ il ne restait du bâtiment qu'un tas de décombres.

rube‡ [ru:b] *n* (*US*) péquenaud‡ *m*.

Rubicon ['ru:bɪkən] *n*: **to cross the** ~ passer *or* franchir le Rubicon.

rubicund ['ru:bɪkənd] *adj complexion* rubicond, rougeaud.

ruble ['ru:bl] *n* (*US*) = **rouble**.

rubric ['ru:brɪk] *n* rubrique *f*.

ruby ['ru:bɪ] 1 *n* rubis *m*; (*colour*) couleur *f* de rubis. 2 *cpd* (*colour*) *wine* (couleur de) rubis *inv*; *lips* vermeil; (*made of rubies*) *necklace, ring* de rubis.

ruck[1] [rʌk] *n* (*Racing*) peloton *m*. (*fig*) **the (common)** ~ les masses *fpl*, la foule, le peuple; (*fig*) **to get out of the** ~ se distinguer du commun des mortels.

ruck[2] [rʌk], **ruckle** ['rʌkl] 1 *n* (*crease*) faux pli, godet *m*. 2 *vi* se froisser, se chiffonner. 3 *vt* froisser, chiffonner.

rucksack ['rʌksæk] *n* sac *m* à dos, sac de camping.

ruckus‡ ['rʌkəs] *n* (*US*) chahut *m*, grabuge* *m*.

ruction* ['rʌkʃən] *n* (*gen pl*) (*rows*) disputes *fpl*, grabuge* *m*; (*riots*) troubles *mpl*, bagarres *fpl*. **there'll be** ~**s if you break that glass** si tu casses ce verre tu vas te faire sonner les cloches* *or* il va y avoir du grabuge*.

rudder ['rʌdə^r] *n* (*Aviat, Naut, fig*) gouvernail *m*. (*Aviat*) **vertical/horizontal** ~ gouvernail de direction/de profondeur.

rudderless ['rʌdəlɪs] *adj* (*lit*) sans gouvernail, à la dérive; (*fig*) à la dérive.

ruddiness ['rʌdɪnɪs] *n* rougeur *f*, teint vif *or* coloré.

ruddy ['rʌdɪ] *adj* (a) *complexion* coloré, rouge de santé, vif; *sky, glow* rougeoyant, rougeâtre. (b) (*: *Brit euph for* **bloody**) fichu*, sacré*. **he's a** ~ **fool** c'est un sacré* *or* fichu* imbécile; **you're a** ~ **nuisance** tu me casses les pieds*, tu m'enquiquines*.

rude [ru:d] *adj* (a) *person, speech, behaviour, reply, gesture* (*impolite*) impoli, mal élevé, (*stronger*) insolent; (*coarse*) grossier; (*improper*) inconvenant, indécent; *story* scabreux; *song* grivois; *gesture* obscène, indécent. ~ **remarks** grossièretés *fpl*; **to be** ~ **to sb** se conduire grossièrement envers qn, être grossier *or* très impoli envers qn; **he's always** ~ c'est un malappris; **would it be** ~ **to ask you your address?** sans indiscrétion peut-on savoir votre adresse?; **it's** ~ **to stare** c'est très mal élevé de dévisager les gens; **there's nothing** ~ **about that picture** ce tableau n'a rien d'inconvenant *or* d'indécent; ~ **word** gros mot.

(b) (*sudden*) *shock* brusque, violent, rude. (*fig*) **to receive a** ~ **awakening** être rappelé brusquement *or* brutalement à la réalité.

(c) (*primitive*) *way of living, peasant* primitif, rude; (*simply made*) *implement* grossier, primitif, rudimentaire.

(d) (*vigorous*) *strength* robuste, vigoureux. **he's in** ~ **health** il a une santé robuste *or* de fer.

rudely ['ru:dlɪ] *adv* (*V* **rude**) impoliment; insolemment; grossièrement; violemment, brusquement. ~**-fashioned object** objet grossièrement fabriqué, objet fabriqué sans art.

rudeness ['ru:dnɪs] *n* (*V* **rude**) impolitesse *f*; insolence *f*; grossièreté *f*; violence *f*, brusquerie *f*; caractère primitif, rudesse *f*.

rudiment ['ru:dɪmənt] *n* (*Anat*) rudiment *m*. (*fig*) ~**s** rudiments *mpl*, éléments *mpl*, notions *fpl* élémentaires.

rudimentary [,ru:dɪ'mentərɪ] *adj* rudimentaire.

rue[1] [ru:] *vt* (*liter*) se repentir de, regretter amèrement.

rue[2] [ru:] *n* (*Bot*) rue *f*.

rueful ['ru:fʊl] *adj look* triste, lugubre; *situation* triste, attristant.

ruefully ['ru:fəlɪ] *adv* d'un air piteux, avec regret.

ruff[1] [rʌf] *n* (a) (*Dress*) fraise *f*; [*bird, animal*] collier *m*, collerette *f*. (b) (*Orn*) (*sandpiper*) combattant *m*; (*pigeon*) pigeon capucin.

ruff[2] [rʌf] (*Cards*) 1 *n* action *f* de couper (avec un atout). 2 *vti* couper (avec un atout).

ruffian ['rʌfɪən] *n* voyou *m*, brute *f*. **you little** ~**!*** petit polisson!

ruffianly ['rʌfɪənlɪ] *adj person* brutal; *behaviour* de voyou, de brute; *looks, appearance* de brigand, de voyou.

ruffle ['rʌfl] 1 *n* (*on wrist*) manchette *f* (*en dentelle etc*); (*on chest*) jabot *m*; (*round neck*) fraise *f*; (*ripple: on water*) ride *f*, ondulation *f*.

2 *vt* (a) (*disturb*) *hair, feathers* ébouriffer; *surface, water* agiter, troubler, rider; *one's clothes* déranger, froisser, chiffonner. **the bird** ~**d (up) its feathers** l'oiseau a hérissé ses plumes.

(b) (*fig*) (*upset*) froisser; (*disturb*) troubler; (*annoy*) contrarier, irriter. **she wasn't at all** ~**d** elle n'a jamais perdu son calme.

rug [rʌg] *n* (a) (*for floor*) petit tapis; (*bedside*) descente *f* de lit, carpette *f*; (*fireside*) carpette. (b) (*woollen cover*) couverture *f*; (*in tartan*) plaid *m*; *V* **travelling**.

rugby ['rʌgbɪ] 1 *n* (*also* ~ **football**) rugby *m*. 2 *cpd*: **rugby league** (le) rugby *m* à treize; **rugby footballer, rugby player** rugbyman *m*, joueur *m* de rugby.

rugged ['rʌgɪd] *adj country, ground, landscape* accidenté; *road* raboteux, rocailleux; *cliff, coast* déchiqueté; *mountains* aux contours déchiquetés; *bark* rugueux; *features* irrégulier, rude; *workmanship, statue* fruste; *character, manners* rude, sans raffinement; *person* bourru, rude; *determination, resistance* acharné, farouche. **covered with** ~ **rocks** hérissé de rochers.

ruggedness ['rʌgɪdnɪs] *n* [*surface*] aspérité *f*, rugosité *f*; [*rock*] anfractuosités *fpl*; [*character*] rudesse *f*; [*features*] irrégularité *f*, rudesse. **the** ~ **of the ground** les accidents *mpl* *or* les aspérités du terrain.

rugger* ['rʌgə^r] *n* (*Brit*) rugby *m*.

Ruhr [rʊə^r] *n* Ruhr *f*.

ruin ['ru:ɪn] 1 *n* (a) (*U*) ruine *f*; (*thing, event, person*) ruine, perte *f*. **the palace was going to** ~ *or* **falling into** ~ le palais tombait en ruine *or* menaçait ruine *or* se délabrait; **he was on the brink of** ~, **stared him in the face** il était au bord de la ruine; **the** ~ **of my hopes** la ruine *or* la faillite de mes espérances; **drink was his** ~ l'alcool a été sa perte; **it will be the** ~ **of him** ça sera sa ruine; **you will be the** ~ **of me** tu seras ma perte *or* ma ruine; *V* **rack**[3].

(b) (*gen pl*) [*building, hopes, beauty etc*] ruine(s) *f(pl)*. (*lit, fig*) **in** ~**s** en ruine; **the castle is now a** ~ le château est maintenant une ruine.

2 *vt building, reputation, hopes, health, person* ruiner; *clothes* abîmer; *event, enjoyment* gâter.

ruination [,ru:ɪ'neɪʃən] *n* ruine *f*, perte *f*. **to be the** ~ **of** ruiner.

ruined ['ru:ɪnd] *adj building* en ruine; *person* ruiné.

ruinous ['ru:ɪnəs] *adj* ruineux. **that trip proved** ~ **for his firm** ce voyage a entraîné la ruine de *or* a ruiné sa compagnie; **the price of butter is** ~* le prix du beurre est exorbitant *or* ruineux.

ruinously ['ru:ɪnəslɪ] *adv*: ~ **expensive** ruineux.

rule [ru:l] 1 *n* (a) (*guiding principle*) règle *f*; (*regulation*) règlement *m*; (*Jur*) décision *f*, ordonnance *f*; (*Gram, Rel*) règle. **the** ~**s of the game** la règle du jeu; **it's against the** ~**s** c'est contraire à la règle *or* au règlement; **running is against the** ~**s, it's against the** ~**s to run** il est contraire à la règle *or* il n'est pas permis de courir; (*lit, fig*) **to play by the** ~**s** jouer suivant *or* selon les règles; ~**s and regulations** statuts *mpl*; **standing** ~ règlement; **it's a** ~ **that ...** il est de règle que ... + *subj*; ~ **of the road** (*Aut*) règle générale de la circulation; (*Naut*) règles générales du trafic maritime; **to do sth by** ~ faire qch selon les règles; (*Math*) **the** ~ **of three** la règle de trois; **by** ~ **of thumb** empiriquement, d'une façon empirique; **golden** ~ règle d'or; *V* **exception, work** *etc*.

(b) (*custom*) coutume *f*, habitude *f*. **ties are the** ~ **in this hotel** les cravates sont de règle dans cet hôtel; **bad weather is the** ~ **in winter** le mauvais temps est habituel *or* normal en hiver; **he makes it a** ~ **to get up early** il a pour règle de se lever tôt; **to make tidiness a** ~ faire de l'ordre une règle; **as a** ~ en règle générale, normalement, en principe.

(c) (*U: authority*) autorité *f*, empire *m*. **under British** ~ sous l'autorité britannique; **under a tyrant's** ~ sous l'empire *or* la domination d'un tyran; (*Pol etc*) **majority** ~, **the** ~ **of the majority** le gouvernement par la majorité; **the** ~ **of law** l'autorité de la loi; *V* **home**.

(d) (*for measuring*) règle *f* (graduée). **a foot** ~ une règle d'un pied; **folding** ~ mètre pliant; *V* **slide**.

(e) (*Rel*) règle *f*.

2 *cpd*: **the rule book** le règlement; (*fig*) **to throw the rule book at sb‡** remettre qn à sa place, rembarrer qn*.

3 *vt* (a) *country* gouverner; (*fig*) *passions, emotion* maîtriser; *person* dominer, mener. (*fig*) **to** ~ **the roost** faire la loi; **he** ~**d the company for 30 years** il a dirigé la compagnie *or* il a été à la tête de la compagnie pendant 30 ans; **to be** ~**d by jealousy** être mené *or* dominé par la jalousie; **to** ~ **one's passions** maîtriser ses passions; **he is** ~**d by his wife** il est mené par sa femme; **if you would only be** ~**d by what I say ...** si seulement tu voulais consentir à écouter mes conseils ...; **I won't be** ~**d by what he wants** je ne veux pas me plier à ses volontés.

(b) (*Jur, Sport etc: give decision*) décider, déclarer (*that* que). (*Jur*) **the judge** ~**d the defence out of order** le juge a déclaré non recevables les paroles de l'avocat pour la défense; **the judge** ~**d that the child should go to school** le juge a décidé que l'enfant irait à l'école.

(c) (*draw lines on*) *paper* régler; *line* tirer à la règle. ~**d paper** papier réglé.

4 *vi* (a) (*reign*) régner (*over* sur).

(b) **the prices ruling in Paris** les cours (pratiqués) à Paris.

(c) (*Jur*) statuer (*against* contre, *in favour of* en faveur de, *on* sur).

rule off *vt* (*Comm*) *account* clore, arrêter. **to rule off a column of figures** tirer une ligne sous une colonne de chiffres.

rule out *vt sep word, sentence* barrer, rayer, biffer; (*fig*) *possibility, suggestion, date, person* exclure, écarter. **the age limit rules him out** il est exclu du fait de la limite d'âge; **murder can't be ruled out** il est impossible d'écarter *or* d'exclure l'hypothèse d'un meurtre.

ruler ['ru:lə^r] *n* (a) (*sovereign*) souverain(e) *m(f)*; (*political leader*) chef *m* (d'État). **the country's** ~**s** les dirigeants *mpl* du pays. (b) (*for measuring*) règle *f*.

ruling ['ru:lɪŋ] 1 *adj principle* souverain; *factor, passion*

price pratiqué, actuel. **the ~ class** la classe dirigeante; (*Pol*) **the ~ party** le parti au pouvoir.

2 *n* (*Admin, Jur*) décision *f*, jugement *m*; *[judge]* décision. **to get/give a ~** obtenir/rendre un jugement.

rum[1] [rʌm] *n* rhum *m*. **~ toddy** grog *m*.

rum[2]* [rʌm] *adj* (*Brit: odd*) bizarre, drôle; *idea* biscornu*.

Rumania [ruːˈmeɪnɪə] *n* = **Romania.**

Rumanian [ruːˈmeɪnɪən] = **Romanian.**

rumba [ˈrʌmbə] *n* rumba *f*.

rumble [ˈrʌmbl] **1** *n [thunder, cannon]* grondement *m*; *[train, lorry]* roulement *m*, grondement; *[pipe, stomach]* gargouillement *m*, borborygme *m*.

2 *vi [thunder, cannon]* gronder; *[stomach, pipes]* gargouiller. *[vehicle]* **to ~ past** passer avec fracas.

3 *vt* **(a)** (*also* **~ out**) *comments, remarks* dire en grondant, grommeler.

(b) (*‡: see through*) *swindle* flairer, subodorer*; *trick* piger‡; *person* voir venir. **I soon ~d him *or* his game *or* what he was up to** j'ai tout de suite pigé sa combine!‡

rumbling [ˈrʌmblɪŋ] *n [thunder]* grondement *m*; *[vehicle]* roulement *m*, grondement; *[stomach, pipe]* gargouillement *m*. **tummy ~s*** gargouillis *mpl*, borborygmes *mpl*.

rumbustious [rʌmˈbʌstʃəs] *adj* bruyant, exubérant.

ruminant [ˈruːmɪnənt] *adj, n* ruminant (*m*).

ruminate [ˈruːmɪneɪt] **1** *vi* (*lit, fig*) ruminer. (*fig*) **to ~ over *or* about *or* on sth** ruminer qch, retourner qch dans sa tête. **2** *vt* ruminer.

rumination [ˌruːmɪˈneɪʃən] *n* (*lit, fig*) rumination *f*.

ruminative [ˈruːmɪnətɪv] *adj* (*fig*) pensif, méditatif, réfléchi.

ruminatively [ˈruːmɪnətɪvlɪ] *adv* pensivement.

rummage [ˈrʌmɪdʒ] **1** *n* **(a)** (*action*) **to have a good ~ round** bien fouiller partout.

(b) (*jumble*) vieilleries *fpl*, objets divers.

2 *cpd*: **rummage sale** vente *f* de charité (*de bric-à-brac*).

3 *vi* (*also* **~ about, ~ around**) farfouiller*, fouiller (*among, in* dans, *for* pour trouver).

rummy[1]‡ [ˈrʌmɪ] *adj* = **rum**[2].

rummy[2] [ˈrʌmɪ] *n* (*Cards*) rami *m*.

rumour, (*US*) **rumor** [ˈruːməʳ] **1** *n* rumeur *f*, bruit *m* (qui court). **~ has it that ...** on dit que ..., le bruit court que ...; **there is a ~ of war** le bruit court *or* on dit qu'il va y avoir la guerre.

2 *vt*: **it is ~ed that ...** on dit que ..., le bruit court que ...; **he is ~ed to be in London** il serait à Londres, le bruit court qu'il est à Londres; **he is ~ed to be rich** on le dit riche.

rump [rʌmp] **1** *n [animal]* croupe *f*; *[fowl]* croupion *m*; (*Culin*) culotte *f* (de bœuf); (*) *[person]* derrière *m*, postérieur* *m*. **2** *cpd*: (*Brit Hist*) **the Rump Parliament** le Parlement Croupion; **rumpsteak** romsteck *m or* rumsteck *m*.

rumple [ˈrʌmpl] *vt clothes* chiffonner, froisser, friper; *paper* froisser, chiffonner; *hair* ébouriffer.

rumpus* [ˈrʌmpəs] **1** *n chahut m*; (*noise*) tapage *m*, boucan‡ *m*; (*quarrel*) prise *f* de bec*. **to make a ~** faire du chahut *or* du boucan; **to have a ~ with sb** se chamailler* avec qn, avoir une prise de bec avec qn*, s'engueuler avec qn‡.

2 *cpd*: (*esp US*) **rumpus room** salle *f* de jeux.

run [rʌn] (*vb: pret* **ran**, *ptp* **run**) **1** *n* **(a)** (*act of running*) action *f* de courir, course *f*. **to go for a 2-km ~** faire 2 km de course à pied; **at a ~** au pas de course, en courant; **to break into a ~** se mettre à courir, prendre le pas de course; (*Baseball, Cricket*) **he made 3 ~s** il a marqué 3 points; **to make a ~ for it** prendre la fuite, se sauver, filer*; **to have the ~ of a place** avoir un endroit à son entière disposition; **to give sb the ~ of a place** mettre un endroit à l'entière disposition de qn; **you have the entire ~ of my garden** mon jardin est à votre entière disposition, vous pouvez aller partout *or* où bon vous semble dans mon jardin; **a criminal on the ~ (from the police)** un criminel recherché par la police; **he is still on the ~** il court encore; **he was on the ~ for several months** il a réussi à rester en liberté plusieurs mois, il n'a été repris qu'au bout de plusieurs mois; **to have the enemy on the ~** mettre l'ennemi en fuite; **to keep the enemy on the ~** harceler l'ennemi; **she has so much to do she's always on the ~*** elle a tant à faire qu'elle est tout le temps à courir *or* en train de courir; (*fig*) **we've given him a good ~ for his money, he has had a good ~ for his money** nous ne nous sommes pas avoués vaincus d'avance; (*on sb's retirement, death etc*) **he's had a good ~** il a bien profité de l'existence; **to have the ~s‡** (*diarrhoea*) avoir la courante‡.

(b) (*outing*) tour *m*, promenade *f*, excursion *f*. **to go for a ~ in the car** faire un tour *or* une promenade en voiture; **they went for a ~ in the country** ils ont fait un tour *or* une excursion *or* une promenade à la campagne; **we had a pleasant ~ down** le voyage a été agréable; **to take a ~ up to London** faire un tour *or* une virée* à Londres, pousser une pointe jusqu'à Londres; **I'll give you a ~ up to town** je vais vous conduire *or* vous emmener en ville; *V* **trial.**

(c) (*distance travelled*) *[bus, tram, boat, plane]* parcours *m*; *[car]* trajet *m*. **it's a 30-minute ~** il y a une demi-heure de trajet; **it's a 30-minute bus ~** il y a une demi-heure d'autobus; **it's a short car ~** le trajet n'est pas long en voiture, on n'en a pas pour longtemps en voiture; **the boat no longer does that ~** le bateau ne fait plus cette traversée, ce service n'existe plus; **on the outward ~ the ferry ...** pendant le parcours aller le ferry ...; **the ferries on the Dover-Calais ~** les ferrys sur le parcours Douvres-Calais *or* qui assurent le service Douvres-Calais; **the ships on the China ~** les paquebots qui font la Chine.

(d) (*series*) succession *f*, série *f*, suite *f*; (*Cards*) séquence *f*. (*Roulette*) **a ~ on the red** une série à la rouge; **the ~ of the cards** le hasard du jeu; **that fashion has had a long ~** cette mode a duré longtemps; (*Theat*) **when the London ~ was over** quand la saison à Londres *or* la série de représentations à Londres s'est terminée; (*Theat*) **the play had a long ~** la pièce a tenu longtemps l'affiche; **there was no difference in the long ~** en fin de compte il n'y a pas eu de différence; **things will sort themselves out in the long ~** les choses s'arrangeront à la longue *or* avec le temps; **to have a ~ of luck** être en veine*; **a ~ of bad luck** une période de malchance *or* de déveine*; **a ~ of misfortunes** une suite de malheurs, une série noire*.

(e) (*rush, great demand*) ruée *f*. (*St Ex*) **a ~ on shares** une très forte demande d'actions; (*Fin*) **there has been a ~ on the pound sterling** il y a eu une ruée sur la livre (sterling); **there was a ~ on the banks** les guichets (des banques) ont été assiégés; (*Comm*) **there has been a ~ on sugar** on s'est rué sur le sucre.

(f) *[tide]* poussée *f*, flux *m*; (*fig: trend*) *[market]* tendance *f*; *[events]* direction *f*, tendance; *[opinion]* tendance, courant *m*. **the (common) ~ of mankind** le commun des mortels; **the ordinary ~ of things** la routine, le train-train habituel; **outside the usual ~ of things** inhabituel, qui sort de l'ordinaire, hors du commun.

(g) (*track for sledging, skiing etc*) piste *f*, descente *f*; (*animal enclosure*) enclos *m*. **ski ~** piste de ski; *V* **chicken.**

(h) (*in stocking*) échelle *f*, maille filée.

(i) (*Mus*) roulade *f*.

(j) (*Typ*) tirage *m*. **a ~ of 5,000 copies** un tirage de 5.000 exemplaires.

2 *cpd*: **runabout** (*car*) petite voiture; (*boat*) runabout *m*; (*Rail etc*) **runabout ticket** billet *m* circulaire; **he gave me the run-around‡** il est resté très évasif, il m'a fait des réponses de Normand; **runaway** *V* **runaway**; **rundown** *V* **rundown**; (*Sport*) **run-off** finale *f* (d'une course); **run-of-the-mill** médiocre, banal, ordinaire; **run-on line** enjambement *m*; **runproof** indémaillable; **run-through** essai *m*, répétition *f*; **run-up** période *f* préparatoire (*to* à); **runway** (*Aviat*) piste *f* (d'envol *or* d'atterrissage); (*Tech*) chemin *m* de roulement, piste, rampe *f*.

3 *vi* **(a)** (*gen*) courir; (*hurry*) courir, se précipiter. **to ~ down/in/off** *etc* descendre/entrer/partir *etc* en courant; **she came ~ning out** elle est sortie en courant; **to ~ down a slope** descendre une pente en courant; **he is always ~ning about the streets** il court toujours dans les rues; **don't ~ across the road** ne traverse pas la rue en courant; **to ~ for all one is worth, to ~ like hell*** courir à toutes jambes; **to ~ for the bus** courir pour attraper l'autobus; **she ran to meet him** elle a couru à sa rencontre, elle s'est précipitée au-devant de lui; **she ran to help him** elle a couru l'aider, elle a couru *or* s'est précipitée *or* a volé à son secours; **she ran over to her neighbour's** elle a couru *or* s'est précipitée chez sa voisine; **he used to ~ for his school** il a disputé des épreuves de course *or* il a couru dans les compétitions d'athlétisme pour son lycée; **the car ran into a tree** la voiture a heurté un arbre (*V also* **run into**).

(b) (*flee*) fuir, se sauver. **to ~ for one's life** se sauver à toutes jambes; **~ for your lives!** sauve-qui-peut!; **~ for it!** sauvez-vous!; *[fox, criminal]* **to ~ to earth** se terrer; **go on then, ~ to mummy!** c'est ça, va (te réfugier) dans les jupes de ta mère!; *V* **cut.**

(c) (*fig*) **the news ran like wildfire through the crowd** la nouvelle s'est répandue comme une traînée de poudre dans la foule; **a rumour ran through the school** un bruit a couru dans l'école; **the order ran down the column** l'ordre a couru *or* a été transmis d'un bout de la colonne à l'autre; **laughter ran round the room** le rire a gagné toute la salle; **a ripple of fear ran through the town** la peur a gagné toute la ville; **how does the last sentence ~?** comment la dernière phrase est-elle rédigée?, rappelez-moi la dernière phrase; **so the story ~s** c'est ainsi que l'histoire est racontée; (*fig: Pol etc*) **to ~ for President, to ~ for the Presidency** être candidat à la présidence; **he isn't ~ning this time** il n'est pas candidat cette fois-ci; **he won't ~ again** il ne se représentera plus.

(d) (*become etc*) **to ~ dry** *[river]* se tarir, être à sec; *[resources etc]* s'épuiser; **my pen's ~ dry** je n'ai plus d'encre; **he ran dry of ideas** il s'est trouvé à court d'idées; **supplies are ~ning short *or* low** les provisions s'épuisent *or* commencent à manquer *or* tirent à leur fin; **to ~ short of sth** se trouver à court de qch, venir à manquer de qch; **to ~ riot** *[people, imagination]* être déchaîné; *[vegetation]* pousser follement; **to ~ to fat** engraisser, prendre de la graisse; **he ~s to sentiment in some of his books** dans quelques-uns de ses livres il a tendance à être sentimental *or* il donne dans le sentimental (*pej*); **to ~ wild** *[person]* faire le fou (*f* la folle)*; *[children]* être déchaîné; *[animals]* courir en liberté; *[plants, garden]* retourner à l'état sauvage; *V* **seed.**

(e) (*move*) filer; *[drawer, curtains]* glisser. **the rope ran through his fingers** la corde lui a filé entre les doigts; (*fig*) **money simply ~s through his fingers** l'argent lui fond entre les mains *or* lui file entre les doigts; **the bed ~s on rollers** le lit a des roulettes; **the drawer ~s smoothly** le tiroir glisse facilement; **this zip doesn't ~ well** cette fermeture éclair ne joue pas bien *or* accroche.

(f) (*flow*) couler; (*drip*) dégoutter; *[river, tears, tap]* couler; *[pen]* fuir, couler; *[sore, abscess]* suppurer; *[butter]* fondre; *[cheese]* couler; *[colour, dye]* s'étaler, se mélanger (à une couleur voisine), baver; (*in washing*) déteindre; *[ink]* baver, faire des bavures. **my ice cream is ~ning** ma glace fond *or* coule; **the river ~s for 30 km** la rivière a 30 km de long; **the river ~s between wooded banks** la rivière coule entre des berges boisées; **rivers ~ into the sea** les fleuves se jettent dans la mer; **the street ~s into the square** la rue débouche dans la place; **to ~ high** *[river]* être haut, couler à pleins bords; *[sea]* être gros (*f* grosse); (*fig*) **feelings were ~ning high** les passions étaient exacerbées; **prices are ~ning high** les prix sont très hauts en ce moment; **a heavy sea was ~ning** la mer était très forte; **where the tide is ~ning strongly** là où la marée monte (*or* descend) très vite; **to leave a tap ~ning** laisser un robinet ouvert; **your bath is ~ning now** votre bain est en train de couler; **the milk ran all over the floor** le lait s'est répandu sur le sol; **the floor was ~ning with water** le plancher était inondé (d'eau); **the walls were ~ning with moisture** les murs ruisselaient d'humidité; **the streets were ~ning with blood** les rues ruisselaient de sang; **his face was ~ning with sweat** sa figure ruisselait de sueur; **tears ran down her cheeks** les larmes coulaient le long de ses joues; **his eyes are ~ning** il a les yeux qui coulent *or* pleurent; **his nose was ~ning** il avait le nez qui coulait; (*fig*) **his blood ran cold** son sang s'est glacé *or* s'est figé dans ses veines.

(g) (*extend, continue*) *[play]* tenir l'affiche, se jouer; *[film]* passer; *[contract]* valoir, être valide; (*Fin*) *[interest]* courir. **the play has been ~ning for a year** la pièce tient l'affiche *or* se joue depuis un an; **this contract has 10 months to ~** ce contrat expire dans 10 mois *or* vaut (encore) pour 10 mois; (*Jur*) **the two sentences to ~ concurrently/consecutively** avec/sans confusion des deux peines; (*Rad, TV*) **the programme ran for an extra 10 minutes** le programme a duré 10 minutes de plus que prévu; **the expenditure ~s into thousands of pounds** les dépenses s'élèvent *or* se chiffrent à des milliers de livres; **the book has ~ into 3 éditions** on a publié 3 éditions de ce livre; **the poem ~s (in)to several hundred lines** le poème comprend plusieurs centaines de vers; **I can't ~ to a new car** je ne peux pas m'offrir *or* me payer* une nouvelle voiture; **the funds won't ~ to a party at the end of term** les fonds ne permettent pas d'organiser une soirée à la fin du trimestre.

(h) (*Naut*) **to ~ before the wind** courir vent arrière; **to ~ ashore** *or* **aground** s'échouer, se jeter à la côte; **to ~ on the rocks** donner *or* se jeter sur les rochers; **to ~ into port** entrer au port; **to ~ foul of another ship** entrer en collision avec *or* aborder un autre navire; (*fig*) **to ~ foul of sb** se disputer avec qn, indisposer qn contre soi.

(i) *[bus, train, coach, ferryboat]* faire le service. **this train ~s between London and Manchester** ce train fait le service Londres-Manchester *or* entre Londres et Manchester; **the buses ~ once an hour** les autobus passent toutes les heures; **the buses aren't ~ning today** il n'y a pas d'autobus *or* les autobus sont supprimés aujourd'hui; **that train doesn't ~ on Sundays** ce train est supprimé le dimanche; **there are no trains ~ning on Christmas Day** le service des trains est suspendu le jour de Noël; **there are no trains ~ning to Birmingham** il n'y a pas de trains en direction de Birmingham.

(j) (*function*) *[machine]* marcher, fonctionner; *[factory]* travailler, marcher; *[wheel]* tourner. **the car is ~ning smoothly** la voiture marche bien; **you mustn't leave the engine ~ning** il ne faut pas laisser tourner le moteur; **this car ~s on diesel** cette voiture marche au gas-oil; **the radio ~s off the mains/off batteries** cette radio marche sur le secteur/sur piles; (*fig*) **things are ~ning smoothly/badly for them** tout va *or* marche bien/mal pour eux.

(k) (*pass*) *[road, river etc]* passer (*through* à travers); *[mountain range]* s'étendre. **the road ~s past our house** la route passe devant notre maison; **the road ~s right into town** la route débouche en plein centre de la ville; **the main road ~s north and south** la route principale va du nord au sud; **he has a scar ~ning across his chest** il a une cicatrice en travers de la poitrine; **a wall ~s round the garden** un mur entoure le jardin; **the river ~s through the valley** la rivière traverse la vallée; (*fig*) **this theme ~s through the whole history of art** ce thème se retrouve *or* est présent dans toute l'histoire de l'art; **asthma ~s in the family** l'asthme est héréditaire dans la famille; **it ~s in the family** ça tient *or* c'est de famille; **that tune is ~ning through my head** cet air me trotte* par la tête; **the idea ran through my head that ...** il m'est venu à l'esprit *or* à l'idée que ...; **the conversation ran on that very subject** la conversation a roulé précisément sur ce sujet; **my thoughts ran on Jenny** je pensais (toujours) à Jenny.

(l) *[stockings]* filer; *[knitting]* se démailler.

4 *vt* **(a)** (*gen*) courir. **he ~s 3 km every day** il fait 3 km de course à pied tous les jours; **he ran 2 km non-stop** il a couru pendant 2 km sans s'arrêter; **he ran the distance in under half an hour** il a couvert la distance en moins d'une demi-heure; **to ~ the 100 metres** courir le 100 mètres; **to ~ a race** courir dans une épreuve, participer à une épreuve de course; **you ran a good race** vous avez fait une excellente course; **the first race will be ~ at 2 o'clock** la première épreuve se courra à 2 heures; **this horse will ~ the Grand Prix** ce cheval va courir (dans) le Grand Prix; **to ~ errands** *or* **messages** faire des commissions *or* des courses; *[child, dog]* **to ~ the streets** traîner dans les rues; **to ~ a blockade** forcer un blocus; **they ran the rapids** ils ont franchi les rapides; (*fig*) **to ~ sb close** serrer qn de près; **you're ~ning things a bit close!*** *or* **fine!*** ça va être juste!, tu calcules un peu juste!; **to let events ~ their course** laisser les événements suivre leur cours; **the disease ran its course** la maladie a suivi son cours normal *or* son évolution normale; **to ~ risks** courir des risques; **you're ~ning the risk of being arrested** *or* **of arrest** vous risquez de vous faire arrêter; **to ~ a temperature** *or* **a fever** faire de la température, avoir de la fièvre; **he was ~ning a high temperature** il avait une forte fièvre; **she ran the car into a tree** elle a percuté un arbre, elle est rentrée* dans un arbre (avec sa voiture); *V* **gauntlet.**

(b) (*chase, hunt*) *fox, deer* chasser; (*make run*) *person, animal* faire courir; (*Sport*) *horse* faire courir, engager; (*Pol*) *candidate* poser *or* appuyer la candidature de. **the party is ~ning 100 candidates this year** le parti présente 100 candidats (aux élections) cette année; (*fig*) **we ran him to earth in the library** nous avons fini par le trouver dans la bibliothèque; **he ran the quotation to earth in 'Hamlet'** il a fini par dénicher la citation dans 'Hamlet'; **to ~ a horse in the Derby** engager *or* faire courir un cheval dans le Derby; **the sheriff ran him out of town** le shérif l'a chassé de la ville; **they ran him out of the house** ils l'ont saisi et l'ont chassé de la maison; **to ~ sb off his feet*** fatiguer *or* éreinter qn; **she is absolutely ~ off her feet*** elle est débordée, elle n'en peut plus, elle ne sait plus où donner de la tête; (*fig*) **that will ~ him into trouble** ça lui créera des ennuis; **that will ~ you into a lot of expense** ça va vous causer de grandes dépenses; **to ~ sb into debt** forcer qn à s'endetter.

(c) (*transport*) *person* conduire (en voiture *or* en bateau); *thing* transporter (en voiture *or* en bateau); (*smuggle*) *guns, whisky* passer en contrebande, faire la contrebande de. **he ran her home** il l'a ramenée chez elle (en voiture); **to ~ sb into town** conduire qn en ville; **I'll ~ your luggage to the station** j'emporterai vos bagages à la gare en voiture; **he was ~ning guns to the island** il faisait passer *or* passait des fusils en contrebande dans l'île.

(d) (*operate etc*) *machine* faire marcher, faire aller, faire fonctionner. **to ~ a radio off the mains** faire marcher une radio sur le secteur; **to ~ a machine by compressed air** actionner une machine par air comprimé, faire marcher une machine à l'air comprimé; **to ~ an engine on gas** faire fonctionner un moteur au gaz; **to ~ a lorry on diesel** faire marcher un camion au gas-oil; **I can't afford to ~ a car** je ne peux pas me permettre d'avoir une voiture; **he ~s a Rolls** il a une Rolls; **this car is very cheap to ~** cette voiture est très économique; **to ~ the car into/out of the garage** rentrer la voiture au/sortir la voiture du garage; **to ~ a boat ashore** mettre un bateau à la côte; *V* **ground.**

(e) (*organize, manage*) *business, company, organization, school* diriger, administrer; *shop, mine* diriger, faire marcher; *hotel, club* tenir, diriger; *newspaper* éditer, gérer, administrer; *competition* organiser; *public transport* organiser (le service de). **they ~ trains to London every hour** il y a un train pour Londres toutes les heures; **the company ~s extra buses at rush hours** la compagnie met en service des autobus supplémentaires aux heures de pointe; **the school is ~ning courses for foreign students** le collège organise des cours pour les étudiants étrangers; **he is ~ning the courses for them** il leur fait des cours; **to ~ a house** tenir une maison; **a house which is easy to ~** une maison facile à tenir *or* entretenir; **who will ~ your house now?** qui va tenir votre maison *or* votre ménage maintenant?; **I want to ~ my own life** je veux être maître de ma vie *or* de mes décisions; **she's the one who really ~s everything** en réalité c'est elle qui dirige tout *or* fait tout marcher; (*fig*) **I'm ~ning this show!*** c'est moi qui fais marcher la boutique! *or* la baraque!*; (*fig*) **he ~s the whole show*** c'est lui qui fait la loi.

(f) (*put, move casually or quickly*) **to ~ one's hand over sth** passer *or* promener la main sur qch; **to ~ one's fingers over the piano keys** faire glisser ses doigts sur les touches *or* sur le clavier; **to ~ one's finger down a list** suivre une liste du doigt; **to ~ one's fingers through one's hair** se passer la main dans les cheveux; **to ~ a comb through one's hair** se passer un peigne dans les cheveux, se donner un coup de peigne; **to ~ one's eye over a page** jeter un coup d'œil sur une page; **he ran the vacuum cleaner over the carpet** il a passé rapidement le tapis à l'aspirateur; **she ran her pencil through the word** elle a barré le mot d'un coup de crayon; **she ran a line of stitches along the hem** elle a fait une série de points le long de l'ourlet; **to ~ a rope through a ring** enfiler *or* faire passer une corde dans un anneau; **to ~ a piece of elastic through the waist of a dress** faire passer un élastique dans la ceinture d'une robe; **to ~ a rope round a tree** passer une corde autour d'un arbre; **to ~ a fence round a garden** entourer un jardin d'une barrière; **to ~ a pipe into a room** faire passer un tuyau *or* amener un tuyau dans une pièce.

(g) (*issue*) (*Press*) publier, imprimer, faire paraître; (*Cine*) présenter, donner; (*Comm*) vendre, mettre en vente. **the paper ran a series of articles on the housing situation** le journal a publié *or* fait paraître une série d'articles sur la crise du logement; **the papers ran the story on the front page** les journaux ont imprimé *or* publié l'article en première page; **the supermarket is ~ning a new line in soap powder** le supermarché est en train de lancer une nouvelle lessive.

(h) (*cause to flow*) faire couler. **to ~ water into a bath** faire couler de l'eau dans une baignoire; **I'll ~ you a bath** je vais te faire couler un bain; **he ~s his words together** il mange ses mots.

run about 1 *vi* courir çà et là. **the children were running about all over the house** les enfants couraient partout dans la maison; (*fig*) **she has been running about with him for several months*** elle sort avec lui depuis plusieurs mois.

2 runabout *n, adj V* **run 2.**

run across 1 *vi* traverser en courant.

2 *vt fus* (*meet*) *person* rencontrer par hasard, tomber sur*; (*find*) *object* trouver par hasard; *quotation, reference* trouver *or* rencontrer par hasard.

run after *vt fus* courir après. (*fig*) **she runs after everything in trousers*** elle est très coureuse; (*fig*) **I'm not going to spend my days running after you!** je ne suis pas ton valet de chambre!* *or* ta bonne!*

run along *vi* courir; (*go away*) s'en aller. **run along!** sauvez-vous!, filez!*

run around 1 *vi* = **run about 1.**

2 run-around *n V* **run 2.**

run at *vt fus* (*attack*) se jeter *or* se précipiter sur.

run away 1 *vi* **(a)** partir en courant; (*flee*) *[person]* se sauver, s'enfuir; (*abscond*) décamper; *[horse]* s'emballer. **to run away from home** s'enfuir (de chez soi), faire une fugue; **don't run away, I need your advice** ne te sauve pas, j'ai besoin d'un conseil; **run away and play!** va jouer (et fiche-moi la paix*)!; (*elope*) **to run away with sb** s'enfuir avec qn; **she ran away with**

another man elle est partie *or* elle s'est enfuie avec un autre homme; (*steal*) **he ran away with the funds** il s'est sauvé* *or* enfui avec les fonds; (*fig*) **don't run away with the idea that ...** n'allez pas vous mettre dans la tête que ...; (*fig*) **he lets his temper run away with him** il ne sait pas se contrôler *or* se dominer.

(b) *[water]* s'écouler. **he let the bath water run away** il a laissé la baignoire se vider.

2 *vt sep water* laisser s'écouler.

3 **runaway** *n, adj V* **runaway.**

run away with *vt fus* (*use up*) *funds, money, resources* épuiser; (*Sport etc: win easily*) *race* gagner dans un fauteuil*; *prize* gagner haut la main; *V also* **run away 1a.**

run back 1 *vi* revenir *or* retourner *or* rentrer en courant.

2 *vt sep* **(a)** *person* ramener (en voiture).

(b) (*rewind*) *tape, film* rembobiner.

run down 1 *vi* **(a)** *[person]* descendre en courant.

(b) *[watch etc]* s'arrêter (faute d'être remonté); *[battery]* se décharger.

2 *vt sep* **(a)** (*Aut*) (*knock over*) renverser; (*run over*) écraser.

(b) (*Naut*) *ship* heurter *or* aborder par l'avant *or* par l'étrave; (*in battle*) éperonner.

(c) (*limit, reduce*) *production* restreindre de plus en plus; *factory* restreindre la production de; *shop* réduire peu à peu l'ampleur de. (*Med*) **to be run down** être fatigué *or* surmené; **I feel a little run down** je me sens à plat*, je suis mal fichu*.

(d) (*: *disparage*) *person* décrier, dénigrer, déblatérer* contre; *thing* éreinter, démolir*; *action* critiquer, dénigrer.

(e) (*pursue and capture*) *criminal* découvrir la cachette de; *stag etc* mettre aux abois.

3 **rundown** *n V* **rundown.**

run in 1 *vi* entrer en courant; (*: *call*) passer. **I'll run in and see you tomorrow*** je passerai vous voir demain, je ferai un saut* chez vous demain.

2 *vt sep* **(a)** *car* roder. (*Aut*) **'running in, please pass'** 'en rodage'.

(b) (*: *arrest*) emmener au poste, fourrer au bloc‡ *or* au trou‡.

run into *vt fus* (*meet*) rencontrer par hasard, tomber sur*. (*fig*) **to run into difficulties** *or* **trouble** se heurter à des difficultés; **to run into danger** se trouver exposé à un danger; **to run into debt** s'endetter; **we've run into a problem** nous nous trouvons devant un problème.

run off 1 *vi* = **run away 1.**

2 *vt sep* **(a)** = **run away 2.**

(b) *poem, letter* écrire *or* rédiger en vitesse; (*Typ*) tirer. **to run off an article** écrire un article au fil de la plume; **to run off 600 copies** tirer 600 exemplaires.

(c) (*Sport*) **to run off the heats** faire (se) disputer les éliminatoires.

3 **run-off** *n V* **run 2.**

run on 1 *vi* **(a)** continuer de courir. (* *fig: in talking etc*) parler sans arrêt, baratiner‡. **he does run on so** c'est un vrai moulin à paroles; **she ran on at great length about her new house** elle n'arrêtait pas *or* elle n'en finissait pas de parler de sa nouvelle maison; **it ran on for 4 hours** ça a duré 4 bonnes heures.

(b) *[letters, words]* ne pas être séparés, être liés; *[line of writing]* suivre sans alinéa; *[verse]* enjamber; *[time]* passer, s'écouler; *[disease etc]* suivre son cours.

2 *vt sep letters, words* faire suivre sans laisser d'espace.

3 **run-on** *adj V* **run 2.**

run out 1 *vi* **(a)** *[person]* sortir en courant; *[rope, chain]* se dérouler; *[liquid]* couler. **the pier runs out into the sea** la jetée s'avance dans la mer.

(b) (*come to an end*) *[lease, contract]* expirer; *[supplies]* s'épuiser, venir à manquer; *[period of time]* s'écouler, tirer à sa fin. **my patience is running out** je suis à bout de patience; **when the money runs out** quand il n'y a plus d'argent, quand l'argent est épuisé.

2 *vt sep rope, chain* laisser filer.

run out of *vt fus supplies, money, patience* manquer de, être à bout de; *time* manquer de.

run over 1 *vi* **(a)** (*overflow*) *[liquid, container]* déborder; (*Rad, TV etc*) **the play ran over by 10 minutes** la pièce a duré 10 minutes de plus que prévu; (*Rad, TV etc*) **we're running over** nous avons pris du retard.

(b) (*go briefly*) passer, faire un saut*. **she ran over to her neighbour's** elle a fait un saut* (jusque) chez sa voisine, elle est passée chez sa voisine.

2 *vt fus* **(a)** (*recapitulate*) *story, part in play* repasser, revoir. **I'll run over your part with you** je vous ferai répéter *or* repasser *or* revoir votre rôle; **let's just run over it again** revoyons *or* reprenons cela encore une fois.

(b) (*reread*) *notes* jeter un coup d'œil sur, parcourir, revoir.

3 *vt sep* (*Aut*) *person, animal* écraser.

run through 1 *vi* passer *or* traverser en courant.

2 *vt fus* **(a)** (*use up*) *fortune* gaspiller, manger.

(b) (*read quickly*) *notes, text* parcourir, jeter un coup d'œil sur.

(c) (*rehearse*) *play* (faire) répéter; (*recapitulate*) résumer, reprendre. **let's run through it again** reprenons cela (encore une fois); **if I may just run through the principal points once more?** puis-je reprendre *or* rappeler *or* récapituler les points principaux?

3 *vt sep*: **to run sb through (with a sword)** passer une épée à travers le corps de qn.

4 **run-through** *n V* **run 2.**

run up 1 *vi* monter en courant. (*fig*) **to run up against difficulties** se heurter à des difficultés.

2 *vt sep* **(a)** *flag* hisser.

(b) *bill, account* laisser accumuler. **to run up a debt** s'endetter (*of* de).

(c) (*: *sew quickly*) fabriquer*.

3 **run-up** *n V* **run 2.**

runaway ['rʌnəweɪ] **1** *n* fuyard *m*, fugitif *m*, -ive *f*.

2 *adj slave, person* fugitif; *horse* emballé; *car, railway truck* fou (*f* folle). ~ **wedding** mariage clandestin; **the ~ couple** le couple clandestin, les amants; (*Fin*) ~ **inflation** inflation galopante; **he had a ~ victory** il a remporté la victoire haut la main.

rundown ['rʌndaʊn] *n* **(a)** réduction *f*, diminution *f*. **there will be a ~ of staff** il y aura une réduction de personnel. **(b) to give sb a ~ on sth*** mettre qn au courant *or* au parfum‡ de qch.

rune [ru:n] *n* rune *f*.

rung[1] [rʌŋ] *ptp of* **ring**[2].

rung[2] [rʌŋ] *n [ladder]* barreau *m*, échelon *m*, traverse *f*; *[chair]* bâton *m*, barreau.

runic ['ru:nɪk] *adj* runique.

runnel ['rʌnl] *n* (*brook*) ruisseau *m*; (*gutter*) rigole *f*.

runner ['rʌnəʳ] **1** *n* **(a)** (*athlete*) coureur *m*; (*horse*) partant *m*; (*messenger*) messager *m*, courrier *m*; (*smuggler*) contrebandier *m*. (*Brit Hist*) **Bow Street R~** sergent *m* (de ville); *V* **blockade, gun.**

(b) (*sliding part*) *[sledge]* patin *m*; *[skate]* lame *f*; *[turbine]* couronne *f* mobile; *[drawer]* coulisseau *m*; *[curtain]* suspendeur *m*.

(c) (*table-~*) chemin *m* de table; (*hall carpet*) chemin de couloir; (*stair carpet*) chemin d'escalier.

(d) (*Bot: plant*) coulant *m*, stolon *m*.

2 *cpd*: (*Brit*) **runner bean** haricot *m* à rames; (*Scol, Sport etc*) **runner-up** second(e) *m(f)*.

running ['rʌnɪŋ] **1** *n* **(a)** (*action: in race etc*) course *f*. **to make the ~** (*Sport*) faire le lièvre; (*fig*) mener la course, prendre la tête; **to be in the ~*** avoir des chances de réussir; **to be out of the ~*** ne plus être dans la course, n'avoir aucune chance de réussir, ne plus compter; **to be in the ~ for promotion/for the job** être sur les rangs pour obtenir de l'avancement/pour avoir le poste.

(b) (*U: functioning*) *[machine]* marche *f*, fonctionnement *m*; *[train]* marche.

(c) (*U: V* **run 4e**) direction *f*; administration *f*; organisation *f*.

(d) (*U: smuggling*) contrebande *f*; *V* **gun.**

2 *adj*: ~ **jump** saut *m* avec élan; **go and take a ~ jump!**‡ va te faire cuire un œuf!‡; ~ **kick** coup de pied donné en courant; (*fig*) ~ **accompaniment** accompagnement soutenu; (*Fin*) ~ **account** compte courant (*entre banques etc*); **to have** *or* **keep a ~ account with sb** être en compte avec qn; ~ **battle** *combat m où l'un des adversaires est en retraite;* **to keep up a ~ battle** (*Aviat, Naut*) soutenir *or* appuyer la chasse; (*fig*) être en lutte continuelle (*with* avec); (*Naut*) ~ **bowline** laguis *m*; (*Rad, TV*) ~ **commentary** commentaire suivi; (*fig*) **she gave us a ~ commentary on what was going on** elle nous a fait un commentaire détaillé sur ce qui se passait; (*Mil*) ~ **fire** feu roulant; ~ **hand** écriture cursive; ~ **knot** nœud coulant; (*Sewing*) ~ **stitch** point *m* de devant; (*Typ*) ~ **title** titre courant; **4 days ~** 4 jours de suite; **3 times ~** 3 fois de suite; **a ~ stream, ~ water** un cours d'eau; ~ **water (in every room)** eau courante (dans toutes les chambres); ~ **sore** (*Med*) plaie *f* qui suppure; (*fig*) véritable plaie; (*Med*) ~ **cold** rhume *m* de cerveau; ~ **tap** robinet *m* qui coule.

3 *cpd*: *[car, train]* **running board** marchepied *m*; **running costs** frais *mpl* d'exploitation; **the running costs of the car/the central heating are high** la voiture/le chauffage central revient cher; (*US Pol*) **running mate** candidat *m* à la vice-présidence; **in running order** en état de marche; (*Sport*) **running track** piste *f*.

runny ['rʌnɪ] *adj substance* liquide, qui coule, qui a tendance à couler; *omelette* baveux; *nose, eyes* qui coule.

runt [rʌnt] *n* (*animal*) avorton *m*; (*pej: person*) nabot *m*, avorton. **a little ~ of a man** un bonhomme tout riquiqui*.

rupee [ru:'pi:] *n* roupie *f*.

rupture ['rʌptʃəʳ] **1** *n* (*lit, fig*) rupture *f*; (*Med*: hernia*) hernie *f*. **2** *vt* rompre. (*Med*) **to ~ o.s.** se donner une hernie. **3** *vi* se rompre.

rural ['rʊərəl] *adj economy, population* rural; *tranquillity, scenery* de la campagne. (*Brit Rel*) ~ **dean** doyen rural; ~ **depopulation** exode rural.

ruse [ru:z] *n* ruse *f*, stratagème *m*.

rush[1] [rʌʃ] **1** *n* **(a)** (*rapid movement*) course précipitée, ruée *f*; *[crowd]* ruée, bousculade *f*, rush *m*; (*Mil: attack*) bond *m*, assaut *m*. **he was caught in the ~ for the door** il a été pris dans la ruée vers la porte; **it got lost in the ~** ça s'est perdu dans la bousculade *or* dans la confusion; **to make a ~ at** se précipiter sur; **there was a ~ for the empty seats** il y a eu une ruée vers les places libres, on s'est rué vers *or* sur les places libres; **gold ~** ruée vers l'or; (*Comm*) **there's a ~ on matches** on se rue sur les allumettes; **we have a ~ on in the office just now** c'est le coup de feu en ce moment au bureau; **the Christmas ~** la bousculade des fêtes de fin d'année; **we've had a ~ of orders** on nous a submergés de commandes; **a ~ of warm air** une bouffée d'air tiède; **there was a ~ of water** l'eau a jailli; **he had a ~ of blood to the head** il a eu un coup de sang.

(b) (*hurry*) hâte *f*. **the ~ of city life** le rythme effréné de la vie urbaine; **to be in a ~** être extrêmement pressé; **I had a ~ to get here in time** j'ai dû me dépêcher pour arriver à l'heure; **I did it in a ~** je l'ai fait à toute vitesse *or* en quatrième vitesse*; **what's all the ~?** pourquoi est-ce que c'est si pressé?; **is there any ~ for this?** est-ce que c'est pressé? *or* urgent?; **it all happened in a ~** tout est arrivé *or* tout s'est passé très vite.

(c) (*Cine*) (projection *f* d')essai *m*.

2 *cpd*: **rush hours** heures *fpl* de pointe *or* d'affluence; **rush-**

hour traffic circulation *f* des heures de pointe; **rush job** travail *m* d'urgence; **that was a rush job** c'était fait à la va-vite*; (*Comm*) **rush order** commande pressée *or* urgente.

3 *vi [person]* se précipiter, s'élancer, se ruer; *[car]* foncer. **the train went ~ing into the tunnel** le train est entré à toute vitesse dans le tunnel; **they ~ed to help her** ils se sont précipités pour l'aider; **I ~ed to her side** je me suis précipité pour être avec elle; **I'm ~ing to finish it** je me presse *or* je me dépêche pour en avoir fini; **to ~ through** *book* lire à la hâte *or* en diagonale*; *meal* prendre sur le pouce*; *museum* visiter au pas de course; *town* traverser à toute vitesse; *work* expédier; **to ~ in/out/back** *etc* entrer/sortir/rentrer *etc* précipitamment *or* à toute vitesse; **to ~ to the attack** se jeter *or* se ruer à l'attaque; **to ~ to conclusions** conclure à la légère; **the blood ~ed to his face** le sang lui est monté au visage; **memories ~ed into his mind** des souvenirs lui affluèrent à l'esprit; **the wind ~ed through the stable** le vent s'engouffrait dans l'écurie; **a torrent of water ~ed down the slope** un véritable torrent a dévalé la pente; *V* **headlong.**

4 *vt* **(a)** (*cause to move quickly*) entraîner *or* pousser vivement. **to ~ sb to hospital** transporter qn d'urgence à l'hôpital; **they ~ed more troops to the front** ils ont envoyé *or* expédié d'urgence des troupes fraîches sur le front; **they ~ed him out of the room** ils l'ont fait sortir précipitamment *or* en toute hâte de la pièce; **I don't want to ~ you** je ne voudrais pas vous bousculer; **don't ~ me!** laissez-moi le temps de souffler!; **to be ~ed off one's feet** être débordé; **to ~ sb off his feet** ne pas laisser à qn le temps de souffler; **to ~ sb into a decision** forcer *or* obliger qn à prendre une décision à la hâte; **to ~ sb into doing sth** forcer *or* obliger qn à faire qch à la hâte; **they ~ed the bill through Parliament** ils ont fait voter la loi à la hâte.

(b) (*take by storm*) (*Mil*) *town, position* prendre d'assaut; *fence, barrier* franchir (sur son élan). **her admirers ~ed the stage** ses admirateurs ont envahi la scène; **the mob ~ed the line of policemen** la foule s'est élancée contre le cordon de police.

(c) (*do hurriedly*) *job, task* dépêcher; *order* exécuter d'urgence.

(d) (:) (*charge*) faire payer; (*swindle*) faire payer un prix exorbitant à, estamper*. **how much were you ~ed for it?** combien on te l'a fait payer?; **you really** WERE **~ed for that!** tu t'es vraiment fait estamper* pour ça!

rush about, rush around *vi* courir çà et là.

rush at *vt fus* se jeter sur, se ruer sur; *enemy* se ruer sur, fondre sur. **don't rush at the job, take it slowly** ne fais pas ça trop vite, prends ton temps.

rush down *vi [person]* descendre précipitamment; *[stream]* dévaler.

rush through *vt sep* (*Comm*) *order* exécuter d'urgence; *goods, supplies* envoyer *or* faire parvenir de toute urgence. **they rushed medical supplies through to him** on lui a fait parvenir des médicaments de toute urgence.

rush up 1 *vi* (*arrive*) accourir.

2 *vt sep help, reinforcements* faire venir *or* (faire) envoyer d'urgence (*to* à).

rush[2] [rʌʃ] **1** *n* (*Bot*) jonc *m*; (*for chair*) jonc, paille *f*. **2** *cpd*: **rush light** chandelle *f* à mèche de jonc; **rush mat** tapis *m* de sparterie; (*U*) **rush matting** (tapis *m* de) sparterie *f*.

rusk [rʌsk] *n* biscotte *f*.

russet ['rʌsɪt] **1** *n* **(a)** (*colour*) couleur *f* feuille-morte *inv*, brun roux. **(b)** (*apple*) reinette grise. **2** *adj* feuille-morte *inv*, brun roux *inv*.

Russia ['rʌʃə] *n* Russie *f*.

Russian ['rʌʃən] **1** *adj* russe. **~ roulette** roulette *f* russe. **2** *n* **(a)** Russe *mf*. **(b)** (*Ling*) russe *m*.

rust [rʌst] **1** *n* (*on metal; also Bot*) rouille *f*. **2** *cpd*: **rust-coloured** (couleur) rouille *inv*, roux (*f* rousse); **rustproof, rust-resistant** inoxydable. **3** *vt* (*lit, fig*) rouiller. **4** *vi* (*lit, fig*) se rouiller.

rust in *vi [screw]* se rouiller dans son trou.

rust up *vi* se rouiller.

rustic ['rʌstɪk] **1** *n* campagnard(e) *m(f)*, paysan(ne) *m(f)*, rustaud(e) *m(f)* (*pej*), rustre *m* (*pej*). **2** *adj scene* rustique, champêtre; *bench, charm, simplicity* rustique.

rusticate ['rʌstɪkeɪt] **1** *vi* habiter la campagne. **2** *vt* (*Brit Univ*) exclure (temporairement).

rustiness ['rʌstɪnɪs] *n* rouillure *f*, rouille *f*.

rustle ['rʌsl] **1** *n [leaves]* bruissement *m*; *[silk, skirts]* bruissement, frou-frou *m*; *[papers]* froissement *m*.

2 *vi [leaves, wind]* bruire; *[papers]* produire un froissement *or* un bruissement; *[clothes, skirt]* faire frou-frou. **she ~d into the room** elle est entrée en froufroutant dans la pièce; **something ~d in the cupboard** il y a eu un froissement *or* un bruissement dans le placard.

3 *vt* **(a)** *leaves* faire bruire; *paper* froisser; *programme* agiter avec un bruissement; *petticoat, skirt* faire froufrouter.

(b) (*esp US: steal*) *cattle* voler.

rustle up* *vt sep* se débrouiller* pour trouver (*or* faire), préparer (à la hâte). **can you rustle up a cup of coffee?** tu voudrais me (*or* nous etc) donner un café en vitesse?

rustler ['rʌslə^r] *n* **(a)** (*esp US: cattle-thief*) voleur *m* de bétail. **(b)** (*US* *: *energetic person*) type* *m* énergique *or* expéditif.

rusty ['rʌstɪ] *adj* (*lit, fig*) rouillé. (*lit*) **to get** *or* **go ~** se rouiller; (*fig*) **my English is ~** mon anglais est un peu rouillé.

rut[1] [rʌt] (*Zool*) **1** *n* rut *m*. **2** *vi* être en rut. **~ting season** saison *f* du rut.

rut[2] [rʌt] **1** *n* (*in track, path*) ornière *f*; (*fig*) routine *f*, ornière. (*fig*) **to be in a ~,** (*fig*) **to get into a ~** *[person]* suivre l'ornière, s'encroûter; *[mind]* devenir routinier; (*fig*) **to get out of the ~** sortir de l'ornière. **2** *vt* sillonner.

rutabaga [ˌruːtə'beɪgə] *n* (*US*) rutabaga *m*.

ruthless ['ruːθlɪs] *adj* impitoyable, cruel, sans pitié.

ruthlessly ['ruːθlɪslɪ] *adv* sans pitié, sans merci, impitoyablement.

ruthlessness ['ruːθlɪsnɪs] *n* caractère *m* *or* nature *f* impitoyable.

rye [raɪ] **1** *n* **(a)** (*grain*) seigle *m*. **(b)** (*US**) = **~ whisky.**

2 *cpd*: **rye bread** pain *m* de seigle; **ryegrass** ivraie *f* vivace, ray-grass *m*; **rye whisky** whisky *m* (américain *or* canadien).

S

S, s [es] *n* (*letter*) S, s *m*.

Saar [zɑː^r] *n* (*river, region*) **the ~** la Sarre.

sabbatarian [ˌsæbə'tɛərɪən] **1** *n* (*Christian*) partisan(e) *m(f)* de l'observance stricte du dimanche; (*Jew*) personne *f* qui observe le sabbat. **2** *adj* (*Jewish Rel*) de l'observance du sabbat.

Sabbath ['sæbəθ] *n* (*Jewish*) sabbat *m*; (*Christian*: †) dimanche *m*. **to keep/break the ~** observer/violer le sabbat *or* le dimanche; **(witches') s~** sabbat.

sabbatical [sə'bætɪkəl] *adj* sabbatique. (*Univ*) **~ (year)** année *f* sabbatique.

saber ['seɪbə^r] (*US*) = **sabre.**

sable ['seɪbl] **1** *n* **(a)** (*Zool*) zibeline *f*, martre *f*. **(b)** (*Her*) sable *m*. **2** *cpd* **(a)** *fur* de zibeline, de martre; *brush* en poil de martre. **(b)** (*liter: black*) noir.

sabot ['sæbəʊ] *n* (*all wood*) sabot *m*; (*leather etc upper*) socque *m*.

sabotage ['sæbətɑːʒ] **1** *n* (*U*) sabotage *m*. **an act of ~** un sabotage. **2** *vt* (*lit, fig*) saboter.

saboteur [ˌsæbə'tɜː^r] *n* saboteur *m*, -euse *f*.

sabre, (*US*) **saber** ['seɪbə^r] **1** *n* sabre *m*. **2** *cpd*: (*fig*) **sabre rattling** bruit *m* de sabre (*fig*); **sabre-toothed tiger** smilodon *m*, machairodus *m*.

sac [sæk] *n* (*Anat, Bio*) sac *m*.

saccharin(e) ['sækərɪn] *n* saccharine *f*.

saccharine ['sækəriːn] *adj drink* sacchariné; *product* à la saccharine; *pill, flavour* de saccharine; (*fig*) *smile* mielleux, douceâtre.

sacerdotal [ˌsæsə'dəʊtl] *adj* sacerdotal.

sachet ['sæʃeɪ] *n* sachet *m*.

sack[1] [sæk] **1** *n* (*bag*) sac *m*. **coal~** sac à charbon; **~ of coal** sac de charbon; **a ~(ful) of potatoes** un (plein) sac de pommes de terre; **that dress makes her look like a ~ of potatoes** dans cette robe elle ressemble à un sac de pommes de terre; (*fig*) **to give sb the ~*** renvoyer qn, mettre *or* flanquer* qn à la porte, sacquer qn*; **to get the ~*** être renvoyé, être mis *or* flanqué* à la porte, être sacqué*.

2 *cpd*: **sackcloth** grosse toile d'emballage, toile à sac; (*Rel*) **sackcloth and ashes** le sac et la cendre; (*fig*) **to be in sackcloth and ashes** être contrit; **sack dress** robe *f* sac; **sack race** course *f* en sac.

sack[2] [sæk] **1** *n* (*plundering*) sac *m*, pillage *m*. **2** *vt town* mettre à sac, saccager, piller.

sack[3] [sæk] *n* (*wine*) vin blanc sec.

sackbut ['sækbʌt] *n* (*Mus*) saquebute *f*.

sacking[1] ['sækɪŋ] *n* **(a)** (*U: Tex*) grosse toile d'emballage, toile à sac. **(b)** (*: *dismissal*) renvoi *m*.

sacking[2] ['sækɪŋ] *n* (*plundering*) sac *m*, pillage *m*.

sacrament ['sækrəmənt] *n* sacrement *m*; *V* **blessed.**

sacramental [ˌsækrə'mentl] **1** *adj* sacramentel. **2** *n* sacramental *m*.

sacred ['seɪkrɪd] *adj* **(a)** (*Rel*) sacré, saint; *music* sacré, religieux. **the S~ Heart** le Sacré-Cœur; **S~ History** l'Histoire Sainte; **things ~ and profane** le sacré et le profane; **~ writings** livres sacrés.

(b) (*solemn*) *duty* sacré; *moment* solennel, sacré; *promise* sacré, inviolable; (*revered*) sacré. **~ to the memory of** consacré *or* voué à la mémoire de; **the cow is a ~ animal in India** aux Indes la vache est un animal sacré; **to her nothing was ~** pour elle rien n'était sacré, elle ne respectait rien; **is nothing ~?** vous ne respectez donc rien?; (*fig*) **~ cow*** chose sacro-sainte.

sacrifice ['sækrɪfaɪs] **1** *n* (*all senses*) sacrifice *m*. (*Rel*) **the ~ of the mass** le saint sacrifice (de la messe); (*fig*) **to make great ~s** faire de grands sacrifices (*for sb* pour qn, *to do* pour faire); **to sell sth at a ~** sacrifier qch, vendre qch à perte; *V* **self.**

2 *vt* (*all senses*) sacrifier (*to* à). **to ~ o.s. for sb** se sacrifier pour qn; (*in small ads etc*) **'cost £25: ~ for £5'*** 'coût 25 livres: sacrifié à 5 livres'.

sacrificial [,sækrɪ'fɪʃəl] *adj* **(a)** (*Rel*) *rite* sacrificiel. **the ~ lamb** l'agneau *m* du sacrifice. **(b)** (*fig*) *sale* à perte; *price* bas (*f* basse). **goods sold at ~ prices** marchandises sacrifiées.

sacrilege ['sækrɪlɪdʒ] *n* (*lit, fig*) sacrilège *m*.

sacrilegious [,sækrɪ'lɪdʒəs] *adj* sacrilège.

sacrist(an) ['sækrɪst(ən)] *n* sacristain(e) *m(f)*, sacristine *f*.

sacristy ['sækrɪstɪ] *n* sacristie *f*.

sacrosanct ['sækrəʊsæŋkt] *adj* sacro-saint.

sacrum ['sækrəm] *n* sacrum *m*.

sad [sæd] *adj* **(a)** (*unhappy*) triste, affligé; (*depressed*) triste, déprimé; *feeling, look* triste, de tristesse; *smile* triste. **~-eyed** aux yeux tristes; **~-faced** au visage triste; **to make sb ~** attrister qn; **to grow ~** s'attrister, devenir triste; **he eventually departed a ~der and (a) wiser man** finalement il partit ayant appris la dure leçon de l'expérience.

(b) (*deplorable*) *news, duty, occasion* triste, attristant; *loss* douloureux; *state, condition* triste; *mistake* regrettable, fâcheux. **it's a very ~ state of affairs** c'est un triste état de choses *or* un état de choses déplorable; **it's a ~ business** c'est une triste affaire, c'est une affaire lamentable.

sadden ['sædn] *vt* attrister, rendre triste, affliger.

saddle ['sædl] **1** *n* **(a)** *[horse, cycle]* selle *f*. (*lit*) **in the ~** en selle; **he leapt into the ~** il sauta en selle; (*fig*) **when he was in the ~** quand c'était lui qui tenait les rênes; *V* **side** *etc.*

(b) *[hill]* col *m*.

(c) (*Culin*) **~ of lamb** selle *f* d'agneau.

2 *cpd*: **saddle-backed** ensellé; **saddlebag** *[horse]* sacoche *f* de selle; *[cycle]* sacoche de bicyclette; **saddlebow** pommeau *m*, arçon *m*; **saddlecloth** tapis *m* de selle; **saddle horse** cheval *m* de selle; **saddle-sore** meurtri à force d'être en selle.

3 *vt* **(a)** (*also* **~ up**) *horse* seller.

(b) (* *fig*) **to ~ sb with sth** imposer qch à qn, coller qch à qn*; **I've been ~d with organizing the meeting** on m'a collé* l'organisation de la réunion; **we're ~d with it** nous voilà avec ça sur les bras.

saddler ['sædləʳ] *n* sellier *m*.

saddlery ['sædlərɪ] *n* (*articles, business*) sellerie *f*.

sadducee ['sædjʊsi:] *n* saducéen(ne) *m(f)*.

sadism ['seɪdɪzəm] *n* sadisme *m*.

sadist ['seɪdɪst] *adj, n* sadique (*mf*).

sadistic [sə'dɪstɪk] *adj* sadique.

sadly ['sædlɪ] *adv* (*unhappily*) *smile, speak* tristement, avec tristesse; (*regrettably*) fâcheusement. **a ~ incompetent teacher** un professeur bien incompétent; **~ lacking in ...** qui manque fortement de ...; **you are ~ mistaken** vous vous trompez fort; **it's ~ in need of repair** cela a bien besoin d'être réparé.

sadness ['sædnɪs] *n* (*U*) tristesse *f*, mélancolie *f*.

safari [sə'fɑ:rɪ] *n* safari *m*. **to make a ~, to go** *or* **be on ~** faire un safari; **~ park** réserve *f*.

safe [seɪf] **1** *adj* **(a)** (*not in danger*) *person* hors de danger, en sécurité. **~ and sound** sain et sauf; **to be ~ from** être à l'abri de; **all the passengers are ~** tous les passagers sont sains et saufs *or* sont hors de danger; (*fig*) **no girl is ~ with him** les filles courent toujours un risque avec lui; **you'll be quite ~ here** vous êtes en sécurité ici, vous ne courez aucun danger ici; **his life was not ~** sa vie était menacée; **I don't feel very ~ on this ladder** je ne me sens pas très en sécurité sur cette échelle.

(b) (*not dangerous*) *toy, animal* sans danger; *method, vehicle* sûr; *action* sans risque, sans danger; *structure, bridge* solide; (*secure*) *hiding place, harbour* sûr; (*prudent*) *action, choice, guess, estimate* prudent, raisonnable. (*Naut*) **a ~ anchorage** un bon mouillage; **is it ~ to come out?** est-ce qu'on peut sortir sans danger?; **it is quite ~ to go alone** on peut y aller seul sans aucun danger; **it's not ~ to go alone** il est dangereux d'y aller tout seul; **is that dog ~?** ce chien n'est pas méchant?; **that dog isn't ~ with children** il ne faut pas laisser les enfants s'approcher du chien; **the ice isn't ~** la glace n'est pas solide *or* ferme; **is the ladder ~ for the children?** est-ce que l'échelle est assez solide pour les enfants?; **this boat is not ~** *or* **not in a ~ condition** ce bateau n'est pas en état; **is the bathing/the beach ~?** la baignade/la plage n'est pas dangereuse?; **~ journey!** bon voyage!; **~ home!*** bon retour!; **I'll keep it ~ for you** je vais vous le garder en lieu sûr; **in a ~ place** en lieu sûr; **in ~ hands** en mains sûres; **he's ~ in jail for the moment** pour le moment on est tranquille — il est sous les verrous; **it's ~ as houses** (*runs no risk*) cela ne court aucun risque; (*offers no risk*) cela ne présente aucun risque; (*Med*) **the ~ period*** la période sans danger; **a ~ investment** un placement sûr *or* de père de famille; **your reputation is ~** votre réputation est inattaquable; **your secret is ~ with me** avec moi votre secret ne risque rien; **the ~st thing (to do) would be to wait here** le plus sûr serait d'attendre ici; **(just) to be on the ~ side** par précaution, pour plus de sûreté, par acquit de conscience; **it's better to be on the ~ side and take an umbrella** pour être plus sûr il vaut mieux prendre un parapluie; **better ~ than sorry!** mieux vaut être trop prudent!; **he was a ~ choice** *or* **they chose a ~ man for headmaster** en le nommant directeur ils n'ont couru aucun risque; (*Sport*) **a ~ winner** un gagnant certain *or* assuré; **it's a ~ bet he'll win** il gagnera à coup sûr; **he's ~ for re-election** il sera réélu à coup sûr; (*Pol*) **a ~ seat** un siège assuré; **it is ~ to predict ...** on peut prédire sans risque d'erreur *or* en toute tranquillité ...; *V* **play.**

2 *n* **(a)** (*for money, valuables*) coffre-fort *m*.

(b) (*for food*) garde-manger *m inv*.

3 *cpd*: **safe-blower** perceur *m* de coffre-fort (*qui utilise des explosifs*); **safe-breaker** perceur *m* de coffre-fort; (*Mil etc*) **safe-conduct** sauf-conduit *m*; **safe-cracker = safe-breaker; safe deposit** (*vault*) dépôt *m* de coffres-forts; (*box*) coffre *m*; **safeguard** (*vt*) sauvegarder, protéger (*against* contre); (*n*) sauvegarde *f*, garantie *f* (*against* contre); **as a safeguard against ...** comme sauvegarde contre ..., pour éviter ...; **safekeeping** bonne garde, sécurité *f*; **in safekeeping** sous bonne garde, en sécurité; **I gave it to him for safekeeping, I put it in his safekeeping** je le lui ai donné à garder *or* pour qu'il le garde (*subj*); **the key is in his safekeeping** on lui a confié (la garde de) la clef.

safely ['seɪflɪ] *adv* (*without mishap*) sans accident; (*without risk*) sans risque, sans danger; (*securely*) en sûreté, sûrement. **he arrived ~** il est bien arrivé *or* arrivé sain et sauf *or* arrivé à bon port; **'arrived ~'** 'bien arrivé'; **you can walk about quite ~ in this town** vous pouvez vous promener sans risque *or* sans danger dans cette ville; **he's ~ through to the semifinal** il est arrivé (sans encombre) en demi-finale; **to put sth away ~** ranger qch en lieu sûr; **we can ~ say that ...** nous pouvons dire à coup sûr *or* sans risque d'erreur que ... .

safeness ['seɪfnɪs] *n* (*freedom from danger*) sécurité *f*; *[construction, equipment]* solidité *f*.

safety ['seɪftɪ] **1** *n* **(a)** (*freedom from danger*) sécurité *f*. **in a place of ~** en lieu sûr; **to ensure sb's ~** veiller sur *or* assurer la sécurité de qn; **his ~ must be our first consideration** sa sécurité doit être notre premier souci; **this airline is very concerned over the ~ of its passengers** cette compagnie d'aviation se préoccupe beaucoup de la sécurité de ses passagers; **he reached ~ at last** il fut enfin en sûreté *or* en sécurité; **he sought ~ in flight** il chercha le salut dans la fuite; **to play for ~** ne pas prendre de risques, jouer au plus sûr; **there is ~ in numbers** plus on est nombreux moins il y a de danger; **for ~'s sake** pour plus de sûreté, par mesure de sécurité; **~ on the roads/in the factories** la sécurité sur les routes/dans les usines; **~ first!** la sécurité d'abord!; (*Aut*) soyez prudents! (*V also* **2**); *V also* **road.**

(b) *[construction, equipment]* solidité *f*.

2 *cpd*: **safety belt** ceinture *f* de sécurité; **safety blade** lame *f* de sûreté; **safety bolt** verrou *m* de sûreté; **safety catch** cran *m* de sécurité; **safety chain** chaîne *f* de sûreté; (*Theat*) **safety curtain** rideau *m* de fer; **safety device** dispositif *m* de sécurité; (*Aut*) **safety first campaign** campagne *f* de la prévention routière; **safety glass** verre *m* Sécurit ®; **safety lamp** lampe *f* de mineur; **safety lock** serrure *f* de sûreté; **safety margin** marge *f* de sécurité; **safety match** allumette *f* de sûreté *or* suédoise; **safety measure** mesure *f* de sécurité; **as a safety measure** pour plus de sûreté, par mesure de sécurité; **safety mechanism** dispositif *m* de sécurité; **safety net** filet *m* (de protection); **safety pin** épingle *f* de sûreté *or* de nourrice; **safety precaution** mesure *f* de sécurité; **safety razor** rasoir *m* de sûreté *or* mécanique; **safety regulations** règles *fpl* de sécurité; **safety screen** écran *m* de sécurité; (*lit, fig*) **safety valve** soupape *f* de sûreté; (*US Aut*) **safety zone** zone protégée pour piétons.

saffron ['sæfrən] **1** *n* safran *m*. **2** *adj colour* safran *inv*; *flavour* safrané. **~ yellow** jaune safran *inv*.

sag [sæg] **1** *vi [ground, roof, chair]* s'affaisser; *[beam, floorboard]* s'arquer, fléchir; *[cheeks, breasts, hemline]* pendre; *[rope]* pendre au milieu, être détendu; *[gate]* être affaissé; *[prices]* fléchir, baisser.

2 *n* affaissement *m*; fléchissement *m*; *[prices]* fléchissement, baisse *f*.

saga ['sɑ:gə] *n* saga *f*; (*fig*) aventure *f or* caractère *m* épique.

sagacious [sə'geɪʃəs] *adj person* sagace, avisé; *comment* judicieux.

sagaciously [sə'geɪʃəslɪ] *adv* avec sagacité.

sagaciousness [sə'geɪʃəsnɪs] *n*, **sagacity** [sə'gæsɪtɪ] *n* sagacité *f*.

sage[1] [seɪdʒ] *n* (*Bot, Culin*) sauge *f*. **~ and onion stuffing** farce *f* à l'oignon et à la sauge; **~ green** vert cendré *inv*; (*US*) **~brush** armoise *f*.

sage[2] [seɪdʒ] **1** *adj* (*wise*) sage, savant, avisé; (*solemn*) solennel, grave. **2** *n* sage *m*.

sagely ['seɪdʒlɪ] *adv* (*wisely*) avec sagesse; (*solemnly*) d'un air *or* d'un ton solennel.

sagging ['sægɪŋ] *adj ground* affaissé; *beam* arqué, fléchi; *cheek, hemline* pendant; *rope* détendu; *gate* affaissé.

Sagittarius [,sædʒɪ'teərɪəs] *n* (*Astron*) Sagittaire *m*.

sago ['seɪgəʊ] *n* sagou *m*. **~ pudding** sagou au lait.

Sahara [sə'hɑ:rə] *n*: **the ~ (Desert)** le (désert du) Sahara.

sahib ['sɑ:hɪb] *n* (*aux Indes*) Monsieur *m*, maître *m*. **Smith S~** Monsieur Smith; *V* **pukka.**

said [sed] *pret, ptp of* **say.**

sail [seɪl] **1** *n* **(a)** *[boat]* voile *f*. **under ~** à la voile; **the boat has set ~** le bateau a pris la mer; *[boat]* **to set ~ for** partir à destination de; **he has set ~ for America** il est parti pour l'Amérique (en bateau); **there wasn't a ~ in sight** il n'y avait pas une seule voile en vue; *V* **hoist, wind**[1] *etc.*

(b) (*trip*) **to go for a ~** faire un tour en bateau *or* en mer;

Spain is 2 days' ~ from here l'Espagne est à 2 jours de mer.
(c) *[windmill]* aile *f*.
2 *cpd*: (*US*) **sailboat** bateau *m* à voiles, voilier *m*; **sailcloth** toile *f* à voile; **sail maker** voilier *m* (*personne*); **sailplane** planeur *m*.
3 *vi* **(a)** *[boat]* **to ~ into harbour** entrer au port; **the ship ~ed into Cadiz** le bateau arriva à Cadix; **it ~ed round the cape** il doubla le cap; **to ~ at 10 knots** filer 10 nœuds; **the boat ~ed down the river** le bateau descendit la rivière; **the steamer ~s at 6 o'clock** le vapeur prend la mer *or* part à 6 heures.
(b) *[person]* **to ~ away/back** *etc* partir/revenir *etc* en bateau; **to ~ round the world** faire le tour du monde en bateau; **we ~ed for Australia** nous sommes partis pour l'Australie (en bateau); **we ~ed into Southampton** nous sommes entrés dans le port de Southampton; **we ~ at 6 o'clock** nous partons à 6 heures, le bateau part à 6 heures; **he ~s** *or* **goes ~ing every weekend** il fait du bateau *or* de la voile tous les week-ends; (*fig*) **he was ~ing close to** *or* **near the wind** il jouait un jeu dangereux.
(c) (*fig*) *[swan etc]* glisser. **clouds were ~ing across the sky** des nuages glissaient *or* couraient dans le ciel; **the book ~ed across the room and landed at her feet** le livre vola à travers la pièce et atterrit à ses pieds; **the book ~ed out of the window** le livre est allé voler par la fenêtre; **she ~ed into the room*** elle entra dans la pièce toutes voiles dehors (*hum*).
4 *vt* **(a) to ~ the seas** parcourir les mers; **he ~ed the Atlantic last year** l'année dernière il a fait la traversée de *or* il a traversé l'Atlantique (en bateau).
(b) *boat* manœuvrer, piloter, commander. **he ~ed his boat round the cape** il a doublé le cap; **he ~s his own yacht** (*owns it*) il a son propre yacht; (*captains it*) il pilote son yacht lui-même.
sail into *vt fus* **(a)** (*: *scold*) passer un savon à*, laver la tête à*, voler dans les plumes à*.
(b) (*) **he sailed into the work** il attaqua le travail avec entrain.
sail through* **1** *vi* réussir haut la main.
2 *vt fus*: **to sail through one's degree/one's driving test** avoir sa licence/son permis de conduire haut la main.
sailing ['seɪlɪŋ] **1** *n* **(a)** (*U*) navigation *f* (à voile). **a day's ~** une journée de voile *or* en mer; **his hobby is ~** son passe-temps favori est la voile; *V* **plain**.
(b) (*departure*) départ *m*.
2 *cpd*: (*Brit*) **sailing boat** bateau *m* à voiles, voilier *m*; **sailing date** date *f* de départ (d'un bateau); **sailing dinghy** canot *m* à voiles, dériveur *m*; **sailing orders** instructions *fpl* pour appareiller; **sailing ship** voilier *m*, navire *m* à voiles.
sailor ['seɪlə^r] **1** *n* (*gen*) marin *m*; (*before the mast*) matelot *m*. **to be a good/bad ~** avoir/ne pas avoir le pied marin. **2** *cpd*: **sailor hat** canotier *m* (*chapeau*); **sailor suit** costume marin.
sainfoin ['sænfɔɪn] *n* sainfoin *m*.
saint [seɪnt] **1** *n* saint(e) *m(f)*. **~'s day** fête *f* (de saint); **All S~s' (Day)** la Toussaint; **he's no ~*** ce n'est pas un petit saint.
2 *cpd*: **Saint Bernard** (*dog*) saint-bernard *m inv*; **Saint John/Peter** *etc* saint Jean/Pierre *etc*; (*Geog*) **the Saint Lawrence** le Saint-Laurent; **the Saint Lawrence Seaway** la voie maritime du Saint-Laurent; **saint-like** = **saintly**; **Saint Patrick's Day** la Saint-Patrick; **Saint Peter's Church** (l'église *f*) Saint-Pierre; (*Med*) **Saint Vitus' dance** danse *f* de Saint-Guy.
sainted ['seɪntɪd] *adj* sanctifié.
sainthood ['seɪnthʊd] *n* sainteté *f*.
saintliness ['seɪntlɪnɪs] *n* sainteté *f*.
saintly ['seɪntlɪ] *adj quality* de saint; *smile* plein de bonté. **a ~ person** une sainte personne, une personne pleine de bonté.
sake[1] [seɪk] *n*: **for the ~ of sb** pour l'amour de qn, par égard pour qn; **for God's ~** pour l'amour de Dieu; **for my ~** pour moi, par égard pour moi; **for your own ~** pour ton bien; **for their ~(s)** pour eux; **to eat for the ~ of eating** manger pour le plaisir de manger; **for old times' ~** en souvenir du passé; **for argument's ~** à titre d'exemple; **art for art's ~** l'art pour l'art; **for the ~ of peace** pour avoir la paix; *V* **goodness, heaven, pity** *etc*.
sake[2] ['sɑːkɪ] *n* saké *m*.
sal [sæl] *n* sel *m*. **~ ammoniac** sel ammoniac; **~ volatile** sel volatil.
salaam [sə'lɑːm] **1** *n* salutation *f* (à l'orientale). **2** *vi* saluer (à l'orientale).
salable ['seɪləbl] *adj* = **saleable**.
salacious [sə'leɪʃəs] *adj joke, remark* licencieux, grivois; *smile, look* lubrique.
salaciousness [sə'leɪʃəsnɪs] *n* grivoiserie *f*; lubricité *f*.
salad ['sæləd] **1** *n* salade *f*. **ham ~** jambon accompagné de salade; **toma ~** salade de tomates; *V* **fruit, potato** *etc*.
2 *cpd*: **salad bowl** saladier *m*; **salad cream** (*sorte f de*) mayonnaise *f* (*en bouteille etc*); (*fig*) **salad days** années *fpl* de jeunesse et d'inexpérience; **salad dish** = **salad bowl**; **salad dressing** vinaigrette *f*; (*made with egg*) mayonnaise *f*; **salad oil** huile *f* de table; **salad servers** couvert *m* à salade.
salamander ['sæləˌmændə^r] *n* (*Myth, Zool*) salamandre *f*.
salami [sə'lɑːmɪ] *n* salami *m*.
salaried ['sælərɪd] *adj person* qui touche un traitement *or* des appointements; *post* où l'on touche un traitement. (*Ind*) **~ staff** employés *mpl* touchant un traitement *or* des appointements.
salary ['sælərɪ] **1** *n* (*monthly, professional etc*) traitement *m*, appointements *mpl*; (*gen: pay*) salaire *m*.
2 *cpd*: **salary bracket** fourchette *f* des traitements; **salary earner** personne *f* qui touche un traitement; **salary range** éventail *m* des traitements; **salary scale** échelle *f* des traitements.
sale [seɪl] **1** *n* **(a)** (*act*) vente *f*. **'for ~'** 'à vendre'; **'not for ~'** 'cet article n'est pas à vendre'; **to put up for ~** mettre en vente; **our house is up for ~** notre maison est à vendre *or* en vente; **on ~** en vente; **on ~ at all good chemists** en vente dans toutes les bonnes pharmacies; **we made a quick ~** la vente a été vite conclue; **it's going cheap for a quick ~** le prix est bas parce qu'on espère vendre vite; **he finds a ready ~ for his vegetables** il n'a aucun mal à vendre ses légumes; **his vegetables find a ready ~** ses légumes se vendent sans aucun mal; **on ~ or return (basis)** vendu avec possibilité de rendre; **~s are up/down** les ventes ont augmenté/baissé; **~ by auction** vente publique, vente aux enchères; *V* **cash** *etc*.
(b) (*place, event*) (*auction*) vente *f* (aux enchères); (*Comm: also* **~s**) soldes *mpl*. **the ~s are on** c'est la saison des soldes; **the ~ begins** *or* **the ~s begin next week** les soldes commencent la semaine prochaine; **this shop is having a ~ just now** il y a des soldes dans ce magasin en ce moment; **to put in the ~** mettre en solde, solder; **in a ~** en solde; **they are having a ~ in aid of the blind** on organise une vente (de charité) en faveur des aveugles; *V* **bring, clearance, jumble** *etc*.
2 *cpd*: **sale of work** vente *f* de charité; **sale price** prix *m* de solde *or* de rabais; **saleroom** salle *f* des ventes; (*US*) **sales clerk** vendeur *m*, -euse *f*; **sales department** service *m* des ventes; **sales force** ensemble *m* des représentants; **salesman** (*in shop*) vendeur *m*; (*representative*) représentant *m* de commerce; **he's a good salesman** il sait vendre (*V* **door 1a** *etc*); **sales manager** directeur commercial; **salesmanship** art *m* de la vente; **sales promotion** promotion *f* des ventes; **sales resistance** réaction *f* défavorable (à la publicité), résistance *f* (de l'acheteur); (*US*) **salesroom** = **saleroom**; **sales talk*** boniment *m* (*often pej*), baratin* *m*; (*US*) **sales tax** taxe *f* à l'achat; **saleswoman** vendeuse *f*; **sale value** valeur marchande.
saleable ['seɪləbl] *adj* vendable. **highly ~** très demandé.
salient ['seɪlɪənt] *adj, n* saillant (*m*).
salina [sə'liːnə] *n* **(a)** (*marsh etc*) (marais *m*) salant *m*, salin *m*, saline *f*; (*saltworks*) salin, saline(s), raffinerie *f* de sel. **(b)** (*mine*) mine *f* de sel.
saline ['seɪlaɪn] **1** *adj solution* salin. **2** *n* **(a)** = **salina a. (b)** (*Chem: solution*) solution *f* isotonique de sel(s) alcalin(s); (*Med*) purgatif salin.
salinity [sə'lɪnɪtɪ] *n* salinité *f*.
saliva [sə'laɪvə] *n* salive *f*.
salivary ['sælɪvərɪ] *adj* salivaire.
salivate ['sælɪveɪt] *vi* saliver.
salivation [ˌsælɪ'veɪʃən] *n* salivation *f*.
sallow[1] ['sæləʊ] *adj complexion* jaunâtre, cireux.
sallow[2] ['sæləʊ] *n* (*Bot*) saule *m*.
sallowness ['sæləʊnɪs] *n* teint *m* jaunâtre.
sally ['sælɪ] *n* **(a)** (*Mil*) sortie *f*. **(b)** (*flash of wit*) saillie *f*, boutade *f*. **to make a ~** dire une boutade.
sally forth, sally out *vi* (*Mil*) faire une sortie; (*gen*) sortir gaiement.
salmon ['sæmən] **1** *n* saumon *m*; *V* **rock**[2], **smoke**. **2** *cpd*: **salmon fishing** pêche *f* au saumon; **salmon pink** (rose) saumon *inv*; **salmon steak** darne *f* de saumon; **salmon trout** truite saumonée.
salmonella [ˌsælmə'nelə] *n* salmonellose *f*.
salon ['sælɔ̃ːŋ] *n* (*all senses*) salon *m*; *V* **beauty, hair**.
saloon [sə'luːn] **1** *n* **(a)** salle *f*, salon *m*; *V* **billiard**.
(b) (*US*) bar *m*, saloon *m*.
(c) (*Naut*) salon *m*, cabine *f*. **to travel ~** voyager en première classe.
(d) (*Brit: car*) conduite intérieure, berline *f*. **5-seater ~** berline 5 places.
2 *cpd*: (*Brit*) **saloon bar** bar *m*; **saloon car** (*Brit Aut*) conduite intérieure, berline *f*; (*US Rail*) wagon-salon *m*; (*Naut*) **saloon deck** pont *m* des premières (classes).
salsify ['sælsɪfɪ] *n* salsifis *m*.
salt [sɔːlt] **1** *n* **(a)** (*U: Chem, Culin*) sel *m*. **kitchen/table ~** sel de cuisine/de table; **there's too much ~ in the potatoes** les pommes de terre sont trop salées; **I don't like ~ in my food** je n'aime pas manger salé; (*fig*) **to rub ~ in the wound** retourner le couteau dans la plaie; (*fig*) **he's not worth his ~** il ne vaut pas grand-chose; (*fig*) **to take sth with a pinch** *or* **grain of ~** ne pas prendre qch au pied de la lettre; (*fig*) **the ~ of the earth** le sel de la terre; (*fig*) **to sit above/below the ~** être en faveur/défaveur.
(b) ~s sels *mpl*; *V* **bath, smell** *etc*.
(c) (*Naut*) **an old ~** un vieux loup de mer.
2 *cpd water, butter, beef* salé; *taste* salé, de sel. **saltcellar** salière *f*; **salt flats** salants *mpl*; **salt-free** sans sel; **salt lake** lac salé; **salt marsh** (marais) salant, salin *m*, saline *f*; **salt mine** mine *f* de sel; **salt pan** puits salant; **salt pork** petit salé; **salt spoon** cuiller *f* à sel; (*Hist*) **salt tax** gabelle *f*; (*fig*) **salt tears** larmes amères; **saltwater fish** poisson *m* de mer; **saltworks** salin *m*, saline(s) *f(pl)*, raffinerie *f* de sel.
3 *vt meat, one's food* saler.
salt away *vt sep meat* saler; (*fig*) *money* mettre à gauche*.
salt down *vt fus* saler, conserver dans le sel.
saltiness ['sɔːltɪnɪs] *n* *[water]* salinité *f*; *[food]* goût salé.
salting ['sɔːltɪŋ] *n* salaison *f*.
saltpetre, (*US*) saltpeter ['sɔːltˌpiːtə^r] *n* salpêtre *m*.
salty ['sɔːltɪ] *adj taste* salé; *deposit* saumâtre.
salubrious [sə'luːbrɪəs] *adj* salubre, sain. (*fig*) **not a very ~ district** un quartier peu recommandable.
salubrity [sə'luːbrɪtɪ] *n* salubrité *f*.
salutary ['sæljʊtərɪ] *adj* salutaire.
salutation [ˌsæljʊ'teɪʃən] *n* salut *m*; (*exaggerated*) salutation *f*. **in ~** pour saluer.
salute [sə'luːt] **1** *n* (*with hand*) salut *m*; (*with guns*) salve *f*. **military ~** salut militaire; **to give (sb) a ~** faire un salut (à qn); **to return sb's ~** répondre au salut de qn; **to take the ~** passer les troupes en revue; *V* **fire, gun. 2** *vt* (*lit*) saluer (de la main); (*fig: acclaim*) saluer (*as* comme). **to ~ the flag** saluer le drapeau. **3** *vi* (*Mil etc*) faire un salut.
salvage ['sælvɪdʒ] **1** *n* (*U*) **(a)** (*saving*) *[ship, cargo]* sauvetage *m*; (*for re-use*) récupération *f*.

(b) (*things saved from fire, wreck*) objets *or* biens sauvés *or* récupérés; (*things for re-use*) objets récupérables. **to collect old newspapers for ~** récupérer les vieux journaux.
(c) (*payment*) prime *f or* indemnité *f* de sauvetage.
2 *cpd operation, work, company, vessel* de sauvetage.
3 *vt ship* sauver, effectuer le sauvetage de; *material, cargo* sauver (*from* de); (*for re-use*) récupérer.
salvation [sælˈveɪʃən] **1** *n* (*Rel etc*) salut *m*; (*economic*) relèvement *m*. (*fig*) **work has been his ~** c'est le travail qui l'a sauvé, il a trouvé son salut dans le travail; *V* **mean**[2].
2 *cpd*: **Salvation Army** Armée *f* du Salut; **Salvation Army band** fanfare *f* de l'Armée du Salut.
salvationist [sælˈveɪʃənɪst] *n* salutiste *mf*.
salve[1] [sælv] **1** *n* (*lit, fig*) baume *m*. **2** *vt* soulager, calmer, apaiser. **to ~ his conscience he ...** pour être en règle avec sa conscience il ... .
salve[2] [sælv] *vt* (*salvage*) sauver.
salver [ˈsælvəʳ] *n* plateau *m* (*de métal*).
salvo[1] [ˈsælvəʊ] *n* (*Mil*) salve *f*; *V* **fire.**
salvo[2] [ˈsælvəʊ] *n* (*Jur*) réserve *f*, réservation *f*.
salvor [ˈsælvəʳ] *n* sauveteur *m* (*en mer*).
Sam [sæm] *n* (*dim of* **Samuel**) Sam *m*; *V* **uncle.**
Samaritan [səˈmærɪtən] **1** *n* Samaritain(e) *m(f)*. (*Rel*) **the Good ~** le bon Samaritain; **he was a good ~** il faisait le bon Samaritain; (*organization*) **the S~s** ≃ S.O.S. Amitié. **2** *adj* samaritain.
samba [ˈsæmbə] *n* samba *f*.
sambo [ˈsæmbəʊ] *n* (*pej*) noiraud(e) *m(f)*, moricaud(e) *m(f)* (*pej*).
same [seɪm] **1** *adj* même; (*Jur: aforementioned*) susdit. **the ~ books as** *or* **that** les mêmes livres que; **the ~ day** le même jour; **the very ~ day** le jour même, exactement le même jour; **that ~ day** ce même jour, ce jour même; **in the ~ way ...** de même ...; **in the ~ way as** *or* **that** de la même façon que; **we sat at the ~ table as usual** nous nous sommes assis à notre table habituelle; **how are you? — ~ as usual!*** comment vas-tu? — comme d'habitude! *or* toujours pareil!*; **is that the ~ man (that) I saw yesterday?** est-ce bien le même homme que celui que j'ai vu hier?; **they turned out to be one and the ~ person** en fin de compte il s'agissait d'une seule et même personne; **he always says the ~ old thing** il répète toujours la même chose; **it comes to the ~ thing** cela revient au même (*V* **one**); **they both arrived at the ~ time** ils sont arrivés tous les deux en même temps; **don't all talk at the ~ time** ne parlez pas tous en même temps *or* à la fois; **at the ~ time we must remember that ...** en même temps il faut se rappeler que ...; **at the very ~ time as ...** au moment même *or* précis où ...; **to go the ~ way as sb** (*lit*) aller dans la même direction que qn; (*fig*) suivre les traces *or* marcher sur les traces de qn (*iro*); **I'm afraid he'll go the ~ way as his brother** je crains qu'il ne suive l'exemple de son frère; (*in health*) **she's much about the ~** son état est inchangé, elle est pareille*.
2 *pron* le même, la même; (*Jur: aforementioned*) le susdit, la susdite. **the film is the ~ as before** le film est le même qu'avant; **the price is the ~ as last year** c'est le même prix que l'année dernière; **we must all write the ~** il faut que nous écrivions (*subj*) tous la même chose; **do the ~ as your brother** fais comme ton frère; **he left and I did the ~** il est parti et j'ai fait de même *or* j'en ai fait autant; **I would do the ~ again** je recommencerais; **don't do the ~ again!** ne recommence pas!; (*in bar etc*) **the ~ again please** la même chose s'il vous plaît, remettez ça*; **I don't feel the ~ about it as I did** maintenant je vois la chose différemment; **I still feel the ~ about you** mes sentiments à ton égard n'ont pas changé; **it's all** *or* **just the ~ to me** cela m'est égal; **all** *or* **just the ~** tout de même, quand même; **things go on just the ~** (*monotonously*) rien ne change; (*in spite of everything*) rien n'est changé, la vie continue (quand même); **it's not the ~ as before** ce n'est plus pareil, ce n'est plus comme avant; **it's the ~ everywhere** c'est partout pareil; **and the ~ to you!** à vous aussi, à vous de même; (*as retort: in quarrel etc*) et je te souhaite la pareille!; **~ here!*** moi aussi!; **it's the ~ with us** (et) nous aussi!; (*Comm: on invoice*) **to repairing ~** réparation du même *or* de la même.
sameness [ˈseɪmnɪs] *n* identité *f*, similitude *f*; (*monotony*) monotonie *f*, uniformité *f*.
samovar [ˌsæməʊˈvɑːʳ] *n* samovar *m*.
sampan [ˈsæmpæn] *n* sampan(g) *m*.
sample [ˈsɑːmpl] **1** *n* (*gen*) échantillon *m*; (*Med*) *[urine]* échantillon; *[blood, tissue]* prélèvement *m*. **as a ~** à titre d'échantillon; **to take a ~** prélever un échantillon, faire un prélèvement (*also Geol*); **to take a blood ~** faire une prise *or* un prélèvement de sang (*from* à); **to choose from ~s** choisir sur échantillons; (*Comm*) **all the goods are up to ~** toutes les marchandises sont d'aussi bonne qualité que les échantillons; (*Comm*) **free ~** échantillon gratuit; *V* **random** *etc*.
2 *cpd*: (*Comm*) **sample book** collection *f* d'échantillons; **sample bottle, sample cigarette, sample selection** *etc* échantillon *m*; **sample line, sample sentence, sample verse** *etc* exemple *m*; **a sample section of the population** une section représentative de la population; **sample survey** enquête *f* par sondage.
3 *vt food, wine* goûter.
sampler [ˈsɑːmpləʳ] *n* marque *f* (*broderie représentant un début dans les travaux d'aiguille*).
sampling [ˈsɑːmplɪŋ] *n* prélèvement *m* d'échantillons, choix *m* d'échantillons, échantillonnage *m*. (*Comm etc*) **~ technique** technique *f* d'échantillonnage.
Samson [ˈsæmsn] *n* Samson *m*.
Samuel [ˈsæmjʊəl] *n* Samuel *m*.
sanatorium [ˌsænəˈtɔːrɪəm] *n, pl* **sanatoria** [ˌsænəˈtɔːrɪə] sanatorium *m*; (*Scol*) infirmerie *f*.
sanctification [ˌsæŋktɪfɪˈkeɪʃən] *n* sanctification *f*.
sanctify [ˈsæŋktɪfaɪ] *vt* sanctifier.
sanctimonious [ˌsæŋktɪˈməʊnɪəs] *adj* moralisateur (*f* -trice).
sanctimoniously [ˌsæŋktɪˈməʊnɪəslɪ] *adv* d'une manière moralisatrice; *speak* d'un ton moralisateur *or* prêcheur.
sanctimoniousness [ˌsæŋktɪˈməʊnɪəsnɪs] *n* caractère *or* ton moralisateur, attitude moralisatrice.
sanction [ˈsæŋkʃən] **1** *n* **(a)** (*U: authorization*) sanction *f*, approbation *f*. **with the ~ of sb** avec le consentement de qn; **he gave it his ~** il a donné son approbation.
(b) (*enforcing measure*) sanction *f*. **to impose economic ~s on** prendre des sanctions économiques contre.
2 *vt law, conduct* sanctionner, approuver. **I will not ~ such a thing** je ne peux pas approuver *or* sanctionner une chose pareille; **this expression has been ~ed by usage** cette expression est consacrée par l'usage.
sanctity [ˈsæŋktɪtɪ] *n [person, behaviour]* sainteté *f*; *[oath, place]* caractère sacré; *[property, marriage]* inviolabilité *f*. **odour of ~** odeur *f* de sainteté.
sanctuary [ˈsæŋktjʊərɪ] *n* (*holy place*) sanctuaire *m*; (*refuge*) asile *m*; (*for wild life*) réserve *f*. **right of ~** droit *m* d'asile; **to seek ~** chercher asile; *V* **bird.**
sanctum [ˈsæŋktəm] *n* **(a)** (*holy place*) sanctuaire *m*.
(b) (*: *sb's study etc*) retraite *f*, tanière *f*. (*hum*) **the (inner) ~** le saint des saints (*hum*).
sand [sænd] **1** *n* **(a)** sable *m*. **a grain of ~** un grain de sable; **this resort has miles and miles of golden ~(s)** cette station balnéaire a des kilomètres de plages de sable doré; (*fig*) **the ~s are running out** nos instants sont comptés; **~s** *[beach]* plage *f* (de sable); *[desert]* désert *m* (de sable).
(b) (*US**: *courage*) cran* *m*.
2 *cpd*: **sandbag** (*n*) sac *m* de sable *or* de terre; (*vt: stun*) assommer; **sandbank** banc *m* de sable; **sand bar** barre *f* (*de rivière*); **sandblast** (*n*) jet *m* de sable; (*vt*) décaper à la sableuse; **sandblasting** décapage *m* à la sableuse; **sandblasting machine** sableuse *f*; (*US*) **sandbox** tas *m* de sable; **happy as a sandboy** gai comme un pinson; **sandcastle** château *m* de sable; **sand desert** désert *m* de sable; **sand dune** dune *f* (de sable); **sand flea** (*beach flea*) puce *f* de mer; (*tropical*) chique *f*; **sand fly** phlébotome *m*; (*biting midge*) simulie *f*; **sandglass** sablier *m*; (*fig*) **sandman** marchand *m* de sable; **sandpaper** (*n*) papier *m* de verre; (*vt: also* **sandpaper down**) frotter *or* poncer au papier de verre; **sandpapering** ponçage *m* au papier de verre; **sandpiper** bécasseau *m*; (*esp Brit*) **sandpit** sablonnière *f*, carrière *f* de sable; (*for children*) tas *m* de sable; **sandshoes** (*rubber-soled*) tennis *mpl*; (*rope-soled*) espadrilles *fpl*; **sandstone** grès *m*; **sandstone quarry** grésière *f*; **sandstorm** tempête *f* de sable.
3 *vt* **(a)** *path* sabler, couvrir de sable; (*against ice*) sabler.
(b) (*also* **~ down**) frotter *or* poncer au papier de verre.
sandal [ˈsændl] *n* sandale *f*.
sandal(wood) [ˈsændl(wʊd)] **1** *n* santal *m*. **2** *cpd box, perfume* de santal.
sanding [ˈsændɪŋ] *n [road]* sablage *m*; (*sandpapering*) ponçage *m* au papier de verre.
sandwich [ˈsænwɪdʒ] **1** *n* sandwich *m*. **cheese ~** sandwich au fromage; **open ~** canapé *m*.
2 *cpd*: **sandwich board** panneau *m* publicitaire (*porté par un homme-sandwich*); (*Ind*) **sandwich course** ≃ cours *mpl* de promotion professionnelle *or* sociale, cours de formation professionnelle; **sandwich loaf** pain *m* de mie; **sandwich man** homme-sandwich *m*.
3 *vt* (*also* **~ in**) *person, appointment* intercaler. **to be ~ed (between)** être pris en sandwich (entre)*.
sandy [ˈsændɪ] *adj* **(a)** *soil, path* sablonneux; *water, deposit* sableux; *beach* de sable.
(b) (*colour*) couleur (de) sable *inv*. **~ hair** cheveux *mpl* blond roux.
sane [seɪn] *adj person* sain d'esprit; *judgment* sain, raisonnable, sensé. **he isn't quite ~** il n'a pas toute sa raison.
sanely [ˈseɪnlɪ] *adv* sainement, raisonnablement, judicieusement.
Sanforized [ˈsænfəraɪzd] *adj* ® irrétrécissable, qui ne rétrécit pas au lavage.
sang [sæŋ] *pret of* **sing.**
sangfroid [ˈsɑ̃ːŋˈfrwɑː] *n* sang-froid *m*.
sanguinary [ˈsæŋgwɪnərɪ] *adj battle, struggle* sanglant; *ruler* sanguinaire, altéré de sang (*liter*).
sanguine [ˈsæŋgwɪn] *adj* **(a)** *person* optimiste, plein d'espoir; *temperament, outlook* optimiste; *prospect* encourageant. **we are ~ about our chances of success** nous sommes optimistes quant à nos chances de succès; **of ~ disposition** d'un naturel optimiste, porté à l'optimisme.
(b) *complexion* sanguin, rubicond.
sanguinely [ˈsæŋgwɪnlɪ] *adv* avec optimisme, avec confiance.
sanguineous [sæŋˈgwɪnɪəs] *adj* sanguinolent.
sanitarium [ˌsænɪˈtɛərɪəm] *n* (*esp US*) = **sanatorium.**
sanitary [ˈsænɪtərɪ] **1** *adj* **(a)** (*clean*) hygiénique, salubre.
(b) *system, equipment* sanitaire. **there are poor ~ arrangements** les conditions sanitaires laissent *or* le sanitaire laisse à désirer.
2 *cpd*: **sanitary engineer** ingénieur *m* sanitaire; **sanitary inspector** inspecteur *m*, -trice *f* de la Santé publique; (*Brit*) **sanitary towel,** (*US*) **sanitary napkin** serviette *f* hygiénique.
sanitation [ˌsænɪˈteɪʃən] *n* (*in house*) installations *fpl* sanitaires; (*in town*) système *m* sanitaire; (*science*) hygiène publique.
sanity [ˈsænɪtɪ] *n [person]* santé mentale; *[judgment, reasoning]* rectitude *f*. **he was restored to ~** il retrouva sa santé mentale *or* sa raison; **~ demands that ...** le bon sens exige que ... + *subj*; **fortunately ~ prevailed** heureusement le bon sens l'emporta.
sank [sæŋk] *pret of* **sink**[1].

Sanskrit [ˈsænskrɪt] *adj, n* sanscrit (*m*).
Santa Claus [ˌsæntəˈklɔːz] *n* le père Noël.
sap^1 [sæp] *n* (*Bot*) sève *f*.
sap^2 [sæp] **1** *n* (*Mil: trench*) sape *f*. **2** *vt strength, confidence* saper, miner.
sap^3‡ [sæp] *n* (*fool*) cruche* *f*, gogo* *m*.
sapless [ˈsæplɪs] *adj plant* sans sève, desséché.
sapling [ˈsæplɪŋ] *n* jeune arbre *m*; (*fig*) jeune homme *m*. **~s** boisage *m*.
sapper [ˈsæpəʳ] *n* sapeur *m*. (*Brit Mil*) **the S~s*** le génie.
sapphic [ˈsæfɪk] *adj* saphique.
sapphire [ˈsæfaɪəʳ] **1** *n* (*jewel, gramophone needle*) saphir *m*. **2** *cpd ring* de saphir(s). **sapphire (blue) sky** un ciel de saphir.
sappiness [ˈsæpɪnɪs] *n* abondance *f* de sève.
sappy^1 [ˈsæpɪ] *adj leaves* plein de sève; *wood* vert.
sappy^2‡ [ˈsæpɪ] *adj* (*foolish*) cruche*.
saraband [ˈsærəbænd] *n* sarabande *f*.
Saracen [ˈsærəsn] **1** *adj* sarrasin. **2** *n* Sarrasin(e) *m(f)*.
sarcasm [ˈsɑːkæzəm] *n* (*U*) sarcasme *m*, raillerie *f*.
sarcastic [sɑːˈkæstɪk] *adj* sarcastique. **~ remarks** sarcasmes *mpl*.
sarcastically [sɑːˈkæstɪkəlɪ] *adv* avec sarcasme, railleusement, sarcastiquement.
sarcophagus [sɑːˈkɒfəgəs] *n, pl* **sarcophagi** [sɑːˈkɒfəgaɪ] sarcophage *m*.
sardine [sɑːˈdiːn] *n* sardine *f*. **tinned** *or* (*US*) **canned ~s** sardines en boîte *or* en conserve, ≃ sardines à l'huile; *V* **pack**.
Sardinia [sɑːˈdɪnɪə] *n* Sardaigne *f*.
Sardinian [sɑːˈdɪnɪən] **1** *adj* sarde. **2** *n* **(a)** Sarde *mf*. **(b)** (*Ling*) sarde *m*.
sardonic [sɑːˈdɒnɪk] *adj* sardonique.
sardonically [sɑːˈdɒnɪkəlɪ] *adv* sardoniquement.
sari [ˈsɑːrɪ] *n* sari *m*.
sarky‡ [ˈsɑːkɪ] *adj* sarcastique.
sarong [səˈrɒŋ] *n* sarong *m*.
sarsaparilla [ˌsɑːsəpəˈrɪlə] *n* salsepareille *f*.
sartorial [sɑːˈtɔːrɪəl] *adj elegance, matters* vestimentaire. **~ art** art *m* du tailleur.
sash^1 [sæʃ] *n* (*on uniform*) écharpe *f*; (*on dress etc*) large ceinture *f* à nœud.
sash^2 [sæʃ] **1** *n* [*window*] châssis *m* à guillotine. **2** *cpd*: **sash cord** corde *f* (d'une fenêtre); **sash window** fenêtre *f* à guillotine.
sass‡ [sæs] (*US*) **1** *n* toupet* *m*, culot* *m*. **2** *vt* répondre d'un ton insolent à.
Sassenach [ˈsæsənæx] *n* (*Scot: gen pej*) *nom donné aux Anglais par les Écossais*.
sassy* [ˈsæsɪ] *adj* (*US*) = **saucy**.
sat [sæt] *pret, ptp of* **sit**.
Satan [ˈseɪtn] *n* Satan *m*; *V* **limb**.
satanic [səˈtænɪk] *adj* satanique, démoniaque.
satanically [səˈtænɪkəlɪ] *adv* d'une manière satanique.
Satanism [ˈseɪtənɪzəm] *n* satanisme *m*.
satchel [ˈsætʃəl] *n* cartable *m*.
sate [seɪt] *vt* = **satiate**.
sateen [sæˈtiːn] **1** *n* satinette *f*. **2** *cpd* en satinette.
satellite [ˈsætəlaɪt] **1** *n* (*Astron, Pol, Space*) satellite *m*. **2** *cpd town, country* satellite.
satiate [ˈseɪʃɪeɪt] *vt* assouvir, rassasier (*with* de); (*fig*) gaver (*with* de), blaser (*with* par).
satiation [ˌseɪʃɪˈeɪʃən] *n* (*lit, fig*) assouvissement *m*. **to ~ (point)** (jusqu')à satiété.
satiety [səˈtaɪətɪ] *n* satiété *f*.
satin [ˈsætɪn] **1** *n* satin *m*; *V* **silk**. **2** *cpd dress, slipper* en *or* de satin; *paper, finish* satiné. **satin stitch** plumetis *m*; **satinwood** bois satiné de l'Inde.
satinette [ˌsætɪˈnet] **1** *n* satinette *f*. **2** *cpd* en satinette.
satire [ˈsætaɪəʳ] *n* satire *f* (*on* contre).
satiric(al) [səˈtɪrɪk(əl)] *adj* satirique.
satirically [səˈtɪrɪkəlɪ] *adv* d'une manière satirique.
satirist [ˈsætərɪst] *n* (*writer*) écrivain *m* satirique; (*cartoonist*) caricaturiste *mf*; (*in cabaret etc*) ≃ chansonnier *m*. **he's TV's greatest ~** il n'a pas son pareil à la télévision pour la satire.
satirize [ˈsætəraɪz] *vt* faire la satire de.
satisfaction [ˌsætɪsˈfækʃən] *n* **(a)** (*pleasure*) satisfaction *f*, contentement *m* (*at* de). **to feel ~/great ~** éprouver de la satisfaction/une satisfaction profonde; **it was a great ~ to us to hear that ...** nous avons appris avec beaucoup de satisfaction que ...; **one of his greatest ~s was his son's success** le succès de son fils lui a apporté l'une de ses plus grandes satisfactions; **to note with ~** constater avec satisfaction; **to my (great) ~ he ...** à ma grande satisfaction il ...; **to everybody's ~** à la satisfaction générale; **it has not been proved to my ~** cela n'a pas été prouvé de façon à me convaincre; **has the repair been done to your ~?** est-ce que vous êtes satisfait de la réparation?; *V* **job**.
(b) [*demand, need*] satisfaction *f*; [*wrong*] réparation *f*, dédommagement *m*; [*appetite*] assouvissement *m*; [*debt*] règlement *m*, acquittement *m*. **to give/obtain ~** donner/obtenir satisfaction; **I demand ~** j'exige qu'on me donne (*subj*) satisfaction.
satisfactorily [ˌsætɪsˈfæktərɪlɪ] *adv* d'une manière satisfaisante *or* acceptable.
satisfactory [ˌsætɪsˈfæktərɪ] *adj result, report, work* satisfaisant. **to bring sth to a ~ conclusion** mener qch à bien; **his work is/isn't ~** son travail est satisfaisant/laisse à désirer.
satisfy [ˈsætɪsfaɪ] **1** *vt* **(a)** *person* satisfaire, contenter, faire plaisir à. **he is never satisfied** il n'est jamais content *or* satisfait; **he was satisfied to remain ...** il a accepté de rester ..., il a trouvé suffisant de rester ...; **in a satisfied voice** d'un ton satisfait *or* content; **I am not satisfied with your answer** votre réponse ne me satisfait pas; (*iro*) **are you satisfied now?** vous voilà satisfait!; (*Scol, Univ*) **to ~ the examiners** être reçu (à un examen).
(b) *hunger, need, want, creditor* satisfaire; *condition* satisfaire, remplir; *objection* répondre à; *debt, obligation* s'acquitter de; (*Comm*) *demand* satisfaire à.
(c) (*convince*) convaincre, assurer (*sb that* qn que, *of* de). **to ~ o.s. of sth** s'assurer de qch; **I am satisfied that you have done your best** je suis convaincu *or* persuadé que vous avez fait de votre mieux.
2 *vi* donner satisfaction.
satisfying [ˈsætɪsfaɪɪŋ] *adj report, result, experience* satisfaisant; *food* nourrissant, substantiel.
saturate [ˈsætʃəreɪt] *vt* saturer (*with* de). (*Comm*) **to ~ the market** saturer le marché; **my shoes are ~d** mes chaussures sont trempées.
saturation [ˌsætʃəˈreɪʃən] **1** *n* saturation *f*. **2** *cpd*: **saturation bombing** tactique *f* de saturation (par bombardement); **saturation point** point *m* de saturation; **to reach saturation point** arriver à saturation.
Saturday [ˈsætədɪ] *n* samedi *m*. **on ~** samedi; **on ~s** le samedi; **next ~, ~ next** samedi prochain *or* qui vient; **last ~** samedi dernier; **the first/last ~ of the month** le premier/dernier samedi du mois; **every ~** tous les samedis, chaque samedi; **every other ~, every second ~** un samedi sur deux; **it is ~ today** nous sommes aujourd'hui samedi; **~ December 18th** samedi 18 décembre; **on ~ January 23rd** le samedi 23 janvier; **the ~ after next** samedi en huit; **a week on ~, ~ week** samedi en huit; **a fortnight on ~, ~ fortnight** samedi en quinze; **a week/fortnight past on ~** il y a huit/quinze jours samedi dernier; **the following ~** le samedi suivant; **the ~ before last** l'autre samedi; **~ morning** samedi matin; **~ afternoon** samedi après-midi; **~ evening** samedi soir; **~ night** samedi soir, (*overnight*) la nuit de samedi; (*TV*) **~ evening viewing** émissions *fpl* du samedi soir; (*Comm*) **~ closing** fermeture *f* le samedi; (*Press*) **the ~ edition** l'édition de *or* du samedi; *V* **holy**.
Saturn [ˈsætən] *n* (*Myth*) Saturne *m*; (*Astron*) Saturne *f*.
Saturnalia [ˌsætəˈneɪlɪə] *n* (*fig*) saturnale(s) *f(pl)*.
saturnine [ˈsætənaɪn] *adj* saturnien (*liter*), sombre, mélancolique.
satyr [ˈsætəʳ] *n* satyre *m*.
sauce [sɔːs] **1** *n* **(a)** (*Culin*) sauce *f*. **mint ~** sauce à la menthe; (*Prov*) **what's ~ for the goose is ~ for the gander** ce qui est bon pour l'un l'est pour l'autre; *V* **apple, tomato, white** *etc*.
(b) (‡: *impudence*) toupet* *m*. **none of your ~!** (*to child*) petit(e) impertinent(e)!; (*to adult*) assez d'impertinence!
2 *cpd*: **sauceboat** saucière *f*; **saucepan** casserole *f* (*V* **double 4**).
saucer [ˈsɔːsəʳ] *n* soucoupe *f*. **~-eyed, with eyes like ~s** avec des yeux comme des soucoupes; **~-shaped** en forme de soucoupe; *V* **flying**.
saucily [ˈsɔːsɪlɪ] *adv behave, speak* avec impertinence, impertinemment; *dress* avec coquetterie; *look* d'un air coquin.
sauciness [ˈsɔːsɪnɪs] *n* (*cheekiness*) toupet* *m*; impertinence *f*; (*smartness*) coquetterie *f*.
saucy [ˈsɔːsɪ] *adj* (*cheeky*) impertinent; *look* coquin; (*smart*) coquet, coquin. **hat at a ~ angle** chapeau coquettement posé sur l'oreille.
Saudi Arabia [ˈsaʊdɪəˈreɪbɪə] *n* Arabie *f* Séoudite *or* Saoudite.
sauerkraut [ˈsaʊəkraʊt] *n* (*U*) choucroute *f*.
sauna [ˈsɔːnə] *n* (*also* **~ bath**) sauna *m or f*.
saunter [ˈsɔːntəʳ] **1** *vi* flâner, se balader*. **to ~ in/out/away** *etc* entrer/sortir/s'éloigner *etc* d'un pas nonchalant. **2** *n* balade* *f*, flânerie *f*. **to go for a ~** faire une petite promenade *or* une balade*.
saurian [ˈsɔːrɪən] *adj, n* saurien (*m*).
sausage [ˈsɒsɪdʒ] **1** *n* saucisse *f*; (*pre-cooked*) saucisson *m*. **beef/pork ~** saucisse de bœuf/de porc; (*Brit*) **not a ~**‡ rien, des clous‡; *V* **cocktail, garlic, liver**^{1} *etc*.
2 *cpd*: **sausage dog*** teckel *m*, saucisson *m* à pattes (*hum*); **sausage machine** machine *f* à saucisses; **sausage meat** chair *f* à saucisse; (*esp Brit*) **sausage roll** friand *m*.
sauté [ˈsəʊteɪ] **1** *vt potatoes, meat* faire sauter. **2** *adj*: **~ potatoes** pommes (de terre) sautées.
savage [ˈsævɪdʒ] **1** *adj* **(a)** (*cruel, fierce*) *person* brutal; *dog* méchant, féroce; *attack, criticism* virulent, féroce; *look* furieux, féroce. **to have a ~ temper** être très colérique, avoir un caractère de chien*; **to deal a ~ blow (to)** frapper brutalement.
(b) (*primitive*) *tribe, life, customs* primitif, sauvage, barbare.
2 *n* sauvage *mf*.
3 *vt* [*dog etc*] attaquer férocement; (*fig*) [*critics etc*] éreinter, attaquer violemment.
savagely [ˈsævɪdʒlɪ] *adv* sauvagement, brutalement.
savageness [ˈsævɪdʒnɪs] *n*, **savagery** [ˈsævɪdʒrɪ] *n* (*cruelty*) sauvagerie *f*, brutalité *f*, férocité *f*; (*primitiveness*) barbarie *f*.
savanna(h) [səˈvænə] *n* savane *f*.
savant [ˈsævənt] *n* érudit(e) *m(f)*, homme *m* de science, lettré(e) *m(f)*.
save^1 [seɪv] **1** *vt* **(a)** (*rescue*) *person, animal, jewels, building etc* sauver (*from* de); (*Rel*) *sinner* sauver, délivrer. (*Rel*) **to ~ one's soul** sauver son âme; (*fig*) **I couldn't do it to ~ my soul** je ne le ferais pour rien au monde; **to ~ sb from death/drowning** *etc* sauver qn de la mort/de la noyade *etc*; **to ~ sb from falling** empêcher qn de tomber; **to ~ sb's life** sauver la vie à *or* de qn; **to ~ sb from himself** protéger qn de *or* contre lui-même; **to ~ the situation** sauver la situation; (*fig*) **to ~ one's bacon*** se tirer du pétrin; **to ~ one's skin*** *or* **neck*** *or* **hide*** sauver sa peau*; **to ~ face** sauver la face; **God ~ the Queen!** vive la reine!; **to ~ sth from the wreck/the fire** *etc* sauver qch du naufrage/de l'in-

cendie *etc*; (*fig*) **things look black but we must try to ~ something from the wreckage** la situation est sombre mais il faut essayer de sauver les meubles*; **to ~ a building from demolition** sauver un bâtiment de la démolition, empêcher la démolition d'un bâtiment; **they ~d the palace for posterity** on a préservé le palais pour la postérité.

(b) (*store away: also* ~ **up**) *money* mettre de côté; *food* mettre de côté, garder. **I've ~d you a piece of cake** je t'ai gardé un morceau de gâteau; **to ~ o.s. (up) for sth** se réserver pour qch; **he was saving (up) the cherry till last** il gardait la cerise pour la bonne bouche; **I ~d your letter till the last** j'ai gardé ta lettre pour la bonne bouche; **to ~ (up) old newspapers for charity** garder les vieux journaux pour les bonnes œuvres; (*collect*) **to ~ stamps/matchboxes** *etc* collectionner les timbres/les boîtes d'allumettes *etc*.

(c) (*not spend, not use*) *money, labour* économiser; (*time*) (faire) gagner. **you have ~d me a lot of trouble** vous m'avez épargné *or* évité bien des ennuis; **to ~ time let's assume that ...** pour aller plus vite *or* pour gagner du temps admettons que ... + *subj*; **this route will ~ you 10 miles** cet itinéraire vous fera gagner 10 milles; **that will ~ my going** *or* **me from going** cela m'évitera d'y aller; **think of all the money you'll ~** pensez à tout l'argent que vous économiserez *or* à toutes les économies que vous ferez; (*Comm*) **'~ 10p on this packet'** '10 pence d'économie sur ce paquet'; **you ~ £1 if you buy 3 packets** vous économisez une livre si vous achetez 3 paquets; **to ~ petrol** faire des économies d'essence, économiser l'essence; **he's saving his strength** *or* **himself for tomorrow's race** il se ménage pour la course de demain; *V* **penny, stitch.**

(d) (*Sport*) **to ~ a goal** empêcher de marquer, faire un blocage, sauver un but.

2 *vi* **(a)** (*also* ~ **up**) mettre de l'argent de côté, faire des économies, épargner. **to ~ (up) for the holidays/for a new bike** mettre de l'argent de côté pour les vacances/pour (acheter) un nouveau vélo.

(b) to ~ on sth économiser sur qch, faire des économies sur qch.

3 *n* (*Sport*) arrêt *m* (du ballon), blocage *m*. **what a brilliant ~!** c'est un arrêt de toute première classe!

save up 1 *vi* = **save[1] 2a.**

2 *vt sep* = **save[1] 1b.**

save[2] [seɪv] *prep* sauf, à l'exception de. **~ that ...** sauf que ..., à cette exception près que ..., à ceci près que ... .

saveloy [ˈsævəlɔɪ] *n* cervelas *m*.

saving [ˈseɪvɪŋ] **1** *n* **(a)** (*rescue*) sauvetage *m*; *[sinner]* salut *m*; *V* **face, life.**

(b) *[time]* économie *f*; *[money]* économie, épargne *f*. **we must make ~s** il faut économiser *or* faire des économies; **this means a great ~ of time/petrol** *etc* cela représente une grande économie de temps/d'essence *etc*; **a great ~ of money** une grande économie; **the government is trying to encourage ~(s)** le gouvernement cherche à encourager l'épargne; **small ~s** la petite épargne; **to live on one's ~s** vivre de ses économies; *V* **national, post office.**

2 *cpd*: **savings bank** caisse *f* d'épargne; **savings stamp** timbre-épargne *m*.

3 *adj* (*Jur*) **~ clause** avenant *m*; **generosity is his ~ grace** il se rachète par sa générosité; *V* **labour** *etc*.

4 *prep* (†) sauf. **~ your presence** sauf votre respect.

saviour [ˈseɪvjəʳ] *n* sauveur *m*. (*Rel*) **the S~** le Sauveur.

savor [ˈseɪvəʳ] *etc* (*US*) = **savour** *etc*.

savory [ˈseɪvərɪ] **1** *n* **(a)** (*herb*) sarriette *f*. **(b)** (*US*) = **savoury 2.** **2** *adj* (*US*) = **savoury 1.**

savour, (*US*) **savor** [ˈseɪvəʳ] **1** *n* (*flavour*) saveur *f*, goût *m*; (*fig*) pointe *f*, trace *f*, soupçon *m*. **2** *vt food, drink* savourer, déguster. **3** *vi*: **to ~ of sth** sentir qch; **his attitude ~s of pedantry** son attitude sent le pédantisme.

savouriness, (*US*) **savoriness** [ˈseɪvərɪnɪs] *n* saveur *f*, succulence *f*.

savourless, (*US*) **savorless** [ˈseɪvəlɪs] *adj* sans saveur, sans goût, insipide, fade.

savoury, (*US*) **savory** [ˈseɪvərɪ] **1** *adj smell, taste* savoureux, appétissant; *dish* salé (*par opposition à sucré*). (*fig*) **not a very ~ subject** un sujet peu appétissant *or* peu ragoûtant; **not a very ~ district** un quartier peu recommandable.

2 *n* (*Culin*) mets non sucré, (*on toast*) canapé chaud.

Savoy [səˈvɔɪ] **1** *n* Savoie *f*. **2** *adj* savoyard. **~ cabbage** chou frisé de Milan.

savvy‡ [ˈsævɪ] **1** *n* jugeote* *f*, bon sens. **2** *vi* (†) **no ~** sais pas, moi‡.

saw[1] [sɔː] (*vb: pret* **sawed,** *ptp* **sawed** *or* **sawn) 1** *n* scie *f*; *V* **circular** *etc*.

2 *cpd*: (*pej*) **sawbones***† chirurgien *m*, charcutier‡ *m* (*pej*); (*US*) **sawbuck‡** billet *m* de dix dollars; (*U*) **sawdust** sciure *f* (de bois); **saw edge** lame dentée; **saw-edged knife** couteau-scie *m*; **sawfish** poisson *m* scie, scie *f*; **sawhorse** chevalet *m* de scieur de bois; **sawmill** scierie *f*.

3 *vt* scier, débiter à la scie; *V also* **sawn.**

4 *vi*: **to ~ through a log** scier une bûche en deux; **to ~ through a plank/the bars of a cell** scier une planche/les barreaux d'une cellule.

saw away *vi* (* *pej*) **to saw away at the violin** racler du violon.

saw off 1 *vt sep* enlever à la scie.

2 sawn-off *adj V* **sawn 2.**

saw up *vt sep* débiter à la scie.

saw[2] [sɔː] *n* (*saying*) dicton *m*.

saw[3] [sɔː] *pret of* **see[1]**.

sawn [sɔːn] **1** *ptp of* **saw[1]**. **2** *adj* scié. **~ timber** bois *m* de sciage; **~-off shotgun** carabine *f* à canon scié.

sawyer [ˈsɔːjəʳ] *n* scieur *m*.

sax* [sæks] *n* (*abbr of* **saxophone**) saxo* *m*.

saxifrage [ˈsæksɪfrɪdʒ] *n* saxifrage *f*.

Saxon [ˈsæksn] **1** *adj* saxon. **2** *n* **(a)** Saxon(ne) *m(f)*. **(b)** (*Ling*) saxon *m*.

Saxony [ˈsæksənɪ] *n* Saxe *f*.

saxophone [ˈsæksəfəʊn] *n* saxophone *m*.

saxophonist [ˌsækˈsɒfənɪst] *n* saxophoniste *mf*, saxo* *m*.

say [seɪ] *pret, ptp* **said 1** *vt* **(a)** (*speak, utter, pronounce*) dire (*sth to sb* qch à qn); *lesson, poem* réciter. (*Rel*) **to ~ mass** dire *or* célébrer la messe; **to ~ a prayer** faire *or* dire une prière; **to ~ thank you** dire merci; **to ~ goodbye to sb** dire au revoir à qn; (*more formally*) faire ses adieux à qn; (*fig*) **you can ~ goodbye to peace and quiet!** tu peux dire adieu à ta tranquillité!; (*fig*) **to ~ yes/no to an invitation** accepter/refuser une invitation (*V also* **1f**); **your father said no** ton père a dit (que) non; **~ after me ...** répétez après moi ...; **could you ~ that again?** pourriez-vous répéter ce que vous venez de dire?; **I've got nothing to ~** (*can't think of anything*) je n'ai rien à dire; (*to police, judge etc: no formal statement*) je n'ai pas de déclaration à faire; (*to press etc: no comment*) pas de commentaire, je n'ai rien à dire; **I've got nothing more to ~** je n'ai rien à ajouter; **all of that can be said in 2 sentences** tout cela tient en 2 phrases; **something was said about it** on en a parlé, il en a été question; **I should like to ~ a few words about** j'aimerais dire quelques mots au sujet de *or* à propos de; **I should like to ask Mr X to ~ a few words** je voudrais prier M X de prendre la parole; **he said I was to give you this** il m'a dit de vous donner ceci; **he said to wait here** il a dit d'attendre ici; **to ~ one's say** dire ce qu'on a à dire (*V also* **3**); **so ~ing, he sat down** sur ces mots *or* sur ce, il s'assit; *V* **least, less** *etc.*

(b) (*assert, state*) dire; (*claim*) prétendre. **as I said yesterday** comme je l'ai dit hier; **as I said in my letter/on the phone** comme je vous l'ai dit dans ma lettre/au téléphone; **it ~s in the rules, the rules ~** il est dit dans le règlement; **it ~s on the radio there's going to be snow** la radio annonce de la neige; (*expressing doubt*) **that's what you ~!, so you ~!** que vous dites!*, c'est ce que vous dites!, c'est vous qui le dites!; **he got home at 6 so he ~s** il est rentré à 6 heures à ce qu'il dit *or* prétend; **it is said that ...** on dit que ...; **he is said to have an artificial leg** on dit qu'il a une jambe artificielle.

(c) (*suppose; think; assume; estimate*) dire, penser. **what will people ~?** qu'est-ce que les gens vont dire?; **he doesn't care what people ~** il se moque du qu'en-dira-t-on; **I ~ he should take it** je suis d'avis qu'il le prenne; **I should ~ she's intelligent** je pense qu'elle est intelligente; **I would ~ she was 50** je lui donnerais 50 ans; **what would you ~ is the population of Paris?** quelle est à votre avis *or* d'après vous la population de Paris?; **to see him you would ~ he was drunk** à le voir on dirait qu'il est ivre; **let us ~ for argument's sake that ...** mettons à titre d'exemple que ...; **~ someone left you a fortune, what would you do with it?** si vous héritiez d'une fortune qu'en feriez-vous?; *V also* **1f.**

(d) (*admit*) dire, reconnaître. **I must ~ (that) she's very pretty** je dois dire *or* reconnaître qu'elle est très jolie.

(e) (*register*) *[dial, gauge etc]* marquer. **my watch ~s 10 o'clock** ma montre marque 10 heures; **the thermometer ~s 30°** le thermomètre marque 30°.

(f) (*in phrases*) dire. **I can't ~ I'm fond of anchovies** je ne peux pas dire que j'aime (*subj*) les anchois; **'10 o'clock' he said to himself** '10 heures' se dit-il; **would you really ~ so?** (le pensez-vous) vraiment?; **is he right? — I should ~ he is** *or* **I should ~ so** (*emphatic: expressing certainty*) est-ce qu'il a raison? — et comment! *or* pour avoir raison il a raison!; (*expressing doubt*) est-ce qu'il a raison? — il me semble *or* je pense que oui; **I should ~ he IS right!** il a bien raison, c'est moi qui vous le dis!; **didn't I ~ so?** je l'avais bien dit n'est-ce pas?; **and so ~ all of us** nous sommes tous d'accord là-dessus; **to ~ nothing of ...** (+ *n*) sans parler de ...; (+ *vb*) sans parler du fait que ..., sans compter que ...; **that's ~ing a lot*** ce n'est pas peu dire; **he's cleverer than his brother but that isn't ~ing much*** *or* **a lot*** il est plus intelligent que son frère mais ça ne veut pas dire grand-chose*; **that doesn't ~ much for him** ce n'est pas à son honneur; **that doesn't ~ much for his intelligence** cela ne dénote pas beaucoup d'intelligence de sa part, cela en dit long (*iro*) sur son intelligence; **it ~s much** *or* **a lot for his courage that he stayed** il a bien prouvé son courage en restant; **she hasn't much to ~ for herself** elle n'a jamais grand-chose à dire; **he always has a lot to ~ for himself** il parle toujours beaucoup, il a toujours son mot à dire; **what have you (got) to ~ for yourself?** qu'avez-vous comme excuse?; **you might as well ~ the earth is flat!** autant dire que la terre est plate!; **don't ~ it's broken!*** ne me dis pas que c'est cassé!; **you can ~ THAT again!*** c'est le cas de le dire!, à qui le dites-vous!*; (*emphatic*) **you('ve) said it!*** tu l'as dit!*; (*hum*) **though I ~s‡** *or* **sez‡ it as shouldn't ...** ce n'est pas à moi de dire ça mais ...; **~ no more** (= *I understand*) (vous n'avez) pas besoin d'en dire plus; **let's ~ no more about it!** n'en parlons plus!; **enough said!*, 'nuff said!‡** (ça) suffit!, assez parlé!, en voilà assez!; **to ~ the least** c'est le moins qu'on puisse dire; **she was not very wise, to ~ the least** elle était pour le moins imprudente; **it wasn't a very good meal, to ~ the least of it** c'était un repas assez médiocre pour ne pas dire plus; **it goes without ~ing that ...** il va sans dire que ..., il va de soi que ...; **shall we ~ £5?** disons 5 livres?; **shall we ~ Tuesday?** mettons mardi?; **just ~ the word and I'll go** vous n'avez qu'un mot à dire pour que je parte; **he hadn't a good word to ~ for her** il n'a rien trouvé à dire en sa faveur; **there's something to be said for it** cela a des mérites *or* du bon *or* des avantages; **there's something to be said for waiting** il y aurait peut-être intérêt à attendre, on ferait peut-être mieux d'attendre; **it's easier** *or* **sooner said than done!** c'est plus facile à dire qu'à faire!, facile à dire!*; **when all is said and done** tout compte fait, au bout du compte; **what do you ~ to a cup of tea? — I won't ~ no (to it)*** que diriez-vous d'une tasse de thé? — j'en boirais bien une *or* ce ne serait pas de refus* *or* je ne dirais pas non; **what would you ~ to a round of golf?** si on faisait une partie de golf?; **there's no ~ing what he'll do** (il est) impossible de dire *or* on ne peut pas savoir ce qu'il fera.

2 *vi* dire. **so to ~** pour ainsi dire; **that is to ~** c'est-à-dire; **it is (as) one** *or* **you might ~ a new method** c'est comme qui dirait* une nouvelle méthode; **(I) ~!*** dites donc!; (*iro*) **you don't ~!*** sans blague!* (*iro*), pas possible! (*iro*); **~*, what time is it?** dites, quelle heure est-il?; **if there were, ~, 500 people** s'il y avait, mettons *or* disons, 500 personnes; (*iro*) **~s** *or* **sez you!‡** que tu dis!*; **~s who?‡, sez who?‡** ah oui? (*iro*); **as they ~** comme on dit, comme dirait l'autre*; **it seems rather rude, I must ~** cela ne me paraît guère poli, je l'avoue; (*expressing indignation*) **well, I must ~!** ça alors!*; **it's not for me to ~** (*not my responsibility*) ce n'est pas à moi de décider *or* de juger; (*not my place*) ce n'est pas à moi de le dire.

3 *n*: **to have one's ~** dire son mot, dire ce qu'on a à dire; **to have a ~/no ~ in the matter** avoir/ne pas avoir voix au chapitre; *V also* **1a.**

saying ['seɪɪŋ] *n* dicton *m*, proverbe *m*, adage *m*. **as the ~ goes** comme dit le proverbe, comme on dit.

say-so* ['seɪsəʊ] *n*: **on your ~** parce que vous le dites (*or* l'aviez dit *etc*); **on his ~** parce qu'il le dit (*or* l'a dit *etc*), sur ses dires.

scab [skæb] **1** *n* **(a)** *[wound]* croûte *f*, escarre *f*. **(b)** (*U*) = **scabies. (c)** (‡ *pej: Ind*) jaune* *m* (*pej*). **2** *vi* **(a)** se cicatriser, former une croûte. **(b)** (‡ *pej: Ind*) refuser de se mettre en grève, faire le jaune*.

scabbard ['skæbəd] *n [dagger]* gaine *f*; *[sword]* fourreau *m*.

scabby ['skæbɪ] *adj skin* croûteux; (*Med*) scabieux; (‡) *behaviour* moche*, méprisable.

scabies ['skeɪbiːz] *n* (*U: Med*) gale *f*.

scabious[1] ['skeɪbɪəs] *adj* (*Med*) scabieux.

scabious[2] ['skeɪbɪəs] *n* (*Bot*) scabieuse *f*.

scabrous ['skeɪbrəs] *adj* **(a)** *question, topic* scabreux, risqué. **(b)** (*Bot, Zool*) rugueux.

scads‡ [skædz] *npl* (*US*) **to have ~ of** avoir beaucoup de *or* plein* de.

scaffold ['skæfəld] *n* **(a)** (*gallows*) échafaud *m*. **(b)** (*Constr*) échafaudage *m*.

scaffolding ['skæfəldɪŋ] *n* (*U*) (*structure*) échafaudage *m*; (*material*) matériel *m* pour échafaudages.

scalawag* ['skæləwæg] *n* (*US*) = **scallywag*.**

scald [skɔːld] **1** *vt jar, teapot, tomatoes* échauder, ébouillanter; (*sterilize*) stériliser. **to ~ one's hand** s'ébouillanter la main; **to ~ o.s.** s'ébouillanter; (*Culin*) **to ~ the milk** chauffer le lait sans le faire bouillir.

2 *n* brûlure *f* (causée par l'eau bouillante).

scalding ['skɔːldɪŋ] *adj* brûlant. **~ hot** bouillant; (*fig*) **~ tears** larmes brûlantes.

scale[1] [skeɪl] **1** *n* **(a)** *[thermometer, ruler]* graduation *f*, échelle *f* (graduée); *[numbers]* série *f*; *[wages]* barème *m*, échelle. **~ of charges** tableau *m* des tarifs; **social ~** échelle sociale; *V* **centigrade, Fahrenheit, sliding.**

(b) *[map, drawing]* échelle *f*. **(drawn) to ~** à l'échelle; **drawn to a ~ of** rapporté à l'échelle de; **on a ~ of 5 km to the centimetre** à une échelle de 5 km pour un centimètre *or* de 1/500.000; **this map is not to ~** *or* **is out of ~** les distances ne sont pas respectées sur cette carte; **on a large ~** sur une grande échelle, en grand; **on a small ~** sur une petite échelle, en petit; **on a national ~** à l'échelle nationale.

(c) (*Mus*) gamme *f*. **to practise one's ~s** faire ses gammes.

2 *cpd*: **scale drawing** dessin *m* à l'échelle; **scale model** modèle réduit; *V* **full-scale** *etc*.

3 *vt* **(a)** *wall, mountain* escalader.

(b) *map* dessiner à l'échelle.

scale down *vt sep salary*, (*Scol*) *marks* réduire proportionnellement; *drawing* réduire l'échelle de; *production* réduire, baisser.

scale up *vt sep* augmenter proportionnellement.

scale[2] [skeɪl] **1** *n* (*for weighing*) plateau *m* (de balance). **(a pair of) ~s** une balance; (*for heavy weights*) une bascule; (*Astron*) **the S~s** la Balance; (*fig*) **to turn the ~s (in sb's favour/against sb)** faire pencher la balance (du côté de qn/contre qn); *V* **bathroom, platform, tip**[3] *etc*.

2 *cpd*: **scale maker** fabricant *m* de balances; **scale pan** plateau *m* de balance.

3 *vti* peser.

scale[3] [skeɪl] **1** *n* **(a)** *[fish, reptile, rust]* écaille *f*; *[skin]* squame *f*. **metal ~** écaille métallique; (*fig*) **the ~s fell from his eyes** les écailles lui sont tombées des yeux.

(b) (*U*) *[water pipes, kettle]* tartre *m*, dépôt *m* calcaire; *[teeth]* tartre.

2 *vt* **(a)** *fish* écailler.

(b) *teeth* détartrer.

scale off *vi* s'en aller en écailles, s'écailler.

scallion ['skælɪən] *n* échalote *f*.

scallop ['skɒləp] **1** *n* **(a)** coquille *f* Saint-Jacques, pétoncle *m*. **~ shell** coquille.

(b) (*Sewing*) **~s** festons *mpl*.

2 *vt* **(a) ~ed fish/lobster** coquille *f* de poisson/de homard.

(b) *hem etc* festonner. (*Sewing*) **~ed edge** bordure festonnée *or* à festons; (*Culin*) **to ~ (the edges of) a pie** canneler le bord d'une tourte.

scallywag* ['skælɪwæg] *n*, (*US*) **scalawag*** *n* (*hum*) petit(e) polisson(ne) *m(f)*.

scalp [skælp] **1** *n* cuir chevelu; (*Red Indian trophy*) scalp *m*. **2** *vt* scalper.

scalpel ['skælpəl] *n* bistouri *m*, scalpel *m*.

scaly ['skeɪlɪ] *adj fish* écailleux; *skin* squameux; *kettle, pipe* entartré.

scamp[1]* [skæmp] *n* galopin* *m*, coquin(e) *m(f)*, vaurien(ne) *m(f)*.

scamp[2] [skæmp] *vt one's work etc* bâcler*.

scamper ['skæmpə^r] **1** *n* galopade *f*; *[mice]* trottinement *m*.

2 *vi [children]* galoper; *[mice]* trottiner. *[children]* **to ~ in/out** *etc* entrer/sortir *etc* au galop.

scamper about *vi [children]* gambader; *[mice]* trottiner çà et là.

scamper away, scamper off *vi [children, mice]* s'enfuir, détaler*.

scan [skæn] **1** *vt* **(a)** (*examine closely*) *horizon* scruter; *crowd* fouiller du regard.

(b) (*glance quickly over*) *horizon* promener son regard sur; *crowd* parcourir des yeux; *newspaper* parcourir rapidement, feuilleter.

(c) (*Radar, TV*) balayer.

(d) (*Poetry*) scander.

2 *vi* se scander. **this line does not ~** ce vers est faux.

scandal ['skændl] **1** *n* **(a)** (*disgrace*) scandale *m*; (*Jur*) diffamation *f*. **to cause a ~** causer un scandale; **the groundnuts ~** le scandale des arachides; **it's a (real) ~** c'est scandaleux, c'est une honte; **it's a ~ that ...** c'est un scandale *or* une honte que ... + *subj*.

(b) (*U: gossip*) médisance *f*, cancans *mpl*, ragots* *mpl*. **to talk ~** colporter des cancans *or* des ragots*; **have you heard the latest ~?** avez-vous entendu les derniers potins?*; **there's a lot of ~ going around about him** il y a beaucoup de ragots* qui circulent sur son compte.

2 *cpd*: **scandalmonger** mauvaise langue, colporteur *m*, -euse *f* de ragots*.

scandalize ['skændəlaɪz] *vt* scandaliser, indigner. **to be ~d by** se scandaliser de, s'indigner de; **she was quite ~d** elle était vraiment scandalisée *or* indignée.

scandalous ['skændələs] *adj talk, behaviour* scandaleux; (*Jur*) diffamatoire. **that's a ~ price** c'est scandaleux de demander ce prix-là; **it's simply ~** c'est vraiment scandaleux, c'est un vrai scandale.

scandalously ['skændələslɪ] *adv* scandaleusement.

Scandinavia [ˌskændɪ'neɪvɪə] *n* Scandinavie *f*.

Scandinavian [ˌskændɪ'neɪvɪən] **1** *adj* scandinave. **2** *n* Scandinave *mf*.

scanner ['skænə^r] *n* (*Phot*) projecteur *m*; (*Aerial Phot*) déchiffreur *m*; (*Med*) tomographe *m*, scanner *m*.

scansion ['skænʃən] *n* scansion *f*.

scant [skænt] *adj* peu abondant, insuffisant. **to pay ~ attention** faire à peine attention; **~ praise** éloge des plus brefs.

scantily ['skæntɪlɪ] *adv* insuffisamment. **~ clad** vêtu du strict minimum, en tenue légère (*hum*).

scantiness ['skæntɪnɪs] *n* insuffisance *f*.

scanty ['skæntɪ] *adj meal, harvest* peu abondant, insuffisant; *swimsuit* minuscule, réduit à sa plus simple expression (*hum*). **a ~ income** de maigres revenus *mpl*.

scapegoat ['skeɪpgəʊt] *n* bouc *m* émissaire.

scapegrace ['skeɪpgreɪs] *n* coquin(e) *m(f)*, vaurien(ne) *m(f)*.

scapula ['skæpjʊlə] *n* omoplate *f*.

scapular ['skæpjʊlə^r] *adj, n* scapulaire (*m*).

scar[1] [skɑː^r] **1** *n* (*mark: lit, fig*) cicatrice *f*; (*knife wound, esp on face*) balafre *f*. **it left a ~ on his face** cela a laissé une cicatrice sur son visage; (*fig*) **the quarrying left a ~ on the hillside** l'exploitation de la carrière a laissé une cicatrice sur *or* a mutilé le flanc de la colline; (*fig*) **it left a deep ~ on his mind** il en est resté profondément marqué (*fig*).

2 *cpd*: **Scarface** le Balafré.

3 *vt* marquer d'une cicatrice, (*with knife*) balafrer. **he was ~red with many wounds** il portait les cicatrices de nombreuses blessures; **face ~red by smallpox** figure grêlée par la petite vérole; **war-~red town** ville qui porte des cicatrices de la guerre; **walls ~red by bullets** des murs portant des traces de balles.

scar[2] [skɑː^r] *n* (*crag*) rocher escarpé.

scarab ['skærəb] *n* (*beetle, gem*) scarabée *m*.

scarce [skɛəs] **1** *adj food, money* peu abondant; *copy, edition* rare. **money/corn is getting ~** l'argent/le blé se fait rare; **such people are ~** de telles gens sont rares, on ne rencontre pas souvent de telles gens; **to make o.s. ~*** s'esquiver, se sauver*.

2 *adv* (††) = **scarcely.**

scarcely ['skɛəslɪ] *adv* à peine. **it ~ touched him** cela l'a à peine touché; **I could ~ stand** je pouvais à peine tenir debout, j'avais de la peine *or* du mal à tenir debout; **~ anybody knows** il y a très peu de gens qui savent; **he ~ ever goes there** il n'y va presque jamais, il n'y va guère; **I ~ know what to say** je ne sais trop que dire; **I can ~ believe it** j'ai peine à *or* du mal à le croire.

scarceness ['skɛəsnɪs] *n*, **scarcity** ['skɛəsɪtɪ] *n [corn, money etc]* manque *m*, pénurie *f*, disette *f*. **there is a ~ of good artists today** il n'y a plus guère de bons artistes; **the ~ of the metal** la rareté du métal; **this item has a certain scarcity value** cet objet a une certaine valeur à cause de sa rareté.

scare [skɛə^r] **1** *n* peur *f*. **to give sb a ~** effrayer qn, faire peur à qn, donner la frousse à qn*; **what a ~ he gave me!** il m'a fait une de ces peurs! *or* une de ces frousses!*; **to raise a ~** semer l'alarme, faire courir des bruits alarmants; **the invasion ~** les bruits alarmistes d'invasion; **because of the war ~** à cause des rumeurs de guerre; **there have been several war ~s this year** à plusieurs reprises cette année les gens ont craint la guerre.

2 *cpd*: (*lit, fig*) **scarecrow** épouvantail *m*; (*US Press*) **scarehead‡** manchette *f* à sensation; **scaremonger** alarmiste *mf*.

3 *vt* effrayer, faire peur à. **to ~ sb stiff*** faire une peur bleue à qn; **to be ~d stiff*** avoir une peur bleue, avoir la frousse* *or* la trouille‡; **to be ~d out of one's wits*** être complètement affolé *or* paniqué*; **he's ~d to death of women*** il a une peur terrible *or* mortelle des femmes; *V* **living.**
scare away, scare off *vt sep*: **the dog scared him away** la peur du chien l'a fait fuir, il a fui par peur du chien; (*fig*) **the price scared him away** le prix lui a fait peur.
scared [skɛəd] *adj* effrayé, affolé (*of* par).
scarf [skɑːf] *n, pl* **scarves** *or* **~s** écharpe *f*; (*square*) foulard *m*. **~-ring** coulant *m or* anneau *m* pour foulard; *V* **head.**
scarify ['skɛərɪfaɪ] *vt* (*Agr, Med*) scarifier; (*fig*) éreinter.
scarlatina [ˌskɑːlə'tiːnə] *n* scarlatine *f*.
scarlet ['skɑːlɪt] **1** *adj* écarlate. **to go** *or* **blush ~ (with shame)** devenir rouge *or* écarlate (de honte). **2** *cpd*: **scarlet fever** scarlatine *f*; **scarlet pimpernel** mouron *m* rouge; **scarlet runner (bean)** haricot grimpant. **3** *n* écarlate *f*.
scarp [skɑːp] *n* escarpement *m*.
scarper‡ ['skɑːpəʳ] *vi* (*Brit*) ficher le camp*.
scarves [skɑːvz] *npl of* **scarf.**
scary* ['skɛərɪ] *adj* qui met mal à l'aise, qui donne des frissons.
scat‡ [skæt] *excl* allez ouste!*
scathing ['skeɪðɪŋ] *adj remark, criticism* acerbe, caustique, cinglant. **to be ~ about sth** critiquer qch de façon cinglante; **to give sb a ~ look** jeter un regard noir à qn, foudroyer qn du regard.
scathingly ['skeɪðɪŋlɪ] *adv* d'une manière acerbe *or* cinglante. **to look ~ at sb** foudroyer qn du regard.
scatter ['skætəʳ] **1** *vt* **(a)** (*also* **~ about, ~ around**) *crumbs, papers* éparpiller; *seeds* semer à la volée; *sand, salt, sawdust* répandre. (*fig*) **to ~ sth to the four winds** semer qch aux quatre vents; **he ~ed pennies among the children** il a jeté à la volée des piécettes aux enfants; **to ~ cushions on a divan** jeter des coussins çà et là sur un divan.
(b) *clouds, crowd* disperser; *enemy* mettre en déroute; *light* diffuser. **my relatives are ~ed all over the country** ma famille est dispersée aux quatre coins du pays.
2 *vi* [*clouds, crowd*] se disperser. **the onlookers ~ed at the approach of the police** les badauds se sont dispersés à l'arrivée de la police.
3 *n* (*Math, Tech*) dispersion *f*. **a ~ of houses** des maisons dispersées *or* éparses; **a ~ of raindrops** quelques gouttes de pluie éparses.
4 *cpd*: **scatterbrain** écervelé(e) *m*, hurluberlu* *m*; **scatter-brained** écervelé, hurluberlu*; **scatter cushions** petits coussins.
scattered ['skætəd] *adj books* éparpillés; *houses* dispersés, éparpillés; *population* dispersé, disséminé; *light* diffus. **the village is very ~** les maisons du village sont très dispersées.
scattering ['skætərɪŋ] *n* [*clouds, crowd*] dispersion *f*; [*light*] diffusion *f*. **there was a ~ of people in the hall** il y avait quelques personnes dispersées *or* çà et là dans la salle.
scattiness* ['skætɪnɪs] *n* (*Brit*) loufoquerie* *f*.
scatty* ['skætɪ] *adj* (*Brit*) loufoque*, farfelu.
scavenge ['skævɪndʒ] **1** *vt streets* enlever les ordures de. **2** *vi*: **to ~ (in the dustbins) for sth** fouiller (dans les poubelles) pour trouver qch.
scavenger ['skævɪndʒəʳ] **1** *n* **(a)** (*Zool*) insecte *m or* animal *m* nécrophage *or* coprophage. **(b)** (*street cleaner*) éboueur *m*. **2** *cpd*: **scavenger hunt** chasse *f* au trésor, rallye *m*.
scenario [sɪ'nɑːrɪəʊ] *n* scénario *m*.
scenarist ['siːnərɪst] *n* scénariste *mf*.
scene [siːn] **1** *n* **(a)** (*Theat etc*) (*part of play*) scène *f*; (*setting*) scène, décor *m*; (*fig*) incident *m*. **the garden ~ in 'Richard II'** la scène du jardin dans 'Richard II'; (*Cine, TV*) **outdoor** *or* **outside ~** extérieur *m*; **~ from a film** scène *or* séquence *f* (tirée) d'un film; **the big ~ in the film** la grande scène du film; **it was his big ~** c'était sa grande scène; **the ~ is set in Paris** la scène se passe à Paris, l'action se déroule à Paris; (*fig*) **the ~ was set for their romance** toutes les conditions étaient réunies pour leur idylle; **this set the ~ for the discussion** ceci a ouvert la voie à *or* préparé le terrain pour les discussions; (*fig*) **now let our reporter set the ~ for you** notre reporter va maintenant vous mettre au courant de la situation; (*Theat, fig*) **behind the ~s** dans les coulisses; **~s of violence** scènes de violence; **there were angry ~s at the meeting** des incidents violents ont eu lieu au cours de la réunion; *V* **change.**
(b) (*place*) lieu(x) *m(pl)*, endroit *m*. **the ~ of the crime/accident** le lieu du crime/de l'accident; (*Mil*) **~ of operations** théâtre *m* des opérations; **he needs a change of ~** il a besoin de changer d'air *or* de décor*; **they were soon on the ~** ils furent vite sur les lieux; **to appear** *or* **come on the ~** faire son apparition; **when I came on the ~** quand je suis arrivé; **he has disappeared from the political ~** il a disparu de la scène politique; **the political ~ in France** la situation politique en France; **the drug ~ in our big cities** la situation de la drogue dans nos grandes villes; **it's not my ~‡** ça n'est pas mon genre, ça n'est pas dans mes goûts.
(c) (*sight, view*) spectacle *m*, vue *f*, tableau *m*. **the ~ from the top is marvellous** du sommet la vue *or* le panorama est magnifique; **the ~ spread out before you** la vue *or* le panorama qui s'offre à vous; **the hills make a lovely ~** les collines offrent un très joli spectacle *or* tableau; **picture the ~ ...** représentez-vous la scène ...; **it was a ~ of utter destruction** c'était un spectacle de destruction totale.
(d) (*: *fuss*) scène *f*. **try not to make a ~ about it** tâche de ne pas en faire (toute) une scène *or* toute une histoire; **to have a ~ with sb** avoir une scène avec qn; **I hate ~s** je déteste les scènes.
(e) (‡: *sexually*) **to have a ~ with sb** avoir une liaison avec qn.
2 *cpd*: (*Theat*) **scene change** changement *m* de décor(s); **scene painter** peintre *m* de décors; **scene shift** changement *m* de décor(s); **scene shifter** machiniste *mf*.
scenery ['siːnərɪ] *n* **(a)** paysage *m*, vue *f*. **the ~ is very beautiful** le paysage est très beau, la vue est très belle; **mountain ~** paysage de montagnes; (*fig*) **a change of ~ will do you good** un changement d'air *or* de cadre *or* de décor* vous fera du bien.
(b) (*Theat*) décor(s) *m(pl)*.
scenic ['siːnɪk] *adj* scénique. (*esp US Rail*) **~ car** voiture *f* panoramique; **~ railway** (*panoramic*) petit train (d'agrément); (*Brit: switchback*) montagnes *fpl* russes; (*US*) **~ road** route *f* touristique; **an area of great ~ beauty** une région qui offre de très beaux panoramas.
scenography [siː'nɒgrəfɪ] *n* scénographie *f*.
scent [sent] **1** *n* **(a)** (*odour*) parfum *m*, odeur *f*.
(b) (*liquid perfume*) parfum *m*. **to use ~** se parfumer.
(c) (*animal's track*) fumet *m*; (*fig*) piste *f*, voie *f*. (*Hunting, fig*) **to lose the ~** perdre la piste; **to throw** *or* **put sb off the ~** dépister *or* déjouer qn; **to put** *or* **throw dogs off the ~** dépister les chiens, brouiller *or* faire perdre la piste aux chiens; **to be on the (right) ~** être sur la bonne piste *or* voie; **he got the ~ of something suspicious** il a flairé quelque chose de louche.
(d) (*sense of smell*) [*person*] odorat *m*; [*animal*] flair *m*.
2 *cpd*: **scent bottle** flacon *m* à parfum; **scent spray** vaporisateur *m* (à parfum); (*aerosol*) atomiseur *m* (à parfum).
3 *vt* **(a)** (*put ~ on*) *handkerchief, air* parfumer (*with* de). **the ~ed air** l'air parfumé *or* odorant.
(b) (*smell*) *game* flairer; (*fig*) *danger, trouble* flairer, pressentir.
scentless ['sentlɪs] *adj* inodore, sans odeur.
scepter ['septəʳ] *n* (*US*) = **sceptre.**
sceptic, (*US*) **skeptic** ['skeptɪk] *adj, n* sceptique (*mf*).
sceptical, (*US*) **skeptical** ['skeptɪkəl] *adj* sceptique (*of, about* sur). **I'm rather ~ about it** cela me laisse sceptique.
sceptically, (*US*) **skeptically** ['skeptɪkəlɪ] *adv* avec scepticisme.
scepticism, (*US*) **skepticism** ['skeptɪsɪzəm] *n* scepticisme *m*.
sceptre, (*US*) **scepter** ['septəʳ] *n* sceptre *m*.
schedule ['ʃedjuːl, *US* 'skedjuːl] **1** *n* **(a)** [*work, duties*] programme *m*, plan *m*; [*trains etc*] horaire *m*; [*events*] calendrier *m*. **production/building** *etc* **~** prévisions *fpl or* programme pour la production/la construction *etc*; **to make out a ~** établir un programme *or* un plan *or* un horaire; **the whole ceremony went off according to ~** toute la cérémonie s'est déroulée selon le programme *or* les prévisions; (*fig*) **it all went according to ~** tout s'est passé comme prévu; **the train is on** *or* **up to ~** le train est à l'heure; **the train is behind ~** le train a du retard; **the preparations are on ~/behind ~** il n'y a pas de retard/il y a du retard dans les préparatifs; **our work has fallen behind ~** nous sommes en retard dans notre travail *or* sur notre plan de travail; **the ceremony will take place on ~** la cérémonie aura lieu à l'heure prévue (*or* à la date prévue *etc*); **our ~ does not include the Louvre** notre programme ne comprend pas le Louvre; **to be ahead of ~** (*in work*) avoir de l'avance sur son programme; [*train*] avoir de l'avance; **to work to a very tight ~** avoir un programme de travail très serré.
(b) (*list*) [*goods, contents*] liste *f*, inventaire *m*; [*prices*] barème *m*; (*Customs, Income Tax etc*) tarif *m*. **~ of charges** tarif *or* liste *or* barème des prix.
2 *vt* **(a)** (*gen pass*) *activity* établir le programme *or* l'horaire de. **his ~d speech** le discours qu'il doit (*or* devait *etc*) prononcer; **his ~d departure** son départ prévu; **at the ~d time/date** *etc* à l'heure/à la date *etc* prévue *or* indiquée; **~d price** prix tarifé; **as ~d** comme prévu; [*train, bus etc*] **~d service** service régulier; **this stop is not ~d** cet arrêt n'est pas indiqué dans l'horaire; **he is ~d to leave at midday** son départ est fixé pour midi; **you are ~d to speak after him** d'après le programme c'est à vous de parler après lui; **the train is ~d for 11 o'clock** *or* **to arrive at 11 o'clock** selon l'horaire le train doit arriver à 11 heures.
(b) *object* inscrire sur une liste. (*Brit: Admin, Archit*) **~d building** bâtiment classé (*comme monument historique*).
schema ['skiːmə] *n, pl* **schemata** [skiː'mɑːtə] schéma *m*.
schematic [skɪ'mætɪk] *adj* schématique.
scheme [skiːm] **1** *n* **(a)** (*plan*) plan *m*, projet *m*; (*method*) procédé *m* (*for doing* pour faire). **he's got a ~ for re-using plastic bottles** il a un plan *or* un projet *or* un procédé pour réutiliser les bouteilles en plastique; **a ~ of work** un plan de travail; **profit-sharing ~** système *m* de participation (aux bénéfices); **a ~ for greater productivity** un plan destiné à augmenter la productivité; **the ~ for the new bridge** le projet pour le nouveau pont; **it's some crazy ~ of his** c'est une de ses idées invraisemblables; **it's not a bad ~*** ça n'est pas une mauvaise idée.
(b) (*plot*) complot *m*, machination(s) *f(pl)*; (*dishonest plan*) procédé *m* malhonnête, combine‡ *f*. **it's a ~ to get him out of the way** c'est un complot pour l'éliminer.
(c) (*arrangement*) classification *f*, arrangement *m*, combinaison *f*; *V* **colour, rhyme.**
2 *vt* combiner, machiner.
3 *vi* comploter, conspirer, intriguer (*to do* pour faire).
schemer ['skiːməʳ] *n* (*on small scale*) intrigant(e) *m(f)*; (*on large scale*) conspirateur *m*, -trice *f*, comploteur *m*, -euse *f*.
scheming ['skiːmɪŋ] **1** *adj* intrigant, rusé. **2** *n* machinations *fpl*, intrigues *fpl*.
scherzo ['skɜːtsəʊ] *n* scherzo *m*.
schism ['sɪzəm] *n* schisme *m*.
schismatic [sɪz'mætɪk] *adj, n* schismatique (*mf*).
schist [ʃɪst] *n* schiste *m*.
schizo‡ ['skɪtsəʊ] *adj, n* (*abbr of* **schizophrenic**) schizophrène (*mf*).
schizoid ['skɪtsɔɪd] *adj, n* schizoïde (*mf*).

schizophrenia [ˌskɪtsəʊˈfriːnɪə] *n* schizophrénie *f*.
schizophrenic [ˌskɪtsəʊˈfrenɪk] *adj, n* schizophrène (*mf*).
schmaltz* [ʃmɔːlts] *n* (*US*) sentimentalisme excessif.
schnapps [ʃnæps] *n* schnaps *m*.
schnorkel [ˈʃnɔːkl] *n* = **snorkel.**
scholar [ˈskɒləʳ] *n* **(a)** lettré(e) *m(f)*, érudit(e) *m(f)*. **a ~ and a gentleman** un homme cultivé et raffiné; **a Dickens ~** un(e) spécialiste de Dickens; **I'm not much of a ~** je ne suis pas bien savant *or* instruit.
(b) (*scholarship holder*) boursier *m*, -ière *f*; (†: *pupil*) écolier *m*, -ière *f*.
scholarly [ˈskɒləlɪ] *adj account, work, man* érudit, savant.
scholarship [ˈskɒləʃɪp] **1** *n* **(a)** (*U*) érudition *f*, savoir *m*. **(b)** (*award*) bourse *f* (d'études). **to win a ~ to Cambridge** obtenir une bourse pour Cambridge (*par concours*). **2** *cpd*: **scholarship holder** boursier *m*, -ière *f*.
scholastic [skəˈlæstɪk] **1** *adj philosophy* scolastique; *work, achievement* scolaire. **~ agency** bureau *m* de placement pour professeurs. **2** *n* (*Philos*) scolastique *m*.
scholasticism [skəˈlæstɪsɪzəm] *n* scolastique *f*.
school[1] [skuːl] **1** *n* **(a)** (*gen*) école *f*; (*primary ~*) école; (*secondary ~*) collège *m*; (*grammar ~*) lycée *m*; (*of dancing*) école, académie *f*; (*of music*) école, conservatoire *m*. **~ of motoring** auto-école *f*; **to go to ~** aller à l'école (*or* au collège *or* au lycée *etc*); **to leave ~** quitter l'école *etc*; **at** *or* **in ~** à l'école *etc*; **we were at ~ together** nous étions à la même école *etc*; **he wasn't at ~ yesterday** il n'était pas à l'école *etc or* en classe hier, il était absent hier; **the whole ~ wish(es) you well** toute l'école *etc* vous souhaite du succès; *V* **boarding, high, old, summer** *etc*.
(b) (*lessons*) classe(s) *f(pl)*, (*gen secondary*) cours *mpl*. **~ reopens in September** la rentrée scolaire *or* la rentrée des classes est en septembre; **there's no ~ this morning** il n'y a pas classe *or* pas de classes ce matin, il n'y a pas (de) cours ce matin.
(c) (*Univ*) faculté *f*, collège *m*; (*Oxford and Cambridge*) salle *f* d'examens. (*Oxford and Cambridge*) **S~s** les examens *mpl* (*V also* **1e**); **he's at law/medical ~** il fait son droit/sa médecine; **S~ of Linguistics/African Studies** *etc* Institut *m or* (*smaller*) Département *m* de Linguistique/d'Études africaines *etc*.
(d) (*fig*) école *f*. **the hard ~ of poverty** la dure école de la pauvreté; **he learnt that in a good ~** il a appris cela à bonne école.
(e) (*Hist: scholasticism*) **the ~s** l'École, la scolastique.
(f) *[painting, philosophy etc]* école *f*. (*Art*) **the Dutch ~** l'école hollandaise; **the Freudian ~** l'école freudienne; **a ~ of thought** une école de pensée; **an aristocrat/doctor** *etc* **of the old ~** un aristocrate/un docteur *etc* de la vieille école; **he's one of the old ~** il est de la vieille école *or* de la vieille garde, c'est un traditionaliste.
2 *cpd equipment, edition* scolaire. **school-age child** enfant *mf* d'âge scolaire; **school attendance** scolarisation *f*, scolarité *f*; **school attendance officer** fonctionnaire *mf* chargé(e) de faire respecter les règlements de la scolarisation; **schoolbag** cartable *m*; **schoolbook** livre *m* scolaire *or* de classe; **schoolboy** (*V* **1a**) élève *m*, écolier *m*, lycéen *m*, collégien *m* (*V also* **public**); **schoolboy slang** argot *m* des écoles *or* des lycées; **school bus** autobus *m or* car *m* de ramassage scolaire; **school bus service** service *m* de ramassage scolaire; **schoolchild** écolier *m*, -ière *f*, lycéen(ne) *m(f)*, collégien(ne) *m(f)*; **school crossing patrol** *V* **crossing b**; **schooldays** années *fpl* de scolarité *or* d'école; **during my schooldays** du temps où j'allais en classe; **school doctor** médecin *m* scolaire; **school fees** frais *mpl* de scolarité; **schoolfellow** camarade *mf* de classe; **schoolgirl** (*V* **1a**) élève *f*, écolière *f*, lycéenne *f*, collégienne *f*; **schoolgirl complexion** teint *m* de jeune fille; **schoolgirl crush*** béguin* *m* (*on* pour); **school holidays** vacances *fpl* scolaires; **during school hours** pendant les heures de classe; **schoolhouse** (*school building*) école *f*; (*for headmaster*) maison *f* du directeur; (*Brit*) **school leaver** jeune *mf* qui a terminé ses études secondaires, jeune libéré(e) de l'obligation scolaire (*Admin*); **school-leaving age** âge *m* de fin de scolarité; **school life** vie *f* scolaire; (*pej*) **schoolmarm** institutrice *f*; (*pej*) **she is very schoolmarmish** elle fait *or* est très maîtresse d'école; **schoolmaster** (*primary*) instituteur *m*; (*secondary*) professeur *m*; **schoolmate** = **schoolfellow**; **schoolmistress** (*primary*) institutrice *f*; (*secondary*) professeur *m*; **school officer** = **school attendance officer**; **school report** bulletin *m* (scolaire); **schoolroom** salle *f* de classe; **in the schoolroom** dans la (salle de) classe, en classe; **schoolteacher** (*primary*) instituteur *m*, -trice *f*; (*secondary*) professeur *m*; **schoolteaching** enseignement *m*; **in school time** pendant les heures de classe; **school year** année *f* scolaire.
3 *vt animal* dresser; *feelings, reactions* contrôler. **to ~ o.s. to do** s'astreindre à faire.
school[2] [skuːl] *n [fish]* banc *m*.
schooling [ˈskuːlɪŋ] *n* **(a)** (*Scol*) instruction *f*, études *fpl*. **~ is free** les études sont gratuites; **compulsory ~** scolarité *f* obligatoire; **~ is compulsory up to 16** la scolarité est obligatoire jusqu'à 16 ans; **he had very little formal ~** il a reçu très peu d'instruction.
(b) *[horse]* dressage *m*.
schooner [ˈskuːnəʳ] *n* **(a)** (*Naut*) schooner *m*, goélette *f*. **(b)** (*Brit: sherry glass*) grand verre *m* (à Xérès); (*US: beer glass*) demi *m* (de bière).
sciatic [saɪˈætɪk] *adj* sciatique.
sciatica [saɪˈætɪkə] *n* sciatique *f*.
science [ˈsaɪəns] **1** *n* **(a)** science(s) *f(pl)*. **we study ~ at school** nous étudions les sciences au lycée; **gardening for him is quite a ~** pour lui le jardinage est une véritable science; (*Univ*) **the Faculty of S~, the S~ Faculty** la faculté des sciences; (*Brit*) **Secretary (of State) for S~, Minister of S~** ministre *m* de la Recherche scientifique; **Department** *or* **Ministry of S~** ministère *m* de la Recherche scientifique; *V* **applied, natural, social** *etc*.
(b) (††: *knowledge*) savoir *m*, connaissances *fpl*. **to blind sb with science** éblouir qn de sa science.
2 *cpd*: *equipment, subject* scientifique; *exam* de sciences. **science fiction** (*n*) science-fiction *f*; (*adj*) de science-fiction; **science teacher** professeur *m* de sciences.
scientific [ˌsaɪənˈtɪfɪk] *adj investigation, method, studies* scientifique; *gifts* pour les sciences; *instrument* de précision. **~ farming** l'agriculture *f* scientifique; **he's a very ~ footballer** il joue au football avec science.
scientifically [ˌsaɪənˈtɪfɪkəlɪ] *adv* scientifiquement.
scientist [ˈsaɪəntɪst] *n* scientifique *mf*. **my daughter is a ~** ma fille est une scientifique; **one of our leading ~s** l'un de nos plus grands savants; *V* **Christian, social** *etc*.
Scillies [ˈsɪlɪz] *npl*, **Scilly Isles** [ˈsɪlɪaɪlz] *npl* Sorlingues *fpl*.
scimitar [ˈsɪmɪtəʳ] *n* cimeterre *m*.
scintillate [ˈsɪntɪleɪt] *vi [star, jewel]* scintiller; (*fig*) *[person]* briller (*dans une conversation*), pétiller d'esprit.
scintillating [ˈsɪntɪleɪtɪŋ] *adj star* scintillant; *jewel* scintillant, étincelant; *conversation, wit, remark* brillant, pétillant, étincelant.
scion [ˈsaɪən] *n* (*person*) descendant(e) *m(f)*; (*Bot*) scion *m*.
scissor [ˈsɪzəʳ] **1** *n*: **~s** ciseaux *mpl*; **a pair of ~s** une paire de ciseaux; *V* **kitchen, nail** *etc*. **2** *cpd*: **scissor bill** bec *m* en ciseaux. **3** *vt* (*) couper avec des ciseaux.
sclerosis [sklɪˈrəʊsɪs] *n* sclérose *f*; *V* **multiple.**
scoff[1] [skɒf] *vi* se moquer. **to ~ at** se moquer de, mépriser; **he was ~ed at by the whole town** il a été l'objet de risée de toute la ville.
scoff[2]* [skɒf] *vti* (*esp Brit*) bouffer‡.
scoffer [ˈskɒfəʳ] *n* moqueur *m*, -euse *f*, railleur *m*, -euse *f*.
scoffing [ˈskɒfɪŋ] *adj remark, laugh* moqueur, railleur.
scold [skəʊld] **1** *vt* réprimander, attraper, passer un savon à* (*for doing* pour avoir fait); *child* gronder, attraper, tirer les oreilles à* (*for doing* pour avoir fait). **he got ~ed** il s'est fait attraper.
2 *vi* grogner, rouspéter*.
3 *n* (*woman*) mégère *f*, chipie *f*.
scolding [ˈskəʊldɪŋ] *n* gronderie *f*, réprimande *f*. **to get a ~ from sb** se faire gronder *or* attraper par qn; **to give sb a ~** réprimander *or* gronder qn.
scollop [ˈskɒləp] = **scallop.**
scone [skɒn] *n* (sorte *f* de) petit pain au lait.
scoop [skuːp] **1** *n* **(a)** (*for flour, sugar*) pelle *f* (à main); (*for water*) écope *f*; (*for ice cream*) cuiller *f* à glace; (*for mashed potatoes*) cuiller à purée; *[bulldozer]* lame *f*; *[dredger]* benne *f* preneuse; (*also* **~ful**) pelletée *f*. **at one ~** en un seul coup de pelle; (*with hands*) d'un seul coup.
(b) (*Press*) reportage exclusif *or* à sensation, scoop *m*; (*Comm*) bénéfice important. **to make a ~** (*Comm*) faire un gros bénéfice; (*Press*) publier une nouvelle à sensation en exclusivité, faire un scoop; (*Press*) **it was a ~ for the 'Globe'** le 'Globe' l'a publié en exclusivité, cela a été un scoop pour le 'Globe'.
2 *vt* (*Comm*) *market* s'emparer de; *competitor* devancer; *profit* ramasser; (*Press*) *story* publier en exclusivité.
scoop out *vt sep*: **to scoop water out of a boat** écoper un bateau; **he scooped the sand out (of the bucket)** il a vidé le sable (du seau); **he had to scoop the water out of the sink** il a dû se servir d'un récipient pour vider l'eau de l'évier; **he scooped out a hollow in the soft earth** il a creusé un trou dans la terre molle.
scoop up *vt sep earth, sweets* ramasser, (*with instrument*) ramasser à la pelle. **the eagle scooped up the rabbit** l'aigle a saisi le lapin dans ses serres; **he scooped up the child and ran for his life** il a ramassé l'enfant en vitesse et s'est enfui à toutes jambes.
scoot‡ [skuːt] *vi* se sauver*, filer*. **~!** allez-vous-en!, fichez le camp!*, filez!*; **to ~ in/out** *etc* entrer/sortir *etc* rapidement *or* en coup de vent.
scoot away‡, scoot off‡ *vi* se sauver*, filer*.
scooter [ˈskuːtəʳ] *n* (*also* **motor ~**) scooter *m*; (*child's*) trottinette *f*.
scope [skəʊp] *n* (*opportunity: for activity, action etc*) possibilité *f*, occasion *f*; (*range*) *[law, regulation]* étendue *f*, portée *f*; (*capacity*) *[person]* compétence *f*, moyens *mpl* (intellectuels), capacité(s) *f(pl)*; *[undertaking]* envergure *f*. **a programme of considerable ~** un programme d'une envergure considérable; **to extend the ~ of one's activities** élargir le champ de ses activités, étendre son rayon d'action; **his job gave him plenty of ~ (for his ability)** son travail lui offrait beaucoup de possibilités pour montrer ses compétences; **he wants a job with more ~** il voudrait un travail avec un champ d'activité plus varié; **it gave him full ~ to decide for himself** cela lui a permis de prendre les décisions lui-même; **this work is within/beyond his ~** ce travail entre dans ses compétences/dépasse ses compétences; **the subject is within/beyond the ~ of this book** le sujet entre dans les limites/dépasse les limites de ce livre; **that is within the ~ of the new regulations** ceci est prévu par le nouveau règlement.
scorbutic [skɔːˈbjuːtɪk] *adj* scorbutique.
scorch [skɔːtʃ] **1** *n* (*also* **~ mark**) brûlure légère. **there was a ~ on her dress** sa robe avait été roussie.
2 *vt linen* roussir, brûler légèrement; *grass [fire etc]* brûler; *[sun]* dessécher, roussir. **~ed earth policy** tactique *f* de la terre brûlée.
3 *vi* roussir.
scorch along* *vi [car]* rouler à toute vitesse; *[driver]* conduire à un train d'enfer; *[cyclist]* pédaler à fond de train *or* comme un fou* (*f* une folle*).
scorcher* [ˈskɔːtʃəʳ] *n* journée *f* torride. **it was a (real) ~ (of a day)** il faisait une chaleur caniculaire *or* une de ces chaleurs*.

scorching ['skɔːtʃɪŋ] *adj* **(a)** *heat* torride; *sand* brûlant. ~ **sun** soleil *m* de plomb.

(b) (*: *also* ~ **hot)** *food* brûlant; *liquid* bouillant; *weather* très chaud. **it was a ~ (hot) day** il faisait une de ces chaleurs*.

score [skɔːʳ] **1** *n* **(a)** (*Sport*) score *m*; (*Cards*) marque *f*. **to keep (the) ~** (*gen*) compter *or* marquer les points; (*Cards*) tenir la marque; (*Tennis*) tenir le score; (*Ftbl*) **there's no ~ yet** on n'a pas encore marqué (de but); **there was no ~ in the match between X and Y** X et Y ont fait match nul *or* zéro à zéro; **what's the ~?** (*Sport*) où en est le jeu? *or* la partie? *or* le match?; (* *fig*) où en sommes-nous?; (*fig*) **to know the ~*** en connaître un bout*, connaître la musique* (*fig*); *V* **half** *etc.*

(b) (*debt*) compte *m*, dette *f*. (*fig*) **to settle a ~ with sb** régler son compte à qn; **he's got a ~** *or* **an old ~ to settle with him** il a un compte à régler avec lui.

(c) (*subject, account*) titre *m*. **on the ~ of** pour cause de, en raison de; **on more ~s than one** à plus d'un titre; **on that ~** à cet égard, sur ce chapitre, à ce titre; **on what ~?** à quel titre?; **on several ~s** à plusieurs titres.

(d) (*cut*) (*on metal, wood*) rayure *f*; (*deeper*) entaille *f*; (*on rock*) strie *f*; (*on skin, leather*) (*accidental*) éraflure *f*; (*deliberate*) incision *f*.

(e) (*Mus*) partition *f*. **piano ~** partition de piano; **to follow the ~** suivre la partition; *V* **vocal**.

(f) (*twenty*) **a ~** vingt; **a ~ of people** une vingtaine de personnes; **three ~ and ten**†† soixante-dix; (*fig*) **~s of times** trente-six fois*; **there were ~s of mistakes** il y avait un grand nombre de *or* des tas* de fautes.

2 *cpd*: **scoreboard** tableau *m*; **scorecard** (*Shooting*) carton *m*; (*Golf*) carte *f* du parcours; (*Cards*) feuille *f* de marque; **scorekeeper** marqueur *m*; (*Games*) **scoresheet** feuille *f* de marque.

3 *vt* **(a)** *goal, point* marquer. (*Scol etc*) **to ~ 70% (in an exam)** avoir 70 sur 100 (à un examen); **to ~ well in a test** avoir *or* obtenir un bon résultat à un test; (*Tennis*) **he went 5 games without scoring a point** il n'a pas marqué un seul point pendant 5 jeux; **they had 14 goals ~d against them** leurs adversaires ont marqué 14 buts; **to ~ a hit** (*Fencing*) toucher; (*Shooting*) viser juste; (*fig*) **to ~ a great success** *or* **a hit** remporter *or* se tailler un grand succès; **he certainly ~d a hit with her*** il a vraiment eu une touche*; (*fig*) **to ~ a point (over** *or* **off sb)** prendre le dessus (sur qn), l'emporter (sur qn), marquer un point (aux dépens de qn).

(b) (*cut*) *stick* entailler; *rock* strier; *ground* entamer; *wood, metal* rayer; *leather, skin* inciser, (*accidentally*) érafler; (*Culin*) inciser.

(c) (*Mus*) (*arrange*) adapter (*for* pour); (*orchestrate*) orchestrer (*for* pour); (*US: compose*) composer. **the film was ~d by X** la musique du film a été composée par X; **it is ~d for piano and cello** c'est écrit pour piano et violoncelle.

4 *vi* (*Sport*) *[player]* marquer un *or* des point(s); *[footballer etc]* marquer un but; (*keep the score*) marquer les points. (*Ftbl*) **they failed to ~** ils n'ont pas réussi à marquer (un but); (*fig*) **that is where he ~s** c'est là qu'il a le dessus *or* l'avantage; **to ~ over** *or* **off sb** marquer un point aux dépens de qn, damer le pion à qn.

score off, score out *vt sep* rayer, barrer, biffer.

score up *vt sep points* marquer, faire; *debt* porter en compte, inscrire. (*fig*) **that remark will be scored up against you** on ne vous pardonnera pas cette réflexion.

scorer ['skɔːrəʳ] *n* (*keeping score*) marqueur *m*; (*also* **goal ~**) marqueur (de but).

scoring ['skɔːrɪŋ] *n* (*U*) **(a)** (*Sport*) buts *mpl*; (*Cards*) points *mpl*. (*Ftbl etc*) **all the ~ was in the second half** tous les buts ont été marqués pendant la deuxième mi-temps; **'rules for ~'** 'comment marquer les points'; **the rules for ~ should be changed** il faudrait changer la règle pour marquer les points.

(b) (*cut*) incision *f*, striage *m*; (*Culin*) incision.

(c) (*Mus*) arrangement *m*.

scorn [skɔːn] **1** *n* (*U*) mépris *m*, dédain *m*. **to be filled with ~ (for)** éprouver un grand mépris (pour), n'avoir que du mépris (pour); *V* **finger, laugh.**

2 *vt person* mépriser; *action* dédaigner, mépriser; *advice* faire fi de, négliger; *suggestion* rejeter, passer outre à. **he ~s telling lies** *or* **to tell a lie** mentir est au-dessous de lui.

scornful ['skɔːnfʊl] *adj person, look, laugh, remark* méprisant, dédaigneux. **to be ~ about sth** traiter *or* considérer qch avec mépris *or* dédain.

scornfully ['skɔːnfəlɪ] *adv say, wave, point* avec mépris, avec dédain, d'un air méprisant *or* dédaigneux; *speak* d'un ton méprisant *or* dédaigneux.

Scorpio ['skɔːpɪəʊ] *n* (*Astron*) Scorpion *m*.

scorpion ['skɔːpɪən] *n* scorpion *m*.

Scot [skɒt] *n* Écossais(e) *m(f)*. **the ~s** les Écossais.

Scotch [skɒtʃ] **1** *n* **(a)** (*also* **~ whisky**) whisky *m*, scotch *m*. **(b)** (*abusivement pour* **Scottish** *ou* **Scots**) **the ~** les Écossais *mpl*. **2** *cpd*: **Scotch broth** potage *m* (*de mouton, de légumes et d'orge*); (*Brit*) **Scotch egg** *œuf dur enrobé de chair à saucisse*; **Scotch mist** bruine *f*, crachin *m*; **Scotch tape** ® scotch *m* ®, ruban adhésif; **Scotch terrier** scotch-terrier *m*. **3** *adj* (*abusivement pour* **Scottish** *ou* **Scots**) écossais.

scotch [skɒtʃ] *vt rumour* étouffer; *plan, attempt* faire échouer; *revolt, uprising* réprimer; *claim* démentir.

scot-free ['skɒt'friː] *adj* (*unpunished*) sans être puni; (*not paying*) sans payer, gratis; (*unhurt*) indemne.

Scotland ['skɒtlənd] *n* Écosse *f*. **Secretary of State for ~** ministre *m* chargé de l'Écosse; *V* **yard**².

Scots [skɒts] **1** *n* (*Ling*) écossais *m*. **2** *cpd*: **Scotsman** Écossais *m*; **Scotswoman** Écossaise *f*. **3** *adj* écossais. (*Mil*) **~ Guards** la Garde écossaise; **~ law** le droit écossais.

Scotticism ['skɒtɪsɪzəm] *n* expression écossaise.

Scottie ['skɒtɪ] *n* (*abbr of* **Scotch terrier**) scotch-terrier *m*.

Scottish ['skɒtɪʃ] *adj* écossais. **~ country dancing** danses folkloriques écossaises; **~ Nationalism** nationalisme écossais; **~ Nationalist** (*n*) nationaliste *mf* écossais(e); (*adj*) de *or* des nationaliste(s) écossais; **the ~ Office** le ministère des Affaires écossaises.

scoundrel ['skaʊndrəl] *n* vaurien *m*, gredin *m*; (*child*) coquin *m*, (petit) chenapan *m*. **he's a thorough ~** c'est un fieffé gredin; **you little ~!** (espèce de) petit coquin!

scoundrelly ['skaʊndrəlɪ] *adj* de gredin, de vaurien.

scour ['skaʊəʳ] **1** *vt* **(a)** *pan, sink* récurer; *metal* décaper; *table, floor* frotter; (*with water*) nettoyer à grande eau.

(b) *channel* creuser, éroder.

(c) (*search*) parcourir. **they ~ed the town for the murderer** ils ont parcouru toute la ville à la recherche de l'assassin; **to ~ the area/the woods/the countryside** battre le secteur/les bois/toute la région.

2 *cpd*: **scouring powder** poudre *f* à récurer.

scour about *vi*: **to scour about for sb** chercher qn partout.

scour off *vt sep* enlever en frottant.

scour out *vt sep* récurer.

scourer ['skaʊərəʳ] *n* (*powder*) poudre *f* à récurer; (*pad*) tampon abrasif *or* à récurer.

scourge [skɜːdʒ] **1** *n* (*fig*) fléau *m*; (*whip*) discipline *f*, fouet *m*. **2** *vt* (*fig*) châtier, être un fléau pour; (*whip*) fouetter. **to ~ o.s.** se flageller.

scouse* [skaʊs] *n* patois *m* de Liverpool.

scout [skaʊt] **1** *n* **(a)** (*Mil*) éclaireur *m*. **he's a good ~***† c'est un chic type*; *V* **talent**.

(b) (*gen Catholic*) scout *m*; (*gen non-Catholic*) éclaireur *m*; *V* **cub** *etc.*

(c) (*) **to have a ~ round** reconnaître le terrain; **have a ~ round to see if he's there** allez jeter un coup d'œil pour voir s'il est là.

(d) (*Brit Univ*) domestique *m*.

2 *cpd*: **scout camp** camp *m* scout; (*Mil*) **scout car** voiture *f* de reconnaissance; **scoutmaster** chef *m* scout; **scout movement** mouvement *m* scout; **scout uniform** uniforme *m* de scout.

3 *vi* (*Mil*) aller en reconnaissance.

scout about, scout around *vi* (*Mil*) aller en reconnaissance. (*fig*) **to scout about for** chercher, aller *or* être à la recherche de.

scouting ['skaʊtɪŋ] *n* (*U*) **(a)** (*youth movement*) scoutisme *m*. **(b)** (*Mil*) reconnaissance *f*.

scow [skaʊ] *n* chaland *m*.

scowl [skaʊl] **1** *n* air *m* de mauvaise humeur, mine renfrognée. **he said with a ~** dit-il en se renfrognant *or* d'un air renfrogné.

2 *vi* se renfrogner, faire la grimace, froncer les sourcils. **to ~ at sb/sth** jeter un regard mauvais à qn/qch; **'shut up!' he ~ed** 'tais-toi!' dit-il en se renfrognant *or* l'œil mauvais.

scowling ['skaʊlɪŋ] *adj face, look* renfrogné, maussade.

scrabble ['skræbl] **1** *vi* (*also* **~ about, ~ around**) **to ~ in the ground for sth** gratter la terre pour trouver qch; **she ~d (about** *or* **around) in the sand for the keys she had dropped** elle cherchait à tâtons dans le sable les clefs qu'elle avait laissé tomber; **he ~d (about** *or* **around) for a pen in the drawer** il a tâtonné dans le tiroir à la recherche d'un stylo.

2 *n* (*game*) **S~** ® Scrabble *m* ®.

scrag [skræg] **1** *n* (*Culin: also* **~ end**) collet *m* (de mouton). **2** *vt* (‡) *person* tordre le cou à*.

scragginess ['skrægɪnɪs] *n* *[neck, body, person]* aspect décharné, maigreur *f* squelettique; *[animal]* aspect famélique.

scraggy ['skrægɪ] *adj person, animal* efflanqué, décharné; *arm* décharné. **~ cat** chat *m* famélique; **~ chicken** poulet *m* étique; **~ neck** cou *m* de poulet* (*fig*).

scram‡ [skræm] *vi* ficher le camp*. **~!** fiche(-moi) le camp!*; **I'd better ~** je dois filer*.

scramble ['skræmbl] **1** *vi* **(a)** (*clamber*) **to ~ up/down** grimper/descendre tant bien que mal; **he ~d along the cliff** il a avancé avec difficulté le long de la falaise; **they ~d over the rocks/up the cliff** en s'aidant des pieds et des mains ils ont avancé sur les rochers/escaladé la falaise; **he ~d into/out of the car** il est monté dans/est descendu de la voiture à toute vitesse, il s'est précipité dans/hors de la voiture; **he ~d down off the wall** il a dégringolé du mur; **he ~d through the hedge** il s'est frayé tant bien que mal un passage à travers la haie; **to ~ for** *coins, seats* se bousculer pour (avoir), se disputer; *jobs etc* faire des pieds et des mains pour (avoir)*.

(b) (*Sport*) **to go scrambling** faire du moto-cross.

(c) (*Aviat*) décoller sur alerte.

2 *vt* (*Culin, Telec*) brouiller. **~d eggs** œufs brouillés.

3 *n* **(a)** bousculade *f*, ruée *f*, curée *f*. **the ~ for seats** la ruée pour les places; **there was a ~ for seats** (*lit*) on s'est rué sur les places; (*fig*) on s'est arraché les places.

(b) (*also* **motorcycle ~**) (réunion *f* de) moto-cross *m*.

scrambler ['skræmbləʳ] *n* (*Telec*) brouilleur *m*.

scrambling ['skræmblɪŋ] *n* (*Sport*) moto-cross *m*.

scrap¹ [skræp] **1** *n* **(a)** (*small piece*) *[paper, cloth, bread, string]* (petit) bout *m*; *[verse, writing]* quelques lignes *fpl*; *[conversation]* bribe *f*; *[news]* fragment *m*. **~s** (*broken pieces*) débris *mpl*; (*food remnants*) restes *mpl*; (*fig*) **there isn't a ~ of evidence** il n'y a pas la moindre preuve; **it wasn't a ~ of use** cela n'a servi absolument à rien; **there wasn't a ~ of truth in it** il n'y avait pas un brin de vérité là-dedans; **not a ~** pas du tout.

(b) (*U:* **~ iron**) ferraille *f*. **to collect ~** récupérer de la ferraille; **I put it out for ~** je l'ai envoyé à la ferraille; **to sell a car/ship for ~** vendre une voiture/un bateau à la casse; **what is it worth as ~?** qu'est-ce que cela vaudrait (vendu) à la casse?

2 *cpd*: **scrapbook** album *m* (*de coupures de journaux etc*); **scrap car** voiture mise à la ferraille; **scrap dealer** marchand *m* de ferraille, ferrailleur *m*; **scrap heap** tas *m* de ferraille; (*fig*) **to throw sth on the scrap heap** mettre qch au rebut *or* au rancart*, bazarder qch*; **to throw sb on the scrap heap*** mettre qn au rancart*; **scrap iron** ferraille *f*; **scrap merchant** = **scrap dealer**; **scrap metal** = **scrap iron**; **scrap paper** (*for scribbling on*) (papier *m* de) brouillon *m*; (*old newspapers etc*) vieux papiers *mpl*; **its scrap value is £10** (vendu) à la casse cela vaut 10 livres; **scrap yard** chantier *m* de ferraille; (*for cars*) cimetière *m* de voitures.

3 *vt* jeter, bazarder*; *car, ship* envoyer à la ferraille *or* à la casse; *equipment* mettre au rebut; *project* abandonner, mettre au rancart*. **let's ~ the idea** laissons tomber cette idée.

scrap²* [skræp] 1 *n* (*fight*) bagarre *f*. **to get into *or* have a ~** se bagarrer* (*with* avec).

2 *vi* se bagarrer*.

scrape [skreɪp] 1 *n* **(a)** (*action*) coup *m* de grattoir *or* de racloir; (*sound*) grattement *m*, raclement *m*; (*mark*) éraflure *f*, égratignure *f*. **to give sth a ~** gratter *or* racler qch; **to give one's knee a ~** s'érafler *or* s'égratigner le genou.

(b) *[butter etc]* lichette* *f*.

(c) (*: *trouble*) **to get (o.s.) into a ~** s'attirer des ennuis, se mettre dans un mauvais pas; **he's always getting into ~s** il lui arrive toujours des histoires*; **to get (o.s.) out of a ~** se tirer d'affaire *or* d'embarras *or* du pétrin; **to get sb into a ~** attirer des ennuis à qn, mettre qn dans un mauvais pas; **to get sb out of a ~** tirer qn d'affaire *or* d'embarras *or* du pétrin.

2 *vt* (*clean*) gratter, racler; (*graze*) érafler, égratigner; (*just touch*) frôler, effleurer. **to ~ (the skin off) one's knees** s'érafler les genoux; **to ~ one's plate clean** tout manger, nettoyer *or* racler* son assiette ; **to ~ a living** vivoter; **to ~ a violin*** racler du violon; (*Naut*) **to ~ the bottom** talonner (le fond); (*fig*) **to ~ the bottom of the barrel** en être réduit aux raclures (*fig*); (*Aut*) **I ~d his bumper** je lui ai frôlé *or* éraflé le pare-chocs.

3 *vi* (*make scraping sound*) racler, gratter; (*rub*) frotter (*against* contre). **to ~ along the wall** frôler le mur; **the car ~d past the lamppost** la voiture a frôlé le réverbère; **to ~ through the doorway** réussir de justesse à passer par la porte; (*fig*) **he just ~d clear of a prison sentence** il a frisé la peine de prison, il a tout juste évité une peine de prison; **to ~ through an exam** réussir un examen de justesse; *V* **bow²**.

scrape along *vi*: **she scraped along on £10 per week** elle vivotait avec 10 livres par semaine; **I can just scrape along in Spanish** je me débrouille en espagnol*.

scrape away 1 *vi* (*) **to scrape away at the violin** racler du violon.

2 *vt sep* enlever en grattant *or* en raclant.

scrape off *vt sep* = **scrape away 2**.

scrape out *vt sep contents* enlever en grattant *or* en raclant; *pan* nettoyer en raclant, récurer.

scrape through *vi* passer de justesse; (*fig: succeed*) réussir de justesse.

scrape together *vt sep* **(a) to scrape 2 bits of metal together** frotter 2 morceaux de métal l'un contre l'autre.

(b) *objects* rassembler, ramasser; (*fig*) *money* réunir à grand-peine, amasser à force d'économie(s).

scrape up *vt sep earth, pebbles* ramasser, mettre en tas; (*fig*) *money* réussir à économiser, amasser à grand-peine. **to scrape up an acquaintance with sb** réussir à faire la connaissance de qn.

scraper ['skreɪpəʳ] *n* racloir *m*, grattoir *m*; (*at doorstep*) décrottoir *m*, gratte-pieds *m inv*.

scraping ['skreɪpɪŋ] 1 *adj noise* de grattement, de raclement.

2 *n* **(a)** *[butter]* mince couche *f*, lichette* *f*. **~s** *[food]* restes *mpl*; *[dirt, paint]* raclures *fpl*.

(b) (*action*) grattement *m*, raclement *m*; *V* **bow²**.

scrappy ['skræpɪ] *adj conversation, essay* décousu; *education* incomplet (*f* -ète), présentant des lacunes. **a ~ meal** (*insubstantial*) un repas sur le pouce*; (*from left-overs*) un repas (fait) de restes.

scratch [skrætʃ] 1 *n* **(a)** (*mark*) (*on skin*) égratignure *f*, éraflure *f*; (*on paint*) éraflure; (*on glass, record*) rayure *f*. **they came out of it without a ~** ils s'en sont sortis indemnes *or* sans une égratignure; **it's only a ~** ce n'est qu'une égratignure.

(b) (*action*) grattement *m*; (*by claw*) coup *m* de griffe; (*by fingernail*) coup d'ongle. **the cat gave her a ~** le chat l'a griffée; **to have a good ~*** se gratter un bon coup*.

(c) (*noise*) grattement *m*, grincement *m*.

(d) (*Sport*) **to be on *or* start from ~** être scratch *inv*; (*fig*) **to start from ~** partir de zéro*; **we'll have to start from ~ again** il nous faudra repartir de zéro*; **he didn't come up to ~** il ne s'est pas montré à la hauteur; **my car didn't come up to ~** ma voiture n'a pas été aussi bonne qu'il l'aurait fallu; **to bring up to ~** amener au niveau voulu; **to keep sb up to ~** maintenir qn au niveau voulu.

2 *cpd crew, team* de fortune, improvisé; *vote* par surprise; *golfer* scratch *inv*, de handicap zéro. (*US*) **scratch pad** bloc-sténo *m*; **scratch race course** *f* scratch; (*Golf*) **scratch score** scratch score *m*.

3 *vt* **(a)** (*with nail, claw*) griffer; *varnish* érafler; *record, glass* rayer. **to ~ a hole in sth** creuser un trou en grattant qch; **he ~ed his hand on a nail** il s'est éraflé *or* écorché la main sur un clou; **he ~ed his name on the wood** il a gravé son nom dans le bois; (*fig*) **to ~ the surface of a subject** effleurer un sujet; (*fig*) **to ~ a few lines** griffonner quelques mots.

(b) (*to relieve itch*) gratter. **to ~ o.s.** se gratter; (*lit, fig*) **to ~ one's head** se gratter la tête; (*fig*) **you ~ my back and I'll ~ yours** un petit service en vaut un autre.

(c) (*cancel*) *meeting* annuler; (*Sport etc*) *competitor, horse* scratcher; *match, game* annuler.

4 *vi* **(a)** (*with nail, claw*) griffer; (*to relieve itch*) se gratter; *[hens]* gratter le sol; *[pen]* gratter, grincer. **the dog was ~ing at the door** le chien grattait à la porte.

(b) (*Sport etc*) *[competitor]* se faire scratcher; *[candidate]* se désister.

scratch out *vt sep* **(a)** (*from list*) rayer, effacer.

(b) *hole* creuser en grattant. **to scratch sb's eyes out** arracher les yeux à qn.

scratch together *vt sep* (*fig*) *money* réussir à amasser (en grattant les fonds de tiroir).

scratch up *vt sep bone* déterrer; (*fig*) *money* = **scratch together**.

scratchy ['skrætʃɪ] *adj surface, material* rêche, qui accroche; *pen* qui grince, qui gratte; *drawing* lâche, mou (*f* molle); *handwriting* en pattes de mouche.

scrawl [skrɔːl] 1 *n* gribouillage *m*, griffonnage *m*. **I can't read her ~** je ne peux pas déchiffrer son gribouillage; **the word finished in a ~** le mot se terminait par un gribouillage; **her letter was just a ~** sa lettre était griffonnée.

2 *vt* gribouiller, griffonner. **to ~ a note to sb** griffonner un mot à qn; **there were rude words ~ed all over the wall** il y avait des mots grossiers gribouillés sur tout le mur.

3 *vi* gribouiller.

scrawny ['skrɔːnɪ] *adj person, animal* efflanqué, décharné; *arm* décharné. **~ cat** chat *m* famélique; **~ neck** cou *m* de poulet* (*fig*).

scream [skriːm] 1 *n* **(a)** *[pain, fear]* cri aigu *or* perçant, hurlement *m*; *[laughter]* éclat *m*. **to give a ~** pousser un cri.

(b) (*) **it was a ~** c'était à se tordre, c'était vraiment marrant‡; **he's a ~** il est impayable*.

2 *vi* (*also* **~ out**) *[person]* crier, pousser des cris, hurler; *[baby]* crier, brailler; *[siren, brakes, wind]* hurler. **to ~ with laughter** rire aux éclats *or* aux larmes; **to ~ with pain/with rage** hurler de douleur/de rage; **to ~ for help** crier à l'aide *or* au secours; **to ~ at sb** crier après qn; **to ~ o.s. hoarse** s'enrouer à force de crier, s'égosiller.

3 *vt* (*also* **~ out**) **(a)** *abuse etc* hurler (*at* à). **'shut up' he ~ed** 'taisez-vous' hurla-t-il.

(b) *[headlines, posters]* annoncer en toutes lettres.

scream out 1 *vi* = **scream 2**. **2** *vt sep* = **scream 3**.

screamingly‡ ['skriːmɪŋlɪ] *adv*: **~ funny** à mourir de rire, tordant*.

scree ['skriː] *n* éboulis *m* (*en montagne*).

screech [skriːtʃ] 1 *n* (*gen*) cri strident; (*from pain, fright, rage*) hurlement *m*; *[brakes]* grincement *m*; *[tyres]* crissement *m*; *[owl]* cri (rauque et perçant); *[siren]* hurlement. **she gave a ~ of laughter** elle est partie d'un rire perçant.

2 *cpd*: **screech owl** effraie *f*.

3 *vi* *[person]* pousser des cris stridents, hurler; *[brakes]* grincer; *[tyres]* crisser; *[singer, owl]* crier; *[siren]* hurler.

4 *vt* crier à tue-tête.

screed [skriːd] *n* longue missive. **to write ~s*** écrire des volumes *or* toute une tartine*.

screen [skriːn] 1 *n* **(a)** (*in room*) paravent *m*; (*for fire*) écran *m* de cheminée; (*fig*) *[troops, trees]* rideau *m*; (*pretence*) masque *m*; *V* **safety, smoke** *etc.*

(b) (*Cine, TV etc*) écran *m*. **to show sth on a ~** projeter qch; (*TV*) **a 50-cm ~** un écran de 50 cm; (*Cine*) **the ~** l'écran, le cinéma; (*Cine*) **the big *or* large ~** le grand écran; (*TV*) **the small ~** le petit écran, la télé*; **to write for the ~** écrire des scénarios; *V* **panoramic, television, wide** *etc.*

(c) (*sieve*) crible *m*, claie *f*.

2 *cpd*: **screen actor** acteur *m* de cinéma, vedette *f* de l'écran; **screenplay** scénario *m*; **screen rights** droits *mpl* d'adaptation cinématographique; **screen test** essai *m* à l'écran, essai filmé; **screen writer** scénariste *mf*.

3 *vt* **(a)** (*hide*) masquer, cacher. **the trees ~ed the house** les arbres masquaient *or* cachaient la maison; **to ~ sth from sight *or* view** dérober *or* masquer qch aux regards; **he ~ed the book with his hand** il a caché le livre de sa main; **to ~ sth from the wind/sun** protéger qch du vent/du soleil; **in order to ~ our movements from the enemy** pour cacher *or* masquer nos mouvements à l'ennemi.

(b) (*Cine, TV*) *film* projeter; *book* porter à l'écran, tirer un film de.

(c) (*sieve*) *coal* cribler. (*fig*) **to ~ sb for a job** soumettre qn à une procédure sévère de sélection sur dossier; (*Med*) **to ~ sb for cancer** faire subir à qn un test de dépistage du cancer.

screen off *vt sep*: **the kitchen was screened off from the rest of the room** la cuisine était cachée du reste de la pièce (par un rideau *or* un paravent); **the nurses screened off his bed** les infirmières ont mis un *or* des paravent(s) autour de son lit; **the trees screened off the house from the road** les arbres cachaient la maison de la route, les arbres formaient un écran (de verdure) entre la maison et la route; **a cordon of police screened off the accident from the onlookers** les agents de police ont formé un cordon pour cacher l'accident aux badauds.

screening ['skriːnɪŋ] *n* **(a)** *[film]* projection *f*. **(b)** *[coal]* criblage *m*; (*fig*) *[person]* tri *m*, procédure *f* de sélection sur dossier; (*Med*) *[person]* test *m* or visite *f* de dépistage (*of sb* que l'on fait subir à qn).

screw [skruː] 1 *n* **(a)** vis *f*; (*action*) tour *m* de vis. (*Brit*) **a ~ of tea/sweets/tobacco** *etc* un cornet de thé/de bonbons/de tabac *etc*; (*fig*) **he's got a ~ loose*** il lui manque une case*; **to put the ~(s) on sb*** forcer la main à qn; *V* **thumb** *etc.*

(b) (*Aviat, Naut*) hélice *f*; *V* **air, twin**.

(c) (*Brit‡: income*) salaire *m*. **he gets a good ~** son boulot paie bien‡.

(d) (*Prison sl: warder*) garde-chiourme *m*, maton *m* (*sl*).

(e) (*∵*) **it was a good ~** on a bien baisé∵; **she's a good ~** elle baise bien∵.

2 *cpd:* (*US*) **screwball:** (*adj, n*) cinglé(e)**:** *m(f)*, tordu(e)**:** *m(f)*; **screw bolt** boulon *m* à vis; **screwdriver** tournevis *m*; **screw joint** joint *m* à vis; **screw propeller** hélice *f*; **screw thread** filet *m* de vis; **screw top** (*n*) couvercle *m* à pas de vis; (*adj: also* **screw-topped**) avec couvercle à pas de vis.

3 *vt* **(a)** visser (*on* sur, *to* à), fixer avec une vis. **to ~ sth tight** visser qch à bloc; (*fig*) **to ~ one's face into a smile** grimacer un sourire; **to ~ sb's neck:** tordre le cou à qn*. **(b)** (*extort*) *money* extorquer, soutirer (*out of* à); *information* arracher (*out of* à). **(c)** (**) *woman* baiser**.

4 *vi* se visser.

screw down 1 *vi* se visser.
2 *vt sep* visser (à fond).

screw off 1 *vi* se dévisser.
2 *vt sep* dévisser.

screw on 1 *vi* se visser.
2 *vt sep* visser, fixer avec des vis; *lid* visser. (*fig*) **he's got his head screwed on all right:** *or* **the right way:** il a la tête sur les épaules*.

screw round *vt sep* tourner, visser. (*fig*) **to screw one's head round** se dévisser la tête *or* le cou*.

screw together *vt sep two parts* fixer avec une vis. **to screw sth together** assembler qch avec des vis.

screw up *vt sep* **(a)** visser (à fond), resserrer (à fond). **(b)** *paper* chiffonner, froisser; *handkerchief* rouler, tortiller. **to screw up one's eyes** plisser les yeux; **to screw up one's face** faire la grimace; (*fig*) **to screw up (one's) courage** prendre son courage à deux mains* (*to do* pour faire). **(c)** (**:** *spoil*) bousiller*.

screwed: [skru:d] *adj* (*Brit*) soûl, paf**:** *inv*, bourré**:**.

screwy: [ˈskru:ɪ] *adj* (*mad*) cinglé**:**, tordu**:**.

scribble [ˈskrɪbl] **1** *vi* gribouiller.
2 *vt* gribouiller, griffonner. **to ~ a note to sb** griffonner un mot à qn; **there were comments ~d all over the page** il y avait des commentaires griffonnés *or* gribouillés sur toute la page.
3 *n* gribouillage *m*, griffonnage *m*. **I can't read her ~** je ne peux pas déchiffrer son gribouillage; **the word ended in a ~** le mot se terminait par un gribouillage; **her letter was just a ~** sa lettre était griffonnée.

scribble down *vt sep notes* griffonner.

scribble out *vt sep* **(a)** (*erase*) rayer, raturer. **(b)** *essay, draft* jeter sur le papier, ébaucher.

scribbler [ˈskrɪbləʳ] *n* (*lit*) gribouilleur *m*, -euse *f*; (*fig: bad author*) plumitif *m*.

scribbling [ˈskrɪblɪŋ] *n* gribouillage *m*, gribouillis *m*. (*Brit*) **~ pad** bloc-notes *m*.

scribe [skraɪb] *n* (*all senses*) scribe *m*.

scrimmage [ˈskrɪmɪdʒ] *n* (*Brit*) mêlée *f*, bagarre *f*.

scrimp [skrɪmp] *vi* lésiner (*on* sur), être chiche (*on* de). **to ~ and save** économiser sur tout.

scrimpy [ˈskrɪmpɪ] *adj amount, supply* microscopique; *garment* étriqué.

scrimshank [ˈskrɪmʃæŋk] (*Brit Mil sl*) **1** *n* = **scrimshanker**. **2** *vi* (**:**) tirer au flanc*.

scrimshanker [ˈskrɪm,ʃæŋkəʳ] *n* (*Brit Mil sl*) tire-au-flanc* *m inv*.

scrip [skrɪp] *n* (*Fin*) titre *m* provisoire (d'action).

script [skrɪpt] **1** *n* **(a)** (*Cine*) scénario *m*; (*Rad, Theat, TV*) texte *m*; (*in exam*) copie *f*; (*Jur*) document original. **(b)** (*U*) (*handwriting*) script *m*, écriture *f* script; (*Typ*) scriptes *fpl*; *V* **italic**.
2 *cpd:* (*Cine*) **script girl** script(-girl) *f*; **scriptwriter** scénariste *mf*, dialoguiste *mf*.
3 *vt film* écrire le scénario de. (*Rad, TV*) **~ed talk/discussion** *etc* conversation/discussion *etc* préparée d'avance.

scriptural [ˈskrɪptʃərəl] *adj* scriptural, biblique.

Scripture [ˈskrɪptʃəʳ] *n* (*also* **Holy ~(s)**) Écriture sainte, Saintes Écritures. (*Scol*) **~ (lesson)** (cours *m* d')instruction religieuse.

scrofula [ˈskrɒfjʊlə] *n* scrofule *f*.

scrofulous [ˈskrɒfjʊləs] *adj* scrofuleux.

scroll [skrəʊl] *n* **(a)** *[parchment]* rouleau *m*; (*ancient book*) manuscrit *m*; *V* **dead**. **(b)** (*Archit*) volute *f*, spirale *f*; (*in writing*) enjolivement *m*; *[violin]* volute *f*.

Scrooge [skru:dʒ] *n* harpagon *m*.

scrotum [ˈskrəʊtəm] *n* scrotum *m*.

scrounge* [skraʊndʒ] **1** *vt meal, clothes etc* se faire payer (*from or off sb* par qn). **to ~ money from sb** taper qn*; **he ~d £5 off him** il l'a tapé de 5 livres*; **can I ~ your pen?** je peux te chiper ton stylo?*
2 *vi:* **to ~ on sb** vivre aux crochets de qn; **he's always scrounging** c'est un parasite; (*for meals*) c'est un pique-assiette.
3 *n:* **to be on the ~ for sth** essayer d'emprunter qch; **he's always on the ~** c'est un parasite.

scrounger* [ˈskraʊndʒəʳ] *n* parasite *m*; (*for meals*) pique-assiette *mf inv*.

scrub[1] [skrʌb] **1** *n* nettoyage *m* à la brosse, bon nettoyage. **to give sth a good ~** bien nettoyer qch (à la brosse *or* avec une brosse); **give your face a ~!** lave-toi bien la figure!; **it needs a ~** cela a besoin d'être bien nettoyé.
2 *cpd:* **scrubbing brush** brosse dure; (*US*) **scrubwoman** femme *f* de ménage.
3 *vt* **(a)** *floor* nettoyer *or* laver à la brosse; *washing* frotter; *pan* récurer. **to ~ one's hands** se brosser les mains, se nettoyer les mains à la brosse; **she ~bed the walls clean** elle a nettoyé les murs à fond. **(b)** (**:** *cancel*) annuler, laisser tomber*.
4 *vi* frotter. **she's been on her knees ~bing all day** elle a passé sa journée à genoux à frotter les planchers; (*fig*) **let's ~ round it:** laissons tomber*, n'en parlons plus.

scrub away *vt sep* enlever en frottant; *stain* faire partir (en frottant).

scrub down *vt sep room, walls* nettoyer à fond *or* à grande eau, se livrer à un nettoyage en règle de. **to scrub oneself down** faire une toilette en règle.

scrub off *vt sep* = **scrub away**.

scrub out *vt sep name* effacer; *stain* faire partir; *pan* récurer.

scrub up *vi [surgeon etc]* se brosser les mains avant d'opérer.

scrub[2] [skrʌb] *n* (*U*) broussailles *fpl*.

scrubber[1] [ˈskrʌbəʳ] *n* (*also* **pan-~**) tampon *m* à récurer.

scrubber[2]: [ˈskrʌbəʳ] *n* sauteuse**:** *f*, putain**:** *f*.

scrubby [ˈskrʌbɪ] *adj tree* rabougri; *countryside* couvert de broussailles.

scruff [skrʌf] *n* **(a) by the ~ of the neck** par la peau du cou. **(b)** (***:** *person*) individu débraillé *or* mal soigné.

scruffiness [ˈskrʌfɪnɪs] *n [person]* débraillé *m*, laisser-aller *m*; *[building]* miteux *m*.

scruffy [ˈskrʌfɪ] *adj appearance* négligé; *person* débraillé; *building* miteux. **he looks ~** il fait sale *or* crado**:**; **a ~ old raincoat** un vieil imperméable fatigué; **~ hair** cheveux sales et mal peignés.

scrum [skrʌm] *n* (*Rugby*) mêlée *f*; (***:** *in crowd*) bousculade *f*, mêlée. **there was a terrible ~ at the sales** il y avait une de ces bousculades aux soldes; (*Rugby*) **~ half** demi *m* de mêlée.

scrummage [ˈskrʌmɪdʒ] **1** *n* = **scrum**. **2** *vi* (*Rugby*) jouer en mêlée; (*fig*) se bousculer.

scrumptious* [ˈskrʌmpʃəs] *adj* succulent, délicieux.

scrunch [skrʌntʃ] = **crunch**.

scruple [ˈskru:pl] **1** *n* scrupule *m*. **to have ~s about sth** avoir des scrupules au sujet de qch; **he has no ~s** il est sans scrupules, il est dénué de scrupules; **to have no ~s about doing sth** n'avoir aucun scrupule à faire qch, ne pas se faire scrupule de faire qch.
2 *vi:* **not to ~ to do** ne pas hésiter à faire, ne pas se faire scrupule de faire.

scrupulous [ˈskru:pjʊləs] *adj person, honesty* scrupuleux; *attention* scrupuleux, méticuleux. **he was very ~ about paying his debts** il payait ses dettes de façon scrupuleuse.

scrupulously [ˈskru:pjʊləslɪ] *adv* scrupuleusement, d'une manière scrupuleuse. **~ honest** d'une honnêteté scrupuleuse; **~ exact** exact jusqu'au scrupule; **~ clean** d'une propreté irréprochable.

scrupulousness [ˈskru:pjʊləsnɪs] *n* (*U*) (*honesty*) scrupules *mpl*, esprit scrupuleux; (*exactitude*) minutie *f*.

scrutineer [,skru:tɪˈnɪəʳ] *n* scrutateur *m*, -trice *f*.

scrutinize [ˈskru:tɪnaɪz] *vt writing, document* scruter, examiner minutieusement; *votes* pointer.

scrutiny [ˈskru:tɪnɪ] *n [document, conduct]* examen minutieux *or* rigoureux; *[votes]* pointage *m*.

scuba [ˈsku:bə] *n* scaphandre *m* autonome.

scud [skʌd] *vi* (*also* **~ along**) *[clouds, waves]* courir (à toute allure); *[boat]* filer (vent arrière). **the clouds were ~ding across the sky** les nuages couraient (à toute allure) dans le ciel.

scuff [skʌf] **1** *vt shoes, furniture* érafler. **~ed shoes** chaussures éraflées; **to ~ one's feet** traîner les pieds. **2** *vi* traîner les pieds.

scuffle [ˈskʌfl] **1** *n* bagarre *f*, échauffourée *f*, rixe *f*. **2** *vi* se bagarrer (*with* avec)*.

scull [skʌl] **1** *n* (*one of a pair of oars*) aviron *m* (de couple); (*single oar for stern*) godille *f*. **2** *vi* (*with 2 oars*) ramer (en couple); (*with single oar*) godiller. **to go ~ing** faire de l'aviron. **3** *vt* (*with 2 oars*) faire avancer à l'aviron; (*with single oar*) faire avancer à la godille.

scullery [ˈskʌlərɪ] *n* (*esp Brit*) arrière-cuisine *f*. **~ maid** fille *f* de cuisine.

sculp(t) [skʌlp(t)] **1** *vt* sculpter (*out of* dans). **2** *vi* sculpter, faire de la sculpture.

sculptor [ˈskʌlptəʳ] *n* sculpteur *m*.

sculptress [ˈskʌlptrɪs] *n* femme *f* sculpteur, sculpteur *m*. **I met a ~** j'ai rencontré une femme sculpteur; **she is a ~** elle est sculpteur.

sculptural [ˈskʌlptʃərəl] *adj* sculptural.

sculpture [ˈskʌlptʃəʳ] **1** *n* sculpture *f*. **a (piece of) ~** une sculpture. **2** *vti* sculpter.

scum [skʌm] *n* **(a)** *[water, soup etc]* écume *f*, mousse *f*. **to remove the ~ (from)** écumer. **(b)** (*pej: people*) rebut *m*, lie *f*. **the ~ of the earth** le rebut du genre humain. **(c)** (**:** *pej: person*) salaud**:** *m*, salope**:** *f*.

scummy [ˈskʌmɪ] *adj* (*lit*) écumeux, couvert d'écume, mousseux; (**:** *pej*) de salaud**:**.

scunner: [ˈskʌnəʳ] *n* (*esp N Engl, Scot*) **to take a ~ to sb/sth** prendre qn/qch en grippe, avoir qn/qch dans le nez**:**.

scupper [ˈskʌpəʳ] **1** *n* (*Naut*) dalot *m or* daleau *m*. **2** *vt* (*Brit**) *plan, effort* saboter. **we're ~ed** nous sommes fichus*.

scurf [skɜ:f] *n [scalp]* pellicules *fpl*; *[skin]* peau morte; (*skin disease*) dartre *f*.

scurfy [ˈskɜ:fɪ] *adj scalp* pelliculeux; *skin* dartreux.

scurrility [skʌˈrɪlɪtɪ] *n* (*V* **scurrilous**) caractère calomnieux; caractère fielleux; virulence *f*; grossièreté *f*, vulgarité *f*.

scurrilous [ˈskʌrɪləs] *adj* (*defamatory*) calomnieux; (*vicious*) fielleux, haineux; (*bitter*) virulent; (*coarse*) grossier, vulgaire.

scurrilously [ˈskʌrɪləslɪ] *adv* (*V* **scurrilous**) calomnieusement; avec virulence; grossièrement, vulgairement.

scurry [ˈskʌrɪ] **1** *n* débandade *f*, sauve-qui-peut *m inv*.
2 *vi* se précipiter, filer* (à toute allure). **to ~ through sth** faire qch à toute vitesse, expédier qch.

scurry away, scurry off *vi* se sauver (à toutes jambes), décamper.

scurvy ['skɜːvɪ] 1 *n* scorbut *m*. 2 *adj* (†† *or liter*) bas (*f* basse), mesquin, vil (*f* vile).
scutcheon ['skʌtʃən] *n* = **escutcheon.**
scuttle[1] ['skʌtl] *n* (*for coal*) seau *m* (à charbon).
scuttle[2] ['skʌtl] *vi* courir précipitamment. **to ~ in/out/through** *etc* entrer/sortir/traverser *etc* précipitamment.
scuttle away, scuttle off *vi* déguerpir, filer*.
scuttle[3] ['skʌtl] 1 *n* **(a)** (*Naut*) écoutille *f*. **(b)** (*US: in ceiling etc*) trappe *f*. 2 *vt* **(a)** (*Naut*) saborder. **to ~ one's own ship** se saborder. **(b)** (*fig*) *hopes, plans* faire échouer.
scythe [saɪð] 1 *n* faux *f*. 2 *vt* faucher.
sea [siː] 1 *n* **(a)** (*not land*) mer *f*. **on the ~** *boat* en mer; *town* au bord de la mer; **by** *or* **beside the ~** au bord de la mer; **over** *or* **beyond the ~(s)** outre-mer; **from over** *or* **beyond the ~(s)** d'outre-mer; **to swim in the ~** nager *or* se baigner dans la mer; **to go to ~** *[boat]* prendre la mer; *[person]* devenir *or* se faire marin; **to put to ~** prendre la mer; **by ~** par mer, en bateau; (*Naut*) **service at ~** service *m* à la mer; **look out to ~** regardez au large; **(out) at ~** en mer; (*fig*) **I'm all at ~** (*in lecture, translation etc*) je nage complètement*; (*after moving house, changing jobs etc*) j'ai perdu le nord*, je suis complètement déboussolé*; **I'm all at ~ over how to answer this question** je ne sais absolument pas comment répondre à cette question, pour ce qui est de répondre à cette question je nage complètement*; **he was all at ~ in the discussion** il était complètement perdu dans la discussion; **it left him all at ~** cela l'a complètement désorienté, cela l'a laissé extrêmement perplexe; (*fig*) **the call of the ~** l'appel *m* du large; *V* **follow, half, high** *etc*.
(b) (*particular area: also on moon*) mer *f*. **the S~ of Galilee** la mer de Galilée; *V* **dead, red, seven** *etc*.
(c) (*U: state of the ~*) (état *m* de la) mer *f*. **what's the ~ like?** (*for sailing*) comment est la mer?, quel est l'état de la mer?; (*for bathing*) est-ce que l'eau est bonne?; **the ~ was very rough** la mer était très houleuse *or* très mauvaise, il y avait une très grosse mer; **a rough** *or* **heavy ~** une mer houleuse; **a calm ~** une mer calme; (*Naut*) **to ship a ~** embarquer un paquet de mer.
(d) (*fig*) *[faces, difficulties]* océan *m*, multitude *f*; *[corn, blood]* mer *f*.
2 *cpd*: **sea air** air marin *or* de la mer; **sea anchor** ancre flottante; **sea anemone** anémone *f* de mer; **sea bathing** bains *mpl* de mer; **sea battle** bataille navale; **sea bed** fond *m* de la mer; **sea bird** oiseau *m* de mer, oiseau marin; **sea biscuit** biscuit *m* de mer; **seaboard** littoral *m*, côte *f*; **sea boot** botte *f* de mer *or* de marin; **seaborne** *goods* transporté par mer; *trade* maritime; **sea bream** daurade *f*; **sea breeze** brise *f* de mer; **sea calf** veau marin, phoque *m*; **sea captain** capitaine *m* (dans la marine marchande); **sea coast** côte *f*; **sea cow** vache marine; **sea crossing** traversée *f* (par mer); **sea dog** (*fish*) roussette *f*, chien *m* de mer; (*seal*) phoque commun; (*sailor*) **(old) sea dog** (vieux) loup *m* de mer; **seafarer, seafaring man** marin *m*; **seafaring** (*also* **seafaring life**) vie *f* de marin; **sea fight** combat naval; **sea fish** poisson *m* de mer; **seafood** fruits *mpl* de mer; **sea front** bord *m* de (la) mer, front *m* de mer; (*liter*) **seagirt** ceint par la mer; **sea god** dieu marin; **seagoing man** marin *m*; **seagoing ship** (navire *m*) long-courrier *m*; **sea-green** vert glauque *inv*; **seagull** mouette *f*; **sea horse** hippocampe *m*; **sea kale** chou marin, crambe *m*; **sea lavender** lavande *f* de mer, statice *m*; **to find** *or* **get one's sea legs** s'amariner, s'habituer à la mer; **he's got his sea legs** il a retrouvé le pied marin; **sea level** niveau *m* de la mer; **sea lion** otarie *f*, lion *or* ours marin; (*Scot*) **sea loch** bras *m* de mer; (*Brit*) **Sea Lord** ≃ amiral *m* de l'état-major de la Marine; **First Sea Lord** ≃ amiral-chef *m* d'état-major de la Marine; **seaman** *V* **seaman**; **sea mile** mille marin; **sea otter** loutre marine; **seaplane** hydravion *m*; **seaplane base** hydrobase *f*; **seaport** port *m* de mer; **sea power** puissance navale; **sea route** route *f* maritime; **sea rover** (*ship*) bateau *m* pirate; (*person*) pirate *m*; **seascape** (*view*) panorama marin; (*Art*) marine *f*; **sea scout** scout marin; **sea serpent** serpent *m* de mer; **sea shanty** chanson *f* de marins; **sea shell** coquillage *m*; **seashore** rivage *m*, plage *f*, bord *m* de (la) mer; **by** *or* **on the seashore** au bord de la mer; **children playing on the seashore** enfants *mpl* qui jouent sur la plage *or* sur le rivage; **to be seasick** avoir le mal de mer; **seasickness** mal *m* de mer; **seaside** *V* **seaside**; **sea transport** transports *mpl* maritimes; **sea trout** truite *f* de mer; **sea urchin** oursin *m*; **sea wall** digue *f*; **sea water** eau *f* de mer; **seaway** route *f* maritime; **seaweed** algue(s) *f(pl)*; **seaworthiness** bon état de navigabilité (*d'un navire*) (*V* **certificate a**); **seaworthy** en état de naviguer.
seal[1] [siːl] 1 *n* phoque *m*. 2 *cpd*: **sealskin** (*n*) peau *f* de phoque; (*adj*) (en peau) de phoque. 3 *vi*: **to go ~ing** chasser le phoque.
seal[2] [siːl] 1 *n* (*stamping device*) sceau *m*, cachet *m*; (*on document*) sceau, cachet; (*on envelope*) cachet; (*on package*) plomb *m*; (*Jur: on door etc*) scellé *m*. (*fig*) **under ~ of secrecy** sous le sceau du secret; **under the ~ of confession** dans le secret de la confession; (*Comm*) **~ of quality** label *m* de qualité; (*Jur*) **given under my hand and ~** signé et scellé par moi; **to put** *or* **set one's ~ to sth** apposer son sceau à qch; (*fig*) **to set one's ~ (of approval) to sth** donner son approbation à qch; (*fig*) **this set the ~ on their alliance** ceci a scellé leur alliance; *V* **privy, self** *etc*.
2 *cpd*: **seal ring** chevalière *f*.
3 *vt* **(a)** (*put ~ on*) *document* sceller, apposer un sceau sur; (*stick down*) *envelope, packet* coller, fermer; (*close with ~*) *envelope* cacheter; *package* plomber; *jar* sceller, fermer hermétiquement; *tin* souder. **~ed orders** instructions secrètes; (*fig*) **my lips are ~ed** mes lèvres sont scellées; (*Culin*) **to ~ a steak** *etc* saisir un bifteck *etc*; *V* **hermetically.**
(b) (*decide*) *fate* régler, décider (de); *bargain* conclure. **this ~ed his fate** cela a décidé (de) *or* a réglé son sort.
seal in *vt sep* enfermer (hermétiquement). **our special process seals the flavour in** notre procédé spécial garde *or* conserve toute la saveur.
seal off *vt sep* (*close up*) *door, room* condamner; (*forbid entry to*) *passage, road, room* interdire l'accès de; (*with troops, police etc*) *district* mettre un cordon autour de, encercler, boucler.
seal up *vt sep window, door* fermer hermétiquement, sceller; *tin* souder.
sealer ['siːləʳ] *n* (*person*) chasseur *m* de phoques; (*ship*) navire équipé pour la chasse au(x) phoque(s).
sealing ['siːlɪŋ] *n [document]* scellage *m*; *[letter]* cachetage *m*; *[package]* plombage *m*. **~ wax** cire *f* à cacheter.
seam [siːm] 1 *n* **(a)** (*in cloth, canvas*) couture *f*; (*in plastic, rubber*) couture, joint *m*; (*in planks, metal*) joint; (*in welding*) soudure *f*. **to come apart at the ~s** se découdre; (*fig*) **the room was bursting at the ~s*** la pièce était bondée de gens *or* pleine à craquer.
(b) (*Min*) filon *m*, veine *f*; (*Geol*) couche *f*.
(c) (*on face*) (*wrinkle*) ride *f*; (*scar*) balafre *f*, couture *f*.
2 *vt* faire une couture *or* un joint à. (*fig*) **a face ~ed with wrinkles/scars** un visage sillonné de rides/couturé (de cicatrices).
seaman ['siːmən], *pl* **seamen** 1 *n* marin *m*; *V* **able, ordinary.** 2 *cpd*: **seamanlike** de bon marin.
seamanship ['siːmənʃɪp] *n* habileté *f* dans la manœuvre, qualités *fpl* de marin.
seamen ['siːmən] *npl of* **seaman.**
seamless ['siːmlɪs] *adj* sans couture(s).
seamstress ['semstrɪs] *n* couturière *f*.
seamy ['siːmɪ] *adj district* mal famé, louche. **the ~ side of life** le côté peu reluisant de la vie, l'envers *m* du décor (*fig*).
séance ['seɪɑ̃ːns] *n [spiritualists]* séance *f* de spiritisme; *[committee etc]* séance *f*, réunion *f*.
sear [sɪəʳ] 1 *adj* desséché, flétri.
2 *vt* (*wither*) *flower, grain, leaves [heat]* dessécher, flétrir; *[frost]* flétrir; (*burn*) brûler; (*Med: cauterize*) cautériser; (*brand*) marquer au fer rouge; (*fig: make callous*) *person, conscience, feelings* endurcir.
sear through *vt fus walls, metal* traverser, percer.
search [sɜːtʃ] 1 *n* **(a)** (*for sth lost*) recherche(s) *f(pl)*. **in ~ of** à la recherche de; **a ~ was made for the child** on a entrepris des recherches pour retrouver l'enfant; **the ~ for the missing man** les recherches entreprises pour retrouver l'homme; **to begin a ~ for** *person* partir à la recherche de; *thing* se mettre à la recherche de; **in my ~ I found an interesting book** au cours de mes recherches j'ai découvert un livre intéressant; *V* **house.**
(b) *[drawer, box, pocket, district]* fouille *f*; (*Admin*) *[luggage etc]* visite *f*; (*Jur*) *[building etc]* perquisition *f*. **the ~ did not reveal anything** la fouille n'a rien donné; **his ~ of the drawer revealed nothing** il a fouillé le tiroir sans rien trouver *or* pour ne rien trouver; **the thieves' ~ of the house** la fouille de la maison par les voleurs; (*Police*) **house ~** perquisition à domicile, visite domiciliaire; (*Jur*) **right of ~** droit *m* de visite; **passengers must submit to a ~** les passagers doivent se soumettre à une fouille.
2 *cpd*: **searchlight** projecteur *m* (*pour éclairer*); **search party** équipe *f* *or* caravane *f* *or* expédition *f* de secours; (*Jur*) **search warrant** mandat *m* de perquisition.
3 *vt* **(a)** (*hunt through*) *house, park, woods, district* fouiller; (*Jur*) *house etc* perquisitionner. **they ~ed the woods for the child** ils ont fouillé les bois *or* ils ont passé les bois au peigne fin à la recherche de l'enfant; **we have ~ed the library for it** nous l'avons cherché partout dans la bibliothèque.
(b) (*examine*) *pocket, drawer, suitcase* fouiller (dans) (*for* pour essayer de retrouver); *luggage* (*gen*) fouiller; (*Customs, Police etc*) visiter; *suspect* fouiller. **they ~ed him for a weapon** ils l'ont fouillé pour s'assurer qu'il n'avait pas d'arme; **~ me!*** je n'en sais rien moi!, je n'en ai pas la moindre idée!
(c) (*scan*) *documents, records, photograph* examiner (en détail) (*for* pour trouver). (*fig*) **he ~ed her face for some sign of affection** il a cherché sur son visage un signe d'affection; **to ~ one's conscience** sonder sa conscience; **to ~ one's memory** chercher dans *or* fouiller dans ses souvenirs.
4 *vi* chercher. **to ~ after** *or* **for sth** chercher qch; **to ~ through sth** fouiller qch, chercher dans qch; **they ~ed through his belongings** ils ont fouillé ses affaires.
search about, search around *vi*: **to search about for sth** chercher qch (un peu) partout, fouiller (un peu) partout pour trouver qch.
search out *vt sep* chercher à trouver; (*and find*) découvrir.
searcher ['sɜːtʃəʳ] *n* chercheur *m*, -euse *f* (*for, after* en quête de).
searching ['sɜːtʃɪŋ] *adj look* pénétrant, scrutateur (*f* -trice); *examination* rigoureux, minutieux; *V* **heart.**
searchingly ['sɜːtʃɪŋlɪ] *adv* de façon pénétrante.
searing ['sɪərɪŋ] *adj pain* aigu (*f* -guë), fulgurant.
seaside ['siːsaɪd] 1 *n* (*U*) bord *m* de la mer. **at** *or* **beside** *or* **by the ~** au bord de la mer, à la mer; **we're going to the ~** nous allons à la mer *or* au bord de la mer.
2 *cpd town* au bord de la mer; *holiday* à la mer; *hotel* en bord de mer, sur le bord de la mer. **seaside resort** station *f* balnéaire.
season ['siːzn] 1 *n* **(a)** (*spring, summer etc*) saison *f*. **the dry ~** la saison sèche; *V* **monsoon, rainy** *etc*.
(b) (*period of activity, availability etc*) saison *f*, époque *f*, temps *m*; (*fig*) moment opportun. **to be in/out of ~** *[food]* être/ne pas être de saison; *[remark etc]* être à propos/hors de propos; **a word in ~** un mot dit à propos *or* au moment opportun; (*fig*) **in (~) and out of ~** à tout bout de champ; **strawberries in/out of ~** fraises en saison/hors de saison; (*fig*) **in due ~** en temps utile, au moment opportun; **it isn't the ~ for lily of the valley** ce n'est pas la saison du muguet; **it was hardly the ~ for joking** ce

n'était guère le moment de plaisanter; **the Christmas ~** la période de Noël *or* des fêtes; **the (social) ~** la saison (mondaine); **the London (social) ~** la saison londonienne; **her first ~** sa première saison, ses débuts *mpl* dans le monde; **the busy ~** (*for shops etc*) la période de grand travail *or* de pointe; (*for hotels etc*) la pleine saison; **the hunting/fishing** *etc* **~** la saison de la chasse/de la pêche *etc*; **the football ~** la saison de football; (*Sport*) **his first ~ in the Celtic team** sa première saison dans l'équipe du Celtic; **the ~ is at its height** la saison bat son plein, c'est le plein de la saison; **the start of the ~** *[tourism, hotels etc]* le début de (la) saison; (*Sport*) l'ouverture *f* de la saison; (*Shooting*) l'ouverture de la chasse; (*social*) le commencement de la saison (mondaine); **'S~'s greetings'** 'Joyeux Noël et Bonne Année'; **early in the ~** (*specific*) au début de la saison; (*non-specific*) en début de saison; **late in the ~** (*specific*) à l'arrière-saison; (*non-specific*) en arrière-saison; **the off-~** la morte-saison; **during the off-~** hors saison; *V* **festive, silly, tourist** *etc*.

(c) (*Theat*) saison *f* (théâtrale). **he did a ~ at the Old Vic** il a joué à l'Old Vic pendant une saison; **the film is here for a short ~** le film sera projeté quelques semaines; (*on notice*) **'for a ~, Laurence Olivier in 'Macbeth''** 'pendant quelque temps, Laurence Olivier dans 'Macbeth''.

(d) = **~ ticket**; *V* **2**.

(e) (*Vet*) **in ~** en chaleur.

2 *cpd*: (*Rail, Theat*) **season ticket** carte *f* d'abonnement; **to take out a season ticket** prendre un abonnement, s'abonner (*for* à); **season ticket holder** personne *f* qui possède une carte d'abonnement.

3 *vt* **(a)** *wood* faire sécher, dessécher; *cask* abreuver; *V also* **seasoned**.

(b) (*Culin*) (*with condiments*) assaisonner; (*with spice*) épicer, relever. **a highly ~ed dish** un plat relevé; (*fig*) **a speech ~ed with humour** un discours assaisonné *or* pimenté d'humour.

seasonable ['si:znəbl] *adj weather* de saison; *advice* à propos, opportun.

seasonal ['si:zənl] *adj* (*all senses*) saisonnier. **it's very ~** c'est très saisonnier, cela dépend beaucoup de la saison; **~ worker** (ouvrier *m*, -ière *f*) saisonnier *m*, -ière *f*.

seasoned ['si:znd] *adj wood* séché, desséché; (*fig*) *worker* expérimenté; *writer, actor, footballer etc* chevronné, expérimenté; *troops* aguerri. **a ~ campaigner for civil rights** un vétéran des campagnes pour les droits civils; (*fig*) **~ campaigner** vieux routier (*fig*); **to be ~ to sth** être habitué à qch; *V also* **season**.

seasoning ['si:znɪŋ] *n* assaisonnement *m*, condiment *m*. **add ~** assaisonnez; **check the ~** vérifiez l'assaisonnement; **there's too much ~** c'est trop assaisonné; (*fig*) **with a ~ of humour** avec un grain d'humour.

seat [si:t] **1** *n* **(a)** (*chair etc*) (*gen*) siège *m*; (*in theatre, cinema*) fauteuil *m*; (*in bus, train*) banquette *f*; (*Aut*) (*individual*) siège; (*for several people*) banquette; (*on cycle*) selle *f*; *V* **back, driver, hot** *etc*.

(b) (*place or right to sit*) place *f*. **to take a ~** s'asseoir; **to take one's ~** prendre place (*V also* **1d**); **to keep one's ~** rester assis; **to lose one's ~** perdre sa place (*V also* **1d, 1f**); (*Cine, Theat*) **I'd like 2 ~s for ...** je voudrais 2 places pour ...; **keep a ~ for me** gardez-moi une place; **there are ~s for 70 people** il y a 70 places assises; *V* **book** *etc*.

(c) *[chair]* siège *m*; *[trousers]* fond *m*; (*: *buttocks*) derrière *m*, postérieur* *m*.

(d) (*Parl*) siège *m*. **to keep/lose one's ~** être/ne pas être réélu; (*Brit*) **to take one's ~ in the Commons/in the Lords** prendre son siège aux Communes/à la Chambre des Lords, ≃ être validé comme député à l'Assemblée nationale/comme sénateur; **the socialists gained/lost 10 ~s** les socialistes ont gagné/perdu 10 sièges; **they won the ~ from the Conservatives** ils ont pris le siège aux conservateurs; **a majority of 50 ~s** une majorité de 50 (députés *etc*); *V* **safe**.

(e) (*location, centre*) *[government]* siège *m*; *[commerce]* centre *m*; (*Med*) *[infection]* foyer *m*. **~ of learning** siège *or* haut lieu du savoir; **he has a (country) ~ in the north** il a un manoir *or* un château dans le nord.

(f) (*Equitation*) **to have a good ~** avoir une bonne assiette, bien se tenir en selle; **to keep one's ~** rester en selle; **to lose one's ~** être désarçonné, vider les étriers.

2 *cpd*: **seat back** dossier *m* (de chaise *etc*); (*Aut, Aviat*) **seat belt** ceinture *f* de sécurité; *V* **fasten**.

3 *vt* **(a)** *child* (faire) asseoir; (*at table*) *guest* placer. **to ~ o.s.** s'asseoir; **please be ~ed** veuillez vous asseoir, asseyez-vous je vous prie; **to remain ~ed** rester assis; **the waiter ~ed him at my table** le garçon l'a placé à ma table; *V* **deep**.

(b) (*have or find room for*) **we cannot ~ them all** nous n'avons pas assez de sièges pour tout le monde; **how many does the hall ~?** combien y a-t-il de places assises *or* à combien peut-on s'asseoir dans la salle?; **this car ~s 6 in comfort** on tient confortablement à 6 dans cette voiture; **this table ~s 8** on peut tenir à 8 à cette table, c'est une table pour 8 personnes *or* couverts.

(c) (*also* **re~**) *chair* refaire le siège de; *trousers* (re)mettre un fond à.

4 *vi*: **this skirt won't ~** cette jupe ne va pas se déformer derrière.

-seater ['si:tə^r] *adj, n ending in cpds*: (*Aut*) **a two-seater** une deux places; **two-seater car/plane** voiture *f*/avion *m* biplace *or* à deux places; **a 50-seater coach** un car de 50 places.

seating ['si:tɪŋ] **1** *n* (*U*) **(a)** (*act*) répartition *f or* allocation *f* des places. **is the ~ (of the guests) all right?** est-ce qu'on a bien placé les invités?

(b) (*seats*) sièges *mpl*; (*as opposed to standing room*) places assises. **~ for 600** 600 places assises.

2 *cpd*: **seating accommodation** nombre *m* de places assises; **we must think about the seating arrangements** il faut penser à placer les gens; **what are the seating arrangements?** comment va-t-on placer les gens?; **seating capacity** = **seating accommodation**; (*at dinner*) **seating plan** plan *m* de table.

seaward ['si:wəd] **1** *adj journey* vers le large; *breeze* de terre. **2** *adv* = **seawards**.

seawards ['si:wədz] *adv* vers le large, vers la mer.

sebaceous [sɪ'beɪʃəs] *adj* sébacé.

sebum ['si:bəm] *n* sébum *m*.

sec‡ [sek] *n abbr of* **second**².

secant ['si:kənt] **1** *n* sécante *f*. **2** *adj* sécant.

secateurs [,sekə'tɜ:z] *npl* (*esp Brit: also* **pair of ~**) sécateur *m*.

secede [sɪ'si:d] *vi* faire sécession, se séparer (*from* de).

secession [sɪ'seʃən] *n* sécession *f*, séparation *f*.

secessionist [sɪ'seʃnɪst] *adj, n* sécessionniste (*mf*).

seclude [sɪ'klu:d] *vt* éloigner *or* isoler (du monde).

secluded [sɪ'klu:dɪd] *adj house* à l'écart, (dans un endroit) retiré; *garden* isolé; *life* retiré (du monde), solitaire. **~ spot** endroit retiré.

seclusion [sɪ'klu:ʒən] *n* solitude *f*. **to live in ~** vivre en solitaire, vivre retiré du monde.

second¹ ['sekənd] **1** *adj* **(a)** (*esp one of many*) deuxième; (*more often one of 2*) second. **to be ~ in the queue** être le (*or* la) deuxième dans la queue; **to be ~ in command** (*Mil*) commander en second; (*gen*) être deuxième dans la hiérarchie (*V also* **2**); (*Scol*) **he was ~ in French** il a été deuxième en français; (*fig*) **he's a ~ Beethoven** c'est un autre Beethoven; **Britain's ~ city** la deuxième ville de Grande-Bretagne; (*Brit Parl*) **the ~ chamber** la Chambre des Lords; **give him a ~ chance to show what he can do** donnez-lui encore une chance de montrer ce dont il est capable; **you won't get a ~ chance to go to Australia** vous ne retrouverez pas l'occasion d'aller en Australie, l'occasion d'aller en Australie ne se représentera pas; **would you like a ~ cup of tea?** voulez-vous encore du thé?; **would you like a ~ cup?** voulez-vous une seconde *or* autre tasse?; **he had a ~ cup of coffee** il a repris du café; **every ~ day** tous les deux jours, un jour sur deux; **every ~ Thursday** un jeudi sur deux; (*Aut*) **~ gear** seconde *f*; (*Theat*) **the ~ house** la deuxième représentation de la journée; (*Med*) **to ask for a ~ opinion** demander l'avis d'un autre *or* d'un deuxième médecin; (*Med*) **I'd like a ~ opinion** je voudrais consulter un deuxième *or* autre médecin, j'aimerais avoir un autre avis; (*Gram*) **in the ~ person** à la deuxième personne; (*Gram*) **~ person singular/plural** deuxième personne du singulier/pluriel; **in the ~ place** deuxièmement, (*more formally*) en second lieu; **in the first place ... in the ~ place** d'abord ... ensuite; **~ teeth** seconde dentition; **for the ~ time** pour la deuxième fois; **for the ~ and last time** pour la seconde et dernière fois; (*Mus*) **~ violin** second violon; **Charles the S~** Charles Deux, Charles II; *V also* **2**; *for other phrases V* **sixth**.

(b) (*fig phrases*) **to be in one's ~ childhood** retomber en enfance; **to play ~ fiddle to sb** jouer un rôle secondaire auprès de qn, (*over longer period*) vivre dans l'ombre de qn; **it's ~ nature to him** c'est une seconde nature chez lui; **it was ~ nature for him to help his friends** aider ses amis était chez lui une seconde nature; **~ to none** sans pareil, sans rival, inégalable; **for elegance of style he is ~ to none** pour ce qui est de l'élégance du style il ne le cède à personne; **~ self** autre soi-même *m*; **my ~ self** un(e) autre moi-même; **to have ~ sight** avoir le don de seconde vue; **he has a ~ string to his bow** il a plus d'une corde à son arc; **I'm having ~ thoughts (about it)** je commence à avoir des doutes (là-dessus); **I've had ~ thoughts about the holiday** pour ce qui est des vacances j'ai changé d'avis; **the director has had ~ thoughts about it** le directeur est revenu sur sa première décision là-dessus; **on ~ thoughts ...** réflexion faite ..., à la réflexion ...; **to get one's ~ wind** (*lit*) retrouver son souffle; (*fig*) reprendre des forces, retrouver ses forces; *V also* **2**; *for other phrases V* **sixth**.

2 *cpd*: **second-best** *V* **second-best**; **second-class** *V* **second-class**; (*Rel*) **the second coming** le second avènement *m* (du Messie); **second cousin** cousin(e) issu(e) de germain; **secondhand** *V* **secondhand** *and also* **second**² **2**; **second-in-command** (*Mil*) commandant *m* en second; (*Naut*) second *m*; (*gen*) second, adjoint *m*; (*Mil*) **second lieutenant** sous-lieutenant *m*; (*Merchant Navy*) **second mate, second officer** commandant *m* en second; **second-rate** de qualité inférieure, de deuxième ordre; **second-rater*** médiocre *mf*, médiocrité *f*.

3 *adv* **(a)** (*in race, exam, competition*) en seconde place *or* position. **he came** *or* **was placed ~** il s'est classé deuxième *or* second.

(b) = **secondly**.

(c) (*Rail etc*) **to travel ~** voyager en seconde.

(d) (*+ superl adj*) **the ~ largest/smallest book** le plus grand/petit livre sauf un.

4 *n* **(a)** deuxième *mf*, second(e) *m(f)*. **he came a good ~** il s'est fait battre de justesse; **he came a poor ~** il a été largement battu (en deuxième place); (*Comm*) **~s** articles *mpl* de second choix, articles comportant un défaut.

(b) (*Boxing*) soigneur *m*; (*in duel*) second *m*, témoin *m*. (*Boxing*) **~s out (of the ring)!** soigneurs hors du ring!

(c) (*Brit Univ*) ≃ licence *f* avec mention (assez) bien. **he got an upper/a lower ~** ≃ il a eu sa licence avec mention bien/assez bien; **many students get a lower ~** de nombreux étudiants sont reçus avec la mention assez bien.

(d) (*Aut*: **~ gear**) seconde *f*. **in ~** en seconde.

5 *vt* **(a)** *motion* appuyer; *speaker* appuyer la motion de. **I'll ~ that** (*at meeting*) j'appuie la proposition *or* la demande; (**gen*) je suis pour*.

(b) [sɪ'kɒnd] (*Brit: Admin, Mil*) affecter provisoirement (*to* à), détacher (*to* à). **he has been ~ed for service abroad** il est en détachement à l'étranger.

second² ['sekənd] **1** *n* seconde *f* (*also Geog, Math etc*); (*fig*) seconde, instant *m*. **it won't take a ~** il y en a pour une seconde *or* un instant; **at that very ~** à cet instant précis; **just a ~!, half a ~!*** un instant!, une (petite) seconde!; **I'm coming in half a ~** j'arrive tout de suite *or* dans une seconde; *V* **split**.

2 *cpd*: **second(s) hand** trotteuse *f*.

secondary ['sekəndərɪ] *adj* (*coming second*) secondaire; *meaning* secondaire, dérivé; *education* secondaire, du second degré; (*minor*) secondaire, accessoire. **of ~ importance** secondaire, peu important; (*Philos*) **~ cause** cause seconde; (*Brit*) **~ modern school** ≃ collège *m* d'enseignement général; **~ road** route départementale *or* secondaire; (*Chem, Ind*) **~ product** sous-produit *m*.

second-best ['sekənd'best] **1** *n* pis-aller *m inv*. **as a ~** faute de mieux, au pis-aller.

2 *adj jacket etc* de tous les jours. **3** *adv*: **to come off ~** perdre, se faire battre.

second-class ['sekənd'klɑːs] **1** *adj* (*lit*) de deuxième classe; *mail* (à) tarif réduit; (*Rail*) *ticket, compartment* de seconde (classe); *hotel* de seconde catégorie, de second ordre; (*pej*) *food, goods etc* de qualité inférieure. **~ citizen** déshérité(e) *m(f)* dans la société; (*Univ*) **~ degree = second¹ 4c**; (*Rail*) **a ~ return to London** un aller et retour de seconde pour Londres; (*Rail*) **~ seat** seconde *f*.

2 *adv* (*Rail etc*) **to travel ~** voyager en seconde.

seconder ['sekəndəʳ] *n* [*motion*] personne *f* qui appuie une motion; [*candidate*] deuxième parrain *m*.

secondhand ['sekənd'hænd] **1** *adj clothes, car* d'occasion, de seconde main; (*fig*) *information, account* de seconde main. **~ bookseller** libraire *m* d'occasion, bouquiniste *mf*; **~ bookshop** librairie *f* d'occasion; **~ dealer** marchand(e) *m(f)* d'occasion.

2 *adv buy* d'occasion. **to hear sth ~** entendre dire qch, entendre qch de quelqu'un d'autre.

secondly ['sekəndlɪ] *adv* deuxièmement, (*more formally*) en second lieu. **firstly ... ~ ...** d'abord ... ensuite ... .

secondment [sɪ'kɒndmənt] *n* (*Brit*) affectation *f* provisoire, détachement *m*. **on ~** (*at home*) en détachement, détaché (*to* à); (*abroad*) en mission (*to* à).

secrecy ['siːkrəsɪ] *n* (*U*) secret *m*. **in ~** en secret, dans le secret; **in strict ~** en grand secret; **under pledge of ~** sous le sceau du secret; **there's no ~ about it** on n'en fait pas (un) mystère; **there was an air of ~ about her** elle avait un petit air mystérieux; **I rely on your ~** je compte sur votre discrétion; *V* **swear**.

secret ['siːkrɪt] **1** *n* **(a)** secret *m*. **to keep a ~** garder un secret; **I told it you as a ~** je vous l'ai dit en confidence; **to let sb into the ~** mettre qn dans le secret; **to let sb into a ~** révéler *or* confier *or* dire un secret à qn; **to be in the ~** être au courant *or* dans le coup*; **there's no ~ about it** cela n'a rien de secret; **to have no ~s from sb** ne pas avoir de secrets pour qn; **he makes no ~ of the fact that** il ne cache pas que; **lovers' ~** confidence *f* d'amoureux; **the ~ of success/successful writing** le secret du succès/de la littérature à succès; **the ~ of being a good teacher is ...** pour être bon professeur le secret est ...; **the ~s of nature** les secrets *or* les mystères *mpl* de la nature; *V* **open, state** *etc*.

(b) (*U: secrecy*) **in ~** en secret, dans le secret.

2 *adj* **(a)** (*concealed*) *place, drawer, marriage, negotiations* secret (*f* -ète); *door, passage* secret, dérobé; (*secluded*) *place* retiré, caché. **to keep one's plans ~** ne pas révéler ses plans, cacher ses plans; **to keep sth ~ from sb** ne pas révéler *or* montrer qch à qn; **it's all highly ~** c'est tout ce qu'il y a de plus secret; **~ agent** agent secret; **~ police** police secrète; **the S~ Service** les services secrets; **~ society** société secrète; *V* **top¹**.

(b) (*secretive*) secret (*f* -ète), dissimulé (*pej*).

secretarial [ˌsekrə'tɛərɪəl] *adj work* de secrétariat, de secrétaire. **~ college** école *f* de secrétariat; **~ course** études *fpl* de secrétaire; **to have a ~ job** être secrétaire.

secretariat [ˌsekrə'tɛərɪət] *n* secrétariat *m* (*personnel, bureau, services*).

secretary ['sekrətrɪ] **1** *n* **(a)** (*in office, of club etc*) secrétaire *mf*; (*also* **company ~**) secrétaire général (*d'une société*). (*Pol*) **S~ of State** (*Brit*) ministre *m* (*of, for* de); (*US*) secrétaire *m* d'État, ≃ ministre des Affaires étrangères; *V* **foreign, parliamentary, under** *etc*.

(b) (*writing desk*) secrétaire *m*.

2 *cpd*: **secretary-general** secrétaire général.

secrete [sɪ'kriːt] *vt* **(a)** (*Anat, Bio, Med*) sécréter. **(b)** (*hide*) cacher.

secretion [sɪ'kriːʃən] *n* (*V* **secrete**) **(a)** sécrétion *f*. **(b)** action *f* de cacher.

secretive ['siːkrətɪv] *adj* (*by nature*) secret (*f* -ète), dissimulé (*pej*), cachottier (*pej*). **to be ~ about sth** faire un secret *or* un mystère de qch, être très réservé à propos de qch.

secretively ['siːkrətɪvlɪ] *adv* d'une façon très réservée, d'une façon dissimulée (*pej*).

secretiveness ['siːkrətɪvnɪs] *n* (*U*) réserve *f*, caractère dissimulé (*pej*) *or* cachottier (*pej*).

secretly ['siːkrətlɪ] *adv* secrètement, en secret, en cachette.

sect [sekt] *n* secte *f*.

sectarian [sek'tɛərɪən] *adj, n* sectaire (*mf*).

sectarianism [sek'tɛərɪənɪzəm] *n* attitude *f or* esprit *m* sectaire, sectarisme *m*.

section ['sekʃən] **1** *n* **(a)** [*book, law, population*] section *f*, partie *f*; [*text, document*] section, article *m*, paragraphe *m*; [*country*] partie; [*road, pipeline*] section, tronçon *m*; [*town*] quartier *m*; [*machine, furniture*] élément *m*; (*Mil*) groupe *m* (de combat). (*Press*) **the financial ~** la *or* les page(s) financière(s); (*Admin, Jur*) **~ 2 of the municipal by-laws** l'article 2 des arrêtés municipaux; **this bookcase comes in ~s** cette bibliothèque se vend par éléments; **there is a ~ of public opinion which maintains ...** il y a une partie *or* une section de l'opinion publique qui maintient ... .

(b) (*Admin, Ind*) section *f*; (*Comm*) rayon *m*; *V* **consular, passport** *etc*.

(c) (*cut*) coupe *f*, section *f*; (*for microscope*) coupe, lamelle *f*. **longitudinal/vertical ~** coupe longitudinale/verticale; *V* **cross**.

(d) (*act of cutting*) section *f*, sectionnement *m*.

2 *cpd*: **section mark** signe *m* de paragraphe.

3 *vt* sectionner.

section off *vt sep* séparer.

sectional ['sekʃənl] *adj* (*made of sections*) *bookcase etc* à éléments, démontable; (*representing a part*) *interests* d'une classe, d'un groupe; *drawing* en coupe.

sector ['sektəʳ] *n* **(a)** secteur *m*; (*Mil*) secteur, zone *f*; (*fig*) secteur, domaine *m*. **private/public ~** secteur privé/public. **(b)** (*Geom*) secteur *m*; (*instrument*) compas *m* (de proportions).

secular ['sekjʊləʳ] *adj authority, clergy* séculier; *teaching, school* laïque; *art, writer, music* profane.

secularism ['sekjʊlərɪzəm] *n* (*policy*) laïcité *f*; (*doctrine*) laïcisme *m*.

secularization [ˌsekjʊləraɪ'zeɪʃən] *n* (*V* **secular**) sécularisation *f*; laïcisation *f*.

secularize ['sekjʊləraɪz] *vt* (*V* **secular**) séculariser; laïciser.

secure [sɪ'kjʊəʳ] **1** *adj* **(a)** (*solid, firm*) *bolt, padlock* solide; *nail, knot* solide, qui tient bien; *rope* bien attaché; *door, window* bien fermé; *structure, ladder* qui ne bouge pas, ferme; *foothold, handhold* bon, sûr. **to make ~** *rope* bien attacher; *door, window* bien fermer; *tile* bien fixer.

(b) (*in safe place*) en sûreté, en sécurité, en lieu sûr; *hideout, place* sûr; (*certain*) *career, future, promotion, fame* assuré. **~ from** *or* **against** à l'abri de.

(c) (*unworried*) tranquille, sans inquiétude. **to feel ~ about** ne pas avoir d'inquiétudes sur *or* au sujet de; **~ in the knowledge that** ayant la certitude que; **a child must be (emotionally) ~** un enfant a besoin de sécurité sur le plan affectif, un enfant a besoin d'être sécurisé.

2 *vt* **(a)** (*get*) *object* se procurer, obtenir; *staff, performer* engager. **to ~ sth for sb** procurer qch à qn, obtenir qch pour qn.

(b) (*fix*) *rope* fixer, attacher; *door, window* bien fermer; *tile* fixer; (*tie up*) *person, animal* attacher.

(c) (*make safe*) (*from danger*) préserver, protéger, garantir (*against, from* de); *debt* garantir; *career, future* assurer.

securely [sɪ'kjʊəlɪ] *adv* (*V* **secure 1**) (*firmly*) solidement, bien; (*safely*) en sécurité.

security [sɪ'kjʊərɪtɪ] **1** *n* **(a)** (*safety, confidence*) sécurité *f*. **in ~** en sécurité; (*Admin, Ind*) **job ~** sécurité de l'emploi; (*Jur*) **~ of tenure** bail assuré; (*Psych*) **a child needs ~** un enfant a besoin de sécurité sur le plan affectif, un enfant a besoin d'être sécurisé.

(b) (*Ind, Pol etc: against spying*) sécurité *f*. **~ was very lax** les mesures de sécurité étaient très relâchées.

(c) (*Fin: for loan*) caution *f*, garantie *f*. **loans without ~** crédit *m* à découvert; **up to £100 without ~** jusqu'à 100 livres sans caution *or* sans garantie; **to stand ~ for sb** se porter garant pour *or* de qn.

(d) (*St Ex*) **securities** valeurs *fpl*, titres *mpl*; **government securities** fonds *mpl* d'État.

2 *cpd*: **Security Council** Conseil *m* de sécurité; **security forces** forces *fpl* de sécurité; **security guard** garde chargé de la sécurité; **security leak** fuite *f* (*de documents, de secrets etc*); **security officer** (*Mil, Naut*) officier chargé de la sécurité; (*Comm, Ind*) inspecteur *m* (chargé) de la sécurité; **security police** services *mpl* de la sûreté; **security risk** *personne f susceptible de compromettre la sûreté de l'État, la sécurité d'une organisation etc*; **that man is a security risk** cet homme n'est pas sûr.

sedan [sɪ'dæn] *n* **(a)** (*also* **~ chair**) chaise *f* à porteurs. **(b)** (*US: car*) conduite intérieure, berline *f*.

sedate [sɪ'deɪt] **1** *adj person* posé, calme, réfléchi; *behaviour* calme, pondéré. **2** *vt* (*Med*) donner des sédatifs à, mettre sous sédation.

sedately [sɪ'deɪtlɪ] *adv* posément, calmement.

sedateness [sɪ'deɪtnɪs] *n* (*V* **sedate**) allure posée *or* réfléchie; calme *m*, pondération *f*.

sedation [sɪ'deɪʃən] *n* sédation *f*. **under ~** sous sédation, sous calmants.

sedative ['sedətɪv] *adj, n* calmant (*m*), sédatif (*m*).

sedentary ['sedntrɪ] *adj work* sédentaire. **~ worker** travailleur *m*, -euse *f* sédentaire.

sedge [sedʒ] *n* laiche *f*, carex *m*. **~ warbler** phragmite *m* des joncs, rousserolle *f*.

sediment ['sedɪmənt] *n* (*Geol, Med*) sédiment *m*; (*in boiler, liquids*) dépôt *m*; (*in wine*) dépôt, lie *f*.

sedimentary [ˌsedɪ'mentərɪ] *adj* sédimentaire.

sedimentation [ˌsedɪmen'teɪʃən] *n* sédimentation *f*.

sedition [sə'dɪʃən] *n* sédition *f*.

seditious [sə'dɪʃəs] *adj* séditieux.

seduce [sɪ'djuːs] *vt* (*also sexually*) séduire. **to ~ sb from sth** détourner qn de qch; **to ~ sb into doing sth** entraîner qn à faire qch.

seducer [sɪ'djuːsəʳ] *n* séducteur *m*, -trice *f*.

seduction [sɪ'dʌkʃən] *n* séduction *f*.

seductive [sɪ'dʌktɪv] *adj person, charms* séduisant, attrayant; *smile, perfume* aguichant, séducteur (*f* -trice); *offer* alléchant.

seductively [sɪ'dʌktɪvlɪ] *adv* d'une manière séduisante, avec séduction.

seductiveness [sɪ'dʌktɪvnɪs] *n* caractère séduisant, qualité séduisante.

seductress [sɪˈdʌktrɪs] *n* séductrice *f*.
sedulous [ˈsedjʊləs] *adj* assidu, persévérant, attentif.
sedulously [ˈsedjʊləslɪ] *adv* assidûment, avec persévérance.
see[1] [siː] *pret* **saw**, *ptp* **seen 1** *vt* **(a)** (*gen*) voir. **I can ~ him** je le vois; **I saw him read/reading the letter** je l'ai vu lire/qui lisait la lettre; **he was ~n to read the letter** on l'a vu lire la lettre; **she saw him knocked down** elle l'a vu (se faire) renverser; **there was no one at all** *or* **not a soul to be ~n** il n'y avait pas un chat* (*fig*), il n'y avait pas âme qui vive; **there was not a house to be ~n** il n'y avait pas une seule maison en vue; (*Brit*) **I could ~ him far enough!*** j'en ai (*or* avais) marre de sa tête!‡, ce qu'il peut (*or* a pu) me casser les pieds!‡; **I could ~ it** *or* **that one coming*** je le sentais venir, je m'y attendais; **to ~ fit to do** juger bon de faire; **will she come? — if she ~s fit** est-ce qu'elle viendra? — oui, si elle le juge bon; **I'll be glad to ~ the back of him*** je serai heureux de le voir partir *or* d'être débarrassé de lui; **let's hope we've ~n the last of him** espérons que nous sommes débarrassés de lui; **I'll be glad to ~ the last of this work** je serai heureux d'arriver au bout de ce travail *or* d'en avoir fini avec ce travail; **~ page 10** voir (à la) page 10; **to ~ double** voir double; (*fig*) **to ~ red** voir rouge; **to ~ sth with one's own eyes** voir qch de ses propres yeux; **to ~ the sights** faire du tourisme, visiter la ville; **to ~ the sights of Paris** visiter (les monuments de) Paris; **we spent a few days in Paris ~ing the sights** nous avons passé quelques jours à Paris à visiter la ville; (*fig*) **to ~ stars** voir trente-six chandelles; **I must be ~ing things*** je dois avoir des visions* *or* des hallucinations; **can you ~ your way without a torch?** est-ce que vous pouvez trouver votre chemin *or* est-ce que vous y voyez assez sans lampe de poche?; (*fig*) **can you ~ your way to helping us?** est-ce que vous trouveriez (le) moyen de nous aider?; **I can't ~ my way to doing that** je ne vois pas comment je pourrais le faire; (*fig*) **he can't ~ the wood for the trees** il se perd dans les détails; **I want to ~ the world** je veux voyager; *V* **remain**.

(b) (*understand, conceive*) voir, comprendre, saisir. **to ~ the joke** comprendre *or* saisir la plaisanterie; **to ~ sense** entendre raison; **he won't ~ sense** il ne veut pas entendre raison, il ne veut pas comprendre; **try to make him ~ sense** essaie de lui faire entendre raison; **I can't ~ the point of it** je n'en vois pas l'intérêt *or* l'utilité; **I don't ~ the point of inviting him** je ne vois pas l'intérêt de l'inviter; **do you ~ what I mean?** voyez-vous *or* vous voyez ce que je veux dire?; **I ~ what you're getting at** je vois *or* je devine où vous voulez en venir; **I fail to ~** *or* **I can't ~ how you're going to do it** je ne vois pas du tout *or* je ne vois vraiment pas comment vous allez le faire; **the way I ~ it, as I ~ it** à mon avis, selon moi; **this is how** *or* **the way I ~ it** voici comment je vois *or* comprends la chose; **the French ~ it differently** les Français voient la chose différemment; **I don't ~ why** je ne vois pas pourquoi.

(c) (*notice, learn, discover*) voir, remarquer, apprendre, découvrir. **I saw in the paper that he is gone** j'ai vu *or* lu dans le journal qu'il est parti; **I ~ they've bought a new car** je vois *or* je remarque *or* j'apprends qu'ils ont acheté une nouvelle voiture; **I ~ nothing wrong in it** je n'y trouve rien à redire; **I don't know what she ~s in him** (*what good qualities*) je ne sais pas ce qu'elle lui trouve (de bien); (*what attracts her*) je ne sais pas ce qui l'attire en lui; **~ who's at the door** allez voir qui est à la porte; **not until I ~ how many there are** pas avant de savoir *or* de voir *or* de découvrir combien il y en a.

(d) (*visit, meet, speak to*) voir; *doctor, lawyer* voir, consulter. **to go and ~ sb, to go to ~ sb** aller voir qn; **I'm ~ing the doctor tomorrow** je vais chez le docteur *or* je vois le docteur demain; **the manager wants to ~ you** le directeur veut vous voir, le directeur vous demande; **I can't ~ you today** je ne peux pas vous voir *or* recevoir aujourd'hui; **I want to ~ you about my son** je voudrais vous voir *or* vous parler au sujet de mon fils; **they ~ a lot of him** ils le voient souvent; **you must ~ less of him** il faut que vous le voyiez (*subj*) moins souvent.

(e) (*: *phrases*) **~ you!, (I'll) be ~ing you!** à bientôt!, salut!*; **~ you later!** à tout à l'heure!; **~ you some time!** à un de ces jours!; **~ you soon!** à bientôt!; **~ you (on) Sunday** *etc* à dimanche *etc*; **~ you next week** *etc* à la semaine prochaine *etc*.

(f) (*experience, know*) voir, éprouver, connaître. **this hat has ~n better days** ce chapeau a connu des jours meilleurs; **I never thought we'd ~ the day when ...** je n'aurais jamais cru qu'un jour ...; **we'll never ~ his like again** nous ne verrons jamais son pareil; (*Mil*) **he saw service in Libya** il a servi en Libye, il a fait la campagne de Libye; **he has ~n service abroad** il a servi à l'étranger; **since she's started going round with that crowd she has certainly ~n life** depuis qu'elle fait partie de cette bande elle en a vu des choses; **I'm going to Australia because I want to ~ life** je pars en Australie parce que je veux voir le monde *or* rouler ma bosse*; **since becoming a social worker she's certainly ~n life** depuis qu'elle est assistante sociale elle a pu se rendre compte de ce que c'est que la vie; **I've ~n some things in my time*** **but ...** j'en ai vu (des choses) dans ma vie* mais ... .

(g) (*accompany, escort*) (re)conduire, (r)accompagner. **to ~ sb to the station** accompagner *or* conduire qn à la gare; **to ~ sb home/to the door** reconduire *or* raccompagner qn jusque chez lui/jusqu'à la porte; **the policeman saw him off the premises** l'agent l'a reconduit (jusqu'à la porte); **to ~ she children to bed** coucher les enfants; **he was so drunk we had to ~ him to bed** il était tellement ivre que nous avons dû l'aider à se coucher; *V also* **see off, see out**.

(h) (*allow to be*) laisser, permettre. **I couldn't ~ her left alone** je ne pouvais pas supporter *or* permettre qu'on la laisse (*subj*) toute seule.

(i) (*ensure*) s'assurer. **~ that he has all he needs** (*make sure*) veillez à ce qu'il ait tout ce dont il a besoin; (*check*) assurez-vous qu'il ne manque de rien; **~ that you have it ready for Monday** faites en sorte que ce soit prêt pour lundi; **I'll ~ he gets the letter** je ferai le nécessaire pour que la lettre lui parvienne, je me charge de lui faire parvenir la lettre; (*Brit*) **I'll ~ you all right‡** (*gen*) je vais arranger ton affaire; (*bribe etc*) je te garantis que tu y trouveras ton compte; **I'll ~ you damned** *or* **in hell first!*** jamais de la vie!, va te faire fiche!*, va te faire foutre!‡; *V also* **see to**.

(j) (*imagine*) (s')imaginer, se représenter, voir. **I can't ~ him as Prime Minister** je ne le vois *or* ne l'imagine pas du tout en Premier ministre; **I can't ~ myself doing that** je me vois mal *or* je m'imagine mal *or* je ne me vois pas du tout faisant cela; **I can't ~ myself being elected** je ne vois pas très bien comment je pourrais être élu.

(k) (*Poker etc*) **(I'll) ~ you** je demande à vous voir, je vous vois.

2 *vi* **(a)** voir. **to ~ in/out/through** *etc* voir à l'intérieur/à l'extérieur/à travers *etc*; **let me ~** montre-moi, fais voir (*V also* 2d); **~ for yourself** voyez vous-même; **as you can ~** comme vous pouvez (le) constater; **so I ~** c'est bien ce que je vois; (*in anger*) **now ~ here!** non, mais dites donc!*, écoutez-moi un peu!; **he couldn't ~ to read** il n'y voyait pas assez clair pour lire; **cats can ~ in the dark** les chats voient clair la nuit; **you can ~ for miles** on y voit à des kilomètres; *V* **eye**.

(b) (*find out*) voir. **I'll go and ~** je vais (aller) voir; **I'll go and ~ if dinner's ready** je vais (aller) voir si le dîner est prêt.

(c) (*understand*) voir, comprendre. **as far as I can ~** à ce que je vois, pour autant que je puisse en juger; **I~!** je vois!, ah bon!; (*in explanations etc*) **... you ~ ...** voyez-vous, ... vous comprenez, ... vous voyez; **it's all over now, ~?‡** c'est fini, compris?*; **but he's dead don't you ~?** tu ne vois pas qu'il est mort?, il est mort tu vois *or* sais bien.

(d) (*think, deliberate*) voir. **let me ~, let's ~** voyons (un peu); **let me ~** *or* **let's ~, what have I got to do?** voyons, qu'est-ce que j'ai à faire?; **can I go out? — we'll ~** est-ce que je peux sortir? — on va voir *or* on verra (ça).

3 *cpd*: **see-through** *blouse etc* transparent.

see about *vt fus* **(a)** (*deal with*) s'occuper de. **he came to see about buying the house** il est venu voir s'il pouvait acheter la maison; **he came to see about the washing machine** il est venu au sujet de la machine à laver.

(b) (*consider*) **to see about sth** voir si qch est possible; **may I go? — we'll see about it** est-ce que je peux y aller? — on va voir *or* on verra (ça); **he said he wouldn't do it — we'll see about that!** il a dit qu'il ne le ferait pas — c'est ce qu'on va voir!; **we must see about (getting) a new television** il va falloir songer à s'acheter une nouvelle télévision.

see after *vt fus* s'occuper de.

see in *vt sep person* faire entrer. **to see the New Year in** fêter la Nouvelle Année, faire le réveillon du Nouvel An.

see into *vt fus* (*study, examine*) s'enquérir de, examiner. **we shall have to see into this** il va falloir examiner la question *or* se renseigner là-dessus.

see off *vt sep*: **I saw him off at the station/airport** *etc* je l'ai accompagné au train *or* à la gare/à l'avion *or* à l'aéroport *etc*; **we'll come and see you off** on viendra vous dire au revoir (à la gare *or* à l'aéroport *or* au bateau *etc*).

see out *vt sep* **(a)** *person* reconduire *or* raccompagner à la porte. **I'll see myself out*** ne vous dérangez pas, je trouverai le chemin, pas la peine de me raccompagner!*; **he saw himself out** il est sorti sans qu'on le raccompagne (*subj*).

(b) this coat will have to see the winter out il faut que ce manteau lui (*or* me *etc*) fasse l'hiver; **he was so ill we wondered whether he'd see the week out** il était si malade que nous nous demandions s'il passerait la semaine; **I saw the third act out then left** je suis resté jusqu'à la fin du troisième acte et je suis parti.

see over *vt fus house, factory, gardens* visiter.

see through 1 *vt fus person* ne pas se laisser tromper *or* duper par, pénétrer les intentions de, voir dans le jeu de; *behaviour, promises* ne pas se laisser tromper *or* duper par, voir clair dans. **I saw through him at once** j'ai tout de suite compris où il voulait en venir, j'ai tout de suite deviné ses intentions *or* vu son jeu.

2 *vt always separate project, deal* mener à bonne fin. **£10 should see you through** 10 livres devraient vous suffire; **don't worry, I'll see you through** ne vous inquiétez pas, vous pouvez compter sur moi.

3 see-through *adj V* **see**[1] **3**.

see to *vt fus* (*deal with*) s'occuper de; veiller à; (*mend*) réparer. **I'll see to the car** je m'occuperai de la voiture; **please see to it that ...** veillez s'il vous plaît à ce que ... + *subj*; **see to it that the door is shut** veillez à ce que la porte soit bien fermée; **the sweets didn't last long, the children saw to that!** les bonbons n'ont pas fait long feu, les enfants se sont chargés de les faire disparaître!

see[2] [siː] *n* [*bishop*] siège épiscopal, évêché *m*; [*archbishop*] archevêché *m*; *V* **holy**.

seed [siːd] **1** *n* **(a)** (*Agr, Bot etc*) graine *f*; (*collective n: for sowing*) graines *fpl*, semence *f*; (*in apple, grape etc*) pépin *m*. **to run** *or* **go to ~** [*plant etc*] monter en graine; [*person*] (*grow slovenly*) se négliger, se laisser aller; (*lose vigour*) se décatir.

(b) (*fig: source, origin*) germe *m*, semence *f*. **the ~s of discontent** les germes du mécontentement; **to sow ~s of doubt in sb's mind** semer le doute dans l'esprit de qn.

(c) (*sperm*) semence *f*, sperme *m*; (*offspring*) progéniture *f*.

(d) (*Tennis etc: also* **~ed player**) tête *f* de série. **first ~** joueur classé premier, joueuse classée première, première tête de série.

2 *cpd*: **seedbed** semis *m*, couche *f*; **seed box** germoir *m*; **seedcake** gâteau *m* au carvi; **seed corn** blé *m* de semence; **seeding machine** semoir *m*; **seed merchant** grainetier *m*; **seed pearls**

semence *f* de perles, très petites perles; **seed potato** pomme *f* de terre de semence; **seedsman** = **seed merchant.**

3 *vt* **(a)** *lawn* ensemencer; *raisin, grape* épépiner. **to ~ clouds** ensemencer les nuages.

(b) (*Tennis*) **he was ~ed third** il était (classé) troisième tête de série; *V also* **1d.**

4 *vi* monter en graine.

seedily ['si:dɪlɪ] *adv dress* minablement, de façon miteuse *or* minable.

seediness ['si:dɪnɪs] *n* **(a)** (*shabbiness*) aspect *m* minable *or* miteux. **(b)** (*: *illness*) indisposition *f*.

seedless ['si:dlɪs] *adj* sans pépins.

seedling ['si:dlɪŋ] *n* semis *m*, (jeune) plant *m*.

seedy ['si:dɪ] *adj* **(a)** (*shabby*) *clothes* râpé, miteux; *person, hotel* minable, miteux. **(b)** (*: *ill*) **I'm feeling ~** je suis *or* je me sens mal fichu*, je me sens patraque*, je ne me sens pas dans mon assiette; **he looks rather ~** il a l'air mal fichu*.

seeing ['si:ɪŋ] **1** *n* vue *f*, vision *f*. (*Prov*) **~ is believing** voir c'est croire. **2** *conj*: **~ (that)** vu que, étant donné que. **3** *cpd*: (*US*) **Seeing Eye dog** chien *m* d'aveugle.

seek [si:k] *pret, ptp* **sought 1** *vt* **(a)** (*look for*) *situation, solution, person, death* chercher; *fame, honours* rechercher, ambitionner; *happiness, peace* chercher, rechercher. **to ~ one's fortune in Canada** chercher *or* tenter fortune au Canada; **they sought shelter from the storm** ils ont cherché un abri *or* un refuge contre la tempête; **we sought shelter in the embassy/under a big tree** nous nous sommes réfugiés à l'ambassade/sous un grand arbre; **the reason is not far to ~** la raison n'est pas difficile à trouver, on n'a pas à chercher loin pour trouver la raison.

(b) (*ask*) demander (*from sb* à qn). **to ~ advice/help from sb** demander conseil/de l'aide à qn, chercher conseil/secours auprès de qn.

(c) (*frm: attempt*) chercher (*to do* à faire). **they sought to kill him** ils ont cherché à le tuer.

2 *vi*: **to ~ for** *or* **after sth/sb** rechercher qch/qn; **much sought after** très recherché, très demandé.

seek out *vt sep person* aller voir, (aller) s'adresser à; *trouble etc* (re)chercher.

seeker ['si:kəʳ] *n* chercheur *m*, -euse *f* (*after* en quête de); *V* **self.**

seem [si:m] *vi* **(a)** sembler, paraître, avoir l'air. **he ~s honest** il semble (être) honnête, il paraît honnête, il a l'air honnête; **she ~s to know you** elle a l'air de vous connaître, elle semble vous connaître, on dirait qu'elle vous connaît; **she ~s not to want to leave** elle semble ne pas vouloir partir, on dirait qu'elle ne veut pas partir; **we ~ to have met before** il me semble *or* j'ai l'impression que nous nous sommes déjà rencontrés; **I ~ to have heard that before** il me semble avoir déjà entendu cela, il me semble que j'ai déjà entendu cela; **I can't ~ to do it** je n'arrive pas à le faire; **I ~ed to be floating** j'avais l'impression de planer; **how did she ~ to you?** comment l'as-tu trouvée?; **how does it ~ to you?** qu'en penses-tu?; **it all ~s like a dream** on croit rêver.

(b) (*impers vb*) paraître, sembler. (*looks to me as if*) **it ~s that** *or* **as if the government is going to fall** il semble bien que le gouvernement va tomber; (*people say*) **it ~s that the government is going to fall** il paraît que le gouvernement va tomber; **I've checked and it ~s she's right** j'ai vérifié et il semble qu'elle a raison *or* on dirait qu'elle a raison *or* elle semble avoir raison; **it ~s she's right for everybody says so** il semble bien qu'elle a raison *or* il y a de fortes chances qu'elle ait raison puisque tout le monde est d'accord là-dessus; **I've checked and it doesn't ~ she's right** *or* **it ~s she's not right** j'ai vérifié et il ne semble pas qu'elle ait raison *or* elle semble avoir tort *or* il y a de fortes chances qu'elle ait tort; **from what people say it doesn't ~ she's right** d'après ce qu'on dit elle semble avoir tort; **does it ~ that she is right?** est-ce qu'il semble qu'elle ait raison?, est-ce qu'elle semble avoir raison?; **the heat was so terrible it ~ed that the whole earth was ablaze** il faisait une chaleur si terrible qu'il semblait que la terre entière fût *or* était en feu; **it ~s to me that he refused** il me semble qu'il a refusé; **it ~s to me that we should leave at once** il me semble qu'il faudrait partir tout de suite; **it does not ~ to me that we can accept** il ne me semble pas que nous puissions accepter; **does it ~ to you as though it's going to rain?** est-ce qu'il te semble qu'il va pleuvoir?, est-ce que tu crois qu'il va pleuvoir?; **they're getting married next week — so it ~s** ils vont se marier *or* ils se marient la semaine prochaine — (à ce qu')il paraît; **it ~s not** il paraît que non; **it ~s that he died yesterday** il paraît qu'il est mort hier; **he died yesterday it ~s** il est mort hier paraît-il; **I did what ~ed best** j'ai fait ce que j'ai jugé bon; **it ~s ages since we last met** il y a des siècles* que nous ne nous sommes vus; **there ~s to be a mistake in this translation** il semble y avoir une erreur dans cette traduction; **there ~s to be a mistake, I'm the one who booked this room** il semble y avoir erreur, c'est moi qui ai retenu cette chambre.

seeming ['si:mɪŋ] *adj* apparent, soi-disant *inv*.

seemingly ['si:mɪŋlɪ] *adv* apparemment. **there has ~ been a rise in inflation** à ce qu'il paraît il y a eu une hausse de l'inflation; **he's left then? — ~** il est donc parti? — (à ce qu')il paraît *or* d'après ce qu'on dit.

seemliness ['si:mlɪnɪs] *n* [*behaviour*] bienséance *f*; [*dress*] décence *f*.

seemly ['si:mlɪ] *adj behaviour* convenable, bienséant; *dress* décent, correct.

seen [si:n] *ptp of* **see**[1].

seep [si:p] *vi* suinter, filtrer. **water was ~ing through the walls** l'eau suintait des murs *or* filtrait à travers les murs, les murs suintaient.

seep away *vi* s'écouler.

seep in *vi* s'infiltrer.

seep out *vi* suinter.

seepage ['si:pɪdʒ] *n* [*water, blood*] suintement *m*; (*from tank*) fuite *f*, déperdition *f*.

seer [sɪəʳ] *n* (*liter*) voyant(e) *m(f)*, prophète *m*, prophétesse *f*.

seersucker ['sɪəˌsʌkəʳ] *n* crépon *m* de coton.

seesaw ['si:sɔ:] **1** *n* (jeu *m* de) bascule *f*. **2** *cpd*: **seesaw motion** mouvement *m* de bascule, va-et-vient *m inv*. **3** *vi* (*lit*) jouer à la bascule; (*fig*) osciller.

seethe [si:ð] *vi* **(a)** [*boiling liquid etc*] bouillir, bouillonner, être en effervescence; [*sea*] bouillonner.

(b) (*fig*) **to ~ with anger** *or* **rage** *or* **fury** bouillir de colère *or* rage *or* fureur; **he was (positively) seething*** il était furibond, il était (fou) furieux; **a country seething with discontent** un pays où le mécontentement fermente; **the crowd ~d round the star** la foule se pressait autour de la vedette; **the streets were seething with people** les rues grouillaient de *or* foisonnaient de monde.

segment ['segmənt] **1** *n* (*Anat, Geom, Zool*) segment *m*; [*orange etc*] quartier *m*, morceau *m*. **2** [seg'ment] *vt* segmenter, couper en segments. **3** [seg'ment] *vi* se segmenter.

segmental [ˌseg'mentl] *adj* segmentaire.

segmentation [ˌsegmən'teɪʃən] *n* segmentation *f*.

segregate ['segrɪgeɪt] *vt* séparer, isoler (*from* de). **to ~ the sexes** séparer les sexes; **they decided to ~ the contagious patients** ils ont décidé d'isoler les (malades) contagieux; **the political prisoners were ~d from the others** les prisonniers politiques ont été séparés *or* isolés des autres.

segregated ['segrɪgeɪtɪd] *adj* (*Pol*) *school, club, bus* où la ségrégation (raciale) est appliquée. **a ~ school system** un système d'enseignement où la ségrégation est appliquée.

segregation [ˌsegrɪ'geɪʃən] *n* (*Pol*) ségrégation *f*; [*group, person, object*] séparation *f*, isolement *m* (*from* de).

segregationist [ˌsegrɪ'geɪʃnɪst] **1** *n* ségrégationniste *mf*. **2** *adj riot, demonstration* ségrégationniste; *policy* de ségrégation, ségrégationniste.

seine [seɪn] *n* seine *f*.

seismic ['saɪzmɪk] *adj* sismique.

seismograph ['saɪzməgrɑ:f] *n* sismographe *m*.

seismography [saɪz'mɒgrəfɪ] *n* sismographie *f*.

seismology [saɪz'mɒlədʒɪ] *n* sismologie *f*.

seize [si:z] **1** *vt* **(a)** (*clutch, grab*) saisir, attraper. **she ~d (hold of) his hand, she ~d him by the hand** elle lui a saisi la main; **he ~d her by the hair** il l'a empoignée par les cheveux; **to ~ sb bodily** attraper qn à bras-le-corps; **to ~ the opportunity to do** saisir l'occasion *or* sauter sur l'occasion de faire; **to be ~d with rage** avoir un accès de rage; **to be ~d with fear** être saisi de peur; **she was ~d with the desire to see him** un désir soudain de le voir s'est emparé d'elle *or* l'a saisie; **he was ~d with a bout of coughing** il a été pris d'un accès de toux, il a eu un accès de toux; *V* **bull**[1].

(b) (*get possession of by force*) s'emparer de, se saisir de; (*Mil*) *territory* s'emparer de; *person, gun, ship* capturer, s'emparer de. **to ~ power** s'emparer du pouvoir.

(c) (*Jur*) *person* arrêter, détenir; *property* saisir; *contraband* confisquer, saisir.

2 *vi* (*Tech*) se gripper.

seize up *vi* (*Tech*) se gripper; (*Med*) s'ankyloser.

seize (up)on *vt fus idea, suggestion, offer, chance* saisir, sauter sur.

seizure ['si:ʒəʳ] *n* **(a)** (*U*) [*goods, gun, property*] saisie *f*; [*city, ship*] capture *f*; [*power, territory*] prise *f*; [*criminal*] capture, arrestation *f*; (*Jur*) appréhension *f* (au corps); [*contraband*] saisie, confiscation *f*.

(b) (*Med*) crise *f*, attaque *f*. **to have a ~** avoir une crise *or* une attaque.

seldom ['seldəm] *adv* rarement, peu souvent. **~ if ever** rarement pour ne pas dire jamais.

select [sɪ'lekt] **1** *vt team, candidate* sélectionner (*from, among* parmi); *gift, book, colour* choisir (*from, among* parmi). **to ~ a sample of rock** prélever un échantillon de; *colours, materials* choisir un échantillon de; **~ed poems** poèmes choisis; **~ed works** œuvres choisies; (*Comm*) **~ed fruit** fruits sélectionnés *or* de premier choix.

2 *adj audience* choisi, d'élite; *club* fermé; *restaurant* chic *inv*, sélect. (*Parl*) **~ committee** commission *f* parlementaire (d'enquête); **a ~ few** quelques privilégiés; **a ~ group of friends** quelques amis choisis; **they formed a small ~ group** ils formaient un petit groupe fermé.

selection [sɪ'lekʃən] **1** *n* sélection *f*, choix *m*. **to make a ~** faire une sélection *or* un choix; (*Literat, Mus*) **~s from** morceaux choisis de; *V* **natural. 2** *cpd*: **selection committee** comité *m* de sélection.

selective [sɪ'lektɪv] *adj recruitment, classification* sélectif. **one must be ~** il faut savoir faire un choix; **~ breeding** élevage *m* à base de sélection; (*Brit*) **~ school** école *f* *or* lycée *m* *or* collège *m* à recrutement sélectif.

selectivity [ˌsɪlek'tɪvɪtɪ] *n* (*Elec, Rad*) sélectivité *f*; (*Scol*) sélection *f*.

selector [sɪ'lektəʳ] *n* (*person*) sélectionneur *m*, -euse *f*; (*Tech*) sélecteur *m*.

self [self] **1** *n, pl* **selves (a)** (*also Philos, Psych*) **the ~** le moi *inv*; **the cult of ~** le culte du moi; **the conscious ~** le moi conscient; **his better ~** le meilleur de lui-même; **her real ~** son vrai moi; **my former ~** le moi *or* la personne que j'étais auparavant; **she's her old ~ again** elle est redevenue complètement elle-même; **she had no thought of ~** elle ne pensait jamais à elle-même *or* à son intérêt personnel; *V* **second**[1], **shadow.**

(b) (*Comm etc*) moi-même *etc*. **your good ~** vous-même;

your good selves vous-mêmes; (*on cheque*) **pay ~** payez à l'ordre de moi-même.

2 *cpd*: **self-abasement** avilissement *m or* abaissement *m* de soi; **self-absorbed** égocentrique; **self-abuse** masturbation *f*; **self-accusation** auto-accusation *f*; **self-acting** automatique; **self-addressed envelope** enveloppe *f* à mon (*or* son *etc*) nom et adresse; **self-adhesive** auto-adhésif; **self-adjusting** à réglage automatique; **to indulge in self-advertisement** faire sa propre réclame; **self-apparent** évident, qui va (*or* allait *etc*) de soi; **he was a self-appointed critic of ...** il a pris sur lui de critiquer ...; **self-assertion** autoritarisme *m*; **self-assertive** autoritaire, impérieux; **self-assurance** assurance *f*, confiance *f* en soi; **self-assured** sûr de soi, plein d'assurance; **self-centred** égocentrique; **self-coloured** uni; **self-composed** posé, calme; **self-composure** calme *m*, sang-froid *m*; **self-conceit** vanité *f*, suffisance *f*; **self-conceited** vaniteux, suffisant; **he is a self-confessed thief** *etc* il est voleur *etc* de son propre aveu; **self-confidence** confiance *f* en soi; **self-confident** sûr de soi, plein d'assurance; **self-conscious** timide, gêné, intimidé; **self-consciousness** gêne *f*, timidité *f*, gaucherie *f*; **self-contained** *person* indépendant; *flat* indépendant, avec entrée particulière; **self-contempt** mépris *m* de soi; **self-contradiction** contradiction *f* avec soi-même; **self-contradictory** *text* contradictoire (*en soi*), *person* qui se contredit; **self-control** maîtrise *f* de soi, sang-froid *m*; **self-controlled** maître (*f* maîtresse) de soi; **self-critical** qui se critique; (*Pol, Rel*) qui fait son autocritique; **self-criticism** critique *f* de soi; (*Pol, Rel*) autocritique *f*; **self-deception** illusion *f*; **self-defeating** qui a un effet contraire à l'effet recherché, infructueux; **(in) self-defence** (en) légitime défense *f* (*V* **noble 1a**); **self-denial** abnégation *f*, sacrifice *m* de soi; **self-denying** *person* qui fait preuve d'abnégation, qui se sacrifie; *decision etc* qui impose le sacrifice de ses intérêts; **self-destruction** autodestruction *f*, suicide *m*; **self-determination** autodétermination *f*; **self-discipline** discipline *f* (personnelle); (*Aut*) **self-drive** sans chauffeur; **self-drive car hire** location *f* de voitures sans chauffeur; **self-educated** autodidacte; **self-effacing** effacé, modeste; **self-employed** qui travaille à son compte; **self-esteem** respect *m* de soi, amour-propre *m*; **self-evident** évident, qui va de soi; **self-examination** examen *m* de conscience; **self-explanatory** qui se passe d'explication, évident (en soi); **self-expression** expression *f* (libre); **self-filling** à remplissage automatique; **self-governing** autonome; **self-government** autonomie *f*; **self-help** efforts personnels, débrouillardise* *f*; **self-importance** suffisance *f*; **self-important** suffisant, m'as-tu-vu* *inv*; **self-indulgence** amour *m* de son propre confort, sybaritisme *m*; **self-indulgent** qui ne se refuse rien, sybarite; **self-inflicted** que l'on s'inflige à soi-même, volontaire; **self-interest** intérêt *m* (personnel); **self-locking** à fermeture automatique; **self-made** qui a réussi par ses propres moyens; **self-made man** self-made man *mu5, fils m* de ses œuvres (*frm*); **self-opinionated** entêté, opiniâtre; **self-pity** apitoiement *m* sur soi-même; **full of self-pity** qui s'apitoie sur son (propre) sort; **self-portrait** autoportrait *m*; **self-possessed** assuré, qui garde son sang-froid; **self-possession** assurance *f*, sang-froid *m*; **self-praise** éloge *m* de soi-même; **self-preservation** instinct *m* de conservation; **self-propelled** autopropulsé; (*Brit*) **self-raising flour** farine *f* à levure; **self-reliant** indépendant; **to be self-reliant** ne compter que sur soi(-même); **self-reproach** repentir *m*, remords *m*; **self-respect** respect *m* de soi, dignité personnelle; **self-respecting** qui se respecte; **no self-respecting teacher would agree that ...** aucun professeur qui se respecte (*subj*) ne conviendrait que ...; **self-restraint** retenue *f*; **self-righteous** pharisaïque, satisfait de soi; **self-righteousness** pharisaïsme *m*, satisfaction *f* de soi; (*Naut*) **self-righting** inchavirable; (*US*) **self-rising flour** = **self-raising flour**; **self-sacrifice** abnégation *f*, dévouement *m*; **self-sacrificing** qui se sacrifie, qui a l'esprit de sacrifice; **selfsame** même; **this is the selfsame book** c'est bien le même livre; **I reached Paris the selfsame day** je suis arrivé à Paris le même jour *or* le jour même; **self-satisfaction** contentement *m* de soi, fatuité *f*; **self-satisfied** *person* content de soi, suffisant; *smile* suffisant, de satisfaction; **self-sealing** *envelope* autocollant, auto-adhésif; *container* à obturation automatique; **self-seeker** égoïste *mf*; **self-seeking** égoïste; **self-service** libre-service *m inv*; **a self-service shop/restaurant** un (magasin/restaurant) libre-service *or* self-service; **a self-service garage** une station *or* un poste (d'essence) libre-service; (*Aut*) **self-starter** démarreur *m* (automatique *or* électrique); **self-styled** soi-disant *inv*, prétendu; **self-sufficiency** indépendance *f*; (*self-confidence*) suffisance *f*; (*economic*) indépendance *f* économique, autarcie *f*; **self-sufficient** indépendant; (*self-confident*) suffisant; (*economically*) économiquement indépendant; **self-supporting** *person* qui subvient à ses (propres) besoins; *firm* financièrement indépendant; **self-taught** autodidacte; **'French self-taught'** 'apprenez le français tout seul'; **self-willed** entêté, volontaire; **self-winding** (à remontage) automatique.

selfish ['selfɪʃ] *adj person, behaviour* égoïste; *motive* intéressé.
selfishly ['selfɪʃlɪ] *adv* égoïstement, en égoïste.
selfishness ['selfɪʃnɪs] *n* égoïsme *m*.
selfless ['selflɪs] *adj* désintéressé, altruiste.
selflessly ['selflɪslɪ] *adv* sans penser à soi, d'une façon désintéressée, par altruisme.
selflessness ['selflɪsnɪs] *n* désintéressement *m*, altruisme *m*.
sell [sel] *pret, ptp* **sold 1** *vt* **(a)** vendre. **'to be sold'** 'à vendre'; **to ~ sth for 2 francs** vendre qch 2 F; **he sold it (to) me for 10 francs** il me l'a vendu 10 F; **he sold the books at 10 francs each** il a vendu les livres 10 F chaque *or* pièce; **he was selling them at** *or* **for 10 francs a dozen** il les vendait 10 F la douzaine; **do you ~ stamps?** avez-vous des timbres?; **are stamps sold here?** est-ce qu'on vend des timbres ici?; **I was sold this in Grenoble** on m'a vendu cela à Grenoble; **he's a commercial traveller who ~s shirts** c'est un voyageur de commerce qui place *or* vend des chemises; **it's not the price but the quality that ~s this item** ce n'est pas le prix mais la qualité qui fait vendre cet article; **we're finding it difficult to ~ our stock of ...** nous avons du mal à écouler notre stock de ...; (*pej*) **to ~ o.s.** se vendre (*V also* **1b**); **to ~ sb into slavery** vendre qn comme esclave; **to ~ a secret** vendre *or* trahir un secret; (*fig*) **to ~ the pass** abandonner *or* trahir la cause; (*St Ex*) **to ~ short** vendre à découvert; (*fig*) **to ~ sb short** (*cheat*) avoir qn*, posséder qn*; (*belittle*) débiner qn*; **to ~ one's life dearly** vendre chèrement sa vie; **he sold his soul for political power** il a vendu son âme contre le pouvoir (politique); **I'd ~ my soul for a coat like that!*** je donnerais n'importe quoi *or* je me damnerais pour avoir un manteau comme ça!; **to ~ sb down the river** trahir qn, lâcher qn*; **to ~ sb a pup‡** rouler qn*.

(b) (*: *put across*) **to ~ sb an idea** faire accepter une idée à qn; **if we can ~ coexistence to Ruritania** si nous arrivons à faire accepter le principe de la coexistence à la Ruritanie; **he doesn't ~ himself** *or* **his personality very well** il n'arrive pas à se faire valoir *or* à se mettre en valeur; **if you can ~ yourself to the voters** si vous arrivez à vous faire accepter par *or* à convaincre les électeurs; **to be sold on* an idea** *etc* être enthousiasmé *or* emballé* par une idée *etc*; **to be sold on sb*** être complètement emballé* par qn *or* entiché de qn.

(c) (*: *cheat, betray*) tromper, attraper, avoir*. **I've been sold!** on m'a eu!*, je me suis fait avoir!*.

2 *vi* se vendre. **these books ~ at** *or* **for 10 francs each** ces livres se vendent 10 F chaque *or* pièce; **they ~ at 10 francs a dozen** ils se vendent 10 F la douzaine; **your car should ~ for 8,000 francs** votre voiture devrait se vendre 8.000 F *or* réaliser 8.000 F; **it ~s well** cela se vend bien; **that line doesn't ~** cet article se vend mal; **~ing price** prix *m* de vente; **the idea didn't ~** l'idée n'a pas été acceptée; *V* **cake**.

3 *n* **(a)** (‡) (*disappointment*) déception *f*; (*fraud*) attrape-nigaud *m*. **what a ~!** ce que je me suis (*or* tu t'es *etc*) fait avoir!*

(b) (*Comm*) *V* **hard, soft.**

sell back *vt sep* revendre (*à la même personne etc*).
sell off *vt sep stock* liquider; *goods* solder; *shares* vendre, liquider.
sell out 1 *vi* (*Comm*) (*sell one's business*) vendre son fonds *or* son affaire; (*sell one's stock*) liquider son stock. (*fig*) **to sell out to the enemy** passer à l'ennemi; **to sell out on sb** trahir qn, laisser tomber qn*.

2 *vt sep* **(a)** (*St Ex*) vendre, réaliser.

(b) (*Comm*) vendre tout son stock de. **this item is sold out** cet article est épuisé; **we are sold out** on n'en a plus; **we are sold out of milk** on n'a plus de lait; (*Theat*) **the house was sold out** toutes les places étaient louées.

3 sellout *n V* **sellout.**

sell up (*esp Brit*) **1** *vi* (*Comm*) vendre son fonds *or* son affaire.

2 *vt sep* **(a)** (*Jur*) *goods* opérer la vente forcée de, saisir; *debtor* vendre les biens de.

(b) (*Comm*) *business* vendre, liquider.

seller ['seləʳ] *n* **(a)** (*person*) vendeur *m*, -euse *f*, marchand(e) *m(f)*. **~'s market** marché vendeur; **onion-~** marchand(e) *m(f)* d'oignons; *V* **book** *etc*.

(b) (*) **this book is a (good) ~** ce livre se vend bien *or* comme des petits pains*; *V* **best.**

sellotape ['seləʊteɪp] ® **1** *n* scotch *m* ®, ruban adhésif. **2** *vt* scotcher, coller avec du ruban adhésif.
sellout ['selaʊt] *n* **(a)** (*Cine, Theat etc*) **the play was a ~** tous les billets (pour la pièce) ont été vendus, on a joué à guichets fermés *or* à bureaux fermés.

(b) (*betrayal*) trahison *f*, capitulation *f*. **a ~ of minority opinion** une trahison de l'opinion de la minorité; (*Pol*) **a ~ to the left** une capitulation devant la gauche.

seltzer ['seltsəʳ] *n* (*also* **~ water**) eau *f* de Seltz.
selvage, selvedge ['selvɪdʒ] *n* lisière *f* (*d'un tissu*).
selves [selvz] *npl of* **self.**
semantic [sɪ'mæntɪk] *adj* sémantique.
semantically [sɪ'mæntɪkəlɪ] *adv* du point de vue de la sémantique.
semanticist [sɪ'mæntɪsɪst] *n* sémanticien(ne) *m(f)*.
semantics [sɪ'mæntɪks] *n* (*U*) sémantique *f*.
semaphore ['seməfɔːʳ] **1** *n* **(a)** signaux *mpl* à bras. **in ~** par signaux à bras. **(b)** (*Rail*) sémaphore *m*. **2** *vt* transmettre par signaux à bras.
semblance ['sembləns] *n* semblant *m*, apparence *f*. **without a ~ of respect** sans le moindre semblant de respect; **to put on a ~ of sorrow** prétendre avoir *or* faire semblant d'avoir de la peine.
semen ['siːmən] *n* sperme *m*, semence *f*.
semester [sɪ'mestəʳ] *n* (*esp US*) semestre *m*.
semi ['semɪ] **1** *pref* semi-, demi-, à demi, à moitié. **semibasement** ≃ rez-de-jardin *m*; (*Mus: esp Brit*) **semibreve** ronde *f*; (*Mus: esp Brit*) **semibreve rest** pause *f*; **semicircle** demi-cercle *m*; **semicircular** demi-circulaire, semi-circulaire, en demi-cercle; **semicolon** point-virgule *m*; **semiconductor** semi-conducteur *m*; **semiconscious** à demi conscient; **semiconsonant** semi-consonne *f*; **semidarkness** pénombre *f*, demi-jour *m*; **semidetached (house)** maison jumelée *or* jumelle; **semifinal** demi-finale *f*; **semifinalist** (*player*) joueur *m*, -euse *f* de demi-finale; (*team*) équipe *f* jouant dans la demi-finale; **semiofficial** semi-officiel, officieux; **semiprecious** semi-précieux; **semiprecious stone** pierre fine *or* semi-précieuse; (*Mus: esp Brit*) **semiquaver** double croche *f*; **semi-skilled** *work* d'ouvrier spécialisé; **semiskilled worker** ouvrier *m*, -ière *f* spécialisé(e), O.S. *mf*; **semitone** demi-ton *m*; **semivowel** semi-voyelle *f*.

2 *n* (*Brit** *abbr of* semidetached house) *V* 1.

seminal ['semɪnl] *adj* (*Anat*) séminal; (*fig*) fécond, fructueux.

seminar ['semɪnɑːʳ] *n* séminaire *m*, colloque *m*; (*Univ*) séminaire, séance *f* de travaux pratiques *or* de T.P.

seminarist ['semɪnərɪst] *n* séminariste *m*.

seminary ['semɪnərɪ] *n* (*priests' college*) séminaire *m*; (*school*) petit séminaire.

Semite ['siːmaɪt] *n* Sémite *mf*.

Semitic [sɪ'mɪtɪk] *adj language* sémitique; *people* sémite.

semolina [ˌsemə'liːnə] *n* semoule *f*. ~ (pudding) semoule au lait.

sempiternal [ˌsempɪ'tɜːnl] *adj* (*liter*) éternel, perpétuel.

sempstress ['sempstrɪs] *n* = **seamstress.**

senate ['senɪt] *n* (a) (*Pol*) sénat *m*. (b) (*Univ*) conseil *m* de l'université.

senator ['senɪtəʳ] *n* sénateur *m*.

senatorial [ˌsenə'tɔːrɪəl] *adj* sénatorial.

send [send] *pret, ptp* **sent 1** *vt* (a) (*dispatch*) envoyer (*to sb* à qn); (*by post*) envoyer *or* expédier (par la poste). **I sent him a letter to say that ...** je lui ai envoyé *or* expédié une lettre pour lui dire que ...; **I sent the letter to him yesterday** je lui ai envoyé *or* expédié la lettre hier; **I wrote the letter but didn't ~ it (off)** j'ai écrit la lettre mais je ne l'ai pas envoyée *or* expédiée *or* mise à la poste; **to ~ good wishes** adresser *or* envoyer ses bons vœux; **John ~s his best wishes** Jean vous (*or* nous *etc*) envoie ses bons vœux; **~ her my regards** faites-lui mes amitiés; **to ~ help** envoyer des secours; **to ~ word that ...** faire savoir que ..., faire dire que ...; **I'll ~ a car (for you)** j'enverrai une voiture (vous chercher); **to ~ washing to the laundry** donner *or* envoyer du linge au blanchissage.

(b) (*cause to go*) *person* envoyer. **to ~ sb for sth** envoyer qn chercher qch; **to ~ sb to do sth** envoyer qn faire qch; **I sent him (along) to see her** je l'ai envoyé la voir; **~ him (along) to see me** dis-lui de venir me voir, envoie-le-moi; **to ~ sb to bed** envoyer qn se coucher; **to ~ sb home** (*through illness*) renvoyer qn chez lui, dire à qn de rentrer chez lui; (*for misbehaviour*) renvoyer qn chez lui; (*from abroad*) rapatrier qn; (*Ind*) **to ~ workers home** mettre des employés en chômage technique; (*lit, fig*) **to ~ sb to sleep** endormir qn; **they sent him to school in London** ils l'ont envoyé *or* mis à l'école (*or* au lycée *etc*) à Londres; **I won't ~ you to school today** je ne t'envoie pas à l'école aujourd'hui, tu n'iras pas à l'école aujourd'hui; **children are sent to school at the age of 5** les enfants doivent aller à l'école à partir de 5 ans; **some children are sent to school without breakfast** il y a des enfants qui vont à l'école *or* qui partent pour l'école sans avoir pris de petit déjeuner; **he was sent to prison** on l'a envoyé en prison; **the rain sent us indoors** la pluie nous a fait rentrer; **they sent the dogs after the escaped prisoner** ils ont envoyé les chiens à la poursuite *or* à la recherche du prisonnier évadé; (*fig*) **to ~ sb packing*** *or* **about his business*** envoyer promener qn*, envoyer paître qn*, envoyer qn sur les roses*; (*fig*) **to ~ sb to Coventry** mettre qn en quarantaine, boycotter qn.

(c) (*propel, cause to move*) *ball* envoyer, lancer; *missile, arrow* lancer. **to ~ an astronaut/a rocket into space** lancer *or* envoyer un astronaute/une fusée dans l'espace; **he sent the ball over the trees** il a envoyé *or* lancé le ballon par-dessus les arbres; **he screwed up the paper and sent it straight into the basket** il a froissé le papier et l'a envoyé *or* l'a lancé tout droit dans la corbeille; **the explosion sent a cloud of smoke into the air** l'explosion a projeté un nuage de fumée (en l'air); **God sent a plague to punish the Egyptians** Dieu envoya *or* infligea un fléau aux Égyptiens pour les punir; **the rain has been sent to save our crops** cette pluie nous a été envoyée *or* donnée pour sauver nos récoltes; (*hum*) **these things are sent to try us!** c'est le Ciel qui nous envoie ces épreuves!; (*fig*) **to ~ a shiver down sb's spine** faire passer un frisson dans le dos de qn; **the news sent a thrill through her** la nouvelle l'a électrisée; **the sight of the dog sent her running to her mother** en voyant le chien elle s'est précipitée vers sa mère; **the blow sent him sprawling** le coup l'a envoyé par terre; **he sent the plate flying** il a envoyé voler *or* valser* l'assiette; **to ~ sb flying** envoyer qn rouler à terre.

(d) (+*adj: cause to become*) rendre. **the noise is ~ing me mad** le bruit me rend fou; **all this worry is ~ing me out of my mind** *or* **crazy** tous ces soucis me rendent fou.

(e) (‡: *make ecstatic*) emballer*, exciter, enthousiasmer. **he ~s me** je le trouve sensationnel; **this music ~s me** cette musique m'emballe* *or* me fait quelque chose.

2 *vi* (*frm, liter*) **they sent to ask if ...** ils envoyèrent demander si ... .

3 *cpd*: **they were given a warm send-off*** on leur a fait des adieux chaleureux; **they gave him a big send-off*** ils sont venus nombreux lui souhaiter bon voyage; (*Brit*) **send-up*** [*person*] mise *f* en boîte*, parodie *f*; [*book*] parodie.

send away 1 *vi*: **to send away for sth** se faire envoyer qch, commander qch par correspondance.

2 *vt sep* (a) faire partir, envoyer. **to send one's children away to school** mettre ses enfants en pension.

(b) (*dismiss*) renvoyer, congédier. **to send sb away with a flea in his ear‡** envoyer promener qn*, envoyer qn sur les roses*.

(c) *parcel, letter, goods* envoyer, expédier; (*post*) mettre à la poste.

send back *vt sep person, thing* renvoyer.

send down *vt sep* (a) (*lit*) *person* faire descendre, envoyer en bas.

(b) *prices, sb's temperature, blood pressure* faire baisser.

(c) (*Brit Univ*) renvoyer (de l'université).

send for *vt fus* (a) *doctor, police etc* faire venir, envoyer chercher, appeler. **to send for help** envoyer chercher de l'aide, se faire envoyer des secours.

(b) (*order by post*) se faire envoyer, commander par correspondance.

send forth *vt sep* (*liter*) *light* émettre; *leaf* produire; *smell* exhaler, répandre; *army* envoyer.

send in *vt sep* (a) *person* faire entrer; *troops etc* envoyer.

(b) *resignation* envoyer, donner; *report, entry form* envoyer, soumettre. **to send in an application** faire une demande; (*for job*) poser sa candidature; **to send in a request** envoyer *or* faire une demande; **send in your name and address if you wish to receive ...** envoyez vos nom et adresse si vous désirez recevoir ... .

send off 1 *vi* = **send away 1.**

2 *vt sep* (a) *person* envoyer. **I sent him off to think it over/get cleaned up** *etc* je l'ai envoyé méditer là-dessus/se débarbouiller *etc*; **she sent the child off to the grocer's** elle a envoyé l'enfant chez l'épicier; **she sent him off with a flea in his ear‡** elle l'a envoyé promener*, elle l'a envoyé sur les roses*.

(b) (*say goodbye to*) dire au revoir à. **there was a large crowd to send him off** une foule de gens était venue *or* étaient venus lui dire au revoir *or* lui souhaiter bon voyage.

(c) *letter, parcel, goods* envoyer, expédier; (*post*) mettre à la poste.

(d) (*Ftbl etc*) *player* expulser *or* renvoyer du terrain.

3 **send-off*** *n V* **send 3.**

send on *vt sep letter* faire suivre; *luggage* (*in advance*) expédier à l'avance; (*afterwards*) faire suivre; *object left behind* renvoyer.

send out 1 *vi*: **to send out for sth** envoyer chercher qch; **prisoners are allowed to send out for meals from a nearby café** les détenus ont le droit d'envoyer chercher leurs repas dans un café voisin.

2 *vt sep* (a) *person, dog etc* faire sortir, mettre à la porte. **she sent the children out to play** elle a envoyé les enfants jouer dehors; **I sent her out for a breath of air** je l'ai envoyée prendre l'air; **they were sent out for talking too loudly** on les a fait sortir *or* on les a mis à la porte parce qu'ils parlaient trop fort.

(b) (*post*) *correspondence, leaflets* envoyer (par la poste).

(c) *scouts, messengers, emissary* envoyer, expédier, dépêcher.

(d) (*emit*) *smell* répandre, exhaler; *heat* émettre, répandre; *light* diffuser, émettre; *smoke* jeter, répandre.

send round *vt sep* (a) *document, bottle etc* faire circuler.

(b) faire parvenir. **I'll send it round to you as soon as it's ready** je vous le ferai parvenir *or* porter dès que cela sera prêt.

(c) *person* envoyer. **I sent him round to the grocer's** je l'ai envoyé chez l'épicier.

send up 1 *vt sep* (a) *person, luggage* faire monter; *smoke* jeter, répandre; *aeroplane* envoyer; *spacecraft, flare* lancer.

(b) (*Brit**: *make fun of*) *person* mettre en boîte*, charrier‡; *book* parodier.

(c) *entry form* envoyer.

(d) (*blow up*) faire sauter*, faire exploser.

2 (*Brit*) **send-up*** *n V* **send 3.**

sender ['sendəʳ] *n* expéditeur *m*, -trice *f*, envoyeur *m*, -euse *f*; *V* **return.**

Seneca ['senɪkə] *n* Sénèque *m*.

Senegal [ˌsenɪ'gɔːl] *n* Sénégal *m*.

Senegalese ['senɪgə'liːz] **1** *adj* sénégalais. **2** *n, pl inv* Sénégalais(e) *m(f)*.

senile ['siːnaɪl] *adj* sénile. **~ decay** dégénérescence *f* sénile; **~ dementia** démence *f* sénile.

senility [sɪ'nɪlɪtɪ] *n* sénilité *f*.

senior ['siːnɪəʳ] **1** *adj* (a) (*older*) aîné, plus âgé. **he is 3 years ~ to me, he is ~ to me by 3 years** il est mon aîné de 3 ans, il est plus âgé que moi de 3 ans, il a 3 ans de plus que moi; **Smith S~** Smith père; **~ citizen** personne âgée; **the problem of ~ citizens** les problèmes des gens âgés *or* du troisième âge; (*Brit*) **~ school** (*oldest classes*) grandes classes; (*secondary school*) collège *m* d'enseignement secondaire; (*US*) **~ high school** (*building*) lycée *m*; (*classes*) classes *fpl* de lycée; (*US: Scol, Univ*) **~ year** dernière année d'études (scolaires *or* universitaires).

(b) (*of higher rank*) *employee* de grade supérieur; *officer* supérieur (*f* -eure); *position, rank* supérieur, plus élevé. **he is ~ to me in the firm** (*in rank*) il est au-dessus de moi dans l'entreprise, son poste dans l'entreprise est plus élevé que le mien; (*in service*) il a plus d'ancienneté que moi dans la maison; **~ clerk** premier commis, commis principal; **~ executive** cadre supérieur *or* d'état-major; (*Brit Scol*) **~ master** professeur principal; **~ partner** associé principal; (*Brit*) **the S~ Service** la marine (de guerre).

2 *n* (a) (*in age*) aîné(e) *m(f)*. **he is my ~ by 3 years, he is 3 years my ~** (*in age*) il est mon aîné de 3 ans, il est plus âgé que moi de 3 ans; (*in service*) il a 3 ans d'ancienneté de plus que moi.

(b) (*US Univ*) étudiant(e) *m(f)* de dernière année. (*Brit Scol*) **the ~s** les grand(e)s *m(f)pl*.

seniority [ˌsiːnɪ'ɒrɪtɪ] *n* (*in age*) priorité *f* d'âge; (*in rank*) supériorité *f*; (*in years of service*) ancienneté *f*. **promotion by ~** avancement *m* à l'ancienneté.

senna ['senə] *n* séné *m*.

sensation [sen'seɪʃən] *n* (a) (*U: feeling*) sensation *f*. **to lose all ~ in one's arm** perdre toute sensation dans le bras.

(b) (*impression*) sensation *f*, impression *f*. **to have a dizzy ~** avoir une sensation de vertige; **I had a gliding ~ or the ~ of gliding** j'avais la sensation *or* l'impression de planer.

(c) (*excitement*) sensation *f*; (*Press*) sensation, scandale *m*. **to create** *or* **cause a ~** faire sensation; **it was a ~ in Paris** cela a fait sensation à Paris; **it's a ~!** c'est sensationnel!

sensational [sen'seɪʃənl] *adj* (a) *event* qui fait sensation, sensationnel; *fashion* qui fait sensation. **~ murder** meurtre *m* qui fait sensation.

(b) *film, novel, newspaper* à sensation. **he gave a ~ account**

of the accident il a fait un récit dramatique de l'accident.

(c) (*: *marvellous*) sensationnel*, formidable*, sensass* *inv.*

sensationalism [sen'seɪʃnəlɪzəm] *n* (*U*) **(a)** (*Press etc*) recherche *f or* exploitation *f* du sensationnel. **(b)** (*Philos*) sensualisme *m.*

sensationalist [sen'seɪʃnəlɪst] **1** *n* colporteur *m*, -euse *f* de nouvelles à sensation; (*writer*) auteur *m* à sensation. **2** *adj* à sensation.

sensationally [sen'seɪʃnəlɪ] *adv report, describe* en recherchant le sensationnel. **it was ~ successful/popular** *etc* cela a connu un succès/une popularité *etc* inouï(e) *or* fantastique.

sense [sens] **1** *n* **(a)** (*faculty*) sens *m.* **~ of hearing** ouïe *f*; **~ of smell** odorat *m*; **~ of sight** vue *f*; **~ of taste** goût *m*; **~ of touch** toucher *m*; **to come to one's ~s** (*regain consciousness*) reprendre connaissance, revenir à soi (*V also* **1d**); *V* **sixth.**

(b) (*awareness*) sens *m*, sentiment *m.* **~ of colour** sens de la couleur; **~ of direction** sens de l'orientation; **~ of duty** sentiment du devoir; **~ of humour** sens de l'humour; **to lose all ~ of time** perdre toute notion de l'heure; **the ~ of my own inadequacy** le sentiment de mon impuissance; **to have no ~ of shame** ne pas savoir ce que c'est que la honte; *V* **business, road, strong.**

(c) (*sensation, impression*) (*physical*) sensation *f*; (*mental*) sentiment *m.* **a ~ of warmth** une sensation de chaleur; **a ~ of guilt** un sentiment de culpabilité.

(d) (*sanity*) **~s** raison *f*; **to take leave of one's ~s** perdre la tête *or* la raison; **to come to one's ~s** (*become reasonable*) revenir à la raison; **to bring sb to his ~s** ramener qn à la raison; **anyone in his ~s would know ...** tout homme sensé *or* tout homme jouissant de sa raison saurait ...; **no one in his ~s would do that** il faudrait être fou pour faire ça.

(e) (*wisdom, sound judgment; also* **common ~**) bon sens, intelligence *f.* **haven't you enough ~** *or* **the (good) ~ to refuse?** n'avez-vous pas assez de bon sens pour refuser?; **there is some ~ in what he says** il y a du bon sens dans ce qu'il dit; **to have more ~ than to do** avoir trop de bon sens pour faire, être trop sensé pour faire; **you should have had more ~ than to do it** vous auriez dû avoir assez de bon sens pour ne pas le faire; *V* **common.**

(f) (*reasonable quality*) sens *m.* **there's no ~ in (doing) that** cela n'a pas de sens, cela ne rime à rien; **what's the ~ of** *or* **in (doing) that?** à quoi bon (faire) cela?; *V* **see**[1], **sound**[2], **talk.**

(g) (*meaning*) *[word, phrase, writing, text etc]* sens *m*, signification *f.* **in the literal/figurative ~** au sens propre/figuré; **in every ~ of the word** dans toute l'acception du terme; **in a ~** dans un (certain) sens, dans une certaine mesure; **to get the ~ of what sb says** saisir l'essentiel de ce que dit qn.

(h) (*rational meaning*) *[words, writing, action, event]* sens *m. [words, speech etc]* **to make ~** avoir du sens; *[words, speech etc]* **not to make ~** ne pas avoir de sens, être dénué de sens; **what she did makes ~** ce qu'elle a fait est logique *or* se tient; **what she did just doesn't make ~** ce qu'elle a fait n'a pas le sens commun *or* n'est pas logique *or* ne tient pas debout*; **why did she do it? — I don't know, it doesn't make ~** pourquoi est-ce qu'elle a fait ça? — je n'en sais rien, ça n'a pas le sens commun *or* ça n'est pas logique *or* ça ne tient pas debout*; **to make ~ of sth** arriver à comprendre qch, saisir la signification de qch.

(i) (*opinion*) **the general ~ of the meeting** l'opinion générale *or* le sentiment de ceux présents.

2 *cpd*: **sense organ** organe des sens *or* sensoriel.

3 *vt* (*become aware of, feel*) sentir (intuitivement), pressentir. **to ~ somebody's presence** se rendre compte d'une présence, sentir une présence; **to ~ danger** pressentir le danger; **I could ~ his eyes on me** je sentais qu'il me regardait; **I ~d his interest in what I was saying** j'ai senti *or* je me suis rendu compte que ce que je disais l'intéressait; **to ~ that one is unwelcome** sentir qu'on n'est pas le bienvenu; **I ~d as much** c'est bien ce que j'ai deviné *or* senti.

senseless ['senslɪs] *adj* **(a)** (*stupid*) *person* insensé; *action, idea* stupide, qui n'a pas le sens commun, (*stronger*) absurde, insensé. **a ~ waste of energy resources** un gâchis insensé des ressources d'énergie; **a ~ waste of human life** des pertes insensées en vies humaines; **what a ~ thing to do!** (*or* **to say!** *etc*) c'est d'une stupidité sans nom!, ça n'a pas le sens commun!

(b) (*unconscious*) sans connaissance. **to fall ~ (to the floor)** tomber sans connaissance; *V* **knock.**

senselessly ['senslɪslɪ] *adv* stupidement, d'une façon insensée.

senselessness ['senslɪsnɪs] *n [person]* manque *m* de bon sens; *[action, idea]* absurdité *f.* **the absolute ~ of the war** l'absurdité totale de la guerre.

sensibility [ˌsensɪ'bɪlɪtɪ] *n* **(a)** (*U*) sensibilité *f.* **(b) sensibilities** susceptibilité *f.*

sensible ['sensəbl] *adj* **(a)** (*wise, of sound judgment*) *person* sensé, raisonnable, sage. **she's a ~ person** *or* **type*** elle est très raisonnable *or* sensée, elle a les deux pieds sur terre*; **try to be ~ about it** sois raisonnable; **that was ~ of you** c'était raisonnable de ta part, tu as fait preuve de bon sens.

(b) (*reasonable, practicable*) *act, decision, choice* judicieux, sage; *clothes* pratique, commode. **the most ~ thing (to do) would be to see her** le plus sage *or* raisonnable serait de la voir; **~ shoes** chaussures *fpl* pratiques.

(c) (*perceptible*) *change, difference, rise in temperature* sensible, appréciable, assez considérable.

(d) (†, *frm: aware*) **I am ~ of the honour you do me** je suis sensible à *or* conscient de l'honneur que vous me faites.

sensibleness ['sensəblnɪs] *n* bon sens, jugement *m.*

sensibly ['sensəblɪ] *adv* **(a)** (*reasonably*) *act, decide* raisonnablement, sagement, judicieusement. **to be ~ dressed** porter des vêtements pratiques. **(b)** (*perceptibly*) sensiblement.

sensitive ['sensɪtɪv] **1** *adj* **(a)** *person* (*emotionally aware, responsive*) sensible; (*easily hurt*) sensible (*to* à); (*easily offended*) facilement blessé (*to* par), susceptible, ombrageux; (*easily influenced*) impressionnable, influençable. **she is ~ about her nose** elle n'aime pas qu'on lui parle (*subj*) de son nez.

(b) *skin, tooth, eyes, (Phot) film* sensible (*to* à); (*Phot*) *paper* sensibilisé. **public opinion is very ~ to hints of corruption** l'opinion publique réagit vivement à tout soupçon de corruption.

(c) (*delicate*) *skin, question* délicat.

2 -sensitive *adj ending in cpds*: **heat-sensitive** sensible à la chaleur.

sensitively ['sensɪtɪvlɪ] *adv* avec sensibilité, d'une manière sensible.

sensitiveness ['sensɪtɪvnɪs] *n* (*V* **sensitive 1a**) sensibilité *f*; susceptibilité *f.*

sensitivity [ˌsensɪ'tɪvɪtɪ] *n* (*V* **sensitive 1a, 1b, 1c**) sensibilité *f*; susceptibilité *f*; délicatesse *f*; (*Fin, St Ex*) instabilité *f.*

sensitize ['sensɪtaɪz] *vt* (*Med, Phot*) sensibiliser.

sensory ['sensərɪ] *adj* des sens; (*Physiol*) *organ, nerve* sensoriel.

sensual ['sensjʊəl] *adj* sensuel.

sensualism ['sensjʊəlɪzəm] *n* sensualité *f*; (*Philos*) sensualisme *m.*

sensualist ['sensjʊəlɪst] *n* personne sensuelle, voluptueux *m*, -euse *f*; (*Philos*) sensualiste *mf.*

sensuality [ˌsensjʊ'ælɪtɪ] *n* sensualité *f.*

sensuous ['sensjʊəs] *adj poetry, music* voluptueux, qui fait appel aux sens, qui affecte les sens; *person, temperament* voluptueux, sensuel.

sensuously ['sensjʊəslɪ] *adv* avec volupté, voluptueusement.

sensuousness ['sensjʊəsnɪs] *n [poetry, music]* qualité voluptueuse *or* évocatrice; *[person, temperament]* volupté *f.*

sent [sent] *pret, ptp of* **send.**

sentence ['sentəns] **1** *n* **(a)** (*Gram*) phrase *f.*

(b) (*Jur*) (*judgment*) condamnation *f*, sentence *f*; (*punishment*) peine *f.* (*lit, fig*) **to pass ~ on sb** prononcer une condamnation *or* une sentence contre qn; **~ of death** arrêt *m* de mort, condamnation à mort; **under ~ of death** condamné à mort; **he got a 5-year ~** il a été condamné à 5 ans de prison; **a long ~** une longue peine; *V* **commute, life, serve** *etc.*

2 *cpd*: (*Gram*) **sentence structure** structure *f* de la phrase.

3 *vt* prononcer une condamnation *or* une sentence contre. **to ~ sb to death/to 5 years** condamner qn à mort/à 5 ans de prison.

sententious [sen'tenʃəs] *adj* sentencieux, pompeux.

sententiously [sen'tenʃəslɪ] *adv* sentencieusement.

sententiousness [sen'tenʃəsnɪs] *n [speech]* ton sentencieux; *[person]* caractère sentencieux.

sentient ['senʃənt] *adj* sensible, doué de sensation.

sentiment ['sentɪmənt] *n* **(a)** (*feeling*) sentiment *m*; (*opinion*) opinion *f*, avis *m.* **my ~s towards your daughter** les sentiments que j'éprouve pour votre fille *or* que m'inspire votre fille.

(b) (*U: sentimentality*) sentimentalité *f*, sentiment* *m*, sensiblerie *f* (*pej*).

sentimental [ˌsentɪ'mentl] *adj person, novel, value* sentimental (*also pej*). (*Literat*) **~ comedy** comédie larmoyante.

sentimentalism [ˌsentɪ'mentəlɪzəm] *n* sentimentalisme *m*, sensiblerie *f* (*pej*).

sentimentalist [ˌsentɪ'mentəlɪst] *n* sentimental(e) *m(f).*

sentimentality [ˌsentɪmen'tælɪtɪ] *n* sentimentalité *f*, sensiblerie *f* (*pej*).

sentimentalize [ˌsentɪ'mentəlaɪz] **1** *vt* rendre sentimental. **2** *vi* faire du sentiment*.

sentimentally [ˌsentɪ'mentəlɪ] *adv* sentimentalement, d'une manière *or* d'une voix sentimentale.

sentinel ['sentɪnl] *n* sentinelle *f*, factionnaire *m.*

sentry ['sentrɪ] **1** *n* (*Mil etc*) sentinelle *f*, factionnaire *m*; (*fig*) sentinelle. **2** *cpd*: **sentry box** guérite *f*; **to be on sentry duty** être en *or* de faction.

sepal ['sepəl] *n* sépale *m.*

separable ['sepərəbl] *adj* séparable.

separate ['seprɪt] **1** *adj section, piece* séparé, distinct; *treaty, peace* séparé; *career, existence* indépendant; *organization, unit* distinct, indépendant; *entrance* particulier; *occasion, day* différent; *question, issue* différent, autre. **the children have ~ rooms** les enfants ont chacun leur (propre) chambre; **Paul and his wife sleep in ~ beds/rooms** Paul et sa femme font lit/chambre à part; (*in restaurant etc*) **we want ~ bills** nous voudrions des additions séparées *or* chacun notre addition; **the two houses though semidetached are quite ~** les deux maisons bien que jumelées sont tout à fait indépendantes (l'une de l'autre); **I wrote it on a ~ sheet** je l'ai écrit sur une feuille séparée *or* sur une feuille à part; **take a ~ sheet for each answer** prenez une nouvelle feuille pour chaque réponse; **there will be ~ discussions on this question** cette question sera discutée à part *or* séparément; **there is a ~ department for footwear** il y a un rayon séparé *or* spécial pour les chaussures; **'with ~ toilet'** 'avec W.-C. séparé'; **keep the novels ~ from the textbooks** séparez les romans des livres de classe; (*Can*) **~ school** école *f* *or* collège *m* privé(e).

2 *n* (*clothes*) **~s** coordonnés *mpl.*

3 ['sepəreɪt] *vt* séparer (*from* de); (*sort out*) séparer, trier; (*divide up*) diviser; *strands* dédoubler; *milk* écrémer. **to ~ truth from error** distinguer le vrai du faux; **they are ~d but not divorced** ils sont séparés mais ils n'ont pas divorcé; *V* **sheep, wheat.**

4 ['sepəreɪt] *vi* **(a)** *[liquids]* se séparer (*from* de); *[metals etc]* se séparer, se détacher (*from* de).

(b) *[people]* se séparer, se quitter; *[fighters]* rompre.

(c) *[married couple]* se séparer; *[non-married couple]* rompre.

separate out *vt sep* séparer, trier.
separately [ˈseprɪtlɪ] *adv* **(a)** (*apart*) séparément, à part. **(b)** (*one by one*) séparément, un par un, un à la fois. **these articles are sold ~** ces articles se vendent séparément.
separation [ˌsepəˈreɪʃən] **1** *n* séparation *f*; *[ore]* triage *m*; (*Pol, Rel*) scission *f*, séparation; (*after marriage*) séparation (*from* d'avec). **judicial ~** séparation de corps.
2 *cpd*: **separation allowance** (*Mil*) allocation *f* militaire; (*Jur: alimony*) pension *f* alimentaire.
separatism [ˈsepərətɪzəm] *n* séparatisme *m*.
separatist [ˈsepərətɪst] *adj, n* séparatiste (*mf*).
separator [ˈsepəreɪtəʳ] *n* (*all senses*) séparateur *m*.
Sephardi [seˈfɑːdɪ] *n, pl* **Sephardim** [seˈfɑːdɪm] Séfardi *mf or* Séfaraddi *mf*.
sepia [ˈsiːpjə] *n* **(a)** (*colour*) sépia *f*. **~ drawing** sépia. **(b)** (*fish*) seiche *f*.
sepoy [ˈsiːpɔɪ] *n* cipaye *m*.
sepsis [ˈsepsɪs] *n* (*Med*) septicité *f*, état *m* septique.
September [sepˈtembəʳ] **1** *n* septembre *m*, mois *m* de septembre. **the first of ~** le premier septembre; **the tenth of ~** le dix septembre; **on the tenth of ~** le dix septembre; **in ~** en septembre; **in the month of ~** au mois de septembre; **each** *or* **every ~** tous les ans *or* chaque année en septembre; **at the beginning of ~** au début (du mois) de septembre, début septembre*; **in the middle of ~, in mid ~** au milieu (du mois) de septembre, à la mi-septembre; **at the end of ~** à la fin (du mois) de septembre, fin septembre*; **during ~** pendant le mois de septembre; **there are 30 days in ~** il y a 30 jours au mois de septembre, septembre a 30 jours; **~ was cold** septembre a été froid, il a fait froid en septembre; **early in ~, in early ~** au début de septembre; **late in ~, in late ~** vers la fin de septembre; **last/next ~** septembre dernier/prochain.
2 *cpd*: **the September holidays/rains** *etc* les congés *mpl*/les pluies *fpl etc* (du mois) de septembre; (*Hist*) **September Riots** massacres *mpl* de septembre; **it's September weather** il fait un temps de septembre.
Septembrist [sepˈtembrɪst] *n* septembriseur *m*.
septet [sepˈtet] *n* septuor *m*.
septic [ˈseptɪk] *adj* septique; *wound* infecté. **to go** *or* **become ~** s'infecter; **~ poisoning** septicémie *f*; **~ tank** fosse *f* septique.
septicaemia, (*US*) **septicemia** [ˌseptɪˈsiːmɪə] *n* septicémie *f*.
septuagenarian [ˌseptjʊədʒɪˈnɛərɪən] *adj, n* septuagénaire (*mf*).
Septuagesima [ˌseptjʊəˈdʒesɪmə] *n* Septuagésime *f*.
Septuagint [ˈseptjʊədʒɪnt] *n* version *f* (biblique) des Septante.
septum [ˈseptəm] *n, pl* **septa** [ˈseptə] (*Anat, Bot*) cloison *f*.
septuplet [sepˈtʌplɪt] *n* septuplé(e) *m(f)*.
sepulchral [sɪˈpʌlkrəl] *adj* sépulcral; (*fig: gloomy*) funèbre, sépulcral.
sepulchre, (*US*) **sepulcher** [ˈsepəlkəʳ] *n* sépulcre *m*, tombeau *m*; (*Rel*) sépulcre. (*fig*) **whited ~** hypocrite *mf*; *V* **holy.**
sequel [ˈsiːkwəl] *n* **(a)** (*consequence*) suite *f*, conséquence *f*; (*to illness etc*) séquelles *fpl*. **it had a tragic ~** cela a eu des suites *or* des conséquences tragiques. **(b)** *[book, film etc]* suite *f*.
sequence [ˈsiːkwəns] *n* **(a)** (*order*) ordre *m*, suite *f*. **in ~** par ordre, les uns à la suite des autres; **in historical ~** par ordre chronologique; **logical ~** ordre *or* enchaînement *m* logique; (*Gram*) **~ of tenses** concordance *f* des temps.
(b) (*series*) suite *f*, succession *f*; (*Cards*) séquence *f*.
(c) **(film) ~** séquence *f*; **(dance) ~** numéro *m* (de danse).
(d) (*Mus*) séquence *f*.
sequential [sɪˈkwenʃəl] *adj* (*in regular sequence*) séquentiel; (*following*) qui suit. **~ upon** *or* **from** qui résulte de.
sequester [sɪˈkwestəʳ] *vt* **(a)** (*isolate*) isoler; (*shut up*) enfermer, séquestrer. **~ed** *life* isolé, retiré; *spot* retiré, peu fréquenté. **(b)** (*Jur*) *property* séquestrer. **~ed** *property* mis *or* placé sous séquestre.
sequestrate [sɪˈkwestreɪt] *vt* (*Jur*) **(a)** = **sequester b. (b)** (*confiscate*) confisquer, saisir.
sequestration [ˌsiːkwesˈtreɪʃən] *n* (*Jur*) **(a)** *[property]* séquestration *f*, mise *f* sous séquestre. **(b)** (*confiscation*) confiscation *f*, saisie *f* conservatoire.
sequin [ˈsiːkwɪn] *n* paillette *f*.
sequoia [sɪˈkwɔɪə] *n* séquoia *m*.
seraglio [seˈrɑːlɪəʊ] *n* sérail *m*.
seraph [ˈserəf] *n, pl* **~s** *or* (*Rel, liter etc*) **seraphim** séraphin *m*.
seraphic [səˈræfɪk] *adj* (*lit, fig*) séraphique.
seraphim [ˈserəfɪm] *npl of* **seraph.**
Serb [sɜːb] **1** *adj* serbe. **2** *n* **(a)** Serbe *mf*. **(b)** (*Ling*) serbe *m*.
Serbia [ˈsɜːbɪə] *n* Serbie *f*.
Serbian [ˈsɜːbɪən] = **Serb.**
Serbo-Croat [ˈsɜːbəʊˈkrəʊæt], **Serbo-Croatian** [ˈsɜːbəʊkrəʊˈeɪʃən] **1** *adj* serbo-croate. **2** *n* **(a)** Serbo-croate *mf*. **(b)** (*Ling*) serbo-croate *m*.
sere [sɪəʳ] *adj* = **sear 1.**
serenade [ˌserəˈneɪd] **1** *n* sérénade *f*. **2** *vt* donner une sérénade à.
serendipity [ˌserənˈdɪpɪtɪ] *n* (*U: hum*) don *m* de faire par hasard des découvertes heureuses.
serene [səˈriːn] *adj person, smile* serein, tranquille, paisible; *sky* serein, clair; *sea* calme. **to become** *or* **grow ~** *[person]* redevenir serein, se rasséréner; *[sky]* redevenir serein; *[sea]* redevenir calme; **His S~ Highness** Son Altesse Sérénissime; **all ~!*** tout va bien!
serenely [səˈriːnlɪ] *adv smile etc* avec sérénité, sereinement; *say* d'un ton serein. **~ indifferent to the noise** suprêmement indifférent au bruit.
serenity [sɪˈrenɪtɪ] *n* (*V* **serene**) sérénité *f*; calme *m*; tranquillité *f*.
serf [sɜːf] *n* serf *m*, serve *f*.
serfdom [ˈsɜːfdəm] *n* servage *m*.
serge [sɜːdʒ] **1** *n* serge *f*. **2** *cpd* de serge. **blue serge suit** complet *m* en serge bleue.
sergeant [ˈsɑːdʒənt] **1** *n* **(a)** (*Mil*) (*Infantry*) sergent *m*; (*Artillery, Cavalry*) maréchal *m* des logis. (*US Mil*) **~ first class** caporal- *or* brigadier-chef *m*; **yes, ~** oui, chef; *V* **colour, drill**[2], **flight**[1] *etc.*
(b) (*US Air Force*) caporal-chef *m*.
(c) (*Police*) (*Brit, US*) brigadier *m*; *V* **detective.**
2 *cpd*: **sergeant at arms** huissier *m* d'armes; (*Mil*) **sergeant-major** (*Infantry*) sergent-major *m*; (*Artillery, Cavalry*) maréchal *m* des logis-chef; *V* **company, regimental.**
serial [ˈsɪərɪəl] **1** *n* **(a)** (*Rad, TV*) feuilleton *m*; (*in magazine etc*: *also* **~ story**) roman-feuilleton *m*, feuilleton. **television/radio ~** feuilleton à la télévision/à la radio, feuilleton télévisé/radiophonique; **13-part ~** feuilleton en 13 épisodes.
(b) (*publication, journal*) publication *f* périodique, périodique *m*.
2 *adj* **(a)** d'une série, formant une série, en série; *music* sériel. **~ number** *[goods, car engine]* numéro *m* de série; *[soldier]* (numéro) matricule *m*; *[cheque, banknote]* numéro.
(b) **~ rights** droits *mpl* de reproduction en feuilleton; **~ writer** feuilletoniste *mf*.
serialize [ˈsɪərɪəlaɪz] *vt* (*Press*) publier en feuilleton; (*Rad, TV*) adapter en feuilleton. **it was ~d in 6 parts** cela a été publié *or* adapté en 6 épisodes; **it has been ~d in the papers** cela a paru *or* été publié en feuilleton dans les journaux.
serially [ˈsɪərɪəlɪ] *adv* **(a)** *number* en série. **(b) to appear/be published ~** *[story]* paraître/être publié en feuilleton; *[magazine, journal]* paraître/être publié en livraisons périodiques.
seriatim [ˌsɪərɪˈeɪtɪm] *adv* successivement, point par point.
sericulture [ˌserɪˈkʌltʃəʳ] *n* sériciculture *f*.
series [ˈsɪərɪz] **1** *n, pl inv* **(a)** (*also Chem, Comm, Elec, Mus*) série *f*; (*succession*) série, suite *f*, succession *f*; (*Math*) série, suite. **in ~** (*also Elec*) en série; **~ of stamps/coins** *etc* série de timbres/de monnaies *etc*; **~ of colours** gamme *f or* échelle *f* de couleurs; **a ~ of volumes on this subject** une série de volumes sur ce sujet; **there has been a ~ of incidents** il y a eu une série *or* une suite *or* une succession d'incidents, il y a eu plusieurs incidents successifs.
(b) (*Rad, TV*) série *f* (d'émissions); (*set of books*) collection *f*; (*set of stamps*) série. (*Rad, TV*) **this is the last in the present ~ (of programmes)** c'est le dernier programme de cette série; (*Publishing*) **a new paperback ~** une nouvelle collection de poche; *V* **world.**
2 *cpd*: (*Elec*) **series connection** montage *m* en série.
serio-comic [ˌsɪərɪəʊˈkɒmɪk] *adj* mi-sérieux mi-comique.
serious [ˈsɪərɪəs] *adj* **(a)** (*in earnest, not frivolous*) *person, offer, suggestion, interest* sérieux, sincère; *publication, conversation, discussion, occasion* sérieux, important; *report, information, account* sérieux, sûr; *attitude, voice, smile, look* plein de sérieux, grave; *tone* sérieux, grave; (*unsmiling*) *person* sérieux, grave, froid; *look* grave, sévère; (*thoughtful*) sérieux, réfléchi, posé; *pupil* sérieux, appliqué. **are you ~?** parlez-vous sérieusement?; **I'm quite ~** je suis sérieux, je parle sérieusement, je ne plaisante pas; **to give ~ thought to sth** (*ponder*) bien réfléchir à qch; (*intend*) songer sérieusement à (faire qch); **to be ~ about one's work** être sérieux dans son travail; **the ~ student of jazz will maintain that ...** quelqu'un qui s'intéresse sérieusement au jazz affirmera que ...; **marriage is a ~ business** le mariage est une affaire sérieuse.
(b) (*causing concern*) *illness, injury, mistake, situation* grave, sérieux; *damage* important, considérable; *threat* sérieux; *loss* grave, lourd. **I have ~ doubts about ...** je doute sérieusement de ..., j'ai de graves doutes sur ...; **the patient's condition is ~** le patient est dans un état grave.
seriously [ˈsɪərɪəslɪ] *adv* **(a)** (*in earnest*) sérieusement, avec sérieux; (*not jokingly*) sérieusement, sans plaisanter, sans blaguer*. **he said it all quite ~** il l'a dit tout à fait sérieusement, en disant ça il ne plaisantait *or* ne blaguait* pas; **yes, but ~ ...** oui, mais sérieusement ...; **~ now ...** sérieusement ..., sans blague* ..., toute plaisanterie *or* blague* (mise) à part ...; **to take sth/sb ~** prendre qch/qn au sérieux.
(b) (*dangerously*) gravement, sérieusement, dangereusement; *ill* gravement; *wounded* grièvement; *worried* sérieusement.
seriousness [ˈsɪərɪəsnɪs] *n* **(a)** *[intention, offer, suggestion, interest]* sérieux *m*, sincérité *f*; *[publication, discussion, conversation, occasion]* sérieux, importance *f*; *[report, information, account]* caractère sérieux *or* sûr; *[attitude, voice, smile, tone, look]* sérieux, gravité *f*; *[character]* sérieux, gravité, froideur *f*; (*thoughtfulness*) sérieux, caractère posé *or* réfléchi. **in all ~** sérieusement, en toute sincérité.
(b) *[situation, illness, mistake, threat, loss, injury]* gravité *f*; *[damage]* importance *f*, ampleur *f*.
serjeant [ˈsɑːdʒənt] = **sergeant.**
sermon [ˈsɜːmən] *n* (*Rel*) sermon *m*; (*fig pej*) sermon, laïus* *m*. **the S~ on the Mount** le Sermon sur la Montagne; (*fig pej*) **to give sb a ~, to preach a ~ to sb** faire un sermon à qn.
sermonize [ˈsɜːmənaɪz] (*fig pej*) **1** *vt* sermonner. **2** *vi* prêcher, faire des sermons.
serous [ˈsɪərəs] *adj* séreux.
serpent [ˈsɜːpənt] *n* (*lit, fig*) serpent *m*; *V* **sea.**
serpentine [ˈsɜːpəntaɪn] **1** *adj river, road* sinueux, tortueux, qui serpente; (*treacherous*) perfide; (*Zool*) de serpent. **2** *n* (*Miner*) serpentine *f*, ophite *m*.
serrate [seˈreɪt] *vt* denteler, découper en dents de scie. **~d** en dents de scie, dentelé.
serration [seˈreɪʃən] *n* dentelure *f*.

serried ['serɪd] *adj* serré. **in ~ ranks** en rangs serrés.
serum ['sɪərəm] *n* sérum *m*.
servant ['sɜːvənt] **1** *n* (*in household*) domestique *mf*; (*maid*) bonne *f*; (*fig*) serviteur *m*, servante *f*. **to keep a ~** avoir un(e) domestique; **a large staff of ~s** une nombreuse domesticité; **the ~s' hall** l'office *f*; **I'm not your ~** je ne suis pas votre domestique; **the government is the ~ of the people** le gouvernement est le serviteur *or* est au service du peuple; (*frm*) **your obedient ~** ≃ je vous prie d'agréer, Monsieur (*or* Madame *etc*), l'expression de ma considération distinguée; *V* **civil, humble, man, public** *etc*.
2 *cpd*: **servant girl** servante *f*, bonne *f*.
serve [sɜːv] **1** *vt* **(a)** (*work for*) *master, employer, family* servir, être au service de; *God, one's country* servir. **he ~d his country well** il a bien servi son pays, il a bien mérité de la patrie (*frm*); **he has ~d the firm well** il a bien servi la compagnie, il a rendu de grands services à la compagnie; **he has ~d our cause well** il a bien servi notre cause; (*fig*) **to ~ two masters** servir deux maîtres à la fois; (*Rel*) **to ~ mass** servir la messe.
(b) (*be used as*) *[object etc]* servir (*as* de); (*be useful to*) rendre service à, être utile à. **it's not very good but it will ~ me** ça n'est pas parfait mais ça fera l'affaire; **it will ~ my** (*or* **your** *etc*) **purpose** *or* **needs** cela fera l'affaire; **it ~s its purpose** *or* **turn** cela fait l'affaire, cela suffit bien; **it ~s a variety of purposes** cela sert à divers usages; **it ~s no useful purpose** cela ne sert à rien (de spécial); **if my memory ~s me (right)** (*V also* 1c) si j'ai bonne mémoire, si je me souviens bien; **his knowledge of history ~d him well** ses connaissances en histoire *or* d'histoire lui ont été très utiles *or* se sont avérées très utiles *or* lui ont bien servi; **that excuse won't ~ you when ...** cette excuse ne vous servira à rien quand ... .
(c) (*phrases*) **(it) ~s him right** c'est bien fait pour lui, il ne l'a pas volé; **(it) ~s you right for being so stupid** cela t'apprendra à être si stupide; **it would have ~d them right if they hadn't got any** ça aurait été bien fait pour eux s'ils n'en avaient pas reçu.
(d) (*in shop, restaurant*) servir. **to ~ sb (with) sth** servir qch à qn; **are you being ~d?** est-ce qu'on vous sert? *or* s'occupe de vous?
(e) *food, meal* servir (*to sb* à qn). **dinner is ~d** le dîner est servi; (*as formal announcement*) Madame est servie, Monsieur est servi; **this fish should be ~d with mustard sauce** ce poisson se sert *or* se mange avec une sauce à la moutarde; (*in recipe etc*) **'~s 5'** '5 portions'; *V* **first**.
(f) (*with transport, church services*) desservir; (*with gas, electricity*) alimenter. **the bus ~s 6 villages** le car dessert 6 villages; **the power station ~s a large district** la centrale alimente une zone étendue.
(g) (*work out*) **to ~ one's apprenticeship** *or* **time (as)** faire son apprentissage (de); **to ~ one's time** (*Mil*) faire son temps de service; (*Prison*) faire son temps de prison; (*in prison*) **to ~ time** faire de la prison; **to ~ a prison sentence** purger une peine (de prison); **he has ~d over 25 years altogether** en tout il a fait plus de 25 ans de prison.
(h) (*Jur*) **to ~ notice on sb (to the effect) that ...** notifier *or* signifier à qn que ...; **to ~ a summons on sb, to ~ sb with a summons** remettre une assignation à qn; **to ~ a warrant on sb, to ~ sb with a warrant** délivrer à qn un mandat; **to ~ a writ on sb, to ~ sb with a writ** assigner qn.
(i) (*Tennis etc*) servir.
(j) *[bull, stallion etc]* servir.
2 *vi* **(a)** *[servant, waiter]* servir. **to ~ at table** servir à table; **is there anyone serving at this table?** est-ce que quelqu'un fait le service de cette table? *or* s'occupe du service à cette table?
(b) (*work, do duty*) servir. **to ~ on a committee/jury** être membre d'un comité/d'un jury; **he has ~d for 2 years as chairman of this society** cela fait 2 ans qu'il exerce la fonction de président de cette société.
(c) (*Mil*) servir. **to ~ in the army** servir dans l'armée; **he ~d in Germany** il a servi en Allemagne; **he ~d as a Sapper in the Engineers** il a servi comme simple soldat dans le génie; **to ~ under sb** servir sous (les ordres de) qn; **he ~d with my brother** mon frère et lui ont été soldats ensemble.
(d) (*be useful*) servir (*for, as* de), être utile. **that table is not exactly what I want but it will ~** cette table n'est pas exactement ce que je veux mais elle fera l'affaire; **it ~s to show/explain** *etc* cela sert à montrer/expliquer *etc*.
(e) (*Rel*) servir; (*Tennis*) servir, être au service.
3 *n* (*Tennis etc*) service *m*. **he has a strong ~** il a un service puissant; **it's your ~** c'est à vous de servir.
serve out *vt sep* **(a)** *meal, soup* servir; *rations, provisions* distribuer.
(b) to serve sb out (for sth) prendre sa revanche sur qn (pour qch), payer qn de retour (pour qch).
serve up *vt sep* servir, mettre sur la table.
server ['sɜːvəʳ] *n* **(a)** (*Rel*) servant *m*; (*Tennis etc*) servant(e) *m(f)*, serveur *m*, -euse *f*. **(b)** (*tray*) plateau *m*; (*utensil*) couvert *m* à servir; *V* **salad**.
servery ['sɜːvərɪ] *n* (*Brit*) office *f*.
service ['sɜːvɪs] **1** *n* **(a)** (*U: act of serving: gen, domestic, Mil etc*) service *m*. (*Mil*) **to see ~ (as)** avoir du service *or* servir (comme); **this coat has seen** *or* **given good ~** ce manteau a fait de l'usage; **10 years' ~** 10 ans de service; **on Her Majesty's ~** au service de Sa Majesté; *[domestic servant]* **to be in ~** être domestique *or* en service; **to be in sb's ~** être au service de qn; **at your ~** à votre service *or* disposition; **our company is always at your ~** notre compagnie est toujours à votre service; **to be of ~ to sb** être utile à qn, rendre service à qn; **can I be of ~?** est-ce que je peux vous aider?; (*in shop*) qu'y a-t-il pour votre service?; **to bring/come into ~** mettre/entrer en service; **this machine is out of ~** cette machine est hors service; (*in shop, hotel etc*) **the ~ is very poor** le service est très mauvais; (*on bill*) **15% ~ included** service 15% compris; *V* **active, military**.
(b) (*department; system*) service *m*. **medical/public/social** *etc* **~s** services médicaux/publics/sociaux *etc*; **customs ~** (service de la) douane *f*; (*Mil*) **when I was in the S~s** quand j'étais dans l'armée (*or* la marine *or* l'aviation *etc*); (*Mil*) **the S~s were represented** il y avait des représentants (des différentes branches) des forces armées; **the train ~ to London is excellent** le service de chemin de fer pour Londres est *or* les trains pour Londres sont excellent(s); **do you know what the train ~ is (to London)?** connaissez-vous l'horaire des trains (pour Londres)?; **the number 4 bus ~** la ligne *or* le service du (numéro) 4; *V* **civil, health, postal** *etc*.
(c) (*help etc rendered*) service *m*. **to do sb a ~** rendre service à qn; **for ~s rendered (to)** pour services rendus (à); **they dispensed with his ~s** ils se sont passés *or* privés de ses services; **do you need the ~s of a lawyer?** avez-vous besoin (des services) d'un avocat?
(d) (*Rel*) (*gen*) service *m*; (*Catholic*) service, office *m*; (*Protestant*) service, culte *m*; *V* **evening, funeral** *etc*.
(e) (*Aut, Comm etc: maintenance work*) révision *f*. (*Aut*) **30,000-km ~** révision des 30.000 km; **to put one's car in for ~** donner sa voiture à réviser; *V* **after** *etc*.
(f) (*set of crockery*) service *m*. **coffee ~** service à café; *V* **dinner, tea** *etc*.
(g) (*Tennis etc*) service *m*.
2 *cpd*: *[motorway]* **service area** aire *f* de services; **the service bus** l'autobus régulier; **service charge** service *m*; **service department** (*office etc*) service *m* des réparations *or* d'entretien; (*repair shop*) atelier *m* de réparations; (*Brit Mil*) **service dress** tenue *f* numéro un; (*US*) **service elevator** = **service lift**; (*Mil*) **service families** familles *fpl* de militaires; (*Brit*) **service flat** appartement *m* avec service (*assuré par le personnel de l'immeuble*); **service hatch** passe-plat *m*; (*Brit*) **service lift** (*for goods*) monte-charge *m inv*; (*for personnel*) ascenseur *m* de service; (*Mil*) **serviceman** militaire *m*; **service module** module *m* de service; (*Mil*) **service rifle** fusil *m* de guerre; (*Brit*) **service road** (*access road*) voie *f or* chemin *m* d'accès; (*for works traffic*) voie de service; (*Aut*) **service station** station-service *f*.
3 *vt car, washing machine etc* réviser; (*Fin*) *debt* servir les intérêts de. **I put my car in to be ~d** j'ai donné ma voiture à réviser.
serviceable ['sɜːvɪsəbl] *adj* (*useful, practical*) *building* commode; *style, clothes* pratique, commode; (*durable*) *building* durable, solide; *clothes* solide, qui fait de l'usage; (*usable, working*) utilisable.
servicing ['sɜːvɪsɪŋ] *n [car, washing machine etc]* révision *f*.
serviette [ˌsɜːvɪ'et] *n* (*esp Brit*) serviette *f* (de table). **~ ring** rond *m* de serviette.
servile ['sɜːvaɪl] *adj person, behaviour* servile, obséquieux, rampant; *flattery etc* servile.
servility [sɜː'vɪlɪtɪ] *n* servilité *f*.
servitude ['sɜːvɪtjuːd] *n* servitude *f*, asservissement *m*; (*slavery*) esclavage *m*; *V* **penal**.
servo ['sɜːvəʊ] *n abbr of* **servo-mechanism, servo-motor**; *V* **servo-**.
servo- ['sɜːvəʊ] *pref* servo... . **~assisted** servocommandé, (servo-)assisté; **~control** servocommande *f*; **~mechanism** servomécanisme *m*; **~motor** servomoteur *m*.
sesame ['sesəmɪ] *n* sésame *m*; *V* **open**.
sesquipedalian [ˌseskwɪpɪ'deɪlɪən] *adj* polysyllabique.
session ['seʃən] *n* **(a)** (*U: Admin, Jur, Parl etc*) séance *f*, session *f*. **to be in ~** siéger; **this court is now in ~** le tribunal est en session *or* en séance, l'audience est ouverte; **to go into secret ~** siéger en séance secrète *or* à huis clos; *V* **quarter** *etc*.
(b) (*gen, Admin, Jur, Parl etc: sitting*) séance *f*. **2 afternoon ~s a week** 2 séances par semaine l'après-midi; **I had a ~ with him yesterday** nous avons travaillé ensemble *or* nous avons eu une (longue) discussion *etc* hier; **he's just had a ~ with the dentist** il vient d'avoir une séance chez le dentiste; **we're in for a long ~** nous n'aurons pas fini de sitôt, cela menace de durer; *V* **jam**[2], **recording**.
(c) (*Scol, Univ*) (*year*) année *f* (universitaire *or* scolaire); (*US: term*) trimestre *m* (universitaire).
set [set] (*vb: pret, ptp* **set**) **1** *n* **(a)** *[objects]* jeu *m*, série *f*, assortiment *m*; (*kit*) trousse *f*; *[sails, oars, keys, golf clubs, knives, spanners, needles]* jeu; *[ties, pens]* jeu, assortiment; *[chairs, coffee tables, rugs, saucepans, weights, numbers, stamps etc]* série; *[books, ornaments, toy cars]* collection *f*; *[bracelets, magazines]* collection, série; *[dishes, plates, mugs etc]* service *m*; *[tyres]* train *m*; *[jewels]* parure *f*; *[theories etc]* corps *m*, ensemble *m*. **a ~ of rooms** un appartement; **a ~ of kitchen utensils** une batterie de cuisine; **I want a new ~ of buttons for my coat** je veux de nouveaux boutons pour mon manteau; **I bought her a ~ of hairclasps** je lui ai acheté des barrettes assorties; **~ of teeth** dentition *f*, denture *f*; **~ of false teeth** dentier *m*; *[teeth]* **top/bottom ~** appareil *m* pour la mâchoire supérieure/inférieure; **a ~ of dining-room furniture** un mobilier *or* un ensemble de salle à manger; **he had a whole ~ of telephones on his desk** il avait toute une collection *or* batterie (*hum*) de téléphones sur son bureau; **in ~s of 3** par séries *or* jeux de 3; **in ~s** en jeux complets, en séries complètes; **it makes a ~ with those over there** cela forme un jeu *or* un ensemble avec les autres là-bas; **I need 2 more to make up the ~** il m'en manque 2 pour avoir tout le jeu *or* toute la série; **sewing ~** trousse *f* de couture; **painting ~** boîte *f* de peinture; **chess/draughts ~** jeu d'échecs/de dames (*objet*); *V* **tea** *etc*.
(b) (*Tennis*) set *m*; (*Math, Philos*) ensemble *m*.
(c) (*Elec*) appareil *m*; (*Rad, TV*) poste *m*; *V* **head, transistor, wireless** *etc*.

(d) (*group of people*) groupe *m*, bande *f* (*also pej*); (*larger*) cercle *m*, monde *m*, milieu *m*. **the golfing ~** le monde du golf; **the literary ~** le monde des lettres, les milieux littéraires; **I'm not in their ~, we're not in the same ~** nous ne sommes pas du même monde *or* milieu, je n'appartiens pas à leur cercle; **a ~ of thieves/gangsters** *etc* une bande de voleurs/gangsters *etc*; **they're just a ~ of fools!** ce n'est qu'une bande d'imbéciles!; *V* **jet**[1] *etc*.

(e) (*Cine*) plateau *m*; (*Theat etc*) (*stage*) scène *f*; (*scenery*) décor *m*. **on (the) ~** sur le plateau, en scène.

(f) (*Hairdressing*) mise *f* en plis. **to have a ~** se faire faire une mise en plis; **I like your ~** j'aime ta coiffure; *V* **shampoo**.

(g) (*U: position, posture, direction etc*) *[body]* position *f*, attitude *f*; *[head]* port *m*; *[shoulders]* position; *[tide, wind]* direction *f*; *[opinion, sb's mind etc]* tendance *f*. (*liter*) **at ~ of sun** au coucher du soleil.

(h) (*Hunting*) arrêt *m*; *V* **dead**.

(i) (*Horticulture*) plante *f* à repiquer. **onion ~s** oignons *mpl* à repiquer.

2 *adj* **(a)** (*unchanging*) *rule, price, time* fixe; *smile etc* figé; *purpose, dogma* fixe, (bien) déterminé; *opinion, idea* (bien) arrêté; *lunch* à prix fixe; (*prearranged*) *time, date* fixe, décidé d'avance; (*Scol etc*) *book, subject* au programme; *speech, talk* étudié, préparé d'avance; *prayer* liturgique. **~ in one's ways** conservateur (*f* -trice), routinier, qui tient à ses habitudes; **~ in one's opinions** immuable dans ses convictions; (*Met*) **~ fair** au beau fixe; **~ phrase** expression consacrée *or* toute faite; **~ piece** (*fireworks*) pièce *f* (de feu) d'artifice; (*Art, Literat, Mus*) morceau traditionnel; (*in music competition etc*) morceau de concours; **the fruit is ~** les fruits ont (bien) noué.

(b) (*determined*) résolu, déterminé; (*ready*) prêt. **to be ~ (up)on sth** vouloir qch à tout prix, avoir jeté son dévolu sur qch; **since you are so ~ on it** puisque vous y tenez tant; **to be ~ on doing** être résolu à faire, vouloir à tout prix faire; **to be (dead) ~ against** s'opposer (absolument *or* formellement) à; **they're all ~!** ils sont fin prêts!; **to be all ~ to do** être prêt pour faire; (*Sport*) **on your marks, get ~, go!** à vos marques, prêts, partez!; (*fig*) **the scene is ~ for...** tout est prêt pour... .

3 *cpd*: **setback** (*hitch*) contretemps *m*, (*more serious*) revers *m*, échec *m*; (*in health*) rechute *f*; **set-in sleeve** manche rapportée; (*Tennis*) **set point** balle *f* de set; **set square** équerre *f* (à dessin); **set-to*** (*fight*) bagarre *f*; (*quarrel*) prise *f* de bec*; **to have a set-to with sb*** se bagarrer avec qn*, avoir une prise de bec avec qn*; **I don't like that setup at all*** je n'aime pas l'allure de tout ça*; **it's an odd setup*** c'est une drôle de situation; **what's the setup?*** comment est-ce que c'est organisé? *or* que ça marche?; **when did he join the setup?*** quand est-ce qu'il est entré là-dedans? *or* dans l'équipe? *or* dans l'affaire?

4 *vt* **(a)** (*place, put*) *object* mettre, poser, placer; *signature etc* apposer; *sentry, guard* poster. **~ it on the table/beside the window/over there** mettez-le *or* posez-le *or* placez-le sur la table/près de la fenêtre/là-bas; **the house is ~ on a hill** la maison est située sur une colline; **his stories, ~ in the Paris of 1890** ses histoires, situées *or* qui se passent *or* qui se déroulent dans le Paris de 1890; **he ~ the scheme before the committee** il a présenté le projet au comité; **I ~ him above Wordsworth** je le place *or* mets au-dessus de Wordsworth, je le considère supérieur à Wordsworth; **what value do you ~ on this?** (*lit*) à quelle valeur *or* à quel prix estimez-vous cela?; (*fig*) quelle valeur accordez-vous à cela?; **we must ~ the advantages against the disadvantages** il faut peser le pour et le contre, il faut mettre en balance les avantages et les inconvénients; **to ~ fire to sth** mettre le feu à qch; *for other phrases V* **foot, heart, store** *etc*.

(b) (*arrange, adjust*) *clock* mettre à l'heure, régler; *mechanism* régler; (*on display*) *specimen, butterfly etc* monter; *eggs, hen* faire couver; *plant* repiquer; (*Typ*) *type, page* composer; (*Med*) *arm, leg* (*in plaster*) plâtrer; (*with splint*) mettre une attelle à; *fracture* réduire. **have you ~ the alarm clock?** est-ce que tu as mis le réveil?; **I've ~ the alarm for 6** *or* **to wake me at 6** j'ai mis le réveil à *or* pour 6 heures; **he ~s his watch by the radio** il règle sa montre sur la radio; **~ your watch to the right time** mettez votre montre à l'heure; **he ~ the needle to zero** il a ramené l'aiguille à zéro; (*Aviat*) **he ~ the controls to automatic** il a mis les commandes sur automatique; **to ~ sb's hair** faire une mise en plis à qn; **to have one's hair ~** se faire faire une mise en plis; *for other phrases V* **sail, table** *etc*.

(c) (*fix, establish*) *date, deadline, limit* fixer. **let's ~ a time for the meeting** fixons l'heure de la réunion; **I've ~ myself a time limit** je me suis fixé une limite (de temps) *or* un délai; **he ~ a new record for the 100 metres** il a établi un nouveau record pour le 100 mètres; **they ~ the pass mark at 10** on a fixé la moyenne à 10; *for other phrases V* **course, fashion, pace** *etc*.

(d) (*give, assign*) *task* donner; *exam, test* composer *or* choisir les questions de; *texts, books* mettre au programme; *subject* donner. **I ~ them a difficult translation** je leur ai donné une traduction difficile (à faire); **to ~ sb a problem** poser un problème à qn; **Molière is not ~ this year** Molière n'est pas au programme cette année; **I ~ him the job of clearing up** je l'ai chargé de ranger *or* du rangement; *for other phrases V* **example** *etc*.

(e) (*cause to be, do, begin etc*) **to ~ a dog on sb** lâcher *or* lancer un chien contre qn (*V also* **set upon**); **they ~ the police on to him** ils l'ont signalé à la police; **she ~ my brother against me** elle a monté mon frère contre moi; **someone has been ~ over him at the office** on a placé quelqu'un au-dessus de lui au bureau; **to ~ sth going** mettre qch en marche; **the news ~ me thinking** la nouvelle m'a fait réfléchir *or* m'a donné à réfléchir; **that ~ him wondering whether ...** cela l'a porté *or* poussé à se demander si ...; **this ~ everyone laughing** cela a fait rire tout le monde, à cela tout le monde s'est mis à rire; **to ~ sb to do sth** faire faire qch à qn, donner à qn la tâche de faire qch; **I ~ him to work at once** je l'ai mis au travail aussitôt; **to ~ o.s. to do** entreprendre de faire.

(f) *gem* sertir (*in* dans), enchâsser (*in* dans), monter (*in* sur). **to ~ sth with jewels** orner *or* incruster qch de pierres précieuses.

(g) *jelly, jam* faire prendre; *concrete* faire prendre, faire durcir; *dye, colour* fixer.

5 *vi* **(a)** *[sun, moon etc]* se coucher.

(b) *[broken bone, limb]* se ressouder; *[jelly, jam]* prendre; *[glue]* durcir; *[concrete]* prendre, durcir; *[fruit]* nouer; (*fig*) *[character]* se former, s'affermir. **quick-~ting cement** ciment prompt *or* à prise rapide; **his face ~ in a hostile expression** son visage s'est figé dans une expression hostile.

(c) (*begin*) se mettre, commencer (*to doing* à faire). **to ~ to work** se mettre au travail, s'y mettre*.

set about 1 *vt fus* **(a)** (*begin*) *task, essay* entreprendre, se mettre à. **to set about doing** se mettre à faire; **I don't know how to set about it** je ne sais pas comment m'y prendre.

(b) (*attack*) attaquer. **they set about each other** (*blows*) ils en sont venus aux coups *or* aux mains; (*words*) ils se sont mis à se disputer.

2 *vt sep rumour etc* faire courir. **he set it about that ...** il a fait courir le bruit que ... .

set apart *vt sep object etc* mettre de côté *or* à part. (*fig*) **that sets him apart from the others** cela le distingue des autres.

set aside *vt sep* **(a)** (*keep, save*) mettre de côté, garder en réserve.

(b) she set her book aside when I came in elle a posé son livre quand je suis entré.

(c) (*reject, annul*) *request, objection, proposal, petition* rejeter; *decree, will* annuler; (*Jur*) *judgment* casser.

set back 1 *vt sep* **(a)** (*replace*) remettre. **set it back on the shelf** remets-le sur l'étagère.

(b) the house was set back from the road la maison était (construite) en retrait de la route; **the dog set its ears back** le chien a couché les oreilles.

(c) (*retard*) *development, progress* retarder; *clock* retarder (*by one hour* d'une heure). **the disaster set back the project by 10 years** le désastre a retardé de 10 ans la réalisation du projet; *V* **clock**.

(d) (*: *cost*) coûter. **that car must have set him back a good deal** *or* **a packet!** cette voiture a dû lui coûter les yeux de la tête; **how much did all that set you back?** combien tu as dû cracher! pour tout ça?

2 setback *n V* **set 3**.

set by *vt sep* = **set aside a.**

set down *vt sep* **(a)** (*put down*) *object* poser, déposer; *[coach, plane, taxi etc]* *passenger* laisser, déposer. (*Aut*) **I'll set you down at the corner** je vais vous laisser *or* déposer au coin.

(b) (*Aviat*) *plane* poser.

(c) (*record*) noter, inscrire. **to set sth down in writing** *or* **on paper** coucher *or* mettre qch par écrit; (*Comm*) **set it down on** *or* **to my account** mettez-le *or* portez-le sur mon compte.

(d) (*attribute*) attribuer (*sth to sth* qch à qch). **I set it down to his stupidity** je l'attribue à sa stupidité; **the accident must be set down to negligence** l'accident doit être imputé à la négligence; **we set it all down to the fact that he was tired** nous avons expliqué tout cela par sa fatigue, nous avons attribué tout cela à sa fatigue.

(e) (*assess, estimate*) **I had already set him down as a liar** je le tenais déjà pour menteur, j'avais déjà constaté qu'il était menteur.

set forth 1 *vi* = **set off 1.**

2 *vt sep idea, plan, opinion* faire connaître, exposer; *conditions, rules* inclure.

set in 1 *vi* (*begin*) *[complications, difficulties]* survenir, surgir; *[disease]* se déclarer. **a reaction set in after the war** une réaction s'est amorcée après la guerre; **the rain will soon set in** il va bientôt commencer à pleuvoir; **the rain has set in for the night** il va pleuvoir toute la nuit; **the rain has really set in now!** la pluie a l'air bien installée!

2 *vt sep* (*Sewing*) *sleeve* rapporter.

3 set-in *adj V* **set 3.**

set off 1 *vi* (*leave*) se mettre en route, partir, s'en aller. **to set off on a journey/an expedition** partir en voyage/en expédition; (*fig*) **he set off on a long explanation** il s'est lancé dans une longue explication.

2 *vt sep* **(a)** *bomb* faire exploser; *firework* faire partir; *mechanism* déclencher. **to set sb off laughing/crying** *etc* faire rire/pleurer *etc* qn; **her remark set him off and she couldn't get a word in edgeways** après sa remarque il s'est lancé et elle n'a pas pu placer un mot.

(b) (*enhance*) *hair, eyes, picture, furnishings etc* mettre en valeur, faire valoir; *complexion, colour* rehausser, mettre en valeur.

(c) (*balance etc*) **to set off profits against losses** balancer les pertes et les profits, opposer les pertes aux profits; **we must set off the expenses against the profits** il faut déduire les dépenses des bénéfices; **the profit on hats will set off the loss on ties** le bénéfice sur les chapeaux compensera le déficit sur les cravates.

set on *vt fus* = **set upon.**

set out 1 *vi* **(a)** (*leave, depart*) se mettre en route (*for* pour), partir (*for* pour, *from* de, *in search of* à la recherche de).

(b) (*intend, propose*) **he set out to explain why it had happened** il a cherché à *or* s'est proposé d'expliquer pourquoi cela s'était produit; **I didn't set out to prove you were wrong** il n'était pas dans mon intention de prouver *or* mon but n'était pas de prouver que vous aviez tort; **I set out to convince him he should**

change his mind j'ai entrepris de le persuader de changer d'avis; **the book sets out to show that ...** ce livre a pour objet *or* but de montrer que ... .

2 *vt sep books, goods* exposer; *chessmen etc on board* disposer; (*fig*) *reasons, ideas* présenter, exposer. **the conditions are set out in paragraph 3** les modalités sont indiquées *or* prévues au paragraphe 3; **it's very clearly set out here** c'est expliqué *or* exposé ici de façon très claire; **the information is well set out on the page** l'information est bien présentée sur la page.

set to 1 *vi* (*start*) commencer, se mettre (*to do* à faire); (*start work*) s'y mettre*. **they set to with their fists** ils en sont venus aux coups (de poing).

2 set-to* *n V* **set 3.**

set up 1 *vi* (*Comm etc*) **to set up in business as a grocer** s'établir épicier; **he set up in business in London** il a monté une affaire *or* une entreprise à Londres.

2 *vt sep* **(a)** (*place in position*) *chairs, table, stall* placer, installer; *tent* dresser; *monument, statue* ériger, dresser. (*Typ*) **to set up type** assembler les caractères, composer; **to set up camp** établir un camp.

(b) (*fig: start, establish*) *school, institution* fonder; *business, company, fund* créer, lancer; *tribunal, government, committee* constituer; *fashion* lancer; *irritation, quarrel* causer, provoquer, susciter; *record* établir; *theory* avancer. **to set up an inquiry** ouvrir une enquête; **to set up house** s'installer (dans ses meubles); **to set up shop** (*Comm*) ouvrir un commerce *or* un magasin, s'établir, s'installer; (*fig*) s'établir, s'installer; **he set up shop as a grocer** il s'est établi épicier, il a ouvert une épicerie; (*fig*) **he set up shop as a doctor*** il s'est établi docteur; **to set up a yell** se mettre à hurler; **to set sb up in business** établir *or* lancer qn dans les affaires; **he's all set up now** il est bien établi *or* lancé maintenant; **I've set it all up for you** je vous ai tout installé *or* préparé.

(c) (*pose*) **I've never set myself up as a scholar** je n'ai jamais prétendu être savant.

(d) (*after illness*) remonter, rétablir, remettre sur pied.

(e) (*equip*) munir, approvisionner (*with* de), monter (*with* en).

3 setup* *n V* **set 3.**

4 setting-up *n V* **setting 2.**

set upon *vt fus* (*attack*) (*physically*) attaquer, se jeter sur; (*verbally*) attaquer.

sett [set] *n* (*in roadway etc*) pavé *m*.

settee [seˈtiː] *n* canapé *m*. **~ bed** canapé-lit *m*.

setter [ˈsetə^r] *n* **(a)** (*dog*) setter *m*, chien *m* d'arrêt. **(b)** (*person*) *[gems]* sertisseur *m*; *V* **type etc.**

setting [ˈsetɪŋ] **1** *n* **(a)** *[jewel]* monture *f*; (*fig*) cadre *m*.

(b) (*Mus*) *[poem etc]* mise *f* en musique. **~ for piano** arrangement *m* pour piano.

(c) (*U*) *[sun etc]* coucher *m*; (*act of placing*) mise *f*; *[machine etc]* réglage *m*; (*Typ*) composition *f*; (*Med*) *[fracture]* réduction *f*; *[limb, bone]* pose *f* d'un plâtre *or* d'une attelle (*of* à); (*hardening*) *[jam]* épaississement *m*; *[cement]* solidification *f*, durcissement *m*.

2 *cpd*: **setting lotion** lotion *f or* fixateur *m* pour mise en plis; **setting-up** *[institution, company etc]* création *f*, lancement *m*; (*Typ*) composition *f*.

settle[1] [ˈsetl] *n* banc *m* à haut dossier.

settle[2] [ˈsetl] **1** *vt* **(a)** (*place carefully*) placer *or* poser délicatement; (*stop wobbling*) stabiliser; (*adjust*) ajuster. **he ~d himself into the chair** il s'est installé confortablement *or* il s'est enfoncé dans le fauteuil; **to ~ an invalid for the night** installer un malade pour la nuit; **he ~d his daughter in a flat** il a installé sa fille dans un appartement; **to get ~d** s'installer.

(b) (*arrange etc*) *question, matter* régler, décider, trancher; *argument* régler; *conditions, terms, details* régler, décider de; *date* fixer; *difficulty* résoudre, trancher; *problem* résoudre; *affairs* régler, mettre en ordre; *debt* rembourser, s'acquitter de; *bill, account* régler. **that ~s it** (*no more problem*) comme ça le problème est réglé; (*that's made my mind up*) ça me décide; **that's ~d then?** alors c'est convenu? *or* entendu?; **nothing is ~d** rien n'est décidé; **~ it among yourselves** arrangez ça entre vous; (*Jur*) **to ~ a case out of court** régler une affaire à l'amiable; **several points remain to be ~d** il reste encore plusieurs points à régler; (*Ftbl etc*) **the result was ~d in the first half** la première mi-temps a décidé du résultat; **I'll ~ him, I'll ~ his hash!** je vais lui régler son compte*; *V* **score.**

(c) (*calm; stabilize*) *nerves* calmer; *doubts* apaiser, dissiper. **he sprinkled water on the floor to ~ the dust** il a aspergé le sol d'eau pour faire retomber la poussière; **to ~ one's stomach** *or* **digestion** calmer *or* soulager les douleurs d'estomac; **the weather is ~d** le temps est au beau fixe; **a man of ~d habits** un homme aux habitudes régulières.

(d) (*Jur*) **to ~ sth on sb** constituer qch à qn.

(e) (*colonize*) *land* coloniser.

2 *vi* **(a)** *[bird, insect]* se poser (*on* sur); *[dust etc]* retomber; *[sediment, coffee grounds etc]* se déposer; *[building]* se tasser; *[emotions]* s'apaiser; *[conditions, situation]* redevenir normal, s'arranger, se tasser*. *[dust, snow]* **to ~ on sth** couvrir qch; (*fig*) **when the dust has ~d we shall be able ...** quand les choses se seront arrangées *or* tassées* nous pourrons ...; **let the grounds ~ before you pour the coffee** laissez le marc se déposer avant de verser le café; **the wind ~d in the east** le vent a définitivement tourné à l'est; **the weather has ~d** le temps s'est mis au beau fixe; **to ~ into an armchair** s'installer confortablement *or* s'enfoncer dans un fauteuil; **to ~ into one's new job** s'habituer *or* se faire à son nouvel emploi; **to ~ into a routine** adopter une routine; **to ~ into a habit** prendre une habitude *or* un pli*; **to ~ to sth** se mettre (sérieusement) à qch, s'appliquer à qch; **I can't ~ to anything** je suis incapable de me concentrer; **let your meal ~ before you go swimming** attends d'avoir digéré avant de te baigner; (*fig*) **things are settling into shape** cela commence à prendre tournure.

(b) (*go to live*) s'installer, se fixer; (*as colonist*) s'établir. **he ~d in London/in France** il s'est installé *or* fixé à Londres/en France; **the Dutch ~d in South Africa** les Hollandais se sont établis en Afrique du Sud.

(c) to ~ with sb for the cost of the meal régler qn pour le prix du repas, régler le prix du repas à qn; **I'll ~ for all of us** je vais régler la note (pour tout le monde); (*Jur*) **to ~ out of court** arriver à un règlement à l'amiable; **he ~d for £200** il s'est contenté de 200 livres, il a accepté 200 livres; **they ~d on £200** ils se sont mis d'accord sur 200 livres; **will you ~ for a draw?** accepteriez-vous un match nul?; **to ~ on sth** fixer son choix sur qch, opter *or* se décider pour qch.

settle down 1 *vi [person]* (*in armchair etc*) s'installer (*in* dans); (*take up one's residence etc*) s'installer, se fixer; (*become calmer*) se calmer; (*after wild youth etc*) se ranger, s'assagir; *[excitement, emotions]* s'apaiser; *[situation, conditions]* s'arranger, redevenir normal, se tasser*. **he settled down to read the document** il s'est installé pour lire tranquillement le document; **to settle down to work** se mettre (sérieusement) au travail; **he has settled down in his new job** il s'est habitué *or* adapté *or* fait à son nouvel emploi; **to settle down at school** s'habituer *or* s'adapter à l'école; **it's time he got married and settled down** il est temps qu'il se marie (*subj*) et qu'il mène (*subj*) une vie stable; **he can't settle down anywhere** il n'arrive à se fixer nulle part; **he took some time to settle down in Australia/to civilian life** il a mis du temps à s'habituer *or* à s'adapter à la vie en Australie/à la vie civile; **when things have settled down again** quand les choses se seront calmées *or* seront redevenues normales *or* se seront tassées*.

2 *vt sep* installer. **to settle o.s. down in an armchair** s'installer confortablement dans un fauteuil; **he settled the child down on the settee** il a installé l'enfant sur le canapé.

settle in *vi* s'installer, s'adapter. **the house is finished and they're quite settled in** la maison est terminée et ils sont tout à fait installés; **we took some time to settle in** nous avons mis du temps à nous adapter.

settle up 1 *vi* régler (la note). **to settle up with sb** (*financially*) régler qn; (*fig*) régler son compte à qn*; **let's settle up** faisons nos comptes.

2 *vt sep bill* régler.

settlement [ˈsetlmənt] *n* **(a)** (*U*) *[question, argument, bill, debt]* règlement *m*; *[conditions, terms, details, date]* décision *f* (*of* concernant); *[problem]* solution *f*. **in ~ of an account** pour *or* en règlement d'un compte.

(b) (*agreement*) accord *m*. **to reach a ~** arriver à *or* conclure un accord.

(c) (*Jur*) (*act of settling*) constitution *f*; (*income*) rente *f*; (*dowry*) dot *f*; *V* **marriage.**

(d) (*colonization*) colonisation *f*; (*colony*) colonie *f*; (*village*) village *m*, hameau *m*; (*homestead*) ferme *f or* habitation *f* (isolée); *V* **penal.**

(e) (*for social work: also* **~ house**) centre *m* d'œuvres sociales.

(f) (*Constr: of building etc*) tassement *m*.

settler [ˈsetlə^r] *n* colon *m*, colonisateur *m*, -trice *f*.

seven [ˈsevn] **1** *adj* sept *inv*. (*liter*) **the ~ seas** toutes les mers *or* tous les océans (du globe); **the ~ deadly sins** les sept péchés capitaux.

2 *n* sept *m inv*; *for other phrases V* **six.**

3 *cpd*: **sevenfold** (*adj*) septuple; (*adv*) au septuple; **seven-league boots** bottes *fpl* de sept lieues.

seventeen [ˈsevnˈtiːn] **1** *adj* dix-sept *inv*. **2** *n* dix-sept *m inv*.

seventeenth [ˈsevnˈtiːnθ] **1** *adj* dix-septième. **2** *n* dix-septième *mf*; (*fraction*) dix-septième *m*; *for phrases V* **sixth.**

seventh [ˈsevnθ] **1** *adj* septième. **S~ Day Adventist** adventiste *mf* du septième jour; *V* **heaven. 2** *n* septième *mf*; (*fraction*) septième *m*; *for other phrases V* **sixth.**

seventieth [ˈsevntɪɪθ] **1** *adj* soixante-dixième. **2** *n* soixante-dixième *mf*; (*fraction*) soixante-dixième *m*.

seventy [ˈsevntɪ] **1** *adj* soixante-dix *inv*. **2** *n* soixante-dix *m inv*. **he's in his seventies** il est septuagénaire, il a plus de soixante-dix ans; *for other phrases V* **sixty.**

sever [ˈsevə^r] **1** *vt rope etc* couper, trancher; (*fig*) *relations* rompre, cesser; *communications* interrompre. **to ~ one's connections with sb** cesser toutes relations avec qn; (*Comm*) se dissocier de qn. **2** *vi [rope etc]* se rompre, casser, céder.

several [ˈsevrəl] **1** *adj* **(a)** (*in number*) plusieurs. **~ times** plusieurs fois.

(b) (*separate*) différent, divers, distinct. **they went their ~ ways** (*lit*) ils sont partis chacun de son côté; (*fig*) la vie les a séparés.

2 *pron* plusieurs *mfpl*. **~ of them** plusieurs d'entre eux (*or* elles); **~ of us saw the accident** plusieurs d'entre nous ont vu l'accident, nous sommes plusieurs à avoir vu l'accident; **~ of us passed the exam** nous sommes plusieurs à avoir été reçus à l'examen.

severally [ˈsevrəlɪ] *adv* séparément, individuellement, respectivement.

severance [ˈsevərəns] **1** *n* séparation *f* (*from* de); *[relations]* rupture *f*; *[communications]* interruption *f*. **2** *cpd*: (*Ind*) **severance pay** indemnité *f* de licenciement.

severe [sɪˈvɪə^r] *adj person* sévère (*with, on, towards* pour, envers), strict, dur (*with, on, towards* avec, envers); *look, measure, criticism, blow, reprimand* sévère; *style, clothes* sévère, austère; *punishment* dur, sévère; *examination, test* dur, difficile; *competition* serré, acharné; *climate, winter* rigoureux, rude, dur; *cold* intense; *pain* vif (*before n*), violent; *wound,* *defeat* grave; *illness* grave, sérieux. ~ **loss** (*of life, troops*) pertes *fpl* sévères *or* lourdes; (*bereavement*) perte cruelle; (*financial*) lourde perte; **a ~ attack of toothache** une rage de dents; (*Med*) **a ~ cold** un gros rhume.

severely [sɪ'vɪəlɪ] *adv punish* durement, sévèrement; *look, speak, criticize, reprimand* sévèrement; *injure, wound* grièvement; *dress, design* sévèrement, avec austérité. ~ **ill** gravement malade; ~ **tried** durement éprouvé; **to leave ~ alone** *object* ne jamais toucher à; *politics, deal* ne pas du tout se mêler de; *person* ignorer complètement.

severity [sɪ'verɪtɪ] *n* (*V* **severe**) sévérité *f*; gravité *f*; rigueur *f*; violence *f*; dureté *f*; austérité *f*; difficulté *f*; intensité *f*.

Seville [sə'vɪl] *n* Séville. ~ **orange** orange amère, bigarade *f*.

sew [səʊ] *pret* **sewed**, *ptp* **sewn, sewed 1** *vt* coudre. **to ~ a button on sth** (re)coudre un bouton à qch. **2** *vi* coudre, faire de la couture.

sew on *vt sep button etc* (re)coudre.

sew up *vt sep tear* recoudre; *seam* faire; *sack* fermer par une couture; *wound* (re)coudre, suturer. **to sew sth up in a sack** coudre qch dans un sac; **we've got the contract all sewn up*** le contrat est dans le sac* *or* dans la poche*; **they've got the match all sewn up*** ils ont le match dans leur poche*; **it's all sewn up now*** l'affaire est dans le sac*.

sewage ['sju:ɪdʒ] **1** *n* (*U*) vidange(s) *f(pl)*. **2** *cpd*: **sewage disposal** évacuation *f* des vidanges; **sewage farm, sewage works** champ *m* d'épandage.

sewer ['sjʊəʳ] *n* égout *m*. ~ **gas** gaz *m* méphitique (d'égouts); *V* **main**.

sewerage ['sjʊərɪdʒ] *n* **(a)** (*disposal*) évacuation *f* des vidanges; (*system*) (système *m* d')égouts *mpl*. **(b)** = **sewage**.

sewing ['səʊɪŋ] **1** *n* (*U*) couture *f*.

2 *cpd*: **sewing basket** boîte *f* à couture; **sewing cotton** fil *m* de coton, fil à coudre; **sewing machine** machine *f* à coudre; **sewing silk** fil *m* de soie.

sewn [səʊn] *ptp of* **sew**.

sex [seks] **1** *n* **(a)** sexe *m*. **the gentle** *or* **weaker ~** le sexe faible; *V* **fair**[1] *etc*.

(b) (**U*) **to have ~ with sb** coucher avec qn*; **all he ever thinks about is ~** il ne pense qu'à coucher*.

2 *cpd discrimination, education, instinct* sexuel. **sex act** acte sexuel; **sex appeal** sex-appeal *m*; **he is sex-crazy*** c'est un obsédé (sexuel); (*Bio*) **sex-linked** sex-linked; **sex-mad* = sex-crazy***; **sex maniac** obsédé(e) sexuel(le) *m(f)*; **sex offender** délinquant(e) sexuel(le) *m(f)*; **sex pot**‡ aguicheuse* *f*, allumeuse* *f*; **sex-ridden** *person* qui ramène tout au sexe; *book* farci de sexe; **sex shop** sex-shop *m*, boutique *f* porno *inv*; **sex-starved*** (sexuellement) frustré*, refoulé*; **sex urge** pulsion sexuelle, instinct sexuel.

3 *vt chick etc* déterminer le sexe de.

sexagenarian [ˌseksədʒɪ'neərɪən] *adj, n* sexagénaire (*mf*).

sexless ['sekslɪs] *adj* asexué.

sexologist [sek'sɒlədʒɪst] *n* sexologue *mf*.

sexology [sek'sɒlədʒɪ] *n* sexologie *f*.

sextant ['sekstənt] *n* sextant *m*.

sextet [seks'tet] *n* sextuor *m*.

sexton ['sekstən] *n* sacristain *m*, bedeau *m*.

sextuplet [seks'tju:plɪt] *n* sextuplé(e) *m(f)*.

sexual ['seksjʊəl] *adj* sexuel. ~ **intercourse** rapports sexuels.

sexuality [ˌseksjʊ'ælɪtɪ] *n* sexualité *f*.

sexually ['seksjʊəlɪ] *adv* sexuellement. ~ **attractive** physiquement *or* sexuellement attirant.

sexy* ['seksɪ] *adj* sexy* *inv*.

sez‡ [sez] = **says** (*V* **say**). (*iro*) ~ **you!** que tu dis!*

shabbily ['ʃæbɪlɪ] *adv dress* pauvrement; *behave, treat* mesquinement, petitement.

shabbiness ['ʃæbɪnɪs] *n [dress]* aspect élimé *or* râpé; *[person]* mise *f* pauvre; *[behaviour, treatment]* mesquinerie *f*, petitesse *f*.

shabby ['ʃæbɪ] **1** *adj garment* râpé, usé, élimé; *furniture* pauvre, minable; *house, district* miteux; *person* pauvrement vêtu *or* mis; *behaviour, excuse* mesquin, méprisable. **a ~ trick** un vilain tour, une mesquinerie.

2 *cpd*: **shabby-genteel** pauvre mais digne; **shabby-looking** de pauvre apparence.

shack [ʃæk] *n* cabane *f*, hutte *f*.

shack up‡ *vi*: **to shack up with sb** se coller avec qn‡; **to shack up together** avoir un collage‡.

shackle ['ʃækl] **1** *n*: ~**s** chaînes *fpl*, fers *mpl*; (*fig*) chaînes, entraves *fpl*. **2** *vt* mettre aux fers, enchaîner; (*fig*) entraver.

shade [ʃeɪd] **1** *n* **(a)** (*U*) ombre *f*. **in the ~ of a tree** à l'ombre *or* sous l'ombrage d'un arbre; **40° in the ~** 40° à l'ombre; (*Art*) **light and ~** les clairs *mpl* et les ombres *or* les noirs *mpl*; (*fig*) **to put sth in(to) the ~** éclipser qch, rejeter qch dans l'ombre.

(b) *[colour]* nuance *f*, ton *m*; *[opinion]* nuance. **several ~s darker than that** plus sombre de plusieurs tons (que cela); **several ~s of red** plusieurs nuances *or* tons de rouge; **a new ~ of lipstick** un nouveau ton *or* une nouvelle couleur de rouge à lèvres; **a ~ of meaning** une nuance (de sens).

(c) (*fig*) **a ~ of vulgarity** un soupçon de vulgarité; **there's not a ~ of difference between them** il n'y a pas la moindre différence entre eux; **a ~ bigger** un tout petit peu *or* légèrement *or* un tantinet* plus grand.

(d) (*lamp~*) abat-jour *m inv*; (*eye~*) visière *f*; (*US: blind*) store *m*; (*US: sunglasses*) ~**s** lunettes *fpl* de soleil.

(e) (*liter: ghost*) ombre *f*, fantôme *m*. **~s of Professor X!*** voilà qui fait penser au Professeur X!, ça rappelle le Professeur X!

2 *vt* **(a)** *[trees, parasol]* donner de l'ombre à, ombrager, abriter du soleil; *[person] one's work etc* abriter du soleil *or* de la lumière. **~d place** endroit ombragé *or* à l'ombre; **he ~d his eyes with his hands** il s'abrita les yeux de la main; **to ~ a light** voiler une lampe.

(b) (*also* ~ **in**) *painting etc* ombrer, nuancer; *outline, drawing etc* hachurer.

3 *vi* (*also* ~ **off**) se dégrader (*into* jusqu'à), se fondre (*into* en). **the red ~s (off) into pink** le rouge se fond en rose.

shade off 1 *vi* = **shade 3**.

2 *vt sep colours etc* estomper.

shadiness ['ʃeɪdɪnɪs] *n* (*U*) (*shade*) ombre *f*; (*fig*) malhonnêteté *f*, caractère suspect *or* louche.

shading ['ʃeɪdɪŋ] *n* (*U*) (*in painting etc*) ombres *fpl*, noirs *mpl*; (*crosshatching*) hachure(s) *f(pl)*.

shadow ['ʃædəʊ] **1** *n* **(a)** ombre *f*. **in the ~ of the tree** à l'ombre de l'arbre; **in the ~ of the porch** dans l'ombre du porche; **he was standing in (the) ~** il se tenait dans l'ombre; (*darkness*) **the ~s** l'obscurité *f*, les ténèbres *fpl*; **I could see his ~ on the wall** je voyais son ombre (projetée) sur le mur; (*fig*) **he's afraid of his own ~** il a peur de son ombre; **to cast a ~ over sth** (*lit*) projeter une ombre sur qch; (*fig*) assombrir qch; **without a ~ of doubt** sans l'ombre d'un doute; **not a ~ of truth** pas le moindre atome de vérité; **he's only a ~ of his former self** il n'est plus que l'ombre de lui-même; **to have (dark) ~s under one's eyes** avoir les yeux cernés, avoir des cernes *mpl* sous les yeux; **five o'clock ~** (*on chin*) la barbe du soir; *V* **wear**.

(b) (*fig: detective etc*) personne *f* (*or* policier *m or* détective *m etc*) qui file quelqu'un. **to put a ~ on sb** faire filer qn, faire prendre qn en filature.

2 *cpd*: **shadow boxing** (*Sport*) boxe *f* à vide; (*fig*) attaque *f* de pure forme, attaque purement rituelle; (*Brit Parl*) **shadow cabinet** cabinet *m* fantôme (*de l'opposition*); (*Brit Parl*) **he is (the) shadow Foreign Secretary** il est le porte-parole de l'opposition pour les affaires étrangères.

3 *vt* (*follow*) filer, prendre en filature.

shadowy ['ʃædəʊɪ] *adj path* ombragé; *woods* sombre, ombreux; *outline, form, idea, plan* vague, indistinct.

shady ['ʃeɪdɪ] *adj* ombragé; (*fig: dishonest etc*) louche, véreux.

shaft [ʃɑ:ft] *n* **(a)** (*stem etc*) *[arrow, spear]* hampe *f*; *[tool, golf club]* manche *m*; *[feather]* tuyau *m*; *[column]* fût *m*; (*on cart, carriage, plough etc*) brancard *m*; (*Aut, Tech*) arbre *m*; *V* **cam** *etc*.

(b) (*liter: arrow*) flèche *f*. **Cupid's ~s** les flèches de Cupidon; (*fig*) **~ of light** rayon *m or* trait *m* de lumière; **~ of lightning** éclair *m*; **~ of sarcasm/wit** trait de raillerie/d'esprit.

(c) (*vertical enclosed space*) *[mine]* puits *m*; *[lift, elevator]* cage *f*; (*for ventilation*) puits, cheminée *f*.

shag[1] [ʃæg] *n* (*tobacco*) tabac très fort.

shag[2] [ʃæg] *n* (*Orn*) cormoran huppé.

shaggy ['ʃægɪ] *adj hair, beard* hirsute; *mane* broussailleux; *eyebrows* hérissé; *animal* à longs poils rudes. (*fig*) **~ dog story** anecdote embrouillée (*qui se termine en queue de poisson*).

shagreen [ʃæ'gri:n] *n* chagrin *m* (*cuir*).

Shah [ʃɑ:] *n* schah *m*.

shake [ʃeɪk] (*vb: pret* **shook**, *ptp* **shaken** ['ʃeɪkən]) **1** *n* secousse *f*, ébranlement *m*; (*quiver*) tremblement *m*. **to give sth a ~** secouer qch; **with a ~ of his head** avec un hochement de tête *or* en hochant la tête en signe de refus; **with a ~ in his voice** la voix tremblante, d'une voix tremblante; **to be all of a ~*** être tout tremblant; **he's got the ~s*** il a la tremblote*; **I'll be there in a ~*** j'arrive dans un instant *or* une seconde; **in a brace of ~s*, in two ~s (of a lamb's tail)*** en un clin d'œil, en moins de deux*; **he/it is no great ~s*** il/cela ne casse rien*; **he's no great ~s* at swimming** *or* **as a swimmer** il n'est pas fameux *or* il ne casse rien* comme nageur; *V* **hand, milk** *etc*.

2 *cpd*: **shakedown** (*bed*) lit *m* de fortune; (*US*‡: *search*) fouille *f*; (*US*‡: *extortion*) extorsion *f*, chantage *m*; **shake-up** grande réorganisation, grand remaniement.

3 *vt* **(a)** *duster, rug, person* secouer; *dice, bottle, medicine, cocktail* agiter; *house, windows etc* ébranler, faire trembler; (*brandish*) *stick etc* brandir. **'~ the bottle'** 'agiter avant emploi'; **to ~ one's head** (*in refusal etc*) dire *or* faire non de la tête, hocher la tête en signe de refus; (*at bad news etc*) secouer la tête; **he shook his finger at me** (*playfully, warningly*) il m'a fait signe du doigt; (*threateningly*) il m'a menacé du doigt; **to ~ one's fist/stick at sb** menacer qn du poing/de sa canne; **to ~ hands with sb** serrer la main à qn; **they shook hands** ils se sont serré la main; **they shook hands on it** ils se sont serré la main en signe d'accord; (*fig*) **~ a leg!*** remue-toi!, remue tes abattis!*; *[person, animal]* **to ~ o.s.** *or* **itself** se secouer; (*to remove sand, water etc*) s'ébrouer.

(b) to ~ apples from a tree secouer un arbre pour en faire tomber les pommes; **he shook the sand out of his shoes** il a secoué ses chaussures pour en vider le sable; **he shook 2 aspirins into his hand** il a fait tomber 2 comprimés d'aspirine dans sa main; **he shook pepper on to his steak** il a saupoudré son bifteck de poivre; **he shook himself free** il s'est libéré d'une secousse.

(c) (*fig: weaken, impair*) *confidence, belief, resolve* ébranler; *opinion* affecter; *health* ébranler, compromettre; *reputation* nuire à, compromettre. **even torture could not ~ him** même la torture ne l'a pas ébranlé.

(d) (*fig*) (*amaze*) stupéfier; (*disturb*) secouer, bouleverser. **he was ~n by the news** il a été très secoué *or* retourné* par la nouvelle, la nouvelle lui a porté un coup*; **this will ~ you!** tu vas en être soufflé!*, ça va t'en boucher un coin!‡; **4 days which shook the world** 4 jours qui ébranlèrent le monde; **he needs to be ~n out of his smugness** il faudrait qu'il lui arrive (*subj*) quelque chose qui lui fasse perdre de sa suffisance.

(e) (*US**) = **shake off b**.

4 *vi* **(a)** *[person, hand, table]* trembler; *[building, windows, walls]* trembler, être ébranlé; *[leaves, grasses]* trembler, être agité; *[voice]* trembler, trembloter. **he was shaking with laughter, his sides were shaking** il se tordait (de rire); to ~ **with cold** trembler de froid, grelotter; to ~ **with fear** trembler de peur; *(fig)* **to ~ in one's shoes** avoir une peur bleue*, avoir la frousse*; **the walls shook at the sound** le bruit a ébranlé les murs.

(b) (~ *hands*) **they shook on the deal** ils ont scellé leur accord d'une poignée de main; **(let's) ~ on it!** tope là!, topez là!

shake down 1 *vi* **(a)** (*: *settle for sleep*) se coucher, se pieuter:. **I can shake down anywhere** je peux pioncer: *or* me pieuter: n'importe où.

(b) *(learn to work etc together)* **they'll be a good team once they've shaken down** ils formeront une bonne équipe quand ils se seront habitués *or* faits les uns aux autres.

2 *vt sep* **(a) to shake down apples from a tree** faire tomber des pommes en secouant l'arbre, secouer l'arbre pour en faire tomber les pommes; **to shake down the contents of a packet** secouer un paquet pour en tasser le contenu.

(b) *(US:)* **to shake sb down for £50** soutirer *or* faire cracher: 50 livres à qn.

(c) *(US: frisk, search) person* fouiller.

3 shakedown *n V* **shake 2.**

shake off *vt sep* **(a) to shake off dust/sand/water from sth** secouer la poussière/le sable/l'eau de qch; *(fig, liter)* **he shook off the dust of that country from his feet** en quittant ce pays il secoua la poussière de ses sandales.

(b) *(fig: get rid of) cold, cough* se débarrasser de; *yoke etc* se libérer de, s'affranchir de; *habit* se défaire de, perdre; *pursuer* se débarrasser de, semer*.

shake out *vt sep flag, sail* déployer; *blanket* bien secouer; *bag* vider en secouant. **she picked up the bag and shook out its contents** elle a pris le sac et l'a vidé en le secouant; **she shook 50p out of her bag** elle a secoué son sac et en a fait tomber 50 pence.

shake up 1 *vt sep* **(a)** *pillow, cushion* secouer, taper; *bottle, medicine* agiter.

(b) *(fig: disturb)* bouleverser, secouer. **he was considerably shaken up by the news** il a été très secoué *or* il a été bouleversé par la nouvelle, la nouvelle lui a fait un coup*.

(c) *(fig: rouse, stir) person* secouer (les puces à)*; *firm, organization* transformer de fond en comble.

2 shake-up *n V* **shake 2.**

shaker ['ʃeɪkəʳ] *n (for cocktails)* shaker *m*; *V* **flour** *etc.*

Shakespearian [ʃeɪks'pɪərɪən] *adj* shakespearien.

shakily ['ʃeɪkɪlɪ] *adv (gen)* en tremblant; *walk* d'un pas mal assuré, à pas chancelants; *write* d'une main tremblante; *say, reply* d'une voix tremblante *or* chevrotante, *(nervously)* d'une voix mal assurée. **he got ~ to his feet** il s'est levé tout tremblant.

shakiness ['ʃeɪkɪnɪs] *n (U) [hand]* tremblement *m*; *[table etc]* manque *m* de stabilité *or* solidité; *[building]* manque de solidité; *[voice]* chevrotement *m*; *(fig) [position]* instabilité *f*; *[health]* faiblesse *f*; *[knowledge]* insuffisance *f*, faiblesse.

shako ['ʃækəʊ] *n* s(c)hako *m.*

shaky ['ʃeɪkɪ] *adj hand* tremblant, tremblotant; *voice* tremblant, chevrotant, *(nervous)* mal assuré; *writing* tremblé; *table, building* branlant, peu solide; *(fig) health* chancelant, faible. **I feel a bit ~** je ne me sens pas solide sur mes jambes, je me sens faible; *(fig)* **my Spanish is very ~** mes notions d'espagnol sont chancelantes; **his memory is rather ~** sa mémoire n'est pas très sûre, sa mémoire est assez mauvaise.

shale [ʃeɪl] *n* argile schisteuse, schiste argileux. ~ **oil** huile *f* de schiste.

shall [ʃæl] *modal aux vb (2nd pers sg* **shalt**††; *neg* **shall not** *often abbr to* **shan't**; *V also* **should) (a)** *(in 1st person fut tense)* **I shall** *or* **I'll arrive on Monday** j'arriverai lundi; **we shall not** *or* **we shan't be there before 6 o'clock** nous n'y serons pas avant 6 heures; **I'll come in a minute** je vais venir *or* je viens dans un instant.

(b) *(in 1st person questions)* **shall I open the door?** dois-je ouvrir la porte?, voulez-vous que j'ouvre *(subj)* la porte?, j'ouvre la porte?*; **I'll buy 3, shall I?** je vais en acheter 3, n'est-ce pas? *or* d'accord?*; **let's go in, shall we?** entrons, voulez-vous?; **shall we ask him to come with us?** si on lui demandait de venir avec nous?

(c) *(indicating command, guarantee etc)* **it shall be done this way and no other** cela sera fait *or* doit être fait de cette façon et d'aucune autre; *(Bible)* **thou shalt not kill** tu ne tueras point; **you** SHALL **obey me** vous m'obéirez, vous devez m'obéir; **you shan't have that job!** tu n'auras pas ce poste!

shallot [ʃə'lɒt] *n* échalote *f.*

shallow ['ʃæləʊ] **1** *adj* **(a)** *water, dish* peu profond. ~ **breathing** respiration superficielle.

(b) *(fig) mind, character, person* superficiel, sans profondeur; *conversation* futile, superficiel. **to be ~-minded** manquer de profondeur d'esprit.

2 *n*: **~s** bas-fond *m*, haut-fond *m.*

shallowness ['ʃæləʊnɪs] *n (lit)* manque *m* de profondeur; *(fig) [person]* esprit superficiel; *[character]* manque de profondeur; *[conversation]* futilité *f*; *[knowledge]* caractère superficiel.

shalt†† [ʃælt] *2nd pers sg of* **shall.**

sham [ʃæm] **1** *n (pretence)* comédie *f*, frime* *f*; *(person)* imposteur *m*; *(jewellery, furniture)* imitation *f*. **this diamond is a ~** ce diamant est faux *or* de l'imitation *or* du toc*; **the election was a ~** l'élection n'était qu'une comédie *or* était de la frime*; **his promises were a ~** ses promesses n'étaient que du vent; **the whole organization was a ~** l'entière organisation n'était qu'une imposture.

2 *adj jewellery* faux *(f* fausse), en toc*; *piety* feint; *title* faux; *illness* feint, simulé; *fight* simulé. ~ **Louis XVI** de l'imitation *or* du faux Louis XVI.

3 *vt* feindre, simuler. **to ~ ill** *or* **illness** feindre *or* simuler une maladie, faire semblant d'être malade; **she ~med dead** elle a fait la morte, elle a fait semblant d'être morte.

4 *vi* faire semblant, jouer la comédie. **he is only ~ming** il fait seulement semblant.

shamateur* ['ʃæmətəʳ] *n (Sport)* athlète *mf (or* joueur *m*, -euse *f etc)* prétendu(e) amateur *(qui se fait rémunérer)*.

shamble ['ʃæmbl] *vi* marcher en traînant les pieds. **to ~ in/out/away** *etc* entrer/sortir/s'éloigner *etc* en traînant les pieds.

shambles ['ʃæmblz] *n (no pl)* **(a)** *(scene of bloodshed)* scène *f* de carnage; *(scene of devastation)* scène de ravages; *(ruined place)* ruine(s) *f(pl)*. **after the fire the house was a ~** après l'incendie la maison offrait un spectacle de dévastation.

(b) *(muddle)* confusion *f*, désordre *m*, pagaïe* *f*. **what a ~!** quelle (belle) pagaïe!*; **his room was (in) a ~** sa chambre était sens dessus dessous *or* tout en l'air; **the match degenerated into a ~** le match a tourné au désastre *or* à la catastrophe; **your essay is a ~*** votre dissertation est un fouillis sans nom*.

shame [ʃeɪm] **1** *n* **(a)** *(U) (feeling)* honte *f*, confusion *f*; *(humiliation)* honte. **to my eternal** *or* **lasting ~** à ma très grande honte; **he hung his head in ~** il a baissé la tête de honte *or* de confusion; **to bring ~ (up)on sb** être *or* faire la honte de qn, déshonorer qn; **to put sb/sth to ~** faire honte à qn/qch; **~ on you!** quelle honte!, c'est honteux de votre part!; **the ~ of it!** quelle honte!, c'est honteux!; **the ~ of that defeat** la honte de cette défaite, cette défaite déshonorante; **the street is the ~ of the town** cette rue déshonore la ville; **she has no sense of ~** elle ne sait pas ce que c'est que la honte, elle n'a aucune pudeur; **he has lost all sense of ~** il a perdu toute honte, il a toute honte bue *(liter)*; *V* **cry, crying.**

(b) *(no pl)* dommage *m*. **it is a ~** c'est dommage *(that* que+*subj, to do* de faire); **it's a dreadful ~!** c'est tellement dommage!; **it would be a ~ if he were to refuse** *or* **if he refused** il serait dommage qu'il refuse *(subj)*; **what a ~!** (quel) dommage!; **what a ~ he isn't here** (quel) dommage qu'il ne soit pas ici.

2 *vt (bring disgrace on)* couvrir de honte, faire la honte de, déshonorer; *(make ashamed)* faire honte à, humilier, mortifier. **to ~ sb into doing sth** obliger qn à faire qch en lui faisant honte, piquer l'amour-propre de qn pour qu'il fasse qch; **to be ~d into doing sth** faire qch par amour-propre *or* pour conserver son amour-propre.

shamefaced ['ʃeɪmfeɪst] *adj (ashamed)* honteux, penaud; *(confused)* confus, timide. **he was rather ~ about it** il en était tout honteux *or* penaud.

shamefacedly ['ʃeɪmfeɪsɪdlɪ] *adv (V* **shamefaced)** d'un air honteux *or* penaud; avec confusion, timidement.

shamefacedness ['ʃeɪmfeɪstnɪs] *n (V* **shamefaced)** air penaud; confusion *f*, timidité *f.*

shameful ['ʃeɪmfʊl] *adj* honteux, scandaleux. **it's ~ to spend so much on drink** c'est une honte de tant dépenser pour la boisson.

shamefully ['ʃeɪmfəlɪ] *adv* honteusement, scandaleusement, abominablement. **he is ~ ignorant** il est d'une ignorance crasse, il est si ignorant que c'en est une honte.

shameless ['ʃeɪmlɪs] *adj* **(a)** *(unashamed) person* éhonté, effronté; *behaviour* effronté, impudent. **he is a ~ liar** c'est un menteur éhonté, c'est un effronté menteur, il ment sans vergogne; **he is quite ~ about it** il n'en a pas du tout honte.

(b) *(immodest) person* sans pudeur, impudique; *act* impudique.

shamelessly ['ʃeɪmlɪslɪ] *adv (V* **shameless)** effrontément, sans honte, sans vergogne; sans pudeur, de façon impudique.

shamelessness ['ʃeɪmlɪsnɪs] *n (V* **shameless)** effronterie *f*, impudence *f*; impudeur *f.*

shaming ['ʃeɪmɪŋ] *adj* mortifiant, humiliant. **it's too ~!** quelle humiliation!

shammy* ['ʃæmɪ] *n (also* **~ leather)** peau *f* de chamois.

shampoo [ʃæm'puː] **1** *n (product, process)* shampooing *m*. **~ and set** shampooing (et) mise *f* en plis; **to give o.s. a ~** se faire un shampooing, se laver la tête; *V* **dry.**

2 *vt* faire un shampooing à. **to have one's hair ~ed and set** se faire faire un shampooing (et) mise en plis.

shamrock ['ʃæmrɒk] *n* trèfle *m (emblème national de l'Irlande)*.

shandy ['ʃændɪ] *n (Brit)* panaché *m (bière)*.

shanghai [ʃæŋ'haɪ] *vt (Naut*††) embarquer de force comme membre d'équipage, shangailler *(rare)*. *(fig)* **to ~ sb into doing*** contraindre qn à faire.

Shangri-la ['ʃæŋgrɪ'lɑː] *n* paradis *m* terrestre.

shank [ʃæŋk] *n (Anat)* jambe *f*; *[horse]* canon *m*; *(Culin)* jarret *m*; *(handle etc)* manche *m*. *(fig)* **to go** *or* **ride on S~s' pony** *or* **mare** aller à pied, prendre le train onze:.

shan't [ʃɑːnt] = **shall not**; *V* **shall.**

shantung [ˌʃæn'tʌŋ] *n* shant(o)ung *m.*

shanty[1] ['ʃæntɪ] *n (hut)* baraque *f*, cabane *f*, bicoque* *f*. **~town** bidonville *m.*

shanty[2] ['ʃæntɪ] *n (Brit) (also* **sea ~)** chanson *f* de marins.

shape [ʃeɪp] **1** *n* **(a)** *(form, outline)* forme *f*. **what ~ is the room?, what is the ~ of the room?** quelle est la forme de la pièce?, de quelle forme est la pièce?; **stamps of all ~s** des timbres de toutes formes; **of all ~s and sizes** de toutes les formes et de toutes les tailles; **children of all ~s and sizes** des enfants d'allures diverses; **his nose is a funny ~** son nez a une drôle de forme; **this hat has lost its ~** ce chapeau s'est déformé; **it's like a mushroom in ~** cela a la forme d'un champignon, cela ressemble à un champignon; **it's triangular in ~** c'est en forme de triangle, c'est triangulaire; **in the ~ of a cross** en forme de croix; **a prince in the ~ of a swan** un prince sous la forme d'un cygne; **a monster in human ~** un monstre à figure humaine; **I can't stand racism in any ~ or form** je ne peux pas tolérer le racisme sous quelque forme que ce soit; (*lit, fig*) to take the ~ of sth prendre la forme de qch; the news reached him in the ~ of a telegram from his brother c'est par un télégramme de son frère qu'il a appris la nouvelle; that's the ~ of things to come cela donne une idée de ce qui nous attend; who knows what ~ the future will take? qui sait comment se présentera l'avenir?; *[dress, vase, project]* to take ~ prendre forme *or* tournure; to be in good ~ *[person]* être en (bonne) forme; *[business etc]* marcher bien; in poor ~ *person, business* mal en point; he carved the wood into ~ il a façonné le bois; he beat the silver into ~ il a façonné l'argent; (*fig*) to knock *or* lick* into ~ *assistant* former, dresser*; *soldier* entraîner, dresser*; to knock *or* lick* sth into ~ arranger qch, rendre qch présentable; he managed to knock *or* lick* the team into ~ il a réussi à mettre l'équipe au point; to get (o.s.) into ~ (re)trouver la forme; to keep o.s. in good ~ rester *or* se maintenir en forme; to get one's ideas into ~ formuler *or* préciser ses idées.

(b) (*human figure*) forme *f*, figure *f*; (*silhouette*) forme, silhouette *f*; (*thing dimly seen*) forme vague *or* imprécise; (*ghost etc*) fantôme *m*, apparition *f*. a ~ loomed up out of the darkness une forme imprécise surgit de l'obscurité.

(c) (*for jellies etc*) moule *m*; (*in hat-making*) forme *f*.

(d) (*Culin*) rice ~ gâteau *m* de riz; meat ~ pain *m* de viande.

2 *vt clay* façonner, modeler; *stone, wood* façonner, tailler; (*fig*) *statement, explanation* formuler. he ~d the clay into a tree, he ~d a tree out of the clay il a façonné l'argile en arbre; oddly ~d d'une forme bizarre; a nicely ~d stone une pierre d'une jolie forme; to ~ sb's ideas/character former les idées/le caractère de qn; to ~ sb's life déterminer le destin de qn; to ~ the course of events influencer la marche des événements.

3 *vi* (*fig*) prendre forme *or* tournure. our plans are shaping (up) well nos projets prennent tournure *or* s'annoncent bien *or* sont en bonne voie; things are shaping (up) well tout marche bien, on avance; how is he shaping? comment s'en sort-il?*, est-ce qu'il se fait?; how is he shaping in *or* at Spanish? comment marche-t-il *or* s'en sort-il* en espagnol?; he is shaping (up) nicely as a goalkeeper il est en train de devenir un bon gardien de but.

shape up *vi [person]* faire des progrès; *V also* shape 3.

-shaped ['ʃeɪpt] *adj ending in cpds* en forme de. heart-shaped en forme de cœur; *V* egg *etc.*

shapeless ['ʃeɪplɪs] *adj mass, lump* informe; *dress, hat, shoes* informe, sans forme. *[clothes, shoes]* to become ~ se déformer, s'avachir.

shapeliness ['ʃeɪplɪnɪs] *n* belles proportions, beauté *f* (de forme), galbe *m*.

shapely ['ʃeɪplɪ] *adj vase, building, person* bien proportionné, beau (*f* belle). a ~ woman une femme bien faite *or* bien tournée *or* bien roulée*; a ~ pair of legs des jambes bien galbées *or* bien faites.

shard [ʃɑːd] *n* tesson *m* (de poterie).

share [ʃɛəʳ] 1 *n* (a) part *f*. here's your ~ voici votre part, voici ce qui vous est dû; my ~ is £5 (*receiving*) ma (quote-)part s'élève à *or* j'ai droit à *or* je dois recevoir 5 livres; (*paying*) ma (quote-)part s'élève à *or* je dois (payer) 5 livres; his ~ of the inheritance sa part *or* sa portion de l'héritage; his ~ of *or* in the profits sa part des bénéfices; he will get a ~ of *or* in the profits il aura part aux bénéfices; he has a ~ in the business il est l'un des associés dans cette affaire; he has a half-~ in the firm il possède la moitié de l'entreprise; to have a ~ in doing sth contribuer à faire qch; he had some ~ in it il y était pour quelque chose; I had no ~ in that je n'y étais pour rien; to take a ~ in sth participer à qch; to pay one's ~ payer sa (quote-)part; to bear one's ~ of the cost participer aux frais; he wants more than his ~ il veut plus qu'il ne lui est dû, il tire la couverture à lui (*fig*); he isn't doing his ~ il ne fournit pas sa part d'efforts; he's had more than his (fair) ~ of misfortune il a eu plus que sa part de malheurs; to take one's ~ of the blame accepter sa part de responsabilité; he does his full ~ of work il fournit toute sa (quote-)part de travail; they went ~s in the cost of the holiday ils ont payé les vacances à deux (*or* trois *etc*), ils ont partagé le coût des vacances entre eux; *V* fair[1], lion.

(b) (*Fin etc*) action *f*. he has 500 ~s in an oil company il a 500 actions d'une compagnie de pétrole; *V* ordinary, preference *etc.*

(c) (*Agr: plough~*) soc *m* (*de charrue*).

2 *cpd*: (*Fin*) share capital capital *m* actions; (*Brit Fin etc*) share certificate titre *m or* certificat *m* d'actions; (*US Agr*) sharecropper métayer *m*, -ère *f*; sharecropping métayage *m*; (*Fin etc*) shareholder actionnaire *mf*; (*St Ex*) share index indice *m* de la Bourse; share-out partage *m*, distribution *f*; (*St Ex*) share prices prix *mpl* des actions.

3 *vt* (a) *room, prize* partager (*with sb* avec qn); *expenses, work* partager (*with sb* avec qn), participer à; *profits* avoir part à; *sorrow, joy* partager, prendre part à; *responsibility, blame, credit* partager. they ~d the money between them ils se sont partagé l'argent; (*Telec*) ~d line ligne partagée; they ~ certain characteristics ils ont certaines caractéristiques en commun; I do not ~ that view je ne partage pas cette opinion; I ~ your hope that ... j'espère avec *or* comme vous que ... .

(b) (*also* ~ out) partager, répartir (*among, between* entre).

4 *vi* partager. (*loc*) ~ and ~ alike à chacun sa part; to ~ in *sorrow, joy* partager, prendre part à; *responsibility* partager; *profits* avoir part à; *expenses, work* participer à, partager.

share out 1 *vt sep* = share 3b.

2 share-out *n V* share 2.

shark [ʃɑːk] *n* (*fish; also fig Fin*) requin *m*; (*swindler*) escroc *m*, aigrefin *m*. ~skin (*Tex*) peau *f* d'ange; *V* bask *etc.*

sharp [ʃɑːp] 1 *adj* (a) *razor, knife* tranchant, bien affilé, bien aiguisé; *point* aigu (*f* -guë), acéré; *fang* acéré; *needle, pin, nail* pointu, acéré; *pencil* bien taillé, pointu. take a ~ knife prenez un couteau qui coupe bien *or* bien tranchant; the ~ edge *[blade, knife]* le côté coupant, le (côté) tranchant; *[tin etc]* le bord tranchant *or* coupant.

(b) (*pointed etc*) *nose, chin* pointu; *features* anguleux; *corner, angle* aigu (*f* -guë); *bend in road* aigu, brusque. the car made a ~ turn la voiture a tourné brusquement.

(c) (*abrupt*) *descent* raide; *fall in price, change* brusque, soudain.

(d) (*well-defined*) *outline* net, distinct; (*TV*) *contrast, picture* net; *difference, contrast* marqué, prononcé.

(e) (*shrill, piercing*) *cry, voice* perçant, aigu (*f* -guë).

(f) (*Mus*) C ~ do dièse; that note was a little ~ cette note était un peu trop haute.

(g) (*harsh, bitter*) *wind, cold* pénétrant, vif; *frost* fort; *pain* violent, cuisant, vif; *smell, taste, cheese, sauce, perfume* piquant, âpre (*pej*), âcre (*pej*); *words, retort* cinglant, mordant; *rebuke* sévère; *tone* acerbe. to have a ~ tongue avoir la langue acérée.

(h) (*brisk etc*) *pace, quarrel* vif. that was ~ work! ça n'a pas traîné!*, ça n'a pas pris longtemps!, ça a été vite fait!; look *or* be ~ (about it)! fais vite!, dépêche-toi!, grouille-toi!‡

(i) (*acute*) *eyesight* perçant; *hearing, smell* fin; *intelligence, mind* délié, vif, pénétrant; *person* vif, malin (*f* -igne), dégourdi*; *child* vif, éveillé. to have ~ ears avoir l'ouïe fine; to have ~ eyes avoir une vue perçante; (*fig*) he has a ~ eye for a bargain il sait repérer *or* flairer une bonne affaire; to keep a ~ look-out for sb/sth guetter qn/qch avec vigilance *or* d'un œil attentif; he is as ~ as a needle (*clever*) il est malin comme un singe; (*missing nothing*) il est très perspicace, rien ne lui échappe.

(j) (*pej: unscrupulous*) *person* peu scrupuleux, malhonnête. ~ practice procédés déloyaux *or* (*stronger*) malhonnêtes.

2 *adv* (a) (*Mus*) *sing, play* trop haut.

(b) (*abruptly*) *stop* brusquement, net. turn *or* take ~ left tournez à gauche à angle droit *or* tout à fait à gauche.

(c) (*punctually*) at 3 o'clock ~ à 3 heures précises *or* sonnantes, à 3 heures pile.

3 *n* (*Mus*) dièse *m*.

4 *cpd*: (*fig*) sharp-eared à l'ouïe fine; sharp-eyed à qui rien n'échappe; sharp-faced, sharp-featured aux traits anguleux; sharpshooter tireur *m* d'élite; sharp-sighted = sharp-eyed; sharp-tempered coléreux, soupe au lait* *inv*; sharp-tongued qui a la langue acérée; sharp-witted à l'esprit vif *or* prompt.

sharpen ['ʃɑːpən] 1 *vt* (a) *blade, knife, razor, tool* aiguiser, affûter, affiler; *scissors* aiguiser; *pencil* tailler. the cat was ~ing its claws on the chair leg le chat aiguisait ses griffes *or* se faisait les griffes sur le pied de la chaise.

(b) (*fig*) *outline, (TV) contrast, picture, focus* rendre plus net; *difference, contrast* rendre plus marqué; *appetite* aiguiser; *desire* exciter; *pain* aggraver, aviver; *feeling* aviver; *intelligence* affiner, rendre plus fin. to ~ one's wits se dégourdir.

(c) (*esp Brit Mus*) diéser.

2 *vi [voice]* devenir plus perçant; *[desire, pain]* s'accroître, devenir plus vif, s'aviver.

sharpener ['ʃɑːpnəʳ] *n* (*knife~*) (*on wall, on wheel etc*) aiguisoir *m* à couteaux, affiloir *m*; (*long, gen with handle*) fusil *m* à repasser les couteaux; (*pencil* ~) taille-crayons *m inv*.

sharpening ['ʃɑːpnɪŋ] *n* aiguisage *m*, affilage *m*, affûtage *m*.

sharper ['ʃɑːpəʳ] *n* escroc *m*, filou *m*, aigrefin *m*; (*card* ~) tricheur *m*, -euse *f* (*professionnel(le)*).

sharply ['ʃɑːplɪ] *adv* (a) (*lit*) ~ pointed *knife, scissors* à pointe effilée *or* acérée; *nose* pointu, en quart de Brie (*hum*).

(b) (*abruptly*) *change, rise* brusquement, soudain; *turn* brusquement, court; *stop* brusquement, net. (*Aut*) to corner ~ prendre un virage à la corde; the road goes up/down ~ la route monte brusquement *or* raide/descend brusquement *or* en pente abrupte.

(c) (*harshly*) *criticize, reproach* sévèrement, vivement; *observe, comment, retort* sèchement, avec brusquerie, d'un ton acerbe. to speak ~ to sb about sth faire des observations sévères *or* parler sans ménagements à qn au sujet de qch.

(d) (*distinctly*) *show up, stand out* nettement; *differ* nettement, clairement. ~ in focus bien net; the black contrasts ~ with the white le noir forme un contraste très net avec le blanc.

(e) (*acutely, alertly*) *say, ask* vivement, avec intérêt. he looked at me ~ il m'a regardé soudain avec intérêt.

sharpness ['ʃɑːpnɪs] *n* (a) *[razor, knife]* tranchant *m*; *[pencil, needle, nail]* pointe aiguë.

(b) (*fig*) *[turn, bend]* angle *m* brusque; *[outline etc]* netteté *f*; *[pain]* violence *f*, acuité *f*; *[criticism, reproach, rebuke]* sévérité *f*, tranchant *m*; *[tone, voice]* brusquerie *f*, aigreur *f*; *[taste, smell]* piquant *m*, âcreté *f* (*pej*); *[wind, cold]* âpreté *f*. there's a ~ in the air il fait frais *or* frisquet*, le fond de l'air* est frais.

shat✱ [ʃæt] *pret, ptp of* shit✱.

shatter ['ʃætəʳ] 1 *vt window, door* fracasser (*against* contre); *health* ruiner, briser; *self-confidence* briser; *faith* détruire; (*fig*) *hopes, chances* ruiner, détruire; *career* briser. the sound ~ed the glasses le bruit a brisé les verres; to ~ sb's nerves démolir les nerfs de qn; (*fig*) she was ~ed by his death sa mort l'a anéantie; to be ~ed* (*aghast*) être bouleversé *or* très secoué *or* complètement retourné*; (*exhausted*) être éreinté *or* sur les rotules‡. 2 *vi [glass, windscreen, cup]* voler en éclats; *[box etc]* se fracasser (*against* contre). 3 *cpd*: shatterproof glass verre *m* sécurit *inv* ®.

shattering ['ʃætərɪŋ] *adj* (*fig*) *attack* destructeur (*f* -trice); *defeat* écrasant, accablant; *news* bouleversant, renversant*; *experience, disappointment* bouleversant. this was a ~ blow to our hopes/plans nos espoirs/nos projets ont été gravement compromis.

shave [ʃeɪv] (*vb*: *pret* **shaved,** *ptp* **shaved, shaven**††) **1** *n*: **to give sb a ~ raser qn; to have** *or* **give o.s. a ~** se raser, se faire la barbe; (*fig*) **to have a close** *or* **narrow ~** l'échapper belle, y échapper de justesse; **that was a close** *or* **narrow ~!** il était moins une!*, on l'a échappé belle!; *V* **after** *etc.*
2 *vt person, face, legs etc* raser; *wood* raboter, planer; (*fig: graze*) raser, frôler.
3 *vi* se raser.
shave off *vt sep* **(a) to shave off one's beard** se raser la barbe.
(b) the joiner shaved some of the wood off le menuisier a enlevé un peu du bois au rabot.
shaven [ˈʃeɪvn] **1** (††) *ptp of* **shave. 2** *adj* rasé; *V* **clean** *etc.*
shaver [ˈʃeɪvəʳ] *n* **(a)** rasoir *m* électrique. **(b) (young) ~***† gosse* *m*, gamin *m*.
Shavian [ˈʃeɪvɪən] *adj* à la *or* de Bernard Shaw.
shaving [ˈʃeɪvɪŋ] **1** *n* **(a)** (*piece of wood, metal etc*) copeau *m*.
(b) (*U*: *with razor etc*) rasage *m*. **~ is a nuisance** c'est ennuyeux *or* embêtant* de se raser.
2 *cpd*: **shaving brush** blaireau *m*; **shaving cream** crème *f* à raser; **shaving soap** savon *m* à barbe; **shaving stick** bâton *m* de savon à barbe.
shawl [ʃɔːl] *n* châle *m*.
she [ʃiː] **1** *pers pron* **(a)** (*stressed, unstressed*) elle. **~ has come** elle est venue; **here ~ is** la voici; **~ is a doctor** elle est médecin, c'est un médecin; **~ is a small woman** elle est petite; **it is ~** c'est elle; (*frm*) **if I were ~** si j'étais elle, si j'étais à sa place; SHE **didn't do it** ce n'est pas elle qui l'a fait; **younger than ~** plus jeune qu'elle; **~'s a fine boat/car** c'est un beau bateau/une belle voiture.
(b) (+*rel pron*) celle. **~ who** *or* **that can ...** celle qui peut ... .
2 *cpd* femelle. **she-bear** ourse *f*; (*fig*) **she-cat** mégère *f*, furie *f*; (*fig*) **she-devil** démon *m*, furie *f*; **she-hedgehog** hérisson *m* femelle; *V* **wolf** *etc.*
3 *n* (*) femelle *f*. **it's a ~** (*animal*) c'est une femelle; (*baby*) c'est une fille.
sheaf [ʃiːf] *n, pl* **sheaves** *[corn]* gerbe *f*; *[papers]* liasse *f*; *[arrows]* faisceau *m*.
shear [ʃɪəʳ] (*vb*: *pret* **sheared,** *ptp* **sheared** *or* **shorn**). **1** *npl*: **~s** (*Horticulture*) cisaille(s) *f(pl)*; (*Sewing, gen*) grands ciseaux; *V* **pruning** *etc.*
2 *vt sheep* tondre. (*fig*) **shorn of** dépouillé de.
shear off 1 *vi [branch etc]* partir, se détacher.
2 *vt sep wool* tondre; *projecting part, nail* faire partir, arracher; *branch* couper, élaguer. **the ship had its bow shorn off in the collision** dans la collision l'avant du navire a été emporté.
shear through *vt fus paper, cloth* trancher; *wood, metal* fendre; (*fig*) *the waves, the crowd* fendre.
shearer [ˈʃɪərəʳ] *n* (*person*) tondeur *m*, -euse *f*; (*machine*) tondeuse *f*.
shearing [ˈʃɪərɪŋ] *n* (*process*) tonte *f*. (*wool etc*) **~s** tonte.
sheath [ʃiːθ] **1** *n* **(a)** *[dagger]* gaine *f*; *[sword]* fourreau *m*; *[scissors etc]* étui *m*; *[electric cable, flex]* gaine; (*Bio*) gaine, enveloppe *f*; (*Bot*) enveloppe; (*contraceptive*) préservatif *m*.
(b) (*also* **~ dress**) fourreau *m* (*robe*).
2 *cpd*: **sheath knife** couteau *m* à gaine.
sheathe [ʃiːð] *vt* **(a)** *sword, dagger* rengainer; *cable* gainer; *[cat etc] claws* rentrer. **(b)** (*cover*) recouvrir, revêtir (*with* de).
sheaves [ʃiːvz] *npl of* **sheaf.**
Sheba [ˈʃiːbə] *n* Saba.
shebang* [ʃəˈbæŋ] *n* (*US*) **the whole ~** toute l'affaire, tout le tremblement*.
shebeen [ʃɪˈbiːn] *n* (*Ir*) débit *m* de boissons clandestin.
shed¹ [ʃed] *n* (*in garden, on farm, for tools etc*) remise *f*, resserre *f*, (*smaller*) hutte *f*, cabane *f*; (*for cattle etc*) étable *f*; (*rough shelter*) hutte, cabane; (*part of factory*) atelier *m*; *V* **cattle, tool** *etc.*
shed² [ʃed] *pret, ptp* **shed** *vt* **(a)** (*lose, get rid of*) *petals, leaves, fur, horns* perdre; *shell* dépouiller; *[truck] load* déverser, perdre; *tears* verser, répandre; *coat etc* enlever, se dépouiller de (*frm*); *unwanted thing, assistant* se débarrasser de, se défaire de. **the snake ~s its skin** le serpent mue; **to ~ blood** (*one's own*) verser son sang; (*other people's*) faire couler le sang, verser *or* répandre le sang; **I'm trying to ~ 5 kilos** j'essaie de perdre 5 kilos.
(b) (*send out*) *light* répandre, diffuser; *warmth, happiness* répandre. **to ~ light on** (*lit*) éclairer; (*fig*) *sb's motives etc* jeter de la lumière sur; *problem* éclaircir; *little-known subject* éclairer.
she'd [ʃiːd] = **she had, she would;** *V* **have, would.**
sheen [ʃiːn] *n* (*on silk*) lustre *m*, luisant *m*; (*on hair*) brillant *m*, éclat *m*. **to take the ~ off sth** (*lit*) délustrer qch; (*fig*) diminuer l'éclat de qch.
sheep [ʃiːp] **1** *n, pl inv* mouton *m* (*animal*); (*ewe*) brebis *f*. **they followed him like a lot of ~** ils l'ont suivi comme des moutons, ils l'ont suivi comme les moutons de Panurge; (*fig*) **to make ~'s eyes at** faire les yeux doux à; **we must divide** *or* **separate the ~ from the goats** il ne faut pas mélanger les torchons et les serviettes* (*fig*); *V* **black, lost** *etc.*
2 *cpd*: **sheep-dip** bain *m* parasiticide (*pour moutons*); **sheepdog** chien *m* de berger (*V* **trial**); **sheep farm** ferme *f* d'élevage de moutons; **sheep farmer** éleveur *m* de moutons; **sheep farming** élevage *m* de moutons; **sheepfold** parc *m* à moutons, bergerie *f*; (*Naut*) **sheepshank** jambe *f* de chien; **sheepshearer** (*person*) tondeur *m*, -euse *f* (de moutons); (*machine*) tondeuse *f* (à moutons); (*U*) **sheepshearing** tonte *f* (des moutons); **sheepskin** (*n*) peau *f* de mouton; (*adj*) en peau de mouton; **sheepskin jacket** canadienne *f*; **sheep track** piste *f* à moutons; **sheep-worrying** harcèlement *m* des moutons (*par des chiens*).
sheepish [ˈʃiːpɪʃ] *adj* penaud.
sheepishly [ˈʃiːpɪʃlɪ] *adv* d'un air penaud.
sheepishness [ˈʃiːpɪʃnɪs] *n* timidité *f*, air penaud.
sheer¹ [ʃɪəʳ] **1** *adj* **(a)** (*utter*) *chance, kindness, malice* pur; *impossibility, necessity* absolu. **it was ~ mud/rock** *etc* ce n'était que de la boue/du roc *etc*; **by (a) ~ accident** tout à fait par hasard, par pur hasard; **in ~ amazement** absolument stupéfait, bouche bée de stupéfaction; **~ carelessness** pure étourderie, étourderie pure et simple; **in ~ desperation** en désespoir de cause; **by ~ hard work** uniquement grâce au travail *or* aux efforts; **it's ~ madness** c'est de la folie pure *or* douce*; **it's ~ robbery** c'est du vol manifeste; **a ~ waste of time** une véritable perte de temps, une perte de temps absolue.
(b) *stockings, material* extrêmement fin.
(c) *rock, cliff* à pic, abrupt. **a ~ drop** *or* **fall** un à-pic.
2 *adv* à pic, abruptement.
sheer² [ʃɪəʳ] (*Naut: swerve*) **1** *n* embardée *f*. **2** *vi* faire une embardée.
sheer off *vi [ship]* faire une embardée; (*gen*) changer de direction.
sheet [ʃiːt] **1** *n* **(a)** (*on bed*) drap *m*; (*shroud*) linceul *m*; (*dust ~*) housse *f*; (*tarpaulin*) bâche *f*; *V* **water, white** *etc.*
(b) (*piece*) *[plastic, rubber]* morceau *m*; *[paper, notepaper]* feuille *f*; *[iron, steel]* tôle *f*; *[glass, metal etc]* feuille, plaque *f*; (*fig: expanse*) *[water, snow]* étendue *f*. **an odd** *or* **loose ~** une feuille volante; **baking ~** plaque à gâteaux *or* de four; **a ~ of ice** (*large*) une plaque *or* nappe de glace; (*thin film*) une couche de glace; (*on road*) une plaque de verglas; **a ~ of flame** un rideau de flammes; **the rain came down in ~s** il pleuvait à torrents; *V* **balance** *etc.*
(c) (*periodical*) périodique *m*; (*newspaper*) journal *m*.
(d) (*Naut*) écoute *f*; *V* **main** *etc.*
2 *cpd*: **sheet anchor** (*Naut*) ancre *f* de veille; (*fig*) ancre de salut; (*U*) **sheet lightning** éclair *m* en nappe(s); (*U*) **sheet metal** tôle *f*; (*U*) **sheet music** partitions *fpl*.
sheik(h) [ʃeɪk] *n* cheik *m*; *V* **oil.**
sheik(h)dom [ˈʃeɪkdəm] *n* tribu *f or* territoire *m* sous l'autorité d'un cheik.
shekel [ˈʃekl] *n* sicle *m*. (*fig*) **~s*** argent *m*, fric‡ *m*, écus *mpl* (*iro*).
shelf [ʃelf] *pl* **shelves 1** *n* **(a)** étagère *f*, planche *f*, rayon *m*; (*in shop*) rayon; (*in oven*) plaque *f*. **a ~ of books** un rayon de livres; **a set of shelves** une étagère, un rayonnage; (*Comm*) **there are more luxury goods on the shelves nowadays** il y a plus d'articles de luxe sur les rayons *or* dans les magasins aujourd'hui; (*fig: postponed*) **to be on the ~** être en suspens *or* en sommeil; *[woman]* **to be (left) on the ~** monter en graine (*fig*), être laissée pour compte; *V* **book** *etc.*
(b) (*edge*) (*in rock*) rebord *m*, saillie *f*; (*underwater*) écueil *m*; *V* **continental.**
2 *cpd*: (*Comm*) **shelf life** durée *f* de conservation avant vente; (*Libraries*) **shelf mark** cote *f*.
shell [ʃel] **1** *n* **(a)** *[egg, nut, oyster, snail etc]* coquille *f*; *[tortoise, lobster, crab]* carapace *f*; (*on beach, in collection etc*) coquillage *m*; *[peas]* cosse *f*. (*lit, fig*) **to come out of/go back into one's ~** sortir de/rentrer dans sa coquille; *V* **cockle** *etc.*
(b) *[building]* carcasse *f*; *[ship]* coque *f*. (*Culin*) **pastry ~** fond *m* de tarte.
(c) (*Mil*) obus *m*; (*US: cartridge*) cartouche *f*.
(d) (*racing boat*) outrigger *m*.
2 *cpd necklace, ornament etc* de *or* en coquillages. (*Mil*) **shellfire** bombardement *m* par obus; **shellfish** (*pl inv*) (*lobster, crab*) crustacé *m*; (*pl: molluscs*) coquillages *mpl*; (*pl: Culin*) fruits *mpl* de mer; (*Mil*) **shellproof** blindé; (*Med*) **shell shock** psychose *f* traumatique, commotion cérébrale (*à la suite d'éclatements d'obus*); (*Med*) **shell-shocked** commotionné (par des éclatements d'obus); **shell-shocked ex-serviceman** commotionné *m* de guerre.
3 *vt* **(a)** *peas* écosser; *nut* décortiquer, écaler; *oyster* écailler, retirer de sa coquille; *crab, prawn, shrimp* décortiquer; *lobster* retirer de sa carapace.
(b) (*Mil*) bombarder (d'obus).
shell out 1 *vi* (*) casquer‡, payer. **to shell out for sth** payer qch, casquer‡ pour qch.
2 *vt sep* (‡) cracher‡, aligner*.
she'll [ʃiːl] = **she will;** *V* **will.**
shellac [ʃəˈlæk] **1** *n* (*U*) (gomme *f*) laque *f*. **2** *vt* laquer.
shelling [ˈʃelɪŋ] *n* (*U: Mil*) bombardement *m* (*par obus*).
shelter [ˈʃeltəʳ] **1** *n* **(a)** (*U*) abri *m*, couvert *m*. **under the ~ of** sous l'abri de; **to take ~, to get under ~** se mettre à l'abri *or* à couvert; **to take ~ from/under** s'abriter de/sous; **to seek/offer ~** chercher/offrir un abri (*from* contre); **she gave him ~ for the night** elle lui a donné (un) asile pour la nuit; **we must find ~ for the night** nous devons trouver un abri pour cette nuit; (*Brit*) S~ *organisation f bénévole qui cherche à loger les sans-logis.*
(b) (*hut etc*) (*on mountain*) abri *m*, refuge *m*; (*for sentry*) guérite *f*; (*bus ~*) abribus *m*; (*air-raid ~*) abri.
2 *vt* **(a)** (*protect*) (*from wind, rain, sun, shells etc*) abriter (*from* de), protéger (*from* de, contre); (*from blame etc*) protéger (*from* de); *criminal etc* protéger; (*hide*) cacher. **~ed from the wind** à l'abri du vent; *V also* **sheltered.**
(b) (*give lodging to*) recueillir, donner un asile *or* le couvert à; *fugitive etc* donner asile à, recueillir.
3 *vi* s'abriter (*from* de, *under* sous), se mettre à l'abri *or* à couvert.
sheltered [ˈʃeltəd] *adj place* abrité; (*fig*) *life* bien protégé, retiré; *conditions, environment* protégé; (*Econ*) *industry* protégé (*contre la concurrence étrangère*). (*Ind*) **~ workshop** centre *m* d'aide, atelier protégé (*réservé aux travailleurs handicapés*); **he had a ~ childhood** son enfance s'est écoulée à

l'abri des soucis, on lui a fait une enfance sans soucis.
shelve [ʃelv] **1** *vt* **(a)** (*fig: postpone*) *plan, project, problem* mettre en sommeil *or* en suspens. **(b)** (*lit*) *cupboard, wall* garnir de rayons *or* d'étagères. **2** *vi* (*slope*: *also* ~ **down**) descendre en pente douce.
shelves [ʃelvz] *npl of* **shelf.**
shelving ['ʃelvɪŋ] *n* (*U*) rayonnage(s) *m(pl)*, étagères *fpl*.
shemozzle* [ʃə'mɒzl] *n* (*Brit*) bagarre* *f*, chamaillerie* *f*. **there was quite a ~!** ça a bardé!‡
shenanigan(s)* [ʃə'nænɪgən(z)] *n* (*U*) comédie* *f*, histoires* *fpl*.
shepherd ['ʃepəd] **1** *n* **(a)** berger *m*; (*Rel*) pasteur *m*. (*Rel*) **the Good S~** le bon Pasteur.
(b) (*also* ~ **dog**) chien *m* de berger.
2 *cpd*: **shepherd boy** jeune pâtre *m* (*liter*), jeune berger *m*; **shepherd's check** = **shepherd's plaid; shepherd's crook** houlette *f*; (*esp Brit Culin*) **shepherd's pie** hachis *m* Parmentier; **shepherd's plaid** plaid noir et blanc; (*Bot*) **shepherd's purse** bourse-à-pasteur *f*.
3 *vt sheep* garder, soigner. **the dog ~ed the flock into the field** le chien a fait entrer le troupeau dans le pré; (*fig*) **to ~ sb in** faire entrer qn; **to ~ sb out** escorter qn jusqu'à la porte; **he ~ed us round Paris** il nous a escortés *or* nous a guidés *or* nous a servi de guide dans Paris.
shepherdess ['ʃepədɪs] *n* bergère *f*.
sherbet ['ʃɜːbət] *n* **(a)** (*Brit*) (*fruit juice*) jus *m* de fruit glacé; (*fizzy*) boisson gazeuse; (*powder*) poudre acidulée *or* de sorbet. **(b)** (*US: water ice*) sorbet *m*.
sheriff ['ʃerɪf] **1** *n* (*Jur: Brit, US*) shérif *m*.
2 *cpd*: (*Scot*) **S~ Court** ≈ tribunal *m* de grande instance.
sherry ['ʃerɪ] *n* xérès *m*, sherry *m*.
she's [ʃiːz] = **she is, she has;** *V* **be, have.**
Shetland ['ʃetlənd] **1** *adj, n*: **the ~ Islands** *or* **Isles, the ~s** les îles *fpl* Shetland. **2** *cpd*: **Shetland pony** poney shetlandais; **Shetland pullover** pull-over *m* en shetland; **Shetland wool** shetland *m*.
shew [ʃəʊ] *vti* = **show.**
shhh [ʃː] *excl* chut!
shibboleth ['ʃɪbəleθ] *n* (*Bible*) schibboleth *m*; (*fig*) (*doctrine*) doctrine *f or* principe *m* arbitraire; (*password*) mot *m* de passe; (*characteristic*) caractéristique *f*, signe distinctif.
shield [ʃiːld] **1** *n* (*gen*) bouclier *m*; (*not round*) écu *m*; (*Her*) écu, blason *m*; (*on gun*) bouclier; (*on or around machine*) écran *m* de protection, tôle protectrice; (*against radiation*) écran; (*fig*) (*safeguard*) sauvegarde *f*, bouclier (*liter*) (*against* contre); (*person*) protecteur *m*, -trice *f*; *V* **dress, wind**[1] *etc*.
2 *vt* protéger (*from* de, contre); *fugitive, criminal* protéger, couvrir; (*Tech*) *machine operator* protéger; *gun/machine* fixer un bouclier *or* un écran de protection à. **to ~ one's eyes from the sun** se protéger les yeux du soleil; **to ~ sb with one's body** faire à qn un bouclier *or* un rempart de son corps.
shieling ['ʃiːlɪŋ] *n* (*Scot: hut etc*) petite cabane de berger.
shift [ʃɪft] **1** *n* **(a)** (*change*) changement *m* (*in* de), modification *f* (*in* de); (*Ling*) mutation *f*; (*movement: of cargo, load etc*) déplacement *m* (*in* de). **there has been a ~ in policy/emphasis/attitude** la politique/l'accent/l'attitude a changé; **a sudden ~ in policy/attitude** un retournement *or* un bouleversement de la politique/de l'attitude; **a sudden ~ in the wind** une saute de vent; **he asked for a ~ to London/to another department/to an easier job** il a demandé à être muté à Londres/affecté à une autre section/affecté à un emploi plus facile; **it's time he made a ~** il est temps qu'il change (*subj*) d'horizon; *V* **scene, vowel** *etc*.
(b) (*Ind etc*) (*period of work*) poste *m*, période *f* de travail d'une équipe; (*people*) poste, équipe (de relais). **he works ~s, he's on ~s*** il travaille par roulement; **they used to work a 10-hour ~ in that factory** ils avaient des postes de 10 heures dans cette usine; **I work an 8-hour ~** je fais un poste *or* un roulement de 8 heures; **this factory operates on 3 ~s per 24-hour period** dans cette usine 3 équipes *or* 3 postes se relaient sur 24 heures; **which ~ do you prefer?** quel poste préférez-vous?; **the next ~ were late in coming on** le poste suivant *or* l'équipe suivante était en retard pour prendre le relais *or* la relève; **they worked in ~s to release the injured man** ils se sont relayés pour (essayer de) libérer le blessé; *V* **day, night** *etc*.
(c) (*expedient*) expédient *m*, stratagème *m*, truc* *m*, ruse *f* (*pej*), tour *m* (*pej*). **to make ~ with sth/sb** se contenter de *or* s'accommoder de *or* se débrouiller* avec qch/qn; **to make ~ without sth/sb** se passer de qch/qn, se débrouiller* sans qch/qn; **to make ~ to do** se débrouiller* pour faire; **as a last desperate ~ he ...** en désespoir de cause il ... .
(d) (*US Aut*: *gear~*) levier *m* de (changement de) vitesse.
(e) (*straight dress*) robe droite; (†: *woman's slip*) chemise *f*.
2 *cpd*: [*typewriter*] **shift key** touche *f* de majuscule; (*Ind etc*) **shift work** travail *m* en équipe *or* par relais *or* par roulement; **to do shift work, to be on shift work** travailler en équipe *or* par relais.
3 *vt* **(a)** (*move*) *object, furniture* déplacer, changer de place; *one's head, arm etc* bouger, remuer; *chair, car etc* déplacer, changer de place, bouger; (*Theat*) *scenery* changer; *screw* débloquer, faire bouger; *lid, top, cap* faire bouger; *employee* (*to another town*) muter (*to* à); (*to another job, department*) affecter (*to* à); *pupil* transférer, faire passer (*to another class* dans une autre classe); (*fig*) *blame, responsibility* rejeter (*on, on to* sur). **he ~ed his chair nearer the fire** il a approché sa chaise du feu; **to ~ sth in/out/away** *etc* rentrer/sortir/écarter qch; **we couldn't ~ him (from his opinion)** nous n'avons pas réussi à le faire changer d'avis *or* à l'ébranler; **I can't ~ this cold*** je n'arrive pas à me débarrasser de ce rhume.
(b) (*change; exchange*) changer de. (*lit, fig*) **to ~ position** changer de position; (*US Aut*) **to ~ gears** changer de vitesse, passer les vitesses; *V* **ground**[1].
4 *vi* **(a)** (*go*) aller; (*move house*) déménager; (*change position, stir*) [*person, animal, planet etc*] changer de place *or* de position, bouger; [*limb*] remuer, bouger; [*wind*] tourner; [*ballast, cargo, load*] se déplacer; [*opinions, ideas*] changer, se modifier; (*fig: change one's mind*) changer d'avis. **he ~ed over to the window** il s'est approché de la fenêtre; **~ a minute to let me past** pousse-toi *or* bouge-toi* une minute pour me laisser passer; **~ off the rug** va-t-en du tapis; (*on seat etc*) **can you ~ down *or* up *or* along a little?** pourriez-vous vous pousser un peu?; **he has ~ed to London** (*gen*) il est à Londres maintenant; (*moved house*) il a déménagé à Londres; (*changed job*) il a trouvé un nouvel emploi à Londres; (*within same firm*) il a été muté à Londres; **he has ~ed into another class** il a été transféré *or* il est passé dans une autre classe; (*Theat etc*) **the scene ~s to Paris** la scène est maintenant à Paris; (*Aut*) **to ~ into second (gear)** passer la deuxième; **he won't ~** (*lit*) il ne bougera pas; (*fig*: *change opinion*) il est inébranlable, il ne bougera pas; **the government has not ~ed from its original position** le gouvernement n'a pas modifié sa première position; **he/that car certainly ~s*** il/cette voiture ne traîne pas!; **come on, ~!*** allez, remue-toi!* *or* grouille-toi!‡
(b) to ~ for o.s. se débrouiller* tout seul.
shift about, shift around 1 *vi* **(a)** (*move house*) déménager souvent; (*change job*) changer souvent d'emploi; (*within same firm*) être muté plusieurs fois.
(b) (*fidget*) bouger, remuer.
2 *vt sep furniture etc* déplacer, changer de place.
shift away *vi* (*move house*) déménager. **they've shifted away from here** ils n'habitent plus par ici.
shift back 1 *vi* **(a)** (*move house*) **they've shifted back to London** ils sont retournés *or* revenus habiter (à) Londres.
(b) (*withdraw*) (se) reculer.
2 *vt sep chair etc* reculer.
shift over *vi* s'écarter, se déplacer, se pousser. **shift over!** pousse-toi!
shiftily ['ʃɪftɪlɪ] *adv* (*V* **shifty**) sournoisement; de façon évasive.
shiftiness ['ʃɪftɪnɪs] *n* (*V* **shifty**) manque *m* de franchise, caractère *m or* aspect *m* louche, sournoiserie *f*; caractère évasif.
shifting ['ʃɪftɪŋ] *adj scene, opinion* changeant; *sand* mouvant.
shiftless ['ʃɪftlɪs] *adj* (*idle*) fainéant, paresseux, flemmard*; (*unresourceful*) empoté*, qui n'est pas débrouillard*.
shiftlessness ['ʃɪftlɪsnɪs] *n* (*V* **shiftless**) fainéantise *f*, paresse *f*, flemme* *f*; manque *m* de débrouillardise*.
shifty ['ʃɪftɪ] *adj person, behaviour* louche, qui manque de franchise, sournois; *answer* évasif; *look* fuyant. **~-eyed** aux yeux fuyants.
shillelagh [ʃə'leɪlə] *n* (*Ir*) gourdin irlandais.
shilling ['ʃɪlɪŋ] *n* (*Brit*) shilling *m* (*ancienne pièce valant le vingtième de la livre*).
shilly-shally ['ʃɪlɪ,ʃælɪ] **1** *vi* hésiter; (*deliberately*) tergiverser, atermoyer. **stop ~ing!** décide-toi enfin! **2** *n* = **shilly-shallying.**
shilly-shallying ['ʃɪlɪ,ʃælɪɪŋ] *n* (*U*) hésitations *fpl*, valse-hésitation *f*; (*deliberate*) tergiversations *fpl*, atermoiements *mpl*.
shimmer ['ʃɪməʳ] **1** *vi* [*satin, jewels*] chatoyer; [*water, lake, heat haze, road surface*] miroiter. **the moonlight ~ed on the lake** le clair de lune se reflétait sur le lac *or* faisait miroiter le lac.
2 *n* [*satin, jewels*] chatoiement *m*; [*water, lake*] miroitement *m*.
shimmering ['ʃɪmərɪŋ] *adj*, **shimmery** ['ʃɪmərɪ] *adj material, jewel* chatoyant; *water, lake* miroitant. **the ~ moonlight on the lake** le clair de lune qui faisait miroiter le lac.
shin [ʃɪn] **1** *n* tibia *m*.
2 *cpd*: **shinbone** tibia *m*; **shin guard, shin pad** jambière *f*.
3 *vi*: **to ~ up a tree** grimper à un arbre; **to ~ down a tree** dégringoler lestement d'un arbre; **to ~ over a wall** escalader un mur.
shin down *vi* dégringoler* lestement.
shin up *vi* grimper lestement.
shindig* ['ʃɪndɪg] *n* (*dance, party etc*) fiesta *f*, soirée joyeuse.
shindy* ['ʃɪndɪ] *n* **(a)** (*brawl*) bagarre *f*; (*row, commotion*) tapage *m*, boucan* *m*. **to kick up *or* make a ~** faire du boucan*.
(b) = **shindig.**
shine [ʃaɪn] (*vb*: *pret, ptp* **shone**) **1** *n* [*sun*] éclat *m*; [*metal*] éclat, brillant *m*; [*shoes*] brillant. **to give sth a ~** faire briller qch, faire reluire qch; **to take the ~ off** *brass, shoes* rendre mat *or* terne (*pej*); *trouser seat* délustrer; (* *fig*) *success, news* diminuer l'attrait de, faire tomber à plat; *sb else's achievement* éclipser; **the ~ on his trousers** son pantalon lustré; **to take a ~ to sb‡** se toquer de qn*; *V* **moon, rain** *etc*.
2 *vi* [*sun, stars, lamp*] briller; [*metal, shoes*] briller, reluire; (*fig*: *excel*) briller. **the sun is shining** il fait (du) soleil, il y a du soleil, le soleil brille; **the moon is shining** il y a clair de lune; **to ~ on sth** éclairer *or* illuminer qch; **the light was shining in my eyes** j'avais la lumière dans les yeux; **her face shone with happiness** son visage rayonnait de bonheur; **her eyes shone with pleasure/envy** ses yeux brillaient de plaisir/luisaient d'envie; (*fig*) **to ~ at football/Spanish** briller *or* faire des étincelles* au football/en espagnol.
3 *vt* **(a) ~ your torch *or* ~ the light over here** éclairez par ici; **he shone his torch on the car** il a braqué sa lampe de poche sur la voiture, il a éclairé la voiture.
(b) (*pret, ptp* **shone** *or* **shined**) *furniture, brass, shoes* faire briller, faire reluire, astiquer.
shine down *vi* [*sun, moon, stars*] briller.
shine through *vi* [*light etc*] passer, filtrer; (*fig*) [*courage etc*] transparaître.

shiner [ˈʃaɪnəʳ] *n* **(a)** (*: *black eye*) œil poché, œil au beurre noir*. **(b)** *V* **shoe**.

shingle [ˈʃɪŋgl] **1** *n* (*U: on beach etc*) galets *mpl*; (*U: on roof*) bardeaux *mpl*; (*US*: signboard*) petite enseigne (*de docteur, de notaire etc*); (†: *hairstyle*) coupe *f* à la garçonne. **2** *cpd*: **shingle beach** plage *f* de galets. **3** *vt* (†) *hair* couper à la garçonne.

shingles [ˈʃɪŋglz] *n* (*U*) zona *m*.

shingly [ˈʃɪŋglɪ] *adj beach* (couvert) de galets.

shininess [ˈʃaɪnɪnɪs] *n* éclat *m*, brillant *m*.

shining [ˈʃaɪnɪŋ] *adj furniture, car, floor* luisant, reluisant; (*clean*) reluisant (de propreté); (*happy*) *face* rayonnant; *eyes, hair* brillant; *example* resplendissant; *V* **improve**.

shinny [ˈʃɪnɪ] *vi* = **shin 3**.

Shinto [ˈʃɪntəʊ] *n* shintô *m*.

Shintoism [ˈʃɪntəʊɪzəm] *n* shintoïsme *m*.

shinty [ˈʃɪntɪ] *n* (*Ir, Scot*) *sorte f de hockey sur gazon*.

shiny [ˈʃaɪnɪ] *adj surface etc* brillant; *car, furniture* brillant, reluisant; *coin, nose* brillant; *clothes* lustré.

ship [ʃɪp] **1** *n* (*gen*) bateau *m*; (*large*) navire *m*; (*vessel*) vaisseau *m*, bâtiment *m*. **His** (*or* **Her**) **Majesty's S~** (*abbr* **HMS**) **Maria/Falcon** (le HMS) la Maria/le Falcon; (†, *liter*) **the good ~ Caradoc** la nef† Caradoc, le Caradoc; (*Hist*) **~ of the line** bâtiment de ligne; **~'s biscuit** biscuit *m* (de mer); **~'s boat** chaloupe *f*; **~'s company** équipage *m*, hommes *mpl* du bord; **~'s papers** papiers *mpl* de bord *or* d'un navire; (*fig*) **when my ~ comes home** quand j'aurai fait fortune; (*fig*) **the ~ of the desert** le vaisseau du désert, le chameau; *V* **board, jump, war** *etc*.

2 *cpd*: **shipbuilder** constructeur *m* de navires; **shipbuilding** construction navale; **ship canal** canal *m* maritime *or* de navigation; **shipload** (*lit*) charge *f*; (*fig*) grande quantité, masse* *f*; **tourists were arriving by the shipload** les touristes arrivaient par bateaux entiers; **shipmate** camarade *m* de bord; **shipowner** armateur *m*; **ship('s) chandler** fournisseur *m* d'équipement maritime, shipchandler *m*; **shipshape** bien rangé, en ordre; (*loc*) **all shipshape and Bristol fashion** arrangé d'une façon impeccable; **ship-to-shore radio** liaison *f* radio avec la côte; **shipwreck** *V* **shipwreck**; **shipwright** (*builder*) constructeur *m* de navires; (*carpenter*) charpentier *m* (de chantier naval); **shipyard** chantier naval.

3 *vt* **(a)** (*transport*) transporter; (*send by ~*) expédier (par bateau); (*send by any means*) expédier.

(b) (*put or take on board*) *cargo* embarquer, charger; *water* embarquer. **to ~ the oars** rentrer les avirons.

ship off, ship out 1 *vi* s'embarquer (*to* pour).

2 *vt sep* **(a)** (*send by ship*) *goods, troops etc* envoyer (par bateau *or* par mer).

(b) (*: *send*) *goods, person* expédier*.

shipment [ˈʃɪpmənt] *n* cargaison *f*, fret *m*.

shipper [ˈʃɪpəʳ] *n* expéditeur *m*, affréteur *m*.

shipping [ˈʃɪpɪŋ] **1** *n* (*U*) **(a)** (*ships collectively*) navires *mpl*; (*traffic*) navigation *f*. (*Rad*) **attention all ~!** avis à la navigation!; **it was a danger to ~** cela constituait un danger pour la navigation; **the canal is closed to British ~** le canal est fermé aux navires britanniques.

(b) (*act of loading*) chargement *m*, embarquement *m*.

2 *cpd*: **shipping agent** agent *m* maritime; **shipping company, shipping line** compagnie *f* de navigation; **shipping lane** voie *f* de navigation; **shipping losses during 1944** les pertes en navires pendant 1944.

shipwreck [ˈʃɪprek] **1** *n* (*event*) naufrage *m*; (*wrecked ship*) épave *f*. **2** *vt* (*lit*) faire sombrer; (*fig*) ruiner, anéantir. **to be ~ed** faire naufrage; **~ed on a desert island** échoué sur une île déserte; **a ~ed person** un(e) naufragé(e); **~ed sailor/vessel** marin/vaisseau naufragé.

shire [ˈʃaɪəʳ] *n* (*Brit*) comté *m*. **the S~s** les comtés du centre de l'Angleterre; **~ horse** shire *m*, cheval *m* de gros trait.

shirk [ʃɜːk] **1** *vt task, work* ne pas faire; *obligation, duty* esquiver, se dérober à; *difficulty, problem, issue* escamoter, éluder, esquiver. **to ~ doing** éviter de faire, s'arranger pour ne pas faire. **2** *vi* tirer au flanc*.

shirker [ˈʃɜːkəʳ] *n* tire-au-flanc* *m inv*.

shirr [ʃɜːʳ] *vt* froncer, bouillonner (*Couture*). **~ing elastic** (fil *m*) élastique *m* à froncer.

shirt [ʃɜːt] **1** *n* (*man's*) chemise *f*; (*woman's*) chemisier *m*. (*fig*) **keep your ~ on!** ne vous mettez pas en rogne* *or* en pétard*; (*Betting etc*) **to put one's ~ on sth** jouer (toute) sa fortune *or* tout ce qu'on a sur qch; (*Betting etc*) **to lose one's ~** perdre (toute) sa fortune *or* tout ce qu'on a, y laisser sa chemise; *V* **boil, night, stuff** *etc*.

2 *cpd*: **shirt front** plastron *m*; **in (one's) shirt sleeves** en bras *or* manches de chemise; **shirttail** pan *m* de chemise; **in (one's) shirttails** en (pans de) chemise; **shirtwaist(ed) dress, shirtwaister,** (*US*) **shirtwaist** robe *f* chemisier.

shirting [ˈʃɜːtɪŋ] *n* (*U*) shirting *m*.

shirty* [ˈʃɜːtɪ] *adj* (*esp Brit*) en rogne*, de mauvais poil*. **to get ~** se mettre en rogne*, prendre la mouche.

shit✱ [ʃɪt] (*vb*: *pret, ptp* **shat**) **1** *n* (*excrement*) merde✱ *f*; (*fig*) connerie✱ *f*. (*excl*) **~!** merde!✱. **2** *vi* chier✱.

shiver[1] [ˈʃɪvəʳ] **1** *vi* (*with cold*) frissonner, trembler (*with* de); (*with fear*) frissonner, trembler, tressaillir (*with* de); (*with pleasure*) frissonner, tressaillir (*with* de); *V* **shoe**.

2 *n* (*from cold*) frisson *m*; (*from fear, pleasure*) frisson, tressaillement *m*. **it sent ~s down his spine** cela lui a donné froid dans le dos; **he gave a ~** il a frissonné, il a eu un frisson; **to give sb the ~s** donner le frisson à qn.

shiver[2] [ˈʃɪvəʳ] **1** *n* (*fragment*) éclat *m*, fragment *m*. **2** *vi* (*shatter*) voler en éclats, se fracasser. **3** *vt* fracasser.

shivery [ˈʃɪvərɪ] *adj* (*from cold*) frissonnant, qui a des frissons; (*from fever*) fiévreux; (*from fear/emotion etc*) tremblant *or* frissonnant (de peur/d'émotion *etc*).

shoal[1] [ʃəʊl] *n* [*fish*] banc *m* (*de poissons*). (*fig*) **they came in (their) ~s** ils sont venus en foule; **~s of*** une grande quantité de, une masse de*; **~s of applications** une avalanche de demandes.

shoal[2] [ʃəʊl] *n* (*shallows*) haut-fond *m*, bas-fond *m*; (*sandbank*) banc *m* de sable, écueil *m*.

shock[1] [ʃɒk] **1** *n* **(a)** (*impact*) [*collision etc*] choc *m*, heurt *m*; [*earthquake, explosion*] secousse *f*.

(b) (*Elec*) décharge *f* (électrique). **to get a ~** recevoir une décharge (électrique), prendre le jus*; **she got a ~ from the refrigerator, the refrigerator gave her a ~** elle a reçu une décharge en touchant le réfrigérateur.

(c) (*to emotions, sensibilities etc*) choc *m*, coup *m*, secousse *f*; (*U: disgust*) dégoût *m*. **he got such a ~ when he heard that ...** cela lui a donné un tel choc *or* un tel coup *or* une telle secousse d'apprendre que ...; **he hasn't yet got over the ~ of her death** il ne s'est pas encore remis du choc que lui a causé sa mort; **the ~ of the election results** les résultats stupéfiants de l'élection; **their refusal came as a ~ to me** leur refus m'a stupéfié *or* ébahi; **it comes as a ~ to hear that ...** il est stupéfiant d'apprendre que ...; **you gave me a ~!** vous m'avez fait peur!; **I got such a ~!** j'ai eu une de ces émotions!*; **pale with ~** pâle de saisissement; **my feeling is one of ~ at the idea that ...** j'éprouve un sentiment d'horreur à l'idée que ..., je suis bouleversé à l'idée que ...

(d) (*Med*) commotion *f*, choc *m*. **to be suffering from ~** être sous le coup du choc, être commotionné; **in a state of ~** en état de choc; *V* **shell** *etc*.

2 *cpd* (*Mil etc*) *tactics, troops* de choc. (*Aut*) **shock absorber** amortisseur *m*; **shockproof** (*Tech*) anti-choc *inv*; (* *fig*) *person* difficile à choquer; **shock resistant** résistant aux chocs; (*Med*) **shock therapy, shock treatment** (traitement *m* par) électrochoc *m*; (*Phys*) **shock wave** onde *f* de choc.

3 *adj* (*) *result, reaction* stupéfiant.

4 *vt* (*take aback*) secouer, retourner*; (*stronger*) bouleverser; (*disgust*) dégoûter; (*scandalize*) choquer, scandaliser. **his mother's death ~ed him into going to see his father** bouleversé par la mort de sa mère il est allé voir son père; **to ~ sb out of his complacency** secouer (*fig*) qn jusqu'à ce qu'il perde sa suffisance.

shock[2] [ʃɒk] *n*: **a ~ of hair** une tignasse*.

shocker [ˈʃɒkəʳ] *n* **(a)** (*) **he's a ~** il est impossible *or* imbuvable*; **his essay's a ~** sa dissertation est une catastrophe*; **what a ~ of a day!** quel temps épouvantable! *or* de cochon!* **(b)** (*cheap book*) livre *m* à sensation.

shocking [ˈʃɒkɪŋ] **1** *adj* **(a)** (*appalling*) *crime, cruelty* affreux, atroce, odieux; *news, sight* atroce, bouleversant; (*scandalizing*) *book, behaviour* choquant, scandaleux; *decision, waste of money* scandaleux; *price* exorbitant, scandaleux. **the film wasn't really ~** le film n'avait rien de vraiment choquant.

(b) (*very bad*) *weather, results, cold, cough* affreux, terrible, épouvantable; *handwriting* épouvantable; *meal* infect. **she has ~ taste** son manque de goût est atroce.

2 *adv* (*) terriblement, affreusement.

shockingly [ˈʃɒkɪŋlɪ] *adv unfair, expensive, difficult* terriblement, affreusement; *behave* (*appallingly*) épouvantablement, de façon terrible; (*scandalously*) scandaleusement, de façon choquante; (*very badly*) très mal, odieusement; *play, act etc* de façon lamentable.

shod [ʃɒd] *pret, ptp of* **shoe 3**.

shoddily [ˈʃɒdɪlɪ] *adv made* mal, à la six-quatre-deux*; *behave* de façon mesquine.

shoddiness [ˈʃɒdɪnɪs] *n* [*work, goods*] mauvaise qualité; [*behaviour*] bassesse *f*, mesquinerie *f*.

shoddy [ˈʃɒdɪ] **1** *adj work* de mauvaise qualité; *goods* de mauvaise qualité, mal fait, mal fini; *behaviour* mesquin. **2** *n* (*cloth*) tissu *m* fait d'effiloché.

shoe [ʃuː] (*vb*: *pret, ptp* **shod**) **1** *n* chaussure *f*, soulier *m*; (*horse~*) fer *m* (à cheval); (*brake ~*) sabot *m* (de frein). **to have one's ~s on/off** être chaussé/déchaussé; **to put on one's ~s** mettre ses chaussures, se chausser; **to take off one's ~s** enlever ses chaussures, se déchausser; (*fig*) **to shake** *or* **shiver in one's ~s** avoir une peur bleue, (*less strong*) être dans ses petits souliers*; (*fig*) **I wouldn't like to be in his ~s** je n'aimerais pas être à sa place; (*fig*) **to step into sb's ~s** succéder à qn; **he's waiting for dead men's ~s** il attend que quelqu'un meure pour prendre sa place; (*fig*) **you'll know where the ~ pinches when ...** vous vous trouverez serré *or* à court quand ...; (*fig*) **that's another pair of ~s** c'est une autre paire de manches; *V* **court** *etc*.

2 *cpd*: **shoeblack** cireur *m* de chaussures; **shoebrush** brosse *f* à chaussures; **shoe cream** crème *f* pour chaussures; **shoehorn** chausse-pied *m*; **shoelace** lacet *m* de soulier; (*fig*) **you are not fit** *or* **worthy to tie his shoelaces** vous n'êtes pas digne de délier le cordon de ses souliers; **shoe leather** cuir *m* pour chaussures; (*fig*) **I wore out a lot of shoe leather, it cost me a lot in shoe leather** ça m'est revenu cher en chaussures, j'ai dû faire des kilomètres à pied; **shoemaker** (*cobbler*) cordonnier *m*; (*manufacturer*) fabricant *m* de chaussures; (*shoeshop owner*) chausseur *m*; **shoe polish** cirage *m*; **shoe repair** réparation *f* de chaussures; **shoe repairer** cordonnier *m*; **shoe repairer's (shop)** cordonnerie *f*; (*U*) **shoe repairing** cordonnerie *f*; **shoeshine (boy), shoeshiner** cireur *m* de chaussures; **shoeshop** magasin *m* de chaussures; (*lit*) **shoestring = shoelace**; (*fig*) **to do sth on a shoestring** faire qch à peu de frais *or* avec peu d'argent; **they're living on a shoestring** ils sont gênés, ils doivent se serrer la ceinture*; **shoestring budget** budget *m* minime *or* infime; **shoetree** embauchoir *m*.

3 *vt horse* ferrer. [*person*] **to be well/badly shod** être bien/mal chaussé; (*Prov*) **the cobbler's children are always the worst**

shod ce sont les cordonniers qui sont les plus mal chaussés (*Prov*).

shone [ʃɒn] *pret, ptp of* **shine.**

shoo [ʃuː] **1** *excl* (*to animals*) pschtt!; (*to person*) ouste!* **2** *vt* (*also* ~ **away,** ~ **off**) chasser.

shook [ʃʊk] *pret of* **shake.**

shoot [ʃuːt] (*vb: pret, ptp* **shot**) **1** *n* **(a)** (*on branch etc*) pousse *f*, scion *m*, rejeton *m*; (*seedling*) pousse.

(b) (*chute*) glissière *f*, déversoir *m*.

(c) (*shooting party*) partie *f* de chasse; (*land*) (terrain *m* de) chasse *f*. (*fig*) **the whole (bang)** ~‡ (*things*) absolument tout, le tout, tout le tremblement* *or* le bataclan*; (*people*) tout le monde, tout le tremblement*.

2 *cpd*: **shoot-out*** fusillade *f*.

3 *vt* **(a)** *game* (*hunt*) chasser; (*kill*) abattre, tirer; *injured horse etc* abattre; *person* (*hit*) atteindre *or* (*wound*) blesser *or* (*kill*) tuer d'un coup de fusil (*or* de revolver *etc*), abattre, descendre*; (*execute*) fusiller. **to be shot in the head** être atteint *or* blessé *or* tué d'une balle dans la tête; **to be shot in the arm** recevoir une balle dans le bras, être atteint d'une balle au bras; **he had been shot through the heart** il avait reçu une balle en plein cœur; **to** ~ **sb dead** abattre qn; **he was shot as a spy** il a été fusillé pour espionnage; (*hum*) **people have been shot for less*** c'est se mettre la corde au cou*; (*hum*) **you'll get shot for that!*** tu vas te faire incendier pour ça!‡

(b) (*fire*) *gun* tirer *or* lâcher un coup de (*at* sur); *arrow* décocher, lancer, tirer (*at* sur); *bullet* tirer (*at* sur); *rocket, missile* lancer (*at* sur). (*fig*) **the volcano shot lava high into the air** le volcan projetait *or* lançait de la lave dans les airs; **they shot the coal into the cellar** ils ont déversé le charbon dans la cave; **to** ~ **rubbish** déverser des ordures; **to** ~ **a goal, to** ~ **the ball into the net** marquer *or* shooter un but; **he shot the bolt** (*fastened*) il a mis *or* poussé le verrou; (*opened*) il a tiré le verrou; (*fig*) **he has shot his bolt** il a joué sa dernière carte; (*fig*) **to** ~ **a line**‡ faire de l'épate*, en mettre plein la vue*; (*Brit fig*) **to** ~ **a line about**‡ raconter des histoires *or* des bobards* à propos de; (*US fig*) **to** ~ **the works**‡ risquer le tout pour le tout; **to** ~ **dice** jeter les dés; *V* **pool**².

(c) (*fig*) *look, glance* décocher, lancer (*at* à); *[searchlight etc] beam of light* braquer (*at* sur); *[sun] ray of light* lancer, darder. **he shot a smile at her** il lui a jeté un sourire, il lui a souri rapidement; **to** ~ **questions at sb** bombarder *or* mitrailler qn de questions.

(d) (*Cine etc*) *film, scene* tourner; *subject of snapshot etc* prendre (en photo).

(e) *rapids* franchir, descendre; *bridge* passer rapidement sous.

4 *vi* **(a)** (*with gun, bow*) tirer (*at* sur); (*Sport*) (*at target*) tirer (à la cible). (*at game*) **to go** ~**ing** chasser, aller à la chasse, tirer le gibier; **to** ~ **to kill** tirer pour abattre; **to** ~ **on sight** tirer à vue; **he can't** ~ **straight** il tire mal *or* comme un pied*.

(b) (*move quickly*) *[person, car, ball etc]* **to** ~ **in/out/past** *etc* entrer/sortir/passer *etc* en flèche; **to** ~ **along** filer; **he shot to the door** il n'a fait qu'un bond jusqu'à la porte; **the car shot out of a side street** la voiture est sortie *or* a débouché à toute vitesse d'une rue transversale; **he shot across the road** il a traversé la rue comme une flèche; **the ball shot over the wall** le ballon a été projeté par-dessus le mur; **the bullet shot past his ears** la balle lui a sifflé aux oreilles; **the cat shot up the tree** le chat a grimpé à l'arbre à toute vitesse; **the pain went** ~**ing up his arm** la douleur au bras le lancinait, son bras l'élançait; (*in class etc*) **he has shot ahead in the last few weeks** il a fait des progrès énormes depuis quelques semaines.

(c) (*Ftbl etc*) shooter, tirer. **to** ~ **at goal** shooter, faire un shoot; (*fig: in conversation*) ~**!**‡ vas-y!, dis ce que tu as à dire!, dis!*.

(d) (*Bot*) bourgeonner, pousser.

shoot away 1 *vi* **(a)** (*Mil etc: fire*) continuer à tirer, tirer sans arrêt.

(b) (*move*) partir comme une flèche, s'enfuir à toutes jambes.

2 *vt sep* = **shoot off 2b.**

shoot back *vi* **(a)** (*Mil etc*) retourner le (*or* son *etc*) feu (*at* à).

(b) (*move*) retourner *or* rentrer *or* revenir en flèche.

shoot down *vt sep* **(a)** *plane* abattre, descendre. (*Aviat*) **he was shot down in flames** son avion s'est abattu en flammes; (*fig*) **to shoot down in flames*** *project* démolir; *person* descendre en flammes*.

(b) (*kill*) *person* abattre, descendre*.

shoot off 1 *vi* = **shoot away 1b.**

2 *vt sep* **(a)** *gun* décharger, faire partir. (*fig*) **he's always shooting his mouth off**‡ il faut toujours qu'il ouvre (*subj*) le bec* *or* sa grande gueule‡; **to shoot off (one's mouth) about sth** raconter des histoires *or* des bobards* au sujet de qch.

(b) he had a leg shot off il a eu une jambe emportée par un éclat d'obus, un éclat d'obus lui a emporté la jambe.

shoot out 1 *vi [person, car etc]* sortir comme une flèche; *[flame, water]* jaillir.

2 *vt sep* **(a) to shoot out one's tongue** *[person]* tirer la langue; *[snake]* darder sa langue; **he shot out his arm and grabbed my stick** il a avancé brusquement le bras et a attrapé ma canne; **he was shot out of the car** il a été éjecté de la voiture; *V* **neck.**

(b) to shoot it out avoir un règlement de compte (à coups de revolver).

3 shoot-out* *n V* **shoot 2.**

shoot up 1 *vi* **(a)** *[flame, water]* jaillir; *[rocket, price etc]* monter en flèche.

(b) (*grow quickly*) *[tree, plant]* pousser vite; *[child]* pousser comme un champignon.

2 shot up‡ *adj V* **shot 3.**

-shooter [ʃuːtəʳ] *n ending in cpds V* **pea, six** *etc.*

shooting [ˈʃuːtɪŋ] **1** *n* **(a)** (*U*) (*shots*) coups *mpl* de feu; (*continuous*) fusillade *f*. **I heard some** ~ **over there** j'ai entendu des coups de feu par là-bas; **the** ~ **caused 10 deaths** la fusillade a fait 10 morts.

(b) (*act*) (*murder*) meurtre *m or* assassinat *m* (avec une arme à feu); (*execution*) fusillade *f*, exécution *f*. **the** ~ **of a policeman in the main street** le meurtre d'un agent de police abattu dans la grand-rue.

(c) (*Hunting*) chasse *f*. **rabbit** ~ la chasse au lapin; **there's good** ~ **there** il y a une bonne chasse là-bas.

(d) (*Cine*) *[film, scene]* tournage *m*.

2 *adj pain* lancinant. ~ **star** étoile filante.

3 *cpd*: (*Brit Aut*) **shooting brake** break *m*; **shooting gallery** tir *m*, stand *m* (de tir); **there were a few shooting incidents last night** la nuit dernière il y a eu quelques échanges de coups de feu; (*fig*) **the whole shooting match*** tout le bataclan*, tout le tremblement*; **shooting range** tir *m*, stand *m* (de tir); **within shooting range** à portée de fusil (*or* de canon *etc*); **shooting stick** canne-siège *f*.

shop [ʃɒp] **1** *n* **(a)** (*Comm*) magasin *m*, (*small*) boutique *f*. **wine** ~ marchand *m* de vins; **at the butcher's** ~ à la boucherie, chez le boucher; **'The Toy S~'** 'la Maison du Jouet'; **mobile** *or* **travelling** ~ épicerie *etc* roulante; (*lit, fig*) **to shut up** ~ fermer boutique; (*fig*) **you've got** *or* **come to the wrong** ~* tu te trompes d'adresse* (*fig*); (*fig*) **to talk** ~ parler boutique *or* affaires *or* métier; (*fig*) **all over the** ~* (*everywhere*) partout; (*in confusion*) en désordre, en pagaïe*; *V* **back, corner, grocer, set up** *etc.*

(b) (*Ind*) (*workshop*) atelier *m*; (*factory*) usine *f*, fabrique *f*; (*business*) commerce *m*. **assembly** ~ atelier de montage; *V* **closed, machine** *etc.*

2 *cpd*: (*Brit*) **shop assistant** vendeur *m*, -euse *f*, employé(e) *m(f)* (de magasin); (*Ind*) **he works on the shop floor** c'est un ouvrier; (*Ind*) **the shop-floor (workers)** les ouvriers *mpl*; (*Brit*) **shopgirl** vendeuse *f*; **shopkeeper** marchand(e) *m(f)*, commerçant(e) *m(f)*; **shoplift** voler à l'étalage; **shoplifter** voleur *m*, -euse *f* à l'étalage; (*U*) **shoplifting** vol *m* à l'étalage; (*Brit*) **shop-soiled** qui a fait l'étalage *or* la vitrine, défraîchi; (*Ind*) **shop steward** délégué(e) syndical(e) *m(f)*; (*jargon*) **shoptalk*** jargon *m* (de métier); **I'm getting tired of shoptalk*** je commence à en avoir assez de parler affaires *or* métier; (*Brit*) **shopwalker**† chef *m* de rayon; **shop window** vitrine *f*; (*US*) **shopworn** = **shop-soiled.**

3 *vi*: **to** ~ **at Harrods** faire ses courses *or* ses achats chez Harrods; (*sign*) **'**~ **at Brown's'** 'achetez chez Brown'; **to go** ~**ping** (*locally etc*) faire les courses; (*on shopping expedition*) faire des courses, courir les magasins; **I was** ~**ping for a winter coat** je cherchais un manteau d'hiver.

4 *vt* (‡: *esp Brit: betray*) vendre, donner*.

shop around *vi* comparer les prix. **to shop around for sth** faire les magasins pour acheter qch au prix le plus avantageux; (*fig*) **you ought to shop around before you decide on a university** vous devriez vous renseigner à droite et à gauche avant de choisir une université.

shopper [ˈʃɒpəʳ] *n* **(a)** (*person*) personne *f* qui fait ses courses.

(b) (*) = **shopping bag**; *V* **shopping 2.**

shopping [ˈʃɒpɪŋ] **1** *n* (*U*) **(a)** ~ **is very tiring** faire les courses est très fatigant; **'open Thursdays for late evening** ~**'** 'ouvert le jeudi en nocturne', 'nocturne le jeudi'; *V* **window** *etc.*

(b) (*goods*) achats *mpl*.

2 *cpd street, district* commerçant. **shopping bag** sac *m* (à provisions), cabas *m*; **shopping basket** panier *m* (à provisions); **shopping centre** centre commercial; **shopping precinct** zone commerciale (piétonnière).

shore¹ [ʃɔːʳ] **1** *n [sea]* rivage *m*, bord *m*; *[lake]* rive *f*, bord; (*coast*) côte *f*, littoral *m*; (*beach*) plage *f*. (*fig liter*) **these** ~**s** ces rives; (*esp Naut*) **on** ~ à terre; (*Naut*) **to go on** ~ débarquer.

2 *cpd*: (*Naut*) **shore leave** permission *f* à terre; **shoreline** littoral *m*; **shoreward(s)** *V* **shoreward(s).**

shore² [ʃɔːʳ] **1** *n* (*for wall, tunnel*) étai *m*, étançon *m*; (*for tree*) étai; (*for ship*) accore *m*, étançon.

2 *vt* étayer, étançonner; accorer.

shore up *vt sep* **(a)** = **shore**² **2.**

(b) (*fig*) consolider.

shoreward [ˈʃɔːwəd] *adj, adv* vers le rivage *or* la côte *or* la rive.

shorewards [ˈʃɔːwədz] *adv* = **shoreward.**

shorn [ʃɔːn] *ptp of* **shear.**

short [ʃɔːt] **1** *adj* **(a)** *stick, skirt, hair, grass, arms* court; *person* petit, de petite taille; *step, walk* petit; *visit, message, conversation* court, bref; *programme* court; (*Ling*) *vowel, syllable* bref. **the** ~**est route** le chemin le plus court; **the** ~**est distance between two points** le plus court chemin d'un point à un autre; **a** ~ **distance away, a** ~ **way off** à peu de distance, à une faible distance; ~ **trousers** culottes courtes (*de petit garçon*); **he is rather** ~ **in the leg, he's got rather** ~ **legs** il est plutôt court de jambes *or [dog etc]* court sur pattes; **these trousers are** ~ **in the leg** ce pantalon est court de jambes; **one** ~ **year of happiness** une petite *or* brève année de bonheur; **to take a** ~ **holiday** prendre quelques jours de vacances; **a** ~ **time** *or* **while ago** il y a peu de temps; **in a** ~ **time** *or* **while** dans peu de temps, bientôt, sous peu; **time is getting** ~ il ne reste plus beaucoup de temps; **the days are getting** ~**er** les jours raccourcissent; **make the skirt** ~**er** raccourcis la jupe; (*fig*) **the** ~ **answer is that he ...** tout simplement il ...; ~ **and to the point** bref et précis; (*hum*) **that was** ~ **and sweet** ça n'a pas traîné (*hum*), ça a été du vite fait*; (*lit, fig*) ~**cut** raccourci *m*; **I took a** ~**cut through the fields** j'ai pris un raccourci *or* j'ai coupé *or* j'ai pris au plus court à travers champs; **you'll have to do it all with no** ~**cuts** il faudra que tu fasses le tout sans rien omettre; **a** ~ **drink** un petit verre d'apéritif (*or* d'alcool); ~ **drinks** des apéritifs, de l'alcool; (*fig*) **he got the ~ end of the stick** c'est lui qui en a pâti; **to win by a ~ head** (*Racing*) gagner d'une courte tête; (*fig*) gagner de justesse; (*Ind*) **~er hours and better pay** une réduction des heures de travail et une augmentation de salaire; **they want a ~er working week** on veut réduire la semaine de travail; **at ~ notice** dans un court *or* bref délai; **to have a ~ temper** être coléreux *or* soupe au lait* *inv*; (*Ind*) **to be on ~ time, to work ~ time** être en chômage partiel (*V also* **2**); (*fig*) **to make ~ work of sth** ne pas mettre beaucoup de temps à faire qch; (*fig*) **to make ~ work of sb*** envoyer promener qn*; *V also* **2** *and* **hair, shrift, story, term** *etc.*

(b) (*phrases*) **in ~** (enfin) bref; **'TV' is ~ for 'television'** 'TV' est l'abréviation de 'television'; **Fred is ~ for Frederick** Fred est le diminutif de Frederick; **he's called Fred for ~** son diminutif est Fred; **to be ~ of sugar** être à court de sucre, manquer de sucre; **I'm a bit ~ this month*** je suis un peu fauché* *or* à court ce mois-ci; **we're ~ of 3, we're 3 ~** il nous en manque 3, il s'en faut de 3; **I'm £2 ~** il me manque 2 livres; **we're not ~ of volunteers** nous ne manquons pas de volontaires; **not far ~ of £100** pas loin de 100 livres, presque 100 livres; **we are £2,000 ~ of our target** il nous manque encore 2.000 livres pour arriver à la somme que nous nous sommes fixée; **he fell 10 metres ~ of the winning post** il est tombé à 10 mètres du poteau d'arrivée; **it's little ~ of suicide** c'est presque un suicide, peu s'en faut que ce ne soit un suicide; **it's nothing ~ of robbery** c'est du vol ni plus ni moins; **nothing ~ of a revolution will satisfy them** seule la révolution saura les satisfaire, il ne leur faudra rien moins que la révolution pour les satisfaire; **I don't see what you can do ~ of asking him yourself** je ne vois pas ce que vous pouvez faire à moins de *or* si ce n'est lui demander vous-même; **he did everything ~ of asking her to marry him** il a tout fait sauf *or* hormis lui demander de l'épouser; **he's long on muscle but a bit ~ on brains*** il a beaucoup de muscle mais pas tellement de cervelle; *V* **breath** *etc.*

(c) (*insufficient etc*) insuffisant, incomplet (*f* -ète). **petrol is ~** *or* **in ~ supply at the moment** on manque d'essence en ce moment; **to give sb ~ change** ne pas rendre la monnaie juste à qn, ne pas rendre assez à qn; (*deliberately*) tricher en rendant la monnaie à qn; **to give ~ weight** *or* **~ measure** ne pas donner le poids juste; (*deliberately*) tricher sur le poids; *V* **commons.**

(d) (*curt*) *reply, manner* brusque, sec (*f* sèche). **he was rather ~ with me** il m'a répondu (*or* parlé *etc*) assez sèchement *or* brusquement, il s'est montré assez sec *or* brusque à mon égard.

(e) (*Fin*) *bill* à courte échéance; *loan* à court terme. **~ sale** vente *f* à découvert.

2 *cpd*: (*Culin*) **shortbread** sablé *m*; (*US*) **strawberry** *etc* **shortcake** tarte sablée aux fraises *etc*; (*lit, fig*) **short-change** ne pas donner son dû à, rouler*; (*Elec*) **short-circuit** (*n*) court-circuit *m*; (*vt*) (*Elec, fig*) court-circuiter; (*vi*) se mettre en court-circuit; **shortcoming** défaut *m*; (*Culin*) **short(crust) pastry** pâte brisée; (*Fin*) **short-dated** à courte échéance; **shortfall** manque *m*; **short-haired** *person* aux cheveux courts; *animal* à poil ras; **shorthand** *V* **shorthand**; **short-handed** à court de personnel *or* de main-d'œuvre; **short-haul** (*n*) camionnage *m*, zone courte; (*adj*) à courte distance; (*Zool*) **shorthorns** race *f* shorthorn; **short list** liste *f* de(s) candidats sélectionnés; **short-list** mettre sur la liste des candidats sélectionnés; **short-lived** *animal* à la vie éphémère; *happiness* de courte durée; **short-range** *shot, gun* de *or* à courte portée; *aircraft* à court rayon d'action; (*fig*) *plan, weather forecast* à court terme; **short sight** myopie *f*; **short-sighted** (*lit: esp Brit*) myope; (*fig*) *person* myope, qui manque de perspicacité; *policy, measure* qui manque de vision; **short-sightedness** (*lit*) myopie *f*; (*fig*) *[person]* myopie intellectuelle, manque *m* de perspicacité; *[policy, measure]* manque de vision; **short-sleeved** à manches courtes; **to be short-staffed** manquer de personnel, souffrir d'une pénurie de personnel; **short story** nouvelle *f*; **short-story writer** nouvelliste *mf*, conteur *m*, -euse *f*; **to be short-tempered** (*in general*) être coléreux *or* soupe au lait* *inv*, s'emporter facilement; (*in a bad temper*) être d'humeur irritable; **short-term** à court terme; (*Ind*) **short-time working** chômage partiel; (*Rad*) **shortwave** (*n*) ondes courtes; (*adj*) *radio* à ondes courtes; *transmission* sur ondes courtes; **short-winded** qui manque de souffle, au souffle court.

3 *adv*: **to cut ~** *speech, TV etc programme* couper court à, abréger; *class, visit, holiday* écourter, abréger; *person* couper la parole à (*V also* **cut 4a**); **the ball fell ~** le ballon n'est pas tombé assez loin (*V also* **fall 2i**); **to go ~ of sth** manquer de qch, se priver de qch; **sugar is running ~** le sucre commence à manquer; **to run ~ of sth** se trouver à court de qch, venir à manquer de qch; **the car stopped ~ of the house** la voiture s'est arrêtée avant (d'arriver au niveau de) la maison; (*fig*) **I'd stop ~ of murder** je n'irais pas jusqu'au meurtre (*V also* **stop 3b**); **to take sb up ~** couper la parole à qn; **to be taken ~*** être pris d'un besoin pressant*; *V* **sell.**

4 *n* **(a)** (*) (*Cine*) court métrage; (*Elec*) court-circuit *m*. (*drinks*) **~s** des apéritifs, de l'alcool; *V* **long**[1].

(b) (*Dress*) **(a pair of) ~s** un short.

5 *vt* (*Elec*) court-circuiter.

6 *vi* (*Elec*) se mettre en court-circuit.

shortage ['ʃɔːtɪdʒ] *n [corn, coal, energy, cash etc]* manque *m*, pénurie *f*; *[resources]* manque, insuffisance *f*. **in times of ~** en période de pénurie; **there was no ~ of water** on ne manquait pas d'eau; **owing to the ~ of staff** à cause d'une crise *or* pénurie de personnel; **the food ~** la disette *or* pénurie de vivres, la disette; **the housing ~** la crise du logement; **the ~ of £100 in the amount** l'absence *f or* le déficit de 100 livres dans la somme.

shorten ['ʃɔːtn] **1** *vt skirt, rope* raccourcir; *visit, holiday, journey* écourter; *life* abréger; *book, programme, letter* raccourcir, abréger; *syllabus* alléger; *distance, time* réduire.

2 *vi [days etc]* raccourcir. **the odds are ~ing** (*lit*) la cote s'affaiblit; (*fig*) les chances s'amenuisent *or* deviennent moindres.

shortening ['ʃɔːtnɪŋ] *n* (*U*) **(a)** (*V* **shorten**) raccourcissement *m*; abrègement *m*; allègement *m*; réduction *f*. **(b)** (*Culin*) matière grasse.

shorthand ['ʃɔːthænd] **1** *n* sténographie *f*. **to take sth down in ~** prendre qch en sténo, sténographier qch.

2 *cpd*: **shorthand notebook** carnet *m* de sténo; **shorthand notes** notes *fpl* en *or* de sténo; (*Brit*) **shorthand typing** sténodactylo *f*; (*Brit*) **shorthand typist** sténodactylo *mf*; **shorthand writer** sténo(graphe) *mf*.

shortish ['ʃɔːtɪʃ] *adj* (*V* **short**) plutôt court; assez petit; assez bref.

shortly ['ʃɔːtlɪ] *adv* **(a)** (*soon*) bientôt, dans peu de temps; (*in a few days*) prochainement, sous peu. **~ after** peu (de temps) après; **~ before twelve** peu avant midi. **(b)** (*concisely*) brièvement; (*curtly*) sèchement, brusquement.

shortness ['ʃɔːtnɪs] *n* **(a)** *[stick, skirt, hair, grass, arms]* peu *m or* manque *m* de longueur; *[person]* petite taille, petitesse *f*; *[visit, message, conversation, programme]* brièveté *f*, courte durée; *[vowel, syllable]* brévité *f*.

(b) (*curtness*) brusquerie *f*, sécheresse *f*.

shorty* ['ʃɔːtɪ] *n* courtaud(e) *m(f)*. **hey ~!** hé toi le *or* la petit(e)!

shot [ʃɒt] **1** *n* **(a)** (*act of firing*) coup *m*, décharge *f*; (*causing wound*) coup; (*sound*) coup (de feu *or* de fusil *etc*); (*bullet*) balle *f*; (*U: pellets: also* **lead ~**) plomb *m*. **not a single ~ was fired** on n'a pas tiré un seul coup; **to take ~** *or* **have** *or* **fire a ~ at sb/sth** tirer sur qn/qch; **good ~!** (c'était) bien visé! (*V also* **1c**); **a ~ across the bows, a warning ~** (*Naut*) un coup de semonce; (*fig*) un avertissement; **at the first ~** du premier coup; **the first ~ killed him** la première balle l'a tué; **I've got 4 ~s left** il me reste 4 coups *or* balles; **he is a good/bad ~** il est bon/mauvais tireur; (*fig*) **big ~*** huile‡ *f*, grosse légume‡, gros bonnet*; (*fig*) **Parthian ~** flèche *f* du Parthe; (*fig*) **to make a ~ in the dark** tenter le coup, deviner à tout hasard; (*fig*) **that was just a ~ in the dark** c'était dit à tout hasard; **he was off like a ~** il est parti comme une flèche; **he agreed like a ~*** il y a consenti sans hésiter *or* avec empressement; **would you go? — like a ~!*** est-ce que tu irais? — sans hésiter! *or* et comment!*; (*Sport*) **to put the ~** lancer le poids; *V* **crack, long**[1], **parting** *etc.*

(b) (*Space*) lancement *m*; *V* **moon, space.**

(c) (*Sport*) (*Ftbl, Golf, Hockey, Tennis etc*) coup *m*; (*throw*) lancer *m*. **good ~!** (c'était) bien joué!; **a ~ at goal** un shoot, un tir au but.

(d) (*attempt*) essai *m*, tentative *f*, coup *m*; (*guess*) hypothèse *f*; (*turn to play*) tour *m*. **to have a ~ at (doing) sth** essayer de faire qch; **have a ~ at it!** (*try it*) tentez le coup!; (*guess*) devinez!, dites voir!*

(e) (*Phot*) photo(graphie) *f*; (*Cine*) prise *f* de vues.

(f) (*injection*) piqûre *f* (*against* contre); (*of alcohol*) coup *m*. (*fig*) **a ~ in the arm** un coup de fouet, un stimulant.

2 *cpd*: **shotgun** fusil *m* de chasse; (*fig*) **shotgun marriage** *or* **wedding** régularisation *f* (précipitée), mariage forcé; (*Sport*) **shot put** lancer *m* du poids.

3 *pret, ptp of* **shoot. to get/be ~ of‡** se débarrasser/être débarrassé de; (*exhausted*) **to be (all) ~ up‡** être exténué *or* sur les rotules‡.

4 *adj*: **~ silk** soie changeante; **~ with yellow** strié de jaune.

should [ʃʊd] *modal aux vb* (*cond of* **shall**: *neg* **should not** *abbr* **shouldn't**) **(a)** (*indicating obligation, advisability, desirability*) **I should go and see her** je devrais aller la voir, il faudrait que j'aille la voir; **should I go too? — yes you should** devrais-je y aller aussi? — oui vous devriez *or* ça vaudrait mieux; **he thought he should tell you** il a pensé qu'il ferait bien de vous le dire *or* qu'il devrait vous le dire; (*frm*) **you should know that we have spoken to him** il faut que vous sachiez que nous lui avons parlé; **you should have been a teacher** vous auriez dû être professeur; **shouldn't you go and see her?** est-ce que vous ne devriez pas aller la voir?, est-ce que vous ne feriez pas bien d'aller la voir?; **everything is as it should be** tout est comme il se doit, tout est en ordre; **... which is as it should be** ... comme il se doit; **how should I know?** comment voulez-vous que je (le) sache?

(b) (*indicating probability*) **he should win the race** il devrait gagner la course, il va probablement gagner la course; **he should have got there by now I expect** je pense qu'il est arrivé *or* qu'il a dû arriver; **that should be John at the door now** ça doit être Jean (qui frappe *or* qui sonne); **this should do the trick*** ça devrait faire l'affaire; **why should he suspect me?** pourquoi me soupçonnerait-il?

(c) (*often used to form cond tense in 1st person*) **I should** *or* **I'd go if he invited me** s'il m'invitait, j'irais; **we should have come if we had known** si nous avions su, nous serions venus; **will you come? — I should like to** est-ce que vous viendrez? — j'aimerais bien; **I shouldn't be surprised if he comes** *or* **came** *or* **were to come** ça ne m'étonnerait pas qu'il vienne; **I should think there were about 40** (je pense qu')il devait y en avoir environ 40; **was it a good film? — I should think it was!** est-ce que c'était un bon film? — je pense bien! *or* et comment!*; **he's coming to apologize — I should think so too!** il vient présenter ses excuses — j'espère bien!; **I should hope not!** il ne manquerait plus que ça!*; **I should say so!** et comment!*

(d) (*subj uses*) (*frm*) **it is necessary that he should be told** il faut qu'on le lui dise; (*frm*) **lest he should change his mind** de crainte qu'il ne change (*subj*) d'avis; **it is surprising that he should be so young** c'est étonnant qu'il soit si jeune; **who should come in but Paul!** et devinez qui est entré? Paul!

shoulder ['ʃəʊldəʳ] **1** *n* **(a)** (*Anat, Culin, Dress etc*) épaule *f*. **to have broad ~s** (*lit*) être large d'épaules *or* de carrure; (*fig*) avoir les reins solides (*fig*); **the ~s are too wide, it's too wide across the ~s** c'est trop large d'épaules *or* de carrure; **put my jacket round your ~s** mets *or* jette ma veste sur tes épaules *or* sur ton dos; (*lit, fig*) **to cry** *or* **weep on sb's ~** pleurer sur l'épaule de qn; **she had her bag on** *or* **over one ~** elle portait son sac à l'épaule; **they stood ~ to ~** (*lit*) ils étaient coude à coude *or* côte à côte; (*fig*) ils se serraient les coudes, ils s'entraidaient, ils unissaient leurs efforts; (*fig*) **all the responsibilities had fallen on his ~s** toutes les responsabilités étaient retombées sur lui *or* sur ses épaules; (*fig*) **to put** *or* **set one's ~ to the wheel** s'atteler à la tâche; *V* **cold, head, rub, straighten** *etc.*

(b) *[road]* accotement *m*, bas-côté *m*; *[hill]* contrefort *m*, épaulement *m*. *[road]* **hard/soft ~** accotement stabilisé/non stabilisé.

2 *cpd*: **shoulder bag** sac *m* à bandoulière; **shoulder blade** omoplate *f*; **it hit him between the shoulder blades** cela l'a atteint en plein entre les deux épaules; **to carry sb shoulder-high** porter qn en triomphe; **shoulder-length hair** cheveux mi-longs *or* jusqu'aux épaules; **shoulder pad** épaulette *f* (*rembourrage d'épaules de vêtement*); **shoulder strap** *[garment]* bretelle *f*; *[bag]* bandoulière *f*; (*Mil*) patte *f* d'épaule.

3 *vt* **(a)** *load, case etc* charger sur son épaule; *child etc* hisser sur ses épaules; (*fig*) *responsibility* endosser; *task* se charger de. (*Mil*) **to ~ arms** porter l'arme; **~ arms!** portez arme!

(b) to ~ sb aside *or* **out of the way** écarter qn d'un coup d'épaule; **to ~ one's way through the crowd** se frayer un chemin à travers *or* dans la foule à coups d'épaules.

shouldn't ['ʃʊdnt] = **should not**; *V* **should.**

shout [ʃaʊt] **1** *n* cri *m* (*of joy etc* de joie *etc*). **there were ~s of applause/protest/laughter** des acclamations/des protestations bruyantes/des éclats de rire retentirent; **he gave a ~ of laughter** il a éclaté de rire; **to give sb a ~** appeler qn; **~s of 'long live the queen' could be heard** on entendait crier 'vive la reine'; **it's my ~‡** c'est ma tournée*.

2 *vt order, slogan* crier. **'no' he ~ed** 'non' cria-t-il; **to ~ o.s. hoarse** s'enrouer à force de crier; *V* **head.**

3 *vi* crier, pousser des cris (*for joy etc* de joie *etc*). **stop ~ing, I'm not deaf!** ne crie pas comme ça, je ne suis pas sourd!; **to ~ with laughter** éclater de rire; **to ~ for help** crier *or* appeler au secours; **she ~ed for Jane to come** elle a appelé Jane en criant *or* à grands cris; **she ~ed for someone to come and help her** elle a appelé pour qu'on vienne l'aider; **he ~ed to** *or* **at me to throw him the rope** il m'a crié de lui lancer la corde; **he's always ~ing at me** il crie tout le temps après moi, il me crie tout le temps après*; (*fig*) **it's nothing to ~ about*** ça n'a rien d'extraordinaire, il n'y a pas de quoi en faire un plat*.

shout down *vt sep speaker* huer. **they shouted down the proposal** ils ont rejeté la proposition avec de hauts cris.

shout out 1 *vi* pousser un cri.

2 *vt sep order* crier; *slogan* crier, lancer.

shouting ['ʃaʊtɪŋ] *n* (*U*) cris *mpl*, clameur *f*; (*noise of quarrelling*) éclats *mpl* de voix. (*fig*) **it's all over bar the ~** l'important est fait (il ne reste plus que les détails).

shove [ʃʌv] **1** *n* poussée *f*. **to give sb/sth a ~** pousser qn/qch; **give it a good ~** poussez-le un bon coup.

2 *cpd*: (*Brit*) **shove-ha'penny** jeu *m* de palet de table.

3 *vt* **(a)** (*push*) pousser; (*with effort*) pousser avec peine *or* effort; (*thrust*) *stick, finger etc* enfoncer (*into* dans, *between* entre); *rag* fourrer (*into* dans); (*jostle*) bousculer. **to ~ sth in/out/down** *etc* faire entrer/sortir/descendre *etc* qch en poussant; **to ~ sth/sb aside** pousser qch/qn de côté, écarter qch/qn (d'un geste); **to ~ sth into a drawer/one's pocket** fourrer qch dans un tiroir/sa poche; **stop shoving me!** arrêtez de me pousser! *or* bousculer!; **to ~ sb into a room** pousser qn dans une pièce; **to ~ sb against a wall** pousser *or* presser qn contre un mur; **to ~ sb off the pavement** pousser qn du trottoir, (*by jostling*) obliger qn à descendre du trottoir (en le bousculant); **to ~ sb/sth out of the way** écarter qn/qch en poussant, pousser qn/qch à l'écart; **he ~d the box under the table** (*moved*) il a poussé *or* fourré la boîte sous la table; (*hid*) il a vite caché la boîte sous la table; **they ~d the car off the road** ils ont poussé la voiture sur le bas-côté; **she ~d the books off the table** elle a poussé *or* balayé les livres de dessus la table; **he ~d his finger into my eye** il m'a mis le doigt dans l'œil; **he ~d his head through the window** il a mis *or* passé la tête par la fenêtre; **he ~d the book into my hand** il m'a fourré le livre dans la main; **to ~ a door open** ouvrir une porte en poussant *or* d'une poussée, pousser une porte (pour l'ouvrir); **to ~ one's way through the crowd** se frayer un chemin dans *or* à travers la foule, s'ouvrir un passage dans la foule en poussant.

(b) (*: *put*) mettre, poser, ficher*, flanquer*.

4 *vi* pousser. **stop shoving!** arrêtez de pousser!, ne bousculez pas!; **he ~d (his way) past me** il m'a dépassé en me bousculant; **two men ~d (their way) past** deux hommes sont passés en jouant des coudes *or* en bousculant les gens; **he ~d (his way) through the crowd** il s'est frayé un chemin dans *or* à travers la foule.

shove about, shove around *vt sep* (*lit*) *object* pousser çà et là *or* dans tous les sens; *person* bousculer; (**fig: treat high-handedly*) en prendre à son aise avec.

shove away *vt sep person, object* repousser.

shove back *vt sep* (*push back*) *person, chair* repousser; (*replace*) remettre (à sa place); (*into pocket etc*) fourrer de nouveau, remettre.

shove down* *vt sep object* poser. **he shoved down a few notes before he forgot** il a griffonné *or* gribouillé quelques notes pour ne pas oublier.

shove off 1 *vi* (*Naut*) pousser au large; (*: *leave*) ficher le camp*, filer*, se tirer‡.

2 *vt sep boat* pousser au large, déborder.

shove on* *vt sep* **(a)** *one's coat etc* enfiler; *hat* enfoncer.

(b) shove on another record mets donc un autre disque.

shove out *vt sep boat* pousser au large, déborder; *person* mettre à la porte.

shove over 1 *vi* (*: *move over*) se pousser.

2 *vt sep* **(a)** (*knock over*) *chair etc* renverser; *person* faire tomber (par terre).

(b) (*over cliff etc*) pousser.

(c) shove it over to me* passe-le-moi.

shove up* *vi* = **shove over 1.**

shovel ['ʃʌvl] **1** *n* pelle *f*; (*mechanical*) pelleteuse *f*, pelle mécanique.

2 *vt coal, grain* pelleter; (*also* **~ out**) *snow, mud* enlever à la pelle. **to ~ earth into a pile** pelleter la terre pour en faire un tas; (*fig*) **he ~led the food into his mouth*** il fourrait* *or* enfournait* la nourriture dans sa bouche.

shovel up *vt sep sth spilt etc* ramasser avec une pelle *or* à la pelle; *snow* enlever à la pelle.

shovelful ['ʃʌvlfʊl] *n* pelletée *f*.

show [ʃəʊ] (*vb: pret* **showed**, *ptp* **shown** *or* **showed**) **1** *n* **(a)** *[hatred etc]* manifestation *f*, démonstration *f*; *[affection etc]* démonstration, témoignage *m*; (*semblance*) apparence *f*, semblant *m*; (*ostentation*) parade *f*. **there were some fine pieces on ~** quelques beaux objets étaient exposés; **an impressive ~ of power** un impressionnant étalage de force; **a ~ of hands** un vote à main levée; **to vote by ~ of hands** voter à main levée; **the dahlias make** *or* **are a splendid ~** les dahlias sont splendides (à voir) *or* offrent un spectacle splendide; **they make a great ~ of their wealth** ils font parade *or* étalage de leur richesse; **with a ~ of emotion** en affectant l'émotion, en affectant d'être ému; **they made a ~ of resistance** ils ont fait semblant de résister, ils ont offert un simulacre de résistance; **to make a ~ of doing** faire semblant *or* mine de faire; **just for ~** pour l'effet.

(b) (*exhibition*) (*Agr, Art, Tech etc*) exposition *f*; (*Comm*) foire *f*; (*Agr: contest*) concours *m*. **flower ~** floralies *fpl*; (*smaller*) exposition de fleurs; **dress ~** défilé *m* de couture; *[artist etc]* **he's holding his first London ~** il a sa première exposition à Londres, il expose à Londres pour la première fois; **the Boat S~** le Salon de la Navigation; *V* **dog, fashion, motor** *etc.*

(c) (*Theat etc*) spectacle *m*; (*variety* **~**) show *m*. **there are several good ~s on in London** on donne plusieurs bons spectacles à Londres en ce moment; **I often go to a ~** je vais souvent au spectacle; **the last ~ starts at 9** (*Theat*) la dernière représentation *or* (*Cine*) la dernière séance commence à 21 heures; **there is no ~ on Sundays** (*Theat*) pas de représentation le dimanche; (*Cine*) pas de séance le dimanche; **on with the ~!** que la représentation commence (*subj*)! *or* continue (*subj*)!; **the ~ goes on** (*Theat*) le spectacle continue; (*fig*) il faut continuer malgré tout.

(d) (*phrases*) (*esp Brit*) **good ~!*** bravo!; **to put up a good ~** faire bonne figure, bien se défendre*; **to make a poor ~** faire triste *or* piètre figure; **it's a poor ~*** c'est lamentable, il n'y a pas de quoi être fier; **it's a poor ~* that ...** il est malheureux que ...+*subj*; **this is Paul's ~*** c'est Paul qui commande ici; **to run the ~*** faire marcher l'affaire; **to give the ~ away*** vendre la mèche*; *V* **steal** *etc.*

2 *cpd*: **show biz‡** = **show business; show business** le monde du spectacle, l'industrie *f* du spectacle; (*lit, fig*) **showcase** vitrine *f*; **showdown** épreuve *f* de force; (*Brit*) **show flat** appartement *m* témoin; **show girl** girl *f*; **showground** champ *m* de foire; (*Brit*) **showhouse** maison *f* témoin; (*U*) **show jumping** concours *m* hippique, jumping *m*; **showman** (*in fair, circus etc*) forain *m*; (*fig*) **he's a real showman** il a vraiment le sens de la mise en scène (*fig*); **showmanship** art *m or* don *m or* sens *m* de la mise en scène; **show-off** m'as-tu-vu(e)* *m(f)* (*pl inv*); **showpiece** (*of exhibition etc*) trésor *m*, joyau *m*, clou* *m*; **this vase is a real showpiece** ce vase est une pièce remarquable; **the new school is a showpiece** *or* **showplace** la nouvelle école est un modèle du genre; **showplace** (*tourist attraction*) lieu *m* de grand intérêt touristique; **showroom** magasin *m or* salle *f* d'exposition; (*Aut*) **in showroom condition** à l'état *m* de neuf; **he/it was a show-stopper*** il était/c'était le clou* du spectacle.

3 *vt* **(a)** (*display, make visible*) montrer, faire voir; *ticket, passport* montrer, présenter; (*exhibit*) *goods for sale, picture, dog* exposer. **~ it me!** faites voir!, montrez-le moi!; **we're going to ~ (you) some slides** nous allons (vous) passer *or* projeter quelques diapositives; **they ~ a film during the flight** on passe un film *or* il y a une projection de cinéma pendant le vol; **what is ~ing at that cinema/at the Odeon?** qu'est-ce qu'on donne *or* qu'est-ce qui passe dans ce cinéma/à l'Odéon?; **the film was first ~n in 1974** ce film est sorti en 1974; **it has been ~n on television** c'est passé à la télévision; (*in shop*) **what can I ~ you?** que puis-je vous montrer?, que désirez-vous voir?; **as ~n by the graph** comme le montre *or* l'indique le graphique; **as ~n in the illustration on page 4** voir l'illustration page 4; (*fig*) **there's nothing to ~ for it** on ne le dirait pas, ça ne se voit *or* ne se remarque pas; **he has nothing to ~ for it** il n'en a rien tiré, ça ne lui a rien donné *or* apporté; **he has nothing to ~ for all the effort he has put into it** les efforts qu'il y a consacrés n'ont rien donné; **I ought to ~ myself at Paul's party** il faudrait que je fasse acte de présence à la soirée de Paul; **he daren't ~ himself** *or* **his face there again** il n'ose plus s'y montrer *or* montrer son nez là-bas*; (*fig*) **to ~ one's hand** *or* **cards** dévoiler ses intentions, abattre son jeu *or* ses cartes; (*fig*) **to ~ a clean pair of heels** se sauver à toutes jambes; (*Brit fig*) **~ a leg!*** lève-toi!, debout!; (*lit, fig*) **to ~ one's teeth** montrer les dents; (*fig*) **to ~ sb the door** mettre qn à la porte; (*fig*) **to ~ the flag** être là pour le principe, faire acte de présence.

(b) (*indicate*) *[dial, clock etc]* indiquer, marquer; (*gen*) montrer, indiquer. **what time does your watch ~?** quelle heure est-il à votre montre?; (*Comm, Fin*) **to ~ a loss/profit** indiquer une perte/un bénéfice; **the figures ~ a rise over last year's sales** les chiffres montrent *or* indiquent que les ventes ont augmenté par rapport à l'année dernière; **the roads are ~n in red** les routes sont marquées en rouge.

(c) (*demonstrate*) montrer, faire voir; (*reveal*) montrer, laisser voir; (*explain*) montrer, expliquer; (*prove*) montrer, prouver; *one's intelligence, kindness, courage, tact* montrer, faire preuve de; *one's interest, surprise, agreement* montrer, manifester; *one's approval* montrer, indiquer; *one's gratitude, respect* témoigner. **to ~ loyalty** se montrer loyal (*to sb* envers qn); **that dress ~s her bra** cette robe laisse voir son soutien-gorge; **this skirt ~s the dirt** cette jupe est salissante; **it's ~ing signs of wear** cela porte des signes d'usure; **he was ~ing signs of tiredness** il montrait des signes de fatigue; **it ~ed signs of having been used** il était visible qu'on s'en était servi, manifestement on s'en était servi; **it was ~ing signs of rain** il avait l'air de vouloir pleuvoir; **to ~ fight** faire montre de combativité; **her choice of clothes ~s good taste** sa façon de s'habiller témoigne de son bon goût; **he ~ed that he was angry** il a montré *or* manifesté *or* laissé voir *or* laissé paraître sa colère; **she's beginning to ~ her age** elle commence à faire son âge; **this ~s great intelligence** cela montre *or* révèle *or* dénote beaucoup d'intelligence; **he ~ed himself (to be) a coward** il s'est montré *or* révélé lâche; **to ~ sth to be true** démontrer la vérité de qch, montrer que qch est vrai; **it all goes to ~ that ...** tout cela montre *or* prouve bien que ...; **it only *or* just goes to ~!*** tu m'en diras tant!*, c'est bien ça la vie!; **I ~ed him that it was impossible** je lui ai prouvé *or* démontré que c'était impossible; **he ~ed me how it works** il m'a montré *or* il m'a fait voir comment cela fonctionne; (*fig*) **I'll ~ him!*** je lui apprendrai!; **to ~ sb the way** montrer *or* indiquer le chemin à qn; **I'll ~ you the way** suivez-moi (je vais vous montrer le chemin); *V* **willing** *etc.*

(d) (*guide, conduct*) **to ~ sb into the room** faire entrer qn dans la pièce; **to ~ sb to his seat** placer qn; **to ~ sb to the door** reconduire qn jusqu'à la porte; **to ~ sb over *or* round a house** faire visiter une maison à qn.

4 *vi* **(a)** *[emotion]* être visible; *[stain, scar]* se voir; *[underskirt etc]* dépasser. **it doesn't ~** cela ne se voit pas, on ne dirait pas; **don't worry, it won't ~** ne t'inquiète pas, ça ne se verra pas; **his fear ~ed on his face** la peur se voyait *or* se lisait sur son visage.

(b) (‡) = **show up 1b.**

show in *vt sep visitor etc* faire entrer.

show off 1 *vi* crâner*, poser (pour la galerie). **she's always showing off** c'est une crâneuse* *or* une poseuse; **stop showing off** (*gen*) arrête de crâner* *or* d'en fiche plein la vue*; (*showing off knowledge*) arrête d'étaler ta science*.

2 *vt sep* **(a)** *sb's beauty, complexion etc* faire valoir, mettre en valeur.

(b) (*pej*) *one's wealth, knowledge etc* faire parade *or* étalage de, étaler.

3 show-off *n V* **show 2.**

4 showing-off *n V* **showing 2.**

show out *vt sep visitor etc* accompagner *or* reconduire (jusqu'à la porte).

show through *vi* se voir au travers.

show up 1 *vi* **(a)** (*stand out*) *[feature]* ressortir; *[mistake]* être visible *or* manifeste; *[stain]* se voir (nettement). **the tower showed up clearly against the sky** la tour se détachait nettement sur le ciel.

(b) (*appear*) arriver, venir, se pointer*.

2 *vt sep* **(a)** *visitor etc* faire monter.

(b) *fraud, imposter* démasquer, dénoncer; *flaw, defect* faire ressortir.

(c) (*embarrass*) faire honte à (en public).

shower ['ʃaʊəʳ] **1** *n* **(a)** *[rain]* averse *f*; (*fig*) *[blows]* volée *f*, avalanche *f*, grêle *f*; *[sparks, stones, arrows]* pluie *f*; *[blessings]* déluge *m*; *[insults]* torrent *m*, flot *m*.

(b) (*also* **~ bath**) douche *f*. **to have *or* take a ~** prendre une douche.

(c) (*Brit: pej: people*) bande *f* de crétins*.

(d) (*before wedding*) **to give a ~ for sb** organiser une soirée pour donner ses cadeaux à qn.

2 *cpd*: **shower cap** bonnet *m* de douche; **showerproof** imperméable; **shower unit** bloc-douche *m*.

3 *vt* (*fig*) **to ~ sb with gifts/praise, to ~ gifts/praise on sb** combler qn de cadeaux/de louanges; **to ~ blows on sb** faire pleuvoir des coups sur qn; **to ~ abuse *or* insults on sb** accabler *or* couvrir qn d'injures.

showery ['ʃaʊərɪ] *adj day* pluvieux. **it will be ~** il y aura des averses.

showing ['ʃəʊɪŋ] **1** *n* **(a)** *[pictures etc]* exposition *f*; *[film]* projection *f*. (*Cine*) **the first ~ is at 8 p.m.** la première séance est à 20 heures; (*Cine, TV*) **another ~ of this film** une nouvelle projection de ce film.

(b) (*performance*) performance *f*. **on this ~ he doesn't stand much chance** si c'est là ce dont il est capable, il n'a pas de grandes chances.

(c) on his own ~ de son propre aveu.

2 *cpd*: (*U*) **showing-off** pose *f*, crânerie* *f*.

shown [ʃəʊn] *ptp of* **show.**

showy ['ʃəʊɪ] *adj garment, material, décor* qui attire l'attention, voyant (*pej*), tape-à-l'œil* *inv* (*pej*); *colour* éclatant, voyant (*pej*), criard (*pej*); (*pej*) *manner* ostentatoire, prétentieux; (*pej*) *ceremony* plein d'ostentation.

shrank [ʃræŋk] *pret of* **shrink.**

shrapnel ['ʃræpnl] *n* (*U*) éclats *mpl* d'obus.

shred [ʃred] **1** *n [cloth, paper, skin, plastic sheeting]* lambeau *m*; (*fig*) *[truth]* parcelle *f*, grain *m*; *[commonsense]* once *f*, atome *m*, grain. **not a ~ of evidence** pas la plus petite preuve; **her dress hung in ~s** sa robe était en lambeaux; **without a ~ of clothing on** nu comme un ver, complètement nu; **to tear to ~s** mettre en lambeaux, déchiqueter; (*fig*) *argument etc* démolir entièrement, ne rien laisser subsister de.

2 *vt paper etc* mettre en lambeaux, déchiqueter; *carrots etc* râper; *cabbage, lettuce* couper en lanières.

shredder ['ʃredəʳ] *n* (*for vegetables etc*) moulin *m* à légumes, moulinette *f*; (*for documents etc*) destructeur *m* (de documents).

shrew [ʃruː] *n* **(a)** (*Zool*) musaraigne *f*. **(b)** (*woman*) mégère *f*, chipie* *f*; *V* **taming.**

shrewd [ʃruːd] *adj person* perspicace, habile, astucieux; *assessment* perspicace; *plan* astucieux. **I have a ~ idea that ...** je soupçonne fortement que ..., j'ai l'impression très nette que ...; **I've a ~ idea of what he will say** je vois d'ici *or* je sais d'avance ce qu'il va dire; **I can make a ~ guess at how many there were** je peux deviner à peu près combien il y en avait.

shrewdly ['ʃruːdlɪ] *adv* avec perspicacité, habilement, astucieusement.

shrewdness ['ʃruːdnɪs] *n [person]* perspicacité *f*, habileté *f*, sagacité *f*; *[assessment]* perspicacité; *[plan]* astuce *f*.

shrewish ['ʃruːɪʃ] *adj* acariâtre, de mégère, de chipie*.

shriek [ʃriːk] **1** *n* hurlement *m*, cri perçant *or* aigu. **to give a ~** pousser un hurlement *or* un cri; **with ~s of laughter** en riant à gorge déployée.

2 *vi* hurler, crier (*with* de). **to ~ with laughter** rire à gorge déployée, se tordre de rire; (*fig*) **the colour simply ~s at one** cette couleur hurle *or* est vraiment criarde.

3 *vt* hurler, crier. **to ~ abuse at sb** hurler des injures à qn; **'no' he ~ed** 'non' hurla-t-il.

shrift [ʃrɪft] *n*: **to give sb short ~** expédier qn sans ménagement, envoyer promener qn*; **I got short ~ from him** il m'a traité sans ménagement, il m'a envoyé promener*.

shrike [ʃraɪk] *n* pie-grièche *f*.

shrill [ʃrɪl] **1** *adj voice* criard, perçant, aigu (*f* -guë); *cry* perçant, aigu; *whistle, laugh, music* strident. **2** *vi [whistle etc]* retentir. **3** *vt*: **'stop!' she ~ed** 'arrête!' cria-t-elle d'une voix perçante *or* stridente.

shrillness ['ʃrɪlnɪs] *n* (*U*) ton aigu *or* perçant.

shrilly ['ʃrɪlɪ] *adv* d'un ton aigu *or* perçant.

shrimp [ʃrɪmp] **1** *n* crevette *f*. (*fig*) **he's just a little ~** il n'est pas plus haut que trois pommes. **2** *cpd*: (*Culin*) **shrimp cocktail** hors-d'œuvre *m* de crevettes; **shrimp sauce** sauce *f* crevette. **3** *vi*: **to go ~ing** aller pêcher la crevette.

shrine [ʃraɪn] *n* (*reliquary*) châsse *f*; (*place*) lieu saint, lieu de pèlerinage; (*fig*) haut lieu.

shrink [ʃrɪŋk] *pret* **shrank**, *ptp* **shrunk 1** *vi* **(a)** (*get smaller*) *[clothes]* rétrécir; *[area]* se réduire; *[boundaries]* se resserrer; *[piece of meat]* réduire; *[body, person]* se ratatiner, rapetisser; *[wood]* se contracter; *[quantity, amount]* diminuer. (*on label*) **'will not ~'** 'irrétrécissable'.

(b) (*also* **~ away, ~ back**) reculer, se dérober (*from sth* devant qch, *from doing* devant l'idée de faire). **she shrank (away *or* back) from him** elle a eu un mouvement de recul; **he did not ~ from saying that ...** il n'a pas craint de dire que ... .

2 *vt wool* (faire) rétrécir; *metal* contracter.

3 *n* (‡: *esp US*) psychiatre *mf*, psy* *mf*.

shrinkage ['ʃrɪŋkɪdʒ] *n* (*V* **shrink**) rétrécissement *m*; contraction *f*; diminution *f*. **allowing for ~** compte tenu du rétrécissement.

shrinking ['ʃrɪŋkɪŋ] *adj* craintif. (*fig*) **~ violet** sensitive *f*, personne *f* sensible et timide.

shrive†† [ʃraɪv] *pret* **shrived** *or* **shrove**, *ptp* **shrived** *or* **shriven** *vt* confesser et absoudre.

shrivel ['ʃrɪvl] (*also* **~ up**) **1** *vi [apple, body]* se ratatiner; *[skin]* se rider, se flétrir; *[leaf]* se flétrir, se racornir; *[steak]* se racornir, se ratatiner. (*fig*) **her answer made him ~ (up)** sa réponse lui a donné envie de rentrer sous terre.

2 *vt* ratatiner; rider; flétrir; racornir.

shriven ['ʃrɪvn] *ptp of* **shrive.**

shroud [ʃraʊd] **1** *n* **(a)** linceul *m*, suaire *m* (*liter*); (*fig*) *[mist]* voile *m*, linceul (*liter*); *[snow]* linceul (*liter*); *[mystery]* voile.

(b) (*Naut*) hauban *m*.

2 *vt corpse* envelopper dans un linceul, ensevelir. (*fig*) **~ed in mist/snow** enseveli sous la brume/la neige, sous un linceul de brume/de neige (*liter*); **~ed in mystery** enveloppé de mystère.

shrove [ʃrəʊv] **1** *pret of* **shrive. 2** *cpd*: **Shrovetide** les jours gras (*les trois jours précédant le Carême*); **Shrove Tuesday** (le) Mardi gras.

shrub [ʃrʌb] *n* arbrisseau *m*; (*small*) arbuste *m*; *V* **flowering.**

shrubbery ['ʃrʌbərɪ] *n* (massif *m* d')arbustes *mpl*.

shrug [ʃrʌg] **1** *n* haussement *m* d'épaules. **to give a ~ of contempt** hausser les épaules (en signe) de mépris; **... he said with a ~** ... dit-il en haussant les épaules *or* avec un haussement d'épaules.

2 *vti*: **to ~ (one's shoulders)** hausser les épaules.

shrug off *vt sep suggestion, warning* dédaigner, faire fi de; *remark* ignorer, ne pas relever; *infection, a cold* se débarrasser de.

shrunk [ʃrʌŋk] *ptp of* **shrink.**

shrunken ['ʃrʌŋkən] *adj person, body* ratatiné, rabougri. **~ head** tête réduite.

shuck [ʃʌk] (*US*) **1** *n* (*pod*) cosse *f*; *[nut]* écale *f*; *[chestnut]* bogue *f*; *[corn]* spathe *f*. **2** *excl*: **~s!*** mince alors!*, zut alors!* **3** *vt bean* écosser; *nut* écaler; *chestnut* éplucher; *corn* égrener. **to ~ one's clothes** se déshabiller à la va-vite.

shudder ['ʃʌdəʳ] 1 n (from cold) frisson m; (from horror) frisson, frémissement m; [vehicle, ship, engine] vibration f, trépidation f. to give a ~ [person] frissonner, frémir; [vehicle, ship] avoir une forte secousse, être ébranlé; it gives me the ~s* ça me donne des frissons; he realized with a ~ that ... il a frissonné or frémi, comprenant que ... .
2 vi (from cold) frissonner; (from horror) frémir, frissonner; [engine, motor] vibrer, trépider; [vehicle, ship] (on striking sth) avoir une forte secousse, être ébranlé; (for mechanical reasons) vibrer, trépider. I ~ to think what might have happened je frémis rien qu'à la pensée de ce qui aurait pu se produire; what will he do next? — I ~ to think! qu'est-ce qu'il va encore faire? — j'en frémis d'avance!

shuffle ['ʃʌfl] 1 n (a) the ~ of footsteps le bruit d'une démarche traînante.
(b) (Cards) battage m; (fig) réorganisation f. give the cards a good ~ bats bien les cartes; (Parl) a cabinet (re)~ un remaniement ministériel.
2 vt (a) to ~ one's feet traîner les pieds.
(b) cards battre; dominoes mêler, brouiller; papers remuer, déranger.
3 vi (a) traîner les pieds. to ~ in/out/along etc entrer/sortir/avancer etc d'un pas traînant or en traînant les pieds.
(b) (Cards) battre (les cartes).

shuffle off 1 vi s'en aller or s'éloigner d'un pas traînant or en traînant les pieds.
2 vt sep garment enlever maladroitement; (fig) responsibility rejeter (on to sb sur qn), se dérober à.

shun [ʃʌn] vt place, temptation fuir; person, publicity fuir, éviter; work, obligation éviter, esquiver. I ~ned his company j'ai fui sa présence; to ~ doing éviter de faire.

shunt [ʃʌnt] 1 vt (a) (Rail) (direct) aiguiller; (divert) dériver, détourner; (move about) manœuvrer; (position) garer.
(b) (*fig) conversation, discussion aiguiller, détourner (on to sur); person expédier* (to à). (fig) they ~ed the visitors to and fro between the factory and the offices* ils ont fait faire la navette aux visiteurs entre l'usine et les bureaux; ~ that book over to me!‡ passe-moi or file-moi ce bouquin!*
(c) (Elec) shunter, dériver.
2 vi (*fig) [person, object, document] to ~ (to and fro) faire la navette (between entre).

shunter ['ʃʌntəʳ] n (Brit Rail) (person) aiguilleur m (de train); (engine) locomotive f de manœuvre.

shunting ['ʃʌntɪŋ] (Rail) 1 n manœuvres fpl d'aiguillage. 2 cpd: (Brit) shunting operation opération f de triage; shunting yard voies fpl de garage et de triage.

shush [ʃʊʃ] 1 excl chut! 2 vt (*) faire chut à; (silence: also ~ up) faire taire.

shut [ʃʌt] pret, ptp shut 1 vt eyes, door, factory, shop fermer; drawer (re)fermer, repousser. the shop is ~ now le magasin est fermé maintenant; the shop is ~ on Sundays le magasin ferme or est fermé le dimanche; we're ~ting the office for 2 weeks in July nous fermons le bureau pour 2 semaines au mois de juillet; to ~ one's finger in a drawer se pincer or se prendre le doigt dans un tiroir; to ~ sb in a room enfermer qn dans une pièce; ~ your mouth!‡ ferme-la!‡, boucle-la!‡; ~ your face!‡ ta gueule!‡, la ferme!‡; V door, ear¹, eye, open, stable² etc.
2 vi [door, box, lid, drawer] fermer, se fermer; [museum, theatre, shop] fermer. the door ~ la poote s'est (re)fermée; the door ~s badly la porte ferme mal; the shop ~s on Sundays/at 6 o'clock le magasin ferme le dimanche/à 18 heures.
3 cpd: shutdown fermeture f; to get a bit of shut-eye‡ or some shut-eye‡ piquer un roupillon‡, dormir un peu; shut-in enfermé, confiné; shutoff interrupteur m automatique, dispositif m de débranchement automatique; shut-out (Ind) lock-out m inv; (US Sport) victoire éclatante (au cours de laquelle une équipe ne marque pas de points); (Bridge) shut-out bid (annonce f de) barrage m.

shut away vt sep person, animal enfermer; valuables mettre sous clef. he shuts himself away il s'enferme chez lui, il vit en reclus.

shut down 1 vi [business, shop, theatre] fermer (définitivement), fermer ses portes.
2 vt sep lid fermer, rabattre; business, shop, theatre fermer (définitivement); machine arrêter.
3 shutdown n V shut 3.

shut in 1 vt sep person, animal enfermer; (surround) entourer (with de). to feel shut in se sentir enfermé or emprisonné (fig).
2 shut-in adj V shut 3.

shut off 1 vt sep (a) (stop, cut) electricity, gas couper, fermer; engine couper; supplies arrêter, couper.
(b) (isolate) person isoler, séparer (from de). we're very shut off here nous sommes coupés de tout ici or très isolés ici.
2 shutoff n V shut 3.

shut out 1 vt sep (a) he found that they had shut him out, he found himself shut out il a trouvé qu'il était à la porte or qu'il ne pouvait pas entrer; don't shut me out, I haven't got a key ne ferme pas la porte, je n'ai pas de clef; I shut the cat out at night je laisse or mets le chat dehors pour la nuit; close the door and shut out the noise ferme la porte pour qu'on n'entende pas le bruit; he shut them out of his will il les a exclus de son testament; you can't shut him out of your life tu ne peux pas l'exclure or le bannir de ta vie.
(b) (block) view boucher; memory chasser de son esprit.
2 shut-out n, adj V shut 3.

shut to 1 vi [door] se (re)fermer.
2 vt sep (re)fermer.

shut up 1 vi (*: be quiet) se taire. shut up! tais-toi!, ferme-la!‡, boucle-la!‡; better just shut up and get on with it mieux vaut se taire or ne rien dire et continuer.
2 vt sep (a) factory, business, theatre, house fermer; V shop.
(b) person, animal enfermer; valuables mettre sous clef. to shut sb up in prison emprisonner qn, mettre qn en prison.
(c) (*: silence) faire taire, clouer le bec à*.

shutter ['ʃʌtəʳ] 1 n volet m; (Phot) obturateur m. to put up the ~s mettre les volets; (Comm) fermer (le magasin); (fig: permanently) fermer boutique, fermer définitivement. 2 cpd: shutter speed vitesse f d'obturation.

shuttered ['ʃʌtəd] adj house etc aux volets fermés.

shuttle ['ʃʌtl] 1 n [loom, sewing machine] navette f; (fig: plane/train etc) (avion m/train m etc qui fait la) navette.
2 cpd: shuttlecock volant m (Badminton); (Tech) shuttle movement mouvement alternatif; (Aviat, Rail etc) shuttle service (service m de) navette f.
3 vi [person, vehicle, boat] faire la navette (between entre).
4 vt: to ~ sb to and fro envoyer qn à droite et à gauche; he was ~d (back and forth) between the factory and the office on l'a renvoyé de l'usine au bureau et vice versa, il a dû faire la navette entre l'usine et le bureau; the papers ~d (backwards and forwards) from one department to another les documents ont été renvoyés d'un service à l'autre.

shy¹ [ʃaɪ] 1 adj person timide; (reserved) réservé; (unsociable) sauvage; animal timide, peureux; look, smile timide; (self-conscious) embarrassé, gauche. he's a ~ person, he's ~ of people c'est un timide, il est mal à l'aise avec les gens, il est sauvage; he's ~ with or of women il est timide avec les femmes or auprès des femmes, les femmes l'intimident; to make sb (feel) ~ intimider qn, gêner qn, embarrasser qn; don't be ~ ne fais pas le (or la) timide; don't be ~ of telling me what you want n'ayez pas peur de or n'hésitez pas à or ne craignez pas de me dire ce que vous voulez; I'm rather ~ of inviting him je n'ose guère l'inviter, j'ai un peu peur de l'inviter; V bite, fight, work etc.
2 vi [horse] se cabrer (at devant).

shy away vi (fig) to shy away from doing répugner à faire, s'effaroucher à l'idée de faire.

shy² [ʃaɪ] 1 vt (throw) lancer, jeter. 2 n (lit) to take or have a ~ at sth lancer un projectile (or une pierre etc) vers qch; '2p a ~' '2 pence le coup'; (fig: try) to have a ~ at doing tenter de faire; V coconut.

shyly ['ʃaɪlɪ] adv (V shy¹ 1) timidement; avec réserve; gauchement.

shyness ['ʃaɪnɪs] n (V shy¹ 1) timidité f; réserve f; sauvagerie f; embarras m, gaucherie f.

shyster* ['ʃaɪstəʳ] n escroc m; (US: lawyer) avocat véreux or marron.

Siam [saɪ'æm] n Siam m.

Siamese [ˌsaɪə'miːz] 1 adj siamois. ~ cat chat siamois; ~ twins (frères) siamois, (sœurs) siamoises. 2 n (a) (pl inv) Siamois(e) m(f). (b) (Ling) siamois m.

Siberia [saɪ'bɪərɪə] n Sibérie f.

Siberian [saɪ'bɪərɪən] 1 adj sibérien, de Sibérie. 2 n Sibérien(ne) m(f).

sibilant ['sɪbɪlənt] 1 adj (also Ling) sifflant. 2 n (Ling) sifflante f.

sibling ['sɪblɪŋ] 1 n: ~s enfants mfpl de mêmes parents; one of his ~s l'un de ses frères et sœurs; Paul and Lucy are ~s Paul et Lucie sont de mêmes parents or sont frère et sœur. 2 cpd: (Psych) sibling rivalry rivalité fraternelle.

sibyl ['sɪbɪl] n sibylle f.

sibylline ['sɪbɪlaɪn] adj sibyllin.

Sicilian [sɪ'sɪlɪən] 1 adj sicilien. 2 n (a) Sicilien(ne) m(f). (b) (Ling) sicilien m.

Sicily ['sɪsɪlɪ] n Sicile f.

sick [sɪk] 1 adj (a) (ill) person malade; pallor maladif. he's a ~ man c'est un malade; he's (away or off) ~ (il n'est pas là) il est malade; to go ~ se faire porter malade; to fall or take ~ tomber malade; to be ~ of a fever† avoir la fièvre; V home, off etc.
(b) (nauseated, vomiting) to be ~ vomir; to feel ~ avoir mal au cœur, avoir des nausées, avoir envie de vomir; melon makes me ~ le melon me fait mal au cœur or (stronger) me fait vomir (V also 1c); I get ~ in planes j'ai mal au cœur or je suis malade en avion, j'ai le mal de l'air; ~ headache migraine f; V sea etc.
(c) (fig) mind, imagination, fancies malsain. ~ humour humour noir; ~ joke plaisanterie macabre or malsaine; ~ comedian comédien porté sur l'humour noir; to be ~ at heart avoir la mort dans l'âme; to be ~ of sth/sb* en avoir assez de qch/qn, en avoir marre* de qch/qn; to be ~ and tired of sth/sb* en avoir par-dessus la tête de qch/qn; to be ~ to death* or to the (back) teeth‡ of en avoir par-dessus la tête de, en avoir ras le bol‡ or plein le dos* de; to be ~ of the sight of sth/sb* en avoir assez or marre* de voir qch/qn; it's enough to make you ~ il y a de quoi vous écœurer or vous rendre malade*; it makes me ~ to think that ... ça m'écœure or me dégoûte de penser que ...; you make me ~!* tu m'écœures!, tu me dégoûtes!; he was really ~ at failing the exam‡ il était vraiment écœuré d'avoir échoué à l'examen; he really looked ~‡ il avait l'air écœuré, il faisait une de ces têtes!*
2 npl: the ~ les malades mpl.
3 cpd: sick bay infirmerie f; sickbed lit m de malade; (Brit) sick benefit (prestations fpl de l')assurance f maladie; (on) sick leave (en) congé m de maladie; to be on the sick list (Admin) être porté malade; (*) être malade; sick-making‡ dégoûtant; sick pay indemnité f de maladie (versée par l'employeur); sickroom chambre f de malade.

sick up* vt sep vomir, rendre.

sicken ['sɪkn] 1 vt rendre malade, donner mal au cœur à; (fig) dégoûter, écœurer. 2 vi tomber malade. [person] to ~ for sth couver qch; (fig) to ~ of se lasser de, en avoir assez de.

sickening ['sɪknɪŋ] adj sight, smell écœurant, qui soulève le cœur; (*fig*) *cruelty, crime* répugnant, ignoble; *waste* dégoûtant, révoltant; (*: *annoying*) *person, behaviour* agaçant, exaspérant.

sickeningly ['sɪknɪŋlɪ] *adv*: **it is ~ sweet** c'est tellement sucré que c'en est écœurant; **~ polite*** d'une politesse écœurante.

sickle ['sɪkl] **1** *n* faucille *f*. **2** *cpd*: (*Med*) **sickle-cell anaemia** anémie *f* à hématies falciformes.

sickliness ['sɪklɪnɪs] *n* *[person]* état maladif; *[cake]* goût écœurant.

sickly ['sɪklɪ] *adj person* maladif, souffreteux; *complexion* blafard, pâle; *climate* malsain; *plant* étiolé; *smile* pâle, faible; *colour, smell, cake* écœurant. **~ sweet** douceâtre.

sickness ['sɪknɪs] **1** *n* (*U*) (*illness*) maladie *f*. **there's a lot of ~ in the village** il y a beaucoup de malades dans le village; **there's ~ on board** il y a des cas de maladie à bord; (*vomiting*) **bouts of ~** vomissements *mpl*; **mountain ~** mal *m* des montagnes; *V* **travel** *etc*.

2 *cpd*: (*Brit*) **sickness benefit** (prestations *fpl* de l')assurance *f* maladie.

side [saɪd] **1** *n* **(a)** *[person]* côté *m*; *[animal]* flanc *m*. **wounded in the ~** blessé au côté; **to sleep on one's ~** dormir sur le côté; **he had the telephone by his ~** il avait le téléphone à côté de lui *or* à portée de la main; **his assistant was at *or* by his ~** son assistant était à ses côtés; (*fig*) **she remained by his ~ through thick and thin** elle est restée à ses côtés *or* elle l'a soutenu à travers toutes leurs épreuves; **~ by ~** côte à côte; (*Culin*) **a ~ of bacon** une flèche de lard; **a ~ of beef/mutton** un quartier de bœuf/mouton; *V* **split** *etc*.

(b) (*as opposed to top, bottom etc*) *[box, house, car, triangle etc]* côté *m*; *[ship]* flanc *m*, côté; *[hill, mountain]* flanc, versant *m*; (*inside*) *[cave, ditch, box]* paroi *f*. **by the ~ of the church** à côté de *or* tout près de l'église; **set the box on its ~** pose la caisse sur le côté; **go round the ~ of the house** contournez la maison; **you'll find him round the ~ (of the house)** tournez le coin de la maison et vous le verrez; **she is like the ~ of a house*** c'est un monument*, elle est colossale; *V* **near, off** *etc*.

(c) (*outer surface*) *[cube, record, coin]* côté *m*, face *f*; *[square]* côté; *[garment, cloth, slice of bread, sheet of paper]* côté; (*fig*) *[matter, problem etc]* aspect *m*; *[sb's character]* facette *f*. *[garment, cloth]* **the right ~** l'endroit *m*; **the wrong ~** l'envers *m*; *[cloth]* **right/wrong ~ out** à l'endroit/l'envers; **right/wrong ~ up** dans le bon/mauvais sens; (*on box etc*) **'this ~ up'** 'haut'; **write on both ~s of the paper** écrivez au recto et au verso, écrivez recto verso; **I've written 6 ~s** j'ai écrit 6 pages; (*fig*) **the other ~ of the coin *or* picture** le revers de la médaille; **there are two ~s to every quarrel** dans toute querelle il y a deux points de vue; (*fig*) **look at it from his ~ (of it)** considère cela de son point de vue; **he's got a nasty ~* to him *or* to his nature** il a un côté très déplaisant, il a quelque chose de très déplaisant; *V* **bright, flip, right, wrong** *etc*.

(d) (*edge*) *[road, lake, river]* bord *m*; *[wood, forest]* lisière *f*, bord; *[field, estate]* bord, côté *m*. **by the ~ of the road/lake** *etc* au bord de la route/du lac *etc*.

(e) (*lateral part*) côté *m*. **on the other ~ of the street/room** de l'autre côté de la rue/la pièce; **he crossed to the other ~ of the room** il a traversé la pièce; **the east ~ of the town** le côté est *or* la partie est de la ville; **he is paralysed down one ~ of his face** il a un côté du visage paralysé; (*fig*) **the science ~ of the college** la section sciences du collège; (*Brit Parl*) **members on the other ~ of the House** (*the government*) les députés de la majorité; (*the opposition*) les députés de l'opposition; **from all ~s, from every ~** de tous côtés, de toutes parts; **from ~ to ~** d'un côté à l'autre; **he moved to one ~** il s'est écarté *or* poussé; **to take sb on one ~** prendre qn à part; **to put sth to *or* on one ~** mettre qch de côté; **it's on this ~ of London** c'est de notre côté de Londres; (*between here and London*) c'est avant Londres, c'est entre ici et Londres; (*fig*) **he's on the wrong ~ of fifty** il a passé la cinquantaine; (*fig*) **he's on the right ~ of 50** il n'a pas encore 50 ans; **he makes a bit (of money) on the ~*** il se fait un peu d'argent en plus, il fait de la gratte* (*pej*); **a cousin on his mother's ~** un cousin du côté de sa mère; **my grandfather on my mother's ~** mon grand-père maternel; (*TV*) **on the other ~** sur l'autre chaîne; (*fig*) **it's on the heavy/cold ~** c'est plutôt lourd/froid; *V* **safe, sunny** *etc*.

(f) (*group, team, party*) (*gen*) camp *m*, côté *m*; (*Sport*) équipe *f*; (*Pol etc*) parti *m*. **he's on our ~** il est de notre camp *or* avec nous; **God was on their ~** Dieu était avec eux; **we have time on our ~** nous avons le temps pour nous, le temps joue en notre faveur; **whose ~ are you on?** qui soutenez-vous?, qui défendez-vouz?; **there are faults on both ~s** les deux côtés *or* camps ont des torts *or* sont fautifs; **with a few concessions on the government ~** avec quelques concessions de la part du gouvernement; **to take ~s (with sb)** prendre parti (pour qn); **to pick *or* choose ~s** former les camps; (*Sport*) **they've picked *or* chosen the England ~** on a sélectionné l'équipe d'Angleterre; *V* **change**.

(g) (*Brit*: conceit*) **he's got no ~, there's no ~ about him** il est très simple, ce n'est pas un crâneur*; **to put on ~** prendre des airs supérieurs, crâner*.

2 *cpd chapel, panel, elevation, seat* latéral; (*fig*) *effect* secondaire. **sideboard** buffet *m*; (*Brit*) **sideboards,** (*Brit, US*) **sideburns** pattes *fpl*, rouflaquettes* *fpl*; **sidecar** side-car *m*; **side dish** plat *m* d'accompagnement; **side door, side entrance** entrée latérale, petite porte; (*Phot: adj, adv*) **side face** de profil; **side glance** regard *m* de côté; **side issue** question *f* secondaire, à-côté *m*; **sidekick*** (*assistant*) sous-fifre* *m*; (*friend*) copain* *m*, copine* *f*; (*Aut*) **sidelight** lanterne *f*; (*fig*) **it gives us a sidelight on ...** cela nous donne un aperçu de ..., cela révèle un côté *or* aspect inattendu de ...; **sideline** *V* **sideline; sidelong** (*adj*) oblique, de côté; (*adv*) de côté, en oblique; (*Brit Rel*) **sidesman** adjoint *m* au bedeau; **side plate** petite assiette; **side road** petite route, route transversale; (*in town*) petite rue, rue transversale; **to ride sidesaddle** monter en amazone; **side shows** attractions *fpl*; (*Aviat*) **sideslip** (*n*) glissade *f or* glissement *m* sur l'aile; (*vi*) glisser sur l'aile; **side-splitting*** tordant*; **side-step** (*vt*) *blow* éviter, esquiver; *question* éviter, éluder; (*vi*) (*lit*) faire un pas de côté; (*fig*) rester évasif; (*Boxing*) esquiver; **side street** petite rue, rue transversale; **sidetable** desserte *f*; **sidetrack** *train* dériver, dérouter; (*fig*) *person* faire dévier de son sujet; (*fig*) **to get sidetracked** s'écarter de son sujet; **side view** vue *f* de côté; (*US*) **sidewalk** trottoir *m*; **sideways** *V* **sideways; side whiskers** favoris *mpl*.

3 *vi*: **to ~ with sb** se ranger du côté de qn, prendre parti pour qn, faire cause commune avec qn.

-sided ['saɪdɪd] *adj ending in cpds*: **three-sided** à trois côtés, trilatéral; **many-sided** multilatéral; *V* **one** *etc*.

sideline ['saɪdlaɪn] *n* **(a)** (*Sport*) (ligne *f* de) touche *f*. **on the ~s** (*Sport*) sur la touche; (*fig*) dans les coulisses, sur la touche.

(b) activité *f* (*or* travail *m etc*) secondaire. **he sells wood as a ~** il a aussi un petit commerce de bois; (*Comm*) **it's just a ~** ce n'est pas notre spécialité.

sidereal [saɪ'dɪərɪəl] *adj* sidéral.

sideways ['saɪdweɪz] **1** *adj* oblique, de côté. **2** *adv look* de côté, obliquement; *walk* en crabe; *stand* de profil. **it goes in ~** ça rentre de côté; **car parked ~ on to the kerb** voiture garée le long du trottoir.

siding ['saɪdɪŋ] *n* (*Rail*) voie *f* de garage; *V* **goods.**

sidle ['saɪdl] *vi*: **to ~ along** marcher de côté, avancer de biais; **to ~ in/out** *etc* entrer/sortir *etc* furtivement; **he ~d into the room** il s'est faufilé dans la pièce; **he ~d up to me** il s'est glissé vers moi.

siege [si:dʒ] *n* (*Mil, fig*) siège *m*. **in a state of ~** en état de siège; **to lay ~ to a town** assiéger une ville, mettre le siège devant une ville; **to raise *or* lift the ~** lever le siège (*lit*).

sienna [sɪ'enə] *n* (*earth*) terre *f* de Sienne *or* d'ombre; (*colour*) ocre brun; *V* **burnt.**

sierra [sɪ'erə] *n* sierra *f*.

Sierra Leone [sɪ'erəlɪ'əʊn] *n* Sierra Leone *m*.

siesta [sɪ'estə] *n* sieste *f*. **to have *or* take a ~** faire une *or* la sieste.

sieve [sɪv] **1** *n* (*for coal, stones*) crible *m*; (*for sugar, flour, sand, soil*) tamis *m*; (*for wheat*) van *m*; (*for liquids*) passoire *f*. (*Culin*) **to rub *or* put through a ~** passer au tamis; **he's got a head *or* memory like a ~*** sa mémoire est une (vraie) passoire.

2 *vt fruit, vegetables* passer; *sugar, flour, sand, soil* tamiser; *coal, stones* passer au crible, cribler.

sift [sɪft] **1** *vt* **(a)** *flour, sugar, sand* tamiser, passer au tamis; *coal, stones* cribler, passer au crible; *wheat* vanner; (*fig*) *evidence* passer au crible *or* au tamis. **to ~ flour on to sth** saupoudrer qch de farine (au moyen d'un tamis).

(b) (*also* **~ out**) *cinders etc* séparer (à l'aide d'un crible); (*fig*) *facts, truth* dégager.

2 *vi* (*fig*) **to ~ through sth** passer qch en revue, examiner qch.

sifter ['sɪftə'] *n* (*V* **sift 1**) tamis *m*; crible *m*; (*machine*) cribleuse *f*; (*for flour, sugar*) saupoudreuse *f*.

sigh [saɪ] **1** *n* soupir *m*. **to heave *or* give a ~** soupirer, pousser un soupir.

2 *vt*: **'if only he'd come' she ~ed** 'si seulement il arrivait' dit-elle en soupirant *or* soupira-t-elle.

3 *vi* soupirer, pousser un soupir; *[wind]* gémir. **he ~ed with relief** il a poussé un soupir de soulagement; **to ~ for sth** soupirer après *or* pour qch; (*for sth lost*) regretter qch; **to ~ over sth** se lamenter sur qch, regretter qch.

sighing ['saɪɪŋ] *n* *[person]* soupirs *mpl*; *[wind]* gémissements *mpl*.

sight [saɪt] **1** *n* **(a)** (*faculty; act of seeing; range of vision*) vue *f*. **to have good/poor ~** avoir une bonne/mauvaise vue; **to lose one's ~** devenir aveugle, perdre la vue; **to get back *or* regain one's ~** recouvrer la vue; **to know sb by ~** connaître qn de vue; **to shoot on ~ *or* at ~** tirer à vue; **he translated it at ~** il l'a traduit à livre ouvert; **he played the music at ~** il a déchiffré le morceau de musique; **at first ~ it seems to be ...** à première vue *or* au premier abord cela semble être ...; **at the ~ of** à la vue de, en voyant, au spectacle de; **the train was still in ~** on voyait encore le train, le train était encore visible; **the end is (with)in ~** la fin est en vue, on entrevoit la fin; **we are within ~ of a solution** nous entrevoyons une solution; **we live within ~ of the sea** de chez nous on voit *or* aperçoit la mer; **to come into ~** apparaître; **keep the luggage in ~, keep ~ of the luggage, don't let the luggage out of your ~** ne perdez pas les bagages de vue, surveillez les bagages; **out of ~** hors de vue; **to keep out of ~** (*vi*) se cacher, ne pas se montrer; (*vt*) cacher, ne pas montrer; **it is out of ~** on ne le voit pas, ce n'est pas visible, ce n'est pas à portée de vue; **he never lets it out of his ~** il le garde toujours sous les yeux; (*liter*) **out of my ~!** hors de ma vue!; **keep out of his ~!** qu'il ne te voie pas!; (*Prov*) **out of ~ out of mind** loin des yeux loin du cœur (*Prov*); **to catch ~ of** apercevoir; (*lit, fig*) **to lose ~ of sb/sth** perdre qn/qch de vue; **it was my first ~ of Paris** c'était la première fois que je voyais Paris; **I got my first ~ of that document yesterday** j'ai vu ce document hier pour la première fois; **their first ~ of land came after 30 days at sea** la terre leur est apparue pour la première fois au bout de 30 jours en mer; **the ~ of the cathedral** la vue de la cathédrale; **I can't bear *or* stand the ~ of blood** je ne peux pas supporter la vue du sang; **I can't bear *or* stand the ~ of him, I hate the ~ of him** je ne peux pas le voir (en peinture*) *or* le sentir*; (*fig liter*) **to find favour in sb's ~** trouver grâce aux yeux de qn; **all men are equal in the ~ of God** tous les hommes sont égaux devant Dieu; **in the ~ of the law** aux yeux de la loi, devant la loi; *V* **heave, second[1], short** *etc*.

(b) (*spectacle*) spectacle *m* (*also pej*). **the tulips are a wonderful** ~ les tulipes sont magnifiques; **it is a** ~ **to see** *or* **a** ~ **to be seen** cela vaut la peine d'être vu, il faut le voir; **the Grand Canyon is one of the** ~**s of the world** le Grand Canyon constitue l'un des plus beaux spectacles du monde *or* est l'un des plus beaux paysages du monde; **it's one of the** ~**s of Paris** c'est l'une des attractions touristiques de Paris, c'est l'une des choses à voir à Paris; **it's a sad** ~ c'est triste (à voir), ça fait pitié; **it's not a pretty** ~ ça n'est guère joli (à voir); **it was a** ~ **for sore eyes** (*welcome*) c'était un spectacle à réjouir le cœur; (**pej*) c'était à en pleurer; **his face was a** ~**!** (*amazed etc*) il faisait une de ces têtes!*; (*after injury etc*) il avait une tête à faire peur*; (*pej*) **I must look a** ~**!** je dois avoir une de ces allures!* *or* l'air de Dieu sait quoi!*; **doesn't she look a** ~ **in that hat!** elle a l'air d'un épouvantail avec ce chapeau!; *V* **see**[1].

(c) (*on gun*) mire *f*. **to take** ~ viser; **to have sth in one's** ~**s** avoir qch dans sa ligne de tir; (*fig*) **to set one's** ~**s too high** viser trop haut (*fig*); **to set one's** ~**s on sth** viser qch, décider d'obtenir qch.

(d) (*phrases*) **not by a long** ~ loin de là, bien au contraire; **it's a (far** *or* **long)** ~ **better than the other*** c'est infiniment mieux que l'autre; **he's a** ~ **too clever*** il est par *or* bien trop malin.

2 *cpd*: (*Mus*) **sight-read** déchiffrer; **sight-reading** déchiffrage *m*; **sightseeing** tourisme *m*; **to go sightseeing, to do some sightseeing** (*gen*) faire le (*or* la) touriste, faire du tourisme; (*in town*) visiter la ville; **sightseer** touriste *mf*.

3 *vt* **(a)** (*see*) *land, person* apercevoir.

(b) to ~ **a gun** (*aim*) prendre sa visée, viser; (*adjust*) régler le viseur d'un canon.

sighted ['saɪtɪd] 1 *adj* qui voit, doué de vue *or* de vision. **to be partially** ~ avoir un certain degré de vision. 2 *npl*: **the** ~ les voyants *mpl* (*lit*), ceux qui voient.

-sighted ['saɪtɪd] *adj ending in cpds*: **weak-sighted** à la vue faible; *V* **clear, short** *etc.*

sighting ['saɪtɪŋ] *n*: **numerous**~**s of the monster have been reported** de nombreuses personnes ont déclaré avoir vu le monstre; **Mr X has reported 6** ~**s** M X déclare l'avoir vu 6 fois.

sightly ['saɪtlɪ] *adj*: **it's not very** ~ ce n'est pas beau à voir.

sign [saɪn] 1 *n* **(a)** (*with hand etc*) signe *m*, geste *m*. **he made a** ~ **of recognition** il m'a (*or* lui a *etc*) fait signe qu'il me (*or* le *etc*) reconnaissait; **they communicated by** ~**s** ils se parlaient par signes; **to make a** ~ **to sb** faire signe à qn (*to do* de faire); **to make the** ~ **of the Cross** faire le signe de la croix (*over sb/sth* sur qn/qch); **he made a rude** ~ il a fait un geste grossier.

(b) (*symbol: Astron, Math, Mus etc*) signe *m*. **the** ~**s of the zodiac** les signes du zodiaque; **this** ~ **means 'do not machine-wash'** ce signe *or* ce symbole signifie 'ne pas laver à la machine'; *V* **minus** *etc.*

(c) (*indication*) signe *m*, preuve *f*, indication *f*; (*Med*) symptôme *m*; (*trace*) signe, trace *f*, marque *f*. **as a** ~ **of** en signe de; **it's a good/bad** ~ c'est bon/mauvais signe; **those clouds are a** ~ **of rain** ces nuages sont un signe de pluie *or* présagent la pluie; **violence is a** ~ **of fear** la violence est (un) signe *or* une preuve de peur, la violence dénote *or* indique *or* révèle la peur; **it's a** ~ **of the times** c'est un signe des temps; **it's a sure** ~ c'est un signe infaillible; **at the slightest** ~ **of disagreement** au moindre signe de désaccord; **there is no** ~ **of his agreeing** rien ne laisse à penser *or* rien n'indique qu'il va accepter; **he gave no** ~ **of wishing to come with us** il ne donnait aucun signe de *or* il n'avait pas du tout l'air de vouloir venir avec nous; **there was no** ~ **of life** il n'y avait aucun signe de vie; **there's no** ~ **of him anywhere** on ne le trouve nulle part, il n'y a aucune trace de lui; **there's no** ~ **of it anywhere** c'est introuvable, je (*or* il *etc*) n'arrive pas à le (re)trouver; *V* **show.**

(d) (*notice*) panneau *m*; (*on inn, shop*) enseigne *f*; (*Aut: traffic warnings etc*) panneau (de signalisation); (*Aut: directions on motorways etc*) panneau (indicateur); (*writing on signpost*) direction *f*, indication *f*.

2 *cpd*: **sign language** langage *m* par signes; **to talk in sign language** parler *or* communiquer par signes; **signpost** (*n*) poteau indicateur; (*vt*) signaliser, flécher; **it is signposted** c'est indiqué *or* fléché; **the signposting is very bad in that town** la signalisation est très mauvaise dans cette ville; **sign writer** peintre *m* d'enseignes.

3 *vt* **(a)** *letter, document, register, visitors' book* signer. (*fig*) **it was** ~**ed, sealed and delivered by twelve noon** à midi, l'affaire était entièrement réglée; **to** ~ **one's name** signer; **he** ~**s himself John Smith** il signe 'John Smith'; *V* **pledge.**

(b) (*Ftbl etc*) **to** ~ **a player** engager un joueur.

4 *vi* **(a)** signer. **you have to** ~ **for the key** vous devez signer pour obtenir la clef; **he** ~**ed for the parcel** il a signé le reçu de livraison du paquet; (*Ftbl*) **Smith has** ~**ed for Celtic** Smith a signé un contrat d'engagement avec le Celtic; *V* **dot.**

(b) to ~ **to sb to do sth** faire signe à qn de faire qch.

sign away *vt sep*: **to sign away sth** signer sa renonciation à qch, signer l'abandon de son droit sur qch.

sign in *vi* (*in factory*) pointer; (*in hotel*) signer le registre.

sign off *vi* (*Rad, TV*) terminer l'émission. **this is Jacques Dupont signing off** c'est Jacques Dupont qui vous dit au revoir.

sign on 1 *vi* **(a)** (*Ind etc*) se faire embaucher (*as* comme, en tant que); (*Mil*) s'engager (*as* comme, en tant que).

(b) (*on arrival at work*) pointer.

(c) (*enrol*) s'inscrire. **I've signed on for German conversation** je me suis inscrit au cours de conversation allemande.

2 *vt sep employee* embaucher; (*Mil*) engager.

sign over *vt sep* céder par écrit (*to* à).

sign up 1 *vi* = **sign on 1a.**

2 *vt sep* = **sign on 2.**

signal ['sɪgnl] 1 *n* **(a)** (*gen, Ling, Naut, Psych, Rail etc*) signal *m*. **at a prearranged** ~ à un signal convenu; **the** ~ **for departure** le signal du départ; (*Naut*) **flag** ~**s** signaux par pavillons; **(traffic)** ~**s** feux *mpl* de circulation; (*Rail*) **the** ~ **is at red** le signal est au rouge; *V* **distress** *etc.*

(b) (*electronic impulse; message: Rad, Telec, TV*) signal *m*. **I'm getting the engaged** ~ ça sonne occupé *or* pas libre; **send a** ~ **to HQ to the effect that ...** envoyez un signal *or* message au Q.G. pour dire que ...; (*TV*) **the** ~ **is very weak** (*sound*) le son est très faible; (*picture*) l'image est très faible; (*Mil*) **the S**~**s** les Transmissions *fpl.*

2 *cpd*: (*Naut*) **signal book** code international de signaux, livre *m* des signaux; (*Rail*) **signal box** cabine *f* d'aiguillage, poste *m* d'aiguillage *or* de signalisation; (*Naut*) **signal flag** pavillon *m* de signalisation; **signalman** (*Rail*) aiguilleur *m*; (*Naut*) signaleur *m*.

3 *adj* (*avant n*) *success* remarquable, insigne; *importance* capital.

4 *vt message* communiquer par signaux. **to** ~ **sb on/through** *etc* faire signe à qn d'avancer/de passer *etc.*

5 *vi* faire des signaux. **to** ~ **to sb** faire signe à qn (*to do* de faire).

signalize ['sɪgnəlaɪz] *vt* (*mark, make notable*) marquer; (*point out*) distinguer, signaler.

signally ['sɪgnəlɪ] *adv* singulièrement, extraordinairement. **he has** ~ **failed to do it** il a manifestement échoué *or* bel et bien échoué dans sa tentative.

signatory ['sɪgnətərɪ] 1 *adj* signataire. 2 *n* signataire *mf* (*to* de).

signature ['sɪgnətʃə'] 1 *n* **(a)** signature *f*. **to set** *or* **put one's** ~ **to sth** apposer sa signature à qch. **(b)** (*Mus: key* ~) armature *f*. 2 *cpd*: (*esp Brit*) **signature tune** indicatif musical.

signer ['saɪnə'] *n* signataire *mf*.

signet ['sɪgnɪt] *n* sceau *m*, cachet *m*. ~ **ring** chevalière *f*; *V* **writer.**

significance [sɪg'nɪfɪkəns] *n* (*meaning*) signification *f*; (*importance*) *[event, speech]* importance *f*, portée *f*. **a lookofdeep** ~ u regard lourd de eene; **what he thinks is of no** ~ peu importe ce qu'il pense.

significant [sɪg'nɪfɪkənt] *adj achievement, increase, amount* considérable; *event* important, de grande portée; *look* significatif. **it is** ~ **that ...** il est significatif *or* révélateur que ... + *subj.*

significantly [sɪg'nɪfɪkəntlɪ] *adv smile, wink, nudge* d'une façon significative. **she looked at me** ~ elle m'a jeté un regard lourd de sens; ~**, he refused** fait révélateur, il a refusé; **he was** ~ **absent** son absence était significative; **it has improved** ~ l'amélioration est considérable; **it is not** ~ **different** la différence est insignifiante.

signification [,sɪgnɪfɪ'keɪʃən] *n* signification *f*, sens *m*.

signify ['sɪgnɪfaɪ] 1 *vt* **(a)** (*mean*) signifier, vouloir dire (*that* que); (*indicate*) signifier, être (un) signe de, indiquer. **it signifies intelligence** cela indique *or* dénote *or* révèle de l'intelligence.

(b) (*make known*) signifier, indiquer, faire comprendre (*that* que); *one's approval* signifier; *one's opinion* faire connaître.

2 *vi* avoir de l'importance. **it does not** ~ cela n'a aucune importance, cela importe peu.

silage ['saɪlɪdʒ] *n* (*fodder*) fourrage ensilé *or* vert; (*method*) ensilage *m*.

silence ['saɪləns] 1 *n* silence *m*. **he called for** ~ il a demandé *or* réclamé le silence; **when he finished speaking, there was** ~ quand il a fini de parler, le silence a régné *or* on a gardé le silence *or* personne n'a soufflé mot; **they listened in** ~ ils ont écouté en silence *or* sans rien dire; **your** ~ **on this matter ...** le silence *or* le mutisme que vous gardez sur ce sujet ...; (*fig*) **there is** ~ **in official circles** dans les milieux autorisés on garde le silence; (*fig*) **to pass sth over in** ~ passer qch sous silence; (*Prov*) ~ **gives** *or* **means consent** qui ne dit mot consent (*Prov*); (*Prov*) ~ **is golden** le silence est d'or (*Prov*); *V* **dead, radio, reduce** *etc.*

2 *vt person, critic, guns* réduire au silence, faire taire; *noise* étouffer; *conscience* faire taire. **to** ~ **criticism** faire taire les critiques, imposer silence aux critiques; **to** ~ **the opposition** réduire l'opposition au silence.

silencer ['saɪlənsə'] *n* (*on gun,* (*Brit*) *on car*) silencieux *m*.

silent ['saɪlənt] 1 *adj person* silencieux; (*taciturn*) silencieux, peu communicatif, taciturne; *engine, movement* silencieux; *step* silencieux, feutré; *room* silencieux, tranquille; *film, letter, wish, reproach* muet. **it was (as)** ~ **as the grave** *or* **the tomb** il y avait un silence de mort; **to fall** *or* **become** ~ se taire; **to keep** *or* **be** ~ garder le silence, se taire; **be** ~**!** taisez-vous!, silence!; **to remain** ~ **about sth** se taire *or* garder le silence *or* ne rien dire au sujet de qch; ~ **'h'** 'h' muet; **the** ~ **majority** la majorité silencieuse; (*US Comm*) ~ **partner** (associé *m*) commanditaire *m*.

2 *n* (*Cine: gen pl*) **the** ~**s** les films muets, le (cinéma) muet.

silently ['saɪləntlɪ] *adv* (*noiselessly*) silencieusement, sans (faire de) bruit; (*without speaking*) silencieusement, en silence.

silex ['saɪleks] *n* silex *m*.

silhouette [,sɪlu:'et] 1 *n* silhouette *f* (*sur l'horizon etc*); (*Art*) silhouette. 2 *vt*: **to be** ~**d against** se découper contre, se profiler sur, se silhouetter sur; ~**d against** se découpant contre, se profilant sur, silhouetté sur.

silica ['sɪlɪkə] *n* silice *f*.

silicate ['sɪlɪkɪt] *n* silicate *m*.

siliceous [sɪ'lɪʃəs] *adj* siliceux.

silicon ['sɪlɪkən] *n* silicium *m*. ~ **chip** plaquette *f* de silicium.

silicone ['sɪlɪkəʊn] *n* silicone *f*.

silicosis [,sɪlɪ'kəʊsɪs] *n* silicose *f*.

silk [sɪlk] 1 *n* **(a)** (*material*) soie *f*; (*thread*) (fil *m* de) soie. **they**

were all in their ~s and satins elles étaient toutes en grande toilette; the shelves were full of ~s and satins les rayonnages regorgeaient de soierie et de satin; V artificial, raw, sewing etc.

(b) (*Brit Jur*) *[person]* to take ~ être nommé avocat de la couronne.

2 *cpd blouse etc* de *or* en soie. silk factory soierie *f* (*fabrique*); with a silk finish *cloth* similisé, mercerisé; *paintwork* satiné; silk hat haut-de-forme *m*; silk industry soierie *f* (*industrie*); silk manufacturer fabricant *m* en soierie; (*in Lyons*) soyeux *m*; (*U*) silkscreen printing sérigraphie *f*; silk stocking bas *m* de soie; silk thread fil *m* de soie, soie *f* à coudre; silkworm ver *m* à soie; silkworm breeding sériciculture *f*, élevage *m* des vers à soie.

silken ['sɪlkən] *adj dress, hair* soyeux; *skin* soyeux, satiné; *voice* doucereux. it has a ~ sheen cela a des reflets soyeux.

silkiness ['sɪlkɪnɪs] *n* qualité *or* douceur soyeuse, soyeux *m*.

silky ['sɪlkɪ] *adj hair, dress* (à l'aspect) soyeux; *voice* doucereux.

sill [sɪl] *n [window, door]* rebord *m*, appui *m*; (*Aut*) bas *m* de marche.

silliness ['sɪlɪnɪs] *n* sottise *f*, stupidité *f*, niaiserie *f*.

silly ['sɪlɪ] **1** *adj person* bête, idiot, sot (*f* sotte); *behaviour, answer* stupide, idiot, bête; *clothes, shoes* peu pratique, ridicule. you ~ fool! espèce d'idiot(e)!, quel(le) imbécile!; don't be ~ ne fais pas l'idiot(e) *or* l'imbécile; I felt ~ when he said ... je me suis senti bête *or* ridicule quand il a dit ...; I feel ~ in this hat je me sens ridicule *or* je dois avoir l'air idiot avec ce chapeau; he'll do something ~ il va faire une bêtise; that was a ~ thing to do c'était bête *or* idiot de faire cela; (*Press*) the ~ season la période creuse (*où les nouvelles manquent d'intérêt*); V knock.

2 *n* (*also* ~ billy*) idiot(e) *m(f)*. you big ~! espèce d'imbécile!, gros bêta (*f* grosse bêtasse)!*

silo ['saɪləʊ] *n* silo *m*.

silt [sɪlt] *n* vase *f*; (*alluvium*) limon *m*.

silt up **1** *vi* (*with mud*) s'envaser; (*with sand*) s'ensabler.

2 *vt sep [mud]* envaser; *[sand]* ensabler; (*gen*) boucher, engorger.

silver ['sɪlvəʳ] **1** *n* (*U*) **(a)** (*metal*) argent *m*; (~*ware, cutlery etc*) argenterie *f*.

(b) (*money*) argent *m* (monnayé), monnaie *f* (*en pièces d'argent*). have you got any ~? — sorry, only notes and coppers est-ce que vous avez de la monnaie? — désolé, je n'ai que des billets ou alors de la petite monnaie; £2 in ~ 2 livres en pièces d'argent.

2 *cpd cutlery, jewellery etc* d'argent, en argent. silver birch bouleau argenté; 'there will be a silver collection' 'vous êtes priés de contribuer généreusement à la quête'; silver fir sapin argenté; silverfish poisson *m* d'argent; silver foil = silver paper; silver fox renard argenté; silver gilt plaqué *m* argent; silver-grey argenté; silver-haired aux cheveux argentés; silver jubilee (célébration *f* du) vingt-cinquième anniversaire *m* (*d'un événement*); (*Prov*) every cloud has a silver lining après la pluie le beau temps (*Prov*); silver paper papier *m* d'argent *or* d'étain; (*U*) silver plate (*objects*) argenterie *f*; (*material*) plaqué *m* argent; silver-plated argenté, plaqué argent *inv*; silver plating argenture *f*; (*Cine*) the silver screen le grand écran; (*Brit Culin*) silverside tende *f* de tranche; silversmith orfèvre *mf*; (*fig*) to be born with a silver spoon in one's mouth naître fortuné, naître avec une cuiller d'argent dans la bouche; silver-tongued à la langue déliée, éloquent; (*U*) silverware argenterie *f*; silver wedding noces *fpl* d'argent.

3 *vt mirror, fork* argenter.

silvery ['sɪlvərɪ] *adj light, colour* argenté; *sound* argentin. ~ grey gris argenté *inv*.

simian ['sɪmɪən] *adj, n* simien(ne) *m(f)*.

similar ['sɪmɪləʳ] *adj* semblable (*to* à); (*less strongly*) similaire, comparable (*to* à). we have a ~ house notre maison est presque la même *or* presque pareille; the 2 houses are ~ in size les 2 maisons sont de dimensions similaires *or* comparables; the 2 houses are so ~ that ... les 2 maisons sont si semblables que ... *or* se ressemblent à un point tel que ...; on a ~ occasion dans des circonstances semblables *or* similaires, en semblable occasion; your case is ~ votre cas est semblable *or* similaire *or* analogue; paint removers and ~ products les décapants et produits similaires *or* voisins; vehicles ~ to the bicycle véhicules voisins de *or* apparentés à la bicyclette; it is ~ in colour ce n'est pas exactement la même couleur mais presque *or* mais c'est dans les mêmes tons; it is ~ in colour to ruby c'est d'une couleur semblable *or* comparable à celle du rubis.

similarity [ˌsɪmɪ'lærɪtɪ] *n* ressemblance *f* (*to* à, *between* entre), similitude *f* (*between* entre), similarité *f* (*between* entre).

similarly ['sɪmɪləlɪ] *adv* de la même façon. and ~, ... et de même ... .

simile ['sɪmɪlɪ] *n* (*Literat*) comparaison *f*. style rich in ~ style qui abonde en comparaisons.

similitude [sɪ'mɪlɪtjuːd] *n* similitude *f*, ressemblance *f*; (*Literat etc*) comparaison *f*.

simmer ['sɪməʳ] **1** *n* faible ébullition *f*, frémissement *m*, mijotage *m*. the stew was just on the ~ le ragoût cuisait à feu doux *or* mijotait.

2 *vi [water]* frémir; *[vegetables]* cuire à feu doux; *[soup, stew]* cuire à feu doux, mijoter, mitonner; (*fig*) (*with excitement*) être en ébullition; (*with anticipation*) être tout excité d'avance; (*with discontent*) bouillir de mécontentement; *[revolt]* couver, fermenter; *[anger]* couver, monter. he was ~ing (with rage) il bouillait (de rage).

3 *vt water, dye* laisser frémir; *soup, stew* faire cuire à feu doux, mijoter, mitonner; *vegetables* faire cuire à feu doux.

simmer down* *vi* (*fig*) s'apaiser, se calmer. simmer down! calme-toi!, un peu de calme!

simnel cake ['sɪmnlkeɪk] *n* (*Brit*) gâteau *m* aux raisins recouvert de pâte d'amandes (*généralement servi à Pâques*).

Simon ['saɪmən] *n* Simon *m*.

simonize ['saɪmənaɪz] *vt* ® lustrer, polir.

simony ['saɪmənɪ] *n* simonie *f*.

simper ['sɪmpəʳ] **1** *n* sourire affecté. ~s minauderie(s) *f(pl)*. **2** *vti* minauder. 'yes' she ~ed 'oui' dit-elle en minaudant.

simpering ['sɪmpərɪŋ] **1** *n* minauderies *fpl*, mignardises *fpl*. **2** *adj* minaudier, affecté, mignard.

simperingly ['sɪmpərɪŋlɪ] *adv* d'une manière affectée, avec affectation.

simple ['sɪmpl] **1** *adj* **(a)** (*not compound*) *substance, machine, fracture, sentence* simple; *tense* simple, non composé; *form of life* simple, élémentaire. ~ division division *f* simple; ~ equation équation *f* du premier degré; (*Fin, Math*) ~ interest intérêts *mpl* simples; V pure.

(b) (*uncomplicated, easy*) simple, facile; (*plain*) *furniture, way of dressing, style* simple, sans recherche; *dress* simple, sans apprêt; *attitude, answer* simple, franc (*f* franche). it's as ~ as ABC c'est simple comme bonjour; it's very ~! c'est très simple!, c'est tout ce qu'il y a de plus simple!; it's a ~ matter to have the clock repaired il est tout à fait simple *or* très simple de faire réparer la pendule; the ~ life la vie simple; she likes the ~ life elle aime vivre simplement *or* avec simplicité; a ~ little black dress une petite robe noire toute simple *or* très sobre; he's a ~ labourer c'est un simple ouvrier; they're ~ people ce sont des gens simples *or* sans façons; I'm a ~ soul je suis tout simple *or* sans façons (*V also* 1c); to make ~(r) simplifier; in ~ terms, in ~ English, in ~ language pour parler simplement *or* clairement, ≃ en bon français; the ~ fact that ... le simple fait que ...; the ~ truth la vérité pure et simple; for the ~ reason that ... pour la seule *or* simple raison que ...; a dangerously ~ way of ... une façon dangereusement simpliste de ... .

(c) (*innocent*) simple, ingénu, naïf (*f* naïve); (*foolish*) simple, sot (*f* sotte), niais. ~ Simon nigaud *m*, naïf *m*; he's a ~ soul c'est une âme simple, c'est un naïf; (*iro*) c'est une bonne âme; he's a bit ~ il est un peu simplet *or* un peu simple d'esprit.

2 *cpd*: simple-hearted (qui a le cœur) candide, franc (*f* franche), ouvert; simple-minded simplet, simple d'esprit, naïf (*f* naïve); simple-mindedness simplicité *f* d'esprit, naïveté *f*.

simpleton ['sɪmpltən] *n* nigaud(e) *m(f)*, niais(e) *m(f)*.

simplicity [sɪm'plɪsɪtɪ] *n* simplicité *f*. it's ~ itself c'est tout ce qu'il y a de plus simple, c'est la simplicité même, rien de plus simple.

simplifiable ['sɪmplɪfaɪəbl] *adj* simplifiable.

simplification [ˌsɪmplɪfɪ'keɪʃən] *n* simplification *f*.

simplify ['sɪmplɪfaɪ] *vt* simplifier.

simply ['sɪmplɪ] *adv* **(a)** *talk* simplement, avec simplicité; *live, dress* simplement, avec simplicité, sans prétention.

(b) (*only*) simplement, seulement; (*absolutely*) absolument. it ~ isn't possible, it is ~ impossible c'est absolument *or* tout simplement impossible; I ~ said that ... j'ai simplement *or* seulement dit que ...; she could ~ refuse elle pourrait refuser purement et simplement; you ~ MUST come! il faut absolument que vous veniez! (*subj*).

simulacrum [ˌsɪmjʊ'leɪkrəm] *n, pl* **simulacra** [ˌsɪmjʊ'leɪkrə] simulacre *m*.

simulate ['sɪmjʊleɪt] *vt passion, enthusiasm, grief* simuler, feindre, affecter; *illness* simuler, feindre.

simulation [ˌsɪmjʊ'leɪʃən] *n* simulation *f*, feinte *f*.

simulator ['sɪmjʊleɪtəʳ] *n* (*Aut, Space*) simulateur *m*; (*Aviat: also* flight ~) simulateur *m* de vol.

simultaneity [ˌsɪməltə'nɪətɪ] *n* simultanéité *f*.

simultaneous [ˌsɪməl'teɪnɪəs] *adj event, translation* simultané. (*Math*) ~ equations équations équivalentes.

simultaneously [ˌsɪməl'teɪnɪəslɪ] *adv* simultanément, en même temps. ~ with en même temps que.

sin [sɪn] **1** *n* péché *m*. ~s of omission/commission péchés par omission/par action; a ~ against (the law of) God un manquement à la loi de Dieu; it's a ~ to do that (*Rel*) c'est un péché que de faire cela; (* *fig*: † *or hum*) c'est une honte *or* un crime de faire cela; (*fig*) to live in ~ with sb vivre en concubinage avec qn; they are living in ~ ils vivent en concubinage; V seven, ugly etc.

2 *vi* pécher (*against* contre). (*fig*) he was more ~ned against than ~ning il était plus victime que coupable.

Sinai ['saɪneɪaɪ] *n* Sinaï *m*.

since [sɪns] **1** *conj* **(a)** (*in time*) depuis que. ~ I have been here depuis que je suis ici; ever ~ I met him depuis que *or* depuis le jour où je l'ai rencontré; it's a week ~ I saw him cela fait une semaine que je ne l'ai (pas) vu, je ne l'ai pas vu depuis une semaine; it's ages ~ I saw you cela fait des siècles qu'on ne s'est pas vus*.

(b) (*because*) puisque, comme, vu que, étant donné que.

2 *adv* depuis. he has not been here ~ il n'est pas venu depuis; he has been my friend ever ~ il est resté mon ami depuis (ce moment-là); a short time ~, not long ~ il y a peu de temps; it's many years ~ il y a bien des années de cela, cela fait bien des années.

3 *prep* depuis. ~ arriving *or* his arrival depuis son arrivée, depuis qu'il est arrivé; I have been waiting ~ 10 o'clock j'attends depuis 10 heures; ~ then depuis (lors); ever ~ 1900 France has attempted to ... depuis 1900 la France tente de *or* a sans cesse tenté de ...; ever ~ that we've been afraid that ... depuis que cela s'est produit nous redoutons *or* avons constamment craint que ... + *subj*; how long is it ~ the accident? combien de temps s'est passé *or* il s'est passé combien de temps depuis l'accident?, l'accident remonte à quand?

sincere [sɪn'sɪəʳ] *adj person, letter, apology* sincère; *emotion,*

offer, attempt sincère, réel, vrai. **it is my ~ belief that ...** je crois sincèrement que ...; **are they ~ in their desire to help us?** est-ce que leur désir de nous aider est (vraiment) sincère?
sincerely [sɪn'sɪəlɪ] *adv* sincèrement. (*letter-ending*) **Yours ~** ≃ Je vous prie d'agréer, Monsieur (*or* Madame *etc*), l'expression de mes sentiments les meilleurs; (*man to woman*) je vous prie d'agréer, Madame, mes très respectueux hommages; (*less formally*) cordialement à vous, bien à vous.
sincerity [sɪn'serɪtɪ] *n [person]* sincérité *f*, bonne foi; *[emotion]* sincérité. **in all ~** en toute sincérité.
sine [saɪn] *n* (*Math*) sinus *m*.
sinecure ['saɪnɪkjʊəʳ] *n* sinécure *f*.
sinew ['sɪnju:] *n* (*Anat*) tendon *m*. **~s** (*muscles*) muscles *mpl*; (*strength*) force(s) *f(pl)*; (*energy*) vigueur *f*, nerf *m*; **money is the ~s of war** l'argent est le nerf de la guerre; **a man of great moral ~** un homme d'une grande force morale.
sinewy ['sɪnjʊɪ] *adj body* musclé, nerveux; *meat* tendineux, nerveux; *fibres* tendineux.
sinful ['sɪnfʊl] *adj pleasure, desire, thought* coupable, inavouable; *act, waste* scandaleux, honteux; *town* immonde (*fig*). **~ person** pécheur *m*, -eresse *f*.
sinfully ['sɪnfəlɪ] *adv behave, think* d'une façon coupable; *waste etc* scandaleusement.
sinfulness ['sɪnfʊlnɪs] *n* (*U*) *[person]* péchés *mpl*; *[deed]* caractère coupable *or* scandaleux.
sing [sɪŋ] *pret* **sang**, *ptp* **sung 1** *vt [person, bird]* chanter; (*fig*) *sb's beauty etc* chanter, célébrer. **she sang the child to sleep** elle a chanté jusqu'à ce que l'enfant s'endorme; **she was ~ing the child to sleep** elle chantait pour que l'enfant s'endorme; **to ~ mass** chanter la messe; **sung mass** messe chantée, grand-messe *f*; (*fig*) **to ~ another tune** déchanter, changer de ton; (*fig*) **to ~ sb's praises** chanter les louanges de qn.
2 *vi* **(a)** *[person, bird, kettle, violin]* chanter; *[ears]* bourdonner, tinter; *[wind]* siffler. **to ~ like a lark** chanter comme un rossignol; **to ~ soprano** chanter soprano; **to ~ small*** se faire tout petit, filer doux*.
(b) (*US‡*) moucharder*, se mettre à table‡.
3 *cpd*: **to have a singsong** chanter en chœur; **to repeat sth in a singsong (voice)** répéter qch sur deux tons; **singsong voice** voix chantante *or* qui psalmodie.
sing out *vi* chanter fort; (**fig*) crier, parler fort, se faire entendre. **if you want anything just sing out*** si vous voulez quoi que ce soit vous n'avez qu'à appeler (bien fort); **to sing out for sth*** réclamer qch à grands cris.
sing up *vi* chanter plus fort. **sing up!** plus fort!
Singapore [ˌsɪŋgə'pɔ:ʳ] *n* Singapour *m*.
singe [sɪndʒ] **1** *vt* brûler légèrement; *cloth, clothes* roussir; *poultry* flamber. (*fig*) **to ~ one's wings** se brûler les ailes *or* les doigts. **2** *n* (*also* **~ mark**) légère brûlure; (*on cloth*) tache *f* de roussi, roussissure *f*.
singer ['sɪŋəʳ] *n* chanteur *m*, -euse *f*; *V* **opera** *etc*.
Singhalese [ˌsɪŋgə'li:z] **1** *adj* cingalais. **2** *n* **(a)** (*pl inv*) Cingalais(e) *m(f)*. **(b)** (*Ling*) cingalais *m*.
singing ['sɪŋɪŋ] **1** *n* (*U*) *[person, bird, violin]* chant *m*; *[kettle, wind]* sifflement *m*; (*in ears*) bourdonnement *m*, tintement *m*.
2 *cpd*: **to have singing lessons** prendre des leçons de chant, apprendre le chant; **singing teacher** professeur *m* de chant.
single ['sɪŋgl] **1** *adj* **(a)** (*only one*) seul, unique. **there was a ~ rose in the garden** il y avait une seule rose dans le jardin; **he gave her a ~ rose** il lui a donné une rose; **if there is a ~ or one ~ objection to this proposal** s'il y a une seule *or* la moindre objection à cette proposition; **he was the ~ survivor** il était le seul *or* l'unique survivant; **a ~ diamond** un diamant monté seul; (*as ring*) un solitaire; (*Rail*) **a ~ track** une voie unique (*V also* 3); **every ~ day** tous les jours sans exception; **not a ~ person spoke** pas une seule personne n'a parlé; **I didn't see a ~ soul** je n'ai vu personne, je n'ai pas vu âme qui vive; **I haven't a ~ moment to lose** je n'ai pas une minute à perdre; **a *or* one ~ department should deal with all of these matters** un service unique *or* un même service devrait traiter toutes ces affaires.
(b) (*not double etc*) *knot, flower* simple. (*Brit*) **a ~ ticket to London** un aller (simple) *or* un billet simple pour Londres; (*Brit*) **~ fare** prix *m* d'un aller (simple); **in ~ file** *stand* en file indienne; *move* à la *or* en file indienne; **~ bed** lit *m* d'une personne; **~ room** chambre *f* à un lit *or* particulière *or* pour une personne; **to type sth in ~ spacing** taper qch à simple interligne.
(c) (*unmarried*) célibataire. **~ people** célibataires *mpl*; **she's a ~ woman** elle est célibataire, c'est une célibataire; (*Soc*) **the ~ homeless** les gens seuls et sans abri; **the ~ state, the ~ life** le célibat.
2 *n* **(a)** (*Sport: pl*) **~s** simple *m*; **ladies' ~s** simple dames.
(b) (*Brit Rail: ticket*) aller *m* (simple), billet *m* simple.
(c) (*in cinema, theatre*) **there are only ~s left** il ne reste que des places séparées *or* isolées.
(d) (*record*) **a ~** un 45 tours; **his latest ~** son dernier 45 tours.
3 *cpd*: **single-barrelled** à un canon; (*Dress*) **single-breasted** droit; **single-celled** unicellulaire; **in single combat** en combat singulier; (*Brit*) **single-decker** (*adj*) sans impériale; (*n*) autobus *m or* tramway *m etc* sans impériale; **single-engined** monomoteur (*f*-trice); **single-entry book-keeping** comptabilité *f* en partie simple; **single-handed** (*adv*) tout seul, sans (aucune) aide; (*adj*) *achievement* fait sans aide; (*Naut*) *sailing, voyage, race* en solitaire; *[person]* **to be single-handed** n'avoir aucune aide, être tout seul; **single-masted** à un mât; **single-minded** *person* résolu, ferme; *attempt* énergique, résolu; *determination* tenace; **to be single-minded about sth** concentrer tous ses efforts sur qch; **to be single-minded in one's efforts to do sth** tout faire en vue de faire qch; (*Pol*) **single-party** *state, government* à parti unique; (*Aviat*) **single-seater (aeroplane)** (avion *m*) monoplace *m*; (*Rail*) **single-track** à voie unique; (*fig*) **to have a single-track mind** n'avoir qu'une idée en tête, être obsédé (par une seule idée).
single out *vt sep* (*distinguish*) distinguer; (*pick out*) choisir. **I don't want to single anyone out** je ne veux pas faire de distinctions; **he's singled out for all the nasty jobs** on le choisit pour toutes les corvées; **to single o.s. out** se singulariser.
singleness ['sɪŋglnɪs] *n*: **~ of purpose** persévérance *f*, ténacité *f*, unité *f* d'intention.
singlet ['sɪŋglɪt] *n* (*Brit*) maillot *m or* tricot *m* de corps.
singleton ['sɪŋgltən] *n* (*Cards*) singleton *m*.
singly ['sɪŋglɪ] *adv* (*one by one*) séparément, un(e) à un(e); (*unaided*) tout(e) seul(e), sans (aucune) aide.
singular ['sɪŋgjʊləʳ] **1** *adj* **(a)** (*Gram*) *noun, verb* au singulier, singulier; *form, ending* du singulier. **the masculine ~** le masculin singulier. **(b)** (*outstanding*) singulier, remarquable; (*unusual*) singulier, rare; (*strange*) singulier, étrange, bizarre; (*surprising*) singulier, extraordinaire, surprenant. **2** *n* (*Gram*) singulier *m*. **in the ~** au singulier.
singularity [ˌsɪŋgjʊ'lærɪtɪ] *n* **(a)** (*U*: *V* **singular 1b**) singularité *f*; rareté *f*; étrangeté *f*, bizarrerie *f*. **(b)** (*singular feature*) singularité *f*.
singularize ['sɪŋgjʊləraɪz] *vt* singulariser.
singularly ['sɪŋgjʊləlɪ] *adv* (*V* **singular 1b**) singulièrement; remarquablement; étrangement, bizarrement; extraordinairement.
Sinhalese [ˌsɪŋə'li:z] = **Singhalese.**
sinister ['sɪnɪstəʳ] *adj* **(a)** *omen, sign, silenre* sinistre, funeste, de mauvais augure; *plan, plot, appearance, figure* sinistre, menaçant. **(b)** (*Her*) sénestre.
sinisterly ['sɪnɪstəlɪ] *adv* sinistrement.
sink[1] [sɪŋk] *pret* **sank**, *ptp* **sunk 1** *vi* **(a)** (*go under*) *[ship]* couler, sombrer; *[person, object]* couler. **to ~ to the bottom** couler *or* aller au fond; **to ~ like a stone** couler à pic; (*fig*) **they left him to ~ or swim** ils l'ont laissé s'en sortir* *or* s'en tirer* tout seul; (*fig*) **it was ~ or swim** il fallait bien s'en sortir* *or* s'en tirer*; **~ or swim he'll have to manage by himself** il n'a qu'à se débrouiller comme il peut.
(b) *[ground]* s'affaisser; *[foundation, building]* s'affaisser, se tasser; *[level, river, fire]* baisser. **the land ~s towards the sea** le terrain descend en pente vers la mer; **the sun was ~ing** le soleil se couchait; **the sun sank below the horizon** le soleil a disparu *or* s'est enfoncé au-dessous de l'horizon; **to ~ out of sight** disparaître; **to ~ to one's knees** tomber à genoux; **to ~ to the ground** s'affaisser, s'écrouler; **he sank into a chair** il s'est laissé tomber *or* s'est affaissé *or* s'est effondré dans un fauteuil; **he sank into the mud up to his knees** il s'est enfoncé *or* il a enfoncé dans la boue jusqu'aux genoux; **she let her head ~ into the pillow** elle a laissé retomber sa tête sur l'oreiller; **the water slowly sank into the ground** l'eau a pénétré *or* s'est infiltré lentement dans le sol; (*fig: dying*) **he is ~ing fast** il décline *or* il baisse rapidement.
(c) (*fig*) **to ~ into a deep sleep** tomber *or* sombrer dans un sommeil profond; **to ~ into despondency** tomber dans le découragement, se laisser aller au découragement; **to ~ into insignificance/poverty/despair** sombrer dans l'insignifiance/la misère/le désespoir; **he has sunk in my estimation** il a baissé dans mon estime; **his voice sank** sa voix s'est faite plus basse; **his voice sank to a whisper** il s'est mis à chuchoter, sa voix n'a plus été qu'un murmure; **his heart *or* his spirits sank** le découragement *or* l'accablement s'est emparé de lui, il en a eu un coup de cafard*; **his heart sank at the thought** il a eu un serrement de cœur *or* son cœur s'est serré à cette pensée, il a été pris de découragement à cette idée; **it's enough to make your heart ~** c'est à vous démoraliser *or* à vous donner le cafard*.
(d) *[prices, value, temperature]* tomber très bas, baisser beaucoup; *[sales, numbers]* baisser beaucoup. (*St Ex*) **the shares have sunk to 3 dollars** les actions sont tombées à 3 dollars; (*Fin*) **the pound has sunk to a new low** la livre est tombée plus bas que jamais *or* a atteint sa cote la plus basse.
2 *vt* **(a)** *ship* couler, faire sombrer; *object* faire couler (au fond); (*fig*) *theory* démolir; *business, project* ruiner, couler; *play, book* couler, démolir; (*) *person* couler, ruiner la réputation de. (*fig*) **they sank their differences** ils ont enterré *or* oublié *or* mis de côté leurs querelles; **to be sunk in thought/depression/despair** être plongé dans ses pensées/la dépression/le désespoir; **I'm sunk*** je suis fichu* *or* perdu.
(b) *mine, well* creuser, forer; *foundations* creuser; *pipe etc* noyer. **to ~ a post 2 metres in the ground** enfoncer un pieu 2 mètres dans le sol; **the dog sank his fangs into my leg** le chien a enfoncé *or* planté ses crocs dans ma jambe; **he sank his teeth into the sandwich** il a mordu (à belles dents) dans le sandwich; **he can ~ a glass of beer in 5 seconds*** il peut avaler *or* s'envoyer‡ une bière en 5 secondes; (*Golf*) **to ~ the ball** faire entrer la balle dans le trou; (*fig*) **to ~ a lot of money in a project** (*invest*) investir *or* placer beaucoup d'argent dans une entreprise; (*lose*) perdre *or* engloutir *or* engouffrer beaucoup d'argent dans une entreprise.
sink back *vi* (se laisser) retomber, se renverser. **it sank back into the water** c'est retombé dans l'eau; **he managed to sit up but soon sank back exhausted** il a réussi à s'asseoir mais s'est bientôt laissé retomber épuisé; **he sank back into his chair** il s'est enfoncé dans son fauteuil.
sink down *vi [building]* s'enfoncer, s'affaisser; *[post]* s'enfoncer. **to sink down into a chair** s'affaisser dans un fauteuil; **to sink down on one's knees** tomber à genoux; **he sank down (out of sight) behind the bush** il a disparu derrière le buisson.
sink in *vi* **(a)** *[person, post etc]* s'enfoncer; *[water, ointment etc]* pénétrer.

(b) (*fig*) *[explanation]* rentrer; *[remark]* faire son effet. **when the facts sank in, he ...** quand il a pleinement compris les faits, il ...; **as it hadn't really sunk in yet he ...** comme il n'arrivait pas encore à s'en rendre compte il ..., comme il ne réalisait* pas encore il ...; **my explanation took a long time to sink in** j'ai eu du mal à lui (*or* leur *etc*) faire rentrer *or* pénétrer l'explication dans la tête, il a (*or* ils ont *etc*) mis longtemps à comprendre mon explication.

sink[2] [sɪŋk] **1** *n* évier *m.* (*fig*) **a ~ of iniquity** un cloaque du *or* de vice; *V* **kitchen. 2** *cpd*: **sink tidy** coin *m* d'évier (*ustensile ménager*); **sink unit** bloc-évier *m.*

sinker [ˈsɪŋkəʳ] *n* plomb *m*; *V* **hook.**

sinking [ˈsɪŋkɪŋ] **1** *adj*: **with ~ heart** le cœur serré; (*stronger*) la mort dans l'âme; **that ~ feeling** ce serrement de cœur; (*stronger*) ce sentiment de désastre imminent; **to have a ~ feeling** avoir un serrement de cœur; (*stronger*) avoir la mort dans l'âme; **I had a ~ feeling that he would come back again** j'avais le pénible *or* fâcheux pressentiment qu'il reviendrait.

2 *n* (*shipwreck*) naufrage *m.* **the submarine's ~ of the cruiser made possible ...** quand le sous-marin a coulé le croiseur cela a permis... .

3 *cpd*: (*Fin*) **sinking fund** caisse *f* d'amortissement.

sinless [ˈsɪnlɪs] *adj* sans péché, pur, innocent.

sinner [ˈsɪnəʳ] *n* pécheur *m*, -eresse *f.*

Sino- [ˈsaɪnəʊ] *pref* sino-. **~Soviet** sino-soviétique.

Sinologist [ˌsaɪˈnɒlədʒɪst] *n* sinologue *mf.*

Sinology [ˌsaɪˈnɒlədʒɪ] *n* sinologie *f.*

sinuosity [ˌsɪnjʊˈɒsɪtɪ] *n* sinuosité *f.*

sinuous [ˈsɪnjʊəs] *adj* (*lit, fig*) sinueux.

sinus [ˈsaɪnəs] *n* sinus *m inv* (*Med*).

sinusitis [ˌsaɪnəˈsaɪtɪs] *n* (*U*) sinusite *f.*

Sioux [suː] **1** *adj* sioux *inv.* **2** *n* **(a)** (*pl inv*) Sioux *mf.* **(b)** (*Ling*) sioux *m.*

sip [sɪp] **1** *n* petite gorgée. **do you want a ~ of rum?** voulez-vous une goutte de rhum?; **he took a ~** il a bu une petite gorgée. **2** *vt* boire à petites gorgées *or* à petits coups; (*with enjoyment*) siroter*.

siphon [ˈsaɪfən] **1** *n* siphon *m*; *V* **soda.**

2 *vt* siphonner.

siphon off *vt sep* (*lit*) siphonner; (*fig*) *people etc* séparer; *profits, funds* canaliser; (*illegally*) détourner.

sir [sɜːʳ] *n* monsieur *m.* **yes ~** oui Monsieur; (*to army officer*) oui mon capitaine (*or* mon lieutenant *etc*); (*to surgeon*) oui docteur; (*in letter*) **Dear S~** (Cher) Monsieur; (*to newspaper editor*) **S~** Monsieur (le Directeur); (*iro*) **my dear/good ~** mon cher/bon Monsieur; (*Brit*) **S~ John Smith** sir John Smith.

sire [ˈsaɪəʳ] **1** *n* (*Zool*) père *m*; (††: *father*) père; (††: *ancestor*) aïeul *m.* (*to king*) **yes ~** oui sire. **2** *vt* engendrer.

siren [ˈsaɪərən] **1** *n* (*all senses*) sirène *f.* **2** *adj* (*liter*) *charms* séducteur (*f* -trice); *song* de sirène, enchanteur (*f* -teresse).

sirloin [ˈsɜːlɔɪn] *n* aloyau *m.* **a ~ steak** un bifteck dans l'aloyau *or* d'aloyau.

sirocco [sɪˈrɒkəʊ] *n* sirocco *m.*

sis‡ [sɪs] *n* (*abbr of* **sister**) sœurette *f*, frangine‡ *f.*

sisal [ˈsaɪsəl] **1** *n* sisal *m.* **2** *cpd* en *or* de sisal.

sissy* [ˈsɪsɪ] **1** *n* (*coward*) poule mouillée. (*effeminate*) **he's a bit of a ~** il est un peu efféminé, il fait un peu tapette‡. **2** *adj* efféminé. **that's ~!** ça fait fille!

sister [ˈsɪstəʳ] **1** *n* **(a)** sœur *f.* **her younger ~** sa (sœur) cadette, sa petite sœur; *V* **half, step** *etc.*

(b) (*Rel*) religieuse *f*, (bonne) sœur *f.* **yes ~** oui ma sœur; **S~ Mary Margaret** sœur Marie Marguerite; **the S~s of Charity** les sœurs de la Charité.

(c) (*Brit Med*) infirmière *f* en chef. **yes ~** oui Madame (*or* Mademoiselle).

(d) (*US*) **listen ~!**‡ écoute ma vieille!*

2 *cpd*: **sister-in-law** belle-sœur *f.*

3 *adj*: **~ nations/organizations** nations *fpl*/organisations *fpl* sœurs; **~ peoples/countries** peuples *mpl*/pays *mpl* frères; **~ ship** sister-ship *m.*

sisterhood [ˈsɪstəhʊd] *n* (*gen*) fraternité *f*; (*Rel*) communauté *f* (religieuse).

sisterly [ˈsɪstəlɪ] *adj* de sœur, fraternel.

Sistine [ˈsɪstiːn] *adj*: **the ~ Chapel** la chapelle Sixtine.

sit [sɪt] *pret, ptp* **sat 1** *vi* **(a)** s'asseoir. **to be ~ting** être assis; (*to dog*) **~!** assis!; **~ by me** assieds-toi près de moi; **he was ~ting at his desk/at table** il était (assis) à son bureau/à table; **they spent the evening ~ting at home** ils ont passé la soirée (tranquillement) à la maison; **she just ~s at home all day** elle reste chez elle toute la journée à ne rien faire; **he was ~ting over his books all evening** il a passé toute la soirée dans ses livres; **to ~ through a lecture/play** *etc* assister à une conférence/à une pièce jusqu'au bout; **don't just ~ there, do something!** ne reste pas là à ne rien faire!; **to ~ still** rester *or* se tenir tranquille, ne pas bouger; **to ~ straight** *or* **upright** se tenir droit; (*lit, fig: stay put*) **to ~ tight** ne pas bouger; (*fig*) **to be ~ting pretty*** avoir le bon filon*, tenir le bon bout*; (*fig: hum or liter*) **to ~ at sb's feet** suivre l'enseignement de qn; (*Art, Phot*) **to ~ for one's portrait** poser pour son portrait; **she sat for Picasso** elle a posé pour Picasso; **to ~ on a committee/jury** être membre *or* faire partie d'un comité/jury; (*fig*) **to ~ for an exam** passer un examen, se présenter à un examen; **he sat for Sandhurst** il s'est présenté au concours d'entrée de Sandhurst; (*Brit Parl*) **he ~s for Brighton** il est (le) député de Brighton.

(b) *[bird, insect]* se poser, se percher. **to be ~ting** être perché; (*on eggs*) couver; **the hen is ~ting on 12 eggs** la poule couve 12 œufs.

(c) *[committee, assembly etc]* être en séance; siéger. **the committee is ~ting now** le comité est en séance; **the House ~s from November to June** la Chambre siège de novembre à juin; **the House sat for 16 hours** la Chambre a été en séance pendant 16 heures.

(d) *[dress, coat etc]* tomber (*on sb* sur qn). **the jacket ~s badly across the shoulders** la veste tombe mal aux épaules; (*liter*) **it sat heavy on his conscience** cela lui pesait sur la conscience; (*liter*) **how ~s the wind?** d'où vient *or* souffle le vent?

2 *vt* **(a)** (*also* **~ down**) asseoir, installer; (*invite to ~*) faire asseoir. **he sat the child (down) on his knee** il a assis *or* installé l'enfant sur ses genoux; **they sat him (down) in a chair** (*placed him in it*) ils l'ont assis *or* installé dans un fauteuil; (*invited him to sit*) ils l'ont fait asseoir dans un fauteuil.

(b) **to ~ a horse well/badly** monter bien/mal, avoir une bonne/mauvaise assiette.

(c) (*esp Brit*) *exam* passer, se présenter à.

3 *cpd*: **he had a 10-minute sit-down*** il s'est assis 10 minutes (pour se reposer); **we had a sit-down lunch*** nous avons déjeuné à table; **sit-down strike** grève *f* sur le tas; **sit-in** *[demonstrators etc]* sit-in *m inv*, manifestation *f* avec occupation de locaux; *[workers]* grève *f* sur le tas; **the workers held a sit-in** les ouvriers ont organisé une grève sur le tas; **the students held a sit-in in the university offices** les étudiants ont occupé les bureaux de l'université; **sit-upon*** derrière *m*, fesses *fpl.*

sit about, sit around *vi* rester assis (à ne rien faire), traîner.

sit back *vi*: **to sit back in an armchair** s'enfoncer *or* se carrer *or* se caler dans un fauteuil; **to sit back on one's heels** s'asseoir sur les talons; **just sit back and listen to this** installe-toi bien et écoute un peu (ceci); (*fig*) **he sat back and did nothing about it** il s'est abstenu de faire quoi que ce soit, il n'a pas levé le petit doigt; (*fig*) **I can't just sit back and do nothing!** je ne peux quand même pas rester là à ne rien faire! *or* à me croiser les bras!; **the Government sat back and did nothing to help them** le gouvernement n'a pas fait le moindre geste pour les aider.

sit down 1 *vi* s'asseoir. **to be sitting down** être assis; **he sat down to a huge dinner** il s'est attablé devant un repas gigantesque; (*fig*) **to sit down under an insult** supporter une insulte sans broncher, encaisser* une insulte.

2 *vt sep* = **sit 2a.**

3 **sit-down** *n, adj V* **sit 3.**

sit in 1 *vi* **(a)** **she sat in all day waiting for him to come** elle est restée à la maison toute la journée à l'attendre, elle a passé la journée chez elle à l'attendre; **to sit in on a discussion** assister à une discussion (sans y prendre part); (*fig: replace*) **to sit in for sb** remplacer qn.

(b) **the demonstrators sat in in the director's office** les manifestants ont occupé le bureau du directeur.

2 **sit-in** *n V* **sit 3.**

sit on* *vt fus* (*fig*) **(a)** (*keep secret, not publish etc*) *news, facts, report* garder secret, garder le silence sur, garder sous le boisseau; (*not pass on*) *file, document* garder (pour soi), accaparer.

(b) *person* (*silence*) faire taire, fermer *or* clouer le bec à*; (*snub etc*) remettre à sa place, rabrouer, rembarrer*. **he won't be sat on** il ne se laisse pas marcher sur les pieds.

(c) (*reject*) *idea, proposal* rejeter, repousser.

sit out 1 *vi* (*sit outside*) (aller) s'asseoir dehors, se mettre *or* s'installer dehors.

2 *vt sep* **(a)** **to sit a lecture/play** *etc* **out** rester jusqu'à la fin d'une conférence/d'une pièce *etc*, assister à une conférence/à une pièce *etc* jusqu'au bout.

(b) **she sat out the waltz** elle n'a pas dansé la valse.

sit up 1 *vi* **(a)** (*sit upright*) se redresser, s'asseoir bien droit. **to be sitting up** être assis bien droit, se tenir droit; **he was sitting up in bed** il était assis dans son lit; **you can sit up now** vous pouvez vous asseoir maintenant; (*fig*) **to make sb sit up** secouer *or* étonner qn; (*fig*) **to sit up (and take notice)** se secouer, se réveiller; (*after illness*) **he began to sit up and take notice** il a commencé à reprendre intérêt à la vie *or* à refaire surface.

(b) (*stay up*) rester debout, ne pas se coucher. **to sit up late** se coucher tard, veiller tard; **to sit up all night** ne pas se coucher de la nuit; **don't sit up for me** couchez-vous sans m'attendre; **the nurse sat up with him** l'infirmière est restée à son chevet *or* l'a veillé.

2 *vt sep doll, child* asseoir, redresser.

sit upon* 1 *vt fus* = **sit on*.**

2 **sit-upon*** *n V* **sit 3.**

sitcom* [ˈsɪtkɒm] *n* (*Rad, TV etc: abbr of* **situation comedy**) comédie *f* de situation.

site [saɪt] **1** *n [town, building]* emplacement *m*; (*Archeol*) site *m*; (*Constr*) chantier *m* (de construction *or* de démolition *etc*); (*Camping*) (terrain *m* de) camping *m.* **the ~ of the battle** le champ de bataille; *V* **building, launching** *etc.*

2 *vt town, building, gun* placer. **they want to ~ the steelworks in that valley** on veut placer *or* construire l'aciérie dans cette vallée; **the factory is very badly ~d** l'usine est très mal située *or* placée.

siting [ˈsaɪtɪŋ] *n*: **the ~ of the new town there was a mistake** c'était une erreur de bâtir *or* placer la ville nouvelle à cet endroit; **the ~ of the new factories has given rise to many objections** le choix de l'emplacement pour les nouvelles usines a soulevé de nombreuses critiques.

sitter [ˈsɪtəʳ] *n* (*Art*) modèle *m*; (*baby-~*) baby-sitter *m*; (*hen*) couveuse *f.* (*Sport*) **he missed a ~**‡ il a raté un coup enfantin; **it's a ~!**‡ tu ne peux pas (*or* il ne peut pas *etc*) le rater!

sitting [ˈsɪtɪŋ] **1** *n [committee, assembly etc]* séance *f*; (*for portrait*) séance de pose; (*in canteen etc*) service *m.* **they served 200 people in one ~/in 2 ~s** ils ont servi 200 personnes à la fois/en 2 services; **2nd ~ for lunch** 2e service pour le déjeuner.

2 *adj committee* en séance; *game bird* posé, au repos.

3 *cpd*: **sitting and standing room** places debout et assises;

(fig) **sitting duck‡** victime *f or* cible *f* facile; *(Brit Parl)* **sitting member** député *m* en exercice; **sitting room** salon *m*; **sitting tenant** locataire *mf* en possession des lieux *or* en place.

situate ['sɪtjʊeɪt] *vt (locate) building, town* placer; *(put into perspective) problem, event* situer. **the house is ~d in the country** la maison se trouve *or* est située à la campagne; **the shop is well ~d** le magasin est bien situé *or* bien placé; **we are rather badly ~d as there is no bus service** nous sommes assez mal situés car il n'y a pas d'autobus; *(fig)* **he is rather badly ~d at the moment** il est dans une situation assez défavorable *or* en assez mauvaise posture en ce moment; *(financially)* il est assez gêné *or* il a des ennuis d'argent en ce moment; **I am well ~d to appreciate the risks** je suis bien placé pour apprécier les risques; **how are you ~d for money?** est-ce que tu as l'argent qu'il te faut?, est-ce que tu as besoin d'argent?

situation [ˌsɪtjʊ'eɪʃən] **1** *n* **(a)** *(location) [town, building etc]* situation *f*, emplacement *m*. **the house has a fine ~** la maison est bien située. **(b)** *(circumstances)* situation *f (also Literat)*. **he was in a very difficult ~** il se trouvait dans une situation très difficile; **they managed to save the ~** ils ont réussi à sauver *or* redresser la situation; **the international ~** la situation internationale, la conjoncture internationale. **(c)** *(job)* situation *f*, emploi *m*, poste *m*. **'~s vacant/wanted'** 'offres *fpl*/demandes *fpl* d'emploi'. **2** *cpd*: *(Theat etc)* **situation comedy** comédie *f* de situation.

six [sɪks] **1** *adj* six *inv*. **he is ~ (years old)** il a six ans (*V also* 3); **he'll be ~ on Saturday** il aura six ans samedi; **he lives in number ~** il habite au (numéro) six; **~ times six** six fois six.

2 *n* six *m inv*. **there were about ~** il y en avait six environ *or* à peu près; **~ of the girls came** six des filles sont venues; **there are ~ of us** nous sommes *or* on est* six; **all ~ (of us) left** nous sommes partis tous les six; **all ~ (of them) left** tous les six sont partis, ils sont partis tous les six; **it is ~ o'clock** il est six heures; **come at ~** venez à six heures; **it struck ~** six heures ont sonné; **they are sold in ~es** c'est vendu *or* cela se vend par (lots *or* paquets de) six; **the children arrived in ~es** les enfants sont arrivés par groupes de six; **he lives at ~ Churchill Street** il habite (au) six rue Churchill; *(Brit)* **~ of the best*** six grands coups; *(fig)* **to be at ~es and sevens** *[books, house etc]* être en désordre *or* en pagaïe*, être sens dessus dessous; *[person]* être retourné*; *(hum)* **to be ~ foot under*** manger les pissenlits par la racine*; *(fig)* **it's ~ of one and half a dozen of the other** c'est blanc bonnet et bonnet blanc, c'est du pareil au même*, c'est kif-kif*; *V* **knock**.

3 *cpd*: *(Aut)* **six-cylinder** *(adj)* à six cylindres; *(n)* (voiture *f* à) six cylindres *f*; *(Mus)* **in six-eight time** en mesure à six-huit; **sixfold** *(adj)* sextuple; *(adv)* au sextuple; **a six-footer*** un grand d'un mètre quatre-vingts; *(US)* **six-pack** pack *m or* emballage *m* de six; *(Brit)* **sixpence** *(coin)* (ancienne) pièce *f* de six pence; *(value)* six pence *mpl*; **sixpenny** *(adj)* à six pence; **six-seater** *(adj)* à six places; *(n) (car etc)* (voiture *f etc* à) six places *f*; *(plane etc)* (avion *m etc* à) six places *m*; **six-shooter** pistolet *m* automatique; **six-sided** hexagonal; *(Aut)* **six-speed gearbox** boîte *f* à six vitesses; **six-storey** à six étages; **six-year-old** *(adj) child, horse* de six ans; *house, car* vieux (*f* vieille) de six ans; *(n) (child)* enfant (âgé) de six ans; *(horse)* cheval *m* de six ans.

sixish ['sɪksɪʃ] *adj*: **he is ~** il a dans les six ans, il a six ans environ; **he came at ~** il est venu vers (les) six heures.

sixteen ['sɪks'tiːn] **1** *adj* seize *inv*. **she was sweet ~** c'était une fraîche jeune fille (de seize ans). **2** *n* seize *m inv*; *for phrases V* **six**.

sixteenth ['sɪks'tiːnθ] **1** *adj* seizième. **2** *n* seizième *mf*; *(fraction)* seizième *m*; *for phrases V* **sixth**.

sixth [sɪksθ] **1** *adj* sixième. **to be ~ in an exam/in German** être sixième à un concours/en allemand; **she was the ~ to arrive** elle est arrivée la sixième; **Charles the S~** Charles six; **the ~ of November, November the ~** le six novembre; *(fig)* **~ sense** sixième sens *m*.

2 *n* sixième *mf*; *(fraction)* sixième *m*; *(Mus)* sixte *f*. **he wrote the letter on the ~** il a écrit la lettre le six, sa lettre est du six; **your letter of the ~** votre lettre du six (courant); *(Brit Scol)* **the ~ = the ~ form** (*V* 4).

3 *adv* **(a)** *(in race, exam, competition)* en sixième position *or* place. **he came** *or* **was placed ~** il s'est classé sixième.
(b) = **sixthly**.

4 *cpd*: *(Brit Scol)* **sixth form** ≃ classes *fpl* de première et terminale; **to be in the sixth form** ≃ être en première *or* en terminale; **sixth-form pupil, sixth-former** ≃ élève *mf* de première *or* de terminale.

sixthly ['sɪksθlɪ] *adv* sixièmement, en sixième lieu.

sixtieth ['sɪkstɪɪθ] **1** *adj* soixantième. **2** *n* soixantième *mf*; *(fraction)* soixantième *m*.

sixty ['sɪkstɪ] **1** *adj* soixante *inv*. **he is about ~** il a une soixantaine d'années, il a dans les soixante ans; **about ~ books** une soixantaine de livres.

2 *n* soixante *m inv*. **about ~** une soixantaine, environ soixante; **to be in one's sixties** avoir entre soixante et soixante-dix ans, être sexagénaire; **he is in his early sixties** il a un peu plus de soixante ans; **he is in his late sixties** il approche de soixante-dix ans; **she's getting on** *or* **going on for ~** elle approche de la soixantaine, elle va sur ses soixante ans; **(1960s etc) in the sixties** dans les années soixante; **in the early/late sixties** au début/vers la fin des années soixante; **the temperature was in the sixties** il faisait entre quinze et vingt degrés; **the numbers were in the sixties** le nombre s'élevait à plus de soixante; *(Aut)* **to do ~*** faire du soixante milles (à l'heure), ≃ faire du cent (à l'heure); *for other phrases V* **six**.

3 *cpd*: **sixty-first** soixante et unième; *(fig)* **that's the sixty-four (thousand) dollar question*** c'est la question cruciale, c'est toute la question; **there were sixty-odd*** il y en avait soixante et quelques*, il y en avait une soixantaine; **sixty-odd books** un peu plus de soixante livres, soixante et quelques livres; **sixty-one** soixante et un; **sixty-second** soixante-deuxième; **sixty-two** soixante-deux.

sizable ['saɪzəbl] *adj* = **sizeable**.

sizably ['saɪzəblɪ] *adv* = **sizeably**.

size¹ [saɪz] **1** *n (for plaster, paper)* colle *f*; *(for cloth)* apprêt *m*. **2** *vt* encoller; apprêter.

size² [saɪz] **1** *n* **(a)** *[person, animal, sb's head, hands]* taille *f*; *[room, building]* grandeur *f*, dimensions *fpl*; *[car, chair]* dimensions; *[egg, fruit, jewel]* grosseur *f*; *[parcel]* grosseur, dimensions; *[book, photograph, sheet of paper, envelope]* taille, dimensions; *(format)* format *m*; *[sum]* montant *m*; *[estate, park, country]* étendue *f*, superficie *f*; *[problem, difficulty, obstacle]* ampleur *f*, étendue; *[operation, campaign]* ampleur, envergure *f*. *[packet, tube etc]* **the small/large ~** le petit/grand modèle; **the ~ of the town** l'importance *f* de la ville; **a building of vast ~** un bâtiment de belles dimensions; **the ~ of the farm** *(building)* les dimensions de la ferme; *(land)* l'étendue de la ferme; **the ~ of the fish you caught** la taille du poisson que tu as attrapé; **the ~ of the sum involved was so large that ...** la somme en question était d'une telle importance que ...; **sort them according to ~** triez-les selon la grosseur (*or* le format *etc*); **it's the ~ of a brick** c'est de la taille d'une brique; **it's the ~ of a walnut** c'est de la grosseur d'une noix; **it's the ~ of a house/elephant** c'est grand comme une maison/un éléphant; **a child of that ~ shouldn't be allowed to do that** un enfant de cette taille *or* de cet âge ne devrait pas avoir le droit de faire ça; **he's about your ~** il est à peu près de la même taille que vous; *(fig)* **that's about the ~ of it!** c'est à peu près ça!, quelque chose dans ce genre-là!; **he cut the wood to ~** il a coupé le bois à la dimension voulue; **they are all of a ~** ils sont tous de la même grosseur (*or* de la même taille *etc*); *V* **cut down, shape** *etc*.

(b) *[coat, skirt, dress, trousers etc]* taille *f*; *[shoes, gloves]* pointure *f*; *[shirt]* encolure *f*. **what ~ are you?, what ~ do you take?** *(in dress etc)* quelle taille faites-vous?; *(in shoes, gloves)* quelle pointure faites-vous?; *(in hats)* quel est votre tour de tête?; **what ~ of collar?** *or* **shirt?** quelle encolure?; **I take ~ 12** je prends du 12 *or* la taille 12; **what ~ of waist are you?** quel est votre tour de taille?; **hip ~** tour *m* de hanches; **what ~ (of) shoes do you take?** quelle pointure faites-vous?, vous chaussez du combien?; **I take ~ 5 (shoes)** ≃ je chausse *or* je fais du 38; **we are out of ~ 5 (shoes)** ≃ nous n'avons plus de (chaussures en) 38; **try this for ~** essayez ceci pour la taille (*or* la pointure *etc*); **I need a ~ smaller** il me faut la taille (*or* la pointure *etc*) en-dessous; **it's 2 ~s too big for me** c'est 2 tailles au-dessus de ce qu'il me faut; **we haven't got your ~** nous n'avons pas votre taille (*or* pointure *etc*).

2 *vt* classer *or* trier selon la grosseur (*or* la dimension *or* la taille *etc*).

size up *vt sep person* juger, jauger; *situation* mesurer. **to size up the problem** mesurer l'étendue du problème; **I can't quite size him up** *(know what he is worth)* je n'arrive pas vraiment à le juger *or* à décider ce qu'il vaut; *(know what he wants)* je ne vois pas vraiment où il veut en venir.

-size(d) [saɪz(d)] *adj ending in cpds* (*V* **size² 1**) **medium-size(d)** de taille (*or* grandeur *or* grosseur *or* pointure *etc*) moyenne; *V* **life** *etc*.

sizeable ['saɪzəbl] *adj dog, building, car, book, estate* assez grand; *egg, fruit, jewel* assez gros (*f* grosse); *sum, problem, operation* assez important, assez considérable.

sizeably ['saɪzəblɪ] *adv* considérablement, de beaucoup.

sizzle ['sɪzl] **1** *vi* grésiller. **2** *n* grésillement *m*.

sizzler* ['sɪzləʳ] *n* journée *f* torride *or* caniculaire.

sizzling ['sɪzlɪŋ] **1** *adj fat, bacon* grésillant. **a ~ noise** un grésillement. **2** *adv*: **~ hot** brûlant; **it was a ~ hot day*** on étouffait *or* il faisait une chaleur étouffante ce jour-là.

skate¹ [skeɪt] *n (fish)* raie *f*.

skate² [skeɪt] **1** *n* patin *m*. *(fig)* **put** *or* **get your ~s on!*** dépêche-toi!, grouille-toi!‡, magne-toi!‡; *V* **ice, roller**.

2 *cpd*: **skateboard** *(n)* skateboard *m*, planche *f* à roulettes; *(vi)* faire de la planche à roulettes.

3 *vi* patiner. **to go skating** *(ice)* faire du patin *or* du patinage; *(roller)* faire du patin à roulettes *or* du skating; **he ~d across the pond** il a traversé l'étang (en patinant *or* à patins); *(fig)* **it went skating across the room** cela a glissé à travers la pièce; *V* **ice, roller**.

skate over, skate round *vt fus problem, difficulty, objection* esquiver autant que possible.

skater ['skeɪtəʳ] *n (ice)* patineur *m*, -euse *f*; *(roller)* personne *f* qui fait du skating.

skating ['skeɪtɪŋ] **1** *n (ice)* patinage *m*; *(roller)* skating *m*. **2** *cpd champion, championship, display (ice)* de patinage; *(roller)* de skating. **skating rink** *(ice)* patinoire *f*; *(roller)* skating *m*.

skean dhu [skiːən'duː] *n (Scot)* poignard *m*.

skedaddle* [skɪ'dædl] *vi* décamper*, déguerpir.

skein [skeɪn] *n [wool etc]* écheveau *m*.

skeletal ['skelɪtl] *adj* squelettique.

skeleton ['skelɪtn] **1** *n (Anat)* squelette *m*; *[building, ship, model etc]* squelette, charpente *f*; *[plan, scheme, suggestion, novel etc]* schéma *m*, grandes lignes. **he was a mere ~** *or* **a walking ~** *or* **a living ~** c'était un véritable cadavre ambulant; **he was reduced to a ~** il n'était plus qu'un squelette, il était devenu (d'une maigreur) squelettique; **the staff was reduced to a ~** le personnel était réduit au strict minimum; *(fig)* **the ~ at the feast** le *or* la trouble-fête *inv*, le rabat-joie *inv*; *(fig)* **the ~ in the cupboard, the family ~** la honte cachée *or* le honteux secret de la famille.

2 *cpd army, crew, staff* squelettique *(fig)*, réduit au strict minimum. **skeleton key** passe(-partout) *m inv*, crochet *m*, rossignol *m*; **skeleton map** carte *f* schématique; **skeleton outline** *[drawing, map, plan etc]* schéma simplifié; *[proposals, report etc]* résumé *m*, grandes lignes.

skeptic(al) ['skeptɪk(əl)] (*US*) = **sceptic(al).**

sketch [sketʃ] **1** *n* **(a)** (*drawing*) croquis *m*, esquisse *f*; (*fig*) *[ideas, proposals etc]* résumé *m*, aperçu *m*, ébauche *f*. **a rough ~** (*drawing*) une ébauche; (*fig*) **he gave me a (rough) ~ of what he planned to do** il m'a donné un aperçu de *or* il m'a dit en gros ce qu'il comptait faire.

(b) (*Theat*) sketch *m*, saynète *f*.

2 *cpd*: **sketch(ing) book** carnet *m* à croquis *or* à dessins; **sketch(ing) pad** bloc *m* à dessins; **sketch map** carte faite à main levée.

3 *vi* faire des croquis *or* des esquisses. **to go ~ing** aller *or* partir faire des croquis.

4 *vt view, castle, figure* faire un croquis *or* une esquisse de, croquer, esquisser; *map* faire à main levée; (*fig*) *ideas, proposals, novel, plan* ébaucher, esquisser.

sketch in *vt sep detail in drawing* ajouter, dessiner; (*fig*) *details* ajouter; *facts* indiquer.

sketch out *vt sep plans, proposals, ideas* ébaucher, esquisser. (*lit, fig*) **to sketch out a picture of sth** ébaucher qch, dessiner les grandes lignes de qch.

sketchily ['sketʃɪlɪ] *adv* (*V* **sketchy**) incomplètement, superficiellement.

sketchy ['sketʃɪ] *adj answer, account* incomplet (*f* -ète), sommaire; *piece of work* incomplet, peu détaillé. **his knowledge of geography is ~** il n'a que des connaissances superficielles *or* insuffisantes en géographie, il a de grosses lacunes en géographie.

skew [skjuː] **1** *n*: **to be on the ~** être de travers *or* en biais *or* mal posé.

2 *adj* (*squint*) de travers, oblique, de guingois*; (*slanting*) penché, de travers.

3 *cpd*: **skewbald** (*adj*) fauve et blanc, pie *inv*; (*n*) cheval *m* fauve et blanc, cheval pie *inv*; **skew-eyed*** qui louche, qui a un œil qui dit zut à l'autre*; (*Brit*) **(on the) skew-whiff*** de travers, de guingois*, de traviole‡.

4 *vi* **(a)** (*also* **~ round**) obliquer.

(b) (*squint*) loucher.

skewer ['skjʊəʳ] **1** *n* (*for roast etc*) broche *f*; (*for kebabs*) brochette *f*. **2** *vt meat* embrocher, mettre en brochette; (*fig*) transpercer, embrocher*.

ski [skiː] **1** *n* ski *m* (*équipement*); (*Aviat*) patin *m*; *V* **water.**

2 *cpd school, clothes* de ski. **ski boot** chaussure *f* de ski; **ski instructor** moniteur *m*, -trice *f* de ski; **skijump** (*action*) saut *m* à skis; (*place*) tremplin *m* de ski; **skijumping** saut *m* à skis; **skilift** télésiège *m*, remonte-pente *m inv*; **ski pants** fuseau *m* (de ski); **ski pole** = **ski stick; ski resort** station *f* de ski *or* de neige, station de sports d'hiver; **ski run** piste *f* de ski; **ski slopes** pentes *fpl* de ski; **ski stick** bâton *m* de ski; **ski-touring** ski *m* de randonnée; **ski tow** téléski *m*, remonte-pente *m inv*; **ski trousers** = **ski pants; ski wax** fart *m*.

3 *vi* faire du ski, skier. **to go ~ing** (aller) faire du ski; **I like ~ing** j'aime le ski *or* faire du ski *or* skier; **to ~ down a slope** descendre une pente à ski(s).

skid [skɪd] **1** *n* **(a)** (*Aut*) dérapage *m*. **to get** *or* **go into a ~** déraper, faire un dérapage; **to get out of a ~, to correct a ~** redresser *or* contrôler un dérapage.

(b) (*on wheel*) cale *f*.

(c) (*under heavy object*) (*rollers, logs etc*) traîneau *m*. (*cause to fail*) **to put the ~s‡ on** *or* **under** *person* faire un croc-en-jambe à (*fig*); *plan etc* faire tomber à l'eau*; (*US*) **to hit the ~s*** devenir clochard(e)*.

2 *cpd*: **skidlid*** casque *m* (de moto); **skidmark** trace *f* de dérapage; **skidpan** chaussée *f or* terrain *m* de dérapages (*pour apprendre à contrôler un véhicule*); **skidproof** antidérapant; (*US*) **skid row** quartier *m* de clochards, cour *f* des miracles; (*US fig*) **he's heading for skid row** il finira clochard*.

3 *vi* (*Aut*) déraper; *[person]* déraper, glisser. **the car ~ded to a halt** la voiture s'est arrêtée en dérapant; (*Aut*) **I ~ded into a tree** j'ai dérapé et percuté contre un arbre; **he went ~ding into the bookcase** il a glissé *or* dérapé et est allé se cogner contre la bibliothèque; **the toy ~ded across the room** le jouet a glissé jusqu'à l'autre bout de la pièce.

skier ['skiːəʳ] *n* skieur *m*, -euse *f*.

skiff [skɪf] *n* skiff *m*, yole *f*.

skiing ['skiːɪŋ] **1** *n* (*U*) ski *m* (*sport*); *V* **water. 2** *cpd clothes, school* de ski. **skiing holiday** vacances *fpl* aux sports d'hiver, vacances de neige; **to go on a skiing holiday** partir aux sports d'hiver; **skiing instructor** moniteur *m*, -trice *f* de ski; **skiing pants** fuseau *m* (de ski); **skiing resort** station *f* de ski *or* de neige, station de sports d'hiver; **skiing trousers** = **skiing pants.**

skilful, (*US*) skillful ['skɪlfʊl] *adj person* habile, adroit (*at doing* à faire); *gesture, action* habile.

skilfully, (*US*) skillfully ['skɪlfəlɪ] *adv* habilement, adroitement.

skilfulness, (*US*) skillfulness ['skɪlfʊlnɪs] *n* (*U*) habileté *f*, adresse *f*.

skill [skɪl] *n* **(a)** (*U: competence, ability*) habileté *f*, adresse *f*; (*gen manual*) dextérité *f*; (*talent*) savoir-faire *m*, talent *m*. **the ~ of the dancers** l'adresse *or* l'habileté *or* le talent des danseurs; **the ~ of the juggler** l'adresse *or* la dextérité *or* le talent du jongleur; **his ~ at billiards** son habileté *or* son adresse au billard; **his ~ in negotiation** son savoir-faire *or* son talent *or* son habileté en matière de négociations; **his ~ in persuading them** l'habileté dont il a fait preuve en les persuadant; **lack of ~** maladresse *f*.

(b) (*in craft etc*) technique *f*. **~s** capacités *fpl*, compétences *fpl*; **it's a ~ that has to be acquired** c'est une technique qui s'apprend; **we could make good use of his ~s** ses capacités *or* ses compétences nous seraient bien utiles; **what ~s do you have?** quelles sont vos compétences?; **learning a language is a question of learning new ~s** apprendre une langue consiste à acquérir de nouveaux automatismes.

skilled [skɪld] *adj* **(a)** *person* habile, adroit (*in, at doing* pour faire, *in or at sth* en qch); *movement, stroke* adroit. **he's a ~ driver** c'est un conducteur habile *or* adroit; **~ in diplomacy** expert en diplomatie, qui a beaucoup d'habileté *or* d'expérience en diplomatie; **~ in the art of negotiating** versé *or* maître (*f inv*) dans l'art de la négociation.

(b) (*Ind*) *worker, engineer etc* qualifié; *work* de technicien, de spécialiste. **~ labour** main-d'œuvre qualifiée.

skillet ['skɪlɪt] *n* poêlon *m*.

skillful ['skɪlfʊl] *adj* (*US*) = **skilful.**

skillfully ['skɪlfəlɪ] *adv* (*US*) = **skilfully.**

skillfulness ['skɪlfʊlnɪs] *n* (*US*) = **skilfulness.**

skim [skɪm] **1** *vt* **(a)** *milk* écrémer; *soup* écumer. **to ~ the cream/scum/grease from sth** écrémer/écumer/dégraisser qch.

(b) *[bird etc]* **to ~ the ground/water** raser *or* effleurer *or* frôler le sol/la surface de l'eau; **to ~ a stone across the pond** faire ricocher une pierre sur l'étang.

2 *vi*: **to ~ across the water/along the ground** raser l'eau/le sol; **the stone ~med across the pond** la pierre a ricoché d'un bout à l'autre de l'étang; (*fig*) **to ~ through a book** parcourir *or* feuilleter un livre; **he ~med over the difficult passages** il s'est contenté de parcourir rapidement les passages difficiles.

3 *cpd*: **skim(med) milk** lait écrémé.

skim off *vt sep cream, grease* enlever. (*fig*) **they skimmed off the brightest pupils** ils ont mis à part les élèves les plus brillants.

skimp [skɪmp] **1** *vt butter, cloth, paint etc* lésiner sur; *money* économiser; *praise, thanks* être chiche de; *piece of work* faire à la va-vite, bâcler*. **2** *vi* lésiner, économiser.

skimpily ['skɪmpɪlɪ] *adv serve, provide* avec parcimonie; *live* chichement.

skimpiness ['skɪmpɪnɪs] *n [meal, helping, allowance]* insuffisance *f*; *[dress etc]* ampleur insuffisante; *[person]* avarice *f*.

skimpy ['skɪmpɪ] *adj meal, allowance* insuffisant, maigre, chiche; *dress* étriqué, trop juste; *person* avare, radin*.

skin [skɪn] **1** *n* **(a)** *[person, animal]* peau *f*. **she has a good/bad ~** elle a une jolie/vilaine peau; **to wear wool next (to) the ~** porter de la laine sur la peau *or* à même la peau; **wet** *or* **soaked to the ~** trempé jusqu'aux os; **the snake casts** *or* **sheds its ~** le serpent mue; **rabbit ~** peau de lapin; (*fig*) **to be (all** *or* **only) ~ and bone** n'avoir que la peau sur les os; (*fig*) **with a whole ~** indemne, sain et sauf, sans une écorchure; (*fig*) **to escape by the ~ of one's teeth** l'échapper belle; (*fig*) **we caught the last train by the ~ of our teeth** nous avons attrapé le dernier train de justesse; (*fig*) **to have a thick ~** être insensible; **to have a thin ~** être susceptible, avoir l'épiderme sensible; (*fig*) **to get under sb's ~*** porter *or* taper* sur les nerfs à qn; (*fig*) **I've got you under my ~*** je t'ai dans la peau‡, je suis amoureux fou (*f* amoureuse folle) de toi; (*fig*) **it's no ~ off my nose‡** (*does not hurt me*) pour ce que ça me coûte!; (*does not concern me*) ce n'est pas mon problème; *V* **pig, save**[1] *etc.*

(b) (*fig*) *[fruit, vegetable, milk pudding, sausage, drum]* peau *f*; *[boat, aircraft]* revêtement *m*; (*for duplicating*) stencil *m*; (*for wine*) outre *f*. **to cook potatoes in their ~(s)** faire cuire des pommes de terre en robe des champs *or* en robe de chambre; **a banana ~** une peau de banane.

2 *cpd colour, texture* de (la) peau. **skin-deep** superficiel (*V also* **beauty**); **it's only skin-deep** ça ne va pas (chercher) bien loin; **skin disease** maladie *f* de (la) peau; **skin diver** plongeur *m*, -euse *f* sous-marin(e); **skin diving** plongée sous-marine; (*Cine*) **skinflick‡** film *m* porno* *inv*; **skinflint** grippe-sou *m*, radin(e)* *m(f)*; (*US*) **skin game*** escroquerie *f*; **skin graft** greffe *f* de la peau; **skin grafting** greffe *f or* greffage *m* de la peau; **skinhead** jeune homme *m* aux cheveux tondus ras; (*Brit: thug*) skinhead *m*, jeune voyou *m* (aux cheveux tondus ras); **skin test** cuti(-réaction) *f*; **skintight** collant, ajusté.

3 *vt* **(a)** *animal* dépouiller, écorcher; *fruit, vegetable* éplucher. (*fig*) **I'll ~ him alive!*** je vais l'écorcher tout vif!; **to ~ one's knee** s'érafler *or* s'écorcher le genou; *V* **eye.**

(b) (‡: *fleece*) estamper*, plumer*.

skinful‡ ['skɪnfʊl] *n*: **to have (had) a ~** être bourré‡, être noir‡; **he's got a ~ of whisky** il s'est soûlé* *or* il a pris une biture‡ au whisky.

-skinned [skɪnd] *adj ending in cpds*: **fair-skinned** à (la) peau claire; *V* **thick, thin** *etc.*

skinner ['skɪnəʳ] *n* peaussier *m*.

skinny ['skɪnɪ] *adj* maigrelet, maigrichon. (*Fashion*) **the ~ look** la mode ultra-mince; **~-rib (sweater)*** pull-chaussette *m*.

skint‡ [skɪnt] *adj* (*Brit*) fauché*, sans le rond*.

skip[1] [skɪp] **1** *n* petit bond, petit saut. **to give a ~** faire un petit bond *or* saut.

2 *cpd*: (*US*) **skip rope** corde *f* à sauter.

3 *vi* **(a)** gambader, sautiller; (*with rope*) sauter à la corde. **to ~ with joy** sauter *or* bondir de joie; **the child ~ped in/out** *etc* l'enfant est entré/sorti *etc* en gambadant *or* en sautillant; **she ~ped lightly over the stones** elle sautait légèrement par-dessus les pierres; **he ~ped out of the way of the cycle** il a bondi pour éviter le vélo, il a évité le vélo d'un bond; (*fig*) **he ~ped over that point** il est passé sur ce point, il a sauté par-dessus *or* a glissé sur ce point; **to ~ from one subject to another** sauter d'un sujet à un autre; **the author** *or* **book ~s about a lot** l'auteur papillonne beaucoup dans ce livre.

(b) (*fig*) **I ~ped up to London yesterday** j'ai fait un saut à Londres hier; **he ~ped off without paying** il a décampé *or* filé* sans payer; **I ~ped round to see her** j'ai fait un saut chez elle, je suis passé la voir en vitesse; **he ~ped across to Spain** il a fait un saut *or* une virée* en Espagne.

4 *vt* (*omit*) *chapter, page, paragraph* sauter, passer; *class, meal* sauter. **I'll ~ lunch** je vais sauter le déjeuner, je ne vais pas déjeuner, je vais me passer de déjeuner; **~ it!*** laisse tomber!*; **~ the details!** laisse tomber les détails!*, épargne-nous les détails!; **to ~ school** sécher les cours.

skip[2] [skɪp] *n* (*container*) benne *f*.

skipper [ˈskɪpəʳ] **1** *n* (*Naut*) capitaine *m*, patron *m*; (*Sport**) capitaine, chef *m* d'équipe. **2** *vt* (*) *boat* commander; *team* être le chef de, mener.

skipping [ˈskɪpɪŋ] *n* saut *m* à la corde. (*Brit*) **~ rope** corde *f* à sauter.

skirl [skɜːl] *n* son aigu (*de la cornemuse*).

skirmish [ˈskɜːmɪʃ] **1** *n* (*Mil*) échauffourée *f*, escarmouche *f*, accrochage *m*; (*fig*) escarmouche, accrochage*. **2** *vi* (*Mil*) s'engager dans une escarmouche. (*fig*) **to ~ with sb** avoir un accrochage* avec qn.

skirt [skɜːt] **1** *n* jupe *f*; [*frock coat*] basque *f*. (*fig: girl*) **a bit of ~:** une nana:.

2 *cpd*: **a skirt length** une hauteur de jupe.

3 *vt* (*also* **~ round**) (*go round*) contourner, longer; (*miss, avoid*) *town, obstacle* contourner, éviter; *problem, difficulty* esquiver, éluder. **the road ~s (round) the forest** la route longe *or* contourne la forêt; **we ~ed (round) Paris to the north** nous sommes passés au nord de Paris, nous avons contourné Paris par le nord.

4 *vi*: **to ~ round** *V* **3**.

skirting [ˈskɜːtɪŋ] *n* (*Brit: also* **~ board**) plinthe *f*.

skit [skɪt] *n* parodie *f* (*on* de); (*Theat*) sketch *m* satirique.

skitter [ˈskɪtəʳ] *vi*: **to ~ across the water/along the ground** [*bird*] voler en frôlant l'eau/le sol; [*stone*] ricocher sur l'eau/le sol.

skittish [ˈskɪtɪʃ] *adj* (*playful*) espiègle; (*coquettish*) coquet, frivole; *horse* ombrageux.

skittishly [ˈskɪtɪʃlɪ] *adv* (*V* **skittish**) avec espièglerie; en faisant la coquette; d'une manière ombrageuse.

skittle [ˈskɪtl] **1** *n* quille *f*. (*esp Brit*) **~s** (jeu *m* de) quilles; *V* **beer**.

2 *cpd*: **skittle alley** piste *f* de jeu *m* de quilles, bowling *m*.

skive* [skaɪv] (*Brit*) **1** *vi* tirer au flanc*.

2 *n*: **to be on the ~** tirer au flanc*.

skive off* *vi* (*Brit*) se défiler*.

skiver* [ˈskaɪvəʳ] *n* (*Brit*) tire-au-flanc* *m inv*.

skivvy* [ˈskɪvɪ] *n* (*Brit pej*) boniche *f* (*pej*), bonne *f* à tout faire.

skua [ˈskjuːə] *n* stercoraire *m*.

skulduggery* [skʌlˈdʌgərɪ] *n* (*U*) maquignonnage *m*, trafic *m*. **a piece of ~** un maquignonnage.

skulk [skʌlk] *vi* (*also* **~ about**) rôder en se cachant, rôder furtivement. **to ~ in/away** *etc* entrer/s'éloigner *etc* furtivement.

skull [skʌl] **1** *n* crâne *m*. **~ and crossbones** (*emblem*) tête *f* de mort; (*flag*) pavillon *m* à tête de mort; **I can't get it into his (thick) ~* that ...** pas moyen de lui faire comprendre que ..., je n'arrive pas à lui faire entrer dans le crâne* que ... .

2 *cpd*: **skullcap** calotte *f*.

skunk [skʌŋk] *n* (*animal*) mouffette *f*; (*fur*) sconse *m*; (**pej: person*) mufle* *m*, canaille *f*, salaud: *m*.

sky [skaɪ] **1** *n* ciel *m*. **the skies** le(s) ciel(s); (*fig*) les cieux; **there was a clear blue ~** le ciel était clair et bleu; **in the ~** dans le ciel; **under the open ~** à la belle étoile; **under a blue ~, under blue skies** sous des ciels bleus, sous un ciel bleu; **the skies over** *or* **of England** les ciels d'Angleterre; **the skies of Van Gogh** les ciels de Van Gogh; **under warmer skies** sous des cieux plus cléments; **to praise sb to the skies** porter qn aux nues; (*fig*) **it came out of a clear (blue) ~** c'est arrivé de façon tout à fait inattendue, on ne s'y attendait vraiment pas; (*fig*) **the ~'s the limit*** tout est possible.

2 *cpd*: **sky-blue** (*adj, n*) bleu ciel (*m*) *inv*; **skydive** saut *m* (en parachute) en chute libre; **skydiver** parachutiste *mf* (faisant de la chute libre); **skydiving** parachutisme *m* (en chute libre); **sky-high** très haut (dans le ciel); (*fig*) extrêmement haut; **he hit the ball sky-high** il a envoyé le ballon très haut (dans le ciel); **the bridge was blown sky-high** le pont a sauté, le pont a volé en morceaux; **to blow a theory sky-high** démolir une théorie; **prices are sky-high** les prix sont exorbitants; **the crisis sent sugar prices sky-high** la crise a fait monter en flèche le prix du sucre; **skyjack*** détourner, pirater (*un avion*); **skyjacker*** pirate *m* de l'air; (*Space*) **Skylab** laboratoire spatial, Skylab *m*; **skylark** (*n: bird*) alouette *f* (des champs); (*vi:**) chahuter, faire le fou (*f* la folle); **skylarking*** rigolade* *f*, chahut *m*; **skylight** lucarne *f*; **skyline** ligne *f* d'horizon; [*city*] ligne des toits; [*buildings*] profil *m*, silhouette *f*; (*fig*) **sky pilot:** aumônier *m*, curé *m*; **skyrocket** (*n*) fusée volante *or* à baguette; (*vi*) [*prices*] monter en flèche; **skyscraper** gratte-ciel *m inv*; **skyway** (*Aviat**) route *or* voie aérienne; (*US Aut*) route surélevée; **skywriting** publicité tracée (dans le ciel) par un avion.

3 *vt* *ball* envoyer très haut *or* en chandelle.

skyward [ˈskaɪwəd] *adj,adv* vers le ciel.

skywards [ˈskaɪwədz] *adv* vers le ciel.

slab [slæb] **1** *n* **(a)** (*large piece*) [*stone, wood, slate*] bloc *m*; (*flat*) plaque *f*; [*meat*] pièce *f*; (*smaller*) carré *m*, pavé *m*; [*cake*] pavé; (*smaller*) grosse tranche; [*chocolate*] plaque; (*smaller*) tablette *f*.

(b) (*paving ~*) dalle *f*; (*table, surface*) (*in butcher's etc*) étal *m*; (*in mortuary*) table *f* de dissection *or* d'autopsie.

2 *cpd*: **slab cake** grand cake rectangulaire.

slack [slæk] **1** *adj* **(a)** (*loose*) *rope* lâche, mal tendu; *joint* desserré; *hold, grip* faible. **to be ~** [*screw etc*] avoir du jeu; [*rope etc*] avoir du mou; (*of rope etc*) **keep it ~!** laissez du mou!; (*fig*) **~ water** eau(x) morte(s) *or* dormante(s); (*between tides*) mer *f* étale, étale *m*.

(b) (*inactive*) *demand* faible; *market, trade* faible, stagnant. **during ~ periods** (*weeks, months etc*) pendant les jours *or* mois creux, pendant les périodes creuses; (*in the day*) aux heures creuses; **the ~ season** la morte-saison; **business is ~ this week** les affaires marchent au ralenti *or* ne vont pas fort* cette semaine.

(c) *person* (*lacking energy*) mou (*f* molle), indolent; (*lax*) négligent; *student* inappliqué, peu sérieux; *worker* peu sérieux, peu consciencieux. **to be ~ about one's work** négliger son travail, se relâcher dans son travail; **he has grown very ~** (*in general*) il se laisse aller; (*in work etc*) il fait preuve de mollesse dans *or* il n'est plus consciencieux dans son travail; **this pupil is very ~** cet élève est très peu sérieux *or* ne travaille pas assez *or* ne s'applique pas assez; **he is ~ in answering letters** il met longtemps à répondre aux lettres qu'il reçoit.

2 *n* **(a)** (*in rope*) mou *m*; (*in cable*) ballant *m*; (*in joint etc*) jeu *m*. **to take up the ~ in a rope** raidir un cordage; (*fig*) **to take up the ~ in the economy** relancer les secteurs affaiblis de l'économie.

(b) (*Dress: pl*) **~s** pantalon *m*.

(c) (*Min*) poussier *m*.

3 *vi* (*) ne pas travailler comme il le faudrait.

slack off **1** *vi* **(a)** (*: *stop working/trying etc*) se relâcher (dans son travail/dans ses efforts *etc*).

(b) [*business, trade, demand*] ralentir.

2 *vt sep* *rope, cable* détendre, donner du mou à.

slack up* *vi* ralentir (ses efforts *or* son travail).

slacken [ˈslækn] **1** *vt* (*also* **~ off**) *rope* relâcher, donner du mou à; *cable* donner du ballant à; *reins* relâcher; *screw* desserrer; *pressure etc* diminuer, réduire. **to ~ one's pace** ralentir l'allure; (*Aut*) **to ~ speed** diminuer de vitesse, ralentir.

2 *vi* (*also* **~ off**) [*rope*] se relâcher, prendre du mou; [*cable*] prendre du ballant; [*screw*] se desserrer; [*gale*] diminuer de force; [*speed*] diminuer; [*activity, business, trade*] ralentir, diminuer; [*effort, enthusiasm, pressure*] diminuer, se relâcher.

slacken off **1** *vi* **(a)** = **slacken 2**.

(b) [*person*] se relâcher, se laisser aller.

2 *vt sep* = **slacken 1**.

slacken up *vi* = **slacken off 1b**.

slackening [ˈslæknɪŋ] *n* (*also* **~ off**; *V* **slacken**) ralentissement *m*; relâchement *m*; desserrement *m*; diminution *f*.

slacker* [ˈslækəʳ] *n* flemmard(e)* *m(f)*, fainéant(e) *m(f)*.

slackly [ˈslæklɪ] *adv* *hang* lâchement, mollement; (*fig*) *work* négligemment.

slackness [ˈslæknɪs] *n* [*rope etc*] manque *m* de tension; (*) [*person*] négligence *f*, laisser-aller *m*. **the ~ of trade** le ralentissement *or* la stagnation *or* (*stronger*) le marasme des affaires.

slag [slæg] *n* (*Metal*) scories *fpl*, crasses *fpl*. **~ heap** (*Metal*) crassier *m*; (*Min*) terril *m*.

slain [sleɪn] (*liter*) **1** *ptp of* **slay**. **2** *n* (*Mil*) **the ~** les morts, les soldats tombés au champ d'honneur.

slake [sleɪk] *vt* *lime* éteindre; *one's thirst* étancher; (*fig*) *desire for revenge etc* assouvir, satisfaire.

slalom [ˈslɑːləm] *n* slalom *m*.

slam [slæm] **1** *n* **(a)** [*door*] claquement *m*. **(b)** (*Bridge*) chelem *m*. **to make a grand/little ~** faire un grand/petit chelem.

2 *vt* **(a)** *door* (faire) claquer, fermer violemment; *lid* (faire) claquer, rabattre violemment. **to ~ the door shut** claquer la porte; **she ~med the books on the table** elle a jeté brutalement *or* a flanqué* les livres sur la table; **he ~med the ball into the grandstand** d'un coup violent il a envoyé le ballon dans la tribune; (*fig*) **our team ~med yours*** notre équipe a écrasé la vôtre.

(b) (:) *play, singer* critiquer, éreinter*, démolir*.

3 *vi* [*door*] claquer. **the door ~med shut** la porte s'est refermée en claquant.

slam down *vt sep* poser d'un geste violent, jeter brutalement, flanquer*.

slam on *vt sep*: **to slam on the brakes** freiner à mort.

slam to **1** *vi* se refermer en claquant.

2 *vt sep* refermer en claquant.

slander [ˈslɑːndəʳ] **1** *n* calomnie *f*; (*Jur*) diffamation *f*. **it's a ~ to suggest that ...** c'est de la calomnie que de suggérer que ... . **2** *vt* calomnier, dire du mal de; (*Jur*) diffamer.

slanderer [ˈslɑːndərəʳ] *n* calomniateur *m*, -trice *f*; (*Jur*) diffamateur *m*, -trice *f*.

slanderous [ˈslɑːndərəs] *adj* calomnieux, calomniateur (*f* -trice); (*Jur*) diffamatoire.

slanderously [ˈslɑːndərəslɪ] *adv* calomnieusement; (*Jur*) de façon diffamatoire.

slang [slæŋ] **1** *n* (*U*) argot *m*. **in ~** en argot; **in army/school ~** en argot militaire/d'écolier, dans l'argot des armées/des écoles; **that word is ~** c'est un mot d'argot *or* argotique, c'est un argotisme; **to talk ~** parler argot; **he uses a lot of ~** il emploie beaucoup d'argot, il s'exprime dans une langue très verte; *V* **rhyme**. **2** *cpd* *word, expression* d'argot, argotique. (*Brit*) **slanging match*** échange *m* d'insultes, prise *f* de bec*. **3** *vt* (*) traiter de tous les noms.

slangily* [ˈslæŋɪlɪ] *adv*: **to talk ~** parler argot, employer beaucoup d'argot.

slangy* [ˈslæŋɪ] *adj* *person* qui parle argot, qui emploie beaucoup d'argot; *style, language* argotique.

slant [slɑːnt] **1** *n* inclinaison *f*, aspect penché; (*fig*) angle *m*, perspective *f*, point *m* de vue. (*fig*) **his mind has a curious ~** il a une curieuse tournure *or* forme d'esprit; **to give/get a new ~* on sth** présenter/voir qch sous un angle *or* jour nouveau.

2 *cpd*: **slant-eyed** aux yeux bridés; **slantwise** obliquement, de biais.

3 *vi [line, handwriting]* pencher, être incliné, ne pas être droit; *[light, sunbeam]* passer obliquement.

4 *vt line, handwriting* faire pencher, incliner; *(fig) account, news* présenter avec parti-pris. **a ~ed report** un rapport orienté *or* tendancieux.

slanting ['slɑːntɪŋ] *adj roof, surface* en pente, incliné; *handwriting* penché, couché; *line* penché, oblique. **~ rain** pluie *f* (qui tombe en) oblique.

slap [slæp] **1** *n* claque *f*; *(on face)* gifle *f*; *(on back)* grande tape, *(stronger)* grande claque. **a ~ on the bottom** une fessée; *(lit, fig)* **a ~ in the face** une gifle; **a ~ on the back** une grande tape *or* claque dans le dos.

2 *cpd*: *(Brit)* **they were having a bit of the old slap and tickle**‡ ils étaient en train de se peloter*; **slap-bang* into the wall** en plein *or* tout droit dans le mur; **he ran slap-bang(-wallop)* into his mother** il s'est cogné en plein contre sa mère; *(fig: met)* il est tombé tout d'un coup sur sa mère, il s'est retrouvé tout d'un coup nez à nez avec sa mère; **slapdash** *(adj) person* insouciant, négligent; *work* bâclé*, fait à la va-vite *or* sans soin *or* n'importe comment; *(adv)* à la va-vite, sans soin, n'importe comment; **slap-happy*** *(carelessly cheerful)* insouciant, décontracté*, relaxe*; *(US: punch-drunk)* groggy, abruti de coups; **slapstick (comedy)** grosse farce, comédie *or* farce bouffonne; *(Brit)* **a slap-up meal*** un repas fameux* *or* extra*.

3 *adv* (*) en plein, tout droit. **he ran ~ into the wall** il est rentré en plein dans *or* tout droit dans le mur; **~ in the middle** en plein *or* au beau milieu.

4 *vt* **(a)** *(hit) person* donner une tape *or* *(stronger)* claque à. **to ~ sb on the back** donner une tape *or* une claque dans le dos à qn; **to ~ a child's bottom** donner une fessée à un enfant; **to ~ sb's face** *or* **sb in the face** gifler qn; *(in amusement etc)* **to ~ one's knees** se taper sur les cuisses.

(b) *(put)* mettre brusquement, flanquer*; *(apply)* appliquer *or* mettre à la va-vite *or* sans soin. **he ~ped the book on the table** il a flanqué* le livre sur la table; **he ~ped a coat of paint on the wall** il a flanqué* un coup de peinture *or* il a donné un coup de pinceau au mur; **he ~ped £5 on to the price*** il a collé* 5 livres de plus sur le prix, il a gonflé son prix de 5 livres; **she ~ped some foundation on her face*** elle s'est collé du fond de teint n'importe comment *or* à la va-vite.

slap down *vt sep object* poser brusquement *or* violemment. *(fig)* **to slap sb down*** rembarrer* qn, envoyer qn sur les roses*.

slap on *vt sep paint etc* appliquer à la va-vite *or* n'importe comment. **to slap on make-up** se maquiller n'importe comment *or* à la va-vite.

slash [slæʃ] **1** *n* entaille *f*, taillade *f*; *(on face)* entaille, balafre *f*; *(Sewing: in sleeve)* crevé *m*.

2 *vt* **(a)** *(with knife, sickle etc)* entailler, *(several cuts)* taillader; *rope* couper net, trancher; *face* balafrer; *(with whip, stick)* cingler; *(Sewing) sleeve* faire des crevés dans. **to ~ sb** taillader qn; **his attacker ~ed his face/his jacket** son assaillant lui a balafré le visage/a tailladé sa veste; **~ed sleeves** manches *fpl* à crevés.

(b) *(fig) prices* casser*, écraser*; *costs, expenses* réduire radicalement; *speech, text* couper *or* raccourcir radicalement. **'prices ~ed'** 'prix cassés', 'on casse les prix'.

(c) (*: *condemn) book, play* éreinter*, démolir*.

3 *vi*: **he ~ed at me with his stick** il m'a flanqué* un *or* des coup(s) de bâton; **he ~ed at the grass with his stick** il cinglait l'herbe de sa canne.

slashing ['slæʃɪŋ] *adj (fig) criticism, attack* cinglant, mordant.

slat [slæt] *n [blind]* lamelle *f*; *[bed-frame, room divider etc]* lame *f*.

slate [sleɪt] **1** *n (substance, object: Constr, Scol etc)* ardoise *f*; *(fig: US Pol)* liste *f* provisoire de candidats. *(Brit Comm)* **put it on the ~*** mettez-le sur mon compte, ajoutez ça sur mon ardoise*; *V* **wipe**.

2 *cpd industry* ardoisier, de l'ardoise; *roof* en ardoise, d'ardoise. **slate-blue** *(adj, n)* bleu ardoise *(m) inv*; **slate-coloured** ardoise *inv*; **slate-grey** *(adj, n)* gris ardoise *(m) inv*; **slate quarry** ardoisière *f*, carrière *f* d'ardoise.

3 *vt* **(a)** *roof* ardoiser.

(b) *(US Pol) candidate* proposer.

(c) *(Brit*) book, play, actor, politician* éreinter*, démolir*; *(scold)* attraper*, engueuler‡.

slater ['sleɪtəʳ] *n* **(a)** *(in quarry)* ardoisier *m*; *[roof]* couvreur(-ardoisier) *m*. **(b)** *(woodlouse)* cloporte *m*.

slattern ['slætən] *n* souillon *f*.

slatternly ['slætənlɪ] *adj woman, appearance* peu soigné, négligé; *behaviour, habits* de souillon.

slaty ['sleɪtɪ] *adj (in texture)* ardoisier, semblable à l'ardoise; *(in colour)* (couleur) ardoise *inv*.

slaughter ['slɔːtəʳ] **1** *n [animals]* abattage *m*; *[people]* carnage *m*, massacre *m*, tuerie *f*. **the ~ on the roads** les hécatombes *fpl* sur la route; **there was great ~** cela a été un carnage *or* un massacre *or* une tuerie.

2 *cpd*: **slaughterhouse** abattoir *m*.

3 *vt animal* abattre; *person* tuer sauvagement; *people* massacrer. **our team really ~ed them*** notre équipe les a écrasés *or* massacrés*.

slaughterer ['slɔːtərəʳ] *n [animals]* tueur *m*, assommeur *m*; *[person]* meurtrier *m*; *[people]* massacreur *m*.

Slav [slɑːv] **1** *adj* slave. **2** *n* Slave *mf*.

slave [sleɪv] **1** *n (lit, fig)* esclave *mf*. *(fig)* **to be a ~ to** être (l')esclave de; *V* **white**.

2 *cpd*: **slave driver** *(lit)* surveillant *m* d'esclaves; *(fig)* négrier *m*, -ière *f*; **slave labour** *(exploitation)* exploitation *f* des esclaves; *(work)* travail fait par les esclaves; (**fig*) travail de forçat *or* de galérien; **slave labour camp** camp *m* de travaux forcés; **slave ship** (vaisseau *m*) négrier *m*; **slave trade** commerce *m* des esclaves, traite *f* des noirs; **slave trader** marchand *m* d'esclaves, négrier *m*; **slave traffic** trafic *m* d'esclaves.

3 *vi* (*also* **~ away**) travailler comme un nègre, trimer. **to ~ (away) at sth/at doing** s'escrimer sur qch/à faire.

slaver[1] ['sleɪvəʳ] *n (person)* marchand *m* d'esclaves, négrier *m*; *(ship)* (vaisseau *m*) négrier.

slaver[2] ['slævəʳ] *(dribble)* **1** *n* bave *f*, salive *f*.

2 *vi* baver.

slavery ['sleɪvərɪ] *n (lit, fig)* esclavage *m*. **housework is nothing but ~** le ménage est un véritable esclavage *or* une perpétuelle corvée; *V* **sell**.

slavey* ['sleɪvɪ] *n* boniche* *f*.

Slavic ['slævɪk] *adj, n* slave *(m)*.

slavish ['sleɪvɪʃ] *adj subjection* d'esclave; *imitation, devotion* servile.

slavishly ['sleɪvɪʃlɪ] *adv* servilement.

Slavonic [slə'vɒnɪk] *adj, n* slave *(m)*.

slay [sleɪ] *pret* **slew**, *ptp* **slain** *vt (liter)* tuer. *(fig)* **he ~s me!**‡ il me fait mourir *or* crever* de rire!; *V also* **slain**.

slayer ['sleɪəʳ] *n (liter)* tueur *m*, -euse *f*.

sleazy* ['sliːzɪ] *adj* minable, miteux*, dégueulasse‡.

sled [sled] *n* = **sledge 1**.

sledge [sledʒ] **1** *n* luge *f*; *(drawn by horse or dog)* traîneau *m*. **2** *vi*: **to go sledging** faire de la luge, se promener en traîneau; **to ~ down/across** *etc* descendre/traverser *etc* en luge *or* en traîneau.

sledgehammer ['sledʒ,hæməʳ] *n* marteau *m* de forgeron. *(fig)* **to strike sb/sth a ~ blow** assener un coup violent *or* magistral à qn/qch.

sleek [sliːk] *adj hair, fur* lisse, brillant, luisant; *cat* au poil soyeux *or* brillant; *person (in appearance)* (trop) soigné, bichonné; *(in manner)* onctueux; *manners* onctueux, doucereux; *car, plane* aérodynamique; *boat* aux lignes pures.

sleek down *vt sep*: **to sleek one's hair down** se lisser les cheveux.

sleekly ['sliːklɪ] *adv smile, reply* doucereusement, avec onction.

sleekness ['sliːknɪs] *n [hair etc]* brillant *m*, luisant *m*; *[person]* allure (trop) soignée, air bichonné; *[manner]* onctuosité *f*; *[car, plane]* ligne *f* aérodynamique; *[boat]* finesse *f* *or* pureté *f* (de lignes).

sleep [sliːp] *(vb: pret, ptp* **slept**) **1** *n* sommeil *m*. **to be in a deep** *or* **sound ~** dormir profondément; **to be in a very heavy ~** dormir d'un sommeil de plomb; **to talk in one's ~** parler en dormant *or* dans son sommeil; **to walk in one's ~ = to sleepwalk** (*V* 2); **to sleep the ~ of the just** dormir du sommeil du juste; **overcome by ~** ayant succombé au sommeil; **to have a ~, to get some ~** dormir; *(for a short while)* faire un somme; **to get** *or* **go to ~** s'endormir; **my leg has gone to ~** j'ai la jambe engourdie; **I didn't get a wink of ~** *or* **any ~ all night** je n'ai pas fermé l'œil de la nuit; **to put** *or* **send sb to ~** endormir qn; *(euph: put down)* **to put a cat to ~** faire piquer un chat; **I need 8 hours' ~ a night** il me faut (mes) 8 heures de sommeil chaque nuit; **a 3-hour ~** 3 heures de sommeil; **to have a good night's ~** passer une bonne nuit; **a ~ will do you good** cela vous fera du bien de dormir; **let him have his ~ out** laisse-le dormir tant qu'il voudra; *V* **beauty, lose** *etc*.

2 *cpd*: **sleep-learning** hypnopédie *f*; **sleepwalk** marcher en dormant; **he sleepwalks** il est somnambule; **sleepwalker** somnambule *mf*; *(U)* **sleepwalking** somnambulisme *m*; *(U: Comm etc)* **sleepwear** vêtements *mpl* *or* lingerie *f* de nuit.

3 *vi* **(a)** dormir. **to ~ tight** *or* **like a log** *or* **like a top** dormir à poings fermés *or* comme une souche *or* comme un loir; **~ tight!** dors bien!; **to ~ heavily** dormir d'un sommeil de plomb; **he was ~ing deeply** *or* **soundly** il dormait profondément, il était profondément endormi; **to ~ soundly** *(without fear)* dormir sur ses deux oreilles; **to ~ lightly** *(regularly)* avoir le sommeil léger; *(on one occasion)* dormir d'un sommeil léger; **I didn't ~ a wink all night** je n'ai pas fermé l'œil de la nuit; **to ~ the clock round** faire le tour du cadran; *(fig)* **he was ~ing on his feet** il dormait debout.

(b) *(spend night)* coucher. **he slept in the car** il a passé la nuit *or* dormi dans la voiture; **he slept at his aunt's** il a couché chez sa tante; **he ~s on a hard mattress** il couche *or* dort sur un matelas dur; *(euph)* **to ~ with sb** coucher avec qn*.

4 *vt*: **the house ~s 8 (people)** on peut loger *or* coucher 8 personnes dans cette maison; **this room will ~ 4 (people)** on peut coucher 4 personnes *or* coucher à 4 dans cette chambre; **the hotel ~s 500** l'hôtel peut loger *or* contenir 500 personnes; **can you ~ us all?** pouvez-vous nous coucher tous?

sleep around* *vi* coucher avec n'importe qui*, coucher à droite et à gauche*.

sleep away *vt sep*: **to sleep the morning away** passer la matinée à dormir, ne pas se réveiller de la matinée.

sleep in *vi* **(a)** *(lie late)* faire la grasse matinée, dormir tard; *(oversleep)* ne pas se réveiller à temps, dormir trop tard.

(b) *[nurse, servant etc]* être logé sur place.

sleep off *vt sep*: **to sleep sth off** dormir pour faire passer qch, se remettre de qch en dormant; **go to bed and sleep it off** va te coucher et cela te passera en dormant; **to sleep off a hangover, to sleep it off*** dormir pour faire passer sa gueule de bois‡, cuver son vin*.

sleep on 1 *vi*: **he slept on till 10** il a dormi jusqu'à 10 heures, il ne s'est pas réveillé avant 10 heures; **let him sleep on for another hour** laisse-le dormir encore une heure.

2 *vt fus*: **to sleep on a problem/a letter/a decision** attendre le lendemain pour résoudre un problème/répondre à une lettre/prendre une décision; **let's sleep on it** nous verrons demain, la nuit porte conseil; **I'll have to sleep on it** il faut que j'attende demain pour décider.

sleep out *vi* **(a)** *(in open air)* coucher à la belle étoile; *(in tent)* coucher sous la tente.

(b) *[nurse, servant etc]* ne pas être logé (sur place).
sleep through 1 *vi*: **I slept through till the afternoon** j'ai dormi comme une souche *or* sans me réveiller jusqu'à l'après-midi.
2 *vt fus*: **he slept through the storm** l'orage ne l'a pas réveillé; **he slept through the alarm clock** il n'a pas entendu son réveil (sonner).
sleeper ['sliːpəʳ] *n* **(a)** (*person*) dormeur *m*, -euse *f*; (*fig: spy*) espion(ne) *m(f)* en sommeil. **to be a light/heavy ~** avoir le sommeil léger/lourd; **that child is a good ~** cet enfant dort très bien *or* fait sa nuit sans se réveiller.
(b) (*Rail*) (*Brit: on track*) traverse *f*; (*bed*) couchette *f*; (*train*) train couchettes *m*. **I took a ~ to Marseilles** j'ai pris une couchette pour aller à Marseille, je suis allé à Marseille en couchette.
(c) (*esp Brit: earring*) clou *m*.
sleepily ['sliːpɪlɪ] *adv* d'un air *or* ton endormi.
sleepiness ['sliːpɪnɪs] *n [person]* envie *f* de dormir, torpeur *f*; *[town]* somnolence *f*, torpeur.
sleeping ['sliːpɪŋ] 1 *adj person* qui dort, endormi. (*Prov*) **let ~ dogs lie** il ne faut pas réveiller le chat qui dort (*Prov*); **the S~ Beauty** la Belle au bois dormant.
2 *cpd*: **sleeping bag** sac *m* de couchage; **sleeping berth** couchette *f*; (*Rail*) **sleeping car** wagon-couchettes *m*, voiture-lit *f*; **sleeping draught** soporifique *m*; (*Brit Comm*) **sleeping partner** (associé *m*) commanditaire *m*; **sleeping pill** somnifère *m*; **sleeping quarters** chambres *fpl* (à coucher); (*in barracks*) chambrées *fpl*; (*dormitory*) dortoir *m*; **sleeping sickness** maladie *f* du sommeil; **sleeping suit** pyjama *m* (pour enfant); **sleeping tablet = sleeping pill.**
sleepless ['sliːplɪs] *adj person* qui ne dort pas, éveillé; (*fig: alert*) infatigable, inlassable. **to have a ~ night** ne pas dormir de la nuit, passer une nuit blanche; **he spent many ~ hours worrying about it** il a passé bien des heures sans sommeil à se faire du souci à ce sujet.
sleeplessly ['sliːplɪslɪ] *adv* sans dormir.
sleeplessness ['sliːplɪsnɪs] *n* insomnie *f*.
sleepy ['sliːpɪ] 1 *adj person* qui a envie de dormir, somnolent; (*not alert*) endormi; *voice, look, village* endormi, somnolent. **to be** *or* **feel ~** avoir sommeil, avoir envie de dormir. 2 *cpd*: **sleepyhead*** endormi(e) *m(f)*.
sleet [sliːt] 1 *n* neige fondue. 2 *vi*: **it is ~ing** il tombe de la neige fondue.
sleeve [sliːv] 1 *n [garment]* manche *f*; *[record]* pochette *f*; *[cylinder etc]* chemise *f*. (*fig*) **he's always got something up his ~** il a plus d'un tour dans son sac; **he's bound to have something up his ~** il a certainement quelque chose en réserve, il garde certainement un atout caché; **I don't know what he's got up his ~** je ne sais pas ce qu'il nous réserve (comme surprise); **I've got an idea up my ~** j'ai une petite idée en réserve *or* dans la tête; *V* **heart, laugh, shirt** *etc*.
2 *cpd*: **sleeveboard** jeannette *f*.
-sleeved [sliːvd] *adj ending in cpds*: **long-sleeved** à manches longues.
sleeveless ['sliːvlɪs] *adj* sans manches.
sleigh [sleɪ] 1 *n* traîneau *m*. 2 *cpd*: **sleigh bell** grelot *m or* clochette *f* (de traîneau); **to go for a sleigh ride** faire une promenade en traîneau. 3 *vi* aller en traîneau.
sleight [slaɪt] *n*: **~ of hand** (*skill*) habileté *f*, dextérité *f*; (*trick*) tour *m* de passe-passe; **by (a) ~ of hand** par un tour de passe-passe.
slender ['slendəʳ] *adj figure, person* svelte, mince; *stem, hand* fin; *wineglass* élancé; *neck* fin, gracieux; *waist* fin, délié; *fingers* fin, effilé; (*fig*) *hope* ténu, faible; l)ctanre,possibility faible; *excuse* faible, peu convaincant; *income, means* maigre, insuffisant, modeste; *knowledge, resources* maigre, limité, insuffisant. *[person]* **tall and ~** élancé; **small and ~** menu; **a ~ majority** une faible majorité.
slenderize ['slendəraɪz] *vt* (*US*) amincir.
slenderly ['slendəlɪ] *adv*: **~ built** svelte, mince.
slenderness ['slendənɪs] *n* (*V* **slender**) sveltesse *f*, minceur *f*; finesse *f*; faiblesse *f*; insuffisance *f*.
slept [slept] *pret, ptp of* **sleep.**
sleuth [sluːθ] 1 *n* (*dog: also* **~ hound**) limier *m* (*chien*); (*: *detective*) limier, détective *m*. 2 *vi* (*: *also* **~ around**) fureter, fouiner*.
slew[1] [sluː] *pret of* **slay.**
slew[2] [sluː] (*also* **~ round**) 1 *vi* virer, pivoter; (*Naut*) virer; *[car]* déraper lar l'arrière; **right round** faire un tête-à-queue. **the car ~ed (round) to a stop** la voiture s'est arrêtée après un tête-à-queue. 2 *vt* faire pivoter, faire virer. **he ~ed the car (round)** il a fait déraper la voiture par l'arrière; (*right round*) il a fait un tête-à-queue.
slice [slaɪs] 1 *n* **(a)** *[cake, bread, meat]* tranche *f*; *[lemon, cucumber, sausage]* rondelle *f*, tranche. **~ of bread and butter** tranche de pain beurré, tartine beurrée.
(b) (*fig*) (*part*) partie *f*; (*share*) part *f*. **it took quite a ~ of our profits** cela nous a pris une bonne partie de nos bénéfices; **a large ~ of the credit** une grande part du mérite; **~ of life** tranche *f* de vie; **~ of luck** coup *m* de chance.
(c) (*kitchen utensil*) spatule *f*, truelle *f*.
(d) (*Sport*) coup *m* en sifflet.
2 *vt* **(a)** *bread, cake, meat* couper (en tranches); *lemon, sausage, cucumber* couper (en rondelles); *rope etc* couper net, trancher. **to ~ sth thin** couper qch en tranches *or* rondelles fines; **a ~d loaf** un pain en tranches.
(b) (*Sport*) *ball* couper, slicer.
3 *vi*: **this knife won't ~** ce couteau coupe très mal; **this bread won't ~** ce pain se coupe très mal *or* est très difficile à couper.
slice off *vt sep piece of rope, finger etc* couper net. **to slice off a piece of sausage** couper une rondelle de saucisson; **to slice off a steak** couper *or* tailler un bifteck.
slice through *vt fus rope* couper net, trancher; (*fig*) *restrictions etc* (réussir à) passer au travers de, court-circuiter*. (*fig*) **to slice through the air/the waves** fendre l'air/les flots.
slice up *vt sep* couper *or* débiter en tranches *or* en rondelles.
slicer ['slaɪsəʳ] *n* couteau *m* mécanique, machine *f* à couper (*la viande ou le pain*); (*in shop etc*) coupe-jambon *m inv*.
slick [slɪk] 1 *adj* **(a)** *hair* lissé et brillant, luisant; *road, surface* glissant, gras (*f* grasse).
(b) (*pej*) *explanation* trop prompt; *excuse* facile; *style* superficiel, brillant en apparence; *manners* doucereux, mielleux; *person* (*glib*) qui a la parole facile, qui a du bagout*; (*cunning*) astucieux, rusé; *business deal* mené rondement, mené bon train. **he always has a ~ answer** il a toujours la réponse facile, il a toujours réponse à tout; **a ~ customer*** une fine mouche, un(e) fin(e) rusé(e).
2 *n* (*oil~*) nappe *f* de pétrole; (*larger*) marée noire.
3 *vt*: **to ~ (down) one's hair** (*with comb etc*) se lisser les cheveux; (*with hair cream*) se brillantiner les cheveux.
slicker* ['slɪkəʳ] *n* combinard(e)* *m(f)*; *V* **city.**
slickly ['slɪklɪ] *adv answer* habilement.
slickness ['slɪknɪs] *n* (*V* **slick**) **(a)** brillant *m*; nature glissante.
(b) (*pej*) excès *m* de promptitude; qualité superficielle; caractère doucereux; parole *f* facile, bagout* *m*; astuce *f*, ruse *f*.
slide [slaɪd] (*vb: pret, ptp* **slid**) 1 *n* **(a)** (*action*) glissade *f*; (*land~*) glissement *m* (de terrain); (*fig: in prices, temperature etc*) baisse *f*, chute *f* (*in* de).
(b) (*in playground, pool etc*) toboggan *m*; (*polished ice etc*) glissoire *f*; (*for logs etc*) glissoir *m*.
(c) *[microscope]* porte-objet *m*; (*Phot*) diapositive *f*, diapo* *f*. **illustrated with ~s** accompagné de diapositives; **a film for ~s** une pellicule à diapositiges; *V* **colour, lantern.**
(d) (*Tech: runner*) coulisse *f*; (*on trombone etc*) coulisse; (*Mus: between notes*) coulé *m*; (*hair ~*) barrette *f*.
2 *cpd*: (*Phot*) **slide box** classeur *m* pour diapositives, boîte *f* à diapositives; (*Dress etc*) **slide fastener** fermeture *f* éclair ®, fermeture à glissière; (*Phot*) **slide projector** projecteur *m* de diapositives; **slide rule** règle *f* à calcul.
3 *vi* **(a)** *[person, object]* glisser; (*on ice etc*) *[person]* faire des glissades, glisser. **to ~ down the bannisters** descendre en glissant sur la rampe; **to ~ down a slope** descendre une pente en glissant, glisser le long d'une pente; **the drawer ~s in and out easily** le tiroir glisse bien, le tiroir s'ouvre et se ferme facilement; **the top ought to ~ gently into place** on devrait pouvoir mettre le haut en place en le faisant glisser doucement; **the book slid off my knee** le livre a glissé de mon genou; **to let things ~** laisser les choses aller à la dérive; **he let his studies ~** il a négligé ses études.
(b) (*move silently*) se glisser. **he slid into the room** il s'est glissé dans la pièce; (*fig*) **to ~ into bad habits** prendre insensiblement de mauvaises habitudes.
4 *vt* faire glisser, glisser. **he slid the chair across the room** il a fait glisser la chaise à travers la pièce; **he slid the packing case into a corner** il a glissé la caisse dans un coin; **he slid the photo into his pocket** il a glissé la photo dans sa poche; **to ~ the top (back) onto a box** (re)mettre le couvercle sur une boîte (en le faisant glisser); **~ the drawer into place** remets le tiroir en place; **he slid the gun out of the holster** il a sorti le revolver de l'étui.
slide down *vi [person, animal, vehicle]* descendre en glissant; *[object]* glisser.
slide off *vi* **(a)** *[top, lid etc]* s'enlever facilement *or* en glissant.
(b) (*fig: leave quietly*) *[guest]* s'en aller discrètement, s'éclipser*; *[thief]* s'éloigner furtivement.
sliding ['slaɪdɪŋ] 1 *adj movement* glissant; *part* qui glisse, mobile; *panel, door, seat* coulissant. (*Aut*) **~ roof** toit ouvrant; (*Admin, Comm, Ind etc*) **~ scale** échelle *f* mobile. 2 *n* glissement *m*.
slight [slaɪt] 1 *adj* **(a)** *person, figure* (*slim*) mince, menu; (*frail*) frêle; *framework* fragile.
(b) (*small*) *movement, increase, pain, difference, wind, accent* petit, léger (*before n only*); (*trivial, negligible*) *increase, difference* faible, insignifiant, négligeable; *pain* faible; *error* insignifiant, sans importance. **he showed some ~ optimism** il a fait preuve d'un peu d'optimisme; **to a ~ extent** dans une faible mesure; **not the ~est danger** pas le moindre danger; **not in the ~est** pas le moins du monde, pas du tout; **I haven't the ~est idea** je n'(en) ai pas la moindre idée; **just the ~est bit short** un tout petit peu trop court; **there's not the ~est possibility** *or* **chance of that** il n'y en a pas la moindre possibilité, c'est tout à fait impossible; **he takes offence at the ~est thing** il se pique pour un rien; **the wound is only ~** la blessure est légère *or* sans gravité.
2 *vt* (*ignore*) ignorer, manquer d'égards envers; (*offend*) blesser, offenser. **he felt (himself) ~ed** il s'est senti blessé *or* offensé.
3 *n* manque *m* d'égards, humiliation *f*, offense *f*. **this is a ~ on all of us** c'est un affront qui nous touche tous.
slighting ['slaɪtɪŋ] *adj* blessant, offensant, désobligeant.
slightingly ['slaɪtɪŋlɪ] *adv* avec peu d'égards, d'une manière blessante *or* offensante *or* désobligeante.
slightly ['slaɪtlɪ] *adv* **(a)** *sick, cold, better* légèrement, un peu. **I know her ~** je la connais un peu. **(b) ~ built** mince, menu.
slightness ['slaɪtnɪs] *n* (*slimness*) minceur *f*; (*frailty*) fragilité *f*; *[difference, increase etc]* caractère insignifiant *or* négligeable.
slim [slɪm] 1 *adj person, figure, waist* mince, svelte; *ankle, book, volume* mince; (*fig*) *hope, chance* faible; *excuse* mince, médiocre, faible; *evidence* insuffisant, peu convaincant; *resources* maigre, insuffisant, faible.

2 *vi* maigrir; (*diet*) suivre un régime amaigrissant. **she's ~ming** elle essaie de maigrir, elle suit un régime pour maigrir.
3 *vt* (*also* **~ down**) *[diet etc]* faire maigrir; *[dress etc]* amincir.
slim down 1 *vi* maigrir, perdre du poids.
2 *vt sep* = **slim 3.**
slime [slaɪm] *n* (*mud*) vase *f*; (*on riverbeds*) limon *m*; (*sticky substance*) dépôt visqueux *or* gluant; (*from snail*) bave *f*.
sliminess ['slaɪmɪnɪs] *n* (*V* **slimy**) nature vaseuse *or* limoneuse; viscosité *f*; suintement *m*; obséquiosité *f*; servilité *f*.
slimmer ['slɪmə^{r}] *n* personne *f* suivant un régime amaigrissant.
slimming ['slɪmɪŋ] **1** *n* fait *m* de suivre un régime amaigrissant, amaigrissement *m*. **~ can be very tiring** un régime amaigrissant peut être très fatigant, ça peut être très fatigant de se faire maigrir *or* d'être au régime.
2 *adj diet, pills* amaigrissant, pour maigrir; *food* qui ne fait pas grossir; *dress etc* amincissant.
slimness ['slɪmnɪs] *n* (*V* **slim**) minceur *f*, sveltesse *f*; faiblesse *f*; insuffisance *f*.
slimy ['slaɪmɪ] *adj mud* vaseux; (*on riverbeds*) limoneux; *stone, hands* (*muddy*) couvert de vase, boueux; (*sticky*) visqueux, gluant; *liquid, secretion, mark, deposit* visqueux, gluant; *fish, slug* visqueux; *walls* suintant; (*fig*) *manners, smile* doucereux, obséquieux, servile; *person* rampant, servile, visqueux. **he's really ~** c'est un lécheur *or* un lèche-bottes*.
sling [slɪŋ] (*vb*: *pret, ptp* **slung**) **1** *n* **(a)** (*weapon*) fronde *f*; (*child's*) lance-pierre(s) *m inv*.
(b) (*hoist*) cordages *mpl*, courroies *fpl*; (*for oil drums etc*) courroie; (*Naut*: *for loads, casks, boats*) élingue *f*; (*Naut*: *for mast*) cravate *f*; (*for rifle*) bretelle *f*; (*Med*) écharpe *f*. **to have one's arm in a ~** avoir le bras en écharpe.
2 *cpd*: (*US*) **slingshot** lance-pierre(s) *m inv*.
3 *vt* **(a)** (*throw*) *objects, stones* lancer, jeter (*at sb, to sb* à qn, *at sth* sur qch); *insults, accusations* lancer (*at sb* à qn).
(b) (*hang*) *hammock etc* suspendre; *load etc* hisser; (*Naut*) élinguer. **to ~ across one's shoulder** *rifle* mettre en bandoulière *or* à la bretelle; *satchel* mettre en bandoulière; *load, coat* jeter par derrière l'épaule; **with his rifle slung across his shoulder** avec son fusil en bandoulière *or* à la bretelle.
sling away* *vt sep* (*get rid of*) jeter, se débarrasser de, ficher en l'air*.
sling out* *vt sep* (*put out*) *person* flanquer* à la porte *or* dehors; *object* jeter, se débarrasser de, ficher en l'air*.
sling over* *vt sep* (*pass*) passer, envoyer, balancer*.
sling up *vt sep* suspendre.
slink [slɪŋk] *pret, ptp* **slunk** *vi*: **to ~ away/out** *etc* s'en aller/sortir *etc* furtivement *or* sournoisement *or* honteusement.
slinkily* ['slɪŋkɪlɪ] *adv walk* d'une démarche ondoyante *or* ondulante, avec un mouvement onduleux.
slinky* ['slɪŋkɪ] *adj woman* séduisant, provocant, aguichant; *body* sinueux, ondoyant; *walk* ondoyant, ondulant; *dress* moulant, collant.
slip [slɪp] **1** *n* **(a)** (*slide*) dérapage *m*; (*trip*) faux pas; (*of earth*) éboulement *m*; (*fig*: *mistake*) erreur *f*, bévue *f*, gaffe* *f*; (*oversight*) étourderie *f*, oubli *m*; (*moral*) écart *m*, faute légère. (*Prov*) **there's many a ~ 'twixt cup and lip** il y a loin de la coupe aux lèvres (*Prov*); **~ of the tongue, ~ of the pen** lapsus *m*; **it was a ~ of the tongue** c'était un lapsus, la langue lui a (*or* m'a *etc*) fourché; **he made several ~s** il a fait *or* commis plusieurs lapsus; **to give sb the ~** fausser compagnie à qn.
(b) (*pillow~*) taie *f* (d'oreiller); (*underskirt*) combinaison *f*; (*dog lead*) laisse *f*; *V* **gym**.
(c) the ~s (*Naut*) la cale; (*Theat*) les coulisses *fpl*; **in the ~s** (*Naut*) sur cale; (*Theat*) dans les coulisses.
(d) (*plant-cutting*) bouture *f*; (*paper*: *in filing system*) fiche *f*. **a ~ of paper** (*small sheet*) une petite feuille *or* un bout *or* un morceau de papier; (*strip*) une bande de papier; (*fig*) **a (mere) ~ of a boy/girl** un gamin/une gamine, un jeune homme/une jeune fille gracile.
(e) (*U*: *Pottery*) engobe *m*.
(f) (*Aviat*: *side~*) glissade *f or* glissement *m* sur l'aile.
2 *cpd*: **slipcovers** housses *fpl*; **slipknot** nœud coulant; **slip-on** (*adj*) facile à mettre *or* à enfiler*; **slipover*** pull-over *m* sans manches, débardeur *m*; (*Brit*) **slip road** (*to motorway*) bretelle *f* d'accès; (*bypass road*) voie *f* de déviation; **slipshod** *person* (*in dress etc*) débraillé, négligé; (*in work*) négligent; *work, style* négligé, peu soigné; **slipslop*** (*liquor*) lavasse* *f*, bibine* *f*; (*talk, writing*) bêtises *fpl*; (*Knitting*) **slip stitch** maille glissée; (*Aviat*) **slipstream** sillage *m*; **slip-up*** bévue *f*, cafouillage* *m*; **there has been a slip-up somewhere*** quelqu'un a dû faire une gaffe*, quelque chose a cafouillé*, il y a eu un cafouillage*; **a slip-up in communication(s)*** une défaillance *or* un cafouillage* dans les communications; (*Naut*) **slipway** (*for building, repairing*) cale *f* (de construction); (*for launching*) cale de lancement.
3 *vi* **(a)** (*slide*) *[person, foot, hand, object]* glisser. **he ~ped on the ice** il a glissé *or* dérapé sur la glace; **my foot/hand ~ped** mon pied/ma main a glissé; (*Aut*) **the clutch ~ped** l'embrayage a patiné; **the knot has ~ped** le nœud a glissé *or* coulissé; **the fish ~ped off the hook** le poisson s'est détaché de l'hameçon; **the drawer ~s in and out easily** le tiroir glisse bien, le tiroir s'ouvre et se ferme facilement; **the top ought to ~ gently into place** on devrait pouvoir mettre le haut en place en le faisant glisser doucement; **the saw ~ped and cut my hand** la scie a glissé *or* dérapé et m'a entaillé la main; **the book ~ped out of his hand/off the table** le livre lui a glissé des doigts/a glissé de la table; **the beads ~ped through my fingers** les perles m'ont glissé entre les doigts; (*fig*) **money ~s through her fingers** l'argent lui file entre les doigts; **the thief ~ped through their fingers** le voleur leur a filé entre les doigts; **several errors had ~ped into the report** plusieurs erreurs s'étaient glissées dans le rapport; **to let an opportunity ~, to let ~ an opportunity** laisser passer *or* laisser échapper une occasion; **he let ~ an oath** il a laissé échapper un juron; **he let (it) ~ that ...** il a laissé échapper que ...; **he's ~ping*** (*getting old, less efficient*) il baisse, il n'est plus ce qu'il était, il perd les pédales*; (*making more mistakes*) il ne fait pas assez attention, il ne doit plus assez se concentrer.
(b) (*move quickly*) *[person]* se glisser, passer, se faufiler; *[vehicle]* se faufiler, passer. **he ~ped into/out of the room** il s'est glissé *or* coulé dans/hors de la pièce; **he ~ped through the corridors** il s'est faufilé dans les couloirs; **I'll just ~ through the garden** je vais passer par le jardin; **the motorbike ~ped through the traffic** la motocyclette s'est faufilée à travers la circulation; **to ~ into bed** se glisser *or* se couler dans son lit; **to ~ into a dress** se glisser dans *or* enfiler (rapidement) une robe; **to ~ out of a dress** enlever (rapidement) une robe; (*fig*) **he ~ped easily into his new role** il s'est ajusté *or* adapté *or* fait facilement à son nouveau rôle; **to ~ into bad habits** prendre insensiblement de mauvaises habitudes.
4 *vt* **(a)** (*slide*) glisser. **to ~ a coin to sb/into sb's hand** glisser une pièce à qn/dans la main de qn; **he ~ped the book back on the shelf** il a glissé *or* remis le livre à sa place sur l'étagère; **he ~ped the ring on her finger** il lui a glissé *or* passé la bague au doigt; **he ~ped the photo into his pocket** il a glissé la photo dans sa poche; **to ~ the top (back) onto a box** (re)mettre le couvercle sur une boîte (en le faisant glisser); **~ the drawer (back) into place** remets le tiroir en place; **he ~ped the gun out of its holster** il a retiré *or* sorti le revolver de son étui; **a question on Proust was ~ped into the exam** l'épreuve a comporté une question inattendue sur Proust; (*Med*) **a ~ped disc** une hernie discale.
(b) (*escape*) échapper à; (*Naut*) *anchor, cable, moorings* filer. **the dog ~ped its collar** le chien s'est dégagé de son collier; **he ~ped the dog's leash** il a lâché le chien; (*Knitting*) **to ~ a stitch** glisser une maille; **that ~ped his attention** *or* **his notice** cela lui a échappé; **it ~ped his notice that ...** il ne s'est pas aperçu que ..., il n'a pas remarqué que ..., il lui a échappé que ...; **it ~ped my memory** *or* **my mind** j'avais complètement oublié cela, cela m'était complètement sorti de la tête.
slip along *vi* faire un saut, passer. **he has just slipped along to the shops** il a fait un saut jusqu'aux magasins; **slip along to Mary's and ask her ...** fais un saut *or* passe chez Marie et demande-lui ... .
slip away *vi [car, boat]* s'éloigner doucement; *[guest]* partir discrètement, s'esquiver, s'éclipser*; *[thief]* s'en aller furtivement, filer*, s'esquiver. **I slipped away for a few minutes** je me suis esquivé *or* éclipsé* pour quelques minutes; **her life was slipping away (from her)** la vie la quittait.
slip back 1 *vi [car, boat]* revenir *or* retourner doucement; *[guest]* revenir *or* retourner discrètement; *[thief, spy]* revenir *or* retourner furtivement *or* subrepticement. **I'll just slip back and get it** je retourne le chercher.
2 *vt sep V* **slip 4a.**
slip by *vi* = **slip past.**
slip down *vi [object, car]* glisser; *[person]* glisser et tomber. **I'll just slip down and get it** je descends le chercher.
slip in 1 *vi [car, boat]* entrer doucement; *[person]* entrer discrètement *or* sans se faire remarquer; *[thief]* entrer furtivement *or* subrepticement; *[cat etc]* entrer inaperçu. **several errors have slipped in** plusieurs erreurs s'y sont glissées; **I'll just slip in and tell him** je vais juste entrer le lui dire; **I've only slipped in for a minute** je ne fais que passer, je ne fais qu'entrer et sortir.
2 *vt sep object* glisser, placer; *part, drawer* glisser à sa place; *remark, comment* glisser, placer. (*Aut*) **to slip in the clutch** embrayer.
slip off 1 *vi* **(a)** = **slip away.**
(b) *[coat, lid, cover]* glisser.
2 *vt sep cover, ring, bracelet, glove, shoe* enlever; *garment* enlever, ôter.
slip on 1 *vt sep garment* passer, enfiler*; *ring, bracelet, glove* mettre, enfiler; *shoe* mettre; *lid, cover* (re)mettre, placer.
2 slip-on *adj V* **slip 2.**
slip out 1 *vi [guest]* sortir discrètement, s'esquiver, s'éclipser*; *[thief]* sortir furtivement, filer*, s'esquiver. **I must just slip out for some cigarettes** il faut que je sorte un instant chercher des cigarettes; **she slipped out to the shops** elle a fait un saut jusqu'aux magasins; **the secret slipped out** le secret a été révélé par mégarde; **the words slipped out before he realized it** les mots lui ont échappé avant même qu'il ne s'en rende compte.
2 *vt sep* sortir doucement (*or* discrètement *etc*).
slip over 1 *vi* = **slip along.**
2 *vt sep*: **to slip one over on sb*** rouler qn*.
3 slipover* *n V* **slip 2.**
slip past *vi [person, vehicle]* passer, se faufiler. **the years slipped past** les années passèrent.
slip round *vi* = **slip along.**
slip through *vi [person]* passer quand même; *[error etc]* ne pas être remarqué.
slip up* 1 *vi* (*make mistake*) gaffer*, cafouiller*, se ficher dedans*.
2 slip-up *n V* **slip 2.**
slipper ['slɪpə^{r}] *n* pantoufle *f*, (*warmer*) chausson *m*; (*mule*) mule *f*; *V* **glass.**
slippery ['slɪpərɪ] *adj surface, road, stone, fish* glissant; (*fig pej*) *person* (*evasive*) fuyant, insaisissable; (*unreliable*) sur qui on ne peut pas compter. **it's ~ underfoot** le sol est glissant, on glisse en marchant; (*fig pej*) **he's as ~ as an eel** il glisse *or* il

échappe comme une anguille; (*fig*) **to be on ~ ground** être sur un terrain glissant; (*fig*) **to be on a ~ slope** être sur un terrain glissant *or* une pente savonneuse*.

slippy* ['slɪpɪ] *adj fish, stone* glissant; *road, floor* glissant, casse-gueule: *inv*. (*Brit*) **look ~ (about it)!** grouille-toi!:

slit [slɪt] (*vb*: *pret, ptp* **slit**) **1** *n* (*opening*) fente *f*; (*cut*) incision *f*; (*tear*) déchirure *f*. **to make a ~ in sth** fendre *or* inciser *or* déchirer qch; **the skirt has a ~ up the side** la jupe a une fente *or* est fendue sur le côté.

2 *cpd*: **slit-eyed** aux yeux bridés.

3 *vt* (*make an opening in*) fendre; (*cut*) inciser, couper, faire une fente dans; (*tear*) déchirer. **to ~ sb's throat** couper *or* trancher la gorge à qn; **to ~ a letter open** ouvrir une lettre (*avec un objet tranchant*); **to ~ a sack open** éventrer *or* fendre un sac.

slither ['slɪðəʳ] *vi [person, animal]* glisser; *[snake]* onduler. **he ~ed about on the ice** il dérapait sur la glace, il essayait de se tenir en équilibre sur la glace; **the car ~ed (about) all over the place** la voiture a dérapé dans tous les sens; **he ~ed down the slope/down the rope** il a dégringolé* la pente/le long de la corde; **the snake ~ed across the path** le serpent a traversé le sentier en ondulant.

sliver ['slɪvəʳ] *n [glass]* éclat *m*; *[wood]* éclat, écharde *f*; *[cheese, ham etc]* lamelle *f*, petit morceau.

slivovitz ['slɪvəʊvɪts] *n* (*U*) slivowitz *m*.

slob: [slɒb] *n* rustaud(e) *m(f)*, plouc: *mf*.

slobber ['slɒbəʳ] **1** *vi [person, dog etc]* baver. **to ~ over sth** (*lit*) baver sur qch; (*fig pej*) s'attendrir *or* s'extasier exagérément sur qch; **to ~ over sb** *[dog]* couvrir qn de grands coups de langue; (*fig pej*: *kiss etc*) *[person]* faire des mamours* à qn, donner une fricassée de museau à qn:. **2** *n* (*U*) bave *f*, salive *f*; (*fig pej*) sensiblerie *f*, attendrissement exagéré.

sloe [sləʊ] **1** *n* prunelle *f*. **2** *cpd*: **sloe-eyed** aux yeux de biche; **sloe gin** liqueur *f* de prunelle.

slog [slɒg] **1** *n* (*work*) long travail pénible, travail de Romain* *or* de nègre*; (*effort*) gros effort. **the programme was one long ~** le programme exigeait un grand effort *or* représentait un travail de Romain*; **it was a (hard) ~ to pass the exam** il a fallu fournir un gros effort *or* travailler comme un nègre* pour réussir à l'examen; **after a long ~ he reached the top of the hill** après un gros effort il a atteint le sommet de la colline; **he found it nothing but a ~** c'était une vraie corvée pour lui.

2 *vt ball* donner un grand coup à; *opponent* donner un grand coup à, donner un gnon: à.

3 *vi* **(a)** (*work etc*) travailler très dur *or* comme un nègre*. **he ~ged through the book** il s'est forcé à lire le livre, il a poursuivi péniblement la lecture du livre.

(b) (*walk etc*) marcher d'un pas lourd, avancer avec obstination. **he ~ged up the hill** il a gravi la colline avec effort *or* avec obstination *or* d'un pas lourd.

slog along *vi* marcher d'un pas lourd, avancer avec obstination. **we slogged along for 10 km** nous nous sommes traînés sur 10 km.

slog away *vi* travailler dur *or* comme un nègre*. **to slog away at sth** trimer sur qch.

slog on *vi* = **slog along.**

slogan ['sləʊgən] *n* slogan *m*.

slogger* ['slɒgəʳ] *n* (*hard worker*) bourreau *m* de travail, bûcheur *m*, -euse *f*, bosseur: *m*, -euse: *f*; (*Boxing*) cogneur *m*.

sloop [slu:p] *n* sloop *m*.

slop [slɒp] **1** *n*: **~s** (*dirty water*) eaux sales; (*in teacup etc*) fond *m* de tasse; (*liquid food*) (*for invalids etc*) bouillon *m*, aliment *m* liquide; (*for pigs*) pâtée *f*, soupe *f*.

2 *cpd*: **slop basin** vide-tasses *m inv*; **slop bucket, slop pail** (*in kitchen etc*) boîte *f* à ordures, poubelle *f*; (*in bedroom*) seau *m* de toilette; (*on farm*) seau à pâtée.

3 *vt liquid* (*spill*) renverser, répandre; (*tip carelessly*) répandre (*on to* sur, *into* dans). **you've ~ped paint all over the floor** tu as éclaboussé tout le plancher de peinture.

4 *vi* (*also* **~ over**) *[water, tea etc]* déborder, se renverser (*into* dans, *on to* sur); *[bowl, bucket]* déborder.

slop about, slop around 1 *vi* **(a) the water was slopping about in the bucket** l'eau clapotait dans le seau; **they were slopping about in the mud** ils pataugeaient dans la boue.

(b) (*fig*) **she slops about in a dressing gown all day*** elle traîne *or* traînasse toute la journée en robe de chambre.

2 *vt sep* renverser *or* mettre un peu partout.

slop out *vi* (*Prison*) vider les seaux hygiéniques.

slop over 1 *vi* = **slop 4.**

2 *vt sep* renverser, répandre.

slope [sləʊp] **1** *n* **(a)** *[roof, floor, ground, surface]* inclinaison *f*, pente *f*, déclivité *f*; *[handwriting etc]* inclinaison. **roof with a slight/steep ~** toit (qui descend) en pente douce/raide; **road with a ~ of 1 in 8** route avec une pente de 12,5%; (*Mil*) **rifle at the ~** fusil sur l'épaule.

(b) (*rising ground, gentle hill*) côte *f*, pente *f*; (*mountainside*) versant *m*, flanc *m*. **~ up** montée *f*; **~ down** descente *f*; **the car got stuck on a ~** la voiture est restée en panne dans une côte; **halfway up *or* down the ~** à mi-côte, à mi-pente; **on the ~s of Mount Etna** sur les flancs de l'Etna; **the southern ~s of the Himalayas** le versant sud de l'Himalaya; *V* **ski.**

2 *vi [ground, roof]* être en pente, être incliné; *[handwriting]* pencher.

3 *vt* incliner, pencher. (*Mil*) **to ~ arms** mettre l'arme sur l'épaule; **'~ arms!'** 'portez arme!'

slope away, slope down *vi [ground]* descendre en pente (*to* jusqu'à).

slope off* *vi* se sauver*, se tirer:, se barrer:.

slope up *vi [road, ground]* monter.

sloping ['sləʊpɪŋ] *adj ground, roof etc* en pente, incliné; *handwriting etc* penché; *shoulders* tombant.

sloppily* ['slɒpɪlɪ] *adv* (*carelessly*) *dress* de façon négligée, sans soin; *work* sans soin; (*sentimentally*) *talk, behave* avec sensiblerie.

sloppiness ['slɒpɪnɪs] *n* (*V* **sloppy**) état liquide *or* détrempé; manque *m* de soin; négligé *m*; sensiblerie *f*; excès *m* de sentimentalité.

sloppy ['slɒpɪ] *adj food* (trop) liquide; *ground, field* détrempé; (*) *work* peu soigné, bâclé*, saboté*; (*) *appearance* négligé, débraillé; (*) *garment* trop grand, mal ajusté; (*) *smile, look* pâmé, débordant de sensiblerie; (*) *book, film* fadement sentimental. **don't be ~!*** pas de sensiblerie!; **~ talk*** fadaises *fpl*; **~ English*** anglais négligé; **~ joe*** (*sweater*) gros pull vague; (*US Culin*) hamburger servi en sandwich.

slosh [slɒʃ] *vt* **(a)** (*Brit:*: *hit*) flanquer* un coup *or* un gnon: à.

(b) (*: *spill*) renverser, répandre; (*apply lavishly*) répandre (*on to, over* sur, *into* dans). **to ~ paint on a wall** barbouiller un mur de peinture, flanquer* de la peinture sur un mur; **he ~ed water over the floor** (*deliberately*) il a répandu de l'eau par terre; (*accidentally*) il a renversé *or* fichu* de l'eau par terre.

slosh about*, slosh around* 1 *vi* = **slop about 1a.**

2 *vt sep* = **slop about 2.**

sloshed: [slɒʃt] *adj* (*esp Brit*: *drunk*) bourré:, paf: *inv*, noir:. **to get ~** se soûler la gueule:, prendre une cuite*.

slot [slɒt] **1** *n* (*slit*) fente *f*; (*groove*) rainure *f*; (*fig*: *in programme, timetable etc*) heure *f*. **to put a coin in the ~** mettre *or* introduire une pièce dans la fente; (*Rad, TV etc*) **they are looking for something to fill the early-evening comedy ~*** on cherche de quoi remplir l'heure (réservée aux programmes) *or* le créneau de comédie en début de soirée.

2 *cpd*: **slot machine** (*for tickets, cigarettes etc*) distributeur *m* (automatique); (*in fair etc*) appareil *m* *or* machine *f* à sous.

3 *vt*: **to ~ a part into another part** emboîter *or* encastrer une pièce dans une autre pièce; (*fig*) **to ~ sth into a programme/timetable** insérer *or* faire rentrer qch dans une grille de programmes/d'horaires.

4 *vi*: **this part ~s into that part** cette pièce-ci s'emboîte *or* s'encastre dans celle-là; (*fig*) **the song will ~ into the programme here** on peut insérer *or* faire figurer la chanson à ce moment-là du programme.

slot in 1 *vi [piece, part]* s'emboîter, s'encastrer; (*fig*) *[item on programme etc]* s'insérer, figurer.

2 *vt sep piece, part* emboîter, encastrer; (*fig*) *item on programme* insérer, faire figurer.

slot together 1 *vi [pieces, parts]* s'emboîter *or* s'encastrer les un(e)s dans les autres.

2 *vt sep pieces, parts* emboîter *or* encastrer les un(e)s dans les autres.

sloth [sləʊθ] *n* **(a)** (*U*) paresse *f*, fainéantise *f*, indolence *f*. **(b)** (*Zool*) paresseux *m*.

slothful ['sləʊθfʊl] *adj* paresseux, fainéant, indolent.

slothfully ['sləʊθfəlɪ] *adv* avec indolence, avec paresse.

slouch [slaʊtʃ] **1** *n* **(a) to walk with a ~** mal se tenir en marchant.

(b) he's no ~* il n'est pas empoté*.

2 *cpd*: **slouch hat** chapeau *m* (mou) à larges bords.

3 *vi*: **he was ~ing in a chair** il était affalé dans un fauteuil; **she always ~es** elle ne se tient jamais droite, elle est toujours avachie; **stop ~ing!** redresse-toi!, tiens-toi droit!; **he ~ed in/out** *etc* il entra/sortit *etc* en traînant les pieds, le dos voûté.

slouch about, slouch around *vi* traîner à ne rien faire.

slough[1] [slaʊ] *n* (*swamp*) bourbier *m*, marécage *m*. (*fig*) **the S~ of Despond** l'abîme *m* du désespoir.

slough[2] [slʌf] **1** *n [snake]* dépouille *f*, mue *f*.

2 *vt* (*also* **~ off**) **the snake ~ed (off) its skin** le serpent a mué.

slough off *vt sep* **(a)** = **slough**[2] **2.**

(b) (*fig*) *habit etc* perdre, se débarrasser de.

Slovak ['sləʊvæk], **Slovakian** [sləʊ'vækɪən] **1** *adj* slovaque. **2** *n* Slovaque *mf*.

sloven ['slʌvn] *n* (*dirty*) souillon *f* (*woman only*), personne sale *or* négligée dans sa tenue; (*careless*) personne sans soin.

Slovene ['sləʊvi:n] **1** *adj* slovène. **2** *n* **(a)** Slovène *mf*. **(b)** (*Ling*) slovène *m*.

slovenliness ['slʌvnlɪnɪs] *n* (*V* **slovenly**) négligé *m*, débraillé *m*; manque *m* de soin, négligence *f*.

slovenly ['slʌvnlɪ] *adj person, appearance* sale, négligé, débraillé; *work* qui manque de soin, négligé, bâclé*. **she's ~** c'est une souillon.

slow [sləʊ] **1** *adj* **(a)** *person, vehicle, movement, pulse, voice, progress* lent. **it's ~ but sure** c'est lent mais sûr, cela avance (*or* fonctionne *etc*) lentement mais sûrement; (*Brit*) **a ~ train** un (train) omnibus; **at a ~ speed** à petite vitesse; (*lit, fig*) **it was ~ going** on n'avançait que lentement; **it's ~ work** c'est un travail qui avance lentement; **he's a ~ worker** il est lent dans son travail, il travaille lentement; **he's a ~ learner** il apprend lentement, il est lent à apprendre.

(b) (*not prompt*) long (*f* longue), lent. **to be ~ of speech** avoir la parole lente; **he is ~ to anger** il est lent à se mettre en colère, il lui en faut beaucoup pour se mettre en colère; **he is ~ to make up his mind** il est long à se décider, il lui faut beaucoup de temps pour se décider; **they were ~ to act** ils ont tardé à agir, ils ont été longs à agir; **he was ~ to understand** il a été lent à comprendre, il lui a fallu longtemps pour comprendre; **he was not ~ to notice *or* in noticing ...** il a vite remarqué ..., il n'a pas mis longtemps à remarquer ...; *V* **up.**

(c) (*fig*) *pitch, track, surface* collant, lourd; *market, trading* trop calme, stagnant; (*boring*) *party, evening* ennuyeux, qui manque d'entrain; *novel, plot, play* qui avance lentement, ennuyeux; *person* (*phlegmatic*) flegmatique, à l'allure posée; (*stupid*) lent, lourd, endormi. **my watch is ~** ma montre retarde; **my watch is 10 minutes ~** ma montre retarde de 10 minutes; **in a ~ oven** à four doux; **business is ~** les affaires stagnent; **life here is ~** la vie s'écoule lentement ici, ici on vit au ralenti.

2 *adv* lentement. (*Naut*) **~ astern!** (en) arrière doucement!; **to go ~** *[walker, driver, vehicle]* aller *or* avancer lentement; (*fig: be cautious*) y aller doucement; (*fig: be less active, do less*) ralentir (ses activités), ne pas en faire trop; (*Ind*) faire la grève perlée; *[watch etc]* prendre du retard; **to go ~er** ralentir (le pas).

3 *cpd*: **slow-acting/-burning** *etc* à action/combustion *etc* lente; **it is slow-acting/-burning** *etc* cela agit/brûle *etc* lentement; (*US*) **he did a slow burn‡** sa colère a couvé *or* monté; (*Brit*) **slowcoach** (*dawdler*) lambin(e)* *m(f)*; (*dullard*) esprit lent; **slowdown** ralentissement *m*; (*Ind*) grève perlée; **slow match** mèche *f* à combustion lente; (*Cine etc*) **in slow motion** au ralenti; **slow-motion film/shot** *etc* (film *m*/prise *f* de vues *etc* au) ralenti *m*; **slow-moving** *person, animal* lent, aux mouvements lents; *vehicle* lent; *play* lent, dont l'action est lente; (*US*) **slowpoke*** = **slowcoach; slow-speaking, slow-spoken** à la parole lente, au débit lent; **slow-witted** lourdaud, qui a l'esprit lent *or* lourd; (*Zool*) **slow worm** orvet *m*, serpent *m* de verre.

4 *vt* (*also* **~ down, ~ up**) *person* (*in walk*) faire ralentir; (*in activity*) ralentir, retarder; *vehicle, machine* ralentir (la marche de); *traffic* ralentir; *horse* ralentir l'allure *or* le pas de; *progress, production, negotiations, reaction* ralentir, retarder. **his injury ~ed him down** *or* **up** sa blessure l'a ralenti *or* l'a diminué; **all these interruptions have ~ed us down** *or* **up** toutes ces interruptions nous ont retardés.

5 *vi* (*also* **~ down, ~ off, ~ up**) *[driver, vehicle, machine, one's reactions, production, progress]* ralentir; *[walker etc]* ralentir (le pas); *[worker]* ralentir (ses efforts). (*Aut*) '**~**' 'ralentir'; (*Aut*) **a '~' signal** un signal de ralentissement; (*fig*) **you must ~ down or you will make yourself ill** il faut que vous ralentissiez (*subj*) (vos activités) sinon vous allez tomber malade; **since his retirement his life has ~ed down** depuis qu'il a pris sa retraite il vit au ralenti.

slow down 1 *vi, vt sep* = **slow 5, 4.**

2 slowdown *n V* **slow 3.**

slow off *vi* = **slow 5.**

slow up *vi, vt sep* = **slow 5, 4.**

slowly ['sləʊlɪ] *adv think, work* lentement; *walk* lentement, à pas lents; *talk* lentement, d'une voix lente; (*little by little*) peu à peu. **~ but surely** lentement mais sûrement; *[car etc]* **to go** *or* **drive** *or* **move ~** aller lentement *or* au pas; **to go** (*or* **speak** *or* **work** *or* **drive** *etc*) **more ~** ralentir.

slowness ['sləʊnɪs] *n [person, vehicle, movement etc]* lenteur *f*; *[pitch, track]* lourdeur *f*; *[party, evening]* manque *m* d'entrain *or* d'intérêt; *[novel, plot, play]* lenteur, manque de mouvement *or* d'action; (*lack of energy etc*) allure posée; (*stupidity*) lenteur d'esprit, stupidité *f*. **~ of mind** lenteur *or* lourdeur d'esprit; **his ~ to act** *or* **in acting** la lenteur avec laquelle *or* le retard avec lequel il a agi.

sludge [slʌdʒ] *n* (*U*) (*mud*) boue *f*, vase *f*, bourbe *f*; (*sediment*) boue, dépôt *m*; (*sewage*) vidanges *fpl*; (*melting snow*) neige fondante *or* fondue.

slug [slʌg] **1** *n* (*Zool*) limace *f*; (*bullet*) balle *f*; (*blow*) coup *m*; (*Min, Typ*) lingot *m*; (*esp US: metal token*) jeton *m*. (*US*) **a ~ of whisky‡** un peu *or* un coup* de whisky sec.

2 *vt* (*: *hit*) frapper comme une brute.

slug out* *vt sep*: **to slug it out** se taper dessus* (pour régler une question).

sluggard ['slʌgəd] *n* paresseux *m*, -euse *f*, indolent(e) *m(f)*, fainéant(e) *m(f)*.

sluggish ['slʌgɪʃ] *adj person, temperament* mou (*f* molle), lent, apathique; (*slow-moving*) lent; (*lazy*) paresseux; *reaction, movement, circulation, digestion* lent; *liver* paresseux; *engine* peu nerveux; *market, business* (trop) calme, stagnant; *sales* difficile.

sluggishly ['slʌgɪʃlɪ] *adv* (*V* **sluggish**) mollement; lentement; paresseusement. (*Aut*) **the engine picks up ~** le moteur n'est pas nerveux.

sluggishness ['slʌgɪʃnɪs] *n* (*V* **sluggish**) mollesse *f*, lenteur *f*, apathie *f*, paresse *f*; *[engine]* manque *m* de nervosité.

sluice [sluːs] **1** *n* **(a)** (*whole structure*) écluse *f*; (*gate: also* **~ gate, ~ valve**) vanne *f*, porte *f* d'écluse; (*channel: also* **~way**) canal *m* (à vannes); (*water held back*) eaux retenues par la vanne.

(b) to give sth/o.s. a ~ (down) laver qch/se laver à grande eau.

2 *cpd*: **sluice gate** *V* **sluice 1a; sluice valve** = **sluice gate; sluiceway** *V* **sluice 1a.**

3 *vt* (*also* **~ down**) laver à grande eau.

slum [slʌm] **1** *n* (*house*) taudis *m*. **the ~s** les quartiers *mpl* pauvres *or* misérables, les bas quartiers; (*in suburb*) la zone.

2 *cpd*: **slum area** quartier *m* pauvre; **slum clearance** lutte *f* contre les taudis, aménagement *m* des quartiers insalubres; **slum clearance area** zone *f* de quartiers insalubres en voie d'aménagement; **slum dwelling** taudis *m*.

3 *vi* **(a)** (*visit ~s: also go* **~ming**) visiter les taudis.

(b) (*: *live cheaply: also (esp Brit)* **~ it**) vivre à la dure, manger de la vache enragée*. (*iro*) **we don't see you often round here — I'm ~ming (it) today!** on ne te voit pas souvent ici — aujourd'hui je m'encanaille!

4 *vt* (*) **to ~ it** *V* **3b.**

slumber ['slʌmbəʳ] **1** *n* (*liter: also* **~s**) sommeil *m* (paisible).

2 *cpd*: (*Comm*) **slumber wear** vêtements *mpl or* lingerie *f* de nuit.

3 *vi* dormir paisiblement.

slumb(e)rous ['slʌmb(ə)rəs] *adj* (*liter*) (*drowsy*) somnolent; (*soporific*) assoupissant (*liter*).

slummy ['slʌmɪ] *adj house, district, background, kitchen, appearance* sordide, misérable. **the ~ part (of the town)** les bas quartiers, les quartiers pauvres.

slump [slʌmp] **1** *n* (*in numbers, popularity, morale etc*) forte baisse, baisse soudaine (*in* de); (*Econ*) récession *f*, crise *f* (économique *or* monétaire), marasme *m*; (*St Ex*) effondrement *m* (des cours); (*Comm: in sales etc*) crise, baisse soudaine (*in* de); (*in prices*) effondrement (*in* de). **the 1929 ~** la crise (économique) de 1929.

2 *vi* **(a)** *[popularity, morale, production, trade]* baisser brutalement; *[prices, rates]* s'effondrer. **business has ~ed** les affaires sont en crise *or* en récession.

(b) (*also* **~ down**) s'effondrer, s'écrouler, s'affaisser (*into* dans, *onto* sur). **he lay ~ed on the floor** il gisait effondré *or* écroulé par terre; **he was ~ed over the wheel** il était affaissé sur le volant.

(c) (*stoop*) avoir le dos rond *or* voûté.

slump back *vi [person]* retomber en arrière.

slump down *vi* = **slump 2b.**

slung [slʌŋ] *pret, ptp of* **sling.**

slunk [slʌŋk] *pret, ptp of* **slink.**

slur [slɜːʳ] **1** *n* **(a)** (*stigma*) tache *f* (*on* sur), atteinte *f* (*on* à), insinuation *f* (*on* contre); (*insult*) insulte *f*, affront *m*. **to be a ~ on sb's reputation** porter atteinte à *or* être une tache sur la réputation de qn; **that is a ~ on him** cela porte atteinte à son intégrité; **to cast a ~ on sb** porter atteinte à la réputation de qn; **it's no ~ on him to say ...** ce n'est pas le calomnier que de dire ... .

(b) (*Mus*) liaison *f*.

2 *vt* (*join*) *several sounds, words* lier à tort; (*Mus*) lier; (*enunciate indistinctly*) *word etc* mal articuler, ne pas articuler. **his speech was ~red, he ~red his words** il n'arrivait pas à articuler, il n'articulait pas.

3 *vi [sounds etc]* être *or* devenir indistinct.

slur over *vt fus incident, mistake, differences, discrepancies* passer sous silence, glisser sur.

slurp [slɜːp] *vti* boire à grand bruit.

slush [slʌʃ] **1** *n* (*U*) (*snow*) neige fondante *or* fondue; (*mud*) gadoue *f*; (*fig: sentiment*) sensiblerie *f*. **2** *cpd*: (*US*) **slush fund** fonds *mpl* servant à des pots-de-vin.

slushy ['slʌʃɪ] *adj* (*V* **slush**) *snow* fondant, fondu; *mud* détrempé; *streets* couvert de neige fondante *or* de neige fondue *or* de gadoue; (*fig*) *novel, film* fadement sentimental, fadasse*.

slut [slʌt] *n* (*dirty*) souillon *f*; (*immoral*) fille *f* (*pej*), salope‡ *f*.

sluttish ['slʌtɪʃ] *adj appearance* sale, de souillon; *morals, behaviour* de salope. **a ~ woman** une souillon.

sly [slaɪ] **1** *adj* (*wily*) rusé; (*secretive*) dissimulé; (*underhand*) sournois; (*mischievous*) espiègle, malin (*f* -igne). **a ~ look** un regard rusé *or* sournois *or* espiègle *or* par en dessous; **he's a ~ dog*** (*wily*) c'est une fine mouche *or* un fin matois; (*not as pure as he seems*) ce n'est pas un petit saint, ce n'est pas un enfant de chœur; *V* **fox.**

2 *cpd*: **slyboots*** malin *m*, -igne *f*.

3 *n*: **on the ~** en cachette, en secret, en douce*; sournoisement (*pej*).

slyly ['slaɪlɪ] *adv plan, act* de façon rusée *or* dissimulée, sournoisement; *say, smile, suggest* sournoisement (*pej*); (*mischievously*) avec espièglerie; (*in secret*) en cachette, en secret, en douce*.

slyness ['slaɪnɪs] *n* (*V* **sly**) ruse *f*; dissimulation *f*; sournoiserie *f*; espièglerie *f*.

smack[1] [smæk] **1** *vi* (*lit, fig*) **to ~ of sth** sentir qch. **2** *n* léger *or* petit goût; (*fig*) soupçon *m*.

smack[2] [smæk] **1** *n* (*slap*) tape *f*, (*stronger*) claque *f*; (*on face*) gifle *f*; (*sound*) bruit sec, claquement *m*; (**fig: kiss*) gros baiser (qui claque). **he gave the ball a good ~** il a donné un grand coup dans le ballon; (*fig: esp Brit*) **it was a ~ in the eye for them*** (*snub*) c'était une gifle pour eux; (*setback*) c'était un revers pour eux; (*fig: esp Brit*) **to have a ~ at doing sth*** essayer (un coup*) de faire qch; **I'll have a ~ at it** je vais essayer, je vais tenter le coup*.

2 *vt person* donner une tape *or* (*stronger*) une claque à; (*on face*) gifler. **to ~ sb's face** gifler qn, donner une paire de gifles à qn; **I'll ~ your bottom!** je vais te donner la fessée!, tu vas avoir la fessée!; **he ~ed the table (with his hand)** il a frappé sur la table (de la main); **to ~ one's lips** se lécher les babines.

3 *adv* (*) en plein. **~ in the middle** en plein milieu; **he kissed her ~ on the lips** il l'a embrassée en plein sur la bouche; **he ran ~ into the tree** il est rentré en plein *or* tout droit dans l'arbre.

smack[3] [smæk] *n* (*also* **fishing ~**) smack *m*, semaque *m*.

smacker‡ ['smækəʳ] *n* (*kiss*) gros baiser, grosse bise*; (*blow*) grand coup (retentissant); (*Brit: pound*) livre *f*; (*US: dollar*) dollar *m*.

smacking ['smækɪŋ] *n* fessée *f*. **to give sb a ~** donner une *or* la fessée à qn.

small [smɔːl] **1** *adj* **(a)** *child, table, town, quantity, organization, voice* petit; *person* petit, de petite taille; *family* petit, peu nombreux; *audience, population* peu nombreux; *income, sum* petit, modeste; *stock, supply* petit, limité; *meal* petit, léger; *garden, room* petit, de dimensions modestes; (*unimportant*) *mistake, worry, difficulty* petit, insignifiant, mineur; (*pej: morally mean*) *person, mind* petit, bas (*f* basse), mesquin. **a ~ waist** une taille mince *or* svelte; **the ~est details** les moindres détails; **the ~est possible number of books** le moins de livres possible; **a ~ proportion of the business comes from abroad** un pourcentage limité *or* restreint des affaires vient de l'étranger; **to grow** *or* **get ~er** *[income, difficulties, population, amount, supply]* diminuer; *[town, organization]* décroître; **to make ~er** *income, amount, supply* diminuer; *organization* réduire; *garden, object, garment* rapetisser; (*Typ*) **in ~ letters** en (lettres) minuscules *fpl*; **he is a ~ eater** il ne mange pas beaucoup, il a un petit appétit; **~ shopkeeper/farmer** petit commerçant/cultivateur;

he felt ~ when he was told that ... il ne s'est pas senti fier *or* il s'est senti tout honteux quand on lui a dit que ...; **to make sb feel ~** humilier qn, rabaisser qn; *V also* 4 *and* **hour, look, print, way** *etc.*

(b) (*in negative sense: little or no*) **to have ~ cause** *or* **reason to do** n'avoir guère de raisons de faire; **a matter of no ~ consequence** une affaire d'une grande importance *or* qui ne manque pas d'importance; *V* **wonder** *etc.*

2 *adv*: **to cut up ~** *paper* couper en tout petits morceaux; *meat* hacher menu.

3 *n*: **the ~ of the back** le creux des reins; (*Dress: esp Brit*) **~s*** dessous *mpl*, sous-vêtements *mpl.*

4 *cpd*: (*Brit Press*) **small ads** petites annonces; (*Mil*) **small-arms** armes portatives, petites armes; (*Brit fig*) **it is small beer** c'est de la petite bière*; **he is small beer** il ne compte pas, il est insignifiant; **small change** petite *or* menue monnaie; (*Aut*) **small end** pied *m* de bielle; **the small fry** le menu fretin; **he's just small fry** c'est du menu fretin, il ne compte pas, il est insignifiant; (*Brit Agr*) **smallholder** ≃ petit cultivateur; (*Brit Agr*) **smallholding** ≃ petite ferme (*de moins de deux hectares*); (*Anat*) **small intestine** intestin *m* grêle; **small-minded** d'esprit bas, mesquin; **small-mindedness** petitesse *f* d'esprit, mesquinerie *f*; **smallpox** variole *f*, petite vérole; **small-scale** (*adj*) peu important; *undertaking* de peu d'importance, de peu d'envergure; (*TV*) **the small screen** le petit écran; (*U*) **small talk** papotage *m*, menus propos; **he's got plenty of small talk** il a de la conversation, il a la conversation facile; **small-time** (*adj*) peu important, de troisième ordre; **a small-time crook** un escroc à la petite semaine; **small-timer*** moins *m* que rien, individu insignifiant; (*pej*) **small-town** (*adj*) provincial, qui fait province.

smallish ['smɔːlɪʃ] *adj* (*V* **small 1a**) plutôt *or* assez petit (*or* modeste *etc*); assez peu nombreux.

smallness ['smɔːlnɪs] *n [person]* petite taille; *[hand, foot, object]* petitesse *f*; *[income, sum, contribution etc]* modicité *f*; (*small-mindedness*) petitesse (d'esprit), mesquinerie *f.*

smarm* [smɑːm] *vi* (*Brit*) flatter, flagorner. **to ~ over sb** flagorner qn, lécher les bottes* à qn, passer de la pommade* à qn.

smarmy* ['smɑːmɪ] *adj* (*Brit*) *person* flagorneur, lécheur*; *words, manner* obséquieux. **he's always so ~** ce qu'il est flagorneur! *or* lèche-bottes *inv*!*.

smart [smɑːt] **1** *adj* **(a)** (*not shabby*) *person, clothes* chic *inv*, élégant, qui a de l'allure; *hotel, shop, car, house* élégant; *neighbourhood, party, dinner* élégant, chic *inv*, select (*f inv*); (*fashionable*) à la mode, dernier cri *inv*. **she was looking very ~** elle était très élégante *or* très chic, elle avait beaucoup d'allure; **the ~ set** le grand monde, le monde select, la haute‡†; **it's considered ~ these days to do that** de nos jours on trouve que ça fait bien *or* chic de faire ça.

(b) *person* (*clever*) intelligent, habile, dégourdi*; (*shrewd*) astucieux, malin (*f* -igne); (*pej*) retors, roublard*; *deed, act* intelligent, astucieux; *answer* spirituel, bien envoyé. **a ~ lad***, (*US*) **a ~ guy*** un malin, un finaud; **he's trying to be ~** il fait le malin; **he's too ~ for me** il est beaucoup trop futé pour moi; **don't get ~ with me!*** ne la ramène pas!‡; **he thinks it ~ to do that** il trouve (ça) bien *or* intelligent de faire cela; **that was ~ of you!, that was ~ work!** c'était futé de ta part! (*V also* **1c**).

(c) (*quick*) *pace* vif, rapide; *action* prompt; *work* rapide. **that was ~ work!** tu n'as pas (*or* il n'a pas *etc*) perdu de temps! *or* mis longtemps! *or* traîné!; **look ~ (about it)!** remue-toi!*; grouille-toi!‡; **a ~ rebuke** une verte semonce.

2 *cpd*: (*pej*) **smart-alec(k)*** bêcheur* *m*, cuistre *m*, (Monsieur *or* Madame *or* Mademoiselle) je-sais-tout* *mf inv.*

3 *vi* **(a)** *[cut, graze]* faire mal, brûler; *[iodine etc]* piquer. **my eyes were ~ing** j'avais les yeux irrités *or* qui me brûlaient *or* qui me piquaient; **the smoke made his throat ~** la fumée lui irritait la gorge, la gorge lui cuisait *or* lui brûlait à cause de la fumée.

(b) (*fig*) être piqué au vif. **he was ~ing under the insult** il ressentait vivement l'insulte, l'insulte l'avait piqué au vif; **you'll ~ for this!** il vous en cuira!, vous me le payerez!

smarten ['smɑːtn] *vt* (*beautify*) embellir, donner plus d'allure à; (*speed up*) accélérer.

smarten up 1 *vi* **(a)** *[person]* devenir plus élégant *or* soigné; *[town]* devenir plus élégant *or* pimpant. **you'd better smarten up for dinner** il faut que tu t'arranges (*subj*) (un peu) *or* que tu te fasses beau (*f* belle) pour le dîner.

(b) (*speed up*) *[production, pace]* s'accélérer.

2 *vt sep person* rendre plus élégant *or* plus soigné; *child* pomponner, bichonner; *house, room, town* (bien) arranger, rendre élégant *or* pimpant. **to smarten o.s. up** se faire beau (*f* belle) *or* élégant.

smartly ['smɑːtlɪ] *adv* (*elegantly*) *dress* avec beaucoup de chic *or* d'élégance *or* d'allure; (*cleverly*) *act, say* habilement, astucieusement; (*quickly*) *move* promptement, vivement; *answer* du tac au tac. **he rebuked her ~** il lui a fait un reproche cinglant *or* une verte semonce.

smartness ['smɑːtnɪs] *n* (*U*) (*in appearance etc*) chic *m*, élégance *f*, allure *f*; (*cleverness*) intelligence *f*, habileté *f*, astuce *f*; (*pej*) roublardise *f*; (*quickness*) promptitude *f*, rapidité *f.*

smarty* ['smɑːtɪ] *n* (*also* **~-pants***) bêcheur* *m*, -euse* *f*, (Monsieur *or* Madame *or* Mademoiselle) je-sais-tout* *mf inv.*

smash [smæʃ] **1** *n* **(a)** (*sound*) fracas *m*; (*blow*) coup violent; (*Tennis etc*) smash *m*. **the ~ as the car hit the lamppost** le choc quand la voiture a percuté le réverbère; **the cup fell with a ~** la tasse s'est fracassée (en tombant) par terre; **he fell and hit his head a nasty ~ on the kerb** en tombant il s'est violemment cogné la tête contre le trottoir.

(b) (*also* **~-up***) (*accident*) accident *m*; (*Aut, Rail: collision*) collision *f*, tamponnement *m*; (*very violent*) télescopage *m*. **car/rail ~** accident de voiture/de chemin de fer.

(c) (*Econ, Fin: collapse*) effondrement *m* (financier), débâcle *f* (financière); (*St Ex*) krach *m*; (*bankruptcy*) faillite *f*; (*ruin*) ruine *f*, débâcle complète.

(d) whisky/brandy ~ whisky/cognac glacé à la menthe.

2 *cpd*: **smash-and-grab (raid)** cambriolage *m* (commis en brisant une devanture); **there was a smash-and-grab (raid) at the jeweller's** des bandits ont brisé la vitrine du bijoutier et raflé les bijoux; **it was a smash hit*** cela a eu un succès foudroyant, cela a fait fureur; **it was the smash hit of the year*** c'était le succès de l'année; **smash-up*** *V* **smash 1b.**

3 *adv* (*) **to run ~ into a wall** heurter un mur de front *or* de plein fouet, rentrer en plein* dans un mur; **the cup fell ~ to the ground** la tasse s'est fracassée par terre; (*Fin*) **to go ~** faire faillite.

4 *vt* **(a)** (*break*) casser, briser; (*shatter*) fracasser. **I've ~ed my watch** j'ai cassé ma montre; **the waves ~ed the boat on the rocks** les vagues ont fracassé le bateau contre les rochers; **to ~ sth to pieces** *or* **to bits** briser qch en mille morceaux, mettre qch en miettes; **when they ~ed the atom*** quand on a désintégré *or* fissionné l'atome; **to ~ a door open** enfoncer une porte; **he ~ed his fist into Paul's face** il a écrasé son poing sur la figure de Paul; (*Tennis*) **to ~ the ball** faire un smash, smasher; (*Tennis*) **he ~ed the ball into the net** il a envoyé son smash dans le filet.

(b) (*fig*) *spy ring etc* briser, détruire; *hopes* ruiner; *enemy* écraser; *opponent* battre à plate(s) couture(s), pulvériser*. (*Sport etc*) **he ~ed* the record in the high jump** il a pulvérisé* le record du saut en hauteur.

5 *vi* **(a)** se briser (en mille morceaux), se fracasser. **the cup ~ed against the wall** la tasse s'est fracassée contre le mur; **the car ~ed into the tree** la voiture s'est écrasée contre l'arbre; **his fist ~ed into my face** son poing s'est écrasé *or* il a écrasé son poing sur ma figure, il m'a assené son poing sur la figure.

(b) (*Fin*) *[person, firm]* faire faillite.

smash down *vt sep door, fence* fracasser.

smash in *vt sep door* enfoncer. **to smash sb's face in‡** casser la gueule à qn‡.

smash up 1 *vt sep room, house, shop* tout casser dans, tout démolir dans; *car* accidenter, bousiller*. **he was smashed up* in a car accident** il a été grièvement blessé *or* sérieusement amoché‡ dans un accident de voiture.

2 smash-up* *n V* **smash 1b.**

smasher‡ ['smæʃəʳ] *n* (*esp Brit*) (*in appearance*) **he's a ~** il est vachement‡ beau; **she's a ~** elle est vachement‡ jolie *or* bien roulée*; (*in character etc*) **to be a ~** être épatant* *or* vachement chouette‡; **it's a ~** c'est épatant* *or* sensationnel* *or* formidable*.

smashing‡ ['smæʃɪŋ] *adj* (*esp Brit*) formidable*, du tonnerre*, terrible*. **they had a ~ time** ils se sont épatamment* *or* formidablement* bien amusés.

smattering ['smætərɪŋ] *n* connaissances vagues *or* superficielles. **he has a ~ of German** il sait un peu l'allemand, il sait quelques mots d'allemand; **I've got a ~ of maths** j'ai quelques connaissances vagues *or* quelques notions en maths.

smear [smɪəʳ] **1** *n* (*mark*) trace *f*, (*longer*) traînée *f*; (*stain*) (légère) tache *f*, salissure *f*; (*fig: on reputation etc*) tache (*on* sur), atteinte (*on* à); (*insult*) insulte *f*, calomnie *f*; (*Med*) frottis *m*. **a long ~ of ink** une traînée d'encre; **there is a ~ on this page** il y a une légère tache *or* une salissure sur cette page, cette page est tachée *or* salie; *V* **cervical.**

2 *cpd*: **smear campaign** campagne *f* de diffamation; **it is a smear word** c'est un mot d'insulte.

3 *vt* **(a) to ~ cream on one's hands, to ~ one's hands with cream** s'enduire les mains de crème; **he ~ed his face with mud, he ~ed mud on his face** il s'est barbouillé le visage de boue; **his hands were ~ed with ink** il avait les mains barbouillées *or* tachées d'encre, il avait des traînées d'encre sur les mains; **he ~ed butter on the slice of bread** il a étalé du beurre sur la tranche de pain.

(b) *page of print* maculer; *wet paint* faire une trace *or* une marque sur; *lettering* étaler (accidentellement); (*fig*) *reputation, integrity* salir, entacher, porter atteinte à. **to ~ sb** porter atteinte à la réputation de qn, calomnier qn.

4 *vi [ink, paint]* se salir.

smeary ['smɪərɪ] *adj face* barbouillé; *printed page* plein de macules; *window* couvert de taches *or* de traînées; *ink, paint* sali.

smell [smel] (*vb: pret, ptp* **smelled** *or* **smelt**) **1** *n* (*sense of ~*) odorat *m*; *[animal]* odorat, flair *m*; (*odour*) odeur *f*; (*stench*) mauvaise odeur. **he has a keen sense of ~** il a l'odorat très développé, il a le nez très fin; **he has no sense of ~** il n'a pas d'odorat; **the mixture has no ~** le mélange est inodore *or* n'a pas d'odeur *or* ne sent rien; **a gas with no ~** un gaz inodore *or* sans odeur; **it has a nice/nasty ~** cela sent bon/mauvais; **what a ~ in here!** que ça sent mauvais ici!, ça pue ici!; **there was a ~ of burning in the room** il y avait une odeur de brûlé dans la pièce, la pièce sentait le brûlé; **to have a ~ at sth** *[person]* sentir qch, (*more carefully*) renifler qch; *[dog etc]* flairer *or* renifler qch.

2 *cpd*: **smelling salts** sels *mpl.*

3 *vt* sentir; (*sniff at*) sentir, renifler. **he could ~** *or* **he smelt something burning** il sentait que quelque chose brûlait; **he smelt the meat to see if it were bad** il a senti *or* reniflé la viande pour voir si elle était encore bonne; **the dog could ~** *or* **the dog smelt the bone** le chien a flairé *or* éventé l'os; **the dog smelt the bone suspiciously** le chien a flairé *or* reniflé l'os d'un air soupçonneux; (*fig*) **I ~ a rat!** je soupçonne quelque chose!, il y a anguille sous roche!; **he ~ed danger and refused to go on** il a flairé *or* deviné *or* pressenti le danger et a refusé de continuer; **I (can) ~ danger!** je pressens un danger!

4 *vi* (a) since the accident he cannot ~ depuis l'accident il n'a plus d'odorat; to ~ at sth *[person]* sentir *or* renifler qch; *[dog etc]* renifler *or* flairer qch.

(b) that mixture doesn't ~ (at all) ce mélange ne sent rien *or* n'a pas (du tout) d'odeur; this gas doesn't ~ ce gaz est inodore; these socks ~! ces chaussettes sentent mauvais! *or* sentent!*; (*stink*) ces chaussettes puent!; this room ~s! cette pièce sent mauvais! *or* pue!; his breath ~s il a mauvaise haleine; that ~s like chocolate ça sent le chocolat, on dirait du chocolat; to ~ of onions/burning *etc* sentir l'oignon/le brûlé *etc*; to ~ good *or* sweet sentir bon; to ~ bad sentir mauvais; it ~s delicious! ça embaume!; it ~s dreadful! ça pue!; that deal ~s a bit* cette affaire semble plutôt louche *or* ne semble pas très catholique*; (*fig*) that idea ~s!‡ cette idée ne vaut rien!, c'est une idée catastrophique!*; (*fig*) I think he ~s!‡ je trouve que c'est un sale type!*

smell out *vt sep* (a) (*discover*) *[dog etc]* découvrir en flairant *or* en reniflant; *[person] criminal, traitor* découvrir, dépister; *treachery, plot* découvrir.

(b) it's smelling the room out ça empeste la pièce.

smelliness ['smelɪnɪs] *n* (*U*) mauvaise odeur, (*stronger*) puanteur *f*.

smelly ['smelɪ] *adj* (a) qui sent mauvais, malodorant. to be ~ sentir mauvais, (*stronger*) puer; it's ~ in here ça sent mauvais ici, ça sent* ici. (b) (‡*fig: unpleasant*) *person, object, idea* moche*.

smelt¹ [smelt] *pret, ptp of* **smell.**

smelt² [smelt] *n* (*fish*) éperlan *m*.

smelt³ [smelt] *vt ore* fondre; *metal* extraire par fusion.

smelting ['smeltɪŋ] *n* (*V* smelt³) fonte *f*; extraction *f* par fusion. ~ furnace haut-fourneau *m*; ~ works fonderie *f*.

smile [smaɪl] 1 *n* sourire *m*. with a ~ on his lips le sourire aux lèvres; ... he said with a ~ ... dit-il en souriant; ...he said with a nasty ~ ... dit-il en souriant méchamment *or* avec un mauvais sourire; he had a happy ~ on his face il avait un sourire heureux, il souriait d'un air heureux; to give sb a ~ faire *or* adresser un sourire à qn, sourire à qn; to be all ~s être tout souriant *or* tout sourire; take that ~ off your face! arrête donc de sourire comme ça!; I'll wipe *or* knock the ~ off his face! il verra s'il a encore envie de sourire!, je vais lui faire passer l'envie de sourire!; *V* raise, wear, wreathe.

2 *vi* sourire (*at or to sb* à qn). to ~ sadly avoir un sourire triste, sourire tristement *or* d'un air triste; to keep smiling garder le sourire; he ~d at my efforts il a souri de mes efforts; (*fig*) fortune ~d on him la fortune lui sourit.

3 *vt*: to ~ a bitter smile avoir un sourire amer, sourire amèrement *or* avec amertume; to ~ one's thanks remercier d'un sourire.

smiling ['smaɪlɪŋ] *adj* souriant.

smilingly ['smaɪlɪŋlɪ] *adv* en souriant, avec un sourire.

smirch [smɜːtʃ] 1 *vt* (*lit*) salir, souiller; (*fig liter*) ternir, entacher.

2 *n* (*lit, fig*) tache *f*.

smirk [smɜːk] 1 *n* (*self-satisfied smile*) petit sourire satisfait *or* suffisant; (*knowing*) petit sourire narquois; (*affected*) petit sourire affecté. 2 *vi* sourire d'un air satisfait *or* suffisant *or* narquois *or* affecté.

smite [smaɪt] *pret* **smote,** *ptp* **smitten** 1 *vt* (a) (†† *or liter*) (*strike*) frapper (d'un grand coup); (*punish*) châtier (*liter*); (*fig*) *[pain]* déchirer; *[one's conscience]* tourmenter; *[light]* frapper.

(b) (*fig*) to be smitten with *or* by *remorse, desire, urge* être pris de; *terror, deafness* être frappé de; *sb's beauty* être enchanté par; *idea* s'enthousiasmer pour; he was really smitten* with her il en était vraiment toqué* *or* amoureux.

2 *n* coup violent.

smith [smɪθ] *n* (*shoes horses*) maréchal-ferrant *m*; (*forges iron*) forgeron *m*; *V* gold, silver *etc*.

smithereens ['smɪðə'riːnz] *npl*: to smash sth to ~ briser qch en mille morceaux, faire voler qch en éclats; it lay in ~ cela s'était brisé en mille morceaux, cela avait volé en éclats.

smithy ['smɪðɪ] *n* forge *f*.

smitten ['smɪtn] *ptp of* **smite.**

smock [smɒk] 1 *n* (*dress, peasant's garment etc*) blouse *f*; (*protective overall*) blouse, sarrau *m*; (*maternity top*) blouse de grossesse; (*maternity dress*) robe *f* de grossesse. 2 *vt* faire des smocks à.

smocking ['smɒkɪŋ] *n* (*U*) smocks *mpl*.

smog [smɒg] *n* brouillard dense mélangé de fumée, smog *m*. ~ mask masque *m* antibrouillard.

smoke [sməʊk] 1 *n* (a) (*U*) fumée *f*. (*Prov*) there's no ~ without fire il n'y a pas de fumée sans feu (*Prov*); to go up in ~ *[house etc]* brûler; *[plans, hopes etc]* partir en fumée, tomber à l'eau; (*Brit*) the S~‡ Londres; *V* cloud, holy, puff *etc*.

(b) to have a ~ fumer une cigarette (*or* une pipe *etc*); have a ~!* prends une cigarette! *or* une sèche!‡; I've no ~s‡ je n'ai plus de sèches‡.

2 *cpd*: smoke bomb bombe *f* fumigène; smoke-dry (*vt*) fumer; smoke-filled (*during fire*) rempli de fumée; (*from smoking etc*) enfumé; smokeless *V* smokeless; smoke screen (*Mil*) rideau *m or* écran *m* de fumée; (*fig*) paravent *m* (*fig*); smoke signal signal *m* de fumée; smokestack cheminée *f* (*extérieure*).

3 *vi* (a) *[chimney, lamp etc]* fumer.

(b) *[person]* fumer. he ~s like a chimney* il fume comme un sapeur.

4 *vt* (a) *cigarette etc* fumer. he ~s cigarettes/a pipe il fume la cigarette/la pipe.

(b) *meat, fish, glass* fumer. ~d salmon/trout *etc* saumon *m*/truite *f etc* fumé(e); *V* haddock *etc*.

smoke out *vt sep insects, snake etc* enfumer; (*fig*) *traitor, culprit etc* dénicher, débusquer. it was smoking the room out c'était en train d'enfumer la pièce.

smokeless ['sməʊklɪs] *adj* sans fumée. ~ fuel combustible non polluant; ~ zone zone *f* où l'usage de combustibles solides est réglementé (*en vue de limiter la pollution atmosphérique*).

smoker ['sməʊkəʳ] *n* (a) (*person*) fumeur *m*, -euse *f*. he has a ~'s cough il a une toux de fumeur; *V* heavy. (b) (*Rail*) = smoking car *or* carriage; *V* smoking 3.

smoking ['sməʊkɪŋ] 1 *n*: 'no ~ ' 'défense de fumer'; ~ can damage your health le tabac est nuisible à *or* est mauvais pour la santé; to give up ~ arrêter de fumer.

2 *adj* fumant.

3 *cpd*: (*Rail*) smoking carriage, (*US*) smoking car wagon *m* fumeurs; smoking jacket veste *f* d'intérieur *or* d'appartement; smoking room fumoir *m*.

smoky ['sməʊkɪ] *adj atmosphere, room* enfumé; *fire* qui fume; *flame* fumeux; *surface* sali *or* noirci par la fumée; *stain* produit *or* laissé par la fumée; *glass* fumé; (*colour: also* ~ grey, ~-coloured) gris fumée *inv*.

smolder ['sməʊldəʳ] *vi* (*US*) = **smoulder.**

smoldering ['sməʊldərɪŋ] *adj* (*US*) = **smouldering.**

smooch‡ [smuːtʃ] *vi* (*kiss*) se bécoter*; (*pet*) se peloter‡.

smooth [smuːð] 1 *adj* (a) *surface* lisse, uni, égal; *road* à la surface égale *or* unie; *sea, lake* lisse, plat; *stone* lisse, poli; *fabric* lisse, soyeux; (*Aut*) *tyre* lisse, qui n'a plus de stries; *hair* lisse; *skin* lisse, satiné, doux (*f* douce); *cheek, brow* lisse, sans rides; (*hairless*) *face, chin* glabre, lisse; *paste, sauce* homogène, onctueux; *flavour, wine, whisky* moelleux; *voice* doux; *sound* doux.

(b) *running of machinery etc* régulier, sans secousses, sans à-coups; *takeoff* en douceur; *flight* confortable; (*Naut*) *crossing, trip* par mer calme; *breathing, heartbeat, pulse* régulier; *verse, style* coulant, harmonieux; (*fig*) *day, life* calme, paisible, sans heurts. *[machinery, organization, business]* ~ running bon fonctionnement, bonne marche (*V also* 2); (*fig*) to make things *or* the way ~ for sb aplanir les difficultés pour qn; (*fig*) the way is now ~ il n'y a plus d'obstacles maintenant; (*Parl*) the bill had a ~ passage on n'a pas fait obstacle au projet de loi.

(c) (*suave*) *person* doucereux, mielleux; *manners* doucereux, mielleux, onctueux (*pej*). he's a ~ operator* il sait s'y prendre; he is a ~ talker c'est un beau parleur, il parle de façon insinuante *or* un peu trop persuasive; I didn't like his rather ~ suggestion that ... je n'ai pas aimé la façon insinuante *or* un peu trop persuasive dont il a suggéré que ... .

2 *cpd*: smooth-faced au visage glabre *or* lisse; (*fig: slightly pej*) trop poli, doucereux; smooth-running (*adj*) *engine, machinery* qui fonctionne sans à-coups *or* à un rythme uniforme, qui tourne rond*; *car* qui ne secoue pas, qui ne donne pas d'à-coups; *business, organization, scheme* qui marche bien *or* sans heurts; smooth-shaven rasé de près; smooth-spoken, smooth-tongued enjôleur, doucereux.

3 *vt sheets, cloth, piece of paper, skirt* lisser, défroisser; *pillow, hair, feathers* lisser; *wood* rendre lisse, planer; *marble* rendre lisse, polir. to ~ cream into one's skin faire pénétrer la crème dans la peau (en massant doucement); (*fig*) to ~ the way *or* the path for sb aplanir le terrain *or* les obstacles pour qn.

smooth back *vt sep one's hair* ramener doucement en arrière; *sheet* rabattre en lissant *or* en défroissant.

smooth down *vt sep hair, feathers* lisser; *sheet, cover* lisser, défroisser; (*fig*) *person* calmer, apaiser.

smooth out *vt sep material, dress* défroisser; *wrinkles, creases* faire disparaître; (*fig*) *anxieties* chasser, faire disparaître; *difficulties* aplanir, faire disparaître.

smooth over *vt sep soil* aplanir, égaliser; *sand* égaliser, rendre lisse; *wood* rendre lisse, planer. (*fig*) to smooth things over arranger les choses, aplanir des difficultés.

smoothie‡ ['smuːðɪ] *n* (*pej*) beau parleur. to be a ~ savoir un peu trop bien y faire‡, être un peu trop poli.

smoothly ['smuːðlɪ] *adv* (*easily*) facilement; (*gently*) doucement; *move* sans secousses, sans à-coups; *talk* doucereusement. ... he said ~ ... dit-il sans sourciller *or* doucereusement (*pej*); everything is going ~ il n'y a pas de difficultés, tout marche comme sur des roulettes; the journey went off ~ le voyage s'est bien passé *or* s'est passé sans incident.

smoothness ['smuːðnɪs] *n* (*U*: *V* smooth) (a) qualité *f or* aspect *m* lisse *or* uni(e) *or* égal(e) *or* poli(e); douceur *f*; moelleux *m*; aspect glabre; *[road]* surface égale *or* unie; *[sea]* calme *m*. the ~ of the tyre caused the accident c'est parce que le pneu était complètement lisse que l'accident est arrivé.

(b) rythme régulier; douceur *f*; régularité *f*; harmonie *f*; calme *m*.

(c) (*slightly pej: suaveness*) caractère doucereux *or* mielleux; *[voice]* ton doucereux *etc*.

smoothy‡ ['smuːðɪ] *n* = **smoothie‡.**

smote [sməʊt] *pret of* **smite.**

smother ['smʌðəʳ] 1 *vt* (a) (*stifle*) *person* étouffer; *flames* étouffer, éteindre; *noise* étouffer, amortir; *scandal, feelings* étouffer, cacher; *criticism, doubt, yawn* étouffer, réprimer; *one's anger* contenir, réprimer.

(b) (*cover*) (re)couvrir (*with* de). she ~ed the child with kisses elle a couvert *or* dévoré l'enfant de baisers; books ~ed in dust des livres enfouis sous la poussière *or* tout (re)couverts de poussière; a child ~ed in dirt un enfant tout sale *or* tout couvert de crasse; a face ~ed in make-up une figure toute emplâtrée de maquillage; he was ~ed in blankets il était tout emmailloté de couvertures, il était tout emmitouflé dans ses couvertures.

2 *vi [person]* être étouffé, mourir étouffé.

3 *cpd*: (*iro*) smother-love* amour maternel possessif *or* dévorant.

smoulder, (*US*) **smolder** ['sməʊldəʳ] *vi [fire, emotion]* couver.

smouldering, (*US*) **smoldering** ['sməʊldərɪŋ] *adj fire, emo-*

tion qui couve; *ashes, rubble* fumant; *expression, look* provocant, aguichant. **his ~ hatred** la haine qui couve (*or* couvait *etc*) en lui.
smudge [smʌdʒ] **1** *n* (*on paper, cloth*) (légère) tache *f*, traînée *f*; (*in text, print etc*) bavure *f*, tache. **2** *vt face* salir; *print* maculer; *paint* faire une trace *or* une marque sur; *lettering, writing* étaler accidentellement. **3** *vi* se salir; se maculer; s'étaler.
smudgy ['smʌdʒɪ] *adj page* sali, taché, maculé; *writing* à moitié effacé; *face* sali, taché; *eyelashes, eyebrows* épais (*f* -aisse); *outline* brouillé, estompé.
smug [smʌg] *adj person, smile, voice* suffisant, avantageux; *optimism, satisfaction* béat. **don't be so ~!** ne fais pas le (*or* la) suffisant(e)!, ne prends pas ton air supérieur!
smuggle ['smʌgl] **1** *vt tobacco, drugs* faire la contrebande de, passer en contrebande *or* en fraude. **to ~ in/out** *etc contraband* faire entrer/sortir *etc*; *goods* faire entrer/sortir *etc* en contrebande; (*fig*) *letters etc* faire entrer/ sortir *etc* clandestinement *or* en fraude; *person* faire entrer/sortir *etc* clandestinement; **to ~ sth past *or* through the customs** passer qch en contrebande *or* sans le déclarer à la douane; **~d goods** contrebande *f*; **~d whisky** whisky *m* de contrebande.
2 *vi* faire de la contrebande.
smuggler ['smʌgləʳ] *n* contrebandier *m*, -ière *f*.
smuggling ['smʌglɪŋ] **1** *n* (*U*) *[goods]* contrebande *f* (*action*). **2** *cpd*: **smuggling ring** réseau *m* de contrebandiers.
smugly ['smʌglɪ] *adv* d'un air *or* d'un ton suffisant *or* avantageux, avec suffisance.
smugness ['smʌgnɪs] *n [person]* suffisance *f*; *[voice, reply]* ton suffisant *or* avantageux.
smut [smʌt] *n* (*dirt*) petite saleté; (*soot*) flocon *m* de suie; (*in eye*) escarbille *f*; (*dirty mark*) tache *f* de suie; (*Bot*) charbon *m* du blé; (*U: obscenity*) obscénité(s) *f(pl)*, cochonneries* *fpl*. **programme full of ~** programme cochon* *or* salé.
smuttiness ['smʌtɪnɪs] *n* (*U: fig*) obscénité *f*, grossièreté *f*.
smutty ['smʌtɪ] *adj face, object* noirci, sali, taché; (*fig*) *joke, film* cochon*, salé, grossier.
snack [snæk] *n* casse-croûte *m inv*. **to have a ~** casser la croûte, manger (un petit) quelque chose; **~ bar** snack-bar *m*, snack *m*.
snaffle ['snæfl] **1** *n* (*also* **~ bit**) mors brisé. **2** *vt* (*Brit*: steal*) chiper*, faucher*.
snafu‡ [snæ'fuː] (*US*) **1** *adj* en pagaïe*. **2** *vt* mettre la pagaïe* dans.
snag [snæg] **1** *n* (*hidden obstacle*) obstacle caché; (*stump of tree, tooth etc*) chicot *m*; (*tear*) (*in cloth*) accroc *m*; (*in stocking*) fil tiré; (*fig: drawback*) inconvénient *m*, obstacle, difficulté *f*, écueil *m*. **there's a ~ in it somewhere** il y a sûrement un inconvénient *or* une difficulté *or* un os* là-dedans; **to run into *or* hit a ~** tomber sur un os* *or* sur un bec*; **that's the ~!** voilà la difficulté! *or* l'os!* *or* le hic!*; **the ~ is that you must ...** l'embêtant* c'est que vous devez ... .
2 *vt cloth* faire un accroc à; *stocking* déchirer, accrocher (*on sth* contre qch), tirer un fil à.
3 *vi [rope etc]* s'accrocher (à quelque chose).
snail [sneɪl] **1** *n* escargot *m*. **at a ~'s pace** *walk* comme un escargot, à un pas de tortue; (*fig*) *progress, continue* à un pas de tortue. **2** *cpd*: **snail shell** coquille *f* d'escargot.
snake [sneɪk] **1** *n* serpent *m*; (*fig pej: person*) traître(sse) *m(f)*, faux frère. (*fig*) **a ~ in the grass** (*person*) ami(e) *m(f)* perfide, traître(sse) *m(f)*; (*danger*) serpent caché sous les fleurs; (*Pol Econ*) **the S~** le serpent (monétaire); *V* **grass, water** *etc*.
2 *cpd*: **snakebite** morsure *f* de serpent; **snake charmer** charmeur *m* de serpent; **snake pit** fosse *f* aux serpents; **snakes and ladders** (espèce *f* de) jeu *m* de l'oie; **snakeskin** (*n*) peau *f* de serpent; (*cpd*) *handbag etc* en (peau de) serpent.
3 *vi [road, river]* serpenter (*through* à travers). **the road ~d down the mountain** la route descendait en lacets *or* en serpentant au flanc de la montagne; **the whip ~d through the air** la lanière du fouet a fendu l'air en ondulant.
snake along *vi [road, river]* serpenter; *[rope, lasso etc]* fendre l'air en ondulant.
snaky ['sneɪkɪ] *adj place* infesté de serpents; (*fig*) *road, river* sinueux; (*pej*) *person* perfide; *cunning, treachery* de vipère, perfide.
snap [snæp] **1** *n* **(a)** (*noise*) *[fingers, whip, elastic]* claquement *m*; *[sth breaking]* bruit sec, craquement *m*; *[sth shutting]* bruit sec, claquement; (*action*) *[whip]* claquement; *[breaking twig etc]* rupture *or* cassure soudaine. **he closed the lid with a ~** il a refermé le couvercle avec un bruit sec *or* d'un coup sec; **with a ~ of his fingers he ...** faisant claquer ses doigts il ...; **the dog made a ~ at my leg** le chien a essayé de me mordre la jambe; (*Met*) **a cold ~** une brève vague de froid, un coup de froid; (*fig*) **put some ~ into it!** allons, un peu de nerf!* *or* de dynamisme! *or* d'énergie!; **he has plenty of ~** il a du nerf*, il est très dynamique; *V* **brandy, ginger** *etc*.
(b) (*also* **~shot**) photo *f* (d'amateur); (*not posed*) instantané *m*. **here are our holiday ~s** voici nos photos de vacances; **it's only a ~** ce n'est qu'une photo d'amateur.
(c) (*US: ~ fastener*) pression *f*, bouton-pression *m*.
(d) (*Brit: Cards*) (*sorte f de jeu de*) bataille *f*.
2 *adj vote, strike* subit, décidé à l'improviste; *judgment, answer, remark* fait sans réflexion, irréfléchi. **to make a ~ decision** (se) décider tout d'un coup *or* subitement.
3 *adv*: **to go ~** se casser net *or* avec un bruit sec.
4 *excl* tiens! on est *or* fait pareil!; (*Cards*) = bataille!
5 *cpd*: (*Bot*) **snapdragon** gueule-de-loup *f*; **snap fastener** (*on clothes*) pression *f*, bouton-pression *m*; (*on handbag, bracelet etc*) fermoir *m*; **snap-in, snap-on** *hood, lining* amovible (à pressions); **snapshot** *V* **1b**.
6 *vi* **(a)** (*break*) se casser net *or* avec un bruit sec.
(b) *[whip, elastic, rubber band]* claquer. **to ~ shut/open** se fermer/s'ouvrir avec un bruit sec *or* avec un claquement; **the rubber band ~ped back into place** l'élastique est revenu à sa place avec un claquement.
(c) **to ~ at sb** *[dog]* essayer de mordre qn; *[person]* parler à qn d'un ton brusque, rembarrer* qn; **the dog ~ped at the bone** le chien a essayé de happer l'os.
7 *vt* **(a)** (*break*) casser net *or* avec un bruit sec.
(b) *whip, rubber band etc* faire claquer. **to ~ one's fingers** faire claquer ses doigts; **to ~ one's fingers at** *person* faire la nique à; (*fig*) *suggestion, danger* se moquer de; **to ~ sth open/shut** ouvrir/fermer qch d'un coup sec *or* avec un bruit sec.
(c) (*Phot*) prendre un instantané de.
(d) **'shut up!' he ~ped** 'silence!' fit-il avec brusquerie *or* d'un ton brusque.
snap back *vi* **(a)** *[elastic, rope etc]* revenir en place brusquement *or* avec un claquement.
(b) (*fig: after illness, accident*) se remettre très vite.
(c) (*in answering*) répondre d'un ton brusque.
snap off **1** *vi* se casser *or* se briser net.
2 *vt sep* casser net. (*fig*) **to snap sb's head off** rabrouer qn, rembarrer* qn, envoyer qn au diable.
snap out **1** *vi* (*) **to snap out of** *gloom, lethargy, self-pity* se sortir de, se tirer de, ne pas se laisser aller à; *bad temper* contrôler, dominer; **snap out of it!** (*gloom etc*) secoue-toi!*, réagis!, ne te laisse pas aller!; (*bad temper*) contrôle-toi *or* domine-toi un peu!
2 *vt sep question/order* poser/lancer d'un ton brusque *or* cassant.
snap up *vt sep [dog etc]* happer, attraper. (*fig*) **to snap up a bargain** sauter sur *or* se jeter sur une occasion, faire une bonne affaire; **they are snapped up as soon as they come on the market** on se les arrache *or* on saute dessus dès qu'ils sont mis en vente.
snappish ['snæpɪʃ] *adj dog* toujours prêt à mordre; *person* hargneux, cassant; *reply, tone* brusque, mordant, cassant.
snappishness ['snæpɪʃnɪs] *n [person]* caractère hargneux *or* cassant, (*temporary*) brusquerie *f*, mauvaise humeur; *[voice, reply]* ton brusque *or* mordant *or* cassant.
snappy* ['snæpɪ] *adj* **(a)** *reply* prompt, bien envoyé; *phrase, slogan* qui a du punch*. **look ~!, make it ~!** grouille-toi!‡, magne-toi!‡ **(b)** = **snappish**.
snare [snɛəʳ] **1** *n* piège *m*; (*fig*) piège, traquenard *m*. (*fig*) **these promises are a ~ and a delusion** ces promesses ne servent qu'à allécher *or* appâter. **2** *vt* (*lit, fig*) attraper, prendre au piège.
snarky‡ ['snɑːkɪ] *adj* désagréable, de mauvais poil*, râleur*.
snarl[1] [snɑːl] **1** *n [dog]* grondement *m* féroce. **to give a ~ of fury** *[dog]* gronder férocement; *[person]* pousser un rugissement de fureur; **... he said with a ~ ...** dit-il d'une voix rageuse *or* avec hargne.
2 *vi [dog]* gronder en montrant les dents *or* férocement; *[person]* lancer un grondement (*at sb* à qn), gronder. **when I went in the dog ~ed at me** quand je suis entré le chien a grondé en montrant les dents.
3 *vt order* lancer d'un ton hargneux *or* d'une voix rageuse. **to ~ a reply** répondre d'un ton hargneux *or* d'une voix rageuse; **'no' he ~ed** 'non' dit-il avec hargne *or* d'une voix rageuse.
snarl[2] [snɑːl] **1** *n* (*in wool, rope, hair etc*) nœud *m*, enchevêtrement *m*. (*fig*) **a traffic ~(-up)** un embouteillage.
2 *cpd*: **snarl-up** *[vehicles]* embouteillage *m*; (* *fig*) *[plans etc]* pagaïe* *f*.
3 *vi* (*also* **~ up, get ~ed up**) *[wool, rope, hair]* s'emmêler, s'enchevêtrer; *[traffic]* se bloquer; (*) *[plans, programme]* tomber dans la pagaïe*.
4 *vt* (*also* **~ up**) *wool, rope, hair* emmêler, enchevêtrer.
snarl up **1** *vi* = **snarl[2] 3**.
2 *vt sep* **(a)** = **snarl[2] 4**.
(b) *traffic* bloquer; (*) *plans, programme* mettre la pagaïe* dans.
3 **snarl-up** *n V* **snarl[2] 2**.
snatch [snætʃ] **1** *n* **(a)** (*action*) geste vif (pour saisir quelque chose); (*fig*) *[jewellery, wages etc]* vol *m* (à l'arraché); *[child etc]* enlèvement *m*. **there was a jewellery/wages ~ yesterday** hier des voleurs se sont emparés de bijoux/de salaires.
(b) (*small piece*) fragment *m*. **a ~ of music/poetry** quelques mesures *fpl*/vers *mpl*; **a ~ of conversation** des bribes *fpl* *or* un fragment de conversation; **a few ~es of Mozart** quelques mesures *or* un fragment de Mozart; **to work in ~es** travailler de façon intermittente *or* par accès *or* par à-coups.
2 *vt* (*grab*) *object* saisir, s'emparer (brusquement) de; *a few minutes' peace, a short holiday* réussir à avoir; *opportunity* saisir, sauter sur; *kiss* voler, dérober (*from sb* à qn); *sandwich, drink* avaler à la hâte; (*steal*) voler, chiper* (*from sb* à qn), saisir; (*kidnap*) enlever. **she ~ed the book from him** elle lui a arraché le livre; **he ~ed the child from the railway line just in time** il a saisi *or* attrapé *or* empoigné l'enfant et l'a tiré hors de la voie juste à temps; **to ~ some sleep/rest** (réussir à) dormir/se reposer un peu; **to ~ a meal** déjeuner (*or* dîner) à la hâte.
3 *vi*: **to ~ at** *object, end of rope etc* essayer de saisir, faire un geste vif pour saisir; *opportunity, chance* saisir, sauter sur.
snatch away, snatch off *vt sep* enlever d'un geste vif *or* brusque.
snatch up *vt sep object, child* saisir, ramasser vivement.
-snatcher ['snætʃəʳ] *n ending in cpds V* **cradle 3** *etc*.
snatchy* ['snætʃɪ] *adj work* fait par à-coups, fait de façon intermittente; *conversation* à bâtons rompus.
snazzy‡ ['snæzɪ] *adj* chouette‡. **a ~ suit/hotel** un chouette‡ complet/hôtel, un complet/un hôtel drôlement chouette‡; **a ~ new car** une nouvelle voiture drôlement chouette‡; **she's a ~ dresser** elle est toujours drôlement bien sapée‡ *or* fringuée‡.
sneak [sniːk] (*vb*: *pret, ptp* **sneaked** *or* (*US**) **snuck**) **1** *n* (*)

faux jeton*; (*Brit Scol*) mouchard(e)* *m(f)*, rapporteur* *m*, -euse* *f*.

2 *adj attack, visit* furtif, subreptice. (*US Cine*) ~ **preview** avant-première *f*; ~ **thief** chapardeur *m*, -euse *f*.

3 *vi* **(a) to ~ in/out** *etc* entrer/sortir *etc* furtivement *or* subrepticement *or* à la dérobée; **he ~ed into the house** il s'est faufilé *or* s'est glissé dans la maison.

(b) (*Brit Scol**) moucharder*, cafarder* (*on sb* qn).

4 *vt* **(a) I ~ed the letter onto his desk** j'ai glissé la lettre discrètement *or* furtivement *or* en douce* sur son bureau; **he ~ed the envelope from the table** il a enlevé furtivement *or* subrepticement l'enveloppe de la table; **to ~ a look at sth** lancer un coup d'œil furtif à qch, regarder qch à la dérobée; **he was ~ing* a cigarette** il était en train de fumer en cachette.

(b) (*: *pilfer*) chiper*, faucher‡, piquer‡.

sneak away, sneak off *vi* s'esquiver, s'éclipser*, s'en aller furtivement.

sneaker* [ˈsniːkəʳ] *n* (chaussure *f* de) tennis *m*.

sneaking [ˈsniːkɪŋ] *adj dislike, preference* caché, secret (*f* -ète), inavoué. **I had a ~ feeling that ...** je ne pouvais m'empêcher de penser que ..., j'avais (comme qui dirait*) l'impression que ...; **to have a ~ suspicion that ...** soupçonner secrètement *or* à part soi que ...; **I have a ~ respect for him** je ne peux pas m'empêcher de le respecter.

sneaky* [ˈsniːkɪ] *adj person, character* sournois, dissimulé; *action* sournois.

sneer [snɪəʳ] **1** *vi* ricaner, sourire d'un air méprisant *or* sarcastique. **to ~ at sb** se moquer de qn d'un air méprisant; **to ~ at sth** tourner qch en ridicule.

2 *n* (*act*) ricanement *m*; (*remark*) remarque moqueuse, sarcasme *m*, raillerie *f*. **... he said with a ~** ... dit-il d'un ton ricaneur *or* en ricanant *or* avec un sourire de mépris.

sneerer [ˈsnɪərəʳ] *n* ricaneur *m*, -euse *f*, moqueur *m*, -euse *f*, persifleur *m*, -euse *f*.

sneering [ˈsnɪərɪŋ] (*V* **sneer** 2) **1** *adj* ricaneur; moqueur, sarcastique, railleur. **2** *n* (*U*) ricanement(s) *m(pl)*; sarcasme(s) *m(pl)*, raillerie(s) *f(pl)*.

sneeringly [ˈsnɪərɪŋlɪ] *adv* d'un air *or* d'un ton ricaneur, avec un ricanement; de façon sarcastique, en raillant.

sneeze [sniːz] **1** *n* éternuement *m*. **2** *vi* éternuer. (*fig*) **it is not to be ~d at** ce n'est pas à dédaigner, il ne faut pas cracher dessus*.

snick [snɪk] **1** *n* petite entaille, encoche *f*. **2** *vt stick etc* faire une petite entaille *or* une encoche dans, entailler légèrement, encocher; (*Sport*) *ball* juste toucher.

snicker [ˈsnɪkəʳ] **1** *n* **(a)** *[horse]* petit hennissement. **(b)** = **snigger 1**. **2** *vi* **(a)** *[horse]* hennir doucement. **(b)** = **snigger 2**.

snide [snaɪd] *adj* sarcastique, moqueur, narquois.

sniff [snɪf] **1** *n* (*from cold, crying etc*) reniflement *m*. **to give a ~** renifler (une fois); (*disdainfully*) faire la grimace *or* la moue; **... he said with a ~** ... dit-il en reniflant; (*disdainfully*) ... dit-il en faisant la grimace *or* la moue; **I got a ~ of gas** j'ai senti l'odeur du gaz; **to have** *or* **take a ~ at sth** *[person]* renifler qch, (*suspiciously*) flairer qch; *[dog]* renifler *or* flairer qch; **one ~ of that is enough to kill you** il suffit de respirer cela une fois pour en mourir; (*fig*) **I didn't get a ~* of the whisky** je n'ai pas eu droit à une goutte de whisky.

2 *vi* (*from cold, crying*) renifler; (*disdainfully*) faire la grimace *or* la moue; *[dog]* renifler. **to ~ at sth** *[dog]* renifler *or* flairer qch; *[person]* renifler qch; (*fig*) faire la grimace *or* la moue à qch; **it's not to be ~ed at** ce n'est pas à dédaigner, il ne faut pas cracher dessus*.

3 *vt* *[dog]* renifler, flairer; *[person] food, bottle* renifler, sentir l'odeur de, (*suspiciously*) flairer; *air, perfume, aroma* humer; *drug* aspirer; *smelling salts* respirer; (*Pharm*) *inhalant etc* aspirer. **to ~ glue** respirer de la colle.

sniffle [ˈsnɪfl] **1** *n* (*sniff*) reniflement *m*; (*slight cold*) petit rhume de cerveau. **... he said with a ~** ... dit-il en reniflant; **to have a ~** *or* **the ~s*** avoir un petit rhume, être légèrement enrhumé.

2 *vi* *[person, dog]* renifler; (*from catarrh etc*) avoir le nez bouché, renifler.

sniffy‡ [ˈsnɪfɪ] *adj* **(a)** (*disdainful*) dédaigneux, pimbêche (*f only*). **to be ~ about sth** faire le *or* la dégoûté(e) devant qch. **(b)** (*smelly*) qui sent plutôt mauvais, qui a une drôle d'odeur.

snifter‡ [ˈsnɪftəʳ] *n* petit (verre d')alcool. **to have a ~** prendre un petit verre, boire la goutte*.

snigger [ˈsnɪgəʳ] **1** *n* petit rire moqueur; (*cynical*) ricanement *m*.

2 *vi* pouffer de rire; (*cynically*) ricaner. **to ~ at** *remark, question* pouffer de rire *or* ricaner en entendant; *sb's appearance etc* se moquer de; **stop ~ing!** arrête de rire *or* de ricaner comme ça!

snip [snɪp] **1** *n* (*cut*) petit coup (de ciseaux *etc*), petite entaille; (*small piece*) petit bout (*d'étoffe etc*), échantillon *m*; (*Brit* ‡: *bargain*) bonne affaire, (bonne) occasion *f*.

2 *vt* couper (à petits coups de ciseaux *etc*).

snip off *vt sep* couper *or* enlever *or* détacher (à coups de ciseaux *etc*).

snipe [snaɪp] **1** *n* (*pl inv*: *Orn*) bécassine *f*. **2** *vi* (*shoot*) tirer (en restant caché), canarder*. **to ~ at sb/sth** (*shoot*) canarder* qn/qch; (*fig: verbally*) critiquer par en dessous *or* sournoisement.

sniper [ˈsnaɪpəʳ] *n* tireur embusqué, canardeur* *m*.

snippet [ˈsnɪpɪt] *n* *[cloth, paper]* petit bout; *[conversation, news, information]* fragment *m*, bribes *fpl*.

snitch‡ [snɪtʃ] **1** *vi* moucharder* (*on sb* qn). **2** *vt* chiper*, chaparder*, piquer‡. **3** *n* (*nose*) pif‡ *m*. (*fig*) **it's a ~!** (*easy job*) c'est un jeu d'enfant!, c'est du billard!‡; (*bargain*) c'est une bonne affaire!, c'est une occasion!

snivel [ˈsnɪvl] **1** *vi* (*whine*) pleurnicher, larmoyer; (*sniff*) renifler; (*have a runny nose*) avoir le nez qui coule, avoir la morve au nez (*pej*). **2** *n* pleurnicherie(s) *f(pl)*, larmoiement(s) *m(pl)*; reniflement(s) *m(pl)*.

sniveller [ˈsnɪvləʳ] *n* pleurnicheur *m*, -euse *f*.

snivelling [ˈsnɪvlɪŋ] **1** *adj* pleurnicheur, larmoyant. **2** *n* pleurnicherie(s) *f(pl)*, larmoiement(s) *m(pl)*, reniflement(s) *m(pl)*.

snob [snɒb] *n* snob *mf*. **he's a terrible ~** il est terriblement snob; *[lowly placed person]* il se laisse impressionner par *or* il est à plat ventre devant les gens importants.

snobbery [ˈsnɒbərɪ] *n* snobisme *m*.

snobbish [ˈsnɒbɪʃ] *adj* snob *inv*; *lowly placed person* très impressionné par les gens importants (*or* riches *etc*); *accent, manner, district* snob *inv*.

snobbishness [ˈsnɒbɪʃnɪs] *n* snobisme *m*.

snobby* [ˈsnɒbɪ] *adj* snob *inv*.

snog‡ [snɒg] *vi* (*Brit*) se peloter*.

snood [snuːd] *n* résille *f*.

snook[1] [snuːk] *n* (*fish*) brochet *m* de mer.

snook[2] [snuːk] *n* *V* **cock 2b**.

snooker [ˈsnuːkəʳ] **1** *n sorte f de jeu de billard*. **2** *vt* (*Brit*‡) *person* coincer*, mettre en mauvaise posture.

snoop [snuːp] **1** *n*: **to have a ~ around** jeter un coup d'œil discret; **I had a ~ around the kitchen** j'ai fureté discrètement *or* sans être vu dans la cuisine.

2 *vi* se mêler des affaires des autres. **to ~ (around)** rôder *or* fureter *or* fouiller en essayant de passer inaperçu; **he's been ~ing (around) here again** il est revenu fourrer son nez* par ici; **to ~ on sb** surveiller qn, espionner qn; **he was ~ing into her private life** il fourrait son nez* dans *or* il se mêlait de sa vie privée.

snooper [ˈsnuːpəʳ] *n* (*pej*) *personne f qui fait une enquête furtive sur quelqu'un*. **all the ~s from the Ministry** tous les espions du ministère, tous les inspecteurs du ministère qui fourrent leur nez* partout.

snooty* [ˈsnuːtɪ] *adj* snob *inv*, prétentieux, hautain. **to be ~** se donner de grands airs.

snooze* [snuːz] **1** *n* petit somme, roupillon* *m*. **afternoon ~** sieste *f*; **to have a ~ = to snooze**; *V* 2. **2** *vi* sommeiller, piquer un roupillon*; faire la sieste.

snore [snɔːʳ] **1** *n* ronflement *m* (*d'un dormeur*). **2** *vi* ronfler.

snorer [ˈsnɔːrəʳ] *n* ronfleur *m*, -euse *f*.

snoring [ˈsnɔːrɪŋ] *n* (*U*) ronflement(s) *m(pl)*.

snorkel [ˈsnɔːkl] *n* *[submarine]* schnorchel *m*; *[swimmer]* tuba *m* (*pour masque sous-marin*).

snort [snɔːt] **1** *n* **(a)** *[person]* grognement *m*; *[horse etc]* ébrouement *m*. **(b)** (‡) = **snorter b**. **2** *vi* *[horse etc]* s'ébrouer; *[person]* (*angrily, contemptuously*) grogner, ronchonner; (*laughing*) s'étrangler de rire. **3** *vt* (*angrily etc*) grogner, dire en grognant; (*laughing*) dire en s'étranglant de rire.

snorter‡ [ˈsnɔːtəʳ] *n* **(a) a ~ of a question/problem** une question/un problème vache‡; **a ~ of a game** un match formidable*; **a ~ of a storm** une tempête terrible. **(b)** (*drink*) petit (verre d')alcool. **to have a ~** prendre un petit verre, boire la goutte*.

snot* [snɒt] *n* (*U*) morve *f*.

snotty* [ˈsnɒtɪ] **1** *adj* (*) *nose* qui coule; *face* morveux; *child* morveux, qui a le nez qui coule.

2 *cpd*: **snotty-faced*** morveux, qui a le nez qui coule; **snotty-nosed*** (*lit*) = **snotty-faced***; (*fig*) morveux* (*fig*).

3 *n* (*Naut*‡: *midshipman*) midshipman *m*, midship* *m*, aspirant *m*.

snout [snaʊt] *n* **(a)** (*gen*) museau *m*; *[pig]* museau, groin *m*; (* *pej*) *[person]* pif‡ *m*. **(b)** (*Prison sl*: *U*) tabac *m*, perlot‡ *m*.

snow [snəʊ] **1** *n* **(a)** neige *f*. **hard/soft ~** neige dure/molle; **the eternal ~s** les neiges éternelles; *V* **fall, white** *etc*.

(b) (*fig*) (*on TV screen*) neige *f*; (*Drugs sl*) neige‡, cocaïne *f*. (*Culin*) **apple** *etc* **~** purée *f* de pommes *etc* (*aux blancs d'œufs battus en neige*).

2 *cpd*: **snowball** *V* **snowball**; **snow bank** talus *m* de neige, congère *f*; **to be snow-blind** souffrir de *or* être atteint de la cécité des neiges; **snow blindness** cécité *f* des neiges; **snowbound** *road, country* complètement enneigé; *village, house, person* bloqué par la neige; **snow-capped** couronné de neige; (*Aut*) **snowcat** autoneige *f*; (*liter*) **snow-clad, snow-covered** enneigé, enfoui sous la neige; **snowdrift** congère *f*, amoncellement *m* de neige; (*Bot*) **snowdrop** perce-neige *m inv*; **snowfall** chute *f* de neige; **snowfield** champ *m* de neige; **snowflake** flocon *m* de neige; **snow goose** oie *f* des neiges; **snow line** limite *f* des neiges (éternelles); **snowman** bonhomme *m* de neige (*V* **abominable**); (*US*) **snowmobile = snowcat**; **snowplough**, (*US*) **snowplow** chasse-neige *m inv* (*also Ski*); (*Met*) **snow report** bulletin *m* d'enneigement; **snowshoe** raquette *f* (*pour marcher sur la neige*); (*US*) **snowslide** avalanche *f*; **snowstorm** tempête *f* de neige; **snowsuit** combinaison *f or* ensemble *m* matelassé(e); **snow-white** blanc (*f* blanche) comme neige, d'une blancheur de neige; **Snow White** Blanche-Neige *f*.

3 *vi* neiger. **it is ~ing** il neige, il tombe de la neige.

snow in *vt* (*pass only*) **to be snowed in** être bloqué par la neige.

snow under *vt* (*fig: pass only*) **he was snowed under with work** il était complètement submergé *or* débordé de travail, il avait tellement de travail qu'il ne savait pas où donner de la tête; **to be snowed under with letters/offers** être submergé de lettres/d'offres, recevoir une avalanche de lettres/d'offres.

snow up *vt* (*pass only*) **to be snowed up** *[road]* être complètement enneigé, être bloqué par la neige; *[village, farm, person]* être bloqué par la neige.

snowball [ˈsnəʊbɔːl] **1** *n* boule *f* de neige. **it hasn't got a ~'s chance in hell*** ça n'a pas l'ombre d'une chance; **~ fight** bataille *f* de boules de neige.

2 *vt* lancer des boules de neige à, bombarder de boules de neige.

3 *vi* (*lit*) se lancer des *or* se bombarder de boules de neige; (*fig*) *[project etc]* faire boule de neige.

snowy ['snəʊɪ] *adj weather, valley, climate, region* neigeux; *countryside, hills, roof* enneigé, couvert de neige; *day etc* de neige; (*fig*) *linen* neigeux; *hair, beard* de neige. **it was very ~ yesterday** il a beaucoup neigé hier.

snub[1] [snʌb] **1** *n* rebuffade *f.* **2** *vt person* snober; *offer* repousser, rejeter. **to be ~bed** essuyer une rebuffade.

snub[2] [snʌb] *adj nose* retroussé, camus (*pej*). **~-nosed** au nez retroussé *or* camus (*pej*).

snuck* [snʌk] (*US*) *pret, ptp of* **sneak.**

snuff[1] [snʌf] **1** *n* tabac *m* à priser. **pinch of ~** prise *f*; **to take ~** priser. **2** *cpd*: **snuffbox** tabatière *f.* **3** *vti* = **sniff 2, 3.**

snuff[2] [snʌf] *vt candle* moucher. (*euph: die*) **to ~ it**‡ mourir, casser sa pipe*.

snuff out 1 *vi* (‡: *die*) mourir, casser sa pipe*.

2 *vt sep candle* moucher; (*fig*) *enthusiasm* éteindre; (‡: *kill*) zigouiller‡.

snuffer ['snʌfəʳ] *n* (*also* **candle-~**) éteignoir *m.* **~s** mouchettes *fpl.*

snuffle ['snʌfl] **1** *n* **(a)** = **sniffle 1. (b) to speak in a ~** parler du nez *or* d'une voix nasillarde, nasiller. **2** *vi* **(a)** = **sniffle 2. (b)** parler (*or* chanter) d'une voix nasillarde, nasiller. **3** *vt* dire *or* prononcer d'une voix nasillarde.

snug [snʌg] **1** *adj* (*cosy*) *room, house* confortable, douillet; *bed* douillet; *garment* (*cosy*) douillet, moelleux et chaud; (*close-fitting*) bien ajusté; (*compact*) *boat, cottage* petit mais confortable, bien agencé; (*safe etc*) *harbour* bien abrité; *hideout* très sûr; (*fig*) *income etc* gentil, confortable. **it's a ~ fit** *[garment]* c'est bien ajusté; *[object in box etc]* cela rentre juste bien; **it's nice and ~ here** il fait bon ici; **he was ~ in bed** il était bien au chaud dans son lit; **to be as ~ as a bug in a rug*** être bien au chaud, être douillettement installé (*or* couché *etc*).

2 *n* (*Brit*) = **snuggery.**

snuggery ['snʌgərɪ] *n* (*Brit*) (*gen*) petite pièce douillette *or* confortable; (*in pub*) petite arrière-salle.

snuggle ['snʌgl] **1** *vi* se blottir, se pelotonner (*into sth* dans qch, *beside sb* contre qn).

2 *vt child etc* serrer *or* attirer contre soi.

snuggle down *vi* se blottir, se pelotonner (*beside sb* contre qn); se rouler en boule. **snuggle down and go to sleep** installe-toi bien confortablement et dors.

snuggle together *vi* se serrer *or* se blottir l'un contre l'autre.

snuggle up *vi* se serrer, se blottir (*to sb* contre qn).

snugly ['snʌglɪ] *adv* chaudement, confortablement, douillettement. **~ tucked in** bien au chaud dans ses couvertures, bordé bien au chaud; **to fit ~** *[garment]* être bien ajusté; *[object in box etc]* rentrer juste bien.

so [səʊ] **1** *adv* **(a)** (*degree: to such an extent*) si, tellement, aussi. **is it really ~ tiring?** est-ce vraiment si *or* tellement fatigant?, est-ce vraiment aussi fatigant (que cela)?; **do you really need ~ long?** vous faut-il vraiment si longtemps *or* tellement de temps *or* aussi longtemps (que cela)?; **~ early** si tôt, tellement tôt, d'aussi bonne heure; **~ ... that** si *or* tellement ... que; **he was ~ clumsy (that) he broke the cup, he broke the cup he was ~ clumsy*** il était si *or* tellement maladroit qu'il a cassé la tasse; **the body was ~ burnt that it was unidentifiable** *or* **~ burnt as to be unidentifiable** le cadavre était brûlé à un point tel *or* à (un) tel point qu'il était impossible de l'identifier; **he ~ loves her that he would give his life for her** il l'aime tant *or* tellement *or* à un point tel qu'il donnerait sa vie pour elle; **~ ... as to**+*infin* assez ... pour+*infin*; **he was ~ stupid as to tell her what he'd done** il a eu la stupidité de *or* il a été assez stupide pour lui raconter ce qu'il avait fait; **he was not ~ stupid as to say that to her** il n'a pas été bête au point de lui dire cela, il a eu l'intelligence de ne pas lui dire cela; (*frm*) **would you be ~ kind as to open the door?** auriez-vous l'amabilité *or* la gentillesse *or* l'obligeance d'ouvrir la porte?; **not ~ ... as** pas si *or* aussi ... que; **he is not ~ clever as his brother** il n'est pas aussi *or* si intelligent que son frère; **it's not ~ big as all that!** ce n'est pas si grand que ça!; **it's not ~ big as I thought it would be** ce n'est pas aussi grand que je le pensais *or* que je l'imaginais; **it's not nearly ~ difficult as you think** c'est loin d'être aussi difficile que vous le croyez; **it's not ~ early as you think** il n'est pas aussi *or* si tôt que vous le croyez; **he's not ~ good a teacher as his father** il n'est pas aussi bon professeur que son père, il ne vaut pas son père comme professeur; **he's not ~ stupid as he looks** il n'est pas aussi *or* si stupide qu'il en a l'air.

(b) (*so as to, so that ...*) **~ as to** afin de faire, pour faire; **he hurried ~ as not to be late** il s'est dépêché pour ne pas être *or* afin de ne pas être en retard; **~ that** (*purpose*) pour+*infin*, afin de+*infin*, pour que+*subj*, afin que+*subj*; (*result*) si bien que+*indic*, de (telle) sorte que +*indic*; **I'm going early ~ that I'll get a ticket** j'y vais tôt pour obtenir *or* afin d'obtenir un billet; **I brought it ~ that you could read it** je l'ai apporté pour que *or* afin que vous le lisiez; **he arranged the timetable ~ that the afternoons were free** il a organisé l'emploi du temps de façon à laisser les après-midi libres *or* de telle sorte que les après-midi étaient libres; **he refused to move, ~ that the police had to carry him away** il a refusé de bouger, si bien que *or* de sorte que les agents ont dû l'emporter de force.

(c) (*very, to a great extent*) si, tellement. **I'm ~ tired!** je suis si *or* tellement fatigué!; **I'm ~ very tired!** je suis vraiment si *or* tellement fatigué!; **there's ~ much to do** il y a tellement *or* tant (de choses) à faire; **his speech was ~ much nonsense** son discours était complètement stupide; **thanks ~ much*, thanks ever ~**‡ merci bien *or* beaucoup *or* mille fois; **it's not ~ very difficult!** cela n'est pas si difficile que ça!; **he who ~ loved France** lui qui aimait tant la France; *V also* **ever.**

(d) (*manner: thus, in this way*) ainsi, comme ceci *or* cela, de cette façon. **you should stand (just) ~** vous devriez vous tenir ainsi *or* comme ceci, voici comment vous devriez vous tenir; **he likes everything (to be) just ~** il aime que tout soit fait d'une certaine façon *or* fait comme ça et pas autrement*, il est très maniaque; **as A is to B ~ C is to D** C est à D ce que A est à B; **as he failed once ~ he will fail again** il échouera comme il a déjà échoué; **you don't believe me but it is ~** vous ne me croyez pas mais il en est bien ainsi; **~ it was that ...** c'est ainsi que ...; (*frm*) **~ be it** soit; **it ~ happened that ...** il s'est trouvé que ...; (*frm, Jur etc*) **~ help me God!** que Dieu me vienne en aide!

(e) (*used as substitute for phrase, word etc*) **~ saying ...** ce disant ..., sur ces mots ...; **~ I believe** c'est ce que je crois, c'est ce qu'il me semble; **is that ~?** pas possible?, tiens!; (*iro*) vraiment?, vous croyez?, pensez-vous!; **that is ~** c'est bien ça, c'est exact, c'est bien vrai; **if that is ~ ...** s'il en est ainsi ...; **if ~** si oui; **perhaps ~** peut-être bien (que oui), cela se peut; **just ~!, quite ~!** exactement!, tout à fait!, c'est bien ça!; **I told you ~ yesterday** je vous l'ai dit hier; **I told you ~!** je vous l'avais bien dit!; **~ it seems!** à ce qu'il paraît!; **he certainly said ~** il l'a bien dit, il a bien dit ça; **please do ~** faites-le, faites ainsi; **I think ~** je (le) crois, je (le) pense; **I hope ~** je l'espère bien, j'espère bien; **... only more ~** ... mais encore plus; **how ~?** comment (ça se fait)?; **why ~?** pourquoi (donc)?; **he said they would be there and ~ they were** il a dit qu'ils seraient là, et en effet ils y étaient; **~ do I!, ~ have I!, ~ am I!** *etc* moi aussi!; **he's going to bed, and ~ will I** il va se coucher et moi aussi *or* et je vais en faire autant; **if you do that ~ will I** si tu fais ça, j'en ferai autant; **I'm tired — ~ am I!** je suis fatigué — moi aussi! *or* et moi donc!; **he said he was French — ~ he did!** il a dit qu'il était français — mais oui (c'est vrai)! *or* en effet!; **it's raining — ~ it is!** il pleut — en effet! *or* c'est vrai!; **I want to see that film — ~ you shall!** je veux voir ce film — eh bien tu le verras!

(f) (*phrases*) **I didn't say that! — you did so!*** je n'ai pas dit ça! — mais si tu l'as dit! *or* c'est pas vrai* tu l'as dit!; **twenty or ~** à peu près vingt, environ vingt, une vingtaine; **25 or ~** à peu près 25, environ 25; **~ to speak, ~ to say** pour ainsi dire; **and ~ on (and ~ on** *or* **and ~ forth)** et ainsi de suite; **~ long!*** au revoir!, à bientôt!, à un de ces jours!; *V* **far, many, much.**

2 *conj* **(a)** (*therefore*) donc, par conséquent. **he was late, ~ he missed the train** il est arrivé en retard, donc il a *or* par conséquent il a *or* aussi a-t-il (*liter*) manqué le train; **the roads are busy, ~ be careful** il y a beaucoup de circulation, alors fais bien attention.

(b) (*exclamatory*) **~ there he is!** le voilà donc!; **~ you're selling it?** alors vous le vendez?; **~ he's come at last!** il est donc enfin arrivé!; **and ~ you see ...** alors comme vous voyez ...; **I'm going home — ~?** je rentre — (bon) et alors?; **well ~ what?*** (bon) et alors?, et après?.

3 *cpd*: **Mr so-and-so*** Monsieur un tel; **Mrs so-and-so*** Madame une telle; **then if so-and-so says ...** alors si quelqu'un *or* Machin Chouette* dit ...; **he's an old so-and-so*** c'est un vieux schnock‡; **if you ask me to do so-and-so** si vous me demandez de faire ci et ça; **so-called** soi-disant *inv*, prétendu; **so-so*** comme ci comme ça, couci-couça*; **his work is only so-so*** son travail n'est pas fameux*.

soak [səʊk] **1** *n* **(a) to give sth a (good) ~** (bien) faire tremper qch, (bien) laisser tremper qch; **the sheets are in ~** les draps sont en train de tremper.

(b) (‡: *drunkard*) soûlard* *m*, poivrot‡ *m.*

2 *vt* **(a)** faire *or* laisser tremper (*in* dans). **to be/get ~ed to the skin** être trempé/se faire tremper jusqu'aux os *or* comme une soupe*; **bread ~ed in milk** pain imbibé de lait *or* qui a trempé dans du lait; (*fig*) **he ~ed himself in the atmosphere of Paris** il s'est plongé dans l'atmosphère de Paris.

(b) (‡: *take money from*) (*by overcharging*) estamper*; (*by taxation*) faire payer de lourds impôts à. **the government's policy is to ~ the rich** la politique du gouvernement est de faire casquer‡ les riches.

3 *vi* **(a)** tremper (*in* dans). **to put sth in to ~** faire tremper qch, mettre qch à tremper.

(b) (‡: *drink*) boire comme une éponge, avoir la dalle en pente*.

soak in *vi [liquid]* pénétrer, s'infiltrer, être absorbé. (* *fig*) **I told him what I thought and left it to soak in** je lui ai donné mon opinion et je l'ai laissé la digérer *or* je l'ai laissé méditer dessus.

soak out 1 *vi [stain etc]* partir (*au trempage*).

2 *vt sep stains* faire partir (en trempant le linge *etc*).

soak through 1 *vi [liquid]* traverser, filtrer au travers, s'infiltrer.

2 *vt sep*: **to be soaked through** *[garment etc]* être trempé; *[person]* être trempé (jusqu'aux os).

soak up *vt sep* (*lit, fig*) absorber.

soaking ['səʊkɪŋ] **1** *n* trempage *m.* **to get a ~** se faire tremper (jusqu'aux os); **to give sth a ~** faire *or* laisser tremper qch. **2** *adj*: **to be ~ (wet)** *[object]* être trempé; *[person]* être trempé (jusqu'aux os).

soap [səʊp] **1** *n* savon *m*; (**fig*: *also* **soft ~**) flatterie(s) *f(pl)*, flagornerie *f* (*pej*). (*US fig*) **no ~!**‡ rien à faire!, des clous!‡; *V* **shaving, toilet** *etc.* **2** *vt* savonner.

3 *cpd*: (*fig*) **soapbox** (caisse *f* servant de) tribune improvisée (*en plein air*); **he got up on his soapbox and harangued the crowd** il est monté sur sa tribune improvisée *or* sur la caisse qui lui servait de tribune et s'est mis à haranguer la foule; **soapbox orator** orateur *m* de carrefour, harangueur *m*, -euse *f* de foules; **soapbox oratory** harangue(s) *f(pl)* de démagogue; **soap bubble** bulle *f* de savon; **soapdish** porte-savon *m*; **soapflakes** savon *m* en paillettes, paillettes *fpl* de savon; (*fig*) **soap opera** mélo* *m* à épisodes; **soap powder** lessive *f*, détergent *m*; **soapstone** stéatite *f*; **soapsuds** (*lather*) mousse *f* de savon; (*soapy water*) eau savonneuse.

soap down *vt sep* savonner.
soapy ['səʊpɪ] *adj water* savonneux; *taste* de savon; (* *fig pej*) *person* mielleux, doucereux, lécheur*; *manner* onctueux. **that smells ~** ça sent le savon.
soar [sɔːʳ] *vi* (*often* **~ up**) *[bird, aircraft]* monter (en flèche); *[ball etc]* voler (*over the wall etc* par-dessus le mur *etc*); (*fig*) *[tower, cathedral]* s'élancer (vers le ciel); *[prices, costs, profits]* monter en flèche, (*suddenly*) faire un bond; *[ambitions, hopes]* grandir démesurément; *[spirits, morale]* remonter en flèche.
soar up *vi V* **soar.**
soaring ['sɔːrɪŋ] **1** *n [bird]* essor *m*; *[plane]* envol *m*. **2** *adj spire* élancé; *price* qui monte en flèche; *ambition, pride, hopes* grandissant.
sob [sɒb] **1** *n* sanglot *m*. ... **he said with a ~** ... dit-il en sanglotant.
2 *cpd*: **sob story*** histoire mélodramatique *or* d'un pathétique facile *or* larmoyante; (*Press etc*) **the main item was a sob story* about a puppy** l'article principal était une histoire à vous fendre le cœur concernant un chiot; **he told us a sob story* about his sister's illness** il a cherché à nous apitoyer *or* à nous avoir au sentiment* en nous parlant de la maladie de sa sœur; **there's too much sob stuff* in that film** il y a trop de sensiblerie *or* de mélo* dans ce film; **he gave us a lot of sob stuff*** il nous a fait tout un baratin‡ larmoyant.
3 *vt*: **'no' she ~bed** 'non' dit-elle en sanglotant; **to ~ o.s. to sleep** s'endormir à force de sangloter *or* en sanglotant.
sob out *vt sep story* raconter en sanglotant. (*fig*) **to sob one's heart out** pleurer à chaudes larmes *or* à gros sanglots.
sobbing ['sɒbɪŋ] **1** *n* sanglots *mpl*. **2** *adj* sanglotant.
sober ['səʊbəʳ] **1** *adj* **(a)** (*moderate, sedate*) *person* sérieux, posé, sensé; *estimate, statement* modéré, mesuré; *judgment* sensé; *occasion* plein de gravité *or* de solennité; *suit, style, colour* sobre, discret (*f* -ète). **in ~ earnest** sans plaisanterie, bien sérieusement; **to be in ~ earnest** être tout à fait sérieux, ne pas plaisanter; **in ~ fact** en réalité, si l'on regarde la réalité bien en face; **the ~ truth, the ~ fact of the matter** la vérité toute simple, les faits tels qu'ils sont; **as ~ as a judge** sérieux comme un pape* (*V also* **1b**); **to be in a ~ mood** être plein de gravité.
(b) (*not drunk*) **I'm perfectly ~** je n'ai vraiment pas trop bu; **he's never ~** il est toujours ivre, il ne dessoûle* pas; **he is ~ now** il est dégrisé *or* dessoûlé* maintenant; **to be as ~ as a judge, to be stone-cold ~** n'être absolument pas ivre.
2 *cpd*: **sober-headed** *person* sérieux, posé, sensé; *decision* réfléchi, posé; **sober-minded** sérieux, sensé; **sober-sided** sérieux, grave, qui ne rit pas souvent; **sobersides*** bonnet *m* de nuit (*fig*).
3 *vt* **(a)** (*also* **~ down, ~ up**) (*calm*) calmer; (*deflate*) dégriser.
(b) (*also* **~ up**: *stop being drunk*) désenivrer, dessoûler*.
sober down 1 *vi* (*calm down*) se calmer; (*grow sadder*) être dégrisé.
2 *vt sep* = **sober 3a.**
sober up 1 *vi* désenivrer, dessoûler*.
2 *vt sep* = **sober 3a, 3b.**
soberly ['səʊbəlɪ] *adv speak, say* avec modération *or* mesure *or* calme, d'un ton posé; *behave, act* de façon posée *or* sensée; *furnish, dress* sobrement, discrètement.
soberness ['səʊbənɪs] *n*, **sobriety** [səʊ'braɪətɪ] *n* **(a)** (*calm etc*: *V* **sober 1a**) sérieux *m*, caractère mesuré *or* posé *or* sensé; modération *f*, mesure *f*; gravité *f*; sobriété *f*.
(b) (*not drunk*) **to return to ~** désenivrer, dessoûler*; **his ~ was in question** on le soupçonnait d'être ivre.
sobriquet ['səʊbrɪkeɪ] *n* sobriquet *m*.
soccer ['sɒkəʳ] **1** *n* football *m*, foot* *m*.
2 *cpd match, pitch, team* de football, de foot*. **soccer player** footballeur *m or* footballer *m*; **the soccer season** la saison du football *or* du foot*.
sociability [ˌsəʊʃə'bɪlɪtɪ] *n* sociabilité *f*.
sociable ['səʊʃəbl] *adj person* (*gregarious*) sociable, qui aime la compagnie, liant; (*friendly*) sociable, aimable; *animal* sociable; *evening, gathering* amical, agréable. **I'll have a drink just to be ~** je prendrai un verre rien que pour vous (*or* lui *etc*) faire plaisir; **I'm not feeling very ~ this evening** je n'ai pas envie de voir des gens ce soir.
sociably ['səʊʃəblɪ] *adv behave* de façon sociable, aimablement; *invite, say* amicalement.
social ['səʊʃəl] **1** *adj* **(a)** (*Soc etc*) *behaviour, class, relationship, customs, reforms* social. **man is a ~ animal** l'homme est un animal social; **a ~ outcast** une personne mise au ban de la société, un paria; *V also* **3.**
(b) (*in or of society*) *engagements, obligations* mondain. **~ climber** (*still climbing*) arriviste *mf*; (*arrived*) parvenu(e) *m(f)*; (*Press*) **~ column** carnet mondain, mondanités *fpl*; **his ~ equals** ses pairs *mpl*; **a gay ~ life** une vie très mondaine; **we've got almost no ~ life** nous ne menons une vie très retirée, nous ne menons pas une vie très mondaine, nous ne sortons presque jamais; **the ~ life in this town is non-existent** c'est vraiment une ville morte, il n'y a pas de vie mondaine dans cette ville; **how's your ~ life?*** est-ce que tu vois des amis?, est-ce que tu sors beaucoup?
(c) (*gregarious*) *person* sociable; *evening* agréable. **~ club** association amicale (*qui n'est pas spécialisée dans une activité précise*).
2 *n* (petite) fête *f*.
3 *cpd*: **social anthropologist** spécialiste *mf* de l'anthropologie sociale; **social anthropology** anthropologie sociale; **social contract** contrat social; **Social Democracy** social-démocratie *f*; **Social Democrat** social-démocrate *mf*; **Social Democratic** social-démocrate; **social disease** maladie vénérienne; **social engineering** manipulation *f* des structures sociales; (*US*) **social insurance** sécurité sociale; **social science** sciences humaines; (*Univ*) **Faculty of Social Science** faculté *f* des sciences humaines; **social scientist** spécialiste *mf* des sciences humaines; **social security** (*n*) aide sociale; (*cpd*) *benefits etc* de la sécurité sociale; **to be on social security*** recevoir l'aide sociale; **social service = social work; the social services** les services sociaux; **Secretary of State for/Department of Social Services** ministre *m*/ministère *m* des Affaires sociales; **social studies** sciences sociales; **social welfare** sécurité sociale; **social work** assistance sociale; **social worker** assistant(e) *m(f)* de service social, assistant social.
socialism ['səʊʃəlɪzəm] *n* socialisme *m*.
socialist ['səʊʃəlɪst] *adj, n* socialiste (*mf*).
socialistic [ˌsəʊʃə'lɪstɪk] *adj* socialiste.
socialite ['səʊʃəlaɪt] *n* personnalité *f* en vue dans la haute société. **a Paris ~** un membre du Tout-Paris.
sociality [ˌsəʊʃɪ'ælɪtɪ] *n* socialité *f*, sociabilité *f*.
socialization [ˌsəʊʃəlaɪ'zeɪʃən] *n* socialisation *f* (*Pol*).
socialize ['səʊʃəlaɪz] **1** *vt* (*Pol, Psych*) socialiser.
2 *vi* (*be with people*) fréquenter des gens; (*make friends*) se faire des amis; (*chat*) s'entretenir, bavarder (*with sb* avec qn).
socially ['səʊʃəlɪ] *adv interact, be valid* socialement; *acceptable* en société. **I know him** (*or* **her** *etc*) **~** nous nous rencontrons en société.
society [sə'saɪətɪ] **1** *n* **(a)** (*social community*) société *f*. **to live in ~** vivre en société; **for the good of ~** dans l'intérêt social *or* de la société *or* de la communauté; **it is a danger to ~** cela constitue un danger social, cela met la société en danger; **modern industrial societies** les sociétés industrielles modernes.
(b) (*U: high ~*) (haute) société *f*, grand monde. **polite ~** la bonne société; **the years she spent in ~** ses années de vie mondaine.
(c) (*U: company, companionship*) société *f*, compagnie *f*. **in the ~ of** dans la société de, en compagnie de; **I enjoy his ~** je me plais en sa compagnie, j'apprécie sa compagnie.
(d) (*organized group*) société *f*, association *f*; (*charitable ~*) œuvre *f* de charité, association de bienfaisance; (*Scol, Univ etc*) club *m*, association. **dramatic ~** club théâtral, association théâtrale; **learned ~** société savante; (*Rel*) **the S~ of Friends** la Société des Amis, les Quakers *mpl*; (*Rel*) **the S~ of Jesus** la Société de Jésus, les Jésuites *mpl*; *V* **royal** *etc*.
2 *cpd correspondent, news, photographer, wedding* mondain, de la haute société. (*Press*) **society column** carnet mondain, mondanités *fpl*.
socio... ['səʊsɪəʊ] *pref* socio... . **~cultural** socioculturel; **~economic** socio-économique; *V also* **sociological** *etc*.
sociological [ˌsəʊsɪə'lɒdʒɪkəl] *adj* sociologique.
sociologist [ˌsəʊsɪ'ɒlədʒɪst] *n* sociologue *mf*.
sociology [ˌsəʊsɪ'ɒlədʒɪ] *n* sociologie *f*.
sociometry [ˌsəʊsɪ'ɒmɪtrɪ] *n* sociométrie *f*.
sociopath ['səʊsɪəʊpæθ] *n* inadapté(e) social(e).
sociopathic [ˌsəʊsɪəʊ'pæθɪk] *adj* socialement inadapté, sociopathe.
sock[1] [sɒk] *n* **(a)** (*US*) *pl* **~s** *or* **sox** (*short stocking*) chaussette *f*, (*shorter*) socquette *f*; (*inner sole*) semelle *f* (intérieure). (*fig*) **to pull up one's ~s*** retrousser ses manches (*fig*); (*fig*) **put a ~ in it!‡** la ferme!‡, ta gueule!‡ **(b)** (*wind~*) manche *f* à air.
sock[2]‡ [sɒk] **1** *n* (*blow*) coup *m*, beigne‡ *f*, gnon‡ *m*. **to give sb a ~ on the jaw** flanquer un coup *or* son poing sur la gueule‡ à qn. **2** *vt* flanquer une beigne‡ *or* un gnon‡ à. **~ him one!** cogne dessus!*, fous-lui une beigne!‡
socket ['sɒkɪt] **1** *n* (*gen*) cavité *f*, trou *m* (*où qch s'emboîte*); *[hipbone]* cavité articulaire; *[eye]* orbite *f*; *[tooth]* alvéole *f*; (*Elec: for light bulb*) douille *f*; (*Elec: also* **wall ~**) prise *f* de courant, prise femelle; (*Carpentry*) mortaise *f*; (*in candlestick etc*) trou. **to pull sb's arm out of its ~** désarticuler *or* démettre l'épaule à qn.
2 *cpd*: (*Carpentry*) **socket joint** joint *m* à rotule *or* à genou; (*Tech*) **socket wrench** clef *f* à pipe.
Socrates ['sɒkrətiːz] *n* Socrate *m*.
Socratic [sɒ'krætɪk] *adj* socratique.
sod[1] [sɒd] *n* (*U: turf*) gazon *m*; (*piece of turf*) motte *f* (de gazon).
sod[2]∵ [sɒd] (*Brit*) **1** *n* con∵ *m*, couillon∵ *m*; (*pej*) salaud‡ *m*, salopard‡ *m*. **the poor ~s who tried** les pauvres cons∵ *or* couillons∵ *or* bougres* qui l'ont essayé; **poor little ~!** pauvre petit bonhomme!; **he's a real ~** c'est un salaud‡ *or* un salopard‡.
2 *vt*: **~ it!** merde (alors)!∵; **~ him!** il m'emmerde!∵, qu'il aille se faire foutre!∵.
sod off∵ *vi* foutre le camp‡. **sod off!** fous le camp!‡, va te faire foutre!∵
soda ['səʊdə] **1** *n* **(a)** (*Chem*) soude *f*; (*also* **washing ~, ~ crystals**) soude du commerce, cristaux *mpl* (de soude); *V* **baking, caustic** *etc*.
(b) (*also* **~ water**) eau *f* de Seltz. **whisky and ~** whisky *m* soda *or* à l'eau de Seltz; *V* **ice.**
2 *cpd*: (*Chem*) **soda ash** soude *f* du commerce; **soda crystals** *V* **1a**; (*US*) **soda fountain** buvette *f*; (*US*) **soda pop** soda *m*; **soda siphon** siphon *m* (d'eau gazeuse); **soda water** *V* **1b.**
sodality [səʊ'dælɪtɪ] *n* camaraderie *f*, (*association, also Rel*) confrérie *f*.
sodden ['sɒdn] *adj ground* détrempé; *clothes* trempé. (*fig*) **~ with drink** hébété *or* abruti par l'alcool.
sodium ['səʊdɪəm] **1** *n* sodium *m*. **2** *cpd*: **sodium bicarbonate** bicarbonate *m* de soude; **sodium carbonate** carbonate *m* de sodium; **sodium light,** (*US*) **sodium-vapor lamp** lampe *f* à vapeur de sodium.
sodomite ['sɒdəmaɪt] *n* sodomite *m*, pédéraste *m*.
sodomy ['sɒdəmɪ] *n* sodomie *f*, pédérastie *f*.
sofa ['səʊfə] *n* sofa *m*, canapé *m*. **~ bed** canapé-lit *m*.
soft [sɒft] **1** *adj* **(a)** (*in texture, consistency: not hard etc*) *bed, mattress, pillow* doux (*f* douce), moelleux, mou (*f* molle) (*pej*);

mud, snow, clay, ground, pitch mou; *substance* mou, malléable; *wood, stone, pencil, paste* tendre; *metal, iron* doux, tendre; *butter* mou, (r)amolli; *leather, brush, toothbrush* souple, doux; *collar, hat* mou; *material* doux, soyeux, satiné; *silk, hand* doux; *skin, cheek* doux, fin, satiné; *hair* doux, soyeux; (*pej: flabby*) *person, muscle* flasque, avachi. **as ~ as butter** mou comme du beurre; **as ~ as silk/velvet** doux comme de la soie/du velours; **book in ~ covers** livre broché, (*paperback*) livre de poche (*V also* 3); **~ fruit** baies *fpl* comestibles, ≃ fruits *mpl* rouges; **a ~ cheese** un fromage mou *or* à pâte molle; (*Brit Comm*) **~ furnishings** tissus *mpl* d'ameublement (*rideaux, tentures, housses etc*); (*Brit Comm*) **~ goods** textiles *mpl*, tissus *mpl*; (*Anat*) **~ palate** voile *m* du palais; **~ toy** jouet *m* de peluche *or* de chiffon; **to grow** *or* **get** *or* **become ~(er)** *[butter, snow, mud, ground, pitch]* devenir mou, se ramollir; *[leather]* s'assouplir; *[bed, mattress, pillow]* s'amollir, devenir plus moelleux *or* trop mou (*pej*); *[skin]* s'adoucir; *[person, body, muscle]* s'avachir, devenir flasque; **to make ~(er)** *butter, snow, clay, ground* (r)amollir; *leather* assouplir; *bed, mattress, pillow* amollir, rendre moelleux; *skin* adoucir; **this sort of life makes you ~** ce genre de vie vous (r)amollit *or* vous enlève votre énergie; *V also* 3 *and* **coal, margarine, roe², solder** *etc.*

(b) (*gentle, not strong or vigorous*) *tap, touch, pressure* doux (*f* douce), léger; *breeze, day, rain, climate* doux. (*Aviat, Space*) **~ landing** atterrissage *m* en douceur; **~ weather** temps doux, temps mou (*pej*).

(c) (*not harsh*) *words, expression, look, glance* doux (*f* douce), aimable, gentil; *answer* aimable, gentil; *heart* tendre, compatissant; *life* doux, facile, tranquille; *job, option* facile; *person* indulgent (*with or on sb* envers qn). **you're too ~!** tu es trop indulgent! *or* trop bon!; **he has a ~ time of it*** il se la coule douce*; **to have a ~ spot for** avoir un faible pour; **the ~er side of his nature** le côté moins sévère *or* moins rigoureux de son tempérament.

(d) (*not loud*) *sound, laugh* doux (*f* douce), léger; *tone* doux; *music, voice* doux, mélodieux, harmonieux; *steps* ouaté, feutré. **in a ~ voice** d'une voix douce, doucement; **the radio/orchestra/brass section is too ~** la radio/l'orchestre/les cuivres ne joue(nt) pas assez fort; **the music is too ~** la musique n'est pas assez forte, on n'entend pas assez la musique; *V also* 3.

(e) (*fig*) *light* doux (*f* douce), pâle; *colour* doux, pastel *inv*; *outline* doux, estompé, flou. **~ lights, ~ lighting** un éclairage doux *or* tamisé; **~ pastel shades** de doux tons pastel; (*Phot*) **~ focus** flou *m* artistique; (*lens*) objectif *m* pour flou artistique; (*Ling*) **~ consonant** consonne douce; (*Fin*) **the market is ~** le marché est lourd.

(f) (*: *stupid*) stupide, bête, débile*. **to go ~** perdre la boule*; **he must be ~ (in the head)*** il doit être cinglé✝ *or* débile*; **he is ~ on her*** il en est toqué*.

(g) (*: *unmanly; without stamina*) mollasson, qui manque de nerf. **he's ~** c'est une mauviette *or* un mollasson, il n'a pas de nerf.

2 *adv* doucement. (*excl*) **~!**†† silence!

3 *cpd*: (*US*) **softball** espèce *f* de base-ball (*joué sur un terrain plus petit avec une balle plus grande et plus molle*); **soft-boiled egg** œuf *m* à la coque; **soft-cover book** livre broché, (*paperback*) livre de poche; (*Fin*) **soft currency** devise *f* faible; **soft drinks** boissons non alcoolisées; **soft drugs** drogues douces; **soft-footed** à la démarche légère, qui marche à pas feutrés *or* sans faire de bruit; **soft-headed*** faible d'esprit, cinglé✝; **soft-hearted** au cœur tendre, compatissant; **soft pedal** (*n: Mus*) pédale douce; **soft-pedal** (*vi: Mus*) mettre la pédale douce; (*vt: fig*) ne pas trop insister sur; (*Comm*) **soft sell** promotion (de vente) discrète; (*fig*) **he's a master of the soft sell** il est maître dans l'art de persuader discrètement les gens; **soft-shelled** *egg, mollusc* à coquille molle; *crustacean, turtle* à carapace molle; **soft soap** (*n*) (*lit*) savon vert; (*fig*) flatterie *f*, flagornerie *f* (*pej*); **soft-soap** (*vt: fig pej*) flatter, passer de la pommade à, lécher les bottes à*; **soft-spoken** à la voix douce; (*fig*) **to be a soft touch*** se faire avoir* (facilement), se faire refaire* *or* rouler*; (*Aut*) **soft verges** accotements non stabilisés; (*Computers: U*) **software** software* *m*, logiciel *m* (*frm*); **soft water** eau *f* qui n'est pas calcaire, eau douce; **softwood** bois *m* tendre; **soft X-rays** rayons X mous.

soften ['sɒfn] **1** *vt butter, clay, ground, pitch* (r)amollir; *collar, leather* assouplir; *skin* adoucir; *sound* adoucir, atténuer, étouffer; *lights, lighting* adoucir, tamiser; *outline* adoucir, estomper, rendre flou; *colour* adoucir, atténuer; *pain, anxiety* adoucir, atténuer, soulager; *sb's anger, reaction, effect, impression* adoucir, atténuer; *resistance* amoindrir, réduire. (*fig*) **to ~ the blow** adoucir *or* amortir le choc.

2 *vi [butter, clay, ground, pitch]* devenir mou, se ramollir; *[collar, leather]* s'assouplir; *[skin]* s'adoucir; *[outline]* s'adoucir, devenir flou, s'estomper; *[colour]* s'adoucir, s'atténuer; *[sb's anger]* s'atténuer. **his heart ~ed at the sight of her** il s'attendrit en la voyant; **his eyes ~ed as he looked at her** son regard s'est adouci à sa vue.

soften up 1 *vi [butter, clay, ground, pitch]* devenir mou, se ramollir; *[collar, leather]* s'assouplir; *[skin]* s'adoucir; (*grow less stern*) s'adoucir. **we must not soften up towards** *or* **on these offenders** nous ne devons pas faire preuve d'indulgence envers ces délinquants.

2 *vt sep* **(a)** *butter, clay, pitch, ground* (r)amollir; *collar, leather* assouplir; *skin* adoucir.

(b) *person* attendrir; (*: *by cajoling*) *customer etc* bonimenter*, baratiner✝; (*: *by bullying*) intimider, malmener; *resistance, opposition* réduire; (*Mil: by bombing etc*) affaiblir par bombardement intensif.

softener ['sɒfnəʳ] *n* (*water ~*) adoucisseur *m*; (*fabric ~*) adoucissant *m*.

softening ['sɒfnɪŋ] *n* (*V* **soften 1**) (r)amollissement *m*; assouplissement *m*; adoucissement *m*; atténuation *f*; soulagement *m*. (*Med*) **~ of the brain** ramollissement cérébral; (*fig*) **he's got ~ of the brain*** il devient ramollo✝ *or* débile*; **there has been a ~ of their attitude** ils ont modéré leur attitude.

softie* ['sɒftɪ] *n* (*too tender-hearted*) tendre *mf*; (*no stamina etc*) mauviette *f*, mollasson(ne) *m(f)*; (*coward*) poule mouillée, dégonflé(e)* *m(f)*. **you silly ~, stop crying!** ne pleure plus grand(e) nigaud(e)!

softly ['sɒftlɪ] *adv* (*quietly*) *say, call, sing* doucement; *walk* à pas feutrés, sans (faire de) bruit; (*gently*) *touch, tap* légèrement, doucement; (*tenderly*) *smile, look* tendrement, gentiment.

softness ['sɒftnɪs] *n* (*V* **soft**) **(a)** *[bed, mattress, pillow]* douceur *f*, moelleux *m*, mollesse *f* (*pej*); *[mud, snow, ground, pitch, butter]* mollesse; *[substance]* mollesse, malléabilité *f*; *[leather, brush]* souplesse *f*, douceur; *[collar]* souplesse; *[material, silk, hand, skin, hair]* douceur; (*pej*) *[person, muscle]* avachissement *m*.

(b) *[tap, touch, pressure]* douceur *f*, légèreté *f*; *[breeze, wind, rain, climate]* douceur.

(c) *[words, expression, glance]* douceur *f*, amabilité *f*, gentillesse *f*; *[answer]* amabilité, gentillesse; *[life]* douceur, facilité *f*; *[job]* facilité; (*gentleness, kindness*) douceur, affabilité *f*; (*indulgence*) manque *m* de sévérité (*towards* envers).

(d) *[sound, tone, voice, music]* douceur *f*.

(e) *[light, colour]* douceur *f*; *[outline, photograph]* flou *m*.

(f) (*: *stupidity*) stupidité *f*, bêtise *f*.

softy* ['sɒftɪ] *n* = **softie***.

soggy ['sɒgɪ] *adj ground* détrempé; *clothes* trempé; *bread* mal cuit, pâteux; *heat, atmosphere, pudding* lourd.

soh [səʊ] *n* (*Mus*) sol *m*.

soil¹ [sɔɪl] *n* sol *m*, terre *f*. **rich/chalky ~** sol *or* terre riche/calcaire; **cover it over with ~** recouvre-le de terre; (*liter*) **a man of the ~** un terrien, un homme de la terre; (*fig*) **my native ~** ma terre natale, mon pays natal; **on French ~** sur le sol français, en territoire français.

soil² [sɔɪl] **1** *vt* (*lit*) salir; (*fig*) *reputation, honour* souiller, salir, entacher. **this dress is easily ~ed** cette robe se salit vite *or* est salissante; **~ed linen** linge *m* sale; (*Comm*) **~ed copy** exemplaire défraîchi; *V* **shop.**

2 *vi [material, garment]* se salir, être salissant.

3 *n* (*excrement*) excréments *mpl*, ordures *fpl*; (*sewage*) vidange *f*.

4 *cpd*: **soil pipe** tuyau *m* d'écoulement; (*vertical*) tuyau de descente.

soirée ['swɑːreɪ] *n* soirée *f* (*à but culturel, souvent organisée par une association*).

sojourn ['sɒdʒɜːn] (*liter*) **1** *n* séjour *m*. **2** *vi* séjourner, faire un séjour.

solace ['sɒlɪs] (*liter*) **1** *n* consolation *f*, réconfort *m*. **2** *vt person* consoler; *pain* soulager, adoucir.

solanum [səʊ'leɪnəm] *n* solanacée *f*.

solar ['səʊləʳ] *adj warmth, rays* du soleil, solaire; *cycle, energy, system* solaire. **~ battery** batterie *f* solaire, photopile *f*; **~ cell** cellule *f* photovoltaïque; **~ eclipse** éclipse *f* du soleil; **~ flare** facule *f* solaire; **~ furnace** four *m* solaire; (*Anat*) **~ plexus** plexus *m* solaire; **~ wind** vent *m* solaire.

solarium [səʊ'lɛərɪəm] *n* solarium *m*.

sold [səʊld] *pret, ptp of* **sell.**

solder ['səʊldəʳ] **1** *n* soudure *f*. **hard ~** brasure *f*; **soft ~** claire soudure. **2** *vt* souder. **~ing iron** fer *m* à souder.

soldier ['səʊldʒəʳ] **1** *n* soldat *m* (*also fig*), militaire *m*; (*girl ~*) femme *f* soldat. **~s and civilians** (les) militaires et (les) civils; **Montgomery was a great ~** Montgomery était un grand homme de guerre *or* un grand soldat; **he wants to be a ~** il veut se faire soldat *or* être militaire de carrière *or* entrer dans l'armée; **to play (at) ~s** (*pej*) jouer à la guerre; *[children]* jouer aux soldats; **~ of fortune** soldat de fortune, mercenaire *m*; **old ~** vétéran *m*; (*fig*) **to come the old ~ with sb*** prendre des airs supérieurs avec qn, vouloir en imposer à qn; *V* **foot, private** *etc.*

2 *cpd*: **soldier ant** (fourmi *f*) soldat *m*.

3 *vi* servir dans l'armée, être militaire *or* soldat. **he ~ed for 10 years in the East** il a servi (dans l'armée) pendant 10 ans en Orient; **after 6 years' soldiering** après 6 ans dans l'armée; **to be tired of ~ing** en avoir assez d'être soldat *or* d'être militaire *or* d'être dans l'armée.

soldier on *vi* (*Brit fig*) persévérer (malgré tout).

soldierly ['səʊldʒəlɪ] *adj* (typiquement) militaire.

soldiery ['səʊldʒərɪ] *n* (*collective*) soldats *mpl*, militaires *mpl*, soldatesque *f* (*pej*).

sole¹ [səʊl] *n, pl inv* (*fish*) sole *f*; *V* **lemon.**

sole² [səʊl] **1** *n [shoe, sock, stocking]* semelle *f*; *[foot]* plante *f*; *V* **inner. 2** *vt* ressemeler. **to have one's shoes ~d** faire ressemeler ses chaussures.

sole³ [səʊl] *adj* **(a)** (*only, single*) seul, unique. **the ~ season** la seule *or* l'unique saison, la seule et unique saison.

(b) (*exclusive*) *right* exclusif. (*Comm*) **~ agent for ..., ~ stockist of ...** concessionnaire *mf* de ..., dépositaire exclusif (*or* dépositaire exclusive) de ...; (*Jur*) **~ legatee** légataire universel(le).

solecism ['sɒləsɪzəm] *n* (*Ling*) solécisme *m*; (*social offence*) manque *m* de savoir-vivre, faute *f* de goût.

solely ['səʊllɪ] *adv* seulement, uniquement. **I am ~ to blame** je suis seul coupable, je suis entièrement coupable.

solemn ['sɒləm] *adj occasion, promise, silence, music* solennel; *duty* sacré; *plea, warning* formel, plein de solennité *or* de gravité; *person, face* sérieux, grave, solennel (*often pej*).

solemnity [sə'lemnɪtɪ] *n* (*V* **solemn**) solennité *f*; caractère sacré; sérieux *m*, gravité *f*. **with all ~** très solennellement; **the**

solemnities les fêtes solennelles, les solennités.
solemnization [ˌsɒləmnaɪ'zeɪʃən] *n [marriage]* célébration *f.*
solemnize ['sɒləmnaɪz] *vt marriage* célébrer; *occasion, event* solenniser.
solemnly ['sɒləmlɪ] *adv swear, promise, utter* solennellement; *say, smile, nod* gravement, avec sérieux, d'un ton *or* air solennel (*often pej*). (*Jur*) **I do ~ swear to tell the truth** je jure de dire la vérité.
solenoid ['səʊlənɔɪd] *n* (*Elec*) solénoïde *m.*
sol-fa [ˌsɒl'fɑː] *n* solfège *m.*
solicit [sə'lɪsɪt] **1** *vt* solliciter (*sb for sth, sth from sb* qch de qn); *vote* solliciter, briguer. **2** *vi* (*Jur*) *[prostitute]* racoler.
solicitation [səˌlɪsɪ'teɪʃən] *n* (*V* **solicit**) sollicitation *f*; (*Jur*) racolage *m.*
solicitor [sə'lɪsɪtə^{r}] *n* **(a)** (*Jur*) (*Brit*) ≃ avocat *m*; (*US*) ≃ juriste conseil *or* avocat conseil attaché à une municipalité *etc.* **S~ General** (*Brit*) adjoint *m* du procureur général; (*US*) adjoint *or* substitut *m* du ministre de la Justice. **(b)** (*US*) (*for contribution*) solliciteur *m*, -euse *f*; (*for trade*) courtier *m*, placier *m.*
solicitous [sə'lɪsɪtəs] *adj* plein de sollicitude; (*anxious*) inquiet (*f* -ète), préoccupé (*for, about* de); (*eager*) désireux, avide (*of de, to do* de faire).
solicitude [sə'lɪsɪtjuːd] *n* sollicitude *f.*
solid ['sɒlɪd] **1** *adj* **(a)** (*not liquid or gas*) solide. **a ~ body** un corps solide; **~ food** aliments *mpl* solides; **frozen ~** complètement gelé; **to become ~** se solidifier; **this soup is rather ~** cette soupe est un peu trop épaisse *or* n'est pas assez liquide; *V also* **3.**
(b) (*not hollow etc*) *ball, block, tyre* plein; *crowd etc* compact, dense; *row, line* continu, ininterrompu. **cut out of** *or* **in ~ rock** taillé à même la pierre; **6 metres of ~ rock** 6 mètres de roche massive; **of** *or* **in ~ gold/oak** en or/chêne massif; (*fig*) **the garden was a ~ mass of colour** le jardin resplendissait d'une profusion de couleurs; **a ~ stretch of yellow** une étendue de jaune uni.
(c) *bridge, house etc* solide; *car* solide, robuste; *reasons, scholarship, piece of work, character* solide, sérieux; *business firm* solide, sain; *vote, voters* unanime; *meal* copieux, consistant, substantiel. **he was 6 ft 2 of ~ muscle** c'était un homme de 2 mètres de haut et tout en muscles; **on ~ ground** (*lit*) sur la terre ferme; (*fig: in discussion etc*) en terrain sûr; **a man of ~ build** un homme bien bâti *or* bien charpenté; **~ (common) sense** solide *or* gros bon sens; **he is a good ~ worker** c'est un bon travailleur, c'est un travailleur sérieux; **he's a good ~ bloke*** c'est quelqu'un sur qui on peut compter, il a les reins solides (*fig*); **the square was ~ with cars*** la place était complètement embouteillée; **he was stuck ~ in the mud** il était complètement pris *or* enlisé dans la boue; **we are ~ for peace** nous sommes unanimes à vouloir la paix; **Newtown is ~ for Labour** Newtown vote massivement *or* presque à l'unanimité pour les travaillistes; (*US Pol*) **the S~ South** *états du Sud des États-Unis qui votent traditionnellement pour le parti démocrate;* **I waited a ~ hour** j'ai attendu une heure entière; **he slept 10 ~ hours** *or* **10 hours ~** il a dormi 10 heures d'affilée; **they worked for 2 ~ days** *or* **2 days ~** ils ont travaillé 2 jours sans s'arrêter *or* sans relâche; **it will take a ~ day's work** cela exigera une journée entière de travail.
(d) (*Math*) **~ angle** angle *m* solide *or* polyèdre; **~ figure** solide *m*; **~ geometry** géométrie *f* dans l'espace.
2 *n* (*gen, Chem, Math, Phys*) solide *m.* (*food*) **~s** aliments *mpl* solides.
3 *cpd*: (*Ling*) **solid compound** composé *m* dont les termes sont graphiquement soudés; **solid fuel** (*coal etc*) combustible *m* solide; (*for rockets etc: also* **solid propellant**) mélange *m* de comburant et de carburant; **solid-fuel (central) heating** chauffage central au charbon *or* à combustibles solides; **solid-state** (*Phys*) des solides; (*Electronics*) en état solide; (*Ling*) **solid word** mot *m or* lexie *f* simple.
solidarity [ˌsɒlɪ'dærɪtɪ] *n* (*U*) solidarité *f.* (*Ind*) **~ strike** grève *f* de solidarité.
solidification [səˌlɪdɪfɪ'keɪʃən] *n* (*V* **solidify**) solidification *f*; congélation *f.*
solidify [sə'lɪdɪfaɪ] **1** *vt liquid, gas* solidifier; *oil* congeler. **2** *vi* se solidifier; se congeler.
solidity [sə'lɪdɪtɪ] *n* solidité *f.*
solidly ['sɒlɪdlɪ] *adv build etc* solidement; (*fig*) *vote* massivement, en masse, presque à l'unanimité. **they are ~ behind him** ils le soutiennent unanimement *or* à l'unanimité.
soliloquize [sə'lɪləkwaɪz] *vi* soliloquer, monologuer. **'perhaps' he ~d** 'peut-être' dit-il, se parlant à lui-même.
soliloquy [sə'lɪləkwɪ] *n* soliloque *m*, monologue *m.*
solipsism ['səʊlɪpsɪzəm] *n* solipsisme *m.*
solitaire [ˌsɒlɪ'tɛə^{r}] *n* (*stone, game*) solitaire *m*; (*Cards*) réussite *f*, patience *f.*
solitary ['sɒlɪtərɪ] **1** *adj* **(a)** (*alone*) *person, life, journey* solitaire; *hour* de solitude; *place* solitaire, retiré; (*lonely*) seul. (*Jur*) **(in) ~ confinement** (au) régime cellulaire; **to take a ~ walk** se promener tout seul *or* en solitaire.
(b) (*only one*) seul, unique. **a ~ case of hepatitis** un seul *or* unique cas d'hépatite; **not a ~ one** pas un seul.
2 *n* (*) = **~ confinement**; *V* **1a.**
solitude ['sɒlɪtjuːd] *n* solitude *f.*
solo ['səʊləʊ], *pl* **~s** *or* **soli** ['səʊliː] **1** *n* **(a)** (*Mus*) solo *m.* **piano ~** solo de piano.
(b) (*Cards: also* **~ whist**) whist-solo *m.*
2 *adv* (*Mus*) *play* en solo; *fly* en solitaire.
3 *cpd violin etc* solo *inv*; *flight etc* en solitaire.
soloist ['səʊləʊɪst] *n* soliste *mf.*
Solomon ['sɒləmən] *n* Salomon *m.*
solstice ['sɒlstɪs] *n* solstice *m.* **summer/winter ~** solstice d'été/d'hiver.
solubility [ˌsɒljʊ'bɪlɪtɪ] *n* solubilité *f.*
soluble ['sɒljʊbl] *adj substance* soluble; *problem* (ré)soluble.
solution [sə'luːʃən] *n* **(a)** (*to problem etc*) solution *f* (*to* de). **(b)** (*Chem*) (*act*) solution *f*, dissolution *f*; (*liquid*) solution; (*Pharm*) solution, soluté *m*; *V* **rubber**[1].
solvable ['sɒlvəbl] *adj* (ré)soluble.
solve [sɒlv] *vt equation, difficulty* résoudre; *problem* résoudre, trouver la solution de; *crossword puzzle* réussir; *mystery* éclaircir, débrouiller. **to ~ a riddle** trouver la solution d'une énigme *or* d'une devinette, trouver le mot d'une énigme; **that question remains to be ~d** cette question est encore en suspens.
solvency ['sɒlvənsɪ] *n* solvabilité *f.*
solvent ['sɒlvənt] **1** *adj* (*Fin*) solvable; (*Chem*) dissolvant. **2** *n* (*Chem*) solvant *m*, dissolvant *m.*
Somali [səʊ'mɑːlɪ] **1** *adj* somali, somalien. **2** *n* **(a)** Somali(e) *m(f)*, Somalien(ne) *m(f).* **(b)** (*Ling*) somali *m.*
Somalia [səʊ'mɑːlɪə] *n* (République *f* de) Somalie *f.*
Somaliland [səʊ'mɑːlɪlænd] *n* Somalie *f.*
somatic [səʊ'mætɪk] *adj* somatique.
somato... ['səʊmətəʊ] *pref* somato... .
sombre, (*US*) **somber** ['sɒmbə^{r}] *adj colour, outlook, prediction, prospect* sombre; *mood, person* sombre, morne; *day, weather* morne, maussade.
sombrely, (*US*) **somberly** ['sɒmbəlɪ] *adv* sombrement.
sombreness, (*US*) **somberness** ['sɒmbənɪs] *n* caractère *m or* aspect *m* sombre; (*colour*) couleur *f* sombre; (*darkness*) obscurité *f.*
some [sʌm] **1** *adj* **(a)** (*a certain amount or number of*) **~ tea/ice/water/cakes** du thé/de la glace/de l'eau/des gâteaux; **there are ~ children outside** il y a des enfants *or* quelques enfants dehors; **~ old shoes** de vieilles chaussures; **~ dirty shoes** des chaussures sales; **have you got ~ money?** est-ce que tu as de l'argent?; **will you have ~ more meat?** voulez-vous encore de la viande? *or* encore un peu de viande?
(b) (*unspecified, unknown*) quelconque, quelque (*frm*). **~ woman was asking for her** il y avait une dame qui la demandait; **I read it in ~ book (or other)** je l'ai lu quelque part dans un livre; je l'ai lu dans un livre quelconque; **at ~ place in Africa** quelque part en Afrique; **give it to ~ child** donnez-le à un enfant *or* à quelque enfant (*frm*); **~ day** un de ces jours, un jour ou l'autre; **~ day next week** (dans le courant de) la semaine prochaine; **~ other day** un autre jour; **~ other time!** pas maintenant!; **~ time last week** (un jour) la semaine dernière; **~ more talented person** quelqu'un de plus doué; **there must be ~ solution** il doit bien y avoir une solution (quelconque).
(c) (*contrasted with others*) **~ children like school** certains enfants aiment l'école, il y a des enfants qui aiment l'école; **~ few people** quelques rares personnes; **~ people say that ...** certaines personnes disent que ..., il y a des gens qui disent que ..., on dit que ...; **~ people like spinach, others don't** certaines personnes *or* certains aiment les épinards et d'autres non, il y a des gens qui aiment les épinards et d'autres non; **~ people just don't care** il y a des gens qui ne s'en font pas *or* qui se fichent* de tout; **~ butter is salty** certains beurres sont salés, certaines sortes de beurre sont salées; **in ~ ways, he's right** dans un (certain) sens, il a raison; **in ~ way or (an)other** d'une façon ou d'une autre.
(d) (*a considerable amount of*) pas mal de*, certain, quelque. **it took ~ courage to refuse** il a fallu un certain courage *or* pas mal de* courage pour refuser; **he spoke at ~ length** il a parlé assez longuement *or* pas mal de* temps *or* un certain temps; **~ distance away** à quelque distance; **I haven't seen him for ~ years** cela fait quelques *or* plusieurs années que je ne l'ai pas vu; *V* **time.**
(e) (*emphatic: a little*) un peu. **we still have SOME money left** il nous reste quand même un peu d'argent; **the book was SOME help but not much** le livre m'a aidé un peu mais pas beaucoup; **that's SOME consolation!** c'est quand même une petite consolation!
(f) (*: *intensive*) **that's ~ fish!** quel poisson!, c'est un fameux* poisson!, voilà ce qu'on appelle un poisson!; **she's ~ girl!** c'est une fille formidable!* *or* sensass!*; **that was ~ film!** quel film!, c'était un film formidable.
(g) (**iro*) **you're ~ help!** tu parles* d'une aide!, que tu m'aides ou non c'est du pareil au même; **I'm trying to help! — ~ help!** j'essaie de t'aider! — tu parles!* *or* tu appelles ça aider?; **~ garage that is!** vous parlez* d'un garage!
2 *pron* **(a)** (*a certain number*) quelques-un(e)s *m(f)pl*, certain(e)s *m(f)pl.* **~ went this way and others went that** il y en a qui sont partis par ici et d'autres par là; **~ (of them) have been sold** certains (d'entre eux) ont été vendus, on en a vendu quelques-uns *or* un certain nombre; **I've still got ~ of them** j'en ai encore quelques-uns *or* plusieurs; **~ of them were late** certains d'entre eux *or* quelques-uns d'entre eux étaient en retard; **~ of us knew him** quelques-uns d'entre nous le connaissaient; **~ of my friends** certains *or* quelques-uns de mes amis; **I've got ~** j'en ai (quelques-uns *or* certains *or* plusieurs).
(b) (*a certain amount*) **I've got ~** j'en ai; **have ~!** prenez-en!, servez-vous!; **have ~ more** reprenez-en, resservez-vous; **give me ~!** donnez-m'en!; **if you find ~ tell me** si vous en trouvez dites-le-moi; **have ~ of this cake** prenez un peu de (ce) gâteau, prenez un morceau de (ce) gâteau; **~ (of it) has been eaten** on en a mangé (un morceau *or* une partie); **~ of this work is good** une partie de ce travail est bonne, ce travail est bon en partie; **I liked ~ of what you said in that speech** j'ai aimé certaines parties de votre discours *or* certaines choses dans votre discours; **~ of what you say is true** il y a du vrai dans ce que vous dites; **and then ~!*** et plus (encore)!, et pas qu'un peu!*; *V* **time.**
3 *adv* **(a)** (*about*) quelque, environ. **there were ~ twenty**

houses il y avait quelque *or* environ vingt maisons, il y avait une vingtaine de maisons.

(b) (*) *sleep, speak, wait* (*a bit*) un peu; (*a lot*) beaucoup. **you'll have to run ~ to catch him** tu vas vraiment devoir courir pour le rattraper, il va falloir que tu fonces* (*subj*) pour le rattraper; **Edinburgh-London in 30 minutes, that's going ~!** Édimbourg-Londres en 30 minutes, (il) faut le faire!‡

...some [səm] *n ending in cpds* groupe *m* de .... **threesome** groupe de trois personnes; **we went in a threesome** nous y sommes allés à trois; *V* **four** *etc.*

somebody [ˈsʌmbədɪ] *pron* **(a)** (*some unspecified person*) quelqu'un. **there is ~ at the door** il y a quelqu'un à la porte; **there is ~ knocking at the door** on frappe à la porte; **~ else** quelqu'un d'autre; **he was talking to ~ tall and dark** il parlait à quelqu'un de grand aux cheveux sombres; **we need ~ really strong to do that** il nous faut quelqu'un de vraiment fort *or* quelqu'un qui soit vraiment fort pour faire cela; **ask ~ French** demande à un Français (quelconque); **they've got ~ French staying with them** ils ont un Français *or* quelqu'un de français chez eux en ce moment; **~ from the audience** quelqu'un dans l'auditoire *or* l'assemblée; **~ or other** quelqu'un, je ne sais qui; **Mr S~-or-other** Monsieur Chose *or* Machin*; **you must have seen** SOMEBODY! tu as bien dû voir quelqu'un!

(b) (*important person*) personnage important. **she thinks she's ~** elle se prend pour quelqu'un, elle se croit quelqu'un; **they think they are ~ or somebodies** ils se prennent pour *or* ils se croient des personnages importants.

somehow [ˈsʌmhaʊ] *adv* **(a)** (*in some way*) d'une façon ou d'une autre, d'une manière ou d'une autre. **it must be done ~ (or other)** il faut que ce soit fait d'une façon *or* manière ou d'une autre; **he managed it ~** il y est arrivé tant bien que mal; **we'll manage ~** on se débrouillera*; **we saved him ~ or other** nous l'avons sauvé je ne sais comment; **~ or other we must find £100** d'une façon ou d'une autre nous devons nous procurer 100 livres, nous devons nous débrouiller* pour trouver 100 livres.

(b) (*for some reason*) pour une raison ou pour une autre. **~ he's never succeeded** pour une raison ou pour une autre *or* pour une raison quelconque *or* je ne sais pas pourquoi il n'a jamais réussi; **it seems odd ~** je ne sais pas pourquoi mais ça semble bizarre.

someone [ˈsʌmwʌn] *pron* = **somebody.**

someplace [ˈsʌmpleɪs] *adv* (*US*) = **somewhere a.**

somersault [ˈsʌməsɔːlt] **1** *n* culbute *f* (*also accidental*); (*Gymnastics etc: in air*) saut périlleux; (*by car*) tonneau *m*. **to turn a ~** faire la culbute *or* un saut périlleux *or* un tonneau. **2** *vi* [*person*] faire la culbute, faire un *or* des saut(s) périlleux; [*car*] faire un *or* plusieurs tonneau(x).

something [ˈsʌmθɪŋ] **1** *pron* **(a)** quelque chose *m*. **~ moved over there** il y a quelque chose qui a bougé là-bas; **~ must have happened to him** il a dû lui arriver quelque chose; **~ unusual** quelque chose d'inhabituel; **there must be ~ wrong** il doit y avoir quelque chose qui ne va pas; **did you say ~?** pardon?, comment?, vous dites?; **I want ~ to read** je veux quelque chose à lire; **I need ~ to eat** j'ai besoin de manger quelque chose; **would you like ~ to drink?** voulez-vous boire quelque chose?; **give him ~ to drink** donnez-lui (quelque chose) à boire; **he has ~ to live for at last** il a enfin une raison de vivre; **I have ~ else to do** j'ai quelque chose d'autre à faire, j'ai autre chose à faire; **I'll have to tell him ~ or other** il faudra que je lui dise quelque chose *or* que je trouve (*subj*) quelque chose à lui dire; **he whispered ~ or other in her ear** il lui chuchota quelque chose *or* on ne sait quoi à l'oreille; **~ of the kind** quelque chose dans ce genre-là; **there's ~ about her or she's got ~ about her I don't like** il y a chez elle *or* en elle quelque chose que je n'aime pas; **there's ~ in what you say** il y a du vrai dans ce que vous dites; **here's ~ for your trouble** voici pour votre peine; **give him ~ for himself** donnez-lui la pièce* *or* un petit quelque chose; **you've got ~ there!*** là tu n'as pas tort!, c'est vrai ce que tu dis là!; **that really is ~!*** c'est pas rien!*, ça se pose là!*; **she has a certain ~*** elle a un petit quelque chose, elle a un certain je ne sais quoi; **that certain ~* which makes all the difference** ce petit je ne sais quoi qui fait toute la différence; **he's called Paul ~** il s'appelle Paul Chose *or* Paul quelque chose; **that has ~ to do with accountancy** ça a quelque chose à voir avec la comptabilité; **he is ~ to do with Brown and Co.** il a quelque chose à voir avec Brown et Cie.; **he is ~ (or other) in aviation** il est quelque chose dans l'aéronautique; **I hope to see ~ of you** j'espère vous voir un peu; **it is really ~ to find good coffee nowadays** ça n'est pas rien* de trouver du bon café aujourd'hui; **he scored 300 points, and that's ~!** il a marqué 300 points et ça c'est quelque chose!* *or* et ça n'est pas rien!*; **that's always ~** c'est toujours quelque chose, c'est toujours ça, c'est mieux que rien; **he thinks himself ~*** il se croit quelque chose, il se prend pour quelqu'un.

(b) or ~ ou quelque chose dans ce genre-là, ou quelque chose comme ça; **he's got flu or ~** il a la grippe ou quelque chose comme ça *or* dans ce genre-là; **do you think you're my boss or ~?** tu te prends pour mon patron ou quoi?*; **he fell off a wall or ~** il est tombé d'un mur ou quelque chose dans ce genre-là*, je crois qu'il est tombé d'un mur.

(c) he is ~ of a miser il est quelque peu *or* plutôt avare; **he is ~ of a pianist** il est assez bon pianiste, il joue assez bien du piano, il est assez doué pour le piano.

2 *adv* **(a) he left ~ over £5,000** il a laissé plus de 5.000 livres, il a laissé dans les 5.000 livres et plus; **~ under £10** un peu moins de 10 livres; **he won ~ like 10,000 francs** il a gagné quelque chose comme 10.000 F, il a gagné dans les 10.000 F; **it's ~ like 10 o'clock** il est 10 heures environ, il est quelque chose comme 10 heures; **it weighs ~ around 5 kilos** ça pèse 5 kilos environ, ça pèse dans les 5 kilos, ça fait quelque chose comme 5 kilos; **there were ~ like 80 people there** 80 personnes environ étaient présentes, il y avait quelque chose comme 80 personnes; **he talks ~ like his father** il parle un peu comme son père; **now that's ~ like a claret!** voilà ce que j'appelle un bordeaux!, ça au moins c'est du bordeaux!; **now that's ~ like it!*** ça au moins c'est bien! *or* c'est vraiment pas mal!*

(b) it was ~ dreadful! c'était vraiment épouvantable!; **the weather was ~ shocking!** comme mauvais temps ça se posait là!*; **the dog was howling ~ awful** le chien hurlait que c'en était abominable*, le chien hurlait fallait voir comme‡.

sometime [ˈsʌmtaɪm] **1** *adv* **(a)** (*in past*) **~ last month** le mois dernier, au cours du mois dernier; **~ last May** au (cours du) mois de mai dernier; **it was ~ last winter** c'était durant *or* pendant *or* au cours de l'hiver dernier (je ne sais plus exactement quand); **it was ~ before 1950** c'était avant 1950 (je ne sais pas *or* plus exactement quand).

(b) (*in future*) un de ces jours, un jour ou l'autre. **~ soon** bientôt, avant peu; **~ before January** d'ici janvier; **~ next year** (dans le courant de) l'année prochaine; **~ after my birthday** après mon anniversaire; **~ or (an)other it will have to be done** il faudra (bien) le faire à un moment donné *or* tôt ou tard *or* un jour ou l'autre.

2 *adj* (*former*) ancien.

sometimes [ˈsʌmtaɪmz] *adv* **(a)** quelquefois, parfois, de temps en temps. **(b) ~ happy ~ sad** tantôt gai tantôt triste; **~ he agrees and ~ not** tantôt il est d'accord et tantôt non.

somewhat [ˈsʌmwɒt] *adv* quelque peu, un peu, assez.

somewhere [ˈsʌmweəʳ] *adv* **(a)** (*in space*) quelque part. **~ else** autre part, ailleurs; **he's ~ about** il est quelque part par ici, il n'est pas loin; **~ about or around here** (quelque part) par ici, pas loin d'ici; **~ near Paris** (quelque part) pas bien loin de Paris; **~ or other** je ne sais où, quelque part; **~ (or other) in France** quelque part en France; **he's in the garden or ~** il est dans le jardin ou quelque part.

(b) (*approximately*) environ. **~ about 10 o'clock** vers 10 heures, à 10 heures environ *or* à peu près; **she's ~ about fifty** elle a environ cinquante ans, elle a une cinquantaine d'années, elle a dans les cinquante ans; **he paid ~ about £12** il a payé environ 12 livres *or* dans les 12 livres.

somnambulism [sɒmˈnæmbjʊlɪzəm] *n* somnambulisme *m*.

somnambulist [sɒmˈnæmbjʊlɪst] *n* somnambule *mf*.

somniferous [sɒmˈnɪfərəs] *adj* somnifère, soporifique.

somnolence [ˈsɒmnələns] *n* somnolence *f*.

somnolent [ˈsɒmnələnt] *adj* somnolent.

son [sʌn] **1** *n* fils *m*. (*Rel*) **S~ of God/Man** Fils de Dieu/de l'Homme; (*liter*) **the ~s of men** les hommes *mpl*; **he is his father's ~** (*in looks*) c'est tout le portrait de son père; (*in character*) c'est bien le fils de son père; **I've got 3 ~s** j'ai 3 fils *or* 3 garçons; **every mother's ~ of them** tous tant qu'ils sont (*or* étaient *etc*); **come here ~!*** viens ici mon garçon! *or* mon gars!* *or* fiston!*; *V* **father** *etc.*

2 *cpd*: **son-in-law** gendre *m*, beau-fils *m*; **son-of-a-bitch**‡ salaud‡ *m*, fils *m* de garce‡; **son-of-a-gun**‡ (espèce *f* de) vieille fripouille *or* vieux coquin.

sonata [səˈnɑːtə] *n* sonate *f*.

sonatina [ˌsɒnəˈtiːnə] *n* sonatine *f*.

sonde [sɒnd] *n* (*Met, Space*) sonde *f*.

sone [səʊn] *n* sone *f*.

song [sɒŋ] **1** *n* (*ditty, ballad, folksong etc*) chanson *f*; (*more formal*) chant *m*; [*birds*] chant, ramage *m*. **festival of French ~** festival *m* de chant français *or* de la chanson française; **to burst into ~** se mettre à chanter (une chanson *or* un air), entonner une chanson *or* un air; **give us a ~** chante-nous quelque chose; **~ without words** romance *f* sans paroles; **the S~ of S~s, the S~ of Solomon** le cantique des cantiques; (*fig*) **it was going for a ~** c'était à vendre pour presque rien *or* pour une bouchée de pain (*fig*); **what a ~ and dance* there was!** ça a fait une de ces histoires!*; **there's no need to make a ~ and dance* about it** il n'y a pas de quoi en faire toute une histoire* *or* tout un plat*; *V* **march**[1], **sing** *etc.*

2 *cpd*: **songbird** oiseau chanteur; **songbook** recueil *m* de chansons; **song cycle** cycle *m* de chansons; **song hit** chanson *f* à succès, tube* *m*; **song thrush** grive musicienne; **song writer** (*words*) parolier *m*, -ière *f*, auteur *m* de chansons; (*music*) compositeur *m*, -trice *f* de chansons; (*both*) auteur-compositeur *m*.

songster [ˈsɒŋstəʳ] *n* (*singer*) chanteur *m*; (*bird*) oiseau chanteur.

songstress [ˈsɒŋstrɪs] *n* chanteuse *f*.

sonic [ˈsɒnɪk] **1** *adj speed* sonique. **~ barrier** mur *m* du son, barrière *f* sonique; **~ boom** détonation *f* supersonique, bang *m* (super)sonique; **~ depth-finder** sonde *f* à ultra-sons; **~ mine** mine *f* acoustique.

2 *n* (*U*) **~s** l'acoustique *f* (*dans le domaine transsonique*).

sonnet [ˈsɒnɪt] *n* sonnet *m*.

sonny* [ˈsʌnɪ] *n* mon (petit) gars*, fiston* *m*. **~ boy, ~ Jim** mon gars*, fiston*.

sonority [səˈnɒrɪtɪ] *n* sonorité *f*.

sonorous [ˈsɒnərəs] *adj* sonore.

sonorousness [ˈsɒnərəsnɪs] *n* sonorité *f*.

soon [suːn] *adv* **(a)** (*shortly, before long*) bientôt, vite. **we shall ~ be in Paris** nous serons bientôt à Paris, nous serons à Paris dans peu de temps *or* sous peu; **you would ~ get lost** vous seriez vite perdu; **he ~ changed his mind** il a vite changé d'avis, il n'a pas mis longtemps *or* il n'a pas tardé à changer d'avis; **I'll ~ finish that!** j'aurai bientôt terminé!, j'aurai vite *or* tôt fait!; **(I'll) see you ~!** à bientôt!; **very ~** très vite, très bientôt*; **quite ~** dans assez peu de temps, assez vite; **~ afterwards** peu après; **quite ~ afterwards** assez peu de temps après; **all too ~ it was over** ce ne fut que trop vite fini.

(b) (*early*) tôt. **why have you come so ~?** pourquoi êtes-vous venu si tôt?; **I expected you much ~er than this** je vous attendais bien plus tôt (que cela) *or* bien avant; **I couldn't get here any ~er** je n'ai pas pu arriver plus tôt; **how ~ can you get here?** dans combien de temps au plus tôt peux-tu être ici?, quel jour (*or* à quelle heure *etc*) peux-tu venir au plus tôt?; **how ~ will it be ready?** dans combien de temps *or* quand est-ce que ce sera prêt?; **Friday is too ~** vendredi c'est trop tôt; **we were none too ~** il était temps que nous arrivions (*subj*), nous sommes arrivés juste à temps; **must you leave so ~?** faut-il que vous partiez (*subj*) déjà? *or* si tôt?, quel dommage que vous deviez (*subj*) partir déjà! *or* si tôt!; **so ~?** déjà?; **on Friday at the ~est** vendredi au plus tôt, pas avant vendredi; **in 5 years or at his death, whichever is the ~er** dans 5 ans ou à sa mort, s'il meurt avant 5 ans *or* si celle-ci survient avant.

(c) (*in phrases*) **as ~ as possible** dès que possible, aussitôt que possible; **I'll do it as ~ as I can** je le ferai dès que je le pourrai *or* aussitôt que je le pourrai *or* aussitôt que possible; **let me know as ~ as you've finished** prévenez-moi dès que *or* aussitôt que vous aurez fini; **as ~ as he spoke to her he knew ...** aussitôt qu'il lui a parlé il a su ...; **as ~ as 7 o'clock** dès 7 heures; **the ~er we get started the ~er we'll be done** plus tôt nous commencerons plus tôt nous finirons, plus tôt commencé plus tôt fini; **the ~er the better!** le plus tôt sera le mieux!; (*iro*) il serait grand temps!, ça ne serait pas trop tôt!; **~er or later** tôt ou tard; **no ~er had he finished than his brother arrived** à peine avait-il fini que son frère est arrivé; **no ~er said than done!** aussitôt dit aussitôt fait!; **he could (just) as ~ fly to the moon as pass that exam** il a autant de chances de réussir cet examen que d'aller sur la lune.

(d) (*expressing preference*) **I'd as ~/I'd ~er you didn't tell him** j'aimerais autant/je préférerais que vous ne le lui disiez (*subj*) pas; **I would ~er stay here than go** je préférerais rester ici (plutôt) que d'y aller; **I would just as ~ stay here with you** j'aimerais tout autant rester ici avec vous, cela me ferait tout autant plaisir de rester ici avec vous; **he would as ~ die as betray his friends** il préférerait mourir plutôt que de trahir ses amis; **will you go? — I'd ~er not!** *or* **I'd as ~ not!** est-ce que tu iras? — je n'y tiens pas *or* je préférerais pas*; **I'd ~er die!** plutôt mourir!; **what would you ~er do?** qu'est-ce que vous aimeriez mieux (faire)? *or* vous préféreriez (faire)?; **~er than have to speak to her, he left** plutôt que d'avoir à lui parler il est parti; **she'd marry him as ~ as not** elle l'épouserait volontiers, elle aimerait bien l'épouser; **~er you than me!*** je n'aimerais pas être à ta place, je te souhaite bien du plaisir!* (*iro*).

soot [sʊt] *n* (*U*) suie *f*. **soot up** (*Aut*) **1** *vi* [*sparking plugs*] s'encrasser. **2** *vt sep* encrasser.

sooth [suːθ] **1** *n* (††) vérité *f*. **in ~** en vérité. **2** *cpd*: **soothsayer** devin *m*, devineresse *f*; **soothsaying** divination *f*.

soothe [suːð] *vt person* calmer, apaiser; *nerves, mind, pain* calmer; *anger, anxieties* apaiser; *sb's vanity* flatter. **to ~ sb's fears** apaiser les craintes de qn, tranquilliser qn.

soothing [ˈsuːðɪŋ] *adj medicine, ointment* lénitif; *tone, voice, words* apaisant. **I find her presence ~** sa présence me rassure *or* me tranquillise; **I find a hot drink at night ~** une boisson chaude le soir m'aide à me détendre.

soothingly [ˈsuːðɪŋlɪ] *adv* d'une manière apaisante; *say, whisper* d'un ton apaisant.

sooty [ˈsʊtɪ] *adj surface, hands* couvert *or* noir de suie; *mixture, dust* fuligineux. **~ black** charbonneux.

sop [sɒp] *n* **(a)** (*Culin*) pain trempé (*dans du lait, du jus de viande etc*), mouillette *f*. **he can eat only ~s** il ne peut rien manger de trop solide, il doit se nourrir d'aliments semi-liquides; (*fig*) **it's just a ~ to Cerberus** c'est simplement pour le (*or* les *etc*) ramener à de meilleures dispositions *or* pour l'amadouer (*or* les *etc* amadouer); **he gave the guard £10 as a ~** il a donné 10 livres au gardien pour s'acheter ses bons services *or* pour lui graisser la patte*; **it's a ~ to my conscience** c'est pour faire taire ma conscience; **as a ~ to his pride, I agreed** j'ai accepté pour flatter son amour-propre; **he only said that as a ~ to the unions** il a dit cela uniquement pour amadouer les syndicats.

(b) (*: *sissy*) (*man*) poule mouillée, lavette* *f*; (*woman*) femme *f* très fleur bleue.

sop up *vt sep spilt liquid* [*sponge, rag*] absorber; [*person*] éponger (*with* avec). **he sopped up the gravy with some bread** il a saucé son assiette avec un morceau de pain.

Sophia [səʊˈfaɪə] *n* Sophie *f*.

sophism [ˈsɒfɪzəm] *n* = **sophistry**.

sophist [ˈsɒfɪst] *n* sophiste *mf*. (*Hist Philos*) **S~s** sophistes *mpl*.

sophistical [səˈfɪstɪkəl] *adj* sophistique, captieux.

sophisticated [səˈfɪstɪkeɪtɪd] *adj person* (*in taste, life style*) raffiné, blasé (*pej*); (*in appearance*) élégant, sophistiqué (*slightly pej*); *mind, style, tastes* raffiné, recherché; *clothes, room* d'une élégance raffinée *or* étudiée, plein de recherche; *play, film, book* plein de complexité, avancé; *song, revue* plein de recherche; *machinery, machine, method* hautement perfectionné, sophistiqué; *philosophy* développé, avancé; *discussion* subtil (*f* subtile); *wine* élégant. **he's very ~** il est très raffiné, il a beaucoup de savoir-vivre; **he's not very ~** il est très simple; **the author's ~ approach to this problem** la façon très mûre dont l'auteur aborde ce problème; **a ~ little black dress** une petite robe noire toute simple *or* d'un style très dépouillé.

sophistication [səˌfɪstɪˈkeɪʃən] *n* (*V* **sophisticated**) raffinement *m*, caractère blasé; élégance *f*, sophistication *f*; recherche *f*; complexité *f*, caractère avancé; subtilité *f*; [*machine etc*] degré *m* de perfectionnement, complexité, sophistication.

sophistry [ˈsɒfɪstrɪ] *n* (*U*) sophistique *f*; (*instance of this*) sophisme *m*. (*Hist Philos*) **S~** sophistique *f*.

Sophocles [ˈsɒfəkliːz] *n* Sophocle *m*.

sophomore [ˈsɒfəmɔːʳ] *n* (*US*) étudiant(e) *m(f)* de seconde année.

soporific [ˌsɒpəˈrɪfɪk] **1** *adj* soporifique. **2** *n* somnifère *m*.

sopping [ˈsɒpɪŋ] *adj* (*also* **~ wet**) *clothes* tout trempé, à tordre; *person* trempé (jusqu'aux os).

soppy* [ˈsɒpɪ] *adj* (*Brit*) **(a)** (*sentimental*) *person* sentimental, fleur bleue *inv*; *film, book, scene* sentimental, à l'eau de rose.

(b) (*unmanly; without stamina*) mollasson, qui manque de nerf. **he's ~** c'est une mauviette *or* un mollasson, il manque de nerf.

(c) (*silly*) *person* bébête*; *action* bête, idiot.

soprano [səˈprɑːnəʊ] **1** *n,pl* **~s** (*singer*) soprano *mf*; (*voice, part*) soprano *m*; *V* **boy**. **2** *adj voice* de soprano.

sorb [sɔːb] *n* (*tree*) sorbier *m*; (*fruit*) sorbe *f*.

sorbet [ˈsɔːbɪt] *n* = **sherbet**.

sorbic [ˈsɔːbɪk] *adj*: **~ acid** acide *m* sorbique.

sorbitol [ˈsɔːbɪtɒl] *n* sorbitol *m*.

sorcerer [ˈsɔːsərəʳ] *n* sorcier *m*. **the ~'s apprentice** l'apprenti-sorcier *m*.

sorceress [ˈsɔːsəres] *n* sorcière *f*.

sorcery [ˈsɔːsərɪ] *n* sorcellerie *f*.

sordid [ˈsɔːdɪd] *adj conditions, surroundings* sordide, misérable, repoussant; (*fig*) *behaviour, motive, method* sordide, honteux, abject; *agreement, deal* honteux, infâme; *crime, greed, gains* sordide; *film, book* sale, dégoûtant, ignoble. **a ~ little room** une petite pièce sordide *or* d'une saleté repoussante *or* qui est un véritable taudis; **in ~ poverty** dans la misère la plus noire; **it's a pretty ~ business** c'est une affaire assez sordide *or* ignoble; **I found the whole thing quite ~** je suis écœuré par cette affaire; **all the ~ details** tous les détails sordides *or* répugnants; **they had a ~ little affair** ils ont eu ensemble une misérable petite aventure.

sordidness [ˈsɔːdɪdnɪs] *n* [*conditions, surroundings*] aspect *m* sordide, misère *f*, saleté repoussante; (*fig*) [*behaviour, motive, method*] bassesse *f*; [*agreement, deal*] caractère honteux; [*crime, greed, gains*] caractère sordide; [*film, book*] saleté.

sore [sɔːʳ] **1** *adj* **(a)** (*painful*) douloureux, endolori, sensible; (*inflamed*) irrité, enflammé. **his ~ leg** sa jambe douloureuse *or* endolorie *or* qui lui fait (*or* faisait*etc*) mal; **this spot is very ~** cet endroit est très sensible *or* douloureux; **ouch! that's ~!** aïe! ça me fait mal!, aïe! tu me fais mal!; **where is it ~?** où est-ce que vous avez mal?; **tell me if it's ~** dites-moi si cela vous fait mal; **I'm ~ all over** j'ai mal partout; **I have a ~ finger/foot** j'ai mal au doigt/au pied; **I have a ~ head** j'ai mal à la tête, j'ai un mal de tête; (*fig*) **it's a ~ point** c'est un point délicat; (*liter*) **to be ~ at heart** être affligé *or* désolé; *V* **bear**[2], **sight, throat** *etc*.

(b) (*: *offended*) contrarié, vexé (*about sth* par qch), fâché (*with sb* contre qn), en rogne* (*about sth* à cause de, *with sb* contre qn). **he was feeling very ~ about it** il en était vraiment ulcéré, ça l'a vraiment mis en rogne*; **to get ~** râler*, être en rogne* (*about sth* à cause de qch, *with sb* contre qn), prendre la mouche; **don't get ~!** ne te vexe pas!, ne te fâche pas!, ne râle* pas!; **what are you so ~ about?** pourquoi es-tu si fâché?, qu'est-ce que tu as à râler?*

(c) († *or liter*) **to be in ~ need of** avoir grandement besoin de; **a ~ temptation** une tentation difficile à vaincre.

2 *cpd*: (*US*) **sorehead*** râleur* *m*, -euse* *f*, rouspéteur* *m*, -euse* *f*.

3 *adv* († *or liter*) cruellement, péniblement. **~ distressed** cruellement affligé; **to be ~ afraid** avoir grand-peur.

4 *n* (*Med*) plaie *f*. (*fig*) **to open up old ~s** rouvrir *or* raviver d'anciennes blessures (*fig*); *V* **running**.

sorely [ˈsɔːlɪ] *adv wounded* gravement, grièvement; *missed, regretted* amèrement. **it is ~ needed** on en a grandement besoin; **he/his patience was ~ tried** il/sa patience a été soumis(e) à rude *or* cruelle épreuve; **~ tempted** fortement *or* très tenté.

soreness [ˈsɔːnɪs] *n* (*painfulness*) endolorissement *m*; (* *fig*) (*irritation*) contrariété *f*, irritation *f*; (*bitterness*) amertume *f*; (*anger*) colère *f*, rogne* *f*.

sorghum [ˈsɔːgəm] *n* sorgho *m*.

soroptimist [sɒˈrɒptɪmɪst] *n membre m d'une association internationale pour les femmes dans les professions libérales*.

sorority [səˈrɒrɪtɪ] *n* (*US Univ*) club féminin, club d'étudiantes.

sorrel [ˈsɒrəl] **1** *n* **(a)** (*Bot*) oseille *f*. **(b)** (*horse*) alezan clair *m*; (*colour*) roux *m*, brun rouge *m*. **2** *adj horse* alezan clair *inv*.

sorrow [ˈsɒrəʊ] **1** *n* peine *f*, chagrin *m*, tristesse *f*; (*stronger*) douleur *f*. **his ~ at the loss of his son** la peine *or* le chagrin *or* la douleur qu'il a éprouvé(e) à la mort de son fils; **to my (great) ~** à mon grand chagrin, à ma grande tristesse *or* douleur; **this was a great ~ to me** j'en ai eu beaucoup de peine *or* de chagrin *or* de tristesse; **he was a great ~ to her** il lui a causé beaucoup de peine *or* de chagrin; **more in ~ than in anger** avec plus de peine *or* de tristesse que de colère; **the ~s of their race** les afflictions *fpl or* les peines qui pèsent sur leur race; (*Rel*) **the Man of S~s** l'Homme de douleur; *V* **drown**.

2 *vi*: **to ~ over** *sb's death, loss* pleurer; *news* déplorer, se lamenter de; **she sat ~ing by the fire** elle était assise au coin du feu toute à son chagrin.

sorrowful [ˈsɒrəʊfʊl] *adj person* triste, (*stronger*) affligé; *expression, look, smile, face* triste, attristé, (*stronger*) désolé; *news* pénible, triste, affligeant; *music* triste, mélancolique.

sorrowfully [ˈsɒrəʊflɪ] *adv* tristement, avec chagrin, d'un air triste *or* désolé; *say* d'un ton triste *or* désolé.

sorrowing [ˈsɒrəʊɪŋ] *adj* affligé.

sorry [ˈsɒrɪ] *adj* **(a)** (*regretful*) désolé. **I was ~ to hear of your accident** j'étais désolé *or* très peiné *or* navré d'apprendre que vous aviez eu un accident; **I am ~ I cannot come** je regrette *or* je suis désolé de ne (pas) pouvoir venir; **I am ~ she cannot come** je regrette *or* je suis désolé qu'elle ne puisse (pas) venir; **I am ~ to have to tell you that ...** je regrette d'avoir à vous dire que ...; (*frm*) **we are ~ to inform you ...** nous avons le regret de vous informer ...; **he didn't pass, I'm ~ to say** il a échoué hélas *or* malheureusement; **(I am) ~ I am late, I'm ~ to be late** excusez-moi *or* je suis désolé d'être en retard; **say you're ~!** dis *or* demande pardon!; **~!, ~ about that!*** pardon!, excusez-moi!, je suis désolé!; **I'm very *or* terribly ~** je suis vraiment désolé *or* navré; **awfully ~!, so ~!** oh pardon!, excusez-moi!, je suis vraiment désolé!; **will you go? — I'm ~ I can't** est-ce que tu vas y aller? — impossible hélas *or* (je suis) désolé mais je ne peux pas; **can you do it? — no, ~** est-ce que tu peux le faire? — non, désolé *or* désolé, je ne peux pas *or* malheureusement pas; **I am ~ to disturb you** je suis désolé de vous déranger, excusez-moi de vous déranger; **I am *or* feel ~ about all the noise yesterday** je regrette beaucoup qu'il y ait eu tellement de bruit hier; **~ about that vase!** excusez-moi pour ce vase!; **you'll be ~ for this!** vous le regretterez!, vous vous en repentirez!

(b) (*pitying*) **to be *or* feel ~ for sb** plaindre qn; **I feel so ~ for her since her husband died** elle me fait pitié depuis la mort de son mari; **I'm ~ for you but you should have known better** je suis désolé pour vous *or* je vous plains mais vous auriez dû être plus raisonnable; (*iro*) **if he can't do better than that then I'm ~ for him** s'il ne peut pas faire mieux, je regrette pour lui *or* je le plains; **there's no need to feel *or* be ~ for him** il est inutile de le plaindre, il n'est pas à plaindre; **to be *or* feel ~ for o.s.** se plaindre (de son sort), s'apitoyer sur soi-même *or* sur son propre sort; **he looked very ~ for himself** il faisait piteuse mine.

(c) (*woeful*) *condition* triste, déplorable, lamentable; *excuse* piètre, mauvais, lamentable. **to be in a ~ plight** être dans une triste situation, être en fâcheuse posture; **to be in a ~ state** être dans un triste état, être en piteux état; **he was a ~ figure** il faisait triste *or* piteuse figure; **a ~ sight** un triste spectacle, un spectacle désolant *or* affligeant; **it was a ~ tale of mismanagement and inefficiency** c'était une lamentable *or* déplorable histoire de mauvaise gestion et d'inefficacité.

sort [sɔːt] **1** *n* **(a)** (*class, variety, kind, type*) genre *m*, espèce *f*, sorte *f*; (*make*) *[car, machine, coffee etc]* marque *f*. **this ~ of book** ce genre de *or* cette espèce de *or* cette sorte de livre; **books of all ~s** des livres de tous genres *or* de toutes espèces *or* de toutes sortes; **this ~ of thing(s)** ce genre de chose(s); **what ~ of flour do you want? — the ~ you gave me last time** quelle sorte *or* quelle espèce *or* quel genre de farine voulez-vous? — la même que vous m'avez donnée (*or* le même que vous m'avez donné) la dernière fois; **what ~ do you want?** vous en (*or* le *or* la *etc*) voulez de quelle sorte?; **what ~ of car is it?** quelle marque de voiture est-ce?; **what ~ of man is he?** quel genre *or* type d'homme est-ce?; **what ~ of dog is he?** qu'est-ce que c'est comme (race de) chien?; **he is not the ~ of man to refuse** ce n'est pas le genre d'homme à refuser, il n'est pas homme à refuser; **he's not that ~ of person** ce n'est pas son genre; **I'm not that ~ of girl!*** je ne suis pas celle que vous croyez!, ce n'est pas mon genre!, mais pour qui me prenez-vous?; **that's the ~ of person I am** c'est comme ça que je suis (fait); **what ~ of people does he think we are?** (mais enfin) pour qui nous prend-il?; **what ~ of a fool does he take me for?** (non mais*) il me prend pour un imbécile!; **what ~ of behaviour is this?** qu'est-ce que c'est que cette façon de se conduire?; **what ~ of an answer do you call that?** vous appelez ça une réponse?; **classical music is the ~ she likes most** c'est la musique classique qu'elle préfère; **and all that ~ of thing** et autres choses du même genre, et tout ça*; **you know the ~ of thing I mean** vous voyez (à peu près) ce que je veux dire; **I don't like that ~ of talk/behaviour** je n'aime pas ce genre de conversation/de conduite; **he's the ~ that will cheat** il est du genre à tricher; **I know his ~!** je connais les gens de son genre *or* espèce; **your ~* never did any good** les gens de votre genre *or* espèce ne font rien de bien; **they're not our ~*** ce ne sont pas des gens comme nous; **it's my ~* of film** c'est le genre de film que j'aime *or* qui me plaît.

(b) (*in phrases*) **something of the ~** quelque chose de ce genre(-là) *or* d'approchant; **this is wrong — nothing of the ~!** c'est faux — pas le moins du monde!; **I shall do nothing of the ~!** je n'en ferai rien!, certainement pas!; **I will have nothing of the ~!** je ne tolérerai pas cela!; (*pej*) **it was beef of a ~** c'était quelque chose qui pouvait passer pour du bœuf; **he is a painter of ~s** c'est un peintre si l'on peut dire; **after a ~, in some ~** dans une certaine mesure, en quelque sorte, jusqu'à un certain point; **to be out of ~s** ne pas être dans son assiette; (*Prov*) **it takes all ~s (to make a world)** il faut de tout pour faire un monde (*Prov*); (*fig*) **a good ~*** un brave garçon, un brave type*; une brave fille.

(c) a ~ of une sorte *or* espèce de, un genre de; **there was a ~ of box in the middle of the room** il y avait une sorte *or* une espèce *or* un genre de boîte au milieu de la pièce, il y avait quelque chose qui ressemblait à une boîte au milieu de la pièce; **there was a ~ of tinkling sound** il y avait une sorte *or* une espèce de bruit de grelot, on entendait quelque chose qui ressemblait à un bruit de grelot; **in a ~ of way* I'm sorry** d'une certaine façon je le regrette; **I had a ~ of fear that ..., I was ~ of* frightened that ...** j'avais comme peur que ... + ne + *subj*; **I ~ of* thought that he would come** j'avais un peu l'idée qu'il viendrait; **he was ~ of* worried-looking** il avait un peu l'air inquiet, il avait l'air comme qui dirait* inquiet; **it's ~ of* blue** c'est plutôt bleu; **aren't you pleased? — ~ of!*** tu n'es pas content? — assez! *or* ben si!:

2 *cpd*: (*Post*) **sorting office** bureau *m* de tri; **to have a sort-out*** faire du rangement; **I've had a sort-out* of all these old newspapers** j'ai trié tous ces vieux journaux.

3 *vt* **(a)** (*also* **~ out**) (*classify*) *documents, stamps* classer; (*select those to keep*) *documents, clothes, apples* trier, faire le tri de; (*Post etc*) *letters, parcels etc* trier; (*separate*) séparer (*from* de). **he spent the morning ~ing his stamp collection** il a passé la matinée à classer *or* trier les timbres de sa collection; **to ~ things (out) into sizes *or* according to size** trier des objets selon leur taille; (*Cards*) **to ~ out one's cards *or* one's hand** arranger ses cartes, mettre de l'ordre dans ses cartes; **to ~ the clothes (out) into clean and dirty** séparer les vêtements sales des propres, mettre les vêtements sales à part; **can you ~ out the green ones and keep them aside?** pourriez-vous les trier et mettre les verts à part?

(b) (*Scot**: *mend*) arranger. **I've ~ed your bike** j'ai arrangé ton vélo.

sort out 1 *vt sep* **(a) = sort 3a.**

(b) (*fig*) (*tidy*) *papers, toys, clothes* ranger, mettre de l'ordre dans; *ideas* mettre de l'ordre dans; (*solve*) *problem* régler, résoudre; *difficulties* venir à bout de; (*fix, arrange*) arranger. **I just can't sort the twins out* (one from the other)** je ne peux pas distinguer les jumeaux (l'un de l'autre); **can you sort this out for me?** est-ce que vous pourriez débrouiller ça pour moi?; **we've got it all sorted out now** nous avons réglé *or* résolu la question; **we'll soon sort it out** nous aurons vite fait d'arranger ça *or* de régler ça; **things will sort themselves out** les choses vont s'arranger d'elles-mêmes; **he was so excited I couldn't sort out what had happened** il était tellement excité que je n'ai pas pu débrouiller *or* comprendre ce qui s'était passé; **did you sort out with him when you had to be there?** est-ce que tu as décidé *or* fixé avec lui l'heure à laquelle tu dois y être?; (*Brit*) **to sort sb out*** (*by punishing, threatening etc*) régler son compte à qn*; (*get him out of difficulty etc*) tirer qn d'affaire; (*after depression, illness etc*) aider qn à reprendre pied (*fig*).

2 sort-out* *n V* **sort 2.**

sorter [ˈsɔːtəʳ] *n* **(a)** (*person*) trieur *m*, -euse *f*. **(b)** (*machine*) (*for letters*) trieur *m*; (*for punched cards*) trieuse *f*; (*for grain*) trieur; (*for wool, coke etc*) trieur, trieuse.

sortie [ˈsɔːtɪ] *n* (*Aviat, Mil*) sortie *f*. **they made *or* flew 400 ~s** ils ont fait 400 sorties.

sot [sɒt] *n* ivrogne invétéré.

sottish [ˈsɒtɪʃ] *adj* abruti par l'alcool.

sotto voce [ˈsɒtəʊˈvəʊtʃɪ] *adv* (tout) bas, à mi-voix; (*Mus*) sotto-voce.

sou' [saʊ] *adj* (*Naut: in cpds*) = **south.**

Soudan [suˈdɑːn] *n* = **Sudan.**

Soudanese [ˌsuːdəˈniːz] = **Sudanese.**

soufflé [ˈsuːfleɪ] **1** *n* soufflé *m*. **cheese/fish ~** soufflé au fromage/au poisson. **2** *cpd*: **soufflé dish** moule *m* à soufflé; **soufflé omelette** omelette soufflée.

sough [saʊ] (*liter*) **1** *n* murmure *m* (du vent). **2** *vi [wind]* murmurer.

sought [sɔːt] *pret, ptp of* **seek.**

soul [səʊl] **1** *n* **(a)** âme *f*. **with all one's ~** de toute son âme, de tout son cœur; **All S~s' Day** le jour des Morts; **upon my ~!*†** grand Dieu!; **he cannot call his ~ his own** il ne s'appartient pas, il est complètement dominé; (*fig*) **he was the ~ of the movement** c'était lui l'âme *or* l'animateur *m or* la cheville ouvrière du mouvement; **he is the ~ of discretion** c'est la discrétion même *or* personnifiée *or* en personne; **he has no ~** il est trop terre à terre, il a trop les pieds sur terre; *V* **body, heart, sell** *etc.*

(b) (*person*) âme *f*, personne *f*. **a village of 300 ~s** un village de 300 âmes *or* habitants; **the ship sank with 200 ~s** le bateau a sombré avec 200 personnes à bord; **the ship sank with all ~s** le bateau a péri corps et biens; **I didn't see a (single *or* living) ~** je n'ai vu personne, je n'ai pas vu âme qui vive; **(you) poor ~!** mon (*or* ma) pauvre!; **he's a good ~** c'est une excellente personne, il est bien brave*; **lend me your pen, there's a good ~*** sois gentil *or* sois un ange, prête-moi ton stylo; *V* **simple** *etc.*

(c) (*US**) *abbr of* **soul food*** *and* **soul music**; *V* **2.**

2 *cpd*: (*US*) **soul brother*** frère *m* (*terme employé par un Noir des États-Unis parlant d'un autre Noir*); **soul-destroying** (*boring*) abrutissant; (*depressing*) démoralisant; (*US*) **soul food*** nourriture *f* bon marché; **soul mate*** âme *f* sœur; (*US*) **soul music** soul music *f*; **soul-searching** introspection *f*; **after a lot of soul-searching ...** après avoir bien fait son (*or* mon *etc*) examen de conscience ...; **soul-stirring** très émouvant.

soulful [ˈsəʊlfʊl] *adj expression, performance, music* sentimental, attendrissant; *eyes, glance* expressif, éloquent.

soulfully [ˈsəʊlfəlɪ] *adv sing, write* de façon sentimentale *or* attendrissante; *look* d'un air expressif *or* éloquent.

soulless [ˈsəʊllɪs] *adj person* sans cœur; *cruelty* inhumain; *task* abrutissant.

sound[1] [saʊnd] **1** *n* (*Ling, Mus, Phys, Rad, TV etc*) son *m*; *[sea, storm, breaking glass, car brakes etc]* bruit *m*; *[sb's voice, bell, violins etc]* son. **the speed of ~** la vitesse du son; **within ~ of** à portée du son de; **to the ~(s) of the national anthem** au(x) son(s) de l'hymne national; **there was not a ~ to be heard** on n'entendait pas le moindre bruit; **without (making) a ~** sans bruit, sans faire le moindre bruit; **we heard the ~ of voices** nous avons entendu un bruit de voix; **the Glenn Miller ~** la musique de Glenn Miller; (*fig*) **I don't like the ~ of it** (*it doesn't attract me*) ça ne me dit rien, ça ne me plaît pas; (*it's worrying*) ça m'inquiète; (*fig*) **I don't like the ~ of his plans** ses projets ne me disent rien qui vaille; (*fig*) **the news has a depressing ~** les nouvelles semblent déprimantes.

2 *cpd film, recording* sonore. **sound archives** phonothèque *f*; **sound barrier** mur *m* du son; (*Rad etc*) **sound effects** bruitage *m*; (*Cine, Rad etc*) **sound engineer** ingénieur *m* du son; **sound(ing) board** *V* **sounding**[1]; **soundproof** (*vt*) insonoriser; (*adj*) insonorisé; **soundproofing** insonorisation *f*; (*Cine*) **sound track** piste *f or* bande *f* sonore; (*US*) **sound truck** camionnette équipée d'un haut-parleur; (*Phys*) **sound wave** onde *f* sonore.

3 *vi* **(a)** *[bell, trumpet, voice]* sonner, retentir; *[car horn, siren, signal, order]* retentir. **footsteps/a gun ~ed a long way off** on entendit un bruit de pas/un coup de canon dans le lointain;

(*fig*) **a note of warning ~s through his writing** un avertissement retentit dans ses écrits; **it ~s better if you read it slowly** c'est mieux si vous le lisez lentement.

(b) (*suggest by sound*) **that instrument ~s like a flute** le son de cet instrument ressemble à celui de la flûte, on dirait le son de la flûte; **it ~s empty** (au son) on dirait que c'est vide; **a language which ~ed (to me) like Dutch** une langue qui aurait pu être *or* qui (me) semblait être du hollandais; **he ~s (like an) Australian** à l'entendre parler on dirait un Australien; **the train ~ed a long way off, it ~ed as if** *or* **as though the train were a long way off** le train semblait être encore bien loin; **it ~ed as if someone were coming in** on aurait dit que quelqu'un entrait; **that ~s like Paul arriving** ça doit être Paul qui arrive; **she ~s tired** elle semble fatiguée; **you ~ like your mother when you say things like that** quand tu parles comme ça, tu me rappelles ta mère *or* on croirait entendre ta mère; (*to sick person*) **you ~ terrible** (à t'entendre) tu sembles en triste état.

(c) (*fig: seem, appear*) sembler (être). **that ~s like an excuse** cela a l'air d'une excuse, cela ressemble à une excuse; **how does it ~ to you?** qu'en penses-tu?; **it ~s like a good idea** ça a l'air d'(être) une bonne idée, ça semble être une bonne idée; **it doesn't ~ too good** cela n'annonce rien de bon, ce n'est pas très prometteur; **it ~s as if she isn't coming** il semble qu'elle ne vienne pas, elle ne semble pas venir; **you don't ~ like the kind of person we need** (à en juger par ce que vous dites) vous ne semblez pas être le genre de personne qu'il nous faut.

4 *vt* **(a)** *bell, alarm* sonner; *trumpet, bugle* sonner de; (*Mil*) *reveille, retreat* sonner. (*Mil*) **to ~ the last post** envoyer la sonnerie aux morts; (*Aut*) **to ~ the** *or* **one's horn** klaxonner; (*Aut*) **~ing the horn** l'usage *m* du klaxon; (*fig*) **to ~ a (note of) warning** donner *or* sonner l'alarme; **to ~ sb's praises** faire l'éloge de qn, chanter les louanges de qn.

(b) (*Ling*) **to ~ one's 't's** faire sonner ses 't'; **the 'n' in 'hymn' is not ~ed** le 'n' de 'hymn' ne se prononce pas.

(c) (*examine*) *rails, train wheels* vérifier au marteau. (*Med*) **to ~ sb's chest** ausculter qn.

sound off *vi* **(a)** (:) (*proclaim one's opinions*) faire de grands laïus* (*about* sur); (*boast*) se vanter (*about* de), la ramener: (*about* à propos de); (*grumble*) rouspéter*, râler* (*about* à propos de). **to sound off at sb** engueuler: qn.

(b) (*US Mil: number off*) se numéroter.

sound[2] [saʊnd] **1** *adj* **(a)** (*healthy; robust*) *person* en bonne santé, bien portant; *heart* solide; *constitution, teeth, lungs, fruit, tree* sain; *timber* sain, solide; *structure, floor, bridge* solide, en bon état; (*fig*) *firm, business, financial position* sain, solide; *bank, organization* solide; *alliance, investment* bon, sûr, sans danger. **the bullet struck his ~ leg** la balle a atteint sa jambe valide; **of ~ mind** sain d'esprit; **~ in body and mind** sain de corps et d'esprit; **to be ~ in wind and limb** avoir bon pied bon œil; **to be as ~ as a bell** être en parfait état; *V* **safe**.

(b) (*competent, judicious, sensible*) *reasoning, judgment* solide, juste, sain; *doctrine* orthodoxe, solide; *argument* solide, valable; *decision, step, advice, opinion* sensé, valable, judicieux; *case, training* solide; *rule, policy, behaviour, tactics* sensé, valable; *claim, title* valable, sérieux; *statesman, player etc* compétent. **he is a ~ worker** il sait travailler, il est compétent dans son travail; **he is a ~ socialist** c'est un bon socialiste, c'est un socialiste bon teint; **he is ~ enough on theory ...** il connaît très bien la théorie ...; **he is a ~ chap** (*sensible*) il est très sérieux *or* sensé; (*we can trust him*) c'est quelqu'un en qui on peut avoir confiance; **~ sense** bon sens, sens pratique; **that was a ~ move** c'était une action judicieuse *or* sensée.

(c) (*thorough*) *defeat* complet (*f* -ète), total; *sleep* profond. **a ~ thrashing** une bonne *or* belle correction; **he is a ~ sleeper** il a un bon sommeil, il dort bien.

2 *adv*: **to be ~ asleep** être profondément endormi, dormir à poings fermés; **to sleep ~** bien dormir.

sound[3] [saʊnd] **1** *n* (*Med: probe*) sonde *f*.

2 *cpd*: **sound(ing) line** *V* **sounding[2] 2**.

3 *vt* (*gen, Med, Naut etc*) sonder; (*fig: also* **~ out**) *person* sonder (*on, about* sur). **to ~ sb's opinions/feelings on sth** sonder qn sur ses opinions/ses sentiments à propos de qch.

4 *vi* sonder.

sound[4] [saʊnd] *n* (*Geog*) détroit *m*, bras *m* de mer.

sounding[1] ['saʊndɪŋ] **1** *n* **(a)** *[trumpet, bell etc]* son *m*. **the ~ of the retreat/the alarm** le signal de la retraite/de l'alerte.

(b) (*Med*) auscultation *f*.

2 *cpd*: **sounding board** (*Mus*) table *f* d'harmonie; (*behind rostrum etc*) abat-voix *m inv*; (*fig*) **he used the committee as a sounding board for his new idea** il a d'abord essayé sa nouvelle idée sur les membres du comité.

sounding[2] ['saʊndɪŋ] **1** *n* (*Aviat, Naut, Space etc*) (*act*) sondage *m*. (*measurement, data*) **~s** sondages; **to take ~s** (*lit*) faire des prélèvements; (*fig*) faire un *or* des sondage(s), sonder l'opinion.

2 *cpd*: **sounding line** ligne *f* de sonde.

soundless ['saʊndlɪs] *adj* silencieux.

soundlessly ['saʊndlɪslɪ] *adv* sans bruit, en silence.

soundly ['saʊndlɪ] *adv sleep* profondément; *advise, reason, argue* de façon sensée *or* valable, judicieusement, avec justesse *or* bon sens; *organize, manage* bien, de façon saine *or* sûre; *invest* bien, sans danger; (*Sport*) *play* de façon compétente. **~ based** *business, firm* sain, solide; *financial position* sain, solide, sans danger; **he was ~ beaten** (*defeated*) il a été complètement battu, il a été battu à plate(s) couture(s); (*thrashed*) il a reçu une bonne *or* belle correction; *V* **sleep**.

soundness ['saʊndnɪs] *n* (*V* **sound[2]**) *[body]* santé *f*; *[mind]* équilibre *m*, santé; *[business]* solidité *f*; (*solvency*) solvabilité *f*; *[argument]* solidité; *[judgment]* justesse *f*; *[doctrine]* orthodoxie *f*; *[sleep]* profondeur *f*.

soup [su:p] **1** *n* soupe *f*; (*thinner or sieved*) potage *m*; (*very smooth*) velouté *m*. **clear ~** potage clair; **mushroom/tomato ~** velouté de champignons/de tomates; **onion ~** soupe à l'oignon; **vegetable ~** soupe *or* potage aux légumes; (*fig*) **to be in the ~*** être dans le pétrin* *or* dans de beaux draps; *V* **pea** *etc*.

2 *cpd*: **soup cube** potage *m* en cube; (*stock cube*) cube *m* de bouillon; **soup kitchen** soupe *f* populaire; **soup plate** assiette creuse *or* à soupe; **soupspoon** cuiller *f* à soupe; **soup tureen** soupière *f*.

soup up* *vt sep* (*Aut*) *engine* gonfler*. **he was driving a souped-up Mini ®** il conduisait une Mini ® au moteur gonflé* *or* poussé.

soupçon ['su:psɔ̃:ŋ] *n [garlic, malice]* soupçon *m*, pointe *f*.

soupy ['su:pɪ] *adj liquid* (*thick*) épais (*f* -aisse); (*unclear*) trouble; *fog, atmosphere* épais, dense; (* *fig: sentimental*) *film, story, voice* sirupeux.

sour ['saʊəʳ] **1** *adj flavour, fruit, wine etc* aigre, acide, sur; *milk* tourné, aigre; *soil* trop acide; (*fig*) *person, voice* acerbe, revêche, aigre; *face* revêche, rébarbatif; *remark* aigre, acerbe. **the juice is too ~** le jus est trop acide *or* n'est pas assez sucré; **~(ed) cream** ≃ crème *f* aigre; **to go** *or* **turn ~** *[milk]* tourner, devenir aigre; *[relationship, discussion]* tourner au vinaigre; *[plans]* mal tourner; **to be in a ~ mood** être d'humeur revêche *or* massacrante; (*fig*) **it was clearly ~ grapes on his part** il l'a manifestement fait (*or* dit *etc*) par dépit *or* par rancœur.

2 *cpd*: **sour-faced** à la mine revêche *or* rébarbative; **sourpuss*** grincheux *m*, -euse *f*.

3 *vt* aigrir (*also fig*); *milk* faire tourner.

4 *vi* s'aigrir (*also fig*); *[milk]* tourner.

5 *n*: **whisky** *etc* **~** cocktail *m* de whisky *etc* au citron.

source [sɔ:s] **1** *n [river]* source *f*; (*fig*) source, origine *f*. (*Literat etc*) **~s** sources; **a ~ of heat** une source de chaleur; (*Med*) **a ~ of infection** un foyer d'infection; **we have other ~s of supply** nous avons d'autres sources d'approvisionnement, nous pouvons nous approvisionner ailleurs; **what is the ~ of this information?** quelle est l'origine *or* la provenance de cette nouvelle?; **I have it from a reliable ~ that ...** je tiens de bonne source *or* de source sûre que ... .

2 *cpd*: (*Ling*) **source language** langue *f* de départ; (*Literat etc*) **source materials** sources *fpl*.

sourish ['saʊərɪʃ] *adj* (*lit, fig*) aigrelet.

sourly ['saʊəlɪ] *adv* aigrement, avec aigreur.

sourness ['saʊənɪs] *n* (*V* **sour 1**) aigreur *f*, acidité *f*; humeur *f or* aspect *m or* ton *m* revêche.

souse [saʊs] *vt* **(a)** (*immerse*) tremper (*in* dans); (*soak*) faire *or* laisser tremper (*in* dans). **to ~ sth with water** inonder qch d'eau; (*fig: drunk*) **~d:** rond*, noir:.

(b) (*Culin*) mariner. **~d herrings** harengs marinés; (*rolled up*) rollmops *mpl*.

south [saʊθ] **1** *n* sud *m*. **(to the) ~ of** au sud de; **in the ~ of Scotland** dans le sud de l'Écosse; **house facing the ~** maison exposée au sud *or* au midi; *[wind]* **to veer to the ~, to go into the ~** tourner au sud; **the wind is in the ~** le vent est au sud; **the wind is from the ~** le vent vient *or* souffle du sud; **to live in the ~** habiter dans le Sud; (*in France*) habiter dans le Midi; **the S~ of France** le Sud de la France, le Midi; (*US Hist*) **the S~** le Sud, les États *mpl* du Sud; *V* **deep** *etc*.

2 *adj* sud *inv*, du *or* au sud. **~ wind** vent *m* du sud; **~ coast** côte sud *or* méridionale; **on the ~ side** du côté sud; **room with a ~ aspect** pièce exposée au sud *or* au midi; (*Archit*) **~ transept/door** transept/portail sud *or* méridional; **in the ~ Atlantic** dans l'Atlantique Sud; *V also* **4**.

3 *adv* au sud, vers le sud. **the town lies ~ of the border** la ville est située au sud de la frontière; **we drove ~ for 100 km** nous avons roulé pendant 100 km en direction du sud *or* du midi; **go ~ till you get to Crewe** allez en direction du sud jusqu'à Crewe; **to sail due ~** aller droit vers le sud; (*Naut*) avoir le cap au sud; **~ by ~ -west** sud quart sud-ouest.

4 *cpd*: **South Africa** Afrique *f* du Sud; **South African** (*adj*) sud-africain, d'Afrique du Sud; (*n*) Sud-Africain(e) *m(f)*; **South America** Amérique *f* du Sud; **South American** (*adj*) sud-américain, d'Amérique du Sud; (*n*) Sud-Américain(e) *m(f)*; **southbound** *traffic, vehicles* (se déplaçant) en direction du sud; *carriageway* sud *inv*; **South Carolina** Caroline *f* du Sud; **South Dakota** Dakota *m* du Sud; **south-east** (*n*) sud-est *m*; (*adj*) (du *or* au) sud-est *inv*; (*adv*) vers le sud-est; **South-East Asia** le Sud-Est asiatique, l'Asie *f* du Sud-Est; **south-easter** vent *m* du sud-est; **south-easterly** (*adj*) *wind, direction* du sud-est; *situation* au sud-est; (*adv*) vers le sud-est; **south-eastern** (du *or* au) sud-est; **south-eastward(s)** vers le sud-est; **south-facing** exposé au sud *or* au midi; **South Pacific** le Pacifique Sud; (*Boxing*) **southpaw** gaucher *m*; **South Pole** Pôle *m* Sud, pôle austral; **South Sea Islands** l'Océanie *f*; **the South Seas** les Mers *fpl* du Sud; **south-south-east** (*n*) sud-sud-est *m*; (*adj*) (du *or* au) sud-sud-est *inv*; (*adv*) vers le sud-sud-est; **south-south-west** (*n*) sud-sud-ouest *m*; (*adj*) (du *or* au) sud-sud-ouest *inv*; (*adv*) vers le sud-sud-ouest; **south-west** (*n*) sud-ouest *m*; (*adj*) (du *or* au) sud-ouest *inv*; (*adv*) vers le sud-ouest; **south-wester** vent *m* du sud-ouest, suroît *m*; **south-westerly** (*adj*) *wind, direction* du sud-ouest; *situation* au sud-ouest; (*adv*) vers le sud-ouest; **south-western** (du *or* au) sud-ouest *inv*; **south-westward(s)** vers le sud-ouest; *V* **Korea, Vietnam** *etc*.

southerly ['sʌðəlɪ] **1** *adj wind* du sud; *situation* au sud, au midi. **in a ~ direction** en direction du sud *or* du midi, vers le sud *or* le midi; **~ latitudes** latitudes australes; **~ aspect** exposition *f* au sud *or* au midi.

2 *adv* vers le sud.

southern ['sʌðən] **1** *adj* du sud. **the ~ coast** la côte sud *or* méridionale; **house with a ~ outlook** maison exposée au sud *or* au midi; **~ wall** mur exposé au sud *or* au midi; **~ hemisphere** hémisphère sud *inv or* austral; **S~ Africa** Afrique australe; **~**

France le Sud de la France, le Midi; **in ~ Spain** dans le Sud de l'Espagne, en Espagne méridionale. 2 *cpd*: **the Southern Cross** la Croix-du-Sud; **southernmost** le plus au sud, à l'extrême sud.

southerner ['sʌðənəʳ] *n* **(a)** homme *m or* femme *f* du Sud, habitant(e) *m(f)* du Sud; (*in France*) Méridional(e) *m(f)*. **he is a ~** il vient du Sud; **the ~s** les gens du Sud. **(b)** (*US Hist*) sudiste *mf*.

southward ['saʊθwəd] 1 *adj* au sud. 2 *adv* (*also* **~s**) vers le sud.

souvenir [ˌsuːvəˈnɪəʳ] *n* souvenir *m* (*objet*).

sou'wester [saʊ'westəʳ] *n* (*hat*) suroît *m*; (*wind*) = **southwester**; *V* **south 4.**

sovereign ['sɒvrɪn] 1 *n* souverain(e) *m(f)*; (*Brit: coin*) souverain (*ancienne pièce d'or qui valait 20 shillings*).

2 *adj power, authority* souverain (*after n*), suprême; *rights* de souveraineté; (*fig*) *contempt, indifference* souverain (*before n*), absolu. (*Pol*) **~ state** état souverain; (*fig*) **~ remedy** remède souverain *or* infaillible.

sovereignty ['sɒvrəntɪ] *n* souveraineté *f*.

soviet ['səʊvɪət] 1 *n* soviet *m*. **the Supreme S~** le Soviet Suprême; (*people*) **the S~s** les Soviétiques *mpl*. 2 *adj* soviétique. 3 *cpd*: **Soviet Russia** Russie *f* soviétique; **the Soviet Union** l'Union *f* soviétique.

sovietize ['səʊvɪətaɪz] *vt* soviétiser.

sow¹ [saʊ] *n* (*pig*) truie *f*.

sow² [səʊ] *pret* **sowed**, *ptp* **sown** *or* **sowed** 1 *vt seed, grass* semer; *field* ensemencer (*with* en); (*fig*) *mines, pebbles, doubt, discord* semer. (*Prov*) **~ the wind and reap the whirlwind** qui sème le vent récolte la tempête (*Prov*); *V* **seed, wild** *etc.*

2 *vi* semer.

sower ['səʊəʳ] *n* (*person*) semeur *m*, -euse *f*; (*machine*) semoir *m*.

sowing ['səʊɪŋ] 1 *n* **(a)** (*work*) semailles *fpl*; (*period, seeds*) semailles; (*young plants*) semis *mpl*. **(b)** (*U: act*) *[field]* ensemencement *m*. **the ~ of seeds** les semailles. 2 *cpd*: **sowing machine** semoir *m*.

sown [səʊn] *ptp of* **sow²**.

sox [sɒks] *n* (*US*) *pl of* **sock¹**.

soy [sɔɪ] *n* **(a)** (*also* **~ sauce**) sauce *f* au soja. **(b)** (*US*) = **soya**. **~bean** = **soya bean**; *V* **soya**.

soya ['sɔɪə] *n* (*esp Brit: also* **~ bean**) (*plant*) soja *m or* soya *m*; (*bean*) graine *f* de soja. **~ flour** farine *f* de soja.

sozzled‡ ['sɒzld] *adj* paf‡ *inv*, noir‡.

spa [spɑː] *n* (*town*) station thermale, ville *f* d'eau; (*spring*) source minérale.

space [speɪs] 1 *n* **(a)** (*U: gen, Astron, Phys etc*) espace *m*. **the rocket vanished into ~** la fusée a disparu dans l'espace; **he was staring into ~** il regardait dans l'espace *or* dans le vide; *V* **outer.**

(b) (*U: room*) espace *m*, place *f*. **to clear (a** *or* **some) ~ for sth** faire de la place pour qch; **to take up a lot of ~** *[car, books, piece of furniture]* prendre une grande place *or* beaucoup de place, être encombrant; *[building]* occuper un grand espace; **the ~ occupied by a car/a building** l'encombrement *m* d'une voiture/d'un bâtiment; **there isn't enough ~ for it** il n'y a pas assez de place pour ça; **I haven't enough ~ to turn the car** je n'ai pas assez de place pour *or* je n'ai pas la place de tourner la voiture; **to buy ~ in a newspaper (for an advertisement)** acheter de l'espace (publicitaire) dans un journal.

(c) (*gap, empty area*) espace *m*, place *f* (*U*); (*Mus*) interligne *m*; (*Typ: between two words etc*) espace *m*, blanc *m*; (*Typ: blank type*) espace *f*. **in the ~s between the trees** (dans les espaces) entre les arbres; **a ~ of 10 metres between the buildings** un espace *or* un écart *or* une distance de 10 mètres entre les bâtiments; **leave a ~ for the name** laisse de la place *or* un espace *or* un blanc pour le nom; **in the ~ provided** dans la partie (*or* la case) réservée à cet effet; **in an enclosed ~** dans un espace clos *or* fermé; **I'm looking for a ~ to park the car in** *or* **a parking ~** je cherche une place (pour me garer); *V* **blank, open** *etc.*

(d) (*interval, period*) laps *m* de temps, période *f* (de temps), espace *m* (de temps). **after a ~ of 10 minutes** après un intervalle de 10 minutes; **for the ~ of a month** pendant une durée *or* une période d'un mois; **a ~ of 5 years** une période de 5 ans; **in the ~ of 3 generations/one hour** en l'espace de 3 générations/d'une heure; **a short ~ of time** un court laps de temps *or* espace de temps; **for a ~** pendant un certain temps.

2 *cpd journey, programme, research, rocket* spatial. **the Space Age** l'ère spatiale; **space-age** de l'ère spatiale, de l'an 2000; *[typewriter]* **space bar** barre *f* d'espacement; **space capsule** capsule spatiale; **spacecraft** engin *or* vaisseau spatial; **space fiction** science-fiction *f* (*sur le thème des voyages dans l'espace*); **space flight** (*journey*) voyage spatial *or* dans l'espace; (*U*) voyages *or* vols spatiaux; **space heater** radiateur *m*; **space helmet** casque *m* d'astronaute *or* de cosmonaute; **space lab** laboratoire spatial; **spaceman** astronaute *m*, cosmonaute *m*; **space platform = space station**; **spaceport** base *f* de lancement (d'engins spatiaux); **space probe** sonde spatiale; **space-saving** qui économise *or* gagne de la place; **spaceship = spacecraft**; **space shot** (*launching*) lancement *m* d'un engin spatial; (*flight*) vol spatial; **space shuttle** navette spatiale; **space station** station orbitale *or* spatiale; **spacesuit** scaphandre *m* de cosmonaute; **space-time (continuum)** Espace-Temps *m*; **space travel** voyages spatiaux *or* interplanétaires *or* dans l'espace; **spacewalk** (*n*) marche *f* dans l'espace; (*vi*) marcher dans l'espace; **spacewalker** marcheur *m* de l'espace; **spacewoman** astronaute *f*, cosmonaute *f*; (*Press*) **space writer** journaliste *mf* payé(e) à la ligne.

3 *vt* (*also* **~ out**) *chairs, words, visits, letters* espacer; *payments* échelonner (*over* sur). **~ the posts (out) evenly** espacez les poteaux régulièrement, plantez les poteaux à intervalles réguliers; **you'll have to ~ them further out** *or* **further apart, you'll have to ~ them out more** il faudra laisser plus d'espace entre eux *or* les espacer davantage; **to ~ type out to fill a line** espacer *or* répartir les caractères sur toute une ligne; **the houses were well ~d (out)** les maisons étaient bien *or* largement espacées; (*Drugs sl*) **to be ~d (out)** flipper‡, être sous l'influence de la drogue.

spacing ['speɪsɪŋ] *n* (*esp Typ*) espacement *m*; (*between two objects*) espacement, écartement *m*, intervalle *m*; (*also* **~ out**: *of payments, sentries*) échelonnement *m*. (*Typ*) **in single/double ~** avec un interligne simple/double.

spacious ['speɪʃəs] *adj room, car* spacieux, grand; *garden* grand, étendu; *garment* ample. **~ living** *or* **accommodation** logement spacieux.

spaciousness ['speɪʃəsnɪs] *n* grandes dimensions, grandeur *f*.

spade [speɪd] 1 *n* **(a)** bêche *f*, pelle *f*; (*child's*) pelle. (*fig*) **to call a ~ a ~** appeler un chat un chat.

(b) (*Cards*) pique *m*. **to play ~s** jouer pique; **he played a ~** il a joué pique *or* un pique *or* du pique; **the six of ~s** le six de pique; **~s are trumps** atout pique, pique est l'atout.

(c) (‡ *pej*) nègre *m*, négresse *f*.

2 *cpd*: (*fig*) **spadework** gros *m* du travail.

spadeful ['speɪdfʊl] *n* pelletée *f*. (*fig*) **by the ~** en grandes quantités.

spaghetti [spə'getɪ] 1 *n* spaghetti *mpl*. 2 *cpd*: (*Aut*) **spaghetti junction** échangeur *m* à niveaux multiples; (*Cine: esp US*) **spaghetti western*** western *m* spaghetti* *inv*.

Spain [speɪn] *n* Espagne *f*.

spake†† [speɪk] *pret of* **speak.**

span¹ [spæn] 1 *n* **(a)** *[hands, arms]* envergure *f*; *[girder]* portée *f*; *[bridge]* travée *f*; *[arch]* portée, ouverture *f*; *[roof]* portée, travée; *[plane, bird]* (*also* **wing~**) envergure. **a bridge with 3 ~s** un pont à 3 travées; **single-~ bridge** pont à travée unique; **the bridge has a ~ of 120 metres** le pont a une travée *or* une portée de 120 mètres; (*fig*) **the whole ~ of world affairs** l'horizon international.

(b) (*in time*) espace *m* (de temps), durée *f*. **the average ~ of life** la durée moyenne de vie; (*liter*) **man's ~ is short** la vie humaine est brève; **for a brief** *or* **short ~ (of time)** pendant un bref moment, pendant un court espace de temps; *V* **life.**

(c) (††: *measure*) empan *m*.

(d) (*yoke: of oxen etc*) paire *f*.

2 *vt* **(a)** *[bridge, rope, plank etc] stream, ditch* enjamber, franchir, traverser; *[bridge-builder]* jeter *or* construire un pont sur. **he could ~ her waist with his hands** il pouvait lui entourer la taille de ses deux mains; (*fig*) **Christianity ~s almost 2,000 years** le christianisme embrasse presque 2.000 ans; **his life ~s almost the whole of the 18th century** sa vie couvre *or* embrasse presque tout le 18e siècle.

(b) (*measure*) mesurer à l'empan.

span² [spæn] *pret of* **spin.**

spangle ['spæŋgl] 1 *n* paillette *f*. **dress with ~s on it** robe pailletée *or* à paillettes. 2 *vt* orner de paillettes. (*fig*) **~d with** pailleté de; *V* **star.**

Spaniard ['spænjəd] *n* Espagnol(e) *m(f)*.

spaniel ['spænjəl] *n* épagneul *m*.

Spanish ['spænɪʃ] 1 *adj language, cooking* espagnol; *king, embassy* d'Espagne; *teacher* d'espagnol; (*Culin*) *omelette, rice* à l'espagnole. **the ~ way of life** la vie espagnole, la façon de vivre des Espagnols; **~ onion** oignon *m* d'Espagne; **the ~ people** les Espagnols *mpl*.

2 *n* **(a) the ~** les Espagnols *mpl*.

(b) (*Ling*) espagnol *m*.

3 *cpd*: **Spanish America** les pays *mpl* d'Amérique du Sud de langue espagnole; **Spanish-American** hispano-américain; (*Hist*) **the Spanish Armada** l'Invincible Armada *f*; **Spanish chestnut** châtaigne *f*, marron *m*; (*Geog*) **the Spanish Main** la mer des Antilles.

spank [spæŋk] 1 *n*: **to give sb a ~** donner un coup *or* une claque à qn sur les fesses.

2 *vt* donner une fessée à.

3 *vi [horse, vehicle, ship]* **to be** *or* **go ~ing along** aller *or* filer à bonne allure.

spanking ['spæŋkɪŋ] 1 *n* fessée *f*. **to give sb a ~** donner une fessée à qn. 2 *adj* **(a)** *breeze* fort, bon. **to go at a ~ pace** aller *or* filer à bonne allure. **(b)** (*†: *splendid*) épatant*.

spanner ['spænəʳ] *n* (*esp Brit*) clef *f or* clé *f* (à écrous). (*fig*) **to put a ~ in the works** mettre des bâtons dans les roues.

spar¹ [spɑːʳ] *n* (*Geol*) spath *m*.

spar² [spɑːʳ] *n* (*Naut*) espar *m*.

spar³ [spɑːʳ] 1 *vi* (*Boxing*) s'entraîner (à la boxe) (*with sb* avec qn); (*rough and tumble*) se bagarrer* amicalement (*with sb* avec qn); *[two people]* échanger des coups de poing pour rire; (*fig: argue*) se disputer (*with sb* avec qn); *[two people]* se défier en paroles.

2 *cpd*: **sparring partner** sparring-partner *m*.

spare [speəʳ] 1 *adj* **(a)** dont on ne se sert pas; (*reserve*) de réserve, de rechange; (*surplus*) de *or* en trop, dont on n'a pas besoin, disponible. **take a ~ pen in case that one doesn't work** prends un stylo de réserve *or* de rechange au cas où celui-ci ne marcherait pas; **I've a ~ pen if you want it** je peux te prêter un stylo, tu peux prendre mon stylo de rechange; **have you any ~ cups?** est-ce que tu as des tasses dont tu ne te sers pas? *or* de réserve? *or* en trop?; **take some ~ clothes** prends des vêtements de rechange, prends de quoi te changer; **there are 2 going ~** il y en a 2 en trop *or* de trop *or* de reste *or* dont on peut disposer; **we've 2 ~ seats for the film** nous avons 2 places disponibles pour le film; **~ bed/(bed)room** lit *m*/chambre *f* d'ami; **~ cash** (*small amount*) argent *m* en trop *or* de reste; (*larger*) argent disponible; **I have very little ~ time** j'ai très peu de loisirs *or* de temps libre; **in my ~ time** à mes heures perdues, pendant mes moments de loisir (*V also* 2); (*Aut, Tech*) **~ part** pièce *f* de rechange, pièce détachée (*V also* 2); **~ tyre** (*Aut*) pneu *m* de rechange; (** fig: fat*) bourrelet *m* (de graisse); (*Aut*) **~ wheel** roue *f* de secours.

(b) (*lean*) *person* maigre; *diet, meal* frugal.

2 *cpd*: **spare-part surgery*** chirurgie *f* des greffes; (*Culin*) **sparerib** côtelette *f* (de porc) dans l'échine; **spare-time** (fait) à temps perdu *or* pendant les moments de loisir.

3 *n* (*part*) pièce *f* de rechange, pièce détachée; (*tyre*) pneu *m* de rechange; (*wheel*) roue *f* de secours.

4 *vt* **(a)** (*do without*) se passer de. **we can't ~ him** *or* **we can ill ~ him just now** nous ne pouvons pas nous passer de lui en ce moment; **can you ~ it?** pouvez-vous vous en passer?, vous n'en avez pas besoin?, ça ne vous dérange pas trop (de vous en passer)? (*also iro*); **can you ~ £10?** est-ce que tu as 10 livres en trop? *or* de disponibles?; **I can only ~ a few minutes, I've only a few minutes to ~** je ne dispose que de quelques minutes, je n'ai que quelques minutes de libres *or* devant moi; **I can't ~ the time (to do it)** je n'ai pas le temps (de le faire), je n'ai pas une minute (à y consacrer); **he had time to ~ so he went to the pictures** il n'était pas pressé *or* il avait du temps devant lui, alors il est allé au cinéma; **did you have a rush to get here? — no, I had time (and) to ~** est-ce que tu as dû te dépêcher pour arriver? — non, j'ai eu plus de temps qu'il ne m'en fallait; **I can only ~ an hour for my piano practice** je peux seulement consacrer une heure à *or* je ne dispose que d'une heure pour mes exercices de piano; **I can ~ you 5 minutes** je peux vous accorder *or* consacrer 5 minutes; **can you ~ me £5?** est-ce que tu peux me passer 5 livres?; **to ~ a thought for** penser à, dédier une pensée à; **there are 3 to ~** il y en a 3 de trop *or* en surplus, il y en a 3 qui ne servent pas; **I've got none to ~** j'en ai juste ce qu'il me faut, je n'en ai pas de trop; **I've enough and to ~** j'en ai plus qu'il ne m'en faut; **she had a metre to ~** elle en avait un mètre de trop *or* de plus que nécessaire; **with 2 minutes to ~** avec 2 minutes d'avance; **we did it with £5 to ~** nous l'avons fait et il nous reste encore 5 livres.

(b) (*show mercy to*) *person, sb's life, tree etc* épargner. (*lit, fig*) **he ~d no one** il n'a épargné personne, il n'a fait grâce à personne; **the plague ~d no one** la peste n'a épargné personne; **if I'm ~d*** si Dieu me prête vie; **to ~ sb's feelings** ménager (les sentiments de) qn; **~ my blushes!** épargnez ma modestie!, ne me faites pas rougir!; **he doesn't ~ himself** il ne se ménage pas.

(c) *suffering, grief* épargner (*to sb* à qn). **to ~ sb embarrassment** épargner *or* éviter de l'embarras à qn; **I wanted to ~ him trouble** je voulais lui éviter de se déranger; **you could have ~d yourself the trouble** vous auriez pu vous épargner tout ce mal; **I'll ~ you the details** je vous fais grâce des détails.

(d) (*refrain from using etc: gen neg*) *one's strength, efforts* ménager. **he ~d no expense to do it** il a dépensé sans compter pour le faire; **'no expense ~d'** 'sans considération de frais *or* de prix'; **he didn't ~ himself, he ~d no pains** il s'est donné beaucoup de mal; **he could have ~d his pains, he could have ~d himself the trouble** il s'est donné du mal pour rien; **~ your pains, it's too late now** pas la peine de te donner du mal, c'est trop tard maintenant; (*Prov*) **~ the rod and spoil the child** qui aime bien châtie bien (*Prov*).

sparing ['spɛərɪŋ] *adj amount* limité, modéré. **his ~ use of colour** la façon discrète dont il emploie les couleurs, son emploi restreint des couleurs; **~ of words/praise** avare *or* chiche de paroles/compliments; **he was ~ with** *or* **of the wine** il a ménagé le vin, il n'y est pas allé trop fort avec le vin, il a lésiné sur le vin (*pej*); **you must be more ~ of your strength** vous devez économiser *or* ménager vos forces.

sparingly ['spɛərɪŋlɪ] *adv eat, live* frugalement; *spend, drink, praise* avec modération; *use* avec modération, au compte-gouttes* (*fig*).

spark [spɑːk] **1** *n* (*also Elec*) étincelle *f*; (*fig*) *[intelligence, wit, life]* étincelle; *[common sense, interest]* lueur *f*. (*fig*) **to make the ~s fly** (*start a row*) mettre le feu aux poudres (*fig*); (*fight*) se bagarrer un bon coup*; (*Telec: person*) **~s** radio *m* (du bord); *V* **bright**.

2 *cpd*: (*Elec*) **spark gap** écartement *m* des électrodes; (*Aut*) **spark(ing) plug** bougie *f*.

3 *vi* jeter des étincelles.

4 *vt* (*also* **~ off**) *rebellion, complaints, quarrel* provoquer, déclencher; *interest, enthusiasm* susciter, éveiller (*in sb* chez qn).

sparkle ['spɑːkl] **1** *n* (*U*) *[stars, dew, tinsel]* scintillement *m*, étincellement *m*; *[diamond]* éclat *m*, feux *mpl*; (*in eye*) étincelle *f*, éclair *m*; (*fig*) vie *f*, éclat.

2 *vi [glass, china, drops of water, snow etc]* étinceler, briller; *[surface of water, lake etc]* scintiller, miroiter; *[diamond]* étinceler, jeter des feux, scintiller; *[fabric]* chatoyer; *[wine]* pétiller; *[eyes]* étinceler, pétiller (*with* de); *[person]* briller; *[conversation, play, book]* étinceler, pétiller (*with* de), être brillant *or* étincelant.

sparkler ['spɑːklə^r] *n* (*firework*) allumette *f* bengale; (*‡: diamond*) diam‡ *m*.

sparkling ['spɑːklɪŋ] **1** *adj* (*V* **sparkle 2**) étincelant (*with* de), brillant; scintillant; miroitant; chatoyant; pétillant (*with* de); *soft drink* pétillant, gazeux; *wine* pétillant, mousseux. **2** *adv*: **~ clean** étincelant de propreté.

sparrow ['spærəʊ] **1** *n* moineau *m*; *V* **hedge**. **2** *cpd*: **sparrow-grass** asperge(s) *f(pl)*; **sparrowhawk** épervier *m*.

sparse [spɑːs] *adj* clairsemé.

sparsely ['spɑːslɪ] *adv wooded, furnished* peu. **~ populated** peu peuplé, qui a une population clairsemée.

Sparta ['spɑːtə] *n* Sparte *f*.

Spartan ['spɑːtən] **1** *n* Spartiate *mf*. **2** *adj* (*also fig*) spartiate.

spasm ['spæzəm] *n* (*Med*) spasme *m*; (*fig*) accès *m* (*of* de). **a ~ of coughing** un accès *or* une quinte de toux; **to work in ~s** travailler par à-coups *or* par accès.

spasmodic [spæz'mɒdɪk] *adj* (*Med*) spasmodique; (*fig*) *work, attempt, desire* irrégulier, intermittent.

spasmodically [spæz'mɒdɪkəlɪ] *adv work, try* par à-coups, de façon intermittente *or* irrégulière.

spastic ['spæstɪk] **1** *adj* (*Med*) *movement, colon, paralysis* spasmodique; *child etc* handicapé moteur (*f* handicapée moteur).

2 *n* (*Med*) handicapé(e) *m(f)* moteur (*f inv*).

spasticity [spæs'tɪsɪtɪ] *n* (*Med*) paralysie *f* spasmodique.

spat[1] [spæt] *pret, ptp of* **spit**[1].

spat[2] [spæt] *n* (*gaiter*) demi-guêtre *f*.

spat[3] [spæt] *n* (*oyster*) naissain *m*.

spat[4]***** [spæt] *n* (*US: quarrel*) prise *f* de bec*.

spate [speɪt] *n* (*Brit: of river*) crue *f*; (*fig*) *[letters, orders etc]* avalanche *f*; *[words, abuse]* torrent *m*. **in ~** en crue; **to have a ~ of work** être débordé *or* submergé de travail.

spatial ['speɪʃəl] *adj* (*Philos, Psych*) spatial.

spatiotemporal ['speɪʃɪəʊ'tempərəl] *adj* spatio-temporel.

spatter ['spætə^r] **1** *vt* (*accidentally*) éclabousser (*with* de); (*deliberately*) asperger (*with* de). **to ~ mud on** *or* **over a dress** éclabousser de boue une robe.

2 *vi* (*splash*) gicler (*on* sur); (*sound*) crépiter (*on* sur).

3 *n* (*mark*) éclaboussure(s) *f(pl)*; (*sound*) crépitement *m*.

spatula ['spætjʊlə] *n* spatule *f*.

spavin ['spævɪn] *n* éparvin *m*.

spawn [spɔːn] **1** *n [fish, frog]* frai *m*, œufs *mpl*; *[mushroom]* mycélium *m*; blanc *m*; (*pej: person*) progéniture *f* (*iro*). **2** *vt* pondre; (*fig pej*) engendrer. **3** *vi* frayer; (*fig pej*) se reproduire, se multiplier.

spawning ['spɔːnɪŋ] *n* (*U*) frai *m*. **~ place** frayère *f*.

spay [speɪ] *vt animal* châtrer, enlever les ovaires de.

speak [spiːk] *pret* **spoke, spake**††, *ptp* **spoken 1** *vi* **(a)** (*talk*) parler (*to* à, *of, about* de); (*converse*) parler, s'entretenir (*with* avec); (*be on speaking terms*) parler, adresser la parole (*to* à); (*fig*) *[gun, trumpet etc]* retentir, se faire entendre. **to ~ in a whisper** chuchoter; **~, don't shout!** parle sans crier!; **to ~ to o.s.** parler tout seul; **I'll ~ to him about it** je vais lui en parler, je vais lui en toucher un mot *or* deux mots; **I don't know him to ~ to** je ne le connais pas assez bien pour lui parler *or* pour lui adresser la parole; **I'll never ~ to him again** je ne lui adresserai plus jamais la parole; **did you ~?*** pardon?, tu m'as parlé?, tu dis?*; **you have only to ~** tu n'as qu'un mot à dire; **so to ~** pour ainsi dire; **biologically ~ing** biologiquement parlant; **~ing personally** pour ma part, personnellement, en ce qui me concerne; **~ing as a member of the society I ...** en tant que membre de la société je ...; (*Telec*) **who's (that) ~ing?** qui est à l'appareil?; (*passing on call*) c'est de la part de qui?; (*Telec*) **(this is) Paul ~ing** ici Paul, (c'est) Paul à l'appareil; (*Telec*) **~ing!** lui- *or* elle-même!, c'est moi-même!; *V* **action, roughly** *etc*.

(b) (*make a speech*) parler (*on or about sth* de qch); (*begin to ~*) prendre la parole. **to ~ in public** parler en public; **he rose to ~** il s'est levé pour prendre la parole *or* pour parler; **Mr X will ~ next** ensuite c'est M X qui prendra la parole; **the chairman asked him to ~** le président lui a donné la parole; **Mr X will now ~ on 'The Incas'** M X va maintenant (nous) parler des Incas; **it's years since he spoke in the House** cela fait des années qu'il n'a pas fait *or* prononcé de discours à l'Assemblée; **to ~ in a debate** *[proposer, seconder]* faire un discours *or* prendre la parole au cours d'un débat; (*from floor of house*) participer à un débat, intervenir dans un débat.

(c) (*phrases*) **to ~ for sb** (*be spokesman for*) parler pour qn *or* au nom de qn; (*give evidence for*) parler *or* témoigner en faveur de qn; **~ing for myself** personnellement, pour ma part, en ce qui me concerne; **~ for yourself!*** parle pour toi!*; **let him ~ for himself** laisse-le s'exprimer, laisse-le dire lui-même ce qu'il a à dire; **it ~s for itself** c'est évident, c'est tout ce qu'il y a de plus clair; **the facts ~ for themselves** les faits parlent d'eux-mêmes *or* se passent de commentaires; **I can ~ for** *or* **to his honesty** je peux témoigner de *or* répondre de son honnêteté; **that ~s well for his generosity** ceci montre bien *or* prouve bien qu'il est généreux; **that is already spoken for** c'est déjà réservé *or* retenu; **he always ~s well of her** il dit toujours du bien d'elle; **he is very well spoken of** on dit beaucoup de bien de lui; **~ing of holidays** à propos de vacances, puisqu'on parle de vacances; **he has no money to ~ of** il n'a pour ainsi dire pas d'argent; **it's nothing to ~ of** ce n'est pas grand-chose, cela ne vaut pas la peine qu'on en parle (*subj*), c'est trois fois rien*; **everything spoke of wealth** tout indiquait *or* révélait *or* dénotait la richesse; **everything spoke of fear/hatred** tout révélait *or* trahissait la peur/la haine; **you must ~ to the point** *or* **to the subject** vous devez vous en tenir au sujet; (*Parl etc*) **to ~ to a motion** soutenir une motion.

2 *vt* **(a)** *language* parler. **'English spoken'** 'ici on parle anglais'; **French is spoken all over the world** le français se parle dans le monde entier.

(b) (*liter*) *a poem, one's lines, the truth* dire. **to ~ one's mind** dire ce que l'on pense; **I didn't ~ a word** je n'ai rien dit; (*fig*) **it ~s volumes for ...** cela en dit long sur ..., cela témoigne bien de ... .

3 *cpd*: (*US*) **speakeasy*** bar clandestin (*pendant la période de prohibition*).

speak out *vi* = **speak up b**.

speak up *vi* **(a)** (*talk loudly*) parler fort *or* haut; (*raise one's voice*) parler plus fort *or* plus haut. **speak up!** (parle) plus fort! *or* plus haut!; (*don't mumble*) parle plus clairement!

(b) (*fig*) parler franchement, ne pas mâcher ses mots. **he's not afraid to speak up** il n'a pas peur de dire ce qu'il pense *or* de parler franchement, il ne mâche pas ses mots; **I think you ought to speak up** je crois que vous devriez dire franchement ce que vous pensez; **to speak up for sb** parler en faveur de qn, défendre qn; **to speak up against sth** s'élever contre qch.

speaker ['spi:kəʳ] *n* **(a)** (*gen*) celui (*or* celle) qui parle; (*in dialogue, discussion*) interlocuteur *m*, -trice *f*; (*in public*) orateur *m*; (*lecturer*) conférencier *m*, -ière *f*. **he's a good/poor ~** il parle bien/mal, c'est un bon/mauvais orateur *or* conférencier; **the previous ~** la personne qui a parlé la dernière, l'orateur *or* le conférencier précédent; (*Brit Parl*) **the S~** le Speaker (*Président de la Chambre des Communes*).
(b) French ~ personne *f* qui parle français; (*as native or official language*) francophone *mf*; **he is not a Welsh ~** il ne parle pas gallois; *V* **native**.
(c) (*loudspeaker*) haut-parleur *m*.

speaking ['spi:kɪŋ] **1** *adj doll etc* parlant; (*fig*) *proof* parlant, criant; *likeness* criant; *portrait* parlant, très ressemblant. **he has a pleasant ~ voice** il est agréable à entendre parler.
2 *n* (*skill*) art *m* de parler; *V* **public** *etc*.
3 *cpd*: **to be on speaking terms with sb** parler à qn, adresser la parole à qn; **they're not on speaking terms** ils ne s'adressent plus la parole, ils ne se parlent plus; **speaking tube** tuyau *m* acoustique.

-speaking ['spi:kɪŋ] *adj ending in cpds*: **English-speaking** (*with English as native or official language*) *person, country* anglophone; (*knowing English*) *person* parlant anglais; **slow-speaking** au débit lent, à la parole lente.

spear [spɪəʳ] **1** *n* **(a)** *[warrior, hunter]* lance *f*.
(b) *[broccoli, asparagus]* pointe *f*.
2 *vt* transpercer d'un coup de lance. **he ~ed a potato with his fork** il a piqué une pomme de terre avec sa fourchette.
3 *cpd*: (*Brit*) **spear grass** chiendent *m*; **spear gun** fusil sous-marin *or* à harpon; **spearhead** (*n*) fer *m* de lance (*also fig Mil*); (*vt*) *attack, offensive* être le fer de lance de; *campaign* mener; **spearmint** (*n*) (*Bot*) menthe verte; (*: *chewing gum*) chewing-gum *m* (à la menthe); (*cpd*) *sweet* à la menthe; *flavour* de menthe.

spec* [spek] *n* (*abbr of* **speculation**) **to buy sth on ~** risquer *or* tenter le coup* en achetant qch; **I went along on ~** j'y suis allé à tout hasard.

special ['speʃəl] **1** *adj* **(a)** (*specific*) *purpose, use, equipment* spécial, particulier; *notebook, box, room* spécial, réservé (à cet usage); *arrangement, order, permission, fund, edition* spécial. **are you thinking of any ~ date?** est-ce que tu penses à une date particulière? *or* en particulier?; **I've no ~ person in mind** je ne pense à personne en particulier; **~ to that country** spécial *or* particulier *or* propre à ce pays; **by ~ command of** sur ordre spécial *or* exprès de.
(b) (*exceptional*) *attention, pleasure, effort* (tout) particulier; *favour, price, study, skill* (tout) spécial; *occasion* spécial, extraordinaire, exceptionnel; *case, circumstances* extraordinaire, exceptionnel; (*Pol etc*) *powers, legislation* extraordinaire. **take ~ care of it** fais-y particulièrement attention, prends-en un soin tout particulier; (*Comm*) **~ offer** réclame *f*; **it's a ~ case** c'est un cas spécial *or* particulier *or* à part; **it's rather a ~ situation** ce n'est pas une situation ordinaire, c'est une situation plutôt exceptionnelle; **in this one ~ instance** dans ce cas bien particulier; **he has a ~ place in our affections** nous sommes tout particulièrement attachés à lui; **her ~ friend** sa meilleure amie, une amie qui lui est particulièrement chère *or* intime; **he's a very ~ person to her** il lui est tout particulièrement cher; **you're extra ~!*** tu es quelqu'un à part!; **this is rather a ~ day for me** c'est une journée particulièrement importante pour moi; **to ask for ~ treatment** demander à être considéré comme un cas à part; **it's a ~ feature of the village** c'est une caractéristique *or* une particularité du village; (*Press*) **~ feature** article spécial; **he has his own ~ way with the children** il a une façon toute particulière *or* bien à lui de s'y prendre avec les enfants; **my ~ chair** mon fauteuil préféré, le fauteuil que je me réserve; (*Univ etc*) **~ subject** sujet spécialisé; **nothing ~** rien de spécial *or* de particulier; **what's so ~ about her?** qu'est-ce qu'elle a de spécial? *or* de particulier? *or* d'extraordinaire?; *V also* **3**.
2 *n* (*train*) train *m* supplémentaire; (*newspaper*) édition spéciale; (*policeman*) auxiliaire *m* bénévole de police; (*: *Rad or TV programme*) émission spéciale. **the chef's ~** la spécialité du chef *or* de la maison; *V* **football**.
3 *cpd*: **special agent** (*Comm etc*) concessionnaire *mf*; (*spy*) agent secret; (*Brit*) **special constable** auxiliaire *m* bénévole de police; (*Press, Rad, TV*) **special correspondent** envoyé(e) *m(f)* spécial(e); (*Post*) **by special delivery** en exprès; (*Post*) **special-delivery letter** lettre *f* exprès; (*US Post*) **special handling** acheminement *m* rapide; (*Jur*) **special jury** jury spécial; (*Jur*) **special licence** dispense spéciale; **by special messenger** par messager spécial.

specialist ['speʃəlɪst] **1** *n* (*also Med*) spécialiste *mf* (*in* de). (*Med*) **an eye/heart ~** un(e) ophtalmologiste/cardiologue; (*gen*) **you need a ~ to tell you that** seul un spécialiste *or* un expert peut vous dire cela. **2** *cpd knowledge, dictionary* spécial. **it's specialist work** cela requiert un spécialiste *or* un professionnel, un amateur ne peut pas le faire.

speciality [ˌspeʃɪ'ælɪtɪ] *n* **(a)** (*U: V* **special 1b**) caractère (tout) particulier *or* (tout) spécial (*or* extraordinaire *or* exceptionnel).
(b) (*special quality or activity etc*) spécialité *f*. **to make a ~ of sth** se spécialiser dans qch; **his ~ is Medieval English** il est spécialisé dans *or* c'est un spécialiste de l'anglais du moyen-âge; **it is a ~ of the village** c'est une spécialité du village; **armchairs are this firm's ~** cette firme se spécialise dans les fauteuils; **the chef's ~** la spécialité du chef *or* de la maison.

specialization [ˌspeʃəlaɪ'zeɪʃən] *n* spécialisation *f* (*in* dans).

specialize ['speʃəlaɪz] **1** *vi [student, firm, chef etc]* se spécialiser (*in* dans). **2** *vt*: **~d knowledge** connaissances spéciales.

specially ['speʃəlɪ] *adv* **(a)** (*specifically*) spécialement, particulièrement, surtout. **~ written for children** écrit spécialement pour les enfants; **he is ~ interested in Proust** il s'intéresse tout spécialement *or* tout particulièrement à Proust; **we would ~ like to see the orchard** nous aimerions particulièrement *or* surtout voir le verger; **a ~ difficult task** une tâche particulièrement difficile.
(b) (*on purpose*) spécialement, exprès. **I had it ~ made** je l'ai fait faire exprès *or* tout spécialement; **I asked for it ~** je l'ai demandé exprès *or* tout spécialement, j'avais bien dit *or* spécifié que je le voulais.

specialty ['speʃəltɪ] *n* = **speciality b.**

specie ['spi:ʃi:] *n* (*Fin*) espèces *fpl* (monnayées).

species ['spi:ʃi:z] *n, pl inv* (*all senses*) espèce *f*.

specific [spə'sɪfɪk] **1** *adj statement, instruction* précis, explicite, clair; *purpose, reason, plan, meaning, case* précis, particulier, déterminé; *example* précis; (*Bio, Bot, Chem, Phys*) spécifique. **he was very ~ on that point** il s'est montré très explicite sur ce point; (*Phys*) **~ gravity** densité *f*; (*Phys*) **~ heat** chaleur *f* spécifique; (*Bio*) **~ name** nom *m* d'espèce.
2 *n* **(a)** (*Med*) (remède *m*) spécifique *m* (*for* de, contre); (*fig*) remède spécifique.
(b) (*pl: details etc*) **let's get down to ~s** entrons dans les détails, prenons des exemples précis.

specifically [spə'sɪfɪkəlɪ] *adv warn, order, state, explain, mention* expressément, explicitement, de façon précise. **I told you quite ~** je vous l'avais bien précisé *or* spécifié; **designed ~ for** conçu tout particulièrement pour; **we asked for that one ~** nous avons bien spécifié *or* précisé que nous voulions celui-là; **the law does not ~ refer to ...** la loi ne se rapporte pas explicitement à ....

specification [ˌspesɪfɪ'keɪʃən] *n* **(a)** (*U: act of specifying*) spécification *f*, précision *f*.
(b) (*item in contract etc*) stipulation *f*, prescription *f*. **this ~ was not complied with** cette stipulation *or* cette prescription n'a pas été respectée; (*for building, machine etc*) **~s** spécification *f*, caractéristiques *fpl*.

specify ['spesɪfaɪ] *vt* spécifier, préciser. **unless otherwise specified** sauf indication contraire.

specimen ['spesɪmɪn] **1** *n [rock, species, style]* spécimen *m*; *[blood, tissue]* prélèvement *m*; *[urine]* échantillon *m*; (*fig: example*) spécimen, exemple *m* (*of* de). **that trout is a fine ~** cette truite est un magnifique spécimen *or* est magnifique; (*fig*) **an odd ~*** (*man or woman*) un drôle d'échantillon d'humanité; (*man*) un drôle de type*; (*woman*) une drôle de bonne femme*; **you're a pretty poor ~*** tu es un (*or* une) pas grand-chose*.
2 *cpd*: **specimen copy** spécimen *m*; **specimen page** page *f* spécimen; **specimen signature** spécimen *m* de signature.

specious ['spi:ʃəs] *adj logic, argument* spécieux; *beauty* illusoire, trompeur.

speciousness ['spi:ʃəsnɪs] *n* (*V* **specious**) caractère spécieux; apparence illusoire *or* trompeuse.

speck [spek] **1** *n [dust, soot]* grain *m*; *[dirt, mud, ink]* toute petite tache; (*on fruit, leaves, skin*) tache, tavelure *f*; (*tiny amount*) *[sugar, butter]* tout petit peu; *[truth etc]* grain, atome *m*. **it has got black ~s all over it** c'est entièrement couvert de toutes petites taches noires; **I've got a ~ in my eye** j'ai une poussière *or* une escarbille dans l'œil; **just a ~ on the horizon/in the sky** rien qu'un point noir à l'horizon/dans le ciel; **cream? — just a ~*, thanks** de la crème? — rien qu'un tout petit peu, merci.
2 *vt* (*gen pass*) tacheter, moucheter; *fruit* tacheter, taveler.

speckle ['spekl] **1** *n* tacheture *f*, moucheture *f* (*d'un animal*). **2** *vt* tacheter, moucheter.

specs* [speks] *npl* (*abbr of* **spectacles**) lunettes *fpl*.

spectacle ['spektəkl] *n* **(a)** (*sight*) spectacle *m* (*also pej*); (*Cine/Theat etc*) superproduction *f*, film *m*/revue *f etc* à grand spectacle. **the coronation was a great ~** le couronnement a été un spectacle somptueux; (*pej*) **to make a ~ of o.s.** se donner en spectacle.
(b) (pair of) ~s lunettes *fpl*.

spectacled ['spektəkld] *adj* (*also Zool*) à lunettes.

spectacular [spek'tækjʊləʳ] **1** *adj sight, act, results, change, fall* spectaculaire, impressionnant; *defeat, victory* spectaculaire. **a ~ success** un succès fou. **2** *n* (*Cine/Theat*) superproduction *f*, film *m*/revue *f* à grand spectacle.

spectator [spek'teɪtəʳ] **1** *n* spectateur *m*, -trice *f*. **the ~s** les spectateurs, le public, l'assistance *f*.
2 *cpd*: **it is one of the great spectator sports** c'est l'un des sports qui attirent un très grand nombre de spectateurs; **this tends to be rather a spectator sport** c'est un sport qui attire plus de spectateurs que de joueurs.

specter ['spektəʳ] *n* (*US*) = **spectre.**

spectra ['spektrə] *npl of* **spectrum.**

spectral ['spektrəl] *adj* (*all senses*) spectral.

spectre, (*US*) **specter** ['spektəʳ] *n* spectre *m*, fantôme *m*.

spectrogram ['spektrəʊgræm] *n* spectrogramme *m*.

spectrograph ['spektrəʊgrɑ:f] *n* spectrographe *m*.

spectroscope ['spektrəʊskəʊp] *n* spectroscope *m*.

spectroscopy [spek'trɒskəpɪ] *n* spectroscopie *f*.

spectrum ['spektrəm] **1** *n, pl* **spectra** (*Phys*) spectre *m*; (*fig*) gamme *f* (*fig*). **2** *cpd analysis, colours* spectral.

speculate ['spekjʊleɪt] *vi* **(a)** (*Philos*) spéculer (*about, on* sur); (*gen: ponder*) s'interroger (*about, on* sur, *whether* pour savoir si). **he was speculating about going** il se demandait s'il devait y aller ou non.
(b) (*Fin*) spéculer; (*St Ex*) spéculer *or* jouer à la Bourse.

speculation [ˌspekjʊˈleɪʃən] *n* **(a)** (*U*) (*Philos*) spéculation *f*; (*gen: guessing*) conjecture(s) *f(pl)*, supposition(s) *f(pl)* (*about* sur). **it is the subject of much ~** cela donne lieu à bien des conjectures; **it is pure ~** ce n'est qu'une supposition; **after all the ~ about ...** après toutes ces conjectures *or* suppositions sur ... .
(b) (*Fin, St Ex, gen*) spéculation *f* (*in, on* sur). **he bought it as a ~** il a spéculé en achetant cela; **it proved a good ~** ce fut une spéculation réussie *or* une bonne affaire; **that picture he bought was a good ~** il a fait une bonne affaire en achetant ce tableau, il a eu du nez en achetant ce tableau.
speculative [ˈspekjʊlətɪv] *adj* (*all senses*) spéculatif.
speculator [ˈspekjʊleɪtəʳ] *n* spéculateur *m*, -trice *f*.
speculum [ˈspekjʊləm] *n* *[telescope]* miroir *m*; (*Med*) spéculum *m*.
sped [sped] *pret, ptp of* **speed.**
speech [spiːtʃ] **1** *n* **(a)** (*U*) (*faculty*) parole *f*; (*enunciation*) articulation *f*, élocution *f*; (*manner of speaking*) façon *f* de parler; (*as opposed to writing*) parole; (*language: of district or group*) parler *m*; (*Gram*) discours *m*. **to lose the power of ~** perdre (l'usage de) la parole; **his ~ was very indistinct** il parlait *or* articulait très indistinctement, sa façon de parler *or* son élocution était très indistincte; (*on one occasion*) il parlait très indistinctement; **he expresses himself better in ~ than in writing** il s'exprime mieux oralement que par écrit; **the ~ of the playground is different from that of the classroom** le langage *or* le parler des enfants qui jouent diffère de celui des enfants en classe; **his ~ betrays his origins** son langage *or* sa façon de s'exprimer trahit ses origines; (*Prov*) **~ is silver but silence is golden** la parole est d'argent mais le silence est d'or (*Prov*); **free ~, freedom of ~** liberté *f* de parole *or* d'expression; (*Gram*) **direct/indirect ~** discours direct/indirect; *V* **figure, part** *etc*.
(b) (*formal address*) discours *m* (*on* sur); (*short, less formal*) speech* *m*, allocution *f*. **to make a ~** faire un discours; **~, ~!** un discours!; *V* **maiden** *etc*.
2 *cpd:* **speech clinic** centre *m* d'orthophonie; (*Ling*) **speech community** communauté *f* linguistique; (*Brit Scol etc*) **speech day** distribution *f* des prix; **speech defect, speech disorder, speech impediment** défaut *m* d'élocution; **speechmaker** orateur *m*; (*U: slightly pej*) **speechmaking** discours *mpl*, beaux discours (*pej*); (*Anat*) **speech organ** organe *m* de la parole; (*Ling*) **speech sound** phonème *m*; **speech therapist** orthophoniste *mf*; **speech therapy** orthophonie *f*; **speech training** leçons *fpl* d'élocution.
speechify [ˈspiːtʃɪfaɪ] *vi* (*pej*) discourir, pérorer.
speechifying [ˈspiːtʃɪfaɪɪŋ] *n* (*pej*) laïus* *mpl*, beaux discours.
speechless [ˈspiːtʃlɪs] *adj person* (*from surprise, shock*) muet, interloqué, tout interdit; (*from horror, anger, terror, delight*) muet. **~ with rage/shock** muet de rage/sous le choc; **it left him ~** il en est resté sans voix, il en a perdu la parole; **I'm ~!*** j'en suis sans voix!
speed [spiːd] (*vb: pret, ptp* **sped** *or* **speeded**) **1** *n* **(a)** (*rate of movement*) vitesse *f*; (*rapidity*) rapidité *f*; (*promptness*) promptitude *f*. **the ~ of light/sound** la vitesse de la lumière/du son; **his reading ~ is low** il lit lentement; **shorthand/typing ~s** nombre *m* de mots-minute en sténo/en dactylo; **a secretary with good ~s** une secrétaire qui a une bonne vitesse (de frappe et de sténo); (*Aut*) **what ~ were you going at?** *or* **doing?** quelle vitesse faisiez-vous?, à quelle vitesse rouliez-vous?; **at a ~ of 80 km/h** à une vitesse de 80 km/h; **at a great ~** à toute vitesse; **at (full** *or* **top) ~** *go, run, move, row* à toute vitesse *or* allure; *do sth* très vite, en quatrième vitesse*; **with all possible ~** le plus vite possible; **with such ~** si vite; **to pick up** *or* **gather ~** aller de plus en plus vite; *V* **air, cruise, full, high** *etc*.
(b) (*Aut, Tech: gear*) vitesse *f*. **4 forward ~s** 4 vitesses avant; **a 3-~ gear** une boîte à 3 vitesses.
(c) (*U: Phot*) *[film]* rapidité *f*; (*width of aperture*) degré *m* d'obturation; (*length of exposure*) durée *f* d'exposition.
(d) (*U: Drugs sl*) speed *m* (*sl*), amphétamines *fpl*.
(e) good ~!†† Dieu vous garde!†
2 *cpd:* **speedboat** vedette *f*, (*with outboard motor*) hors-bord *m inv*; (*Brit*) **speed cop*** motard* *m*; (*Brit*) **speed limit** limitation *f* de vitesse; **the speed limit is 80 km/h** la vitesse maximale permise est 80 km/h; **speed merchant*** fou *m* de la route, mordu(e)* *m(f)* de la vitesse; (*Aut*) **speed restriction** limitation *f* de vitesse; (*Aut*) **speed trap** piège *m* de police pour contrôle de vitesse; **speed-up** accélération *f*; (*Ind: of production*) amélioration *f* de rendement; (*US*) **speedwalk** tapis roulant; **speedway** (*Sport: racetrack*) piste *f* de vitesse pour motos; (*US Aut: road*) voie *f* express; (*Sport: U*) **speedway racing** course(s) *f(pl) or* épreuve(s) *f(pl)* de vitesse de motos.
3 *vt pret, ptp* **sped** *or* **speeded** (*liter*) *arrow etc* lancer, décocher. **to ~ sb on his way** souhaiter bon voyage à qn; **to ~ the parting guest** précipiter *or* brusquer le départ de l'invité; **God ~ you!**†† Dieu vous garde!†
4 *vi* **(a)** *pret, ptp* **sped** (*move fast*) *[person, vehicle, horse, boat, plane etc]* **to ~ along** aller à toute vitesse *or* à toute allure, filer comme un éclair; (*liter*) **the arrow sped from his bow** la flèche jaillit de son arc.
(b) *pret, ptp* **speeded** (*Aut: go too fast*) conduire trop vite, excéder la limitation de vitesse. **you're ~ing!** tu vas trop vite!, tu fais un *or* des excès de vitesse!
speed along 1 *vi [person, vehicle, horse, boat, plane]* aller à toute allure *or* à toute vitesse, filer comme l'éclair.
2 *vt sep work, production* activer.
speed up *pret, ptp* **speeded up 1** *vi* (*gen*) aller plus vite; *[walker/worker/singer/pianist/train etc]* marcher/travailler/chanter/jouer/rouler *etc* plus vite; (*Aut*) accélérer; *[engine, machine etc]* tourner plus vite. **do speed up!** plus vite!, active!*
2 *vt sep machine* faire tourner plus vite; *service, work, delivery* activer, accélérer; *production* accélérer, augmenter; *person* faire aller *or* faire travailler plus vite, presser; *film* accélérer. **to speed things up** activer les choses.
3 speed-up *n V* **speed 2.**
speeder [ˈspiːdəʳ] *n* (*Aut*) fou *m* de la vitesse, mordu(e)* *m(f)* de la vitesse.
speedily [ˈspiːdɪlɪ] *adv progress, move, finish, work* vite, rapidement; *reply, return* promptement; (*soon*) bientôt. **as ~ as possible** le plus vite *or* rapidement possible; **he replied very ~** il a répondu très promptement, il s'est dépêché de répondre.
speediness [ˈspiːdɪnɪs] *n* (*V* **speedy**) rapidité *f*; promptitude *f*; vitesse *f*.
speeding [ˈspiːdɪŋ] **1** *n* (*Aut*) excès *m* de vitesse. **2** *cpd:* (*Jur*) **speeding conviction/fine** condamnation *f*/contravention *f* pour excès de vitesse.
speedometer [spɪˈdɒmɪtəʳ] *n* (*Aut*) compteur *m* (de vitesse), indicateur *m* de vitesse.
speedster* [ˈspiːdstəʳ] *n* (*Aut*) fou *m* de la route, mordu(e)* *m(f)* de la vitesse.
speedwell [ˈspiːdwel] *n* (*Bot*) véronique *f*.
speedy [ˈspiːdɪ] *adj reply, recovery, service, decision* rapide, prompt; *vehicle, movement* rapide.
speleologist [ˌspiːlɪˈɒlədʒɪst] *n* spéléologue *mf*.
speleology [ˌspiːlɪˈɒlədʒɪ] *n* spéléologie *f*.
spell[1] [spel] **1** *n* (*magic power*) charme *m* (*also fig*), sortilège *m*; (*magic words*) formule *f* magique, incantation *f*. **an evil ~** un maléfice; **to put** *or* **cast** *or* **lay a ~ on** *or* **over sb, to put sb under a ~** jeter un sort à qn, ensorceler qn, envoûter qn; (*fig*) ensorceler qn, envoûter qn; **under a ~** ensorcelé, envoûté, sous le charme; (*fig*) **under the ~ of** ensorcelé par, envoûté par; **to break the ~** rompre le charme (*also fig*); (*fig*) **the ~ of the East** le charme *or* les sortilèges de l'Orient.
2 *cpd:* (*fig*) **spellbinder** (*speaker*) orateur fascinant, ensorceleur *m*, -euse *f*; **that film was a spellbinder** ce film était ensorcelant *or* était envoûtant *or* vous tenait en haleine; **spellbound** (*lit*) ensorcelé, envoûté, enchanté; (*fig*) subjugué, envoûté, sous le charme; (*fig*) **to hold sb spellbound** subjuguer qn, fasciner qn, tenir qn sous le charme.
spell[2] [spel] **1** *n* **(a)** (*period of work; turn*) tour *m*. **we each took a ~ at the wheel** nous nous sommes relayés au volant, nous avons conduit chacun à notre tour; **~ of duty** tour de service.
(b) (*brief period*) (courte) période *f*. (*Met*) **cold/sunny ~s** périodes de froid/ensoleillées; **for/after a ~** pendant/après un certain temps; **for a short ~** pendant un petit moment; **he has done a ~ in prison** il a été en prison pendant un certain temps, il a fait de la prison; **he's going through a bad ~** il traverse une mauvaise période, il est dans une mauvaise passe.
2 *vt* relayer. **to ~ sb at the wheel/at the oars** relayer qn au volant/aux avirons.
spell[3] [spel] *pret, ptp* **spelt** *or* **spelled 1** *vt* **(a)** (*in writing*) écrire, orthographier; (*aloud*) épeler. **how do you ~ it?** comment est-ce que cela s'écrit?, comment écrit-on cela?; **can you ~ it for me?** pouvez-vous me l'épeler?; **he spelt 'address' with one 'd'** il a écrit 'address' avec un seul 'd'.
(b) *[letters]* former, donner; (*fig*) (*mean*) signifier, représenter (*for sb* pour qn); (*entail*) mener à. **d-o-g ~s 'dog'** d-o-g forment *or* donnent *or* font (le mot) 'dog'; (*fig*) **that would ~ ruin for him** cela signifierait *or* représenterait *or* serait la ruine pour lui; **effort ~s success** l'effort mène au succès.
2 *vi* épeler. **to learn to ~** apprendre à épeler, apprendre l'orthographe; **he can't ~, he ~s badly** il fait des fautes d'orthographe, il ne sait pas l'orthographe, il a une mauvaise orthographe.
spell out *vt sep* **(a)** (*read letter by letter*) épeler; (*decipher*) déchiffrer.
(b) (*fig*) *consequences, alternatives* expliquer bien clairement (*for sb* à qn). **let me spell it out for you** laissez-moi vous expliquer bien clairement, laissez-moi mettre les points sur les i; **do I have to spell it out for you?** faut-il que je mette les points sur les i?, faut-il que je te fasse un dessin?*
speller [ˈspeləʳ] *n* **(a)** *[person]* **to be a good/bad ~** savoir/ne pas savoir l'orthographe. **(b)** (*book*) méthode *f* de lecture.
spelling [ˈspelɪŋ] **1** *n* orthographe *f*. **reformed ~** nouvelle orthographe. **2** *cpd test, practice* d'orthographe. **spelling bee** concours *m* d'orthographe; **spelling book** méthode *f* de lecture; **spelling error, spelling mistake** faute *f* d'orthographe; **spelling pronunciation** prononciation *f* orthographique.
spelt[1] [spelt] *pret, ptp of* **spell**[3].
spelt[2] [spelt] *n* (*Bot*) épeautre *m*.
spend [spend] *pret, ptp* **spent 1** *vt* **(a)** *money* dépenser. **he ~s a lot (of money) on food/bus fares/clothes** *etc* il dépense beaucoup en nourriture/tickets d'autobus/vêtements *etc*; **he ~s a lot (of money) on his house/car/girlfriend** il dépense beaucoup *or* il fait de grosses dépenses pour sa maison/sa voiture/sa petite amie; **he spent a fortune on having the roof repaired** il a dépensé une somme folle *or* une fortune pour faire réparer le toit; **without ~ing a penny** *or* **a ha'penny** sans dépenser un sou, sans bourse délier; (*Brit fig euph*) **to ~ a penny*** aller au petit coin*.
(b) (*pass*) *holiday, evening, one's life* passer; (*devote*) *labour, care* consacrer (*on sth* à qch, *doing, in doing* à faire); *time, afternoon* passer, consacrer, employer. **to ~ time on sth** passer du temps sur qch, consacrer du temps à qch; **to ~ time (in) doing** passer *or* consacrer *or* employer du temps à faire; **he ~s his time reading** il passe son temps à lire, il consacre son temps à la lecture; **I spent 2 hours on that letter** j'ai passé 2 heures sur cette lettre, cette lettre m'a pris 2 heures; **he spent a lot of effort (in) getting it just right** il a fait beaucoup d'efforts pour que ce soit juste comme il faut.

(c) (*consume, exhaust*) *ammunition, provisions* épuiser. *[fury, hatred, enthusiasm]* **to be spent** être tombé; (*liter*) **the storm had spent its fury** la tempête s'était calmée; *V also* **spent.**
2 *vi* dépenser.
3 *cpd*: **spendthrift** (*n*) dépensier *m*, -ière *f*, panier percé* *m*; (*adj*) *habits, attitude etc* de prodigalité; **he's a spendthrift** il est très dépensier, il jette l'argent par les fenêtres.

spender ['spendəʳ] *n*: **to be a big ~** dépenser beaucoup.

spending ['spendɪŋ] **1** *n* (*U*) dépenses *fpl*. **government ~** dépenses publiques.
2 *cpd*: **spending money** argent *m* de poche; **spending power** pouvoir *m* d'achat; **to go on a spending spree** dépenser beaucoup (en une seule fois), faire de folles dépenses.

spent [spent] **1** *pret, ptp of* **spend. 2** *adj match, cartridge etc* utilisé. **that movement is a ~ force** ce mouvement n'a plus l'influence *or* le pouvoir qu'il avait; **he was quite ~** il n'en pouvait plus, il était épuisé; (*permanently*) il était fini.

sperm [spɜːm] *n* sperme *m*. **~ whale** cachalot *m*.

spermaceti [ˌspɜːmə'setɪ] *n* spermaceti *m*, blanc *m* de baleine.

spermatozoon [ˌspɜːmətəʊ'zəʊɒn] *n, pl* **spermatozoa** [ˌspɜːmətəʊ'zəʊə] spermatozoïde *m*.

spew [spjuː] *vt* (*also* **~ up**) vomir; (*fig: also* **~ forth, ~ out**) *fire, lava, curses* vomir. **it makes me ~**‡ ça (me) donne envie de vomir, c'est dégueulasse‡.

sphagnum ['sfægnəm] *n* sphaigne *f*.

sphere [sfɪəʳ] *n* (*gen, Astron, Math etc*) sphère *f*; (*fig*) sphère, domaine *m*. **the music of the ~s** la musique des sphères célestes; **~ of interest/influence** sphère d'intérêt/d'influence; **the ~ of poetry** le domaine de la poésie; **in the social ~** dans le domaine social; **distinguished in many ~s** renommé dans de nombreux domaines; **that is outside my ~** cela n'entre pas dans mes compétences.

spherical ['sferɪkəl] *adj* (*also Math*) sphérique. (*hum*) **he was perfectly ~*** il était gros comme une barrique*.

spheroid ['sfɪərɔɪd] **1** *n* sphéroïde *m*. **2** *adj* sphéroïdal.

sphincter ['sfɪŋktəʳ] *n* sphincter *m*.

sphinx [sfɪŋks] *n* (*also fig*) sphinx *m*.

spice [spaɪs] **1** *n* (*Culin*) épice *f*; (*fig*) piquant *m*, sel *m*. (*Culin*) **mixed ~(s)** épices mélangées; (*Culin*) **there's too much ~ in it** c'est trop épicé; **the papers like a story with a bit of ~ to it** les journaux aiment les nouvelles qui ont du piquant *or* qui ne manquent pas de sel; **a ~ of irony/humour** une pointe d'ironie/d'humour.
2 *vt* (*Culin*) épicer, relever (*with* de); (*fig*) relever, pimenter (*with* de).

spiciness ['spaɪsɪnɪs] *n* (*U*) *[food]* goût épicé *or* relevé; *[story]* piquant *m*.

spick-and-span ['spɪkən'spæn] *adj room, object* impeccable de propreté, propre comme un sou neuf; *person* qui a l'air de sortir d'une boîte, tiré à quatre épingles.

spicy ['spaɪsɪ] *adj food, flavour* épicé, relevé; (*fig*) *story, detail* piquant, salé, croustillant.

spider ['spaɪdəʳ] **1** *n* araignée *f*. **2** *cpd*: **spider crab** araignée *f* de mer; (*Constr*) **spiderman** ouvrier *m* travaillant sur un bâtiment élevé; **spider's web,** (*US*) **spider web** toile *f* d'araignée.

spidery ['spaɪdərɪ] *adj shape* en forme d'araignée; *writing* tremblé.

spiel* [spiːl] **1** *n* laïus* *m inv*, baratin‡ *m*; (*Advertising etc*) boniment(s)* *m(p)*, baratin‡. **2** *vi* faire un laïus* *or* du boniment*, baratiner‡ (*about* sur).

spiffing*† ['spɪfɪŋ] *adj* épatant*.

spigot ['spɪgət] *n* (*plug for barrel*) fausset *m*; (*Tech: valve*) clef *f or* clé *f* (*d'un robinet*).

spike [spaɪk] **1** *n* (*wooden, metal*) pointe *f*; (*on railing*) pointe de fer, (fer *m* de) lance *f*; (*on shoe*) pointe, crampon *m*; (*for letters, bills etc*) pique-notes *m inv*; (*nail*) gros clou à large tête; (*tool*) pointe; *[antler]* dague *f*; (*Bot*) épi *m*. (*Sport: shoes*) **~s*** chaussures *fpl* à pointes *or* à crampons.
2 *cpd*: **spike file** pique-notes *m inv*; (*Bot*) **spike lavender** (lavende *f*) aspic *m*.
3 *vt* (*pierce*) transpercer; (*put ~s on*) garnir de pointes *or* de crampons *or* de clous; (*fig: frustrate*) *plan, hope* contrarier; (*) *drink* corser (*with* de). (*Sport*) **~d shoes** chaussures *fpl* à pointes *or* à crampons; (*fig*) **to ~ sb's guns** mettre des bâtons dans les roues à qn.

spikenard ['spaɪknɑːd] *n* (*U*) nard *m* (indien).

spiky ['spaɪkɪ] *adj branch, top of wall* garni *or* hérissé de pointes; (*fig: quick-tempered*) prompt à prendre la mouche, chatouilleux.

spill[1] [spɪl] (*vb: pret, ptp* **spilt** *or* **spilled**) **1** *n* (*from horse, cycle*) chute *f*, culbute *f*; (*Aut*) accident *m*. **to have a ~** faire une chute *or* une culbute, avoir un accident.
2 *cpd*: **spillover** quantité renversée; (*US*) **spillway** déversoir *m*.
3 *vt water, sand, salt* renverser, répandre; *rider, passenger* jeter à terre. **she spilt the salt** elle a renversé le sel; **she spilt wine all over the table** elle a renversé *or* répandu du vin sur toute la table; **you're ~ing water from that jug** tu laisses tomber de l'eau de cette cruche; **to ~ blood** verser *or* faire couler le sang; (*fig*) **to ~ the beans*** vendre la mèche; (*Naut*) **to ~ (wind from) a sail** étouffer une voile.
4 *vi [liquid, salt etc]* se répandre.

spill out 1 *vi* se répandre; (*fig*) *[people etc]* sortir avec précipitation. **after school the children spilled out into the streets** à la sortie de l'école, un flot d'enfants se précipita *or* se déversa dans la rue.
2 *vt sep contents, sand, liquid* répandre; (*fig*) *story, truth, details* révéler, raconter (précipitamment).

spill over 1 *vi [liquids]* déborder, se répandre; (*fig*) *[population]* déborder, se déverser (*into* dans).
2 spillover *n V* **spill**[1] **2; overspill** *n, adj V* **over 3.**

spill[2] [spɪl] *n* (*for lighting with*) longue allumette (*de papier etc*).

spilt [spɪlt] *pret, ptp of* **spill**[1].

spin [spɪn] (*vb: pret* **spun** *or* **span**††, *ptp* **spun**) **1** *n* **(a)** (*turning motion*) tournoiement *m*; (*Aviat*) (chute *f* en) vrille *f*. **to give a wheel a ~** faire tourner une roue; (*on washing machine*) **long/short ~** essorage complet/léger; (*Sport*) **to put a ~ on a ball** donner de l'effet à une balle; (*Aviat*) **to go into a ~** tomber en vrille *or* en vrillant; (*Aviat*) **to pull** *or* **get out of a ~** se sortir d'une (chute en) vrille; (*fig*) *[person]* **to get into a ~** s'affoler, perdre la tête, paniquer*; **everything was in such a ~** c'était la pagaïe* complète; (*fig: try out*) **to give sth a ~**‡ essayer qch; *V* **flat**[1] *etc.*
(b) (*: *ride*) petit tour, balade* *f*. **to go for a ~** faire un petit tour *or* une balade* (en voiture *or* à bicyclette *etc*).
2 *cpd*: **spindrift** embrun(s) *m(pl)*, poudrin *m*; **spin-dry** essorer (à la machine); **spin-dryer** essoreuse *f*; (*U*) **spin-drying** essorage *m* à la machine; **spin-off** profit *or* avantage inattendu; (*Ind, Tech etc*) sous-produit *m*, application *f* secondaire; **this TV series is a spin-off from the famous film** ce feuilleton télévisé est tiré *or* issu du célèbre film.
3 *vt* **(a)** *wool, yarn, fibres, glass* filer (*into* en, pour en faire); *thread etc* fabriquer, produire; *[spider, silkworm]* filer, tisser; (*fig*) *story etc* inventer, fabriquer, débiter (*pej*). (*fig*) **to ~ a yarn** (*make up*) inventer *or* débiter (*pej*) une (longue) histoire; (*tell*) raconter une (longue) histoire; **he spun me a yarn about his difficulties/about having been ill** il m'a inventé *or* débité (*pej*) une longue histoire sur ses problèmes/comme quoi il avait été malade; **spun glass** verre filé; **hair like spun gold** des cheveux ressemblant à de l'or filé; **spun silk** schappe *m or f*; (*Naut*) **spun yarn** bitord *m*; *V* **fine**[2].
(b) *wheel, nut, revolving stand etc* faire tourner; *top* lancer, fouetter; (*Sport*) *ball* donner de l'effet à. **to ~ a coin** jouer à pile ou face.
(c) = **spin-dry**; *V* **2.**
4 *vi* **(a)** *[spinner etc]* filer; *[spider]* filer, tisser.
(b) (*often* **~ round**) *[person, suspended object]* tourner, tournoyer, pivoter; *[top, dancer]* tourner, tournoyer; *[planet, spacecraft]* tourner (sur soi-même); *[machinery wheel]* tourner; *[car wheel]* patiner; *[aircraft]* vriller, tomber en vrillant; (*Sport*) *[ball]* tournoyer. **to ~ round and round** continuer à tourner (*or* tournoyer *etc*); **to send sth/sb ~ning** envoyer rouler qch/qn; **the disc went ~ning away over the trees** le disque s'envola en tournoyant par-dessus les arbres; **he spun round as he heard me come in** il s'est retourné vivement *or* sur ses talons en m'entendant entrer; (*fig*) **my head is ~ning (round)** j'ai la tête qui tourne; (*fig*) **the room was ~ning (round)** la chambre tournait (autour de moi *or* lui *etc*).
(c) (*move quickly*) *[vehicle]* **to ~** *or* **go ~ning along** rouler à toute vitesse, filer (à toute allure).
(d) (*Fishing*) **to ~ for trout** *etc* pêcher la truite *etc* au lancer.

spin out *vt sep story, explanation* faire durer, délayer; *visit etc* faire durer; *money, food* faire durer, économiser, ménager.

spin round 1 *vi V* **spin 4b.**
2 *vt sep wheel, nut, revolving stand* faire tourner; *person* faire pivoter; *dancing partner* faire tourner *or* tournoyer.

spinach ['spɪnɪdʒ] *n* (*plant*) épinard *m*; (*Culin*) épinards.

spinal ['spaɪnl] *adj* (*Anat*) *nerve, muscle* spinal; *ligament, column, disc* vertébral; *injury* à la colonne vertébrale. **~ anaesthesia** rachianesthésie *f*; **~ anaesthetic** rachianesthésique *m*; **~ cord** moelle épinière; **~ meningitis** méningite cérébro-spinale.

spindle ['spɪndl] **1** *n* **(a)** (*Spinning*) fuseau *m*; (*on machine*) broche *f*. **(b)** (*Tech*) *[pump]* axe *m*; *[lathe]* arbre *m*; *[valve]* tige *f*. **2** *cpd*: (*person*) **spindlelegs*, spindleshanks*** faucheux *m* (*fig*).

spindly ['spɪndlɪ] *adj legs, arms* grêle, maigre comme une *or* des allumette(s); *person* grêle, chétif; *chair leg* grêle; *plant* étiolé.

spine [spaɪn] **1** *n* (*Anat*) colonne vertébrale, épine dorsale; *[fish]* épine; *[hedgehog]* piquant *m*, épine; (*Bot*) épine, piquant; *[book]* dos *m*; *[hill etc]* crête *f*. **2** *cpd*: **spine-chilling** à vous glacer le sang.

spineless ['spaɪnlɪs] *adj* (*Zool*) invertébré; (*fig*) mou (*f* molle), flasque (*fig*), sans caractère.

spinelessly ['spaɪnlɪslɪ] *adv* (*fig*) lâchement, mollement.

spinet [spɪ'net] *n* (*Mus*) épinette *f*.

spinnaker ['spɪnəkəʳ] *n* spinnaker *m*, foc-ballon *m*.

spinner ['spɪnəʳ] *n* (*person*) fileur *m*, -euse *f*; (*Fishing*) cuiller *f*; (*spin-dryer*) essoreuse *f*. (*Baseball, Cricket*) **he sent down a ~*** il a donné de l'effet à la balle.

spinneret [ˌspɪnə'ret] *n* (*Tex, Zool*) filière *f*.

spinney ['spɪnɪ] *n* (*Brit*) bosquet *m*, petit bois.

spinning ['spɪnɪŋ] **1** *n* (*by hand*) filage *m*; (*by machine*) filature *f*; (*Fishing*) pêche *f* au lancer. **2** *cpd*: **spinning jenny** jenny *f*; **spinning machine** machine *f or* métier *m* à filer; **spinning mill** filature *f*; **spinning top** toupie *f*; **spinning wheel** rouet *m*.

spinster ['spɪnstəʳ] *n* célibataire *f* (*also Admin*), vieille fille (*pej*). **she is a ~** elle est célibataire, elle n'est pas mariée.

spiny ['spaɪnɪ] *adj* (*V* **spine**) épineux (*also fig*), couvert d'épines *or* de piquants. **~ lobster** langouste *f*.

spiracle ['spɪrəkl] *n* (*airhole*) orifice *m* d'aération; *[whale etc]* évent *m*; *[insect etc]* stigmate *m*; (*Geol*) cassure *f*.

spiral ['spaɪərəl] **1** *adj curve, shell* en spirale, spiroïdal; *movement, dive, decoration* en spirale; *spring* en spirale, à boudin; *nebula, galaxy* spiral; (*Aviat*) en vrille. **~ staircase** escalier tournant *or* en colimaçon.
2 *n* spirale *f*. **in a ~** en spirale; (*fig*) **the price ~** la montée inexorable des prix; **the inflationary ~** la spirale inflationniste.
3 *vi [staircase, smoke]* former une spirale; *[ball, missile etc]* tourner en spirale; *[plane]* vriller; (*fig*) *[prices]* monter en

flèche; *[prices and wages]* former une spirale.
spiral down *vi* (*Aviat*) descendre en vrille.
spiral up *vi* (*Aviat*) monter en vrille; *[staircase, smoke, missile]* monter en spirale; *[prices]* monter en flèche.
spirally ['spaɪərəlɪ] *adv* en spirale, en hélice.
spire ['spaɪəʳ] *n* (*Archit*) flèche *f*, aiguille *f*; *[tree, mountain]* cime *f*; *[grass, plant]* brin *m*, pousse *f*.
spirit ['spɪrɪt] **1** *n* **(a)** (*soul*) esprit *m*, âme *f*. **the life of the ~** la vie de l'esprit, la vie spirituelle; **he was there in ~** il était présent en esprit *or* de cœur; **the ~ is willing but the flesh is weak** l'esprit est prompt mais la chair est faible; **God is pure ~** Dieu est un pur esprit; *V* **holy, move** *etc.*
(b) (*supernatural being*) esprit *m*; (*ghost*) esprit, revenant *m*, fantôme *m*; (*Spiritualism*) esprit. **evil ~** esprit malin *or* du mal.
(c) (*person*) esprit *m*, âme *f*. **one of the greatest ~s of his day** un des plus grands esprits de son temps; **the courageous ~ who ...** l'esprit courageux *or* l'âme courageuse qui ...; **a few restless ~s** quelques mécontents; **the leading ~ in the party** l'âme du parti; *V* **kindred, moving** *etc.*
(d) (*attitude etc*) esprit *m*, disposition *f*; *[proposal, regulations etc]* esprit, intention *f*, but *m*. **he's got the right ~** il a la disposition *or* l'attitude qu'il faut; **in a ~ of forgiveness** dans un esprit *or* une intention de pardon; **he has great fighting ~** il ne se laisse jamais abattre; **you must take it in the ~ in which it was meant** prenez-le dans l'esprit où c'était dit *or* voulu; **to take sth in the right/wrong ~** prendre qch en bonne/mauvaise part *or* du bon/mauvais côté; **you must enter into the ~ of the thing** il faut y participer de bon cœur; **in a ~ of revenge** par esprit de vengeance; **in a ~ of mischief** *etc* par espièglerie *etc*; **the ~, not the letter of the law** l'esprit et non la lettre de la loi; **the film is certainly in the ~ of the book** le film est certainement conforme à l'esprit du livre; **the ~ of the times** l'esprit des temps *or* de l'époque; **that's the ~!** c'est ça!, voilà comment il faut réagir!, voilà l'attitude à prendre!; **community ~** civisme *m*; *V* **public, team** *etc.*
(e) (*frame of mind*) humeur *f*, état *m* d'esprit; (*morale*) moral *m*. **in good ~s** de bonne humeur; **in poor** *or* **low ~s, out of ~s** déprimé, qui n'a pas le moral; **to keep one's ~s up** ne pas se laisser abattre, garder le moral; **my ~s rose** j'ai repris courage; **to raise sb's ~s** remonter le moral à qn; *V* **animal, high** *etc.*
(f) (*courage*) courage *m*, caractère *m*, cran* *m*; (*energy*) énergie *f*; (*vitality*) entrain *m*. **man of ~** homme *m* énergique *or* de caractère; **he replied with ~** il a répondu courageusement *or* énergiquement *or* avec fougue; **he sang/played with ~** il a chanté/joué avec fougue *or* brio.
(g) (*Chem*) alcool *m*. **preserved in ~(s)** conservé dans de l'alcool; **~(s) of ammonia** sel *m* ammoniaque; **~(s) of salt** esprit-de-sel *m*; **~(s) of turpentine** (essence *f* de) térébenthine *f*; (*drink*) **~s** spiritueux *mpl*, alcool; **raw ~s** alcool pur; *V* **methylated, surgical** *etc.*
2 *cpd lamp, stove, varnish* à alcool; (*Spiritualism*) *help, world* des esprits. **spirit gum** colle gomme *f*; **spirit level** niveau *m* à bulle.
3 *vt*: **he was ~ed out of the castle** on l'a fait sortir du château comme par enchantement *or* magie; **the documents were mysteriously ~ed off his desk** les documents ont été mystérieusement escamotés *or* subtilisés de son bureau.
spirit away, spirit off *vt sep person* faire disparaître comme par enchantement; *object, document etc* escamoter, subtiliser.
spirited ['spɪrɪtɪd] *adj person* vif, fougueux, plein d'entrain; *horse* fougueux; *reply, speech* plein de verve, fougueux; *conversation* animé; *music* plein d'allant; *undertaking, defence* courageux, qui montre du cran*. (*Mus*) **he gave a ~ performance** il a joué avec fougue *or* avec brio; *V* **high, low**[1], **public** *etc.*
spiritless ['spɪrɪtlɪs] *adj person* sans entrain, sans énergie, sans vie; *acceptance, agreement* veule, lâche.
spiritual ['spɪrɪtjʊəl] **1** *adj* (*not material etc*) *life, power, welfare* spirituel; (*religious*) *music etc* spirituel, religieux; *heir, successor* spirituel. **he is a very ~ person** c'est vraiment une nature élevée; (*Rel*) **~ adviser** conseiller spirituel, directeur *m* de conscience; (*Brit*) **the lords ~** les lords spirituels (*évêques siégeant à la Chambre des pairs*).
2 *n* chant religieux; (*also* **Negro ~**) (negro-)spiritual *m*.
spiritualism ['spɪrɪtjʊəlɪzəm] *n* (*Rel*) spiritisme *m*; (*Philos*) spiritualisme *m*.
spiritualist ['spɪrɪtjʊəlɪst] *adj, n* (*Rel*) spirite (*mf*); (*Philos*) spiritualiste (*mf*).
spirituality [ˌspɪrɪtjʊ'ælɪtɪ] *n* **(a)** (*U*) spiritualité *f*, qualité spirituelle.
(b) (*Rel*) **spiritualities** biens *mpl* et bénéfices *mpl* ecclésiastiques.
spiritually ['spɪrɪtjʊəlɪ] *adv* spirituellement, en esprit.
spirituous ['spɪrɪtjʊəs] *adj* spiritueux, alcoolique. **~ liquor** spiritueux *mpl*.
spirt [spɜːt] = **spurt.**
spit[1] [spɪt] (*vb: pret, ptp* **spat**) **1** *n* (*spittle*) crachat *m*; (*saliva*) *[person]* salive *f*; *[animal]* bave *f*; (*Bot*) écume printanière, crachat de coucou; (*action*) crachement *m*. (*esp Mil*) **~ and polish** briquage *m*, astiquage *m*; **there was just a ~ of rain** il tombait quelques gouttes de pluie; (*fig*) **he's the dead** *or* **very ~* of his uncle** c'est le portrait craché* de son oncle, son oncle et lui se ressemblent comme deux gouttes d'eau; *V* **frog**[1].
2 *cpd*: *[person]* **to be a spitfire** s'emporter pour un rien.
3 *vt blood, curses, flames etc* cracher.
4 *vi [person, cat etc]* cracher (*at sb* sur qn); *[fire, fat]* crépiter. **she spat in his face** elle lui a craché à la figure; **it was ~ting (with rain)** il tombait quelques gouttes de pluie.
spit out *vt sep pip, pill* (re)cracher; *tooth, curses, information* cracher. (*fig say it*) **spit it out!*** allons, accouche!‡ *or* vide ton sac!* (*fig*).
spit up *vt sep blood etc* cracher.
spit[2] [spɪt] **1** *n* (*Culin*) broche *f*; (*Geog*) pointe *f or* langue *f* (de terre). **2** *cpd*: **spitroast** faire rôtir à la broche; **spitroasted** (rôti) à la broche. **3** *vt* embrocher.
spit[3] [spɪt] *n* (*Horticulture*) **to dig sth 2 ~s deep** creuser qch à une profondeur de 2 fers de bêche.
spite [spaɪt] **1** *n* (*U*) **(a)** (*ill-feeling*) rancune *f*, dépit *m*. **out of pure ~** par pure rancune *or* malveillance; **to have a ~ against sb*** avoir une dent contre qn, en vouloir à qn.
(b) in ~ of malgré, en dépit de; **in ~ of the fact that he has seen me** bien qu'il m'ait vu, malgré qu'il m'ait vu; **in ~ of everyone** envers et contre tous.
2 *vt* vexer, contrarier.
spiteful ['spaɪtfʊl] *adj person* méchant, malveillant, rancunier; *comment* malveillant; *tongue* venimeux. **a ~ remark** une rosserie*.
spitefully ['spaɪtfəlɪ] *adv* par méchanceté, par rancune, par dépit.
spitefulness ['spaɪtfʊlnɪs] *n* méchanceté *f*, malveillance *f*, rancune *f*.
spitting ['spɪtɪŋ] *n*: **'~ prohibited'** 'défense de cracher'; *V* **image.**
spittle ['spɪtl] *n* (*ejected*) crachat *m*; (*dribbled*) *[person]* salive *f*; *[animal]* bave *f*.
spittoon [spɪ'tuːn] *n* crachoir *m*.
spiv* [spɪv] *n* (*Brit*) chevalier *m* d'industrie.
splash [splæʃ] **1** *n* (*act*) éclaboussement *m*; (*sound*) floc *m*, plouf *m*; (*series of sounds*) clapotement *m*; (*mark*) éclaboussure *f*, tache *f*; (*fig: of colour*) tache. **he dived in with a ~** il a plongé dans un grand éclaboussement *or* en faisant une grande gerbe; **it made a great ~ as it hit the water** c'est tombé dans l'eau avec un gros plouf *or* en faisant une grande gerbe; (*fig*) **to make a ~*** faire sensation, faire du bruit; (*fig*) **a great ~ of publicity** un grand étalage de *or* une débauche de publicité.
2 *cpd*: (*Aut etc*) **splashboard** garde-boue *m inv*; (*Space*) **splashdown** amerrissage *m*; **splash guard** garde-boue *m inv*.
3 *vt* éclabousser (*sth over sb/sth* qch sur qn/qch, *sb/sth with sth* qn/qch de qch). **to ~ milk on the floor** renverser du lait par terre; **he ~ed paint on the floor** il a fait des éclaboussures de peinture par terre; (*in swimming etc*) **don't ~ me!** ne m'éclabousse pas!; **to ~ one's way through a stream** traverser un ruisseau en éclaboussant *or* en pataugeant; (*Press*) **the news was ~ed across the front page** la nouvelle a été mise en manchette, la nouvelle a fait cinq colonnes à la une.
4 *vi* **(a)** *[liquid, mud etc]* faire des éclaboussures. **the milk ~ed on** *or* **over the tablecloth** le lait a éclaboussé la nappe; **tears ~ed on to her book** les larmes s'écrasaient sur son livre.
(b) *[person, animal]* barboter, patauger (*in* dans). **to ~ across a stream** traverser un ruisseau en éclaboussant *or* en pataugeant; **the dog ~ed through the mud** le chien pataugeait dans la boue; **to ~ into the water** *[person]* plonger dans l'eau dans un grand éclaboussement *or* en faisant une grande gerbe; *[stone etc]* tomber dans l'eau avec un gros floc *or* plouf.
splash about 1 *vi [person, animal]* barboter, patauger (*in* dans).
2 *vt sep ink, mud* faire des éclaboussures de; (*fig*) *money* faire étalage de.
splash down 1 *vi [spacecraft]* amerrir.
2 splashdown *n V* **splash 2.**
splash out* *vi* (*spend money*) faire une folie.
splash up 1 *vi* gicler (*on sb* sur qn).
2 *vt sep* faire gicler.
splay [spleɪ] **1** *vt window frame* ébraser; *end of pipe etc* évaser; *feet, legs* tourner en dehors.
2 *vi* (*also* **~ out**) *[window frame]* s'ébraser; *[end of pipe etc]* se tourner en dehors.
3 *cpd*: **splayfeet** pieds tournés en dehors; **splayfooted** *person* aux pieds plats; *horse* panard.
spleen [spliːn] *n* (*Anat*) rate *f*; (*fig: bad temper*) mauvaise humeur, humeur noire; (††: *melancholy*) spleen *m*. **to vent one's ~ on** décharger sa bile sur.
splendid ['splendɪd] *adj* (*imposing etc*) *ceremony, view, beauty* splendide, superbe, magnifique; (*excellent*) *holiday, result, idea* excellent, magnifique, formidable*; *teacher, mother etc* excellent. **in ~ isolation** dans un splendide isolement; **that's simply ~!** c'est parfait! *or* épatant!* *or* formidable!*
splendidly ['splendɪdlɪ] *adv* (*V* **splendid**) splendidement, superbement, magnifiquement; de façon excellente, épatamment*, formidablement*. **~ dressed** superbement *or* magnifiquement habillé; **you did ~** tu as été merveilleux *or* épatant*; **it all went ~** tout a marché comme sur des roulettes; **it's coming along ~** ça avance très bien *or* formidablement* bien.
splendiferous* [splen'dɪfərəs] *adj* magnifique, merveilleux, mirobolant*.
splendour, (US) splendor ['splendəʳ] *n* splendeur *f*, magnificence *f*, éclat *m*.
splenetic [splɪ'netɪk] *adj* (*bad-tempered*) atrabilaire, morose; (††: *melancholy*) porté au spleen.
splice [splaɪs] **1** *vt rope, cable, film, tape* épisser; *timbers* enter, abouter. **to ~ the mainbrace** (*Naut*) distribuer une ration de rhum; (**fig: have a drink*) boire un coup*; (*fig*) **to get ~d‡** convoler*. **2** *n* (*in rope, film*) épissure *f*; (*in wood*) enture *f*.
splint [splɪnt] *n* (*Med*) éclisse *f*, attelle *f*. **to put sb's arm in ~s** éclisser le bras de qn; **she had her leg in ~s** elle avait la jambe éclissée.
splinter ['splɪntəʳ] **1** *n [glass, shell, wood]* éclat *m*; *[bone]* esquille *f*; (*in one's finger etc*) écharde *f*.

2 *cpd:* **splinter group** groupe dissident *or* scissionniste; **splinterproof glass** verre *m* sécurit *inv* ®.
3 *vt wood* fendre en éclats; *glass, bone* briser en éclats; (*fig*) *party etc* scinder, fragmenter.
4 *vi [wood]* se fendre en éclats; *[glass, bone]* se briser en éclats; (*fig*) *[party]* se scinder, se fragmenter.

split [splɪt] (*vb: pret, ptp* **split**) **1** *n* **(a)** (*in garment, fabric, canvas*) (*at seam*) fente *f*; (*tear*) déchirure *f*; (*in wood, rock*) crevasse *f*, fente; (*in earth's surface*) fissure *f*, crevasse, fente; (*in skin*) fissure, déchirure, (*from cold*) gerçure *f*, crevasse; (*fig: quarrel*) rupture *f*; (*Pol*) scission *f*, schisme *m*. **there was a 3-way ~ in the committee** le comité s'est trouvé divisé en 3 clans; **they did a 4-way ~ of the profits** ils ont partagé les bénéfices en 4; (*fig: share*) **I want my ~*** je veux ma part (du gâteau*); **to do the ~s** faire le grand écart.
(b) (*small bottle*) **soda/lemonade ~** petite bouteille d'eau gazeuse/de limonade; (*cake*) **jam/cream ~** gâteau fourré à la confiture/à la crème; (*ice cream etc*) **banana ~** banana split *m*.
2 *cpd:* **split-cane** en osier; (*Boxing etc*) **split decision** match nul; (*Gram*) **split infinitive** *infinitif m où un adverbe est intercalé entre 'to' et le verbe*; **split-level cooker** cuisinière *f* à plaques de cuisson et four indépendants; **split-level house** maison *f* à deux niveaux; **split mind** = **split personality**; **split-new** tout neuf (*f* toute neuve); **split-ofn** séparation *f*, scission *f* (*from* de); **split peas** pois cassés; **split-pea soup** soupe *f* de pois cassés; **split personality** double personnalité *f*; **split pin** clavette fendue; **split ring** anneau brisé; **a split second** une fraction de seconde; **in a split second** en un rien de temps; **split-second timing** *[military operation etc]* précision *f* à la seconde près; *[actor, comedian]* sens *m* du moment; **split-up** *[engaged couple, friends]* rupture *f*; *[married couple]* séparation *f*; *[political party]* scission *f*, schisme *m*.
3 *vt* **(a)** (*cleave*) *wood, pole* fendre; *slate, diamond* cliver; *stones* fendre, casser; *fabric, garment* déchirer; *seam* fendre; *[lightning, frost, explosion, blow]* fendre; (*fig*) *party etc* diviser, créer une scission *or* un schisme dans. **to ~ the atom** fissionner l'atome; **to ~ sth open** ouvrir qch en le coupant en deux *or* en fendant; **he ~ his head open as he fell** il s'est fendu le crâne en tombant; **the sea had ~ the ship in two** la mer avait brisé le bateau en deux; **he ~ the block into three** il a coupé le bloc en trois; **~ the loaf lengthwise** fendez le pain dans le sens de la longueur; (*fig*) **to ~ hairs** couper les cheveux en quatre, chercher la petite bête; (*Gram*) **to ~ an infinitive** *intercaler un adverbe entre 'to' et le verbe*; (*fig*) **to ~ one's sides (laughing** *or* **with laughter)** se tordre de rire; **this decision ~ the radical movement** cette décision a divisé le mouvement radical, cette décision a provoqué une scission *or* un schisme dans le mouvement radical; **it ~ the party down the middle** cela a littéralement divisé le parti en deux.
(b) (*divide, share*) *work, profits, booty, the bill* (se) partager, (se) répartir. **let's ~ a bottle of wine** si on prenait une bouteille de vin à deux (*or* trois *etc*)?; **they ~ the money 3 ways** ils ont divisé l'argent en 3; **to ~ the difference** partager la différence; **they ~ the work/the inheritance** ils se sont partagé le travail/l'héritage.
4 *vi* **(a)** *[wood, pole, seam]* se fendre; *[stones]* se fendre, se casser; *[fabric, garment]* se déchirer; (*fig*) *[party, Church, government]* se diviser, se désunir. **he ~ it in two** il l'a fendu (en deux); **he ~ it into three** il l'a coupé en trois; **to ~ open** ouvrir en fendant; (*fig*) **my head is ~ting** j'ai atrocement mal à la tête; **the party ~ over nationalization** le parti s'est divisé sur la question des nationalisations, il y a eu une scission *or* un schisme dans le parti à propos de la question des nationalisations.
(b) (*divide: also* **~ up**) *[cells]* diviser; *[people, party etc]* se diviser, se séparer. **the crowd ~ into smaller groups** la foule s'est divisée *or* séparée en petits groupes; **Latin ~ into the Romance languages** le latin s'est divisé *or* ramifié en langues romanes.
(c) (*Brit**: *tell tales, inform*) vendre la mèche. **to ~ on sb** donner qn, vendre qn, cafarder qn*.
(d) (*‡: depart*) filer*, mettre les bouts‡.

split off 1 *vi [piece of wood, branch etc]* se détacher en se fendant (*from* de); (*fig*) *[group, department, company etc]* se séparer (*from* de). **a small group of children split off and wandered away** un petit groupe d'enfants s'est séparé des autres et est parti de son côté.
2 *vt sep branch, splinter, piece* enlever (en fendant *or* en cassant) (*from* de); (*fig*) *company, group, department* séparer (*from* de).
3 split-off *n V* **split 2**.

split up 1 *vi [ship]* se briser; *[boulder, block of wood etc]* se fendre; (*fig*) *[meeting, crowd]* se disperser; *[party, movement]* se diviser, se scinder; *[friends]* rompre, se brouiller; *[married couple]* se séparer; *[engaged couple]* rompre.
2 *vt sep wood, stones* fendre (*into* en); *money, work* partager, répartir; *compound* diviser (*into* en); *party, group, organization* diviser, scinder (*into* en); *meeting* mettre fin à; *crowd* disperser; *friends* séparer. **we must split the work up amongst us** nous devons nous partager *or* nous répartir le travail; **you'll have to split up those two boys if you want them to do any work** il faut que vous sépariez (*subj*) ces deux garçons si vous voulez qu'ils travaillent (*subj*).
3 split-up *n V* **split 2**.

splitting ['splɪtɪŋ] **1** *n* (*V* **split 3a, 3b, 4a, 4b**) fendage *m*; clivage *m*; cassage *m*; déchirement *m*; division *f*, scission *f*, schisme *m*; partage *m*, répartition *f*; séparation *f*. **the ~ of the atom** la fission de l'atome; *V* **hair** *etc*.
2 *adj:* **I have a ~ headache** j'ai atrocement mal à la tête; *V* **ear**[1], **side** *etc*.

splodge [splɒdʒ], **splotch** [splɒtʃ] **1** *n [ink, paint, colour, dirt, mud]* éclaboussure *f*, tache *f*. **strawberries with a great ~ of cream** des fraises avec un monceau de crème.
2 *vt windows, dress etc* éclabousser, barbouiller (*with* de); *mud, ink etc* faire des taches *or* des éclaboussures de (*on* sur).
3 *vi [mud etc]* gicler (*on* sur).

splurge* [splɜːdʒ] **1** *n* (*ostentation*) tralala* *m*; (*spending spree*) folles dépenses, folie *f*. **the wedding reception was** *or* **made a great ~** la réception de mariage était à grand tralala*; **she had a ~ and bought a Rolls** elle a fait une vraie folie et s'est payé* une Rolls.
2 *vi* (*also* **~ out**) faire une *or* des folie(s) (*on* en achetant).
3 *vt* dépenser (en un seul coup) (*on sth* pour qch), engloutir (*on sth* dans qch).

splutter ['splʌtəʳ] **1** *n [person]* bredouillement *m*, bafouillage* *m*; *[engine]* bafouillage*; *[fire, frying pan, fat, candle]* crépitement *m*.
2 *vi [person]* (*spit*) crachoter, postillonner; (*stutter*) bredouiller, bafouiller*; *[pen]* cracher; *[engine]* bafouiller*, tousser; *[fire, frying pan, fat, candle]* crépiter. **he ~ed indignantly** il a bredouillé *or* bafouillé* d'indignation.
3 *vt* (*also* **~ out**) *words, excuse* bredouiller, bafouiller*.

spoil [spɔɪl] (*vb: pret, ptp* **spoiled** *or* **spoilt**) **1** *n* **(a)** (*gen pl*) **~(s)** (*booty*) butin *m*; (*fig: after business deal etc*) bénéfices *mpl*, profits *mpl*; (*US Pol*) poste *m or* avantage *m* reçu en récompense de services politiques rendus; **the ~s of war** le butin *or* les dépouilles *fpl* de la guerre; (*fig*) **he wants his share of the ~s** il veut sa part du gâteau*.
(b) (*U: from excavations etc*) déblais *mpl*.
2 *cpd:* **spoilsport** trouble-fête *mf inv*, rabat-joie *m inv*; **don't be such a spoilsport!** ne joue pas les trouble-fête! *or* les rabat-joie!; (*US Pol*) **spoils system** système *m* des dépouilles (*consistant à distribuer des postes administratifs à des partisans après une victoire électorale*).
3 *vt* **(a)** (*damage*) *paint, dress etc* abîmer. **to ~ one's eyes** s'abîmer la vue; **fruit ~ed by insects** des fruits abîmés par les insectes; **the drought has really ~t the garden** la sécheresse a vraiment fait des dégâts dans le jardin; **to ~ a ballot paper** rendre un bulletin de vote nul.
(b) (*detract from*) *view, style, effect* gâter; *holiday, occasion, pleasure* gâter, gâcher. **these weeds quite ~ the garden** ces mauvaises herbes enlaidissent *or* défigurent le jardin; **his peace of mind was ~t by money worries** sa tranquillité était empoisonnée par des soucis d'argent; **to ~ sb's fun** gâter *or* gâcher l'amusement de qn; **to ~ one's appetite** s'enlever *or* se couper l'appétit; **if you eat that now you'll ~ your lunch** si tu manges ça maintenant tu n'auras plus d'appétit pour le déjeuner; **don't ~ your life by doing that** ne gâche pas ta vie en faisant cela; **if you tell me the ending you'll ~ the film for me** si vous me racontez la fin vous me gâcherez tout l'intérêt du film; **she ~t the meal by overcooking the meat** elle a gâté le repas en faisant trop cuire la viande; **she ~t the meal by telling him the bad news** elle a gâché le repas en lui racontant la triste nouvelle; **the weather ~ed our holiday** le temps nous a gâté *or* gâché nos vacances; (*Prov*) **to ~ the ship for a ha'p'orth of tar** faire des économies de bouts de chandelle.
(c) (*pamper*) *child, one's spouse, dog etc* gâter. **to ~ sb rotten‡** pourrir qn; *V* **spare**.
4 *vi* **(a)** *[food]* s'abîmer; (*in ship's hold, warehouse, shop*) s'avarier.
(b) to be ~ing for a fight brûler de se battre, chercher la bagarre*.

spoilage ['spɔɪlɪdʒ] *n* (*U*) (*process*) détérioration *f*; (*thing, amount spoilt*) déchet(s) *m(pl)*.

spoiler ['spɔɪləʳ] *n* (*Tech*) aérofrein *m*.

spoilt [spɔɪlt] **1** *pret, ptp of* **spoil**. **2** *adj* **(a)** (*V* **spoil 3a, 3b**), abîmé; gâté, gâché; *ballot paper* nul. **(b)** *child etc* gâté; *desire, refusal* d'enfant gâté.

spoke[1] [spəʊk] **1** *n [wheel]* rayon *m*; *[ladder]* barreau *m*, échelon *m*. (*Brit fig*) **to put a ~ in sb's wheel** mettre des bâtons dans les roues à qn. **2** *cpd:* (*Tech*) **spokeshave** vastringue *f*.

spoke[2] [spəʊk] *pret of* **speak**.

spoken ['spəʊkən] **1** *ptp of* **speak**. **2** *adj dialogue, recitative* parlé. **the ~ language** la langue parlée; **~ French** le français parlé; *V* **well**[2] *etc*.

spokesman ['spəʊksmən] *n, pl* **spokesmen** ['spəʊksmən] porte-parole *m inv* (*of, for* de).

spoliation [ˌspəʊlɪ'eɪʃən] *n* (*esp Naut*) pillage *m*, spoliation *f*.

spondaic [spɒn'deɪɪk] *adj* spondaïque.

spondee ['spɒndiː] *n* spondée *m*.

sponge [spʌndʒ] **1** *n* **(a)** (*Zool, gen*) éponge *f*. **to give sth a ~** donner un coup d'éponge à *or* sur qch; (*fig*) **to throw in** *or* **up the ~*** s'avouer vaincu, abandonner la partie.
(b) (*Culin: also* **~ cake**) gâteau *m* de Savoie.
2 *cpd:* (*Brit*) **sponge bag** sac *m* de toilette; **sponge bath** toilette *f* à l'éponge; (*Culin*) **sponge cake** *V* **1b**; **sponge-down** *[person]* toilette *f* à l'éponge; *[walls]* coup *m* d'éponge; (*Culin*) **sponge finger** boudoir *m*; (*Culin*) **sponge pudding** ≃ pudding *m* (*sorte de gâteau de Savoie*); **sponge rubber** caoutchouc *m* mousse ®.
3 *vt* **(a)** *face, person, carpet* éponger, essuyer *or* nettoyer à l'éponge; *wound* éponger; *liquid* éponger, étancher.
(b) (**: cadge*) *meal* se faire payer* (*from or off sb* par qn). **to ~ money from sb** taper* qn; **he ~d £10 off his father** il a tapé* son père de 10 livres.
4 *vi* (**: cadge*) **to ~ on sb** vivre aux crochets de qn; **he's always sponging** c'est un parasite; (*for meals*) c'est un pique-assiette.

sponge down 1 *vt sep person* laver à l'éponge; *horse* éponger; *walls etc* nettoyer *or* laver *or* essuyer à l'éponge. **to sponge o.s. down** se laver à l'éponge, s'éponger.

2 sponge-down n V sponge 2.
sponge out vt sep wound éponger; stain, writing effacer à l'éponge.
sponge up vt sep liquid éponger, étancher.
sponger* ['spʌndʒəʳ] n (pej) parasite m; (for meals) pique-assiette mf inv.
sponginess ['spʌndʒɪnɪs] n spongiosité f.
spongy ['spʌndʒɪ] adj spongieux.
sponsor ['spɒnsəʳ] 1 n (gen: of appeal, proposal, announcement etc) personne f qui accorde son patronage, membre m d'un comité de patronage; (Fin: for loan etc) répondant(e) m(f); (Rel: godparent) parrain m, marraine f; (for club membership) parrain, marraine; (Rad, TV) personne or organisme m qui assure le patronage; (for fund-raising event) donateur m, -trice f (à l'occasion d'un 'sponsored walk' etc; V 2). (Fin) to be sb's ~, to stand ~ to sb, to act as ~ for sb être le (or la) répondant(e) de qn, se porter caution pour qn.
2 vt appeal, proposal, announcement patronner, présenter; (Fin) borrower se porter caution pour; (Rel) être le parrain (or la marraine) de; club member parrainer; (Rad, TV) programme patronner; fund-raising walker, swimmer etc s'engager à rémunérer (en fonction de sa performance). (in fund-raising) ~ed walk etc marche f etc entreprise pour procurer des donations à une œuvre de charité, les participants étant rémunérés par les donateurs en fonction de leur performance.
sponsorship ['spɒnsəʃɪp] n [loan] cautionnement m; [child, member] parrainage m; (Rad, TV) commande f publicitaire; [appeal, announcement] patronage m.
spontaneity [ˌspɒntəˈneɪətɪ] n spontanéité f.
spontaneous [spɒnˈteɪnɪəs] adj (all senses) spontané. ~ combustion combustion vive.
spontaneously [spɒnˈteɪnɪəslɪ] adv spontanément.
spoof‡ [spu:f] 1 n blague* f, tour m, canular* m. 2 adj prétendu (before n), fait par plaisanterie.
spook [spu:k] 1 n (*hum) apparition f, revenant m. 2 vt (US‡) person, house hanter.
spooky* ['spu:kɪ] adj qui donne la chair de poule or le frisson, qui fait froid dans le dos.
spool [spu:l] n [camera, film, tape, thread, typewriter ribbon] bobine f; [fishing reel] tambour m; [sewing machine, weaving machine] canette f; [wire] rouleau m.
spoon [spu:n] 1 n cuiller f or cuillère f; (Golf) spoon m, bois m trois; V dessert, silver etc. 2 cpd: (Orn) spoonbill spatule f; (lit) to spoonfeed sb nourrir qn à la cuiller; (fig) he needs to be spoonfed all the time il faut toujours qu'on lui mâche (subj) le travail. 3 vt: to ~ sth into a plate/out of a bowl etc verser qch dans une assiette/enlever qch d'un bol etc avec une cuiller. 4 vi (*†) flirter.
spoon off vt sep fat, cream etc enlever avec une cuiller.
spoon out vt sep (take out) verser avec une cuiller; (serve out) servir avec une cuiller.
spoon up vt sep food, soup manger avec une cuiller; spillage ramasser avec une cuiller.
spoonerism ['spu:nərɪzəm] n contrepèterie f.
spoonful ['spu:nfʊl] n cuillerée f.
spoor [spʊəʳ] n (U) foulées fpl, trace f, piste f.
sporadic [spəˈrædɪk] adj sporadique. ~ fighting engagements isolés, échauffourées fpl.
sporadically [spəˈrædɪkəlɪ] adv sporadiquement.
spore [spɔ:ʳ] n spore f.
sporran ['spɒrən] n (Scot) escarcelle f en peau (portée avec le kilt).
sport [spɔ:t] 1 n (a) sport m. he is good at ~ il est doué pour le sport, il est très sportif; he is good at several ~s il est doué pour plusieurs sports; outdoor/indoor ~s sports de plein air/d'intérieur; (meeting) ~s réunion sportive; school ~s réunion or compétition sportive scolaire; V field etc.
(b) (U: fun, amusement) divertissement m, amusement m; (fig liter: plaything) jouet m. it was great ~ c'était très divertissant or amusant; in ~ pour rire, pour s'amuser; we had (some) good ~ nous nous sommes bien divertis or amusés; (liter) to make ~ of sb se moquer de qn, tourner qn en ridicule; V spoil.
(c) (*: person) chic* or brave type* m, chic* or brave fille f. be a ~! sois chic!*; (Australia) come on, ~! allez, mon vieux!* or mon pote!‡
(d) (Bio, Zool) variété anormale.
2 cpd: sports programme, reporting, newspaper etc de sport, sportif; commentator, reporter, news, editor, club sportif; clothes sport inv; sports car voiture f de sport; (US: Rad, TV) sportscast émission sportive; (US: Rad, TV) sportscaster reporter sportif; sports coat = sports jacket; (Brit Scol etc) sports day réunion or compétition sportive scolaire; sports enthusiast, sports fan* fanatique mf de sport; sports ground terrain m de sport, stade m; sports jacket veste f sport inv; sportsman sportif m, amateur m de sport; (fig) he's a real sportsman il est beau joueur, il est très sport inv; (lit, fig) sportsmanlike sportif, chic* inv; (lit, fig) sportsmanship sportivité f, esprit sportif; (Press) sports page page sportive or des sports; (U) sportswear vêtements mpl de sport; sportswoman sportive f, athlète f.
3 vi (liter) folâtrer, batifoler.
4 vt tie, hat, beard, buttonhole arborer, exhiber; black eye exhiber.
sporting ['spɔ:tɪŋ] adj (lit, fig) sportif. (fig) there's a ~ chance that she will be on time il est possible qu'elle soit à l'heure, elle a des chances d'arriver à l'heure; that gave him a ~ chance to do ... cela lui a donné une certaine chance de faire ...; it's very ~ of you c'est très chic* de votre part.
sportingly ['spɔ:tɪŋlɪ] adv (fig) très sportivement, avec beaucoup de sportivité.
sportive ['spɔ:tɪv] adj folâtre, badin.
sporty* ['spɔ:tɪ] adj (lit) sportif; (fig) chic* inv, sportif.
spot [spɒt] 1 n (a) [blood, ink, paint] (mark, dot etc) tache f; (splash) éclaboussure f; (on fruit) tache, tavelure f; (polka dot) pois m; (on dice, domino) point m; [leopard etc] tache, moucheture f; (pimple) bouton m; (freckle-type) tache (de son); (fig: on reputation etc) tache, souillure f (on sur). a ~ of dirt une tache, une salissure; a ~ of red une tache or un point rouge; a dress with red ~s une robe à pois rouges; a ~ of rain quelques gouttes fpl de pluie; to have ~s before one's eyes or the eyes voir des mouches volantes devant les yeux; he came out in ~s il a eu une éruption de boutons; these ~s are measles ce sont des taches de rougeole; (Cards) the ten ~ of spades le dix de pique; (fig liter) without a ~ or stain sans la moindre tache or souillure; V beauty, knock, sun etc.
(b) (esp Brit: small amount) a ~ of un peu de; [whisky, coffee etc] une goutte de; [irony, jealousy, truth, common sense] un grain de, une pointe de; a ~ of sleep will do you good cela te fera du bien de dormir un peu, un petit somme te fera du bien; he did a ~ of work il a travaillé un peu, il a fait quelques bricoles* fpl; brandy? — just a ~ du cognac? — juste une goutte or un soupçon; there's been a ~ of trouble il y a eu un petit incident or un petit problème; how about a ~ of lunch? et si on déjeunait?, et si on mangeait un morceau?; we had a ~ of lunch nous avons déjeuné légèrement, nous avons mangé un morceau; V bother.
(c) (place) endroit m. show me the ~ on the map montrez-moi l'endroit sur la carte; a good ~ for a picnic un bon endroit or coin pour un pique-nique; it's a lovely ~! c'est un endroit or un coin ravissant!; there's a tender ~ on my arm j'ai un point sensible au bras; the ~ in the story where ... l'endroit or le moment dans l'histoire où ...; V high, hit, soft etc.
(d) (phrases) the police were on the ~ in 2 minutes la police fut sur les lieux en 2 minutes; it's easy if you're on the ~ c'est facile si vous êtes sur place or si vous êtes là; leave it to the man on the ~ to decide laissez décider la personne qui est sur place; (Press etc) our man on the ~ notre envoyé spécial; an on-the-~ broadcast/report une émission/un reportage sur place; he decided on the ~ il s'est décidé sur le coup or sur le champ or tout de suite; now I'm really on the ~* cette fois-ci je suis vraiment coincé (fig); to be in a (bad or tight) ~* être dans le pétrin*, être dans de beaux draps.
(e) (*: Rad, Theat, TV: in show) numéro m; (Rad, TV: also ~ advertisement) spot m, message m publicitaire. a solo ~ in cabaret un numéro individuel dans une revue; he got a ~ in the Andy Williams Show il a fait un numéro dans le show d'Andy Williams; Glo-kleen had a ~ (advertisement) before the news Glo-kleen a fait passer un spot or un message publicitaire avant les informations; there was a ~ (announcement) about the referendum il y a eu une brève annonce au sujet du referendum.
(f) (*: also night~) boîte f de nuit.
(g) = spotlight.
(h) (Billiards, Snooker) mouche f.
2 cpd transaction, goods, price payé comptant; count, test intermittent, fait à l'improviste. spot advertisement, spot announcement V 1e; spot cash argent comptant or liquide; spot check contrôle intermittent, vérification f de sondage; spot-check contrôler or vérifier de façon intermittente; spotlight V spotlight; (Brit) what he said was spot-on* ce qu'il a dit était en plein dans le mille*; (Brit) he guessed spot-on* il est tombé en plein dans le mille*; spot remover détachant m; spot survey sondage m.
3 vt (a) (speckle, stain) tacher (with de). a tie ~ted with fruit stains une cravate portant des taches de fruit; V also spotted.
(b) (recognize, notice) person, object, vehicle apercevoir, repérer*; mistake trouver, remarquer, relever; bargain, winner, sb's ability déceler, découvrir. can you ~ any bad apples in this tray? est-ce que tu vois or tu trouves des pommes gâtées sur cette claie?; (Brit) train/plane ~ting passe-temps m inv consistant à identifier le plus grand nombre possible de types de locomotives/d'avions.
4 vi (a) [material, garment etc] se tacher, se salir.
(b) it is ~ting (with rain) il commence à pleuvoir, il tombe quelques gouttes de pluie.
(c) (Mil etc: act as spotter) observer.
spotless ['spɒtlɪs] adj impeccable or reluisant de propreté; (fig) sans tache.
spotlessly ['spɒtlɪslɪ] adv: ~ clean impeccable or reluisant de propreté.
spotlessness ['spɒtlɪsnɪs] n propreté f.
spotlight ['spɒtlaɪt] 1 n (Theat: beam) rayon m or feu m de projecteur; (Theat: lamp) projecteur m, spot m; (Aut) phare m auxiliaire. in the ~ (Theat) sous le feu du or des projecteur(s), dans le rayon du or des projecteur(s); (fig) en vedette, sous le feu des projecteurs; (fig) the ~ was on him il était en vedette; (Theat, fig) to turn the ~ on sb/sth = to spotlight sb/sth (V 2).
2 vt (Theat) diriger les projecteurs sur; (fig) mettre en vedette.
spotted ['spɒtɪd] adj animal tacheté, moucheté; fabric à pois; fruit taché, tavelé; (dirty) taché, sali. (Culin) ~ dick pudding m aux raisins de Corinthe; ~ fever fièvre éruptive.
spotter ['spɒtəʳ] n (a) (Brit: as hobby) train/plane ~ passionné(e) m(f) de trains/d'avions; V also spot 3b. (b) (Mil etc) (for enemy aircraft) guetteur m; (during firing) observateur m. (c) (US Comm*) surveillant(e) m(f) du personnel.
spotty ['spɒtɪ] adj face, skin, person boutonneux; (patterned) fabric à pois; (dirty) tie taché, sali; mirror piqueté.
spouse [spaʊz] n (frm or hum) époux m, épouse f; (Jur) conjoint(e) m(f).
spout [spaʊt] 1 n [teapot, jug, can] bec m; (for tap) brise-jet m

inv; *[gutter, pump etc]* dégorgeoir *m*; *[pipe]* orifice *m*; *[fountain]* jet *m*, ajutage *m*; (*stream of liquid*) jet, colonne *f*. (*Brit fig*) **to be up the ~:** *[plans, timetable etc]* être fichu* *or* foutu:; *[person]* (*in trouble*) être dans un mauvais cas, être dans de beaux draps; (*talking nonsense*) dire des bêtises, débloquer:; *V* **water.**

2 *vi* **(a)** *[liquid]* jaillir, sortir en jet (*from, out of* de); *[whale]* lancer un jet d'eau, souffler.

(b) (**fig pej: harangue*) pérorer, laïusser: (*about* sur).

3 *vt* (*also* **~ out**) **(a)** *liquid* faire jaillir, laisser échapper un jet de; *smoke, lava etc* lancer *or* émettre un jet de, vomir.

(b) (**fig*) *poem etc* débiter, déclamer. **he can ~ columns of statistics** il peut débiter *or* dévider des colonnes entières de statistiques.

sprain [spreɪn] **1** *n* entorse *f*, (*less serious*) foulure *f*. **2** *vt muscle, ligament* fouler, étirer. **to ~ one's ankle** se donner une entorse à la cheville, (*less serious*) se fouler la cheville.

sprang [spræŋ] *pret of* **spring.**

sprat [spræt] *n* sprat *m*.

sprawl [sprɔːl] **1** *vi* (*also* **~ out**) (*fall*) tomber, s'étaler*; (*lie*) être affalé *or* vautré; *[handwriting]* s'étaler (dans tous les sens); *[plant]* ramper, s'étendre (*over* sur); *[town]* s'étaler (*over* dans). **he was ~ing *or* lay ~ed in an armchair** il était affalé *or* vautré dans un fauteuil; **to send sb ~ing** faire tomber qn de tout son long *or* les quatre fers en l'air*, envoyer qn rouler par terre.

2 *n* (*position*) attitude affalée; *[building, town]* étendue *f*. **an ugly ~ of buildings down the valley** d'affreux bâtiments qui s'étalent dans la vallée; **London's suburban ~** l'étalement *m* *or* l'extension *f* de la banlieue londonienne; **the seemingly endless ~ of suburbs** l'étendue apparemment infinie des banlieues, les banlieues tentaculaires.

sprawling [ˈsprɔːlɪŋ] *adj person, position, body* affalé; *handwriting* étalé, informe; *city* tentaculaire.

spray[1] [spreɪ] **1** *n* **(a)** (*gen*) (nuage *m* de) gouttelettes *fpl*; (*from sea*) embruns *mpl*; (*from hose pipe*) pluie *f*; (*from atomizer*) spray *m*; (*from aerosol*) pulvérisation *f*. **wet with the ~ from the fountain** aspergé par le jet de la fontaine.

(b) (*container*) (*aerosol*) bombe *f*, aérosol *m*; (*for scent etc*) atomiseur *m*, spray *m*; (*refillable*) vaporisateur *m*; (*larger: for garden etc*) pulvérisateur *m*. **insecticide ~** (*aerosol*) bombe (d')insecticide; (*contents*) insecticide *m* (*en bombe*); *V* **hair** *etc.*

(c) (*also* **~ attachment, ~ nozzle**) pomme *f*, ajutage *m*.

2 *cpd deodorant, insecticide etc* (présenté) en bombe *etc* (*V* **1b**). **spray can** bombe *f* *etc* (*V* **1b**); **spray gun** pistolet *m*; (*Agr*) **spraying machine** pulvérisateur *m*.

3 *vt* **(a)** *roses, garden, crops* faire des pulvérisations sur; *room* faire des pulvérisations dans; *hair* vaporiser (*with* de). **to ~ the lawn with weedkiller** faire des pulvérisations de désherbant sur la pelouse; **they ~ed the oil slick with detergent** ils ont répandu du détergent sur la marée noire; (*fig*) **to ~ sth/sb with bullets** arroser qch/qn de balles, envoyer une grêle de balles sur qch/qn.

(b) *water* vaporiser, pulvériser (*on* sur); *scent* vaporiser; *insecticide, paint* pulvériser. **they ~ed foam on the flames** ils ont projeté de la neige carbonique sur les flammes.

spray out *vi [liquid etc]* jaillir (*onto, over* sur). **water sprayed out all over them** ils ont été complètement aspergés d'eau.

spray[2] [spreɪ] *n [flowers]* gerbe *f*; *[greenery]* branche *f*; (*brooch*) aigrette *f*.

sprayer [ˈspreɪəʳ] *n* **(a)** = **spray**[1] **1b. (b)** (*aircraft: also* **crop-~**) avion-pulvérisateur *m*.

spread [spred] (*vb: pret, ptp* **spread**) **1** *n* **(a)** (*U*) *[fire, disease, infection]* propagation *f*, progression *f*; *[nuclear weapons]* prolifération *f*; *[idea, knowledge]* diffusion *f*, propagation. **to stop the ~ of a disease** empêcher une maladie de s'étendre, arrêter la propagation d'une maladie; **the ~ of education** le progrès de l'éducation.

(b) (*extent, expanse*) *[wings]* envergure *f*; *[arch]* ouverture *f*, portée *f*; *[bridge]* travée *f*; *[marks, prices, ages etc]* gamme *f*, échelle *f*; *[wealth etc]* répartition *f*, distribution *f*. (*Naut*) **a ~ of canvas *or* of sail** un grand déploiement de voiles; **he's got a middle-age ~** il a pris de l'embonpoint avec l'âge.

(c) (*cover*) (*for table*) dessus *m* *or* tapis *m* de table; (*for meals*) nappe *f*; (*bed~*) dessus-de-lit *m inv*, couvre-lit *m*.

(d) (*Culin*) pâte *f* (à tartiner). **cheese ~** fromage *m* à tartiner; **anchovy ~** pâte d'anchois.

(e) (**fig: meal*) festin *m*, banquet *m*.

(f) (*Cards*) séquence *f*.

(g) (*Press, Typ*) (*two pages*) double page *f*; (*across columns*) deux (*or* trois *etc*) colonnes *fpl*.

2 *cpd:* (*Her*) **spread eagle** aigle éployée; (*US*) **spread-eagle*** chauvin (*employé à propos d'un Américain*); **to spread-eagle sb** envoyer rouler qn les quatre fers en l'air*; **to be *or* lie spread-eagled** être étendu bras et jambes écartés, être vautré.

3 *vt* **(a)** (*also* **~ out**) *cloth, sheet, map* étendre, étaler (*on sth* sur qch); *carpet, rug* étendre, dérouler; *wings, bird's tail, banner, sails* déployer; *net* étendre, déployer; *fingers, toes, arms, legs* écarter; *fan* ouvrir. **to ~ the table** mettre le couvert *or* la table; **the peacock ~ its tail** le paon a fait la roue; (*fig*) **to ~ one's wings** élargir ses horizons; **to ~ o.s.** (*lit: also* **~ o.s. out**) s'étaler, prendre plus de place; (*speak etc at length*) s'étendre, s'attarder (*on* sur); (*extend one's activities*) s'étendre.

(b) *bread etc* tartiner (*with* de); *butter, jam, glue* étaler (*on* sur); *face cream* étendre (*on* sur). **~ both surfaces with glue, ~ glue on both surfaces** étalez de la colle sur les deux côtés, enduisez les deux côtés de colle; **to ~ butter on a slice of bread, to ~ a slice of bread with butter** tartiner de beurre une tranche de pain, beurrer une tartine.

(c) (*distribute*) *sand etc* répandre (*on, over* sur); *fertilizer* épandre, étendre (*over, on* sur); (*also* **~ out**) *objects, cards, goods* étaler (*on* sur); *soldiers, sentries etc* disposer, échelonner (*along* le long de). **he ~ sawdust on the floor** il a répandu de la sciure sur le sol, il a couvert le sol de sciure; **he ~ his books (out) on the table** il a étalé ses livres sur la table; **there were policemen ~ (out) all over the hillside** il y avait des agents de police éparpillés *or* dispersés sur toute la colline; **the wind ~ the flames** le vent a propagé les flammes.

(d) (*diffuse, distribute*) *disease, infection* propager; *germs* disséminer; *wealth* distribuer; *rumours* faire courir; *news* faire circuler, communiquer; *knowledge* répandre, diffuser; *panic, fear, indignation* répandre, semer; (*in time: also* **~ out**) *payment, studies etc* échelonner, étaler (*over* sur). **his visits were ~ (out) over 3 years** ses visites se sont échelonnées *or* étalées sur une période de 3 ans; **he ~ his degree (out) over 5 years** il a échelonné ses études de licence sur 5 ans, il a mis 5 ans à finir sa licence; **his research was ~ over many aspects of the subject** ses recherches embrassaient *or* recouvraient de nombreux aspects du sujet; **our resources are ~ very thinly** nous n'avons plus aucune marge dans l'emploi de nos ressources.

4 *vi* **(a)** (*widen, extend further*) *[river, stain]* s'élargir, s'étaler; *[flood, oil slick, weeds, fire, infection, disease]* gagner du terrain, s'étendre; *[water]* se répandre; *[pain]* s'étendre; *[panic, indignation, news, rumour]* s'étendre, se répandre, se propager; *[knowledge]* se répandre, se disséminer, se propager. **to ~ into *or* over sth** *[river, flood, water, oil slick]* se répandre dans *or* sur qch; *[fire, pain]* se communiquer à qch, atteindre qch; *[weeds, panic]* envahir qch; *[disease]* atteindre qch, contaminer qch; *[news, education]* atteindre qch, se répandre dans *or* sur qch; **under the ~ing chestnut tree** sous les branches étendues du marronnier.

(b) (*stretch, reach: also* **~ out**) *[lake, plain, oil slick, fire etc]* s'étendre (*over* sur). **the desert ~s (out) over 500 square miles** le désert s'étend sur *or* recouvre 500 milles carrés; **his studies ~ (out) over 4 years** ses études se sont étendues sur 4 ans *or* ont duré 4 ans.

(c) *[butter, paste etc]* s'étaler.

spread out 1 *vi* **(a)** *[people, animals]* se disperser, s'éparpiller. **spread out!** dispersez-vous!

(b) (*open out*) *[fan]* s'ouvrir; *[wings]* se déployer; *[valley]* s'élargir.

(c) = **spread 4b.**

2 *vt sep:* **the valley lay spread out before him** la vallée s'étendait à ses pieds; **he was spread out on the floor** il était étendu de tout son long par terre; *V also* **spread 3a, 3c, 3d.**

spreader [ˈspredəʳ] *n* (*for butter etc*) couteau *m* à tartiner; (*for glue etc*) couteau à palette; (*Agr: for fertilizer*) épandeur *m*, épandeuse *f*.

spree [spriː] *n* fête *f*. **to go on *or* have a ~** faire la fête *or* la noce*; *V* **spending.**

sprig [sprɪg] *n* rameau *m*, brin *m*.

sprightliness [ˈspraɪtlɪnɪs] *n* (*V* **sprightly**) activité *f*; vivacité *f*.

sprightly [ˈspraɪtlɪ] *adj* (*physically*) alerte, actif; (*mentally*) alerte, vif, fringant.

spring [sprɪŋ] (*vb: pret* **sprang**, *ptp* **sprung**) **1** *n* **(a)** (*leap*) bond *m*, saut *m*. **in *or* with *or* at one ~** d'un bond, d'un saut; **to give a ~** bondir, sauter.

(b) (*for chair, mattress, watch; also Tech*) ressort *m*. (*Aut*) **the ~s** la suspension; *V* **hair, main** *etc.*

(c) (*U: resilience*) *[mattress]* élasticité *f*; *[bow, elastic band]* détente *f*. **he had a ~ in his step** il marchait d'un pas élastique *or* souple.

(d) *[water]* source *f*. **hot ~** source chaude.

(e) (*fig*) **~s** (*cause, motive*) mobile *m*, motif *m*, cause *f*; (*origin*) source *f*, origine *f*.

(f) (*season*) printemps *m*. **in (the) ~** au printemps; **~ is in the air** il fait un temps printanier *or* de printemps, on sent venir le printemps.

2 *cpd weather, day, flowers* printanier, de printemps; *mattress* à ressorts. **spring balance** balance *f* à ressort; (*file*) **spring binder** classeur *m* à ressort; *[file etc]* **spring binding** reliure *f* à ressort; (*lit, fig*) **springboard** tremplin *m*; (*Culin*) **spring chicken** poussin *m*; **spring-clean** (*n: U: also* **spring-cleaning**) grand nettoyage (de printemps); (*vt*) nettoyer de fond en comble; **spring fever** malaises *mpl* des premières chaleurs; **spring gun** piège *m* à fusil; **spring-like** printanier, de printemps; (*Brit*) **spring onion** ciboule *f*, cive *f*; (*liter*) **springtide** = **springtime;** (*Naut*) **spring tide** marée *f* de vive eau *or* de syzygie; **springtime** printemps *m*; **spring water** eau *f* de source.

3 *vi* **(a)** (*leap*) bondir, sauter. **to ~ in/out/across** *etc* entrer/sortir/traverser *etc* d'un bond; **to ~ at sth/sb** bondir *or* sauter *or* se jeter sur qch/qn; **to ~ to one's feet** se lever d'un bond.

(b) (*fig*) **to ~ to attention** bondir au garde-à-vous; **to ~ to sb's help** bondir *or* se précipiter à l'aide de qn; **to ~ to the rescue** se précipiter pour porter secours; **he sprang into action** il est passé à l'action; **they sprang into the public eye** ils ont tout à coup attiré l'attention du public; **to ~ into existence** apparaître du jour au lendemain; **to ~ into view** apparaître soudain, surgir; **to ~ to mind** venir *or* se présenter à l'esprit; **tears sprang to her eyes** les larmes lui sont venues *or* montées aux yeux; **a denial sprang to his lips** une dénégation lui est venue *or* montée aux lèvres; **his hand sprang to his gun** il a saisi *or* attrapé son pistolet; **the door sprang open** la porte s'est brusquement ouverte; **where did you ~ from?*** d'où est-ce que tu sors?; (*loc*) **hope ~s eternal** l'espoir fait vivre.

(c) (*originate from*) provenir, découler (*from* de). **the oak sprang from a tiny acorn** le chêne est sorti d'un tout petit gland; **all his actions ~ from the desire to ...** toutes ses actions proviennent *or* découlent de son désir de ...; **it sprang from his**

inability to cope with the situation c'est venu *or* né de son incapacité à faire face à la situation.

(d) *[timbers etc]* (*warp*) jouer, se gondoler; (*split*) se fendre.

4 *vt* **(a)** (*leap over*) *ditch, fence etc* sauter, franchir d'un bond.

(b) *trap, lock* faire jouer; *mine* faire sauter. (*fig*) **to ~ a surprise on sb** surprendre qn; **to ~ a question on sb** poser une question à qn à brûle-pourpoint *or* de but en blanc; **to ~ a piece of news on sb** annoncer une nouvelle à qn de but en blanc; **he sprang the suggestion on me suddenly** il me l'a suggéré de but en blanc *or* à l'improviste; **he sprang it on me** il m'a pris de court *or* au dépourvu.

(c) (*put ~s in*) *mattress* pourvoir de ressorts; *car* suspendre. (*Aut*) **well-sprung** bien suspendu.

(d) (*Hunting*) *game* lever; (*‡fig*) *prisoner* faire sauter le mur à, aider à faire la belle‡. **he was sprung‡ from Dartmoor** on l'a aidé à faire la cavale‡ de Dartmoor.

(e) *timbers, mast* (*warp*) gondoler, faire jouer; (*split*) fendre; *V* **leak.**

spring up *vi [person]* se lever d'un bond *or* précipitamment; *[flowers, weeds]* surgir de terre; *[corn]* se lever brusquement; *[new buildings, settlements]* surgir de terre, apparaître brusquement; *[wind, storm]* se lever brusquement; *[rumour]* naître, s'élever; *[doubt, fear]* naître, jaillir; *[friendship, alliance]* na ître, s'établir; *[problem, obstacle, difficulty]* se dresser, se présenter, surgir.

springbok ['sprɪŋbɒk] *n* springbok *m.*

springe [sprɪndʒ] *n* collet *m.*

springiness ['sprɪŋɪnɪs] *n* (*V* **springy**) élasticité *f*; souplesse *f*; flexibilité *f.*

springy ['sprɪŋɪ] *adj rubber, mattress* élastique, souple; *carpet* souple; *plank* flexible, qui fait ressort; *ground, turf* souple; *step* alerte, souple.

sprinkle ['sprɪŋkl] *vt:* **to ~ sth with water, to ~ water on sth** asperger qch d'eau; **to ~ water on the garden** arroser légèrement le jardin; **a rose ~d with dew** une rose couverte de rosée; **to ~ sand on** *or* **over sth, to ~ sth with sand** répandre une légère couche de sable sur qch, couvrir qch d'une légère couche de sable; **to ~ sand/grit on the roadway** sabler/cendrer la route; (*Culin*) **to ~ sugar over a dish, to ~ a dish with sugar** saupoudrer un plat de sucre; **lawn ~d with daisies** pelouse parsemée *or* émaillée (*liter*) de pâquerettes; (*fig*) **they are ~d about here and there** ils sont éparpillés *or* disséminés ici et là.

sprinkler ['sprɪŋkləʳ] **1** *n (for lawn etc)* arroseur *m*; (*for sugar etc*) saupoudroir *m*; (*for fire-fighting*) diffuseur *m* (d'extincteur automatique d'incendie). **2** *cpd:* **sprinkler system** (*for lawn*) combiné *m* d'arrosage; (*for fire-fighting*) installation *f* d'extinction automatique d'incendie.

sprinkling ['sprɪŋklɪŋ] *n* (*V* **sprinkle**) aspersion *f*; arrosage *m*; légère couche. **to give sth a ~ (of) = to sprinkle sth (with)** (*V* **sprinkle**); **a ~ of water** quelques gouttes d'eau; **a ~ of sand** une légère couche de sable; (*fig*) **there was a ~ of young people** il y avait quelques jeunes (gens) çà et là.

sprint [sprɪnt] **1** *n* (*Sport*) sprint *m.* **to make a ~ for the bus** piquer* un sprint *or* foncer pour attraper l'autobus. **2** *vi* (*Sport*) sprinter; (*gen*) foncer, piquer* un sprint. **to ~ down the street** descendre la rue à toutes jambes.

sprinter ['sprɪntəʳ] *n* (*Sport*) sprinter *m*, sprinteur *m*, -euse *f.*

sprit [sprɪt] *n* (*Naut*) livarde *f*, baleston *f.*

sprocket ['sprɒkɪt] *n* pignon *m.* **~ wheel** pignon (d'engrenage).

sprout [spraʊt] **1** *n* (*Bot*) (*on plant, branch etc*) pousse *f*; (*from bulbs, seeds*) germe *m.* **(Brussels) ~s** choux *mpl* de Bruxelles.

2 *vi* **(a)** *[bulbs, onions etc]* germer, pousser.

(b) (*also* **~ up:** *grow quickly*) *[plants, crops, weeds]* bien pousser; *[child]* grandir *or* pousser* vite.

(c) (*also* **~ up:** *appear*) *[mushrooms etc]* pousser, apparaître, surgir; *[weeds]* surgir de terre; *[new buildings]* surgir de terre, pousser comme des champignons.

3 *vt:* **to ~ new leaves** pousser *or* produire de nouvelles feuilles; *[potatoes, bulbs]* **to ~ shoots** germer; **the wet weather has ~ed the barley** le temps humide a fait germer l'orge; **the deer has ~ed horns** les cornes du cerf ont poussé, le cerf a mis ses bois; **Paul has ~ed* a moustache** Paul s'est laissé pousser la moustache.

spruce[1] [spruːs] *n* (*also* **~ tree**) épicéa *m* spruce. (*Can*) **white/black ~** épinette blanche/noire.

spruce[2] [spruːs] *adj person* net, pimpant, soigné; *garment* net, impeccable; *house* impeccable, pimpant.

spruce up *vt sep child* faire beau (*f* belle); *house* bien astiquer. **all spruced up** *person* tiré à quatre épingles, sur son trente et un; *house* bien astiqué, reluisant de propreté; **to spruce o.s. up** se faire tout beau (*or* toute belle).

sprucely ['spruːslɪ] *adv:* **~ dressed** tiré à quatre épingles, sur son trente et un.

spruceness ['spruːsnɪs] *n [person]* élégance *f*, mise soignée; *[house]* propreté *f.*

sprung [sprʌŋ] **1** *ptp of* **spring. 2** *adj seat, mattress* à ressorts.

spry [spraɪ] *adj* alerte, vif, plein d'entrain.

spud [spʌd] **1** *n* (*tool*) sarcloir *m*; (*: *potato*) patate* *f.* **2** *cpd:* (*Mil sl*) **spud-bashing** la corvée de patates*.

spume [spjuːm] *n* (*liter*) écume *f.*

spun [spʌn] *pret, ptp of* **spin.**

spunk‡ [spʌŋk] *n* (*U*) cran* *m*, courage *m.*

spunky‡ ['spʌŋkɪ] *adj* plein de cran*.

spur [spɜːʳ] **1** *n* **(a)** *[horse, fighting cock; also mountain, masonry etc]* éperon *m*; *[bone]* saillie *f*; (*fig*) aiguillon *m.* **to win** *or* **gain one's ~s** (*Hist*) gagner ses éperons; (*fig*) faire ses preuves; **on the ~ of the moment** sous l'impulsion du moment, sur un coup de tête; **the ~ of hunger** l'aiguillon de la faim; **it will be a ~ to further achievements** cela nous (*or* les *etc*) poussera *or* incitera *or* encouragera à d'autres entreprises.

(b) (*Rail: also* **~ track**) (*siding*) voie latérale, voie de garage; (*branch*) voie de desserte, embranchement *m.*

2 *cpd:* **spur gear, spur wheel** roue *f* à dents droites.

3 *vt* (*also* **~ on**) *horse* éperonner; (*fig*) éperonner, aiguillonner. **he ~red his horse on** (*applied spurs once*) il a éperonné son cheval, il a donné de l'éperon à son cheval; (*sped on*) il a piqué des deux; **~red on by ambition** éperonné *or* aiguillonné par l'ambition; **to ~ sb (on) to do sth** pousser *or* encourager *or* inciter qn à faire qch; **this ~red him (on) to greater efforts** ceci l'a encouragé à redoubler d'efforts.

spurge [spɜːdʒ] *n* euphorbe *f.* **~ laurel** daphné *m.*

spurious ['spjʊərɪəs] *adj* (*gen*) faux (*f* fausse); *document, writings* faux, apocryphe; *claim* fallacieux; *interest, affection, desire* simulé, feint.

spuriously ['spjʊərɪəslɪ] *adv* faussement.

spurn [spɜːn] *vt* repousser *or* rejeter (avec mépris).

spurt [spɜːt] **1** *n [water, flame]* jaillissement *m*, jet *m*; *[anger, enthusiasm, energy]* sursaut *m*, regain *m*; (*burst of speed*) accélération *f*; (*fig: at work etc*) effort soudain, coup *m* de collier. (*Racing*) **final ~** emballage *m*, rush *m*; **to put on a ~** (*Sport*) démarrer, sprinter; (*in running for bus etc*) piquer* un sprint, foncer; (*fig: in work etc*) faire un soudain *or* suprême effort, donner un coup de collier.

2 *vi* **(a)** (*also* **~ out, ~ up**) *[water, blood]* jaillir, gicler (*from* de); *[flame]* jaillir (*from* de).

(b) *[runner]* piquer* un sprint, foncer; (*Sport*) démarrer, sprinter.

3 *vt* (*also* **~ out**) *flame, lava* lancer, vomir; *water* laisser jaillir, projeter.

sputnik ['spʊtnɪk] *n* spoutnik *m.*

sputter ['spʌtəʳ] *vi, vt* = **splutter 2, 3.**

sputum ['spjuːtəm] *n* crachat *m*, expectorations *fpl.*

spy [spaɪ] **1** *n* (*gen, Ind, Pol*) espion(ne) *m(f).* **police ~** indicateur *m*, -trice *f* de police.

2 *cpd film, story etc* d'espionnage. **spyglass** lunette *f* d'approche; **spyhole** petit trou, espion *m.*

3 *vi* (*gen*) espionner, épier; (*Ind, Pol*) faire de l'espionnage (*for a country* au service *or* au compte d'un pays). **to ~ on sb/sth** espionner *or* épier qn/qch; **stop ~ing on me!** arrête de m'espionner! *or* de me surveiller!; **to ~ into sth** chercher à découvrir qch subrepticement.

4 *vt* (*catch sight of*) apercevoir, découvrir, remarquer. **I spied him coming** je l'ai vu qui arrivait *or* s'approchait.

spy out *vt sep* reconnaître. (*lit, fig*) **to spy out the land** reconnaître le terrain.

spying ['spaɪɪŋ] *n* (*U*) espionnage *m.*

squab [skwɒb] *n* **(a)** (*Orn*) pigeonneau *m.* **(b)** (*Brit: cushion*) coussin *m* (*dur*).

squabble ['skwɒbl] **1** *n* querelle *f*, chamaillerie* *f*, prise *f* de bec. **2** *vi* se chamailler*, se disputer, se quereller (*over sth* à propos de qch).

squabbler ['skwɒbləʳ] *n* chamailleur* *m*, -euse* *f*, querelleur *m*, -euse *f.*

squabbling ['skwɒblɪŋ] *n* (*U*) chamaillerie(s)* *f(pl).*

squad [skwɒd] **1** *n [soldiers, policemen, workmen, prisoners]* escouade *f*, groupe *m*; (*Mil*) groupe; (*US Sport*) équipe *f.* (*Ftbl*) **the England ~** le contingent anglais; *V* **firing, flying** *etc.* **2** *cpd:* (*Police*) **squad car** voiture *f* de police.

squadron ['skwɒdrən] **1** *n* (*Mil*) escadron *m*; (*Aviat, Naut*) escadrille *f.* **2** *cpd:* (*Brit Aviat*) **squadron leader** commandant *m.*

squalid ['skwɒlɪd] *adj room, conditions* misérable, sordide; *motive* vil (*f* vile), ignoble; *dispute* mesquin, sordide. **it was a ~ business** c'était une affaire ignoble *or* sordide; **they had a ~ little affair** ils ont eu une petite liaison pitoyable *or* minable*.

squall [skwɔːl] **1** *n* **(a)** (*Met*) rafale *f or* bourrasque *f* (de pluie); (*at sea*) grain *m.* (*fig*) **there are ~s ahead** il y a de l'orage dans l'air, il va y avoir du grabuge*. **(b)** (*cry*) hurlement *m*, braillement *m.* **2** *vi [baby]* hurler, brailler.

squalling ['skwɔːlɪŋ] *adj* criard, braillard*.

squally ['skwɔːlɪ] *adj wind* qui souffle en rafales; *weather* à bourrasques, à rafales; *day* entrecoupé de bourrasques.

squalor ['skwɒləʳ] *n* (*U*) conditions *fpl* sordides, misère noire. **to live in ~** vivre dans des conditions sordides *or* dans la misère noire; (*pej*) vivre comme un cochon*.

squander ['skwɒndəʳ] *vt time, money, talents* gaspiller; *fortune, inheritance* dissiper, dilapider; *opportunity, chances* perdre.

square [skwɛəʳ] **1** *n* **(a)** (*shape: also Geom, Mil*) carré *m*; *[chessboard, crossword, graph paper]* case *f*; (**~ piece**) *[fabric, chocolate, toffee etc]* carré; *[cake]* carré, part *f*; (*window pane*) carreau *m.* **to fold paper into a ~** plier une feuille de papier en carré; **divide the page into ~s** divisez la page en carrés, quadrillez la page; **she was wearing a silk (head)~** elle portait un carré *or* un foulard de soie; **linoleum with black and white ~s on it** du linoléum en damier noir et blanc *or* à carreaux noirs et blancs; **the troops were drawn up in a ~** les troupes avaient formé le carré; **form (yourselves into) a ~** placez-vous en carré, formez un carré; (*fig*) **now we're back to ~ one*** nous nous retrouvons à notre point de départ, nous repartons à zéro*.

(b) (*in town*) place *f*; (*with gardens*) square *m*; (*esp US: block of houses*) pâté *m* de maisons; (*Mil: also* **barrack ~**) cour *f* (de caserne). **the town ~** la (grand-)place.

(c) (*drawing instrument*) équerre *f.* **out of ~** qui n'est pas d'équerre; **to cut sth on the ~** équarrir qch; (*fig*) **to be on the ~** *[offer, deal]* être honnête *or* régulier*; *[person]* jouer franc jeu, jouer cartes sur table; *V* **set, T** *etc.*

(d) (*Math*) carré *m.* **four is the ~ of two** quatre est le carré de deux.

(e) (**pej: conventional person*) **he's a real ~** il est vraiment vieux jeu *or* vraiment rétro*, il retarde*; **don't be such a ~!** ne sois pas si vieux jeu! *or* si rétro*!, tu retardes!*

2 *adj* **(a)** (*in shape*) *figure, sheet of paper, shoulders, chin, face* carré. **of ~ build** trapu, ramassé; **to cut sth ~** équarrir qch, couper qch au carré *or* à angle droit; **a ~ corner** un coin à angle droit; (*Typ*) **~ bracket** crochet *m*; (*fig*) **he is a ~ peg in a round hole** il n'est pas à son affaire, il n'est pas taillé pour cela; (*fig*) **a ~ meal** un repas convenable; *V also* **3.**

(b) (*even, balanced*) *books, accounts, figures* en ordre. **to get one's accounts ~** mettre ses comptes en ordre, balancer ses comptes; **to get ~ with sb** (*financially*) régler ses comptes avec qn; (*fig: get even with*) régler son compte à qn, faire son affaire à qn; (*fig*) **to be all ~** être quitte; (*Sport*) être à égalité.

(c) (*honest*) *dealings* honnête, régulier*; (*unequivocal*) *refusal, denial* net, catégorique. **he is absolutely ~** il est l'honnêteté même, il joue franc jeu; **a ~ deal** un arrangement équitable *or* honnête; **to get** *or* **have a ~ deal** être traité équitablement; **to give sb a ~ deal** agir honnêtement avec qn; *V* **fair**[1].

(d) (*Math etc*) *number* carré. **6 ~ metres** 6 mètres carrés; **6 metres ~** (de) 6 mètres sur 6; **~ root** racine carrée.

(e) (**pej: conventional*) *person* vieux jeu *inv*, rétro* *inv*, qui retarde*; *habit* vieux jeu, rétro*.

3 *adv* (*at right angles*) **~ to** *or* **with** à angle droit avec, d'équerre avec; **the ship ran ~ across our bows** le navire nous a complètement coupé la route; **~ in the middle** en plein milieu; **to look sb ~ in the face** regarder qn bien en face; **he hit me ~ on the jaw** il m'a frappé en plein sur la mâchoire; *V* **fair**[1].

4 *cpd:* (*Brit Mil sl*) **square-bashing** exercice *m*; **square-built** trapu; **square-cut** coupé à angle droit, équarri; **square dance** quadrille *m*; (*U*) **square-dancing** quadrille *m*; **square-faced** au visage carré; **square-jawed** à la mâchoire carrée; (*US*) **square knot** nœud plat; (*Naut*) **square-rigged** gréé (en) carré; **square-shouldered** aux épaules carrées, carré d'épaules; **square-toed** *shoes* à bout carré.

5 *vt* **(a)** (*make ~*) *figure, shape* rendre carré, carrer; *stone, timber* équarrir, carrer; *corner* couper au carré *or* à angle droit. **to ~ one's shoulders** redresser les épaules; (*fig*) **to try to ~ the circle** chercher à faire la quadrature du cercle.

(b) (*settle etc*) *books, accounts* mettre en ordre, balancer; *debts* acquitter, régler; *creditors* régler, payer; (*reconcile*) concilier, faire cadrer (*A with B* A avec B). **to ~ one's account with sb** (*lit*) régler ses comptes avec qn; (*fig*) régler son compte à qn, faire son affaire à qn; **to ~ o.s. with sb** régler ses comptes avec qn; **I can't ~ that with what he told me yesterday** ça ne cadre pas avec ce qu'il m'a dit hier; **he managed to ~ it with his conscience** il s'est arrangé avec sa conscience; **can you ~* it with the boss?** est-ce que vous pouvez arranger ça avec le patron?; **I can ~* him** (*get him to agree*) je m'occupe de lui, je me charge de lui; (*bribe him*) je peux lui graisser la patte*.

(c) (*Math*) *number* carrer, élever au carré. **four ~d is sixteen** quatre au carré fait seize.

6 *vi* cadrer, correspondre, s'accorder. **that doesn't ~ with the facts** ceci ne cadre pas *or* ne s'accorde pas avec les faits, ceci ne correspond pas aux faits, ceci n'est pas en rapport avec les faits; **that ~s!** ça cadre!, ça colle!‡

square off *vt sep paper, plan* diviser en carrés, quadriller; *wood, edges* équarrir.

square up 1 *vi* **(a)** *[boxers, fighters]* se mettre en garde (*to sb* devant qn). (*fig*) **to square up to a problem** faire face à un problème.

(b) (*pay debts*) régler ses comptes (*with sb* avec qn).

2 *vt sep* **(a)** (*make square*) *paper* couper au carré *or* à angle droit; *wood* équarrir.

(b) *account, debts* régler, payer. **I'll square things up*** for you j'arrangerai les choses pour vous.

squarely ['skwɛəlɪ] *adv* **(a)** (*completely*) carrément. **we must face this ~** nous devons carrément y faire face; **~ in the middle** en plein milieu, carrément* au milieu; **to look sb ~ in the eyes** regarder qn droit dans les yeux.

(b) (*honestly*) honnêtement, régulièrement*. (*fig*) **he dealt with us very ~** il a agi très honnêtement avec nous, il a été parfaitement régulier avec nous*.

squash[1] [skwɒʃ] **1** *n* **(a)** (*crowd*) cohue *f*, foule *f*; (*crush*) cohue, bousculade *f*. **a great ~ of people** une cohue, une foule; **I lost him in the ~ at the exit** je l'ai perdu dans la cohue *or* dans la bousculade à la sortie.

(b) (*Brit*) **lemon/orange ~** citronnade *f*/orangeade *f* (concentrée).

(c) (*Sport: also* **~ rackets**) squash *m*.

2 *vt fruit, beetle, hat, box* écraser; (*fig*) *argument* réfuter; (*snub*) *person* remettre à sa place, rabrouer, rembarrer*. **to ~ flat** *fruit, beetle* écraser, écrabouiller*; *hat, box* aplatir; **he ~ed his nose against the window** il a écrasé son nez contre la vitre; **you're ~ing me!** tu m'écrases!; **she ~ed the shoes into the suitcase** elle a réussi à faire rentrer les chaussures dans la valise; **can you ~ 2 more people in the car?** est-ce que tu peux introduire *or* faire tenir 2 personnes de plus dans la voiture?

3 *vi* **(a)** *[people]* **they ~ed into the elevator** ils se sont serrés *or* entassés dans l'ascenseur; **they ~ed through the gate** ils sont sortis (*or* entrés) en se pressant *or* s'écrasant *or* se bousculant près du portail.

(b) *[fruit, parcel etc]* s'écraser. **will it ~?** est-ce que cela risque de s'écraser?

squash in 1 *vi [people]* s'empiler, s'entasser. **when the car arrived they all squashed in** quand la voiture est arrivée ils se sont tous empilés *or* entassés dedans; **can I squash in?** est-ce que je peux me trouver une petite place?

2 *vt sep* (*into box, suitcase etc*) réussir à faire rentrer.

squash together 1 *vi [people]* se serrer (les uns contre les autres).

2 *vt sep objects* serrer, tasser. **we were all squashed together** nous étions très serrés *or* entassés.

squash up 1 *vi [people]* se serrer, se pousser. **can't you squash up a bit?** pourriez-vous vous serrer *or* vous pousser un peu?

2 *vt sep object* écraser; *paper* chiffonner en boule.

squash[2] [skwɒʃ] *n* (*gourd*) gourde *f*; (*US*) courge *f*.

squashy ['skwɒʃɪ] *adj fruit* mou (*f* molle), qui s'écrase facilement; *ground* bourbeux, boueux.

squat [skwɒt] **1** *adj person* ramassé, courtaud; *building* écrasé, lourd; *object* petit et épais (*f* -aisse). **a ~ parcel** un petit paquet épais *or* rebondi.

2 *vi* **(a)** (*also* **~ down**) *[person]* s'accroupir, s'asseoir sur ses talons; *[animal]* se tapir, se ramasser. **to be ~ting (down)** *[person]* être accroupi, être assis sur ses talons; *[animal]* être tapi *or* ramassé.

(b) *[squatters]* faire du squattage*. **to ~ in a house** squatter* *or* squatteriser* une maison.

squatter ['skwɒtəʳ] *n* squatter *m*.

squaw [skwɔː] *n* squaw *f*, femme *f* peau-rouge.

squawk [skwɔːk] **1** *vi [hen, parrot]* pousser un *or* des gloussement(s); *[baby]* brailler; *[person]* pousser un *or* des cri(s) rauque(s); (**fig: complain*) râler*, gueuler‡. **2** *n* gloussement *m*, braillement *m*, cri *m* rauque.

squeak [skwiːk] **1** *n [hinge, wheel, pen, chalk]* grincement *m*; *[shoes]* craquement *m*; *[mouse, doll]* petit cri aigu, vagissement *m*; *[person]* petit cri aigu, glapissement *m*. **to let out** *or* **give a ~ of fright/surprise** *etc* pousser un petit cri *or* glapir de peur/de surprise *etc*; **not a ~*, mind!** pas un murmure hein!, n'en souffle pas mot!; **I don't want another ~ out of you** je ne veux plus t'entendre; *V* **narrow.**

2 *vi [hinge, wheel]* grincer, crier; *[pen, chalk]* grincer; *[shoe]* crier, craquer; *[mouse, doll]* vagir, pousser un *or* des petit(s) cri(s) aigu(s); *[person]* glapir.

3 *vt:* **'no' she ~ed** 'non' glapit-elle.

squeaker ['skwiːkəʳ] *n* (*in toy etc*) sifflet *m*.

squeaky ['skwiːkɪ] *adj hinge, wheel, pen* grinçant; *doll* qui crie; *shoes* qui crient, qui craquent.

squeal [skwiːl] **1** *n [person, animal]* cri aigu *or* perçant; *[brakes]* grincement *m*, hurlement *m*; *[tyres]* crissement *m*. **to let out** *or* **give a ~ of pain** pousser un cri de douleur; **... he said with a ~ of laughter** ... dit-il avec un rire aigu.

2 *vi* **(a)** *[person, animal]* pousser un *or* des cri(s) aigu(s) *or* perçant(s); *[brakes]* grincer, hurler; *[tyres]* crisser. **he ~ed like a (stuck) pig** il criait comme un cochon qu'on égorge; **she tickled the child and he ~ed** elle a chatouillé l'enfant et il a poussé un petit cri.

(b) (‡: *inform*) vendre la mèche. **to ~ on sb** dénoncer qn, vendre qn, donner* qn; **somebody ~ed to the police** quelqu'un les (*or* nous *etc*) a donnés* à la police.

3 *vt:* **'help' he ~ed** 'au secours' cria-t-il d'une voix perçante.

squeamish ['skwiːmɪʃ] *adj* (*easily nauseated*) délicat, facilement dégoûté; (*queasy*) qui a mal au cœur, qui a la nausée; (*very fastidious*) facilement dégoûté; (*easily shocked*) qui s'effarouche facilement. **I'm not ~** j'ai l'estomac solide, je ne suis pas facilement dégoûté; **I'm too ~ to do that** je n'ose pas faire cela; **don't be so ~!** ne joue pas aux petits délicats!; **spiders make me feel ~** les araignées me dégoûtent.

squeamishness ['skwiːmɪʃnɪs] *n* (*U*) délicatesse exagérée; (*queasiness*) nausée *f*; (*prudishness*) pruderie *f*.

squeegee [ˌskwiːˈdʒiː] **1** *n* (*mop*) raclette *f* (à bord de caoutchouc).

2 *adv; adj* (‡) de travers, de guingois*.

squeeze [skwiːz] **1** *n* **(a)** (*act, pressure*) pression *f*, compression *f*; (*U: in crowd*) cohue *f*, bousculade *f*. **to give sth a ~** = **to squeeze sth** (*V* **2a**); **he gave her a big ~** il l'a serrée très fort dans ses bras; **a ~ of lemon** quelques gouttes de citron; **a ~ of toothpaste** un peu de dentifrice; **there was a great** *or* **tight ~ in the bus** on était serrés comme des sardines* *or* on était affreusement tassés dans l'autobus; **it was a (tight) ~ to get through** il y avait à peine la place de passer; (*fig*) **to put the ~ on sb‡** presser qn, harceler qn.

(b) (*Econ: also* **credit ~**) restrictions *fpl* de crédit.

(c) (*Bridge*) squeeze *m* (*in clubs* à trèfle).

2 *vt* **(a)** (*press*) *handle, tube, plastic bottle, lemon* presser; *sponge, cloth* presser, tordre, comprimer; *doll, teddy bear* appuyer sur; *sb's hand, arm* serrer. **he ~d his finger in the door** il s'est pris *or* pincé le doigt dans la porte; **she ~d another jersey into the case** elle a réussi à faire rentrer un autre chandail dans la valise; (*fig*) **he ~d his victim dry*** il a saigné sa victime à blanc.

(b) (*extract: also* **~ out**) *water, juice, toothpaste* exprimer (*from, out of* de).

(c) (**fig*) *names, information, money, contribution* soutirer, arracher, extorquer (*out of* à). **you won't ~ a penny out of me for that type of thing** tu ne me feras pas lâcher* un sou pour ce genre de chose; **the government hopes to ~ more money out of the taxpayers** le gouvernement espère obtenir *or* tirer plus d'argent des contribuables.

3 *vi:* **he ~d past me** il s'est glissé devant moi en me poussant un peu; **he managed to ~ into the bus** il a réussi à se glisser *or* à s'introduire dans l'autobus en poussant; **they all ~d into the car** ils se sont entassés *or* empilés dans la voiture; **can you ~ underneath the fence?** est-ce que tu peux te glisser sous la barrière?; **he ~d through the crowd** il a réussi à se faufiler à travers la foule; **she ~d through the window** elle s'est glissée par la fenêtre; **the car ~d into the empty space** il y avait juste assez de place pour se garer.

squeeze in 1 *vi [person]* trouver une petite place; *[car etc]*

rentrer tout juste, avoir juste la place. **can I squeeze in?** est-ce qu'il y a une petite place pour moi?

2 *vt sep object into box,* (**fig*) *item on programme etc* réussir à faire rentrer, trouver une petite place pour. **can you squeeze 2 more people in?** est-ce que vous avez de la place pour 2 autres personnes?, est-ce que vous pouvez prendre 2 autres personnes?; **I can squeeze you in* tomorrow at 9** je peux vous prendre (en vitesse) demain à 9 heures.

squeeze past *vi [person]* passer en se faufilant *or* en poussant; *[car]* se faufiler, se glisser.

squeeze through *vi [person]* se faufiler, se frayer un chemin; *[car]* se faufiler, se glisser (*between* entre).

squeeze up* *vi [person]* se serrer, se pousser.

squeezer ['skwiːzəʳ] *n* presse-fruits *m inv.* **lemon ~** presse-citron *m inv.*

squelch [skweltʃ] **1** *n* **(a)** bruit *m* de succion *or* de pataugeage. **I heard the ~ of his footsteps in the mud** je l'ai entendu patauger dans la boue; **the tomato fell with a ~** la tomate s'est écrasée par terre avec un bruit mat.

(b) (*‡fig: crushing retort*) réplique *f* qui coupe le sifflet*.

2 *vi [mud etc]* faire un bruit de succion. *[person]* **to ~ in/out** *etc* entrer/sortir *etc* en pataugeant; **to ~ (one's way) through the mud** avancer en pataugeant dans la boue; **the water ~ed in his boots** l'eau faisait flic flac* dans ses bottes.

3 *vt* (*crush underfoot*) piétiner, écraser; (*‡fig: snub*) clouer le bec à*, couper le sifflet à*.

squib [skwɪb] *n* pétard *m*; *V* **damp.**

squid [skwɪd] *n* calmar *m*, encornet *m.*

squiffy* ['skwɪfɪ] *adj* (*Brit*) éméché*, pompette*.

squiggle ['skwɪgl] **1** *n* (*scrawl*) gribouillis *m*; (*wriggle*) tortillement *m.* **2** *vi* (*in writing etc*) gribouiller, faire des gribouillis; *[worm etc]* se tortiller.

squint [skwɪnt] **1** *n* (*Med*) strabisme *m*; (*sidelong look*) regard *m* de côté; (*quick glance*) coup *m* d'œil. (*Med*) **to have a ~** loucher, être atteint de strabisme; **to take a ~ at sth** (*obliquely*) regarder qch du coin de l'œil, lorgner qch; (*quickly*) jeter un coup d'œil à qch; **let's have a ~!*** donne voir!, montre voir!*; **have a ~* at this** jette un coup d'œil là-dessus, zyeute ça‡.

2 *vi* (*Med*) loucher. **he ~ed in the sunlight** il grimaçait un peu à cause du soleil; **he ~ed down the tube** il a plongé son regard dans le tube; **to ~ at sth** (*obliquely*) regarder qch du coin de l'œil, lorgner qch; (*quickly*) jeter un coup d'œil à qch; **he ~ed at me quizzically** il m'a interrogé du regard.

3 *cpd:* **squint-eyed** qui louche, atteint de strabisme.

squire ['skwaɪəʳ] **1** *n* (*landowner*) propriétaire terrien; (*Hist: knight's attendant*) écuyer *m.* **the ~ told us ...** le châtelain nous a dit ...; **the ~ of Barcombe** le seigneur† *or* le châtelain de Barcombe; (*Brit*) **yes ~!‡** oui chef!* *or* patron!*

2 *vt lady* escorter, servir de cavalier à. **she was ~d by** elle était escortée par.

squirearchy ['skwaɪərɑːkɪ] *n* (*U*) hobereaux *mpl*, propriétaires terriens.

squirm [skwɜːm] *vi* **(a)** *[worm etc]* se tortiller. *[person]* **to ~ through a window** passer par une fenêtre en faisant des contorsions.

(b) (*fig*) *[person]* (*from embarrassment*) ne pas savoir où se mettre, être au supplice; (*from distaste*) avoir un haut-le-corps. **spiders make me ~** j'ai un haut-le-corps quand je vois une araignée; **her poetry makes me ~** ses poèmes me donnent mal au cœur.

squirrel ['skwɪrəl] **1** *n* écureuil *m.* **red ~** écureuil; **grey ~** écureuil gris.

2 *cpd coat etc* en petit-gris.

squirrel away *vt sep nuts etc* amasser.

squirt [skwɜːt] **1** *n* **(a)** *[water, detergent]* jet *m*; *[scent]* quelques gouttes *fpl.*

(b) (*) (*person*) petit bout* de rien du tout, petit morveux* (*pej*); (*child*) mioche* *mf.*

2 *vt water* faire jaillir, faire gicler (*at, on, onto* sur, *into* dans); *detergent* verser un jet de; *scent* faire tomber quelques gouttes de. **he ~ed the insecticide onto the roses** il a pulvérisé de l'insecticide sur les roses; **to ~ sb with water** asperger *or* arroser qn d'eau; **to ~ sb with scent** asperger qn de parfum.

3 *vi [liquid]* jaillir, gicler. **the water ~ed into my eye** j'ai reçu une giclée d'eau dans l'œil; **water ~ed out of the broken pipe** l'eau jaillissait du tuyau cassé.

Sri Lanka [ˌsriːˈlæŋkə] *n* Sri Lanka *m or f.*

stab [stæb] **1** *n* **(a)** (*with dagger/knife etc*) coup *m* (de poignard/de couteau *etc*). (*fig*) **a ~ in the back** un coup bas *or* déloyal; **a ~ of pain** un élancement; **a ~ of remorse/grief** un remords/une douleur lancinant(e).

(b) (**: attempt*) **to have a ~ at (doing) sth** s'essayer à (faire) qch; **I'll have a ~ at it** je vais tenter le coup.

2 *cpd:* **stab-wound** coup *m* de poignard (*or* couteau *etc*); (*mark*) trace *f* de coup de poignard (*or* couteau *etc*).

3 *vt* (*with dagger*) poignarder. **to ~ sb with a knife** frapper qn d'un coup de couteau, donner un coup de couteau à qn; **to ~ sb to death** tuer qn d'un coup de *or* à coups de poignard *etc*; **he was ~bed through the heart** il a reçu un coup de poignard *etc* dans le cœur; (*lit, fig*) **to ~ sb in the back** poignarder qn dans le dos; **he ~bed his penknife into the desk** il a planté son canif dans le bureau; **he ~bed the pencil through the map** il a transpercé la carte d'un coup de crayon.

4 *vi:* **he ~bed at the book with his finger** il a frappé le livre du doigt.

stabbing ['stæbɪŋ] **1** *n* agression *f* (à coups de couteau *etc*). **there was another ~ last night** la nuit dernière une autre personne a été attaquée à coups de couteau *etc.*

2 *adj gesture* comme pour frapper; *sensation* lancinant. **~ pain** douleur lancinante, élancement *m.*

stability [stəˈbɪlɪtɪ] *n* (*V* **stable**[1]) stabilité *f*; fermeté *f*; solidité *f*; équilibre *m.*

stabilization [ˌsteɪbəlaɪˈzeɪʃən] *n* stabilisation *f.*

stabilize ['steɪbəlaɪz] *vt* stabiliser.

stabilizer ['steɪbəlaɪzəʳ] *n* (*Aut, Naut*) stabilisateur *m*; (*Aviat*) empennage *m.*

stable[1] ['steɪbl] *adj scaffolding, ladder* stable; (*Chem, Phys*) stable; *government* stable, durable; *job* stable, permanent; *prices* stable, (*St Ex*) ferme; *relationship, marriage* solide; *character, conviction* constant, ferme; (*Psych etc*) *person* équilibré. **he is not very ~** il n'est pas très équilibré, il est plutôt instable.

stable[2] ['steɪbl] **1** *n* (*building*) écurie *f*; (*racehorses: also* **racing ~**) écurie (de courses). **(riding) ~(s)** centre *m* d'équitation, manège *m*; (*Prov*) **to shut *or* close the ~ door after the horse has gone** prendre des précautions après coup.

2 *cpd:* **stableboy** palefrenier *m*; (*Brit*) **stablelad** lad *m*; **stablemate** (*horse*) compagnon *m* de stalle; (*fig: person*) camarade *mf* d'études (*or* de travail *etc*).

3 *vt horse* mettre dans une *or* à l'écurie.

staccato [stəˈkɑːtəʊ] **1** *adv* (*Mus*) staccato. **2** *adj* (*Mus*) *note* piqué; (*gen*) *sounds, firing, voice, style* saccadé, coupé.

stack [stæk] **1** *n* **(a)** (*Agr*) meule *f*; *[rifles]* faisceau *m*; *[wood, books, papers]* tas *m*, pile *f.* **~s* of** un tas* de, plein* de; **I've got ~s* *or* a ~* of things to do** j'ai des tas* de choses *or* plein* de choses à faire; **to have ~s* of money** rouler sur l'or, être bourré de fric‡; **we've got ~s* of time** on a tout le temps, on a plein* de temps; *V* **hay** *etc.*

(b) (*group of chimneys*) souche *f* de cheminée; (*on factory/boat etc*) (tuyau *m* de) cheminée *f* (d'usine/de bateau *etc*).

(c) (*in library, bookshop*) **~s** rayons *mpl*, rayonnages *mpl.*

2 *vt* **(a)** (*Agr*) mettre en meule; (*also* **~ up**) *books, wood* empiler, entasser; *dishes* empiler; (*Aviat*) *aircraft* faire attendre (sur niveaux différents).

(b) (*) (*pej*) *jury, committee etc* sélectionner avec partialité (*in favour of* pour favoriser, *against* pour défavoriser). **to ~ the cards *or* (*US*) the deck** tricher en battant les cartes; (*fig*) **the cards are ~ed against me** les jeux sont faits d'avance contre moi, je suis défavorisé.

stadium ['steɪdɪəm] *n* stade *m.*

staff [stɑːf] **1** *n* **(a)** (*pl* **~s**: *work force*) (*Comm, Ind*) personnel *m*; (*Scol, Univ*) personnel enseignant, professeurs *mpl*; (*servants*) domestiques *mpl*; (*Mil*) état-major *m.* **a large ~** un personnel *etc* nombreux; **to be on the ~** faire partie du personnel; **we have 30 typists on the ~** notre personnel comprend 30 dactylos; **he's left our ~** il nous a quittés, il est parti, il ne fait plus partie de notre personnel; **he joined our ~ in 1974** il est entré chez nous en 1974, il a commencé à travailler chez nous en 1974; *V* **chief, editorial.**

(b) (*pl* **staves** *or* **~s**: *liter: rod, pole*) bâton *m*, (*longer*) perche *f*; (*walking stick*) bâton; (*shepherd's*) houlette *f*; (*weapon*) bâton, gourdin *m*; (*symbol of authority*) bâton de commandement; (*Rel*) crosse *f*, bâton pastoral; (*also* **flag~**) mât *m*; (††) *[spear, lance etc]* hampe *f*; (*fig: support*) soutien *m.* **their only weapons were long staves** ils n'étaient armés que de longs bâtons; (*fig*) **a ~ for my old age** mon bâton de vieillesse; (*fig*) **bread is the ~ of life** le pain est l'aliment vital *or* le soutien de la vie.

(c) (*pl* **staves**: *Mus*) portée *f.*

2 *cpd:* (*Mil*) **staff college** école supérieure de guerre; (*Scol, Univ*) **staff meeting** conseil *m* des professeurs; (*Mil*) **staff officer** officier *m* d'état-major; (*Scol, Univ*) **staffroom** salle *f* des professeurs; (*Comm, Ind etc*) **staff training** formation *f* du personnel.

3 *vt school, hospital etc* pourvoir en personnel. **it is ~ed mainly by immigrants** le personnel se compose surtout d'immigrants; **the hotel is well-~ed** l'hôtel est pourvu d'un personnel nombreux; *V* **over, short, under** *etc.*

stag [stæg] **1** *n* (*deer*) cerf *m*; (*other animal*) mâle *m.* **2** *cpd:* **stag beetle** cerf-volant *m*, lucane *f*; **staghunt(ing)** chasse *f* au cerf; **stag party*** réunion *f* entre hommes.

stage [steɪdʒ] **1** *n* **(a)** (*Theat: place*) scène *f.* (*profession etc*) **the ~** le théâtre; **on ~** sur scène; **to go on ~** entrer en scène; **to go on the ~** entrer *or* monter sur la scène; (*fig: as career*) monter sur les planches, commencer à faire du théâtre, devenir acteur (*or* actrice); **on the ~ as in real life** au théâtre comme dans la vie ordinaire; **she has appeared on the ~** elle a fait du théâtre; **to write for the ~** écrire des pièces de théâtre; **the book was adapted for the ~** le livre a été adapté pour le théâtre *or* porté à la scène; **his play never reached the ~** sa pièce n'a jamais été jouée; (*fig*) **to hold the ~** être le point de mire, être en vedette, occuper le devant de la scène; (*fig*) **it was the ~ of a violent confrontation** cela a été le cadre *or* le théâtre (*liter*) d'une violente confrontation; *V* **down**[1] *etc.*

(b) (*platform: in hall etc*) estrade *f*; *[rocket]* étage *m*; (*Constr: scaffolding*) échafaudage *m*; (*also* **landing ~**) débarcadère *m*; *[microscope]* platine *f.* **a 4-~ rocket** une fusée à 4 étages; **the second ~ fell away** le deuxième étage s'est détaché.

(c) (*point, section*) *[journey]* étape *f*; *[road, pipeline]* section *f*; *[operation, process, disease]* étape, stade *m*, phase *f.* **a critical ~** un point *or* une phase *or* un stade critique; **the first ~ of his career** le premier échelon de sa carrière; **in ~s** par étapes, par degrés; **in *or* by easy ~s** (*travel*) par *or* à petites étapes; (*study*) par degrés; **by ~s** (*travel*) par étapes; (*study*) par degrés; **the reform was carried out in ~s** la réforme a été appliquée en plusieurs étapes *or* temps; **in the early ~s** au début; **at an early ~ in its history** vers le début de son histoire; **at this ~ in the negotiations** à ce point *or* à ce stade des négociations; **what ~ is your project at?** à quel stade *or* à quel point *or* où en est votre projet?; **it has reached the ~ of being translated** c'en est au stade de la traduction, on en est à le traduire; **we have reached a ~ where ...** nous (en) sommes arrivés à un point *or* à un stade où ...; **the child has reached the talking ~** l'enfant en est au point *or* au stade où il commence à parler; **he's going through a difficult ~** il passe par une période difficile; **it's just a ~ in his development** ce n'est qu'une phase *or* un stade dans son développement; *V* **fare** *etc.*

(d) (*also* **~coach**) diligence *f.*

2 *cpd:* (*Theat: U*) **stagecraft** technique *f* de la scène; **stage designer** décorateur *m*, -trice *f* de théâtre; **stage direction** (*instruction*) indication *f* scénique; (*U: art, activity*) (art *m* de la) mise *f* en scène; **stage director** metteur *m* en scène; **stage door** entrée *f* des artistes; **stage effect** effet *m* scénique; **stage fright** trac* *m*; **stagehand** machiniste *m*; **stage-manage** *play, production* être régisseur pour; (*fig*) *event, confrontation etc* monter, manigancer (*pej*); (*Theat*) **stage manager** régisseur *m*; **stage name** nom *m* de théâtre; **to be stage-struck** brûler d'envie de faire du théâtre; (*fig*) **stage whisper** aparté *m*; **in a stage whisper** en aparté.

3 *vt* (*Theat*) monter, mettre en scène. (*fig*) **they ~d an accident/a reconciliation** (*organize*) ils ont organisé *or* manigancé un accident/une réconciliation; (*feign*) ils ont monté un accident/fait semblant de se réconcilier; **they ~d a demonstration** (*organize*) ils ont organisé une manifestation; (*carry out*) ils ont manifesté; **to ~ a strike** (*organize*) organiser une grève; (*go on strike*) faire la grève, se mettre en grève; **that was no accident, it was ~d** ce n'était pas un accident, c'était un coup monté; *V* **come** *etc.*

stager ['steɪdʒəʳ] *n:* **old ~** vétéran *m*, vieux routier.

stagey* ['steɪdʒɪ] *adj* (*pej*) *habits* du théâtre, de la scène; *appearance, diction, mannerisms* théâtral; *person* cabotin.

stagger ['stægəʳ] **1** *vi* chanceler, tituber. **he ~ed to the door** il est allé à la porte d'un pas chancelant *or* titubant; **to ~ along/in/out** *etc* avancer/entrer/sortir *etc* en chancelant *or* titubant; **he was ~ing about** il se déplaçait en chancelant *or* titubant, il vacillait sur ses jambes.

2 *vt* **(a)** (*cause to* ~) faire chanceler *or* tituber *or* vaciller; (*amaze*) stupéfier, renverser; (*upset*) atterrer, bouleverser. **this will ~ you** tu vas trouver cela stupéfiant *or* renversant; **I was ~ed to learn** j'ai été atterré *or* bouleversé d'apprendre.

(b) *spokes, objects* espacer; *visits, payments* échelonner; *holidays* étaler. **they work ~ed hours** leurs heures de travail sont étalées *or* échelonnées.

3 *n* allure chancelante *or* titubante. (*Vet*) **~s** vertigo *m.*

staggering ['stægərɪŋ] **1** *adj* (*fig*) *news, suggestion* renversant, atterrant; *amount, size* renversant, stupéfiant. (*lit, fig*) **~ blow** coup *m* de massue.

2 *n* **(a)** (*action*) démarche chancelante *or* titubante.

(b) *[hours, visits etc]* échelonnement *m*; *[holidays]* étalement *m.*

stagnancy ['stægnənsɪ] *n* stagnation *f.*

stagnant ['stægnənt] *adj water* stagnant; (*fig*) *business* stagnant, dans le marasme; *career* stagnant; *mind* inactif.

stagnate [stæg'neɪt] *vi [water]* être stagnant, croupir; (*fig*) *[business]* stagner, être dans le marasme; *[person]* stagner, croupir; *[mind]* être inactif.

stagnation [stæg'neɪʃən] *n* stagnation *f.*

stagy* ['steɪdʒɪ] *adj* = **stagey***.

staid [steɪd] *adj person* posé, rassis; *opinion, behaviour* pondéré, sérieux; *appearance* collet monté *inv.*

staidness ['steɪdnɪs] *n* (*V* **staid**) caractère posé *or* rassis; sérieux *m*; aspect *m* collet monté.

stain [steɪn] **1** *n* **(a)** (*lit, fig: mark*) tache *f* (*on* sur). **blood/grease ~** tache de sang/graisse; **without a ~ on his character** sans une tache à sa réputation.

(b) (*colouring*) colorant *m*. **wood ~** couleur *f* pour bois.

2 *cpd:* **stain remover** détachant *m.*

3 *vt* **(a)** (*mark, soil*) tacher; (*fig*) *reputation etc* tacher, souiller, ternir. **~ed with blood** taché de sang.

(b) (*colour*) *wood* teinter, teindre; *glass* colorer. **~ed glass** (*substance*) verre coloré; (*windows collectively*) vitraux *mpl*; **~ed-glass window** vitrail *m*, verrière *f.*

4 *vi:* **this material will ~** ce tissu se tache facilement *or* est très salissant.

stainless ['steɪnlɪs] *adj* sans tache, pur. **~ steel** acier *m* inoxydable, inox *m.*

stair [steəʳ] **1** *n* (*step*) marche *f*; (*also* **~s, flight of ~s**) escalier *m*. **to pass sb on the ~(s)** rencontrer qn dans l'escalier; **below ~s** à l'office.

2 *cpd carpet* d'escalier. **staircase** escalier *m* (*V* **moving, spiral** *etc*); **stair rod** tringle *f* d'escalier; **stairway** escalier *m*; **stairwell** cage *f* d'escalier.

stake [steɪk] **1** *n* **(a)** (*for fence, tree etc*) pieu *m*, poteau *m*; (*as boundary mark*) piquet *m*, jalon *m*; (*for plant*) tuteur *m*; (*Hist*) bûcher *m*. **to die** *or* **be burnt at the ~** mourir sur le bûcher; (*US fig*) **to pull up ~s*** déménager.

(b) (*Betting*) enjeu *m*; (*fig: share*) intérêt *m*. (*horse-race*) **~s** course *f* de chevaux; (*Horse-racing*) **the Newmarket ~s** le Prix de Newmarket; **to play for high ~s** (*lit*) jouer gros jeu; (*fig*) jouer gros jeu, risquer gros; **the issue at ~** ce dont il s'agit, ce qui est en jeu, ce qui se joue ici; **our future is at ~** notre avenir est en jeu, il s'agit de *or* il y va de notre avenir; **there is a lot at ~** l'enjeu est considérable, il y a gros à perdre; **there is a lot at ~ for him** il a gros à perdre; **he has got a lot at ~** il joue gros jeu, il risque gros, il a misé gros; (*fig*) **to have a ~ in sth** avoir des intérêts dans qch; **he has got a ~ in the success of the firm** il est intéressé matériellement *or* financièrement au succès de l'entreprise; **Britain has a big ~ in North Sea oil** la Grande-Bretagne a de gros investissements *or* a engagé de gros capitaux dans le pétrole de la mer du Nord.

2 *cpd:* **stakeholder** dépositaire *mf* d'enjeux.

3 *vt* **(a)** (*also* **~ out**) *territory, area* marquer *or* délimiter avec des piquets, jalonner; *claim* établir. (*fig*) **to ~ one's claim to sth** revendiquer qch, établir son droit à qch.

(b) (*also* **~ up**) *fence* soutenir à l'aide de poteaux *or* de pieux; *plants* mettre un tuteur à, soutenir à l'aide d'un tuteur.

(c) (*bet*) *money, jewels etc* jouer, miser (*on* sur); (*fig*) *one's reputation, life* risquer, jouer (*on* sur). (*fig*) **he ~d everything** *or* **his all on the committee's decision** il a joué le tout pour le tout *or* il a joué son va-tout sur la décision du comité; **I'd ~ my life on it** j'en mettrais ma tête à couper.

stalactite ['stæləktaɪt] *n* stalactite *f.*

stalagmite ['stæləgmaɪt] *n* stalagmite *f.*

stale [steɪl] **1** *adj meat, eggs, milk* qui n'est plus frais (*f* fraîche); *cheese* desséché, dur; *bread* rassis, (*stronger*) dur; *beer* éventé, plat; *air* confiné; (*fig*) *news* déjà vieux (*f* vieille); *joke* rebattu, éculé; *writer, musician, actor* usé, qui n'a plus d'inspiration; *athlete* surentraîné. **the bread has gone ~** le pain a rassis *or* s'est rassis; **the room smells ~** cette pièce sent le renfermé; **the room smelt of ~ cigar smoke** la pièce avait une odeur de cigares refroidie; **I'm getting ~** je perds mon entrain *or* mon enthousiasme *or* mon inspiration.

2 *vi* (*liter*) *[pleasures etc]* perdre de sa (*or* leur) fraîcheur *or* nouveauté.

stalemate ['steɪlmeɪt] **1** *n* (*Chess*) pat *m*; (*fig*) impasse *f*. **the discussions have reached ~** les discussions sont dans l'impasse; **the ~ is complete** c'est l'impasse totale; **to break the ~** sortir de l'impasse.

2 *vt* (*Chess*) faire pat *inv*; (*fig*) *project* contrecarrer; *adversary* paralyser, neutraliser.

staleness ['steɪlnɪs] *n* (*V* **stale 1**) manque *m* de fraîcheur; dureté *f*; caractère déjà vieux (*or* rebattu *or* éculé); perte *f* d'inspiration; surentraînement *m.*

stalk¹ [stɔːk] **1** *n [plant]* tige *f*; *[fruit]* queue *f*; *[cabbage]* trognon *m*; (*Zool*) pédoncule *m*. (*fig*) **his eyes were out on ~s*** il ouvrait des yeux ronds, il écarquillait les yeux. **2** *cpd:* (*Zool*) **stalk-eyed** aux yeux pédonculés.

stalk² [stɔːk] **1** *vt* **(a)** *game, prey* traquer; *suspect* filer.

(b) *[fear, disease, death]* **to ~ the streets/town** *etc* régner dans les rues/la ville *etc.*

2 *vi:* **to ~ in/out/off** *etc* entrer/sortir/partir *etc* d'un air digne *or* avec raideur; **he ~ed in haughtily/angrily/indignantly** il est entré d'un air arrogant/furieux/indigné.

3 *cpd:* (*fig*) **stalking-horse** prétexte *m.*

stall [stɔːl] **1** *n* (*in stable, cowshed*) stalle *f*; (*in market, street, at fair*) éventaire *m*, boutique *f* (en plein air); (*in exhibition*) stand *m*; (*Rel*) stalle; (*Brit Theat*) (fauteuil *m* d')orchestre *m*. (*Brit Theat*) **the ~s** l'orchestre; **newspaper/flower ~** kiosque *m* à journaux/de fleuriste; (*in station*) **book~** librairie *f* (de gare); **coffee ~** buvette *f*; *V* **choir, finger.**

2 *cpd:* (*Agr*) **stall-fed** engraissé à l'étable; **stallholder** marchand(e) *m(f)* en plein air, marchand(e) tenant un kiosque.

3 *vi* **(a)** *[car, engine, driver]* caler; *[aircraft]* être en perte de vitesse, décrocher.

(b) (*fig*) **to ~ (for time)** essayer de gagner du temps, atermoyer; **he managed to ~ until ...** il a réussi à trouver des faux-fuyants jusqu'à ce que ...; **stop ~ing!** cesse de te dérober!

4 *vt* **(a)** (*Aut*) *engine, car* caler; (*Aviat*) causer une perte de vitesse *or* un décrochage à.

(b) (*also* **~ off**) *person* tenir à distance. **I managed to ~ him until ...** j'ai réussi à le tenir à distance *or* à esquiver ses questions jusqu'à ce que ...; **try to ~ him (off) for a while** essaie de gagner du temps.

stallion ['stæljən] *n* étalon *m.*

stalwart ['stɔːlwət] **1** *adj* (*in build*) vigoureux, bien charpenté, costaud‡; (*in spirit*) vaillant, résolu, déterminé. **to be a ~ supporter of** soutenir vaillamment *or* de façon inconditionnelle. **2** *n* brave homme *m* (*or* femme *f*).

stamen ['steɪmen] *n* (*Bot*) étamine *f.*

stamina ['stæmɪnə] *n* (*U*) (*physical*) vigueur *f*, résistance *f*, endurance *f*; (*intellectual*) vigueur; (*moral*) résistance, endurance. **he's got ~** il est résistant, il a du nerf*.

stammer ['stæməʳ] **1** *n* bégaiement *m*, balbutiement *m*; (*Med*) bégaiement. **to have a ~** bégayer, être bègue.

2 *vi* bégayer, balbutier; (*Med*) bégayer, être bègue.

3 *vt* (*also* **~ out**) *name, facts* bégayer, balbutier. **to ~ (out) a reply** bégayer *or* balbutier une réponse, répondre en bégayant *or* balbutiant; **'n-not t-too m-much' he ~ed** 'p-pas t-trop' bégaya-t-il.

stammerer ['stæmərəʳ] *n* bègue *mf.*

stammering ['stæmərɪŋ] **1** *n* (*U*) bégaiement *m*, balbutiement *m*; (*Med*) bégaiement.

2 *adj person* (*from fear, excitement*) bégayant, balbutiant; (*Med*) bègue; *answer* bégayant, hésitant.

stammeringly ['stæmərɪŋlɪ] *adv* en bégayant, en balbutiant.

stamp [stæmp] **1** *n* **(a)** timbre *m*; (*postage ~*) timbre(-poste); (*fiscal ~, revenue ~*) timbre (fiscal); (*savings ~*) timbre (-épargne); (*trading ~*) timbre(-prime). **(National) Insurance ~** cotisation *f* à la Sécurité sociale; **to put** *or* **stick a ~ on a letter** coller un timbre sur une lettre, timbrer une lettre; **used/unused ~** timbre oblitéré/non-oblitéré.

(b) (*implement*) (*rubber ~*) timbre *m*, tampon *m*; (*date ~*) timbre dateur; (*for metal*) étampe *f*, poinçon *m.*

(c) (*mark, impression*) (*on document etc*) cachet *m*; (*on metal*) empreinte *f*, poinçon *m*; (*Comm: trademark etc*) estampille *f*. **look at the date ~** regardez la date sur le cachet; **here's his address ~** voici le cachet indiquant son adresse; **it's got a receipt ~ on it** il y a un cachet accusant paiement; (*fig*) **he gave the project his ~ of approval** il a approuvé le projet; **the ~ of genius/truth** la marque *or* le sceau du génie/de la vérité; **men of**

his ~ des hommes de sa trempe *or* de son envergure *or* de son acabit (*pej*).

(d) *[foot]* (*from cold*) battement *m* de pied; (*from rage*) trépignement *m*. **with a ~ (of his foot)** en tapant du pied.

2 *cpd:* (*Brit Hist*) **Stamp Act** loi *f* sur le timbre; **stamp album** album *m* de timbres(-poste); **stamp-book** carnet *m* de timbres (-poste); (*U*) **stamp collecting** philatélie *f*; **stamp collection** collection *f* de timbres(-poste); **stamp collector** collectionneur *m*, -euse *f* de timbres(-poste), philatéliste *mf*; **stamp dealer** marchand(e) *m(f)* de timbres(-poste); **stamp duty** droit *m* de timbre; (*fig*) **stamping ground*** lieu favori, royaume *m* (*fig*); **stamp machine** distributeur *m* (automatique) de timbres (-poste).

3 *vt* **(a)** **to ~ one's foot** taper du pied; **to ~ one's feet** (*in rage*) trépigner; (*in dance*) frapper du pied; (*to keep warm*) battre la semelle; **he ~ed the peg into the ground** il a tapé du pied sur le piquet pour l'enfoncer en terre.

(b) (*stick a ~ on*) *letter, parcel* timbrer, affranchir; *savings book, insurance card* timbrer, apposer un *or* des timbre(s) sur; (*put fiscal ~ on*) timbrer. **this letter is not sufficiently ~ed** cette lettre n'est pas suffisamment affranchie; **~ed addressed envelope** enveloppe timbrée pour la réponse.

(c) (*mark with ~*) tamponner, timbrer; *passport, document* viser; *metal* estamper, poinçonner. **to ~ a visa on a passport** apposer un visa sur un passeport; **to ~ the date on a form, to ~ a form with the date** apposer la date au tampon sur un formulaire; **he ~ed a design on the metal** il a estampillé le métal d'un motif; (*fig*) **to ~ sth on one's memory** graver qch dans sa mémoire; **his accent ~s him (as) a Belgian** son accent montre bien *or* indique bien qu'il est belge; *V* **die**[2] *etc.*

4 *vi* **(a)** taper du pied; (*angrily*) taper du pied, trépigner; *[horse]* piaffer. **he ~ed on my foot** il a fait exprès de me marcher sur le pied; **he ~ed on the burning wood** il a piétiné les tisons, il a éteint les tisons du pied; (*fig*) **to ~ on a suggestion*** rejeter *or* repousser une suggestion.

(b) (*angrily*) **to ~ in/out** *etc* entrer/sortir *etc* en tapant du pied; **to ~ about** *or* **around** (*angrily*) marcher de long en large en tapant du pied; (*to keep warm*) marcher de long en large en battant la semelle.

stamp down *vt sep peg etc* enfoncer du pied; (*fig*) *rebellion* écraser, étouffer; *protests* refouler.

stamp out *vt sep* **(a)** *fire* piétiner, éteindre en piétinant; *cigarette* écraser sous le pied; (*fig*) *rebellion* enrayer, juguler; *custom, belief, tendency* déraciner, détruire.

(b) *coin etc* frapper; *design* découper à l'emporte-pièce.

(c) *rhythm* marquer en frappant du pied.

stampede [stæm'piːd] **1** *n [animals, people]* débandade *f*, fuite précipitée, sauve-qui-peut *m inv*; *[retreating troops]* débâcle *f*, déroute *f*; (*fig: rush*) ruée *f*. **there was a ~ for the door** on s'est précipité *or* rué vers la porte; **he got knocked down in the ~ for seats** il a été renversé dans la ruée vers les sièges.

2 *vi [animals, people]* s'enfuir en désordre *or* à la débandade (*from* de), fuir en désordre *or* à la débandade (*towards* vers); (*fig: rush*) se ruer.

3 *vt animals, people* jeter la panique parmi. (*fig*) **they ~d him into agreeing** il a accepté parce qu'ils ne lui ont pas laissé le temps de la réflexion; **we mustn't let ourselves be ~d** il faut que nous prenions (*subj*) le temps de réfléchir.

stance [stæns] *n* (*lit, fig*) position *f*. **to take up a ~** (*lit*) se mettre en position; (*fig*) prendre position.

stanch [stɑːntʃ] *vt* = **staunch**[1].

stanchion ['stɑːnʃən] *n* (*as support*) étançon *m*, étai *m*; (*for cattle*) montant *m*.

stand [stænd] (*vb: pret, ptp* **stood**) **1** *n* **(a)** (*position: lit, fig*) position *f*; (*resistance: Mil, fig*) résistance *f*, opposition *f*; (*Theat: stop, performance*) représentation *f*. **to take (up) one's ~** (*lit*) prendre place *or* position; (*fig*) adopter une attitude (*on sth* envers *or* sur qch), prendre position (*against sth* contre qch); **he took (up) his ~ beside me** (*lit*) il s'est placé *or* mis *or* posté à côté de moi, il a pris position à côté de moi; (*fig*) il m'a soutenu, il a pris la même position *or* adopté la même attitude que moi; (*fig*) **I admired the firm ~ he took on that point** j'ai admiré la fermeté de son attitude *or* de sa position sur ce point; **I make my ~ upon these principles** je fonde *or* je base mon attitude sur ces principes; (*fig*) **to make** *or* **take a ~ against sth** prendre position contre qch, s'élever contre qch, s'opposer à qch, résister à qch; (*Mil*) **they turned and made a ~** ils se sont arrêtés et ont résisté; (*Mil*) **the ~ of the Australians at Tobruk** la résistance des Australiens à Tobrouk; **Custer's last ~** la dernière bataille de Custer; *V* **hand, one** *etc.*

(b) (*taxi ~*) station *f* (de taxis).

(c) (*structure*) (*for plant, bust etc*) guéridon *m*; (*lamp~*) support *m or* pied *m* (de lampe); (*hat~*) porte-chapeaux *m inv*; (*coat~*) portemanteau *m*; (*music ~*) pupitre *m* à musique; (*Comm: for displaying goods*) étal *m*, étalage *m*; (*newspaper ~*) kiosque *m* à journaux; (*market stall*) étalage, boutique *f* en plein air; (*at exhibition, trade fair*) stand *m*; (*at fair*) barraque *f*; (*US: witness ~*) barre *f*; (*band~*) kiosque (à musique); (*Sport; also along procession route etc*) tribune *f*. (*Sport*) **I've got a ticket for the ~(s)** j'ai un billet de tribune(s), j'ai une tribune; (*esp US*) **to take the ~** venir à la barre; *V* **grand, hall, wash** *etc.*

(d) (*Agr*) *[wheat etc]* récolte *f* sur pied; *[trees]* bouquet *m*, groupe *m*.

(e) = **standstill**.

2 *cpd:* **stand-by** *V* **stand-by**; **stand-in** remplaçant(e) *m(f)*; (*Cine*) doublure *f*; **stand-offish** *V* **stand-offish**; **standpipe** colonne *f* d'alimentation; (*lit, fig*) **standpoint** point *m* de vue; **standstill** *V* **standstill**; (*Mil*) **stand-to** alerte *f*; **stand-up** *V* **stand-up**.

3 *vt* **(a)** (*place*) *object* mettre, poser (*on* sur). **he stood the child on the chair** il a mis l'enfant debout sur la chaise; **to ~ sth (up) against a wall** dresser *or* mettre *or* placer qch contre le mur; **to ~ sth on its end** faire tenir qch debout.

(b) (*tolerate*) *heat, pain* supporter; *insolence, attitude* supporter, tolérer. **I can't ~ it any longer** (*pain etc*) je ne peux plus le supporter; (*boredom etc*) j'en ai assez, j'en ai plein le dos*, j'en ai par-dessus la tête*; **I can't ~ (the sight of) her** je ne peux pas la supporter *or* la sentir* *or* la voir*, je la trouve insupportable; **she can't ~ being laughed at** elle ne supporte pas *or* ne tolère pas qu'on se moque (*subj*) d'elle; **I can't ~ gin/Debussy/wet weather** je déteste le gin/Debussy/la pluie.

(c) (*withstand*) *pressure, heat* supporter, résister à. **to ~ the strain** *[rope/beam etc]* supporter la tension/le poids *etc*; *[person]* supporter la tension, tenir le coup*; **she stood the journey quite well** elle a bien supporté le voyage; **these cheap shoes won't ~ much wear** ces chaussures bon marché ne vont pas faire beaucoup d'usage; **it won't ~ close examination** cela ne résiste pas à un examen serré; **it won't ~ much more rubbing like that** cela ne résistera pas longtemps si on continue à le frotter comme ça; **the town stood constant bombardment for 2 days** la ville a résisté 2 jours à un bombardement continuel; *V* **test**.

(d) (*pay for*) payer, offrir. **to ~ sb a meal** payer à déjeuner (*or* dîner) à qn; **to ~ sb a drink** payer à boire à qn; **I'll ~ you an ice cream** je te paie *or* je t'offre une glace; **he stood the next round of drinks** il a payé *or* offert la tournée suivante; **to ~ the cost of sth** payer le coût de qch; *V* **treat**.

(e) (*phrases*) **to ~ a chance** avoir une bonne chance (*of doing* de faire); **to ~ no chance** ne pas avoir la moindre chance (*of doing* de faire); **to ~ one's ground** (*lit*) tenir bon, ne pas reculer; (*fig*) tenir bon *or* ferme, ne pas lâcher pied; **to ~ (one's) trial** passer en jugement.

4 *vi* **(a)** (*be upright; also ~* **up**) *[person, animal]* être *or* se tenir debout; *[pole, table etc]* être debout. **the child has learnt to ~** l'enfant sait se tenir debout maintenant; **he is too weak to ~** il est trop faible pour se tenir debout *or* se tenir sur ses jambes; **we had to ~ as far as Calais** nous avons dû rester *or* voyager debout jusqu'à Calais; **you must ~ (up)** *or* **stay ~ing (up) till the music stops** vous devez rester debout jusqu'à ce que la musique s'arrête (*subj*); **to ~ erect** (*stay upright*) rester debout; (*straighten up*) se redresser; **~ (up) straight!** tiens-toi droit(e)!; (*fig*) **to ~ on one's own (two) feet** voler de ses propres ailes, se débrouiller* tout seul; **he ~s over 6 feet in his socks** il mesure *or* fait plus de 1 mètre 80 sans chaussures; **the tree ~s 30 metres high** l'arbre mesure *or* fait 30 mètres (de haut); **the chair won't ~ (up) properly** cette chaise ne tient pas bien debout, cette chaise est bancale; **the post must ~ upright** le pieu doit être *or* rester droit; **the house is still ~ing** la maison est encore debout *or* existe toujours *or* est toujours là; **not much still ~s of the walls** il ne reste plus grand-chose des murs; **they didn't leave a stone ~ing of the old town** ils n'ont rien laissé debout dans la vieille ville; *V* **attention, easy, hair** *etc.*

(b) (*rise: also ~* **up**) se lever, se mettre debout. **all ~!** tout le monde debout!; (*more frm*) levez-vous s'il vous plaît!; (*fig*) **to ~ (up) and be counted** déclarer ouvertement sa position.

(c) (*~ still*) rester (debout), être (debout). **we stood talking for an hour** nous sommes restés là à parler pendant une heure; **he stood in the doorway** il se tenait dans l'embrasure de la porte; **don't ~ there, do something!** ne reste pas là à ne rien faire!; **I left him ~ing on the bridge** je l'ai laissé sur le pont; (*fig*) **he left the others ~ing** il dépassait les autres d'une tête; **the man ~ing over there** cet homme là-bas; **~ over there till I'm ready** mets-toi *or* reste là-bas jusqu'à ce que je sois prêt; **he stood there ready to shoot** il était là prêt à tirer; **they stood patiently in the rain** ils attendaient patiemment sous la pluie; **they stood in a circle around the grave** ils se tenaient en cercle autour de la tombe; (*esp US*) **to ~ in line** faire la queue; **the car stood abandoned by the roadside** la voiture était abandonnée au bord de la route; **beads of perspiration stood on his brow** des gouttes de sueur perlaient sur son front; **tears stood in her eyes** elle avait les larmes aux yeux; **~ still!** tenez-vous tranquille!, ne bougez pas!, restez là!; (*fig*) **time seemed to ~ still** le temps semblait s'être arrêté; **~ and deliver!** la bourse ou la vie!; (*lit, fig*) **to ~ fast** *or* **firm** tenir bon *or* ferme, ne pas lâcher pied; (*lit*) **to ~ in sb's way** bloquer *or* barrer le passage à qn; (*fig*) **I won't ~ in your way** je ne vous ferai pas obstacle, je ne vous barrerai pas la route; **nothing now ~s in our way** maintenant la voie est libre; **his age ~s in his way** son âge constitue un sérieux handicap; **to ~ in the way of progress** constituer un obstacle au progrès; **to ~ clear** s'écarter; **you're ~ing on my foot** tu me marches sur le pied; **he stood on the beetle** il a marché sur *or* écrasé le scarabée; (*Aut*) **to ~ on the brakes** appuyer à fond sur *or* écraser la pédale de frein, freiner à mort; (*fig*) **to ~ on ceremony** faire des manières; **to ~ on one's dignity** garder ses distances, faire grand cas de sa dignité; **I won't ~ on my right to do so** je n'insisterai pas sur le fait que j'ai le droit de le faire; **it ~s to reason that ...** il va sans dire que ..., il va de soi que ...; **where do you ~ on this question?** quelle est votre position *or* quel est votre point de vue sur cette question?; **I like to know where I ~** j'aime savoir où j'en suis, j'aime connaître ma situation; **where do you ~ with him?** où en êtes-vous avec lui?, quels sont vos rapports avec lui?; **he ~s alone in this matter** personne ne partage son avis sur cette question; **this ~s alone** c'est unique en son genre; (*fig*) **he ~s (head and shoulders) above all the others** il dépasse tous les autres d'une tête (*fig*).

(d) (*be placed*) *[town, building, tree]* se trouver; *[object, vehicle]* se trouver, être. **the village ~s in the valley** le village se trouve *or* est (situé) dans la vallée; **the house ~s in its own grounds** la maison est entourée d'un parc *or* se dresse au milieu d'un parc; **3 chairs stood against the wall** il y avait 3 chaises contre le mur; **to let sth ~ in the sun** laisser *or* exposer qch au soleil; (*fig*) **nothing ~s between you and success** rien ne s'oppose à votre réussite; **that was all that stood between him and ruin** c'était tout ce qui le séparait de la ruine.

(e) (*be mounted, based*) *[statue etc]* reposer (*on* sur); (*fig*) *[argument, case]* reposer, être basé (*on* sur). **the lamp ~s on an alabaster base** la lampe a un pied *or* un support d'albâtre.

(f) (*be at the moment; have reached*) to ~ at *[thermometer, clock]* indiquer; *[offer, price, bid]* être à, avoir atteint; *[score]* être de; **you must accept the offer as it ~s** il faut que vous acceptiez (*subj*) l'offre telle quelle; **the record ~s unbeaten** le record n'a pas encore été battu; **the record stood at 4 minutes for several years** pendant plusieurs années le record est resté à 4 minutes; **sales ~ at 5% up on last year** les ventes sont pour le moment en hausse de 5% sur l'année dernière; (*Banking*) **to have £500 ~ing to one's account** avoir 500 livres en banque *or* à son compte (bancaire); **the amount ~ing to your account** la somme que vous avez à votre compte (bancaire), votre solde *m* de crédit; **as things ~ at the moment** étant donné l'état actuel des choses, les choses étant ce qu'elles sont en ce moment; **how do things ~ between them?** où en sont-ils?; **how do things ~?** où en sont les choses?

(g) (*remain undisturbed, unchanged*) *[liquid, mixture, dough etc]* reposer; *[tea, coffee]* infuser; *[offer, law, agreement, objection]* rester sans changement, demeurer valable. **let the matter ~ as it is** laissez les choses comme elles sont; **they agreed to let the regulation ~** ils ont décidé de ne rien changer au règlement; **to ~ or fall by sth** reposer sur qch.

(h) (*be*) être. **to ~ accused/convicted of murder** être accusé/déclaré coupable de meurtre; **to ~ in fear of sb/sth** craindre *or* redouter qn/qch; **I ~ corrected** je reconnais m'être trompé, je reconnais mon erreur; **to ~ opposed to sth** être opposé à qch, s'opposer à qch; **they were ~ing ready to leave at a moment's notice** ils étaient *or* se tenaient prêts à partir dans la minute; **to ~ well with sb** être bien vu de qn.

(i) (*act as*) remplir la fonction de, être. **to ~ guard over sth** monter la garde près de qch, veiller sur qch; **to ~ godfather to sb** être parrain de qn; **to ~ security for sb** se porter caution pour qn; (*Brit Parl*) **to ~ (as a candidate)** être *or* se porter candidat; (*Brit Parl*) **he stood (as candidate) for Gloomville** il a été candidat *or* s'est présenté à Gloomville; **to ~ for election** se présenter aux élections, être candidat; **he stood for the council but wasn't elected** il était candidat au poste de conseiller mais n'a pas été élu, il était candidat dans l'élection du conseil mais a été battu.

(j) (*be likely*) **to ~ to lose** risquer de perdre; **to ~ to win** risquer* de *or* avoir des chances de gagner; **he ~s to make a fortune on it** il pourrait bien faire fortune ainsi.

(k) (*Naut*) **to ~ (out) to sea** (*move*) mettre le cap sur le large; (*stay*) être *or* rester au large.

stand about, stand around *vi* rester là, traîner (*pej*). **don't stand about doing nothing!** ne reste pas là à ne rien faire!, ne traîne pas sans rien faire!; **they were standing about wondering what to do** ils restaient là à se demander ce qu'ils pourraient bien faire; **they kept us standing about for hours** ils nous ont fait attendre debout *or* fait faire le pied de grue pendant des heures.

stand aside *vi* s'écarter, se pousser. **he stood aside to let me pass** il s'est écarté *or* poussé *or* effacé pour me laisser passer; **stand aside!** poussez-vous!, écartez-vous!; (*fig*) **to stand aside in favour of sb** laisser la voie libre à qn, ne pas faire obstacle à qn; **he never stands aside if there is work to be done** il est toujours prêt à travailler quand il le faut.

stand back *vi [person]* reculer, s'écarter. (*fig*) **you must stand back and get the problem into perspective** il faut que vous preniez (*subj*) du recul pour voir le problème dans son ensemble; **the farm stands back from the motorway** la ferme est à l'écart *or* en retrait de l'autoroute.

stand by 1 *vi* **(a)** (*be onlooker*) rester là (à ne rien faire), se tenir là. **I could not stand by and see him beaten** je ne pouvais rester là à le voir se faire battre sans intervenir; **how could you stand by while they attacked him?** comment pouviez-vous rester là sans rien faire alors qu'ils l'attaquaient?; **he stood by and let me get on with it** il s'est contenté d'assister et m'a laissé faire.

(b) *[troops]* être en état d'alerte; *[person, ship, vehicle]* (*be ready*) être *or* se tenir prêt; (*be at hand*) attendre *or* être sur place. (*gen*) **stand by!** attention!; (*Aviat*) **stand by for takeoff** paré pour le décollage; (*Naut*) **stand by to drop anchor** paré à mouiller l'ancre; **stand by for further news** tenez-vous prêt à recevoir d'autres nouvelles.

2 *vt fus promise* tenir; *sb else's decision* accepter; *one's own decision* réaffirmer, s'en tenir à; *friend* être fidèle à, ne pas abandonner; *colleague etc* soutenir, défendre. **I stand by what I have said** je m'en tiens à ce que j'ai dit.

3 stand-by *V* **stand-by.**

stand down *vi* (*Mil*) *[troops]* être déconsigné (en fin d'alerte); (*Jur*) *[witness]* quitter la barre; (*fig: withdraw*) *[candidate]* se désister; *[chairman etc]* démissionner. **he stood down in favour of his brother** il s'est désisté en faveur de son frère *or* pour laisser la voie libre à son frère.

stand for *vt fus* **(a)** (*represent*) représenter. **what does U.N.O. stand for?** qu'est-ce que les lettres U.N.O. représentent *or* veulent dire *or* signifient?; **our party stands for equality of opportunity** notre parti est synonyme d'égalité des chances; **I dislike all he stands for** je déteste tout ce qu'il représente *or* incarne; *V also* **stand 4i.**

(b) (*tolerate*) supporter, tolérer. **I won't stand for it!** je ne le supporterai *or* tolérerai *or* permettrai pas!

stand in 1 *vi:* **to stand in for sb** remplacer qn; **I offered to stand in when he was called away** j'ai proposé d'assurer le remplacement *or* de le remplacer quand il a dû s'absenter.

2 stand-in *n V* **stand 2.**

stand off 1 *vi* **(a)** (*Naut*) mettre le cap sur le large.

(b) (*move away*) s'écarter; (*fig: keep one's distance*) se tenir à l'écart, garder ses distances.

2 *vt sep* (*Brit*) *workers* mettre temporairement au chômage.

stand out *vi* **(a)** (*project*) *[ledge, buttress]* avancer (*from* sur), faire saillie; *[vein etc]* ressortir, saillir (*on* sur). **to stand out in relief** ressortir, être en relief.

(b) (*be conspicuous, clear*) ressortir, se détacher, trancher, se découper. **to stand out against the sky** ressortir *or* se détacher sur le ciel; **the yellow stands out against the dark background** le jaune ressort *or* se détache *or* tranche sur le fond sombre; **his red hair stands out in the crowd** ses cheveux roux le font remarquer dans la foule; (*fig*) **his ability stands out** son talent ressort *or* est manifeste; (*fig*) **he stands out above all the rest** il surpasse *or* surclasse tout le monde; (*fig*) **that stands out a mile!*** cela saute aux yeux!, cela crève les yeux!

(c) (*remain firm*) tenir bon, tenir ferme. **how long can you stand out?** combien de temps peux-tu tenir *or* résister?; **to stand out for sth** revendiquer qch, s'obstiner à demander qch; **to stand out against** *attack* résister à; *demand* s'opposer fermement à.

stand over 1 *vi [items for discussion]* rester en suspens, être remis à plus tard. **let the matter stand over until next week** remettons la question à la semaine prochaine.

2 *vt fus person* surveiller, être sur *or* derrière le dos de. **I hate people standing over me while I work** je déteste avoir quelqu'un sur *or* derrière le dos quand je travaille; **I'll stand over you till you do it** je ne te lâcherai pas jusqu'à ce que tu l'aies fait; **stop standing over him and let him do it himself** arrête de le surveiller et laisse-le faire cela tout seul.

stand to (*Mil*) **1** *vi* se mettre en état d'alerte.

2 stand-to *n V* **stand 2.**

stand up 1 *vi* (*rise*) se lever, se mettre debout; (*be upright*) *[person]* être debout; *[chair, structure]* être (encore) debout. **she had nothing but the clothes she was standing up in** elle ne possédait que les vêtements qu'elle avait sur le dos; **the soup was so thick the spoon could stand up in it** la soupe était si épaisse qu'on pouvait y faire tenir la cuiller debout; (*fig*) **that argument won't stand up in court** cet argument ne sera pas valable en justice, cet argument sera démoli par l'avocat de la partie adverse; *V also* **stand 4a, 4b.**

2 *vt sep* **(a)** (*place upright*) **to stand sth up (on its end)** mettre qch debout; **to stand sth up against a wall** appuyer *or* mettre qch contre un mur; **he stood the child up on the table** il a mis l'enfant debout sur la table.

(b) (**fig*) poser un lapin à*, faire faux bond à. **she stood me up twice last week** elle m'a fait faux bond deux fois la semaine dernière.

3 stand-up *adj V* **stand-up.**

stand up for *vt fus person* défendre, prendre le parti de, prendre fait et cause pour; *principle, belief* défendre. **you must stand up for what you think is right** vous devez défendre ce qui vous semble juste; **stand up for me if he asks you what you think** prenez ma défense *or* soutenez-moi s'il vous demande votre avis; **to stand up for o.s.** se défendre.

stand up to *vt fus opponent* affronter; (**fig: in argument etc*) tenir tête à; *heat, cold etc* résister à. **it won't stand up to that sort of treatment** cela ne résistera pas à ce genre de traitement; **the report won't stand up to close examination** le rapport ne résistera pas *or* ne supportera pas un examen serré.

standard ['stændəd] **1** *n* **(a)** (*flag*) étendard *m*; (*Naut*) pavillon *m*.

(b) (*norm*) norme *f*; (*criterion*) critère *m*; (*for weights and measures*) étalon *m*; (*for silver*) titre *m*; (*fig: moral, intellectual etc*) niveau voulu, degré *m* d'excellence. **monetary ~** titre de monnaie; **the metre is the ~ of length** le mètre est l'unité *f* de longueur; (*fig*) **to be or come up to ~** *[person]* être à la hauteur, être du niveau voulu; *[thing]* être de la qualité voulue; **I'll never come up to his ~** je n'arriverai jamais à l'égaler; **judging by that ~** si l'on en juge selon ce critère; **you are applying a double ~** vous appliquez deux mesures; **his ~s are high** il cherche l'excellence, il ne se contente pas de l'à-peu-près; (*morally, artistically*) **he has set us a high ~** il a établi un modèle difficile à surpasser; **the exam sets a high ~** cet examen exige un niveau élevé; **the ~ of the exam was low** le niveau de l'examen était bas; **to be first-year university ~** être du niveau de première année d'université; **high/low ~ of living** niveau de vie élevé/bas; **their ~ of culture** leur niveau de culture; **to have high moral ~s** avoir un sens moral très développé; **I couldn't accept their ~s** je ne pouvais pas accepter leur échelle de valeurs; *V* **gold** *etc.*

(c) (*support*) support *m*; (*for lamp, street light*) pied *m*; (*water/gas pipe*) tuyau vertical d'eau/de gaz; (*tree, shrub*) arbre *m* de haute tige; *V* **lamp.**

2 *adj* **(a)** *size, height, procedure* ordinaire, normal; (*Comm: model*) standard *inv*; *metre, kilogram, measure, weight etc* étalon *inv*; *reference book, work* classique, de base; (*Ling*) *pronunciation, usage* correct. **it is now ~ practice to do so** c'est maintenant courant *or* la norme (de faire ainsi); **the practice became ~ in the 1940s** cette pratique s'est généralisée *or* répandue dans les années 40; **a ~ model car** une voiture de série; (*Rail*) **~ gauge** écartement normal (*V also* 3); **he's below ~ height for the police** il n'a pas la taille requise pour être agent de police; **~ time** (l')heure légale; **~ English** (l')anglais correct; **~ French** (le) français correct *or* de l'Académie; (*Statistics*) **~ deviation/error** écart *m*/erreur *f* type.

(b) *shrub, rose* de haute tige.

3 *cpd:* standard bearer porte-étendard *m inv*; (*Rail*) standard-gauge d'écartement normal; (*Brit*) standard lamp lampadaire *m*.
standardization [ˌstændədaɪˈzeɪʃən] *n* standardisation *f*.
standardize [ˈstændədaɪz] *vt* standardiser.
stand-by [ˈstændbaɪ] 1 *n* (*person*) remplaçant(e) *m(f)*; (*car/battery/boots*) voiture *f*/pile *f*/bottes *fpl* de réserve *or* de secours. if you are called away you must have a ~ si vous vous absentez, vous devez avoir un(e) remplaçant(e) *or* quelqu'un qui puisse vous remplacer en cas de besoin; aspirin is a useful ~ l'aspirine est toujours bonne à avoir *or* peut toujours être utile; to be on ~ *[troops]* être sur pied d'intervention; *[plane]* se tenir prêt à décoller (en permanence); *[doctor]* être de garde; (*Mil*) to be on 24-hour ~ être prêt à intervenir dans les 24 heures; (*Mil*) to put on ~ mettre sur pied d'intervention.
2 *adj car, battery etc* de réserve, de secours. (*Aviat*) a ~ ticket billet *m* sans garantie; ~ passenger voyageur *m*, -euse *f* sans garantie.
standee* [stænˈdiː] *n* (*US*) (*at match etc*) spectateur *m*, -trice *f* debout; (*on bus etc*) voyageur *m*, -euse *f* debout.
standing [ˈstændɪŋ] 1 *adj* (a) (*upright*) *passenger* debout *inv*; *statue* en pied; *corn, crop* sur pied. (*in bus, theatre*) ~ room places *fpl* debout; ~ stone pierre levée *or* dressée; he got a ~ ovation ils lui ont fait une ovation, ils se sont levés pour l'ovationner *or* l'applaudir; (*Sport*) ~ jump saut *m* à pieds joints; (*Sport*) ~ start départ *m* debout.
(b) (*permanent*) *army, committee* permanent; *rule* fixe; *custom* établi, courant; *grievance, reproach* constant, de longue date. ~ expenses frais généraux; it's a ~ joke that he wears a wig on plaisante constamment à son sujet en prétendant qu'il porte une perruque; it's a ~ joke c'est un sujet de plaisanterie continuel; (*Banking*) ~ order virement *m* automatique; (*Mil, Parl*) ~ orders règlement *m*; to place a ~ order for a newspaper passer une commande permanente pour un journal.
2 *n* (a) (*position, importance etc*) *[person]* importance *f*, rang *m*, standing *m*; *[restaurant, business]* réputation *f*, standing; *[newspaper]* importance, réputation, influence *f*. social ~ rang *or* position *f* social(e), standing; professional ~ rang *or* standing professionnel; what's his financial ~? quelle est sa situation financière?; what's his ~? quelle est sa réputation?, que pense-t-on de lui?; firms of that ~ des compagnies aussi réputées; a man of (high *or* some *or* good) ~ un homme considéré *or* estimé; he has no ~ in this matter il n'a aucune autorité *or* son opinion ne compte pas *or* il n'a pas voix au chapitre dans cette affaire.
(b) (*duration*) durée *f*. of 10 years' ~ *friendship* qui dure depuis 10 ans; *agreement, contract* qui existe depuis 10 ans; *doctor, teacher* qui a 10 ans de métier; of long ~ de longue *or* vieille date; he has 30 years' ~ in the firm il a 30 ans d'ancienneté dans la compagnie, il travaille dans la compagnie depuis 30 ans; *V* long[1].
stand-offish [ˌstændˈɒfɪʃ] *adj* (*pej*) distant, réservé, froid. don't be so ~! ne prends pas ton air supérieur!
stand-offishly [ˌstændˈɒfɪʃlɪ] *adv* (*pej*) d'une manière réservée *or* distante, avec froideur.
stand-offishness [ˌstændˈɒfɪʃnɪs] *n* (*pej*) froideur *f*, réserve *f*.
standstill [ˈstændstɪl] *n* arrêt *m*. to come to a ~ *[person, car]* s'immobiliser; *[production, discussions]* s'arrêter. to bring to a ~ *car* arrêter; *production, discussion* paralyser; to be at a ~ *[person, car]* être immobile; *[production, discussion]* être paralysé, être au point mort; trade is at a ~ les affaires sont dans le marasme complet.
stand-up [ˈstændʌp] *adj collar* droit; *meal etc* (pris) debout. a ~ fight (*fisticuffs*) une bagarre en règle *or* violente; (*argument*) une discussion en règle *or* violente.
stank [stæŋk] *pret of* stink.
stannic [ˈstænɪk] *adj* stannique.
stanza [ˈstænzə] *n* (*Poetry*) strophe *f*; (*in song*) couplet *m*.
staphylococcus [ˌstæfɪləˈkɒkəs] *n, pl* staphylococci [ˌstæfɪləˈkɒkaɪ] staphylocoque *m*.
staple[1] [ˈsteɪpl] 1 *adj* (*basic*) *food, crop, industry* principal; *products, foods* de base. ~ commodity article *m* de première nécessité; ~ diet nourriture *f* de base.
2 *n* (a) (*Econ*) (*chief commodity*) produit *m or* article *m* de base; (*raw material*) matière première.
(b) (*chief item*) (*Comm: held in stock*) produit *m or* article *m* de base; (*gen: of conversation etc*) élément *or* sujet principal; (*in diet etc*) aliment *m or* denrée *f* de base.
(c) (*Tex: fibre*) fibre *f*.
staple[2] [ˈsteɪpl] 1 *n* (*for papers*) agrafe *f*; (*Tech*) crampon *m*, cavalier *m*. 2 *vt* (*also* ~ together) *papers* agrafer; *wood, stones* cramponner. to ~ sth on to sth agrafer qch à qch.
stapler [ˈsteɪplər] *n* agrafeuse *f*.
star [stɑːr] 1 *n* (a) (*Astron*) étoile *f*, astre *m*; (*Typ etc: asterisk*) astérisque *m*; (*Scol: for merit*) bon point. morning/evening ~ étoile du matin/du soir; (*US*) the S~s and Stripes la Bannière étoilée; S~ of David étoile de David; the ~ of Bethlehem l'étoile de Bethléem (*V also* 2); he was born under a lucky ~ il est né sous une bonne étoile; you can thank your (lucky) ~s* that ... tu peux remercier le ciel *or* bénir ton étoile de ce que ...; (*fig*) to see ~s* voir trente-six chandelles; (*horoscope*) the ~s l'horoscope *m*; it was written in his ~s that he would do it il était écrit qu'il le ferait; *V* guiding, pole[2], shooting *etc*.
(b) (*Cine, Sport etc: person*) vedette *f*; (*actress*) star *f*. the film made him into a ~ le film en a fait une vedette *or* l'a rendu célèbre; *V* all, film *etc*.
2 *cpd:* 3-star hotel hôtel *m* 3 étoiles; (*Brit*) 4-star petrol super* *m*; (*US*) four-star general général *m* à quatre étoiles; starfish étoile *f* de mer; (*hum*) stargazer (*astronomer*) astronome *mf*; (*astrologer*) astrologue *mf*; to be stargazing regarder les étoiles; (*fig: daydream*) rêvasser, être dans la lune; (*Bot*) stargrass herbe étoilée; by starlight à la lumière des étoiles; starlit *night, sky* étoilé; *countryside, scene* illuminé par les étoiles; (*Bot*) star-of-Bethlehem ornithogale *m*, dame-d'onze-heures; (*Cine, Theat*) star part premier rôle; (*Cine, Theat*) a star(ring) role l'un des principaux rôles; (*US Post*) star route liaison postale; (*Mil*) star shell fusée éclairante; star-spangled parsemé d'étoiles; (*US: flag, anthem*) the Star-Spangled Banner la Bannière étoilée; star-studded *sky* parsemé d'étoiles; (*fig: play, cast*) à vedettes; (*Theat, fig*) the star turn la vedette.
3 *vt* (a) (*decorate with* ~s) étoiler. lawn ~red with daisies pelouse parsemée *or* émaillée (*liter*) de pâquerettes.
(b) (*put asterisk against*) marquer d'un astérisque.
(c) (*Cine, Theat*) avoir pour vedette. the film ~s John Wayne John Wayne est la vedette du film; ~ring Greta Garbo as ... avec Greta Garbo dans le rôle de ... .
4 *vi* (*Cine, Theat*) être la vedette (*in a film* d'un film); (*fig*) briller. he ~red as Hamlet c'est lui la vedette qui a joué le rôle de Hamlet.
starboard [ˈstɑːbəd] (*Naut*) 1 *n* tribord *m*. to ~ à tribord; land to ~! terre par tribord! 2 *adj guns, lights* de tribord. on the ~ beam par le travers tribord; on the ~ side à tribord; *V* watch[2]. 3 *vt:* to ~ the helm mettre la barre à tribord.
starch [stɑːtʃ] 1 *n* (*U*) (*in food*) amidon *m*, fécule *f*; (*for stiffening*) amidon; (*fig: formal manner*) raideur *f*, manières apprêtées *or* empesées. he was told to cut out all ~(es) on lui a dit de supprimer tous les féculents.
2 *cpd:* starch-reduced *bread* de régime; *diet* pauvre en féculents.
3 *vt collar* amidonner, empeser.
starchy [ˈstɑːtʃɪ] *adj food* féculent; (*fig pej*) *person, attitude* guindé, apprêté, raide.
stardom [ˈstɑːdəm] *n* (*U: Cine, Sport, Theat etc*) célébrité *f*. to rise to ~, achieve ~ devenir célèbre *or* vedette, atteindre la célébrité.
stare [stɛər] 1 *n* regard *m* (fixe). cold/curious/vacant ~ (long) regard froid/curieux/vague.
2 *vi:* to ~ at sb dévisager qn, fixer qn du regard, regarder qn fixement; to ~ at sth regarder qch fixement, fixer qch du regard; to ~ at sb/sth in surprise regarder qn/qch avec surprise *or* d'un air surpris, écarquiller les yeux devant qn/qch; they all ~d in astonishment ils ont tous regardé d'un air ébahi *or* en écarquillant les yeux; he ~d at me stonily il m'a regardé d'un air dur; what are you staring at? qu'est-ce que tu regardes comme ça?; it's rude to ~ il est mal élevé de regarder les gens fixement; to ~ into space regarder dans le vide *or* dans l'espace, avoir le regard perdu dans le vague.
3 *vt:* to ~ sb in the face dévisager qn, fixer qn du regard, regarder qn dans le blanc des yeux; where are my gloves? — here, they're staring you in the face! où sont mes gants? — ils sont là devant ton nez *or* tu as le nez dessus!; they're certainly in love, that ~s you in the face ils sont vraiment amoureux, cela crève les yeux; ruin ~d him in the face il était au bord de la ruine; the truth ~d him in the face la vérité lui crevait les yeux *or* lui sautait aux yeux.
stare out *vt sep* faire baisser les yeux à.
staring [ˈstɛərɪŋ] *adj crowd* curieux; (*fig*) *colour* criard, voyant, gueulard‡. his ~ eyes son regard fixe; (*in surprise*) son regard étonné *or* ébahi; (*in fear*) son regard effrayé; *V* stark.
stark [stɑːk] 1 *adj* (a) (*stiff*) raide, rigide; (*bleak*) *countryside* désolé, morne; *cliff etc* à pic *inv*, escarpé; *décor* austère. (*fig*) the ~ truth la vérité telle qu'elle est.
(b) (*utter*) pur, absolu, complet (*f* -ète). it is ~ folly c'est de la folie pure.
2 *adv:* ~ (raving *or* staring) mad* complètement fou (*f* folle) *or* dingue* *or* cinglé‡; ~ naked complètement nu, à poil‡.
starkers‡ [ˈstɑːkəz] *adj* (*Brit*) nu comme un ver*, à poil‡.
starkness [ˈstɑːknɪs] *n* (*V* stark 1a) raideur *f*, rigidité *f*; désolation *f*.
starless [ˈstɑːlɪs] *adj* sans étoiles.
starlet [ˈstɑːlɪt] *n* (*Cine*) starlette *f*.
starling [ˈstɑːlɪŋ] *n* étourneau *m*, sansonnet *m*.
starry [ˈstɑːrɪ] 1 *adj sky* étoilé, parsemé d'étoiles; *night* étoilé.
2 *cpd:* starry-eyed *person* (*idealistic*) idéaliste; (*innocent*) innocent, ingénu; (*from wonder*) éberlué; (*from love*) éperdument amoureux, ébloui; in starry-eyed wonder le regard plein d'émerveillement, complètement ébloui.
start [stɑːt] 1 *n* (a) (*beginning*) *[speech, book, film, career etc]* commencement *m*, début *m*; *[negotiations]* ouverture *f*, amorce *f*; (*Sport*) *[race etc]* départ *m*; (*starting line*) (point *m* de) départ. the ~ of the academic year la rentrée universitaire et scolaire; that was the ~ of all the trouble c'est là que tous les ennuis ont commencé; at the ~ au commencement, au début; from the ~ dès le début, dès le commencement; for a ~ d'abord, pour commencer; from ~ to finish du début jusqu'à la fin, de bout en bout, d'un bout à l'autre; to get off to a good ~ bien commencer, prendre un bon départ; to get a good ~ in life bien débuter dans la vie; they gave their son a good ~ in life ils ont fait ce qu'il fallait pour que leur fils débute (*subj*) bien dans la vie; that was a good ~ to his career cela a été un bon début *or* un début prometteur pour sa carrière; to make a ~ commencer; to make an early ~ commencer de bonne heure; (*in journey*) partir de bonne heure; to make a fresh ~ recommencer (à zéro*); (*Sport*) to be lined up for the ~ être sur la ligne de départ; (*Sport*) the whistle blew for the ~ of the race le coup de sifflet a annoncé le départ de la course; (*Sport*) wait for the ~ attendez le signal du départ; *V* false *etc*.
(b) (*advantage*) (*Sport*) avance *f*; (*fig*) avantage *m*. will you

give me a ~? est-ce que vous voulez bien me donner une avance?; to give sb 10 metres' ~ or a 10-metre ~ donner 10 mètres d'avance à qn; (fig) that gave him a ~ over the others in the class cela lui a donné un avantage sur les autres élèves de sa classe, cela l'a avantagé par rapport aux autres élèves de sa classe.

(c) (sudden movement) sursaut m, tressaillement m. to wake with a ~ se réveiller en sursaut; to give a ~ sursauter, tressaillir; to give sb a ~ faire sursauter or tressaillir qn; you gave me such a ~! ce que vous m'avez fait peur!; V fit[2].

2 cpd: (Racing) starting gate barrière f, starting-gate m; (Brit Aut) starting handle manivelle f; (Sport) starting line ligne f de départ; starting point (point m de) départ m; (Sport) starting post ligne f de départ; starting price (St Ex) prix initial; (Racing) cote f de départ.

3 vt (a) (begin) commencer (to do, doing à faire, de faire); se mettre (to do, doing à faire); work commencer, se mettre à; task entreprendre; song commencer (à chanter), entonner; attack déclencher; bottle entamer, déboucher; book, letter [writer] commencer (à écrire); [reader] commencer (à lire). to ~ a cheque book/a page commencer or prendre un nouveau carnet de chèques/une nouvelle page; to ~ a journey partir en voyage; he ~ed the day with a glass of milk il a bu un verre de lait pour bien commencer la journée; to ~ the day right bien commencer la journée, se lever du pied droit; to ~ life as débuter dans la vie comme; that doesn't (even) ~ to compare with ... cela est loin d'être comparable à ..., cela n'a rien de comparable avec ...; it soon ~ed to rain il n'a pas tardé à pleuvoir; I'd ~ed to think you were not coming je commençais à croire que tu ne viendrais pas; to ~ again or afresh recommencer (to do à faire), recommencer à zéro*; don't ~ that again! tu ne vas pas recommencer!; 'it's late' he ~ed 'il est tard' commença-t-il.

(b) (originate, initiate: often ~ off, ~ up) discussion commencer, ouvrir; conversation amorcer, engager; quarrel, argument, dispute faire naître; reform, movement, series of events déclencher; fashion lancer; phenomenon, institution donner naissance à; custom, policy inaugurer; war causer; rumour faire naître. to ~ (up) a fire (in grate etc) allumer un feu, faire du feu; (accidentally) mettre le feu, provoquer un incendie; you'll ~ a fire if you go on doing that! tu vas mettre le feu à la maison or tu vas provoquer un incendie si tu fais ça!; she has ~ed a baby* elle est enceinte.

(c) (cause to ~; also ~ up) engine, vehicle mettre en marche, démarrer; clock mettre en marche; (also ~ off) race donner le signal du départ. (fig) he ~ed the ball rolling by saying ... pour commencer, il a dit ...; he blew the whistle to ~ the runners (off) il a sifflé pour donner le signal du départ; he ~ed the new clerk (off) in the sales department il a d'abord mis or affecté le nouvel employé au service des ventes; they ~ed her (off) as a typist d'abord or pour commencer ils l'ont employée comme dactylo; to ~ sb (off or out) on a career lancer or établir qn dans une carrière; if you ~ him (off) on that subject ... si tu le lances sur ce sujet ...; that ~ed him (off) sneezing/remembering etc alors il s'est mis à éternuer/à se souvenir etc; (lit, fig) to ~ a hare lever un lièvre.

4 vi (a) (also ~ off) [person] commencer, s'y mettre; [speech, programme, meeting, ceremony] commencer (with par). let's ~!, let's get ~ed! commençons!, allons-y!, on s'y met!*; we must ~ at once il faut commencer or nous y mettre immédiatement; well, to ~ at the beginning eh bien, pour commencer par le commencement; it's ~ing (off) rather well/badly cela s'annonce plutôt bien/mal; to ~ (off) well in life bien débuter dans la vie; to ~ in business se lancer dans les affaires; just where the hair ~s à la naissance des cheveux; before October ~s avant le début d'octobre; to ~ again or afresh recommencer (à zéro*); classes ~ on Monday les cours commencent or reprennent lundi; the classes ~ again soon les cours reprennent bientôt, c'est bientôt la rentrée; ~ing from Monday à partir de lundi; to ~ (off) by doing commencer par faire; ~ by putting everything away commence par tout ranger; to ~ with sth commencer or débuter par qch; ~ with me! commencez par moi!; to ~ with there were only 3 of them, but later ... (tout) d'abord ils n'étaient que 3, mais plus tard ...; this is false to ~ with pour commencer or d'abord c'est faux; we only had 100 francs to ~ with nous n'avions que 100 F pour commencer or au début; ~ on a new page prenez une nouvelle page.

(b) (broach) to ~ on a book [writer] commencer (à écrire) un livre; [reader] commencer (à lire) un livre; to ~ on a course of study commencer or entreprendre un programme d'études; they had ~ed on a new bottle ils avaient débouché or entamé une nouvelle bouteille; I ~ed on the job last week j'ai commencé à travailler or j'ai débuté dans mon travail la semaine dernière.

(c) (also ~ up) [music, noise, guns] commencer, retentir; [fire] commencer, prendre; [river] prendre sa source; [road] partir (at de); [political party, movement, custom] commencer, naître. that's when the trouble ~s c'est alors or là que les ennuis commencent; it all ~ed when he refused to pay toute cette histoire a commencé or tout a commencé quand il a refusé de payer.

(d) (leave: also ~ off, ~ out) [person] partir, se mettre en route; [ship] partir; [train] partir, démarrer, se mettre en marche. to ~ (off or out) from London/for Paris/on a journey partir de Londres/pour Paris/en voyage; (Sport) 10 horses ~ed and only 3 finished 10 chevaux ont pris le départ mais 3 seulement ont fini la course; he ~ed (off or out) along the corridor il s'est engagé dans le couloir; he ~ed (off or out) down the street il a commencé à descendre la rue; (fig) he ~ed (off) in the sales department/as a clerk il a débuté dans le service des ventes/comme employé; he ~ed (off or out) as a Marxist il a commencé par être marxiste, au début or au départ il a été marxiste; he ~ed (off) with the intention of writing a thesis au début son intention était d'écrire or il avait l'intention d'écrire une thèse; he ~ed (out) to say that ... son intention était de dire que ....

(e) (also ~ up) [car, engine, machine] démarrer, se mettre en route; [clock] se mettre à marcher. my car won't ~ ma voiture ne veut pas démarrer*.

(f) (jump nervously) [person] sursauter, tressaillir; [animal] tressaillir, avoir un soubresaut. to ~ to one's feet sauter sur ses pieds, se lever brusquement; he ~ed forward il a fait un mouvement brusque en avant; (fig) his eyes were ~ing out of his head les yeux lui sortaient de la tête; tears ~ed to her eyes les larmes lui sont montées aux yeux.

(g) [timbers] jouer.

start back vi (a) (return) prendre le chemin du retour, repartir.

(b) (recoil) [person, horse etc] reculer soudainement, faire un bond en arrière.

start in vi s'y mettre, s'y coller*. start in! allez-y!

start off 1 vi V start 4a, 4d.

2 vt sep V start 3b, 3c.

start out vi V start 4d.

start up 1 vi V start 4c, 4e.

2 vt sep V start 3b, 3c.

starter ['stɑːtər] n (a) (Sport) (official) starter m; (horse, runner) partant m. (Sport) to be under ~'s orders [runner] être à ses marques; [horse] être sous les ordres du starter; (fig) to be a slow ~ être lent au départ or à démarrer; (Scol etc) the child was a late ~ cet enfant a mis du temps à se développer; (fig) it's a non-~* ça ne vaut rien, ça n'a pas l'ombre d'une chance.

(b) (also ~ button) (Aut) démarreur m; (on machine etc) bouton m de démarrage; (also ~ motor) démarreur.

(c) (*) (Culin) ~s hors-d'œuvre m inv; for ~s (Culin) comme hors-d'œuvre; (fig: for a start) pour commencer, d'abord.

starting ['stɑːtɪŋ] cpd V start 2.

startle ['stɑːtl] vt [sound, sb's arrival] faire sursauter or tressaillir or tressauter; [news, telegram] alarmer. it ~d him out of his sleep cela l'a réveillé en sursaut; to ~ sb out of his wits donner un (drôle* de) choc à qn; you ~d me! vous m'avez fait peur!

startled ['stɑːtld] adj animal effarouché; person très surpris, saisi, ahuri; expression, voice très surpris.

startling ['stɑːtlɪŋ] adj (surprising) surprenant, saisissant, ahurissant; (alarming) alarmant.

starvation [stɑː'veɪʃən] 1 n (U) inanition f. they are threatened with ~ ils risquent de mourir d'inanition or de faim, la famine les menace.

2 cpd rations, wages de famine. to be on a starvation diet être sérieusement or dangereusement sous-alimenté; (fig) I am on a starvation diet this week* je suis un régime draconien cette semaine; to be living at starvation level = to be on a starvation diet.

starve [stɑːv] 1 vt (a) faire souffrir de la faim; (deliberately) affamer. to ~ sb to death laisser qn mourir de faim; she ~d herself to feed her children elle s'est privée de nourriture pour donner à manger à ses enfants; you don't have to ~ yourself in order to slim tu peux maigrir sans te laisser mourir de faim; to ~ sb into submission soumettre qn par la faim; (Mil) to ~ a town into surrender amener une ville à se rendre par la famine.

(b) (deprive) priver (sb of sth qn de qch). ~d of affection privé d'affection.

2 vi manquer de nourriture, être affamé. to ~ (to death) mourir de faim; V also starving.

starve out vt sep person, animal obliger à sortir en l'affamant.

starving ['stɑːvɪŋ] adj affamé, famélique. I'm ~* je meurs de faim, j'ai une faim de loup.

stash‡ [stæʃ] vt (also ~ away) (hide) cacher, planquer‡; (save up, store away) mettre à gauche*, mettre de côté. he had £500 ~ed away il avait 500 livres en lieu sûr.

state [steɪt] 1 n (a) (condition) état m. ~ of alert/emergency/siege/war état d'alerte/d'urgence/de siège/de guerre; in your ~ of health/mind dans votre état de santé/d'esprit; he was in an odd ~ of mind il était d'une humeur étrange; you're in no ~ of mind to reply vous n'êtes pas en état de répondre; (fig) what's the ~ of play? où en est-on?; in a good/bad ~ of repair bien/mal entretenu; to be in a good/bad ~ [chair, car, house] être en bon/mauvais état; [person, relationship, marriage] aller bien/mal; you should have seen the ~ the car was in vous auriez dû voir l'état de la voiture; it wasn't in a (fit) ~ to be used c'était hors d'état de servir, c'était inutilisable; he's not in a (fit) ~ to drive il est hors d'état or il n'est pas en état de conduire; what a ~ you're in! vous êtes dans un bel état!; he got into a terrible ~ about it* ça l'a mis dans tous ses états; don't get into such a ~!* ne vous affolez pas!; V affair, declare etc.

(b) (Pol) État m. the S~ l'État; (US) the S~s les États-Unis; (US) the S~ of Virginia l'État de Virginie; the affairs of ~ les affaires de l'État; a ~ within a ~ un État dans l'État; V evidence, minister, police, secretary etc.

(c) (rank) rang m. every ~ of life tous les rangs sociaux.

(d) (U: pomp) pompe f, apparat m. the robes of ~ les costumes mpl d'apparat; in ~ en grande pompe, en grand apparat; to live in ~ mener grand train; V lie[1] etc.

2 cpd business, documents, secret d'État; security, control de l'État; medicine étatisé; (US: often S~) law, policy, prison, university d'État. state apartments appartements officiels; state banquet banquet m de gala; (US) State Capitol = State House; (Brit) state coach carrosse m d'apparat (de cérémonie officielle); state control contrôle m de l'État; under state con-

trol, state-controlled étatisé; (*U*) **statecraft** habileté *f* politique; (*US*) **State Department** Département *m* d'État, ≃ ministère *m* des Affaires étrangères; (*Brit*) **state education** enseignement public; (*Brit*) **state-enrolled nurse** infirmier *m*, -ière *f* auxiliaire, aide-soignante *mf*; (*US*) **State House** Capitole *m*; (*US*) **the State line** la frontière entre les états; **state-owned** étatisé; (*Brit*) **state-registered nurse** infirmier *m*, -ière *f* diplômé(e) d'État; **stateroom** *[palace]* grande salle de réception; *[ship, train]* cabine *f* de luxe; (*US*) **State's attorney** procureur *m*; (*Brit*) **state school** école publique; (*US*) **stateside*** aux États-Unis, ≃ chez nous; **statesman** *V* **statesman;** (*Pol Econ*) **state socialism** socialisme *m* d'État; (*US*) **State('s) rights** droits particuliers de l'État; **state-subsidised** subventionné par l'État; (*US*) **state trooper** ≃ CRS *m*; **to go on** *or* **make a state visit to a country** aller en visite officielle *or* faire un voyage officiel dans un pays; (*US*) **state-wide** (*adj, adv*) d'un bout à l'autre de l'État.

3 *vt* déclarer, affirmer (*that* que); *one's views, the facts* exposer, donner, formuler; *time, place* fixer, spécifier; *conditions* poser, formuler; *theory, restrictions* formuler; *problem* énoncer, poser. **I also wish to ~ that ...** je voudrais ajouter que ...; **it is ~d in the records that ...** il est écrit *or* mentionné dans les archives que ...; **I have seen it ~d that ...** j'ai lu quelque part que ...; **as ~d above** ainsi qu'il est dit plus haut; **~ your name and address** déclinez vos nom, prénoms et adresse; (*written*) inscrivez vos nom, prénoms et adresse; **cheques must ~ the sum clearly** les chèques doivent indiquer la somme clairement; **he was asked to ~ his case** on lui a demandé de présenter ses arguments; (*Jur*) **to ~ the case for the prosecution** présenter le dossier de l'accusation.

stated ['steɪtɪd] *adj date, sum* fixé; *interval* fixe; *limit* prescrit. **at the ~ time, at the time ~** à l'heure dite.

statehood ['steɪthʊd] *n* (*U*) **to achieve ~** devenir un État.

stateless ['steɪtlɪs] *adj* apatride. **~ person** apatride *mf*.

stateliness ['steɪtlɪnɪs] *n* majesté *f*, caractère imposant.

stately ['steɪtlɪ] *adj* majestueux, imposant. (*Brit*) **~ home** château *m* (*de l'aristocratie*).

statement ['steɪtmənt] *n* **(a)** (*U*) *[one's views, the facts]* exposition *f*, formulation *f*; *[time, place]* spécification *f*; *[theory, restrictions, conditions]* formulation; *[problem]* énonciation *f*.

(b) (*written, verbal*) déclaration *f*; (*Jur*) déposition *f*. **official ~** communiqué officiel; **to make a ~** (*gen, Press*) faire une déclaration; (*Jur*) faire une déposition, déposer.

(c) (*Fin: of accounts etc: bill*) relevé *m*; (*Comm: bill*) facture *f*; (*also* **bank ~**) relevé de compte.

statesman ['steɪtsmən] *n, pl* **statesmen** homme *m* d'État. (*fig*) **he is a real ~** il est extrêmement diplomate; *V* **elder**[1].

statesmanlike ['steɪtsmənlaɪk] *adj* diplomatique.

statesmanship ['steɪtsmənʃɪp] *n* (*U*) habileté *f* politique, diplomatie *f*.

statesmen ['steɪtsmən] *npl of* **statesman.**

static ['stætɪk] **1** *adj* (*all senses*) statique.

2 *n* **(a)** (*U*) **~s** statique *f*.

(b) (*Elec, Rad, TV etc: also* **~s**) parasites *mpl*.

station ['steɪʃən] **1** *n* **(a)** (*place*) poste *m*, station *f*; (*fire* **~**) caserne *f* de pompiers; (*lifeboat* **~**) centre *m* *or* poste (de secours en mer); (*Mil*) poste (militaire); (*Police*) poste *or* commissariat *m* (de police), gendarmerie *f*; (*Elec: power* **~**) centrale *f* (électrique); (*Rad*) station de radio, poste émetteur; (*Australia: sheep/cattle ranch*) élevage *m* (de moutons/de bétail), ranch *m*. **naval ~** station navale; (*Rad*) **foreign ~s** stations étrangères; (*Telec*) **calling all ~s** appel à tous les émetteurs; (*Rel*) **the S~s of the Cross** le Chemin de (la) Croix; *V* **frontier, petrol, pump**[1]**, service** *etc.*

(b) (*Rail*) gare *f*; *[underground]* station *f*. **bus** *or* **coach ~** gare routière; **the train came into the ~** le train est entré en gare; (*in underground*) la rame est entrée dans la station; *V* **change** *etc.*

(c) (*position*) poste *m* (*also Mil*), place *f*, position *f*. **to take up one's ~** prendre position, se placer; **from my ~ by the window** de la fenêtre où je m'étais posté *or* où je me trouvais.

(d) (*rank*) condition *f*, rang *m*. **one's ~ in life** son rang *or* sa situation social(e), sa place dans la société; **to get ideas above one's ~** avoir des idées de grandeur; **to marry beneath one's ~**† faire une mésalliance.

2 *cpd* (*Rail*) *staff, bookstall etc* de (la) gare. (*US Rad*) **station break** page *f* de publicité; (*Rail*) **station master** chef *m* de gare; (*Aut*) **station wag(g)on** break *m*.

3 *vt people* placer, mettre, poster; *look-out, troops, ship* poster; *tanks, guns* placer, installer, mettre. **to ~ o.s.** se placer, se poster; **to be ~ed at** *[troops, regiment]* être en *or* tenir garnison à; *[ships, sailors]* être en station à.

stationary ['steɪʃənərɪ] *adj* (*motionless*) *person, ship, vehicle etc* stationnaire, immobile; (*fixed*) *crane etc* fixe.

stationer ['steɪʃənəʳ] *n* papetier *m*, -ière *f*. **~'s (shop)** papeterie *f*.

stationery ['steɪʃənərɪ] **1** *n* (*U*) papier *m* et petits articles de bureau; (*writing paper*) papier à lettres.

2 *cpd:* (*Brit*) **the Stationery Office** ≃ Imprimerie nationale (*fournit aussi de la papeterie à l'administration et publie une gamme étendue d'ouvrages et de brochures didactiques*).

statistic [stə'tɪstɪk] **1** *n* **(a)** (*gen pl*) **~s** statistiques *fpl*, chiffres *mpl*; (*hum: woman's*) mensurations *fpl*; **a set of ~s** une statistique; **these ~s are not reliable** on ne peut pas se fier à ces chiffres *or* à ces statistiques; **~s suggest that ...** la statistique *or* les statistiques suggère(nt) que ...; *V* **vital.**

(b) (*U: subject*) **~s** statistique *f*.

2 *adj* = **statistical.**

statistical [stə'tɪstɪkəl] *adj error* de statistique(s); *probability, table* statistique; *expert* en statistique(s).

statistically [stə'tɪstɪkəlɪ] *adv* statistiquement.

statistician [ˌstætɪs'tɪʃən] *n* statisticien(ne) *m(f)*.

stator ['steɪtəʳ] *n* stator *m*.

statuary ['stætjʊərɪ] **1** *adj* statuaire. **2** *n* (*art*) statuaire *f*; (*statues collectively*) statues *fpl*.

statue ['stætjuː] *n* statue *f*. **the S~ of Liberty** la Statue de la Liberté.

statuesque [ˌstætjʊ'esk] *adj* sculptural.

statuette [ˌstætjʊ'et] *n* statuette *f*.

stature ['stætʃəʳ] *n* stature *f*, taille *f*; (*fig*) calibre *m*, importance *f*, envergure *f*. **of short ~** court de stature *or* de taille; **he is a writer of some ~** c'est un écrivain d'une certaine envergure *or* d'un certain calibre; **his ~ as a painter increased when ...** il a pris de l'envergure *or* de l'importance en tant que peintre quand ...; **moral/intellectual ~** envergure sur le plan moral/intellectuel.

status ['steɪtəs] **1** *n* (*U*) **(a)** (*economic etc position*) situation *f*, position *f*; (*Admin, Jur*) statut *m*. **social ~** standing *m*; **civil ~** état civil; **what is his (official) ~?** quel est son titre officiel?, quelle est sa position officielle?; **the economic ~ of the country** la situation *or* position économique du pays; **the financial ~ of the company** l'état financier de la compagnie; **the ~ of the black population** le statut *or* la condition sociale de la population noire; **his ~ as an assistant director** son standing de directeur-adjoint.

(b) (*prestige*) *[person]* prestige *m*, standing *m*; *[job, post]* prestige. **it is the ~ more than the salary that appeals to him** c'est le prestige plus que le salaire qui a de l'attrait pour lui; **he hasn't got enough ~ for the job** il ne fait pas le poids* pour le poste.

2 *cpd:* **status symbol** marque *f* de standing, signe extérieur de richesse.

status quo ['steɪtəs'kwəʊ] *n* statu quo *m*.

statute ['stætjuːt] **1** *n* (*Jur etc*) loi *f*. **by ~** selon la loi. **2** *cpd:* **statute book** code *m*; **statute law** droit écrit.

statutory ['stætjʊtərɪ] *adj duty, right, control* statutaire; *holiday* légal; *offence, rape* prévu *or* défini par un article de loi. **to have ~ effect** faire force de loi.

staunch[1] [stɔːntʃ] *vt flow* contenir, arrêter; *blood* étancher; *wound* étancher le sang de.

staunch[2] [stɔːntʃ] *adj* sûr, loyal, dévoué; *friend, ally* à toute épreuve.

staunchly ['stɔːntʃlɪ] *adv* avec dévouement, loyalement.

staunchness ['stɔːntʃnɪs] *n* dévouement *m*, loyauté *f*.

stave [steɪv] (*vb: pret, ptp* **stove** *or* **staved**) *n [barrel etc]* douve *f*; (*Mus*) portée *f*; (*Poetry*) stance *f*, strophe *f*.

stave in *vt sep* défoncer, enfoncer.

stave off *vt sep danger* écarter, conjurer; *threat* dissiper, conjurer; *ruin, disaster, defeat* éviter, conjurer; *hunger* tromper; *attack* parer.

staves [steɪvz] *npl of* **staff 1b, 1c** *and* **stave.**

stay[1] [steɪ] **1** *n* **(a)** séjour *m*. **he is in Rome for a short ~** il est à Rome pour une courte visite *or* un bref séjour; **a ~ in hospital** un séjour à l'hôpital; **will it be a long ~?** est-ce qu'il restera (*or* vous resterez *etc*) longtemps?

(b) (*Jur*) suspension *f*. **~ of execution** sursis *m* à l'exécution (d'un jugement); **to put a ~ on proceedings** surseoir aux poursuites.

2 *cpd:* **stay-at-home** casanier *m*, -ière *f*, pantouflard(e)* *m(f)*; **staying power** résistance *f*, endurance *f*; **he hasn't a lot of staying power** il se décourage facilement.

3 *vt* **(a)** (*check*) arrêter; *disease, epidemic* enrayer; *hunger* tromper; (*delay*) retarder; (*Jur*) *judgment* surseoir à, différer; *proceedings* suspendre; *decision* ajourner, remettre. **to ~ one's hand** se retenir.

(b) (*last out*) *race* terminer, aller jusqu'au bout de; *distance* tenir. **to ~ the course** (*Sport*) aller jusqu'au bout; (*fig*) tenir bon, tenir le coup*.

4 *vi* **(a)** (*remain*) rester; demeurer. **~ there!** restez là!; **here I am and here I ~** j'y suis j'y reste; **to ~ still, to ~ put*** ne pas bouger; **to ~ for** *or* **to dinner** rester (à) dîner; **to ~ faithful** rester *or* demeurer fidèle; (*Rad*) **~ tuned!** restez à l'écoute, ne quittez pas l'écoute; **to ~ ahead of the others** garder son avance sur les autres; **it is here to ~** c'est là pour de bon; **things can't be allowed to ~ that way** on ne peut pas laisser les choses comme ça; **if the weather ~s fine** si le temps se maintient (au beau); **he ~ed (for) the whole week** il est resté toute la semaine; **he ~ed a year in Paris** il est resté un an à Paris, il a séjourné un an à Paris.

(b) (*on visit*) **has she come to ~?** est-ce qu'elle est venue avec l'intention de rester?; **she came to ~ (for) a few weeks** elle est venue passer quelques semaines; **I'm ~ing with my aunt** je loge chez ma tante; **to ~ in a hotel** descendre à l'hôtel; **where do you ~ when you go to London?** où logez-vous quand vous allez à Londres?; **he was ~ing in Paris when he fell ill** il séjournait à Paris quand il est tombé malade.

(c) (*Scot: live permanently*) habiter.

(d) (*persevere*) tenir. **to ~ to the finish** tenir jusqu'à la ligne d'arrivée; **to ~ with a scheme*** ne pas abandonner un projet; **~ with it!*** tenez bon!

(e) (*liter: pause*) s'arrêter.

stay away *vi:* **he stayed away for 3 years** il n'est pas rentré avant 3 ans; **he stayed away from the meeting** il n'est pas allé (*or* venu) *or* il s'est abstenu d'aller à la réunion; **to stay away from school** ne pas aller à l'école; (*play truant*) faire l'école buissonnière.

stay behind *vi* rester en arrière *or* à la fin. **you'll stay behind after school!** tu resteras après la classe!

stay down *vi* **(a)** rester en bas; (*bending*) rester baissé; (*lying down*) rester couché; (*under water*) rester sous l'eau; (*fig Scol*) redoubler.

(b) *[food etc]* **nothing he eats will stay down** il n'assimile rien *or* il ne garde rien de ce qu'il mange.
stay in *vi* **(a)** *[person]* (*at home*) rester à la maison, ne pas sortir; (*Scol*) être en retenue.
(b) *[nail, screw, tooth filling]* tenir.
stay out *vi* **(a)** *[person]* (*away from home*) ne pas rentrer; (*outside*) rester dehors. **get out and stay out!** sortez et ne revenez pas!; **he always stays out late on Fridays** il rentre toujours tard le vendredi; **he stayed out all night** il a découché, il n'est pas rentré de la nuit; **don't stay out after 9 o'clock** rentrez avant 9 heures.
(b) (*Ind: on strike*) rester en grève.
(c) (*fig*) **to stay out of sth** ne pas se mêler de qch; **you stay out of this!** mêlez-vous de vos (propres) affaires!
stay over *vi* s'arrêter (un *or* plusieurs jour(s)), faire une halte. **can you stay over till Thursday?** est-ce que vous pouvez rester jusqu'à jeudi?
stay up *vi* **(a)** *[person]* rester debout, ne pas se coucher. **don't stay up for me** ne m'attendez pas pour aller vous coucher; **you can stay up to watch the programme** vous pouvez voir l'émission avant de vous coucher; **we always stay up late on Saturdays** nous veillons *or* nous nous couchons toujours tard le samedi.
(b) (*not fall*) *[trousers, fence etc]* tenir.
stay[2] [steɪ] **1** *n* **(a)** (*for pole, flagstaff etc: also Naut*) étai *m*, hauban *m*; (*for wall*) étai, étançon *m*; (*fig*) soutien *m*, support *m*. **(b)** (†: *corsets*) ~s corset *m*. **2** *vt* (*also* ~ **up**) haubaner (*also Naut*); étayer.
stayer ['steɪəʳ] *n* (*horse*) stayer *m*, cheval *m* qui a du fond; (*runner*) coureur *m* qui a du fond *or* de la résistance physique. **he's a** ~ (*Sport*) il a du fond, il est capable d'un effort prolongé; (*fig*) il n'abandonne pas facilement, il va jusqu'au bout de ce qu'il entreprend.
stead [sted] *n*: **in my/his** *etc* ~ à ma/sa *etc* place; **to stand sb in good** ~ rendre grand service à qn, être très utile à qn.
steadfast ['stedfəst] *adj person* (*unshakeable*) ferme, résolu, inébranlable; (*constant*) constant, loyal; *intention, desire* ferme; *gaze* ferme, résolu. ~ **in adversity/danger** inébranlable au milieu des infortunes/du danger; ~ **in love** constant en amour.
steadfastly ['stedfəstlɪ] *adv* fermement, résolument.
steadfastness ['stedfəstnɪs] *n* fermeté *f*, résolution *f* (*liter*). ~ **of purpose** ténacité *f*.
steadily ['stedɪlɪ] *adv* **(a)** (*firmly*) *walk* d'un pas ferme; *hold* d'une main ferme; *gaze, look* longuement, sans détourner les yeux; *stay, reply, insist* fermement, avec fermeté. **to stand** ~ *[person]* se tenir bien droit sur ses jambes; *[chair]* être stable.
(b) (*constantly, regularly*) *improve, decrease, rise* progressivement, régulièrement; *rain, work, sob, continue* sans arrêt, sans interruption. **the engine ran** ~ le moteur marchait sans à-coups.
steadiness ['stedɪnɪs] *n* **(a)** (*firmness: V* **steady 1a**) stabilité *f*, solidité *f*; fermeté *f*, sûreté *f*; caractère pondéré *or* posé *or* travailleur; application *f* au travail; calme *m*.
(b) (*regularity etc: V* **steady 1b**) constance *f*, uniformité *f*, régularité *f*, stabilité *f*.
steady ['stedɪ] **1** *adj* **(a)** (*firm*) *chair, table, pole* stable, solide; *boat* stable; *hand* ferme, sûr; *gaze* franc (*f* franche); *nerves* solide; *person* (*not changeable*) posé, pondéré; (*hard-working*) travailleur, appliqué; (*not nervous*) imperturbable, calme. **he isn't very** ~ **(on his feet)** il n'est pas très solide sur ses jambes; **the car is not very** ~ **on corners** la voiture ne tient pas très bien la route dans les tournants; **he plays a very** ~ **game** il a un jeu très régulier, il n'y a pas de surprise avec lui; ~ **(on)!*** doucement!, du calme!; (*Naut*) ~ **as she goes!, keep her** ~! comme ça droit!; *V* **ready**.
(b) (*regular, uninterrupted*) *temperature, purpose, wind* constant; *improvement, decrease* uniforme, constant; *pace, speed, progress* régulier, constant; *job, prices, sales, market* stable; *demand* régulier, constant. **we were doing a** ~ **60 km/h** nous roulions à une vitesse régulière *or* constante de 60 km/h; **there was a** ~ **downpour for 3 hours** il n'a pas cessé de pleuvoir pendant 3 heures; **a** ~ **boyfriend** un petit ami; **a** ~ **girlfriend** une petite amie.
2 *adv* (*) **to go** ~ **with sb** sortir avec qn; **they've been going** ~ **for 6 months** ils sortent ensemble depuis 6 mois.
3 *n* (‡) petit(e) ami(e) *m(f)*.
4 *vt wobbling object* assujettir; *chair, table* maintenir, (*wedge*) caler; *nervous person, horse* calmer. **to** ~ **o.s.** reprendre son aplomb (*also fig*), se retenir de tomber; **to** ~ **one's nerves** se calmer; **to have a** ~**ing effect on sb** (*make less nervous*) calmer qn; (*make less wild*) assagir qn, mettre du plomb dans la cervelle de qn*.
5 *vi* (*also* ~ **up**) (*regain balance*) reprendre son aplomb; (*grow less nervous*) se calmer; (*grow less wild*) se ranger, s'assagir; *[prices, market]* se stabiliser.
steak [steɪk] **1** *n* bifteck *m*, steak *m*; (*of meat other than beef*) tranche *f*; (*of fish*) tranche, darne *f*. **frying** ~ bifteck; **stewing** ~ bœuf *m* à braiser; *V* **fillet, rump** *etc*.
2 *cpd*: **steak and kidney pie** tourte *f* à la viande de bœuf et aux rognons; **steakhouse** ≃ grill-room *m*; **steak knife** couteau *m* à viande *or* à steak.
steal [stiːl] *pret* **stole**, *ptp* **stolen 1** *vt object, property* voler, dérober (*liter*) (*from sb* à qn); (*fig*) *kiss* voler (*from sb* à qn). **he stole a book from the library** il a volé un livre à la bibliothèque; **he stole money from the till/drawer** *etc* il a volé de l'argent dans la caisse/dans le tiroir *etc*; **to** ~ **the credit for sth** s'attribuer tout le mérite de qch; **to** ~ **a glance at** jeter un coup d'œil furtif à, lancer un regard furtif à; **to** ~ **a march on sb*** gagner *or* prendre qn de vitesse; (*fig*) **he stole the show** il n'y en a eu que pour lui, on n'a eu d'yeux que pour lui; **to** ~ **sb's thunder** éclipser qn en lui coupant l'herbe sous le pied.
2 *vi* **(a)** voler. (*Bible*) **thou shalt not** ~ tu ne voleras point.
(b) (*move silently*) **to** ~ **up/down/out** *etc* monter/descendre/sortir à pas furtifs *or* feutrés *or* de loup; **he stole into the room** il s'est glissé *or* faufilé dans la pièce; (*fig*) **a smile stole across her lips** un sourire erra sur ses lèvres; **a tear stole down her cheek** une larme furtive glissa sur sa joue; **the light was** ~**ing through the shutters** la lumière filtrait à travers les volets.
steal away 1 *vi* s'esquiver.
2 *vt sep child etc* prendre, enlever (*from sb* à qn); *sb's husband* voler, prendre (*from sb* à qn); *sb's affections* détourner.
stealing ['stiːlɪŋ] *n* (*U*) vol *m*. ~ **is wrong** c'est mal de voler.
stealth [stelθ] *n*: **by** ~ furtivement, à la dérobée.
stealthily ['stelθɪlɪ] *adv remove, exchange* furtivement, à la dérobée; *walk, enter, leave* furtivement, à pas furtifs *or* feutrés *or* de loup.
stealthiness ['stelθɪnɪs] *n* caractère furtif, manière furtive.
stealthy ['stelθɪ] *adj action* fait en secret *or* à la dérobée, furtif; *entrance, look, movement* furtif. ~ **footsteps** pas furtifs *or* feutrés *or* de loup.
steam [stiːm] **1** *n* (*U*) vapeur *f*; (*condensation: on window etc*) buée *f*. **it works by** ~ ça marche *or* fonctionne à la vapeur; (*Naut*) **full** ~ **ahead!** en avant toute!; (*fig*) **the building project is going full** ~ **ahead** le projet de construction va de l'avant à plein régime; **to get up** ~ *[train, ship]* chauffer; *[driver etc]* mettre la chaudière sous pression; (*fig*) *[worker, programme, project]* démarrer vraiment* (*fig*); (*fig*) **to run out of** ~ *[speaker, worker]* s'essouffler (*fig*); *[programme, project]* tourner court, tomber à plat; (*fig*) **under one's own** ~ par ses propres moyens; (*fig*) **to let off** *or* **blow off** ~* (*energy*) se défouler*; (*anger*) épancher sa bile.
2 *cpd boiler, iron, turbine* à vapeur; *bath* de vapeur. **steamboat** (bateau *m* à) vapeur *m*; **steam-driven** à vapeur; (*fig*) **to get steamed up*** se mettre dans tous ses états (*about sth* à propos de qch); **don't get so steamed up about it!*** ne te mets pas dans tous tes états pour ça!; (*Rail*) **steam engine** locomotive *f* à vapeur; **steam heat** chaleur fournie par la vapeur; **steamroller** (*n*) rouleau compresseur; (*vt: fig*) *opposition etc* écraser, briser; *obstacles* aplanir; **to steamroller a bill through Parliament** faire approuver un projet de loi au Parlement sans tenir compte de l'opposition; (*fig*) **steamroller tactics** tactiques dictatoriales; **steamship** paquebot *m*; **steamship company** ligne *f* de paquebots.
3 *vt* passer à la vapeur; (*Culin*) cuire à la vapeur. ~**ed pudding** pudding cuit à la vapeur; **to** ~ **open an envelope** décacheter une enveloppe à la vapeur; **to** ~ **off a stamp** décoller un timbre à la vapeur.
4 *vi* **(a)** *[kettle, liquid, horse, wet clothes]* fumer. ~**ing hot** fumant.
(b) **to** ~ **along/away** *etc [steamship, train]* avancer/partir *etc*; (**fig*) *[person, car]* avancer/partir *etc* à toute vapeur*; **they were** ~**ing along at 12 knots** ils filaient 12 nœuds; **the ship** ~**ed up the river** le vapeur remontait la rivière; **the train** ~**ed out of the station** le train est sorti de la gare dans un nuage de fumée; **to** ~ **ahead** *[steamship]* avancer; (*) *[person]* avancer à toute vapeur*; (**fig: make great progress*) faire des progrès à pas de géant.
steam up 1 *vi [window, mirror]* se couvrir de buée; *[bathroom]* se remplir de buée.
2 *vt sep* embuer.
3 steamed-up* *adj V* **steam 2**.
steamer ['stiːməʳ] *n* **(a)** (*Naut*) (bateau *m* à) vapeur *m*; (*liner*) paquebot *m*. **(b)** (*Culin*) ≃ couscoussier *m*.
steamy ['stiːmɪ] *adj atmosphere, heat* humide; *room, window* embué.
steed [stiːd] *n* (*liter*) coursier *m* (*liter*).
steel [stiːl] **1** *n* **(a)** (*U*) acier *m*. (*fig*) **to be made of** ~ être de bronze (*fig*); **nerves of** ~ nerfs *mpl* d'acier; *V* **stainless** *etc*.
(b) (*sharpener*) aiguisoir *m*, fusil *m*; (*for striking sparks*) briquet† *m*, fusil†; (*liter: sword/dagger*) fer *m*; *V* **cold** *etc*.
2 *cpd knife, tool* d'acier; *industry* sidérurgique; (*St Ex*) *shares, prices* de l'acier. **steel band** steel band *m*; **steel-clad** bardé de fer; **steel engraving** gravure *f* sur acier; **steel grey** gris acier *inv*, gris métallisé *inv*; **steel guitar** guitare *f* aux cordes d'acier; **steel helmet** casque *m*; **steel mill** = **steelworks**; **steel-plated** revêtu d'acier; (*Carpentry etc*) **steel tape** mètre *m* à ruban métallique; (*U*) **steel wool** paille *f* de fer; **steelworks** (*pl inv*) aciérie *f*; **steelyard** balance *f* romaine.
3 *vt* (*fig*) **to** ~ **o.s.** *or* **one's heart to do** s'armer de courage pour faire; **to** ~ **o.s. against** se cuirasser contre.
steely ['stiːlɪ] **1** *adj material, substance* dur comme l'acier; *appearance* de l'acier; *colour* acier *inv*; (*fig*) *person* dur, insensible; *eyes* dur; *gaze, expression* d'acier, dur; *refusal, attitude* inflexible, inébranlable.
2 *cpd*: **steely blue** bleu acier *inv*; **steely-eyed** au regard d'acier; **steely grey** gris acier *inv*, gris métallisé *inv*; **steely-hearted** au cœur d'acier *or* de bronze.
steep[1] [stiːp] *adj* **(a)** *slope* raide, abrupt, escarpé; *cliff* à pic, abrupt; *hill* escarpé; *road* raide, escarpé; *stairs* raide. **it's a** ~ **climb to the top** la montée est raide pour atteindre le sommet; **a** ~ **path** un raidillon.
(b) (**fig*) *price* élevé, excessif; *bill* salé*; *story* raide*. **it's rather** ~ **if he can't even go and see her** c'est un peu raide* *or* fort* qu'il ne puisse même pas aller la voir.
steep[2] [stiːp] **1** *vt* (*in water, dye etc*) tremper (*in* dans); *washing* faire tremper, mettre à tremper; (*Culin*) macérer, mariner (*in* dans). (*fig*) ~**ed in ignorance/vice** croupissant dans l'ignorance/le vice; ~**ed in prejudice** imbu de préjugés; **a town** ~**ed in**

history une ville imprégnée d'histoire; **a scholar ~ed in the classics** un érudit imprégné des auteurs classiques.
2 *vi [clothes etc]* tremper; (*Culin*) macérer, mariner.
steeple ['stiːpl] **1** *n* clocher *m*. **2** *cpd*: **steeplechase** steeple(-chase) *m* (*course*); **steeplechasing** steeple(-chase) *m* (*sport*); **steeplejack** réparateur *m* de hautes cheminées et de clochers.
steeply ['stiːplɪ] *adv*: **to rise** *or* **climb ~** *[road etc]* monter en pente raide; *[prices etc]* monter en flèche.
steepness ['stiːpnɪs] *n [road etc]* pente *f* (raide); *[slope]* abrupt *m*.
steer[1] [stɪəʳ] *n* (*ox*) bœuf *m*; (*esp US: castrated*) bouvillon *m*.
steer[2] [stɪəʳ] **1** *vt ship* gouverner; *boat* diriger, barrer; *car* conduire; (*fig*) *person* guider. (*Naut*) **to ~ a** *or* **one's course to** faire route vers *or* sur; **to ~ one's way through a crowd** se frayer un passage à travers une foule; **he ~ed her over to the bar** il l'a guidée vers le bar.
2 *vi* (*Naut*) tenir le gouvernail *or* la barre, gouverner. **to ~ by the stars** se guider sur les étoiles; **he ~ed for the lighthouse** il a fait route vers *or* il a mis le cap sur le phare; **~ due north!** cap au nord!; **this boat doesn't ~ well** ce bateau gouverne mal; (*fig*) **to ~ clear of** se tenir à l'écart de, éviter.
steerage ['stɪərɪdʒ] (*Naut*) **1** *n* entrepont *m*. **2** *adv* dans l'entrepont, en troisième classe. **3** *cpd*: **steerageway** vitesse minimale de manœuvre.
steering ['stɪərɪŋ] **1** *n* (*U*) (*Aut etc*) conduite *f*; (*Naut*) conduite, pilotage *m*.
2 *cpd*: (*Aut*) **steering arm** bras *m* de direction; (*Aut*) **steering column** colonne *f* de direction; (*Admin etc*) **steering committee** comité *m* d'organisation; **steering gear** (*Aut*) boîte *f* de direction; (*Naut*) servomoteur *m* de barre *or* de gouvernail; (*Aviat*) direction *f*; (*Aut*) **steering (gear) lock** antivol *m* de direction; **steering wheel** (*Aut*) volant *m*; (*Naut*) roue *f* de barre *or* de timonerie.
steersman ['stɪəzmən] *n*, *pl* **steersmen** ['stɪəzmən] (*Naut*) timonier *m*, homme *m* de barre.
stellar ['steləʳ] *adj* stellaire.
stem[1] [stem] **1** *vt* **(a)** (*stop*) *flow* contenir, arrêter, endiguer; *flood, river* contenir, endiguer; *course of disease* enrayer, juguler; *attack* juguler, stopper, briser. (*fig*) **to ~ the course of events** endiguer la marche des événements; (*fig*) **to ~ the tide** *or* **flow of** endiguer (le flot de).
(b) *ski* ramener *or* écarter en chasse-neige.
2 *cpd*: (*Ski*) **stem turn** virage *m* en chasse-neige.
stem[2] [stem] **1** *n* **(a)** *[flower, plant]* tige *f*; *[tree]* tronc *m*; *[fruit, leaf]* queue *f*; *[glass]* pied *m*; *[tobacco pipe]* tuyau *m*; *[feather]* tige, tuyau; (*Handwriting, Printing: of letter*) hampe *f*; (*Mus: of note*) queue; (*Ling: of word*) radical *m*, thème *m*.
(b) (*Naut*) (*timber*) étrave *f*; (*part of ship*) avant *m*, proue *f*. **from ~ to stern** de bout en bout.
2 *vi*: **to ~ from** provenir de, découler de, dériver de.
stench [stentʃ] *n* puanteur *f*, odeur nauséabonde *or* fétide.
stencil ['stensl] **1** *n* (*of metal, cardboard*) pochoir *m*; (*of paper*) poncif *m*; (*in typing etc*) stencil *m*; (*decoration*) peinture *f* *or* décoration *f* au pochoir. (*Typing*) **to cut a ~** préparer un stencil. **2** *vt lettering, name* peindre *or* marquer au pochoir; (*in typing etc*) *document* polycopier, tirer au stencil.
stenographer [ste'nɒgrəfəʳ] *n* sténographe *mf*.
stenography [ste'nɒgrəfɪ] *n* sténographie *f*.
stentorian [sten'tɔːrɪən] *adj* de stentor.
step [step] **1** *n* **(a)** (*movement, sound, track*) pas *m*. **to take a ~ back/forward** faire un pas en arrière/en avant; **with slow ~s** à pas lents; (*lit, fig*) **at every ~** à chaque pas; **~ by ~** (*lit*) pas à pas, (*fig*) petit à petit (*V also* **2**); **he didn't move a ~** il n'a pas bougé d'un pas; **a waltz ~** un pas de valse; **we heard ~s in the lounge** nous avons entendu des pas *or* un bruit de pas dans le salon; **we followed his ~s in the snow** nous avons suivi (la trace de) ses pas dans la neige; (*fig*) **to follow in sb's ~s** marcher sur les pas *or* suivre les brisées de qn; (*fig: distance*) **it's a good ~*** *or* **quite a ~* to the village** il y a un bon bout de chemin *or* ça fait une bonne trotte* d'ici au village; *V* **retrace, watch**[2] *etc*.
(b) (*fig*) pas *m* (*towards* vers); (*measure*) disposition *f*, mesure *f*. **it is a great ~ for the nation to take** c'est pour la nation un grand pas à faire *or* à franchir; **that's a ~ in the right direction** c'est un pas dans la bonne voie; **the first ~s in one's career** les premiers pas *or* les débuts *mpl* de sa carrière; **it's a ~ up in his career** c'est une promotion pour lui; **to take ~s (to do)** prendre des dispositions *or* des mesures (pour faire); **what's the next ~?** qu'est-ce qu'il faut faire maintenant? *or* ensuite?; **the first ~ is to decide ...** la première chose à faire est de décider ...; *V* **false** *etc*.
(c) (*U: in marching, dancing*) pas *m*. **to keep (in) ~** (*in marching*) marcher au pas; (*in dance*) danser en mesure; (*lit, fig*) **to keep ~ with sb** ne pas se laisser distancer par qn; **to fall into ~** se mettre au pas; **to get out of ~** rompre le pas; (*fig*) **in ~/out of ~ with** *[regulation etc]* conforme/non conforme à; *[person]* qui se conforme/ne se conforme pas à, qui agit/n'agit pas conformément à.
(d) (*stair*) marche *f*; (*doorstep*) pas *m* de la porte, seuil *m*; (*on bus etc*) marchepied *m*. **(flight of) ~s** (*indoors*) escalier *m*; (*outdoors*) perron *m*, escalier; **(pair of) ~s** escabeau *m*; **mind the ~** attention à la marche.
2 *cpd*: **stepbrother** demi-frère *m*; **step-by-step instructions** mode *m* d'emploi point par point; **stepchild** beau-fils *m*, belle-fille *f*; **stepdaughter** belle-fille *f*; **stepfather** beau-père *m*; **stepladder** escabeau *m*; **stepmother** belle-mère *f*; **stepped-up** *campaign, efforts* intensifié; *production, sales* augmenté, accru; **stepping stone** (*lit*) pierre *f* de gué; (*fig*) tremplin *m* (*to* pour obtenir, pour arriver à); **stepsister** demi-sœur *f*; **stepson** beau-fils *m*.
3 *vt* **(a)** (*place at intervals*) échelonner.
(b) (*Naut*) *mast* arborer, mettre dans son emplanture.
4 *vi* faire un *or* des pas, aller, marcher. **~ this way** venez par ici; **to ~ off sth** descendre de qch, quitter qch; **he ~ped into the car/on to the pavement** il est monté dans la voiture/sur le trottoir; **he ~ped into his slippers/trousers** il a mis ses pantoufles/son pantalon; **to ~ on sth** marcher sur qch; **to ~ on the brakes** donner un coup de frein; (*US Aut*) **to ~ on the gas*** appuyer sur le champignon*; (*fig*) **~ on it!*** dépêche-toi!, grouille-toi!*; **to ~ out of line** (*lit*) sortir des rangs; (*fig*) s'écarter du droit chemin (*iro*); *V* **shoe** *etc*.
step aside *vi* s'écarter, se ranger.
step back *vi* (*lit*) faire un pas en arrière, reculer. (*fig*) **we stepped back into Shakespeare's time** nous nous sommes reportés quatre siècles en arrière à l'époque shakespearienne.
step down *vi* (*lit*) descendre (*from* de); (*fig*) se retirer, se désister (*in favour of sb* en faveur de qn).
step forward *vi* faire un pas en avant; (*fig*) s'avancer, se faire connaître.
step in *vi* entrer; (*fig*) intervenir, s'interposer.
step inside *vi* entrer.
step out 1 *vi* (*go outside*) sortir; (*hurry*) allonger le pas; (*US* fig*) faire la bombe*.
2 *vt sep* (*measure*) *distance* mesurer en comptant les pas.
step up 1 *vi*: **to step up to sb/sth** s'approcher de qn/qch.
2 *vt sep production, sales* augmenter, accroître; *campaign* intensifier; *attempts, efforts* intensifier, multiplier; (*Elec*) *current* augmenter.
3 stepped-up *adj V* **step 2**.
Stephen ['stiːvn] *n* Étienne *m*.
steppe [step] *n* steppe *f*.
stereo... ['stɪərɪəʊ] *pref* stéréo... .
stereo ['stɪərɪəʊ] **1** *n* **(a)** (*abbr of* **stereophonic**) (*system*) stéréo *f*, stéréophonie *f*; (*record player/radio etc*) chaîne *f*/radio *f etc* stéréophonique *or* stéréo *inv*; (*record/tape etc*) disque *m*/bande *f* magnétique *etc* stéréophonique *or* stéréo. **recorded in ~** enregistré en stéréo(phonie).
(b) *abbr of* **stereoscope, stereotype** *etc*.
2 *cpd record player, cassette recorder, record, tape etc* stéréophonique, stéréo *inv*; *broadcast, recording* en stéréophonie. **stereo effects** effet stéréo(phonique); **stereo sound** audition stéréophonique; **stereovision** vision *f* stéréoscopique.
stereochemistry [ˌstɪərɪə'kemɪstrɪ] *n* stéréochimie *f*.
stereogram ['stɪərɪəgræm] *n*, **stereograph** ['stɪərɪəgræf] *n* stéréogramme *m*.
stereophonic [ˌstɪərɪə'fɒnɪk] *adj* stéréophonique. **~ sound** audition *f* stéréophonique.
stereoscope ['stɪərɪəskəʊp] *n* stéréoscope *m*.
stereoscopic [ˌstɪərɪəs'kɒpɪk] *adj* stéréoscopique.
stereotype ['stɪərɪətaɪp] **1** *n* (*Typ*) cliché *m*; (*process*) clichage *m*; (*fig: Psych, Soc etc*) stéréotype *m*. **2** *vt* (*Printing*) clicher; (*fig*) stéréotyper.
sterile ['steraɪl] *adj* (*all senses*) stérile.
sterility [ste'rɪlɪtɪ] *n* stérilité *f*.
sterilization [ˌsterɪlaɪ'zeɪʃən] *n* stérilisation *f*.
sterilize ['sterɪlaɪz] *vt* stériliser.
sterling ['stɜːlɪŋ] **1** *n* (*U*) **(a)** (*Econ*) livres *fpl* sterling *inv*.
(b) (*also* **~ silver**) argent fin *or* de bon aloi.
2 *adj* **(a)** *gold, silver* fin, de bon aloi; (*fig*) *qualities, principles, worth, sense* solide, sûr, à toute épreuve; *person* de confiance. **pound ~** livre *f* sterling *inv*; **the ~ area** la zone sterling.
(b) (*also* **~ silver**) d'argent fin *or* de bon aloi.
stern[1] [stɜːn] *n* (*Naut*) arrière *m*, poupe *f*; (*) *[horse etc]* croupe *f*; (*) *[person]* derrière *m*, postérieur* *m*. (*Naut*) **~ foremost** par l'arrière, en marche arrière; *V* **stem**[2].
stern[2] [stɜːn] *adj person, character* sévère, dur; *glance, expression, face, speech* sévère, sombre; *discipline* sévère, strict; *punishment* sévère, rigoureux; *warning* grave. **he was made of ~er stuff** il était d'une autre trempe, il n'était pas aussi faible qu'on le pensait.
sternly ['stɜːnlɪ] *adv* sévèrement, durement, sombrement, strictement, rigoureusement, gravement.
sternness ['stɜːnnɪs] *n* (*V* **stern**[2]) sévérité *f*; dureté *f*; rigueur *f*; gravité *f*.
sternum ['stɜːnəm] *n* sternum *m*.
steroid ['stɪərɔɪd] *n* stéride *m*.
stertorous ['stɜːtərəs] *adj* stertoreux, ronflant.
stet [stet] **1** *impers vb* (*frm: Typ*) bon, à maintenir. **2** *vt* maintenir.
stethoscope ['steθəskəʊp] *n* stéthoscope *m*.
Stetson ['stetsən] *n* ® chapeau *m* d'homme à larges bords.
stevedore ['stiːvɪdɔːʳ] *n* (*Naut*) arrimeur *m*, débardeur *m*, docker *m*.
Steven ['stiːvn] *n* Étienne *m*.
stew [stjuː] **1** *n [meat]* ragoût *m*; *[rabbit, hare]* civet *m*. (*fig*) **to be/get in a ~*** être/se mettre dans tous ses états; *V* **Irish**.
2 *cpd*: **stewpan, stewpot** cocotte *f*.
3 *vt meat* cuire en ragoût; *rabbit, hare* cuire en civet; *fruit* faire cuire. **~ed fruit** fruits cuits; (*pej*) **~ed tea** thé trop infusé; (*fig: drunk*) **to be ~ed**: être soûl*; *V* **steak**.
4 *vi [meat]* cuire à l'étouffée; *[fruit]* cuire; *[tea]* devenir trop infusé. (*fig*) **to let sb ~ in his own juice** laisser qn cuire *or* mijoter dans son jus.
steward ['stjuːəd] (*on estate etc*) intendant *m*, régisseur *m*; (*on ship, plane*) steward *m*; (*in club, college*) intendant, économe *m*; (*at meeting*) membre *m* du service d'ordre; (*at dance*) organisateur *m*; *V* **shop**.
stewardess ['stjuədes] *n* hôtesse *f*.
stewardship ['stjuədʃɪp] *n* (*duties*) intendance *f*, économat *m*,

fonctions *fpl* de régisseur. under his ~ quand il était intendant *or* régisseur *or* économe.

stick [stɪk] (*vb: pret, ptp* **stuck**) **1** *n* **(a)** (*length of wood*) bâton *m*; (*twig*) petite branche, brindille *f*; (*walking* ~) canne *f*; (*support for peas, flowers etc*) bâton, tuteur *m*, rame *f*; (*for lollipop etc*) bâton; (*Mil, Mus*) baguette *f*; (*Aviat: joy*~) manche *m* à balai; (*Hockey, Lacrosse*) crosse *f*; (*Ice Hockey*) stick *m*. ~s (*for fire*) du petit bois; (*Sport: hurdles*) haies *fpl*; **a few ~s of furniture** quelques pauvres meubles *mpl*; **every ~ of furniture** chaque meuble; (*pej: backwoods*) **(out) in the ~s*** dans l'arrière-pays, en pleine cambrousse*; (*fig*) **to use** *or* **wield the big ~** manier la trique (*fig*); (*Pol*) faire de l'autoritarisme; **the policy of the big ~** la politique du bâton; (*fig*) **to give sb (the) ~** éreinter qn (*fig*); (*fig*) **to get (hold of) the wrong end of the ~** mal comprendre; *V* **cleft, drum, shooting** *etc.*

(b) *[chalk, charcoal, sealing wax, candy]* bâton *m*, morceau *m*; *[dynamite]* bâton; *[chewing gum]* tablette *f*; *[celery]* branche *f*; *[rhubarb]* tige *f*. **a ~ of bombs** un chapelet de bombes; *V* **grease.**

(c) (*Brit*: person*) **he is a dull** *or* **dry old ~** il est rasoir*; **he's a funny old ~** c'est un numéro*.

(d) (*Drugs sl*) stick *m*, joint *m* (*sl*).

2 *cpd:* (*U*) **sticking plaster** sparadrap *m*; **stick insect** phasme *m*; **stick-in-the-mud*** (*adj, n*) sclérosé(e) *m(f)*, encroûté(e) *m (f)*; **stick-on** (*adj*) adhésif; (*US*) **stickpin** épingle *f* de cravate; (*US Aut*) **stick shift** biellette *f* de commande de vitesses; **stick-up*** hold-up *m*; (*US*) **stickweed** jacobée *f*; **his stickwork is very good** *[hockey player etc]* il manie bien la crosse *or* le stick; *[drummer]* il manie bien les baguettes; *[conductor]* il manie bien la baguette.

3 *vt* **(a)** (*thrust, stab*) *pin, needle, fork* piquer, enfoncer, planter (*into* dans); *knife, dagger, bayonet* plonger, enfoncer, planter (*into* dans); *spade, rod* planter, enfoncer (*into* dans). **to ~ a pin through sth** transpercer qch avec une épingle; **we found this place by ~ing a pin into the map** nous avons trouvé ce coin en plantant une épingle au hasard sur la carte; **a board stuck with drawing pins/nails** un panneau couvert de punaises/hérissé de clous; **to ~ a pig** égorger un cochon; **to squeal like a stuck pig** brailler comme un cochon qu'on égorge; **I've stuck the needle into my finger** je me suis piqué le doigt avec l'aiguille.

(b) (*put*) mettre; poser; placer; fourrer. **he stuck it on the shelf/under the table** il l'a mis *or* posé sur l'étagère/sous la table; **to ~ sth into a drawer** mettre *or* fourrer qch dans un tiroir; **to ~ one's hands in one's pockets** mettre *or* fourrer ses mains dans ses poches; **he stuck his head through the window/round the door** il a passé la tête par la fenêtre/dans l'embrasure de la porte; **he stuck his finger into the hole** il a mis *or* fourré son doigt dans le trou; **he stuck the lid on the box** il a mis *or* placé le couvercle sur la boîte; **to ~ one's hat on one's head** mettre son chapeau sur sa tête; **I'll have to ~ a button on that shirt*** il faudra que je mette *or* couse un bouton à cette chemise; **he had stuck £3 on the price*** il avait majoré le prix de 3 livres; **to ~ an advertisement in the paper*** mettre *or* passer une annonce dans le journal; **they stuck him on the committee*** ils l'ont mis (*or* collé*) au comité; (*fig*) **you know where you can ~ that!‡** tu sais où tu peux te le mettre!‡; *V* **nose** *etc.*

(c) (*with glue etc*) coller. **to ~ a poster on the wall/a door** coller une affiche au mur/sur une porte; **to ~ a stamp on a letter** coller un timbre sur une lettre, timbrer une lettre; **you'll have to ~ it with glue/sellotape** il vous faudra le fixer avec de la colle/du scotch ®; '**~ no bills**' 'défense d'afficher'; **it was stuck fast** c'était bien collé *or* indécollable (*V also* 3e); (*fig*) **he tried to ~ the murder on his brother‡** il a essayé de mettre le meurtre sur le dos de son frère; (*fig*) **you can't ~ that on me!‡** vous ne pouvez pas me mettre ça sur le dos!

(d) (*esp Brit: tolerate*) *sb's presence, mannerisms etc* supporter; *person* souffrir, sentir*, pifer‡. **I can't ~ it any longer** je ne peux plus le supporter, j'en ai plein le dos*, j'en ai ras le bol‡; **I wonder how he ~s it at all** je me demande comment il peut tenir le coup*.

(e) to be stuck *[wheels]* être embourbé *or* enlisé; *[key, lock, door, drawer, gears, valve, lid]* être coincé, être bloqué; *[machine, lift]* être bloqué, être en panne; **to be stuck fast** être bien coincé *or* bloqué; **to get stuck in the mud** s'embourber, s'enliser dans la boue; **to get stuck in the sand** s'enliser dans le sable; **to be stuck in the lift** être coincé *or* bloqué dans l'ascenseur; **a bone got stuck in my throat** une arête s'est mise en travers de ma gorge; **the train was stuck at the station** le train était bloqué *or* immobilisé en gare; **the car was stuck between two trucks** la voiture était bloquée *or* coincée entre deux camions; (*fig*) **I was stuck* in a corner and had to listen to him** j'étais coincé dans un coin et j'ai dû l'écouter; **he was stuck in town all summer** il a été obligé de rester en ville tout l'été; **I'm stuck at home all day** je suis cloué à la maison toute la journée; **we're stuck here for the night** nous allons être obligés de passer la nuit ici; **the second question stuck me*** j'ai séché* sur la deuxième question; **to be stuck for an answer** ne pas savoir que répondre; (*in crossword puzzle, guessing game, essay etc*) **I'm stuck*** je sèche*; **I'll help you if you're stuck*** je t'aiderai si tu as un problème *or* si tu ne sais pas le faire; **I'm stuck for £10*** il me manque 10 livres; **he's not stuck for money*** ce n'est pas l'argent qui lui manque; **I was stuck* with the job of organizing it all** on m'a collé *or* refilé le boulot de tout organiser*; **he stuck* me with the bill** il m'a collé* la note; **I was stuck* with the bill** j'ai récolté la note, j'ai dû me farcir la note‡; **he stuck‡ me (for) £10 for that old book** il m'a fait payer *or* il m'a pris 10 livres pour ce vieux bouquin; **I was stuck* with him all evening** je l'ai eu sur le dos *or* sur les bras toute la soirée.

4 *vi* **(a)** (*embed itself etc*) *[needle, spear]* se planter, s'enfoncer (*into* dans). **he had a knife ~ing in(to) his back** il avait un couteau planté dans le dos.

(b) (*adhere*) *[glue, paste]* tenir; *[stamp, label]* être collé, tenir (*to* à); (*fig*) *[habit, name etc]* rester. **the paper stuck to the table** le papier a collé *or* s'est collé *or* est resté collé à la table; **the eggs have stuck to the pan** les œufs ont attaché à la casserole; (*fig*) **the nickname stuck to him** le surnom lui est resté; (*fig*) **to make a charge ~** prouver la culpabilité de quelqu'un.

(c) (*remain, stay*) rester; (*remain loyal*) rester fidèle (*to* à). **to ~ close to sb** rester aux côtés de qn, ne pas quitter *or* laisser qn; **they stuck to the fox's trail** ils sont restés sur les traces du renard; **I'll ~ in the job for a bit longer** pour le moment je garde ce boulot* *or* je vais rester où je suis; (*fig*) **to ~ to** *or* **by sb through thick and thin** rester fidèle à qn envers et contre tout; **will you ~ by me?** vous ne m'abandonnerez pas?, est-ce que vous me soutiendrez?; (*fig*) **to ~ to sb like a limpet** *or* **a leech** se cramponner à qn, coller à qn comme une sangsue; **she stuck to him all through the tour** elle ne l'a pas lâché d'une semelle pendant toute la tournée; **to ~ to one's word** *or* **promise** tenir parole; **to ~ to one's principles** rester fidèle à ses principes; **to ~ to** *or* **at a job** rester dans un emploi; **~ at it!** persévère!, tiens bon!, ne te laisse pas décourager!; **to ~ to one's post** rester à son poste; (*fig*) **to ~ to one's last** s'en tenir à ce que l'on sait faire; **to ~ to one's guns*** ne pas en démordre; (*fig*) **he stuck to his story** il a maintenu ce qu'il avait dit; **decide what you're going to say then ~ to it** décidez ce que vous allez dire et tenez-vous-y *or* n'en démordez pas; (*fig*) **to ~ to the facts** s'en tenir aux faits; **~ to the point!** ne vous éloignez pas *or* ne sortez pas du sujet!; **to ~ with sb*** (*stay beside*) rester avec qn, ne pas quitter qn; (*stay loyal*) rester fidèle à qn; **~ with him!*** ne le perdez pas de vue!

(d) (*get jammed etc*) *[wheels]* être embourbé *or* enlisé; *[key, lock, door, drawer, gears, valve, lid]* être coincé, être bloqué; *[machine, lift]* être bloqué, être en panne. **to ~ fast** être bien coincé *or* bloqué; **the car stuck in the mud** la voiture s'est enlisée dans la boue *or* s'est embourbée; **a bone stuck in my throat** une arête s'est mise en travers de ma gorge; (*fig*) **that ~s in my throat** *or* **gizzard*** je ne digère* pas ça!; (*fig*) **the bidding stuck at £100** les enchères se sont arrêtées à 100 livres; **I got halfway through and stuck there** je suis resté coincé à mi-chemin; (*fig*) **he stuck halfway through the second verse** il est resté court *or* en carafe* au milieu de la deuxième strophe.

(e) (*balk*) reculer, regimber (*at, on* devant). **he will ~ at nothing to get what he wants** il ne recule devant rien pour obtenir ce qu'il veut; **he wouldn't ~ at murder** il irait jusqu'au meurtre; **they may ~ on** *or* **at that clause** il se peut qu'ils regimbent (*subj*) devant cette clause.

(f) (*extend, protrude*) **the nail was ~ing through the plank** le clou dépassait *or* sortait de la planche; **the rod was ~ing into the next garden** la barre dépassait dans le jardin d'à côté.

stick around* *vi* rester dans les parages. **stick around for a few minutes** restez dans les parages un moment; **I was tired of sticking around doing nothing** j'en avais assez de poireauter* sans rien faire.

stick away *vt sep* cacher, planquer‡. **he stuck it away behind the bookcase** il l'a caché *or* planqué‡ derrière la bibliothèque.

stick back *vt sep* **(a)** (*replace*) remettre (*into* dans, *on to* sur).

(b) (*with glue etc*) recoller.

stick down 1 *vi [envelope etc]* se coller.

2 *vt sep* **(a)** *envelope etc* coller.

(b) (*put down*) poser, mettre. **he stuck it down on the table** il l'a posé *or* mis sur la table.

(c) (*) *notes, details* noter en vitesse. **he stuck down a few dates before he forgot** avant d'oublier il a rapidement noté quelques dates.

stick in 1 *vi* (*) s'y mettre sérieusement; persévérer. **you'll have to stick in if you want to succeed** vous devrez vous y mettre sérieusement si vous voulez réussir; **he stuck in at his maths** il a persévéré en maths.

2 *vt sep* **(a)** (*put in*) *needle, pin, fork* piquer, enfoncer, planter; *dagger, knife, bayonet, spade* planter, enfoncer; *photo in album etc* coller. (*fig*) **he stuck in a few quotations*** il a collé* quelques citations par-ci par-là; **try to stick in a word about our book** essaie de glisser un mot sur notre livre; *V* **oar** *etc.*

(b) (*fig*) **to get stuck in*** s'y mettre sérieusement.

stick on 1 *vi [label, stamp etc]* rester collé.

2 *vt sep* **(a)** *label* coller; *stamp* mettre, coller.

(b) (*put on*) *hat, coat, lid* mettre. **stick on another record** mets un autre disque; (*fig: put the price up*) **to stick it on‡** augmenter les prix.

3 stick-on *adj V* **stick 2.**

stick out 1 *vi* **(a)** (*protrude*) *[ears]* décoller; *[teeth]* avancer; *[shirttails]* dépasser, sortir; *[rod etc]* dépasser; *[balcony etc]* faire saillie. **I could see his legs sticking out from under the car** je pouvais voir ses jambes qui sortaient de dessous la voiture; **to stick out beyond sth** dépasser qch; (*fig*) **it sticks out a mile*** ça crève les yeux (*that* que).

(b) (*persevere etc*) tenir (bon). **can you stick out a little longer?** est-ce que vous pouvez tenir un peu plus longtemps?; **to stick out for more money** tenir bon dans ses revendications pour une augmentation de salaire.

2 *vt sep* **(a)** *rod etc* faire dépasser; *one's arm, head* sortir (*of* de). **to stick one's chest out** bomber la poitrine; **to stick one's tongue out** tirer la langue; *V* **neck.**

(b) (*: *tolerate*) supporter. **to stick it out** tenir le coup.

stick through 1 *vi* (*protrude*) dépasser.

2 *vt sep pen, rod, one's finger etc* passer à travers.

stick together 1 *vi* **(a)** *[labels, pages, objects]* coller ensemble. **the pieces won't stick together** les morceaux ne veulent pas rester collés *or* se coller ensemble.

(b) (*not separate*) rester ensemble; (*fig*) se serrer les coudes.

stick together till you get through the park restez ensemble jusqu'à *or* ne vous séparez pas avant la sortie du parc; (*fig*) **we must all stick together!** nous devons nous serrer les coudes!

2 *vt* coller (ensemble).

stick up 1 *vi* **(a) there was a mast sticking up out of the water** il y avait un mât qui sortait *or* dépassait de l'eau; **his head was sticking up above the crowd** sa tête était visible au-dessus de la foule; **your hair is sticking up** vos cheveux rebiquent*.

(b) to stick up for sb* prendre la défense *or* le parti de qn; **to stick up for o.s.*** défendre ses intérêts, ne pas se laisser faire; **to stick up for one's rights*** défendre ses droits, ne pas se laisser faire; **to stick up to sb**: tenir tête à qn.

2 *vt sep* **(a)** *notice etc* afficher.

(b) to stick up one's hand lever la main; **stick 'em up!*** haut les mains!; **to stick sb up**: dévaliser qn (sous la menace d'un revolver); **they stuck up the bank**: ils ont attaqué la banque (à main armée).

3 **stick-up*** *n V* **stick 2.**

4 **stuck-up*** *adj V* **stuck 2.**

sticker ['stɪkə^r] *n* (*label*) (badge *m*) auto-collant *m*, vignette adhésive. (*fig*) **he's a ~*** il n'abandonne pas facilement, il va jusqu'au bout de ce qu'il entreprend; *V* **bill**[1].

stickiness ['stɪkɪnɪs] *n* (*V* **sticky a**) caractère poisseux *or* gluant *or* collant; viscosité *f*; moiteur *f*; chaleur *f* et humidité *f*.

stickleback ['stɪklbæk] *n* épinoche *f*.

stickler ['stɪklə^r] *n*: **to be a ~ for** *discipline, obedience, correct clothing, good manners* insister sur, tenir rigoureusement à; *etiquette* être à cheval sur, être pointilleux sur; *grammar, spelling* être rigoriste en matière de; *figures, facts* être pointilleux sur le chapitre de, insister sur; **to be a ~ for detail** être tatillon.

sticky ['stɪkɪ] *adj* **(a)** *paste, substance* poisseux, gluant; *label* gommé, adhésif; *paint, toffee, syrup* poisseux; *oil* visqueux; *road, surface, pitch* gluant; (*sweaty*) *hands, palm* moite; (*fig*) *climate* chaud et humide. **~ tape** scotch *m* ®, papier collant, ruban adhésif; **it was a ~ day** il faisait une chaleur moite (ce jour-là).

(b) (**fig*) *problem* épineux, délicat; *situation* délicat; *person* peu accommodant, difficile. (*Brit fig*) **to be on a ~ wicket** être dans une situation délicate; **to come to a ~ end** mal finir; **to have a ~ time** passer un mauvais quart d'heure; (*longer*) connaître des moments difficiles; **he's very ~ about lending his car** il répugne à prêter sa voiture.

stiff [stɪf] **1** *adj* **(a)** (*gen*) raide, rigide; *arm, leg* raide, ankylosé; *joint, shoulder, knee* ankylosé; *corpse* rigide, raide; *collar, shirt front* dur, raide; (*starched*) empesé; *door, lock, brush* dur; *dough, paste* dur, ferme, consistant. (*Culin*) **~ eggwhite** blanc d'œuf battu en neige très ferme; **as ~ as a poker** *or* **a ramrod** raide comme un piquet *or* un échalas *or* la justice; **my leg is ~ today** j'ai une jambe raide aujourd'hui, je remue mal ma jambe aujourd'hui; **you'll be** *or* **feel ~ tomorrow** vous aurez des courbatures *or* vous serez courbatu demain; **he's getting ~ as he grows older** il se raidit avec l'âge, il perd de sa souplesse en vieillissant; **to have a ~ back** avoir mal au dos; **to have a ~ neck** avoir le torticolis (*V also* 2); **to be ~ with cold** être frigorifié, être engourdi par le froid; **he was ~ with boredom** il s'ennuyait à mort; (*fig*) **to keep a ~ upper lip** rester impassible, garder son flegme; *V* **bore**[2], **frozen, scare** *etc*.

(b) (*fig*) *bow, smile* froid; *reception* froid, distant; *person* guindé, froid, distant; *resistance* opiniâtre, tenace; *exam, test* difficile; *climb* raide, pénible; *programme, course, task* ardu; *wind, breeze* fort; *price* élevé, excessif; *bill* salé*. **I could do with a ~ drink** je boirais bien quelque chose de fort; **he had a ~ whisky** il a pris un grand verre de whisky; **this book is ~ reading** ce livre n'est pas d'une lecture facile.

2 *cpd*: (*fig*) **stiff-necked** opiniâtre, entêté.

3 *n* (: *corpse*) macchabée: *m*. (*fool*) **big ~** gros balourd *or* bêta.

stiffen ['stɪfn] (*also* **~ up**) **1** *vt card, fabric* raidir, renforcer; (*starch*) empeser; *dough, paste* donner de la consistance à; *limb* raidir; *joint* ankyloser; (*fig*) *morale, resistance etc* renforcer, affermir.

2 *vi* [*card, fabric*] devenir raide *or* rigide; [*dough, paste*] prendre de la consistance, devenir ferme; [*limb*] se raidir; [*joint*] s'ankyloser; [*door, lock*] devenir dur; [*breeze*] augmenter d'intensité, fraîchir; [*resistance*] devenir opiniâtre; [*morale*] s'affermir. **he ~ed when he heard the noise** il s'est raidi quand il a entendu le bruit.

stiffly ['stɪflɪ] *adv move, turn, bend* raidement, avec raideur; (*fig*) *smile, bow, greet* froidement; *say* sèchement, froidement. **they stood ~ to attention** ils se tenaient au garde-à-vous sans bouger un muscle.

stiffness ['stɪfnɪs] *n* (*V* **stiff**) raideur *f*; rigidité *f*; dureté *f*; fermeté *f*, consistance *f*; difficulté *f*; caractère ardu; froideur *f*, caractère guindé *or* distant.

stifle ['staɪfl] **1** *vt person* étouffer, suffoquer; *fire* étouffer; *sobs* étouffer, retenir, réprimer; *anger, smile, desire réprimer*. **to ~ a yawn/sneeze** réprimer une envie de bâiller/d'éternuer. **2** *vi* étouffer, suffoquer.

stifling ['staɪflɪŋ] *adj smoke, fumes* suffocant; *heat* étouffant, suffocant. **it's a ~ day*** on étouffe aujourd'hui; **it's ~ in here** on étouffe ici.

stigma ['stɪgmə] *n, pl* (*Bot, Med, Rel*) **stigmata** [stɪg'mɑːtə], (*fig*) **~s** stigmate *m*.

stigmatism ['stɪgmətɪzəm] *n* (*Opt*) stigmatisme *m*.

stigmatize ['stɪgmətaɪz] *vt* (*all senses*) stigmatiser.

stile [staɪl] *n* (*in fence*) échalier *m*; (*turn~*) tourniquet *m* (*porte*).

stiletto [stɪ'letəʊ] *n, pl* **~s** *or* **~es** (*weapon*) stylet *m*; (*Brit: also* **~ heel**) talon *m* aiguille.

still[1] [stɪl] **1** *adv* **(a)** (*up to this time*) encore, toujours. **he is ~ in bed** il est encore *or* toujours au lit; **I can ~ remember it** je m'en souviens encore; **he ~ hasn't arrived** il n'est pas encore arrivé, il n'est toujours pas arrivé; **you ~ don't believe me** vous ne me croyez toujours pas; **I ~ have 10 francs left** il me reste encore 10 F; **he's ~ as stubborn as ever** il est toujours aussi entêté.

(b) (+ *comp adj: even*) encore. **~ better, better ~** encore mieux; **he is tall but his brother is taller ~** *or* **~ taller** lui est grand, mais son frère l'est encore plus.

(c) (*nonetheless*) quand même, tout de même. **even if it's cold, you'll ~ come** même s'il fait froid vous viendrez, s'il fait froid vous viendrez quand même *or* tout de même; **he's ~ your brother** il n'en est pas moins votre frère.

2 *conj* néanmoins, quand même. **it's fine — ~, you should take your umbrella** il fait beau — néanmoins, vous devriez prendre votre parapluie *or* vous devriez prendre votre parapluie quand même.

still[2] [stɪl] **1** *adj* (*motionless*) immobile; (*peaceful, quiet*) calme, tranquille, silencieux; (*not fizzy*) *lemonade* non gazeux. **keep ~!** reste tranquille!, ne bouge pas!; **all was ~** tout était calme *or* tranquille *or* silencieux; **the ~ waters of the lake** les eaux calmes *or* tranquilles du lac; (*Prov*) **~ waters run deep** il n'est pire eau que l'eau qui dort; **be ~!**† taisez-vous!; (*fig*) **a** *or* **the ~ small voice** la voix de la conscience.

2 *adv sit, stand, hold* sans bouger.

3 *cpd*: **stillbirth** (*birth*) mort *f* à la naissance; (*child*) enfant *m(f)* mort-né(e); **stillborn** mort-né (*f* mort-née); (*Art*) **still life** nature morte.

4 *n* **(a)** (*liter*) silence *m*, calme *m*. **in the ~ of the night** dans le silence de la nuit.

(b) (*Cine*) photo *f*.

5 *vt anger, fear* calmer; *person* apaiser, tranquilliser; (*silence*) faire taire.

still[3] [stɪl] **1** *n* (*apparatus*) alambic *m*; (*place*) distillerie *f*. **2** *vt* distiller.

stillness ['stɪlnɪs] *n* (*V* **still**[2]) immobilité *f*; calme *m*, tranquillité *f*, silence *m*.

stilt [stɪlt] *n* échasse *f*; (*Archit*) pilotis *m*.

stilted ['stɪltɪd] *adj person, wording, style* guindé, emprunté; *manners* guindé, contraint, emprunté; *book etc* qui manque de naturel *or* d'aisance.

stimulant ['stɪmjʊlənt] **1** *adj* stimulant. **2** *n* (*also fig*) stimulant *m*. (*fig*) **to be a ~ to** stimuler.

stimulate ['stɪmjʊleɪt] *vt* (*also Physiol*) stimuler. **to ~ sb to sth/to do** inciter *or* pousser qn à qch/à faire.

stimulating ['stɪmjʊleɪtɪŋ] *adj air* stimulant, vivifiant; *medicine, drink* stimulant, fortifiant; *person, book, film, experience* stimulant, enrichissant, qui fait penser *or* réfléchir; *music* stimulant, exaltant.

stimulation [ˌstɪmjʊ'leɪʃən] *n* (*stimulus*) stimulant *m*; (*state*) stimulation *f*.

stimulus ['stɪmjʊləs] *n, pl* **stimuli** ['stɪmjʊlaɪ] (*Physiol*) stimulus *m*; (*fig*) stimulant *m*. (*fig*) **to be a ~ to** *or* **for** *exports, efforts* stimuler; *imagination* stimuler, enflammer; **it gave trade a new ~** cela a donné une nouvelle impulsion *or* un coup de fouet au commerce; **under the ~ of** stimulé par.

stimy ['staɪmɪ] = **stymie.**

sting [stɪŋ] (*vb: pret, ptp* **stung**) **1** *n* **(a)** [*insect*] dard *m*, aiguillon *m*. (*fig*) **but there's a ~ in the tail** mais il y a une mauvaise surprise à la fin.

(b) (*pain, wound, mark*) [*insect, nettle etc*] piqûre *f*; [*iodine etc*] brûlure *f*; [*whip*] douleur cuisante; (*fig*) [*attack*] mordant *m*, vigueur *f*; [*criticism, remark*] causticité *f*, mordant. **I felt the ~ of the rain on my face** la pluie me cinglait le visage; **the ~ of salt water in the cut** la brûlure de l'eau salée dans la plaie.

2 *cpd*: **stingray** pastenague *f*.

3 *vt* **(a)** [*insect, nettle*] piquer; [*iodine, ointment*] brûler; [*rain, hail, whip*] cingler, fouetter; (*fig*) [*remark, criticism*] piquer au vif, blesser. (*fig*) **stung by remorse** bourrelé de remords; **my remark stung him into action** ma remarque (l'a piqué au vif et) l'a poussé à agir; **he was stung into replying brusquely** piqué *or* blessé, il répondit brusquement; *V* **quick.**

(b) (:) avoir*, estamper*. **he stung me for £10 for that meal** il m'a eu* *or* estampé* en me faisant payer ce repas 10 livres, il a eu le toupet* de me faire payer ce repas 10 livres; **I've been stung!** je me suis fait avoir!* *or* estamper!*, c'était le coup de fusil!*

4 *vi* **(a)** [*insect, nettle*] piquer; [*iodine, ointment*] brûler; [*blow, slap, whip*] provoquer une sensation cuisante; [*remark, criticism*] être cuisant. **that ~s!** ça pique!, ça brûle!

(b) [*eyes*] cuire, piquer; [*cut, skin*] cuire, brûler. **the fumes made his eyes ~** les fumées picotaient ses yeux.

stingily ['stɪndʒɪlɪ] *adv praise* chichement; *spend* avec avarice; *serve* en lésinant.

stinginess ['stɪndʒɪnɪs] *n* [*person*] ladrerie *f*, avarice *f*; [*portion*] insuffisance *f*.

stinging ['stɪŋɪŋ] **1** *adj cut, blow, pain* cuisant; (*fig*) *remark, criticism* cuisant, mordant. **~ nettle** ortie *f* brûlante *or* romaine. **2** *n* (*sensation*) sensation cuisante.

stingy ['stɪndʒɪ] *adj person* avare, ladre; *portion, amount* misérable, insuffisant. **to be ~ with** *food, wine* lésiner sur; *praise* être chiche de; **to be ~ with money** être avare *or* ladre; **he/she is ~** il/elle est pingre, c'est un/une pingre.

stink [stɪŋk] (*vb: pret* **stank**, *ptp* **stunk**) **1** *n* **(a)** puanteur *f*, odeur infecte. **what a ~!** ce que ça pue!; (*fig*) **there's a ~ of corruption** cela pue la corruption, cela sent la corruption à plein nez.

(b) (:*fig: row, trouble*) esclandre *m*, grabuge* *m*. **there was a dreadful ~ about the broken windows** il y a eu du grabuge* à propos des carreaux cassés; **to cause** *or* **make** *or* **kick up a ~** faire toute une scène, râler*; **to kick up a ~ about sth** causer un esclandre à propos de qch, faire du grabuge* à cause de qch.

2 *cpd*: **stink-bomb** boule puante; **stink-horn** phallus *m* impudique, satyre puant; **stinkpot‡** salaud‡ *m*, salope‡ *f*; **stinkweed** diplotaxis *m*.

3 *vi* **(a)** puer, empester. **it ~s of fish** cela pue *or* empeste le poisson; **it ~s in here!** cela pue *or* empeste ici!; (*lit, fig*) **it ~s to high heaven*** cela sent à plein nez; (*fig*) **it ~s of corruption** cela pue la corruption, cela sent la corruption à plein nez; (*fig*) **the whole business ~s** toute l'affaire pue *or* est infecte *or* est ignoble; **they're ~ing with money‡** ils sont bourrés de fric‡.

(b) (‡: *be bad*) *[book, film, idea, plan]* être déplorable, ne rien valoir; *[person]* être déplorable. **as a boss, he ~s** comme patron il est déplorable *or* une catastrophe ambulante*.

4 *vt room etc* empester.

stink out *vt sep fox etc* enfumer; *room* empester.

stinker‡ ['stɪŋkər] *n* (*pej*) (*person*) salaud‡ *m*, salope‡ *f*; (*exam, question, essay etc*) vacherie‡ *f*; (*meeting/afternoon/task etc*) sale réunion *f*/après-midi *m*/corvée *f etc*; (*letter*) lettre *f* d'engueulade‡. **you ~!** espèce de salaud!‡ *or* salope!‡.

stinking ['stɪŋkɪŋ] **1** *adj substance* puant; (‡ *fig*) infect, ignoble, vache‡. **what a ~‡ thing to do** quelle vacherie!‡; **to have a ~‡ cold** avoir un rhume épouvantable *or* un sale rhume.

2 *adv*: **to be ~ rich‡** être bourré de fric‡, être plein aux as‡.

stint [stɪnt] **1** *n* **(a)** ration *f* de travail, besogne assignée. **to do one's ~** (*daily work*) faire son travail quotidien; (*do one's share*) faire sa part de travail; **he does a ~ in the gym/at the typewriter every day** il passe un certain temps chaque jour au gymnase/à la machine; **I've done my ~ at the wheel** j'ai pris mon tour au volant; **I've finished my ~ for today** j'ai fini ce que j'avais à faire aujourd'hui.

(b) without ~ *spend* sans compter; *give, lend* généreusement, avec largesse.

2 *vt food* lésiner sur; *compliments* être chiche de. **to ~ sb of sth** mesurer qch à qn; **he ~ed himself in order to feed the children** il s'est privé afin de nourrir les enfants; **he didn't ~ himself** il ne s'est privé de rien.

3 *vi*: **to ~ on** *food* lésiner sur; *compliments* être chiche de; **to ~ on money** être avare *or* ladre.

stipend ['staɪpend] *n* (*esp Rel*) traitement *m*.

stipendiary [staɪ'pendɪərɪ] **1** *adj services, official* rémunéré. **2** *n* personne *f* qui reçoit une rémunération *or* un traitement fixe. (*Brit Jur: also* **~ magistrate**) juge *m* de tribunal de police correctionnelle.

stipple ['stɪpl] *vt* pointiller.

stipulate ['stɪpjʊleɪt] **1** *vt* stipuler (*that* que); *amount, price etc* stipuler, convenir expressément de; *quantity* prescrire. **2** *vi*: **to ~ for sth** stipuler qch, spécifier qch, convenir expressément de qch.

stipulation [ˌstɪpjʊ'leɪʃən] *n* stipulation *f*. **on the ~ that ...** à la condition expresse que ... (+*future or subj*).

stir[1] [stɜːr] **1** *n* **(a) to give sth a ~** remuer *or* tourner qch.

(b) (*fig: excitement etc*) agitation *f*, sensation *f*. **there was a great ~ in Parliament about ...** il y a eu beaucoup d'agitation au Parlement à propos de ...; **it caused** *or* **made quite a ~** cela a fait une certaine sensation, cela a eu un grand retentissement, cela a fait du bruit.

2 *vt* **(a)** *tea, soup* remuer, tourner; *mixture* tourner; *fire* tisonner. **he ~red sugar into his tea** il a remué *or* tourné son thé après y avoir mis du sucre; **she ~red milk into the mixture** elle a ajouté du lait au mélange.

(b) (*move*) agiter, (faire) bouger, remuer. **the wind ~red the leaves** le vent a agité *or* remué *or* fait trembler les feuilles; **he didn't ~ a finger (to help)** il n'a pas levé *or* remué le petit doigt (pour aider); **nothing could ~ him from his chair** rien ne pouvait le tirer de son fauteuil; **to ~ o.s.*** se secouer, se bouger‡; (*fig*) **to ~ one's stumps*** se grouiller‡, agiter ses abattis‡.

(c) (*fig*) *curiosity, passions* exciter; *emotions* éveiller; *imagination* stimuler, exciter; *person* émouvoir, exalter. **to ~ sb to do sth** inciter qn à faire qch; **to ~ a people to revolt** inciter un peuple à la révolte; **to ~ sb to pity** émouvoir la compassion de qn; **it ~red his heart** cela lui a remué le cœur; **to ~ sb's blood** réveiller l'enthousiasme de qn; **it was a song to ~ the blood** c'était une chanson enthousiasmante.

3 *vi* *[person]* remuer, bouger; *[leaves, curtains etc]* remuer, trembler; *[feelings]* être excité. **I will not ~ from here** je ne bougerai pas d'ici; **he hasn't ~red from the spot** il n'a pas quitté l'endroit; **he wouldn't ~ an inch** il ne voulait pas bouger d'un centimètre; (*fig*) il ne voulait pas faire la moindre concession; **to ~ in one's sleep** bouger en dormant *or* dans son sommeil; **nobody is ~ring yet** personne n'est encore levé, tout le monde dort encore; **nothing was ~ring in the forest** rien ne bougeait dans la forêt; **the curtains ~red in the breeze** la brise a agité les rideaux; **anger ~red within her** la colère est montée en elle.

stir in *vt sep milk etc* ajouter en tournant.

stir round *vt sep* (*Culin etc*) tourner.

stir up *vt sep soup etc* tourner, remuer; *fire* tisonner; (*fig*) *curiosity, attention, anger* exciter; *imagination* exciter, stimuler; *memories, the past* réveiller; *revolt* susciter; *hatred* attiser; *mob* ameuter; *opposition, discord* fomenter; *trouble* provoquer; *person* secouer (*fig*). **to stir sb up to sth/to do** pousser *or* inciter qn à qch/à faire.

stir[2]**‡** [stɜːr] *n* (*prison*) taule‡ *f or* tôle‡ *f*. **in ~** en taule‡, au bloc*.

stirring ['stɜːrɪŋ] *adj speech, tale, music* excitant, enthousiasmant; *years, period* passionnant.

stirrup ['stɪrəp] **1** *n* (*all senses*) étrier *m*. **to put one's feet in the ~s** chausser les étriers.

2 *cpd*: **stirrup cup** coup *m* de l'étrier; **stirrup leather** étrivière *f*; **stirrup pump** pompe *f* à main portative; **stirrup strap = stirrup leather**.

stitch [stɪtʃ] **1** *n* (*Sewing*) point *m*; (*Knitting*) maille *f*; (*Surgery*) point de suture; (*sharp pain*) point de côté. (*Prov*) **a ~ in time saves nine** un point à temps en vaut cent; **she put a few ~es in the tear** elle a fait un point à la déchirure; **to put ~es in a wound** suturer *or* recoudre une plaie; (*Med*) **he had 10 ~es** on lui a fait 10 points de suture; (*Med*) **to get one's ~es out** se faire retirer ses fils (de suture); (*fig*) **he hadn't a ~ on*** il était à poil‡; **he hadn't a dry ~ on him** il n'avait pas un fil de sec sur le dos; (*fig*) **to be in ~es*** se tenir les côtes, rire à s'en tenir les côtes; **her stories had us in ~es*** ses anecdotes nous ont fait rire à nous en tordre; *V* **cable, drop** *etc*. **2** *vt seam, hem, garment* coudre; *leather* piquer; *book* brocher; (*Med*) suturer; *V* **hand, machine**. **3** *vi* coudre.

stitch down *vt sep* rabattre.

stitch on *vt sep pocket, button* coudre; (*mend*) recoudre.

stitch up *vt sep* coudre; (*mend*) recoudre; (*Med*) suturer.

stoat [stəʊt] *n* hermine *f* (*d'été*).

stock [stɒk] **1** *n* **(a)** (*supply*) *[cotton, sugar, books, goods]* réserve *f*, provision *f*, stock *m* (*Comm*); *[money]* réserve. (*Comm*) **in ~** en stock, en magasin; **out of ~** épuisé; **the shop has a large ~** le magasin est bien approvisionné *or* achalandé*; **coal ~s are low** les réserves *or* les stocks de charbon sont réduit(e)s; (*Theat*) **~ of plays** répertoire *m*; **I've got a ~ of cigarettes** j'ai une provision *or* un stock* de cigarettes; **to get in** *or* **lay in a ~ of** s'approvisionner de, faire provision de; **it adds to our ~ of facts** cela est un complément à toutes nos données; **a great ~ of learning** un grand fonds d'érudition; **to take ~** (*Comm*) faire l'inventaire; (*fig*) faire le point; (*fig*) **to take ~ of** *situation, prospects etc* faire le point de; *person* jauger, évaluer les mérites de; *V* **dead, surplus** *etc*.

(b) (*Agr: animals and equipment*) cheptel *m* (vif et mort); (*Agr: also* **live~**) cheptel vif, bétail *m*; (*Rail*) matériel roulant; (*Ind: raw material*) matière première; (*for paper-making*) pâte *f* à papier; (*Cards*) talon *m*; (*Culin*) bouillon *m*. **chicken ~** bouillon de poulet; *V* **fat, live**[2]**, rolling** *etc*.

(c) (*Fin*) valeurs *fpl*, titres *mpl*; (*also* **government ~s**) fonds publics *or* d'État; (*company shares*) actions *fpl*. **~s and shares** valeurs (mobilières), titres; **to have money in the ~s** avoir de l'argent placé en fonds d'État; **railway ~(s)** actions de chemin de fer; (*fig*) **to put ~ in sth** faire cas de qch; *V* **preference, registered** *etc*.

(d) (*tree trunk*) tronc *m*; (*tree stump*) souche *f*; (*Horticulture: for grafting*) porte-greffe *m*, ente *f*; (*flower*) giroflée *f*, matthiole *f*; (*matthiola incana*) giroflée rouge. (*Hist*) **the ~s** le pilori; **to be on the ~s** *[ship]* être sur cale; (*fig*) *[book, piece of work, scheme]* être en chantier; *V* **laughing** *etc*.

(e) (*base, stem*) *[anvil]* billot *m*; *[plough]* fût *m*; *[rifle]* fût et crosse *f*; *[plane]* fût, bois *m*; *[whip]* manche *m*; *[fishing rod]* gaule *f*; *[anchor]* jas *m*; *V* **lock**[1] *etc*.

(f) (*descent, lineage*) souche *f*, lignée *f*, famille *f*. **of good Scottish ~** de bonne souche écossaise; **he comes of farming ~** il vient d'une famille d'agriculteurs, il est d'origine *or* de souche paysanne.

2 *adj* **(a)** (*Comm*) *goods, model* de série; (*Theat*) du répertoire; (*fig: stereotyped*) *argument, joke, excuse, comment* classique, banal. (*Comm*) **~ line** article suivi; **~ size** taille courante *or* normalisée; **she is not ~ size** elle n'est pas une taille courante; **~ phrase** cliché *m*, expression toute faite.

(b) (*for breeding*) destiné à la reproduction. **~ mare** jument poulinière.

3 *cpd*: **stock book** livre *m* de magasin; **stockbreeder** éleveur *m*, -euse *f*; **stockbreeding** élevage *m*; **stockbroker** agent *m* de change; **stockbroking** commerce *m* des valeurs en bourse; **stock car** (*Rail*) wagon *m* à bestiaux; (*Aut Sport*) stock-car *m*; (*Aut Sport*) **stock-car racing** course *f* de stock-cars; (*Fin*) **stock certificate** titre *m*; **stock company** (*Fin*) société *f* par actions, société anonyme (*V also* **joint**); (*US Theat*) compagnie *f or* troupe *f* (de théâtre) de répertoire; (*Culin*) **stock cube** bouillon-cube *m*; **stock dividend** dividende *m*; **stock exchange** Bourse *f* (des valeurs); **stockfish** stockfisch *m*; **stockholder** actionnaire *mf*; **stock-in-trade** (*goods*) marchandises *fpl* en magasin *or* en stock; (*tools, materials; also fig*) outils *mpl* du métier; **stockjobber** (*Brit*) *intermédiaire mf qui traite directement avec l'agent de change*; (*US: often pej*) agent *m* de change, agioteur *m* (*often pej*); **stock list** (*Fin*) cours *m* de la Bourse; (*Comm*) liste *f* des marchandises en stock, inventaire commercial; **stockman** gardien *m* de bestiaux; **stock market** Bourse *f*, marché financier; **stock market closing report** compte rendu des cours de clôture; (*US Fin*) **stock option** droit *m* (préférentiel) de souscription; **stockpile** (*vt*) *food etc* stocker, faire *or* constituer des stocks de; *weapons* amasser, accumuler; (*vi*) faire des stocks; (*n*) stock *m*, réserve *f*; **stockpiling** stockage *m*; (*Culin*) **stockpot** marmite *f* de bouillon; **stockroom** magasin *m*, réserve *f*, resserre *f*; **to stand** *or* **be stock-still** rester planté comme une borne; (*in fear, amazement*) rester cloué sur place; (*Comm*) **stocktaking** (acte *m* de faire l')inventaire *m*; **to do stocktaking, to be stocktaking** (*Comm*) faire l'inventaire; (*fig*) faire le point; **stockyard** parc *m* à bestiaux.

4 *vt* **(a)** (*supply*) *shop, larder, cupboard* approvisionner (*with* de); *library/farm* monter en livres/en bétail; *river, lake* peupler (*with* de), empoissonner. **well-~ed** *shop etc* bien approvisionné; *library, farm* bien fourni *or* pourvu *or* monté; *garden* bien fourni; **his memory is ~ed with facts** sa mémoire a emmagasiné des tas de connaissances.

(b) (*Comm*) *milk, hats, tools etc* avoir, rendre.

stock up **1** *vi* s'approvisionner, faire ses provisions (*with, on* de, *for* pour).

2 *vt sep shop, larder, cupboard, freezer* garnir; *library* accroître le stock de livres de; *farm* accroître le cheptel de; *river, lake* aleviner, empoissonner.

stockade [stɒ'keɪd] **1** *n* palanque *f*, palissade *f*. **2** *vt* palanquer.
stockily ['stɒkɪlɪ] *adv*: ~ **built** trapu, râblé.
stockiness ['stɒkɪnɪs] *n* aspect trapu *or* râblé.
stockinet(te) [ˌstɒkɪ'net] *n* (*fabric*) jersey *m*; (*knitting stitch*) (point *m* de) jersey.
stocking ['stɒkɪŋ] **1** *n* bas *m*; *V* **Christmas, nylon** *etc*. **2** *cpd*: **in one's stocking feet** sans chaussures; **stocking-filler** tout petit cadeau de Noël; (*Knitting*) **stocking stitch** (point *m* de) jersey *m*.
stockist ['stɒkɪst] *n* (*Brit*) stockiste *m*; *V* **sole**³.
stocky ['stɒkɪ] *adj* trapu, râblé.
stodge* [stɒdʒ] *n* (*Brit: U*) (*food*) aliment bourratif, étouffe-chrétien *m inv*; (*in book etc*) littérature *f* indigeste.
stodgy ['stɒdʒɪ] *adj* (*filling*) *food, diet* bourratif; (*heavy*) *cake* pâteux, lourd; (**fig*) *book* indigeste; (*) *person* rassis, sans imagination.
stoic ['stəʊɪk] **1** *n* stoïque *mf*. (*Philos*) S~ stoïcien *m*. **2** *adj* stoïque. (*Philos*) S~ stoïcien.
stoical ['stəʊɪkəl] *adj* stoïque.
stoicism ['stəʊɪsɪzəm] *n* stoïcisme *m*.
stoke [stəʊk] **1** *vt* (*also* ~ **up**) *fire* garnir, entretenir; *furnace* alimenter; *engine, boiler* chauffer.
2 *cpd*: **stokehole** (*Naut*) chaufferie *f*; [*boiler, furnace*] porte *f* de chauffe.
stoke up 1 *vi* (*furnace*) alimenter la chaudière; (*open fire*) entretenir le feu; (**fig: eat*) se garnir *or* se remplir la panse*.
2 *vt sep* = **stoke 1**.
stoker ['stəʊkəʳ] *n* (*Naut, Rail etc*) chauffeur *m*.
stole¹ [stəʊl] *n* (*Dress*) étole *f*, écharpe *f*; (*Rel*) étole.
stole² [stəʊl] *pret of* **steal**.
stolen ['stəʊlən] *ptp of* **steal**.
stolid ['stɒlɪd] *adj person* flegmatique, impassible; *manner, voice* imperturbable, impassible.
stolidity [stɒ'lɪdɪtɪ] *n*, **stolidness** ['stɒlɪdnɪs] *n* (*V* **stolid**) flegme *m*, impassibilité *f*.
stomach ['stʌmək] **1** *n* (*Anat*) estomac *m*; (*belly*) ventre *m*. **he was lying on his** ~ il était couché *or* allongé sur le ventre, il était à plat ventre; **to have a pain in one's** ~ avoir mal à l'estomac *or* au ventre; (*fig*) **I have no** ~ **for this journey** je n'ai aucune envie de faire ce voyage; **an army marches on its** ~ une armée ne se bat pas le ventre creux; *V* **empty, full, lie**¹ *etc*.
2 *cpd disease* de l'estomac; *ulcer* à l'estomac. **stomach ache** mal *m* à l'estomac *or* au ventre; **stomach pump** pompe stomacale; **he has stomach trouble** il a des ennuis gastriques.
3 *vt* (*fig*) supporter, tolérer, digérer*.
stomp [stɒmp] *vi*: **to** ~ **in/out** *etc* entrer/sortir *etc* d'un pas lourd et bruyant; **we could hear him** ~**ing about** on entendait le bruit lourd de ses pas.
stone [stəʊn] **1** *n* **(a)** (*substance*; *single piece*; *also gem*) pierre *f*; (*pebble*) caillou *m*; (*on beach etc*) galet *m*; (*commemorative*) plaque *f* (commémorative); (*gravestone*) pierre tombale, stèle *f*. **(made) of** ~ de pierre; (*fig*) **within a** ~**'s throw (of)** à deux pas (de); (*fig*) **to leave no** ~ **unturned** remuer ciel et terre (*to do* pour faire); **to turn to** ~, **to change into** ~ (*vt*) pétrifier, changer en pierre; (*vi*) se pétrifier; *V* **paving, precious, stand, tomb** *etc*.
(b) (*in fruit*) noyau *m*.
(c) (*Med*) calcul *m*. **to have a** ~ **in the kidney** avoir un calcul dans le rein; *V* **gall**¹ *etc*.
(d) (*Brit: weight: pl gen inv*) = *14 livres* = *6,348 kg*.
2 *cpd building* de *or* en pierre. **Stone Age** l'âge *m* de (la) pierre; **stone-blind** complètement aveugle; **stonebreaker** (*person*) casseur *m* de pierres; (*machine*) casse-pierre(s) *m*, concasseur *m*; (US) **stone-broke*** = **stony-broke*** (*V* **stony 2**); (*Orn*) **stonechat** traquet *m*; **stone-cold** complètement froid; **stone-cold sober*** pas du tout ivre; (*Bot*) **stonecrop** orpin *m*; **stonecutter** (*person*) tailleur *m* de pierre(s) précieuse(s), lapidaire *m*; (*machine*) sciotte *f*, scie *f* (de carrier); **stone-dead** raide mort; **stone-deaf** sourd comme un pot; **stone fruit** fruit *m* à noyau; **stonemason** tailleur *m* de pierre(s); **stonewall** (*Cricket*) jouer très prudemment; (*fig*) donner des réponses évasives; **stoneware** poterie *f* de grès; **stonework** maçonnerie *f*.
3 *vt* **(a)** *person, object* lancer *or* jeter des pierres sur, bombarder de pierres. **to** ~ **sb to death** lapider qn, tuer qn à coups de pierre.
(b) *date, olive* dénoyauter.
stoned‡ [stəʊnd] *adj* (*drunk*) soûl*, complètement rond‡; (*Drugs*) défoncé‡.
stonily ['stəʊnɪlɪ] *adv* avec froideur, froidement; *stare, look* d'un œil froid.
stony ['stəʊnɪ] **1** *adj path, road, soil* pierreux, caillouteux, rocailleux; *beach* de galets; *substance, texture* pierreux; (*fig*) *person, attitude* dur, insensible; *heart* de pierre, dur; *look, welcome* glacial.
2 *cpd*: (*Brit*) **stony-broke*** fauché comme les blés*; **stony-faced** au visage impassible.
stood [stʊd] *pret, ptp of* **stand**.
stooge [stu:dʒ] *n* (*Theat*) comparse *mf*, faire-valoir *m*; (*pej*) laquais *m*.
stooge about‡, stooge around‡ *vi* rôder, errer.
stook [stu:k] **1** *n* moyette *f*. **2** *vi* moyetter.
stool [stu:l] **1** *n* **(a)** tabouret *m*; (*folding*) pliant *m*; (*foot*~) tabouret, marchepied† *m*. (*fig*) **to fall between two** ~**s** s'asseoir entre deux chaises, se retrouver le bec dans l'eau*; *V* **music, piano** *etc*.
(b) (*fig*) [*window*] rebord *m*; (*Med*) selle *f*; (*Bot*) pied *m* (*de plante*), plante *f* mère.
2 *cpd*: **stool pigeon*** indicateur *m*, -trice *f*, mouchard(e) *m(f)*; (*in prison*) mouton *m*.
stoop¹ [stu:p] **1** *n*: **to have a** ~ avoir le dos voûté *or* rond.
2 *vi* **(a)** (*state*) avoir le dos voûté *or* rond, être voûté.
(b) (*also* ~ **down**) se baisser, se pencher, se courber; (*fig*) s'abaisser (*to sth* jusqu'à qch, *to do, to doing* jusqu'à faire). (*fig*) **he would** ~ **to anything** il est prêt à toutes les bassesses.
3 *vt* baisser, courber, incliner.
stoop² [stu:p] *n* (*US*) véranda *f*.
stooping ['stu:pɪŋ] *adj person* penché, courbé; *back* voûté.
stop [stɒp] **1** *n* **(a)** (*halt*) arrêt *m*; (*short stay*) halte *f*. **we had a** ~ **of a few days in Arles** nous avons fait une halte de quelques jours à Arles; **we had a** ~ **for coffee** nous avons fait une pause café*; **they worked for 6 hours without a** ~ ils ont travaillé 6 heures d'affilée *or* sans discontinuer; **a 5-minute** ~, **5 minutes'** ~ 5 minutes d'arrêt; **to be at a** ~ [*traffic, vehicle*] être à l'arrêt; [*work, progress, production*] s'être arrêté, avoir cessé; **to come to a** ~ [*traffic, vehicle*] s'arrêter; [*work, progress, production*] cesser; **to bring to a** ~ *traffic, vehicle* arrêter; *work, progress, production* faire cesser; **to make a** ~ [*bus, train*] s'arrêter; [*plane, ship*] faire escale; **to put a** ~ **to sth** mettre un terme à qch; **I'll put a** ~ **to all that!** je vais mettre un terme *or* le holà à tout ça!
(b) (*stopping place*) [*bus, train*] arrêt *m*; [*plane, ship*] escale *f*; *V* **bus, request** *etc*.
(c) (*Mus*) [*flute, trumpet etc*] clef *f or* clé *f*; [*organ*] jeu *m*. (*fig*) **to pull out all the** ~**s** faire un suprême effort, remuer ciel et terre (*to do* pour faire).
(d) (*Punctuation*) point *m*; (*in telegrams*) stop *m*; *V also* **full**.
(e) (*device*) (*on drawer, window*) taquet *m*; (*on typewriter: also* **margin** ~) margeur *m*; (*Tech*) mentonnet *m*.
(f) (*Ling*) occlusive *f*.
(g) (*Phot*) diaphragme *m*.
2 *cpd button, lever, signal* d'arrêt; (*Phot*) *bath, solution* de rinçage. (*US*) **stop-and-go** = **stop-go**; **stopcock** robinet *m* d'arrêt; (*Ling*) **stop consonant** (consonne *f*) occlusive *f*; **stopgap** (*n*) bouche-trou *m*; (*adj*) *measure, solution* intérimaire; (*gen, Econ*) **a period of stop-go** une période d'activité intense suivie de relâchement; **stoplight** (*traffic light*) feu *m* rouge; (*brake light*) stop *m*; **stop-off** arrêt *m*, courte halte; (*St Ex*) **stop order** ordre *m* stop; **stopover** halte *f*; (*Aviat, Rail etc*) **stopover ticket** billet *m* avec faculté d'arrêt; (*Brit Press*) **stop-press** (*news*) nouvelles *fpl* de dernière heure; (*as heading*) 'dernière heure'; (*Aut*) **stop sign** (panneau *m*) stop *m*; **stop street** rue *f* non prioritaire; **stopwatch** chronomètre *m*.
3 *vt* **(a)** (*block*) *hole, pipe* boucher, obturer; (*accidentally*) boucher, bloquer; *leak* boucher, colmater; *jar, bottle* boucher; *tooth* plomber. **to** ~ **one's ears** se boucher les oreilles; (*fig*) **to** ~ **one's ears to sth** rester sourd à qch; **to** ~ **a gap** (*lit*) boucher un trou *or* un interstice; (*fig*) combler une lacune (*V also* **stop 2**); **to** ~ **the way** barrer le chemin.
(b) (*halt*) *person, vehicle, ball, machine, process* arrêter; *traffic* arrêter, interrompre; *progress* interrompre; *light* empêcher de passer; *pain, worry, enjoyment* mettre fin à; (*fig: Sport etc: beat*) battre. **to** ~ **sb short** (*lit*) arrêter qn net *or* brusquement; (*fig: silence*) couper la parole à qn; **to** ~ **sb in his tracks** (*lit*) arrêter qn net *or* brusquement; (*fig*) couper qn dans son élan; **he** ~**ped a bullet*** il a reçu une balle; **the walls** ~ **some of the noise** les murs arrêtent *or* étouffent *or* absorbent une partie du bruit.
(c) (*cease*) arrêter, cesser (*doing* de faire). ~ **it!** assez!, ça suffit!; ~ **that noise!** assez de bruit!; **to** ~ **work** arrêter *or* cesser de travailler, cesser le travail.
(d) (*interrupt*) *activity, building, production* interrompre, arrêter; (*suspend*) suspendre; (*Boxing*) *fight* suspendre; *allowance, leave, privileges* supprimer; *wages* retenir; *gas, electricity, water supply* couper. **rain** ~**ped play** la pluie a interrompu *or* arrêté la partie; **they** ~**ped £2 out of his wages** ils ont retenu 2 livres sur son salaire; **to** ~ **one's subscription** résilier son abonnement; **to** ~ **(payment on) a cheque** faire opposition au paiement d'un chèque; [*bank*] **to** ~ **payment** suspendre ses paiements; **he** ~**ped the milk for a week** il a fait interrompre *or* il a annulé la livraison du lait pendant une semaine.
(e) (*prevent*) empêcher (*sb's doing, sb from doing* qn de faire, *sth happening, sth from happening* que qch (n')arrive (*subj*)). **there's nothing to** ~ **you** rien ne vous empêche; **he** ~**ped the house (from) being sold** il a empêché que la maison (ne) soit vendue *or* la vente de la maison.
(f) (*Mus*) *string* presser; [*trumpet etc*] *hole* boucher, mettre le doigt sur.
4 *vi* **(a)** [*person, vehicle, machine, clock, sb's heart*] s'arrêter. ~ **thief!** au voleur!; (*in work etc*) **you can** ~ **now** vous pouvez (vous) arrêter maintenant; (*in lesson etc*) **we'll** ~ **here for today** nous nous arrêterons *or* nous nous en tiendrons là pour aujourd'hui; **he** ~**ped (dead) in his tracks** il s'est arrêté net *or* pile*; **he** ~**ped in mid sentence** il s'est arrêté au beau milieu d'une phrase; (*fig*) **he never knows where to** ~ il ne sait pas s'arrêter; (*fig*) **he will** ~ **at nothing** il est prêt à tout, il ne recule devant rien (*to do* pour faire); *V* **dead, short** *etc*.
(b) [*supplies, production, process, music*] s'arrêter, cesser; [*attack, pain, worry, enjoyment, custom*] cesser; [*allowance, privileges*] être supprimé; [*play, programme, concert*] finir, se terminer; [*conversation, discussion, struggle*] cesser, se terminer.
(c) (*) (*remain*) rester; (*live temporarily*) loger. ~ **where you are!** restez là où vous êtes!; **I'm** ~**ping with my aunt** je loge chez ma tante.
stop away* *vi*: **he stopped away for 3 years** il est resté 3 ans sans revenir *or* 3 ans absent; **he stopped away from the meeting** il n'est pas allé (*or* venu) à la réunion, il s'est tenu à l'écart de la réunion.
stop behind* *vi* rester en arrière *or* à la fin.
stop by* *vi* s'arrêter en passant.

stop down* *vi* (*bending*) rester baissé; (*lying down*) rester couché; (*under water*) rester sous l'eau.
stop in* *vi* **(a)** (*at home*) rester à la maison *or* chez soi, ne pas sortir.
(b) = **stop by***.
stop off 1 *vi* s'arrêter; (*on journey*) s'arrêter, faire une courte halte, interrompre son voyage.
2 stop-off *n V* **stop 2.**
stop out* *vi* rester dehors, ne pas rentrer. **he always stops out late on Fridays** il rentre toujours tard le vendredi.
stop over 1 *vi* s'arrêter (un *or* plusieurs jour(s)), faire une halte.
2 stopover *n, adj V* **stop 2.**
stop up 1 *vi* (*Brit**) ne pas se coucher, rester debout. **don't stop up for me** ne m'attendez pas pour aller vous coucher.
2 *vt sep hole, pipe* boucher; (*accidentally*) boucher, bloquer, obstruer; *jar, bottle* boucher. **my nose is stopped up** j'ai le nez bouché.
stoppage ['stɒpɪdʒ] *n* **(a)** (*in traffic, work, game*) arrêt *m*, interruption *f*, suspension *f*; (*strike*) grève *f*; *[leave, wages, payment]* suspension; (*deduction*) retenue *f*. **(b)** (*blockage*) obstruction *f*, engorgement *m*; (*Med*) occlusion *f*.
stopper ['stɒpə^{r}] **1** *n [bottle, jar]* bouchon *m*; *[bath, basin]* bouchon, bonde *f*. **to take the ~ out of a bottle** déboucher une bouteille; (*fig*) **to put a ~ on sth*** mettre une terme *or* le holà à qch; *V* **conversation. 2** *vt* boucher.
stopping ['stɒpɪŋ] **1** *n* **(a)** (*U: halting etc: V* **stop 3b, 3c, 3d**) arrêt *m*, interruption *f*; suspension *f*; cessation *f*; *[cheque]* arrêt de paiement; (*Mus*) *V* **double.**
(b) (*U: blocking: V* **stop 3a**) obturation *f*, bouchage *m*.
(c) *[tooth]* plombage *m*.
2 *cpd*: (*lay-by etc*) **stopping place** parking *m*; **we were looking for a stopping place** nous cherchions un coin où nous arrêter; **stopping train** (train *m*) omnibus *m*.
storage ['stɔːrɪdʒ] **1** *n* (*U*) *[goods, fuel, food]* entreposage *m*, emmagasinage *m*; *[heat, electricity]* accumulation *f*; *[documents]* conservation *f*; (*Computers*) mise *f* en réserve. **to put in(to) ~** entreposer, emmagasiner; *V* **cold.**
2 *cpd capacity, problems* d'entreposage, d'emmagasinage; *charges* de magasinage. **storage battery** accumulateur *m*, accu* *m*; **(electric) storage heater** radiateur *m* électrique par accumulation; **storage space** espace *m* de rangement; **storage tank** *[oil etc]* réservoir *m* d'emmagasinage; *[rainwater]* citerne *f*.
store [stɔː^{r}] **1** *n* **(a)** (*supply, stock, accumulation*) provision *f*, réserve *f*, stock *m*; *[learning, information]* fonds *m*. **to get in** *or* **lay in a ~ of sth** faire provision de qch; **to keep a ~ of sth** avoir une provision de qch, stocker qch; (*fig*) **to set great ~/little ~ by sth** faire grand cas/peu de cas de qch, attacher du prix/peu de prix à qch.
(b) (*pl: supplies*) **~s** provisions *fpl*; **to take on** *or* **lay in ~s** s'approvisionner, faire des provisions.
(c) (*depot, warehouse*) entrepôt *m*; (*furniture ~*) garde-meuble *m*; (*in office, factory etc: also* **~s**) réserve *f*, (*larger*) service *m* des approvisionnements. **ammunition ~** dépôt *m* de munitions; **to put in(to) ~** *goods etc* entreposer; *furniture* mettre au garde-meuble; **I am keeping this in ~ for winter** je garde cela en réserve pour l'hiver; (*fig*) **I've got a surprise in ~ for you** j'ai une surprise en réserve pour vous, je vous réserve une surprise; (*fig*) **what does the future hold** *or* **have in ~ for him?** que lui réserve l'avenir?
(d) (*shop*) magasin *m*, commerce *m*; (*large*) grand magasin; (*small*) boutique *f*. **book ~** magasin de livres, librairie *f*; *V* **chain, department, general** *etc*.
2 *cpd item, line* de série; *clothes* de confection *or* de série; *cake* du commerce. **storehouse** entrepôt *m*, magasin *m*; (*fig: of information etc*) mine *f*; **storekeeper** magasinier *m*; (*esp US: shopkeeper*) commerçant(e) *m(f)*; **storeroom** réserve *f*, magasin *m*.
3 *vt* **(a)** (*keep in reserve, collect: also* **~ up**) *food, fuel, goods* mettre en réserve; *documents* conserver; *electricity, heat* emmagasiner; (*fig: in one's mind*) *facts, information* noter *or* enregistrer dans sa mémoire. **this cellar can ~ enough coal for the winter** cette cave peut contenir assez de charbon pour passer l'hiver.
(b) (*place in ~: also* **~ away**) *food, fuel, goods* emmagasiner, entreposer; *one's furniture* mettre au garde-meuble; *crops* mettre en grange, engranger; (*Computers*) mettre en réserve. **he ~d the information (away)** (*in filing system etc*) il rangea *or* classa le renseignement; (*in his mind*) il nota le renseignement; **I've got the camping things ~d (away) till we need them** j'ai rangé *or* mis de côté les affaires de camping en attendant que nous en ayons besoin.
(c) (*equip, supply*) *larder etc* approvisionner, pourvoir, munir (*with* de); *mind, memory* meubler (*with* de).
4 *vi*: **these apples ~ well/badly** ces pommes se conservent bien/mal.
store away *vt sep V* **store 3b.**
store up *vt sep V* **store 3a.**
storey, (*US*) **story**[2] ['stɔːrɪ] *n* étage *m*. **on the 3rd ~** au 3e (étage); **a 4-~(ed)** *or* (*US*) **4-storied building** un bâtiment à *or* de 4 étages.
-storeyed, (*US*) **-storied** ['stɔːrɪd] *adj ending in cpds V* **storey.**
stork [stɔːk] *n* cigogne *f*.
storm [stɔːm] **1** *n* **(a)** tempête *f*; (*thunderstorm*) orage *m*; (*on Beaufort scale*) violente tempête. **~ of rain/snow** tempête de pluie/de neige; **magnetic ~** orage magnétique; (*Brit fig*) **it was a ~ in a teacup** c'était une tempête dans un verre d'eau; *V* **dust, hail**[1], **sand** *etc*.
(b) (*fig*) *[arrows, missiles]* pluie *f*, grêle *f*; *[insults, abuse]* torrent *m*; *[cheers, protests, applause, indignation]* tempête *f*. **there was a political ~** les passions politiques se sont déchaînées; **his speech caused** *or* **raised quite a ~** son discours a provoqué une véritable tempête *or* un ouragan; **to bring a ~ about one's ears** soulever un tollé (général); **a period of ~ and stress** une période très orageuse *or* très tourmentée.
(c) (*Mil*) **to take by ~** prendre *or* emporter d'assaut; (*fig*) **the play took London by ~** la pièce a obtenu un succès foudroyant *or* fulgurant à Londres; **he took her by ~** il a eu un succès foudroyant *or* fulgurant auprès d'elle, elle a eu le coup de foudre pour lui.
2 *cpd signal, warning* de tempête. **storm belt** zone *f* des tempêtes; **stormbound** bloqué par la tempête; (*US*) **storm cellar** abri *m* tempête, abri cyclonique; **storm centre** centre *m* de dépression; (*fig*) centre de l'agitation; **storm cloud** nuage orageux; (*fig*) nuage noir *or* menaçant; **storm cone** cône *m* de tempête; **storm door** double porte *f* (*à l'extérieur*); **storm drain** bouche *f* d'égout; **storm lantern** lampe-tempête *f*, lanterne-tempête *f*; **storm-lashed** battu par l'orage *or* la tempête; (*Orn, fig*) **storm petrel = stormy petrel** (*V* **stormy**); **stormproof** à l'épreuve de la tempête; **storm-tossed** ballotté *or* battu par la tempête; (*Mil*) **storm trooper** membre *m* des sections d'assaut nazies; **storm troops** troupes *fpl* d'assaut; **storm window** double fenêtre *f* (*à l'extérieur*).
3 *vt* (*Mil*) prendre *or* emporter d'assaut. (*fig*) **angry ratepayers ~ed the town hall** les contribuables en colère ont pris d'assaut *or* ont envahi la mairie.
4 *vi [wind]* souffler en tempête, faire rage; *[rain]* tomber à torrents, faire rage; (*fig*) *[person]* fulminer (*with rage etc* de colère *etc*). **to ~ at sb** tempêter *or* fulminer contre qn; **to ~ (one's way) in/out** *etc* entrer/sortir *etc* comme un ouragan.
stormy ['stɔːmɪ] *adj weather, sky* orageux; *sea* houleux, démonté; (*fig*) *discussion, meeting* houleux, orageux; *glance* noir, fulminant; *temperament, person* violent, emporté. **~ petrel** (*Orn*) pétrel *m*; (*fig*) enfant *mf* terrible.
story[1] ['stɔːrɪ] **1** *n* **(a)** (*account*) histoire *f*. **it's a long ~** c'est toute une histoire, c'est une longue histoire; **that's not the whole** *or* **full ~** mais ce n'est pas tout; **according to your ~** d'après ce que vous dites, selon vous; **I've heard his ~** j'ai entendu sa version des faits; (*fig*) **it's quite another ~** *or* **a very different ~** c'est une tout autre histoire; (*fig*) **it's the same old ~** c'est toujours la même histoire *or* la même chanson; (*fig*) **these scars tell their own ~** ces cicatrices parlent d'elles-mêmes *or* en disent long; (*fig hum*) **that's the ~ of my life!** c'est l'histoire de ma vie!
(b) (*tale*) histoire *f*, conte *m*; (*legend*) histoire, légende *f*; (*Literat*) histoire, récit *m*; (*short*) nouvelle *f*; (*anecdote, joke*) histoire, anecdote *f*. **there's an interesting ~ attached to that** on raconte une histoire intéressante à ce sujet; **so the ~ goes** d'après ce que l'on raconte, d'après les on-dit; **he writes stories** il écrit des histoires *or* des nouvelles; **she told the children a ~** elle a raconté une histoire aux enfants; **do you know the ~ about ...?** connaissez-vous l'histoire de ...?; **what a ~ this house could tell!** que de choses cette maison pourrait nous (*or* vous *etc*) raconter!; *V* **bedtime, fairy, short** *etc*.
(c) (*Cine, Literat, Theat etc: plot: also* **~ line**) action *f*, intrigue *f*, scénario *m*. **the ~ of the play is taken from his book** l'action *or* l'intrigue *or* le scénario de la pièce est emprunté(e) à son livre; **he did the ~ for the film** il a écrit le scénario du film.
(d) (*Press, Rad, TV*) (*article*) article *m*; (*event*) nouvelle *f*. **he was sent to cover the ~ of the refugees** on l'a envoyé faire un reportage sur les réfugiés; **they daren't print that ~** ils n'osent pas publier cette nouvelle.
(e) (** fig*) histoire *f*. **to tell stories** raconter des histoires.
2 *cpd*: **storybook** (*n*) livre *m* de contes *or* d'histoires; (*adj: fig*) *situation, love affair* de roman *or* de livre d'histoires; **a meeting with a storybook ending** une rencontre qui se termine comme dans les romans; **story line** *V* **1c**; **storyteller** conteur *m*, -euse *f*; (**: fibber*) menteur *m*, -euse *f*; **story-writer** nouvelliste *mf*.
story[2] ['stɔːrɪ] *n* (*US*) = **storey.**
stoup [stuːp] *n* (*Rel*) bénitier *m*; (††: *tankard*) pichet *m*.
stout [staʊt] **1** *adj* **(a)** (*fat*) gros (*f* grosse), corpulent. **to get** *or* **grow ~** prendre de l'embonpoint.
(b) (*strong*) *stick* solide; *coat* épais (*f* -aisse), solide; *shoes* robuste, solide; *horse* vigoureux, puissant; *resistance, defence* intrépide, énergique; *soldier* vaillant, intrépide. **with ~ hearts** vaillamment; **he is a ~ fellow*** c'est un brave type*, on peut compter sur lui.
2 *cpd:* **stout-hearted** vaillant, intrépide.
3 *n* (*beer*) stout *m*, bière brune (*épaisse et forte*).
stoutly ['staʊtlɪ] *adv fight, defend, resist* vaillamment, intrépidement; *deny* catégoriquement; *believe, maintain* dur comme fer. **~ built** *hut etc* solidement bâti; *person* (*strong*) costaud, bien bâti *or* charpenté, de forte carrure; (*fat*) corpulent, gros (*f* grosse).
stoutness ['staʊtnɪs] *n* (*V* **stout**) corpulence *f*, embonpoint *m*; solidité *f*, robustesse *f*; vigueur *f*; puissance *f*; intrépidité *f*; vaillance *f*.
stove[1] [stəʊv] **1** *n* **(a)** (*heater*) poêle *m*. **(b)** (*cooker*) (*solid fuel*) fourneau *m*; (*gas, electricity*) cuisinière *f*; (*small*) réchaud *m*. **(c)** (*Ind, Tech*) four *m*, étuve *f*. **2** *cpd:* (*lit, also fig: hat*) **stovepipe** tuyau *m* de poêle.
stove[2] [stəʊv] *pret, ptp of* **stave.**
stow [stəʊ] **1** *vt* ranger, mettre; (*out of sight: also* **~ away**) faire disparaître, cacher; (*Naut*) *cargo* arrimer; (*also* **~ away**) *ropes, tarpaulins etc* ranger. **where can I ~ this?** où puis-je déposer ceci?; **~ it!‡** la ferme!‡, ferme-la!‡
2 *cpd:* **stowaway** passager clandestin, passagère clandestine.
stow away 1 *vi* voyager clandestinement.

2 *vt sep* (*put away*) ranger, déposer, mettre; (*put in its place*) ranger, placer; (*put out of sight*) faire disparaître, cacher; (*:fig*) *meal, food* enfourner*; *V also* **stow 1**.

3 stowaway *n V* **stow 2**.

stowage ['stəʊɪdʒ] *n* (*Naut*) (*action*) arrimage *m*; (*space*) espace *m* utile; (*costs*) frais *mpl* d'arrimage.

strabismus [strə'bɪzməs] *n* strabisme *m*.

strabotomy [strə'bɒtəmɪ] *n* strabotomie *f*.

straddle ['strædl] **1** *vt horse, cycle* enfourcher; *chair* se mettre à califourchon *or* à cheval sur; *fence, ditch* enjamber. **to be straddling sth** être à califourchon *or* à cheval sur qch; **the village ~s the border** le village est à cheval sur la frontière; **the enemy positions ~d the river** l'ennemi avait pris position des deux côtés de la rivière; (*Mil: gunnery*) **to ~ a target** encadrer un objectif; (*US fig*) **to ~ an issue** nager entre deux eaux, ménager la chèvre et le chou.

2 *vi* être à califourchon; (*US* fig*) nager entre deux eaux, ménager la chèvre et le chou. **straddling legs** jambes écartées.

strafe* [strɑːf] *vt* (*Mil etc*) (*with machine guns*) mitrailler; (*with shellfire, bombs*) bombarder, marmiter; (*fig*) (*punish*) punir; (*reprimand*) semoncer vertement.

straggle ['strægl] *vi* **(a)** *[vines, plants]* pousser tout en longueur, pousser au hasard; *[hair]* être *or* retomber en désordre; *[houses, trees etc]* être épars *or* disséminés; *[village etc]* s'étendre en longueur. **the branches ~d along the wall** les branches tortueuses grimpaient le long du mur; **the village ~s for miles along the road** les maisons du village s'égrènent *or* le village s'étend sur des kilomètres le long de la route; **her hair was straggling over her face** ses cheveux rebelles *or* des mèches folles retombaient en désordre sur son visage.

(b) *[people, cars, planes]* **to ~ in/out** *etc* entrer/sortir *etc* les uns après les autres *or* par petits groupes (détachés) *or* petit à petit.

straggle away, straggle off *vi* se débander *or* se disperser petit à petit.

straggler ['strægləʳ] *n* (*person*) traînard(e) *m(f)* (*also Mil*); (*plane etc*) avion *etc* isolé (qui traîne derrière les autres); (*Bot*) branche gourmande, gourmand *m*.

straggling ['stræglɪŋ] *adj*, **straggly** ['stræglɪ] *adj* qui traîne en longueur; *plant* (qui pousse) tout en longueur; *village* tout en longueur. **~ hair** cheveux fins rebelles *or* en désordre *or* décoiffés; **a ~ row of houses** un rang de maisons disséminées; **a long ~ line** une longue ligne irrégulière.

straight [streɪt] **1** *adj* **(a)** (*not curved, twisted etc*) *line, stick, limb, edge* droit; *road* droit, rectiligne; *course, route* direct, en ligne droite; *tree, tower* droit, vertical; *chair* à dossier droit; *hair* raide; *stance, posture, back* bien droit; (*Geom*) *angle* plat; *picture* d'aplomb, droit; *rug, tablecloth* droit; *hat* droit, d'aplomb, bien mis. **to put** *or* **set ~** *picture* redresser, remettre d'aplomb; *hat, tie* ajuster; **the picture/your tie isn't ~** le tableau/votre cravate est de travers; **your hem isn't ~** votre ourlet n'est pas rond; (*fig*) **to keep a ~ face** garder son sérieux (*V also* **4**).

(b) (*in order*) *room, house, books, one's affairs, accounts* en ordre. **to put** *or* **set** *or* **get ~** *house, room, books* mettre en ordre, mettre de l'ordre dans; *one's affairs, accounts* mettre de l'ordre dans; (*fig*) **let's get this ~** entendons-nous bien sur ce point; **to put** *or* **set sb ~ about sth** éclairer qn sur qch; **to keep sb ~ about sth** empêcher qn de se tromper sur qch; **to put** *or* **set o.s. ~ with sb** faire en sorte de ne pas être en reste avec qn; **now we're ~** maintenant on est quitte; *V* **record**.

(c) (*direct, frank*) *person* honnête, franc (*f* franche), loyal; *dealing* loyal, régulier; *answer, question* franc; *look* franc, droit; *denial, refusal* net (*f* nette), catégorique. **to give sb a ~ look** regarder qn droit dans les yeux; **~ speaking, ~ talking** franc-parler *m*; **to play a ~ game** agir loyalement, jouer franc jeu; (*Racing, St Ex etc*) **~ tip** tuyau* *m* de bonne source.

(d) (*plain, uncomplicated, undiluted*) *whisky etc* sec, sans eau; (*Theat*) *part, actor* sérieux. **a ~ play** une pièce de théâtre proprement dite; (*Pol*) **a ~ fight** une campagne électorale où ne s'affrontent que deux candidats; (*US Pol*) **to vote a ~ ticket** voter le programme du parti sans modification; (*Cards*) **~ flush** quinte *f* flush.

(e) (*:*) (*not homosexual*) qui n'est pas homosexuel; (*not a drug addict*) qui ne se drogue pas; (*not a criminal*) qui n'est pas véreux.

2 *n* **(a)** *[racecourse, railway line, river etc]* **the ~** la ligne droite; (*fig*) **now we're in the ~** ça va aller comme sur des roulettes (à partir de) maintenant.

(b) to cut sth on the ~ couper qch (de) droit fil; **out of the ~** de travers, en biais.

(c) (*fig*) **to follow** *or* **keep to the ~ and narrow** rester dans le droit chemin.

3 *adv* **(a)** (*in a ~ line*) *walk, drive, fly* droit, en ligne droite; *grow, stand* (bien) droit; *sit* correctement. **he came ~ at me** il est venu (tout) droit vers moi; **to shoot ~** tirer juste; **I can't see ~*** j'y vois trouble*; **the cork shot ~ up in the air** le bouchon est parti droit en l'air; **hold yourself ~** redressez-vous, tenez-vous droit; **~ above us** juste au-dessus de nous; **~ across from the house** juste en face de la maison; **to go ~ ahead** *or* **~ on** aller tout droit; **he looked ~ ahead** il a regardé droit devant lui; **to look sb ~ in the face** *or* **the eye** regarder qn bien en face *or* droit dans les yeux; **the bullet went ~ through his chest** la balle lui a traversé la poitrine de part en part.

(b) (*directly*) tout droit, tout de suite, sur-le-champ, aussitôt. **he went ~ to London** il est allé directement *or* tout droit à Londres; **go ~ to bed** va droit au lit, va tout de suite te coucher; **~ after this** tout de suite après; **~ away, ~ off** tout de suite, sur-le-champ; **~ out, ~ off** (*without hesitation*) sans hésiter; (*without beating about the bush*) sans ambages, sans mâcher ses mots; **he read 'Hamlet' ~ off** il a lu 'Hamlet' d'une seule traite; **to come ~ to the point** en venir droit au fait; (*fig*) **~ from the horse's mouth** de source sûre; (*fig*) **I let him have it ~ from the shoulder** je le lui ai dit carrément *or* sans mâcher mes mots *or* sans ambages, je le lui ai dit tout cru; **I'm telling you ~, I'm giving it to you ~*** je vous le dis tout net; **give it to me ~*** n'y va pas par quatre chemins*.

(c) (*phrases*) **to drink one's whisky ~** boire son whisky sec *or* sans eau; (*Theat*) **he played the role ~** il a joué le rôle de façon classique *or* sans modification; *[criminal]* **he's been going ~ for a year now** voilà un an qu'il est resté dans le droit chemin *or* qu'il vit honnêtement.

4 *cpd*: **straight-cut tobacco** tabac coupé dans la longueur de la feuille; **straightedge** règle large et plate, limande *f* (*Carpentry*); **straight-faced** en gardant son (*or* mon *etc*) sérieux; **straightforward** *V* **straightforward**; **straight-line** *depreciation* constant; (*Theat*) **straight man** comparse *m*, faire-valoir *m*; **straight-out*** *answer, denial, refusal* net (*f* nette), catégorique; *supporter, enthusiast, communist* sans réserve; *liar, thief* fieffé (*before n*); **straightway**†† tout de suite, sur-le-champ.

straighten ['streɪtn] **1** *vt wire, nail* redresser, défausser; *road* refaire en éliminant les tournants; *hair* défriser, aplatir; *tie, hat* ajuster; *picture* redresser, remettre d'aplomb; *room* mettre de l'ordre dans, mettre en ordre; *papers* ranger. **to ~ one's back** *or* **shoulders** se redresser, se tenir droit; **to ~ the hem of a skirt** arrondir une jupe.

2 *vi* (*also* **~ out**) *[road etc]* devenir droit; (*also* **~ out, ~ up**) *[growing plant etc]* pousser droit; (*also* **~ up**) *[person]* se redresser.

straighten out 1 *vi V* **straighten 2**.

2 *vt sep wire, nail* redresser, défausser; *road* refaire en éliminant les tournants; (*fig*) *situation* débrouiller; *problem* résoudre; *one's ideas* mettre de l'ordre dans, débrouiller. **he managed to straighten things out*** il a réussi à arranger les choses; **I'm trying to straighten out how much I owe him*** j'essaie de démêler combien je lui dois; **to straighten sb out**: remettre qn dans la bonne voie; **I'll soon straighten him out!**: je vais aller le remettre à sa place!, je vais lui apprendre!

straighten up 1 *vi* **(a)** *V* **straighten 2**.

(b) (*tidy up*) mettre de l'ordre, ranger.

2 *vt sep room, books, papers* ranger, mettre de l'ordre dans.

straightforward [,streɪt'fɔːwəd] *adj* (*frank*) honnête, franc (*f* franche); (*plain-spoken*) franc, direct; (*simple*) simple. **it's very ~** c'est tout ce qu'il y a de plus simple.

straightforwardly [,streɪt'fɔːwədlɪ] *adv answer* franchement, sans détour; *behave* avec droiture, honnêtement. **everything went quite ~** tout s'est passé sans anicroche.

straightforwardness [,streɪt'fɔːwədnɪs] *n* (*V* **straightforward**) honnêteté *f*, franchise *f*; simplicité *f*.

strain[1] [streɪn] **1** *n* **(a)** (*Tech etc*) tension *f*, effort *m*, pression *f*, traction *f*. **the ~ on the rope** la tension de la corde, l'effort *m or* la force exercé(e) sur la corde; **it broke under the ~** cela s'est rompu sous la tension *or* sous l'effort de traction; **that puts a great ~ on the beam** cela exerce une forte pression *or* traction sur la poutre; **to take the ~ off sth** soulager qch, diminuer la tension de qch; **can you take some of the ~?** pouvez-vous nous (*or* les *etc*) aider à soutenir ceci?; (*fig*) **it put a great ~ on their friendship** cela a mis leur amitié à rude épreuve; **it was a ~ on the economy** cela grevait l'économie; **it was a ~ on his purse** cela faisait mal à son portefeuille, cela grevait son budget; *V* **breaking, stand**.

(b) (*physical*) effort *m* (physique); (*mental*) tension nerveuse; (*overwork*) surmenage *m*; (*tiredness*) fatigue *f*. **the ~(s) of city life** la tension de la vie urbaine; **the ~ of 6 hours at the wheel** la fatigue nerveuse engendrée par 6 heures passées au volant; **listening for 3 hours is a ~** écouter pendant 3 heures demande un grand effort; **all the ~ and struggle of bringing up the family** toutes les tensions et les soucis qui sont le lot du chef de famille; **the ~ of climbing the stairs** l'effort requis pour monter l'escalier; **he has been under a great deal of ~** ses nerfs ont été mis à rude épreuve; **the situation put a great ~ on him** *or* **put him under a great ~** la situation l'a mis dans un état de tension nerveuse; *V* **stress**.

(c) (*Med: sprain*) entorse *f*, foulure *f*; *V* **eye** *etc*.

(d) ~s (*Mus*) accords *mpl*, accents *mpl*; (*Poetry*) accents, chant *m*; **to the ~s of the 'London March'** aux accents de la 'Marche Londonienne'.

2 *vt* **(a)** *rope, beam* tendre fortement *or* excessivement; (*Med*) *muscle* froisser, claquer; *arm, ankle* fouler; (*fig*) *friendship, relationship, marriage* mettre à l'épreuve; *resources, savings, budget, the economy* grever; *meaning* forcer; *word* forcer le sens de; *sb's patience* mettre à l'épreuve; *one's authority* outrepasser, excéder. (*Med*) **to ~ one's back** se donner un tour de reins; **to ~ one's heart** se fatiguer le cœur; **to ~ one's shoulder** se claquer un muscle dans l'épaule; **to ~ one's voice** forcer sa voix; **to ~ one's eyes** s'abîmer *or* se fatiguer les yeux; **he ~ed his eyes to make out what it was** il plissa les yeux pour mieux distinguer ce que c'était; **to ~ one's ears to hear sth** tendre l'oreille pour entendre qch; **to ~ every nerve to do** fournir un effort intense pour faire; **to ~ o.s.** (*physically*) faire un faux mouvement; (*mentally*) se surmener; (*iro*) **don't ~ yourself!** surtout ne te fatigue pas!

(b) (†† *or liter*) **to ~ sb to o.s.** *or* **one's heart** serrer qn contre son cœur, étreindre qn.

(c) (*filter*) *liquid* passer, filtrer; *soup, gravy* passer; *vegetables* (*free*) égoutter.

3 *vi*: **to ~ to do** (*physically*) peiner pour faire, fournir un gros effort pour faire; (*mentally*) s'efforcer de faire; **to ~ at sth** (*pushing/pulling*) pousser/tirer qch de toutes ses forces; (*fig: jib at*) renâcler à qch; (*Prov*) **to ~ at a gnat (and swallow a**

camel) faire une histoire pour une vétille et passer sur une énormité; (*fig*) to ~ after sth faire un grand effort pour obtenir qch; to ~ under a weight ployer sous un poids.
strain off *vt sep liquid* vider.
strain² [streɪn] *n* (*breed, lineage*) race *f*, lignée *f*; *[animal etc]* race *f*; *[virus]* souche *f*; (*tendency, streak*) tendance *f*. there is a ~ of madness in the family il y a dans la famille des tendances à *or* une prédisposition à la folie; (*fig*) there was a lot more in the same ~ il y en avait encore beaucoup du même genre; he continued in this ~ il a continué sur ce ton *or* dans ce sens.
strained [streɪnd] *adj* (a) *arm, ankle* foulé; *muscle* froissé, claqué; *eyes* fatigué; *voice* forcé; *smile, laugh, cough* forcé, contraint; *look* contraint; *relations, atmosphere, nerves* tendu; *style* affecté. he has a ~ shoulder/back il s'est claqué un muscle dans l'épaule/le dos.
(b) *soup, gravy* passé; *vegetables* égoutté; *baby food* en purée.
strainer ['streɪnəʳ] *n* (*Culin*) passoire *f*; (*Tech*) épurateur *m*.
strait [streɪt] 1 *n* (a) (*Geog: also* ~s) détroit *m*. the S~s of Gibraltar le détroit de Gibraltar; the S~s of Dover le Pas de Calais.
(b) (*fig*) ~s situation *f* difficile; to be in financial ~s avoir des ennuis d'argent; *V* dire.
2 *adj* (††) étroit.
3 *cpd*: strait jacket camisole *f* de force; strait-laced collet monté *inv*.
straitened ['streɪtnd] *adj*: in ~ circumstances dans la gêne.
strand¹ [strænd] 1 *n* (*liter: shore*) grève *f*, rivage *m*, rive *f*.
2 *vt ship* échouer; (*also* to leave ~ed) *person* laisser en rade *or* en plan. they were (left) ~ed without passports or money ils se sont retrouvés en rade *or* coincés sans passeport ni argent; he took the car and left me ~ed il a pris la voiture et m'a laissé en plan *or* en rade.
strand² [strænd] *n* *[thread, wire]* brin *m*; *[rope]* toron *m*; *[fibrous substance]* fibre *f*; *[pearls]* rang *m*; (*fig: in narrative etc*) fil *m*, enchaînement *m*. a ~ of hair une mèche; (*fig*) the ~s of one's life le fil de sa vie.
strange [streɪndʒ] *adj* (a) (*alien, unknown*) *language, country* inconnu. there were several ~ people there il y avait plusieurs personnes que je ne connaissais pas (*or* qu'il ne connaissait pas *etc*); don't talk to any ~ men n'adresse pas la parole à des inconnus; I never sleep well in a ~ bed je ne dors jamais bien dans un lit autre que le mien.
(b) (*odd, unusual*) étrange, bizarre, insolite, surprenant. it is ~ that il est étrange *or* bizarre *or* surprenant que + *subj*; ~ to say I have never met her chose curieuse *or* chose étrange je ne l'ai jamais rencontrée; ~ as it may seem aussi étrange que cela puisse paraître; I heard a ~ noise j'ai entendu un bruit insolite.
(c) (*unaccustomed*) *work, activity* inaccoutumé. you'll feel rather ~ at first vous vous sentirez un peu dépaysé pour commencer.
strangely ['streɪndʒlɪ] *adv* étrangement, curieusement, bizarrement. ~ enough I have never met her chose curieuse *or* chose étrange je ne l'ai jamais rencontrée.
strangeness ['streɪndʒnɪs] *n* étrangeté *f*, bizarrerie *f*, nouveauté *f*.
stranger ['streɪndʒəʳ] 1 *n* (*unknown*) inconnu(e) *m(f)*; (*from another place*) étranger *m*, -ère *f*. he is a perfect ~ (to me) il m'est totalement inconnu; I'm a ~ here je ne suis pas d'ici; I am a ~ to Paris je ne connais pas Paris; a ~ to politics un novice en matière de politique; (*liter*) he was no ~ to misfortune il connaissait bien le malheur, il avait l'habitude du malheur; you're quite a ~! vous vous faites *or* vous devenez rare!, on ne vous voit plus!
2 *cpd*: (*Brit Parl*) Strangers' Gallery tribune réservée au public.
strangle ['stræŋgl] 1 *vt* étrangler; (*fig*) *free speech* étrangler, museler; *protests* étouffer. ~d *person, voice* étranglé; *sneeze, sob* étouffé, réprimé. 2 *cpd*: to have a stranglehold on (*lit*) tenir à la gorge; (*fig*) tenir à la gorge *or* à sa merci.
strangler ['stræŋgləʳ] *n* étrangleur *m*, -euse *f*.
strangling ['stræŋglɪŋ] *n* (*lit*) strangulation *f*, étranglement *m*; (*fig*) étranglement. there have been several ~s in Boston plusieurs personnes ont été étranglées à Boston.
strangulate ['stræŋgjʊleɪt] *vt* (*Med*) étrangler.
strangulation [ˌstræŋgjʊ'leɪʃən] *n* (*U*) strangulation *f*.
strap [stræp] 1 *n* (*of leather*) lanière *f*, courroie *f*, sangle *f*; (*of cloth*) sangle, bande *f*, courroie; (*on shoe*) lanière; (*on harness etc*) sangle, courroie; (*on suitcase, around book*) sangle, courroie, lanière; (*on garment*) bretelle *f*; (*watch* ~) bracelet *m*; (*for razor*) cuir *m*; (*in bus, tube*) poignée *f* de cuir; (*Scol*) lanière de cuir; (*Tech*) lien *m*. (*Scol*) to give sb the ~ administrer une correction à qn (avec une lanière de cuir).
2 *cpd*: straphang voyager debout (dans le métro *etc*); straphanger voyageur *m*, -euse *f* debout *inv*.
3 *vt* (a) (*tie*) attacher (*sth to sth* qch à qch).
(b) (*also* ~ up) *sb's ribs etc* bander *or* maintenir avec une sangle; *suitcase, books* attacher avec une sangle *or* une courroie.
(c) *child etc* administrer une correction à.
strap down *vt sep* attacher avec une sangle *or* une courroie.
strap in *vt sep object* attacher avec une sangle *or* une courroie; *child in car, pram etc* attacher avec une ceinture de sécurité *or* un harnais. he isn't properly strapped in il est mal attaché, sa ceinture de sécurité *or* son harnais est mal mis(e).
strap on *vt sep object* attacher; *watch* mettre, attacher.
strap up *vt sep* = strap 3b.
strapless ['stræplɪs] *adj dress, bra* sans bretelles.
strapper* ['stræpəʳ] *n* gaillard(e) *m(f)*.
strapping ['stræpɪŋ] *adj* costaud, bien découplé *or* charpenté.
strata ['strɑːtə] *npl of* stratum.
stratagem ['strætɪdʒəm] *n* stratagème *m*.
strategic(al) [strə'tiːdʒɪk(əl)] *adj* stratégique.
strategist ['strætɪdʒɪst] *n* stratège *m*.
strategy ['strætɪdʒɪ] *n* stratégie *f*.
stratification [ˌstrætɪfɪ'keɪʃən] *n* stratification *f*.
stratify ['strætɪfaɪ] *vti* stratifier.
stratocruiser ['strætəʊˌkruːzəʳ] *n* avion *m* stratosphérique.
stratosphere ['strætəʊsfɪəʳ] *n* stratosphère *f*.
stratospheric [ˌstrætəʊs'ferɪk] *adj* stratosphérique.
stratum ['strɑːtəm] *n*, *pl* strata (*Geol*) strate *f*, couche *f*; (*fig*) couche.
straw [strɔː] 1 *n* paille *f*. to drink sth through a ~ boire qch avec une paille; (*fig*) man of ~ homme *m* de paille; (*fig*) to clutch *or* catch *or* grasp at a ~ *or* ~s se raccrocher désespérément à un semblant d'espoir; (*fig*) it's a ~ in the wind c'est une indication des choses à venir; (*fig*) that's the last ~ *or* the ~ that breaks the camel's back c'est la goutte d'eau qui fait déborder le vase; I don't care a ~* je m'en fiche*; *V* draw.
2 *cpd baskets etc* de *or* en paille; *roof* en paille, en chaume. strawberry *V* strawberry; straw-coloured paille *inv*; straw hat chapeau *m* de paille; straw mattress paillasse *f*; (*fig*) straw vote sondage *m* d'opinion, vote *m* d'essai.
strawberry ['strɔːbərɪ] 1 *n* (*fruit*) fraise *f*; (*plant*) fraisier *m*. wild ~ fraise des bois, fraise sauvage.
2 *cpd jam* de fraises; *ice cream* à la fraise; *tart* aux fraises. strawberry bed fraiseraie *f* *or* fraisière *f*; strawberry blonde blond vénitien *inv*; (*Anat*) strawberry mark fraise *f*, envie *f*; strawberry roan rouan vineux.
stray [streɪ] 1 *n* (a) (*dog, cat, etc*) animal errant *or* perdu; (*sheep, cow etc*) animal égaré; (*child*) enfant *mf* perdu(e) *or* abandonné(e). this dog is a ~ c'est un chien perdu *or* errant; *V* waif.
(b) (*Rad*) ~s parasites *mpl*, friture *f*.
2 *adj dog, cat* perdu, errant; *sheep, cow* égaré; *child* perdu, abandonné; (*fig*) *plane, taxi, shot etc* isolé; *thought* inopiné. a few ~ houses quelques maisons isolées *or* éparses; a few ~ cars quelques rares voitures; he was picked up by a ~ motorist il a été pris par un des rares automobilistes.
3 *vi* (*also* ~ away) *[person, animal]* s'égarer; *[thoughts]* vagabonder, errer. (*lit, fig*) to ~ (away) from *village, plan, subject* s'écarter de; *course, route* dévier de; they ~ed into enemy territory ils se sont égarés *or* ont fait fausse route et se sont retrouvés en territoire ennemi; his thoughts ~ed to the coming holidays il se prit à penser aux vacances prochaines.
streak [striːk] 1 *n* (a) (*line, band*) raie *f*, bande *f*; *[ore, mineral]* veine *f*; *[light]* raie, filet *m*; *[blood, paint]* filet. his hair had ~s of grey in it ses cheveux commençaient à grisonner; she had (blond) ~s put in her hair elle s'est fait faire des mèches (blondes); a ~ of cloud across the sky une traînée nuageuse dans le ciel; a ~ of lightning un éclair; he went past like a ~ (of lightning) il est passé comme un éclair.
(b) (*fig: tendency*) tendance(s) *f(pl)*, propension *f*. he has a jealous ~ *or* a ~ of jealousy il a des tendances *or* une propension à la jalousie; she has a ~ of Irish blood elle a une goutte de sang irlandais dans les veines; a ~ of luck/bad luck une période de chance/malchance.
2 *vt* zébrer, strier (*with* de). mirror ~ed with dirt miroir zébré de longues traînées sales; sky ~ed with red ciel strié *or* zébré de bandes rouges; cheeks ~ed with tear-marks joues sillonnées de larmes; clothes ~ed with mud/paint vêtements maculés de longues traînées de boue/de peinture; his hair was ~ed with grey ses cheveux commençaient à grisonner; rock ~ed with quartz roche veinée de quartz; meat ~ed with fat viande persillée.
3 *vi* (a) (*rush*) to ~ in/out/past *etc* entrer/sortir/passer *etc* comme un éclair.
(b) (*: *dash naked*) courir tout nu en public.
streaker* ['striːkəʳ] *n* streaker *m*, -euse *f*.
streaky ['striːkɪ] *adj colour* marbré; *window, mirror* zébré; *rock etc* veiné. (*Culin*) ~ bacon bacon pas trop maigre.
stream [striːm] 1 *n* (a) (*brook*) ruisseau *m*.
(b) (*current*) courant *m*. to go with the ~ (*lit*) suivre le fil de l'eau; (*fig*) suivre le courant *or* le mouvement, faire comme tout le monde; (*lit, fig*) to go against the ~ aller contre le courant *or* à contre-courant; *V* down¹, up.
(c) (*flow*) *[water etc]* flot *m*, jet *m*; *[lava]* flot, torrent *m*; *[blood, light]* flot; *[tears]* torrent, ruisseau *m*; *[cold air etc]* courant *m*; *[oaths, curses, excuses]* flot, torrent, déluge *m*; *[cars, trucks]* flot, succession *f*, défilé ininterrompu; (*Scol*) classe *f* de niveau. a thin ~ of water un mince filet d'eau; the water flowed out in a steady ~ l'eau s'écoulait régulièrement; *[oil]* to be on ~ être en service; to come on ~ être mis en service; ~s of people were coming out des flots de gens sortaient, les gens sortaient à flots; (*Brit Scol*) divided into 5 ~s réparti en 5 classes de niveau; (*Brit Scol*) the B ~ la classe B, le groupe B; (*Literat, Psych*) the ~ of consciousness la vie mouvante et insaisissable de la conscience, le 'stream of consciousness'.
2 *cpd*: streamline (*Aut, Aviat*) donner un profil aérodynamique à; (*fig*) rationaliser; streamlined (*Aviat*) fuselé, profilé; (*Aut*) aérodynamique; (*fig*) rationalisé.
3 *vi* (a) *[water, tears, oil, milk]* ruisseler; *[blood]* ruisseler, dégouliner. to ~ with blood/tears *etc* ruisseler de sang/de larmes *etc*; the fumes made his eyes ~ les émanations l'ont fait pleurer à chaudes larmes; cold air/sunlight ~ed through the window l'air froid/le soleil entra à flots par la fenêtre.
(b) (*in wind etc: also* ~ out) flotter au vent.
(c) *[people, cars etc]* to ~ in/out/past *etc* entrer/sortir/passer *etc* à flots.
4 *vt* (a) to ~ blood/water *etc* ruisseler de sang/d'eau *etc*.

(b) (*Scol*) *pupils* répartir par niveau. **to ~ French** *or* **the French classes** répartir les élèves par niveau en français.
streamer ['stri:mə^r] *n* (*of paper*) serpentin *m*; (*banner*) banderole *f*; (*Astron*) flèche lumineuse; (*Press*) manchette *f*.
streaming ['stri:mɪŋ] **1** *n* (*Scol*) répartition *f* des élèves par niveau. **2** *adj:* **I've got a ~ cold** je n'arrête pas de me moucher avec ce rhume.
street [stri:t] **1** *n* rue *f*. **I saw him in the ~** je l'ai vu dans la rue; (*fig*) **the man in the ~** l'homme de la rue, l'homme moyen; a **woman of the ~s** une prostituée; **she is on the ~s** elle fait le trottoir*; (*Brit fig*) **that is right up my ~*** cela est tout à fait dans mes cordes; (*Brit fig*) **he is not in the same ~ as you*** il ne vous vient pas à la cheville; (*Brit fig*) **to be ~s ahead of sb*** dépasser qn de loin; (*fig*) **~s better*** beaucoup mieux; *V* **back, high, queer** *etc*.
2 *cpd:* **street arab** gamin(e) *m(f)* des rues; (*US*) **streetcar** tramway *m*; **street cleaner** balayeur *m*; **street directory** = **street guide; street door** porte *f* sur la rue; (*U: Mil*) **street fighting** combats *mpl* de rue; **street guide** guide *m or* répertoire *m or* index *m* des rues; **street lamp** réverbère *m*; **at street level** au rez-de-chaussée; (*U*) **street lighting** éclairage *m* des rues *or* de la voie publique; **street map** plan *m* des rues; **street market** marché *m* à ciel ouvert; **street musician** musicien *m* des rues; **street photographer** photostoppeur *m*, -euse *f*; **street sweeper** (*person*) balayeur *m*; (*machine*) balayeuse *f*; **street urchin** = **street arab; street vendor** marchand ambulant; **streetwalker** prostituée *f*, putain: *f*.
strength [streŋθ] *n* (*U*) **(a)** *[person, animal, hand, voice, magnet, lens]* force *f*, puissance *f*; (*health*) forces, robustesse *f*; *[enemy, team, nation, one's position]* force; *[building, wall, wood]* solidité *f*; *[shoes, material]* solidité, robustesse; *[wind]* force; *[current]* intensité *f*; *[character, accent, emotion, influence, attraction]* force; *[belief, opinion]* force, fermeté *f*; *[arguments, reasons]* force, solidité; *[protests]* force, vigueur *f*; *[claim, case]* solidité; *[tea, coffee, cigarette]* force; *[sauce]* goût relevé; *[drink]* teneur *f* en alcool; *[solution]* titre *m*. **he hadn't the ~ to lift it** il n'avait pas la force de le soulever; **his ~ failed him** ses forces l'ont abandonné; **give me ~!*** Dieu qu'il faut être patient!; **to get one's ~ back** reprendre des forces, recouvrer ses forces; **~ of character** force de caractère; **~ of purpose** résolution *f*, détermination *f*; **~ of will** volonté *f*, fermeté; (*Fin*) **the ~ of the pound** la solidité de la livre; **the pound has gained in ~** la livre s'est consolidée; (*fig*) **on the ~ of** sur la foi de, en vertu de; *V* **tensile** *etc*.
(b) (*Mil, Naut*) effectif(s) *m(pl)*. **fighting ~** effectif(s) mobilisable(s); **they are below** *or* **under ~** leur effectif n'est pas au complet; **to bring up to ~** compléter l'effectif de; **in** *or* **at full ~** au grand complet; (*fig*) **his friends were there in ~** ses amis étaient là en grand nombre; **to be on the ~** (*Mil*) figurer sur les contrôles; (*gen*) faire partie du personnel.
strengthen ['streŋθən] **1** *vt muscle, limb* fortifier, rendre fort; *eyesight* améliorer; *person* fortifier, remonter, tonifier; (*morally*) fortifier, tonifier, enhardir; *enemy, nation, team, one's position, protest, case* renforcer; (*Fin*) *the pound, stock market* consolider; *building, table, shoes* consolider, renforcer; *wall* étayer; *fabric, material* renforcer; *affection, emotion, effect* augmenter, renforcer; *opinion, belief* confirmer, renforcer.
2 *vi [muscle, limb]* devenir fort *or* vigoureux, se fortifier; *[wind]* augmenter, redoubler; *[desire, influence, characteristic]* augmenter.
strengthening ['streŋθənɪŋ] (*V* **strengthen**) **1** *n* renforcement *m*; consolidation *f*; augmentation *f*. **2** *adj* fortifiant, remontant, tonifiant. **to have a ~ effect on sth** avoir l'effet de consolider (*or* renforcer *etc*) qch.
strenuous ['strenjʊəs] *adj exercise, work, training* ardu; *game, march* fatigant, qui nécessite *or* exige de l'effort; *life, holiday* très actif; *effort, attempt* acharné, vigoureux; *protest* vigoureux, énergique; *attack, conflict, opposition, resistance* acharné. **I have had a ~ day** je me suis beaucoup dépensé aujourd'hui; **it was all too ~ for me** cela nécessitait trop d'effort pour moi; **I'd like to do something a little less ~** j'aimerais faire quelque chose qui exige (*subj*) un peu moins d'effort; **to make ~ efforts to do** faire des efforts acharnés pour faire, s'efforcer avec acharnement de faire.
strenuously ['strenjʊəslɪ] *adv* (*V* **strenuous**) énergiquement, vigoureusement, avec acharnement.
streptococcal [ˌstreptəʊ'kɒkl] *adj*, **streptococcic** [ˌstreptəʊ'kɒksɪk] *adj* streptococcique.
streptococcus [ˌstreptəʊ'kɒkəs] *n, pl* **streptococci** [ˌstreptəʊ'kɒkaɪ] streptocoque *m*.
streptomycin [ˌstreptəʊ'maɪsɪn] *n* streptomycine *f*.
stress [stres] **1** *n* **(a)** (*pressure etc*) pression *f*, contrainte *f*, agression *f*, stress *m*; (*Med*) stress; (*also* **mental ~, nervous ~**) tension *f* (nerveuse). **in times of ~** à des moments *or* à une période de grande tension; **under the ~ of circumstances** poussé par les circonstances, sous la pression des circonstances; **the ~es and strains of modern life** toutes les pressions et les tensions de la vie moderne, les agressions de la vie moderne; **to be under ~** être très tendu, être sous tension; **this put him under great ~** cela a mis ses nerfs à rude épreuve; **he reacts well under ~** il réagit bien dans des conditions difficiles.
(b) (*emphasis*) insistance *f*. **to lay ~ on** *good manners, academic subjects etc* insister sur, mettre l'accent sur; *fact, detail* insister sur, faire ressortir.
(c) (*Ling, Poetry*) (*accent*) accent *m* d'intensité; (*accented syllable*) syllabe accentuée; (*Mus*) accent. (*Ling*) **the ~ is on the first syllable** l'accent tombe sur la première syllabe.
(d) (*Tech*) effort *m*; charge *f*; travail *m*. **tensile ~** tension *f*; **the ~ acting on a metal** l'effort qui agit sur un métal; **the ~ produced in the metal** le travail du métal; *[beam, metal]* **to be in ~** travailler; **the ~ to which a beam is subjected** la charge qu'on fait subir à une poutre; **a ~ of 500 kilos per square millimetre** une charge de 500 kilos par millimètre carré.
2 *cpd:* (*Ling*) **stress mark** accent *m*.
3 *vt* **(a)** (*emphasize*) *good manners, one's innocence* insister sur; *fact, detail* faire ressortir, souligner, attirer l'attention sur.
(b) (*Ling, Mus, Poetry*) accentuer.
(c) (*Tech*) fatiguer, faire travailler.
stressful ['stresfʊl] *adj way of life, circumstances* difficile, qui engendre beaucoup de tension nerveuse.
stretch [stretʃ] **1** *n* **(a)** (*act, gesture*) étirement *m*; (*distance, span: of wing etc*) envergure *f*. **with a ~ of his arm** en étendant le bras; **to give a rope a ~** étirer une corde; **to give shoes a ~** élargir des chaussures; **there's not much ~ left in this elastic** cet élastique a beaucoup perdu de son élasticité; **there's a lot of ~ in this material** ce tissu donne *or* prête bien; **to be at full ~** *[arms, rope etc]* être complètement tendu; (*fig*) *[engine etc]* tourner à plein; *[factory]* tourner à plein (rendement); *[person]* donner son plein; (*Med*) **~ mark** vergeture *f*; **by a ~ of the imagination** en faisant un effort d'imagination; **by no ~ of the imagination can one say ...** même en faisant un gros effort d'imagination on ne peut pas dire ...; **not by a long ~!** loin de là!
(b) (*period of time*) période *f*. **for a long ~ of time** (pendant) longtemps; **for hours at a ~** (pendant) des heures d'affilée *or* sans discontinuer *or* sans interruption; **he read it all in one ~** il l'a tout lu d'une seule traite, il l'a lu (tout) d'une traite; (*Prison sl*) **to do a ~** faire de la prison *or* de la taule:; **he's done a 10-year ~** il a fait 10 ans de prison *or* taule:.
(c) (*distance*) **there's a straight ~ (of road) after you pass the lake** la route est toute droite *or* il y a un bout tout droit une fois que vous avez dépassé le lac; **a magnificent ~ of country** une campagne magnifique; **in that ~ of the river** dans cette partie de la rivière; **for a long ~ the road runs between steep hills** sur des kilomètres la route serpente entre des collines escarpées; *V* **home**.
(d) (*Naut*) bordée *f* (courue sous les mêmes amures).
2 *adj fabric, socks, trousers* extensible; (*elasticated*) élastique.
3 *vt* **(a)** (*make longer, wider etc*) *rope, spring* tendre; *elastic* étirer; *shoe, glove, hat* élargir; (*Med*) *muscle, tendon* distendre; (*fig*) *law, rules* tourner; *meaning* forcer; *one's principles* adapter; *one's authority* outrepasser, excéder. (*fig*) **to ~ a point** faire une concession; **to ~ the truth** forcer la vérité, exagérer.
(b) (*extend: often* **~ out**) *wing* déployer; *rope, net, canopy* tendre (*between* entre, *above* au-dessus de); *rug* étendre, étaler; *linen* étendre; (*fig*) *athlete, student* pousser, exiger le maximum d'effort de. **he had to ~ his neck to see** il a dû tendre le cou pour voir; **he ~ed (out) his arm to grasp the handle** il tendit *or* allongea le bras pour saisir la poignée; **he ~ed his arms and yawned** il s'étira et bâilla; **he ~ed his leg to ease the cramp** il a étendu *or* allongé la jambe pour atténuer la crampe; (*fig: go for a walk*) **I'm just going to ~ my legs** je vais me dégourdir les jambes; **to be fully ~ed** *[rope etc]* être complètement tendu; (*fig*) *[engine]* tourner à plein; *[factory]* tourner à plein (rendement); *[person]* donner son plein; **his income was ~ed to the full** son revenu n'était pas élastique et il ne lui restait rien à la fin du mois; **to ~ o.s.** (*after sleep etc*) s'étirer; (*fig: one's abilities etc*) travailler à la limite de ses possibilités; **the work he is doing does not ~ him enough** le travail qu'il fait n'exige pas assez de lui.
(c) (*knock down: also* **~ out**) étendre. **the blow ~ed him (out) cold** le coup l'a mis K.-O.*
4 *vi* **(a)** *[person, animal]* s'étirer. **he ~ed lazily** il s'est étiré paresseusement; **he ~ed across me to get the book** il a tendu le bras devant moi pour prendre le livre.
(b) (*lengthen*) s'allonger; (*widen*) s'élargir; *[elastic]* s'étirer, se tendre; *[fabric, jersey, gloves, shoes]* prêter, donner.
(c) (*extend, reach, spread out: often* **~ out**) *[rope etc]* s'étendre, aller; *[forest, plain, procession, sb's authority, influence]* s'étendre. **the rope won't ~ to that post** la corde ne va pas jusqu'à ce poteau; **how far will it ~?** jusqu'où ça va?; (*fig*) **my money won't ~* to a new car** mon budget ne me permet pas d'acheter une nouvelle voiture; **the festivities ~ed (out) into January** les festivités se sont prolongées sur une partie de janvier; **a life of misery ~ed (out) before her** une vie de misère s'étendait *or* s'étalait devant elle.
stretch across *vi:* **he stretched across and touched her cheek** il a tendu la main et touché sa joue.
stretch down *vi:* **she stretched down and picked up the book** elle a tendu la main et ramassé le livre, elle a allongé le bras pour ramasser le livre.
stretch out 1 *vi [person, arm etc]* s'étendre, s'allonger; *[countryside etc]* s'étendre. **he stretched out on the bed** il s'est étendu *or* allongé sur le lit; *V also* **stretch 4c**.
2 *vt sep* **(a)** (*reach*) *arm, hand, foot* tendre, allonger; (*extend*) *leg etc* allonger, étendre; *wing* déployer; *net, canopy, rope* tendre; *rug* étendre, étaler; *linen* étendre; (*lengthen*) *meeting, discussion* prolonger; *story, explanation* allonger; *V also* **stretch 3b**.
(b) = **stretch 3c**.
stretch over *vi* = **stretch across**.
stretch up *vi:* **he stretched up to reach the shelf** il s'est levé sur la pointe des pieds pour atteindre l'étagère.
stretcher ['stretʃə^r] **1** *n* **(a)** (*Med*) brancard *m*, civière *f*.
(b) (*device*) (*for gloves*) ouvre-gants *m inv*; (*for shoes*) forme *f*; (*for fabric*) cadre *m*; (*for artist's canvas*) cadre, châssis *m*; (*on umbrella*) baleine *f*.
(c) (*Constr: brick*) panneresse *f*, carreau *m*; (*crosspiece in*

framework) traverse *f*; (*crossbar in chair, bed etc*) barreau *m*, bâton *m*; (*cross-plank in canoe etc*) barre *f* de pieds.

2 *cpd:* (*Med*) **stretcher-bearer** brancardier *m*; **stretcher case** malade *mf or* blessé(e) *m(f)* qui ne peut pas marcher; **stretcher party** détachement *m* de brancardiers.

stretchy ['stretʃɪ] *adj* extensible, qui donne, qui prête.

strew [struː] *pret* **strewed,** *ptp* **strewed** *or* **strewn** [struːn] *vt straw, sand, sawdust* répandre, éparpiller (*on, over* sur); *flowers, objects* éparpiller, semer (*on, over* sur); *wreckage etc* éparpiller, disséminer (*over* sur); *ground, floor* joncher, parsemer (*with* de); *room, table* joncher (*also fig*).

striate [straɪ'eɪt] *vt* strier.

stricken ['strɪkən] **1** (*rare*) *ptp of* **strike.**

2 *adj person, animal* (*wounded*) gravement blessé; (*ill*) atteint *or* touché par un mal; (*afflicted*) affligé; (*in dire straits*) *person, country, army* très éprouvé; (*damaged*) *city* dévasté, ravagé; *ship* très endommagé; *V also* **strike.**

-stricken ['strɪkən] *adj ending in cpds* frappé de, atteint de, accablé de. **plague-stricken** pestiféré, atteint de la peste, frappé par la peste; *V* **grief** *etc.*

strict [strɪkt] *adj* **(a)** (*severe, stern*) *person, principle, views* strict, sévère; *discipline* strict, sévère, rigoureux; *ban, rule* strict, rigoureux; *order* formel; *etiquette* rigide. **to be ~ with sb** être strict *or* sévère avec *or* à l'égard de qn.

(b) (*precise*) *meaning* strict (*after n*); *translation* précis, exact; (*absolute*) *accuracy, secrecy* strict (*before n*), absolu; *mentality, privacy* strict (*before n*). **in the ~ sense of the word** au sens strict du mot; **there is a ~ time limit on ...** il y a un délai impératif *or* de rigueur en ce qui concerne ...; **the ~ truth** la stricte vérité, l'exacte vérité; *V* **confidence.**

strictly ['strɪktlɪ] *adv* **(a)** (*sternly, severely*) *treat, bring up* strictement, d'une manière stricte, sévèrement, avec sévérité, avec rigueur.

(b) (*precisely*) strictement, exactement, rigoureusement; (*absolutely*) strictement, absolument. **~ confidential/personal** strictement confidentiel/privé; **~ between ourselves** strictement entre nous; **~ speaking** à strictement *or* à proprement parler; **'smoking ~ prohibited'** 'défense formelle de fumer'; **smoking was ~ prohibited** il était formellement interdit de fumer; *V* **bird.**

strictness ['strɪktnɪs] *n [person, principles, views]* sévérité *f*; *[discipline]* sévérité, rigueur *f*; *[translation]* exactitude *f*, précision *f*.

stricture ['strɪktʃə^r] *n* (*criticism*) critique *f* (hostile) (*on* de); (*restriction*) restriction *f* (*on* de); (*Med*) sténose *f*, rétrécissement *m*.

stridden ['strɪdn] *ptp of* **stride.**

stride [straɪd] (*vb: pret* **strode,** *ptp* **stridden**) **1** *n* grand pas, enjambée *f*; *[runner]* foulée *f*. **with giant ~s** à pas de géant; **in** *or* **with a few ~s he had caught up with the others** il avait rattrapé les autres en quelques enjambées *or* foulées; (*fig*) **to make great ~s** faire de grands progrès (*in French* en français, *in her studies* dans ses études, *in doing* pour ce qui est de faire); **to get into one's ~** prendre le rythme *or* la cadence; **to take in one's ~** *changes etc* accepter avec équanimité; *exam/interrogation etc* passer/subir *etc* sans le moindre effort.

2 *vi* marcher à grands pas *or* à grandes enjambées. **to ~ along/in/away** *etc* avancer/entrer/s'éloigner *etc* à grands pas *or* à grandes enjambées; **he was striding up and down the room** il arpentait la pièce.

3 *vt* **(a)** *deck, yard, streets* arpenter.

(b) (†) = **bestride.**

stridency ['straɪdənsɪ] *n* stridence *f*.

strident ['straɪdənt] *adj* strident.

stridently ['straɪdəntlɪ] *adv announce, declare* d'une voix stridente; *hoot, sound, whistle* d'une façon stridente.

strife [straɪf] **1** *n* (*U*) conflit *m*, dissensions *fpl*, luttes *fpl*, (*less serious*) querelles *fpl*. (*Pol*) **party crippled by internal ~** parti paralysé par des dissensions *or* des querelles intestines; **industrial ~** conflits sociaux; **domestic ~** querelles de ménage, dissensions domestiques; (*liter*) **to cease from ~** déposer les armes.

2 *cpd:* **strife-ridden** déchiré par les luttes *or* les conflits.

strike [straɪk] (*vb: pret* **struck,** *ptp* **struck,** (*rare*) **stricken**) **1** *n* **(a)** (*act*) coup *m* (frappé); (*Aviat, Mil*) raid *m* (aérien).

(b) (*Ind*) grève *f* (*of, by* de). **to be (out) on ~** être en grève, faire grève (*for* pour obtenir, *against* pour protester contre); **to go on ~, to come out on ~** se mettre en grève, faire grève; *V* **general, hunger, sympathy** *etc.*

(c) (*Min, Miner etc: discovery*) découverte *f*. **the rich ~ of oil** la découverte d'un riche gisement de pétrole; **to make a ~** découvrir un gisement; (*fig*) **a lucky ~** un coup de chance.

(d) (*Fishing: by angler*) ferrage *m*; (*Fishing: by fish*) touche *f*, mordage *m*; (*Baseball, Bowling*) strike *m*. (*US fig*) **to have two ~s against one*** être mal-en-point.

(e) *[clock]* sonnerie *f* des heures.

2 *cpd* (*Ind*) *committee, fund* de grève. **strikebound** immobilisé par une grève; (*Ind*) **strikebreaker** briseur *m* de grève; **he was accused of strikebreaking** on l'a accusé d'être un briseur de grève; (*Aviat, Mil*) **strike force** détachement *m* d'avions; (*Ind*) **strike leader** leader *m or* dirigeant *m* des grévistes; (*Ind*) **strike pay** salaire *m* de gréviste.

3 *vt* **(a)** (*hit*) *person* frapper, donner un *or* des coup(s) à; *ball* toucher, frapper; *nail, table* frapper sur, taper sur, donner un coup sur, cogner sur; (*Mus*) *string* toucher, pincer; *[snake]* mordre, piquer. **to ~ sth with one's fist, to ~ one's fist on sth** frapper du poing *or* donner un coup de poing sur qch; **to ~ sth with a hammer** frapper *or* taper *or* cogner sur qch avec un marteau, donner un coup de marteau sur qch; **to ~ a man when he is down** frapper un homme à terre; **he struck me (a blow) on the chin** il m'a frappé au menton, il m'a donné un coup de poing au menton; **to ~ the first blow** donner le premier coup, frapper le premier (*or* la première); (*fig*) **to ~ a blow for freedom** rompre une lance pour la liberté; (*fig*) **he struck his rival a shrewd blow by buying the land** il a porté à son rival un coup subtil en achetant la terre; **he struck the knife from his assailant's hand** d'un coup de poing il a fait tomber le couteau de la main de son assaillant; **the pain struck him as he bent down** la douleur l'a saisi quand il s'est baissé; **disease struck the city** la maladie a frappé la ville *or* s'est abattue sur la ville; **to be stricken by** *or* **with remorse** être pris de remords; (*fig*) **the news struck him all of a heap‡** la nouvelle lui a coupé bras et jambes *or* l'a éberlué*; (*fig*) **he was struck all of a heap‡** il en est resté baba*; **the city was struck** *or* **stricken by fear** la ville a été prise de peur, la peur s'est emparée de la ville; **to ~ fear into sb('s heart)** remplir (le cœur de) qn d'effroi; **it struck terror and dismay into the whole population** cela terrorisa la population tout entière.

(b) (*knock against*) *[person, one's shoulder etc, spade]* cogner contre, heurter; *[car etc]* heurter, rentrer dans*; (*Naut*) *rocks, the bottom* toucher, heurter; (*fig*) *[lightning, light]* frapper. **he struck his head on** *or* **against the table as he fell** sa tête a heurté la table quand il est tombé, il s'est cogné la tête à *or* contre la table en tombant; **the stone struck him on the head** la pierre l'a frappé *or* l'a heurté à la tête; **he was struck by 2 bullets** il a reçu 2 balles; **to be struck by lightning** être frappé par la foudre, être foudroyé; **a piercing cry struck his ear** un cri perçant lui frappa l'oreille *or* les oreilles; **the horrible sight that struck his eyes** le spectacle horrible qui lui frappa les yeux *or* le regard *or* la vue.

(c) (*find, discover*) *gold* découvrir, trouver; (*fig*) *hotel, road* tomber sur, trouver; (*fig*) *difficulty, obstacle* rencontrer. **to ~ oil** (*Miner*) trouver du pétrole; (*fig*) trouver le filon; (*fig*) **to ~ it rich** faire fortune; *V* **patch.**

(d) (*make, produce etc*) *coin, medal* frapper; *sparks, fire* faire jaillir (*from* de); *match* frotter, gratter; (*fig*) *agreement, truce* arriver à, conclure. **to ~ a light** allumer une allumette (*or* un briquet *etc*); (*Bot*) **to ~ roots** prendre racine; (*Horticulture*) **to ~ cuttings** faire prendre racine à des boutures; **to ~ an average** établir une moyenne; **to ~ a balance** trouver le juste milieu; **to ~ a bargain** conclure un marché; **to ~ an attitude of surprise** faire l'étonné(e); *V* **pose.**

(e) *chord, note* sonner, faire entendre; *[clock]* sonner. (*fig*) **that ~s a chord** cela me dit *or* me rappelle quelque chose; (*fig*) **to ~ a false note** sonner faux; **to ~ a note of warning** donner *or* sonner l'alarme; **the clock struck 3** la pendule a sonné 3 heures; **it has just struck 6** 6 heures viennent juste de sonner; (*Naut*) **to ~ 4 bells** piquer 4.

(f) (*take down*) *tent* démonter, plier; *sail* amener; *camp* lever; *flag* baisser, amener. (*Theat*) **to ~ the set** démonter le décor.

(g) (*delete*) *name* rayer (*from* de); *person* (*from list*) rayer; (*from professional register*) radier (*from* de). **the judge ordered the remark to be struck** *or* **stricken from the record** le juge a ordonné que la remarque soit rayée du procès-verbal.

(h) (*cause to be or become*) rendre (subitement). (*lit, fig*) **to ~ sb dumb** rendre qn muet; **to ~ sb dead** porter un coup mortel à qn; (*fig*) **~ me pink!‡** j'en suis soufflé!*

(i) (*make impression on*) frapper; sembler, paraître (*sb* à qn). **I was struck by his intelligence** j'étais frappé par son intelligence; **I wasn't very struck* with him** il ne m'a pas fait très bonne impression; **to be struck on sb‡** (*impressed by*) être très impressionné par qn; (*in love with*) être toqué* de qn; **the funny side of it struck me later** le côté drôle de la chose m'est apparu *or* m'a frappé plus tard; **that ~s me as a good idea** cela me semble *or* paraît une bonne idée; **an idea suddenly struck him** soudain il eut une idée, une idée lui vint soudain à l'esprit; **it ~s me that** *or* **~s me* he is lying** j'ai l'impression qu'il ment, à mon avis il ment; **how did he ~ you?** quelle impression *or* quel effet vous a-t-il fait?; **how did the film ~ you?** qu'avez-vous pensé du film?

(j) (*Fishing*) *[angler]* ferrer. **the fish struck the bait** le poisson a mordu à l'appât.

4 *vi* **(a)** (*hit*) frapper; (*attack*) (*Mil*) attaquer; *[snake]* mordre, piquer; *[tiger]* sauter sur sa proie; (*fig*) *[disease etc]* frapper; *[panic]* s'emparer des esprits. (*lit, fig*) **to ~ home** frapper *or* toucher juste, faire mouche; **he struck at his attacker** il porta un coup à son assaillant; **we must ~ at the root of this evil** nous devons attaquer *or* couper ce mal dans sa racine; (*fig*) **it ~s at the root of our parliamentary system** cela porte atteinte aux fondements mêmes de notre système parlementaire; **his speech ~s at the heart of the problem** son discours porte sur le fond même du problème; **he struck at the heart of the problem** il a mis le doigt sur le fond du problème; **his foot struck against** *or* **on a rock** son pied a buté contre *or* heurté un rocher; **when the ship struck** quand le bateau a touché; **the sun was striking through the mist** le soleil perçait la brume; **the chill struck through to his very bones** le froid pénétra jusqu'à la moelle de ses os; *V* **iron.**

(b) *[match]* s'allumer.

(c) *[clock]* sonner. **has 6 o'clock struck?** est-ce que 6 heures ont sonné?; (*fig*) **his hour has struck** son heure est venue *or* a sonné.

(d) (*Ind: go on ~*) faire grève (*for* pour obtenir, *against* pour protester contre).

(e) (*turn, move, go*) aller, prendre. **~ left on leaving the forest** prenez à gauche en sortant de la forêt; **to ~ uphill** se mettre à grimper la côte.

(f) (*Horticulture: take root*) prendre racine; (*Fishing: seize bait*) mordre.
strike back *vt* (*Mil, gen*) rendre les coups (*at sb* à qn), se venger (*at sb* de qn), user de représailles (*at sb* à l'égard de qn).
strike down *vt sep* (*fig*) *[person, disease]* terrasser.
strike in *vi* (*fig: interrupt*) interrompre.
strike off 1 *vi* (*change direction*) prendre, aller. **he struck off across the fields** il a pris *or* il s'en est allé à travers champs.
2 *vt sep* **(a)** *sb's head* trancher, couper; *branch* couper.
(b) (*score out, delete*) (*from list*) rayer. *[doctor etc]* **to be struck off** être radié.
(c) (*Typ*) tirer.
strike on *vt fus idea* avoir; *solution* tomber sur, trouver.
strike out 1 *vi* **(a)** (*hit out*) se débattre. **he struck out wildly** il s'est débattu furieusement; **he struck out at his attackers** il lança une volée de coups dans la direction de ses attaquants.
(b) (*set off*) **to strike out for the shore** *[swimmer]* se mettre à nager *or [rower]* se mettre à ramer vers le rivage; (*fig*) **he left the firm and struck out on his own** il a quitté l'entreprise et s'est mis à son compte.
2 *vt sep* (*delete*) *word, question* rayer.
strike through *vt sep* = **strike out 2.**
strike up 1 *vi [band etc]* commencer à jouer; *[music]* commencer.
2 *vt sep* (*Mus*) *[band]* se mettre à jouer; *[singers]* se mettre à chanter. **strike up the band!** faites jouer l'orchestre!; **to strike up an acquaintance** faire *or* lier connaissance (*with sb* avec qn); **to strike up a friendship** lier amitié (*with sb* avec qn).
strike upon *vt fus* = **strike on.**
striker ['straɪkəʳ] *n* **(a)** (*Ind*) gréviste *mf*. **(b)** (*clapper*) frappeur *m*; (*on clock*) marteau *m*; (*on gun*) percuteur *m*; (*Ftbl*) buteur *m*.
striking ['straɪkɪŋ] **1** *adj* **(a)** (*impressive, outstanding*) frappant, saisissant.
(b) *clock* qui sonne les heures. **the ~ mechanism** la sonnerie des heures.
(c) (*Mil*) *force, power* de frappe. (*Mil, fig*) **within ~ distance** *or* **range of sth** à portée de qch.
(d) (*Ind*) *workers* en grève, gréviste.
2 *n* **(a)** *[coins]* frappe *f*.
(b) *[clock]* sonnerie *f* des heures.
strikingly ['straɪkɪŋlɪ] *adv* d'une manière frappante *or* saisissante, remarquablement. **~ beautiful** d'une beauté frappante *or* saisissante, remarquablement beau (*f* belle).
string [strɪŋ] (*vb: pret, ptp* **strung**) **1** *n* **(a)** (*cord*) ficelle *f*; *[violin, piano, bow, racket etc]* corde *f*; *[puppet]* ficelle, fil *m*; *[apron, bonnet, anorak]* cordon *m*; (*Bot: on bean etc*) fil(s). **a piece of ~** un bout de ficelle; (*fig*) **with no ~s attached** sans condition(s); (*fig*) **there are no ~s attached** cela ne vous (*or* nous *etc*) engage à rien; **he has got her on a ~** il la tient, il la mène par le bout du nez; **to have more than one ~ to one's bow** avoir plus d'une corde à son arc; **his first ~** sa première ressource; **his second ~** sa deuxième ressource, la solution de rechange; (*Mus*) **the ~s** les cordes, les instruments *mpl* à cordes; *V* **apron, heart, pull** *etc.*
(b) *[beads, pearls]* rang *m*; *[onions]* chapelet *m*; *[garlic]* chaîne *f*; (*fig*) *[people, vehicles]* file *f*; *[racehorses]* écurie *f*; *[curses, lies, insults, excuses]* kyrielle *f*, chapelet.
2 *cpd* (*Mus*) *orchestra, quartet* à cordes; *serenade, piece* pour cordes. **string bag** filet *m* à provisions; **string bean** haricot vert; (*Mus*) **string(ed) instrument** instrument *m* à cordes; (*Mus*) **string player** musicien(ne) *m(f)* qui joue d'un instrument à cordes; **string-puller** = **wire-puller** (*V* **wire**); **string-pulling** = **wire-pulling** (*V* **wire**); **string vest** gilet *m or* tricot *m* (de corps) de coton à grosses mailles.
3 *vt* **(a)** *violin etc* monter; *bow* garnir d'une corde; *racket* corder; *V* **highly.**
(b) *beads, pearls* enfiler; *rope* tendre (*across* en travers de, *between* entre). **they strung lights in the trees** ils ont suspendu *or* attaché des (guirlandes de) lampions dans les arbres.
(c) *beans* enlever les fils de.
string along* 1 *vi* suivre. **to string along with sb** (*accompany*) accompagner qn, aller *or* venir avec qn; (*fig: agree with*) se ranger du côté de *or* à l'avis de qn.
2 *vt sep* (*pej*) faire marcher, bercer de fausses espérances.
string out 1 *vi [people, things]* s'échelonner (*along a road* le long d'une route). **string out a bit more!** espacez-vous un peu plus!
2 *vt sep lanterns, washing etc* suspendre; *guards, posts* échelonner. *[people, things]* **to be strung out along the road** être échelonnés *or* s'échelonner le long de la route.
string up *vt sep* **(a)** *lantern, onions, nets* suspendre (au moyen d'une corde).
(b) (*fig*) **he had strung himself up to do it** il avait aiguisé toutes ses facultés en vue de le faire; **to be strung up (about sth)** être très tendu *or* nerveux (à la pensée de qch).
(c) (*: *hang; lynch*) pendre.
stringed [strɪŋd] *adj V* **string 2.**
-stringed [strɪŋd] *adj ending in cpds:* **4-stringed** à 4 cordes.
stringency ['strɪndʒənsɪ] *n* (*V* **stringent**) rigueur *f*; irrésistibilité *f*. **in times of economic ~** en période d'austérité.
stringent ['strɪndʒənt] *adj* (*strict*) *rule, order, law* strict, rigoureux; *measures* énergique, rigoureux; (*compelling*) *reasons, arguments* irrésistible; *necessity* impérieux. (*Fin*) **~ money market** marché financier tendu *or* serré.
stringently ['strɪndʒəntlɪ] *adv* rigoureusement, strictement.
stringy ['strɪŋɪ] *adj beans, celery, meat* filandreux; *molasses, cooked cheese* filant, qui file; *plant, seaweed* tout en longueur; (*fig*) *person* filiforme.
strip [strɪp] **1** *n* **(a)** *[metal, wood, paper, grass]* bande *f*; *[fabric]* bande, bandelette *f*; *[ground]* bande, langue *f*; *[water, sea]* bras *m*. **a ~ of garden** un petit jardin tout en longueur; **to tear sb off a ~‡, to tear a ~ off sb‡** bien sonner les cloches à qn*.
(b) (*Aviat: also* **landing ~**) piste *f* d'atterrissage.
(c) (*also* **comic ~**) = **~ cartoon;** *V* **2.**
(d) (*Brit Sport: clothes*) tenue *f*.
(e) (*) = **~tease;** *V* **2.**
2 *cpd:* (*Brit*) **strip cartoon** bande dessinée; (*Agr*) **strip cropping** *cultures alternées selon les courbes de niveaux;* (*Brit*) **strip lighting** éclairage *m* au néon *or* fluorescent; (*US*) **strip mining** extraction *f* à ciel ouvert; **strip poker** strip-poker *m*; **strip show, striptease** strip-tease *m*; **striptease artist** strip-teaseuse *f*.
3 *vt* **(a)** (*remove everything from: often* **~ down**) *person* déshabiller, dévêtir; *room, house* démeubler, vider; *[thieves]* dévaliser, vider; *car, engine, gun* démonter complètement; (*Tech*) *nut, screw, gears* arracher le filet de; *[wind, people, birds] branches, bushes* dépouiller, dégarnir. **to ~ sb naked** *or* **to the skin** déshabiller *or* dévêtir qn complètement; **to ~ a bed (down)** défaire un lit complètement; **to ~ (down) the walls** *or* **wallpaper** enlever *or* arracher le papier peint.
(b) (*deprive etc*) *person, object* dépouiller (*of* de). **to ~ a tree of its bark, to ~ the bark from a tree** dépouiller un arbre de son écorce; **to ~ a room of all its pictures** enlever tous les tableaux dans une pièce; (*Fin*) **to ~ a company of its assets** cannibaliser* une compagnie; *V also* **asset.**
4 *vi* se déshabiller, se dévêtir; *[striptease artist]* faire du strip-tease. **to ~ naked** *or* **to the skin** se mettre nu; **to ~ to the waist** se déshabiller *or* se dévêtir jusqu'à la ceinture; **to be ~ped to the waist** être nu jusqu'à la ceinture.
strip down 1 *vi* = **strip off 1.**
2 *vt sep* (*Tech etc*) *machine, engine, gun* démonter complètement; *V also* **strip 3a.**
strip off 1 *vi* se déshabiller *or* se dévêtir complètement, se mettre nu.
2 *vt sep buttons, ornaments* enlever, ôter (*from* de); *paper* enlever, arracher (*from* de); *leaves* faire tomber (*from* de); *berries* prendre (*from* de).
stripe [straɪp] *n* **(a)** (*of one colour: also Zool*) raie *f*, rayure *f*. (*pattern*) **~s** (*gen*) rayures; (*Zool*) rayures, zébrures *fpl*; **yellow with a white ~** jaune rayé de blanc; *V* **pin, star** *etc.*
(b) (*Mil*) galon *m*. **to get one's ~s** gagner ses galons; **to lose one's ~s** être dégradé.
(c) (†) (*lash*) coup *m* de fouet; (*weal*) marque *f* (d'un coup de fouet).
striped [straɪpt] *adj fabric, garment* rayé, à raies, à rayures; (*Zool*) rayé, tigré. **~ with red** à raies *or* rayures rouges, rayé de rouge.
stripling ['strɪplɪŋ] *n* adolescent *m*, tout jeune homme, gringalet *m* (*pej*).
stripper ['strɪpəʳ] *n* **(a)** (*also* **paint-~**) décapant *m*. **(b)** (*: *striptease artist*) strip-teaseuse *f*.
strive [straɪv] *pret* **strove,** *ptp* **striven** ['strɪvn] *vi* **(a)** (*try hard*) s'efforcer (*to do* de faire), faire son possible (*to do* pour faire), s'évertuer (*to do* à faire). **to ~ after** *or* **for sth** s'efforcer de *or* faire son possible pour *or* s'évertuer à obtenir qch.
(b) (*liter: struggle, fight*) lutter, se battre (*against, with* contre).
stroboscope ['strəʊbəskəʊp] *n* stroboscope *m*.
strode [strəʊd] *pret of* **stride.**
stroke [strəʊk] **1** *n* **(a)** (*movement; blow: gen, Billiards, Cricket, Golf, Tennis etc*) coup *m*; (*Swimming: movement*) mouvement *m* des bras (*pour nager*); (*Rowing, Swimming: style*) nage *f*; (*Rowing: movement*) coup de rame *or* d'aviron. **he gave the cat a ~** il a fait une caresse au chat; **with a ~ of his axe** d'un coup de hache; **with a ~ of the pen** d'un trait de plume; **~ of lightning** coup de foudre; (*Golf, Tennis etc*) **good ~!** bien joué!; **to row at 38 ~s to the minute** ramer *or* nager à une cadence de 38 coups d'aviron minute; (*Rowing, fig*) **to set the ~** donner la cadence; (*Sport, fig*) **to put sb off his ~** faire perdre sa cadence *or* son rythme à qn; **he swam the pool with powerful ~s** il a traversé le bassin d'une manière puissante; *V* **back, breast** *etc.*
(b) (*fig*) **at a ~, at one ~** d'un (seul) coup; **it was a tremendous ~ to get the committee's agreement** cela a été un coup de maître que d'obtenir l'accord du comité; **he hasn't done a ~ (of work)** il n'a rien fait du tout, il n'en a pas fichu une rame*; **~ of diplomacy** chef-d'œuvre *m* de diplomatie; **~ of genius** trait *m* de génie; **~ of luck** coup de chance *or* de veine; *V* **master** *etc.*
(c) (*mark*) *[pen, pencil]* trait *m*; *[brush]* touche *f*; (*Typ*) barre *f*. **thick ~s of the brush** des touches épaisses; (*Typ*) 5 ~ 6 5 barre 6; *V* **brush** *etc.*
(d) *[bell, clock]* coup *m*. **on the ~ of 10** sur le coup de 10 heures, à 10 heures sonnantes; **he arrived on the ~** il est arrivé à l'heure exacte; **in the ~ of time** juste à temps.
(e) (*Med*) attaque *f* (d'apoplexie). **to have a ~** avoir une attaque (d'apoplexie); *V* **heat, sun.**
(f) (*Tech: of piston*) course *f*. **a two-/four-~ engine** un moteur à deux/quatre temps; *V also* **two.**
(g) (*Rowing: person*) chef *m* de nage. **to row ~** être chef de nage, donner la nage.
2 *vt* **(a)** *cat, sb's hand, one's chin* caresser; *sb's hair* caresser, passer la main dans. (*fig*) **to ~ sb (up) the wrong way** prendre qn à rebrousse-poil *or* à contre-poil.
(b) (*Rowing*) **to ~ a boat** être chef de nage, donner la nage.
(c) (*draw line through: also* **~ out**) barrer, biffer, rayer.
(d) (*Sport*) *ball* frapper.
3 *vi* (*Rowing*) être chef de nage, donner la nage.
stroke down *vt sep cat's fur* caresser; *hair* lisser. (*fig*) **to**

stroke sb down apaiser *or* amadouer qn.
stroke out *vt sep* = **stroke 2c.**
stroke up *vt sep V* **stroke 2a.**
stroll [strəʊl] **1** *n* petite promenade. **to have** *or* **take a ~, to go for a ~** aller faire un tour.
2 *vi* se promener nonchalamment, flâner. **to ~ in/out/away** *etc* entrer/sortir/s'éloigner *etc* sans se presser *or* nonchalamment; **to ~ up and down the street** descendre et remonter la rue en flânant *or* sans se presser *or* nonchalamment.
stroller ['strəʊlər] *n* **(a)** (*person*) promeneur *m*, -euse *f*, flâneur *m*, -euse *f*. **(b)** (*US: push chair*) poussette *f*.
strolling ['strəʊlɪŋ] *adj player, minstrel* ambulant.
strong [strɒŋ] **1** *adj* **(a)** (*powerful*) fort (*also Mil, Pol, Sport etc*), vigoureux, puissant; (*healthy*) fort, robuste, vigoureux; *heart* robuste, solide; *nerves* solide; *eyesight* très bon (*f* bonne); *leg* vigoureux; *arm, limb* fort, vigoureux; *voice* fort, puissant; (*morally*) fort, courageux; *candidate, contender* sérieux, qui a des chances de gagner; *magnet* puissant; *wind* fort; (*Elec*) *current* intense; *lens, spectacles* fort, puissant; (*solid, robust*) *building, wall* solide; *table, shoes, bolt, nail* solide, robuste; *glue* fort; *fabric, material* solide, résistant. **to be (as) ~ as a horse** (*powerful*) être fort comme un bœuf *or* comme un Turc; (*healthy*) avoir une santé de fer; (*in circus etc*) **~ man** hercule *m*; **do you feel ~?** est-ce que vous avez des forces?, est-ce que vous vous sentez en forme?; (*in health*) **when you are ~ again** quand vous aurez repris des forces, quand vous aurez retrouvé vos forces; **she has never been very ~** elle a toujours eu une petite santé; (*in courage etc*) **you must be ~** soyez courageux, vous devez faire preuve de courage; (*mentally etc*) **he's a very ~ person** c'est un homme bien trempé *or* un homme qui a du ressort; **you need a ~ stomach for that job** il faut avoir l'estomac solide *or* bien accroché pour faire ce travail; **we are in a ~ position to make them obey** nous sommes bien placés pour les faire obéir; **his ~ suit** (*Cards*) sa couleur forte; (*fig: also* **his ~ point**) son fort; **to be ~ in maths** être fort en maths; *V* **constitution** *etc.*
(b) (*fig*) *character, personality* fort, puissant; *characteristic* marqué, frappant; *accent* fort, marqué; *emotion, desire, interest* vif (*f* vive); *reasons, argument, evidence* solide, sérieux; (*St Ex*) *market* ferme; (*Econ*) *the pound, dollar* solide; *letter* bien senti; *protest* énergique, vigoureux, vif; *measures, steps* énergique; *influence, attraction* fort, profond; (*Mus*) *beat* fort. **in ~ terms** en termes non équivoques; **~ language** grossièretés *fpl*, propos grossiers; **there are ~ indications that ...** tout semble indiquer que ...; **a ~ effect** beaucoup d'effet; **I had a ~ sense of ...** je ressentais vivement ...; **I've a ~ feeling that ...** j'ai bien l'impression que ...; **he's got ~ feelings on this matter** cette affaire lui tient à cœur; **it is my ~ opinion** *or* **belief that** je suis fermement convaincu *or* persuadé que; **a ~ socialist** un socialiste fervent; **~ supporters of** d'ardents partisans de, des fervents de; **I am a ~ believer in** je crois fermement à *or* profondément à; *V* **case**[1] *etc.*
(c) (*affecting senses powerfully*) *coffee, cheese, wine, cigarette* fort; (*pej*) *butter* rance; *sauce, taste* fort, relevé; *solution* concentré; *light* fort, vif (*f* vive). **~ drink** alcool *m*, liqueurs fortes, spiritueux *mpl*; **his breath is very ~** il a l'haleine forte; **it has a ~ smell** ça sent fort.
(d) (*in numbers*) **an army 500 ~** une armée (forte) de 500 hommes; **they were 100 ~** ils étaient au nombre de 100.
2 *cpd:* (*fig*) **strong-arm** (*adj*) *method* fort, brutal; *tactics* faisant appel à la force; (*vt*) (*) faire violence à; **to strong-arm* sb into doing sth** forcer la main à qn pour qu'il fasse qch; **strong-armed** aux bras forts; **strongbox** coffre-fort *m*; (*on Beaufort scale*) **strong breeze** vent frais; (*on Beaufort scale*) **strong gale** fort coup de vent; **stronghold** (*Mil*) forteresse *f*, fort *m*; (*fig*) bastion *m*; **strong-limbed** aux membres forts *or* vigoureux; **strong-minded** *V* **strong-minded; strongroom** chambre forte; (*Gram*) **strong verb** verbe irrégulier; **strong-willed** résolu; **to be strong-willed** avoir de la volonté.
3 *adv:* **to be going ~** *[person]* être toujours solide; *[car etc]* marcher toujours bien; **that's pitching it** *or* **coming it** *or* **going it a bit ~*** il pousse (*or* vous poussez *etc*) un peu*, il y va (*or* vous y allez *etc*) un peu fort.
strongly ['strɒŋlɪ] *adv fight, attack* avec force, énergiquement; *play* efficacement; *attract, interest, influence, desire* fortement, vivement; *accentuate, remind, indicate* fortement; *protest, defend* énergiquement, vigoureusement; *believe* fermement, profondément; *feel, sense* profondément; *answer* en termes sentis; *constructed, made* solidement. **~ built** *wall, table* solide, robuste; *person* bien bâti, de forte constitution; **a ~-worded letter** une lettre bien sentie; **it smells very ~** cela sent très fort; **it smells ~ of onions** cela a une forte odeur d'oignons.
strong-minded ['strɒŋ'maɪndɪd] *adj* résolu, qui a beaucoup de volonté, qui sait ce qu'il veut.
strong-mindedly ['strɒŋ'maɪndɪdlɪ] *adv* avec une persévérance tenace, avec ténacité.
strong-mindedness ['strɒŋ'maɪndɪdnɪs] *n* volonté *f*, force *f* de caractère.
strontium ['strɒntɪəm] *n* strontium *m*. **~ 90** strontium 90, strontium radio-actif.
strop [strɒp] **1** *n* cuir *m* (à rasoir). **2** *vt razor* repasser sur le cuir.
strophe ['strəʊfɪ] *n* strophe *f*.
stroppy‡ ['strɒpɪ] *adj* (*Brit*) contrariant, difficile. **to get ~** monter sur ses grands chevaux.
strove [strəʊv] *pret of* **strive.**
struck [strʌk] *pret, ptp of* **strike.**
structural ['strʌktʃərəl] *adj* **(a)** (*Anat, Bot, Chem etc*) structural. **~ psychology/linguistics** psychologie/linguistique structurale; **~ complexity** complexité structurale *or* de structure.
(b) (*Constr*) *fault etc* de construction. **~ alterations** modifications *fpl* des parties portantes; **~ steel** acier *m* (de construction); **~ engineering** ponts et chaussées *mpl.*
structuralism ['strʌktʃərəlɪzəm] *n* structuralisme *m*.
structuralist ['strʌktʃərəlɪst] *adj, n* structuraliste (*mf*).
structurally ['strʌktʃərəlɪ] *adv* (*Anat, Bot, Chem etc*) du point de vue de la structure; (*Constr*) du point de vue de la construction, du point de vue des fondations et des murs. **there is nothing ~ wrong with the building** il n'y a rien à redire quant aux fondations et aux murs; (*Constr*) **~ sound** d'une construction solide.
structure ['strʌktʃər] *n* **(a)** (*Anat, Bot, Chem, Geol, Ling, Math, Philos, Phys, Psych etc*) structure *f*; (*Literat, Poetry*) structure, composition *f*. **social/administrative ~** structure sociale/administrative.
(b) (*Constr*) *[building etc]* ossature *f*, carcasse *f*, armature *f*; (*the building, bridge etc itself*) construction *f*, édifice *m*.
struggle ['strʌgl] **1** *n* (*lit, fig*) lutte *f* (*for* pour, *against* contre, *with* avec, *to do* pour faire). **to put up a ~** résister (*also fig*), se débattre; **he lost his glasses in the ~** il a perdu ses lunettes dans la mêlée; (*Mil*) **they surrendered without a ~** ils n'ont opposé aucune résistance; **you won't succeed without a ~** vous ne réussirez pas sans vous battre, il faudra vous battre si vous voulez réussir; **her ~ to feed her children** sa lutte quotidienne pour nourrir ses enfants; **the ~ to find somewhere to live** les difficultés qu'on a à trouver *or* le mal qu'il faut se donner pour trouver un logement; **I had a ~ to persuade him** j'ai eu beaucoup de mal à le persuader, je ne l'ai persuadé qu'au prix de grands efforts; **it was a ~ but we made it** cela nous a demandé beaucoup d'efforts mais nous y sommes arrivés.
2 *vi* **(a)** (*fight*) lutter, se battre, résister; (*thrash around*) se débattre, se démener; (*fig: try hard*) se démener, se décarcasser* (*to do* pour faire), s'efforcer (*to do* de faire). **he was struggling with the thief** il était aux prises *or* se battait avec le voleur; **he ~d fiercely as they put on the handcuffs** il a résisté avec acharnement quand on lui a passé les menottes; **he ~d to get free from the ropes** il s'est débattu *or* démené pour se dégager des cordes; **they were struggling for power** ils se disputaient le pouvoir; (*fig*) **he was struggling to make ends meet** il avait beaucoup de mal à joindre les deux bouts, il tirait le diable par la queue; **he is struggling to finish it before tomorrow** il se démène *or* il se décarcasse* pour le terminer avant demain.
(b) (*move with difficulty*) **to ~ in/out** *etc* entrer/sortir *etc* avec peine *or* à grand-peine; **he ~d up the cliff** il s'est hissé péniblement *or* à grand-peine jusqu'au sommet de la falaise; **he ~d through the tiny window** il s'est contorsionné pour passer par la minuscule fenêtre; **to ~ through the crowd** se frayer péniblement un chemin à travers la foule; **he ~d to his feet** (*from armchair etc*) il s'est levé non sans peine; (*during fight etc*) il s'est relevé péniblement; **he ~d into a jersey** il a enfilé non sans peine un pullover.
struggle along *vi* (*lit*) avancer avec peine *or* à grand-peine; (*fig: financially*) subsister *or* se débrouiller tant bien que mal.
struggle back *vi* (*return*) revenir (*or* retourner) avec peine *or* à grand-peine. (*fig*) **to struggle back to solvency** s'efforcer de redevenir solvable.
struggle on *vi* **(a)** = **struggle along.**
(b) (*continue the struggle*) continuer de lutter, poursuivre la lutte (*against* contre).
struggle through *vi* (*fig*) venir à bout de ses peines, s'en sortir.
strum [strʌm] **1** *vt* **(a)** *piano* tapoter de; *guitar, banjo etc* gratter de, racler (de). **(b)** (*also* **~ out**) *tune* (*on piano*) tapoter; (*on guitar etc*) racler. **2** *vi:* **to ~ on** = **1a. 3** *n* (*also* **~ming**) *[guitar etc]* raclement *m*.
strumpet†† ['strʌmpɪt] *n* catin *f*.
strung [strʌŋ] *pret, ptp of* **string;** *V also* **highly, string up** *etc.*
strut[1] [strʌt] *vi* (*also* **~ about, ~ around**) se pavaner. **to ~ in/out/along** *etc* entrer/sortir/avancer *etc* en se pavanant *or* en se rengorgeant *or* d'un air important.
strut[2] [strʌt] *n* (*support*) étai *m*, support *m*; (*for wall, trench, mine*) étrésillon *m*; (*more solid*) étançon *m*; (*Carpentry*) contrefiche *f*, (*between uprights*) lierne *f*, traverse *f*, entretoise *f*; (*Constr: in roof*) jambe *f* de force.
strychnine ['strɪkniːn] *n* strychnine *f*.
stub [stʌb] **1** *n [tree, plant]* souche *f*, chicot *m*; *[pencil, broken stick]* bout *m*, morceau *m*; *[cigarette, cigar]* bout, mégot* *m*; *[tail]* moignon *m*; *[cheque, ticket]* talon *m*. **2** *vt:* **to ~ one's toe/one's foot** se cogner le doigt de pied/le pied (*against* contre).
stub out *vt sep cigar, cigarette* écraser.
stubble ['stʌbl] *n* (*U*) (*Agr*) chaume *m*, éteule *f*; (*on chin*) barbe *f* de plusieurs jours. **field of ~** chaume, éteule.
stubbly ['stʌblɪ] *adj field* couvert de chaume; *chin, face* mal rasé; *beard* de plusieurs jours; *hair* court et raide, en brosse.
stubborn ['stʌbən] *adj person* entêté, têtu, obstiné, opiniâtre; *animal* rétif; *campaign, resistance* opiniâtre, obstiné, acharné; *denial, refusal, insistence* obstiné, opiniâtre; *fever, disease* rebelle, persistant, opiniâtre; *V* **mule**[1].
stubbornly ['stʌbənlɪ] *adv* obstinément, opiniâtrement. **he ~ refused** il a obstinément *or* opiniâtrement refusé, il s'est obstiné à refuser.
stubbornness ['stʌbənnɪs] *n* (*V* **stubborn**) entêtement *m*, obstination *f*, opiniâtreté *f*; acharnement *m*; persistance *f*.
stubby ['stʌbɪ] *adj person* trapu, courtaud, boulot (*f* -otte); *finger* épais (*f* -aisse), boudiné; *pencil, crayon* gros et court. **a ~ tail** un bout de queue.

stucco ['stʌkəʊ] 1 *n* stuc *m*. 2 *cpd* de *or* en stuc, stuqué. 3 *vt* stuquer.

stuck [stʌk] 1 *pret, ptp of* **stick**. 2 *cpd:* **stuck-up*** prétentieux; **to be stuck-up*** se croire*, faire du chiqué*.

stud¹ [stʌd] 1 *n* (*knob, nail*) clou *m* à grosse tête; (*on door, shield etc*) clou décoratif; (*on boots*) clou à souliers, caboche *f*; (*on football boots*) crampon *m*; (*on tyre, roadway*) clou; (*Aut: cat's-eye*) clou à catadioptre; (*also* **collar ~**) bouton *m* de col; (*in chain*) étai *m*; (*Constr*) montant *m*; (*Tech: double-headed screw*) goujon *m*; (*pivot screw*) tourillon *m*.
2 *vt boots, shield, door, tyre* clouter. (*fig*) **~ded with** parsemé de, émaillé de; **sky ~ded with stars** ciel constellé, ciel parsemé *or* semé *or* piqueté *or* criblé d'étoiles.

stud² [stʌd] 1 *n* (*racing* **~**) écurie *f* (de courses); (**~** *farm*) haras *m*. **to be at ~** étalonner.
2 *cpd:* **studbook** stud-book *m*; **stud farm** haras *m*; **stud fee** prix *m* de la saillie; **studhorse** étalon *m*; **stud mare** (jument *f*) poulinière *f*; (*Cards*) **stud poker** *variété f de poker*.

student ['stju:dənt] 1 *n* (*Univ*) étudiant(e) *m(f)*; (*Scol, esp US*) élève *mf*, lycéen(ne) *m(f)*. (*Univ*) **medical ~** étudiant(e) en médecine; **he is a ~ of bird life** il étudie la vie des oiseaux; **he is a keen ~** il est très studieux.
2 *cpd* (*Univ*) *life* étudiant, estudiantin; *residence, restaurant* universitaire; *power, unrest* étudiant; *attitudes, opinions* des étudiants. **the student community** les étudiants *mpl*; (*US*) **student lamp** lampe *f* de bureau (*orientable*); **student teacher** élève *mf* professeur.

studentship ['stju:dəntʃɪp] *n* bourse *f* (d'études).

studied ['stʌdɪd] *adj calm, politeness* étudié, calculé; *insult, avoidance* délibéré, voulu; (*pej*) *pose, style* affecté.

studio ['stju:dɪəʊ] 1 *n* [*artist, photographer, musician etc*] studio *m*, atelier *m*. (*Cine, Rad, Recording, TV etc*) studio; *V* **mobile, recording** *etc*. 2 *cpd:* **studio couch** divan *m*; (*Phot*) **studio portrait** portrait *m* photographique.

studious ['stju:dɪəs] *adj person* studieux, appliqué; *piece of work, inspection* sérieux, soigné; *effort* assidu, soutenu; *calm, politeness* étudié, calculé; *insult, avoidance* délibéré, voulu.

studiously ['stju:dɪəslɪ] *adv* (*with care etc*) studieusement; (*deliberately*) d'une manière étudiée *or* calculée *or* délibérée, soigneusement. **he ~ avoided her** il prenait soin de l'éviter.

studiousness ['stju:dɪəsnɪs] *n* application *f* (*à l'étude*), amour *m* de l'étude.

study ['stʌdɪ] 1 *n* **(a)** (*gen, Art, Mus, Phot, Soc etc*) étude *f*. **to make a ~ of sth** faire une étude de qch, étudier qch; **it is a ~ of women in industry** c'est une étude sur les femmes dans l'industrie; **his studies showed that ...** ses recherches *fpl* ont montré que ...; (*fig hum*) **his face was a ~** il fallait voir son visage, son visage était un poème*; *V* **brown** *etc*.
(b) (*U*) étude *f*; (*Scol*) études *fpl*. **he spends all his time in ~** il consacre tout son temps à l'étude *or* à ses études, il passe tout son temps à étudier.
(c) (*room*) bureau *m*, cabinet *m* de travail.
2 *cpd visit, hour* d'étude; *group* de travail. (*Scol*) **study room,** (*US*) **study hall** étude *f*, salle *f* d'études.
3 *vt nature, an author, text* étudier; (*Scol, Univ*) *maths etc* faire des études de, étudier; *project, proposal, map, ground* étudier, examiner soigneusement; *person, sb's face, reactions* étudier, observer attentivement; *stars* observer; *V also* **studied**.
4 *vi* (*gen*) étudier; (*Scol, Univ etc*) étudier, faire ses études. **to ~ hard** travailler dur; **to ~ under sb** [*undergraduate*] suivre les cours de qn; [*postgraduate*] travailler *or* faire des recherches sous la direction de qn; [*painter, composer*] être l'élève de qn; **to ~ for an exam** préparer un examen; **he is ~ing to be a doctor/a pharmacist** il fait des études de médecine/de pharmacie; **he is ~ing to be a teacher** il fait des études pour entrer dans l'enseignement *or* pour devenir professeur.

stuff [stʌf] 1 *n* (*U*) **(a)** (*material, substance*) chose *f*, truc* *m*. **radioactive waste is dangerous ~** les déchets radioactifs sont une substance dangereuse *or* constituent un réel danger; **do you call this ~ wine?** vous appelez ça du vin?; **what's this ~ in this jar?** qu'est-ce que c'est que ça *or* que ce truc* dans ce pot?; **his new book is good ~** son nouveau livre est bien; **there's some good ~ in what he writes** il y a de bonnes choses dans ce qu'il écrit; **his painting is poor ~** sa peinture ne vaut pas grand-chose; **I can't listen to his ~ at all** je ne peux pas souffrir sa musique (*or* sa poésie *etc*); (*pej*) **all that ~ about how he wants to help us** toutes ces promesses en l'air comme quoi il veut nous aider; **that's the ~ (to give them** *or* **to give the troops)!*** bravo, c'est ça!; **~ and nonsense!*** balivernes!; **he is the ~ that heroes are made from,** (*liter*) **he is the ~ of heroes** il a l'étoffe d'un héros; **he knows his ~*** il connaît son sujet (*or* son métier), il s'y connaît; **do your ~!*** vas-y!, c'est à toi!; **he did his ~ very well*** il s'en est bien sorti; **she's a nice bit of ~‡** c'est une jolie môme* *or* nana‡; *V* **green, hot, stern²** *etc*.
(b) (*miscellaneous objects*) choses *fpl*; (*jumbled up*) fatras *m*; (*possessions*) affaires *fpl*, fourbi* *m*; (*tools etc*) [*workman*] attirail *m*, affaires, fourbi*. **he brought back a lot of ~ from China** il a rapporté des tas de choses de Chine.
(c) (*fabric, cloth*) étoffe *f* (*surtout de laine*).
2 *cpd* (†) *dress etc* en laine, en lainage.
3 *vt* **(a)** (*fill, pack*) *cushion, quilt, chair, toy, mattress* rembourrer (*with* avec); (*Taxidermy*) *animal* empailler; *sack, box, pockets* bourrer, remplir (*with* de); (*Culin*) *chicken, tomato* farcir (*with* avec); *hole* boucher (*with* avec); (*cram, thrust*) *objects, clothes, books* fourrer (*in, into* dans). **to ~ one's ears** se boucher les oreilles; **to ~ one's fingers into one's ears** fourrer ses doigts dans ses oreilles; **he ~ed the papers down the drain** il a fait disparaître les papiers dans le tuyau de descente; **he ~ed some money into my hand** il m'a fourré de l'argent dans la main; (*fig*) **he is a ~ed shirt*** il est pompeux; **~ed toy** jouet *m* de peluche; **to ~ o.s. with food, to ~ food into one's mouth** se gaver *or* se bourrer de nourriture; **he was ~ing himself*** il s'empiffrait*; **they ~ed him with morphine** ils l'ont bourré de morphine; **to ~ one's head with useless facts** se farcir *or* se bourrer la tête *or* la mémoire de connaissances inutiles; **he's ~ing you** *or* **your head with silly ideas** il te bourre le crâne *or* il te farcit la cervelle d'idées niaises; **the museum is ~ed with interesting things** le musée est bourré de choses intéressantes; (*US Pol*) **to ~ a ballot box** mettre des bulletins de vote truqués dans une urne; **get ~ed!‡** va te faire cuire un œuf!, va te faire foutre!**
(b) (*: *put*) mettre, poser, laisser. **~ your books on the table** mets *or* pose *or* laisse tes livres sur la table; (*fig*) **(you know where) you can ~ that!‡** tu sais où tu peux te le mettre!‡
4 *vi* (*guzzle*) se gaver, se gorger.

stuff away* *vt sep food* enfourner*, engloutir.

stuff up *vt sep hole* boucher. **my nose is stuffed up, I'm stuffed up*** j'ai le nez bouché.

stuffily ['stʌfɪlɪ] *adv say etc* d'un ton désapprobateur.

stuffiness ['stʌfɪnɪs] *n* (*in room*) manque *m* d'air; [*person*] pruderie *f*, esprit *m* étriqué *or* vieux jeu.

stuffing ['stʌfɪŋ] *n* [*quilt, cushion, toy, mattress, chair*] bourre *f*, rembourrage *m*, rembourrure *f*; (*Taxidermy*) paille *f*; (*Culin*) farce *f*. (*fig*) **he's got no ~** c'est une chiffe molle; **to knock the ~ out of sb** [*boxer, blow*] dégonfler qn; [*illness, defeat, news*] mettre qn à plat; (*take down a peg*) remettre qn à sa place.

stuffy ['stʌfɪ] *adj* **(a)** *room* mal ventilé, mal aéré. **it's ~ in here** on manque d'air *or* on étouffe ici; **it smells ~** ça sent le renfermé. **(b)** *person* collet monté *inv*, vieux jeu *inv*; *book, programme etc* ennuyeux et moralisant.

stultify ['stʌltɪfaɪ] *vt person* abrutir, déshumaniser; *sb's efforts, action* rendre vain; *argument, reasoning, claim* enlever toute valeur à.

stultifying ['stʌltɪfaɪɪŋ] *adj work* abrutissant, déshumanisant; *atmosphere* débilitant.

stumble ['stʌmbl] 1 *n* **(a)** (*in walking*) faux pas *m*, trébuchement *m*; [*horse*] faux pas.
(b) he recited it without a ~ il l'a récité sans trébucher *or* se reprendre une seule fois.
2 *cpd:* **stumbling block** pierre *f* d'achoppement.
3 *vi* **(a)** trébucher (*over* sur, contre), faire un faux pas; [*horse*] broncher. **he ~d against the table** il a trébuché *or* fait un faux pas et a heurté la table; **to ~ in/out/along** *etc* entrer/sortir/avancer *etc* en trébuchant.
(b) (*in speech*) trébucher (*at, over* sur). **he ~d through the speech** il a récité (*or* lu) le discours d'une voix hésitante *or* trébuchante.

stumble across, stumble (up)on *vt fus* (*fig*) tomber sur.

stump [stʌmp] 1 *n* [*tree*] souche *f*, chicot *m*; [*limb, tail*] moignon *m*; [*tooth*] chicot *m*; [*cigar*] bout *m*, mégot* *m*; [*pencil, chalk, sealing wax, crayon etc*] bout (*qui reste de qch*); (*Cricket*) piquet *m*. (*fig: legs*) **~s‡** guiboles‡ *fpl*; *V* **stir¹**.
2 *vt* **(a)** (*: *puzzle*) coller*, faire sécher*. **to be ~ed by sth** être incapable de *or* ne savoir que répondre à qch, sécher* sur qch; (*during quiz, crossword etc*) **I'm ~ed** je sèche*.
(b) (*Cricket*) mettre hors jeu.
3 *vi:* **to ~ in/out/along** *etc* entrer/sortir/avancer *etc* à pas lourds (*heavily*) *or* clopin-clopant* (*limping*).

stump up* (*Brit*) 1 *vi* casquer‡.
2 *vt sep* cracher*, y aller de.

stumpy ['stʌmpɪ] *adj person* courtaud, boulot (*f* -otte); *object* épais (*f* -aisse) et court.

stun [stʌn] *vt* étourdir, assommer; (*fig: amaze*) abasourdir, stupéfier.

stung [stʌŋ] *pret, ptp of* **sting.**

stunk [stʌŋk] *ptp of* **stink.**

stunner‡ ['stʌnəʳ] *n* (*girl/dress/car etc*) fille *f*/robe *f*/voiture *f etc* fantastique *or* sensationnelle*.

stunning ['stʌnɪŋ] *adj blow* étourdissant; (*overwhelming*) *news, announcement, event* stupéfiant, renversant; (*: *terrific*) *girl, dress, car* sensationnel*, fantastique.

stunningly ['stʌnɪŋlɪ] *adv dressed etc* d'une manière éblouissante *or* sensationnelle*.

stunt¹ [stʌnt] 1 *n* (*feat*) tour *m* de force, exploit *m* (*destiné à attirer l'attention du public*); (*Aviat*) acrobatie *f*; [*students*] canular* *m*; (*trick*) truc* *m*, coup monté, combine‡ *f*; (*publicity* **~**) truc* publicitaire. **it's a ~ to get your money** c'est un truc* *or* c'est un coup monté pour avoir votre argent; **that was a good ~** c'était un truc* ingénieux *or* une combine‡ ingénieuse.
2 *cpd:* (*Aviat*) **stunt flier** aviateur *m* qui fait de l'acrobatie, aviateur *m* de haute voltige; **stunt flying** acrobatie aérienne, haute voltige; (*Cine, TV*) **stuntman** cascadeur *m*.

stunt² [stʌnt] *vt growth* retarder, arrêter; *person, plant* retarder la croissance de.

stunted ['stʌntɪd] *adj person, plant* rabougri, rachitique, chétif.

stupefaction [ˌstju:pɪ'fækʃən] *n* stupéfaction *f*, stupeur *f*.

stupefy ['stju:pɪfaɪ] *vt* [*blow*] étourdir; [*drink, drugs, lack of sleep*] abrutir; (*fig: astound*) stupéfier, abasourdir.

stupefying ['stju:pɪfaɪɪŋ] *adj* (*fig*) stupéfiant, ahurissant.

stupendous [stju(:)'pendəs] *adj ceremony, beauty* prodigieux; (**fig*) *film, holiday* fantastique, sensationnel*, formidable*.

stupendously [stju(:)'pendəslɪ] *adv* formidablement*, d'une manière sensationnelle* *or* fantastique.

stupid ['stju:pɪd] *adj* stupide, bête, idiot; (*from sleep, drink etc*) abruti, hébété. **don't be ~** ne sois pas bête *or* stupide *or* idiot, ne fais pas l'idiot; **I've done a ~ thing** j'ai fait une bêtise *or* une sottise; **come on, ~*** allez viens, gros bêta* (*f* grosse bêtasse*); **you ~ idiot!*** espèce d'idiot(e)!; **the blow knocked him ~** le coup l'a étourdi; **he drank himself ~** il s'est abruti d'alcool.

stupidity [stjuːˈpɪdɪtɪ] *n* stupidité *f*, sottise *f*, bêtise *f*.
stupidly [ˈstjuːpɪdlɪ] *adv* stupidement, sottement. **I ~ told him your name** j'ai eu la sottise de *or* j'ai été assez bête pour lui dire votre nom.
stupidness [ˈstjuːpɪdnɪs] *n* = **stupidity.**
stupor [ˈstjuːpəʳ] *n* stupeur *f*.
sturdily [ˈstɜːdɪlɪ] *adv* (*V* **sturdy**) robustement; vigoureusement; énergiquement; solidement. **~ built** *person, child* robuste; *chair, cycle* robuste, solide; *house* de construction solide.
sturdiness [ˈstɜːdɪnɪs] *n* (*V* **sturdy**) robustesse *f*; solidité *f*; vigueur *f*.
sturdy [ˈstɜːdɪ] *adj person, tree* robuste, vigoureux; *cycle, chair* robuste, solide; (*fig*) *resistance, defence, refusal* énergique, vigoureux. **~ common sense** gros *or* robuste bon sens.
sturgeon [ˈstɜːdʒən] *n* esturgeon *m*.
stutter [ˈstʌtəʳ] **1** *n* bégaiement *m*. **to have a ~** bégayer. **2** *vi* bégayer. **3** *vt* (*also* **~ out**) bégayer, dire en bégayant.
stutterer [ˈstʌtərəʳ] *n* bègue *mf*.
stuttering [ˈstʌtərɪŋ] **1** *n* (*U*) bégaiement *m*. **2** *adj* bègue, qui bégaie.
sty[1] [staɪ] *n* [*pigs*] porcherie *f*.
sty[2], **stye** [staɪ] *n* (*Med*) orgelet *m*, compère-loriot *m*.
Stygian [ˈstɪdʒɪən] *adj* (*fig*) sombre *or* noir comme le Styx, ténébreux. **~ darkness** ténèbres *fpl* impénétrables, nuit noire.
style [staɪl] **1** *n* **(a)** (*gen, Art, Literat, Mus, Sport, Typ etc*) style *m*. **in the ~ of Mozart** dans le style *or* à la manière de Mozart; **building in the Renaissance ~** édifice *m* (de) style Renaissance; **March 6th, old/new ~** 6 Mars vieux/nouveau style; **~ of life** *or* **living** style de vie; **he won in fine ~** il l'a emporté haut la main; **I like his ~ of writing** j'aime sa manière d'écrire *or* son style; (*fig*) **I don't like his ~** je n'aime pas son genre; **that house is not my ~*** ce n'est pas mon genre de maison; **that's the ~!*** bravo!; *V* **cramp**[1] *etc*.
(b) (*Dress etc*) mode *f*, genre *m*, modèle *m*; (*Hairdressing*) coiffure *f*. **in the latest ~** (*adv*) à la dernière mode; (*adj*) du dernier cri; **these coats are made in 2 ~s** ces manteaux sont confectionnés en 2 genres *or* en 2 modèles; **the 4 ~s are all the same price** les 4 modèles sont tous au même prix; **I want something in that ~** je voudrais quelque chose dans ce genre *or* dans ce goût-là.
(c) (*U: distinction, elegance*) [*person*] allure *f*, chic *m*; [*building, car, film, book*] style *m*, cachet *m*. **that writer lacks ~** cet écrivain manque de style *or* d'élégance, le style de cet écrivain manque de tenue; **to live in ~** mener grand train, vivre sur un grand pied; **he does things in ~** il fait bien les choses; **they got married in ~** ils se sont mariés en grande pompe; **he certainly travels in ~** quand il voyage il fait bien les choses, il voyage dans les règles de l'art.
(d) (*sort, type*) genre *m*. **just the ~ of book/car I like** justement le genre de livre/de voiture que j'aime.
(e) (*form of address*) titre *m*.
2 *cpd:* (*Typ*) **style book** manuel *m* des règles typographiques.
3 *vt* **(a)** (*call, designate*) appeler. **he ~s himself 'Doctor'** il se fait appeler 'Docteur'; **the headmaster is ~d 'rector'** le directeur a le titre de 'recteur'; *V* **self-styled.**
(b) (*design etc*) *dress, car, boat* créer, dessiner. **to ~ sb's hair** créer une nouvelle coiffure pour qn; **it is ~d for comfort not elegance** c'est un modèle conçu en fonction du confort et non de l'élégance.
(c) (*Typ*) *manuscript* préparer (*selon le style de l'éditeur*).
styling [ˈstaɪlɪŋ] *n* (*U*) [*dress*] forme *f*, ligne *f*, façon *f*; [*car*] ligne *f*; (*Hairdressing*) coupe *f*.
stylish [ˈstaɪlɪʃ] *adj person* élégant, qui a du chic; *garment, hotel, district* chic *inv*; *film, book, car* qui a une certaine élégance.
stylishly [ˈstaɪlɪʃlɪ] *adv live, dress* élégamment; *travel* dans les règles de l'art.
stylishness [ˈstaɪlɪʃnɪs] *n* élégance *f*, chic *m*.
stylist [ˈstaɪlɪst] *n* (*Literat*) styliste *mf*; (*Dress etc*) modéliste *mf*; (*Hairdressing*) coiffeur *m*, -euse *f*, artiste *mf* (capillaire).
stylistic [staɪˈlɪstɪk] **1** *adj* (*Literat etc*) stylistique, du style. **~ device** procédé *m* stylistique *or* de style. **2** *n* (*U*) **~s** stylistique *f*.
stylize [ˈstaɪlaɪz] *vt* styliser.
stylus [ˈstaɪləs] *n* (*tool*) style *m*; [*record player*] pointe *f* de lecture.
stymie [ˈstaɪmɪ] **1** *n* (*Golf*) trou barré. **2** *vt* (*Golf*) barrer le trou à; (**fig*) coincer*. **I'm ~d*** je suis coincé*, je suis dans une impasse.
styptic [ˈstɪptɪk] **1** *adj* styptique. **~ pencil** crayon *m* de glycérine.
2 *n* styptique *m*.
suasion [ˈsweɪʒən] *n* (*also* **moral ~**) pression morale.
suave [swɑːv] *adj person* doucereux; *manner, voice* doucereux, onctueux (*pej*). **I didn't like his rather ~ suggestion that ...** je n'ai pas aimé la façon insinuante *or* un peu trop persuasive dont il a suggéré que ... .
suavely [ˈswɑːvlɪ] *adv* doucereusement, onctueusement (*pej*).
suavity [ˈswɑːvɪtɪ] *n* (*U*) manières doucereuses *or* onctueuses (*pej*).
sub* [sʌb] *abbr of* **subaltern, sub-edit, sub-editor, sub-lieutenant, submarine** (*n*), **subscription, substitute.**
sub... [sʌb] **1** *pref* sub..., sous-; *V* **subculture** *etc*.
2 *cpd:* (*Jur*) **sub judice** devant le tribunal *or* les tribunaux; **this is at present sub judice** l'affaire passe à présent devant les tribunaux; **sub rosa** en confidence, sous le sceau du secret; **sub specie** sous l'aspect de.
subagent [sʌbˈeɪdʒənt] *n* sous-agent *m*.
subalpine [ˈsʌbˈælpaɪn] *adj* subalpin.
subaltern [ˈsʌbltən] **1** *n* (*Brit Mil*) lieutenant *m*; sous-lieutenant *m*. **2** *adj* subalterne.
subaqueous [ˈsʌbˈeɪkwɪəs] *adj* subaquatique, aquatique.
subarctic [ˈsʌbˈɑːktɪk] *adj* sub-arctique; (*fig*) presque arctique.
subassembly [ˌsʌbəˈsemblɪ] *n* sous-assemblée *f*.
subatomic [ˈsʌbəˈtɒmɪk] *adj* plus petit que l'atome.
sub-basement [ˈsʌbˈbeɪsmənt] *n* second sous-sol.
sub-branch [ˈsʌbˈbrɑːntʃ] *n* sous-embranchement *m*.
subclass [ˈsʌbˈklɑːs] *n* sous-classe *f*.
subcommittee [ˈsʌbkəˌmɪtɪ] *n* sous-comité *m*; (*larger*) sous-commission *f*. **the Housing S~** la sous-commission du logement.
subconscious [ˈsʌbˈkɒnʃəs] *adj, n* subconscient (*m*).
subconsciously [ˈsʌbˈkɒnʃəslɪ] *adv* de manière subconsciente, inconsciemment.
subcontinent [ˈsʌbˈkɒntɪnənt] *n* subcontinent *m*. **the (Indian) S~** le subcontinent des Indes.
subcontract [ˈsʌbˈkɒntrækt] **1** *n* sous-traité *m*. **2** [ˌsʌbkənˈtrækt] *vt* sous-traiter.
subcontractor [ˈsʌbkənˈtræktəʳ] *n* sous-entrepreneur *m*, sous-traitant *m*.
subculture [ˈsʌbˈkʌltʃəʳ] *n* (*Soc*) subculture *f*; (*Bacteriology*) culture repiquée.
subcutaneous [ˈsʌbkjʊˈteɪnɪəs] *adj* sous-cutané.
subdistrict [ˈsʌbˌdɪstrɪkt] *n* subdivision *f* d'un quartier.
subdivide [ˌsʌbdɪˈvaɪd] **1** *vt* subdiviser. **2** *vi* se subdiviser.
subdivision [ˈsʌbdɪˌvɪʒən] *n* subdivision *f*.
subdominant [ˌsʌbˈdɒmɪnənt] *n* (*Ecol*) (espèce *f*); sous-dominante *f*. (*Mus*) sous-dominante *f*.
subdue [səbˈdjuː] *vt people, country* subjuguer, assujettir, soumettre; *feelings, passions, desire* contenir, refréner, maîtriser; *light, colour* adoucir, atténuer; *voice* baisser; *pain* atténuer, amortir.
subdued [səbˈdjuːd] *adj emotion* contenu; *reaction, response* faible, pas très marqué; *voice, tone* bas (*f* basse); *conversation, discussion* à voix basse; *light, lighting* tamisé, voilé. **she was very ~** elle avait perdu sa vivacité *or* son entrain *or* son exubérance.
sub-edit [ˈsʌbˈedɪt] *vt* (*Brit: Press, Typ*) corriger, mettre au point, préparer pour l'impression.
sub-editor [ˈsʌbˈedɪtəʳ] *n* (*Brit: Press, Typ*) secrétaire *mf* de (la) rédaction.
sub-entry [ˈsʌbˌentrɪ] *n* sous-entrée *f*.
subfamily [ˈsʌbˌfæmɪlɪ] *n* sous-famille *f*.
subgroup [ˈsʌbˌgruːp] *n* sous-groupe *m*.
subhead(ing) [ˈsʌbˌhed(ɪŋ)] *n* sous-titre *m*.
subhuman [ˈsʌbˈhjuːmən] *adj* pas tout à fait humain, moins qu'humain.
subject [ˈsʌbdʒɪkt] **1** *n* **(a)** (*citizen etc*) sujet(te) *m(f)*; ressortissant(e) *m(f)*, national(e) *m(f)*. **the king and his ~s** le roi et ses sujets; **British ~** sujet britannique; **he is a French ~** (*in France*) il est de nationalité française; (*elsewhere*) c'est un ressortissant *or* un national français.
(b) (*Med, Phot, Psych etc: person*) sujet *m*. **he's a good ~ for treatment by hypnosis** c'est un sujet qui répond bien au traitement par l'hypnose; **he's a good ~ for research into hypnosis** c'est un bon sujet d'expérience pour une étude de l'hypnose.
(c) (*matter, topic: gen, Art, Literat, Mus etc*) sujet *m* (*of, for* de); (*Scol, Univ*) matière *f*, discipline *f*. **to get off the ~** sortir du sujet; **that's off the ~** c'est hors du sujet *or* à côté du sujet; **let's get back to the ~** revenons à nos moutons; **on the ~ of** au sujet de, sur le sujet de; **while we're on the ~ of ...** pendant que nous parlons de ..., à propos de ...; (*Scol, Univ*) **his best ~** sa matière *or* sa discipline forte; *V* **change, drop** *etc*.
(d) (*reason, occasion*) sujet *m*, motif *m* (*of, for* de). **it is not a ~ for rejoicing** il n'y a pas lieu de se réjouir.
(e) (*Gram, Logic, Philos*) sujet *m*.
2 *cpd:* **subject heading** rubrique *f*; **subject index** (*in book*) index *m* des matières; (*in library*) fichier *m* par matières; **subject matter** (*theme*) sujet *m*; (*content*) contenu *m*; (*Gram*) **subject pronoun** pronom *m* sujet.
3 *adj people, tribes, state* soumis. **~ to** (*liable to*) (*disease etc*) sujet à; (*flooding, subsidence etc*) exposé à; (*the law, taxation*) soumis à; (*conditional upon*) sous réserve de, à condition de; (*except for*) sous réserve de, sauf; **~ to French rule** sous (la) domination française; **nations ~ to communism** nations *fpl* d'obédience communiste; **our prices are ~ to alteration** nos prix peuvent être modifiés *or* sont donnés sous réserve de modifications; **~ to the approval of the committee** sous réserve de l'approbation du comité; **you may leave the country ~ to producing the necessary documents** vous pouvez quitter le pays à condition de fournir les documents nécessaires; **~ to prior sale** sous réserve de *or* sauf vente antérieure.
4 [səbˈdʒekt] *vt* (*subdue*) *country* soumettre, assujettir (*liter*). **to ~ sb to sth** soumettre qn à qch, faire subir qch à qn; **to ~ sth to heat/cold** exposer qch à la chaleur/au froid; **he was ~ed to much criticism** il a été en butte à de nombreuses critiques, il a été très critiqué; **to ~ o.s. to criticism** s'exposer à la critique.
subjection [səbˈdʒekʃən] *n* sujétion *f*, soumission *f*. **to hold** *or* **keep in ~** maintenir dans la sujétion *or* sous son joug; **to bring into ~** soumettre, assujettir (*liter*); **they were in a state of complete ~** ils vivaient dans la sujétion *or* dans la soumission *or* dans les chaînes.
subjective [səbˈdʒektɪv] **1** *adj* subjectif; (*Gram*) *case, pronoun* sujet; *genitive* subjectif. **2** *n* (*Gram*) nominatif *m*.
subjectively [səbˈdʒektɪvlɪ] *adv* subjectivement.
subjectivism [səbˈdʒektɪvɪzəm] *n* subjectivisme *m*.
subjectivity [ˌsʌbdʒekˈtɪvɪtɪ] *n* subjectivité *f*.
subjoin [ˈsʌbˈdʒɔɪn] *vt* adjoindre, ajouter.
subjugate [ˈsʌbdʒʊgeɪt] *vt people, country* subjuguer,

soumettre, assujettir; *animal, feelings* dompter.

subjugation [ˌsʌbdʒʊˈgeɪʃən] *n* subjugation *f*, assujettissement *m*.

subjunctive [səbˈdʒʌŋktɪv] *adj, n* subjonctif (*m*). **in the ~ (mood)** au (mode) subjonctif.

subkingdom [ˈsʌbˌkɪŋdəm] *n* (*Bot, Zool etc*) embranchement *m*.

sublease [ˈsʌbˈliːs] **1** *n* sous-location *f*. **2** *vti* sous-louer (*to* à, *from* à).

sublet [ˈsʌbˈlet] (*vb: pret, ptp* **sublet**) **1** *n* sous-location *f*. **2** *vti* sous-louer (*to* à).

sub-librarian [ˈsʌblaɪˈbrɛərɪən] *n* bibliothécaire *mf* adjoint(e).

sub-lieutenant [ˈsʌblefˈtenənt] *n* (*Brit Naut*) enseigne *m* de vaisseau.

sublimate [ˈsʌblɪmeɪt] **1** *vt* (*all senses*) sublimer. **2** [ˈsʌblɪmɪt] *adj, n* (*Chem*) sublimé (*m*).

sublimation [ˌsʌblɪˈmeɪʃən] *n* sublimation *f*.

sublime [səˈblaɪm] **1** *adj* **(a)** *being, beauty, work, scenery* sublime; (*: *excellent*) *dinner, hat, person* divin, fantastique, sensationnel*.

(b) *contempt, indifference, impertinence* suprême (*before n*), souverain (*before n*), sans pareil.

2 *n* sublime *m*. **from the ~ to the ridiculous** du sublime au grotesque.

sublimely [səˈblaɪmlɪ] *adv* **(a) ~ beautiful** d'une beauté sublime. **(b)** *contemptuous, indifferent* au plus haut point, suprêmement, souverainement. **~ unaware** *or* **unconscious of** dans une ignorance absolue de.

subliminal [ˌsʌbˈlɪmɪnl] *adj* subliminal. **~ advertising** publicité insidieuse.

subliminally [ˌsʌbˈlɪmɪnəlɪ] *adv* au-dessous du niveau de la conscience.

sublimity [səˈblɪmɪtɪ] *n* sublimité *f*.

sublingual [sʌbˈlɪŋgwəl] *adj* sublingual.

submachine gun [ˈsʌbməˈʃiːngʌn] *n* mitraillette *f*.

submarine [ˌsʌbməˈriːn] *adj, n* sous-marin (*m*). **~ chaser** chasseur *m* de sous-marins.

submariner [ˌsʌbˈmærɪnəʳ] *n* sous-marinier *m*.

submaxillary [ˌsʌbˈmæksɪlərɪ] *adj* sous-maxillaire.

submediant [ˌsʌbˈmiːdɪənt] *n* (*Mus*) sixte *f*.

submerge [səbˈmɜːdʒ] *vt [flood, tide, sea]* submerger. **~d** *rock/wreck etc* submergé; (*fig*) *poor people* déshérité, indigent; **to ~ sth in sth** immerger qch dans qch; (*fig*) **~d in work** submergé *or* débordé de travail.

submersible [səbˈmɜːsəbl] *adj* submersible.

submersion [səbˈmɜːʃən] *n* (*V* **submerge**) submersion *f*; immersion *f*.

submission [səbˈmɪʃən] *n* **(a)** (*Mil, fig*) soumission (*to* à). **starved/beaten into ~** réduit par la faim/les coups; **to make one's ~ to sb** faire sa soumission à qn.

(b) (*U: submissiveness*) soumission *f*, docilité *f*.

(c) (*U: V* **submit 1b**) soumission *f*.

(d) (*Jur etc*) thèse *f*. **his ~ was that ...** il a allégué *or* avancé que ..., sa thèse était que ...; **in my ~** selon ma thèse.

submissive [səbˈmɪsɪv] *adj person, answer, smile* soumis, docile.

submissively [səbˈmɪsɪvlɪ] *adv* avec soumission, docilement.

submissiveness [səbˈmɪsɪvnɪs] *n* soumission *f*, docilité *f*.

submit [səbˈmɪt] **1** *vt* **(a) to ~ o.s. to sb/sth** se soumettre à qn/qch.

(b) (*put forward*) *documents, sample, proposal, report, evidence* soumettre (*to* à). **to ~ that** suggérer que; **I ~ that** ma thèse est que.

2 *vi* (*Mil*) se soumettre (*to* à); (*fig*) se soumettre, se plier (*to* à).

subnormal [ˈsʌbˈnɔːməl] *adj temperature* au-dessous de la normale; *person* arriéré.

suborbital [ˈsʌbˈɔːbɪtəl] *adj* (*Space*) sous-orbital.

sub-order [ˈsʌbˈɔːdəʳ] *n* sous-ordre *m*.

subordinate [səˈbɔːdnɪt] **1** *adj member of staff, rank, position* subalterne; (*Gram*) subordonné.

2 *n* subordonné(e) *m(f)*, subalterne *mf*.

3 [səˈbɔːdɪneɪt] *vt* subordonner (*to* à). (*Gram*) **subordinating conjunction** conjonction *f* de subordination.

subordination [səˌbɔːdɪˈneɪʃən] *n* subordination *f*.

suborn [sʌˈbɔːn] *vt* suborner.

subplot [ˈsʌbˌplɒt] *n* (*liter*) intrigue *f* secondaire.

subpoena [səbˈpiːnə] (*Jur*) **1** *n* citation *f*, assignation *f*. **2** *vt* citer *or* assigner (à comparaître).

subpopulation [ˈsʌbˌpɒpjʊˈleɪʃən] *n* subpopulation *f*.

sub post office [sʌbˈpəʊstˌɒfɪs] *n* petit bureau de poste secondaire *or* de quartier *or* de village.

subregion [ˈsʌbˌriːdʒən] *n* sous-région *f*.

subroutine [ˌsʌbruːˈtiːn] *n* (*Computers*) sous-programme *m*.

subscribe [səbˈskraɪb] **1** *vt* **(a)** *money* donner, verser (*to* à).

(b) *one's signature, name* apposer (*to* au bas de); *document* signer. **he ~s himself John Smith** il signe John Smith.

2 *vi* verser une somme d'argent, apporter une contribution, cotiser*. **to ~ to** *book, new publication, fund* souscrire à; *newspaper* s'abonner à, être abonné à; *opinion, idea, project, proposal* souscrire à, donner son adhésion à.

subscriber [səbˈskraɪbəʳ] **1** *n* (*to fund, new publication etc*) souscripteur *m*, -trice *f* (*to* de); (*to newspaper, also Telec*) abonné(e) *m(f)* (*to* de); (*to opinion, idea*) adepte *mf*, partisan *m* (*to* de).

2 *cpd:* (*Brit Telec*) **subscriber trunk dialling** (*abbr* **STD**) automatique *m*.

subscript [ˈsʌbskrɪpt] **1** *adj* inférieur (*f* -eure). **2** *n* indice *m*.

subscription [səbˈskrɪpʃən] **1** *n* (*to fund, charity*) souscription *f*; (*to club*) cotisation *f*; (*to newspaper*) abonnement *m*. **to pay one's ~** (*to club*) payer *or* verser sa cotisation; (*to newspaper*) payer *or* régler son abonnement; (*Press*) **to take out a ~ to** s'abonner à.

2 *cpd:* (*Press*) **subscription rate** tarif *m* d'abonnement.

subsection [ˈsʌbˌsekʃən] *n* (*Jur etc*) subdivision *f*, article *m*.

subsequent [ˈsʌbsɪkwənt] *adj* **(a)** (*following*) ultérieur (*f* -eure), postérieur (*f* -eure), suivant, subséquent (*frm, Jur*). **on a ~ visit** lors d'une visite postérieure *or* ultérieure; **his ~ visit** sa visite suivante; **~ to his speech** à la suite de son discours; **~ to this** par la suite. **(b)** (*resultant*) consécutif, résultant.

subserve [səbˈsɜːv] *vt* (*frm*) favoriser.

subservience [səbˈsɜːvɪəns] *n* (*V* **subservient a**) caractère *m* subalterne; obséquiosité *f*, servilité *f*; asservissement *m* (*to* à).

subservient [səbˈsɜːvɪənt] *adj* **(a)** *role* subalterne; (*pej*) *person, manner* obséquieux (*pej*), servile (*pej*); (*to taste, fashion*) asservi (*to* à). **(b)** (*frm: useful*) utile (*to* à).

subset [ˈsʌbˌset] *n* sous-ensemble *m*.

subside [səbˈsaɪd] *vi [land, pavement, foundations, building]* s'affaisser, se tasser; *[flood, river]* baisser, décroître; *[wind, anger, excitement]* tomber, se calmer; *[threat]* s'éloigner; *[person]* (*into armchair etc*) s'affaisser, s'écrouler (*into* dans, *on to* sur); (*: *keep quiet*) se taire.

subsidence [səbˈsaɪdəns] *n [land, pavement, foundations, building]* affaissement *m*. **'road liable to ~'** = 'chaussée instable'; **the crack in the wall is caused by ~** la faille dans le mur est due à l'affaissement du terrain.

subsidiary [səbˈsɪdɪərɪ] **1** *adj motive, reason* subsidiaire; *advantage, income* accessoire. (*Fin*) **~ company** filiale *f*. **2** *n* (*Fin*) filiale *f*.

subsidize [ˈsʌbsɪdaɪz] *vt* subventionner.

subsidy [ˈsʌbsɪdɪ] *n* subvention *f*. **government** *or* **state ~** subvention de l'État; **there is a ~ on butter** l'État subventionne le beurre.

subsist [səbˈsɪst] *vi* subsister. **to ~ on bread/£60 a week** vivre de pain/avec 60 livres par semaine.

subsistence [səbˈsɪstəns] **1** *n* **(a)** existence *f*, subsistance *f*. **means of ~** moyens *mpl* d'existence *or* de subsistance.

(b) (*also* **~ allowance**) frais *mpl or* indemnité *f* de subsistance.

2 *cpd:* **subsistence crops** cultures vivrières de base; **to live at subsistence level** avoir tout juste de quoi vivre; **subsistence wage** salaire tout juste suffisant pour vivre.

subsoil [ˈsʌbsɔɪl] *n* (*Agr, Geol*) sous-sol *m*.

subsonic [ˈsʌbˈsɒnɪk] *adj* subsonique.

subspecies [ˈsʌbˈspiːʃiːz] *n* sous-espèce *f*.

substance [ˈsʌbstəns] *n* (*matter, material*) substance *f* (*also Chem, Philos, Phys, Rel etc*); (*essential meaning, gist*) substance, fond *m*, essentiel *m*; (*solid quality*) solidité *f*; (*consistency*) consistance *f*; (*wealth etc*) biens *mpl*, fortune *f*. **that is the ~ of his speech** voilà la substance *or* l'essentiel de son discours; **I agree with the ~ of his proposals** je suis d'accord sur l'essentiel de ses propositions; **the meal had not much ~ (to it)** le repas n'était pas très substantiel; **to lack ~** *[film, book, essay]* manquer d'étoffe; *[argument]* être plutôt mince; *[accusation, claim, allegation]* être sans grand fondement; *V* **sum**.

substandard [ˌsʌbˈstændəd] *adj goods* de qualité inférieure; *performance* médiocre; *housing* inférieur aux normes exigées; (*Ling*) non conforme à la langue correcte.

substantial [səbˈstænʃəl] *adj* **(a)** (*great, large*) *amount, proportion, load, loan, part, progress* important, considérable, substantiel (*fig*); *proof* solide, concluant; *difference* appréciable; *argument* de poids; *meal* substantiel, copieux; *firm* solide, bien assis; *landowner, farmer, businessman* riche, cossu; *house etc* grand, important. **to be in ~ agreement** être d'accord sur l'essentiel *or* dans l'ensemble.

(b) (*real*) substantiel, réel.

substantially [səbˈstænʃəlɪ] *adv* **(a)** (*considerably*) *improve, contribute, progress* considérablement. **~ bigger** beaucoup plus grand; **~ different** très différent; **not ~ different** pas réellement différent.

(b) (*to a large extent*) en grande partie. **this is ~ true** c'est en grande partie vrai; **it is ~ the same book** c'est en grande partie le même livre, ce n'est guère différent de l'autre livre.

(c) *built, constructed* solidement.

substantiate [səbˈstænʃɪeɪt] *vt* fournir des preuves à l'appui de, justifier.

substantiation [səbˌstænʃɪˈeɪʃən] *n* preuve *f*, justification *f*.

substantival [ˌsʌbstənˈtaɪvəl] *adj* (*Gram*) substantif, à valeur de substantif.

substantive [ˈsʌbstəntɪv] **1** *n* (*Gram*) substantif *m*. **2** *adj* **(a)** (*Gram*) substantif. **(b)** indépendant, autonome.

substation [ˈsʌbˌsteɪʃən] *n* sous-station *f*.

substitute [ˈsʌbstɪtjuːt] **1** *n* (*person: gen, Sport*) remplaçant(e) *m(f)*, suppléant(e) *m(f)* (*for* de); (*thing*) produit *m* de remplacement, succédané *m* (*gen pej*), ersatz *m inv* (*gen pej*) (*for* de); (*Gram*) terme suppléant. **you must find a ~ (for yourself)** vous devez vous trouver un remplaçant, il faut vous faire remplacer; **~s for rubber, rubber ~s** succédanés *or* ersatz de caoutchouc; (*Comm*) **'beware of ~s'** 'refusez toutes imitations *or* contrefaçons'; **there is no ~ for wool** rien ne peut remplacer la laine; *V* **turpentine** *etc*.

2 *adj* (*Sport*) (à titre de) remplaçant. **~ coffee** ersatz *m inv or* succédané *m* de café.

3 *vt* substituer (*A for B* A à B), remplacer (*A for B* B par A).

4 *vi*: **to ~ for sb** remplacer *or* suppléer qn.

substitution [ˌsʌbstɪˈtjuːʃən] *n* substitution *f* (*also Chem, Ling, Math etc*), remplacement *m*. **~ of x for y** substitution de x à y, remplacement de y par x.

substratum [ˈsʌbˈstrɑːtəm] *n* (*gen, Geol, Soc etc*) substrat m; (*Agr*) sous-sol *m*; (*fig*) fond *m*.

substructure ['sʌbˌstrʌktʃəʳ] *n* infrastructure *f*.
subsume [səb'sjuːm] *vt* subsumer.
subsystem [ˌsʌb'sɪstəm] *n* sous-système *m*.
subtemperate [ˌsʌb'tempərɪt] *adj* subtempéré.
subtenancy ['sʌb'tenənsɪ] *n* sous-location *f*.
subtenant ['sʌb'tenənt] *n* sous-locataire *mf*.
subtend [səb'tend] *vt* sous-tendre.
subterfuge ['sʌbtəfjuːdʒ] *n* subterfuge *m*.
subterranean [ˌsʌbtə'reɪnɪən] *adj* souterrain.
subtilize ['sʌtɪlaɪz] *vti* subtiliser.
subtitle ['sʌbˌtaɪtl] *(Cine)* **1** *n* sous-titre *m*.
2 *vt* sous-titrer.
subtitling ['sʌbˌtaɪtlɪŋ] *n* sous-titrage *m*.
subtle ['sʌtl] *adj person* subtil (*f* subtile), perspicace, qui a beaucoup de finesse; *mind, intelligence* subtil, fin, pénétrant; *argument, suggestion, analysis, reply* subtil, ingénieux, astucieux; *irony, joke* subtil, fin; *distinction* subtil, ténu; *allusion* subtil, discret (*f* -ète); *charm* subtil, indéfinissable; *perfume* subtil, délicat. (*Cine, Literat, Theat etc*) **it wasn't very ~** c'était un peu gros, c'était cousu de fil blanc.
subtleness ['sʌtlnɪs] *n* = **subtlety a.**
subtlety ['sʌtltɪ] *n* **(a)** (*U: V* **subtle**) subtilité *f*; perspicacité *f*; finesse *f*; ingéniosité *f*; délicatesse *f*. **(b)** **a ~** une subtilité.
subtly ['sʌtlɪ] *adv* subtilement.
subtonic [ˌsʌb'tɒnɪk] *n* sous-tonique *f*.
subtopic ['sʌb'tɒpɪk] *n* sous-thème *m*, subdivision *f* d'un thème.
subtotal [ˌsʌb'təʊtl] *n* total partiel.
subtract [səb'trækt] *vt* soustraire, retrancher, déduire (*from* de).
subtraction [səb'trækʃən] *n* soustraction *f*.
subtropical ['sʌb'trɒpɪkəl] *adj* subtropical.
suburb ['sʌbɜːb] *n* faubourg *m*. **the ~s** la banlieue; **in the ~s** en banlieue; **the outer ~s** la grande banlieue; **it is now a ~ of London** c'est maintenant un faubourg de Londres, ça fait partie de la banlieue de Londres.
suburban [sə'bɜːbən] *adj house, square, shops, community, development, train* suburbain, de banlieue; (*pej*) *person, attitude, accent* banlieusard* (*pej*).
suburbanite [sə'bɜːbənaɪt] *n* habitant(e) *m(f)* de la banlieue, banlieusard(e)* *m(f)* (*pej*).
suburbanize [sə'bɜːbənaɪz] *vt* donner le caractère *or* les caractéristiques de la banlieue à, transformer en banlieue.
suburbia [sə'bɜːbɪə] *n* (*U*) la banlieue.
subvention [səb'venʃən] *n* subvention *f*.
subversion [səb'vɜːʃən] *n* subversion *f*, renversement *m*.
subversive [səb'vɜːsɪv] *adj* subversif.
subvert [səb'vɜːt] *vt the law, tradition* bouleverser, renverser; (*corrupt*) *person* corrompre, pervertir.
subway ['sʌbweɪ] *n* (*underpass: esp Brit*) passage souterrain; (*railway: esp US*) métro *m*.
sub-zero ['sʌb'zɪərəʊ] *adj temperature* au-dessous de zéro.
succeed [sək'siːd] **1** *vi* **(a)** (*be successful*) réussir (*in sth* dans qch); (*prosper*) réussir, avoir du succès; *[plan, attempt]* réussir. **to ~ in doing** réussir *or* parvenir *or* arriver à faire; **he ~s in all he does** tout lui réussit, il réussit tout ce qu'il entreprend; (*Prov*) **nothing ~s like success** un succès en entraîne un autre; **to ~ in business/as a politician** réussir *or* avoir du succès en affaires/en tant qu'homme politique; **to ~ in life/one's career** réussir dans la vie/sa carrière.
(b) (*follow*) succéder (*to* à). **he ~ed (to the throne) in 1911** il a succédé (à la couronne) en 1911; **there ~ed a period of peace** il y eut ensuite une période de paix.
2 *vt [person]* succéder à, prendre la suite de; *[event, storm, season etc]* succéder à, suivre. **he ~ed his father as leader of the party** il a succédé à *or* pris la suite de son père à la direction du parti; **he was ~ed by his son** son fils lui a succédé; **as year ~ed year** comme les années passaient, comme les années se succédaient.
succeeding [sək'siːdɪŋ] *adj* (*in past*) suivant, qui suit; (*in future*) à venir, futur. **each ~ year brought ...** chaque année qui passait apportait ...; **each ~ year will bring ...** chacune des années à venir apportera ...; **on 3 ~ Saturdays** 3 samedis consécutifs *or* de suite; **in the ~ chaos** dans la confusion qui a suivi.
success [sək'ses] **1** *n [plan, venture, attempt, person]* succès *m*, réussite *f* (*in an exam* à un examen, *in one's aim* dans son but). **his ~ in doing sth** le fait qu'il ait réussi à faire qch; **his ~ in his attempts** la réussite qui a couronné ses efforts; **without ~** sans succès, en vain; **to meet with ~** avoir *or* obtenir *or* remporter du succès; **to have great ~** faire fureur, avoir un succès fou; **to make a ~ of** *project, enterprise* faire réussir, mener à bien; *job, meal, dish* réussir; **he was a ~ at last** il avait enfin réussi, il était enfin arrivé, il avait enfin du succès; **he was a great ~ at the dinner/as Hamlet/as a writer/in business** il a eu beaucoup de succès au dîner/dans le rôle de Hamlet/en tant qu'écrivain/en affaires; **it was a ~** *[holiday, meal, evening, attack]* c'était une réussite, c'était réussi; *[play, book, record]* ça a été couronné de succès; **the hotel was a great ~** on a été très content de l'hôtel; *V* **succeed.**
2 *cpd:* **success story** histoire *f* d'une réussite.
successful [sək'sesfʊl] *adj plan, venture* couronné de succès, qui a réussi; *businessman* prospère, qui a du succès *or* qui est heureux en affaires; *writer, painter, book* à succès; *candidate* (*in exam*) reçu, admis; (*in election*) élu; *application* couronné de succès; *visit, deal, effort* fructueux, couronné de succès; *marriage, outcome* heureux; *career, business, firm* prospère. **to be ~** réussir (*in an exam/competition etc* à un examen/concours *etc, in one's attempts/life/one's career etc* dans ses efforts/la vie/sa carrière *etc*); *[performer, play etc]* avoir un succès fou; **to be ~ in doing** réussir *or* parvenir *or* arriver à faire.
successfully [sək'sesfəlɪ] *adv* avec succès. **to do sth ~** faire qch avec succès, réussir à faire qch.
succession [sək'seʃən] *n* **(a)** *[victories, disasters, delays, kings]* succession *f*, série *f*, suite *f*. **in ~** (*one after the other*) successivement, l'un(e) après l'autre; (*by turns*) successivement, tour à tour, alternativement; (*on each occasion*) successivement, progressivement; **4 times in ~** 4 fois de suite; **for 10 years in ~** pendant 10 années consécutives *or* 10 ans de suite; **in close** *or* **rapid ~** à la file, coup sur coup; **the ~ of days and nights** la succession *or* l'alternance *f* des jours et des nuits.
(b) (*U*) (*act of succeeding: to title, throne, office, post*) succession *f* (*to* à); (*Jur: heirs collectively*) héritiers *mpl*. **he is second in ~ (to the throne)** il occupe la deuxième place dans l'ordre de succession (à la couronne); **in ~ to his father** à la suite de son père.
successive [sək'sesɪv] *adj generations, discoveries* successif; *days, months* consécutif. **on 4 ~ days** pendant 4 jours de suite *or* 4 jours consécutifs; **with each ~ failure** à chaque nouvel échec.
successively [sək'sesɪvlɪ] *adv* (*by turns*) successivement, tour à tour, alternativement; (*on each occasion*) successivement, progressivement; (*one after the other*) successivement, l'un(e) après l'autre.
successor [sək'sesəʳ] *n* (*person, thing*) successeur *m* (*to, of* de). **the ~ to the throne** l'héritier *m*, -ière *f* de la couronne; **to be sb's ~** succéder à qn.
succinct [sək'sɪŋkt] *adj* succinct, concis, bref.
succinctly [sək'sɪŋktlɪ] *adv* succinctement, brièvement, en peu de mots.
succinctness [sək'sɪŋktnɪs] *n* concision *f*.
succour, (*US*) **succor** ['sʌkəʳ] (*liter*) **1** *n* (*U*) secours *m*, aide *f*.
2 *vt* secourir, soulager, venir à l'aide de.
succulence ['sʌkjʊləns] *n* succulence *f*.
succulent ['sʌkjʊlənt] **1** *adj* (*also Bot*) succulent. **2** *n* (*Bot*) plante grasse. **~s** cactées *fpl*.
succumb [sə'kʌm] *vi* (*to temptation etc*) succomber (*to* à); (*die*) mourir (*to* de), succomber.
such [sʌtʃ] **1** *adj* **(a)** (*of that sort*) tel, pareil. **~ a book** un tel livre, un livre pareil, un pareil livre, un livre de cette sorte; **~ books** de tels livres, des livres pareils, de pareils livres, des livres de cette sorte; **~ people** de telles gens, des gens pareils, de pareilles gens; **we had ~ a case last year** nous avons eu un cas semblable l'année dernière; **in ~ cases** en pareil cas; **did you ever hear of ~ a thing?** avez-vous jamais entendu une chose pareille?; **there's no ~ thing!** ça n'existe pas! (*V also* **1b**); **there is no ~ thing in France** (il n'y a) rien de tel en France; **I said no ~ thing!** je n'ai jamais dit cela!, je n'ai rien dit de la sorte!; **no ~ thing!** pas du tout!; **or some ~ thing** ou une chose de ce genre; **no ~ book exists** un tel livre n'existe pas; **Robert was ~ a one** Robert était comme ça; **~ was my reply** telle a été ma réponse, c'est ce que j'ai répondu; **~ is not the case** ce n'est pas le cas ici; **~ is life!** c'est la vie!; **it was SUCH weather!** quel temps il a fait!, il a fait un de ces temps!
(b) **~ as** tel que, comme. **a friend ~ as Paul, ~ a friend as Paul** un ami tel que *or* comme Paul; **only ~ a fool as Martin would do that** il fallait un idiot comme Martin *or* quelqu'un d'aussi bête que Martin pour faire cela; **~ writers as Molière, Corneille etc** des écrivains tels (que) Molière, Corneille etc; **~ a book as this, a book ~ as this** un livre tel que *or* comme celui-ci; **he's not ~ a fool as you think** il n'est pas aussi *or* si bête que vous croyez; **I'm not ~ a fool as to believe that!** je ne suis pas assez bête pour croire ça!; **there are no ~ things as unicorns** les licornes n'existent pas; **have you ~ a thing as a penknife?** auriez-vous un canif par hasard?; **I must buy some more things — ~ as?** je dois acheter plusieurs choses encore — quel genre de choses? *or* quoi encore?; **it is not ~ as to cause concern** cela ne doit pas être une raison d'inquiétude; **his health was ~ as to alarm his wife** son état de santé était de nature à alarmer sa femme; **it caused ~ scenes of grief as are rarely seen** cela a provoqué des scènes de douleur telles qu'on *or* comme on en voit peu; **~ books as I have** le peu de livres *or* les quelques livres que je possède; **you can take my car, ~ as it is** vous pouvez prendre ma voiture pour ce qu'elle vaut; *V* **time** *etc*.
(c) (*so much*) tellement, tant. **embarrassed by ~ praise** embarrassé par tant *or* tellement de compliments; **he was in ~ pain** il souffrait tellement; **don't be in ~ a rush** ne soyez pas si pressé; **we had SUCH a surprise!** quelle surprise nous avons eue!, nous avons été drôlement surpris!*; **there was ~ a noise that ...** il y avait tellement *or* tant de bruit que ...; **his rage was ~ that ..., ~ was his rage that ...** il était tellement *or* si furieux que ... .
2 *adv* **(a)** (*so very*) si, tellement. **he gave us ~ good coffee** il nous a offert un si bon café; **it was SUCH a long time ago!** il y a si *or* tellement longtemps de ça!; **he bought ~ an expensive car that ...** il a acheté une voiture si *or* tellement chère que ... .
(b) (*in comparisons*) aussi. **I haven't had ~ good coffee for years** ça fait des années que je n'ai pas bu un aussi bon café; **~ lovely children as his** des enfants aussi gentils que les siens.
3 *pron* ceux *mpl*, celles *fpl*. **~ as wish to go** ceux qui veulent partir; **all ~** tous ceux; **I'll give you ~ as I have** je vous donnerai ceux que j'ai *or* le peu que j'ai; **I know of no ~** je n'en connais point; **there are no houses as ~** il n'y a pas de maisons à proprement parler; **and as ~ he was promoted** et en tant que tel il a obtenu de l'avancement; **he was a genius but not recognized as ~** c'était un génie mais il n'était pas reconnu pour tel *or* considéré comme tel; **teachers and doctors and ~(like)*** les professeurs et les docteurs et autres (gens de la sorte); **rabbits and hares and ~(like)*** les lapins, les lièvres et autres animaux de ce genre *or* de la sorte; **shoes and gloves and ~(like)*** les souliers, les gants et autres choses de ce genre *or* de la sorte.
4 *cpd:* **Mr such-and-such*** Monsieur un tel; **in such-and-such**

a street dans telle rue; **suchlike*** (*adj*) de la sorte, de ce genre; (*pron*) *V* 3.

suck [sʌk] **1** *n* **(a)** **to have a ~ at sth** sucer qch.
(b) (*at breast*) tétée *f*. **to give ~** to allaiter, donner le sein à.
2 *cpd:* **sucking-pig** cochon *m* de lait.
3 *vt fruit, pencil* sucer; *juice, poison* sucer (*from* de); (*through straw*) *drink* aspirer (*through* avec); *sweet* sucer, suçoter; *[baby] breast, bottle* téter; *[leech]* sucer; *[pump, machine]* aspirer (*from* de). **to ~ one's thumb** sucer son pouce; **child ~ing its mother's breast** enfant qui tète sa mère; **to ~ dry** *orange etc* sucer tout le jus de; (*fig*) *person* (*of money*) sucer jusqu'au dernier sou; (*of energy*) sucer jusqu'à la moelle.
4 *vi* **(a)** *[baby]* téter.
(b) **to ~ at** *fruit, pencil* sucer; *sweet* sucer, suçoter; *pipe* sucer.

suck down *vt sep [sea, mud, sands]* engloutir.

suck in 1 *vi* (*:fig*) **to suck in with sb** faire de la lèche à qn:, lécher les bottes de qn.
2 *vt sep [sea, mud, sands]* engloutir; *[porous surface]* absorber; *[pump, machine]* aspirer; (*fig*) *knowledge, facts* absorber, assimiler.

suck out *vt sep [person]* sucer, faire sortir en suçant (*of, from* de); *[machine]* refouler à l'extérieur (*of, from* de).

suck up 1 *vi* (*:fig*) **to suck up to sb** faire de la lèche à qn:, lécher les bottes de qn.
2 *vt sep [person]* aspirer, sucer; *[pump, machine]* aspirer; *[porous surface]* absorber.

sucker ['sʌkəʳ] *n* **(a)** (*on machine*) ventouse *f*, suceuse *f*, suçoir *m*; (*plunger*) piston *m*; (*Bot*) surgeon *m*, drageon *m*; *[leech, octopus]* ventouse; *[insect]* suçoir.
(b) (*:* *person*) poire* *f*, gogo* *m*. **to be a ~ for sth** ne pouvoir résister à qch.

suckle ['sʌkl] **1** *vt child* allaiter, donner le sein à; *young animal* allaiter. **2** *vi* téter.

suckling ['sʌklɪŋ] *n* (*act*) allaitement *m*; (*child*) nourrisson *m*, enfant *mf* à la mamelle.

sucrose ['suːkrəʊz] *n* saccharose *f*.

suction ['sʌkʃən] **1** *n* succion *f*. **it works by ~** cela marche par succion; **to adhere by ~ (on)** faire ventouse (sur).
2 *cpd apparatus, device* de succion. **suction disc** ventouse *f*; **suction pump** pompe aspirante; (*Min*) **suction shaft** puits *m* d'appel d'air; **suction valve** clapet *m* d'aspiration.

Sudan [sʊ'dɑːn] *n* Soudan *m*.

Sudanese [ˌsuːdə'niːz] **1** *n* **(a)** (*pl inv*) Soudanais(e) *m(f)*. **(b)** (*Ling*) soudanais *m*. **2** *adj* soudanais.

sudden ['sʌdn] *adj movement, pain, emotion, change, decision* soudain, subit, brusque; *death, inspiration* subit; *bend in road, marriage, appointment* imprévu, inattendu. **all of a ~** soudain, tout à coup, tout d'un coup, brusquement; **it's all so ~!** on s'y attendait tellement peu!, c'est arrivé tellement vite!; (*fig Sport*) **~ death** verdict instantané.

suddenly ['sʌdnlɪ] *adv* brusquement, soudainement, subitement, tout à coup, tout d'un coup, soudain. **to die ~** mourir subitement.

suddenness ['sʌdnnɪs] *n* (*V* **sudden**) soudaineté *f*, brusquerie *f*; caractère imprévu *or* inattendu.

suds [sʌdz] *npl* (*also* **soap~**) (*lather*) mousse *f* de savon; (*soapy water*) eau savonneuse.

sue [suː] **1** *vt* (*Jur*) poursuivre en justice, entamer une action contre, intenter un procès à (*for* pour obtenir, *over, about* au sujet de). **to ~ sb for damages** poursuivre qn en dommages-intérêts; **to ~ sb for libel** intenter un procès en diffamation à qn; **to be ~d for damages/libel** être poursuivi en dommages-intérêts/en diffamation; **to ~ sb for divorce** entamer une procédure de divorce contre qn.
2 *vi* **(a)** (*Jur*) intenter un procès, engager des poursuites. **to ~ for divorce** entamer une procédure de divorce.
(b) (*liter*) **to ~ for peace/pardon** solliciter la paix/le pardon.

suede [sweɪd] **1** *n* daim *m*, cuir suédé. **imitation ~** suédine *f*. **2** *cpd shoes, handbag, coat, skirt* de daim; *gloves* de suède; *leather* suédé.

suet [sʊɪt] *n* (*Culin*) graisse *f* de rognon *or* de bœuf. **~ pudding** *gâteau sucré ou salé à base de farine et de graisse de bœuf.*

Suez ['suːɪz] *n*: **~ Canal** canal *m* de Suez; **Gulf of ~** golfe *m* de Suez.

suffer ['sʌfəʳ] **1** *vt* **(a)** (*undergo*) *hardship, hunger, bereavement, martyrdom, torture* souffrir, subir; *punishment, change in circumstances, loss* subir; *damage, setback* éprouver, essuyer, subir; *pain, headaches* éprouver, ressentir. **he ~ed a lot of pain** il a beaucoup souffert; (*liter*) **to ~ death** mourir; **her popularity ~ed a decline** sa popularité a souffert *or* a décliné.
(b) (*bear*) *pain* endurer, tolérer, supporter; (*allow*) *opposition, sb's rudeness, refusal etc* tolérer, permettre. **I can't ~ it a moment longer** je ne peux plus le souffrir *or* le tolérer, c'est intolérable, c'est insupportable; **he doesn't ~ fools gladly** il n'a aucune patience pour les imbéciles; (*liter*) **to ~ sb to do** souffrir que qn fasse.
2 *vi* **(a)** *[person]* souffrir. **to ~ in silence** souffrir en silence; **to ~ for one's sins** expier ses péchés; **he ~ed for it later** il en a souffert les conséquences *or* il en a pâti plus tard; **you'll ~ for this** il vous en cuira, vous me le paierez; **I'll make him ~ for it!** il me le paiera!
(b) (*be afflicted by*) **to ~ from** *rheumatism, heart trouble, the cold, hunger* souffrir de; *deafness* être atteint de; *a cold, influenza, frostbite, pimples, bad memory* avoir; **he ~s from a limp/stammer** *etc* il boite/bégaie *etc*; **he was ~ing from shock** il était commotionné; **to ~ from the effects of** *fall, illness* se ressentir de, souffrir des suites de; *alcohol, drug* subir le contrecoup de; **to be ~ing from having done** souffrir *or* se ressentir d'avoir fait; **the child was ~ing from its environment** l'enfant subissait les conséquences fâcheuses de son milieu *or* était la victime de son milieu; **she ~s from lack of friends** son problème c'est qu'elle n'a pas d'amis; **the house is ~ing from neglect** la maison se ressent d'avoir été négligée *or* du manque d'entretien; **his style ~s from overelaboration** son style souffre *or* a le défaut d'être trop élaboré; *V* **delusion** *etc.*
(c) (*be injured, impaired*) *[limb]* souffrir, être blessé; *[eyesight, haring, speech]* souffrir, se détériorer; *[health, reputation, plans, sales, wages]* souffrir, pâtir; *[car, town, house]* souffrir, être endommagé; *[business]* souffrir, péricliter. **your health will ~** votre santé en souffrira *or* en pâtira; **the regiment ~ed badly** le régiment a essuyé de grosses pertes.

sufferance ['sʌfərəns] *n* tolérance *f*, souffrance *f* (*Jur*). **on ~** par tolérance.

sufferer ['sʌfərəʳ] *n* (*from illness*) malade *mf*; (*from misfortune*) victime *f*; (*from accident*) accidenté(e) *m(f)*, victime. **~s from diabetes, diabetes ~s** diabétiques *mfpl*; (*hum*) **my fellow ~s at the concert** mes compagnons *mpl* d'infortune au concert.

suffering ['sʌfərɪŋ] **1** *n* souffrance(s) *f(pl)*. **'after much ~ patiently borne'** 'après de longues souffrances patiemment endurées'; **her ~ was great** elle a beaucoup souffert. **2** *adj* souffrant, qui souffre.

suffice [sə'faɪs] (*frm*) **1** *vi* suffire, être suffisant. **~ it to say** qu'il (me) suffise de dire, je me contenterai de dire. **2** *vt* suffire à, satisfaire.

sufficiency [sə'fɪʃənsɪ] *n* (*frm*) quantité suffisante. **a ~ of coal** une quantité suffisante de charbon, suffisamment de charbon, du charbon en quantité suffisante *or* en suffisance; *V* **self.**

sufficient [sə'fɪʃənt] *adj books, money, food, people* assez de, suffisamment de; *number, quantity* suffisant. **to be ~** être suffisant *or* assez (*for* pour), suffire (*for* à); **I've got ~** j'en ai assez *or* suffisamment; **~ to eat** assez à manger; **he earns ~ to live on** il gagne de quoi vivre; **one meal a day is ~** un repas par jour est suffisant; **one song was ~ to show he couldn't sing** une chanson a suffi à *or* pour démontrer qu'il ne savait pas chanter; **that's quite ~ thank you** cela me suffit, je vous remercie; *V* **self.**

sufficiently [sə'fɪʃəntlɪ] *adv* suffisamment, assez. **he is ~ clever to do so** il est suffisamment *or* assez intelligent pour le faire; **a ~ large number/quantity** un nombre/une quantité suffisant(e).

suffix ['sʌfɪks] **1** *n* suffixe *m*. **2** [sʌ'fɪks] *vt* suffixer (*to* à).

suffocate ['sʌfəkeɪt] **1** *vi* suffoquer, étouffer; (*fig: with anger, indignation, surprise*) suffoquer (*with* de).
2 *vt* suffoquer, étouffer; (*fig*) *[anger, indignation, surprise]* suffoquer. **he felt ~d in that small town atmosphere** il étouffait dans cette atmosphère de petite ville.

suffocating ['sʌfəkeɪtɪŋ] *adj heat, atmosphere* étouffant, suffocant; *fumes* suffocant, asphyxiant; (*fig*) étouffant. **it's ~ in here** on étouffe ici.

suffocation [ˌsʌfə'keɪʃən] *n* suffocation *f*, étouffement *m*; (*Med*) asphyxie *f*. **to die from ~** mourir asphyxié.

suffragan ['sʌfrəgən] **1** *adj* suffragant. **2** *n*: **~ (bishop)** (évêque *m*) suffragant *m*.

suffrage ['sʌfrɪdʒ] *n* **(a)** (*franchise*) droit *m* de suffrage *or* de vote *or* de voter. **universal ~** suffrage universel. **(b)** (*frm: vote*) suffrage *m*, vote *m*.

suffragette [ˌsʌfrə'dʒet] *n* suffragette *f*. (*Hist*) **the S~ Movement** le Mouvement des Suffragettes.

suffragist ['sʌfrədʒɪst] *n* partisan(e) *m(f)* du droit de vote pour les femmes.

suffuse [sə'fjuːz] *vt [light]* baigner, se répandre sur; *[emotion]* envahir. **the room was ~d with light** la pièce baignait dans une lumière douce; **~d with red** rougi, empourpré; **eyes ~d with tears** yeux baignés de larmes.

sugar ['ʃʊgəʳ] **1** *n* (*U*) sucre *m*. **come here ~!*** viens ici chéri(e)! *or* mon petit lapin en sucre!; *V* **icing** *etc.*
2 *vt food, drink* sucrer; *V* **pill.**
3 *cpd:* **sugar basin** sucrier *m*; **sugar beet** betterave sucrière *or* à sucre; **sugar bowl = sugar basin; sugar cane** canne *f* à sucre; **sugar-coated** dragéifié; **sugar cube** morceau *m* de sucre; (*fig*) **sugar daddy**‡ vieux protecteur; **sugar(ed) almond** dragée *f*; **sugar-free** sans sucre; **sugar loaf** pain *m* de sucre; **sugar lump = sugar cube;** (*Can, US*) **sugar maple** érable *m* à sucre; **sugar pea** mange-tout *m inv*; **sugar plantation** plantation *f* de canne à sucre; **sugarplum** bonbon *m*, dragée *f*; **sugar refinery** raffinerie *f* de sucre; **sugar sifter** saupoudreuse *f*, sucrier verseur; **sugar tongs** pince *f* à sucre.

sugarless ['ʃʊgəlɪs] *adj* sans sucre.

sugary ['ʃʊgərɪ] *adj food, drink* (très) sucré; *taste* de sucre, sucré; (*fig pej*) *person, smile* doucereux; *voice* mielleux. (*pej*) **she is rather ~** elle a un petit air sucré, elle est tout sucre tout miel.

suggest [sə'dʒest] *vt* **(a)** (*propose*) suggérer, proposer (*sth to sb* qch à qn); (*pej: hint*) insinuer (*sth to sb* qch à qn). **I ~ that we go to the museum** je suggère *or* je propose qu'on aille au musée; **he ~ed that they (should) go to London** il leur a suggéré *or* proposé d'aller à Londres; **an idea ~ed itself (to me)** une idée m'est venue à l'esprit; **what are you trying to ~?** que voulez-vous dire par là?, qu'insinuez-vous? (*pej*); (*esp Jur*) **I ~ to you that ...** mon opinion est que ... . **(b)** (*imply*) *[facts, data, sb's actions]* suggérer, laisser supposer, sembler indiquer (*that* que); (*evoke*) suggérer, évoquer, faire penser à. **what does that smell ~ to you?** à quoi cette odeur vous fait-elle penser?, qu'est-ce que cette odeur vous suggère? *or* évoque pour vous?; **the coins ~ a Roman settlement** les monnaies suggèrent l'existence d'un camp romain, les monnaies donnent à penser *or* laissent supposer qu'il y a eu un camp romain; **it doesn't exactly ~ a careful man** on ne peut pas dire que cela dénote un homme soigneux.

suggestible [sə'dʒestɪbl] *adj* suggestible, influençable.

suggestion [sə'dʒestʃən] *n* **(a)** (*proposal*) suggestion *f*, proposition *f*; (*insinuation*) allusion *f*, insinuation *f*. **to make** *or* **offer a ~** faire une suggestion *or* une proposition; **if I may make a ~** si je peux me permettre de faire une suggestion; **have you any ~s?** avez-vous quelque chose à suggérer?; **my ~ is that ...** je suggère *or* je propose que ...; **there is no ~ of corruption** il ne saurait être question de corruption, rien n'autorise à penser qu'il y ait eu corruption.

(b) (*U: Psych etc*) suggestion *f*. **the power of ~** la force de suggestion.

(c) (*trace*) soupçon *m*, pointe *f*.

suggestive [sə'dʒestɪv] *adj* suggestif (*also pej*). **to be ~ of** = **suggest b.**

suggestively [sə'dʒestɪvlɪ] *adv* (*pej*) de façon suggestive.

suggestiveness [sə'dʒestɪvnɪs] *n* (*pej*) caractère suggestif, suggestivité *f*.

suicidal [ˌsuɪ'saɪdl] *adj person, tendency, carelessness* suicidaire. **I feel ~ this morning** j'ai envie de me jeter par la fenêtre (*or* sous un train *or* à l'eau *etc*) ce matin; (*fig*) **that would be absolutely ~!** ce serait un véritable suicide!; **he drives in this ~ way** il conduit comme un fou, s'il voulait se suicider il ne conduirait pas autrement.

suicide ['suɪsaɪd] **1** *n* (*act: lit, fig*) suicide *m*; (*person*) suicidé(e) *m(f)*. **there were 2 attempted ~s** il y a eu 2 tentatives *fpl* de suicide, 2 personnes ont tenté de se suicider; **such an act was political ~** un tel acte représentait un véritable suicide politique, il se suicidait politiquement en faisant cela; (*fig*) **it would be ~ to do so** le faire équivaudrait à un suicide, ce serait se suicider que de le faire; *V* **attempt, commit** *etc*.

2 *cpd*: **suicide attempt, suicide bid** tentative *f* de suicide.

suit [suːt] **1** *n* **(a)** (*garment*) (*for man*) costume *m*, complet *m*; (*for woman*) tailleur *m*, ensemble *m*. **~ of clothes** tenue *f*; **~ of armour** armure complète; (*Naut*) **a ~ of sails** un jeu de voiles; *V* **lounge, trouser** *etc*.

(b) (*frm: request*) requête *f*, pétition *f*; (*liter: for marriage*) demande *f* en mariage; *V* **press.**

(c) (*Jur*) poursuite *f*, procès *m*, action *f*. **to bring a ~** intenter un procès (*against sb* à qn), engager des poursuites (*against sb* contre qn); **criminal ~** action criminelle; *V* **file**[2], **law, party** *etc*.

(d) (*Cards*) couleur *f*. **long** *or* **strong ~** couleur longue; (*fig*) fort *m*; **short ~** couleur courte; *V* **follow.**

2 *cpd*: **suitcase** valise *f*.

3 *vt* **(a)** (*be convenient, satisfactory for*) *[arrangements, date, price, suggestion]* convenir à, arranger, aller à; *[climate, food, occupation]* convenir à. **it doesn't ~ me to leave now** cela ne m'arrange pas de partir maintenant; **I'll do it when it ~s me** je le ferai quand ça m'arrangera; **such a step ~ed him perfectly** *or* **just ~ed his book*** une telle mesure lui convenait parfaitement *or* l'arrangeait parfaitement *or* faisait tout à fait son affaire; **~ yourself!*** c'est comme vous voudrez!, faites comme vous voudrez! *or* voulez!, faites à votre gré! *or* à votre idée!; **~s me!*** ça me va!, ça me botte!‡; **it ~s me here** je suis bien ici; *V* **ground.**

(b) (*be appropriate to*) convenir à, aller à. **the job doesn't ~ him** l'emploi ne lui convient pas, ce n'est pas un travail fait pour lui; **such behaviour hardly ~s you** une telle conduite ne vous va guère *or* n'est guère digne de vous; (*Theat*) **the part ~ed him perfectly** le rôle lui allait comme un gant *or* était fait pour lui; **he is not ~ed to teaching** il n'est pas fait pour l'enseignement; **the hall was not ~ed to such a meeting** la salle n'était pas faite pour *or* ne se prêtait guère à une telle réunion; **they are well ~ed (to one another)** ils sont faits l'un pour l'autre, ils sont très bien assortis.

(c) *[garment, colour, hairstyle]* aller à. **it ~s her beautifully** cela lui va à merveille.

(d) (*adapt*) adapter, approprier (*sth to sth* qch à qch). **to ~ the action to the word** joindre le geste à la parole.

4 *vi* convenir, aller, faire l'affaire. **will tomorrow ~?** est-ce que demain vous convient? *or* vous va? *or* est à votre convenance?

suitability [ˌsuːtə'bɪlɪtɪ] *n* (*V* **suitable**) fait *m* de convenir *or* d'aller *or* d'être propice *etc*; *[action, remark, reply, example, choice]* à-propos *m*, pertinence *f*. **I doubt the ~ of these arrangements** je doute que ces dispositions conviennent (*subj*).

suitable ['suːtəbl] *adj climate, food* qui convient; *colour, size* qui va; *place, time* propice, adéquat; *action, reply, example, remark, choice* approprié, pertinent; *clothes* approprié, adéquat; (*socially*) convenable. **the most ~ man for the job** l'homme le plus apte à faire *or* le plus à même de faire ce travail, l'homme le plus indiqué pour faire ce travail; **I can't find anything ~** je ne trouve rien qui me convienne; (*clothes*) je ne trouve rien qui m'aille; **the 25th is the most ~ for me** c'est le 25 qui m'arrange *or* me convient le mieux; **he is not a ~ teacher for such a class** quelqu'un comme lui ne devrait pas enseigner dans une telle classe; **he is not at all a ~ person** ce n'est pas du tout l'homme qu'il faut; **the hall is quite ~ for the meeting** c'est une salle qui se prête bien à ce genre de réunion; **the film isn't ~ for children** ce n'est pas un film pour les enfants; **this gift isn't ~ for my aunt** ce cadeau ne plaira pas à ma tante *or* ne sera pas au goût de ma tante.

suitably ['suːtəblɪ] *adv reply* à propos; *explain* de manière adéquate; *thank, apologize* comme il convient (*or* convenait *etc*), comme il se doit (*or* devait *etc*); *behave* convenablement, comme il faut. **he was ~ impressed** il a été favorablement impressionné.

suite [swiːt] *n* (*furniture*) mobilier *m*; (*rooms*) suite *f*; (*retainers*) suite, escorte *f*; (*Mus*) suite; *V* **bedroom, bridal** *etc*.

suiting ['suːtɪŋ] *n* (*U*) tissu *m* pour complet.

suitor ['suːtəʳ] *n* soupirant *m*, prétendant *m*; (*Jur*) plaideur *m*, -euse *f*.

sulfa ['sʌlfə] *etc* (*US*) = **sulpha** *etc*.

sulk [sʌlk] **1** *n* bouderie *f*, maussaderie *f*. **to be in the ~s, to have (a fit of) the ~s** bouder, faire la tête.

2 *vi* bouder.

sulkily ['sʌlkɪlɪ] *adv* en boudant, d'un air *or* d'un ton maussade.

sulkiness ['sʌlkɪnɪs] *n* (*state*) bouderie *f*; (*temperament*) caractère boudeur *or* maussade.

sulky ['sʌlkɪ] *adj* boudeur, maussade. **to be** *or* **look ~** faire la tête.

sullen ['sʌlən] *adj person, look, smile* maussade, renfrogné; *comment, silence* renfrogné; *horse* rétif; *clouds* menaçant; *sky, countryside, lake* maussade, morne.

sullenly ['sʌlənlɪ] *adv say, reply, refuse, deny* d'un ton maussade; *promise, agree* de mauvaise grâce. **he remained ~ silent** il ne s'est pas départi de son air renfrogné *or* maussade et n'a pas ouvert la bouche.

sullenness ['sʌlənnɪs] *n* (*V* **sullen**) maussaderie *f*, humeur *f* maussade, air renfrogné; aspect menaçant *or* morne *or* maussade.

sully ['sʌlɪ] *vt* (*liter*) souiller.

sulpha, (*US*) **sulfa** ['sʌlfə] *n*: **~ drug** sulfamide *m*.

sulphate, (*US*) **sulfate** ['sʌlfeɪt] *n* sulfate *m*. **copper ~** sulfate de cuivre.

sulphide, (*US*) **sulfide** ['sʌlfaɪd] *n* sulfure *m*.

sulphonamide, (*US*) **sulfonamide** [sʌl'fɒnəmaɪd] *n* sulfamide *m*.

sulphur, (*US*) **sulfur** ['sʌlfəʳ] **1** *n* soufre *m*. **2** *cpd*: **sulphur dioxide** anhydride sulfureux; **sulphur spring** source sulfureuse.

sulphureous, (*US*) **sulfureous** [sʌl'fjʊərɪəs] *adj* sulfureux; (*in colour*) couleur de soufre, soufré.

sulphuric, (*US*) **sulfuric** [sʌl'fjʊərɪk] *adj* sulfurique.

sulphurous, (*US*) **sulfurous** ['sʌlfərəs] *adj* sulfureux.

sultan ['sʌltən] *n* sultan *m*.

sultana [sʌl'tɑːnə] **1** *n* **(a)** (*fruit*) raisin sec de Smyrne. **(b)** (*woman*) sultane *f*. **2** *cpd*: (*Culin*) **sultana cake** cake *m* (aux raisins secs de Smyrne).

sultanate ['sʌltənɪt] *n* sultanat *m*.

sultriness ['sʌltrɪnɪs] *n* (*heat*) chaleur étouffante; *[weather]* lourdeur *f*.

sultry ['sʌltrɪ] *adj heat* étouffant, suffocant; *weather, air* lourd; *atmosphere* étouffant, pesant; (*fig*) *voice* chaud, sensuel; *person, character* passionné; *look, smile* plein de passion, sensuel, provocant.

sum [sʌm] **1** *n* (*total after addition*) somme *f*, total *m* (*of* de); (*amount of money*) somme (d'argent); (*Math: problem*) calcul *m*, opération *f*. (*Scol: arithmetic*) **~s** le calcul; **to do a ~ in one's head** faire un calcul mental *or* de tête; **he is good at ~s** il est bon en calcul; **the ~ of our experience** la somme de notre expérience; **the ~ and substance of what he said** les grandes lignes de ce qu'il a dit; **in ~** en somme, somme toute; *V* **lump**[1], **round** *etc*.

2 *cpd*: **summing-up** récapitulation *f*, résumé *m* (*also Jur*); **sum total** (*amount*) somme totale; (*money*) montant *m* (global); (*fig*) **the sum total of all this was that he ...** le résultat de tout cela a été qu'il ... .

sum up 1 *vi* récapituler, faire un *or* le résumé; (*Jur*) résumer. **to sum up, let me say that ...** en résumé *or* pour récapituler je voudrais dire que ... .

2 *vt sep* **(a)** (*summarize*) *speech, facts, arguments* résumer, récapituler; *book etc* résumer. **that sums up all I felt** cela résume tout ce que je ressentais.

(b) (*assess*) *person* jauger, se faire une idée de; *situation* apprécier d'un coup d'œil.

3 summing-up *n V* **sum 2.**

sumac(h) ['suːmæk] *n* sumac *m*.

summarily ['sʌmərɪlɪ] *adv* sommairement.

summarize ['sʌməraɪz] *vt book, text* résumer; *facts, arguments* récapituler; *speech, debate* récapituler, résumer.

summary ['sʌmərɪ] **1** *n* **(a)** (*U: V* **summarize**) résumé *m*; récapitulation *f*.

(b) (*printed matter, list etc*) sommaire *m*, résumé *m*; (*Fin: of accounts*) relevé *m*. (*Rad, TV*) **here is a ~ of the news** voici les nouvelles *fpl* en bref.

2 *adj* (*all senses*) sommaire.

summat‡ ['sʌmət] *n* (*dial*) = **something.**

summation [sʌ'meɪʃən] *n* (*addition*) addition *f*; (*summing-up*) récapitulation *f*, résumé *m* (*also Jur*).

summer ['sʌməʳ] **1** *n* été *m*. **in ~** en été; **in the ~ of 1977** en été 1977; (*liter*) **a girl of 17 ~s** une jeune fille de 17 printemps; *V* **high, Indian** *etc*.

2 *cpd weather, heat, day, season, activities* d'été, estival; *residence* d'été. **summer camp** colonie *f* de vacances; **summer clothes** vêtements *mpl* d'été, tenue estivale *or* d'été; **summer holidays** grandes vacances; **summerhouse** pavillon *m* (dans un jardin); **summer lightning** éclair *m* de chaleur; **summer resort** station estivale; **summer school** cours *mpl* de vacances; **summertime** (*season*) été *m*; **summer time** (*by clock*) heure *f* d'été; **summer visitor** estivant(e) *m(f)*.

3 *vi* (*rare*) passer l'été.

summery ['sʌmərɪ] *adj* d'été.

summit ['sʌmɪt] **1** *n [mountain]* sommet *m*, cime *f*, faîte *m*; (*fig*) *[power, honours, glory]* sommet, apogée *m*, faîte; *[ambition]* summum *m*; (*Pol*) sommet. **2** *cpd* (*Pol*) *meeting, talks* au sommet. **summit conference** (conférence *f* au) sommet *m*.

summon ['sʌmən] *vt servant, police* appeler, faire venir; (*to meeting*) convoquer (*to* à); *[monarch, president, prime minister]* mander (*to* à); (*Jur*) citer, assigner, appeler en justice (*as* comme); *help, reinforcements* requérir. **the Queen ~ed**

Parliament la reine a convoqué le Parlement; **to ~ sb to do** sommer qn de faire; *(Jur)* **to ~ sb to appear** citer *or* assigner qn; *(Mil)* **they ~ed the town to surrender** ils ont sommé la ville de *or* ils ont mis la ville en demeure de se rendre; **I was ~ed to his presence** j'ai été requis de paraître devant lui, il m'a mandé auprès de lui; **to ~ sb in/down** *etc* sommer qn d'entrer/de descendre *etc*.

summon up *vt sep one's energy, strength* rassembler, faire appel à; *interest, enthusiasm* faire appel à. **to summon up (one's) courage** faire appel à *or* rassembler tout son courage, s'armer de courage, prendre son courage à deux mains (*to do* pour faire); **he summoned up the courage to fight back** il a trouvé le courage de riposter.

summons ['sʌmənz] **1** *n* sommation *f* (*also Mil*), injonction *f*; *(Jur)* assignation *f*, citation *f*. *(Jur)* **to take out a ~ against sb** faire assigner qn; **he got a ~ for drunken driving** il a reçu une citation *or* une assignation pour conduite en état d'ivresse; *(Mil)* **they sent him a ~ to surrender** ils lui ont fait parvenir une sommation de se rendre; *V* **issue, serve.**

2 *vt* *(Jur)* citer, assigner (*à comparaître*), appeler en justice (*for sth* pour qch).

sump [sʌmp] *n* *(Tech)* puisard *m*; *(Brit Aut)* carter *m*. **~ oil** huile *f* de carter.

sumptuary ['sʌmptjʊərɪ] *adj* *(frm)* somptuaire.

sumptuous ['sʌmptjʊəs] *adj* somptueux, fastueux, luxueux.

sumptuously ['sʌmptjʊəslɪ] *adv* somptueusement.

sumptuousness ['sʌmptjʊəsnɪs] *n* somptuosité *f*.

sun [sʌn] **1** *n* soleil *m* (*also Astron*). **the ~ is shining** il fait (du) soleil, le soleil brille; **in the ~** au soleil; **right in the ~** en plein soleil; **a place in the ~** *(lit)* un endroit ensoleillé *or* au soleil; *(fig)* une place au soleil; **in the July ~** au soleil de juillet; **come out of the ~** ne restez pas au soleil; **the ~ is in my eyes** j'ai le soleil dans les yeux; **he rose with the ~** il se levait avec le soleil; **everything under the ~** tout ce qu'il est possible d'imaginer; **nothing under the ~** rien au monde; **there's no prettier place under the ~** il n'est pas de plus joli coin au monde *or* sur la terre; **no reason under the ~** pas la moindre raison; **there is nothing new under the ~** il n'y a rien de nouveau sous le soleil; *V* **midnight** *etc*.

2 *vt*: **to ~ o.s.** *[lizard, cat]* se chauffer au soleil; *[person]* prendre un bain de soleil, lézarder au soleil.

3 *cpd*: **sunbaked** brûlé par le soleil; **sunbath** bain *m* de soleil; **sunbathe** prendre un bain *or* des bains de soleil, se (faire) bronzer; **sunbather** personne *f* qui prend un bain de soleil; **sunbathing** bains *mpl* de soleil; **sunbeam** rayon *m* de soleil; **sunbed** fauteuil *m* bain de soleil; **sunblind** store *m*; **sun bonnet** capeline *f*; **sunburn** *(tan)* bronzage *m*, hâle *m*; *(painful)* coup *m* de soleil; **sunburned, sunburnt** *(tanned)* bronzé, hâlé; *(painfully)* brûlé par le soleil; **to get sunburnt** *(tan)* (se faire) bronzer; *(painfully)* prendre un coup de soleil; **sunburst** échappée *f* de soleil; **sunburst clock** pendule *f* soleil; **Sunday** *V* **Sunday**; **sun deck** *[house, hotel etc]* véranda *f*; *(Naut)* pont supérieur *or* des embarcations; **sundial** cadran *m* solaire; **sundown = sunset; sundowner*** *(Australia: tramp)* chemineau *m*, clochard *m*; *(Brit: drink)* *boisson alcoolique prise au coucher du soleil*; **sun-drenched** inondé de soleil; **sundried** séché au soleil; **sun-filled** ensoleillé, rempli de soleil; *(Zool)* **sunfish** poisson lune *m*; *(Bot)* **sunflower** tournesol *m*, soleil *m*; *(Culin)* **sunflower oil/seeds** huile *f*/graines *fpl* de tournesol; **sunglasses** lunettes *fpl* de soleil; **sun-god** dieu *m* soleil; **sun hat** chapeau *m* de soleil *or* de plage; **sun helmet** casque colonial; **sun lamp** lampe *f* à rayons ultraviolets; **sunlight** (lumière *f* du) soleil *m*; **in the sunlight** au soleil, à la lumière du soleil; **sunlit** ensoleillé; **sun lotion = suntan lotion; sun lounge** véranda *f*; **sunlounger = sunbed; sun oil = suntan oil; sun porch** petite véranda (à l'entrée); *(Med)* **sunray lamp = sun lamp; sunray treatment** héliothérapie *f*; **sunrise** lever *m* du soleil; *(Aut)* **sun roof** toit ouvrant; **sunset** coucher *m* du soleil; **sunshade** *lady's parasol* ombrelle *f*; *(for eyes)* visière *f*; *(for table, on pram)* parasol *m*; *(in car)* pare-soleil *m inv*; *(Aut)* **sun-shield** pare-soleil *m inv*; **sunshine** *V* **sunshine; sunspecs* = sunglasses; sunspot** tache *f* solaire; *(Med)* **sunstroke** insolation *f*, coup *m* de soleil; **sunsuit** costume *m* bain de soleil; **suntan** bronzage *m*; **to get a suntan** (se faire) bronzer; **suntan lotion** lotion *f or* lait *m* solaire; **suntanned** bronzé; **suntan oil** huile *f* solaire; **suntrap** coin très ensoleillé; **sun umbrella** parasol *m*; **sunup* = sunrise; sun visor** *(for eyes, on cap)* visière *f*; *(Aut)* pare-soleil *m inv*; *(Rel)* **sun-worship** culte *m* du Soleil; **sun-worshipper** *(Rel)* adorateur *m*, -trice *f* du Soleil; *(fig)* adepte *mf or* fanatique *mf* du soleil.

sundae ['sʌndeɪ] *n* dessert *m* à la glace et aux fruits. **peach ~** ≃ pêche *f* melba.

Sunday ['sʌndɪ] **1** *n* **(a)** dimanche *m*; *for phrases V* **Saturday**; *V also* **Easter, month, palm**[2].

(b) *(fig: ~ papers)* **the ~s*** les journaux *mpl* du dimanche.

2 *cpd clothes, paper* du dimanche; *walk, rest, peace* dominical. **in one's Sunday best** tout endimanché, en habits du dimanche; *(*pej)* **Sunday driver, Sunday motorist** chauffeur *m* du dimanche; **Sunday school** école *f* du dimanche, ≃ catéchisme *m*.

sunder ['sʌndəʳ] *(liter)* **1** *vt* séparer, fractionner, scinder. **2** *n*: **in ~** *(apart)* écartés; *(in pieces)* en morceaux.

sundry ['sʌndrɪ] **1** *adj* divers, différent. **all and ~** tout le monde, n'importe qui; **to all and ~** à tout venant, à tout le monde, à n'importe qui. **2** *npl*: **sundries** articles *mpl* divers.

sung [sʌŋ] *ptp of* **sing.**

sunk [sʌŋk] *ptp of* **sink**[1].

sunken ['sʌŋkən] *adj ship, rock* submergé; *eyes* creux, cave; *cheeks* creux; *garden* en contrebas; *bath* encastré (*au ras du sol*).

sunless ['sʌnlɪs] *adj* sans soleil.

sunny ['sʌnɪ] *adj room, situation, month, morning* ensoleillé; *side* (*of street, building etc*) exposé au soleil; ensoleillé; *(fig) smile* radieux, épanoui; *person, personality* heureux, épanoui. **it is ~** *or* **a ~ day** il fait (du) soleil; *(Brit Met)* **'~ intervals** *or* **periods'** 'éclaircies' *(frm)*; *(Met)* **the outlook is ~** on prévoit (le retour) du soleil, on peut s'attendre à un temps ensoleillé; *(fig)* **he always sees the ~ side of things** il voit tout en rose, il voit tout du bon côté; **he's on the ~ side of fifty*** il est du bon côté de la cinquantaine.

sunshine ['sʌnʃaɪn] **1** *n* *(U)* (lumière *f* du) soleil *m*. **in the ~** au soleil; *(Met)* **5 hours of ~** 5 heures d'ensoleillement; *(iro)* **he's a real ray of ~ today** il est gracieux comme une porte de prison aujourd'hui; **hallo ~!*** bonjour mon rayon de soleil!

2 *cpd*: *(Aut)* **sunshine roof** toit ouvrant.

sup [sʌp] **1** *vi* souper (*on, off* de). **2** *vt* (*also* **~ up**) boire *or* avaler à petites gorgées. **3** *n* petite gorgée.

super ['suːpəʳ] **1** *adj* (*) formidable*, sensationnel*. **2** *cpd*: **super-duper‡** formid* *inv*, sensass* *inv*, terrible*. **3** *n* (*) *abbr of* **superintendent** (*of police*) *and* (*Cine*) **supernumerary.**

super... ['suːpəʳ] *pref* super..., sur..., hyper... . **~-salesman** super-vendeur *m*; *(Pol)* **~power** superpuissance *f*, grande puissance; **~human** surhumain; **~sensitive** hypersensible; *V also* **superannuate** *etc*.

superable ['suːpərəbl] *adj* surmontable.

superabundant [ˌsuːpərə'bʌndənt] *adj* surabondant.

superannuate [ˌsuːpə'rænjʊeɪt] *vt* mettre à la retraite. **~d** retraité, à la *or* en retraite; *(fig)* suranné, démodé.

superannuation [ˌsuːpəˌrænjʊ'eɪʃən] *n* *(act)* (mise *f* à la) retraite *f*; *(pension)* pension *f* de retraite; (*also* **~ contribution**) versements *mpl or* cotisations *fpl* pour la pension. **~ fund** caisse *f* de retraite.

superb [suː'pɜːb] *adj* superbe, magnifique.

superbly [suː'pɜːblɪ] *adv* superbement, magnifiquement. **he is ~ fit** il est en pleine forme *or* dans une forme éblouissante.

supercargo ['suːpəˌkɑːgəʊ] *n* *(Naut)* subrécargue *m*.

supercharged ['suːpətʃɑːdʒd] *adj* surcomprimé.

supercharger ['suːpətʃɑːdʒəʳ] *n* compresseur *m*.

supercilious [ˌsuːpə'sɪlɪəs] *adj* hautain, dédaigneux.

superciliously [ˌsuːpə'sɪlɪəslɪ] *adv* avec dédain, dédaigneusement, d'un air *or* d'un ton hautain.

superciliousness [ˌsuːpə'sɪlɪəsnɪs] *n* hauteur *f*, arrogance *f*.

super-class ['suːpəˌklɑːs] *n* super-classe *f*.

superconductivity ['suːpəˌkɒndʌk'tɪvɪtɪ] *n* supraconductivité *f*.

superego [ˌsuːpər'iːgəʊ] *n* sur-moi *m*.

supererogation ['suːpərˌerə'geɪʃən] *n* surérogation *f*.

superficial [ˌsuːpə'fɪʃəl] *adj* superficiel.

superficiality ['suːpəˌfɪʃɪ'ælɪtɪ] *n* caractère superficiel, manque *m* de profondeur.

superficially [ˌsuːpə'fɪʃəlɪ] *adv* superficiellement.

superficies [ˌsuːpə'fɪʃiːz] *n* superficie *f*.

superfine ['suːpəfaɪn] *adj goods, quality* extra fin, superfin, surfin; *(pej) distinction* trop ténu, bien mince.

superfluity [ˌsuːpə'flʊɪtɪ] *n* **(a)** surabondance *f* (*of* de). **(b)** = **superfluousness.**

superfluous [sʊ'pɜːflʊəs] *adj goods, explanation* superflu. **~ hair** poils superflus; **it is ~ to say that ...** je n'ai pas besoin de dire que ..., inutile de dire que ...; **he felt rather ~*** il se sentait de trop.

superfluously [sʊ'pɜːflʊəslɪ] *adv* d'une manière superflue.

superfluousness [sʊ'pɜːflʊəsnɪs] *n* caractère superflu.

supergiant [ˌsuːpə'dʒaɪənt] *n* *(Astron)* supergéante *f*.

superhuman [ˌsuːpə'hjuːmən] *adj* surhumain.

superimpose [ˌsuːpərɪm'pəʊz] *vt* superposer (*on* à). *(Cine, Phot, Typ)* **~d** en surimpression.

superintend [ˌsuːpərɪn'tend] *vt work, shop, department* diriger; *exam* surveiller; *production* contrôler; *vote-counting* présider à.

superintendence [ˌsuːpərɪn'tendəns] *n* (*V* **superintend**) direction *f*; surveillance *f*; contrôle *m*.

superintendent [ˌsuːpərɪn'tendənt] *n [institution, orphanage]* directeur *m*, -trice *f*; *[department]* chef *m*. **~ of police** ≃ commissaire *m* de (police).

superior [sʊ'pɪərɪəʳ] **1** *adj* **(a)** supérieur (*f* -eure) (*to* à); *product, goods* de qualité supérieure; *(pej: smug) person* condescendant, suffisant; *air, smile* supérieur, de supériorité, suffisant. **~ in number** to supérieur en nombre à, numériquement supérieur à; **in ~ numbers** en plus grand nombre, plus nombreux; *(Typ)* **~ letter/number** lettre *f*/nombre *m* supérieur(e); **he felt rather ~** il a éprouvé un certain sentiment de supériorité; **in a ~ voice** d'un ton supérieur *or* suffisant; *V* **mother.**

(b) *(Bio, Bot etc)* supérieur (*f* -eure).

2 *n* (*also Rel*) supérieur(e) *m(f)*.

superiority [sʊˌpɪərɪ'ɒrɪtɪ] *n* supériorité *f* (*to, over* par rapport à). **~ complex** complexe *m* de supériorité.

superlative [sʊ'pɜːlətɪv] **1** *adj condition, quality, achievement* sans pareil; *happiness, indifference* suprême; *(Gram)* superlatif. **2** *n* *(Gram)* superlatif *m*. **in the ~** au superlatif; *(fig)* **he tends to talk in ~s** il a tendance à exagérer.

superlatively [sʊ'pɜːlətɪvlɪ] *adv* extrêmement, au suprême degré, au plus haut point. **he was ~ fit** il était on ne peut plus en forme; *(iro)* **he is ~ stupid** c'est le roi des imbéciles.

superman ['suːpəmæn] *n, pl* **supermen** surhomme *m*.

supermarket ['suːpəˌmɑːkɪt] *n* supermarché *m*.

supermen ['suːpəmen] *npl of* **superman.**

supernal [suː'pɜːnəl] *adj* *(liter)* céleste, divin.

supernatural [ˌsuːpə'nætʃərəl] *adj, n* surnaturel (*m*).

supernormal [ˌsuːpə'nɔːməl] *adj* au-dessus de la normale.

supernova [ˌsuːpəˈnəʊvə] *n* (*Astron*) supernova *f*.

supernumerary [ˌsuːpəˈnjuːmərərɪ] **1** *adj* (*Admin, Bio etc*) surnuméraire; (*superfluous*) superflu. **2** *n* (*Admin etc*) surnuméraire *mf*; (*Cine*) figurant(e) *m(f)*.

superphosphate [ˌsuːpəˈfɒsfeɪt] *n* superphosphate *m*.

superpose [ˌsuːpəˈpəʊz] *vt* (*also Geom*) superposer (*on* à).

superposition [ˈsuːpəpəˈzɪʃən] *n* superposition *f*.

superscription [ˌsuːpəˈskrɪpʃən] *n* suscription *f*.

supersede [ˌsuːpəˈsiːd] *vt belief, object, order* remplacer; *person* supplanter, prendre la place de. **this edition ~s previous ones** cette édition remplace et annule les précédentes; **~d idea/method** idée/méthode périmée.

supersonic [ˈsuːpəˈsɒnɪk] *adj* supersonique. **~ bang** *or* **boom** bang *m* (supersonique).

supersonically [ˈsuːpəˈsɒnɪkəlɪ] *adv* en supersonique.

superstition [ˌsuːpəˈstɪʃən] *n* superstition *f*.

superstitious [ˌsuːpəˈstɪʃəs] *adj* superstitieux.

superstitiously [ˌsuːpəˈstɪʃəslɪ] *adv* superstitieusement.

superstructure [ˈsuːpəˌstrʌktʃəʳ] *n* superstructure *f*.

supertanker [ˈsuːpəˌtæŋkəʳ] *n* pétrolier géant, tanker géant.

supervene [ˌsuːpəˈviːn] *vi* survenir.

supervise [ˈsuːpəvaɪz] **1** *vt person, worker* surveiller, avoir l'œil sur; *organization, department* diriger; *work* surveiller, diriger, superviser; *exam* surveiller; (*Univ*) *research* diriger. **2** *vi* exercer la surveillance, surveiller.

supervision [ˌsuːpəˈvɪʒən] *n* surveillance *f*, contrôle *m*, direction *f* (*esp Comm*). **under the ~ of** sous la surveillance de; **to keep sth under strict ~** exercer une surveillance *or* un contrôle sévère sur qch.

supervisor [ˈsuːpəvaɪzəʳ] *n* (*gen*) surveillant(e) *m(f)*; (*Comm*) chef *m* de rayon; (*at exam*) surveillant(e); (*Univ*) directeur *m*, -trice *f or* patron *m* de thèse.

supervisory [ˈsuːpəvaɪzərɪ] *adj post, duty* de surveillance. **in a ~ capacity** à titre de surveillant.

supine [ˈsuːpaɪn] *adj* (*lit: also* **lying ~, in a ~ position**) couché *or* étendu sur le dos; (*fig pej*) mou (*f* molle), indolent, mollasse.

supper [ˈsʌpəʳ] **1** *n* (*main evening meal*) dîner *m*; (*after theatre etc*) souper *m*; (*snack*) collation *f*. **to have ~** dîner (*or* souper *etc*); (*Rel*) **the Last S~** la Cène; *V* **lord**. **2** *cpd*: **suppertime** l'heure *f* du souper; **at suppertime** au souper.

supplant [səˈplɑːnt] *vt person* supplanter, évincer; *object* supplanter, remplacer.

supple [ˈsʌpl] *adj* souple; (*fig*) souple, servile (*pej*). **to become ~(r)** s'assouplir.

supplement [ˈsʌplɪmənt] **1** *n* (*also Press*) supplément *m* (*to* à); *V* **colour**. **2** [ˌsʌplɪˈment] *vt income* augmenter, arrondir (*by doing* en faisant); *book, information, one's knowledge* ajouter à, compléter.

supplementary [ˌsʌplɪˈmentərɪ] *adj* supplémentaire, additionnel; (*Geom, Mus*) supplémentaire. **~ to** en plus de; (*Brit Admin*) **~ benefit** allocation *f* supplémentaire; (*Parl*) **~ question** question orale.

suppleness [ˈsʌplnɪs] *n* (*V* **supple**) souplesse *f*; servilité *f*.

suppletion [səˈpliːʃən] *n* (*Ling*) suppléance *f*.

suppletive [səˈpliːtɪv] *adj* (*Ling*) supplétif.

suppliant [ˈsʌplɪənt] *adj, n,* **supplicant** [ˈsʌplɪkənt] *adj, n* suppliant(e) *m(f)*.

supplicate [ˈsʌplɪkeɪt] **1** *vt* supplier, implorer (*sb to do* qn de faire); *mercy etc* implorer (*from sb* de qn). **2** *vi*: **to ~ for sth** implorer qch.

supplication [ˌsʌplɪˈkeɪʃən] *n* supplication *f*; (*written*) supplique *f*.

supplier [səˈplaɪəʳ] *n* (*Comm*) fournisseur *m*.

supply¹ [səˈplaɪ] **1** *n* **(a)** (*amount, stock*) provision *f*, réserve *f*, stock *m* (*also Comm*). **a good ~ of coal** une bonne provision *or* réserve de charbon, un bon stock de charbon; **to get** *or* **lay in a ~ of** s'approvisionner de, faire des provisions de; **to get in a fresh ~ of sth** renouveler sa provision *or* sa réserve *or* son stock de qch, se réapprovisionner de qch; **supplies** (*gen*) provisions, réserves; (*food*) vivres *mpl*; (*Mil*) subsistances *fpl*, approvisionnements *mpl*; **electrical supplies** matériel *m* électrique; **office supplies** fournitures *fpl or* matériel de bureau.

(b) (*U*) alimentation *f*. **the ~ of fuel to the engine** l'alimentation du moteur en combustible; **the electricity/gas ~** l'alimentation en électricité/gaz; (*Econ*) **~ and demand** l'offre et la demande; (*Brit*) **Ministry of S~** ≃ services *mpl* de l'Intendance; *V* **short, water** *etc*.

(c) (*person: temporary substitute*) remplaçant(e) *m(f)*, suppléant(e) *m(f)*. **to teach** *or* **be on ~** faire des suppléances *or* des remplacements.

(d) (*Parl*) **supplies** crédits *mpl*.

2 *cpd train, wagon, truck, convoy* préposé au ravitaillement, ravitailleur; *pharmacist etc* intérimaire. **supply ship** navire ravitailleur; **supply teacher** suppléant(e) *m(f)*, remplaçant(e) *m(f)*.

3 *vt* **(a)** (*provide, furnish*) *tools, books, goods* fournir, procurer (*to sb* à qn); (*Comm*) fournir, approvisionner; (*equip*) *person, city* fournir, approvisionner (*with sth* en *or* de qch); (*Mil: with provisions*) ravitailler, approvisionner. (*Comm*) **we ~ most of the local schools** nous fournissons *or* nous approvisionnons la plupart des écoles locales, nous sommes les fournisseurs de la plupart des écoles locales; **sheep ~ wool** les moutons donnent de la laine; **we ~ the tools for the job** nous fournissons *or* nous procurons les outils nécessaires pour faire le travail; **to ~ electricity/gas/water to the town** alimenter la ville en électricité/gaz/eau; **to ~ sb with food** nourrir *or* alimenter qn; **they kept us supplied with milk** grâce à eux nous n'avons jamais manqué de lait; **the car was supplied with a radio** la voiture était munie *or* pourvue d'une radio; **a battery is not supplied with the torch** une pile n'est pas livrée avec la torche; **to ~ sb with information/details** fournir des renseignements/des détails à qn.

(b) (*make good*) *need, deficiency* suppléer à, remédier à; *sb's needs* subvenir à; *loss* réparer, compenser.

supply² [ˈsʌplɪ] *adv move, bend* avec souplesse, souplement.

support [səˈpɔːt] **1** *n* **(a)** (*U: lit, fig*) appui *m*, soutien *m*. **he couldn't stand without ~** il ne pouvait pas se soutenir (sur ses jambes); **he leaned on me for ~** il s'est appuyé sur moi; **to give ~ to sb/sth** soutenir qn/qch; **this bra gives good ~** ce soutien-gorge maintient bien la poitrine; (*fig*) **he looked to his friends for ~** il a cherché un soutien *or* un appui auprès de ses amis; **he needs all the ~ he can get** il a bien besoin de tout l'appui qu'on pourra lui donner; **the proposal got no ~** personne n'a parlé en faveur de la proposition; **he spoke in ~ of the motion** il a parlé en faveur de la motion; **in ~ of his theory/claim** à l'appui de sa théorie/revendication; **have I your ~ in this?** est-ce que je peux compter sur votre appui *or* soutien en la matière?; **to give** *or* **lend one's ~ to** prêter son appui à; **that lends ~ to his theory** ceci corrobore *or* vient corroborer sa théorie; **they demonstrated in ~ of the prisoners** ils ont manifesté en faveur des prisonniers, ils ont fait une manifestation de soutien aux prisonniers; **they stopped work in ~** ils ont cessé le travail par solidarité; **he depends on his father for (financial) ~** il dépend financièrement de son père; (*financial*) **he has no visible means of ~** il n'a pas de moyens d'existence connus; **what means of ~ has he got?** quelles sont ses ressources?; *V* **moral**.

(b) (*object*) (*gen*) appui *m*; (*Constr, Tech*) support *m*, soutien *m*; (*fig: moral, financial etc*) soutien; (*US Econ: subsidy*) subvention *f*. **use the stool as a ~ for your foot** prenez le tabouret comme appui pour votre pied; **he is the sole (financial) ~ of his family** il est le seul soutien (financier) de sa famille; **he has been a great ~ to me** il a été pour moi un soutien précieux.

2 *cpd* (*Mil etc*) *troops, convoy, vessel* de soutien.

3 *vt* **(a)** (*hold up*) *[pillar, beam]* supporter, soutenir; *[bridge]* porter; *[person, neck]* soutenir. **the elements necessary to ~ life** les éléments nécessaires à l'entretien de la vie, les éléments vitaux.

(b) (*uphold*) *motion, theory, cause, party* être pour, être en faveur de, être partisan de; *candidate* soutenir, appuyer, être partisan de; *sb's application, action, protest* soutenir, appuyer; *team* être supporter de, supporter*. **with only his courage to ~ him** avec son seul courage comme soutien, n'ayant de soutien que son courage; **his friends ~ed him in his refusal to obey** ses amis l'ont soutenu *or* l'ont appuyé *or* ont pris son parti lorsqu'il a refusé d'obéir; **the socialists will ~ it** les socialistes seront *or* voteront pour; **I cannot ~ what you are doing** je ne peux pas approuver ce que vous faites; (*Cine, Theat*) **~ed by a cast of thousands** avec le concours de milliers d'acteurs et figurants; **the proofs that ~ my case** les preuves à l'appui de ma cause; (*Econ*) **a subsidy to ~ the price of beef** une subvention pour maintenir le prix du bœuf; (*Ftbl*) **he ~s Celtic** c'est un supporter du Celtic, il supporte* le Celtic.

(c) (*financially*) subvenir aux besoins de. **he has a wife and 3 children to ~** il doit subvenir aux besoins de sa femme et de ses 3 enfants; **to ~ o.s.** gagner sa vie, subvenir à ses propres besoins; **the school is ~ed by money from ...** l'école reçoit une aide financière de ... .

(d) (*endure*) supporter, tolérer.

supportable [səˈpɔːtəbl] *adj* supportable, tolérable.

supporter [səˈpɔːtəʳ] *n* **(a)** (*Constr, Tech*) soutien *m*, support *m*; (*Her*) tenant *m*.

(b) (*person*) *[party]* partisan(e) *m(f)*, tenant *m*; *[theory, cause, opinion]* adepte *mf*, partisan(e), tenant; (*Sport*) supporter *m*. **football ~s** supporters de football.

supporting [səˈpɔːtɪŋ] *adj wall* d'appui, de soutènement; (*Cine, Theat*) *role, part* secondaire, de second plan; *actor* qui a un rôle secondaire *or* de second plan. **~ cast** partenaires *mpl*; **~ film** film *m* qui passe en premier; *V* **self**.

suppose [səˈpəʊz] **1** *vt* **(a)** (*imagine*) supposer (*that* que+*subj*); (*assume, postulate*) supposer (*that* que+*indic*). **~ he doesn't come? — he will — yes but just ~!** et s'il ne vient pas? — il viendra — oui mais à supposer qu'il ne vienne pas? *or* oui mais au cas où il ne viendrait pas?; **if we ~ that the two are identical** si nous supposons que les deux sont identiques; (*Math*) **~ A equals B** soit A égale B; **~ ABC a triangle** soit un triangle ABC.

(b) (*believe, think*) supposer, croire, penser, imaginer (*that* que). **what do you ~ he wants?** à votre avis que peut-il bien vouloir?; **he is (generally) ~d to be rich, it is (generally) ~d that he is rich** il passe pour être riche, on dit qu'il est riche; **I never ~d him (to be) a hero** je n'ai jamais pensé *or* imaginé qu'il fût un héros; **I don't ~ he'll agree, I ~ he won't agree** cela m'étonnerait qu'il soit d'accord, je ne crois pas *or* je ne pense pas qu'il soit d'accord; **I ~ so** probablement; **I don't ~ so, I ~ not** je ne (le) pense *or* crois pas, probablement pas; **wouldn't you ~ he'd be sorry?** n'auriez-vous pas pensé qu'il le regretterait?

(c) (*modal use in pass: 'ought'*) **to be ~d to do sth** être censé faire qch; **she was ~d to telephone this morning** elle était censée *or* elle devait téléphoner ce matin; **he isn't ~d to know** il n'est pas censé le savoir; **you're not ~d to do that** il ne vous est pas permis de faire cela.

(d) (*in imperative: 'I suggest'*) **~ we go for a walk?** et si nous allions nous promener?; **~ I tell him myself?** et si c'était moi qui le lui disais?

(e) (*in prp as conj: 'if'*) **supposing** si+*indic*, à supposer que+*subj*, supposé que+*subj*; **supposing he can't do it?** et s'il ne peut pas le faire?, et à supposer *or* et supposé qu'il ne puisse le faire?; **even supposing that** à supposer même que+*subj*; **always supposing that** en supposant que+*subj*, en admettant que+*subj*.

(f) (*presuppose*) supposer. **that ~s unlimited resources** cela suppose des ressources illimitées.

2 *vi:* **you'll come, I ~?** vous viendrez, j'imagine? *or* je suppose?; **don't spend your time supposing, do something!** ne passe pas ton temps à faire des suppositions, fais quelque chose!

supposed [sə'pəʊzd] *adj* (*presumed*) présumé, supposé; (*so-called*) prétendu, soi-disant *inv*; *V also* **suppose.**

supposedly [sə'pəʊzɪdlɪ] *adv* soi-disant, à ce que l'on suppose (*or* supposait *etc*). **they were ~ aware of what had happened** ils étaient soi-disant conscients *or* ils étaient censés être conscients de ce qui était arrivé; **he had ~ gone to France** il était censé être allé en France; **did he go? — ~!** est-ce qu'il y est allé? — à ce que l'on suppose! *or* soi-disant!; **~ not** apparemment pas.

supposing [sə'pəʊzɪŋ] *conj V* **suppose 1e.**

supposition [ˌsʌpə'zɪʃən] *n* supposition *f*, hypothèse *f*. **that is pure ~** c'est une pure supposition; **on the ~ that ...** à supposer que ...+*subj*, dans la supposition que ...+*subj*; **on this ~** dans cette hypothèse.

suppositional [ˌsʌpə'zɪʃənəl] *adj*, **suppositious** [ˌsʌpə'zɪʃəs] *adj* hypothétique.

supposititious [səˌpɒzɪ'tɪʃəs] *adj* supposé, faux (*f* fausse), apocryphe.

suppository [sə'pɒzɪtərɪ] *n* suppositoire *m*.

suppress [sə'pres] *vt abuse, crime* supprimer, mettre fin à; *revolt* réprimer, étouffer; *one's feelings* réprimer, contenir, refouler, maîtriser; *yawn* étouffer; *facts, truth, scandal* étouffer, dissimuler, cacher; *newspaper, publication* interdire, supprimer; (*Psych*) refouler; (*Elec, Rad etc*) éliminer; (*: *silence*) *heckler etc* faire taire. **to ~ a cough/sneeze** *etc* se retenir de *or* réprimer une envie de tousser/d'éternuer *etc*.

suppression [sə'preʃən] *n* (*V* **suppress**) suppression *f*; répression *f*; étouffement *m*; dissimulation *f*; interdiction *f*; (*Psych*) refoulement *m*; (*Elec, Rad etc*) élimination *f*.

suppressive [sə'presɪv] *adj* répressif.

suppressor [sə'presə^r] *n* (*Elec etc*) dispositif *m* antiparasite.

suppurate ['sʌpjʊəreɪt] *vi* suppurer.

suppuration [ˌsʌpjʊə'reɪʃən] *n* suppuration *f*.

supra... ['su:prə] *pref* supra..., sur... . **~national** supranational; **~renal** surrénal.

supremacy [sʊ'preməsɪ] *n* suprématie *f* (*over* sur).

supreme [sʊ'pri:m] *adj* (*all senses*) suprême. (*Rel*) **the S~ Being** l'Être suprême; (*Mil*) **S~ Commander** commandant *m* en chef *or* suprême, généralissime *m*; (*Can, US Jur*) **S~ Court** Cour *f* suprême; **to make the ~ sacrifice** faire le sacrifice de sa vie; *V* **reign, soviet** *etc*.

supremo* [sʊ'pri:məʊ] *n* (*Brit*) grand patron*.

sura ['sʊərə] *n* surate *f*.

surcharge ['sɜ:tʃɑ:dʒ] **1** *n* (*extra payment, extra load, also Elec; also Post: overprinting*) surcharge *f*; (*extra tax*) surtaxe *f*. **import ~** surtaxe à l'importation. **2** [sɜ:'tʃɑ:dʒ] *vt* surcharger; surtaxer.

surd [sɜ:d] **1** *adj* (*Math*) irrationnel; (*Ling*) sourd. **2** *n* (*Math*) quantité *f or* nombre *m* irrationnel(le); (*Ling*) sourde *f*.

sure [ʃʊə^r] **1** *adj* **(a)** (*infallible; reliable; safe etc*) *aim, shot, marksman, judgment, method, friend, footing* sûr; *solution, remedy* sûr, infaillible; *facts* sûr, indubitable; *success* assuré, certain.

(b) (*definite, indisputable*) sûr, certain. **it is ~ that he will come, he is ~ to come** il est sûr *or* certain qu'il viendra; **it is not ~ that he will come, he is not ~ to come** il n'est pas sûr *or* certain qu'il vienne; **it's not ~ yet** ça n'a encore rien de sûr; **it's ~ to rain** il va pleuvoir à coup sûr *or* c'est sûr et certain*; **be ~ to tell me, be ~ and tell me** ne manquez pas de me le dire; **you're ~ of a good meal** un bon repas vous est assuré; **he's ~ of success** il est sûr *or* certain de réussir; **you can't be ~ of him** vous ne pouvez pas être sûr de lui; **I want to be ~ of seeing him** je veux être sûr *or* certain de le voir; **to make ~ of a seat** s'assurer (d')une place; **to make ~ of one's facts** vérifier *or* s'assurer de ce qu'on avance; **better get a ticket beforehand and make ~** il vaut mieux prendre un billet à l'avance pour plus de sûreté *or* pour être sûr*; **did you lock it? — I think so but I'd better make ~** l'avez-vous fermé à clef? — je crois, mais je vais vérifier *or* m'en assurer; **I've made ~ of having enough coffee for everyone** j'ai veillé à ce qu'il y ait assez de café pour tout le monde; **nothing is ~ in this life** dans cette vie on n'est sûr de rien; **~ thing!*** oui bien sûr!; **he is, to be ~, rather tactless** il manque de tact, c'est certain; (*excl*) **well, to be ~!*** bien, ça alors!; **he'll leave for ~** il partira sans aucun doute; **and that's for ~*** ça ne fait aucun doute; **I'll find out for ~** je me renseignerai pour savoir exactement ce qu'il en est; **do you know for ~?** êtes-vous absolument sûr? *or* certain?; **I'll do it next week for ~** je le ferai la semaine prochaine sans faute.

(c) (*positive, convinced, assured*) sûr (*of* de), certain. **I'm** *or* **I feel ~ I've seen him** je suis sûr *or* certain de l'avoir vu; **I'm ~ he'll help us** je suis sûr qu'il nous aidera; **I'm not ~** je ne suis pas sûr *or* certain (*that* que+*subj*); **I'm not ~ how/why/when** *etc* je ne sais pas très bien comment/pourquoi/quand *etc*; **I'm not ~ (if) he can** je ne suis pas sûr *or* certain qu'il puisse; **I'm ~ I didn't mean to** je ne l'ai vraiment pas fait exprès; **he says he did it but I'm not so ~ (about that)** il dit que c'est lui qui l'a fait mais je n'en suis pas si sûr (que ça); **I'm going alone! — I'm not so ~ about that!** *or* **don't be so ~ about that!** j'irai seul! — ne le dis pas si vite!; **to be/feel ~ of o.s.** être/se sentir sûr de soi.

2 *adv* **(a)** (*: *esp US: certainly*) pour sûr*. **he can ~ play the piano** pour sûr*, il sait jouer du piano; **he was ~ drunk, he ~ was drunk** pour sûr*, il était ivre, il était drôlement ivre; **will you do it? — ~!** le ferez-vous? — bien sûr! *or* pour sûr!*

(b) **~ enough** (*confirming*) effectivement, en effet, de fait; (*promising*) assurément, sans aucun doute; **and ~ enough he did arrive** et effectivement *or* en effet *or* de fait il est arrivé; **it's petrol, ~ enough** c'est effectivement de l'essence, c'est de l'essence en effet; **~ enough!** assurément!; (*US**) **he ~ enough made a hash of that** pour sûr qu'il a tout gâché*.

(c) **as ~ as** aussi sûr que; **as ~ as my name's Smith** aussi sûr que je m'appelle Smith; **as ~ as fate, as ~ as anything, as ~ as guns*, as ~ as eggs is eggs‡** aussi sûr que deux et deux font quatre.

3 *cpd:* (*US*) **sure enough*** réel; **sure-fire*** certain, infaillible; **sure-footed** au pied sûr; **sure-footedly** d'un pied sûr.

surely ['ʃʊəlɪ] *adv* **(a)** (*expressing confidence: assuredly*) sûrement, certainement; (*expressing incredulity*) tout de même. **~ we've met before?** je suis sûr que nous nous sommes déjà rencontrés?; **~ he didn't say that!** il n'a pas pu dire ça, tout de même!; **there is ~ some mistake** il doit sûrement *or* certainement y avoir quelque erreur; **~ you can do something to help?** il doit bien y avoir quelque chose que vous puissiez faire pour aider; **~ you didn't believe him?** vous ne l'avez pas cru, j'espère; **it must rain soon, ~** il va bien pleuvoir, tout de même; **that's ~ not true** ça ne peut pas être vrai, ça m'étonnerait que ce soit vrai; **~ not!** pas possible!; (*US: with pleasure*) **~!** bien volontiers!

(b) (*inevitably*) sûrement, à coup sûr. **justice will ~ prevail** la justice prévaudra sûrement.

(c) *advance, move* (*safely*) sûrement; (*confidently*) avec assurance; *V* **slowly.**

sureness ['ʃʊənɪs] *n* (*certainty*) certitude *f*; (*sure-footedness*) sûreté *f*; (*self-assurance*) assurance *f*, sûreté de soi; *[judgment, method, footing, grip]* sûreté; *[aim, shot]* justesse *f*, précision *f*. **the ~ of his touch** sa sûreté de main.

surety ['ʃʊərətɪ] *n* **(a)** (*Jur*) (*sum*) caution *f*; (*person*) caution, garant(e) *m(f)*. **to go** *or* **stand ~ for sb** se porter caution *or* garant pour qn; **in his own ~ of £100** après avoir donné une sûreté personnelle de 100 livres.

(b) (††) certitude *f*. **of a ~** certainement.

surf [sɜ:f] **1** *n* (*U*) (*waves*) vague déferlante, ressac *m*; (*foam*) écume *f*; (*spray*) embrun *m*.

2 *vi* (*also* **go ~ing**) surfer, pratiquer le surf.

3 *cpd:* **surfboard** (*n*) planche *f* (de surf); (*vi*) surfer; **surfboarder** surfeur *m*, -euse *f*; **surfboarding** surf *m*; **surf boat** surf-boat *m*; **surfride** surfer; **surfrider** = **surfboarder; surfriding** = **surfboarding.**

surface ['sɜ:fɪs] **1** *n* **(a)** *[earth, sea, liquid, object etc]* surface *f*; (*fig*) surface, extérieur *m*, dehors *m*. *[sea, lake etc]* **under the ~** sous l'eau; **he rose to the ~** il est remonté à la surface; **on the ~** (*Naut*) en surface; (*Min: also* **at the ~**) au jour, à la surface; (*fig*) à première vue, au premier abord; en apparence; **on the ~ of the table** sur la surface de la table; **his faults are all on the ~** il a des défauts mais il a bon fond; (*fig*) **I can't get below the ~ with him** je n'arrive pas à le connaître vraiment *or* à aller au-delà des apparences avec lui; **the road ~ is icy** la chaussée est verglacée.

(b) (*Math*) (*area*) surface *f*, superficie *f*, aire *f*; (*side: of solid*) côté *m*, face *f*.

2 *cpd tension* superficiel (*also fig*); (*Naut*) *vessel etc* de surface; (*Min*) *work* au jour, à la surface. (*Math etc*) **surface area** surface *f*, superficie *f*, aire *f*; (*Post*) **surface mail** courrier *m* par voie de terre, courrier maritime; **by surface mail** par voie de terre, par voie maritime; (*on record player*) **surface noise** grésillements *mpl*; (*Mil*) **surface-to-air** sol-air *inv*; (*Mil*) **surface-to-surface** sol-sol *inv* ; (*Min*) **surface workers** personnel *m* qui travaille au jour *or* à la surface.

3 *vt* **(a)** *road* revêtir (*with* de); *paper* calandrer, glacer.

(b) (*Naut*) *submarine, object, wreck* amener à la surface.

4 *vi [swimmer, diver, whale]* revenir *or* remonter à la surface; *[submarine]* faire surface; (**fig*) (*after absence*) réapparaître; (*after hard work*) faire surface.

surfeit ['sɜ:fɪt] **1** *n* excès *m* (*of* de); (*U: satiety*) satiété *f*. **to have a ~ of** avoir une indigestion de (*fig*); **there is a ~ of** il y a par trop de. **2** *vt:* **to be ~ed with pleasure** être repu de plaisir.

surfing ['sɜ:fɪŋ] *n* surf *m*.

surge [sɜ:dʒ] **1** *n* mouvement puissant; *[rage, fear, enthusiasm]* vague *f*, montée *f*. **the ~ of the sea** la houle; **he felt a ~ of anger** il a senti la colère monter en lui; **there was a ~ of sympathy for him** il y a eu un vif mouvement *or* une vague de sympathie pour lui; **the ~ of people around the car** la foule qui se pressait autour de la voiture; **he was carried along by the ~ of the crowd** il était porté par le mouvement de la foule.

2 *vi* **(a)** *[waves]* s'enfler; *[flood, river]* déferler. **the sea ~d against the rocks** la houle battait *or* heurtait les rochers; **the surging sea** la mer houleuse; **the ship ~d at anchor** le bateau amarré était soulevé par la houle; (*fig*) **a surging mass of demonstrators** une foule déferlante de manifestants; (*Elec*) **the power ~d suddenly** il y a eu une brusque surtension de courant; **the blood ~d to his cheeks** le sang lui est monté *or* lui a reflué au visage; **anger ~d (up) within him** la colère monta en lui.

(b) *[crowd, vehicles etc]* déferler. **to ~ in/out** *etc* entrer/sortir *etc* à flots; **they ~d round the car** ils se pressaient autour de la voiture; **they ~d forward** ils se sont lancés en avant.

surgeon ['sɜ:dʒən] *n* chirurgien *m*. **she is a ~** elle est chirurgien; **a woman ~** une femme chirurgien; *V* **dental, house, veterinary** *etc*.

surgery ['sɜ:dʒərɪ] **1** *n* **(a)** (*U: skill; study; operation*) chirurgie *f*. **it is a fine piece of ~** le chirurgien a fait du beau travail; *V* **plastic** *etc*.

(b) (*Brit: consulting room*) cabinet *m* (de consultation); (*interview*) consultation *f*. **come to the ~ tomorrow** venez à mon cabinet demain, venez à la consultation demain; **when is his ~?** à quelle heure sont ses consultations?, à quelle heure consulte-t-il?; **during his ~** pendant ses heures de consultation; **there is an afternoon ~** il consulte l'après-midi.

2 *cpd:* **surgery hours** heures *fpl* de consultation.

surgical ['sɜːdʒɪkəl] *adj operation, intervention, treatment* chirurgical; *instruments* chirurgical, de chirurgie. **~ cotton** coton *m* hydrophile; **~ dressing** pansement *m*; **~ shock** choc *m* opératoire; (*Brit*) **~ spirit** alcool *m* à 90 (degrés).

surliness ['sɜːlɪnɪs] *n* caractère *or* air revêche *or* maussade *or* renfrogné.

surly ['sɜːlɪ] *adj* revêche, maussade, renfrogné, bourru.

surmise ['sɜːmaɪz] 1 *n* conjecture *f*, hypothèse *f*. **it was nothing but ~** c'était entièrement conjectural. 2 [sɜː'maɪz] *vt* conjecturer, présumer (*from sth* d'après qch, *that* que). **I ~d as much** je m'en doutais.

surmount [sɜː'maʊnt] *vt* **(a)** (*Archit etc*) surmonter. **~ed by a statue** surmonté d'une statue. **(b)** (*overcome*) *obstacle, difficulties, problems* surmonter, venir à bout de.

surmountable [sɜː'maʊntəbl] *adj* surmontable.

surname ['sɜːneɪm] 1 *n* nom *m* de famille. **name and ~** nom et prénoms.

2 *vt:* **~d Jones** nommé *or* dénommé Jones, dont le nom de famille est (*or* était) Jones.

surpass [sɜː'pɑːs] *vt* surpasser (*in* en); *hopes, expectations* dépasser. (*also iro*) **to ~ o.s.** se surpasser (*also iro*).

surpassing [sɜː'pɑːsɪŋ] *adj* incomparable, sans pareil.

surplice ['sɜːpləs] *n* surplis *m*.

surplus ['sɜːpləs] 1 *n* (*Comm, Econ, gen*) surplus *m*, excédent *m*; (*Fin*) boni *m*, excédent. **a tea ~** un surplus *or* un excédent de thé.

2 *adj* (*gen*) *food, boxes etc* en surplus, en trop, de reste; (*Comm, Econ*) en surplus, excédentaire; (*Fin*) de boni, excédentaire. **it is ~ to (our) requirements** cela excède nos besoins; *[book, document etc]* **~ copies** exemplaires *mpl* de passe; **~ stock** surplus *mpl*, stocks *mpl* excédentaires; **American ~ wheat** excédent *or* surplus de blé américain; **his ~ energy** son surcroît d'énergie.

3 *cpd:* **surplus store** magasin *m* de surplus américains.

surprise [sə'praɪz] 1 *n* (*emotion: U*) surprise *f*, étonnement *m*; (*event etc*) surprise. **much to my ~, to my great ~** à ma grande surprise, à mon grand étonnement; **he stopped in ~** il s'est arrêté sous l'effet de la surprise, étonné il s'est arrêté; **to take by ~** *person* surprendre, prendre au dépourvu; (*Mil*) *fort, town* prendre par surprise; **a look of ~** un regard surpris *or* traduisant la surprise; **imagine my ~ when ...** imaginez quel a été mon étonnement *or* quelle a été ma surprise quand ...; **what a ~!** quelle surprise!; **to give sb a ~** faire une surprise à qn, surprendre qn; **it was a lovely/nasty ~ for him** cela a été pour lui une agréable/mauvaise surprise; **it came as a ~ (to me) to learn that ...** j'ai eu la surprise d'apprendre que ... .

2 *adj defeat, gift, visit, decision* inattendu, inopiné. **~ attack** attaque *f* par surprise, attaque brusquée.

3 *vt* **(a)** (*astonish*) surprendre, étonner. **he was ~d to hear that ...** il a été surpris *or* étonné d'apprendre que ..., cela l'a surpris *or* étonné d'apprendre que ...; **I shouldn't be ~d if it snowed** cela ne m'étonnerait pas qu'il neige (*subj*); **don't be ~d if he refuses** ne soyez pas étonné *or* surpris s'il refuse, ne vous étonnez pas s'il refuse; **it's nothing to be ~d at** cela n'a rien d'étonnant, ce n'est pas *or* guère étonnant; **I'm ~d at *or* by his ignorance** son ignorance me surprend; **I'm ~d at you!** je ne m'attendais pas à cela de vous!, cela me surprend de votre part!; **it ~d me that he agreed** j'ai été étonné *or* surpris qu'il accepte (*subj*), je ne m'attendais pas à ce qu'il accepte (*subj*); (*iro*) **go on, ~ me!** allez, étonne-moi!; **he ~d me into agreeing to do it** j'ai été tellement surpris que j'ai accepté de le faire.

(b) (*catch unawares*) *army, sentry* surprendre, attaquer par surprise; *thief* surprendre, prendre sur le fait; (*gen*) surprendre.

surprised [sə'praɪzd] *adj* surpris, étonné; *V also* **surprise.**

surprising [sə'praɪzɪŋ] *adj* surprenant, étonnant. **it is ~ that** il est surprenant *or* étonnant que+*subj*.

surprisingly [sə'praɪzɪŋlɪ] *adv big, sad etc* étonnamment, étrangement. **you look ~ cheerful for someone who ...** vous m'avez l'air de bien bonne humeur pour quelqu'un qui ...; **~ enough, ...** chose étonnante, ...; **not ~ he didn't come** comme on pouvait s'y attendre il n'est pas venu, il n'est pas venu, ce qui n'a rien d'étonnant.

surrealism [sə'rɪəlɪzəm] *n* surréalisme *m*.

surrealist [sə'rɪəlɪst] *adj, n* surréaliste (*mf*).

surrealistic [sə,rɪə'lɪstɪk] *adj* surréaliste.

surrender [sə'rendəʳ] 1 *vi* (*Mil*) se rendre (*to* à), capituler (*to* devant). **to ~ to the police** se livrer à la police, se constituer prisonnier; (*fig*) **to ~ to despair** s'abandonner *or* se livrer au désespoir.

2 *vt* **(a)** (*Mil*) *town, hill* livrer (*to* à).

(b) *firearms* rendre (*to* à); *stolen property, documents, photos* remettre, restituer (*to* à); *insurance policy* racheter; *lease* céder; *one's rights, claims, powers, liberty* renoncer à, abdiquer; *hopes* abandonner. (*fig*) **to ~ o.s. to despair/to the delights of sth** s'abandonner *or* se livrer au désespoir/aux plaisirs de qch.

3 *n* **(a)** (*Mil etc*) reddition *f* (*to* à), capitulation *f* (*to* devant). **no ~!** on ne se rend pas!; *V* **unconditional.**

(b) (*giving up*) *[firearms, stolen property, documents]* remise *f* (*to* à); *[insurance policy]* rachat *m*; *[one's rights, claims, powers, liberty]* renonciation *f* (*of* à), abdication *f* (*of* de, *to* en faveur de); *[hopes]* abandon *m*; *[lease]* cession *f*; (*return*) restitution *f* (*of* de, *to* à).

4 *cpd:* (*Insurance*) **surrender value** valeur *f* de rachat.

surreptitious [,sʌrəp'tɪʃəs] *adj entry, removal* subreptice, clandestin; *movement, gesture* furtif.

surreptitiously [,sʌrəp'tɪʃəslɪ] *adv* subrepticement, clandestinement, furtivement, sournoisement (*pej*).

surrogate ['sʌrəgeɪt] *n* (*frm*) substitut *m*, représentant *m*; (*Rel*) *évêque m auxiliaire à qui l'on délègue le pouvoir d'autoriser les mariages sans publication de bans*; (*Psych*) substitut.

surround [sə'raʊnd] 1 *vt* entourer; (*totally*) cerner, encercler. **~ed by** entouré de; (*Mil, Police etc*) **you are ~ed** vous êtes cerné *or* encerclé. 2 *n* bordure *f*, encadrement *m*; (*Brit: on floor: also* **~s**) bordure (entre le tapis et le mur).

surrounding [sə'raʊndɪŋ] 1 *adj* environnant. **the ~ countryside** les environs *mpl*, les alentours *mpl*.

2 *npl:* **~s** (*surrounding country*) alentours *mpl*, environs *mpl*; (*setting*) cadre *m*, décor *m*; **the ~s of Glasgow are picturesque** les alentours *or* les environs de Glasgow sont pittoresques, Glasgow est située dans un cadre *or* un décor pittoresque; **he found himself in ~s strange to him** il s'est retrouvé dans un cadre *or* décor qu'il ne connaissait pas; **animals in their natural ~s** des animaux dans leur cadre naturel.

surtax ['sɜːtæks] *n* (*income tax*) impôt *m* supplémentaire (au-dessus d'un certain revenu).

surveillance [sɜː'veɪləns] *n* surveillance *f*. **to keep sb under ~** garder qn à vue; **under constant ~** sous surveillance continue, gardé à vue.

survey ['sɜːveɪ] 1 *n* **(a)** (*comprehensive view*) *[countryside, prospects, development etc]* vue générale *or* d'ensemble (*of* de). **he gave a general ~ of the situation** il a fait un tour d'horizon de la situation, il a passé la situation en revue.

(b) (*investigation, study*) *[reasons, prices, situation, sales, trends]* enquête *f* (*of* sur), étude *f* (*of* de). **to carry out *or* make a ~ of** enquêter sur, faire une étude de; **~ of public opinion** sondage *m* d'opinion.

(c) (*Surv: of land, coast etc*) (*act*) relèvement *m*, levé *m*; (*report*) levé; *V* **aerial, ordnance.**

(d) (*in housebuying*) (*act*) visite *f* d'expert, inspection *f*, examen *m*; (*report*) (rapport *m* d')expertise *f*.

2 *cpd:* **survey ship** bateau *m* hydrographique.

3 [sɜː'veɪ] *vt* **(a)** (*look around at*) *countryside, view, crowd* embrasser du regard; *prospects, trends* passer en revue. **he ~ed the scene with amusement** il regardait la scène d'un œil amusé; **the Prime Minister ~ed the situation** le Premier ministre a fait un tour d'horizon de *or* a passé en revue la situation; **the book ~s the history of the motorcar** le livre passe en revue *or* étudie dans les grandes lignes l'histoire de l'automobile.

(b) (*examine, study*) *ground before battle etc* inspecter; *developments, needs, prospects* enquêter sur, faire une étude de.

(c) (*Surv*) *site, land* arpenter, faire le levé de, relever; *house, building* inspecter, examiner; *country, coast* faire levé topographique de; *seas* faire le levé hydrographique de.

surveying [sɜː'veɪɪŋ] 1 *n* (*V* **survey 3c**) **(a)** (*act*) arpentage *m*, levé *m*; inspection *f*, examen *m*.

(b) (*science, occupation*) arpentage *m*; topographie *f*; hydrographie *f*.

2 *cpd instrument* d'arpentage; *studies* d'arpentage *or* de topographie *or* d'hydrographie.

surveyor [sə'veɪəʳ] *n [property, buildings etc]* expert *m*; *[land, site]* (arpenteur *m*) géomètre *m*; *[country, coastline]* topographe *mf*; *[seas]* hydrographe *mf*; *V* **quantity** *etc.*

survival [sə'vaɪvəl] 1 *n* (*act*) survie *f* (*also Jur, Rel*); (*relic: of custom, beliefs etc*) survivance *f*, vestige *m*. **the ~ of the fittest** la persistance du plus apte. 2 *cpd:* **survival course/kit** cours *m*/kit *m* de survie.

survive [sə'vaɪv] 1 *vi [person]* survivre; *[house, jewellery, book, custom]* survivre, subsister. **he ~d to tell the tale** il a survécu et a pu raconter ce qui s'était passé; **only 3 volumes ~** il ne reste *or* il ne subsiste plus que 3 tomes; (*iro*) **you'll ~!** vous n'en mourrez pas!

2 *vt person* survivre à; *injury, disease* réchapper de; *fire, accident, experience, invasion* survivre à, réchapper de. **he is ~d by a wife and 2 sons** sa femme et 2 fils lui survivent.

survivor [sə'vaɪvəʳ] *n* survivant(e) *m(f)*.

Susan ['suːzn] *n* Suzanne *f*.

susceptibility [sə,septə'bɪlɪtɪ] *n* (*sensitiveness*) vive sensibilité, émotivité *f*, impressionnabilité *f*; (*touchiness*) susceptibilité *f*; (*Med*) prédisposition *f* (*to* à). **his ~ to hypnosis** la facilité avec laquelle on l'hypnotise; **his susceptibilities** ses cordes *fpl* sensibles.

susceptible [sə'septəbl] *adj* (*sensitive, impressionable*) sensible, émotif, impressionnable; (*touchy*) susceptible, ombrageux. **to be ~ to** *pain* être (très) sensible à, craindre; *kindness* être sensible à; *suggestion, sb's influence* être ouvert à, être accessible à; (*Med*) *disease* être prédisposé à; *treatment* répondre à; **~ of** susceptible de.

suspect ['sʌspekt] 1 *n* suspect(e) *m(f)*.

2 *adj evidence, act* suspect.

3 [səs'pekt] *vt* **(a)** soupçonner (*that* que); *person* soupçonner, suspecter (*pej*) (*of a crime* d'un crime, *of doing* de faire *or* d'avoir fait); *ambush, swindle* flairer, soupçonner. **I ~ him of being the author** *[book etc]* je le soupçonne d'en être l'auteur; *[anonymous letter]* je le soupçonne *or* je le suspecte d'en être l'auteur.

(b) (*think likely*) soupçonner, avoir dans l'idée, avoir le sentiment (*that* que). **I ~ he knows who did it** je soupçonne *or* j'ai dans l'idée *or* j'ai le sentiment qu'il sait qui est le coupable; **I ~ed as much** je m'en doutais; **he'll come, I ~** il viendra, j'imagine.

(c) (*doubt*) suspecter, douter de. **I ~ the truth of what he says**

je doute de *or* je suspecte la vérité de ce qu'il dit.

suspend [səs'pend] *vt* **(a)** (*hang*) suspendre (*from* à). *[particles etc]* **to be ~ed in sth** être en suspension dans qch; **a column of smoke hung ~ed in the still air** une colonne de fumée flottait dans l'air immobile.

(b) (*stop temporarily; defer etc*) *publication* suspendre, surseoir; *decision, payment, regulation, meetings, discussions* suspendre; *licence, permission* retirer provisoirement; *bus service* interrompre provisoirement. **to ~ judgment** suspendre son jugement; (*Jur*) **~ed sentence** condamnation *f* avec sursis; (*Jur*) **he received a ~ed sentence of 6 months in jail** il a été condamné à 6 mois de prison avec sursis; **to be in a state of ~ed animation** (*Med*) être dans le coma; (*fig hum*) *[committee etc]* ne donner aucun signe de vie.

(c) *employee, office-holder, officer etc* suspendre (*from* de); (*Scol, Univ*) exclure *or* renvoyer temporairement.

suspender [səs'pendəʳ] **1** *n* **(a)** (*Brit*) (*for stockings*) jarretelle *f*; (*for socks*) fixe-chaussette *m*. **(b)** (*US*) **~s** bretelles *fpl*. **2** *cpd:* (*Brit*) **suspender belt** porte-jarretelles *m inv*.

suspense [səs'pens] **1** *n* (*U*) **(a)** incertitude *f*, attente *f*; (*in book, film, play*) suspense *m*. **we waited in great ~** nous avons attendu haletants; **to keep sb in ~** tenir qn en suspens, laisser qn dans l'incertitude; *[film]* tenir en suspens *or* en haleine; **to put sb out of (his) ~** mettre fin à l'incertitude *or* à l'attente de qn; **the ~ is killing me!*** ce suspense me tue! (*also iro*).

(b) (*Admin, Jur*) **to be *or* remain in ~** être (laissé) *or* rester en suspens.

2 *cpd:* (*Book-keeping*) **suspense account** compte *m* d'attente.

suspension [səs'penʃən] **1** *n* **(a)** (*V* **suspend b**) suspension *f*; retrait *m* provisoire; interruption *f* provisoire.

(b) (*V* **suspend c**) suspension *f*; renvoi *m or* exclusion *f* temporaire.

(c) (*Aut, Chem, Tech etc*) suspension *f*. (*Chem*) **in ~** en suspension.

2 *cpd:* **suspension bridge** pont suspendu; (*Gram*) **suspension points** points *mpl* de suspension.

suspensory [səs'pensərɪ] *adj ligament* suspenseur (*m only*); *bandage* de soutien.

suspicion [səs'pɪʃən] *n* **(a)** soupçon *m*; (*U*) soupçon(s). **an atmosphere laden with ~** une atmosphère chargée de soupçons; **above ~** au-dessus *or* à l'abri de tout soupçon; **under ~** considéré comme suspect; **he was regarded with ~** on s'est montré soupçonneux à son égard; (*Jur*) **to arrest sb on ~** arrêter qn sur des présomptions; **on ~ of murder** sur présomption de meurtre; **I had a ~ that he wouldn't come back** je soupçonnais *or* quelque chose me disait *or* j'avais le sentiment qu'il ne reviendrait pas; **I had no ~ that ...** je ne me doutais pas du tout que ...; **I had (my) ~s about that letter** j'avais mes doutes quant à cette lettre; **I have my ~s about it** j'ai des doutes là-dessus, cela me semble suspect; **he was right in his ~ that ...** il avait raison de soupçonner que ..., c'est à juste titre qu'il soupçonnait que ... .

(b) (*fig: trace, touch*) soupçon *m*.

suspicious [səs'pɪʃəs] *adj* **(a)** (*feeling suspicion*) soupçonneux, méfiant. **to be ~ about sb/sth** avoir des soupçons à l'égard de qn/quant à qch, tenir qn/qch pour suspect; **to be ~ of** se méfier de.

(b) (*causing suspicion: also* **~-looking**) *person, vehicle, action* suspect, louche.

suspiciously [səs'pɪʃəslɪ] *adv* **(a)** (*with suspicion*) *examine, glance, ask etc* avec méfiance, soupçonneusement.

(b) (*causing suspicion*) *behave, run away etc* d'une manière suspecte *or* louche. **it looks ~ like measles** ça m'a tout l'air d'être la rougeole; **it sounds ~ as though he won't give it back** ça m'a tout l'air de signifier qu'il ne le rendra pas; **he arrived ~ early** il me paraît suspect qu'il soit arrivé si tôt; **he was ~ eager** il était d'un empressement suspect.

suspiciousness [səs'pɪʃəsnɪs] *n* (*U*) (*feeling suspicion*) caractère soupçonneux *or* méfiant; (*causing suspicion*) caractère suspect.

suss* [sʌs] *vt* (*Brit*) **to ~ out** dénicher.

sustain [səs'teɪn] *vt* **(a)** *weight, beam etc* supporter; *body* nourrir, sustenter†; *life* maintenir; (*Mus*) *note* tenir, soutenir; *effort, role* soutenir; *pretence* poursuivre, prolonger; *assertion, theory* soutenir, maintenir; *charge* donner des preuves à l'appui de. **that food won't ~ you for long** ce n'est pas cette nourriture qui va vous donner beaucoup de forces; (*Jur*) **objection ~ed** ≃ (objection) accordée; (*Jur*) **the court ~ed his claim *or* ~ed him in his claim** le tribunal a fait droit à sa revendication; **~ed** *effort, attack* soutenu, prolongé; *applause* prolongé.

(b) (*suffer*) *attack* subir; *loss* éprouver, essuyer; *damage* subir, souffrir; *injury* recevoir. **he ~ed concussion** il a été commotionné.

sustaining [səs'teɪnɪŋ] *adj food* nourrissant, nutritif. (*US: Rad, TV*) **sustaining program** émission non patronnée.

sustenance ['sʌstɪnəns] *n* (*U*) **(a)** (*nourishing quality*) valeur nutritive; (*food and drink*) alimentation *f*, nourriture *f*. **there's not much ~ in melon** le melon n'est pes très nourrissant *or* nutritif, le melon n'a pas beaucoup de valeur nutritive; **they depend for ~ on, they get their ~ from** ils se nourrissent de; **roots and berries were *or* provided their only ~** les racines et les baies étaient leur seule nourriture, pour toute nourriture ils avaient des racines et des baies.

(b) (*means of livelihood*) moyens *mpl* de subsistance.

suttee [sʌ'tiː] *n* (*widow*) (veuve *f*) satî *f inv*; (*rite*) satî *m*.

suture ['suːtʃəʳ] *n* suture *f*.

suzerain ['suːzəreɪn] *n* suzerain(e) *m(f)*.

suzerainty ['suːzəreɪntɪ] *n* suzeraineté *f*.

svelte [svelt] *adj* svelte.

swab [swɒb] **1** *n* (*mop, cloth*) serpillière *f*; (*Naut*) faubert *m*; (*for gun-cleaning*) écouvillon *m*; (*Med: cotton wool etc*) tampon *m*; (*Med: specimen*) prélèvement *m*. (*Med*) **to take a ~ of sb's throat** faire un prélèvement dans la gorge de qn.

2 *vt* **(a)** (*also* **~ down**) *floor etc* nettoyer, essuyer; (*Naut*) *deck* passer le faubert.

(b) (*also* **~ out**) *gun* écouvillonner; (*Med*) *wound* tamponner, essuyer *or* nettoyer avec un tampon.

swaddle ['swɒdl] **1** *vt* (*in bandages*) emmailloter (*in* de); (*in blankets etc*) emmitoufler* (*in* dans); *baby* emmailloter, langer. **2** *cpd:* (*liter*) **swaddling bands, swaddling clothes** maillot *m*, lange *m*.

swag [swæg] *n* **(a)** (*‡: loot*) butin *m*. **(b)** (*Australia*) bal(l)uchon* *m*.

swagger ['swægəʳ] **1** *n* air fanfaron; (*gait*) démarche assurée. **to walk with a ~** marcher en plastronnant *or* d'un air important.

2 *cpd:* (*Mil*) **swagger cane** badine *f*, jonc *m*; **swagger coat** manteau *m* trois quarts; (*US*) **swagger stick = swagger cane.**

3 *adj* (*Brit**) chic *inv*.

4 *vi* **(a)** (*also* **~ about, ~ along**) plastronner, parader. **to ~ in/out *etc*** entrer/sortir *etc* d'un air fanfaron *or* en plastronnant.

(b) (*boast*) se vanter (*about* de).

swaggering ['swægərɪŋ] **1** *adj gait* assuré; *person* fanfaron, qui plastronne; *look, gesture* fanfaron. **2** *n* (*strutting*) airs plastronnants; (*boasting*) fanfaronnades *fpl*.

swain [sweɪn] *n* (†† *or liter etc*) amant† *m*, soupirant† *m*.

swallow¹ ['swɒləʊ] **1** *n* (*Orn*) hirondelle *f*. (*Prov*) **one ~ doesn't make a summer** une hirondelle ne fait pas le printemps (*Prov*).

2 *cpd:* (*Brit*) **swallow dive** saut *m* de l'ange; **swallowtail (butterfly)** machaon *m*; **swallow-tailed coat** (habit *m* à) queue *f* de pie.

swallow² ['swɒləʊ] **1** *n* (*act*) avalement *m*; (*amount*) gorgée *f*. **at *or* with one ~** d'un trait, d'un seul coup.

2 *vi* avaler. (*emotionally*) **he ~ed hard** sa gorge se serra.

3 *vt* **(a)** *food, drink, pill* avaler; *oyster* gober. (*fig*) **to ~ the bait** se laisser prendre (à l'appât).

(b) (*fig*) *story* avaler, gober; *insult* avaler, encaisser*; *one's anger, pride* ravaler. **that's a bit hard to ~** c'est plutôt dur à avaler; **they ~ed it whole** ils ont tout avalé *or* gobé.

swallow down *vt sep* avaler.

swallow up *vt sep* (*fig*) engloutir. **the ground seemed to swallow them up** le sol semblait les engloutir; **he was swallowed up in the crowd** il s'est perdu *or* il a disparu dans la foule; **the mist swallowed them up** la brume les a enveloppés; **taxes swallow up half your income** les impôts engloutissent *or* engouffrent la moitié de vos revenus.

swam [swæm] *prét of* **swim**.

swami ['swɑːmɪ] *n* pandit *m*.

swamp [swɒmp] **1** *n* marais *m*, marécage *m*.

2 *cpd:* (*US*) **swamp buggy** voiture *f* amphibie; **swamp fever** paludisme *m*, malaria *f*; (*U*) **swampland** marécages *mpl*.

3 *vt* (*flood*) inonder; (*sink*) submerger; *boat* emplir d'eau; (*fig*) submerger (*with* de). (*fig*) **he was ~ed with requests/letters** il était submergé de requêtes/lettres; **I'm absolutely ~ed* (with work)** je suis débordé (de travail); (*Ftbl etc*) **towards the end of the game they ~ed us** vers la fin de la partie ils ont fait le jeu.

swampy ['swɒmpɪ] *adj* marécageux.

swan [swɒn] **1** *n* cygne *m*. **the S~ of Avon** le cygne de l'Avon (*Shakespeare*). **2** *cpd:* (*US*) **swan dive** saut *m* de l'ange; **swan-necked** au cou de cygne; (*U*) **swansdown** (*feathers*) (duvet *m* de) cygne *m*; (*Tex*) molleton *m*; (*fig*) **swan song** chant *m* du cygne; (*Brit*) **swan-upping** *recensement annuel des cygnes de la Tamise*.

3 *vi* (*Brit**) **he ~ned off to London before the end of term** il est parti à Londres sans s'en faire* *or* il est tranquillement parti à Londres avant la fin du trimestre; **he's ~ning around in Paris somewhere** il se balade* quelque part dans Paris sans s'en faire*.

swank* [swæŋk] **1** *n* **(a)** (*U*) esbroufe* *f*. **out of ~** pour épater*, pour faire de l'esbroufe*. **(b)** (*person*) esbroufeur* *m*, -euse* *f*. **2** *vi* faire de l'esbroufe*, chercher à épater* *or* à en mettre plein la vue*. **to ~ about sth** se vanter de qch.

swanky* ['swæŋkɪ] *adj* rupin‡, qui en impose*.

swannery ['swɒnərɪ] *n* colonie *f* de cygnes.

swap* [swɒp] **1** *n* troc *m*, échange *m*. **it's a fair ~** ça se vaut; (*stamps etc*) **~s** doubles *mpl*.

2 *vt* échanger, troquer (*A for B* A contre B); *stamps, stories* échanger (*with sb* avec qn). **Paul and Martin have ~ped hats** Paul et Martin ont échangé leurs chapeaux; **let's ~ places** changeons de place (l'un avec l'autre); **I'll ~ you!** tu veux échanger avec moi?; *V* **wife**.

3 *vi* échanger. **let's ~!** échangeons!

sward†† [swɔːd] *n* gazon *m*, pelouse *f*.

swarm¹ [swɔːm] **1** *n [bees, flying insects]* essaim *m*; *[ants, crawling insects]* fourmillement *m*, grouillement *m*; *[people]* essaim, nuée *f*, troupe *f*. (*fig*) **in a ~, in ~s** en masse.

2 *vi* **(a)** *[bees]* essaimer.

(b) *[crawling insects]* fourmiller, pulluler, grouiller. *[people]* **to ~ in/out *etc*** entrer/sortir *etc* en masse; **they ~ed round *or* over *or* through the palace** ils ont envahi le palais en masse; **the children ~ed round his car** les enfants s'agglutinaient autour de sa voiture.

(c) (*lit, fig*) *[ground, town, streets]* fourmiller, grouiller (*with* de).

swarm² [swɔːm] *vt* (*also* **~ up**) *tree, pole* grimper à toute vitesse à (*en s'aidant des pieds et des mains*).

swarthiness ['swɔːðɪnɪs] *n* teint basané *or* bistré.

swarthy ['swɔːðɪ] *adj* basané, bistré.

swashbuckler ['swɒʃˌbʌkləʳ] *n* fier-à-bras *m*.

swashbuckling ['swɒʃˌbʌklɪŋ] *adj* fanfaron, qui plastronne.

swastika ['swɒstɪkə] *n* svastika *m or* swastika *m*; (*Nazi*) croix gammée.

swat [swɒt] **1** *vt fly, mosquito* écraser; (*: *slap*) *table etc* donner un coup sur, taper sur. **2** *n* **(a)** **to give a fly a ~, to take a ~ at a fly** donner un coup de tapette à une mouche. **(b)** (*also* **fly ~**) tapette *f*.

swath [swɔːθ] *n, pl* **~s** [swɔːðs] (*Agr*) andain *m*. **to cut corn in ~s** couper le blé en andains; **to cut a ~ through sth** ouvrir une voie dans qch.

swathe [sweɪð] *vt* emmailloter (*in* de), envelopper (*in* dans). **~d in bandages** emmailloté de bandages; **~d in blankets** enveloppé *or* emmitouflé* dans des couvertures.

swatter ['swɒtə^r] *n* (*also* **fly ~**) tapette *f*.

sway [sweɪ] **1** *n* (*U*) **(a)** (*motion*) *[rope, hanging object, trees]* balancement *m*, oscillation *f*; *[boat]* balancement, oscillations; *[tower block, bridge]* mouvement *m* oscillatoire, oscillation.

(b) (*liter*) emprise *f*, empire *m* (*over* sur), domination *f* (*over* de). **to hold ~ over** avoir de l'emprise *or* de l'empire sur, tenir sous son emprise *or* son empire *or* sa domination.

2 *cpd:* **sway-backed** ensellé.

3 *vi [tree, rope, hanging object, boat]* se balancer, osciller; *[tower block, bridge]* osciller; *[train]* tanguer; *[person]* tanguer, osciller; (*fig: vacillate*) osciller, balancer (*liter*) (*between* entre). **he stood ~ing (about *or* from side to side *or* backwards and forwards)** il oscillait (sur ses jambes *or* de droite à gauche *or* d'arrière en avant), il tanguait; **to ~ in/out** *etc* (*from drink, injury*) entrer/sortir *etc* en tanguant; (*regally*) entrer/sortir *etc* majestueusement; **he ~ed towards leniency** il a penché pour la clémence.

4 *vt* **(a)** *hanging object* balancer, faire osciller; *hips* rouler, balancer; *[wind]* balancer, agiter; *[waves]* balancer, ballotter.

(b) (*influence*) influencer, avoir une action déterminante sur. **these factors finally ~ed the committee** ces facteurs ont finalement influencé le choix *or* la décision du comité; **I allowed myself to be ~ed** je me suis laissé influencer; **his speech ~ed the crowd** son discours a eu une action déterminante sur la foule.

swear [swɛə^r] *pret* **swore**, *ptp* **sworn 1** *vt* **(a)** jurer (*on sth* sur qch, *that* que, *to do* de faire); *fidelity, allegiance* jurer. **I ~ it!** je le jure!; **to ~ an oath** (*solemnly*) prêter serment; (*curse*) lâcher *or* pousser un juron; **to ~ (an oath) to do sth** faire (le) serment *or* jurer de faire qch; (*Jur*) **to ~ a charge against sb** accuser qn sous serment; **I could have sworn he touched it** j'aurais juré qu'il l'avait touché; **I ~ he said so!** il l'a dit je vous le jure, je vous jure qu'il l'a dit; **I ~ I've never enjoyed myself more** ma parole, je ne me suis jamais autant amusé; *V also* **black, oath, sworn** *etc*.

(b) *witness, jury* faire prêter serment à. **to ~ sb to secrecy** faire jurer le secret à qn.

2 *vi* **(a)** (*take solemn oath etc*) jurer. (*Jur*) **do you so ~? — I ~** = dites 'je le jure' — je le jure; **he swore on the Bible/by all that he held dear** il a juré sur la Bible/sur tout ce qu'il avait de plus cher; **to ~ to the truth of sth** jurer que qch est vrai; **would you ~ to having seen him?** est-ce que vous jureriez que vous l'avez vu?; **I think he did but I couldn't *or* wouldn't ~ to it** il me semble qu'il l'a fait mais je n'en jurerais pas.

(b) (*curse*) jurer, pester (*at* contre, après); (*blaspheme*) blasphémer. **don't ~!** ne jure pas!, ne sois pas grossier!; **to ~ like a trooper** jurer comme un charretier; **it's enough to make you ~*** il y a de quoi vous faire râler*.

3 *cpd:* **swearword** gros mot, juron *m*.

swear by *vt fus* (*fig*) **he swears by vitamin C tablets** il ne jure que par les vitamines C; **I swear by whisky as a cure for flu** pour moi il n'y a rien de tel que le whisky pour guérir la grippe.

swear in *vt sep jury, witness, president etc* assermenter, faire prêter serment à.

swear off *vt fus alcohol, tobacco* jurer de renoncer à. **he has sworn off stealing** il a juré de ne plus voler.

swear out *vt sep* (*US Jur*) **to swear out a warrant for sb's arrest** obtenir un mandat d'arrêt contre qn en l'accusant sous serment.

sweat [swet] **1** *n* **(a)** sueur *f*, transpiration *f*; (*fig: on walls etc*) humidité *f*, suintement *m*; (*state*) sueur(s). **by the ~ of his brow** à la sueur de son front; **to be dripping *or* covered with ~** ruisseler de sueur, être en nage; **to be in a ~** (*lit*) être en sueur, être couvert de sueur; (**fig*) avoir des sueurs froides; **he was in a great ~ about it** ça lui donnait des sueurs froides; *V* **cold**.

(b) (*: *piece of work etc*) corvée *f*. **it was an awful ~** on en a bavé‡; **no ~!‡** pas de problème!

(c) (‡) **an old ~** un vétéran, un vieux routier.

2 *cpd:* **sweatband** (*in hat*) cuir intérieur; (*Sport*) bandeau *m*; **sweat gland** glande *f* sudoripare; **sweat shirt** sweat-shirt *m*; **sweat shop** atelier *m or* usine *f* où les ouvriers sont exploités; **sweat-stained** taché *or* maculé de sueur.

3 *vi [person, animal]* suer (*with, from* de), être en sueur; *[walls]* suer, suinter; *[cheese etc]* suer. **he was ~ing profusely** il suait à grosses gouttes; **to ~ like a bull** suer comme un bœuf; (*fig*) **he was ~ing over his essay*** il suait sur sa dissertation.

4 *vt* **(a)** *person, animal* faire suer *or* transpirer; (*fig*) *workers* exploiter. **~ed goods** marchandises produites par une main d'œuvre exploitée; **~ed labour** main d'œuvre exploitée.

(b) to ~ blood* (*work hard*) suer sang et eau (*over sth* sur qch); (*be anxious*) avoir des sueurs froides; **he was ~ing blood over *or* about the exam*** l'examen lui donnait des sueurs froides.

sweat out *vt sep cold etc* guérir en transpirant. (*fig*) **you'll just have to sweat it out*** il faudra t'armer de patience; **they left him to sweat it out*** ils n'ont rien fait pour l'aider.

sweater ['swetə^r] **1** *n* tricot *m*, pullover *m*, pull* *m*. **2** *cpd:* **sweater girl** fille bien roulée*.

sweating ['swetɪŋ] *n [person, animal]* transpiration *f*; (*Med*) sudation *f*; *[wall]* suintement *m*.

sweaty ['swetɪ] *adj body* en sueur; *feet* qui suent; *hand* moite (de sueur); *smell* de sueur; *shirt, sock* mouillé *or* maculé de sueur.

swede [swiːd] *n* (*esp Brit*) rutabaga *m*.

Swede [swiːd] *n* Suédois(e) *m(f)*.

Sweden ['swiːdn] *n* Suède *f*.

Swedish ['swiːdɪʃ] **1** *adj* suédois. **2** *n* **(a) the S~** les Suédois *mpl*. **(b)** (*Ling*) suédois *m*.

sweep [swiːp] (*vb: pret, ptp* **swept**) **1** *n* **(a)** (*with broom etc*) coup *m* de balai. **to give a room a ~ (out)** donner un coup de balai à *or* balayer une pièce; *V* **clean**.

(b) (*also* **chimney ~**) ramoneur *m*; *V* **black**.

(c) (*movement*) *[arm]* grand geste; *[sword]* grand coup; *[scythe]* mouvement *m* circulaire; *[net]* coup; *[lighthouse beam, radar beam]* trajectoire *f*; *[tide]* progression *f* irrésistible; (*fig*) *[progress, events]* marche *f*. **in *or* with one ~** d'un seul coup; **with a ~ of his arm** d'un geste large; **to make a ~ of the horizon** (*with binoculars*) parcourir l'horizon; *[lighthouse beam]* balayer l'horizon; **to make a ~ for mines** draguer des mines; **the police made a ~ of the district** la police a ratissé le quartier.

(d) (*range*) *[telescope, gun, lighthouse, radar]* champ *m*. **with a ~ of 180°** avec un champ de 180°.

(e) (*curve, line*) *[coastline, hills, road, river]* grande courbe; (*Archit*) courbure *f*, voussure *f*; *[curtains, long skirt]* drapé *m*. **a wide ~ of meadowland** une vaste étendue de prairie; (*Aut, Aviat, Naut etc*) **the graceful ~ of her lines** sa ligne aérodynamique *or* son galbe plein(e) de grâce.

(f) (*) *abbr of* **sweepstake**; *V* **2**.

2 *cpd:* *[aircraft wing etc]* **sweepback** dessin *m* en flèche arrière, angle *m* flèche; *[clock etc]* **sweep hand** trotteuse *f*; **sweepstake** sweepstake *m*.

3 *vt* **(a)** *room, floor, street etc* balayer; *chimney* ramoner; (*Naut*) *river, channel* draguer; (*fig*) *[waves, hurricane, bullets, searchlights, skirts]* balayer. **to ~ a room clean** donner un bon coup de balai dans une pièce; (*Naut*) **to ~ sth clean of mines** déminer qch; (*fig*) **he swept the horizon with his binoculars** il a parcouru l'horizon avec ses jumelles; **his eyes/his glance swept the room** il a parcouru la pièce des yeux/du regard; **their fleet swept the seas in search of ...** leur flotte a sillonné *or* parcouru les mers à la recherche de ...; **a wave of indignation swept the city** une vague d'indignation a déferlé sur la ville; *V* **broom** *etc*.

(b) *dust, snow etc* balayer; (*Naut*) *mines* draguer, enlever. **he swept the rubbish off the pavement** il a enlevé les ordures du trottoir d'un coup de balai; **she swept the snow into a heap** elle a balayé la neige et en a fait un tas; (*fig*) **to ~ sth under the carpet** tirer le rideau sur qch; **to ~ sth off the table on to the floor** faire tomber qch par terre d'un geste large; **to ~ sth into a bag** faire glisser qch d'un geste large dans un sac; (*fig*) **to ~ everything before one** remporter un succès total, réussir sur toute la ligne; (*fig*) **to ~ the board** remporter un succès complet, tout rafler; **the socialists swept the board at the election** les socialistes ont remporté l'élection haut la main; (*fig*) **he swept the obstacles from his path** il a balayé *or* écarté les obstacles qui se trouvaient sur son chemin; **the army swept the enemy before them** l'armée a balayé l'ennemi devant elle; **the crowd swept him into the square** la foule l'a emporté *or* entraîné sur la place, il a été pris dans le mouvement de la foule et il s'est retrouvé sur la place; **the wave swept him overboard** la vague l'a jeté par-dessus bord; **the gale swept the caravan over the cliff** la rafale a emporté la caravane et l'a précipitée du haut de la falaise; **the current swept the boat downstream** le courant a emporté le bateau; **to be swept off one's feet** (*by wind, flood etc*) être emporté (*by* par); (*fig*) être enthousiasmé *or* emballé (*by* par); **the water swept him off his feet** le courant lui a fait perdre pied; (*fig*) **he swept her off her feet** elle a eu le coup de foudre pour lui.

4 *vi* **(a)** (*pass swiftly*) *[person, vehicle, convoy]* **to ~ in/out/along** *etc* entrer/sortir/avancer *etc* rapidement; **the car swept round the corner** la voiture a pris le virage comme un bolide; **the planes went ~ing across the sky** les avions sillonnaient le ciel; **the rain swept across the plain** l'orage a balayé la plaine; **panic swept through the city** la panique s'est emparée de la ville; **plague swept through the country** la peste a ravagé le pays.

(b) (*move impressively*) *[person, procession]* **to ~ in/out/along** *etc* entrer/sortir/avancer *etc* majestueusement; **she came ~ing into the room** elle a fait une entrée majestueuse dans la pièce; **the royal car swept down the avenue** la voiture royale a descendu l'avenue d'une manière imposante; (*fig*) **the motorway ~s across the hills** l'autoroute s'élance à travers les collines; **the forests ~ down to the sea** les forêts descendent en pente douce jusqu'au bord de la mer; **the bay ~s away to the south** la baie décrit une courbe majestueuse vers le sud; **the Alps ~ down to the coast** les Alpes descendent majestueusement vers la côte.

sweep along 1 *vi V* **sweep 4a, 4b**.

2 *vt sep [crowd, flood, current, gale]* emporter, entraîner; *leaves* balayer.

sweep aside *vt sep object, person* repousser, écarter; *suggestion, objection* repousser, rejeter; *difficulty, obstacle* écarter.

sweep away 1 *vi* (*leave*) (*rapidly*) s'éloigner rapidement; (*impressively*) s'éloigner majestueusement *or* d'une manière imposante; *V also* **sweep 4b**.

2 *vt sep dust, snow, rubbish* balayer; *[crowd, flood, current, gale]* entraîner. **they swept him away to lunch** ils l'ont entraîné pour aller déjeuner.

sweep down 1 *vi V* **sweep 4b**.

2 *vt sep walls etc* nettoyer avec un balai; *[flood, gale etc]* emporter. **the river swept the logs down to the sea** les bûches ont flotté sur la rivière jusqu'à la mer.
sweep off = **sweep away.**
sweep out 1 *vi V* **sweep 4a, 4b.**
2 *vt sep room, dust, rubbish* balayer.
sweep up 1 *vi* **(a)** (*with broom etc*) **to sweep up after sb** balayer les débris *or* les saletés de qn; **to sweep up after a party** balayer quand les invités sont partis.
(b) he swept up to me il s'est approché de moi (*angrily*) avec furie *or* (*impressively*) majestueusement; **the car swept up to the house** la voiture a remonté l'allée jusqu'à la maison (*fast*) rapidement *or* (*impressively*) d'une manière imposante.
2 *vt sep snow, leaves, dust etc* balayer. **she swept up the letters and took them away** elle a ramassé les lettres d'un geste brusque et les a emportées.
sweeper ['swi:pəʳ] *n* (*person*) balayeur *m*; (*machine*) balayeuse *f*; (*carpet* ~) balai *m* mécanique; (*vacuum cleaner*) aspirateur *m*; *V* **street.**
sweeping ['swi:pɪŋ] **1** *adj* **(a)** *movement, gesture* large; *bow, curtsy* profond; *glance* circulaire; *coastline* qui décrit une courbe majestueuse; *skirts* qui balaient le sol.
(b) *change, reorganization* radical, fondamental; *reduction* considérable; *price cut* imbattable. ~ **statement,** ~ **generalization** généralisation hâtive; **that's pretty** ~! c'est beaucoup dire!
2 *npl:* ~**s** balayures *fpl*, ordures *fpl*; (*fig: of society etc*) rebut *m*.
sweet [swi:t] **1** *adj* **(a)** (*not sour*) *apple, orange, cider, wine* doux (*f* douce); *tea, coffee, biscuit* sucré; *taste* sucré, douceâtre (*pej*). **to have a** ~ **tooth** être friand de sucreries; **I love** ~ **things** j'aime les sucreries *fpl*; (*Culin*) ~ **and sour** aigre-doux (*f* aigre-douce); **a sickly** ~ **smell** une odeur fétide.
(b) (*fig*) *milk, air, breath* frais (*f* fraîche); *water* pur; *soil* sain; *scent* agréable, suave; *sound, voice* harmonieux, mélodieux; *running of engine, machine* sans à-coups; *money, revenge, success, character, face, smile* doux (*f* douce). (*fig*) **the** ~ **smell of success** la douceur exquise du succès; **it was** ~ **to his ear** c'était doux à son oreille; (*pej*) ~ **words** flagorneries *fpl*; **she is a very** ~ **person** elle est vraiment très gentille, elle est tout à fait charmante; **that was very** ~ **of her** c'était très gentil de sa part; **he carried on in his own** ~ **way** il a continué comme il l'entendait; **he'll do it in his own** ~ **time** il le fera quand ça lui dira*; **at his own** ~ **will** à son gré; **to be** ~ **on sb*** avoir le béguin pour qn*, être amoureux de qn; ~ **Fanny Adams‡** rien de rien, que dalle‡; *V* **nothing, sixteen** *etc.*
(c) (*: *attractive*) *child, dog* mignon, adorable, gentil; *house, hat, dress* mignon, gentillet. **a** ~ **old lady** une adorable vieille dame; **what a** ~ **little baby!** le mignon petit bébé!
2 *adv:* **to smell** ~ sentir bon; **to taste** ~ avoir un goût sucré.
3 *n* (*esp Brit: candy*) bonbon *m*; (*Brit: dessert*) dessert *m*. (*fig*) **the** ~**s of success/solitude** *etc* les délices *fpl* de la réussite/de la solitude *etc*; **come here, (my)** ~* viens ici, mon ange.
4 *cpd:* **sweetbread** ris *m* de veau *or* d'agneau; **sweetbriar, sweetbrier** églantier odorant; **sweet chestnut** châtaigne *f*, marron *m*; **sweet corn** maïs sucré; **sweetheart** ami(e) *m(f)*, bien-aimé(e)† *m(f)*; **yes sweetheart** oui chéri(e) *or* mon ange *or* mon cœur; **sweet herbs** fines herbes; **sweetmeat** sucrerie *f*, confiserie *f*; **sweet-natured** d'un naturel doux; **sweetpea** pois *m* de senteur; **sweet potato** patate *f* (douce); **sweet-scented** parfumé, odoriférant, odorant; (*Brit*) **sweetshop** confiserie *f*; **sweet-smelling** = **sweet-scented; sweet talk** flagorneries *fpl*; **sweet-talk** flagorner; **sweet-tempered** = **sweet-natured; sweet william** œillet *m* de poète.
sweeten ['swi:tn] **1** *vt coffee, sauce etc* sucrer; *air* purifier; *room* assainir; (*fig*) *person, sb's temper, task* adoucir; (*: *bribe*) graisser la patte à*; *V* **pill. 2** *vi [person, sb's temper]* s'adoucir.
sweetener ['swi:tnəʳ] *n* (*Culin*) édulcorant *m*, sucrette* *f*; (**fig: bribe*) pot-de-vin *m*.
sweetening ['swi:tnɪŋ] *n* (*U*) **(a)** (*substance*) édulcorant *m*. **(b)** (*V* **sweeten**) sucrage *m*; adoucissement *m*.
sweetie* ['swi:tɪ] *n* **(a)** (*person: also* ~**-pie‡**) **he's/she's a** ~ il/elle est chou*, c'est un ange; **yes** ~ oui mon chou* *or* mon ange. **(b)** (*esp Scot: candy*) bonbon *m*.
sweetish ['swi:tɪʃ] *n* au goût sucré, douceâtre.
sweetly ['swi:tlɪ] *adv sing, play* mélodieusement; *smile, answer* gentiment. **the engine is running** ~ le moteur marche sans à-coups.
sweetness ['swi:tnɪs] *n* (*to taste*) goût sucré; (*in smell*) odeur *f* suave; (*to hearing*) son mélodieux *or* harmonieux; *[person, nature, character, expression]* douceur *f*.
swell [swel] (*vb: pret* **swelled,** *ptp* **swollen** *or* **swelled**) **1** *n* **(a)** *[sea]* houle *f*. **heavy** ~ forte houle; *V* **ground.**
(b) (*Mus*) crescendo *m inv* (et diminuendo *m inv*); (*on organ*) boîte expressive.
(c) (*†: *stylish person*) personne huppée*, gandin *m* (*pej*). **the** ~**s** les gens huppés*, le gratin*.
2 *adj* **(a)** (*: *stylish*) *clothes* chic *inv*; *house, car, restaurant* chic, rupin‡; *relatives, friends* huppé*.
(b) (*: *esp US: excellent*) sensationnel*, formidable*. **a** ~ **guy** un type sensationnel* *or* vachement bien*; **that's** ~ c'est formidable* *or* sensass* *inv.*
3 *cpd:* (*Mus*) **swell box** boîte expressive; (*esp US*) **swellhead*** bêcheur* *m*, -euse* *f*; **swellheaded*** bêcheur*; **swellheadedness*** vanité *f*, suffisance *f*.
4 *vi* **(a)** (*also* ~ **up**) *[balloon, tyre, airbed]* (se) gonfler; *[sails]* se gonfler; *[ankle, arm, eye, face]* enfler; *[wood]* gonfler. (*fig*) **to** ~ **(up) with pride** se gonfler d'orgueil; **to** ~ **(up) with rage/indignation** s'emplir de rage/d'indignation.
(b) (*increase*) *[river]* grossir; *[sound, music, voice]* s'enfler; *[numbers, population, membership]* grossir, augmenter. **the numbers soon** ~**ed to 500** les nombres ont vite augmenté *or* grossi pour atteindre 500, les nombres se sont vite élevés à 500; **the little group soon** ~**ed into a crowd** le petit groupe est vite devenu une foule; **the murmuring** ~**ed to a roar** le murmure s'enfla pour devenir un rugissement.
5 *vt sail* gonfler; *sound* enfler; *river, lake* grossir; *number* augmenter. **this** ~**ed the membership/population to 1,500** ceci a porté à 1.500 le nombre des membres/le total de la population; **population swollen by refugees** population grossie par les réfugiés; **river swollen by rain** rivière grossie par les pluies, rivière en crue; **a second edition swollen by a mass of new material** une deuxième édition augmentée par une quantité de documents nouveaux; **to be swollen with pride** être gonflé *or* bouffi d'orgueil; **to be swollen with rage** bouillir de rage; *V also* **swollen** *etc.*
swell out 1 *vi [sails etc]* se gonfler.
2 *vt sep* gonfler.
swell up *vi* = **swell 4a.**
swelling ['swelɪŋ] **1** *n* **(a)** (*Med*) enflure *f*; (*lump*) grosseur *f*; (*bruising*) enflure, tuméfaction *f*; (*on tyre etc*) hernie *f*. **(b)** (*U: V* **swell 4**) enflement *m*; gonflement *m*. **2** *adj jaw etc* qui enfle; *sail* gonflé; *sound, chorus, voices* qui enfle; *line, curve* galbé.
swelter ['sweltəʳ] *vi* étouffer de chaleur.
sweltering ['sweltərɪŋ] *adj weather, heat, afternoon* étouffant, oppressant. **it's** ~ **in here** on étouffe de chaleur ici.
swept [swept] **1** *pret, ptp of* **sweep. 2** *cpd:* **sweptback** (*Aviat*) en flèche; *hair* rejeté en arrière.
swerve [swɜ:v] **1** *vi [boxer, fighter]* faire un écart; *[ball]* dévier; *[vehicle, ship]* faire une embardée; *[driver]* donner un coup de volant; (*fig*) dévier (*from* de). **the car** ~**d away from the lorry on to the verge** la voiture a fait une embardée pour éviter le camion et est montée sur l'accotement; **he** ~**d round the bollard** il a viré sur les chapeaux de roues autour de la borne lumineuse.
2 *n [vehicle, ship]* embardée *f*; *[boxer, fighter]* écart *m*.
swift [swɪft] **1** *adj reaction, response, revenge, victory* prompt, rapide; *vehicle, journey* rapide; *movement* vif, leste. **they were** ~ **to act** ils ont été prompts à agir, ils ont agi sans tarder; (*liter*) ~ **to anger** prompt à la colère *or* à se mettre en colère.
2 *cpd:* **swift-flowing** au cours rapide; (*liter*) **swift-footed** au pied léger.
3 *n* (*Orn*) martinet *m*.
swiftly ['swɪftlɪ] *adv* rapidement, vite.
swiftness ['swɪftnɪs] *n* (*V* **swift 1**) rapidité *f*, vitesse *f*, promptitude *f*.
swig* [swɪg] **1** *n* lampée* *f*, (*larger*) coup *m*. **to take a** ~ **at a bottle** boire un coup à même la bouteille.
2 *vt* lamper*.
swig down* *vt sep* avaler d'un trait.
swill [swɪl] **1** *n* **(a)** (*U*) (*for pigs etc*) pâtée *f*; (*garbage, slops*) eaux grasses. **(b) to give sth a** ~ **(out** *or* **down)** = **to swill sth (out** *or* **down)**; *V* **2a. 2** *vt* **(a)** (*also* ~ **out,** ~ **down**) laver à grande eau, rincer. **(b)** boire avidement, boire à grands traits.
swim [swɪm] (*vb: pret* **swam,** *ptp* **swum**) **1** *n:* **to go for a** ~, **to have** *or* **take a** ~ (*in sea etc*) aller nager *or* se baigner; (*in swimming baths*) aller à la piscine; **it's time for our** ~ c'est l'heure de la baignade; **after a 2-km** ~ après avoir fait 2 km à la nage; **Channel** ~ traversée *f* de la Manche à la nage; **it's a long** ~ voilà une bonne *or* longue distance à parcourir à la nage; **I had a lovely** ~ ça m'a fait du bien de nager comme ça; (*fig*) **to be in the** ~ être dans le bain.
2 *cpd:* **swimsuit** maillot *m* (de bain).
3 *vi* **(a)** *[person]* nager, (*as sport*) faire de la natation; *[fish, animal]* nager. **to go** ~**ming** (*in sea etc*) aller nager, aller se baigner; (*in swimming baths*) aller à la piscine; **to** ~ **away/back** *etc [person]* s'éloigner/revenir *etc* à la nage; *[fish]* s'éloigner/revenir *etc*; **to** ~ **across a river** traverser une rivière à la nage; **he swam under the boat** il est passé sous le bateau (à la nage); **to** ~ **under water** nager sous l'eau; **he had to** ~ **for it** son seul recours a été de se sauver à la nage *or* de se jeter à l'eau et de nager; (*fig*) **to** ~ **with the tide** suivre le courant.
(b) (*fig*) **the meat was** ~**ming in gravy** la viande nageait *or* baignait dans la sauce; **her eyes were** ~**ming (with tears)** ses yeux étaient noyés *or* baignés de larmes; **the bathroom was** ~**ming** la salle de bains était inondée; **the room was** ~**ming round** *or* ~**ming before his eyes** la pièce semblait tourner autour de lui; **his head was** ~**ming** la tête lui tournait.
4 *vt lake, river* traverser à la nage. **it was first swum in 1900** la première traversée à la nage a eu lieu en 1900; **he can** ~ **10 km** il peut faire 10 km à la nage; **he can** ~ **2 lengths** il peut nager *or* faire 2 longueurs; **before he had swum 10 strokes** avant qu'il ait pu faire *or* nager 10 brasses; **I can't** ~ **a stroke** je suis incapable de faire une brasse; **can you** ~ **the crawl?** savez-vous nager *or* faire le crawl?
swimmer ['swɪməʳ] *n* nageur *m*, -euse *f*.
swimming ['swɪmɪŋ] **1** *n* nage *f*, natation *f*.
2 *cpd:* **swimming bath(s)** piscine *f*; **swimming cap** bonnet *m* de bain; (*Brit*) **swimming costume** maillot *m* (de bain) une pièce; **swimming gala** fête *f* de natation; **swimming pool** = **swimming bath(s); swimming ring** bouée *f*; **swimming suit** maillot *m* (de bain); **swimming trunks** maillot *m or* caleçon *m or* slip *m* de bain.
swimmingly ['swɪmɪŋlɪ] *adv:* **to go** ~ se dérouler sans accrocs *or* à merveille; **it's all going** ~ tout marche comme sur des roulettes.
swindle ['swɪndl] **1** *n* escroquerie *f*. **it's a** ~ c'est du vol, nous nous sommes fait estamper* *or* rouler*.
2 *vt* escroquer, estamper*, rouler*. **to** ~ **sb out of his money, to** ~ **sb's money out of him** escroquer de l'argent à qn.
swindler ['swɪndləʳ] *n* escroc *m*.

swine [swaɪn] **1** *n, pl inv* (*Zool*) pourceau *m*, porc *m*; (*:fig: person*) salaud: *m*. **you ~!:** espèce de salaud!: **2** *cpd:* **swineherd**†† porcher *m*, -ère *f*.

swing [swɪŋ] (*vb: pret, ptp* **swung**) **1** *n* **(a)** (*movement*) balancement *m*; [*pendulum*] (*movement*) mouvement *m* de va-et-vient, oscillations *fpl*; (*arc, distance*) arc *m*; [*instrument pointer, needle*] oscillations; (*Boxing, Golf*) swing *m*. **the ~ of the boom sent him overboard** le retour de la bôme l'a jeté par-dessus bord; **he gave the starting handle a ~** il a donné un tour de manivelle; **the golfer took a ~ at the ball** le joueur de golf a essayé de frapper *or* a frappé la balle avec un swing; **to take a ~ at sb** décocher *or* lancer un coup de poing à qn; (*fig*) **the ~ of the pendulum brought him back to power** le mouvement du pendule l'a ramené au pouvoir; (*Pol*) **the socialists need a ~ of 5% to win the election** il faudrait aux socialistes un revirement d'opinion en leur faveur de l'ordre de 5% pour qu'ils remportent (*subj*) l'élection; (*Pol*) **a ~ to the left** un revirement en faveur de la gauche; (*St Ex*) **the ~s of the market** les fluctuations *fpl or* les hauts et les bas *mpl* du marché.

(b) (*rhythm*) [*dance etc*] rythme *m*; [*jazz music*] swing *m*. **to walk with a ~ (in one's step)** marcher d'un pas rythmé; **music/poetry with a ~ to it** *or* **that goes with a ~** musique/poésie rythmée *or* entraînante; (*fig*) **to go with a ~** [*evening, party*] marcher du tonnerre*; [*business, shop*] très bien marcher; **to be in full ~** [*party, election, campaign*] battre son plein; [*business*] être en plein rendement, gazer*; **to get into the ~ of things** se mettre dans le bain.

(c) (*scope, freedom*) **they gave him full ~ in the matter** ils lui ont donné carte blanche en la matière; **he was given full ~ to make decisions** on l'a laissé entièrement libre de prendre des décisions; **he gave his imagination full ~** il a donné libre cours à son imagination.

(d) (*seat for ~ing*) balançoire *f*. **to have a ~** se balancer, faire de la balançoire; **to give a child a ~** pousser un enfant qui se balance; (*fig*) **what you gain on the ~s you lose on the roundabouts** ce qu'on gagne d'un côté on perd de l'autre.

(e) (*also* **~ music**) swing *m*.

2 *cpd:* (*Mus*) **swing band** orchestre *m* de swing; **swing bridge** pont tournant; (*Brit*) **swing door** porte battante; **swing music** *V* **swing 1e**; (*Aviat*) **swing-wing** à géométrie variable.

3 *vi* **(a)** (*hang, oscillate*) [*arms, legs*] se balancer, être ballant; [*object on rope etc*] se balancer, pendiller, osciller; [*hammock*] se balancer; [*pendulum*] osciller; (*on a swing*) se balancer; (*pivot: also* **~ round**) tourner, pivoter; [*person*] se retourner, virevolter. **he was left ~ing by his hands** il s'est retrouvé seul suspendu par les mains; **to ~ to and fro** se balancer; **the load swung (round) through the air as the crane turned** comme la grue pivotait la charge a décrit une courbe dans l'air; **the ship was ~ing at anchor** le bateau rappelait sur son ancre; **he swung across on the rope** agrippé à la corde il s'élança et passa de l'autre côté; **the monkey swung from branch to branch** le singe se balançait de branche en branche; **he swung up the rope ladder** il grimpa prestement à l'échelle de corde; **he swung (up) into the saddle** il a sauté en selle; **the door swung open/shut** la porte s'ouvrit/se referma; **he swung (round) on his heel** il a virevolté.

(b) (*move rhythmically*) **to ~ along/away** *etc* avancer/s'éloigner *etc* d'un pas rythmé *or* allègre; **the regiment went ~ing past the king** le régiment a défilé au pas cadencé devant le roi; **to ~ into action** [*army etc*] se mettre en branle; (*fig*) passer à l'action; (*fig*) **music that really ~s** musique *f* au rythme entraînant.

(c) (*change direction: often* **~ round**) [*plane, vehicle*] virer (*to the south etc* au sud *etc*). **the convoy swung (round) into the square** le convoi a viré pour aller sur la place; **the river ~s north here** ici la rivière décrit une courbe *or* oblique vers le nord; (*fig Pol*) **the country has swung to the right** le pays a viré *or* effectué un virage à droite.

(d) to ~ at a ball frapper *or* essayer de frapper une balle avec un swing; **to ~ at sb** décocher *or* lancer un coup de poing à qn; **he swung at me with the axe** il a brandi la hache pour me frapper.

(e) (*: be hanged*) être pendu. **he'll ~ for it** on lui mettra la corde au cou pour cela; **I'd ~ for him** je le tuerais si je le tenais.

4 *vt* **(a)** (*move to and fro*) *one's arms, legs, umbrella, hammock* balancer; *object on rope* balancer, faire osciller; *pendulum* faire osciller; *child on swing* pousser; (*brandish*) brandir. **he swung his sword above his head** il a fait un moulinet avec l'épée au-dessus de sa tête; **he swung his axe at the tree** il a brandi sa hache pour frapper l'arbre; **he swung his racket at the ball** il a ramené sa raquette pour frapper la balle; **he swung the box (up) on to the roof of the car** il a envoyé la boîte sur le toit de la voiture; **he swung the case (up) on to his shoulders** il a balancé la valise sur ses épaules; **he swung himself across the stream/over the wall** *etc* il s'est élancé et a franchi le ruisseau/et a sauté par-dessus le mur *etc*; **to ~ o.s. (up) into the saddle** sauter en selle; **to ~ one's hips** rouler *or* balancer les hanches, se déhancher; (*Brit fig*) **to ~ the lead*** tirer au flanc*; *V* **room**.

(b) (*turn: often* **~ round**) *propeller* lancer; *starting handle* tourner. **to ~ a door open/shut** ouvrir/fermer une porte; **he swung the ship (round) through 180°** il vira de 180°, il fit virer (le bateau) de 180°; **he swung the car round the corner** il a viré au coin.

(c) (*fig: influence*) *election, decision* influencer; *voters* faire changer d'opinion. **his speech swung the decision against us** son discours a provoqué un revirement et la décision est allée contre nous; **he managed to ~ the deal*** il a réussi à emporter l'affaire; **to ~ it on sb:** tirer une carotte à qn*, pigeonner qn*.

(d) (*Mus*) *a tune, the classics etc* jouer de manière rythmée.

swing round 1 *vi* [*person*] se retourner, virevolter; [*crane etc*] tourner, pivoter; [*car, ship, plane, convoy, procession*] virer; (*fig*) [*voters*] virer de bord; [*opinions etc*] connaître un revirement; *V also* **swing 3a, 3c**.

2 *vt sep object on rope etc* faire tourner; *sword, axe* brandir, faire des moulinets avec; *crane etc* faire pivoter; *car, ship, plane, convoy, procession* faire tourner *or* virer; *V also* **swing 4b**.

swing to *vi* [*door*] se refermer.

swingeing ['swɪndʒɪŋ] *adj blow, attack* violent; *defeat, majority* écrasant; *damages, taxation, price increases* considérable, énorme.

swinging ['swɪŋɪŋ] *adj step* rythmé; *music* rythmé, entraînant; *rhythm* entraînant, endiablé; (*:fig*) (*lively*) dynamique; (*modern, fashionable etc*) dans le vent, à la page. (*US*) **~ door** porte battante; **the party was really ~** la surprise-partie était du tonnerre* *or* à tout casser*; **~ London** le 'swinging London'; **London was really ~ then** on rigolait* bien à Londres dans ce temps-là.

swinish: ['swaɪnɪʃ] *adj* dégueulasse:.

swipe [swaɪp] **1** *n* (*) (*at ball etc*) grand coup; (*slap*) gifle *f*, calotte* *f*, baffe: *f*. **to take a ~ at** = **to swipe at**; *V* **3**.

2 *vt* **(a)** (*: hit*) *ball* frapper à toute volée; *person* calotter *or* gifler à toute volée.

(b) (*: steal: often hum*) calotter:, piquer: (*sth from sb* qch à qn).

3 *vi* (*) **to ~ at** *ball etc* frapper *or* essayer de frapper à toute volée; *person* flanquer* une gifle *or* une calotte* à.

swirl [swɜːl] **1** *n* (*in river, sea*) tourbillon *m*, remous *m*; [*dust, sand*] tourbillon; [*smoke*] tourbillon, volute *f*; (*fig*) [*cream, ice cream etc*] volute; [*lace, ribbons etc*] tourbillon. **the ~ of the dancers' skirts** le tourbillon *or* le tournoiement des jupes des danseuses.

2 *vi* [*water, river, sea*] tourbillonner, faire des remous *or* des tourbillons; [*dust, sand, smoke, skirts*] tourbillonner, tournoyer.

3 *vt* [*river etc*] **to ~ sth along/away** entraîner/emporter qch en tourbillonnant; **he ~ed his partner round the room** il a fait tournoyer *or* tourbillonner sa partenaire autour de la salle.

swish [swɪʃ] **1** *n* [*whip*] sifflement *m*; [*water, person in long grass*] bruissement *m*; [*grass in wind*] frémissement *m*, bruissement; [*tyres in rain*] glissement *m*; [*skirts*] bruissement, froufrou soyeux.

2 *vt* **(a)** *whip, cane* faire siffler.

(b) (*: beat, cane*) administrer *or* donner des coups de trique à.

3 *vi* [*cane, whip*] siffler, cingler l'air; [*water*] bruire; [*long grass*] frémir, bruire; [*skirts*] bruire, froufrouter.

4 *adj* (*esp Brit*: *smart*) rupin:.

swishy: ['swɪʃɪ] *adj* (*Brit: smart*) rupin:; (*US: effeminate*) efféminé, du genre tapette:.

Swiss [swɪs] **1** *adj* suisse. **~ French/German** suisse romand/allemand; **the ~ Guards** la garde (pontificale) suisse; (*Brit Culin*) **~ roll** gâteau roulé. **2** *n, pl inv* Suisse(sse) *m(f)*. **the ~** les Suisses.

switch [swɪtʃ] **1** *n* **(a)** (*Elec*) bouton *m* électrique, interrupteur *m*, commutateur *m*; (*Aut: also* **ignition ~**) contact *m*. (*Elec*) **the ~ was on/off** le bouton était sur la position ouvert/fermé, c'était allumé/éteint.

(b) (*Rail: points*) aiguille *f*, aiguillage *m*.

(c) (*transfer*) [*opinion*] changement *m*, revirement *m*, retournement *m*; [*allegiance etc*] changement; [*funds*] transfert *m* (*from* de, *to* en faveur de). **his ~ to Labour** son revirement en faveur des travaillistes; (*Bridge: in bidding*) **the ~ to hearts/clubs** (le changement de couleur et) le passage à cœur/trèfle; **the ~ of the 8.30 from platform 4** le changement de voie du train de 8.30 attendu au quai 4; **the ~ of the aircraft from Heathrow to Gatwick because of fog** le détournement sur Gatwick à cause du brouillard de l'avion attendu à Heathrow.

(d) (*stick*) baguette *f*; (*cane*) canne *f*; (*riding crop*) cravache *f*; (*whip*) fouet *m*.

(e) [*hair*] postiche *m*.

2 *cpd:* **switchback** (*n*) (*Brit: at fair; also road*) montagnes *fpl* russes; (*adj*) (*up and down*) tout en montées et descentes; (*zigzag*) en épingles à cheveux; (*US*) **switchblade (knife)** couteau *m* à cran d'arrêt; **switchboard** (*Elec*) tableau *m* de distribution; (*Telec*) standard *m*; (*Telec*) **switchboard operator** standardiste *mf*; (*Rail*) **switchman** aiguilleur *m*; **the switch-over from A to B** le passage de A à B; **the switchover to the metric system** l'adoption *f* du système métrique; (*US Rail*) **switchyard** gare *f* de triage.

3 *vt* **(a)** (*transfer*) *one's support, allegiance, attention* reporter (*from* de, *to* sur). (*Ind*) **to ~ production to another model** (cesser de produire l'ancien modèle et) se mettre à produire un nouveau modèle; **to ~ the conversation to another subject** détourner la conversation, changer de sujet de conversation.

(b) (*exchange*) échanger (*A for B* A contre B, *sth with sb* qch avec qn); (*also* **~ over, ~ round**) *two objects, letters in word, figures in column* intervertir, permuter; (*rearrange: also* **~ round**) *books, objects* changer de place. **we had to ~ taxis when the first broke down** nous avons dû changer de taxi quand le premier est tombé en panne; **to ~ plans** changer de projet; **we have ~ed all the furniture round** nous avons changé tous les meubles de place.

(c) (*Rail*) aiguiller (*to another track* sur une autre voie).

(d) (*Elec etc*) **to ~ the heater to 'low'** mettre le radiateur sur 'doux'; **to ~ the radio/TV to another programme** changer de station/de chaîne; *V also* **switch back, switch on** *etc*.

(e) to ~ the grass with one's cane cingler l'herbe avec sa canne; **the cow ~ed her tail** la vache fouettait l'air de sa queue; **he ~ed it out of my hand** il me l'a arraché de la main.

4 *vi* **(a)** (*transfer: also* ~ over) **Paul ~ed (over) to Conservative** Paul a voté conservateur cette fois; **we ~ed (over) to oil central heating** (nous avons changé et) nous avons maintenant fait installer le chauffage central au mazout; **many have ~ed (over) to teaching** beaucoup se sont recyclés dans l'enseignement.

(b) *[tail etc]* battre l'air.

switch back 1 *vi* (*to original plan, product, allegiance etc*) revenir, retourner (*to* à). (*Rad, TV*) **to switch back to the other programme** remettre l'autre émission.

2 *vt sep*: **to switch the heater back to 'low'** remettre le radiateur sur 'doux'; **to switch the light back on** rallumer; **to switch the heater/oven back on** rallumer le radiateur/le four.

3 switchback *n, adj V* **switch 2.**

switch off 1 *vi* **(a)** (*Elec*) éteindre; (*Rad, TV*) éteindre *or* fermer le poste. (*fig*) **when the conversation is boring, he just switches off*** quand la conversation l'ennuie, il décroche*.

(b) *[heater, oven etc]* **to switch off automatically** s'éteindre tout seul *or* automatiquement.

2 *vt sep light* éteindre; *electricity, gas* éteindre, fermer; *radio, television, heater* éteindre, fermer, arrêter. (*Rad, TV*) **he switched the programme off** il a fermé *or* éteint le poste; (*Aut*) **to switch off the engine** couper l'allumage, arrêter le moteur; **the oven switches itself off** le four s'éteint automatiquement; (*fig*) **he seems to be switched off* most of the time** il semble être détaché des autres la plupart du temps.

switch on 1 *vi* **(a)** (*Elec*) allumer; (*Rad, TV*) allumer le poste.

(b) *[heater, oven etc]* **to switch on automatically** s'allumer tout seul *or* automatiquement.

2 *vt sep gas, electricity* allumer; *water supply* ouvrir; *radio, television, heater* allumer, brancher; *engine, machine* mettre en marche. **to switch on the light** allumer; (*fig*) **his music switches me on‡** sa musique m'excite *or* me rend euphorique; (*fig*) **to be switched on‡** (*up-to-date*) être dans le vent *or* à la page; (*by drugs*) planer*, être sous l'influence de la drogue; (*sexually*) être tout excité *or* émoustillé (*by* par).

switch over 1 *vi* **(a)** = **switch 4a.**

(b) (*TV/Rad*) changer de chaîne/de station. (*TV/Rad*) **to switch over to the other programme** mettre l'autre chaîne/station.

2 *vt sep* **(a)** *V* **switch 3b.**

(b) (*TV/Rad*) **to switch the programme over** changer de chaîne/de station.

3 switchover *n V* **switch 2.**

switch round 1 *vi [two people]* changer de place (l'un avec l'autre).

2 *vt sep V* **switch 3b.**

Switzerland ['swɪtsələnd] *n* Suisse *f*. **French-/German-/Italian-speaking ~** la Suisse romande/allemande/italienne.

swivel ['swɪvl] **1** *n* pivot *m*, tourillon *m*.

2 *cpd seat, mounting etc* pivotant, tournant. **swivel chair** fauteuil pivotant.

3 *vt* (*also* ~ **round**) faire pivoter, faire tourner.

4 *vi [object]* pivoter, tourner.

swivel round 1 *vi* pivoter.

2 *vt sep* = **swivel 3.**

swizz‡ [swɪz] *n* (*Brit: swindle*) escroquerie *f*. (*disappointment*) **what a ~!** on est eu!*, on s'est fait avoir!*

swizzle ['swɪzl] **1** *n* (*Brit‡*) = **swizz‡. 2** *cpd*: **swizzle stick** fouet *m*.

swollen ['swəʊlən] **1** *ptp of* **swell.**

2 *adj arm, eye, jaw, face* enflé; *stomach* gonflé, ballonné; *river, lake* en crue; *population* accru. **eyes ~ with tears** yeux gonflés de larmes; **to have ~ glands** avoir (une inflammation) des ganglions; *V also* **swell.**

3 *cpd*: **swollen-headed*** *etc* = **swellheaded*** *etc*; *V* **swell 3.**

swoon [swu:n] **1** *vi* († *or hum: faint*) se pâmer († *or hum*); (*fig*) se pâmer d'admiration (*over sb/sth* devant qn/qch). **2** *n* († *or hum*) pâmoison *f*. **in a ~** en pâmoison.

swoop [swu:p] **1** *n [bird, plane]* descente *f* en piqué; (*attack*) attaque *f* en piqué (*on* sur); *[police etc]* descente, rafle *f* (*on* dans). **at one (fell) ~** d'un seul coup.

2 *vi* (*also* ~ **down**) *[bird]* fondre, piquer; *[aircraft]* descendre en piqué, piquer; *[police etc]* faire une descente. **the plane ~ed (down) low over the village** l'avion est descendu en piqué au-dessus du village; **the eagle ~ed (down) on the rabbit** l'aigle a fondu *or* s'est abattu sur le lapin; **the soldiers ~ed (down) on the terrorists** les soldats ont fondu sur les terroristes.

swoosh* [swu(:)ʃ] **1** *n [water]* bruissement *m*; *[stick etc through air]* sifflement *m*; *[tyres in rain]* glissement *m*.

2 *vi [water]* bruire. **he went ~ing through the mud** il est passé avec un bruit de boue qui gicle *or* en faisant gicler bruyamment la boue.

swop [swɒp] = **swap.**

sword [sɔ:d] **1** *n* épée *f*. **to wear a ~** porter l'épée; **to put sb to the ~** passer qn au fil de l'épée; **to put up one's ~** rengainer son épée, remettre son épée au fourreau; **those that live by the ~ die by the ~** quiconque se servira de l'épée périra par l'épée; *V* **cross, point** *etc*.

2 *cpd scar, wound* d'épée. **sword arm** bras droit; **sword dance** danse *f* du sabre; **swordfish** espadon *m*; **there was a lot of swordplay in the film** il y avait beaucoup de duels *or* ça ferraillait dur* dans le film; **at sword-point** à la pointe de l'épée; **to be a good swordsman** être une fine lame; **swordsmanship** habileté *f* dans le maniement de l'épée; **swordstick** canne *f* à épée; **sword-swallower** avaleur *m* de sabres.

swore [swɔ:ʳ] *pret of* **swear.**

sworn [swɔ:n] **1** *ptp of* **swear. 2** *adj evidence, statement* donné sous serment; *enemy* juré; *ally, friend* à la vie et à la mort.

swot* [swɒt] (*Brit*) **1** *n* (*pej*) bûcheur *m*, -euse *f*, bosseur‡ *m*. **2** *vt* bûcher*, potasser*. **3** *vi* bûcher*, potasser*, bosser‡. **to ~ for an exam** bachoter; **to ~ at maths** potasser* *or* bûcher* ses maths.

swot up* *vi, vt sep*: **to swot up (on) sth** potasser* qch.

swotting* ['swɒtɪŋ] *n* bachotage *m*. **to do some ~** bosser‡, bachoter.

swum [swʌm] *ptp of* **swim.**

swung [swʌŋ] **1** *pret, ptp of* **swing. 2** *adj* (*Typ*) ~ **dash** tilde *m*.

sybarite ['sɪbəraɪt] *n* sybarite *mf*.

sybaritic [,sɪbə'rɪtɪk] *adj* sybarite.

sycamore ['sɪkəmɔ:ʳ] *n* sycomore *m*, faux platane.

sycophancy ['sɪkəfənsɪ] *n* flagornerie *f*.

sycophant ['sɪkəfənt] *n* flagorneur *m*, -euse *f*.

sycophantic [,sɪkə'fæntɪk] *adj* flagorneur.

syllabary ['sɪləbərɪ] *n* syllabaire *m*.

syllabic [sɪ'læbɪk] *adj* syllabique.

syllabify [sɪ'læbɪfaɪ] *vt* décomposer en syllabes.

syllable ['sɪləbl] *n* syllabe *f*.

syllabub ['sɪləbʌb] *n* (espèce *f* de) sabayon *m*.

syllabus ['sɪləbəs] *n* (*Scol, Univ*) programme *m*. **on the ~** au programme.

syllogism ['sɪlədʒɪzəm] *n* syllogisme *m*.

syllogistic [,sɪlə'dʒɪstɪk] *adj* syllogistique.

syllogize ['sɪlədʒaɪz] *vi* raisonner par syllogismes.

sylph [sɪlf] **1** *n* sylphe *m*; (*fig: woman*) sylphide *f*. **2** *cpd*: **sylph-like** *woman* gracile, qui a une taille de sylphide; *figure* de sylphide.

sylvan ['sɪlvən] *adj* (*liter*) sylvestre, des bois.

symbiosis [,sɪmbɪ'əʊsɪs] *n* (*also fig*) symbiose *f*.

symbol ['sɪmbəl] *n* symbole *m*.

symbolic(al) [sɪm'bɒlɪk(əl)] *adj* symbolique.

symbolically [sɪm'bɒlɪkəlɪ] *adv* symboliquement.

symbolism ['sɪmbəlɪzəm] *n* symbolisme *m*.

symbolist ['sɪmbəlɪst] *adj, n* symboliste (*mf*).

symbolization [,sɪmbəlaɪ'zeɪʃən] *n* symbolisation *f*.

symbolize ['sɪmbəlaɪz] *vt* symboliser.

symmetric(al) [sɪ'metrɪk(əl)] *adj* symétrique.

symmetrically [sɪ'metrɪkəlɪ] *adv* symétriquement, avec symétrie.

symmetry ['sɪmɪtrɪ] *n* symétrie *f*.

sympathetic [,sɪmpə'θetɪk] *adj* (*showing pity*) *person* compatissant (*to, towards* envers); *words, smile, gesture* de sympathie, compatissant; (*kind*) bien disposé, bienveillant (*to* envers, à l'égard de), compréhensif; (*Anat etc*) sympathique. **they were ~ but could not help** ils ont compati mais n'ont rien pu faire pour aider; **you will find him very ~** vous le trouverez bien disposé à votre égard *or* tout prêt à vous écouter; **they are ~ to actors** ils sont bien disposés à l'égard des acteurs.

sympathetically [,sɪmpə'θetɪkəlɪ] *adv* (*showing pity*) avec compassion; (*kindly*) avec bienveillance; (*Anat etc*) par sympathie.

sympathize ['sɪmpəθaɪz] *vi*: **I do ~ with you!** je vous plains!; **her cousin called to ~** sa cousine est venue témoigner sa sympathie; **I ~ with you in your grief** je m'associe *or* je compatis à votre douleur; **I ~ with you** *or* **what you feel** *or* **what you say** je comprends votre point de vue.

sympathizer ['sɪmpəθaɪzəʳ] *n* **(a)** (*in adversity*) personne *f* qui compatit. **he was surrounded by ~s** il était entouré de personnes qui lui témoignaient leur sympathie. **(b)** (*fig: esp Pol*) sympathisant(e) *m(f)* (*with* de).

sympathy ['sɪmpəθɪ] **1** *n* **(a)** (*pity*) compassion *f*. **please accept my (deepest) ~** *or* **sympathies** veuillez agréer mes condoléances; **to feel ~ for** éprouver *or* avoir de la compassion pour; **to show one's ~ for sb** témoigner sa sympathie à *or* pour qn.

(b) (*fellow feeling*) solidarité *f* (*for* avec). **the sympathies of the crowd were with him** il avait le soutien de la foule, la foule était pour lui; **I have no ~ with lazy people** je n'ai aucune indulgence pour les gens qui sont paresseux; **he is in ~ with the workers** il est du côté des ouvriers; **I am in ~ with your proposals but ...** je suis en accord avec *or* je ne désapprouve pas vos propositions mais ...; **to come out** *or* **strike in ~ with sb** faire grève en solidarité avec qn.

2 *cpd*: (*Ind*) **sympathy strike** grève *f* de solidarité.

symphonic [sɪm'fɒnɪk] *adj* symphonique.

symphony ['sɪmfənɪ] **1** *n* symphonie *f*. **2** *cpd concert, orchestra* symphonique. **symphony writer** symphoniste *mf*.

symposium [sɪm'pəʊzɪəm] *n* (*all senses*) symposium *m*.

symptom ['sɪmptəm] *n* (*Med, fig*) symptôme *m*, indice *m*.

symptomatic [,sɪmptə'mætɪk] *adj* symptomatique (*of* de).

synagogue ['sɪnəgɒg] *n* synagogue *f*.

synchromesh [,sɪŋkrəʊ'meʃ] *n* (*Aut*) synchronisation *f*. **~ on all gears** boîte *f* de vitesse avec tous les rapports synchronisés.

synchronism ['sɪŋkrənɪzəm] *n* synchronisme *m*.

synchronization [,sɪŋkrənaɪ'zeɪʃən] *n* synchronisation *f*.

synchronize ['sɪŋkrənaɪz] **1** *vt* synchroniser. **2** *vi [events]* se passer *or* avoir lieu simultanément; *[footsteps etc]* être synchronisés. **to ~ with sth** être synchrone avec qch, se produire en même temps que qch.

synchronous ['sɪŋkrənəs] *adj* synchrone.

syncline ['sɪŋklaɪn] *n* synclinal *m*.

syncopate ['sɪŋkəpeɪt] *vt* syncoper.

syncopation [,sɪŋkə'peɪʃən] *n* (*Mus*) syncope *f*.

syncope ['sɪŋkəpɪ] *n* (*Ling, Med*) syncope *f*.

syncretism ['sɪŋkrɪtɪzəm] *n* syncrétisme *m*.

syndic ['sɪndɪk] *n* (*government official*) administrateur *m*, syndic *m*; (*Brit Univ*) membre *m* d'un comité administratif.

syndicalism ['sɪndɪkəlɪzəm] *n* syndicalisme *m*.

syndicalist ['sɪndɪkəlɪst] *n* syndicaliste *mf*.

syndicate ['sɪndɪkɪt] **1** *n* (*Comm etc*) syndicat *m*, coopérative *f*. **2** ['sɪndɪkeɪt] *vt* (*US Press*) *article etc* vendre *or* publier par l'intermédiaire d'un syndicat de distribution.
syndrome ['sɪndrəʊm] *n* (*also fig*) syndrome *m*.
synecdoche [sɪ'nekdəkɪ] *n* synecdoque *f*.
synod ['sɪnəd] *n* synode *m*.
synonym ['sɪnənɪm] *n* synonyme *m*.
synonymous [sɪ'nɒnɪməs] *adj* synonyme (*with* de).
synonymy [sɪ'nɒnəmɪ] *n* synonymie *f*.
synopsis [sɪ'nɒpsɪs] *n, pl* **synopses** [sɪ'nɒpsi:z] résumé *m*, précis *m*; (*Cine, Theat*) synopsis *m or f*.
synoptic [sɪ'nɒptɪk] *adj* synoptique.
syntactic(al) [sɪn'tæktɪk(əl)] *adj* syntaxique *or* syntactique.
syntagmatic [ˌsɪntæg'mætɪk] *adj* syntagmatique.
syntax ['sɪntæks] *n* syntaxe *f*.
synthesis ['sɪnθəsɪs] *n, pl* **syntheses** ['sɪnθəsi:z] synthèse *f*.
synthesize ['sɪnθəsaɪz] *vt* synthétiser; (*Chem*) produire synthétiquement *or* par une synthèse, faire la synthèse de.
synthetic [sɪn'θetɪk] **1** *adj* (*all senses*) synthétique. **2** *n* produit *m* synthétique. (*Tex*) ~**s** fibres *fpl* synthétiques, textiles artificiels.
syphilis ['sɪfɪlɪs] *n* syphilis *f*.
syphilitic [ˌsɪfɪ'lɪtɪk] *adj, n* syphilitique (*mf*).
syphon ['saɪfən] = **siphon.**
Syria ['sɪrɪə] *n* Syrie *f*.
Syrian ['sɪrɪən] **1** *adj* syrien.
2 *n* Syrien(ne) *m(f)*.
syringe [sɪ'rɪndʒ] **1** *n* seringue *f*. **2** *vt* seringuer.
syrup ['sɪrəp] *n* sirop *m*; (*Culin: also* **golden** ~) mélasse raffinée.
syrupy ['sɪrəpɪ] *adj* (*lit, fig*) sirupeux.
system ['sɪstəm] **1** *n* **(a)** système *m*; (*Anat: body*) organisme *m*. **solar/nervous/political** ~ système solaire/nerveux/politique; **railway** ~ réseau *m* de chemin de fer; **digestive** ~ appareil digestif; **it was a shock to his** ~ cela a été une secousse pour son organisme, cela a ébranlé son organisme; (*Pol*) **down with the** ~! à bas le système!; (*fig*) **to get sth out of one's** ~ se purger *or* se libérer de qch; *V* **feudal** *etc.*
(b) (*U: order*) méthode *f* (*U*). **to lack** ~ manquer de méthode.
2 *cpd*: **systems analyst** analyste-programmeur *mf*.
systematic [ˌsɪstə'mætɪk] *adj reasoning, work* systématique, méthodique; *failures* systématique.
systematically [ˌsɪstə'mætɪkəlɪ] *adv* (*V* **systematic**) systématiquement; méthodiquement.
systematization [ˌsɪstəmətaɪ'zeɪʃən] *n* systématisation *f*.
systematize ['sɪstəmətaɪz] *vt* systématiser.

T

T, t [ti:] **1** *n* (*letter*) T, t *m*. (*fig*) **that's it to a T** c'est exactement cela; **it fits him to a T** cela lui va comme un gant; *V* **dot.**
2 *cpd*: **T-junction** intersection *f* en T; **T-shaped** en forme de T, en équerre; **T-shirt** T-shirt *m or* tee-shirt *m*; **T-square** équerre *f* en T.
ta: [tɑ:] *excl* (*Brit*) merci!
tab [tæb] *n* (*part of garment*) patte *f*; (*loop on garment etc*) attache *f*; (*label*) étiquette *f*; (*on shoelace*) ferret *m*; (*marker: on file etc*) languette *f*, étiquette; (*US*: café check*) addition *f*, note *f*. **to keep** ~**s** *or* **a** ~ **on*** *person* avoir *or* tenir à l'œil*; *thing* avoir l'œil sur*; (*US: lit, fig*) **to pick up the** ~* payer la note *or* l'addition.
tabard ['tæbəd] *n* tabard *m*.
tabby ['tæbɪ] *n* (*also* ~ **cat**) chat(te) *m(f)* tigré(e) *or* moucheté(e).
tabernacle ['tæbənækl] *n* tabernacle *m*.
table ['teɪbl] **1** *n* **(a)** (*furniture, food on it*) table *f*; (*people at* ~) tablée *f*, table. **ironing/bridge/garden** ~ table à repasser/de bridge/de jardin; **at** ~ à table; **to sit down to** ~ se mettre à table; **to lay** *or* **set the** ~ mettre la table *or* le couvert; (*Parl*) **to lay sth on the** ~ remettre *or* ajourner qch; (*Parl*) **the bill lies on the** ~ la discussion du projet de loi a été ajournée; (*fig*) **he slipped me £5 under the** ~* il m'a passé 5 livres de la main à la main; (*fig*) **he was nearly under the** ~ un peu plus et il roulait sous la table*; *V* **clear, turn** *etc.*
(b) *[facts, statistics]* table *f* (*also Math*); *[prices, fares, names]* liste *f*; (*Sport: also* **league** ~) classement *m*. ~ **of contents** table des matières; (*Math*) **the two-times** ~ la table de (multiplication par) deux; (*Sport*) **we are in fifth place in the** ~ nous sommes classés cinquièmes, nous sommes cinquièmes au classement; *V* **log**[2] *etc.*
(c) (*Geog*) = **tableland;** *V* **3.**
(d) (*Rel*) **the T**~**s of the Law** les Tables de la Loi.
2 *vt* **(a)** (*Parl*) *bill, motion etc* (*Brit: submit*) présenter; (*postpone*) ajourner.
(b) (*tabulate*) dresser une liste *or* une table de; *results* classifier.
3 *cpd wine, grapes, knife, lamp* de table. **tablecloth** nappe *f*; **table-cover** tapis *m* de table; **table d'hôte** (*adj*) à prix fixe; (*n*) repas *m* à prix fixe; (*Geog*) **tableland** (haut) plateau *m*; **table leg** pied *m* de table; **table linen** linge *m* de table; **he has good table manners** il sait se tenir à table; **tablemat** (*of linen etc*) napperon *m*; (*heat-resistant*) dessous-de-plat *m inv*; (*Geog*) **Table Mountain** la Montagne de la Table; **table napkin** serviette *f* (de table); **table runner** chemin *m* de table; **table salt** sel fin; **tablespoon** cuiller *f* de service; (*measurement: also* **tablespoonful**) cuillerée *f* à soupe (*US Culin = 29,5 ml*); (*U*) **table talk** menus propos; **table tennis** (*n*) ping-pong *m*, tennis *m* de table; (*cpd*) de ping-pong; **table-tennis player** joueur *m*, -euse *f* de ping-pong, pongiste *mf*; **tabletop** dessus *m* de table; (*U*) **table turning** (spiritisme *m* par les) tables tournantes; (*U*) **tableware** vaisselle *f*.
tableau ['tæbləʊ] *n, pl* ~**x** ['tæbləʊz] (*Theat*) tableau vivant; (*fig*) tableau.
tablet ['tæblɪt] *n* (*stone: inscribed*) plaque *f* (commémorative); (*Hist: of wax, slate etc*) tablette *f*; *[soap, chocolate etc]* pain *m*; (*Pharm*) comprimé *m*, cachet *m*; (*for sucking*) pastille *f*.
tabloid ['tæblɔɪd] **1** *n* (*Press: also* ~ **newspaper**) tabloïd *m*; (*US Pharm* ®) comprimé *m*, cachet *m*. **2** *adj* (*also* **in** ~ **form**) en raccourci, condensé.
taboo [tə'bu:] **1** *adj, n* (*Rel, fig*) tabou (*m*). **2** *vt* proscrire, interdire.
tabor ['teɪbə[r]] *n* tambourin *m*.
tabu [tə'bu:] = **taboo.**
tabular ['tæbjʊlə[r]] *adj* tabulaire.
tabulate ['tæbjʊleɪt] *vt facts, figures* mettre sous forme de table; *results etc* classifier; (*Typing*) mettre en colonnes.
tabulation [ˌtæbjʊ'leɪʃən] *n* (*V* **tabulate**) disposition *f* en listes *or* tables; classification *f*; tabulation *f*.
tabulator ['tæbjʊleɪtə[r]] *n [typewriter]* tabulateur *m*.
tachometer [tæ'kɒmɪtə[r]] *n* tachymètre *m*.
tachymeter [tæ'kɪmɪtə[r]] *n* tachéomètre *m*.
tacit ['tæsɪt] *adj* tacite.
tacitly ['tæsɪtlɪ] *adv* tacitement.
taciturn ['tæsɪtɜ:n] *adj* taciturne.
taciturnity [ˌtæsɪ'tɜ:nɪtɪ] *n* taciturnité *f*.
tack [tæk] **1** *n* **(a)** (*for wood, lino, carpets etc*) broquette *f*; (*for upholstery*) semence *f*; (*US: also* **thumb**~) punaise *f*; *V* **brass.**
(b) (*Sewing*) point *m* de bâti.
(c) (*Naut*) bord *m*, bordée *f*. **to make a** ~ faire *or* courir *or* tirer un bord *or* une bordée; **to be on a port/starboard** ~ être bâbord/tribord amures; (*fig*) **to be on the right/wrong** ~ être sur la bonne/mauvaise voie; (*fig*) **to try another** ~ essayer une autre tactique.
(d) (*U: for horse*) sellerie *f* (*articles*).
2 *cpd*: **tackroom** sellerie *f* (*endroit*).
3 *vt* **(a)** (*also* ~ **down**) *wood, lino, carpet* clouer (*avec des broquettes*).
(b) (*Sewing*) faufiler, bâtir.
4 *vi* (*Naut: make a* ~) faire *or* courir *or* tirer un bord *or* une bordée. **they** ~**ed back to the harbour** ils sont rentrés au port en louvoyant *or* en tirant des bordées.
tack down *vt sep* (*Sewing*) maintenir en place au point de bâti; *V also* **tack 3a.**
tack on *vt sep* (*Sewing*) bâtir, appliquer au point de bâti; (*fig*) ajouter (après coup) (*to* à).
tacking ['tækɪŋ] (*Sewing*) **1** *n* bâtissage *m*, faufilure *f*. **to take out the** ~ **from sth** défaufiler qch. **2** *cpd*: **tacking stitch** point *m* de bâti.
tackle ['tækl] **1** *n* **(a)** (*U*) (*esp Naut: ropes, pulleys*) appareil *m* de levage; (*gen: gear, equipment*) équipement *m*. **fishing** ~ articles *mpl or* matériel *m* de pêche.
(b) (*Ftbl, Hockey, Rugby, etc*) plaquage *m*.
2 *vt* (*Ftbl, Hockey, Rugby etc*) plaquer; *thief, intruder* saisir (à bras le corps); *task* s'attaquer à; *problem, question, subject* aborder, s'attaquer à; (*) *meal, food* attaquer*. **I'll** ~ **him about it at once** je vais lui en parler *or* lui en dire deux mots tout de suite; **I** ~**d him about what he had done** je l'ai questionné sur ce qu'il avait fait; **he** ~**d Hebrew on his own** il s'est mis à l'hébreu tout seul.
tacky[1] ['tækɪ] *adj glue* qui commence à prendre; *paint* pas tout à fait sec (*f* sèche); *surface* poisseux, collant.
tacky[2]* ['tækɪ] *adj* (*US*) *person* mal fagoté*, mal ficelé*; *clothes* démodé.

tact [tækt] *n* (*U*) tact *m*, doigté *m*, délicatesse *f*.
tactful ['tæktfʊl] *adj person* délicat, plein de tact; *hint* subtil (*f* subtile), fin; *inquiry, reference* discret (*f* -ète); *answer* plein de tact, diplomatique* (*fig*); *suggestion* plein de tact, délicat. **be ~!** du tact!, un peu de diplomatie!*; **to be ~ with sb** agir envers qn avec tact *or* doigté, ménager qn; **you could have been a bit more ~** tu aurais pu avoir un peu plus de tact *or* de doigté.
tactfully ['tæktfəlɪ] *adv* avec tact, avec doigté, avec délicatesse.
tactfulness ['tæktfʊlnɪs] *n* = **tact**.
tactic ['tæktɪk] *n* (*Mil, fig*) tactique *f*. (*U: Mil*) **~s** la tactique.
tactical ['tæktɪkəl] *adj* (*Mil, fig*) *exercise, weapon, value* tactique; *error etc* de tactique; (*skilful*) adroit.
tactically ['tæktɪkəlɪ] *adv* (*Mil, fig*) d'un *or* du point de vue tactique.
tactician [tæk'tɪʃən] *n* (*Mil, fig*) tacticien *m*.
tactile ['tæktaɪl] *adj* tactile.
tactless ['tæktlɪs] *adj person* peu délicat, qui manque de tact; *hint* grossier; *inquiry, reference* indiscret (*f* -ète); *answer* qui manque de tact, peu diplomatique* (*fig*); *suggestion* peu délicat.
tactlessly ['tæktlɪslɪ] *adv* sans tact, sans doigté, sans délicatesse.
tadpole ['tædpəʊl] *n* têtard *m*.
taffeta ['tæfɪtə] *n* (*U*) taffetas *m*.
taffrail ['tæfreɪl] *n* (*Naut*) couronnement *m*; (*rail*) lisse *f* de couronnement.
Taffy* ['tæfɪ] *n* (*also* **~ Jones**) *sobriquet donné à un Gallois*.
taffy ['tæfɪ] *n* (*US*) bonbon *m* au caramel.
tag [tæg] **1** *n* **(a)** *[shoelace, cord etc]* ferret *m*; (*on garment etc*) patte *f*, marque *f*; (*label*) étiquette *f*; (*marker: on file etc*) languette *f*, étiquette. **all uniforms must have name ~s** chaque uniforme doit être marqué au nom de son propriétaire; *V* **price** *etc*.
(b) (*Ling*) (*quotation*) citation *f*; (*cliché*) cliché *m*, lieu commun; (*catchword*) slogan *m*; *V* **question**.
(c) (*U: game*) (jeu *m* de) chat *m*.
2 *cpd*: (*US*) **tagboard** carton *m* (pour étiquettes); (*US*) **tag day** journée *f* de vente d'insignes (*pour une œuvre*); **tag end** *[speech, performance, programme etc]* fin *f*; *[goods for sale]* restes *mpl*; **tag line** *[play]* dernière réplique; *[poem]* dernier vers.
3 *vt* **(a)** *garment* marquer; *bag, box, file* étiqueter; (*US* fig*) *car* mettre un papillon* sur; *driver* mettre une contravention à.
(b) (*: *follow*) suivre; *[detective]* filer.
tag along *vi* suivre le mouvement*. **the children tagged along behind their mother** les enfants suivaient leur mère comme des petits poussins; **the others came tagging along behind** les autres traînaient derrière *or* étaient à la traîne derrière; **she usually tags along (with us)** la plupart du temps elle vient avec nous.
tag on* **1** *vi*: **to tag on to sb** coller aux talons de qn*; **he came tagging on behind** il traînait derrière.
2 *vt sep* (*fig*) ajouter (après coup) (*to* à).
tagmeme ['tægmiːm] *n* tagmème *m*.
tagmemics [tæg'miːmɪks] *n* (*U*) tagmémique *f*.
Tahiti [tɑː'hiːtɪ] *n* Tahiti *m*.
tail [teɪl] **1** *n* **(a)** *[animal, aircraft, comet, kite, procession, hair]* queue *f*; *[shirt]* pan *m*; *[coat]* basque *f*; *[coin]* pile *f*; (**hum: buttocks*) postérieur* *m* (*hum*). **~s*** (*Dress*) queue de pie; **~s I win!** pile je gagne!; (*lit, fig*) **with his ~ between his legs** la queue entre les jambes; (*fig*) **he was right on my ~** il me suivait de très près; *V* **nose, sting, turn** *etc*.
(b) (‡) **to put a ~ on sb** faire filer qn.
2 *cpd*: (*Aviat*) **tail assembly** dérive *f*; (*Aut*) **tailback** bouchon *m*; (*Aut etc*) **tailboard** hayon *m*; **tail coat** habit *m*; **tail end** *[piece of meat, roll of cloth etc]* bout *m*; *[procession etc]* queue *f*; *[storm, debate, lecture]* toutes dernières minutes, fin *f*; (*Aut*) **tailgate** hayon *m*; (*US Aut*) **to tailgate sb*** coller au pare-chocs de qn; (*Aut, Rail etc*) **tail lamp, taillight** feu *m* arrière *inv*; **tail-piece** (*to speech etc*) appendice *m*; (*to letter*) post-scriptum *m*; (*Typ*) cul-de-lampe *m*; *[violin]* cordier *m*; (*Aut*) **tailpipe** tuyau *m* d'échappement; (*Aviat*) **tail skid** béquille *f* de queue; (*Aviat*) **tailspin** vrille *f*; (*Aviat*) **to be in a tailspin** vriller; **tailwind** vent *m* arrière *inv*.
3 *vt* **(a)** (*) *suspect etc* suivre, filer.
(b) (*cut ~ of*) *animal* couper la queue à; *V* **top**[1].
4 *vi*: **to ~ after sb** suivre qn tant bien que mal.
tail away *vi [sounds]* se taire (peu à peu); *[attendance, interest, numbers]* diminuer, baisser (petit à petit).
tail back **1** *vi*: **the traffic tailed back to the bridge** le bouchon remontait jusqu'au pont.
2 tailback *n V* **tail 2**.
tail off *vi* = **tail away**.
-tailed [teɪld] *adj ending in cpds*: **long-tailed** à la queue longue.
tailor ['teɪlə[r]] **1** *n* tailleur *m*. **~'s chalk** craie *f* de tailleur; **~'s dummy** mannequin *m*; (*fig pej*) fantoche *m*.
2 *cpd*: **tailor-made** *garment* fait sur mesure; (*fig*) **the building was tailor-made for this purpose** le bâtiment était fonctionnalisé, le bâtiment était construit spécialement pour cet usage; **a lesson tailor-made for that class** une leçon conçue *or* préparée spécialement pour cette classe; **the job was tailor-made for him** le poste était fait pour lui.
3 *vt garment* façonner; (*fig*) *speech, book* adapter (*to, to suit* à, *for* pour). **a ~ed skirt** une jupe ajustée.
taint [teɪnt] **1** *vt meat, food* gâter; *water* infecter, polluer; *air, atmosphere* vicier, infecter, polluer; (*fig liter*) *sb's reputation* ecc souiller (*liter*).
2 *n* (*U*) (*infection*) infection *f*, souillure *f*; (*decay*) corruption *f*, décomposition *f*; (*fig: of insanity, sin, heresy etc*) tache *f* (*fig*), souillure (*fig liter*).
tainted ['teɪntɪd] *adj food* gâté; *meat* avarié; *water* infecté, pollué; *air, atmosphere* vicié, infecté, pollué; *action, motive* impur; *reputation* entaché, sali, souillé (*liter*); *money* mal acquis; *blood* impur; *family, lineage* sali, souillé (*liter*). **to become ~** *[food]* se gâter; *[meat]* s'avarier; *[water, air etc]* s'infecter, se polluer.
take [teɪk] (*vb: pret* **took**, *ptp* **taken**) **1** *n* (*Cine, Phot*) prise *f* de vue(s); (*Sound recording*) enregistrement *m*; (*Fishing, Hunting etc*) prise *f*.
2 *cpd*: **takeaway** (*food shop*) café *m* qui fait des plats à emporter; **takeaway food** plats préparés (à emporter); **takeaway meal** repas *m* à emporter; **takedown*** *toy, weapon etc* démontable; **take-home pay** salaire net; **takeoff** (*Aviat*) décollage *m*; (*fig: Econ etc*) démarrage *m*; (*imitation*) imitation *f*, pastiche *m*; (*US*) **takeout** = **takeaway**; (*Bridge*) **takeout (bid)** réponse *f* de faiblesse; (*Fin etc*) **takeover** rachat *m*; **takeover bid** offre publique d'achat, O.P.A. *f*.
3 *vt* **(a)** (*gen*) prendre; (*seize*) prendre, saisir. **to ~ sb's hand** prendre la main de qn; **he took me by the arm, he took my arm** il m'a pris le bras; **he took her in his arms** il l'a prise dans ses bras; **to ~ sb by the throat** prendre *or* saisir qn à la gorge.
(b) (*extract*) prendre (*from sth* dans qch), tirer (*from sth* de qch); (*remove*) prendre, enlever, ôter (*from sb* à qn); (*without permission*) prendre; (*steal*) prendre, voler. **to ~ sth from one's pocket** prendre qch dans *or* tirer qch de sa poche; **to ~ sth from a drawer** prendre qch dans un tiroir; **the devil ~ it!***† au diable!; **he ~s his examples from real life** il tire ses exemples de la réalité; **I took these statistics from a government report** j'ai tiré ces statistiques d'un rapport gouvernemental; *V* **hand** *etc*.
(c) (*Math etc: subtract*) soustraire, retrancher, retirer (*from* de). **he took 10 francs off the price** il a rabattu 10 F sur le prix.
(d) (*capture etc*) (*Mil*) *city, district, hill* prendre, s'emparer de; (*gen*) *suspect, wanted man* prendre, capturer; *fish etc* prendre, attraper; (*sexually*) *woman* prendre; (*Chess*) prendre; *prize* avoir, obtenir, remporter; *degree* avoir, obtenir. **he must be ~n alive** il faut le prendre *or* capturer vivant; (*Cards*) **to ~ a trick** faire une levée; **my ace took his king** j'ai pris son roi avec mon as; **the grocer ~s about £500 per day** l'épicier (se) fait à peu près 500 livres de recette par jour; *V* **fancy, prisoner, surprise** *etc*.
(e) (*make, have, undertake etc*) *notes, letter, photo, temperature, measurements, lessons, bath, decision, holiday etc* prendre. **the policeman took his name and address** l'agent a pris *or* relevé ses nom et adresse; **he ~s 'The Times'** il prend 'The Times'; (*Phot*) **he took the cathedral from the square** il a pris la cathédrale vue de la place; **to ~ a ticket for a concert** prendre un billet *or* une place pour un concert; **I'll ~ that one** je prends *or* prendrai celui-là; **to ~ a wife**† prendre femme†; **~ your partners for a waltz** invitez vos partenaires et en avant pour la valse; **you'll have to ~ your chance** il va falloir que tu prennes le risque; **to ~ sth (up)on o.s.** prendre qch sur soi; **to ~ it (up)on o.s. to do** prendre sur soi *or* sous son bonnet de faire; (*Med*) **to ~ cold** prendre froid; **to ~ ill, to be ~n ill** tomber malade; **to ~ fright** prendre peur; *V* **advantage, opportunity, possession** *etc*.
(f) (*ingest, consume*) *food, drink* prendre. **he ~s sugar in his tea** il prend du sucre dans son thé; **to ~ tea**† **with sb** prendre le thé avec qn; **to ~ drugs** *[patient]* prendre des médicaments; (*gen*) se droguer; **to ~ morphine** se droguer à la morphine, prendre de la morphine; (*Med*) **'not to be ~n (internally)'** 'pour usage externe'; **he took no food for 4 days** il n'a rien mangé *or* pris pendant 4 jours; **how much alcohol has he ~n?** combien d'alcool a-t-il bu? *or* absorbé?; **I can't ~ alcohol** je ne supporte pas l'alcool.
(g) (*occupy*) *chair, seat* prendre, s'asseoir sur; (*rent*) *house, flat etc* prendre, louer. **to ~ one's seat** s'asseoir; **is this seat ~n?** cette place est-elle prise? *or* occupée?
(h) (*go by*) *bus, train, plane, taxi* prendre; *road* prendre, suivre. **~ the first on the left** prenez la première à gauche.
(i) (*negotiate*) *bend* prendre; *hill* grimper; *fence* sauter; (*sit*) *exam, test* passer, se présenter à; (*study*) *subject* prendre, faire. **he took that corner too fast** il a pris ce virage trop vite; (*Scol, Univ*) **what are you taking next year?** qu'est-ce que tu prends *or* fais l'an prochain (comme matière)?
(j) (*tolerate*) accepter. **he won't ~ no for an answer** il n'acceptera pas un refus; **he won't ~ that reply from you** il n'acceptera jamais une telle réponse venant de vous; **I'll ~ no nonsense!** on ne me raconte pas d'histoires!; **I'm not taking any!‡** je ne marche pas!*; **I can't ~ it any more** je n'en peux plus; **we can ~ it!** on ne se laissera pas abattre!, on (l')encaissera!*; (*fig*) **he/the car took a lot of punishment** il/la voiture en a beaucoup vu*; *V* **beating, lie down** *etc*.
(k) (*have as capacity*) contenir, avoir une capacité de. **the bus ~s 60 passengers** l'autobus a une capacité de 60 places; **the hall will ~ 200 people** la salle contient jusqu'à 200 personnes; **the bridge will ~ 10 tons** le pont supporte un poids maximal de 10 tonnes.
(l) (*receive, accept*) *gift, payment* prendre, accepter; *a bet* accepter; *news* prendre, supporter. **he won't ~ less than £50 for it** il en demande au moins 50 livres; **~ it from me!** croyez-moi!, croyez-moi sur parole!; **(you can) ~ it or leave it** c'est à prendre ou à laisser; **whisky? I can ~ it or leave it*** le whisky? j'aime ça mais sans plus; **she took his death quite well** elle s'est montrée très calme en apprenant sa mort; **she took his death very badly** elle a été très affectée par sa mort; **I wonder how she'll ~ it** je me demande comment elle prendra cela; **you must ~ us as you find us** vous devez nous prendre comme nous sommes; **to ~ things as they come** prendre les choses comme elles viennent*; **you must ~ things as they are** il faut prendre les choses comme elles sont*; **to ~ things** *or* **it** *or* **life easy*** ne

pas s'en faire, se la couler douce*; ~ **it easy!*** du calme!, t'en fais pas!*; (*handing over task etc*) **will you ~ it from here?** pouvez-vous prendre la suite? *or* la relève?; *V* **amiss, lamb, word** *etc.*

(m) (*assume*) supposer, imaginer. **I ~ it that ...** je suppose *or* j'imagine que ...; **how old do you ~ him to be?** quel âge lui donnez-vous?; **what do you ~ me for?** pour qui me prenez-vous?; **do you ~ me for a fool?** vous me prenez pour un imbécile?; **I took him for** *or* **to be a doctor** je l'ai pris pour un médecin; **I took him to be foreign** je le croyais étranger; **to ~ A for B** prendre A pour B, confondre A et B; *V* **grant, read**[1] *etc.*

(n) (*consider*) prendre. **now ~ Ireland** prenons par exemple l'Irlande; **~ the case of ...** prenons *or* prenez le cas de ...; **taking one thing with another ...** tout bien considéré ... .

(o) (*require*) prendre, demander; (*Gram*) être suivi de. **it ~s time** cela prend *or* demande du temps; **the journey ~s 5 days** le voyage prend *or* demande 5 jours; **it took me 2 hours to do it, I took 2 hours to do it** j'ai mis 2 heures à le faire; (*US*) **~ five*** pause de cinq minutes, on s'arrête cinq minutes; **~ your time!** prenez votre temps!; **it won't ~ long** cela ne prendra pas longtemps; **that ~s a lot of courage** cela demande beaucoup de courage; **it ~s a brave man to do that** il faut être courageux pour faire cela; **it ~s some doing*** cela n'est pas facile (à faire); **it ~s some believing*** c'est à peine croyable; **it took 3 policemen to hold him down** il a fallu 3 gendarmes pour le tenir; (*Prov*) **it ~s two to make a quarrel** il faut être au moins deux pour se battre; **he has got what it ~s to do the job** il a toutes les qualités requises pour ce travail; (*courage*) **he's got what it ~s!*** il en a!:.

(p) (*carry*) *child, object* porter, apporter, emporter; *one's gloves, umbrella* prendre, emporter (avec soi); (*lead*) emmener, conduire; (*accompany*) accompagner. **he took her some flowers** il lui a apporté des fleurs; **~ his suitcase upstairs** montez sa valise; **he ~s home £60 a week** il gagne *or* se fait* 60 livres net (*inv*) par semaine; **he took her to the cinema** il l'a emmenée au cinéma; **I'll ~ you to dinner** je vous emmènerai dîner; **they took him over the factory** ils lui ont fait visiter l'usine; **to ~ sb to hospital** transporter qn à l'hôpital; **he took me home in his car** il m'a ramené *or* raccompagné dans sa voiture; **this road will ~ you to Paris** cette route vous mènera à Paris; **this bus will ~ you to the town hall** cet autobus vous conduira à la mairie; (*fig*) **what took you to Lille?** qu'est-ce qui vous a fait aller à Lille?; *V* **post**[3], **walk** *etc.*

4 *vi [fire, vaccination, plant cutting etc]* prendre. (*Phot*) **he ~s well, he ~s a good photo*** il est très photogénique; *V* **kindly** *etc.*

take aback *vt sep V* **aback.**

take after *vt fus* ressembler à, tenir de.

take along *vt sep person* emmener; *camera etc* emporter, prendre.

take apart 1 *vi [toy, machine etc]* se démonter.

2 *vt sep machine, engine, toy* démonter; (**fig: criticize harshly*) *plan, suggestion* démanteler, démolir*. **I'll take him apart* if I get hold of him!** si je l'attrape je l'étripe* *or* je lui fais sa fête!:

take aside *vt sep person* prendre à part, emmener à l'écart.

take away 1 *vi*: **it takes away from its value** cela diminue *or* déprécie sa valeur; **that doesn't take away from his merit** cela n'enlève rien à son mérite.

2 *vt sep* **(a)** (*carry, lead away*) *object* emporter; *person* emmener. (*on book etc*) **'not to be taken away'** 'à consulter sur place'.

(b) (*remove*) *object* prendre, retirer, enlever (*from sb* à qn); *sb's child, wife, sweetheart* enlever (*from sb* à qn). **she took her children away from the school** elle a retiré ses enfants de l'école.

(c) (*Math*) soustraire, retrancher, ôter (*from* de). (*in counting*) **if you take 3 away from 6 ...** 6 moins 3 ... .

3 takeaway *adj, n V* **take 2.**

take back *vt sep* **(a)** *gift, promise, one's wife etc* reprendre.

(b) (*return*) *book, goods* rapporter (*to* à); (*accompany*) *person* raccompagner, reconduire (*to* à). (*fig*) **it takes me back to my childhood** cela me rappelle mon enfance; **that takes me back a few years!** ça me rappelle de vieux souvenirs!

take down 1 *vt sep* **(a)** *vase from shelf etc* descendre (*from, off* de); *trousers* baisser; *picture* décrocher, descendre; *poster* décoller; *V* **peg.**

(b) (*dismantle*) *scaffolding, machine* démonter; *building* démolir.

(c) (*write etc*) *notes, letter* prendre; *address, details* prendre, noter, inscrire.

2 takedown* *adj V* **take 2.**

take from *vt fus* = **take away from;** *V* **take away.**

take in *vt sep* **(a)** *chairs, harvest* rentrer; *person* faire entrer; *lodgers* prendre; *friend* recevoir; *orphan, stray dog* recueillir; *newspaper etc* prendre, recevoir. **she takes in sewing** elle fait *or* prend de la couture à domicile.

(b) *skirt, dress, waistband* reprendre; *knitting* diminuer.

(c) (*include, cover*) couvrir, inclure, englober, embrasser. **we cannot take in all the cases** nous ne pouvons pas couvrir *or* inclure tous les cas; **this takes in all possibilities** ceci englobe *or* embrasse toutes les possibilités; (*fig*) **we took in Venice on the way home** nous avons visité Venise sur le chemin du retour.

(d) (*grasp, understand*) saisir, comprendre. **that child takes everything in** rien n'échappe à cet enfant; **the children were taking it all in** les enfants étaient tout oreilles; **she couldn't take in his death at first** dans les premiers temps elle ne pouvait pas se faire à l'idée de sa mort; **he hadn't fully taken in that she was dead** il n'avait pas (vraiment) réalisé qu'elle était morte; **he took in the situation at a glance** il a apprécié la situation en un clin d'œil.

(e) (*: *cheat, deceive*) avoir*, rouler*. **I've been taken in** je me suis laissé avoir*, j'ai été roulé*; **he's easily taken in** il se fait facilement avoir*; **to be taken in by appearances** se laisser prendre aux *or* tromper par les apparences; **I was taken in by his disguise** je me suis laissé prendre à son déguisement.

take off 1 *vi [person]* partir (*for* pour); *[aircraft]* décoller; *[high jumper etc]* s'élancer. **the plane took off for Berlin** l'avion s'est envolé pour Berlin.

2 *vt sep* **(a)** (*remove*) *garment* enlever, ôter, retirer; *buttons, price tag, lid* enlever; *telephone receiver* décrocher; *item on menu, train, bus* supprimer. (*Med*) **they had to take his leg off** on a dû l'amputer d'une jambe; (*Comm*) **he took £5 off** il a baissé le prix de *or* il a fait un rabais de 5 livres, il a rabattu 5 livres sur le prix.

(b) (*lead etc away*) *person, car* emmener. **he took her off to lunch** il l'a emmenée déjeuner; **to take sb off to jail** emmener qn en prison; **he was taken off to hospital** on l'a transporté à l'hôpital; **after the wreck a boat took the crew off** une embarcation est venue sauver l'équipage du navire naufragé; **to take o.s. off** s'en aller.

(c) (*imitate*) imiter, pasticher.

3 takeoff *n V* **take 2.**

take on 1 *vi* **(a)** *[song, fashion etc]* prendre, marcher*.

(b) (*: *be upset*) s'en faire*.

2 *vt sep* **(a)** *work, responsibility* prendre, accepter, se charger de; *bet* accepter; *challenger* (*for game/fight*) accepter de jouer/de se battre contre. **I'll take you on** (*Betting*) je parie avec vous; (*Sport*) je joue contre vous; **he has taken on more than he bargained for** il n'avait pas compté prendre une si lourde responsabilité.

(b) *employee* prendre, embaucher; *cargo, passenger* embarquer, prendre; *form, qualities* prendre, revêtir.

take out 1 *vt sep* **(a)** (*lead, carry outside*) *prisoner* faire sortir; *chair etc* sortir. **they took us out to see the sights** ils nous ont emmenés visiter la ville; **he took her out to lunch/the theatre** il l'a emmenée déjeuner/au théâtre; **he has often taken her out** il l'a souvent sortie; **I'm going to take the children/dog out** je vais sortir les enfants/le chien.

(b) (*from pocket, drawer*) prendre (*from, of* dans); (*remove*) sortir, retirer, enlever, ôter (*from, of* de); *tooth* arracher; *appendix, tonsils* enlever; *stain* ôter, enlever (*from* de). **take your hands out of your pockets** sors *or* enlève *or* retire tes mains de tes poches; (*fig*) **that will take you out of yourself a little** cela vous changera un peu les idées; (*fig*) **that sort of work certainly takes it out of you*** il n'y a pas de doute que ces choses-là fatiguent* beaucoup; **when he got the sack he took it out on the dog*** quand il a été mis à la porte il s'est défoulé* sur le chien; **don't take it out on me!*** ce n'est pas la peine de t'en prendre à moi!; **don't take your bad temper out on me*** ne passez pas votre mauvaise humeur sur moi.

(c) *insurance* prendre, contracter; *patent* prendre; *licence* se procurer.

2 takeout *adj, n V* **take 2.**

take over 1 *vi [dictator, army, political party etc]* prendre le pouvoir. **to take over from sb** prendre la relève *or* le relai de qn; **let him take over** cédez-lui la place.

2 *vt sep* **(a)** (*escort or carry across*) **he took me over to the island in his boat** il m'a transporté jusqu'à l'île dans son bateau; **will you take me over to the other side?** voulez-vous me faire traverser?

(b) (*assume responsibility for*) *business, shop, materials, goods, furniture etc* reprendre; *new car* prendre livraison de; *sb's debts* prendre à sa charge. **he took over the shop from his father** il a pris la suite de son père dans le magasin; **he took over the job from X** c'est lui qui a pris la succession de X; **I took over his duties** je l'ai remplacé dans ses fonctions; **he took over the leadership of the party when Smith resigned** il a remplacé Smith à la tête du parti après la démission de celui-ci.

(c) (*Fin*) *another company* racheter. (*fig*) **the tourists have taken over Venice** les touristes ont envahi Venise.

3 takeover *n, adj V* **take 2.**

take to *vt fus* **(a)** (*conceive liking for*) *person* se prendre d'amitié pour, se prendre de sympathie pour, sympathiser avec; *game, action, study* prendre goût à, mordre à:. **I didn't take to the idea** l'idée ne m'a rien dit; **they took to each other at once** ils se sont plu immédiatement; **I didn't take to him** il ne m'a pas beaucoup plu.

(b) (*start, adopt*) *habit* prendre; *hobby* se mettre à. **to take to drink/drugs** se mettre à boire/à se droguer; **she took to telling everyone ...** elle s'est mise à dire à tout le monde ... .

(c) to take to one's bed s'aliter; **to take to the woods** *[walker]* passer par les bois; *[hunted man]* s'enfuir à travers bois; (*Naut*) **to take to the boats** abandonner *or* évacuer le navire; *V* **heel**[1] *etc.*

take up 1 *vi*: **to take up with sb** se lier avec qn, se prendre d'amitié pour qn.

2 *vt sep* **(a)** (*lead, carry upstairs, uphill etc*) *person* faire monter; *object* monter.

(b) (*lift*) *object from ground etc* ramasser, prendre; *carpet* enlever; *roadway, pavement* dépaver; *dress, hem, skirt* raccourcir; *passenger* prendre; (*fig: after interruption*) *one's work, book etc* reprendre, se remettre à, continuer; *conversation, discussion, story* reprendre (le fil de); *V* **cudgel** *etc.*

(c) (*occupy*) *space* occuper, tenir, prendre; *time* prendre, demander; *attention* occuper, absorber. **he's very taken up** il est très pris; **he's quite taken up with her** il ne pense plus qu'à elle; **he's completely taken up with his plan** il est tout entier à son projet; **it takes up too much room** cela prend *or* occupe trop de place; **it takes up all my free time** cela (me) prend tout mon temps libre.

(d) (*absorb*) *liquids* absorber. **to take up the slack in a rope** tendre une corde.

(e) (*raise question of*) *subject* aborder. **I'll take that up with him** je lui en parlerai.

(f) (*start learning, doing etc*) *hobby, subject, sport, languages etc* se mettre à; *career* embrasser; *method* adopter, retenir; *challenge* relever; *shares* souscrire à; *person* (*as friend*) adopter; (*as protégé*) prendre en main. (*fig*) **I'll take you up on your promise** je mettrai votre parole à l'épreuve; **I'll take you up on that some day** je m'en souviendrai à l'occasion, un jour je vous prendrai au mot.

(g) (*understand*) comprendre. **you've taken me up wrongly** vous m'avez mal compris.

taken ['teɪkən] **1** *ptp of* take.

2 *adj* **(a)** *seat, place* pris, occupé.

(b) to be very ~ with sb/sth être très impressionné par qn/qch; **I'm not very ~ with him** il ne m'a pas fait une grosse impression; **I'm quite ~ with** *or* **by that idea** cette idée me plaît énormément.

taker ['teɪkəʳ] *n*: **~s of snuff** les gens qui prisent; **drug-~s** les drogués *mpl*; **at £5 he found no ~s** il n'a pas trouvé d'acheteurs *or* de preneurs pour 5 livres; **this suggestion found no ~s** cette suggestion n'a été relevée par personne.

taking ['teɪkɪŋ] **1** *adj person, manners* engageant, attirant, séduisant. **2** *n* **(a) it is yours for the ~** tu n'as qu'à (te donner la peine de) le prendre. **(b)** (*Comm*) **~s** recette *f*. **(c)** (*Mil: capture*) prise *f*.

talc [tælk] *n*, **talcum (powder)** ['tælkəm(ˌpaʊdəʳ)] *n* talc *m*.

tale [teɪl] **1** *n* (*story*) conte *m*, histoire *f*; (*legend*) histoire, légende *f*; (*account*) récit *m*, histoire (*pej*). **'T~s of King Arthur'** 'La Légende du Roi Arthur'; **he told us the ~ of his adventures** il nous a fait le récit de ses aventures; **I've heard that ~ before** j'ai déjà entendu cette histoire-là quelque part; **I've been hearing ~s about you** on m'a dit *or* raconté des choses sur vous; **to tell ~s** rapporter, cafarder*; (*fig*) **to tell ~s out of school** vendre la mèche, raconter ce qu'on devait (*or* doit *etc*) taire; *V* **fairy, old, woe** *etc*.

2 *cpd*: **talebearer** rapporteur *m*, -euse *f*, cafard* *m*; **talebearing, taletelling** rapportage *m*, cafardage* *m*.

talent ['tælənt] **1** *n* **(a)** don *m*, talent *m*; (*U*) talent. **to have a ~ for drawing** être doué pour le dessin, avoir un don *or* du talent pour le dessin; **a writer of great ~** un écrivain de grand talent *or* très talentueux; **he encourages young ~** il encourage les jeunes talents; **he is looking for ~ amongst the schoolboy players** il cherche de futurs grands joueurs parmi les lycéens; (*attractive people*) **there's not much ~ here tonight**‡ (*amongst the girls*) il n'y a pas grand-chose comme minettes‡ *or* nénettes‡ ici ce soir; (*amongst the boys*) il n'y a pas grand-chose comme types bien* ici ce soir.

(b) (*coin*) talent *m*.

2 *cpd*: **talent scout, talent spotter** (*Cine, Theat*) dénicheur *m*, -euse *f* de vedettes; (*Sport*) dénicheur, -euse de futurs grands joueurs.

talented ['tæləntɪd] *adj person* talentueux, doué; *book, painting etc* plein de talent.

talisman ['tælɪzmən] *n* talisman *m*.

talk [tɔːk] **1** *n* **(a)** conversation *f*, discussion *f*; (*more formal*) entretien *m*; (*chat*) causerie *f*. **during his ~ with the Prime Minister** pendant son entretien avec le Premier ministre; **I enjoyed our (little) ~** notre causerie *or* notre petite conversation m'a été très agréable; **we've had several ~s about this** nous en avons parlé *or* discuté plusieurs fois; **I must have a ~ with him** (*gen*) il faut que je lui parle (*subj*); (*warning, threatening etc*) j'ai à lui parler; **we must have a ~ some time** il faudra que nous nous rencontrions (*subj*) un jour pour discuter *or* causer.

(b) (*informal lecture*) exposé *m* (*on* sur); (*less academic or technical*) causerie *f* (*on* sur). **to give a ~** faire un exposé, donner une causerie (*on* sur); **Mr X has come to give us a ~ on ...** M X est venu nous parler de ...; **to give a ~ on the radio** parler à la radio.

(c) (*U*) propos *mpl*; (*gossip*) bavardage(s) *m(pl)*; (*pej*) racontars *mpl*. **the ~ was all about the wedding** les propos tournaient autour du mariage; **you should hear the ~!** si tu savais ce qu'on raconte!; **there is (some) ~ of his returning** (*it is being discussed*) il est question qu'il revienne; (*it is being rumoured*) on dit qu'il va peut-être revenir, le bruit court qu'il va revenir; **there was no ~ of his resigning** il n'a pas été question qu'il démissionne (*subj*); **it's common ~ that ...** on dit partout que ..., tout le monde dit que ...; **it's just ~** ce ne sont que des on-dit *or* des racontars *or* des bavardages; **there has been a lot of ~ about her** il a beaucoup été question d'elle; on a raconté beaucoup d'histoires sur elle (*pej*); **I've heard a lot of ~ about the new factory** j'ai beaucoup entendu parler de la nouvelle usine; **all that ~ about what he was going to do!** toutes ces vaines paroles sur ce qu'il allait faire!; (*pej*) **he's all ~** c'est un grand vantard *or* hâbleur; **it was all (big) ~** tout ça c'était du vent*; **she's/it's the ~ of the town** on ne parle que d'elle/de cela; *V* **baby, idle, small** *etc*.

2 *cpd*: (*Rad/TV*) **talk show** causerie *f or* tête à tête *m or* entretien *m* (radiodiffusé(e)/télévisé(e)).

3 *vi* **(a)** (*speak*) parler (*about, of* de); (*chatter*) bavarder, causer. **he can't ~ yet** il ne parle pas encore; **after days of torture he finally ~ed** après plusieurs jours de torture, il a enfin parlé; **I'll make you ~!** (avec moi) tu vas parler!; **now you're ~ing!*** voilà qui devient intéressant!; **it's easy** *or* **all right for him to ~!** il peut parler!; **look who's ~ing!*** tu peux toujours parler, toi!; (*fig*) **to ~ through one's hat*** dire n'importe quoi; **he was just ~ing for the sake of ~ing** il parlait pour ne rien dire; **he ~s too much** (*too loquacious*) il parle trop; (*indiscreet*) il ne sait pas se taire; **don't ~ to me like that!** ne me parle pas sur ce ton!; **do what he tells you because he knows what he's ~ing about** fais ce qu'il te demande parce qu'il sait ce qu'il dit; **he knows what he's ~ing about when he's on the subject of cars** il s'y connaît quand il parle (de) voitures; **he doesn't know what he's ~ing about** il ne sait pas ce qu'il dit; **I'm not ~ing about you** ce n'est pas de toi que je parle, il ne s'agit pas de toi; **he was ~ing of** *or* **about going to Greece** il parlait d'aller en Grèce; **the marriage was much ~ed of in the town** toute la ville parlait du mariage; **his much ~ed-of holiday never happened** ses fameuses vacances ne sont jamais arrivées; **I'm not ~ing to him any more** je ne lui adresse plus la parole, je ne lui cause plus*; **~ing of films, have you seen ...?** en parlant de *or* à propos de films, avez-vous vu ...?; **~ about a stroke of luck!*** tu parles d'une aubaine!*; *V* **big**.

(b) (*converse*) parler (*to* à, *with* avec), discuter (*to, with* avec); (*more formally*) s'entretenir (*to, with* avec); (*chat*) causer (*to, with* avec); (*gossip*) parler, causer (*about* de), jaser (*pej*) (*about* sur). **who were you ~ing to?** à qui parlais-tu?; **I saw them ~ing (to each other)** je les ai vus en conversation l'un avec l'autre; **to ~ to o.s.** se parler tout seul; **I'll ~ to you about that tomorrow** je t'en parlerai demain; (*threateningly*) j'aurai deux mots à te dire là-dessus demain; **we were just ~ing of** *or* **about you** justement nous parlions de toi; **the Foreign Ministers ~ed about the crisis in China** les ministres des Affaires étrangères se sont entretenus de la crise chinoise; **I have ~ed with him several times** j'ai eu plusieurs conversations avec lui; **try to keep him ~ing** essaie de le faire parler aussi longtemps que possible; **to get o.s. ~ed about** faire parler de soi; *V* **nineteen** *etc*.

4 *vt* **(a)** *a language, slang* parler. **to ~ business/politics** parler affaires/politique; **to ~ nonsense** *or* **rubbish*** *or* **tripe**‡ raconter des idioties, dire n'importe quoi *or* des conneries‡; **he's ~ing sense** c'est la voix de la raison qui parle, ce qu'il dit est le bon sens même; **~ sense!** ne dis pas n'importe quoi!; *V* **hind**[2], **shop, turkey** *etc*.

(b) to ~ sb into doing sth amener qn à *or* persuader qn de faire qch (*à force de paroles*); **I managed to ~ him out of doing it** je suis arrivé à le dissuader de le faire (en lui parlant); **she ~ed him into a better mood** elle l'a remis de meilleure humeur en lui parlant; **he ~ed himself into the job** il a si bien parlé qu'on lui a offert le poste.

talk away *vi* parler *or* discuter sans s'arrêter, ne pas arrêter de parler. **we talked away for hours** nous avons passé des heures à parler *or* discuter; **she was talking away about her plans when suddenly ...** elle était partie à parler de ses projets quand soudain ... .

talk back *vi* répondre (insolemment) (*to sb* à qn).

talk down 1 *vi*: **to talk down to sb** parler à qn comme à un enfant.

2 *vt sep* **(a)** (*silence*) **they talked him down** leurs flots de paroles l'ont réduit au silence.

(b) (*Aviat*) *pilot, aircraft* aider à atterrir par radio-contrôle.

talk on *vi* parler *or* discuter sans s'arrêter, ne pas arrêter de parler. **she talked on and on about it** elle en a parlé pendant des heures et des heures.

talk out *vt sep* (*Parl*) **to talk out a bill** prolonger la discussion d'un projet de loi jusqu'à ce qu'il soit trop tard pour le voter.

talk over *vt sep* **(a)** *question, problem* discuter (de), débattre. **let's talk it over** discutons-en entre nous; **I must talk it over with my wife first** je dois d'abord en parler à ma femme.

(b) = **talk round 1**.

talk round 1 *vt sep*: **to talk sb round** amener qn à changer d'avis, gagner qn à son avis, convaincre *or* persuader qn.

2 *vt fus problem, subject* tourner autour de. **they talked round it all evening** ils ont tourné autour du pot toute la soirée.

talkative ['tɔːkətɪv] *adj* bavard, loquace, volubile.

talkativeness ['tɔːkətɪvnɪs] *n* volubilité *f*, loquacité *f* (*liter*).

talker ['tɔːkəʳ] *n* parleur *m*, -euse *f*, causeur *m*, -euse *f*, bavard(e) *m(f)* (*sometimes pej*). **he's a great ~** c'est un grand bavard *or* un causeur intarissable, il a la langue bien pendue*; **he's a terrible ~** c'est un vrai moulin à paroles.

talkie* ['tɔːkɪ] *n* (*Cine*) film parlant. **the ~s** le cinéma parlant; *V* **walkie-talkie**.

talking ['tɔːkɪŋ] **1** *n* bavardage *m*. **he did all the ~** il a fait tous les frais de la conversation; **that's enough ~!** assez de bavardages!, assez bavardé!

2 *adj doll, parrot, film* parlant.

3 *cpd*: **talking book** livre enregistré; **talking point** sujet *m* de discussion *or* de conversation; **talking-to*** attrapade* *f*; **to give sb a (good) talking-to*** passer un bon savon à qn*.

tall [tɔːl] **1** *adj person* grand, de haute taille; *building etc* haut, élevé. **how ~ is that mast?** quelle est la hauteur de ce mât?; **how ~ are you?** combien mesurez-vous?; **he is 6 feet ~** ≃ il mesure 1 mètre 80; **~ and slim** élancé; **he is ~er than his brother** il est plus grand que son frère; **she is ~er than me by a head** elle me dépasse de la tête; **she wears high heels to make herself look ~er** elle porte des talons hauts pour se grandir; (*fig*) **he told me a ~ story about ...** il m'a raconté une histoire à dormir debout sur ...; **that's a ~ story!** elle est forte, celle-là!*; **that's a ~ order!** c'est demander un peu trop!, c'est pousser (un peu)!*

2 *cpd*: (*Brit*) **tallboy** commode *f*.

tallness ['tɔːlnɪs] *n* [*person*] grande taille; [*building etc*] hauteur *f*.

tallow ['tæləʊ] *n* suif *m*. **~ candle** chandelle *f*.

tally ['tælɪ] **1** *n* (*Hist: stick*) taille *f* (*latte de bois*); (*count*) compte *m*. **to keep a ~ of** (*count*) tenir le compte de; (*mark off on list*) pointer.

2 *vi* s'accorder (*with* avec), correspondre (*with* à).

tallyho ['tælɪ'həʊ] *excl, n* taïaut (*m*).
talon ['tælən] *n* **(a)** *[eagle etc]* serre *f*; *[tiger etc, person]* griffe *f*. **(b)** (*Archit, Cards*) talon *m*.
tamable ['teɪməbl] *adj* = **tameable.**
tamarin ['tæmərɪn] *n* tamarin *m* (*Zool*).
tamarind ['tæmərɪnd] *n* (*fruit*) tamarin *m*; (*tree*) tamarinier *m*.
tamarisk ['tæmərɪsk] *n* tamaris *m*.
tambour ['tæm,bʊəʳ] *n* (*Archit, Mus*) tambour *m*; (*Embroidery*) métier *m or* tambour à broder.
tambourine [ˌtæmbə'riːn] *n* tambour *m* de basque, tambourin *m*.
tame [teɪm] **1** *adj bird, animal* apprivoisé; (*fig*) *story, match* insipide, fade. **to become** *or* **grow ~(r)** s'apprivoiser; **the sparrows are quite ~** les moineaux sont presque apprivoisés *or* ne sont pas farouches; (*hum*) **let's ask our ~ American** demandons-le à notre Américain de service (*hum*); (*hum*) **I really need a ~ osteopath** ce qu'il me faudrait vraiment c'est un ostéopathe à demeure.
2 *vt bird, wild animal* apprivoiser; *large or fierce animal* dresser; *esp lion, tiger* dompter; (*fig*) *passion* maîtriser; *person* mater, soumettre.
tameable ['teɪməbl] *adj* (*V* **tame 2**) apprivoisable; dressable; domptable.
tamely ['teɪmlɪ] *adv agree* docilement. **the story ends ~** l'histoire finit en eau de boudin.
tamer ['teɪməʳ] *n* dresseur *m*, -euse *f*. **lion-~** dompteur *m*, -euse *f* (de lions), belluaire *m*.
taming ['teɪmɪŋ] *n* (*U*) (*gen*) apprivoisement *m*; *[circus animals]* dressage *m*, domptage *m*. **'The T~ of the Shrew'** 'La Mégère Apprivoisée'.
tam o'shanter [ˌtæmə'ʃæntəʳ] *n* béret écossais.
tamp [tæmp] *vt earth* damer, tasser; *tobacco* tasser. (*in blasting*) **to ~ a drill hole** bourrer un trou de mine à l'argile *or* au sable.
tamper ['tæmpəʳ] *vi*: **to ~ with** *machinery, car, brakes, safe etc* toucher à (*sans permission*); *lock* essayer de crocheter; *document, text* altérer, fausser, falsifier; (*Jur*) *evidence* falsifier; *sb's papers, possessions* toucher à, mettre le nez dans*.
tampon ['tæmpən] *n* (*Med*) tampon *m*.
tan [tæn] **1** *n* (*also* **sun~**) bronzage *m*, hâle *m*. **she's got a lovely ~** elle a un beau bronzage, elle est bien bronzée.
2 *adj* ocre, brun roux *inv*.
3 *vt* **(a)** *skins* tanner. (*fig*) **to ~ sb*, to ~ sb's hide (for him)*** rosser qn*, tanner le cuir à qn‡.
(b) *[sun] sunbather, holiday-maker* brunir, bronzer, hâler; *sailor, farmer etc* hâler, basaner, tanner. **to get ~ned = to tan;** *V* **4.**
4 *vi* bronzer, brunir.
tandem ['tændəm] **1** *n* tandem *m*. **2** *adv* (*also fig*) en tandem.
tang [tæŋ] *n* **(a)** (*taste*) saveur forte (et piquante); (*smell*) senteur *or* odeur forte (et piquante). **the salt ~ of the sea air** l'odeur caractéristique de la marée. **(b)** *[file, knife]* soie *f*.
tangent ['tændʒənt] *n* (*Math*) tangente *f*. (*fig*) **to go off** *or* **fly off at a ~** partir dans une digression.
tangential [tæn'dʒenʃəl] *adj* tangentiel.
tangerine [ˌtændʒə'riːn] **1** *n* (*also* **~ orange**) mandarine *f*. **2** *adj* (*colour*) mandarine *inv*.
tangibility [ˌtændʒɪ'bɪlɪtɪ] *n* tangibilité *f*.
tangible ['tændʒəbl] *adj* tangible, palpable; (*fig*) *proof, result* tangible; *assets* matériel, réel.
tangibly ['tændʒəblɪ] *adv* tangiblement, manifestement.
Tangier [tæn'dʒɪəʳ] *n*, **Tangiers** [tæn'dʒɪəz] *n* Tanger.
tangle ['tæŋgl] **1** *n [wool, string, rope]* enchevêtrement *m*; *[creepers, bushes, weeds]* fouillis *m*, enchevêtrement; (*fig: muddle*) confusion *f*. **to get into a ~** *[string, rope, wool]* s'entortiller, s'embrouiller, s'enchevêtrer; *[hair]* s'emmêler, s'enchevêtrer; (*fig*) *[accounts etc]* s'embrouiller; *[traffic]* se bloquer; *[person]* s'embrouiller, être empêtré; **he got into a ~ when he tried to explain** il s'est embrouillé dans ses explications; **I'm in a ~ with the accounts** je suis empêtré dans les comptes; **the whole affair was a hopeless ~** toute cette histoire était affreusement confuse *or* était affreusement embrouillée *or* était un véritable embrouillamini*.
2 *vt* (*also* **~ up**: *lit, fig*) enchevêtrer, embrouiller, emmêler. **~d** *string, rope, wool* embrouillé, enchevêtré, entortillé; *hair* emmêlé, enchevêtré; (*fig*) **a ~d web of lies** un inextricable tissu de mensonges; **to get ~d (up) = to get into a tangle** (*V* **1**).
3 *vi* (**fig*) **to ~ with sb** se frotter à qn, se colleter avec qn*; **they ~d over whose fault it was** ils se sont colletés* sur la question de savoir à qui était la faute.
tango ['tæŋgəʊ] **1** *n, pl* **~s** tango *m*. **2** *vi* danser le tango.
tank [tæŋk] **1** *n* **(a)** (*container*) (*for storage*) réservoir *m*, cuve *f*; (*esp for rainwater*) citerne *f*; (*for gas*) réservoir; (*Aut: petrol* ~) réservoir (à essence); (*for transporting*) réservoir, cuve, (*esp oil*) tank *m*; (*for fermenting, processing etc*) cuve (*also Phot*); (*for fish*) aquarium *m*. **fuel ~** réservoir à carburant; *V* **septic** *etc*.
(b) (*Mil*) char *m* (d'assaut *or* de combat), tank *m*.
2 *cpd*: (*US Rail*) **tank car** wagon-citerne *m*; (*US fig*) **tank town** petite ville (perdue); (*Mil*) **tank trap** fossé *m* antichar; (*US*) **tank truck** camion-citerne *m*.
tank up 1 *vi* (*Aut**) faire le plein; (*‡fig: drink a lot*) boire un bon coup*.
2 *vt sep* (***) *car etc* remplir d'essence. (*fig*) **to be tanked up‡** être soûl* *or* bituré‡.
tankard ['tæŋkəd] *n* chope *f*, pot *m* à bière.
tanker ['tæŋkəʳ] *n* (*truck*) camion-citerne *m*; (*ship*) pétrolier *m*, tanker *m*; (*aircraft*) avion-ravitailleur *m*; (*Rail*) wagon-citerne *m*.
tankful ['tæŋkfʊl] *n*: **a ~ of petrol** un réservoir (plein) d'essence; **a ~ of water** une citerne (pleine) d'eau.
tanned [tænd] *adj* (*also* **sun~**) *sunbather, holiday-maker* bronzé, bruni, hâlé; *sailor, farmer* hâlé, basané, tanné.
tanner[1] ['tænəʳ] *n* tanneur *m*.
tanner[2]* ['tænəʳ] *n* (*Brit*) (ancienne) pièce *f* de six pence.
tannery ['tænərɪ] *n* tannerie *f* (*établissement*).
tannic ['tænɪk] *adj* tannique.
tannin ['tænɪn] *n* tan(n)in *m*.
tanning ['tænɪŋ] *n [hides]* tannage *m*; (*‡fig: beating*) tannée‡ *f*, raclée* *f*, correction *f*.
tannoy ['tænɔɪ] *n* ® système *m* de haut-parleurs. **on** *or* **over the ~** par le(s) haut-parleur(s).
tansy ['tænzɪ] *n* tanaisie *f*.
tantalize ['tæntəlaɪz] *vt* mettre au supplice (*fig*), tourmenter (*par de faux espoirs*).
tantalizing ['tæntəlaɪzɪŋ] *adj offer, suggestion* terriblement tentant; *smell* terriblement appétissant; *slowness etc* désespérant. **it's ~!** c'est terriblement tentant!, (*stronger*) c'est le supplice de Tantale!
tantalizingly ['tæntəlaɪzɪŋlɪ] *adv* d'une façon cruellement tentante. **~ slowly** avec une lenteur désespérante.
tantamount ['tæntəmaʊnt] *adj*: **~ to** équivalent à; **it's ~ to failure** autant dire un échec, cela équivaut à un échet.
tantrum ['tæntrəm] *n* (*also* **temper ~**) crise *f* de colère *or* de rage. **to have** *or* **throw a ~** piquer une colère *or* une crise (de rage).
Tanzania [ˌtænzə'nɪə] *n* Tanzanie *f*.
Tanzanian [ˌtænzə'nɪən] **1** *adj* tanzanien. **2** *n* Tanzanien(ne) *m(f)*.
tap[1] [tæp] **1** *n* (*Brit: for water, gas etc*) robinet *m*; (*Brit: ~ on barrel etc*) cannelle *f*, robinet, chantepleure *f*; (*plug for barrel*) bonde *f*. **beer on ~** bière *f* en fût; (*fig*) **there are funds/resources on ~** il y a des fonds/des ressources disponibles; **he seems to have unlimited money on ~** il a l'air d'avoir de l'argent en veux-tu en voilà*; **there are plenty of helpers on ~*** il y a autant d'assistants que l'on veut.
2 *cpd*: **taproom** salle *f* (de bistro); (*Bot*) **taproot** pivot *m*, racine pivotante; (*Brit*) **tap water** eau *f* du robinet.
3 *vt cask, barrel* percer, mettre en perce; *pine* gemmer; *other tree* inciser; (*Elec*) *current* capter; *wire* brancher; *telephone* mettre sur écoute; *telephone line* brancher (*pour mettre un téléphone sur écoute*); (*fig*) *resources, supplies* exploiter, utiliser. **to ~ a tree for its rubber, to ~ (off) rubber from a tree** inciser un arbre pour en tirer le latex; **my phone is being ~ped** mon téléphone est sur écoute; (*fig*) **to ~ sb for money*** emprunter *or* taper* de l'argent à qn; **they ~ped her for a loan*** ils lui ont demandé un prêt; **to ~ sb for information** soutirer des informations à qn.
tap[2] [tæp] **1** *n* **(a)** petit coup, petite tape. **there was a ~ at the door** on a frappé doucement *or* légèrement à la porte.
(b) (*Mil*) **~s** (sonnerie *f* de) l'extinction *f* des feux.
2 *cpd*: **tap-dance** (*n*) claquettes *fpl*; (*vi*) faire des claquettes; **tap-dancer** danseur *m*, -euse *f* de claquettes.
3 *vi* frapper légèrement *or* doucement, taper (doucement), tapoter. **to ~ on** *or* **at the door** frapper doucement *or* légèrement à la porte.
4 *vt* frapper légèrement *or* doucement, taper (doucement), tapoter. **she ~ped the child on the cheek** elle a tapoté la joue de l'enfant; **he ~ped me on the shoulder** il m'a tapé sur l'épaule; **to ~ in/out a nail** enfoncer/enlever un clou à petits coups.
tap out *vt sep* **(a)** *one's pipe* débourrer; *V also* **tap**[2] **4.**
(b) to tap out a message in Morse transmettre un message en morse.
tape [teɪp] **1** *n* **(a)** (*gen: of cloth, paper, metal*) ruban *m*, bande *f*; (*Sewing: decoration*) ruban, ganse *f*; (*Sewing: for binding*) extra-fort *m*; (*for parcels, documents*) bolduc *m*; (*sticky ~*) scotch *m* ®, ruban adhésif; (*Med*) sparadrap *m*; (*for recording*) bande (magnétique); (*Sport*) fil *m* d'arrivée; (*at opening ceremonies*) ruban. **ticker-~** ruban (de papier) perforé; **the message was coming through on the ~** le message nous parvenait sur ruban perforé; *V* **insulate, red** *etc*.
(b) = tape measure; *V* **2.**
2 *cpd*: **tape deck** platine *f* de magnétophone; (*Brit*) **tape machine** téléscripteur *m*, téléimprimeur *m*; **tape measure** mètre *m* à ruban, centimètre *m* (*esp Sewing*); **tape-record** enregistrer (au magnétophone *or* sur bande); **tape recorder** magnétophone *m*; **tape recording** enregistrement *m* (magnétique *or* au magnétophone); **tapeworm** ténia *m*, ver *m* solitaire.
3 *vt* **(a)** (*also* **~ up**) *parcel etc* attacher *or* ficeler avec du ruban *or* du bolduc; (*with sticky tape*) scotcher*, coller avec du scotch ® *or* du ruban adhésif; (*also* **~ up, ~ together**) *broken vase etc* recoller avec du scotch *etc*. (*Brit fig*) **I've got him ~d*** je sais ce qu'il vaut; **I've got it all ~d*** je sais parfaitement de quoi il retourne*; **they had the game/situation ~d*** ils avaient le jeu/la situation bien en main; **he's got the job ~d*** il sait parfaitement ce qu'il y a à faire, il peut le faire les doigts dans le nez‡.
(b) (*record*) *song, message* enregistrer (sur bande *or* au magnétophone); *video material* enregistrer.
taper ['teɪpəʳ] **1** *n* (*for lighting*) bougie fine (*pour allumer les cierges, bougies etc*); (*Rel: narrow candle*) cierge *m*.
2 *vt column, table leg, trouser leg, aircraft wing* fuseler; *stick, end of belt* tailler en pointe, effiler; *hair* effiler; *structure, shape* terminer en pointe.
3 *vi [column, table leg, trouser leg]* finir en fuseau; *[stick, end of belt]* s'effiler; *[hair]* être effilé; *[structure, outline]* se terminer en pointe, s'effiler.
taper off 1 *vi [sound]* se taire peu à peu; *[storm]* s'estomper, aller en diminuant; *[speech, conversation]* s'effilocher. **the end**

tapers off to a point le bout se termine en pointe.
2 *vt sep* finir en pointe.
tapered ['teɪpəd] *adj*, **tapering** ['teɪpərɪŋ] *adj column, table leg, trouser leg* fuselé, en fuseau; *stick* pointu; *hair* effilé; *structure, outline* en pointe. ~ **fingers** doigts fuselés.
tapestry ['tæpɪstrɪ] *n* tapisserie *f*.
tapioca [,tæpɪ'əʊkə] *n* tapioca *m*.
tapir ['teɪpəʳ] *n* tapir *m*.
tappet ['tæpɪt] *n* (*Tech*) poussoir *m* (de soupape).
tar[1] [tɑːʳ] **1** *n* (*U*) goudron *m*; (*on roads*) goudron, bitume *m*.
2 *vt fence etc* goudronner; *road* goudronner, bitumer. **to ~ and feather sb** passer qn au goudron et à la plume; (*fig*) **they're all ~red with the same brush** ils sont tous à mettre dans le même sac*.
tar[2]*† [tɑːʳ] *n* (*sailor*) mathurin† *m*; *V* **jack**.
tarantella [,tærən'telə] *n* tarentelle *f*.
tarantula [tə'ræntjʊlə] *n* tarentule *f*.
tardily ['tɑːdɪlɪ] *adv* (*belatedly*) tardivement; (*slowly*) lentement; (*late*) en retard.
tardiness ['tɑːdɪnɪs] *n* (*U*) (*slowness*) lenteur *f*, manque *m* d'empressement (*in doing* à faire); (*unpunctuality*) manque de ponctualité.
tardy ['tɑːdɪ] *adj* (*belated*) tardif; (*unhurried*) lent, nonchalant; (*late*) en retard.
tare[1] [tɛəʳ] *n* (*weeds*) **~s**†† ivraie *f* (*U: liter*).
tare[2] [tɛəʳ] *n* (*Comm: weight*) tare *f* (*poids*).
target ['tɑːgɪt] **1** *n* (*Mil, Sport: for shooting practice; fig: of criticism etc*) cible *f*; (*Mil: in attack or mock attack; fig: objective*) but *m*, objectif *m*. **to be on ~** [*rocket, missile, bombs etc*] suivre la trajectoire prévue; (*fig*) [*remark, criticism*] mettre (en plein) dans le mille; (*in timing etc*) être (*or* arriver) à l'heure prévue; **dead on ~!** pile!; **they set themselves a ~ of £100** ils se sont fixés comme but *or* objectif de réunir (*or* de gagner *etc*) 100 livres; **the ~s for production** les objectifs de production.
2 *cpd date, amount etc* fixé, prévu. **target language** langue *f* d'arrivée, langue cible *inv*; (*Mil, Sport*) **target practice** exercices *mpl* de tir; (*Space*) **target vehicle** vaisseau-cible *m*.
tariff ['tærɪf] **1** *n* (*Econ: taxes*) tarif douanier; (*Comm: price list*) tarif, tableau *m* des prix. **2** *cpd*: (*Econ*) **tariff reform** réforme *f* des tarifs douaniers.
tarmac ['tɑːmæk] *n* ® (*esp Brit: U*) (*substance*) macadam *m* goudronné; (*airport runway*) piste *f*; (*airport apron*) aire *f* d'envol.
tarn [tɑːn] *n* petit lac (de montagne).
tarnish ['tɑːnɪʃ] **1** *vt* [*metal*] ternir; [*gilded frame etc*] dédorer; [*mirror*] désargenter; (*fig*) [*reputation, memory*] ternir. **2** *vi* se ternir; se dédorer; se désargenter. **3** *n* (*U*) ternissure *f*; dédorage *m*; désargentage *m*.
tarot ['tærəʊ] *n* (*U*) tarot(s) *m(pl)*. ~ **card** tarot.
tarpaulin [tɑː'pɔːlɪn] *n* **(a)** (*U*) toile goudronnée. **(b)** (*sheet*) bâche *f* (goudronnée); (*on truck, over boat cargo*) prélart *m*.
tarpon ['tɑːpɒn] *n* tarpon *m*.
tarragon ['tærəgən] *n* estragon *m*. ~ **vinegar** vinaigre *m* à l'estragon.
tarry[1] ['tɑːrɪ] *adj substance* goudronneux, bitumeux; (*tar-stained*) taché *or* plein de goudron.
tarry[2] ['tærɪ] *vi* (*liter*) (*stay*) rester, demeurer; (*delay*) s'attarder, tarder.
tarsus ['tɑːsəs] *n, pl* **tarsi** ['tɑːsaɪ] tarse *m*.
tart[1] [tɑːt] *adj flavour, fruit* âpre, aigrelet, acidulé; *wine* aigrelet; (*fig*) acerbe.
tart[2] [tɑːt] *n* **(a)** (*esp Brit Culin*) tarte *f*; (*small*) tartelette *f*. **apple ~** tarte(lette) aux pommes.
(b) (*: prostitute*) poule*: *f*, grue*: *f*.
tart up*: *vt sep* (*Brit pej*) *house, car, design, scheme* rénover, retaper, rajeunir. **to tart o.s. up** (*dress*) s'attifer (comme une grue*:); (*make up*) se maquiller outrageusement.
tartan ['tɑːtən] **1** *n* tartan *m*. **2** *adj garment, fabric* écossais. ~ (**travelling**) **rug** plaid *m*.
tartar ['tɑːtəʳ] *n* (*U: Chem etc*) tartre *m*; *V* **cream**.
Tartar ['tɑːtəʳ] **1** *n* **(a)** Tartare *mf or* Tatar(e) *m(f)*.
(b) t~ personne *f* difficile *or* intraitable; (*woman*) mégère *f*, virago *f*; (*fig*) **to catch a t~** trouver à qui parler.
2 *adj* **(a)** (*Geog*) tartare *or* tatar.
(b) (*Culin*) **t~(e) sauce** sauce *f* tartare; **steak t~(e)** (steak *m*) tartare *m*.
tartaric [tɑː'tærɪk] *adj* tartrique.
tartly ['tɑːtlɪ] *adv* aigrement, d'une manière acerbe.
tartness ['tɑːtnɪs] *n* (*lit, fig*) aigreur *f*.
task [tɑːsk] **1** *n* tâche *f*, besogne *f*, travail *m*; (*Scol*) devoir *m*. **to take sb to ~** prendre qn à partie, réprimander qn (*for, about* pour).
2 *vt sb's brain, patience, imagination* mettre à l'épreuve; *sb's strength* éprouver. **it didn't ~ him too much** cela ne lui a pas demandé trop d'effort.
3 *cpd*: (*Mil etc*) **task force** détachement spécial (*affecté à un travail particulier*); (*Prov*) **poverty is a hard taskmaster** la misère est un tyran implacable; **he is a hard taskmaster** il ne plaisante pas avec le travail.
Tasmania [tæz'meɪnɪə] *n* Tasmanie *f*.
Tasmanian [tæz'meɪnɪən] **1** *adj* tasmanien. **2** *n* Tasmanien(ne) *m(f)*.
tassel ['tæsəl] *n* gland *m*; (*pompon*) pompon *m*.
taste [teɪst] **1** *n* **(a)** (*flavour*) goût *m*, saveur *f*. **it has an odd ~** cela a un drôle de goût; **it has no ~** cela n'a aucun goût *or* aucune saveur; **it left a bad ~ in the mouth** (*lit*) cela m'a (*or* lui a *etc*) laissé un goût déplaisant dans la bouche; (*fig*) j'en ai (*or* il en a *etc*) gardé une amertume.
(b) (*U: sense*) goût *m* (*also fig*). **sweet to the ~** (au goût) sucré; (*fig*) **to have (good) ~** avoir du goût, avoir bon goût; **he has no ~** il n'a aucun goût, il a très mauvais goût; **in good/bad ~** de bon/mauvais goût; **in poor** *or* **doubtful ~** d'un goût douteux; **people of ~** les gens de goût.
(c) to have a ~ of sth (*lit*) goûter (à) qch; (*fig*) goûter de qch; **would you like a ~ (of it)?** voulez-vous (y) goûter?; **he had a ~ of the cake** il a goûté au gâteau; **I gave him a ~ of the wine** je lui ai fait goûter le vin; (*fig*) **it gave him a ~ of military life/of the work** cela lui a donné un aperçu *or* un échantillon de la vie militaire/du travail; (*fig*) **to give sb a ~ of the whip** montrer à qn ce qui l'attend s'il ne marche pas droit; **a ~ of happiness** une idée du bonheur; **we got a ~ of his anger** il nous a donné un échantillon de sa colère; **it was a ~ of things to come** c'était un avant-goût de l'avenir.
(d) (*small amount, trace*) **a ~ of** (*gen*) un (tout) petit peu de; [*salt etc*] une pincée de; [*vinegar, cream, brandy*] une goutte de.
(e) (*liking*) goût *m*, penchant *m* (*for* pour). **it is to my ~** ça correspond à mon *or* mes goût(s); **to have a ~ for** avoir un penchant pour; **to get** *or* **acquire** *or* **develop a ~ for** prendre goût à; (*Culin*) **sweeten to ~** sucrer à volonté; **it's a matter of ~** c'est affaire de goût; **there's no accounting for ~** des goûts et des couleurs on ne discute pas; **each to his own ~, ~s differ** chacun son goût; **one's ~(s) in music** ses goûts musicaux; **she has expensive ~s** elle a un goût *or* un penchant pour tout ce qui est cher; **he has expensive ~s in cars** il a le goût des voitures de luxe.
2 *cpd*: **taste bud** papille gustative.
3 *vt* **(a)** (*perceive flavour of*) goûter, sentir. **I can't ~ the garlic** je ne sens pas (le goût de) l'ail; **I can't ~ anything when I have a cold** je trouve tout insipide quand j'ai un rhume; **you won't ~ it** tu n'en sentiras pas le goût.
(b) (*sample*) *food, drink* goûter à; (*esp for first time*) goûter de; (*to test quality*) *food* goûter; *wine* déguster; (*fig*) *power, freedom, success* goûter à, connaître. **just ~ this!** goûtez à ça!; **I haven't ~d salmon for years** ça fait des années que je n'ai pas mangé *or* goûté de saumon; **I have never ~d snails** je n'ai jamais mangé d'escargots; **he had not ~d food for a week** il n'avait rien mangé depuis une semaine; **~ the sauce before adding salt** goûtez la sauce avant d'ajouter du sel; **you must ~ my marmalade** je vais vous faire goûter de ma confiture d'oranges.
4 *vi* avoir un goût. **it doesn't ~ at all** cela n'a aucun goût; **to ~ bitter** avoir un goût amer; **to ~ good/bad** avoir bon/mauvais goût; **to ~ of** *or* **like sth** avoir un goût de qch; **it doesn't ~ of anything in particular** cela n'a pas de goût spécial; **it ~s all right to me** d'après moi cela a un goût normal.
tasteful ['teɪstfʊl] *adj* de bon goût, d'un goût sûr, élégant.
tastefully ['teɪstfəlɪ] *adv* avec goût.
tastefulness ['teɪstfʊlnɪs] *n* bon goût, goût sûr.
tasteless ['teɪstlɪs] *adj* sans saveur, fade (*pej*), insipide (*pej*); (*fig*) *remark etc* de mauvais goût.
tastelessly ['teɪstlɪslɪ] *adv* sans goût.
tastelessness ['teɪstlɪsnɪs] *n* manque *m* de saveur, fadeur *f* (*pej*); (*fig*) mauvais goût.
taster ['teɪstəʳ] *n* dégustateur *m*, -trice *f*.
tastiness ['teɪstɪnɪs] *n* saveur *f* agréable, goût *m* (délicieux).
tasty ['teɪstɪ] *adj* (*tasting good*) savoureux, délicieux; (*well-seasoned*) relevé, bien assaisonné.
tat[1] [tæt] **1** *vi* faire de la frivolité (*dentelle*). **2** *vt* faire en frivolité.
tat[2]* [tæt] *n* (*U: Brit pej: shabby clothes*) friperies *fpl*; (*goods*) camelote* *f*.
ta-ta*: ['tæ'tɑː] *excl* (*Brit*) au revoir!
tattered ['tætəd] *adj clothes, flag* en lambeaux, en loques, dépenaillé*; *book, handkerchief* en morceaux, tout déchiré; *sheet of paper, bed linen* en lambeaux, en morceaux; *person* déguenillé, dépenaillé*, loqueteux; *reputation* en miettes.
tatters ['tætəz] *npl* lambeaux *mpl*, loques *fpl*. **in ~ = tattered**.
tatting ['tætɪŋ] *n* (*U*) frivolité *f* (*dentelle*).
tattle ['tætl] **1** *vi* jaser, cancaner. **2** *n* (*U*) bavardage *m*, commérages *mpl*.
tattler ['tætləʳ] *n* (*man or woman*) commère *f* (*pej*), concierge* *mf* (*fig pej*).
tattoo[1] [tə'tuː] **1** *vt* tatouer. **2** *n* tatouage *m*.
tattoo[2] [tə'tuː] *n* (*Mil: on drum, bugle*) retraite *f*; (*Brit Mil: spectacle*) parade *f* militaire; (*gen: drumming*) battements *mpl*. **to beat a ~ on the drums** battre le tambour; (*fig*) **his fingers were beating a ~ on the table** il pianotait *or* tambourinait sur la table.
tatty* ['tætɪ] *adj* (*esp Brit*) *clothes, shoes, leather goods, furniture* fatigué; *paint* écaillé; *house* délabré; *plant, flowers* défraîchi; *poster, book* écorné. **she looked rather ~** elle était plutôt défraîchie.
taught [tɔːt] *pret, ptp of* **teach**.
taunt [tɔːnt] **1** *n* raillerie *f*, sarcasme *m*. **2** *vt* railler, persifler (*liter*). **to ~ sb with cowardice** taxer qn de lâcheté sur un ton railleur *or* persifleur.
taunting ['tɔːntɪŋ] *adj* railleur, persifleur, sarcastique.
tauntingly ['tɔːntɪŋlɪ] *adv* d'un ton railleur *or* persifleur *or* sarcastique.
tauromachy ['tɔːrəmækɪ] *n* (*liter*) tauromachie *f*.
Taurus ['tɔːrəs] *n* (*Astron*) le Taureau.
taut [tɔːt] *adj* (*lit, fig*) tendu.
tauten ['tɔːtn] **1** *vt* tendre. **2** *vi* se tendre.
tautness ['tɔːtnɪs] *n* tension *f* (*d'un cordage etc*).
tautological [,tɔːtə'lɒdʒɪkəl] *adj* tautologique.
tautology [tɔː'tɒlədʒɪ] *n* tautologie *f*.
tavern† ['tævən] *n* taverne† *f*, auberge *f*.
tawdriness ['tɔːdrɪnɪs] *n* [*goods*] qualité *f* médiocre; [*clothes*] mauvais goût tapageur; [*jewellery*] clinquant *m*; (*fig*) [*motive etc*] indignité *f*.
tawdry ['tɔːdrɪ] *adj goods* de camelote*; *clothes* criard,

tapageur, voyant; *jewellery* clinquant; (*fig*) *motive, affair etc* indigne.

tawny ['tɔːnɪ] *adj* fauve (*couleur*).

tax [tæks] **1** *n* (*on goods, services*) taxe *f*, impôt *m*; (*income* ~) impôts, contributions *fpl*. **before/after** ~ avant/après l'impôt; **half of it goes in** ~ j'en perds (*or* il en perd *etc*) la moitié en impôts *or* en contributions; **how much** ~ **do you pay?** combien d'impôts payez-vous?, à quoi se montent vos contributions?; **I paid £1,000 in** ~ **last year** j'ai payé 1.000 livres d'impôts *or* de contributions l'an dernier; **free of** ~ exempt d'impôt, exonéré; **to put** *or* **place** *or* **levy a** ~ **on sth** mettre une taxe *or* un impôt sur qch, taxer *or* imposer qch; **petrol** ~, ~ **on petrol** taxe *or* droit *m* sur l'essence; (*fig*) **it was a** ~ **on his strength** cela a mis ses forces à l'épreuve.

2 *cpd authorities, privilege, system etc* fiscal. **tax accountant** conseiller fiscal; **tax avoidance** évasion fiscale; **tax coding** indice *m* d'abattement fiscal; **tax-collecting** perception *f* (des impôts); **tax collector** percepteur *m*, -trice *f*; **tax-deductible** sujet à dégrèvements (d'impôts); **tax evader** fraudeur *m*, -euse *f* fiscal(e); **tax evasion** fraude fiscale, évasion fiscale; (*US*) **tax-exempt** = **tax-free**; **tax form** feuille *f* d'impôts; (*Brit*) **tax-free** exempt d'impôts, exonéré; **tax haven** refuge fiscal; **the taxman*** le percepteur; **taxpayer** contribuable *mf*; **for tax purposes** pour des raisons fiscales; **tax return** (feuille *f* de) déclaration *f* de revenus *or* d'impôts; (*US*) **tax shelter** échappatoire fiscale.

3 *vt* **(a)** *goods etc* taxer, imposer; *income, profits, person* imposer; (*fig*) *patience* mettre à l'épreuve; *strength* éprouver. **he is very heavily** ~**ed** il paie beaucoup d'impôts, il est lourdement imposé; **they are being** ~**ed out of existence** ils paient tant d'impôts qu'ils ont de la peine à survivre.

(b) to ~ **sb with sth** taxer *or* accuser qn de qch; **to** ~ **sb with doing** accuser qn de faire.

taxable ['tæksəbl] *adj* imposable.

taxation [tæk'seɪʃən] **1** *n* (*U*) (*act*) taxation *f*; (*taxes*) impôts *mpl*, contributions *fpl*. **2** *cpd authority, system* fiscal.

taxeme ['tæksiːm] *n* taxème *m*.

taxi ['tæksɪ] **1** *n* taxi *m*. **by** ~ en taxi.

2 *cpd charges etc* de taxi. **taxicab** taxi *m*; (*US*) **taxi dancer*** taxi-girl *f*; **taxi driver** chauffeur *m* de taxi; **taxi fare** tarif *m* de taxi; **taxi man*** = **taxi driver**; **taximeter** taximètre *m*, compteur *m* (de taxi); **taxi rank**, (*US*) **taxi stand** station *f* de taxis.

3 *vi* **(a)** *[aircraft]* se déplacer *or* rouler (lentement) au sol. **the plane** ~**ed along the runway** l'avion a roulé *or* s'est déplacé lentement le long de la piste.

(b) (*go by taxi*) aller en taxi.

taxidermist ['tæksɪdɜːmɪst] *n* empailleur *m*, -euse *f*, naturaliste *mf*.

taxidermy ['tæksɪdɜːmɪ] *n* empaillage *m*, naturalisation *f*, taxidermie *f*.

taxonomist [tæk'sɒnəmɪst] *n* taxonomiste *mf*.

taxonomy [tæk'sɒnəmɪ] *n* taxonomie *f*.

tea [tiː] **1** *n* **(a)** (*plant, substance*) thé *m*. **she made a pot of** ~ elle a fait du thé; (*fig*) **I wouldn't do it for all the** ~ **in China** je ne le ferais pour rien au monde; *V* **cup** *etc*.

(b) (*esp Brit: meal*) thé *m*; (*for children*) ≈ goûter *m*. **to have** ~ prendre le thé; *[children]* goûter; *V* **high** *etc*.

(c) (*herbal*) infusion *f*, tisane *f*; *V* **beef** *etc*.

2 *cpd*: **tea bag** sachet *m* de thé; (*Brit*) **tea break** pause(-)thé *f*; **to have a tea break** faire la pause(-)thé; **tea caddy** boîte *f* à thé; (*Brit*) **teacake** petit pain brioché; (*US*) **teacart** = **tea trolley**; **tea chest** caisse *f* (à thé); **teacloth** (*for dishes*) torchon *m* (à vaisselle); (*for table*) nappe *f* (à thé); (*for trolley, tray*) napperon *m*; (*Brit*) **tea cosy** couvre-théière *m*; **teacup** tasse *f* à thé (*V also* **read**[1], **storm**); **teacupful** tasse *f* (à thé *or* à café) (*mesure*); **tea dance** thé dansant; **teahouse** maison *f* de thé (*en Chine ou au Japon*); **teakettle** bouilloire *f*; **tea leaf** feuille *f* de thé (*V also* **read**[1]); **tea party** thé *m* (*réception*); **tea-plant** arbre *m* à thé; **tea plate** petite assiette; **teapot** théière *f*; **tearoom** salon *m* de thé; **tea service, tea set** service *m* à thé; **teashop** pâtisserie-salon de thé *f*; **teaspoon** petite cuiller, cuiller à thé *or* à café; **teaspoonful** cuillerée *f* à café; **tea strainer** passoire *f* (à thé), passe-thé *m inv*; **they sat at the tea table** ils étaient assis autour de la table mise pour le thé; **the subject was raised at the tea table** on en a discuté pendant le thé; **to set the tea table** mettre la table pour le thé; **where are the tea-things?*** où est le service à thé?; **to wash up the tea-things** faire la vaisselle après le thé; **teatime** l'heure *f* du thé; (*Brit*) **tea towel** torchon *m* (à vaisselle); **tea tray** plateau *m* (à thé); (*Brit*) **tea trolley** table roulante; **tea urn** fontaine *f* à thé; (*US*) **tea wagon** = **tea trolley**.

teach [tiːtʃ] *pret, ptp* **taught** **1** *vt* (*gen*) apprendre (*sb sth, sth to sb* qch à qn); (*Scol, Univ etc*) enseigner (*sb sth, sth to sb* qch à qn). **to** ~ **sb (how) to do** apprendre à qn à faire; **I'll** ~ **you what to do** je t'apprendrai ce qu'il faut faire; **he** ~**es French** il enseigne le français; **he taught her French** il lui a appris *or* enseigné le français; (*US*) **to** ~ **school** (*in primary school*) être instituteur (*or* institutrice); (*in secondary school*) être professeur; **to** ~ **o.s. (to do) sth** apprendre (à faire) qch tout seul; (*fig*) **to** ~ **sb a lesson** donner une leçon à qn (*fig*); **that will** ~ **him a lesson!, that will** ~ **him (a thing or two)!** ça lui apprendra (à vivre)!; **that will** ~ **you to mind your own business!** ça t'apprendra à te mêler de tes affaires!; **I'll** ~ **you (not) to speak to me like that!** je vais t'apprendre à me parler sur ce ton!; **you can't** ~ **him anything about cars** il n'a rien à apprendre de personne en matière de voitures; (*Brit*) **go and** ~ **your grandmother to suck eggs!‡** on n'apprend pas à un vieux singe à faire des grimaces!*

2 *vi* enseigner. **he always wanted to** ~ il a toujours eu le désir d'enseigner; **he had been** ~**ing all morning** il avait fait cours *or* fait la classe toute la matinée; **what does he do? — he** ~**es** que fait-il? — il enseigne.

3 *cpd*: **teach-in** séance *f* d'études, séminaire *m* (*sur un thème*).

teachability [ˌtiːtʃə'bɪlɪtɪ] *n* (*esp US*) *[child]* aptitude *f* à apprendre.

teachable ['tiːtʃəbl] *adj* (*esp US*) *child* qui apprend facilement; *subject* enseignable.

teacher ['tiːtʃə[r]] **1** *n* (*in secondary school; also private tutor*) professeur *m*; (*in primary school*) instituteur *m*, -trice *f*, maître *m* d'école, maîtresse *f* d'école; (*gen: member of teaching profession*) enseignant(e) *m(f)*. **she is a maths** ~ elle est professeur de maths; **the** ~**s accepted the government's offer** les enseignants ont accepté l'offre du gouvernement.

2 *cpd*: **teacher's handbook** livre *m* du maître; **teacher(s') training college** établissement *m* de formation pédagogique (*non-universitaire*); **to be at teacher(s') training college** suivre une formation pédagogique (*non-universitaire*); **teacher training** formation *f* pédagogique; **to do one's teacher training** suivre une formation pédagogique; **teacher training certificate** diplôme *m* habilitant à enseigner; **to get one's teacher training certificate** (*primary schools*) ≈ sortir de l'École Normale (primaire); (*secondary schools*) ≈ avoir son C.A.P.E.S. *etc*; **to get one's teacher training qualification** = **to get one's teacher training certificate**.

teaching ['tiːtʃɪŋ] **1** *n* **(a)** (*U: act, profession*) enseignement *m*. **to go into** ~ entrer dans l'enseignement; *V* **team**.

(b) (*also* ~**s**) *[philosopher, sage etc]* enseignements *mpl* (*liter*) (*on, about* sur).

2 *cpd*: **teaching aids** matériel *m* pédagogique; **teaching hospital** centre *m* hospitalo-universitaire (*abbr* C.H.U. *m*); **teaching machine** machine *f* à enseigner; **the teaching profession** (*activity*) l'enseignement *m*; (*in secondary schools only*) le professorat; (*teachers collectively*) le corps enseignant, les enseignants *mpl*; **the teaching staff** le personnel enseignant, les enseignants *mpl*.

teak [tiːk] *n* teck *m* *or* tek *m*.

teal [tiːl] *n, pl inv* sarcelle *f*.

team [tiːm] **1** *n* (*Sport, gen*) équipe *f*; *[horses, oxen]* attelage *m*. **football** ~ équipe de football; **our research** ~ notre équipe de chercheurs.

2 *cpd*: **team games** jeux *mpl* d'équipe; **team-mate** coéquipier *m*, -ière *f*; **team member** équipier *m*, -ière *f*; (*U*) **team spirit** esprit *m* d'équipe; (*U*) **team teaching** enseignement coordonné pour groupes; (*U*) **teamwork** collaboration *f* (d'équipe).

3 *vt* (*also* ~ **up**) *actor, worker* mettre en collaboration (*with* avec); *clothes, accessories* associer (*with* avec).

team up **1** *vi [people]* faire équipe (*with* avec); *[colours]* s'harmoniser (*with* avec); *[clothes, accessories, furnishings etc]* s'associer (*with* avec).

2 *vt sep* = **team 3**.

teamster ['tiːmstə[r]] *n* (*US*) routier *m*, camionneur *m*.

tear[1] [tεə[r]] (*vb: pret* **tore**, *ptp* **torn**) **1** *n* déchirure *f*, accroc *m*. **to make a** ~ **in sth** déchirer qch; **it has a** ~ **in it** c'est déchiré, il y a un accroc dedans.

2 *cpd*: (*Brit*) **tearaway** casse-cou *m inv*; **tear-off** amovible; **tear-off calendar** éphéméride *f*.

3 *vt* **(a)** (*rip*) *cloth, garment* déchirer, faire un trou *or* un accroc à; *flesh, paper* déchirer. **to** ~ **a hole in** faire une déchirure *or* un accroc à, faire un trou dans; **he tore it along the dotted line** il l'a déchiré en suivant le pointillé; **to** ~ **to pieces** *or* **to bits*** *paper* déchirer en menus morceaux; *garment* mettre en pièces *or* lambeaux; *prey* mettre en pièces; (*fig*) *play, performance* éreinter; *argument, suggestion* démolir; **to** ~ **open** *envelope* déchirer; *letter* déchirer l'enveloppe de; *parcel* ouvrir en déchirant l'emballage de; **clothes torn to rags** vêtements mis en lambeaux; **to** ~ **one's hair** s'arracher les cheveux; (*Med*) **to** ~ **a muscle** se déchirer un muscle; **I tore my hand on a nail** je me suis ouvert la main sur un clou; (*fig*) **that's torn it!***, (*US*) **that** ~**s it!*** voilà qui flanque tout par terre!*; *V* **shred**.

(b) (*fig*) **to be torn by war/remorse** *etc* être déchiré par la guerre/le remords *etc*; **to be torn between two things/people** être tiraillé par *or* balancer entre deux choses/personnes; **I'm very much torn** j'hésite beaucoup (entre les deux).

(c) (*snatch*) arracher (*from sb* à qn, *out of or off or from sth* de qch). **he tore it out of her hand** il le lui a arraché des mains; **he was torn from his seat** il a été arraché de son siège.

4 *vi* **(a)** *[cloth etc]* se déchirer.

(b) he tore at the wrapping paper il a déchiré l'emballage (impatiemment); **he tore at the earth with his bare hands** il a griffé la terre de ses mains nues.

(c) (*rush*) **to** ~ **out/down** *etc* sortir/descendre *etc* à toute allure *or* à toute vitesse; **he tore up the stairs** il a monté l'escalier quatre à quatre; *[person, car]* **to** ~ **along the road** filer à toute allure le long de la route; **they tore after him** ils se sont lancés *or* précipités à sa poursuite; (*fig*) **to** ~ **into sb*** (*attack verbally*) s'en prendre violemment à qn; (*scold*) passer un savon à qn*.

tear away **1** *vi [person]* partir comme un bolide; *[car]* démarrer en trombe.

2 *vt sep* (*lit, fig*) arracher (*from sb* à qn, *from sth* de qch). (*fig*) **I couldn't tear myself away from it/him** je n'arrivais pas à m'en arracher/à m'arracher à lui.

3 tearaway *n V* **tear 2**.

tear down *vt sep poster, flag* arracher (*from* de); *building* démolir.

tear off **1** *vi* = **tear away 1**.

2 *vt sep* **(a)** *label, wrapping* arracher (*from* de); *perforated page, calendar leaf* détacher (*from* de); *V* **strip**.

(b) (*: *write hurriedly*) *letter etc* bâcler*, torcher*.

3 tear-off *adj V* **tear 2**.

tear out **1** *vi V* **tear 4c**. **2** *vt sep* arracher (*from* de); *cheque*, *ticket* détacher (*from* de). **to tear sb's eyes out** arracher les yeux à qn.

tear up *vt sep* **(a)** *paper etc* déchirer, mettre en morceaux *or* en pièces; (*fig*) *contract* déchirer (*fig*); *offer* reprendre.

(b) *stake, weed, shrub* arracher; *tree* déraciner.

tear^2 [tɪəʳ] **1** *n* larme *f*. **in ~s** en larmes; **there were ~s in her eyes** elle avait les larmes aux yeux; **she had ~s of joy in her eyes** elle pleurait de joie; **near** *or* **close to ~s** au bord des larmes; **to burst** *or* **dissolve into ~s** fondre en larmes; **the memory/thought/sight brought ~s to his eyes** à ce souvenir/cette pensée/ce spectacle il eut les larmes aux yeux; **the film/book/experience brought ~s to his eyes** le film/le livre/cette expérience lui fit venir les larmes aux yeux; *V* **shed**^{2} *etc*.

2 *cpd*: **tear bomb** grenade *f* lacrymogène; **teardrop** larme *f*; **teargas** gaz *m* lacrymogène; **the film/book** *etc* **was a real tear-jerker*** c'était un film/roman *etc* tout à fait du genre à faire pleurer dans les chaumières; **tear-stained** barbouillé de larmes.

tearful ['tɪəfʊl] *adj look* larmoyant, (*stronger*) éploré; *face* en larmes; (*whining*) *voice, story, plea* larmoyant (*pej*), pleurnichard* (*pej*). **she was very ~** elle a beaucoup pleuré; **in a ~ voice** avec des larmes dans la voix, (*whining*) d'une voix pleurnicharde* (*pej*).

tearfully ['tɪəfəlɪ] *adv* les larmes aux yeux, en pleurant; (*whining*) en pleurnichant* (*pej*).

tearing ['tεərɪŋ] **1** *n* déchirement *m*. **2** *adj*: **a ~ sound** un craquement; (*fig*) **to be in a ~ hurry*** être terriblement pressé.

tearless ['tɪəlɪs] *adj* sans larmes.

tearlessly ['tɪəlɪslɪ] *adv* sans larmes, sans pleurer.

tease [ti:z] **1** *n* (*person*) taquin(e) *m(f)*.

2 *vt* **(a)** (*playfully*) taquiner; (*cruelly*) tourmenter.

(b) (*Tech*) *cloth* peigner; *wool* carder.

tease out *vt sep tangle of wool, knots, matted hair* débrouiller *or* démêler (patiemment).

teasel ['ti:zl] *n* (*Bot*) cardère *f*; (*Tech*) carde *f*.

teaser ['ti:zəʳ] *n* (*person*) taquin(e) *m(f)*; (*problem*) problème *m* (difficile); (*tricky question*) colle* *f*.

teasing ['ti:zɪŋ] **1** *n* (*U*) taquineries *fpl*. **2** *adj* taquin.

teat [ti:t] *n [animal]* tétine *f*, tette *f*; *[esp cow]* trayon *m*; *[woman]* mamelon *m*, bout *m* de sein; *[baby's bottle]* tétine; (*dummy*) tétine; (*Tech*) téton *m*.

technical ['teknɪkəl] *adj* (*all senses*) technique. **~ college** collège *m* technique; **~ hitch** incident *m or* ennui *m* technique; (*Jur*) **~ offence** contravention *f*; (*Jur*) **judgment quashed on a ~ point** arrêt cassé pour vice de forme.

technicality [,teknɪ'kælɪtɪ] *n* **(a)** (*U*) technicité *f*.

(b) (*detail/word/difficulty/fault*) détail *m*/terme *m*/difficulté *f*/ennui *m* technique. **I don't understand all the technicalities** certains détails techniques m'échappent.

technically ['teknɪkəlɪ] *adv* techniquement. (*fig*) **~ we shouldn't be here** en principe on ne devrait pas être là.

technician [tek'nɪʃən] *n* technicien(ne) *m(f)*.

Technicolor ['teknɪ,kʌləʳ] *n* ® Technicolor *m* ®. **in ~** en Technicolor.

technique [tek'ni:k] *n* technique *f*.

techno... ['teknəʊ] *pref* techno...

technocracy [tek'nɒkrəsɪ] *n* technocratie *f*.

technocrat ['teknəʊkræt] *n* technocrate *mf*.

technological [,teknə'lɒdʒɪkəl] *adj* technologique.

technologist [tek'nɒlədʒɪst] *n* technologue *mf*.

technology [tek'nɒlədʒɪ] *n* technologie *f*. (*Brit*) **Minister/Ministry of T~** ministre *m*/ministère *m* des Affaires technologiques.

techy ['tetʃɪ] *adj* = **tetchy**.

Ted [ted] *n* **(a)** (*dim of* **Edward** *or* **Theodore**) Ted *m*. **(b)** (*) = **teddy-boy**; *V* **Teddy**.

ted [ted] *vt* faner.

tedder ['tedəʳ] *n* (*machine*) faneuse *f*; (*person*) faneur *m*, -euse *f*.

Teddy ['tedɪ] **1** *n* (*dim of* **Edward** *or* **Theodore**) Teddy *m*. **2** *cpd*: **teddy (bear)** nounours *m* (*baby talk*), ours *m* en peluche; (*Brit*) **teddy-boy**† = blouson noir.

tedious ['ti:dɪəs] *adj* ennuyeux, assommant*.

tediously ['ti:dɪəslɪ] *adv* d'une façon ennuyeuse *or* assommante*. **~ long** d'une longueur assommante*.

tediousness ['ti:dɪəsnɪs] *n*, **tedium** ['ti:dɪəm] *n* (*U*) ennui *m*.

tee [ti:] (*Golf*) **1** *n* tee *m*.

2 *vt ball* placer sur le tee.

tee off 1 *vi* partir du tee. **2** *vt sep* (‡) (*US: annoy*) embêter*, casser les pieds à*; (*US fig: begin*) démarrer*.

tee up *vi* placer la balle sur le tee.

tee-hee ['ti:'hi:] (*vb: pret, ptp* **tee-heed**) **1** *excl* hi-hi! **2** *n* (petit) ricanement *m*. **3** *vi* ricaner.

teem [ti:m] *vi* **(a)** *[crowds, fish, snakes etc]* grouiller, fourmiller, pulluler. *[river, street etc]* **to ~ with** grouiller de, fourmiller de; **his brain ~s with ideas** il déborde d'idées. **(b) it was ~ing (with rain), the rain was ~ing down** il pleuvait à verse *or* à seaux.

teeming ['ti:mɪŋ] *adj crowd* grouillant, fourmillant, pullulant; *street* grouillant de monde, fourmillant; *river* grouillant de poissons. **~ rain** pluie battante *or* diluvienne.

teenage ['ti:neɪdʒ] *adj boy, girl* jeune, adolescent (*de 13 à 19 ans*); *behaviour, view* adolescent, d'adolescent, de jeune; *fashions* pour jeunes, pour adolescents.

teenager ['ti:n,eɪdʒəʳ] *n* jeune *mf*, adolescent(e) *m(f)*.

teens [ti:nz] *npl* jeunesse *f*, adolescence *f* (*de 13 à 19 ans*). **he is still in his ~** il est encore adolescent; **he is just out of his ~** il a à peine vingt ans; **he is in his early/late ~** il a un peu plus de treize ans/un peu moins de vingt ans.

teensy(weensy)‡ ['ti:nzɪ('wi:nzɪ)] *adj* = **teeny 1**.

teeny ['ti:nɪ] **1** *adj* (*: *also* **~weeny‡**) minuscule, tout petit, tout petit petit*. **2** *cpd*: **teeny-bopper‡** (jeune) minet(te)* *m(f)*.

tee-shirt ['ti:ʃɜ:t] *n* = **T-shirt**; *V* **T**.

teeter ['ti:təʳ] *vi [person]* chanceler; *[pile]* vaciller. (*fig*) **to ~ on the edge** *or* **brink of** être prêt à tomber dans.

teeth [ti:θ] *npl of* **tooth**.

teethe [ti:ð] *vi* faire *or* percer ses dents.

teething ['ti:ðɪŋ] **1** *n* poussée *f* des dents, dentition *f*. **2** *cpd*: **teething ring** anneau *m* (*de bébé qui perce ses dents*); (*fig*) **teething troubles** difficultés *fpl* de croissance (*fig*).

teetotal ['ti:'təʊtl] *adj person* qui ne boit jamais d'alcool; *league* antialcoolique.

teetotaler ['ti:'təʊtləʳ] *n* (*US*) = **teetotaller**.

teetotalism [ti:'təʊtəlɪzəm] *n* abstention *f* de toute boisson alcoolique.

teetotaller, (*US*) **teetotaler** ['ti:'təʊtləʳ] *n* personne *f* qui ne boit jamais d'alcool.

tegument ['tegjʊmənt] *n* tégument *m*.

te-hee ['ti:'hi:] = **tee-hee**.

tele... ['telɪ] *pref* télé...

telecast ['telɪkɑ:st] **1** *n* émission *f* de télévision. **2** *vt* diffuser.

telecommunication ['telɪkə,mju:nɪ'keɪʃən] ən] *n* (*gen pl*) télécommunication *f*; *V* **post**^{3}.

telefilm ['telɪfɪlm] *n* film *m* pour la télévision.

telegenic [,telɪ'dʒenɪk] *adj* télégénique.

telegram ['telɪgræm] *n* télégramme *m*; (*Diplomacy, Press*) dépêche *f*, câble *m*.

telegraph ['telɪgrɑ:f] **1** *n* télégraphe *m*. **2** *cpd message, wires* télégraphique. **telegraph pole** *or* **post** poteau *m* télégraphique. **3** *vti* télégraphier.

telegrapher [tɪ'legrəfəʳ] *n* télégraphiste *mf*.

telegraphese ['telɪgrɑ:'fi:z] *n* (*U*) style *m* télégraphique.

telegraphic [,telɪ'græfɪk] *adj* télégraphique.

telegraphically [,telɪ'græfɪkəlɪ] *adv* télégraphiquement.

telegraphist [tɪ'legrəfɪst] *n* télégraphiste *mf*.

telegraphy [tɪ'legrəfɪ] *n* télégraphie *f*.

telekinesis [,telɪkɪ'ni:sɪs] *n* (*U*) télékinésie *f*.

telemeter ['telɪmi:təʳ] *n* télémètre *m*.

teleology [,telɪ'ɒlədʒɪ] *n* téléologie *f*.

telepathic [,telɪ'pæθɪk] *adj* télépathique. (*iro*) **I'm not ~!*** je ne suis pas devin!

telepathically [,telɪ'pæθɪkəlɪ] *adv* télépathiquement.

telepathist [tɪ'lepəθɪst] *n* télépathe *mf*.

telepathy [tɪ'lepəθɪ] *n* télépathie *f*.

telephone ['telɪfəʊn] **1** *n* téléphone *m*. **on the ~** au téléphone; **to be on the ~** (*speaking*) être au téléphone; (*be a subscriber*) avoir le téléphone (chez soi).

2 *vt person* téléphoner à, appeler (au téléphone); *message, telegram* téléphoner (*to* à).

3 *vi* téléphoner.

4 *cpd*: **telephone book** = **telephone directory**; **telephone booth, telephone box** cabine *f* téléphonique; **telephone call** coup *m* de téléphone*, appel *m* téléphonique; **telephone directory** annuaire *m* (du téléphone); **telephone exchange** central *m* téléphonique; **telephone kiosk** = **telephone booth**; **telephone line** ligne *f* téléphonique; **telephone message** message *m* téléphonique; **telephone number** numéro *m* de téléphone; **telephone operator** standardiste *mf*, téléphoniste *mf*; **the telephone service** le service des téléphones; **our country has an excellent telephone service** le téléphone marche très bien dans notre pays; **telephone subscriber** abonné(e) *m(f)* au téléphone; **telephone-tapping** mise *f* sur écoute (téléphonique).

telephonic [,telɪ'fɒnɪk] *adj* téléphonique.

telephonist [tɪ'lefənɪst] *n* (*esp Brit*) téléphoniste *mf*.

telephony [tɪ'lefənɪ] *n* téléphonie *f*.

telephoto ['telɪ'fəʊtəʊ] *adj*: **~ lens** téléobjectif *m*.

telephotograph [,telɪ'fəʊtəgræf] *n* téléphotographie *f*.

telephotography [,telɪfə'tɒgrəfɪ] *n* (*U*) téléphotographie *f*.

teleprint ['telɪ,prɪnt] *vt* (*Brit*) transmettre par téléscripteur.

teleprinter ['telɪ,prɪntəʳ] *n* (*Brit*) téléscripteur *m*, télétype *m*.

teleprompter ['telɪ,prɒmptəʳ] *n* (télé)prompter *m*.

telescope ['telɪskəʊp] **1** *n* (*reflecting*) télescope *m*; (*refracting*) lunette *f* d'approche, longue-vue *f*; (*Astron*) lunette astronomique, télescope. **2** *vi [railway carriages etc]* se télescoper. **3** *vt* télescoper.

telescopic [,telɪs'kɒpɪk] *adj* télescopique. **~ lens** téléobjectif *m*.

teletype ['telɪtaɪp] *vt* ® (*US*) transmettre par téléscripteur *or* télétype.

teletypewriter [,telɪ'taɪpraɪtəʳ] *n* ® (*US*) téléscripteur *m*, télétype *m*.

televiewer ['telɪ,vju:əʳ] *n* téléspectateur *m*, -trice *f*.

televiewing ['telɪ,vju:ɪŋ] *n* (*U: watching TV*) la télévision. **this evening's ~ contains ...** le programme de (la) télévision pour ce soir comprend ... .

televise ['telɪvaɪz] *vt* téléviser.

television ['telɪ,vɪʒən] **1** *n* télévision *f*; (**~ *set***) télévision, téléviseur *m*, poste *m* (de télévision). **on ~** à la télévision, à la télé*; **colour ~** télévision (en) couleur.

2 *cpd actor, camera, studio* de télévision; *play, report, news, serial* télévisé. *[hotel etc]* **television lounge** salle *f* de télévision; **television programme** émission *f* de télévision; **television room** = **television lounge**; **television screen** écran *m* de télévision *or* de téléviseur; **on the television screen** sur le petit écran; **television set** télévision *f*, téléviseur *m*, poste *m* (de télévision).

telex ['teleks] **1** *n* télex *m*. **2** *vt* envoyer par télex.

tell [tel] *pret, ptp* **told 1** *vt* **(a)** (*gen sense*) dire (*that* que). **~ me your name** dites-moi votre nom; **I told him how pleased I was** je lui ai fait part de *or* dit ma joie; **I told him what/where/how/why**

je lui ai dit *or* expliqué ce que/où/comment/pourquoi; **I told him the way to London, I told him how to get to London** je lui ai expliqué comment aller à Londres; **I am glad to ~ you that ...** je suis heureux de pouvoir vous dire *or* annoncer que ...; **to ~ sb sth again** répéter *or* redire qch à qn; **something ~s me he won't be pleased** quelque chose me dit qu'il ne sera pas content; **let me ~ you that you are quite mistaken** permettez-moi de vous dire que vous vous trompez lourdement; **I won't go, I ~ you!** je n'irai pas, te dis-je!, puisque je te dis que je n'irai pas!; **there was terrible trouble, I can ~ you!** il y avait des tas de difficultés, c'est moi qui te le dis!*; **don't ~ me you've lost it!** tu ne vas pas me dire que *or* ne me dis pas que tu l'as perdu!; **I told you so!** je te l'avais bien dit!; **... or so I've been told** ... ou du moins c'est ce qu'on m'a dit; **I could ~ you a thing or two about him** je pourrais vous en dire long sur lui; **I('ll) ~ you what*, let's go for a swim!** tiens, si on allait se baigner!*; **you're ~ing me!*** à qui le dis-tu!; **~ me another!*** à d'autres!*

(b) (*relate*) dire, raconter; *story, adventure* raconter (*to* à); *a lie, the truth* dire; (*divulge*) *secret* dire, révéler; *sb's age* révéler; *the future* prédire. **to ~ sb's fortune** dire la bonne aventure à qn; **to ~ fortunes** dire la bonne aventure; **to ~ (you) the truth, truth to ~** à vrai dire; (*fig*) **every picture ~s a story** *or* **a tale** on en apprend des choses quand on regarde autour de soi; **can you ~ the time?** sais-tu lire l'heure?; **can you ~ me the time?** peux-tu me dire l'heure (qu'il est)?; **clocks ~ the time** les horloges indiquent l'heure; **that ~s me all I need to know** maintenant je sais tout ce qu'il me faut savoir; **his actions ~ us a lot about his motives** ses actes nous en disent long sur ses motifs; **she was ~ing him about it** elle lui en parlait; **I told him about what had happened** je lui ai dit *or* raconté ce qui était arrivé; *V* **tale.**

(c) (*distinguish*) distinguer, voir; (*recognize*) reconnaître; (*know*) savoir. **to ~ right from wrong** démêler *or* distinguer le bien du mal; **I can't ~ them apart** je ne peux pas les distinguer (l'un de l'autre); **how can I ~ what he will do?** comment puis-je savoir ce qu'il va faire?; **there's no ~ing what he might do** impossible de dire *or* savoir ce qu'il pourrait faire; **I couldn't ~ how it was done** je ne pourrais pas dire comment ça a été fait; **no one can ~ what he'll say** personne ne peut savoir ce qu'il va dire; **you can ~ he's clever by the way he talks** on voit bien qu'il est intelligent à la façon dont il parle; **I can't ~ the difference** je ne vois pas la différence (*between* entre); **you can't ~ much from his letter** sa lettre n'en dit pas très long.

(d) (*command*) dire, ordonner (*sb to do* à qn de faire). **do as you are told** fais ce qu'on te dit; **I told him not to do it** je lui ai dit de ne pas le faire, je lui ai défendu de le faire.

(e) (††: *count*) compter, dénombrer. (*emploi courant*) **there were 30 books all told** il y avait 30 livres en tout; **to ~ one's beads** dire *or* égrener *or* réciter son chapelet.

2 *vi* **(a)** parler (*of, about* de). (*fig*) **the ruins told of a long-lost civilization** les ruines témoignaient d'une civilisation depuis longtemps disparue; **his face told of his sorrow** sa douleur se lisait sur son visage; **more than words can ~** plus qu'on ne peut (*or* que je ne peux *etc*) dire.

(b) (*know*) savoir. **how can I ~?** comment le saurais-je?; **I can't ~** je n'en sais rien; **who can ~?** qui sait?; **you never can ~** on ne sait jamais; **you can't ~ from his letter** on ne peut pas savoir d'après sa lettre.

(c) (*be talebearer*) **I won't ~!** je ne le répéterai à personne!; **to ~ on sb*** rapporter *or* cafarder* contre qn; **don't ~ on us!*** ne nous dénonce pas!

(d) (*have an effect*) se faire sentir (*on sb/sth* sur qn/qch). **breeding ~s** quand on a de la classe cela se sent toujours; **his influence must ~** son influence ne peut que se faire sentir; **his age is beginning to ~** il commence à accuser son âge; **his age told against him** il était handicapé par son âge.

3 *cpd*: **telltale** (*n*) rapporteur *m*, -euse *f*, cafard* *m*; (*adj*) *mark etc* révélateur (*f* -trice), éloquent.

tell off 1 *vt sep* **(a)** (*: *reprimand*) gronder, attraper* (*sb for sth* qn pour qch, *for doing* pour avoir fait).

(b) (*select etc*) *person* affecter (*for sth* à qch), désigner (*to do* pour faire); (†: *check off*) dénombrer.

2 telling-off* *n V* **telling.**

teller ['telə^r] *n* (*Banking*) caissier *m*, -ière *f*; [*votes*] scrutateur *m*, -trice *f*; *V* **story** *etc.*

telling ['telɪŋ] **1** *adj figures, point, detail* révélateur (*f* -trice), éloquent; *argument, style* efficace; *blow* bon, bien assené.

2 *n* (*U*) [*story etc*] récit *m*, narration *f*. **it lost nothing in the ~** c'était encore mieux quand on l'entendait raconter.

3 *cpd*: **telling-off*** attrapade* *f*; **to get/give a good telling-off*** recevoir/passer un bon savon* (*from* de, *to* à).

telly* ['telɪ] *n* (*Brit abbr of* **television**) télé* *f*. **on the ~** à la télé.

temerity [tɪ'merɪtɪ] *n* (*U*) audace *f*, témérité *f*.

temp* [temp] *n* (*abbr of* **temporary**) intérimaire *mf*, secrétaire *mf etc* qui fait de l'intérim.

temper ['tempə^r] **1** *n* **(a)** (*U: nature, disposition*) tempérament *m*, caractère *m*, humeur *f*; (*U: mood*) humeur *f*; (*fit of bad ~*) (accès *m or* crise *f* de) colère *f*. **he has a very even ~** il est d'un caractère *or* d'un tempérament *or* d'une humeur très égal(e); **to have a hot** *or* **quick ~** être soupe au lait; **to have a nasty** *or* **foul** *or* **vile ~** avoir un sale caractère; **he was in a foul ~** il était d'une humeur massacrante; **to be in a good/bad ~** être de bonne/mauvaise humeur; **to keep one's ~** garder son calme, se maîtriser; **to lose one's ~** se mettre en colère; **to be in/get into a ~** être/se mettre en colère (*with sb* contre qn, *over or about sth* à propos de qch); **to put sb into a ~** mettre qn en colère; **~, ~!** ne nous mettons pas en colère!; **in a fit of ~ he ...** dans un accès de colère il ...; **he flew into a ~** il a explosé *or* éclaté; *V* **tantrum.**

(b) [*metal*] trempe *f*.

2 *vt metal* tremper; (*fig*) *effects, rigours, passions* tempérer (*with* par).

tempera ['tempərə] *n* (*U: Art*) détrempe *f*.

temperament ['tempərəmənt] *n* (*U*) (*nature*) tempérament *m*, nature *f*; (*moodiness, difficult ~*) humeur *f*, tendance *f* au caprice. **the artistic ~** le tempérament artiste; **outburst of ~** saute *f* d'humeur.

temperamental [,tempərə'mentl] *adj* **(a)** *person, horse* fantasque, capricieux, d'humeur instable; (*fig*) *machine, device* capricieux. **(b)** (*innate*) *reluctance, ability, tendency* naturel, inné.

temperance ['tempərəns] **1** *n* (*U*) modération *f*; (*in drinking*) tempérance *f*. **2** *cpd movement, league* antialcoolique; *hotel* où l'on ne sert pas de boissons alcoolisées.

temperate ['tempərɪt] *adj* (*all senses*) tempéré.

temperature ['temprɪtʃə^r] **1** *n* température *f*. **to have** *or* **run a ~** avoir de la température *or* de la fièvre; **to take sb's ~** prendre la température de qn. **2** *cpd change etc* de température. (*Med*) **temperature chart** feuille *f* de température.

-tempered ['tempəd] *adj ending in cpds*: **even-tempered** d'humeur égale; *V* **bad, good** *etc.*

tempest ['tempɪst] *n* (*liter*) tempête *f*, orage *m*.

tempestuous [tem'pestjʊəs] *adj weather* de tempête; *wind* de tempête, violent; (*fig*) *meeting, scene* orageux, agité; *character, person* passionné.

tempi ['tempiː] *npl of* **tempo.**

Templar ['templə^r] *n* = **Knight Templar;** *V* **knight.**

template ['templɪt] *n* patron *m*, gabarit *m*, calibre *m*.

temple[1] ['templ] *n* (*Rel*) temple *m*. (*Brit Jur*) **the T~** ≈ le Palais (de Justice).

temple[2] ['templ] *n* (*Anat*) tempe *f*.

templet ['templɪt] *n* = **template.**

tempo ['tempəʊ] *n, pl* **~s** *or* **tempi** (*Mus, fig*) tempo *m*.

temporal ['tempərəl] *adj* (*Gram, Rel*) temporel; (*Anat*) temporal.

temporarily ['tempərərɪlɪ] *adv agree, appoint, decide* provisoirement, temporairement; *lame, blind, disappointed* pendant un certain temps, pendant un moment.

temporary ['tempərərɪ] *adj job, worker* temporaire; *secretary* intérimaire; *teacher* suppléant; *ticket, licence* valide à titre temporaire; *decision, solution, method, powers* provisoire, temporaire; *building* provisoire; *relief, improvement* passager. **~ road surface** revêtement *m* provisoire.

temporize ['tempəraɪz] *vi* **(a)** (*procrastinate*) atermoyer, tergiverser (*liter*); (*parley, deal*) transiger, composer par expédient (*with sb* avec qn, *about sth* sur qch); (*effect compromise*) pactiser, transiger, composer (*with sb* avec qn). **to ~ between two people** faire accepter un compromis à deux personnes.

(b) (*pej: bend with circumstances*) faire de l'opportunisme.

tempt [tempt] *vt* **(a)** tenter, séduire. **to ~ sb to do** *or* **into doing** induire qn à faire, donner à qn l'envie *or* la tentation de faire; **try and ~ her to eat a little** tâchez de la persuader de manger un peu; **may I ~ you to a little more wine?** puis-je vous offrir un petit peu plus de vin?; **I am very ~ed to accept** je suis très tenté d'accepter; **I'm very ~ed** c'est très tentant; (*hum*) **don't ~ me!** n'essaie pas de me tenter!; *V* **sorely.**

(b) († *or Bible: test*) tenter, induire en tentation. (*emploi courant*) **to ~ Providence** *or* **fate** tenter la Providence.

temptation [temp'teɪʃən] *n* tentation *f*. **to put ~ in sb's way** exposer qn à la tentation; **lead us not into ~** ne nous laissez pas succomber à la tentation; **there is a great ~ to assume ...** il est très tentant de supposer ...; **there is no ~ to do so** on n'est nullement tenté de le faire.

tempter ['temptə^r] *n* tentateur *m*.

tempting ['temptɪŋ] *adj* tentant.

temptingly ['temptɪŋlɪ] *adv* d'une manière tentante, d'un air tentant.

temptress ['temptrɪs] *n* tentatrice *f*.

ten [ten] **1** *adj* dix *inv*. **about ~ books** une dizaine de livres; **the T~ Commandments** les dix commandements *mpl*.

2 *n* dix *m inv*. **there were about ~** il y en avait une dizaine; **~s of thousands of ...** des milliers (et des milliers) de ...; **hundreds, ~s and units** les centaines, les dizaines et les unités; **to count in ~s** compter par dizaines; (*fig*) **~ to one he won't come** je parie qu'il ne viendra pas; (*fig*) **they're ~ a penny** il y en a tant qu'on en veut, il y en a à la pelle*; (*Aut*) **to drive with one's hands at ~ to two** conduire avec les mains à dix heures dix; *for other phrases V* **six.**

3 *cpd*: (*US*) **ten-cent store** bazar *m*; **tenfold** (*adj*) décuple; (*adv*) au décuple; **to increase tenfold** décupler; (*US*) **ten-gallon hat** ≈ chapeau *m* de cowboy; **tenpin bowling, tenpins** bowling *m* (à dix quilles).

tenacious [tɪ'neɪʃəs] *adj* tenace, obstiné, entêté.

tenaciously [tɪ'neɪʃəslɪ] *adv* avec ténacité, obstinément.

tenacity [tɪ'næsɪtɪ] *n* (*U*) ténacité *f*.

tenancy ['tenənsɪ] *n*: **during my ~ of the house** pendant que j'étais locataire de la maison.

tenant ['tenənt] **1** *n* locataire *mf*. **2** *cpd*: **tenant farmer** métayer *m*, tenancier *m*. **3** *vt property* habiter comme locataire.

tenantry ['tenəntrɪ] *n* (*U: collective*) (ensemble *m* des) tenanciers *mpl* (d'un domaine).

tench [tentʃ] *n* tanche *f*.

tend[1] [tend] *vt sheep, shop* garder; *invalid* soigner; *machine* surveiller.

tend[2] [tend] *vi* [*person*] avoir tendance, tendre, incliner (*to do* à faire); [*thing*] avoir tendance (*to do* à faire). **to ~ towards** avoir des tendances à, incliner à *or* vers; **he ~s to be lazy** il a tendance *or* il tend à être paresseux, il est enclin à la paresse; **he ~s to(wards) fascism** il a des tendances fascistes, il incline au *or* vers le fascisme; **I ~ to think that ...** j'incline *or* j'ai tendance à penser que ...; **that ~s to be the case with such people** c'est en général le cas avec des gens de cette sorte; **it is a grey ~ing to blue** c'est un gris tirant sur le bleu.

tendency ['tendənsɪ] *n* tendance *f*. **to have a ~ to do** avoir tendance à faire; **there is a ~ for business to improve** les affaires ont tendance *or* tendent à s'améliorer; *(St Ex)* **a strong upward ~** une forte tendance à la hausse; **the present ~ to(wards) socialism** les tendances socialistes actuelles.

tendentious [ten'denʃəs] *adj* tendancieux.

tendentiously [ten'denʃəslɪ] *adv* tendancieusement.

tendentiousness [ten'denʃəsnɪs] *n* caractère tendancieux.

tender[1] ['tendər] *n (Rail)* tender *m*; *(Naut) (for passengers)* tender *m*; *(for supplies)* bâtiment *m* de servitude.

tender[2] ['tendər] **1** *vt (proffer) object* tendre, offrir; *money, thanks, apologies* offrir. **to ~ one's resignation** donner sa démission *(to sb* à qn).

2 *vi (Comm)* faire une soumission *(for sth* pour qch).

3 *n* **(a)** *(Comm)* soumission *f*. **to make *or* put in a ~ for sth** faire une soumission pour qch, soumissionner qch; **to invite ~s for sth, to put sth out to ~** mettre qch en adjudication.

(b) *(Fin)* **legal ~** cours légal; **that coin is no longer legal ~** cette pièce n'a plus cours.

tender[3] ['tendər] **1** *adj* **(a)** *skin* tendre, délicat; *flower* délicat, fragile; *meat, vegetable, shoots* tendre; *spot, bruise, heart* sensible; *conscience, subject* délicat. *(liter)* **of ~ years *or* age** d'âge tendre.

(b) *(affectionate) person, memories, thoughts, words* tendre, doux *(f* douce); *look, voice* tendre, caressant; *greeting, farewell, embrace* tendre.

2 *cpd*: **tenderfoot** *(pl* **~s)** novice *mf*, nouveau *m*, nouvelle *f*; **tender-hearted** sensible, compatissant; **to be tender-hearted** être un cœur tendre; *(U)* **tender-heartedness** compassion *f*, sensibilité *f*; *(Culin)* **tenderloin** filet *m*.

tenderize ['tendəraɪz] *vt (Culin)* attendrir.

tenderly ['tendəlɪ] *adv* tendrement, avec tendresse.

tenderness ['tendənɪs] *n (U)* **(a)** *[skin etc]* tendresse *f*; *[flower etc]* fragilité *f*; *[meat etc]* tendreté *f*; *[bruise etc]* sensibilité *f*. **(b)** *(emotion)* tendresse *f (towards* envers).

tendon ['tendən] *n* tendon *m*.

tendril ['tendrɪl] *n (Bot)* vrille *f*.

tenebrous ['tenɪbrəs] *adj (liter)* ténébreux.

tenement ['tenɪmənt] *n (apartment)* logement *m*, appartement *m*; *(block: also* **~ house)** bâtiment *m*.

tenet ['tenət] *n* principe *m*, doctrine *f*.

tenner* ['tenər] *n (Brit)* (billet *m* de) dix livres; *(US)* (billet de) dix dollars.

tennis ['tenɪs] **1** *n (U)* tennis *m*. **a game of ~** une partie de tennis.

2 *cpd player, racket, club* de tennis. **tennis ball** balle *f* de tennis; **tennis court** (court *m or* terrain *m* de) tennis *m inv*; *(Med)* **tennis elbow** synovite *f* du coude; **tennis shoe** (chaussure *f* de) tennis *m*.

tenon ['tenən] *n* tenon *m*.

tenor ['tenər] **1** *n* **(a)** *(general sense, course) [speech, discussion]* sens *m*, substance *f*; *[one's life, events, developments]* cours *m*.

(b) *(exact wording)* teneur *f*.

(c) *(Mus)* ténor *m*.

2 *adj (Mus) voice, part* de ténor; *aria* pour ténor; *recorder, saxophone etc* ténor *inv*.

tense[1] [tens] *n (Gram)* temps *m*. **in the present ~** au temps présent.

tense[2] [tens] **1** *adj rope, muscles, person, voice* tendu; *period* de tension; *smile* crispé; *(Ling) vowel* tendu. **in a voice ~ with emotion** d'une voix étranglée par l'émotion; **they were ~ with fear/anticipation** *etc* ils étaient crispés de peur/par l'attente *etc*; **things were getting rather ~** l'atmosphère devenait plutôt électrique; **the evening was rather ~** tout le monde était très tendu toute la soirée.

2 *vt muscles* tendre. **to ~ o.s.** se tendre.

tensely ['tenslɪ] *adv say* d'une voix tendue. **they waited/watched ~** ils attendaient/regardaient, tendus.

tenseness ['tensnɪs] *n (U: lit, fig)* tension *f*.

tensile ['tensaɪl] *adj material* extensible, élastique. **~ strength** force *f* de tension; **high-~ steel** acier *m* de haute tension; *V* **stress.**

tension ['tenʃən] **1** *n (U)* tension *f*. **2** *cpd*: *(Med)* **tension headache** mal *m* de tête (dû à la tension nerveuse).

tent [tent] **1** *n* tente *f*. **2** *cpd*: **tent peg/pole** piquet *m*/montant *m* de tente. **3** *vi* camper.

tentacle ['tentəkl] *n (also fig)* tentacule *m*.

tentative ['tentətɪv] *adj suggestion, gesture, smile* timide; *offer, voice* hésitant; *scheme* expérimental; *conclusion, solution* provisoire. **everything is very ~ at the moment** rien n'est encore décidé pour le moment; **she is a very ~ person** elle n'a aucune confiance en elle-même.

tentatively ['tentətɪvlɪ] *adv try, act* expérimentalement; *decide* provisoirement; *say, suggest, smile, walk* timidement.

tenterhooks ['tentəhʊks] *npl*: **to be/keep sb on ~** être/tenir qn sur des charbons ardents *or* au supplice.

tenth [tenθ] **1** *adj* dixième. **2** *n* dixième *mf*; *(fraction)* dixième *m*. **nine-~s of the book** les neuf dixièmes du livre; **nine-~s of the time** la majeure partie du temps; *for other phrases V* **sixth.**

tenuity [te'njʊɪtɪ] *n (U)* ténuité *f*.

tenuous ['tenjʊəs] *adj* ténu.

tenure ['tenjʊər] *n (feudal)* tenure *f*; *[land, property]* bail *m*. *[appointment etc]* **the ~ is for 2 years** la période de jouissance est de 2 ans; **during his ~ of office** pendant qu'il était en fonction; *V* **security.**

tepee ['tiːpiː] *n* wigwam *m*.

tepid ['tepɪd] *adj (lit, fig)* tiède.

tepidity [te'pɪdɪtɪ] *n*, **tepidness** ['tepɪdnɪs] *n (U: lit, fig)* tiédeur *f*.

tercentenary [ˌtɜːsen'tiːnərɪ] *adj, n* tricentenaire *(m)*.

tercet ['tɜːsɪt] *n (Poetry)* tercet *m*; *(Mus)* triolet *m*.

term [tɜːm] **1** *n* **(a)** *(gen, Admin, Fin, Jur, Med) (limit)* terme *m*; *(period)* période *f*, terme *(Jur)*. **to put *or* set a ~ to sth** mettre *or* fixer un terme à qch; *(Fin, Med)* **at ~** à terme; **in the long ~** à long terme; **in the short ~** dans l'immédiat; **a long-/short-~ loan** un prêt à long/court terme; **the long-/short-~ view** la vue à longue/brève échéance; **during his ~ of office** pendant la période où il exerçait ses fonctions; **elected for a 3-year ~** élu pour une durée *or* période de 3 ans; **~ of imprisonment** peine *f* de prison.

(b) *(Scol, Univ)* trimestre *m*; *(Jur)* session *f*. *(Scol, Univ)* **the autumn/spring/summer ~** le premier/second *or* deuxième/troisième trimestre; **in ~(time), during ~(time)** pendant le trimestre; **out of ~(time)** pendant les vacances (scolaires *or* universitaires).

(c) *(Math, Philos)* terme *m*. **A expressed in ~s of B** A exprimé en fonction de B; *(fig)* **in ~s of production we are doing well** sur le plan de la production nous avons de quoi être satisfaits; **he sees art in ~s of human relationships** pour lui l'art est fonction des relations humaines.

(d) *(conditions)* **~s** *(gen)* conditions *fpl*; *[contracts etc]* termes *mpl*; *(Comm etc)* prix *m(pl)*, tarif *m*; **you can name your own ~s** vous êtes libre de stipuler vos conditions; **on what ~s?** à quelles conditions?; **not on any ~s** à aucun prix, à aucune condition; **they accepted him on his own ~s** ils l'ont accepté tel qu'il était; **to lay down *or* dictate ~s to sb** imposer des conditions à qn; **to come to ~s with *person*** arriver à un accord avec; *problem etc* faire face à; *(Jur)* **~s and conditions** modalités *fpl*; **~s of surrender** conditions *or* termes de la reddition; **it is not within our ~s of reference** cela n'entre pas dans les termes de notre mandat; **~s of sale** conditions de vente; **~s of payment** conditions *or* modalités de paiement; **credit ~s** conditions de crédit; *(Comm)* **we offer it on easy ~s** nous offrons des facilités *fpl* de paiement; **our ~s for full board** notre tarif pension complète; **'inclusive ~s: £20'** '20 livres tout compris'.

(e) *(relationship)* **to be on good/bad ~s with sb** être en bons/mauvais termes *or* rapports avec qn; **they are on the best of ~s** ils sont au mieux, ils sont en excellents termes; **they're on fairly friendly ~s** ils ont des rapports assez amicaux *or* des relations assez amicales; *V* **equal, speaking.**

(f) *(expression, word)* terme *m*, expression *f*, mot *m*. **technical/colloquial ~** terme technique/familier; **in plain *or* simple ~s** en termes simples *or* clairs; **he spoke of her in glowing ~s** il a parlé d'elle en termes très chaleureux.

2 *cpd exams etc* trimestriel. **termtime** *V* **1b.**

3 *vt* appeler, nommer. **what we ~ happiness** ce que nous nommons *or* appelons le bonheur; **it was ~ed a compromise** ce fut qualifié de compromis.

termagant ['tɜːməgənt] *n* harpie *f*, mégère *f*.

terminal ['tɜːmɪnl] **1** *adj* **(a)** *(last) part, stage* terminal; *illness, cancer* dans sa phase terminale; *patient* en phase terminale. *(Rail)* **~ point, ~ station** terminus *m*.

(b) *(termly)* trimestriel.

2 *n* **(a)** *(Rail, Coach)* (gare *f*) terminus *m inv*; *(Underground: terminus)* (gare) terminus; *(Underground: at beginning of line)* tête *f* de ligne. **air ~** aérogare *f*; **container ~** terminus de containers; **oil ~** terminal *m* de conduites pétrolières.

(b) *(Elec)* borne *f*.

terminate ['tɜːmɪneɪt] **1** *vt* terminer, mettre fin à, mettre un terme à; *contract* résilier, résoudre, révoquer. **2** *vi* se terminer, finir *(in* en, par).

termination [ˌtɜːmɪ'neɪʃən] *n* fin *f*, conclusion *f*; *[contract]* résiliation *f*, résolution *f*, révocation *f*; *(Gram)* terminaison *f*. *(Med)* **~ of pregnancy** interruption *f* de grossesse.

termini ['tɜːmɪnaɪ] *npl of* **terminus.**

terminological [ˌtɜːmɪnə'lɒdʒɪkəl] *adj* de terminologie.

terminology [ˌtɜːmɪ'nɒlədʒɪ] *n* terminologie *f*.

terminus ['tɜːmɪnəs] *n*, *pl* **termini** terminus *m inv*.

termite ['tɜːmaɪt] *n* termite *m*, fourmi blanche.

tern [tɜːn] *n* hirondelle *f* de mer, sterne *f*.

ternary ['tɜːnərɪ] *adj* ternaire.

terrace ['terəs] **1** *n (Agr, Geol etc)* terrasse *f*; *(raised bank)* terre-plein *m*; *(patio, veranda, balcony, roof)* terrasse; *(row of houses)* rangée *f* de maisons *(attenantes les unes aux autres)*. *(Sport)* **the ~s** les gradins *mpl*.

2 *cpd*: **terrace cultivation** culture *f* en terrasses.

3 *vt hillside* arranger en terrasses. **~d** *garden, hillside* en terrasses; **they live in a ~d house** leur maison est attenante aux maisons voisines.

terracotta ['terə'kɒtə] **1** *n* terre cuite. **2** *cpd (made of* **~)** en terre cuite; *(colour)* ocre brun *inv*.

terrain [te'reɪn] *n* terrain *m (sol)*.

terrapin ['terəpɪn] *n* tortue *f* d'eau douce.

terrazzo [te'rætsəʊ] *n* sol *m* de mosaïque.

terrestrial [tɪ'restrɪəl] *adj* terrestre.

terrible ['terəbl] *adj accident, disaster* terrible, effroyable, atroce; *heat, pain* atroce, affreux, terrible; *poverty, conditions* effroyable; *holiday, disappointment, report* affreux, abominable, épouvantable.

terribly ['terəblɪ] *adv* **(a)** *(very)* drôlement*, rudement*, terriblement; *(pej)* atrocement*, affreusement, horriblement. **(b)** *(very badly) play, sing* affreusement *or* épouvantablement mal.

terrier ['terɪər] *n* **(a)** terrier *m*. **(b)** *(Brit Mil sl)* **the ~s** la territoriale*, les territoriaux *mpl*.

terrific [tə'rɪfɪk] *adj* **(a)** *(terrifying)* terrifiant, épouvantable.

(b) (*: *extreme etc) amount, size, height* énorme, fantastique; *speed* fou (*f* folle), incroyable*; *noise* énorme, épouvantable, incroyable*; *hill, climb* terriblement *or* incroyablement raide; *heat, cold* terrible, épouvantable; *anxiety* terrible; *pleasure* énorme, formidable*, terrible*.

(c) (*: *excellent) result, news, game* formidable*, sensationnel*.

terrifically* [tə'rɪfɪkəlɪ] *adv* **(a)** (*extremely*) terriblement, incroyablement; (*pej*) horriblement, épouvantablement. **(b)** (*very well*) *sing, play* formidablement bien*.

terrify ['terɪfaɪ] *vt* terrifier. **to ~ sb out of his wits** rendre qn fou (*f* folle) de terreur; **to be terrified of** avoir une terreur folle de.

terrifying ['terɪfaɪɪŋ] *adj* terrifiant, épouvantable, terrible.

terrifyingly ['terɪfaɪɪŋlɪ] *adv loud, near* épouvantablement; *bellow etc* de façon terrifiante.

territorial [ˌterɪ'tɔːrɪəl] **1** *adj* territorial. **~ waters** eaux territoriales; **T~ Army** armée territoriale. **2** *n* (*Brit Mil*) **T~** territorial *m*; **the T~s** l'armée territoriale, la territoriale*, les territoriaux.

territory ['terɪtərɪ] *n* territoire *m*.

terror ['terə^r] **1** *n* **(a)** (*U*) terreur *f*, épouvante *f*. **they were living in ~** ils vivaient dans la terreur; **he went in ~ of his life** il craignait fort pour sa vie, il avait la terreur d'être assassiné; **I have a ~ of flying** j'ai la terreur de monter en avion; *V* **reign**.

(b) terreur* *f*. **he was the ~ of the younger boys** il était la terreur des plus petits*; **he's a ~ on the roads*** c'est un danger public sur les routes; **that child is a (real *or* little *or* holy) ~*** cet enfant est une vraie (petite) terreur*.

2 *cpd*: **terror-stricken** épouvanté.

terrorism ['terərɪzəm] *n* (*U*) terrorisme *m*. **an act of ~** un acte de terrorisme.

terrorist ['terərɪst] *adj, n* terroriste (*mf*).

terrorize ['terəraɪz] *vt* terroriser.

terry ['terɪ] *n* (*also* **~ cloth, ~ towelling**) tissu *m* éponge.

terse [tɜːs] *adj* laconique, brusque (*pej*).

tersely ['tɜːslɪ] *adv* laconiquement, avec brusquerie (*pej*).

terseness ['tɜːsnɪs] *n* caractère *m* laconique, brusquerie *f* (*pej*).

tertiary ['tɜːʃərɪ] **1** *adj* tertiaire. **2** *n* (*Geol*) tertiaire *m*; (*Rel*) tertiaire *mf*.

terylene ['terəliːn] **1** *n* ® térylène *m* ®. **2** *cpd* en térylène.

tessellated ['tesɪleɪtɪd] *adj pavement* en mosaïque.

tessellation [ˌtesɪ'leɪʃən] *n* (*U*) mosaïque *f*.

test [test] **1** *n* **(a)** (*practical*) essai *m*; (*physical, mental, moral*) épreuve *f*; (*Med, Pharm*) analyse *f*, examen *m*; (*Chem*) analyse, test *m*; (*Physiol, Psych etc*) test; (*Scol*) interrogation *f* (*écrite ou orale*); (*driving ~*) (examen du) permis *m* de conduire; (*on vehicle, weapon, machine*) essai; (*criterion*) critère *m*. (*Pharm etc*) **to do a ~ for sugar** faire une recherche de sucre; **urine ~** analyse d'urine; **hearing ~** examen de l'ouïe; **they did a ~ for diphtheria** ils ont fait une analyse pour voir s'il s'agissait de la diphtérie; (*Med*) **he sent a specimen to the laboratory for ~s** il a envoyé un échantillon au laboratoire pour analyses; **they did ~s on the water to see whether ...** ils ont analysé l'eau pour voir si ...; **the aircraft has been grounded for ~s** l'avion a été retiré de la circulation pour (être soumis à) des essais; (*Med*) **the Wasserman ~** la réaction Wasserman; **they are trying to devise a ~ to find suitable security staff** ils essaient de concevoir un test permettant de sélectionner le personnel de gardiennage; (*Scol*) **they have a French ~ every month** ils ont une interrogation de français tous les mois; **it wasn't a fair ~ of her linguistic abilities** cela n'a pas permis d'évaluer correctement ses aptitudes linguistiques; **if we apply the ~ of visual appeal** si nous utilisons le critère de l'attrait visuel; *V* **acid, driving, endurance** *etc*.

(b) (*U*) **to put to the ~** mettre à l'essai *or* à l'épreuve; **to stand the ~** *[person]* se montrer à la hauteur*; *[machine, vehicle]* résister aux épreuves; **it has stood the ~ of time** cela a (bien) résisté au passage du temps.

(c) = ~ match; *V* **2**.

2 *cpd shot etc* d'essai; *district, experiment, year* test *inv*. (*Nucl Phys, Pol*) **test ban treaty** traité *m* d'interdiction d'expériences *or* d'essais nucléaires; *[oil]* **test bore** sondage *m* de prospection; (*Brit TV*) **test card** mire *f*; (*Jur*) **test case** conflit-test *m or affaire-test f* (destiné(e) à faire jurisprudence); **the strike is a test case** c'est une grève-test; (*Aut*) **test drive** (*n*) essai *m* de route; **test-drive** (*vt*) faire faire un essai de route à; (*Aviat*) **test flight** vol *m* d'essai; **testing-bench** banc *m* d'essai; **testing ground** terrain *m* d'essai; (*Brit: Cricket, Rugby*) **test match** ≃ match international; **test paper** (*Scol*) interrogation écrite; (*Chem*) (papier) réactif *m*; (*US TV*) **test pattern = test card**; (*Mus*) **test piece** morceau imposé; (*Aviat*) **test pilot** pilote *m* d'essai; **test tube** éprouvette *f*; **test-tube baby** bébé-éprouvette *m*.

3 *vt machine, weapon, tool* essayer; *vehicle* essayer, mettre à l'essai; *aircraft* essayer, faire faire un vol d'essai à; (*Comm*) *goods* vérifier; (*Chem*) *metal, water* analyser; (*Pharm*) *blood* faire une (*or* des) analyse(s) de; *new drug etc* expérimenter; (*Psych*) *person, animal* tester; (*gen*) *person* mettre à l'épreuve; *sight, hearing* examiner; *intelligence* mettre à l'épreuve, mesurer; *sb's reactions* mesurer; *patience, nerves* éprouver, mettre à l'épreuve. **they ~ed the material for resistance to heat** ils ont soumis le matériau à des essais destinés à vérifier sa résistance à la chaleur; **to ~ metal for impurities** analyser un métal pour déterminer la proportion d'impuretés qu'il contient; (*Med*) **they ~ed him for diabetes** ils l'ont soumis à des analyses pour une recherche de diabète; **they ~ed the child for hearing difficulties** ils ont fait passer à l'enfant un examen de l'ouïe; **they ~ed the children in geography** ils ont fait subir aux enfants une interrogation de contrôle en géographie; **they ~ed him for the job** ils lui ont fait passer des tests d'aptitude pour le poste; (*fig*) **it is a ~ing time for us all** c'est une période éprouvante pour nous tous.

4 *vi*: **to ~ for sugar** faire une recherche de sucre; **they were ~ing for a gas leak** ils faisaient des essais pour voir s'il y avait une fuite de gaz; (*Telec etc*) **'~ing, ~ing'** ≃ 'un, deux, trois'.

test out *vt sep machine, weapon, tool* essayer; *vehicle* essayer, mettre à l'essai; *aircraft* essayer, faire faire un vol d'essai à.

testament ['testəmənt] *n* (*all senses*) testament *m*. **the Old/New T~** l'Ancien/le Nouveau Testament.

testamentary [ˌtestə'mentərɪ] *adj* testamentaire.

testator [tes'teɪtə^r] *n* testateur *m*.

testatrix [tes'teɪtrɪks] *n* testatrice *f*.

tester[1] ['testə^r] *n* (*person*) contrôleur *m*, -euse *f*; (*machine etc*) appareil *m* de contrôle.

tester[2] ['testə^r] *n* (*over bed*) baldaquin *m*, ciel *m* de lit.

testes ['testiːz] *npl of* **testis**.

testicle ['testɪkl] *n* testicule *m*.

testification [ˌtestɪfɪ'keɪʃən] *n* déclaration *or* affirmation solennelle.

testify ['testɪfaɪ] **1** *vt* (*Jur etc*) témoigner, déclarer *or* affirmer sous serment (*that* que).

2 *vi* (*Jur etc*) porter témoignage, faire une déclaration sous serment. **to ~ against/in favour of sb** déposer contre/en faveur de qn; **to ~ to sth** (*Jur*) attester qch; (*gen*) témoigner de qch.

testily ['testɪlɪ] *adv* d'un ton *or* d'un air grincheux.

testimonial [ˌtestɪ'məʊnɪəl] *n* (*character etc reference*) recommandation *f*, certificat *m*; (*gift*) témoignage *m* d'estime (*offert à qn par ses collègues etc*). **as a ~ to our gratitude** en témoignage de notre reconnaissance.

testimony ['testɪmənɪ] *n* (*Jur*) témoignage *m*, déposition *f*; (*statement*) déclaration *f*, attestation *f*. **in ~ whereof** en foi de quoi.

testis ['testɪs] *n, pl* **testes** testicule *m*.

testy ['testɪ] *adj* irritable, grincheux.

tetanus ['tetənəs] **1** *n* tétanos *m*. **2** *cpd symptom* tétanique; *epidemic* de tétanos; *vaccine, injection* antitétanique.

tetchily ['tetʃɪlɪ] *adv* irritablement.

tetchiness ['tetʃɪnɪs] *n* (*U*) irritabilité *f*.

tetchy ['tetʃɪ] *adj* irritable, grincheux.

tête-à-tête ['teɪtɑː'teɪt] **1** *adv* en tête à tête, seul à seul. **2** *n* tête à tête *m*.

tether ['teðə^r] **1** *n* longe *f*. (*fig*) **to be at the end of one's ~** être à bout (de patience *or* de nerfs), être au bout de son rouleau*. **2** *vt* (*also* **~ up**) *animal* attacher (*to* à).

tetragon ['tetrəgən] *n* quadrilatère *m*.

tetrahedron [ˌtetrə'hiːdrən] *n* tétraèdre *m*.

tetrameter [te'træmɪtə^r] *n* tétramètre *m*.

Teutonic [tjʊ'tɒnɪk] *adj* teutonique.

text [tekst] **1** *n* (*all senses*) texte *m*. **2** *cpd*: **textbook** manuel *m*, cours *m*; (*fig*) **a textbook case of ...** un exemple classique *or* typique de ....

textile ['tekstaɪl] *adj, n* textile (*m*). **~ industry** (industrie *f*) textile *m*.

textual ['tekstjʊəl] *adj error* de texte; *copy, translation* textuel.

textually ['tekstjʊəlɪ] *adv* textuellement, mot à mot.

texture ['tekstʃə^r] *n [cloth]* contexture *f*; *[minerals, soil]* texture *f*, structure *f*, contexture; *[skin, wood, paper, silk etc]* grain *m*; (*fig*) structure, contexture.

Thai [taɪ] **1** *adj* thaïlandais; (*Ling*) thaï *inv*. **2** *n* **(a)** Thaïlandais(e) *m(f)*. **(b)** (*Ling*) thaï *m*.

Thailand ['taɪlænd] *n* Thaïlande *f*.

thalidomide [θə'lɪdəʊmaɪd] ® **1** *n* thalidomide *f* ®. **2** *cpd*: **thalidomide baby** (petite) victime *f* de la thalidomide.

Thames [temz] *n* Tamise *f*. (*fig*) **he'll never set the ~ on fire** il n'a pas inventé la poudre, il n'a pas inventé le fil à couper le beurre.

than [ðæn, *weak form* ðən] *conj* **(a)** que. **I have more ~ you** j'en ai plus que toi; **he is taller ~ his sister** il est plus grand que sa sœur; **he has more brains ~ sense** il a plus d'intelligence que de bon sens; **more unhappy ~ angry** plus malheureux que fâché; **you'd be better going by car ~ by bus** tu ferais mieux d'y aller en voiture plutôt qu'en autobus; **I'd do anything rather ~ admit it** je ferais tout plutôt que d'avouer cela; **no sooner did he arrive ~ he started to complain** il n'était pas plus tôt arrivé *or* il était à peine arrivé qu'il a commencé à se plaindre; **it was a better play ~ we expected** la pièce était meilleure que nous ne l'avions prévu; **it was nothing more ~ a lie** cela n'était qu'un mensonge.

(b) (*with numerals*) de. **more/less ~ 20** plus/moins de 20; **less ~ half** moins de la moitié; **more ~ once** plus d'une fois.

thank [θæŋk] **1** *vt* remercier, dire merci à (*sb for sth* qn de qch, *for doing* de faire, d'avoir fait). **I cannot ~ you enough** je ne saurais assez vous remercier; **~ you** merci; **~ you very much** merci bien (*also iro*), merci beaucoup, merci mille fois; **~ you for the book/for helping us** merci pour le livre/de nous avoir aidés; **no ~ you** (non) merci; **without so much as a ~ you** sans même dire merci; **~ you for nothing!*** je te remercie! (*iro*); **~ goodness*, ~ heaven(s)*, ~ God*** Dieu merci; **~ goodness you've done it!*** Dieu merci tu l'as fait!; (*fig*) **you've got him to ~ for that** c'est à lui que tu dois cela; **he's only got himself to ~** il ne peut s'en prendre qu'à lui-même; **I'll ~ you to mind your own business!** je vous prierai de vous mêler de ce qui vous regarde!

2 *npl*: **~s** remerciements *mpl*; (*excl*) **~s!*** merci!; **~s very much!, ~s a lot!*** merci bien (*also iro*), merci beaucoup, merci mille fois; **~s a million*** merci mille fois; **many ~s for all you've done** merci mille fois pour ce que vous avez fait; **many ~s for helping us** merci mille fois de nous avoir aidés; **with my warmest *or* best ~s** avec mes remerciements les plus sincères; **give him my ~s** transmettez-lui mes remerciements, remerciez-le de ma part; **to give ~s to God** rendre grâces à

Dieu; ~s be to God! Dieu soit loué!; that's all the ~s I get! c'est comme ça qu'on me remercie!; ~s to you grâce à toi; no ~s to you! ce n'est pas grâce à toi!

3 *cpd*: thanksgiving action *f* de grâce(s); (*Can, US*) Thanksgiving Day jour *m* d'action de grâce; thanks offering action *f* de grâce(s) (*don*).

thankful ['θæŋkfʊl] *adj* reconnaissant (*for* de). he was ~ to sit down il s'est assis avec soulagement; we were ~ for your umbrella! nous avons vraiment béni votre parapluie!; let us be ~ that he didn't know estimons-nous heureux qu'il ne l'ait pas su; I was ~ that he hadn't seen me j'ai été bien content *or* je me suis félicité qu'il ne m'ait pas vu; *V* mercy.

thankfully ['θæŋkfəlɪ] *adv* (*gratefully*) avec reconnaissance; (*with relief*) avec soulagement.

thankfulness ['θæŋkfʊlnɪs] *n* (*U*) gratitude *f*, reconnaissance *f*.

thankless ['θæŋklɪs] *adj* ingrat.

that [ðæt, *weak form* ðət] 1 *dem adj, pl* those (a) (*unstressed*) ce, (*before vowel and mute 'h'*) cet, *f* cette, *pl* ces. what's ~ noise? qu'est-ce que c'est que ce bruit?; ~ man cet homme; ~ car cette voiture; those books ces livres; how's ~ work of yours getting on? et ce travail, comment ça va?*; I love ~ house of yours! votre maison, je l'adore!; ~ awful dog of theirs ce sale chien qu'ils ont*; where's ~ son of his? où est-il, ce fameux fils?, où est-il, son fichu* fils? (*pej*); what about ~ £5 I lent you? et ces 5 livres que je t'ai prêtées?

(b) (*stressed; or as opposed to* this, these) ce *or* cet *or* cette *or* ces ... -là. I mean THAT book c'est de ce livre-là que je parle; I like ~ photo better than this one je préfère cette photo-là à celle-ci; ~ hill over there la *or* cette colline là-bas; (on) ~ Saturday ce samedi-là; everyone agreed on ~ point tout le monde était d'accord là-dessus; the leaf was blowing this way and ~ la feuille tournoyait de-ci de-là; she ran this way and ~ elle courait dans tous les sens; there's little to choose between this author and ~ (one) il n'y a pas grande différence entre cet auteur-ci et l'autre.

2 *dem pron, pl* those (a) cela, ça; ce. what's ~? qu'est-ce que c'est que ça?; who's ~? qui est-ce?; is ~ you Paul? c'est toi Paul?; ~'s what they've been told c'est *or* voilà ce qu'on leur a dit; ~'s the boy I told you about c'est *or* voilà le garçon dont je t'ai parlé; those are my children ce sont mes enfants, voilà mes enfants; do you like ~? vous aimez cela?; ~'s fine! c'est parfait!; ~'s enough! ça suffit!; what do you mean by ~? qu'est-ce que vous voulez dire (par là)?; she's not as stupid as (all) ~ elle n'est pas si bête que ça; I prefer ~ to this je préfère cela à ceci; as for ~! pour ce qui est de ça!, quant à cela!; you're not going and ~'s ~! tu n'y vas pas, un point c'est tout!; well, ~'s ~! eh bien voilà!; so ~ was ~ les choses se sont arrêtées là; if it comes to ~, why did you go? mais en fait, est-ce que tu avais besoin d'y aller?; so it has come to ~! on en est donc là!, voilà donc où on en est (arrivé)!; before/after ~ avant/après cela; with *or* at ~ she burst into tears là-dessus *or* sur ce, elle a éclaté en sanglots; and there were 6 of them at ~! et en plus ils étaient 6!; ~ is (to say) ... c'est-à-dire ... ; we were talking of this and ~ nous bavardions de choses et d'autres; do it like ~ fais-le comme ça; let's leave it at ~ for today ça suffit pour aujourd'hui; he went on about loyalty and all ~* il parlait de loyauté et patati et patata*; did he go? — ~ he did!† y est-il allé? — pour sûr!†

(b) (~ *one*) celui-là *m*, celle-là *f*, ceux-là *mpl*, celles-là *fpl*. I prefer this to ~ je préfère celui-ci à celui-là (*or* celle-ci à celle-là); those over there ceux-là (*or* celles-là) là-bas; not THOSE! pas ceux-là (*or* celles-là)!

(c) (*before rel pron*) celui *m*, celle *f*, ceux *mpl*, celles *fpl*. those who came ceux qui sont venus; there are those who say certains disent, il y a des gens qui disent.

3 *adv* (a) (*so*) si, aussi. it's ~ high c'est haut comme ça; it's not ~ cold! il ne fait pas si froid que ça!; I couldn't go ~ far je ne pourrais pas aller aussi loin que ça; I can't carry ~ much je ne peux pas porter autant que ça; he was at least ~ much taller than me il me dépassait de ça au moins.

(b) (*: *so very*) it was ~ cold! il faisait un de ces froids!; it was ~ cold we had to stay indoors il faisait tellement froid que nous avons dû rester à la maison; I was ~ tired I fell asleep je me suis endormi tellement j'étais fatigué; he was ~ ill! il était vraiment malade, il n'était pas bien du tout.

4 *rel pron* (a) (*nominative*) qui; (*accusative*) que. the man ~ came to see you l'homme qui est venu vous voir; the letter ~ I sent yesterday la lettre que j'ai envoyée hier; and Martin, idiot ~ he is, didn't tell me et Martin, cet imbécile, ne me l'a pas dit; fool ~ I am! imbécile que je suis!

(b) (*with prep*) lequel *m*, laquelle *f*, lesquels *mpl*, lesquelles *fpl*. the men ~ I was speaking to les hommes auxquels je parlais; the box ~ you put it in la boîte dans laquelle vous l'avez mis; the girl/the book ~ I told you about la jeune fille/le livre dont je vous ai parlé; not ~ I know of pas que je sache.

(c) (*in expressions of time*) où. the evening ~ we went to the opera le soir où nous sommes allés à l'opéra; during the years ~ he'd been abroad pendant les années où il était à l'étranger; the summer ~ it was so hot l'été où il a fait si chaud, l'été qu'il a fait si chaud*.

5 *conj* (a) que. he said ~ he had seen her il a dit qu'il l'avait vue, il a dit l'avoir vue; he was speaking so softly ~ I could hardly hear him il parlait si bas que je l'entendais à peine; not ~ I want to do it non (pas) que je veuille le faire; what's the matter? — it's ~ I don't know the way qu'est-ce qu'il y a? — c'est que je ne sais pas comment y aller; supposing ~ à supposer que + *subj*; it is natural ~ he should refuse il est normal qu'il refuse (*subj*); in ~ he might refuse en ce sens qu'il pourrait refuser; ~ he should behave like this is incredible il est incroyable qu'il se conduise de cette façon; ~ he should behave like this! dire qu'il peut se conduire ainsi!; oh ~ we could! si seulement nous pouvions!; *V* would *etc.*

(b) (*so that: liter, frm*) afin que + *subj*. so ~, in order ~ pour que + *subj*, afin que + *subj*.

thatch [θætʃ] 1 *n* (*U*) chaume *m*. (*fig*) his ~ of hair sa crinière. 2 *vt roof* couvrir de chaume; *cottage* couvrir en chaume. ~ed roof toit *m* de chaume; ~ed cottage chaumière *f*, chaumine† *f*.

thaw [θɔː] 1 *n* (*Met*) dégel *m*; (*fig : Pol etc*) détente *f*.

2 *vt* (*also* ~ out) *ice* faire dégeler, faire fondre; *snow* faire fondre; *frozen food* décongeler, dégeler.

3 *vi* (*also* ~ out) [*ice*] fondre, dégeler; [*snow*] fondre; [*frozen food*] décongeler, dégeler; [*person*] (*: *get warmer*) (se) dégeler*; (**fig: grow friendlier*) dégeler*, se dérider. (*Met*) it's ~ing il dégèle.

the [ðiː, *weak form* ðə] 1 *def art* (a) le, la, (*before vowel or mute 'h'*) l', les. of ~, from ~ du, de la, de l', des; to ~, at ~ au, à la, à l', aux; ~ prettiest le plus joli, la plus jolie, les plus joli(e)s; ~ poor les pauvres *mpl*.

(b) (*neuter*) ~ good and ~ beautiful le bien et le beau; translated from ~ German traduit de l'allemand; it is ~ unusual that is frightening c'est ce qui est inhabituel qui fait peur.

(c) (*with musical instruments*) to play ~ piano jouer du piano.

(d) (*with sg n denoting whole class*) ~ aeroplane is an invention of our century l'avion est une invention de notre siècle.

(e) (*distributive use*) 50p ~ pound 50 pence la livre; 2 dollars to ~ pound 2 dollars la livre; paid by ~ hour payé à l'heure; 30 miles to ~ gallon ≃ 9.3 litres au 100 (km).

(f) (*with names etc*) Charles ~ First/Second/Third Charles premier/deux/trois; ~ Browns les Brown; ~ Bourbons les Bourbons.

(g) (*stressed*) THE Professor Smith le célèbre professeur Smith; he's THE surgeon here c'est lui le grand chirurgien ici; it's THE restaurant in this part of town c'est le meilleur restaurant du quartier; he's THE man for the job c'est le candidat idéal pour ce poste; it was THE colour last year c'était la couleur à la mode l'an dernier; it's THE book just now c'est le livre à lire en ce moment.

(h) (*other special uses*) ~ cheek of it! ce toupet!*; he hasn't ~ sense to refuse il n'a pas assez de bon sens pour refuser; I'll see him in ~ summer je le verrai cet été; the dictionary for ~ eighties le dictionnaire des années quatre-vingt; he's got ~ measles* il a la rougeole; well, how's ~ leg?* eh bien, et cette jambe?*

2 *adv*: ~ more he works ~ more he earns plus il travaille plus il gagne d'argent; ~ sooner ~ better le plus tôt sera le mieux; all ~ better! tant mieux!; it will be all ~ more difficult cela sera d'autant plus difficile; it makes me all ~ more proud je n'en suis que plus fier; he was none ~ worse for it il ne s'en est pas trouvé plus mal pour ça.

theater (*US*), **theatre** ['θɪətəʳ] 1 *n* (a) (*place*) théâtre *m*, salle *f* de spectacle; (*drama*) théâtre. I like the ~ j'aime le théâtre; to go to the ~ aller au théâtre *or* au spectacle; it makes good ~ c'est du bon théâtre.

(b) (*large room*) salle *f* de conférences. (*Univ etc*) lecture ~ amphithéâtre *m*; *V* operating.

(c) (*Mil etc*) théâtre *m*. ~ of operations/war théâtre des opérations/des hostilités.

2 *cpd visit* au théâtre; *management* du théâtre. theatregoer habitué(e) *m(f)* du théâtre; London's theatreland le Londres des théâtres; theatre lover amateur *m* de théâtre.

theatrical [θɪ'ætrɪkəl] 1 *adj* théâtral (*also fig pej*). ~ company troupe *f* de théâtre.

2 *npl*: ~s théâtre *m* (d'amateurs); he does a lot of (amateur) ~s il fait beaucoup de théâtre d'amateurs; (*fig pej*) what were all those ~s about? pourquoi toute cette comédie?

theatrically [θɪ'ætrɪkəlɪ] *adv* théâtralement (*also fig pej*).

thee [ðiː] *pron* (††, *liter, dial*) te; (*before vowel*) t'; (*stressed; after prep*) toi.

theft [θeft] *n* vol *m*.

their [ðɛəʳ] *poss adj* leur (*f inv*).

theirs [ðɛəz] *poss pron* le leur, la leur, les leurs. this car is ~ cette voiture est à eux (*or* à elles) *or* leur appartient *or* est la leur; a friend of ~ un de leurs amis, un ami à eux (*or* à elles)*; I think it's one of ~ je crois que c'est un(e) des leurs; your house is better than ~ votre maison est mieux que la leur; it's no fault of ~ ce n'est pas de leur faute; (*pej*) that car of ~ leur fichue* voiture; that stupid son of ~ leur idiot de fils; the house became ~ la maison est devenue la leur; no advice of ~ could prevent him ... aucun conseil de leur part ne pouvait l'empêcher de ...; (*frm*) it is not ~ to decide il ne leur appartient pas de décider; ~ is a specialized department leur section est une section spécialisée.

theism ['θiːɪzəm] *n* théisme *m*.

theist ['θiːɪst] *adj, n* théiste (*mf*).

theistic(al) [θiː'ɪstɪk(əl)] *adj* théiste.

them [ðem, *weak form* ðəm] *pers pron pl* (a) (*direct*) (*unstressed*) les; (*stressed*) eux *mpl*, elles *fpl*. I have seen ~ je les ai vu(e)s; I know HER but I don't know THEM je la connais, elle, mais eux (*or* elles) je ne les connais pas; if I were ~ si j'étais à leur place, si j'étais eux (*or* elles); it's ~! ce sont eux (*or* elles)!, les voilà!

(b) (*indirect*) leur. I gave ~ the book je leur ai donné le livre; I'm speaking to ~ je leur parle.

(c) (*after prep etc*) eux, elles. I'm thinking of ~ je pense à eux (*or* elles); as for ~ quant à eux (*or* elles); younger than ~ plus jeune qu'eux (*or* elles).

(d) (*phrases*) both of ~ tous (*or* toutes) les deux; several of ~ plusieurs d'entre eux (*or* elles); give me a few of ~ donnez-m'en quelques-un(e)s; every one of ~ was lost ils furent tous perdus, elles furent toutes perdues; **I don't like either of ~** je ne les aime ni l'un(e) ni l'autre; **none of ~ would do it** aucun d'entre eux (*or* aucune d'entre elles) n'a voulu le faire; **it was very good of ~** c'était très gentil de leur part; **he's one of ~*** je (*or* tu) vois le genre!*

thematic [θɪ'mætɪk] *adj* thématique.

theme [θi:m] **1** *n* thème *m*, sujet *m*; (*Mus*) thème, motif *m*; (*US Scol: essay*) (courte) dissertation *f*. **2** *cpd*: **theme song** chanson principale (*d'un film etc*); (*US: signature tune*) indicatif *m* (musical); (*fig*) refrain *m* (habituel), leitmotiv *m*.

themselves [ðəm'selvz] *pers pron pl* (*reflexive: direct and indirect*) se; (*emphatic*) eux-mêmes *mpl*, elles-mêmes *fpl*; (*after prep*) eux, elles. **they've hurt ~** ils se sont blessés, elles se sont blessées; **they said to ~** ils (*or* elles) se sont dit; **they saw it ~** ils l'ont vu eux-mêmes; **they were talking amongst ~** ils discutaient entre eux; **(all) by ~** tout seuls, toutes seules.

then [ðen] **1** *adv* **(a)** (*at that time*) alors, à cette époque(-là), à ce moment(-là), en ce temps(-là). **we had 2 dogs ~** nous avions alors 2 chiens, nous avions 2 chiens à cette époque-là *or* à ce moment-là *or* en ce temps-là; **I'm going to London and I'll see him ~** je vais à Londres et je le verrai à ce moment-là; **(every) now and ~** de temps en temps, de temps à autre; **~ and there, there and ~** sur-le-champ, séance tenante.

(b) (*after prep*) **from ~ on(wards)** dès lors, dès cette époque(-là) *or* ce moment(-là) *or* ce temps(-là), à partir de cette époque(-là) *or* ce moment(-là); **before ~** avant cela *or* ce moment-là *or* ce temps-là; **since ~** depuis ce moment-là *or* cette époque-là *or* ce temps-là *or* lors; **between now and ~** d'ici là; **(up) until ~** jusque-là, jusqu'alors.

(c) (*next, afterwards*) ensuite, puis, alors. **he went first to London ~ to Paris** il est allé d'abord à Londres, puis *or* et ensuite à Paris; **and ~ what?** et puis après?; **now this u40that** tantôt ceci, tantôt cela.

(d) (*in that case*) en ce cas, donc, alors. **~ it must be in the sitting room** alors ça doit être au salon; **if you don't want that ~ what do you want?** si vous ne voulez pas de ça, alors que voulez-vous donc?; **but ~ that means that ...** mais c'est donc que ... ; **someone had already warned you ~?** on vous avait donc déjà prévenu?; **now ~ what's the matter?** alors qu'est-ce qu'il y a?

(e) (*furthermore; and also*) et puis, d'ailleurs, aussi. **(and) ~ there's my aunt** et puis il y a ma tante; **... and ~ it's none of my business** ... et d'ailleurs *or* ... et puis cela ne me regarde pas; **... and ~ again** *or* **... but ~ he might not want to go** ... remarquez, il est possible qu'il ne veuille pas y aller; **... and ~ again** *or* **... but ~ he has always tried to help us** ... et pourtant, il faut dire qu'il a toujours essayé de nous aider.

2 *adj* (*before n*) d'alors, de l'époque, du moment. **the ~ Prime Minister** le premier ministre d'alors *or* de l'époque.

thence [ðens] (†, *frm, liter*) **1** *adv* (*from there*) de là, de ce lieu-là; (*therefore*) par conséquent, pour cette raison. **2** *cpd*: **thenceforth, thenceforward** dès lors.

theocracy [θɪ'ɒkrəsɪ] *n* théocratie *f*.

theocratic [θɪə'krætɪk] *adj* théocratique.

theodolite [θɪ'ɒdəlaɪt] *n* théodolite *m*.

theologian [θɪə'ləʊdʒɪən] *n* théologien(ne) *m(f)*.

theological [θɪə'lɒdʒɪkəl] *adj* théologique. **~ college** séminaire *m*.

theology [θɪ'ɒlədʒɪ] *n* théologie *f*.

theorem ['θɪərəm] *n* théorème *m*.

theoretic(al) [θɪə'retɪk(əl)] *adj* théorique.

theoretically [θɪə'retɪkəlɪ] *adv* théoriquement.

theoretician [,θɪərə'tɪʃən] *n*, **theorist** ['θɪərɪst] *n* théoricien(ne) *m(f)*.

theorize ['θɪəraɪz] *vi* [*scientist, psychologist etc*] élaborer une (*or* des) théorie(s) (*about* sur). **it's no good just theorizing about it** ce n'est pas la peine de faire des grandes théories là-dessus*.

theory ['θɪərɪ] *n* théorie *f*. **in ~** en théorie.

theosophical [θɪə'sɒfɪkəl] *adj* théosophique.

theosophist [θɪ'ɒsəfɪst] *n* théosophe *mf*.

theosophy [θɪ'ɒsəfɪ] *n* théosophie *f*.

therapeutic(al) [,θerə'pju:tɪk(əl)] *adj* thérapeutique.

therapeutics [,θerə'pju:tɪks] *n* (*U*) thérapeutique *f*.

therapist ['θerəpɪst] *n* thérapeute *mf*; *V* **occupational** *etc*.

therapy ['θerəpɪ] *n* thérapie *f*.

there [ðɛəʳ] **1** *adv* **(a)** (*place*) y, là. **we shall soon be ~** nous y serons bientôt, nous serons bientôt là, nous serons bientôt arrivés; **put it ~** posez-le là; **when we left ~** quand nous en sommes partis, quand nous sommes partis de là; **on ~** là-dessus; **in ~** là-dedans; **back** *or* **down** *or* **over ~** là-bas; **about** *or* **around ~** (par *or* vers) là-bas; **here and ~** çà et là, par-ci par-là; **from ~** de là; **they went ~ and back in 2 hours** ils ont fait l'aller et retour en 2 heures; *V* **here**.

(b) ~ is il y a, il est (*liter*); **~ are** il y a; **once upon a time ~ was a princess** il y avait *or* il était une fois une princesse; **~ will be dancing later** plus tard on dansera; **~ is a page missing** il y a une page qui manque; **~ are 3 apples left** il reste 3 pommes, il y a encore 3 pommes; **~ comes a time when ...** il vient un moment où ...; **~'s no denying it** c'est indéniable.

(c) (*other uses*) **~'s my brother!** voilà mon frère!; **~ are the others!** voilà les autres!; **~ he is!** le voilà!; **~ they go!** les voilà partis!; **that man ~ saw it all** cet homme-là a tout vu; **hey you ~!*** hé *or* ho toi, là-bas!*; **hurry up ~!*** dépêchez-vous, là-bas!; **~'s my mother calling me** il y a *or* voilà ma mère qui m'appelle; **~'s the problem** là est *or* c'est *or* voilà le problème; **I disagree with you ~** là je ne suis pas d'accord avec vous; **you've got me ~!*** alors là, ça me dépasse!*; **you press this switch and ~ you are!*** tu appuies sur ce bouton et ça y est!; **~ you are*, I told you that would happen** voilà *or* tiens, je t'avais dit que ça allait arriver; (*fig*) **~ you go again*, complaining about ...** ça y est, tu recommences à te plaindre de ...; (*fig*) **~ he goes again!*** ça y est, il recommence!; (*fig*) **he's all ~*** c'est un malin, il n'est pas idiot; **he's not all ~*** il est un peu demeuré.

2 *excl*: **~*, what did I tell you?** alors, qu'est-ce que je t'avais dit?; **~, ~, don't cry!** allons, allons, ne pleure pas!; **~, drink this** allez *or* tenez, buvez ceci; **but ~, what's the use?** (mais) enfin, à quoi bon?

3 *cpd*: **thereabouts** (*place*) par là, près de là, dans le voisinage; (*degree etc*) à peu près, environ; **£5 or thereabouts** environ 5 livres; (*frm*) **thereafter** par la suite; (*frm*) **thereat** (*place*) là; (*time*) là-dessus; **thereby** de cette façon, de ce fait, par ce moyen; **thereby hangs a tale!** c'est toute une histoire!; **therefore** donc, par conséquent, pour cette raison; (*frm*) **therefrom** de là; (*frm*) **therein** (*in that regard*) à cet égard, en cela; (*inside*) (là-)dedans; (*frm*) **thereof** de cela, en; **he ate thereof** il en mangea; (*frm*) **thereon** (là-)dessus; (*frm*) **thereto** y; (*frm*) **theretofore** jusque-là; (*frm*) **thereunder** (là) en-dessous; **thereupon** (*then*) sur ce; (*on that subject*) là-dessus, à ce sujet; (*frm*) **therewith** (*with that*) avec cela, en outre; (*at once*) sur ce.

there's [ðɛəz] = **there is, there has;** *V* **be, have.**

therm [θɜ:m] *n* = 1,055 × 10^8 joules; (*formerly*) thermie *f*.

thermal ['θɜ:məl] **1** *adj* thermal; (*Elec, Phys*) thermique. **~ baths** thermes *mpl*; **~ spring** source thermale; **British T~ Unit** (*abbr* **BTU**) = 252 calories.

2 *n* (*Met*) courant ascendant (d'origine thermique), ascendance *f* thermique.

thermic ['θɜ:mɪk] *adj* = **thermal 1.**

thermionic [,θɜ:mɪ'ɒnɪk] **1** *adj effect, emission* thermoionique. **~ valve,** (*US*) **~ tube** tube *m* électronique. **2** *n* (*U*) **~s** thermoionique *f*.

thermo... ['θɜ:məʊ] *pref* therm(o)... .

thermocouple ['θɜ:məʊkʌpl] *n* thermocouple *m*.

thermodynamic ['θɜ:məʊdaɪ'næmɪk] **1** *adj* thermodynamique. **2** *n* (*U*) **~s** thermodynamique *f*.

thermoelectric ['θɜ:məʊɪ'lektrɪk] *adj* thermoélectrique.

thermometer [θə'mɒmɪtəʳ] *n* thermomètre *m*.

thermonuclear ['θɜ:məʊ'nju:klɪəʳ] *adj* thermonucléaire.

thermopile ['θɜ:məʊpaɪl] *n* pile *f* thermoélectrique.

Thermos ['θɜ:məs] *n* ® thermos *m or f inv* ®. **~ flask** bouteille *f* thermos.

thermostat ['θɜ:məstæt] *n* thermostat *m*.

thermostatic [,θɜ:məs'tætɪk] *adj* thermostatique.

thesaurus [θɪ'sɔ:rəs] *n* (*gen*) trésor *m* (*fig*); (*lexicon etc*) dictionnaire *m* synonymique; (*Computers*) thesaurus *m*.

these [ði:z] *dem adj, dem pron: pl of* **this.**

thesis ['θi:sɪs] *n, pl* **theses** ['θi:si:z] thèse *f*.

Thespian ['θespɪən] *adj* (*liter or hum*) dramatique, de Thespis.

they [ðeɪ] *pers pron pl* **(a)** ils *mpl*, elles *fpl*; (*stressed*) eux *mpl*, elles *fpl*. **~ have gone** ils sont partis, elles sont parties; **there ~ are!** les voilà!; **~ are teachers** ce sont des professeurs; **THEY know nothing about it** eux, ils n'en savent rien.

(b) (*people in general*) on. **~ say that ...** on dit que ... .

they'd [ðeɪd] = **they had, they would;** *V* **have, would.**

they'll [ðeɪl] = **they will;** *V* **will.**

they're [ðɛəʳ] = **they are;** *V* **be.**

they've [ðeɪv] = **they have;** *V* **have.**

thiamine ['θaɪəmi:n] *n* thiamine *f*.

thick [θɪk] **1** *adj* **(a)** (*in shape*) *finger, wall, line, slice, layer, glass, waist, jersey, cup* épais (*f* -aisse); *thread, book, lips, nose, wool, string* épais, gros (*f* grosse); *print* épais, gras (*f* grasse). **a wall 50 cm ~** un mur de 50 cm d'épaisseur, un mur épais de 50 cm; **the ice was 10 cm ~** la glace avait 10 cm d'épaisseur; (*with pen, brush etc*) **a ~ stroke** un trait épais, un gros trait; (*Brit*) **to give sb a ~ ear*** frotter les oreilles à qn*; (*Brit fig*) **that's a bit ~!*** ça c'est un peu fort!* *or* violent!* *or* raide!*; *V* **skin.**

(b) (*in consistency etc*) *soup, cream, gravy* épais (*f* -aisse), consistant; *honey* dur; *oil, mud, eyelashes, eyebrows* épais; *fog, smoke* dense, épais; *forest, vegetation, foliage* épais, touffu, dense; *hedge* (bien) fourni, touffu; *beard, hair* épais, touffu; *crowd* dense. **the air is very ~ in here** on manque d'air ici; **the air was ~ with smoke** (*at a party etc*) la pièce était enfumée; (*during fire etc*) l'air était plein d'une fumée épaisse; **the air was ~ with insults** les insultes volaient; **the furniture was ~ with dust** les meubles étaient couverts d'une épaisse couche de poussière; **the road was ~ with cars** la rue était encombrée de voitures; **the town was ~ with tourists** la ville était envahie de touristes; **the leaves were ~ on the ground** les feuilles couvraient le sol d'une couche épaisse; (*fig*) **antique shops are ~ on the ground around here*** il y a pléthore de magasins d'antiquités par ici; **in a ~ voice** (*from headcold, fear*) d'une voix voilée; (*from drink*) d'une voix pâteuse; (*fig*) **they are as ~ as thieves** ils s'entendent comme larrons en foire; **he's very ~* with Paul, Paul and he are very ~*** lui et Paul sont comme les deux doigts de la main.

(c) (*: *stupid*) bête, obtus, borné. **he's as ~ as a brick‡** il est bête comme ses pieds*.

2 *adv spread, lie etc* en couche épaisse; *cut* en tranches épaisses. **the snow fell ~** la neige tombait dru; **blows/arrows fell ~ and fast** les coups/flèches pleuvaient (de partout); (*fig*) **he lays it on a bit ~*** il exagère *or* pousse‡ un peu.

3 *n* [*finger, leg etc*] partie charnue. **in the ~ of the crowd** au plus fort *or* épais de la foule; **in the ~ of the fight** en plein cœur de la mêlée; **they were in the ~ of it** ils étaient en plein dedans; **through ~ and thin** à travers toutes les épreuves, contre vents et marées.

4 *cpd*: **thickheaded*** bête, obtus, borné; **thick-knit** (*adj*) gros (*f* grosse), en grosse laine; (*n*) gros chandail, chandail en grosse laine; **thick-lipped** aux lèvres charnues, lippu; **thickset** (*and small*) trapu, râblé; (*and tall*) bien bâti, costaud*; **thickskinned** *orange* à la peau épaisse; (*fig*) *person* peu sensible; **he's very**

thickskinned c'est un dur, rien ne le touche; thick-skulled*, thick-witted* = thickheaded*.

thicken ['θɪkən] 1 vt sauce épaissir, lier. 2 vi [branch, waist, hair, line etc] s'épaissir; [crowd] grossir; [sauce etc] épaissir; (fig) [mystery] s'épaissir; V plot.

thicket ['θɪkɪt] n fourré m, hallier m.

thickly ['θɪklɪ] adv spread en une couche épaisse; cut en tranches épaisses, en morceaux épais; speak, say (from headcold, fear) d'une voix voilée; (from drink) d'une voix pâteuse. ~ spread with butter couvert d'une épaisse couche de beurre; ~ covered with or in dust couvert d'une épaisse couche de poussière; the snow fell ~ la neige tombait dru; ~ populated region région f à forte concentration de population; ~ wooded très boisé.

thickness ['θɪknɪs] n (a) (U) [wall etc] épaisseur f; [lips etc] épaisseur, grosseur f; [fog, forest] épaisseur, densité f; [hair] épaisseur, abondance f. (b) (layer) épaisseur f. 3 ~es of material 3 épaisseurs de tissu.

thief [θi:f] n, pl thieves voleur m, -euse f. (Prov) once a ~ always a ~ qui a volé volera (Prov); (Prov) set a ~ to catch a ~ à voleur voleur et demi (Prov); stop ~! au voleur!; thieves' cant argot m du milieu; thieves' kitchen repaire m de brigands; V honour, thick etc.

thieve [θi:v] vti voler.

thievery ['θi:vərɪ] n (U) vol m.

thieves [θi:vz] npl of thief.

thieving ['θi:vɪŋ] 1 adj voleur. 2 n (U) vol m.

thievish† ['θi:vɪʃ] adj voleur, de voleur.

thigh [θaɪ] 1 n cuisse f. 2 cpd: thighbone fémur m; thigh boots cuissardes fpl.

thimble ['θɪmbl] n dé m (à coudre).

thimbleful ['θɪmblfʊl] n (fig) doigt m, goutte f.

thin [θɪn] 1 adj (a) finger, wall, slice, layer, line, wool, ice mince; cup, glass fin; paper, waist, lips, nose mince, fin; fabric, garment, blanket mince, léger; arm, leg, person mince, maigre (slightly pej). ~ string petite ficelle; [person] to get ~(ner) maigrir, s'amaigrir; as ~ as a rake or a lath maigre comme un clou; (with pen) a ~ stroke un trait mince or fin, un délié; (fig) it's the ~ end of the wedge c'est s'engager sur la pente savonneuse; V ice, skin etc.

(b) soup, gravy clair, clairet, peu épais (f -aisse); cream, honey liquide; mud peu épais, liquide; oil peu épais; beard, hair, eyelashes, eyebrows, hedge clairsemé; fog, smoke fin, léger; crowd épars; voice grêle, fluet; blood appauvri, anémié. he's rather ~ on top* il perd ses cheveux, il a un début de tonsure*; at 20,000 metres the air is ~ à 20.000 mètres l'air est raréfié; (fig) to disappear or vanish into ~ air disparaître (d'un seul coup) sans laisser de traces; doctors are ~ on the ground here* les médecins sont rares par ici.

(c) (fig) profits maigre; excuse, story, argument peu convaincant; plot squelettique. his disguise was rather ~ son déguisement a été facilement percé à jour; to have a ~ time of it* passer un moment or (longer) passer par une période plutôt pénible.

2 adv spread en une couche mince; cut en tranches or morceaux minces.

3 cpd: thin-lipped aux lèvres minces or fines; (with rage etc) les lèvres pincées; thin-skinned orange etc à la peau mince or fine; (fig) person susceptible.

4 vt paint étendre, délayer; sauce allonger, délayer, éclaircir; trees, hair éclaircir.

5 vi [fog, crowd] se disperser, s'éclaircir; [numbers] se réduire, s'amenuiser. his hair is ~ning il a maintenant les cheveux clairsemés.

thin down 1 vi [person] maigrir.

2 vt sep paint étendre, délayer; sauce allonger.

thin out 1 vi [crowd, fog] se disperser, s'éclaircir.

2 vt sep seedlings, trees éclaircir; numbers, population réduire; crowd disperser.

thine [ðaɪn] (†† or liter) 1 poss pron le tien, la tienne, les tiens, les tiennes. 2 poss adj ton, ta, tes.

thing [θɪŋ] n (a) (gen sense) chose f; (object) chose, objet m. surrounded by beautiful ~s entouré de belles choses or de beaux objets; ~ of beauty bel objet, belle chose; such ~s as money, fame ... des choses comme l'argent, la gloire ...; he's interested in ideas rather than ~s ce qui l'intéresse ce sont les idées et non pas les objets; ~s of the mind appeal to him il est attiré par les choses de l'esprit; the ~ he loves most is his car ce qu'il aime le plus au monde c'est sa voiture; what's that ~? qu'est-ce que c'est que cette chose-là? or ce machin-là?* or ce truc-là?*; what sort of (a) ~ is that to say to anyone? ça n'est pas une chose à dire (aux gens); the good ~s in life les plaisirs mpl de la vie; he thinks the right ~s il pense comme il faut; she likes sweet ~s elle aime les sucreries fpl; she has been seeing ~s elle a eu des visions; you've been hearing ~s! tu as dû entendre des voix!

(b) (belongings etc) ~s affaires fpl; have you put away your ~s? as-tu rangé tes affaires?; to take off one's ~s se débarrasser de son manteau etc; (undress completely) se déshabiller; do take your ~s off! débarrassez-vous (donc)!; have you got your swimming ~s? as-tu tes affaires de bain?; have you got any swimming ~s? as-tu ce qu'il faut pour aller te baigner?; where are the first-aid ~s? où est la trousse de secours?

(c) (affair, item, circumstance) chose f. I've 2 ~s still to do j'ai encore 2 choses à faire; the ~s she said! les choses qu'elle a pu dire!; the next ~ to do is ... ce qu'il y a à faire maintenant c'est ...; the best ~ would be to refuse le mieux serait de refuser; (iro) that's a fine or nice ~ to do! c'est vraiment la chose à faire! (iro); the last ~ on the agenda le dernier point à l'ordre du jour; you take the ~ too seriously tu prends la chose trop au sérieux; you worry about ~s too much tu te fais trop de soucis; I must think ~s over il faut que j'y réfléchisse; how are ~s with you? et vous, comment ça va?; how's ~s?* comment va?*; ~s are going from bad to worse les choses vont de mal en pis; since that's how ~s are puisque c'est comme ça, puisqu'il en est ainsi; to expect great ~s of sb/sth attendre beaucoup de qn/qch; they were talking of one ~ and another ils parlaient de choses et d'autres; taking one ~ with another à tout prendre, somme toute; the ~ is to know when he's likely to arrive ce qu'il faut c'est savoir or la question est de savoir à quel moment il devrait en principe arriver; the ~ is she'd already seen him (ce qu'il y a) c'est qu'elle l'avait déjà vu, mais elle l'avait déjà vu; it's a strange ~, but ... c'est drôle, mais ... ; for one ~ it doesn't make sense d'abord or en premier lieu ça n'a pas de sens; and (for) another ~, I'd already spoken to him et en plus, je lui avais déjà parlé; it's a good ~ I came heureusement que je suis venu; he's on to a good ~* il a trouvé le filon*; it's the usual ~, he hadn't checked the petrol c'est le truc* or le coup* classique, il avait oublié de vérifier l'essence; that was a near or close ~ vous l'avez (or il l'a etc) échappé belle; it's just one of those ~s ce sont des choses qui arrivent; it's just one damn ~ after another* les embêtements se succèdent; I didn't understand a ~ of what he was saying je n'ai pas compris un mot de ce qu'il disait; I hadn't done a ~ about it je n'avais strictement rien fait; he knows a ~ or two il s'y connaît; he's in London doing his own ~* il est à Londres et fait ce qui lui plaît or chante*; she's gone off to do her own ~* elle est partie trouver or chercher sa voie; she has got a ~ about spiders* elle a horreur des araignées, elle a la phobie des araignées; he has got a ~ about blondes* il est obsédé par les blondes; he made a great ~ of my refusal* quand j'ai refusé il en a fait toute une histoire or tout un plat*; don't make a ~ of it!* n'en fais pas tout un plat!*, ne monte pas ça en épingle!; Mr T~* rang up Monsieur Chose* or Monsieur Machin* a téléphoné; V equal, first, such etc.

(d) (person, animal) créature f. (you) poor little ~! pauvre petit(e)!; poor ~, he's very ill le pauvre, il est très malade; she's a spiteful ~ c'est une rosse*; you horrid ~!* chameau!*; I say, old ~* dis donc (mon) vieux.

(e) (best, most suitable etc ~) that's just the ~ for me c'est or voilà justement ce qu'il me faut; just the ~!, the very ~! (of object) voilà justement ce qu'il me (or nous etc) faut!; (of idea, plan) c'est l'idéal!; yoga is the ~ nowadays le yoga c'est la grande mode aujourd'hui; it's the in ~* c'est le truc* à la mode; that's not the ~ to do cela ne se fait pas; it's quite the ~ nowadays ça se fait beaucoup aujourd'hui; I don't feel quite the ~ today je ne suis pas dans mon assiette aujourd'hui; this is the latest ~ in ties c'est une cravate dernier cri.

thingamabob*, **thingumabob*** ['θɪŋəmɪbɒb] n, **thingumajig*** ['θɪŋəmɪdʒɪg] n, **thingummy*** ['θɪŋəmɪ] n machin* m, truc* m, trucmuche* m.

think [θɪŋk] (vb: pret, ptp thought) 1 n (*) I'll have a ~ about it j'y penserai; to have a good ~ about sth bien réfléchir à qch; you'd better have another ~ about it tu ferais bien d'y repenser; he's got another ~ coming! il se fait des illusions!, il faudra qu'il y repense! (subj).

2 cpd: think tank* groupe m d'experts.

3 vi (a) (gen sense) penser, réfléchir. ~ carefully réfléchissez bien; ~ twice before agreeing réfléchissez-y à deux fois avant de donner votre accord; ~ again! (reflect on it) repensez-y!; (have another guess) ce n'est pas ça, recommencez!; let me ~ que je réfléchisse*, laissez-moi réfléchir; to ~ aloud penser tout haut; to ~ big* avoir de grandes idées; (iro) I don't ~!* ça m'étonnerait!

(b) (devote thought to) penser, songer, réfléchir (of, about à). I was ~ing about or of you yesterday je pensais or songeais à vous hier; I ~ of you always je pense toujours à toi; you can't ~ of everything on ne peut pas penser à tout; I've too many things to ~ of or about just now j'ai trop de choses en tête en ce moment; he's always ~ing of or about money, he ~s of or about nothing but money il ne pense qu'à l'argent; what else is there to ~ about? c'est ce qu'il y a de plus important or intéressant; (you) ~ about it!, († or liter) ~ on it! pensez-y!, songez-y!; I'll ~ about it j'y penserai, j'y songerai, je vais y réfléchir; I'll have to ~ about it il faudra que j'y réfléchisse or pense (subj); that's worth ~ing about cela mérite réflexion; it's not worth ~ing about ça ne vaut pas la peine d'y penser; there's so much to ~ about il y a tant de choses à prendre en considération; you've given us so much to ~ about vous nous avez tellement donné matière à réfléchir; what are you ~ing about? à quoi pensez-vous?; what were you ~ing of! or about! où avais-tu la tête?; it doesn't bear ~ing of! c'est trop affreux d'y penser; I'm ~ing of or about resigning je pense à donner ma démission; he was ~ing of or about suicide il pensait au suicide; you ought to ~ twice about it il faudrait y réfléchir bien sérieusement; I wouldn't ~ of such a thing! ça ne me viendrait jamais à l'idée!; would YOU ~ of letting him go alone? vous le laisseriez partir seul, vous?; I didn't ~ to ask or of asking if you ... je n'ai pas eu l'idée de demander si tu ... .

(c) (remember, take into account) penser (of à). he ~s of nobody but himself il ne pense qu'à lui; he's got his children to ~ of or about il faut qu'il pense (subj) à ses enfants; to ~ of or about sb's feelings considérer les sentiments de qn; that makes me ~ of the day when ... cela me fait penser au or me rappelle le jour où ...; I can't ~ of her name je n'arrive pas à me rappeler son nom; I couldn't ~ of the right word le mot juste ne me venait pas.

(d) (imagine) to ~ of imaginer, se rendre compte de; ~ of me in a bikini! imagine-moi en bikini!; ~ of what might have happened imagine ce qui aurait pu arriver; just ~! imagine un peu!; **(just) ~, we could go to Spain** rends-toi compte, nous pourrions aller en Espagne; **~ of the cost of it all!** rends-toi compte de la dépense!; **and to ~ of her going there alone!** quand on pense qu'elle y est allée toute seule!, (et) dire qu'elle y est allée toute seule!

(e) (*devise etc*) **to ~ of** avoir l'idée de; **I was the one who thought of inviting him** c'est moi qui ai eu l'idée de l'inviter; **what will he ~ of next?** qu'est-ce qu'il va encore inventer?; **he has just thought of a clever solution** il vient de trouver une solution astucieuse; **~ of a number** pense à un chiffre.

(f) (*have as opinion*) penser (*of* de). **to ~ well *or* highly *or* a lot of sb/sth** penser le plus grand bien de qn/qch, avoir une haute opinion de qn/qch; **he is very well thought of in France** il est très respecté en France; **I don't ~ much of him** je n'ai pas une haute opinion de lui; **I don't ~ much of that idea** cette idée ne me dit pas grand-chose; **to ~ better of doing sth** décider à la réflexion de ne pas faire qch; **he thought (the) better of it** il a changé d'avis; **~ nothing of it!** je vous en prie!; **he thought nothing of walking both ways** il trouvait tout naturel de faire l'aller et retour à pied; *V* **fit**[1].

4 *vt* **(a)** (*be of opinion, believe*) penser, croire, trouver. **I ~ so/not** je pense *or* crois que oui/non; **I rather ~ so** j'ai plutôt l'impression que oui; **I thought as much!, I thought so!** je m'y attendais!, je m'en doutais!; **I hardly ~ it likely that ...** cela m'étonnerait beaucoup que ... + *subj*; **she's pretty, don't you ~?** elle est jolie, tu ne trouves pas?; **I don't know what to ~** je ne sais (pas) qu'en penser; **I ~ it will rain** je pense *or* crois qu'il va pleuvoir; **I don't ~ he came** je ne pense *or* crois pas qu'il soit venu; **I don't ~ he will come** je ne pense pas qu'il vienne *or* qu'il viendra; **what do you ~?** qu'est-ce que tu (en) penses?; (*iro*) **what do YOU ~?** qu'est-ce que tu crois, toi?; **what do you ~ of him?** comment le trouves-tu?; **I can guess what you are ~ing** je devine ta pensée; **what do you ~ I should do?** que penses-tu *or* crois-tu que je doive faire?; **who do you ~ you are?** pour qui te prends-tu?; **I never thought he'd look like that** ce n'est pas comme ça que je l'avais imaginé; **you must ~ me very rude** vous devez me trouver très impoli; **he ~s he is intelligent, he ~s himself intelligent** il se croit *or* se trouve intelligent; **they are thought to be rich** ils passent pour être riches; **to ~ the worst of sb** avoir une très mauvaise opinion de qn; **she ~s the world of him** elle le met sur un piédestal, elle trouve qu'il n'a pas son pareil; **I didn't ~ to see you here** je ne m'attendais pas à vous voir ici; **he ~s money the whole time*** il ne pense qu'argent*.

(b) (*conceive, imagine*) (s')imaginer. **~ what we could do with that house!** imagine ce que nous pourrions faire de cette maison!; **I can't ~ what he means!** je ne vois vraiment pas ce qu'il veut dire!; **you would ~ he'd have known that already** on aurait pu penser qu'il le savait déjà; **who would have thought it!** qui l'aurait dit!; **to ~ that she's only 10** et dire qu'elle n'a que 10 ans, quand on pense qu'elle n'a que 10 ans; **I didn't ~ to let him know** il ne m'est pas venu à l'idée *or* je n'ai pas eu l'idée de le mettre au courant; **to ~ evil thoughts** avoir de mauvaises pensées.

(c) (*reflect*) penser à. **just ~ what you're doing!** pense un peu à ce que tu fais!; **we must ~ how we may do it** il faut nous demander comment nous allons pouvoir le faire; **I was ~ing (to myself) how ill he looked** je me disais qu'il avait l'air bien malade.

think back *vi* repenser (*to* à), essayer de se souvenir *or* se rappeler. **he thought back, and replied ...** il a fait un effort de mémoire, et a répliqué ... .

think out *vt sep problem, proposition* réfléchir sérieusement à, étudier; *plan* élaborer, préparer; *answer, move* réfléchir sérieusement à, préparer. **that needs thinking out** il faut y réfléchir à fond.

think over *vt sep offer, suggestion* (bien) réfléchir à, peser. **think things over carefully first** pèse bien le pour et le contre auparavant; **I'll have to think it over** il va falloir que j'y réfléchisse.

think through *vt sep plan, proposal* examiner en détail *or* par le menu, considérer dans tous ses détails.

think up *vt sep plan, scheme, improvement* avoir l'idée de; *answer, solution* trouver; *excuse* inventer. **who thought up that idea?** qui a eu cette idée?; **what will he think up next?** qu'est-ce qu'il va encore bien pouvoir inventer?

thinkable ['θɪŋkəbl] *adj* concevable, imaginable. **it's not ~ that** il n'est pas pensable *or* concevable *or* imaginable que + *subj*.

thinker ['θɪŋkəʳ] *n* penseur *m*, -euse *f*.

thinking ['θɪŋkɪŋ] **1** *adj being, creature* rationnel. **to any ~ person** pour toute personne qui réfléchit; **to put on one's ~ cap** réfléchir, cogiter* (*hum*).

2 *n* (*act*) pensée *f*, réflexion *f*; (*thoughts collectively*) opinions *fpl* (*on, about* sur). **I'll have to do some (hard) ~ about it** il va falloir que j'y réfléchisse sérieusement; **to my way of ~** à mon avis; **that may be his way of ~, but ...** c'est peut-être comme ça qu'il voit les choses, mais ...; **current ~ on this** les opinions actuelles là-dessus; *V* **wishful**.

thinly ['θɪnlɪ] *adv cut* en tranches minces *or* fines; *spread* en une couche mince. **he sowed the seeds ~** il a fait un semis clair; **a ~ populated district** une région à la population éparse *or* clairsemée; **~ clad** insuffisamment vêtu; **~ wooded area** zone peu boisée; **a criticism ~ disguised as a compliment** une critique à peine déguisée en compliment.

thinness ['θɪnnɪs] *n* (*U: V* **thin 1a**) minceur *f*; finesse *f*; légèreté *f*; maigreur *f*.

third [θɜːd] **1** *adj* troisième. **in the presence of a ~ person** en présence d'un tiers *or* d'une tierce personne; (*Gram*) **in the ~ person** à la troisième personne; **~ time lucky!** la troisième fois sera (*or* a été *etc*) la bonne; **the ~ finger** le majeur, le médius; **the T~ Estate** le Tiers État; **the T~ World** le Tiers-Monde; *V also* 4; *for other phrases V* **sixth**.

2 *n* **(a)** troisième *mf*; (*fraction*) tiers *m*; (*Mus*) tierce *f*; *for phrases V* **sixth**.

(b) (*Univ*) ≃ licence *f* sans mention.

(c) (*Aut:* **~ gear**) troisième vitesse *f*. **in ~** en troisième.

3 *adv* **(a)** (*in race, exam, competition*) en troisième place *or* position. **he came *or* was placed ~** il s'est classé troisième.

(b) (*Rail*) **to travel ~** voyager en troisième.

(c) = **thirdly**.

4 *cpd*: **third-class** *V* **third-class**; **to give sb the third degree*** (*torture*) passer qn à tabac‡; (*question closely*) cuisiner‡ qn; (*Med*) **third-degree burns** brûlures *fpl* au troisième degré; (*Jur*) **third party** tierce personne, tiers *m*; **third-party insurance** assurance *f* au tiers; **third-rate** de qualité très inférieure.

third-class ['θɜːd'klɑːs] **1** *adj* (*lit*) de troisième classe; *hotel* de troisième catégorie, de troisième ordre; (*Rail*) *ticket, compartment* de troisième (classe); (*fig pej*) *meal, goods* de qualité tres inférieure. (*Rail*) **~ seat** troisième *f*; (*Univ*) **~ degree** *V* **2**.

2 *n* (*Univ: also* **~ degree**) ≃ licence *f* sans mention.

3 *adv* (*Rail*) **to travel ~** voyager en troisième.

thirdly ['θɜːdlɪ] *adv* troisièmement, en troisième lieu.

thirst [θɜːst] **1** *n* (*lit, fig*) soif *f* (*for* de). **I've got a real ~ on (me)*** j'ai la pépie*.

2 *vi* (*lit, fig: liter*) avoir soif (*for* de). **~ing for revenge** assoiffé de vengeance; **~ing for blood** altéré *or* assoiffé de sang.

thirsty ['θɜːstɪ] *adj person, animal* qui a soif, (*stronger*) assoiffé; (*fig*) *land* desséché. **to be ~** avoir soif (*for* de); **it makes you ~, it's ~ work** ça donne soif.

thirteen ['θɜː'tiːn] **1** *adj* treize *inv*. **2** *n* treize *m inv*; *for phrases V* **six**.

thirteenth ['θɜː'tiːnθ] **1** *adj* treizième. **2** *n* treizième *mf*; (*fraction*) treizième *m*; *for phrases V* **sixth**.

thirtieth ['θɜːtɪɪθ] **1** *adj* trentième. **2** *n* trentième *mf*; (*fraction*) trentième *m*; *for phrases V* **sixth**.

thirty ['θɜːtɪ] **1** *adj* trente *inv*. **about ~ books** une trentaine de livres. **2** *n* trente *m inv*. **about ~** une trentaine; *for other phrases V* **sixty**.

this [ðɪs] **1** *dem adj, pl* **these (a)** ce, (*before vowel and mute 'h'*) cet, *f* cette, *pl* ces. **who is ~ man?** qui est cet homme?; **whose are these books?** à qui sont ces livres?; **these photos you asked for** les photos que vous avez réclamées; **~ week** cette semaine; **~ time last week** la semaine dernière à pareille heure; **~ time next year** l'année prochaine à la même époque; **~ coming week** la semaine prochaine *or* qui vient; **it all happened ~ past half-hour** tout est arrivé dans la demi-heure qui vient de s'écouler; **I've been waiting ~ past half-hour** voilà une demi-heure que j'attends, j'attends depuis une demi-heure; **how's ~ hand of yours?** et votre main, comment va-t-elle?

(b) (*stressed; or as opposed to* **that, those**) ce *or* cet *or* cette *or* ces ... -ci. **I mean THIS book** c'est de ce livre-ci que je parle; **I like ~ photo better than that one** je préfère cette photo-ci à celle-là; **~ chair (over) here** cette chaise-ci; **the leaf was blowing that way and ~** la feuille tournoyait de-ci de-là; **she ran that way and ~** elle courait dans tous les sens.

2 *dem pron, pl* **these (a)** ceci, ce. **what is ~?** qu'est-ce que c'est (que ceci)?; **whose is ~?** à qui appartient ceci?; **who's ~?** qui est-ce?; **~ is my son** (*in introduction*) je vous présente mon fils; (*in photo etc*) c'est mon fils; **~ is the boy I told you about** c'est *or* voici le garçon dont je t'ai parlé; (*on phone*) **~ is Joe Brown** ici Joe Brown, Joe Brown à l'appareil; **~ is Tuesday** nous sommes mardi; **but ~ is May** mais nous sommes en mai; **~ is what he showed me** voici ce qu'il m'a montré; **~ is where we live** c'est ici que nous habitons; **I didn't want you to leave like ~!** je ne voulais pas que tu partes comme ça!; **it was like ~ ...** voici comment les choses se sont passées ...; **do it like ~** faites-le comme ceci; **after ~ things got better** après ceci les choses se sont arrangées; **before ~ I'd never noticed him** je ne l'avais jamais remarqué auparavant; **it ought to have been done before ~** cela devrait être déjà fait; **we were talking of ~ and that** nous parlions de choses et d'autres; **so it has come to ~!** nous en sommes donc là!; **at ~ she burst into tears** sur ce, elle éclata en sanglots; **with ~ he left us** sur ces mots il nous a quittés; **what's all ~ I hear about your new job?** qu'est-ce que j'apprends, vous avez un nouvel emploi?

(b) (**~ one**) celui-ci *m*, celle-ci *f*, ceux-ci *mpl*, celles-ci *fpl*. **I prefer that to ~** je préfère celui-là à celui-ci (*or* celle-là à celle-ci); **how much is ~?** combien coûte celui-ci (*or* celle-ci)?; **these over here** ceux-ci (*or* celles-ci); **not THESE!** pas ceux-ci (*or* celles-ci)!

3 *adv*: **it was ~ long** c'était aussi long que ça; **he had come ~ far** il était venu jusqu'ici; (*in discussions etc*) il avait fait tant de progrès; **~ much is certain ...** un point est acquis ...; **I can't carry ~ much** je ne peux pas porter (tout) ceci; **he was at least ~ much taller than me** il était plus grand que moi d'au moins ça.

thistle ['θɪsl] **1** *n* chardon *m*. **2** *cpd*: **thistledown** duvet *m* de chardon.

thistly ['θɪslɪ] *adj ground* couvert de chardons.

thither ['ðɪðəʳ] (†, *liter, frm*) **1** *adv* là, y; *V* **hither**. **2** *cpd*: **thitherto** jusqu'alors.

tho' [ðəʊ] *abbr of* **though**.

thole[1] [θəʊl] *n* (*Naut*) tolet *m*.

thole[2] [θəʊl] *vt* (††, *dial*) supporter.

Thomas ['tɒməs] *n* Thomas *m*. **he's a doubting ~** c'est saint Thomas.

thong [θɒŋ] *n [whip]* lanière *f*, longe *f*; (*on garment*) lanière, courroie *f*.

thoracic [θɔː'ræsɪk] *adj* thoracique.

thorax ['θɔːræks] *n* thorax *m*.

thorium ['θɔːrɪəm] *n* thorium *m.*
thorn [θɔːn] **1** *n* (*spike*) épine *f*; (*U: hawthorn*) aubépine *f.* (*fig*) **to be a ~ in sb's side** *or* **flesh** être une épine dans le pied de qn; *V* **rose²**. **2** *cpd*: (*fish*) **thornback** raie bouclée; **thorn bush** buisson *m* d'épine.
thornless ['θɔːnlɪs] *adj* sans épines, inerme (*Bot*).
thorny ['θɔːnɪ] *adj* (*lit, fig*) épineux.
thorough ['θʌrə] **1** *adj work, worker* consciencieux; *search, research* minutieux; *knowledge, examination* profond, approfondi, ample. **to give sth a ~ cleaning/wash** *etc* nettoyer/laver *etc* qch à fond; **he's a ~ rascal** c'est un coquin fieffé; **he's making a ~ nuisance of himself** il se rend totalement insupportable; **I felt a ~ idiot** je me sentais complètement idiot.
2 *cpd*: **thoroughbred** (*adj*) *horse* pur-sang *inv*; *other animal* de race; (*n*) (*horse*) (cheval *m*) pur-sang *m inv*; (*other animal*) bête *f* de race; (*fig: person*) **he's a real thoroughbred** il a vraiment de la classe *or* de la branche; **thoroughfare** (*street*) rue *f*; (*public highway*) voie publique; **'no thoroughfare'** 'passage interdit'; **thoroughgoing** *examination, revision, believer* convaincu; *hooligan* vrai (*before n*); *rogue, scoundrel* fieffé.
thoroughly ['θʌrəlɪ] *adv wash, clean* à fond; *examine, investigate, study* à fond, minutieusement, dans le détail; *understand* parfaitement; (*very*) tout à fait, tout, tout ce qu'il y a de*. **to search ~** *house* fouiller de fond en comble; *drawer* fouiller à fond; **I ~ agree** je suis tout à fait d'accord; **~ clean** tout propre, tout à fait propre; **he's ~ nasty** il est tout ce qu'il y a de* déplaisant.
thoroughness ['θʌrənɪs] *n* (*U*) *[worker]* minutie *f*; *[knowledge]* ampleur *f*. **the ~ of his work/research** la minutie qu'il apporte à son travail/sa recherche.
those [ðəʊz] *dem adj, dem pron: pl of* **that.**
thou¹ [ðaʊ] *pers pron* (†, *liter*) tu; (*stressed*) toi.
thou²* [θaʊ] *abbr of* **thousand, thousandth.**
though [ðəʊ] **1** *conj* **(a)** (*despite the fact that*) bien que +*subj*, quoique +*subj*, malgré le fait que +*subj*, encore que +*subj*. **~ it's raining** bien qu'il pleuve, malgré la pluie; **~ poor they were honest** ils étaient honnêtes bien que *or* quoique *or* encore que pauvres.
(b) (*even if*) **I will do it ~ I (should) die in the attempt** je le ferai, dussé-je y laisser la vie; **strange ~ it may seem** si *or* pour bizarre *or* étrange que cela puisse paraître; **(even) ~ I shan't be there I'll think of you** je ne serai pas là mais je n'en penserai pas moins à toi; (*liter*) **what ~ they are poor** malgré *or* nonobstant (*liter*) leur misère.
(c) as ~ comme si; *V* **as.**
2 *adv* pourtant, cependant. **it's not easy ~** ce n'est pourtant pas facile, pourtant ce n'est pas facile; **did he ~!*** ah bon!, tiens tiens!
thought [θɔːt] **1** *pret, ptp of* **think.**
2 *n* **(a)** (*U*) (*gen*) pensée *f*; (*reflection*) pensée, réflexion *f*, méditation *f*; (*daydreaming*) rêverie *f*; (*thoughtfulness*) considération *f*. **to be lost** *or* **deep in ~** être absorbé par ses pensées (*or* par la rêverie), être plongé dans une méditation (*or* dans une rêverie); **after much ~** après mûre réflexion, après y avoir beaucoup réfléchi; **he acted without ~** il a agi sans réfléchir; **without ~ for** *or* **of himself he ...** sans considérer son propre intérêt il ...; **he was full of ~ for her welfare** il se préoccupait beaucoup de son bien-être; **you must take ~ for the future** il faut penser à l'avenir; **he took** *or* **had no ~ for his own safety** il n'avait aucun égard pour sa propre sécurité; **to give ~ to sth** bien réfléchir à qch, mûrement réfléchir sur qch; **I gave it no more ~, I didn't give it another ~** je n'y ai pas repensé; **I didn't give it a moment's ~** je n'y ai pas pensé une seule seconde; **don't give it another ~** n'y pensez plus; **contemporary/scientific ~ on the subject** les opinions des contemporains/des scientifiques sur la question; **the ~ of Nietzsche** la pensée de Nietzsche.
(b) (*idea*) pensée *f*, idée *f*; (*opinion*) opinion *f*, avis *m*; (*intention*) intention *f*, idée. **it's a happy ~** voilà une idée qui fait plaisir; **what a ~!*** imagine un peu!; **what a horrifying ~!*** quel cauchemar!; **what a frightening ~!*** c'est à faire peur!*; **what a lovely ~!*** comme ça serait bien!; **what a brilliant ~!*** quelle idée de génie!; **that's a ~!*** tiens, mais c'est une idée!; **it's only a ~** ce n'est qu'une idée; **the mere ~ of it frightens me** rien que d'y penser *or* rien qu'à y penser j'ai peur; **he hasn't a ~ in his head** il n'a rien dans la tête; **my ~s were elsewhere** j'avais l'esprit ailleurs; **he keeps his ~s to himself** il garde ses pensées pour lui, il ne laisse rien deviner *or* paraître de ses pensées; **the T~s of Chairman Mao** les pensées du Président Mao; **I had ~s** *or* **some ~ of going to Paris** j'avais vaguement l'idée *or* l'intention d'aller à Paris; **he gave up all ~(s) of marrying her** il a renoncé à toute idée de l'épouser; **his one ~ is to win the prize** sa seule pensée *or* idée est de remporter le prix; **it's the ~ that counts** c'est l'intention qui compte; **to read sb's ~s** lire (dans) la pensée de qn; *V* **collect², penny, second¹** *etc.*
(c) (*adv phrase*) **a ~** un peu, un tout petit peu; **it is a ~ too large** c'est un (tout petit) peu trop grand.
3 *cpd*: **thought-provoking** qui pousse à la réflexion; **thought-reader** liseur *m*, -euse *f* de pensées; (*fig*) **he's a thought-reader** il lit dans la pensée des gens; (*fig*) **I'm not a thought-reader** je ne suis pas devin; **thought reading** divination *f* par télépathie; **thought transference** transmission *f* de pensée.
thoughtful ['θɔːtfʊl] *adj* **(a)** *person* (*pensive*) pensif, méditatif; (*in character*) sérieux, réfléchi; *book, remark, research* profond, sérieux, (bien) réfléchi. **he was looking ~ about it** il avait l'air de méditer là-dessus; **at this, he looked ~** à ces mots il a pris un air pensif; **he's a ~ boy** c'est un garçon réfléchi *or* sérieux.
(b) (*considerate*) *person* prévenant, attentionné; *act, remark* plein de délicatesse; *invitation* gentil. **how ~ of you!** comme c'est (*or* c'était) gentil à vous!; **to be ~ of others** être plein d'égards pour autrui, être attentif à autrui.
thoughtfully ['θɔːtfəlɪ] *adv* **(a)** (*pensively*) *ask, say* pensivement. **(b)** (*considerately*) avec prévenance. **he ~ booked tickets for us as well** il a eu la prévenance de louer des places pour nous aussi.
thoughtfulness ['θɔːtfʊlnɪs] *n* (*U: V* **thoughtful**) **(a)** (*look*) air pensif *or* méditatif; (*character*) caractère réfléchi *or* sérieux. **(b)** (*consideration*) prévenance *f*, considération *f*.
thoughtless ['θɔːtlɪs] *adj behaviour, words, answer* étourdi, irréfléchi, inconsidéré; *person* étourdi, léger, malavisé. **a ~ action** une étourderie; **he's very ~** il se soucie fort peu des autres.
thoughtlessly ['θɔːtlɪslɪ] *adv* (*carelessly*) à l'étourdie, étourdiment, à la légère; (*inconsiderately*) négligemment, insouciamment.
thoughtlessness ['θɔːtlɪsnɪs] *n* (*U*) (*carelessness*) étourderie *f*, légèreté *f*; (*lack of consideration*) manque *m* de prévenance *or* d'égards.
thousand ['θaʊzənd] **1** *adj* mille *inv*. **a ~ men** mille hommes; **about a ~ men** un millier d'hommes; **a ~ years** mille ans, un millénaire; **a ~ thanks!** mille fois merci!; **two ~ pounds** deux mille livres.
2 *n* mille *m inv*. **a ~, one ~** mille; **a** *or* **one ~ and one** mille (et) un; **a ~ and two** mille deux; **five ~** cinq mille; **about a ~, a ~ odd** un millier; (*Comm*) **sold by the ~** vendu par mille; **~s of people** des milliers de gens; **they came in their ~s** ils sont venus par milliers.
3 *cpd*: **thousandfold** (*adj*) multiplié par mille; (*adv*) mille fois autant.
thousandth ['θaʊzəntθ] **1** *adj* millième. **2** *n* millième *mf*; (*fraction*) millième *m*.
thraldom ['θrɔːldəm] *n* (*U: liter*) servitude *f*, esclavage *m*.
thrall [θrɔːl] *n* (*liter: lit, fig*) (*person*) esclave *mf*; (*state*) servitude *f*, esclavage *m*. (*fig*) **to be in ~ to** être esclave de.
thrash [θræʃ] **1** *vt* **(a)** (*beat*) rouer de coups, rosser; (*as punishment*) donner une bonne correction à; (*: *Sport etc*) battre à plate(s) couture(s), donner une bonne correction à. **they nearly ~ed the life out of him, they ~ed him to within an inch of his life** ils ont failli le tuer à force de coups.
(b) (*move wildly*) **the bird ~ed its wings (about)** l'oiseau battait *or* fouettait l'air de ses ailes; **he ~ed his arms/legs (about)** il battait des bras/des jambes.
(c) (*Agr*) = **thresh.**
2 *vi* battre violemment (*against* contre).
thrash about 1 *vi* (*struggle*) se débattre. **he thrashed about with his stick** il battait l'air de sa canne.
2 *vt sep one's legs, arms* battre de; *stick* agiter; *V also* **thrash 1b.**
thrash out* *vt sep problem, difficulty* débattre de. **they managed to thrash it out** ils ont réussi à démêler le problème (*or* aplanir la difficulté *etc*).
thrashing ['θræʃɪŋ] *n* correction *f*, rossée* *f*; (*: *Sport etc*) correction (*fig*), dérouillée: *f*. **to give sb a good ~** rouer qn de coups; (*as punishment; also Sport*) donner une bonne correction à qn.
thread [θred] **1** *n* **(a)** (*most senses*) fil *m*. **nylon ~** fil de nylon; (*fig*) **to hang by a ~** ne tenir qu'à un fil; (*fig*) **to lose the ~ (of what one is saying)** perdre le fil de son discours; (*fig*) **to pick up** *or* **take up the ~ again** retrouver le fil; (*fig*) **a ~ of light** un (mince) rayon de lumière.
(b) *[screw]* pas *m*, filetage *m*. **screw with left-hand ~** vis filetée à gauche.
2 *vt needle, beads* enfiler. **to ~ sth through a needle/over a hook/into a hole** faire passer qch à travers le chas d'une aiguille/par un crochet/par un trou; **to ~ a film on to a projector** monter un film sur un projecteur; **he ~ed his way through the crowd** il s'est faufilé à travers la foule; **the car ~ed its way through the narrow streets** la voiture s'est faufilée dans les petites rues étroites.
3 *vi* **(a) = to ~ one's way;** *V* **2.**
(b) *[needle, beads]* s'enfiler; *[tape, film]* passer.
4 *cpd*: **threadbare** *rug, clothes* usé, râpé, élimé; *room* défraîchi; (*fig*) *joke, argument, excuse* usé, rebattu; (*Med*) **threadworm** oxyure *m*.
threat [θret] *n* (*lit, fig*) menace *f*. **to make a ~ against sb** proférer une menace à l'égard de qn; **under (the) ~ of** menacé de; **it is a grave ~ to civilization** cela constitue une sérieuse menace pour la civilisation, cela menace sérieusement la civilisation.
threaten ['θretn] **1** *vt* menacer (*sb with sth* qn de qch, *to do* de faire). **to ~ violence** proférer des menaces de violence; **~ed with extinction** menacé de disparition; (*fig*) **it is ~ing to rain** la pluie menace. **2** *vi [storm, war, danger]* menacer.
threatening ['θretnɪŋ] *adj gesture, tone, words* de menace, menaçant; (*fig*) *weather, clouds* menaçant; *news* de mauvais augure. (*Psych*) **to find sb ~** se sentir menacé par qn.
threateningly ['θretnɪŋlɪ] *adv say* d'un ton menaçant, avec des menaces dans la voix; *gesticulate* d'une manière menaçante.
three [θriː] **1** *adj* trois *inv*.
2 *n* trois *m inv*. (*Pol*) **the Big T~** les Trois Grands; (*Sport*) **let's play best of ~** (*after first game*) jouons la revanche et la belle; (*after second game*) jouons la belle; **they were playing best of ~** ils jouaient deux jeux et la belle; **~'s a crowd*** on n'a que faire d'un tiers; *for other phrases V* **six.**
3 *cpd*: **three-act play** pièce *f* en trois actes; **three-cornered** triangulaire; **three-cornered hat** tricorne *m*; **three-dimensional** (*abbr 3-D*) *object* à trois dimensions; *picture, film* en relief; **threefold** (*adj*) triple, triplé; (*adv*) trois fois autant; **three-legged** *table* à trois pieds; *animal* à trois pattes; (*Sport*)

three-legged race course *f* de pieds liés; **three-line** *V* **whip; threepence** *V* **threepence; threepenny** *V* **threepenny;** (*Elec*) **three-phase** triphasé; **three-piece suite** salon *m* comprenant canapé et deux fauteuils; **three-ply** *wool* trois fils *inv*; (*Aviat*) **three-point landing** atterrissage *m* trois points; (*Aut*) **three-point turn** demi-tour *m* en trois manœuvres; **three-quarter** (*adj*) *portrait* de trois-quarts; *sleeve* trois-quarts *inv*; (*n: Rugby*) trois-quarts *m inv*; **three-quarters** trois quarts *mpl*; († *or liter*) **threescore** (*adj, n*) soixante (*m*); († *or liter*) **threescore and ten** (*adj, n*) soixante-dix (*m*); **three-sided** *object* à trois côtés, à trois faces; *discussion* à trois; **threesome** (*people*) groupe *m* de trois, trio *m*; (*game*) partie *f* à trois; **we went in a threesome** nous y sommes allés à trois; **three-way** *split, division* en trois; *discussion* à trois; **three-wheeler** (*car*) voiture *f* à trois roues; (*tricycle*) tricycle *m*.

threepence [ˈθrepəns] *n* (*Brit*) trois anciens pence.

threepenny [ˈθrepənɪ] (*Brit*) **1** *adj* à trois pence. **2** *n* (*also* **~ bit** *or* **piece**) ancienne pièce de trois pence.

threnody [ˈθrenədɪ] *n* chant *m* funèbre.

thresh [θreʃ] *vt* (*Agr*) battre.

thresher [ˈθreʃəʳ] *n* (*person*) batteur *m*, -euse *f* (en grange); (*machine*) batteuse.

threshing [ˈθreʃɪŋ] (*Agr*) **1** *n* battage *m*. **2** *cpd*: **threshing machine** batteuse *f*.

threshold [ˈθreʃhəʊld] *n* seuil *m*, pas *m* de la porte. **to cross the ~** franchir le seuil; (*fig*) **on the ~ of** au bord *or* au seuil de; (*Psych*) **above the ~ of consciousness** supraliminaire; **below the ~ of consciousness** subliminaire; **to have a high/low pain ~** avoir un seuil de tolérance à la douleur élevé/peu élevé.

threw [θruː] *pret of* **throw**.

thrice [θraɪs] *adv* trois fois.

thrift [θrɪft] **1** *n* (*U*) économie *f*. **2** *cpd*: **thrift shop** *petite boutique gérée au profit d'œuvres charitables*.

thriftiness [ˈθrɪftɪnɪs] *n* = **thrift**.

thriftless [ˈθrɪftlɪs] *adj* imprévoyant, dépensier.

thriftlessness [ˈθrɪftlɪsnɪs] *n* (*U*) imprévoyance *f*.

thrifty [ˈθrɪftɪ] *adj* économe.

thrill [θrɪl] **1** *n* frisson *m*, sensation *f*, émotion *f*. **a ~ of joy** un frisson de joie; **with a ~ of joy he ...** en frissonnant de joie, il ...; **what a ~!** quelle émotion!; **she felt a ~ as his hand touched hers** un frisson l'a traversée *or* elle s'est sentie électrisée quand il lui a touché la main; **it gave me a big ~** ça m'a vraiment fait quelque chose!*; **to get a ~ out of doing sth** se procurer des sensations fortes en faisant qch; **the film was packed with** *or* **full of ~s** c'était un film à sensations *or* émotions.

2 *vt person, audience, crowd* électriser, transporter. **his glance ~ed her** son regard l'a enivrée; **I was ~ed!** j'étais aux anges!*; **I was ~ed to meet him** ça m'a vraiment fait plaisir *or* fait quelque chose* de le rencontrer.

3 *vi* tressaillir *or* frissonner (de joie).

thriller [ˈθrɪləʳ] *n* (*novel/play/film*) roman *m*/pièce *f*/film *m* à suspense.

thrilling [ˈθrɪlɪŋ] *adj play, film, journey* palpitant; *news* saisissant.

thrive [θraɪv] *pret* **throve** *or* **thrived**, *ptp* **thriven** [ˈθrɪvn] *or* **thrived** *vi* [*person, animal*] se développer bien, être florissant de santé; [*plant*] pousser *or* venir bien; [*business, industry*] prospérer; [*businessman*] prospérer, réussir. **children ~ on milk** le lait est excellent pour les enfants; **he ~s on hard work** le travail lui réussit.

thriving [ˈθraɪvɪŋ] *adj person, animal* robuste, florissant de santé; *plant* robuste; *industry, businessman* prospère, florissant.

throat [θrəʊt] *n* (*external*) gorge *f*; (*internal*) gorge, gosier *m*. **to take sb by the ~** prendre qn à la gorge; **I have a sore ~** j'ai mal à la gorge, j'ai une angine; **he had a fishbone stuck in his ~** il avait une arête de poisson dans le gosier; (*fig*) **that sticks in my ~** je n'arrive pas à accepter *or* avaler* ça; (*fig*) **to thrust** *or* **ram** *or* **force** *or* **shove* sth down sb's ~** rebattre les oreilles de qn avec qch; *V* **clear, cut, frog[1], jump.**

throaty [ˈθrəʊtɪ] *adj* guttural, de gorge.

throb [θrɒb] **1** *n* [*heart*] pulsation *f*, battement *m*; [*engine*] vibration *f*; [*drums, music*] rythme *m* (fort); [*pain*] élancement *m*. **a ~ of emotion** un frisson d'émotion.

2 *vi* [*heart*] palpiter; [*voice, engine*] vibrer; [*drums*] battre (en rythme); [*pain*] lanciner. **a town ~bing with life** une ville vibrante d'animation; **the wound ~bed** la blessure me (*or* lui *etc*) causait des élancements; **my head/arm is ~bing** j'ai des élancements dans la tête/dans le bras; **we could hear the music ~bing in the distance** nous entendions au loin le rythme marqué *or* les flonflons *mpl* de la musique.

throes [θrəʊz] *npl*: **in the ~ of death** à l'agonie; **in the ~ of war/disease/a crisis** *etc* en proie à la guerre/la maladie/une crise *etc*; **in the ~ of an argument/quarrel/debate** au cœur d'une discussion/d'une dispute/d'un débat; **while he was in the ~ of (writing) his book** pendant qu'il était aux prises avec la rédaction de son livre; **while we were in the ~ of deciding what to do** pendant que nous débattions de ce qu'il fallait faire.

thrombosis [θrɒmˈbəʊsɪs] *n* thrombose *f*.

throne [θrəʊn] *n* (*all senses*) trône *m*. **to come to the ~** monter sur le trône; **on the ~** sur le trône; *V* **power.**

throng [θrɒŋ] **1** *n* foule *f*, multitude *f*, cohue *f* (*pej*).

2 *vi* affluer, se presser (*towards* vers, *round* autour de, *to see* pour voir).

3 *vt*: **people ~ed the streets** la foule se pressait dans les rues; **to be ~ed (with people)** [*streets, town, shops*] être grouillant de monde; [*room, bus, train*] être plein de monde, être bondé *or* comble.

thronging [ˈθrɒŋɪŋ] *adj crowd, masses* grouillant, pullulant.

throttle [ˈθrɒtl] **1** *n* (*Aut, Tech: valve*) papillon *m* des gaz; (*Aut: accelerator*) accélérateur *m*. **to give an engine full ~** accélérer à fond; **at full ~** à pleins gaz; **to open the ~** accélérer, mettre les gaz; **to close the ~** réduire l'arrivée des gaz.

2 *vt person* étrangler (*also fig*), serrer la gorge de.

throttle back, throttle down 1 *vi* mettre le moteur au ralenti.

2 *vt sep engine* mettre au ralenti.

through, (*US*) **thru** [θruː] *phr vb elem* **1** *adv* **(a)** (*place, time, process*) **the nail went (right) ~** le clou est passé à travers; **just go ~** passez *or* entrez donc; **to let sb ~** laisser passer qn; **you can get a train right ~ to London** on peut attraper un train direct pour Londres; (*in exam*) **did you get ~?, are you ~?** as-tu été reçu?, as-tu réussi?; **did you stay all ~?** es-tu resté jusqu'à la fin?; **we're staying ~ till Tuesday** nous restons jusqu'à mardi; **he slept all night ~** il ne s'est pas réveillé de la nuit; **I knew all ~ that this would happen** je savais depuis le début que cela se produirait; **to be wet ~** [*person*] être trempé (jusqu'aux os); [*clothes*] être trempé, être (bon) à essorer; **soaked ~ and ~** complètement trempé; **I know it ~ and ~** je le connais par cœur; **he's a liar ~ and ~** il ment comme il respire; **he's a Scot ~ and ~** il est écossais jusqu'au bout des ongles; **read it (right) ~ to the end, read it right ~** lis-le en entier *or* jusqu'au bout *or* de bout en bout; **I read the letter ~ quickly** j'ai lu la lettre rapidement; *V* **go through, see through** *etc*.

(b) (*Brit Telec*) **to put sb ~** passer qn à qn; **I'll put you ~ to her** je vous la passe; **you're ~** now vous avez votre correspondant; **you're ~ to Mr X** M X est en ligne.

(c) (*: *finished*) **I'm ~** ça y est (j'ai fini)*; **are you ~?** ça y est (tu as fini)?*; **I'm not ~ with you yet** je n'en ai pas encore fini *or* terminé avec vous; **are you ~ with that book?** ce livre, c'est fini?, tu n'as plus besoin de ce livre?; **he told me we were ~** il m'a dit qu'on allait casser* *or* que c'était fini entre nous; **he's ~ with her** il l'a plaquée*, lui et elle, c'est fini; **I'm ~ with football!** le football, (c'est) fini!*

2 *prep* **(a)** (*place*) à travers. **a stream flows ~ the garden** un ruisseau traverse le jardin *or* coule à travers le jardin; **water poured ~ the roof** le toit laissait passer des torrents d'eau; **to go ~ a forest** traverser une forêt; **to get ~ a hedge** passer au travers d'une haie; **he went right ~ the red light** il a carrément grillé le feu rouge; **to hammer a nail ~ a plank** enfoncer un clou à travers une planche; **he was shot ~ the head** on lui a tiré une balle dans la tête; **to look ~ a window/telescope** regarder par une fenêtre/dans un télescope; **I can hear them ~ the wall** je les entends de l'autre côté du mur; **to go ~ sb's pockets** fouiller les poches de qn, faire les poches de qn*; **he has really been ~ it*** il en a vu de dures*; **he is ~ the first part of the exam** il a réussi à la première partie de l'examen; **I'm half-way ~ the book** j'en suis à la moitié du livre; **to speak ~ one's nose** parler du nez; *V* **get through, go through, see through** *etc*.

(b) (*time*) pendant, durant. **all** *or* **right ~ his life, all his life ~** pendant *or* durant toute sa vie, sa vie durant; **he won't live ~ the night** il ne passera pas la nuit; (*US*) **(from) Monday ~ Friday** de lundi (jusqu')à vendredi; **he lives there ~ the week** il habite là pendant la semaine.

(c) (*indicating means, agency*) par, par l'entremise *or* l'intermédiaire de, grâce à, à cause de. **to send ~ the post** envoyer par la poste; **it was all ~ him that I got the job** c'est grâce à lui *or* par son entremise *or* par son intermédiaire que j'ai eu le poste; **it was all ~ him that I lost the job** c'est à cause de lui que j'ai perdu le poste; **I heard it ~ my sister** je l'ai appris par ma sœur; **~ his own efforts** par ses propres efforts; **it happened ~ no fault of mine** ce n'est absolument pas de ma faute si c'est arrivé; **absent ~ illness** absent pour cause de maladie; **to act ~ fear** agir par peur *or* sous le coup de la peur; **~ not knowing the way he ...** parce qu'il ne connaissait pas le chemin il ... .

3 *adj carriage, traffic, train, ticket* direct. [*train*] **~ portion** rame directe; **'no ~ way'** 'impasse'.

4 *cpd*: **throughout** *V* **throughout**; **throughput** (*Computers*) débit *m*; (*Ind*) consommation *f* de *or* en matières premières (*en un temps donné*); (*US*) **through street** rue *f* prioritaire; (*US*) **throughway** autoroute *f* à péage.

throughout [θruˈaʊt] **1** *prep* **(a)** (*place*) partout dans. **~ the world** partout dans le monde, dans le monde entier.

(b) (*time*) pendant, durant. **~ his life** durant toute sa vie, sa vie durant.

2 *adv* (*everywhere*) partout; (*the whole time*) tout le temps.

throve [θrəʊv] *pret of* **thrive**.

throw [θrəʊ] (*vb: pret* **threw**, *ptp* **thrown**) **1** *n* [*ball, javelin, discus*] jet *m*; (*Wrestling*) mise *f* à terre. **it was a good ~** c'était un bon jet; **with one ~ of the ball he ...** d'un seul coup il ... ; (*in table games*) **you lose a ~** vous perdez un tour; *V* **stone.**

2 *cpd*: **throwaway** (*adj*) *bottle, packaging* à jeter; *remark, line* qui n'a l'air de rien; (*n: leaflet etc*) prospectus *m*, imprimé *m*; [*characteristic, custom etc*] **it's a throwback to** ça remonte à; (*Ftbl*) **throw-in** remise *f* en jeu.

3 *vt* **(a)** (*cast*) *object, stone* lancer, jeter (*to* à); *ball, javelin, discus, hammer* lancer; *dice* jeter. **he threw a towel at her** il lui a jeté *or* envoyé une serviette à la tête; **they were ~ing stones at the cat** ils jetaient *or* lançaient des pierres au chat; **he threw the ball 50 metres** il a lancé la balle à 50 mètres; **he threw it across the room** il l'a jeté *or* lancé à l'autre bout de la pièce; (*at dice*) **to ~ a six** avoir un six; (*fig*) **to ~ the book at sb*** chapitrer qn vertement, passer un savon* à qn; *V* **water** *etc*.

(b) (*hurl violently*) projeter; (*in fight, wrestling*) envoyer au sol (*or* au tapis); [*horse*] *rider* démonter, désarçonner. **the force of the explosion threw him into the air/across the room** la force de l'explosion l'a projeté en l'air/à l'autre bout de la pièce; **he was ~n clear of the car** il a été projeté hors de la voiture; **to ~ o.s. to the ground/at sb's feet/into sb's arms** se jeter à terre/aux pieds de qn/dans les bras de qn; **to ~ o.s. on sb's mercy** s'en remettre à la merci de qn; (*fig*) **she really threw herself at him*** *or* **at his head*** elle s'est vraiment jetée à sa tête; (*fig*) **he threw himself into the job** il s'est mis *or* attelé à la tâche avec enthousiasme; **he threw himself into the task of clearing up** il y est allé de tout son courage pour mettre de l'ordre.

(c) (*direct*) *light, shadow, glance* jeter; *slides, pictures* projeter; *kiss* envoyer (*to* à); *punch* lancer (*at* à). **to ~ one's voice** *faire en sorte que la voix semble provenir d'une grande distance; V* **light[1]** *etc.*

(d) (*put suddenly, hurriedly*) jeter (*into* dans, *over* sur). **to ~ sb into jail** jeter qn en prison; **to ~ a bridge over a river** jeter un pont sur une rivière; **he threw the switch** il a allumé (*or* éteint) d'un geste rapide *or* brusquement; **to ~ a question at sb** poser une question à qn à brûle-pourpoint; **to ~ sb into confusion** jeter la confusion dans l'esprit de qn; **it ~s the emphasis on ...** cela met l'accent sur ...; **it threw the police off the trail** cela a dépisté la police; **to ~ open** *door, window* ouvrir tout grand; (*fig*) *house, gardens* ouvrir au public; *race, competition etc* ouvrir à tout le monde; **to ~ a party*** organiser *or* donner une petite fête (*for sb* en l'honneur de qn); (*lose deliberately*) **to ~ a race*** *etc* perdre délibérément une course *etc*; *V* **blame, doubt, fit[2], relief** *etc.*

(e) *pottery* tourner; *silk* tordre.

(f) (*: *disconcert*) déconcerter, décontenancer, désorienter, dérouter. **I was quite ~n when he ...** je n'en suis pas revenu *or* je suis resté baba* quand il ... .

throw about, throw around *vt sep litter, confetti* éparpiller. **don't throw it about or it might break** ne t'amuse pas à le lancer, ça peut se casser; **they were throwing a ball about** ils jouaient à la balle; **to throw one's money about** jeter son argent par les fenêtres; (*fig*) **to throw one's weight about** faire l'important; **to throw o.s. about** se débattre.

throw aside *vt sep* (*lit*) jeter de côté; (*fig*) rejeter, repousser.

throw away 1 *vt sep* **(a)** *rubbish, cigarette end* jeter; (*fig*) *one's life, happiness, talents, health* gâcher; *sb's affection* perdre; *money, time* gaspiller, perdre; *chance* gâcher, perdre, laisser passer. **she is throwing herself away on a man like that** elle est en train de gâcher sa vie avec un homme comme lui; **you're throwing yourself away if you take that job** tu vas gaspiller tes dons si tu acceptes cet emploi.

(b) (*esp Theat*) *line, remark* (*say casually*) laisser tomber; (*lose effect of*) perdre tout l'effet de.

2 throwaway *adj, n V* **throw 2.**

throw back 1 *vt sep* **(a)** (*return*) *ball etc* renvoyer (*to* à); *fish* rejeter; (*fig*) *image* renvoyer, réfléchir.

(b) *head, hair* rejeter en arrière; *shoulders* redresser. **to throw o.s. back** se (re)jeter en arrière.

(c) *enemy etc* repousser. (*fig*) **to be thrown back upon sth** être obligé de se rabattre sur qch.

2 throwback *n V* **throw 2.**

throw down *vt sep object* jeter; *weapons* déposer. **to throw o.s. down** se jeter à terre; **to throw down a challenge** lancer *or* jeter un défi; *[rain]* **it's really throwing it down*** il pleut à seaux, il tombe des cordes.

throw in 1 *vt sep* **(a)** *object into box etc* jeter; (*Ftbl*) *ball* remettre en jeu; *one's cards* jeter (sur la table). (*fig*) **to throw in one's hand** *or* **the sponge** *or* **the towel** abandonner (la partie); *V* **lot.**

(b) (*fig*) *remark, question* interposer. **he threw in a reference to it** il l'a mentionné en passant.

(c) (*fig: as extra*) **with £5 thrown in** avec 5 livres en plus *or* par-dessus le marché; **if you buy a washing machine they throw in a packet of soap powder** si vous achetez une machine à laver ils vous donnent un paquet de lessive en prime; **we had a cruise of the Greek Islands with a day in Athens thrown in** nous avons fait une croisière autour des îles grecques avec en prime un arrêt d'un jour à Athènes.

2 throw-in *n V* **throw 2.**

throw off *vt sep* **(a)** (*get rid of*) *burden, yoke* rejeter, se libérer de, se débarrasser de; *clothes* enlever *or* quitter *or* ôter (en hâte), se débarrasser brusquement de; *disguise* jeter; *pursuers, dogs* perdre, semer*; *habit, tendency, cold, infection* se débarrasser de.

(b) (*) *poem, composition* faire *or* écrire au pied levé.

throw on *vt sep coal, sticks* ajouter; *clothes* enfiler *or* passer à la hâte. **she threw on some lipstick*** elle s'est vite mis *or* passé un peu de rouge à lèvres.

throw out *vt sep* **(a)** jeter dehors; *rubbish, old clothes etc* jeter, mettre au rebut; *person* (*lit*) expulser, mettre à la porte, vider*; (*fig: from army, school etc*) expulser, renvoyer; *suggestion* rejeter, repousser; (*Parl*) *bill* repousser. (*fig*) **to throw out one's chest** bomber la poitrine.

(b) (*say*) *suggestion, hint, idea, remark* laisser tomber; *challenge* jeter, lancer.

(c) (*make wrong*) *calculation, prediction, accounts, budget* fausser; (*disconcert*) *person* désorienter, déconcerter.

throw over *vt sep plan, intention* abandonner, laisser tomber*; *friend, boyfriend etc* laisser tomber*, lâcher*, plaquer: (*for sb else* pour qn d'autre).

throw together *vt sep* **(a)** (*pej: make hastily*) *furniture, machine* faire à la six-quatre-deux*; (*) *essay* torcher. **he threw a few things together and left at once** il a rassemblé quelques affaires *or* jeté quelques affaires dans un sac et il est parti sur-le-champ.

(b) (*fig: by chance*) *people* réunir (par hasard). **they were thrown together, fate had thrown them together** le hasard les avait réunis.

throw up 1 *vi* (*vomit*) vomir.

2 *vt sep* **(a)** (*into air*) *ball etc* jeter *or* lancer en l'air. **he threw the book up to me** il m'a jeté *or* lancé le livre; **he threw up his hands in despair** il a levé les bras de désespoir; (*fig*) **the meeting threw up several good ideas** quelques bonnes idées sont sorties de la réunion.

(b) (*vomit*) vomir.

(c) (*: *abandon, reject*) *job, task, studies* lâcher, abandonner; *opportunity* laisser passer.

thrower [ˈθrəʊəʳ] *n* lanceur *m*, -euse *f*; *V* **discus** *etc.*

thrown [θrəʊn] *ptp of* **throw.**

thru [θruː] (*US*) = **through.**

thrum [θrʌm] *vti* = **strum.**

thrush[1] [θrʌʃ] *n* (*Orn*) grive *f*.

thrush[2] [θrʌʃ] *n* (*Med*) muguet *m*; (*Vet*) échauffement *m* de la fourchette.

thrust [θrʌst] (*vb: pret, ptp* **thrust**) **1** *n* **(a)** (*push*) poussée *f* (*also Mil*); (*stab: with knife, dagger, stick etc*) coup *m*; (*with sword*) botte *f*; (*fig: remark*) pointe *f*. (*fig*) **that was a ~ at you** ça c'était une pointe dirigée contre vous, c'est vous qui étiez visé; *V* **cut.**

(b) (*U*) *[propeller, jet engine, rocket]* poussée *f*; (*Archit, Tech*) poussée; (*fig: drive, energy*) dynamisme *m*, initiative *f*.

2 *vt* **(a)** pousser brusquement *or* violemment; *finger, stick* enfoncer; *dagger* plonger, enfoncer (*into* dans, *between* entre); *rag etc* fourrer* (*into* dans). **he ~ the box under the table** (*moved*) il a poussé *or* fourré* la boîte sous la table; (*hid*) il a vite caché la boîte sous la table; **he ~ his finger into my eye** il m'a mis le doigt dans l'œil; **he ~ the letter at me** il m'a brusquement mis la lettre sous le nez; **to ~ one's hands into one's pockets** enfoncer les mains dans ses poches; **he had a knife ~ into his belt** il avait un couteau glissé dans sa ceinture; **he ~ his head through the window** il a mis *or* passé la tête par la fenêtre; **he ~ the book into my hand** il m'a fourré le livre dans la main; **to ~ one's way** *V* **3a.**

(b) (*fig*) *job, responsibility* imposer (*upon sb* à qn); *honour* conférer (*on* à). **some have greatness ~ upon them** certains ont de la grandeur sans la rechercher; **I had the job ~ (up)on me** on m'a imposé ce travail; **to ~ o.s. (up)on sb** imposer sa présence à qn.

3 *vi* **(a)** (*also* **~ one's way**) **to ~ in/out** *etc* entrer/sortir *etc* en se frayant un passage; **he ~ past me** il a réussi à passer (*or* il m'a dépassé) en me bousculant; **to ~ through a crowd** se frayer un passage dans la foule.

(b) (*Fencing*) allonger une botte.

thrust aside *vt sep object, person* écarter brusquement, pousser brusquement à l'écart; (*fig*) *objection, suggestion* écarter *or* rejeter violemment.

thrust forward *vt sep object, person* pousser en avant (brusquement). **to thrust o.s. forward** s'avancer brusquement, se frayer *or* s'ouvrir un chemin; (*fig*) se mettre en avant, se faire valoir.

thrust in 1 *vi* (*lit: also* **thrust one's way in**) s'introduire de force; (*fig: interfere*) intervenir.

2 *vt sep stick, pin, finger* enfoncer; *rag* fourrer dedans*; *person* pousser (violemment) à l'intérieur *or* dedans.

thrust out *vt sep* **(a)** (*extend*) *hand* tendre brusquement; *legs* allonger brusquement; *jaw, chin* projeter en avant.

(b) (*push outside*) *object, person* pousser dehors. **he opened the window and thrust his head out** il a ouvert la fenêtre et passé la tête dehors.

thrust up *vi [plants etc]* pousser vigoureusement.

thruster [ˈθrʌstəʳ] *n* (*pej*) **to be a ~** se mettre trop en avant, être arriviste.

thrustful* [ˈθrʌstfʊl] *adj* = **thrusting.**

thrustfulness* [ˈθrʌstfʊlnɪs] *n* (*U*) dynamisme *m*, initiative *f*, arrivisme *m* (*pej*).

thrusting [ˈθrʌstɪŋ] *adj* dynamique, entreprenant; (*pej*) arriviste, qui se fait valoir, qui se met trop en avant.

thud [θʌd] **1** *n* bruit sourd, son mat. **I heard the ~ of gunfire** j'entendais gronder sourdement les canons.

2 *vi* faire un bruit sourd, rendre un son mat (*on, against* en heurtant); *[guns]* gronder sourdement; (*fall*) tomber avec un bruit sourd. *[person]* **to ~** *or* **to go ~ding in/out** *etc* entrer/sortir *etc* à pas pesants.

thug [θʌg] *n* voyou *m*, gangster *m*; (*at demonstrations*) casseur *m*; (*term of abuse*) brute *f*.

thumb [θʌm] **1** *n* pouce *m*. (*fig*) **to be under sb's ~** être sous la coupe de qn; **she's got him under her ~** elle le mène par le bout du nez; (*fig*) **to be all ~s** être très maladroit; **he gave me the ~s up (sign)*** (*all going well*) il m'a fait signe que tout allait bien; (*to wish me luck*) il m'a fait signe pour me souhaiter bonne chance; **he gave me the ~s down (sign)*** il m'a fait signe que ça n'allait pas (*or* que ça n'avait pas bien marché); *V* **finger, rule, twiddle** *etc.*

2 *cpd nail, print* du pouce. **thumb index** répertoire *m* à onglets; (*fig*) **thumbnail sketch** croquis *m* sur le vif; **thumbscrew** (*Tech*) vis *f* à papillon *or* à ailettes; (*Hist: torture*) poucettes *fpl*; (*US*) **thumbtack** punaise *f*.

3 *vt* **(a)** *book, magazine* feuilleter. **well ~ed** tout écorné (par l'usage); **to ~ one's nose** faire un pied de nez (*at sb* à qn).

(b) (*) **to ~ a lift** *or* **a ride** faire du stop* *or* de l'auto-stop; **he ~ed a lift to Paris** il est allé à Paris en stop* *or* en auto-stop; **I managed at last to ~ a lift** je suis enfin arrivé à arrêter *or* à avoir une voiture.

thumb through *vt fus book* feuilleter. **he thumbed through the card index** il a fait défiler les fiches sous ses doigts.

thump [θʌmp] **1** *n* (*blow: with fist/stick etc*) (grand) coup *m* de poing/de canne *etc*; (*sound*) bruit lourd et sourd. **to fall with a ~** tomber lourdement; **to give sb a ~** assener un coup à qn.

2 *vt person* assener un *or* des coup(s) à; *table* cogner sur, taper sur; *door* cogner à, taper à. **I could have ~ed him!*** je l'aurais giflé! *or* bouffé!:

3 *vi* **(a)** cogner, frapper (*on* sur, *at* à); *[heart]* battre fort, (*with fear*) battre la chamade. **he was ~ing on the piano** il tapait (comme un sourd) sur le piano, il jouait comme un forcené.

(b) *[person]* **to ~ in/out** *etc* entrer/sortir *etc* en martelant le pavé (*or* le plancher); (*at a run*) entrer/sortir *etc* en courant bruyamment.

thump out *vt sep*: **to thump out a tune on the piano** marteler un air au piano.

thumping‡ [ˈθʌmpɪŋ] *adj* (*also* **~ great**) énorme, monumental*, phénoménal.

thunder [ˈθʌndəʳ] **1** *n* (*U*) tonnerre *m*; *[applause]* tonnerre, tempête *f*; *[hooves]* retentissement *m*, fracas *m*; *[passing vehicles, trains]* fracas, bruit *m* de tonnerre. **there's ~ about** le temps est à l'orage; **there's ~ in the air** il y a de l'orage dans l'air; **I could hear the ~ of the guns** j'entendais tonner les canons; *V* **peal, steal.**

2 *cpd*: **thunderbolt** coup *m* de foudre; (*fig*) coup de tonnerre; **thunderclap** coup *m* de tonnerre (*lit*); **thundercloud** nuage orageux; (*fig*) nuage noir; **thunderstorm** orage *m*; (*fig*) **thunderstruck** abasourdi, ahuri, stupéfié.

3 *vi* (*Met*) tonner; *[guns]* tonner; *[hooves]* retentir. **the train ~ed past** le train est passé dans un grondement de tonnerre.

4 *vt* (*also* **~ out**) *threat, order* proférer d'une voix tonitruante. **'no!' he ~ed** 'non!' tonna-t-il *or* dit-il d'une voix tonitruante; **the crowd ~ed their approval** la foule a exprimé son approbation dans un tonnerre d'applaudissements et de cris.

thunderer [ˈθʌndərəʳ] *n*: **the T~** le dieu de la Foudre et du Tonnerre, Jupiter tonnant.

thundering [ˈθʌndərɪŋ] *adj* **(a) in a ~ rage** *or* **fury** dans une colère noire, fulminant; **in a ~ temper** d'une humeur massacrante. **(b)** (*: *also* **~ great**) énorme, monumental*, phénoménal. **it was a ~ success** ça a eu un succès fou *or* un succès monstre.

thunderous [ˈθʌndərəs] *adj welcome, shouts* étourdissant. **~ acclaim** ovation *f*; **~ applause** tonnerre *m* d' applaudissements.

thundery [ˈθʌndərɪ] *adj* orageux.

thurible [ˈθjʊərɪbl] *n* encensoir *m*.

thurifer [ˈθjʊərɪfəʳ] *n* thuriféraire *m*.

Thursday [ˈθɜːzdɪ] *n* jeudi *m*; *for phrases V* **Saturday.**

thus [ðʌs] *adv* (*in this way*) ainsi, comme ceci, de cette façon, de cette manière; (*consequently*) ainsi, donc, par conséquent. **~ far** (*up to here*) jusqu'ici; (*up to there*) jusque-là.

thwack [θwæk] **1** *n* (*blow*) grand coup; (*with hand*) claque *f*, gifle *f*; (*sound*) claquement *m*, coup sec. **2** *vt* frapper vigoureusement, donner un coup sec à; (*slap*) donner une claque à.

thwart[1] [θwɔːt] *vt plan* contrecarrer, contrarier; *person* contrecarrer *or* contrarier les projets de. **to be ~ed at every turn** voir tous ses plans contrariés l'un après l'autre.

thwart[2] [θwɔːt] *n* (*Naut*) banc *m* de nage.

thy [ðaɪ] *poss adj* (††, *liter, dial*) ton, ta, tes.

thyme [taɪm] *n* thym *m*. **wild ~** serpolet *m*.

thyroid [ˈθaɪrɔɪd] **1** *n* (*also* **~ gland**) thyroïde *f*. **2** *adj* thyroïde.

thyself [ðaɪˈself] *pers pron* (††, *liter, dial*) (*reflexive*) te; (*emphatic*) toi-même.

ti [tiː] *n* (*Mus*) si *m*.

tiara [tɪˈɑːrə] *n [lady]* diadème *m*; *[Pope]* tiare *f*.

Tiber [ˈtaɪbəʳ] *n* Tibre *m*.

Tibet [tɪˈbet] *n* Tibet *m*.

Tibetan [tɪˈbetən] **1** *adj* tibétain, du Tibet. **2** *n* **(a)** Tibétain(e) *m(f)*. **(b)** (*Ling*) tibétain *m*.

tibia [ˈtɪbɪə] *n* tibia *m*.

tic [tɪk] *n* tic *m* (nerveux).

tich‡ [tɪtʃ] *n* bout *m* de chou*, microbe* *m* (*also pej*).

tichy‡ [ˈtɪtʃɪ] *adj* (*also* **~ little**) minuscule.

tick[1] [tɪk] **1** *n* **(a)** *[clock]* tic-tac *m*.

(b) (*Brit**: *instant*) instant *m*. **just a ~!, half a ~!** une minute!, un instant!; **in a ~, in a couple of ~s** en un rien de temps, en moins de deux, en un clin d'œil; **it won't take a ~** *or* **two ~s** c'est l'affaire d'un instant, il y en a pour une seconde; **I shan't be a ~** j'en ai pour une seconde.

(c) (*mark*) coche *f*. **to put** *or* **mark a ~ against sth** cocher qch.

2 *cpd*: (*Racing*) **ticktack** signaux *mpl* (des bookmakers); (*Brit*) **ticktack man** aide *m* de bookmaker; (*US*) **tick-tack-toe** ≈ (jeu *m* de) morpion *m*; *[clock]* **tick-tock** tic-tac *m*.

3 *vt* (*Brit*) *name, item, answer* cocher; (*Scol: mark right*) marquer juste.

4 *vi [clock, bomb etc]* faire tic-tac, tictaquer. (*fig*) **I don't understand what makes him ~*** il est un mystère pour moi.

tick away 1 *vi [clock etc]* continuer son tic-tac; *[taximeter]* tourner.

2 *vt sep*: **the clock ticked the hours away** la pendule marquait les heures.

tick off 1 *vt sep* **(a)** (*Brit*) *name, item* cocher.

(b) (*Brit**: *reprimand*) attraper, passer un savon à*.

(c) (*US**: *annoy*) embêter*, casser les pieds à*.

2 ticking-off* *n V* **ticking**[2] **2.**

tick over *vi* (*Brit*) *[engine]* tourner au ralenti; *[taximeter]* tourner; *[business etc]* aller *or* marcher doucettement.

tick[2] [tɪk] *n* (*Zool*) tique *f*.

tick[3]* [tɪk] *n* (*Brit: credit*) crédit *m*. **on ~** à crédit; **to give sb ~** faire crédit à qn.

tick[4] [tɪk] *n* (*U: cloth*) toile *f* (à matelas); (*cover*) housse *f* (pour matelas).

ticker [ˈtɪkəʳ] **1** *n* **(a)** (*esp US*) téléscripteur *m*, téléimprimeur *m*.

(b) (‡) (*watch*) tocante* *f*; (*heart*) palpitant‡ *m*.

2 *cpd*: (*U*) **ticker-tape** bande *f* de téléscripteur *or* téléimprimeur; (*US: at parades etc*) ≈ serpentin *m*; (*US*) **to get a ticker-tape welcome** être accueilli par une pluie de serpentins.

ticket [ˈtɪkɪt] **1** *n* **(a)** (*Aviat, Cine, Rail, Theat etc: also for football match etc*) billet *m*; (*for bus, tube*) ticket *m*; (*Comm: label*) étiquette *f*; (*counterfoil*) talon *m*; (*from cash register*) ticket, reçu *m*; (*for cloakroom*) ticket, numéro *m*; (*for left-luggage*) bulletin *m*; (*for library*) carte *f*; (*from pawnshop*) reconnaissance *f* (du mont-de-piété). **coach ~** billet de car; **admission by ~ only** entrée réservée aux personnes munies d'un billet; (*fig*) **that's the ~!*** c'est ça!, voilà ce qu'il nous faut!; *V* **return, season** *etc.*

(b) (*Aut**) P.-V. *m*, papillon *m*. **I found a ~ on the windscreen** j'ai trouvé un papillon sur le pare-brise; **to get a ~ for parking** attraper un P.-V. pour stationnement illégal; **to give sb a ~ for parking** mettre un P.-V. à qn pour stationnement illégal.

(c) (*certificate*) *[pilot]* brevet *m*. *[ship's captain]* **to get one's ~** passer capitaine.

(d) (*US Pol: list*) liste *f* (électorale). **he is running on the Democratic ~** il se présente sur la liste des démocrates; *V* **straight.**

2 *cpd*: **ticket agency** (*Theat*) agence *f* de spectacles; (*Rail etc*) agence de voyages; **ticket collector** contrôleur *m*; **ticket holder** personne munie d'un billet; **ticket inspector** = **ticket collector**; **ticket office** bureau *m* de vente des billets, guichet *m*; (*Brit Jur*) **ticket-of-leave**† libération conditionnelle; (*Brit Jur*) **ticket-of-leave man**† libéré conditionnel; **ticket tout** *V* **tout 1.**

3 *vt goods* étiqueter; (*US*) *traveller etc* donner un billet à; (*US Aut**) mettre un P.-V. à.

ticking[1] [ˈtɪkɪŋ] *n* (*U: Tex*) toile *f* (à matelas).

ticking[2] [ˈtɪkɪŋ] **1** *n [clock]* tic-tac *m*. **2** *cpd*: (*Brit**) **ticking-off** attrapade* *f*; **to give sb a ticking-off** passer un savon à qn*, attraper qn; **to get a ticking-off** recevoir un bon savon*, se faire attraper.

tickle [ˈtɪkl] **1** *vt* (*lit*) *person, dog* chatouiller; (*please*) *sb's vanity, palate etc* chatouiller; (*: *delight*) *person* plaire à, faire plaisir à; (*: *amuse*) amuser, faire rire. **to ~ sb's ribs, to ~ sb in the ribs** chatouiller les côtes à qn; **to be ~d to death‡, to be ~d pink‡** être heureux comme tout, être aux anges; *V* **fancy** *etc.*

2 *vi* chatouiller.

3 *n* chatouillement *m*, chatouilles* *fpl*. **he gave the child a ~** il a chatouillé l'enfant, il a fait des chatouilles* à l'enfant; **to have a ~ in one's throat** avoir un chatouillement dans la gorge; *V* **slap.**

tickler* [ˈtɪkləʳ] *n* (*Brit*) (*question, problem*) colle* *f*; (*situation*) situation délicate *or* épineuse.

tickling [ˈtɪklɪŋ] **1** *n* chatouillement *m*, chatouille(s)* *f(pl)*. **2** *adj sensation* de chatouillement; *blanket* qui chatouille; *cough* d'irritation.

ticklish [ˈtɪklɪʃ] *adj*, **tickly*** [ˈtɪklɪ] *adj* **(a)** *sensation* de chatouillement; *blanket* qui chatouille; *cough* d'irritation. *[person]* **to be ~** être chatouilleux, craindre les chatouilles*.

(b) (*touchy*) *person, sb's pride* chatouilleux; (*difficult*) *situation, problem, task* épineux, délicat.

ticky-tacky [ˈtɪkɪˌtækɪ] (*US*) **1** *adj* de pacotille. **2** *n* pacotille *f*.

tidal [ˈtaɪdl] *adj force* de la marée; *river, inland sea, estuary* qui a des marées. **~ wave** raz-de-marée *m inv*; (*fig: of enthusiasm, protest etc*) immense vague *f*, flot *m*.

tidbit [ˈtɪdbɪt] *n* (*esp US*) = **titbit.**

tiddler* [ˈtɪdləʳ] *n* (*Brit*) (*stickleback*) épinoche *f*; (*tiny fish*) petit poisson; (*small child*) petit(e) mioche* *m(f)*.

tiddly [ˈtɪdlɪ] **1** *adj* (*: *esp Brit*) pompette*, éméché*. **2** *cpd*: **tiddlywinks** jeu *m* de puce.

tide [taɪd] **1** *n* marée *f*. **at high/low ~** à marée haute/basse; **the ~ is on the turn** la mer est étale; **the ~ turns at 3 o'clock** la marée commence à monter (*or* à descendre) à 3 heures; (*fig*) **the ~ has turned, there has been a turn of the ~** la chance a tourné, la chance est passée de notre (*or* leur *etc*) côté; (*fig*) **to go with the ~** suivre le courant; (*fig*) **to go against the ~** aller à contre-courant; **the ~ of events** le cours *or* la marche des événements; **the rising ~ of public impatience** l'exaspération grandissante et généralisée du public; *V* **time.**

2 *cpd*: **tideland** laisse *f*; **tidemark** laisse *f* de haute mer, ligne *f* de (la) marée haute; (*hum: on neck, in bath*) ligne de crasse; **tidewater** (eaux *fpl* de) marée *f*; **tideway** (*channel*) chenal *m* de marée; (*tidal part of river*) section (d'un cours d'eau) soumise à l'influence des marées.

3 *vt*: **to ~ sb over a difficulty** dépanner qn lors d'une difficulté, tirer qn d'embarras provisoirement; **it ~d him over the week till payday** ça l'a dépanné en attendant d'être payé *or* ça lui a permis d'attendre le jour de paye à la fin de la semaine.

tide over *vt sep* dépanner. **£5 should tide me over until ...** avec 5 livres je devrais m'en sortir *or* m'en tirer* jusqu'à ... .

... tide [taɪd] *n ending in cpds* saison *f*. **Eastertide** (la saison de) Pâques *m*; *V* **Whit** *etc.*

tidily [ˈtaɪdɪlɪ] *adv arrange, fold* soigneusement, avec soin; *write* proprement. **she is always ~ dressed** elle est toujours correctement vêtue *or* toujours mise avec soin; **try to dress more ~** tâche de t'habiller plus correctement *or* d'apporter plus de soin à ta tenue.

tidiness [ˈtaɪdɪnɪs] *n* (*U*) *[room, drawer, desk, books]* belle ordonnance; *[handwriting, schoolwork]* propreté *f*. **the ~ of his appearance** sa tenue soignée.

tidings [ˈtaɪdɪŋz] *npl* (*liter*) nouvelle(s) *f(pl)*.

tidy [ˈtaɪdɪ] **1** *adj* **(a)** *room, drawer, cupboard* bien rangé, ordonné, en ordre; *desk, objects, books* bien rangé, en ordre; *dress, appearance, hair* net, soigné; *handwriting, schoolwork* net, propre; *habits* d'ordre; *person* (*in appearance*) soigné; (*in character*) ordonné, méthodique. **to make** *or* **get a room ~** ranger une pièce, mettre de l'ordre dans une pièce; **try to make your writing tidier** tâche d'écrire plus proprement; **to make o.s.**

~s'arranger, remettre de l'ordre dans sa toilette; **to have a ~ mind** avoir l'esprit méthodique.

(b) (*) *sum, amount, income* rondelet, coquet, joli; *speed* bon. **it cost a ~ bit** *or* **a ~ penny** ça lui (*or* nous *etc*) a coûté une jolie somme; **it took a ~ bit of his salary** ça lui a pris un bon morceau de son salaire.

2 *n* vide-poches *m inv*; *V* **sink**[2] *etc*.

3 *cpd*: **to have a tidy-out*** *or* **tidy-up*** faire une séance de rangement *or* du rangement; **to give sth a (good) tidy-out*** *or* **tidy-up*** ranger qch à fond.

4 *vt* (*also* ~ **up**) *drawer, cupboard, books, clothes* ranger, mettre de l'ordre dans; *desk* ranger, mettre de l'ordre sur. **to ~ o.s. (up)** s'arranger, remettre de l'ordre dans sa toilette; **to ~ (up) one's hair** arranger sa coiffure, remettre de l'ordre dans sa coiffure.

tidy away *vt sep* ranger.

tidy out 1 *vt sep cupboard, drawer* vider pour y mettre de l'ordre.

2 tidy-out* *n V* **tidy 3.**

tidy up 1 *vi* (*tidy room etc*) (tout) ranger; (*tidy o.s.*) s'arranger.

2 *vt sep* = **tidy 4.**

3 tidy-up* *n V* **tidy 3.**

tie [taɪ] **1** *n* **(a)** (*cord etc*) *[garment, curtain]* attache *f*; *[shoe]* lacet *m*, cordon *m*; (*neck~*) cravate *f*; (*fig: bond, link*) lien *m*; (*fig: restriction*) entrave *f*; (*Mus*) liaison *f*; (*Archit*) tirant *m*, entrait *m*; (*US Rail*) traverse *f*. (*Dress*) **black ~** smoking *m*; (*Dress*) **white ~** habit *m*; (*fig*) **the ~s of blood** les liens du sang; **family ~s** (*links*) liens de famille *or* de parenté; (*responsibilities*) attaches familiales; **she finds the children a great ~** avec les enfants elle n'est pas libre, les enfants l'accaparent beaucoup; *V* **old.**

(b) (*esp Sport*) (*draw*) égalité *f* (de points); (*drawn match*) match nul; (*drawn race/competition*) course *f*/concours *m* dont les vainqueurs sont ex æquo. **the match ended in a ~, the result (of the match) was a ~** les deux équipes ont fait match nul *or* ont terminé le match à égalité; **to play off a ~** (*second match*) rejouer un match nul; (*third match*) jouer la belle; (*Scol, Sport etc*) **there was a ~ for second place** il y avait deux ex æquo en seconde position.

(c) (*Sport: match*) match *m* de championnat; *V* **cup.**

2 *cpd*: **tie-(and-)dye** *n* méthode *f* nouer-lier-teindre (*procédé consistant à cacher certaines parties en nouant ou en liant*); (*in quiz etc*) **tie-breaker** question *f* subsidiaire; **tie-clasp, tie-clip** fixe-cravate *m*; **tie-in** (*link*) lien *m*, rapport *m* (*with* avec); (*US Comm: sale*) vente jumelée *or* par lots; (*US Comm: article*) lot *m*; **tie-on** *label* à œillet; **tiepin** épingle *f* de cravate; (*Archit, Aut*) **tie-rod** tirant *m*; (*US*) **tie-tack** = **tie-clasp**; **tie-up** (*connection*) lien *m* (*with* avec, *between* entre); (*Fin: merger*) fusion *f* (*with* avec, *between* entre); (*US: stoppage*) difficultés *fpl*, problèmes *mpl*.

3 *vt* **(a)** (*fasten*) attacher (*to* à); *shoelace, necktie, rope* attacher, nouer; *parcel* attacher, ficeler; *ribbon* nouer, faire un nœud à; *shoes* lacer. **to ~ sb's hands** (*lit*) attacher *or* lier les mains de qn; (*fig*) lier les mains de *or* à qn; (*lit, fig*) **his hands are ~d** il a les mains liées; (*lit, fig*) **to be ~d hand and foot** avoir pieds et poings liés; **to ~ sth in a bow, to ~ a bow in sth** faire un nœud avec qch; **to ~ a knot in sth** faire un nœud à qch; *[rope etc]* **to get ~d in knots** se nouer, faire des nœuds; (*fig*) **to get ~d in knots*, to ~ o.s. in knots*** s'embrouiller; *V* **apron.**

(b) (*link*) lier (*to* à); (*restrict*) restreindre, limiter. **the house is ~d to her husband's job** la maison est liée au travail de son mari; (*Brit Agr etc*) **~d cottage** logement *m* de fonction (*d'ouvrier agricole etc*); (*Brit: of pub*) **it is a ~d house** ils ne vendent qu'une sorte de bière; **I'm ~d to the house/my desk all day** je suis retenu *or* cloué à la maison/mon bureau toute la journée; **are we ~d to this plan?** sommes-nous obligés de nous en tenir à ce projet?; **we are very ~d in the evenings** nous sommes rarement libres le soir; **she is very ~d by the children** elle est très prise par les enfants; **he isn't ~d at all** il n'a aucune attache, rien ne le retient.

4 *vi* **(a)** *[shoelace, necktie, rope]* se nouer.

(b) (*draw*) (*Sport etc*) faire match nul; (*in competition*) être ex æquo; (*in election*) obtenir le même nombre de voix, faire le même score (électoral). (*Sport*) **we ~d with them 4-all** nous avons fait match nul 4 partout; (*in race, exam, competition*) **they ~d for first place** ils ont été premiers ex æquo.

tie back *vt sep curtains* attacher sur les côtés; *hair* retenir (en arrière).

tie down *vt sep object, person, animal* attacher. (*fig*) **he didn't want to be tied down** il ne voulait pas perdre sa liberté; **to tie sb down to a promise** obliger qn à tenir sa promesse; **can you tie him down to these conditions?** pouvez-vous l'astreindre à ces conditions?; **we can't tie him down to a date/a price** nous n'arrivons pas à lui faire fixer une date/un prix; **I shan't tie you down to 6 o'clock** il n'est pas nécessaire que ce soit à 6 heures; **I don't want to tie myself down to going** je ne veux pas m'engager à y aller *or* me trouver contraint d'y aller.

tie in 1 *vi* **(a)** (*be linked*) être lié (*with* à). **it all ties in with what they plan to do** tout est lié à ce qu'ils projettent de faire; **this fact must tie in somewhere** ce fait doit bien avoir un rapport quelque part.

(b) (*be consistent*) correspondre (*with* à), concorder, cadrer (*with* avec). **it doesn't tie in with what I was told** ça ne correspond pas à *or* ça ne cadre pas avec *or* ça ne concorde pas avec ce qu'on m'a dit.

2 *vt sep*: **I'm trying to tie that in with what he said** j'essaie de voir la liaison *or* le rapport entre ça et ce qu'il a dit; **can you tie the visit in with your trip to London?** pouvez-vous combiner la visite et *or* avec votre voyage à Londres?

3 tie-in *n V* **tie 2.**

tie on 1 *vt sep label etc* attacher (avec une ficelle). (*US*) **to tie one on‡** se cuiter‡.

2 tie-on *adj V* **tie 2.**

tie together *vt sep objects, people* attacher ensemble.

tie up 1 *vi* (*Naut*) accoster.

2 *vt sep* **(a)** (*bind*) *parcel* ficeler; *prisoner* attacher, ligoter; (*tether*) *boat, horse* attacher (*to* à). (*fig*) **there are a lot of loose ends to tie up** il y a beaucoup de points de détail à régler avant d'en avoir fini; (*fig: muddled*) **to get (o.s.) all tied up*** s'embrouiller.

(b) *capital, money* immobiliser.

(c) (*fig: conclude*) *business deal etc* conclure. **it's all tied up now** tout est réglé maintenant, c'est une chose réglée maintenant, nous avons (*or* il a *etc*) tout réglé.

(d) (*: *pass only: occupied*) **he is tied up all tomorrow** il est pris *or* occupé toute la journée de demain; **he is tied up with the manager** il est occupé avec le directeur; **we are tied up for months to come** nous avons un emploi du temps très chargé pour les mois qui viennent; **he's rather tied up with a girl in Dover** une jeune fille de Douvres l'accapare en ce moment.

(e) (*pass only: linked*) **this company is tied up with an American firm** cette compagnie a des liens avec *or* est liée à une firme américaine; **his illness is tied up* with the fact that his wife has left him** sa maladie est liée au fait que sa femme l'a quitté.

(f) (*US: obstruct, hinder*) *traffic* obstruer, entraver; *production, sales* arrêter momentanément; *project, programme* entraver. **to get tied up** *[traffic]* se bloquer; *[production, sales]* s'arrêter; *[project, programme]* être suspendu.

3 tie-up *n V* **tie 2.**

tier [tɪər] **1** *n* (*in stadium, amphitheatre*) gradin *m*; (*part of cake*) étage *m*. (*Theat*) **grand ~** balcon *m*; (*Theat*) **upper ~** seconde galerie; **to arrange in ~s** (*gen*) étager, disposer par étages; *seating* disposer en gradins; **to rise in ~s** s'étager.

2 *vt seats etc* disposer en gradins. **~ed seating** places assises en gradins *or* en amphithéâtre; **three-~ed cake** ≈ pièce montée à trois étages.

Tierra del Fuego [tɪˌerədel'fweɪgəʊ] *n* Terre de Feu *f*.

tiff [tɪf] *n* prise *f* de bec*.

tiffin† ['tɪfɪn] *n* (*mot anglo-indien*) repas *m* de midi.

tig [tɪg] *n* = **tag 1c.**

tiger ['taɪgər] **1** *n* tigre *m* (*also fig*). **she fought like a ~** elle s'est battue comme une tigresse; (*fig*) **he has a ~ by the tail** il a déclenché quelque chose dont il n'est plus maître.

2 *cpd*: **tiger lily** lis tigré; **tiger moth** écaille *f* (*papillon*); **tiger's eye (stone)** œil *m* de tigre.

tight [taɪt] **1** *adj* **(a)** (*not loose*) *rope* raide, tendu; *coat, skirt, trousers* ajusté, étroit; (*too ~*) étriqué, (trop) juste, trop étroit; *belt, shoes* qui serre, trop juste; *tap, screw, lid, drawer* dur; *bend in road* raide; *knot, weave, knitting* serré; *restrictions, control* sévère, strict, rigoureux; *programme, schedule* serré, minuté, très chargé. **as ~ as a drum** tendu comme un tambour; **my shoes are (too) ~** mes chaussures me serrent; **it should be fairly ~ over the hips** cela devrait être relativement ajusté sur les hanches; **it's a ~ fit** c'est juste; **to keep (a) ~ hold** *or* **a ~ grasp on sth** (*lit*) bien tenir qch, serrer qch; (*fig*) avoir *or* tenir qch en main; **it will be ~ but I think we'll make it in time** ce sera juste mais je crois que nous y arriverons; (*fig*) **to be in a ~ corner** *or* **situation** se trouver dans une situation difficile; *V* **skin, spot, squeeze** *etc.*

(b) (*not leaky*) *boat, container, joint* étanche. **air~** hermétique, étanche (à l'air); *V* **water** *etc.*

(c) *credit* serré, resserré; *business* difficile; *budget* juste, serré; *transaction, deal* qui laisse peu de marge. **money is very ~** (*Econ*) l'argent est rare; (*at home*) les finances sont très justes *or* serrées; *[person]* **to be ~ (with one's money)** être avare *or* radin*, ne pas les lâcher facilement*.

(d) (*: *drunk*) soûl*, gris*, rond*. **to get ~** prendre une cuite*, se cuiter‡.

2 *adv grasp* bien, solidement; *close* bien, hermétiquement; *squeeze* très fort. **screw the nut up ~** serrez l'écrou à bloc; **don't fasten** *or* **tie it too ~** ne le serrez pas trop (fort); *V* **hold, sit, sleep** *etc.*

3 *cpd*: **tight-fisted** avare, radin*, près de son argent*; **tight-fitting** *garment* ajusté, collant; *lid, stopper* qui ferme bien; **tight-knit** *jersey etc* tricoté serré; (*fig*) *family* uni; *programme, schedule* serré; **to maintain a tight-lipped silence, to be very tight-lipped** ne pas desserrer les lèvres *or* les dents (*about sth* au sujet de qch); (*from anger etc*) **he stood there tight-lipped** il se tenait là avec un air pincé; **in tight-lipped disapproval** d'un air de réprobation; **tightrope** corde *f* raide, fil *m*; **tightrope walker** funambule *mf*; (*US*) **tightwad‡** radin(e)* *m(f)*.

4 *npl*: **~s** collant *m*.

tighten ['taɪtn] **1** *vt* (*often ~* **up**) *rope* tendre; *coat, skirt, trousers* ajuster, rétrécir; *screw, wheel, grasp, embrace* resserrer; *legislation, restrictions, regulations, control* renforcer. (*lit, fig*) **to ~ one's belt** se serrer la ceinture.

2 *vi* (*also ~* **up**) *[rope]* se tendre, se raidir; *[screw, wheel]* se resserrer; *[restrictions, regulations]* être renforcé.

tighten up 1 *vi* **(a)** = **tighten 2.**

(b) (*fig*) **to tighten up on security/immigration** devenir plus strict *or* sévère en matière de sécurité/d'immigration; **the police are tightening up on shoplifters** la police renforce la lutte contre les voleurs à l'étalage.

2 *vt sep V* **tighten 1.**

tightly ['taɪtlɪ] *adv* = **tight 2.**

tightness ['taɪtnɪs] *n [dress, trousers]* étroitesse *f*; *[screw, lid, drawer]* dureté *f*; *[restrictions, control]* rigueur *f*, sévérité *f*. **he felt a ~ in his chest** il s'est senti la poitrine oppressée.

tigress ['taɪgrɪs] *n* tigresse *f*.

Tigris ['taıgrıs] *n* Tigre *m*.
tilde ['tıldı] *n* tilde *m*.
tile [taıl] **1** *n* (*on roof*) tuile *f*; (*on floor, wall, fireplace*) carreau *m*. (*Brit fig*) **to be out on the ~s*, to spend** *or* **have a night on the ~s*** faire la noce* *or* la bombe*; (*fig*) **he's got a ~ loose‡** il y a quelque chose qui ne tourne pas rond dans sa cervelle* *or* là-haut‡.
2 *vt roof* couvrir de tuiles; *floor, wall, fireplace* carreler. **~d** *roof* en tuiles; *floor, room etc* carrelé.
till[1] [tıl] = **until.**
till[2] [tıl] *n* caisse *f* (enregistreuse); (*old-fashioned type*) tiroir-caisse *m*; (*takings*) caisse. **pay at the ~** payez à la caisse; (*fig*) **caught with one's hand in the ~** pris sur le fait, pris en flagrant délit.
till[3] [tıl] *vt* (*Agr*) labourer.
tillage ['tılıdʒ] *n* (*act*) labour *m*, labourage *m*; (*land*) labour, guéret *m*.
tiller[1] ['tılər] *n* (*Agr*) laboureur *m*.
tiller[2] ['tılər] *n* (*Naut*) barre *f* (*du gouvernail*).
tilt [tılt] **1** *n* **(a)** (*tip, slope*) inclinaison *f*. **it has a ~ to it, it's on a** *or* **the ~** c'est incliné, ça penche.
(b) (*Hist*) (*contest*) joute *f*; (*thrust*) coup *m* de lance. (*fig*) **to have a ~ at** décocher des pointes à; **(at) full ~** à toute vitesse, à fond de train.
2 *cpd*: **tilt-top table** table *f* rabattable (*toutes inclinaisons*).
3 *vt* (*often* **~ over**) *object, one's head* pencher, incliner. **to ~ one's hat over one's eyes** rabattre son chapeau sur les yeux.
4 *vi* **(a)** (*also* **~ over**) pencher, être incliné.
(b) (*Hist*) jouter (*at* contre); *V* **wind**[1].
tilth [tılθ] *n* (*soil*) couche *f* arable; (*tilling*) labourage *m*.
timber ['tımbər] **1** *n* **(a)** (*U*) (*wood*) bois *m* d'œuvre, bois de construction; (*trees collectively*) arbres *mpl*, bois. (*excl*) **~!** attention (à l'arbre qui tombe)!, gare!; **land under ~** futaie *f*, terre boisée (*pour l'abattage*).
(b) (*beam*) madrier *m*, poutre *f*; (*Naut*) membrure *f*.
2 *cpd fence etc* en bois. (*U*) **timberland** région boisée (*pour l'abattage*); **timber line** ligne supérieure de la forêt; (*Brit*) **timber merchant** marchand *m* de bois, négociant *m* en bois; **timber wolf** loup *m* (gris); (*Brit*) **timberyard** chantier *m* de bois.
3 *vt tunnel etc* boiser. **~ed** *house* en bois; *land, hillside* boisé; *V* **half.**
timbering ['tımbərıŋ] *n* (*U*) boisage *m*.
timbre ['tæmbrə, 'tımbər] *n* timbre *m*.
timbrel ['tımbrəl] *n* tambourin *m*.
Timbuktu [ˌtımbʌk'tuː] *n* Tombouctou *m* (*also fig*).
time [taım] **1** *n* **(a)** (*U: gen*) temps *m*. **~ and space** le temps et l'espace; **~ flies** le temps passe vite; **only ~ will tell** ≃ qui vivra verra; **~ will show if ...** le temps dira si ..., on saura avec le temps si ... ; **in ~, with ~, in process of ~, in the course of ~, as ~ goes** (*or* **went**) **by** avec le temps, à la longue; **it takes ~ for it to change** (*a few minutes*) ça ne change pas tout de suite; (*longer*) ça ne change pas du jour au lendemain; **it takes ~ to change people's ideas** changer les idées des gens demande *or* prend du temps; **at this point in ~** à l'heure qu'il est, en ce moment; **from ~ out of mind** de temps immémorial, de toute éternité; (*Prov*) **~ and tide wait for no man** les événements n'attendent personne; (*Prov*) **~ is money** le temps c'est de l'argent; (*liter*) **to take T~ by the forelock** saisir l'occasion aux cheveux; *V* **immemorial, test, unity** *etc*.
(b) (*U: more specifically*) temps *m*. **I've no ~ for that sort of thing** (*lit*) je n'ai pas le temps de faire ce genre de chose; (*fig*) ce genre de chose m'agace; **it didn't leave him much ~ for sleep** ça ne lui a guère laissé le temps de dormir; **I've enough ~** *or* **I have the ~ to go there** j'ai le temps d'y aller; **we've got plenty of ~, we've all the ~ in the world** nous avons tout notre temps; **you've got plenty of ~ to wait for me** vous avez bien le temps de m'attendre; **I can't find ~ to do** *or* **for (doing) the garden** je n'arrive pas à trouver le temps de m'occuper du jardin; **to make up for lost ~** rattraper le temps perdu; **what a waste of ~!** quelle perte de temps!, que de temps perdu!; **in no ~ at all, in less than no ~** en un rien de temps, en moins de deux*; **he had ~ on his hands** *or* **~ to spare** il avait du temps de reste *or* du temps devant lui; **~ hung heavy (on his hands)** le temps lui durait *or* pesait, il trouvait le temps long; **I spent a lot of ~ preparing this, it took me a lot of ~ to prepare this** il m'a fallu pas mal de temps pour le préparer*, le préparer m'a pris pas mal de temps*; **he spent all/half his ~ reading** il a passé tout son temps/la moitié de son temps à lire; **I had to stand for part** *or* **some of the ~** j'ai dû rester debout (pendant) une partie du temps; **part** *or* **some of the ~ he looks cheerful but most of the ~ he doesn't** parfois *or* quelquefois *or* par moments il a l'air gai, mais la plupart du temps il a l'air triste; **he spends the best part of his ~ in London** il passe la meilleure partie *or* la plus grande partie de son temps à Londres, il passe le plus clair de son temps à Londres; **the letter was in my pocket all the ~** la lettre était dans ma poche (pendant) tout ce temps-là; **all the ~ he knew who had done it** il savait dès le début qui l'avait fait; **I can't be impartial all (of) the ~** je ne peux pas être tout le temps impartial; **take your ~** prenez votre temps; **take your ~ over it!** mettez-y le temps qu'il faudra!; (*fig*) **it took me all my ~ to finish it** j'ai eu du mal à le finir; **your ~ is up** (*in exam, prison visit etc*) c'est l'heure; (*Telec*) votre temps de communication est écoulé; **my ~ is my own** mon temps m'appartient, je suis maître de mon temps; **free ~, ~ off** temps libre; **he'll tell you in his own good ~** il vous le dira quand bon lui semblera; **all in good ~!** chaque chose en son temps!; **let me know in good ~** prévenez-moi à temps; **he arrived in good ~ for the start of the match** il est arrivé en avance pour le début du match; **a race against ~** une course contre la montre; **he was working against ~ to finish it** il travaillait d'arrache-pied pour le terminer à temps; **for the ~ being** pour le moment; *V* **bide, play, spare** *etc*.
(c) (*U: period, length of ~*) **for a ~** pendant un (certain) temps; **a long ~** longtemps; **a short ~** peu de temps; **a short ~ later** peu (de temps) après; **for a short ~ we thought that ...** nous avons (pendant) un moment pensé que ...; **he hasn't been seen for a long ~** on ne l'a pas vu depuis longtemps, ça fait longtemps qu'on ne l'a pas vu; **it's a long ~ since he left** il y a bien longtemps qu'il est parti; **what a (long) ~ you've been!** vous y avez mis le temps!, il vous en a fallu du temps!; **it took a very long ~ for that to happen** ceci n'est arrivé que très longtemps après, il a fallu attendre longtemps pour que cela arrive (*subj*); **in a short ~ they were all gone** quelques moments plus tard ils avaient tous disparu; **for a long ~ (to come) he will wonder ...** il se demandera (pendant) longtemps ...; **for a long ~ (past) he has been unable to work** il a longtemps été hors d'état de travailler; **I waited for some ~** j'ai attendu assez longtemps *or* pas mal de temps*; **I waited for some considerable ~** j'ai attendu un temps considérable; **after some little ~** après un certain temps; **some ~ ago** il y a quelque temps *or* un certain temps; **it won't be ready for some ~ (yet)** ce ne sera pas prêt avant un certain temps *or* avant pas mal de temps*; **some ~ before the war** quelque temps avant la guerre; **he did it in half the ~ it took you** il l'a fait deux fois plus vite *or* en deux fois moins de temps que vous; **he is coming in 2 weeks' ~** il vient dans 2 semaines; (*frm*) **within the agreed ~** dans les délais convenus; (*US*) **to buy sth on ~** acheter qch à tempérament; **what ~ did he do it in?** il a mis combien de temps?; **the winner's ~ was 12 seconds** le temps du gagnant était 12 secondes; **cooking ~ 25 minutes** temps de cuisson 25 minutes; *[prisoner]* **to do ~*** faire de la taule‡; (*US*) **to make ~ with sb‡** tomber qn‡; *V* **extra, record, serve** *etc*.
(d) (*U: period worked*) **to be on** *or* **to work full ~** travailler à plein temps *or* à temps plein (*V also* **full 4**); **to be on ~ and a half** faire des heures supplémentaires payées une fois et demie le tarif normal *or* à 150%; **Sunday working is paid at double ~** les heures du dimanche sont payées *or* comptées double; **in the firm's ~, in company ~** pendant les heures de service; **in one's own ~** après les heures de service; *V* **half, part-time, short** *etc*.
(e) (*epoch, era: often pl*) époque *f*. **in medieval ~s** à l'époque médiévale; **in Gladstone's ~** du temps de Gladstone; **in olden ~s, in ~s past, in former ~s** dans le temps, jadis; **~ was when one could ...** il fut un temps où l'on pouvait ...; **in my ~ it was all different** de mon temps c'était complètement différent; **I've seen some queer things in my ~** j'ai vu des choses étranges dans ma vie; **that was before my ~** (*before I was born*) c'était avant ma naissance *or* que je (ne) sois né; (*before I came here*) c'était avant que je (ne) vienne ici; **in ~(s) of peace** en temps de paix; **peace in our ~** la paix de notre vivant; **it will last our ~** cela durera aussi longtemps que nous; (*fig*) **he is ahead of** *or* **before his ~, he was born before his ~** il est en avance sur son époque; **to keep up with the ~s** être de son époque, vivre avec son époque, être à la page; **to be behind the ~s** être vieux jeu* *inv*; **the ~s we live in** l'époque où nous vivons; **at the best of ~s** (déjà) quand tout va bien; **~s are hard** les temps sont durs; **those were tough ~s** la vie n'était pas facile de ce temps-là; **they lived through some terrible ~s in the war** ils ont connu des moments terribles *or* ils en ont vu de dures* pendant la guerre; **to have a poor** *or* **rough** *or* **bad** *or* **thin** *or* **tough* ~ (of it)** en voir de dures*; **I gave him a bad ~ of it** je lui ai fait passer un mauvais quart d'heure; (*longer*) je lui ai fait *or* mené la vie dure; **what great ~s we've had!** c'était la belle vie! *or* le bon temps!; **to have a good ~ (of it)** bien s'amuser; **it was a tense ~ for all of us** cela a été une période très tendue pour nous tous; *V* **big, injury, sign.**
(f) (*by clock*) heure *f*. **what is the ~?, what ~ is it?** quelle heure est-il?; **what ~ do you make it?, what do you make the ~?** quelle heure avez-vous?; **have you got the right ~?** est-ce que vous avez l'heure exacte *or* juste?; **the ~ is 4.30** il est 4 heures et demie; **what ~ is he arriving at?** à quelle heure est-ce qu'il arrive?; **he looked at the ~** il a regardé l'heure; **that watch keeps good ~** cette montre est toujours à l'heure; **there's a ~ and a place for everything** il y a un temps pour tout; (*fig*) **to pass the ~ of day** bavarder un peu, échanger quelques mots (*with sb* avec qn); **at this ~ of (the) night** à cette heure de la nuit; **at any ~ of the day or night** à n'importe quelle heure du jour ou de la nuit; **at any ~ during school hours** n'importe quand pendant les heures d'ouverture de l'école; **open at all ~s** ouvert à toute heure; (*Brit: in pub*) **~ gentlemen please!** on ferme!; (*US*) **it's midnight by Eastern ~** il est minuit, heure de la côte est; **ahead of ~** en avance; **behind ~** en retard; **just in ~** juste à temps (*for sth* pour qch, *to do* pour faire); **on ~** à l'heure; **the trains are on ~** *or* **up to ~, the trains are running to ~** les trains sont à l'heure; **it's near my train ~** c'est presque l'heure de mon train; **it's ~ for tea, it's tea~** c'est l'heure du thé; **it's ~ to go** c'est l'heure de partir; **it's ~ I was going, it's ~ for me to go** il est temps que je m'en aille; **it's about ~ he was here** il serait temps *or* il commence à être temps qu'il arrive (*subj*); **it's ~ somebody taught him a lesson** il est grand temps que quelqu'un lui donne (*subj*) une bonne leçon; **and about ~ too!** et ce n'est pas trop tôt!; *V* **Greenwich, high, tell** *etc*.
(g) (*moment, point of ~*) moment *m*. **at the** *or* **that ~** à ce moment-là; **at this ~** en ce moment; **at the present ~** en ce moment, actuellement; **at this particular ~** à ce moment précis; **at one ~** à un moment donné; **sometimes ... at other ~s** quelquefois ... d'autres fois; **at all ~s** à tous moments; **I have at no ~ said that** je n'ai jamais dit cela, à aucun moment je n'ai dit cela; **at ~s** par moments; **I could hit him at ~s, there are ~s when I could hit him** il y a des moments où je pourrais le gifler; **at his ~ of life** à son âge; **he came at a very inconvenient ~** il est

arrivé à un moment tout à fait inopportun, il a mal choisi son moment pour arriver; **he may come (at) any ~** il peut arriver d'un moment à l'autre; **come (at) any ~** venez n'importe quand, venez quand vous voudrez; **it may happen any ~ now** cela peut arriver d'un moment à l'autre; **at this ~ of year** à cette époque de l'année, à cette saison; **to do two things at the same ~** faire deux choses à la fois; **they arrived at the same ~ as we did** ils sont arrivés en même temps que nous; **but at the same ~, you must admit that ...** mais pourtant *or* cependant, il faut avouer que ...; **by the ~ I had finished** le temps que je termine (*subj*), quand j'eus *or* j'ai eu (enfin) terminé; **by this *or* that ~ they had drunk all the wine** à ce moment-là ils avaient déjà bu tout le vin; **you must be cold by this ~** vous devez avoir froid maintenant; **by this ~ next year** dans un an; **this ~ tomorrow** demain à cette heure-ci; **this ~ last year** l'année dernière à cette époque-ci; **this ~ last week** il y a exactement huit jours; **(in) between ~s** entre temps; **from ~ to ~** de temps en temps; **from that ~ *or* this ~ on he was ...** à partir de ce moment il fut ...; **from this ~ on I shall do what you tell me** désormais *or* dorénavant je ferai ce que tu me diras; **until such ~ as** jusqu'à ce que + *subj*, en attendant que + *subj*; **this is no ~ for quarrelling** ce n'est pas le moment de se disputer; **to choose one's ~** choisir son moment; **now's your ~ to tell him** c'est maintenant que vous devriez (le) lui dire; **now's the ~ to do it** c'est maintenant le moment de le faire; **at Christmas ~** à (la) Noël; **to die before one's ~** mourir avant l'âge; **his ~ has come** son heure est venue *or* est arrivée *or* a sonné; **when the ~ comes** quand le moment viendra; **the ~ has come to do ...** il est temps de faire ...; **the ~ has come for us to leave** il est temps que nous partions (*subj*); **it's ~ to get up** c'est l'heure de nous (*or* vous *etc*) lever; *V* **given, proper** *etc*.

(h) (*occasion*) fois *f*. **this ~** cette fois; **(the) next ~ you come** la prochaine fois que vous viendrez; **every *or* each ~** chaque fois; **give me beer every ~!*** rien ne vaut une bonne bière!, donnez-moi de la bière à tous les coups!*; **several ~s** plusieurs fois; **at other ~s** d'autres fois; **at various ~s in the past** plusieurs fois déjà; **at odd ~s I've wondered ...** il m'est arrivé parfois de me demander ...; **many a ~, many ~s** maintes fois, bien des fois, très souvent; **~ after ~, ~s without number, ~ and (~) again** maintes et maintes fois, à plusieurs reprises; **hundreds of ~s*** vingt *or* trente-six *or* cent fois; **(the) last ~** la dernière fois; **there's always a first ~** il y a un début à tout; **the previous ~, the ~ before** la fois d'avant, la dernière fois; **come back some other ~** revenez une autre fois; **some ~ or other I'll do it** un jour ou l'autre je le ferai; **I remember the ~ when he told me about it** je me rappelle le jour où il me l'a dit; **one at a ~** un(e) par un(e), un(e) à un(e); **for weeks at a ~** pendant des semaines entières; **one can use the machine for 10 francs a ~** ça coûte 10 F chaque fois qu'on se sert de la machine.

(i) (*multiplying*) fois *f*. **2 ~s 3 is 6** 2 fois 3 (font) 6; **10 ~s as big as, 10 ~s the size of** 10 fois plus grand que; **it's worth 10 ~s as much** ça vaut 10 fois plus.

(j) (*Mus etc*) mesure *f*. **in ~** en mesure; **three-four ~** mesure à trois temps; **to keep ~** rester en mesure; *V* **beat, mark**[1].

2 *vt* **(a)** (*choose ~ of*) *invasion, visit* fixer (*for* à), prévoir (*for* pour); *remark, interruption* choisir *or* calculer le moment de. **the bomb was ~d to go off at midnight** l'explosion de la bombe était fixée à *or* prévue pour minuit; **you ~d that perfectly!** c'est tombé à point nommé!, vous ne pouviez pas mieux calculer *or* choisir votre moment!; **well-~d** *remark, entrance* tout à fait opportun, tombé à point nommé; *blow* bien calculé.

(b) (*count ~ of*) *race, runner, worker etc* chronométrer; *programme, ceremony, piece of work* minuter. **to ~ sb over 1,000 metres** chronométrer (le temps de) qn sur 1.000 mètres; **~ how long it takes you** calculez le temps qu'il vous faut pour le faire; **to ~ an egg** minuter la cuisson d'un œuf.

3 *cpd*: (*Ind*) **time and motion study** étude *f* des cadences; **time bomb** bombe *f* à retardement; **time capsule** capsule *f* témoin (*devant servir de document historique*); (*Ind etc*) **time clock** (*machine itself*) enregistreur *m* de temps; **they were standing near the time clock** ils se tenaient près du pointage; **time-consuming** qui prend du temps; (*US Fin*) **time deposit** dépôt *m* à terme; (*US Comm*) **time discount** remise *f* pour paiement anticipé; (*US Fin*) **time draft** traite *f* à délai de date; (*Phot*) **time exposure** pose *f*; **time fuse** détonateur *m or* fusée *f* à retard *or* à retardement; **time-honoured** consacré (par l'usage); **timekeeper** (*watch*) montre *f*; (*stopwatch*) chronomètre *m*; *[person]* **to be a good timekeeper** être toujours à l'heure; **time-lag** (*between events etc*) décalage *m*, retard *m*; (*between countries*) décalage horaire; **time-lapse photography** accéléré *m*; **to put *or* set a time limit on sth** fixer un délai *or* une limite de temps pour qch; **within a certain time limit** dans un certain délai; **without a time limit** sans limitation de temps; (*US Fin*) **time loan** emprunt *m* à terme; (*US*) **timeout** arrêt *m*, pause *f*; (*Ftbl*) mi-temps *f*; **timepiece** (*gen*) mécanisme *m* d'horlogerie; (*watch*) montre *f*; (*clock*) horloge *f*; **it is a great time-saver** ça fait gagner beaucoup de temps; **time-saving** (*adj*) qui fait gagner du temps; (*n*) économie *f or* gain *m* de temps; (*pej*) **timeserver** opportuniste *mf*; (*pej*) **time-serving** (*adj*) opportuniste; (*n*) opportunisme *m*; (*Computers*) **time-sharing** time-sharing *m*, temps partagé; (*Ind etc*) **time sheet** feuille *f* de présence; (*Rad*) **time signal** signal *m* horaire; (*Mus*) **time signature** indication *f* de la mesure; **time study = time and motion study**; **time switch** *[electrical apparatus]* minuteur *m*; (*for lighting*) minuterie *f*; **timetable** (*Rail etc*) (indicateur *m*) horaire *m*; (*Scol*) emploi *m* du temps; **timeworn** *stones etc* usé par le temps; *idea* rebattu; **time zone** fuseau *m* horaire.

timeless ['taɪmlɪs] *adj* éternel.

timeliness ['taɪmlɪnɪs] *n* (*U*) à-propos *m*, opportunité *f*.

timely ['taɪmlɪ] *adj* à propos, opportun.

timer ['taɪmə^r] *n* (*Culin etc*) compte-minutes *m inv*; (*egg ~*) sablier *m*; (*on machine, electrical device etc*) minuteur *m*; (*Aut*) distributeur *m* d'allumage; *V* **old.**

timid ['tɪmɪd] *adj* (*shy*) timide; (*unadventurous*) timoré, craintif; (*cowardly*) peureux.

timidity [tɪ'mɪdɪtɪ] *n* (*U*: *V* **timid**) timidité *f*; caractère timoré *or* craintif; caractère peureux.

timidly ['tɪmɪdlɪ] *adv* (*V* **timid**) timidement; craintivement; peureusement.

timidness ['tɪmɪdnɪs] *n* = **timidity.**

timing ['taɪmɪŋ] **1** *n* **(a)** *[musician etc]* sens *m* du rythme. **a good comedian depends on his (sense of) ~** un bon comédien doit minuter très précisément son débit; **the actors' ~ was excellent throughout the play** le minutage des acteurs était excellent tout au long de la pièce; **~ is very important in formation flying** la synchronisation est capitale dans les vols en formation; **the ~ of this demonstration** (*date/hour*) la date/l'heure de cette manifestation; (*programme of various stages*) le minutage de cette manifestation; **he arrived just when the meal was ready: I had to admire his ~** il est arrivé au moment précis où le repas était prêt, il ne pouvait pas mieux *or* je dois dire qu'il a su choisir son moment.

(b) (*Aut*) réglage *m* de l'allumage.

(c) (*Ind, Sport*) chronométrage *m*.

2 *cpd*: **timing device, timing mechanism** *[bomb etc]* mouvement *m* d'horlogerie; *[electrical apparatus]* minuteur *m*.

timorous ['tɪmərəs] *adj* timoré, craintif.

Timothy ['tɪməθɪ] *n* Timothée *m*.

timpani ['tɪmpənɪ] *npl* timbales *fpl*.

timpanist ['tɪmpənɪst] *n* timbalier *m*.

tin [tɪn] **1** *n* **(a)** (*U*) étain *m*; (*~plate*) fer-blanc *m*.

(b) (*esp Brit: container*) boîte *f* (*en fer-blanc*); (*mould*) moule *m*; (*dish*) plat *m*. **~ of salmon** boîte de saumon; **cake ~** (*for storing*) boîte à gâteaux; (*for baking*) moule à gâteau; **meat *or* roasting ~** plat à rôtir.

2 *vt* **(a)** (*put in ~s*) *food etc* mettre en boîte(s) *or* en conserve. **~ned fruit/salmon** fruits *mpl*/saumon *m* en boîte *or* en conserve; **~ned goods** conserves *fpl*.

(b) (*coat with ~*) étamer.

3 *cpd* (*made of ~*) en étain, d'étain; (*made of ~plate*) en *or* de fer-blanc. **tin can** boîte *f* (en fer-blanc); (*U*) **tinfoil** papier *m* d'étain, papier (d')aluminium; **tin hat** casque *m*; (*Aut*) **tin lizzie*** (petite) chignole* *f*; **tin mine** mine *f* d'étain; (*Brit*) **tin opener** ouvre-boîte(s) *m*; (*U*) **tinplate** fer-blanc *m*; **tinpot*** *car, bike* qui ne vaut pas grand-chose, en fer-blanc; **a tinpot little town*** un petit bled*; **tinsmith** ferblantier *m*; **tin soldier** soldat *m* de plomb; (*Brit*) **tintack** clou *m* de tapissier, semence *f*.

tincture ['tɪŋktʃə^r] **1** *n* (*Pharm*) teinture *f*; (*fig*) nuance *f*, teinte *f*. **~ of iodine** teinture d'iode. **2** *vt* (*lit, fig*) teinter (*with* de).

tinder ['tɪndə^r] **1** *n* (*U*) (*in tinderbox*) amadou *m*; (*small sticks*) petit bois (*U*). **as dry as ~** sec (*f* sèche) comme de l'amadou. **2** *cpd*: **tinderbox** briquet *m* (à amadou); (*fig: esp Pol*) poudrière *f*.

tine [taɪn] *n [fork]* dent *f*, fourchon *m*; *[antler]* andouiller *m*.

ting [tɪŋ] **1** *n* tintement *m*. **2** *vi* tinter. **3** *vt* faire tinter. **4** *cpd*: **ting-a-ling** *[telephone, doorbell]* dring dring *m*; *[handbell, tiny bells]* drelin drelin *m*.

tinge [tɪndʒ] (*lit, fig*) **1** *n* teinte *f*, nuance *f*. **2** *vt* teinter (*with* de).

tingle ['tɪŋgl] **1** *vi* (*prickle*) picoter, fourmiller; (*fig: thrill*) vibrer, frissonner. **her face was tingling** le visage lui picotait *or* lui cuisait; **her cheeks were tingling with cold** le froid lui piquait *or* lui brûlait les joues; **my fingers are tingling** j'ai des picotements *or* des fourmis dans les doigts; **the toothpaste makes my tongue ~** le dentifrice me pique la langue; **he was tingling with impatience** il brûlait d'impatience.

2 *n* (*sensation*) picotement *m*, fourmillement *m*, sensation cuisante; (*thrill*) frisson *m*. (*sound*) **to have a ~ in one's ears** avoir les oreilles qui tintent.

tingling ['tɪŋglɪŋ] **1** *n* (*U*) = **tingle 2. 2** *adj* = **tingly.**

tingly ['tɪŋglɪ] *adj sensation* cuisant, de picotement, de fourmillement. **my arm is *or* feels ~** j'ai des fourmis *or* des fourmillements dans le bras.

tinker ['tɪŋkə^r] **1** *n* (*gen*) romanichel(le) *m(f)* (*often pej*); (*specifically*) rétameur *m* (ambulant); (*: *child*) polisson(ne) *m(f)*. (*fig*) **it's not worth a ~'s cuss *or* ~'s damn** ça ne vaut pas tripette* *or* un clou*; **I don't care *or* give a ~'s cuss *or* ~'s damn** je m'en fiche*, je m'en soucie comme de l'an quarante; **~, tailor, soldier, sailor ...** ≃ il m'aime un peu, beaucoup, passionnément ... .

2 *vi* (*also ~ about*) bricoler, s'occuper à des bricoles. **he was ~ing (about) with the car** il bricolait la voiture; **stop ~ing with that watch!** arrête de tripoter cette montre!

tinkle ['tɪŋkl] **1** *vi* tinter. **2** *vt* faire tinter. **3** *n* tintement *m*. (*Brit Telec*) **to give sb a ~*** donner *or* passer un coup de fil à qn*.

tinkling ['tɪŋklɪŋ] **1** *n* (*U*) tintement *m*. **2** *adj bell* qui tinte; *stream* qui clapote, qui gazouille.

tinny ['tɪnɪ] *adj sound* métallique, grêle; *taste* métallique; (**pej*) *car, typewriter etc* de camelote*. **~ piano** casserole* *f*.

tinsel ['tɪnsəl] *n* (*U*) guirlandes *fpl* de Noël (argentées), clinquant *m* (*also fig pej*).

tint [tɪnt] **1** *n* teinte *f*, nuance *f*; (*for hair*) shampooing colorant; *V* **flesh. 2** *vt* teinter (*with* de). **to ~ one's hair** se faire un shampooing colorant.

tintinnabulation ['tɪntɪˌnæbjʊ'leɪʃən] *n* tintinnabulement *m*.

tiny ['taɪnɪ] *adj* tout petit, minuscule. **a ~ little man** un tout petit bonhomme.

tip[1] [tɪp] **1** *n [stick, pencil, ruler, wing, finger, nose]* bout *m*; *[sword, knife, asparagus]* pointe *f*; *[shoe]* bout, pointe; *[cigarette]* bout; (*filter ~*) bout (filtre); *[umbrella]* embout *m*; *[billiard cue]* procédé *m*. **from ~ to toe** de la tête aux pieds; **he stood on the ~s of his toes** il s'est dressé sur la pointe des pieds; **he touched it with the ~ of his toe** il l'a touché du bout de l'orteil; (*fig*) **I've got it on** *or* **it's on the ~ of my tongue** je l'ai sur le bout de la langue; (*fig*) **it's just the ~ of the iceberg** c'est seulement la partie émergée de l'iceberg; *V* **fingertip, wing** *etc.*

2 *vt* (*put ~ on*) mettre un embout à; (*cover ~ of*) recouvrir le bout de. **~ped cigarettes** cigarettes *fpl* (à bout) filtre *inv*; **~ped with steel, steel-~ped** ferré, qui a un embout de fer.

3 *cpd*: **on tiptoe** sur la pointe des pieds; **to tiptoe in/out** *etc* entrer/sortir *etc* sur la pointe des pieds; **tiptop*** de premier ordre, excellent, de toute première*.

tip[2] [tɪp] **1** *n* **(a)** (*tap*) tape *f*, petit coup.

(b) (*gratuity*) pourboire *m*.

(c) (*hint*) suggestion *f*; (*advice*) conseil *m*; (*Racing*) tuyau* *m*. **that horse is a hot ~ for the 3.30** ce cheval a une première chance dans la course de 15h 30; **take my ~** suivez mon conseil.

2 *cpd*: **to give sb a tip-off** (*gen*) prévenir qn, donner *or* filer un tuyau* à qn; (*Police*) avertir *or* prévenir qn (*par une dénonciation*).

3 *vt* **(a)** (*tap, touch*) toucher (légèrement), effleurer. **to ~ one's hat to sb** mettre *or* porter la main à son chapeau pour saluer qn.

(b) (*reward*) donner un pourboire à. **he ~ped the waiter 5 francs** il a donné un pourboire de 5 F au garçon; **to ~ sb the wink*** **about sth** filer un tuyau* à qn sur qch.

(c) (*Racing, gen*) pronostiquer. **to ~ the winner** pronostiquer le cheval gagnant; **he ~ped Blue Streak for the 3.30** il a pronostiqué la victoire de Blue Streak dans la course de 15h 30; (*fig*) **they are ~ped to win the next election** on pronostique qu'ils vont remporter les prochaines élections; **Paul was ~ped for the job** on avait pronostiqué que Paul serait nommé.

tip off 1 *vt sep* (*gen*) donner *or* filer un tuyau* à (*about sth* sur qch); *police* prévenir *or* avertir (*par une dénonciation*).

2 tip-off *n V* **tip**[2] **2**.

tip[3] [tɪp] **1** *n* (*Brit*) (*for coal*) terril *m*; (*for rubbish*) décharge *f*, dépotoir *m*; (**fig: untidy place*) dépotoir.

2 *cpd*: **tip-cart** tombereau *m*; **tipcat** (jeu *m* du) bâtonnet *m*; **tipstaff** *V* **tipstaff**; **tip-up seat** (*in theatre etc*) siège *m* rabattable; (*in taxi, underground etc*) strapontin *m*; **tip-up truck** camion *m* à benne (basculante).

3 *vt* (*incline, tilt*) pencher, incliner; (*overturn*) faire basculer, renverser; (*pour, empty*) *liquid* verser (*into* dans, *out of* de); *load, sand, rubbish* déverser, déposer; *clothes, books etc* déverser (*into* dans, *out of* de). **he ~ped the water out of the bucket** il a vidé le seau; **to ~ sb off his chair** renverser *or* faire basculer qn de sa chaise; **they ~ped him into the water** ils l'ont fait basculer *or* tomber dans l'eau; **the car overturned and they were ~ped into the roadway** la voiture s'est retournée et ils se sont retrouvés sur la chaussée; **to ~ the scales at 90 kg** peser 90 kg; (*fig*) **to ~ the scales** faire pencher la balance (*in sb's favour* en faveur de qn, *against sb* au détriment de qn).

4 *vi* (*incline*) pencher, être incliné; (*overturn*) se renverser, basculer. **'no ~ping', '~ping prohibited'** 'défense de déposer des ordures'.

tip back, tip backward(s) 1 *vi* [*chair*] se rabattre en arrière; [*person*] se pencher en arrière, basculer (en arrière).

2 *vt sep chair* rabattre *or* faire basculer (en arrière).

tip forward(s) 1 *vi* [*chair*] se rabattre en avant; [*person*] se pencher en avant.

2 *vt sep chair* rabattre *or* faire basculer (en avant); *car seat* rabattre (en avant).

tip out *vt sep liquid, contents* vider; *load* décharger, déverser. **they tipped him out of his chair/out of bed** ils l'ont fait basculer de sa chaise/du lit.

tip over 1 *vi* (*tilt*) pencher; (*overturn*) basculer.

2 *vt sep* faire basculer.

tip up 1 *vi* [*table etc*] (*tilt*) pencher, être incliné; (*overturn*) basculer; [*box, jug*] se renverser; [*seat*] se rabattre; [*truck*] basculer.

2 *vt sep* (*tilt*) *table etc* incliner; *jug, box* pencher, incliner; *person* faire basculer.

3 tip-up *adj V* **tip**[3] **2**.

tipper ['tɪpəʳ] *n* **(a)** (*vehicle*) camion *m* à benne (basculante); (*back of vehicle*) benne *f* (basculante). **(b) he is a good** *or* **big ~*** il a le pourboire facile.

tippet ['tɪpɪt] *n* (*also* **fur ~**) étole *f* (de fourrure).

tipple ['tɪpl] **1** *vi* picoler*. **2** *n* (*hum*) **gin is his ~** ce qu'il préfère boire c'est du gin.

tippler ['tɪpləʳ] *n* picoleur* *m*, -euse* *f*.

tipsily ['tɪpsɪlɪ] *adv walk* en titubant légèrement; *talk* d'un ton qui dénote une légère ivresse.

tipstaff ['tɪpstɑːf] *n* (*Brit Jur*) huissier *m*.

tipster ['tɪpstəʳ] *n* (*Racing*) pronostiqueur *m*.

tipsy ['tɪpsɪ] *adj* gai, éméché*, parti*. **to get ~** devenir gai; (*Brit*) **~ cake** (sorte *f* de) baba *m* au rhum.

tirade [taɪ'reɪd] *n* diatribe *f*.

tire[1] ['taɪəʳ] *n* (*US*) = **tyre**.

tire[2] ['taɪəʳ] **1** *vt* fatiguer; (*weary*) fatiguer, lasser.

2 *vi* se fatiguer; se lasser. **he ~s easily** il se fatigue vite, il est vite fatigué; **he never ~s of telling us how ...** il ne se lasse jamais de nous dire comment ... .

tire out *vt sep* épuiser, éreinter, claquer*, crever*. **to be tired out** être épuisé *or* éreinté *or* claqué* *or* crevé*, ne plus tenir debout.

tired ['taɪəd] *adj person* fatigué; (*weary*) las (*f* lasse); *movement, voice* las. **I'm ~ of waiting** j'en ai assez d'attendre, je suis las *or* fatigué d'attendre; **to be ~ of sth/sb** en avoir assez de qch/qn; **to get ~ of** commencer à en avoir assez de, se lasser de; **I'm ~ of telling you** je me tue à vous le répéter; **you make me ~!*** tu me fatigues!, tu me casses les pieds!*; **the same ~ clichés** les mêmes clichés rebattus.

tiredly ['taɪədlɪ] *adv reply* d'une voix fatiguée; *walk* d'un pas lourd, avec une démarche fatiguée.

tiredness ['taɪədnɪs] *n* (*V* **tired**) fatigue *f*; lassitude *f*.

tireless ['taɪəlɪs] *adj* infatigable, inlassable.

tirelessly ['taɪəlɪslɪ] *adv* infatigablement, inlassablement.

tiresome ['taɪəsəm] *adj* (*annoying*) agaçant, ennuyeux; (*boring*) ennuyeux, assommant.

tiresomeness ['taɪəsəmnɪs] *n* (*V* **tiresome**) caractère agaçant *or* ennuyeux.

tiring ['taɪərɪŋ] *adj* fatigant.

tiro ['taɪərəʊ] *n* = **tyro**.

Tirol [tɪ'rəʊl] *n* = **Tyrol**.

tisane [tɪ'zæn] *n* tisane *f*.

tissue ['tɪʃuː] **1** *n* (*cloth*) tissu *m*, étoffe *f*; (*Anat, Bio*) tissu; (*paper handkerchief*) mouchoir *m* en papier, kleenex *m* ®; (*fig: web, mesh*) tissu, enchevêtrement *m*. **a ~ of lies** un tissu de mensonges.

2 *cpd*: **tissue culture** culture *f* de tissus; (*U*) **tissue paper** papier *m* de soie.

tit[1] [tɪt] *n* (*Orn*) mésange *f*; *V* **blue** *etc.*

tit[2] [tɪt] *n*: **~ for tat!** un prêté pour un rendu!

tit[3]** [tɪt] *n* (*breast*) sein *m*, nichon: *m*, néné: *m*.

Titan ['taɪtən] *n* (*also fig*: **t~**) Titan *m*.

titanic [taɪ'tænɪk] *adj* **(a)** titanesque. **(b)** (*Chem*) au titane.

titanium [tɪ'teɪnɪəm] *n* titane *m*.

titbit ['tɪtbɪt] *n* (*esp Brit*) [*food*] friandise *f*, bon morceau; [*gossip*] potin *m*; (*in newspaper*) entrefilet croustillant.

tithe [taɪð] *n* dîme *f*.

Titian ['tɪʃɪən] **1** *n* le Titien. **2** *adj*: **t~** blond vénitien *inv*.

titillate ['tɪtɪleɪt] *vt* titiller.

titillation [ˌtɪtɪ'leɪʃən] *n* titillation *f*.

titivate ['tɪtɪveɪt] **1** *vi* se pomponner, se bichonner. **2** *vt* bichonner, pomponner.

title ['taɪtl] **1** *n* **(a)** (*gen, also Sport*) titre *m*. **under the ~ of** sous le titre de; **what ~ should I give him?** comment dois-je l'appeler?; **I don't know his exact ~** je ne connais pas son titre exact; **George III gave him a ~** Georges III lui a conféré un titre *or* l'a titré *or* l'a anobli; **this earned him the ~ of 'King of the Ring'** cela lui a valu le titre de 'Roi du Ring'; (*Cine, TV*) **~s** titres.

(b) (*Jur*) droit *m*, titres *mpl* (*to sth* à qch).

2 *cpd*: **title deed** titre *m* (constitutif) de propriété; (*Sport*) **title holder** détenteur *m*, -trice *f or* tenant(e) *m(f)* du titre; **title page** page *f* de titre; (*Cine, Theat*) **title role** rôle *m* du personnage qui donne son nom à la pièce, ≃ rôle principal.

3 *vt book etc* intituler.

titled ['taɪtld] *adj person* titré.

titmouse ['tɪtmaʊs] *n* mésange *f*.

titrate ['taɪtreɪt] *vt* titrer (*Chem*).

titter ['tɪtəʳ] **1** *vi* rire sottement (*at* de), glousser. **2** *n* gloussement *m*, petit rire sot.

tittle ['tɪtl] **1** *n* brin *m*, grain *m*; *V* **jot**. **2** *cpd*: **tittle-tattle** (*n: U*) cancans *mpl*, potins *mpl*; (*vi*) cancaner, jaser.

titular ['tɪtjʊləʳ] *adj possessions, estate* titulaire; *ruler, leader* nominal.

tizzy* ['tɪzɪ] *n* affolement* *m*, panique* *f*. **to be in/get into a ~** être/se mettre dans tous ses états.

to [tuː, *weak form* tə] (*phr vb elem*) **1** *prep* **(a)** (*direction, movement*) à; vers; en; chez. **he went ~ the door** il est allé à la porte; **he was walking slowly ~ the door** il marchait lentement vers la porte; **to go ~ school/town** aller à l'école/en ville; **to go ~ France/Canada** aller en France/au Canada; **to go ~ London/Le Havre** aller à Londres/au Havre; **he came over ~ where I was standing** il est venu (jusqu')à l'endroit où je me trouvais; **to go ~ the doctor('s)** aller chez le docteur; **let's go ~ John's** allons chez Jean; **~ the left** à gauche; **~ the west** à l'ouest; **the road ~ London** la route de Londres; **on the way ~ Paris** sur la route de Paris, en allant à Paris; **to fall ~ the ground** tomber par *or* à terre; **to turn a picture ~ the wall** retourner un tableau contre le mur; **he was sitting with his back ~ me** il était assis le dos tourné vers moi.

(b) (*as far as*) (jusqu')à. **to count (up) ~ 20** compter jusqu'à 20; **it comes ~ £20** ça fait 20 livres en tout, ça s'élève à 20 livres; **it is 90 km ~ Paris** nous sommes à 90 km de Paris; **it's correct ~ a millimetre** c'est exact à un millimètre près; **they perished ~ a man** pas un seul n'a survécu; **8 years ago ~ the day** il y a 8 ans jour pour jour; **~ this day** jusqu'à ce jour, jusqu'à aujourd'hui; **I didn't stay ~ the end** je ne suis pas resté jusqu'à la fin; **from morning ~ night** du matin (jusqu')au soir; **from Monday ~ Friday** du lundi au vendredi; **from day ~ day** de jour en jour; **from town ~ town** de ville en ville; **from time ~ time** de temps en temps; **from bad ~ worse** de mal en pis; **there were 50 ~ 60 people** il y avait (de) 50 à 60 personnes, il y avait entre 50 et 60 personnes.

(c) (*marking dative*) à. **to give sth ~ sb** donner qch à qn; **I gave them ~ him** je les lui ai donnés; **give it ~ me** donnez-le-moi; **the man I sold it ~** l'homme à qui *or* auquel je l'ai vendu; **she said ~ herself** elle s'est dit; **that belongs ~ him** cela lui appartient; **what's it ~ you?, what does it matter ~ you?** qu'est-ce que cela peut vous faire?; **be nice ~ her** sois gentil avec elle; **it's a great help ~ me** cela m'est très utile; **known ~ the Ancients** connu des anciens.

(d) (*in dedications etc*) **'~ my wife Anne'** 'à ma femme, Anne'; **dedicated ~ the memory of** dédié à la mémoire de; **here's ~ you!** à la vôtre!; **~ absent friends!** (buvons) à la santé des absents!; **to erect a statue ~ sb** ériger une statue en l'honneur de qn.

(e) (*against, next to*) à; contre. **back ~ back** dos à dos; **bumper ~ bumper** pare-chocs contre pare-chocs; **to clasp sb ~ one's heart** serrer qn sur son cœur.

(f) (*in time phrases*) **20 (minutes) ~ 2** 2 heures moins 20; **at (a) quarter ~ 4** à 4 heures moins le quart; **it's (a) quarter ~** il est moins le quart; **it was 10 ~** il était moins 10.

(g) (*in proportions etc*) **A is ~ B as C is ~ D** A est à B ce que C est à D; **to bet 10 ~ 1** parier 10 contre 1; **by a majority of 10 ~ 7** avec une majorité de 10 contre 7; **they won by 4 goals ~ 2** ils ont gagné 4 (buts) à 2; **one person ~ a room** une personne par chambre; **200 people ~ the square km** 200 personnes au km carré; **how many miles ~ the gallon?** ≃ combien de litres au cent?

(h) (*in comparison with*) **inferior/superior ~** inférieur (*f* -eure)/supérieur (*f* -eure) à; **that's nothing ~ what is to come** ce n'est rien à côté de ce qui va venir; **he's famous (compared) ~ what he used to be 10 years ago** il est célèbre en comparaison de *or* à côté de ce qu'il était il y a 10 ans; **I prefer bridge ~ chess** je préfère le bridge aux échecs.

(i) (*concerning*) **what would you say ~ a beer?** que diriez-vous d'une bière?; **there's nothing ~ it** il n'y a rien de plus facile; **that's all there is ~ it** (*it's easy*) ça n'est pas plus difficile que ça; (*no ulterior motive etc*) c'est aussi simple que ça; (*Comm*) **'~ repairing cooker: 100 francs'** 'remise en état d'une cuisinière: 100 F'; (*Comm*) **~ services rendered** pour services rendus.

(j) (*according to*) **~ the best of my recollection** (pour) autant que je m'en souvienne; **~ all intents and purposes** à toutes fins utiles; **~ all appearances** selon toute apparence; **~ my mind, ~ my way of thinking** à mon avis; **it's not ~ my taste** ce n'est pas à mon goût; **in time ~ the music** en mesure avec la musique; **cheque ~ the value of £100** chèque de 100 livres; (*Math*) **3 ~ the 4th, 3 ~ the power 4** 3 (à la) puissance 4; **~ some degree** dans une certaine mesure.

(k) (*of*) de. **assistant ~ the manager** adjoint(e) *m(f)* du directeur; **secretary ~ the board** secrétaire *mf* (auprès) du comité de gestion; **ambassador ~ France** ambassadeur *m* en France; **ambassador ~ King Paul** ambassadeur auprès du roi Paul; **wife ~ Mr Milton** femme *f* de M Milton; **he has been a good friend ~ us** il a été pour nous un ami fidèle.

(l) (*of purpose, result*) **~ my delight** à ma grande joie; **~ this end** à cet effet, dans ce but; **it is ~ his credit** c'est tout à son honneur; **the water had changed ~ ice** l'eau s'était changée en glace *or* avait gelé; **his love turned ~ hatred** son amour a tourné à la haine; **frozen ~ death** mort de froid; **it comes ~ the same thing** ça revient au même *or* à la même chose.

2 *particle* (*forming infin*) **(a)** (*shown in French by vb ending*) **~ be** être; **~ eat** manger.

(b) (*with ellipsis of vb*) **he asked me to come but I didn't want ~** il m'a demandé de venir mais je n'ai pas voulu; **I'll try ~** j'essaierai; **I'd love ~** ce sera(it) avec plaisir; **I didn't mean ~** je ne l'ai pas fait exprès; **I forgot ~** j'ai oublié.

3 *adv*: **to push the door ~** fermer la porte (en la poussant); **when the door is ~** quand la porte est fermée; **to go ~ and fro** *[person]* aller et venir; *[machine part etc]* avoir un mouvement de va-et-vient; *[train, bus etc]* faire la navette (*between* entre); **he was walking ~ and fro** il faisait les cent pas, il se promenait de long en large; *V* **come to** *etc*.

4 *cpd*: **-to-be** (*cpd ending*) futur (*V* **mother** *etc*); **husband-to-be** futur mari; **to make a to-do*** faire des embarras *or* des histoires*; **she made a great to-do about it*** elle en a fait tout un plat!*; **what a to-do!*** quelle histoire!, quelle affaire!; **to-ing and fro-ing** allées et venues *fpl*.

toad [təʊd] **1** *n* crapaud *m* (*also fig*).

2 *cpd*: (*Culin*) **toad-in-the-hole** *saucisses cuites au four dans de la pâte à crêpes*; **toadstool** champignon *m*, (*poisonous*) champignon vénéneux.

toady ['təʊdɪ] **1** *n* flagorneur *m*, -euse *f*, lèche-bottes* *mf inv*. **2** *vi*: **to ~ to sb** flatter qn bassement, lécher les bottes de qn*.

toadying ['təʊdɪɪŋ] *n*, **toadyism** ['təʊdɪɪzəm] *n* (*U*) flagornerie *f*.

toast [təʊst] **1** *n* **(a)** (*U: Culin*) pain grillé, toast *m*. **you've burnt the ~** tu as laissé brûler le pain *or* les toasts; **a piece *or* slice of ~** une tartine grillée, un (morceau de) toast, une rôtie; **sardines on ~** sardines *fpl* sur toast *or* sur canapé; (*fig*) **you've got him on ~*** vous le tenez; *V* **warm**.

(b) (*drink, speech*) toast *m*. **to drink a ~ to sb** porter un toast à qn *or* en l'honneur de qn, boire à la santé *or* au succès de qn; **they drank his ~ in champagne** ils lui ont porté un toast au champagne; **here's a ~ to all who ...** levons nos verres en l'honneur de tous ceux qui ... ; **to propose *or* give a ~ to sb** porter un toast à qn *or* en l'honneur de qn; **she was the ~ of the town** elle était la vedette de la ville.

2 *cpd*: **toasting fork** fourchette *f* à griller le pain; **toastmaster** animateur *m* pour réceptions et banquets; **toast rack** porte-toast *m*.

3 *vt* **(a)** *bread etc* (faire) griller. (*fig*) **he was ~ing his toes by the fire** il se chauffait *or* se rôtissait les pieds auprès du feu.

(b) (*propose ~ to*) porter un toast à; (*drink ~ to*) *person* boire à la santé de *or* au succès de, porter un toast à; *event, victory* arroser (*in champagne etc* au champagne *etc*).

toaster ['təʊstəʳ] *n* grille-pain *m inv* (*électrique*).

tobacco [tə'bækəʊ] **1** *n* **(a)** (*U*) tabac *m*.

(b) (*also* **~ plant**) (pied *m* de) tabac *m*.

2 *cpd leaf, smoke, plantation, company* de tabac; *pouch* à tabac; *industry* du tabac. **tobacco jar** pot *m* à tabac; **tobacco planter** propriétaire *m* d'une plantation de tabac.

tobacconist [tə'bækənɪst] *n* (*esp Brit*) marchand(e) *m(f)* de tabac, buraliste *mf*. **~'s (shop)** (bureau *m or* débit *m* de) tabac *m*.

toboggan [tə'bɒgən] **1** *n* toboggan *m*; (*child's*) luge *f*.

2 *cpd race* de toboggan. **toboggan run** piste *f* de toboggan.

3 *vi* **(a)** (*also* **go ~ing**) faire du toboggan *or* de la luge. **he ~ed down the hill** il a descendu la colline en toboggan *or* en luge.

(b) (*fig*) *[prices, sales, numbers etc]* dégringoler.

tocsin ['tɒksɪn] *n* tocsin *m*.

todᵵ [tɒd] *n* (*Brit*) **on one's ~** tout seul (*f* toute seule).

today [tə'deɪ] **1** *adv* aujourd'hui (*also fig*). **it rained all (day) ~** il a plu toute la journée aujourd'hui; **a week (past) ~** il y a huit jours aujourd'hui; **~ week, a week (from) ~** aujourd'hui en huit; **early ~** aujourd'hui de bonne heure; **what day is it ~?** quel jour est-on *or* est-ce aujourd'hui?; **what date is it ~?** quelle est la date aujourd'hui?; (*fig*) **~ you can't dismiss anyone without a good reason** aujourd'hui on ne peut renvoyer personne sans motif; (*fig*) **here ~ and gone tomorrow** ça va ça vient.

2 *n* aujourd'hui *m* (*also fig*). **what day is ~?** quel jour sommes-nous?, quel jour est-ce aujourd'hui?; **~ is Friday** aujourd'hui c'est vendredi; **what is ~'s date?** quelle est la date d'aujourd'hui?; **~ is the 4th** aujourd'hui c'est le 4; **~ is very wet** il pleut beaucoup aujourd'hui; **~ was a bad day for me** aujourd'hui ça s'est mal passé pour moi; **~'s paper** le journal d'aujourd'hui; (*fig*) **the writers of ~** les écrivains d'aujourd'hui.

toddle ['tɒdl] **1** *vi* **(a)** *[child]* **to ~ in/out** *etc* entrer/sortir *etc* à pas hésitants; **he has begun to ~, he is just toddling** il fait ses premiers pas.

(b) (**hum*) (*go*) aller; (*stroll*) se balader*; (*leave: also* **~ off**) se sauver*, se trotterᵵ.

2 *n* (*hum*) **to go for a ~**ᵵ aller faire un petit tour *or* une petite balade*.

toddler ['tɒdləʳ] *n* tout(e) petit(e) *m(f)* (qui commence à marcher), bambin* *m*. **he's only a ~** il est encore tout petit; **she has one baby and one ~** elle a un bébé et un petit qui commence juste à marcher.

toddy ['tɒdɪ] *n* ≃ grog *m*.

toe [təʊ] **1** *n* (*Anat*) orteil *m*, doigt *m* de pied; *[sock, shoe]* bout *m*. **big/little ~** gros/petit orteil; **to tread *or* step on sb's ~s** (*lit*) marcher sur les pieds de qn; (*fig*) froisser *or* blesser qn; (*fig*) **to keep sb on his ~s** forcer qn à rester vigilant *or* alerte; (*fig*) **that will keep you on your ~s!** ça t'empêchera de t'endormir!, ça te fera travailler!; *V* **tip**[1], **top**[1].

2 *cpd*: **reinforced toecap** bout dur *or* renforcé (*de soulier*); **toehold** prise *f* (pour le pied); **toenail** ongle *m* de l'orteil *or* du pied.

3 *vt* (*touch/push*) toucher/pousser du bout de l'orteil. **to ~ the line** *or* (*US*) **mark** (*in race*) se ranger sur la ligne de départ; (*fig*) obéir, être docile, se plier; *V* **party**.

-toed [təʊd] *adj ending in cpds*: **three-toed** à trois orteils.

toffᵵ† [tɒf] *n* (*Brit*) aristoᵵ *m*, dandy* *m*.

toffee ['tɒfɪ] (*Brit*) **1** *n* caramel *m*. (*fig*) **he can't do it for ~*** il n'est pas fichu* de le faire. **2** *cpd*: **toffee apple** pomme caramélisée; (*pej*) **toffee-nosed**ᵵ bêcheur*, qui fait du chiqué*.

tog* [tɒg] **1** *vt*: **to ~ up *or* out** nipper*, fringuerᵵ. **to be all ~ged up *or* out (in one's best clothes)** être bien fringuéᵵ *or* sapéᵵ, être sur son trente et un. **2** *n*: **~s** fringuesᵵ *fpl*.

toga ['təʊgə] *n* toge *f*.

together [tə'geðəʳ] (*phr vb elem*) *adv* **(a)** ensemble. **I've seen them ~** je les ai vus ensemble; (*fig*) **we're in this ~** nous sommes logés à la même enseigne; (*fig pej*) **they were both in it ~** ils avaient partie liée tous les deux; **you must keep ~** vous devez rester ensemble, vous ne devez pas vous séparer; **tie the ropes ~** nouez les cordes; **all ~ now!** (*shouting, singing*) tous en chœur maintenant!; (*pulling*) (oh!) hisse!; **~ with what you bought yesterday that makes ...** avec ce que vous avez acheté hier ça fait ... ; **(taken) ~ with the previous figures, these show that ...** ces chiffres, considérés conjointement avec les précédents, indiquent que ... ; **if you look at the reports ~** si vous considérez les rapports conjointement; **they belong ~** *[objects]* ils vont ensemble; *[people]* ils sont faits l'un pour l'autre; *V* **bang together, gather together, live together** *etc*.

(b) (*simultaneously*) en même temps, à la fois, simultanément; *sing, play, recite* à l'unisson. **the shots were fired ~** les coups de feu ont été tirés simultanément *or* en même temps; **they both stood up ~** ils se sont tous les deux levés en même temps; **don't all speak ~** ne parlez pas tous à la fois; (*Mus*) **you're not ~** vous n'êtes pas à l'unisson.

(c) (*continuously*) **for days/weeks ~** (pendant) des jours entiers/des semaines entières; **for 5 weeks ~** (pendant) 5 semaines de suite *or* d'affilée.

togetherness [tə'geðənɪs] *n* (*U*) (*unity*) unité *f*; (*friendliness*) camaraderie *f*.

toggle ['tɒgl] **1** *n* (*Naut*) cabillot *m*; (*on garment*) bouton *m* de duffel-coat. **2** *cpd*: (*Tech*) **toggle joint** genouillère *f*; (*Elec*) **toggle switch** bouton *m* (à levier).

Togo ['təʊgəʊ] *n* Togo *m*.

toil[1] [tɔɪl] **1** *n* (*U*) (dur) travail *m*, labeur *m* (*liter*).

2 *vi* **(a)** (*work hard: also* **~ away**) travailler dur (*at, over* à, *to do* pour faire), peiner (*at, over* sur, *to do* pour faire).

(b) (*move with difficulty*) *[person, horse, vehicle]* **to ~ along/up** *etc* avancer/monter *etc* péniblement *or* avec peine.

toil[2] [tɔɪl] *n* (*fig liter: snare, net*) **~s** rets *mpl*.

toilet ['tɔɪlɪt] **1** *n* **(a)** (*dressing etc, dress*) toilette *f*.

(b) (*lavatory*) toilettes *fpl*, cabinets *mpl*, waters* *mpl*. **'T~s'** 'Toilettes'; **to go to the ~** aller aux toilettes *or* aux cabinets *or* aux waters*; **to put sth down the ~** jeter qch dans la cuvette des cabinets.

2 *cpd*: **toilet bag, toilet case** trousse *f* de toilette; (*U*) **toilet paper** papier *m* hygiénique; (*Comm*) **toilet requisites** articles *mpl* de toilette; **toilet roll** rouleau *m* de papier hygiénique; **toilet seat** siège *m* des cabinets; **toilet soap** savonnette *f*, savon *m* de toilette; **toilet table** table *f* de toilette; (*U*) **toilet tissue** = **toilet paper**; **to toilet-train a child** apprendre à un enfant à être propre; **toilet training** apprentissage *m* de la propreté; **toilet water** eau *f* de toilette.

toiletries ['tɔɪlɪtrɪz] *npl* articles *mpl* de toilette.
toilette [twɑː'let] *n* = **toilet 1a.**
toilsome ['tɔɪlsəm] *adj* (*liter*) pénible, épuisant.
token ['təʊkən] **1** *n* (*sign, symbol*) marque *f*, témoignage *m*, gage *m*; (*keepsake*) souvenir *m*; (*metal disc: for travel, telephone etc*) jeton *m*; (*voucher, coupon*) bon *m*, coupon *m*; (*gift* ~) bon-cadeau *m*. **milk** ~ bon de lait; **as a** ~ **of, in** ~ **of** en témoignage de, en gage de; *(fig)* **by the same** ~ de même; *V* **book, record** *etc.*
2 *cpd payment, strike* symbolique. **they put up a token resistance** ils ont opposé un semblant de résistance pour la forme; (*Parl*) **token vote** vote *m* de crédits (dont le montant n'est pas définitivement fixé).
told [təʊld] *pret, ptp of* **tell.**
tolerable ['tɒlərəbl] *adj* **(a)** (*bearable*) tolérable, supportable. **(b)** (*fairly good*) passable, assez bon. **the food is** ~ on y mange passablement, on n'y mange pas trop mal.
tolerably ['tɒlərəblɪ] *adv* passablement, assez. ~ **certain** à peu près certain; **he plays** ~ **(well)** il joue passablement, il ne joue pas trop mal.
tolerance ['tɒlərəns] *n* tolérance *f*, indulgence *f*; (*Med, Tech*) tolérance.
tolerant ['tɒlərənt] *adj* tolérant, indulgent (*of* à l'égard de). **to be** ~ **of sth** tolérer qch.
tolerantly ['tɒlərəntlɪ] *adv* d'une manière tolérante, avec indulgence.
tolerate ['tɒləreɪt] *vt heat, pain* supporter; *insolence, injustice* tolérer, supporter; (*Med, Tech*) tolérer.
toleration [ˌtɒlə'reɪʃən] *n* (*U*) tolérance *f*.
toll[1] [təʊl] **1** *n* (*tax, charge*) péage *m*. *(fig)* **the war took a heavy** ~ **of** *or* **among the young men** la guerre a fait beaucoup de victimes parmi les jeunes, les jeunes ont payé un fort tribut à la guerre; **it took (a) great** ~ **of his strength** cela a sérieusement ébranlé *or* sapé ses forces; **we must reduce the accident** ~ **on the roads** il nous faut réduire le nombre des victimes de la route; **the** ~ **of dead and injured has risen** le nombre des morts et des blessés a augmenté.
2 *cpd*: **tollbar** barrière *f* de péage; **tollbridge** pont *m* à péage; **tollgate** = **tollbar**; **tollkeeper** péager *m*, -ère *f*; **toll road, tollway** route *f* à péage.
toll[2] [təʊl] **1** *vi [bell]* sonner. **for whom the bell** ~**s** pour qui sonne le glas. **2** *vt bell, the hour* sonner; *sb's death* sonner le glas pour.
Tom [tɒm] **1** *n* (*dim of* **Thomas**) Thomas *m*. *(fig)* **(any)** ~, **Dick or Harry** n'importe qui, le premier venu; *V* **peep**[1]. **2** *cpd*: **Tom Thumb** Tom-pouce *m*; (*in French tale*) le petit Poucet.
tom [tɒm] *n* (*also* ~**cat**) matou *m*.
tomahawk ['tɒməhɔːk] *n* tomahawk *m*, hache *f* de guerre.
tomato [tə'mɑːtəʊ, (*US*) tə'meɪtəʊ] *pl* ~**es 1** *n* (*fruit, plant*) tomate *f*. **2** *cpd*: **tomato juice** jus *m* de tomates; **tomato ketchup** ketchup *m*; **tomato plant** tomate *f*; **tomato sauce** sauce *f* tomate.
tomb [tuːm] **1** *n* tombeau *m*, tombe *f*. **2** *cpd*: **tombstone** pierre tombale, tombe *f*.
tombac, tombak ['tɒmbæk] *n* (*U*) tombac *m*, laiton *m*.
tombola [tɒm'bəʊlə] *n* (*Brit*) tombola *f*.
tomboy ['tɒmbɔɪ] *n* garçon manqué.
tomboyish ['tɒmbɔɪɪʃ] *adj* de garçon manqué.
tomboyishness ['tɒmbɔɪɪʃnɪs] *n* (*U*) manières *fpl* de garçon manqué.
tome [təʊm] *n* tome *m*, gros volume.
tomfool [tɒm'fuːl] *adj* absurde, idiot.
tomfoolery [tɒm'fuːlərɪ] *n* (*U*) niaiserie(s) *f(pl)*, âneries *fpl*.
Tommy ['tɒmɪ] (*dim of* **Thomas**) **1** *n* Thomas *m*; (*Brit Mil**: *also* **t**~) tommy* *m*, soldat *m* britannique. **2** *cpd*: **tommy gun** mitraillette *f*; (*U*) **tommyrot*** bêtises *fpl*, âneries *fpl*.
tomorrow [tə'mɒrəʊ] **1** *adv* demain (*also fig*). **all (day)** ~ toute la journée (de) demain; **a week (past)** ~ il y aura huit jours demain; **a week from** ~ demain en huit; **he'll have been here a week** ~ cela fera huit jours demain qu'il est là; **see you** ~! à demain!; **early** ~ demain de bonne heure; **what day will it be** ~? quel jour sera-t-on demain?; **what date will it be** ~? quelle sera la date demain?; *(fig)* ~ **we will see cities where forests stand today** demain nous verrons des villes là où se dressent des forêts aujourd'hui; *V* **today.**
2 *n* demain *m* (*also fig*). **the day after** ~ après-demain; **what day will** ~ **be?** quel jour serons-nous demain?; ~ **will be Saturday** demain ce sera samedi; **what date will** ~ **be?** quelle est la date de demain?; ~ **will be the 5th** demain ce sera le 5; **I hope** ~ **will be dry** j'espère qu'il ne pleuvra pas demain; ~ **will be a better day for you** les choses iront mieux pour vous demain; (*loc*) ~ **never comes** demain n'arrive jamais; (*loc*) ~ **is another day!** on n'est pas encore à demain!; ~**'s paper** le journal de demain; *(fig)* **the writers of** ~ les écrivains *mpl* de demain *or* de l'avenir.
3 *cpd*: **tomorrow morning/afternoon/evening** demain matin/après-midi/soir; **tomorrow week** demain en huit.
tomtit ['tɒmtɪt] *n* mésange *f*.
tomtom ['tɒmtɒm] *n* tam-tam *m*.
ton [tʌn] **1** *n* **(a)** (*weight*) tonne *f* (*Brit* = *1016,06 kg*; *Can, US etc* = *907,20 kg*). **metric** ~ tonne (= *1000 kg*); **a 7-**~ **truck** un camion de 7 tonnes; *(fig)* **it weighs a** ~, **it's a** ~ **weight** c'est du plomb; (**fig*) ~**s of** beaucoup de, des tas de*.
(b) (*Naut*) (*also* **register** ~) tonneau *m* (= *2,83 m*^{3}); (*also* **displacement** ~) tonne *f*; **a 60,000-**~ **steamer** un paquebot de 60.000 tonnes.
(c) (*Aut*‡ *etc*) **to do a** ~ **(up)** faire du cent soixante à l'heure.
2 *cpd*: (*Brit: motorcyclists*) **the ton-up boys**‡ les motards* *mpl*, les fous *mpl* de la moto.
tonal ['təʊnl] *adj* tonal.
tonality [təʊ'nælɪtɪ] *n* tonalité *f*.
tone [təʊn] **1** *n* **(a)** (*in sound: also Ling, Mus*) ton *m*; (*Telec: also of radio, record player etc*) tonalité *f*; *[musical instrument]* sonorité *f*. **to speak in low** ~**s** *or* **in a low** ~ parler à voix basse *or* doucement; **to speak in angry** ~**s, to speak in an angry** ~ **(of voice)** parler sur le ton de la colère; **don't speak to me in that** ~ **(of voice)!** ne me parlez pas sur ce ton!; (*Ling*) **rising/falling** ~ ton montant/descendant; *V* **dialling, engaged** *etc.*
(b) (*in colour*) ton *m*. **a two-**~ **car** une voiture de deux tons.
(c) (*general character*) ton *m*. **what was the** ~ **of his letter?** quel était le ton de sa lettre?; **in friendly** ~**s, in a friendly** ~ sur un ton amical; **we were impressed by the whole** ~ **of the school** nous avons été impressionnés par la tenue générale de l'école; (*Fin*) **the** ~ **of the market** la tenue du marché; **to raise/lower the** ~ **of sth** rehausser/rabaisser le ton de qch.
(d) (*U: class, elegance*) classe *f*. **it gives the restaurant** ~, **it adds** ~ **to the restaurant** cela donne de la classe au restaurant.
(e) (*Med, Physiol: of muscles etc*) tonus *m*, tonicité *f*.
2 *cpd*: *[record player]* **tone arm** bras *m* de lecture; *[record player etc]* **tone control (knob)** bouton *m* de tonalité; **to be tone-deaf** ne pas avoir d'oreille; **tone-deafness** manque *m* d'oreille; (*Ling*) **tone language** langue *f* à ton; **tone poem** poème *m* symphonique.
3 *vi [colour]* s'harmoniser (*with* avec).
tone down *vt sep colour* adoucir; *sound* baisser; *radio etc* baisser (le son de); *(fig) criticism, effect* atténuer, adoucir.
tone in *vi* s'harmoniser (*with* avec).
tone up *vt sep muscles, the system* tonifier.
toneless ['təʊnlɪs] *adj voice* blanc (*f* blanche), sans timbre.
tonelessly ['təʊnlɪslɪ] *adv speak* d'une voix blanche.
tongs [tɒŋz] *npl* (*also* **pair of** ~) pinces *fpl*; (*for coal*) pincettes *fpl*; (*for sugar*) pince *f* (à sucre); (*curling* ~) fer *m* (à friser); *V* **hammer.**
tongue [tʌŋ] **1** *n* **(a)** (*Anat, Culin*) langue *f*; *[shoe]* languette *f*; *[bell]* battant *m*; (*fig: of flame, land; also on tool, machine etc*) langue. **to put out** *or* **stick out one's** ~ tirer la langue (*at sb* à qn); *[dog, person]* **his** ~ **was hanging out** il tirait la langue; *[hounds]* **to give** ~ donner de la voix; *(fig)* **to lose/find one's** ~ perdre/retrouver sa langue; **with his** ~ **in his cheek,** ~ **in cheek** ironiquement, en plaisantant; **keep a civil** ~ **in your head!** tâchez d'être plus poli!; *(fig)* **I can't get my** ~ **round it** je n'arrive pas à le prononcer correctement; *V* **hold, tip**[1], **wag**[1] *etc.*
(b) (*language*) langue *f*. (*Rel*) **to speak in** ~**s** avoir le don (surnaturel) de s'exprimer dans des langues inconnues; *V* **mother** *etc.*
2 *cpd*: (*Carpentry*) **tongue-and-groove boarding** *or* **strips** planches *fpl* à rainure et languette; **tongue-and-groove joint** assemblage *m* à rainure et languette; *(fig)* **tongue-tied** muet (*fig*); *(fig)* **tongue-tied from shyness/fright/astonishment** *etc* muet de timidité/peur/stupeur *etc*, trop timide/effrayé/abasourdi *etc* pour parler; **tongue twister** phrase *f* très difficile à prononcer.
tonic ['tɒnɪk] **1** *adj* (*Ling, Med, Mus, Physiol*) tonique. ~ **water** *V* **2b**; ~ **wine** vin *m* tonique; (*Mus*) ~ **solfa** solfège *m*.
2 *n* **(a)** (*Med*) tonique *m*, fortifiant *m*. (*lit, fig*) **you need a** ~ il vous faut un bon tonique; *(fig)* **it was a real** ~ **to see him** cela m'a vraiment remonté le moral de le voir.
(b) (*also* ~ **water**) ≈ Schweppes *m*®; **gin and** ~ gin-tonic *m*.
(c) (*Mus*) tonique *f*.
tonicity [tɒ'nɪsɪtɪ] *n* tonicité *f*.
tonight [tə'naɪt] *adv, n* (*before bed*) ce soir; (*during sleep*) cette nuit.
tonnage ['tʌnɪdʒ] *n* (*Naut: all senses*) tonnage *m*.
tonneau ['tʌnəʊ] *n* (*Aut: also* ~ **cover**) bâche *f* (*de voiture de sport*).
-tonner ['tʌnəʳ] *n ending in cpds*: **a 10-tonner** (*truck*) un (camion de) 10 tonnes.
tonometer [təʊ'nɒmɪtəʳ] *n* (*Mus*) diapason *m* de Scheibler; (*Med*) tonomètre *m*.
tonsil ['tɒnsl] *n* amygdale *f*. **to have one's** ~**s out** *or* **removed** être opéré des amygdales.
tonsillectomy [ˌtɒnsɪ'lektəmɪ] *n* amygdalectomie *f*.
tonsillitis [ˌtɒnsɪ'laɪtɪs] *n* (*U*) amygdalite *f*. **he's got** ~ il a une angine, il a une amygdalite (*frm*).
tonsorial [tɒn'sɔːrɪəl] *adj* (*hum*) de barbier.
tonsure ['tɒnʃəʳ] **1** *n* tonsure *f*. **2** *vt* tonsurer.
tontine [tɒn'tiːn] *n* tontine *f*.
Tony ['təʊnɪ] *n* (*dim of* **Anthony**) Antoine *m*.
too [tuː] *adv* **(a)** (*excessively*) trop, par trop (*liter*). **it's** ~ **hard for me** c'est trop difficile pour moi; **it's** ~ **hard for me to explain** c'est trop difficile pour que je puisse vous l'expliquer; **that case is** ~ **heavy to carry** cette valise est trop lourde à porter; **it's** ~ **heavy for me to carry** c'est trop lourd à porter pour moi; **he's** ~ **mean to pay for it** il est trop pingre pour le payer; **that's** ~ **kind of you!** vous êtes vraiment trop aimable!; **I'm not** ~ **sure about that** je n'en suis pas très certain; ~ **true!***, ~ **right!*** que oui!*, et comment!*; **it's just**~**-**~**!**‡ en voilà un chichi!*; *V* **good, many, much, none** *etc.*
(b) (*also*) aussi; (*moreover*) en plus, par-dessus le marché, de plus, en outre. **I went** ~ moi aussi j'y suis allé; **you** ~ **can own a car like this** vous aussi vous pouvez être le propriétaire d'une voiture comme celle-ci; HE **can swim** ~ lui aussi sait nager; **he can** SWIM ~ il sait nager aussi, il sait aussi *or* également nager; **they asked for a discount** ~! et en plus *or* et par-dessus le marché ils ont demandé un rabais!; **and then,** ~, **there's the question of ...** et puis, de plus *or* en outre, il y a la question de ... .
took [tʊk] *pret of* **take.**
tool [tuːl] **1** *n* (*gen, Tech*) outil *m*; (*fig: book etc*) outil, instrument *m*. **set of** ~**s** panoplie *f* d'outils; **garden** ~**s** outils *or* ustensiles *mpl* de jardinage; (*lit, fig*) **these are the** ~**s of my trade** voilà les outils de mon métier; **he was merely a** ~ **of the**

revolutionary party il n'était que l'outil *or* l'instrument du parti révolutionnaire; (*fig*) **a ~ in the hands of** un instrument dans les mains de; *V* **down**[1], **machine, workman** *etc.*

2 *cpd*: **toolbag** trousse *f* à outils; **toolbox** boîte *f or* caisse *f or* coffre *m* à outils; **toolcase** = **toolbag, toolbox**; **toolchest** = **toolbox**; **toolhouse** = **toolshed**; **toolkit** trousse *f* à outils; (*Ind*) **toolmaker** outilleur *m*; (*Ind*) **toolmaking** montage *m* et réglage *m* des machines-outils; (*Ind*) **toolroom** atelier *m* d'outillage; **toolshed** cabane *f* à outils.

3 *vt* travailler, ouvrager; *book-cover* ciseler, repousser. **~ed leather** cuir repoussé.

4 *vi* (*Aut*) **to ~ along/past*** rouler/passer tranquillement *or* pépère‡.

tooling ['tu:lɪŋ] *n* (*on book-cover etc*) repoussé *m*, ciselure *f*.

toot [tu:t] **1** *n* [*car-horn*] coup *m* de klaxon; [*whistle*] coup de sifflet; [*trumpet, flute*] note *f* (brève). **2** *vi* klaxonner, corner; donner un coup de sifflet; jouer une note. **3** *vt* (*Aut*) **to ~ the horn** klaxonner, corner.

tooth [tu:θ] **1** *n, pl* **teeth** [*person, animal, comb, saw etc*] dent *f*. **front ~** dent de devant; **back ~** molaire *f*; **to have a ~ out** se faire arracher une dent; **to mutter sth between one's teeth** *or* **between clenched teeth** grommeler qch entre ses dents; **to set** *or* **grit one's teeth** serrer les dents; (*lit, fig*) **to bare** *or* **show one's teeth** montrer les dents; **in the teeth of the wind** contre le vent; **in the teeth of the opposition** en dépit de *or* malgré l'opposition; **~ and nail** avec acharnement, farouchement; (*fig*) **to get one's teeth into sth** se mettre à fond à qch, se mettre à faire qch pour de bon; **there's nothing you can get your teeth into** (*of food etc*) ce n'est pas très substantiel; (*fig*) il n'y a là rien de substantiel *or* solide; (*fig*) **the legislation has no teeth** la législation est impuissante; (*fig*) **to give a law teeth** renforcer le pouvoir d'une loi; (*fig*) **to cast** *or* **throw sth in sb's teeth** jeter qch à la tête de qn, reprocher qch à qn; **to be fed up** *or* **sick to the (back) teeth of sth‡** en avoir marre* *or* ras le bol‡ de qch; *V* **chatter, edge, long**[1] *etc.*

2 *cpd*: **toothache** mal *m or* rage *f* de dents; **to have toothache** avoir mal aux dents; **toothbrush** brosse *f* à dents; **toothbrush moustache** moustache *f* en brosse; **toothcomb** peigne fin; (*fig*) **to go through sth with a (fine) toothcomb** passer qch au peigne fin; **toothpaste** (pâte *f*) dentifrice *m*; **toothpick** cure-dent *m*; **tooth powder** poudre *f* dentifrice.

toothed ['tu:θt] *adj wheel, leaf* denté.

-toothed ['tu:θt] *adj ending in cpds*: **big-toothed** aux grandes dents.

toothless ['tu:θlɪs] *adj* édenté.

toothsome ['tu:θsəm] *adj* savoureux, succulent.

toothy ['tʊθɪ] *adj* [*person*] **to be ~** arborer une belle rangée de dents, avoir des dents de cheval (*pej*); **he gave me a ~ smile** il m'a souri découvrant largement ses dents.

tootle ['tu:tl] **1** *n* [*trumpet, flute, car-horn*] notes *fpl* (brèves); (*tune*) petit air.

2 *vi* **(a)** (*toot: Aut*) klaxonner, corner; (*Mus*) jouer un petit air.

(b) (*Aut**) **to ~ along/past** *etc* rouler/passer *etc* gaiement *or* sans s'en faire*.

3 *vt trumpet, flute etc* jouer un peu de.

toots‡ ['tu:ts] *n* ma belle*.

tootsy‡ ['tu:tsɪ] *n* **(a)** (*toe*) doigt *m* de pied; (*foot*) peton* *m*, pied *m*. **(b)** (*girl*) jolie nana‡. **hi ~!** salut ma belle!*

top[1] [tɒp] **1** *n* **(a)** (*highest point*) [*mountain, tree*] sommet *m*, faîte *m*, cime *f*; [*hill, head*] sommet, haut *m*; [*ladder, stairs, page, wall, cupboard*] haut; [*wave*] crête *f*; [*box, container*] dessus *m*; [*list, table, classification, queue*] tête *f*; (*surface*) surface *f*. **at the ~ of** *hill, mountain* au sommet de; *stairs, ladder, building, page* en haut de; *list, queue, division, league* en tête de; *street etc* en haut de, au bout de; *garden* au fond de; *profession, career* au faîte de; **it's near the ~ of the pile** c'est vers le haut de la pile; **it's at the ~ of the pile** c'est en haut *or* au sommet de la pile; **6 lines from the ~ of page 7** 6e ligne à partir du haut de la page 7; (*Scol*) **to be at the ~ of the class** être premier de la classe; **it's ~ of the pops this week** c'est en tête du hit-parade cette semaine; **the men at the ~** les dirigeants *mpl*, les responsables *mpl*, ceux qui sont au pouvoir *or* à la tête; **the men at the ~ don't care about it** en haut lieu ils ne s'en soucient guère; **he was sitting at the ~ of the table** il était assis à la place d'honneur; **at the ~ of one's voice** à tue-tête; **to come** *or* **rise** *or* **float to the ~** remonter à la surface, surnager; **it was floating on ~ of the water** cela flottait sur l'eau; (*Mil*) **to go over the ~** monter à l'assaut; (*fig: too many*) **we've got 5 over the ~*** nous en avons 5 de trop; **on (the) ~ of** sur; **it's the one on (the) ~** c'est celui qui est en dessus; **take the plate on the ~** prends l'assiette du dessus; (*fig*) **he came out on ~** il a eu le dessus, il l'a emporté; (*fig*) **to be on ~ of the world** être aux anges; **to be on the ~ of one's form** être au meilleur de sa forme; (*in career etc*) **he'll get to the ~** il réussira, il ira loin; (*fig*) **he's on ~ of things now*** il s'en sort très bien *or* il domine bien la situation maintenant; (*after breakdown, bereavement*) il a repris le dessus maintenant; **things are getting on ~ of her*** elle est dépassée, elle ne sait plus où donner de la tête; **he bought another car on ~ of the one he's got already** il a acheté une autre auto en plus de celle qu'il a déjà; **then on ~ of all that he refused to help us** et puis par-dessus le marché il a refusé de nous aider; **from ~ to toe, from the ~ of his head to the tip of his toes** de la tête (jusqu')aux pieds; **from ~ to bottom** de fond en comble; **he's saying that off the ~ of his head*** il dit ça comme ça (mais il n'en est pas certain), il parle sans savoir ce qu'il dit (*pej*); **the system is rotten from ~ to bottom** le système tout entier est pourri; **the ~ of the morning to you!*** je vous souhaite bien le bonjour!; (*Brit Aut*) **in ~ = in top gear** (*V* 2); **he's the ~s‡** il est champion*; *V* **blow**[1], **up** *etc.*

(b) (*upper part, section*) [*car etc*] toit *m*; [*bus*] étage supérieur; (*open ~*) impériale *f*; [*plant, vegetable*] fane *f*. (*Aut*) **a sliding** *or* **sunshine ~** un toit ouvrant; (*on bus*) **seats on ~** places *fpl* à l'étage supérieur; **we saw London from the ~ of a bus** nous avons vu Londres du haut d'un bus; **let's go up on ~** (*in bus*) on va en haut; (*in ship*) on va sur le pont; **my pyjama ~** la veste de mon pyjama; **I want a ~ to go with this skirt** je voudrais un haut qui aille avec cette jupe; **the table ~ is made of oak** le plateau de la table est en chêne; **the table ~ is scratched** le dessus de la table est rayé; *V* **big** *etc.*

(c) (*cap, lid*) [*box*] couvercle *m*; [*bottle*] (*screw-on*) bouchon *m*; (*snap-on*) capsule *f*; [*pen*] capuchon *m*.

2 *adj* (*highest*) *shelf, drawer* du haut; *floor, storey* dernier; (*highest in rank etc*) premier; (*best*) (le) meilleur. **the ~ step** la dernière marche (d'en haut); [*paint*] **the ~ coat** la dernière couche (*V also* 3); **the ~ right-hand corner** le coin en haut à droite; (*fig*) **he's out of the ~ drawer*** il est de bonne famille, il fait partie du gratin*; (*Mus*) **the ~ note** la note la plus haute; **~ prices** prix *mpl* maximums *or* maxima; **we pay ~ price(s) for old clocks** nous offrons les meilleurs prix pour les vieilles horloges; **at ~ speed** à toute vitesse; (*Brit Aut*) **in ~ gear** (*four-speed box*) en quatrième; (*five-speed box*) en cinquième; **in ~ form** en pleine forme; (*Scol*) **he was** *or* **came ~ in maths** il a été premier en maths; **the ~ mark** la meilleure note; (*fig*) **~ marks for efficiency** vingt sur vingt pour efficacité; (*Scol*) **in the ~ class** (*secondary school*) ≃ en terminale; (*primary*) ≃ au cours moyen 2; (*~ stream*) dans le premier groupe; (*Mus*) **the ~ 20** les 20 premiers du hit-parade; **the ~ men in the party** les dirigeants *mpl* du parti; **one of the ~ pianists** un des plus grands pianistes; **a ~ job, one of the ~ jobs** un des postes les plus prestigieux; **the newspaper for ~ people** le journal de l'élite; (*fig*) **the ~ brass*** les huiles* *fpl*; (*fig*) **he's ~ dog* around here** c'est lui qui commande ici *or* qui fait la pluie et le beau temps ici.

3 *cpd*: **top boots** bottes *fpl* à revers; (*Dress*) **topcoat** pardessus *m*, manteau *m*; (*Agr*) **top-dress** fumer en surface; **top dressing** fumure *f* en surface; **topflight*** de premier ordre, excellent; **top hat** (chapeau *m*) haut-de-forme *m*; **top-hatted** en (chapeau) haut-de-forme; **top-heavy** *structure etc* trop lourd du haut; (*fig*) *organization* mal équilibré; (*Brit*) **top-hole*†** de première*, au poil*; **topknot** (*hair*) toupet *m*, houppe *f*; (*ribbons etc*) coque *f*; (*bird's feathers*) aigrette *f*; **top-level** *meeting, talks, discussion* au sommet; *decision* pris au sommet; (*Naut*) **topmast** mât *m* de hune; **topmost** le plus haut, le plus élevé; **topnotch*†** = **topflight***; **top-ranking** (très) haut placé; (*Naut*) **topsail** hunier *m*; **top-secret** ultra-secret (*f* ultra-secrète), top secret (*f* top secrète); [*prison*] **top-security wing** quartier *m* sous surveillance spéciale; **topside** (*Brit Culin*) gîte *m* (à la noix); (*Naut*) haut *m*, accastillage *m*; **topsoil** couche *f* arable.

4 *vt* **(a)** (*remove ~ from*) *tree* étêter, écimer; *plant* écimer; *radish, carrot etc* couper *or* enlever les fanes de; (‡: *behead*) *person* couper le cou à*. **to ~ and tail fruit** préparer des fruits (*en les équeutant etc*).

(b) (*form ~ of*) surmonter. **~ped by a dome** surmonté d'un dôme.

(c) (*exceed*) dépasser. **we have ~ped last year's sales figures** nous avons dépassé les chiffres de vente de l'année dernière; **the fish ~ped 10 kg** le poisson pesait *or* faisait plus de 10 kg; **to ~ sb in height** dépasser qn en hauteur; (*fig*) **and to ~ it all ...** et pour couronner le tout ..., et pour comble ...; **that ~s the lot!*** c'est le bouquet!*

(d) (*pass ~ of*) *hill* franchir le sommet de; *ridge* franchir.

(e) (*be at ~ of*) *pile* être au sommet de; *list, queue* être en *or* à la tête de. (*Theat*) **to ~ the bill** être en tête d'affiche, tenir la vedette.

top off 1 *vi* (*reach peak*) [*sales, production etc*] atteindre son (*or* leur) maximum (et se stabiliser).

2 *vt sep* terminer, compléter. **we topped off the meal with a glass of cognac** nous avons couronné *or* complété le repas par un verre de cognac.

top out *vi* (*Constr*) terminer le gros œuvre d'un gratte-ciel.

top up (*Brit*) **1** *vi* (*Aut*) **to top up with oil** remettre *or* rajouter de l'huile.

2 *vt sep cup, glass* remplir (à nouveau); (*Aut*) *battery* remettre de l'eau dans; *coffee, oil, petrol* rajouter, remettre. **can I top you up?*** je vous en remets?

top[2] [tɒp] *n* (*toy*) toupie *f*; *V* **sleep, spinning.**

topaz ['təʊpæz] *n* topaze *f*.

tope† [təʊp] *vi* boire.

topee ['təʊpi:] *n* casque colonial.

toper† ['təʊpə^r] *n* grand buveur.

topic ['tɒpɪk] *n* [*essay, speech*] sujet *m*; (*for discussion*) sujet de discussion, thème *m*.

topical ['tɒpɪkəl] *adj* d'actualité.

topicality [ˌtɒpɪ'kælɪtɪ] *n* (*U*) actualité *f*.

topless ['tɒplɪs] *adj costume* sans haut; *girl* aux seins nus. **~ swimsuit** monokini* *m*.

topographer [tə'pɒgrəfə^r] *n* topographe *mf*.

topographic(al) [ˌtɒpə'græfɪk(l)] *adj* topographique.

topography [tə'pɒgrəfɪ] *n* topographie *f*.

topper* ['tɒpə^r] *n* (chapeau *m*) haut-de-forme *m*.

topping ['tɒpɪŋ] **1** *adj* (*Brit*†*) épatant*. **2** *n* (*U: Culin*) **chocolate/orange ~** crème *f* au chocolat/à l'orange (*dont on nappe un dessert*).

topple ['tɒpl] **1** *vi* (*lose balance*) [*person*] basculer, culbuter, perdre l'équilibre; [*pile*] basculer; (*fall: also ~ over, ~ down*) [*person*] tomber; [*pile etc*] s'effondrer, se renverser; [*empire, dictator, government*] tomber. **to ~ over a cliff** tomber du haut d'une falaise. **2** *vt sep object* faire tomber, faire basculer, renverser; *government, ruler* renverser, faire tomber.

topsy-turvy ['tɒpsɪ'tɜːvɪ] *adj, adv* sens dessus dessous, à l'envers. **everything is ~** tout est sens dessus dessous; (*fig*) c'est le monde à l'envers *or* renversé.
toque [təʊk] *n* toque *f*.
tor [tɔːʳ] *n* butte *f* (rocheuse).
torch [tɔːtʃ] **1** *n* (*flaming*) torche *f*, flambeau *m* (*also fig*); (*Brit: electric*) lampe *f* de poche, torche électrique. (*fig*) **he still carries a ~ for her*** il en pince toujours pour elle*; *V* **Olympic**.
2 *cpd*: **torchbearer** porteur *m* de flambeau *or* de torche; **by torchlight** à la lumière des flambeaux (*or* d'une lampe de poche); **torchlight procession** retraite *f* aux flambeaux.
tore ['tɔːʳ] *pret of* **tear**[1].
toreador ['tɒrɪədɔːʳ] *n* toréador *m*.
torero [tə'rɛərəʊ] *n* torero *m*.
torment ['tɔːment] **1** *n* tourment *m* (*liter*), supplice *m*. **to be in ~** être au supplice; **the ~s of jealousy** les affres *fpl* de la jalousie; **to suffer ~s** souffrir le martyre.
2 [tɔː'ment] *vt* (*cause pain to*) tourmenter, torturer, martyriser; (*harass*) *person, animal* harceler, tourmenter. **~ed by jealousy** torturé *or* rongé par la jalousie.
tormentor [tɔː'mentəʳ] *n* persécuteur *m*, -trice *f*, (*stronger*) bourreau *m*.
torn [tɔːn] *ptp of* **tear**[1].
tornado [tɔː'neɪdəʊ] *n, pl* **~es** tornade *f*.
Toronto [tə'rɒntəʊ] *n* Toronto.
torpedo [tɔː'piːdəʊ] **1** *n, pl* **~es** torpille *f*. **2** *cpd*: **torpedo boat** torpilleur *m*, vedette *f* lance-torpilles; **torpedo tube** (tube *m*) lance-torpilles *m inv*. **3** *vt* torpiller (*also fig*).
torpid ['tɔːpɪd] *adj* engourdi, torpide.
torpidity [tɔː'pɪdɪtɪ] *n*, **torpor** ['tɔːpəʳ] *n* torpeur *f*, engourdissement *m*.
torque [tɔːk] **1** *n* (*Aut, Phys*) moment *m* de torsion; (*Hist: collar*) torque *m*.
2 *cpd*: (*Aut*) **torque converter** convertisseur *m* de couple; **torque wrench** clef *f* dynamométrique.
torrent ['tɒrənt] *n* torrent *m* (*also fig*). **the rain was coming down in ~s** il pleuvait à torrents.
torrential [tɒ'renʃəl] *adj* torrentiel.
torrid ['tɒrɪd] *adj climate, heat* torride; (*fig*) *passion, love affair* ardent. (*Geog*) **the T~ Zone** la zone intertropicale.
torsion ['tɔːʃən] **1** *n* torsion *f*. **2** *cpd*: **torsion balance/bar** balance *f*/barre *f* de torsion.
torso ['tɔːsəʊ] *n* (*Anat*) torse *m*; (*Sculp*) buste *m*.
tort [tɔːt] *n* (*Jur*) acte délictuel *or* quasi-délictuel.
tortoise ['tɔːtəs] **1** *n* tortue *f*. **2** *cpd*: **tortoiseshell** (*n*) écaille *f* (de tortue); (*cpd*) *ornament, comb* en *or* d'écaille; *spectacles* à monture d'écaille.
tortuous ['tɔːtjʊəs] *adj path* tortueux, sinueux; *methods, argument* tortueux, détourné; *mind* tortueux, retors (*pej*).
torture ['tɔːtʃəʳ] **1** *n* torture *f*, supplice *m*. **to put sb to (the) ~** torturer qn, faire subir des tortures à qn; (*fig*) **it was sheer ~!** c'était un vrai supplice!
2 *cpd*: **torture chamber** chambre *f* de torture.
3 *vt* (*lit*) torturer; (*fig*) torturer, mettre à la torture *or* au supplice; *senses etc* mettre au supplice; *language* écorcher; *meaning* dénaturer; *tune* massacrer. **~d by doubt** torturé *or* tenaillé par le doute.
torturer ['tɔːtʃərəʳ] *n* tortionnaire *m*, bourreau *m*.
Tory ['tɔːrɪ] (*Brit Pol*) **1** *n* tory *m*, conservateur *m*, -trice *f*. **2** *adj party, person, policy* tory *inv*, conservateur (*f* -trice).
Toryism ['tɔːrɪɪzəm] *n* (*Brit Pol*) torysme *m*.
tosh* [tɒʃ] *n* (*U*) bêtises *fpl*, blagues *fpl*. (*excl*) **~!** allons (donc)!
toss [tɒs] **1** *n* **(a)** (*throw*) lancement *m*; (*by bull*) coup *m* de cornes. (*from horse*) **to take a ~** faire une chute, être désarçonné; **with a ~ of his head** d'un mouvement brusque de la tête.
(b) [*coin*] coup *m* de pile ou face. **they decided it by the ~ of a coin** ils l'ont décidé à pile ou face; **to win/lose the ~** gagner/perdre à pile ou face; *V* **argue**.
2 *cpd*: [*coin*] **toss-up** coup *m* de pile ou face; (*fig*) **it was a toss-up between the theatre and the cinema** le théâtre ou le cinéma ça nous (*or* leur *etc*) était égal *or* c'était kif-kif*; **it's a toss-up whether I go or stay** que je parte ou que je reste (*subj*), c'est un peu à pile ou face.
3 *vt ball etc* lancer, jeter (*to* à); *pancake* faire sauter; *head, mane* rejeter en arrière; [*bull*] projeter en l'air; [*horse*] désarçonner, démonter. **to ~ sb in a blanket** faire sauter qn dans une couverture; **they ~ed a coin to decide who should stay** ils ont joué à pile ou face pour décider qui resterait; **I'll ~ you for it** on le joue à pile ou face; **the sea ~ed the boat against the rocks** la mer a projeté *or* envoyé le bateau sur les rochers; **the boat was ~ed by the waves** le bateau était agité *or* ballotté par les vagues; *V* **caber**.
4 *vi* **(a)** (*often* **~ about, ~ around**) [*person*] s'agiter; [*plumes, trees*] se balancer; [*boat*] tanguer. **he was ~ing (about *or* around) in his sleep** il s'agitait dans son sommeil, son sommeil était agité; **he was ~ing and turning all night** il n'a pas arrêté de se tourner et se retourner toute la nuit.
(b) (*often* **~ up**) jouer à pile ou face. **let's ~ (up) for it** on le joue à pile ou face; **I'll ~ you for the drinks** on joue à pile ou face et le perdant paie à boire; **they ~ed (up) to see who would stay** ils ont joué à pile ou face pour savoir qui resterait.
toss about, toss around **1** *vi V* **toss 4a**.
2 *vt sep boat etc* ballotter, faire tanguer; *plumes, branches* agiter. (*fig*) **to toss one's money about** jeter l'argent par les fenêtres.
toss aside *vt sep object* jeter de côté; (*fig*) *person, helper* repousser; *suggestion, offer* rejeter, repousser; *scheme* rejeter.
toss away *vt sep* jeter.
toss back *vt sep ball etc* renvoyer; *hair, mane* rejeter en arrière. (*fig*) **they were tossing ideas back and forth** ils échangeaient toutes sortes d'idées.
toss off *vt sep drink* lamper, avaler d'un coup; *essay, letter, poem* écrire au pied levé, torcher (*pej*).
toss out *vt sep rubbish* jeter; *person* mettre à la porte, jeter dehors.
toss over *vt sep* lancer. **toss it over!** envoie!, lance!
toss up **1** *vi V* **toss 4b**.
2 *vt sep object* lancer, jeter (*into the air* en l'air).
3 toss-up *n V* **toss 2**.
tot[1] [tɒt] *n* **(a)** (*child: also* **tiny ~**) petit(e) enfant *m(f)*, tout(e) petit(e) *m(f)*, bambin *m*. **(b)** (*esp Brit: drink*) **a ~ of whisky** un petit verre de whisky; **just a ~** juste une goutte *or* une larme.
tot[2]* [tɒt] (*esp Brit*) **1** *vt* (*also* **~ up**) additionner, faire le total de. **2** *vi*: **it ~s up to £5** ça fait 5 livres en tout, ça se monte *or* ça s'élève à 5 livres; **I'm just ~ting up** je fais le total.
total ['təʊtl] **1** *adj sum, amount, quantity* total, global; *eclipse, war* total; *failure, silence* total, complet (*f* -ète), absolu. **the ~ losses/sales/debts** le total des pertes/ventes/dettes; **it was a ~ loss** on a tout perdu; **to be in ~ ignorance of sth** être dans l'ignorance la plus complète de qch, ignorer complètement qch; **they were in ~ disagreement** ils étaient en complet désaccord; (*Psych*) **~ recall** remémoration totale; *V* **abstainer, abstinence**.
2 *n* (montant *m*) total *m*, somme *f* (totale). **it comes to a ~ of £5, the ~ comes to £5** le total s'élève à 5 livres, cela fait 5 livres en tout; *V* **grand, sum**.
3 *vt* **(a)** (*add: also* **~ up**) *figures, expenses* totaliser, faire le total de, additionner.
(b) (*amount to*) s'élever à. **that ~s £5** cela fait 5 livres (en tout), cela s'élève à 5 livres; **the class ~led 40** il y avait 40 élèves en tout dans la classe.
totalitarian [ˌtəʊtælɪ'tɛərɪən] *adj, n* totalitaire (*mf*).
totalitarianism [ˌtəʊtælɪ'tɛərɪənɪzəm] *n* totalitarisme *m*.
totality [təʊ'tælɪtɪ] *n* totalité *f*.
totalizator ['təʊtəlaɪzeɪtəʳ] *n* **(a)** (*adding etc machine*) (appareil *m*) totalisateur *m*, machine totalisatrice. **(b)** (*Betting: esp Brit*) pari mutuel.
totalize ['təʊtəlaɪz] *vt* totaliser, additionner.
totalizer ['təʊtəlaɪzəʳ] *n* = **totalizator**.
totally ['təʊtəlɪ] *adv* totalement, entièrement, complètement.
tote[1]* [təʊt] *n abbr of* **totalizator b**.
tote[2] [təʊt] **1** *vt* (*: *carry*) *gun, object* porter. **I ~d it around all day** je l'ai coltiné* *or* trimballé* toute la journée. **2** *cpd*: (*US*) **tote bag** (sac *m*) fourre-tout* *m*.
totem ['təʊtəm] *n* totem *m*. **~ pole** mât *m* totémique.
totemic [təʊ'temɪk] *adj* totémique.
totter ['tɒtəʳ] *vi* [*person*] chanceler, vaciller, tituber; [*object, column, chimney stack*] chanceler, vaciller; (*fig*) [*company, government*] chanceler. **to ~ in/out *etc*** entrer/sortir *etc* en titubant *or* d'un pas chancelant.
tottering ['tɒtərɪŋ] *adj*, **tottery** ['tɒtərɪ] *adj* chancelant.
toucan ['tuːkən] *n* toucan *m*.
touch [tʌtʃ] **1** *n* **(a)** (*sense of* **~**) toucher *m*. **Braille is read by ~** le braille se lit au toucher; **soft to the ~** doux (*f* douce) au toucher; **the cold ~ of marble** le toucher froid du marbre.
(b) (*act of* **~ing**) contact *m*, toucher *m*; (*light brushing*) frôlement *m*, effleurement *m*; [*instrumentalist, typist*] toucher; [*artist*] touche *f*. **the slightest ~ might break it** le moindre contact pourrait le casser; **to give sb a ~ on the arm** toucher le bras de qn; **at the ~ of her hand, he ...** au contact de sa main, il ... ; **with the ~ of a finger** à la simple pression d'un doigt; **at the ~ of a switch** au simple contact d'un bouton; **she felt the ~ of the wind on her cheek** elle sentait le contact *or* la caresse du vent sur sa joue; **he altered it with a ~ of the brush/pen** il l'a modifié d'un coup de pinceau/d'un trait de plume; **to have a light ~** [*pianist, typist*] avoir le toucher léger; [*typewriter*] avoir une frappe légère; **you can see the master's ~ in this portrait** vous pouvez voir la touche du maître dans ce portrait; (*lit, fig*) **to put the final *or* finishing ~(es) to sth, to give sth the final *or* finishing ~(es)** mettre la dernière touche à qch; **it has the ~ of genius** cela porte le sceau du génie; **he lacks the human *or* personal ~** il est trop impersonnel *or* froid, il manque de chaleur humaine; **it's the human *or* personal ~ that makes his speeches so successful** c'est la note personnelle qui fait que ses discours ont tant de succès; **that's the Nelson ~** c'est du Nelson (tout pur); **you've got the right ~ with him** vous savez vous y prendre avec lui.
(c) (*small amount*) **a ~ of** un tout petit peu de; **a ~ of colour/gaiety** une touche de couleur/de gaieté; **a ~ of sadness/humour** une pointe *or* une note de tristesse/d'humour; **there's a ~ of spring in the air** il y a du printemps dans l'air; **there's a ~ of frost/cold in the air** il pourrait bien geler/faire froid; **he got a ~ of the sun** il a pris un petit coup de soleil; **to have a ~ of flu** être un peu grippé; **to have a ~ of rheumatism** faire un peu de rhumatisme; **it needs a ~ of paint** il faudrait y passer une petite couche de peinture.
(d) (*contact, communication*) contact *m*, rapport *m*, relation *f*. **to be/keep in ~ with sb** être/rester en contact *or* en rapport *or* en relation avec qn; **I'll be in ~!** je t'écrirai! (*or* je te téléphonerai!); **keep in ~!** tiens-nous au courant!; **to be out of ~ with sb, to have lost ~ with sb** avoir perdu le contact avec qn, ne plus être en contact *or* en rapport *or* en relation avec qn; **to be out of ~ *or* to have lost ~ with the political situation** ne plus être au courant de la situation politique, être déphasé en matière de politique*; (*fig*) **he's completely out of ~, he has lost ~ with what is going on** il est complètement déphasé*; **we're very much out of ~ here** nous sommes coupés de tout ici; **to get in(to) ~ with sb** se mettre en rapport *or* en relation *or* en contact avec qn, prendre contact avec qn, joindre *or* contacter* qn; **you can**

get in(to) ~ with me at this number vous pouvez me joindre *or* m'atteindre *or* me contacter* à ce numéro; **you ought to get in ~ with the police** vous devriez prendre contact avec *or* contacter* la police; **to lose ~ with sb** perdre le contact avec qn; **they lost ~ (with each other) long ago** il y a bien longtemps qu'ils ne sont plus en relation *or* en rapport; **I'll put you in ~ with him** je vous mettrai en rapport *or* en relation avec lui.

(e) (*Ftbl, Rugby*) touche *f.* **the ball went into ~** le ballon est sorti en touche; **it is in ~** il y a touche; **to kick for ~, to kick the ball into ~** envoyer le ballon en touche.

(f) (*: *borrowing etc*) **he has made a ~** il a tapé* quelqu'un; **he's good for a ~, he's a soft** *or* **an easy ~** il est toujours prêt à se laisser taper*.

2 *cpd*: **it's touch-and-go with the sick man** le malade est entre la vie et la mort; **it was touch-and-go whether she did it** elle a été à deux doigts de ne pas le faire; **it was touch-and-go until the last minute** l'issue est restée incertaine jusqu'au bout; **touchdown** (*Aviat, Space*) (*on land*) atterrissage *m*; (*on sea*) amerrissage *m*; (*on moon*) alunissage *m*; (*US*) **touch football** *variante f du jeu de football*; (*Ftbl etc*) **touchline** (ligne *f* de) touche *f*; **touchpaper** papier nitraté; (*lit, fig*) **touchstone** pierre *f* de touche; **touch-type** taper au toucher; **touch-typing** dactylographie *f* au toucher; **touch-typist** dactylo* *f* qui tape au toucher; **touchwood** amadou *m.*

3 *vt* **(a)** (*come into contact with*) toucher; (*brush lightly*) frôler, effleurer. **'do not ~ the goods'** 'ne touchez pas les *or* aux marchandises'; **he ~ed it with his finger** il l'a touché du doigt; **he ~ed her arm** il lui a touché le bras, il l'a touchée au bras; **his hand ~ed mine** sa main a touché *or* frôlé *or* effleuré la mienne; **to ~ one's hat to sb** saluer qn en portant la main à son chapeau; **I can ~ the bottom** je peux toucher le fond, j'ai pied; **the ship ~ed the bottom** le bateau a touché; **his feet are not ~ing the ground** ses pieds ne touchent pas terre; (*Aviat*) **to ~ ground** atterrir, toucher le sol; *V* **wood.**

(b) (*tamper with*) toucher à. **don't ~ that switch!** ne touchez pas à ce bouton!; **don't ~ that!** n'y touchez pas!; **the burglars didn't ~ the safe** les cambrioleurs n'ont pas touché au coffre-fort; **I didn't ~ it!** je n'y ai pas touché!; **I didn't ~ him!** je n'ai pas touché (à) un cheveu de sa tête, je ne lui ai rien fait; **~ nothing till the police arrive** ne touchez à rien avant l'arrivée de la police.

(c) (*fig*) **their land ~es ours** leur terre touche à *or* est contiguë à la nôtre; **Switzerland ~es Italy** la Suisse et l'Italie sont limitrophes *or* ont une frontière commune; **the ship ~ed Bordeaux** le bateau a fait escale à *or* a touché Bordeaux; **he merely ~ed the problem of racism** il n'a fait qu'effleurer le problème du racisme; **the frost ~ed the plants** la gelée a abîmé les plantes; **the fire didn't ~ the paintings** l'incendie a épargné les tableaux; **they can't ~ you if you don't break the law** ils ne peuvent rien contre vous *or* rien vous faire si vous respectez la loi; (*in exam*) **I didn't ~ the 3rd question** je n'ai pas touché à la 3e question; **he won't ~ anything illegal** si c'est illégal il n'y touchera pas; **water won't ~ these stains** l'eau n'agira pas sur ces taches; **the steak is so tough the knife just won't ~ it** le bifteck est si dur que le couteau n'arrive pas à l'entamer *or* à y pénétrer; **clouds ~ed with pink** nuages à reflets roses; *V* **barge.**

(d) (*gen neg*) *food, drink* toucher à. **he didn't ~ his meal** il n'a pas touché à son repas; **I never ~ onions** je ne mange jamais d'oignons; **I won't ~ gin** je ne boirai pas *or* je ne prendrai pas de gin.

(e) (*equal, rival*) valoir, égaler. **her cooking doesn't** *or* **can't ~ yours** sa cuisine est loin de valoir la tienne; **there's no pianist to ~ him, there's nobody to ~ him as a pianist, nobody can ~ him as a pianist** personne ne peut l'égaler *or* il est sans égal comme pianiste; **there's nothing to ~ hot whisky for a cold** rien ne vaut un grog au whisky pour guérir un rhume.

(f) (*concern*) toucher, concerner, regarder. **it ~es us all closely** cela nous touche *or* nous concerne tous de très près; **if it ~es the national interest** s'il y va de l'intérêt national.

(g) (*move emotionally*) toucher. **we were very ~ed by your letter** nous avons été très touchés de votre lettre.

(h) (*) **to ~ sb for a loan** taper* qn; **I ~ed him for £10** je l'ai tapé* de 10 livres.

4 *vi* **(a)** *[hands, ends etc]* se toucher; *[lands, gardens, areas]* se toucher, être contigus (*f* -guës). (*fig*) **to ~ (up)on a subject** effleurer un sujet.

(b) (*meddle*) **don't ~!** n'y touchez pas!, ne touchez pas!; **'do not ~'** 'défense de toucher'.

touch at *vt fus* (*Naut*) toucher (à), faire escale à.

touch down 1 *vi* **(a)** (*Aviat, Space*) (*on land*) atterrir; (*on sea*) amerrir; (*on moon*) alunir.

(b) (*Rugby etc*) marquer un essai; (*behind one's own goal-line*) toucher dans son en-but.

2 *vt sep* (*Rugby etc*) **to touch the ball down** marquer un essai; (*behind one's own goal-line*) toucher la balle dans l'en-but.

3 touchdown *n V* **touch 2.**

touch off *vt sep fuse, firework* faire partir; *mine etc* faire exploser *or* détoner *or* partir; *explosion* déclencher; (*fig*) *crisis, riot* faire éclater, déclencher; *reaction, scene, argument* provoquer, déclencher.

touch up *vt sep* retoucher.

touché [tuːˈʃeɪ] *excl* (*Fencing*) touché!; (*fig*) très juste!

touched [tʌtʃt] *adj* (*moved*) touché (*by* de); (*: *mad*) toqué*, timbré*.

touchiness [ˈtʌtʃɪnɪs] *n* (*U*) susceptibilité *f.*

touching [ˈtʌtʃɪŋ] **1** *adj* touchant, attendrissant. **2** *prep* concernant, touchant (†, *liter*).

touchingly [ˈtʌtʃɪŋlɪ] *adv* d'une manière touchante.

touchy [ˈtʌtʃɪ] *adj person* susceptible (*about* sur la question *or* le chapitre de), chatouilleux, ombrageux; *business, situation* délicat. **he's very ~** il se vexe *or* s'offense pour un rien.

tough [tʌf] **1** *adj* **(a)** (*strong*) *cloth, steel, leather, garment etc* solide, résistant; *person* dur, robuste, résistant, endurant, costaud*; (*pej*) *meat* dur, coriace. **you have to be ~ to do that kind of work** il faut de la résistance pour faire ce genre de travail.

(b) (*hard, stubborn*) *resistance, struggle, opposition* acharné, âpre; *journey* rude, fatigant, pénible; *task* dur, rude, pénible; *obstacle* rude, sérieux; *problem* épineux; *regulations, conditions* dur, sévère; *person* dur, tenace; (*pej*) coriace. **it's ~ work** c'est un travail dur *or* pénible, ce n'est pas du gâteau* *or* de la tarte*; **rugby is a ~ game** le rugby n'est pas un sport de *or* pour fillettes; **he is a ~ man to deal with** il ne fait pas souvent de concessions; **~ guy** dur *m*; (*pej*) **they're a ~ lot, they're ~ customers** ce sont des durs à cuire*; **to get ~ with sb*** (commencer à) se montrer dur pour *or* envers qn; **to have a ~ time of it*** en voir de dures*.

(c) (*) **that's ~** c'est vache*; **it was ~ on the others** c'était vache* pour les autres; **~ luck** déveine* *f*, manque *m* de pot*; **~ luck!** (*pity*) pas de veine!, manque de pot!*; (*you'll have to put up with it*) tant pis pour vous!; **that's ~ luck on him** il n'a pas de veine *or* de pot*.

2 *n* (*) dur *m.*

toughen [ˈtʌfn] (*also* **~ up**) **1** *vt metal, glass, cloth, leather* rendre plus solide, renforcer; *person* endurcir, aguerrir; *conditions* rendre plus sévère.

2 *vi [metal, glass, cloth, leather]* devenir plus solide; *[person]* s'endurcir, s'aguerrir; *[conditions, regulations]* devenir plus sévère.

toughly [ˈtʌflɪ] *adv fight, oppose* avec acharnement, âprement; *speak, answer* durement, sans ménagement. **it is ~ made** c'est du solide.

toughness [ˈtʌfnɪs] *n* (*U*: *V* **tough**) solidité *f*, résistance *f*; dureté *f*, endurance *f*; acharnement *m*, âpreté *f*; caractère *m* pénible *or* rude; caractère épineux; sévérité *f*; ténacité *f.*

toupee [ˈtuːpeɪ] *n* postiche *m.*

tour [tʊəʳ] **1** *n* (*journey*) voyage *m*, périple *m*; (*by team, actors, musicians etc*) tournée *f*; (*of town, factory, museum etc*) visite *f*, tour *m*; (*package ~*) voyage organisé. (*Hist*) **the Grand T~** le tour de l'Europe; **they went on a ~ of the Lake District** ils ont fait un voyage *or* un périple dans la région des Lacs; **we went on** *or* **made a ~ of the Loire castles** nous avons visité *or* fait* les châteaux de la Loire; **they went on a ~ to Spain** ils sont allés en voyage organisé *or* ils ont fait un voyage organisé en Espagne; **the ~ includes 3 days in Venice** le voyage comprend 3 jours à Venise; **to go on a ~ round the world** faire le tour du monde; **to go on a walking/cycling ~** faire une randonnée à pied/en bicyclette; (*sign on coach*) **'on ~'** 'excursion'; (*Sport, Theat etc*) **to go on ~** faire une tournée; **to be on ~** être en tournée; (*Theat etc*) **to take a company on ~** emmener une troupe en tournée; **to take a play on ~** donner une pièce en tournée; **~ of inspection** tournée d'inspection; **~ of duty** ronde *f*; *V* **conduct** *etc.*

2 *cpd*: **tour operator** (*bus company*) compagnie *f* de cars (faisant des voyages organisés); (*travel agency*) organisateur(s) *m(pl)* de voyages.

3 *vt district, town, exhibition, museum, factory* visiter. **they are ~ing France** ils visitent la France, ils font du tourisme en France; (*Sport, Theat*) ils sont en tournée en France; **the play is ~ing the provinces** la pièce tourne en province *or* est en tournée en province.

4 *vi*: **to go ~ing** voyager, faire du tourisme; **they went ~ing in Italy** ils sont allés visiter l'Italie, ils ont fait du tourisme en Italie.

tourer [ˈtʊərəʳ] *n* voiture *f* de tourisme.

touring [ˈtʊərɪŋ] **1** *n* (*U*) tourisme *m*, voyages *mpl* touristiques. **2** *adj team* en tournée. **~ car** voiture *f* de tourisme; (*Theat*) **~ company** (*permanently*) troupe ambulante; (*temporarily*) troupe en tournée.

tourism [ˈtʊərɪzəm] *n* tourisme *m.*

tourist [ˈtʊərɪst] **1** *n* touriste *mf.* **'T~s' Guide to London'** 'Guide touristique de Londres'.

2 *cpd class, ticket* touriste *inv*; *season* des touristes. **tourist agency** agence *f* de tourisme; **tourist bureau** syndicat *m* d'initiative; (*US*) **tourist court** motel *m*; (*US*) **tourist home** *maison dans laquelle des chambres sont louées aux touristes*; **tourist office = tourist bureau**; **the tourist trade** le tourisme; **tourist traffic** flot *m or* influx *m* des touristes (en voiture).

3 *adv travel* en classe touriste.

touristy* [ˈtʊərɪstɪ] *adj* (*pej*) trop touristique.

tournament [ˈtʊənəmənt] *n* (*Hist, gen*) tournoi *m.* **chess/tennis ~** tournoi d'échecs/de tennis.

tourney [ˈtʊənɪ] *n* (*Hist*) tournoi *m.*

tourniquet [ˈtʊənɪkeɪ] *n* (*Med*) tourniquet *m*, garrot *m.*

tousle [ˈtaʊzl] *vt hair* ébouriffer; *clothes* chiffonner, friper, froisser; *bed, bedclothes* mettre en désordre.

tousled [ˈtaʊzld] *adj person* échevelé; *hair* ébouriffé, échevelé; *clothes* chiffonné, fripé, froissé; *bed, bedclothes* en désordre.

tout [taʊt] **1** *n* (*gen*) vendeur ambulant; (*Racing*) pronostiqueur *m*; (*also* **ticket ~**) revendeur *m* de billets (*au marché noir*).

2 *vt wares* vendre (avec insistance); *tickets* revendre (*au marché noir*).

3 *vi* raccrocher les passants; (*Racing*) vendre des pronostics. **to ~ for custom** raccrocher *or* racoler *or* accoster les clients, courir après la clientèle; **the taxi drivers were ~ing for the hotels** les chauffeurs de taxi racolaient des clients pour les hôtels.

tout about, tout (a)round *vt sep wares* vendre (avec insistance). **he has been touting those books about for weeks*** ça fait des semaines qu'il essaie de placer *or* de caser* ces livres.

tow[1] [təʊ] **1** *n* (*act*) remorque *f*; (*line*) (câble *m* de) remorque; (*vehicle etc towed*) véhicule *m* en remorque. (*lit*) **to give sb a ~,**

to have sb in ~ remorquer qn; (*fig*) **he had a couple of girls in ~*** il avait deux filles dans son sillage (*fig*); **to be on ~** être en remorque; (*sign*) **'on ~'** 'véhicule en remorque'; **to take a car in ~** prendre une voiture en remorque.

2 *cpd*: **towboat** remorqueur *m*; (*US*) **tow car** voiture remorqueuse; **towing-line, towline, towing-rope, towrope** (câble *m* de) remorque *f*; **towpath** chemin *m* de halage; (*Aut*) **to give sb a tow-start** faire démarrer qn en remorque; **towing-truck,** (*US*) **tow truck** dépanneuse *f*.

3 *vt boat, vehicle* remorquer (*to, into* jusqu'à); *caravan, trailer* tirer, tracter; *barge* haler.

tow away *vt sep vehicle* remorquer; *[police]* mettre en fourrière.

tow[2] [təʊ] **1** *n* (*Tex*) filasse *f*, étoupe *f* (blanche). **2** *cpd*: **tow-haired, tow-headed** aux cheveux (blond) filasse.

towage ['təʊɪdʒ] *n* remorquage *m*.

toward(s) [tə'wɔːd(z)] *prep* **(a)** (*of direction*) vers, du côté de, dans la direction de. **if he comes ~ you** s'il vient vers vous *or* dans votre direction *or* de votre côté; **his back was ~ the door** il tournait le dos à la porte; (*fig*) **we are moving ~ a solution/war** *etc* nous nous acheminons vers une solution/la guerre *etc*; **he is saving ~ a new car** il fait des économies pour (acheter) une nouvelle voiture.

(b) (*of time*) vers. **~ 10 o'clock** vers *or* sur le coup de 10 heures, sur les 10 heures; **~ the end of the century** vers la fin du siècle.

(c) (*of attitude*) envers, à l'égard de. **his attitude ~ them** son attitude envers eux *or* à leur égard; **my feelings ~ him** mes sentiments à son égard *or* envers lui *or* pour lui.

towel ['taʊəl] **1** *n* serviette *f* (de toilette); (*dish ~, tea ~*) torchon *m*; (*for hands*) essuie-main(s) *m*; (*for glasses*) essuie-verres *m inv*; (*sanitary ~*) serviette hygiénique; *V* **bath** *etc*.

2 *cpd*: **towel rail** porte-serviettes *m inv*.

3 *vt* frotter avec une serviette. **to ~ o.s. dry** se sécher *or* s'essuyer avec une serviette.

towelling ['taʊəlɪŋ] **1** *n* (*U*) tissu *m* éponge. **2** *cpd robe etc* en *or* de tissu éponge.

tower ['taʊəʳ] **1** *n* tour *f*. **the T~ of Babel** la tour de Babel; **the T~ of London** la Tour de Londres; (*fig*) **he is a ~ of strength** il est ferme comme un roc, c'est un roc; **he proved a ~ of strength to me** il s'est montré un soutien précieux pour moi.

2 *cpd*: (*Brit*) **tower block** immeuble-tour *m*, tour *f* (d'habitation).

3 *vi [building, mountain, cliff, tree]* se dresser de manière imposante; *[person]* se tenir de manière imposante. **the new block of flats ~s above** *or* **over the church** le nouvel immeuble écrase l'église; **he ~ed over her** elle était toute petite à côté de lui; (*fig*) **he ~s above** *or* **over his colleagues** il domine de très haut ses collègues.

tower up *vi [building, cliff etc]* se dresser de manière imposante, s'élever très haut.

towering ['taʊərɪŋ] *adj building, mountain, cliff* très haut, imposant; *tree* énorme, imposant. **he saw a ~ figure** il vit une silhouette imposante; (*fig*) **in a ~ rage** dans une colère noire.

town [taʊn] **1** *n* ville *f*. **he lives in (a) ~** il habite en ville *or* à la ville; **she lives in a little ~** elle habite (dans) une petite ville; **there is more work in the ~ than in the country** il y a plus de travail en ville *or* à la ville qu'à la campagne; **guess who's in ~!** devine qui vient d'arriver en ville!; **he's out of ~** il est en province; **to go (in)to ~, to go down~** aller en ville; **to go up to ~** monter en ville; **the whole ~ is talking about it** toute la ville en parle; (*Univ*) **~ and gown** les citadins *mpl* et les étudiants *mpl*; **a country ~** une ville de province; **let's go out on the ~*** on va faire une descente en ville* (*hum*); (*fig*) **to have a night on the ~*** faire la noce* *or* la bombe*; (*fig*) **he really went to ~ on that essay*** il a mis le paquet* quand il a écrit cette dissertation; **they went to ~ on their daughter's wedding*** ils n'ont pas fait les choses à moitié *or* ils n'ont pas lésiné pour le mariage de leur fille; *V* **man, new, talk** *etc*.

2 *cpd*: **town-and-country planning** aménagement *m* du territoire; **town centre** centre *m* de la ville; **town clerk** ≃ secrétaire *m* de mairie; (*Brit*) **town council** conseil municipal; (*Brit*) **town councillor** conseiller *m*, -ère *f* municipal(e); (*Hist*) **town crier** crieur public; **town-dweller** citadin(e) *m(f)*; **town hall** ≃ mairie *f*, hôtel *m* de ville; **town house** maison *f* en ville; (*more imposing*) hôtel particulier; **town life** vie urbaine; (*Brit*) **town planner** urbaniste *mf*; (*Brit*) **town planning** urbanisme *m*; **townsfolk = townspeople**; **township** *V* **township**; **townsman** citadin *m*, habitant *m* de la ville *or* des villes; **my fellow townsmen** mes concitoyens *mpl*; **townspeople** citadins *mpl*, habitants *mpl* de la ville *or* des villes.

townee* [taʊ'niː] *n*, (*US*) **townie*** ['taʊnɪ] *n* (*pej*) pur citadin; (*Univ sl*) citadin.

township ['taʊnʃɪp] *n* commune *f*, municipalité *f*.

toxaemia, (*US*) **toxemia** [tɒk'siːmɪə] *n* toxémie *f*.

toxic ['tɒksɪk] *adj* toxique.

toxicological [ˌtɒksɪkə'lɒdʒɪkəl] *adj* toxicologique.

toxicology [ˌtɒksɪ'kɒlədʒɪ] *n* toxicologie *f*.

toxin ['tɒksɪn] *n* toxine *f*.

toy [tɔɪ] **1** *n* jouet *m*.

2 *cpd house, truck, stove, railway* miniature; *trumpet* d'enfant. **toybox** boîte *f* *or* coffre *m* à jouets; **toy car** petite auto; **toychest = toybox**; (*fig*) **toy dog** chien *m* d'appartement; **toy maker** fabricant *m* de jouets; **toyshop** magasin *m* de jouets; **toy soldier** petit soldat; **toy train** petit train; (*electric*) train électrique.

3 *vi*: **to ~ with** *object, pen, sb's affections etc* jouer avec; *idea, scheme* caresser; **to ~ with one's food** manger du bout des dents, chipoter, picorer.

trace[1] [treɪs] **1** *n* trace *f*. **there were ~s of the cave having been lived in** il y avait des traces d'habitation dans la grotte; **the police could find no ~ of the thief** la police n'a trouvé aucune trace du voleur; **~s of an ancient civilization** la trace *or* les vestiges *mpl* d'une ancienne civilisation; **to vanish/sink without ~** disparaître/sombrer sans laisser de traces; **there is no ~ of it now** il n'en reste plus trace maintenant; **we have lost all ~ of them** nous avons complètement perdu leur trace; **~s of arsenic in the stomach** traces d'arsenic dans l'estomac; **without a ~ of ill-feeling** sans la moindre rancune.

2 *cpd*: **trace element** oligo-élément *m*.

3 *vt* **(a)** (*draw*) *curve, line etc* tracer, esquisser, dessiner; (*with tracing paper etc*) décalquer.

(b) (*follow trail of*) suivre la trace de; (*and locate*) *person* retrouver, dépister; *object* retrouver. **ask the police to help you ~ him** demandez à la police de vous aider à le retrouver; **I can't ~ your file at all** je ne trouve pas (de) trace de votre dossier; **I can't ~ his having been in touch with us** je n'ai aucune indication *or* mention du fait qu'il nous ait contactés.

trace back *vt sep*: **to trace back one's ancestry** *or* **descent** *or* **family to** faire remonter sa famille à, établir que sa famille remonte à; **they traced the murder weapon back to a shop in Leeds** ils ont réussi à établir que l'arme du crime provenait d'un magasin de Leeds; **we traced him back to Paris, then the trail ended** (en remontant la filière) nous avons retrouvé sa trace à Paris, mais là, la piste s'est perdue.

trace[2] [treɪs] *n [harness]* trait *m*; *V* **kick**.

traceable ['treɪsəbl] *adj*: **it is ~** on peut le retrouver.

tracer ['treɪsəʳ] *n* (*person*) traceur *m*, -euse *f*; (*instrument*) roulette *f*, traçoir *m*; (*Biochemistry*) traceur; (*also* **~ bullet**) balle traçante; (*also* **~ shell**) obus traçant.

tracery ['treɪsərɪ] *n* (*U*) (*Archit*) réseau *m* (*de fenêtre ajourée*); *[veins on leaves]* nervures *fpl*; *[frost on window etc]* dentelles *fpl*.

trachea [trə'kɪə] *n* trachée *f*.

tracheotomy [ˌtrækɪ'ɒtəmɪ] *n* trachéotomie *f*.

trachoma [træ'kəʊmə] *n* trachome *m*.

tracing ['treɪsɪŋ] **1** *n* (*process: U*) calquage *m*; (*result*) calque *m*. **2** *cpd*: **tracing paper** papier-calque *m inv*, papier *m* à décalquer.

track [træk] **1** *n* **(a)** (*mark, trail*) trace *f*; *[animal]* trace, piste *f*, foulée *f*; *[person]* trace, piste; *[tyres, wheels]* trace; *[boat]* sillage *m*; (*route: on radar screen; also of bullet, comet, rocket, hurricane etc*) trajectoire *f*. **the hurricane destroyed everything in its ~** l'ouragan a tout détruit sur son passage; **a ~ of muddy footprints across the floor** des traces de pas boueuses sur tout le plancher; **to follow in sb's ~s** (*lit*) suivre la trace de qn; (*fig*) suivre la voie tracée par qn, suivre *or* marcher sur les traces de qn; **to be on sb's ~(s)** être sur la piste de qn; **he had the police on his ~(s)** la police était sur sa piste; **they got on to his ~ very quickly** ils ont très vite trouvé sa piste; **to put** *or* **throw sb off the ~** désorienter qn; **to keep ~ of** *spacecraft etc* suivre; (*fig*) *events* suivre (la marche *or* le fil de); *developments, situation* suivre, rester au courant de; **they kept ~ of him till they reached the wood** ils ont suivi sa trace jusqu'au bois; (*fig*) **I kept ~ of her until she got married** je suis resté en contact avec elle jusqu'à son mariage; **I've lost ~ of what he's doing** je ne suis plus au courant de ce qu'il fait; **to lose ~ of** *spacecraft etc* perdre; (*fig*) *developments, situation* ne plus suivre, ne plus être au courant de; *events* perdre le fil de; **they lost ~ of him in the woods** ils ont perdu sa trace une fois arrivés au bois; **I lost ~ of her after the war** j'ai perdu tout contact avec elle *or* je l'ai perdue de vue après la guerre; **don't lose ~ of him** (*lit*) ne perdez pas sa trace; (*fig*) ne le perdez pas de vue; **I've lost ~ of those books** je ne sais plus *or* j'ai oublié où sont ces livres; **to lose all ~ of time** perdre la notion du temps; **keep ~ of the time** n'oubliez pas l'heure; **I've lost ~ of what he is saying** j'ai perdu le fil de ce qu'il dit, je ne suis plus ce qu'il dit; (*fig*) **we must be making ~s*** il faut qu'on se sauve* (*subj*); **he made ~s for the hotel*** il a filé à l'hôtel; *V* **stop**.

(b) (*path*) chemin *m*, sentier *m*, piste *f*. **sheep ~** piste à moutons; **mule ~** chemin *or* sentier muletier; **from there on, the road became nothing but a ~** à partir de là, la route n'était plus carrossable; (*fig*) **to be on the right ~** être sur la bonne voie; **to put sb on the right ~** mettre qn dans la bonne voie; (*fig*) **to be on the wrong ~, to be off the ~** faire fausse route; (*fig*) **you're away off the ~!** vous êtes tout à fait à côté!, vous n'y êtes pas du tout!; *V* **beaten, cart, dirt** *etc*.

(c) (*Rail*) voie *f* (ferrée), rails *mpl*. **to leave the ~(s)** quitter les rails, dérailler; **to cross the ~** traverser la voie; **single-~ line** ligne *f* à voie unique; (*US fig*) **to live on the wrong side of the ~s** vivre dans les quartiers pauvres; *V* **one**.

(d) (*Sport*) piste *f*. **motor-racing ~** autodrome *m*; **dog-racing ~** cynodrome *m*; *V* **race**[1] *etc*.

(e) *[sound tape, computer tape]* piste *f*; *[long-playing record]* morceau *m*. **4-~ tape** bande *f* à 4 pistes; *V* **sound**[1].

(f) (*Aut etc*) (*tyre tread*) chape *f*; (*space between wheels*) écartement *m*; (*also* **caterpillar ~**) chenille *f*.

(g) (*US Scol*) **divided into 5 ~s** répartis en 5 classes de niveau; **the B ~** la classe B, le groupe B.

2 *cpd*: (*Sport*) **track athletics** athlétisme *m* sur piste; **tracked vehicle** véhicule *m* à chenille; (*Sport*) **track event** épreuves *fpl* sur piste; (*Cine*) **track(ing) shot** travel(l)ing *m*; (*Space*) **tracking station** station *f* d'observation; (*US Rail*) **tracklayer = trackman**; (*Rail*) **track maintenance** entretien *m* de la voie; (*US Rail*) **trackman** responsable *m* de l'entretien de la voie; (*US Sport*) **track meet** réunion sportive sur piste; (*Sport*) **track race/racing** course *f*/courses *fpl* sur piste; (*Sport, also fig*) **to have a good track record** avoir eu de bons résultats; **tracksuit** survêtement *m*; (*US Scol*) **track system** système *m* de répartition des élèves par niveau; (*US Rail*) **trackwalker = trackman**.

3 *vt animal* suivre à la piste *or* à la trace, suivre la trace de; *person, vehicle* suivre la trace de; *hurricane, rocket, spacecraft, comet* suivre la trajectoire de. **to ~ dirt over the floor** laisser des traces sales sur le plancher.

4 *vi [camera]* faire un travel(l)ing.

track down *vt sep animal, wanted man* traquer et capturer; *lost object, lost person, reference, quotation* (finir par) trouver *or* localiser.

tracker ['trækəʳ] **1** *n* (*Hunting*) traqueur *m*; (*gen*) poursuivant(e) *m(f)*. **2** *cpd*: **tracker dog** chien policier.

trackless ['trækləs] *adj forest, desert* sans chemins; *vehicle* sans chenilles.

tract[1] [trækt] **1** *n* **(a)** *[land, water]* étendue *f*; *[coal etc]* gisement *m*; (*US: housing estate*) résidence *f*, domaine *m*. **vast ~s of wilderness** de vastes zones *fpl or* étendues désertiques.

(b) (*Anat*) **digestive/respiratory ~** appareil *or* système digestif/respiratoire.

2 *cpd*: (*US*) **tract house** pavillon *m* (*dans un lotissement*).

tract[2] [trækt] *n* (*pamphlet*) tract *m*.

tractable ['træktəbl] *adj person* accommodant, souple; *animal* docile; *material* malléable; *problem* soluble, résoluble.

traction ['trækʃən] **1** *n* (*U: all senses*) traction *f*. (*Tech*) **electric/steam ~** traction électrique/à vapeur. **2** *cpd*: **traction engine** locomobile *f*.

tractive ['træktɪv] *adj* de traction.

tractor ['træktəʳ] **1** *n* tracteur *m*. **2** *cpd*: **tractor driver** conducteur *m*, -trice *f* de tracteur; (*US*) **tractor-trailer** tracteur *m* à remorque.

trad* [træd] *adj* (*esp Mus*) *abbr of* **traditional.**

trade [treɪd] **1** *n* **(a)** (*U: commerce*) commerce *m*, affaires *fpl*. (*Econ*) **overseas ~** commerce extérieur; **the wool ~, the ~ in wool** le commerce de la laine; **he's in the wool ~** il est négociant en laine; **the drug ~, the ~ in drugs** le trafic de la drogue; **they do a lot of ~ with** ils font beaucoup de commerce avec, ils commercent beaucoup avec; **~ has been good *or* brisk** les affaires ont été bonnes, le commerce a bien marché; **to do a good *or* brisk *or* roaring ~** vendre beaucoup (*in* de); (*Brit*) **Board of T~**, (*US*) **Department of T~** ministère *m* du Commerce; **Secretary (of State) for T~, Minister of T~** ministre *m* du Commerce; *V* **rag**[1], **tourist** *etc.*

(b) (*job, skill*) métier *m*. **he is a butcher by ~** il est boucher de son métier *or* de son état; (*hum*) **he's a doctor by ~** il est médecin de son état; **to put sb to a ~**† mettre qn en apprentissage; **she wants him to learn a ~** elle veut qu'il apprenne un métier; (*fig*) **he's in the ~** il est du métier; (*lit, fig*) **as we say in the ~** comme on dit dans le jargon du métier; pour employer un terme technique; **known in the ~ as ...** que les gens du métier appellent ... ; **special terms for the ~** tarif spécial pour les membres de la profession; *V* **stock, tool, trick** *etc.*

(c) = **trade wind**; *V* 2.

(d) (*swap*) échange *m*. **to do a ~ with sb for sth** faire l'échange de qch avec qn.

2 *cpd*: **trade association** association commerciale; **trade barriers** barrières douanières; **trade deficit** balance *f* (commerciale) déficitaire, déficit extérieur; (*Brit*) **the Trade Descriptions Act** *la loi protégeant les consommateurs contre la publicité et les appellations mensongères;* **trade discount** remise *f* au détaillant; **trade fair** foire(-exposition) commerciale; (*Econ*) **trade figures** résultats *mpl* (financiers); (*Comm*) **trade-in** reprise *f*; **he took my old machine as a trade-in** il m'a repris ma vieille machine; **trade-in price/value** prix *m*/valeur *f* à la reprise; **trade journal** revue (commerciale) spécialisée; **trademark** (*n*) marque *f* (de fabrique), label *m*; **registered trademark** marque déposée; (*vt*) *product, goods* apposer une marque *or* un label sur; *symbol, word* déposer; **trade name** marque déposée; (*US*) **trade-off** échange *m*; **trade paper** = **trade journal**; **trade price** prix *m* de gros; (*Econ*) **trade returns** = **trade figures**; **trade route** route commerciale; **trade school** collège *m* technique; (*Comm, Ind, also fig*) **trade secret** secret *m* de fabrication; **tradesman** commerçant *m*; **tradesman's entrance** entrée *f* de service *or* des fournisseurs; **tradespeople** commerçants *mpl*; **trade(s) union** syndicat *m*; (*Brit*) **the Trades Union Congress** la confédération des syndicats britanniques; **trade(s) unionism** syndicalisme *m*; **trade(s) unionist** syndicaliste *mf*; (*Geog*) **trade wind** (vent) alizé *m*.

3 *vi* **(a)** *[firm, country, businessman]* faire le commerce (*in* de); commercer, avoir *or* entretenir des relations commerciales (*with* avec). **he ~s as a wool merchant** il est négociant en laine; (*fig*) **to ~ (up)on sb's kindness** abuser de la gentillesse de qn.

(b) (*exchange*) échanger *or* troquer (*with sb* avec qn).

4 *vt* (*exchange*) **to ~ A for B** échanger *or* troquer A contre B; **I ~d my knife with him for his marbles** je lui ai donné mon canif en échange de ses billes.

trade in *vt sep car, television etc* faire reprendre. **I've traded it in for a new one** je l'ai fait reprendre quand j'en ai acheté un nouveau.

trader ['treɪdəʳ] *n* **(a)** commerçant(e) *m(f)*, marchand(e) *m(f)*; (*bigger*) négociant(e) *m(f)*; (*street* ~) vendeur *m*, -euse *f* de rue; (*US St Ex*) contrepartiste *m*. **wool ~** négociant en laine; *V* **slave** *etc.*

(b) (*ship*) navire marchand *or* de la marine marchande.

tradescantia [ˌtrædəs'kæntɪə] *n* tradescantia *m*.

trading ['treɪdɪŋ] **1** *n* (*U*) commerce *m*, affaires *fpl*, négoce *m*.

2 *cpd port, centre* de commerce. (*Brit*) **trading estate** zone industrielle; **trading nation** nation commerçante; (*esp Can, US*) **trading post** comptoir *m* (commercial); (*Fin, Ind*) **trading profits for last year** bénéfices obtenus pour l'exercice de l'année écoulée; **trading stamp** timbre-prime *m*.

tradition [trə'dɪʃən] *n* tradition *f*. **according to ~** selon la tradition *or* la coutume; (*fig*) **it's in the best ~** c'est dans la plus pure tradition (*of* de).

traditional [trə'dɪʃənl] *adj* traditionnel. **it is ~ for them to do that** chez eux il est de tradition de faire ça; **they wore the ~ red cloaks** ils portaient les capes rouges traditionnelles *or* les traditionnelles capes rouges.

traditionalism [trə'dɪʃnəlɪzəm] *n* traditionalisme *m*.

traditionalist [trə'dɪʃnəlɪst] *adj, n* traditionaliste (*mf*).

traditionally [trə'dɪʃnəlɪ] *adv* traditionnellement.

traduce [trə'djuːs] *vt* (*frm*) calomnier, diffamer.

traffic ['træfɪk] (*vb: pret, ptp* **trafficked**) **1** *n* (*U*) **(a)** (*Aut*) circulation *f*; (*Aviat, Naut, Rail, Telec*) trafic *m*. **road ~** circulation routière; **rail ~** trafic ferroviaire; (*Aut*) **holiday ~** circulation des grands départs *or* des grandes rentrées, rush *m* des vacances; **there's a lot of ~ *or* the ~ is heavy this morning** (*Aut*) il y a beaucoup de circulation ce matin; (*Aviat, Naut, Rail*) le trafic est intense ce matin; **the bridge is closed to heavy ~ *or* is open to light ~ only** l'accès au pont est interdit aux poids lourds; **~ is building up/falling off** (*Aut*) la circulation s'intensifie/se dégage; (*Aviat, Naut, Rail*) le trafic s'intensifie/se raréfie; (*Aut*) **the build-up *or* backlog of ~ extends to the bridge** le bouchon s'étire jusqu'au pont; **~ coming into London should avoid Putney Bridge** il est recommandé aux automobilistes se rendant à Londres d'éviter Putney Bridge; **~ in and out of Heathrow Airport** le trafic à destination et en provenance de l'aéroport de Heathrow; (*Naut*) **~ in *or* using the Channel** trafic *or* navigation *f* en Manche; *V* **tourist** *etc.*

(b) (*trade*) commerce *m* (*in* de); (*pej*) trafic *m* (*in* de). **the drug ~** le trafic de la drogue.

2 *cpd*: (*US*) **traffic circle** rond-point *m*, sens *m* giratoire; **traffic control** (*Aut*) prévention routière; (*Aviat, Naut, Rail*) contrôle *m* du trafic; (*Aviat*) **traffic controller** contrôleur *m*, -euse *f* de la navigation aérienne, aiguilleur *m* du ciel; (*Aviat*) **traffic control tower** tour *f* de contrôle; (*esp US*) **traffic cop*** = **traffic policeman**; **traffic diversion** déviation *f*; **traffic holdup** bouchon *m* (*de circulation*); (*Brit*) **traffic island** refuge *m*; **traffic jam** embouteillage *m*, bouchon *m*; **traffic light** feu *m* (de signalisation); **to go through the traffic lights at red** passer au rouge, griller le feu rouge; **the traffic lights were (at) green** le feu était (au) vert; (*Jur*) **traffic offence** infraction *f* au code de la route; **traffic police** police *f* de la route; **traffic policeman** agent *m* de la circulation; **traffic regulations** réglementation *f* de la circulation; **traffic sign** panneau *m* de signalisation, poteau indicateur; **international traffic signs** signalisation routière internationale; **traffic signal** = **traffic light**; (*Brit*) **traffic warden** contractuel(le) *m(f)*.

3 *vi*: **to ~ in sth** faire le commerce *or* le trafic (*pej*) de.

trafficator† ['træfɪkeɪtəʳ] *n* (*Brit*) flèche *f* (de direction)†.

trafficker ['træfɪkəʳ] *n* trafiquant(e) *m(f)* (*in* en).

tragedian [trə'dʒiːdɪən] *n* (*writer*) auteur *m* tragique; (*actor*) tragédien *m*.

tragedienne [trəˌdʒiːdɪ'en] *n* tragédienne *f*.

tragedy ['trædʒɪdɪ] *n* (*gen, Theat*) tragédie *f*. **the ~ of it is that ...** ce qui est tragique, c'est que ... ; **it is a ~ that ...** il est tragique que ... + *subj*.

tragic ['trædʒɪk] *adj* (*gen, Theat*) tragique.

tragically ['trædʒɪkəlɪ] *adv* tragiquement.

tragicomedy ['trædʒɪ'kɒmɪdɪ] *n* tragi-comédie *f*.

tragicomic ['trædʒɪ'kɒmɪk] *adj* tragi-comique.

trail [treɪl] **1** *n* **(a)** (*of blood, smoke: from meteor, comet etc*) traînée *f*; (*tracks: gen*) trace *f*; (*Hunting*) piste *f*, trace(s), foulée *f*. **a long ~ of refugees** une longue file *or* colonne de réfugiés; **to leave a ~ of destruction** tout détruire sur son passage; **his illness brought a series of debts in its ~** sa maladie a amené dans son sillage une série de dettes; (*lit, fig*) **to be on the ~ of sb** être sur la piste de qn; **I'm on the ~ of that book you want** j'ai trouvé trace *or* j'ai retrouvé la trace du livre que vous voulez; *V* **hot, vapour** *etc.*

(b) (*path, road*) sentier *m*, chemin *m*; *V* **blaze**[2].

2 *cpd*: (*fig*) **trailblazer** pionnier *m*, -ière *f*.

3 *vt* **(a)** (*follow*) suivre la piste de.

(b) (*drag, tow*) *object on rope, toy cart etc* tirer, traîner; (*Aut*) *caravan, trailer, boat* tirer, tracter. **he was ~ing his schoolbag behind him** il traînait son cartable derrière lui; **the children ~ed dirt all over the carpet** les enfants ont couvert le tapis de traces sales; **to ~ one's fingers through *or* in the water** laisser traîner ses doigts dans l'eau; **don't ~ your feet!** ne traîne pas les pieds!

(c) (*Mil*) *rifle etc* porter à la main.

4 *vi* **(a)** *[object]* traîner; *[plant]* ramper. **your coat is ~ing in the mud** ton manteau traîne dans la boue; **smoke ~ed from the funnel** une traînée de fumée s'échappait de la cheminée; (*fig Sport*) **they were ~ing by 13 points** ils étaient en retard de 13 points; (*Ftbl*) **they are ~ing at the bottom of the league** ils traînent en bas de division.

(b) to ~ along/in/out *etc* (*move in straggling line*) passer/entrer/sortir *etc* à la queue leu leu *or* en file; (*move wearily*) passer/entrer/sortir *etc* en traînant les pieds.

trail away, trail off *vi [voice, music]* s'estomper.

trailer ['treɪləʳ] **1** *n* **(a)** (*Aut*) remorque *f*; (*esp US: caravan*) caravane *f*. **(b)** (*Cine, TV*) film *m* publicitaire, publicité* *f* (*for a film* pour un film). **2** *cpd*: (*US*) **trailer camp, trailer court, trailer park** camp *m* de caravaning.

trailing ['treɪlɪŋ] *adj hair, blanket etc* traînant; *plant* rampant. (*Aviat*) **~ edge** bord *m* de fuite.

train [treɪn] **1** *n* **(a)** (*Rail*) train *m*; (*in underground*) rame *f*, métro *m*. **to go by ~** prendre le train; **on *or* in the ~** dans le train; **to transport by ~** transporter par voie ferroviaire; *V* **express, freight, slow** *etc.*

(b) (*procession*) file *f*; (*entourage*) suite *f*, équipage *m*;

[camels] caravane *f*, file; *[mules]* train *m*, file; *[vehicles etc]* cortège *m*, file. **he arrived with 50 men in his ~** il arriva avec un équipage de 50 hommes; (*fig*) **the war brought famine in its ~** la guerre amena la famine dans son sillage *or* entraîna la famine; *V* **baggage** *etc*.

(c) (*line, series*) suite *f*, série *f*, succession *f*; *[gunpowder]* traînée *f*. **in an unbroken ~** en succession ininterrompue; **a ~ of events** une suite d'événements; **it broke** *or* **interrupted his ~ of thought** cela est venu interrompre le fil de sa *or* ses pensée(s); **I've lost my ~ of thought** je ne retrouve plus le fil de ma *or* mes pensée(s); (*fig*) **it is in ~** c'est en préparation, c'est en marche; **to set sth in ~** mettre qch en marche *or* en mouvement.

(d) *[dress, robe]* traîne *f*.

(e) (*Tech*) train *m*. **~ of gears** train de roues d'engrenage.

2 *cpd*: (*Hist*) **trainband** milice *f*; **trainbearer** dame *f* *or* demoiselle *f* d'honneur; (*little boy*) page *m*; (*US Rail*) **trainman** cheminot *m*; **train oil** huile *f* de baleine; **there is a very good train service to London** les trains pour Londres sont très fréquents; **there is an hourly train service to London** il y a un train pour Londres toutes les heures; **do you know what the train service is to London?** connaissez-vous l'horaire des trains pour Londres?; **train set** train *m* électrique; **train-spotter** passionné(e) *m(f)* de trains; **to go train-spotting** observer les trains (*pour identifier les divers types de locomotives*).

3 *vt* **(a)** (*instruct*) *person, engineer, doctor, nurse, teacher, craftsman, apprentice* former; *employee, soldier* former, instruire; (*Sport*) *player* entraîner, préparer; *animal* dresser; *voice* travailler; *ear, mind, memory* exercer. **he is ~ing someone to take over from him** il forme son successeur; (*housetrain*) **to ~ a puppy/child** apprendre à un chiot/à un enfant à être propre; **to ~ an animal to do** apprendre à *or* dresser un animal à faire; **to ~ sb to do** apprendre à qn à faire; (*professionally*) former qn à faire, préparer qn à faire; **to ~ o.s. to do** s'entraîner *or* s'exercer à faire; **to ~ sb in a craft** apprendre un métier à qn, préparer qn à un métier; **he was ~ed in weaving** *or* **as a weaver** il a reçu une formation de tisserand; **to ~ sb in the use of sth** *or* **to use sth** apprendre à qn à utiliser qch, instruire qn dans le maniement de qch; **where were you ~ed?** où avez-vous reçu votre formation?; *V also* **trained**.

(b) (*direct etc*) *gun, camera, telescope etc* braquer (*on* sur). **to ~ a plant along a wall** faire grimper une plante le long d'un mur.

4 *vi* **(a)** recevoir une (*or* sa) formation; (*Sport*) s'entraîner (*for* pour), se préparer (*for* à). **to ~ as** *or* **~ to be a teacher/secretary** *etc* recevoir une formation de professeur/de secrétaire *etc*; **where did you ~?** où avez-vous reçu votre formation?

(b) (*Rail: go by ~*) aller en train.

train up *vt sep* former, préparer.

trained [treɪnd] *adj person* compétent, qualifié (*for* pour, en matière de); *engineer* diplômé, breveté; *nurse* diplômé, qualifié; *teacher* habilité à enseigner; *animal* dressé. **to the ~ eye/ear** pour un œil/une oreille exercé(e); **he isn't ~ for this job** il n'a pas la formation voulue pour ce poste, il n'est pas qualifié pour ce poste; **we need a ~ person for the job** nous avons besoin de quelqu'un qui soit qualifié pour ce poste *or* qui ait la compétence voulue pour ce poste; **they employ only ~ personnel** ils n'emploient que du personnel qualifié; **he is not ~ at all** il n'a reçu aucune formation professionnelle; **well-~** *employee, worker* qui a reçu une bonne formation; *butler, valet, maid* stylé; *child* bien élevé; *animal* bien dressé; (*iro*) **she's got a well-~ husband** son mari est bien dressé.

trainee [treɪ'niː] **1** *n* (*gen*) stagiaire *mf*; (*in trades*) apprenti(e) *m(f)*. **sales/management ~** stagiaire de vente/de direction.

2 *adj* (*gen*) stagiaire, en stage; (*in trades*) en apprentissage. **~ typist** dactylo* *f* stagiaire; **~ hairdresser** apprenti(e) coiffeur *m*, -euse *f*.

trainer ['treɪnəʳ] *n* **(a)** *[athlete, football team, racehorse]* entraîneur *m*, -euse *f*; (*in circus*) dresseur *m*, -euse *f*, (*esp of lions*) dompteur *m*, -euse *f*.

(b) (*Aviat*) (*flight simulator*) simulateur *m* de vol; (*also* **~ aircraft**) avion-école *m*.

(c) (*shoe*) chaussure *f* de sport.

training ['treɪnɪŋ] **1** *n [person, engineer, doctor, nurse, teacher, craftsman]* formation *f*; *[employee, soldier]* formation, instruction *f*; (*Sport*) entraînement *m*, préparation *f*; *[animal]* dressage *m*. (*Sport*) **to be out of ~** avoir perdu la forme; (*Sport*) **to be in ~** (*preparing o.s.*) être en cours d'entraînement *or* de préparation; (*on form*) être en forme; (*Sport*) **to be in ~ for sth** s'entraîner pour *or* se préparer à qch; **staff ~** formation du personnel; **she has had some secretarial ~** elle a suivi quelques cours de secrétariat; *V* **teacher, toilet, voice** *etc*.

2 *cpd*: **training camp** camp *m* d'entraînement; **training centre** (*gen*) centre *m* de formation; (*Sport*) centre (d'entraînement) sportif; **training college** (*gen*) école spécialisée *or* professionnelle; **(teacher) training college** *V* **teacher 2**; **training course** cours *m(pl)* professionnel(s); **training manual** manuel *m* *or* cours *m* d'instruction; **training plane** avion-école *m*; **training scheme** programme *m* de formation *or* d'entraînement; **training ship** navire-école *m*.

traipse* [treɪps] *vi*: **to ~ in/out** *etc* entrer/sortir *etc* d'un pas traînant *or* en traînassant*; **they ~d in wearily** ils sont entrés en traînant les pieds; **to ~ around** *or* **about** se balader*, déambuler; **we've been traipsing about the shops all day** nous avons traîné *or* traînassé* dans les magasins toute la journée.

trait [treɪt] *n* trait *m* (*de caractère*).

traitor ['treɪtəʳ] *n* traître *m*. **to be a ~ to one's country/to a cause** trahir sa patrie/une cause.

traitorous ['treɪtərəs] *adj* traître (*f* traîtresse), déloyal, perfide.

traitorously ['treɪtərəslɪ] *adv* traîtreusement, perfidement, en traître (*or* en traîtresse).

traitress ['treɪtrɪs] *n* traîtresse *f*.

trajectory [trə'dʒektərɪ] *n* trajectoire *f*.

tram [træm] **1** *n* **(a)** (*Brit: also* **~car**) tram(way) *m*. **to go by ~** prendre le tram. **(b)** (*Min*) berline *f*, benne roulante. **2** *cpd*: (*Brit*) **tramline, tramway** (*rails*) voie *f* de tramway; (*route*) ligne *f* de tramway.

trammel ['træməl] (*liter*) **1** *vt* entraver. **2** *npl*: **~s** entraves *fpl*.

tramp [træmp] **1** *n* **(a)** (*sound*) martèlement *m* de pas, pas *m(pl)* lourd(s).

(b) (*hike*) randonnée *f*, excursion *f*, promenade *f*. **to go for a ~** (aller) faire une randonnée *or* une excursion; **after a 10-hour ~** après 10 heures de marche (à pied); **it's a long ~** c'est long à faire à pied.

(c) (*vagabond*) chemineau *m*, clochard(e) *m(f)*, vagabond(e) *m(f)*. (*fig pej*) **she's a ~*** elle est coureuse*.

(d) (*also* **~ steamer**) tramp *m*.

2 *vi*: **to ~ along** (*hike*) poursuivre son chemin à pied; (*walk heavily*) marcher d'un pas lourd; **to ~ up and down** faire les cent pas; **he was ~ing up and down the platform** il arpentait le quai d'un pas lourd.

3 *vt*: **to ~ the streets** battre le pavé; **I ~ed the town looking for the church** j'ai parcouru la ville à pied pour trouver l'église.

tramp down, tramp in *vt sep* tasser du pied.

trample ['træmpl] **1** *vt*: **to ~ sth (underfoot)** (*lit*) piétiner qch, fouler qch aux pieds; (*fig*) *person, conquered nation* fouler aux pieds, bafouer; *sb's feelings* bafouer; *objections etc* passer outre à. **he ~d the stone into the ground** il a enfoncé du pied la pierre dans le sol; **he was ~d by the horses** il a été piétiné par les chevaux. **2** *vi*: **to ~ in/out** *etc* entrer/sortir *etc* d'un pas lourd; (*lit, fig*) **to ~ on = to trample (underfoot)**; *V* **1**. **3** *n* (*act*) piétinement *m*; (*sound*) bruit *m* de pas.

trampoline ['træmpəlɪn] *n* tremplin *m* (*de gymnastique*).

trance [trɑːns] *n* (*Hypnosis, Rel, Spiritualism etc*) transe *f*; (*Med*) catalepsie *f*; (*fig: ecstasy*) transe, extase *f*. **to go** *or* **fall into a ~** (*Hypnosis, Rel, Spiritualism etc*) entrer en transe; (*Med*) tomber en catalepsie; (*fig*) entrer en transe, tomber en extase; *[hypnotist]* **to put sb into a ~** faire entrer qn en transe.

tranny‡ ['trænɪ] *n abbr of* **transistor (radio)**.

tranquil ['træŋkwɪl] *adj* tranquille, paisible, serein.

tranquillity, (*US*) *also* **tranquility** [træŋ'kwɪlɪtɪ] *n* tranquillité *f*, calme *m*.

tranquillize, (*US*) *also* **tranquilize** ['træŋkwɪlaɪz] *vt* tranquilliser, calmer.

tranquillizer, (*US*) *also* **tranquilizer** ['træŋkwɪlaɪzəʳ] *n* tranquillisant *m*, calmant *m*.

trans... [trænz] *pref* trans... . **the T~-Canada Highway** la route transcanadienne.

transact [træn'zækt] *vt business* traiter, régler, faire.

transaction [træn'zækʃən] *n* (*Econ, Fin, St Ex*) transaction *f*; (*gen*) opération *f*, affaire *f*; (*U*) conduite *f*, gestion *f*. **we have had some ~s with that firm** nous avons fait quelques opérations *or* quelques affaires avec cette société; **cash ~** opération au comptant; **the ~s of the Royal Society** (*proceedings*) les travaux *mpl* de la Royal Society; (*minutes*) les actes *mpl* de la Royal Society.

transactional [træn'zækʃənl] *adj* transactionnel.

transalpine ['trænz'ælpaɪn] *adj* transalpin.

transatlantic ['trænzət'læntɪk] *adj* transatlantique.

transceiver [træn'siːvəʳ] *n* (*Rad*) émetteur-récepteur *m*.

transcend [træn'send] *vt belief, knowledge, description* transcender, dépasser; (*excel over*) surpasser; (*Philos, Rel*) transcender.

transcendence [træn'sendəns] *n*, **transcendency** [træn'sendənsɪ] *n* transcendance *f*.

transcendent [træn'sendənt] *adj* transcendant.

transcendental [ˌtrænsen'dentl] *adj* transcendantal. **~ meditation** méditation transcendantale.

transcendentalism [ˌtrænsen'dentəlɪzəm] *n* transcendantalisme *m*.

transcontinental ['trænzˌkɒntɪ'nentl] *adj* transcontinental.

transcribe [træn'skraɪb] *vt* transcrire.

transcript ['trænskrɪpt] *n* transcription *f*.

transcription [træn'skrɪpʃən] *n* transcription *f*.

transect [træn'sekt] *vt* sectionner (transversalement).

transept ['trænsept] *n* transept *m*.

transfer [træns'fɜːʳ] **1** *vt employee, civil servant, diplomat* transférer, muter (*to* à); *soldier, player, prisoner* transférer (*to* à); *passenger* transférer (*to* à), transborder; *object, goods* transférer (*to sb* à qn, *to a place* à un lieu), transporter (*to a place* dans un lieu), transmettre (*to sb* à qn); *power* faire passer (*from* de, *to* à); *ownership, money* transférer (*from* de, *to* à); *design, drawing* reporter, décalquer (*to* sur). (*Telec*) **to ~ the charges** téléphoner en P.C.V.; (*Telec*) **~red charge call** communication *f* en P.C.V.; (*notice*) **business ~red to ...** (*office*) bureaux transférés à ... ; (*shop*) magasin transféré à ... ; **to ~ one's affection to sb** reporter son *or* ses affection(s) sur qn.

2 *vi [employee, civil servant, diplomat]* être transféré *or* muté (*to* à); *[soldier, player, prisoner, offices]* être transféré (*to* à). (*Univ etc*) **he's ~red from Science to Geography** il ne fait plus de science, il s'est réorienté en géographie; **to ~ from one train/plane** *etc* **to another** être transféré *or* transbordé d'un train/avion *etc* à un autre.

3 ['trænsfɜːʳ] *n* **(a)** (*V* **1**) transfert *m*, mutation *f* (*to* à); transbordement *m*; transport *m*, transmission *f*; (*Pol: of power*) passation *f*; (*Jur: document*) transfert, translation *f* (*Jur*). **to pay sth by bank ~** payer qch par virement bancaire; (*Jur*) **~ of ownership** transfert *or* translation de propriété (*from* de, *to* à); (*Ftbl etc*) **to ask for a ~** demander un transfert.

(b) (*picture, design etc*) (*rub-on type*) décalcomanie *f*; (*stick-on*) autocollant *m*.

(c) (*Coach, Rail: also* ~ **ticket**) billet *m* de correspondance.
4 ['trænsfɜː ʳ] *cpd*: (*Ftbl etc*) **transfer fee** (prix *m* du) transfert *m*.

transferable [træns'fɜːrəbl] *adj* transmissible. **not** ~ personnel.

transferee [ˌtrænsfɜː'riː] *n* (*Jur*) cessionnaire *mf*, bénéficiaire *mf*.

transference ['trænsfərəns] *n* (*U*) **(a)** = **transfer 3**; *V* **thought. (b)** (*Psych*) transfert *m*.

transferor, transferrer [træns'fɜːrəʳ] *n* (*Jur*) cédant(e) *m(f)*.

transfiguration [ˌtrænsfɪgə'reɪʃən] *n* transfiguration *f*.

transfigure [træns'fɪgəʳ] *vt* transfigurer.

transfix [træns'fɪks] *vt* (*lit*) transpercer. (*fig*) **to be** *or* **stand** ~**ed** être cloué sur place; **to be** ~**ed with horror** être cloué au sol d'horreur, être paralysé par l'horreur.

transform [træns'fɔːm] **1** *vt* (*gen*) transformer, métamorphoser (*into* en); (*Chem, Elec, Math, Phys*) convertir, transformer (*into* en). **to be** ~**ed into** se transformer en. **2** ['trænsfɔːm] *n* (*US Ling*) transformation *f*.

transformation [ˌtrænsfə'meɪʃən] *n* (*V* **transform 1**) transformation *f*, métamorphose *f*; conversion *f*; (*Ling*) transformation.

transformational [ˌtrænsfə'meɪʃənl] *adj* (*Ling*) transformationnel.

transformer [træns'fɔːməʳ] **1** *n* (*Elec*) transformateur *m*. **2** *cpd*: **transformer station** poste *m* de transformateurs.

transfuse [træns'fjuːz] *vt* (*Med, fig*) transfuser.

transfusion [træns'fjuːʒən] *n* (*Med, fig*) transfusion *f*. **blood** ~ transfusion sanguine *or* de sang; **to give sb a** ~ faire une transfusion à qn.

transgress [træns'gres] **1** *vt* transgresser, violer. **2** *vi* pécher.

transgression [træns'greʃən] *n* (*sin*) péché *m*, faute *f*; (*U*) transgression *f*.

transgressor [træns'gresəʳ] *n* transgresseur *m* (*liter*); (*Rel*) pécheur *m*, -eresse *f*.

tranship [træn'ʃɪp] *vt* = **transship.**

transhipment [træn'ʃɪpmənt] *n* = **transshipment.**

transience ['trænzɪəns] *n* caractère *m* éphémère *or* transitoire.

transient ['trænzɪənt] **1** *adj* transitoire, éphémère, passager. **2** *n* (*US: in hotel etc*) client(e) *m(f)* de passage.

transistor [træn'zɪstəʳ] *n* (*Elec*) transistor *m*; (*also* ~ **radio,** ~ **set**) transistor.

transistorize [træn'zɪstəraɪz] *vt* transistoriser. ~**d** transistorisé, à transistors.

transit ['trænzɪt] **1** *n* (*U*) (*gen*) transit *m*; (*Astron*) passage *m*. **in** ~ en transit. **2** *cpd goods, passengers* en transit; *documents, port, visa* de transit. (*Mil etc*) **transit camp** camp volant; (*Aviat*) **transit lounge** salle *f* de transit.

transition [træn'zɪʃən] **1** *n* transition *f* (*from* de, *to* à). **2** *cpd period* de transition.

transitional [træn'zɪʃənəl] *adj period, government* de transition; *measures* transitoire.

transitive ['trænzɪtɪv] *adj* transitif.

transitively ['trænzɪtɪvlɪ] *adv* transitivement.

transitory ['trænzɪtərɪ] *adj* transitoire, éphémère, passager.

translatable [trænz'leɪtəbl] *adj* traduisible.

translate [trænz'leɪt] **1** *vt* **(a)** (*gen, Ling*) traduire (*from* de, *into* en). **how do you** ~ **'weather'?** quelle est la traduction de 'weather'?, comment traduit-on 'weather'?; **the word is** ~**d as ...** le mot se traduit par ... ; **which when** ~**d means ...** ce qu'on peut traduire par ... ; (*fig*) **to** ~ **ideas into actions** passer des idées aux actes; **the figures,** ~**d in terms of hours lost, mean ...** exprimés *or* traduits en termes d'heures perdues, ces chiffres signifient ... .
(b) (*Rel*) *bishop, relics* transférer; (*convey to heaven*) ravir.
2 *vi* [*person*] traduire; [*word, book*] se traduire. **it won't** ~ c'est intraduisible.

translation [trænz'leɪʃən] *n* **(a)** traduction *f*; (*Scol etc*) version *f*. **the poem loses in** ~ le poème perd à la traduction; **it is a** ~ **from the Russian** c'est traduit du russe.
(b) (*Rel*) [*bishop*] translation *f*; [*relics*] transfert *m*; (*conveying to heaven*) ravissement *m*.

translator [trænz'leɪtəʳ] *n* traducteur *m*, -trice *f*.

transliterate [trænz'lɪtəreɪt] *vt* translit(t)érer.

transliteration [ˌtrænzlɪtə'reɪʃən] *n* translit(t)ération *f*.

translucence [trænz'luːsns] *n* translucidité *f*.

translucent [trænz'luːsnt] *adj*, **translucid** [trænz'luːsɪd] *adj* translucide.

transmigrate ['trænzmaɪ'greɪt] *vi* [*soul*] transmigrer; [*people*] émigrer.

transmigration [ˌtrænzmaɪ'greɪʃən] *n* [*soul*] transmigration *f*; [*people*] émigration *f*.

transmissible [trænz'mɪsəbl] *adj* transmissible.

transmission [trænz'mɪʃən] **1** *n* (*all senses*) transmission *f*. **2** *cpd*: (*Aut*) **transmission shaft** arbre *m* de transmission.

transmit [trænz'mɪt] **1** *vt* (*gen, Aut, Med, Phys etc*) transmettre; (*Rad, Telec, TV*) émettre, diffuser. **2** *vi* (*Rad, Telec, TV*) émettre, diffuser.

transmitter [trænz'mɪtəʳ] *n* (*Telec*) transmetteur *m*, poste émetteur; (*capsule*) capsule *f* microphonique; (*Rad, TV*) émetteur *m*, station émettrice.

transmitting [trænz'mɪtɪŋ] **1** *adj* (*Telec*) *set, station* émetteur (*f* -trice). **2** *n* (*gen, Med, Phys*) = **transmission 1.**

transmogrify [trænz'mɒgrɪfaɪ] *vt* (*hum*) métamorphoser, transformer (*into* en).

transmutable [trænz'mjuːtəbl] *adj* transmuable *or* transmutable.

transmutation [ˌtrænzmjuː'teɪʃən] *n* transmutation *f*.

transmute [trænz'mjuːt] *vt* transmuer *or* transmuter (*into* en).

transom ['trænsəm] *n* traverse *f*.

transonic [træn'sɒnɪk] *adj* = **transsonic.**

transparency [træns'peərənsɪ] *n* **(a)** (*U*) transparence *f*. **(b)** (*Phot*) diapositive *f*. **colour** ~ diapositive en couleur.

transparent [træns'peərənt] *adj* (*all senses*) transparent.

transpierce [træns'pɪəs] *vt* transpercer.

transpiration [ˌtrænspɪ'reɪʃən] *n* transpiration *f*.

transpire [træns'paɪəʳ] **1** *vi* **(a)** (*impers vb*) (*become known*) s'ébruiter; (*happen*) se passer, arriver. **it** ~**d that ...** on a appris par la suite que ... . **(b)** (*Bot, Physiol*) transpirer. **2** *vt* transpirer.

transplant [træns'plɑːnt] **1** *vt plant, kidney, population* transplanter; *seedlings etc* repiquer. **2** ['trænsplɑːnt] *n* (*Med*) transplantation *f*. **he's had a heart** ~ on lui a fait une greffe* du cœur *or* une transplantation cardiaque.

transplantation [ˌtrænsplɑːn'teɪʃən] *n* (*V* **transplant 1**) transplantation *f*; repiquage *m*.

transport ['trænspɔːt] **1** *n* **(a)** [*goods, parcels etc*] transport *m*. **road/rail** ~ transport par route/par chemin de fer; **by road** ~ par route; **by rail** ~ par chemin de fer; (*Brit*) **Minister/Ministry of T**~ ministre *m*/ministère *m* des Transports; **have you got any** ~ **for this evening?*** tu as une voiture pour ce soir?
(b) (*esp Mil: ship/plane/train*) navire *m*/avion *m*/train *m* de transport.
(c) (*fig*) [*delight etc*] transport *m*; [*fury etc*] accès *m*.
2 *cpd costs, ship, plane etc* de transport; *system* des transports. (*Brit*) **transport café** routiers* *m* (*sg*), restaurant *m* de routiers.
3 [træns'pɔːt] *vt* (*lit, fig*) transporter.

transportable [træns'pɔːtəbl] *adj* transportable.

transportation [ˌtrænspɔː'teɪʃən] *n* (moyen *m* de) transport *m*; [*criminals*] transportation *f*. (*US*) **Secretary/Department of T**~ ministre *m*/ministère *m* des Transports.

transporter [træns'pɔːtəʳ] *n* (*person, object*) transporteur *m*; *V* **car.**

transpose [træns'pəʊz] *vt* transposer.

transposition [ˌtrænspə'zɪʃən] *n* transposition *f*.

transship [træns'ʃɪp] *vt* transborder.

transshipment [træns'ʃɪpmənt] *n* transbordement *m*.

trans-Siberian [trænzsaɪ'bɪərɪən] *adj* transsibérien.

transsonic [trænz'sɒnɪk] *adj* transsonique.

transubstantiate [ˌtrænsəb'stænʃɪeɪt] *vt* transsubstantier.

transubstantiation ['trænsəbˌstænʃɪ'eɪʃən] *n* transsubstantiation *f*.

transversal [trænz'vɜːsəl] (*Geom*) **1** *adj* transversal. **2** *n* (ligne *f*) transversale *f*.

transversally [trænz'vɜːsəlɪ] *adv* transversalement.

transverse ['trænzvɜːs] **1** *adj* (*gen, Geom*) transversal; (*Anat*) transverse. **2** *n* (*gen*) partie transversale; (*Geom*) axe transversal.

transversely [trænz'vɜːslɪ] *adv* transversalement.

transvestism ['trænzˌvestɪzəm] *n* travestisme *m*.

transvestite [trænz'vestaɪt] *n* travesti(e) *m(f)*.

trap [træp] **1** *n* **(a)** (*gen*) piège *m*; (*snare*) collet *m*, traquenard *m*; (*covered hole*) trappe *f*; (*fig*) piège, traquenard. **lion** *etc* ~ piège à lions *etc*; (*lit, fig*) **to set** *or* **lay a** ~ tendre un piège (*for sb* à qn); (*lit, fig*) **to catch in a** ~ prendre au piège; **we were caught like rats in a** ~ nous étions faits comme des rats; (*fig*) **he fell into the** ~ il est tombé dans le piège; **it's a** ~ c'est un piège; *V* **man, mouse, radar** *etc.*
(b) (~ *door*) trappe *f* (*also Theat*); (*greyhound racing*) box *m* de départ; (*in drainpipe*) siphon *m*; (*‡: mouth*) gueule‡ *f*. **shut your** ~**!‡** ta gueule!‡, la ferme!‡; **keep your** ~ **shut (about it)‡** ferme ta gueule‡ (là-dessus).
(c) (*carriage*) charrette anglaise, cabriolet *m*.
2 *cpd*: **trap door** trappe *f*; **trapshooting** ball-trap *m*.
3 *vt* **(a)** (*lit, fig: snare*) *animal, person* prendre au piège. **they** ~**ped him into admitting that ...** il est tombé dans leur piège et a admis que ... .
(b) (*immobilize, catch, cut off*) *person, vehicle, ship* bloquer, immobiliser; *gas, liquid* retenir; *object* coincer (*in sth* dans qch). **20 miners were** ~**ped** 20 mineurs étaient bloqués *or* murés (au fond); **the climbers were** ~**ped on a ledge** les alpinistes étaient bloqués sur une saillie; **to** ~ **one's finger in the door** se coincer *or* se pincer le doigt dans la porte; (*Sport*) **to** ~ **the ball** bloquer le ballon.

trapeze [trə'piːz] **1** *n* trapèze *m* (*de cirque*). **2** *cpd*: **trapeze artist** trapéziste *mf*, voltigeur *m*, -euse *f*.

trapezium [trə'piːzɪəm] *n* trapèze *m* (*Math*).

trapezoid ['træpɪzɔɪd] **1** *n* trapèze *m* (*Math*). **2** *adj* trapézoïdal.

trapper ['træpəʳ] *n* trappeur *m*.

trappings ['træpɪŋz] *npl* (*for horse*) harnachement *m*; (*dress ornaments*) ornements *mpl*, apparat *m*, atours† *mpl*. (*fig*) **shorn of all its** ~ débarrassé de toutes ses fioritures; (*fig*) **if you look beneath the** ~ si on regarde derrière la façade; **with all the** ~ **of kingship** avec tout le cérémonial afférent à la royauté; **all the** ~ **of success** tous les signes extérieurs du succès.

Trappist ['træpɪst] **1** *n* trappiste *m*. **2** *adj* de la Trappe.

trapse* [treɪps] *vi* = **traipse.**

trash [træʃ] **1** *n* (*refuse: esp US*) ordures *fpl*; (*‡pej: people*) racaille *f* (*U*). (*fig*) **this is** ~ ça ne vaut rien (du tout); (*esp goods*) c'est de la camelote*; (*message, letter, remark etc*) c'est de la blague*; **he talks a lot of** ~ il ne raconte que des inepties, ce qu'il dit c'est de la blague*; [*people*] **they're just** ~**‡** c'est de la racaille; **he's** ~**‡** c'est un moins que rien; *V* **white.**
2 *cpd*: (*US*) **trash can** poubelle *f*, boîte *f* à ordures.

trashy ['træʃɪ] *adj goods* de camelote*, de pacotille; *novel, play* de quatre sous; *film, speech, opinion, ideas* qui ne vaut rien (du tout).

trauma ['trɔːmə] *n* (*Med, Psych*) trauma *m*; (*fig*) traumatisme *m*.

traumatic [trɔːˈmætɪk] *adj* (*Med*) traumatique; (*Psych, fig*) traumatisant.
traumatism [ˈtrɔːmətɪzəm] *n* traumatisme *m*.
travail†† [ˈtræveɪl] 1 *n* labeur *m*; (*in childbirth*) douleurs *fpl* de l'enfantement. 2 *vi* peiner; (*in childbirth*) être en couches.
travel [ˈtrævl] 1 *vi* (a) (*journey*) voyager, faire un *or* des voyage(s), aller. **they have ~led a lot** ils ont beaucoup voyagé, ils ont fait beaucoup de voyages; **they have ~led a long way** ils sont venus de loin; (*fig*) ils ont fait beaucoup de chemin; **he is ~ling in Spain just now** il est en voyage en Espagne en ce moment; **as he was ~ling across France** pendant qu'il voyageait à travers la France; **to ~ round the world** faire le tour du monde; **to ~ light** voyager avec peu de bagages; **I like ~ling by car** j'aime voyager en voiture; **he ~s to work by car** il va au travail en voiture; *[food, wine]* **it ~s well** ça supporte bien le voyage.
(b) (*Comm*) voyager, être représentant. **he ~s for a Paris firm** il voyage pour *or* il représente une société parisienne; **he ~s in soap** il est représentant en savon.
(c) (*move, go*) *[person, animal, vehicle]* aller; *[object]* aller, passer; *[machine part, bobbin, piston etc]* se déplacer. **to ~ at 80 km/h** faire du 80 km/h; **you were ~ling too fast** vous alliez trop vite; **he was really ~ling!*** il roulait drôlement vite!*; **this car can certainly ~*** c'est une voiture qui a du nerf*; **light ~s at (a speed of) ...** la vitesse de la lumière est de ... ; **news ~s fast** les nouvelles circulent vite; **the boxes ~ along a moving belt** les boîtes passent sur une *or* se déplacent le long d'une chaîne; **this part ~s 3 cm** cette pièce se déplace de 3 cm *or* a une course de 3 cm; (*fig*) **his eyes ~led over the scene** son regard se promenait *or* il promenait son regard sur le spectacle; **her mind ~led over recent events** elle a revu en esprit les événements récents.
2 *vt*: **to ~ a country/district** parcourir un pays/une région; **they ~ the road to London every month** ils font la route de Londres tous les mois; **a much-~led road** une route très fréquentée; **they ~led 300 km** ils ont fait *or* parcouru 300 km.
3 *n* (a) (*U*) voyage(s) *m(pl)*. **to be fond of ~** aimer voyager, aimer le(s) voyage(s); **~ was difficult in those days** les voyages étaient difficiles *or* il était difficile de voyager à l'époque; **~ broadens the mind** les voyages ouvrent l'esprit.
(b) **~s** voyages *mpl*; **his ~s in Spain** ses voyages en Espagne; **he's off on his ~s again** il repart en voyage; **if you meet him on your ~s** (*lit*) si vous le rencontrez au cours de vos voyages; (*fig hum*) si vous le rencontrez au cours de vos allées et venues.
(c) *[machine part, piston etc]* course *f*.
4 *cpd allowance, expenses* de déplacement; *scholarship etc* de voyage. **travel agency** agence *f* de voyages *or* de tourisme; **travel agent** agent *m* de tourisme; **travel book** récit *m* de voyage; **travel brochure** dépliant *m* touristique; **travel bureau** = **travel agency**; **travel film** film *m* de voyage; (*documentary*) documentaire *m* touristique; **travel organization** organisme *m* de tourisme; **to be travel-sick, to suffer from travel sickness** (*in car/plane/boat*) avoir le mal de la route/de l'air/de mer; **travel-sickness pills** médicament *m* contre le mal de la route (*or* de l'air *etc*); **travel-stained** sali par le(s) voyage(s); **travel-weary, travel-worn** fatigué par le(s) voyage(s).
travelator [ˈtrævəleɪtəʳ] *n* tapis roulant.
travelled, (*US*) **traveled** [ˈtrævld] *adj* (*also* **well-~**) *person* qui a beaucoup voyagé; *V also* **travel 2**.
traveller, (*US*) **traveler** [ˈtrævləʳ] 1 *n* voyageur *m*, -euse *f*; (*commercial ~*) voyageur *m or* représentant *m* de commerce. (*Comm*) **he is a ~ in soap** il est représentant en savon.
2 *cpd*: **traveller's cheque**, (*US*) **traveler's check** chèque *m* de voyage; (*Bot*) **travel(l)er's joy** clématite *f* des haies.
travelling, (*US*) **traveling** [ˈtrævlɪŋ] 1 *n* (*U*) voyage(s) *m(pl)*.
2 *adj circus, troupe* ambulant; *crane* mobile. (*Comm*) **~ salesman** voyageur *m or* représentant *m* de commerce.
3 *cpd bag, rug, scholarship* de voyage; *expenses, allowance* de déplacement. **travelling clock** réveil *m or* pendulette *f* de voyage.
travelogue, (*US*) *also* **travelog** [ˈtrævəlɒg] *n* (*talk*) compte rendu *m* de voyage; (*film*) documentaire *m* touristique; (*book*) récit *m* de voyage.
traverse [ˈtrævəs] 1 *vt* (*Alpinism, Ski*) traverser; *[searchlights]* balayer.
2 *vi* (*Alpinism, Ski*) faire une traversée, traverser.
3 *n* (*line*) transversale *f*; (*crossbar, crossbeam; also across rampart, trench etc*) traverse *f*; (*Archit*) galerie transversale; (*Alpinism, Ski*) traversée *f*.
travesty [ˈtrævɪstɪ] 1 *n* (*Art, Literat etc*) parodie *f*, pastiche *m*; (*pej*) parodie *f*, simulacre *m*, travestissement *m*. (*pej*) **it was a ~ of freedom/peace** c'était un simulacre de liberté/de paix; **it was a ~ of justice** c'était un simulacre de justice *or* un travestissement de la justice *or* une parodie de la justice, la justice était bafouée.
2 *vt* travestir, déformer, falsifier.
trawl [trɔːl] 1 *n* (*also* **~ net**) chalut *m*. 2 *vi* pêcher au chalut. **to ~ for herring** pêcher le hareng au chalut. 3 *vt net* traîner, tirer.
trawler [ˈtrɔːləʳ] 1 *n* (*ship, man*) chalutier *m*. 2 *cpd*: **trawler fisherman** pêcheur *m* au chalut; **trawler owner** propriétaire *mf* de chalutier.
trawling [ˈtrɔːlɪŋ] *n* (*U*) chalutage *m*, pêche *f* au chalut.
tray [treɪ] 1 *n* (*for carrying things*) plateau *m*; (*for storing things*) (*box-type*) boîte *f* (de rangement); (*basket-type*) corbeille *f* (de rangement); (*drawer-type*) tiroir *m*; *V* **ash²**, **ice** *etc.*
2 *cpd*: **traycloth** napperon *m*.
treacherous [ˈtretʃərəs] *adj person, action, answer* traître (*f* traîtresse), déloyal, perfide; (*fig*) *ground, surface, weather* traître; *memory* infidèle. **road conditions are ~** il faut se méfier de l'état des routes.
treacherously [ˈtretʃərəslɪ] *adv* traîtreusement, perfidement.
treachery [ˈtretʃərɪ] *n* traîtrise *f*, déloyauté *f*.
treacle [ˈtriːkl] (*Brit*) 1 *n* mélasse *f*. 2 *cpd*: **treacle pudding/tart** pudding *m*/tarte *f* à la mélasse raffinée.
treacly [ˈtriːklɪ] *adj* (*fig*) sirupeux.
tread [tred] (*vb*: *pret* **trod**, *ptp* **trodden**) 1 *n* (a) (*U: gait*) pas *m*, démarche *f*; (*sound*) bruit *m* de pas.
(b) *[tyre]* chape *f*; *[stair]* giron *m*; *[shoe]* semelle *f*; (*belt over tractor etc wheels*) chenille *f*.
2 *cpd*: **treadmill** (*mill*) trépigneuse *f*; (*Hist: punishment*) manège *m* de discipline; (*fig*) **he hated the treadmill of life in the factory** il détestait la morne *or* mortelle routine du travail d'usine.
3 *vi* marcher. **to ~ on sth** mettre le pied sur qch, marcher sur qch; **he trod on the cigarette end** il a écrasé le mégot du pied; (*fig*) **to ~ on sb's heels** suivre *or* serrer qn de près, talonner qn; (*lit, fig*) **to ~ carefully** *or* **warily** avancer avec précaution; *V* **toe** *etc.*
4 *vt path, road* suivre, parcourir (*à pieds*). **he trod the streets looking for somewhere to live** il a erré dans les rues *or* il a battu le pavé à la recherche d'un logis; **to ~ sth underfoot** fouler qch aux pieds, piétiner qch; **to ~ grapes** fouler du raisin; **~ the earth (in** *or* **down) round the roots** tassez la terre du pied autour des racines; **he trod his cigarette end into the mud** il a enfoncé du pied son mégot dans la boue; **you're ~ing mud into the carpet** tu mets *or* tu étales de la boue sur le tapis; **to ~ water** (*pret, ptp gen* **treaded**) nager en chien; (*Theat*: †† *or liter*) **to ~ the boards** faire du théâtre; (†† *or liter: dance*) **to ~ a measure** danser.
tread down *vt sep* tasser *or* presser du pied.
tread in *vt sep root, seedling* consolider en tassant tout autour la terre du pied.
treadle [ˈtredl] 1 *n* pédale *f* (*de tour, de machine à coudre etc*). 2 *cpd machine* à pédale. 3 *vi* actionner la pédale, pédaler.
treason [ˈtriːzn] *n* trahison *f*. **high ~** haute trahison.
treasonable [ˈtriːzənəbl] *adj thought, action* qui constitue une trahison.
treasure [ˈtreʒəʳ] 1 *n* trésor *m* (*also fig*). **yes my ~** oui mon trésor; **~s of medieval art** les trésors *or* les joyaux *mpl* de l'art médiéval; **our charlady is a real ~** notre femme de ménage est une perle*.
2 *cpd*: **treasure-house** (*lit*) trésor *m* (*lieu*); (*fig: of library, museum etc*) mine *f*, trésor; **she's a real treasure-house of information** c'est un puits de science, c'est une mine d'érudition; **treasure hunt** chasse *f* au trésor; (*U*) **treasure-trove** trésor *m* (*dont le propriétaire est inconnu*).
3 *vt* (a) (*value greatly*) *object, sb's friendship, opportunity etc* tenir beaucoup à, attacher une grande valeur à.
(b) (*keep carefully: also* **~ up**) *object, money, valuables* garder précieusement, prendre grand soin de; *memory, thought* conserver précieusement, chérir.
treasurer [ˈtreʒərəʳ] *n* trésorier *m*, -ière *f* (*d'une association etc*).
treasury [ˈtreʒərɪ] 1 *n* (a) **the T~** la Trésorerie, ≈ le ministère des Finances; (*US*) **Secretary/Department of the T~** ministre *m*/ministère *m* des Finances.
(b) (*place*) trésorerie *f*; (*fig: book etc*) trésor *m*.
(2) *cpd*: **treasury bill** ≈ bon *m* du Trésor; (*Brit Parl*) **Treasury bench** banc *m* des ministres.
treat [triːt] 1 *vt* (a) *person* traiter, agir envers, se conduire envers; *animal* traiter; *object, theme, suggestion* traiter, examiner. **to ~ sb well** bien traiter qn, bien agir *or* se conduire envers qn; **to ~ sb badly** mal agir *or* se conduire envers qn, traiter qn fort mal; **to ~ sb like a child** traiter qn en enfant; **he ~ed me as though I was to blame** il s'est conduit envers moi comme si c'était ma faute; **you should ~ your mother with more respect** vous devriez montrer plus de respect envers votre mère; **you should ~ your books with more care** tu devrais faire plus attention à *or* prendre plus de soin de tes livres; **the article ~s the problems of race relations with fresh insight** cet article traite *or* analyse *or* examine les problèmes des rapports interraciaux avec beaucoup de pénétration; **he ~s the subject very objectively** il traite le sujet avec beaucoup d'objectivité; **he ~ed the whole thing as a joke** il a pris tout cela à la plaisanterie.
(b) *wood, soil, substance* traiter (*with sth* à qch); (*Med*) traiter, soigner (*sb for sth* qn pour qch). **they ~ed him/the infection with penicillin** ils l'ont soigné/ont soigné l'infection à la pénicilline.
(c) (*pay for etc*) **to ~ sb to sth** offrir *or* payer* qch à qn; **to ~ o.s. to sth** s'offrir *or* se payer* qch; **I'll ~ you to a drink** je t'offre *or* te paie* un verre, je régale*.
2 *vi* (a) (*negotiate*) **to ~ with sb** traiter avec qn (*for sth* pour qch); **to ~ for peace** engager des pourparlers en vue de la paix.
(b) (*discuss*) *[book, article etc]* **to ~ of** traiter (de), examiner.
3 *n* (a) (*pleasure*) plaisir *m*; (*outing*) sortie *f*; (*entertainment*) distraction *f*; (*present*) cadeau *m*. **what a ~!** quelle aubaine!, chouette* alors!; **it's a ~ in store** c'est un plaisir à venir; **it was a great ~ (for us) to see them again** ça nous a vraiment fait plaisir de les revoir, ça a été une joie de les revoir; **it is a ~ for her to go out to a meal** elle se fait une joie de *or* c'est tout un événement* pour elle de dîner en ville; **let's give the children a ~** faisons (un) plaisir *or* une gâterie aux enfants, gâtons un peu les enfants; **I want to give her a ~** je veux lui faire plaisir; **the school ~ was a visit to the seaside** la fête de l'école a consisté en une excursion au bord de la mer; **to stand ~** inviter; **to stand sb a ~** (*gen*) offrir *or* payer* quelque chose à qn; (*food, drink only*) régaler* qn; **this is to be my ~** c'est moi qui offre *or* qui paie*; (*food, drink only*) c'est moi qui régale*.
(b) (*Brit*: adv phrase*) **a ~** à merveille; **the garden is coming**

on a ~ le jardin avance à merveille; **the plan worked a ~** le projet a marché comme sur des roulettes.
treatise ['triːtɪz] *n* (*Literat*) traité *m* (*on* de).
treatment ['triːtmənt] *n* (*gen, Chem, Med etc*) traitement *m*. **his ~ of his parents/the dog** la façon dont il traite ses parents/le chien; **his ~ of this subject in his book** la façon dont il traite ce sujet dans son livre; **he got very good ~ there** (*gen*) on l'a très bien traité là-bas; (*Med*) il a été très bien traité *or* soigné là-bas; **to give sb preferential ~** accorder à qn un traitement préférentiel *or* un régime de faveur; **he needs medical ~** il a besoin de soins médicaux *or* d'un traitement; **they refused him ~** ils ont refusé de le soigner; **he is having (a course of) ~ for kidney trouble** il suit un traitement *or* il est sous traitement pour ennuis rénaux; (*fig*) **to give sb the ~**‡ en faire voir de dures* *or* de toutes les couleurs* à qn; *V* **respond.**
treaty ['triːtɪ] *n* **(a)** traité *m* (*with* avec, *between* entre). (*Pol*) **to make a ~ with sb** conclure *or* signer un traité avec qn.
(b) (*U*) **to sell a house by private ~** vendre une maison par accord privé.
treble ['trebl] **1** *adj* **(a)** (*triple*) triple. (*in numerals*) **~ seven five four** (77754) triple sept cinq quatre; **the amount is in ~ figures** le montant dépasse la centaine; (*in football pools*) **the ~ chance** *méthode f de pari en football.*
(b) (*Mus*) *voice* de soprano (*voix d'enfant*); *part* pour *or* de soprano. the **~ clef** la clef de sol.
2 *n* (*Mus: part, singer*) soprano *m*.
3 *adv* (*thrice*) trois fois plus que.
4 *vti* tripler.
trebly ['treblɪ] *adv* triplement, trois fois plus.
tree [triː] (*vb: pret, ptp* **treed**) **1** *n* **(a)** arbre *m*. **cherry ~** cerisier *m*; (*Bible*) **the ~ of life** l'arbre de vie; (*Bible*) **the ~ of knowledge** l'arbre de la science du bien et du mal; (*Rel*††: *the Cross*) the **~** l'arbre de la Croix; (*fig*) **to be** *or* **to have reached the top of the ~** être arrivé au haut de l'échelle (*fig*); (*fig*) **to be up a ~**‡ être dans le pétrin; *V* **apple, bark¹, bark², family, plum** *etc.*
(b) (*shoe ~*) embauchoir *m*; (*cobbler's last*) forme *f*.
2 *cpd*: **tree-covered** boisé; **tree fern** fougère arborescente; **tree frog** rainette *f*, grenouille *f* arboricole; **tree house** cabane construite dans un arbre; (*US*) **tree lawn** plate-bande plantée d'arbres (*entre la rue et le trottoir*); **tree-lined** bordé d'arbres; (*Bot*) **tree of heaven** ailante *m*; **tree surgeon** arboriculteur *m*, -trice *f* (qui s'occupe du traitement des arbres malades); **tree surgery** arboriculture *f* (spécialisée dans le traitement des arbres malades); **treetop** cime *f* d'un arbre; **tree trunk** tronc *m* d'arbre.
3 *vt* forcer à se réfugier dans un arbre.
treeless ['triːlɪs] *adj* sans arbres, dépourvu d'arbres, déboisé.
trefoil ['trefɔɪl] *n* (*Archit, Bot*) trèfle *m*.
trek [trek] **1** *vi* **(a)** (*go slowly*) cheminer, avancer avec peine; (*as holiday*) faire de la randonnée; (*Hist: go by oxcart*) voyager en char à bœufs. **they ~ked out to India** pour aller en Inde ils ont voyagé à la dure *or* avec le minimum de confort; *V* **pony.**
(b) (*: *walk*) se traîner. **I had to ~ over to the library** il a fallu que je me traîne (*subj*) jusqu'à la bibliothèque.
2 *n* (*journey on foot*) randonnée *f*; (*leg of journey*) étape *f*; (*by oxcart*) voyage *m* en char à bœufs; (*: *walk*) balade* *f*. **during their ~ to India** pendant leur voyage aventureux en Inde; **it was quite a ~* to the hotel** il y avait un bon bout de chemin* à faire jusqu'à l'hôtel.
trellis ['trelɪs] **1** *n* treillis *m*, (*stronger*) treillage *m*; (*U: also* **~work**) treillage. **2** *vt* treillisser, treillager.
tremble ['trembl] **1** *vi* (*from fear*) trembler, frémir, frissonner; (*from excitement, passion*) frémir, trembler; (*from cold*) trembler, frissonner, grelotter; *[hand]* trembler; *[voice]* (*with fear, age*) trembler, chevroter; (*with passion*) vibrer; *[ground, building]* trembler, être secoué; *[engine, ship]* vibrer, trépider. **I ~ to think what might have happened** je frémis rien qu'à la pensée de ce qui aurait pu arriver; **what will he do next? — I ~ to think!** qu'est-ce qu'il va encore faire? — j'en frémis d'avance; **he ~d at the thought** il a frémi rien que d'y penser.
2 *n* (*V1*) tremblement *m*; frémissement *m*; frissonnement *m*; vibration(s) *f(pl)*; trépidation(s) *f(pl)*. **to be all of a ~*** trembler comme une feuille, trembler de la tête aux pieds.
trembling ['tremblɪŋ] (*V* **tremble 1**) **1** *adj* tremblant, frémissant, frissonnant; grelottant; chevrotant; vibrant; trépidant. **2** *n* (*U*) tremblement *m*; frémissement *m*; frissonnement *m*; vibration(s) *f(pl)*; *V* **fear.**
tremendous [trə'mendəs] *adj difference, size, change, number* énorme, fantastique; *storm, explosion, blow* terrible, épouvantable; *victory* foudroyant; *speed* fou (*f* folle); (*: *excellent*) formidable*, sensationnel*, sensass*. **a ~ crowd** un monde fou; a **~ success** un succès fou *or* à tout casser*; **we had a ~ time*** on s'est drôlement bien amusé*.
tremendously [trə'mendəslɪ] *adv* formidablement*, terriblement, extrêmement, drôlement*, vachement‡.
tremolo ['treməlәu] *n* (*Mus*) trémolo *m*.
tremor ['tremәʳ] *n* tremblement *m*; *V* **earth.**
tremulous ['tremjʊləs] *adj* (*timid*) *person* timide, craintif, effarouché; *smile* timide, incertain; (*trembling*) (*from fear*) *person* tremblant, frissonnant, frémissant; *voice* tremblant, chevrotant; (*from excitement, passion*) *person* frémissant, frissonnant; *voice* vibrant; *hand* tremblant; *handwriting* tremblé.
tremulously ['tremjʊləslɪ] *adv say, answer, suggest* en tremblant, en frémissant, timidement; *smile* d'une façon incertaine, timidement.
trench [trentʃ] **1** *n* tranchée *f* (*also Mil*); (*wider*) fossé *m*. **he fought in the ~es** il était dans les tranchées *or* a fait la guerre des tranchées.
2 *cpd*: **trench coat** trench-coat *m*; (*Med*) **trench fever** rickettsiose *f*, typhus *m* exanthématique; **trench knife** couteau *m* (à double tranchant); (*Mil*) **trench warfare** guerre *f* de tranchées.
3 *vt* (*dig trenches in*) creuser une *or* des tranchée(s) dans; (*Mil: surround with trenches*) *one's position etc* retrancher.
4 *vi* creuser une *or* des tranchée(s).
trenchant ['trentʃənt] *adj* d'un ton incisif *or* mordant.
trencher ['trentʃәʳ] **1** *n* tranchoir *m*. **2** *cpd*: **he is a good** *or* **great** *or* **hearty trencherman** il a un sacré coup de fourchette*.
trend [trend] **1** *n* (*tendency*) tendance *f* (*towards* à); (*Geog*) *[coast, river, road]* direction *f*, orientation *f*; (*fashion*) mode *f*, vogue *f*. (*Fin etc*) **upward/downward ~** tendance à la hausse/à la baisse; **there is a ~ towards doing/away from doing** on a tendance à faire/à ne plus faire; **the latest ~s in swimwear** la mode la plus récente en maillots de bain; **the ~ of events** le cours *or* la tournure des événements; **~s in popular music** les tendances de la musique populaire; *V* **market, reverse** *etc.*
2 *cpd*: **trendsetter** (*person*) personne *f* qui donne le ton *or* qui lance une mode; (*article*) article *m* dernier cri *inv*.
3 *vi [river, road]* **to ~ northwards/southwards** *etc* aller vers le nord/le sud *etc*; *[events, opinions]* **to ~ towards sth** tendre vers qch.
trendy* ['trendɪ] **1** *adj clothes* dernier cri *inv*, à la dernière mode; *opinions* dans le vent, d'avant-garde, avancé; *behaviour, religion* à la mode, dans le vent. **he's got quite a ~ image** il donne l'impression d'être tout à fait dans le vent *or* à la page.
2 *n* personne *f* dans le vent.
trepan [trɪ'pæn] **1** *vt metal plate etc* forer; (*Med*) trépaner. **2** *n* (*for quarrying etc*) foreuse *f*, trépan *m*; (*Med*) trépan *m*.
trephine [tre'fiːn] (*Med*) **1** *vt* trépaner. **2** *n* trépan *m*.
trepidation [ˌtrepɪ'deɪʃən] *n* (*fear*) vive inquiétude; (*excitement*) agitation *f*.
trespass ['trespəs] **1** *n* **(a)** (*U: Jur: illegal entry*) entrée non autorisée.
(b) (††, *Rel: sin*) offense *f*, péché *m*. **forgive us our ~es** pardonnez-nous nos offenses.
2 *vi* **(a)** s'introduire sans permission. **'no ~ing'** 'entrée interdite', 'propriété privée'; **you're ~ing** vous êtes dans une propriété privée; **to ~ on** *sb's land* s'introduire *or* se trouver sans permission dans; (*fig*) *sb's hospitality, time* abuser de; *sb's privacy* s'ingérer dans; *sb's rights* empiéter sur.
(b) (††, *Rel*) **to ~ against** *person* offenser; *law* enfreindre; **as we forgive them that ~ against us** comme nous pardonnons à ceux qui nous ont offensés.
trespasser ['trespəsәʳ] *n* **(a)** intrus(e) *m(f)* (dans une propriété privée). **'~s will be prosecuted'** 'défense d'entrer sous peine de poursuites'. **(b)** (††, *Rel: sinner*) pécheur *m*, -eresse *f*.
tress [tres] *n* (*liter*) boucle *f* de cheveux. **~es** chevelure *f*.
trestle ['tresl] **1** *n* tréteau *m*, chevalet *m*. **2** *cpd*: **trestle bridge** pont *m* sur chevalets; **trestle table** table *f* à tréteaux.
trews [truːz] *npl* pantalon écossais (étroit).
tri... [traɪ] *pref* tri... .
triad ['traɪəd] *n* (*gen*) triade *f*; (*Mus*) accord parfait.
trial ['traɪəl] **1** *n* **(a)** (*Jur*) (*proceedings*) procès *m*; (*U*) jugement *m*. **the ~ lasted a month** le procès a duré un mois; **a new ~ was ordered** la révision du procès a été demandée; **at the ~ it emerged that ...** au cours du procès *or* à l'audience il est apparu que ...; **during his ~ he claimed that ...** pendant son procès il a affirmé que ...; **~ by jury** jugement par jury; **to be** *or* **go on ~** passer en jugement *or* en justice; **to be on ~ for theft** être jugé pour vol; **he was on ~ for his life** il encourait la peine de mort; **to bring sb to ~** faire passer qn en jugement *or* en justice; **to come up for ~** *[case]* passer au tribunal; *[person]* passer en jugement; *V* **commit, stand.**
(b) (*test*) *[machine, vehicle, drug etc]* essai *m*. **~s** (*Ftbl etc*) match *m* de sélection; (*Athletics etc*) épreuve *f* de sélection; **sheepdog ~s** concours *m* de chiens de berger; **horse ~s** concours hippique; **~ of strength** épreuve de force; **to have a ~ of strength with sb** lutter de force avec qn, se mesurer à qn; **by (a system of) ~ and error** par tâtonnements, en tâtonnant; **it was all ~ and error** on a procédé uniquement par tâtonnements; **to take sb/sth on ~** prendre qn/qch à l'essai; *[machine, method, employee]* **to be on ~** être à l'essai; **to give sb a ~** mettre qn à l'essai.
(c) (*hardship*) épreuve *f*; (*nuisance*) souci *m*. **the ~s of old age** les afflictions *fpl or* les vicissitudes *fpl* de la vieillesse; **the interview was a great ~** l'entrevue a été une véritable épreuve *or* a été très éprouvante; **he is a ~ to his mother** il est un souci perpétuel pour sa mère, il donne beaucoup de souci à sa mère; **what a ~ you are!** ce que tu es agaçant! *or* exaspérant!; *V* **tribulation.**
2 *cpd flight, period etc* d'essai; *offer, marriage* à l'essai. (*Fin*) **trial balance** balance *f* d'inventaire; **trial run** (*lit*) essai *m*; (*fig*) période *f* d'essai.
triangle ['traɪæŋgl] *n* (*Math, Mus, fig*) triangle *m*; (*drawing instrument*) équerre *f*; *V* **eternal.**
triangular [traɪ'æŋgjʊlәʳ] *adj* triangulaire.
triangulate [traɪ'æŋgjʊleɪt] *vt* trianguler.
triangulation [traɪˌæŋgjʊ'leɪʃən] *n* triangulation *f*.
tribal ['traɪbəl] *adj customs, dance, system* tribal; *life* de la tribu; *warfare* entre tribus.
tribalism ['traɪbəlɪzəm] *n* tribalisme *m*.
tribe [traɪb] **1** *n* (*gen, Bot, Zool*) tribu *f*; (* *fig*) tribu, smala* *f*. **2** *cpd*: **tribesman** membre *m* d'une (*or* de la) tribu.
tribo... ['traɪbәu] *pref* tribo... . **~electricity** tribo-électricité *f*.
tribulation [ˌtrɪbjʊ'leɪʃən] *n* affliction *f*, souffrance *f*. **(trials and) ~s** tribulations *fpl*; **in times of ~** en période d'adversité, en temps de malheurs.
tribunal [traɪ'bjuːnl] *n* (*gen, Jur, fig*) tribunal *m*. **~ of inquiry** commission *f* d'enquête.

tribune ['trɪbjuːn] *n* (*platform*) tribune *f* (*also fig*); (*Hist, gen: person*) tribun *m*.
tributary ['trɪbjʊtərɪ] **1** *adj* tributaire. **2** (*river*) affluent *m*; (*state, ruler*) tributaire *m*.
tribute ['trɪbjuːt] *n* tribut *m*, hommage *m*; (*esp Hist: payment*) tribut. **to pay ~** to payer tribut à, rendre hommage à; (*Hist etc*) payer (le) tribut à; **it is a ~ to his generosity that nobody went hungry** qu'aucun n'ait souffert de la faim témoigne de sa générosité; *V* **floral**.
trice [traɪs] **1** *n*: **in a ~** en un clin d'œil, en moins de deux* *or* de rien.
2 *vt* (*Naut: also* **~ up**) hisser.
Tricel ['traɪsel] ® **1** *n* Tricel *m* ®. **2** *cpd shirt etc* de *or* en Tricel.
tricentennial [ˌtraɪsen'tenɪəl] *adj, n* tricentenaire (*m*).
triceps ['traɪseps] *n* triceps *m*.
trick [trɪk] **1** *n* **(a)** (*dodge, ruse*) ruse *f*, astuce *f*, truc* *m*; (*prank, joke, hoax*) tour *m*, farce *f*, blague* *f*; *[conjurer, juggler, dog etc]* tour. **it's a ~ to make you believe ...** c'est une ruse *or* une astuce *or* un truc* pour vous faire croire ...; **he got it all by a ~** il a tout obtenu par une ruse *or* un stratagème *or* une combine*; **a dirty** *or* **low** *or* **shabby** *or* **nasty ~** un sale tour, un tour de cochon*; **a ~ of the trade** une ficelle du métier; **it's a ~ of the light** c'est une illusion d'optique; **he's up to his (old) ~s again*** il fait de nouveau des siennes*; (*fig*) **he knows a ~ or two*** il a plus d'un tour dans son sac; **I know a ~ worth two of that*** je connais un tour *or* un truc* bien meilleur encore que celui-là; **that will do the ~*** ça fera l'affaire, c'est juste ce qu'il faut; **I'll soon get the ~ of it*** je vais bientôt prendre le pli *or* le truc*; (*US*) **~ or treat!** donnez-moi quelque chose ou je vous joue un tour! (*expression employée par les enfants qui font la quête la veille de la Toussaint*); *V* **bag, card¹, conjuring, play etc.**
(b) (*peculiarity*) particularité *f*; (*habit*) habitude *f*, manie *f*; (*mannerism*) tic *m*. **he has a ~ of scratching his ear when puzzled** il a le tic de se gratter l'oreille quand il est perplexe; **he has a ~ of arriving just when I'm making coffee** il a le don d'arriver *or* il faut toujours qu'il arrive (*subj*) au moment où je fais du café; **this horse has a ~ of stopping suddenly** ce cheval a la manie de s'arrêter brusquement; **these things have a ~ of happening just when you don't want them to** ces choses-là se produisent comme par magie *or* ont le don de se produire juste quand on ne le veut pas; **history has a ~ of repeating itself** l'histoire a le don de se répéter.
(c) (*Cards*) levée *f*, pli *m*. **to take a ~** faire une levée *or* un pli; (*fig*) **he never misses a ~** rien ne lui échappe.
2 *cpd*: **trick-cyclist** cycliste-acrobate *mf*; (*Brit*: psychiatrist*) psy* *m*, psychiatre *mf*; **trick photograph** photographie truquée; **trick photography** truquage *m* photographique; **trick question** question-piège *f*; (*on horse*) **trick rider** voltigeur *m*, -euse *f* (à cheval); **trick riding** voltige *f* (à cheval).
3 *vt* (*deceive*) attraper, avoir*, rouler*; (*swindle*) escroquer. **I've been ~ed!** on m'a eu!* *or* roulé!*; **to ~ sb into doing** amener qn à faire par la ruse; **to ~ sb out of sth** obtenir qch de qn *or* soutirer qch à qn par la ruse.
trick out, trick up *vt sep* parer (*with* de). **the ladies tricked out in all their finery** les dames sur leur trente et un *or* tout endimanchées.
trickery ['trɪkərɪ] *n* (*U*) ruse *f*, supercherie *f*, fourberie *f*. **by ~** par ruse.
trickiness ['trɪkɪnɪs] *n* (*U*) (*V* **tricky**) caractère délicat *or* épineux, difficulté *f*; caractère rusé *or* retors.
trickle ['trɪkl] **1** *n [water, blood etc]* filet *m*. **the stream has shrunk to a mere ~** le ruisseau n'est plus qu'un filet d'eau; **a ~ of people** quelques (rares) personnes *fpl*; **there was a ~ of news from the front line** il y avait de temps en temps des nouvelles du front; **there was a steady ~ of cash/offers/letters** l'argent/les offres/les lettres arrivai(en)t en petit nombre mais régulièrement.
2 *cpd*: (*Elec*) **trickle charger** chargeur *m* à régime lent.
3 *vi [water etc]* (*drop slowly*) couler *or* tomber goutte à goutte; (*flow slowly*) dégoutter, dégouliner, couler en un filet. **tears ~d down her cheeks** les larmes coulaient *or* dégoulinaient le long de ses joues; **the rain ~d down his neck** la pluie lui dégoulinait dans le cou; **the stream ~d along over the rocks** le ruisseau coulait faiblement sur les rochers; (*fig*) *[people]* **to ~ in/out/away** *etc* entrer/sortir/s'éloigner *etc* par petits groupes *or* les uns après les autres; (*Ftbl*) **the ball ~d into the net** le ballon a roulé doucement dans le filet; **money ~d into the fund** les contributions au fonds arrivaient lentement; **money ~d out of his account** son compte se dégarnissait lentement (mais régulièrement), une succession de petites sorties (d'argent) dégarnissait lentement son compte; **letters of complaint are still trickling into the office** quelques lettres de réclamation continuent à arriver au bureau.
4 *vt liquid* faire couler goutte à goutte, faire dégouliner *or* dégoutter (*into* dans, *out of* de).
trickle away *vi [water etc]* s'écouler doucement *or* lentement *or* goutte à goutte; *[money etc]* disparaître *or* être utilisé peu à peu; *V also* **trickle 3**.
trickster ['trɪkstəʳ] *n* filou *m*; *V* **confidence**.
tricky ['trɪkɪ] *adj problem, situation* délicat, épineux, difficile; *job, task* difficile, délicat, plein de pièges *or* de complications; (*pej*) *person* rusé, retors. **he's a ~ man to deal with** (*scheming*) avec lui il faut se méfier; (*difficult, touchy*) il n'est pas commode.
tricolo(u)r ['trɪkələʳ] *n* (drapeau *m*) tricolore *m*.
tricorn ['traɪkɔːn] **1** *adj* à trois cornes. **2** *n* tricorne *m*.
trictrac ['trɪktræk] *n* trictrac *m*.
tricuspid [traɪ'kʌspɪd] *adj* tricuspide.
tricycle ['traɪsɪkl] *n* tricycle *m*; (*for invalid*) tricyclecar *m*.
trident ['traɪdənt] *n* trident *m*.
tridentine [traɪ'dentaɪn] *adj* tridentin.
tridimensional [ˌtraɪdɪ'menʃənl] *adj* tridimensionnel, à trois dimensions.
triennial [traɪ'enɪəl] **1** *adj* triennal; (*Bot*) trisannuel. **2** *n* (*Bot*) plante trisannuelle.
triennially [traɪ'enɪəlɪ] *adv* tous les trois ans.
trier ['traɪəʳ] *n*: **to be a ~** être persévérant, ne pas se laisser rebuter, être toujours prêt à essayer.
trifle ['traɪfl] **1** *n* **(a)** bagatelle *f*. **it's only a ~** (*object, sum of money etc*) c'est une bagatelle, ce n'est rien, c'est bien peu de chose; (*remark, event etc*) c'est une vétille, il n'y a pas de quoi fouetter un chat; **he worries over ~s** il se fait du mauvais sang pour un rien; **£5 is a mere ~** 5 livres est une bagatelle *or* une misère *or* trois fois rien; **he bought it for a ~** il l'a acheté pour une bagatelle *or* une bouchée de pain *or* trois fois rien.
(b) (*adv phrase*) **a ~** un peu, un rien, un tantinet; **it's a ~ difficult** c'est un peu *or* un rien *or* un tantinet difficile.
(c) (*Culin*) diplomate *m* (à l'anglaise).
2 *vi*: **to ~ with** *person, sb's affections, trust etc* traiter à la légère, se jouer de; **he's not to be ~d with** il ne faut pas le traiter à la légère; **to ~ with one's food** manger du bout des dents, chipoter.
trifle away *vt sep time* perdre; *money* gaspiller.
trifler ['traɪfləʳ] *n* (*pej*) fantaisiste *mf*, fumiste *mf*.
trifling ['traɪflɪŋ] *adj* insignifiant, dérisoire.
trifocal ['traɪ'fəʊkəl] **1** *adj* à triple foyer, trifocal. **2** *n* (*lens*) verre *m* à triple foyer. **~s** lunettes à triple foyer *or* trifocales.
trifoliate [traɪ'fəʊlɪɪt] *adj* à trois feuilles, trifolié.
triforium [traɪ'fɔːrɪəm] *n* triforium *m*.
triform ['traɪfɔːm] *adj* à *or* en trois parties.
trigger ['trɪgəʳ] **1** *n [gun]* détente *f*, gâchette *f*; *[tool]* déclic *m*. **to press** *or* **pull** *or* **squeeze the ~** appuyer sur la détente *or* la gâchette; **he's quick** *or* **fast on the ~*** (*lit*) il n'attend pas pour tirer; (*fig*) il réagit vite.
2 *cpd*: **trigger finger** index *m* (*avec lequel on appuie sur la gâchette*); **trigger-happy*** *person* prêt à tirer pour un rien; (*fig*) *nation etc* prêt à déclencher la guerre pour un rien.
3 *vt* (*also* **~ off**) *explosion* déclencher; *revolt, protest* déclencher, provoquer; *reaction* provoquer.
trigonometric(al) [ˌtrɪgənə'metrɪk(əl)] *adj* trigonométrique.
trigonometry [ˌtrɪgə'nɒmɪtrɪ] *n* trigonométrie *f*.
trigraph ['traɪgræf] *n* trigramme *m*.
trike* [traɪk] *n abbr of* **tricycle**.
trilateral [ˌtraɪ'lætərəl] *adj* trilatéral.
trilby ['trɪlbɪ] *n* (*Brit: also* **~ hat**) (chapeau *m* en) feutre *m*.
trilingual [ˌtraɪ'lɪŋgwəl] *adj* trilingue.
trilith(on) ['traɪlɪθ(ɒn)] *n* trilithe *m*.
trill [trɪl] **1** *n* (*Mus: also of bird*) trille *m*; (*Ling*) consonne roulée. **2** *vi* (*Mus: also of bird*) triller. **3** *vt* triller. (*Ling*) **to ~ one's rs** rouler les r; **'come in' she ~ed** 'entrez' roucoula-t-elle.
trillion ['trɪljən] *n* (*Brit*) trillion *m*; (*US*) billion *m*.
trilogy ['trɪlədʒɪ] *n* trilogie *f*.
trim [trɪm] **1** *adj appearance, person, clothes* net, soigné; *ship, garden, house* bien tenu, en bon ordre, coquet. **she has a ~ figure** elle a la taille svelte *or* bien prise; **the car has ~ lines** cette voiture a une ligne très pure; **it's a ~ little boat** c'est un petit bateau coquet *or* pimpant.
2 *n* **(a)** (*U*) (*condition*) état *m*, ordre *m*. **in (good) ~** *garden, house etc* en (bon) état *or* ordre; *person, athlete* en (bonne) forme; *[athlete etc]* **to get into ~** se remettre en forme; **to get things into ~** mettre de l'ordre dans les choses; (*Naut*) **the ~ of the sails** l'orientation *f* des voiles.
(b) (*cut*) **to give sth a ~ = to trim sth**; *V* **3a**.
(c) (*around window, door*) moulures *fpl*; (*Aut: inside*) aménagement intérieur; (*Aut: outside*) finitions extérieures; (*on dress etc*) garniture *f*. **car with blue (interior) ~** voiture à intérieur bleu.
3 *vt* **(a)** (*cut*) *beard* tailler *or* couper légèrement; *hair* rafraîchir; *wick, lamp* tailler, moucher; *branch, hedge, roses* tailler légèrement; *piece of wood, paper* couper les bords de, rogner. **to ~ the edges of sth** couper *or* rogner les bords de qch; **to ~ the ragged edge off sth** ébarber qch.
(b) (*decorate*) *hat, dress* garnir, orner (*with* de); *Christmas tree* décorer (*with* de). **to ~ the edges of sth with sth** border qch de qch; (*US*) **to ~ a store window** composer un étalage, décorer une vitrine de magasin.
(c) *boat, aircraft* équilibrer; *sail* gréer, orienter.
trim away *vt sep* enlever aux ciseaux (*or* au couteau *or* à la cisaille).
trim down *vt sep wick* tailler, moucher.
trim off *vt sep* = **trim away**.
trimaran ['traɪməræn] *n* trimaran *m*.
trimester [trɪ'mestəʳ] *n* trimestre *m*.
trimmings ['trɪmɪŋz] *npl* (*ornamentation*) garniture(s) *f(pl)*; (*edging*) bordure *f*; (*accessories*) accessoires *mpl*; (*cuttings*) chutes *fpl*. **it costs over £100 without the ~** cela coûte plus de 100 livres sans les accessoires; **roast beef and all the ~** du rosbif avec la garniture habituelle.
trimness ['trɪmnɪs] *n [garden, boat, house]* aspect net *or* soigné. **the ~ of his appearance** son aspect soigné *or* coquet *or* pimpant; **the ~ of her figure** la sveltesse de sa silhouette.
trinary ['traɪnərɪ] *adj* trinaire.
Trinidad ['trɪnɪdæd] *n* (l'île *f* de) la Trinité. **~ and Tobago** Trinité-et-Tobago *m*.
Trinidadian [ˌtrɪnɪ'dædɪən] **1** *adj* de la Trinité. **2** *n* habitant(e) *m(f)* de la Trinité.
trinitrotoluene [traɪˌnaɪtrəʊ'tɒljʊiːn] *n* trinitrotoluène *m*.
trinity ['trɪnɪtɪ] **1** *n* trinité *f*. (*Rel*) **the Holy T~** la Sainte Trinité.
2 *cpd*: **Trinity (Sunday)** la fête de la Trinité; (*Univ*) **Trinity**

term troisième trimestre *m* (de l'année universitaire).

trinket ['trɪŋkɪt] *n* (*gen*) bibelot *m*, babiole *f* (*also pej*), bricole *f* (*pej*); (*specifically jewel*) colifichet *m* (*also pej*); (*on chain*) breloque *f*.

trinomial [traɪ'nəʊmɪəl] *n* (*Math*) trinôme *m*.

trio ['triəʊ] *n* trio *m*.

trip [trɪp] **1** *n* **(a)** (*journey*) voyage *m*; (*excursion*) excursion *f*. **he's away on a ~** il est (parti) en voyage; **we did the ~ in 10 hours** nous avons fait le voyage *or* le trajet en 10 heures; **there are cheap ~s to Spain** on organise des voyages à prix réduit en Espagne; **we went on** *or* **took a ~ to Malta** nous sommes allés (en voyage) à Malte; **we took** *or* **made a ~ into town** nous sommes allés en ville; **he does 3 ~s to Scotland a week** il va en Écosse 3 fois par semaine; **I don't want another ~ to the shops today** je ne veux pas retourner dans les magasins aujourd'hui; **after 4 ~s to the kitchen he ...** après 4 voyages à la cuisine il ...; *V* **business, coach, day, round** *etc*.

(b) (*Drugs sl*) trip *m* (*sl*). **to be on a ~** faire un trip (*sl*), flipper‡; **to have a bad ~** faire un trip (*sl*) qui tourne mal.

(c) (*stumble*) faux pas; (*in wrestling etc*) croche-pied *m*, croc-en-jambe *m*; (*fig: mistake*) faux pas, erreur *f*, gaffe* *f*.

2 *cpd*: **tripwire** fil *m* de détente.

3 *vi* **(a)** (*stumble: also* **~ up**) trébucher (*on, over* contre, sur), buter (*on, over* contre), faire un faux pas. **he ~ped and fell** il a trébuché *or* il a fait un faux pas et il est tombé.

(b) (*go lightly and quickly*) **to ~ along/in/out** *etc* marcher/entrer/sortir *etc* d'un pas léger *or* sautillant; **the words came ~ping off her tongue** elle l'a dit sans la moindre hésitation; (*hum*) **to ~ the light fantastic*** danser.

(c) (*Drugs sl*) faire un trip (*sl*), flipper‡.

trip over *vi* trébucher, faire un faux pas.

trip up 1 *vi* **(a)** = **trip 3a.**

(b) (*fig*) faire une erreur, gaffer*.

2 *vt sep* faire trébucher; (*deliberately*) faire un croche-pied *or* un croc-en-jambe à; (*fig: in questioning etc*) prendre en défaut, désarçonner (*fig*).

tripartite [ˌtraɪ'pɑːtaɪt] *adj* triparti, tripartite.

tripe [traɪp] *n* (*U*) (*Culin*) tripes *fpl*; (*: *nonsense*) bêtises *fpl*, idioties *fpl*. **what absolute ~!*** quelles bêtises!, quelles foutaises!‡

triphase ['traɪfeɪz] *adj* (*Elec*) triphasé.

triphthong ['trɪfθɒŋ] *n* triphtongue *f*.

triplane ['traɪpleɪn] *n* triplan *m*.

triple ['trɪpl] **1** *adj* triple. **the T~ Alliance** la Triple-Alliance; (*Mus*) **in ~ time** à trois temps. **2** *n* triple *m*. **3** *adv* trois fois plus que. **4** *vti* tripler.

triplet ['trɪplɪt] *n* (*Mus*) triolet *m*; (*Poetry*) tercet *m*. (*persons*) **~s** triplé(e)s *m(f)pl*.

triplex ['trɪpleks] **1** *adj* triple. **2** *n* ® (*also* **~ glass**) triplex *m* ®, verre sécurit *m* ®.

triplicate ['trɪplɪkɪt] **1** *adj* en trois exemplaires. **2** *n* **(a) in ~** en trois exemplaires. **(b)** (*third copy*) triplicata *m*. **3** *vt* faire *or* tirer trois exemplaires de.

triply ['trɪplɪ] *adv* triplement.

tripod ['traɪpɒd] *n* trépied *m*.

tripos ['traɪpɒs] *n* (*Cambridge Univ*) examen *m* pour le diplôme de B.A. avec mention.

tripper ['trɪpəʳ] *n* (*Brit*) touriste *mf*, vacancier *m*, -ière *f*; (*on day trip*) excursionniste *mf*.

triptych ['trɪptɪk] *n* triptyque *m*.

trireme ['traɪriːm] *n* trirème *f*.

trisect [traɪ'sekt] *vt* diviser en trois parties (égales).

trisyllabic ['traɪsɪ'læbɪk] *adj* trisyllabe, trisyllabique.

trisyllable [ˌtraɪ'sɪləbl] *n* trisyllabe *m*.

trite [traɪt] *adj* banal, plat, rebattu.

tritely ['traɪtlɪ] *adv* banalement, platement.

triteness ['traɪtnɪs] *n* (*U*) banalité *f*, platitude *f*.

tritium ['trɪtɪəm] *n* tritium *m*.

triton ['traɪtn] *n* (*all senses*) triton *m*.

tritone ['traɪtəʊn] *n* (*Mus*) triton *m*.

triturate ['trɪtʃəreɪt] *vt* triturer, piler.

trituration [ˌtrɪtʃə'reɪʃən] *n* trituration *f*, pilage *m*.

triumph ['traɪʌmf] **1** *n* (*emotion*) sentiment *m* de triomphe; (*victory*) triomphe *m*, victoire *f*; (*success*) triomphe, réussite *f*, succès triomphal; (*Roman Hist*) triomphe. **in ~** en triomphe; **it was a ~ for ...** cela a été un triomphe *or* un succès triomphal pour ...; **it is a ~ of man over nature** c'est le triomphe de l'homme sur la nature; **his ~ at having succeeded** sa satisfaction triomphante d'avoir réussi.

2 *vi* (*lit, fig*) triompher (*over* de).

triumphal [traɪ'ʌmfəl] *adj* triomphal.

triumphant [traɪ'ʌmfənt] *adj homecoming* triomphal; *team, army* triomphant, victorieux; *look, smile* triomphant, de triomphe.

triumphantly [traɪ'ʌmfəntlɪ] *adv return, march* en triomphe, triomphalement; *answer, announce* d'un ton triomphant, triomphalement.

triumvirate [traɪ'ʌmvɪrɪt] *n* triumvirat *m*.

triune ['traɪjuːn] *adj* trin.

trivet ['trɪvɪt] *n* (*over fire*) trépied *m*, chevrette *f*; (*on table*) dessous-de-plat *m inv*.

trivia ['trɪvɪə] *npl* bagatelles *fpl*, futilités *fpl*, fadaises *fpl*.

trivial ['trɪvɪəl] *adj sum, amount, loss* insignifiant, dérisoire; *reason, excuse* insignifiant, sans valeur; *remark, comment* sans importance *or* valeur; *film, book* banal, sans originalité *or* intérêt. **a ~ mistake** une faute légère *or* sans gravité, une peccadille.

triviality [ˌtrɪvɪ'ælɪtɪ] *n* **(a)** (*U: V* **trivial**) caractère insignifiant *or* dérisoire; manque *m* d'importance *or* de valeur *or* d'intérêt; banalité *f*.

(b) trivialities bagatelles *fpl*, futilités *fpl*, fadaises *fpl*.

triweekly ['traɪ'wiːklɪ] **1** *adv* (*thrice weekly*) trois fois par semaine; (*every three weeks*) toutes les trois semaines. **2** *adj event, visit* qui se produit trois fois par semaine (*or* toutes les trois semaines).

trochaic [trɒ'keɪɪk] *adj* trochaïque.

trochee ['trəʊkiː] *n* trochée *m*.

trod [trɒd] *pret of* **tread.**

trodden ['trɒdn] *ptp of* **tread.**

troglodyte ['trɒglədaɪt] *n* troglodyte *m*.

Trojan ['trəʊdʒən] **1** *adj* troyen; *horse, war* de Troie. **2** *n* Troyen(ne) *m(f)*; *V* **work.**

troll [trəʊl] *n* troll *m*.

trolley ['trɒlɪ] **1** *n* (*esp Brit*) (*for luggage*) chariot *m* (à bagages), (*two-wheeled*) diable *m*; (*for shopping*) poussette *f*, (*in supermarket*) chariot; (*tea ~*) table roulante, chariot à desserte, (*in office*) chariot à boissons; (*for stretcher etc*) chariot; (*in mine, quarry etc*) benne roulante; (*Rail*) wagonnet *m*; (*on tramcar*) trolley *m*; (*US: tramcar*) tramway *m*, tram *m*.

2 *cpd*: **trolley bus** trolleybus *m*; (*US*) **trolley car** tramway *m*, tram *m*; (*US*) **trolley line** (*rails*) voie *f* de tramway; (*route*) ligne *f* de tramway; **trolley pole** perche *f* de trolley.

trollop ['trɒləp] *n* putain‡ *f*, garce‡ *f*.

trombone [trɒm'bəʊn] *n* trombone *m* (*Mus*).

trombonist [trɒm'bəʊnɪst] *n* tromboniste *mf*.

troop [truːp] **1** *n* [*people*] bande *f*, groupe *m*; [*animals*] bande, troupe *f*; [*scouts*] troupe; (*Mil: of cavalry*) escadron *m*. (*Mil*) **~s** troupes.

2 *cpd movements etc* de troupes. **troop carrier** (*Aut*) transport *m* de troupes; (*Naut*) transport *m* (*navire*); (*Aviat*) avion *m* de transport militaire; **troopship** transport *m* (*navire*); **troop train** train *m* militaire.

3 *vi*: **to ~ in/past** *etc* entrer/passer *etc* en bande *or* en groupe; **they all ~ed over to the window** ils sont tous allés s'attrouper près de la fenêtre.

4 *vt* (*Brit Mil*) **to ~ the colour** faire la parade du drapeau; (*ceremony*) **~ing the colour** le salut au drapeau.

trooper ['truːpəʳ] *n* (*Mil*) soldat *m* de cavalerie; (*US: state ~*) ≃ C.R.S. *m*; *V* **swear.**

trope [trəʊp] *n* trope *m*.

trophy ['trəʊfɪ] *n* (*Hunting, Mil, Sport*) trophée *m*; (*gen: memento*) souvenir *m*.

tropic ['trɒpɪk] **1** *n* tropique *m*. **T~ of Cancer/Capricorn** tropique du cancer/du capricorne; **in the ~s** sous les tropiques. **2** *adj* (*liter*) = **tropical.**

tropical ['trɒpɪkəl] *adj plant, region* tropical, des tropiques; *heat, rain* tropical.

tropism ['trəʊpɪzəm] *n* tropisme *m*.

troposphere ['trɒpəsfɪəʳ] *n* troposphère *f*.

trot [trɒt] **1** *n* (*pace*) trot *m*. **to go at a ~** [*horse*] aller au trot, trotter; [*person*] trotter; **to go for a ~** (aller) faire du cheval; (*fig*) **5 days/whiskies etc on the ~*** 5 jours/whiskies *etc* de suite *or* d'affilée; **he is always on the ~*** il court tout le temps, il n'a pas une minute de tranquillité; **to keep sb on the ~** ne pas accorder une minute de tranquillité à qn; **to have the ~s‡** (*diarrhoea*) avoir la courante‡.

2 *vi* [*horse*] trotter; [*person*] trotter, courir. [*person*] **to ~ in/past** *etc* entrer/passer *etc* au trot *or* en courant *or* d'un pas pressé.

3 *vt horse* faire trotter.

trot along *vi* **(a)** = **trot over.**

(b) = **trot away.**

trot away, trot off *vi* partir *or* s'éloigner (au trot *or* en courant), filer*.

trot out 1 *vi* sortir (au trot *or* en courant).

2 *vt sep excuses, reasons* débiter; *names, facts etc* réciter d'affilée.

trot over, trot round *vi* aller, courir. **she trotted over** *or* **round to the grocer's** elle a fait un saut *or* a couru chez l'épicier.

troth†† [trəʊθ] *n* promesse *f*, serment *m*; *V* **plight**².

trotter ['trɒtəʳ] *n* **(a)** (*horse*) trotteur *m*, -euse *f*. **(b)** (*Culin*) **pig's/sheep's ~s** pieds *mpl* de porc/de mouton.

troubadour ['truːbədɔːʳ] *n* troubadour *m*.

trouble ['trʌbl] **1** *n* **(a)** (*U: difficulties, unpleasantness*) ennuis *mpl*, difficulté *f*. **to be in ~** avoir des ennuis, être en difficulté; **you're in ~ now** ce coup-ci tu as des ennuis *or* tu as des problèmes; **he's in ~ with the boss** il a des ennuis avec le patron, il s'est fait réprimander par le patron; **to get into ~** s'attirer des ennuis; **he got into ~ for doing that** il a eu *or* il s'est attiré des ennuis pour (avoir fait) cela, il s'est fait attraper pour (avoir fait) ça; **to get sb into ~** causer des ennuis à qn, mettre qn dans le pétrin; (*euph*) **to get a girl into ~*** mettre une (jeune) fille dans une position intéressante (*euph*); **to get out of ~** se tirer d'affaire; **to make ~** causer des ennuis (*for sb* à qn); **you're making ~ for yourself** tu t'attires des ennuis; **I don't want any ~** je ne veux pas d'ennuis; **it's asking for ~** c'est se chercher des ennuis; **he goes around looking for ~** il cherche les ennuis; **here comes ~!*** aïe! des ennuis en perspective!; *V* **meet**¹ *etc*.

(b) (*U: bother, effort*) mal *m*, peine *f*. **it's no ~** cela ne me dérange pas; **it's no ~ to do it properly** ce n'est pas difficile de le faire comme il faut; **it's not worth the ~** cela ne *or* n'en vaut pas la peine; **nothing is too much ~ for her** elle se dévoue *or* se dépense sans compter; **I had all that ~ for nothing** je me suis donné tout ce mal pour rien; **you could have saved yourself the ~** tu aurais pu t'éviter cette peine; **he went to enormous ~ to help us** il s'est donné un mal fou *or* il s'est mis en quatre pour nous aider; **to go to the ~ of doing, to take the ~ to do** se donner la peine *or* le mal de faire; **he went to** *or* **took a lot of ~ over his essay** il s'est vraiment donné beaucoup de mal pour sa dissertation, il s'est vraiment beaucoup appliqué à sa dissertation; **I**

don't want to put you to the ~ of writing je ne veux pas qu'à cause de moi vous vous donniez (*subj*) le mal d'écrire; **I'm putting you to** *or* **giving you a lot of ~** je vous donne beaucoup de mal, je vous dérange beaucoup; **it's no ~ at all!** je vous en prie!, ça ne me dérange pas du tout!

(c) (*difficulty, problem*) difficulté *f*, problème *m*; (*misfortune*) ennui *m*, souci *m*, peine *f*; (*nuisance*) souci, embarras *m*, ennui. **what's the ~?** qu'est-ce qu'il y a?, qu'est-ce qui ne va pas?, qu'est-ce que tu as?; **that's (just) the ~!** c'est ça l'ennui!; **the ~ is that ...** l'ennui *or* le problème (c')est que ...; **the ~ with you is that you can never face the facts** l'ennui avec toi *or* ton défaut c'est que tu ne regardes jamais les choses en face; **the carburettor is giving us ~** nous avons des problèmes *or* des ennuis de carburateur; **the technician is trying to locate the ~** le technicien essaie de localiser la panne *or* le problème; **there has been ~ between them ever since** depuis, ils s'entendent mal; **he caused ~ between them** il a semé la discorde entre eux; **I'm having ~ with my eldest son** mon fils aîné me donne des soucis *or* me cause des ennuis; **the child is a ~ to his parents** l'enfant est un souci pour ses parents; **he had ~ in tying his shoelace** il a eu du mal à attacher son lacet; **did you have any ~ in getting here?** est-ce que vous avez eu des difficultés *or* des problèmes en venant?; **now your ~s are over** vous voilà au bout de vos peines; **his ~s are not yet over** il n'est pas encore au bout de ses peines, il n'est pas encore sorti de l'auberge; **family ~s** ennuis domestiques *or* de famille; **money ~s** soucis *or* ennuis d'argent *or* financiers; (*Med*) **I have back ~, my back is giving me ~** j'ai mal au dos, mon dos me fait souffrir; **kidney/chest ~** ennuis rénaux/pulmonaires; (*Aut*) **we've got engine ~** nous avons des ennuis de moteur, il y a quelque chose qui ne va pas dans le moteur; *V* **heart.**

(d) (*political, social unrest*) conflits *mpl*, troubles *mpl*. **they're having a lot of ~ in Southern Africa** il y a des troubles étendus *or* il y a beaucoup d'agitation *or* la situation est très tendue en Afrique australe; (*Ir Hist*) **the T~s** les troubles; **labour ~s** conflits du travail, troubles sociaux; **there's ~ brewing** le malaise s'accroît, l'orage couve (*fig*); **he caused a lot of ~ between unions and management** il a causé de nombreux désaccords *or* beaucoup de friction entre les syndicats et le patronat; **there's ~ at the factory** ça chauffe* à l'usine.

2 *cpd*: **trouble-free** *period, visit* sans ennuis *or* problèmes *or* soucis; *car* qui ne tombe jamais en panne; *university* non-contestataire; **troublemaker** fauteur *m*, -trice *f* de troubles, provocateur *m*, -trice *f*; **troubleshooter** (*Tech*) expert *m* (appelé en cas de crise); (*Ind, Pol*) conciliateur *m*, médiateur *m*; **troublesome** *V* **troublesome; trouble spot** point *m* de conflit, point chaud *or* névralgique.

3 *vt* **(a)** (*grieve*) affliger, peiner; (*worry*) inquiéter, préoccuper; (*inconvenience*) gêner; (*disturb*) troubler. **his eyes ~ him** il a des ennuis d'yeux; **the heat ~d us** la chaleur nous a gênés; **do these headaches ~ you often?** est-ce que vous souffrez souvent de ces maux de tête?; *V also* **troubled.**

(b) (*bother*) déranger. **I am sorry to ~ you** je suis désolé de vous déranger; **does it ~ you if ...** est-ce que cela vous dérange si ... + *indic or* que ... + *subj*; **don't ~ yourself!** ne vous dérangez pas!, ne vous tracassez pas!; **he didn't ~ himself to reply** il ne s'est pas donné la peine de répondre; **may I ~ you for a light?** puis-je vous demander du feu?; **I'll ~ you to show me the letter!** vous allez me faire le plaisir de me montrer la lettre!; **I shan't ~ you with the details** je vous ferai grâce des détails, je vous passerai les détails.

4 *vi* se déranger. **please don't ~!** ne vous dérangez pas!, ne vous donnez pas cette peine-là!; **to ~ to do** se donner la peine *or* le mal de faire.

troubled ['trʌbld] *adj person* inquiet (*f* -ète), préoccupé; *look, voice* inquiet; *life* agité, orageux; *water* trouble. **to be ~ about sth** s'inquiéter de qch, être préoccupé par qch; **we live in ~ times** nous vivons à une époque agitée *or* mouvementée *or* de troubles; *V* **fish, oil.**

troublesome ['trʌblsəm] *adj person* fatigant, pénible, difficile (à supporter); *request* gênant, embarrassant; *task* ennuyeux, pénible; *cough* gênant, incommodant. **how ~!** quel ennui!

troublous ['trʌbləs] *adj* (*liter*) trouble, agité.

trough [trɒf] *n* **(a)** (*depression*) dépression *f*, creux *m*; (*between waves*) creux (d'une vague); (*channel*) chenal *m*; (*fig*) point bas. (*Met*) **~ of low pressure** dépression, zone *f* dépressionnaire.

(b) (*drinking ~*) abreuvoir *m*; (*feeding ~*) auge *f*; (*kneading ~*) pétrin *m*.

trounce [traʊns] *vt* (*thrash*) rosser, rouer de coups; (*Sport: defeat*) écraser, battre à plate(s) couture(s); (*reprimand*) tancer, réprimander.

troupe [truːp] *n* (*Theat*) troupe *f*.

trouper ['truːpəʳ] *n* (*Theat*) acteur *m*, -trice *f*, artiste *mf* (*qui fait partie d'une troupe de théâtre*).

trouser ['traʊzəʳ] **1** *npl*: **~s** pantalon *m*; **a pair of ~s** un pantalon; **long ~s** pantalon long; **short ~s** culottes courtes; *V* **wear. 2** *cpd*: **trouser clip** pince *f* à pantalon; **trouser leg** jambe *f* de pantalon; **trouser press** presse *f* à pantalons; **trouser suit** tailleur-pantalon *m*.

trousseau ['truːsəʊ] *n* trousseau *m* (*de jeune mariée*).

trout [traʊt] **1** *n, pl inv* truite *f*. **2** *cpd*: **trout fisherman** pêcheur *m* de truites; **trout fishing** pêche *f* à la truite.

trove [trəʊv] *n V* **treasure 2.**

trow†† [traʊ] *vti* croire.

trowel ['traʊəl] *n* (*Constr*) truelle *f*; (*gardening*) déplantoir *m*; *V* **lay on.**

Troy [trɔɪ] *n* Troie.

troy [trɔɪ] *n* (*also* **~ weight**) troy *m*, troy-weight *m*, poids *m* de Troy.

truancy ['truənsɪ] *n* (*Scol*) absence non autorisée (*d'un élève*). **he was punished for ~** il a été puni pour avoir manqué les cours *or* pour s'être absenté; **~ is increasing in inner city schools** le nombre d'élèves qui s'absentent sans autorisation augmente dans les établissements du centre des villes.

truant ['truənt] **1** *n* (*Scol*) élève *mf* qui fait l'école buissonnière. **to play ~** manquer *or* sécher* les cours, faire l'école buissonnière; **he's playing ~ from the office today** (il n'est pas au bureau aujourd'hui,) il fait l'école buissonnière.

2 *adj* (*liter*) *thought* vagabond.

3 *cpd*: (*US*) **truant officer** *fonctionnaire chargé de faire respecter les règlements de la scolarisation.*

truce [truːs] *n* trêve *f*. (*fig*) **to call a ~ to sth** faire trêve à qch.

truck[1] [trʌk] **1** *n* (*U*) (*barter*) troc *m*, échange *m*; (*payment*) paiement *m* en nature; (*US: vegetables*) produits maraîchers. (*fig*) **to have no ~ with** refuser d'avoir affaire à.

2 *cpd*: (*US*) **truck farm** jardin maraîcher; **truck farmer** maraîcher *m*, -ère *f*; **truck garden = truck farm.**

truck[2] [trʌk] **1** *n* (*lorry*) camion *m*; (*Rail*) wagon *m* à plateforme, truck *m*; (*luggage handcart*) chariot *m* à bagages, (*two-wheeled*) diable *m*.

2 *vt* (*esp US*) camionner.

3 *cpd*: **truckdriver** camionneur *m*, routier *m*; **truckload** plein camion; (*US*) **truckman = truckdriver.**

truckage ['trʌkɪdʒ] *n* (*US*) camionnage *m*.

trucker ['trʌkəʳ] *n* (*US*) camionneur *m*, routier *m*.

trucking ['trʌkɪŋ] *n* (*US*) camionnage *m*.

truckle ['trʌkl] **1** *vi* s'humilier, s'abaisser (*to* devant). **2** *cpd*: **truckle bed** lit *m* gigogne *inv*.

truculence ['trʌkjʊləns] *n* brutalité *f*, agressivité *f*.

truculent ['trʌkjʊlənt] *adj* brutal, agressif.

truculently ['trʌkjʊləntlɪ] *adv* brutalement, agressivement.

trudge [trʌdʒ] **1** *vi*: **to ~ in/out/along** *etc* entrer/sortir/marcher *etc* péniblement *or* en traînant les pieds; **we ~d round the shops** nous nous sommes traînés de magasin en magasin; **he ~d through the mud** il pataugeait (péniblement) dans la boue.

2 *vt*: **to ~ the streets/the town** *etc* se traîner de rue en rue/dans toute la ville *etc.*

3 *n* marche *f* pénible.

true [truː] **1** *adj* **(a)** (*exact, accurate*) *story, news, rumour, statement* vrai, véridique; *description, account, report* fidèle, exact, véridique; *copy* conforme; *statistics, measure* exact. **it all turned out to be ~** il s'est finalement trouvé que tout était vrai; **that's ~!** c'est vrai!; **too ~!*** ah oui alors!, je ne te le fais pas dire!; **we mustn't generalize, it's ~, but ...** il ne faut pas généraliser, d'accord *or* c'est vrai, mais ...; **that's wrong! — ~, but ...** c'est faux! — d'accord, *or* c'est juste, *or* c'est vrai, mais ...; **can it be ~ that** est-il possible que +*subj*; **it is ~ that** il est vrai que +*indic*; **is it ~ that** est-il vrai que+*indic or subj*; **it's not ~ that** il n'est pas vrai que+ *indic or subj*; **if it is ~ that** s'il est vrai que+*indic or subj*; **to come ~** se réaliser; **the same holds ~ for** il en va *or* est de même pour, c'est aussi vrai pour; **I certify that this is a ~ likeness of X** je certifie que cette photographie présente une parfaite ressemblance avec X; *V* **good** *etc.*

(b) (*real, genuine*) *repentance, sympathy, friendship* réel, vrai, véritable, authentique. **what is the ~ situation?** quelle est la situation réelle?, quelle est en réalité la situation?; **the one ~ God** le seul vrai Dieu, le seul Dieu véritable; **the frog is not a ~ reptile** la grenouille n'est pas vraiment un reptile; **he is a ~ scholar** c'est un vrai *or* véritable savant; **he has been a ~ friend to me** il a été un vrai *or* véritable ami pour moi; **spoken like a ~ Englishman!** voilà qui est parler en vrai *or* véritable Anglais!; **~ love** (*emotion*) le grand amour; (*lover*) bien-aimé(e) *m(f)*; **~ north** le nord vrai *or* géographique.

(c) (*faithful*) **to be ~ to sb/sth** être fidèle à qn/qch; **there were 60 of them, all good men and ~** ils étaient 60, tous loyaux et braves; **~ to life** réaliste; **to be** *or* **run ~ to type** être conforme au type; **~ to type, he refused to help** comme on aurait pu s'y attendre, il a refusé de prêter son aide; **the horse ran ~ to form** le cheval a fait une course digne de lui.

(d) *surface, join* plan, uniforme; *wall, upright* vertical, d'aplomb; *beam* droit; *wheel* dans l'axe; (*Mus*) *voice, instrument, note* juste.

2 *n*: **out of ~** *upright, wall* pas d'aplomb; *beam* tordu, gauchi; *surface* gondolé; *join* mal aligné; *wheel* voilé, faussé.

3 *adv aim, sing* juste. **to breed ~** se reproduire selon le type parental; **tell me ~** dis-moi la vérité; *V* **ring**[2].

4 *cpd*: **true-blue*** loyal; **true-born** véritable, vrai, authentique; **true-bred** de race pure, racé; **true-false test** questionnaire *m or* test *m* du type 'vrai ou faux'; **true-hearted** loyal; sincère; **true-life** vrai, vécu.

truffle ['trʌfl] *n* truffe *f*.

trug [trʌg] *n* (*Brit*) corbeille *f* de jardinier.

truism ['truːɪzəm] *n* truisme *m*.

truly ['truːlɪ] *adv* (*truthfully*) sans mentir, franchement; (*genuinely*) vraiment, réellement; (*faithfully*) fidèlement. **tell me ~** dis-moi la vérité; **I ~ believe that ...** je crois vraiment *or* réellement que ...; **to love sb ~** aimer vraiment qn; **he did say so, ~ (he did)!** il l'a dit, je te jure!*; **really and ~?** vraiment?, vraiment vrai?*; **it reflects public opinion very ~** c'est un reflet très fidèle de *or* cela reflète parfaitement l'opinion publique; **he's a ~ great writer** c'est véritablement un grand écrivain; **a ~ terrible film** un vrai *or* véritable navet, un film vraiment mauvais; **well and ~** bel et bien; (*letter ending*) **yours ~** je vous prie d'agréer l'expression de mes sentiments respectueux *or* (*man to woman*) de mes très respectueux hommages; **nobody knows it better than yours ~*** personne ne le sait mieux que votre humble serviteur (*hum*).

trump[1] [trʌmp] **1** *n* (*Cards*) atout *m*. **spades are ~(s)** l'atout est pique, c'est atout pique; **what's ~(s)?** quel est l'atout?; **the three**

of ~(s) le trois d'atout; (*fig*) **he had a ~ up his sleeve** il avait un atout en réserve; (*fig*) **he was holding all the ~s** il avait tous les atouts dans son jeu; (*Brit fig*) **to turn up ~s*** faire des merveilles; *V* **no.**

2 *cpd*: (*fig*) **his trump card** sa carte maîtresse, son atout.

3 *vt* (*Cards*) couper, prendre avec l'atout. (*fig*) **to ~ sb's ace** faire encore mieux que qn.

trump up *vt sep charge, excuse* forger *or* inventer (de toutes pièces).

trump[2] [trʌmp] *n* (*liter*) trompette *f*. **the Last T~** la trompette du Jugement (dernier).

trumpery ['trʌmpərɪ] **1** *n* (*U*) (*showy trash*) camelote* *f* (*U*); (*nonsense*) bêtises *fpl*. **2** *adj* (*showy*) criard; (*paltry*) insignifiant, sans valeur.

trumpet ['trʌmpɪt] **1** *n* **(a)** (*instrument*) trompette *f*; (*player*) trompette *m*, trompettiste *mf*; (*~-shaped object*) cornet *m*; *V* **ear**[1].

(b) *[elephant]* barrissement *m*.

2 *cpd*: **trumpet blast** coup *m or* sonnerie *f* de trompette; **trumpet call** (*lit*) = **trumpet blast**; (*fig*) vibrant appel (*for* pour).

3 *vi [elephant]* barrir.

4 *vt* trompeter.

trumpeter ['trʌmpɪtə[r]] *n* trompettiste *mf*.

trumpeting ['trʌmpɪtɪŋ] *n [elephant]* barrissement(s) *m(pl)*.

truncate [trʌŋ'keɪt] *vt* tronquer.

truncheon ['trʌntʃən] *n* (*weapon*) matraque *f*; (*Brit: for directing traffic*) bâton *m* (*d'agent de police*).

trundle ['trʌndl] **1** *vt* (*push/pull/roll*) pousser/traîner/faire rouler bruyamment.

2 *vi*: **to ~ in/along/down** entrer/passer/descendre lourdement *or* bruyamment.

trunk [trʌŋk] **1** *n* (*Anat, Bot*) tronc *m*; *[elephant]* trompe *f*; (*case*) malle *f*; (*US Aut*) coffre *m*, malle. **~s** (*swimming*) slip *m or* maillot *m* de bain; (*underwear*) slip (d'homme); (*Telec*†) l'inter *m*; *V* **subscriber.**

2 *cpd*: (*Brit Telec*) **trunk call** communication interurbaine; **trunk line** (*Telec*) inter *m*, téléphone interurbain; (*Rail*) grande ligne; (*Brit*) **trunk road** (route *f*) nationale *f*.

trunnion ['trʌnɪən] *n* tourillon *m*.

truss [trʌs] **1** *n [hay etc]* botte *f*; *[flowers, fruit on branch]* grappe *f*; (*Constr*) ferme *f*; (*Med*) bandage *m* herniaire. **2** *vt hay* botteler; *chicken* trousser; (*Constr*) armer, renforcer.

truss up *vt sep chicken* trousser; *prisoner* ligoter.

trust [trʌst] **1** *n* **(a)** (*U: faith, reliance*) confiance *f* (*in* en). **position of ~** poste *m* de confiance; **breach of ~** abus *m* de confiance; **to have ~ in sb/sth** avoir confiance en qn/qch; **to put** *or* **place one's ~ in sb/sth** faire confiance *or* se fier à qn/qch; **to take sth on ~** accepter qch de confiance *or* les yeux fermés; **you'll have to take what I say on ~** il vous faudra me croire sur parole; (*without payment*) **he gave it to me on ~** il me l'a donné sans me faire payer tout de suite.

(b) (*Jur*) fidéicommis *m*. **to hold sth/leave money in ~ for one's children** tenir qch/faire administrer un legs par fidéicommis à l'intention de ses enfants.

(c) (*charge, responsibility*) charge *f*, devoir *m*, obligation *f*. **to give sth into sb's ~** confier qch à la charge de qn.

(d) (*Comm, Fin*) trust *m*, cartel *m*; *V* **brain, investment, unit** *etc*.

2 *cpd*: (*Banking*) **trust account** compte *m* en fidéicommis; (*US*) **trust company** société *f* fiduciaire; **trust fund** fonds *m* en fidéicommis; (*Pol*) **trust territory** *territoire confié à un pays par les Nations Unies*; **trustworthy** *V* **trustworthy.**

3 *vt* **(a)** (*believe in, rely on*) *person, object* avoir confiance en, se fier à; *method, promise* se fier à. **don't you ~ me?** tu n'as pas confiance (en moi)?; **he is not to be ~ed** on ne peut pas lui faire confiance; **you can ~ me** vous pouvez avoir confiance en moi; **you can ~ me with your car** tu peux me confier ta voiture, tu peux me prêter ta voiture en toute confiance; **he's not to be ~ed with a knife** il ne serait pas prudent de le laisser manipuler un couteau; **can we ~ him to do it?** peut-on compter sur lui pour le faire?; **the child is too young to be ~ed on the roads** l'enfant est trop petit pour qu'on le laisse (*subj*) aller dans la rue tout seul; **I can't ~ him out of my sight** j'ai si peu confiance en lui que je ne le quitte pas des yeux; (*iro*) **~ you!*** ça ne m'étonne pas de toi!, (pour) ça on peut te faire confiance! (*iro*); (*iro*) **~ him to break it!*** pour casser quelque chose on peut lui faire confiance!; **he can be ~ed to do his best** on peut être sûr qu'il fera de son mieux; **you can't ~ a word he says** impossible de croire deux mots de ce qu'il raconte; **I wouldn't ~ him as far as I can throw him*** je n'ai absolument aucune confiance en lui.

(b) (*entrust*) confier (*sth to sb* qch à qn).

(c) (*hope*) espérer (*that* que). **I ~ not** j'espère que non.

4 *vi*: **to ~ in sb** se fier à qn, s'en remettre à qn; **let's ~ to luck** *or* **to chance** essayons tout de même, tentons notre chance, tentons le coup*; **I'll have to ~ to luck to find the house** il faudra que je m'en remette à la chance pour trouver la maison.

trusted ['trʌstɪd] *adj friend, servant* en qui l'on a toute confiance; *method* éprouvé.

trustee [trʌs'tiː] **1** *n* **(a)** (*Jur*) fidéicommissaire *m*, curateur *m*, -trice *f*, fiduciaire *m*. **(b)** *[institution, school]* administrateur *m*, -trice *f*. **the ~s** le conseil d'administration. **2** *cpd*: (*Brit*) **Trustee Savings Bank** ≈ Caisse *f* d'Épargne.

trusteeship [trʌs'tiːʃɪp] *n* **(a)** (*Jur*) fidéicommis *m*, curatelle *f*. **(b)** *[institution etc]* poste *m* d'administrateur. **during his ~** pendant qu'il était administrateur.

trustful ['trʌstfʊl] *adj* confiant.

trustfully ['trʌstfəlɪ] *adv* avec confiance.

trusting ['trʌstɪŋ] *adj* = **trustful.**

trustworthiness ['trʌst,wɜːðɪnɪs] *n* (*U*) *[person]* loyauté *f*, fidélité *f*; *[statement]* véracité *f*.

trustworthy ['trʌst,wɜːðɪ] *adj person* digne de confiance; *report, account* fidèle, exact.

trusty ['trʌstɪ] *adj* († *or hum*) sûr, loyal, fidèle. **my ~ sword** ma fidèle épée.

truth [truːθ] *pl* **~s** [truːðz] **1** *n* **(a)** (*U*) vérité *f*. **you must always tell the ~** il faut toujours dire la vérité; **to tell the ~,** *or* **~ to tell, he ...** à vrai dire, *or* à dire vrai, il ... ; **the ~ of it is that** la vérité c'est que; **there's no ~ in what he says** il n'y a pas un mot de vrai dans ce qu'il dit; **there's some ~ in that** il y a du vrai dans ce qu'il dit (*or* dans ce que vous dites *etc*); (*Prov*) **~ will out** la vérité finira (toujours) par se savoir; (*Jur*) **the ~, the whole ~ and nothing but the ~** la vérité, toute la vérité et rien que la vérité; **the plain unvarnished ~** la vérité toute nue, la vérité sans fard; **in ~** en vérité.

(b) vérité *f*; *V* **home.**

2 *cpd*: **truth drug** sérum *m* de vérité.

truthful ['truːθfʊl] *adj person* qui dit la vérité; *statement, account* véridique, vrai.

truthfully ['truːθfəlɪ] *adv answer* véridiquement, sans mentir. **I don't mind, ~** sincèrement, ça m'est égal.

truthfulness ['truːθfʊlnɪs] *n* (*U*) véracité *f*.

try [traɪ] **1** *n* **(a)** (*attempt*) essai *m*, tentative *f*. **to have a ~** essayer (*at doing* de faire); **to give sth a ~** essayer qch; **he had a ~ for the job** il s'est présenté pour le poste; **it was a good ~** il a (*or* tu as *etc*) vraiment essayé; **it's worth a ~** cela vaut le coup d'essayer; **to do sth at the first ~** faire qch du premier coup; **after 3 tries he gave up** après avoir essayé 3 fois, il a abandonné.

(b) (*Rugby*) essai *m*. **to score a ~** marquer un essai.

2 *cpd*: **it's a try-on*** c'est du bluff; **tryout** essai *m*.

3 *vt* **(a)** (*attempt*) essayer, tâcher (*to do* de faire); (*seek*) chercher (*to do* à faire). **~ to eat** *or* **~ and eat some of it** essaie *or* tâche d'en manger un peu; **he was ~ing to understand** il essayait de *or* tâchait de *or* cherchait à comprendre; **it's ~ing to rain*** il a l'air de vouloir pleuvoir*; **I'll ~ anything once** je suis toujours prêt à faire un essai; (*warning*) **just you ~ it!** essaie donc un peu!, essaie un peu pour voir!*; **you've only tried 3 questions** vous avez seulement essayé de répondre à 3 questions; **have you ever tried the high jump?** as-tu déjà essayé le saut en hauteur?; **to ~ one's best** *or* **one's hardest** faire de son mieux, faire tout son possible (*to do* pour faire); **to ~ one's hand at (doing) sth** s'essayer à (faire) qch.

(b) (*sample, experiment with*) *method, recipe, new material, new car etc* essayer. **have you tried these olives?** avez-vous goûté à *or* essayé ces olives?; **won't you ~ me for the job?** vous ne voulez pas me faire faire un essai?; **have you tried aspirin?** avez-vous essayé (de prendre de) l'aspirine?; **~ pushing that button** essayez de presser ce bouton; **~ this for size** essaie cela pour voir si c'est ta taille (*garment*) *or* si c'est ta pointure (*shoe*) *or* si ça marche (*spanner, screw etc*); (*‡fig: offering any object*) essaie ça pour voir.

(c) (*test, put strain on*) *person, sb's patience, strength, endurance, eyes, eyesight* mettre à l'épreuve, éprouver; *vehicle, plane* tester; *machine, gadget* tester, mettre à l'essai. **to ~ one's strength against sb** se mesurer à qn; **to ~ one's luck** tenter sa chance, tenter le coup; **this material has been tried and tested** ce tissu a subi tous les tests; **he was tried and found wanting** il ne s'est pas montré à la hauteur, il n'a pas répondu à ce qu'on attendait de lui; **they have been sorely tried** ils ont été durement éprouvés.

(d) (*Jur*) *person, case* juger. **to ~ sb for theft** juger qn pour vol; (*Mil*) **he was tried by court-martial** il est passé en conseil de guerre.

4 *vi* essayer. **~ again!** recommence!, refais un essai!; **I didn't even ~ (to)** je n'ai même pas essayé; **to ~ for a job/a scholarship** essayer d'obtenir un poste/une bourse.

try on 1 *vt sep* **(a)** *garment, shoe* essayer.

(b) (*) **to try it on with sb** essayer de voir jusqu'où on peut pousser qn; **he's trying it on** il essaie de voir jusqu'où il peut aller (*fig*); **he's trying it on to see how you'll react** il essaie de voir comment tu vas réagir; **don't try anything on!** ne fais pas le malin!

2 try-on* *n V* **try 2.**

try out 1 *vt sep machine, new material* essayer, faire l'essai de; *new drug, new recipe, method, solution* essayer; *new teacher, employee etc* mettre à l'essai. **try it out on the cat first** essaie d'abord de voir quelle est la réaction du chat.

2 tryout *n V* **try 2.**

try over *vt sep* (*Mus*) essayer.

trying ['traɪɪŋ] *adj person* fatigant, pénible; *work* ennuyeux, fastidieux, pénible; *experience* pénible, douloureux. **to have a ~ time** passer un (*or* des) moment(s) difficile(s) *or* pénible(s); (*longer*) avoir une mauvaise période.

tryst†† [trɪst] *n* rendez-vous *m* (d'amour).

tsar [zɑː[r]] *n* tsar *m*.

tsarina [zɑː'riːnə] *n* tsarine *f*.

tsetse fly ['tsetsɪflaɪ] *n* mouche *f* tsé-tsé *inv*.

tub [tʌb] **1** *n* (*gen*) cuve *f*; (*for washing clothes*) baquet *m*, bac *m*; (*also* **bath~**) tub *m*, (*in bathroom*) baignoire *f*; (*: *boat*) sabot* *m*, rafiau* *m or* rafiot* *m*; (*for cream etc*) (petit) pot *m*. (*Brit*) **to have a ~*** prendre un bain (*or* un tub).

2 *cpd*: (*Brit fig*) **tub-thumper** orateur *m* démagogue; (*Brit fig*) **tub-thumping** (*n: U*) démagogie *f*; (*adj*) démagogique.

tuba ['tjuːbə] *n* tuba *m*.

tubby* ['tʌbɪ] *adj* rondelet, dodu, boulot (*f* -otte) (*esp of woman*).

tube [tjuːb] **1** *n* (*gen, Anat, Telec, TV*) tube *m*; *[tyre]* chambre *f* à air. (*Brit: the underground*) **the ~** le métro; (*Brit*) **to go by ~** prendre le métro; (*US: television*) **the ~*** la télé*; *V* **inner** *etc*.

2 *cpd*: (*Brit*) **tube station** station *f* de métro.

tubeless ['tju:blɪs] *adj tyre* sans chambre à air.

tuber ['tju:bər] *n* (*Bot*) tubercule *m*.

tubercle ['tju:bɜ:kl] *n* (*Anat, Bot, Med*) tubercule *m*.

tubercular [tjʊ'bɜ:kjʊlər] *adj* (*Anat, Bot, Med*) tuberculeux.

tuberculin [tjʊ'bɜ:kjʊlɪn] *n* tuberculine *f*. **~-tested cows** vaches tuberculinisées.

tuberculosis [tjʊ,bɜ:kjʊ'ləʊsɪs] *n* tuberculose *f*.

tuberculous [tjʊ'bɜ:kjʊləs] *adj* = **tubercular.**

tubing ['tju:bɪŋ] *n* (*U*) tube(s) *m(pl)*, tuyau(x) *m(pl)*.

tubular ['tju:bjʊlər] *adj* tubulaire. (*Mus*) **~ bells** carillon *m* (d'orchestre).

tuck [tʌk] **1** *n* **(a)** (*Sewing etc*) rempli *m*. **to put** *or* **take a ~ in sth** faire un rempli dans qch.

(b) (*Brit* :: *U: food*) boustifaille: *f*.

2 *cpd*: (*Brit Scol*) **tuckbox** boîte *f* à provisions; **tuck-in*** bon repas, festin *m* (*hum*); **they had a (good) tuck-in*** ils ont vraiment bien mangé; (*Brit Scol*) **tuck-shop** comptoir *m or* boutique *f* à provisions.

3 *vt* **(a)** (*gen*) mettre. **he ~ed the book under his arm** il a mis *or* rangé le livre sous son bras; **he ~ed his shirt into his trousers** il a rentré sa chemise dans son pantalon; **he was sitting with his feet ~ed under him** il avait les pieds repliés sous lui.

(b) (*Sewing*) faire un rempli dans.

4 *vi*: **to ~ into a meal*** attaquer un repas.

tuck away *vt sep* **(a)** (*put away*) mettre, ranger. **tuck it away out of sight** cache-le; **the hut is tucked away among the trees** la cabane se cache *or* est cachée *or* est perdue parmi les arbres.

(b) (*: *eat*) bouffer:.

tuck in 1 *vi* (*: *eat*) (bien) boulotter*. **tuck in!** allez(-y)!, attaquez!*

2 *vt sep shirt, flap, stomach* rentrer; *bedclothes* border. **to tuck sb in** border qn.

3 tuck-in* *n V* **tuck 2.**

tuck under *vt sep flap* rentrer.

tuck up *vt sep skirt, sleeves* remonter; *hair* relever; *legs* replier. **to tuck sb up (in bed)** border qn (dans son lit).

tucker¹†† ['tʌkər] *n* (*Dress*) fichu *m*; *V* **bib.**

tucker²* ['tʌkər] *vt* (*US*) fatiguer, crever*.

Tudor ['tju:dər] *adj* (*Archit*) Tudor *inv*; (*period*) des Tudors.

Tuesday ['tju:zdɪ] *n* mardi *m*; *V* **shrove**; *for other phrases V* **Saturday.**

tufa ['tju:fə] *n* tuf *m* calcaire.

tuffet ['tʌfɪt] *n* [*grass*] touffe *f* d'herbe; (*stool*) (petit) tabouret *m*.

tuft [tʌft] *n* touffe *f*. (*Orn*) **~ of feathers** huppe *f*, aigrette *f*.

tufted ['tʌftɪd] *adj grass* en touffe; *bird* huppé.

tug [tʌg] **1** *n* **(a)** (*pull*) (petite) saccade *f*, (petit) coup *m*. **to give sth a ~** tirer sur qch; **I felt a ~ at my sleeve/on the rope** j'ai senti qu'on me tirait par la manche/qu'on tirait sur la corde; (*fig*) **parting with them was quite a ~** les quitter a été un vrai déchirement.

(b) (*also* **~boat**) remorqueur *m*.

2 *cpd*: **tug-of-love*** *lutte acharnée entre les parents pour avoir la garde d'un enfant*; **tug-of-war** (*Sport*) lutte *f* à la corde; (*fig*) lutte (acharnée *or* féroce).

3 *vt* (*pull*) *rope, sleeve etc* tirer sur; (*drag*) tirer, traîner; (*Naut*) remorquer. **to ~ sth up/down** faire monter/faire descendre qch en le tirant *or* traînant.

4 *vi* tirer fort *or* sec (*at, on* sur).

tuition [tjʊ'ɪʃən] *n* (*U*) cours *mpl*. **private ~** cours particuliers (*in* de).

tulip ['tju:lɪp] *n* tulipe *f*. **~ tree** tulipier *m*.

tulle [tju:l] *n* tulle *m*.

tumble ['tʌmbl] **1** *n* **(a)** (*fall*) chute *f*, culbute *f*; [*acrobat etc*] culbute, cabriole *f*. **to have** *or* **take a ~** faire une chute *or* une culbute; (*fig*) **they had a ~ in the hay** ils ont folâtré dans le foin.

(b) (*confusion*) désordre *m*; (*confused heap*) amas *m*.

2 *cpd*: **tumbledown** en ruine(s), délabré; **tumble dryer** tambour *m or* séchoir *m* (à linge) à air chaud; **tumbleweed** (espèce *f* d')amarante *f*.

3 *vi* **(a)** (*fall*) faire une chute, tomber, dégringoler; (*trip*) trébucher (*over* sur); (*fig*) [*person, ruler etc*] faire la culbute; [*acrobat etc*] faire des culbutes *or* des cabrioles. **to ~ head over heels** faire la culbute, culbuter; **to ~ downstairs** culbuter *or* dégringoler dans l'escalier; **he ~d over a chair** il a trébuché sur une chaise; **he ~d over the cliff/into the river** il est tombé du haut de la falaise/dans la rivière.

(b) (*rush*) se jeter. **he ~d into bed** il s'est jeté au lit; **he ~d out of bed** (*fell*) il est tombé du lit; (*rushed*) il a bondi hors du lit; **they ~d out of the car** ils ont déboulé de la voiture; **the clothes ~d out of the cupboard** la pile de vêtements a dégringolé quand on a ouvert le placard.

(c) (*Brit* fig: realize*) **to ~ to sth** réaliser* qch.

4 *vt pile, heap* renverser, faire tomber, faire culbuter; *hair* ébouriffer; *books, objects* jeter en tas *or* en vrac.

tumble about, tumble around 1 *vi* [*puppies, children*] gambader, s'ébattre, folâtrer; [*acrobat*] cabrioler.

2 *vt sep books, objects* mélanger.

tumble down 1 *vi* [*person*] faire une chute *or* une culbute, culbuter. [*building etc*] **to be tumbling down** tomber en ruine(s), menacer ruine.

2 tumbledown *adj V* **tumble 2.**

tumble out 1 *vi* [*objects, contents*] tomber en vrac, s'éparpiller.

2 *vt sep objects, contents* faire tomber en vrac.

tumble over 1 *vi* culbuter.

2 *vt sep* renverser, faire tomber, faire culbuter.

tumbler ['tʌmblər] *n* (*glass*) verre *m* (droit); (*of plastic, metal*) gobelet *m*; (*in lock*) gorge *f* (de serrure); (*tumble dryer*) tambour *m or* séchoir *m* (à linge) à air chaud; (*Tech etc: revolving drum*) tambour rotatif; (*acrobat*) acrobate *mf*; (*pigeon*) pigeon culbutant.

tumbrel ['tʌmbrəl] *n*, **tumbril** ['tʌmbrɪl] *n* tombereau *m*.

tumefaction [,tju:mɪ'fækʃən] *n* tuméfaction *f*.

tumescent [tju:'mesnt] *adj* tumescent.

tumid ['tju:mɪd] *adj* (*Med*) tuméfié; (*fig*) ampoulé.

tumy* ['tʌmɪ] *n* ventre *m*. **~ache** mal *m* de ventre.

tumour, (*US*) **tumor** ['tju:mər] *n* tumeur *f*.

tumuli ['tju:mjʊlaɪ] *npl of* **tumulus.**

tumult ['tju:mʌlt] *n* (*uproar*) tumulte *m*; (*emotional*) émoi *m*. **in a ~** dans le tumulte; (*emotionally*) en émoi.

tumultuous [tju:'mʌltjʊəs] *adj* tumultueux.

tumultuously [tju:'mʌltjʊəslɪ] *adv* tumultueusement.

tumulus ['tju:mjʊləs] *n, pl* **tumuli** tumulus *m*.

tun [tʌn] *n* fût *m*, tonneau *m*.

tuna ['tju:nə] *n* (*also* **~ fish**) thon *m*.

tundra ['tʌndrə] *n* toundra *f*.

tune [tju:n] **1** *n* **(a)** (*melody*) air *m*. **he gave us a ~ on the piano** il nous a joué un air au piano; **there's not much ~ to it** ce n'est pas très mélodieux; **to the ~ of** *sing* sur l'air de; *march, process* aux accents de; (*fig*) **to the ~ of £30** et c'est (*or* c'était) la coquette somme de 30 livres; (*fig*) **to change one's ~, to sing another ~** changer de ton.

(b) (*U*) **to be in ~** [*instrument*] être accordé; [*singer*] chanter juste; **to be out of ~** [*instrument*] être désaccordé; [*singer*] chanter faux; **to sing/play in ~** chanter/jouer juste; **to sing/play out of ~** chanter/jouer faux; (*fig*) **to be in/out of ~ with** être en accord/désaccord avec.

2 *cpd*: (*Aut*) **tune-up** réglage *m*, mise *f* au point.

3 *vt* (*Mus*) accorder; (*Rad, TV: also* **~ in**) régler (*to* sur); (*Aut*) régler, mettre au point. (*Rad*) **you are ~d (in) to ...** vous êtes à l'écoute de ... ; *V* **stay**[1].

tune in (*Rad, TV*) **1** *vi* se mettre à l'écoute (*to* de). **tune in again tomorrow** soyez de nouveau à l'écoute demain.

2 *vt sep* régler (*to* sur). (*fig*) **he is/isn't tuned in:** il est/n'est pas dans la course*; *V also* **tune 3.**

tune up 1 *vi* (*Mus*) accorder son (*or* ses) instrument(s).

2 *vt sep* (*Mus*) accorder; (*Aut*) mettre au point.

3 tune-up *n V* **tune 2.**

tuneful ['tju:nfʊl] *adj voice, music, instrument, opera* mélodieux; *singer* à la voix mélodieuse.

tunefully ['tju:nfəlɪ] *adv* mélodieusement.

tunefulness ['tju:nfʊlnɪs] *n* (*V* **tuneful**) caractère mélodieux; voix mélodieuse.

tuneless ['tju:nlɪs] *adj* peu mélodieux, discordant.

tunelessly ['tju:nlɪslɪ] *adv sing, play* faux.

tuner ['tju:nər] **1** *n* (*person*) accordeur *m*; (*Rad: also* **stereo ~**) radio-préamplificateur *m*; (*knob*) bouton *m* de réglage; *V* **piano. 2** *cpd*: **tuner amplifier** radio-ampli *m*.

tungsten ['tʌŋstən] *n* (*U*) tungstène *m*.

tunic ['tju:nɪk] *n* tunique *f*.

tuning ['tju:nɪŋ] **1** *n* (*Mus*) accord *m*; (*Rad, TV*) réglage *m*; (*Aut*) réglage(s), mise *f* au point. **2** *cpd*: (*Mus*) **tuning fork** diapason *m*; (*Rad etc*) **tuning knob** bouton *m* de réglage.

Tunis ['tju:nɪs] *n* Tunis.

Tunisia [tju:'nɪzɪə] *n* Tunisie *f*.

Tunisian [tju:'nɪzɪən] **1** *adj* tunisien. **2** *n* Tunisien(ne) *m(f)*.

tunnel ['tʌnl] **1** *n* (*gen, Rail*) tunnel *m*; (*Min*) galerie *f*. **to make a ~ = to tunnel** (*V* 3); *V also* **channel.**

2 *cpd*: (*Opt*) **tunnel vision** rétrécissement *m* du champ visuel; (*fig*) **to have tunnel vision** voir les choses avec des œillères.

3 *vi* [*people, rabbits etc*] percer *or* creuser un *or* des tunnel(s) *or* des galeries (*in* dans, *under* sous). **to ~ in/out** *etc* entrer/sortir *etc* en creusant un tunnel.

4 *vt* percer *or* creuser un *or* des tunnel(s) dans. **a mound ~led by rabbits** un monticule dans lequel les lapins ont percé *or* creusé des galeries; **shelters ~led out of the hillside** des abris creusés à flanc de colline; **to ~ one's way in** *etc* = **to tunnel in** *etc* (*V* 3).

tunny ['tʌnɪ] *n* = **tuna.**

tuppence ['tʌpəns] *n* (*abbr of* **twopence**) deux pence *mpl*. (*fig*) **it's not worth ~*** ça ne vaut pas un radis*; **I don't care ~*** je m'en fiche (comme de l'an quarante)*.

tuppenny ['tʌpənɪ] *adj* (*abbr of* **twopenny**) à *or* de deux pence. (*fig*) **~-ha'penny** de rien du tout*, de deux sous.

turban ['tɜ:bən] *n* turban *m*.

turbid ['tɜ:bɪd] *adj* turbide.

turbidity [tɜ:'bɪdɪtɪ] *n* turbidité *f*.

turbine ['tɜ:baɪn] *n* turbine *f*. **steam/gas ~** turbine à vapeur/à gaz.

turbo... ['tɜ:bəʊ] *pref* turbo... .

turbofan ['tɜ:bəʊ,fæn] *n* (*fan*) turbofan *m*; (*also* **~ engine**) turbofan *m*, turboventilateur *m*.

turbogenerator ['tɜ:bəʊ,dʒenəreɪtər] *n* turbogénérateur *m*.

turbojet ['tɜ:bəʊ'dʒet] *n* (*also* **~ engine**) turboréacteur *m*; (*also* **~ aircraft**) avion *m* à turboréacteur.

turboprop ['tɜ:bəʊ'prɒp] *n* (*also* **~ engine**) turbopropulseur *m*; (*also* **~ aircraft**) avion *m* à turbopropulseur.

turbosupercharger [,tɜ:bəʊ'su:pətʃɑ:dʒər] *n* turbocompresseur *m* de suralimentation.

turbot ['tɜ:bət] *n* turbot *m*.

turbulence ['tɜ:bjʊləns] *n* (*U*) turbulence *f* (*also Aviat*); [*waves, sea*] agitation *f*.

turbulent ['tɜ:bjʊlənt] *adj crowd, class, passions, person, personality, mood* turbulent; *waves, sea* agité.

turd∵ [tɜ:d] *n* merde∵ *f*; (*person*) con∵ *m*, couillon∵ *m*.

tureen [tə'ri:n] *n* soupière *f*.

turf [tɜ:f] **1** *n* (*U*) (*grass*) gazon *m*; (*peat*) tourbe *f*; (*Sport*) turf *m*. (*Sport*) **the T~** le turf.

2 *cpd*: (*Brit*) **turf accountant** bookmaker *m*.

3 vt (a) (also ~ over) land gazonner.
(b) (Brit*) (throw) balancer*, jeter; (push) pousser; (put) mettre, flanquer*.

turf in* vt sep (Brit) objects balancer* dedans. (fig: give up) he turfed it all in‡ il a tout laissé tomber*.

turf out* vt sep (Brit) objects sortir; (throw away) bazarder*; person flanquer à la porte*, virer*; (‡) suggestion démolir*.

turgid ['tɜːdʒɪd] adj turgide; (fig) style, language boursouflé, ampoulé.

Turk [tɜːk] n Turc m, Turque f. (fig: esp Pol) young ~ jeune loup m, jeune homme m aux dents longues.

Turkey ['tɜːkɪ] n Turquie f.

turkey ['tɜːkɪ] 1 n dindon m, dinde f; (Culin) dinde; (US Theat‡: flop) four* m. (US fig) to talk ~* parler net or franc; (Drugs sl) cold ~ manque m. 2 cpd: turkey buzzard vautour m aura; turkey cock dindon m.

Turkish ['tɜːkɪʃ] 1 adj turc (f turque). 2 cpd: Turkish bath bain turc; (Culin: U) Turkish delight lo(u)koum m; Turkish towel serviette f éponge inv; (U) Turkish towelling tissu m éponge (U). 3 n (Ling) turc m.

turmeric ['tɜːmərɪk] n (U) curcuma m, safran m des Indes.

turmoil ['tɜːmɔɪl] n agitation f, trouble m; (emotional) trouble, émoi m. everything was in a ~ c'était le bouleversement or le chambardement* le plus complet.

turn [tɜːn] 1 n (a) (movement: of wheel, handle etc) tour m. to give sth a ~ tourner qch; to give a screw a ~ donner un tour de vis; with a ~ of his head he could see ... en tournant la tête il voyait ... ; (Culin) done to a ~ à point; V hand.
(b) (change: of direction, condition) tournure f; (bend: in road etc) tournant m, virage m. to make a ~ [person, vehicle] tourner; [road, ship] virer; 'no left ~' 'défense de tourner à gauche'; take the next left ~ prenez la prochaine route à gauche; (walk) to go for or take a ~ in the park aller faire un tour dans le parc; the milk is on the ~ le lait commence à tourner; at the ~ of the century en début (or en fin) de siècle; (specifically) fin dix-neuvième et début vingtième etc; at the ~ of the year vers la fin de l'année, en fin d'année; (fig) at every ~ à tout instant; things took a new ~ les choses ont pris une nouvelle tournure; events took a tragic ~ les événements ont pris un tour or une tournure tragique; [events] to take a ~ for the worse s'aggraver; to take a ~ for the better s'améliorer; the patient took a ~ for the worse/better l'état du malade s'est aggravé/amélioré; V tide.
(c) (Med: crisis) crise f, attaque f; (fright) coup m. he had one of his ~s last night il a eu une nouvelle crise or attaque la nuit dernière; she has giddy ~s elle a des vertiges; it gave me quite a ~*, it gave me a nasty ~* ça m'a fait un coup*.
(d) (action etc) to do sb a good ~ rendre un service à qn; to do sb a bad ~ jouer un mauvais tour à qn; that's my good ~ for the day j'ai fait ma bonne action or B.A.* pour la journée; (Prov) one good ~ deserves another un prêté pour un rendu (Prov); it has served its ~ ça a fait son temps.
(e) (Theat etc) numéro m. to do a ~ faire un numéro; V star.
(f) (in game, queue, series) tour m. it's your ~ c'est votre tour, c'est à vous; it's your ~ to play (c'est) à vous de jouer; whose ~ is it? c'est à qui de jouer?, c'est à qui le tour?; wait your ~ attendez votre tour; they answered in ~ ils ont répondu chacun à leur tour, ils ont répondu à tour de rôle; they played in ~ or by ~s ils ont joué à tour de rôle; I feel hot and cold by ~s or in ~ j'ai tour à tour trop chaud et trop froid; ~ (and ~) about à tour de rôle; to take it ~ (and ~) about to do sth, to take ~s at doing sth, to take it in ~(s) to do sth faire qch à tour de rôle; take it in ~s! chacun son tour!; to take ~s at the wheel se relayer au volant; to take a ~ at the wheel faire un bout de conduite; (fig) to speak or talk out of ~ commettre une indiscrétion.
(g) (tendency etc) tendance f, tournure f d'esprit, mentalité f. to be of or have a scientific ~ of mind avoir l'esprit or une tournure d'esprit scientifique; to be of or have a cheerful ~ of mind être d'une disposition or d'une nature joyeuse; to have a strange ~ of mind avoir une mentalité bizarre; ~ of phrase, ~ of style tournure, tour m de phrase; there's an old-fashioned ~ to her speech sa façon de parler a un tour démodé; to have a good ~ of speed être rapide.
2 cpd: (lit, fig) turnabout volte-face f inv; turnaround (lit, fig) volte-face f inv; (place for turning vehicle) endroit m pour ma nœuvrer; (Naut: time required for unloading, refuelling etc) estarie f or starie f; turncoat renégat(e) m(f); turndown (n) (rejection) refus m; (downward tendency) tendance f à la baisse; (adj) flap à rabattre; turndown collar col rabattu; turnkey geôlier m, -ière f; (Aut) turnoff embranchement m (où il faut tourner); (fig) it's a real turn-off‡ c'est vraiment à vous rebuter or dégoûter; it's a turn-on!‡ c'est excitant!; turnout V turnout; turnover V turnover; turnpike (barrier) barrière f de péage; (US: road) autoroute f à péage; turnstile tourniquet m; turntable [record player] platine f; (for trains, cars etc) plaque tournante; turntable ladder échelle pivotante; (Brit) turn-up [trousers] revers m; (Brit fig) that was a turn-up for the book!‡ ça été une belle surprise!
3 vt (a) handle, knob, screw, key, wheel tourner; (mechanically etc) faire tourner. ~ it to the left tournez-le vers la gauche; ~ the wheel right round faites faire un tour complet à la roue; what ~s the wheel? qu'est-ce qui fait tourner la roue?; (Aut) he ~ed the wheel sharply il a donné un brusque coup de volant; you can ~ it through 90° on peut le faire pivoter de 90°; ~ the key in the lock ferme (la porte) à clef; V somersault.
(b) page tourner; mattress, pillow, collar, the soil, steak, record retourner. to ~ one's ankle se tordre la cheville; it ~s my stomach cela me soulève le cœur, cela m'écœure; V inside, upside down.
(c) (change position of, direct) car, object tourner (towards vers); thoughts, attention tourner, diriger (towards vers). to ~ a picture to the wall tourner un tableau face au mur; to ~ a gun on sb braquer un revolver sur qn; they ~ed hoses on the demonstrators ils ont aspergé les manifestants avec des lances d'incendie; ~ the switch to 'on' ouvrez le commutateur; ~ the knob to 'high' tournez le bouton jusqu'à 'fort'; ~ it to 'wash' mettez-le en position 'lavage'; to ~ the lights low baisser les lumières; ~ your face this way tourne le visage de ce côté-ci; he ~ed his back on us (lit) il nous a tourné le dos; (fig) il s'est mis à nous battre froid; he ~ed his back on the past il a tourné la page (fig); as soon as he ~s his back, as soon as his back is ~ed dès qu'il a le dos tourné; without ~ing a hair sans sourciller, sans broncher; (fig) to ~ the other cheek tendre l'autre joue; he ~ed his hand to writing il s'est mis à écrire; he can ~ his hand to anything il sait tout faire; (fig) to ~ the tables renverser les rôles, retourner la situation (on sb aux dépens de qn); he ~ed his steps to the sea il a dirigé ses pas vers la mer; they ~ed his argument against him ils ont retourné son raisonnement contre lui; they ~ed him against his father ils l'ont fait se retourner contre or ils l'ont monté contre son père; V account, advantage, heat etc.
(d) (deflect) blow parer, détourner. he ~ed the beggar from the door il a chassé le mendiant; nothing will ~ him from his purpose rien ne l'écartera or ne le détournera de son but; to ~ sb from doing dissuader qn de faire.
(e) (shape) wood, metal tourner. a well-~ed leg une jambe faite au tour; (fig) well-~ed phrase expression bien tournée.
(f) (go round) to ~ the corner (lit) tourner au or le coin de la rue; (fig) passer le moment critique; he has or is ~ed 40 il a 40 ans passés; it's ~ed 3 o'clock il est 3 heures passées.
(g) (transform) changer, transformer (into en); (translate) traduire (into en); milk faire tourner. the experience ~ed him into an old man cette expérience a fait de lui un vieillard; an actor ~ed writer un acteur devenu écrivain; (fig) ~ your talents into hard cash faites travailler vos talents pour vous; to ~ a book into a play/film adapter un livre pour la scène/l'écran; to ~ verse into prose mettre de la poésie en prose; to ~ sth black noircir qch; it ~ed him green with envy cela l'a fait verdir de jalousie, il en était vert de jalousie; we were ~ed sick by the sight le spectacle nous a rendus malades; to ~ a boat adrift faire partir un bateau à la dérive; V loose etc.
4 vi (a) (move round; rotate, revolve) [handle, knob, wheel, screw, key] tourner; [person] se tourner, se retourner. ~ to face me tourne-toi vers moi; he ~ed and saw me il s'est retourné et m'a vu; he ~ed to me and smiled il s'est tourné vers moi et a souri; he ~ed to lie on his other side il s'est tourné sur son autre côté; the earth ~s on its axis la terre tourne autour de son axe; (fig) my head is ~ing j'ai la tête qui tourne; his stomach ~ed at the sight le spectacle lui a retourné l'estomac or soulevé le cœur; it all ~s on whether he has the money tout dépend s'il a l'argent ou non; to ~ tail (and run) prendre ses jambes à son cou; he would ~ in his grave if he knew ... il se retournerait dans sa tombe s'il savait ...; V toss, turtle.
(b) [person] se tourner (towards vers), se retourner; [person, vehicle, aircraft] (change course) tourner; (reverse direction) faire demi-tour; [ship] virer; [road, river] faire un coude; [wind] tourner, changer; [tide] changer de direction. he ~ed to look at me il s'est retourné pour me regarder; (Mil) right ~! à droite!, droite!; to ~ (to the) left tourner à gauche; ~ first right prenez la première à droite; they ~ed and came back ils ont fait demi-tour or fait volte-face et ils sont revenus (sur leurs pas); the car ~ed at the end of the street (turned round) la voiture a fait demi-tour au bout de la rue; (turned off) la voiture a tourné au bout de la rue; (Aut) there's nowhere to ~ il n'y a pas d'endroit où faire demi-tour; the car ~ed into a side street la voiture a tourné dans une rue transversale; our luck has ~ed la chance a tourné pour nous; the conversation ~ed on the election la conversation en est venue à l'élection; the dog ~ed on him le chien l'a attaqué; they ~ed on him and accused him of treachery ils s'en sont pris à lui et l'ont accusé de trahison; (fig) to ~ against sb se retourner contre qn; (fig) he didn't know which way to ~ il ne savait plus où donner de la tête; he ~ed to me for advice il s'est tourné vers or adressé à moi pour me demander conseil; where can I ~ for money? où pourrais-je trouver de l'argent?; he ~ed to politics il s'est tourné vers la politique; he ~ed to drink il s'est mis à boire; our thoughts ~ to those who ... nos pensées vont à or se tournent vers ceux qui ...; V tide.
(c) (change; become) devenir, tourner à; [leaves] jaunir; [milk] tourner; [weather] changer. he ~ed into a frog il se changea or se métamorphosa en grenouille; he ~ed into an old man overnight il est devenu vieux en l'espace d'une nuit; to ~ to stone se changer en pierre, se pétrifier; his admiration ~ed to scorn son admiration se changea en or tourna au or fit place au mépris; (fig) his knees ~ed to water or jelly ses genoux se sont dérobés sous lui; the weather has ~ed cold le temps s'est rafraîchi; to ~ black noircir; to ~ angry se mettre en colère; to ~ traitor (Mil, Pol) se vendre à l'ennemi; (gen) se mettre à trahir; to ~ communist devenir communiste; to ~ Catholic se convertir au catholicisme; to ~ professional passer or devenir professionnel.

turn about, turn around 1 vi [person] se retourner, faire volte-face; [vehicle] faire demi-tour; [object] tourner. (Mil) about turn! demi-tour!
2 vt sep tourner (dans l'autre sens).
3 turnabout n, turnaround n V turn 2.

turn aside 1 vi (lit, fig) se détourner (from de).
2 vt sep détourner.

turn away 1 vi se détourner (from de).
2 vt sep (a) head, face, eyes, gun détourner. turn the photo-

graph away from the light tourne la photographie de telle façon qu'elle ne soit pas exposée à la lumière.
(b) (*reject*) *person, customer* renvoyer; *beggar* chasser; *offer* refuser, rejeter. they're turning business away ils refusent des clients.

turn back 1 *vi* (a) *[traveller]* revenir, rebrousser chemin, faire demi-tour; *[vehicle]* faire demi-tour.
(b) to turn back to page 100 revenir à la page 100.
2 *vt sep* (a) (*fold, bend*) *bedclothes* rabattre; *corner of page* relever, replier.
(b) (*send back*) *person, vehicle* faire faire demi-tour à.
(c) *clock, hands of clock* reculer (*to* jusqu'à). (*fig*) if only we could turn the clock back si seulement on pouvait remonter le (cours du) temps; it has turned the clock back 50 years cela nous (*or* vous *etc*) a fait revenir en arrière de 50 ans.

turn down 1 *vt sep* (a) (*fold, bend*) *bedclothes* rabattre, retourner; *collar* rabattre. to turn down the corner of the page corner la page.
(b) (*reduce*) *gas, heat, lighting, radio, music* baisser.
(c) (*refuse*) *offer, suggestion, loan, suitor* rejeter, repousser; *candidate, volunteer* refuser.
(d) (*place upside down*) *playing card* retourner (face contre table).
2 turndown *n, adj V* turn 2.

turn in 1 *vi* (a) *[car, person]* to turn in to a driveway entrer *or* tourner dans une allée.
(b) his toes turn in il a les pieds tournés en dedans.
(c) (*: *go to bed*) aller se coucher.
2 *vt sep* (a) to turn in the ends of sth rentrer les bouts de qch; to turn one's toes in tourner les pieds en dedans.
(b) (*: *surrender, return*) *borrowed goods, equipment* rendre (*to* à); *wanted man* livrer (à la police); *stolen goods* apporter à la police.

turn off 1 *vi* (a) *[person, vehicle]* tourner.
(b) *[heater, oven etc]* to turn off automatically s'éteindre automatiquement.
2 *vt sep water* fermer, (*at main*) couper; *tap* fermer; *light* éteindre; *electricity, gas* éteindre, fermer, (*at main*) couper; *radio, television, heater* éteindre, fermer, arrêter. (*Rad, TV*) he turned the programme off il a fermé *or* éteint le poste; (*Aut*) to turn off the engine couper l'allumage, arrêter le moteur; the oven turns itself off le four s'éteint tout seul *or* automatiquement; (*fig*) the way he smiled turned me off‡ sa façon de sourire m'a totalement rebuté.
3 turnoff *n V* turn 2.

turn on 1 *vi* (a) *[heater, oven etc]* to turn on automatically s'allumer automatiquement.
(b) (*Rad, TV*) allumer *or* ouvrir le poste.
2 *vt sep tap* ouvrir; *water* faire couler, (*at main*) mettre, brancher; *gas, electricity* allumer, (*at main*) mettre, brancher; *radio, television, heater* allumer, brancher; *engine, machine* mettre en marche. to turn on the light allumer; (*fig*) to turn on the charm* (se mettre à) faire du charme*; (*fig*) this music turns me on‡ cette musique me fait quelque chose*; (*fig*) to be turned on‡ (*up-to-date*) être dans le vent *or* à la page; (*by drugs*) planer*; (*sexually*) être (tout) excité *or* émoustillé* (*by* par).
3 turn-on‡ *n V* turn 2.

turn out 1 *vi* (a) (*from bed*) se lever; (*from house*) sortir; *[guard]* (aller) prendre la faction; *[troops etc]* aller au rassemblement. not many people turned out to see her peu de gens sont venus la voir.
(b) *[car, pedestrian]* to turn out of a driveway sortir d'une allée.
(c) his toes turn out il tourne les pieds en dehors, il a les pieds en canard.
(d) (*transpire; end*) s'avérer. it turned out that she had not seen her il s'est avéré qu'elle ne l'avait pas vue; it turned out to be true cela s'est avéré juste; it turned out to be wrong cela s'est révélé faux; it turned out to be harder than we thought cela s'est avéré plus difficile que l'on ne pensait; he turned out to be a good student il s'est révélé bon étudiant; as it turned out, nobody came en l'occurrence personne n'est venu; it all depends how things turn out tout dépend de la façon dont les choses vont se passer; everything will turn out all right tout finira bien.
2 *vt sep* (a) *light* éteindre; *gas* éteindre, fermer.
(b) to turn one's toes out marcher en canard, tourner les pieds en dehors.
(c) (*empty out*) *pockets, suitcase* retourner, vider; *contents* vider (*of* de); *room, cupboard* nettoyer à fond; *cake, jelly* démouler (*on to* sur, *of* de); (*expel*) *person* mettre à la porte; *tenant* expulser. they turned him out of the house ils l'ont mis à la porte; to turn sb out of his job renvoyer qn.
(d) *troops, police* envoyer. to turn out the guard faire donner la garde.
(e) (*produce*) *goods* fabriquer, produire. the college turns out good teachers le collège forme de bons professeurs.
(f) to be well turned out être élégant.
3 turnout *n V* turnout.

turn over 1 *vi* (a) *[person]* se retourner; *[car etc]* se retourner, faire un tonneau; *[boat]* se retourner, chavirer. turn over and go to sleep! (re)tourne-toi et dors!; the barrel turned over and over le tonneau faisait des tours sur lui-même; my stomach turned over (*at gruesome sight*) j'ai eu l'estomac retourné; (*from fright etc*) mon sang n'a fait qu'un tour; (*Aut*) the engine was turning over le moteur était *or* tournait au ralenti.
(b) (*in letter etc*) please turn over (*abbr* PTO) tournez s'il vous plaît (*abbr* T.S.V.P.).
2 *vt sep* (a) *page* tourner; *mattress, earth, playing card, plate* retourner. (*fig*) to turn over an idea in one's mind retourner *or* ressasser une idée dans sa tête; *V* leaf.
(b) (*hand over*) *object* rendre; *person* livrer (*to* à).
3 turnover *n V* turnover.

turn round 1 *vi* *[person]* se retourner, faire volte-face; *[vehicle]* faire demi-tour; *[object]* tourner. to turn round and round tourner *or* tournoyer sur soi-même; turn round and look at me retournez-vous et regardez-moi; he turned round and came back il a fait demi-tour et est revenu.
2 *vt sep one's head* tourner; *person, object* tourner, retourner; *vehicle, ship, aircraft* faire faire demi-tour à.

turn up 1 *vi* (a) (*arrive*) arriver, venir; (*be found*) être trouvé *or* retrouvé; *[playing card]* sortir. something will turn up on va bien trouver quelque chose; I've lost my job — something will turn up (for you) j'ai perdu mon poste — tu finiras par trouver quelque chose; *V* trump[1].
(b) (*point upwards*) remonter, être relevé. his nose turns up il a le nez retroussé *or* en trompette.
2 *vt sep* (a) *collar, sleeve* remonter. to have a turned-up nose avoir le nez retroussé *or* en trompette; (*fig: disgust*) it really turns me up‡ ça me débecte‡; (*Brit fig: stop*) turn it up!‡ y en a marre!‡, la ferme!‡; *V also* nose.
(b) *buried object* déterrer; (*fig: find*) *lost object, reference* déterrer, dénicher.
(c) *heat, gas* monter, mettre plus fort; *radio, television* mettre plus fort. (*Rad, TV etc*) to turn up the sound augmenter *or* monter le volume.
3 turn-up *n V* turn 2.

turner ['tɜ:nəʳ] *n* tourneur *m*.
turnery ['tɜ:nərɪ] *n* atelier *m* de tournage.
turning ['tɜ:nɪŋ] 1 *n* (a) (*side road*) route (*or* rue) latérale; (*fork*) embranchement *m*; (*bend in road, river*) coude *m*. take the second ~ on the left prenez la deuxième à gauche.
(b) (*U: Tech*) tournage *m*.
2 *cpd*: (*Aut*) turning circle rayon *m* de braquage; (*Tech*) turning lathe tour *m*; (*fig*) he was at a turning point in his career il était à un tournant de sa carrière; that was the turning point in her life ce fut le moment décisif de sa vie.
turnip ['tɜ:nɪp] *n* navet *m*.
turnout ['tɜ:naʊt] *n* (a) (*attendance*) assistance *f*. what sort of a ~ was there? combien y avait-il de gens (dans l'assistance)?; there was a good ~ beaucoup de gens sont venus.
(b) (*clean-out*) nettoyage *m*. to have a good ~ of a room/cupboard nettoyer une pièce/un placard à fond.
(c) (*Ind: output*) production *f*.
(d) (*Dress*) tenue *f*.
turnover ['tɜ:n,əʊvəʳ] *n* (a) (*Comm etc*) *[stock, goods]* roulement *m*; *[shares]* mouvement *m*; (*total business done*) chiffre *m* d'affaires. a profit of £4,000 on a ~ of £40,000 un bénéfice de 4.000 livres pour un volume de vente de 40.000 livres; he sold them cheaply hoping for a quick ~ il les a vendus bon marché pour les écouler rapidement.
(b) *[staff, workers]* mouvement *m*. there is a high *or* rapid (rate of) ~ in that firm cette maison connaît de fréquents changements *or* renouvellements de personnel.
(c) (*Culin*) chausson *m*. apple ~ chausson aux pommes.
turpentine ['tɜ:pəntaɪn] *n* (essence *f* de) térébenthine *f*. ~ substitute white-spirit *m*.
turpitude ['tɜ:pɪtju:d] *n* turpitude *f*.
turps* [tɜ:ps] *n abbr of* turpentine.
turquoise ['tɜ:kwɔɪz] 1 *n* (*stone*) turquoise *f*; (*colour*) turquoise *m*. 2 *adj necklace, ring* de turquoise(s); (*colour*) turquoise *inv*.
turret ['tʌrɪt] 1 *n* (*Archit, Mil, Phot, Tech*) tourelle *f*. 2 *cpd*: turret gun canon *m* de tourelle.
turreted ['tʌrɪtɪd] *adj* à tourelles.
turtle ['tɜ:tl] 1 *n* tortue marine. (*fig*) to turn ~ chavirer, se renverser; *V* mock. 2 *cpd*: turtledove tourterelle *f*; turtleneck (sweater) (pullover *m* à) col montant.
Tuscan ['tʌskən] 1 *adj* toscan. 2 *n* (a) Toscan(e) *m(f)*. (b) (*Ling*) toscan *m*.
Tuscany ['tʌskənɪ] *n* Toscane *f*.
tush [tʌʃ] *excl* bah!
tusk [tʌsk] *n* défense *f* (*d'éléphant etc*).
tussle ['tʌsl] 1 *n* (*struggle*) lutte *f* (*for* pour); (*scuffle*) mêlée *f*. to have a ~ with sb en venir aux mains avec qn; (*verbally*) avoir une prise de bec* avec qn.
2 *vi* se battre (*with sb* avec qn, *for sth* pour qch).
tussock ['tʌsək] *n* touffe *f* d'herbe.
tut [tʌt] (*also* ~-~) 1 *excl* allons allons!, allons donc! 2 *vi*: he (~-) ~ted at the idea à cette idée il a eu une exclamation désapprobatrice.
tutelage ['tju:tɪlɪdʒ] *n* tutelle *f*.
tutelary ['tju:tɪlərɪ] *adj* tutélaire.
tutor ['tju:təʳ] 1 *n* (*private teacher*) précepteur *m*, -trice *f*; (*Brit Univ*) directeur *m*, -trice *f* d'études; (*US Univ*) assistant(e) *m(f)* (*en faculté*).
2 *vt* donner des leçons particulières *or* des cours particuliers à. to ~ sb in Latin donner des cours particuliers de latin à qn.
tutorial [tju:'tɔ:rɪəl] 1 *adj system, class* de travaux pratiques; *duties* de directeur d'études. 2 *n* (*Univ*) travaux pratiques *or* dirigés (*in* de).
tutti-frutti ['tʊtɪ'frʊtɪ] *n* plombières *f*.
tutu ['tu:tu:] *n* tutu *m*.
tuwhit-tuwhoo [tʊ'wɪttʊ'wu:] *n* hou-hou *m*.
tuxedo [tʌk'si:dəʊ] *n* (*US*) smoking *m*.
TV* [,ti:'vi:] *n* (*abbr of* television) télé* *f*.
twaddle ['twɒdl] *n* (*U*) âneries *fpl*, balivernes *fpl*, fadaises *fpl*.
twain [tweɪn] *npl*: the ~†† les deux; (*loc*) and never the ~ shall meet les deux sont inconciliables.
twang [twæŋ] 1 *n* *[wire, string]* son *m* (de corde pincée); (*tone of*

voice) ton nasillard, nasillement *m.* **to speak with a ~** nasiller, parler du nez; **he has an American ~** il a le nasillement américain dans la voix.

2 *vt guitar etc* pincer les cordes de, gratter de.

3 *vi [wire, bow]* vibrer.

twangy ['twæŋɪ] *adj noise* de corde pincée; *voice, tone* nasillard.

'twas†† [twɒz] = **it was;** *V* **be.**

tweak [twiːk] **1** *vt sb's ear, nose* tordre; *rope etc, sb's hair* tirer (d'un coup sec). **2** *n* coup sec. **to give sth a ~ = to tweak sth;** *V* 1.

twee* [twiː] *adj (Brit pej) person* chichiteux, mignard; *room etc* à la décoration maniérée; *decoration* maniéré, un peu cucul:.

tweed [twiːd] **1** *n* tweed *m. (suit)* **~s** costume *m* de tweed. **2** *cpd jacket etc* de *or* en tweed.

tweedy ['twiːdɪ] *adj material* qui ressemble au tweed. (**pej*) **she's one of these ~ ladies** elle a le genre dame bien et tweeds cossus.

'tween [twiːn] *prep (liter)* = **between.**

tweeny* ['twiːnɪ] *n (Brit)* bonne *f.*

tweet [twiːt] **1** *n (also* **~-~***)* gazouillis *m,* gazouillement *m,* pépiement *m.* **2** *vi* gazouiller, pépier.

tweeter ['twiːtəʳ] *n* tweeter *m.*

tweeze* [twiːz] *vt eyebrows etc* épiler.

tweezers ['twiːzəz] *npl (also* **pair of ~***)* pinces fines, pinces à épiler.

twelfth [twelfθ] **1** *adj* douzième. **T~ Night** la fête des Rois. **2** *n* douzième *mf; (fraction)* douzième *m; for phrases V* **sixth.**

twelve [twelv] **1** *adj* douze *inv.* **2** *n* douze *m inv; V* **o'clock;** *for other phrases V* **six. 3** *cpd:* **twelvemonth††** année *f,* an *m; (Mus)* **twelve-tone** dodécaphonique.

twentieth ['twentɪɪθ] **1** *adj* vingtième. **2** *n* vingtième *mf; (fraction)* vingtième *m; for phrases V* **sixth.**

twenty ['twentɪ] **1** *adj* vingt *inv.* **about ~ books** une vingtaine de livres. **2** *n* vingt *m.* **about ~** une vingtaine; *for other phrases V* **sixty.**

twerp: [twɜːp] *n* andouille: *f.*

twice [twaɪs] *adv* deux fois. **~ as much, ~ as many** deux fois plus; **~ as much bread** deux fois plus de pain; **~ as long as ...** deux fois plus long que ...; **she is ~ your age** elle a deux fois votre âge, elle a le double de votre âge; **~ 2 is 4** deux fois 2 font 4; **~ weekly, ~ a week** deux fois la *or* par semaine; *(fig)* **he didn't have to be asked ~** il ne s'est pas fait prier; **he's ~ the man you are** il te vaut bien, il vaut beaucoup mieux que toi; *V* **once, think.**

twiddle ['twɪdl] **1** *vt knob* tripoter, manier. *(fig)* **to ~ one's thumbs** se tourner les pouces. **2** *vi:* **to ~ with sth** jouer avec *or* tripoter qch. **3** *n:* **to give sth a ~** donner plusieurs petits tours à qch.

twig¹ [twɪg] *n* brindille *f,* petite branche.

twig²* [twɪg] *vti (Brit)* piger*.

twilight ['twaɪlaɪt] **1** *n (evening)* crépuscule *m (also fig); (morning)* aube naissante. **at ~** *(evening)* au crépuscule, à la tombée du jour; *(morning)* à l'aube naissante; **in the ~** dans le demi-jour *or* la semi-obscurité *or* la pénombre; *(fig)* **in the ~ of history** dans les brumes *fpl* de l'histoire.

2 *cpd:* **a twilight world** un monde nébuleux.

twill [twɪl] *n (Tex)* sergé *m.*

'twill [twɪl] = **it will;** *V* **will.**

twin [twɪn] **1** *n* jumeau *m,* -elle *f; V* **identical, Siamese.**

2 *adj son, brother* jumeau; *daughter, sister* jumelle; *town* jumelé. **~ boys** jumeaux *mpl;* **~ girls** jumelles *fpl.*

3 *cpd:* **twin beds** lits jumeaux; **twin-cylinder** *(adj)* à deux cylindres; *(n)* moteur *m* à deux cylindres; **twin-engined** bimoteur; **twin-screw** à deux hélices; **twinset** twin-set *m.*

4 *vt town etc* jumeler *(with* avec).

twine [twaɪn] **1** *n (U)* ficelle *f.*

2 *vt (weave)* tresser; *(roll)* entortiller, enrouler *(round* autour de). **she ~d her arms round his neck** elle lui a enlacé le cou de ses bras.

3 *vi [plant, coil]* s'enrouler *(round* autour de); *[river, road]* serpenter, zigzaguer.

twinge [twɪndʒ] *n:* **a ~ (of pain)** un élancement, un tiraillement; **a ~ of sadness** un pincement au cœur; **a ~ of conscience** *or* **remorse** *or* **guilt** un (petit) remords; **to feel a ~ of remorse/shame** éprouver un certain remords/une certaine honte; **to feel a ~ of regret** *or* **sadness** avoir un pincement au cœur.

twining ['twaɪnɪŋ] *adj plant* volubile *(Bot).*

twinkle ['twɪŋkl] **1** *vi [star, lights]* scintiller, briller; *[eyes]* briller, pétiller.

2 *n [star, lights]* scintillement *m; [eyes]* éclat *m,* pétillement *m.* ... **he said with a ~ (in his eye)** ... dit-il avec un pétillement (malicieux) dans les yeux; **he had a ~ in his eye** il avait les yeux pétillants (de malice); **in a ~, in the ~ of an eye** en un clin d'œil.

twinkling ['twɪŋklɪŋ] **1** *adj (V* **twinkle** 1) scintillant, brillant; pétillant. **2** *n:* **in the ~ of an eye** en un clin d'œil.

twirl [twɜːl] **1** *n [body]* tournoiement *m; (in writing)* fioriture *f.* **to give sth a ~ = to twirl sth;** *V* 3.

2 *vi (also* **~ round***) [cane, lasso, dancer]* tournoyer; *[handle, knob]* pivoter.

3 *vt (also* **~ round***) cane, lasso* faire tournoyer; *knob, handle* faire pivoter.

twirp: [twɜːp] *n* = **twerp:.**

twist [twɪst] **1** *n* **(a)** *(action)* torsion *f; (Med)* entorse *f,* foulure *f.* **to give a ~ to** *knob, handle* faire pivoter, faire tourner; *wire* tordre; *one's ankle* se tordre, se fouler; **he gave a ~ to the ball** il a imprimé une rotation à la balle; **with a quick ~ (of the hand)** d'un rapide tour de poignet.

(b) *(coil)* rouleau *m; (in road)* tournant *m,* virage *m; (in river)* coude *m; (in wire, flex, cord)* tortillon *m; (fig) (of mind, events)* tournure *f; (of meaning)* distorsion *f.* **a ~ of yarn** une torsade *or* un cordonnet de fil; **sweets in a ~ of paper** des bonbons dans un tortillon de papier *or* une papillote; **a ~ of tobacco** une torsade de tabac; **a ~ of lemon** un zeste de citron; **the road is full of ~s and turns** la route est pleine de tournants *or* de virages, la route serpente beaucoup; **to take a ~ round a post with a rope** faire passer une corde autour d'un poteau; **the story has an unexpected ~ to it** l'histoire comporte un coup de théâtre; **he gave a new ~ to this old plot** il a donné un tour nouveau à cette vieille intrigue; *(fig)* **you'll get yourself into a ~* if you do that** tu vas te retrouver en difficulté si tu fais cela; *(fig)* **to go round the ~:** devenir dingue:, perdre la boule:; **to drive sb round the ~:** faire tourner qn en bourrique*.

(c) *(: cheat)* **what a ~!** on a été eus!*; **it's a ~!** c'est de la triche!*

(d) *(dance)* twist *m.* **to do the ~** twister.

2 *vt* **(a)** *(interweave) threads, strands, ropes, wires* entortiller, tresser; *(turn round on itself) thread, rope, wire, one's handkerchief* tordre; *(coil)* enrouler *(round* autour de); *knob, handle* tourner; *top, cap* tourner, visser; *(Sport) ball* imprimer une rotation à; *(fig) meaning* déformer, fausser, altérer; *words* déformer. **he ~ed the strands into a cord** il a entortillé *or* tressé les fils pour en faire une corde; **he ~ed the paper into a ball** il a tirebouchonné le papier pour en faire une boule; **you've ~ed it out of shape** tu l'as déformé en le tordant, tu l'as tordu; **~ the cap clockwise** vissez la capsule dans le sens des aiguilles d'une montre; **to ~ the top off a jar** dévisser le couvercle d'un bocal (pour l'enlever); **to ~ one's ankle** se tordre *or* se fouler la cheville; **to ~ one's neck** attraper le torticolis; **to ~ sb's arm** tordre le bras à qn; *(fig)* forcer la main à qn; **he ~ed his mouth scornfully** il eut un rictus méprisant; **limbs ~ed by arthritis** des membres tordus par l'arthrite; **his face was ~ed with pain/rage** ses traits étaient tordus par la douleur/la fureur; **you're ~ing everything I say** tu déformes tout ce que je dis; *V* **finger, twisted** *etc.*

(b) *(: cheat)* rouler*, avoir*.

3 *vi* **(a)** *[flex, rope etc]* s'entortiller, s'enrouler; *[socks, trousers]* vriller, tirebouchonner; *[one's ankle etc]* se tordre. **to ~ round sth** s'enrouler autour de qch; **the road ~s (and turns) through the valley** la route tortille *or* zigzague *or* serpente à travers la vallée; **the motorbike ~ed through the traffic** la moto louvoyait *or* zigzaguait parmi la circulation.

(b) *(dance the ~)* twister.

twist about, twist around *vi [rope etc]* tortiller; *[road etc]* tortiller, zigzaguer, serpenter.

twist off 1 *vi:* **the top twists off** le couvercle se dévisse.

2 *vt sep branch* enlever en tordant; *bottle-top* enlever en dévissant.

twist out 1 *vi:* **he twisted out of their grasp** il s'est dégagé de leur étreinte.

2 *vt sep object* enlever en tournant.

twist round 1 *vi [road etc]* tortiller, zigzaguer, serpenter; *[person]* se retourner.

2 *vt sep rope, wire* enrouler; *knob, handle,* tourner; *top, cap* tourner, visser; *one's head, chair* tourner.

twist up 1 *vi [ropes etc]* s'entortiller, s'emmêler; *[smoke]* monter en volutes.

2 *vt sep ropes, threads* entortiller, emmêler.

twisted ['twɪstɪd] *adj key, rod* tordu; *wire, rope, flex, cord* tordu, emmêlé, entortillé; *wrist, ankle* tordu, foulé; *(fig) logic* faux *(f* fausse); *mind* tordu, mal tourné; *(dishonest)* malhonnête; *lawyer, politician* véreux.

twister* ['twɪstəʳ] *n (Brit)* escroc *m (lit, fig); (US)* tornade *f.*

twit¹ [twɪt] *vt (tease)* taquiner *(about, with* sur, à propos de).

twit²: [twɪt] *n (Brit: fool)* idiot(e) *m(f),* crétin(e) *m(f).*

twitch [twɪtʃ] **1** *n (nervous movement)* tic *m; (pull)* coup sec, saccade *f.* **I've got a ~ in my eyelid** j'ai la paupière qui se convulse; **he has a (nervous) ~ in his cheek** il a un tic à la joue; **with one ~ (of his hand) he freed the rope** il a dégagé la corde d'une saccade; **he gave the rope a ~** il a tiré d'un coup sec sur la corde; **a ~ of the whip** un (petit) coup de fouet.

2 *vi [person, animal, hands]* avoir un mouvement convulsif; *(permanent condition)* avoir un tic; *[face, mouth, cheek, eyebrow, muscle]* se convulser, se contracter (convulsivement); *[dog's nose etc]* remuer, bouger.

3 *vt rope etc* tirer d'un coup sec, donner un coup sec à. **he ~ed it out of her hands** il le lui a arraché des mains; **the horse ~ed its ears** les oreilles du cheval ont bougé *or* ont remué, le cheval a chauvi des oreilles; **the dog ~ed its nose** le nez du chien a remué *or* a bougé.

twitch away *vt sep* arracher d'un petit geste *(from sb* à qn).

twitter ['twɪtəʳ] **1** *vi [bird]* gazouiller, pépier; *[person] (chatter)* babiller, jacasser *(pej) (about* sur); *(be nervous)* s'agiter (nerveusement).

2 *n [birds]* gazouillis *m,* gazouillement *m,* pépiement *m. (fig)* **to be in a ~(about sth)*** être tout sens dessus dessous* (à cause de qch).

'twixt [twɪkst] *prep (†† or liter)* = **betwixt.**

two [tuː] **1** *adj* deux *inv; V* **mind** *etc.*

2 *n* deux *m inv.* **to cut sth in ~** couper qch en deux; **~ by ~** deux par deux, deux à deux; **in ~s** par deux; **in ~s and threes** deux ou trois à la fois, par petits groupes; **they're ~ of a kind** ils se ressemblent (tous les deux); *(fig)* **to put ~ and ~ together** faire le rapport (entre deux *or* plusieurs choses); **~'s company** on est mieux à deux; *V* **one;** *for other phrases V* **six.**

3 *cpd:* *(US fig pej)* **two-bit*** de quatre sous; *(Parl)* **the two-chamber system** le bicamérisme; *(US)* **two-cycle = two-stroke;** *(Aut)* **two-cylinder** à deux cylindres; *(Aut)* **two-door** à deux portes; *(lit, fig)* **two-edged** à double tranchant; *(fig)* **two-faced** hypocrite; **twofold** *(adj)* double; *(adv)* au double; **two-handed** *sword* à deux mains; *saw* à deux poignées; *card game* à deux joueurs; **two-legged** bipède; *(Pol)* **two-party** biparti *or*

bipartite; (*Brit*) **twopence** deux pence (*V also* **tuppence**); (*Brit*) **twopenny** à *or* de deux pence; (*Brit fig*) **twopenny-halfpenny*** de rien du tout*, de deux sous; **twopenny piece** pièce *f* de deux pence; (*Elec*) **two-phase** diphasé; **two-piece (suit)** (*man's*) costume *m* (deux-pièces); (*woman's*) tailleur *m* (deux-pièces); **two-piece (swimsuit)** deux-pièces *m inv*, bikini *m*; **two-ply** *cord, rope* à deux brins; *wool* à deux fils; *wood* à deux épaisseurs; **two-seater** (*adj*) à deux places; (*n*) (*car*) voiture *f or* (*plane*) avion *m* à deux places; (*fig*) **this is a two-sided problem** ce problème peut être appréhendé de deux façons; **twosome** (*people*) couple *m*; (*game*) jeu *m or* partie *f* à deux; **we went in a twosome** nous y sommes allés à deux; **two-storey** à deux étages; (*Aut*) **two-stroke (engine)** moteur *m* à deux temps, deux-temps *m inv*; **two-stroke (mixture/fuel)** mélange *m*/carburant *m* pour moteur à deux-temps; **to two-time‡ sb** doubler* qn; **two-tone** (*in colour*) de deux tons; (*in sound*) à deux tons; **two-way** (*Elec*) *switch* à deux départs; (*Aut*) *street* à double sens; *traffic* dans les deux sens; *exchange* bilatéral; **a two-way radio** un émetteur-récepteur; **two-wheeler** deux-roues *m inv*.

'twould†† [twʊd] = **it would**; *V* **would**.

tycoon [taɪ'kuːn] *n*: **(business** *or* **industrial)** ~ gros *or* important homme d'affaires; **oil** *etc* ~ magnat *m or* roi *m* du pétrole *etc*.

tyke* [taɪk] *n* (*dog*) cabot *m* (*pej*); (*child*) môme *mf*.

tympani ['tɪmpənɪ] *n* = **timpani**.

tympanist ['tɪmpənɪst] *n* = **timpanist**.

tympanum ['tɪmpənəm] *n* (*Anat, Archit, Zool*) tympan *m*; (*Mus*) tymbale *f*.

type [taɪp] **1** *n* **(a)** (*typical example*) type *m* (même), exemple *m* même. **to deviate from the ~** s'éloigner du type ancestral; **she was the very ~ of English beauty** c'était le type même *or* l'exemple même de la beauté anglaise; *V* **revert, true**.

(b) (*class, variety, sort*) genre *m*, espèce *f*, sorte *f*; (*make of machine, coffee etc*) marque *f*; *[aircraft, car]* modèle *m*. **books of all ~s** des livres de toutes sortes *or* de tous genres *or* de toutes espèces; **a new ~ of plane, a new ~ plane*** un nouveau modèle d'avion; **a gruyère-~ cheese** un fromage genre gruyère*; **what ~ do you want?** vous en (*or* le *or* la *etc*) voulez de quelle sorte?; **what ~ of car is it?** quel modèle de voiture est-ce?; **what ~ of man is he?** quel genre *or* type d'homme est-ce?; **what ~ of dog is he?** qu'est-ce que c'est comme (race de) chien?; **you know the ~ of thing I mean** vous voyez (à peu près) ce que je veux dire; **he's not that ~ of person** ce n'est pas son genre; **I know his ~!** je connais les gens de son genre *or* espèce; **he's not my ~*** il n'est pas mon genre*; **it's my ~ of film** c'est le genre de film que j'aime *or* qui me plaît.

(c) (*: *person*) type* *m*. **he's/she's an odd ~** c'est un drôle de numéro* *or* d'oiseau*.

(d) (*Typ*) type *m*, caractère *m*; (*collectively*) caractères. **to set ~** composer; **to set sth (up) in ~** composer qch; **in ~** composé; **to keep the ~ set up** conserver la forme; **in large/small ~** en gros/petits caractères; **in italic ~** en italiques; *V* **bold** *etc*.

2 *cpd*: (*Theat etc*) **to be type-cast** se voir toujours attribuer les mêmes rôles; (*Typ*) **typeface** œil *m* de caractère; (*U*) **typescript** manuscrit *or* texte dactylographié; **typeset** composer; **typesetter** (*person*) compositeur *m*, -trice *f*; (*machine*) linotype *f*; (*U*) **typesetting** composition *f*; **typewrite** taper (à la machine); **typewriter** machine *f* à écrire; **typewriting** dactylographie *f*; **typewritten** tapé (à la machine), dactylographié.

3 *vt* **(a)** *blood sample etc* classifier. (*Theat etc*) **he is now ~d as the kindly old man** on ne lui donne plus que les rôles de doux vieillard; (*Theat*) **I don't want to be ~d** je ne veux pas me cantonner dans un (seul) rôle.

(b) *letter etc* taper (à la machine).

4 *vi [typist etc]* taper à la machine. **'clerk: must be able to ~'** 'employé(e) de bureau sachant la dactylo'.

type out *vt sep* **(a)** *notes, letter* taper (à la machine).

(b) *error* effacer (à la machine).

type over *vt sep* = **type out b**.

type up *vt sep notes* taper (à la machine).

typhoid ['taɪfɔɪd] **1** *n* (*also* **~ fever**) (fièvre *f*) typhoïde *f*. **2** *cpd symptom, victim* de la typhoïde; *inoculation* anti-typhoïdique.

typhoon [taɪ'fuːn] *n* typhon *m*.

typhus ['taɪfəs] *n* typhus *m*.

typical ['tɪpɪkəl] *adj behaviour, speech* typique, caractéristique (*of* de); *case, example* typique, type *inv*. **~ of** typique de; **it was a ~ day in spring** c'était un jour de printemps comme il y en a tant; **the ~ Frenchman** le Français type *or* typique; **he's a ~ teacher** c'est le type même du professeur; **with ~ modesty he said ...** avec sa modestie habituelle il a dit ...; **this is ~ rudeness on his part** c'est une grossièreté qui est bien de lui; **that's ~ of him!** c'est bien *or* tout à fait (de) lui!; (*iro*) **~!** étonnant! (*iro*), ça ne m'étonne pas!, le coup classique!*

typically ['tɪpɪkəlɪ] *adv* typiquement. **he is ~ English** il est typiquement anglais, c'est l'Anglais type *or* typique; **it's ~ French to do that** c'est très *or* bien français de faire ça; **it was ~ wet that day** il pleuvait beaucoup ce jour-là, comme d'habitude; **he was ~ rude to us** il s'est conduit envers nous avec sa grossièreté habituelle.

typify ['tɪpɪfaɪ] *vt [behaviour, incident, object]* être caractéristique de; *[person]* avoir le type même de.

typing ['taɪpɪŋ] **1** *n* (*U*) **(a)** (*skill*) dactylo *f*, dactylographie *f*. **to learn ~** apprendre à taper (à la machine), apprendre la dactylo *or* la dactylographie.

(b) there were several pages of ~ to read il y avait plusieurs pages dactylographiées à lire.

2 *cpd lesson, teacher* de dactylo, de dactylographie. **typing error** faute *f* de frappe; **typing paper** papier *m* machine; **typing pool** bureau *m or* pool *m* des dactylos, dactylo* *f*; **she works in the typing pool** elle est à la dactylo*; **to send sth to the typing pool** envoyer qch à la dactylo*.

typist ['taɪpɪst] *n* dactylo *mf*, dactylographe *mf*; *V* **shorthand**.

typographer [taɪ'pɒgrəfəʳ] *n* typographe *mf*.

typographic(al) [ˌtaɪpə'græfɪk(əl)] *adj* typographique.

typography [taɪ'pɒgrəfɪ] *n* typographie *f*.

typological [ˌtaɪpə'lɒdʒɪkəl] *adj* typologique.

typology [taɪ'pɒlədʒɪ] *n* typologie *f*.

tyrannic(al) [tɪ'rænɪk(əl)] *adj* tyrannique.

tyrannically [tɪ'rænɪkəlɪ] *adv* tyranniquement.

tyrannicide [tɪ'rænɪsaɪd] *n* (*act*) tyrannicide *m*; (*person*) tyrannicide *mf*.

tyrannize ['tɪrənaɪz] **1** *vi*: **to ~ over sb** tyranniser qn. **2** *vt* tyranniser.

tyranny ['tɪrənɪ] *n* tyrannie *f*.

tyrant ['taɪərənt] *n* tyran *m*.

tyre, (*US*) **tire** ['taɪəʳ] **1** *n* pneu *m*; *V* **spare** *etc*. **2** *cpd*: **tyre gauge** manomètre *m* (pour pneus); **tyre lever** démonte-pneu *m inv*; **tyre pressure** pression *f* (de gonflage); **tyre valve** valve *f* (de gonflage).

tyro ['taɪərəʊ] *n* novice *mf*, débutant(e) *m(f)*.

Tyrol [tɪ'rəʊl] *n* Tyrol *m*.

Tyrolean [ˌtɪrə'liː(ː)ən] **1** *adj* tyrolien.

2 *n* Tyrolien(ne) *m(f)*.

tzar [zɑːʳ] *n* = **tsar**.

tzarina [zɑːˈriːnə] *n* = **tsarina**.

U

U, u [juː] **1** *n* (*letter*) U, u *m*.

2 *cpd*: **U-bend** (*in pipe*) coude *m*; (*in road*) coude, virage *m* en épingle à cheveux; **U-boat** sous-marin allemand; **U-shaped** en (forme de) U; (*Aut*) **U-turn** demi-tour *m*; **'no U-turns'** 'défense de faire demi-tour'.

3 *adj* (*Brit**: *upper-class*) *word, accent, behaviour* distingué. **non-U** commun; **it's not very U to do that** cela manque de distinction que de faire ça.

ubiquitous [juː'bɪkwɪtəs] *adj* doué d'ubiquité, omniprésent.

ubiquity [juː'bɪkwɪtɪ] *n* ubiquité *f*, omniprésence *f*.

udder ['ʌdəʳ] *n* pis *m*, mamelle *f*.

Uganda [juː'gændə] *n* Ouganda *m*.

ugh [ɜːh] *excl* pouah!

ugli ['ʌglɪ] *n* tangelo *m*.

uglify ['ʌglɪfaɪ] *vt* enlaidir, rendre laid.

ugliness ['ʌglɪnɪs] *n* (*U*) laideur *f*.

ugly ['ʌglɪ] *adj person, appearance* laid, vilain; *custom, vice etc* particulièrement déplaisant, répugnant; *situation, war* qui n'est pas beau à voir; *expression* menaçant; *news* très inquiétant; *wound* vilain. **as ~ as sin** laid comme un pou *or* un singe; **an ~ rumour** de vilains bruits; **it is an ~ sight** ce n'est pas beau à voir; **'blackmail' is an ~ word** 'chantage' est un bien vilain mot; **~ customer*** sale individu *m*, sale type* *m*; (*fig*) **~ duckling** vilain petit canard; **he gave me an ~ look** il m'a regardé d'un sale œil; **to grow** *or* **turn ~, to cut up ~*** se faire menaçant, montrer les dents; **the whole business is growing ~** l'affaire prend une sale tournure; *V* **mood**.

uh-huh ['ʌˌhʌ] *excl* (*agreeing*) oui oui.

uh-uh ['ʌˌʌ] *excl* (*warning*) hé!

uke‡ [juːk] *n abbr of* **ukulele**.

Ukraine [juː'kreɪn] *n* Ukraine *f*.

ukulele [ˌjuːkə'leɪlɪ] *n* guitare hawaïenne.

ulcer ['ʌlsəʳ] *n* (*Med*) ulcère *m*; (*fig*) plaie *f*.

ulcerate ['ʌlsəreɪt] **1** *vt* ulcérer. **~d** ulcéreux. **2** *vi* s'ulcérer.

ulceration [ˌʌlsə'reɪʃən] *n* ulcération *f*.

ulcerative ['ʌlsəˌreɪtɪv] *adj* ulcératif.

ulcerous [ˈʌlsərəs] *adj* (*having ulcers*) ulcéreux; (*causing ulcers*) ulcératif.
ullage [ˈʌlɪdʒ] *n* (*U*) creux *m* du réservoir.
ulna [ˈʌlnə] *n*, *pl* **ulnae** [ˈʌlniː] cubitus *m*.
Ulster [ˈʌlstəʳ] **1** *n* **(a)** (province *f* de l')Ulster *m*. **(b)** (*coat*) **u~** ulster *m*. **2** *cpd* de l'Ulster. **Ulsterman** habitant *m or* natif *m* de l'Ulster; **Ulsterwoman** habitante *f or* native *f* de l'Ulster.
ulterior [ʌlˈtɪərɪəʳ] *adj* ultérieur (*f* -eure). **~ motive** arrière-pensée *f*.
ultimata [ˌʌltɪˈmeɪtə] *npl of* **ultimatum**.
ultimate [ˈʌltɪmɪt] *adj* (*furthest*) le plus éloigné; (*final*) ultime, final; *destination, outcome* final, définitif; *authority* suprême; *principle, truth, cause* fondamental. (*Mil*) **the ~ deterrent** l'ultime moyen de dissuasion; (*fig*) **the ~ (in) luxury/generosity** le summum du luxe/de la générosité; **the ~ (in) selfishness** le comble de l'égoïsme.
ultimately [ˈʌltɪmɪtlɪ] *adv* (*in the end, at last*) finalement, à la fin; (*fundamentally*) en fin de compte, en définitive, en dernière analyse. **he did ~ arrive** il a fini par arriver, il est finalement arrivé; **we will ~ build a block of flats here** nous envisageons de construire un immeuble ici par la suite; **it may ~ be possible** ce n'est pas impossible à une date ultérieure; **it ~ depends on you** en définitive *or* en dernière analyse *or* en fin de compte cela dépend de vous.
ultimatum [ˌʌltɪˈmeɪtəm] *n*, *pl* **~s** *or* **ultimata** ultimatum *m*. **to deliver** *or* **issue an ~** adresser un ultimatum (*to* à).
ultimo [ˈʌltɪməʊ] *adv* (*Comm*) du mois dernier. **the 25th ~** le 25 du mois dernier.
ultra... [ˈʌltrə] *pref* ultra..., hyper... . **~fashionable** du tout dernier cri, très à la mode; **~sensitive** ultra-sensible, hypersensible; **~short** ultra-court; **~red** infrarouge; **~rich** richissime.
ultrahigh [ˈʌltrəˈhaɪ] *adj*: **~ frequency** très haute fréquence.
ultramarine [ˌʌltrəməˈriːn] *adj*, *n* (bleu) outremer (*m*) *inv*.
ultramodern [ˈʌltrəˈmɒdən] *adj* ultramoderne.
ultramontane [ˌʌltrəˈmɒnteɪn] *adj*, *n* ultramontain(e) *m(f)*.
ultramontanism [ˌʌltrəˈmɒntɪnɪzəm] *n* ultramontanisme *m*.
ultrasonic [ˌʌltrəˈsɒnɪk] **1** *adj* ultrasonique. **2** *n* (*U*) **~s** science *f* des ultrasons.
ultraviolet [ˌʌltrəˈvaɪəlɪt] *adj* ultra-violet. (*Med*) **to have ~ treatment** se faire traiter aux rayons ultra-violets.
ultra vires [ˌʌltrəˈvaɪəriːz] *adv*, *adj* (*Jur*) au-delà des pouvoirs.
ululate [ˈjuːljʊleɪt] *vi* [*owl*] hululer *or* ululer; [*dog*] hurler.
ululation [ˌjuːljʊˈleɪʃən] *n* (*V* **ululate**) hululement *m or* ululement *m*; hurlement *m*.
Ulysses [juːˈlɪsiːz] *n* Ulysse *m*.
umber [ˈʌmbəʳ] *adj*, *n* (terre *f* d')ombre (*f*), terre (*f*) de Sienne; *V* **burnt**.
umbilical [ˌʌmbɪˈlaɪkəl] *adj* ombilical.
umbilicus [ˌʌmbɪˈlaɪkəs] *n* ombilic *m*, nombril *m*.
umbrage [ˈʌmbrɪdʒ] *n* (*U*) ombrage *m* (*fig*), ressentiment *m*. **to take ~** prendre ombrage, se froisser (*at* de).
umbrella [ʌmˈbrelə] **1** *n* parapluie *m*; (*fig*) protection *f*. (*Mil*) **air ~** écran *m or* rideau *m* de protection aérienne; (*fig*) **under the ~ of** sous les auspices *or* l'égide de. **2** *cpd*: **umbrella stand** porte-parapluies *m inv*.
umlaut [ˈʊmlaʊt] *n* (*vowel change*: *U*) inflexion *f* vocalique; (*diaeresis*) tréma *m*.
umpire [ˈʌmpaɪəʳ] **1** *n* arbitre *m*. **2** *vt* arbitrer. **3** *vi* servir d'arbitre, être l'arbitre.
umpteen* [ˈʌmptiːn] *adj* beaucoup de, je ne sais combien de. **I've told you ~ times** je te l'ai dit maintes et maintes fois *or* je ne sais combien de fois *or* trente-six fois *or* cent fois; **he had ~ books** il avait je ne sais combien de livres *or* des quantités de livres.
umpteenth* [ˈʌmptiːnθ] *adj* (é)nième.
'un [ən] *pron* (*abbr of* **one**) **he's a good ~** c'est un brave type; **little ~** petiot(e) *m(f)*.
un... [ʌn] *pref* dé..., dés..., dis..., in..., mal... .
unabashed [ˈʌnəˈbæʃt] *adj* nullement décontenancé *or* intimidé. **'yes' he said ~** 'oui' dit-il sans se décontenancer *or* sans perdre contenance *or* sans se laisser intimider.
unabated [ˈʌnəˈbeɪtɪd] *adj* non diminué. **with ~ interest** avec toujours autant d'intérêt.
unabbreviated [ˈʌnəˈbriːvɪeɪtɪd] *adj* non abrégé, sans abréviation.
unable [ˈʌnˈeɪbl] *adj*: **to be ~ to do** (*have no means, power, opportunity*) être incapable de faire, ne (pas) pouvoir faire, être dans l'impossibilité de faire, ne pas être en mesure de faire; (*not know how to*) ne (pas) savoir faire.
unabridged [ˈʌnəˈbrɪdʒd] *adj* intégral, non abrégé. **~ edition/version** édition/version intégrale.
unaccented [ˈʌnækˈsentɪd] *adj*, **unaccentuated** [ˈʌnækˈsentjʊeɪtɪd] *adj voice, speech* sans accent; *syllable* inaccentué, non accentué, atone.
unacceptable [ˈʌnəkˈseptəbl] *adj offer, suggestion* inacceptable; *amount, degree, extent* inadmissible.
unaccommodating [ˈʌnəˈkɒmədeɪtɪŋ] *adj* (*disobliging*) désobligeant; (*not easy to deal with*) peu accommodant.
unaccompanied [ˈʌnəˈkʌmpənɪd] *adj person, child, luggage* non accompagné; (*Mus*) *singing* sans accompagnement, a cappella; *instrument* seul.
unaccomplished [ˌʌnəˈkʌmplɪʃt] *adj* **(a)** (*unfinished*) *work, task, journey* inaccompli, inachevé; *project, desire* inaccompli, non réalisé. **(b)** (*untalented*) *person* sans talents; *performance* médiocre.
unaccountable [ˈʌnəˈkaʊntəbl] *adj* inexplicable.
unaccountably [ˈʌnəˈkaʊntəblɪ] *adv* inexplicablement.
unaccounted [ˈʌnəˈkaʊntɪd] *adj*: **2 passengers are still ~ for** 2 passagers n'ont toujours pas été retrouvés; **£5 is still ~ for** il manque encore 5 livres.
unaccustomed [ˈʌnəˈkʌstəmd] *adj slowness, charm* inaccoutumé, inhabituel. **to be ~ to (doing) sth** ne pas avoir l'habitude de (faire) qch.
unacknowledged [ˈʌnəkˈnɒlɪdʒd] *adj letter* resté sans réponse, dont on n'a pas accusé réception; *help, services* non reconnu (publiquement); *child* non reconnu.
unacquainted [ˈʌnəˈkweɪntɪd] *adj*: **to be ~ with sth** ignorer qch, ne pas être au courant de qch; **to be ~ with sb** ne pas avoir fait la connaissance de qn; **they are ~** ils ne se connaissent pas.
unadaptable [ˈʌnəˈdæptəbl] *adj* inadaptable, peu adaptable.
unadapted [ˈʌnəˈdæptɪd] *adj* mal adapté, inadapté (*to* à).
unaddressed [ˈʌnəˈdrest] *adj* sans adresse, qui ne porte pas d'adresse.
unadopted [ˈʌnəˈdɒptɪd] *adj*: **~ road** route non prise en charge par la commune.
unadorned [ˈʌnəˈdɔːnd] *adj* sans ornement, tout simple; (*fig*) *truth* pur, tout nu. **beauty ~** la beauté toute simple *or* sans artifice *or* sans fard.
unadulterated [ˈʌnəˈdʌltəreɪtɪd] *adj* pur, naturel; *wine* non frelaté; (*fig*) *bliss, nonsense* pur.
unadvertised [ˈʌnˈædvətaɪzd] *adj meeting, visit* sans publicité, discret (*f* -ète).
unadvised [ˈʌnədˈvaɪzd] *adj person* qui n'a pas reçu de conseils; (*ill-advised*) *person* malavisé, imprudent; *measures* inconsidéré, imprudent.
unaesthetic [ˌʌniːsˈθetɪk] *adj* inesthétique, peu esthétique.
unaffected [ˈʌnəˈfektɪd] *adj* **(a)** (*sincere*) *person* naturel, simple; *behaviour* non affecté; *style* sans recherche, simple. **(b)** non affecté. **~ by damp/cold** non affecté par l'humidité/le froid, qui résiste à l'humidité/au froid; **~ by heat** inaltérable à la chaleur; **they are ~ by the new legislation** ils ne sont pas affectés *or* touchés par la nouvelle législation; **he was quite ~ by her sufferings** ses souffrances ne l'ont pas touché *or* l'ont laissé froid.
unaffectedly [ˈʌnəˈfektɪdlɪ] *adv behave* sans affectation; *dress* simplement.
unaffiliated [ˈʌnəˈfɪlɪeɪtɪd] *adj* non affilié (*to* à).
unafraid [ˈʌnəˈfreɪd] *adj* sans peur, qui n'a pas peur. **to be ~ of (doing) sth** ne pas avoir peur de (faire) qch.
unaided [ˈʌnˈeɪdɪd] **1** *adv* sans aide, tout seul. **2** *adj*: **by his own ~ efforts** par ses propres efforts *or* moyens.
unaired [ˌʌnˈɛəd] *adj* non aéré.
unalloyed [ˈʌnəˈlɔɪd] *adj happiness* sans mélange, parfait.
unalterable [ʌnˈɒltərəbl] *adj rule* invariable, immuable; *fact* certain; *emotion, friendship* inaltérable.
unalterably [ʌnˈɒltərəblɪ] *adv* invariablement, immuablement.
unaltered [ˈʌnˈɒltəd] *adj* inchangé, non modifié, tel quel. **his appearance was ~** physiquement il n'avait pas changé *or* il était toujours le même.
unambiguous [ˈʌnæmˈbɪgjʊəs] *adj wording* non ambigu (*f* -guë), non équivoque, clair; *order, thought* clair.
unambiguously [ˈʌnæmˈbɪgjʊəslɪ] *adv* sans ambiguïté, sans équivoque.
unambitious [ˈʌnæmˈbɪʃəs] *adj person* sans ambition, peu ambitieux; *plan* modeste.
un-American [ˈʌnəˈmerɪkən] *adj* antiaméricain; (*not typical*) peu *or* pas américain.
unamiable [ˈʌnˈeɪmɪəbl] *adj* désagréable, peu aimable.
unanimity [ˌjuːnəˈnɪmɪtɪ] *n* (*U*) unanimité *f*.
unanimous [juːˈnænɪməs] *adj group, decision* unanime. **the committee was ~ in its condemnation of this** *or* **in condemning this** les membres du comité ont été unanimes pour *or* à condamner cela, les membres du comité ont condamné cela à l'unanimité; **it was accepted by a ~ vote** cela a été voté à l'unanimité.
unanimously [juːˈnænɪməslɪ] *adv agree, condemn* à l'unanimité, unanimement; *vote* à l'unanimité.
unannounced [ˈʌnəˈnaʊnst] *adj* sans se faire annoncer, sans tambour ni trompette.
unanswerable [ʌnˈɑːnsərəbl] *adj question* à laquelle il est impossible de répondre; *argument* irréfutable, incontestable.
unanswered [ˈʌnˈɑːnsəd] *adj letter, request, question* (qui reste) sans réponse; *problem, puzzle* non résolu; *criticism, argument* non réfuté; (*Jur*) *charge* irréfuté.
unappealing [ˈʌnəˈpiːlɪŋ] *adj* peu attirant, peu attrayant.
unappetizing [ˈʌnˈæpɪtaɪzɪŋ] *adj* (*lit, fig*) peu appétissant.
unappreciated [ˈʌnəˈpriːʃɪeɪtɪd] *adj person* méconnu, incompris; *offer, help* non apprécié.
unappreciative [ˈʌnəˈpriːʃɪətɪv] *adj audience* froid, indifférent. **to be ~ of sth** ne pas apprécier qch, rester indifférent à qch.
unapproachable [ˈʌnəˈprəʊtʃəbl] *adj* d'un abord difficile, inabordable.
unarmed [ˈʌnˈɑːmd] *adj person* non armé; *combat* sans armes.
unashamed [ˈʌnəˈʃeɪmd] *adj pleasure, greed* effronté, impudent. **he was quite ~ about it** il n'en avait absolument pas honte; **he was an ~ believer in magic** il croyait à la magie et ne s'en cachait pas.
unashamedly [ˈʌnəˈʃeɪmɪdlɪ] *adv say, suggest* sans honte, sans vergogne. **he was ~ delighted about it** il ne cherchait nullement à déguiser la joie que cela lui procurait; **he was ~ selfish** il était d'un égoïsme éhonté, il était égoïste sans vergogne; **he was ~ a liar** c'était un menteur éhonté *or* effronté, il mentait sans vergogne *or* effrontément.
unasked [ˈʌnˈɑːskt] *adj*: **she did it ~** elle l'a fait sans qu'on le lui ait demandé *or* de son propre chef; **he came in ~** il est entré sans y avoir été invité.
unassailable [ˌʌnəˈseɪləbl] *adj fortress* imprenable; *position, reputation* inattaquable; *argument, reason* irréfutable,

inattaquable. **he is quite ~ on that point** ses arguments sont irréfutables sur ce point, on ne peut pas l'attaquer sur ce point.
unassisted ['ʌnə'sɪstɪd] *adj* sans aide, tout seul.
unassuming ['ʌnə'sjuːmɪŋ] *adj* sans prétentions, modeste.
unassumingly ['ʌnə'sjuːmɪŋlɪ] *adv* modestement, sans prétentions.
unattached ['ʌnə'tætʃt] *adj part etc* non attaché, libre; (*fig*) *person, group* indépendant (*to* de); (*not married etc*) libre, sans attaches; (*Jur*) non saisi.
unattainable ['ʌnə'teɪnəbl] *adj place, objective, person* inaccessible.
unattended ['ʌnə'tendɪd] *adj* **(a)** (*not looked after*) *luggage, shop, machine* sans surveillance; *child* sans surveillance, (tout) seul. **do not leave your luggage ~** surveillez toujours vos bagages; **~ to** négligé.
(b) (*unaccompanied*) *king etc* seul, sans escorte.
unattractive ['ʌnə'træktɪv] *adj appearance, house, idea* peu attrayant, peu séduisant; *person, character* déplaisant, peu sympathique.
unattractiveness ['ʌnə'træktɪvnɪs] *n* (*U*) manque *m* d'attrait *or* de beauté.
unauthenticated ['ʌnɔː'θentɪkeɪtɪd] *adj evidence* non établi; *signature* non authentifié.
unauthorized ['ʌn'ɔːθəraɪzd] *adj* non autorisé, sans autorisation.
unavailable ['ʌnə'veɪləbl] *adj funds* indisponible; (*Comm*) *article* épuisé, qu'on ne peut se procurer; *person* indisponible, qui n'est pas disponible *or* libre.
unavailing ['ʌnə'veɪlɪŋ] *adj effort* vain, inutile; *remedy, method* inefficace.
unavailingly ['ʌnə'veɪlɪŋlɪ] *adv* en vain, sans succès.
unavoidable [ˌʌnə'vɔɪdəbl] *adj* inévitable. **it is ~ that** il est inévitable que+*subj*.
unavoidably [ˌʌnə'vɔɪdəblɪ] *adv* inévitablement. **he was ~ delayed** il a été retardé pour des raisons indépendantes de sa volonté.
unaware ['ʌnə'wɛəʳ] *adj*: **to be ~ of sth** ignorer qch, ne pas être conscient de qch, ne pas avoir conscience de qch; **to be ~ that** ignorer que, ne pas savoir que; **'stop' he said, ~ of the danger** 'arrête' dit-il, ignorant *or* inconscient du danger; **I was not ~ that** je n'étais pas sans savoir que; **he is politically quite ~** il n'a aucune conscience politique, il n'est pas politisé; **he is socially quite ~** il n'est pas sensibilisé aux problèmes sociaux.
unawares ['ʌnə'wɛəz] *adv* **(a)** (*by surprise*) à l'improviste, au dépourvu. **to catch** *or* **take sb ~** prendre qn à l'improviste *or* au dépourvu. **(b)** (*not realizing*) inconsciemment, par mégarde.
unbacked ['ʌn'bækt] *adj* (*Fin*) à découvert.
unbalance ['ʌn'bæləns] **1** *vt* déséquilibrer. **2** *n* déséquilibre *m*.
unbalanced ['ʌn'bælənst] *adj* **(a)** mal équilibré; (*mentally*) déséquilibré. **his mind was ~** il était déséquilibré. **(b)** (*Fin*) *account* non soldé.
unbandage ['ʌn'bændɪdʒ] *vt limb, wound* débander; *person* ôter ses bandages *or* ses pansements à.
unbaptized ['ʌnbæp'taɪzd] *adj* non baptisé.
unbar ['ʌn'bɑːʳ] *vt door* débarrer, enlever la barre de.
unbearable [ʌn'bɛərəbl] *adj* insupportable.
unbearably [ʌn'bɛərəblɪ] *adv* insupportablement. **~ selfish** d'un égoïsme insupportable.
unbeatable ['ʌn'biːtəbl] *adj* imbattable.
unbeaten ['ʌn'biːtn] *adj army, player, team* invaincu; *record, price* non battu.
unbecoming ['ʌnbɪ'kʌmɪŋ] *adj garment* peu seyant, qui ne va *or* ne sied pas; (*fig*) *behaviour* malséant, inconvenant.
unbeknown(st) ['ʌnbɪ'nəʊn(st)] *adv*: **~ to** à l'insu de.
unbelief ['ʌnbɪ'liːf] *n* (*also Rel*) incrédulité *f*. **in ~, with an air of ~** d'un air incrédule.
unbelievable [ˌʌnbɪ'liːvəbl] *adj* incroyable. **it is ~ that** il est incroyable que+*subj*.
unbelievably [ˌʌnbɪ'liːvəblɪ] *adv* incroyablement. **~ selfish** d'un égoïsme incroyable.
unbeliever ['ʌnbɪ'liːvəʳ] *n* (*also Rel*) incrédule *mf*.
unbelieving ['ʌnbɪ'liːvɪŋ] *adj* (*also Rel*) incrédule.
unbelievingly ['ʌnbɪ'liːvɪŋlɪ] *adv* d'un air incrédule.
unbend ['ʌn'bend] *pret, ptp* **unbent 1** *vt pipe, wire* redresser, détordre. **2** *vi* [*person*] se détendre. **he unbent enough to ask me how I was** il a daigné me demander comment j'allais.
unbending ['ʌn'bendɪŋ] *adj* non flexible, rigide; (*fig*) *person, attitude* inflexible, intransigeant.
unbias(s)ed ['ʌn'baɪəst] *adj* impartial.
unbidden ['ʌn'bɪdn] *adj*: **she did it ~** elle l'a fait sans qu'on le lui ait demandé *or* de son propre chef; **he came in ~** il est entré sans y avoir été invité.
unbind ['ʌn'baɪnd] *pret, ptp* **unbound** *vt* (*free*) délier; (*untie*) dénouer, défaire; (*unbandage*) débander; *V also* **unbound**.
unbleached ['ʌn'bliːtʃt] *adj linen* écru; *hair* non décoloré.
unblemished [ʌn'blemɪʃt] *adj* (*lit, fig*) sans tache.
unblinking [ʌn'blɪŋkɪŋ] *adj person* imperturbable, impassible. **he gave me an ~ stare, he looked at me with ~ eyes** il m'a regardé sans ciller (des yeux).
unblock ['ʌn'blɒk] *vt sink, pipe* déboucher; *road, harbour, traffic* dégager.
unblushing [ʌn'blʌʃɪŋ] *adj* effronté, éhonté.
unblushingly [ʌn'blʌʃɪŋlɪ] *adv* sans rougir (*fig*), effrontément.
unbolt ['ʌn'bəʊlt] *vt door* déverrouiller, tirer le verrou de; *beam* déboulonner.
unborn ['ʌn'bɔːn] *adj child* qui n'est pas encore né; *generation* à venir, futur.
unbosom [ʌn'bʊzəm] *vt*: **to ~ o.s. to sb** ouvrir son cœur à qn, se confier à qn.
unbound ['ʌn'baʊnd] **1** *pret, ptp of* **unbind**. **2** *adj prisoner, hands, feet* non lié; *seam* non bordé; *book* broché, non relié; *periodical* non relié.
unbounded [ʌn'baʊndɪd] *adj joy, gratitude* sans borne, illimité; *conceit, pride* démesuré.
unbowed ['ʌn'baʊd] *adj* (*fig*) insoumis, invaincu. **with head ~** la tête haute.
unbreakable ['ʌn'breɪkəbl] *adj* incassable; (*fig*) *promise, treaty* sacré.
unbreathable ['ʌn'briːðəbl] *adj* irrespirable.
unbribable ['ʌn'braɪbəbl] *adj* incorruptible, qui ne se laisse pas acheter.
unbridled [ʌn'braɪdld] *adj* (*fig*) débridé, déchaîné, effréné.
unbroken ['ʌn'brəʊkən] *adj crockery, limb* non cassé; *seal* intact, non brisé; *skin* intact, non déchiré; *ice* non rompu, continu, intact; (*fig*) *promise* tenu; *series, silence, sleep* ininterrompu; *record* non battu; *horse* indompté; *voice* qui n'a pas mué. **his spirit remained ~** il ne se découragea pas; (*Aut*) **~ line** ligne continue; **descended in an ~ line from Edward VII** descendu en ligne directe d'Édouard VII.
unbuckle ['ʌn'bʌkl] *vt* déboucler.
unburden [ʌn'bɜːdn] *vt conscience* soulager; *heart* épancher. **to ~ o.s.** s'épancher (*to sb* avec qn, dans le sein de qn), se livrer (*to sb* à qn); **to ~ o.s. of sth** se décharger de qch.
unburied ['ʌn'berɪd] *adj* non enterré, non enseveli.
unbusinesslike [ʌn'bɪznɪslaɪk] *adj trader, dealer* qui n'a pas le sens des affaires, peu commerçant; *transaction* irrégulier; (*fig*) *person* qui manque de méthode *or* d'organisation; *report* peu méthodique.
unbutton ['ʌn'bʌtn] **1** *vt coat* déboutonner. (**fig*) **to ~ o.s.** se déboutonner. **2** *vi* (**fig*) [*person*] se déboutonner.
uncalled-for [ʌn'kɔːldfɔːʳ] *adj criticism* injustifié; *remark* déplacé. **that was quite ~** vous n'aviez nullement besoin de faire (*or* dire) ça.
uncannily [ʌn'kænɪlɪ] *adv silent, cold* mystérieusement, sinistrement; *alike* étrangement.
uncanny [ʌn'kænɪ] *adj sound* mystérieux, étrange, inquiétant; *atmosphere* étrange, qui donne le frisson; *mystery, event, question, resemblance, accuracy, knack* troublant. **it's ~ how he does it** je ne m'explique vraiment pas comment il peut le faire.
uncap ['ʌn'kæp] *vt bottle* décapsuler.
uncared-for ['ʌn'kɛədfɔːʳ] *adj garden, building* négligé, (laissé) à l'abandon; *appearance* négligé, peu soigné; *child* laissé à l'abandon, délaissé.
uncarpeted ['ʌn'kɑːpɪtɪd] *adj* sans tapis.
uncatalogued ['ʌn'kætəlɒgd] *adj* qui n'a pas été catalogué.
uncaught ['ʌn'kɔːt] *adj criminal* qui n'a pas été appréhendé *or* pris.
unceasing [ʌn'siːsɪŋ] *adj* incessant, continu, continuel.
unceasingly [ʌn'siːsɪŋlɪ] *adv* sans cesse, continuellement.
uncensored ['ʌn'sensəd] *adj letter* non censuré; *film, book* non censuré, non expurgé.
unceremonious ['ʌnˌserɪ'məʊnɪəs] *adj* brusque.
unceremoniously ['ʌnˌserɪ'məʊnɪəslɪ] *adv* sans cérémonie, brusquement, avec brusquerie.
uncertain [ʌn'sɜːtn] *adj person* incertain, qui n'est pas sûr *or* certain; *voice, smile, steps* incertain, mal assuré, hésitant; *age, date, result, weather* incertain; *temper* inégal. **it is ~ whether** il n'est pas certain *or* sûr que+*subj*; **he is ~ whether** il ne sait pas au juste si+*indic*, il n'est pas sûr que+*subj*; **to be ~ about sth** être incertain de qch, ne pas être certain *or* sûr de qch, avoir des doutes sur qch; **he was ~ about what he was going to do** il était incertain de ce qu'il allait faire, il ne savait pas au juste ce qu'il allait faire; **in no ~ terms** en des termes on ne peut plus clairs.
uncertainly [ʌn'sɜːtnlɪ] *adv* d'une manière hésitante.
uncertainty [ʌn'sɜːtntɪ] *n* incertitude *f*, doute(s) *m(pl)*. **in order to remove any ~** pour dissiper des doutes éventuels; **in view of this ~** *or* **these uncertainties** en raison de l'incertitude dans laquelle nous nous trouvons *or* de ces incertitudes.
uncertificated ['ʌnsə'tɪfɪkeɪtɪd] *adj* (*gen*) non diplômé; *secondary teacher* non certifié.
unchain ['ʌn'tʃeɪn] *vt* (*lit, fig*) déchaîner.
unchallengeable ['ʌn'tʃælɪndʒəbl] *adj* indiscutable, incontestable.
unchallenged ['ʌn'tʃælɪndʒd] *adj leader, rights, superiority* incontesté, indiscuté; *statement, figures* non contesté, non controversé; (*Jur*) *witness* non récusé. **I cannot let that go ~** je ne peux pas laisser passer ça sans protester; **he slipped ~ through the enemy lines** il a passé au travers des lignes ennemies sans être interpellé.
unchangeable [ʌn'tʃeɪndʒəbl] *adj* invariable, immuable.
unchanged ['ʌn'tʃeɪndʒd] *adj* inchangé.
unchanging [ʌn'tʃeɪndʒɪŋ] *adj* invariable, immuable.
uncharged ['ʌn'tʃɑːdʒd] *adj* (*Elec*) non chargé; (*Jur*) non accusé; *gun* non chargé.
uncharitable [ʌn'tʃærɪtəbl] *adj* peu charitable.
uncharted [ʌn'tʃɑːtɪd] *adj* inexploré, qui n'est pas sur la carte.
unchaste ['ʌn'tʃeɪst] *adj* non chaste, lascif.
unchecked ['ʌn'tʃekt] *adj* **(a)** (*unrestrained*) *anger* non maîtrisé, non réprimé. (*Mil*) **they advanced ~ for several kilometres** ils ont fait plusieurs kilomètres sans rencontrer d'opposition; **this practice continued ~ for several years** cette pratique s'est poursuivie sans la moindre opposition *or* s'est poursuivie impunément pendant des années.
(b) (*not verified*) *figures, statement* non vérifié; *typescript* non relu.
unchivalrous ['ʌn'ʃɪvəlrəs] *adj* peu galant, discourtois.
unchristian ['ʌn'krɪstjən] *adj* peu chrétien, contraire à l'esprit chrétien; (**fig: uncivilized*) impossible*. **at an ~ hour** à une heure indue *or* impossible*.

uncial [ˈʌnsɪəl] 1 *adj* oncial.
2 *n* onciale *f*.
uncircumcised [ˈʌnˈsɜːkəmsaɪzd] *adj* incirconcis.
uncivil [ˈʌnˈsɪvɪl] *adj* incivil (*f* incivile), impoli (*to sb* envers qn).
uncivilized [ˈʌnˈsɪvɪlaɪzd] *adj country* inculte, barbare; *behaviour* barbare, grossier; (*fig*) impossible*. ~ **hour** heure indue.
unclad [ˈʌnˈklæd] *adj* sans vêtements, nu.
unclaimed [ˈʌnˈkleɪmd] *adj property, prize* non réclamé; *right* non revendiqué.
unclasp [ˈʌnˈklɑːsp] *vt necklace* défaire, dégrafer; *hands* ouvrir.
unclassed [ˈʌnˈklɑːst] *adj* non classé.
unclassified [ˈʌnˈklæsɪfaɪd] *adj items, papers* non classé, non classifié; *road* non classé; (*fig: not secret*) *information* non secret (*f* -ète).
uncle [ˈʌŋkl] *n* oncle *m*. **yes** ~ oui tonton, oui mon oncle; (*US*) **U~ Sam** l'oncle Sam (*personnification des U.S.A.*); (*US pej*) **U~ Tom** bon nègre; *V* **Dutch**.
unclean [ˈʌnˈkliːn] *adj* (*lit*) sale, malpropre; (*fig, Rel*) impur.
unclear [ˌʌnˈklɪəʳ] *adj* qui n'est pas clair *or* évident; *result, outcome* incertain. **it is** ~ **whether he is coming or not** il n'est pas clair s'il va venir ou pas.
unclench [ˈʌnˈklentʃ] *vt* desserrer.
uncloak [ˈʌnˈkləʊk] *vt* (*fig*) *person* démasquer; *mystery, plot* dévoiler.
unclog [ˈʌnˈklɒg] *vt pipe* déboucher; *wheel* débloquer.
unclothe [ˈʌnˈkləʊð] *vt* déshabiller, dévêtir.
unclothed [ˈʌnˈkləʊðd] *adj* sans vêtements, nu.
unclouded [ˈʌnˈklaʊdɪd] *adj sky* sans nuages, dégagé; *liquid* clair, limpide; (*fig*) *happiness* sans nuages, parfait; *future* sans nuages.
unco [ˈʌŋkəʊ] *adv* (*Scot*) très, extrêmement.
uncoil [ˈʌnˈkɔɪl] 1 *vt* dérouler. 2 *vi* se dérouler.
uncollected [ˈʌnkəˈlektɪd] *adj tax* non perçu; *bus fare* non encaissé; *luggage, lost property* non réclamé; *refuse* non ramassé, non enlevé.
uncoloured, (*US*) **uncolored** [ˈʌnˈkʌləd] *adj* (*colourless*) incolore; (*black and white*) en noir et blanc; *hair* non teint; (*fig*) *judgment, description* objectif, impartial. (*fig*) ~ **by** non déformé *or* faussé par.
uncombed [ˈʌnˈkəʊmd] *adj hair, wool* non peigné.
un-come-at-able* [ˈʌnkʌmˈætəbl] *adj* inaccessible.
uncomely [ˈʌnˈkʌmlɪ] *adj person* laid, peu joli; *clothes* peu seyant.
uncomfortable [ʌnˈkʌmfətəbl] *adj shoes, lodgings* inconfortable, peu confortable; *position* inconfortable, incommode; *person* (*physically*) qui n'est pas bien *or* à l'aise; (*uneasy*) mal à l'aise; *afternoon etc* désagréable, pénible. **this chair is very** ~ on est très mal dans ce fauteuil, ce fauteuil n'est pas du tout confortable; **you look** ~ **in that chair** vous n'avez pas l'air bien (assis) dans ce fauteuil; (*fig*) **to feel** ~ **about sth** se sentir gêné *or* mal à l'aise au sujet de qch; **I had an** ~ **feeling that he was watching me** j'avais l'impression déconcertante qu'il me regardait; **I had an** ~ **feeling that he would change his mind** je ne pouvais pas m'empêcher de penser qu'il allait changer d'avis; **to make things** *or* **life** ~ **for sb** faire *or* créer des ennuis à qn; **to have an** ~ **time** passer un mauvais quart d'heure; (*longer*) connaître des moments difficiles.
uncomfortably [ʌnˈkʌmfətəblɪ] *adv hot* désagréablement; *seated, dressed* inconfortablement, peu confortablement, mal; (*uneasily*) *think* avec une certaine inquiétude; *say* avec gêne. **the bullet went past** ~ **close** la balle est passée un peu trop près à mon (*or* son *etc*) goût.
uncommitted [ˈʌnkəˈmɪtɪd] *adj person, party* non engagé, libre; *literature* non engagé; *attitude* neutraliste.
uncommon [ʌnˈkɒmən] 1 *adj* (*unusual*) rare, peu commun, peu fréquent; (*outstanding*) rare, singulier, extraordinaire. **it is not** ~ **for this to happen** il n'est pas rare que cela arrive (*subj*), cela arrive assez souvent.
2 *adv* (*) singulièrement, extraordinairement.
uncommonly [ʌnˈkɒmənlɪ] *adv kind, hot* singulièrement, extraordinairement. **not** ~ assez souvent.
uncommunicative [ˈʌnkəˈmjuːnɪkətɪv] *adj* peu communicatif, peu expansif, renfermé.
uncomplaining [ˈʌnkəmˈpleɪnɪŋ] *adj* qui ne se plaint pas, patient, résigné.
uncomplainingly [ˈʌnkəmˈpleɪnɪŋlɪ] *adv* sans se plaindre, patiemment.
uncompleted [ˈʌnkəmˈpliːtɪd] *adj* inachevé.
uncomplicated [ʌnˈkɒmplɪkeɪtɪd] *adj* peu compliqué, simple.
uncomplimentary [ˈʌnˌkɒmplɪˈmentərɪ] *adj* peu flatteur.
uncompromising [ʌnˈkɒmprəmaɪzɪŋ] *adj person, attitude* intransigeant, inflexible.
uncompromisingly [ʌnˈkɒmprəmaɪzɪŋlɪ] *adv say* en se refusant à toute concession. ~ **loyal** d'une loyauté intransigeante.
unconcealed [ˈʌnkənˈsiːld] *adj object* non caché, non dissimulé; *joy* évident, non dissimulé.
unconcern [ˈʌnkənˈsɜːn] *n* (*calm*) calme *m*; (*in face of danger*) sang-froid *m*; (*lack of interest*) indifférence *f*, insouciance *f*.
unconcerned [ˈʌnkənˈsɜːnd] *adj* (*unworried*) imperturbable (*by* devant), qui ne s'inquiète pas (*by, about* de); (*unaffected*) indifférent (*by* à), insouciant (*by* de). **he went on speaking,** ~ il continua de parler sans se laisser troubler.
unconcernedly [ˈʌnkənˈsɜːnɪdlɪ] *adv* sans s'inquiéter, sans se laisser troubler, avec indifférence, avec insouciance.
unconditional [ˈʌnkənˈdɪʃənl] *adj* inconditionnel, sans condition, sans réserve. (*Jur*) ~ **discharge** libération inconditionnelle; (*Mil*) ~ **surrender** reddition *f* sans condition.
unconditionally [ˈʌnkənˈdɪʃnəlɪ] *adv* inconditionnellement, sans condition.
unconfined [ˈʌnkənˈfaɪnd] *adj* illimité, sans bornes.
unconfirmed [ˈʌnkənˈfɜːmd] *adj report, rumour* non confirmé.
uncongenial [ˈʌnkənˈdʒiːnɪəl] *adj person* peu sympathique, antipathique; *work, surroundings* peu agréable.
unconnected [ˈʌnkəˈnektɪd] *adj events, facts* sans rapport; *languages* sans connexion, d'origine différente; *ideas* décousu, sans suite; (*Elec*) débranché.
unconquerable [ʌnˈkɒŋkərəbl] *adj army, nation* invincible; *difficulty* insurmontable; *tendency* irrépressible, incorrigible.
unconquered [ʌnˈkɒŋkəd] *adj* qui n'a pas été conquis.
unconscionable [ʌnˈkɒnʃnəbl] *adj* déraisonnable.
unconscious [ʌnˈkɒnʃəs] 1 *adj* **(a)** (*Med*) sans connaissance, évanoui. **he was** ~ **for 3 hours** il est resté sans connaissance *or* évanoui pendant 3 heures; **to become** ~ perdre connaissance; **knocked** ~ assommé.
(b) (*unaware*) *person* inconscient (*of* de); *humour etc* inconscient, involontaire; *desire, dislike* inconscient. **to be** ~ **of sth** être inconscient de qch, ne pas avoir conscience de qch; (*Psych*) **the** ~ **mind** l'inconscient *m*.
2 *n* (*Psych*) inconscient *m*.
unconsciously [ʌnˈkɒnʃəslɪ] *adv* inconsciemment, sans s'en rendre compte. **he made an** ~ **funny remark** il a fait une remarque dont l'humour lui a échappé.
unconsciousness [ʌnˈkɒnʃəsnɪs] *n* (*U*) **(a)** (*Med*) évanouissement *m*, perte *f* de connaissance. **(b)** (*unawareness*) inconscience *f*.
unconsidered [ˈʌnkənˈsɪdəd] *adj remark, action* inconsidéré, irréfléchi. ~ **trifles** des vétilles sans importance.
unconstitutional [ˈʌnˌkɒnstɪˈtjuːʃənl] *adj* inconstitutionnel, anticonstitutionnel.
unconstitutionally [ʌnˌkɒnstɪˈtjuːʃnəlɪ] *adv* inconstitutionnellement, anticonstitutionnellement.
unconstrained [ˈʌnkənˈstreɪnd] *adj person* non contraint, libre; *behaviour* aisé; *act* spontané.
uncontested [ˈʌnkənˈtestɪd] *adj* incontesté; (*Parl*) *seat* non disputé, remporté sans opposition.
uncontrollable [ˈʌnkənˈtrəʊləbl] *adj child, animal* indiscipliné, impossible; *desire, emotion* irrésistible, irrépressible, qui ne peut être contenu *or* maîtrisé; *epidemic, price rise, inflation* qui ne peut être enrayé, qui ne peut être freiné. **he was seized with** ~ **laughter** le fou rire l'a pris; ~ **fits of rage** emportements *mpl*; **to have an** ~ **temper** ne pas être toujours maître de soi, ne pas savoir se contrôler.
uncontrollably [ˈʌnkənˈtrəʊləblɪ] *adv skid etc* sans pouvoir se reprendre. **to laugh** ~ avoir le fou rire.
uncontrolled [ˈʌnkənˈtrəʊld] *adj emotion, desire* non contenu, non maîtrisé, effréné; *price rises* effréné; *inflation* rampant, incontrôlé.
uncontroversial [ˈʌnˌkɒntrəˈvɜːʃəl] *adj* qui ne prête pas à controverse, non controversable.
unconventional [ˈʌnkənˈvenʃənl] *adj* peu conventionnel, original.
unconventionally [ˈʌnkənˈvenʃnəlɪ] *adv* de manière peu conventionnelle.
unconverted [ˈʌnkənˈvɜːtɪd] *adj* (*Fin, Rel, gen*) non converti.
unconvinced [ˈʌnkənˈvɪnst] *adj* non convaincu, sceptique. **to be** *or* **remain** ~ ne pas être convaincu *or* persuadé (*of sth* de qch), avoir des doutes (*of sth* sur qch).
unconvincing [ˈʌnkənˈvɪnsɪŋ] *adj* peu convaincant.
unconvincingly [ˈʌnkənˈvɪnsɪŋlɪ] *adv speak, argue* d'un ton *or* d'une manière peu convaincant(e).
uncooked [ˈʌnˈkʊkt] *adj* non cuit, cru.
uncooperative [ˈʌnkəʊˈɒpərətɪv] *adj* peu coopératif.
uncoordinated [ˈʌnkəʊˈɔːdɪneɪtɪd] *adj* non coordonné.
uncork [ˈʌnˈkɔːk] *vt* déboucher, enlever le bouchon de.
uncorrected [ˈʌnkəˈrektɪd] *adj* non corrigé.
uncorroborated [ˈʌnkəˈrɒbəreɪtɪd] *adj* non corroboré, sans confirmation.
uncorrupted [ˈʌnkəˈrʌptɪd] *adj* non corrompu.
uncountable [ˈʌnˈkaʊntəbl] *adj* innombrable, incalculable. (*Ling*) ~ **noun** nom *m* non comptable.
uncounted [ˈʌnˈkaʊntɪd] *adj* qui n'a pas été compté; (*fig: innumerable*) innombrable.
uncouple [ˈʌnˈkʌpl] *vt carriage* dételer; *train, engine* découpler; *trailer* détacher.
uncouth [ʌnˈkuːθ] *adj person, behaviour* grossier, fruste.
uncover [ʌnˈkʌvəʳ] *vt* découvrir.
uncovered [ʌnˈkʌvəd] *adj* découvert; (*Fin*) à découvert.
uncritical [ˈʌnˈkrɪtɪkəl] *adj person* dépourvu d'esprit critique; *attitude, approach, report* non critique. **to be** ~ **of** manquer d'esprit critique à l'égard de.
uncross [ˈʌnˈkrɒs] *vt* décroiser.
uncrossed [ˈʌnˈkrɒst] *adj* décroisé; *cheque* non barré.
uncrowded [ˈʌnˈkraʊdɪd] *adj* où il n'y a pas trop de monde.
uncrowned [ˈʌnˈkraʊnd] *adj* non couronné, sans couronne. (*fig*) **the** ~ **king of** le roi sans couronne de.
uncrushable [ˈʌnˈkrʌʃəbl] *adj fabric, dress* infroissable.
unction [ˈʌŋkʃən] *n* (*all senses*) onction *f*.
unctuous [ˈʌŋktjʊəs] *adj* (*pej*) onctueux, mielleux.
unctuously [ˈʌŋktjʊəslɪ] *adv* (*pej*) onctueusement, avec onction.
unctuousness [ˈʌŋktjʊəsnɪs] *n* (*U: pej*) manières onctueuses.
uncultivated [ˈʌnˈkʌltɪveɪtɪd] *adj land, person, mind* inculte; *voice, accent* qui manque de raffinement.
uncultured [ˈʌnˈkʌltʃəd] *adj person, mind* inculte; *voice, accent* qui manque de raffinement.
uncurl [ˈʌnˈkɜːl] 1 *vt wire, snake* dérouler. **to** ~ **one's legs** déplier ses jambes. 2 *vi* se dérouler.

uncut [ˈʌnˈkʌt] *adj* (*gen*) non coupé; *hedge* non taillé; *crops* sur pied; *diamond* brut; *gem, stone* non taillé; *edition, film, play* sans coupures, intégral.

undamaged [ʌnˈdæmɪdʒd] *adj goods* non endommagé, en bon état; *reputation* intact.

undamped [ˈʌnˈdæmpt] *adj* (*fig*) *enthusiasm, courage* non refroidi.

undated [ˈʌnˈdeɪtɪd] *adj* non daté, sans date.

undaunted [ˈʌnˈdɔːntɪd] *adj* non intimidé, non effrayé (*by* par), inébranlable. **he was ~ by their threats** leurs menaces ne l'effrayaient pas; **he carried on ~** il a continué sans se laisser intimider *or* démonter.

undeceive [ˈʌndɪˈsiːv] *vt* détromper, désabuser (*liter*).

undecided [ˈʌndɪˈsaɪdɪd] *adj person* indécis, irrésolu; *question* indécis; *weather* incertain. **that is still ~** cela n'a pas encore été décidé; **I am ~ whether to go or not** je n'ai pas décidé si j'irai ou non.

undeclared [ˈʌndɪˈklɛəd] *adj* (*Customs*) non déclaré.

undefeated [ˈʌndɪˈfiːtɪd] *adj* invaincu.

undefended [ˈʌndɪˈfendɪd] *adj* (*Mil etc*) sans défense, non défendu; (*Jur*) *suit* où on ne présente pas de défense, où le défendeur s'abstient de plaider.

undefiled [ˈʌndɪˈfaɪld] *adj* (*liter: lit, fig*) pur, sans tache. **~ by any contact with ...** qui n'a pas été contaminé *or* souillé par le contact de ... .

undefined [ˌʌndɪˈfaɪnd] *adj word, condition* non défini; *sensation etc* indéterminé, vague.

undelivered [ˈʌndɪˈlɪvəd] *adj* non remis, non distribué. **if ~ return to sender** ≃ en cas d'absence prière de retourner à l'expéditeur.

undemonstrative [ˈʌndɪˈmɒnstrətɪv] *adj* réservé, peu démonstratif, peu expansif.

undeniable [ˌʌndɪˈnaɪəbl] *adj* indéniable, incontestable.

undeniably [ˌʌndɪˈnaɪəblɪ] *adv* incontestablement, indiscutablement. **it is ~ true that** il est incontestable *or* indiscutable que.

undenominational [ˈʌndɪˌnɒmɪˈneɪʃənl] *adj* non confessionnel.

undependable [ˈʌndɪˈpendəbl] *adj person* sur qui on ne peut compter, à qui on ne peut se fier; *information* peu sûr; *machine* peu fiable.

under [ˈʌndəʳ] **1** *adv* **(a)** (*beneath*) au-dessous, en dessous. **he stayed ~ for 3 minutes** (*under water*) il est resté sous l'eau pendant 3 minutes; (*under anaesthetic*) il est resté sous l'effet de l'anesthésie *or* il est resté anesthésié pendant 3 minutes; (*Comm etc*) **as ~** comme ci-dessous; **he lifted the rope and crawled ~** il a soulevé la corde et il est passé par-dessous en se traînant; *V* **down**[1], **go under** *etc*.

(b) (*less*) au-dessous. **children of 15 and ~** les enfants de 15 ans et au-dessous; **10 degrees ~** 10 degrés au-dessous de zéro.

2 *prep* **(a)** (*beneath*) sous. **~ the table/sky/umbrella** sous la table/le ciel/le parapluie; **he came out from ~ the bed** il est sorti de dessous le lit; **the book slipped from ~ his arm** le livre a glissé de sous son bras; **it's ~ there** c'est là-dessous; **he went and sat ~ it** il est allé s'asseoir dessous; **to stay ~ water** rester sous l'eau; **~ the microscope** au microscope; *for other phrases V* **breath, cover, wing** *etc*.

(b) (*less than*) moins de, au-dessous de. **to be ~ age** avoir moins de dix-huit ans; être mineur; **children ~ 15** enfants de moins de *or* enfants au-dessous de 15 ans (*V also* 3); **it sells at ~ £10** cela se vend à moins de 10 livres; **there were ~ 50 of them** il y en avait moins de 50; **any number ~ 10** un chiffre au-dessous de 10; **in ~ 2 hours** en moins de 2 heures; **those ~ the rank of captain** ceux au-dessous du grade de capitaine.

(c) (*fig*) sous. **~ the Tudors** sous les Tudors; **~ the circumstances** dans les circonstances; **~ an assumed name** sous un faux nom; **you'll find him ~ 'plumbers' in the book** vous le trouverez sous 'plombiers' dans l'annuaire; **sent ~ plain cover** envoyé sous pli discret; (*Agr*) **~ wheat** en blé; **~ sentence of death** condamné à mort; (*Mil etc*) **to serve ~ sb** servir sous les ordres de qn; **he had 50 men ~ him** il avait 50 hommes sous ses ordres; **~ the command of** sous les ordres de; **to study ~ sb** *[undergraduate]* suivre les cours de qn; *[postgraduate]* faire des recherches *or* travailler sous la direction de qn; *[painter, composer]* être l'élève de qn; **this department comes ~ his authority** cette section relève de sa compétence; *for other phrases V* **control, impression, obligation** *etc*.

(d) (*according to*) en vertu de, conformément à, selon. **~ article 25** en vertu de *or* conformément à l'article 25; **~ French law** selon la législation française; **~ the terms of the contract** aux termes du contrat, selon *or* suivant les termes du contrat; **~ his will** selon son testament.

3 *cpd* (*insufficiently*) sous-; (*junior*) aide-, sous-. **underachieve** ne pas donner toute sa mesure à l'école; (*Theat*) **underact** jouer (un rôle) avec beaucoup de sobriété *or* très sobrement; **under-age drinking** consommation *f* d'alcool par les mineurs; **underarm** (*adv, adj*) par en-dessous; **underbelly** (*Anat*) bas-ventre *m*; (*fig*) point vulnérable; (*Bridge*) **to underbid (one's hand)** annoncer au-dessous de sa force; **underbody** dessous *m*; (*U*) **underbrush** sous-bois *m inv*, broussailles *fpl*; (*Fin*) **to be undercapitalized** être sous-financé; (*Aviat*) **undercarriage** train *m* d'atterrissage; **undercharge** ne pas faire payer assez à; **he undercharged me by £2** il aurait dû me faire payer 2 livres de plus; **underclothes,** (*U*) **underclothing** (*gen, also men's*) sous-vêtements *mpl*; (*women's only*) dessous *mpl*, lingerie *f* (*U*); *[paint]* **undercoat** *[paint]* couche *f* de fond; (*US Aut*) couche *f* antirouille (du châssis); (*Culin*) **undercooked** pas assez cuit; **undercover** secret (*f* -ète), clandestin; **undercover agent** agent secret; **undercurrent** (*lit*) courant *m* (sous-marin); (*fig*) courant sous-jacent; **underdeveloped** (*Anat*) qui n'est pas complètement développé *or* formé; (*Econ*) sous-développé; (*fig*) **the underdog** (*in game, fight*) celui qui perd, le perdant; (*economically, socially*) l'opprimé *m*; (*Culin*) **underdone** saignant; (*pej*) pas assez cuit; (*US*) **underdrawers** caleçon *m*, slip *m* (*pour homme*); **to be underdressed** ne pas être vêtu avec l'élégance requise; **underemployed** *person, equipment, building* sous-employé; *resources* sous-exploité; **underemployment** *[person etc]* sous-emploi *m*; *[resources]* sous-exploitation *f*; **underestimate** (*n*) sous-estimation *f*; (*vt*) sous-estimer, mésestimer, méconnaître; (*U*) **underestimation** sous-estimation *f*; (*Phot*) **underexpose** sous-exposer; (*Phot*) **underexposed** sous-exposé; (*Phot*) **underexposure** sous-exposition *f*; **underfeed** sous-alimenter; **underfeeding** sous-alimentation *f*; **underfelt** assise *f* de feutre; **under-floor heating** chauffage *m* par le plancher *or* le sol; **underfoot** sous les pieds; **it is wet underfoot** le sol est humide; **to trample sth underfoot** fouler qch aux pieds; **under-gardener** aide-jardinier *m*; **undergarment** sous-vêtement *m*; **undergraduate** (*n*) étudiant(e) *m(f)* (*qui prépare la licence*); (*cpd*) *life* étudiant, estudiantin; *circles* étudiant; *rooms* pour étudiants, d'étudiants; *opinion* des étudiants; *attitude* d'étudiant; **underground** *V* **underground;** (*U*) **undergrowth** broussailles *fpl*, sous-bois *m inv*; (*Sport*) **underhand** (*adj, adv*) par en-dessous; (*fig*) **underhand(ed)** *V* **underhand(ed); underlay** = **underfelt;** (*fig*) **underlie** être à la base de, sous-tendre; (*lit, fig*) **underline** souligner; (*U*) **underlining** soulignage *m*, soulignement *m*; **underlying** (*lit*) sous-jacent; (*fig*) (*basic*) fondamental, de base; (*hidden*) sous-jacent, profond; **undermanned** *ship, plane* à court d'équipage; *office, tank etc* à court de personnel; **undermentioned** (cité) ci-dessous; **undermine** (*lit*) *cliffs* miner, saper; (*fig*) *influence, power, authority* saper, ébranler; *health* miner, user; *effect* amoindrir; **undermost** (*adj*) le plus bas; (*adv*) tout en bas; **undernourish** sous-alimenter; **undernourishment** sous-alimentation *f*; **underpaid** sous-payé, sous-rémunéré; **underpants** caleçon *m*, slip *m* (*pour homme*); **underpart** partie inférieure; (*Aut*) **underpass** (*for cars*) passage inférieur (*de l'autoroute*); (*for pedestrians*) passage souterrain; **underpay** sous-payer, sous-rémunérer; **underpin** *wall* étayer; *building* reprendre en sous-œuvre; (*fig*) étayer; **underplay** minimiser; (*Theat*) **to underplay a role** jouer un rôle sans en tirer l'effet maximum; **underpopulated** sous-peuplé; **underprice** mettre un prix trop bas à; **at £2 this book is underpriced** le prix de 2 livres est trop bas pour ce livre; **underprivileged** (*gen*) défavorisé; (*Econ*) économiquement faible; **the underprivileged** les économiquement faibles; (*Econ, Ind*) **underproduce** sous-produire; **underproduction** sous-production *f*; **underrate** sous-estimer, mésestimer, méconnaître; **underripe** vert, qui n'est pas mûr; **underscore** souligner; **under-sea** (*adj*) sous-marin; (*adv*) sous la mer; (*Brit Aut*) **underseal** (*vt*) traiter contre la rouille (le châssis de); (*n*) couche *f* antirouille (du châssis); **undersecretary** sous-secrétaire *m*; (*Brit*) **Undersecretary of State** sous-secrétaire d'État; **undersell** *competitor* vendre moins cher que; *goods* vendre au-dessous du prix minimum légal; **undersexed** de faible libido; (*US*) **undershirt** tricot *m* de corps; (*Aviat*) **to undershoot the runway** atterrir avant d'atteindre la piste; (*US*) **undershorts** = **underpants; undershot** à aubes; **underside** dessous *m*; (*frm*) **undersigned** soussigné; (*frm*) **I the undersigned declare ...** je soussigné(e) déclare ...; **undersized** de (trop) petite taille, trop petit; **underskirt** jupon *m*; (*Aut*) **underslung** *car* à carrosserie surbaissée; *chassis* suspendu; **undersoil** sous-sol *m*; **understaffed** à court de personnel; **understand** *V* **understand; understate** minimiser; **understatement** *V* **understatement; understood** *V* **understand;** (*Theat*) **understudy** (*n*) doublure *f*; (*vt*) doubler; **undertake** *V* **undertake; undertaker** ordonnateur *m or* entrepreneur *m* des pompes funèbres, croque-mort* *m*; **undertaker's** (service *m* des) pompes funèbres *fpl*; **undertaking** *V* **undertaking;** (*in age*) **the under-10's** les moins de 10 ans; **under-the-counter** (*adj*) clandestin, au marché noir; (*adv*) clandestinement, au marché noir; **in an undertone** à mi-voix; (*fig*) **an undertone of criticism** des critiques sous-jacentes; **undervalue** *object* sous-évaluer, ne pas estimer à sa juste valeur; (*fig*) *person* sous-estimer, mésestimer, méconnaître; *sb's help* sous-estimer; **these houses are undervalued** ces maisons valent plus que leur prix; **undervest** tricot *m* de corps; **underwater** (*adj*) sous-marin; (*adv*) sous l'eau; (*U*) **underwear** = **underclothes; underweight** *goods* d'un poids insuffisant; *[person]* **to be underweight** ne pas peser assez, être trop maigre; **underworld** (*n*) (*hell*) enfers *mpl*; (*criminals*) milieu *m*, pègre *f*; (*cpd*) *organization* du milieu; *connections etc* avec le milieu; **underwrite** (*gen*) garantir; (*Insurance, St Ex*) souscrire; (*fig*) garantir, assurer; **underwriter** (*St Ex*) souscripteur *m*; (*Insurance*) membre *m* d'un syndicat de garantie, souscripteur *m*.

undercut [ˌʌndəˈkʌt] *pret, ptp* **undercut 1** *vt* (*Comm*) vendre moins cher que; (*Sport*) *ball* lifter. **2** *n* (*Culin*) (morceau *m* de) filet *m*.

undergo [ˈʌndəˈgəʊ] *pret* **underwent,** *ptp* **undergone** *vt test, change, modification,* (*Med*) *operation* subir; *suffering* éprouver; (*Med*) *treatment* suivre. **it is ~ing repairs** c'est en réparation.

underground [ˈʌndəgraʊnd] **1** *adj work* sous terre, souterrain; *explosion, cable* souterrain; (*fig*) *organization, press* clandestin, secret (*f* -ète); (*Art, Cine*) underground *inv*, d'avant-garde. **~ railway** métro *m*; (*fig*) **~ movement** mouvement clandestin; (*in occupied country*) résistance *f*.

2 *adv* sous (la) terre; (*fig*) clandestinement, secrètement. **it is 3 metres ~** c'est à 3 mètres sous (la) terre; *[wanted man]* **to go ~** entrer dans la clandestinité; *[guerilla]* prendre le maquis.

3 *n* (*Brit Rail*) métro *m*. **the ~** (*Mil, Pol etc*) la résistance; (*Art etc*) mouvement *m* underground *or* d'avant-garde.

underhand [ˌʌndəˈhænd] *adj*, **underhanded** [ˌʌndəˈhændɪd] *adj* (*pej*) en sous-main, en dessous, sournois. ~ **trick** fourberie *f*.

underhandedly [ˌʌndəˈhændɪdlɪ] *adv* (*pej*) sournoisement, en dessous, en sous-main.

underling [ˈʌndəlɪŋ] *n* (*pej*) subalterne *m*, sous-fifre* *m inv* (*pej*).

underneath [ˌʌndəˈniːθ] **1** *prep* sous, au-dessous de. **stand ~ it** mettez-vous dessous; **from ~ the table** de dessous la table. **2** *adv* (en) dessous. **the one ~** celui d'en dessous. **3** *adj* d'en dessous. **4** *n* dessous *m*.

understand [ˌʌndəˈstænd] *pret, ptp* **understood 1** *vt* **(a)** *person, words, meaning, painting, difficulty* comprendre; *action, event* comprendre, s'expliquer. **this can be understood in several ways** cela peut se comprendre de plusieurs façons; **that is easily understood** c'est facile à comprendre, cela se comprend facilement; **to make o.s. understood** se faire comprendre; **do I make myself understood?** est-ce que je me fais bien comprendre?; **that's quite understood!** c'est entendu!; **it must be understood that** il faut (bien) comprendre que; (*frm*) **it being understood that your client is responsible** à condition que votre client accepte (*subj*) la responsabilité; **do you ~ why/how/what?** est-ce que vous comprenez pourquoi/comment/ce que?; **that's what I can't ~** voilà ce que je ne comprends pas *or* ce qui me dépasse; **I can't ~ it!** je ne comprends pas!; **I can't ~ a word of it** je n'y comprends rien; **I can't ~ his agreeing to do it** je n'arrive pas à comprendre *or* je ne m'explique pas qu'il ait accepté de le faire; **I quite ~ that you don't want to come** je comprends très bien que vous n'ayez pas envie de venir; **you don't ~ the intricacies of the situation** vous ne comprenez pas *or* vous ne vous rendez pas compte de la complexité de la situation; **my wife doesn't ~ me** ma femme ne me comprend pas.

(b) (*believe etc*) (croire) comprendre. **I understood we were to be paid** j'ai cru comprendre que nous devions être payés; **I ~ you are leaving today** il paraît que vous partez aujourd'hui, si je comprends bien vous partez aujourd'hui; **am I to ~ that ...?** dois-je comprendre que ...?; **she is understood to have left the country, it is understood that she has left the country** il paraît *or* on pense généralement *or* on croit qu'elle a quitté le pays; **he let it be understood that** il a donné à entendre *or* il a laissé entendre que; **we were given to ~ that ...** on nous a donné à entendre que ..., on nous a fait comprendre que ... .

(c) (*imply, assume*) *word etc* sous-entendre. **to be understood** *[arrangement, price, date]* ne pas être spécifié; (*Gram*) être sous-entendu; **it was understood that he would pay for it** on présumait qu'il le paierait; **it's understood that he will pay** il est entendu qu'il paiera.

2 *vi* comprendre. **now I ~!** je comprends *or* j'y suis maintenant!; **there's to be no noise, do you ~!** pas de bruit, c'est bien compris! *or* tu entends!; **he was a widower, I ~** il était veuf, si j'ai bien compris *or* si je ne me trompe (pas).

understandable [ˌʌndəˈstændəbl] *adj person, speech* compréhensible, intelligible; *behaviour* compréhensible, naturel, normal; *pride, sorrow etc* compréhensible, naturel. **it is ~ that** on comprend *or* il est normal que+*subj*; **that's ~** ça se comprend.

understandably [ˌʌndəˈstændəblɪ] *adv* naturellement. **he's ~ angry** il est en colère et ça se comprend *or* ça n'a rien de surprenant.

understanding [ˌʌndəˈstændɪŋ] **1** *adj person* compréhensif (*about* à propos de); *smile, look* compatissant, bienveillant.

2 *n* **(a)** (*U*) compréhension *f*, entendement *m*, intelligence *f*. **he has good ~** il comprend vite; **he had a good ~ of the problems** il comprenait bien les problèmes; **his ~ of the problems/of children** sa compréhension des problèmes/des enfants, sa faculté de comprendre les problèmes/les enfants; **the age of ~** l'âge *m* de discernement.

(b) (*agreement*) accord *m*, arrangement *m*. **to come to an ~ with sb** s'entendre *or* s'arranger avec qn; **I have an ~ with the local shop** je me suis entendu avec le magasin du coin; **there is an ~ between us that ...** il est entendu entre nous que ...; **on the ~ that** à condition que + *subj*.

(c) (*U: concord*) entente *f*, bonne intelligence. **this will encourage ~ between our nations** ceci favorisera l'entente entre nos nations.

understandingly [ˌʌndəˈstændɪŋlɪ] *adv* avec bienveillance, avec compassion, en faisant preuve de compréhension.

understatement [ˈʌndəˌsteɪtmənt] *n* affirmation *f* en dessous de la vérité; (*Ling*) litote *f*. **to say he is clever is rather an ~** dire qu'il est intelligent n'est pas assez dire *or* ne suffit pas; **that's an ~** c'est peu dire, vous pouvez le dire, le terme est faible; **that's the ~ of the year!*** c'est bien le moins qu'on puisse dire!

understood [ˌʌndəˈstʊd] **1** *ptp of* **understand. 2** *adj* (*agreed*) entendu, convenu; (*Gram*) sous-entendu. **it is an ~ thing that he can't always be there** il est bien entendu qu'il ne peut pas toujours être là.

undertake [ˌʌndəˈteɪk] *pret* **undertook,** *ptp* **undertaken** *vt task* entreprendre; *duty* se charger de; *responsibility* assumer; *obligation* contracter. **to ~ to do** promettre *or* se charger de faire, s'engager à faire.

undertaking [ˌʌndəˈteɪkɪŋ] *n* **(a)** (*task, operation*) entreprise *f*. **it is quite an ~** ce n'est pas une petite affaire, c'est toute une entreprise.

(b) (*promise*) promesse *f*, engagement *m*. **to give an ~** promettre (*that* que, *to do* de faire); **I can give no such ~** je ne peux rien promettre de la sorte.

undeserved [ˈʌndɪˈzɜːvd] *adj* immérité.

undeservedly [ˈʌndɪˈzɜːvɪdlɪ] *adv reward, punish* à tort, indûment; *be rewarded, punished* sans l'avoir mérité, indûment.

undeserving [ˈʌndɪˈzɜːvɪŋ] *adj person* peu méritant; *cause* peu méritoire. **~ of** indigne de, qui ne mérite pas.

undesirable [ˈʌndɪˈzaɪərəbl] **1** *adj* peu souhaitable, (*stronger*) indésirable. **it is ~ that** il est peu souhaitable que + *subj*; (*Admin, Jur*) **~ alien** étranger *m*, -ère *f* indésirable. **2** *n* indésirable *mf*.

undetected [ˈʌndɪˈtektɪd] *adj* non décelé, non détecté, non découvert. **to go ~** passer inaperçu.

undetermined [ˈʌndɪˈtɜːmɪnd] *adj* (*unknown*) indéterminé, non connu; (*uncertain*) irrésolu, indécis.

undeterred [ˈʌndɪˈtɜːd] *adj* non découragé. **to carry on ~** continuer sans se laisser décourager *or* comme si de rien n'était.

undeveloped [ˈʌndɪˈveləpt] *adj fruit, intelligence, part of body* qui ne s'est pas développé; *film* non développé; *land, resources* non exploité.

undeviating [ʌnˈdiːvɪeɪtɪŋ] *adj path* droit; *policy, course* constant.

undies* [ˈʌndɪz] *npl* dessous *mpl*, lingerie *f* (*U*).

undigested [ˈʌndaɪˈdʒestɪd] *adj* non digéré.

undignified [ʌnˈdɪgnɪfaɪd] *adj* qui manque de dignité.

undiluted [ˈʌndaɪˈluːtɪd] *adj concentrate* non dilué; *pleasure* sans mélange; *nonsense* pur.

undiminished [ˈʌndɪˈmɪnɪʃt] *adj* non diminué.

undimmed [ˈʌnˈdɪmd] *adj lamp* qui n'a pas été mis en veilleuse; *headlight* qui n'a pas été mis en code; *colour, metal, beauty* non terni; *sight* aussi bon qu'auparavant. **my memory of it is ~** je m'en souviens avec précision.

undiplomatic [ˈʌnˌdɪpləˈmætɪk] *adj person* peu diplomate; *action, answer* peu diplomatique.

undipped [ˈʌnˈdɪpt] *adj* (*Aut*) *headlight* non en code. **his headlights were ~** il était en phares*, il n'était pas en code; **to drive on ~ headlights** conduire avec ses phares allumés.

undiscerning [ˈʌndɪˈsɜːnɪŋ] *adj* qui manque de discernement.

undischarged [ˈʌndɪsˈtʃɑːdʒd] *adj bankrupt* non réhabilité; *debt* non acquitté, impayé.

undisciplined [ʌnˈdɪsɪplɪnd] *adj* indiscipliné.

undisclosed [ˈʌndɪsˈkləʊzd] *adj* non révélé, non divulgué.

undiscovered [ˈʌndɪsˈkʌvəd] *adj* (*not found*) non découvert; (*unknown*) inconnu. **the treasure remained ~ for 700 years** le trésor n'a été découvert que 700 ans après.

undiscriminating [ˈʌndɪsˈkrɪmɪneɪtɪŋ] *adj* qui manque de discernement.

undisguised [ˈʌndɪsˈgaɪzd] *adj* (*lit, fig*) non déguisé.

undismayed [ˈʌndɪsˈmeɪd] *adj* non découragé, non consterné. **he was quite ~ by the news** la nouvelle ne l'a nullement consterné; **... he said ~ ...** dit-il sans se laisser décourager *or* intimider.

undisputed [ˈʌndɪsˈpjuːtɪd] *adj* incontesté.

undistinguished [ˈʌndɪsˈtɪŋgwɪʃt] *adj* (*in character*) médiocre, quelconque; (*in appearance*) peu distingué.

undisturbed [ˈʌndɪsˈtɜːbd] *adj* **(a)** (*untouched*) *papers, clues* non dérangé, non déplacé; (*uninterrupted*) *person* qui n'a pas été dérangé; *sleep* non troublé, paisible. **to work ~** travailler sans être dérangé.

(b) (*unworried*) non inquiet (*f* -ète), calme. **he was ~ by the news** la nouvelle ne l'a pas inquiété.

undivided [ˈʌndɪˈvaɪdɪd] *adj* indivisé, entier; (*unanimous*) unanime. **your ~ attention** toute votre attention.

undo [ˈʌnˈduː] *pret* **undid,** *ptp* **undone** *vt button, garment, knot, parcel, box, knitting* défaire; *good effect* détruire, annuler; *mischief, wrong* réparer; *V also* **undone.**

undoing [ˈʌnˈduːɪŋ] *n* (*U*) ruine *f*, perte *f*. **that was his ~** c'est ce qui l'a perdu, c'est ce qui a causé sa perte.

undomesticated [ˈʌndəˈmestɪkeɪtɪd] *adj animal* non domestiqué; *woman* qui n'est pas bonne maîtresse de maison; *man* qui ne sait pas faire le ménage.

undone [ˈʌnˈdʌn] **1** *ptp of* **undo. 2** *adj button, garment, knot, parcel* défait; *task* non accompli. **to come ~** se défaire; **to leave sth ~** ne pas faire qch; (†† *or hum*) **I am ~!** je suis perdu!

undoubted [ʌnˈdaʊtɪd] *adj* indubitable, certain.

undoubtedly [ʌnˈdaʊtɪdlɪ] *adv* indubitablement, sans aucun doute.

undramatic [ˈʌndrəˈmætɪk] *adj* peu dramatique.

undreamed-of [ʌnˈdriːmdɒv] *adj,* **undreamt-of** [ʌnˈdremtɒv] *adj* insoupçonné, qui dépasse l'imagination.

undress [ˈʌnˈdres] **1** *vt* déshabiller. **to get ~ed** se déshabiller. **2** *vi* se déshabiller. **3** *n* (*also Mil*) **in a state of ~** en petite tenue.

undrinkable [ˈʌnˈdrɪŋkəbl] *adj* (*unpalatable*) imbuvable; (*poisonous*) non potable.

undue [ˈʌnˈdjuː] *adj* indu, excessif.

undulate [ˈʌndjʊleɪt] *vi* onduler, ondoyer.

undulating [ˈʌndjʊleɪtɪŋ] *adj movement* ondoyant, onduleux; *aspect* onduleux; *line* sinueux, onduleux; *countryside* vallonné.

undulation [ˌʌndjʊˈleɪʃən] *n* ondulation *f*, ondoiement *m*.

undulatory [ˈʌndjʊlətrɪ] *adj* ondulatoire.

unduly [ˈʌnˈdjuːlɪ] *adv* trop, excessivement. **he was not ~ worried** il n'était pas inquiet outre mesure.

undying [ʌnˈdaɪɪŋ] *adj* (*fig*) éternel.

unearned [ˈʌnˈɜːnd] *adj money* non gagné; (*fig*) *praise, reward* immérité. **~ income** rentes *fpl*; **~ increment** plus-value *f*.

unearth [ˈʌnˈɜːθ] *vt* déterrer; (*fig*) déterrer, dénicher, découvrir.

unearthly [ʌnˈɜːθlɪ] *adj* surnaturel, sinistre, mystérieux; (**fig*) impossible*. **~ hour** heure indue.

uneasily [ʌnˈiːzɪlɪ] *adv* (*V* **uneasy**) *answer, gaze* avec inquiétude, d'un air gêné, avec gêne; *sleep* mal, d'un sommeil agité.

uneasiness [ʌnˈiːzɪnɪs] *n* (*U*) inquiétude *f*.

uneasy [ʌnˈiːzɪ] *adj calm, peace, truce* troublé, difficile; *silence* gêné; *sleep, night* agité; *conscience* non tranquille; *person* (*ill-at-ease*) mal à l'aise, gêné; (*worried*) inquiet (*f* -ète), anxieux. **to**

grow *or* **become ~ about sth** commencer à s'inquiéter au sujet de qch; **I have an ~ feeling that he's watching me** j'ai l'impression déconcertante qu'il me regarde; **I had an ~ feeling that he would change his mind** je ne pouvais m'empêcher de penser qu'il allait changer d'avis.
uneatable ['ʌn'iːtəbl] *adj* immangeable.
uneaten ['ʌn'iːtn] *adj* non mangé, non touché.
uneconomic(al) ['ʌn,iːkə'nɒmɪk(əl)] *adj machine, car* peu économique; *work, method* peu économique, peu rentable. **it is ~ to do that** il n'est pas économique *or* rentable* de faire cela.
unedifying [ʌn'edɪfaɪɪŋ] *adj* peu édifiant.
unedited [ʌn'edɪtɪd] *adj film* non monté; *essays, works* non édité; *tape* non mis au point.
uneducated ['ʌn'edjʊkeɪtɪd] *adj person* sans éducation; *speech, accent* populaire.
unemotional ['ʌnɪ'məʊʃənl] *adj* (*having little emotion*) peu émotif, peu émotionnable; (*showing little emotion*) *person, voice, attitude* qui ne montre *or* ne trahit aucune émotion, impassible; *reaction* peu émotionnel; *description, writing* neutre, dépourvu de passion.
unemotionally ['ʌnɪ'məʊʃnəlɪ] *adv* avec impassibilité.
unemployable ['ʌnɪm'plɔɪəbl] *adj* qui ne peut pas travailler, qui ne peut pas être embauché.
unemployed ['ʌnɪm'plɔɪd] **1** *adj person* sans travail, en chômage; *object, machine* inutilisé, dont on ne se sert pas; (*Fin*) *capital* qui ne travaille pas. **2** *n*: **the ~** les chômeurs *mpl.*
unemployment ['ʌnɪm'plɔɪmənt] **1** *n* (*U*) chômage *m.* **to reduce** *or* **cut ~** réduire le chômage *or* le nombre des chômeurs.
2 *cpd*: (*Brit*) **unemployment benefit,** (*US*) **unemployment compensation** allocation *f* de chômage; **the unemployment figures** les statistiques *fpl* du chômage, le nombre des chômeurs.
unencumbered ['ʌnɪn'kʌmbəd] *adj* non encombré (*with* de).
unending [ʌn'endɪŋ] *adj* interminable, sans fin.
unendurable ['ʌnɪn'djʊərəbl] *adj* insupportable, intolérable.
unengaged ['ʌnɪn'geɪdʒd] *adj* libre.
un-English ['ʌn'ɪŋglɪʃ] *adj* peu anglais, pas anglais.
unenlightened ['ʌnɪn'laɪtnd] *adj* peu éclairé, rétrograde.
unenterprising ['ʌn'entəpraɪzɪŋ] *adj person* peu entreprenant, qui manque d'initiative; *policy, act* qui manque d'audacité *or* de hardiesse.
unenthusiastic ['ʌnɪn,θuːzɪ'æstɪk] *adj* peu enthousiaste. **you seem rather ~ about it** ça n'a pas l'air de vous enthousiasmer *or* de vous emballer*.
unenthusiastically ['ʌnɪn,θuːzɪ'æstɪkəlɪ] *adv* sans enthousiasme.
unenviable [ʌn'envɪəbl] *adj* peu enviable.
unequal ['ʌn'iːkwəl] *adj size, opportunity, work* inégal. **to be ~ to a task** ne pas être à la hauteur d'une tâche.
unequalled ['ʌn'iːkwəld] *adj skill, enthusiasm, footballer, pianist* inégalé, sans égal, qui n'a pas son égal; *record* inégalé.
unequally ['ʌn'iːkwəlɪ] *adv* inégalement.
unequivocal ['ʌnɪ'kwɪvəkəl] *adj* sans équivoque. **he gave him an ~ 'no'** il lui a opposé un 'non' catégorique *or* sans équivoque.
unequivocally ['ʌnɪ'kwɪvəkəlɪ] *adv* sans équivoque.
unerring ['ʌn'ɜːrɪŋ] *adj judgment, accuracy* infaillible; *aim, skill, blow* sûr.
unerringly ['ʌn'ɜːrɪŋlɪ] *adv* infailliblement; d'une manière sûre.
unessential ['ʌnɪ'senʃəl] **1** *adj* non essentiel, non indispensable. **2** *npl*: **the ~s** tout ce qui n'est pas essentiel *or* indispensable, le superflu.
unesthetic [,ʌniːs'θetɪk] *adj* = **unaesthetic.**
unethical ['ʌn'eθɪkəl] *adj* peu éthique, immoral.
uneven ['ʌn'iːvən] *adj surface* inégal; *path* inégal, raboteux; *ground* inégal, accidenté; *quality, pulse, work* inégal, irrégulier; *number* impair. (*Aut*) **the engine sounds ~** il y a des à-coups dans le moteur, le moteur ne tourne pas rond.
unevenly ['ʌn'iːvənlɪ] *adv* (*V* **uneven**) inégalement; irrégulièrement.
unevenness ['ʌn'iːvənnɪs] *n* (*U*: *V* **uneven**) inégalité *f*; irrégularité *f.*
uneventful ['ʌnɪ'ventfʊl] *adj day, meeting, journey* sans incidents, peu mouvementé; *life* calme, tranquille, peu mouvementé; *career* peu mouvementé.
unexceptionable [,ʌnɪk'sepʃnəbl] *adj* irréprochable.
unexceptional [,ʌnɪk'sepʃənl] *adj* qui n'a rien d'exceptionnel.
unexciting ['ʌnɪk'saɪtɪŋ] *adj time, life, visit* peu passionnant, peu intéressant; *food* ordinaire.
unexpected ['ʌnɪks'pektɪd] *adj arrival* inattendu, inopiné; *result, change* inattendu, imprévu; *success, happiness* inattendu, imprévu, inespéré. **it was all very ~** on ne s'y attendait pas du tout.
unexpectedly ['ʌnɪks'pektɪdlɪ] *adv* alors qu'on ne s'y attend (*or* attendait *etc*) pas, subitement. **to arrive ~** arriver à l'improviste *or* inopinément.
unexpired ['ʌnɪks'paɪəd] *adj* non expiré, encore valide.
unexplained ['ʌnɪks'pleɪnd] *adj* inexpliqué.
unexploded ['ʌnɪks'pləʊdɪd] *adj* non explosé, non éclaté.
unexploited ['ʌnɪks'plɔɪtɪd] *adj* inexploité.
unexplored ['ʌnɪks'plɔːd] *adj* inexploré.
unexposed ['ʌnɪks'pəʊzd] *adj* (*Phot*) *film* vierge.
unexpressed ['ʌnɪks'prest] *adj* inexprimé.
unexpurgated ['ʌn'ekspɜːgeɪtɪd] *adj* non expurgé, intégral.
unfading [ʌn'feɪdɪŋ] *adj* (*fig*) impérissable, ineffaçable.
unfailing [ʌn'feɪlɪŋ] *adj supply* inépuisable, intarissable; *zeal* inépuisable; *optimism* inébranlable; *remedy* infaillible.
unfailingly [ʌn'feɪlɪŋlɪ] *adv* infailliblement, immanquablement.
unfair ['ʌn'fɛəʳ] *adj person* injuste (*to sb* envers qn, à l'égard de qn); *decision, arrangement, deal* injuste, inéquitable; *competition, play, tactics* déloyal. **it's ~ that** ce n'est pas juste *or* c'est injuste que +*subj*; **it is ~ of her to do so** il est injuste qu'elle agisse ainsi, ce n'est pas juste de sa part d'agir ainsi.
unfairly ['ʌn'fɛəlɪ] *adv decide* injustement; *play* déloyalement.
unfairness ['ʌn'fɛənɪs] *n* (*V* **unfair**) injustice *f*; déloyauté *f.*
unfaithful ['ʌn'feɪθfʊl] *adj* infidèle (*to* à).
unfaithfully ['ʌn'feɪθfəlɪ] *adv* infidèlement, avec infidélité.
unfaithfulness ['ʌn'feɪθfʊlnɪs] *n* infidélité *f.*
unfaltering [ʌn'fɔːltərɪŋ] *adj step, voice* ferme, assuré.
unfalteringly [ʌn'fɔːltərɪŋlɪ] *adv speak* d'une voix ferme *or* assurée; *walk* d'un pas ferme *or* assuré.
unfamiliar ['ʌnfə'mɪljəʳ] *adj place, sight* peu familier, étrange, inconnu; *person, subject* peu familier, inconnu, mal connu. **to be ~ with sth** mal connaître qch, ne pas être au fait de qch.
unfamiliarity ['ʌnfə,mɪlɪ'ærɪtɪ] *n* (*U*) aspect étrange *or* inconnu.
unfashionable ['ʌn'fæʃnəbl] *adj dress, subject* démodé, qui n'est plus à la mode, passé de mode; *district, shop, hotel* peu chic *inv.* **it is ~ to speak of ...** ça ne se fait plus de parler de ... .
unfasten ['ʌn'fɑːsn] *vt garment, buttons, rope* défaire; *door* ouvrir, déverrouiller; *bonds* défaire, détacher; (*loosen*) desserrer.
unfathomable [ʌn'fæðəməbl] *adj* (*lit, fig*) insondable.
unfathomed ['ʌn'fæðəmd] *adj* (*lit, fig*) insondé.
unfavourable, (*US*) **unfavorable** ['ʌn'feɪvərəbl] *adj conditions, report, outlook, weather* défavorable; *moment* peu propice, inopportun; *wind* contraire.
unfavourably, (*US*) **unfavorably** ['ʌn'feɪvərəblɪ] *adv* défavorablement. **I was ~ impressed** j'ai eu une impression défavorable; **to regard sth ~** être défavorable *or* hostile à qch.
unfeeling [ʌn'fiːlɪŋ] *adj* insensible, impitoyable, dur.
unfeelingly [ʌn'fiːlɪŋlɪ] *adv* sans pitié, impitoyablement.
unfeigned [ʌn'feɪnd] *adj* non simulé, sincère.
unfeignedly [ʌn'feɪnɪdlɪ] *adv* sincèrement, vraiment.
unfeminine [ʌn'femɪnɪn] *adj* peu féminin.
unfettered ['ʌn'fetəd] *adj* (*liter: lit, fig*) sans entrave. **~ by** libre de.
unfilial ['ʌn'fɪljəl] *adj* peu filial.
unfinished ['ʌn'fɪnɪʃt] *adj task, essay* inachevé, incomplet (*f* -ète). **I have 3 ~ letters** j'ai 3 lettres à finir; **we have some ~ business** nous avons quelques affaires pendantes; (*threatening*) nous avons une affaire à régler; *[piece of handcraft etc]* **it looks rather ~** c'est mal fini, la finition laisse à désirer.
unfit ['ʌn'fɪt] **1** *adj* (*incompetent*) inapte, impropre (*for* à, *to do* à faire); (*unworthy*) indigne (*to do* de faire); (*ill*) qui n'est pas en forme, qui n'est pas bien, (*stronger*) souffrant. **he is ~ to be a teacher** il ne devrait pas enseigner; **he was ~ to drive** il n'était pas en état de conduire; **he is ~ for work** il n'est pas en état de reprendre le travail; **~ for military service** inapte au service militaire; **the doctor declared him ~ for the match** le docteur a déclaré qu'il n'était pas en état de jouer; **~ for habitation** inhabitable; **~ for consumption** impropre à la consommation; **~ to eat** (*unpalatable*) immangeable; (*poisonous*) non comestible; **~ for publication** impropre à la publication, impubliable; **road ~ for lorries** route impraticable aux camions.
2 *vt* rendre inapte (*for* à, *to do* à faire).
unfitness ['ʌn'fɪtnɪs] *n* inaptitude *f* (*for* à, *to do* à faire); (*ill-health*) incapacité *f.*
unfitted [ʌn'fɪtɪd] *adj* inapte (*for* à, *to do* à faire).
unfitting [ʌn'fɪtɪŋ] *adj language, behaviour* peu *or* guère convenable, inconvenant; *ending, result* mal approprié.
unfix ['ʌn'fɪks] *vt* détacher, enlever; (*Mil*) *bayonets* remettre.
unflagging [ʌn'flægɪŋ] *adj person, devotion, patience* infatigable, inlassable; *enthusiasm* inépuisable; *interest* soutenu jusqu'au bout.
unflaggingly [ʌn'flægɪŋlɪ] *adv* infatigablement, inlassablement.
unflappable* ['ʌn'flæpəbl] *adj* imperturbable, qui ne perd pas son calme.
unflattering ['ʌn'flætərɪŋ] *adj person, remark, photo, portrait* peu flatteur. **he was very ~ about it** ce qu'il en a dit n'avait rien de flatteur *or* n'était pas flatteur; **she wears ~ clothes** elle porte des vêtements qui ne la mettent guère en valeur *or* qui ne l'avantagent guère.
unflatteringly ['ʌn'flætərɪŋlɪ] *adv* d'une manière peu flatteuse.
unfledged ['ʌn'fledʒd] *adj* (*fig*) *person, organization, movement* qui manque d'expérience. **an ~ youth** un garçon sans expérience, un blanc-bec (*pej*).
unflinching ['ʌn'flɪntʃɪŋ] *adj* stoïque, qui ne bronche pas.
unflinchingly ['ʌn'flɪntʃɪŋlɪ] *adv* stoïquement, sans broncher.
unflyable ['ʌn'flaɪəbl] *adj plane* qu'on ne peut pas faire voler.
unfold [ʌn'fəʊld] **1** *vt napkin, map, blanket* déplier; *wings* déployer; (*fig*) *plans, ideas* exposer; *secret* dévoiler, révéler. **to ~ a map on a table** étaler une carte sur une table; **to ~ one's arms** décroiser les bras.
2 *vi [flower]* s'ouvrir, s'épanouir; *[view, countryside]* se dérouler, s'étendre; *[story, film, plot]* se dérouler.
unforeseeable ['ʌnfɔː'siːəbl] *adj* imprévisible.
unforeseen ['ʌnfɔː'siːn] *adj* imprévu.
unforgettable ['ʌnfə'getəbl] *adj* inoubliable.
unforgivable ['ʌnfə'gɪvəbl] *adj* impardonnable.
unforgivably ['ʌnfə'gɪvəblɪ] *adv* impardonnablement.
unforgiven ['ʌnfə'gɪvən] *adj* non pardonné.
unforgiving ['ʌnfə'gɪvɪŋ] *adj* implacable, impitoyable.
unforgotten ['ʌnfə'gɒtn] *adj* inoublié.
unformed ['ʌn'fɔːmd] *adj* informe.

unforthcoming [ˈʌnfɔːθˈkʌmɪŋ] *adj reply, person* réticent. **he was very ~ about it** il s'est montré très réticent, il s'est montré peu disposé à en parler.

unfortified [ˈʌnˈfɔːtɪfaɪd] *adj* (*Mil*) sans fortifications, non fortifié.

unfortunate [ʌnˈfɔːtʃnɪt] **1** *adj person* malheureux, malchanceux; *coincidence* malheureux, fâcheux, regrettable; *circumstances* triste; *event* fâcheux, malencontreux; *remark* malheureux, malencontreux. **it is most ~ that** il est très malheureux *or* regrettable que+*subj*; **he has been ~** il n'a pas eu de chance.

2 *n* malheureux *m*, -euse *f*.

unfortunately [ʌnˈfɔːtʃnɪtlɪ] *adv* malheureusement, par malheur. **an ~ worded document** un document rédigé de façon malencontreuse.

unfounded [ˈʌnˈfaʊndɪd] *adj rumour, allegation, belief* dénué de tout fondement, sans fondement; *criticism* injustifié.

unframed [ˈʌnˈfreɪmd] *adj picture* sans cadre.

unfreeze [ˈʌnˈfriːz] *pret* **unfroze,** *ptp* **unfrozen 1** *vt* (*lit*) dégeler; (*Econ, Fin*) débloquer.

2 *vi* dégeler.

unfrequented [ˈʌnfrɪˈkwentɪd] *adj* peu fréquenté.

unfriendliness [ˈʌnˈfrendlɪnɪs] *n* (*U*) froideur *f* (*towards* envers).

unfriendly [ˈʌnˈfrendlɪ] *adj person, reception* froid; *attitude, behaviour, act, remark* inamical, (*stronger*) hostile. **to be ~ to(wards) sb** manifester de la froideur *or* de l'hostilité à qn, ne pas être très gentil avec qn.

unfrock [ˈʌnˈfrɒk] *vt* défroquer.

unfroze [ˈʌnˈfrəʊz] *pret of* **unfreeze.**

unfrozen [ˈʌnˈfrəʊzn] *ptp of* **unfreeze.**

unfruitful [ˈʌnˈfruːtfʊl] *adj* stérile, infertile; (*fig*) infructueux.

unfruitfully [ˈʌnˈfruːtfʊlɪ] *adv* (*fig*) en vain, sans succès.

unfulfilled [ˈʌnfʊlˈfɪld] *adj promise* non tenu; *ambition* inaccompli, non réalisé; *desire* insatisfait; *condition* non rempli; *prophecy* non réalisé. *[person]* **to feel ~** se sentir frustré, éprouver un sentiment d'insatisfaction.

unfunny* [ˈʌnˈfʌnɪ] *adj* qui n'est pas drôle, qui n'a rien de drôle.

unfurl [ʌnˈfɜːl] **1** *vt* déployer. **2** *vi* se déployer.

unfurnished [ˈʌnˈfɜːnɪʃt] *adj* non meublé.

ungainliness [ʌnˈgeɪnlɪnɪs] *n* (*U*) gaucherie *f*.

ungainly [ʌnˈgeɪnlɪ] *adj* gauche, disgracieux, dégingandé.

ungallant [ˈʌnˈgælənt] *adj* peu *or* guère galant, discourtois.

ungenerous [ˈʌnˈdʒenərəs] *adj* peu généreux, parcimonieux.

ungentlemanly [ʌnˈdʒentlmənlɪ] *adj* peu *or* guère galant, discourtois.

un-get-at-able* [ˈʌngetˈætəbl] *adj* inaccessible.

ungird [ˈʌnˈgɜːd] *pret, ptp* **ungirt** *vt* détacher.

unglazed [ˈʌnˈgleɪzd] *adj door, window* non vitré; *picture* qui n'est pas sous verre; *pottery* non vernissé, non émaillé; *photograph* mat; *cake* non glacé.

ungodliness [ʌnˈgɒdlɪnɪs] *n* (*U*) impiété *f*.

ungodly [ʌnˈgɒdlɪ] *adj person, action, life* impie, irréligieux; (* *fig*) impossible*. **~ hour** heure indue.

ungovernable [ʌnˈgʌvənəbl] *adj people, country* ingouvernable; *desire, passion* irrépressible. **he has an ~ temper** il n'est pas toujours maître de lui-même.

ungracious [ˈʌnˈgreɪʃəs] *adj person* peu gracieux, incivil (*f* incivile); *smile, remark* peu gracieux, peu aimable.

ungraciously [ˈʌnˈgreɪʃəslɪ] *adv* avec mauvaise grâce.

ungrammatical [ˈʌngrəˈmætɪkəl] *adj* incorrect, non grammatical, agrammatical.

ungrammatically [ˈʌngrəˈmætɪkəlɪ] *adv* incorrectement, agrammaticalement.

ungrateful [ʌnˈgreɪtfʊl] *adj person* ingrat, peu reconnaissant (*towards* envers); *task* ingrat.

ungratefully [ʌnˈgreɪtfəlɪ] *adv* avec ingratitude.

ungrudging [ˈʌnˈgrʌdʒɪŋ] *adj person, contribution* généreux; *help* donné sans compter; *praise, gratitude* très sincère.

ungrudgingly [ʌnˈgrʌdʒɪŋlɪ] *adv give* généreusement; *help* de bon cœur, sans compter.

unguarded [ˈʌnˈgɑːdɪd] *adj* (*Mil etc*) sans surveillance; (*fig*) *remark* irréfléchi, imprudent. **in an ~ moment** dans un moment d'inattention.

unguent [ˈʌŋgwənt] *n* onguent *m*.

ungulate [ˈʌŋgjʊleɪt] **1** *adj* ongulé. **2** *n* animal ongulé. **~s** ongulés *mpl*.

unhallowed [ʌnˈhæləʊd] *adj* non consacré, profane.

unhampered [ˈʌnˈhæmpəd] *adj* non entravé (*by* par), libre.

unhand [ʌnˈhænd] *vt* (†† *or hum*) lâcher.

unhandy* [ʌnˈhændɪ] *adj* gauche, maladroit.

unhappily [ʌnˈhæpɪlɪ] *adv* (*miserably*) d'un air malheureux, sur un ton malheureux; (*unfortunately*) malheureusement.

unhappiness [ʌnˈhæpɪnɪs] *n* (*U*) tristesse *f*, chagrin *m*.

unhappy [ʌnˈhæpɪ] *adj person* (*sad*) triste, malheureux; (*ill-pleased*) mécontent; (*worried*) inquiet (*f* -ète); (*unfortunate*) malheureux, malchanceux; *childhood* malheureux; *remark, choice* malheureux, malencontreux; *coincidence* malheureux, regrettable, fâcheux; *circumstances* triste. **to make sb ~** causer du chagrin à qn, rendre qn malheureux; **this ~ state of affairs** cette situation regrettable *or* déplorable *or* fâcheuse; **we are ~ about the decision** la décision nous inquiète; **I feel ~ about leaving him alone** je n'aime pas le laisser seul, cela m'inquiète de le laisser seul.

unharmed [ˈʌnˈhɑːmd] *adj person* sain et sauf, indemne; *thing* intact, non endommagé. **he escaped ~** il en est sorti indemne *or* sain et sauf.

unharness [ˈʌnˈhɑːnɪs] *vt* dételer (*from* de).

unhealthy [ʌnˈhelθɪ] *adj person, appearance, complexion* maladif; *air, place* malsain; (*fig*) *curiosity* malsain, morbide. (*fig: dangerous*) **it's getting rather ~ around here*** les choses commencent à se gâter par ici; **the car sounds a bit ~*** le moteur fait un bruit qui ne me plaît pas.

unheard [ˈʌnˈhɜːd] **1** *adj* non entendu. **he was condemned ~** il a été condamné sans avoir été entendu.

2 *cpd*: **unheard-of** inouï, sans précédent; **it's quite unheard-of for such a thing to happen** ce genre de chose n'arrive pratiquement jamais *or* est sans précédent.

unheeded [ˈʌnˈhiːdɪd] *adj* (*ignored*) négligé, ignoré; (*unnoticed*) inaperçu. **this warning went ~** on n'a pas prêté attention à *or* on n'a pas tenu compte de *or* on a ignoré cet avertissement.

unheeding [ˈʌnˈhiːdɪŋ] *adj* insouciant (*of* de), indifférent (*of* à). **they passed by ~** ils sont passés à côté sans faire attention.

unhelpful [ˈʌnˈhelpfʊl] *adj person* peu secourable, peu serviable, peu obligeant; *advice, book, tool* qui n'aide guère, qui n'apporte rien d'utile. **I found that very ~** ça ne m'a pas aidé du tout, je ne suis pas plus avancé.

unhelpfully [ˈʌnˈhelpfʊlɪ] *adv say, suggest* sans apporter quoi que ce soit d'utile.

unheralded [ˈʌnˈherəldɪd] *adj* sans tambour ni trompette.

unhesitating [ʌnˈhezɪteɪtɪŋ] *adj reply, reaction* immédiat, prompt; *person* résolu, ferme, qui n'hésite pas. **his ~ generosity** sa générosité spontanée.

unhesitatingly [ʌnˈhezɪteɪtɪŋlɪ] *adv* sans hésitation, sans hésiter.

unhindered [ˈʌnˈhɪndəd] *adj progress* sans obstacles, sans encombre, sans entrave; *movement* libre, sans encombre. **to go ~** passer librement *or* sans rencontrer d'obstacles *or* sans encombre; **he worked ~** il a travaillé sans être dérangé (*by* par).

unhinge [ʌnˈhɪndʒ] *vt* enlever de ses gonds, démonter; (*fig*) *mind* déranger; *person* déséquilibrer, désaxer.

unhitch [ˈʌnˈhɪtʃ] *vt rope* décrocher, détacher; *horse* dételer.

unholy [ʌnˈhəʊlɪ] *adj* impie, profane; (* *fig*) impossible*. **~ hour** heure indue.

unhook [ˈʌnˈhʊk] *vt picture from wall* décrocher (*from* de); (*undo*) *garment* dégrafer.

unhoped-for [ʌnˈhəʊptfɔːʳ] *adj* inespéré.

unhopeful [ʌnˈhəʊpfʊl] *adj prospect, start* peu prometteur; *person* pessimiste, qui n'a guère d'espoir.

unhorse [ˈʌnˈhɔːs] *vt* désarçonner, démonter.

unhurried [ˈʌnˈhʌrɪd] *adj person* posé, pondéré, qui prend son temps; *steps, movement* lent; *reflection* mûr (*before n*), long (*f* longue); *journey* fait sans se presser. **after ~ consideration** après avoir longuement *or* posément considéré; **they had an ~ meal** ils ont mangé sans se presser.

unhurriedly [ˈʌnˈhʌrɪdlɪ] *adv* posément, en prenant son temps, sans se presser.

unhurt [ˈʌnˈhɜːt] *adj* indemne, sain et sauf. **to escape ~** sortir indemne *or* sain et sauf.

unhygienic [ˈʌnhaɪˈdʒiːnɪk] *adj* contraire à l'hygiène, non hygiénique.

uni... [ˈjuːnɪ] *pref* uni..., mono... .

unicameral [ˈjuːnɪˈkæmərəl] *adj* (*Parl*) unicaméral.

unicellular [ˈjuːnɪˈseljʊləʳ] *adj* unicellulaire.

unicorn [ˈjuːnɪkɔːn] *n* licorne *f*.

unidentified [ˈʌnaɪˈdentɪfaɪd] *adj butterfly, person* non identifié. **~ flying object** (*abbr* **UFO**) objet volant non identifié (*abbr* **O.V.N.I.** *m*).

unidirectional [ˌjuːnɪdɪˈrekʃənl] *adj* unidirectionnel.

unification [ˌjuːnɪfɪˈkeɪʃən] *n* unification *f*.

uniform [ˈjuːnɪfɔːm] **1** *n* uniforme *m*. **in ~** en uniforme; (*Mil etc*) **in full ~** en grand uniforme; **out of ~** *policeman, soldier* en civil; *schoolboy* en habits de tous les jours. **2** *adj length* uniforme; *colour, shade* pareil, même; *temperature* constant. **to make ~** uniformiser. **3** *cpd trousers etc* d'uniforme.

uniformed [ˈjuːnɪfɔːmd] *adj policeman etc* en uniforme; *organization* qui porte un uniforme.

uniformity [ˌjuːnɪˈfɔːmɪtɪ] *n* (*U*) uniformité *f*.

uniformly [ˈjuːnɪfɔːmlɪ] *adv* uniformément, sans varier.

unify [ˈjuːnɪfaɪ] *vt* unifier.

unilateral [ˈjuːnɪˈlætərəl] *adj* unilatéral. **~ declaration of independence** (*abbr* **UDI**) proclamation unilatérale d'indépendance; **~ disarmament** désarmement unilatéral.

unilaterally [ˈjuːnɪˈlætərəlɪ] *adv* unilatéralement.

unimaginable [ˌʌnɪˈmædʒnəbl] *adj* inimaginable, inconcevable.

unimaginative [ˈʌnɪˈmædʒnətɪv] *adj* peu imaginatif, qui manque d'imagination.

unimaginatively [ˈʌnɪˈmædʒnətɪvlɪ] *adv* d'une manière peu imaginative, sans imagination.

unimaginativeness [ˈʌnɪˈmædʒnətɪvnɪs] *n* manque *m* d'imagination.

unimpaired [ˈʌnɪmˈpeəd] *adj quality* non diminué; *health, mental powers, hearing* aussi bon qu'auparavant; *prestige* intact, entier. **his sight is ~** sa vue ne s'est pas détériorée *or* n'a pas été affectée, sa vue est aussi bonne qu'auparavant, il a conservé toute sa vue.

unimpeachable [ˌʌnɪmˈpiːtʃəbl] *adj reputation, conduct, honesty* irréprochable, inattaquable; *references* irréprochable, impeccable; *evidence* irrécusable; *source* sûr.

unimpeded [ˈʌnɪmˈpiːdɪd] *adj* libre d'entraves.

unimportant [ˈʌnɪmˈpɔːtənt] *adj* peu important, sans importance, insignifiant.

unimposing [ˈʌnɪmˈpəʊzɪŋ] *adj* peu imposant, peu impressionnant.

unimpressed [ˈʌnɪmˈprest] *adj* (*by sight, size, pleas etc*) peu impressionné (*by* par); (*by explanation, argument*) peu convaincu (*by* par). **I was** ~ ça ne m'a pas impressionné *or* convaincu.

unimpressive ['ʌnɪm'presɪv] *adj person, amount* peu *or* guère impressionnant, insignifiant; *sight, achievement, result* peu *or* guère impressionnant, peu frappant; *argument, performance* peu convaincant.

unimproved ['ʌnɪm'pruːvd] *adj situation, position, work, health, appearance, condition* qui ne s'est pas amélioré, inchangé; *method* non amélioré; *team* qui ne joue pas mieux qu'avant. *[invalid]* **he is** ~ son état de santé ne s'est pas amélioré *or* demeure inchangé.

unincorporated [ˌʌnɪn'kɔːpəreɪtɪd] *adj* non incorporé (*in* dans); (*Comm, Jur*) non enregistré.

uninfluential ['ʌnɪnflʊ'enʃəl] *adj* sans influence, qui n'a pas d'influence.

uninformed ['ʌnɪn'fɔːmd] *adj person* mal informé, mal renseigné (*about* sur), qui n'est pas au courant (*about* de); *opinion* mal informé.

uninhabitable ['ʌnɪn'hæbɪtəbl] *adj* inhabitable.

uninhabited ['ʌnɪn'hæbɪtɪd] *adj* inhabité.

uninhibited ['ʌnɪn'hɪbɪtɪd] *adj person* sans inhibitions, qui n'a pas d'inhibitions; *impulse, desire* non refréné; *dance* sans retenue.

uninitiated ['ʌnɪ'nɪʃɪeɪtɪd] **1** *adj* non initié (*into* à), qui n'est pas au courant (*into* de).

2 *n* (*Rel etc*) **the** ~ les non-initiés *mpl*, les profanes *mpl*; (*fig*) **it is complicated for the** ~ c'est bien compliqué pour ceux qui ne s'y connaissent pas *or* qui ne sont pas au courant.

uninjured ['ʌn'ɪndʒəd] *adj* qui n'est pas blessé, indemne, sain et sauf. **he was** ~ **in the accident** il est sorti indemne *or* sain et sauf de l'accident.

uninspired ['ʌnɪn'spaɪəd] *adj* qui n'est pas inspiré, qui manque d'inspiration.

uninspiring ['ʌnɪn'spaɪərɪŋ] *adj* qui n'est pas *or* guère inspirant.

uninsured ['ʌnɪn'ʃʊəd] *adj* non assuré (*against* contre).

unintelligent ['ʌnɪn'telɪdʒənt] *adj* inintelligent.

unintelligible ['ʌnɪn'telɪdʒɪbl] *adj* inintelligible.

unintelligibly ['ʌnɪn'telɪdʒəblɪ] *adv* inintelligiblement.

unintended ['ʌnɪn'tendɪd] *adj*, **unintentional** ['ʌnɪn'tenʃənl] *adj* involontaire, non intentionnel, inconscient. **it was quite** ~ ce n'était pas fait exprès.

unintentionally ['ʌnɪn'tenʃnəlɪ] *adv* involontairement, sans le vouloir, sans le faire exprès.

uninterested [ʌn'ɪntrɪstɪd] *adj* indifférent (*in* à).

uninteresting ['ʌn'ɪntrɪstɪŋ] *adj book, account, activity* inintéressant, dépourvu d'intérêt; *person* ennuyeux; *offer* non intéressant.

uninterrupted ['ʌnˌɪntə'rʌptɪd] *adj* ininterrompu, continu.

uninterruptedly ['ʌnˌɪntə'rʌptɪdlɪ] *adv* sans interruption.

uninvited ['ʌnɪn'vaɪtɪd] *adj person* qui n'a pas été invité; *criticism* gratuit. **to arrive** ~ arriver sans avoir été invité *or* sans invitation; **to do sth** ~ faire qch sans y avoir été invité.

uninviting ['ʌnɪn'vaɪtɪŋ] *adj* peu attirant, peu attrayant; *food* peu appétissant.

union ['juːnjən] **1** *n* **(a)** (*gen, Pol*) union *f*; (*Ind: trade* ~) syndicat *m*; (*marriage*) union, mariage *m*. **postal/customs** ~ union postale/douanière; (*US*) **the U**~ les États-Unis *mpl*; **U**~ **of Soviet Socialist Republics** (*abbr* **USSR**) Union des républiques socialistes soviétiques (*abbr* U.R.S.S. *f*); (*Univ*) **the (Students') U**~ l'Association *f* des Étudiants; (*fig*) **in perfect** ~ en parfaite harmonie.

(b) (*Tech*) raccord *m*.

2 *cpd* (*Ind*) *card, leader, movement* syndical; *headquarters* du syndicat. (*Brit*) **Union Jack** Union Jack *m* (*drapeau du Royaume-Uni*); (*Ind*) **union member** syndiqué(e) *m(f)*, membre *m* du syndicat; (*US*) **union shop** atelier *m* d'ouvriers syndiqués; (*US*) **union suit** combinaison *f*.

unionism ['juːnjənɪzəm] *n* (*Ind*) syndicalisme *m*; (*Pol*) unionisme *m*.

unionist ['juːnjənɪst] *n* **(a)** (*Ind: trade* ~) syndiqué(e) *m(f)*, membre *m* d'un syndicat. **the militant** ~**s** les syndicalistes *mpl*, les militants syndicaux. **(b)** (*Pol: Ir, US etc*) unioniste *mf*.

unionize ['juːnjənaɪz] (*Ind*) **1** *vt* syndiquer. **2** *vi* se syndiquer.

uniparous [juː'nɪpərəs] *adj* (*Zool*) unipare; (*Bot*) à axe principal unique.

unique [juː'niːk] *adj* (*sole*) unique; (*outstanding*) unique, exceptionnel.

uniquely [juː'niːklɪ] *adv* exceptionnellement.

uniqueness [juː'niːknɪs] *n* (*V* **unique**) caractère unique *or* exceptionnel.

unisex* ['juːnɪseks] *adj* unisexe.

unison ['juːnɪzn] *n* (*Mus, fig*) unisson *m*. **in** ~ à l'unisson; (*fig*) **'yes' they said in** ~ 'oui' dirent-ils en chœur *or* tous ensemble.

unit ['juːnɪt] **1** *n* **(a)** (*gen, Admin, Elec, Math, Measure, Mil, Pharm*) unité *f*. **administrative/linguistic/monetary** ~ unité administrative/linguistique/monétaire; ~ **of length** unité de longueur; *V* **thermal** *etc*.

(b) (*complete section, part*) bloc *m*, groupe *m*, élément *m*. **compressor** ~ groupe *m* compresseur; **generative** ~ groupe *m* électrogène; **the lens** ~ **of a camera** l'objectif *m* d'un appareil photographique; **you can buy the furniture in** ~**s** vous pouvez acheter le mobilier par éléments; **the research people form a** ~ **in themselves** les chercheurs constituent un groupe indépendant *or* une cellule indépendante; **they are building a new assembly** ~ ils construisent un nouveau bloc de montage; **where will you house the new research** ~? où logerez-vous le nouveau groupe *or* service de recherches?; *V* **kitchen, sink**² *etc*.

2 *cpd*: **unit furniture** mobilier *m* par éléments; **unit price** prix *m* unitaire; (*Brit Fin*) **unit trust** société *f* d'investissement.

Unitarian [ˌjuːnɪ'tɛərɪən] (*Rel*) *adj, n* unitaire (*mf*), unitarien(ne) *m(f)*.

Unitarianism [ˌjuːnɪ'tɛərɪənɪzəm] *n* (*Rel*) unitarisme *m*.

unitary ['juːnɪtərɪ] *adj* unitaire.

unite [juː'naɪt] **1** *vt countries, groups, objects* unir; *party, country* unifier; (*marry*) unir, marier. **to** ~ **A and B/A with B** unir A et B/A à B.

2 *vi* s'unir (*with sth* à qch, *with sb* à *or* avec qn, *against* contre, *in doing, to do* pour faire). **women of the world** ~! femmes du monde entier, unissez-vous!

united [juː'naɪtɪd] **1** *adj* (*Pol, gen*) uni; (*unified*) unifié; *front* uni; *efforts* conjugué. **by a** ~ **effort they...** en unissant *or* en conjuguant leurs efforts ils ..., par leurs efforts conjugués ils ...; (*Prov*) ~ **we stand, divided we fall** l'union fait la force.

2 *cpd*: **United Arab Republic** (*abbr* **U.A.R.**) République Arabe Unie (*abbr* R.A.U. *f*); **United Kingdom** Royaume-Uni *m*; **United Nations (Organization)** (*abbr* **UN** *or* **UNO**) (Organisation *f* des) Nations unies (*abbr* O.N.U. *f*); **United States (of America)** (*abbr* **US** *or* **USA**) États-Unis *mpl*.

unity ['juːnɪtɪ] *n* unité *f*; (*fig*) harmonie *f*, accord *m*. (*Theat*) ~ **of time/place/action** unité de temps/de lieu/d'action; (*Prov*) ~ **is strength** l'union fait la force; **to live in** ~ vivre en harmonie (*with* avec).

univalent ['juːnɪ'veɪlənt] *adj* univalent.

univalve ['juːnɪvælv] **1** *adj* univalve.

2 *n* mollusque *m* univalve.

universal [ˌjuːnɪ'vɜːsəl] **1** *adj language, remedy, suffrage, protest* universel. **such beliefs are** ~ de telles croyances sont universelles *or* sont répandues dans le monde entier; **its use has become** ~ son emploi s'est répandu *or* s'est généralisé dans le monde entier, son emploi s'est universalisé *or* est devenu universel; **to make sth** ~ universaliser qch, rendre qch universel, généraliser qch; ~ **joint** (joint *m* de) cardan *m*.

2 *n* universel *m*.

universality [ˌjuːnɪvɜː'sælɪtɪ] *n* (*U*) universalité *f*.

universalize [ˌjuːnɪ'vɜːsəlaɪz] *vt* universaliser, rendre universel.

universally [ˌjuːnɪ'vɜːsəlɪ] *adv* universellement, dans le monde entier.

universe ['juːnɪvɜːs] *n* univers *m*.

university [ˌjuːnɪ'vɜːsɪtɪ] **1** *n* université *f*. **to be at/go to** ~ être/aller à l'université *or* à la Fac*; **to study at** ~ faire des études universitaires; *V* **open**. **2** *cpd degree, town, library* universitaire; *professor, student* d'université, de Fac*. **he has a university education** il a fait des études universitaires.

unjust ['ʌn'dʒʌst] *adj* injuste (*to* envers).

unjustifiable [ʌn'dʒʌstɪfaɪəbl] *adj* injustifiable.

unjustifiably [ʌn'dʒʌstɪfaɪəblɪ] *adv* sans justification.

unjustified ['ʌn'dʒʌstɪfaɪd] *adj* injustifié.

unjustly ['ʌn'dʒʌstlɪ] *adv* injustement.

unkempt ['ʌn'kempt] *adj appearance* négligé, débraillé; *hair* mal peigné, ébouriffé; *clothes, person* débraillé.

unkind [ʌn'kaɪnd] *adj person, behaviour* peu aimable, pas gentil, (*stronger*) cruel, méchant; *remark* méchant, peu gentil; *climate* rigoureux, rude; *fate* cruel. **to be** ~ être peu aimable *or* pas gentil *or* cruel (*to sb* avec *or* envers qn); (*verbally*) être méchant (*to sb* avec *or* envers qn).

unkindly [ʌn'kaɪndlɪ] **1** *adv speak, say* méchamment, (*stronger*) avec malveillance; *behave* méchamment, (*stronger*) cruellement. **don't take it** ~ **if ...** ne soyez pas offensé si ..., ne le prenez pas en mauvaise part si ...; **to take** ~ **to sth** accepter qch difficilement.

2 *adj person* peu aimable, peu gentil; *remark* méchant, peu gentil; *climate* rude. **in an** ~ **way** méchamment, avec malveillance.

unkindness [ʌn'kaɪndnɪs] *n* **(a)** (*U*) *[person, behaviour]* manque *m* de gentillesse, (*stronger*) méchanceté *f*; *[words, remark]* méchanceté; *[fate]* cruauté *f*; *[weather]* rigueur *f*.

(b) (*act of* ~) méchanceté *f*, action *or* parole méchante.

unknot ['ʌn'nɒt] *vt* dénouer, défaire (le nœud de).

unknowable ['ʌn'nəʊəbl] *adj* inconnaissable.

unknowing ['ʌn'nəʊɪŋ] *adj* inconscient. **... he said, all** ~ ... dit-il, sans savoir ce qui se passait.

unknowingly ['ʌn'nəʊɪŋlɪ] *adv* inconsciemment.

unknown ['ʌn'nəʊn] **1** *adj* inconnu. **it was** ~ **to him** cela lui était inconnu, il l'ignorait, il n'en savait rien; ~ **to him the plane had crashed** l'avion s'était écrasé, ce qu'il ignorait; **a substance** ~ **to science** une substance inconnue de *or* ignorée de la science; (*Math, fig*) ~ **quantity** inconnue *f*; **he's an** ~ **quantity** il représente une inconnue; (*Mil*) **the U**~ **Soldier** *or* **Warrior** le Soldat inconnu; (*Jur*) **murder by person or persons** ~ meurtre *m* dont l'auteur est (*or* les auteurs sont) inconnu(s).

2 *n* **(a) the** ~ (*Philos, gen*) l'inconnu *m*; (*Math, fig*) l'inconnue *f*; **voyage into the** ~ voyage dans l'inconnu; **in space exploration there are many** ~**s** dans l'exploration de l'espace il y a de nombreuses inconnues.

(b) (*person, actor etc*) inconnu(e) *m(f)*. **they chose an** ~ **for the part of Macbeth** ils ont choisi un inconnu pour jouer le rôle de Macbeth.

unlace ['ʌn'leɪs] *vt* délacer, défaire (le lacet de).

unladen ['ʌn'leɪdn] *adj ship* à vide. ~ **weight** poids *m* à vide.

unladylike ['ʌn'leɪdɪlaɪk] *adj girl, woman* mal élevée, qui manque de distinction; *manners, behaviour* peu distingué. **it's** ~ **to yawn** une jeune fille bien élevée ne bâille pas.

unlamented ['ʌnlə'mentɪd] *adj* non regretté. **he died** ~ on ne pleura pas sa mort.

unlatch ['ʌn'lætʃ] *vt* ouvrir, soulever le loquet de.

unlawful ['ʌn'lɔːfʊl] *adj act, means* illégal, illicite; *marriage* illégitime. (*Jur*) ~ **assembly** (*outdoors*) attroupement séditieux; (*indoors*) réunion illégale.

unlawfully [ˈʌnˈlɔːfəlɪ] *adv* illégalement, illicitement.
unlearn [ˈʌnˈlɜːn] *vt* désapprendre.
unlearned [ˈʌnˈlɜːnɪd] *adj* ignorant, illettré.
unleash [ˈʌnˈliːʃ] *vt dog* détacher, lâcher; *hounds* découpler; (*fig*) déchaîner, déclencher.
unleavened [ˈʌnˈlevnd] *adj* sans levain, azyme (*Rel*).
unless [ənˈles] *conj* à moins que ... (ne)+*subj*, à moins de+*infin*. **~ you can find another** à moins que vous n'en trouviez un autre, à moins d'en trouver un autre; **~ I am mistaken** à moins que je (ne) me trompe, si je ne me trompe (pas); **~ I hear to the contrary** sauf avis contraire, sauf contrordre; (*Admin, Comm, Pharm etc*) **~ otherwise stated** sauf indication contraire.
unlettered [ˈʌnˈletəd] *adj* illettré.
unlicensed [ˈʌnˈlaɪsənst] *adj activity* illicite, non autorisé; *vehicle* sans vignette. (*Brit*) **~ premises** commerce non patenté pour la vente des spiritueux.
unlikable [ˈʌnˈlaɪkəbl] *adj* = **unlikeable.**
unlike [ˈʌnˈlaɪk] **1** *adj* dissemblable (*also Math, Phys*), différent. **they are quite ~** ils ne se ressemblent pas du tout.
2 *prep* à la différence de, contrairement à. **~ his brother, he ...** à la différence de *or* contrairement à son frère, il ...; **it's quite ~ him to do that** ça ne lui ressemble pas *or* ça n'est pas dans ses habitudes *or* ça n'est pas (du tout) son genre de faire cela; **how ~ George!** on ne s'attendait pas à ça de la part de Georges!; **your house is quite ~ mine** votre maison n'est pas du tout comme la mienne *or* est très différente de la mienne; **the portrait is quite ~ him** le portrait ne lui ressemble pas, le portrait est très peu ressemblant.
unlikeable [ˈʌnˈlaɪkəbl] *adj person* peu sympathique; *town, thing* peu agréable.
unlikelihood [ʌnˈlaɪklɪhʊd] *n*, **unlikeliness** [ʌnˈlaɪklɪnɪs] *n* (*U*) improbabilité *f*.
unlikely [ʌnˈlaɪklɪ] *adj happening, outcome* improbable, peu probable; *explanation* peu plausible, invraisemblable; (*hum*) *hat etc* invraisemblable. **it is ~ that she will come, she is ~ to come** il est improbable *or* peu probable qu'elle vienne, il y a peu de chances pour qu'elle vienne; **she is ~ to succeed** elle a peu de chances de réussir; **that is ~ to happen** cela ne risque guère d'arriver; **it is most ~** c'est fort *or* très improbable; **it is not ~ that** il est assez probable que+*subj*, il n'est pas impossible que+*subj*; **in the ~ event of his accepting** au cas *or* dans le cas fort improbable où il accepterait; **it looks an ~ place for mushrooms** ça ne me paraît pas être un endroit à champignons; **the most ~ men have become prime minister** des hommes que rien ne semblait destiner à de telles fonctions sont devenus premier ministre; **she married a most ~ man** on ne s'attendait vraiment pas à ce qu'elle épouse (*subj*) un homme comme lui; **she wears the most ~ clothes** elle s'habille d'une façon on ne peut plus invraisemblable.
unlimited [ʌnˈlɪmɪtɪd] *adj time, resources, opportunities* illimité; *patience, power* illimité, sans bornes.
unlined [ˈʌnˈlaɪnd] *adj garment, curtain* sans doublure; *face* sans rides; *paper* uni, non réglé.
unlisted [ˈʌnˈlɪstɪd] *adj* qui ne figure pas sur une liste; (*St Ex*) non inscrit à la cote. **~ building** édifice non classé.
unlit [ˈʌnˈlɪt] *adj lamp* non allumé; *road* non éclairé; *vehicle* sans feux.
unload [ˈʌnˈləʊd] **1** *vt ship, cargo, truck, rifle, washing machine* décharger; (*fig: get rid of*) se débarrasser de, se défaire de; (*St Ex*) se défaire de. **to ~ sth on (to) sb** se décharger de qch sur qn.
2 *vi [ship, truck]* être déchargé, déposer son chargement.
unloading [ˈʌnˈləʊdɪŋ] *n* déchargement *m*.
unlock [ˈʌnˈlɒk] *vt door, box* ouvrir; (*fig*) *heart* ouvrir; *mystery* résoudre; *secret* révéler. **the door is ~ed** la porte n'est pas fermée à clef.
unlooked-for [ʌnˈlʊktfɔːʳ] *adj* inattendu, inespéré.
unloose [ˈʌnˈluːs] *vt*, **unloosen** [ʌnˈluːsn] *vt rope* relâcher, détendre; *knot* desserrer; *prisoner* libérer, relâcher; *grasp* relâcher, desserrer.
unlovable [ˈʌnˈlʌvəbl] *adj* peu *or* guère attachant.
unlovely [ˈʌnˈlʌvlɪ] *adj* déplaisant.
unloving [ˈʌnˈlʌvɪŋ] *adj* peu affectueux, froid.
unluckily [ʌnˈlʌkɪlɪ] *adv* malheureusement, par malheur. **~ for him** malheureusement pour lui; **the day started ~** la journée a mal commencé.
unluckiness [ʌnˈlʌkɪnɪs] *n* manque *m* de chance *or* de veine*.
unlucky [ʌnˈlʌkɪ] *adj person* malchanceux, qui n'a pas de chance; *coincidence, event* malencontreux; *choice, decision* malheureux; *moment* mal choisi, mauvais; *day* de malchance, de déveine*; *omen* néfaste, funeste; *object, colour, number, action* qui porte malheur. **he is always ~** il n'a jamais de chance; **he tried to get a seat but he was ~** il a essayé d'avoir une place mais il n'y est pas arrivé; **he was just ~** il n'a pas eu de chance *or* de veine*; **he was ~ enough to meet her** il a eu la malchance *or* la déveine* de la rencontrer; **how ~ for you!** vous n'avez pas de chance! *or* de veine!*, ce n'est pas de chance pour vous!; **it was ~ (for her) that her husband should walk in just then** malheureusement pour elle son mari est entré à cet instant précis, elle n'a pas eu de chance *or* de veine* que son mari soit entré à cet instant précis; **it is ~ to walk under a ladder** ça porte malheur de passer sous une échelle.
unmade [ˈʌnˈmeɪd] **1** *pret, ptp of* **unmake. 2** *adj bed* non encore fait, défait; *road* non goudronné.
un-made-up [ˈʌnmeɪdˈʌp] *adj face, person* non maquillé, sans maquillage.
unmake [ˈʌnˈmeɪk] *pret, ptp* **unmade** *vt* défaire; (*destroy*) détruire, démolir.
unman [ˈʌnˈmæn] *vt* faire perdre courage à, émasculer (*fig*).
unmanageable [ʌnˈmænɪdʒəbl] *adj vehicle, boat* difficile à manœuvrer, peu maniable; *animal* indocile; *person, child* impossible, difficile; *parcel, size, amount* peu maniable; *hair* difficile à coiffer.
unmanly [ˈʌnˈmænlɪ] *adj* (*cowardly*) lâche; (*effeminate*) efféminé.
unmanned [ˈʌnˈmænd] *adj tank, ship* sans équipage; *spacecraft* inhabité. (*Space*) **~ flight** vol *m* sans équipage; **the machine was left ~ for 10 minutes** il n'y a eu personne au contrôle de la machine pendant 10 minutes; **the telephone was left ~** il n'y avait personne pour prendre les communications; **he left the desk ~** il a laissé le guichet sans surveillance; **3 of the positions were ~** 3 des positions n'étaient pas occupées; *V also* **unman.**
unmannerliness [ʌnˈmænəlɪnɪs] *n* (*U*) manque *m* de savoir-vivre, impolitesse *f*.
unmannerly [ʌnˈmænəlɪ] *adj* mal élevé, impoli, discourtois.
unmapped [ˈʌnˈmæpt] *adj* dont on n'a pas établi *or* dressé la carte.
unmarked [ˈʌnˈmɑːkt] *adj* (*unscratched etc*) sans tache, sans marque; *body, face* sans marque; (*unnamed*) *linen, suitcase* non marqué, sans nom; (*uncorrected*) *essay* non corrigé; (*Ling*) non marqué; (*Sport*) *player* démarqué. **~ police car** voiture (de police) banalisée.
unmarketable [ˈʌnˈmɑːkɪtəbl] *adj* invendable.
unmarriageable [ˈʌnˈmærɪdʒəbl] *adj* immariable.
unmarried [ˈʌnˈmærɪd] *adj* célibataire, qui n'est pas marié. **~ mother** mère *f* célibataire, fille-mère *f* (*pej*); **the ~ state** le célibat.
unmask [ˈʌnˈmɑːsk] **1** *vt* (*lit, fig*) démasquer. **2** *vi* ôter son masque.
unmatched [ˈʌnˈmætʃt] *adj* sans pareil, sans égal, incomparable.
unmeant [ˈʌnˈment] *adj* qui n'est pas voulu, involontaire.
unmentionable [ʌnˈmenʃnəbl] **1** *adj object* dont il ne faut pas faire mention; *word* qu'il ne faut pas prononcer. **it is ~** il ne faut pas en parler. **2** *n* (*hum*) **~s*** sous-vêtements *mpl*, dessous *mpl*.
unmerciful [ʌnˈmɜːsɪfʊl] *adj* impitoyable, sans pitié (*towards* pour).
unmercifully [ʌnˈmɜːsɪfəlɪ] *adv* impitoyablement, sans pitié.
unmerited [ˈʌnˈmerɪtɪd] *adj* immérité.
unmethodical [ˈʌnmɪˈθɒdɪkəl] *adj* peu méthodique.
unmindful [ʌnˈmaɪndfʊl] *adj*: **~ of** oublieux de, indifférent à, inattentif à.
unmistakable [ˈʌnmɪsˈteɪkəbl] *adj evidence, sympathy* indubitable; *voice, accent, walk* qu'on ne peut pas ne pas reconnaître. **the house is quite ~** vous ne pouvez pas ne pas reconnaître la maison, vous ne pouvez pas vous tromper de maison.
unmistakably [ˈʌnmɪsˈteɪkəblɪ] *adv* manifestement, sans aucun doute, indubitablement.
unmitigated [ʌnˈmɪtɪgeɪtɪd] *adj terror, admiration* non mitigé, absolu; *folly* pur. **it is ~ nonsense** c'est complètement idiot *or* absurde; **he is an ~ scoundrel/liar** c'est un fieffé coquin/menteur.
unmixed [ˈʌnˈmɪkst] *adj* pur, sans mélange.
unmolested [ˈʌnməˈlestɪd] *adj* (*unharmed*) indemne, sain et sauf; (*undisturbed*) (laissé) en paix, tranquille.
unmortgaged [ˈʌnˈmɔːgɪdʒd] *adj* libre d'hypothèques, non hypothéqué.
unmotivated [ˈʌnˈməʊtɪveɪtɪd] *adj* immotivé, sans motif.
unmounted [ˈʌnˈmaʊntɪd] *adj* (*without horse*) sans cheval, à pied; *gem* non serti, non monté; *picture, photo* non monté *or* collé sur carton; *stamp* non collé dans un album.
unmourned [ˈʌnˈmɔːnd] *adj* non regretté. **he died ~** on ne pleura pas sa mort.
unmoved [ˈʌnˈmuːvd] *adj* insensible, indifférent (*by* à), qui n'est pas ému (*by* par). **he was ~ by her tears** ses larmes ne l'ont pas ému *or* touché; **it leaves me ~** cela me laisse indifférent *or* froid.
unmusical [ˈʌnˈmjuːzɪkəl] *adj sound* peu mélodieux, peu harmonieux; *person* peu musicien, qui n'a pas d'oreille.
unnam(e)able [ˈʌnˈneɪməbl] *adj* innommable.
unnamed [ˈʌnˈneɪmd] *adj fear, object* innommé; *author, donor* anonyme.
unnatural [ʌnˈnætʃrəl] *adj* anormal, non naturel; *habit, vice, love* contre nature, pervers; *relationship* contre nature; (*affected*) *style, manner* affecté, forcé, qui manque de naturel. **it is ~ for her to be so unpleasant** il n'est pas normal *or* naturel qu'elle soit si désagréable.
unnaturally [ʌnˈnætʃrəlɪ] *adv* anormalement; (*affectedly*) d'une manière affectée *or* forcée. **it was ~ silent** un silence anormal régnait; **not ~ we were worried** nous étions naturellement inquiets, bien entendu, nous étions inquiets.
unnavigable [ˈʌnˈnævɪgəbl] *adj* non navigable.
unnecessarily [ʌnˈnesɪsərɪlɪ] *adv do, say* inutilement, pour rien. **he is ~ strict** il est sévère sans nécessité.
unnecessary [ʌnˈnesɪsərɪ] *adj* (*useless*) inutile; (*superfluous*) superflu. **all this fuss is quite ~** c'est faire beaucoup d'histoires pour rien; **it is ~ to add that ...** (il est) inutile d'ajouter que ...; **it is ~ for you to come** il n'est pas nécessaire *or* il est inutile que vous veniez (*subj*).
unneighbourly, (*US*) **unneighborly** [ˈʌnˈneɪbəlɪ] *adj* peu sociable, qui n'agit pas en bon voisin. **this ~ action** cette action mesquine de la part de mon (*or* son *etc*) voisin.
unnerve [ˈʌnˈnɜːv] *vt* faire perdre courage à, démonter (*fig*), déconcerter, dérouter.
unnerving [ˈʌnˈnɜːvɪŋ] *adj* déconcertant, déroutant.
unnoticed [ˈʌnˈnəʊtɪst] *adj* inaperçu, inobservé. **to go ~** passer inaperçu.
unnumbered [ˈʌnˈnʌmbəd] *adj page* sans numéro, qui n'a pas été numéroté; *house* sans numéro; (*liter: innumerable*) innombrable.
unobjectionable [ˈʌnəbˈdʒekʃnəbl] *adj* acceptable.

unobservant [ˈʌnəbˈzɜːvənt] *adj* peu observateur (*f* -trice), peu perspicace.
unobserved [ˈʌnəbˈzɜːvd] *adj* inaperçu, inobservé. **he escaped ~** il s'est échappé sans être vu; **to go ~** passer inaperçu.
unobstructed [ˈʌnəbˈstrʌktɪd] *adj pipe* non bouché, non obstrué; *path, road* dégagé, libre. **the driver has an ~ view to the rear** le conducteur a une excellente visibilité à l'arrière.
unobtainable [ˈʌnəbˈteɪnəbl] *adj* (*Comm etc*) impossible à obtenir *or* à se procurer. (*Telec*) **the number is ~** il est impossible d'obtenir le numéro.
unobtrusive [ˈʌnəbˈtruːsɪv] *adj person* discret (*f* -ète), effacé; *object* discret, pas trop visible; *smell, remark* discret.
unobtrusively [ˈʌnəbˈtruːsɪvlɪ] *adv* discrètement.
unoccupied [ˈʌnˈɒkjʊpaɪd] *adj person* inoccupé, désœuvré, qui n'a rien à faire; *house* inoccupé, inhabité; *seat* libre, qui n'est pas pris; *post* vacant; (*Mil*) *zone* libre.
unofficial [ˈʌnəˈfɪʃəl] *adj report, information, news* officieux, non officiel; *visit* privé. **in an ~ capacity** à titre privé *or* personnel *or* non officiel; (*Ind*) **~ strike** grève *f* sauvage.
unofficially [ˈʌnəˈfɪʃəlɪ] *adv* (*V* **unofficial**) officieusement, non officiellement.
unopened [ˈʌnˈəʊpənd] *adj* non ouvert, qui n'a pas été ouvert. **the book lay ~ all day** le livre est resté fermé toute la journée; **the bottle was ~** la bouteille n'avait pas été ouverte.
unopposed [ˈʌnəˈpəʊzd] *adj* (*Parl, gen*) sans opposition; (*Mil*) sans rencontrer de résistance. (*Parl*) **the bill was given an ~ second reading** le projet de loi a été accepté sans opposition à la deuxième lecture.
unorganized [ˈʌnˈɔːgənaɪzd] *adj* (*gen, Bio, Ind*) inorganisé; (*badly organized*) mal organisé.
unoriginal [ˈʌnəˈrɪdʒɪnəl] *adj person, work* qui manque d'originalité, peu original; *style, remark* banal; *idea* peu original, banal.
unorthodox [ˈʌnˈɔːθədɒks] *adj* (*gen*) peu orthodoxe; (*Rel*) hétérodoxe.
unostentatious [ˈʌnˌɒstənˈteɪʃəs] *adj* discret (*f* -ète), sans ostentation, simple.
unostentatiously [ˈʌnˌɒstənˈteɪʃəslɪ] *adv* discrètement, sans ostentation.
unpack [ˈʌnˈpæk] **1** *vt suitcase* défaire; *belongings* déballer. **to get ~ed** déballer ses affaires. **2** *vi* défaire sa valise, déballer ses affaires.
unpacking [ˈʌnˈpækɪŋ] *n* (*U*) déballage *m*. **to do one's ~** déballer ses affaires.
unpaid [ˈʌnˈpeɪd] *adj bill* impayé; *debt* non acquitté; *work, helper* non rétribué. **to work ~** travailler à titre bénévole, travailler gracieusement *or* gratuitement.
unpalatable [ʌnˈpælɪtəbl] *adj food* qui n'a pas bon goût, peu agréable à manger; (*fig*) *fact, report* désagréable, dur à digérer* *or* à avaler*; *truth* désagréable à entendre.
unparalleled [ʌnˈpærəleld] *adj* (*unequalled*) *beauty, wit* incomparable, sans égal; *success* hors pair; (*unprecedented*) *event* sans précédent.
unpardonable [ʌnˈpɑːdnəbl] *adj* impardonnable, inexcusable.
unpardonably [ʌnˈpɑːdnəblɪ] *adv* inexcusablement. **~ rude** d'une impolitesse impardonnable *or* inexcusable.
unparliamentary [ˈʌnˌpɑːləˈmentərɪ] *adj* antiparlementaire, indigne d'un parlementaire; (*fig*) injurieux, grossier.
unpatented [ˈʌnˈpeɪtntɪd] *adj invention* non breveté.
unpatriotic [ˈʌnˌpætrɪˈɒtɪk] *adj person* peu patriote; *act, speech* antipatriotique.
unpatriotically [ˈʌnˌpætrɪˈɒtɪkəlɪ] *adv* antipatriotiquement.
unpaved [ˈʌnˈpeɪvd] *adj* non pavé.
unperceived [ˈʌnpəˈsiːvd] *adj* inaperçu.
unperturbed [ˈʌnpəˈtɜːbd] *adj* non déconcerté, non découragé. **he was ~ by this failure** cet échec ne l'a pas découragé; **~ by this failure, he ...** sans se laisser décourager par cet échec, il ....
unpick [ˈʌnˈpɪk] *vt seam* découdre; *stitch* défaire.
unpin [ˈʌnˈpɪn] *vt* détacher (*from* de); *sewing, one's hair* enlever les épingles de.
unplaced [ˈʌnˈpleɪst] *adj* (*Sport*) *horse* non placé; *athlete* non classé.
unplanned [ˈʌnˈplænd] *adj occurrence* imprévu; *baby* non prévu.
unplayable [ˈʌnˈpleɪəbl] *adj* injouable.
unpleasant [ʌnˈpleznt] *adj person* déplaisant, désagréable; *house, town* peu attrayant, déplaisant; *smell, taste* désagréable; *surprise, weather* désagréable, mauvais; *remark* désagréable, déplaisant, désobligeant; *experience, situation* désagréable, fâcheux. **he was very ~ to her** il a été très désagréable *or* déplaisant avec elle, il a été très désobligeant envers elle; **he had an ~ time** il a passé un mauvais quart d'heure; (*longer*) il a passé de mauvais moments.
unpleasantly [ʌnˈplezntlɪ] *adv reply* désagréablement; *behave, smile* de façon déplaisante. **the bomb fell ~ close** la bombe est tombée un peu trop près à mon (*or* son *etc*) goût.
unpleasantness [ʌnˈplezntnɪs] *n* [*experience, person*] caractère *m* désagréable; [*place, house*] aspect *or* caractère déplaisant; (*quarrelling*) discorde *f*, friction *f*, dissension *f*. **there has been a lot of ~ recently** il y a eu beaucoup de frictions *or* dissensions ces temps derniers; **after that ~ at the beginning of the meeting** après cette fausse note au début de la réunion.
unpleasing [ʌnˈpliːzɪŋ] *adj* déplaisant.
unplug [ˈʌnˈplʌg] *vt* (*Elec*) débrancher.
unplumbed [ˈʌnˈplʌmd] *adj depth, mystery* non sondé.
unpoetic(al) [ˈʌnpəʊˈetɪk(əl)] *adj* peu poétique.
unpolished [ˈʌnˈpɒlɪʃt] *adj furniture* non ciré, non astiqué; *floor, shoes* non ciré; *glass* dépoli; *silver* non fourbi, non astiqué; *diamond* non poli; (*fig*) *person* qui manque d'éducation *or* de savoir-vivre; *manners* peu raffiné; *style* qui manque de poli.
unpolluted [ˈʌnpəˈluːtɪd] *adj air, river* non pollué; (*fig*) *mind* non contaminé, non corrompu.
unpopular [ˈʌnˈpɒpjʊləʳ] *adj person, decision, style, model* impopulaire. **this measure was ~ with the workers** cette mesure était impopulaire chez les ouvriers, les ouvriers n'ont pas bien accueilli cette mesure; **to make o.s. ~** se rendre impopulaire; **he is ~ with his colleagues** ses collègues ne l'aiment pas beaucoup, il n'est pas très populaire *or* il est impopulaire auprès de ses collègues; **I'm rather ~ with him just now*** je ne suis pas très bien vu de lui *or* je n'ai pas la cote* auprès de lui en ce moment.
unpopularity [ˈʌnˌpɒpjʊˈlærɪtɪ] *n* (*U*) impopularité *f*.
unpractical [ˈʌnˈpræktɪkəl] *adj method, tool* peu pratique. **he's very ~** il manque tout à fait de sens pratique, il n'a pas du tout l'esprit pratique.
unpractised, (*US*) **unpracticed** [ʌnˈpræktɪst] *adj person* inexpérimenté, inexpert; *movement etc* inexpert, inhabile; *eye, ear* inexercé.
unprecedented [ʌnˈpresɪdəntɪd] *adj* sans précédent.
unpredictable [ˈʌnprɪˈdɪktəbl] *adj event, consequence, reaction* imprévisible, impossible à prévoir; *person* aux réactions imprévisibles; *weather* incertain. **he is quite ~** on ne sait jamais ce qu'il va faire *or* comment il va réagir.
unprejudiced [ʌnˈpredʒʊdɪst] *adj* impartial, sans parti pris, sans prévention(s), sans préjugés.
unpremeditated [ˈʌnprɪˈmedɪteɪtɪd] *adj* non prémédité.
unprepared [ˈʌnprɪˈpeəd] *adj meal etc* qui n'est pas préparé *or* prêt; *speech* improvisé. **I was ~ for the exam** je n'avais pas suffisamment préparé l'examen; **he began it quite ~** il l'a commencé sans préparation *or* sans y être préparé; **to catch sb ~** prendre qn au dépourvu; **he was ~ for the news** il ne s'attendait pas à la nouvelle, la nouvelle l'a pris au dépourvu *or* l'a surpris.
unpreparedness [ˈʌnprɪˈpeərɪdnɪs] *n* (*U*) impréparation *f*.
unprepossessing [ˈʌnˌpriːpəˈzesɪŋ] *adj appearance* peu avenant. **he is ~** il n'est guère avenant, il présente* mal, il fait mauvaise impression.
unpresentable [ˈʌnprɪˈzentəbl] *adj person, thing* qui n'est pas présentable.
unpretentious [ˈʌnprɪˈtenʃəs] *adj* sans prétention(s).
unpriced [ˈʌnˈpraɪst] *adj goods* dont le prix n'est pas marqué.
unprincipled [ʌnˈprɪnsɪpld] *adj* peu scrupuleux, sans scrupules.
unprintable [ˈʌnˈprɪntəbl] *adj* (*lit*) impubliable; (*fig*) licencieux, obscène, scabreux. (*hum*) **his comments were quite ~** je ne peux vraiment pas répéter ce qu'il a dit.
unprivileged [ˈʌnˈprɪvɪlɪdʒd] *adj* (*gen*) défavorisé; (*Econ*) économiquement faible.
unproductive [ˈʌnprəˈdʌktɪv] *adj capital, soil* improductif; *discussion, meeting, work* stérile, improductif.
unprofessional [ˈʌnprəˈfeʃənl] *adj* contraire au code professionnel.
unpunctual [ˈʌnˈpʌŋktjʊəl] *adj* peu ponctuel, qui n'est jamais à l'heure.
unpunctuality [ˈʌnˌpʌŋktjʊˈælɪtɪ] *n* (*U*) manque *m* de ponctualité.
unpunished [ˈʌnˈpʌnɪʃt] *adj* impuni. **to go ~** rester impuni.
unqualified [ˈʌnˈkwɒlɪfaɪd] *adj* **(a)** *craftsman, player* non qualifié; *teacher, engineer, nurse* non diplômé. **no ~ person will be considered** les candidats n'ayant pas les diplômes requis ne seront pas considérés; **he is ~ for the job** (*no paper qualifications*) il n'a pas les titres *or* le(s) diplôme(s) requis *or* il ne remplit pas les conditions requises pour ce poste; (*unsuitable*) il n'a pas les qualités requises pour tenir le poste; **he is ~ to judge** il n'est pas qualifié *or* compétent pour juger.
(b) (*absolute*) *acceptance, support, approval* inconditionnel, sans réserve; *praise* non mitigé, sans réserve; *success* formidable, fou (*f* folle); (*: *utter*) *idiot* fini, achevé, parfait (*before n*); *rogue, liar* fieffé (*before n*).
(c) (*Gram*) *adjective* non modifié.
unquenchable [ʌnˈkwentʃəbl] *adj* (*lit, fig*) insatiable.
unquenched [ʌnˈkwentʃt] *adj fire* non éteint; *desire* inassouvi. **~ thirst** soif non étanchée; (*fig*) soif inassouvie.
unquestionable [ʌnˈkwestʃənəbl] *adj fact, authority* incontestable, indiscutable; *honesty, sincerity* hors de doute, certain.
unquestionably [ʌnˈkwestʃənəblɪ] *adv* indiscutablement.
unquestioned [ʌnˈkwestʃənd] *adj* qui n'est pas mis en question *or* en doute, incontesté, indiscuté.
unquestioning [ʌnˈkwestʃənɪŋ] *adj acceptance* inconditionnel; *belief, faith, obedience* aveugle, total.
unquiet [ˈʌnˈkwaɪət] **1** *adj person, mind* inquiet (*f* -ète), tourmenté; *times* agité, troublé. **2** *n* inquiétude *f*; agitation *f*.
unquote [ˈʌnˈkwəʊt] *vi* (*imper only*) (*in dictation*) fermez lez guillemets; (*in report, lecture*) fin de citation.
unquoted [ˈʌnˈkwəʊtɪd] *adj* (*St Ex*) non coté.
unravel [ʌnˈrævəl] **1** *vt material* effiler, effilocher; *knitting* défaire; *threads* démêler; (*fig*) *mystery* débrouiller, éclaircir; *plot* dénouer. **2** *vi* s'effiler, s'effilocher.
unread [ˈʌnˈred] *adj book, newspaper* qui n'a pas été lu. **he left the letter ~** il a laissé la lettre sans la lire; **the book lay ~ on the table** le livre est resté sur la table sans avoir été lu.
unreadable [ˈʌnˈriːdəbl] *adj handwriting* illisible; *book* illisible, pénible à lire.
unreadiness [ˈʌnˈredɪnɪs] *n* (*U*) impréparation *f*.
unready [ˈʌnˈredɪ] *adj* mal préparé, qui n'est pas prêt. **he was ~ for what happened next** il ne s'attendait pas à ce qui est arrivé ensuite, ce qui est arrivé ensuite l'a pris au dépourvu.
unreal [ˈʌnˈrɪəl] *adj* irréel, imaginaire. **it all seemed rather ~ to me** tout cela me paraissait quelque peu irréel, j'avais l'impression de rêver.

unrealistic ['ʌnrɪə'lɪstɪk] *adj* peu réaliste.
unreality ['ʌnrɪ'ælɪtɪ] *n* (*U*) irréalité *f*.
unrealizable ['ʌnrɪə'laɪzəbl] *adj* irréalisable.
unrealized ['ʌn'riːəlaɪzd] *adj plan, ambition* qui n'a pas été réalisé; *objective* qui n'a pas été atteint.
unreason ['ʌn'riːzn] *n* (*U*) déraison *f*, manque *m* de bon sens.
unreasonable [ʌn'riːznəbl] *adj person, suggestion* qui n'est pas raisonnable, déraisonnable; *demand, length of time* excessif, démesuré; *price* qui n'est pas raisonnable, exorbitant, exagéré. **at this ~ hour** à cette heure indue; **it is ~ to expect him to accept** on ne peut pas raisonnablement compter qu'il acceptera.
unreasonableness [ʌn'riːznəblnɪs] *n* (*U*) *[person]* attitude *f* déraisonnable; *[demand, price]* caractère exorbitant *or* excessif.
unreasonably [ʌn'riːznəblɪ] *adv* déraisonnablement, excessivement, exagérément.
unreasoning [ʌn'riːznɪŋ] *adj emotion, action* irraisonné; *person* qui ne raisonne pas.
unreclaimed ['ʌnrɪ'kleɪmd] *adj land* (*from forest*) non défriché; (*from sea*) non asséché.
unrecognizable ['ʌn'rekəgnaɪzəbl] *adj* méconnaissable, qui n'est pas reconnaissable.
unrecognized ['ʌn'rekəgnaɪzd] *adj value, worth, talent* méconnu; (*Pol*) *government, régime* non reconnu. **he walked ~ down the street** il a descendu la rue (à pied) san. être reconnu *or* sans que personne ne le reconnaisse.
unrecorded ['ʌnrɪ'kɔːdɪd] *adj* **(a)** *event, deed, decision* non mentionné, qui n'est pas dans les archives, non enregistré. **(b)** (*on tape etc*) *song, programme* non enregistré.
unredeemed ['ʌnrɪ'diːmd] *adj object from pawn* non dégagé; *debt* non remboursé, non amorti; *bill* non honoré; *mortgage* non purgé; *promise* non tenu; *obligation* non rempli; *sinner* non racheté; *fault* non réparé; *failing* non racheté, non compensé (*by* par).
unreel [ʌn'rɪəl] **1** *vt film* dérouler; *thread* dérouler, dévider; *fishing line* dérouler, lancer. **2** *vi* se dérouler; se dévider.
unrefined ['ʌnrɪ'faɪnd] *adj petroleum, metal* brut, non raffiné; *sugar* non raffiné; *person, manners, speech* qui manque de raffinement, fruste.
unreflecting ['ʌnrɪ'flektɪŋ] *adj* **(a)** *person* irréfléchi; impulsif; *act, emotion* irraisonné. **(b)** *surface* non réfléchissant.
unreformed ['ʌnrɪ'fɔːmd] *adj* non amendé.
unregarded ['ʌnrɪ'gɑːdɪd] *adj* dont on ne tient pas compte, dont on ne fait pas cas. **his generosity went quite ~** sa générosité est passée inaperçue.
unregistered ['ʌn'redʒɪstəd] *adj birth* non déclaré; *car* non immatriculé; (*Post*) non recommandé.
unregretted ['ʌnrɪ'gretɪd] *adj person, act, words* que l'on ne regrette pas. **he died ~** on ne pleura pas sa mort.
unrehearsed ['ʌnrɪ'hɜːst] *adj performance* sans répétition; *speech, reply* improvisé, spontané; *incident* imprévu, inattendu.
unrelated ['ʌnrɪ'leɪtɪd] *adj*: **to be ~ to** *[facts, events]* n'avoir aucun rapport avec, être sans rapport avec; *[person]* n'avoir aucun lien de parenté avec; **the two events are quite ~** il n'y a aucun rapport entre les deux événements; **the two Smiths are ~** il n'y a aucun lien de parenté entre les deux Smith, les deux Smith ne sont pas parents entre eux.
unrelenting ['ʌnrɪ'lentɪŋ] *adj* implacable.
unreliability ['ʌnrɪ,laɪə'bɪlɪtɪ] *n* (*U*) *[person]* manque *m* de sérieux; *[machine]* manque *m* de fiabilité.
unreliable ['ʌnrɪ'laɪəbl] *adj person* sur qui on ne peut compter, en qui on ne peut avoir confiance; *company, firm* qui n'est pas sérieux, qui n'inspire pas confiance; *car, machine* peu fiable; *news* sujet à caution, de source douteuse; *source of information* douteux. **he's very ~** on ne peut vraiment pas compter sur lui *or* se fier à lui *or* avoir confiance en lui; **my watch is ~** je ne peux pas me fier à ma montre.
unrelieved ['ʌnrɪ'liːvd] *adj pain* constant, que rien ne soulage; *gloom, anguish* constant, que rien ne vient dissiper. **~ grey/black** gris/noir uniforme; **~ boredom** ennui mortel; **bare landscape ~ by any trees** paysage nu dont l'uniformité n'est même pas rompue par la présence d'arbres.
unremarkable ['ʌnrɪ'mɑːkəbl] *adj* médiocre, non remarquable, quelconque.
unremarked ['ʌnrɪ'mɑːkt] *adj* inaperçu.
unremitting ['ʌnrɪ'mɪtɪŋ] *adj kindness, help, effort* inlassable, infatigable; *hatred* opiniâtre, constant. **he was ~ in his attempts to help us** il s'est inlassablement efforcé de nous aider.
unremittingly ['ʌnrɪ'mɪtɪŋlɪ] *adv* sans cesse, sans relâche, inlassablement.
unremunerative ['ʌnrɪ'mjuːnərətɪv] *adj* peu rémunérateur (*f* -trice), mal payé; (*fig*) peu fructueux, peu rentable.
unrepaid ['ʌnrɪ'peɪd] *adj loan* non remboursé.
unrepealed ['ʌnrɪ'piːld] *adj* non abrogé.
unrepeatable ['ʌnrɪ'piːtəbl] *adj offer, bargain* unique, exceptionnel; *comment* trop grossier pour être répété. **what she said is ~** je n'ose répéter ce qu'elle a dit.
unrepentant ['ʌnrɪ'pentənt] *adj* impénitent. **he is quite ~ about it** il ne manifeste pas le moindre repentir, il n'en a nullement honte.
unrepresentative ['ʌn,reprɪ'zentətɪv] *adj* peu représentatif (*of* de).
unrepresented ['ʌn,reprɪ'zentɪd] *adj* non représenté, sans représentant.
unrequited ['ʌnrɪ'kwaɪtɪd] *adj* non partagé, qui n'est pas payé de retour.
unreserved ['ʌnrɪ'zɜːvd] *adj* non réservé.
unreservedly ['ʌnrɪ'zɜːvɪdlɪ] *adv speak* franchement, sans réserve; *approve, agree, accept* sans réserve, entièrement.
unresisting ['ʌnrɪ'zɪstɪŋ] *adj* qui ne résiste pas, soumis.
unresolved ['ʌnrɪ'zɒlvd] *adj* non résolu.
unresponsive ['ʌnrɪs'pɒnsɪv] *adj* (*physically*) insensible (*to* à); (*emotionally, intellectually*) insensible, sourd (*to* à); *audience* qui ne réagit pas. **he was fairly ~ when I spoke to him about it** il n'a pas beaucoup réagi quand je lui en ai parlé.
unrest [ʌn'rest] *n* (*U*) agitation *f*, troubles *mpl*, remous *mpl*.
unrestrained ['ʌnrɪ'streɪnd] *adj feelings* non contenu, non refréné; *language, behaviour* outrancier.
unrestricted ['ʌnrɪ'strɪktɪd] *adj time, power* sans restriction, illimité; *access* libre.
unrevealed ['ʌnrɪ'viːld] *adj* non révélé.
unrewarded ['ʌnrɪ'wɔːdɪd] *adj person, effort* non récompensé, sans récompense. **to go ~** rester sans récompense.
unrewarding ['ʌnrɪ'wɔːdɪŋ] *adj* ingrat, qui n'en vaut pas la peine; (*financially*) peu rémunérateur (*f* -trice).
unrighteous [ʌn'raɪtʃəs] **1** *adj* impie, pervers. **2** *npl*: **the ~** les impies *mpl*.
unrighteousness [ʌn'raɪtʃəsnɪs] *n* (*U*) perversité *f*.
unripe ['ʌn'raɪp] *adj* vert, qui n'est pas mûr.
unrivalled, (*US*) *also* **unrivaled** [ʌn'raɪvəld] *adj* sans égal, sans concurrence, incomparable.
unroadworthy ['ʌn'rəʊd,wɜːðɪ] *adj car* qui n'est pas en état de marche.
unrobe ['ʌn'rəʊb] **1** *vi* se dévêtir, se dépouiller de ses vêtements (*de cérémonie*); (*undress*) se déshabiller.
2 *vt* dépouiller de ses vêtements (*de cérémonie*), dévêtir; (*undress*) déshabiller.
unroll ['ʌn'rəʊl] **1** *vt* dérouler. **2** *vi* se dérouler.
unromantic ['ʌnrə'mæntɪk] *adj place, landscape, words* peu romantique; *person* terre à terre, prosaïque, peu romantique.
unruffled ['ʌn'rʌfld] *adj hair* lisse; *water* lisse, non ridé; *person* calme, qui ne se départ pas de son calme. **to carry on ~** continuer sans se laisser déconcerter *or* sans sourciller.
unruled ['ʌn'ruːld] *adj paper* uni, non réglé.
unruly [ʌn'ruːlɪ] *adj child* indiscipliné, turbulent; *hair* indiscipliné. **~ behaviour** indiscipline *f*.
unsaddle ['ʌn'sædl] *vt horse* desseller; *rider* désarçonner.
unsafe ['ʌn'seɪf] *adj* **(a)** (*dangerous*) *machine, car* dangereux, peu sûr; *ladder* dangereux, instable; *structure, bridge* dangereux, non solide; *journey* périlleux, risqué; *toy* dangereux; *method* peu sûr. **~ to eat** impropre à la consommation; **~ to drink** non potable. **(b)** (*in danger*) en danger. **to feel ~** ne pas se sentir en sécurité.
unsaid ['ʌn'sed] *adj* inexprimé, passé sous silence. **much was left ~** on a passé beaucoup de choses sous silence, il restait beaucoup de choses à dire; **that would have been better left ~** il aurait mieux valu passer cela sous silence *or* ne pas dire cela, ce n'était pas une chose à dire.
unsalaried ['ʌn'sæləriːd] *adj* non rémunéré.
unsaleable ['ʌn'seɪləbl] *adj* invendable.
unsatisfactory ['ʌn,sætɪs'fæktərɪ] *adj* peu satisfaisant, qui laisse à désirer.
unsatisfied ['ʌn'sætɪsfaɪd] *adj person* insatisfait, mécontent; (*unconvinced*) non convaincu, non persuadé; *desire* insatisfait, inassouvi; *curiosity, need, demand, appetite* non satisfait.
unsatisfying ['ʌn'sætɪsfaɪɪŋ] *adj result* peu satisfaisant; *work* ingrat, qui donne peu de satisfaction; *food* peu nourrissant.
unsaturated ['ʌn'sætʃəreɪtɪd] *adj* (*Chem*) non saturé.
unsavoury, (*US*) **unsavory** ['ʌn'seɪvərɪ] *adj food* peu savoureux, désagréable à manger; *smell* nauséabond; (*fig*) *person, district* peu recommandable; *reputation* équivoque, louche; *subject* plutôt répugnant, très déplaisant.
unscathed ['ʌn'skeɪðd] *adj* indemne. **to escape ~** s'en sortir sans une égratignure *or* sain et sauf *or* indemne.
unscholarly ['ʌn'skɒləlɪ] *adj person* peu érudit, peu savant; *work* qui manque d'érudition.
unschooled ['ʌn'skuːld] *adj person* qui n'a pas d'instruction. **~ in** qui n'a rien appris de, ignorant en matière de *or* pour ce qui est de.
unscientific ['ʌn,saɪən'tɪfɪk] *adj method, approach* peu scientifique; *person* qui manque d'esprit scientifique; (*fig*) peu méthodique.
unscramble ['ʌn'skræmbl] *vt* (*Telec*) déchiffrer.
unscratched ['ʌn'skrætʃt] *adj surface* non rayé, intact; *person* indemne, sain et sauf. **to escape ~** s'en sortir sans une égratignure.
unscrew ['ʌn'skruː] **1** *vt* dévisser. **2** *vi* se dévisser.
unscripted ['ʌn'skrɪptɪd] *adj* (*Rad, TV*) improvisé, non préparé d'avance.
unscrupulous [ʌn'skruːpjʊləs] *adj person* dénué de scrupules, sans scrupules, malhonnête, indélicat; *act* malhonnête, indélicat.
unscrupulously [ʌn'skruːpjʊləslɪ] *adv* sans scrupule(s), peu scrupuleusement.
unscrupulousness [ʌn'skruːpjʊləsnɪs] *n* (*U*) *[person]* manque *m* de scrupules *or* de délicatesse; *[act]* malhonnêteté *f*, manque de délicatesse.
unseal ['ʌn'siːl] *vt* (*open*) ouvrir, décacheter; (*take seal off*) desceller.
unseasonable [ʌn'siːznəbl] *adj fruit etc* hors de saison. **the weather is ~** ce n'est pas un temps de saison.
unseasoned ['ʌn'siːznd] *adj timber* vert, non conditionné; *food* non assaisonné.
unseat ['ʌn'siːt] *vt rider* désarçonner; (*Parl*) faire perdre son siège à.
unseaworthy ['ʌn'siː,wɜːðɪ] *adj* qui n'est pas en état de naviguer *or* en mesure de tenir la mer.

unsecured [ˈʌnsɪˈkjʊəd] *adj* (*Fin*) à découvert, sans garantie.
unseeing [ˈʌnˈsiːɪŋ] *adj* (*lit, fig*) aveugle.
unseemliness [ʌnˈsiːmlɪnɪs] *n* (*V* **unseemly**) inconvenance *f*, manque *m* de bienséance; indécence *f*; grossièreté *f*.
unseemly [ʌnˈsiːmlɪ] *adj behaviour* inconvenant, malséant; *dress* inconvenant, indécent; *language* inconvenant, grossier.
unseen [ˈʌnˈsiːn] **1** *adj* (*invisible*) invisible; (*unnoticed*) inaperçu. **he escaped ~** il s'est échappé sans être vu; (*esp Brit: Scol, Univ*) **~ translation** version *f* (*sans préparation*).
2 *n* **(a)** (*esp Brit: Scol, Univ*) version *f* (*sans préparation*). **(b) the ~** le monde occulte.
unselfconscious [ˈʌnˌselfˈkɒnʃəs] *adj* naturel. **he was very ~ about it** cela ne semblait nullement le gêner *or* l'intimider.
unselfconsciously [ˈʌnˌselfˈkɒnʃəslɪ] *adv* avec naturel, sans la moindre gêne.
unselfish [ˈʌnˈselfɪʃ] *adj person* non égoïste; *act* désintéressé.
unselfishly [ˈʌnˈselfɪʃlɪ] *adv* sans penser à soi, généreusement.
unselfishness [ˈʌnˈselfɪʃnɪs] *n* (*U*) *[person]* absence *f* d'égoïsme; *[act]* désintéressement *m*.
unserviceable [ˈʌnˈsɜːvɪsəbl] *adj* inutilisable, hors d'état de fonctionner.
unsettle [ˈʌnˈsetl] *vt person, weather* perturber.
unsettled [ˈʌnˈsetld] *adj person* perturbé; *weather, future* incertain; *market* instable; *question* pendant, qui n'a pas été décidé; *account* impayé, non acquitté. **he feels ~ in his job** il n'est pas vraiment satisfait de son emploi.
unsettling [ˈʌnˈsetlɪŋ] *adj news* inquiétant; *influence, effect* perturbateur (*f* -trice).
unsex [ˈʌnˈseks] *vt* faire perdre sa masculinité (*or* féminité) à; (*make impotent*) rendre impuissant.
unsexed [ˈʌnˈsekst] *adj chicks* dont on n'a pas procédé au sexage.
unshackle [ˈʌnˈʃækl] *vt* ôter les fers à, désenchaîner; (*fig*) émanciper, libérer.
unshaded [ˈʌnˈʃeɪdɪd] *adj* (*in sunlight*) non ombragé, en plein soleil; *lamp* sans abat-jour; *part of drawing or map etc* non hachuré.
unshakeable [ˈʌnˈʃeɪkəbl] *adj* inébranlable.
unshaken [ˈʌnˈʃeɪkən] *adj* inébranlable.
unshaven [ˈʌnˈʃeɪvn] *adj* non rasé; (*bearded*) barbu.
unsheathe [ˈʌnˈʃiːð] *vt* dégainer.
unship [ˈʌnˈʃɪp] *vt cargo* décharger, débarquer.
unshod [ˈʌnˈʃɒd] *adj horse* déferré; *person* déchaussé, pieds nus.
unshrinkable [ˈʌnˈʃrɪŋkəbl] *adj* irrétrécissable (au lavage).
unsighted [ˈʌnˈsaɪtɪd] *adj* qui n'est pas en vue, que l'on n'a pas vu.
unsightliness [ʌnˈsaɪtlɪnɪs] *n* (*U*) aspect disgracieux, laideur *f*.
unsightly [ʌnˈsaɪtlɪ] *adj* disgracieux, laid. **he has an ~ scar on his face** une cicatrice lui dépare le visage.
unsigned [ˈʌnˈsaɪnd] *adj* non signé, sans signature.
unsinkable [ˈʌnˈsɪŋkəbl] *adj* insubmersible.
unskilful, (*US*) **unskillful** [ˈʌnˈskɪlfʊl] *adj* (*clumsy*) maladroit; (*inexpert*) malhabile, inexpert.
unskilfully, (*US*) **unskillfully** [ˈʌnˈskɪlfəlɪ] *adv* (*clumsily*) avec maladresse; (*inexpertly*) malhabilement.
unskilled [ˈʌnˈskɪld] *adj* (*gen*) inexpérimenté, inexpert; (*Ind*) *work* de manœuvre, ne nécessitant pas de connaissances professionnelles spéciales. **~ worker** manœuvre *m*, ouvrier *m*,-ière *f* non spécialisé(e).
unskimmed [ˈʌnˈskɪmd] *adj milk* non écrémé, entier.
unsociability [ˈʌnˌsəʊʃəˈbɪlɪtɪ] *n* (*U*) insociabilité *f*.
unsociable [ʌnˈsəʊʃəbl] *adj* insociable. **I'm feeling rather ~ this evening** je n'ai guère envie de voir des gens ce soir.
unsold [ˈʌnˈsəʊld] *adj* invendu.
unsoldierly [ˈʌnˈsəʊldʒəlɪ] *adj behaviour, emotion* indigne d'un soldat; *appearance* peu militaire, peu martial; *person* qui n'a pas l'esprit *or* la fibre militaire.
unsolicited [ˈʌnsəˈlɪsɪtɪd] *adj* non sollicité.
unsolvable [ˈʌnˈsɒlvəbl] *adj* insoluble, qu'on ne peut résoudre.
unsolved [ˈʌnˈsɒlvd] *adj* non résolu, inexpliqué; *crossword* non terminé. **one of the great ~ mysteries** une des grandes énigmes.
unsophisticated [ˈʌnsəˈfɪstɪkeɪtɪd] *adj person* (*in taste, lifestyle*) simple; (*in attitude*) simple, naturel; (*in appearance*) qui n'est pas sophistiqué; *style, room* simple; *film, book, song, machine* simple, qui n'est pas compliqué. **an ~ wine** un petit vin sans prétention.
unsought [ˈʌnˈsɔːt] *adj* (*also* **~-for**) non recherché, non sollicité.
unsound [ˈʌnˈsaʊnd] *adj health* précaire, chancelant; *heart* non solide; *constitution, teeth, lungs, fruit, tree* qui n'est pas sain; *timber* pourri, gâté; *structure, floor, bridge* en mauvais état, peu solide; *bank, organization* peu solide; *alliance, investment* peu sûr, hasardeux; *reasoning, judgment, argument* mal fondé, spécieux, boiteux, peu valable; *policy, decision, step, advice, opinion* peu sensé, peu judicieux; *case, training* peu solide; *claim, title* peu valable, peu acceptable; *statesman, player* incompétent. (*Jur*) **of ~ mind** qui ne jouit pas de toutes ses facultés mentales; **the book is ~ on some points** certains aspects de ce livre sont discutables, certains arguments de ce livre sont spécieux *or* boiteux.
unsparing [ʌnˈspeərɪŋ] *adj* **(a)** (*lavish*) prodigue (*of* de), généreux. **to be ~ in one's efforts to do** ne pas ménager ses efforts pour faire. **(b)** (*cruel*) impitoyable, implacable.
unsparingly [ʌnˈspeərɪŋlɪ] *adv give* généreusement, avec prodigalité, avec largesse; *work* inlassablement.
unspeakable [ʌnˈspiːkəbl] *adj* (*good*) indicible, ineffable, indescriptible; (*bad*) indescriptible, innommable.
unspeakably [ʌnˈspiːkəblɪ] *adv* d'une manière indescriptible. **to suffer ~** souffrir l'inexprimable; **~ bad** affreusement mauvais, exécrable.
unspecified [ˈʌnˈspesɪfaɪd] *adj* non spécifié.
unspent [ˈʌnˈspent] *adj money, funds* non dépensé, qui reste.
unspoiled [ˈʌnˈspɔɪld] *adj,* **unspoilt** [ˈʌnˈspɔɪlt] *adj paint, dress etc* intact, qui n'est pas abîmé; *countryside, beauty, view* qui n'est pas déparé *or* défiguré; *style* naturel; *child* qui reste naturel. **~ by** non gâché par; **he remained ~ by his great success** malgré son grand succès il restait aussi simple qu'avant.
unspoken [ˈʌnˈspəʊkən] *adj word* non prononcé; *thought* inexprimé; *consent* tacite.
unsporting [ˈʌnˈspɔːtɪŋ] *adj,* **unsportsmanlike** [ˈʌnˈspɔːtsmənlaɪk] *adj* (*Sport, gen*) déloyal. **to be ~** (*not play fair*) être déloyal, ne pas jouer franc jeu, ne pas être sport *inv*; (*be bad loser*) être mauvais joueur; **that's very ~ of you** ce n'est pas très chic de votre part.
unspotted [ˈʌnˈspɒtɪd] *adj* (*lit, fig*) sans tache, immaculé.
unstable [ˈʌnˈsteɪbl] *adj* (*all senses*) instable.
unstained [ˈʌnˈsteɪnd] *adj* (*not coloured*) *furniture, floor* non teinté; (*clean*) *garment, surface* immaculé, sans tache; *reputation* non terni, sans tache.
unstamped [ˈʌnˈstæmpt] *adj letter* non affranchi, non timbré; *document, passport* non tamponné.
unstatesmanlike [ˈʌnˈsteɪtsmənlaɪk] *adj* peu diplomatique.
unsteadily [ˈʌnˈstedɪlɪ] *adv walk* d'un pas chancelant *or* incertain; *say* d'une voix mal assurée, avec hésitation, en cherchant ses mots.
unsteadiness [ˈʌnˈstedɪnɪs] *n* (*V* **unsteady**) manque *m* de stabilité; manque d'assurance; irrégularité *f*.
unsteady [ˈʌnˈstedɪ] *adj ladder, structure* instable, branlant; *hand* mal assuré, tremblant; *step, gait, voice* mal assuré, chancelant; *flame* vacillant; *rhythm* irrégulier; (*fig: unreliable*) peu sûr, inconstant, changeant; *mind* irrésolu, instable. **to be ~ on one's feet** *[invalid, old person, child]* ne pas très bien tenir sur ses jambes, marcher d'un pas chancelant *or* incertain; *[drunkard]* tituber, chanceler.
unstick [ˈʌnˈstɪk] *pret, ptp* **unstuck 1** *vt* décoller. **to come unstuck** *[stamp, notice]* se décoller; (*) *[plan]* tomber à l'eau*; **he certainly came unstuck* over that scheme** il est vraiment tombé sur un bec* pour ce qui est de ce projet.
2 *vi* se décoller.
unstinted [ʌnˈstɪntɪd] *adj praise* sans réserve; *generosity* sans bornes; *efforts* illimité, incessant.
unstinting [ʌnˈstɪntɪŋ] *adj person* prodigue (*of* de), généreux; *praise* sans réserve; *kindness, generosity* sans bornes. **to be ~ in one's efforts to do** ne pas ménager ses efforts pour faire; **to be ~ in one's praise of** chanter les louanges de.
unstitch [ˈʌnˈstɪtʃ] *vt* découdre. **to come ~ed** se découdre.
unstop [ˈʌnˈstɒp] *vt sink* déboucher, désobstruer; *bottle* déboucher, décapsuler.
unstoppable* [ˈʌnˈstɒpəbl] *adj* qu'on ne peut pas arrêter.
unstrap [ˈʌnˈstræp] *vt*: **to ~ A from B** détacher A de B, défaire les sangles qui attachent A à B.
unstressed [ˈʌnˈstrest] *adj syllable* inaccentué, atone.
unstring [ˈʌnˈstrɪŋ] *pret, ptp* **unstrung** *vt violin* enlever *or* détendre les cordes de; *beads* désenfiler.
unstrung [ˈʌnˈstrʌŋ] *adj* (*fig*) *person* qui a les nerfs à fleur de peau.
unstudied [ˈʌnˈstʌdɪd] *adj* naturel, spontané.
unsubdued [ˈʌnsəbˈdjuːd] *adj* (*lit, fig*) indompté.
unsubmissive [ˈʌnsəbˈmɪsɪv] *adj* insoumis, indocile.
unsubsidized [ˈʌnˈsʌbsɪdaɪzd] *adj* non subventionné, qui ne reçoit pas de subvention.
unsubstantial [ˈʌnsəbˈstænʃəl] *adj structure* peu solide, léger; *meal* peu substantiel, peu nourrissant; *argument* peu solide, sans substance; *evidence* insuffisant.
unsubstantiated [ˈʌnsəbˈstænʃɪeɪtɪd] *adj accusation* non prouvé; *testimony, rumour* non confirmé, non corroboré.
unsuccessful [ˈʌnsəkˈsesfʊl] *adj negotiation, venture, visit, meeting* infructueux, qui est un échec; *attempt* vain, infructueux; *candidate* refusé, malheureux; *application* refusé, non retenu; *writer, painter, book* qui n'a pas de succès; *firm* qui ne prospère pas; *marriage, outcome* malheureux. **to be ~** échouer, ne pas réussir; **to be ~ in doing sth** ne pas réussir *or* ne pas arriver à faire qch; **he is ~ in everything he does** rien ne lui réussit; **he was ~ in his exam** il a échoué à *or* il n'a pas été reçu à son examen; **I tried to speak to him but I was ~** j'ai essayé de lui parler mais sans succès *or* mais en vain *or* mais je n'ai pas pu; **after 3 ~ attempts he ...** après avoir essayé 3 fois sans succès il ..., après avoir échoué 3 fois il ... .
unsuccessfully [ˈʌnsəkˈsesfəlɪ] *adv* en vain, sans succès.
unsuitability [ˈʌnˌsuːtəˈbɪlɪtɪ] *n*: **he was rejected on the grounds of ~ (for the job)** il n'a pas été retenu parce qu'il n'avait pas le profil requis pour l'emploi.
unsuitable [ˈʌnˈsuːtəbl] *adj climate, food, place, time, arrangement* qui ne convient pas; *moment* inopportun; *colour, size* qui ne va pas; *clothes* peu approprié, inadéquat, (*socially*) non convenable; *action, reply, example, device* peu approprié, inopportun; *language, attitude* inconvenant. **to be ~ for** *[clothes, language, date]* ne pas convenir à; *[film, book]* ne pas être (conseillé) pour; **he is ~ for the post** ce n'est pas l'homme qu'il faut pour le poste; **to marry a very ~ person** faire une mésalliance.
unsuited [ˈʌnˈsuːtɪd] *adj*: **~ to** *or* **for** impropre à; **~ to do** impropre *or* inapte à faire; **they are ~ (to each other)** ils ne sont pas compatibles.
unsullied [ˈʌnˈsʌlɪd] *adj* sans souillure, sans tache.
unsung [ˈʌnˈsʌŋ] *adj* (*liter*) *hero, exploits* méconnu.
unsupported [ˈʌnsəˈpɔːtɪd] *adj structure* non soutenu, non étayé; *statement* non confirmé, non corroboré; *hypothesis* non

vérifié, non soutenu; *candidate* sans appui, sans soutien; *troops* non soutenu; *mother, family* sans soutien financier.

unsure [ʌnˈʃʊəʳ] *adj person* incertain (*of, about* de); *memory* peu fidèle. **to be ~ of o.s.** ne pas être sûr de soi, manquer d'assurance.

unsurmountable [ˈʌnsəˈmaʊntəbl] *adj* insurmontable.

unsurpassable [ˈʌnsəˈpɑːsəbl] *adj* insurpassable.

unsurpassed [ˈʌnsəˈpɑːst] *adj* non surpassé (*in* en).

unsuspected [ˈʌnsəsˈpektɪd] *adj* insoupçonné.

unsuspecting [ˈʌnsəsˈpektɪŋ] *adj* qui ne se méfie pas, qui ne se doute de rien. **and he, quite ~, said ...** et lui, ne se doutant de rien *or* sans la moindre méfiance, dit ... .

unsuspicious [ˈʌnsəsˈpɪʃəs] *adj* (*feeling no suspicion*) peu soupçonneux, peu méfiant; (*causing no suspicion*) qui n'a rien de suspect, qui n'éveille aucun soupçon. **~-looking** tout à fait ordinaire.

unsweetened [ˈʌnˈswiːtnd] *adj* non sucré, sans sucre.

unswerving [ʌnˈswɜːvɪŋ] *adj resolve* inébranlable; *loyalty* inébranlable, à toute épreuve.

unswervingly [ʌnˈswɜːvɪŋlɪ] *adv*: **~ loyal** totalement dévoué (*to* à); **to hold ~ to one's course** poursuivre inébranlablement son but, ne pas se laisser détourner de son but.

unsympathetic [ˈʌnˌsɪmpəˈθetɪk] *adj* indifférent (*to* à), peu compatissant, incompréhensif; (*unlikeable*) antipathique. **he was quite ~ when we ...** il n'a pas du tout compati *or* il n'a pas manifesté la moindre compassion quand nous ... .

unsympathetically [ˈʌnˌsɪmpəˈθetɪkəlɪ] *adv* sans (manifester) beaucoup de compassion; (*stronger*) sans (manifester) la moindre compassion.

unsystematic [ˈʌnˌsɪstɪˈmætɪk] *adj work, reasoning* peu systématique, peu méthodique.

unsystematically [ˈʌnˌsɪstɪˈmætɪkəlɪ] *adv* sans système, sans méthode.

untainted [ˈʌnˈteɪntɪd] *adj* (*lit*) *meat, butter* frais (*f* fraîche); (*fig*) *reputation* intact, non terni, sans tache; *person, mind* non corrompu (*by* par), pur.

untam(e)able [ˈʌnˈteɪməbl] *adj bird, wild animal* inapprivoisable; *large or fierce animal* non dressable; *esp lion, tiger* indomptable.

untamed [ˈʌnˈteɪmd] *adj animal etc* sauvage, inapprivoisé, farouche; *esp lion, tiger* indompté; *passion* violent, fougueux.

untangle [ˈʌnˈtæŋgl] *vt rope, wool, hair* démêler; *mystery* débrouiller, éclaircir; *plot* dénouer.

untanned [ˈʌnˈtænd] *adj hide* non tanné; *person* non bronzé.

untapped [ˈʌnˈtæpt] *adj resources* inexploité.

untarnished [ˈʌnˈtɑːnɪʃt] *adj* (*lit, fig*) non terni, sans tache.

untasted [ˈʌnˈteɪstɪd] *adj food, delights* auquel on n'a pas goûté. **the food lay ~ on the plate** le repas restait dans l'assiette; **he left the meal ~** il n'a pas goûté au repas.

untaught [ˈʌnˈtɔːt] *adj* (*uneducated*) sans instruction, ignorant; (*natural, innate*) spontané, inné, naturel.

untaxable [ˈʌnˈtæksəbl] *adj income* non imposable; *goods* exempt de taxes.

untaxed [ˈʌnˈtækst] *adj goods* exempt de taxes, non imposé; *income* non imposable, exempté d'impôts; *car* sans vignette.

unteachable [ˈʌnˈtiːtʃəbl] *adj person* à qui on ne peut rien apprendre; *pupil* réfractaire à tout enseignement; *subject* impossible à enseigner, qui ne se prête pas à l'enseignement.

untempered [ˈʌnˈtempəd] *adj steel* non revenu.

untenable [ˈʌnˈtenəbl] *adj position* intenable; *opinion* insoutenable.

untenanted [ˈʌnˈtenəntɪd] *adj* inoccupé, sans locataire(s).

untested [ˈʌnˈtestɪd] *adj person, theory, method* qui n'a pas été mis à l'épreuve; *product, weapon, invention* qui n'a pas été essayé; *new drug* non encore expérimenté; (*Psych*) non testé.

unthinkable [ʌnˈθɪŋkəbl] *adj* impensable, inconcevable. **it is ~ that** il est impensable *or* inconcevable que + *subj*.

unthinking [ˈʌnˈθɪŋkɪŋ] *adj* irréfléchi, étourdi.

unthinkingly [ˈʌnˈθɪŋkɪŋlɪ] *adv* sans réfléchir, étourdiment.

unthought-of [ʌnˈθɔːtɒv] *adj* auquel on n'a pas pensé *or* songé.

unthread [ˈʌnˈθred] *vt needle, pearls* désenfiler.

untidily [ʌnˈtaɪdɪlɪ] *adv work, live* sans méthode, sans ordre; *write* sans soin, de manière brouillonne. **to dress ~** s'habiller sans soin; **to be ~ dressed** être débraillé; **his books lay ~ about the room** ses livres jonchaient la pièce.

untidiness [ʌnˈtaɪdɪnɪs] *n* (*U*) [*room*] désordre *m*; [*dress*] débraillé *m*; [*person*] (*in dress, appearance*) débraillé *m*; (*in habits*) manque *m* d'ordre.

untidy [ʌnˈtaɪdɪ] *adj appearance* négligé, désordonné; *clothes* débraillé, mal tenu; *hair* ébouriffé, mal peigné; *person* désordonné, brouillon; *writing* brouillon; *work, page* sale, brouillon; *room* en désordre, en pagaïe*; *desk* en désordre, mal rangé.

untie [ˈʌnˈtaɪ] *vt knot* défaire; *string* dénouer, défaire; *parcel* défaire, ouvrir; *prisoner, hands* délier, détacher; *bonds* défaire, détacher.

until [ənˈtɪl] **1** *prep* jusqu'à. **~ such time as** (*in future*) jusqu'à ce que+*subj*, en attendant que +*subj*; (*in past*) avant que+*subj*; **~ the next day** jusqu'au lendemain; **from morning ~ night** du matin (jusqu')au soir; **~ now** jusqu'ici, jusqu'à maintenant; **~ then** jusque-là; **not ~** (*in future*) pas avant; (*in past*) ne ... que; **it won't be ready ~ tomorrow** ce ne sera pas prêt avant demain; **he didn't leave ~ the following day** il n'est parti que le lendemain; **the work was not begun ~ 1970** ce n'est qu'en 1970 que les travaux ont commencé; **I had heard nothing of it ~ 5 minutes ago** j'en ai seulement entendu parler *or* j'en ai entendu parler pour la première fois il y a 5 minutes.

2 *conj* (*in future*) jusqu'à ce que+*subj*, en attendant que+*subj*; (*in past*) avant que+*subj*. **wait ~ I come** attendez (jusqu'à ce) que je vienne; **~ they built the new road** avant qu'ils (ne) fassent la nouvelle route; **~ they build the new road** en attendant qu'ils fassent la nouvelle route; **he laughed ~ he cried** il a ri aux larmes; **not ~** (*in future*) pas avant que+*subj*, tant que ... ne ... pas +*indic*; (*in past*) tant que ... ne ... pas+*indic*; **he won't come ~ you invite him** il ne viendra pas avant que vous (ne) l'invitiez, il ne viendra pas tant que vous ne l'inviterez pas; **they did nothing ~ we came** ils n'ont rien fait tant que nous n'avons pas été là; **do nothing ~ I tell you** ne faites rien avant que je (ne) vous le dise *or* tant que je ne vous l'aurai pas dit; **do nothing ~ you get my letter** ne faites rien avant d'avoir reçu ma lettre; **don't start ~ I come** ne commencez pas avant que j'arrive, attendez-moi pour commencer; **wait ~ you get my letter** attendez d'avoir reçu ma lettre.

untilled [ˈʌnˈtɪld] *adj* non labouré, non cultivé, inculte.

untimely [ʌnˈtaɪmlɪ] *adj spring, weather* prématuré, précoce; *moment* inopportun, mal choisi; *arrival* inopportun, intempestif; *remark* inopportun, déplacé, intempestif. **to come to an ~ end** [*person*] mourir prématurément *or* avant son temps; [*project*] être enterré prématurément.

untiring [ʌnˈtaɪərɪŋ] *adj person, efforts* infatigable, inlassable. **to be ~ in one's efforts to do** s'efforcer infatigablement *or* inlassablement de faire.

untiringly [ʌnˈtaɪərɪŋlɪ] *adv* infatigablement, inlassablement.

unto [ˈʌntʊ] *prep* (*liter*) = **to, towards.**

untold [ˈʌnˈtəʊld] *adj story* non raconté; *secret* jamais dévoilé *or* divulgué; *amount, loss, wealth* incalculable; *agony* indicible; *delights* indescriptible.

untouchable [ʌnˈtʌtʃəbl] **1** *adj* intouchable. **2** *n* (*in India*) intouchable *mf*, paria *m*; (*fig*) paria.

untouched [ˈʌnˈtʌtʃt] *adj* **(a)** auquel on n'a pas touché. (*Comm*) **~ by hand** sans manipulation directe; **he left his meal ~, his meal lay ~** il n'a pas touché à son repas. **(b)** (*safe*) *person* indemne; *thing* intact; (*unaffected*) insensible, indifférent (*by* à).

untoward [ˌʌntəˈwɔːd] *adj* fâcheux, malencontreux.

untrained [ˈʌnˈtreɪnd] *adj worker, teacher* qui n'a pas reçu de formation professionnelle; *animal* non dressé. **to the ~ ear** à l'oreille inexercée.

untrammelled [ʌnˈtræməld] *adj* non entravé (*by* par), libre (*by* de).

untranslatable [ˈʌntrænzˈleɪtəbl] *adj* intraduisible.

untravelled [ˈʌnˈtrævld] *adj road* peu fréquenté; *person* qui n'a pas voyagé.

untried [ˈʌnˈtraɪd] *adj product, weapon, invention* qui n'a pas été essayé; *person, method* qui n'a pas été mis à l'épreuve; (*Jur*) *case, person* non jugé. **he was condemned ~** il a été condamné sans jugement.

untrodden [ˈʌnˈtrɒdn] *adj* (*liter*) *path* peu fréquenté; *region, territory* inexploré, vierge; *snow* non foulé, vierge.

untroubled [ˈʌnˈtrʌbld] *adj* tranquille, calme, paisible. **~ by the thought of ...** nullement troublé à la pensée de ...; **to be ~ by the news** rester impassible en apprenant la nouvelle.

untrue [ˈʌnˈtruː] *adj statement, rumour* faux (*f* fausse), erroné, inexact; *instrument* qui n'est pas juste, inexact; *reading* erroné, inexact; *lover etc* infidèle (*to* à), déloyal (*to* envers). **it is ~ that** il est faux *or* il n'est pas vrai que+*subj*.

untrustworthy [ˈʌnˈtrʌstˌwɜːðɪ] *adj person* indigne de confiance; *book* auquel on ne peut se fier; *source of information* douteux.

untruth [ˈʌnˈtruːθ] *n, pl* **~s** [ˈʌnˈtruːðz] contre-vérité *f*, (*stronger*) mensonge *m*; (*U*) fausseté *f*.

untruthful [ˈʌnˈtruːθfʊl] *adj statement* mensonger; *person* menteur, qui ne dit pas la vérité.

untruthfully [ˈʌnˈtruːθfəlɪ] *adv* mensongèrement, en mentant.

untruthfulness [ˈʌnˈtruːθfʊlnɪs] *n* (*U*) fausseté *f*, caractère mensonger.

untuneful [ˈʌnˈtjuːnfʊl] *adj* peu harmonieux.

untutored [ˈʌnˈtjuːtəd] *adj person* peu instruit, dont les connaissances sont rudimentaires; *work* qui dénote des connaissances rudimentaires; *taste* non formé.

untwine [ˈʌnˈtwaɪn] *vt* défaire, détortiller.

untwist [ˈʌnˈtwɪst] *vt* (*untangle*) *rope, threads, wool* démêler, détortiller; (*straighten out*) *flex, rope* détordre; (*unravel*) *rope, wool* défaire; (*unscrew*) *bottle-top* dévisser.

unusable [ˈʌnˈjuːzəbl] *adj* inutilisable.

unused [ˈʌnˈjuːzd] *adj* **(a)** (*new*) *clothes* neuf (*f* neuve), qui n'a pas été porté; *machine* neuf, qui n'a pas servi; (*not in use*) *resources, talent* inutilisé; (*Ling*) inusité.

(b) [ˈʌnˈjuːst] **to be ~ to (doing) sth** être peu habitué à (faire) qch; ne pas avoir l'habitude de (faire) qch; **I am quite ~ to it now** j'en ai perdu l'habitude, je n'en ai plus l'habitude.

unusual [ʌnˈjuːʒʊəl] *adj shape, name* insolite, étrange, bizarre; *talents, size* exceptionnel. **it is ~ for him to be early** il est exceptionnel *or* rare qu'il arrive (*subj*) de bonne heure, il n'arrive pas de bonne heure d'habitude, il n'est pas dans ses habitudes d'arriver de bonne heure; **it's not ~ for him to be late** *or* **that he should be late** il n'est pas rare qu'il soit en retard, il lui arrive souvent d'être en retard; **that's ~ for him!** ce n'est pas dans ses habitudes!, on ne s'attend pas à ça de lui!

unusually [ʌnˈjuːʒʊəlɪ] *adv* (*unaccustomedly*) exceptionnellement, anormalement; (*exceedingly*) exceptionnellement, extraordinairement. **~ quiet/happy** anormalement silencieux/gai; **~ difficult/gifted** exceptionnellement difficile/doué; **~ early** plus tôt que de coutume *or* d'habitude *or* d'ordinaire.

unutterable [ʌnˈʌtərəbl] *adj joy, boredom* indicible, indescriptible; (*) *idiot, fool* fini, achevé.

unvaried [ʌnˈveərɪd] *adj* uniforme, qui manque de variété, monotone (*pej*). **the menu was ~ from one week to the next** le menu ne changeait pas d'une semaine à l'autre.

unvarnished [ˈʌnˈvɑːnɪʃt] *adj wood* non verni; *pottery* non vernissé; (*fig*) *account, description* simple, sans fard, sans embellissements. **the ~ truth** la vérité pure et simple, la vérité toute nue.

unvarying [ʌn'vɛərɪɪŋ] *adj* invariable, constant.

unvaryingly [ʌn'vɛərɪɪŋlɪ] *adv* invariablement.

unveil [ʌn'veɪl] *vt* dévoiler.

unveiling [ʌn'veɪlɪŋ] *n* dévoilement *m*; (*ceremony*) inauguration *f*.

unventilated ['ʌn'ventɪleɪtɪd] *adj* sans ventilation.

unverifiable ['ʌn'verɪfaɪəbl] *adj* invérifiable.

unverified ['ʌn'verɪfaɪd] *adj* non vérifié.

unversed ['ʌn'vɜːst] *adj*: **~ in** peu versé dans.

unvoiced ['ʌn'vɔɪst] *adj opinion, sentiment* inexprimé; (*Ling*) non voisé, sourd.

unwanted ['ʌn'wɒntɪd] *adj clothing, article* superflu, dont on ne se sert pas, dont on n'a pas besoin; *child* non désiré, non souhaité; *effect* non recherché.

unwarlike ['ʌn'wɔːlaɪk] *adj* peu guerrier, peu belliqueux, pacifique.

unwarranted [ʌn'wɒrəntɪd] *adj* injustifié.

unwary [ʌn'wɛərɪ] *adj* qui n'est pas sur ses gardes, sans méfiance, imprudent.

unwashed ['ʌn'wɒʃt] **1** *adj hands, object* non lavé; *person* qui ne s'est pas lavé. **2** *n*: **the Great U~** la racaille, la populace.

unwavering [ʌn'weɪvərɪŋ] *adj faith, resolve, devotion* inébranlable; *gaze* fixe; *concentration* qui ne faiblit pas. **to follow an ~ course** poursuivre inébranlablement son but, aller droit au but, ne pas se laisser détourner de son but.

unwaveringly [ʌn'weɪvərɪŋlɪ] *adv follow, continue* inébranlablement; *say* fermement; *gaze* fixement.

unweaned ['ʌn'wiːnd] *adj* non sevré.

unwearable ['ʌn'wɛərəbl] *adj clothes, colour* non portable, pas mettable.

unwearied [ʌn'wɪərɪd] *adj*, **unwearying** [ʌn'wɪərɪɪŋ] *adj* infatigable, inlassable. **to be ~ in one's efforts to do** s'efforcer infatigablement *or* inlassablement de faire.

unwed ['ʌn'wed] *adj* = **unmarried**.

unwelcome [ʌn'welkəm] *adj visitor, gift* importun; *news, delay, change* fâcheux. **the money was not ~** l'argent était le bienvenu; **they made us feel most ~** ils nous ont très mal accueillis, ils nous ont bien fait sentir que nous les importunions.

unwell ['ʌn'wel] *adj* indisposé, souffrant. **to feel ~** se sentir mal, ne pas se sentir très bien.

unwholesome ['ʌn'həʊlsəm] *adj atmosphere, climate* malsain, insalubre; *thoughts, interest* malsain, morbide; *influence* mal sain, pernicieux, nocif; *food* mal sain.

unwieldy [ʌn'wiːldɪ] *adj tool, sword* peu maniable, difficile à manier; *person* lourd, qui se déplace avec peine.

unwilling ['ʌn'wɪlɪŋ] *adj*: **to be ~ to do** (*reluctant*) être peu disposé à faire, faire à contrecœur *or* de mauvaise grâce *or* contre son gré; (*refuse*) ne pas vouloir faire, refuser de faire; **I am ~ for him to go** je ne veux pas qu'il y aille; **her ~ helper/ accomplice** son aide/complice malgré lui.

unwillingly ['ʌn'wɪlɪŋlɪ] *adv* à contrecœur, de mauvaise grâce, contre son gré, malgré soi.

unwillingness [ʌn'wɪlɪŋnɪs] *n* (*U*) **his ~ to help is surprising** il est étonnant qu'il ne soit pas disposé à aider.

unwind ['ʌn'waɪnd] *pret, ptp* **unwound 1** *vt* dérouler. **2** *vi* se dérouler; (**fig: relax*) se détendre, se relaxer.

unwisdom ['ʌn'wɪzdəm] *n* (*U*) manque *m* de bon sens, imprudence *f*.

unwise ['ʌn'waɪz] *adj person* imprudent, malavisé; *move, decision* imprudent, peu judicieux. **it would be ~ to do** on serait malavisé de faire, il serait imprudent de faire.

unwisely ['ʌn'waɪzlɪ] *adv* imprudemment.

unwitting [ʌn'wɪtɪŋ] *adj* involontaire; *action* non intentionnel, involontaire. **he was the ~ victim of** il a été la victime involontaire de, il a été sans le savoir la victime de.

unwittingly [ʌn'wɪtɪŋlɪ] *adv* involontairement, sans le savoir, par mégarde.

unwomanly [ʌn'wʊmənlɪ] *adj* peu féminin.

unwonted [ʌn'wəʊntɪd] *adj* peu commun, inaccoutumé.

unworkable ['ʌn'wɜːkəbl] *adj scheme, idea* impraticable; *mine* inexploitable; *substance, fabric* rebelle.

unworldly ['ʌn'wɜːldlɪ] *adj person* détaché de ce monde, qui n'a pas les pieds sur terre, peu réaliste, naïf (*f* naïve); *beauty* céleste, qui n'est pas de ce monde; *idealism, preoccupations* détaché de ce monde.

unworthiness [ʌn'wɜːðɪnɪs] *n* manque *m* de mérite.

unworthy [ʌn'wɜːðɪ] *adj* indigne (*of* de, *to do* de faire). **it is ~ of you** c'est indigne de vous.

unwounded ['ʌn'wuːndɪd] *adj* non blessé, indemne, valide.

unwrap ['ʌn'ræp] *vt* défaire, ouvrir.

unwritten ['ʌn'rɪtn] *adj song, folk tale* non écrit; *agreement* verbal. **it is an ~ law** *or* **rule that...** il est tacitement admis que...

unyielding [ʌn'jiːldɪŋ] *adj person* inflexible, qui ne cède pas; *substance* très dur; *structure* très solide.

unyoke ['ʌn'jəʊk] *vt* dételer.

unzip ['ʌn'zɪp] *vt* ouvrir la fermeture éclair ® de. **can you ~ me?** peux-tu défaire ma fermeture éclair?

up [ʌp] (*phr vb elem*) **1** *adv* **(a)** (*gen*) en haut, en l'air. **he threw the ball ~** il a jeté la balle en l'air; **hold it ~ higher** tiens-le plus haut; **~ there** là-haut; **~ in the air** en l'air; **~ in the sky** (là-haut) dans le ciel; **~ in the mountains** dans les montagnes; **from ~ on the hill** (du haut) de la colline; **~ on deck** sur le pont; **~ on top of the cupboard** sur le placard; **~ at the top of the tree** en haut *or* au sommet de l'arbre; **it's ~ on top** c'est là-haut (dessus); **~ above** au-dessus; **~ above sth** au-dessus de qch; **he lives 5 floors ~** il habite au 5e étage; **the people 3 floors ~ from me** les gens qui habitent 3 étages au-dessus de chez moi; **all the way ~** jusqu'en haut, jusqu'au sommet; **I met him on my way ~** je l'ai rencontré en montant; **I was on my way ~ to see you** je montais vous voir; **halfway ~** (*on hill*) à mi-côte, à mi-chemin; (*in pipe, tree, stairs etc*) à mi-hauteur; **a little farther ~** (*on wall etc*) un peu plus haut; (*along bench etc*) un peu plus loin; **sit close ~ to me** assieds-toi tout près de moi; **his hand has been ~ for a long time** il a la main levée depuis longtemps; **with his head ~ (high)** la tête haute; **the blinds were ~** les stores étaient levés; **the ladder was ~ against the wall** l'échelle était appuyée contre le mur (*V also* **1h**); **set the box ~ on end** mets la boîte debout; **it was ~ on end** c'est était debout; (*on parcel*) **'this side ~'** 'haut'; **sit still for a while, you've been ~ and down all evening** assieds-toi un moment, tu n'as pas arrêté (de) toute la soirée; **to jump ~ and down** sauter; **to walk ~ and down** faire les cent pas; *V also* **climb, face up to, hand up** *etc*.

(b) (*out of bed*) **to be ~** être levé, être debout *inv*; **(get) ~!** debout!, levez-vous!; **we were ~ at 7** nous étions levés *or* debout à 7 heures; **I was still ~ at midnight** j'étais encore debout *or* je ne m'étais toujours pas couché à minuit; **he's always ~ early** il est toujours levé *or* il se lève toujours de bonne heure; **I was ~ late this morning** je me suis levé tard ce matin; **I was ~ late last night** je me suis couché tard hier soir; **he was ~ all night** il ne s'est pas couché de la nuit; **she was ~ all night looking after her child** elle ne s'est pas couchée de la nuit *or* elle a veillé toute la nuit pour s'occuper de son enfant; **he was ~ and down all night** il n'a pas arrêté de se lever toute la nuit; **she was ~ and about** *or* **~ and doing* at 7 o'clock** elle était debout *or* sur pied et à l'ouvrage à 7 heures; **to be ~ and about again** ne plus être alité; *V also* **get up**.

(c) (*fig*) **when the sun was ~** quand le soleil était levé, après le lever du soleil; **the tide is ~** la marée est haute; **the river is ~** la rivière a monté; **the road is ~** la route est en travaux; (*Parl*) **the House is ~** la Chambre ne siège pas; **the temperature was ~ in the forties** la température dépassait quarante degrés; **~ with Joe Bloggs!** vive Joe Bloggs!; **~ with Celtic!** allez Celtic!, tous pour Celtic!; **to be ~ (on horseback)** être à cheval; **a horse with Smith ~** un cheval monté par Smith; **he's ~ at the top of the class** il est en tête de (sa) classe; **he was ~ with** *or* **~ among the leaders** il était dans les premiers; **he's well ~ in Latin** (*place in class*) il a une bonne place *or* il est bien placé en latin; (*knows a lot*) il est fort *or* calé* en latin; **I'm ~ with him in maths** nous nous valons en maths*, nous sommes au même niveau *or* de la même force en maths*; **I'm not very well ~ in what's been going on** je ne suis pas vraiment au fait de ce qui s'est passé; (*Univ*) **when I was ~*** quand j'étais étudiant *or* à la Fac*; **~ in London** à Londres; **~ in Scotland** en Écosse; **he's ~ from Birmingham** il vient *or* il arrive de Birmingham; **he's ~ in Leeds for the weekend** il passe le weekend à Leeds; **I come ~ to town every week** je viens en ville toutes les semaines; **we're ~ for the day** nous sommes venus passer la journée; **I was on my way ~ to London** j'allais à Londres, j'étais en route pour Londres; **~ north** dans le nord; **I'll play you 100 ~** je vous fais une partie en 100, le premier qui a 100 points gagne; **Chelsea were 3 goals ~** Chelsea menait par 3 buts; **we were 20 points ~ on them** nous avions 20 points d'avance sur eux; **to be one ~ on sb*** faire mieux que qn; **to be** *or* **come ~ before Judge X** *[accused person]* comparaître devant le juge X; *[case]* être jugé par le juge X; **his blood is ~** il a le sang qui bout; **his temper is ~** il est en colère; *[invalid]* **he's been rather ~ and down recently** il a eu des hauts et des bas récemment; **what's ~?*** (*what's happening*) qu'est-ce qu'il y a?; (*what's wrong*) qu'est-ce qui ne va pas?; **what's ~ with him?*** qu'est-ce qu'il a?, qu'est-ce qui lui prend?; **what's ~ with the car/your leg?*** qu'est-ce qu'elle a votre voiture?/votre jambe?; **I know there's something ~*** (*happening*) je sais qu'il se passe quelque chose; (*wrong*) je sais qu'il y a quelque chose qui ne va pas; **there's something ~ with Paul*** il y a quelque chose qui ne va pas *or* qui ne tourne pas rond* chez Paul; **there's something ~ with the engine*** il y a quelque chose qui ne tourne pas rond* dans le moteur; **there's something ~ with my leg*** j'ai quelque chose à la jambe, ma jambe me tracasse; *for other phrases V* **arm**[2], **hard** *etc*.

(d) (*more, higher etc*) **to be ~** *[prices, salaries, shares, numbers]* avoir augmenté, avoir monté (*by* de); *[temperature, water level]* avoir monté (*by* de); **potatoes are ~ again** les pommes de terre ont encore augmenté; **the standard is ~** le niveau est plus élevé; **it is ~ on last year** cela a augmenté par rapport à l'an dernier.

(e) (*upwards*) **from £2 ~** à partir de 2 livres; **from (the age of) 13 ~** à partir de (l'âge de) 13 ans; **from his youth ~** dès sa jeunesse.

(f) (*installed, built etc*) **we've got the curtains/ pictures ~ at last** nous avons enfin posé les rideaux/accroché les tableaux; **the shutters are ~** les volets sont posés *or* (*closed*) mis *or* fermés; **the new building isn't ~ yet** le nouveau bâtiment n'est pas encore construit; **the tent isn't ~ yet** la tente n'est pas encore plantée; **look, the flag is ~!** regarde, le drapeau est hissé!; **the notice about the outing is ~** l'excursion est affichée.

(g) (*finished*) **his leave/visit is ~** sa permission/sa visite est terminée; **it is ~ on the 20th** ça se termine *or* ça finit le 20; **when 3 days were ~** au bout de 3 jours; **time's ~!** c'est l'heure!; **it's all ~ with him*** il est fichu*; *V* **game**[1] *etc*.

(h) to be ~ against difficulties se heurter à *or* être aux prises avec des difficultés; **you don't know what you're ~ against!** tu n'as pas idée des difficultés qui t'attendent!; **he's ~ against stiff competition** il a affaire à forte partie *or* à des concurrents sérieux; **he's ~ against a very powerful politician** il a contre lui un homme politique très puissant; **we're really ~ against it** nous allons avoir du mal à nous en sortir.

(i) (*as far as*) ~ to jusqu'à; ~ to now jusqu'à maintenant, jusqu'ici; ~ to here jusqu'ici; ~ to there jusque-là; what page are you ~ to? à quelle page en êtes-vous?; ~ to and including chapter 5 jusqu'au chapitre 5 inclus; to count ~ to 100 compter jusqu'à 100; he'll pay ~ to £10 il paiera jusqu'à 10 livres.

(j) (*depending on*) it's ~ to you to decide c'est à vous de décider; it's ~ to you whether you go or not c'est à vous de décider si vous y allez ou non; shall I do it? — it's ~ to you je le fais? — faites comme vous voulez *or* faites commes vous l'entendez *or* (c'est) à vous de décider *or* ça ne tient qu'à vous; if it were ~ to me... s'il n'en tenait qu'à moi..., si c'était moi qui décidais...; it's ~ to us to help him c'est à nous de l'aider, il nous appartient de l'aider.

(k) (*busy doing etc*) what is he ~ to? qu'est-ce qu'il fait? *or* fabrique?*, qu'est-ce qu'il peut bien faire?; he's ~ to something il manigance *or* mijote quelque chose, il a quelque chose en tête; what have you been ~ to recently? qu'est-ce que vous devenez ces temps-ci?; what have you been ~ to? qu'est-ce que tu as manigancé? *or* fabriqué?*; what are you ~ to with that knife? qu'est-ce que tu fais *or* fabriques* avec ce couteau?; he's ~ to no good *[child]* il prépare quelque sottise; *[adult]* il mijote quelque mauvais coup.

(l) (*equal to*) to be ~ to a task être à la hauteur d'une tâche; is he ~ to advanced work? est-il capable de faire des études supérieures?; it isn't ~ to his usual standard d'habitude il fait mieux que ça, il nous a habitués à mieux; are you feeling ~ to going for a walk? est-ce que tu te sens d'attaque à faire une promenade?; I just don't feel ~ to it je ne m'en sens pas le courage; he really isn't ~ to going back to work yet il n'est vraiment pas encore en état de reprendre le travail; it's not ~ to much ça ne vaut pas grand-chose; *V* mischief *etc*.

2 *prep*: to be ~ a tree/~ a ladder être dans un arbre/sur une échelle; to go ~ the stairs monter les marches d'un escalier, monter l'escalier; to go ~ the street monter la rue; to climb ~ a cliff escalader une falaise; to climb ~ a tree grimper dans *or* sur un arbre; to run ~ a hill monter une colline en courant; to sail ~ a river remonter une rivière en bateau; he pointed ~ the hill/the stairs il indiqua du doigt le haut de la colline/de l'escalier; the car drove ~ the road la voiture a remonté la rue; the house is ~ that road la maison est dans cette rue; they live just ~ the road ils habitent un peu plus haut *or* plus loin dans la (même) rue; put it ~ your sleeve mets-le dans ta manche; ~ hill and down dale par monts et par vaux; he travelled ~ and down the country il parcourait le pays; people ~ and down the country are saying... un peu partout dans le pays *or* aux quatre coins du pays il y a des gens qui disent...; he walked ~ and down the street il a fait les cent pas dans la rue, il a arpenté la rue; I've been ~ and down the stairs all evening je n'ai pas arrêté de monter et descendre les escaliers de toute la soirée; further ~ the page plus haut sur la même page; halfway ~ the hill à mi-chemin du sommet (de la colline), à mi-côte; halfway ~ the pipe/stairs à mi-hauteur du tuyau/de l'escalier; halfway ~ the road à mi-chemin (de la rue).

3 *n* (a) ~s and downs (*in oad etc*) accidents *mpl*; (*fig: in life, health etc*) hauts *mpl* et bas *mpl*; after many ~s and downs après maintes vicissitudes; his career had its ~s and downs il a connu des hauts et des bas *or* des succès et des revers dans sa carrière, sa carrière a connu des hauts et des bas.

(b) he's on the ~* il fait des *or* il est en progrès; he is on the ~ and ~* tout va de mieux en mieux pour lui.

4 *adj* (*Brit Rail*) the ~ train le train qui va à Londres; the ~ platform le quai du train pour Londres.

5 *vi* (*: hum*) he ~ped and hit him il a bondi et l'a frappé; I ~ped and told him what I thought of him sans plus attendre je lui ai dit ses quatre vérités; he ~ped and offed sans faire ni une ni deux il a fichu le camp*.

6 *vt* (*) *price etc* augmenter, monter.

7 *cpd*: up-and-coming plein d'avenir, plein de promesses; up-and-down *movement* ascendant et descendant, de va-et-vient; (*fig*) *career, business* qui a des hauts et des bas; *progress* en dents de scie; (*Mus*) upbeat levé *m*; (*fig: adj*) up-beat* optimiste; upbraid *V* upbraid; upbringing éducation *f*; he owed his success to his upbringing il devait son succès à l'éducation qu'il avait reçue *or* à la manière dont il avait été élevé; (*US*) upcoming imminent, prochain; upcountry (*adv*) *go* vers l'intérieur (*d'un pays*); *be* à l'intérieur; (*adj*) de l'intérieur; (*Aviat*) up-current courant (d'air) ascendant; update mettre à jour; (*US*) up-draft = up-current; upend *box etc* mettre debout; (* *fig*) *system etc* renverser; upgrade *V* upgrade; upheld *V* uphold; uphill *V* uphill; uphold *V* uphold; upholder défenseur *m*; upkeep *[family, house, car, garden]* entretien *m*; upland (*n: also* uplands) hautes terres, hauteurs *fpl*, plateau(x) *m(pl)*; (*adj*) des hautes terres, du plateau, des plateaux, des hauteurs; uplift *V* uplift; upmost = uppermost; upon (*prep*) = on 2; upraise élever, lever; upright *etc V* upright *etc*; uprising soulèvement *m*, insurrection *f*, révolte *f* (*against* contre); upriver = upstream; uproar *etc V* uproar *etc*; (*lit, fig*) uproot déraciner; upset *etc V* upset *etc*; upshot résultat *m*, aboutissement *m*, conséquence *f*; the upshot of it all was... le résultat de tout cela a été...; in the upshot à la fin, en fin de compte; upside down *V* upside down; (*Brit*) to get upsides* with sb (*catch up*) rattraper qn; (*take revenge*) se venger de qn, rendre la pareille à qn; upstage *V* upstage; upstairs *V* upstairs; upstanding (*erect*) qui se tient droit; (*well-built*) bien bâti, bien campé; (*honest*) droit, honnête, probe; a fine upstanding young man un honnête gaillard; (*frm*) to be upstanding se lever; (*pej*) upstart (*n*) parvenu(e) *m(f)*, prétentieux *m*, -euse *f*; (*adj*) parvenu; (*presumptuous*) prétentieux; (*US*) upstate (*adv*) *go* vers l'intérieur (d'un État des États Unis); *be* à l'intérieur; (*adj*) de l'intérieur; upstream (*adv*) *be* en amont (*from* de); *sail* vers l'amont; *swim* contre le courant; (*adj*) d'amont; with arms upstretched les bras tendus en l'air; upstroke (*with pen*) délié *m*; *[piston etc]* course ascendante; upsurge *[feeling]* vague *f*, accès *m*; *[interest]* renaissance *f*, recrudescence *f*, regain *m*; (*Aut, Aviat*) upswept profilé; upswept hair cheveux relevés sur la tête; upswing mouvement ascendant, montée *f*; (*fig*) amélioration *f* notable; to be quick on the uptake avoir l'esprit vif *or* délié, comprendre *or* saisir vite; to be slow on the uptake être lent à comprendre *or* à saisir; upthrust (*gen, Tech*) poussée ascendante; (*Geol*) soulèvement *m*; uptight* très tendu, crispé; to get uptight* se crisper (*about* à propos de); up-to-date *report, assessment, information* très récent; *building* moderne; *attitude, person* moderne, dans le vent, à la page (*V also* date[1] 1c); uptorn *tree* déraciné, arraché; up-to-the-minute de dernière heure; (*US*) uptown (*adv*) dans les beaux quartiers; (*adj*) des beaux quartiers; upturn retourner, mettre à l'envers; (*overturn*) renverser; upturned nose nez retroussé; upward(s) *V* upward(s); upwind (*adv*) contre le vent, du côté du vent; to be upwind of être dans le vent par rapport à.

upbraid [ʌp'breɪd] *vt* réprimander, morigéner, faire des reproches à. to ~ sb for doing reprocher à qn de faire (*or* d'avoir fait).

upgrade ['ʌpgreɪd] 1 *n* rampe *f*, montée *f*. (*fig*) to be on the ~ *[business]* être en progrès; *[price]* augmenter, être en hausse; *[sick person]* être en voie de guérison.

2 ['ʌp'greɪd] *adv* = uphill 1.

3 [ʌp'greɪd] *vt employee* promouvoir; *job, post* revaloriser. I have been ~d je suis monté en grade, j'ai été promu.

upheaval [ʌp'hiːvəl] *n* (*Geol*) soulèvement *m*; (*fig*) bouleversement *m*; (*esp Pol*) perturbation(s) *f(pl)*, crise *f*; (*esp in home, family*) branle-bas *m*, remue-ménage *m*; (*from volcano, earthquake*) cataclysme *m*. it caused a lot of ~ cela a tout perturbé.

uphill ['ʌp'hɪl] 1 *adv*: to go ~ *[road]* aller en montant, monter; *[car]* monter (la côte). 2 *adj road* qui monte; (*fig*) *task* pénible, difficile, ardu. it's ~ all the way ça monte tout le long; (*fig*) c'est une lutte continuelle.

uphold [ʌp'həʊld] *pret, ptp* upheld *vt institution, person* soutenir, donner son soutien à; *law* faire respecter, maintenir; (*Jur*) *verdict* confirmer, maintenir.

upholster [ʌp'həʊlstəʳ] *vt* rembourrer, capitonner, recouvrir. (*fig hum*) she is fairly well ~ed* elle est assez bien rembourrée*.

upholsterer [ʌp'həʊlstərəʳ] *n* tapissier *m*.

upholstery [ʌp'həʊlstərɪ] *n* (*U*) (*trade*) tapisserie *f* (*art, métier*); (*material*) rembourrage *m*, capitonnage *m*; (*in car*) garniture *f*.

uplift ['ʌplɪft] 1 *n* (*fig*) sentiment *m* d'élévation morale *or* spirituelle.

2 *cpd*: uplift bra soutien-gorge *m* qui maintient bien la poitrine.

3 [ʌp'lɪft] *vt soul* élever; *person* élever (l'âme *or* l'esprit *or* les sentiments de), grandir. to feel ~ed se sentir grandi.

upper ['ʌpəʳ] 1 *adj part, section, floor* supérieur (*f* -eure), du dessus, au-dessus; *lip, jaw, stratum, deck* supérieur; (*in geographical names*) haut; (*fig: in rank etc*) supérieur. the temperature is in the ~ thirties la température dépasse trente-cinq degrés; the ~ (reaches of the) Thames la haute Tamise; the ~ classes les couches supérieures de la société (*V also* 3).

2 *n [shoe]* empeigne *f*. (*fig*) to be (down) on one's ~s* manger de la vache enragée, être dans la purée*.

3 *cpd*: (*Typ*) upper case haut *m* de casse; upper-case letter majuscule *f*; (*Brit Cine, Theat*) upper circle deuxième balcon *m*; upper-class (*adj*) aristocratique; (*fig*) the upper crust* le gratin*; upper-crust* (*adj*) aristocratique; (*Boxing*) uppercut uppercut *m*; (*Parl*) the Upper House (*gen*) la Chambre haute; (*Brit*) la Chambre des Lords; (*France, US etc*) le Sénat; the upper-income bracket la tranche des revenus élevés; the upper middle class la haute bourgeoisie; (*Scol*) the upper school les grandes classes.

uppermost ['ʌpəməʊst] 1 *adj* (*highest*) le plus haut, le plus élevé; (*on top*) en dessus. the thought of it was ~ in my mind j'y pensais avant tout autre chose, c'était au premier plan de mes pensées. 2 *adv* en dessus.

uppish* ['ʌpɪʃ] *adj*, (*Brit*) **uppity**: ['ʌpɪtɪ] *adj* prétentieux, bêcheur*, arrogant, crâneur*. to get ~ monter sur ses ergots; to get ~ with sb traiter qn de haut.

upright ['ʌpraɪt] 1 *adj* (*erect*) *person, structure* droit, vertical; *piano* droit; (*fig: honest*) droit, honnête, probe.

2 *adv stand* droit; *place* droit, verticalement.

3 *n* (a) *[door, window]* montant *m*, pied-droit *m* (*Archit*); *[goal-post]* montant de but.

(b) (*piano*) piano droit.

uprightly ['ʌp,raɪtlɪ] *adv* honnêtement, avec droiture.

uprightness ['ʌp,raɪtnɪs] *n* (*U*) honnêteté *f*, droiture *f*.

uproar ['ʌprɔːʳ] *n* (*U*) tumulte *m*, vacarme *m*, tapage *m*. this caused an ~, at this there was (an) ~ (*shouting*) cela a déclenché un véritable tumulte; (*protesting*) cela a déclenché une tempête de protestations; the hall was in (an) ~ (*shouting*) le tumulte régnait dans la salle; (*protesting*) toute la salle protestait bruyamment; (*disturbance*) la plus vive agitation régnait dans la salle; the meeting ended in (an) ~ la réunion s'est terminée dans le tumulte.

uproarious [ʌp'rɔːrɪəs] *adj* (*noisy*) *meeting, crowd* tumultueux, tapageur; (*hilarious*) *joke, mistake* hilarant; *laughter* éclatant. ~ success succès fou *or* monstre *or* bœuf* *inv*.

uproariously [ʌp'rɔːrɪəslɪ] *adv* tumultueusement, avec vacarme. to laugh ~ rire aux éclats, se tordre de rire; ~ funny désopilant.

upsa-daisy* ['ʌpsə,deɪzɪ] *excl* (*baby talk*) allez, hop!

upset [ʌp'set] *pret, ptp* upset 1 *vt* (a) (*overturn*) *cup etc* renverser; *boat* faire chavirer; (*spill*) *milk, contents* renverser, répandre. (*fig*)**that ~ the applecart*** ça a tout fichu par terre*, ça a chamboulé* tous mes (*or* ses *etc*) projets.

(b) (*fig*) *plan, timetable* déranger, bouleverser; *system* déranger; *calculation* fausser; *stomach, digestion* déranger; *person* (*offend*) vexer; (*grieve*) faire de la peine à; (*annoy*) contrarier, fâcher, indisposer; (*make ill*) rendre malade. **don't ~ yourself** ne vous tracassez pas, ne vous en faites pas*, ne vous frappez pas*, ne vous faites pas de bile*; **now you've ~ him** maintenant il est vexé; **onions always ~ me** *or* **my digestion** *or* **my stomach** les oignons me rendent malade, je ne supporte pas les oignons.

2 *adj* **(a)** *person* (*offended*) vexé; (*grieved*) peiné, attristé, triste; (*annoyed*) fâché, contrarié, ennuyé; (*ill*) indisposé, souffrant. **to get ~** se vexer; se fâcher; devenir triste; **he looked terribly ~** il avait l'air bouleversé *or* tout chaviré*; **what are you so ~ about?** qu'est-ce qui ne va pas?

(b) *stomach, digestion* dérangé.

3 [ˈʌpset] *cpd*: **upset price** mise *f* à prix.

4 [ˈʌpset] *n* (*upheaval*) désordre *m*, remue-ménage *m*; (*in plans etc*) renversement *m*, dérangement *m* (*in* de); (*emotional*) chagrin *m*; (*: *quarrel*) brouille *f*. **to have a stomach ~** avoir l'estomac dérangé, avoir une indigestion.

upsetting [ʌpˈsetɪŋ] *adj* (*offending*) vexant; (*saddening*) triste, (*stronger*) affligeant; (*annoying*) contrariant, fâcheux, ennuyeux.

upside down [ˈʌpsaɪdˈdaʊn] **1** *adv* à l'envers. **to hold a book ~** tenir un livre à l'envers; **to turn ~** *box, book* retourner; (*fig*) *room, drawer, cupboard* mettre sens dessus dessous; (*) *plans* flanquer à l'eau*.

2 *adj* à l'envers, retourné; (*in disorder*) *room etc* sens dessus dessous. (*Culin*) **pineapple ~ cake** gâteau renversé à l'ananas.

upstage [ˈʌpˈsteɪdʒ] **1** *adv* (*Theat*) *be, stand* au fond de la scène; *go* vers le fond de la scène; *enter* par le fond de la scène. **2** *adj* (* *fig*) hautain, prétentieux, crâneur*. **3** *vt* éclipser.

upstairs [ˈʌpˈstɛəz] **1** *adv* en haut. **he's ~** il est en haut; **to go ~** monter (l'escalier); **he ran ~** il monta l'escalier quatre à quatre; **to take ~** *person* faire monter; *luggage etc* monter; **the people ~** les gens du dessus; (*fig*) **he's not got much ~*** il n'est pas très intelligent, ça ne tourne pas très fort là-haut*; *V* **kick**.

2 *n*: **the house has no ~** la maison est de plain-pied *or* n'a pas d'étage; **the ~ belongs to another family** l'étage *m* appartient à une autre famille.

3 [ˈʌpstɛəz] *adj flat, neighbour* du dessus; *room* d'en haut, de l'étage. **I prefer an ~ room** je préfère une chambre à l'étage *or* en étage.

upsy-daisy* [ˈʌpsəˌdeɪzɪ] *excl* = **upsa-daisy**.

upward [ˈʌpwəd] **1** *adj movement* ascendant, ascensionnel; *pull, thrust* vers le haut, ascensionnel; *trend* à la hausse; *slope* qui monte; *glance* levé. **2** *adv* = **upwards**.

upwards [ˈʌpwədz] (*phr vb elem*) *adv move, walk* en montant, vers le haut. **to look ~** regarder en haut *or* vers le haut; **looking ~** les yeux levés, la tête levée; **place the book face ~** posez le livre face en dessus, posez le livre à l'endroit; **he was lying face ~** il était couché sur le dos; **to slope gently ~** monter en pente douce; (*fig*) **prices from 10 francs ~** prix à partir de 10 F; **from childhood ~** dès sa jeunesse; **and ~** et plus, et au-dessus; **~ of 3,000** 3.000 et plus.

Urals [ˈjʊərəlz] *npl*: **the ~** les monts *mpl* Oural, l'Oural *m*.

uranium [jʊəˈreɪnɪəm] *n* uranium *m*.

Uranus [jʊəˈreɪnəs] *n* (*Myth*) Uranus *m*; (*Astron*) Uranus *f*.

urban [ˈɜːbən] *adj* urbain. **in ~ areas** dans les zones urbaines; **~ guerilla** guérillero *m* urbain; **~ renewal** rénovations urbaines; **~ sprawl** étalement urbain.

urbane [ɜːˈbeɪn] *adj* urbain, courtois.

urbanity [ɜːˈbænɪtɪ] *n* (*U*) urbanité *f*, courtoisie *f*.

urbanization [ˌɜːbənaɪˈzeɪʃən] *n* urbanisation *f*.

urbanize [ˈɜːbənaɪz] *vt* urbaniser.

urchin [ˈɜːtʃɪn] *n* polisson(ne) *m(f)*, garnement *m*; *V* **sea, street**.

Urdu [ˈʊəduː] *n* ourdou *m*.

urea [ˈjʊərɪə] *n* urée *f*.

ureter [jʊəˈriːtəʳ] *n* uretère *m*.

urethra [jʊəˈriːθrə] *n* urètre *m*.

urge [ɜːdʒ] **1** *n* désir ardent, forte envie, démangeaison* *f* (*to do* de faire). **to feel** *or* **have the ~ to do** éprouver une forte envie de faire, avoir vivement envie de faire, être démangé* par une envie de faire; *V* **sex**.

2 *vt person* pousser, exhorter (*to do* à faire), presser, conseiller vivement (*to do* de faire); *caution, remedy, measure* préconiser, conseiller vivement, recommander avec insistance. **I ~d him not to go** je lui ai vivement déconseillé d'y aller; **he needed no urging** il ne s'est pas fait prier; **to ~ that sth (should) be done** recommander vivement que *or* insister pour que qch soit fait; **'do it now!' he ~d** 'faites-le tout de suite!' insista-t-il; **he ~d acceptance of the report** il a vivement recommandé *or* préconisé l'acceptation du rapport; **to ~ patience on sb** exhorter qn à la patience; **they ~d this policy on the Government** ils ont fait pression sur le gouvernement pour qu'il adopte (*subj*) cette politique; **to ~ sb back/in/out** *etc* presser qn de revenir/d'entrer/de sortir *etc*.

urge on *vt sep horse* presser, pousser, talonner; *person* faire avancer; *troops* pousser en avant, faire avancer; (*fig*) *worker* aiguillonner, presser; *work* activer, hâter; (*Sport*) *team* animer, encourager. **to urge sb on to (do) sth** inciter qn à (faire) qch.

urgency [ˈɜːdʒənsɪ] *n* (*U*) [*case etc*] urgence *f*; [*tone, entreaty*] insistance *f*. **a matter of ~** une affaire urgente; **there's no ~** ce n'est pas urgent, cela ne presse pas; **with a note of ~ in his voice** avec insistance.

urgent [ˈɜːdʒənt] *adj need, case, attention* urgent; *tone, entreaty* insistant. **it's ~!** c'est urgent!, ça urge!*; **it's not ~** ce n'est pas urgent, cela ne presse pas, cela peut attendre; **it is ~ that he should go** il doit y aller d'urgence, il est urgent qu'il y aille; **to be in ~ need of** avoir un besoin urgent de.

urgently [ˈɜːdʒəntlɪ] *adv need* d'urgence, sans délai; *plead* instamment.

uric [ˈjʊərɪk] *adj* urique.

urinal [ˈjʊərɪnl] *n* (*place*) urinoir *m*; (*in street*) vespasienne *f*; (*receptacle*) urinal *m*.

urinary [ˈjʊərɪnərɪ] *adj* urinaire.

urinate [ˈjʊərɪneɪt] *vi* uriner.

urine [ˈjʊərɪn] *n* urine *f*.

urn [ɜːn] *n* **(a)** (*for ashes*) urne *f*. **(b) tea ~** fontaine *f* à thé.

urogenital [ˌjʊərəʊˈdʒenɪtl] *adj* urogénital.

urological [ˌjʊərəʊˈlɒdʒɪkl] *adj* urologique.

urologist [jʊəˈrɒlədʒɪst] *n* urologue *mf*.

urology [jʊəˈrɒlədʒɪ] *n* urologie *f*.

Ursa [ˈɜːsə] *n* (*Astron*) **~ Major/Minor** la Grande/Petite Ourse.

Uruguay [ˈjʊərəgwaɪ] *n* Uruguay *m*.

Uruguayan [ˌjʊərəˈgwaɪən] **1** *adj* uruguayen, de l'Uruguay. **2** *n* Uruguayen(ne) *m(f)*.

us [ʌs] *pers pron* **(a)** nous. **he hit ~** il nous a frappés; **give it to ~** donnez-le-nous; **in front of ~** devant nous; **let ~** *or* **let's go!** allons-y!; **younger than ~** plus jeune que nous; **both of ~** nous deux, tous (*or* toutes) les deux; **several of ~** plusieurs d'entre nous; **he is one of ~** il est des nôtres; **as for ~ English, we...** nous autres Anglais, nous... .

(b) (:) me, moi. **give ~ a bit!** donne-m'en un morceau!, donne-moi-z-en!:; **give ~ a look!** fais voir!

usable [ˈjuːzəbl] *adj* utilisable. **no longer ~** hors d'usage.

usage [ˈjuːzɪdʒ] *n* (*U*) **(a)** (*custom*) usage *m*, coutume *f*; (*Ling*) usage. **(b)** (*treatment*) [*tool, machine, chair etc*] manipulation *f*; [*person*] traitement *m*. **it's had some rough ~** ça a été bousculé, on s'en est mal servi; **kind ~** gentillesse *f*.

use [juːs] **1** *n* **(a)** (*U: employment*) usage *m*, emploi *m*, utilisation *f*. **the ~ of steel in industry** l'emploi de l'acier dans l'industrie; **to learn the ~ of** apprendre à se servir de; **care is necessary in the ~ of firearms** il faut prendre des précautions quand on utilise des *or* on se sert d'armes à feu; **directions for ~** mode *m* d'emploi; **'for the ~ of teachers only'** *book, equipment* 'à l'usage des professeurs seulement'; *room* 'réservé aux professeurs'; **to keep sth for one's own ~** réserver qch à son usage personnel; **for ~ in case of emergency** à utiliser en cas d'urgence; **fit for ~** en état de servir; **ready for ~** prêt à servir; (*Med*) **for external ~** à usage externe; **to improve with ~** s'améliorer à l'usage; **in ~** *machine* en usage, utilisé; *word* en usage, usité; **no longer in ~, now out of ~** *machine* hors d'usage, qui n'est plus utilisé; *word* qui ne s'emploie plus, inusité; (*on machine, lift etc*) **'out of ~'** 'en dérangement'; **in general ~** d'usage *or* d'emploi courant; **it is in daily ~** on s'en sert tous les jours; **to come into ~** entrer en usage; **to go out of ~** tomber en désuétude; **to put sth into ~** commencer à se servir de qch; **to make ~ of** se servir de, faire usage de, utiliser; **to make good ~ of, to put to good ~** *machine, time, money* faire un bon emploi de, tirer parti de; *opportunity, facilities* mettre à profit, tirer parti de.

(b) (*way of using*) emploi *m*, utilisation *f*; (*need*) besoin *m*. **a new ~ for** un nouvel emploi de, une nouvelle utilisation de; **it has many ~s** cela a beaucoup d'emplois; **I'll find a ~ for it** je trouverai un moyen de m'en servir, j'en trouverai l'emploi; **I've no further ~ for it** je ne m'en sers plus, je n'en ai plus besoin; (*fig*) **I've no ~ for that sort of behaviour!*** je n'ai que faire de ce genre de conduite!; **I've no ~ for him at all!*** il m'embête!*

(c) (*U: usefulness*) **to be of ~** servir, être utile (*for or to sth* à qch, *to sb* à qn); **to be (of) no ~** ne servir à rien; **this is no ~ any more** ce n'est plus bon à rien; **what's the ~ of all this?** à quoi sert tout ceci?; **is this (of) any ~ to you?** est-ce que cela peut vous être utile? *or* vous servir?; **can I be (of) any ~?** puis-je être utile?; **he's no ~** il est incapable, il est nul; **he's no ~ as a goalkeeper** il ne vaut rien comme gardien de but; **you're no ~ to me if you can't spell** vous ne m'êtes d'aucune utilité si vous faites des fautes d'orthographe; **a lot of ~ that will be to you*** ça te fera une belle jambe!*; **there's** *or* **it's no ~ you(r) protesting** il ne vous sert à rien de protester; **it's no ~ trying to reason with him** il ne sert à rien d'essayer de le raisonner, on perd son temps à essayer de le raisonner; **it's no ~, he won't listen** ça ne sert à rien *or* c'est inutile, il ne veut rien entendre; **it's no ~, we must start work** tout ça c'est bien joli mais il faut nous mettre au travail; **you won't get it, it is no ~** tu ne l'auras pas, rien à faire; **what's the ~ of telling him not to, he never takes any notice** à quoi bon lui dire d'arrêter, il ne prête jamais attention; **I've told him fifty times already, what's the ~?** je le lui ai dit trente-six fois déjà, pour ce que ça a servi.

(d) (*U*) usage *m*. **to have the ~ of a garage** avoir l'usage d'un garage, pouvoir se servir d'un garage; **he gave me the ~ of his car** il m'a permis de me servir de sa voiture; **to have lost the ~ of one's arm** avoir perdu l'usage de son bras; **to have the full ~ of one's faculties** jouir de toutes ses facultés.

(e) (*custom*) usage *m*, coutume *f*.

2 [juːz] *vt* **(a)** *object, tool* se servir de, utiliser, employer; *force, discretion* user de; *opportunity* profiter de; *method, means* employer; *sb's name* faire usage de. **he ~d a knife to open it** il s'est servi d'un couteau *or* il a utilisé un couteau *or* il a pris un couteau pour l'ouvrir; **it is ~d for opening bottles** on s'en sert pour ouvrir les bouteilles; **are you using this?** vous servez-vous de ceci?, avez-vous besoin de ceci?; **have you ~d a gun before?** vous êtes-vous déjà servi d'un fusil?; **the money is to be ~d to build a new hospital** l'argent servira à construire un nouvel hôpital *or* à la construction d'un nouvel hôpital; **he ~d his shoe as a hammer** il s'est servi de son soulier comme marteau; **I ~ that as a table** ça me sert de table; **ointment to be ~d sparingly** crème à utiliser en couche légère; **I don't ~ my French much** je ne me sers pas beaucoup de mon français; **I don't want to ~ the car** je ne veux pas prendre la voiture; **he said I could ~ his car** il a dit que je pouvais me servir de *or* prendre sa voiture; **no longer ~d** *tool, machine, room* qui ne sert plus; *word* qui ne s'emploie plus, inusité; **~ your head!** *or* **brains!** réfléchis un peu!, tu as une tête, c'est pour t'en servir!; **~ your eyes!** ouvre l'œil!; **I feel I've just been ~d** j'ai l'impression qu'on s'est tout bonnement servi de moi; **I could ~ a drink!*** je prendrais bien un verre!; **this house could ~ a bit of paint!*** une couche de peinture ne ferait pas de mal à cette maison!; *V also* **used.**

(b) (*also* **~ up**) user, consommer; prendre. **this car ~s (up) too much petrol** cette voiture use *or* consomme trop d'essence; **have you ~d (up) all the sellotape ®?** avez-vous pris tout le scotch ®? *or* fini le scotch?; **you can ~ (up) the left-overs in a casserole** vous pouvez utiliser les restes pour faire un ragoût.

(c) (*treat*) *person* traiter, agir envers. **to ~ sb well** bien traiter qn, bien agir envers qn; **he was badly ~d** on a mal agi envers lui, on a abusé de sa bonne volonté.

3 *aux vb*: **I ~d to see her every week** je la voyais toutes les semaines; **I ~d to swim every day** je me baignais *or* j'avais l'habitude de me baigner tous les jours; **I ~d not** *or* **I use(d)n't*** *or* **I didn't ~* to smoke** (autrefois) je ne fumais pas; **what ~d he to** *or* **what did he ~* to do on Sundays?** qu'est-ce qu'il faisait (d'habitude) le dimanche?; **things aren't what they ~d to be** les choses ne sont plus ce qu'elles étaient.

use up *vt sep food* consommer entièrement, finir; *objects, ammunition, one's strength, resources, surplus* épuiser; *money* dépenser. **to use up the scraps** utiliser les restes; **it is all used up** c'est épuisé, il n'en reste plus; *V also* **use 2b.**

used [ju:zd] *adj* **(a)** *stamp* oblitéré; *car* d'occasion.

(b) [ju:st] (*accustomed*) **to be ~ to (doing) sth** être habitué à (faire) qch, avoir l'habitude de (faire) qch; **I'm not ~ to it** je n'en ai pas l'habitude, je n'y suis pas habitué; **to get ~ to** s'habituer à; **you'll get ~ to it** vous vous y ferez.

use(d)n't ['ju:snt] = **used not;** *V* **use 3.**

useful ['ju:sfʊl] *adj tool, chair, book* utile; *discussion, time* utile, profitable; *attempt* honorable. **it is ~ for him to be able to ...** il est très utile qu'il puisse ...; **to make o.s. ~** se rendre utile, donner un coup de main*; **to come in ~** être utile; **that knife will come in ~** ce couteau pourra nous rendre service; **to be ~ to sb** *[person]* rendre service à qn; *[advice, knowledge, tool]* être utile à qn, rendre service à qn; (*iro*) **that's ~!** nous voilà bien avancés!; **this machine has a ~ life of 10 years** cette machine peut donner 10 ans de satisfaction *or* de service; **he's a ~ man to know** c'est un homme utile à connaître *or* qu'il est bon de connaître; **it's a ~ thing to know** c'est bon à savoir; **he's a ~ player** c'est un joueur compétent; **he's quite ~ with his fists** il sait bien se servir de ses poings; **he's ~ with a gun** il sait manier un fusil.

usefully ['ju:sfəlɪ] *adv* utilement.

usefulness ['ju:sfʊlnɪs] *n* (*U*) utilité *f*; *V* **outlive.**

useless ['ju:slɪs] *adj tool* inutile; (*unusable*) inutilisable; *advice, suggestion* inutile, qui ne vaut rien; *person* incompétent; *remedy* inefficace; *volunteer* incapable; *effort* inutile, vain. **this is a ~ machine** c'est une machine inutile *or* qui ne sert à rien; **this machine is ~ without a handle** cette machine est inutilisable sans une manivelle, on ne peut pas se servir de cette machine sans une manivelle; **shouting is ~** (il est) inutile de crier, il ne sert à rien de crier, ce n'est pas la peine de crier; **he's ~ as a goalkeeper** il ne vaut rien comme gardien de but; **he's absolutely ~*** c'est un cas désespéré, il est complètement nul.

uselessly ['ju:slɪslɪ] *adv* inutilement.

uselessness ['ju:slɪsnɪs] *n* (*U*) *[tool, advice etc]* inutilité *f*; *[remedy]* inefficacité *f*; *[person]* incompétence *f*.

user ['ju:zəʳ] *n [machine, dictionary etc]* utilisateur *m*, -trice *f*; *[public service, telephone, road, train]* usager *m*. **gas ~s** usagers *or* utilisateurs du gaz; **car ~s** automobilistes *mpl*.

usher ['ʌʃəʳ] **1** *n* (*in law courts etc*) huissier *m*; (*doorkeeper*) portier *m*; (*at public meeting*) membre *m* du service d'ordre; (*in theatre, church*) placeur *m*.

2 *vt*: **to ~ sb out/along** *etc* faire sortir/avancer *etc* qn; **to ~ sb into a room** introduire *or* faire entrer qn dans une salle; **to ~ sb to the door** reconduire qn à la porte.

usher in *vt sep person* introduire, faire entrer; (*fig*) *period, season* inaugurer, commencer. **it ushers in a new era** cela annonce *or* inaugure une nouvelle époque, cela marque le début d'une ère nouvelle; **it ushered in a new reign** cela inaugura un nouveau règne, ce fut l'aurore d'un nouveau règne; **the spring was ushered in by storms** le début du printemps fut marqué par des orages.

usherette [,ʌʃə'ret] *n* (*Cine, Theat*) ouvreuse *f*.

usual ['ju:ʒʊəl] **1** *adj drink, crowd, time* habituel; *price* courant. **my ~ grocer** mon épicier habituel; **it is the ~ practice** c'est ce qui se fait d'habitude; **his ~ practice was to rise at 6** il avait l'habitude de se lever à 6 heures; **as is ~ with such machines it broke down** comme toutes les machines de ce genre elle est tombée en panne; **as is ~ on these occasions** comme le veut la coutume en ces occasions; **he was on his ~ good behaviour** il se tenait bien, comme d'habitude; **he'll soon be his ~ self again** il retrouvera bientôt sa santé (*or* sa gaieté *etc*); **as ~, as per ~*** comme d'habitude, comme à l'ordinaire; (*Comm*) **'business as ~'** 'la vente *or* les affaires continue(nt)'; **more than ~** plus que d'habitude *or* d'ordinaire *or* de coutume; **it's not ~ for him to be late** il est rare qu'il soit en retard, il n'est pas en retard d'habitude; *V* **channel.**

2 *n* (*: *drink*) **you know my ~** vous savez ce que je prends d'habitude; **the ~ please!** comme d'habitude s'il vous plaît!

usually ['ju:ʒʊəlɪ] *adv* habituellement, d'habitude, généralement, ordinairement, d'ordinaire, à l'ordinaire. **I ~ go on Wednesdays** j'y vais généralement *or* ordinairement le mercredi, habituellement *or* d'habitude *or* d'ordinaire j'y vais le mercredi; **what do you ~ do?** qu'est-ce que vous faites d'habitude? *or* d'ordinaire? *or* à l'ordinaire?; **more than ~ careful** encore plus prudent que d'habitude *or* d'ordinaire *or* de coutume.

usufruct ['ju:zjʊfrʌkt] *n* (*Jur*) usufruit *m*.

usufructuary [,ju:zjʊ'frʌktjʊərɪ] (*Jur*) **1** *n* usufruitier *m*, -ière *f*. **2** *adj* usufruitier.

usurer ['ju:ʒərəʳ] *n* usurier *m*, -ière *f*.

usurious [ju:'zjʊərɪəs] *adj* usuraire.

usurp [ju:'zɜ:p] *vt* usurper.

usurpation [,ju:zɜ:'peɪʃən] *n* (*U*) usurpation *f*.

usurper [ju:'zɜ:pəʳ] *n* usurpateur *m*, -trice *f*.

usurping [ju:'zɜ:pɪŋ] *adj* usurpateur (*f* -trice).

usury ['ju:ʒʊrɪ] *n* (*U: Fin*) usure *f*.

utensil [ju:'tensl] *n* ustensile *m*; *V* **kitchen.**

uterine ['ju:təraɪn] *adj* utérin.

uterus ['ju:tərəs] *n* utérus *m*.

utilitarian [,ju:tɪlɪ'tɛərɪən] **1** *adj* utilitaire. **2** *n* utilitariste *mf*.

utilitarianism [,ju:tɪlɪ'tɛərɪənɪzəm] *n* (*U*) utilitarisme *m*.

utility [ju:'tɪlɪtɪ] **1** *n* **(a)** (*U*) utilité *f*. **(b)** (*public ~*) service public. **2** *adj goods* utilitaire, fonctionnel; *vehicle* utilitaire. **3** *cpd*: **utility room** *pièce réservée à des travaux de couture, repassage etc.*

utilizable ['ju:tɪlaɪzəbl] *adj* utilisable, employable.

utilization [,ju:tɪlaɪ'zeɪʃən] *n* (*V* **utilize**) utilisation *f*; exploitation *f*.

utilize ['ju:tɪlaɪz] *vt object* utiliser, se servir de; *situation, resources, person* utiliser, tirer parti de, exploiter.

utmost ['ʌtməʊst] **1** *adj* **(a)** (*greatest*) le plus grand; *skill* suprême; *danger* extrême. **with the ~ speed** à toute vitesse; **with the ~ candour** en toute franchise, avec la plus grande franchise; **with the ~ possible care** avec le plus grand soin possible, aussi soigneusement que possible; **it is of the ~ importance that ...** il est extrêmement important que ... + *subj*; **it's a matter of the ~ importance** c'est une affaire de la plus haute importance *or* d'une importance capitale.

(b) (*furthest*) le plus éloigné, extrême. **to the ~ ends of the earth** aux quatre coins de la terre.

2 *n*: **to do one's ~ to do** faire tout son possible *or* tout ce qu'on peut pour faire; **to the ~ of one's ability** à la limite de ses capacités, au mieux de ses possibilités; **that is the ~ I can do** c'est absolument tout ce que je peux faire, je ne peux absolument pas faire plus *or* mieux; **to the ~** au plus haut degré, au plus haut point; **at the ~** au maximum, tout au plus.

Utopia [ju:'təʊpɪə] *n* utopie *f*.

Utopian [ju:'təʊpɪən] **1** *adj* utopique.

2 *n* utopiste *mf*.

utricle ['ju:trɪkl] *n* utricule *m*.

utter¹ ['ʌtəʳ] *adj candour, sincerity, disaster* complet (*f* -ète), total, absolu; *madness* pur; *idiot, brute, fool* fini, parfait (*before n*), achevé. **an ~ rogue/liar** un fieffé coquin/menteur; **it was ~ nonsense!** c'était complètement absurde, ça n'avait aucun sens; **he's an ~ stranger** il m'est complètement inconnu.

utter² ['ʌtəʳ] *vt word* prononcer, proférer; *cry* pousser; *threat, insult* proférer; *libel* publier; *counterfeit money* émettre, mettre en circulation. **he didn't ~ a word** il n'a pas dit un seul mot, il n'a pas soufflé mot.

utterance ['ʌtərəns] *n* **(a)** (*remark etc*) paroles *fpl*, déclaration *f*. **(b)** (*U*) *[facts, theory]* énonciation *f*; *[feelings]* expression *f*. **to give ~ to** exprimer. **(c)** (*style of speaking*) élocution *f*, articulation *f*. **to have a clear/defective ~** bien/mal articuler.

utterly ['ʌtəlɪ] *adv* complètement, totalement, tout à fait.

uttermost ['ʌtəməʊst] = **utmost.**

uvula ['ju:vjələ] *n, pl* **uvule** ['ju:vjəli:] luette *f*, uvule *f*.

uvular ['ju:vjələʳ] *adj* (*Anat, Ling*) uvulaire.

uxorious [ʌk'sɔ:rɪəs] *adj* excessivement dévoué *or* soumis à sa femme.

uxoriousness [ʌk'sɔ:rɪəsnɪs] *n* (*U*) dévotion excessive à sa femme.

V

V, v [viː] *n* (*letter*) V, v *m*. **V-neck** décolleté *m* en V *or* en pointe; **V-necked** à encolure en V *or* en pointe; **V-shaped** en (forme de) V; **to give the V-sign** faire le V de la victoire; (*rudely*) faire un geste obscène de la main.

vac* [væk] *n* (*Brit Univ*) vacances *fpl* (universitaires).

vacancy [ˈveɪkənsɪ] *n* **(a)** (*room*) chambre *f* à louer; (*job*) vacance *f*, poste vacant. ~ **for a typist** poste de dactylo à suppléer; (*notice*) 'on cherche dactylo'; **'no vacancies'** (*of jobs*) 'pas d'embauche'; (*in hotel*) 'complet'.
(b) (*U: emptiness*) vide *m*.
(c) (*U: lack of intelligence*) esprit *m* vide, stupidité *f*.

vacant [ˈveɪkənt] *adj* **(a)** (*unoccupied*) *job* vacant, libre, à remplir; *room, house* inoccupé, libre; *seat* libre, disponible. (*Jur*) **with ~ possession** avec libre possession, avec jouissance immédiate.
(b) (*empty*) *hours* creux, de loisir; *mind* inoccupé, vide; *stare* vague; *person* (*stupid*) stupide, niais; (*dreamy*) sans expression, rêveur, distrait.

vacantly [ˈveɪkəntlɪ] *adv* (*V* **vacant b**) d'un air niais *or* absent, d'une manière stupide. **to gaze ~ into space** fixer le vide, avoir le regard perdu dans le vide.

vacate [vəˈkeɪt] *vt room, seat, job* quitter. **to ~ a house** quitter une maison, déménager (d'une maison); **to ~ one's post** démissionner; **to ~ the premises** vider les lieux.

vacation [vəˈkeɪʃən] **1** *n* **(a)** (*esp Brit*) (*Univ*) vacances *fpl*; (*Jur*) vacations *fpl or* vacances judiciaires; *V* **long**[1] *etc*.
(b) (*US*) vacances *fpl*. **on ~** en vacances; **to take a ~** prendre des vacances.
2 *cpd*: **vacation course** cours *mpl* de vacances.
3 *vi* (*US*) passer des *or* ses vacances.

vacationist [vəˈkeɪʃənɪst] *n* (*US*) vacancier *m*, -ière *f*.

vaccinate [ˈvæksɪneɪt] *vt* vacciner (*against* contre). **to be** *or* **get ~d** se faire vacciner.

vaccination [ˌvæksɪˈneɪʃən] *n* vaccination *f*. **smallpox ~** vaccination contre la variole.

vaccine [ˈvæksiːn] *n* vaccin *m*. **polio ~** vaccin contre la polio; **~-damaged** victime d'encéphalo-myélite vaccinale.

vacillate [ˈvæsɪleɪt] *vi* vaciller, hésiter, (*between* entre).

vacillating [ˈvæsɪleɪtɪŋ] **1** *adj* irrésolu, indécis, qui hésite. **2** *n* vacillation *f*, irrésolution *f*, indécision *f*.

vacillation [ˌvæsɪˈleɪʃən] *n* indécision *f*, vacillation *f*.

vacuity [væˈkjuːɪtɪ] *n* vacuité *f*. **vacuities** niaiseries *fpl*, remarques *fpl* stupides.

vacuous [ˈvækjʊəs] *adj face, eyes, stare* vide, sans expression; *remark* bête, vide de sens.

vacuum [ˈvækjʊm] **1** *n* **(a)** vide *m*; (*Phys*) vacuum *m*; *V* **nature**.
(b) = **vacuum cleaner**; *V* **2**.
2 *cpd brake, pump, tube* à vide. (*US*) **vacuum bottle** = **vacuum flask**; **vacuum cleaner** aspirateur *m*; **vacuum flask** bouteille *f* thermos ®, thermos *m inv*; **vacuum-packed** emballé sous vide.
3 *vt* (*also* **~-clean**) *carpet* passer à l'aspirateur.

vade mecum [ˈvɑːdɪˈmeɪkʊm] *n* vade-mecum *m inv*.

vagabond [ˈvægəbɒnd] **1** *n* vagabond(e) *m(f)*; (*tramp*) chemineau *m*, clochard(e) *m(f)*. **2** *adj life* errant, de vagabondage; *thoughts* vagabond; *habits* irrégulier.

vagary [ˈveɪgərɪ] *n* caprice *m*, fantaisie *f*.

vagina [vəˈdʒaɪnə] *n* vagin *m*.

vaginal [vəˈdʒaɪnəl] *adj* vaginal. **~ discharge** pertes blanches.

vagrancy [ˈveɪgrənsɪ] *n* (*also Jur*) vagabondage *m*.

vagrant [ˈveɪgrənt] **1** *n* vagabond(e) *m(f)*; (*tramp*) clochard(e) *m(f)*, mendiant(e) *m(f)*, chemineau *m*; (*Jur*) vagabond(e). **2** *adj* vagabond, errant.

vague [veɪg] *adj* **(a)** (*not clear*) *outline, photograph* flou, imprécis; *direction, question, account* vague, imprécis *memory, impression* flou, confus. **I haven't the vaguest idea (about it)** je n'en ai pas la moindre idée; **her reply was ~** sa réponse manquait de clarté *or* de précision; **I had a ~ idea she would come** je pensais vaguement *or* j'avais comme une idée* qu'elle viendrait; **he was ~ about the time of his arrival** (*didn't say exactly*) il n'a pas (bien) précisé l'heure de son arrivée; (*didn't know exactly*) il n'était pas sûr de l'heure à laquelle il arriverait.
(b) (*absent-minded*) *looks, behaviour* vague, indécis; *person* distrait. **to look ~** avoir l'air vague *or* distrait; **to have a ~ look in one's eyes** avoir l'air vague.

vaguely [ˈveɪglɪ] *adv speak, remember, look* vaguement; *understand* confusément, vaguement.

vagueness [ˈveɪgnɪs] *n* **(a)** *[photograph etc]* imprécision *f*, manque *m* de précision *or* de netteté. **(b)** (*absent-mindedness*) **his ~ is very annoying** c'est agaçant qu'il soit si étourdi *or* tête en l'air*.

vain [veɪn] *adj* **(a)** (*useless, empty*) *attempt* inutile, vain; *hope* vain, futile; *promise* vide, illusoire; *words* creux; *display, ceremony* futile. **in ~** en vain, vainement, inutilement; **she tried in ~ to open the door** elle a essayé en vain d'ouvrir la porte; **I looked for him in ~, he had already left** j'ai eu beau le chercher, il était déjà parti; **all his (or my *etc*) efforts were in ~** c'était peine perdue; **to take God's name in ~** blasphémer le nom de Dieu; (*hum*) **we've been taking your name in ~!** nous venons de parler de vous!
(b) (*conceited*) vaniteux.

vainglorious [veɪnˈglɔːrɪəs] *adj* orgueilleux, vaniteux, prétentieux.

vainglory [veɪnˈglɔːrɪ] *n* (*U*) orgueil *m*, vanité *f*, prétention *f*.

vainly [ˈveɪnlɪ] *adv* **(a)** (*to no effect*) en vain, vainement, inutilement. **(b)** (*conceitedly*) vaniteusement, avec vanité.

valance [ˈvæləns] *n* (*round bed frame*) tour *m or* frange *f* de lit; (*round bed canopy*) lambrequin *m*.

vale [veɪl] *n* (*liter*) val *m* (*liter*), vallée *f*. (*fig*) **this ~ of tears** cette vallée de larmes.

valediction [ˌvælɪˈdɪkʃən] *n* **(a)** (*farewell*) adieu(x) *m(pl)*. **(b)** (*US Scol*) discours *m* d'adieu.

valedictorian [ˌvælɪdɪkˈtɔːrɪən] *n* (*US Scol*) élève *mf* qui prononce le discours d'adieu.

valedictory [ˌvælɪˈdɪktərɪ] **1** *adj* d'adieu. **2** *n* (*US Scol*) discours *m* d'adieu.

valence [ˈveɪləns] *n* **(a)** (*Chem*) valence *f*. **(b)** (*Bio*) atomicité *f*.

valency [ˈveɪlənsɪ] *n* = **valence a**.

valentine [ˈvæləntaɪn] *n* **(a)** **V~** Valentin(e) *m(f)*; **St V~'s Day** la Saint-Valentin. **(b)** (*also* **~ card**) carte *f* de la Saint-Valentin (*envoyée comme gage d'amour*).

valerian [vəˈlɪərɪən] *n* valériane *f*.

valet [ˈvæleɪ] **1** *n* valet *m* de chambre. **2** [ˈvælɪt] *vt man* servir comme valet de chambre; *clothes* entretenir. **dry cleaner with ~ing service** pressing *m*.

valetudinarian [ˈvælɪˌtjuːdɪˈnɛərɪən] *adj, n* valétudinaire (*mf*).

Valhalla [vælˈhælə] *n* Walhalla *m*.

valiant [ˈvæljənt] *adj soldier, action* courageux, brave, valeureux (*liter*), vaillant (*liter*). **he made a ~ effort to save the child** il a tenté avec courage de sauver l'enfant; **he made a ~ effort to smile** il a fait un gros effort pour sourire.

valiantly [ˈvæljəntlɪ] *adv* vaillamment, courageusement.

valid [ˈvælɪd] *adj* **(a)** (*Jur etc*) *claim, contract, document* valide, valable. **passport ~ for all countries** passeport valable pour tous pays; **~ passport** passeport valable *or* valide *or* en règle; **ticket ~ for one week** billet bon *or* valable *or* valide pour une semaine.
(b) *excuse* valable; *argument, reasoning* solide, valable, bien fondé.

validate [ˈvælɪdeɪt] *vt claim, document* valider; *argument* prouver la justesse de.

validation [ˌvælɪˈdeɪʃən] *n* validation *f*.

validity [vəˈlɪdɪtɪ] *n [document, claim]* validité *f*; *[argument]* force *f*, justesse *f*.

valise [vəˈliːz] *n* (*US*) sac *m* de voyage; (*Mil*) sac (de soldat).

Valium [ˈvælɪəm] *n* ® valium *m* ®.

Valkyrie [ˈvælkɪrɪ] *n* Walkyrie *f*, Valkyrie *f*.

valley [ˈvælɪ] *n* vallée *f*, val *m* (*liter*); (*small, narrow*) vallon *m*. **the Seine/Rhône *etc* ~** la vallée de la Seine/du Rhône *etc*; **the Loire ~** le Val de Loire; *V* **lily**.

valor [ˈvæləʳ] *n* (*US*) = **valour**.

valorous [ˈvælərəs] *adj* (*liter*) valeureux (*liter*), vaillant (*liter*).

valour, (*US*) valor [ˈvæləʳ] *n* (*liter*) vaillance *f* (*liter*), bravoure *f*, valeur *f*.

valuable [ˈvæljʊəbl] **1** *adj jewel, painting* de valeur, d'une grande valeur, de grand prix; *help, advice, time* précieux.
2 *n*: **~s** objets *mpl* de grande valeur; **all her ~s were stolen** on lui a volé tous les objets de valeur *or* tout ce qui avait de la valeur.

valuation [ˌvæljʊˈeɪʃən] *n [house, painting]* évaluation *f*, estimation *f*; (*Comm, Jur*) *[property]* expertise *f*; (*fig*) *[person's character]* appréciation *f*; (*value decided upon*) appréciation. **to have a ~ made of a picture** faire évaluer *or* expertiser un tableau; **the ~ is too high/too low** l'appréciation est trop élevée/trop faible; **to make a correct ~ of sth** estimer qch à sa juste valeur; (*fig*) **to take sb at his own ~** prendre qn pour celui qu'il croit être.

valuator [ˈvæljʊeɪtəʳ] *n* expert *m* (en estimations de biens mobiliers).

value [ˈvæljuː] **1** *n* **(a)** (*gen*) valeur *f*, (*usefulness, worth*) valeur, utilité *f*. **her education has been of no ~ to her** son éducation ne lui a rien valu *or* ne lui a servi à rien.
(b) (*worth in money*) valeur *f*, prix *m*. **to gain (in) ~** prendre de la valeur; **to lose (in) ~** se déprécier; **loss of ~** perte *f or* diminution *f* de valeur; **he paid the ~ of the cup he broke** il a remboursé (le prix de) la tasse qu'il a cassée; **of little ~** de peu de valeur; **of no ~** sans valeur; **to be of great ~** valoir cher; **to get good ~ for money** en avoir pour son argent; **the large packet is the best ~** le grand paquet est le plus avantageux; **to put a ~ on sth** évaluer qch; **to set a low ~ on sth** attacher peu de valeur à qch; **to put too high/too low a ~ on sth** surestimer/sous-estimer qch; **goods to the ~ of £100** marchandises d'une valeur de 100 livres.
(c) (*moral worth*) *[esp person]* valeur *f*, mérite *m*. **to appreciate sb at his proper ~** estimer *or* apprécier qn à sa

juste valeur; (*moral standards*) ~s valeurs *fpl.*
2 *cpd*: **value added tax** (*abbr* **V.A.T.**) taxe *f* sur la valeur ajoutée (*abbr* T.V.A.); (*fig*) **value judgment** jugement *m* de valeur.
3 *vt* **(a)** *house, jewels, painting* évaluer, expertiser (*at* à).
(b) *friendship, comforts* apprécier, priser; *liberty, independence* tenir à.
valued ['vælju:d] *adj friend* précieux; *colleague* estimé.
valueless ['væljʊlɪs] *adj* sans valeur.
valuer ['væljʊə^{r}] *n* expert *m* (en estimations de biens mobiliers).
valve [vælv] *n* (*Anat*) valvule *f*; (*Bot, Zool*) valve *f*; (*Tech*) *[machine]* soupape *f*, valve; *[air chamber, tyre]* valve; (*Electronics, Rad*) lampe *f*; *[musical instrument]* piston *m*. **inlet/outlet** ~ soupape d'admission/d'échappement; **exhaust** ~ clapet *m* de refoulement; *V* **safety, suction** *etc.*
valvular ['vælvjʊlə^{r}] *adj* valvulaire.
vamoose‡ [və'mu:s] *vi* filer*, décamper*. ~! fiche le camp!*
vamp[1] [væmp] **1** *n* (*woman*) vamp *f*. **2** *vt* vamper*. **3** *vi* jouer la femme fatale.
vamp[2] [væmp] **1** *vt* (*repair*) rafistoler; (*fig: also* ~ **up**) bâcler; (*Mus*) improviser. **2** *vi* (*Mus*) improviser des accompagnements.
vampire ['væmpaɪə^{r}] *n* (*lit, fig*) vampire *m*. ~ **bat** vampire (*chauve-souris*).
van[1] [væn] **1** *n* **(a)** (*Brit Aut*) camionnette *f*, fourgonnette *f*; *V* **removal** *etc.* **(b)** (*Brit Rail*) fourgon *m*; *V* **guard, luggage** *etc.* **(c)** (*: *abbr of* **caravan**) caravane *f*; (*gipsy's*) roulotte *f*. **2** *cpd*: **van-boy** livreur *m*.
van[2] [væn] *n abbr of* **vanguard.**
van[3] [væn] *n* (*Tennis: abbr of* **advantage 1b**) ~ **in/out** avantage *m* dedans/dehors.
vanadium [və'neɪdɪəm] *n* vanadium *m*.
vandal ['vændəl] *n* (*fig*) vandale *mf*. (*Hist*) **V**~ Vandale *mf*.
vandalism ['vændəlɪzəm] *n* vandalisme *m*.
vandalistic [,vændə'lɪstɪk] *adj* destructeur (*f* -trice), de vandale.
vandalize ['vændəlaɪz] *vt painting, building* saccager.
vane [veɪn] *n [windmill]* aile *f*; *[propeller]* pale *f*; *[turbine]* aube *f*; *[quadrant etc]* pinnule *f*, lumière *f*; *[feather]* barbe *f*; (*also* **weather** ~) girouette *f*.
vanguard ['vængɑ:d] *n* **(a)** (*Mil, Naut*) avant-garde *f*. **in the** ~ **(of)** en tête (de).
(b) (*fig*) avant-garde *f*. **in the** ~ **of progress** à l'avant-garde *or* à la pointe du progrès.
vanilla [və'nɪlə] **1** *n* vanille *f*. **2** *cpd cream, ice* à la vanille. **vanilla pod** gousse *f* de vanille; **vanilla sugar** sucre vanillé.
vanillin [væ'nɪlɪn] *n* vanilline *f*.
vanish ['vænɪʃ] **1** *vi* disparaître; *[obstacles, fears]* disparaître, se dissiper. **to** ~ **into thin air** se volatiliser, disparaître sans laisser de traces.
2 *cpd*: **vanishing cream** crème *f* de jour; **vanishing point** point *m* de fuite; **vanishing trick** tour *m* de passe-passe.
vanity ['vænɪtɪ] **1** *n* (*U*) **(a)** (*conceit*) vanité *f*; (*pride*) orgueil *m*. **I may say without** ~ je peux dire sans (vouloir) me vanter.
(b) (*worthlessness*) vanité *f*, futilité *f*. **all is** ~ tout est vanité.
2 *cpd*: **vanity bag** sac *m* (de soirée); **vanity case** sac *m* de toilette.
vanquish ['væŋkwɪʃ] *vt* vaincre.
vanquisher ['væŋkwɪʃə^{r}] *n* vainqueur *m*.
vantage ['vɑ:ntɪdʒ] **1** *n* **(a)** avantage *m*, supériorité *f*. **(b)** (*Tennis*) = **van**[3]. **2** *cpd*: (*Mil*) **vantage ground** position stratégique *or* avantageuse; (*fig*) **vantage point** position avantageuse, bonne place.
vapid ['væpɪd] *adj remark, conversation* fade, sans intérêt, insipide; *style* plat.
vapidity [væ'pɪdɪtɪ] *n [conversation]* insipidité *f*; *[style]* platitude *f*.
vapor ['veɪpə^{r}] *n* (*US*) = **vapour.**
vaporization [,veɪpəraɪ'zeɪʃən] *n* vaporisation *f*.
vaporize ['veɪpəraɪz] **1** *vt* vaporiser. **2** *vi* se vaporiser.
vaporizer ['veɪpəraɪzə^{r}] *n* vaporisateur *m*, vaporiseur *m*; (*for perfume*) atomiseur *m*.
vaporous ['veɪpərəs] *adj* vaporeux.
vapour, (*US*) **vapor** ['veɪpə^{r}] **1** *n* **(a)** (*Phys: also mist etc*) vapeur *f*; (*on glass*) buée *f*. **(b) to have the** ~**s**† avoir des vapeurs†. **2** *cpd*: **vapour bath** bain *m* de vapeur; (*Aviat*) **vapour trail** traînée *f* de condensation. **3** *vi* (*US*‡: *boast*) fanfaronner.
variability [,vɛərɪə'bɪlɪtɪ] *n* (*also Bio*) variabilité *f*.
variable ['vɛərɪəbl] **1** *adj* (*gen, Bot, Math, Tech*) variable; *weather* variable, incertain, changeant; *mood* changeant. ~-**pitch propeller** hélice *f* à pas variable. **2** *n* (*Chem, Math, Phys*) variable *f*.
variance ['vɛərɪəns] *n* **(a)** désaccord *m*, différend *m*. *[people]* **to be at** ~ être en désaccord; **to be at** ~ **with sb about sth** avoir un différend avec qn sur qch; **this is at** ~ **with what he said earlier** ceci ne s'accorde pas avec *or* ceci contredit ce qu'il a dit auparavant.
(b) (*Math*) variance *f*.
(c) (*Jur*) différence *f*, divergence *f*. **there is a** ~ **between the two statements** les deux dépositions ne s'accordent pas *or* ne concordent pas.
variant ['vɛərɪənt] **1** *n* variante *f*. **2** *adj* **(a)** (*alternative*) différent. ~ **reading** variante *f*. **(b)** (*diverse*) différent, divers, varié.
variation [,vɛərɪ'eɪʃən] *n* (*gen, Bio, Chem, Met, Mus, Phys*) variation *f*; (*in opinions, views*) fluctuation(s) *f(pl)*, changements *mpl.*
varicoloured, (*US*) **varicolored** ['værɪ'kʌləd] *adj* multicolore, bigarré; (*fig*) divers.
varicose ['værɪkəʊs] *adj* variqueux. ~ **veins** varices *fpl.*
varied ['vɛərɪd] *adj* varié, divers.
variegated ['vɛərɪgeɪtɪd] *adj* bigarré, diapré (*liter*); (*Bot*) panaché.
variegation [,vɛərɪ'geɪʃən] *n* bigarrure *f*, diaprure *f* (*liter*).
variety [və'raɪətɪ] **1** *n* **(a)** (*diversity*) variété *f*, diversité *f*; (*quantity*) quantité *f*, nombre *m*. **for a** ~ **of reasons** pour diverses raisons; **a large** ~ **of** un grand choix de.
(b) (*Bio, Bot: species*) variété *f*.
(c) (*U: esp Brit Theat*) variétés *fpl.*
2 *cpd*: **variety artiste** artiste *mf* de variétés *or* de music-hall; **variety show** (*Theat, TV*) spectacle *m* de variétés; (*Rad, TV*) émission *f* de variétés; (*US*) **variety store** grand magasin; **variety theatre** (théâtre *m* de) variétés *fpl*; (*Brit*) **variety turn** numéro *m*.
variola [və'raɪələ] *n* variole *f*, petite vérole.
various ['vɛərɪəs] *adj* (*different*) divers, différent; (*several*) divers, plusieurs. **the** ~ **meanings of a word** les divers sens d'un mot; **at** ~ **times** (*different*) en diverses occasions; (*several*) à plusieurs reprises; ~ **people have told me ...** plusieurs *or* diverses personnes m'ont dit ... .
variously ['vɛərɪəslɪ] *adv* diversement, de différentes *or* diverses façons.
varmint*† ['vɑ:mɪnt] *n* polisson(ne) *m(f)*, vaurien(ne) *m(f)*.
varnish ['vɑ:nɪʃ] **1** *n* (*lit, fig*) vernis *m*; (*on pottery*) émail *m*; *V* **nail, spirit. 2** *vt furniture, painting* vernir; *pottery* vernisser. (*fig*) **to** ~ **the truth** maquiller la vérité.
varnishing ['vɑ:nɪʃɪŋ] *n* vernissage *m*. (*Art*) ~ **day** (le jour du) vernissage.
varsity ['vɑ:sɪtɪ] *n* (*Brit Univ**) fac* *f*. (*Sport*) ~ **match** match *m* (entre les universités d'Oxford et de Cambridge).
vary ['vɛərɪ] **1** *vi* varier, se modifier, changer. **to** ~ **with the weather** changer selon le temps; **to** ~ **from sth** différer de qch; **opinions** ~ **on this point** les opinions varient sur ce point. **2** *vt* (faire) varier.
varying ['vɛərɪɪŋ] *adj* qui varie, variable. **with** ~ **degrees of success** avec plus ou moins de succès.
vascular ['væskjʊlə^{r}] *adj* vasculaire.
vase [vɑ:z] *n* vase *m*. **flower** ~ vase à fleurs.
vasectomy [væ'sektəmɪ] *n* vasectomie *f*.
vaseline ['væsɪli:n] ® **1** *n* vaseline *f*. **2** *vt* enduire de vaseline.
vasomotor [,veɪzəʊ'məʊtə^{r}] *adj* vaso-moteur (*f* -trice).
vassal ['væsəl] *adj, n* (*Hist, fig*) vassal (*m*).
vassalage ['væsəlɪdʒ] *n* vassalité *f*, vasselage *m*.
vast [vɑ:st] *adj* **(a)** *size, area, bulk* vaste, immense. **a** ~ **expanse** une vaste étendue.
(b) (*great*) vaste, énorme. ~ **knowledge** de vastes connaissances; **to a** ~ **extent** dans une très large *or* grande mesure; **a** ~ **success** un succès énorme; ~ **sums (of money)** des sommes folles.
vastly ['vɑ:stlɪ] *adv grateful, amused* infiniment; *rich* extrêmement, immensément. **he was** ~ **mistaken** il se trompait du tout au tout.
vastness ['vɑ:stnɪs] *n* immensité *f*.
vat [væt] *n* cuve *f*, bac *m*.
Vatican ['vætɪkən] **1** *n* Vatican *m*. **2** *cpd policy etc* du Vatican. **Vatican City** la Cité du Vatican; **the Vatican Council** le Concile du Vatican.
vaudeville ['vəʊdəvɪl] (*esp US*) **1** *n* spectacle *m* de variétés *or* de music-hall. **2** *cpd show, singer* de music-hall.
vault[1] [vɔ:lt] *n* **(a)** (*cellar*) cave *f*, cellier *m*; (*tomb*) caveau *m*; (*in bank*) coffre-fort *m*, chambre forte. **(b)** (*Archit*) voûte *f*. (*liter*) **the** ~ **of heaven** la voûte céleste (*liter*).
vault[2] [vɔ:lt] **1** *vi* sauter. **to** ~ **over sth** sauter qch; *V* **pole**[1]. **2** *vt* sauter d'un bond. **3** *n* saut *m*.
vaulted ['vɔ:ltɪd] *adj* (*Archit*) voûté, en voûte.
vaulting[1] ['vɔ:ltɪŋ] *n* (*Archit*) voûte(s) *f(pl)*.
vaulting[2] ['vɔ:ltɪŋ] *n* (*Sport*) exercice *m or* pratique *f* du saut. ~ **horse** cheval *m* d'arçons.
vaunt [vɔ:nt] (*liter*) **1** *vt* vanter, se vanter de; se targuer de. **2** *vi* se vanter, fanfaronner.
veal [vi:l] *n* veau *m* (*Culin*). ~ **cutlet** escalope *f* de veau; *V* **fillet.**
vector ['vektə^{r}] **1** *n* **(a)** (*Bio, Math*) vecteur *m*. **(b)** (*Aviat*) direction *f*. **2** *cpd* (*Math*) vectoriel. **3** *vt* (*Aviat*) radioguider.
vectorial [vek'tɔ:rɪəl] *adj* vectoriel.
veep‡ [vi:p] *n* (*US*) = **vice-president;** *V* **vice-.**
veer [vɪə^{r}] **1** *vi [wind]* tourner (*to* vers, à), changer de direction; *[ship]* virer (de bord); *[car, road]* virer. **the car** ~**ed off the road** la voiture a quitté la route; (*fig*) **he** ~**ed round to my point of view** changeant d'opinion il s'est rallié à mon point de vue; **he** ~**ed off** *or* **away from his subject** il s'est éloigné de son sujet.
2 *vt* **(a)** (*Naut*) *cable* filer.
(b) *ship, car* faire virer.
vegetable ['vedʒɪtəbl] **1** *n* **(a)** légume *m*. **early** ~**s** primeurs *fpl*; (*fig: brain-damaged*) **he's just a** ~* il n'a pas toutes ses facultés *or* l'usage de ses facultés.
(b) (*generic term: plant*) végétal *m*, plante *f*.
2 *cpd oil, matter* végétal. **vegetable dish** plat *m* à légumes, légumier *m*; **vegetable garden** (jardin) potager *m*; **vegetable kingdom** règne végétal; **vegetable knife** couteau *m* à éplucher; (*esp Brit*) **vegetable marrow** courge *f*; **vegetable salad** salade *f or* macédoine *f* de légumes; **vegetable slicer** coupe-légumes *m inv*; **vegetable soup** soupe *f* aux *or* de légumes.
vegetarian [,vedʒɪ'tɛərɪən] *adj, n* végétarien(ne) *m(f)*.
vegetarianism [,vedʒɪ'tɛərɪənɪzəm] *n* végétarisme *m*; (*excluding eggs etc*) végétalisme *m*.
vegetate ['vedʒɪteɪt] *vi* végéter, moisir*.
vegetation [,vedʒɪ'teɪʃən] *n* (*U*) végétation *f*.
vegetative ['vedʒɪtətɪv] *adj* (*Bio, fig*) végétatif.
vehemence ['vi:ɪməns] *n [feelings]* ardeur *f*, intensité *f*, véhé-

mence *f*; *[actions]* violence *f*, fougue *f*, véhémence.

vehement ['viːɪmənt] *adj feelings, speech* ardent, passionné, véhément; *wind, attack* violent, impétueux.

vehemently ['viːɪməntlɪ] *adv speak* avec passion, avec véhémence; *attack* avec violence.

vehicle ['viːɪkl] *n* (*Aut, Med, Painting, Pharm, fig*) véhicule *m*; *V* **commercial.**

vehicular [vɪ'hɪkjʊlə^r] *adj* de véhicules, de voitures. ~ **traffic** circulation *f*.

veil [veɪl] **1** *n* voile *m*, voilette *f*, (*fig*) voile. (*Rel*) **to take the** ~ prendre le voile; (*fig liter*) **beyond the** ~ dans l'au-delà; **to wear a** ~ être voilé; (*fig*) **to draw/throw a** ~ **over** mettre/jeter un voile sur; **under the** ~ **of** sous le voile de; ~ **of mist** voile de brume.

2 *vt* voiler, couvrir d'un voile; (*fig*) *truth, facts* voiler; *feelings* voiler, dissimuler. **the clouds** ~**ed the moon** les nuages voilaient la lune.

veiled [veɪld] *adj person, hint, reference* voilé; *meaning* voilé, caché.

veiling ['veɪlɪŋ] *n* (*on hat etc*) voilage *m*; (*fig*) *[truth, facts]* dissimulation *f*.

vein [veɪn] *n* **(a)** (*Anat*) veine *f*; (*in leaf*) nervure *f*; (*in insect wing, stone*) veine; *[silver etc]* filon *m*, veine. (*fig*) **there is a** ~ **of truth in what he says** il y a un fond de vérité dans ce qu'il dit; *V* **varicose.**

(b) (*fig: mood*) esprit *m*, humeur *f*, disposition *f*. **in (a) humorous** ~ dans un esprit humoristique; **in the same** ~ dans le même esprit.

veined [veɪnd] *adj hand* veiné; *leaf* nervuré.

velar ['viːlə^r] *adj* vélaire.

veld(t) [velt] *n* veld(t) *m*.

vellum ['veləm] **1** *n* vélin *m*. **2** *cpd binding* de vélin. **vellum paper** papier *m* vélin.

velocipede† [və'lɒsɪpiːd] *n* vélocipède† *m*.

velocity [vɪ'lɒsɪtɪ] *n* vélocité *f*, vitesse *f*.

velour(s) [və'lʊə^r] *n* velours épais.

velum ['viːləm] *n* (*Anat*) voile *m* du palais.

velvet ['velvɪt] **1** *n* velours *m*. (*fig*) **to be on** ~* jouer sur le *or* du velours*; *V* **black, iron. 2** *cpd dress* de velours. (*fig*) **with a velvet tread** à pas de velours, à pas feutrés.

velveteen ['velvɪtiːn] *n* velvet *m*.

velvety ['velvɪtɪ] *adj surface, texture, material* velouteux, velouté; *sauce, voice* velouté.

venal ['viːnl] *adj* vénal.

venality [viː'nælɪtɪ] *n* vénalité *f*.

vend [vend] *vt* (*Jur*) vendre.

vendetta [ven'detə] *n* vendetta *f*.

vending ['vendɪŋ] *n* vente *f*. ~ **machine** distributeur *m* automatique.

vendor ['vendɔː^r] *n* vendeur *m*, -euse *f*; *V* **news, street.**

veneer [və'nɪə^r] **1** *n* placage *m*; (*fig*) vernis *m*. **with** *or* **under a** ~ **of** sous un vernis de. **2** *vt* plaquer.

venerable ['venərəbl] *adj* vénérable.

venerate ['venəreɪt] *vt* vénérer.

veneration [ˌvenə'reɪʃən] *n* vénération *f*.

venereal [vɪ'nɪərɪəl] *adj* vénérien. ~ **disease** (*abbr* **V.D.**) maladie vénérienne.

Venetian [vɪ'niːʃən] **1** *adj* vénitien, de Venise. ~ **glass** cristal *m* de Venise; ~ **blind** store vénitien. **2** *n* Vénitien(ne) *m(f)*.

Venezuela [ˌvene'zweɪlə] *n* Venezuela *m*.

Venezuelan [ˌvene'zweɪlən] **1** *adj* vénézuélien. **2** *n* Vénézuélien(ne) *m(f)*.

vengeance ['vendʒəns] *n* vengeance *f*. **to take** ~ **(up)on** se venger de *or* sur; **to take** ~ **for** tirer vengeance de; (*fig*) **with a** ~ pour de bon*; **to work with a** ~ travailler d'arrache-pied.

vengeful ['vendʒfʊl] *adj* vindicatif.

venial ['viːnɪəl] *adj* (*also Rel*) véniel.

veniality [ˌviːnɪ'ælɪtɪ] *n* caractère véniel.

Venice ['venɪs] *n* Venise.

venison ['venɪsən] *n* venaison *f*.

venom ['venəm] *n* (*lit, fig*) venin *m*.

venomous ['venəməs] *adj* (*lit, fig*) venimeux. (*fig*) ~ **tongue** langue *f* de vipère.

venomously ['venəməslɪ] *adv* d'une manière venimeuse, haineusement.

venous ['viːnəs] *adj* (*Anat, Bot*) veineux.

vent [vent] **1** *n* (*for gas, liquid*) orifice *m*, conduit *m*; (*in chimney*) tuyau *m*; (*in barrel*) trou *m*; (*in coat*) fente *f*. (*fig*) **to give** ~ **to** donner *or* laisser libre cours à. **2** *vt barrel* pratiquer un trou dans; (*fig*) *one's anger etc* décharger (*on* sur).

ventilate ['ventɪleɪt] *vt room* ventiler, aérer; *blood* oxygéner; (*fig*) *question* livrer à la discussion; *grievance* étaler au grand jour. *room* **badly** ~**d** mal aéré.

ventilation [ˌventɪ'leɪʃən] *n* aération *f*, ventilation *f*. ~ **shaft** conduit *m or* bouche *f* d'aération.

ventilator ['ventɪleɪtə^r] *n* ventilateur *m*; (*Aut*) déflecteur *m*.

ventricle ['ventrɪkl] *n* ventricule *m*.

ventriloquism [ven'trɪləkwɪzəm] *n* ventriloquie *f*.

ventriloquist [ven'trɪləkwɪst] *n* ventriloque *mf*. ~**'s dummy** poupée *f* de ventriloque.

venture ['ventʃə^r] **1** *n* aventure *f*, entreprise *f* (*risquée, hasardeuse*). **at a** ~ au hasard; **it's a bit of a (risky)** ~ c'est une entreprise assez risquée *or* assez hasardeuse; **his** ~ **into business proved disastrous** son incursion dans les affaires a été un désastre; **all his business** ~**s failed** toutes ses entreprises en matière de commerce *or* toutes ses tentatives commerciales ont échoué; **this is a new** ~ **in publishing** ceci constitue quelque chose de nouveau *or* un coup d'essai en matière d'édition.

2 *vt life* risquer, exposer, hasarder (*liter*); *fortune, opinion, reputation* risquer, hasarder (*liter*); *explanation, estimate* hasarder, avancer. **when I asked him that, he** ~**d a guess** quand je lui ai posé la question, il a hasardé *or* avancé une réponse; **to** ~ **to do** oser faire, se permettre de faire; **he** ~**d the opinion that** il a hasardé une opinion selon laquelle, il s'est permis d'observer que, il a osé observer que; **I** ~**d to write to you** je me suis permis de vous écrire (à tout hasard); **... but he did not** ~ **to speak** ... mais il n'a pas osé parler; (*Prov*) **nothing** ~ **nothing gain** qui ne risque rien n'a rien (*Prov*).

3 *vi* s'aventurer, se risquer. **to** ~ **in/out/through** *etc* se risquer à entrer/sortir/traverser *etc*; **to** ~ **out of doors** se risquer à sortir; **to** ~ **into town/into the forest** s'aventurer *or* se hasarder dans la ville/dans la forêt; **they** ~**d on a programme of reform** ils ont essayé de mettre sur pied *or* d'entreprendre un ensemble de réformes; **when we** ~**d on this** quand nous avons entrepris cela, quand nous nous sommes lancés là-dedans.

venture forth *vi* (*liter*) se risquer à sortir.

venturesome ['ventʃəsəm] *adj person* aventureux, entreprenant; *action* risqué, hasardeux.

venue ['venjuː] *n* (*meeting place*) lieu *m* (de rendez-vous); (*Jur*) lieu du procès, juridiction *f*.

Venus ['viːnəs] *n* (*Astron, Myth*) Vénus *f*. (*Bot*) ~ **fly-trap** dionée *f*.

veracious [və'reɪʃəs] *adj* véridique.

veracity [və'ræsɪtɪ] *n* véracité *f*.

veranda(h) [və'rændə] *n* véranda *f*.

verb [vɜːb] *n* (*Gram*) verbe *m*; *V* **auxiliary** *etc.*

verbal ['vɜːbəl] *adj statement, agreement, promise, error* verbal; *confession* oral; *translation* mot à mot, littéral; (*Gram*) verbal. ~ **memory** mémoire auditive.

verbalize ['vɜːbəlaɪz] *vt feelings etc* traduire en paroles, exprimer.

verbally ['vɜːbəlɪ] *adv* verbalement, oralement.

verbatim [vɜː'beɪtɪm] **1** *adj* textuel, mot pour mot. **2** *adv* textuellement, mot pour mot.

verbena [vɜː'biːnə] *n* (*genus*) verbénacées *fpl*; (*plant*) verveine *f*.

verbiage ['vɜːbɪɪdʒ] *n* verbiage *m*.

verbose [vɜː'bəʊs] *adj* verbeux, prolixe.

verbosely [vɜː'bəʊslɪ] *adv* avec verbosité, verbeusement.

verbosity [vɜː'bɒsɪtɪ] *n* verbosité *f*.

verdant ['vɜːdənt] *adj* verdoyant.

verdict ['vɜːdɪkt] *n* **(a)** (*Jur*) verdict *m*. ~ **of guilty/not guilty** verdict de culpabilité/de non-culpabilité; *V* **bring in. (b)** *[doctor, electors, press etc]* verdict *m*, jugement *m*, décision *f*. **to give one's** ~ **about** *or* **on** se prononcer sur.

verdigris ['vɜːdɪgrɪs] *adj, n* vert-de-gris (*m*) *inv*.

verdure ['vɜːdjʊə^r] *n* (*liter*) verdure *f*.

verge [vɜːdʒ] **1** *n [road]* (*Brit*) bord *m*, accotement *m*; *[forest]* orée *f*; (*around flower bed*) bordure *f* en gazon. **to be on the** ~ **of ruin/death** être à deux doigts de *or* frôler la ruine/la mort; **on the** ~ **of a discovery** à la veille d'une découverte; **on the** ~ **of tears** sur le point de pleurer, au bord des larmes; **on the** ~ **of doing** sur le point de faire.

2 *vi* incliner, tendre (*towards* vers).

verge on *vt fus [ideas, actions]* approcher de, côtoyer. **he's verging on bankruptcy** il est au bord de la faillite; **she is verging on fifty** elle frise la cinquantaine; **she was verging on madness** elle frôlait la folie.

verger ['vɜːdʒə^r] *n* (*Rel*) bedeau *m*; (*ceremonial*) huissier *m* à verge.

Vergil ['vɜːdʒɪl] *n* Virgile *m*.

Vergilian [və'dʒɪlɪən] *adj* virgilien.

verifiable ['verɪfaɪəbl] *adj* vérifiable.

verification [ˌverɪfɪ'keɪʃən] *n* (*check*) vérification *f*, contrôle *m*; (*proof*) vérification.

verify ['verɪfaɪ] *vt statements, information, spelling* vérifier; *documents* contrôler; *suspicions, fears* vérifier, confirmer.

verisimilitude [ˌverɪsɪ'mɪlɪtjuːd] *n* vraisemblance *f*.

veritable ['verɪtəbl] *adj* véritable, vrai.

verity ['verɪtɪ] *n* (*liter*) vérité *f*.

vermicelli [ˌvɜːmɪ'selɪ] *n* vermicelle(s) *m(pl)*.

vermicide ['vɜːmɪsaɪd] *n* vermicide *m*.

vermifugal ['vɜːmɪfjuːgəl] *adj* vermifuge.

vermifuge ['vɜːmɪfjuːdʒ] *n* vermifuge *m*.

vermilion [və'mɪljən] *adj,n* vermillon (*m*) *inv*.

vermin ['vɜːmɪn] *collective n* (*animals*) animaux *mpl* nuisibles; (*insects*) vermine *f* (*U*), parasites *mpl*; (*pej: people*) vermine (*U*), racaille *f* (*U*), parasites *mpl*.

verminous ['vɜːmɪnəs] *adj person, clothes* pouilleux, couvert de vermine; *disease* vermineux.

vermouth ['vɜːməθ] *n* vermout(h) *m*.

vernacular [və'nækjʊlə^r] **1** *n* (*native speech*) langue *f* vernaculaire, dialecte *m*; (*jargon*) jargon *m*.

2 *adj crafts* indigène, du pays; *language* vernaculaire, du pays.

vernal ['vɜːnl] *adj equinox* vernal; (*liter*) *flowers* printanier.

veronica [və'rɒnɪkə] *n* véronique *f*.

verruca [və'ruːkə] *n* verrue *f* (*gen plantaire*).

versatile ['vɜːsətaɪl] *adj person* aux talents variés, doué en tous genres; *mind* souple; *genius* universel, encyclopédique; (*Bot, Zool*) versatile.

versatility [ˌvɜːsə'tɪlɪtɪ] *n [person]* variété *f* de talents, faculté *f* d'adaptation; *[mind]* souplesse *f*; (*Bot, Zool*) versatilité *f*.

verse [vɜːs] *n* **(a)** (*stanza*) strophe *f*, couplet *m*. **(b)** (*U: poetry*) poésie *f*, vers *mpl*. **in** ~ en vers; ~ **drama** drame *m* en vers; *V* **blank, free** *etc.* **(c)** *[Bible, Koran]* verset *m*; *V* **chapter.**

versed [vɜːst] *adj* (*also* **well-**~) versé (*in* dans). **not (well-)**~ peu versé.

versification [ˌvɜːsɪfɪ'keɪʃən] *n* versification *f*, métrique *f*.

versifier ['vɜːsɪfaɪə^r] *n* (*pej*) versificateur *m*, -trice *f* (*pej*).

versify ['vɜːsɪfaɪ] 1 *vt* versifier, mettre en vers. 2 *vi* faire des vers.

version ['vɜːʃən] *n* **(a)** (*account*) *[event]* version *f*; *[facts]* interprétation *f*. **(b)** (*variant*) *[text]* version *f*, variante *f*; *[car]* modèle *m*. **(c)** (*translation*) version *f*, traduction *f*.

verso ['vɜːsəʊ] *n* verso *m*.

versus ['vɜːsəs] *prep* (*Jur, Sport, gen*) contre.

vertebra ['vɜːtɪbrə] *n, pl* **vertebrae** ['vɜːtibriː] vertèbre *f*.

vertebral ['vɜːtɪbrəl] *adj* vertébral.

vertebrate ['vɜːtɪbrət] *adj, n* vertébré (*m*).

vertex ['vɜːteks] *n, pl* **vertices** ['vɜːtɪsiːz] (*gen, Geom*) sommet *m*; (*Anat*) vertex *m*.

vertical ['vɜːtɪkəl] 1 *adj line, plane* vertical. ~ **cliff** falaise *f* à pic; ~ **take-off aircraft** avion *m* à décollage vertical. 2 *n* verticale *f*. **out of** *or* **off the** ~ décalé par rapport à *or* écarté de la verticale.

vertically ['vɜːtɪkəlɪ] *adv* verticalement.

vertiginous [vɜː'tɪdʒɪnəs] *adj* vertigineux.

vertigo ['vɜːtɪgəʊ] *n* (*U*) vertige *m*. **to suffer from** ~ avoir des vertiges.

verve [vɜːv] *n* verve *f*, brio *m*.

very ['verɪ] 1 *adv* **(a)** (*extremely*) très, fort, bien. ~ **amusing** très *or* fort *or* bien amusant; **to be** ~ **careful** faire très attention; **I am** ~ **cold/hot** j'ai très froid/chaud; **are you tired?** — ~**/not** ~ êtes-vous fatigué? — très*/pas très*; ~ **well written/made** très bien écrit/fait; ~ **well, if you insist** (très) bien, si vous insistez; ~ **little** très peu; ~ **little milk** très peu de lait; **it is not** ~ **likely** ce n'est pas très probable, c'est peu probable; (*Rel*) **the V**~ **Reverend ...** le Très Révérend ...; ~ **high frequency** (*Rad*) (ondes *fpl*) ultra-courtes *fpl*; (*Electronics*) très haute fréquence.

(b) (*absolutely*) tout, de loin. ~ **best quality** toute première qualité; ~ **last/first** tout dernier/premier; **she is the** ~ **cleverest in the class** c'est elle la plus intelligente de la classe; **give it me tomorrow at the** ~ **latest** donnez-le-moi demain au plus tard *or* demain dernier délai; **at midday at the** ~ **latest** à midi au plus tard; **at the** ~ **most/least** tout au plus/moins; **to be in the** ~ **best of health** être en excellente santé; **they are the** ~ **best of friends** ils sont les meilleurs amis du monde.

(c) ~ **much** beaucoup, bien; **thank you** ~ **much** merci beaucoup; **I liked it** ~ **much** je l'ai beaucoup aimé; **he is** ~ **much better** il va beaucoup mieux; ~ **much bigger** beaucoup *or* bien plus grand; ~ **much respected** très *or* fort respecté; **he is** ~ **much the more intelligent of the two** il est de beaucoup *or* de loin le plus intelligent des deux; **he doesn't work** ~ **much** il ne travaille pas beaucoup, il travaille peu.

(d) (*for emphasis*) **the** ~ **same day** le jour même, ce jour-là; **the** ~ **same hat** exactement le même chapeau; **the** ~ **next day** le lendemain même, dès le lendemain; *V* **own**.

2 *adj* **(a)** (*precise, exact*) même, exactement. **that** ~ **day/moment** ce jour/cet instant même; **on the** ~ **spot** à l'endroit même; **his** ~ **words** ses propos mêmes; **the** ~ **thing/man I need** tout à fait la chose/ l'homme qu'il me faut; **to catch in the** ~ **act** prendre en flagrant délit (*of stealing etc* de vol *etc*).

(b) (*extreme*) tout. **at the** ~ **end** *[play, year]* tout à la fin; *[garden, road]* tout au bout; **at the** ~ **back** tout au fond; **to the** ~ **end** jusqu'au bout; **in the** ~ **depths of the sea/forest** au plus profond de la mer/la forêt.

(c) (*mere*) seul. **the** ~ **thought of** la seule pensée de, rien que de penser à; **the** ~ **idea!** quelle idée alors!

(d) (*liter*) **he is a** ~ **rascal** *or* **the veriest rascal** c'est un fieffé coquin.

Very ['vɪərɪ] *adj* (*Mil*) ~ **light** fusée éclairante; ~ **pistol** pistolet *m* lance-fusées.

vesicle ['vesɪkl] *n* vésicule *f*.

vesper ['vespəʳ] *n*: ~**s** vêpres *fpl*; **to ring the** ~ **bell** sonner les vêpres.

vessel ['vesl] *n* **(a)** (*Naut*) vaisseau *m*, navire *m*, bâtiment *m*. **(b)** (*Anat, Bot*) vaisseau *m*; *V* **blood**. **(c)** (*liter: receptacle*) vaisseau *m* (*liter*), récipient *m*, vase *m*. **drinking** ~ vaisseau.

vest[1] [vest] 1 *n* **(a)** (*Brit*) tricot *m* de corps. **(b)** (*US*) gilet *m*. 2 *cpd*: **vest pocket** poche *f* de gilet.

vest[2] [vest] *vt* (*frm*) **to** ~ **sb with sth, to** ~ **sth in sb** investir qn de qch, assigner qch à qn; **the authority** ~**ed in me** l'autorité dont je suis investi; (*Comm, Fin*) ~**ed interests** droits *mpl* acquis; (*fig*) **he has a** ~**ed interest in the play since his daughter is acting in it** il est directement intéressé dans la pièce, étant donné que sa fille y joue.

vestal ['vestl] *adj*: ~ **virgin** vestale *f*.

vestibule ['vestɪbjuːl] 1 *n [house, hotel]* vestibule *m*, hall *m* d'entrée; *[church]* vestibule; (*Anat*) vestibule. 2 *cpd*: (*US*) **vestibule train** train *m* à compartiments.

vestige ['vestɪdʒ] *n* (*trace, remnant*) vestige *m*; (*Anat*) organe rudimentaire *or* atrophié. (*fig*) **not a** ~ **of truth/common sense** pas un grain de vérité/de bon sens; **a** ~ **of hope** un reste d'espoir.

vestigial [ves'tɪdʒɪəl] *adj* rudimentaire, atrophié.

vestment ['vestmənt] *n [priest]* vêtement sacerdotal; (*ceremonial robe*) habit *m* de cérémonie.

vestry ['vestrɪ] *n* (*part of church*) sacristie *f*; (*meeting*) assemblée paroissiale, conseil paroissial.

vesture ['vestʃəʳ] *n* (*U: liter*) vêtements *mpl*.

Vesuvius [vɪ'suːvɪəs] *n* Vésuve *m*.

vet [vet] 1 *n* (*abbr of* **veterinary surgeon, veterinarian**) vétérinaire *mf*. 2 *vt* (*) *text* corriger, revoir; *application* examiner de près *or* minutieusement; *person* examiner soigneusement *or* de près. **the director** ~**ted him for the job** le directeur l'a examiné sous tous les angles avant de lui offrir le poste; **we have** ~**ted him thoroughly** nous nous sommes renseignés de façon approfondie à son sujet.

vetch [vetʃ] *n* vesce *f*.

veteran ['vetərən] 1 *n* vétéran *m*. **war** ~ ancien combattant.

2 *cpd* (*experienced*) expérimenté. **she is a veteran campaigner for women's rights** elle fait campagne depuis toujours pour les droits de la femme; **a veteran car** une voiture d'époque (*avant 1916*); **a veteran teacher/ golfer** un vétéran de l'enseignement/du golf.

veterinarian [ˌvetərɪ'nɛərɪən] *n* vétérinaire *mf*.

veterinary ['vetərɪnərɪ] *adj medicine, science* vétérinaire. (*esp Brit*) ~ **surgeon** vétérinaire *mf*.

veto ['viːtəʊ] 1 *n, pl* ~**es** veto *m*. **to use one's** ~ exercer son droit de veto; **to put a** ~ **on** mettre son veto à. 2 *vt* (*Pol etc, also fig*) mettre *or* opposer son veto à.

vex [veks] *vt* contrarier, ennuyer, fâcher. **to be** ~**ed with sb** être fâché contre *or* avec qn; **to get** ~**ed** se fâcher; **a** ~**ed question** une question controversée.

vexation [vek'seɪʃən] *n* (*U*) ennui *m*, tracas *m*.

vexatious [vek'seɪʃəs] *adj thing* contrariant, ennuyeux; *person* tracassier, contrariant.

vexing ['veksɪŋ] *adj* contrariant, ennuyeux.

via ['vaɪə] *prep* par, via.

viability [ˌvaɪə'bɪlɪtɪ] *n* viabilité *f*.

viable ['vaɪəbl] *adj* viable.

viaduct ['vaɪədʌkt] *n* viaduc *m*.

vial ['vaɪəl] *n* (*liter*) fiole *f*.

viands ['vaɪəndz] *npl* (*liter*) aliments *mpl*.

viaticum [vaɪ'ætɪkəm] *n* viatique *m*.

vibes‡ [vaɪbz] *npl abbr of* **vibrations, vibraphone. the** ~ **are wrong** ça ne gaze pas.

vibrant ['vaɪbrənt] *adj* vibrant. (*fig*) **to be** ~ **with** vibrer de.

vibraphone ['vaɪbrəfəʊn] *n* vibraphone *m*.

vibrate [vaɪ'breɪt] *vi* (*quiver*) vibrer (*with* de); (*resound*) retentir (*with* de); (*fig*) frémir, vibrer (*with* de).

vibration [vaɪ'breɪʃən] *n* vibration *f*.

vibrator [vaɪ'breɪtəʳ] *n* **(a)** (*Elec*) vibrateur *m*. **(b)** (*massager*) vibromasseur *m*.

vibratory ['vaɪbrətərɪ] *adj* vibratoire.

viburnum [vaɪ'bɜːnəm] *n* viorne *f*.

vicar ['vɪkəʳ] *n* **(a)** pasteur *m* (*de l'Église anglicane*). **good evening** ~ bonsoir pasteur, ≃ bonsoir monsieur le curé. **(b)** ~ **apostolic** vicaire *m* apostolique; ~ **general** grand vicaire, vicaire général; **the V**~ **of Christ** le vicaire de Jésus-Christ.

vicarage ['vɪkərɪdʒ] *n* presbytère *m* (*de l'Église anglicane*).

vicarious [vɪ'kɛərɪəs] *adj* **(a)** (*delegated*) délégué. **to give** ~ **authority** to déléguer son autorité à.

(b) (*for others*) *work* fait à la place d'un autre. **the** ~ **suffering of Christ** les souffrances que le Christ subit pour autrui; **I got** ~ **pleasure out of it** j'en ai retiré indirectement du plaisir.

vicariously [vɪ'kɛərɪəslɪ] *adv experience* indirectement; *authorize* par délégation, par procuration.

vice[1] [vaɪs] 1 *n* (*U: depravity*) vice *m*; (*evil characteristic*) vice; (*less strong*) défaut *m*. *[dog, horse etc]* **he has no** ~**s** il n'est pas vicieux. 2 *cpd*: (*Police*) **vice squad** brigade mondaine *or* des mœurs.

vice[2], (*US*) **vise** [vaɪs] *n* (*Tech*) étau *m*; *V* **grip** *etc*.

vice[3] ['vaɪsɪ] *prep* (*frm*) à la place de.

vice- [vaɪs] *pref* vice-. ~**admiral** vice-amiral *m*; ~**chairman** vice-président(e) *m(f)*; ~**chairmanship** vice-présidence *f*; ~**chancellor** (*Univ*) recteur *m*; (*Jur*) vice-chancelier *m*; ~**consul** vice-consul *m*; ~**presidency** vice-présidence *f*; ~**president** vice-président(e) *m(f)*.

viceroy ['vaɪsrɔɪ] *n* vice-roi *m*.

vice versa ['vaɪsɪ'vɜːsə] *adv* vice versa, inversement.

vicinity [vɪ'sɪnɪtɪ] *n* **(a)** (*nearby area*) voisinage *m*, environs *mpl*, alentours *mpl*. **in the** ~ dans les environs, à proximité; **in the** ~ **of** aux alentours de, à proximité de; **in the immediate** ~ dans les environs immédiats; **the immediate** ~ **of the town** les abords *mpl* de la ville. **(b)** (*closeness*) proximité *f*.

vicious ['vɪʃəs] *adj remark, look, criticism* méchant, malveillant, haineux; *kick, attack* brutal, violent; *habit* vicieux, pervers; *animal* vicieux, rétif. **to have a** ~ **tongue** être mauvaise langue, avoir une langue de vipère; ~ **circle** cercle vicieux.

viciously ['vɪʃəslɪ] *adv* (*V* **vicious**) méchamment, avec malveillance, haineusement; brutalement, violemment.

viciousness ['vɪʃəsnɪs] *n* (*V* **vicious**) méchanceté *f*, malveillance *f*; brutalité *f*, violence *f*.

vicissitude [vɪ'sɪsɪtjuːd] *n* vicissitude *f*.

victim ['vɪktɪm] *n* (*lit, fig*) victime *f*. **to be the** ~ **of** être victime de; **to fall (a)** ~ **to** devenir la victime de; (*fig: to sb's charms etc*) succomber à.

victimization [ˌvɪktɪmaɪ'zeɪʃən] *n* représailles *fpl* (*subies par un ou plusieurs des responsables*). **the dismissed worker alleged** ~ l'ouvrier qu'on avait licencié a prétendu être victime de représailles.

victimize ['vɪktɪmaɪz] *vt* faire une victime de, prendre pour *or* en victime; (*Ind*) exercer des représailles sur.

victor ['vɪktəʳ] *n* vainqueur *m*.

Victoria [vɪk'tɔːrɪə] 1 *n* **(a)** Victoria *f*. **(b)** (*carriage*) **v**~ victoria *f*. 2 *cpd*: **Victoria Falls** chutes *fpl* de Victoria; (*Brit Mil*) **Victoria Cross** (*abbr* **V.C.**) Croix *f* de Victoria (*la plus haute décoration militaire*).

Victorian [vɪk'tɔːrɪən] 1 *n* Victorien(ne) *m(f)*. 2 *adj* victorien.

Victoriana [vɪkˌtɔːrɪ'ɑːnə] *n* (*U*) objets victoriens, antiquités victoriennes.

victorious [vɪk'tɔːrɪəs] *adj army* victorieux, vainqueur (*m only*); *shout* de victoire. **to be** ~ **(in)** sortir victorieux (de).

victoriously [vɪk'tɔːrɪəslɪ] *adv* victorieusement.

victory ['vɪktərɪ] *n* victoire *f*. **to gain** *or* **win a** ~ **over** remporter une victoire sur; *V* **winged**.

victual ['vɪtl] **1** *vt* approvisionner, ravitailler. **2** *vi* s'approvisionner, se ravitailler. **3** *n*: ~s victuailles *fpl*, vivres *mpl*.
victualler ['vɪtləʳ] *n* fournisseur *m* (de provisions); *V* **license**[1].
vide ['vɪdeɪ] *impers vb* (*frm*) voir, Cf.
videlicet [vɪ'di:lɪset] *adv* (*frm*) c'est-à-dire, à savoir.
video ['vɪdɪəʊ] **1** *n* (*US*) télévision *f*. **2** *cpd*: **video (cassette) recorder** magnétoscope *m*; **videophone** vidéophone *m*; (*TV*) **video recording** enregistrement *m* sur magnétoscope; **video tape** (bande *f* de) magnétoscope *m*.
vie [vaɪ] *vi* rivaliser, lutter. **to ~ with sb for sth** lutter avec qn pour (avoir) qch, disputer qch à qn; **to ~ with sb in doing** rivaliser avec qn pour faire; **they ~d with each other in their work** ils travaillaient à qui mieux mieux.
Vienna [vɪ'enə] **1** *n* Vienne. **2** *cpd* viennois, de Vienne.
Viennese [ˌvɪə'ni:z] **1** *adj* viennois. **2** *n, pl inv* Viennois(e) *m(f)*.
Vietnam ['vjet'næm] *n* Viet-Nam *m*. **North/South ~** Viet-Nam du Nord/du Sud; **the ~ war** la guerre du Viet-Nam.
Vietnamese [ˌvjetnə'mi:z] **1** *adj* vietnamien. **North/South ~** nord-/sud-vietnamien. **2** *n* **(a)** (*pl inv*) Vietnamien(ne) *m(f)*. **North/South ~** Nord-/Sud-Vietnamien(ne) *m(f)*. **(b)** (*Ling*) vietnamien *m*.
view [vju:] **1** *n* **(a)** (*U: range of vision*) vue *f*. **in full ~ of** aux yeux de; **to come into ~** apparaître; *[person]* **to come into ~ of** arriver en vue de; **the house is within ~ of the sea** de la maison on voit la mer; **hidden from ~** caché; (*lit, fig*) **to keep sth in ~** ne pas perdre qch de vue; *[exhibits]* **on ~** exposé; **the house will be on ~ tomorrow** on pourra visiter la maison demain; *V* **bird, front** *etc*.
(b) (*scenery, photograph*) vue *f*, panorama *m*. **there is a splendid ~ from here** d'ici la vue est splendide; **a ~ over** une vue sur; **a good ~ of the tower** une belle vue *or* un beau panorama de la tour; **50 ~s of Paris** 50 vues *or* photos de Paris; **a room with a ~** une chambre avec une belle vue.
(c) (*opinion*) vue *f*, avis *m*, opinion *f*. **in my ~** à mon avis; **to hold ~s on** avoir des opinions *or* des idées sur; **to take a dim*** *or* **a poor ~ of sb's conduct** apprécier médiocrement la conduite de qn; **to fall in with sb's ~s** tomber d'accord avec qn; *V* **point**.
(d) (*survey*) vue *f*, aperçu *m*. **a general** *or* **overall ~ of a problem** une vue d'ensemble d'un problème; **clear ~ of the facts** idée claire des faits; **in ~ of** étant donné, vu; **in ~ of the fact that** étant donné que, vu que; **at first ~** à première vue.
(e) (*intention, plan*) vue *f*, but *m*. **with this in ~** dans ce but, à cette fin; **with the ~ of doing, with a ~ to doing** dans l'intention de faire, afin de faire; **he has in ~ the purchase of the house** il envisage d'acheter la maison; **he has the holiday in ~ when he says ...** il pense aux vacances *or* il n'oublie pas les vacances quand il dit ... .
2 *cpd*: (*Phot*) **viewfinder** viseur *m*; **viewpoint** point *m* de vue.
3 *vt* **(a)** (*examine*) *house* visiter, inspecter.
(b) (*consider*) *problem, prospect* envisager, considérer, regarder.
4 *vi* (*TV*) regarder la télévision.
viewer ['vju:əʳ] *n* **(a)** spectateur *m*, -trice *f*; (*TV*) téléspectateur *m*, -trice *f*. **(b)** (*for slides*) visionneuse *f*; (*viewfinder*) viseur *m*.
vigil ['vɪdʒɪl] *n* (*gen*) veille *f*; (*by sickbed, corpse etc*) veillée *f*; (*Rel*) vigile *f*. **to keep ~ over sb** veiller qn; **a long ~** une longue veille, de longues heures sans sommeil.
vigilance ['vɪdʒɪləns] *n* vigilance *f*.
vigilant ['vɪdʒɪlənt] *adj* vigilant, attentif.
vigilante [ˌvɪdʒɪ'læntɪ] *n membre m d'un groupe non-officiel qui se charge de veiller à l'ordre public.*
vigilantly ['vɪdʒɪləntlɪ] *adv* avec vigilance, attentivement.
vignette [vɪ'njet] *n* (*in books*) vignette *f*; (*Painting, Phot*) portrait *m* en buste dégradé; (*character sketch*) esquisse *f* de caractère.
vigor ['vɪgəʳ] *n* (*US*) = **vigour.**
vigorous ['vɪgərəs] *adj* (*lit, fig*) vigoureux.
vigorously ['vɪgərəslɪ] *adv* (*lit, fig*) vigoureusement, avec vigueur.
vigour, (*US*) **vigor** ['vɪgəʳ] *n* (*physical or mental strength*) vigueur *f*, énergie *f*, ardeur *f*; (*health*) vigueur, vitalité *f*.
Viking ['vaɪkɪŋ] **1** *adj* viking. **2** *n* Viking *m*.
vile [vaɪl] *adj* **(a)** (*base, evil*) *motive, action, traitor etc* vil (*f* vile), infâme, ignoble.
(b) (*extremely bad*) *food, drink, taste, play* abominable, exécrable; *smell* abominable, infect; (*) *weather* infect, abominable. **to be in a ~ temper** être d'une humeur massacrante.
vilely ['vaɪllɪ] *adv* vilement, bassement.
vileness ['vaɪlnɪs] *n* vilenie *f*, bassesse *f*.
vilification [ˌvɪlɪfɪ'keɪʃən] *n* diffamation *f*, calomnie *f*.
vilify ['vɪlɪfaɪ] *vt* calomnier, diffamer.
villa ['vɪlə] *n* (*in town*) pavillon *m* (*de banlieue*); (*in country*) maison *f* de campagne; (*by sea*) villa *f*.
village ['vɪlɪdʒ] **1** *n* village *m*, bourgade *f*, patelin* *m*. **2** *cpd well, school* du village. **village green** pré communal; **village idiot** idiot *m* du village.
villager ['vɪlɪdʒəʳ] *n* villageois(e) *m(f)*.
villain ['vɪlən] *n* (*scoundrel*) scélérat *m*, vaurien *m*; (*in drama, novel*) traître(sse) *m* (*f*); (*: *rascal*) coquin(e) *m(f)*; (*Police etc sl: criminal*) bandit *m*.
villainous ['vɪlənəs] *adj act, conduct* ignoble, infâme; (*: *bad*) *coffee, weather* abominable, infect. **~ deed** infamie *f*.
villainously ['vɪlənəslɪ] *adv* d'une manière ignoble.
villainy ['vɪlənɪ] *n* infamie *f*, bassesse *f*.
villein ['vɪlɪn] *n* (*Hist*) vilain(e) *m(f)*, serf *m*, serve *f*.
vim* [vɪm] *n* (*U*) énergie *f*, entrain *m*. **full of ~** plein d'entrain.
vindicate ['vɪndɪkeɪt] *vt opinion, person, action* justifier, défendre avec succès; *rights* faire valoir.
vindication [ˌvɪndɪ'keɪʃən] *n* justification *f*, défense *f*. **in ~ of** en justification de, pour justifier.
vindictive [vɪn'dɪktɪv] *adj* vindicatif.
vindictively [vɪn'dɪktɪvlɪ] *adv* vindicativement.
vindictiveness [vɪn'dɪktɪvnɪs] *n* caractère vindicatif.
vine [vaɪn] **1** *n* (*grapevine*) vigne *f*; (*similar plant*) plante grimpante *or* rampante. **2** *cpd leaf, cutting* de vigne. **vine grower** viticulteur *m*, vigneron *m*; **vine-growing district** région *f* viticole; **vine harvest** vendange(s) *f(pl)*; **vineyard** *V* **vineyard.**
vinegar ['vɪnɪgəʳ] *n* vinaigre *m*, *V* **cider, oil** *etc*.
vinegary ['vɪnɪgərɪ] *adj* acide, qui a le goût du vinaigre, qui sent le vinaigre; (*fig*) *remark* acide, acidulé.
vineyard ['vɪnjəd] *n* vignoble *m*.
vintage ['vɪntɪdʒ] **1** *n* (*harvesting*) vendange(s) *f(pl)*, récolte *f*; (*season*) vendanges *fpl*; (*year*) année *f*, millésime *m*. **what ~ is this wine?** ce vin est de quelle année?; **1966 was a good ~** 1966 était une bonne année (*pour le vin*); (*wine*) **the 1972 ~** le vin de 1972.
2 *cpd*: **vintage car** voiture *f* d'époque (*construite entre 1917 et 1930*); (*fig hum*) **this typewriter is a vintage model** cette machine à écrire est une antiquité *or* une pièce de musée; **vintage wine** grand vin, vin de grand cru; **a vintage year for burgundy** une bonne année pour le bourgogne.
vintner ['vɪntnəʳ] *n* négociant *m* en vins.
vinyl ['vaɪnɪl] **1** *n* vinyle *m*. **2** *cpd tiles* de *or* en vinyle; *paint* de vinyle.
viol ['vaɪəl] *n* viole *f*. **~ da gamba** viole de gambe; **~ player** violiste *mf*.
viola[1] [vɪ'əʊlə] *n* (*Mus*) alto *m*. **~ player** altiste *mf*.
viola[2] ['vaɪ'əʊlə] *n* (*Bot*) (*flower*) (*sorte de*) pensée *f*; (*genus*) violacée *f*.
violate ['vaɪəleɪt] *vt* (*all senses*) violer.
violation [ˌvaɪə'leɪʃən] *n* (*gen*) violation *f*; (*rape*) viol *m*.
violator ['vaɪəleɪtəʳ] *n* violateur *m*, -trice *f*.
violence ['vaɪələns] *n* (*all senses*) violence *f*. **to use ~ against** employer la violence contre; **there was an outbreak of ~** des bagarres *fpl or* de violents incidents ont éclaté; **racial ~** violents incidents raciaux; **by ~** par la violence; **crime of ~** voie *f* de fait; **act of ~** acte *m* de violence; (*Jur*) **robbery with ~** vol *m* avec coups et blessures; (*fig*) **to do ~** to faire violence à.
violent ['vaɪələnt] *adj person, death, emotion, contrast, pain* violent; *attack, blow* violent, brutal; *colour* criard. **to have a ~ temper** avoir un tempérament violent; **to be in a ~ temper** être dans une colère noire *or* dans une rage folle; **by ~ means** par la violence; **a ~ dislike (for)** une vive aversion (pour *or* envers).
violently ['vaɪələntlɪ] *adv struggle, criticize, react* violemment, avec violence; (*severely*) *ill, angry* terriblement. **to behave ~** se montrer violent; **to fall ~ in love with** tomber follement amoureux de.
violet ['vaɪəlɪt] **1** *n* (*Bot*) violette *f*; (*colour*) violet *m*. **2** *adj* violet.
violin [ˌvaɪə'lɪn] **1** *n* violon *m*; *V* **first.** **2** *cpd sonata, concerto* pour violon. **violin case** étui *m* à violon.
violinist [ˌvaɪə'lɪnɪst] *n* violoniste *mf*.
violoncellist [ˌvaɪələn'tʃelɪst] *n* violoncelliste *mf*.
violoncello [ˌvaɪələn'tʃeləʊ] *n* violoncelle *m*.
viper ['vaɪpəʳ] *n* (*Zool, fig*) vipère *f*.
viperish ['vaɪpərɪʃ] *adj* de vipère (*fig*).
virago [vɪ'rɑ:gəʊ] *n* mégère *f*, virago *f*.
viral ['vaɪərəl] *adj* viral.
Virgil ['vɜ:dʒɪl] *n* Virgile *m*.
virgin ['vɜ:dʒɪn] **1** *n* (fille *f*) vierge *f*; garçon *m* vierge. **she/he is a ~** elle/il est vierge; (*Rel*) **the (Blessed) V~** la (Sainte) Vierge.
2 *adj person* vierge; (*fig*) *forest, land* vierge; *freshness, sweetness* virginal. **~ snow** neige fraîche; (*Geog*) **the V~ Isles** les Îles *fpl* Vierges.
virginal ['vɜ:dʒɪnl] **1** *n* (*Mus*) virginal *m*. **2** *adj* virginal.
Virginia [və'dʒɪnjə] *n* Virginie *f*. (*Brit*) **~ creeper** vigne *f* vierge; **~ tobacco** Virginie *m*, tabac blond.
Virginian [və'dʒɪnjən] **1** *n* Virginien(ne) *m(f)*. **2** *adj* de Virginie.
virginity [vɜ:'dʒɪnɪtɪ] *n* virginité *f*.
Virgo ['vɜ:gəʊ] *n* (*Astron*) la Vierge.
virile ['vɪraɪl] *adj* (*lit, fig*) viril (*f* virile).
virility [vɪ'rɪlɪtɪ] *n* virilité *f*.
virologist [ˌvaɪə'rɒlədʒɪst] *n* spécialiste *mf* en virologie.
virology [ˌvaɪə'rɒlədʒɪ] *n* virologie *f*.
virtual ['vɜ:tjʊəl] *adj*: **he is the ~ leader** en fait c'est lui le chef, c'est lui le vrai chef; **it was a ~ failure** de fait ce fut un échec; **this reply is a ~ insult** cette réponse équivaut à une insulte.
virtually ['vɜ:tjʊəlɪ] *adv* en fait, en pratique, pratiquement. **he ~ confessed** il a pratiquement avoué; **he is ~ the boss** en pratique *or* en fait c'est lui le chef; **it's ~ the same** en fait c'est le même, cela revient au même; **to be ~ certain** être pratiquement certain.
virtue ['vɜ:tju:] *n* **(a)** (*moral quality*) vertu *f*. **to make a ~ of necessity** faire de nécessité vertu.
(b) (*U: chastity*) vertu *f*, chasteté *f*. **a woman of easy ~** une femme de petite vertu.
(c) (*advantage*) mérite *m*, avantage *m*. **this set has the ~ of being portable** ce poste a l'avantage d'être portatif; **he has the ~ of being easy to understand** il a le mérite d'être facile à comprendre; **there is no ~ in doing that if it is unnecessary** il n'y a aucun mérite à faire cela si ce n'est pas nécessaire.
(d) (*U: power*) pouvoir *m*,cefficacité *f*. **healing ~** pouvoir thérapeutique; **in** *or* **by ~ of** en vertu de.
virtuosity [ˌvɜ:tjʊ'ɒsɪtɪ] *n* virtuosité *f*.
virtuoso [ˌvɜ:tjʊ'əʊzəʊ] **1** *n* (*esp Mus*) virtuose *mf*. **a violin ~** un(e) virtuose du violon. **2** *adj performance* de virtuose.
virtuous ['vɜ:tjʊəs] *adj* vertueux.

virtuously ['vɜːtjʊəslɪ] *adv* vertueusement.
virulence ['vɪrʊləns] *n* virulence *f.*
virulent ['vɪrʊlənt] *adj* virulent.
virulently ['vɪrʊləntlɪ] *adv* avec virulence.
virus ['vaɪərəs] *n* virus *m* (*also fig*). **rabies ~** virus de la rage *or* rabique; **~ disease** maladie virale *or* à virus.
visa ['viːzə] 1 *n* visa *m* (*de passeport*). **entrance/exit ~** visa d'entrée/de sortie. 2 *vt* viser.
visage ['vɪzɪdʒ] *n* (*liter*) visage *m*, figure *f.*
vis-à-vis ['viːzəviː] 1 *prep* vis-à-vis de. 2 *adv* face à face, vis-à-vis†. 3 *n* (*person placed opposite*) vis-à-vis *m*; (*person of similar status*) homologue *mf.*
viscera ['vɪsərə] *npl* viscères *mpl.*
visceral ['vɪsərəl] *adj* viscéral.
viscid ['vɪsɪd] *adj* visqueux (*lit*).
viscose ['vɪskəʊs] 1 *n* viscose *f.* 2 *adj* visqueux (*lit*).
viscosity [vɪs'kɒsɪtɪ] *n* viscosité *f.*
viscount ['vaɪkaʊnt] *n* vicomte *m.*
viscountcy ['vaɪkaʊntsɪ] *n* vicomté *f.*
viscountess ['vaɪkaʊntɪs] *n* vicomtesse *f.*
viscounty ['vaɪkaʊntɪ] *n* = **viscountcy.**
viscous ['vɪskəs] *adj* visqueux, gluant.
vise [vaɪs] (*US*) = **vice[2].**
visé ['viːzeɪ] (*US*) = **visa.**
visibility [ˌvɪzɪ'bɪlɪtɪ] *n* visibilité *f.* (*Met*) **good/poor** *or* **low ~** bonne/mauvaise visibilité; **~ is down to** *or* **is only 20 metres** la visibilité ne dépasse pas 20 mètres.
visible ['vɪzəbl] *adj* (**a**) (*able to be seen*) visible. **~ to the naked eye** visible à l'œil nu; **to become ~** apparaître.
(**b**) (*obvious*) visible, manifeste. **with ~ impatience** avec une impatience manifeste; (*Jur*) **with no ~ means of support** sans ressources apparentes.
visibly ['vɪzəblɪ] *adv* visiblement.
Visigoth ['vɪzɪgɒθ] *n* Wisigoth *mf.*
vision ['vɪʒən] *n* (**a**) (*U*) vision *f*, vue *f*; (*fig: foresight*) vision, prévoyance *f.* **his ~ is very bad** sa vue est très mauvaise; **within/outside range of ~** à portée de/hors de vue; (*fig*) **a man of great ~** un homme qui voit loin; *V* **field.**
(**b**) (*in dream, trance*) vision *f*, apparition *f.* **it came to me in a ~** j'en ai eu une vision; **to have ~s of wealth** avoir des visions de richesses; **she had ~s of being drowned** elle s'est vue noyée.
visionary ['vɪʒənərɪ] *adj, n* visionnaire (*mf*).
visit ['vɪzɪt] 1 *n* (*call, tour*) visite *f*; (*stay*) séjour *m.* **to pay sb a ~** rendre visite à qn; **he went on a two-day ~ to Paris** il est allé passer deux jours à Paris; **I'm going on a ~ to Glasgow next week** j'irai à Glasgow la semaine prochaine; **on a private/official ~** en visite privée/officielle; **to be on a ~ to London** séjourner à Londres, faire un séjour à Londres; **his ~ to Paris lasted 3 days** son séjour à Paris a duré 3 jours; *V* **pay.**
2 *vt* (**a**) (*go and see*) *person* aller voir; (*more formally*) rendre visite à; *town* aller à, faire un petit tour à; *museum, zoo* aller à, (*more thorough*) visiter; *theatre* aller à.
(**b**) (*go and stay with*) *person* faire un séjour chez; (*go and stay in*) *town, country* faire un séjour à *or* en.
(**c**) (*inspect*) inspecter, faire une visite d'inspection à; *troops* passer en revue. (*Jur*) **to ~ the scene of the crime** se rendre sur les lieux du crime.
(**d**) (*afflict; inflict*) *person* punir (*with* de). **to ~ the sins of the father upon the children** punir les enfants pour les péchés de leurs pères.
visit with *vt fus* (*US*) *person* passer voir.
visitation [ˌvɪzɪ'teɪʃən] *n* (**a**) (*by official*) visite *f* d'inspection; [*bishop*] visite pastorale; (*pej hum: prolonged visit*) visite trop prolongée. (*Rel*) **the V~** la Visitation. (**b**) (*calamity*) punition *f* du ciel.
visiting ['vɪzɪtɪŋ] 1 *n*: **I find ~ a nuisance** cela m'ennuie de faire des visites.
2 *cpd*: (*Brit*) **visiting card** carte *f* de visite; **visiting hours** heures *fpl* de visite; (*Univ*) **visiting professor** professeur associé; (*Sport*) **the visiting team** les visiteurs *mpl*; **I know him but I'm not on visiting terms with him** je le connais, mais nous ne nous rendons pas visite; **visiting time** = **visiting hours.**
visitor ['vɪzɪtə[r]] *n* (*guest; tourist; also at exhibition etc*) visiteur *m*, -euse *f*; (*in hotel*) client(e) *m(f)*, voyageur *m*, -euse *f.* **~s' book** livre *m* d'or; (*in hotel*) registre *m*; **to have a ~/~s** avoir une visite/de la visite; *V* **health** *etc.*
visor ['vaɪzə[r]] *n* visière *f*; *V* **sun.**
vista ['vɪstə] *n* (**a**) (*view*) panorama *m*, vue *f.* (**b**) (*survey*) (*of past*) vue *f*; (*of future*) perspective *f*, horizon *m.*
visual ['vɪzjʊəl] *adj field, memory* visuel; *nerve* optique. **to teach with ~ aids** enseigner par des méthodes visuelles.
visualize ['vɪzjʊəlaɪz] *vt* (**a**) (*recall*) *person, sb's face* se représenter, évoquer.
(**b**) (*imagine*) s'imaginer, se représenter. **try to ~ a million pounds** essayez de vous imaginer un million de livres; **I ~d him working at his desk** je me le suis représenté travaillant à son bureau.
(**c**) (*foresee*) envisager, prévoir. **we do not ~ many changes** nous n'envisageons pas beaucoup de changements.
visually ['vɪzjʊəlɪ] *adv* visuellement.
vital ['vaɪtl] 1 *adj* (**a**) (*of life*) vital. **~ force** force vitale; **~ parts** organes vitaux; **~ statistics** [*population*] statistiques *fpl* démographiques; (*: *woman's*) mensurations *fpl.*
(**b**) (*essential*) *supplies, resources* vital, essentiel, indispensable; (*very important*) *problem, matter, question* vital, fondamental. **of ~ importance** d'une importance capitale; **your support is ~ to us** votre soutien nous est indispensable; **it is ~ that ...** il est indispensable *or* vital que ...+*subj.*
(**c**) (*fatal*) *wound* mortel; *error* fatal.
(**d**) (*lively*) énergique, plein d'entrain.
2 *n*: **the ~s** (*Anat*) les organes vitaux; (*fig*) les parties essentielles.
vitality [vaɪ'tælɪtɪ] *n* (*lit, fig*) vitalité *f.*
vitalize ['vaɪtəlaɪz] *vt* (*lit*) vivifier; (*fig*) mettre de la vie dans, animer.
vitally ['vaɪtəlɪ] *adv necessary, urgent* absolument, extrêmement. **this problem is ~ important** ce problème est d'une importance capitale; **it is ~ important that we arrive on time** il est absolument indispensable *or* il faut absolument que nous arrivions (*subj*) à l'heure.
vitamin ['vɪtəmɪn] 1 *n* vitamine *f.* **~ A/B** *etc* vitamine A/B *etc*; **with added ~s** vitaminé.
2 *cpd content* en vitamines; *tablets* de vitamines. **vitamin deficiency** carence *f* en vitamines; **vitamin deficiency disease** avitaminose *f.*
vitaminize ['vɪtəmɪnaɪz] *vt* incorporer des vitamines dans. **~d food** nourriture vitaminée.
vitiate ['vɪʃɪeɪt] *vt* (*all senses*) vicier.
viticulture ['vɪtɪkʌltʃə[r]] *n* viticulture *f.*
vitreous ['vɪtrɪəs] *adj china, rock, electricity* vitreux; *enamel* vitrifié.
vitrifaction [ˌvɪtrɪ'fækʃən] *n*, **vitrification** [ˌvɪtrɪfɪ'keɪʃən] *n* vitrification *f.*
vitrify ['vɪtrɪfaɪ] 1 *vt* vitrifier. 2 *vi* se vitrifier.
vitriol ['vɪtrɪəl] *n* (*Chem, fig*) vitriol *m.*
vitriolic [ˌvɪtrɪ'ɒlɪk] *adj* (*Chem*) de vitriol; (*fig*) venimeux, mordant.
vitriolize ['vɪtrɪəlaɪz] *vt* vitrioler.
vituperate [vɪ'tjuːpəreɪt] 1 *vt* injurier, vitupérer contre. 2 *vi* vitupérer.
vituperation [vɪˌtjuːpə'reɪʃən] *n* vitupération *f.*
vituperative [vɪ'tjuːpərətɪv] *adj* injurieux.
viva[1] ['viːvə] 1 *excl* vive! 2 *n* vivat *m.*
viva[2] ['vaɪvə] *n* (*Brit*) = **viva voce 3.**
vivacious [vɪ'veɪʃəs] *adj* vif, enjoué, qui a de la vivacité, animé; (*Bot*) vivace.
vivaciously [vɪ'veɪʃəslɪ] *adv* avec vivacité, avec verve.
vivacity [vɪ'væsɪtɪ] *n* vivacité *f*; (*in words*) verve *f.*
vivarium [vɪ'veərɪəm] *n* vivarium *m*; (*for fish, shellfish*) vivier *m.*
viva voce ['vaɪvə'vəʊsɪ] 1 *adj* oral, verbal. 2 *adv* de vive voix, oralement. 3 *n* (*Brit Univ*) épreuve orale, oral *m.*
vivid ['vɪvɪd] *adj light* vif; *colour* vif, éclatant; *tie etc* voyant; (*lively*) *imagination, recollection* vif; (*clear*) *description* vivant, frappant. **a ~ blue dress** une robe d'un bleu éclatant.
vividly ['vɪvɪdlɪ] *adv describe, recount* d'une manière vivante *or* colorée; *imagine* de façon précise. **to remember sth ~** avoir un vif souvenir de qch.
vividness ['vɪvɪdnɪs] *n* [*colour*] vivacité *f*, éclat *m*; [*light*] éclat, clarté *f*; [*style*] clarté, vigueur *f.*
vivify ['vɪvɪfaɪ] *vt* vivifier, ranimer.
viviparous [vɪ'vɪpərəs] *adj* vivipare.
vivisect [ˌvɪvɪ'sekt] *vt* pratiquer la vivisection sur.
vivisection [ˌvɪvɪ'sekʃən] *n* vivisection *f.*
vivisectionist [ˌvɪvɪ'sekʃənɪst] *n* (*Vet*) vivisecteur *m*; (*supporter*) partisan(e) *m(f)* de la vivisection.
vixen ['vɪksn] *n* (*Zool*) renarde *f*; (*fig pej*) mégère *f*, garce: *f.*
vizier [vɪ'zɪə[r]] *n* vizir *m.*
vocable ['vəʊkəbl] *n* vocable *m.*
vocabulary [vəʊ'kæbjʊlərɪ] *n* (*gen*) vocabulaire *m*; (*in textbook*) lexique *m*, glossaire *m.*
vocal ['vəʊkəl] *adj* (**a**) (*Anat*) vocal. **~ c(h)ords** cordes vocales.
(**b**) *communication* oral, verbal. **~ music** musique vocale; (*Mus*) **~ score** partition chorale.
(**c**) (*voicing one's opinions*) *group, person* qui se fait entendre; (*noisy*) bruyant. **Women's Lib are getting very ~** le M.L.F. commence à faire du bruit *or* à se faire entendre.
vocalic [vəʊ'kælɪk] *adj* vocalique.
vocalist ['vəʊkəlɪst] *n* chanteur *m*, -euse *f* (*dans un groupe*).
vocalize ['vəʊkəlaɪz] 1 *vt one's opinions* exprimer; *consonant* vocaliser; *language* écrire en marquant des points-voyelles. 2 *vi* (*Ling*) se vocaliser; (*Mus*) vocaliser, faire des vocalises.
vocally ['vəʊkəlɪ] *adv* vocalement, oralement.
vocation [vəʊ'keɪʃən] *n* (*Rel etc*) vocation *f.* **to have a ~ for teaching** avoir la vocation de l'enseignement.
vocational [vəʊ'keɪʃənl] *adj* professionnel. **~ guidance/school/training** orientation/école/formation professionnelle.
vocative ['vɒkətɪv] 1 *n* vocatif *m.* **in the ~** au vocatif. 2 *adj*: **~ case** vocatif *m.*
vociferate [vəʊ'sɪfəreɪt] *vi* vociférer, brailler*.
vociferation [vəʊˌsɪfə'reɪʃən] *n* vocifération *f.*
vociferous [vəʊ'sɪfərəs] *adj* bruyant, criard.
vociferously [vəʊ'sɪfərəslɪ] *adv* bruyamment, en vociférant.
vodka ['vɒdkə] *n* vodka *f.*
vogue [vəʊg] *n* (**a**) (*fashion*) mode *f*, vogue *f.* **wigs were the ~** *or* **in ~** then les perruques étaient alors à la mode *or* en vogue; **to be all the ~** faire fureur; **to come into ~** devenir à la mode; **to go out of ~** passer de mode.
(**b**) (*popularity*) vogue *f*, popularité *f.* **to have a great ~** être très en vogue.
voice [vɔɪs] 1 *n* (**a**) (*faculty of speech*) voix *f*; (*pitch, quality*) voix, ton *m.* **to lose one's ~** perdre sa voix; **to be in good ~** être en voix; **in a deep ~** d'une voix grave; (*fig*) **he likes the sound of his own ~** il aime s'écouter parler; **his ~ has broken** il a mué; **a ~ could be heard at the back of the room** on entendait une voix au fond de la salle; **three ~s were raised in protest about the heating** trois personnes se sont plaintes du chauffage; (*Mus*) **tenor/bass ~** voix *f* de ténor/de basse; (*Mus*) **a piece for ~ and piano** un morceau pour voix et piano; *V* **loud, raise** *etc.*
(**b**) (*fig*) avis *m*, voix *f.* **to have a ~ in the matter** avoir voix au

chapitre; **they acclaimed him with one ~** ils ont été unanimes à l'acclamer; **to give ~** to exprimer; (*liter*) **to listen to the ~ of a friend** écouter les conseils *or* la voix d'un ami; **the ~ of reason** la voix de la raison; **the ~ of God** la voix de Dieu.
(c) (*Gram*) **active/passive ~** voix active/passive.
(d) (*Phon*) voix *f*.
2 *cpd*: (*Mus*) **voice parts** parties vocales; **voice production** diction *f*, élocution *f*; **voice range** étendue *f* de la voix; **voice training** *[actor etc]* cours *mpl* de diction *or* d'élocution; *[singer]* cours *m* de chant *m*.
3 *vt* **(a)** (*express*) *feelings, opinion* exprimer, formuler.
(b) (*Ling*) *consonant* voiser, sonoriser. **~d consonant** consonne sonore *or* voisée.
(c) (*Mus*) accorder.
-voiced [vɔɪst] *adj ending in cpds*: **low-/warm-voiced** à voix basse/chaude.
voiceless ['vɔɪslɪs] *adj* aphone, sans voix; (*Ling*) *consonant* sourd, non-voisé.
void [vɔɪd] **1** *n* (*lit, fig*) vide *m*.
2 *adj* **(a)** (*frm: vacant*) *space* vide; *job* vacant. **~ of** vide de, dépourvu de.
(b) (*Jur*) nul. **to make ~** rendre nul; *V* **null**.
(c) (*Cards*) **to be ~ in** avoir chicane à.
3 *vt* **(a)** (*remove*) évacuer (*from* de).
(b) (*excrete*) évacuer; (*vomit*) vomir.
(c) (*Jur*) annuler, rendre nul.
voile [vɔɪl] *n* voile *m* (*Tex*).
volatile ['vɒlətaɪl] *adj* (*Chem*) volatil (*f* volatile); (*fig*) *political situation* explosif; (*changeable*) *person* versatile; (*lively*) pétillant de vie; (*transient*) fugace.
volatility [ˌvɒlə'tɪlɪtɪ] *n* (*Chem*) volatilité *f*; (*fickleness*) inconstance *f*, versatilité *f*; (*liveliness*) entrain *m*.
volatilize [vɒ'lætəlaɪz] **1** *vt* volatiliser. **2** *vi* se volatiliser, s'évaporer.
volcanic [vɒl'kænɪk] *adj* (*lit, fig*) volcanique.
volcano [vɒl'keɪnəʊ] *n* volcan *m*.
vole[1] [vəʊl] *n* (*Zool*) campagnol *m*.
vole[2] [vəʊl] (*Cards*) **1** *n* vole *f*. **2** *vi* faire la vole.
volition [vɒ'lɪʃən] *n* volition *f*, volonté *f*. **of one's own ~** de son propre gré.
volley ['vɒlɪ] **1** *n* **(a)** (*Mil*) volée *f*, salve *f*; (*fig*) *[insults]* bordée *f*, torrent *m*; *[applause]* salve. **to fire a ~** tirer une salve.
(b) (*Sport*) volée *f*. **half ~** demi-volée *f*.
2 *cpd*: **volleyball** volley(-ball) *m*.
3 *vt* **(a)** (*Mil*) tirer une volée de; (*fig*) *insults* lâcher un torrent *or* une bordée de.
(b) (*Sport*) reprendre en volée, attraper à la volée.
4 *vi* **(a)** (*Mil*) tirer par salves.
(b) (*Sport*) renvoyer une volée.
volt [vəʊlt] **1** *n* volt *m*.
2 *cpd*: **volt meter** voltmètre *m*.
voltage ['vəʊltɪdʒ] *n* voltage *m*, tension *f*. **high/low ~** haute/basse tension.
voltaic [vɒl'teɪɪk] *adj* voltaïque.
volte-face ['vɒlt'fɑːs] *n* volte-face *f inv*. (*lit, fig*) **to make a ~** faire volte-face.
volubility [ˌvɒljʊ'bɪlɪtɪ] *n* volubilité *f*, loquacité *f*.
voluble ['vɒljʊbl] *adj* volubile, loquace.
volubly ['vɒljʊblɪ] *adv* avec volubilité, avec faconde.
volume ['vɒljuːm] **1** *n* **(a)** (*book*) volume *m*, tome *m*. **in 6 ~s** en 6 volumes; **a 6-~ dictionary** un dictionnaire en 6 volumes.
(b) (*size*) volume *m*. **production ~** volume de la production.
(c) (*sound*) volume *m*, puissance *f*. (*Rad, TV*) **to turn the ~ up/down** augmenter/diminuer le volume.
(d) (*large amount*) **~s of smoke** nuages *mpl* de fumée; **~s of tears** flots *mpl* de larmes; **to write ~s** écrire des volumes; *V* **speak.**
2 *cpd*: (*Rad, TV*) **volume control** bouton *m* de réglage du volume.
volumetric [ˌvɒljʊ'metrɪk] *adj* volumétrique.
voluminous [və'luːmɪnəs] *adj* volumineux.
voluntarily ['vɒləntərɪlɪ] *adv* (*willingly*) volontairement, de mon (*or* son *etc*) plein gré; (*without payment*) bénévolement.
voluntary ['vɒləntərɪ] **1** *adj* **(a)** (*not forced*) *confession, statement* volontaire, spontané; *contribution, movement* volontaire.
(b) (*unpaid*) *help, service, work* bénévole. **~ worker** travailleur *m* bénévole. **2** *n* (*Mus, Rel*) morceau *m* d'orgue.
volunteer [ˌvɒlən'tɪəʳ] **1** *n* (*gen, Mil*) volontaire *mf*.
2 *cpd army, group* de volontaires; *helper* bénévole.
3 *vt* donner *or* offrir de son plein gré. **to ~ information** fournir (spontanément) un renseignement; **'there were 7 of them' he ~ed** 'ils étaient 7' dit-il spontanément.
4 *vi* s'offrir, se proposer (*for sth* pour qch, *to do* pour faire); (*Mil*) s'engager comme volontaire (*for* dans).
voluptuous [və'lʌptjʊəs] *adj* voluptueux, sensuel.
voluptuously [və'lʌptjʊəslɪ] *adv* voluptueusement.
voluptuousness [və'lʌptjʊəsnɪs] *n* volupté *f*, sensualité *f*.
volute [və'luːt] *n* (*Archit*) volute *f*.
voluted [və'luːtɪd] *adj* (*Archit*) en volute.
vomit ['vɒmɪt] **1** *n* vomissement *m*, vomi* *m*. **2** *vt* (*lit, fig*) vomir. **to ~ out** *or* **up** *or* (*liter*) **forth** vomir. **3** *vi* vomir.
voodoo ['vuːduː] **1** *adj* vaudou *inv*. **2** *n* vaudou *m*. **3** *vt* envoûter.
voracious [və'reɪʃəs] *adj appetite, person* vorace; *reader* avide.
voraciously [və'reɪʃəslɪ] *adv eat* voracement, avec voracité; *read* avidement, avec voracité.
voracity [vɒ'ræsɪtɪ] *n* (*lit, fig*) voracité *f*.
vortex ['vɔːteks] *n* (*lit*) vortex *m*, tourbillon *m*; (*fig*) tourbillon.
votary ['vəʊtərɪ] *n* (*liter*) fervent(e) *m(f)* (*of* de).
vote [vəʊt] **1** *n* **(a)** (*expression of opinion*) vote *m*, suffrage *m*; (*franchise*) droit *m* de vote *or* de suffrage. **to give the ~ to the under twenty-ones** accorder le droit de vote aux moins de vingt-et-un ans; **~s for women!** droit de vote pour les femmes!; **to put to the ~** mettre au vote *or* aux voix; **to take a ~ (on)** procéder au vote (sur); **~ of censure** *or* **no confidence** motion *f* de censure; **to pass a ~ of censure** voter la censure; **~ of confidence** vote de confiance; **to ask for a ~ of confidence** poser la question de confiance; **to pass a ~ of confidence (in)** passer un vote de confiance (à l'égard de); **~ of thanks** discours *m* de remerciement.
(b) (*vote cast*) voix *f*, vote *m*. **to give one's ~ to** donner sa voix à, voter pour; **to win ~s** gagner des voix; **to count the ~s** compter les voix *or* les votes; (*Pol*) dépouiller le scrutin; **~ for/against sth** voix pour/contre qch; (*Pol*) **the Labour ~** les voix travaillistes; *V* **casting, floating** *etc.*
(c) (*money allotted*) crédits votés.
2 *vt* **(a)** (*approve*) *bill, treaty* voter. **the committee ~d to request a subsidy** le comité a voté une demande d'une subvention.
(b) (*elect*) élire. **he was ~d chairman** il a été élu président; (*fig*) **the group ~d her the best cook** le groupe l'a proclamée la meilleure cuisinière; **I ~* we go to the pictures** je propose qu'on aille au cinéma.
3 *vi* voter, donner sa voix (*for* pour, *against* contre); *[general election etc]* aller aux urnes, voter. **the country ~s in 3 weeks** les élections ont lieu dans 3 semaines; **to ~ Socialist/for the Socialists** voter socialiste/pour les socialistes.
vote down *vt sep* rejeter (*par le vote*).
vote in *vt sep law* adopter, voter; *person* élire.
vote out *vt sep amendment* ne pas voter, ne pas adopter, rejeter, repousser. **the M.P. was voted out by a large majority** le député a été battu aux élections à une forte majorité; **the electors voted the Conservative government out** les électeurs ont rejeté le gouvernement conservateur.
vote through *vt sep bill, motion* voter, ratifier.
voter ['vəʊtəʳ] *n* électeur *m*, -trice *f*.
voting ['vəʊtɪŋ] **1** *n* vote *m*; scrutin *m*. **the ~ went against him** le vote lui a été défavorable; **the ~ took place yesterday** le scrutin a eu lieu hier. **2** *cpd*: **voting booth** isoloir *m*; (*US*) **voting machine** machine *f* pour enregistrer les votes; **voting paper** bulletin *m* de vote.
votive ['vəʊtɪv] *adj* votif.
vouch [vaʊtʃ] *vi*: **to ~ for sb/sth** se porter garant de qn/qch, répondre de qn/qch; **to ~ for the truth of** garantir la vérité de.
voucher ['vaʊtʃəʳ] *n* **(a)** (*for cash, meals, petrol*) bon *m*; *V* **luncheon. (b)** (*receipt*) reçu *m*, récépissé *m*; (*for debt*) quittance *f*. **(c)** (*proof*) pièce justificative.
vouchsafe [vaʊtʃ'seɪf] *vt reply* accorder; *help* octroyer. (*frm*) **to ~ to do** accepter gracieusement de faire; (*pej*) condescendre à faire.
vow [vaʊ] **1** *n* vœu *m*, serment *m*. **to take a ~ to do** faire le vœu *or* le serment de faire; **to make a ~ (to do)** faire vœu (de faire); (*Rel*) **to take one's ~s** prononcer ses vœux; **~ of celibacy** vœu de célibat; *V* **break** *etc.*
2 *vt* jurer (*to do* de faire, *that* que); *obedience, loyalty* vouer. **to ~ vengeance on sb** jurer de se venger de qn.
vowel ['vaʊəl] **1** *n* voyelle *f*. **2** *cpd system, sound* vocalique. **vowel shift** mutation *f* vocalique.
voyage ['vɔɪɪdʒ] **1** *n* (*Naut*) voyage *m* par mer, traversée *f*; (*fig*) voyage. **to go on a ~** partir en voyage (par mer); **the ~ across the Channel** la traversée de la Manche; **the ~ out** le voyage d'aller; **the ~ back** *or* **home** le voyage de retour; **~ of discovery** voyage d'exploration.
2 *vt* (*Naut*) traverser, parcourir.
3 *vi* **(a)** (*Naut*) voyager par mer. **to ~ across** traverser.
(b) (*US Aviat*) voyager par avion.
voyager ['vɔɪədʒəʳ] *n* passager *m*, -ère *f*, voyageur *m*, -euse *f*.
voyeur [vwɑː'jɜːʳ] *n* voyeur *m*.
▲ **voyeurism** [vwɑː'jɜːrɪzəm] *n* voyeurisme *m*.
vulcanite ['vʌlkənaɪt] *n* ébonite *f*.
vulcanization [ˌvʌlkənaɪ'zeɪʃən] *n* vulcanisation *f*.
vulcanize ['vʌlkənaɪz] *vt* vulcaniser.
vulgar ['vʌlgəʳ] *adj* **(a)** (*pej: unrefined*) *person, action, language, clothes* vulgaire, grossier. **~ ostentation** ostentation grossière; **~ word** gros mot, grossièreté *f*.
(b) (††: *of the common people*) vulgaire, commun. **~ Latin** latin *m* vulgaire; **the ~ tongue** la langue commune.
(c) (*Math*) **~ fraction** fraction *f* ordinaire.
vulgarian [vʌl'geərɪən] *n* (*pej*) personne *f* vulgaire, parvenu *m*.
vulgarism ['vʌlgərɪzəm] *n* (*uneducated expression*) vulgarisme *m*; (*swearword*) gros mot, grossièreté *f*.
vulgarity [vʌl'gærɪtɪ] *n* vulgarité *f*, grossièreté *f*.
vulgarize ['vʌlgəraɪz] *vt* **(a)** (*make known*) vulgariser, populariser. **(b)** (*make coarse*) rendre vulgaire.
vulgarly ['vʌlgəlɪ] *adv* **(a)** (*generally*) vulgairement, communément. **(b)** (*coarsely*) vulgairement, grossièrement.
Vulgate ['vʌlgɪt] *n* Vulgate *f*.
vulnerability [ˌvʌlnərə'bɪlɪtɪ] *n* (*also Bridge*) vulnérabilité *f*.
vulnerable ['vʌlnərəbl] *adj* (*also Bridge*) vulnérable. **to find sb's ~ spot** trouver le point faible de qn.
vulture ['vʌltʃəʳ] *n* (*also fig*) vautour *m*.
vulva ['vʌlvə] *n* vulve *f*.
vying ['vaɪɪŋ] *n* rivalité *f*, concurrence *f*.

W

W, w ['dʌbljʊ] *n* (*letter*) W, w *m*.
wackyː ['wækɪ] *adj* (*US*) farfelu*, fou-fou* (*f* fofolle*).
wad [wɒd] **1** *n* **(a)** (*plug, ball*) *[cloth, paper]* tampon *m*; *[putty, chewing gum]* boulette *f*; (*for gun*) bourre *f*; *[straw]* bouchon *m*. **a ~ of cotton wool** un tampon d'ouate; **a ~ of tobacco** (*uncut*) une carotte de tabac; (*for chewing*) une chique de tabac.
(b) (*bundle*) *[papers, documents]* paquet *m*, tas *m*, pile *f*, (*tied together*) liasse *f*; *[banknotes]* liasse.
2 *vt* **(a)** (*also* **~ up**) *paper etc* faire un tampon de; *putty etc* faire une boulette de.
(b) *garment* doubler d'ouate, ouater; *quilt* rembourrer.
(c) (*also* **~ up**) *hole, crack* boucher avec un tampon *or* avec une boulette.
wadding ['wɒdɪŋ] *n* (*U*) (*raw cotton or felt; also for gun*) bourre *f*; (*gen: for lining or padding*) rembourrage *m*, capiton *m*; (*for garments*) ouate *f*.
waddle ['wɒdl] **1** *vi [duck]* se dandiner; *[person]* se dandiner, marcher comme un canard. **to ~ in/out/across** *etc* entrer/sortir/traverser *etc* en se dandinant. **2** *n* dandinement *m*.
wade [weɪd] **1** *vi* **(a) to ~ through water/mud** avancer *or* marcher *or* patauger dans l'eau/la boue; **to ~ through long grass** avancer *or* marcher dans l'herbe haute; **he ~d ashore** il a regagné la rive à pied; (*fig*) **to ~ into sb*** (*attack physically*) se jeter *or* tomber *or* se ruer sur qn; (*attack verbally*) tomber sur qn, prendre qn à partie; (*scold*) engueulerː qn; **to ~ into a meal*** attaquer un repas*; **I managed to ~ through his book*** j'ai réussi à lire son livre, mais ça a été laborieux; **it took me an hour to ~ through your essay*** il m'a fallu une heure pour venir à bout de votre dissertation; **he was wading through his homework*** il faisait ses devoirs lentement et méthodiquement.
(b) (*paddle: for fun*) barboter.
2 *vt stream* passer *or* traverser à gué.
wade inː *vi* (*in fight/argument etc*) se mettre de la partie (*dans une bagarre/dispute etc*).
wader ['weɪdəʳ] *n* (*boot*) cuissarde *f*, botte *f* de pêche; (*bird*) échassier *m*.
wadi ['wɒdɪ] *n* oued *m*.
wading ['weɪdɪŋ] **1** *n* (*U*) barbotage *m*, pataugeage *m*. **2** *cpd*: **wading bird** échassier *m*.
wafer ['weɪfəʳ] **1** *n* (*Culin*) gaufrette *f*; (*Rel*) (pain *m* d')hostie *f*; (*seal*) cachet *m* (*de papier rouge*).
2 *cpd*: **wafer-thin** mince comme du papier à cigarette *or* comme une pelure d'oignon.
wafery ['weɪfərɪ] *adj* = **wafer-thin**; *V* **wafer 2**.
waffle[1] ['wɒfl] *n* (*Culin*) gaufre *f*. **~ iron** gaufrier *m*.
waffle[2]* ['wɒfl] (*Brit*) **1** *n* (*U*) (*in conversation*) rabâchage *m*; (*in speech, book, essay*) remplissage *m*, délayage *m*, rabâchage. **there's too much ~ in this essay** il y a trop de remplissage dans cette dissertation, vous avez (*or* il a *etc*) trop allongé la sauce* dans cette dissertation.
2 *vi* (*in conversation*) parler pour ne rien dire, parler dans le vague; (*in speech, book, essay*) faire du remplissage, allonger la sauce*. **he was waffling on about the troubles he'd had** il parlait interminablement de ses problèmes.
waft [wɑːft] **1** *vt smell, sound* porter, apporter; (*also* **~ along**) *boat* faire avancer, pousser; *clouds* faire glisser *or* avancer. **2** *vi [sounds, smell]* flotter; *[corn etc]* ondoyer. **3** *n [air, scent]* (petite) bouffée *f*.
wag[1] [wæg] **1** *vt* agiter, remuer. **the dog ~ged its tail (at me)** le chien a agité *or* remué la queue (en me voyant); **he ~ged his finger/his pencil at me** il a agité le doigt/son crayon dans ma direction; **to ~ one's head** hocher la tête.
2 *vi [tail]* remuer, frétiller. **his tongue never stops ~ging** il a la langue bien pendue, il ne s'arrête jamais de bavarder; **the news set tongues ~ging** la nouvelle a fait marcher les langues *or* a fait jaser (les gens).
3 *n [tail]* remuement *m*, frétillement *m*. **with a ~ of its tail** en remuant *or* agitant la queue.
4 *cpd*: (*Orn*) **wagtail** hoche-queue *m* *or* hochequeue *m*, bergeronnette *f*, lavandière *f*.
wag[2] [wæg] *n* (*joker*) plaisantin *m*, farceur *m*, -euse *f*.
wage [weɪdʒ] **1** *n* salaire *m*, paye *f* *or* paie *f*; *[domestic servant]* gages *mpl*. **hourly/weekly ~** salaire horaire/hebdomadaire; **I've lost 2 days' ~s** j'ai perdu 2 jours de salaire *or* de paye; **his week's ~s** son salaire *or* sa paye de la semaine; **his ~ is** *or* **his ~s are £45 per week** il touche un salaire de 45 livres par semaine, il gagne *or* est payé 45 livres par semaine; **he gets a good ~** il est bien payé, il a un bon salaire; (*Bible*) **the ~s of sin is death** la mort est le salaire du péché; *V* **living**.
2 *cpd*: **wage demand** = **wage(s) claim**; (*Ind etc*) **wage earner** salarié(e) *m(f)*; **she is the family wage earner** c'est elle qui fait vivre sa famille *or* qui est le soutien de sa famille; **wage freeze** blocage *m* des salaires; **wage increase** augmentation *f* *or* hausse *f* de salaire; **wage packet** (*lit*) enveloppe *f* de paye; (*fig*) paye *f* *or* paie *f*; **wage scale** échelle *f* des salaires; **wage(s) claim** demande *f* de révision de salaire; **wages clerk** employé(e) *m(f)* aux salaires, ≃ aide-comptable *mf*; **wages slip** bulletin *m* de salaire, fiche *f* de paye; (*US Ind*) **wage worker** = **wage earner**.
3 *vt*: **to ~ war** faire la guerre (*against* à, contre); **to ~ a campaign** partir en campagne (*against* contre), lancer une campagne (*for* pour).
wager ['weɪdʒəʳ] **1** *vt* parier (*on* sur, *that* que). **I'll ~ you £10 that ...** je vous parie 10 livres que ... . **2** *n* pari *m*. **to lay a ~** faire un pari.
waggish ['wægɪʃ] *adj* badin, facétieux.
waggishly ['wægɪʃlɪ] *adv* d'une manière facétieuse, d'un ton facétieux *or* badin.
waggle ['wægl] **1** *vt pencil, branch* agiter; *loose screw, button* faire jouer. **it was waggling its tail** il agitait *or* remuait la queue, il frétillait de la queue; **to ~ one's hips** tortiller des hanches; **my finger hurts if you ~ it like that** j'ai mal quand vous me tortillez le doigt comme ça.
2 *vi [tail]* remuer, frétiller; *[tooth]* branler.
3 *n*: **to give sth a ~** agiter *or* remuer *or* tripoter *or* tortiller *or* faire jouer qch.
waggon ['wægən] **1** *n* (*horse- or ox-drawn*) chariot *m*; (*truck*) camion *m*; (*Brit Rail*) wagon *m* (de marchandises); (*tea trolley*) table roulante, chariot. (*fig*) **to go/be on the ~*** ne plus/ne pas boire (d'alcool), se mettre/être au régime sec; *V* **station** *etc*.
2 *cpd*: **waggonload** (*Agr*) charretée *f*; (*Rail*) wagon *m*; (*US Hist*) **waggon train** convoi *m* de chariots.
waggoner ['wægənəʳ] *n* roulier *m*, charretier *m*.
waggonette [ˌwægə'net] *n* break *m*.
Wagnerian [vɑːg'nɪərɪən] **1** *adj* wagnérien. **2** *n* Wagnérien(ne) *m(f)*.
wagon ['wægən] *n* (*esp US*) = **waggon**.
waif [weɪf] *n* enfant *mf* misérable; (*homeless*) enfant abandonné(e). **~s and strays** enfants abandonnés.
wail [weɪl] **1** *n [person]* gémissement *m*, plainte *f*; *[baby]* vagissement *m*; *[wind]* gémissement, plainte; *[siren]* hurlement *m*. **to give a ~** pousser un gémissement *or* un vagissement, gémir, vagir.
2 *vi [person]* gémir, pousser un *or* des gémissement(s); (*cry*) pleurer; (*whine*) pleurnicher; *[baby]* vagir; *[wind]* gémir; *[siren]* hurler; *[bagpipes etc]* gémir.
wailing ['weɪlɪŋ] **1** *n* (*U*: *V* **wail 1**) gémissements *mpl*; plaintes *fpl*; vagissements *mpl*; hurlements *mpl*. **2** *adj voice, person* gémissant; *sound* plaintif. **the W~ Wall** le mur des Lamentations.
wain [weɪn] *n* (*liter*) chariot *m*. (*Astron*) **Charles's W~** le Chariot de David, la Grande Ourse.
wainscot ['weɪnskət] *n* lambris *m* (*en bois*).
wainscoting ['weɪnskətɪŋ] *n* lambrissage *m* (*en bois*).
waist [weɪst] **1** *n* **(a)** (*Anat, Dress*) taille *f*, ceinture *f*. **he put his arm round her ~** il l'a prise par la taille; **she measures 70 cm round the ~** elle fait 70 cm de tour de taille; **they were stripped to the ~** ils étaient nus jusqu'à la ceinture, ils étaient torse nu; **he was up to the** *or* **his ~ in water** l'eau lui arrivait à la ceinture *or* à mi-corps.
(b) (*fig*) étranglement *m*, resserrement *m*; *[violin]* partie resserrée de la table.
(c) (*US*) (*blouse*) corsage *m*, blouse *f*; (*bodice*) corsage, haut *m*.
2 *vt jacket etc* cintrer.
3 *cpd*: **waistband** ceinture *f* (*de jupe etc*); (*Brit*) **waistcoat** gilet *m*; **waistline** taille *f*; (*hum*) **I've got to think of my waistline** je dois faire attention à ma ligne; **waist measurement, waist size** tour *m* de taille.
-waisted ['weɪstɪd] *adj ending in cpds*: **to be slim-waisted** avoir la taille fine; **high-/low-waisted dress** robe *f* à taille haute/basse; *V* **shirt**.
wait [weɪt] **1** *n* **(a)** attente *f*. **you'll have a 3-hour ~** vous aurez 3 heures d'attente, vous devrez attendre (pendant) 3 heures; **it was a long ~** il a fallu attendre longtemps, l'attente a été longue; **there was a 20-minute ~ between trains** il y avait 20 minutes de battement *or* d'attente entre les trains; (*on coach journey etc*) **there is a half-hour ~ at Leeds** il y a un arrêt d'une demi-heure *or* une demi-heure d'arrêt à Leeds; **during the ~ between the performances** pendant le battement *or* la pause entre les représentations; **to be** *or* **lie in ~** guetter, être à l'affût; **to be** *or* **lie in ~ for sb** *[huntsman, lion]* guetter qn; *[bandits, guerrillas]* dresser un guet-apens *or* une embuscade à qn; **the journalists lay in ~ for him as he left the theatre** les journalistes l'attendaient (au passage) à sa sortie du théâtre *or* le guettaient à sa sortie du théâtre.
(b) (*Brit*) **the ~s** les chanteurs *mpl* de Noël (*qui vont de porte en porte*).
2 *vi* **(a)** attendre. **to ~ for sb/sth** attendre qn/qch; **to ~ for sb to leave, to ~ until sb leaves** attendre le départ de qn, attendre que qn parte; **~ till you're old enough** attends d'être assez grand; **can you ~ till 10 o'clock?** pouvez-vous attendre (jusqu'à) 10 heures?; **I ~ed 2 hours** j'ai attendu (pendant) 2 heures; **~ a moment!** (attendez) un instant! *or* une minute!; (*interrupting, querying*) minute!*; **just you ~!** tu vas voir ce

que tu vas voir!; (*threateningly*) tu ne perds rien pour attendre!; **just ~ till your father finds out!** attends un peu que ton père apprenne ça!; **~ and see!** attends (voir)!; **we'll just have to ~ and see** il va falloir attendre, il va falloir voir venir; **~ and see what happens next** attendez voir ce qui va se passer; **to keep sb ~ing** faire attendre qn; **don't keep us ~ing** ne te fais pas attendre, ne nous fais pas attendre; **I was kept ~ing in the corridor** on m'a fait attendre dans le couloir, j'ai fait le pied de grue dans le couloir; (*loc*) **everything comes to him who ~s** tout vient à point à qui sait attendre (*Prov*); **he didn't ~ to be told twice** il ne se l'est pas fait dire deux fois; **that was worth ~ing for** cela valait la peine d'attendre; **I just can't ~ for next Saturday!** je meurs d'impatience *or* d'envie d'en être à samedi prochain!; **I can't ~ to see him again!** (*longingly*) je meurs d'envie de le revoir!; **I can't ~ for the day when this happens** je rêve du jour où cela arrivera; **the Conservatives can't ~ to reverse this policy** les conservateurs brûlent en de révoquer cette politique; **parcel ~ing to be collected** colis *m* en souffrance; **all that can ~ till tomorrow** tout cela peut attendre jusqu'à demain.

(b) servir. **to ~ (at table)** servir à table, faire le service.

3 *vt* **(a)** *signal, orders, one's turn, chance* attendre. **to ~ one's time** attendre son heure (*to do* pour faire); **we'll ~ lunch for you** nous vous attendrons pour nous mettre à table.

(b) (*US*) **to ~ table** servir à table, faire le service.

wait about, wait around *vi* attendre; (*loiter*) traîner. **to wait about for sb** attendre qn, faire le pied de grue pour qn; **the job involves a lot of waiting about** on perd beaucoup de temps à attendre dans ce métier; **you can't expect him to wait about all day while you ...** tu ne peux pas exiger qu'il traîne (*subj*) toute la journée à t'attendre pendant que tu ... .

wait behind *vi* rester. **to wait behind for sb** rester pour attendre qn.

wait in *vi* rester à la maison (*for sb* pour attendre qn).

wait on *vt fus* **(a)** *[servant]* servir, être de service auprès de; (*at table*) servir. **I'm not here to wait on him!** je ne suis pas sa bonne! (*or* son valet de chambre!); **she waits on him hand and foot** elle est aux petits soins pour lui.

(b) (*frm*) = **wait upon a.**

wait out *vt sep* rester jusqu'à la fin *or* jusqu'au bout de.

wait up *vi* veiller, ne pas se coucher. **we waited up till 2 o'clock** nous avons veillé *or* attendu jusqu'à 2 heures, nous ne nous sommes pas couchés avant 2 heures; **she always waits up for him** elle attend toujours qu'il rentre (*subj*) pour se coucher, elle ne se couche jamais avant qu'il ne soit rentré; **don't wait up for me** couchez-vous sans m'attendre; **you can wait up to see the programme** tu peux voir le programme avant de te coucher, tu peux rester debout pour voir le programme.

wait upon *vt fus* **(a)** (*frm*) *[ambassador, envoy etc]* présenter ses respects à.

(b) = **wait on a.**

waiter ['weɪtə^r] *n* garçon *m* (de café), serveur *m*. **~!** garçon!; *V* **dumb, head, wine.**

waiting ['weɪtɪŋ] **1** *n* (*U*) attente *f*. (*Aut*) **'no ~'** 'stationnement strictement interdit'; **all this ~!** ce qu'on attend!, dire qu'il faut attendre si longtemps!; (*frm*) **to be in ~ on sb** être attaché au service de qn; *V* **lady.**

2 *adj* qui attend.

3 *cpd*: (*fig*) **to play a waiting game** (*gen*) attendre son heure; (*in diplomacy, negotiations etc*) mener une politique d'attente, se conduire en attentiste; **waiting list** liste *f* d'attente; **waiting room** (*Rail*) salle *f* d'attente; *[office, surgery etc]* salon *m* d'attente.

waitress ['weɪtrɪs] *n* serveuse *f*. **~!** Mademoiselle (s'il vous plaît)!

waive [weɪv] *vt* (*Jur*) *claim, right, privilege* renoncer à, abandonner; *condition, age limit* ne pas insister sur, abandonner; *principle* déroger à, renoncer à.

waiver ['weɪvə^r] *n* (*Jur*: *V* **waive**) renonciation *f* (*of* à); abandon *m* (*of* de).

wake[1] [weɪk] *n* (*Naut*) sillage *m*, eaux *fpl*. (*fig*) **in the ~ of the storm** à la suite de l'orage, après l'orage; **in the ~ of the army** dans le sillage *or* sur les traces de l'armée; **the war brought famine in its ~** la guerre a amené la famine dans son sillage; **to follow in sb's ~** marcher sur les traces de qn *or* dans le sillage de qn.

wake[2] [weɪk] (*vb*: *pret* **woke, waked,** *ptp* **waked, woken, woke**) **1** *n* **(a)** (*over corpse*) veillée *f* mortuaire.

(b) (*N Engl*) **W~s (Week)** *semaine f de congé annuel dans le nord de l'Angleterre.*

2 *vi* (*also* **~ up**) se réveiller, s'éveiller (*from* de). **~ up!** réveille-toi!; (**fig*: *think what you're doing*) mais enfin réveille-toi! *or* ouvre les yeux!; **to ~ from sleep** se réveiller, s'éveiller, sortir du sommeil; **to ~ (up) from a nightmare** (*lit*) se réveiller d'un cauchemar; (*fig*) sortir d'un cauchemar; **she woke (up) to find them gone** en se réveillant *or* à son réveil elle s'est aperçue qu'ils étaient partis; **he woke up (to find himself) in prison** il s'est réveillé en prison; **he woke up to find himself rich** à son réveil il était riche; (*fig*) **to ~ (up) to sth** prendre conscience de *or* se rendre compte de *or* s'apercevoir de qch; **to ~ (up) from one's illusions** revenir de ses illusions; (*fig*) **he suddenly woke up* and started to work hard** il s'est tout à coup réveillé *or* remué et s'est mis à travailler dur; (*fig*) **he suddenly woke up* and realized that ...** tout à coup ses yeux se sont ouverts et il s'est rendu compte que ... .

3 *vt* (*also* **~ up**) *person* réveiller (*from* de), tirer du sommeil; (*fig*) *memories* (r)éveiller, ranimer; *desires* éveiller, provoquer, exciter. **a noise that would ~ the dead** un bruit à réveiller les morts.

wakeful ['weɪkfʊl] *adj person* (*awake*) éveillé, qui ne dort pas; (*alert*) vigilant; *hours etc* sans sommeil. **to have** *or* **spend a ~ night** passer une nuit blanche.

wakefulness ['weɪkfʊlnɪs] *n* (*sleeplessness*) insomnie *f*; (*watchfulness*) vigilance *f*.

waken ['weɪkən] *vti* = **wake**[2].

wakey-wakey‡ ['weɪkɪ'weɪkɪ] *excl* réveillez-vous!, debout!

waking ['weɪkɪŋ] **1** *adj*: **in one's ~ hours** pendant les heures de veille; **he devoted all his ~ hours to ...** il consacrait chaque heure de sa journée à ...; **~ or sleeping, he ...** (qu'il soit) éveillé ou endormi, il ... .

2 *n* (état *m* de) veille *f*. **between ~ and sleeping** entre la veille et le sommeil, dans un (état de) demi-sommeil.

wale [weɪl] *n* (*US*) = **weal**[1].

Wales [weɪlz] *n* pays *m* de Galles. **North/South ~** le Nord/le Sud du pays de Galles; (*Brit*) **Secretary of State for ~** ministre *m* chargé du pays de Galles; *V* **prince.**

walk [wɔːk] **1** *n* **(a)** promenade *f*; (*long*) randonnée *f*; (*Sport*) épreuve *f* de marche. **to go for a ~, to take** *or* **have a ~** se promener, faire une promenade, (*shorter*) faire un tour; **let's have a little ~** promenons-nous un peu, allons faire un petit tour; **he had a long ~** il s'est promené longtemps, il a fait une grande promenade, il a fait une vraie randonnée; **we went on a long ~ to see the castle** nous avons fait une excursion (à pied) pour visiter le château; **to take sb for a ~** emmener qn se promener *or* en promenade; **to take the dog for a ~** promener le chien; **he did a 10-km ~ each day** il faisait chaque jour une promenade de 10 km; **the house is 10 minutes' ~ from here** la maison est à 10 minutes de marche d'ici *or* à 10 minutes à pied d'ici; **it's only a short ~ to the shops** il n'y a pas loin à marcher jusqu'aux magasins, il n'y a pas loin pour aller aux magasins; **there's a nice ~ by the river** il y a une jolie promenade à faire le long de la rivière; *V* **sponsor.**

(b) (*gait*) démarche *f*, façon *f* de marcher. **I knew him by his ~** je l'ai reconnu à sa démarche *or* à sa façon de marcher; **he slowed down to a ~** il a ralenti pour aller au pas; **you've plenty of time to get there at a ~** vous avez tout le temps qu'il faut pour y arriver sans courir; **he went at a quick ~** il marchait d'un pas rapide.

(c) (*avenue*) avenue *f*, promenade *f*; (*path in garden*) allée *f*; (*path in country*) chemin *m*, sentier *m*; (*US*: *sidewalk*) trottoir *m*. (*fig*) **from all ~s of life** de toutes conditions sociales.

2 *cpd*: **walkabout*** (*Australia*) voyage *m* (d'aborigène) dans le désert; (*gen*: *of president, celebrity*) bain *m* de foule; *[president, celebrity]* **to go** *or* **be on a walkabout*** prendre un bain de foule; (*US*) **walkaway* (victory** *or* **win)** victoire *f* dans un fauteuil*; **walk-in** *wardrobe, cupboard, larder* de plain-pied; (*Theat etc*) **walk(ing)-on part** rôle *m* de figurant(e); **walkout** (*strike*) grève *f* surprise; (*from meeting, lecture etc*) départ *m* (en signe de protestation); **to stage a walkout** *[workers]* faire une grève surprise; *[students, delegates etc]* partir (en signe de protestation); (*Racing*) **walkover** walk-over *m*; (*fig*) **it was a walkover!*** (*game etc*) c'était une victoire facile! *or* dans un fauteuil!*; (*exam etc*) c'était un jeu d'enfant, c'était simple comme bonjour; (*Sport*) **it was a walkover for Smith*** Smith a gagné dans un fauteuil* *or* haut la main; (*US*) **walk-up** (*house*) immeuble *m* sans ascenseur; (*apartment*) appartement *m* dans un immeuble sans ascenseur; (*US*) **walkway** passage *m* pour piétons.

3 *vi* **(a)** (*gen*) marcher; (*not run*) aller au pas, ne pas courir. **I haven't ~ed since the accident** je n'ai pas (re)marché depuis l'accident; **I can't ~ as I used to** je n'ai plus mes jambes d'autrefois; (*loc*) **you must ~ before you can run** on apprend petit à petit, c'est en forgeant qu'on devient forgeron (*Prov*); **to ~ in one's sleep** être somnambule, marcher en dormant; **don't ~ on the new rug** ne marche pas sur le nouveau tapis; **to ~ across/down** *etc* traverser/descendre *etc* (en marchant *or* sans courir); **he ~ed up/down the stairs** (*gen*) il a monté/descendu l'escalier; (*didn't run*) il a monté/descendu l'escalier sans courir; **he was ~ing up and down** il marchait de long en large, il faisait les cent pas; **you should always WALK across the road** on ne doit jamais traverser la rue en courant; **~, don't run** ne cours pas; (*fig*) **my pen seems to have ~ed*** mon stylo a fichu le camp*.

(b) (*not ride or drive*) aller à pied; (*go for a ~*) se promener, faire une promenade; *[ghost]* apparaître. **they ~ed all the way to London** ils ont fait tout le chemin à pied jusqu'à Londres; **I always ~ home** je rentre toujours à pied; **shall we ~ a little?** si nous faisions quelques pas?, si nous marchions un peu?, si nous nous promenions un peu?; **they were out ~ing** ils étaient partis se promener (à pied).

4 *vt* **(a)** *distance* faire à pied. **he ~s 5 km every day** il fait 5 km (de marche) à pied par jour; **you can ~ it in a couple of minutes** vous y serez en deux minutes à pied, à pied cela vous prendra deux minutes, à pied vous en avez pour deux minutes; **he ~ed it in 10 minutes** il l'a fait à pied en 10 minutes, il lui a fallu 10 minutes à pied; (*fig*: *it was easy*) **he ~ed it*** cela a été un jeu d'enfant pour lui.

(b) parcourir. **to ~ the streets** se promener dans les rues; (*to fill in time*) flâner dans les rues; (*from poverty*) errer dans les rues, battre le pavé; *[prostitute]* faire le trottoir; **he ~ed the town looking for a dentist** il a parcouru la ville en tous sens à la recherche d'un dentiste; **they ~ed the countryside in search of ...** ils ont battu la campagne à la recherche de ...; **to ~ the plank** subir le supplice de la planche (*sur un bateau de pirates*); **the policeman was ~ing his beat** l'agent de police faisait sa ronde; **I've ~ed this road many times** j'ai pris cette route (à pied) bien des fois.

(c) (*cause to ~*) *person* faire marcher, faire se promener, promener; *dog* promener; *horse* conduire à pied. **I ~ed him round the garden till he was calmer** je me suis promené avec lui dans le jardin jusqu'à ce qu'il se calme (*subj*); **the nurse ~ed**

him down the ward to exercise his legs l'infirmière l'a fait marcher *or* se promener dans la salle pour qu'il s'exerce (*subj*) les jambes; **I ~ed him round Paris** je l'ai promené dans Paris; **he seized my arm and ~ed me across the room** il m'a pris par le bras et m'a fait traverser la pièce; **to ~ sb in/out** *etc* faire entrer/sortir *etc* qn; **I'll ~ you to the station** je vais vous accompagner (à pied) à la gare; **to ~ sb home** raccompagner qn; **I had to ~ my cycle home** j'ai dû pousser ma bicyclette jusqu'à la maison; **they ~ed him off his feet** ils l'ont tellement fait marcher qu'il ne tenait plus debout.

walk about 1 *vi* aller et venir, se promener, circuler.

2 walkabout* *n V* **walk 2.**

walk across *vi* (*over bridge etc*) traverser. **to walk across to sb** s'approcher de qn, se diriger vers qn.

walk around *vi* = **walk about 1.**

walk away 1 *vi* partir, filer*. **to walk away from sb** s'éloigner de qn, quitter qn; **he walked away with the wrong coat** il s'est trompé de manteau en partant.

2 walkaway* *n, adj V* **walk 2.**

walk away with* *vt fus* **(a)** (*win easily*) *game, prize* gagner haut la main. **I did the work but he walked away with all the credit** c'est moi qui ai fait tout le travail et c'est lui qui a reçu tous les éloges.

(b) (*steal*) barboter‡, faucher*.

walk back *vi* revenir, rentrer, retourner; (*specifically on foot*) revenir *or* rentrer *or* retourner à pied.

walk in 1 *vi* entrer. **'please walk in'** 'prière d'entrer', 'entrez sans frapper'; **who should walk in but Paul!** et voilà que Paul est entré (à ce moment-là)!, et qui entre sur ces entrefaites? Paul!; **he just walked in and took all my jewels** il n'a eu qu'à (se donner la peine d')entrer pour prendre tous mes bijoux; **he just walked in and gave me the sack** il est entré sans crier gare et m'a annoncé qu'il me mettait à la porte.

2 walk-in *adj V* **walk 2.**

walk into *vt fus* **(a)** *trap, ambush* tomber dans. **you really walked into that one!*** tu es vraiment tombé *or* tu as vraiment donné dans le panneau!; **he wondered what he had walked into** il se demandait dans quelle galère il s'était laissé entraîner.

(b) (*bump into*) *person, lamppost, table* se cogner à, rentrer dans*; (**: meet*) tomber sur.

walk off 1 *vi* = **walk away 1.**

2 *vt sep excess weight* perdre en marchant. **to walk off a headache** prendre l'air *or* faire une promenade pour se débarrasser d'un mal de tête.

walk off with* *vt fus* = **walk away with*.**

walk on 1 *vi* (*Theat*) être figurant(e), jouer les utilités.

2 walk(ing)-on *adj V* **walk 2.**

3 walker-on *n V* **walker 2.**

walk out 1 *vi* (*go out*) sortir; (*go away*) partir; (*from conference etc*) partir (en signe de protestation); (*go on strike*) se mettre en grève, faire grève. (*fig*) **you can't walk out now!** tu ne peux pas partir comme ça!, tu ne peux pas tout laisser tomber* comme ça!; **her husband has walked out** son mari l'a quittée *or* plaquée‡; **they walked out of the discussion** ils ont quitté la séance de discussion (en signe de protestation).

2 walkout *n V* **walk 2.**

walk out on* *vt fus boyfriend, business partner* laisser tomber*, plaquer‡.

walk out with† *vt fus* (*Brit: court*) fréquenter†.

walk over 1 *vi* passer (à pied), faire un saut (à pied). **I'll walk over tomorrow morning** j'y passerai *or* j'y ferai un saut (à pied) demain matin; **he walked over to me and said ...** il s'est approché de moi et a dit ... .

2 *vt fus* (*) **(a)** (*defeat easily*) battre haut la main.

(b) (*treat badly: also* **walk all over**) marcher sur les pieds de. **she lets him walk all over her** elle se laisse marcher sur les pieds (sans jamais lui faire de reproche).

3 walkover *n V* **walk 2.**

walk up 1 *vi* (*go upstairs etc*) monter; (*approach*) s'approcher (*to sb* de qn). (*at fair etc*) **walk up, walk up!** approchez, approchez!

2 walk-up *n V* **walk 2.**

walker ['wɔːkəʳ] **1** *n* **(a)** (*esp Sport*) marcheur *m*, -euse *f*; (*for pleasure*) promeneur *m*, -euse *f*. **he's a good/bad ~** il est bon/mauvais marcheur; **he's a fast ~** il marche vite; *V* **sleep, street** *etc*.

(b) (*support frame*) (*for convalescents etc*) déambulateur *m*; (*for babies*) trotte-bébé *m*.

2 *cpd*: (*Theat*) **walker-on** figurant(e) *m(f)*, comparse *mf*.

walkie-talkie ['wɔːkɪ'tɔːkɪ] *n* talkie-walkie *m*.

walking ['wɔːkɪŋ] **1** *n* (*U*) marche *f* à pied, promenade(s) *f(pl)* (à pied); (*as a constitutional*) footing *m* (*U*); *V* **sleep** *etc*.

2 *adj* ambulant. (*Mil*) **the ~ wounded** les blessés capables de marcher; **he is a ~ encyclopedia** c'est une encyclopédie vivante; **he is a ~ miracle** c'est un miracle ambulant, il revient de loin.

3 *cpd*: **it is within walking distance (of the house)** on peut facilement y aller à pied (de la maison); **we had a walking holiday last year** l'année dernière comme vacances nous avons fait un voyage à pied; (*Theat*) **walking-on** *adj V* **walk 2**; **at a walking pace** au pas; (*US*) **to give sb his walking papers*** renvoyer qn, mettre *or* flanquer* qn à la porte; **walking race** épreuve *f* de marche; **walking shoes** chaussures *fpl* de marche; **walking stick** canne *f*; **to be on a walking tour** *or* **trip** faire une longue randonnée à pied.

wall [wɔːl] **1** *n* (*gen*) mur *m* (*also fig*); (*interior; also of trench, tunnel*) paroi *f*; *[dam]* mur; (*round garden, field*) mur (de clôture); (*round city, castle etc*) murs, remparts *mpl*, murailles *fpl*; (*Anat*) paroi; *[tyre]* flanc *m*; (*fig: of smoke, mountains etc*) muraille *f*. **within the (city) ~s** dans les murs, dans la ville; **the Great W~ of China** la grande muraille de Chine; **the Berlin W~** le mur de Berlin; **the north ~ of the Eiger** la face nord *or* la paroi nord de l'Eiger; (*Econ*) **a high tariff ~** une barrière douanière élevée; (*loc*) **~s have ears** les murs ont des oreilles; *[prisoner]* **to go over the ~** s'évader, faire la belle‡; (*fig*) **to go to the ~** *[person]* céder le pas; *[thing, plan, activity]* disparaître, être sacrifié; **it's always the weakest to the ~** ce sont toujours les plus faibles qui écopent; **it is a case of the weakest to the ~** les plus faibles doivent céder le pas; (*fig*) **he had his back to the ~, he was up against the ~** il avait le dos au mur, il était acculé; **to get sb up against the ~, to drive** *or* **push sb to the ~** acculer qn, mettre qn au pied du mur; (*fig*) **to bang** *or* **knock** *or* **beat one's head against a (brick) ~** se cogner *or* se taper la tête contre les murs; (*fig*) **to come up against a (blank) ~** se heurter à un mur; **to drive** *or* **send sb up the ~*** rendre qn dingue‡, en faire voir de toutes les couleurs* à qn; *V* **party.**

2 *cpd decoration, clock, map* mural. **wall bars** espalier *m* (*pour exercices de gymnastique*); (*US*) **wallboard** plaque *f* de plâtre; **wall chart** planche murale (*gravure*); **wall cupboard** placard mural *or* suspendu; **wall-eyed** qui louche, qui a un œil qui dit zut à l'autre*; (*Bot*) **wallflower** giroflée *f*; (*fig*) **to be a wallflower** faire tapisserie; **wall lamp, wall light** applique *f* (*lampe*); **wall lighting** éclairage *m* par appliques; **wallpaper** (*n*) papier peint; (*vt*) tapisser (de papier peint); (*Elec*) **wall socket** prise *f* (murale); **to carpet sth wall to wall** recouvrir qch de moquette; **wall-to-wall carpeting** moquette *f*.

3 *vt garden* entourer d'un mur, construire un mur autour de; *city* fortifier, entourer de murs *or* de remparts. **~ed garden** jardin clos; **~ed town** ville fortifiée.

wall in *vt sep garden etc* entourer d'un mur.

wall off *vt sep plot of land* séparer par un mur.

wall up *vt sep doorway, window* murer, condamner; *person, relics* murer, emmurer.

wallaby ['wɒləbɪ] *n* wallaby *m*.

wallah ['wɒlə] *n* (*Hist: Anglo-Indian*) ≈ chaouch *m*; (‡†) type* *m*.

wallet ['wɒlɪt] *n* portefeuille *m*; (††: *of pilgrims etc*) besace *f*.

Walloon [wɒ'luːn] **1** *adj* wallon. **2** *n* **(a)** Wallon(ne) *m(f)*. **(b)** (*Ling*) wallon *m*.

wallop ['wɒləp] **1** *n* **(a)** (*: *in fight, as punishment*) coup *m*, beigne‡ *f*, torgnole‡ *f*; (*in accident*) coup, gnon‡ *m*; (*sound*) fracas *m*, boucan* *m*. **to give sb a ~** flanquer une beigne‡ *or* une torgnole‡ à qn; **~!** vlan!; **it hit the floor with a ~** vlan! c'est tombé par terre, c'est tombé par terre avec un grand fracas.

(b) (‡: *speed*) **to go at a fair ~** aller à toute pompe* *or* à fond de train.

(c) (*Brit*‡: *beer*) bière *f*.

2 *vt* (*) *person* rosser*, cogner*; *ball, object* taper sur, donner un *or* des grand(s) coup(s) dans.

3 *adv*: **he went ~ into the wall*** il est rentré* en plein dans le mur.

walloping‡ ['wɒləpɪŋ] **1** *adj* sacré* (*before n*), formidable, phénoménal. **~ big** vachement grand‡.

2 *n* raclée* *f*, rossée* *f*. **to give sb a ~** (*punish*) flanquer une raclée* *or* une rossée* à qn; (*Sport etc: beat*) enfoncer* qn, battre qn à plate(s) couture(s).

wallow ['wɒləʊ] **1** *vi [person, animal]* se vautrer (*in* dans); *[ship]* être ballotté; (*fig*) (*in vice, sin*) se vautrer (*in* dans); (*in self-pity etc*) se complaire (*in* à). **2** *n* mare bourbeuse.

walnut ['wɔːlnʌt] **1** *n* noix *f*; (*also* **~ tree**) noyer *m*; (*U: wood*) noyer. **2** *cpd table etc* de *or* en noyer; *chocolate* aux noix; *oil* de noix.

walrus ['wɔːlrəs] *n* morse *m* (*Zool*). (*hum*) **~ moustache** moustache *f* à la gauloise.

waltz [wɔːlts] **1** *n* valse *f*.

2 *vi* valser, danser la valse. (*fig: move gaily*) **to ~ in/out** *etc* entrer/sortir *etc* d'un pas joyeux *or* dansant; **she ~ed in without even knocking*** elle a fait irruption sans même frapper; **he ~ed off with the prize*** il a gagné le prix haut la main.

3 *vt*: **he ~ed her round the room** il l'a entraînée dans une valse tout autour de la pièce; (*fig: in delight etc*) il s'est mis à danser de joie avec elle.

wampum ['wɒmpəm] *n* wampum *m*.

wan [wɒn] *adj complexion, sky, light* pâle, blême, blafard; *person, look* triste; *smile* pâle, faible. *[sky etc]* **to grow ~** pâlir, blêmir.

wand [wɒnd] *n [conjurer, fairy]* baguette *f* (magique); *[usher, steward, sheriff]* verge *f*, bâton *m*.

wander ['wɒndəʳ] **1** *n* tour *m*, balade* *f*. **to go for a ~ around the town/the shops** aller faire un tour en ville/dans les magasins.

2 *cpd*: **wanderlust** envie *f* de voir le monde, bougeotte* *f*.

3 *vi* **(a)** *[person]* errer, aller sans but; (*for pleasure*) flâner; *[thoughts]* errer, vagabonder, vaguer; *[river, road]* serpenter, faire des méandres. **he ~ed through the streets** il errait *or* allait sans but *or* flânait de par les rues, il se promenait au hasard des rues; **his glance ~ed round the room** son regard errait dans la pièce.

(b) (*stray*) s'égarer. **he ~ed off the path** il s'est écarté du chemin, il s'est égaré; **to ~ from the subject** s'écarter du sujet; **his eyes ~ed from the page** son regard distrait s'est écarté de la page; **his thoughts ~ed back to his youth** ses pensées se sont égarées *or* distraitement reportées à sa jeunesse; **his attention ~ed** il était distrait, il n'arrivait pas à fixer son attention *or* à se concentrer; **sorry, my mind was ~ing** excusez-moi, j'étais distrait; **his mind ~ed to the day when ...** il repensa par hasard au jour où ...; (*pej*) **his mind is ~ing, his wits are ~ing, he's ~ing*** (*from fever*) il délire, il divague; (*from old age*) il divague, il déraille*; **don't take any notice of what he says, he's just ~ing*** ne faites pas attention à ce qu'il dit, il radote.

(c) (*go casually*) **to ~ in/out/away** *etc* entrer/sortir/partir *etc* sans se presser *or* d'un pas nonchalant; **they ~ed round the shop** ils ont flâné dans le magasin; **let's ~ down to the café** descendons tranquillement *or* tout doucement au café.

4 *vt* parcourir au hasard, errer dans. **to ~ the streets** aller au hasard des rues, errer dans les rues; **to ~ the hills/the countryside** se promener au hasard *or* errer dans les collines/dans la campagne; **to ~ the world** courir le monde, rouler sa bosse*.

wander about, wander around *vi (aimlessly)* aller sans but, se promener au hasard, errer; *(casually)* aller sans se presser *or* d'un pas nonchalant, flâner.

wanderer ['wɒndərəʳ] *n* vagabond(e) *m(f)* *(also pej)*.

wandering ['wɒndərɪŋ] **1** *adj way of life, person* errant, vagabond; *river, road* qui serpente, en lacets; *tribe* nomade; *glance* errant, distrait; *imagination, thoughts* vagabond; *(pej) thoughts, speech* délirant. **the W~ Jew** le Juif errant; **~ minstrel** ménestrel ambulant.

2 *npl*: **~s** *(journeyings)* voyages *mpl* à l'aventure, vagabondages *mpl*; *(fig: in speech etc)* divagations *fpl*.

wane [weɪn] **1** *vi [moon]* décroître; *[strength, reputation, popularity, interest]* diminuer, baisser, décliner. **2** *n*: **to be on the ~** = **to wane**; *V* **1**.

wangle* ['wæŋgl] **1** *n* combine‡ *f*. **it's a ~** c'est une combine‡; **he got it by a ~** il se l'est procuré par le système D*, il l'a eu par une combine‡.

2 *vt* **(a)** *(get)* se débrouiller pour avoir; *(without paying)* carotter*, resquiller*. **to ~ sth for sb** se débrouiller pour obtenir qch pour qn, carotter* qch pour qn; **can you ~ me a free ticket?** est-ce que tu peux m'avoir une place gratuite? *or* me resquiller* une place?; **I'll ~ it somehow** je me débrouillerai pour arranger ça, je goupillerai* ça; **he ~d £10 out of his father** il a soutiré *or* carotté* 10 livres à son père; **he ~d his way into the hall** il s'est faufilé dans la salle.

(b) *(fake) results, report, accounts* truquer*, cuisiner*.

3 *vi*: **to ~ in** *etc* = **to ~ one's way in** *etc*; *V* **2a**.

wangler* ['wæŋgləʳ] *n* *(V* **wangle 2a***)* débrouillard(e)* *m(f)*; carotteur* *m*, -euse* *f*, resquilleur* *m*, -euse* *f*.

wangling* ['wæŋglɪŋ] *n* *(U)* système D* *m*, carottage* *m*, resquille* *f*.

waning ['weɪnɪŋ] *(V* **wane***)* **1** *n* *(U)* décroissement *m*; baisse *f*, diminution *f*.

2 *adj* décroissant; en baisse, qui diminue.

wanly ['wɒnlɪ] *adv shine* avec une clarté pâle *or* blême; *smile, look, say* tristement, faiblement.

wanness ['wɒnnɪs] *n [person]* tristesse *f*; *[complexion]* pâleur *f*.

want [wɒnt] **1** *n* **(a)** *(U: lack)* manque *m*. **for ~ of** faute de, par manque de; **for ~ of anything better** faute de mieux; **for ~ of anything better to do** faute d'avoir quelque chose de mieux à faire; **for ~ of something to do he ...** comme il n'avait rien à faire il ..., par désœuvrement il ...; **it wasn't for ~ of trying that he ...** ce n'était pas faute d'avoir essayé qu'il ...; **there was no ~ of enthusiasm** ce n'était pas l'enthousiasme qui manquait, l'enthousiasme ne faisait pas défaut.

(b) *(U: poverty, need)* pauvreté *f*, besoin *m*, misère *f*. **to be** *or* **live in ~** être dans le besoin, être nécessiteux; **to be in ~ of sth** avoir besoin de qch.

(c) *(gen pl: requirement, need)* **~s** besoins *mpl*; **his ~s are few** il a peu de besoins, il n'a pas besoin de grand-chose; **it fills** *or* **meets a long-felt ~** cela comble enfin cette lacune.

2 *cpd*: *(US Press)* **want ad** demande *f* *(for* de).

3 *vt* **(a)** *(wish, desire)* vouloir, désirer *(to do* faire). **what do you ~?** que voulez-vous?, que désirez-vous?; **what do you ~ with** *or* **of him?** qu'est-ce que vous lui voulez?; **what do you ~ to do tomorrow?** qu'est-ce que vous avez envie de faire demain?, qu'est-ce que vous voulez *or* désirez faire demain?; **I don't ~ to!** je n'en ai pas envie!; *(more definite)* je ne veux pas!; **all I ~ is a good sleep** tout ce que je veux, c'est dormir longtemps; **he ~s success/popularity** il veut *or* désire *or* ambitionne le succès/la popularité; **I ~ your opinion on this** je voudrais votre avis là-dessus; **what does he ~ for that picture?** combien veut-il *or* demande-t-il pour ce tableau?; **I ~ you to tell me ...** je veux que tu me dises ...; **I ~ the car cleaned** je veux qu'on nettoie *(subj)* la voiture; **I always ~ed a car like this** j'ai toujours souhaité avoir une *or* j'ai toujours eu envie d'une voiture comme ça; **I was ~ing to leave** j'avais envie de partir; **to ~* in/out** *etc* vouloir entrer/sortir *etc*; *(fig)* **he ~s out*** il ne veut plus continuer, il veut laisser tomber*; **you're not ~ed here** on n'a pas besoin de vous ici, on ne veut pas de vous ici; **I know when I'm not ~ed!*** je me rends compte que je suis de trop; **where do you ~ this table?** où voulez-vous (qu'on mette) cette table?; *(fig)* **you've got him where you ~ him** vous l'avez coincé*, vous le tenez à votre merci; *(iro)* **you don't ~ much!** il n'en faut pas beaucoup pour vous faire plaisir! *or* vous satisfaire! *(iro)*; *(sexually)* **to ~ sb** désirer qn.

(b) *(seek, ask for)* demander. **the manager ~s you in his office** le directeur veut vous voir *or* vous demande dans son bureau; **you're ~ed on the phone** on vous demande au téléphone; **to be ~ed by the police** être recherché par la police; **'~ed for murder'** 'recherché pour meurtre'; **the ~ed man** le suspect, l'homme que la police recherche *(or* recherchait *etc)*; **'good cook ~ed'** 'on demande une bonne cuisinière'.

(c) *(gen Brit) (need) [person]* avoir besoin de; *[thing]* exiger, réclamer; (*: *ought)* devoir. **we have all we ~** nous avons tout ce qu'il nous faut; **you ~ a bigger hammer if you're going to do it properly** tu as besoin de *or* il te faut un marteau plus grand pour faire cela correctement; **what do you ~ with a house that size?** pourquoi as-tu besoin d'une *or* veux-tu une maison aussi grande?; **such work ~s good eyesight** un tel travail exige *or* réclame *or* nécessite une bonne vue; **the car ~s cleaning** la voiture a besoin* d'être lavée, il faudrait laver la voiture; **your hair ~s combing** tu as besoin de te peigner, il faudrait que tu te peignes *(subj)*, tu devrais te peigner; **that child ~s a smacking** cet enfant a besoin d'une *or* mérite une fessée, une fessée ne ferait pas de mal à cet enfant; **you ~ to be careful with that!*** fais attention à ça!, fais gaffe‡ à ça!; **you ~ to see his new boat!*** il faudrait que tu voies son nouveau bateau!, tu devrais voir son nouveau bateau!

(d) *(lack)* **he ~s talent** il manque de talent, le talent lui fait défaut; **this shirt ~s a button** il manque un bouton à cette chemise; **the carpet ~s 5 cm to make it fit** il manque 5 cm pour que le tapis soit de la bonne dimension; **it ~ed only his agreement** il ne manquait que son accord; **it ~s 12 minutes to midnight** dans 12 minutes il sera minuit.

4 *vi* *(be in need)* être dans le besoin *or* la misère, être nécessiteux. *(lack)* **to ~ for sth** manquer de qch, avoir besoin de qch; **they ~ for nothing** il ne leur manque rien, ils ne manquent de rien, ils n'ont besoin de rien; *V* **waste**.

wanting ['wɒntɪŋ] **1** *adj* **(a)** *(missing)* **the end of the poem is ~** il manque la fin du poème, la fin du poème manque; **a sense of compassion is ~ in the novel** le roman manque *or* est dépourvu d'un sens de la charité; **the necessary funds were ~** les fonds nécessaires faisaient défaut *or* manquaient.

(b) *(lacking in, short of)* **~ in** qui manque de, déficient en; **he was ~ in courage** il manquait de courage, le courage lui manquait *or* lui faisait défaut; *(loc)* **he was tried and found ~** il a été mis à l'épreuve et jugé insuffisant; **it was tried and found ~** on s'est aperçu que ce n'était pas suffisamment bien; *(pej)* **he is a bit ~*** il est simplet, il lui manque une case‡.

2 *prep* *(without)* sans; *(minus)* moins.

wanton ['wɒntən] **1** *adj* **(a)** *(pej) woman* dévergondé; *thoughts* impudique, libertin.

(b) *(liter: capricious) person, breeze* capricieux. **a ~ growth of weeds** des mauvaises herbes luxuriantes *or* exubérantes.

(c) *(gratuitous) cruelty, destruction* gratuit, injustifié, absurde.

2 *n* (††) dévergondée *f*, femme légère.

wantonly ['wɒntənlɪ] *adv* *(V* **wanton***)* de façon dévergondée; impudiquement; capricieusement; *destroy, spoil etc* gratuitement, de façon injustifiée.

wantonness ['wɒntənnɪs] *n* *(U: V* **wanton***)* dévergondage *m*; caprices *mpl*; *[cruelty, destruction]* gratuité *f*, absurdité *f*.

war [wɔːʳ] **1** *n* guerre *f*. **to be at ~** être en (état de) guerre *(with* avec); *[country]* **to go to ~** se mettre en guerre, entrer en guerre *(against* contre, *over* à propos de); *[soldier]* **to go (off) to ~** partir pour la guerre, aller à la guerre; *(Mil, also fig)* **to make ~ on** faire la guerre à; **the Great W~** la Grande Guerre, la guerre de 14 *or* de 14–18; **the period between the ~s** *(1918-39)* l'entre-deux-guerres *m inv*; *(Brit)* **the W~ Office**, *(US)* **the W~ Department** le ministère de la Guerre; *(Mil, fig)* **to carry the ~ into the enemy's camp** passer à l'attaque, prendre l'offensive, porter la guerre chez l'ennemi; *(fig)* **it was ~ to the knife** *or* **the death between them** c'était une lutte à couteaux tirés entre eux; *(fig)* **~ of words** guerre de paroles; *(fig)* **you've been in the ~s again*** tu t'es encore fait amocher‡ *or* estropier; *V* **cold, nerve, state** *etc*.

2 *cpd conditions, debt, crime, criminal, orphan, widow, wound, zone* de guerre. *(US Pol etc)* **war chest** caisse spéciale (d'un parti politique pour les élections); *(fig)* **war clouds** nuages avant-coureurs de la guerre; *(Press, Rad, TV)* **war correspondent** correspondant *m* de guerre; **war cry** cri *m* de guerre; **war dance** danse guerrière; **war-disabled** mutilé(e)s *m(f)pl* *or* invalides *mfpl* de guerre; *(U)* **warfare** guerre *f* *(U)*; **war fever** psychose *f* de guerre; **war games** *(Mil: for training)* kriegspiel *m*; *(Mil: practice manoeuvres)* manœuvres *fpl* militaires; *(board games)* jeux *mpl* de stratégie militaire; **warhead** ogive *f*; **atomic warhead** ogive *f* or tête *f* nucléaire; **warhorse** cheval *m* de bataille; *(fig)* **an old warhorse** un vétéran, un(e) dur(e) à cuire*; **warlike** guerrier, belliqueux; **war lord** chef *m* militaire, seigneur *m* de la guerre; **war memorial** monument *m* aux morts; **warmonger(ing)** *V* **warmonger(ing)**; **war paint** peinture *f* de guerre *(des Indiens)*; *(fig hum: make-up)* maquillage *m*, peinturlurage *m (pej)*; **to be on the warpath** être sur le sentier de la guerre; (* *fig hum*) chercher la bagarre*; **warship** navire *m* or vaisseau *m* de guerre; **wartime** *(U: n)* temps *m* de guerre; *(cpd)* de guerre; **in wartime** en temps de guerre; **war-torn** déchiré par la guerre; **war-weary** las *(f* lasse) de la guerre; **the war-wounded** les blessés *mpl* de guerre.

3 *vi* faire la guerre *(against* à).

warble ['wɔːbl] **1** *n* gazouillis *m*, gazouillements *mpl*. **2** *vi [bird]* gazouiller; *[person]* roucouler. **3** *vt* *(also* **~ out***)* chanter en gazouillant.

warbler ['wɔːbləʳ] *n* oiseau chanteur.

warbling ['wɔːblɪŋ] *n* gazouillis *m*, gazouillement(s) *m(pl)*.

ward [wɔːd] **1** *n* **(a)** *(Jur: person)* pupille *mf*. **~ of court** pupille sous tutelle judiciaire; **in ~** sous tutelle judiciaire; *V* **watch²**.

(b) *(Brit: Local Government)* section électorale.

(c) *[prison, hospital]* salle *f*, *(separate building)* pavillon *m*.

2 *cpd*: *(US Pol pej)* **ward heeler** agent *or* courtier électoral; *(Naut)* **wardroom** carré *m*.

ward off *vt sep blow, danger* parer, éviter.

warden ['wɔːdn] *n [institution]* directeur *m*, -trice *f*; *[city, castle]* gouverneur *m*; *[park, game reserve]* gardien *m*, -ienne *f*; *[youth hostel]* père *m* or mère *f* aubergiste; *(US: prison governor)* directeur, -trice; *(Brit Univ)* directeur *m*, -trice *f* de foyer universitaire; *(Brit: on hospital board etc)* membre *m* du conseil d'administration; *(Brit: air-raid ~)* préposé(e) *m(f)* à la défense passive; *(traffic ~)* contractuel(le) *m(f)*. *(Brit)* **W~ of the Cinque Ports** gouverneur des Cinque Ports; *V* **church, fire** *etc*.

warder ['wɔːdəʳ] *n* *(esp Brit)* gardien *m* or surveillant *m* (de prison).

wardress ['wɔːdrɪs] *n* (*esp Brit*) gardienne *f or* surveillante *f* (de prison).

wardrobe ['wɔːdrəʊb] **1** *n* (*cupboard*) armoire *f*, penderie *f*, garde-robe *f*; (*clothes*) garde-robe; (*Theat*) costumes *mpl*. (*Cine, Theat*) **Miss X's ~ by ...** costumes de Mlle X par ..., Mlle X est habillée par ... . **2** *cpd*: (*Theat*) **wardrobe mistress** costumière *f*; **wardrobe trunk** malle *f* penderie.

...ward(s) [wəd(z)] *suf* vers, dans la *or* en direction de. **townward(s)** vers la ville, dans la *or* en direction de la ville; *V* **backward(s), downward(s)** *etc*.

wardship ['wɔːdʃɪp] *n* (*U*) tutelle *f*.

...ware [wɛəʳ] *n ending in cpds*: (*U*) **kitchenware** articles *mpl* de cuisine; (*U*) **silverware** argenterie *f*; *V* **hard** *etc*.

warehouse ['wɛəhaʊs] **1** *n, pl* **warehouses** ['wɛəˌhaʊzɪz] entrepôt *m*, magasin *m*. **2** ['wɛəhaʊz] *vt* entreposer, mettre en magasin, emmagasiner. **3** *cpd*: **warehouseman** magasinier *m*.

wares [wɛəz] *npl* marchandises *fpl*.

warily ['wɛərɪlɪ] *adv* (*V* **wary**) avec prudence, avec circonspection; avec précaution. **... she said ~ ...** dit-elle *or* avança-t-elle avec précaution.

wariness ['wɛərɪnɪs] *n* (*U*: *V* **wary**) prudence *f*, circonspection *f*; précaution *f*.

warlock ['wɔːlɒk] *n* sorcier *m*.

warm [wɔːm] **1** *adj* **(a)** (assez) chaud. **I am ~** j'ai (assez) chaud; **this room is quite ~** il fait (assez) chaud *or* il fait bon dans cette pièce; **a ~ iron/oven** un fer/four moyen; **the iron/oven is ~** le fer/four est (assez) chaud; **I am as ~ as toast** je suis chaud comme une caille*; **it's ~, the weather is ~** il fait chaud; **it's too ~ in here** il fait trop chaud ici, on étouffe ici; **it's nice and ~ in here** il fait bon ici, il fait agréablement chaud ici; **in ~ weather** par temps chaud; (*Met*) **~ front** front chaud; **the water is just ~** l'eau est juste chaude *or* n'est pas très chaude; **this coffee's only ~** ce café n'est pas assez chaud *or* est tiède; **to get sth ~** (ré)chauffer qch; **to get** *or* **grow ~** *[person]* se (ré)chauffer; *[water, object]* chauffer; (*in guessing etc games*) **you're getting ~(er)!** tu chauffes!; **to keep sth ~** *or* **in a ~ place** tenir qch au chaud; **this scarf keeps me ~** cette écharpe me tient chaud; **you've got to keep yourself ~** surtout ne prenez pas froid; **it's ~ work** c'est du travail qui donne chaud; (*fig*) **to make things ~ for sb** mener la vie dure à qn, en faire voir de dures* à qn; **things got too ~ for him** ça chauffait* trop *or* ça bardait‡ trop à son goût.

(b) (*fig*) *colour, shade* chaud; *voice, tone* chaud, chaleureux, entraînant; *dispute, discussion* chaud, vif, animé; *temperament* chaud, vif; *feelings* chaud, chaleureux; *apologies, thanks* vif; *greeting, welcome, congratulations, encouragement* cordial, chaleureux; *applause* chaleureux, enthousiaste; *supporter, admirer* ardent, chaud, enthousiaste. **they have a very ~ relationship** ils ont beaucoup d'affection l'un pour l'autre; **she is a very ~ person, she has a very ~ nature** *or* **heart** elle est très chaleureuse *or* affectueuse (de nature), elle est pleine de chaleur; (*in letter*) **'with ~est wishes'** 'avec tous mes vœux les plus amicaux'.

2 *cpd*: **warm-blooded** (*Zool*) à sang chaud; (*fig*) ardent, sensuel, qui a le sang chaud; **warm-hearted** chaleureux, affectueux; **warming pan** bassinoire *f*; **warming-up exercises** mouvements *mpl or* exercices *mpl* d'échauffement; **warm-up*** (*Sport*) période *f* d'échauffement, mise *f* en train; (*Rad, Theat, TV etc*) mise en train.

3 *n* (*) **to give sth a ~** (ré)chauffer qch; **come and have a ~ by the fire** viens te (ré)chauffer près du feu; **come inside and sit in the ~** entrez vous asseoir au chaud.

4 *vt* (*also* **~ up**) *person, room* réchauffer; *water, food* (ré)chauffer, faire (ré)chauffer; *coat, slippers* (ré)chauffer. **to ~ o.s.** se (ré)chauffer; **to ~ one's feet/hands** se (ré)chauffer les pieds/les mains; (*fig*) **the news ~ed my heart** la nouvelle m'a (ré)chauffé le cœur; *V* **cockle**.

5 *vi* **(a)** (*also* **~ up**) *[person]* se (ré)chauffer; *[water, food, clothing]* chauffer; *[room, bed]* se réchauffer, devenir plus chaud.

(b) (*fig*) **to ~ to an idea** s'enthousiasmer peu à peu pour une idée; **I ~ed to him, my heart ~ed to him** je me suis pris de sympathie pour lui; **to ~ to one's subject** se laisser entraîner par son sujet, traiter son sujet avec un enthousiasme grandissant.

warm over, warm through *vt sep food* faire (ré)chauffer.

warm up 1 *vi* **(a) = warm 5a.**

(b) *[engine, car]* se réchauffer; *[athlete, dancer]* s'échauffer; *[discussion]* s'échauffer, s'animer; *[audience]* devenir animé. **the party was warming up** la soirée commençait à être pleine d'entrain, la soirée chauffait*; **the game is warming up** la partie commence à devenir excitante; **things are warming up** ça commence à s'animer *or* à chauffer*.

2 *vt sep person, room* réchauffer; *water, food* (ré)chauffer, faire (ré)chauffer; *coat, slippers* (ré)chauffer; *engine, car* faire chauffer; *discussion* animer; (*Theat etc*) *audience* mettre en train.

3 warm-up* *n V* **warm 2**.

4 warming-up *adj V* **warm 2**.

warmly ['wɔːmlɪ] *adv clothe, wrap up* chaudement; (*fig*) *congratulate, welcome* chaudement, chaleureusement, cordialement; *applaud* chaleureusement, avec enthousiasme; *thank, recommend* vivement, chaudement. **the sun shone ~** le soleil était chaud; **tucked up ~ in bed** bordé bien au chaud dans son lit.

warmonger ['wɔːˌmʌŋgəʳ] *n* belliciste *mf*.

warmongering ['wɔːˌmʌŋgərɪŋ] **1** *adj* belliciste. **2** *n* (*U*) propagande *f* belliciste.

warmth [wɔːmθ] *n* (*U*: *V* **warm 1a, 1b**) chaleur *f*; vivacité *f*; cordialité *f*.

warn [wɔːn] *vt* prévenir, avertir (*of* de, *that* que). **to ~ the police** alerter la police; **you have been ~ed!** vous êtes averti! *or* prévenu!; **to ~ sb against doing** *or* **not to do** conseiller *or* recommander à qn de ne pas faire, déconseiller à qn de faire; **to ~ sb off** *or* **against sth** mettre qn en garde contre qch, déconseiller qch à qn.

warning ['wɔːnɪŋ] **1** *n* (*act*) avertissement *m*; (*in writing*) avis *m*, préavis *m*; (*signal*) alerte *f*, alarme *f*; (*Met*) avis. **it fell without ~** c'est tombé inopinément; **they arrived without ~** ils sont arrivés à l'improviste *or* sans prévenir; **he left me without ~** il m'a quitté sans me prévenir; **let this be a ~ to you** que cela vous serve d'avertissement; **thank you for the ~** merci de m'avoir prévenu *or* averti; **there was a note of ~ in his voice** il y avait une mise en garde dans le ton qu'il a pris; **to take ~ from** tirer la leçon de; **his employer gave him a ~ about lateness** son patron lui a donné un avertissement à propos de son manque de ponctualité; **to give a week's ~** prévenir huit jours à l'avance; (*more formal*) donner un délai de huit jours; (*in writing*) donner un préavis de huit jours; **I gave you due ~ (that)** je vous avais bien prévenu (que); (*Met*) **gale/storm ~** avis de grand vent/de tempête.

2 *adj glance, cry* d'avertissement. **~ device** dispositif *m* d'alarme, avertisseur *m*; **~ light** voyant *m* (avertisseur), avertisseur lumineux; **~ notice** avis *m*, avertissement *m*; **~ shot** (*gen, Mil*) coup tiré en guise d'avertissement; (*Naut*) coup de semonce; (*fig*) avertissement; **~ sign** panneau avertisseur; **... he said in a ~ tone** *or* **voice ...** dit-il pour mettre en garde.

warp [wɔːp] **1** *n* **(a)** (*Tex*) chaîne *f*; (*fig: essence, base*) fibre *f*.

(b) (*distortion*) (*in wood*) gauchissement *m*, voilure *f*; (*in metal*) voilure.

2 *vt wood* gauchir, voiler; *metal, aircraft wing, tennis racket* voiler; (*fig*) *judgment* fausser, pervertir; *mind, character, person* débaucher, corrompre. **he has a ~ed mind, his mind is ~ed** il a l'esprit tordu; **he has a ~ed sense of humour** il a un sens morbide de l'humour; **he gave us a ~ed account of ...** il nous a fait un récit tendancieux de ... .

3 *vi* gauchir, se voiler; se fausser, se pervertir; devenir débauché *or* corrompu.

warrant ['wɒrənt] **1** *n* **(a)** (*U: justification*) justification *f*, droit *m*. **he has no ~ for saying so** il ne s'appuie sur rien pour justifier cela.

(b) (*Comm, Fin etc: certificate*) (*for payment or services*) bon *m*; (*guarantee*) garantie *f*; (*Mil*) brevet *m*; (*Jur, Police*) mandat *m*. (*Jur*) **there is a ~ out against him, there is a ~ out for his arrest** on a émis un mandat d'arrêt contre lui; (*Police*) **let me see your ~** je veux voir votre mandat (d'arrêt *or* de perquisition *etc*); *V* **death, search**.

2 *cpd*: (*Mil*) **warrant officer** adjudant *m* (*auxiliaire de l'officier*).

3 *vt* **(a)** (*justify*) *action, assumption, reaction, behaviour* justifier, légitimer. **the facts do not ~ it** les faits ne le justifient pas *or* ne le permettent pas.

(b) (*guarantee*) garantir. **I'll ~ (you) he won't do it again!*** je vous assure *or* promets *or* certifie qu'il ne recommencera pas!

warrantable ['wɒrəntəbl] *adj* justifiable, légitime.

warrantee [ˌwɒrən'tiː] *n* (*Jur*) créancier *m*, -ière *f*.

warranter, warrantor ['wɒrəntəʳ] *n* (*Jur*) garant(e) *m(f)*, débiteur *m*, -trice *f*.

warranty ['wɒrəntɪ] *n* autorisation *f*, droit *m*; (*Comm, Jur*) garantie *f*.

warren ['wɒrən] *n [rabbits]* terriers *mpl*, garenne *f*; (*fig*) (*overcrowded house, tenement*) taupinière *f* (*fig*); (*part of town*) dédale *m*, labyrinthe *m*. **a ~ of little streets** un dédale *or* un labyrinthe de petites rues.

warring ['wɔːrɪŋ] *adj nations* en guerre; (*fig*) *interests* contradictoires, contraires; *ideologies* en conflit, en opposition.

warrior ['wɒrɪəʳ] *n* guerrier *m*, -ière *f*; *V* **unknown**.

Warsaw ['wɔːsɔː] *n* Varsovie. **the ~ Pact countries** les pays du pacte de Varsovie.

wart [wɔːt] **1** *n* (*Med*) verrue *f*; (*Bot*) excroissance *f*; (*on wood*) loupe *f*. (*fig*) **~s and all** sans aucune flatterie, sans aucun embellissement. **2** *cpd*: **wart hog** phacochère *m*.

warty ['wɔːtɪ] *adj* couvert de verrues, verruqueux.

wary ['wɛərɪ] *adj person* prudent, sur ses gardes, circonspect; *voice, look* prudent; *manner* précautionneux. **to be ~ about sb/sth** se méfier de qn/qch; **to be ~ of doing sth** hésiter beaucoup à faire qch; **it's best to be ~ here** il vaut mieux être prudent *or* être sur ses gardes *or* prendre ses précautions ici; **to keep a ~ eye on sb/sth** avoir l'œil sur qn/qch, surveiller qn/qch de près.

was [wɒz] *pret of* **be**.

wash [wɒʃ] **1** *n* **(a) to give sth a ~** laver qch; **to have a ~** se laver, faire sa toilette; **to have a quick ~** se débarbouiller, faire un brin de toilette; (*notice*) **'~ and brush-up: 6p'** = 'serviette et savon: 6 pence'; **it needs a ~** cela a besoin d'être lavé, il faut laver cela; **your face needs a ~** il faut que tu te laves (*subj*) la figure *or* que tu te débarbouilles (*subj*); **to send sheets to the ~** envoyer des draps au blanchissage *or* à la laverie; **the colours ran in the ~** cela a déteint à la lessive *or* au lavage; (*fig*) **it will all come out in the ~*** ça finira par être étalé au grand jour, on finira bien par savoir ce qu'il en est; *V* **car**.

(b) = washing 1b.

(c) *[ship]* sillage *m*, remous *m*; (*sound: of waves etc*) clapotis *m*.

(d) (*various liquids*) (*mouth~*) eau *f* dentifrice; (*layer of paint: for walls etc*) badigeon *m*; (*Art*) *[watercolour]* lavis *m*; (*kitchen waste*) eau de vaisselle, eaux grasses. **to give the walls a blue ~** badigeonner les murs en *or* de bleu; *V* **eye, whitewash** *etc*.

2 *cpd*: wash-and-wear *shirt* qui ne nécessite aucun repassage; (*Comm: on label*) 'ne pas repasser'; washbasin (cuvette *f* de) lavabo *m*; washboard planche *f* à laver; washbowl = washbasin; washcloth gant *m* de toilette; washday jour *m* de lessive; wash-hand basin = washbasin; wash house lavoir *m*; (*Brit*) wash leather peau *f* de chamois; wash-out* (*event, play*) fiasco *m*, désastre *m*; (*person*) zéro *m*, nullité *f*; washroom toilettes *fpl*; washstand lavabo *m*; (*unplumbed*) console *f* de toilette; washtub (*bath*) tub *m*; (*for clothes*) baquet *m*, bassine *f*.

3 *vt* (a) (*gen*) laver. to ~ o.s. *[person]* se laver, faire sa toilette; *[cat]* faire sa toilette*; (*fig*) to ~ one's hands of sth se laver les mains de qch; (*fig*) to ~ one's hands of sb se désintéresser de qn; to ~ a child's face laver le visage d'un enfant, débarbouiller un enfant; he ~ed the dirt off his hands il s'est lavé les mains pour (en) enlever la saleté; to ~ the dishes faire la vaisselle; to ~ the clothes faire la lessive; to ~ sth with detergent/in hot water nettoyer qch avec du détergent/ à l'eau chaude; (*fig*) to ~ one's dirty linen in public laver son linge sale en public; he ~ed the floor clean il a bien nettoyé *or* lavé le sol; the rain ~ed it clean la pluie l'a lavé; the rain ~ed the car clean of mud la pluie a fait partir toute la boue de la voiture; (*fig*) to be ~ed clean *or* free of sin être lavé de tout péché.

(b) *[river, sea, waves, current]* (*carry*) emporter, entraîner; (*flow over*) baigner; (*scoop out*) creuser. several barrels were ~ed ashore plusieurs tonneaux ont échoué *or* ont été rejetés sur la côte; to be ~ed out to sea être emporté par la mer, être entraîné vers le large; the raft was ~ed downstream le radeau a été emporté *or* entraîné en aval; the Atlantic ~es its western shores la côte ouest est baignée par l'Atlantique; the water ~ed a channel through the sand l'eau a creusé un chenal dans le sable; *V* overboard.

(c) (*Min*) *earth, gravel, gold, ore* laver; (*Chem*) *gas* épurer. to ~ walls with distemper badigeonner des murs, passer des murs au badigeon, peindre des murs à la détrempe; to ~ brass with gold couvrir du cuivre d'une pellicule d'or.

4 *vi* (a) (*have a ~*) *[person]* se laver, faire sa toilette; *[cat]* faire sa toilette*; (*do the washing*) laver, faire la lessive. he ~ed in cold water il s'est lavé à l'eau froide; this fabric will/won't ~ ce tissu est/n'est pas lavable; (*Brit fig*) that just won't ~!* ça ne prend pas!; that excuse won't ~ with him* cette excuse ne prendra pas *or* ne marchera pas avec lui, on ne lui fera pas avaler cette excuse.

(b) *[waves, sea, flood, river]* to ~ against *cliffs, rocks* baigner; *lighthouse, boat* clapoter contre; to ~ over sth balayer qch.

wash away 1 *vi* (*with soap*) s'en aller *or* partir au lavage; (*with water*) s'en aller *or* partir à l'eau.

2 *vt sep* (a) *[person] stain* enlever *or* faire partir au lavage; *mud* enlever à l'eau; (*fig*) *sins* laver. the rain washed the mud away la pluie a fait partir la boue.

(b) *[river, current, sea]* (*carry away*) emporter; (*destroy*) éroder, dégrader; *footprints etc* balayer, effacer. the boat was washed away le bateau a été emporté; the river washed away part of the bank la rivière a érodé *or* dégradé une partie de la rive.

wash down *vt sep* (a) *deck, car* laver (à grande eau); *wall* lessiver.

(b) *medicine, pill* faire descendre (*with* avec); *food* arroser (*with* de).

(c) *[rain, flood, river]* emporter, entraîner.

wash in *vt sep [sea, tide]* rejeter (sur le rivage).

wash off 1 *vi* (*from clothes*) s'en aller *or* partir au lavage (*with soap*) *or* à l'eau (*with water*); (*from walls*) partir au lessivage. it won't wash off ça ne s'en va pas, ça ne part pas, c'est indélébile; (*from hands*) it will wash off ça partira quand tu te laveras (*or* je me laverai *etc*) les mains.

2 *vt sep* (*from clothes*) faire partir au lavage (*with soap*) *or* à l'eau (*with water*); (*from wall*) faire partir en lessivant.

wash out 1 *vi* (a) *[stain]* s'en aller *or* partir au lavage (*with soap*) *or* à l'eau (*with water*); *[dye, colours]* passer au lavage. this stain won't wash out cette tache ne s'en va pas *or* ne part pas, cette tache est indélébile.

(b) (*US*:) he washed out of university il a échoué à l'université.

2 *vt sep* (a) (*remove*) *stain* enlever *or* faire partir au lavage (*with soap*) *or* à l'eau (*with water*).

(b) (*clean*) *bottle, pan* laver.

(c) (*fig: spoil*) perturber; (*: *cancel*) rendre impossible. (*fig: by rain*) the match was washed out (*prevented*) le match a été annulé *or* n'a pas eu lieu à cause de la pluie; (*halted*) la pluie a perturbé *or* interrompu le match; his illness has washed out* any chance of a holiday this year sa maladie a anéanti toute possibilité de vacances cette année; our plans were washed out* by the change in the exchange rate nos projets sont partis à vau-l'eau avec le nouveau taux de change; (*tired etc*) to be/look/feel washed out* être/avoir l'air/se sentir complètement lessivé*.

3 wash-out* *n V* wash 2.

wash through *vt sep clothes* laver rapidement, passer à l'eau.

wash up 1 *vi* (a) (*Brit: wash dishes*) faire *or* laver la vaisselle.

(b) (*US: have a wash*) se débarbouiller, faire un brin de toilette.

2 *vt sep* (a) (*Brit*) *plates, cups* laver. to wash up the dishes faire *or* laver la vaisselle.

(b) *[sea, tide]* rejeter (sur le rivage).

(c) (*: *finish: gen pass*) to be (all) washed up *[plan, scheme]* être fichu*, être tombé à l'eau*; *[marriage, relationship]* être en ruines; Paul and Anne are all washed up tout est fini entre Paul et Anne; (*tired etc*) to be/feel/look washed up être/se sentir/avoir l'air lessivé*.

3 washing-up *n, adj V* washing 2.

washable ['wɒʃəbl] *adj* lavable.

washer ['wɒʃəʳ] 1 *n* (a) (*Tech*) rondelle *f*, joint *m*; (*in tap*) rondelle. (b) (*washing machine*) machine *f* à laver; *V* dish, wind[1] *etc*. 2 *cpd*: washerwoman laveuse *f* (de linge).

washing ['wɒʃɪŋ] 1 *n* (a) (*act*) *[car]* lavage *m*; *[clothes]* lessive *f*, blanchissage *m*; *[walls]* lessivage *m*; *V* brain.

(b) (*U: clothes*) linge *m*, lessive *f*. to do the ~ faire la lessive, laver le linge; I do a big ~ on Mondays je lave un gros tas de linge le lundi, le lundi est mon jour de grande lessive; put your jeans in the ~ mets tes jeans au sale; your shirt is in the ~ ta chemise est à la lessive.

2 *cpd*: washing day jour *m* de lessive; washing line corde *f* à linge; washing machine machine *f* à laver; washing powder lessive *f* (en poudre), détergent *m*; washing soda cristaux *mpl* de soude; (*Brit*) washing-up vaisselle *f* (*à laver etc*); to do the washing-up faire *or* laver la vaisselle; look at all that washing-up! regarde tout ce qu'il y a comme vaisselle à faire! *or* à laver!; washing-up bowl bassine *f*, cuvette *f*; washing-up liquid lave-vaisselle *m inv*; washing-up water eau *f* de vaisselle.

washy ['wɒʃɪ] *adj* = wishy-washy.

wasn't ['wɒznt] = was not; *V* be.

wasp [wɒsp] 1 *n* (a) guêpe *f*. ~'s nest guêpier *m*. (b) (*US**) W~ (*also* W.A.S.P.) blanc protestant, blanche protestante. 2 *cpd*: wasp-waisted à taille de guêpe.

waspish ['wɒspɪʃ] *adj* grincheux, hargneux.

waspishly ['wɒspɪʃlɪ] *adv* avec hargne.

wassail†† ['wɒseɪl] 1 *n* (*festivity*) beuverie *f*; (*drink*) bière épicée. 2 *vi* faire ribote†.

wast†† [wɒst] *2nd pers sg pret of* be.

wastage ['weɪstɪdʒ] 1 *n* (*U*) *[resources, energy, food, money]* gaspillage *m*; *[time]* perte *f*, gâchage *m*; (*lost from container*) fuites *fpl*, pertes *fpl*; (*rejects*) déchets *mpl*; (*as part of industrial process etc*) déperdition *f*; (*Comm: through pilfering etc*) coulage *m*. such a ~ of good men un tel gaspillage de talent; there is a huge ~ of energy/money on gaspille énormément d'énergie/d'argent; the amount of ~ that goes on in large establishments le gaspillage *or* le gâchis qui se produit dans les grands établissements.

2 *cpd*: the wastage rate among students/entrants to the profession le pourcentage d'étudiants qui abandonnent en cours d'études/de ceux qui abandonnent en début de carrière.

waste [weɪst] 1 *n* (a) (*U*) *[resources, energy, food, money]* gaspillage *m*, gâchis *m*; *[time]* perte *f*. to go *or* run to ~ être gaspillé, se perdre inutilement; *[land]* tomber en friche, être à l'abandon; there's too much ~ in this firm il y a trop de gaspillage dans cette compagnie; we must reduce the ~ in the kitchens nous devons diminuer le gaspillage *or* le gâchis dans les cuisines; it's a ~ of manpower c'est un gaspillage de ressources humaines; it's a ~ of money to do that on gaspille de l'argent en faisant cela, on perd de l'argent à faire cela; that machine was a ~ of money cela ne valait vraiment pas la peine d'acheter cette machine, on a vraiment fichu de l'argent en l'air* en achetant cette machine; it's a ~ of effort c'est un effort inutile *or* perdu; it's a ~ of time! c'est une perte de temps!, c'est du temps perdu!; it's a ~ of time doing that on perd son temps à faire *or* en faisant cela; it's a ~ of time and energy c'est peine perdue; it's a ~ of breath c'est perdre sa salive, c'est dépenser sa salive pour rien; what a ~! quel gaspillage!

(b) (*U: waste material*) déchets *mpl*; (*household* ~) ordures *fpl* (ménagères); (*water*) eaux sales *or* usées. nuclear/metal ~ déchets nucléaires/de métal; *V* cotton.

(c) (*expanse: often pl*) terres désolées, désert *m*; (*in town*) terrain *m* vague. ~s *or* a ~ of snow and ice un désert immense de neige et de glace.

2 *adj material* de rebut; *energy, heat* perdu; *food* superflu, inutilisé; *water* usé, sale; *land, ground* inculte, en friche; *region, district* à l'abandon, désolé. ~ paper vieux papiers, papier(s) de rebut (*V also* 3); ~ products (*Ind*) déchets *mpl* de fabrication; (*Physiol*) déchets (de l'organisme); a piece of ~ land un terrain vague (*V also* 3); 'The W~ Land' 'la Terre désolée'; to lay ~ ravager, dévaster.

3 *cpd*: wastebasket corbeille *f* (à papier); (*Brit*) wastebin (*wastebasket*) corbeille *f* (à papier); (*in kitchen*) boîte *f* à ordures, poubelle *f*; waste disposal unit broyeur *m* d'ordures; wasteland terres *fpl* à l'abandon *or* en friche; (*in town*) terrain *m* vague; wastepaper basket = wastebasket; waste pipe (tuyau *m* de) vidange *f*.

4 *vt* (a) *resources, food, electricity, energy etc* gaspiller; *time* perdre; *opportunity* perdre, laisser passer. to ~ one's money gaspiller de l'argent, ficher de l'argent en l'air* (*on sth* pour qch, *on doing* pour faire); nothing is ~d in this firm il n'y a aucun gaspillage *or* il n'y a aucun gâchis *or* rien ne se perd dans cette entreprise; we ~d 9 litres of petrol nous avons gaspillé *or* perdu 9 litres d'essence, nous avons dépensé 9 litres d'essence pour rien; I ~d a whole day on that journey j'ai perdu toute une journée avec ce voyage; you're wasting your breath! tu dépenses ta salive pour rien!, tu perds ton temps!; I won't ~ my breath discussing that je ne vais pas perdre mon temps *or* me fatiguer à discuter cela; you're wasting your time trying tu essaies en pure perte, tu perds ton temps à essayer; the sarcasm was ~d on him il n'a pas compris *or* saisi le sarcasme; caviar is ~d on him il ne sait pas apprécier le caviar, ça ne vaut pas la peine de lui donner du caviar; ~d effort des efforts inutiles *or* vains; a ~d life une vie gâchée; his attempts to placate her were ~d il a essayé en vain de l'amadouer, ses efforts pour l'amadouer n'ont rien donné *or* ont été en pure perte.

(b) limbs/body ~d by disease membres/corps atrophié(s) par la maladie.

5 *vi [food, goods, resources]* se perdre, être gaspillé. **you mustn't let it** ~ il ne faut pas le laisser perdre; (*Prov*) ~ **not want not** l'économie protège du besoin.
waste away *vi* dépérir. (*iro*) **you're not exactly wasting away!** tu ne fais pas précisément pitié à voir! (*iro*).
wasted ['weɪstɪd] *adj limb* décharné; (*withered*) atrophié.
wasteful ['weɪstfʊl] *adj person* gaspilleur; *process* peu économique, peu rentable. ~ **expenditure** gaspillage *m*, dépenses excessives *or* inutiles; ~ **habits** gaspillage; **to be** ~ **of sth** *[person]* gaspiller qch; *[method, process]* mal utiliser qch.
wastefully ['weɪstfəlɪ] *adv*: **to spend/buy/throw away** ~ faire du gaspillage en dépensant/achetant/jetant, dépenser/acheter/jeter bêtement; **to use sth** ~ ne pas utiliser qch au mieux.
wastefulness ['weɪstfʊlnɪs] *n* (*U*) *[person]* manque *m* d'économie; *[process]* manque de rentabilité.
waster ['weɪstə^{r}] *n* = **wastrel.**
wasting ['weɪstɪŋ] *adj disease* qui ronge, qui mine.
wastrel ['weɪstrəl] *n* (*spendthrift*) dépensier *m*, -ière *f*, panier percé *m*; (*good-for-nothing*) propre *mf* à rien.
watch[1] [wɒtʃ] **1** *n* montre *f*. **by my** ~ à ma montre; *V* **stop, wrist.**
2 *cpd chain, glass* de montre. **watchband** bracelet *m* de montre; **watchmaker** horloger *m*, -ère *f*; **watchmaking** horlogerie *f*; **watch pocket** gousset *m*; **watch strap** = **watchband.**
watch[2] [wɒtʃ] **1** *n* **(a)** (*U*) (*vigilance*) vigilance *f*; (*act of watching*) surveillance *f*. **to keep** ~ faire le guet; **to keep (a) close** ~ **on** *or* **over** surveiller de près *or* avec vigilance; **to set a** ~ **on sth/sb** faire surveiller qch/qn; (*frm*) **to keep** ~ **and ward over sth** surveiller qch avec vigilance; **to be on the** ~ (*Mil etc*) monter la garde; (*gen*) guetter, faire le guet; **to be on the** ~ **for sb/sth** guetter qn/qch; **to be on the** ~ **for danger** être sur ses gardes à cause d'un danger éventuel; **to be on the** ~ **for bargains** être à l'affût des bonnes affaires.
(b) (*Naut: period of duty*) quart *m*. **to be on** ~ être de quart; (*fig:* † *or liter*) **the long** ~**es of the night** les longues nuits sans sommeil; *V* **dog.**
(c) (*Mil*) (*group of men*) garde *f* (*Mil*), quart *m* (*Naut*); (*one man*) sentinelle *f* (*Mil*), homme *m* de quart (*Naut*). (*Naut*) **the port** ~ les bâbordais *mpl*; **the starboard** ~ les tribordais *mpl*; (*Hist*) **the** ~ le guet, la ronde; *V* **officer.**
2 *cpd*: **watchdog** (*lit*) chien *m* de garde; (*fig*) gardien *m*, -ienne *f*; (*Rel*) **watch night service** messe *f* de minuit de la Saint-Sylvestre; **watchtower** tour *f* de guet; **watchword** (*password*) mot *m* de passe; (*fig: motto*) mot d'ordre.
3 *vt* **(a)** *event, match, programme, TV, ceremony* regarder; *person* regarder, observer, (*spy on*) surveiller, observer, épier; *suspect, suspicious object, house, car* surveiller; *movement, expression, birds, insect etc* observer; *notice board, small ads etc* consulter régulièrement; *political situation, developments* surveiller, suivre de près. ~ **me,** ~ **what I do** regarde-moi (faire), regarde ce que je fais, observe-moi; ~ **how he does it** regarde *or* observe comment il s'y prend; ~ **the soup to see it doesn't boil over** surveille la soupe pour qu'elle ne se sauve (*subj*) pas; **to** ~ **sb do** *or* **doing sth** regarder qn faire qch; **have you ever** ~**ed an operation?** avez-vous déjà vu une opération? *or* assisté à une opération?; **we are being** ~**ed** (*gen*) on nous observe *or* surveille *or* épie; (*by police, detective etc*) on nous surveille; **to** ~ **sb's movements** surveiller *or* épier les allées et venues de qn; **he needs** ~**ing** il faut le surveiller, il faut l'avoir à l'œil; ~ **tomorrow's paper** ne manquez pas de lire le journal de demain; (*Prov*) **a** ~**ed pot never boils** marmite surveillée ne bout jamais; *V* **bird.**
(b) (*guard: Mil etc*) monter la garde devant, garder; (*take care of*) *child, dog* surveiller, s'occuper de; *luggage, shop* surveiller, garder.
(c) (*be careful of, mind*) faire attention à. ~ **that knife!** (fais) attention avec ce couteau!; ~ **that sharp edge!** (fais) attention au bord coupant!; ~ **your head!** attention *or* gare à votre tête!; (*fig*) ~ **your step!,** ~ **how you go!*** fais gaffe!‡; **we'll have to** ~ **the money carefully** il faudra que nous fassions attention à *or* surveillions (*subj*) nos dépenses; **I must** ~ **the** *or* **my time as I've a train to catch** il faut que je surveille (*subj*) l'heure car j'ai un train à prendre; **he works well but does tend to** ~ **the clock** il travaille bien mais il a tendance à surveiller la pendule; **to** ~ **one's step** (*lit*) faire attention *or* regarder où on met le pied; (*fig*) se surveiller (*dans ses paroles or ses actes*); **to** ~ **what one says** parler avec précaution, faire attention à ce que l'on dit; ~ **what you're doing!** fais attention (à ce que tu fais)!; ~ **it!*** (*warning*) attention!, fais gaffe!‡; (*threat*) attention!, gare à toi!; ~ **your language!** surveille ton langage!; ~ **you don't burn yourself** faites attention *or* prenez garde de ne pas vous brûler, attention, ne vous brûlez pas!; ~ **(that) he does all his homework** veillez à ce qu'il fasse *or* assurez-vous qu'il fait tous ses devoirs.
(d) (*look for*) *opportunity* guetter. **he** ~**ed his chance and slipped out** il a guetté *or* attendu le moment propice et s'est esquivé.
4 *vi* regarder; (*be on guard*) faire le guet, monter la garde; (*Rel etc: keep vigil*) veiller; (*pay attention*) faire attention. **he has only come to** ~ il est venu simplement pour regarder *or* simplement en spectateur; **to** ~ **by sb's bedside** veiller au chevet de qn; **to** ~ **over** *person* surveiller; *thing* surveiller, garder; *sb's rights, safety* protéger, surveiller; **somebody was** ~**ing at the window** quelqu'un les (*or* me *etc*) regardait de la fenêtre; **to** ~ **for sth/sb** guetter qch/qn; **he's** ~**ing to see what you're going to do** il attend pour voir ce que vous allez faire; ~ **and you'll see how it's done** regarde et tu vas voir comme cela se fait; *V* **brief.**
watch out *vi* (*keep a look-out*) faire le guet; (*fig: take care*) faire attention, prendre garde. **watch out for the signal** guettez *or* attendez le signal; **watch out!** attention!, fais gaffe!‡; (*as menace*) attention!, gare à toi!; **watch out for cars when crossing the road** faites attention *or* prenez garde aux voitures en traversant la rue; **to watch out for thieves** être sur ses gardes contre les voleurs; **watch out for trouble if ...** préparez-vous *or* attendez-vous à des ennuis si ... .
watcher ['wɒtʃə^{r}] *n* (*observer*) guetteur *m*, observateur *m*, -trice *f*; (*spectator*) spectateur *m*, -trice *f*; (*onlooker*) curieux *m*, -euse *f*; *V* **bird.**
watchful ['wɒtʃfʊl] *adj* vigilant, attentif. **to keep a** ~ **eye on sth/sb** garder qch/qn à l'œil, avoir l'œil sur qch/qn; **under the** ~ **eye of ...** sous l'œil vigilant de ... .
water ['wɔːtə^{r}] **1** *n* **(a)** (*U: gen*) eau *f*. **I want a drink of** ~ je voudrais de l'eau *or* un verre d'eau; **to turn on the** ~ (*at main*) ouvrir l'eau; (*from tap*) ouvrir le robinet; **the road is under** ~ la route est inondée, la route est recouverte par les eaux; **to swim under** ~ nager sous l'eau; **to go by** ~ voyager par bateau; **the island across the** ~ l'île de l'autre côté de l'eau; **we spent an afternoon on the** ~ nous avons passé un après-midi sur l'eau; **there's 3 metres of** ~ **here, the** ~ **is 3 metres deep here** ici l'eau est profonde de 3 mètres, il y a ici 3 mètres (de profondeur) d'eau *or* 3 mètres de fond; (*tide*) **at high/low** ~ à marée haute/basse, à mer pleine/basse; *[ship]* **to make** ~ faire eau (*V also* **1c**); **it won't hold** ~ *[container, bucket]* cela n'est pas étanche, l'eau va fuir; (*fig*) *[plan, suggestion, excuse]* cela ne tient pas debout, cela ne vaut rien; (*fig*) **a lot of** ~ **has passed under the bridge since then** il est passé beaucoup d'eau sous les ponts depuis ce temps-là; **he spends money like** ~ il jette l'argent par les fenêtres, l'argent lui fond entre les mains; (*fig*) **to pour** *or* **throw cold** ~ **on sth** se montrer peu enthousiaste pour qch; (*fig*) **it's like** ~ **off a duck's back*** c'est comme si on chantait, c'est comme de l'eau sur le dos d'un canard; **lavender/rose** ~ eau de lavande/de rose; *V* **deep, fire, fish** *etc.*
(b) *[spa, lake, river, sea]* ~**s** eaux *fpl*; **to take** *or* **drink the** ~**s** prendre les eaux, faire une cure thermale; **in French** ~**s** dans les eaux (territoriales) françaises; **the** ~**s of the Rhine** l'eau *or* les eaux du Rhin; *V* **territorial** *etc.*
(c) (*Med, Physiol*) **to make** *or* **pass** ~ uriner; (*in pregnancy*) **the** ~**s** les eaux *fpl*; ~ **on the knee** épanchement *m* de synovie; ~ **on the brain** hydrocéphalie *f*.
2 *cpd level, pressure, pipe, vapour* d'eau; *pump, mill* à eau; *plant etc* aquatique. **water bailiff** garde-pêche *m inv*; **waterbed** matelas *m* d'eau; **water beetle** gyrin *m*, tourniquet *m*; **water bird** oiseau *m* aquatique; **water biscuit** craquelin *m*; (*Med*) **water blister** ampoule *f*, phlyctène *f*; (*Zool*) **water boatman** notonecte *m or f*; **waterborne** flottant; *boats* à flot; *goods* transporté par voie d'eau; *disease* d'origine hydrique; **water bottle** (*gen*) carafe *f* (à eau); *[soldier etc]* bidon *m* (*V* **hot 3**); **water buffalo** (*Indian*) arni *m*; (*Indonesian*) kérabau *m*; **water butt** citerne *f* (à eau de pluie); **water cannon** grande lance à eau; **water carrier** porteur *m*, -euse *f* d'eau; **water cart** (*for streets*) arroseuse *f*; (*for selling*) voiture *f* de marchand d'eau; **water clock** horloge *f* à eau; **water closet** (*abbr* **W.C.**) cabinet(s) *m(pl)*, waters *mpl*, W.-C. *mpl*; **watercolour** (*n: painting*) aquarelle *f*; (*adj*) à l'aquarelle; **watercolours** (*paints*) couleurs *fpl* à l'eau *or* pour aquarelle; **painted in watercolours** peint à l'aquarelle; **watercolourist** aquarelliste *mf*; **water-cooled** à refroidissement par eau; **water-cooler** distributeur *m* d'eau réfrigérée; **water-cooling** refroidissement *m* par eau; **watercourse** cours *m* d'eau; **watercress** cresson *m* (de fontaine); **water diviner** sourcier *m*, -ière *f*, radiesthésiste *mf*; **water divining art** *m* du sourcier, radiesthésie *f*; **waterfall** chute *f* d'eau, cascade *f*; **water fountain** jet *m* d'eau; **waterfowl** (*sg*) oiseau *m* d'eau; (*collective pl*) gibier *m* d'eau; **waterfree** sans eau, anhydre; **waterfront** (*at docks etc*) quais *mpl*; (*sea front*) front *m* de mer; **water gas** gaz *m* à l'eau; (*tumbler*) **water glass** verre *m* à eau; (*U: Chem*) **waterglass** silicate *m* de potasse; **water heater** chauffe-eau *m inv*; **water hen** poule *f* d'eau; **water hole** mare *f*; (*Culin*) **water ice** sorbet *m*; (*Aut etc*) **water jacket** chemise *f* d'eau; (*Racing*) **water jump** rivière *f*, brook *m*; **water lily** nénuphar *m*; **waterline** (*Naut*) ligne *f* de flottaison; (*left by tide, river*) = **watermark; waterlogged** *wood* imprégné d'eau; *shoes* imbibé d'eau; *land, pitch* détrempé; **water main** conduite principale d'eau; **waterman** batelier *m*; **watermark** (*in paper*) filigrane *m*; (*left by tide*) laisse *f* de haute mer; (*left by river*) ligne *f* des hautes eaux; **above/below the watermark** au-dessus/au-dessous de la laisse de haute mer *or* de la ligne des hautes eaux; **water meadow** prairie souvent inondée, noue *f*; **watermelon** melon *m* d'eau, pastèque *f*; **water meter** compteur *m* d'eau; **water nymph** naïade *f*; **water pistol** pistolet *m* à eau; **water polo** water-polo *m*; **water power** énergie *f* hydraulique, houille blanche; **waterproof** (*adj*) *material* imperméable; *watch* étanche; (*n*) imperméable *m*; (*vt*) imperméabiliser; **waterproof sheet** (*for bed*) alaise *f*; (*tarpaulin*) bâche *f*; (*U*) **waterproofing** imperméabilisation; **water purifier** (*device*) épurateur *m* d'eau; (*tablet*) cachet *m* pour purifier l'eau; **water rat** rat *m* d'eau; (*Brit*) **water rate** taxe *f* sur l'eau; **water-repellent** (*adj*) hydrofuge, imperméable; (*n*) hydrofuge *m*; **water-resistant** *ink etc* qui résiste à l'eau, indélébile; *material* imperméable; **watershed** (*Geog*) ligne *f* de partage des eaux; (*fig*) moment critique *or* décisif, grand tournant; **waterside** (*n*) bord *m* de l'eau; (*adj*) *flower, insect* du bord de l'eau; *landowner* riverain; **at** *or* **on** *or* **by the waterside** au bord de l'eau, sur la berge; **along the waterside** le long de la rive; **water ski** (*n*) ski *m* nautique (*objet*); **water-ski** (*vi*) faire du ski nautique; (*U*) **water-skiing** ski *m* nautique (*sport*); **water snake** serpent *m* d'eau; **water softener** adoucisseur *m* d'eau; **water-soluble** soluble dans l'eau; **waterspout** (*on roof etc*) (tuyau *m* de) descente *f*; (*Met*) trombe *f*; **water supply** (*for town*) approvisionnement *m* en eau, distribution *f* des eaux; (*for house etc*) alimentation *f*

en eau; (*for traveller*) provision *f* d'eau; **the water supply was cut off** on avait coupé l'eau; **water system** (*Geog*) réseau *m* hydrographique; (*for house, town*) = **water supply**; (*Geog*) **water table** niveau *m* hydrostatique; **water tank** réservoir *m* d'eau, citerne *f*; **watertight** *container* étanche; (*fig*) *excuse, plan* inattaquable, indiscutable; (*lit*) **watertight compartment** compartiment *m* étanche; (*fig*) **in watertight compartments** séparé par des cloisons étanches; **water tower** château *m* d'eau; **waterway** voie *f* navigable; **waterweed** élodée *f*; **waterwheel** roue *f* hydraulique; **water wings** bouée *f*, flotteurs *mpl* de natation; **waterworks** (*system*) système *m* hydraulique; (*place*) station *f* hydraulique; (*fig: cry*) **to turn on the waterworks*** se mettre à pleurer à chaudes larmes *or* comme une Madeleine*; (*Med euph*) **to have something wrong with one's waterworks*** avoir des ennuis de vessie.

3 *vi [eyes]* larmoyer, pleurer. **his mouth ~ed** il a eu l'eau à la bouche; **it made his mouth ~** cela lui a fait venir l'eau à la bouche.

4 *vt plant, garden* arroser; *animal* donner à boire à, faire boire; *wine, milk* couper (d'eau), baptiser*. (*Tex*) **~ed silk** soie moirée; **the river ~s the whole province** le fleuve arrose *or* irrigue toute la province.

water down *vt sep milk, wine* couper (d'eau), baptiser*; (*fig*) *story* édulcorer; *effect* atténuer, affaiblir. **the film is a watered-down version of the book** le film est une version édulcorée du livre.

watering ['wɔːtərɪŋ] **1** *n [streets, plants]* arrosage *m*; *[fields, region]* irrigation *f*. **frequent ~ is needed** il est conseillé d'arroser fréquemment, des arrosages fréquents sont recommandés.

2 *cpd*: **watering can** arrosoir *m*; **watering place** (*for animals*) abreuvoir *m*; (*spa*) station thermale, ville *f* d'eaux; (*seaside resort*) station *f* balnéaire.

Waterloo [ˌwɔːtə'luː] *n* Waterloo. (*fig*) **to meet one's ~** faire naufrage (*fig*).

watery ['wɔːtərɪ] *adj substance* aqueux, qui contient de l'eau; *eyes* larmoyant, humide; *district, ground* détrempé, saturé d'eau; *sky, moon* qui annonce la pluie; (*pej*) *tea, coffee* trop faible; *soup* trop liquide; *taste* fade, insipide; *colour* délavé, pâle. (*liter*) **in his ~ grave** dans l'onde qui est son tombeau.

watt [wɒt] *n* (*Elec*) watt *m*.

wattage ['wɒtɪdʒ] *n* (*Elec*) puissance *f* *or* consommation *f* en watts.

wattle ['wɒtl] *n* **(a)** (*U: woven sticks*) clayonnage *m*. **~ and daub** clayonnage enduit de torchis. **(b)** *[turkey, lizard]* caroncule *f*; *[fish]* barbillon *m*.

wave [weɪv] **1** *n* **(a)** (*at sea*) vague *f*, lame *f*; (*on lake*) vague; (*on beach*) rouleau *m*; (*on river, pond*) vaguelette *f*; (*in hair*) ondulation *f*, cran *m*; (*on surface*) ondulation; (*fig: of dislike, enthusiasm, strikes, protests etc*) vague. (*liter*) **the ~s** les flots *mpl*, l'onde *f*; **her hair has a natural ~ (in it)** ses cheveux ondulent naturellement *or* ont un cran naturel; (*Mil*) **the first ~ of the attack** la première vague d'assaut; **to come in ~s** *[people]* arriver par vagues; *[explosions etc]* se produire par vagues; (*fig: Cine etc*) **the new ~** la nouvelle vague; *V* **crime, heat, permanent** *etc*.

(b) (*Phys, Rad, Telec etc*) onde *f*. **long ~** grandes ondes; **medium/short ~** ondes moyennes/courtes; *V* **light**[1], **shock**[1], **sound**[1] *etc*.

(c) (*gesture*) geste *m* *or* signe *m* de la main. **he gave me a cheerful ~** il m'a fait un signe joyeux de la main; **with a ~ of his hand** d'un geste *or* signe de la main, en agitant la main.

2 *cpd*: (*Rad etc*) **waveband** bande *f* de fréquences; (*Electronics*) **wave guide** guide *m* d'ondes; (*Phys*) **wavelength** longueur *f* d'ondes; (*fig*) **we're not on the same wavelength** nous ne sommes pas sur la même longueur d'ondes*; (*U: Phys*) **wave mechanics** mécanique *f* ondulatoire.

3 *vi* **(a)** *[person]* faire signe de la main; *[flag]* flotter (au vent); *[branch, tree]* être agité; *[grass, corn]* onduler, ondoyer. **to ~ to sb** (*in greeting*) saluer qn de la main, faire bonjour (*or* au revoir) de la main à qn; (*as signal*) faire signe à qn (*to do* de faire).

(b) *[hair]* onduler, avoir un *or* des cran(s).

4 *vt* **(a)** *flag* agiter, faire claquer, brandir; *handkerchief etc* agiter; (*threateningly*) *stick, sword* brandir. **to ~ one's hand to sb** faire signe de la main à qn; **he ~d the ticket at me furiously** il a agité vivement le ticket sous mon nez; **to ~ goodbye to sb** dire au revoir de la main à qn, agiter la main en signe *or* guise d'adieu; **he ~d his thanks** il a remercié d'un signe de la main, il a agité la main en signe *or* guise de remerciement; **to ~ sb back/through/on** *etc* faire signe à qn de reculer/de passer/d'avancer *etc*.

(b) *hair* onduler.

wave about, wave around *vt sep object* agiter dans tous les sens. **to wave one's arms about** gesticuler, agiter les bras dans tous les sens.

wave aside, wave away *vt sep person, object* écarter *or* éloigner d'un geste; *offer, sb's help etc* rejeter *or* refuser d'un geste.

wave down *vt sep*: **to wave down a car** faire signe à une voiture de s'arrêter.

wavelet ['weɪvlɪt] *n* vaguelette *f*.

waver ['weɪvəʳ] *vi [flame, shadow]* vaciller, osciller; *[voice]* trembler, trembloter; *[courage, determination]* vaciller, chanceler; *[person]* (*weaken*) lâcher pied, flancher*; (*hesitate*) vaciller, hésiter, balancer (*between* entre). **he ~ed in his resolution** sa résolution chancelait; **he is beginning to ~** il commence à ne plus être aussi décidé *or* à flancher*.

waverer ['weɪvərəʳ] *n* indécis(e) *m(f)*, irrésolu(e) *m(f)*.

wavering ['weɪvərɪŋ] **1** *adj flame, shadow* vacillant, oscillant; *voice* tremblant, tremblotant; *courage, determination* vacillant, chancelant.

2 *n* (*U: V* **waver**) vacillation *f*, oscillations *fpl*; tremblement *m*; hésitation(s) *f(pl)*.

wavy ['weɪvɪ] **1** *adj hair, surface* ondulé; *line* onduleux. **2** *cpd*: **wavy-haired** aux cheveux ondulés.

wax[1] [wæks] **1** *n* (*U*) cire *f*; (*for skis*) fart *m*; (*in ear*) cérumen *m*, cire; *V* **bee, sealing** *etc*.

2 *cpd candle, doll, seal, record* de *or* en cire. **wax(ed) paper** papier paraffiné; **waxworks** (*pl: figures*) personnages *mpl* en cire; (*sg: wax museum*) musée *m* de cire.

3 *vt floor, furniture* cirer, encaustiquer; *shoes, moustache* cirer; *thread* poisser; *car* lustrer.

wax[2] [wæks] *vi [moon]* croître. († *or hum*) **to ~ merry/poetic** *etc* devenir d'humeur joyeuse/poétique *etc*; **to ~ eloquent** déployer toute son éloquence (*about, over* à propos de); *V* **enthusiastic**.

waxen ['wæksən] *adj* (*of wax*: †) de *or* en cire; (*like wax*) cireux.

waxy ['wæksɪ] *adj substance, texture* cireux; *complexion, colour* cireux, jaunâtre; *potato* qui ne se défait pas.

way [weɪ] **1** *n* **(a)** (*road etc*) chemin *m*, voie *f*. **follow the ~ across the fields** suivez le chemin qui traverse les champs *or* à travers champs; **they drove a ~ through the hills** ils ont fait un chemin *or* fait une route *or* ouvert un passage à travers les collines; **the Appian W~** la voie Appienne; (*Rel*) **the W~ of the Cross** le chemin de la Croix; **private/public ~** voie privée/publique; **they live over *or* across the ~** ils habitent de l'autre côté de la rue (*from* par rapport à), ils habitent en face; **the ~ is obstructed by roadworks** le chemin *or* la voie *or* le passage est bloqué(e) par les travaux; *V* **parting, pave, permanent** *etc*.

(b) (*route*) chemin *m* (*to* de, vers). **which is the ~ to the town hall?** pouvez-vous m'indiquer le chemin *or* la direction de la mairie?; **he talked all the ~ to the theatre** il a parlé pendant tout le chemin jusqu'au théâtre; **there are houses all the ~** il y a des maisons tout le long du chemin; **it rained all the ~** il a plu pendant tout le chemin; (*fig*) **I'm with you all the ~*** je suis entièrement d'accord avec vous; **we have gone *or* taken the wrong ~** nous nous sommes trompés de chemin, nous avons pris le mauvais chemin; (*fig*) **the ~ to success** le chemin du succès; **the shortest *or* quickest ~ to Leeds** le chemin le plus court pour aller à Leeds; **I went the long ~ round** j'ai pris le chemin le plus long; **on the ~ to London we met ...** en allant à Londres *or* en route pour Londres nous avons rencontré ...; **it's on the ~ to the station** c'est sur le chemin de la gare; **we met several people on the ~** nous avons rencontré plusieurs personnes en route *or* chemin faisant; **on the ~ here I saw ...** en venant (ici) j'ai vu ...; **you pass it on your ~ home** vous passez devant en rentrant chez vous; **I must be on my ~** il faut que je parte *or* que je me mette en route; **to start on one's ~** se mettre en route; **he is on the ~ to fame** il est sur le chemin de la gloire, il est en passe de devenir célèbre; **he went by ~ of Glasgow** il est passé par Glasgow, il y est allé via Glasgow; **they met a tramp by the ~** en chemin *or* sur leur route *or* chemin faisant ils ont rencontré un vagabond; (*fig*) **by the ~, what did he say?** à propos, qu'est-ce qu'il a dit?; **oh and by the ~ ...** oh à propos ..., oh pendant que j'y pense ...; (*fig*) **that is by the ~** tout ceci est secondaire *or* entre parenthèses, je signale ceci au passage *or* en passant; **the village is quite out of the ~** le village est vraiment à l'écart *or* isolé; (*fig*) **it's nothing out of the ~** cela n'a rien de spécial *or* d'extraordinaire, c'est très quelconque; **it's an out-of-the-~ subject** c'est un sujet peu commun, c'est un sujet qui sort des sentiers battus; **I'll take you home if it's not out of my ~** je vous ramènerai si c'est sur mon chemin *or* si cela ne me fait pas faire un détour; (*fig*) **to go out of one's ~ to do sth** se donner du mal pour faire qch, faire un effort particulier pour faire qch; **he went out of his ~ to help us** il s'est donné du mal *or* il s'est coupé en quatre pour nous aider; **don't go out of your ~ to do it** ne vous dérangez pas pour le faire; **to lose the *or* one's ~** perdre son chemin (*to* en allant à); **to ask the *or* one's ~** demander son chemin (*to* pour aller à); **I know the *or* my ~ to the station** je connais le chemin de la gare, je sais comment aller à la gare; (*fig*) **she knows her ~ about** elle sait se retourner *or* se débrouiller*; **he went on his ~, content** il est parti satisfait; **they went their own ~s *or* their separate ~s** (*lit*) ils sont partis chacun de leur côté; (*fig*) chacun a suivi son chemin; (*fig*) **he went his own ~** il a fait à son idée *or* à sa guise, il n'en a fait qu'à sa tête; (*fig*) **he has gone the ~ of his brothers** il a fait comme ses frères; **to make one's ~ towards ...** se diriger vers ...; **he made his ~ through the forest** il a traversé la forêt; (*fig*) **he had to make his own ~ in Hollywood** il a dû faire son chemin tout seul à Hollywood; *V* **find, point, see**[1], **work** *etc*.

(c) (*route*: + *adv or prep*) chemin *m*, route *f*. **the ~ back** le chemin *or* la route du retour; **the ~ back to the station** le chemin pour retourner à la gare; **on the ~ back he met ...** au retour *or* sur le chemin du retour *or* en revenant il a rencontré ...; **he made his ~ back to the car** il est retourné (*or* revenu) vers la voiture; **the ~ down/up** le chemin pour descendre/monter, la descente/montée; **I don't know the ~ down/up** je ne sais pas par où on descend/monte; **the ~ forward is dangerous** le chemin devient dangereux plus loin; **the ~ in** l'entrée *f*; '**~ in**' 'entrée'; **I'm looking for a ~ in/out** je cherche un moyen d'entrer/de sortir; **do you know the ~ into/out of this building?** savez-vous par où on entre dans/sort de ce bâtiment?; *[fashion etc]* **it's on the ~ in** c'est la nouvelle mode; **it's on the ~ out** c'est passé de mode; **the ~ out** la sortie; '**~ out**' 'sortie'; **you'll see it on the *or* your ~ out** vous le verrez en sortant; (*fig*) **there is no ~ out *or* no ~ round this difficulty** il n'y a pas moyen de se sortir de la difficulté *or* de contourner la difficulté; (*fig*) **there's no other ~ out** il n'y a pas d'autre façon de s'en sortir *or* d'autre solution; **the ~ through the forest is clearly marked** le chemin à travers la forêt est clairement indiqué; '**no ~ through**' 'sans issue'.

(d) (*path*) passage *m.* (*fig*) the middle ~ le juste milieu; to be in sb's ~ se trouver *or* être sur le chemin de qn; to be in the ~ (*lit*) bloquer *or* barrer le passage; (*fig*) gêner; am I in the *or* your ~? (*lit*) est-ce que je vous empêche de passer?; (*fig*) est-ce que je vous gêne?; it's not in the ~ *or* it's out of the ~ over there ça ne gêne pas là-bas; to get out of the ~ se ranger, s'écarter (du chemin); (get) out of the *or* my ~! pousse-toi!, écarte-toi!, laisse-moi passer!; to get out of sb's ~ laisser passer qn, céder le pas à qn; I couldn't get out of the ~ of the car in time je n'ai pas pu m'écarter de la voiture à temps; get it out of the ~! poussez-le!, écartez-le!; as soon as I've got the exam out of the ~ dès que je serai débarrassé de l'examen; keep matches out of children's ~ *or* out of the ~ of children ne laissez pas les allumettes à la portée des enfants; to keep out of sb's ~ éviter qn; keep (well) out of his ~ today! ne te frotte pas à lui aujourd'hui!; he kept well out of the ~ il a pris soin de rester à l'écart; to put sth out of the ~ ranger qch, écarter qch; put it out of the ~ in the cupboard range-le dans le placard; he wants his wife out of the ~* il veut se débarrasser de sa femme; to put difficulties in sb's ~ créer des difficultés à qn; he put me in the ~ of one or two good bargains il m'a permis de profiter de *or* il m'a indiqué quelques bonnes affaires; to make ~ for sb faire place à qn, s'écarter pour laisser passer qn; (*fig*) laisser la voie libre à qn; make ~! écartez-vous!; make ~ for the king! place au roi!; he made ~ for the ambulance il s'est écarté pour laisser passer l'ambulance; (*fig*) this made ~ for a return to democracy ceci a ouvert la voie à *or* préparé le terrain pour la restauration de la démocratie; to push *or* force *or* thrust *or* elbow one's ~ through a crowd se frayer un chemin à travers une foule; to hack *or* cut one's ~ through the jungle s'ouvrir un chemin à la hache dans la jungle; to crawl/limp *etc* one's ~ to the door ramper/boiter *etc* jusqu'à la porte; he talked his ~ out of the difficulty il s'est sorti de cette difficulté avec de belles paroles; *V* open, prepare, stand *etc.*

(e) to give ~ [*person*] (*stand back*) s'écarter, se pousser, reculer; (*surrender*) se rendre, céder; (*agree*) donner son accord, consentir; [*troops*] reculer, se retirer; [*car, traffic*] laisser la priorité (*to* à); [*beam, bridge*] céder, s'effondrer; [*rope*] céder, se casser; (*Aut*) 'give ~' 'cédez la priorité'; (*Aut*) 'give ~ to traffic from the right' 'priorité à droite'; he gave ~ to their demands il a cédé *or* consenti à leurs revendications; she gave ~ to tears elle s'est laissée aller à pleurer; don't give ~ to despair ne vous abandonnez pas au désespoir; the storm gave ~ to sunshine l'orage a fait place au soleil; the radio gave ~ to a television set la radio a fait place à un poste de télévision; *V* right *etc.*

(f) (*distance*) distance *f.* a long ~ off *or* away loin; a little ~ away *or* off pas très loin, à une courte distance; it's a long *or* good ~ to London Londres est loin, ça fait loin pour aller à Londres*; it's a long ~ from here to London cela fait loin d'ici à Londres; the roots go a long ~ down les racines descendent loin; it's a long ~ from here c'est loin d'ici; he's a long ~ from home il est loin de chez lui; (*fig*) you're a long ~ out vous êtes loin du compte; we've a long ~ to go (*lit*) nous avons encore une grande distance à parcourir *or* un grand bout de chemin à faire; (*fig*) nous sommes encore très loin du compte, nous ne sommes pas au bout de nos peines; your work has still a long ~ to go vous avez encore de grands efforts à faire dans votre travail; (*fig*) it should go a long ~ towards paying the bill cela devrait couvrir une grande partie de la facture; it should go a long ~ towards improving relations between the two countries cela devrait bien améliorer les rapports entre les deux pays; he makes a little go a long ~ il tire le meilleur parti de ce qu'il a; a little kindness goes a long ~ un peu de gentillesse facilite bien des choses; he is a long ~ from understanding why I did it il est loin d'avoir compris pourquoi je l'ai fait; it's better by a long ~ c'est nettement mieux; not by a long ~! absolument pas!, pas du tout!, pas le moins du monde!

(g) (*direction*) direction *f*, sens *m.* this ~ par ici; 'this ~ for *or* to the cathedral' 'vers la cathédrale'; this ~ and that par-ci par-là, en tous sens, partout; turn round this ~ for a moment tourne-toi par ici un instant; which ~ did he go? par où est-il passé?, dans quelle direction est-il parti?; which ~ do we go from here? (*lit*) par où passons-nous maintenant?, quel chemin prenons-nous maintenant?; (*fig*) quelle voie devons-nous choisir maintenant?, que faire maintenant?; are you going my ~? est-ce que vous allez dans la même direction que moi?; (*fig*) everything's going his ~ just now* tout lui sourit *or* lui réussit en ce moment; he went that ~ il est allé *or* parti par là; she didn't know which ~ to look elle ne savait pas où regarder; he looked the other ~ il a détourné les yeux; he never looks my ~ il ne regarde jamais dans ma direction; I'll be down *or* round your ~ tomorrow je serai près de chez vous *or* dans vos parages demain; if he comes your ~ again s'il revient dans vos parages; if the chance comes your ~ si jamais vous en avez l'occasion; it's out *or* over Oxford ~ c'est du côté d'Oxford; (*fig*) he's in a fair ~ to succeed il est en passe de réussir; you're wearing your hat the wrong ~ round vous avez mis votre chapeau à l'envers *or* dans le mauvais sens; the right ~ up dans le bon sens; the wrong ~ up sens dessus dessous; his jersey is the right/wrong ~ out son chandail est à l'endroit/à l'envers; turn the box the other ~ round tourne la boîte dans l'autre sens; HE didn't hit HER, it was the other ~ round ce n'est pas lui qui l'a frappée, c'est juste le contraire; a one-~ street une rue à sens unique; a three-~ discussion une discussion à trois participants; *V* rub up *etc.*

(h) (*manner, method, course of action*) façon *f*, méthode *f*, manière *f*, moyen *m.* there are ~s and means il y a différents moyens (*of doing* de faire); we haven't the ~s and means to do it nous n'avons pas les ressources suffisantes pour le faire; (*Admin*) W~s and Means Committee la Commission des Finances; we'll find a ~ to do *or* of doing it nous trouverons un moyen *or* une façon de le faire; love will find a ~ l'amour finit toujours par triompher; do it (in) this ~ fais-le comme ceci *or* de cette façon *or* de cette manière; that's the ~ to do it voilà comment il faut s'y prendre, c'est ainsi qu'il faut (le) faire; (*encouraging*) that's the ~! voilà c'est bien!; (*refusing*) no ~!* pas question!*; do it your own ~ fais-le comme tu veux *or* à ta façon; he has his own ~ of doing things il a sa façon à lui de faire les choses; the French ~ of life la manière de vivre des Français, la vie à la française; to get one's own ~ obtenir ce que l'on désire, faire exactement ce que l'on veut; to want one's own ~ vouloir imposer sa volonté, ne vouloir en faire qu'à sa tête; Arsenal had it all their own ~ in the second half Arsenal a complètement dominé le match pendant la deuxième mi-temps; I won't let him have things all his own ~ je ne vais pas faire ses quatre volontés* *or* lui passer tous ses caprices; my ~ is to get the personnel together first ma méthode consiste à rassembler d'abord le personnel; to my ~ of thinking à mon avis; her ~ of looking at it son point de vue sur la question; that's the ~ the money goes c'est à ça que l'argent passe; what an odd ~ to behave! quelle drôle de façon de se conduire!; whatever ~ you like to look at it de quelque façon que vous envisagiez (*subj*) la chose; it's just the ~ things are c'est la vie; that's the ~ of the world! ainsi va le monde!; it's just the ~ I'm made c'est comme ça que je suis; leave it all the ~ it is laisse les choses comme elles sont; the ~ things are going we shall have nothing left du train où vont les choses il ne nous restera rien; that's always the ~ c'est toujours comme ça; that's always the ~ with him c'est toujours comme ça *or* toujours pareil avec lui; it was this ~ ... voici comment cela s'est passé ...; to do sth the right/wrong ~ faire qch bien/mal; there's a right and a wrong ~ of doing everything il y a toujours une bonne et une mauvaise façon de faire quelque chose; he said it in such a ~ that ... il l'a dit d'un tel ton *or* d'une telle façon *or* d'une telle manière que ...; in a general ~ it's true c'est vrai en général; once in a ~ we ... (une fois) de temps en temps nous ...; it was by ~ of being a joke c'était en guise de plaisanterie, c'était entendu comme une plaisanterie; I did it by ~ of discovering what ... je l'ai fait pour découvrir *or* afin de découvrir ce que ...; I met him by the ~ of work je l'ai rencontré dans *or* par mon travail.

(i) (*state; condition; degree*) état *m.* things are in a bad ~ tout va mal; he is in a bad ~ il va mal; the car is in a very bad ~ la voiture est en piteux état; she was in a terrible ~ (*physically*) elle était dans un état terrible; (*agitated*) elle était dans tous ses états; there are no two ~s about it c'est absolument clair; one ~ or (an)other you must ... d'une façon ou d'une autre vous devez ...; (*Racing*) each ~ gagnant ou placé; you can't have it both *or* all ~s il faut choisir; they live in quite a small ~ ils vivent modestement, ils ont un petit train de vie *or* un train de vie modeste; (*fig*) in a small ~ he contributed to ... il a apporté sa petite contribution à ...; in a small ~ it did make a difference cela a quand même fait une petite différence; he deals in quite a big ~ il fait de grosses affaires; he is a bookseller in a big ~ c'est un gros libraire; we lost in a really big ~ nous avons vraiment beaucoup perdu; in the ordinary ~ of things à l'ordinaire, normalement; he's not a plumber in the ordinary ~ ce n'est pas un plombier ordinaire *or* comme les autres *or* au sens traditionnel du mot; *V* family *etc.*

(j) (*custom, habit, manner of behaving*) coutume *f*, habitude *f*, manière *f*, façon *f.* the ~s of the Spaniards les coutumes espagnoles; the good old ~s les coutumes du bon vieux temps; the ~s of God and men les voies *fpl* de Dieu et de l'homme; they mistrusted his foreign ~s ils se méfiaient de ses habitudes d'étranger; he has an odd ~ of scratching his chin when he laughs il a une drôle de façon *or* manière de se gratter le menton quand il rit; he is very slow in his ~s il est très lent dans ce qu'il fait, il fait tout très lentement; he is amusing in his (own) ~ il est amusant à sa façon; in his own small ~ he helped a lot of people dans la mesure de ses modestes moyens il a aidé beaucoup de gens; that's not my ~ ce n'est pas mon genre, ce n'est pas ma façon de faire; it's not my ~ to show my feelings ce n'est pas mon genre *or* dans mes habitudes d'exprimer ce que je ressens; it's only his (little) ~ c'est comme ça qu'il est, voilà comment il est; she has a (certain) ~ with her elle sait persuader; he has a ~ with people il sait (comment) s'y prendre avec les gens, les gens le trouvent sympathique; he has got a ~ with cars il sait (comment) s'y prendre avec les voitures; to mend *or* improve one's ~s s'amender, acheter une conduite*; to get into/out of the ~ of doing prendre/perdre l'habitude de faire.

(k) (*respect, detail, particular*) égard *m*, point *m.* in some ~s à certains égards; in many ~s à bien des égards; can I help you in any ~? puis-je vous aider en quoi que ce soit?, puis-je faire quelque chose pour vous aider?; in every ~ possible, in every possible ~ de toutes les façons possibles; does that in any ~ explain it? est-ce là une explication satisfaisante?; he's in no ~ *or* not in any ~ to blame ce n'est vraiment pas sa faute, ce n'est aucunement sa faute; not in any ~! en aucune façon!; without in any ~ wishing to do so sans vouloir le moins du monde le faire; he's right in a *or* one ~ il a raison dans un certain sens; what is there in the ~ of books? qu'est-ce qu'il y a comme livres?, qu'est-ce qu'il y a à lire?

(l) (*Naut*) to gather/lose ~ prendre/perdre de la vitesse; to have ~ on avoir de l'erre; to be under ~ faire route, être en route; (*fig*) to be under ~ (*Aut etc*) être en marche; [*meeting, discussion*] être en cours; [*plans*] être en voie de réalisation *or* d'exécution; to get under ~ (*Naut*) appareiller, lever l'ancre; (*fig*) [*person*] se mettre en route, partir; (*Aut etc*) se mettre en marche, démarrer; [*meeting, discussion*] démarrer; [*plan, pro-

ject] démarrer, commencer à se réaliser *or* à être exécuté; **they got the ship under ~** ils ont appareillé; **things are getting under ~ at last** cela commence enfin à prendre tournure; **to get sth under ~** *(meeting etc)* faire démarrer qch; *(project etc)* activer qch.

(m) *(Shipbuilding)* **~s** cale *f.*

2 *adv* (*) très loin. **~ over there** très loin là-bas; **~ down below** très loin en bas, bien plus bas; **~ up in the sky** très haut dans le ciel; **~ back/over = away back/over** (*V* **away 1a**); **~ out to sea** loin au large; **you're ~ out in your calculations** tu es très loin de compte dans tes calculs (*V also* **3**).

3 *cpd:* *(Comm)* **waybill** récépissé *m;* **wayfarer** *etc V* **wayfarer** *etc;* **waylay** *V* **waylay;** **way-out*** *clothes, ideas, behaviour* excentrique; *guess* très loin de compte; **wayside** *(n)* bord *m or* côté *m* de la route; *(cpd) plant, café* au bord de la route; **along the wayside** le long de la route; **by the wayside** au bord de la route; *(fig liter)* **to fall by the wayside** quitter le droit chemin; *(US)* **way station** petite gare; *(US)* **way train** omnibus *m.*

wayfarer ['weɪˌfɛərəʳ] *n* voyageur *m,* -euse *f.*

wayfaring ['weɪˌfɛərɪŋ] *n* voyages *mpl.*

waylay [weɪ'leɪ] *pret, ptp* **waylaid** *vt* *(attack)* attaquer, assaillir; *(speak to)* arrêter au passage.

wayward ['weɪwəd] *adj person* capricieux, entêté, rebelle; *horse* rétif.

waywardness ['weɪwədnɪs] *n* *(U)* caractère capricieux *or* rebelle *or* rétif.

W.C. ['dʌblju(ː)'siː] *n* W.-C. *mpl,* waters *mpl.*

we [wiː] *pers pron pl* *(unstressed, stressed)* nous. WE **don't do that** nous, nous ne faisons pas ce genre de choses; **~ went to the pictures** nous sommes allés *or* on est allé* au cinéma; **~ French** nous autres Français; **~ the teachers understand that ...** nous autres professeurs, nous comprenons que ...; **~ three have already discussed it** nous en avons déjà discuté à nous trois, nous trois en avons déjà discuté; **'~ are convinced' said the king** 'nous sommes convaincu' dit le roi.

weak [wiːk] **1** *adj* **(a)** *(physically) person, animal* faible, qui manque de forces; *join, beam, structure, material* faible, fragile, qui manque de solidité; *(morally etc) person* faible, mou *(f* molle); *army, country, team* faible, sans défense; *government* faible, impuissant; *excuse, argument, evidence* faible, réfutable, peu convaincant; *intellect* faible. **his health is ~** il a une santé fragile *or* délicate; **~ from** *or* **with hunger** affaibli par la faim; **~ from** *or* **with fright** les jambes molles de peur; **to have a ~ heart** être cardiaque, avoir le cœur faible *or* malade; **to have ~ lungs** *or* **a ~ chest** avoir les poumons fragiles, être faible des bronches; **to have a ~ stomach** *or* **digestion** avoir l'estomac fragile; **to have ~ eyes** *or* **eyesight** avoir la vue faible, avoir une mauvaise vue; **to have a ~ chin/mouth** avoir le menton fuyant/la bouche tombante; **in a ~ voice** d'une voix fluette *or* faible; **to be ~ in the head*** être faible d'esprit, être débile*; **his knees felt ~, he went ~ at the knees** ses genoux se dérobaient sous lui, il avait les jambes molles *or* comme du coton*; **he is ~ in maths** il est faible en maths; **~ point** point *m* faible; *(fig)* **the ~ link in the chain** le point faible; **you're too ~ with her** tu te montres trop faible envers elle; *V* **constitution, sex, wall** *etc.*

(b) *coffee, tea* léger, faible; *solution, mixture, drug, lens, spectacles, magnet* faible; *(Elec) current* faible; *(Econ) the pound, dollar* faible. *(Gram)* **~ verb** verbe *m* faible.

2 *n:* **the ~** les faibles *mpl.*

3 *cpd:* *(fig)* **weak-kneed** mou *(f* molle), lâche, faible; **weak-minded** faible *or* simple d'esprit; **weak-willed** faible, velléitaire.

weaken ['wiːkən] **1** *vi [person] (in health)* s'affaiblir, faiblir; *(in resolution)* faiblir, flancher*; *[structure, material]* faiblir, commencer à fléchir; *[voice]* faiblir, baisser; *[influence, power]* baisser, diminuer; *[country, team]* faiblir; *[prices]* fléchir.

2 *vt person (physically)* affaiblir, miner; *(morally, politically)* affaiblir; *join, structure, material* enlever de la solidité à; *heart* fatiguer; *country, team, government* affaiblir, rendre vulnérable; *defence, argument, evidence* affaiblir, enlever du poids *or* de la force à; *coffee, solution, mixture* couper, diluer; *(Econ) the pound, dollar* affaiblir, faire baisser.

weakening ['wiːkənɪŋ] **1** *n [health, resolution]* affaiblissement *m; [structure, material]* fléchissement *m,* fatigue *f.* **2** *adj effect* affaiblissant, débilitant; *disease, illness* débilitant, qui mine.

weakling ['wiːklɪŋ] *n* *(physically)* gringalet *m,* mauviette *f;* *(morally etc)* faible *mf,* poule *f* mouillée.

weakly ['wiːklɪ] **1** *adj* faible, maladif, chétif.

2 *adv move* faiblement, sans forces; *speak* faiblement, mollement.

weakness ['wiːknɪs] *n* (*V* **weak**) faiblesse *f;* fragilité *f;* mollesse *f;* impuissance *f.* **it's one of his ~es** c'est là un de ses points faibles; **to have a ~ for** avoir un faible pour.

weal[1] [wiːl] *n* *(wound)* marque *f* d'un coup de fouet *(or* de bâton *etc),* zébrure *f.*

weal[2]†† [wiːl] *n* bien *m,* bonheur *m.* **the common ~** le bien public; **~ and woe** le bonheur et le malheur.

weald [wiːld] *n* *(wooded country)* pays boisé; *(open country)* pays découvert.

wealth [welθ] **1** *n* *(U)* *(money)* richesse(s) *f(pl),* fortune *f;* *(natural resources etc)* richesse(s). **a man of great ~** un homme puissamment riche; **'The W~ of Nations'** 'la Richesse des Nations'; **the ~ of the oceans** les richesses *or* les riches ressources *fpl* des océans; **the mineral ~ of a country** les richesses minières d'un pays; *(fig)* **a ~ of ideas** une profusion *or* une abondance d'idées, des idées en abondance *or* à profusion.

2 *cpd:* **wealth tax** impôt *m* sur la fortune.

wealthy ['welθɪ] **1** *adj person, family* riche, fortuné, nanti; *country* riche. **2** *n:* **the ~** les riches *mpl.*

wean [wiːn] *vt baby* sevrer; *(fig: from bad habits etc)* détacher, détourner *(from, off* de). **I've managed to ~ him off gin** je l'ai habitué à se passer de gin; **I ~ed her off the idea of going to Greece** je l'ai dissuadée de partir pour la Grèce.

weaning ['wiːnɪŋ] *n* sevrage *m.*

weapon ['wepən] *n* *(lit, fig)* arme *f.* **~ of offence/defence** arme offensive/défensive.

weaponry ['wepənrɪ] *n* *(U: collective)* matériel *m* de guerre, armement(s) *m(pl).*

wear [wɛəʳ] *(vb: pret* **wore,** *ptp* **worn)** **1** *n* *(U)* **(a)** *(act of wearing)* port *m,* fait *m* de porter; *(use)* usage *m;* *(deterioration through use)* usure *f.* **clothes for everyday ~** vêtements pour tous les jours; **for evening ~ we suggest ...** comme tenue de soirée nous suggérons ...; **it isn't for town ~** ce n'est pas une tenue de ville, cela ne se porte pas en ville; **it is compulsory ~ for officers** le port en est obligatoire pour les officiers; **what is the correct ~ for these occasions?** quelle est la tenue convenable pour de telles occasions?, qu'est-ce qui est de mise en de telles occasions?; **this carpet has seen** *or* **had some hard ~** ce tapis a beaucoup servi; **to be in constant ~** *[garment]* être porté continuellement; *[tyres etc]* être en usage continuel, être continuellement utilisé; **this material will stand up to a lot of ~** ce tissu fera beaucoup d'usage *or* résistera bien à l'usure; **there is still some ~ left in it** *(garment)* c'est encore mettable; *(carpet, tyre)* cela fera encore de l'usage; **he got 4 years' ~ out of it** cela lui a fait *or* duré 4 ans; **it has had a lot of ~ and tear** c'est très usagé, cela a été beaucoup porté *or* utilisé; **fair** *or* **normal ~ and tear** usure normale; **the ~ and tear on the engine** l'usure du moteur; **to show signs of ~, to look the worse for ~** *[clothes, shoes, carpet]* commencer à être défraîchi *or* fatigué; *[tyres, machine]* commencer à être fatigué *or* usagé; *(fig)* **he was (looking) somewhat the worse for ~*** il n'était pas très frais.

(b) *(esp Comm: clothes collectively)* vêtements *mpl.* **children's ~** vêtements pour enfants; **summer ~** vêtements d'été; *V* **foot, sport** *etc.*

2 *vt* **(a)** *garment, flower, sword, watch, spectacles* porter; *beard, moustache* porter, avoir; *(fig) smile* avoir, arborer; *look* avoir, afficher. **he was ~ing a hat** il avait *or* il portait un chapeau, il avait mis un chapeau; **I never ~ a hat** je ne mets *or* porte jamais de chapeau; **hats are now rarely worn** les chapeaux ne se portent plus guère aujourd'hui; **what shall I ~?** qu'est-ce que je vais mettre?; **I've nothing to ~** je n'ai rien à me mettre; **I haven't worn that for ages** cela fait des siècles que je ne l'ai pas mis *or* porté; **Eskimos don't ~ bikinis** les Esquimaudes ne portent jamais de bikini; **she was ~ing blue** elle était en bleu; **what the well-dressed woman is ~ing this year** ce que la femme élégante porte cette année; **he ~s good clothes** il est bien habillé, il s'habille bien; **she ~s her hair long** elle a les cheveux longs; **she ~s her hair in a bun** elle porte un chignon; **I never ~ scent** je ne me parfume jamais, je ne me mets jamais de parfum; **she was ~ing make-up** elle (s')était maquillée; **she was ~ing lipstick** elle s'était *or* elle avait mis du rouge à lèvres; **to ~ the crown** être sur le trône; *(fig)* **she's the one who ~s the trousers** *or* **the pants*** c'est elle qui porte la culotte* *or* qui commande; **she wore a frown** elle fronçait les sourcils; **he wore a look** *or* **an air of satisfaction, he wore a satisfied look on his face** son visage exprimait la satisfaction, il affichait *or* avait un air de satisfaction; **she ~s her age** *or* **her years well** elle porte bien son âge, elle est encore bien pour son âge; *V* **heart** *etc.*

(b) *(rub etc) clothes, fabric, stone, wood* user; *groove, path* creuser peu à peu. **to ~ a hole in sth** trouer *or* percer peu à peu qch, faire peu à peu un trou à qch; **to ~ sth into holes** faire des trous à qch; **the knife blade was worn thin** la lame du couteau s'était amincie à l'usage; **the rug was worn thin** *or* **threadbare** le tapis était usé jusqu'à la corde *or* complètement râpé; **he had worn himself to a shadow** il s'était fatigué au point de n'être plus que l'ombre de lui-même; **worn with care** usé *or* rongé par les soucis; *V also* **frazzle, work, worn** *etc.*

(c) *(Brit*: tolerate, accept)* tolérer. **he won't ~ that** il ne marchera pas*, cela ne prendra pas avec lui; **the committee won't ~ another £100 on your expenses** vous ne ferez jamais avaler au comité 100 livres de plus pour vos frais*.

3 *vi* **(a)** *(last) [clothes, carpet, tyres etc]* faire de l'usage, résister à l'usure. **a good tweed will ~ forever** un bon tweed ne s'use jamais *or* est inusable; **these shoes will ~ for years** ces chaussures dureront *or* feront des années; **that dress/carpet has worn well** cette robe/ce tapis a bien résisté à l'usure *or* a fait beaucoup d'usage; *(fig)* **theory/friendship that has worn well** théorie/amitié intacte en dépit du temps; **that car has worn well*** cette voiture est quand même encore en bon état; **she has worn well*** elle est bien conservée.

(b) *(rub etc thin) [garment, fabric, stone, wood]* s'user. **the trousers have worn at the knees** le pantalon est usé aux genoux; **to ~ into holes** se trouer; **the rock has worn smooth** la roche a été polie par le temps; **the material has worn thin** le tissu est râpé; *(fig)* **that excuse has worn thin!** cette excuse ne prend plus!; **my patience is ~ing thin** je suis presque à bout de patience.

(c) *[day, year, sb's life]* **to ~ towards its end** *or* **towards a close** tirer à sa fin.

wear away 1 *vi [wood, metal]* s'user; *[cliffs etc]* être rongé *or* dégradé; *[inscription, design]* s'effacer.

2 *vt sep* user; ronger, dégrader; effacer.

wear down 1 *vi [heels, pencil etc]* s'user; *[resistance, courage]* s'épuiser.

2 *vt sep materials* user; *patience, strength* user, épuiser;

courage, resistance miner. (*fig*) **the hard work was wearing him down** le travail l'usait *or* le minait; **they wore him down with constant pestering until he finally agreed** ils n'ont cessé de l'importuner jusqu'à ce qu'il finisse par accepter *or* jusqu'à ce qu'il accepte (*subj*) de guerre lasse.
wear off 1 *vi [colour, design, inscription]* s'effacer, disparaître; *[pain]* disparaître, passer; *[anger, excitement]* s'apaiser, passer; *[effects]* se dissiper, disparaître; *[anaesthetic]* se dissiper. **the novelty has worn off** cela n'a plus l'attrait de la nouveauté.
2 *vt sep* effacer par l'usure, faire disparaître.
wear on *vi [day, year, winter etc]* avancer; *[battle, war, discussions etc]* se poursuivre. **as the years wore on** à mesure que les années passaient, avec le temps.
wear out 1 *vi [clothes, material, machinery]* s'user; *[patience, enthusiasm]* s'épuiser.
2 *vt sep* **(a)** *shoes, clothes* user; *one's strength, reserves, materials, patience* épuiser.
(b) (*exhaust*) *person, horse* épuiser. **to wear one's eyes out** s'user les yeux *or* la vue; **to wear o.s. out** s'épuiser, s'exténuer (*doing* à faire); **to be worn out** être exténué *or* éreinté.
3 **worn-out** *adj V* **worn.**
wear through *vt sep* trouer, percer.
wearable ['wɛərəbl] *adj garment* mettable.
wearer ['wɛərəʳ] *n*: **will the ~ of the green coat please come forward?** la personne vêtue du *or* portant le manteau vert aurait-elle l'obligeance de s'avancer?; **these shoes will delight the ~** ces chaussures feront la joie de la personne *or* de celui (*or* de celle) qui les portera; **as all uniform ~s know ...** comme tous ceux qui portent l'uniforme le savent ...; **direct from maker to ~** directement du fabricant au client.
wearied ['wɪərɪd] *adj* (*tired*) *person, animal, smile, look* las (*f* lasse); *sigh* de lassitude.
wearily ['wɪərɪlɪ] *adv say* d'un ton las *or* fatigué, avec lassitude; *sigh, smile, look* d'un air las *or* fatigué, avec lassitude; *move* péniblement.
weariness ['wɪərɪnɪs] *n* (*V* **weary**) lassitude *f*, fatigue *f*, épuisement *m*; abattement *m*; ennui *m*; *V* **world.**
wearing ['wɛərɪŋ] *adj* épuisant, lassant.
wearisome ['wɪərɪsəm] *adj* (*tiring*) fatigant, épuisant; (*boring*) ennuyeux, lassant, fastidieux.
weary ['wɪərɪ] **1** *adj* (*tired*) *person, animal* las (*f* lasse), fatigué, épuisé; *smile, look* las; (*dispirited*) *person* las, abattu; *sigh* de lassitude; (*tiring*) *journey, wait* fatigant, épuisant; (*irksome*) ennuyeux, lassant. **to be/grow ~ of (doing) sth** être las/se lasser de (faire) qch; **~ of life** dégoûté *or* las de vivre; **~ of waiting** las *or* fatigué d'attendre; **~ with walking** fatigué *or* las à force d'avoir marché; **4 ~ hours** 4 heures mortelles; **10 ~ miles** 10 milles épuisants; *V* **world.**
2 *vi* se lasser (*of sth* de qch, *of doing* de faire).
3 *vt* (*tire*) fatiguer, lasser; (*try patience of*) lasser, agacer, ennuyer (*with* à force de); *V also* **wearied.**
weasel ['wi:zl] *n* belette *f*; (*fig pej: person*) fouine *f* (*fig pej*).
weather ['weðəʳ] **1** *n* temps *m*. **~ permitting** si le temps le permet; **what's the ~ like?, what's the ~ doing?*** quel temps fait-il?; **it's fine/bad ~** il fait beau/mauvais, le temps est beau/mauvais; **I don't like the ~ much** je n'aime pas ce genre de temps; **summer ~** temps d'été *or* estival; **in hot ~** par temps chaud, en période de chaleur; **in all ~s** par tous les temps; (*fig*) **to be under the ~*** être mal fichu*, ne pas être dans son assiette; *V* **heavy, wet.**
2 *vt* **(a)** (*survive*) *tempest, hurricane* essuyer, réchapper à; (*fig*) *crisis* survivre à, réchapper à, surmonter. **to ~ a storm** (*lit*) essuyer une tempête, réchapper à une tempête; (*fig*) tenir le coup, ne pas succomber.
(b) (*expose to ~*) *wood etc* faire mûrir. **~ed rocks** rochers exposés aux intempéries; **rocks ~ed by rain and wind** rochers patinés *or* érodés par la pluie et par le vent.
3 *vi [wood]* mûrir; *[rocks]* s'effriter.
4 *cpd knowledge, map, prospects* météorologique; *conditions, variations* atmosphérique; (*Naut*) *side, sheet* du vent. **weather-beaten** *person, face* hâlé, tanné; *building* dégradé par les intempéries; *stone* effrité par les intempéries; (*U*) **weather-boarding** planches *fpl* de recouvrement; **weather-bound** immobilisé *or* retenu par le mauvais temps; (*US*) **Weather Bureau** Office national de la météorologie; **weather chart** carte *f* du temps, carte météorologique; **weather cock** girouette *f*; (*fig*) **to keep a weather eye on sth** surveiller qch; (*fig*) **to keep one's weather eye open** veiller au grain (*fig*); **weather forecast** prévisions *fpl* météorologiques, météo* *f*; **weatherman*** météorologue *m*, météorologiste *m*; **weatherproof** (*adj*) *clothing* imperméable; *house* étanche; (*vt*) *clothing* imperméabiliser; *house* rendre étanche; **weather report** bulletin *m* météorologique, météo* *f*; **weather ship** navire *m* météo *inv*; **the weather situation** le temps (qu'il fait *or* fera *etc*); **weather station** station *f or* observatoire *m* météorologique; **weather strip** bourrelet *m* (*pour porte etc*); **weather vane = weather cock; weather-worn = weather-beaten.**
weave [wi:v] (*vb: pret* **wove,** *ptp* **woven**) **1** *n* tissage *m*. **loose/tight ~** tissage lâche/serré; **a cloth of English ~** du drap tissé en Angleterre.
2 *vt threads, cloth, web* tisser; *strands* entrelacer; *basket, garland, daisies* tresser; (*fig*) *plot* tramer, tisser; *story* inventer, bâtir. **to ~ flowers into one's hair** entrelacer des fleurs dans ses cheveux; **to ~ details into a story** introduire *or* incorporer des détails dans une histoire; **to ~ one's way** *V* **3c.**
3 *vi* **(a)** (*Tex etc*) tisser.
(b) *[road, river, line]* serpenter.
(c) (*pret, ptp gen* **weaved**) **to ~ (one's way) through the crowd** se faufiler à travers la foule; **the drunk man ~d (his way) across the room** l'ivrogne a titubé *or* zigzagué à travers la pièce; **the car was weaving (its way) in and out through the traffic** la voiture se faufilait *or* se glissait à travers la circulation; **the boxer was weaving in and out skilfully** le boxeur s'engageait et se dégageait adroitement; (*fig*) **let's get weaving!*** allons, remuons-nous!
weaver ['wi:vəʳ] *n* (*person*) tisserand(e) *m(f)*; (*also* **~bird**) tisserin *m*.
weaving ['wi:vɪŋ] **1** *n* (*U: V* **weave**) tissage *m*; tressage *m*; entrelacement *m*. **2** *cpd*: **weaving mill** (atelier *m* de) tissage *m*.
web [web] **1** *n* (*fabric*) tissu *m*; *[spider]* toile *f*; (*between toes etc*) *[animals etc]* palmure *f*; *[humans]* palmature *f*; (*fig: of lies etc*) tissu.
2 *cpd*: **to have web(bed) feet** *or* **toes, to be webfooted** *or* **webtoed** *[animal]* être palmipède, avoir les pieds palmés; *[human]* avoir une palmature.
webbing ['webɪŋ] *n* (*U*) (*fabric*) toile forte en bande; (*on chair*) sangles *fpl*; (*on bird's, animal's foot*) palmure *f*; (*on human foot*) palmature *f*.
we'd [wi:d] = **we had, we should, we would;** *V* **have, should, would.**
wed [wed] *pret* **wedded,** *ptp* **wedded,** (*rare*) **wed 1** *vt* (*marry*) épouser, se marier avec; (*fig*) *things, qualities* allier. (*fig*) *[person]* **to be ~ded to sth** tenir infiniment à qch, se consacrer corps et âme à qch; **his cunning, ~ded to ambition, led to** ... sa ruse, alliée à l'ambition, a conduit à ... .
2 *vi* se marier.
3 *npl*: **the newly-~s** les jeunes *or* nouveaux mariés.
wedded ['wedɪd] *adj person* marié; *bliss, life* conjugal. **his ~ wife** sa légitime épouse; **the ~ couple** les mariés *mpl*.
wedding ['wedɪŋ] **1** *n* (*ceremony*) mariage *m*, noces *fpl* (*frm*). **silver/golden ~** noces d'argent/d'or; **they had a quiet ~** ils se sont mariés dans l'intimité, le mariage a été célébré dans l'intimité; **they had a church ~** ils se sont mariés à l'église, ils ont eu un mariage religieux; *V* **civil.**
2 *cpd cake, night* de noces; *present* de mariage, de noces; *invitation* de mariage; *ceremony, march* nuptial. **wedding anniversary** anniversaire *m* de mariage; **wedding breakfast** lunch *m* de mariage; (*less elegant*) repas *m* de noces; **their wedding day** le jour de leur mariage; **wedding dress** robe *f* de mariée; **wedding ring** alliance *f*, anneau *m* de mariage.
wedge [wedʒ] **1** *n* (*for holding sth steady; under wheel etc*) cale *f*; (*for splitting wood, rock*) coin *m*; (*piece: of cake, pie etc*) part *f*, morceau *m*. (*fig*) **to drive a ~ between two people** brouiller deux personnes; *V* **thin.**
2 *cpd*: **wedge-heeled** à semelles compensées; **wedge-shaped** en forme de coin; **wedge-soled = wedge-heeled.**
3 *vt* (*fix*) *table, wheels* caler; (*stick, push*) enfoncer (*into* dans, *between* entre). **to ~ a door open/shut** maintenir une porte ouverte/fermée à l'aide d'une cale; **the door was ~d** on avait mis une cale à la porte; **he ~d the table leg to hold it steady** il a calé le pied de table; **I can't move this, it's ~d** je n'arrive pas à l'enlever, c'est coincé; **to ~ a stick into a crack** enfoncer un bâton dans une fente; **the car was ~d between two trucks** la voiture était coincée entre deux camions; **he managed to ~ another book into the bookcase** il a réussi à faire rentrer *or* à enfoncer *or* à fourrer* un autre livre dans la bibliothèque.
wedge in 1 *vi [person]* se glisser.
2 *vt sep* (*into case, box etc*) *object* faire rentrer, enfoncer, fourrer*; (*into car, onto seat etc*) *person* faire rentrer, entasser. **to be wedged in** être coincé.
wedlock ['wedlɒk] *n* (*U*) mariage *m*. **to be born out of ~** être (un) enfant naturel.
Wednesday ['wenzdeɪ] *n* mercredi *m*; *V* **ash**²; *for other phrases V* **Saturday.**
wee¹ [wi:] *adj* (*Scot*) tout petit. **a ~ bit** un tout petit peu.
wee²‡ [wi:] *n, vi*: **to (have a) ~** faire pipi*.
weed [wi:d] **1** *n* **(a)** mauvaise herbe; (* *pej: person*) mauviette *f*; (‡: *marijuana*) herbe *f* (*sl*). (*hum*) **the ~*** le tabac.
(b) **(widow's) ~s** vêtements *mpl* de deuil; **in widow's ~s** en deuil.
2 *cpd*: **weed-killer** désherbant *m*, herbicide *m*.
3 *vt* désherber; (*hoe*) sarcler.
weed out *vt sep plant* enlever, arracher; (*fig*) *weak candidates* éliminer (*from* de); *troublemakers* expulser (*from* de).
weeding ['wi:dɪŋ] *n* (*U*) désherbage *m*; (*with hoe*) sarclage *m*. **I've done some ~** j'ai un peu désherbé.
weedy ['wi:dɪ] *adj ground* couvert de mauvaises herbes, envahi par les mauvaises herbes; (*fig pej*) *person* qui a l'air d'une mauviette.
week [wi:k] **1** *n* semaine *f*. **in a ~** dans une semaine *or* une huitaine, dans huit jours; **what day of the ~ is it?** quel jour de la semaine sommes-nous?; **~ in ~ out** chaque semaine, semaine après semaine, pendant des semaines; **~ after ~** semaine après semaine; **this ~** cette semaine; **next/last ~** la semaine prochaine/dernière; **the ~ before last** l'avant-dernière semaine; **the ~ after next** pas la semaine prochaine, celle d'après; **by the end of the ~ he had ...** à la fin de la semaine il avait ...; **in the middle of the ~** vers le milieu *or* dans le courant de la semaine; **twice a ~** deux fois par semaine; **this time next ~** dans huit jours à la même heure; **this time last ~** il y a huit jours à la même heure; **today ~, a ~ today, this day ~** (d')aujourd'hui en huit; **tomorrow ~, a ~ tomorrow** (de) demain en huit; **yesterday ~, a ~ (past) yesterday** il y a eu une semaine hier; **Sunday ~, a ~ on Sunday** (de) dimanche en huit; **every ~** chaque semaine; **two ~s ago** il y a deux semaines, il y a quinze jours; **in 3 ~s' time** dans *or* d'ici 3 semaines; **it lasted for ~s** cela a duré des semaines (et des semaines); **the ~ ending May 6th** la semaine qui se termine le 6 mai; **he owes her 3 ~s' rent** il lui doit 3 semaines de loyer; **paid by the ~** payé à la

semaine; **the working ~** la semaine de travail; **a 36-hour ~** une semaine de 36 heures; **a ~'s wages** le salaire hebdomadaire *or* de la semaine; *V* **Easter.**

2 *cpd*: weekday (*n*) jour *m* de semaine, jour ouvrable (*esp Comm*); **(on) weekdays** en semaine, les jours ouvrables; (*cpd*) *activities, timetable* de la semaine.

weekend ['wi:k'end] 1 *n* week-end *m*, fin *f* de semaine. **at ~s** en fin de semaine, pendant le(s) week-end(s); **what are you doing at the ~?** qu'est-ce que tu vas faire pendant le week-end?; **we're going away for the ~** nous partons en week-end; **to take a long ~** prendre un week-end prolongé; **they had Tuesday off so they made a long ~ of it** comme ils ne devaient pas travailler mardi ils ont fait le pont.

2 *cpd visit, programme* de *or* du week-end. **weekend bag, weekend case** sac *m* de voyage, mallette *f*; **a weekend cottage** une maison de campagne.

3 *vi* passer le week-end.

weekender ['wi:k'endəʳ] *n* personne *f* partant (*or* partie) en week-end. **the village is full of ~s** le village est plein de gens qui sont venus pour le week-end.

weekly ['wi:klɪ] 1 *adj wages, visit* de la semaine, hebdomadaire; *journal* hebdomadaire.

2 *adv* (*once a week*) chaque semaine, une fois par semaine; (*same day each week*) tous les huit jours. **twice ~** deux fois par semaine.

3 *n* (*Press*) hebdomadaire *m*.

weeny* ['wi:nɪ] *adj* tout petit, petit petit*.

weep [wi:p] *pret, ptp* **wept** 1 *vi [person]* pleurer, verser des larmes; *[walls, sore, wound etc]* suinter. **to ~ for joy** pleurer de joie; **to ~ for sb/sth** pleurer qn/qch; **to ~ over sth** pleurer *or* se lamenter sur qch; **she wept to see him leave** elle a pleuré de le voir partir; **I could have wept!** j'en aurais pleuré!

2 *vt tears* pleurer, verser, répandre. **to ~ one's eyes out** pleurer à chaudes larmes; *V* **bucket.**

3 *n*: **to have a good ~** pleurer à chaudes larmes *or* un bon coup; **to have a little ~** pleurer un peu, verser quelques larmes.

weeping ['wi:pɪŋ] 1 *n* (*U*) larmes *fpl*. 2 *adj person* qui pleure; *walls, wound* suintant. **~ willow** saule pleureur.

weepy ['wi:pɪ] *adj voice* larmoyant. **to be** *or* **feel ~** avoir envie de pleurer, avoir les larmes aux yeux.

weevil ['wi:vl] *n* charançon *m*.

weewee* ['wi:wi:] (*baby talk*) 1 *n* pipi* *m*. 2 *vi* faire pipi*.

weft [weft] *n* (*Tex*) trame *f*.

weigh [weɪ] 1 *vt* **(a)** (*lit, fig*) peser. **to ~ o.s.** se peser; **to ~ sth in one's hand** soupeser qch; **it ~s 9 kilos** ça pèse 9 kilos; **how much** *or* **what do you ~?** combien est-ce que vous pesez?; (*fig*) **that argument doesn't ~ anything with me** cet argument n'a aucun poids à mes yeux; **to ~ one's words** peser ses mots; **to ~ (up) A against B** mettre en balance A et B; **to ~ (up) the pros and cons** peser le pour et le contre.

(b) (*Naut*) **to ~ anchor** lever l'ancre.

2 *vi [object, responsibilities]* peser (*on* sur). **this box ~s fairly heavy** cette boîte pèse assez lourd; **the fear of cancer ~s on her** *or* **on her mind all the time** la peur du cancer la tourmente constamment; **there's something ~ing on her mind** quelque chose la préoccupe *or* la tracasse; **these factors do not ~ with him** ces facteurs ne comptent pas *or* n'ont aucun poids à ses yeux.

3 *cpd*: weighbridge pont-bascule *m*; (*Sport*) weigh-in pesage *m*; weighing machine balance *f*.

weigh down 1 *vi* peser *or* appuyer de tout son poids *or* de toutes ses forces (*on sth* sur qch). (*fig*) **this sorrow weighed down on her** ce chagrin la rongeait *or* la minait.

2 *vt sep* faire plier *or* ployer, courber; (*fig*) accabler, tourmenter. **the fruit weighed the branch down** la branche ployait *or* pliait sous le poids des fruits; **he was weighed down with parcels** il pliait sous le poids des paquets; **to be weighed down with responsibilities** être accablé *or* surchargé de responsabilités; **to be weighed down with fears** être en proie à toutes sortes de peurs.

weigh in 1 *vi [boxer, jockey etc]* se faire peser. **to weigh in at 70 kilos** peser 70 kilos avant le match *or* la course; (*fig*) **he weighed in with the fact that ...** il est intervenu dans le débat avec un argument de poids: le fait que ... .

2 *vt sep boxer, jockey* peser (*avant le match or la course*).

3 **weigh-in** *n V* **weigh 3.**

weigh out *vt sep sugar etc* peser.

weigh up *vt sep* (*consider*) examiner, calculer; (*compare*) mettre en balance (*A with B, A against B* A et B). **I'm weighing up whether to go or not** je me tâte pour savoir si j'y vais ou non; *V also* **weigh 1a.**

weight [weɪt] 1 *n* **(a)** (*U*) poids *m*; (*Phys: relative ~*) pesanteur *f*. (*Phys*) **atomic ~** poids atomique; **to be sold by ~** se vendre au poids; **what is your ~?** combien pesez-vous?, quel poids faites-vous?; **my ~ is 60 kilos** je pèse 60 kilos; **it is 3 kilos in ~** ça pèse 3 kilos; **what a ~ it is!** que c'est lourd!; **they are the same ~** ils font le même poids; (*fig*) **it is worth its ~ in gold** cela vaut son pesant d'or; **to be under~/over~** être trop maigre/trop gros (*f* grosse); **to put on** *or* **gain ~** grossir, prendre du poids; **to lose ~** maigrir, perdre du poids; **he put** *or* **leaned his full ~ on the handle** il a pesé *or* appuyé de tout son poids sur la poignée; **he put his full ~ behind the blow** il a frappé de toutes ses forces; **feel the ~ of this box!** soupesez-moi cette boîte !; *V* **pull, throw about** *etc.*

(b) (*fig*) *[argument, words, public opinion, evidence]* poids *m*, force *f*; *[worry, responsibility, years, age]* poids. **to lend** *or* **give ~ to sth** donner du poids à qch; **to carry ~** *[argument, factor]* avoir du poids (*with* pour); *[person]* avoir de l'influence; **we must give due ~ to his arguments** nous devons donner tout leur poids à ses arguments; *V* **mind.**

(c) (*for scales, on clock etc*) poids *m*. **~s and measures** poids et mesures; *V* **paper, put** *etc.*

2 *cpd*: (*Sport*) **weight lifter** haltérophile *m*; **weight lifting** haltérophilie *f*.

3 *vt* (*sink*) lester avec un poids (*or* une pierre *etc*); (*hold down*) retenir *or* maintenir avec un poids (*or* une pierre *etc*). (*fig*) **the situation was heavily ~ed in his favour/against him** la situation lui était nettement favorable/défavorable.

weight down *vt sep* (*sink*) lester avec un poids (*or* une pierre *etc*); (*hold down*) retenir *or* maintenir avec un poids (*or* une pierre *etc*).

weightiness ['weɪtɪnɪs] *n* (*U: V* **weighty**) lourdeur *f*; caractère probant; importance *f*, gravité *f*.

weighting ['weɪtɪŋ] *n* (*on salary*) indemnité *f*, allocation *f*. **London ~** indemnité de résidence pour Londres.

weightless ['weɪtlɪs] *adj* (*Space*) en état d'apesanteur.

weightlessness ['weɪtlɪsnɪs] *n* apesanteur *f*.

weighty ['weɪtɪ] *adj load* pesant, lourd; (*fig*) *burden, responsibility* lourd; *argument, matter* de poids; *reason* probant; *consideration, deliberation* mûr; *problem* grave, important.

weir [wɪəʳ] *n* barrage *m*.

weird [wɪəd] *adj* (*eerie*) surnaturel, mystérieux; (*odd*) bizarre, étrange, curieux, singulier.

weirdly ['wɪədlɪ] *adv* (*V* **weird**) mystérieusement; bizarrement, étrangement, curieusement, singulièrement.

weirdness ['wɪədnɪs] *n* étrangeté *f*.

weirdy‡ ['wɪədɪ] *n* drôle d'oiseau* *m* (*pej*), phénomène* *m*.

welch* [welʃ] *vi* = **welsh*.**

welcome ['welkəm] 1 *adj* **(a)** *reminder, interruption* opportun. *[guest, helper, food, news, decision]* **to be ~** être le (*or* la) bienvenu(e); **~!** soyez le bienvenu (*or* la bienvenue *etc*)!; **~ to our house** nous sommes enchantés de vous avoir chez nous, (*more frm*) bienvenue chez nous; (*on notice*) **'~ to England!'** 'bienvenue en Angleterre!'; **to make sb ~** faire bon accueil à qn; **I didn't feel very ~** j'ai eu l'impression que je n'étais pas le bienvenu, je me suis senti de trop; **a cup of coffee is always ~** une tasse de café est toujours la bienvenue; **it was ~ news/a ~ sight** nous avons été (*or* il a été *etc*) heureux de l'apprendre/de le voir; **it was a ~ gift** ce cadeau était le bienvenu, ce cadeau m'a (*or* lui a *etc*) fait bien plaisir; **it was a ~ change** ce changement tombait à point; **it was a ~ relief** j'ai été (*or* il a été *etc*) vraiment soulagé.

(b) (*answer to thanks*) **you're ~!** il n'y a pas de quoi!, c'est moi qui vous remercie!, de rien!; **you're ~ to try** libre à vous d'essayer; **you're ~ to use my car** n'hésitez pas à prendre ma voiture; **you're ~ to anything you need from here** tout ce qui est ici est à votre entière disposition; **you're ~ to any help I can give you** si je peux vous être utile, ce sera avec plaisir.

2 *n* accueil *m*. **to bid sb ~** souhaiter la bienvenue à qn; **to give sb a warm ~** faire un accueil chaleureux à qn; **they gave him a great ~** ils lui ont fait fête; **I got a fairly cold ~** j'ai été accueilli *or* reçu plutôt froidement; **words of ~** paroles *fpl* d'accueil, mots *mpl* de bienvenue; **what sort of a ~ will this product get from the housewife?** comment la ménagère accueillera-t-elle ce produit?; *V* **out.**

3 *vt person, delegation, group of people* (*greet, receive*) accueillir; (*greet warmly*) faire bon accueil à, accueillir chaleureusement; (*bid welcome*) souhaiter la bienvenue à; *sb's return, news, suggestion, change* se réjouir de. **he ~d me in** il m'a chaleureusement invité à entrer; **I'd ~ a cup of coffee** je prendrais volontiers une tasse de café, je ne dirais pas non à une tasse de café; *V* **open.**

welcome back *vt sep*: **they welcomed him back after his journey** ils l'ont accueilli chaleureusement *or* ils lui ont fait fête à son retour de voyage.

welcoming ['welkəmɪŋ] *adj smile, handshake* accueillant; *ceremony, speeches* d'accueil. **the ~ party was waiting at the airport** la délégation venue les accueillir attendait à l'aéroport.

weld [weld] 1 *n* soudure *f*.

2 *vt metal, rubber, seam, join* souder; (*also* **~ together**) *pieces, parts* souder, assembler; (*fig*) *groups, parties* cimenter l'union de; *ideas* amalgamer, réunir. **to ~ sth on to sth** souder qch à qch; **the hull is ~ed throughout** la coque est complètement soudée; (*fig*) **he ~ed them (together) into a united party** il en a fait un parti cohérent.

3 *vi* souder.

welder ['weldəʳ] *n* (*person*) soudeur *m*; (*machine*) soudeuse *f*.

welding ['weldɪŋ] 1 *n* (*U*) (*Tech*) soudage *m*; (*fig*) *[parties]* union *f*; *[ideas]* amalgame *m*. 2 *cpd process* de soudure, de soudage. **~ torch** chalumeau *m*.

welfare ['welfɛəʳ] 1 *n* **(a)** bien *m*, bien-être *m*. **the nation's ~, the ~ of all** le bien public; **the physical/spiritual ~ of the young** la santé physique/morale des jeunes; **I'm anxious about his ~** je suis inquiet pour son bien *or* bien-être; **to look after sb's ~** avoir la responsabilité de qn; *V* **child** *etc.*

(b) **public/social ~** assistance publique/sociale; **to be on (the) ~‡** toucher les prestations sociales *or* d'économiquement faible; **to live on (the) ~‡** vivre aux dépens de l'État.

2 *cpd milk, meals* gratuit. **welfare centre** centre *m* d'assistance sociale; **the establishment of the Welfare State in Great Britain** l'établissement de l'État-providence *m* en Grande-Bretagne; **thanks to the Welfare State, they ...** grâce à la Sécurité sociale et autres avantages sociaux, ils ...; **Britain is a welfare state** l'État-providence a été institué en Grande-Bretagne; **welfare work** travail social; **welfare worker** ≃ travailleur *m*, -euse *f* social(e).

well[1] [wel] 1 *n* (*for water, oil*) puits *m*; *[staircase, lift]* cage *f*; (*shaft between buildings*) puits, cheminée *f*; (*Brit Jur*) barreau *m*. (*fig*) **this book is a ~ of information** ce livre est une mine de renseignements; *V* **ink, oil** *etc.*

2 *cpd*: **welldigger** puisatier *m*; (*lit, fig*) **wellhead, wellspring** source *f*; **well water** eau *f* de puits.
3 *vi* (*also* ~ **up**) *[tears, emotion]* monter. **tears ~ed (up) in her eyes** les larmes lui montèrent aux yeux; **anger ~ed (up) within him** la colère sourdit (*liter*) *or* monta en lui.
well out *vi [spring]* sourdre; *[tears]* couler; *[blood]* suinter (*from* de).
well[2] [wel] 1 *adv, comp* **better**, *superl* **best** (a) (*satisfactorily, skilfully etc*) *behave, sleep, eat, treat, remember* bien. **he sings as ~ as he plays** il chante aussi bien qu'il joue; **he sings as ~ as she does** il chante aussi bien qu'elle; ~ **done!** bravo!; ~ **played!** bien joué!; **everything is going** ~ tout va bien; **the evening went off very** ~ la soirée s'est très bien passée; **to do** ~ **in one's work** bien réussir dans son travail; **to do** ~ **at school** bien marcher à l'école; **he did very** ~ **for an 8-year-old** il s'est bien débrouillé pour un enfant de 8 ans; **he did quite** ~, **he came out of it quite** ~ il ne s'en est pas mal sorti, il ne s'est pas mal débrouillé; **the patient is doing** ~ le malade est en bonne voie; **you did** ~ **to come at once** vous avez bien fait de venir tout de suite; **you would do** ~ **to think about it** vous feriez bien d'y penser; **to do as** ~ **as one can** faire de son mieux; **he did himself** ~ il ne s'est privé de rien, il s'est traité comme un prince; **to do** ~ **by sb** bien agir *or* être généreux envers qn; **you're** ~ **out of it!** c'est une chance que tu n'aies plus rien à voir avec cela (*or* lui *etc*); **how** ~ **I understand!** comme je vous comprends!; **I know the place** ~ je connais bien l'endroit; ~ **I know it!** je le sais bien!, je ne le sais que trop!; *V also* **5**.
(b) (*intensifying: very much; thoroughly*) bien. **it was** ~ **worth the trouble** cela valait bien le dérangement *or* la peine de se déranger; **he is** ~ **past** *or* **over fifty** il a largement dépassé la cinquantaine; ~ **over 1,000 people** bien plus de 1.000 personnes; **it's** ~ **past 10 o'clock** il est bien plus de 10 heures; ~ **and truly** bel et bien; **he could** ~ **afford to pay for it** il avait largement les moyens de le payer; **lean** ~ **forward** penchez-vous bien en avant.
(c) (*with good reason; with equal reason*) **you may** ~ **be surprised to learn that** vous serez sans aucun doute surpris d'apprendre que; **one might** ~ **ask why** on pourrait à juste titre demander pourquoi; **you might** ~ **ask!** belle question!, c'est vous qui me le demandez!; **you could** ~ **refuse to help them** vous pourriez à juste titre refuser de les aider; **he couldn't very** ~ **refuse** il ne pouvait guère refuser; **we may as** ~ **begin now** autant (vaut) commencer maintenant, nous ferions aussi bien de commencer maintenant; **you might (just) as** ~ **say that ...** autant dire que ...; **you may as** ~ **tell me the truth** autant me dire la vérité, tu ferais aussi bien de me dire la vérité; **shall I go?** — **you may** *or* **might as** ~ j'y vais? — tant qu'à faire, allez-y!*; **we might (just) as** ~ **have stayed at home** autant valait rester à la maison, nous aurions aussi bien fait de ne pas venir; **she apologized, as** ~ **she might** elle a présenté ses excuses, comme il se devait; **she apologized** — ~ **she might!** elle a présenté ses excuses — c'était la moindre des choses!; *V* **pretty**.
(d) (*in addition*) **as** ~ aussi; **I'll take those as** ~ je prendrai ceux-là aussi; **and it rained as** ~! et par-dessus le marché il a plu!; **by night as** ~ **as by day** de jour comme de nuit, aussi bien de jour que de nuit; **as** ~ **as his dog he has 2 rabbits** en plus de son chien il a 2 lapins; **on bikes as** ~ **as in cars** à vélo aussi bien qu'en voiture, à vélo comme en voiture; **I had Paul with me as** ~ **as Lucy** j'avais Paul aussi en même temps que Lucy; **all sorts of people, rich as** ~ **as poor** toutes sortes de gens, tant riches que pauvres.
2 *excl* (*surprise*) tiens!, eh bien!; (*relief*) ah bon!, eh bien!; (*resignation*) enfin! (*resuming after interruption*) ~, **as I was saying ...** donc, comme je disais ..., je disais donc que ...; (*hesitation*) ~ **...** c'est que ...; **he has won the election!** — ~, ~(, ~)! il a été élu! — tiens, tiens(, tiens)!; ~? eh bien?, et alors?; ~, **who would have thought it?** tiens! *or* eh bien! qui l'aurait jamais cru?; ~ **I never!**, ~, **what do you know!*** pas possible!, ça par exemple!, bien ça alors!; **I intended to do it** — ~, **have you?** j'avais l'intention de le faire — et alors?; ~, **what do you think of it?** eh bien! qu'en dites-vous?; ~, **here we are at last!** eh bien! nous voilà enfin!; ~, **there's nothing we can do about it** enfin, on n'y peut rien; ~, **you may be right** qui sait, vous avez peut-être raison; **very** ~ **then** (bon) d'accord; **you know Paul?** ~, **he's getting married** vous connaissez Paul? eh bien il se marie; **are you coming?** — ~ **... I've got a lot to do here** vous venez? — c'est que ... j'ai beaucoup à faire ici.
3 *adj, comp* **better**, *superl* **best (a)** bien; bon. (*Prov*) **all's** ~ **that ends well** tout est bien qui finit bien (*Prov*); (*Mil*) **all's** ~! tout va bien!; **all is not** ~ **with her** il y a quelque chose qui ne va pas, elle traverse une mauvaise passe; **it's all very** ~ **to say that** c'est bien beau *or* joli de dire cela; **that's all very** ~ **but ...**, **that's all** ~ **and good but ...** tout ça c'est bien joli *or* beau mais ...; **if you want to do it,** ~ **and good** si vous voulez le faire je ne vois pas d'inconvénient; **it would be** ~ **to start early** on ferait bien de partir tôt; **it is as** ~ **to remember** il y a tout lieu de se rappeler; **it's as** ~ **not to offend her** il vaudrait mieux ne pas la froisser; **it would be just as** ~ **for you to stay** vous feriez tout aussi bien de rester; **it's** ~ **for you that nobody saw you** heureusement pour vous qu'on ne vous a pas vu, vous avez de la chance *or* c'est heureux pour vous qu'on ne vous ait pas vu.
(b) (*healthy*) **how are you?** — **very** ~, **thank you** comment allez-vous? — très bien, merci; **I hope you're** ~ j'espère que vous allez bien; **to feel** ~ se sentir bien; **to get** ~ se remettre; **get** ~ **soon!** remets-toi vite!; **people who are** ~ **do not realize ...** les bien portants *mpl* ne se rendent pas compte ... .
4 *n*: **to think/speak** ~ **of** penser/dire du bien de; **I wish you** ~! je vous souhaite de réussir!, bonne chance!; **somebody who wishes you** ~ quelqu'un qui vous veut du bien; (*Prov*) **let** *or* **leave** ~ **alone** le mieux est l'ennemi du bien (*Prov*).
5 *cpd*: **well-advised** *action, decision* sage, prudent; **you would be well advised to go** vous feriez bien de partir; **well-aimed** *shot* bien visé; *remark* qui porte; **well-appointed** *house, room* bien équipé; **well-attended** *meeting, lecture* qui attire beaucoup de monde, qui a du succès; *show, play* couru; **well-balanced** (*lit*) bien équilibré; (*fig*) *person, diet* bien équilibré; *paragraph, sentence* bien agencé; **well-behaved** *child* sage, qui se conduit bien; *animal* obéissant, discipliné; **well-being** bien-être *m*; **wellborn** bien né, de bonne famille; **well-bred** (*of good family*) de bonne famille; (*courteous*) bien élevé; *animal* de bonne race; **well-built** *building* bien construit, solide; *person* bien bâti, solide, costaud*; **well-chosen** bien choisi; **in a few well-chosen words** en quelques mots bien choisis; **well-defined** *colours, distinctions* bien défini; *photo, outline* net; *problem* bien défini, précis; **well-deserved** bien mérité; **well-developed** (*Anat*) bien développé; *person* bien fait; *plan* bien développé; *argument, idea* bien exposé; **well-disposed** bien disposé (*towards* envers); **well-dressed** bien habillé, bien vêtu; **well-earned** bien mérité; **well-educated** cultivé, instruit; **well-equipped** bien équipé; (*esp with tools*) bien outillé; **to be well equipped to do** *[person]* avoir ce qu'il faut pour faire; *[factory]* être parfaitement équipé pour faire; **well-favoured**†† beau (*f* belle); **well-fed** bien nourri; **well-founded** *suspicion* bien fondé, légitime; **well-groomed** *person* soigné; *hair* bien coiffé; *horse* bien pansé; **well-grounded** *suspicion* bien fondé, légitime; **he is well grounded in history** il a des bases solides en histoire; **well-heeled*** bien nanti, fort à l'aise; **well-informed** bien informé, bien renseigné (*about* sur); (*knowledgeable*) *person* instruit; (*Pol, Press*) **well-informed sources** milieux bien informés; **well-intentioned** bien intentionné; **well-judged** *remark, criticism* bien vu, judicieux; *shot, throw* bien visé, bien vu; *estimate* juste; **well-kept** *house, garden* bien entretenu, bien tenu; *hands, nails* soigné; *hair* bien entretenu; *secret* bien gardé; **well-knit** (*lit*) bien tricoté; (*fig*) *person, body* bien bâti; *arguments, speech* bien enchaîné; *scheme* bien conçu; **well-known** bien connu, célèbre; **well-made** bien fait; **well-mannered** qui a de bonnes manières, bien élevé; (*fig*) **well-marked** marqué, prononcé, distinct; **well-meaning** *person* bien intentionné; *remark, action* fait avec les meilleures intentions; **well-meant** fait avec les meilleures intentions; **well-nigh** presque; **well-nourished** bien nourri; (*rich*) **to be well-off** vivre dans l'aisance, être riche *or* aisé *or* bien nanti; **the less well-off** ceux qui ont de petits moyens; (*fortunate*) **you don't know when you're well-off** tu ne connais pas ton bonheur; **she's well-off without him** elle se passe fort bien de lui; **well-oiled** (*lit*) bien graissé; (*: *drunk*) pompette*; **well-preserved** *building, person* bien conservé; **well-proportioned** bien proportionné; **well-read** instruit, cultivé; **well-rounded** *style* harmonieux; *sentence* bien tourné; **well-spent** *time* bien employé, bien utilisé; *money* utilement dépensé; **well-spoken** *person* (*courteous*) poli, courtois, qui parle bien; (*with good accent*) qui a une élocution soignée; *words* bien choisi, bien trouvé; **well-spoken-of** dont on dit du bien; **well-stocked** *shop, larder* bien approvisionné; *river, lake* bien empoissonné; **well-thought-of** *person* (bien) considéré, dont on a bonne opinion; *thing* bien considéré, bien apprécié; **well-thought-out** bien conçu; **well-timed** opportun, à propos; **well-to-do** aisé, riche; **to be well-to-do** vivre dans l'aisance, être riche *or* aisé *or* bien nanti; **well-tried** *method* éprouvé; **well-trodden** *path* battu; **well-turned** *phrase* bien tourné; **a crowd of well-wishers had gathered to see him off** de nombreux admirateurs étaient venus lui souhaiter bon voyage; **he got many letters from well-wishers** il a reçu de nombreuses lettres d'encouragement; **well-worn** *path* battu; *carpet, clothes* usagé; (*fig*) *phrase, expression* banal, usagé, rebattu.
we'll [wi:l] = **we shall, we will**; *V* **shall, will**.
wellington ['welɪŋtən] *n* (*also* ~ **boot**) botte *f* de caoutchouc.
Welsh [welʃ] 1 *adj* gallois. (*Brit*) ~ **dresser** vaisselier *m*; (*Pol*) ~ **Nationalism/Nationalist** nationalisme *m*/nationaliste *mf* gallois(e); (*Brit Pol*) **the** ~ **Office** le ministère des Affaires galloises.
2 *n* **(a)** (*pl*) **the** ~ les Gallois *mpl*.
(b) (*Ling*) gallois *m*.
3 *cpd*: **Welshman** Gallois *m*; (*Culin*) **Welsh rabbit, Welsh rarebit** toast *m* au fromage; **Welshwoman** Galloise *f*.
welsh* [welʃ] *vi*: **to** ~ **on sb** (*gen*) lever le pied* en emportant l'argent de qn; (*in gambling*) lever le pied* en emportant l'enjeu de qn.
welt [welt] *n [shoe]* trépointe *f*; (*weal*) marque *f* de coup, zébrure *f*.
welter ['weltəʳ] 1 *n [objects, words, ideas]* fatras *m*. **in a** ~ **of blood** dans un bain de sang; **in a** ~ **of mud** dans un véritable bourbier. 2 *vi* (*in blood*) baigner (*in* dans); (*in mud*) se vautrer, se rouler (*in* dans).
welterweight ['weltəweɪt] (*Boxing*) 1 *n* poids *m* welter. 2 *cpd champion, fight* poids welter *inv*.
wen [wen] *n* loupe *f*, kyste sébacé. (*fig*) **the Great W~** Londres.
wench [wentʃ] († *or hum*) 1 *n* jeune fille *f*, jeune femme *f*. 2 *vi*: **to go** ~**ing** courir le jupon.
wend [wend] *vt*: **to** ~ **one's way** aller son chemin, s'acheminer (*to, towards* vers); **to** ~ **one's way back from** s'en revenir de.
went [went] *pret of* **go**.
wept [wept] *pret, ptp of* **weep**.
were [wɜ:ʳ] *pret of* **be**.
we're [wɪəʳ] = **we are**; *V* **be**.
weren't [wɜ:nt] = **were not**; *V* **be**.
werewolf ['wɪəwʊlf] *n, pl* **werewolves** ['wɪəwʊlvz] loup-garou *m*.
wert†† [wɜ:t] *2nd pers sg pret of* **be**.
Wesleyan ['wezlɪən] 1 *n* disciple *m* de Wesley. 2 *adj* de Wesley.

west [west] 1 *n* ouest *m*. (to the) ~ of à l'ouest de; in the ~ of Scotland dans l'ouest de l'Écosse; house facing the ~ maison exposée à l'ouest *or* au couchant; *[wind]* to veer to the ~, to go into the ~ tourner à l'ouest; the wind is in the ~ le vent est à l'ouest; the wind is from the ~ le vent vient *or* souffle de l'ouest; to live in the ~ habiter dans l'ouest; the W~ (*Pol*) l'Occident *m*, l'Ouest *m*; (*US Geog*) l'Ouest; *V* wild *etc*.

2 *adj* ouest *inv*, de *or* à l'ouest. ~ wind vent *m* d'ouest; ~ coast côte ouest *or* occidentale; on the ~ side du côté ouest; room with a ~ aspect pièce exposée à l'ouest *or* au couchant; (*Archit*) ~ transept/door transept *m*/portail *m* ouest; in the ~ Atlantic dans l'Atlantique ouest; (*in London*) the W~ End le West End (*quartier élégant de Londres*); (*Brit*) the W~ Country le sud-ouest (de l'Angleterre); *V also* 4.

3 *adv* à l'ouest, vers l'ouest. the town lies ~ of the border la ville est située à l'ouest de la frontière; we drove ~ for 100 km nous avons roulé pendant 100 km en direction de l'ouest; go ~ till you get to Crewe allez en direction de l'ouest jusqu'à Crewe; (*fig*) to go ~* *[thing]* être fichu* *or* perdu; *[person]* passer l'arme à gauche*; to sail due ~ aller droit vers l'ouest; (*Naut*) avoir le cap à l'ouest; ~ by south ouest quart sud-ouest.

4 *cpd*: West Africa Afrique occidentale; West African (*adj*) de l'Afrique occidentale, ouest-africain; (*n*) habitant(e) *m(f)* de l'Afrique occidentale; westbound *traffic, vehicles* (se déplaçant) en direction de l'ouest; *carriageway* ouest *inv*; west-facing exposé (*or* orienté) à l'ouest *or* au couchant; West Indian (*adj*) antillais; (*n*) Antillais(e) *m(f)*; West Indies Antilles *fpl*; west-north-west (*n*) ouest-nord-ouest *m*; (*adj*) (de l' *or* à l')ouest-nord-ouest *inv*; (*adv*) vers l'ouest-nord-ouest; west-south-west (*n*) ouest-sud-ouest; (*adj*) (de l' *or* à l')ouest-sud-ouest *inv*; (*adv*) vers l'ouest-sud-ouest; *V* Berlin *etc*.

westerly ['westəlı] 1 *adj wind* de l'ouest; *situation* à l'ouest, au couchant. in a ~ direction en direction de l'ouest, vers l'ouest; ~ longitude longitude *f* ouest *inv*; ~ aspect exposition *f* à l'ouest *or* au couchant.

2 *adv* vers l'ouest.

western ['westən] 1 *adj* (de l')ouest *inv*. in ~ France dans la France de l'ouest; the ~ coast la côte ouest *or* occidentale; house with a ~ outlook maison exposée à l'ouest *or* au couchant; ~ wall mur exposé à l'ouest *or* au couchant; W~ Australia Australie occidentale; W~ Europe Europe occidentale; the W~ Church l'Église *f* d'Occident, l'Église latine; *V* country.

2 *n* (*film*) western *m*; (*novel*) roman *m* d'aventures de cowboys.

3 *cpd*: westernmost le plus à l'ouest, le plus occidental.

westerner ['westənəʳ] *n* homme *m or* femme *f* de l'ouest, habitant(e) *m(f)* de l'ouest. he is a ~ il vient de l'ouest; the ~s les gens *mpl* de l'ouest.

westernization u'westənaı'zeıʃən] *n* occidentalisation *f*.

westernize ['westənaız] *vt* occidentaliser. to become ~d s'occidentaliser.

wet [wet] 1 *adj* (a) *object, roof* (tout) mouillé; *grass* mouillé, (*damp*) humide; *clothes* mouillé, (*stronger*) trempé. the roads are very ~ les routes sont très humides *or* mouillées; the road is slippery when ~ la chaussée est glissante par temps de pluie; the ink is still ~ l'encre n'est pas encore sèche; the paint is ~ la peinture est fraîche; (*notice*) '~ paint' 'attention à *or* prendre garde à la peinture'; *[person]* to be ~ to the skin *or* ~ through être trempé jusqu'aux os; my shirt is wringing ~ ma chemise est complètement trempée *or* est à tordre; to get ~ se mouiller; to get one's feet ~ se mouiller les pieds; don't get your shoes ~ ne mouille pas tes souliers; cheeks ~ with tears joues baignées de larmes; (*fig*) he's still ~ behind the ears* il manque d'expérience, il est encore bleu*; it grows in ~ places ça pousse dans les endroits humides; *V* soaking.

(b) (*of weather*) it is ~ il pleut, le temps est pluvieux; it's going to be ~ le temps est à la pluie, il va pleuvoir; a ~ day un jour de pluie, un jour pluvieux; on ~ days les jours de pluie; it's a very ~ climate c'est un climat très humide *or* pluvieux; in ~ weather quand le temps est pluvieux, par temps humide *or* pluvieux; the ~ season la saison des pluies, la saison pluviale *or* humide.

(c) (‡: *silly, spineless*) he's really ~ c'est une vraie lavette*, il est vraiment nouille*.

(d) (*US: against prohibition*) *town, state* où la vente des boissons alcoolisées est autorisée.

2 *cpd*: (*US*) wetback* ouvrier agricole mexicain (*entré illégalement aux États-Unis*); (*fig*) wet blanket rabat-joie *m inv*, trouble-fête *mf inv*; (*Naut*) wet dock bassin *m* à flot; wet dream pollution *f or* éjaculation *f* nocturne; (*esp US*) the wetlands les marécages *mpl*; wet-nurse (*n*) nourrice *f*; (*vt*) servir de nourrice à, élever au sein; wetsuit combinaison *f* de plongée.

3 *n* (a) the ~ (*rain*) la pluie; (*damp*) l'humidité *f*; it got left out in the ~ c'est resté dehors sous la pluie (*or* à l'humidité); come in out of the ~ ne restez pas sous la pluie, entrez.

(b) (‡*pej: person*) lavette* *f*, nouille* *f*.

4 *vt* mouiller. to ~ one's lips se mouiller les lèvres; (*fig*) to ~ one's whistle*† boire un coup*, en siffler un*; to ~ o.s. *or* one's pants mouiller sa culotte; to ~ the bed mouiller le lit.

5 *vi* (*: *urinate*) faire pipi*.

wether ['weðəʳ] *n* bélier châtré, mouton *m*.

wetness ['wetnıs] *n* humidité *f*. the ~ of the weather le temps pluvieux.

we've [wi:v] = we have; *V* have.

whack [wæk] 1 *n* (a) (*blow*) grand coup; (*sound*) coup sec, claquement *m*. to give sth/sb a ~ donner un grand coup à qch/qn; (*excl*) ~! vlan!

(b) (*: *attempt*) to have a ~ at doing essayer de faire; I'll have a ~ at it je vais tenter le coup*.

(c) (*: *share*) part *f*. you'll get your ~ tu auras ta part.

2 *vt thing, person* donner un (*or* des) grand(s) coup(s) à; (*spank*) fesser; (‡: *defeat*) flanquer une déculottée* *or* une dérouillée‡ à. (*Brit fig: exhausted*) to be ~ed‡ être crevé‡ *or* claqué‡.

whacker‡ ['wækəʳ] *n* (*Brit*) (*fish etc*) poisson *m etc* énorme; (*lie*) mensonge *m* énorme.

whacking ['wækıŋ] 1 *n* (*spanking*) fessée *f*; (*beating: lit, fig*) raclée* *f*. to give sb/sth a ~ = to whack sb/sth; *V* whack. 2 *adj* (*: *esp Brit: also* ~ big*, ~ great*) énorme.

whale [weıl] 1 *n* baleine *f*. (*fig*) we had a ~ of a time* on s'est drôlement* bien amusé; a ~ of a difference* une sacrée* différence; a ~ of a lot of* ... vachement* de ..., une sacrée* quantité de ... .

2 *cpd*: (*Naut*) whaleboat baleinière *f*; whalebone fanon *m* de baleine; (*U: Dress*) baleine *f*; whale oil huile *f* de baleine.

3 *vi* (*also* go whaling) aller à la pêche à la baleine.

whaler ['weıləʳ] *n* (*man*) pêcheur *m* de baleine; (*ship*) baleinier *m*.

whaling ['weılıŋ] 1 *n* (*U*) pêche *f* à la baleine. 2 *cpd industry* baleinier. whaling ship baleinier *m*; whaling station port baleinier.

wham [wæm] *excl* vlan!

whang [wæŋ] 1 *n* bruit retentissant. 2 *vt* donner un coup dur et sonore à. 3 *vi* faire un bruit retentissant.

wharf [wɔ:f] *n, pl* ~s *or* wharves quai *m*.

wharfage ['wɔ:fıdʒ] *n* (*U*) droits *mpl* de quai.

wharves [wɔ:vz] *npl of* wharf.

what [wɒt] 1 *adj* (a) (*interrog, also indirect speech: which*) quel. ~ play did you see? quelle pièce avez-vous vue?; ~ news did he bring? quelles nouvelles vous a-t-il données?; ~ books do you want? quels livres voulez-vous?; ~ time is it? quelle heure est-il?; he told me ~ time it was il m'a dit l'heure (qu'il était); ~ one* are you looking for? lequel (*or* laquelle) cherchez-vous?; she showed me ~ book it was elle m'a montré quel livre c'était.

(b) (*exclamatory*) quel; que. ~ a man! quel homme!; ~ a pity! quel dommage!; ~ a nuisance! que c'est ennuyeux!; ~ fools we are! que nous sommes bêtes!; ~ a huge house! quelle maison immense!; ~ a nice house you have! que vous avez une jolie maison!, quelle jolie maison vous avez!; ~ a lot of people! que de monde!; (*iro*) ~ an excuse! quelle excuse!

(c) (*as much or as many as*) tout ... que. give me ~ books you have about it donnez-moi tous les livres en votre possession qui s'y rapportent; I gave him ~ money I had je lui ai donné tout l'argent que j'avais; ~ little I said le peu que j'ai dit; ~ little help I could give l'aide que j'ai apportée si petite soit-elle.

2 *pron* (a) (*interrog*) (*subject*) (qu'est-ce) qui; (*obj*) (qu'est-ce) que; (*after prep*) quoi. ~ did you do? qu'est-ce que vous avez fait?, qu'avez-vous fait?; ~'s happened?, ~'s up?* qu'est-ce qu'il y a?, qu'est-ce qui arrive? *or* se passe?; ~ does it matter? qu'est-ce que ça fait?; ~ is that? qu'est-ce que c'est que ça?; ~'s that book? quel est ce livre?, qu'est-ce que c'est que ce livre?; ~ is his address? quelle est son adresse?; ~ is this called? comment ça s'appelle?; ~'s the French for 'pen'? comment dit-on 'pen' en français?; ~ can we do? que pouvons-nous faire?; ~ the heck* *or* hell‡ *etc* did he say? qu'est-ce qu'il a bien pu raconter?; oh ~ the hell!‡ oh après tout qu'est-ce que ça peut bien foutre!‡, oh je m'en fous!‡; ~ do 2 and 2 make? que font 2 et 2?; ~'s the use of that? à quoi ça sert?; ~ does he owe his success to? à quoi doit-il son succès?; ~ is wealth without happiness? qu'est-ce que la richesse sans le bonheur?; ~ were you talking about? de quoi parliez-vous?; ~ will it cost? combien est-ce que ça coûtera?, ça coûtera combien?; you told him WHAT? quoi! qu'est-ce que vous lui avez dit?; it's WHAT? c'est quoi?; (*esp Brit*) it's getting late, ~?*† il se fait tard, pas vrai?

(b) (*fixed interrog phrases*) ~ about a drink? si on buvait quelque chose?, si on prenait un verre?; ~ about Robert? et Robert?; ~ about writing that letter? et si vous écriviez cette lettre?; ~ about the money you owe me? et l'argent que vous me devez?; well, ~ about it? *or* ~ of it?, so ~?* et alors?; ~ about *or* of the danger involved? et les risques que l'on court?; ~ for? pourquoi? (*V also* 4); ~ did you do that for? pourquoi avez-vous fait ça?; ... and ~ have you*, ... and ~ not* et je ne sais quoi encore; ~ if we were to go and see him? et si on allait le voir?; ... but ~ if we were to do it all the same? ... que se passerait-il si on le faisait quand même?; ~ if it rains? et s'il pleut?; (*liter*) ~ though there may be *or* there are dangers et qu'importent les dangers!

(c) (*indirect use*) (*subject*) ce qui; (*obj*) ce que. I wonder ~ will happen je me demande ce qui va arriver; tell us ~ you're thinking about dites-nous ce à quoi vous pensez; he asked me ~ she'd told me il m'a demandé ce qu'elle m'avait dit; I don't know ~ that book is je ne sais pas ce que c'est que ce livre *or* quel est ce livre; he knows ~'s ~ il s'y connaît, il connaît son affaire; he just doesn't know ~'s ~ il n'a aucune idée, il est complètement dépassé; I'll show them ~'s ~ je vais leur montrer de quoi il retourne *or* de quel bois je me chauffe*.

(d) (*rel use etc: that which*) (*nominative*) ce qui; (*accusative*) ce que. ~ is done is done ce qui est fait est fait; ~ I need is ... ce dont j'ai besoin c'est ...; ~ can be changed is ... ce que l'on peut changer c'est ...; ~ I like is coffee ce que j'aime c'est le café; I don't know who is doing ~ je ne sais pas qui fait quoi; I know ~ ..., (I'll) tell you ~ ... tu sais quoi ..., j'ai une idée ...; he's not ~ he was 5 years ago il n'est plus ce qu'il était il y a 5 ans; Paris isn't ~ it was Paris n'est plus ce qu'il était; I've no clothes except ~ I'm wearing je n'ai d'autres vêtements que ceux que je porte; do ~ you will faites ce que vous voudrez; say ~ you like vous pouvez dire ce que vous voudrez *or* voulez.

(e) (*fixed phrases*) and ~ is more et qui plus est; and ~ is worse et ce qui est pire; **and, ~ is less common, there was ...** et, ce qui est plus inhabituel *or* et, chose plus inhabituelle, il y avait ...; **~ with the suitcase and the box he could hardly ...** avec la valise et la boîte en plus il ne pouvait guère ...; **~ with the heatwave and the financial crisis** entre la vague de chaleur et la crise financière, étant donné la vague de chaleur et la crise financière; **~ with one thing and another** avec ceci et cela; (*after listing things*) avec tout ça; **never a day passes but ~ it rains*** il ne se passe pas de jour qu'il ne pleuve; **not but ~ that wouldn't be a good thing** non que cela soit une mauvaise chose.

3 *excl*: **~! no butter!** quoi! *or* comment! pas de beurre!; **he's getting married — ~!** il se marie — quoi!; **~-ho!***† ohé bonjour!

4 *cpd*: **what-d'ye-call-her*, what's-her-name*** la fille Machin*; (*married woman*) Madame Machin*; **what-d'ye-call-him*, what's-his-name*** Machin* *m*, Machin Chouette* *m*; **what-d'ye-call-it*, what's-its-name*** machin* *m*, truc* *m*, bidule‡ *m*; (*liter*) **whate'er**, (*liter*) **whatsoe'er**, (*emphatic*) **whatsoever = whatever; whatever** *V* **whatever; to give sb what for*** passer un savon à qn*; **whatnot** (*furniture*) étagère *f*; (*) = **what-d'ye-call-it***.

whatever [wɒt'evəʳ] **1** *adj* **(a)** (*gen*) **~ book you choose** quel que soit le livre que vous choisissiez (*subj*); **any box of ~ size** n'importe quelle boîte quelle qu'en soit la taille; **give me ~ money you've got** donne-moi (tout) ce que tu as comme argent; **he agreed to make ~ repairs might prove necessary** il a accepté de faire toutes réparations reconnues nécessaires (quelles qu'elles soient); **you'll have to change ~ plans you've made** il vous faudra changer les projets que vous avez faits (quels qu'ils soient).

(b) (*: *emphatic interrog*) **~ books have you been reading?** qu'est-ce que vous êtes allé lire?, vous avez lu de drôles de livres!*; **~ time is it?** quelle heure peut-il bien être?

2 *adv*: **~ the weather** quel que soit le temps qu'il fasse; **~ the news from the front, they ...** quelles que soient les nouvelles du front, ils ...; **I'll take anything ~ that you can spare** je prendrai tout ce dont vous n'avez pas besoin (quoi que ce soit); **I've no money ~** je n'ai pas un sou, je n'ai pas le moindre argent; **there's no doubt ~ about it** cela ne fait pas le moindre doute *or* aucun doute *or* pas l'ombre d'un doute; **none ~** pas le moindre; **in no case ~ shall we agree to see ...** en aucun cas nous n'accepterons de voir ...; **has he any chance ~?** a-t-il la moindre chance?

3 *pron* **(a)** (*no matter what*) quoi que+*subj*. **~ happens** quoi qu'il arrive; **~ you (may) find** quoi que vous trouviez; **~ it may be** quoi que ce soit; **~ he may mean** quel que soit ce qu'il veut dire; **I'll pay ~ it costs** je paierai ce que ça coûtera; **~ it costs, get it** achète-le quel qu'en soit le prix; **~ he said before, he won't now do it** quoi qu'il ait dit auparavant, il ne le fera pas maintenant.

(b) (*anything that*) tout ce que. **do ~ you please** faites ce que vous voulez *or* voudrez; **we shall do ~ seems necessary** nous ferons le nécessaire.

(c) (*: *emphatic interrog*) **~ did you do?** qu'est-ce que vous êtes allé faire?; **~ did you say that for?** pourquoi êtes-vous allé dire ça?

wheat [wi:t] **1** *n* (*U*) blé *m*, froment *m*. (*fig*) **to separate *or* divide the ~ from the chaff** séparer le bon grain de l'ivraie.

2 *cpd flour* de blé, de froment; *field* de blé, à blé. **it's wheat country** c'est une terre à blé; (*Orn*) **wheatear** cul-blanc *m*; (*U*) **wheatgerm** germes *mpl* de blé; **wheatmeal** farine brute (*à 80%*); **wheat sheaf** gerbe *f* de blé.

wheaten ['wi:tn] *adj* de blé, de froment.

wheedle ['wi:dl] *vt* cajoler, câliner. **to ~ sth out of sb** obtenir *or* tirer qch de qn par des cajoleries *or* des câlineries; **to ~ sb into doing** cajoler *or* câliner qn pour qu'il fasse, amener qn à force de cajoleries *or* câlineries à faire.

wheedling ['wi:dlɪŋ] **1** *adj* câlin, enjôleur. **2** *n* cajolerie(s) *f(pl)*, câlinerie(s) *f(pl)*.

wheel [wi:l] **1** *n* **(a)** (*gen*) roue *f*; (*Naut*) (roue de) gouvernail *m*; (*Aut: steering ~*) volant *m*; (*spinning ~*) rouet *m*; (*potter's ~*) tour *m* (de potier); (*in roulette etc*) roue; (*Hist: torture instrument*) roue. **~ of fortune** roue de la fortune; **big ~** (*in fairground etc*) grande roue; (*: *important person*) huile* *f*; **at the ~** (*Naut*) au gouvernail; (*Aut*) au volant; **to take the ~** (*Naut*) prendre le gouvernail; (*Aut*) se mettre au volant; (*Hist*) **to break sb on the ~** rouer qn; (*fig*) **the ~s of government** les rouages du gouvernement; (*fig*) **to oil *or* grease the ~s** huiler les rouages; (*fig*) **there are ~s within ~s** c'est plus compliqué que ça ne paraît, il y a toutes sortes de forces en jeu; *V* **shoulder, spoke[1]** *etc*.

(b) (*Mil etc*) **to make a right/left ~** effectuer une conversion à droite/à gauche.

2 *cpd*: **wheelbarrow** brouette *f*; (*Aut*) **wheelbase** empattement *m*; **wheelchair** fauteuil roulant; (*hum*) **when I'm in a wheelchair ...** quand je serai dans une petite voiture* ...; (*Naut*) **wheelhouse** timonerie *f*; **wheelwright** charron *m*.

3 *vt barrow, pushchair, bed* pousser, rouler; *child* pousser (dans un landau *etc*). **to ~ a trolley into/out of a room** rouler *or* pousser un chariot dans/hors d'une pièce; **they ~ed the sick man over to the window** ils ont poussé le malade (dans son fauteuil roulant *or* sur son lit roulant) jusqu'à la fenêtre; (*fig: bring*) **he ~ed‡ out an enormous box** il a sorti une boîte énorme; **~ him in!‡** amenez-le!

4 *vi* (*also* **~ round**) [*birds*] tournoyer; [*windmill sails etc*] tourner (en rond); [*person*] se retourner (brusquement), virevolter; (*Mil*) effectuer une conversion; [*procession*] tourner. (*Mil*) **right ~!** à droite!; (*fig*) **he is always ~ing and dealing*** il est toujours en train de manigancer quelque chose *or* de chercher des combines*; **there has been a lot of ~ing and dealing* over the choice of candidate** le choix du candidat a donné lieu à toutes sortes de manigances *fpl or* combines* *fpl or* micmacs* *mpl*.

wheeled [wi:ld] *adj object* à roues, muni de roues. **three-~** à trois roues.

-wheeler ['wi:ləʳ] *n ending in cpds*: **four-wheeler** voiture *f* à quatre roues; *V* **two** *etc*.

wheeze [wi:z] **1** *n* **(a)** respiration bruyante *or* sifflante.

(b) (‡†: *Brit: scheme*) truc* *m*, combine* *f*.

2 *vi* [*person*] respirer bruyamment *or* comme un asthmatique; [*animal*] souffler, ahaner.

3 *vt* (*also* **~ out**) **'yes,' he ~d** 'oui,' dit-il d'une voix rauque; **the old organ ~d out the tune** le vieil orgue a joué le morceau dans un bruit de soufflerie.

wheezy ['wi:zɪ] *adj person* poussif, asthmatique; *animal* poussif; *organ etc* asthmatique (*fig*).

whelk [welk] *n* buccin *m*.

whelp [welp] **1** *n* (*animal*) petit(e) *m(f)*; (*pej: youth*) petit morveux. **2** *vi* (*of animals*) mettre bas.

when [wen] **1** *adv* quand. **~ did it happen?** quand *or* à quelle époque *or* à quel moment cela s'est-il passé?, cela s'est passé quand?*; **~ does the train leave?** quand *or* à quelle heure part le train?; **~ is your birthday?** quand est votre anniversaire?, quelle est la date de votre anniversaire?; **~ was the wheel invented?** de quand date l'invention de la roue?, quand la roue a-t-elle été inventée?; **~ did Columbus cross the Atlantic?** quand *or* en quelle année Christophe Colomb a-t-il traversé l'Atlantique?; **I don't know ~ we'll see him again** je ne sais pas quand nous le reverrons; **~'s the wedding?** à quand le mariage?; **~ does snow first fall?** vers quelle date la neige commence-t-elle à tomber?; **~ can you use the definite article with this word?** quand peut-on employer l'article défini avec ce mot?; **do you know ~ he first met her?** savez-vous quand il a fait sa connaissance?; **do you know ~ is the best time to call on her?** savez-vous quel est le meilleur moment pour lui rendre visite?; **he didn't tell me ~ she would telephone** il ne m'a pas dit quand *or* quel jour (*or* à quelle heure) elle téléphonerait; **he told me ~ to meet him *or* ~ I should meet him** il m'a dit quand (je devais) le rencontrer; **did he say ~ he'd be back?** a-t-il dit quand il serait de retour?; **let me know ~ you want your holidays** faites-moi savoir quand *or* à quelle date vous voulez vos congés; **till ~?** jusqu'à quand?; **he's got to go by ~?** il faut qu'il soit parti quand?; **since ~ has he got a car?** depuis quand a-t-il une voiture?; (*iro*) **since ~?*** depuis quand?*

2 *conj* **(a)** (*at the time that*) quand, lorsque. **~ I heard his voice I smiled** quand *or* lorsque j'ai entendu sa voix j'ai souri; **he waved ~ he saw me** il a fait signe de la main quand *or* lorsqu'il m'a vu; **~ I was a child there was no TV** quand *or* lorsque j'étais enfant il n'y avait pas de télé*; **~ (he was) just a child he ...** alors qu'il n'était qu'un enfant il ..., tout enfant il ...; **he did it ~ (he was) a student at Oxford** il l'a fait quand *or* lorsqu'il était étudiant à Oxford; **~ (it is) finished the bridge will measure ...** une fois terminé, le pont mesurera ...; **let me know ~ she comes** faites-moi savoir quand elle arrivera; **~ speaking German I often make mistakes** quand je parle allemand je fais souvent des fautes; **~ writing to her, remember to say...** quand vous lui écrirez n'oubliez pas de dire ...; **go ~ you like** partez quand vous voulez *or* voudrez; **I'll still love you ~ you're old and grey** je vous aimerai encore quand vous serez vieille et que vous aurez les cheveux gris; **he's only happy ~ drunk** il n'est heureux que lorsqu'il est ivre.

(b) (*rel use*) où; que. **on the day ~ I met him** le jour où je l'ai rencontré; **at the time ~ I should have been at the station** au moment *or* à l'heure où j'aurais dû être à la gare; **it was in spring, ~ the trees are green** c'était au printemps, à l'époque où les arbres sont verts; **on Saturdays, ~ most people don't work** le samedi, jour où la plupart des gens ne travaillent pas; **he arrived at 8 o'clock, ~ traffic is at its peak** il est arrivé à 8 heures, heure à laquelle la circulation est la plus intense; **at the very moment ~ I was about to leave** juste au moment où j'allais partir; **one day ~ the sun was shining** un jour que *or* où le soleil brillait; **it was one of those days ~ everything is quiet** c'était un de ces jours où tout est calme; **this is a time ~ we must speak up for our principles** c'est dans un moment comme celui-ci qu'il faut défendre nos principes; **there are times ~ I wish I'd never met him** il y a des moments où je regrette de l'avoir jamais connu; **he left in June, since ~ we have not heard from him** il est parti en juin et nous sommes sans nouvelles depuis *or* et depuis lors nous sommes sans nouvelles; **it will be ready on Sunday, until ~ we must ...** ce sera prêt samedi et en attendant nous devons ...; (*pouring drinks etc*) **say ~!*** vous me direz ... .

(c) (*the time that*) **he told me about ~ you got lost in Paris** il m'a raconté le jour *or* la fois* où vous vous êtes perdu dans Paris; **she spoke of ~ they had visited London** elle a parlé de la semaine (*or* du jour) où ils avaient visité Londres; **now is ~ I need you most** c'est maintenant que j'ai le plus besoin de vous; **that's ~ the train leaves** c'est l'heure à laquelle le train part; **that's ~ Napoleon was born** c'est l'année (*or* le jour) où Napoléon est né; **that's ~ you ought to try to be patient** c'est le moment d'essayer de faire preuve de patience; **that was ~ the trouble started** c'est alors que les ennuis ont commencé.

(d) (*after*) quand, une fois que. **~ you've read the book you'll know why** quand vous aurez lu le livre vous saurez pourquoi; **~ they had left he telephoned me** après leur départ *or* après qu'ils furent partis il m'a téléphoné; **~ they had finished the coffee she offered them some brandy** après qu'ils eurent fini *or* quand ils eurent fini le café elle leur a offert du cognac; **~ you've been to Greece you ...** quand *or* une fois que vous êtes allé en Grèce vous ..., après être allé en Grèce vous ...; **~ he had seen her he slipped away** après l'avoir vue il s'est esquivé; **~ he had sat down he began to talk** une fois assis il commença de parler; **you**

may ask questions ~ he's finished vous pouvez poser vos questions quand il aura fini *or* après qu'il aura fini.

(e) (*each time that, whenever*) quand, lorsque, chaque fois que. ~ it rains I wish I were in Italy quand il pleut je regrette de ne pas être en Italie; ~ the moon is full à la pleine lune; I take aspirin ~ I have a headache je prends un cachet d'aspirine quand j'ai mal à la tête; my heart sinks ~ he says 'it reminds me ...' j'ai le cœur qui défaille chaque fois qu'il dit 'ça me rappelle ...'.

(f) (*whereas; although*) alors que. he walked ~ he could have taken the bus il est allé à pied alors qu'il aurait pu prendre le bus; he walked ~ I would have taken the bus il est allé à pied tandis que *or* alors que moi j'aurais pris le bus.

(g) (*considering that*) quand, alors que, étant donné que. what are you doing indoors ~ you could be out in the sun? que fais-tu dans la maison quand *or* alors que tu pourrais profiter du soleil dehors?; how can you understand ~ you won't listen? comment pouvez-vous comprendre quand *or* si vous n'écoutez pas?; what's the good of trying ~ I know I can't do it? à quoi sert d'essayer quand *or* étant donné que je sais que je ne peux pas le faire?; fancy going to Blackpool ~ you could have gone to Mexico! quelle idée d'aller à Blackpool quand vous auriez pu aller au Mexique!

(h) (*and then*) quand. he had just sat down ~ the phone rang il venait juste de s'asseoir quand le téléphone a sonné; hardly had I got back ~ I had to leave again je venais à peine de rentrer quand j'ai dû repartir; I was about to leave ~ I remembered ... j'étais sur le point de partir quand je me suis rappelé ... .

3 *n*: I want to know the ~ and the how of all this je veux savoir quand et comment tout ça est arrivé.

4 *cpd*: (*liter*) whene'er = whenever; whenever *V* whenever; (*liter*) whensoe'er, (*emphatic*) whensoever = whenever.

whence [wens] *adv, conj* (*liter*) d'où.

whenever [wen'evər] 1 *conj* (a) (*at whatever time*) come ~ you wish venez quand vous voulez *or* voudrez; you may leave ~ you're ready vous pouvez partir quand vous serez prêt.

(b) (*every time that*) chaque fois que, toutes les fois que. come and see us ~ you can venez nous voir quand vous le pouvez; ~ I see a black horse I think of Jenny chaque fois que *or* toutes les fois que je vois un cheval noir je pense à Jenny; ~ it rains the roof leaks chaque fois qu'il pleut le toit laisse entrer l'eau; ~ people ask him he says ... quand on lui demande il dit ...; ~ you touch it it falls over on n'a qu'à le toucher et il tombe.

2 *adv* (*) mais quand donc. ~ did you do that? mais quand donc est-ce que vous avez fait ça?*; last Monday, or ~ lundi dernier, ou je ne sais quand; I can leave on Monday, or Tuesday, or ~ je peux partir lundi, ou mardi, ou un autre jour *or* ou n'importe quand.

where [wɛər] 1 *adv* (*in or to what place*) où. ~ do you live? où habitez-vous?; ~ are you going (to)? où allez-vous?; I wonder ~ he is je me demande où il est; ~'s the theatre? où est le théâtre?; ~ are you from?, ~ do you come from? d'où êtes-vous?; I don't know ~ I put it je ne sais pas où je l'ai mis; you saw him near ~? vous l'avez vu près d'où?; he was going towards ~? il allait vers où?; ~ have you got to in the book? où est-ce que vous en êtes de votre livre?; (*fig*) ~ do I come into it? qu'est-ce que je viens faire dans tout ça?, quel est mon rôle dans tout ça?; ~'s the difference? où voyez-vous une différence?; ~ should we be if ...? où serions-nous si ...?

2 *conj* (a) (*gen*) (là) où. stay ~ you are restez (là) où vous êtes; there is a garage ~ the 2 roads intersect il y a un garage au croisement des 2 routes; there is a school ~ our house once stood il y a une école là où *or* à l'endroit où se dressait autrefois notre maison, à l'emplacement de notre maison il y a une école; go ~ you like allez où vous voulez *or* voudrez; it is coldest ~ there are no trees for shelter c'est là où il n'y a pas d'arbre pour abriter (du vent) qu'il fait le plus froid; it's not ~ I expected to see it je ne m'attendais pas à le voir là; Lyons stands ~ the Saône meets the Rhône Lyon se trouve au confluent de la Saône et du Rhône.

(b) (*rel use*) où. the house ~ he was born la maison où il est né, sa maison natale; in the place ~ there used to be a church à l'endroit où il y avait une église; he put it down there, ~ the box is now il l'a mis là, à l'endroit où se trouve maintenant la boîte; England is ~ you'll find this sort of thing most often c'est en Angleterre que vous trouverez le plus fréquemment cela.

(c) (*the place that*) là que. this is ~ the car was found c'est là qu'on a retrouvé la voiture; this is ~ we got to in the book c'est là que nous en sommes du livre; that's ~ you're wrong! c'est là que vous vous trompez!, voilà votre erreur!; so that's ~ my gloves have got to! voilà où sont passés mes gants!; (*fig*) that's ~ *or* there's* ~ things started to go wrong c'est là que les choses se sont gâtées; this is ~ *or* here's* ~ you've got to make your own decision là il faut que tu décides (*subj*) tout seul; that's ~ I meant c'est là que je voulais dire; he went up to ~ she was sitting il s'est approché de l'endroit où elle était assise; I walked past ~ he was standing j'ai dépassé l'endroit où il se tenait; from ~ I'm standing I can see ... d'où *or* de là où je suis je peux voir ... .

(d) (*wherever etc*) là où. you'll always find water ~ there are trees vous trouverez toujours de l'eau là où il y a des arbres; ~ there is kindness, there you will find ... là où il y a de la gentillesse, vous trouverez ... .

(e) (*whereas*) alors que. he walked ~ he could have taken the bus il est allé à pied alors qu'il aurait pu prendre le bus; he walked ~ I would have taken the bus il est allé à pied alors que *or* tandis que moi j'aurais pris le bus.

3 *n*: I want to know the ~ and the why of it je veux savoir où et pourquoi c'est arrivé.

4 *cpd*: whereabouts (*adv*) où (donc); to know sb's/sth's whereabouts savoir où est qn/qch; whereas (*but on the other hand*) alors que, tandis que; (*Jur: in view of the fact that*) attendu que, étant donné que; (*liter*) whereat sur quoi, après quoi, et sur ce, et là-dessus; whereby (*conj: frm*) par quoi, par lequel (*or* laquelle *etc*), au moyen duquel (*or* de laquelle *etc*); (*interrog adv*: ††) par quoi, par quel moyen; wherefore†† (*interrog adv*) pourquoi; (*con*) et donc, et pour cette raison (*V also* why 4); wherein (*interrog adv*: ††) en quoi, dans quoi; (*conj: frm*) où, en quoi, dans quoi, dans lequel (*or* laquelle *etc*); (*frm, liter*) whereof de quoi, dont, duquel (*or* de laquelle *etc*); (*frm, liter*) whereon (*conj*) sur quoi, sur lequel (*or* laquelle *etc*); (*interrog adv*) sur quoi; (*liter*) wheresoe'er, (*emphatic*) wheresoever = wherever; (*frm*) whereto et dans ce but, et en vue de ceci; whereupon sur quoi, après quoi, et sur ce, et là-dessus; wherever *V* wherever; (*frm, liter*) wherewith avec quoi, avec lequel (*or* laquelle *etc*); the wherewithal les moyens *mpl*, les ressources *fpl* nécessaires; he hasn't the wherewithal to buy it il n'a pas les moyens de l'acheter, il n'a pas ce qu'il lui faut pour l'acheter.

wherever [wɛər'evər] 1 *conj* (a) (*no matter where*) où que +*subj*. ~ I am I'll always remember où que je sois, je n'oublierai jamais; ~ you go I'll go too partout où tu iras, j'irai; I'll buy it ~ it comes from je l'achèterai d'où que cela provienne *or* quelle qu'en soit la provenance; ~ it came from, it's here now! peu importe d'où cela vient, c'est là maintenant!

(b) (*anywhere, in or to whatever place*) (là) où. sit ~ you like asseyez-vous (là) où vous voulez; go ~ you please allez où bon vous semblera; we'll go ~ you wish nous irons (là) où vous voudrez; he comes from Barcombe, ~ that is il vient d'un endroit qui s'appellerait Barcombe.

(c) (*everywhere*) partout où. ~ you see this sign, you can be sure that ... partout où vous voyez ce signe, vous pouvez être sûr que ...; ~ there is water available partout où il y a de l'eau.

2 *adv* (*) mais où donc. ~ did you get that hat? mais où donc avez-vous déniché ce chapeau?*; I bought it in London or Liverpool or ~ je l'ai acheté à Londres, Liverpool ou Dieu sait où.

whet [wet] 1 *vt tool* aiguiser, affûter; *desire, appetite, curiosity* aiguiser, stimuler. 2 *cpd*: whetstone pierre *f* à aiguiser.

whether ['weðər] *conj* (a) si. I don't know ~ it's true or not, I don't know ~ or not it's true je ne sais pas si c'est vrai ou non; you must tell him ~ you want him (or not) il faut que tu lui dises si oui ou non tu as besoin de lui; I don't know ~ to go or not je ne sais pas si je dois y aller ou non; it is doubtful ~ il est peu probable que+*subj*; I doubt ~ je doute que+*subj*; I'm not sure ~ je ne suis pas sûr si+*indic* or que+*subj*.

(b) que+*subj*. ~ it rains or (~ it) snows I'm going out qu'il pleuve ou qu'il neige je sors; ~ you go or not, ~ or not you go que tu y ailles ou non.

(c) soit. ~ today or tomorrow soit aujourd'hui soit demain; ~ before or after soit avant soit après; ~ with or without an umbrella avec ou sans parapluie; I shall help you ~ or no de toute façon *or* quoi qu'il arrive (*subj*) je vous aiderai.

whew [hwuː] *excl* (*relief, exhaustion*) ouf!; (*surprise, admiration*) fichtre!*

whey [weɪ] *n* petit-lait *m*.

which [wɪtʃ] 1 *adj* (a) (*interrog*) quel. ~ card did he take? quelle carte a-t-il prise?, laquelle des cartes a-t-il prise?; I don't know ~ book he wants je ne sais pas quel livre il veut; ~ one? lequel (*or* laquelle)?; ~ one of you? lequel (*or* laquelle) d'entre vous?; ~ Smith do you mean? quel Smith voulez-vous dire?

(b) (*rel use*) in ~ case auquel cas; ... Paris, ~ city I know well ... Paris, ville que je connais bien; he spent a week here, during ~ time ... il a passé une semaine ici au cours de laquelle ...; he used 'peradventure', ~ word ... il a employé 'peradventure', mot qui ...

2 *pron* (a) (*interrog*) lequel *m*, laquelle *f*. ~ is the best of these maps?, ~ of these maps is the best? quelle est la meilleure de ces cartes?, laquelle de ces cartes est la meilleure?; ~ of you two is taller? lequel de vous deux est le plus grand?, qui est le plus grand de vous deux?; ~ are the ripest apples? quelles sont les pommes les plus mûres?, quelles pommes sont les plus mûres?; ~ would you like? lequel aimeriez-vous?; ~ of you are married? lesquels d'entre vous sont mariés?; ~ of you owns the red car? lequel d'entre vous est le propriétaire de la voiture rouge?

(b) (*the one or ones that*) celui (*or* celle *or* ceux *or* celles) qui *or* que. I don't mind ~ you give me vous pouvez me donner celui que vous voudrez (ça m'est égal); show me ~ is the cheapest montrez-moi celui qui est le moins cher; I can't tell *or* I don't know ~ is ~ je ne peux pas les distinguer; tell me ~ are the Frenchmen dites-moi lesquels sont les Français; I know ~ I'd rather have je sais celui que je préférerais; ask him ~ of the books he'd like demandez-lui parmi tous les livres lequel il voudrait; I don't mind ~ ça m'est égal.

(c) (*rel: with n antecedent*) (*nominative*) qui; (*accusative*) que; (*after prep*) lequel, laquelle, lesquels, lesquelles. the book ~ is on the table le livre qui est sur la table; the apple ~ you ate la pomme que vous avez mangée; the house towards ~ she was going la maison vers laquelle elle se dirigeait; the film of ~ he was speaking le film dont il parlait; opposite ~ en face duquel (*or* de laquelle *etc*); the book ~ I told you about le livre dont je vous ai parlé; the box ~ you put it in la boîte dans laquelle vous l'avez mis.

(d) (*rel: with clause antecedent*) (*nominative*) ce qui; (*accusative*) ce que; (*after prep*) quoi. he said he knew her, ~ is true il a dit qu'il la connaissait, ce qui est vrai; she said she was 40, ~ I don't believe elle a dit qu'elle avait 40 ans, ce que *or* chose que je ne crois pas *or* mais je n'en crois rien; you're late, ~ reminds me ... vous êtes en retard, ce qui me fait penser ...; ... upon ~ she left the room ... sur quoi *or* et sur ce elle a quitté la pièce; ... **of ~ more later** ... ce dont je reparlerai plus tard, ... mais je reviendrai là-dessus plus tard; **from ~ we deduce that** d'où *or* et de là nous déduisons que; **after ~ we went to bed** après quoi nous sommes allés nous coucher.

whichever [wɪtʃ'evəʳ] **1** *adj* **(a)** (*that one which*) **~ method is most successful should be chosen** on devrait choisir la méthode garantissant les meilleurs résultats, peu importe laquelle; **take ~ book you like best** prenez le livre que vous préférez (,peu importe lequel); **I'll have ~ apple you don't want** je prendrai la pomme que *or* dont vous ne voulez pas; **keep ~ one you prefer** gardez celui que vous préférez; **go by ~ route is the most direct** prenez la route la plus directe, peu importe laquelle; **do it in ~ way you can** faites-le comme vous pourrez.

(b) (*no matter which*) (*nominative*) quel que soit ... qui+*subj*; (*accusative*) quel que soit ... que+*subj*. **~ dress you wear** quelle que soit la robe que tu portes; **~ book is chosen** quel que soit le livre choisi; (*fig*) **~ way you look at it** de quelque manière que vous le considériez (*subj*).

2 *pron* **(a)** (*the one which*) (*nominative*) celui *m* qui, celle *f* qui; (*accusative*) celui *m* que, celle *f* que. **~ is best for him** celui (*or* celle) qui lui convient le mieux; **~ you choose will be sent to you at once** celui (*or* celle) que vous choisirez vous sera expédié(e) immédiatement; **~ of the books is selected** le livre qui sera sélectionné quel qu'il soit; **choose ~ is easiest** choisissez (celui qui est) le plus facile.

(b) (*no matter which one*) (*nominative*) quel *m* que soit celui qui+*subj*, quelle *f* que soit celle qui+*subj*; (*accusative*) quel que soit celui que+*subj*, quelle que soit celle que+*subj*. **~ of the two books he chooses, it won't make a lot of difference** quel que soit le livre qu'il choisisse, cela ne fera pas beaucoup de différence; **~ of the methods is chosen, it can't affect you much** quelle que soit la méthode choisie, ça ne vous affectera pas beaucoup.

whiff [wɪf] *n* (*puff: of smoke, hot air etc*) bouffée *f*; (*smell*) odeur *f*. **a ~ of chloroform** une bouffée *or* petite dose de chloroforme; **a ~ of garlic/seaweed** *etc* une bouffée d'ail/de varech *etc*; **after a few ~s he put out the cigarette** après quelques bouffées il a éteint la cigarette; **one ~ of this is enough to kill you** il suffit de respirer ça une fois pour mourir; **I caught a ~ of gas** j'ai senti l'odeur du gaz; **take a ~ of this!*** renifle ça!; (*pej*) **what a ~!*** ce que ça sent mauvais!

whiffy* ['wɪfɪ] *adj* qui sent mauvais.

Whig [wɪg] *adj, n* (*Brit Pol*) whig (*m*).

while [waɪl] **1** *conj* **(a)** (*during the time that*) pendant que. **it happened ~ I was out of the room** c'est arrivé pendant que *or* alors que j'étais hors de la pièce; **can you wait ~ I telephone?** pouvez-vous attendre pendant que je téléphone?; **she fell asleep ~ reading** elle s'est endormie en lisant; **~ you're away I'll write some letters** pendant ton absence j'écrirai quelques lettres; **don't drink ~ on duty** ne buvez pas pendant le service; **'heels repaired ~ you wait'** 'talon minute' (*V also* 2); **~ you're up you could close the door** pendant que *or* puisque tu es debout tu pourrais fermer la porte; **and ~ you're about it** et pendant que vous y êtes.

(b) (*as long as*) tant que. **~ there's life there's hope** tant qu'il y a de la vie il y a de l'espoir; **it won't happen ~ I'm here** cela n'arrivera pas tant que je serai là; **~ I live I shall make sure that** ... tant que *or* aussi longtemps que je vivrai je ferai en sorte que ... .

(c) (*although*) quoique+*subj*, bien que+*subj*. **~ I admit he is sometimes right** ... tout en admettant *or* quoique j'admette qu'il ait quelquefois raison ...; **~ there are a few people who like that sort of thing** ... bien qu'il y ait un petit nombre de gens qui aiment ce genre de chose ... .

(d) (*whereas*) alors que, tandis que. **she sings quite well, ~ her sister can't sing a note** elle ne chante pas mal alors que *or* tandis que sa sœur ne sait pas chanter du tout.

2 *cpd*: **while-you-wait heel repairs** ≃ talon minute.

3 *n* **(a) a ~** quelque temps; **a short ~, a little ~** un moment, un instant; **a long ~, a good ~** (assez) longtemps; **after a ~** quelque temps après, au bout de quelque temps; **let's stop for a ~** arrêtons un moment *or* (*longer*) quelque temps; **for a ~ I thought** ... j'ai pensé un moment ..., (*longer*) pendant quelque temps j'ai pensé ...; **it takes quite a ~ to ripen** cela met assez longtemps à mûrir; **once in a ~** (une fois) de temps en temps; **(in) between ~s** entre-temps; *V* **worth**.

(b) he looked at me (all) the ~ il m'a regardé pendant tout ce temps-là.

while away *vt sep* (faire) passer.

whiles [waɪlz] *adv* (*dial, esp Scot*) quelquefois, de temps en temps.

whilst [waɪlst] *conj* = **while 1**.

whim [wɪm] *n* caprice *m*, fantaisie *f*, lubie *f*. **to be full of ~s** être capricieux *or* fantasque; **it's just a (passing) ~** c'est une lubie qui lui (*or* te *etc*) passera; **he gives in to her every ~** il lui passe tous ses caprices, il fait ses quatre volontés*; **as the ~ takes him** comme l'idée lui prend.

whimper ['wɪmpəʳ] **1** *n* (faible) gémissement *m*, (faible) geignement *m*, plainte inarticulée. ... **he said with a ~** ... dit-il d'un ton larmoyant, ... gémit-il, ... pleurnicha-t-il (*pej*); (*fig*) **without a ~** sans se plaindre. **2** *vi* [*person, baby*] gémir *or* geindre faiblement, pleurnicher (*pej*); [*dog*] gémir, pousser des cris plaintifs. **3** *vt*: **'no,' he ~ed** 'non,' gémit-il *or* pleurnicha-t-il (*pej*), 'non,' dit-il d'un ton larmoyant.

whimpering ['wɪmpərɪŋ] **1** *n* geignements *mpl*, gémissements *mpl*. **2** *adj tone, voice* larmoyant, pleurnicheur (*pej*); *person, animal* qui gémit faiblement.

whimsical ['wɪmzɪkəl] *adj person* capricieux, fantasque; *smile, look* étrange, curieux; *idea* saugrenu; *story, book* étrange, fantaisiste.

whimsicality [,wɪmzɪ'kælɪtɪ] *n* **(a)** (*U*) caractère capricieux *or* fantasque *or* fantaisiste *or* curieux. **(b) whimsicalities** idées (*or* actions *etc*) bizarres *or* saugrenues.

whimsically ['wɪmzɪkəlɪ] *adv say, suggest* de façon saugrenue; *smile, look* étrangement, curieusement; *muse, ponder* malicieusement.

whimsy ['wɪmzɪ] *n* (*whim*) caprice *m*, fantaisie *f*, lubie *f*; (*U: whimsicality*) caractère *m* fantaisiste.

whin [wɪn] *n* (*Bot*) ajonc *m*.

whine [waɪn] **1** *n* [*person, child, dog*] gémissement prolongé; (*fig: complaint*) plainte *f*; [*bullet, shell, siren, machine*] plainte stridente *or* monocorde. ... **he said in a ~** ... se lamenta-t-il, ... dit-il d'une voix geignarde; (*fig*) **it's another of his ~s about taxes** le voilà qui se répand encore en lamentations sur ses impôts; (*fig*) **I'm tired of all his ~s** j'en ai assez de ses jérémiades *fpl*.

2 *vi* [*person, dog*] geindre, gémir; (*fig: complain*) se lamenter; [*siren*] gémir. (*fig*) **to ~ about sth** se lamenter sur qch; **don't come whining to me about it** ne venez pas vous plaindre à moi, ne venez pas me faire vos doléances.

3 *vt*: **'it's happened again,' he ~d** 'ça a recommencé,' se lamenta-t-il *or* dit-il d'une voix geignarde.

whining ['waɪnɪŋ] **1** *n* [*person, child*] gémissements continus, pleurnicheries *fpl*, jérémiades *fpl*; [*dog*] gémissements; (*fig: complaining*) plaintes continuelles, jérémiades, lamentations *fpl*. **2** *adj voice* geignard, pleurard; *child* geignard, pleurnicheur; *dog* qui gémit.

whinny ['wɪnɪ] **1** *n* hennissement *m*. **2** *vi* hennir.

whip [wɪp] **1** *n* **(a)** fouet *m*; (*riding ~*) cravache *f*.

(b) (*Parl*) (*person*) whip *m*, chef *m* de file (*député chargé par son parti d'assurer la discipline à l'intérieur du groupe parlementaire*); (*Brit: summons*) convocation *f*. **three-line ~** convocation impérative.

(c) (*Culin: dessert*) crème instantanée.

2 *cpd*: (*Tex*) **whipcord** whipcord *m*; (*fig*) **to have the whip hand** être le maître, avoir le dessus; **to have the whip hand over sb** avoir la haute main sur qn; **whiplash** (*blow from whip*) coup *m* de fouet; (*fig: in car accident*) coup *m* du lapin*, syndrome cervical traumatique; **whiplash injury to the neck** lésion *f* traumatique de la colonne vertébrale; (*Brit*) **whip-round*** collecte *f*; **to have a whip-round* for sb/sth** faire une collecte pour qn/qch.

3 *vt* **(a)** *person, animal, child* fouetter; (*Culin*) *cream* fouetter, battre au fouet; *egg white* battre en neige; (*fig*) (*defeat*) battre à plate(s) couture(s); (*criticize severely*) critiquer vivement, cingler, éreinter. **the rain ~ped her face** la pluie lui cinglait *or* fouettait la figure.

(b) (*seize etc*) **to ~ sth out of sb's hands** enlever brusquement *or* vivement qch des mains de qn; **he ~ped a gun out of his pocket** il a brusquement sorti un revolver de sa poche; **he ~ped the letter off the table** il a prestement fait disparaître la lettre qui était (restée) sur la table.

(c) (*Brit**: *steal*) faucher*, piquer‡. **somebody's ~ped my watch!** quelqu'un m'a fauché* *or* piqué‡ ma montre!

(d) *cable, rope* surlier; (*Sewing*) surfiler.

4 *vi*: **to ~ along/back/away** *etc* filer/reculer/partir *etc* à toute allure *or* comme un éclair; **the car ~ped round the corner** la voiture a pris le tournant à toute allure; **the wind ~ped through the trees** le vent s'élançait à travers les arbres; **the rope broke and ~ped across his face** la corde a cassé et lui a cinglé le visage.

whip away 1 *vi V* **whip 4**.

2 *vt sep* (*remove quickly*) [*person*] enlever brusquement *or* vivement, faire disparaître; [*wind etc*] emporter brusquement.

whip back *vi* [*broken rope, cable etc*] revenir brusquement en arrière; *V also* **whip 4**.

whip in 1 *vi* **(a)** [*person*] entrer précipitamment *or* comme un éclair.

(b) (*Hunting*) être piqueur.

2 *vt sep* **(a)** (*Hunting*) *hounds* ramener, rassembler; (*Parl*) *members voting* battre le rappel de; (*fig*) *voters, supporters* rallier.

(b) (*Culin*) **whip in the cream** incorporez la crème avec un fouet.

whip off *vt sep garment etc* ôter *or* enlever en quatrième vitesse; *lid, cover* ôter brusquement.

whip on *vt sep* **(a)** *garment etc* enfiler en quatrième vitesse.

(b) (*urge on*) *horse* cravacher.

whip out 1 *vi* [*person*] sortir précipitamment.

2 *vt sep knife, gun, purse* sortir brusquement *or* vivement (*from* de).

whip over* *vi* = **whip round 1b**.

whip round 1 *vi* **(a)** (*turn quickly*) [*person*] se retourner vivement; [*object*] pivoter brusquement.

(b) (*) **he's just whipped round to the grocer's** il est juste allé faire un saut à l'épicerie; **whip round to your aunt's and tell her** ... va faire un saut *or* cours chez ta tante lui dire ... .

2 whip-round* *n V* **whip 2**.

whip through *vt fus book* parcourir rapidement; *homework, task* expédier, faire en quatrième vitesse.

whip up *vt sep* **(a)** *emotions, enthusiasm, indignation* donner un coup de fouet à, fouetter, attiser; *support, interest* donner un coup de fouet à, stimuler.

(b) *cream, egg whites* fouetter, battre au fouet. (*fig*) **to whip up a meal*** préparer un repas en vitesse; **can you whip us up something to eat?*** est-ce que vous pourriez nous faire à manger* *or* nous préparer un morceau en vitesse?

(c) (*snatch up*) saisir brusquement.

whipper ['wɪpəʳ] *cpd*: **whipper-in** piqueur *m*; **whippersnapper** freluquet *m*.

whippet ['wɪpɪt] n whippet m.
whipping ['wɪpɪŋ] 1 n (as punishment) correction f. to give sb a ~ fouetter qn, donner le fouet à qn, donner des coups de fouet à qn.
2 cpd: (fig) whipping boy bouc m émissaire; (Culin) whipping cream crème fraîche (à fouetter); whipping post poteau m (où étaient attachées les personnes qu'on fouettait); whipping top toupie f.
whippoorwill ['wɪp,pʊə,wɪl] n engoulevent m d'Amérique du Nord.
whir [wɜːʳ] = whirr.
whirl [wɜːl] 1 n [leaves, papers, smoke] tourbillon m, tournoiement m; [sand, dust, water] tourbillon. (fig) a ~ of parties and dances un tourbillon de surprises-parties et de bals; the whole week was a ~ of activity nous n'avons (or ils n'ont etc) pas arrêté de toute la semaine; the social ~ la vie mondaine; her thoughts/emotions were in a ~ tout tourbillonnait dans sa tête/son cœur, ses pensées/émotions étaient en désarroi; my head is in a ~ la tête me tourne; (fig) to give sth a ~* essayer qch.
2 cpd: whirlpool tourbillon m; whirlwind (n) tornade f, trombe f (V also sow²); (adj: fig) éclair* inv.
3 vi (a) (spin: also ~ round) [leaves, papers, smoke, dancers] tourbillonner, tournoyer; [sand, dust, water] tourbillonner; [wheel, merry-go-round, spinning top] tourner. they ~ed past us in the dance ils sont passés près de nous en tourbillonnant pendant la danse; the leaves ~ed down les feuilles tombaient en tourbillonnant; my head is ~ing (round) la tête me tourne; her thoughts/emotions were ~ing tout tourbillonnait dans sa tête/son cœur, ses pensées/ses émotions étaient en désarroi.
(b) (move rapidly) to ~ along aller à toute vitesse or à toute allure; to ~ away or off partir à toute vitesse or à toute allure.
4 vt [wind] leaves, smoke faire tourbillonner, faire tournoyer; dust, sand faire tourbillonner. he ~ed his sword round his head il a fait tournoyer son épée au-dessus de sa tête; they ~ed us round the Louvre ils nous ont fait visiter le Louvre à toute vitesse; the train ~ed us up to London le train nous a emportés à Londres (à toute allure).
whirl round 1 vi (turn suddenly) [person] se retourner brusquement, virevolter; [revolving chair etc] pivoter; V also whirl 3a.
2 vt sep (a) [wind] leaves, smoke faire tourbillonner, faire tournoyer; dust, sand faire tourbillonner.
(b) sword, object on rope etc faire tournoyer; revolving chair etc faire pivoter.
whirligig ['wɜːlɪgɪg] n (toy) moulin m à vent; (merry-go-round) manège m; (beetle) tourniquet m, gyrin m; (fig: of events etc) tourbillon m. the smoke moved in a ~ towards ... la fumée allait en tourbillonnant or en tournoyant dans la direction de ... .
whirlybird* ['wɜːlɪbɜːd] n (US) hélicoptère m, banane* f.
whirr [wɜːʳ] 1 vi [bird's wings, insect's wings] bruire; [cameras, machinery] ronronner, (louder) vrombir; [propellers] vrombir. the helicopter went ~ing off l'hélicoptère est parti en vrombissant.
2 n [bird's wings, insect's wings] bruissement m (d'ailes); [machinery] ronronnement m, (louder) vrombissement m; [propellers] vrombissement.
whisk [wɪsk] 1 n (for sweeping) époussette f; (fly~) émouchoir m, chasse-mouches m inv; (Culin) fouet m. with a ~ of his tail, the horse ... d'un coup de queue, le cheval ...; (Culin) give the mixture a good ~ bien battre le mélange.
2 vt (a) (Culin) (whip) fouetter; (beat) battre. ~ the eggs into the mixture incorporez les œufs dans le mélange avec un fouet or en remuant vigoureusement.
(b) the horse ~ed its tail le cheval fouettait l'air de sa queue.
(c) to ~ sth out of sb's hands enlever brusquement or vivement qch des mains de qn; she ~ed the letter off the table elle a prestement fait disparaître la lettre de la table; he ~ed it out of his pocket il l'a brusquement sorti de sa poche; he ~ed the vacuum cleaner round the flat il a passé l'aspirateur dans l'appartement en deux temps trois mouvements; the lift ~ed us up to the top floor l'ascenseur nous a emportés jusqu'au dernier étage (à toute allure); he was ~ed into a meeting on l'a brusquement entraîné dans une réunion; he ~ed her off to meet his mother il l'a emmenée illico* faire la connaissance de sa mère.
3 vi: to ~ along/in/out etc filer/entrer/sortir etc à toute allure; she ~ed out of the room elle a quitté brusquement la pièce.
whisk away vt sep flies chasser d'un coup d'émouchoir; dust, crumbs enlever d'un coup d'époussette; (fig) cloth, dishes emporter.
whisk off vt sep flies chasser d'un coup d'émouchoir; dust enlever d'un coup d'époussette; lid, cover ôter brusquement; garment enlever or ôter en quatrième vitesse; V also whisk 2c.
whisk together vt sep (Culin) mélanger en fouettant or avec un fouet.
whisk up vt sep (Culin) fouetter; V also whisk 2c.
whisker ['wɪskəʳ] n [animal, man] poil m. ~s (side ~s) favoris mpl; (beard) barbe f; (moustache) moustache(s) f(pl); [animal] moustaches. he won the race by a ~ il s'en est fallu d'un cheveu or d'un poil* qu'il ne perde la course.
whiskered ['wɪskəd] adj (V whisker) man qui a des favoris (or une barbe or des moustaches).
whiskey (Ir, US), **whisky** (Brit, Can) ['wɪskɪ] 1 n whisky m. a ~ and soda un whisky soda; V sour. 2 cpd flavour de whisky.
whisper ['wɪspəʳ] 1 vi [person] chuchoter, parler à voix basse; [leaves, water] chuchoter, murmurer. to ~ to sb parler or chuchoter à l'oreille de qn, parler à voix basse à qn; it's rude to ~ c'est mal élevé de chuchoter à l'oreille de quelqu'un; you'll have to ~ il faudra que vous parliez (subj) bas.
2 vt chuchoter, dire à voix basse (sth to sb qch à qn, that que). he ~ed a word in my ear il m'a dit or soufflé quelque chose à l'oreille; to ~ sweet nothings to sb susurrer des mots doux à (l'oreille de) qn; (fig) I've heard it ~ed that he's gone away j'ai entendu dire qu'il est parti; (fig) it is being ~ed that ... le bruit court que ..., on dit que ... .
3 n (low tone) chuchotement m; [wind, leaves, water] murmure m, bruissement m; (fig: rumour) bruit m, rumeur f. I heard a ~ j'ai entendu un chuchotement, j'ai entendu quelqu'un qui parlait à voix basse; a ~ of voices des chuchotements; to say/answer in a ~ dire/répondre à voix basse; to speak in a ~ parler bas or à voix basse; her voice scarcely rose above a ~ sa voix n'était guère qu'un murmure; (fig) not a ~ to anyone! n'en soufflez mot à personne!; (fig) I've heard a ~ that he won't come back j'ai entendu dire qu'il ne reviendrait pas; there is a ~ that ..., the ~ is going round that ... le bruit court que ..., on dit que ... .
whispering ['wɪspərɪŋ] 1 adj person qui chuchote, qui parle à voix basse; leaves, wind, stream qui chuchote, qui murmure. ~ voices des chuchotements mpl.
2 n [voice] chuchotement m; [leaves etc] chuchotement, bruissement m, murmure m, chuchotis m; (fig) (gossip) médisances fpl; (rumours) rumeurs insidieuses. (fig) there has been a lot of ~ about them toutes sortes de rumeurs insidieuses ont couru sur leur compte.
3 cpd: (fig) whispering campaign campagne (diffamatoire) insidieuse; whispering gallery galerie f à écho.
whist [wɪst] n whist m. ~ drive tournoi m de whist.
whistle ['wɪsl] 1 n (a) (sound) (made with mouth) sifflement m, (jeering) sifflet m; (made with a ~) coup m de sifflet; [train, kettle, blackbird] sifflement. the ~s of the audience (cheering) les sifflements d'admiration du public; (booing) les sifflets du public; to give a ~ [person, train, kettle, blackbird] siffler; (blow a ~) donner un coup de sifflet.
(b) (object: also of kettle etc) sifflet m; (Mus: also penny ~) flûteau m. a blast on a ~ un coup de sifflet strident; the referee blew his ~ l'arbitre a donné un coup de sifflet or a sifflé; the referee blew his ~ for half-time l'arbitre a sifflé la mi-temps; it broke off as clean as a ~ ça a cassé net; (fig) to blow the ~ on sth‡ (inform about it) vendre la mèche à propos de qch; (stop it) mettre un terme à qch; (fig) he blew the ~ on it‡ (informed on it) il a vendu la mèche; (stopped it) il y a mis le holà.
2 cpd: (fig: Pol etc) whistle stop arrêt bref (dans une petite ville au cours d'une campagne électorale); he made a whistle-stop tour of Virginia il a fait à toute allure le tour de la Virginie.
3 vi [person] siffler, (tunefully, light-heartedly) siffloter; (blow a ~) donner un coup de sifflet, siffler; [bird, bullet, wind, kettle, train] siffler. he ~d to his dog il a sifflé son chien; he ~d at or for me to stop il a sifflé pour que je m'arrête (subj); he ~d for a taxi il a sifflé un taxi; the boy was whistling at all the pretty girls le garçon sifflait toutes les jolies filles; the referee ~d for a foul l'arbitre a sifflé une faute; the crowd ~d at the referee la foule a sifflé l'arbitre; the audience booed and ~d les spectateurs ont hué et sifflé; the audience cheered and ~d les spectateurs ont manifesté leur enthousiasme par des acclamations et des sifflements; he strolled along whistling (away) gaily il flânait en sifflotant gaiement; (fig) to ~ in the dark crâner*, faire semblant de ne pas avoir peur; (fig) he can ~ for it!* il peut se fouiller!* or se brosser!*, il peut toujours courir!*; an arrow ~d past his ear une flèche a sifflé à son oreille; the cars ~d by us les voitures passaient devant nous à toute allure.
4 vt tune siffler, (casually, light-heartedly) siffloter. to ~ a dog back/in etc siffler un chien pour qu'il revienne/entre (subj) etc.
whistle up vt sep dog, taxi siffler. (fig) he whistled up 4 or 5 people to give us a hand* il s'est débrouillé pour dégoter* 4 ou 5 personnes prêtes à nous donner un coup de main; can you whistle up another blanket or two?* vous pouvez dégoter* encore une ou deux couvertures?
Whit [wɪt] 1 n la Pentecôte. 2 cpd holiday etc de Pentecôte. Whit Monday/Sunday le lundi/dimanche de Pentecôte; Whitsun(tide) les fêtes fpl de (la) Pentecôte, la Pentecôte; Whit Week la semaine de Pentecôte.
whit [wɪt] n: there was not a ~ of truth in it il n'y avait pas un brin de vérité là-dedans; he hadn't a ~ of sense il n'avait pas un grain de bon sens; it wasn't a ~ better after he'd finished quand il a eu terminé ce n'était pas mieux du tout; I don't care a ~ ça m'est profondément égal, je m'en moque complètement.
white [waɪt] 1 adj (a) (gen) bread, hair, wine, meat, metal, rabbit blanc (f blanche). (Culin) ~ sauce béchamel f, sauce blanche; as ~ as a sheet pâle comme un linge; as ~ as snow blanc comme (la) neige; to be ~ with fear/anger être blanc or blême or pâle de peur/colère; to go or turn ~ (with fear, anger) blêmir, pâlir, blanchir; [hair] blanchir; [object] devenir blanc, blanchir; he went ~ with fear il a blêmi de peur; this detergent gets the clothes ~r than ~ ce détergent lave encore plus blanc; ~ blood cell, ~ corpuscle globule blanc; a ~ Christmas un Noël sous la neige; (fig) it's a ~ elephant c'est tout à fait superflu, on n'en a pas besoin; ~ elephant stall étalage m d'objets superflus; (fig) to show the ~ feather caner*, se dégonfler*; (Mil etc) the ~ flag le drapeau blanc; ~ frost gelée blanche; ~ fox (animal) renard m polaire; (skin, fur) renard blanc; (at sea) ~ horses moutons mpl; (US) the W~ House la Maison Blanche; (fig) a ~ lie un pieux mensonge; (Parl) ~ paper livre blanc (on sur); V also 3 etc.
(b) (racially) person, face, skin, race blanc (f blanche). a ~ man un Blanc; a ~ woman une Blanche; the ~ South Africans les Blancs d'Afrique du Sud; ~ supremacy la suprématie de la race blanche; (pej) ~ trash les petits Blancs pauvres; V also 3 etc.
2 n (a) (colour) blanc m; (whiteness) blancheur f; [egg, eye]

blanc. **to be dressed in** ~ être vêtu de blanc; (*linen etc*) **the** ~**s** le (linge) blanc; (*clothes*) **tennis** ~**s** tenue *f* de tennis; **his face was a deathly** ~ son visage était d'une pâleur mortelle; **the sheets were a dazzling** ~ les draps étaient d'une blancheur éclatante; (*Mil etc*) **don't fire till you see the** ~**s of their eyes** ne tirez qu'au dernier moment; *V* **black** *etc*.

(b) (*person of* ~ *race*) Blanc *m*, Blanche *f*.

3 *cpd*: **whitebait** blanchaille *f*; (*US: at sea*) **whitecaps** moutons *mpl*; **a white-collar job** un emploi dans un bureau; **white-collar worker** employé(e) *m(f)* de bureau; (*fig*) **whited sepulchre** sépulcre blanchi, hypocrite *mf*; (*Astron*) **white dwarf** naine blanche; **white-faced** blême, pâle; **white gold** or blanc; (*Comm*) **white goods** (*linens*) linge blanc; (*US: domestic appliances*) appareils ménagers; **white-haired** *person* aux cheveux blancs; *animal* à poil blanc, aux poils blancs; **Whitehall** *siège m du gouvernement britannique*; **it is thought in Whitehall** ... on pense dans les milieux gouvernementaux ...; **white-headed** *person* aux cheveux blancs; *bird* à tête blanche; (*fig*) **the white-headed boy** l'enfant chéri; (*Phys*) **white heat** chaude blanche, chaleur *f* d'incandescence; **to raise metal to a white heat** chauffer un métal à blanc; (*fig*) **the indignation of the crowd had reached white heat** l'indignation de la foule avait atteint son paroxysme; (*fig*) **to be the white hope of** être le grand espoir de, être l'espoir numéro un de; **white-hot** chauffé à blanc; **white lead** blanc *m* de céruse; (*Phys*) **white light** lumière blanche; (*fig liter*) **white-livered** poltron, couard; **white magic** magie blanche; **the White Nile** le Nil Blanc; (*Acoustics*) **white noise** son blanc; (*Met*) **there is a whiteout** il y a le jour blanc; (*Orn*) **white owl** harfang *m*, chouette blanche; (*US*) **white raisin** raisin sec de Smyrne; **White Russia** Russie Blanche; **White Russian** (*adj*) russe blanc (*f* russe blanche); (*n*) Russe blanc, Russe blanche; (*Comm*) **white sale** vente *f* de blanc; **white sapphire** saphir blanc; **white slavery, the white slave trade** la traite des blanches; (*Brit*) **white spirit** white-spirit *m*; (*Bot*) **whitethorn** aubépine *f*; (*Orn*) **whitethroat** (*Old World warbler*) grisette *f*; (*American sparrow*) moineau *m* d'Amérique; (*Dress*) **white tie** habit *m*; **it was a white-tie affair** l'habit était de rigueur; **whitewash** *V* **whitewash**.

whiten ['waɪtn] *vti* blanchir.

whiteness ['waɪtnɪs] *n* (*V* **white 1**) blancheur *f*, blanc *m*, couleur blanche; pâleur *f*; aspect *m* blême.

whitening ['waɪtnɪŋ] *n* (*U*) **(a)** (*act*) *[wall etc]* blanchiment *m*; *[linen]* blanchiment, décoloration *f*; *[hair]* blanchissement *m*. **(b)** (*substance: for shoes, doorsteps etc*) blanc *m*.

whitewash ['waɪtwɒʃ] **1** *n* **(a)** (*U: for walls etc*) lait *m or* blanc *m* de chaux.

(b) (*fig*) **the whole episode was a** ~ **of the government's inefficiency** tout l'épisode était une mise en scène pour camoufler la carence du gouvernement; (*fig*) **the article in the paper was nothing but a** ~ **of his doubtful character** l'article du journal ne visait qu'à blanchir sa réputation douteuse.

(c) (*US Sport*:) raclée* *f*.

2 *vt* **(a)** *wall etc* blanchir à la chaux, chauler.

(b) (*fig*) *sb's reputation, career, motives* blanchir; *sb's faults, happening* justifier (par des arguments fallacieux); *person* blanchir, disculper, réhabiliter. (*fig*) **they tried to** ~ **the whole episode** ils se sont livrés à une entreprise de justification de toute l'affaire, ils ont essayé de peindre l'affaire sous les traits les plus anodins.

(c) (*US Sport*:) écraser complètement*.

whither ['wɪðə^{r}] *adv* (*liter*) où. (*in headlines, titles etc*) '~ **Leyland now?**' 'où va Leyland?'

whiting[1] ['waɪtɪŋ] *n* (*fish*) merlan *m*.

whiting[2] ['waɪtɪŋ] *n* (*U: for shoes, doorsteps etc*) blanc *m*.

whitish ['waɪtɪʃ] *adj* blanchâtre.

whitlow ['wɪtləʊ] *n* panaris *m*.

whittle ['wɪtl] *vt piece of wood* tailler au couteau. **to** ~ **sth out of a piece of wood, to** ~ **a piece of wood into sth** tailler qch au couteau dans un morceau de bois.

whittle away 1 *vi*: **to whittle away at sth** tailler qch au couteau.

2 *vt sep* = **whittle down**.

whittle down *vt sep wood* tailler; (*fig*) *costs, amount* rogner, réduire.

whiz [wɪz] = **whizz**.

whizz [wɪz] **1** *n* **(a)** (*sound*) sifflement *m*.

(b) (*US*:) champion* *m*, as *m*. **he's a** ~ **at tennis** au tennis il est champion* *or* c'est un as.

2 *cpd*: **whizz-bang** (*Mil sl: shell*) obus *m*; (*firework*) pétard *m*; **whizz kid*** petit prodige.

3 *vi* aller à toute vitesse en sifflant, filer à toute allure *or* comme une flèche. **to** ~ *or* **go** ~**ing through the air** fendre l'air en sifflant; (*Aut*) **to** ~ **along/past** *etc* filer/passer *etc* à toute vitesse *or* à toute allure; **I'll just** ~ **over to see him*** je file* le voir; **he** ~**ed up to town for the day*** il a fait un saut en ville pour la journée.

4 *vt* (:) (*throw*) lancer, filer:; (*transfer quickly*) apporter. ~ **the book over to me** lance-moi le livre, file-moi: le livre; **he** ~**ed it round to us as soon as it was ready** il nous l'a vite apporté *or* passé dès que c'était prêt.

who [hu:] **1** *pron* **(a)** (*interrog: remplace aussi 'whom' dans le langage parlé*) (qui est-ce) qui; (*after prep*) qui. ~**'s there?** qui est là?; ~ **are you?** qui êtes-vous?; ~ **has the book?** (qui est-ce) qui a le livre?; ~ **does he think he is?** pour qui se prend-il?; ~ **came with you?** (qui est-ce) qui est venu avec vous?; ~ **should it be but Robert!** qui vois-je? Robert!; **I don't know** ~**'s** ~ **in the office** je ne connais pas très bien les gens au bureau; '**W**~**'s W**~' = 'Bottin Mondain'; ~**(m) did you see?** vous avez vu qui?; ~**(m) did you speak to?** vous avez parlé à qui?; ~**'s the book by?** le livre est de qui?; ~**(m) were you with?** vous étiez avec qui?; **you-know-**~ **said** ... qui-vous-savez a dit ... .

(b) (*rel*) qui. **my aunt** ~ **lives in London** ma tante qui habite à Londres; **he** ~ **wishes to object must do so now** quiconque désire élever une objection doit le faire maintenant; **those** ~ **can swim** ceux qui savent nager; (*liter*) ~ **is not with me is against me** celui qui *or* quiconque n'est pas pour moi est contre moi.

2 *cpd*: **whodunit*** roman policier, polar* *m*; **whoever** *V* **whoever**;, (*liter*) **whoe'er**, (*liter*) **whosoe'er**, (*emphatic*) **whosoever** = **whoever**.

whoa [wəʊ] *excl* (*also* ~ **there**) ho!, holà!

whoever [hu:'evə^{r}] *pron* (*remplace aussi 'whomever' dans le langage parlé*) **(a)** (*anyone that*) quiconque. ~ **wishes may come with me** quiconque le désire peut venir avec moi; **you can give it to** ~ **wants it** vous pouvez le donner à qui le veut *or* voudra; ~ **finds it can keep it** quiconque *or* celui qui le trouvera pourra le garder; ~ **said that was an idiot** celui qui a dit ça était un imbécile; **ask** ~ **you like** demandez à qui vous voulez *or* voudrez. **(b)** (*no matter who*) (*nominative*) qui que ce soit qui+*subj*; (*accusative*) qui que ce soit que+*subj*. ~ **you are, come in!** qui que vous soyez, entrez!; ~ **he marries, it won't make much difference** qui que ce soit qu'il épouse *or* quelle que soit celle qu'il épouse, ça ne fera pas beaucoup de différence. **(c)** (*: *interrog: emphatic*) qui donc. ~ **told you that?** qui donc vous a dit ça?, qui a bien pu vous dire ça?; ~ **did you give it to?** vous l'avez donné à qui?

whole [həʊl] **1** *adj* **(a)** (*entire*) entier. **the** ~ **world** le monde entier; **along its** ~ **length** sur toute sa longueur; ~ **villages were destroyed** des villages entiers ont été détruits; **the** ~ **road was like that** toute la route était comme ça; **he used a** ~ **notebook** il a utilisé un carnet entier; **he swallowed it** ~ il l'a avalé tout entier; **the pig was roasted** ~ le cochon était rôti tout entier; **we waited a** ~ **hour** nous avons attendu une heure entière *or* toute une heure; **it rained 3** ~ **days** il a plu 3 jours entiers; **but the** ~ **man eludes us** mais l'homme tout entier reste un mystère pour nous; **is that the** ~ **truth?** est-ce que c'est bien toute la vérité?; **but the** ~ **point of it was to avoid that** mais tout l'intérêt de la chose était d'éviter cela; **with my** ~ **heart** de tout mon cœur; **he took the** ~ **lot** il a pris le tout; **it's a** ~ **lot better*** c'est vraiment beaucoup mieux; **there are a** ~ **lot of things I'd like to tell her** il y a tout un tas de choses que j'aimerais lui dire; **to go the** ~ **hog*** aller jusqu'au bout, s'engager à fond (*V also* **3**).

(b) (*intact, unbroken*) intact, complet (*f* -ète). **not a glass was left** ~ **after the party** il ne restait pas un seul verre intact après la surprise-partie; **keep the egg yolks** ~ gardez les jaunes intacts, veillez à ne pas crever les jaunes; **he has a** ~ **set of Dickens** il a une série complète des œuvres de Dickens; **to our surprise he came back** ~ à notre grande surprise il est revenu sain et sauf; **the seal on the letter was still** ~ le sceau sur la lettre était encore intact; (*US fig*) **made out of** ~ **cloth** inventé de toutes pièces; ~ **milk** lait entier; (*Mus*) ~ **note** ronde *f*; (*Math*) ~ **number** nombre entier; (††: *healed*) **his hand was made** ~ sa main a été guérie.

2 *n* **(a)** (*the entire amount of*) totalité *f*. **the** ~ **of the morning** tout le matin; **the** ~ **of the time** tout le temps; **the** ~ **of the apple was bad** la pomme toute entière était gâtée; **the** ~ **of Paris was snowbound** Paris était complètement bloqué par la neige; **the** ~ **of Paris was talking about it** dans tout Paris on parlait de ça; **nearly the** ~ **of our output this year** presque toute notre production *or* presque la totalité de notre production cette année; **he received the** ~ **of the amount** il a reçu la totalité de la somme; **as a** ~, **on the** ~ dans l'ensemble.

(b) (*complete unit*) tout *m*. **four quarters make a** ~ quatre quarts font un tout *or* un entier; **the** ~ **may be greater than the sum of its parts** le tout peut être plus grand que la somme de ses parties; **the estate is to be sold as a** ~ la propriété doit être vendue en bloc; **considered as a** ~ **the play was successful, although some scenes** ... dans l'ensemble *or* prise dans son ensemble la pièce était un succès, bien que certaines scènes ... .

3 *cpd*: **wholehearted** *approval, admiration* sans réserve(s); **they made a wholehearted attempt** ... ils ont essayé de tout cœur ...; **wholeheartedly** de tout cœur, à fond; (*esp US*) **whole-hog**: (*adj*) *support* sans réserve(s), total; *supporter* acharné, ardent (*before n*); (*adv*) à fond, jusqu'au bout; **to be a whole-hogger**: (*gen*) se donner entièrement à ce qu'on fait; (*Pol*) être jusqu'au-boutiste *mf*; (*Brit*) **wholemeal** *flour* brut; *bread* = complet; **wholesale** *V* **wholesale**; (*Comm*) **wholesaler** grossiste *mf*, marchand(e) *m(f)* en gros; **wholesome** *food, life, thoughts, book, person* sain; *air, climate* sain, salubre; *exercise, advice* salutaire; **wholesomeness** (*V* **wholesome**) caractère *m or* nature *f* sain(e); salubrité *f*; caractère salutaire; **whole-wheat** *flour* brut; *bread* = complet.

wholesale ['həʊlseɪl] **1** *n* (*U: Comm*) (vente *f* en) gros *m*. **at** *or* **by** ~ en gros.

2 *adj* **(a)** (*Comm*) *price, firm, trade* de gros. ~ **dealer**, ~ **merchant**, ~ **trader** grossiste *mf*, marchand(e) *m(f)* en gros; ~ **market** marché *m* de gros.

(b) (*fig*) *slaughter, destruction* systématique, en masse; *rejection, criticism, acceptance* en bloc. **there has been** ~ **sacking of unskilled workers** il y a eu des licenciements en masse parmi les manœuvres; **there is a** ~ **campaign in the press against** ... il y a une campagne systématique *or* généralisée dans la presse contre ...; **there was a** ~ **attempt to persuade the public that** ... on a essayé par tous les moyens de persuader le public que ... .

3 *adv* **(a)** (*Comm*) *buy, sell* en gros. **I can get it for you** ~ je peux vous le faire avoir au prix de gros.

(b) (*fig*) en masse, en série, en bloc. **such houses are being destroyed** ~ de telles maisons sont détruites en série; **these proposals were rejected** ~ toutes ces propositions ont été rejetées en bloc; **workers are being dismissed ~** on procède en ce moment à des licenciements en masse.

wholism ['həʊlɪzəm] *n* = **holism.**

wholistic [həʊ'lɪstɪk] *adj* = **holistic.**

wholly ['həʊlɪ] *adv* complètement, entièrement, tout à fait.

whom [hu:m] **1** *pron* **(a)** *(interrog: souvent remplacé par 'who' dans le langage parlé)* **~ did you see?** qui avez-vous vu?; **by ~ is the book?** de qui est le livre?; **with ~?** avec qui?; **to ~?** à qui?; *V also* **who 1a.**

(b) *(rel)* **my aunt ~ I love dearly** ma tante que j'aime tendrement; **those ~ he had seen recently** ceux qu'il avait vus récemment; **the man to ~** l'homme à qui, l'homme auquel; **the man of ~** l'homme dont; *(liter)* **~ the gods love die young** ceux qui sont aimés des dieux meurent jeunes.

2 *cpd*: **whomever,** *(emphatic)* **whomsoever** *accusative case of* **whoever, whosoever.**

whoop [hu:p] **1** *n* cri *m (de joie, de triomphe)*; *(Med)* toux aspirante (de la coqueluche). **with a ~ of glee/triumph** avec un cri de joie/de triomphe.

2 *vi* pousser des cris; *(Med)* avoir des quintes de toux coquelucheuse.

3 *vt*: **to ~ it up‡** faire la noce* *or* la bringue‡, bien se marrer‡.

4 *cpd*: **whooping cough** coqueluche *f.*

whoopee [wʊ'pi:] **1** *excl* hourra!, youpi! **2** *n*: **to make ~‡** faire la noce* *or* la bringue‡, bien se marrer‡.

whoops [wu:ps] *excl (also* **~-a-daisy***) (avoiding fall etc)* oups!, houp-là!; *(lifting child)* houp-là!, hop-là!

whoosh [wu:ʃ] **1** *excl* zoum! **2** *n*: **the ~ of sledge runners in the snow** le bruit des patins de luges glissant sur la neige, le glissement des patins de luges sur la neige. **3** *vi*: **the car ~ed past** la voiture est passée à toute allure dans un glissement de pneus.

whop‡ [wɒp] *vt (beat)* rosser*; *(defeat)* battre à plate(s) couture(s).

whopper* ['wɒpəʳ] *n (car/parcel/nose etc)* voiture *f*/colis *m*/nez *m etc* énorme; *(lie)* mensonge *m* énorme.

whopping ['wɒpɪŋ] **1** *adj (*: also* **~ big, ~ great***)* énorme. **2** *n* (‡) raclée* *f.*

whore [hɔ:ʳ] **1** *n (‡pej)* putain‡ *f.*

2 *cpd*: **whorehouse‡** bordel‡ *m*; **whoremonger†** fornicateur *m*; *(pimp)* proxénète *m*, souteneur *m.*

3 *vi (lit: also* **go whoring***)* courir la gueuse, se débaucher. *(fig liter)* **to ~ after sth** se prostituer pour obtenir qch.

whorish‡ ['hɔ:rɪʃ] *adj* de putain‡, putassier‡.

whorl [wɜ:l] *n [fingerprint]* volute *f*; *[spiral shell]* spire *f*; *(Bot)* verticille *m.* **~s of meringue/cream** des tortillons *mpl* de meringue/crème.

whortleberry ['wɜ:tlbərɪ] *n* myrtille *f.*

whose [hu:z] **1** *poss pron* à qui. **~ is this?** à qui est ceci?; **I know ~ it is** je sais à qui c'est; **~ is this hat?** à qui est ce chapeau?; **here's a lollipop each — let's see ~ lasts longest!** voici une sucette chacun — voyons celle de qui durera le plus longtemps!

2 *poss adj* **(a)** *(interrog)* à qui, de qui. **~ hat is this?** à qui est ce chapeau?; **~ son are you?** de qui êtes-vous le fils?; **~ book is missing?** c'est le livre de qui qui manque?, qui n'a pas *(or* n'a pas remis *etc)* son livre?; **~ fault is it?** à qui la faute?

(b) *(rel use)* dont, de qui. **the man ~ hat I took** l'homme dont j'ai pris le chapeau; **the boy ~ sister I was talking to** le garçon à la sœur duquel *or* à la sœur de qui je parlais; **those ~ passports I've got here** ceux dont j'ai les passeports ici.

whosever [hu:'zevəʳ] *poss pron* = **of whomever** *(V* **whoever***).* **~ book you use, you must take care of it** peu importe à qui est le livre dont tu te sers, il faut que tu en prennes soin.

why [waɪ] **1** *adv (for what reason, with what purpose etc)* pourquoi. **~ did you do it?** pourquoi l'avez-vous fait?; **I wonder ~ he left her** je me demande pourquoi il l'a laissée; **I wonder ~** je me demande pourquoi; **he told me ~ he did it** il m'a dit pourquoi il l'a fait *or* la raison pour laquelle il l'a fait; **~ not?** pourquoi pas?; **~ not phone her?** pourquoi ne pas lui téléphoner?; **~ ask her when you don't have to?** pourquoi le lui demander quand vous n'êtes pas obligé de le faire?

2 *excl* eh bien!, tiens! **~, what's the matter?** eh bien, qu'est-ce qui ne va pas?; **~, it's you!** tiens, c'est vous!; **~, it's quite easy!** voyons donc, ce n'est pas difficile!

3 *conj*: **the reasons ~ he did it** les raisons pour lesquelles il l'a fait; **there's no reason ~ you shouldn't try again** il n'y a pas de raison (pour) que tu n'essayes *(subj)* pas de nouveau; **that is ~ I never spoke to him again** c'est pourquoi je ne lui ai jamais reparlé.

4 *n*: **the ~(s) and the wherefore(s)** les causes *fpl* et les raisons *fpl*; **the ~ and the how** le pourquoi et le comment.

5 *cpd*: *(interrog: emphatic)* **whyever*** pourquoi donc; **whyever did you do it?*** pourquoi donc est-ce que vous avez fait ça?, pourquoi est-ce que vous êtes allé faire ça?*

wibbly-wobbly* [,wɪblɪ'wɒblɪ] *adj* = **wobbly.**

wick [wɪk] *n* mèche *f.* *(fig)* **he gets on my ~‡** il me tape sur le système*, il me court sur le haricot‡.

wicked ['wɪkɪd] *adj* **(a)** *(iniquitous) person* mauvais, méchant, malfaisant; *act, behaviour* mauvais, vilain, inique; *system, policy* inique, pernicieux. **he is a very ~ man** il est foncièrement méchant *or* mauvais; **that was a ~ thing to do!** quelle vilenie!; **it was a ~ attempt to get rid of him** cette tentative d'élimination était dictée par la méchanceté.

(b) *(bad, unpleasant) blow, wound* vilain; *pain* cruel, violent; *satire, criticism, comment* méchant. **a ~ waste** un scandaleux gâchis; **he has a ~ temper** il a un caractère épouvantable; **it's ~ weather*** il fait un temps affreux *or* un très vilain temps; **this is a ~ car to start*** faire démarrer cette voiture est une véritable plaie*.

(c) *(mischievous etc) smile, look, remark, suggestion* malicieux. **he's a ~ little boy** c'est un petit malicieux *or* coquin; **he's got a ~ sense of humour** il a un humour très malicieux *or* espiègle.

(d) *(*: excellent, skilful)* **that was a ~ shot!** quel beau coup!; **he plays a ~ game** il a un jeu du tonnerre*; **the way he got out of that affair was really ~** la façon dont il s'est sorti de cette histoire, chapeau!*

wickedly ['wɪkɪdlɪ] *adv* **(a)** *(evilly) behave* vilainement, très mal. **he ~ destroyed ...** il a eu la vilenie de détruire ... .

(b) *(mischievously) look, smile, suggest* malicieusement.

(c) *(*: skilfully) play, manage etc* comme un chef*.

wickedness ['wɪkɪdnɪs] *n [behaviour, order, decision, person]* méchanceté *f*, cruauté *f*, vilenie *f*; *[murder]* horreur *f*, atrocité *f*; *[look, smile, suggestion]* malice *f*; *[waste]* scandale *m.*

wicker ['wɪkəʳ] **1** *n (U) (substance)* osier *m*; *(objects: also* **~work***)* vannerie *f.* **2** *cpd (also* **~work***) basket, chair* d'osier, en osier.

wicket ['wɪkɪt] **1** *n* **(a)** *(door, gate)* (petite) porte *f*, portillon *m*; *(for bank teller etc)* guichet *m.*

(b) *(Cricket) (stumps etc)* guichet *m*; *(pitch between them)* terrain *m (entre les guichets)*; *V* **sticky.**

2 *cpd*: *(Cricket)* **wicket-keeper** gardien *m* de guichet.

widdershins ['wɪdəʃɪnz] *adv* = **withershins.**

wide [waɪd] **1** *adj road, river, strip* large; *margin* grand; *garment* large, ample, flottant; *ocean, desert* immense, vaste; *circle, gap, space* large, grand; *(fig) knowledge* vaste, grand, très étendu; *survey, study* de grande envergure. **how ~ is the room?** quelle est la largeur de la pièce?, quelle largeur a la pièce?; **it is 5 metres ~** cela a *or* fait 5 mètres de large; **the ~ Atlantic** l'immense *or* le vaste Atlantique; *(Cine)* **the ~ screen** le grand écran *(panoramique)*; **she stared, her eyes ~ with fear** elle regardait, les yeux agrandis de peur *or* par la peur; **... mouth ~ with astonishment ...** bouche bée de stupeur; **a man with ~ views *or* opinions** un homme aux vues larges; **he has ~ interests** il a des goûts très éclectiques; **to a ~ extent** dans une large mesure; **in the widest sense of the word** au sens le plus général *or* le plus large du mot; **it has a ~ variety of uses** cela se prête à une grande variété d'usages; **the shot/ball/arrow was ~** le coup/la balle/la flèche est passé(e) à côté; **it was ~ of the target** c'était loin de la cible; *V* **mark² *etc.***

2 *adv aim, shoot, fall* loin du but. **the bullet went ~** la balle est passée à côté; **he flung the door ~** il a ouvert la porte en grand; **they are set ~ apart** *[trees, houses, posts]* ils sont largement espacés; *[eyes]* ils sont très écartés; **he stood with his legs ~ apart** il se tenait debout les jambes très écartées; *V* **far, open.**

3 *cpd*: *(Phot)* **wide-angle lens** objectif *m* grand-angulaire, objectif grand angle *inv*; **wide-awake** *(lit)* bien *or* tout éveillé; *(fig)* éveillé, alerte, vif; *(Brit pej)* **wide boy‡** escroc *m*, filou *m*, requin* *m*; **wide-eyed** *(adj) (in naïveté)* aux yeux grands ouverts *or* écarquillés; *(in fear, surprise)* aux yeux agrandis *or* écarquillés; *(adv)* les yeux écarquillés; **in wide-eyed amazement** les yeux agrandis par la stupeur; **wide-ranging** *mind, report, survey* de grande envergure; *interests* divers, variés; **widespread** *arms* en croix; *wings* déployé.

-wide [waɪd] *adj, adv ending in cpds V* **country, nation *etc.***

widely ['waɪdlɪ] *adv* **(a)** *scatter, spread* partout, sur une grande étendue; *travel* beaucoup; *differ* largement, radicalement. **~ different cultures** des cultures radicalement différentes; **the trees were ~ spaced** les arbres étaient largement espacés.

(b) *(fig: extensively)* généralement. **it is ~ believed that ...** on pense communément *or* généralement que ...; **~-held opinions** des opinions très répandues; **he is ~ known for his generosity** sa réputation de générosité est bien connue, il est connu partout pour sa générosité; **to be ~ read** *[author, book]* être beaucoup lu; *[reader]* avoir beaucoup lu *(in sth* qch), être très cultivé.

widen ['waɪdn] **1** *vt circle, gap, space* élargir, agrandir; *road, river, strip, garment* élargir; *margin* augmenter; *knowledge* accroître, élargir; *survey, study* accroître la portée de.

2 *vi (also* **~ out***)* s'élargir; s'agrandir.

wideness ['waɪdnɪs] *n* largeur *f.*

widgeon ['wɪdʒən] *n* canard siffleur.

widow ['wɪdəʊ] **1** *n* veuve *f.* **W~ Smith†** la veuve Smith; *(fig)* **she's a golf ~** elle ne voit jamais son mari qui est toujours à jouer au golf, son mari la délaisse pour aller jouer au golf; **~'s peak** pousse *f* de cheveux en V sur le front; *V* **grass, mite, weed *etc.***

2 *vt*: **to be ~ed** *[man]* devenir veuf; *[woman]* devenir veuve; **she was ~ed in 1975** elle est devenue veuve en 1975, elle a perdu son mari en 1975; **she has been ~ed for 10 years** elle est veuve depuis 10 ans; **he lives with his ~ed mother** il vit avec sa mère qui est veuve.

widower ['wɪdəʊəʳ] *n* veuf *m.*

widowhood ['wɪdəʊhʊd] *n* veuvage *m.*

width [wɪdθ] **1** *n* **(a)** *(U) [road, river, strip, bed, ocean, desert, gap, space, margin]* largeur *f*; *[garment]* ampleur *f*; *[circle]* largeur, diamètre *m.* **what is the ~ of the room?** quelle est la largeur de la pièce?, quelle largeur a la pièce?; **it is 5 metres in ~, its ~ is 5 metres, it has a ~ of 5 metres** cela a *or* fait 5 mètres de large; **measure it across its ~** prends la mesure en largeur.

(b) *(of cloth)* largeur *f*, lé *m.* **you'll get it out of one ~** une largeur *or* un lé te suffira.

2 *cpd*: **widthways, widthwise** en largeur.

wield [wi:ld] *vt sword, axe, pen, tool* manier; *(brandish)* brandir; *power, authority, control* exercer.

Wiener schnitzel ['vi:nə'ʃnɪtsəl] *n* escalope viennoise.

wife [waɪf] *pl* **wives 1** *n* **(a)** *(spouse)* femme *f*, épouse *f (esp Admin, frm)*; *(married woman)* femme mariée. **his second ~** sa deuxième *or* seconde femme; **the ~‡** la patronne‡; **he decided to take a ~** il a décidé de se marier *or* de prendre femme†; **to take sb to ~†** prendre qn pour femme; **wives whose husbands have reached the age of 65** les femmes mariées dont les maris ont atteint 65 ans; **'The Merry Wives of Windsor'** 'Les Joyeuses Commères de Windsor'; *V* **working** *etc.*

(b) († *or* **dial: woman*) bonne femme*. **she's a poor old ~** c'est une pauvre vieille; *V* **old** *etc.*

2 *cpd*: **wife-swapping** échange *m* de partenaires (*par deux couples*).

wifely ['waɪflɪ] *adj duties, virtues* conjugal; *feelings, wisdom* d'une bonne épouse.

wig [wɪg] **1** *n* (*full-head*) perruque *f*; (*half-head*) postiche *m*; (✱: *hair*) tignasse* *f*. **2** *cpd*: **wigmaker** perruquier *m*, -ière *f*.

wigeon ['wɪdʒən] *n* = **widgeon.**

wigging✱ ['wɪgɪŋ] *n* (*Brit: scolding*) savon* *m*, attrapade✱ *f*. **to give sb a ~** passer un savon* à qn; **to get a ~** se faire enguirlander*.

wiggle ['wɪgl] **1** *vt pencil, stick* agiter; *toes* agiter, remuer; *loose screw, button, tooth* faire jouer. **to ~ one's hips** tortiller des hanches; **my finger hurts if you ~ it like that** j'ai mal quand vous me tortillez le doigt comme ça; **he ~d his finger at me warningly** il a agité l'index en ma direction en guise d'avertissement.

2 *vi [loose screw etc]* branler; *[tail]* remuer, frétiller; *[rope, snake, worm]* se tortiller. **she ~d across the room** elle a traversé la pièce en se déhanchant *or* en tortillant des hanches.

3 *n*: **to walk with a ~** marcher en se déhanchant, marcher en tortillant des hanches; **to give sth a ~ = to wiggle sth**; *V* **1.**

wiggly ['wɪglɪ] *adj snake, worm* qui se tortille. **a ~ line** un trait ondulé.

wight†† [waɪt] *n* être *m.*

wigwam ['wɪgwæm] *n* wigwam *m.*

wild [waɪld] **1** *adj* **(a)** (*not domesticated etc*) *animal* sauvage; (*wary*) farouche; *plant, tribe, man, land, countryside* sauvage. **~ flowers** fleurs *fpl* des champs, fleurs sauvages; **~ ferret/goat** *etc* furet *m*/chèvre *f etc* sauvage; **~ rabbit** lapin *m* de garenne; **~ boar** sanglier *m*; **he's still too ~ to let you get near him** il est encore trop farouche pour te laisser t'approcher de lui; **the plant in its ~ state** la plante à l'état sauvage; **it was growing ~** ça poussait à l'état sauvage; **a ~ stretch of coastline** une côte sauvage; (*fig*) **~ horses wouldn't make me tell you** je ne te le dirais pour rien au monde; (*fig*) **it proved to be a ~-goose chase** l'aventure a fini en eau de boudin; **he sent me off on a ~-goose chase** il m'a fait courir partout pour rien; (*fig*) **to sow one's ~ oats** jeter sa gourme, faire des frasques *or* fredaines; (*US*) **~ and woolly*** rustre; *V also* **2** *and* **rose²**, **run, strawberry** *etc.*

(b) (*rough*) *wind* violent, furieux, de tempête; *sea* déchaîné, gros (*f* grosse), en furie. **in ~ weather** par gros temps; **the weather was ~** il faisait très gros temps; **it was a ~ night** le vent faisait rage cette nuit-là.

(c) (*unrestrained*) *appearance* farouche; *laughter, anger* fou (*f* folle); *idea, plan* fou, extravagant, abracadabrant; *imagination, enthusiasm* débordant, délirant; *life, evening* mouvementé, fou. **his hair was ~ and uncombed** il avait les cheveux en bataille; **there was ~ confusion at the airport** la confusion la plus totale régnait à l'aéroport; **he took a ~ swing at his opponent** il a lancé le poing en direction de son adversaire; **he had a ~ look in his eyes** il avait une lueur sauvage *or* farouche dans les yeux; **he was ~ in his youth, he had a ~ youth** il a eu quelques années folles quand il était jeune; **a whole gang of ~ kids** toute une bande de casse-cou; **they were leading a fairly ~ life** ils menaient une vie de bâtons de chaise; **he goes to a lot of ~ parties** il passe son temps en folles soirées; **we had some ~ times together** nous avons fait bien des folies ensemble; **those were ~ times** l'époque était rude; **there were moments of ~ indignation** par moments ils étaient fous d'indignation; **he had some ~ scheme for damming the river** il avait un projet fou *or* abracadabrant *or* extravagant pour barrer le fleuve; **there was a lot of ~ talk about ...** on a agité des tas d'idées au sujet de ...; **they made some ~ promises** ils ont fait quelques promesses insensées *or* folles *or* extravagantes; **that is a ~ exaggeration** c'est une énorme exagération; **to make a ~ guess** risquer *or* émettre à tout hasard une hypothèse (*at sth* sur qch).

(d) (*excited*) (*: *enthusiastic*) fou (*f* folle), dingue* (*about* de); (*: *angry*) (fou) furieux, dingue*. **the dog went ~ when he saw his master** le chien est devenu comme fou quand il a vu son maître; **the audience went ~ with delight** le public a hurlé de joie; **his fans went ~ when he appeared** la folie a gagné les fans* quand il est apparu; **he was ~ with joy** il ne se tenait plus de joie; **he was ~ with anger/indignation** il était fou de rage/d'indignation; **to be ~ about sb/sth** être dingue* de qn/qch; **I'm not ~ about it*** ça ne m'emballe* pas beaucoup; **it's enough to drive you ~!*** c'est à vous rendre dingue!*; **he was absolutely ~* when he heard about it** il était absolument hors de lui quand il l'a su.

2 *cpd*: **wildcat** chat *m* sauvage; (*fig*) **wildcat scheme/venture** (*gen*) projet *m*/entreprise *f* insensé(e); (*US: financially*) projet/entreprise mal financé(e); (*fig Ind*) **wildcat strike** grève *f* sauvage; **wild-eyed** aux yeux fous; **in wild-eyed terror** une terreur folle dans les yeux; **to spread like wildfire** se répandre comme une traînée de poudre; **wildfowl** (*one bird*) oiseau *m* sauvage; (*collectively*) oiseaux sauvages; (*Hunting*) gibier *m* à plume; **to go wildfowling** chasser (le gibier à plumes) au tir; **he's interested in wildlife** il s'intéresse à la vie des animaux sauvages; **the wildlife of Central Australia** les animaux *mpl* sauvages *or* la faune d'Australie centrale; (*US*) **the Wild West** le Far West; (*US*) **Wild West show** spectacle *m* sur le thème du Far West.

3 *n*: **the call of the ~** l'appel *m* de la nature; **he went off into the ~s** il est parti vers des régions sauvages *or* reculées; **he lives in the ~s of Alaska** il vit au fin fond de l'Alaska.

wildebeest ['wɪldɪbiːst] *n* gnou *m.*

wilderness ['wɪldənɪs] *n* étendue déserte, région reculée *or* sauvage. **a ~ of snow and ice** de vastes étendues de neige et de glace; **a ~ of empty seas** des kilomètres et des kilomètres de mer; (*fig*) **a ~ of streets/ruins** un désert de rues/de ruines; (*Bible*) **to preach in the ~** prêcher dans le désert; (*fig*) **to be in the ~** faire sa traversée du désert; **this garden is a ~** ce jardin est une vraie jungle.

wildly ['waɪldlɪ] *adv [wind, sea etc] blow, gust, rage* violemment, furieusement; *[person] behave* de façon extravagante; *wave, gesticulate, talk* fiévreusement; *applaud, cheer* follement, frénétiquement; *protest* violemment. **her heart was beating ~** son cœur battait violemment *or* à se rompre; **he looked at them ~** il leur a jeté un regard fou; **he hit out ~** il lançait des coups dans tous les sens *or* au hasard; **to shoot ~** tirer au hasard; **you're guessing ~** tu dis ça tout à fait au hasard; **~ happy** follement heureux; **~ delighted** aux anges; **I'm not ~ pleased about it*** ce n'est pas que ça me fasse très plaisir; **they were rushing about ~** ils se précipitaient dans tous les sens.

wildness ['waɪldnɪs] *n [land, countryside, scenery]* aspect *m* sauvage; *[tribe, people]* sauvagerie *f*; *[wind, sea]* fureur *f*, violence *f*; *[appearance]* désordre *m*; *[imagination]* extravagance *f*; *[enthusiasm]* ferveur *f*. **the ~ of the weather** le sale temps qu'il fait (*or* faisait *etc*).

wile [waɪl] *n* (*trick*) ruse *f*. (*coquetry*) **~s** artifices *mpl.*

wilful, (*US*) **willful** ['wɪlfʊl] *adj person, character* entêté, têtu, obstiné; *action* voulu, volontaire, délibéré; *crime* prémédité; *damage, destruction* commis avec préméditation.

wilfully, (*US*) **willfully** ['wɪlfəlɪ] *adv* (*obstinately*) obstinément, avec entêtement, avec obstination; (*deliberately*) à dessein, délibérément, de propos délibéré.

wilfulness, (*US*) **willfulness** ['wɪlfʊlnɪs] *n [person]* obstination *f*, entêtement *m*; *[action]* caractère délibéré *or* intentionnel.

wiliness ['waɪlɪnɪs] *n* ruse *f* (*U*), astuce *f* (*U*).

will [wɪl] **1** *modal aux vb* (*2nd pers sg* **wilt**††; *neg* **will not** *often abbr to* **won't**; *V also* **would**) **(a)** (*used to form fut tense*) **he will speak** il parlera, il va parler; **don't worry, he will come** ne vous inquiétez pas, il ne manquera pas de venir *or* il viendra sans faute; **you'll regret it some day** tu le regretteras un jour; **we will (***or* **shall) come too** nous viendrons (nous) aussi; **you won't lose it again, will you?** tu ne le perdras plus, n'est-ce pas?; **you will come to see us, won't you?** vous viendrez nous voir, n'est-ce pas?; **will he come too? — yes he will** est-ce qu'il viendra (lui) aussi? — oui; **I'll go with you — no you won't!** je vais vous accompagner — non, certainement pas! *or* en aucun cas!; **they'll arrive tomorrow — will they?** ils arriveront demain — ah bon? *or* c'est sûr?; **I don't think he'll do it tomorrow** je ne pense pas qu'il le fasse demain; (*in commands*) **you will speak to no one** ne parlez à personne, vous ne parlerez à personne.

(b) (*indicating conjecture*) **that will be the postman** ça doit être le facteur, c'est *or* voilà sans doute le facteur; **that will have been last year, I suppose** c'était l'année dernière, sans doute; **she'll be about forty** elle doit avoir quarante ans environ *or* la quarantaine; **she'll have forgotten all about it by now** elle aura tout oublié à l'heure qu'il est.

(c) (*indicating willingness*) **I will help you** je vous aiderai, je veux bien vous aider; **will you help me? — yes I will/no I won't** tu veux m'aider? — oui je veux bien/non je ne veux pas; **if you'll help me I think we can do it** si vous voulez bien m'aider, je crois que nous y arriverons; **won't you come with us?** tu ne veux pas venir (avec nous)?; **will you have a cup of coffee?** voulez-vous *or* prendrez-vous un petit café?; **won't you have a drink?** vous prendrez bien un verre?; (*in requests*) **will you please sit down!** voulez-vous vous asseoir, s'il vous plaît!; (*in commands*) **will you be quiet!** veux-tu (bien) te taire!; **just a moment, will you?** un instant s'il vous plaît; (*in marriage service*) **I will** oui; **I WILL see him!** on ne m'empêchera pas de le voir!; **I won't have it!** je ne tolère pas ça!, je n'admets pas ça!; **the window won't open** la fenêtre ne s'ouvre pas *or* ne veut pas s'ouvrir; **do what you will** faites ce que vous voulez *or* comme vous voulez; **come when you will** venez quand vous voulez; **look where you will** regardez où bon vous semble.

(d) (*indicating habit, characteristic*) **he will sit for hours doing nothing** il reste assis pendant des heures à ne rien faire; **this bottle will hold one litre** cette bouteille contient un litre *or* fait le litre; **the car will do 150 km/h** cette voiture fait 150 km/h; **he WILL talk all the time!** il ne peut pas s'empêcher *or* s'arrêter de parler!; **if you WILL tell her all I say to you** si tu insistes pour *or* si tu t'entêtes à lui raconter tout ce que je te dis; **I WILL call him Richard, though his name's actually Robert** il faut toujours que je l'appelle (*subj*) Richard bien qu'en fait il s'appelle (*subj*) Robert; (*loc*) **boys will be boys** il faut (bien) que jeunesse se passe (*loc*); **accidents will happen** il y aura toujours des accidents, on ne peut pas empêcher les accidents.

2 *pret, ptp* **willed** *vt* **(a)** (*wish, intend*) vouloir (*that* que+*subj*). **God has ~ed it so** Dieu a voulu qu'il en soit ainsi; **it is as God ~s** c'est la volonté de Dieu; **you must ~ it really hard if you wish to succeed** pour réussir il faut le vouloir très fort; **to ~ sb's happiness** vouloir le bonheur de qn.

(b) (*urge etc by willpower*) exercer sa volonté. **he was ~ing her to accept** il désirait ardemment qu'elle accepte (*subj*); **he ~ed himself to stand up** il fit un suprême effort pour se mettre debout.

(c) (*Jur: leave in one's will*) léguer (*sth to sb* qch à qn).

3 *n* **(a)** (*faculty*) volonté *f*; (*wish*) volonté, désir *m*. **he has a strong ~, he has a ~ of his own** il est très volontaire; **a ~ of iron, an iron ~** une volonté de fer; **to have a weak ~** manquer de volonté; **the ~ to live** la volonté de survivre; (*Prov*) **where**

there's a ~ there's a way vouloir c'est pouvoir (*Prov*); **the ~ of God** la volonté de Dieu, la volonté divine; **it is the ~ of the people that ...** la volonté du peuple est que ... + *subj*; (*frm*) **what is your ~?** quelle est votre volonté?; (*frm*) **it is my ~ that he should leave** je veux qu'il parte; **you must take the ~ for the deed** il faut juger la chose sur l'intention; **Thy ~ be done** que Ta volonté soit faite; **to choose/borrow** *etc* **at ~** choisir/emprunter *etc* à volonté; **you are free to leave at ~** vous êtes libre de partir quand vous voulez; **to do sth against one's ~** faire qch à son corps défendant *or* à contre-cœur; **with the best ~ in the world** avec la meilleure volonté du monde; **to work with a ~** travailler avec détermination *or* ardeur; *V* **free, goodwill, ill, sweet** *etc.*

(b) (*Jur*) testament *m.* **the last ~ and testament of ...** les dernières volontés de ...; **he left it to me in his ~** il me l'a légué par testament, il me l'a laissé dans son testament.

4 *cpd*: **willpower** volonté *f*, vouloir *m.*

willful ['wɪlfʊl] *etc* (*US*) = **wilful** *etc.*

William ['wɪljəm] *n* Guillaume *m.* **~ the Conqueror** Guillaume le Conquérant.

willies‡ ['wɪlɪz] *npl*: **to have the ~** avoir les chocottes‡ *fpl*; **it gives me the ~** ça me donne les chocottes‡.

willing ['wɪlɪŋ] **1** *adj* **(a) to be ~ to do** être prêt *or* disposé à faire, vouloir bien faire, faire volontiers; **I'm quite ~ to tell him** je veux bien le lui dire; je ne demande pas mieux que de le lui dire; **he wasn't very ~ to help** il n'était pas tellement prêt à aider; **those who are ~ and able to go** ceux qui veulent et qui peuvent y aller; **God ~** si Dieu le veut.

(b) *helper, worker* bien disposé, de bonne volonté. **a few ~ men** quelques hommes de bonne volonté; **~ hands helped him to his feet** des mains secourables se tendirent et l'aidèrent à se lever; **there were plenty of ~ hands** il y avait beaucoup d'offres d'assistance; (*fig*) **the ~ horse** la bonne âme (qui se sacrifie toujours).

(c) (*voluntary*) *obedience, help, sacrifice* spontané.

2 *n*: **to show ~** faire montre de bonne volonté.

willingly ['wɪlɪŋlɪ] *adv* (*with goodwill*) volontiers, de bon cœur *or* gré; (*voluntarily*) volontairement, spontanément. **will you help? — ~!** peux-tu nous aider? — volontiers!; **did he do it ~ or did you have to make him?** l'a-t-il fait de lui-même *or* volontairement *or* spontanément ou bien vous a-t-il fallu le forcer?

willingness ['wɪlɪŋnɪs] *n* bonne volonté; (*enthusiasm*) empressement *m* (*to do* à faire). **I don't doubt his ~, just his competence** ce n'est pas sa bonne volonté que je mets en doute mais sa compétence; **I was grateful for his ~ to help** je lui étais reconnaissant de bien vouloir m'aider *or* de son empressement à m'aider; **in spite of the ~ with which she agreed** malgré la bonne volonté qu'elle a mise à accepter, malgré son empressement à accepter.

will-o'-the-wisp ['wɪləðə'wɪsp] *n* (*lit, fig*) feu follet *m.*

willow ['wɪləʊ] **1** *n* (*tree*) saule *m*; (*wood*) (bois *m* de) saule (*U*); (*for baskets etc*) osier *m.* (*fig: cricket/baseball bat*) **the ~*** la batte (de cricket/de baseball); *V* **weeping.**

2 *cpd bat etc* de *or* en saule; *basket* d'osier, en osier. (*Bot*) **willowherb** épilobe *m*; **the willow pattern** le motif chinois (dans les tons bleus); **willow pattern china** porcelaine *f* à motif chinois; (*Orn*) **willow warbler** pouillot *m.*

willowy ['wɪləʊɪ] *adj person* svelte, élancé; *object* fin, mince.

willy-nilly ['wɪlɪ'nɪlɪ] *adv* bon gré mal gré.

wilt[1]†† [wɪlt] *2nd pers sg of* **will 1.**

wilt[2] [wɪlt] **1** *vi* [*flower*] se faner, se flétrir; [*plant*] se dessécher, mourir; [*person*] (*grow exhausted*) s'affaiblir, s'alanguir; (*lose courage*) fléchir, être pris de découragement; [*effort, enthusiasm etc*] diminuer. **the guests began to ~ in the heat of the room** la chaleur de la pièce commençait à incommoder les invités; **he ~ed visibly when I caught his eye** son visage s'est décomposé quand il a vu mon regard.

2 *vt flower* faner, flétrir; *plant* dessécher.

wily ['waɪlɪ] *adj* rusé, astucieux, malin (*f* -igne). **he's a ~ old devil* or bird* or fox*, he's as ~ as a fox** c'est un malin *or* un vieux roublard‡ *or* un vieux renard.

wimple ['wɪmpl] *n* guimpe *f.*

win [wɪn] (*vb: pret, ptp* **won**) **1** *n* (*Sport etc*) victoire *f.* **another ~ for Scotland** une nouvelle victoire pour l'Écosse; **it was a convincing ~ for France** la victoire revenait indiscutablement à la France; **to have a ~** gagner; **to back a horse for a ~** jouer un cheval gagnant.

2 *vi* **(a)** (*in war, sport, competition etc*) gagner, l'emporter. **to ~ by a length** gagner *or* l'emporter d'une longueur; **go in and ~!** vas-y et ne reviens pas sans la victoire!; **he was playing to ~** il jouait pour gagner; **who's ~ning?** qui est-ce qui gagne?; **to ~ hands down*** gagner les doigts dans le nez‡, gagner haut la main, (*esp in race*) arriver dans un fauteuil.

(b) to ~ free *or* **loose** se dégager (*from sth* de qch).

3 *vt* **(a)** *war, match, competition, bet, sum of money* gagner; *race* gagner, enlever; *prize* remporter, décrocher; *scholarship* obtenir; *victory* remporter. **he won it for growing radishes** il l'a gagné pour sa culture de radis; **he won £5 from her at cards** il lui a gagné 5 livres aux cartes; **to ~ the day** (*Mil*) remporter la victoire; (*gen*) l'emporter; **his essay won him a trip to France** sa dissertation lui a valu un voyage en France.

(b) (*obtain etc*) *fame, fortune* trouver; *sb's attention* capter, captiver; *sb's friendship* gagner; *sb's esteem* gagner, conquérir; *sympathy, support, admirers, supporters* s'attirer; *coal, ore etc* extraire (*from* de). **to ~ friends** se faire des amis; **to ~ a name or a reputation (for o.s.)** se faire un nom *or* une réputation (*as* en tant que); **this won him the friendship of ...** ceci lui a gagné *or* valu l'amitié de ...; **this won him the attention of the crowd** ça lui a valu l'attention de la foule; **this manoeuvre won him the time he needed** cette manœuvre lui a valu d'obtenir le délai dont il avait besoin; **to ~ sb's love/respect** se faire aimer/respecter de qn; **to ~ sb to one's cause** gagner *or* rallier qn à sa cause; (†) **to ~ a lady or a lady's hand (in marriage)** obtenir la main d'une demoiselle.

(c) (*reach*) *summit, shore, goal* parvenir à, arriver à. **he won his way to the top of his profession** il a durement gagné sa place au sommet de sa profession.

win back *vt sep cup, trophy* reprendre (*from* à); *gaming loss etc* recouvrer; *land* reconquérir (*from* sur), reprendre (*from* à); *sb's favour, support, esteem, girlfriend etc* reconquérir. **I won the money back from him** j'ai repris l'argent qu'il m'avait gagné.

win out *vi* (*esp US*) **(a)** gagner.

(b) = win through.

win over, win round *vt sep* s'attirer, conquérir. **I won him over to my point of view** je l'ai gagné à ma façon de voir; **the figures won him over to our way of thinking** les statistiques l'ont fait se rallier à notre façon de voir; **I won him over eventually** j'ai fini par le convaincre *or* le persuader; **to win sb over to doing sth** convaincre *or* persuader qn de faire qch.

win through *vi* y arriver, y parvenir, réussir (à la fin). **you'll win through all right!** tu y arriveras!, tu en viendras à bout!; (*in competition etc*) **he won through to the second round** il a gagné le premier tour.

wince [wɪns] **1** *vi* (*flinch*) tressaillir, se crisper; (*grimace*) grimacer (de douleur *or* dégoût *etc*). **he ~d at the thought/at the sight** cette pensée/ce spectacle l'a fait tressaillir *or* se crisper; **he ~d as I touched his injured arm** il a sursauté *or* il a fait une grimace de douleur lorsque j'ai touché son bras blessé; **without wincing** sans broncher *or* sourciller.

2 *n* tressaillement *m*, crispation *f*; (*grimace*) grimace *f* (de douleur *or* dégoût *etc*). **to give a ~ = to wince;** *V* **1.**

winch [wɪntʃ] **1** *n* treuil *m.* **2** *vt*: **to ~ sth up/down** *etc* monter/descendre *etc* qch au treuil; **they ~ed him out of the water** ils l'ont hissé hors de l'eau au treuil.

wind[1] [wɪnd] **1** *n* **(a)** vent *m.* **high ~** grand vent, vent violent *or* fort; **following ~** vent arrière; **the ~ is rising/dropping** le vent se lève/tombe; **the ~ was in the east** le vent venait de l'est *or* était à l'est; **where is the ~?, which way is the ~?** d'où vient le vent?; **to go/run like the ~** aller/filer comme le vent; **between ~ and water** (*Naut*) près de la ligne de flottaison; (*fig*) sur la corde raide; (*Naut*) **to sail into the ~** avancer contre le vent; (*Naut*) **to run before the ~** avoir vent arrière; (*fig*) **to take the ~ out of sb's sails** couper l'herbe sous le pied de qn; **to see how the ~ blows** *or* **lies** (*Naut*) prendre l'aire du vent; (*fig*) voir la tournure que prennent (*or* vont prendre *etc*) les choses, prendre le vent; (*fig*) **the ~ of change is blowing** un grand courant d'air frais souffle; (*fig*) **there's something in the u40**il y a quelque chose dans l'air, il se prépare quelque chose; (*fig*) **to get ~ of sth** avoir vent de qch; **he threw caution to the ~s** il a fait fi de toute prudence; *V* **ill, north, sail** *etc.*

(b) (*breath*) souffle *m.* **he has still plenty of ~** il a encore du souffle; **he had lost his ~** il avait perdu le souffle *or* perdu haleine; **to knock the ~ out of sb** [*blow*] couper la respiration *or* le souffle à qn; [*fighter*] mettre qn hors d'haleine; [*fall, exertion*] essouffler qn, mettre qn hors d'haleine; **to get one's ~ back** reprendre (son) souffle, reprendre haleine; (*fig pej*) **it's all ~** ce n'est que du vent, c'est du vent; (*fig*) **to put the ~ up sb*** flanquer la frousse à qn*; **to get/have the ~ up*** attraper/avoir la frousse* (*about* à propos de); *V* **sound**[2] *etc.*

(c) (*Med*) vents *mpl*, gaz *mpl.* **the baby has got ~** le bébé a des vents; **to break ~** lâcher un vent, avoir des gaz; **to bring up ~** avoir un renvoi.

(d) (*Mus*) **the ~(s)** les instruments *mpl* à vent.

2 *cpd erosion etc* éolien. (*fig*) **windbag*** hâbleur *m*, -euse *f*; **wind-bells = wind-chimes; windblown** *person, hair* ébouriffé par le vent; *tree* fouetté par le vent; **windbreak** (*tree, fence etc*) abat-vent *m inv*; (*for camping etc*) pare-vent *m inv*; **Windbreaker ® = windcheater;** (*Med*) **windburn** brûlure *f* épidermique (due au vent); (*Brit*) **windcheater** anorak léger; **wind-chimes** carillon éolien; **wind cone** manche *f* à air; **windfall** (*lit*) fruit(s) abattu(s) par le vent; (*fig*) aubaine *f*, manne *f* (tombée du ciel); **windflower** anémone *f*; **wind gauge** anémomètre *m*; (*Mus*) **wind instrument** instrument *m* à vent; (*Naut*) **windjammer** grand voilier (de la marine marchande); **windmill** moulin *m* à vent; (*fig*) **to tilt at or fight windmills** se battre contre les moulins à vent; (*Anat*) **windpipe** trachée *f*; **windproof** protégeant du vent, qui ne laisse pas passer le vent; (*esp Brit Aut*) **windscreen** pare-brise *m inv*; **windscreen washer** lave-glace *m inv*; **windscreen wiper** essuie-glace *m inv*; (*US*) **windshield = windscreen; windsleeve, windsock = wind cone; windstorm** vent *m* de tempête; **windswept** venteux, battu des vents, balayé par le(s) vent(s); (*Phys*) **wind tunnel** tunnel *m* aérodynamique; **there was a wind tunnel between the two tower blocks** il y avait un courant d'air à renverser les gens entre les deux tours; **windward** *V* **windward.**

3 *vt* **(a) to ~ sb** [*blow etc*] couper la respiration *or* le souffle à qn; [*fighter*] mettre qn hors d'haleine; [*fall, exertion*] essouffler qn, mettre qn hors d'haleine; **he was ~ed by the blow, the blow ~ed him** le coup lui a coupé le souffle *or* la respiration; **he was quite ~ed by the climb** l'ascension l'avait essoufflé *or* mis hors d'haleine; **I'm only ~ed** j'ai la respiration coupée, c'est tout.

(b) *horse* faire *or* laisser souffler.

(c) (*Hunting: scent*) avoir vent de.

wind[2] [wɪnd] *pret, ptp* **winded** *or* **wound** *vt*: **to ~ the horn** sonner du cor; (*Hunting*) sonner de la trompe.

wind[3] [waɪnd] (*vb: pret, ptp* **wound**) **1** *n* **(a)** (*bend: in river etc*) tournant *m*, coude *m.* **(b) to give one's watch a ~** remonter sa montre; **give the handle another ~ or two** donne un ou deux tours de manivelle de plus.

2 *vt* **(a)** *(roll) thread, rope etc* enrouler (*on* sur, *round* autour de); *(wrap)* envelopper (*in* dans). **to ~ wool (into a ball)** enrouler de la laine (pour en faire une pelote); **~ this round your head** enroule-toi ça autour de la tête; **with the rope wound tightly round his waist** la corde bien enroulée autour de la taille, la corde lui ceignant étroitement la taille; **she wound a shawl round the baby, she wound the baby in a shawl** elle a enveloppé le bébé dans un châle; **to ~ one's arms round sb** enlacer qn; **the snake/rope wound itself round a branch** le serpent/la corde s'est enroulé(e) autour d'une branche; **he slowly wound his way home** il s'en revint lentement chez lui, il prit lentement le chemin du retour; *V also* **3** *and* **finger** *etc.*

(b) *clock, watch, toy* remonter; *handle* donner un (*or* des) tour(s) de.

3 *vi* (*also* **~ its way**) *[river, path]* **to ~ along** serpenter, faire des zigzags; **the road ~s through the valley** la route serpente à travers la vallée, la route traverse la vallée en serpentant; **the procession wound through the town** la procession a serpenté à travers la ville; **the line of cars wound slowly up the hill** les voitures ont lentement gravi la colline en une file ondulante *or* sinueuse; **to ~ up/down** *[path etc]* monter/descendre en serpentant *or* en zigzags; *[stairs, steps]* monter/descendre en tournant; *[snake, ivy etc]* **to ~ round sth** s'enrouler autour de qch.

wind down 1 *vi* (*: *relax*) se détendre, se relaxer*; *V also* **wind³ 3.**

2 *vt sep* (*on rope/winch etc*) faire descendre (au bout d'une corde/avec un treuil *etc*).

wind off *vt sep* dérouler, dévider.

wind on *vt sep* enrouler.

wind up 1 *vi [meeting, discussion]* se terminer, finir (*with* par). **they wound up in Cannes** ils ont fini *or* ils se sont retrouvés à Cannes; **he wound up as a doctor** il a fini (comme) médecin; (*in debate*) **he wound up for the Government** c'est lui qui a résumé la position du gouvernement dans le discours de clôture; *V also* **wind³ 3.**

2 *vt sep* **(a)** *object on rope/winch etc* faire monter (au bout d'une corde/avec un treuil *etc*); (*fig: end*) *meeting, speech* clôturer, clore, terminer (*with* par); (*Comm*) *business* liquider. **to wind up one's affairs** liquider ses affaires; (*Banking*) **to wind up an account** clôturer *or* clore un compte.

(b) *watch etc* remonter. (*fig: tense*) **to be wound up*** être tendu *or* crispé (*about* à propos de); **it gets me all wound up (inside)*** ça me retourne*.

3 winding-up *n V* **winding 3.**

winder ['waɪndəʳ] *n [watch etc]* remontoir *m*; (*for thread etc*) dévidoir *m*; (*person*) dévideur *m*, -euse *f*.

winding ['waɪndɪŋ] **1** *adj road* sinueux, tortueux; *river* sinueux, qui serpente. **a ~ staircase** un escalier tournant.

2 *n* **(a)** (*U: V* **wind³ 2**) enroulement *m*; enveloppement *m*; remontage *m*; (*on to bobbin*) bobinage *m*.

(b) ~(s) *[road]* zigzags *mpl*; *[river]* méandres *mpl*.

3 *cpd*: **winding sheet** linceul *m*; **winding-up** *[meeting, account]* clôture *f*; *[business, one's affairs]* liquidation *f*.

windlass ['wɪndləs] *n* guindeau *m*, treuil *m*.

windless ['wɪndlɪs] *adj* sans vent. **it was a ~ day** il n'y avait ce jour-là pas un brin *or* un souffle de vent.

window ['wɪndəʊ] **1** *n* (*gen*) fenêtre *f*; (*in car, train*) vitre *f*, glace *f*; (~ *pane*) vitre, carreau *m*; (*stained-glass* ~) vitrail *m*, (*larger*) verrière *f*; *[shop]* vitrine *f*, devanture *f*, (*more modest*) étalage *m*; *[café etc]* vitrine; (*in post office, ticket office etc*) guichet *m*; (*in envelope*) fenêtre. **I saw her at the ~** je l'ai vue à la fenêtre (*or* à la vitre); **don't lean out of the ~** ne te penche pas par la fenêtre; (*in train, car etc*) ne te penche pas en dehors; **to look/jump** *etc* **out of the ~** regarder/sauter *etc* par la fenêtre; **the ~s look out on to fields** les fenêtres donnent sur *or* ont vue sur des champs; **to break a ~** casser une vitre *or* un carreau; **to clean the ~s** nettoyer *or* laver les carreaux; (*Comm*) **to put sth in the ~** mettre qch en vitrine *or* à la devanture; (*Comm*) **I saw it in the ~** je l'ai vu à l'étalage *or* à la devanture *or* en vitrine; (*Comm*) **the ~s are lovely at Christmas time** les vitrines sont très belles au moment de Noël; (*Comm*) **in the front of the ~** sur le devant de la vitrine.

2 *cpd*: **window box** jardinière *f* (*à plantes*); **window cleaner** (*person*) laveur *m*, -euse *f* de vitres *or* carreaux; (*substance*) produit *m* à nettoyer les vitres *or* carreaux; **to do the window-cleaning** faire les vitres *or* carreaux; (*Comm*) **window dresser** étalagiste *mf*; (*Comm*) **window dressing** composition *f* d'étalage; **she is learning window dressing** elle fait des études d'étalagiste; (*fig pej*) **it's only window dressing** ce n'est qu'une façade; **window envelope** enveloppe *f* à fenêtre; **window frame** châssis *m* (de fenêtre); **window ledge** rebord *m* de fenêtre; **window pane** vitre *f*, carreau *m*; **window seat** (*in room*) banquette *f* (située sous la fenêtre); (*in vehicle*) place *f* côté fenêtre *inv*; (*US*) **window shade** store *m*; **she's a great window-shopper** elle adore faire du lèche-vitrine; **window-shopping** lèche-vitrine *m*; **to go window-shopping** faire du lèche-vitrine; **windowsill** (*inside*) appui *m* de fenêtre; (*outside*) rebord *m* de fenêtre.

windward ['wɪndwəd] **1** *adj* qui est au vent *or* contre le vent, qui est du côté du vent. (*Geog*) **the W~ Islands** les îles *fpl* du Vent.

2 *adv* du côté du vent, au vent, contre le vent.

3 *n* côté *m* du vent. **to look to ~** regarder dans la direction du vent; **to get to ~ of sth** se mettre contre le vent par rapport à qch.

windy ['wɪndɪ] *adj* **(a)** *place* battu *or* balayé par les vents, venteux, exposé au vent, éventé; *day, weather* de (grand) vent. **it's ~ today** il fait *or* il y a du vent aujourd'hui, le vent souffle aujourd'hui.

(b) (*Brit‡ fig: scared*) **to be/get ~ about sth** paniquer* à cause de qch.

wine [waɪn] **1** *n* vin *m*. **elderberry ~** vin de sureau.

2 *vt*: **to ~ and dine sb** emmener qn faire un dîner bien arrosé.

3 *vi*: **to ~ and dine** faire un dîner bien arrosé.

4 *cpd bottle, cellar* à vin; (*colour*) lie de vin *inv or* lie-de-vin *inv*. **winebibber** grand(e) buveur *m*, -euse *f* (de vin); **wine-bottling** mise *f* en bouteilles (du vin); **wine cask** fût *m*, tonneau *m* (à vin); **wine-coloured** lie de vin *inv or* lie-de-vin *inv*; **wine-glass** verre *m* à vin; **wine grower** viticulteur *m*, -trice *f*, vigneron(ne) *m(f)*; **winegrowing** (*n*) viticulture *f*, culture *f* de la vigne; (*adj*) *district, industry* vinicole, viticole; **wine list** carte *f* des vins; (*Brit*) **wine merchant** marchand(e) *m(f)* de vin; (*on larger scale*) négociant(e) *m(f)* en vins; **wine press** pressoir *m* (à vin); **wineshop** boutique *f* du marchand de vin; **wineskin** outre *f* à vin; **wine taster** (*person*) dégustateur *m*, -trice *f* (de vins); (*cup etc*) tâte-vin *m inv*; **wine tasting** dégustation *f* (de vins); **wine vinegar** vinaigre *m* de vin; **wine waiter** sommelier *m*.

wing [wɪŋ] **1** *n* (*gen, Archit, Aut, Mil, Pol, Sport, Zool; also of plane*) aile *f*; (*air force unit*) groupe *m* (de deux ou plusieurs escadrilles); *[armchair]* oreillette *f*. **to be on the ~** être en vol, voler; **to shoot a bird on the ~** tirer un oiseau au vol *or* à la volée; *[bird]* **to take ~** prendre son vol *or* son essor, s'envoler; (*fig*) **he or his heart took ~** son cœur s'emplit de joie; (*fig: vanish*) **to take ~s** disparaître, s'envoler, fondre comme neige au soleil; (*fig*) **to take sb under one's ~** prendre qn sous son aile; (*fig*) **on the ~s of fantasy** sur les ailes de l'imagination; (*fig*) **fear lent or gave him ~s** la peur lui donnait des ailes; (*Theat*) **the ~s** les coulisses *fpl*, la coulisse; **to stand or stay in the ~s** (*Theat*) se tenir en coulisse, se tenir dans les *or* la coulisse(s); (*fig*) rester dans la coulisse; (*Aviat: insignia*) ~s insigne *m* (de pilote); (*fig*) **to earn or win or get one's ~s** faire ses preuves, gagner ses éperons, prendre du grade *or* du galon; (*Pol*) **on the left/right ~ of the party** sur l'aile gauche/droite du parti; (*Sport*) **he plays (on the) left ~** il est ailier gauche; *V* **clip², spread** *etc.*

2 *cpd*: (*Zool*) **wing case** élytre *m*; **wing chair** fauteuil *m* à oreillettes; **wing collar** col cassé; (*Aviat*) **wing commander** lieutenant-colonel *m* (de l'armée de l'air); (*Aviat*) **wing flap** aileron *m*; (*liter*) **wing-footed** aux pieds ailés; (*Brit Aut*) **wing mirror** rétroviseur *m* de côté; **wing nut** papillon *m*, écrou *m* à ailettes; **wingspan, wingspread** envergure *f*; **wing tip** bout *m* de l'aile.

3 *vt* **(a)** (*wound*) *bird* blesser *or* toucher (à l'aile); *person* blesser au bras (*or* à la jambe *etc*).

(b) (*liter*) **to ~ an arrow at sth** darder une flèche en direction de qch; (*liter*) **fear ~ed his steps** la peur lui donnait des ailes; **to ~ one's way** = **to wing**; *V* **4.**

4 *vi* (*also* **~ one's way**) voler. **they ~ed over the sea** ils ont survolé la mer.

winged [wɪŋd] *adj creature, god, statue* ailé. **the W~ Victory of Samothrace** la Victoire de Samothrace.

-winged [wɪŋd] *adj ending in cpds*: **white-winged** aux ailes blanches.

winger ['wɪŋəʳ] *n* (*Sport*) ailier *m*.

wingless ['wɪŋlɪs] *adj* sans ailes; *insect* aptère.

wink [wɪŋk] **1** *n* clin *m* d'œil; (*blink*) clignement *m*. **to give sb a ~** faire un clin d'œil à qn; **in a ~, as quick as a ~** en un clin d'œil; *V* **forty, sleep, tip²** *etc.*

2 *vi [person]* faire un clin d'œil; (*blink*) cligner des yeux; *[star, light]* clignoter. (*fig*) **to ~ at sth** fermer les yeux sur qch.

3 *vt*: **to ~ one's eye** faire un clin d'œil (*at sb* à qn); **to ~ one's eyes** cligner des yeux; **to ~ a tear back or away** cligner de l'œil pour chasser une larme.

winker ['wɪŋkəʳ] *n* (*Brit Aut*) clignotant *m*.

winking ['wɪŋkɪŋ] **1** *adj light, signal* clignotant. **2** *n* clins *mpl* d'œil; (*blinking*) clignements *mpl* d'yeux. **it was as easy as ~** c'était simple comme bonjour.

winkle ['wɪŋkl] **1** *n* bigorneau *m*. **2** *vt* (*also* **fig*) extirper (*sth/sb out of* qch/qn de).

winner ['wɪnəʳ] *n* (*person*) vainqueur *m*; (*Sport; also in competitions etc*) gagnant(e) *m(f)*; (*horse/car/essay etc*) (cheval *m*/voiture *f*/composition *f etc*) gagnant(e) *m(f)*. **to be the ~** gagner; (*Tennis*) **that ball was a ~** cette balle était imparable; (*fig*) **his latest disc/show is a ~*** son dernier album/spectacle va faire un malheur*; (*fig*) **he's a ~!*** il est sensass!‡; **to pick or spot a ~** (*Racing*) choisir un gagneur; (*fig: in business, show business etc*) trouver une locomotive*.

winning ['wɪnɪŋ] **1** *adj* **(a)** (*person, dog, car etc*) gagnant; *blow, stroke, shot etc* décisif, de la victoire. **the ~ goal came in the last 5 minutes** le but qui a décidé de la victoire a été marqué dans les 5 dernières minutes.

(b) (*captivating*) *person* charmant, adorable; *smile, manner* charmeur, engageant. **the child has ~ ways, the child has a ~ way with him** cet enfant a une grâce irrésistible.

2 *npl* (*Betting etc*) ~s gains *mpl*.

3 *cpd*: **winning post** poteau *m* d'arrivée.

winningly ['wɪnɪŋlɪ] *adv* d'une manière charmeuse, d'un air engageant.

winnow ['wɪnəʊ] *vt grain* vanner. (*fig liter*) **to ~ truth from falsehood** démêler le vrai d'avec le faux.

winnower ['wɪnəʊəʳ] *n* (*person*) vanneur *m*, -euse *f*; (*machine*) tarare *m*.

winsome ['wɪnsəm] *adj* séduisant, engageant, charmeur.

winsomely ['wɪnsəmlɪ] *adv* d'une manière séduisante, d'un air engageant.

winsomeness ['wɪnsəmnɪs] *n* (*U*) charme *m*, séduction *f*.

winter ['wɪntəʳ] **1** *n* hiver *m*. **in ~** en hiver; **in the ~ of 1977** pendant l'hiver de 1977; **'A W~'s Tale'** 'Le Conte d'hiver'.

2 *cpd weather, day, season, temperatures, activities, residence* d'hiver, hivernal. **winter clothes** vêtements *mpl* d'hiver; (*Bot*) **wintergreen** gaulthérie *f*; **oil of wintergreen** essence *f* de

wintergreen; **winter holidays** vacances *fpl* d'hiver; **winter sleep** sommeil hibernal, hibernation *f*; **winter sports** sports *mpl* d'hiver; **wintertime** hiver *m*.
3 *vi* hiverner, passer l'hiver.
4 *vt animals* hiverner.
winterize ['wɪntəraɪz] *vt* (*US*) préparer pour l'hiver.
wintry ['wɪntrɪ] *adj sky, weather* d'hiver, hivernal; (*fig*) *smile, gesture* glacial.
wipe [waɪp] **1** *n* coup *m* de torchon (*or* d'éponge *etc*). **to give sth a ~** donner un coup de torchon (*or* d'éponge *etc*) à qch.
2 *vt table, dishes, floor* essuyer (*with* avec). **to ~ one's hands/face/eyes** s'essuyer les mains/le visage/les yeux (*on* sur, *with* avec); **to ~ one's feet** (*with towel*) s'essuyer les pieds; (*on mat*) s'essuyer les pieds, essuyer ses pieds; **to ~ one's nose** se moucher; **to ~ one's bottom** s'essuyer; **he ~d the glass dry** il a soigneusement essuyé le verre; **to ~ the blackboard** effacer *or* essuyer *or* nettoyer le tableau; (*fig*) **to ~ the slate clean** passer l'éponge; (*fig*) **to ~ the floor with sb*** réduire qn en miettes*; **that will ~ the smile off her face!*** après ça on va voir si elle a toujours le sourire!
wipe away *vt sep tears* essuyer; *marks* effacer.
wipe off *vt sep* effacer.
wipe out *vt sep* **(a)** *container* bien essuyer; *writing, error etc* effacer; (*fig*) *insult* effacer, laver; *debt* régler, s'acquitter de; *the past, memory* oublier, effacer. **to wipe out an old score** régler une vieille dette (*fig*).
(b) (*annihilate*) *town, people, army* anéantir. **to wipe sb out*** ratiboiser* qn.
wipe up *vt sep* essuyer.
wiper ['waɪpə^r] *n* (*cloth*) torchon *m*; (*Brit Aut*) essuie-glace *m inv*.
wire ['waɪə^r] **1** *n* **(a)** (*U: substance*) fil *m* (métallique *or* de fer); (*Elec*) fil (électrique); (*piece of ~*) fil; (*snare*) collet *m*, lacet *m*; (*~ fence*) grillage *m*, treillis *m* métallique. **copper ~** fil de cuivre; **telephone ~s** fils téléphoniques; **cheese ~** fil à couper; *V* **barbed, live^2** *etc*.
(b) (*telegram*) télégramme *m*.
2 *cpd object, device* de *or* en fil de fer. **wire brush** brosse *f* métallique; **wire cutters** cisaille *f*, pince coupante; **wire-drawer, wire-drawing machine** étireuse *f*; **wire gauge** calibre *m* (pour fils métalliques); **wire gauze** toile *f* métallique; (*US*) **wire glass** verre armé; **wire-haired terrier** terrier *m* à poils durs; (*U*) **wire netting** treillis *m* métallique, grillage *m*; (*fig*) **he's a wirepuller*** il sait tirer les ficelles; (*fig*) **there's a lot of wirepulling*** il y a pas mal de gens qui tirent les ficelles*; **wire rope** câble *m* métallique; **wiretap** (*vi*) mettre un (*or* des) téléphone(s) sur écoute; (*vt*) mettre sur écoute; **wiretapping** mise *f* sur écoute d'une ligne téléphonique; **wire wool** paille *f* de fer; **wireworks** entreprise *f* produisant du treillis métallique.
3 *vt* **(a)** (*also ~ up*) *opening, fence* grillager; *flowers, beads* monter sur fil de fer; (*Elec*) *house* faire l'installation électrique de; *circuit* installer. **to ~ sth to sth** relier *or* rattacher qch à qch (avec du fil de fer); (*Elec*) brancher qch sur qch, relier qch à qch; **to ~ a room (up) for sound** sonoriser une pièce; **it's all ~d (up) for television** l'antenne (réceptrice *or* émettrice) de télévision est déjà installée.
(b) (*telegraph*) télégraphier (*to* à).
4 *vi* télégraphier.
wire together *vt sep objects* attacher (avec du fil de fer).
wire up *vt sep* = **wire 3a.**
wireless ['waɪəlɪs] **1** *n* **(a)** (*U: ~ telegraphy*) télégraphie *f* sans fil, T.S.F. *f*. **to send a message by ~** envoyer un sans-fil; **they were communicating by ~** ils communiquaient par sans-fil.
(b) (†: *esp Brit: ~ set*) (poste *m* de) T.S.F.† *f*. **on the ~** à la T.S.F.
2 *cpd station, programme* radiophonique. **wireless broadcast** émission *f* de T.S.F.; **wireless message** radiogramme *m*, radio *m*, sans-fil *m*; **wireless operator** radiotélégraphiste *mf*, radio *mf*; **wireless room** cabine *f* radio *inv*; **wireless set** poste *m* de T.S.F.; **wireless telegraph, wireless telegraphy** télégraphie *f* sans fil, T.S.F. *f*, radiotélégraphie *f*; **wireless telephone** téléphone *m* sans fil; **wireless telephony** téléphonie *f* sans fil, radiotéléphonie *f*.
wiring ['waɪərɪŋ] *n* (*U: Elec*) installation *f* (électrique). **to have the ~ redone** faire refaire l'installation électrique (*in* de).
wiry ['waɪərɪ] *adj hair* dru; *animal* nerveux (*fig*); *person* noueux, maigre et nerveux.
wisdom ['wɪzdəm] **1** *n* (*U*) *[person]* sagesse *f*; *[action, remark]* prudence *f*.
2 *cpd*: **wisdom tooth** dent *f* de sagesse.
wise^1 [waɪz] **1** *adj* (*sagacious*) *person* sage; *look, nod* sage, averti; *thoughts, sayings* sage, avisé; (*learned*) savant; (*prudent*) prudent; (*judicious*) *action, remark* judicieux, sensé. **a ~ man** (*sagacious*) un sage; (*learned*) un savant, un érudit; (*Bible*) **the (Three) W~ Men** les (trois) rois mages; **he grew ~r with age** il s'est assagi avec l'âge *or* en vieillissant; **it wasn't very ~ to tell him that** ce n'était pas très judicieux *or* prudent de lui dire ça; **he was ~ enough to refuse** il s'est montré assez sage *or* prudent pour refuser, il a eu la sagesse *or* la prudence de refuser; **how ~ of you!** vous avez eu bien raison; **the wisest thing to do is ...** ce qu'il y a de plus sage à faire est ...; **I'm none the ~r** ça ne m'avance pas beaucoup, je n'en sais pas plus pour autant; **nobody will be any the ~r if you ...** personne n'en saura rien *or* ne s'apercevra de rien *or* n'y verra que du feu si tu ...; **~ guy*** gros malin*, type* *m* qui fait le malin; **to put sb ~ to sth*** mettre qn au courant *or* au parfum* de qch; **to be ~ to sth*** être au courant de qch; **to get ~ to sb*** piger* ce que veut (*or* fait) qn, piger* le petit jeu de qn.
2 *cpd*: **wiseacre** puits *m* de science (*iro*); **wisecrack*** (*n*) vanne‡; (*vi*) faire *or* sortir une (*or* des) vanne(s)‡; **'need any help?' he wisecracked*** 'z'avez besoin de mes services?'* plaisanta-t-il.
wise up‡ *vt sep*: **to wise sb up** mettre qn au parfum* (*about* de); **to get wised up about sth** se faire mettre au parfum* de qch.
wise^2 [waɪz] *n*: **in no ~** aucunement, en aucune façon *or* manière; **in this ~** ainsi, de cette façon *or* manière.
...wise [waɪz] *adv ending in cpds* **(a)** en ce qui concerne, du point de vue de, pour ce qui est de, côté*. **healthwise he's fine but moneywise things aren't too good** du point de vue santé *or* côté* santé ça va, mais pour ce qui est de l'argent *or* côté* argent ça ne va pas trop bien.
(b) à la manière de, dans le sens de *etc*; *V* **clockwise, lengthways** *etc*.
wisely ['waɪzlɪ] *adv* (*sagaciously*) sagement; (*prudently*) prudemment, judicieusement. **he loved her not ~ but too well** il l'aimait follement dans tous les sens du terme; **he didn't behave very ~** sa conduite n'a guère été prudente *or* judicieuse.
wish [wɪʃ] **1** *vt* **(a)** (*desire*) souhaiter, désirer. **I ~ that you**+*cond* je voudrais que vous+*subj*; **I ~ to be told when he comes** je souhaite *or* désire être informé de sa venue; **I ~ to be alone** je souhaite *or* désire *or* voudrais être seul; **he did not ~ it** il ne le souhaitait *or* désirait pas; **what do you ~ him to do?** que voudrais-tu *or* souhaites-tu *or* désires-tu qu'il fasse?; **I ~ I'd gone with you** j'aurais bien voulu vous accompagner, je regrette de ne pas vous avoir accompagné; **I ~ you had left with him** j'aurais bien voulu que tu sois parti avec lui, je regrette que tu ne sois pas parti avec lui; **I ~ I hadn't said that** je regrette d'avoir dit cela; **I ~ you'd stop talking!** tu ne peux donc pas te taire!; **I only ~ I'd known about that before!** si seulement j'avais su ça avant!, comme je regrette de n'avoir pas su ça avant!; **I ~ I could!** si seulement je pouvais!; **I ~ to heaven* he hadn't done it** mais bon sang* pourquoi est-il allé faire ça?; **I ~ it weren't so** si seulement il pouvait ne pas en être ainsi.
(b) (*desire for sb else*) souhaiter, vouloir; (*bid*) souhaiter. **he doesn't ~ her any ill** *or* **harm** il ne lui veut aucun mal; **I ~ you well** *or* **I ~ you (good) luck in what you're trying to do** je vous souhaite de réussir dans ce que vous voulez faire; (*iro*) **I ~ you well of it!, I ~ you luck of it!** je te souhaite bien du plaisir!; **he ~ed us (good) luck as we left** il nous a souhaité bonne chance au moment de partir; **~ me luck!** dis-moi 'merde'!‡ (*esp Scol etc*), souhaite-moi bonne chance!; **to ~ sb good morning** dire bonjour à qn, souhaiter *or* donner le bonjour à qn († *or hum*); **to ~ sb good-bye** dire au revoir à qn; **to ~ sb a happy birthday** souhaiter bon anniversaire à qn; **I ~ you every happiness!** je vous souhaite d'être très heureux!; **he ~ed us every happiness** il nous a fait tous ses souhaits de bonheur.
(c) (* *fig*) **the bike was ~ed on (to) me** je n'ai pas pu faire autrement que d'accepter le vélo; **the job was ~ed on (to) me** c'est un boulot qu'on m'a collé*; **I wouldn't ~ that on (to) anybody** c'est quelque chose que je ne souhaiterais pas à mon pire ennemi; **I got her kids ~ed on (to) me for the holiday** elle m'a laissé ses gosses sur les bras pendant les vacances*.
2 *vi* faire un vœu. **you must ~ as you eat it** fais un vœu en le mangeant; **to ~ for sth** souhaiter qch; **I ~ed for that to happen** j'ai souhaité que cela se produise; **she's got everything she could ~ for** elle a tout ce qu'elle peut désirer; **what more could you ~ for?** que pourrais-tu souhaiter de plus?; **it's not everything you could ~ for** ce n'est pas l'idéal.
3 *n* **(a)** (*desire, will*) désir *m*. **what is your ~?** que désirez-vous?; (*liter or hum*) **your ~ is my command** vos désirs sont pour moi des ordres; **it has always been my ~ to do that** j'ai toujours désiré faire *or* eu envie de faire cela; **he had no great ~ to go** il n'avait pas grande envie d'y aller; **to go against sb's ~es** contrecarrer les désirs de qn; **he did it against my ~es** il l'a fait contre mon gré.
(b) (*specific desire*) vœu *m*, souhait *m*. **to make a ~** faire un vœu, formuler un souhait; **the fairy granted him 3 ~es** la fée lui accorda 3 souhaits; **his ~ came true, his ~ was granted, he got his ~** son vœu *or* souhait s'est réalisé; **you shall have your ~** ton souhait sera réalisé *or* te sera accordé, ton vœu sera exaucé.
(c) give him my good *or* **best ~es** (*in conversation*) faites-lui mes amitiés; (*in letter*) transmettez-lui mes meilleures pensées; **he sends his best ~es** (*in conversation*) il vous fait ses amitiés; (*in letter*) il vous envoie ses meilleures pensées; **best ~es** *or* **all good ~es for a happy birthday** tous mes (*or* nos) meilleurs vœux pour votre anniversaire; (*in letter*) **with best ~es from, with all good ~es from** bien amicalement; **the Queen sent a message of good ~es on Independence Day** la reine a envoyé des vœux pour le jour de l'Indépendance; **they came to offer him their best ~es on the occasion of ...** ils sont venus lui offrir leurs meilleurs vœux pour ... .
4 *cpd*: **wishbone** bréchet *m*; (*Psych*) **wish fulfilment** accomplissement *m* de désir.
wishful ['wɪʃfʊl] *adj*: **to be ~ to do** *or* **of doing** avoir envie de faire; **it's ~ thinking if you believe that** si tu crois cela c'est que tu prends tes désirs pour la réalité.
wishy-washy* ['wɪʃɪˌwɒʃɪ] *adj colour* délavé; *speech, style, taste* fade, insipide, fadasse*; *person* sans aucune personnalité, falot, fadasse*.
wisp [wɪsp] *n [straw]* brin *m*; *[hair]* fine mèche; *[thread]* petit bout; *[smoke]* mince volute *f*. **a little ~ of a girl** une fillette menue.
wispy ['wɪspɪ] *adj straw, hair* fin; *smoke* mince, fin. **a ~ little old lady** une vieille dame menue.
wistaria [wɪs'tɛərɪə] *n*, **wisteria** [wɪs'tɪərɪə] *n* glycine *f*.
wistful ['wɪstfʊl] *adj* nostalgique, mélancolique, rêveur.
wistfully ['wɪstfəlɪ] *adv* avec nostalgie *or* mélancolie, avec une tristesse rêveuse.
wistfulness ['wɪstfʊlnɪs] *n [person]* caractère *m* mélancolique; *[look, smile, voice]* nostalgie *f*, mélancolie *f*, regret *m*.

wit[1] [wɪt] *vi* (*Jur etc*) **to ~ ...** à savoir ..., c'est à dire ... .

wit[2] [wɪt] *n* **(a)** (*gen pl: intelligence*) **~(s)** esprit *m*, intelligence *f*, astuce *f*; **mother ~, native ~** bon sens, sens commun; **he hadn't the ~** *or* **he hadn't enough ~ to hide the letter** il n'a pas eu l'intelligence *or* la présence d'esprit de cacher la lettre; **you'll need all your ~s about you** *or* **you'll need to use all your ~s if you're to avoid being seen** il va te falloir toute ta présence d'esprit pour éviter d'être vu; **keep your ~s about you!** restez attentif!; **use your ~s!** sers-toi de ton intelligence!; **it was a battle of ~s (between them)** ils jouaient au plus fin; **he lives by his ~s** c'est un chevalier d'industrie, il vit d'expédients; **to collect** *or* **gather one's ~s** rassembler ses esprits; **the struggle for survival sharpened his ~s** la lutte pour la vie lui avivait l'esprit; **he was at his ~s' end** il ne savait plus que faire, il ne savait plus à quel saint se vouer; **I'm at my ~s' end to know what to do** je ne sais plus du tout ce que je dois faire; **to be/go out of one's ~s** être/devenir fou (*f* folle); **she was nearly out of her ~s with worry about him** elle était si inquiète pour lui qu'elle en devenait folle.

(b) (*U: wittiness*) esprit *m*. **the book is full of ~** le livre est très spirituel *or* est plein d'esprit; **he has a ready** *or* **pretty ~** il a beaucoup d'esprit, il est très spirituel; **in a flash of ~ he said ...** obéissant à une inspiration spirituelle il a dit ...; **this flash of ~ made them all laugh** ce trait d'esprit les a tous fait rire.

(c) (*person*) homme *m* d'esprit, femme *f* d'esprit; (*Hist, Literat*) bel esprit.

witch [wɪtʃ] **1** *n* sorcière *f*; (*fig: charmer*) ensorceleuse *f*, magicienne *f*. (*fig*) **she's an old ~** c'est une vieille sorcière; **~es' sabbath** sabbat *m* (de sorcières).

2 *cpd*: **witchcraft** sorcellerie *f*; **witch doctor** sorcier *m* (*de tribu*); **witch-elm = wych-elm; witch hazel** hamamélis *m*; (*fig: esp Pol*) **witch hunt** chasse *f* aux sorcières; **the witching hour of midnight!** minuit, l'heure fatale!, minuit, l'heure du crime! (*hum*).

witchery ['wɪtʃərɪ] *n* sorcellerie *f*; (*fig: fascination*) magie *f*, ensorcellement *m*, envoûtement *m*.

with [wɪð, wɪθ] (*phr vb elem*) **1** *prep* **(a)** (*indicating accompaniment, relationship*) avec, à. **I was ~ her** j'étais avec elle; **go ~ your brother** va avec ton frère, accompagne ton frère; **he lives ~ his aunt** (*in his house*) il habite avec sa tante; (*in her house*) il habite chez *or* avec sa tante; **she was staying ~ friends** elle passait quelque temps chez des amis; **I'll be ~ you in a minute** je suis à vous dans un instant; **I have no money ~ me** je n'ai pas d'argent sur moi; **she had her umbrella ~ her** elle avait pris son parapluie; **he took it away ~ him** il l'a emporté avec lui; **she left the child ~ her aunt** elle a laissé l'enfant avec sa tante *or* à la garde de sa tante; **mix the red ~ the blue** mélange le rouge et le bleu; **do you take sugar ~ coffee?** prenez-vous du sucre dans *or* avec votre café?; **that problem is always ~ us** ce problème ne nous lâche pas; **~ 'Hamlet' it's the best play he wrote** c'est, avec 'Hamlet', la meilleure pièce qu'il ait écrite; **fill it up ~ petrol** faites le plein d'essence; **they loaded the truck ~ coal** ils ont chargé le camion de charbon.

(b) (*agreement, harmony*) avec. **to agree ~ sb** être d'accord avec qn; **can you carry the committee ~ you?** le comité vous suivra-t-il?; **the hat doesn't go ~ the dress** le chapeau ne va pas avec la robe; **are you ~ us then?** alors vous êtes des nôtres?; **I'm ~ you in what you say** je suis d'accord avec ce que vous dites; **I'm ~ you all the way** je suis avec vous cent pour cent; **I'm ~ you** (*I agree*) je suis d'accord; (*: *I understand*) je vois*, je vous suis; **he just wasn't ~ us*** (*didn't understand*) il ne voyait* pas du tout; (*wasn't paying attention*) il était tout à fait ailleurs; (*up-to-date*) **to be ~ it‡** [*person*] être dans le vent* *or* dans la course‡; [*clothes etc*] être dans le vent* *or* du dernier cri (*V also* 2); **to get ~ it‡** se mettre dans la course‡.

(c) (*descriptive: having etc*) à, qui a, avec. **the man ~ the beard** le barbu, l'homme à la barbe; **the boy ~ brown eyes** le garçon aux yeux marron; **the house ~ the green shutters** la maison aux volets verts; **I want a coat ~ a fur collar** je veux un manteau à col de fourrure; **a room ~ a view of the sea** une chambre avec vue sur la mer *or* qui a vue sur la mer *or* qui donne sur la mer; **the box ~ the red label** la boîte à étiquette rouge, la boîte qui a une étiquette rouge.

(d) (*manner*) avec, de. **~ my whole heart** de tout mon cœur; **I'll do it ~ pleasure** je le ferai avec plaisir; **~ a shout of joy he sprang up** (en) poussant un cri de joie il a sauté sur ses pieds; **he welcomed us ~ open arms** il nous a accueillis à bras ouverts; **~ all speed** à grande allure, à toute vitesse; **I did it ~ a lot of trouble** je l'ai fait avec beaucoup de difficultés; **~ no trouble at all he ...** sans la moindre difficulté il ...; **he made it ~ great care** il l'a fait avec un soin infini; **... he said ~ a smile ...** dit-il en souriant *or* avec un sourire; **she turned away ~ tears in her eyes** elle s'est détournée, les larmes aux yeux.

(e) (*means, instrument*) avec, de. **cut it ~ a knife** coupe-le avec un couteau; **he was writing ~ a pencil** il écrivait avec un crayon; **I saw it ~ my own eyes** je l'ai vu de mes propres yeux; **take it ~ both hands** prenez-le à deux mains; **he walks ~ a stick** il marche avec une *or* à l'aide d'une canne; **~ God's help** avec l'aide de Dieu; **cover it ~ a cloth** couvre-le d'une *or* avec une serviette.

(f) (*cause*) avec, de. **trembling ~ fear** tremblant de peur; **he jumped ~ joy** il a sauté de joie; **the hills are white ~ snow** les monts sont blancs de neige; **he's in bed ~ flu** il est retenu au lit par la grippe; **he went down ~ measles** il a attrapé la rougeole; **she was sick ~ fear** elle était malade de peur; **~ the price of food these days you can't expect that ...** au prix où est la nourriture de nos jours comment voulez-vous que ... (+ *subj*); **it varies ~ the weather** ça change avec le temps; **this period ended ~ the outbreak of war** cette période s'est terminée avec le début de la guerre; **it all started ~ his attempt to cut prices** tout a commencé quand il a essayé de réduire les prix.

(g) (*opposition*) avec, contre. **they were at war ~ Spain** ils étaient en guerre avec *or* contre l'Espagne; **the war ~ Japan** la guerre avec *or* contre le Japon; **he had an argument ~ his brother** il a eu une dispute avec son frère; **in competition ~** en concurrence avec; **he was struggling ~ the intruder** il était en train de se colleter avec l'intrus.

(h) (*separation*) **to part ~ sb** se séparer de qn; **he won't part ~ it** il ne veut pas s'en séparer; **I can't dispense ~ that** je ne peux pas me passer de ça.

(i) (*in regard to*) avec, de. **the trouble ~ Paul is that** ce qu'il y a avec Paul c'est que; **it's a habit ~ him** c'est une habitude chez lui; **be patient ~ her** sois patient avec elle; **she's good ~ children** elle sait bien s'occuper des enfants; **what do you want ~ that book?** qu'est-ce que tu veux faire de ce livre?; **be honest ~ me** dites-moi les choses franchement; **what's the matter ~ you?** qu'est-ce que tu as?, qu'est-ce qui te prend?; **what's up ~ Paul?***, (*esp US*) **what's ~ Paul?*** qu'est-ce qu'il a, Paul?*, qu'est-ce qui lui prend, Paul?*; **he was pleased ~ what he saw** il était satisfait *or* content de ce qu'il voyait.

(j) (*indicating time*) avec. **he rose ~ the sun** il se levait avec le jour; **~ the approach of winter** à l'approche de l'hiver, l'hiver approchant; **it lessened ~ time** cela a diminué avec le temps; **~ these words he left us** à ces mots *or* sur ces mots *or* là-dessus *or* sur ce il nous a quittés; **~ that he closed the door** sur ce *or* là-dessus il a fermé la porte.

(k) (*despite*) malgré. **~ all his faults I still like him** malgré tous ses défauts je l'aime bien quand même; **~ all that he is still the best we've got** malgré tout ça il est encore le meilleur que nous ayons.

(l) (*in exclamatory phrases*) **away ~ you!** allez-vous-en!; **away ~ him!** qu'on l'emmène (*subj*)!; **down ~ traitors!** à bas les traîtres!; **off ~ his head!** qu'on lui coupe (*subj*) la tête!

2 *cpd*: **with-it‡** *person* dans le vent*, dans la course‡; *ideas, dress, school, firm etc* dans le vent*.

withal†† [wɪ'ðɔːl] *adv* en outre, de plus.

withdraw [wɪθ'drɔː] *pret* **withdrew,** *ptp* **withdrawn 1** *vt person, hand, money, permission, application, help, troops* retirer; *ambassador, representative* rappeler; *accusation, opinion, suggestion, statement* retirer, rétracter; *claim* retirer, renoncer à; *order* annuler; (*Med*) *drugs* arrêter. (*Jur*) **to ~ a charge** retirer une accusation.

2 *vi* [*troops etc*] reculer, se retirer, se replier (*from* de); [*person*] (*move away*) se retirer; (*retract offer, promise etc*) se rétracter, se dédire; [*candidate, competitor*] se retirer, se désister (*from* de, *in favour of sb* en faveur de qn). (*Mil*) **to ~ to a new position** se replier; **he withdrew a few paces** il a reculé de quelques pas; **you can't ~ now!** tu ne peux plus te dédire *or* plus reculer maintenant!; **I ~ from the game** je me retire de la partie, j'abandonne; (*fig*) **to ~ into o.s.** se replier sur soi-même.

withdrawal [wɪθ'drɔːəl] **1** *n* **(a)** (*U: V* **withdraw 1**) retrait *m*; rappel *m*; rétraction *f*; annulation *f*. **they demand the ~ of the troops** ils exigent le retrait des troupes; **the army's ~ to new positions** le repli de l'armée sur de nouvelles positions.

(b) (*Med, Psych*) (état *m* de) manque *m*.

2 *cpd*: (*Med, Psych*) **withdrawal symptoms** symptômes *mpl* de (l'état de) manque.

withdrawn [wɪθ'drɔːn] **1** *ptp of* **withdraw. 2** *adj* (*reserved*) *person* renfermé.

withe [wɪθ] *n* = **withy.**

wither ['wɪðəʳ] **1** *vi* [*plant*] se flétrir, se faner, s'étioler, dépérir; [*person, limb*] (*from illness*) s'atrophier; (*from age*) se ratatiner; (*fig*) [*beauty*] se faner; [*hope, love, enthusiasm*] s'évanouir.

2 *vt plant* flétrir, faner; *limb* atrophier, ratatiner; *beauty* altérer, faner; *hope etc* détruire petit à petit. **he ~ed her with a look** il l'a regardée avec un profond mépris, son regard méprisant lui a donné envie de rentrer sous terre.

wither away *vi* [*plant*] se dessécher, mourir; [*beauty*] se faner complètement, s'évanouir; [*hope etc*] s'évanouir.

withered ['wɪðəd] *adj flower, leaf, plant* flétri, fané, desséché; *arm, leg* atrophié; *face* fané, flétri. **a ~ old woman** une vieille femme toute desséchée.

withering ['wɪðərɪŋ] **1** *n* [*plant*] dépérissement *m*; [*limb*] atrophie *f*; [*beauty*] déclin *m*; [*hope, love, enthusiasm*] évanouissement *m*. **2** *adj heat* desséchant; *tone, look* profondément méprisant; *remark, criticism* cinglant, blessant.

witheringly ['wɪðərɪŋlɪ] *adv say, look* avec un profond mépris.

withers ['wɪðəz] *npl* garrot *m* (*du cheval*).

withershins ['wɪðəʃɪnz] *adv* dans le sens opposé au mouvement apparent du soleil.

withhold [wɪθ'həʊld] *pret, ptp* **withheld** *vt money from pay etc* retenir (*from sth* de qch); *payment, decision* remettre, différer; *one's consent, permission, one's help, support* refuser (*from sb* à qn); *facts, truth, news* cacher, taire (*from sb* à qn). (*US*) **~ing tax** retenue *f* à la source; **he withheld his tax in protest against ...** il a refusé de payer ses impôts pour protester contre ... .

within [wɪð'ɪn] (*phr vb elem*) **1** *adv* dedans, à l'intérieur. **from ~** de l'intérieur.

2 *prep* **(a)** (*inside*) à l'intérieur de. **~ the box** à l'intérieur de la boîte; **~ (the boundary of) the park** à l'intérieur du parc, dans les limites du parc; **here ~ the town** à l'intérieur même de la ville; **~ the city walls** à l'intérieur des murs (de la ville), dans l'enceinte de la ville; **a voice ~ him said ...** une voix en lui dit ... .

(b) (*~ limits of*) **to be ~ the law** être dans (les limites de) la légalité; **to live ~ one's income** vivre selon ses moyens; **~ the range of the guns** à portée de(s) canon(s); **the coast was ~ sight** la côte était à portée de la vue *or* en vue; **they were ~ sight of the town** ils étaient en vue de la ville; (*fig*) **he was ~ reach** *or*

sight of his goal il touchait au but; *V* **call, province, reach.**

(c) (*in measurement, distances*) ~ **a kilometre of the house** à moins d'un kilomètre de la maison; **we were ~ a mile of the town** nous étions à moins d'un mille de la ville; **correct to ~ a centimetre** correct à un centimètre près; *V* **inch.**

(d) (*in time*) ~ **a week of her death they had forgotten about her** moins d'une semaine après sa mort ils ne pensaient plus à elle; **I'll be back ~ an hour** *or* **the hour** je serai de retour d'ici une heure; **he returned ~ the week** il est revenu avant la fin de la semaine; ~ **2 years from now** d'ici 2 ans; ~ **the stipulated period** dans les délais stipulés; *V* **living.**

without [wɪð'aʊt] (*phr vb elem*) **1** *adv* (*liter*) à l'extérieur, au dehors. **from ~** de l'extérieur, de dehors.

2 *prep* **(a)** sans. ~ **a coat** sans manteau; ~ **a coat or hat** sans manteau ni chapeau; ~ **any money** sans argent, sans un *or* le sou*; **he is ~ friends** il n'a pas d'amis; **with or ~ sugar?** avec ou sans sucre?; ~ **a doubt** sans aucun doute; ~ **doubt** sans doute; **not ~ some difficulty** non sans difficulté; **do it ~ fail** ne manquez pas de le faire, faites-le sans faute; **he was quite ~ shame** il n'avait aucune honte; ~ **speaking, he ...** sans parler, il ...; ~ **anybody knowing** sans que personne le sache; **to go ~ sth, to do ~ sth** se passer de qch.

(b) (††: *outside*) au *or* en dehors de, à l'extérieur de.

3 *conj* (*dial or* ‡: *unless*) à moins que+*subj*, à moins de+*infin.*

withstand [wɪθ'stænd] *pret, ptp* **withstood** *vt* résister à.

withy ['wɪðɪ] *n* brin *m* d'osier.

witless ['wɪtlɪs] *adj* sot (*f* sotte), stupide.

witness ['wɪtnɪs] **1** *n* **(a)** (*Jur etc: person*) témoin *m.* (*Jur*) ~ **for the defence/prosecution** témoin à décharge/à charge; **there were 3 ~es to this event** cet événement a eu 3 témoins, 3 personnes ont été témoins de cet événement; **in front of 2 ~es** en présence de 2 témoins; (*Jur*) **to call sb as ~** citer qn comme témoin; (*Jur*) **'your ~'** 'le témoin est à vous'; *V* **eye.**

(b) (*esp Jur: evidence*) témoignage *m.* **in ~ of** en témoignage de; **in ~ whereof** en témoignage de quoi; **to give ~ on behalf of/against** témoigner en faveur de/contre, rendre témoignage pour/contre; **to bear** *or* **be ~ to sth** témoigner de qch, attester qch; **he took this as ~ of her good faith** cela a été pour lui le témoignage *or* l'attestation *f* de sa bonne foi; **I took it as ~ of the fact that ...** j'ai pensé que cela attestait le fait que ...; (*fig*) **her clothes were ~ to her poverty** ses vêtements révélaient *or* attestaient sa pauvreté; **he has his good points, (as) ~ his work for the blind** il a ses bons côtés, témoin *or* comme le prouve *or* à preuve* ce qu'il fait pour les aveugles; ~ **the case of X** voyez *or* regardez *or* témoin le cas de X.

2 *cpd*: (*Jur*) (*Brit*) **witness box,** (*US*) **witness stand** barre *f* des témoins; **in the witness box** *or* **stand** à la barre.

3 *vt* **(a)** (*see*) être le témoin de (*esp Jur*), assister à, voir. **did anyone ~ the theft?** quelqu'un a-t-il été témoin du vol?; **the accident was ~ed by several people** plusieurs personnes ont été témoins de l'accident; (*fig*) **a building/a century which has ~ed ...** un bâtiment/un siècle qui a vu ...

(b) (*esp Jur*) *document* attester *or* certifier l'authenticité de. **to ~ sb's signature** être témoin, signer comme témoin.

4 *vi* (*Jur*) **to ~ to sth** témoigner de qch, attester qch; **he ~ed to having seen the accident** il a témoigné *or* attesté avoir vu l'accident *or* qu'il a vu l'accident.

-witted ['wɪtɪd] *adj ending in cpds* à l'esprit ... . **quick-witted** à l'esprit vif; *V* **slow** *etc.*

witticism ['wɪtɪsɪzəm] *n* mot *m* d'esprit, bon mot.

wittily ['wɪtɪlɪ] *adv* spirituellement, avec beaucoup d'esprit. **...he said wittily** ...dit-il avec beaucoup d'esprit.

wittiness ['wɪtɪnɪs] *n* (*U*) esprit *m*, humour *m.*

wittingly ['wɪtɪŋlɪ] *adv* sciemment, en toute connaissance de cause.

witty ['wɪtɪ] *adj* spirituel, plein d'esprit. ~ **remark** mot *m* d'esprit.

wives [waɪvz] *npl of* **wife.**

wizard ['wɪzəd] *n* magicien *m*, enchanteur *m*, sorcier *m.* (*fig*) **he is a financial ~** il a le génie de la finance, c'est un génie *or* il est génial en matière financière; **he is a ~ with a paintbrush/slide rule** c'est un champion* *or* un as du pinceau/ de la règle à calcul; **he's a ~ at chess** c'est un as *or* un crack* aux échecs; (*Brit: excl*) ~!† au poil!*

wizardry ['wɪzədrɪ] *n* (*U*) magie *f*, sorcellerie *f*; (*fig*) génie *m.* **it is a piece of ~** c'est génial; **this evidence of his financial ~** cette preuve de son génie en matière financière.

wizened ['wɪznd] *adj* ratatiné, desséché.

woa [wəʊ] *excl* = **whoa.**

woad [wəʊd] *n* guède *f.*

wobble ['wɒbl] **1** *vi* **(a)** [*jelly, one's hand, pen, voice*] trembler; [*object about to fall, pile of rocks*] osciller, remuer dangereusement; [*cyclist etc*] osciller; [*tightrope walker, dancer*] chanceler; [*table, chair*] branler, être branlant *or* instable; [*compass needle*] osciller; [*wheel*] avoir du jeu, être voilé. **the cart ~d through the streets** la charrette est passée dans les rues en brinquebalant *or* en cahotant.

(b) (**fig: hesitate*) vaciller, osciller, hésiter (*between* entre).

2 *vt* faire trembler; faire osciller; faire remuer dangereusement; faire branler; faire chanceler.

3 *n*: **to walk with a ~** avoir une démarche chancelante, marcher d'un pas chancelant; **this chair has a ~** cette chaise est bancale; (*Aut*) **wheel ~** shimmy *m.*

wobbly ['wɒblɪ] *adj hand, voice* tremblant; *jelly* qui tremble; *table, chair* bancal, branlant; *object about to fall* qui oscille *or* remue dangereusement, branlant; *wheel* qui a du jeu, voilé. **to be ~ = to wobble** (*V* **wobble 1**); **he's rather ~ still after his illness** il est encore faible après sa maladie; **his legs are a bit ~, he's a bit ~ on his legs** il flageole un peu sur ses jambes; **I'm rather ~ on this bike** je n'arrive pas à trouver mon équilibre *or* je suis en équilibre instable sur cette bicyclette.

wodge [wɒdʒ] *n* (*Brit*) gros morceau.

woe [wəʊ] **1** *n* malheur *m.* († *or hum*) ~ **is me!** pauvre de moi!; ~ **betide the man who ...** malheur à celui qui ...; **he told me his ~s** *or* **his tale of ~** il m'a fait le récit de ses malheurs *or* tribulations *fpl*; **it was such a tale of ~ that** c'était une litanie si pathétique que.

2 *cpd*: **woebegone** désolé, abattu.

woeful ['wəʊfʊl] *adj person, smile, look, gesture* malheureux, très triste; *news, story, sight* affligeant, très triste; *incident, state of affairs* malheureux, cruel.

woefully ['wəʊfəlɪ] *adv say, look* (très) tristement. **the house is ~ lacking in modern conveniences** le confort moderne fait cruellement défaut à cette maison.

wog‡ [wɒg] *n* (*Brit pej*) moricaud(e) *m(f)* (*pej*), métèque* *m* (*pej*).

woke [wəʊk] *pret of* **wake**[2].

woken ['wəʊkn] *ptp of* **wake**[2].

wold [wəʊld] *n* haute plaine, plateau *m.*

wolf [wʊlf] **1** *n, pl* **wolves** loup *m.* **she-~** louve *f*; (*fig*) **a ~ in sheep's clothing** un loup déguisé en brebis; (*fig*) **that will keep the ~ from the door** cela nous (*or* les *etc*) mettra au moins à l'abri du besoin; (*fig*) **he's a ~*** c'est un tombeur de femmes*; *V* **cry, lone** *etc.*

2 *cpd*: (*US*) **wolf call = wolf whistle**; (*also Scouting*†) **wolf cub** louveteau *m*; **wolfhound** chien-loup *m*; **wolf pack** bande *f* de loups; (*Bot*) **wolfsbane** aconit *m*; (*fig*) **wolf whistle** sifflement admiratif (*à l'adresse d'une fille*); **he gave a wolf whistle** il a sifflé la fille.

3 *vt* (*also* ~ **down**) engloutir.

wolfish ['wʊlfɪʃ] *adj* vorace.

wolfishly ['wʊlfɪʃlɪ] *adv* voracement.

wolfram ['wʊlfrəm] *n* wolfram *m*, tungstène *m.*

wolverine ['wʊlvəri:n] *n* (*Zool*) glouton *m*, carcajou *m.*

wolves [wʊlvz] *npl of* **wolf.**

woman ['wʊmən] *pl* **women 1** *n* femme *f.* **young ~** jeune femme; **come along, young ~!** allez mademoiselle, venez!; (*hum: wife*) **the little ~‡** ma (*or* sa *etc*) petite femme*; ~ **of the world** femme du monde; **Paul and all his women** Paul et toutes ses maîtresses; **he runs after women** c'est un coureur de jupons, il court (après) les femmes; ~ **is a mysterious creature** la femme est une créature mystérieuse; (*loc*) **a ~'s place is in the home** la place d'une femme est au foyer (*loc*); (*loc*) **a ~'s work is never done** on n'a jamais fini de faire le ménage; **she's a career ~** c'est une femme qui consacre beaucoup d'énergie à sa carrière, elle est (assez) ambitieuse dans sa vie professionnelle; **I've got a ~ who comes in 3 times a week** j'ai une femme de ménage qui vient 3 fois par semaine; **women's liberation** la libération de la femme; **Women's Liberation Movement, Women's Lib*** mouvement *m* de libération de la femme, M.L.F. *m*; (*Press*) **women's page** la page des lectrices; **women's rights** les droits *mpl* de la femme; **women's suffrage** le droit de vote pour les femmes; **women's team** équipe féminine; *V* **old** *etc.*

2 *adj*: **he's got a ~ music teacher** il a un professeur de musique femme, son professeur de musique est une femme; ~ **worker** ouvrière *f*; **women doctors think that ...** les femmes médecins pensent que ...; **women often prefer women doctors** les femmes préfèrent souvent les médecins femmes; **he's got a ~ driver** son chauffeur est une femme; **women drivers are generally maligned** on calomnie généralement les femmes au volant; ~ **friend** amie *f.*

3 *cpd*: **the womenfolk** les femmes *fpl*; **woman-hater** misogyne *mf*; **womanhood** *V* **womanhood**; **womankind** les femmes *fpl* (*en général*); **womanlike** (*adj*) féminin, de femme; (*adv*) d'une manière très féminine.

womanhood ['wʊmənhʊd] *n* (*U: feminine nature*) féminité *f.* **to reach ~** devenir une femme.

womanish ['wʊmənɪʃ] *adj* (*gen pej*) *man* efféminé; *quality, behaviour* de femme.

womanize ['wʊmənaɪz] *vi* courir les femmes.

womanizer ['wʊmənaɪzə^r] *n* coureur *m* de jupons.

womanliness ['wʊmənlɪnɪs] *n* (*U*) féminité *f*, caractère féminin.

womanly ['wʊmənlɪ] *adj figure, bearing* féminin, de femme; *behaviour* digne d'une femme. ~ **kindness/gentleness** gentillesse/douceur toute féminine.

womb [wu:m] *n* utérus *m*; (*fig*) (*of nature*) sein *m*; (*of earth*) sein, entrailles *fpl.*

wombat ['wɒmbæt] *n* wombat *m*, phascolome *m.*

women ['wɪmɪn] *npl of* **woman.**

won [wʌn] *pret, ptp of* **win.**

wonder ['wʌndə^r] **1** *n* **(a)** (*U*) émerveillement *m*, étonnement *m.* **to be lost in ~** être muet d'étonnement *or* d'admiration, être émerveillé *or* ébloui; **he watched, lost in silent ~** il regardait en silence, émerveillé *or* ébloui; **the sense of ~ that children have** la faculté d'être émerveillé qu'ont les enfants; **... he said in ~** ... dit-il d'une voix remplie d'étonnement.

(b) (*object etc*) merveille *f*, prodige *m*, miracle *m.* **the ~ of electricity** le miracle de l'électricité; **the ~s of science/medicine** les prodiges *or* les miracles de la science/de la médecine; **the Seven W~s of the World** les sept merveilles du monde; **the ~ of it all is that ...** le plus étonnant dans tout cela c'est que ...; **it's a ~ that he didn't fall** c'est extraordinaire qu'il ne soit pas tombé, on se demande comment il a fait pour ne pas tomber; **it's a ~ to me that ...** je n'en reviens pas que ... +*subj*; **he paid cash for a ~!** et miracle, il a payé comptant!; **if for a ~ he ...** si par extraordinaire il ...; **no ~ he came late, it's no ~ (that) he came late** ce n'est pas étonnant qu'il soit arrivé en retard; **no ~!** cela n'a rien d'étonnant!, pas étonnant!*; **he failed, and little** *or* small ~! il a échoué, ce qui n'est guère étonnant!; it's little *or* small ~ that ... il n'est guère étonnant que ... + *subj*; *V* nine, work *etc.*

2 *cpd*: wonderland pays *m* merveilleux; 'Alice in Wonderland' 'Alice au pays des merveilles'; wonderstruck frappé d'étonnement, émerveillé, ébloui; he is a wonder-worker il accomplit de vrais miracles; this drug/cure is a wonder-worker c'est un remède/une cure miracle.

3 *vi* (a) (*marvel*) s'étonner, s'émerveiller. the shepherds ~ed at the angels les bergers émerveillés regardaient les anges; I ~ at your rashness votre audace m'étonne *or* me surprend; I ~ (that) you're still able to work je ne sais pas comment vous faites pour travailler encore; I ~ (that) he didn't kill you cela m'étonne qu'il ne vous ait pas tué; do you ~ *or* can you ~ at it? est-ce que cela vous étonne?; he'll be back, I shouldn't ~ cela ne m'étonnerait pas qu'il revienne.

(b) (*reflect*) penser, songer. his words set me ~ing ce qu'il a dit m'a laissé songeur; I was ~ing about what he said je pensais *or* songeais à ce qu'il a dit; I'm ~ing about going to the pictures j'ai à moitié envie d'aller au cinéma; he'll be back — I ~! il reviendra — je me le demande!

4 *vt* se demander. I ~ who he is je me demande qui il est, je serais curieux de savoir qui il est; I ~ what to do je ne sais pas quoi faire; I ~ where to put it je me demande où (je pourrais) le mettre; he was ~ing whether to come with us il se demandait s'il allait nous accompagner; I ~ why! je me demande pourquoi!

wonderful ['wʌndəfʊl] *adj* (*astonishing*) merveilleux, étonnant, extraordinaire; (*miraculous*) miraculeux; (*excellent*) merveilleux, magnifique, formidable*, sensationnel*. isn't it ~! c'est formidable!* *or* sensationnel!*; (*iro*) ce n'est pas extraordinaire ça! (*iro*).

wonderfully ['wʌndəfəlɪ] *adv* (+*adj*) merveilleusement; (+*vb*) à merveille, admirablement. it was ~ hot all day il a fait merveilleusement chaud toute la journée; she manages ~ considering how handicapped she is elle se débrouille admirablement *or* à merveille si l'on considère combien elle est handicapée; he looks ~ well il a très bonne mine.

wondering ['wʌndərɪŋ] *adj* (*astonished*) étonné; (*thoughtful*) songeur, pensif.

wonderingly ['wʌndərɪŋlɪ] *adv* (*with astonishment*) avec étonnement, d'un air étonné; (*thoughtfully*) songeusement, pensivement.

wonderment ['wʌndəmənt] *n* = wonder 1a.

wondrous ['wʌndrəs] 1 *adj* (*liter*) merveilleux. 2 *adv* († *or liter*) merveilleusement. ~ well à merveille.

wondrously ['wʌndrəslɪ] *adv* (*liter*) = wondrous 2.

wonky* ['wɒŋkɪ] *adj* (*Brit*) *chair, table* bancal; *machine* qui ne tourne pas rond*, déréglé, détraqué. their marriage is rather ~ at the moment leur mariage traverse une mauvaise passe en ce moment; he's feeling rather ~ still il se sent encore un peu patraque* *or* vaseux*; your hat's a bit ~ votre chapeau est mis de travers *or* de traviole*; to go ~ [*car, machine*] se détraquer; [*TV picture etc*] se dérégler; [*piece of handicraft, drawing*] aller de travers.

won't [wəʊnt] = will not; *V* will.

wont [wəʊnt] 1 *adj*: to be ~ to do avoir coutume *or* avoir l'habitude de faire. 2 *n* coutume *f*, habitude *f* (*to do* de faire). as was my ~ ainsi que j'en avais l'habitude, comme de coutume.

wonted [wəʊntɪd] *adj* (*liter*) habituel, coutumier.

woo [wuː] *vt woman* faire la cour à, courtiser; (*fig*) *person* rechercher les faveurs de; *fame, success* rechercher, poursuivre. (*fig*) he ~ed them with promises of ... il cherchait à s'assurer leurs faveurs *or* à leur plaire en leur promettant...

wood [wʊd] 1 *n* (a) (*U: material*) bois *m*. (*fig*) to touch ~, (*US*) to knock on ~ toucher du bois; touch ~!, (*US*) knock on ~! touchons *or* je touche du bois!; *V* dead, hard, soft *etc.*

(b) (*forest*) bois *m*. ~s bois *mpl*; a pine~ un bois de pins, une pinède; (*fig*) he can't see the ~ for the trees les arbres lui cachent la forêt; (*fig*) we're out of the ~ now on est au bout du tunnel maintenant; (*fig*) we're not out of the ~ yet on n'est pas encore tiré d'affaire *or* sorti de l'auberge.

(c) (*cask*) drawn from the ~ tiré au tonneau; aged in the ~ vieilli au tonneau; wine in the ~ vin *m* au tonneau.

(d) (*Mus*) the ~s les bois *mpl*.

(e) (*Golf*) bois *m*; (*Bowls*) boule *f*.

2 *cpd floor, object, structure* de bois, en bois. wood alcohol esprit-de-bois *m*, alcool *m* méthylique; wood anemone anémone *f* des bois; woodbine *V* woodbine; wood block bois *m* de graveur; wood carving (*act: U*) sculpture *f* sur bois; (*object*) sculpture en bois; woodchuck marmotte *f* d'Amérique; (*Orn*) woodcock bécasse *f*; (*U*) woodcraft connaissance *f* des bois; woodcut gravure *f* sur bois; woodcutter bûcheron *m*, -onne *f*; woodcutting (*Art: act, object*) gravure *f* sur bois; (*in forest*) abattage *m* des arbres; wood engraving gravure *f* sur bois; woodland (*n: U*) région boisée, bois *mpl*; (*cpd*) *flower, path etc* des bois; (*Orn*) woodlark alouette *f* des bois; woodlouse (*pl* woodlice) cloporte *m*; woodman forestier *m*; (*Myth*) wood nymph dryade *f*, nymphe *f* des bois; (*Orn*) woodpecker pic *m*; (*Orn*) woodpigeon (pigeon *m*) ramier *m*; woodpile tas *m* de bois; wood pulp pulpe *f*, pâte *f* à papier; wood shavings copeaux *mpl* (de bois); woodshed bûcher *m*; (*US*) woodsman = woodman; (*Mus*) woodwind (*one instrument*) bois *m*; (*collective pl*) bois *mpl*; (*U*) woodwork (*craft, subject*) menuiserie *f*, ébénisterie *f*; (*objects etc*) menuiserie, boiserie *f*; woodworm ver *m* du bois; the table has got woodworm la table est piquée des vers *or* mangée aux vers *or* vermoulue.

woodbine ['wʊdbaɪn] *n* chèvrefeuille *m*.

wooded ['wʊdɪd] *adj* boisé. thickly/sparsely ~ très/peu boisé.

wooden ['wʊdn] *adj* (*lit*) de bois, en bois; (*fig*) *movement, gesture* raide; *look* sans expression, inexpressif; *personality, response* gauche. ~ face visage *m* de bois; ~-headed idiot, imbécile; ~ leg jambe *f* de bois; ~ spoon cuiller *f* de *or* en bois.

woodsy ['wʊdzɪ] *adj* (*US*) *countryside* boisé; *flowers etc* des bois.

woody ['wʊdɪ] *adj countryside* boisé; *plant, stem, texture* ligneux; *odour* de *or* du bois.

wooer† ['wuːəʳ] *n* prétendant *m*.

woof[1] [wʊf] *n* (*Tex*) trame *f*.

woof[2] [wʊf] 1 *n* [*dog*] aboiement *m*. 2 *vi* aboyer. ~, ~! oua, oua!

woofer ['wʊfəʳ] *n* haut-parleur *m* spécial graves.

wool [wʊl] 1 *n* laine *f*; (*‡: hair*) tifs *mpl*. he was wearing ~ il portait de la laine *or* des lainages; a ball of ~ une pelote de laine; knitting/darning ~ laine à tricoter/repriser; (*fig*) to pull the ~ over sb's eyes en faire *or* laisser accroire à qn; the sweater is all ~ *or* pure ~ le pullover est pure laine; *V* dye, steel *etc.*

2 *cpd cloth* de laine; *dress* en *or* de laine. wool fat suint *m*; (*fig*) wool-gathering manque *m* d'attention; (*fig*) to be *or* go wool-gathering être dans les nuages, rêvasser; wool-grower éleveur *m*, -euse *f* de moutons à laine; wool-lined doublé laine; wool merchant négociant(e) *m(f)* en laines, lainier *m*, -ière *f*; (*Brit Parl*) the Woolsack le Sac de Laine (*siège du Lord Chancellor à la chambre des Lords*); woolshed lainerie *f*; wool shop magasin *m* de laines; the wool trade le commerce de la laine.

woollen, (*US*) *also* **woolen** ['wʊlən] 1 *adj cloth* de laine; *garment* en *or* de laine, de *or* en lainage. ~ cloth, ~ material lainage *m*, étoffe *f* de laine; ~ goods lainages; the ~ industry l'industrie lainière; ~ manufacturer fabricant(e) *m(f)* de lainages.

2 *npl*: ~s lainages *mpl*.

woolliness, (*US*) *also* **wooliness** ['wʊlɪnɪs] *n* (*fig: V* woolly) caractère confus *or* nébuleux; verbosité *f*.

woolly, (*US*) *also* **wooly** ['wʊlɪ] 1 *adj material, garment, appearance, sheep* laineux; (*fig*) *clouds* cotonneux; (*also* ~-headed, ~-minded) *ideas* confus, nébuleux; *essay, book, speech* verbeux; *V* wild.

2 *npl*: woollies*, (*US*) *also* woolies* lainages *mpl*; winter woollies* lainages d'hiver.

woops* [wʊps] *excl* = whoops*.

woozy‡ ['wuːzɪ] *adj* dans les vapes‡, tout chose*; (*tipsy*) éméché; *ideas* confus, nébuleux; *outline* estompé, flou. this cold makes me feel ~ je suis complètement abruti par ce rhume.

wop‡ [wɒp] *n* (*pej*) métèque* *m* (*pej*).

word [wɜːd] 1 *n* (a) (*gen*) mot *m*; (*spoken*) mot, parole *f*. [*song etc*] ~s paroles; the written/spoken ~ ce qui est écrit/dit; by ~ of mouth de vive voix (*V also* 2); angry ~s mots prononcés sous le coup de la colère; fine ~s de belles paroles; (*iro*) fine *or* big ~s! belles paroles!, toujours les grands mots!; a man of few ~s un homme peu loquace; in ~ and deed en parole et en fait; ~ for ~ *repeat, copy out* mot pour mot, textuellement; *translate* mot à mot, littéralement; *review, go over* mot par mot (*V also* 2); in other ~s autrement dit; in a ~ en un mot; what's the ~ for 'banana' in German?, what's the German ~ for 'banana'? comment dit-on 'banane' en allemand?; the French have a ~ for it les Français ont un mot pour dire cela; in the ~s of Racine comme dit Racine, selon les mots de Racine; I can't put my thoughts/feelings into ~s je ne trouve pas les mots pour exprimer ce que je pense/ressens; I can't find ~s *or* I have no ~s to tell you how ... je ne saurais vous dire comment ...; ~s fail me! j'en perds la parole!, je ne sais plus que dire!; without a ~, he left the room il a quitté la pièce sans dire un mot; with these ~s, he sat down sur ces mots il s'est assis; it's too stupid for ~s c'est vraiment trop stupide; boring is not the ~ for it! ennuyeux est trop peu dire!; 'negligent' is a better ~ for it 'négligent' serait plus juste *or* serait plus près de la vérité; those were his very ~s ce sont ses propres paroles, c'est ce qu'il a dit mot pour mot *or* textuellement; it all came out in a flood of ~s il (*or* elle *etc*) nous a tout raconté dans un flot *or* déluge de paroles; I told him in so many ~s that ... je lui ai carrément dit que ..., sans y aller par quatre chemins je lui ai dit que ...; he didn't say so in so many ~s ce n'est pas exactement ce qu'il a dit (mais cela revenait au même); I'll give you a ~ of warning je vais vous donner un petit conseil; after these ~s of warning après cette mise en garde; he won't hear a ~ against her il n'admet absolument pas qu'on la critique (*subj*); nobody had a good ~ to say about him (*or* it) personne n'a pris sa défense, personne n'a trouvé la moindre chose à dire en sa faveur; to put in a (good) ~ for sb dire *or* glisser un mot en faveur de qn; I want a ~ with you j'ai à vous parler; I'll have a ~ with him about it je lui en toucherai un mot, je vais lui en parler; I had a ~ with him about it je lui en ai parlé brièvement; I didn't breathe a ~ je n'ai pas soufflé mot; I never said a ~ je n'ai rien dit du tout, je n'ai pas ouvert la bouche; he didn't say a ~ about it il n'en a absolument pas parlé; I can't get a ~ out of him je ne peux rien en tirer (,il reste muet); you took the ~s right out of my mouth c'est exactement ce que j'allais dire, vous avez dit ce que j'avais sur la langue; you put ~s into my mouth! vous me faites dire ce que je n'ai pas dit!; (*quarrel*) to have ~s with sb avoir des mots avec qn*, se disputer avec qn; *V* believe, breathe, eat, edge *etc.*

(b) (*U: news*) nouvelles *fpl*; (*message*) mot *m*. ~ came from headquarters that ... le quartier général nous (*or* leur *etc*) a fait dire *or* nous (*or* les *etc*) a prévenus que ...; ~ came that ... on a appris que ...; there's no ~ from John yet on est toujours sans nouvelles de Jean; I'm hoping for ~ about it tomorrow j'espère que j'aurai des nouvelles demain *or* que demain je saurai ce qui se passe; I hope he'll bring us ~ of Liline j'espère qu'il nous apportera des nouvelles de Liline.

(c) (*promise etc: no pl*) parole *f*, promesse *f*. ~ of honour parole d'honneur; a man of his ~ un homme de parole; his ~ is

his bond il n'a qu'une parole; **he is as good as his** ~ on peut le croire sur parole; **he was as good as his** ~ il a tenu (sa) parole; **to give one's** ~ donner sa parole (d'honneur) (*to sb* à qn, *that* que); **I give you my** ~ **for it** je vous en donne ma parole; **to break one's** ~ manquer à sa parole; **to go back on one's** ~ retirer *or* rendre *or* reprendre sa parole; **to keep one's** ~ tenir (sa) parole; **to hold sb to his** ~ contraindre qn à tenir sa promesse; **to take sb at his** ~ prendre qn au mot; **it was his** ~ **against mine** c'était sa parole contre la mienne; **I've only got her** ~ **for it** c'est elle qui le dit, je n'ai aucune preuve; **you'll have to take his** ~ **for it** il vous faudra le croire sur parole; **take my** ~ **for it, he's a good man** croyez-m'en, c'est un brave homme; (*excl*) **(upon) my** ~**!*** ma parole!

(d) (*command*) (mot *m* d')ordre *m*; (*pass*~) mot *m* de passe. **the** ~ **of command** l'ordre; **his** ~ **is law** c'est lui qui fait la loi; **he gave the** ~ **to advance** il a donné l'ordre *or* le signal d'avancer; *V* **say.**

(e) (*Rel*) **the W**~ (*logos*) le Verbe; (*the Bible, the Gospel; also* **the W**~ **of God**) le Verbe (de Dieu), la parole de Dieu.

(f) (*Computers*) mot *m.*

2 *cpd:* **word-blind** dyslexique; **word-blindness** dyslexie *f*; **wordbook** lexique *m*, vocabulaire *m*; **word-for-word** *analysis* mot par mot; **a word-for-word translation** une traduction mot-à-mot, un mot-à-mot; **word game** jeu *m* avec des mots; **word list** liste *f* de mots; **word-of-mouth** (*adj*) verbal, oral; (*Gram*) **word order** ordre *m* des mots; **to be word-perfect in sth** savoir qch sur le bout du doigt; **to give a word picture of sth** faire le tableau de qch, dépeindre qch; **wordplay** jeu *m* sur les mots, jeu de mots; **word processing** traitement *m* des mots.

3 *vt document, protest* formuler, rédiger, libeller (*Admin*). **he had** ~**ed the letter very carefully** il avait choisi les termes de la lettre avec le plus grand soin; **I don't know how to** ~ **it** je ne sais pas comment le formuler.

wordiness ['wɜːdɪnɪs] *n* verbosité *f.*

wording ['wɜːdɪŋ] *n [letter, speech, statement]* termes *mpl*; *[official document]* libellé *m.* **the** ~ **of the last sentence is clumsy** la dernière phrase est maladroitement exprimée *or* formulée; **the** ~ **is exceedingly important** le choix des termes est extrêmement important; **change the** ~ **slightly** changez quelques mots (ici et là); **a different** ~ **would make it less ambiguous** ce serait moins ambigu si on l'exprimait autrement.

wordy ['wɜːdɪ] *adj* verbeux.

wore [wɔːʳ] *pret of* **wear.**

work [wɜːk] **1** *n* **(a)** (*U: gen*) travail *m*, œuvre *f.* **to be at** ~ travailler, être à l'œuvre *or* au travail; **he was at** ~ **on another picture** il travaillait sur un autre tableau; **there are subversive forces at** ~ **here** des forces subversives sont à l'œuvre; **to start** ~**, to set to** ~ se mettre à l'œuvre; **to set to** ~ **mending** *or* **to mend the fuse** entreprendre de *or* se mettre à réparer le fusible; **they set him to** ~ **mending the fence** ils lui ont donné pour tâche de réparer la barrière; **he does his** ~ **well** il travaille bien, il fait du bon travail; **good** ~**!** bien travaillé!, bravo!; **that's a good piece of** ~ c'est du bon travail; **he's doing useful** ~ **there** il fait œuvre utile là-bas; **she put a lot of** ~ **into it** elle a passé beaucoup de temps dessus; **there's still a lot of** ~ **to be done on it** il reste encore beaucoup à faire; **I've got some more** ~ **for you** j'ai encore du travail pour vous; **I'm trying to get some** ~ **done** j'essaie de travailler un peu; ~ **has begun on the new bridge** les travaux du nouveau pont ont commencé, on a commencé la construction du nouveau pont; **it's women's** ~ c'est un travail de femme; (*iro*) **it's nice** ~ **if you can get it!*** c'est une bonne planque pour ceux qui ont de la veine!*; **it's quite easy** ~ ce n'est pas difficile à faire; **it's hot** ~ ça donne chaud; **to make short** *or* **quick** ~ **of sth** faire qch très rapidement; (*fig*) **to make short** ~ **of sb** envoyer promener qn; **there's been some dirty** ~*** here!** il y a quelque chose de pas catholique là-dessous!; **it's obviously the** ~ **of a professional** c'est manifestement l'œuvre d'un professionnel *or* un travail de professionnel; *V* **cut out, thirsty** *etc.*

(b) (*as employment*) travail *m.* **to go to** ~ aller travailler, aller à l'usine (*or* au bureau *etc*); **he's looking for** ~ il cherche du travail *or* de l'emploi; **he's at** ~ **at the moment** il est au bureau (*or* à l'usine *etc*) en ce moment; **he is in regular** ~ il a un emploi régulier; **to be out of** ~ être en chômage *or* sans emploi; **to put** *or* **throw sb out of** ~ réduire qn au chômage; **this decision threw a lot of men out of** ~ cette décision a fait beaucoup de chômeurs; **600 men were thrown out of** ~ 600 hommes ont été licenciés *or* ont perdu leur emploi; **he's off** ~ **today** il n'est pas allé (*or* venu) travailler aujourd'hui; **he has been off** ~ **for 3 days** il est absent depuis 3 jours; **a day off** ~ un jour de congé; **I've got time off** ~ j'ai du temps libre; **where is his (place of)** ~**?** où est son travail?*, où travaille-t-il?; **domestic** ~ travaux domestiques; **office** ~ travail de bureau; **I've done a full day's** ~ j'ai eu une journée bien remplie, je n'ai pas perdu mon temps aujourd'hui; *V* **day, social** *etc.*

(c) (*product*) ouvrage *m*, œuvre *f*; (*Art, Literat*) œuvre. **the** ~**s of God** les œuvres de Dieu; **good** ~**s** bonnes œuvres; **his life's** ~ l'œuvre de sa vie; **each man will be judged by his** ~**s** chaque homme sera jugé selon ses œuvres; **it was a** ~ **of skill and patience** c'était un ouvrage qui faisait preuve d'habileté et de patience; **a** ~ **of art** une œuvre d'art; **the complete** ~**s of Corneille** les œuvres complètes de Corneille; **it's one of the few** ~**s he has written about ...** c'est l'un des quelques ouvrages qu'il ait écrit sur ...; **one of Beethoven's major** ~**s** une des œuvres majeures de Beethoven; **published** ~**s on this subject** ouvrages publiés sur ce sujet; (*Art, Literat, Mus etc*) **this** ~ **was commissioned by ...** cette œuvre a été commandée par ...; ~**s of fiction/reference** ouvrages de fiction/référence; **he sells a lot of his** ~ il vend beaucoup de tableaux (*or* de livres *etc*).

(d) (*pl*) ~**s** (*gen, Admin, Mil*) travaux *mpl*; *[clock, machine etc]* mécanisme *m.* **Minister/Ministry of W**~**s** ministre *m*/ministère *m* des Travaux publics; **building** ~**s** travaux de construction; **road** ~**s** travaux d'entretien *or* de réfection de la route; (*fig*) **they gave him the** ~**s**‡ ils lui en ont fait voir de dures*, il a eu droit à un interrogatoire (*or* une engueulade‡ *etc*) en règle; (*murdered him*) ils l'ont descendu‡, ils lui ont fait la peau‡; (*fig*) **the whole** ~**s*** tout le tralala*; *V* **public, spanner** *etc.*

(e) (*pl inv: factory*) ~**s** usine *f*; **gas**~**s** usine à gaz; *V* **steel** *etc.*

2 *cpd:* **workaday** *clothes* de travail, de tous les jours; *event* banal, courant; (**hum*) **workaholic** bourreau *m* de travail; **workbag** sac *m* à ouvrage; **workbasket** corbeille *f* à ouvrage; **workbench** établi *m*; **workbook** (*exercise book*) cahier *m* d'exercices; (*manual*) manuel *m*; (*work record book*) cahier de préparations, cahier-journal *m*; **workbox** boîte *f* à ouvrage; **workday** (*adj*) = **workaday**; **a workday of 8 hours** une journée de travail de 8 heures; **Saturday is a workday** (*gen*) on travaille le samedi; (*Comm*) le samedi est un jour ouvrable; **workdesk** bureau *m* de travail; (*Econ, Ind*) **work force** main *f* d'œuvre; **workhorse** cheval *m* de labour (*also fig*); (*Brit Hist*) **workhouse** hospice *m*; **his work load is too heavy** il a trop de travail; **they were discussing work loads** ils discutaient de la répartition du travail; **workman** *V* **workman**; **workmate** camarade *mf* de travail; (*Sport*) **workout** séance *f* d'entraînement; **workpeople** travailleurs *mpl*, ouvriers *mpl*; **work permit** permis *m* de travail; **workroom** salle *f* de travail; **works council** comité *m* d'entreprise; **workshop** atelier *m*; **to be workshy** être rebuté par le travail, être fainéant; **works manager** chef *m* d'exploitation; **worktable** table *f* de travail; (*Brit Ind*) **work-to-rule** grève *f* du zèle; (*US*) **a work week of 38 hours** une semaine de 38 heures; **work-worn** *hands* usé par le travail.

3 *vi* **(a)** (*gen*) travailler. **to** ~ **hard** travailler dur; **to** ~ **like a Trojan** travailler comme un forçat *or* un bœuf; (*Ind*) **to** ~ **to rule** faire la grève du zèle; **they** ~ **a 38-hour week** ils travaillent *or* ils font 38 heures par semaine; **he prefers to** ~ **in wood/clay** il préfère travailler avec le bois/la terre glaise; **he prefers to** ~ **in oils** il aime mieux faire de la peinture à l'huile; **he is** ~**ing at his maths** il travaille ses maths; **he** ~**ed on the car all morning** il a travaillé sur la voiture toute la matinée; (*fig*) **I've been** ~**ing on him but haven't yet managed to persuade him** j'ai bien essayé de le convaincre mais je n'y suis pas encore arrivé; **he's** ~**ing at** *or* **on his memoirs** il travaille à ses mémoires; **the police are** ~**ing on the case** la police enquête sur l'affaire; **have you solved the problem? — we're** ~**ing on it** avez-vous résolu le problème? — on y travaille *or* on cherche; **they are** ~**ing on the principle that ...** ils partent du principe que ...; **there are not many facts/clues** *etc* **to** ~ **on** on manque de faits/d'indices *etc* sur lesquels on puisse se baser *or* qui puissent servir de point de départ; **he has always** ~**ed for/against such a reform** il a toujours lutté pour/contre une telle réforme; **we are** ~**ing towards a solution/agreement** *etc* nous nous dirigeons petit à petit vers une solution/un accord *etc*; **he** ~**ed carefully along to the edge of the cliff** il s'est approché du bord de la falaise en prenant bien garde de ne pas tomber; *V* **overtime** *etc.*

(b) *[mechanism, watch, machine, car, switch]* marcher; *[drug, medicine]* agir, faire effet, opérer; *[yeast]* fermenter; *[scheme, arrangement]* marcher. **the lift isn't** ~**ing** l'ascenseur ne marche pas *or* est en panne; **it** ~**s off the mains/on electricity** ça marche sur le secteur/à l'électricité; **my brain doesn't seem to be** ~**ing today** mon cerveau n'a pas l'air de fonctionner aujourd'hui; **the spell** ~**ed** le charme a fait son effet; **the plan** ~**ed like a charm** tout s'est déroulé exactement comme prévu; **it just won't** ~ ça ne marchera pas *or* jamais; (*fig*) **that** ~**s both ways** c'est à double tranchant.

(c) (*move*) *[face, mouth]* se contracter, se crisper. **his tie had** ~**ed round to the back of his neck** sa cravate avait tourné et lui pendait dans le dos; **dust has** ~**ed into the mechanism** de la poussière s'est introduite *or* s'est glissée dans le mécanisme; **water has** ~**ed through the roof** de l'eau s'est infiltrée par le toit; **the wind has** ~**ed round to the south** le vent a petit à petit tourné au sud; *V* **loose.**

4 *vt* **(a)** (*cause to* ~) *person, staff* faire travailler; *mechanism, machine* faire marcher, actionner. **he** ~**s his staff too hard** il exige trop de travail de son personnel, il surmène son personnel; **he** ~**s himself too hard** il se surmène trop (*V also* **4b**); **he's** ~**ing himself to death** il se tue à la tâche; **can you** ~ **the sewing machine?** sais-tu te servir de la machine à coudre?; **the machine is** ~**ed by electricity** la machine marche à l'électricité.

(b) (*achieve by* ~) *miracle* faire, accomplir; *change* apporter. **to** ~ **wonders** *or* **marvels** *[person]* faire des merveilles; *[drug, medicine, action, suggestion etc]* faire merveille; **he** ~**ed his passage to Australia** il a payé son passage en travaillant à bord du bateau sur lequel il a gagné l'Australie; **to** ~ **one's way through college** travailler pour payer ses études (*V also* **4d**); (*fig*) **he has managed to** ~ **his promotion*** il s'est débrouillé pour obtenir son avancement; **can you** ~ **it* so that she can come too?** pouvez-vous faire en sorte qu'elle puisse venir aussi?; **I'll** ~ **it* if I can** si je peux m'arranger pour le faire je le ferai; **he** ~**ed his audience (up) into a frenzy of enthusiasm** il est arrivé par degrés à soulever l'enthousiasme de son auditoire; **he** ~**ed himself (up) into a rage** il s'est mis dans une colère noire; *V* **oracle.**

(c) (*operate, exploit*) *mine, land* exploiter, faire valoir. (*Comm*) **this representative** ~**s the south-east region** ce représentant couvre la région du sud-est.

(d) (*manoeuvre etc*) **to** ~ **a ship into position** exécuter une manœuvre pour placer un bateau en position (opérationnelle); **he** ~**ed the rope gradually through the hole** il est petit à petit arrivé à faire passer la corde dans le trou; **he** ~**ed his hands**

free il est arrivé à délier ses mains; **to ~ sth loose** arriver à desserrer qch; **he ~ed the lever up and down** il a levé et baissé le levier plusieurs fois; **she ~ed the hook carefully out of the cloth** en s'y prenant minutieusement elle a réussi à enlever le crochet du tissu; **he ~ed the incident into his speech** il s'est arrangé pour introduire *or* parler de l'incident dans son discours; **he ~ed his way along to the edge of the roof** il s'est approché graduellement du rebord du toit; **I saw him ~ing his way round towards me** je l'ai vu qui s'approchait de moi petit à petit.

(e) (*make, shape*) *metal, wood, leather etc* travailler, façonner; *dough, clay* travailler, pétrir; *object* façonner (*out of* dans); (*sew*) coudre; (*embroider*) *design etc* broder. (*Culin*) **~ the butter and sugar together** travaillez bien le beurre et le sucre; **~ the flour in gradually** incorporez la farine petit à petit.

work away *vi:* **they worked away all day** ils ont passé toute la journée à travailler; **she was working away at her embroidery** elle continuait à faire sa broderie.

work down *vi [stockings etc]* glisser.

work in 1 *vi* **(a)** *[dust, sand etc]* s'introduire, s'insinuer.

(b) (*cooperate etc*) **she works in with us as much as possible** elle collabore avec nous autant que possible; **this doesn't work in with our plans for ...** ceci ne cadre pas *or* ne concorde pas avec nos projets pour ...; **that'll work in quite well** ça cadrera très bien.

2 *vt sep bolt, nut, stick etc* introduire petit à petit; *reference, quotation, subject etc* glisser, introduire. **we'll work in a mention of it somewhere** on s'arrangera pour le mentionner quelque part; *V also* **work 4e.**

work off 1 *vi [nut, handle etc]* se détacher.

2 *vt sep* **(a)** *debt, obligation* acquitter en travaillant.

(b) *one's surplus fat* se débarrasser de; *weight* éliminer; *frustration, rage* passer, assouvir. **to work off one's energy** dépenser son surplus d'énergie; **don't work off your annoyance on me!** ne passe pas ta mauvaise humeur sur moi!

work out 1 *vi* **(a)** *[plan, arrangement]* aboutir, réussir, marcher; *[puzzle, problem, sum]* se résoudre exactement, marcher*. **what does the total work out at?** cela s'élève à *or* fait combien en tout?; **it works out at 5 apples per child** ça fait 5 pommes par enfant; **it's all working out as planned** tout se déroule comme prévu; **things didn't work out (well) for her** les choses ont plutôt mal tourné pour elle; **their marriage didn't work out** leur mariage n'a pas marché*; **it will work out (right) in the end** tout finira (bien) par s'arranger; **how did it work out?** comment ça a marché?*

(b) *[athlete, boxer etc]* s'entraîner.

2 *vt sep* **(a)** *calculation, equation* résoudre; *answer, total* trouver; *code* déchiffrer; *problem* résoudre; *puzzle* faire résoudre; *plan, scheme, idea* élaborer, mettre au point. **how much? — I'll have to work it out** combien ça fait? — il faut que je calcule (*subj*); **who worked all this out?** qui a eu l'idée de tout ça?; **can you work out where we are on the map?** peux-tu découvrir où nous sommes sur la carte?; **he worked out why she'd gone** il a fini par découvrir pourquoi elle était partie; **I can't work it out** ça me dépasse.

(b) (*exhaust resources of*) *mine, land* épuiser.

3 workout *n V* **work 2.**

work round *vi* (*in conversation, negotiations etc*) **you'll have to work round to that subject tactfully** il faudra que vous abordiez (*subj*) ce sujet avec tact; **what are you working round to?** où voulez-vous en venir?; *V also* **work 3c.**

work up 1 *vi* **(a) events were working up to a climax** on était au bord de la crise, une crise se préparait; **the book works up to a dramatic ending** l'auteur a su amener un dénouement dramatique; (*in conversation etc*) **to work up to sth** en venir à qch, préparer le terrain pour qch; **what is he working up to?** où veut-il bien en venir?; **I thought he was working up to a proposal** je croyais qu'il préparait le terrain pour faire sa demande.

(b) *[garment etc]* remonter.

2 *vt sep trade, business* développer. **he worked the firm up from almost nothing into a major company** en partant pratiquement de rien il a réussi à faire de cette firme une compagnie de grande envergure; **he worked his way up to the top of his firm** il a gravi un à un tous les échelons de la hiérarchie dans son entreprise; **he worked his way up from nothing** il est parti de rien et s'est élevé à la force du poignet; (*Comm*) **he's trying to work up a connection in Wales** il essaie d'établir une liaison au Pays de Galles; **he worked the crowd up into a fury** il a déchaîné la fureur de la foule; **to work up an appetite** s'ouvrir l'appétit; **I can't work up much enthusiasm for the plan** je n'arrive pas à m'enthousiasmer beaucoup pour ce projet; **can't you work up a little more interest in it?** tu ne pourrais pas t'y intéresser un petit peu plus?; **to work o.s. up, to get worked up** se mettre dans tous ses états, s'énerver.

workable ['wɜːkəbl] *adj* **(a)** *scheme, arrangement, solution, suggestion* possible, réalisable. **it's just not ~** ça ne marchera jamais. **(b)** *mine, land* exploitable.

worker ['wɜːkəʳ] **1** *n* travailleur *m*, -euse *f*, ouvrier *m*, -ière *f*. (*esp Agr, Ind etc*) **woman ~** ouvrière; **he's a good ~** il travaille bien; **he's a fast ~** (*lit*) il travaille vite; (**fig*) il ne perd pas de temps; **all the ~s in this industry** tous ceux qui travaillent dans cette industrie; (*Ind*) **management and ~s** patronat *m* et travailleurs; **we rely on volunteer ~s** nous dépendons de travailleurs bénévoles; **office ~** employé(e) *m(f)* de bureau; **research ~** chercheur *m*, -euse *f*.

2 *cpd:* **worker ant** ouvrière *f*, fourmi *f* neutre; **worker bee** (abeille) ouvrière *f*; (*Ind*) **worker director** ouvrier *m* faisant partie du conseil d'administration; (*Ind*) **worker participation in decisions** participation *f* des ouvriers aux décisions; **worker priest** prêtre-ouvrier *m*.

working ['wɜːkɪŋ] **1** *adj clothes, lunch, dinner* de travail; *model* qui marche; *partner* actif. **~ capital** fonds *mpl* de roulement; **the ~ class** la classe ouvrière (*V also* 2); **the ~ classes** le prolétariat; **a ~ day of 8 hours** une journée de travail de 8 heures; **Saturday is a ~ day** (*gen*) on travaille le samedi; (*Comm*) le samedi est un jour ouvrable; **~ drawing** épure *f*; **good ~ environment** bonnes conditions de travail; **~ expenses** *[mine, factory]* frais *mpl* d'exploitation; *[salesman]* frais; (*Pol etc*) **to have a ~ majority** avoir une majorité suffisante; (*Ind, Soc etc*) **the ~ man will not accept ...** les ouvriers *mpl or* les travailleurs *mpl* n'accepteront pas ...; **he's an ordinary ~ man** c'est un simple ouvrier; **he's a ~ man now** il travaille maintenant, il gagne sa vie maintenant; (*Brit*) **~ party** commission *f* d'enquête; **a ~ wife** une femme mariée qui travaille; **she's an ordinary ~ woman** c'est une simple ouvrière; **she is a ~ woman** elle travaille, elle gagne sa vie; *V* **order.**

2 *cpd*: **working-class** *origins, background, accent, suburb* ouvrier, prolétarien; **he is working-class** il est issu de *or* il appartient à la classe ouvrière.

3 *n* **(a) ~s** *[watch, mechanism]* mécanisme *m*, rouages *mpl*; (*Min*) chantier *m* d'exploitation; **I don't understand the ~s of her mind** je ne comprends pas ce qui se passe dans sa tête.

(b) (*U*) (*work*) travail *m*; *[machine etc]* fonctionnement *m*; *[yeast]* fermentation *f*; *[mine, land]* exploitation *f*; *[metal, wood, leather, clay, dough]* travail; (*Sewing*) couture *f*; (*embroidery*) broderie *f*.

workman ['wɜːkmən] *pl* **workmen 1** *n* **(a)** (*gen, Comm, Ind etc*) ouvrier *m*. **a ~ came to fix the roof** un ouvrier est venu réparer le toit; (*Prov*) **a bad ~ blames his tools** les mauvais ouvriers se plaignent toujours de leurs outils (*Prov*).

(b) to be a good ~ bien travailler, avoir du métier.

2 *cpd*: **workmanlike** *person, attitude* professionnel; *object, product, tool* bien fait, soigné; **it was a workmanlike essay** c'était une dissertation honnête *or* bien travaillée; **he made a workmanlike job of it** il a fait du bon travail; **he set about it in a very workmanlike way** il s'y est pris comme un vrai professionnel.

workmanship ['wɜːkmənʃɪp] *n [craftsman]* métier *m*, maîtrise *f*. **this example of his ~** cet exemple de sa maîtrise *or* de son habileté professionnelle *or* de ce qu'il est capable de faire; **a chair of fine ~** une chaise faite avec art; **a superb piece of ~** un *or* du travail superbe.

workmen ['wɜːkmən] *npl of* **workman.**

world [wɜːld] **1** *n* **(a)** (*gen, Geog etc*) monde *m*. **all over the ~, all the ~ over** dans le monde entier; **to go round the ~, to go on a trip round the ~** *or* **a round-the-~ tour** faire le tour du monde, voyager autour du monde; **a round-the-~ cruise** une croisière autour du monde; **to see the ~** voir du pays, courir le monde; **the most powerful nation in the ~** la nation la plus puissante du monde; **it is known throughout the ~** c'est connu dans le monde entier, c'est universellement connu; **our company leads the ~ in shoe manufacturing** notre compagnie est à la pointe de l'industrie de la chaussure dans le monde; **~s out in space** mondes extra-terrestres; **to be alone in the ~** être seul au monde; **it's a small ~!** (que) le monde est petit!; **the New W~** le Nouveau Monde; **the ancient ~** le monde antique, l'antiquité *f*; **the English-speaking ~** le monde anglophone; **the ~ we live in** le monde où nous vivons; **in the ~ of tomorrow** dans le monde de demain; **since the ~ began, since the beginning of the ~** depuis que le monde est monde; (*Rel*) **~ without end** dans les siècles des siècles; **he is a citizen of the ~** c'est un citoyen du monde; **his childhood was a ~ of hot summers and lazy days** son enfance était un univers d'étés brûlants et de journées oisives; (*fig*) **he lives in a ~ of his own** il vit dans un monde à lui; (*fig*) **to be dead to the ~** (*asleep*) dormir profondément; (*drunk*) être ivre mort; *V* **old, old-world.**

(b) (*emphatic phrases*) **to think the ~ of sb** ne jurer que par qn, avoir la plus haute estime *or* admiration pour qn; **she's all the ~ to him** elle est tout pour lui; **it did him a ~ of good** ça lui a fait énormément de bien *or* un bien fou*; **there's a ~ of difference between Paul and Richard** il y a un monde entre Paul et Richard; **their views are ~s apart** leurs opinions sont diamétralement opposées; **it was for all the ~ as if ...** c'était exactement *or* tout à fait comme si ...; **I'm the ~'s worst cook** il n'y a pas au monde pire cuisinière que moi; **I'd give the ~ to know ...** je donnerais tout au monde pour savoir ...; **it's what he wants most in (all) the ~** c'est ce qu'il veut plus que tout au monde; **in the whole (wide) ~ you won't find a better man than he is** nulle part au monde vous ne trouverez un meilleur homme que lui; **nowhere in the ~, nowhere in the whole (wide) ~** nulle part au monde; **I wouldn't do it for (anything in) the ~, nothing in the ~ would make me do it** je ne le ferais pour rien au monde, je ne le ferais pas pour tout l'or du monde; **what/where/why/how in the ~ ...?** que/où/pourquoi/comment diable* ...?; **where in the ~ has he got to?** où a-t-il bien pu passer?, où diable* est-ce qu'il est passé?

(c) (*this life etc*) monde *m*; (*Rel: as opposed to spiritual life*) siècle *m*, monde; (*domain, realm*) monde, univers *m*. **in this ~** ici-bas, en ce (bas) monde; (*fig*) **it's out of this ~*** c'est extraordinaire, c'est sensationnel*; **the next ~, the ~ to come** l'au-delà, l'autre monde; **he's gone to a better ~** il est parti pour un monde meilleur; **he's not long for this ~** il n'en a plus pour longtemps (à vivre); (*Rel*) **in the ~** dans le siècle; (*Rel*) **the ~, the flesh and the devil** les tentations *fpl* du monde, de la chair et du diable; **to bring a child into the ~** mettre un enfant au monde; **to come into the ~** venir au monde, naître; **the ~ of nature** le monde de la nature; **the business/sporting ~** le monde des affaires/du sport; **in the university ~** dans les milieux universitaires; **in the ~ of music** dans le monde de la musique; **the ~**

of dreams l'univers *or* le monde des rêves; in the best of all possible ~s dans le meilleur des mondes (possibles); *V* best, other.

(d) *(society etc)* monde *m.* a man of the ~ un homme du monde; to go up in the ~ faire du chemin *(fig);* to come down in the ~ déchoir; he has come down in the ~ il a connu de meilleurs jours; to make one's way in the ~ faire son chemin dans le monde; he had the ~ at his feet il avait le monde à ses pieds; you have to take the ~ as you find it il faut prendre le monde comme il est *or* les choses comme elles sont; the ~ and his wife absolument tout le monde, tout le monde sans exception; you know what the ~ will say if ... tu sais ce que les gens diront si ... .

2 *cpd power, war, proportions* mondial; *record, tour* du monde; *language* universel. *(Fin)* the World Bank la Banque internationale pour la reconstruction et le développement; *(fig)* it's a world-beater* cela a eu un succès fou*; world boxing champion champion *m* du monde de boxe; *(Sport)* world champion champion *m* du monde; world championship championnat *m* du monde; *(Jur)* the World Court la Cour internationale de justice; *(Ftbl)* the World Cup la Coupe du monde; *(Comm)* World Fair Exposition Internationale; world-famous de renommée mondiale, célèbre dans le monde entier; World Health Organization *(abbr* WHO*)* Organisation mondiale de la santé *(abbr* O.M.S.); on a world scale à l'échelle mondiale; *(US Baseball)* World Series championnat *m* du monde; world-shaking stupéfiant; World War One/Two la Première/Deuxième *or* Seconde guerre mondiale; world-weariness dégoût *m* du monde; world-weary las (*f* lasse) du monde; world-wide mondial, universel.

worldliness ['wɜ:ldlɪnɪs] *n [person]* attachement *m* aux biens de ce monde; *(Rel)* mondanité *f.*

worldly ['wɜ:ldlɪ] 1 *adj matters, pleasures* de ce monde, terrestre; *attitude* matérialiste; *(also* ~-minded*) person* attaché aux biens de ce monde; *(Rel)* mondain, temporel. his ~ goods sa fortune, ses biens temporels.

2 *cpd:* worldly-wisdom expérience *f* du monde, savoir-faire *m;* worldly-wise qui a l'expérience du monde.

worm [wɜ:m] 1 *n (gen: earth~ etc)* ver *m* (de terre); *(in fruit etc)* ver; *(maggot)* asticot *m; (fig: person)* minable* *mf,* miteux* *m,* -euse* *f. (Med)* ~s vers; *(fig)* the ~ has turned il en a eu *(or* j'en ai eu *etc)* assez de se *(or* me *etc)* faire marcher dessus; *(US fig)* a can of ~s* un véritable guêpier *(fig);* you ~!* misérable!; *V* book, glow, silk *etc.*

2 *cpd:* worm-cast déjections *fpl* de ver; *(Tech)* worm drive transmission *f* par vis sans fin; worm-eaten *fruit* véreux; *furniture* mangé aux vers, vermoulu; *(fig)* désuet (*f* -ète), suranné; *(Tech)* worm gear engrenage *m* à vis sans fin; wormhole piqûre *f or* trou *m* de ver; *(Vet)* worm(ing) powder poudre *f* vermifuge; wormlike vermiculaire, vermiforme; *(fig)* a worm's-eye view of what is going on un humble aperçu de ce qui se passe; wormwood *V* wormwood.

3 *vt* (a) *(wriggle)* to ~ o.s. *or* one's way along/down/across *etc* avancer/descendre/traverser *etc* à plat ventre *or* en rampant; he ~ed his way through the narrow window il a réussi en se tortillant à passer par la lucarne; *(fig)* he ~ed his way into our group il s'est insinué *or* immiscé dans notre groupe.

(b) *(extract)* to ~ sth out of sb soutirer qch à qn; I'll ~ it out of him somehow je m'arrangerai pour lui tirer les vers du nez.

(c) *(rid of ~s) dog etc* débarrasser de ses vers.

wormwood ['wɜ:mwʊd] *n* armoise *f. (fig)* it was ~ to him cela le mortifiait.

wormy ['wɜ:mɪ] *adj fruit* véreux; *furniture* vermoulu, mangé aux vers; *soil* plein de vers; *shape* vermiculaire.

worn [wɔ:n] 1 *ptp of* wear. 2 *adj garment, carpet, tyre, hands, machine part* usé; *person* las (*f* lasse); *V also* wear. 3 *cpd:* worn-out *garment, carpet, tyre* usé jusqu'à la corde; *tool, machine part* complètement usé; *person* épuisé, fourbu, éreinté; *V also* wear.

worried ['wʌrɪd] *adj* inquiet (*f* -ète). to be ~ about sth être inquiet de *or* au sujet de *or* pour qch; ~ to death* fou (*f* folle) d'inquiétude; *V also* worry.

worrier ['wʌrɪəʳ] *n* inquiet *m,* -ète *f.* he's a dreadful ~ c'est un éternel inquiet.

worrisome ['wʌrɪsəm] *adj* inquiétant.

worry ['wʌrɪ] 1 *n* souci *m.* the ~ of having to find the money le souci d'avoir à trouver l'argent; he hasn't any worries il est sans souci; that's the least of my worries c'est le cadet *or* le moindre de mes soucis; what's your ~?* qu'est-ce qui ne va pas?; he is a constant ~ to his parents il est un perpétuel souci pour ses parents; it is a great ~ to us all, it's causing us a lot of ~ cela nous fait faire *or* nous cause *or* nous donne beaucoup de souci(s); what a ~ it all is! tout ça c'est bien du souci!

2 *cpd:* *(US)* worrywart* éternel inquiet, éternelle inquiète.

3 *vi* (a) se faire du souci, s'inquiéter, s'en faire* *(about, over* pour), *(stronger)* se tourmenter, se faire de la bile *or* du mauvais sang *(about, over* pour). don't ~ about me ne vous faites pas de souci *or* ne vous inquiétez pas *or* ne vous en faites pas* pour moi; she worries about her health sa santé la tracasse; *(iro)* I should ~!* je ne vois pas pourquoi je m'en ferais!*; I'll punish him if I catch him, don't you ~!* je le punirai si je l'y prends, (ne) t'en fais pas!*

(b) to ~ at sth = to ~ sth; *V* 4b.

4 *vt* (a) *(make anxious)* inquiéter, tracasser. it worries me that he should believe ... cela m'inquiète qu'il puisse croire ...; the whole business worries me to death* j'en suis fou d'inquiétude; don't ~ yourself about it ne te fais pas de mauvais sang *or* ne te mets pas martel en tête pour ça; she worried herself sick over it all elle s'est rendue malade à force de se faire du souci pour tout ça, elle s'est rongé les sangs à propos de tout ça; what's ~ing you? qu'est-ce qui ne va pas?; *V also* worried.

(b) *[dog etc] bone, rat, ball* prendre entre les dents et secouer, jouer avec; *sheep* harceler. he kept ~ing the loose tooth with his tongue il n'arrêtait pas d'agacer avec sa langue la dent qui branlait.

worry along *vi* continuer à se faire du souci.

worry out *vt sep problem* résoudre à force de retourner dans tous les sens.

worrying ['wʌrɪɪŋ] 1 *adj* inquiétant. the ~ thing is that ... ce qui m'inquiète *or* ce qui est inquiétant c'est qu'il ...; to have a ~ time passer un mauvais quart d'heure, *(longer)* en voir de dures*.

2 *n:* ~ does no good il ne sert à rien de se faire du souci; all this ~ has aged him tout le souci qu'il s'est fait l'a vieilli; *V* sheep.

worse [wɜ:s] 1 *adj, comp of* bad *and* ill pire, plus mauvais. your essay is ~ than his: his is bad but yours is ~ votre dissertation est plus mauvaise que la sienne: la sienne est mauvaise mais la vôtre est pire; you're ~ than he is! tu es pire que lui!; and, (what's) ~ ... et, qui pis est ...; it's ~ than ever c'est pire *or* pis *(liter)* que jamais; it could have been ~ ç'aurait pu être pire; things couldn't be ~ ça ne pourrait pas aller plus mal; ~ things have happened on a vu pire; *(fig hum)* ~ things happen at sea* ce n'est pas le bout du monde; and, to make matters *or* things ~, he ... et, pour comble de malheur, il ...; you've only made matters *or* things *or* it ~ tu n'as fait qu'aggraver la situation *(or* ton cas*) or* qu'envenimer les choses; he made matters ~ for himself by refusing il a aggravé son cas en refusant; things will get ~ before they get better les choses iront plus mal avant d'aller mieux; it gets ~ and ~ ça ne fait qu'empirer, ça va de mal en pis *or* de pis en pis; he is getting ~ *(in behaviour, memory, faculties)* il ne s'améliore *or* s'arrange pas; *(in health)* il va de plus en plus mal, son état ne fait que s'aggraver *or* qu'empirer; to get ~ *[rheumatism etc]* empirer; *[climate, weather, food]* se détériorer, se gâter; *[economic situation, conditions]* se détériorer, empirer; the smell is getting ~ ça sent de plus en plus mauvais; I feel slightly ~ je me sens légèrement moins bien *or* plutôt plus mal; business is ~ than ever les affaires vont plus mal que jamais; it will be the ~ for you if ... c'est vous qui serez perdant si ...; so much the ~ for him! tant pis pour lui!; he's none the ~ for his fall il ne s'est pas ressenti de sa chute; he's none the ~ for it il ne s'en porte pas plus mal; the house would be none the ~ for a coat of paint une couche de peinture ne ferait pas de mal à cette maison; to be the ~ for drink être éméché *or (stronger)* ivre.

2 *adv, comp of* badly *and* ill *sing, play etc* plus mal. he did it ~ than you did il l'a fait plus mal que toi; it hurts ~ than ever ça fait plus mal que jamais; that child behaves ~ and ~ cet enfant se conduit de mal en pis; you might do ~ than to accept accepter n'est pas ce que vous pourriez faire de pire; you might *or* could do ~ vous pourriez faire pire *or* pis *(liter);* he is ~ off than before il se retrouve dans une situation pire qu'avant, il se retrouve encore plus mal en point qu'avant; I like him none the ~ for that je ne l'en aime pas moins pour ça; I shan't think any the ~ of you for it je n'en aurai pas une moins bonne opinion de toi pour ça; it's raining ~ than ever il pleut pire *or* pis que jamais; she hates me ~ than before elle me déteste encore plus qu'avant; he was taken ~ during the night son état a empiré *or* s'est aggravé pendant la nuit.

3 *n* pire *m.* I have ~ to tell you je ne vous ai pas tout dit, il y a pire encore; there's ~ to come on n'a pas vu le pire; ~ followed ensuite cela a été pire; there has been a change for the ~ *(gen)* il y a eu une détérioration très nette de la situation; *(Med)* il y a eu une aggravation très nette de son état; *V* bad.

worsen ['wɜ:sn] 1 *vi [situation, conditions]* empirer, se détériorer; *[sb's state, health]* empirer, s'aggraver; *[rheumatism]* empirer; *[chances of success]* diminuer, se gâter; *[relationship]* se détériorer, se gâter.

2 *vt* empirer, rendre pire.

worship ['wɜ:ʃɪp] 1 *n* (a) *(Rel)* adoration *f,* culte *m,* vénération *f;* *(organized ~)* culte, office *m;* *(gen: of person)* adoration, culte; *(of money, success etc)* culte. *(Rel)* place of ~ édifice consacré au culte, église *f,* temple *m;* *(Rel)* hours of ~ heures *fpl* des offices; *V* hero *etc.*

(b) *(esp Brit: in titles)* His W~ (the Mayor) Monsieur le maire; Your W~ *(to Mayor)* Monsieur le Maire; *(to magistrate)* Monsieur le Juge.

2 *vt* *(Rel)* *God, idol etc* adorer, vénérer, rendre un culte à; *(gen)* adorer, vénérer, avoir un culte pour, vouer un culte à; *money, success etc* avoir le culte de. he ~ped the ground she trod on il vénérait jusqu'au sol qu'elle foulait.

3 *vi* *(Rel)* faire ses dévotions.

worshipful ['wɜ:ʃɪpfʊl] *adj* *(esp Brit: in titles)* the W~ Mayor of ... Monsieur le maire de ...; the W~ Company of Goldsmiths l'honorable compagnie des orfèvres.

worshipper ['wɜ:ʃɪpəʳ] *n* *(Rel, fig)* adorateur *m,* -trice *f.* *(churchgoers)* ~s fidèles *mpl.*

worst [wɜ:st] 1 *adj, superl of* bad *and* ill le *(or* la*)* pire, le *(or* la*)* plus mauvais(e). that was the ~ hotel we found c'est le plus mauvais hôtel que nous ayons trouvé; the ~ film I've ever seen le plus mauvais film *or* le pire navet que j'aie jamais vu; the ~ student in the class le plus mauvais élève de la classe; that was his ~ mistake cela a été son erreur la plus grave; it was the ~ thing he ever did c'est la pire chose qu'il ait jamais faite; it was the ~ winter for 20 years c'était l'hiver le plus rude depuis 20 ans; *(Med)* he felt ~ when ... il s'est senti le plus mal quand ...; she arrived at the ~ possible time elle n'aurait pas pu arriver à un plus mauvais moment *or* à un moment plus inopportun; he chose the ~ possible job for a man with a heart condition pour quelqu'un qui souffre du cœur il n'aurait pas pu choisir un emploi plus contre-indiqué.

2 *adv, superl of* badly *and* ill le plus mal. they all sing badly but he sings ~ of all ils chantent tous mal mais c'est lui qui chante le plus mal de tous; the ~-dressed man in England l'homme le plus mal habillé d'Angleterre; he came off ~ c'est lui qui s'en est le plus mal sorti; such people are the ~ off ce sont ces gens-là qui souffrent le plus *or* sont le plus affectés; it's my leg that hurts ~ of all c'est ma jambe qui me fait le plus mal; that boy behaved ~ of all ce garçon a été le pire de tous.

3 *n* pire *m*, pis *m* (*liter*). the ~ that can happen le pire *or* la pire chose *or* le pis (*liter*) qui puisse arriver; at (the) ~ au pis aller; to be at its (*or* their) ~ *[crisis, storm, winter, epidemic]* être à *or* avoir atteint son (*or* leur) paroxysme *or* son (*or* leur) point culminant; *[situation, conditions, relationships]* n'avoir jamais été aussi mauvais; at the ~ of the storm/epidemic au plus fort de l'orage/de l'épidémie; things *or* matters were at their ~ les choses ne pouvaient pas aller plus mal; the ~ is yet to come il faut s'attendre à pire, on n'a pas encore vu le pire; the ~ was yet to come le pire devait arriver ensuite, on n'avait pas encore vu le pire; he feared the ~ il craignait le pire; the ~ of it is that ... le pire c'est que ...; ... and that's not the ~ of it! ... et il y a pire encore!; that's the ~ of ... ça c'est l'inconvénient de ...; if the ~ comes to the ~ en mettant les choses au pis, même en envisageant le pire; the ~ hasn't come to the ~ yet ce pourrait encore être pire, la situation n'est pas désespérée; to get the ~ of it *or* of the bargain* être le perdant, avoir la mauvaise part; do your ~! vous pouvez toujours essayer!; it brings out the ~ in me ça réveille en moi les pires instincts.

4 *vt* battre, avoir la supériorité sur. to be ~ed avoir le dessous.

worsted ['wʊstɪd] 1 *n* worsted *m*. 2 *cpd suit etc* en worsted.

worth [wɜːθ] 1 *n* (a) (*value*) valeur *f*. what is its ~ in today's money? ça vaut combien *or* quelle est sa valeur en argent d'aujourd'hui?; its ~ in gold sa valeur (en) or; a book/man *etc* of great ~ un livre/homme *etc* de grande valeur; I know his ~ je sais ce qu'il vaut; he showed his true ~ il a montré sa vraie valeur *or* ce dont il était capable.

(b) (*quantity*) he bought 20 pence ~ of sweets il a acheté pour 20 pence de bonbons; 50 pence ~, please (pour) 50 pence s'il vous plaît; *V* money, penny *etc*.

2 *adj* (a) (*equal in value to*) to be ~ valoir; the book is ~ £10 le livre vaut 10 livres; it can't be ~ that! ça ne peut pas valoir autant!; what *or* how much is it ~? ça vaut combien?; I don't know what it's ~ in terms of cash je ne sais pas combien ça vaut en argent *or* quel prix ça pourrait aller chercher; how much is the old man ~? à combien s'élève la fortune du vieux?; it's ~ a great deal ça a beaucoup de valeur, ça vaut cher; it's ~ a great deal to me ça a beaucoup de valeur pour moi; what is his friendship ~ to you? quel prix attachez-vous à son amitié?; it's more than my life is ~ to do that ma vie ne vaudrait pas la peine d'être vécue si je faisais ça; it's as much as my job is ~ to show him that lui montrer ça est un coup à perdre mon emploi*; to be ~ one's weight in gold valoir son pesant d'or; it's not ~ the paper it's written on ça ne vaut pas le papier sur lequel c'est écrit; this pen is ~ 10 of any other make ce stylo en vaut 10 d'une autre marque; one Scotsman's ~ 3 Englishmen un Écossais vaut 3 Anglais; tell me about it — what's it ~ to you?* dites-le-moi — vous donneriez combien pour le savoir? *or* (vous êtes prêt à payer) combien?*; I'll give you my opinion for what it's ~ je vais vous dire ce que j'en pense, prenez-le pour ce que ça vaut; he was running/shouting for all he was ~ il courait/criait comme un perdu *or* de toutes ses forces; to try for all one is ~ to do sth faire absolument tout son possible pour faire qch.

(b) (*deserving, meriting*) it's ~ the effort ça mérite qu'on fasse l'effort; it was well ~ the trouble ça valait bien le dérangement *or* la peine qu'on se dérange (*subj*); it's not ~ the time and effort involved c'est une perte de temps et d'effort; the book is not ~ reading le livre ne vaut pas la peine d'être lu; it's not ~ having ça ne vaut rien*; that's ~ knowing c'est bon à savoir; it's ~ thinking about ça mérite réflexion; it's ~ going to see the film just for the photography rien que pour la photographie le film mérite *or* vaut la peine d'être vu; (*Prov*) what is ~ doing is ~ doing well ce qui vaut la peine d'être fait vaut la peine d'être bien fait (*Prov*); it's ~ it ça vaut la peine *or* le coup*; will you go? — is it ~ it? tu iras? — est-ce que ça en vaut la peine?; life isn't ~ living la vie ne vaut pas la peine d'être vécue; the museum is ~ a visit le musée vaut la visite; it is ~ while to study the text on gagne à étudier le texte, c'est un texte qui mérite d'être étudié; it would be ~ (your) while to go and see him vous gagneriez à aller le voir; it's not ~ (my) while waiting for him je perds (*or* perdrais) mon temps à l'attendre; it's not ~ while ça ne vaut pas le coup*; it wasn't ~ his while to take the job il ne gagnait rien à accepter l'emploi, ça ne valait pas le coup* qu'il accepte (*subj*) l'emploi; I'll make it ~ your while* je vous récompenserai de votre peine, vous ne regretterez pas de l'avoir fait.

3 *cpd:* worthwhile *visit* qui en vaut la peine; *book* qui mérite d'être lu; *film* qui mérite d'être vu; *work, job, occupation, life, career* utile, qui a un sens, qui donne des satisfactions; *contribution* notable, très valable; *cause* louable, digne d'intérêt; he is a worthwhile person to go and see c'est une personne qu'on gagne à aller voir; I want the money to go to someone worthwhile je veux que l'argent aille à quelqu'un qui le mérite *or* à une personne méritante.

worthily ['wɜːðɪlɪ] *adv* dignement.

worthiness ['wɜːðɪnɪs] *n* (*V* worthy 1b) caractère *m* digne *or* brave; caractère louable *or* noble.

worthless ['wɜːθlɪs] *adj object, advice, contribution* qui ne vaut rien; *effort* vain. he's a ~ individual il ne vaut pas cher, il n'est bon à rien; he's not completely ~ il n'est pas complètement dénué de qualités.

worthlessness ['wɜːθlɪsnɪs] *n [object, advice]* absence totale de valeur; *[effort]* inutilité *f*; *[person]* absence totale de qualités.

worthy ['wɜːðɪ] 1 *adj* (a) (*deserving*) digne (*of* de). to be ~ of sth/sb être digne de qch/qn, mériter qch/qn; to be ~ to do être digne de faire, mériter de faire; he found a ~ opponent *or* an opponent ~ of him il a trouvé un adversaire digne de lui; it is ~ of note that ... il est bon de remarquer que ...; nothing ~ of mention rien de notable; ~ of respect digne de respect; ~ of praise louable, digne d'éloge.

(b) (*meritorious*) *person* digne, brave; *motive, cause, aim, effort* louable, noble. the ~ people of Barcombe les dignes *or* braves habitants *mpl* de Barcombe; the ~ poor les pauvres méritants.

2 *n* (*Hist*) notable *m*; (*hum iro*) brave homme *m*, brave femme *f*. a Victorian ~ un notable sous le règne de Victoria; (*hum iro*) the village worthies les dignes *or* braves habitants *mpl* du village.

wot†† [wɒt] *vti* sais, sait. God ~ Dieu sait.

wotcher‡ ['wɒtʃə^r] *excl* (*Brit*) salut!

would [wʊd] 1 *modal aux vb* (*cond of* will: *neg* would not *often abbr to* wouldn't) (a) (*used to form cond tenses*) he would do it if you asked him il le ferait si vous le lui demandiez; he would have done it if you had asked him il l'aurait fait si vous le lui aviez demandé; I wondered if you'd come je me demandais si vous viendriez *or* si vous alliez venir; I thought you'd want to know j'ai pensé que vous aimeriez le savoir; who would have thought it? qui l'aurait pensé?; so it would seem c'est bien ce qu'il semble; you would think she had enough to do without ... on pourrait penser qu'elle a assez à faire sans ... .

(b) (*indicating conjecture*) it would have been about 8 o'clock when he came il devait être 8 heures à peu près quand il est venu, il a dû venir vers 8 heures; he'd have been about fifty if he'd lived il aurait eu la cinquantaine s'il avait vécu; he'd be about 50, but he doesn't look it il doit avoir dans les 50 ans, mais il ne les fait pas*; I saw him come out of the shop — when would this be? je l'ai vu sortir du magasin — quand est-ce que c'était?

(c) (*indicating willingness*) I said I would do it je lui ai dit que je le ferais *or* que je voulais bien le faire; he wouldn't help me il ne voulait pas m'aider, il n'a pas voulu m'aider; the car wouldn't start la voiture n'a pas démarré *or* n'a pas voulu démarrer; if you would come with me, I'd go to see him si vous vouliez bien m'accompagner, j'irais le voir; what would you have me do? que voulez-vous que je fasse?; would you like some tea? voulez-vous *or* voudriez-vous du thé?; would you like to go for a walk? voulez-vous faire une promenade?, est-ce que vous aimeriez faire une promenade?; (*in requests*) would you please leave! voulez-vous partir, s'il vous plaît!; (*frm*) would you be so kind as to tell him auriez-vous l'amabilité *or* la gentillesse de le lui dire; would you mind closing the window please voulez-vous fermer la fenêtre, s'il vous plaît.

(d) (*indicating habit, characteristic*) he would always read the papers before dinner il lisait toujours *or* il avait l'habitude de lire les journaux avant le dîner; 50 years ago the streets would be empty on Sundays il y a 50 ans, les rues étaient vides le dimanche; you WOULD go and tell her! c'est bien de toi d'aller le lui dire!*, il a fallu que tu ailles le lui dire!; you would!* c'est bien de toi!*, ça ne m'étonne pas de toi!; it WOULD have to rain! il pleut, naturellement!, évidemment il fallait qu'il pleuve!

(e) (*subj uses: liter*) would to God she were here! plût à Dieu qu'elle fût ici!; would that it were not so! si seulement cela n'était pas le cas!; would I were younger! si seulement j'étais plus jeune!

2 *cpd:* a would-be poet/teacher une personne qui veut être poète/professeur; (*pej*) un prétendu *or* soi-disant poète/professeur.

wound[1] [wuːnd] 1 *n* (*to person, plant, tree*) blessure *f*, plaie *f*; (*fig: to sb's vanity etc*) blessure. bullet/knife ~ blessure causée par une balle/un couteau; chest/head ~ blessure *or* plaie à la poitrine/tête; *V* lick, salt *etc*. 2 *vt* (*lit, fig*) blesser. he was ~ed in the leg il était blessé à la jambe; the bullet ~ed him in the shoulder la balle l'a atteint *or* l'a blessé à l'épaule; her feelings were *or* she was ~ed by this remark elle a été profondément blessée par cette remarque; *V also* wounded.

wound[2] [waʊnd] *pret, ptp of* wind[2], wind[3].

wounded ['wuːndɪd] 1 *adj soldier* blessé; (*fig*) *vanity etc* blessé. a ~ man un blessé. 2 *npl:* the ~ les blessés *mpl*; *V* walking, war *etc*.

wounding ['wuːndɪŋ] *adj* blessant.

wove [wəʊv] *pret of* weave.

woven ['wəʊvən] *ptp of* weave.

wow‡ [waʊ] 1 *excl* sensass!‡, terrible!* 2 *n:* it's a ~! c'est sensationnel!* *or* terrible!* 3 *vt* emballer*.

wrack[1] [ræk] *vt* = rack[2] 3.

wrack[2] [ræk] *n* = rack[3].

wrack[3] [ræk] *n* (*seaweed*) varech *m*.

wraith [reɪθ] *n* apparition *f*, spectre *m*.

wrangle ['ræŋgl] 1 *n* altercation *f*, dispute *f*. 2 *vi* se disputer, se chamailler* (*about, over* à propos de). they were wrangling over *or* about who should pay ils n'arrivaient pas à s'entendre pour décider qui payerait.

wrangler ['ræŋglə^r] *n* (*Cambridge Univ*) = major *m*; (*US: cowboy*) cowboy *m*.

wrap [ræp] 1 *n* (*shawl*) châle *m*; (*stole, scarf*) écharpe *f*; (*cape*) pèlerine *f*; (*coat*) manteau *m*; (*rug, blanket*) couverture *f*. ~s (*outdoor clothes*) vêtements chauds; (*outer covering: on parcel etc*) emballage *m*; (*fig*) to keep a scheme under ~s* ne pas dévoiler un projet.

2 *cpd:* **wraparound** *or* **wrapover skirt/dress** jupe *f*/robe *f* portefeuille.

3 *vt* (*cover*) envelopper (*in* dans); *parcel* emballer, empaqueter (*in* dans); (*wind*) *tape, bandage* enrouler (*round* autour de). (*Culin*) ~ **the chops in foil** enveloppez les côtelettes dans du papier d'aluminium; **chops ~ped in foil** côtelettes *fpl* en papillotes; (*in shops*) **shall I ~ it for you?** est-ce que je vous l'enveloppe?, est-ce que je vous fais un paquet?; **she ~ped the child in a blanket** elle a enveloppé l'enfant dans une couverture; ~ **the rug round your legs** enroulez la couverture autour de vos jambes, enveloppez vos jambes dans la couverture; **he ~ped his arms round her** il l'a enlacée; **~ped bread/cakes** *etc* pain *m*/gâteaux *mpl* pré-emballé(s) *or* pré-empaqueté(s); (*fig*) **the town was ~ped in mist** la brume enveloppait la ville; **the whole affair was ~ped in mystery** toute l'affaire était enveloppée *or* entourée de mystère; (*fig*) **he ~ped the car round a lamppost**‡ il a encadré* un lampadaire; *V* **gift.**

wrap up 1 *vi* **(a)** (*dress warmly*) s'habiller chaudement, s'emmitoufler. **wrap up well!** couvrez-vous bien!

(b) (*Brit*‡: *be quiet*) se taire, la fermer‡, la boucler‡. **wrap up!** la ferme!‡, boucle-la!‡

2 *vt sep* **(a)** *object* envelopper (*in* dans); *parcel* emballer, empaqueter (*in* dans); *child, person* (*in rug etc*) envelopper, (*in clothes*) emmitoufler; (*fig: conceal*) *one's intentions* dissimuler. **wrap yourself up well!** couvrez-vous bien!; (*fig*) **he wrapped up his meaning in unintelligible jargon** il a entortillé ce qu'il voulait dire dans un jargon tout à fait obscur; **he wrapped it up a bit*, but what he meant was ...** il ne l'a pas dit franchement *or* il l'a enrobé un peu *or* il a quelque peu tourné autour du pot*, mais ce qu'il voulait dire c'est ...; **tell me straight out, don't try to wrap it up*** dis-le moi carrément, n'essaie pas de me dorer la pilule.

(b) (*fig: engrossed*) **to be wrapped up in one's work** être absorbé par *or* ne vivre que pour son travail; **to be wrapped up in sb** penser constamment à qn; **he is quite wrapped up in himself** il ne pense qu'à lui-même.

(c) (*: *conclude*) *deal* conclure. **he hopes to wrap up his business there by Friday evening** il espère conclure *or* régler ce qu'il a à y faire d'ici vendredi soir; **let's get all this wrapped up** finissons-en avec tout ça; **he thought he had everything wrapped up** il pensait avoir tout arrangé *or* réglé.

wrapper ['ræpəʳ] *n* **(a)** *[sweet, chocolate, chocolate bar]* papier *m*; *[parcel]* papier d'emballage; *[newspaper for post]* bande *f*; *[book]* jaquette *f*, couverture *f*. **(b)** (*US: garment*) peignoir *m*.

wrapping ['ræpɪŋ] **1** *n* (*also* **~s**) emballage *m*. **2** *cpd:* **wrapping paper** (*brown paper*) papier *m* d'emballage, papier kraft; (*decorated paper*) papier (pour) cadeau.

wrath [rɒθ] *n* (*liter*) colère *f*, courroux *m* (*liter*).

wrathful ['rɒθfʊl] *adj* (*liter*) courroucé (*liter*).

wrathfully ['rɒθfəlɪ] *adv* (*liter*) avec courroux (*liter*).

wreak [riːk] *vt one's anger etc* assouvir (*upon sb* sur qn); *destruction* entraîner violemment. **to ~ vengeance** *or* **revenge** assouvir une vengeance (*on sb* sur qn); (*lit*) **to ~ havoc** faire des ravages, dévaster; (*fig*) **this ~ed havoc with their plans** cela a bouleversé *or* a chamboulé* tous leurs projets.

wreath [riːθ] *n, pl* **~s** [riːðz] *[flowers]* guirlande *f*, couronne *f*; (*funeral* ~) couronne; *[smoke]* volute *f*, ruban *m*; *[mist]* écharpe *f*. **laurel ~** couronne de laurier.

wreathe [riːð] **1** *vt* **(a)** (*garland*) *person* couronner (*with* de); *window etc* orner (*with* de). (*fig*) **valley ~d in mist** vallée enveloppée de brume; **hills ~d in cloud** collines *fpl* dont le sommet disparaît dans les nuages; **his face was ~d in smiles** son visage était rayonnant.

(b) (*entwine*) *flowers, ribbons* enrouler (*round* autour de), tresser, entrelacer.

2 *vi [smoke]* **to ~ upwards** s'élever en tournoyant.

wreck [rek] **1** *n* **(a)** (**~ed** *ship*) épave *f*, navire naufragé; (*act, event*) naufrage *m*; (*fig: of hopes, plans, ambitions*) naufrage, effondrement *m*, anéantissement *m*. **the ~ of the Hesperus** le naufrage de l'Hespérus; **sunken ~s in the Channel** des épaves englouties au fond de la Manche; **the ship was a total ~** le navire a été entièrement perdu.

(b) (*accident: Aut, Aviat, Rail*) accident *m*; (**~ed** *train/plane/car etc*) train *m*/avion *m*/voiture *f etc* accidenté(e); (*building*) ruines *fpl*, décombres *mpl*; (*person*) épave *f*, loque *f*. (*Rail*) **there has been a ~ near Stratford** il y a eu un accident de chemin de fer près de Stratford; **the car was a complete ~** la voiture était bonne à mettre à la ferraille *or* à envoyer à la casse; **he was a ~** il était l'ombre de lui-même; **he looks a ~** on dirait une loque, il a une mine de déterré.

2 *vt* **(a)** *ship* provoquer le naufrage de; *train* faire dérailler; *plane* détruire; *building* démolir; *mechanism* détraquer, abîmer, bousiller*, esquinter*; *furniture etc* casser, démolir. *[ship, sailor]* **to be ~ed** faire naufrage; **the plane was completely ~ed** il n'est resté que des débris de l'avion; **in his fury he ~ed the whole house** dans sa rage il a tout démoli *or* cassé dans la maison.

(b) (*fig*) *marriage, friendship* briser, être la ruine de; *career* briser; *plans, hopes, ambitions* ruiner, anéantir, annihiler; *negotiations, discussions* faire échouer, saboter; *health* ruiner. **this ~ed his chances of success** cela a anéanti ses chances de succès; **it ~ed my life** cela a brisé ma vie, ma vie en a été brisée.

wreckage ['rekɪdʒ] *n* (*U*) **(a)** (*wrecked ship*) épave *f*, navire naufragé; (*pieces from this*) débris *mpl*; (*Aut, Aviat, Rail etc*) débris; *[building]* décombres *mpl*. (*Aviat, Rail*) **~ was strewn over several kilometres** les débris étaient disséminés sur plusieurs kilomètres; **there are still several bodies in the charred ~** les corps de plusieurs victimes se trouvent encore parmi les débris (*or* décombres) calcinés.

(b) (*act*) *[ship]* naufrage *m*; *[train]* déraillement *m*; (*fig: of hopes, ambitions, plans*) anéantissement *m*.

wrecker ['rekəʳ] *n* **(a)** (*gen*) destructeur *m*, démolisseur *m*; (*Hist: of ships*) naufrageur *m*. **(b)** (*in salvage*) (*person*) sauveteur *m* (d'épave); (*boat*) canot *or* bateau sauveteur; (*truck*) dépanneuse *f*. **(c)** (*in demolition*) *[buildings]* démolisseur *m*; *[cars]* marchand(e) *m(f)* de ferraille.

wrecking ['rekɪŋ] **1** *n* = **wreckage b. 2** *cpd:* **wrecking bar** (pince *f* à) levier *m*.

wren [ren] *n* roitelet *m*. (*Brit Navy*) **W~** Wren *f* (*auxiliaire féminine de la marine royale britannique*).

wrench [rentʃ] **1** *n* **(a)** (*tug*) mouvement violent de torsion; (*Med*) entorse *f*; (*fig: emotional*) déchirement *m*. **he gave the handle a ~** il a tiré de toutes ses forces sur la poignée; **the ~ of parting** le déchirement de la séparation; **it was a ~ when she saw him leave** cela a été un déchirement quand elle l'a vu partir.

(b) (*tool*) clef *f or* clé *f* (à écrous), tourne-à-gauche *m*; *V* **monkey.**

2 *vt handle etc* tirer violemment sur. **to ~ sth (away) from sb** *or* **from sb's grasp** arracher qch des mains de qn; (*Med*) **to ~ one's ankle** se tordre la cheville, se faire une entorse; **to ~ sth off** *or* **out** *or* **away** arracher qch (*of, from* de); **he ~ed himself free** il s'est dégagé avec un mouvement violent; **to ~ a box open** ouvrir de force une boîte.

wrest [rest] *vt object* arracher violemment (*from sb* des mains de qn); *secret, confession* arracher (*from sb* à qn); *power, leadership, title* ravir (*from sb* à qn). **he managed to ~ a living from the poor soil** à force de travail et de persévérance il a réussi à tirer un revenu du maigre sol.

wrestle ['resl] **1** *vi* lutter (corps à corps) (*with sb* contre qn); (*Sport*) lutter à main plate *or* corps à corps, pratiquer la lutte, (*as entertainment*) catcher (*with sb* contre qn). (*fig*) **to ~ with** *problem, one's conscience, sums, device* se débattre avec; *difficulties* se débattre contre, se colleter avec; *temptation, illness, disease* lutter contre; **the pilot ~d with the controls** le pilote se débattait avec les commandes; (*fig*) **she was wrestling with her suitcases** elle peinait avec ses valises, elle avait bien du mal à porter ses valises.

2 *vt opponent* lutter contre; (*Sport*) rencontrer à la lutte *or* au catch.

3 *n* lutte *f*. **to have a ~ with sb** lutter avec qn.

wrestler ['resləʳ] *n* (*Sport*) lutteur *m*, -euse *f*, catcheur *m*, -euse *f*.

wrestling ['reslɪŋ] **1** *n* (*Sport: U*) lutte *f* (à main plate); (*as entertainment*) catch *m*.

2 *cpd:* **wrestling hold** prise *f* de catch *or* de lutte à main plate; **wrestling match** match *m or* rencontre *f* de catch *or* de lutte à main plate.

wretch [retʃ] *n* (*unfortunate*) pauvre hère *m*, pauvre diable *m*, (pauvre) malheureux *m*, -euse *f*; (*pej*) scélérat(e) *m(f)*, misérable *mf*; (*hum*) affreux *m*, -euse *f*, misérable. **he's a filthy ~*** c'est un salaud‡; **you ~!** oh l'affreux!; **cheeky little ~!** petit polisson!, petit misérable!

wretched ['retʃɪd] *adj* **(a)** *person* (*very poor*) misérable; (*unhappy*) malheureux, misérable; (*depressed*) déprimé, démoralisé; (*ill*) malade, mal fichu. **the ~ beggars** les pauvres gueux *mpl*, les miséreux *mpl*; (*conscience-stricken etc*) **I feel ~ about it** je me sens vraiment coupable.

(b) (*poverty-stricken, miserable*) *life, conditions, houses* misérable; (*shamefully small*) *wage* de misère, dérisoire, minable; *sum, amount* misérable (*before n*), insignifiant, minable, dérisoire. **in ~ poverty** dans une misère noire; **~ clothes** vêtements misérables *or* miteux, guenilles *fpl*; **~ slums** taudis *mpl* misérables *or* lamentables.

(c) (*contemptible*) *behaviour, remark* mesquin; (*very bad*) *weather, holiday, meal, results* minable*, lamentable, affreux, pitoyable; (*: *annoying*) maudit (*before n*), fichu* (*before n*). **that was a ~ thing to do** c'était vraiment mesquin de faire ça, il devrait (*or* vous devriez *etc*) avoir honte d'avoir fait ça; **what ~ luck!** quelle déveine!*; **there were some ~ questions in the exam** il y avait quelques questions impossibles *or* épouvantables à l'examen; **I'm a ~ player** je suis un piètre joueur, je joue très mal; **they played a ~ game** ils ont très mal joué; **where's that ~ pencil?*** où est ce fichu* *or* maudit crayon?; **that ~ dog of his*** son maudit chien; **then the ~ woman had to apologize to us!** ensuite la malheureuse femme a dû nous présenter ses excuses!

wretchedly ['retʃɪdlɪ] *adv* (*very poorly*) *live* misérablement, pauvrement; (*unhappily*) *weep, apologize, look* misérablement, pitoyablement; *say, explain* d'un ton pitoyable; (*contemptibly*) *treat, behave* mesquinement, abominablement; *pay* lamentablement, très mal, chichement; (*very badly*) *perform, play, sing* lamentablement, très mal. **~ clad** misérablement vêtu; **his wage is ~ small** son salaire est vraiment dérisoire.

wretchedness ['retʃɪdnɪs] *n* (*extreme poverty*) misère *f*, extrême pauvreté *f*; (*unhappiness*) extrême tristesse *f*; (*shamefulness*) *[amount, wage, sum]* caractère *m* dérisoire *or* pitoyable, extrême modicité *f*; *[act, behaviour]* mesquinerie *f*; (*poor quality*) *[meal, hotel, weather]* extrême médiocrité *f*, caractère minable *or* pitoyable. **his ~ at having to do this** le sentiment de culpabilité et d'impuissance qu'il éprouvait devant la nécessité de faire cela.

wrick [rɪk] **1** *vt* (*Brit*) **to ~ one's ankle** se tordre la cheville; **to ~ one's neck** attraper un torticolis. **2** *n* entorse *f*; (*in neck*) torticolis *m*.

wriggle ['rɪgl] **1** *n:* **with a ~ he freed himself** il s'est dégagé d'un mouvement du corps; **to give a ~** = **to wriggle;** *V* **2.**

2 *vi [worm, snake, eel]* se tortiller; *[fish]* frétiller; *[person]* (*restlessly*) remuer, gigoter*, se trémousser; (*in embarrass-*

ment) se tortiller; (*squeamishly*) frissonner, tressaillir; (*excitedly*) frétiller. **to ~ along/down** *etc [worm etc]* avancer/descendre *etc* en se tortillant; *[person]* avancer/descendre *etc* à plat ventre *or* en rampant; **the fish ~d off the hook** le poisson a réussi à se détacher de l'hameçon, le poisson frétillait tellement qu'il s'est détaché de l'hameçon; **she managed to ~ free** elle a réussi à se dégager en se tortillant *or* en se contorsionnant; **he ~d through the hole in the hedge** il s'est faufilé *or* s'est glissé dans le trou de la haie (en se tortillant); **do stop wriggling (about)!** arrête de te trémousser *or* de gigoter* comme ça!, tiens-toi tranquille!

3 *vt:* **to ~ one's toes/fingers** remuer *or* tortiller les orteils/les doigts; **to ~ one's way along** *etc* = **to ~ along** *etc*; *V* **2.**

wriggle about, wriggle around *vi [worm, snake, eel]* se tortiller; *[fish, tadpole]* frétiller; *[person]* se trémousser, gigoter*; *V also* **wriggle 2.**

wriggle out *vi [worm etc]* sortir; *[person]* se dégager. **the snake wriggled out of the cage** le serpent s'est coulé hors de la cage; **the fish wriggled out of my hand** le poisson m'a glissé des mains *or* m'a glissé entre les doigts; (*fig*) **to wriggle out of a difficulty** esquiver une difficulté; **to wriggle out of a task/a responsibility/the blame** *etc* se dérober à *or* esquiver une tâche/une responsabilité/la réprobation *etc*; **he'll manage to wriggle out of it somehow** il trouvera bien un moyen de s'esquiver *or* de se défiler*, il se ménagera bien une porte de sortie.

wriggler ['rɪglə^r] *n* **(a)** *[child etc]* **he's a dreadful ~** il n'arrête pas de gigoter*, il ne se tient jamais tranquille. **(b)** (*mosquito larva*) larve *f* de moustique.

wriggly ['rɪglɪ] *adj worm, eel, snake* qui se tortille; *fish* frétillant; *child* remuant, qui gigote* *or* se trémousse.

wring [rɪŋ] (*vb: pret, ptp* **wrung**) **1** *n:* **to give clothes a ~** essorer des vêtements.

2 *vt* **(a)** (*squeeze, twist*) serrer, tordre. **to ~ a chicken's neck** tordre le cou à un poulet; **I'll ~ your neck if I catch you!*** je te tordrai le cou si je t'y prends!*; **to ~ one's hands** se tordre les mains (de désespoir); **he wrung my hand, he wrung me by the hand** il m'a serré longuement la main; (*fig*) **a story to ~ one's heart** une histoire à vous fendre le cœur.

(b) (*also* **~ out**) *wet clothes, rag, towel* essorer; *water* exprimer (*from sth* de qch). (*on label*) **'do not ~'** 'ne pas essorer'; **~ a cloth out in cold water and apply to forehead** faites une compresse avec un linge mouillé dans de l'eau froide et appliquez-la sur le front.

(c) (*fig: extort: also* **~ out**) arracher, extorquer. **they wrung a confession/the truth from** *or* **out of him** ils lui ont arraché une confession/la vérité; **he wrung £10 out of me** il m'a extorqué *or* soutiré* 10 livres; **I'll ~ it out of him!** je vais lui tirer les vers du nez!, je vais le faire parler!; **they managed to ~ out of him what had happened** ils sont arrivés non sans peine à lui faire dire *or* avouer ce qui s'était passé.

wring out *vt sep* **(a)** = **wring 2b, 2c.**

(b) (*: *exhausted*) **to be wrung out** être lessivé* *or* vidé* *or* moulu.

wringer ['rɪŋə^r] *n* essoreuse *f.* **to put sth through the ~** essorer qch.

wringing ['rɪŋɪŋ] *adj* (*also* **~ wet**) *garment* trempé, à tordre*; *person* trempé jusqu'aux os.

wrinkle ['rɪŋkl] **1** *n* **(a)** (*on skin, fruit*) ride *f*; (*in stockings, cloth, rug etc*) pli *m.*

(b) (*) (*tip*) bon tuyau*; (*good idea*) combine* *f.*

2 *vt* (*also* **~ up**) *skin* rider; *forehead* plisser; *nose* froncer; *fruit* rider, ratatiner; *rug, sheet* plisser, faire des plis dans.

3 *vi [sb's brow]* se plisser, se contracter; *[nose]* se plisser, se froncer; *[rug]* faire des plis; *[stockings]* faire l'accordéon.

wrinkle down *vi [stockings etc]* tomber en accordéon.

wrinkle up 1 *vi [skirt, sweater]* remonter en faisant des plis; *[rug]* faire des plis; *[sb's brow, nose]* se plisser.

2 *vt sep* = **wrinkle 2.**

wrinkled ['rɪŋkld] *adj skin, face* ridé; *brow, nose* plissé, froncé; *apple* ridé, ratatiné; *sheet, rug, sweater, skirt* qui fait des plis; *stocking, sock* qui fait l'accordéon. **a ~ old woman** une vieille femme toute ratatinée *or* desséchée.

wrist [rɪst] **1** *n* poignet *m.* **2** *cpd*: **wristband** *[shirt etc]* poignet *m*; *[watch etc]* bracelet *m*; **wrist watch** montre-bracelet *f.*

wristlet ['rɪstlɪt] **1** *n* bracelet *m* (de force). **2** *cpd*: **wristlet watch** montre-bracelet *f.*

writ[1] [rɪt] *n* (*Jur*) acte *m* judiciaire; (*for election*) *lettre officielle émanant du président de la Chambre des communes, demandant qu'on procède à des élections.* **to issue a ~ against sb** assigner qn (en justice); **to issue a ~ for libel against sb** assigner qn en justice pour diffamation; **to serve a ~ on sb, to serve sb with a ~** assigner qn; **~ of attachment** commandement *m* de saisie; **~ of execution** titre *m* exécutoire; **~ of habeas corpus** ordre *m* (écrit) d'habeas corpus; **~ of subpoena** assignation *f or* citation *f* (en justice).

writ[2] †† [rɪt] *pret, ptp of* **write.**

write [raɪt] *pret* **wrote,** *ptp* **written 1** *vt* **(a)** (*gen*) écrire; *cheque, list* faire, écrire; *prescription, certificate* rédiger; *bill* faire. **did I ~ that?** j'ai écrit ça, moi?; **how is it written?** comment ça s'écrit?; (*liter*) **it is written 'thou shalt not kill'** il est écrit 'tu ne tueras point'; (*fig*) **his guilt was written all over his face** la culpabilité se lisait sur son visage; (*fig*) **he had 'policeman' written all over him*** cela sautait aux yeux qu'il était policier.

(b) *book, essay, poem* écrire; *music, opera* écrire, composer. **you could ~ a book about all that is going on here** on pourrait écrire *or* il y aurait de quoi écrire un livre sur tout ce qui se passe ici.

2 *vi* **(a)** (*gen*) écrire. **he can read and ~** il sait lire et écrire; **~ on both sides of the paper** écrivez des deux côtés de la feuille; **as I ~, I can see ...** en ce moment même, je peux voir ...; **you must print, not ~ your name** il ne faut pas écrire votre nom en cursive mais en caractères d'imprimerie; **this pen ~s well** ce stylo écrit bien.

(b) (*as author*) **he had always wanted to ~** il avait toujours voulu écrire *or* être écrivain; **he ~s for a living** il est écrivain de métier *or* de profession; **he ~s about social policy** il écrit sur *or* il traite dans ses livres (*or* ses articles) des questions de politique sociale; **he ~s for 'The Times'** il écrit dans le 'Times'; **he ~s on foreign policy for 'The Guardian'** il écrit des articles de politique étrangère dans le 'Guardian'; **what shall I ~ about?** sur quoi est-ce que je vais écrire?

(c) (*correspond*) écrire (*to* à). **he wrote to tell us that ...** il (nous) a écrit pour nous dire que ...; (*Comm*) **~ for our brochure** demandez notre brochure; **I've written for a form** j'ai écrit pour leur demander un formulaire; *V* **home.**

3 *cpd*: (*US Pol*) **write-in** (*insertion of name*) inscription *f*; (*name itself*) nom inscrit; (*Comm*) **write-off** perte sèche; (*fig*) **the car etc was a write-off** la voiture *etc* était bonne pour la ferraille *or* la casse; (*Press*) **write-up** compte rendu; **there's a write-up about it in today's paper** il y a un compte rendu dans le journal d'aujourd'hui; **the play got a good write-up** la pièce a eu de bonnes critiques.

write away *vi* (*Comm etc*) **to write away for** *information, application form, details* écrire pour demander; *goods* commander par lettre.

write back *vi* répondre (*par lettre*).

write down *vt sep* **(a)** écrire; (*note*) noter; (*put in writing*) mettre par écrit. **write it down at once or you'll forget** écrivez-le *or* notez-le tout de suite sinon vous oublierez; **write all your ideas down and send them to me** mettez toutes vos idées par écrit et envoyez-les moi; **it was all written down for posterity** c'était tout consigné pour la postérité; (*fig*) **I had written him down as useless*** je m'étais mis dans la tête qu'il n'était bon à rien.

(b) (*Comm etc: reduce price of*) réduire le prix de.

write in 1 *vi:* **listeners are invited to write in with their suggestions** nos auditeurs sont invités à nous envoyer leurs suggestions; **a lot of people have written in to complain** beaucoup de gens nous ont écrit pour se plaindre; **to write in for sth** écrire pour demander qch.

2 *vt sep word, item on list etc* insérer, ajouter; (*US Pol*) *candidate's name* inscrire.

3 write-in *n V* **write 3.**

write off 1 *vi* = **write away.**

2 *vt sep* **(a)** (*write quickly*) *letter etc* écrire en vitesse *or* d'une traite.

(b) *debt* passer aux profits et pertes, annuler. **they wrote off £20,000** ils ont passé 20.000 livres aux profits et pertes; (*Comm*) **the operation was written off as a total loss** ils ont décidé de mettre un terme à l'opération qui se révélait une perte sèche; (*fig*) **I've written off the whole thing as a dead loss** j'en ai fait mon deuil*, j'ai fait une croix dessus*; (*fig*) **he had been written off as a failure** on avait décidé qu'il ne ferait jamais rien de bon; **they had written off all the passengers (as dead)** ils tenaient tous les passagers pour morts; **the insurance company decided to write off his car** la compagnie d'assurances a décidé que la voiture était irréparable; **he wrote his car off in the accident*** il a complètement bousillé* sa voiture dans l'accident; **the boat was completely written off*** le bateau a été complètement détruit *or* a été une perte totale.

3 write-off *n V* **write 3.**

write out *vt sep* **(a)** *one's name and address, details etc* écrire; *cheque, list* faire, écrire; *prescription, bill* rédiger; *bill* faire.

(b) (*copy*) *notes, essay etc* recopier, mettre au net *or* au propre; *recipe* copier, relever. **write out the words 3 times each** copiez chaque mot 3 fois.

write up 1 *vi* = **write away.**

2 *vt sep* **(a)** *notes, diary* mettre à jour; *happenings, developments* faire un compte rendu de; (*Chem etc*) *experiment* rédiger; (*Archeol etc*) *one's findings* consigner. **he wrote up the day's events in the ship's log** il a inscrit *or* consigné dans le journal de bord les événements de la journée; **she wrote it up for the local paper** elle en a fait le compte rendu pour le journal local.

(b) (*praise*) écrire un article élogieux (*or* une lettre élogieuse) sur.

3 write-up *n V* **write 3.**

writer ['raɪtə^r] *n* (*of letter, book etc*) auteur *m*; (*as profession*) écrivain *m*, auteur. **the (present) ~ believes ...** l'auteur croit ...; **a thriller ~** un auteur de romans policiers; **he is a ~** il est écrivain, c'est un écrivain; **to be a good ~** (*of books*) être un bon écrivain, écrire bien; (*in handwriting*) écrire bien, avoir une belle écriture; **to be a bad ~** (*of books*) écrire mal, être un écrivailleur *or* un écrivassier; (*in handwriting*) écrire mal *or* comme un chat; **~'s cramp** crampe *f* des écrivains; (*Scot Jur*) **W~ to the Signet** ≈ notaire *m*; *V* **hack**[2], **letter** *etc.*

writhe [raɪð] *vi* se tordre; (*fig*) frémir. **it made him ~** (*in pain*) il s'est tordu de douleur; (*from disgust*) il a frémi de dégoût; (*from embarrassment*) il ne savait plus où se mettre; **he ~d under the insult** il a frémi sous l'injure.

writhe about, writhe around *vi* (*in pain*) se tordre dans des convulsions; (*to free o.s.*) se contorsionner en tous sens.

writing ['raɪtɪŋ] **1** *n* **(a)** (*U: hand~, sth written*) écriture *f.* **there was some ~ on the page** il y avait quelque chose d'écrit sur la page; **I could see the ~ but couldn't read it** je voyais bien qu'il y avait quelque chose d'écrit mais je n'ai pas pu le déchiffrer; **I can't read your ~** je n'arrive pas à déchiffrer votre écriture; **in his own ~** écrit de sa main; (*fig*) **he saw the ~ on the**

wall il a vu le signe sur le mur.

(b) (*U: written form*) écrit *m.* **I'd like to have that in ~** j'aimerais avoir cela par écrit; **get his permission in ~** obtenez sa permission par écrit; **evidence in ~ that ...** preuve par écrit *or* littérale que ...; **to put sth in ~** mettre qch par écrit.

(c) (*U: occupation of writer*) **he devoted his life to ~** il a consacré sa vie à son œuvre d'écrivain; **~ is his hobby** écrire est son passe-temps favori; **he earns quite a lot from ~** ses écrits lui rapportent pas mal d'argent.

(d) (*output of writer*) écrits *mpl,* œuvres *fpl.* **there is in his ~ evidence of a desire to ...** on trouve dans ses écrits la manifestation d'un désir de ...; **the ~s of H. G. Wells** les œuvres de H. G. Wells.

(e) (*U: act*) **he learns reading and ~** il apprend à lire et à écrire; **~ is a skill which must be learned** écrire est un art qui requiert un apprentissage; **the ~ of this book took 10 years** écrire ce livre a pris 10 ans.

2 *cpd*: **writing case** correspondancier *m,* nécessaire *m* de correspondance; **writing desk** secrétaire *m* (*bureau*); **writing lesson** leçon *f* d'écriture; **writing pad** bloc *m* de papier à lettres, bloc-notes *m*; **writing paper** papier *m* à lettres; **writing table** table *f* à écrire.

written [ˈrɪtn] **1** *ptp of* **write.**

2 *adj reply, inquiry, request* écrit, par écrit; *evidence* par écrit, littéral. **~ exam** épreuve écrite, écrit *m*; (*Parl*) **~ question** question écrite; *V* **hand** *etc.*

wrong [rɒŋ] **1** *adj* **(a)** (*wicked*) mal; (*unfair*) injuste. **it is ~ to lie, lying is ~** c'est mal de mentir; **it is ~ for her to have to beg, it is ~ that she should have to beg** il est injuste qu'elle soit obligée de mendier; **you were ~ to hit him, it was ~ of you to hit him** tu as eu tort de le frapper; **what's ~ with going to the pictures?** quel mal y a-t-il à aller au cinéma?; **there's nothing ~ with** *or* **in that** il n'y a rien à redire à ça, je n'y vois aucun mal.

(b) (*mistaken, incorrect*) *belief, guess* erroné; *answer, solution, calculation, sum* faux (*f* fausse), inexact, incorrect; *clock, watch* qui n'est pas à l'heure; (*Mus*) *note* faux; (*unsuitable, inconvenient*) qui n'est pas ce qu'il faut (*or* fallait *etc*). **you're quite ~** vous vous trompez, vous avez tort, vous faites erreur; (*iro*) **how ~ can you get!*** comme on peut se tromper!; **he was ~ in deducing that ...** il a eu tort de déduire que ...; **I was ~ about him** je me suis mépris *or* trompé sur son compte; **he got all his sums ~** toutes ses opérations étaient fausses; **the Chancellor got his sums ~*** le chancelier de l'Échiquier a fait une erreur *or* s'est trompé dans ses calculs; **you've got your facts ~** ce que vous avancez est faux, les choses ne se sont pas passées comme ça; **he got the figures ~** il s'est trompé dans les chiffres; **they got it ~ again** ils se sont encore trompés; **he told me the ~ time** (*gen*) il ne m'a pas donné l'heure exacte; (*for appointment etc*) il ne m'a pas donné la bonne heure; **it happened at the ~ time** c'est arrivé à un moment inopportun; **the letter has the ~ date on it** ils se sont trompés de date sur la lettre; **the ~ use of drugs** l'usage abusif des médicaments; (*Telec*) **to get a ~ number** se tromper de numéro; (*Telec*) **that's the ~ number** ce n'est pas le bon numéro; **he got on the ~ train** il s'est trompé de train, il n'a pas pris le bon train; **it's the ~ road for Paris** ce n'est pas la bonne route pour Paris; (*fig*) **you're on the ~ road** *or* **track** vous faites fausse route; **I'm in the ~ job** ce n'est pas le travail qu'il me faut; **she married the ~ man** elle n'a pas épousé l'homme qu'il lui fallait; **you've got** *or* **picked the ~ man if you want someone to mend a fuse** vous tombez mal si vous voulez quelqu'un qui puisse réparer un fusible; **he's got the ~ kind of friends** il a de mauvaises fréquentations; **that's the ~ kind of plug** ce n'est pas la prise qu'il faut, ce n'est pas la bonne sorte de prise; **to say the ~ thing** dire ce qu'il ne fallait pas dire, faire un impair; **you've opened the packet at the ~ end** vous avez ouvert le paquet par le mauvais bout *or* du mauvais côté; **that's quite the ~ way to go about it** ce n'est pas comme ça qu'il faut s'y prendre *or* qu'il faut le faire, vous vous y prenez (*or* il s'y prend *etc*) mal; **a piece of bread went down the ~ way** j'ai (*or* il a *etc*) avalé une miette de pain de travers; **he was on the ~ side of the road** il était du mauvais côté de la route; **he got out of the train on the ~ side** il est descendu du train à contre-voie; (*fig*) **he got out of bed on the ~ side, he got out of the ~ side of the bed** il s'est levé du pied gauche; **the ~ side of the cloth** le mauvais côté *or* l'envers *m* du tissu; **he's on the ~ side of forty** il a dépassé la quarantaine; (*fig*) **to get on the ~ side of sb** se faire mal voir de qn; (*rub sb up the wrong way*) prendre qn à rebrousse-poil; **you've put it back in the ~ place** vous l'avez mal remis, vous ne l'avez pas remis là où il fallait; *V also* **end, side, stick, way** *etc.*

(c) (*amiss*) qui ne va pas. **something's ~, there's something ~ (with it** *or* **him** *etc*) il y a quelque chose qui ne va pas; **something's ~ with my leg** j'ai quelque chose à la jambe, ma jambe me tracasse; **something's ~ with my watch** ma montre ne marche pas comme il faut; **what's ~?** qu'est-ce qui ne va pas?; **there's nothing ~** ça va, tout va bien; **there's something ~ somewhere** il y a quelque chose qui cloche* là-dedans; **what's ~ with you?** qu'est-ce que vous avez?; **what's ~ with your arm?** qu'est-ce que vous avez au bras?; **what's ~ with the car?** qu'est-ce qu'elle a, la voiture?, qu'est-ce qui cloche* dans la voiture?; **he's ~ in the head*** il a le cerveau dérangé *or* fêlé*.

2 *adv answer, guess* mal, incorrectement. **you've spelt it ~** vous l'avez mal écrit; **you're doing it all ~** vous vous y prenez mal; **you did ~ to refuse** vous avez eu tort de refuser; **you've got the sum ~** vous avez fait une erreur de calcul; (*misunderstood*) **you've got it all ~*** vous n'avez rien compris; **don't get me ~*** comprends-moi bien; **she took me up ~** elle n'a pas compris ce que je voulais dire; **to go ~** (*on road*) se tromper de route, faire fausse route; (*in calculations, negotiations etc*) se tromper, faire une faute *or* une erreur; (*morally*) mal tourner; *[plan]* mal tourner; *[business deal etc]* tomber à l'eau; *[machine, car]* tomber en panne; *[clock, watch etc]* battre la breloque; **you can't go ~** (*on road*) c'est très simple, il est impossible de se perdre; (*in method etc*) c'est simple comme bonjour; **you won't go far ~ if you ...** vous ne pouvez guère vous tromper si vous ...; **something went ~ with the gears** quelque chose s'est détraqué *or* a foiré* dans l'embrayage; **something must have gone ~** il a dû arriver quelque chose; **nothing can go ~ now** tout doit marcher comme sur des roulettes maintenant; **everything went ~ that day** tout est allé mal *or* de travers ce jour-là.

3 *n* **(a)** (*evil*) mal *m.* (*Prov*) **two ~s don't make a right** un second tort ne compense pas le premier; **to do ~** mal agir; (*fig*) **he can do no ~ in her eyes** tout ce qu'il fait trouve grâce à ses yeux; *V also* **right.**

(b) (*injustice*) injustice *f,* tort *m.* **he suffered great ~** il a été la victime de graves injustices; **to right a ~** réparer une injustice; **you do me ~ in thinking ...** vous êtes injuste envers moi *or* vous me faites tort en pensant ...; **he did her ~**† il a abusé d'elle.

(c) to be in the ~ être dans son tort, avoir tort; **to put sb in the ~** mettre qn dans son tort.

4 *vt* traiter injustement, faire du tort à. **you ~ me if you believe ...** vous êtes injuste envers moi si vous croyez... .

5 *cpd:* **wrongdoer** malfaiteur *m,* -trice *f*; (*U*) **wrongdoing** méfaits *mpl*; **wrong-headed** buté.

wrongful [ˈrɒŋfʊl] *adj* injustifié. (*Jur*) **~ arrest** arrestation *f* arbitraire; (*Ind*) **~ dismissal** renvoi injustifié.

wrongfully [ˈrɒŋfəlɪ] *adv* à tort.

wrongly [ˈrɒŋlɪ] *adv* (*incorrectly*) *state, allege, multiply* incorrectement, inexactement; *treat* injustement; *accuse* faussement, à tort; *answer, guess, translate* mal, incorrectement, pas comme il faut; *position, insert* mal, pas comme il faut. **the handle has been put on ~** le manche n'a pas été mis comme il faut *or* a été mal mis; **you have been ~ informed** on vous a mal renseigné; **~ dismissed** renvoyé injustement *or* à tort; **he behaved quite ~ when he said that** il a eu tort de dire ça; *V* **rightly.**

wrongness [ˈrɒŋnɪs] *n* (*incorrectness*) *[answer]* inexactitude *f*; (*injustice*) injustice *f*; (*evil*) immoralité *f.*

wrote [rəʊt] *pret of* **write.**

wrought [rɔːt] **1** *pret, ptp* †† of **work** (*liter*) **he ~ valiantly** il a œuvré vaillamment; **the destruction ~ by the floods** les ravages provoqués par l'inondation. **2** *adj iron* forgé; *silver* ouvré.

3 *cpd:* **wrought iron** fer forgé; **wrought-iron** (*adj*) *gate, decoration* en fer forgé; **wrought-ironwork** ferronnerie *f*; **to be wrought-up** être très tendu.

wrung [rʌŋ] *pret, ptp of* **wring.**

wry [raɪ] *adj comment, humour, joke* désabusé, empreint d'une ironie désabusée. **a ~ smile** un sourire forcé *or* désabusé; **with a ~ shrug of his shoulders he ...** d'un haussement d'épaules désabusé il ...; **to make a ~ face** faire la grimace.

wryly [ˈraɪlɪ] *adv* avec une ironie désabusée.

wych-elm [ˈwɪtʃˈelm] *n* orme blanc *or* de montagne.

wynd [waɪnd] *n* (*Scot*) venelle *f.*

X

X, x [eks] (*vb: pret, ptp* **x-ed, x'ed**) **1** *n* (*letter*) X, x *m*; (*Math, fig*) x. **he signed his name with an X** il a signé d'une croix *or* en faisant une croix; **for x years** pendant x années; **Mr X** Monsieur X; **X-certificate film** film interdit aux moins de 18 ans *or* réservé aux adultes; **X marks the spot** l'endroit est marqué d'une croix; *V* **X-ray**. **2** *vt* marquer d'une croix.
x out *vt sep mistake* raturer (par une série de croix).
xenon ['zenɒn] *n* xénon *m*.
xenophobe ['zenəfəʊb] *adj, n* xénophobe (*mf*).
xenophobia [,zenə'fəʊbiə] *n* xénophobie *f*.
xenophobic [,zenə'fəʊbɪk] *adj* xénophobique.
xerography [zɪə'rɒgrəfɪ] *n* xérographie *f*.
Xerox ['zɪərɒks] ® **1** *n* (*machine*) photocopieuse *f*; (*reproduction*) photocopie *f*. **2** *vt* (faire) photocopier, prendre *or* faire une photocopie de, copier*. **3** *vi* se faire *or* se laisser photocopier.
Xmas ['eksməs, 'krɪsməs] *n abbr of* **Christmas**.
X-ray ['eks'reɪ] **1** *n* (*ray*) rayon *m* X; (*photograph*) radiographie *f*, radio* *f*. **to have an ~** se faire radiographier, se faire faire une radio*.
2 *vt heart, envelope* radiographier, faire une radio de*; *person* radiographier, faire une radio à*.
3 *cpd* radioscopique, radiographique. **X-ray diagnosis** radiodiagnostic *m*; **X-ray examination** examen *m* radioscopique, radio* *f*; **X-ray photo, X-ray picture** (*on film*) radiographie *f*, radio* *f*; (*on screen*) radioscopie *f*, radio*; **X-ray treatment** radiothérapie *f*.
xylograph ['zaɪləgrɑːf] *n* xylographie *f*.
xylographic [,zaɪlə'græfɪk] *adj* xylographique.
xylography [zaɪ'lɒgrəfɪ] *n* xylographie *f*.
xylophone ['zaɪləfəʊn] *n* xylophone *m*.

Y

Y, y [waɪ] *n* (*letter*) Y, y *m*. **Y-fronts** ® slip *m* (d'homme); **Y-shaped** en (forme d') Y.
yacht [jɒt] **1** *n* (*sails or motor*) yacht *m*; (*sails*) voilier *m*.
2 *vi* faire du yachting *or* de la voile *or* de la navigation de plaisance.
3 *cpd*: **yacht club** yacht-club *m*, cercle *m* nautique *or* de voile; **yacht race** course *f* de yachts *or* de voiliers; **yachtsman** yacht(s)man *m*, plaisancier *m*.
yachting ['jɒtɪŋ] **1** *n* yachting *m*, navigation *f* de plaisance.
2 *cpd cruise* en yacht; *cap* de marin; *magazine etc* de la voile. **in yachting circles** dans les milieux de la voile *or* de la navigation de plaisance; **it's not a yachting coast** ce n'est pas une côte propice au yachting *or* à la navigation de plaisance.
yackety-yak* ['jækɪtɪ'jæk] **1** *vi* (**pej*) caqueter, jacasser. **2** *n* caquetage *m*.
yah [jɑː] *excl* beuh!
yahoo [jɑː'huː] *n* butor *m*, rustre *m*.
yak[1] [jæk] *n* (*Zool*) yak *m or* yack *m*.
yak[2]* [jæk] = **yackety-yak**.
yam [jæm] *n* (*plant, tuber*) igname *f*; (*US: sweet potato*) patate douce.
yank [jæŋk] **1** *n* coup sec, saccade *f*.
2 *vt* tirer d'un coup sec.
yank off* *vt sep* **(a)** (*detach*) arracher *or* extirper (d'un coup sec).
(b) to yank sb off to jail embarquer* qn en prison.
yank out* *vt sep* arracher *or* extirper (d'un coup sec).
Yank* [jæŋk] (*abbr of* **Yankee**) **1** *adj* amerloque‡, ricain‡ (*pej*). **2** *n* Amerloque‡ *mf*, Ricain(e)‡ *m(f)* (*pej*).
Yankee* ['jæŋkɪ] **1** *n* Yankee *mf*. **2** *adj* yankee (*f inv*). **'~ Doodle'** *chant populaire américain*.
yap [jæp] **1** *vi* [*dog*] japper; [*person*] jacasser. **2** *n* jappement *m*.
yapping ['jæpɪŋ] **1** *adj dog* jappeur; *person* jacasseur. **2** *n* jappements *mpl*; jacasserie *f*.
Yarborough ['jɑːbrə] *n* (*Bridge etc*) *main ne contenant aucune carte supérieure au neuf*.
yard[1] [jɑːd] **1** *n* **(a)** yard *m* (*91,44 cm*), ≃ mètre *m*. **one ~ long** long d'un yard *or* d'un mètre; **20 ~s away from us** à 20 mètres de nous; **he can't see a ~ in front of him** il ne voit pas à un mètre devant lui; (*Sport*) **to run a hundred ~s, to run in the hundred ~s** *or* **hundred ~s' race** ≃ courir le cent mètres; **to buy cloth by the ~** acheter de l'étoffe au mètre; **how many ~s would you like?** quel métrage désirez-vous?
(b) (*fig*) **he pulled out ~s of handkerchief** il a sorti un mouchoir d'une longueur interminable; **a word a ~ long** un mot qui n'en finit plus; **an essay ~s long** une dissertation-fleuve; **with a face a ~ long** faisant un visage long d'une aune, faisant une tête longue comme ça; **sums by the ~** des calculs à n'en plus finir.
(c) (*Naut*) vergue *f*.
2 *cpd*: (*Naut*) **yardarm** bout *m* de vergue; (*fig*) **yardstick** mesure *f*.
yard[2] [jɑːd] *n* **(a)** [*farm, hospital, prison, school etc*] cour *f*; (*surrounded by the building: in monastery, hospital etc*) préau *m*. **back~** cour de derrière; *V* **farm** *etc*.
(b) (*work-site*) chantier *m*; (*for storage*) dépôt *m*. **builder's/shipbuilding ~** chantier de construction/de construction(s) navale(s); **timber~** dépôt de bois; **coal/contractor's ~** dépot de charbon/de matériaux de construction; *V* **dock**[1], **goods** *etc*.
(c) (*Brit*) **the Y~, Scotland Y~** Scotland Yard *m*, ≃ le Quai des Orfèvres; **to call in the Y~** demander l'aide de Scotland Yard.
(d) (*US*) (*garden*) jardin *m*; (*field*) champ *m*.
(e) (*enclosure for animals*) parc *m*; *V* **stock**.
yardage ['jɑːdɪdʒ] *n* longueur *f* en yards, ≃ **métrage** *m*.
yarn [jɑːn] **1** *n* **(a)** fil *m*; (*Tech: for weaving*) filé *m*. **cotton/nylon** *etc* **~** fil de coton/de nylon *etc*. **(b)** (*tale*) longue histoire; *V* **spin**. **2** *vi* raconter *or* débiter des histoires.
yarrow ['jærəʊ] *n* mille-feuille *f*, achillée *f*.
yashmak ['jæʃmæk] *n* litham *m*.
yaw [jɔː] *vi* (*Naut*) (*suddenly*) faire une embardée, embarder; (*gradually*) dévier de la route; (*Aviat, Space*) faire un mouvement de lacet.
yawl [jɔːl] *n* (*Naut*) (*sailing boat*) yawl *m*; (*ship's boat*) yole *f*.
yawn [jɔːn] **1** *vi* **(a)** [*person*] bâiller. **to ~ with boredom** bâiller d'ennui.
(b) [*chasm etc*] s'ouvrir, être béant.
2 *vt*: **to ~ one's head off** bâiller à se décrocher la mâchoire; **'no' he ~ed** 'non' dit-il en bâillant *or* dans un bâillement.
3 *n* bâillement *m*. **to give a ~** bâiller; **the film is one long ~*** le film est ennuyeux de bout en bout *or* fait bâiller; *V* **stifle**.
yawning ['jɔːnɪŋ] **1** *adj chasm* béant; *person* qui bâille. **2** *n* bâillements *mpl*.
yaws [jɔːz] *n* (*Med*) pian *m*.
ye[1] [jiː] *pers pron* (††, *liter, dial*) vous. **~ gods!*** grands dieux!*, ciel! (*hum*).
ye[2] [jiː] (††: *the*) *ancienne forme écrite de* **the**.
yea [jeɪ] (††: *yes*) **1** *particle* oui. **whether ~ or nay** que ce soit oui ou (que ce soit) non. **2** *adv* (*liter: indeed*) voire, et même. **3** *n* oui *m*. **the ~s and the nays** les voix *fpl* pour et les voix contre, les oui *mpl* et les non.
yeah* [jɛə] *particle* (*esp US*) oui. (*iro*) **oh ~?** et puis quoi encore?
year [jɪəʳ] **1** *n* **(a)** an *m*, année *f*. **last ~** l'an dernier, l'année dernière; **this ~** cette année; **next ~** l'an prochain, l'année prochaine, l'année qui vient; (*loc*) **this ~, next ~, sometime, never!** ≃ un peu, beaucoup, passionnément, à la folie, pas du tout!; **every ~, each ~** tous les ans, chaque année; **every other ~, every second ~** tous les deux ans; **3 times a ~** 3 fois l'an

ou par an; in the ~ of grace en l'an de grâce; in the ~ of Our Lord en l'an or en l'année de Notre Seigneur; in the ~ 1969 en 1969; in the ~ one thousand en l'an mille or mil; ~ by ~, from ~ to ~ d'année en année; from one ~ to the other d'une année à l'autre; ~ in ~ out année après année; all the ~ round, from ~('s) end to ~('s) end d'un bout de l'année à l'autre; over the ~s, as (the) ~s go (or went) by au cours or au fil des années; taking one ~ with another, taking the good ~s with the bad bon an mal an; ~s (and ~s) ago il y a (bien) des années; for ~s together plusieurs années de suite; to pay by the ~ payer à l'année; document valid one ~ document valide un an; a ~ last January il y a eu un an au mois de janvier (dernier); a ~ in January, a ~ next January il y aura un an en janvier (prochain); they have not met for ~s ils ne se sont pas vus depuis des années; (fig) I've been waiting for you for ~s* ça fait une éternité que je t'attends; sentenced to 15 ~s' imprisonment condamné à 15 ans de prison; (Prison) he got 10 ~s il a attrapé 10 ans; he is 6 ~s old il a 6 ans; in his fortieth ~ dans sa quarantième année; it costs £10 a ~ cela coûte 10 livres par an; he earns £3,000 a ~ il gagne 3.000 livres par an; a friend of 30 ~s' standing un ami de 30 ans or que l'on connaît (or connaissait etc) depuis 30 ans; it has taken ~s off my life!, it has put ~s on me! cela m'a vieilli de cent ans!; that new hat takes ~s off her ce nouveau chapeau la rajeunit; V after, donkey, New Year etc.

(b) ~s âge m; from his earliest ~s dès son âge le plus tendre; he looks old for his ~s il fait or paraît plus vieux que son âge; young for his ~s jeune pour son âge; well on in ~s d'un âge avancé; to get on in ~s prendre de l'âge; (liter) to grow in ~s avancer en âge; to reach ~s of discretion arriver à l'âge adulte (fig).

(c) (Scol, Univ) année f. he is first in his ~ il est le premier de son année; she was in my ~ at school elle était de mon année au lycée; he's in the second ~ (Univ) il est en deuxième année; (secondary school) ≃ il est en cinquième.

(d) [coin, stamp, wine] année f.

2 cpd: yearbook annuaire m (d'une université, d'un organisme etc); yearlong qui dure (or durait etc) un an.

yearling ['jɪəlɪŋ] 1 n animal m d'un an; (racehorse) yearling m. 2 adj (âgé) d'un an.

yearly ['jɪəlɪ] 1 adj annuel. 2 adv annuellement.

yearn [jɜːn] vi (a) (feel longing) languir (for, after après), aspirer (for, after à). to ~ for home avoir la nostalgie de chez soi or du pays; to ~ to do avoir très envie or mourir d'envie de faire, aspirer à faire.

(b) (feel tenderness) s'attendrir, s'émouvoir (over sur).

yearning ['jɜːnɪŋ] 1 n désir ardent or vif (for, after de, to do de faire), envie f (for, after de, to do de faire), aspiration f (for, after vers, to do à faire). 2 adj desire vif (f vive), ardent; look plein de désir or de tendresse.

yearningly ['jɜːnɪŋlɪ] adv (longingly) avec envie, avec désir; (tenderly) avec tendresse, tendrement.

yeast [jiːst] n (U) levure f. dried ~ levure déshydratée.

yeasty ['jiːstɪ] adj (a) (frothy) écumeux, mousseux; (frivolous) superficiel, sans consistance, frivole. (b) ~ taste goût m de levure.

yell [jel] 1 n hurlement m, cri m. to give a ~ pousser un hurlement or un cri; a ~ of fright un hurlement or un cri d'effroi; a ~ of laughter un grand éclat de rire; (US Univ) college ~ ban m d'étudiants; (fig) it was a ~!‡ c'était à se tordre!*; (fig) he's a ~‡ il est tordant*.

2 vi (a) (also ~ out) hurler (with de). to ~ with laughter rire bruyamment or aux éclats.

(b) (*: weep) beugler‡, hurler.

3 vt (a) (also ~ out) hurler, crier. 'stop it!' he ~ed 'arrêtez!' hurla-t-il.

(b) (*: weep) she was ~ing her head off elle beuglait‡ comme un veau, elle hurlait.

yelling ['jelɪŋ] 1 n hurlements mpl, cris mpl. 2 adj hurlant.

yellow ['jeləʊ] 1 adj (a) (colour) object etc jaune; hair, curls blond. to go or turn or become or grow ~ devenir jaune, jaunir; the ~ races les races fpl jaunes; V also 2 and canary etc.

(b) (fig pej: cowardly) lâche, froussard*, trouillard‡. there was a ~ streak in him il y avait un côté lâche or froussard* or trouillard‡ en lui.

2 cpd: (pej) yellowback† roman m à sensation; (pej) yellow-belly‡ froussard(e)* m(f), trouillard(e)‡ m(f); (Med) yellow fever fièvre f jaune; (Naut) yellow flag pavillon m de quarantaine; (Orn) yellowhammer bruant m jaune; (Naut) yellow jack* = yellow flag; yellow metal (gold) métal m jaune; (brass) cuivre m jaune, métal Muntz; yellow ochre jaune m d'ocre; (Telec) the yellow pages ≃ l'annuaire m des professions; (fig) yellow peril péril m jaune; (pej) the yellow press la presse à sensation; Yellow River le fleuve Jaune; Yellow Sea la mer Jaune; yellow soap savon m de Marseille.

3 n (also of egg) jaune m.

4 vi jaunir.

5 vt jaunir. paper ~ed with age papier jauni par le temps.

yellowish ['jeləʊɪʃ] adj tirant sur le jaune, un peu jaune, jaunâtre (pej).

yellowness ['jeləʊnɪs] n (U) (a) (colour) [object] couleur f jaune, jaune m; [skin] teint m jaune. (b) (*pej: cowardice) lâcheté f, trouillardise‡ f.

yellowy ['jeləʊɪ] adj = yellowish.

yelp [jelp] 1 n [dog] jappement m; [fox, person] glapissement m. 2 vi japper; glapir.

yelping ['jelpɪŋ] 1 n [dog] jappement m; [fox, person] glapissement m. 2 adj dog jappeur; fox, person glapissant.

Yemen ['jemən] n Yémen m.

yen[1] [jen] n (money) yen m.

yen[2] [jen] n désir m intense, grande envie (for de). to have a ~ to do avoir (grande) envie de faire.

yeoman ['jəʊmən] pl yeomen 1 n (a) (Hist: freeholder) franc-tenancier m.

(b) (Brit Mil) cavalier m; V yeomanry.

2 cpd: yeoman farmer (Hist) franc-tenancier m; (modern) propriétaire exploitant; (Brit) Yeoman of the Guard hallebardier m de la garde royale; (fig) to do or give yeoman service rendre des services inestimables.

yeomanry ['jəʊmənrɪ] n (U) (a) (Hist) (classe f des) francs-tenanciers mpl. (b) (Brit Mil) régiment m de cavalerie (volontaire).

yeomen ['jəʊmən] npl of yeoman.

yep‡ [jep] particle ouais‡, oui.

yes [jes] 1 particle (answering affirmative question) oui; (answering neg question) si. do you want some? — ~! en voulez-vous? — oui!; don't you want any? — ~ (I do)! vous n'en voulez pas? — (mais) si!; to say ~ dire oui; he says ~ to everything il dit oui à tout; ~ certainly mais oui, certes oui; ~, rather* bien sûr (que oui); (contradicting) oh ~, you DID say that si si or mais si, vous avez bien dit cela; ~? (awaiting further reply) (ah) oui?, et alors?; (answering knock at door) oui?, entrez!; waiter! — ~ sir? garçon! — (oui) Monsieur?

2 n oui m inv. he gave a reluctant ~ il a accepté de mauvaise grâce; he answered with ~es and noes il n'a répondu que par des oui et des non.

3 cpd: (*pej) yes man béni-oui-oui* m inv (pej); he's a yes man il dit amen à tout.

yesterday ['jestədeɪ] 1 adv (a) hier. it rained ~ il a plu hier; all (day) ~ toute la journée d'hier; he arrived only ~ il n'est arrivé qu'hier; a week (from) ~ d'hier en huit; a week (past) ~ il y a eu hier huit jours; I had to have it by ~ or no later than ~ il fallait que je l'aie hier au plus tard; late ~ hier dans la soirée; V born.

(b) (fig: in the past) hier, naguère. towns which ~ were villages des villes qui étaient hier or naguère des villages.

2 n (a) hier m. ~ was the second c'était hier le deux; ~ was Friday c'était hier vendredi; ~ was very wet il a beaucoup plu hier; ~ was a bad day for him la journée d'hier s'est mal passée pour lui; the day before ~ avant-hier; where's ~'s newspaper? où est le journal d'hier?

(b) (fig) hier m, passé m. the great men of ~ tous les grands hommes du passé or d'hier; all our ~s tout notre passé.

3 cpd: yesterday afternoon hier après-midi; yesterday evening hier (au) soir; yesterday morning hier matin; yesterday week il y a eu hier huit jours.

yesternight ['jestə'naɪt] n, adv (††, liter) la nuit dernière, hier soir.

yesteryear ['jestə'jɪəʳ] n (††, liter) les années passées. the snows of ~ les neiges d'antan.

yet [jet] 1 adv (a) (also as ~) (by this time, still, thus far, till now) encore, toujours, jusqu'ici, jusqu'à présent; (by that time, still, till then) encore, toujours, jusqu'alors, jusque-là. they haven't (as) ~ returned or returned (as) ~ ils ne sont pas encore or ne sont toujours pas revenus; they hadn't (as) ~ managed to do it ils n'étaient pas encore or toujours pas arrivés à le faire; the greatest book (as) ~ written le plus beau livre écrit jusqu'ici or jusqu'à présent; no one has come (as) ~ personne n'est encore venu, jusqu'à présent or jusqu'ici, personne n'est venu; no one had come (as) ~ jusqu'alors or jusque-là personne n'était (encore) venu.

(b) (so far; already; now) maintenant; alors; déjà; encore. has he arrived ~? est-il déjà arrivé?; no, not ~ non, pas encore; I wonder if he's come ~ je me demande s'il est déjà arrivé or s'il est arrivé maintenant; not (just) ~ pas tout de suite, pas encore, pas pour l'instant; don't come in (just) ~ n'entrez pas tout de suite or pas encore or pas pour l'instant; must you go just ~? faut-il que vous partiez (subj) déjà?; I needn't go (just) ~ je n'ai pas besoin de partir tout de suite; that won't happen (just) ~, that won't happen ~ awhile(s) ça n'est pas pour tout de suite.

(c) (still, remaining) encore (maintenant). they have a few days ~ ils ont encore or il leur reste encore quelques jours; there's another bottle ~ il reste encore une bouteille; half is ~ to be built il en reste encore la moitié à construire; places ~ to be seen des endroits qui restent (encore) à voir; he has ~ to learn il a encore à apprendre, il lui reste à apprendre; (liter) she is ~ alive elle est encore vivante, elle vit encore.

(d) (with comp: still, even) encore. this is ~ more difficult ceci est encore plus difficile; he wants ~ more money il veut encore plus or encore davantage d'argent.

(e) (in addition) encore, de plus. ~ once more encore une fois, une fois de plus; another arrived and ~ another il en est arrivé un autre et encore un autre.

(f) (before all is over) encore, toujours. he may come ~ or ~ come il peut encore or toujours venir; he could come ~ il pourrait bien encore or toujours venir; I'll speak to her ~ je finirai bien par lui parler; I'll do it ~ j'y arriverai bien quand même.

(g) (frm) nor ~ ni, et ... non plus, ni même, et ... pas davantage; I do not like him nor ~ his sister je ne les aime ni lui ni sa sœur, je ne l'aime pas et sa sœur non plus or et sa sœur pas davantage; not he nor ~ I ni lui ni moi; they did not come nor ~ (even) write ils ne sont pas venus et ils n'ont même pas écrit.

2 conj (however) cependant, pourtant; (nevertheless) toutefois, néanmoins, malgré tout, tout de même. (and) ~ everyone liked her (et) pourtant or néanmoins tout le monde l'aimait, mais tout le monde l'aimait quand même; (and) ~ I like the house (et) malgré tout or (et) pourtant or (et) néanmoins j'aime bien la maison; it's strange ~ true c'est étrange mais pourtant vrai or mais vrai tout de même.

yeti ['jetɪ] n yéti m.

yew [juː] n (also ~ tree) if m; (wood) (bois m d')if.

Yid: [jɪd] *n (pej)* youpin(e) *m(f) (pej)*, Juif *m*, Juive *f*.
Yiddish ['jɪdɪʃ] **1** *adj* yiddish *inv.* **2** *n (Ling)* yiddish *m*.
yield [ji:ld] **1** *n [earth]* production *f*; *[land, farm, field, orchard, tree]* rendement *m*, rapport *m*, récolte(s) *f(pl)*; *[mine, oil well]* débit *m*; *[labour]* produit *m*, rendement; *[an industry]* production, rendement; *[tax]* recettes *fpl*, rapport, revenu *m*; *[business, shares]* rapport, rendement, revenu. **~ per acre** rendement à l'hectare.
2 *vt* **(a)** (*produce, bear; bring in*) *[earth]* produire; *[farm, field, land, orchard, tree]* rendre, produire, donner, rapporter; *[mine, oil well]* débiter; *[labour, an industry]* produire; *[business, investments, tax, shares]* rapporter. **to ~ a profit** rapporter un profit *or* un bénéfice; **that land ~s no return** cette terre ne rend pas, cette terre ne produit *or* rapporte rien; (*Fin*) **shares ~ing high interest** actions *fpl* à gros rendement; **shares ~ing 10%** actions qui rapportent 10%; **it will ~ the opportunity of** cela fournira l'occasion de; **to ~ results** donner *or* produire des résultats; **this ~ed many benefits** bien des bénéfices en ont résulté.
(b) (*surrender*) *fortress, territory* céder, livrer, abandonner (*to* à); *ownership, rights* céder (*to* à), renoncer à (*to* en faveur de). (*Mil, fig*) **to ~ ground to sb** céder du terrain à qn; (*fig*) **to ~ the floor to sb** laisser la parole à qn; **to ~ a point to sb** concéder un point à qn, céder à qn sur un point; **if he ~s this point** s'il admet *or* concède ce point, s'il cède sur ce point; (*Aut*) **to ~ the right of way to sb** laisser *or* céder la priorité à qn; (*frm*) **to ~ obedience/thanks to sb** rendre obéissance/grâces à qn (*frm*).
3 *vi* **(a)** (*give produce; bring in revenue: V* **2a** *for typical subjects*) rendre; rapporter; donner; produire; débiter. **field that ~s well** champ qui rapporte *or* qui donne un bon rendement, champ qui rend bien; **land that ~s poorly** terre qui rend peu *or* mal.
(b) (*surrender, give way*) céder (*to* devant, à), se rendre (*to* à). **we shall never ~** nous ne céderons jamais, nous ne nous rendrons jamais; **they begged him but he would not ~** ils l'ont supplié mais il n'a pas cédé *or* il ne s'est pas laissé fléchir; (*Mil etc*) **they ~ed to us** ils se rendirent à nous; **to ~ to force** céder devant la force; **to ~ to superior forces** céder devant *or* à des forces supérieures; **to ~ to superior numbers** céder au nombre; **to ~ to reason** se rendre à la raison; **to ~ to sb's entreaties** céder aux prières *or* instances de qn; **to ~ to sb's threats** céder devant les menaces de qn; **to ~ to sb's argument** se rendre aux raisons de qn; **the disease ~ed to treatment** le mal a cédé aux remèdes; **to ~ to temptation** succomber à la tentation; (*liter*) **he ~ed to nobody in courage** il ne le cédait à personne en courage; **I ~ to nobody in my admiration for ...** personne plus que moi n'admire ... .
(c) (*give way*) *[branch, door, ice, rope]* céder; *[beam]* céder, fléchir; *[floor, ground]* s'affaisser; *[bridge]* céder, s'affaisser. **to ~ under pressure** céder à la pression.
yield up *vt sep* (*liter*) abandonner, céder, livrer. **to yield o.s. up to temptation** succomber *or* s'abandonner *or* se livrer à la tentation; **to yield up the ghost** rendre l'âme.
yielding ['ji:ldɪŋ] **1** *adj* **(a)** (*fig*) *person* complaisant, accommodant. **(b)** (*lit: V* **yield 3c**) qui cède, qui fléchit; *ground, surface* mou (*f* molle), élastique. **2** *n [person]* soumission *f*; *[town, fort]* reddition *f*, capitulation *f*; *[right, goods]* cession *f*.
yippee: ['jɪpi:] *excl* hourra!
yob(bo): ['jɒb(əʊ)] *n (Brit pej)* blouson noir (*pej*), petit caïd (*pej*).
yod [jɒd] *n (Ling)* yod *m*.
yodel ['jəʊdl] **1** *vi* jodler *or* iodler, faire des tyroliennes. **2** *n* (*song, call*) tyrolienne *f*.
yoga ['jəʊgə] *n* yoga *m*.
yog(h)ourt, yog(h)urt ['jəʊgət] *n* yog(h)ourt *m or* yaourt *m*.
yogi ['jəʊgɪ] *n* yogi *m*.
yo-heave-ho ['jəʊ'hi:v'həʊ] *excl (Naut)* ho hisse!
yoke [jəʊk] **1** *n* **(a)** (*for oxen*) joug *m*; (*for carrying pails*) palanche *f*, joug; (*on harness*) support *m* de timon.
(b) (*fig: dominion*) joug *m*. **to come under the ~ of** tomber sous le joug de; **to throw off** *or* **cast off the ~** briser *or* secouer *or* rompre le joug.
(c) (*pl inv: pair*) attelage *m*, paire *f*, couple† *m*. **a ~ of oxen** une paire de bœufs.
(d) *[dress, blouse]* empiècement *m*.
(e) (*Constr*) *[beam]* moise *f* (*T*), lien *m*; (*Tech*) bâti *m*, carcasse *f*.
2 *cpd*: **yoke oxen** bœufs *mpl* d'attelage.
3 *vt* (*also* **~ up**) *oxen* accoupler; *ox etc* mettre au joug; *pieces of machinery* accoupler; (*fig: also* **~ together**) unir. **to ~ oxen (up) to the plough** atteler des bœufs à la charrue.
yokel ['jəʊkəl] *n (pej)* rustre *m*, péquenaud *m* (*pej*).
yolk [jəʊk] *n* jaune *m* (d'œuf).
yon [jɒn] *adj* (††, *liter, dial*) = **yonder 2.**
yonder ['jɒndə^r] **1** *adv* là(-bas). **up ~** là-haut; **over ~** là-bas; **down ~** là-bas en bas. **2** *adj* (††, *liter*) ce ... -là, ce ... là-bas. **from ~ house** de cette maison-là, de cette maison là-bas.
yoo-hoo: ['ju:'hu:] *excl* ohé! (vous *or* toi là-bas!), hou hou!
yore [jɔ:^r] *n* (††, *liter*) **of ~** d'antan (*liter*), (d')autrefois; **in days of ~** au temps jadis.
Yorkshire ['jɔ:kʃə^r] *n* Yorkshire *m*. (*Culin*) **~ pudding** *pâte à crêpe cuite qui accompagne un rôti de bœuf*; **~ terrier** yorkshire-terrier *m*.
you [ju:] *pers pron* **(a)** (*nominative*) tu, vous, (*pl*) vous; (*accusative, dative*) te, vous, (*pl*) vous; (*stressed and after prep*) toi, vous, (*pl*) vous. **~ are very kind** tu es très gentil, vous êtes très gentil(s); **I shall see ~ soon** je te *or* je vous verrai bientôt, on se voit bientôt; **this book is for ~** ce livre est pour toi *or* vous; **she is younger than ~** elle est plus jeune que toi *or* vous; **~ and yours** toi et les tiens, vous et les vôtres; **all of ~** vous tous; **all ~ who came here** vous tous qui êtes venus ici; **~ who know him** toi qui le connais, vous qui le connaissez; **~ French** vous autres Français; **~ and I will go together** toi *or* vous et moi, nous irons ensemble; **there ~ are!** (*you've arrived*) te *or* vous voilà!, (*take this*) voici!, tiens!, tenez!; **if I were ~** (si j'étais) à ta *or* votre place, si j'étais toi *or* vous; **between ~ and me** (*lit*) entre toi *or* vous et moi; (*in secret*) entre nous, de toi *or* vous à moi; **~ fool (~)!** imbécile (que tu es)!:, espèce d'imbécile!:; **~ darling!** tu es un amour!; **it's ~** c'est toi *or* vous; **~ there!** toi *or* vous là-bas!; **never ~ mind*** (*don't worry*) ne t'en fais pas*, ne vous en faites pas*; (*it's not your business*) ça ne te *or* vous regarde pas, mêle-toi de tes *or* mêlez-vous de vos affaires; **don't ~ go away** ne pars pas, toi, ne partez pas, vous; **there's a fine house for ~!** en voilà une belle maison!; **now YOU say something** maintenant à toi *or* à vous de parler; (††, *dial*) **sit ~ down** assieds-toi, asseyez-vous.
(b) (*one, anyone*) (*nominative*) on; (*accusative, dative*) vous, tu. **~ never know, ~ never can tell** on ne sait jamais; **~ go towards the church** vous allez *or* tu vas vers l'église; **~ never know your (own) luck** on ne connaît jamais son bonheur *or* sa chance; **fresh air does ~ good** l'air frais (vous *or* te) fait du bien.
you'd [ju:d] = **you had, you would**; *V* **have, would.**
you'll [ju:l] = **you will**; *V* **will.**
young [jʌŋ] **1** *adj, comp* **younger** ['jʌŋgə^r], *superl* **youngest** ['jʌŋgɪst] *man, tree, country* jeune; *moon, grass* nouveau (*before vowel* nouvel; *f* nouvelle); *appearance, smile* jeune, juvénile. **~ people** jeunes *mpl*, jeunes gens *mpl*, jeunesse *f*; **~ lady** (*unmarried*) jeune fille *f*, demoiselle *f*; (*married*) jeune femme *f*; **they have a ~ family** ils ont de jeunes enfants; **listen to me, ~ man** écoutez-moi, jeune homme; **her ~ man*†** son amoureux, son petit ami; **~ in heart** jeune de cœur; **he is ~ for his age** il est jeune pour son âge, il paraît *or* fait plus jeune que son âge; **he is very ~ for this job** il est bien jeune pour ce poste; **to marry ~** se marier jeune; **he is 3 years younger than you** il est plus jeune que vous de 3 ans, il a 3 ans de moins que vous, il est votre cadet de 3 ans; **my younger brother** mon frère cadet; **my younger sister** ma sœur cadette; **the younger son of the family** le cadet de la famille; **I'm not so ~ as I was** je n'ai plus (mes) vingt ans (*fig*); **in my ~ days** dans ma jeunesse, dans mon jeune temps, quand j'étais jeune; **in my younger days** quand j'étais plus jeune; **to grow** *or* **get younger** rajeunir; **if I were younger** si j'étais plus jeune; **if I were 10 years younger** si j'avais 10 ans de moins; **you're only ~ once** jeunesse n'a qu'un temps; **you ~ scoundrel!** petit *or* jeune voyou!; **~ Mr Brown, Mr Brown the younger** le jeune M Brown; (*as opposed to his father*) M Brown fils; **Pitt the Younger** le second Pitt; **Pliny the Younger** Pline le Jeune; **the night is ~** (*liter*) la nuit n'est pas très avancée; (**hum*) on a toute la nuit devant nous*; **the younger generation** la jeune génération, la génération montante; **the ~ idea** (*lit*) ce que pensent les jeunes; (*fig*) la jeune génération; **Y~ France** la jeune génération en France; **he has a very ~ outlook** il a des idées très jeunes; **that dress is too ~ for her** cette robe est *or* fait trop jeune pour elle; **~ wine** vin vert; **~ nation** peuple neuf *or* jeune; (*fig*) **~ blood** sang nouveau *or* jeune; *V* **hopeful** *etc.*
2 *collective npl* **(a)** (*people*) **the ~** les jeunes *mpl*, les jeunes gens *mpl*, la jeunesse; **~ and old** les (plus) jeunes comme les (plus) vieux, tout le monde; **a mother defending her ~** une mère qui défend ses petits *or* sa nichée (*fig*); **books for the ~** livres pour les jeunes *or* la jeunesse.
(b) *[animal]* petits *mpl*. **cat with ~** chatte pleine.
3 *cpd*: **young-looking** qui a (*or* avait *etc*) l'air jeune; **she's very young-looking** elle a l'air *or* elle fait très jeune.
youngish ['jʌŋɪʃ] *adj* assez jeune.
youngster ['jʌŋstə^r] *n* (*boy*) jeune garçon *m*, jeune *m*; (*child*) enfant *mf*.
your [jʊə^r] *poss adj* **(a)** ton, ta, tes; votre, vos. **~ book** ton *or* votre livre; **YOUR book** ton livre à toi, votre livre à vous; **~ table** ta *or* votre table; **~ friend** ton ami(e) *or* votre ami(e); **~ clothes** tes *or* vos vêtements; **this is the best of ~ paintings** c'est ton *or* votre meilleur tableau; **give me ~ hand** donne-moi *or* donnez-moi la main; **you've broken ~ leg!** tu t'es cassé la jambe!; *V* **majesty, worship** *etc.*
(b) (*one's*) son, sa, ses; ton *etc*, votre *etc*. **you give him ~ form and he gives you ~ pass** on lui donne son formulaire et il vous remet votre laissez-passer; **exercise is good for ~ health** l'exercice est bon pour la santé.
(c) (*typical*) ton *etc*, votre *etc*. **so these are ~ country pubs?** alors c'est ça, vos bistro(t)s* de campagne?; **~ ordinary Englishman will always prefer ...** l'Anglais moyen préférera toujours ... .
you're [jʊə^r] = **you are**; *V* **be.**
yours [jʊəz] *poss pron* le tien, la tienne, les tiens, les tiennes; le vôtre, la vôtre, les vôtres. **this is my book and that is ~** voici mon livre et voilà le tien *or* le vôtre; **this book is ~** ce livre est à toi *or* à vous, ce livre est le tien *or* le vôtre; **is this poem ~?** ce poème est-il de toi? *or* de vous?; **when will the house become ~?** quand est-ce que la maison deviendra (la) vôtre?; **she is a cousin of ~** c'est une de tes *or* de vos cousines; **that is no business of ~** cela ne te *or* vous regarde pas, ce n'est pas ton *or* votre affaire; **it's no fault of ~** ce n'est pas de votre faute (à vous); (*Comm*) **~ of the 10th inst.** votre honorée du 10 courant (*Comm*); **no advice of ~ could prevent him** aucun conseil de votre part ne pouvait l'empêcher; **it is not ~ to decide** ce n'est pas à vous de décider, il ne vous appartient pas de décider; **~ is a specialized department** la vôtre *or* votre section est une section spécialisée; (*pej*) **that dog of ~** ton *or* votre sacré* *or* fichu* chien; **that stupid son of ~** ton *or* votre idiot de fils; **that temper of ~** ton *or* votre sale caractère; (*in pub etc*) **what's ~?** qu'est-ce que tu prends? *or* vous prenez?; *V* **affectionately, ever, you** *etc.*

yourself [jəˈself] *pers pron, pl* **yourselves** [jəˈselvz] (*reflexive: direct and indirect*) te, vous, (*pl*) vous; (*after prep*) toi, vous, (*pl*) vous; (*emphatic*) toi-même, vous-même, (*pl*) vous-mêmes. **have you hurt ~?** tu t'es fait mal?, vous vous êtes fait mal?; **are you enjoying ~?** tu t'amuses bien?, vous vous amusez bien?; **were you talking to ~?** tu te parlais à toi-même?, tu te parlais tout seul?, vous vous parliez à vous-même?, vous vous parliez tout seul?; **you never speak of ~** tu ne parles jamais de toi, vous ne parlez jamais de vous; **you ~ told me, you told me ~** tu me l'as dit toi-même, vous me l'avez dit vous-même; **(all) by ~** tout seul; **did you do it by ~?** tu l'as *or* vous l'avez fait tout seul?; **you will see for ~** tu verras toi-même, vous verrez vous-même; **how's ~?‡** et toi, comment (ça) va?*; **you are not (quite) ~ today** tu n'es pas dans ton assiette *or* vous n'êtes pas dans votre assiette aujourd'hui.

youth [juːθ] **1** *n* **(a)** (*U*) jeunesse *f*. **in (the days of) my ~** dans ma jeunesse, lorsque j'étais jeune, au temps de ma jeunesse; **in early ~** dans la première *or* prime jeunesse; **he has kept his ~** il est resté jeune; (*Prov*) **~ will have its way** *or* **its fling** il faut que jeunesse se passe; *V* **first**.

(b) (*pl* **youths** [juːðz]: *young man*) (jeune) homme *m*. **~s** jeunes gens *mpl*.

(c) (*collective: young people*) jeunesse *f*, jeunes *mpl*, jeunes gens *mpl*. **she likes working with (the) ~** elle aime travailler avec les jeunes; **the ~ of a country** la jeunesse d'un pays; **the ~ of today are very mature** les jeunes d'aujourd'hui sont très mûrs, la jeunesse aujourd'hui est très mûre.

2 *cpd* de jeunes, de jeunesse. **youth club** foyer *m or* centre *m* de jeunes; **youth leader** animateur *m*, -trice *f* de groupes de jeunes; **the Hitler Youth Movement** les Jeunesses hitlériennes; *V* **hostel**.

youthful [ˈjuːθfʊl] *adj person, looks, fashion* jeune; *air, mistake* de jeunesse; *quality, freshness* juvénile. **she looks ~** elle a l'air jeune, elle a un air de jeunesse.

youthfulness [ˈjuːθfʊlnɪs] *n* jeunesse *f*. **~ of appearance** air *m* jeune *or* de jeunesse.

you've [juːv] = **you have**; *V* **have**.

yow [jaʊ] *excl* aïe!

yowl [jaʊl] **1** *n [person, dog]* hurlement *m*; *[cat]* miaulement *m*. **2** *vi [person, dog]* hurler (*with, from* de); *[cat]* miauler.

yo-yo [ˈjəʊjəʊ] *n* ® yo-yo *m* ®.

yucca [ˈjʌkə] *n* yucca *m*.

yucky‡ [ˈjʌkɪ] *adj* dégueulasse‡, dégoûtant.

Yugoslav [ˈjuːgəʊˈslɑːv] **1** *adj* yougoslave. **2** *n* Yougoslave *mf*.

Yugoslavia [ˈjuːgəʊˈslɑːvɪə] *n* Yougoslavie *f*.

Yugoslavian [ˈjuːgəʊˈslɑːvɪən] *adj* yougoslave.

Yule [juːl] **1** *n* (†) Noël *m*. **2** *cpd:* **Yule log** bûche *f* de Noël; **Yuletide**† (époque *f* de) Noël *f*.

yummy‡ [ˈjʌmɪ] **1** *adj food* délicieux. **2** *excl* miam, miam!*

yum-yum‡ [ˈjʌmˈjʌm] *excl* = **yummy 2**.

Z

Z, z [zed, (*US*) ziː] *n* (*letter*) Z, z *m*.

Zaire [zɑːˈiːəʳ] *n* Zaïre *m*.

Zambesi [zæmˈbiːzɪ] *n* Zambèze *m*.

Zambia [ˈzæmbɪə] *n* Zambie *f*.

zany [ˈzeɪnɪ] **1** *adj* dingue‡, toqué*, cinglé*. **2** *n* (*Theat*) bouffon *m*, zan(n)i *m* (*Theat Hist*).

Zanzibar [ˈzænzɪbɑːʳ] *n* Zanzibar *m*.

zeal [ziːl] *n* (*U*) **(a)** (*religious fervour*) zèle *m*, ferveur *f*. **(b)** (*enthusiasm*) zèle *m*, ardeur *f* (*for* pour), empressement *m* (*for* à).

zealot [ˈzelət] *n* **(a)** fanatique *mf*, zélateur *m*, -trice *f* (*liter*) (*for* de).

(b) (*Jewish Hist*) **Z~** zélote *mf*.

zealotry [ˈzelətrɪ] *n* fanatisme *m*.

zealous [ˈzeləs] *adj* (*fervent*) zélé; (*devoted*) dévoué, empressé. **~ for the cause** plein de zèle *or* d'ardeur *or* d'enthousiasme pour la cause.

zealously [ˈzeləslɪ] *adv* (*fervently*) avec zèle, avec ferveur, avec ardeur; (*stronger*) avec fanatisme; (*devotedly*) avec zèle, avec empressement.

zebra [ˈziːbrə] **1** *n* zèbre *m*. **2** *cpd:* (*Brit*) **zebra crossing** passage *m* pour piétons; **zebra stripes** zébrures *fpl*; **with zebra stripes** zébré.

zebu [ˈziːbuː] *n* zébu *m*.

zed [zed], (*US*) **zee** [ziː] *n* (la lettre) z *m*.

Zen [zen] *n* Zen *m*.

zenana [zeˈnɑːnə] *n* zenana *m*.

zenith [ˈzenɪθ] *n* (*Astron*) zénith *m*; (*fig*) zénith, apogée *m*, faîte *m*. **at the ~ of his power** au zénith *or* à l'apogée *or* au faîte de son pouvoir.

zephyr [ˈzefəʳ] *n* zéphyr *m*.

zeppelin [ˈzeplɪn] *n* zeppelin *m*.

zero [ˈzɪərəʊ], *pl* **~s** *or* **~es** **1** *n* **(a)** (*point on scale*) zéro *m*. **15 degrees below ~** 15 degrés au-dessous de zéro; **absolute ~** zéro absolu; (*fig*) **his chances of success sank to ~** ses chances de réussite se réduisirent à zéro.

(b) (*esp US: cipher, numeral etc*) zéro *m*. **row of ~s** série *f* de zéros.

2 *cpd tension, voltage* nul (*f* nulle). (*Aviat*) **zero altitude** altitude *f* zéro; **to fly at zero altitude** voler en rase-mottes, faire du rase-mottes; **zero hour** (*Mil*) l'heure *f* H; (*fig*) le moment critique *or* décisif; **zero point** point *m* zéro.

zero in *vi:* **to zero in on sth** se diriger droit vers *or* sur qch, piquer droit sur qch.

zest [zest] *n* (*U*) **(a)** (*gusto*) entrain *m*, élan *m*, enthousiasme *m*. **to fight with ~** combattre avec entrain; **he ate it with great ~** il l'a mangé avec grand appétit; **~ for living** goût *m* pour la vie, appétit *m* de vivre.

(b) (*fig*) saveur *f*; piquant *m*. **story full of ~** histoire savoureuse; **it adds ~ to the episode** cela donne une certaine saveur *or* du piquant à l'histoire.

(c) (*Culin*) *[orange, lemon]* zeste *m*.

zestful [ˈzestfʊl] *adj* plein d'entrain, enthousiaste.

zestfully [ˈzestfəlɪ] *adv* avec entrain *or* enthousiasme *or* élan.

zigzag [ˈzɪgzæg] **1** *n* zigzag *m*.

2 *adj path, course, line* en zigzag; *road* en lacets; *pattern, design* à zigzags.

3 *adv* en zigzag.

4 *vi* zigzaguer, faire des zigzags. **to ~ along** avancer en zigzaguant, marcher *etc* en zigzag; **to ~ out/through** *etc* sortir/traverser *etc* en zigzaguant.

zinc [zɪŋk] **1** *n* (*U*) zinc *m*. **2** *cpd plate, alloy* de zinc; *roof* zingué. **zinc blende** blende *f*; **zinc chloride** chlorure *m* de zinc; **zinc dust** limaille *f* de zinc; **zinc ointment** pommade *f* à l'oxyde de zinc; **zinc oxide** oxyde *m* de zinc; **zinc sulphate** sulfate *m* de zinc; **zinc white** = **zinc oxide**.

zing [zɪŋ] **1** *n* **(a)** (*noise of bullet*) sifflement *m*. **(b)** (**U*) entrain *m*. **2** *vi [bullet, arrow]* siffler. **the bullet ~ed past his ear** la balle lui a sifflé à l'oreille; **the cars ~ed past** les voitures sont passées dans un bruit strident.

zinnia [ˈzɪnɪə] *n* zinnia *m*.

Zion [ˈzaɪən] *n* Sion *m*.

Zionism [ˈzaɪənɪzəm] *n* sionisme *m*.

Zionist [ˈzaɪənɪst] **1** *adj* sioniste. **2** *n* Sioniste *mf*.

zip [zɪp] **1** *n* **(a)** (*also* **~ fastener**) fermeture *f* éclair ®, fermeture à glissière. **pocket with a ~** poche *f* à fermeture éclair, poche zippée*.

(b) (*sound of bullet*) sifflement *m*.

(c) (**U*) entrain *m*, élan *m*.

2 *cpd:* (*US Post*) **zip code** code postal; **zip fastener** = **zip 1a**; **zip-on** à fermeture éclair ®.

3 *vt* **(a)** (*close: also* **~ up**) *dress, bag* fermer avec une fermeture éclair ® *or* à glissière.

(b) she ~ped open her dress/bag *etc* elle a ouvert la fermeture éclair ® *or* à glissière de sa robe/de son sac *etc*.

4 *vi* (*) *[car, person]* **to ~ in/out/past/up** *etc* entrer/sortir/passer/monter *etc* comme une flèche.

zip on **1** *vi* s'attacher avec une fermeture éclair ® *or* fermeture à glissière.

2 *vt sep* attacher avec une fermeture éclair ® *or* fermeture à glissière.

3 zip-on *adj V* **zip 2**.

zip up **1** *vi [dress etc]* se fermer avec une fermeture éclair ® *or* fermeture à glissière.

2 *vt sep V* **zip 3a**.

zipper [ˈzɪpəʳ] *n* = **zip 1a**.

zippy‡ [ˈzɪpɪ] *adj* plein d'entrain, dynamique.

zircon [ˈzɜːkən] *n* zircon *m*.

zither [ˈzɪðəʳ] *n* cithare *f*.

zodiac [ˈzəʊdɪæk] *n* zodiaque *m*; *V* **sign**.

zombie [ˈzɒmbɪ] *n* (**fig pej*) mort(e) *m(f)* vivant(e); (*lit*) zombi *m*.

zonal [ˈzəʊnl] *adj* zonal.

zone [ˈzəʊn] **1** *n* **(a)** (*Astron, Geog, Math etc*) zone *f*; (*esp Mil*) (*area*) zone; (*subdivision of town*) secteur *m*. **it lies within the ~ reserved for ...** cela se trouve dans le secteur *or* la zone réservé(e) à ...; *V* **battle, danger, time** *etc*.

(b) (*US: also* **postal delivery ~**) zone *f* (postale).

2 *vt* **(a)** (*divide into ~s*) *area* diviser en zones; *town* diviser en secteurs.

(b) this district has been ~d for industry c'est une zone réservée à l'implantation industrielle.
zoning ['zəʊnɪŋ] *n* répartition *f* en zones.
zoo [zu:] *n* zoo *m*. **~ keeper** gardien(ne) *m(f)* de zoo.
zoological [ˌzəʊə'lɒdʒɪkəl] *adj* zoologique. **~ gardens** jardin *m* *or* parc *m* zoologique.
zoologist [ˌzəʊ'ɒlədʒɪst] *n* zoologiste *mf*.
zoology [zəʊ'ɒlədʒɪ] *n* zoologie *f*.
zoom [zu:m] **1** *n* **(a)** (*sound*) vrombissement *m*, bourdonnement *m*.
(b) (*Aviat: upward flight*) montée *f* en chandelle.
(c) (*Phot: also* **~ lens**) zoom *m*.
2 *vi* **(a)** *[engine]* vrombir, bourdonner.
(b) to ~ away/through *etc* démarrer/traverser *etc* en trombe*; **the car ~ed past us** la voiture est passée en trombe* devant nous.
(c) (*Aviat*) *[plane]* monter en chandelle.
zoom in *vi* (*Cine*) faire un zoom (*on* sur).
zoomorphic [ˌzəʊəʊ'mɔ:fɪk] *adj* zoomorphe.
Zoroaster [ˌzɒrəʊ'æstəʳ] *n* Zoroastre *m*.
zucchini [zu:'ki:nɪ] *n* (*US*) courgette *f*.
Zuider Zee ['zaɪdəzi:] *n* Zuiderzee *m*.
Zulu ['zu:lu:] **1** *adj* zoulou (*f inv*).
2 *n* **(a)** Zoulou *mf*.
(b) (*Ling*) zoulou *m*.
3 *cpd:* **Zululand** Zoulouland *m*.
zwieback ['zwi:bæk] *n* (*US*) biscotte *f*.
zygote ['zaɪgəʊt] *n* zygote *m*.

ABRÉVIATIONS

ABBREVIATIONS

Abréviations courantes, en anglais et en français
Il n'existe pas de règles précises régissant l'emploi du point dans les abréviations anglaises. Lorsque l'abréviation se compose de plusieurs majuscules — lorsqu'il s'agit, en fait, d'un sigle — la tendance actuelle est d'omettre le(s) point(s), par exemple *BBC*, *FBI* et d'autres sigles désignant des institutions. On garde toutefois le(s) point(s) dans les sigles tels que *A.D.* (= anno domini).

Lorsque l'abréviation est constituée par une partie du mot entier le point est omis lorsque la dernière lettre de l'abréviation se trouve être celle du mot entier, par exemple *Abp* (= Archbishop); dans les autres cas, on fait suivre l'abréviation du point, par exemple *temp.* (= temperature) ou *ult.* (= ultimo).

Le signe & (esperluète) figure à la place alphabétique du mot 'and'.

Les abréviations utilisées pour les besoins de ce dictionnaire, mais qui ne sont pas nécessairement d'emploi courant, figurent à la page xxviii.

Abbreviations commonly used in French and English
There is no firm rule about the use of the point in English abbreviations. Where the abbreviation consists of more than one capital letter, modern usage increasingly tends to omit all points, thus *BBC*, *FBI* (initials of organizations); but the point is mostly retained in such cases as *A.D.* (= Anno Domini). Where the abbreviation consists of part(s) of a single word and the last letter of the original word is retained, no point is written, thus *Abp* (= Archbishop); in all other cases a final point is written, thus *temp.* (= temperature), *ult.* (= ultimo).

The ampersand (&) is placed in the alphabetical position for 'and'.

Abbreviations are generally pronounced letter for letter but those which are spoken as words have been given their phonetic transcription (*eg* NATO ['neɪtəʊ]).

Other abbreviations used in this dictionary, but which are not in general use, are given on page xxviii.

ABRÉVIATIONS FRANÇAISES
FRENCH ABBREVIATIONS

A

A_2 [adø] Antenne$_2$
Ach. Achète
ADN *nm* Acide désoxyribonucléique
AF *fpl* Allocations familiales
AFNOR [afnɔʀ] *nf* Association française de normalisation
AFP *nf* Agence France-Presse
AG *nf* Assemblée générale
ANPE *nf* Agence nationale pour l'emploi
AOC Appellation d'origine contrôlée
Appt Appartement
Ardt Arrondissement
AS *fpl* Assurances sociales
AS . . . *nf* Association sportive . . .
Asc. Ascenseur
ASSEDIC [asedik] *nf* Association pour l'emploi dans l'industrie et le commerce
av. Avenue; avant

B

BA *nm* (*Can*) Baccalauréat ès arts
B.A. *nf* Bonne action (d'un scout)
Bat. Bâtiment
BCG *nm* vaccin bilié de Calmette et Guérin
bd. Boulevard
BE *nm* Brevet élémentaire
BEI *nm* Brevet d'enseignement industriel
BENELUX [benelyks] *nm* Union douanière de la Belgique, du Luxembourg et des Pays-Bas
BEP *nm* Brevet d'études professionnelles
BEPC *nm* Brevet d'études du 1er cycle
BIT *nm* Bureau international du travail
BP *nf* Boîte postale
BSc *nm* (*Can*) Baccalauréat ès Sciences
BT *nm* Brevet de technicien
BTS *nm* Brevet de technicien supérieur

C

C. Celsius, centigrade
CAF [kaf] *nf* Caisse d'allocations familiales
CAP *nm* Certificat d'aptitude professionnelle
CAPES [kapɛs] *nm* Certificat d'aptitude au professorat de l'enseignement du second degré
CC *nm* Corps consulaire
CCP *nm* Compte chèques postaux
CD *nm* Corps diplomatique
CDS *nm* Centre des démocrates sociaux
CE *nm* Conseil de l'Europe
CEE *nf* Communauté économique européenne
CEG *nm* Collège d'enseignement général
CEGEP [seʒep] *nm* (*Québec*) collège d'enseignement général et professionnel; general and vocational college
CEP *nf* Caisse d'épargne et de prévoyance
CERN *nm* Conseil européen de recherches nucléaires
CES *nm* Collège d'enseignement secondaire
Ces. bail Cession bail
CET *nm* Collège d'enseignement technique
CFA *nf* Communauté française d'Afrique
CFDT *nf* Confédération française et démocratique du travail
CFF *mpl* Chemins de fer fédéraux (*suisses*)
CFL *nf* Société nationale des Chemins de fer luxembourgeois
CFTC *nf* Confédération générale des cadres
CGT *nf* Confédération générale du travail
Chbre Chambre
Ch. comp Charges comprises
Chf. cent. Chauffage central
CHU *nm* Centre hospitalier universitaire
Cial Commercial
CIDUNATI [sidynati] *nm* Comité d'information et de défense de l'union nationale des artisans et travailleurs indépendants
CIO *nm* Comité international olympique
CNPF *nm* Conseil national du patronat français
CNRS *nm* Centre national de la recherche scientifique
CNTE *nm* Centre national de télé-enseignement
COMECOM [kɔmekɔm] *nm* Conseil pour l'aide mutuelle économique
Constr. Construction
Cpt Comptant
C.Q.F.D. Ce qu'il fallait démontrer
CROUS [krus] *nm* Centre régional des œuvres universitaires et scolaires
CRS *nm* membre des Compagnies républicaines de sécurité

CV *nm* Curriculum vitae

D

DCA *nf* Défense contre avions
DDT *nm* dichloro-diphényl-trichloréthane
DEA *nm* Diplôme d'études approfondies
DES *nm* Diplôme d'études supérieures
DEUG [døg] *nm* Diplôme d'études universitaires générales
DOM *nm* Département d'outre-mer
DPLG Diplômé par le gouvernement
DST *nf* direction de la surveillance du territoire
DTTAB = TABDT
DUT *nm* Diplôme universitaire de technologie

E

EDF *nf* Électricité de France
EN *nf* École normale
EN . . . *nf* École nationale . . .
ENA [enɑ] *nf* École nationale d'administration
ENI [eni] *nf* École nationale d'ingénieurs
ENS . . . [ənɛs] *nf* École nationale supérieure . . .
ENSI [ɛnsi] *nf* École nationale supérieure d'ingénieurs
EOR *nm* Élève officier de réserve
Et. Étage

F

F Francs
FB Franc belge
FC . . . *nm* Football club . . .
FEN [fɛn] *nf* Fédération de l'éducation nationale
FF frères; franc français
FF . . . *nf* Fédération française . . .
FFI *fpl* Forces françaises de l'intérieur
FLN *nm* Front de libération nationale
F.M. *nf* Fréquence modulée
FMI *nm* Fonds monétaire international
FNSEA *nf* Fédération nationale des syndicats d'exploitants agricoles
FO *nf* Force ouvrière
FPLP *nm* Front populaire pour la libération de la Palestine
FR$_3$ [ɛfɛʀtʀwɑ] France Régions$_3$
FS Franc suisse

G

GDF *nm* Gaz de France
GO Grandes ondes

H

Ha Hectare
HEC *fpl* Hautes études commerciales
HF Haute fréquence
HLM *nf* Habitation à loyer modéré

I

IFOP [ifɔp] *nm* Institut française d'opinion publique
Imm. Immeuble
IN . . . [in] *nm* Institut national . . .
INSEE [inse] *nm* Institut national de la statistique et des études économiques
IPES [ipɛs] *nm* Institut de préparation aux enseignements du second degré
IUT *nm* Institut universitaire de technologie

J

J-C Jésus-Christ
J.F. Jeune fille
J.H. Jeune homme
JO *nm* Journal officiel

K

Km Kilomètre

M

M. Monsieur
Max. Maximum
Me Maître
Messrs Messieurs
MF Modulation de fréquence
Mgr Monseigneur
Min. Minimum
MLF *nm* Mouvement de libération des femmes
Mlle Mademoiselle
MM Messieurs
Mme Madame
M° Métro

N

NB Nota bene
NF Norme française; nouveaux francs

O

OC Ondes courtes
OCDE *nf* Organisation de coopération et de développement économique
OMM *nf* Organisation météorologique mondiale
OMS *nf* Organisation mondiale de la santé
ONU *nf* Organisation des nations unies
OPEP [opɛp] *nf* Organisation des pays exportateurs de pétrole
ORTF *nm* (†) Office de la radiodiffusion et télévision française
ORSEC [ɔʀsɛk] Organisation des secours
OS *nm* Ouvrier spécialisé
OTAN [otɑ̃] *nf* Organisation du traité de l'Atlantique Nord
OUA *nf* Organisation de l'unité africaine
OVNI [ɔvni] *nm* Objet volant non identifié

P

P. Pièce
Park. *nm* Parking
PC *nm* Parti communiste; accusé de réception; poste de commandement
PCC *nm* Pour copie conforme
PCV *nm* (Per-Ce-Voir) communication téléphonique payable par le destinataire
PDG *nm* Président-directeur général
Pl. Place
PME *fpl* Petites et moyennes entreprises
PMI *fpl* Petites et moyennes industries
PMU *nm* Pari mutuel urbain
PNB *nm* Produit national brut
PO Petites ondes
Ppte Propriété
PR *nm* Parti républicain
PS *nm* Parti socialiste; post-scriptum
PSU *nm* Parti socialiste unifié
P et T *fpl* Postes et télécommunications
Pte Porte
PTT *fpl* Postes télégraphes téléphones
P.-V. *nm* Procès-verbal
Px Prix

Q

QG *nm* Quartier général
QI *nm* Quotient intellectuel

R

r. Route; rue
RATP *nf* Régie autonome des transports parisiens
RD *nf* Route départementale
RDA *nf* République Démocratique Allemande
R.d.C. Rez-de-chaussée
Rech. Recherche
Ref. Référence
RER *nm* Réseau express régional
RF République française
RFA *nf* République Fédérale Allemande
RN *nf* Route nationale
RP Recette principale
RPR *nm* Rassemblement pour la république
RSVP Répondez s'il vous plaît
Rte Route
RTL Radio télé(vision) luxembourgeoise
R-V Rendez-vous

S

SA Société anonyme
SARL Société à responsabilité limitée
SDECE [zdɛk] *nm* Service de documentation extérieure et de contre-espionnage
SDN *nf* Société des nations
SECAM [sekɑm] *nm* Séquentiel à mémoire (*procédé TV*)
SEITA [seitɑ] *nf* Service d'exploitation industrielle des tabacs et allumettes
SFIO *nf* Section française de l'internationale ouvrière
SFP *nf* Société française de production
SGDG Sans garantie du gouvernement
SGEN [sgɛn] *nm* Syndicat général de l'éducation nationale
SICAV [sikɑv] *nf* Société d'investissement à capital variable
SMAG [smɑg] *nm* Salaire minimum agricole garanti
SMIC [smik] *nm* Salaire minimum interprofessionnel de croissance
SMIG [smig] *nm* Salaire minimum interprofessionnel garanti
SNCB *nf* Société nationale des chemins de fer belges
SNCF *nf* Société nationale des chemins de fer français
SNI [sni] *nm* Syndicat national des instituteurs
SNES [snɛs] *nm* Syndicat national de l'enseignement secondaire
SNE sup [sne syp] *nm* Syndicat national de l'enseignement supérieur
SOFRES [sɔfʀɛs] *nf* Société française d'enquêtes pour sondage
SOS *nm* Save our souls: message de détresse
SPA *nf* Société protectrice des animaux
SS *nf* Sécurité sociale
Sté Société
SVP S'il vous plaît

T

TABDT *nm* Vaccin antityphoïdique et antiparatypoïdique A et B, antidiphtérique et tétanique
TEE *nm* Trans-Europ-Express
Tél. Téléphone
TF_1 [teɛfœ̃] Télévision française 1
TNP *nm* Théâtre national populaire
TNT *nm* Trinitrotoluène
TOM *nm* Territoire d'outre-mer
TSF *nf* Télégraphie sans fil
TSVP Tournez s'il vous plaît
TTC Toutes taxes comprises
Tt cft Tout confort
TVA *nf* Taxe sur la valeur ajoutée

U

UDF *nf* Union pour la démocratie française
UER *nf* Unité d'enseignement et de recherche
UNEDIC [ynedik] *nf* Union nationale pour l'emploi dans l'industrie et le commerce
UNEF [ynɛf] *nf* Union nationale des étudiants de France
UNESCO [ynɛsko] *nf ou m* United Nations Educational, Scientific and Cultural Organization
UNICEF [ynisɛf] *nf ou m* United Nations International Children's Emergency Fund
URSS *nf* Union des Républiques Socialistes Soviétiques
URSSAF [yʀsɑf] *nf* Union pour le recouvrement des cotisations de la Sécurité sociale et des allocations familiales
US . . . *nf* Union sportive de . . .
UV *nm* Ultra-violet; unité de valeur

V

Vd Vend
VDQS Vin de qualité supérieure
VRP *nm* Voyageurs, représentants, placiers
VSOP Very superieur old pale (très vieil alcool supérieur)

W

WC *mpl* Water-closet

Z

ZAC [zɑk] *nf* Zone d'aménagement concerté
ZAD [zɑd] *nf* Zone d'aménagement différé
ZUP [zyp] *nf* Zone à urbaniser en priorité

ABRÉVIATIONS ANGLAISES
ENGLISH ABBREVIATIONS

A

A	1 answer
	2 (*Brit Cine*) adults
AA	1 Automobile Association
	2 Alcoholics Anonymous
	3 (*Brit Cine*) Restricted
AAA	1 Amateur Athletic Association
	2 American Automobile Association
AAU	(*US*) Amateur Athletic Union
A.A.U.P.	American Association of University Professors
A.B.	1 (*Naut*) able-bodied seaman
	2 (*US Univ*) = **B.A.**
ABA	Amateur Boxing Association
ABC	American Broadcasting Company
Abp	Archbishop
abr	abridged
abs., absol.	absolutely
abs., abstr.	abstract
A/C	account current
a/c	account
AC	1 (*Elec*) alternating current
	2 aircraftman
acc.	(*Fin*) account
ACGB	Arts Council of Great Britain
A.D.	Anno Domini, in the year of our Lord
ADC	aide-de-camp
Adjt	adjutant
ad lib	ad libitum, at pleasure
admin.	administration
advt	advertisement
AEC	(*US*) Atomic Energy Commission
AEF	1 Amalgamated Union of Engineering and Foundry Workers
	2 (*US*) American Expeditionary Forces
AEU	Amalgamated Engineering Union
A.F.C.	(*US*) Air Force Cross
AFL-CIO	American Federation of Labor *and* Congress of Industrial Organizations
A.F.M.	(*US*) Air Force Medal
AFN	American Forces Network
AGM	Annual General Meeting
A1	first class
AI	Amnesty International
A.I.(D.)	artificial insemination (by donor)
Ala.	(*US*) Alabama
Alas.	(*US*) Alaska
Alta.	(*Can*) Alberta
A.M.	(*US Univ*) = **M.A.**
a.m.	ante meridiem, before noon
A.M.A.	American Medical Association
anon.	anonymous
AO(C)B	any other (competent) business
A.P.O.	(*US*) Army Post Office
app.	appendix
appro.	approval
apt	apartment
A.R.A.M.	Associate of the Royal Academy of Music
A.R.C.M.	Associate of the Royal College of Music
A.R.I.B.A.	Associate of the Royal Institute of British Architects
Ariz.	(*US*) Arizona
Ark.	(*US*) Arkansas
arr.	arrives
A/S	account sales
ASLEF	[æzlef] Associated Society of Locomotive Engineers and Firemen
A.S.P.C.A.	American Society for the Prevention of Cruelty to Animals
assn	association
ASTMS	Association of Scientific, Technical and Managerial Staffs
Att., Atty.	Attorney (*US*); sollicitor (*Brit*)
Atty. Gen.	Attorney-General
AUT	Association of University Teachers
A.V.	Authorized Version (of the Bible)
av.	average
Av., Ave.	Avenue
avdp.	avoirdupois
a.w.	atomic weight
AWOL	(*Mil*) absent without leave

B

b.	born
B.A.	1 (*Univ*) Bachelor of Arts
	2 British Academy
	3 British Association (for the Advancement of Science)
b. & b., B. & B.	bed and breakfast
BAOR	British Army of the Rhine
Bart	Baronet
Battn	battalion
BB	Boys' Brigade
BBC	British Broadcasting Corporation
B.C.	1 before Christ
	2 British Columbia
BCG	Bacillus Calmette-Guérin
B.D.	Bachelor of Divinity
Beds.	Bedfordshire
BEF	British Expeditionary Force
B.E.M.	British Empire Medal
Benelux	Belgium, Netherlands, Luxembourg
Berks.	Berkshire
B.F.	(*euph*) bloody fool
b/f	(*Fin*) brought forward
BFI	British Film Institute
B.F.P.O.	British Forces Post Office
biog.	1 biography
	2 biographical
bk	1 book
	2 (*Fin*) bank
B.L.	Bachelor of Law
B/L	bill of lading
bldg	building
B. Litt.	Bachelor of Letters
Blvd.	Boulevard
B.M.	1 Bachelor of Medicine
	2 British Museum
BMA	British Medical Association
B. Mus.	Bachelor of Music
B.O.	(*euph*) body odour
B. of E.	Bank of England
bor.	borough
BOT	Board of Trade
Bp	Bishop
BP	British Petroleum
BR	British Rail
Br	Brother
B/R	bill receivable
Brecon.	Breconshire (Wales)
Brig.	Brigadier
Bros	Brothers
B/S	bill of sale
BSC	British Steel Corporation
B.Sc.	Bachelor of Science
B.Sc. Econ.	Bachelor of Economic Science
BSI	British Standards Institution
BST	1 British Summer Time
	2 British Standard Time
Bucks.	Buckinghamshire

B.V.M. Blessed Virgin Mary

C

C. 1 (*Literat*) chapter
2 (*Geog*) Cape
3 central
4 Centigrade

c. 1 (*US Fin*) cent
2 (*Fin: France*) centime
3 century
4 circa, about
5 (*Math*) cubic

C.A. Chartered Accountant
C/A current account
Caer. Caernarvonshire (Wales)
Cal., Calif. (*US*) California
Cambs. Cambridgeshire
Cantab. (*Univ*) Cantabrigiensis, of Cambridge
CAP Common Agricultural Policy
Capt. Captain
Card. Cardiganshire (Wales)
Carm. Carmarthenshire (Wales)
carr. carriage
CAT College of Advanced Technology
cat. catalogue

C.B. 1 Companion of the Bath
2 (*Mil*) confined to barracks
3 cash book

CBC Canadian Broadcasting Corporation
C.B.E. Commander of the Order of the British Empire
CBI Confederation of British Industries
CBS (*US*) Columbia Broadcasting System

CC 1 Chamber of Commerce
2 County Council
3 Cricket Club

CEGB Central Electricity Generating Board
Cent. centigrade
CENTO ['sentəʊ] Central Treaty Organization
cert. certificate
CEWC Council for Education in World Citizenship
cf. confer, compare
c/f, c/fwd (*Fin*) carried forward
ch. (*Literat*) chapter
Ch.B Chirurgiae Baccalaureus, Bachelor of Surgery
Ches. Cheshire
C.I. Channel Islands
c/i certificate of insurance
CIA (*US*) Central Intelligence Agency
CID Criminal Investigation Department
c.i.f. cost, insurance and freight
C.(I.)G.S. Chief of (Imperial) General Staff
C.-in-C. Commander-in-Chief
CIO (*US*) Congress of Industrial Organizations
C.M. Common Market
C.M.S. Church Missionary Society
CND Campaign for Nuclear Disarmament

Co. 1 (*Comm*) company
2 county

C.O. 1 (*Mil*) Commanding Officer
2 conscientious objector

c/o care of
C.O.D. (*Comm*) cash on delivery
C. of E. Church of England
COI Central Office of Information
Col. (*Mil*) Colonel
col. column
coll. college
Colo. (*US*) Colorado
Com. Communist
Comecon ['kɒmi:kɒn] Council for Mutual Economic Assistance
conj. conjugation
Conn. (*US*) Connecticut
Cons. Conservative
cont., cont'd continued
Co-op Co-operative (Society)
Corn. Cornwall

Corp. 1 (*Comm, Fin*) Corporation
2 (*Pol*) Corporation
3 (*Mil*) Corporal

Coy company

C.P. 1 (*Pol*) Communist Party
2 (*Comm*) carriage paid

cp. compare
c.p. candlepower
C.P.A. (*US*) Certified Public Accountant
Cpl Corporal

Cr. 1 (*Comm*) credit; creditor
2 (*Pol*) councillor

C.R.T. cathode-ray tube
C.S.M. Company Sergeant-Major
C.U. Cambridge University
cu. ft. cubic foot, cubic feet
cu. in. cubic inch(es)
Cumb. Cumberland
c.w.o. cash with order
CWS Cooperative Wholesale Society
cwt hundredweight(s)
C.Z. Canal Zone

D

d. 1 date
2 daughter
3 died
4 (*Rail etc*) departs
5 (*Fin*) denarius, penny

D.A. 1 (*Fin*) deposit account
2 (*US*) District Attorney

dag. decagram(s), decagramme(s)
dal. decalitre(s)
dam. decametre(s)
D.B.E. Dame Commander of the Order of the British Empire

D.C. 1 (*Elec*) direct current
2 (*US*) District of Columbia

D.C.M. Distinguished Conduct Medal
D.D. Doctor of Divinity
D.D.S. Doctor of Dental Surgery
dec. deceased
Del. (*US*) Delaware
Dem. Democrat
Denb. Denbighshire (Wales)
dep. departs
dept department
Derbys. Derbyshire
DES Department of Education and Science
D.F.C. Distinguished Flying Cross
D.F.M. Distinguished Flying Medal
DHSS Department of Health and Social Security
diam. diameter
Dip. Diploma
dist. district
div. dividend
D.I.Y. do-it-yourself

DJ 1 dinner jacket
2 disc jockey

D.Lit. Doctor of Letters
DM Deutschmark
D.M. Doctor of Medicine
D.Mus. Doctor of Music
do. ditto
D.O.A. (*US*) dead on arrival (e.g. at hospital)
dol. dollar(s)

doz.	dozen
D.P.	displaced person
D.Phil.	Doctor of Philosophy
D.P.P.	Director of Public Prosecutions
dpt	department
Dr	1 doctor 2 (*Comm*) debtor
d/s	days after sight
D.S.C.	Distinguished Service Cross
D.Sc.	Doctor of Science
D.S.M.	Distinguished Service Medal
D.S.O.	Distinguished Service Order
DTs	delirium tremens
D.V.	Deo volente, God willing

E

E.	east
ea.	each
E. & O.E.	errors and omissions excepted
ECG	electrocardiogram
ECOSOC	Economic and Social Council
ECSC	European Coal and Steel Community
ed.	1 edition 2 editor 3 edited
E/E	errors excepted
EEC	European Economic Community
EFTA	European Free Trade Association
e.g.	exempli gratia, for example
encl.	enclosure(s)
E.N.E.	east-north-east
E.P.	1 electroplate 2 (*Mus*) extended play
EPU	European Payments Union
E.R.	Elizabeth Regina, Queen Elizabeth
ERNIE	['ɜːnɪ] Electronic Random Number Indicator Equipment
E.S.E.	east-south-east
E.S.N.	(*euph*) educationally subnormal
E.S.P.	extrasensory perception
Esq.	Esquire
est.	established
ETA	estimated time of arrival
et al.	et alii, and others
et seq.	et sequentia, and the following
ETU	Electrical Trades Union
Euratom	[jʊər'ætəm] European Atomic Energy Community
ex.	example
excl.	1 excluding 2 exclusive
ex div.	ex dividend, without dividend
ex int.	ex interest, without interest
ext.	(*Telec*) extension

F

F.	1 Fahrenheit 2 (*Rel*) Father
f.	1 (*Naut*) fathom 2 (*Math*) foot, feet 3 following 4 female
FA	Football Association
FAA	(*US*) Federal Aviation Agency
FAO	Food and Agriculture Organization
FBI	(*US*) Federal Bureau of Investigation
F.C.	Football Club
FCC	(*US*) Federal Communications Commission
F.D.	Fidei Defensor, Defender of the Faith
FDA	(*US*) Food and Drug Administration
ff.	following
FHA	(*US*) Federal Housing Administration
F'hold	freehold
FIFA	Federation of International Football Associations
Fla.	(*US*) Florida
Flint.	Flintshire (Wales)
F/Lt	Flight Lieutenant
F.M.	1 (*Mil*) Field Marshal 2 (*Rad*) frequency modulation
fm	fathom
F.O.	(*Aviat*) Flying Officer
Fo., fol.	folio
f.o.b.	free on board
foll.	following
f.o.r.	free on rail
F.P.	1 fire plug 2 freezing point
Fr	1 Father 2 Friar
fr.	1 (*Fin*) franc(s) 2 from
F.R.I.B.A.	Fellow of the Royal Institute of British Architects
F.R.S.	Fellow of the Royal Society
ft.	foot, feet
FTC	(*US*) Federal Trade Commission

G

G	(*US Cine*) General
g.	gram(s), gramme(s)
Ga.	(*US*) Georgia
gal.	gallon(s)
GATT	General Agreement on Tariffs and Trade
G.B.	Great Britain
G.C.	George Cross
G.C.E.	General Certificate of Education
G.C.F.	greatest common factor
Gdns.	Gardens
GDR	German Democratic Republic
Gen.	General
GHQ	General Headquarters
G.I.	(*US*) government issue
Gib.	Gibraltar
Gk	Greek
Glam.	Glamorgan (Wales)
GLC	Greater London Council
Glos.	Gloucestershire
G.M.	George Medal
gm, gms	gram(s), gramme(s)
GMC	General Medical Council
GMT	Greenwich Mean Time
GMWU	General and Municipal Workers' Union
GNP	gross national product
G.O.C.	General Officer Commanding
G.O.M.	grand old man
G.O.P.	(*US*) Grand Old Party
Gov.	Governor
Govt	Government
G.P.	general practitioner
GP	(*US Cine*) for mature audiences
GPO	General Post Office
G.R.	Georgius Rex, King George
gr.	1 gross (*brut*) 2 gross (= 144)
G.R.T.	gross register tons
G.S.	General Staff
guar.	guaranteed

H

h.	hour(s)
h. & c.	hot and cold (water)
Hants.	Hampshire
H.C.	House of Commons
H.C.F.	highest common factor
H.E.	1 high explosive 2 His Excellency

	3 (*Rel*) His Eminence
Herts.	Hertfordshire
HEW	(*US*) Department of Health, Education and Welfare
H.F.	high frequency
hf.	half
hg.	hectogram(s), hectogramme(s)
HGV	heavy goods vehicle
H.H.	1 His (Her) Highness 2 (*Rel*) His Holiness
H.I.M.	His (Her) Imperial Majesty
H.K.	Hong Kong
hl.	hectolitre(s)
H.L.	House of Lords
hm.	hectometre(s)
H.M.	His (Her) Majesty
H.M.I.	His (Her) Majesty's Inspector
HMS	His (Her) Majesty's Ship
H.M.S.O.	Her Majesty's Stationery Office
HNC/HND	Higher National Certificate/ Higher National Diploma
ho.	house
Hon.	1 Honorary 2 Honourable (*Brit*)
H.P., h.p.	1 (*Comm*) hire purchase 2 (*Tech*) horsepower
HQ	Headquarters
hr(s)	hour(s)
H.R.H.	His (Her) Royal Highness
ht	height
HT	high-tension
Hunts.	Huntingdonshire
HV	high-voltage
H.W.M.	high-water mark

I

I.	Island, Isle
Ia.	(*US*) Iowa
IAAF	International Amateur Athletic Federation
I.A.E.A.	International Atomic Energy Agency
I.B.	1 (*Comm*) invoice book 2 (*Pol*) International Brigade
IBA	Independent Broadcasting Authority
IBM	International Business Machines
I.C.	Intelligence Corps
i/c	in charge (of)
I.C.A.	1 Institute of Chartered Accountants 2 Institute of Contemporary Arts
ICAO	International Civil Aviation Organization
ICBM	intercontinental ballistic missile
I.C.E.	Institute of Civil Engineers
ICFTU	International Confederation of Free Trade Unions
I.C.I.	Imperial Chemical Industries
ID	identification
I.D.A.	International Development Association
Ida.	(*US*) Idaho
i.e.	id est, that is, namely
I.L.E.A.	Inner London Education Authority
I.L.G.W.U.	(*US*) International Ladies' Garment Workers' Union
Ill.	(*US*) Illinois
ill.	1 illustrated 2 illustration
ILO	International Labour Organization
ILP	Independent Labour Party
IMF	International Monetary Fund
in., ins	inch(es)
Inc.	(*US*) Incorporated
incl.	1 including 2 inclusive
Ind.	1 (*US*) Indiana 2 (*Pol*) Independent
ins.	1 insurance 2 inches
Inst.	Institute
inst.	instant, of the present month
I.O.M.	Isle of Man
IOU	I owe you
I.O.W.	Isle of Wight
IPA	1 International Phonetic Association 2 International Phonetic Alphabet
IQ	intelligence quotient
I.R.	Inland Revenue
I.R.A.	Irish Republican Army
IRS	(*US*) Internal Revenue Service
Is.	Isle(s), Island(s)
I.S.B.N.	International Standard Book Number
ITA	Independent Television Authority
i.t.a.	initial teaching alphabet
ITN	Independent Television News
ITV	Independent Television
I.U.D.	intra-uterine device
IUS	International Union of Students

J

J.C.	Jesus Christ
Jn	junction
J.P.	Justice of the Peace
Jr, Jun., Junr	junior

K

Kan.	(*US*) Kansas
K.B.E.	Knight of the British Empire
K.C.	King's Counsel
Ken.	(*US*) Kentucky
K.G.	Knight of the Garter
KGB	*Russian Secret Police*
kHz	Kilohertz
KKK	(*US*) Ku Klux Klan
K.O.	knock-out
Kt	Knight
kw.	kilowatt(s)
kw/h.	kilowatt-hours
Ky.	(*US*) Kentucky

L

L.	1 (*Ling*) Latin 2 Licentiate 3 (*Aut*) learner 4 Lake 5 Large
l.	1 left 2 litre(s)
La.	(*US*) Louisiana
LA	(*US*) Los Angeles
Lab.	1 (*Pol*) Labour 2 (*Can*) Labrador
Lancs.	Lancashire
Lat.	Latin
lat.	latitude
lb.	libra, pound
l.b.w.	(cricket) leg before wicket
L.C.	1 Lord Chancellor 2 (*Comm*) letter of credit
L.C.D.	lowest common denominator
L.C.F.	lowest common factor
L.C.M.	lowest common multiple
L-Cpl	Lance-Corporal
Ld	Lord
LEA	Local Education Authority
Leics.	Leicestershire
l.h.	left hand
L.I.	(*US*) Long Island
Lib.	1 Library 2 (*Pol*) Liberal

Lieut. Lieutenant
Lieut.-Col. Lieutenant-Colonel
Lincs. Lincolnshire
Litt.D. Litterarum Doctor, Doctor of Letters
ll. lines
Ll.B. Legum Baccalaureus, Bachelor of Laws
Ll.D. Legum Doctor, Doctor of Laws
long. longitude
L.P. 1 (*Pol*) Labour Party
2 (*Mus*) long-playing (record)
LPG Liquified Petroleum Gas
L.R.A.M. Licentiate of the Royal Academy of Music
L.s.d. Librae, solidi, denarii; pounds, shillings, and pence
LSD (*Chem*) lysergic acid diethylomide
LSE London School of Economics
Lt. Lieutenant
LT low-tension
Lt.-Col. Lieutenant-Colonel
Ltd Limited
Lt.-Gen. Lieutenant-General
LV luncheon voucher
L.W.M. low-water mark

M

M medium
m. 1 married
2 metre(s)
3 mile(s)
4 male
5 minute(s)
6 million
M.A. Master of Arts
Maj. Major
Maj.-Gen. Major-General
Man., Manit. (*Can*) Manitoba
Mass. (*US*) Massachusetts
max. maximum
M.B. Medicinae Baccalaureus, Bachelor of Medicine
M.B.E. Member of the Order of the British Empire
M.C. 1 Master of Ceremonies
2 (*US*) Member of Congress
3 (*Mil*) Military Cross
MCC Marylebone Cricket Club
M.D. 1 Medicinae Doctor, Doctor of Medicine
2 (*euph*) mentally deficient
Md. (*US*) Maryland
Mddx Middlesex
Me. (*US*) Maine
Med. 1 medieval
2 (*Med*) medical
Mer. Merionethshire (Wales)
Messrs Messieurs
Met. Metropolitan
met. meteorological
mfd manufactured
mfg manufacturing
mfr manufacturer
mfs manufacturers
Mgr Monsignor
M.I.5 Military Intelligence (5)
Mich. (*US*) Michigan
MIDAS [ˈmaɪdəs] Missile Defence Alarm System
Min. 1 Minister
2 Ministry
min. 1 minute(s)
2 minimum
Minn. (*US*) Minnesota
misc. miscellaneous
Miss. (*US*) Mississippi
M.I.T. Massachusetts Institute of Technology
MLA Modern Language Association (of America)
MLR Minimum Lending Rate
M.M. Military Medal
M.N. Merchant Navy
Mo. (*US*) Missouri
M.O. 1 (*Fin*) money order
2 medical officer
M.O.D. Ministry of Defence
mod. cons. modern conveniences
M.O.H. 1 Medical Officer of Health
2 Ministry of Health
mol. wt. molecular weight
Mon. Monmouthshire (Wales)
Mont. 1 Montgomeryshire (Wales)
2 (*US*) Montana
MOT Ministry of Transport
M.P. 1 (*Pol*) Member of Parliament
2 (*Mil*) Military Police
3 Metropolitan Police (London)
M.P.B.W. Ministry of Public Building and Works
m.p.g. miles per gallon
m.p.h. miles per hour
M.P.S. Member of the Pharmaceutical Society
Mr Mister
MRC Medical Research Council
MRP manufacturer's recommended price
Mrs Mistress
M.S. motorship
M.Sc. Master of Science
M.S.L. mean sea-level
Mt Mount
MTB motor torpedo-boat
Mus.B. Musicae Baccalaureus, Bachelor of Music
Mus.D. Musicae Doctor, Doctor of Music
Mx Middlesex

N

N. north
n. 1 neuter
2 name
NAACP (*US*) National Association for the Advancement of Colored People
NAAFI Navy, Army and Air Force Institutes
NALGO National Association of Local Government Officers
NAS 1 National Association of Schoolmasters
2 (*US*) National Academy of Science
NASA (*US*) National Astronautics and Space Administration
Nat. 1 National
2 (*Pol*) Nationalist
Nat. Hist. Natural History
NATO [ˈneɪtəʊ] North Atlantic Treaty Organization
N.B. 1 nota bene, note well
2 (*Can*) New Brunswick
N.C. (*US*) North Carolina
NCB National Coal Board
N.C.O. non-commissioned officer
N.D., N.Dak. (*US*) North Dakota
n.d. no date
N.E. 1 (*US*) New England
2 north-east
Neb., Nebr. (*US*) Nebraska
NEDC (*fam:* **Neddy**) National Economic Development Council
Nev. (*US*) Nevada
N.F. Newfoundland
NF National Front
NFS National Fire Service
NFU National Farmers' Union
N.H. (*US*) New Hampshire

N.H.(I.)	National Health (Insurance)
N.H.S.	National Health Service
NIBMAR	[ˈnɪbmɑːʳ] no independence before majority rule
N.J.	(*US*) New Jersey
NLI	National Lifeboat Institution
N.M., N.Mex.	(*US*) New Mexico
N.N.E.	north-north-east
N.N.W.	north-north-west
No.	1 numero, number 2 north
non seq.	non sequitur, it does not follow
Northants.	Northamptonshire
Northumb.	Northumberland
Nos.	numbers
Notts.	Nottinghamshire
n.p. or d.	no place or date
nr	near
N.S.	(*Can*) Nova Scotia
NSB	National Savings Bank
NSPCC	National Society for the Prevention of Cruelty to Children
N.S.W.	New South Wales
N.T.	New Testament
nt wt	net weight
N.U.I.	National University of Ireland
NUJ	National Union of Journalists
NUM	National Union of Mineworkers
NUR	National Union of Railwaymen
NUS	National Union of Students
NUT	National Union of Teachers
N.W.	north-west
NWAP	National Women's Aid Federation
N.W.T.	North West Territory
N.Y.	New York
N.Y.C.	New York City
N.Z.	New Zealand

O

O.	1 (*US*) Ohio 2 (*Can*) Ontario
O.A.P.	old-age pension(er)
OAS	Organization of American States
O.A.U.	Organization of African Unity
Ob.	Obiit, died
O.B.E.	Officer of the Order of the British Empire
O.C.	Officer Commanding
OECD	Organization for European Cooperation and Development
OEEC	Organization for European Economic Cooperation
O.H.M.S.	On His (Her) Majesty's Service
Okla.	(*US*) Oklahoma
O.M.	Order of Merit
o.n.o.	or near offer
Ont.	(*Can*) Ontario
op. cit.	opere citato, in the work cited
O.P.E.C.	[ˈəʊpek] Organization of Petroleum Exporting Countries
opp.	opposite
O.R.	operational research
ord.	ordinary
Ore.	(*US*) Oregon
orig.	origin, original
O.S.	1 (*Naut*) ordinary seaman 2 (*Geog*) Ordnance Survey 3 outsize
O.T.	Old Testament
Oxon.	1 Oxfordshire 2 (*Univ*) Oxoniensis, of Oxford
oz.	ounce(s)

P

p.	page
p	(*Fin*) penny, pence (*pl*)
P.A.	1 Press Association 2 personal assistant 3 public address system
Pa.	(*US*) Pennsylvania
p.a.	per annum, yearly
p & p	postage and packing
par., para.	paragraph
pat.	patent
PAU	Pan-American Union
P.A.Y.E.	Pay as you earn
P.C.	1 police constable 2 Privy Council 3 Privy Councillor 4 Parish Council
p.c.	1 postcard 2 per cent
pd	paid
P.E.	physical education
P.E.I.	Prince Edward Island
Pemb.	Pembrokeshire
P.E.N. Club	(International Association of) Poets, Playwrights, Editors, Essayists and Novelists
Penn.	(*US*) Pennsylvania
per pro.	per procurationem, by proxy
Pfc.	(*US Mil*) private first class
PF	Patriotic Front
Ph.D.	Doctor of Philosophy
PIB	Prices and Incomes Board
Pl.	Place
P/L	profit and loss
PLO	Palestinian Liberation Organization
P.M.	Prime Minister
p.m.	post meridiem, after noon
P.M.G.	Postmaster General
P.O.	1 post office 2 (*Aviat*) Pilot Officer
p.o.	postal order
P.O.B.	post office box
pop.	population
poss.	1 possible 2 possibly
P.O.W.	prisoner of war
p.p.	per procurationem, by proxy
pp.	pages
PPE	philosophy, politics and economics
PPS	1 Parliamentary Private Secretary 2 post-postscriptum
P.R.	1 (*Pol*) proportional representation 2 (*Comm*) public relations 3 Puerto Rico
pr	pair
Pres.	1 president 2 (*Rel*) Presbyterian
P.R.O.	1 Public Record Office 2 (*Comm etc*) public relations officer
prop.	proprietor
Prot.	Protestant
pro tem.	pro tempore, for the time being
prox.	proximo, in the next month
P.S.	postscript
PSV	public service vehicle
P.T.	physical training
pt	1 part 2 (*Fin*) payment 3 pint(s) 4 point
PTA	Parent-Teacher Association
Pte	Private
PTO	please turn over
Pty	proprietary

PVC	polyvinyl chloride
Pvt.	(*US Mil*) Private
PX	(*US*) Post Exchange

Q

Q.	1 Queen
	2 (*Can*) Quebec
	3 question
q.	1 query
	2 quart(s)
Q.C.	Queen's Counsel
Q.E.D.	quod erat demonstrandum, which was to be proved
Q.E.F.	quod erat faciendum, which was to be done
Q.M.	Quartermaster
qr	1 quarter(s)
	2 quire(s)
qt	quart(s)
qto	quarto
Qu.	Queen
Que.	(*Can*) Quebec
quot.	quotation
q.v.	quod vide, which see

R

R.	1 Rex, King
	2 Regina, Queen
	3 (*Geog*) River
	4 (*Rail*) railway
	5 Réaumur
R	(*US Cine*) Restricted
r.	right
R.A.	1 (*Art*) Royal Academy
	2 (*Art*) Royal Academician
	3 (*Mil*) Royal Artillery
RAC	1 (*Aut*) Royal Automobile Club
	2 (*Mil*) Royal Armoured Corps
Rad.	Radnorshire (Wales)
RADA	Royal Academy of Dramatic Art
RAF	Royal Air Force
R.C.	Roman Catholic
R.C.M.	Royal College of Music
R.C.P.	Royal College of Physicians
R.C.S.	Royal College of Surgeons
Rd	Road
R/D	refer to drawer
R.E.	Royal Engineers
recd	received
ref.	1 reference
	2 (*as prep*) with reference to
regd	1 (*Comm etc*) registered
	2 (*Post*) registered
regt	regiment
REME	Royal Electrical and Mechanical Engineers
Rep.	1 Republic
	2 (*Pol*) Republican
ret.	retired
Rev.	Reverend
Rgt	regiment
r.h.	right hand
R.H.S.	1 Royal Horticultural Society
	2 Royal Humane Society
	3 Royal Historical Society
R.I.	(*US*) Rhode Island
R.I.B.A.	Royal Institute of British Architects
R.I.P.	requiescat in pace, rest in peace
RL	Rugby League
Rly	Railway
R.M.	Royal Marines
R.M.S.	Royal Mail Steamer
RN	1 Royal Navy
	2 (*US*) Registered Nurse
RNIB	Royal National Institute for the Blind
RNLI	Royal National Lifeboat Institution
RNR	Royal Naval Reserve
RNVR	Royal Naval Volunteer Reserve
R.P.	reply paid
R.P.M.	resale price maintenance
R.R.	(*US*) Railroad
RRP	recommended retail price
R.S.	Royal Society
R.S.A.	1 Royal Scottish Academy
	2 Royal Scottish Academician
	3 Royal Society of Arts
	4 Royal Society of Antiquaries
R.S.M.	Regimental Sergeant-Major
RSPCA	Royal Society for the Prevention of Cruelty to Animals
RSVP	répondez s'il vous plaît
Rt Hon.	Right Honourable
Rt Rev.	Right Reverend
RU	Rugby Union
Rutl.	Rutland
R.V.	Revised Version (of the Bible)
r.v.	rateable value
Ry	Rail

S

S.	1 south
	2 (*Rel*) Saint
	3 small
s.	1 second
	2 son
	3 (*Fin*) shilling(s)
S.A.	1 South Africa
	2 South America
	3 South Australia
	4 Salvation Army
s.a.e.	stamped addressed envelope
Salop	Shropshire
SALT	Strategic Arms Limitation Talks
Sask.	(*Can*) Saskatchewan
S.C.	(*US*) South Carolina
Sc.D.	Scientiae Doctor, Doctor of Science
S.C.E.	Scottish Certificate of Education
Sch.	School
S.D., S.Dak.	(*US*) South Dakota
S.E.	south-east
SEATO	[siːtəʊ] South-East Asia Treaty Organization
sec.	1 secondary
	2 section
	3 second(s)
Sec., Secy	Secretary
Sen., Senr.	senior
Serg., Sergt	Sergeant
S.E.T.	Selective Employment Tax
SF	science fiction
s.g.	specific gravity
Sgt	Sergeant
SHAPE	[ʃeɪp] Supreme Headquarters Allied Powers in Europe
S.M.	Sergeant-Major
SNP	Scottish National Party
So.	south
Soc.	1 Society
	2 (*Pol*) Socialist
SOGAT	[ˈsəʊgæt] Society of Graphical and Allied Trades
Som.	Somerset
Sov.	Sovereign
S.P.	starting price
sp. gr.	specific gravity
Sq.	Square
sq.	(*Math*) square
Sr	senior

S.R.N.	state registered nurse
SS	Saints
S.S.	steamship
S.S.E.	south-south-east
S.S.W.	south-south-west
St	1 Saint 2 Strait 3 Street
St.	(*Rail etc*) Station
st.	stone(s)
Sta.	(*Rail etc*) Station
Staffs.	Staffordshire
STD	(*Telec*) subscriber trunk dialling
Std.	standard
stg	sterling
Stn	(*Rail etc*) Station
S.T.U.C.	Scottish Trades Union Congress
supp.	supplement
Supt	Superintendent
S.W.	south-west
SWAPO	['swɑːpəʊ] South West African People's Organization
Sx	Sussex
syn.	1 synonym 2 synonymous

T

t.	ton(s)
T.A.	Territorial Army
TAVR	Territorial Army Volunteer Reserve
TB	tuberculosis
TCD	Trinity College, Dublin
T.D.	1 Territorial Decoration 2 (*US*) Treasury Department
Tel.	telephone
temp.	1 temperature 2 temporary
Tenn.	(*US*) Tennessee
Tex.	(*US*) Texas
TGWU	Transport and General Workers' Union
T.N.T.	trinitrotoluene
T.O.	Telegraph Office
trans.	1 translation 2 translated 3 transactions
Trs.	Treasurer
TT	1 teetotal, teetotaller 2 (*Aut*) Tourist Trophy 3 (*Agr*) tuberculin-tested
TU	Trade Union
TUC	Trades Union Congress
TVA	Tennessee Valley Authority

U

U	(*Cine*) Universal
U.A.R.	United Arab Republic
UDA	Ulster Defence Association
UDI	Unilateral Declaration of Independence
UDR	Ulster Defence Regiment
UFO	['juːfəʊ] Unidentified flying object
UHF	ultra-high frequency
U.K.	United Kingdom
ult.	ultimo, last month
UMW	(*US*) United Mineworkers
UN	United Nations
UNA	United Nations Association
UNESCO	[juː'neskəʊ] United Nations Educational, Scientific and Cultural Organization
UNICEF	['juːnɪsef] United Nations International Children's Emergency Fund
Univ.	University
UNO	United Nations Organization
US	United States
USA	1 United States of America 2 United States Army
USAF	United States Air Force
U.S.C.G.	United States Coast Guard
USDA	United States Department of Agriculture
USDAW	Union of Shop, Distributive and Allied Workers
U.S.M.	1 (*Post*) United States Mail 2 (*Mil*) United States Marines 3 (*Fin*) United States Mint
USN	United States Navy
USNG	United States National Guard
U.S.N.R.	United States Naval Reserve
USS	1 (*Pol*) United States Senate 2 (*Naut*) United States Ship 3 United States Service
USSR	Union of Soviet Socialist Republics
U.S.T.C.	United States Tariff Commission
Ut.	(*US*) Utah

V

V 1	flying bomb
V 2	rocket bomb
v.	1 (*Literat*) verse 2 (*Bible*) verse 3 (*Law, Sport* etc) versus 4 (*Elec*) volt(s) 5 vide, see.
Va.	(*US*) Virginia
VAT	[væt] value-added tax
V.C.	1 (*Mil*) Victoria Cross 2 (*Univ*) Vice-Chancellor 3 Vice-Chairman
V.D.	venereal disease
Ven.	Venerable
v.g.	very good
VHF	very high frequency
VIP	very important person
viz.	videlicet, namely
vol., vols	volume(s)
V.P., V.Pres.	Vice-President
V.R.	Victoria Regina, Queen Victoria
vs	versus, against
VSO	Voluntary Service Overseas
Vt.	(*US*) Vermont
vv.	verses (see v. 1*and* 2)
v.v.	vice-versa

W

W.	west
w.	watt(s)
WAAC	Women's Auxiliary Army Corps
WAAF	Women's Auxiliary Air Force
WAC	(*US*) Women's Army Corps
War., Warwicks.	Warwickshire
Wash.	(*US*) Washington
WAVES	[weɪvz] (*US*) Women's Appointed Volunteer Emergency Service
W.C.	water closet
W.C.C.	World Council of Churches
W.D.	War Department
w./e.	week ending
WEA	Workers' Educational Association
WEU	Western European Union
WFTU	World Federation of Trade Unions
WHO	World Health Organization
W.I.	1 Women's Institute 2 West Indies
Wilts.	Wiltshire
Wis(c).	(*US*) Wisconsin
wk	week
W/L	wavelength
W.N.W.	west-north-west
WMO	World Meteorological Organization

W.O.	1 (*Mil*) War Office
	2 (*Mil, Naut*) Warrant Officer
Worcs.	Worcestershire
W.P.	weather permitting
w.p.m.	words per minute
WRAC	Women's Royal Army Corps
WRAF	Women's Royal Air Force
WRNS	Women's Royal Naval Service
W.R.V.S.	Women's Royal Voluntary Service
W.S.W.	west-south-west
wt.	weight
W/T	wireless telegraphy
WUS	World University Service
W.Va.	(*US*) West Virginia
Wyo.	(*US*) Wyoming
WX	women's extra-large size

X

X	1 (*Cine*) adults only
	2 Cross (as in King's X)
Xmas	Christmas

Y

yd.	yard(s)
YHA	Youth Hostels Association
YMCA	Young Men's Christian Association
YMHA	Young Men's Hebrew Association
Yorks.	Yorkshire
yr	1 year
	2 your
yrs	1 years
	2 yours
YWCA	Young Women's Christian Association
YWHA	Young Women's Hebrew Association

LE VERBE FRANÇAIS THE FRENCH VERB

	Present	*Imperfect*	*Future*	*Past Historic*	*Past Participle*	*Subjunctive*
(1)—**arriver, se reposer** (regular: see tables)						
(2)—**finir** (regular: see table)						
Verbs in **-er**						
(3)—**placer**	je place nous plaçons	je plaçais	je placerai	je plaçai	placé, ée	que je place
	N.B.—Verbs in *-ecer* (e.g. *dépecer*) are conjugated like *placer* and *geler*. Verbs in *-écer* (e.g. *rapiécer*) are conjugated like *céder* and *placer*.					
bouger	je bouge nous bougeons	je bougeais	je bougerai	je bougeai	bougé, ée	que je bouge
	N.B.—Verbs in *-éger* (e.g. *protéger*) are conjugated like *bouger* and *céder*.					
(4)—**appeler**	j'appelle nous appelons	j'appelais	j'appellerai	j'appelai	appelé, ée	que j'appelle
jeter	je jette nous jetons	je jetais	je jetterai	je jetai	jeté, ée	que je jette
(5)—**geler**	je gèle nous gelons	je gelais	je gèlerai	je gelai	gelé, ée	que je gèle
acheter	j'achète nous achetons	j'achetais	j'achèterai	j'achetai	acheté, ée	que j'achète
Also verbs in *-emer* (e.g. *semer*), *-ener* (e.g. *mener*), *-eser* (e.g. *peser*), *-ever* (e.g. *lever*), etc.	N.B.—Verbs in *-ecer* (e.g. *dépecer*) are conjugated like *geler* and *placer*.					
(6)—**céder**	je cède nous cédons	je cédais	je céderai	je cédai	cédé, ée	que je cède
Also verbs in *-é* + *consonant(s)* + *-er* (e.g. *célébrer, lécher, déléguer, préférer*, etc).	N.B.—Verbs in *-éger* (e.g. *protéger*) are conjugated like *céder* and *bouger*. Verbs in *-écer* (e.g. *rapiécer*) are conjugated like *céder* and *placer*.					
(7)—**épier**	j'épie nous épions	j'épiais	j'épierai	j'épiai	épié, ée	que j'épie
(8)—**noyer** Also verbs in *-uyer* (e.g. *appuyer*)	je noie nous noyons	je noyais	je noierai	je noyai	noyé, ée	que je noie
			N.B. *envoyer* has in the future tense *j'enverrai*, and in the conditional *j'enverrais*.			
payer Also all verbs in *-ayer*.	je paie *ou* je paye		je paierai *ou* je payerai			que je paie *ou* paye
(9)—**aller** (see table)						

	Present	Imperfect	Future	Past Historic	Past Participle	Subjunctive
Verbs in **-ir** other than those of the *finir* type.						
(10)—**haïr**	je hais [ʒəɛ] il hait nous haïssons ils haïssent	je haïssais [ʒəaisɛ]	je haïrai	je haïs [ʒəai]	haï, e	que je haïsse
(11)—**courir**	je cours il court nous courons ils courent	je courais	je courrai	je courus	couru, e	que je coure
(12)—**cueillir**	je cueille il cueille nous cueillons ils cueillent	je cueillais	je cueillerai	je cueillis	cueilli, e	que je cueille
(13)—**assaillir**	j'assaille il assaille nous assaillons ils assaillent	j'assaillais	j'assaillirai	j'assaillis	assailli, e	que j'assaille
(14)—**servir**	je sers il sert nous servons ils servent	je servais	je servirai	je servis	servi, e	que je serve
(15)-**bouillir**	je bous il bout nous bouillons ils bouillent	je bouillais	je bouillirai	je bouillis	bouilli, e	que je bouille
(16)—**partir**	je pars il part nous partons ils partent	je partais	je partirai	je partis	parti, e	que je parte
sentir	je sens il sent nous sentons ils sentent	je sentais	je sentirai	je sentis	senti, e N.B. *mentir* has no feminine in the past participle.	que je sente
(17)—**fuir**	je fuis il fuit nous fuyons ils fuient	je fuyais	je fuirai	je fuis	fui (no feminine)	que je fuie
(18)—**couvrir**	je couvre il couvre nous couvrons il couvrent	je couvrais	je couvrirai	je couvris	couvert, e	que je couvre

	Present	Imperfect	Future	Past Historic	Past Participle	Subjunctive
(19)—**mourir**	je meurs il meurt nous mourons ils meurent	je mourais	je mourrai	je mourus	mort, e	que je meure
(20)—**vêtir**	je vêts il vêt nous vêtons ils vêtent	je vêtais	je vêtirai	je vêtis	vêtu, e	que je vête
(21)—**acquérir**	j'acquiers il acquiert nous acquérons il acquièrent	j'acquérais	j'acquerrai	j'acquis	acquis, e	que j'acquière
(22)—**venir**	je viens il vient nous venons ils viennent	je venais	je viendrai	je vins	venu, e	que je vienne
Verbs in -oir						
(23)—**pleuvoir** *(impersonal)*	il pleut	il pleuvait	il pleuvra	il plut	plu (no feminine)	qu'il pleuve
(24)—**prévoir**	je prévois il prévoit nous prévoyons ils prévoient	je prévoyais	je prévoirai	je prévis	prévu, e	que je prévoie
(25)—**pourvoir**	je pourvois il pourvoit nous pourvoyons ils pourvoient	je pourvoyais	je pourvoirai	je pourvus	pourvu, e	que je pourvoie
(26)—**asseoir**	j'assois il assoit nous assoyons ils assoient ou j'assieds il assied nous asseyons ils asseyent	j'assoyais ou j'asseyais	j'assoirai ou j'assiérai *ou* j'asseyerai	j'assis	assis, e	que j'assoie ou que j'asseye
(27)—**mouvoir**	je meus il meut nous mouvons ils meuvent	je mouvais nous mouvions	je mouvrai	je mus	mû, ue	que je meuve que nous mouvions

N.B. *émouvoir* and *promouvoir* have the past participles *ému, e* and *promu, e* respectively.

	Present	Imperfect	Future	Past Historic	Past Participle	Subjunctive
(28)—**recevoir**	je reçois	je recevais	je recevrai	je reçus	reçu, e	que je reçoive
	il reçoit					
	nous recevons	nous recevions				que nous recevions
	ils reçoivent					
devoir					dû, ue	
(29)—**valoir**	je vaux	je valais	je vaudrai	je valus	valu, e	que je vaille
	il vaut					
	nous valons	vous valions				que nous valions
	ils valent					
équivaloir					équivalu (no feminine)	
prévaloir					prévalu (no feminine)	que je prévale
falloir *(impersonal)*	il faut	il fallait	il faudra	il fallut	fallu (no feminine)	qu'il faille
(30)—**voir**	je vois	je voyais	je verrai	je vis	vu, e	que je voie
	il voit					
	nous voyons	nous voyions				que nous voyions
	ils voient					
(31)—**vouloir**	je veux	je voulais	je voudrai	je voulus	voulu, e	que je veuille
	il veut					
	nous voulons	nous voulions				que nous voulions
	ils veulent					
(32)—**savoir**	je sais	je savais	je saurai	je sus	su, e	que je sache
	il sait					
	nous savons	nous savions				que nous sachions
	ils savent					
(33)—**pouvoir**	je peux (ou je puis)	je pouvais	je pourrai	je pus	pu (no feminine)	que je puisse
	il peut					
	nous pouvons	nous pouvions				que nous puissions
	ils peuvent					
(34)—**avoir** (see table)						
Verbs in -re						
(35)—**conclure**	je conclus	je concluais	je conclurai	je conclus	conclu, e	que je conclue
	il conclut					
	nous concluons					
	ils concluent					

N.B. *exclure* is conjugated like *conclure*, past participle *exclu, e. inclure* is conjugated like *conclure* except for the past participle *inclus, e.*

	Present	Imperfect	Future	Past Historic	Past Participle	Subjunctive
(36)—**rire**	je ris	je riais	je rirai	je ris	ri (no feminine)	que je rie
	il rit					
	nous rions					
	ils rient					

	Present	Imperfect	Future	Past Historic	Past Participle	Subjunctive
(37)—**dire**	je dis il dit nous disons vous dites ils disent	je disais	je dirai	je dis	dit, e	que je dise
	N.B. *médire, contredire, dédire, interdire, prédire* are conjugated like *dire* except *médisez, contredisez, dédisez, interdisez, prédisez.*					
suffire	vous suffisez				suffi (no feminine) N.B. *confire* is conjugated like *suffire* except for the past participle *confit, e.*	
(38)—**nuire** Also the verbs *luire, reluire.*	je nuis il nuit nous nuisons ils nuisent	je nuisais	je nuirai	je nuisis	nui (no feminine)	que je nuise
conduire Also the verbs *construire, cuire, déduire, détruire, enduire, induire, instruire, introduire, produire, réduire, séduire, traduire.*					conduit, e	
(39)—**écrire**	j'écris il écrit nous écrivons ils écrivent	j'écrivais	j'écrirai	j'écrivis	écrit, e	que j'écrive
(40)—**suivre**	je suis il suit nous suivons ils suivent	je suivais	je suivrai	je suivis	suivi, e	que je suive
(41)—**rendre** Also the verbs in *-andre* (e.g. *répandre*), *-erdre* (e.g. *perdre*), *-ondre* (e.g. *répondre*), *-ordre* (e.g. *mordre*).	je rends il rend nous rendons ils rendent	je rendais	je rendrai	je rendis	rendu, e	que je rende
rompre	il rompt					
battre	je bats il bat nous battons ils battent	je battais	je battrai	je battis	battu, e	que je batte
(42)—**vaincre**	je vaincs il vainc nous vainquons ils vainquent	je vainquais	je vaincrai	je vainquis	vaincu, e	que je vainque
(43)—**lire**	je lis il lit nous lisons ils lisent	je lisais	je lirai	je lus	lu, e	que je lise

	Present	Imperfect	Future	Past Historic	Past Participle	Subjunctive
(44)—croire	je crois il croit nous croyons ils croient	je croyais	je croirai	je crus	cru, e	que je croie
(45)—clore	je clos il clôt *ou* clot ils closent (rare)	je closais (disputed)	je clorai (rare)	not applicable	clos, e	que je close
(46)—vivre	je vis il vit nous vivons ils vivent	je vivais	je vivrai	je vécus	vécu, e	que je vive
(47)—moudre	je mouds il moud nous moulons ils moulent	je moulais	je moudrai	je moulus	moulu, e	que je moule
(48)—coudre	je couds il coud nous cousons ils cousent	je cousais	je coudrai	je cousis	cousu, e	que je couse
(49)—joindre	je joins il joint nous joignons ils joignent	je joignais	je joindrai	je joignis	joint, e	que je joigne
(50)—traire	je trais il trait nous trayons ils traient	je trayais	je trairai	not applicable	trait, e	que je traie
(51)—absoudre	j'absous il absout nous absolvons ils absolvent	j'absolvais	j'absoudrai	j'absolus (rare)	absous, oute	que j'absolve
				N.B. *dissoudre* is conjugated like *absoudre*. *résoudre* is conjugated like *absoudre*, but the past historic *je résolus* is current. *résoudre* has two past participles, *résolu, e* (current) and *résous, oute* (rare).		
(52)—craindre	je crains il craint nous craignons ils craignent	je craignais	je craindrai	je craignis	craint, e	que je craigne
peindre	je peins il peint nous peignons ils peignent	je peignais	je peindrai	je peignis	peint, e	que je peigne

	Present	Imperfect	Future	Past Historic	Past Participle	Subjunctive
(53)—**boire**	je bois il boit nous buvons ils boivent	je buvais	je boirai	je bus	bu, e	que je boive que nous buvions
(54)—**plaire**	je plais il plaît nous plaisons ils plaisent	je plaisais	je plairai	je plus	plu (no feminine)	que je plaise
					N.B. The past participle of *plaire, complaire, déplaire* is generally invariable.	
taire	il tait				tu, e	
(55)—**croître**	je croîs il croît nous croissons ils croissent	je croissais	je croîtrai	je crûs	crû, ue	que je croisse
					N.B. *accroître, décroître* have the past participles *accru, e* and *décru, e* respectively.	
(56)—**mettre**	je mets il met nous mettons ils mettent	je mettais	je mettrai	je mis	mis, e	que je mette
(57)—**connaître**	je connais il connaît nous connaissons ils connaissent	je connaissais	je connaîtrai	je connus	connu, e	que je connaisse
(58)—**prendre**	je prends il prend nous prenons ils prennent	je prenais	je prendrai	je pris	pris, e	que je prenne que nous prenions
(59)—**naître**	je nais il naît ils naissent	je naissais nous naissons	je naîtrai	je naquis	né, e	que je naisse
					N.B. *renaître* has no past participle.	
(60)—**faire** (see table)						
(61)—**être** (see table)						

1. **arriver** (regular verb)

INDICATIVE

Present

j'arrive
tu arrives
il arrive
nous arrivons
vous arrivez
ils arrivent

Perfect

je suis arrivé
tu es arrivé
il est arrivé
nous sommes arrivés
vous êtes arrivés
ils sont arrivés

Imperfect

j'arrivais
tu arrivais
il arrivait
nous arrivions
vous arriviez
ils arrivaient

Pluperfect

j'étais arrivé
tu étais arrivé
il était arrivé
nous étions arrivés
vous étiez arrivés
ils étaient arrivés

Past Historic

j'arrivai
tu arrivas
il arriva
nous arrivâmes
vous arrivâtes
ils arrivèrent

Past Anterior

je fus arrivé
tu fus arrivé
il fut arrivé
nous fûmes arrivés
vous fûtes arrivés
ils furent arrivés

Future

j'arriverai
tu arriveras
il arrivera
nous arriverons
vous arriverez
ils arriveront

Future Perfect

je serai arrivé
tu seras arrivé
il sera arrivé
nous serons arrivés
vous serez arrivés
ils seront arrivés

CONDITIONAL

Present

j'arriverais
tu arriverais
il arriverait
nous arriverions
vous arriveriez
ils arriveraient

Past I

je serais arrivé
tu serais arrivé
il serait arrivé
nous serions arrivés
vous seriez arrivés
ils seraient arrivés

Past II

je fusse arrivé
tu fusses arrivé
il fût arrivé
nous fussions arrivés
vous fussiez arrivés
ils fussent arrivés

IMPERATIVE

Present

arrive
arrivons
arrivez

Past

sois arrivé
soyons arrivés
soyez arrivés

SUBJUNCTIVE

Present

que j'arrive
que tu arrives
qu'il arrive
que nous arrivions
que vous arriviez
qu'ils arrivent

Imperfect

que j'arrivasse
que tu arrivasses
qu'il arrivât
que nous arrivassions
que vous arrivassiez
qu'ils arrivassent

Past

que je sois arrivé
que tu sois arrivé
qu'il soit arrivé
que nous soyons arrivés
que vous soyez arrivés
qu'ils soient arrivés

Pluperfect

que je fusse arrivé
que tu fusses arrivé
qu'il fût arrivé
que nous fussions arrivés
que vous fussiez arrivés
qu'ils fussent arrivés

INFINITIVE

Present

arriver

Past

être arrivé

PARTICIPLE

Present

arrivant

Past

arrivé
étant arrivé

N.B. The verbs *jouer, tuer*, etc, are regular, e.g. je *joue*, je *jouerai*; je *tue*, je *tuerai*.

1b. **se reposer** (pronominal verb)

INDICATIVE

Present

je me repose
tu te reposes
il se repose
nous nous reposons
vous vous reposez
ils se reposent

Perfect

je me suis reposé
tu t'es reposé
il s'est reposé
nous nous sommes reposés
vous vous êtes reposés
ils se sont reposés

Imperfect

je me reposais
tu te reposais
il se reposait
nous nous reposions
vous vous reposiez
ils se reposaient

Pluperfect

je m'étais reposé
tu t'étais reposé
il s'était reposé
nous nous étions reposés
vous vous étiez reposés
ils s'étaient reposés

Past Historic

je me reposai
tu te reposas
il se reposa
nous nous reposâmes
vous vous reposâtes
ils se reposèrent

Past Anterior

je me fus reposé
tu te fus reposé
il se fut reposé
nous nous fûmes reposés
vous vous fûtes reposés
ils se furent reposés

Future

je me reposerai
tu te reposeras
il se reposera
nous nous reposerons
vous vous reposerez
ils se reposeront

Future Perfect

je me serai reposé
tu te seras reposé
il se sera reposé
nous nous serons reposés
vous vous serez reposés
ils se seront reposés

CONDITIONAL

Present

je me reposerais
tu te reposerais
il se reposerait
nous nous reposerions
vous vous reposeriez
ils se reposeraient

Past I

je me serais reposé
tu te serais reposé
il se serait reposé
nous nous serions reposés
vous vous seriez reposés
ils se seraient reposés

Past II

je me fusse reposé
tu te fusses reposé
il se fût reposé
nous nous fussions reposés
vous vous fussiez reposés
ils se fussent reposés

SUBJUNCTIVE

Present

que je me repose
que tu te reposes
qu'il se repose
que nous nous reposions
que vous vous reposiez
qu'ils se reposent

Imperfect

que je me reposasse
que tu te reposasses
qu'il se reposât
que nous nous reposassions
que vous vous reposassiez
qu'ils se reposassent

Past

que je me sois reposé
que tu te sois reposé
qu'il se soit reposé
que nous nous soyons reposés
que vous vous soyez reposés
qu'ils se soient reposés

Pluperfect

que je me fusse reposé
que tu te fusses reposé
qu'il se fût reposé
que nous nous fussions reposés
que vous vous fussiez reposés
qu'ils se fussent reposés

IMPERATIVE

Present

repose-toi
reposons-nous
reposez-vous

INFINITIVE

Present

se reposer

Past

s'être reposé

PARTICIPLE

Present

se reposant

Past

s'étant reposé

2. **finir** (regular verb)

INDICATIVE

Present

je finis
tu finis
il finit
nous finissons
vous finissez
ils finissent

Perfect

j'ai fini
tu as fini
il a fini
nous avons fini
vous avez fini
ils ont fini

Imperfect

je finissais
tu finissais
il finissait
nous finissions
vous finissiez
ils finissaient

Pluperfect

j'avais fini
tu avais fini
il avait fini
nous avions fini
vous aviez fini
ils avaient fini

Past Historic

je finis
tu finis
il finit
nous finîmes
vous finîtes
ils finirent

Past Anterior

j'eus fini
tu eus fini
il eut fini
nous eûmes fini
vous eûtes fini
ils eurent fini

Future

je finirai
tu finiras
il finira
nous finirons
vous finirez
ils finiront

Future Perfect

j'aurai fini
tu auras fini
il aura fini
nous aurons fini
vous aurez fini
ils auront fini

CONDITIONAL

Present

je finirais
tu finirais
il finirait
nous finirions
vous finiriez
ils finiraient

Past I

j'aurais fini
tu aurais fini
il aurait fini
nous aurions fini
vous auriez fini
ils auraient fini

Past II

j'eusse fini
tu eusses fini
il eût fini
nous eussions fini
vous eussiez fini
ils eussent fini

IMPERATIVE

Present

finis
finissons
finissez

Past

aie fini
ayons fini
ayez fini

SUBJUNCTIVE

Present

que je finisse
que tu finisses
qu'il finisse
que nous finissions
que vous finissiez
qu'ils finissent

Imperfect

que je finisse
que tu finisses
qu'il finît
que nous finissions
que vous finissiez
qu'ils finissent

Past

que j'aie fini
que tu aies fini
qu'il ait fini
que nous ayons fini
que vous ayez fini
qu'ils aient fini

Pluperfect

que j'eusse fini
que tu eusses fini
qu'il eût fini
que nous eussions fini
que vous eussiez fini
qu'ils eussent fini

INFINITIVE

Present

finir

Past

avoir fini

PARTICIPLE

Present

finissant

Past

fini
ayant fini

9. **aller**

INDICATIVE		CONDITIONAL	SUBJUNCTIVE
Present	*Perfect*	*Present*	*Present*
je vais	je suis allé	j'irais	que j'aille
tu vas	tu es allé	tu irais	que tu ailles
il va	il est allé	il irait	qu'il aille
nous allons	nous sommes allés	nous irions	que nous allions
vous allez	vous êtes allés	vous iriez	que vous alliez
ils vont	ils sont allés	ils iraient	qu'ils aillent
Imperfect	*Pluperfect*	*Past I*	*Imperfect*
j'allais	j'étais allé	je serais allé	que j'allasse
tu allais	tu étais allé	tu serais allé	que tu allasses
il allait	il était allé	il serait allé	qu'il allât
nous allions	nous étions allés	nous serions allés	que nous allassions
vous alliez	vous étiez allés	vous seriez allés	que vous allassiez
ils allaient	ils étaient allés	ils seraient allés	qu'ils allassent
Past Historic	*Past Anterior*	*Past II*	*Past*
j'allai	je fus allé	je fusse allé	que je sois allé
tu allas	tu fus allé	tu fusses allé	que tu sois allé
il alla	il fut allé	il fût allé	qu'il soit allé
nous allâmes	nous fûmes allés	nous fussions allés	que nous soyons allés
vous allâtes	vous fûtes allés	vous fussiez allés	que vous soyez allés
ils allèrent	ils furent allés	ils fussent allés	qu'ils soient allés
Future	*Future Perfect*	IMPERATIVE	*Pluperfect*
		Present	
j'irai	je serai allé	va	que je fusse allé
tu iras	tu seras allé	allons	que tu fusses allé
il ira	il sera allé	allez	qu'il fût allé
nous irons	nous serons allés	*Past*	que nous fussions allés
vous irez	vous serez allés	sois allé	que vous fussiez allés
ils iront	ils seront allés	soyons allés	qu'ils fussent allés
		soyez allés	

INFINITIVE		PARTICIPLE	
Present	*Past*	*Present*	*Past*
aller	être allé	allant	allé, ée
			étant allé

34. avoir

INDICATIVE		CONDITIONAL	SUBJUNCTIVE
Present	*Perfect*	*Present*	*Present*
j'ai tu as il a nous avons vous avez ils ont	j'ai eu tu as eu il a eu nous avons eu vous avez eu ils ont eu	j'aurais tu aurais il aurait nous aurions vous auriez ils auraient	que j'aie que tu aies qu'il ait que nous ayons que vous ayez qu'ils aient
Imperfect	*Pluperfect*	*Past I*	*Imperfect*
j'avais tu avais il avait nous avions vous aviez ils avaient	j'avais eu tu avais eu il avait eu nous avions eu vous aviez eu ils avaient eu	j'aurais eu tu aurais eu il aurait eu nous aurions eu vous auriez eu ils auraient eu	que j'eusse que tu eusses qu'il eût que nous eussions que vous eussiez qu'ils eussent
Past Historic	*Past Anterior*	*Past II*	*Past*
j'eus tu eus il eut nous eûmes vous eûtes ils eurent	j'eus eu tu eus eu il eut eu nous eûmes eu vous eûtes eu ils eurent eu	j'eusse eu tu eusses eu il eût eu nous eussions eu vous eussiez eu ils eussent eu	que j'aie eu que tu aies eu qu'il ait eu que nous ayons eu que vous ayez eu qu'ils aient eu
Future	*Future Perfect*	IMPERATIVE *Present*	*Pluperfect*
j'aurai tu auras il aura nous aurons vous aurez ils auront	j'aurai eu tu auras eu il aura eu nous aurons eu vous aurez eu ils auront eu	aie ayons ayez	que j'eusse eu que tu eusses eu qu'il eût eu que nous eussions eu que vous eussiez eu qu'ils eussent eu
INFINITIVE *Present*	*Past*	PARTICIPLE *Present*	*Past*
avoir	avoir eu	ayant	eu ayant eu

60. **faire**

INDICATIVE

Present

je fais
tu fais
il fait
nous faisons
vous faites
ils font

Perfect

j'ai fait
tu as fait
il a fait
nous avons fait
vous avez fait
ils ont fait

Imperfect

je faisais
tu faisais
il faisait
nous faisions
vous faisiez
ils faisaient

Pluperfect

j'avais fait
tu avais fait
il avait fait
nous avions fait
vous aviez fait
ils avaient fait

Past Historic

je fis
tu fis
il fit
nous fîmes
vous fîtes
ils firent

Past Anterior

j'eus fait
tu eus fait
il eut fait
nous eûmes fait
vous eûtes fait
ils eurent fait

Future

je ferai
tu feras
il fera
nous ferons
vous ferez
ils feront

Future Perfect

j'aurai fait
tu auras fait
il aura fait
nous aurons fait
vous aurez fait
ils auront fait

CONDITIONAL

Present

je ferais
tu ferais
il ferait
nous ferions
vous feriez
ils feraient

Past I

j'aurais fait
tu aurais fait
il aurait fait
nous aurions fait
vous auriez fait
ils auraient fait

Past II

j'eusse fait
tu eusses fait
il eût fait
nous eussions fait
vous eussiez fait
ils eussent fait

SUBJUNCTIVE

Present

que je fasse
que tu fasses
qu'il fasse
que nous fassions
que vous fassiez
qu'ils fassent

Imperfect

que je fisse
que tu fisses
qu'il fît
que nous fissions
que vous fissiez
qu'ils fissent

Past

que j'aie fait
que tu aies fait
qu'il ait fait
que nous ayons fait
que vous ayez fait
qu'ils aient fait

Pluperfect

que j'eusse fait
que tu eusses fait
qu'il eût fait
que nous eussions fait
que vous eussiez fait
qu'ils eussent fait

IMPERATIVE

Present

fais
faisons
faites

Past

aie fait
ayons fait
ayez fait

INFINITIVE

Present

faire

Past

avoir fait

PARTICIPLE

Present

faisant

Past

fait
ayant fait

61. être

INDICATIVE		CONDITIONAL	SUBJUNCTIVE
Present	*Perfect*	*Present*	*Present*
je suis	j'ai été	je serais	que je sois
tu es	tu as été	tu serais	que tu sois
il est	il a été	il serait	qu'il soit
nous sommes	nous avons été	nous serions	que nous soyons
vous êtes	vous avez été	vous seriez	que vous soyez
ils sont	ils ont été	ils seraient	qu'ils soient
Imperfect	*Pluperfect*	*Past I*	*Imperfect*
j'étais	j'avais été	j'aurais été	que je fusse
tu étais	tu avais été	tu aurais été	que tu fusses
il était	il avait été	il aurait été	qu'il fût
nous étions	nous avions été	nous aurions été	que nous fussions
vous étiez	vous aviez été	vous auriez été	que vous fussiez
ils étaient	ils avaient été	ils auraient été	qu'ils fussent
Past Historic	*Past Anterior*	*Past II*	*Past*
je fus	j'eus été	j'eusse été	que j'aie été
tu fus	tu eus été	tu eusses été	que tu aies été
il fut	il eut été	il eût été	qu'il ait été
nous fûmes	nous eûmes été	nous eussions été	que nous ayons été
vous fûtes	vous eûtes été	vous eussiez été	que vous ayez été
ils furent	ils eurent été	ils eussent été	qu'ils aient été
Future	*Future Perfect*	IMPERATIVE	*Pluperfect*
		Present	
je serai	j'aurai été		que j'eusse été
tu seras	tu auras été	sois	que tu eusses été
il sera	il aura été	soyons	qu'il eût été
nous serons	nous aurons été	soyez	que nous eussions été
vous serez	vous aurez été		que vous eussiez été
ils seront	ils auront été		qu'ils eussent été
INFINITIVE		PARTICIPLE	
Present	*Past*	*Present*	*Past*
être	avoir été	étant	été
			ayant été

LE VERBE ANGLAIS — THE ENGLISH VERB

L'anglais comprend de nombreux verbes forts ou irréguliers (dont nous donnons la liste ci-dessous) ainsi que de nombreuses variantes orthographiques (voir au paragraphe 7), mais à chaque temps la conjugaison reste la même pour toutes les personnes sauf à la troisième personne du singulier du présent de l'indicatif.

Les notes qui suivent se proposent de résumer la structure et les formes du verbe anglais.

1 Le mode indicatif

(a) Le présent de l'indicatif a la même forme que l'infinitif présent à toutes les personnes sauf à la troisième personne du singulier, à laquelle vient s'ajouter un '*s*', ex: *he sells.* Dans les cas où l'infinitif se termine par une sifflante ou une chuintante on intercale un '*e*', ex: *kisses, buzzes, rushes, touches.*

Les verbes qui se terminent en consonne + *y* changent cet *y* en *ies* à la troisième personne du singulier, ex: *tries, pities, satifies*; là où le *y* est précédé d'une voyelle, on applique la règle générale, ex: *pray — he prays, annoy — she annoys.*

Le verbe *be* a des formes irrégulières pour toutes les personnes:

I am	we are
you are	you are
he is	they are

Trois autres verbes ont une forme irrégulière à la troisième personne du singulier:

do	he does
have	he has
go	he goes

(b) L'imparfait, le passé simple et le participe passé ont la même forme en anglais. On les construit en ajoutant *ed* au radical de l'infinitif, ex: *paint — I painted — painted,* ou en ajoutant *d* à l'infinitif des verbes qui se terminent par un *e* muet, ex: *bare — I bared — bared, move — I moved — moved, revise — I revised — revised.*

Pour les verbes irréguliers, voir la liste ci-dessous.

(c) Les temps composés du passé se forment à l'aide de l'auxiliaire *to have* suivi du participe passé: au passé composé = *I have painted*; au plus-que-parfait = *I had painted.*

(d) Le futur et le conditionnel

Le futur se forme à l'aide de *will* ou de *shall* suivi de l'infinitif: ex: *I will do it; they shall not pass.*

On forme le conditionnel avec *should* ou *would* plus l'infinitif, ex: *I would go, if she should come.*

L'auxiliaire *to have* accompagné de *shall* ou *will* et du participe passé du verbe conjugué s'emploie pour le futur antérieur, ex: *I shall have finished.*

On emploie également l'auxiliaire *to have,* cette fois accompagné de *would* et du participe passé pour former le conditionnel passé, ex: *I would have paid.*

(e) Il existe également en anglais, au mode indicatif, une forme progressive qui se forme avec l'auxiliaire *to be,* conjugué au temps approprié et suivi du participe présent, ex: *I am waiting, we were hoping, they will be buying it, they would have been waiting still, I had been painting all day.*

Ce système diffère dans une certaine mesure du système français, qui a parfois comme équivalent la formule 'être en train de' suivie de l'infinitif.

2 Le mode subjonctif

Le subjonctif est peu utilisé en anglais. Au présent et à toutes les personnes, il a la même forme que l'infinitif, ex: (*that*) *I go,* (*that*) *she go* etc.

À l'imparfait, *to be* est l'unique verbe qui ait une forme irrégulière. Cette forme est *were* pour toutes les personnes: (*that*) *I were,* (*that*) *we were* etc. Il faut cependant noter que le subjonctif s'emploie obligatoirement en anglais dans: *if I were you, were I to attempt it* (l'emploi de *was* étant considéré comme incorrect dans ces expressions, ainsi que dans d'autres expressions analogues).

Le subjonctif se rencontre aussi dans l'expression figée *so be it* et dans le langage juridique ou officiel, ex: *it is agreed that nothing be done, it was resolved that the pier be painted* (quoique *should be done* et *should be painted* soient également corrects).

3 Le gérondif et le participe présent ont la même forme en anglais. Ils s'obtiennent en ajoutant la désinence *ing* au radical de l'infinitif, ex: *washing, sending, passing.*

Pour les variantes orthographiques voir paragraphe 7.

4 La voix passive se forme exactement comme en français avec le temps approprié du verbe *to be* et le participe passé: *we are forced to, he was killed, they had been injured, the company will be taken over, it ought to have been rebuilt, were it to be agreed.*

5 Le mode impératif

Il n'y a qu'une forme de l'impératif, qui est en fait celle de l'infinitif, ex: *tell me, come here, don't do that.*

6 Verbes forts ou irréguliers

Infinitif	*Prétérit*	*Participe passé*
abide	abode *or* abided	abode *or* abided
arise	arose	arisen
awake	awoke	awaked
be	was, were	been
bear	bore	borne
beat	beat	beaten
become	became	become
beget	begot, begat††	begotten
begin	began	begun
bend	bent	bent
beseech	besought	besought
bet	bet *or* betted	bet *or* betted
bid	bade *or* bid	bid *or* bidden
bind	bound	bound
bite	bit	bitten
bleed	bled	bled
blow	blew	blown
break	broke	broken
breed	bred	bred
bring	brought	brought
build	built	built
burn	burned *or* burnt	burned *or* burnt
burst	burst	burst
buy	bought	bought
can	could	—
cast	cast	cast
catch	caught	caught
chide	chid	chidden *or* chid
choose	chose	chosen
cleave[1] *(fendre)*	clove *or* cleft	cloven *or* cleft
cleave[2] *(s'attacher)*	cleaved	cleaved
cling	clung	clung
come	came	come
cost	cost *or* costed	cost *or* costed
creep	crept	crept
cut	cut	cut
deal	dealt	dealt
dig	dug	dug
do	did	done
draw	drew	drawn
dream	dreamed *or* dreamt	dreamed *or* dreamt
drink	drank	drunk
drive	drove	driven
dwell	dwelt	dwelt
eat	ate	eaten
fall	fell	fallen
feed	fed	fed
feel	felt	felt
fight	fought	fought
find	found	found
flee	fled	fled
fling	flung	flung
fly	flew	flown
forbid	forbad(e)	forbidden
forget	forgot	forgotten
forsake	forsook	forsaken

Infinitif	*Prétérit*	*Participe passé*
freeze	froze	frozen
get	got	got, (*US*) gotten
gild	gilded	gilded *or* gilt
gird	girded *or* girt	girded *or* girt
give	gave	given
go	went	gone
grind	ground	ground
grow	grew	grown
hang	hung, (*Jur*) hanged	hung, (*Jur*) hanged
have	had	had
hear	heard	heard
heave	heaved, (*Naut*) hove	heaved, (*Naut*) hove
hew	hewed	hewed *or* hewn
hide	hid	hidden
hit	hit	hit
hold	held	held
hurt	hurt	hurt
keep	kept	kept
kneel	knelt	knelt
know	knew	known
lade	laded	laden
lay	laid	laid
lead	led	led
lean	leaned *or* leant	leaned *or* leant
leap	leaped *or* leapt	leaped *or* leapt
learn	learned *or* learnt	learned *or* learnt
leave	left	left
lend	lent	lent
let	let	let
lie	lay	lain
light	lit *or* lighted	lit *or* lighted
lose	lost	lost
make	made	made
may	might	might
mean	meant	meant
meet	met	met
mow	mowed	mown *or* mowed
pay	paid	paid
put	put	put
quit	quit *or* quitted	quit *or* quitted
read [ri:d]	read [red]	read [red]
rend	rent	rent
rid	rid	rid
ride	rode	ridden
ring[2]	rang	rung
rise	rose	risen
run	ran	run
saw	sawed	sawed *or* sawn
say	said	said
see	saw	seen
seek	sought	sought
sell	sold	sold
send	sent	sent
set	set	set
sew	sewed	sewed *or* sewn
shake	shook	shaken
shave	shaved	shaved *or* shaven

Infinitif	*Prétérit*	*Participe passé*
shear	sheared	sheared *or* shorn
shed	shed	shed
shine	shone	shone
shoe	shod	shod
shoot	shot	shot
show	showed	shown *or* showed
shrink	shrank	shrunk
shut	shut	shut
sing	sang	sung
sink	sank	sunk
sit	sat	sat
slay	slew	slain
sleep	slept	slept
slide	slid	slid
sling	slung	slung
slink	slunk	slunk
slit	slit	slit
smell	smelled *or* smelt	smelled *or* smelt
smite	smote	smitten
sow	sowed	sowed *or* sown
speak	spoke	spoken
speed	speeded *or* sped	speeded *or* sped
spell	spelled *or* spelt	spelled *or* spelt
spend	spent	spent
spill	spilled *or* spilt	spilled *or* spilt
spin	spun *or* span††	spun
spit	spat	spat
split	split	split
spoil	spoiled *or* spoilt	spoiled *or* spoilt
spread	spread	spread
spring	sprang	sprung
stand	stood	stood

Infinitif	*Prétérit*	*Participe passé*
stave	stove *or* staved	stove *or* staved
steal	stole	stolen
stick	stuck	stuck
sting	stung	stung
stink	stank	stunk
strew	strewed	strewed *or* strewn
stride	strode	stridden
strike	struck	struck
string	strung	strung
strive	strove	striven
swear	swore	sworn
sweep	swept	swept
swell	swelled	swollen
swim	swam	swum
swing	swung	swung
take	took	taken
teach	taught	taught
tear	tore	torn
tell	told	told
think	thought	thought
thrive	throve *or* thrived	thriven *or* thrived
throw	threw	thrown
thrust	thrust	thrust
tread	trod	trodden
wake	woke *or* waked	woken *or* waked
wear	wore	worn
weave	wove	woven
weep	wept	wept
win	won	won
wind	wound	wound
wring	wrung	wrung
write	wrote	written

Ne sont pas compris dans cette liste les verbes formés avec un préfixe. Pour leur conjugaison, se référer au verbe de base, ex: pour *forbear* voir *bear*, pour *understand* voir *stand.*

7 Verbes faibles présentant des variantes orthographiques

L'orthographe de nombreux verbes peut varier légèrement au participe passé et au gérondif.

(a) Les verbes se terminant par une seule consonne précédée d'une seule voyelle accentuée redoublent la consonne devant la désinence *ed* ou *ing*:

infinitif	*participe passé*	*gérondif*
sob	sobbed	sobbing
wed	wedded	wedding
lag	lagged	lagging
control	controlled	controlling
dim	dimmed	dimming
tan	tanned	tanning
tap	tapped	tapping
prefer	preferred	preferring
pat	patted	patting

(Par contre *to cook* devient *cooked — cooked* parce qu'il comporte une voyelle longue, et *fear* qui comporte une diphtongue donne *feared — fearing*).

(b) Les verbes qui se terminent en *c* changent le *c* en *ck* devant les désinences *ed* et *ing*:

frolic	frolicked	frolicking
traffic	trafficked	trafficking

(c) Les verbes terminés par la consonne *l* ou *p* précédée d'une voyelle non accentuée redoublent la consonne au participe passé et au gérondif en anglais britannique, mais restent inchangés en anglais américain:

grovel	(*Brit*) grovelled	(*Brit*) grovelling
	(*US*) groveled	(*US*) groveling
travel	(*Brit*) travelled	(*Brit*) travelling
	(*US*) traveled	(*US*) traveling
worship	(*Brit*) worshipped	(*Brit*) worshipping
	(*US*) worshiped	(*US*) worshiping

NB la même différence existe entre les formes substantivées de ces verbes:
(*Brit*) traveller = (*US*) traveler;
(*Brit*) worshipper = (*US*) worshiper.

(d) Lorsque le verbe se termine par un *e* muet à l'infinitif, le *e* muet disparaît en faveur de la désinence *ed* ou *ing*.

invite	invited	inviting
rake	raked	raking
smile	smiled	smiling
move	moved	moving

(le *e* muet se conserve toutefois dans les verbes *dye, singe*, etc et dans une série peu nombreuse de verbes se terminant en *oe*: *dyeing, singeing, hoeing.*

(e) Si le verbe se termine en *y*, le *y* devient *ied* pour former l'imparfait et le participe passé, ex:
worry — worried — worried;
pity — pitied — pitied;
falsify — falsified — falsified;
try — tried — tried.
Le gérondif de ces verbes est parfaitement régulier, ex: *worrying, trying*, etc.

(f) Le gérondif des verbes monosyllabiques *die, lie, vie* s'écrit: *dying, lying, vying.*

NOMBRES, POIDS ET MESURES

NUMERALS, WEIGHTS AND MEASURES

I NUMERALS — LES NOMBRES

1 Cardinal numbers — Les nombres cardinaux

nought	0	zéro
one	1	(*m*) un, (*f*) une
two	2	deux
three	3	trois
four	4	quatre
five	5	cinq
six	6	six
seven	7	sept
eight	8	huit
nine	9	neuf
ten	10	dix
eleven	11	onze
twelve	12	douze
thirteen	13	treize
fourteen	14	quatorze
fifteen	15	quinze
sixteen	16	seize
seventeen	17	dix-sept
eighteen	18	dix-huit
nineteen	19	dix-neuf
twenty	20	vingt
twenty-one	21	vingt et un
twenty-two	22	vingt-deux
twenty-three	23	vingt-trois
thirty	30	trente
thirty-one	31	trente et un
thirty-two	32	trente-deux
forty	40	quarante
fifty	50	cinquante
sixty	60	soixante
seventy	70	soixante-dix
eighty	80	quatre-vingt
ninety	90	quatre-vingt-dix
ninety-nine	99	quatre-vingt-dix-neuf
a (*or* one) hundred	100	cent
a hundred and one	101	cent un
a hundred and two	102	cent deux
a hundred and ten	110	cent dix
a hundred and eighty-two	182	cent quatre-vingt-deux
two hundred	200	deux cents
two hundred and one	201	deux cent un
two hundred and two	202	deux cent deux
three hundred	300	trois cents
four hundred	400	quatre cents
five hundred	500	cinq cents
six hundred	600	six cents
seven hundred	700	sept cents
eight hundred	800	huit cents
nine hundred	900	neuf cents
a (*or* one) thousand)	1000	mille
a thousand and one	1001	mille un
a thousand and two	1002	mille deux
two thousand	2000	deux mille
ten thousand	10000	dix mille
a (*or* one) hundred thousand	100000	cent mille
a (*or* one) million (see note b)	1000000	un million (*V* note b)
two million	2000000	deux millions

Notes on usage of the cardinal numbers

(a) **One**, and the other numbers ending in one, agree in French with the noun (stated or implied): *une maison, un employé, il y a cent une personnes*

(b) **1000000**: In French, the word *million* is a noun, so the numeral takes *de* when there is a following noun: *un million de fiches, trois millions de maisons détruites*
En anglais le mot *million* (ainsi que mille et cent) n'est pas suivi de *of* lorsqu'il accompagne un nom: *a million people, a hundred houses, a thousand people*

(c) To divide the larger numbers clearly, a point is used in French where English places a comma: English 1,000 = French 1.000; English 2,304,770 = French 2.304.770. (This does not apply to dates: see below.)
Alors qu'un point est utilisé en français pour séparer les centaines des milliers, l'anglais utilise la virgule à cet effet; ex: français 1.000 = anglais 1,000; français 2.304.770 = anglais 2,304,770. (*Cette règle ne s'applique pas aux dates. Voir ci-dessous*).

2 Ordinal numbers — Les nombres ordinaux

first	1	(*m*) premier, (*f*) -ière
second	2	deuxième
third	3	troisième
fourth	4	quatrième
fifth	5	cinquième
sixth	6	sixième
seventh	7	septième
eighth	8	huitième
ninth	9	neuvième
tenth	10	dixième
eleventh	11	onzième
twelfth	12	douzième
thirteenth	13	treizième
fourteenth	14	quatorzième
fifteenth	15	quinzième
sixteenth	16	seizième
seventeenth	17	dix-septième
eighteenth	18	dix-huitième
nineteenth	19	dix-neuvième
twentieth	20	vingtième
twenty-first	21	vingt et unième
twenty-second	22	vingt-deuxième
thirtieth	30	trentième

thirty-first	31	trente et unième
fortieth	40	quarantième
fiftieth	50	cinquantième
sixtieth	60	soixantième
seventieth	70	soixante-dixième
eightieth	80	quatre-vingtième
ninetieth	90	quatre-vingt-dixième
hundredth	100	centième
hundred and first	101	cent et unième
hundred and tenth	110	cent-dixième
two hundredth	200	deux centième
three hundredth	300	trois centième
four hundredth	400	quatre centième
five hundredth	500	cinq centième
six hundredth	600	six centième
seven hundredth	700	sept centième
eight hundredth	800	huit centième
nine hundredth	900	neuf centième
thousandth	1000	millième
two thousandth	2000	deux millième
millionth	1000000	millionième
two millionth	2000000	deux millionième

Notes on usage of the ordinal numbers

(a) **first, and the other numbers ending in first, agree in French with the noun (stated or implied):** *la première maison, le premier employé, la cent et unième personne*

(b) **Abbreviations: English 1st, 2nd, 3rd, 4th, 5th, etc. = French (*m*) 1er, (*f*) 1ere, 2e, 3e, 4e, 5e and so on.**

(c) **See also the notes on Dates, below.**
Voir aussi ci-dessous le paragraphe concernant les dates.

3 Fractions — Les fractions

one half, a half	$\frac{1}{2}$	(*m*) un demi, (*f*) une demie
one and a half helpings	$1\frac{1}{2}$	une portion et demie
two and a half kilos	$2\frac{1}{2}$	deux kilos et demi
one third, a third	$\frac{1}{3}$	un tiers
two thirds	$\frac{2}{3}$	deux tiers
one quarter, a quarter	$\frac{1}{4}$	un quart
three quarters	$\frac{3}{4}$	trois quarts
one sixth, a sixth	$\frac{1}{6}$	un sixième
five and five sixths	$5\frac{5}{6}$	cinq et cinq sixièmes
one twelfth, a twelfth	$\frac{1}{12}$	un douzième
seven twelfths	$\frac{7}{12}$	sept douzièmes
one hundredth, a hundredth	$\frac{1}{100}$	un centième
one thousandth, a thousandth	$\frac{1}{1000}$	un millième

4 Decimals — Les décimales

In French, a comma is written where English uses a point: English 3.56 (three point five six) = French 3,56 (trois virgule cinquante six); English .07 (point nought seven) = French ,07 (virgule zéro sept).

Alors que le français utilise la virgule pour séparer les entiers des décimales, le point est utilisé en anglais à cet effet: anglais 3.56 (three point five six) = français 3,56 (trois virgule cinquante six; anglais .07 (point nought seven) = français 0,07 (zéro virgule zéro sept).

5 Nomenclature — Numération

3,684 is a four-digit number / *3.684 est un nombre à quatre chiffres*

It contains 4 units, 8 tens, 6 hundreds and 3 thousands / *4 est le chiffre des unités, 8 celui des dizaines, 6 celui des centaines et 3 celui des milliers*

The decimal .234 contains 2 tenths, 3 hundredths and 4 thousandths / *la fraction décimale 0,234 contient 2 dixièmes, 3 centièmes et 4 millièmes*

6 Percentages — Les pourcentages

$2\frac{1}{2}$% two and a half per cent / *deux et demi pour cent*

18% of the people here are over 65 / *ici dix-huit pour cent des gens ont plus de soixante-cinq ans*

Production has risen by 8% / *la production s'est accrue de huit pour cent*

(See also the main text of the dictionary / *Voir aussi dans le texte.*)

7 Signs — Les signes

English

+	addition sign
+	plus sign (*eg* + 7 = plus seven)
−	subtraction sign
−	minus sign (*eg* − 3 = minus three)
×	multiplication sign
÷	division sign
√	square root sign
∞	infinity
≡	sign of identity, is equal to
=	sign of equality, equals
≈	is approximately equal to
≠	sign of inequality, is not equal to
>	is greater than
<	is less than

français

+	signe plus, signe de l'addition
+	signe plus (*ex*: + 7 = plus 7)
−	signe moins, signe de la soustraction
−	signe moins (*ex*: − 3 = moins 3)
×	signe de la multiplication
:	signe de la division
√	signe de la racine
∞	symbole de l'infini
≡	signe d'identité
=	signe d'égalité
≈	signe d'équivalence
≠	signe de non égalité
>	plus grand que
<	plus petit que

8 Calculations — Le calcul

$8+6=14$ eight and (*or* plus) six are (*or* make) fourteen/*huit et* (ou *plus*) *six font* (ou *égalent*) *quatorze*

$15-3=12$ fifteen take away (*or* fifteen minus) three equals twelve, three from fifteen leaves twelve / *trois ôtés de quinze égalent 12, quinze moins trois égalent 12*

$3\times3=9$ three threes are nine, three times three is nine / *trois fois trois égalent neuf, trois multiplié par trois égalent neuf*

$32\div8=4$ thirty-two divided by eight is (*or* equals) four / *32 divisé par 8 égalent 4*

$3^2=9$ three squared is nine / *trois au carré égale neuf*

$2^5=32$ two to the fifth (*or* to the power of five) is (*or* equals) thirty-two / *2 à la puissance cinq égale trente-deux*

$\sqrt{16}=4$ the square root of sixteen is four / *la racine carrée de seize est quatre*

9 Time — L'heure

2 hours 33 minutes and 14 seconds / *deux heures trente-trois minutes et quatorze secondes*
half an hour / *une demi-heure*
a quarter of an hour / *un quart d'heure*
three quarters of an hour / *trois quarts d'heure*
what's the time? / *quelle heure est-il?*
what time do you make it? / *quelle heure avez-vous?*
have you the right time? / *avez-vous l'heure exacte?*
I make it 2.20 / *d'après ma montre il est 2h 20*
my watch says 3.37 / *il est 3h 37 à ma montre*
it's 1 o'clock / *il est une heure*
it's 2 o'clock / *il est deux heures*
it's 5 past 4 / *il est quatre heures cinq*
it's 10 to 6 / *il est six heures moins dix*
it's half past 8 / *il est huit heures et demie*
it's a quarter past 9 / *il est neuf heures et quart*
it's a quarter to 2 / *il est deux heures moins le quart*
at 10 a.m. / *à dix heures du matin*
at 4 p.m. / *à quatre heures de l'après-midi*
at 11 p.m. / *à onze heures du soir*
at exactly 3 o'clock, at 3 sharp, at 3 on the dot / *à trois heures exactement, à trois heures précises*
the train leaves at 19.32 / *le train part à dix-neuf heures trente-deux*
(at) what time does it start? / *à quelle heure est-ce que cela commence?*
it is just after 3 / *il est trois heures passées*
it is nearly 9 / *il est presque neuf heures*
about 8 o'clock / *aux environs de huit heures*
at (*or* by) 6 o'clock at the latest / *à six heures au plus tard*
have it ready for 5 o'clock / *tiens-le prêt pour 5 heures*
it is full each night from 7 to 9 / *c'est plein chaque soir de 7 à 9*
'closed from 1.30 to 4.30' / *'fermé de une heure et demie à quatre heures et demie'*
until 8 o'clock / *jusqu'à huit heures*
it would be about 11 / *il était environ 11 heures, il devait être environ 11 heures*
it would have been about 10 / *il devait être environ dix heures*
at midnight / *à minuit*
before midday, before noon / *avant midi*

10 Dates — Les dates

N.B. The days of the week and the months are written with small letters in French and with capitals in English; lundi, mardi, février, mars.

NB: *Contrairement au français, les jours de la semaine et les mois prennent une majuscule en anglais: Monday, Tuesday, February, March.*

the 1st of July, July 1st / le 1er juillet
the 2nd of May, May 2nd / *le 2 mai*
on June 21st, on the 21st (of) June / *le 21 juin*
on Monday / *lundi*
he comes on Mondays / *il vient le lundi*
'closed on Fridays' / *'fermé le vendredi'*
he lends it to me from Monday to Friday / *il me le prête du lundi au vendredi*
from the 14th to the 18th / *du 14 au 18*
what's the date?, what date is it today? / *quelle est la date d'aujourd'hui?*
today's the 12th / *aujourd'hui nous sommes le 12*
one Thursday in October / *un jeudi en octobre*
about the 4th of July / *aux environs du 4 juillet*
Heading of letters / *en-tête de lettre*:
19th May 1984 / *le 19 mai 1984*
1978 nineteen (hundred and) seventy-eight / *mille neuf cent soixante dix-huit, dix-neuf cent soixante dix-huit*
4 B.C., B.C. 4 / *4 av. J.-C.*
70 A.D., A.D. 70 / *70 ap. J.-C.*
in the 13th century / *au 13e siècle*
in (*or* during) the 1930s / *dans* (ou *pendant*) *les années 30*
in 1940 something / *en 1940 et quelques*
(See also the main text of the dictionary / *Voir aussi dans le texte.*

II WEIGHTS AND MEASURES — POIDS ET MESURES

1 Metric System — système métrique

Measures formed with the following prefixes are mostly omitted / *la plupart des mesures formées à partir des préfixes suivants ont été omises*:

deca-	10 times	10 fois	*déca-*
hecto-	100 times	100 fois	*hecto-*
kilo-	1000 times	1000 fois	*kilo-*
deci-	one tenth	un dixième	*déci-*
centi-	one hundredth	un centième	*centi-*
mil(l)i-	one thousandth	un millième	*mil(l)i-*

Linear measures — mesures de longueur

1 millimetre (millimètre)	=	0.03937 inch
1 centimetre (centimètre)	=	0.3937 inch
1 metre (mètre)	=	39.37 inches
	=	1.094 yards
1 kilometre (kilomètre)	=	0.6214 mile ($\frac{5}{8}$ mile)

Square measures — mesures de superficie

1 square centimetre (centimètre carré)	=	0.155 square inch
1 square metre (mètre carré)	=	10.764 square feet
	=	1.196 square yards
1 square kilometre (kilomètre carré)	=	0.3861 square mile
	=	247.1 acres
1 are (are)=100 square metres	=	119.6 square yards
1 hectare (hectare)=100 ares	=	2.471 acres

Cubic measures — mesures de volume

1 cubic centimetre (centimètre cube)	=	0.061 cubic inch
1 cubic metre (mètre cube)	=	35.315 cubic feet
	=	1.308 cubic yards

Measures of capacity — mesures de capacité

1 litre (litre)=1000 cubic centimetres	=	1.76 pints
	=	0.22 gallon

Weights — poids

1 gramme (gramme)	=	15.4 grains
1 kilogramme (kilogramme)	=	2.2046 pounds
1 quintal (quintal)=100 kilogrammes	=	220.46 pounds
1 metric ton (tonne)=1000 kilogrammes	=	0.9842 ton

2 British system — système britannique

Linear measures — mesures de longueur

1 inch	=	2,54 centimètres
1 foot (pied)=12 inches	=	30,48 centimètres
1 yard (yard)=3 feet	=	91,44 centimètres
1 furlong=220 yards	=	201,17 mètres
1 mile (mile)=1760 yards	=	1,609 kilomètres

Surveyors' measures — mesures d'arpentage

1 link=7.92 inches	=	20,12 centimètres
1 rod (*or* pole, perch)=25 links	=	5,029 mètres
1 chain=22 yards=4 rods	=	20,12 mètres

Square measures — mesures de superficie

1 square inch	=	6,45 cm^2
1 square foot (pied carré)=144 square inches	=	929,03 cm^2
1 square yard (yard carré)=9 square feet	=	0,836 m^2
1 square rod=30.25 square yards	=	25,29 m^2
1 acre=4840 square yards	=	40,47 ares
1 square mile (mile carré)=640 acres	=	2,59 km^2

Cubic measures — mesures de volume

1 cubic inch	=	16,387 cm^3
1 cubic foot (pied cube)=1728 cubic inches	=	0,028 m^3
1 cubic yard (yard cube)=27 cubic feet	=	0,765 m^3
1 register ton (tonne)=100 cubic feet	=	2,832 m^3

Measures of capacity — mesures de capacité

(a) Liquid — pour liquides

1 gill	=	0,142 litre
1 pint (pinte)=4 gills	=	0,57 litre
1 quart=2 pints	=	1,136 litres
1 gallon (gallon)=4 quarts	=	4,546 litres

(b) Dry — pour matières sèches

1 peck=2 gallons	=	9,087 litres
1 bushel=4 pecks	=	36,36 litres
1 quarter=8 bushels	=	290,94 litres

Weights — Avoirdupois system — Poids — système avoirdupois

1 grain (grain)	=	0,0648 gramme
1 drachm *or* dram=27,34 grains	=	1,77 grammes
1 ounce (once)=16 drachms	=	28,35 grammes
1 pound (livre)=16 ounces	=	453,6 grammes = 0,453 kilogramme
1 stone=14 pounds	=	6,348 kilogrammes
1 quarter=28 pounds	=	12,7 kilogrammes
1 hundredweight=112 pounds	=	50,8 kilogrammes
1 ton (tonne)=2240 pounds=20 hundredweight	=	1,016 kilogrammes

3 US Measures — mesures nord-américaines

In the US, the same system as that which applies in Great Britain is used for the most part; the main differences are mentioned below.
***Les mesures britanniques sont valables pour les USA dans la majeure partie des cas. Les principales différences sont énumérées ci-dessous*:**

Measures of Capacity — mesures de capacité

(a) Liquid — pour liquides

1 US liquid gill	=	0,118 litre
1 US liquid pint=4 gills	=	0,473 litre
1 US liquid quart=2 pints	=	0,946 litre
1 US gallon=4 quarts	=	3,785 litres

(b) Dry — pour matières sèches

1 US dry pint	=	0,550 litre
1 US dry quart=2 dry pints	=	1,1 litres
1 US peck=8 dry quarts	=	8,81 litres
1 US bushel=4 pecks	=	35,24 litres

Weights — poids

1 hundredweight (*or* short hundredweight)=100 pounds	=	45,36 kilogrammes
1 ton (*or* short ton)=2000 pounds=20 short hundredweights	=	907,18 kilogrammes

Abréviations grammaticales et niveaux de langue

Abbreviations, field labels and style labels

abréviation	**abbr, abrév**	abbreviated, abbreviation
adjectif	**adj**	adjective
administration	**Admin**	administration
adverbe	**adv**	adverb
agriculture	**Agr**	agriculture
anatomie	**Anat**	anatomy
antiquité	**Antiq**	ancient history
approximativement	**approx**	approximately
archéologie	**Archeol, Archéol**	archaeology
architecture	**Archit**	architecture
argot	**arg**	slang
article	**art**	article
astrologie	**Astrol**	astrology
astronomie	**Astron**	astronomy
attribut	**attrib**	predicative
automobile	**Aut**	automobiles
auxiliaire	**aux**	auxiliary
aviation	**Aviat**	aviation
biologie	**Bio**	biology
botanique	**Bot**	botany
britannique, Grande-Bretagne	**Brit**	British, Great Britain
canadien, Canada	**Can**	Canadian, Canada
chimie	**Chem, Chim**	chemistry
cinéma	**Cine, Ciné**	cinema
commerce	**Comm**	commerce
comparatif	**comp**	comparative
conditionnel	**cond**	conditional
conjonction	**conj**	conjunction
construction	**Constr**	building trade
mots composés	**cpd**	compound, in compounds
cuisine	**Culin**	cookery
défini	**def, déf**	definite
démonstratif	**dem, dém**	demonstrative
dialectal, régional	**dial**	dialect
diminutif	**dim**	diminutive
direct	**dir**	direct
écologie	**Ecol**	ecology
économique	**Econ, Écon**	economics
écossais, Écosse	**Écos**	Scottish, Scotland
par exemple	**eg**	for example
électricité, électronique	**Elec, Élec**	electricity, electronics
épithète	**épith**	before noun
surtout	**esp**	especially
et cetera	**etc**	etcetera
euphémisme	**euph**	euphemism
par exemple	**ex**	for example
exclamation	**excl**	exclamation
féminin	**f**	feminine
figuré	**fig**	figuratively
finance	**Fin**	finance
féminin pluriel	**fpl**	feminine plural
formel, langue soignée	**frm**	formal language
football	**Ftbl**	football
fusionné	**fus**	fused
futur	**fut**	future
en général, généralement	**gen, gén**	in general, generally
géographie	**Geog, Géog**	geography
géologie	**Geol, Géol**	geology
géométrie	**Geom, Géom**	geometry
grammaire	**Gram**	grammar
gymnastique	**Gym**	gymnastics
héraldique	**Her, Hér**	heraldry
histoire	**Hist**	history
humoristique	**hum**	humorous
impératif	**imper, impér**	imperative
impersonnel	**impers**	impersonal
industrie	**Ind**	industry
indéfini	**indef, indéf**	indefinite
indicatif	**indic**	indicative
indirect	**indir**	indirect
infinitif	**infin**	infinitive
inséparable	**insep**	inseparable
interrogatif	**interrog**	interrogative
invariable	**inv**	invariable
irlandais, Irlande	**Ir**	Irish, Ireland
ironique	**iro**	ironic
irrégulier	**irrég**	irregular
droit, juridique	**Jur**	law, legal
linguistique	**Ling**	linguistics
littéral, au sens propre	**lit**	literally
littéraire	**liter**	literary
littérature	**Literat**	literature
littéraire	**littér**	literary
littérature	**Littérat**	literature
locutions	**loc**	locution